BOOK REVIEW INDEX

ISSN 0524-0581

BOOK REVIEW INDEX

2016 Cumulation

Kristin B. Mallegg
Editor

GALE
CENGAGE Learning

Farmington Hills, Mich • San Francisco • New York • Waterville, Maine
Meriden, Conn • Mason, Ohio • Chicago

GALE
CENGAGE Learning

Book Review Index 2016 Cumulation

Project Editor: Kristin B. Mallegg

Editorial Support Services: Lawrence Gee, Eric Lapuz, Steve Lee, Connie Wan-Querubin

Composition and Electronic Capture: Gary Oudersluys

Manufacturing: Rita Wimberley

© 2016 Gale Cengage Learning

ALL RIGHTS RESERVED. No part of this work covered by the copyright herein may be reproduced, transmitted, stored, or used in any form or by any means graphic, electronic, or mechanical, including but not limited to photocopying, recording, scanning, digitizing, taping, Web distribution, information networks, or information storage and retrieval systems, except as permitted under Section 107 or 108 of the 1976 United States Copyright Act, without the prior written permission of the publisher.

This publication is a creative work fully protected by all applicable copyright laws, as well as by misappropriation, trade secret, unfair competition, and other applicable laws. The authors and editors of this work have added value to the underlying factual material herein through one or more of the following: unique and original selection, coordination, expression, arrangement, and classification of the information.

> For product information and technology assistance, contact us at
> **Gale Customer Support, 1-800-877-4253**
> For permission to use material from this text or product,
> submit all requests online at www.cengage.com/permissions
> Further permissions questions can be emailed to
> **permissionrequest@cengage.com**

While every effort has been made to secure permission to reprint material and to ensure the reliability of the information presented in this publication, Gale Cengage Learning neither guarantees the accuracy of the data contained herein nor assumes any responsibility for errors, omissions or discrepancies. Gale Cengage Learning accepts no payment for listing; and inclusion in the publication of any organization, agency, institution, publication, service, or individual does not imply endorsement of the editors or publisher. Errors brought to the attention of the publisher and verified to the satisfaction of the publisher will be corrected in future editions.

Gale
27500 Drake Rd.
Farmington Hills, MI, 48331-3535

LIBRARY OF CONGRESS CATALOG CARD NUMBER 88-658021

ISBN-13: 978-1-4103-1818-3

ISSN 0524-0581

Printed in Mexico
1 2 3 4 5 6 7 20 19 18 17 16

Contents

Introduction vii
Users Guide ix
Publications Indexed xi
Book Review Index 1
Title Index 513

Introduction

Book Review Index (BRI) is a master key providing access to reviews of thousands of books, audiobooks, and e-books. Representing a wide range of popular, academic, and professional interests, *BRI* guides readers and researchers to reviews appearing in over 400 publications from the United States, Canada, Europe, and Australia. *BRI* includes citations for reviews of any type of book, audiobook, or e-book that has been or is about to be published. *BRI's* definition of "review" is broad, citing reviews that provide a critical comment, a description of the book's contents, or a recommendation regarding the type of library collection for which a book is suited.

This volume cumulates the three issues for 2016. The journals and other reviewing sources have been carefully selected to ensure a wide range of subject coverage and relevancy to those interested in reviews. Sources indexed include:

- reviewing journals such as *Choice, Booklist,* and *School Library Journal;*
- national publications of general interest like *Esquire* and *Newsweek;*
- scholarly and literary journals such as *American Historical Review* and *The Kenyon Review;* and
- electronic publications such as *Law* and *Politics Book Review, H-Net: Humanities and Social Science Online,* and *Reference Reviews.*

Arrangement of BRI

Book Review Index has two major parts. The main section of the book presents book review citations arranged by the name of the author of the reviewed book. The citations include the title, illustrators or readers, name of the reviewing source, date of publication, length of the review, and in some cases the age range for which the reviewer felt the book was appropriate.

There are three size ranges: 1 to 50 words, 51 to 500 words, and over 501 words. This scheme effectively classifies reviews as "small," "medium," and "large."

Following the main section is the Title Index, which gives the user access to the citations by way of the title. This index is useful when the name of the author is unknown. Listings in the title index refer the user to the main entry section. When a title appears without an author it is an indication that the title itself is the main entry form.

For more information on the entries and definitions of codes, please consult the Users Guide following this introduction.

Available in Electronic Formats

Online. *Book Review Index* is available online from Gale Cengage Learning. via two different subscriptions: the index-only offering and the *Book Review Index Online Plus* option. The index-only resource includes more than 5 million review citations, while *Book Review Index Plus* includes not only the 5 million review citations, but also more than 664,000 full-text reviews from InfoTrac OneFile and InfoTrac Expanded Academic. Both *Book Review Index Online* and *Book Review Index Online Plus* include citations from more than 5,800 publications with over 2.5 million titles reviewed; this represents the entire backfile of *Book Review Index* print content, dating back to 1965. For more information, call 1-800-877-GALE. BRI is also available online on DIALOG as File 137, Book Review Index and includes reviews from 1969-2004. For more information, contact The Dialog Corporation, 11000 Regency Parkway, Ste. 10, Cary, NC 27511; phone: (919) 462-8600; toll-free: 800-3-DIALOG.

Acknowledgements

The editors of *Book Review Index* would like to thank the many staff members who helped in the compilation of this issue. We would also like to express our gratitude to the publishers of the journals indexed in *BRI*. Their assistance is invaluable to the publication of *BRI*.

Comments and Suggestions Are Welcome

The editors welcome comments or suggestions on the scope and coverage of *BRI*. Please address all correspondence to:

Editor
Book Review Index
Gale Cengage Learning
27500 Drake Road
Farmington Hills, MI 48331-3535

Phone: 248-699-GALE
Toll-Free: 800-347-GALE
Fax: 248-699-8067

Users Guide

Inclusion Criteria

BRI's broad inclusion criteria are designed to allow searchers to find practically any review that has been published within the time covered by a particular issue. Coverage includes:

- Adult fiction and nonfiction books
- Poetry and song books
- Books that are intended for children
- Audio books and electronic editions (aka books on tape) of books.
- E-books for adults, young adults and children.

Sample Entry

|1| Sattler, Helen R -
|2| The Book of Eagles
|3| (Illus. by Dore, Gustave) or (Read by Prichard, Michael)
|4| c
|5| CCB-B -
|6| v50 - O '96 -
|7| p43(1)
|8| [51-500]

Descriptions of Numbered Elements

|1| Author or Editor of work being reviewed. When a work has multiple authors, only the first or principal author is shown.

|2| Title of work being reviewed. Subtitles are usually included.

|3| Illustrator (if the book is intended for children or young adults) or Reader of an audiobook

|4| Age or Type code. See Explanation of Age and Type Codes below.

|5| Abbreviation of reviewing periodical title. See the "Publications Indexed" section for complete list of abbreviations.

|6| Volume number and date or issue number

|7| Page on which review appears or NA, which indicates the review is only available online. See "Page Number Designations" below for more details.

|8| Approximate number of words in the review. Ranges used are 1-50, 51-500, and 500+.

Explanation of Age and Type Codes

Some entries in BRI include age and/or type codes that help define the kind of work being reviewed.

Age codes

Age designations are determined by the reviewer or publisher.

"c" denotes a book for children (up to age ten)

"y" denotes a book written for young adults (ages eleven through eighteen)

Page Number Designations

Pagination for periodical articles is expressed with a starting page followed by the total number of pages in parentheses, if the article spans more than one page. For academic journals, pagination may be expressed in the same way or by a beginning page and ending page separated by a dash.

Examples

- p10
- p70(5)
- p196-199

Some periodical content that is generated from electronic feed does not contain any pagination information. In these cases, the pagination value "pNA" is used.

Abbreviations for Months and Seasons

Names of individual months and seasons are spelled out, while dates spanning across months or seasons are sometimes abbreviated.

Examples

- Annual
- April-August
- April-Dec
- Autumn
- Autumn-Spring
- Autumn-Wntr

Arrangement of Citations

The main (or Author) section is arranged alphabetically by author names. When the authorship is attributed to a corporate entity, the name of that group is interfiled among the authors. In cases where a book has no author cited, it appears in the main section under its title interfiled among the authors. A user searching for a particular entry in the author or title indexes should note the following guidelines.

- Roman and arabic numerals file in numerical order before the letter A. For example, the title *30-Minute Meals* would file before entries beginning with A; *Thirty-Minute Meals* would file in the T's.

- Acronyms and initialisms file as single words unless periods or spaces divide the letters. Letters following a period or space file as new words. Users should note that variant forms of initialisms would file separately under this arrangement. For example, U.S.A. would appear near the beginning of the U section, while USA would file just before the word "Use."

- Initial articles are ignored in most cases for both English and non-English language titles.

Title Index

The Title Index, which follows the main section, lists all titles for which BRI has citations to reviews. It is arranged alphabetically and follows the same sorting conventions as noted above. A listing in the title index gives the author where the citations will be found in the main section. When no author is listed, the citations are listed under the title in the main (author) section.

Publications Indexed

Preceding the main section is the list of reviewing sources indexed in *BRI*. This section is arranged by the abbreviation used with the main entries to indicate the journal. Each entry in the Publications Indexed section gives the title, subscription address, frequency of publication, ISSN, and URL (Uniform Resource Locater) if the journal's publisher maintains a site on the Internet.

Publications Indexed

The periodical abbreviations used in Book Review Index citations are arranged here alphabetically in letter-by-letter sequence. The full periodical title appears to the right of the abbreviation. The following information is also provided for each publication: frequency, ISSN, subscription address, and URL if the source is available online.

A

ABR: *American Book Review*
Issues per year: 6 ISSN 0149-9408
c/o Unit for Contemporary Literature
Normal, IL 61790-4241 United States

Advocate: *The Advocate (The national gay & lesbian newsmagazine)*
Issues per year: 6 ISSN 0001-8996
10960 Wilshire Boulevard
Los Angeles, CA 90024-3721 United States

Afr Am R: *African American Review*
Issues per year: 4 ISSN 1062-4783
St. Louis University - Humanities 317
St. Louis, MO 63108 United States
http://aar.slu.edu/

Africa T: *Africa Today Magazine*
Issues per year: 4 ISSN 0001-9887
Office of Scholarly Publishing
Bloomington, IN 47405-3907 United States
http://www.iupress.indiana.edu

Afterimage: *Afterimage*
Issues per year: 6 ISSN 0300-7472
31 Prince St.
Rochester, NY 14620 United States
http://vsw.org/

AHR: *American Historical Review*
Issues per year: 5 ISSN 0002-8762
400 A Street SE
Washington, DC 20003-3889 United States

AJE: *American Journal of Education*
Issues per year: 4 ISSN 0195-6744
Journals Division
Chicago, IL 60637-2954 United States
http://www.journals.uchicago.edu

AJP: *American Journal of Philology*
Issues per year: 4 ISSN 0002-9475
2715 N. Charles Street
Baltimore, MD 21218 United States
http://www.press.jhu.edu

AJPsy: *American Journal of Psychology*
Issues per year: 4 ISSN 0002-9556
1325 South Oak St.
Champaign, IL 61820-6903 United States
http://www.press.uillinois.edu/

AJS: *The American Journal of Sociology*
Issues per year: 6 ISSN 0002-9602
Journals Division
Chicago, IL 60637-2954 United States
http://www.journals.uchicago.edu

AL: *American Literature*
Issues per year: 4 ISSN 0002-9831
Box 90660
Durham, NC 27708-0660 United States
http://dukeupress.edu/

AM: *America*
Issues per year: 26 ISSN 0002-7049
106 West 56th St.
New York, NY 10019 United States
http://www.americamagazine.org

Am Ant: *American Antiquity*
Issues per year: 4 ISSN 0002-7316
1111 14th Street NW, Suite 800
Washington, DC 20005-5622 United States

Am Bio T: *The American Biology Teacher*
Issues per year: 8 ISSN 0002-7685
PO BOX 3363
Warrenton, VA 20188 United States
http://www.nabt.org

Am Craft: *American Craft*
Issues per year: 6 ISSN 0194-8008
72 Spring Street
New York, NY 10012 United States

Am Ind CRJ: *American Indian Culture and Research Journal*
Issues per year: 4 ISSN 0161-6463
Box 951548
Los Angeles, CA 90095-1548 United States

Am MT: *American Music Teacher*
Issues per year: 6 ISSN 0003-0112
The Carew Tower
Cincinnati, OH 45202-2814 United States
http://www.mtna.org

Am Q: *American Quarterly*
Issues per year: 4 ISSN 0003-0678
2715 N. Charles Street
Baltimore, MD 21218 United States
http://www.press.jhu.edu

Am Sci: *American Scientist*
Issues per year: 6 ISSN 0003-0996
3106 East NC Highway 54
Research Triangle Park, NC 27709-3975 United States
http://www.sigmaxi.org/

Am St: *American Studies*
Issues per year: 2 ISSN 0026-3079
University of Kansas at Lawrence
Lawrence, KS 66045-2117 United States

Am Theat: *American Theatre*
Issues per year: 11 ISSN 8750-3255
Dist. by Eastern News Distributors, Inc.
Sandusky, OH 44870 United States
http://www.tcg.org/

Amerasia J: *Amerasia Journal*
Issues per year: 3 ISSN 0044-7471
3230 Campbell Hall
Los Angeles, CA 90024-1546 United States

Ams: *Americas: A Quarterly Review of Inter-American Cultural History*
Issues per year: 4 ISSN 0003-1615
1712 Euclid Ave.
Berkeley, CA 94709-1208 United States

Analog: *Analog Science Fiction & Fact*
Issues per year: 13 ISSN 1059-2113
PO Box 54027
Boulder, CO 80322-4027 United States

Ant R: *The Antioch Review*
Issues per year: 4 ISSN 0003-5769
PO Box 148
Yellow Springs, OH 45387 United States

APH: *Air Power History*
Issues per year: 4 ISSN 1044-016X
1535 Command Dr., Suite A122
Andrews Air Force Base, MD 20762-7002 United States

APJ: *Air & Space Power Journal*
Issues per year: 4 ISSN 1555-385X
155 N. Twining Street
Maxwell AFB, AL 36112-6026 United States
http://www.au.af.mil/au/ssq/

Apo: *Apollo*
Issues per year: 12 ISSN 0003-6536
c/o The Spectator
London SW1H 9HP United Kingdom

APR: *The American Poetry Review*
Issues per year: 6 ISSN 0360-3709
The University of the Arts,
Philadelphia, PA 19102-4901 United States

Archiv: *Archivaria*
Issues per year: 2 ISSN 0318-6954
P.O. Box 2596, Station D
Ottawa, Ontario K1P 5W6 Canada

Arm F&S: *Armed Forces & Society: An Interdisciplinary Journal*
Issues per year: 4 ISSN 0095-327X
Rutgers - The State University of New Jersey
Piscataway, NJ 08854-8042 United States
http://www.transactionpub.com/cgi-bin/transactionpublishers.storefront

Art N: *ARTnews*
Issues per year: 4 ISSN 0004-3273
P.O. Box 2083
Knoxville, IA 50197-2083 United States

AS: *The American Scholar*
Issues per year: 4 ISSN 0003-0937
1606 New Hampshire Avenue, NW
Washington, DC 20009 United States
https://www.pbk.org/home/index.aspx

Astron: *Astronomy*
Issues per year: 12 ISSN 0091-6358
21027 Crossroads Circle
Waukesha, WI 53187-1612 United States
http://corporate.kalmbach.com/

Atl: *The Atlantic*
Issues per year: 12 ISSN 1072-7825
600 New Hampshire Ave., N.W.
Washington, DC 20037 United States
http://www.atlanticmedia.com/

Aztlan: *AZTLAN - A Journal of Chicano Studies*
Issues per year: 2 ISSN 0005-2604
University of California
Los Angeles, CA 90024 United States

B

Barron's: *Barron's*
Issues per year: 52 ISSN 1077-8039
Box 300
Princeton, NJ 08543-0300 United States

BHR: *Business History Review*
Issues per year: 4 ISSN 0007-6805
Book Review Coordinator
Boston, MA 02163 United States

Biomag: *Biography*
Issues per year: 4 ISSN 0162-4962
2840 Kolowalu St.
Honolulu, HI 96822 United States
http://www.uhpress.hawaii.edu

BioSci: *BioScience*
Issues per year: 11 ISSN 0006-3568
2000 Center Street, Suite 303
Berkeley, CA 94704-1223 United States

Bkbird: *Bookbird*
Issues per year: 4 ISSN 0006-7377
c/o Barbara A. Lehman, Ed.,
Mansfield, OH 44906 United States

Bks & Cult: *Books & Culture*
Issues per year: 6 ISSN 1082-8931
465 Gunderson Dr.
Carol Stream, IL 60188 United States
http://www.christianitytoday.com/

BL: *Booklist*
Issues per year: 6 ISSN 0006-7385
50 East Huron St.
Chicago, IL 60611-2795 United States
http://www.ala.org

BSA-P: *Papers of the Bibliographical Society of America*
Issues per year: 4 ISSN 0006-128X
P.O. Box 397
New York, NY 10163 United States

Bwatch: *The Bookwatch*
Issues per year: 12 ISSN 0896-4521
278 Orchard Dr.
Oregon, WI 53575 United States
http://www.midwestbookreview.com

C

Callaloo: *Callaloo*
Issues per year: 4 ISSN 0161-2492
2715 N. Charles Street
Baltimore, MD 21218 United States
http://www.press.jhu.edu

Can Hist R: *Canadian Historical Review*
Issues per year: 4 ISSN 0008-3755
340 Nagel Drive
Cheektowaga, NY 14225 United States
http://www.utpjournals.com/

Can Lit: *Canadian Literature*
Issues per year: 4 ISSN 0008-4360
Buchanan E1582
Vancouver, British Columbia V6T 1Z1 Canada
http://www.ubc.ca/

CC: *The Christian Century*
Issues per year: 37 ISSN 0009-5281
104 S. Michigan Avenue, Suite 700
Chicago, IL 60603 United States
http://www.christiancentury.org

CCB-B: *The Bulletin of the Center for Children's Books*
Issues per year: 12 ISSN 0008-9036
Journals Division
Champaign, IL 61820 United States
http://www.press.uillinois.edu/

CEH: *Central European History*
Issues per year: 4 ISSN 0008-9389
165 First Avenue
Atlantic Highlands, NJ 07716-1289 United States

CH: *Church History*
Issues per year: 4 ISSN 0009-6407
Cambridge University Press
New York, NY 10013-2473 United States
http://www.churchhistory.org

CH Bwatch: *Children's Bookwatch*
Issues per year: 12
278 Orchard Dr.
Oregon, WI 53575 United States
http://www.midwestbookreview.com

Ch Today: *Christianity Today*
Issues per year: 14 ISSN 0009-5753
P.O. Box 11617 or 11618?
Des Moines, IA 50340 United States
http://www.christianitytoday.com/

CHE: *The Chronicle of Higher Education*
Issues per year: 49 ISSN 0009-5982
1255 23rd St. N.W. Suite 700
Washington, DC 20037 United States
http://www.chronicle.com

CHR: *The Catholic Historical Review*
Issues per year: 4 ISSN 0008-8080
620 Michigan Ave., N.E.
Washington, DC 20064 United States
http://cuapress.cua.edu/journals.htm

CI: *Catholic Insight*
Issues per year: 10 ISSN 1192-5671
P.O. Box 625
Toronto, Ontario M5C 2J8 Canada
http://www.catholicinsight.com

CJ: *The Classical Journal*
Issues per year: 6 ISSN 0009-8353
St. Olaf College
Northfield, MN 55057-1098 United States
http://www.camws.org

CJR: *Columbia Journalism Review*
Issues per year: 2 ISSN 0010-194X
801 Puiltzer Hall
New York, NY 10027 United States
http://www.journalism.columbia.edu

Class R: *Classical Review*
Issues per year: 1 ISSN 0009-840X
Journals Department
Eynsham, Oxford OX8 1JJ United Kingdom

Clio: *CLIO*
Issues per year: 4 ISSN 0884-2043
2101 E. Coliseum Blvd.
Fort Wayne, IN 46805 United States
http://www.ipfw.edu/engl/clio.html

Col Lit: *College Literature*
Issues per year: 3 ISSN 0093-3139
554 New Main
West Chester, PA 19383 United States
http://www.wcupa.edu/

Comp L: *Comparative Literature*
Issues per year: 4 ISSN 0010-4124
223 Friendly Hall
Eugene, OR 97403-1233 United States

Comw: *Commonweal*
Issues per year: 22 ISSN 0010-3330
15 Dutch Street
New York, NY 10038 United States
http://www.cweal.org/

Cons: *Conscience*
Issues per year: 4 ISSN 0740-6835
1436 U Street N.W., Suite 301
Washington, DC 20009-3997 United States
http://www.catholicsforchoice.org

Cont Pac: *The Contemporary Pacific*
Issues per year: 2 ISSN 1043-898X
2840 Kolowalu St.
Honolulu, HI 96822 United States
http://www.uhpress.hawaii.edu

CQ: *The Carolina Quarterly*
Issues per year: 3 ISSN 0008-6797
CB# 3520, 510 Greenlaw Hall
Chapel Hill, NC 27599-3520 United States
http://www.unc.edu/depts/cqonline

CrimJR: *Criminal Justice Review*
Issues per year: 4 ISSN 0734-0168
Law Review
Atlanta, GA 30303-3098 United States
http://www.gsu.edu

Critm: *Criticism*
Issues per year: 4 ISSN 0011-1589
Attn: Lauren Crocker
Detroit, MI 48201-1309 United States
http://wsupress.wayne.edu/index.html

CS: *Contemporary Sociology*
Issues per year: 6 ISSN 0094-3061
1722 N Street NW
Washington, DC 20036 United States

CSM: *The Christian Science Monitor*
Issues per year: 52 ISSN 0882-7729
PO Box 568
Boston, MA 02117-0568 United States
http://www.spirituality.com/

CWS: *Canadian Woman Studies*
Issues per year: 4 ISSN 0713-3235
212 Founders College
North York, Ontario M3J 1P3 Canada
http://www.yorku.ca/cwscf/

D

Dal R: *The Dalhousie Review*
Issues per year: 3 ISSN 0011-5827
Dalhousie Review
Halifax, Nova Scotia B3H 4R2 Canada
http://www.dal.ca/

Dance: *Dance Magazine*
Issues per year: 12 ISSN 0011-6009
P.O. Box 50470
Cicero, IL 60650 United States
http://www.dancemagazine.com/

Dance RJ: *Dance Research Journal*
Issues per year: 2 ISSN 0149-7677
State University of New York
Brockport, NY 14420 United States

Dbt: *Down Beat*
Issues per year: 12 ISSN 0012-5768
Box 1071
Skokie, IL 60076 United States

Dialogue: *Dialogue: Canadian Philosophical Review*
Issues per year: 4 ISSN 0012-2173
75 University Ave.
W. Waterloo, Ontario N2L 3C5 Canada
http://www.wlupress.wlu.ca

Dis: *Dissent*
Issues per year: 4 ISSN 0012-3846
310 Riverside Drive, Suite 2008
New York, NY 10025 United States

E

E-A St: *Europe-Asia Studies*
Issues per year: 10 ISSN 0966-8136
3 Park Square
Abingdon, Oxfordshire OX14 4RN United Kingdom
http://www.taylorandfrancis.com/

Econ: *The Economist*
Issues per year: 51 ISSN 0013-0613
111 West 57th St.
New York, NY 10019-2211 United States
http://store.eiu.com/

Eight-C St: *Eighteenth-Century Studies*
Issues per year: 4 ISSN 0013-2586
c/o Jeffrey Smitten
Logan, UT 84322-3730 United States

En Jnl: *The Energy Journal*
Issues per year: 4 ISSN 0195-6574
28790 Chagrin Blvd., Suite 350
Cleveland, OH 44122 United States
http://www.iaee.org

ERS: *Ethnic and Racial Studies*
Issues per year: 12 ISSN 0141-9870
ITPS Ltd.
Andover, Hants SP10 5BE United Kingdom

Esq: *Esquire*
Issues per year: 12 ISSN 0194-9535
C.D.S.
Des Moines, IA 50315 United States
http://www.hearst.com

F

Film Cr: *Film Criticism*
Issues per year: 3 ISSN 0163-5069
Film Criticism Office
Meadville, PA 16335 United States

For Aff: *Foreign Affairs*
Issues per year: 6 ISSN 0015-7120
58 East 68th St.
New York, NY 10021 United States
http://www.cfr.org/

Forbes: *Forbes*
Issues per year: 27 ISSN 0015-6914
P.O. Box 10048
Des Moines, IA 50340-0048 United States
http://www.forbes.com

Fortune: *Fortune*
Issues per year: 25 ISSN 0015-8259
Time & Life Building
New York, NY 10020 United States
http://www.timeinc.com

FQ: *Film Quarterly*
Issues per year: 4 ISSN 0015-1386
Journals Division
Berkeley, CA 94704-1223 United States

FR: *The French Review*
Issues per year: 4 ISSN 0016-111X
57 East Armory Avenue
Champaign, IL 61820 United States

FS: *French Studies*
Issues per year: 4 ISSN 0016-1128
c/o Prof. A.W. Raitt, ed., Taylor
Oxford OX1 3NA United Kingdom

G

G&L Rev W: *The Gay & Lesbian Review Worldwide*
Issues per year: 4 ISSN 1532-1118
45 Lawrence Street
Boston, MA 02116 United States
http://www.glreview.com/

Ga R: *The Georgia Review*
Issues per year: 4 ISSN 0016-8386
The University of Georgia
Athens, GA 30602-9009 United States

Ger Q: *The German Quarterly*
Issues per year: 4 ISSN 0016-8831
112 Haddontowne Court
Cherry Hill, NJ 08034-3662 United States
http://www.aatg.org

GR: *The Geographical Review*
Issues per year: 4 ISSN 0016-7428
Ms. Mary Lynn Bird
Brooklyn, NY 11201-4404 United States
https://www.amergeog.org

GSR: *German Studies Review*
Issues per year: 3 ISSN 0149-7952
ASU Foundation
Tempe, AZ 85287-4011 United States
http://www.asu.edu/

H

HAHR: *Hispanic American Historical Review*
Issues per year: 4 ISSN 0018-2168
Box 90660
Durham, NC 27708-0660 United States
http://dukeupress.edu/

Har Bus R: *Harvard Business Review*
Issues per year: 12 ISSN 0017-8012
60 Harvard Way
Boston, MA 02163 United States
http://www.hbsp.harvard.edu

HB: *The Horn Book Magazine*
Issues per year: 6 ISSN 0018-5078
7858 Industrial Parkway
Plain City, OH 43064 United States
http://www.hbook.com/

HB Guide: *The Horn Book Guide*
Issues per year: 2 ISSN 1044-405X
7858 Industrial Parkway
Plain City, OH 43064 United States
http://www.hbook.com/

HER: *Harvard Educational Review*
Issues per year: 4 ISSN 0017-8055
Graduate School of Education
Cambridge, MA 02138 United States

HER: *The English Historical Review*
Issues per year: 6 ISSN 0013-8266
Journals Customer Service Department
Oxford OX2 6DP United Kingdom

Hisp R: *Hispanic Review*
Issues per year: 4 ISSN 0018-2176
Attn: Katherine McGuire
Philadelphia, PA 19104-4112 United States
http://www.upenn.edu/pennpress

Historian: *The Historian*
Issues per year: 4 ISSN 0018-2370
University of South Florida, SOC 107
Tampa, FL 33620-8100 United States

HM: *Harper's Magazine*
Issues per year: 12 ISSN 0017-789X
P.O. Box 7511
Red Oak, IA 51591-0511 United States
http://harpers.org

HNet: *H-Net: Humanities and Social Sciences Online*
Issues per year: 12 ISSN 1538-0661
Michigan State University, 310 Auditorium Bldg
East Lansing, MI 48824 United States

HR: *The Hudson Review*
Issues per year: 4 ISSN 0018-702X
684 Park Avenue
New York, NY 10021 United States

HT: *History Today*
Issues per year: 12 ISSN 0018-2753
20 Old Compton Street
London W1V 5PE United Kingdom

Hum: *The Humanist*
Issues per year: 6 ISSN 0018-7399
1777 "T" Street, NW
Washington, DC 20001-7125 United States
http://www.americanhumanist.org/

I

IBMR: *International Bulletin of Missionary Research*
Issues per year: 4 ISSN 0272-6122
P.O. Box 3000
Denville, NJ 07834 United States

IJAHS: *International Journal of African Historical Studies*
Issues per year: 3 ISSN 0361-7882
270 Bay State Road
Boston, MA 02215 United States

IJCM: *International Journal of Commerce and Management*
Issues per year: 4 ISSN 1056-9219
Box 10812
Birmingham, AL 35201-0812 United States
http://www.emeraldinsight.com/

IJMES: *International Journal of Middle East Studies*
Issues per year: 4 ISSN 0020-7438
32 Avenue of the Americas
New York, NY 10013-2473 United States
http://www.cambridge.org

ILS: *Irish Literary Supplement*
Issues per year: 2 ISSN 0733-3390
2592 North Wading River Road
Wading River, NY 11792-1404 United States

IndRev: *Independent Review*
Issues per year: 4 ISSN 1086-1653
100 Swan Way
Oakland, CA 94621-1428 United States

Intpr: *Interpretation*
Issues per year: 4 ISSN 0020-9643
3401 Brook Road
Richmond, VA 23227 United States
http://www.union-psce.edu/

Isis: *Isis*
Issues per year: 4 ISSN 0021-1753
Journals Division
Chicago, IL 60637-2954 United States
http://www.journals.uchicago.edu

J

J Am St: *Journal of American Studies*
Issues per year: 3 ISSN 0021-8758
32 Avenue of the Americas
New York, NY 10013-2473 United States
http://www.cambridge.org

J Chem Ed: *Journal of Chemical Education*
Issues per year: 12 ISSN 0021-9584
Subscription Department
Easton, PA 18042 United States

J Hi E: *Journal of Higher Education*
Issues per year: 6 ISSN 0022-1546
1070 Carmack Rd.
Columbus, OH 43210-1002 United States
http://www.ohiostatepress.org

J Mil H: *The Journal of Military History*
Issues per year: 4 ISSN 0899-3718
George C. Marshall Library
Lexington, VA 24450 United States
http://www.smh-hq.org/

J Phil: *The Journal of Philosophy*
Issues per year: 12 ISSN 0022-362X
Business Manager
New York, NY 10027 United States

J Rehab: *The Journal of Rehabilitation*
Issues per year: 4 ISSN 0022-4154
633 South Washington Street
Alexandria, VA 22314-4109 United States

J Urban H: *Journal of Urban History*
Issues per year: 6 ISSN 0096-1442
2455 Teller Road
Thousand Oaks, CA 91320 United States
http://www.sagepub.com

JAAR: *Journal of the American Academy of Religion*
Issues per year: 4 ISSN 0002-7189
P.O. Box 15399
Atlanta, GA 30333-0399 United States

JAH: *Journal of American History*
Issues per year: 4 ISSN 0021-8723
Executive Secretary
Bloomington, IN 47408-4199 United States
http://www.oah.org/pubs/index.html

JAS: *The Journal of Asian Studies*
Issues per year: 4 ISSN 0021-9118
University of Michigan at Ann Arbor
Ann Arbor, MI 48109 United States

JE: *Journal of Education*
Issues per year: 3 ISSN 0022-0574
School of Education
Boston, MA 02215 United States

JEGP: *The Journal of English and Germanic Philology*
Issues per year: 4 ISSN 0363-6941
1325 South Oak St.
Champaign, IL 61820-6903 United States
http://www.press.uillinois.edu/

JEH: *The Journal of Economic History*
Issues per year: 4 ISSN 0022-0507
32 Avenue of the Americas
New York, NY 10013-2473 United States
http://www.cambridge.org

JGS: *Journal of Gender Studies*
Issues per year: 6 ISSN 0958-9236
3 Park Square
Abingdon, Oxfordshire OX14 4RN United Kingdom
http://www.taylorandfrancis.com/

JHI: *Journal of the History of Ideas*
Issues per year: 4 ISSN 0022-5037
Attn: Katherine McGuire
Philadelphia, PA 19104-4112 United States
http://www.upenn.edu/pennpress

JIH: *The Journal of Interdisciplinary History*
Issues per year: 4 ISSN 0022-1953
55 Hayward Street
Cambridge, MA 02142-1315 United States
http://www.mitpressjournals.org/

JMH: *The Journal of Modern History*
Issues per year: 4 ISSN 0022-2801
Journals Division
Chicago, IL 60637-2954 United States
http://www.journals.uchicago.edu

JNE: *Journal of Negro Education*
Issues per year: 4 ISSN 0022-2984
1240 Randolph St., N.E.
Washington, DC 20017 United States

JNES: *Journal of Near Eastern Studies*
Issues per year: 4 ISSN 0022-2968
Journals Division
Chicago, IL 60637-2954 United States
http://www.journals.uchicago.edu

JP: *The Journal of Parapsychology*
Issues per year: 4 ISSN 0022-3387
Rhine Research Center
Durham, NC 27705 United States
http://www.rhine.org/

JR: *The Journal of Religion*
Issues per year: 4 ISSN 0022-4189
Journals Division
Chicago, IL 60637-2954 United States
http://www.journals.uchicago.edu

JSH: *Journal of Southern History*
Issues per year: 4 ISSN 0022-4642
Journal of Southern History MS 45
Houston, TX 77251-1892 United States
http://www.uga.edu/~sha

JTWS: *Journal of Third World Studies*
Issues per year: 2 ISSN 8755-3449
P.O. Box 1232
Americus, GA 31709-1232 United States
http://itc.gsw.edu/atws/journal.htm

JWH: *Journal of Women's History*
Issues per year: 3 ISSN 1042-7961
Journals Publishing Division
Baltimore, MD 21211-2190 United States
http://www.press.jhu.edu

K

Ken R: *The Kenyon Review*
Issues per year: 6 ISSN 0163-075X
Kenyon College
Gambier, OH 43022 United States
http://www.kenyonreview.org

Kiplinger: *Kiplinger's Personal Finance Magazine*
Issues per year: 12 ISSN 1528-9729
1100 13th Street, NW, Suite 750
Washington, DC 20005 United States
http://www.kiplinger.com

KR: *Kirkus Reviews*
Issues per year: 24 ISSN 1948-7428
6411 Burleson Road
Austin, TX 78744 United States
http://www.kirkusreviews.com/

L

Lang Soc: *Language in Society*
Issues per year: 4 ISSN 0047-4045
32 Avenue of the Americas
New York, NY 10013-2473 United States
http://www.cambridge.org

Lat Ant: *Latin American Antiquity*
Issues per year: 4 ISSN 1045-6635
1111 14th Street NW, Suite 800
Washington, DC 20005-5622 United States

Law&PolBR: *Law and Politics Book Review*
Issues per year: 12 ISSN 1062-7421
1527 New Hampshire Avenue NW
Washington, DC 20036 United States
http://www.apsanet.org/

LJ: *Library Journal*
Issues per year: 21 ISSN 0363-0277
7858 Industrial Parkway
Plain City, OH 43064 United States

Lon R Bks: *London Review of Books*
Issues per year: 24 ISSN 0260-9592
28-30 Little Russell St.
London WC1A 2HN United Kingdom

LQ: *Library Quarterly*
Issues per year: 4 ISSN 0024-2519
Journals Division
Chicago, IL 60637-2954 United States
http://www.journals.uchicago.edu

LR: *Library Review*
Issues per year: 8 ISSN 0024-2535
Box 10812
Birmingham, AL 35201-0812 United States
http://www.emeraldinsight.com/

LRTS: *Library Resources & Technical Services*
Issues per year: 4 ISSN 0024-2527
50 East Huron St.
Chicago, IL 60611-2795 United States
http://www.ala.org

M

M Ed J: *Music Educators Journal*
Issues per year: 6 ISSN 0027-4321
http://www.sagepub.com

MA: *Modern Age*
Issues per year: 4 ISSN 0026-7457
14 South Bryn Mawr Avenue
Bryn Mawr, PA 19010-3275 United States
http://www.isi.org

Mac: *Maclean's*
Issues per year: 52 ISSN 0024-9262
1 Mount Pleasant Road
Toronto, Ontario M4Y 2Y5 Canada
http://rogerspublishing.ca/

Mag Antiq: *The Magazine Antiques*
Issues per year: 6 ISSN 0161-9284
Box 10547
Des Moines, IA 50340 United States

Magpies: *Magpies*
Issues per year: 5 ISSN 0817-0088
P.O. Box 98
Grange, Queensland 4051 Australia

MAQ: *Medical Anthropology Quarterly*
Issues per year: 4 ISSN 0745-5194
2200 Wilson Blvd., Suite 600
Arlington, VA 22201 United States

Mar Crp G: *Marine Corps Gazette*
Issues per year: 12 ISSN 0025-3170
715 Broadway St.
Quantico, VA 22134 United States

Math T: *Mathematics Teacher*
Issues per year: 9 ISSN 0025-5769
1906 Association Drive
Reston, VA 22091-1593 United States
http://www.nctm.org/

Meanjin: *Meanjin*
Issues per year: 4 ISSN 0815-953X
187 Grattan Street
Carlton, Victoria 3053 Australia
http://www.meanjin.unimelb.edu.au

Med R: *Medieval Review*
Issues per year: 12 ISSN 1096-746X
Western Michigan University, Walwood Hall, 1903 W Michigan,
Kalamazoo, MI 49008-5432 United States

MEQ: *Middle East Quarterly*
Issues per year: 4 ISSN 1073-9467
1500 Walnut St., Suite 1050
Philadelphia, PA 19103-4624 United States
http://www.mequarterly.org/

MFSF: *Modern Fiction Studies*
Issues per year: 4 ISSN 0026-7724
Department of English
West Lafayette, IN 47907 United States

MFSF: *The Magazine of Fantasy and Science Fiction*
Issues per year: 6 ISSN 1095-8258
P.O. Box 3447
Hoboken, NY 07030 United States
https://www.sfsite.com/fsf

MLN: *MLN*
Issues per year: 5 ISSN 0026-7910
2715 N. Charles Street
Baltimore, MD 21218 United States
http://www.press.jhu.edu

MLR: *The Modern Language Review*
Issues per year: 4 ISSN 0026-7937
W.S. Maney & Son Ltd.
Leeds LS9 7DL United Kingdom
http://www.mhra.org.uk/

MP: *Modern Philology*
Issues per year: 4 ISSN 0026-8232
Journals Division
Chicago, IL 60637-2954 United States
http://www.journals.uchicago.edu

Ms: *Ms. Magazine*
Issues per year: 6 ISSN 0047-8318
135 W. 50th St.
New York, NY 10020 United States

MT: *Musical Times*
Issues per year: 4 ISSN 0027-4666
22 Gibson Sq
London N1 0R United Kingdom

N

NACEJou: *NACE Journal*
Issues per year: 4 ISSN 1542-2046
62 Highland Avenue
Bethlehem, PA 18017 United States

NAR: *The North American Review*
Issues per year: 6 ISSN 0029-2397
1222 West 27th Street
Cedar Falls, IA 50614-0516 United States

Nat Post: *National Post*
Issues per year: 52 ISSN 1486-8008
300-1450 Don Mills Rd.
Don Mills, Ontario M3B 2X7 Canada
http://www.canwestglobal.com/home.html

Nat R: *National Review*
Issues per year: 25 ISSN 0028-0038
215 Lexington Ave., 11th Floor
New York, NY 10016 United States
http://www.nationalreview.com/

Nation: *The Nation*
Issues per year: 47 ISSN 0027-8378
33 Irving Place
New York, NY 10003 United States
http://www.thenation.com

Nature: *Nature*
Issues per year: 51 ISSN 0028-0836
The Macmillan Building
London N1 9XW United Kingdom
http://www.nature.com

NEQ: *The New England Quarterly*
Issues per year: 4 ISSN 0028-4866
Northeastern University
Boston, MA 02115 United States

New Or: *New Orleans Magazine*
Issues per year: 12 ISSN 0897-8174
111 Veterans Blvd., 18th Floor
Metairie, LA 70005 United States

New R: *The New Republic*
Issues per year: 12 ISSN 0028-6583
P.O. Box 602
Mount Morris, IL 61054 United States
http://www.thenewrepublic.com/

New Sci: *New Scientist*
Issues per year: 51 ISSN 0262-4079
Quadrant House
Sutton, Surrey SM2 5AS United Kingdom
http://www.reedbusiness.co.uk/

New York: *New York*
Issues per year: 50 ISSN 0028-7369
75 Varick Street, 4th Floor
New York, NY 10013 United States
http://mediakit.nymag.com/

NH: *Natural History*
Issues per year: 12 ISSN 0028-0712
PMB 204
Durham, NC 27713-6650 United States
http://naturalhistorymag.com/

Nine-C Lit: *Nineteenth-Century Literature*
Issues per year: 4 ISSN 0891-9356
Journals Division
Berkeley, CA 94704-1223 United States

Notes: *Notes*
Issues per year: 4 ISSN 0027-4380
8551 Research Way, Suite 180
Middletown, WI 53562 United States
http://www.musiclibraryassoc.org

NS: *New Statesman*
Issues per year: 50 ISSN 1364-7431
John Carpenter House
London EC4Y 0AN United Kingdom
http://www.newstatesman.com/

NW: *Newsweek*
Issues per year: 52 ISSN 0028-9604
7 Hanover Square
New York, NY 10004 United States
http://www.newsweek.com/

NWCR: *Naval War College Review*
Issues per year: 4 ISSN 0028-1484
U.S. Naval War College
Newport, RI 02841-1027 United States
http://www.nwc.navy.mil/press/

NWSA Jnl: *Feminist Formations*
Issues per year: 3 ISSN 2151-7363
Journals Publishing Division
Baltimore, MD 21211-2190 United States
http://www.press.jhu.edu

NY: *The New Yorker*
Issues per year: 47 ISSN 0028-792X
Editorial Assets & Rights
New York, NY 10036 United States
http://www.condenast.com/

NYRB: *The New York Review of Books*
Issues per year: 21 ISSN 0028-7504
P.O. Box 420384
Palm Coast, FL 32142-0384 United States

NYT: *The New York Times*
Issues per year: 365 ISSN 0362-4331
620 8th Avenue, 8th floor
New York, NY 10018 United States
http://www.nytimes.com

NYTBR: *The New York Times Book Review*
Issues per year: 52 ISSN 0028-7806
620 8th Avenue, 8th floor
New York, NY 10018 United States
http://www.nytimes.com

O

Obs: *The Observer (London, England)*
Issues per year: 52 ISSN 0029-7712
Kings Place
London N1 9GU United Kingdom
http://www.guardian.co.uk/

ON: *Opera News*
Issues per year: 10 ISSN 0030-3607
70 Lincoln Center Plaza
New York, NY 10023 United States
http://www.metoperafamily.org/guild/

P

Pac A: *Pacific Affairs*
Issues per year: 4 ISSN 0030-851X
1855 West Mall, Suite 376
Vancouver, British Columbia V6T 1Z2 Canada
http://pacificaffairs.ubc.ca/

PAJ: *PAJ: A Journal of Performance and Art*
Issues per year: 3 ISSN 1520-281X
55 Hayward Street
Cambridge, MA 02142-1315 United States
http://www.mitpressjournals.org/

Par: *Parents Magazine*
Issues per year: 12 ISSN 1083-6373
1716 Locust St.
Des Moines, IA 50309-3023 United States
http://www.meredith.com/

Parabola: *Parabola*
Issues per year: 4 ISSN 0362-1596
656 Broadway
New York, NY 10012 United States

Parameters: *Parameters*
Issues per year: 4 ISSN 0031-1723
122 Forbes Ave.
Carlisle, PA 17013-5238 United States
http://www.carlisle.army.mil/

Pers PS: *Perspectives on Political Science*
Issues per year: 4 ISSN 1045-7097
3 Park Square
Abingdon, Oxfordshire OX14 4RN United Kingdom
http://www.taylorandfrancis.com/

Phil Lit R: *Philatelic Literature Review*
Issues per year: 4 ISSN 0270-1707
P.O. Box 8000
State College, PA 16803 United States

Phil R: *The Philosophical Review*
Issues per year: 4 ISSN 0031-8108
Sage School of Philosophy
Ithaca, NY 14853 United States

PHR: *Pacific Historical Review*
Issues per year: 4 ISSN 0030-8684
Journals Division
Berkeley, CA 94704-1223 United States

Phys Today: *Physics Today*
Issues per year: 12 ISSN 0031-9228
One Physics Ellipse
College Park, MD 20740-3843 United States

PMS: *Popular Music and Society*
Issues per year: 4 ISSN 0300-7766
3 Park Square
Abingdon, Oxfordshire OX14 4RN United Kingdom
http://www.taylorandfrancis.com/

Poet: *Poetry*
Issues per year: 12 ISSN 0032-2032
61 W. SUPERIOR ST.
Chicago, IL 60654-5457 United States
http://www.poetryfoundation.org/

Poetics T: *Poetics Today*
Issues per year: 4 ISSN 0333-5372
Box 90660
Durham, NC 27708-0660 United States
http://dukeupress.edu/

PQ: *Philological Quarterly*
Issues per year: 4 ISSN 0031-7977
Department of Publications
Iowa City, IA 52242-1113 United States
http://www.uiowa.edu/

Pres St Q: *Presidential Studies Quarterly*
Issues per year: 4 ISSN 0360-4918
1020 Nineteenth Street N.W., Suite 250
Washington, DC 20036 United States
http://www.theprisidency.org/

Prog: *The Progressive*
Issues per year: 12 ISSN 0033-0736
409 E. Main St.
Madison, WI 53703 United States

PSQ: *Prairie Schooner*
Issues per year: 4 ISSN 0032-6682
1111 Lincoln Mall
Lincoln, NE 68588-0630 United States
http://www.nebraskapress.unl.edu/

Pub Hist: *Public Historian*
Issues per year: 4 ISSN 0272-3433
Journals Division
Berkeley, CA 94704-1223 United States

Pub Op Q: *Public Opinion Quarterly*
Issues per year: 4 ISSN 0033-362X
Journals Department
Eynsham, Oxford OX8 1JJ United Kingdom

PW: *Publishers Weekly*
Issues per year: 55 ISSN 0000-0019
71 West 23rd Street
New York, NY 10010 United States
http://www.publishersweekly.com

Q

QRB: *Quarterly Review of Biology*
Issues per year: 4 ISSN 0033-5770
Journals Division
Chicago, IL 60637-2954 United States
http://www.journals.uchicago.edu

Quad: *Quadrant*
Issues per year: 10 ISSN 0033-5002
PO Box 1495
Collingwood, Victoria 3066 Australia
http://www.quadrant.org.au/

Queens Q: *Queen's Quarterly*
Issues per year: 4 ISSN 0033-6041
144 Barrie Street
Ottawa, Ontario K7L 3N6 Canada
http://www.queensu.ca/quarterly/

R

R&USQ: *Reference & User Services Quarterly*
Issues per year: 4 ISSN 1094-9054
50 East Huron St.
Chicago, IL 60611-2795 United States
http://www.ala.org

RAH: *Reviews in American History*
Issues per year: 4 ISSN 0048-7511
Journals Publishing Division
Baltimore, MD 21211-2190 United States
http://www.press.jhu.edu

Reason: *Reason Magazine*
Issues per year: 11 ISSN 0048-6906
3415 S. Sepulveda Blvd., Ste. 400
Los Angeles, CA 90034-6060 United States

Rel St: *Religious Studies*
Issues per year: 4 ISSN 0034-4125
32 Avenue of the Americas
New York, NY 10013-2473 United States
http://www.cambridge.org

Ren Q: *Renaissance Quarterly*
Issues per year: 4 ISSN 0034-4338
The Graduate School and University Center
New York, NY 10016-4309 United States
http://www.rsa.org/

RES: *The Review of English Studies*
Issues per year: 5 ISSN 0034-6551
Journals Department
Eynsham, Oxford OX8 1JJ United Kingdom

Res Links: *Resource Links*
Issues per year: 5 ISSN 1201-7647
P.O. Box 9
Pouch Cove, New Foundland A0A 3L0 Canada
http://www.atcl.ca

RM: *The Review of Metaphysics*
Issues per year: 4 ISSN 0034-6632
Catholic University of America
Washington, DC 20064 United States
http://www.reviewofmetaphysics.org/index.php?option=com_content&view=article&id=15&Itemid=16

RocksMiner: *Rocks & Minerals*
Issues per year: 6 ISSN 0035-7529
4 Park Square
Abingdon, Oxfordshire OX14 4RN United Kingdom
http://www.tandf.co.uk/journals/

Roundup M: *Roundup Magazine*
Issues per year: 6 ISSN 1081-2229
P.O. Box 29, Star Route
Encampment, WY 82325 United States

RVBW: *Reviewer's Bookwatch*
Issues per year: 12
278 Orchard Dr.
Oregon, WI 53575 United States
http://www.midwestbookreview.com

S

S Liv: *Southern Living*
Issues per year: 12 ISSN 0038-4305
P.O. Box 830119
Birmingham, AL 35201 United States

S&S: *Science & Society*
Issues per year: 4 ISSN 0036-8237
72 Spring Street
New York, NY 10012 United States

S&T: *Sky & Telescope*
Issues per year: 12 ISSN 0037-6604
New Track Media
Cincinnati, OH 45202 United States
http://newtrackmedia.com/

SAH: *Studies in American Humor*
Issues per year: 1 ISSN 0095-280X
Central Piedmont Community College
Charlotte, NC 28235-5009 United States

Scan St: *Scandinavian Studies*
Issues per year: 4 ISSN 0036-5637
1325 South Oak St.
Champaign, IL 61820-6903 United States
http://www.press.uillinois.edu/

Sch Lib: *School Librarian*
Issues per year: 4 ISSN 0036-6595
Unit 2, Lotmead Business Village
Wanborough, Swindon SN4 0UY United Kingdom
http://www.sla.org.uk/

Sci & Ch: *Science and Children*
Issues per year: 8 ISSN 0036-8148
1840 Wilson Blvd.
Arlington, VA 22201-3000 United States
http://www.nsta.org/

Sci Teach: *The Science Teacher*
Issues per year: 9 ISSN 0036-8555
1840 Wilson Blvd.
Arlington, VA 22201-3000 United States
http://www.nsta.org/

SE: *Social Education*
Issues per year: 6 ISSN 0037-7724
8555 16th Street, Suite 500.
Silver Springs, MD 20910 United States
http://www.ncss.org/

SEP: *Saturday Evening Post*
Issues per year: 6 ISSN 0048-9239
1100 Waterway Blvd.
Indianapolis, IN 46202 United States
http://www.saturdayeveningpost.com/

Sev Cent N: *Seventeenth-Century News*
Issues per year: 2 ISSN 0037-3028
Blocker 227, 4227 TAMU
College Station, TX 77843-4227 United States

Sew R: *The Sewanee Review*
Issues per year: 4 ISSN 0037-3052
Journals Publishing Division
Baltimore, MD 21218-4363 United States
http://www.press.jhu.edu

SF: *Social Forces*
Issues per year: 4 ISSN 0037-7732
Journals Customer Service Department
Oxford OX2 6DP United Kingdom

SFS: *Science Fiction Studies*
Issues per year: 3 ISSN 0091-7729
Arthur B. Evans
Greencastle, IN 46135-0037 United States

Shakes Q: *Shakespeare Quarterly*
Issues per year: 4 ISSN 0037-3222
201 East Capitol Street S.E.
Washington, DC 20003 United States

SHQ: *Southwestern Historical Quarterly*
Issues per year: 4 ISSN 0038-478X
Richardson Hall 2-306
Austin, TX 78712 United States

Si & So: *Sight and Sound*
Issues per year: 12 ISSN 0037-4806
Sight and Sound Subscriptions
Harborough, Leicestershire LE16 9EF United Kingdom

SIAM Rev: *SIAM Review*
Issues per year: 4 ISSN 0036-1445
3600 University City Science
Philadelphia, PA 19104-2688 United States

Signs: *Signs*
Issues per year: 4 ISSN 0097-9740
Journals Division
Chicago, IL 60637-2954 United States
http://www.journals.uchicago.edu

Six Ct J: *The Sixteenth Century Journal*
Issues per year: 4 ISSN 0361-0160
MC 111L
Kirksville, MO 63501 United States

Slav R: *Slavic Review*
Issues per year: 4 ISSN 0037-6779
Jordan Quad-Acacia
Stanford, CA 94305-4130 United States
http://www.fas.harvard.edu/~aaass

SLJ: *School Library Journal*
Issues per year: 12 ISSN 0362-8930
7858 Industrial Parkway
Plain City, OH 43064 United States

Soc: *Society*
Issues per year: 6 ISSN 0147-2011
Van Godewijckstraat 30, P.O. Box 17
Dordrecht 3300 AA Netherlands
http://www.springer.com/

Soc Ser R: *Social Service Review*
Issues per year: 4 ISSN 0037-7961
Journals Division
Chicago, IL 60637-2954 United States
http://www.journals.uchicago.edu

South CR: *South Carolina Review*
Issues per year: 2 ISSN 0038-3163
Department of English
Clemson, SC 29634-1503 United States

SPBW: *Small Press Bookwatch*
Issues per year: 12
278 Orchard Dr.
Oregon, WI 53575 United States
http://www.midwestbookreview.com

Spec: *Spectator*
Issues per year: 52 ISSN 0038-6952
22 Old Queen Street
London SW1H 9HP United Kingdom
http://www.spectator.co.uk

Specu: *Speculum: A Journal of Medieval Studies*
Issues per year: 4 ISSN 0038-7134
1430 Massachusetts Avenue
Cambridge, MA 02138 United States

SSJ: *Sociology of Sport Journal*
Issues per year: 4 ISSN 0741-1235
P.O. Box 5076
Champaign, IL 61825-5076 United States

Stud Hum: *Studies in the Humanities*
Issues per year: 2 ISSN 0039-3800
110 Leonard Hall - Room 110
Indiana, PA 15705-1094 United States
http://www.iup.edu/english/default.aspx

T

T&C: *Technology and Culture*
Issues per year: 4 ISSN 0040-165X
Journals Division
Chicago, IL 60637-2954 United States
http://www.journals.uchicago.edu

TC Math: *Teaching Children Mathematics*
Issues per year: 9 ISSN 1073-5836
1906 Association Drive
Reston, VA 22091-1593 United States
http://www.nctm.org/

TDR: *TDR (Cambridge, Mass.)*
Issues per year: 4 ISSN 1054-2043
55 Hayward Street
Cambridge, MA 02142-1315 United States
http://www.mitpressjournals.org/

Teach Lib: *Teacher Librarian*
Issues per year: 5 ISSN 1481-1782
P.O. Box 958
Bowie, MD 20718-0958 United States
http://www.kurdylapublishing.com/

Teach Mus: *Teaching Music*
Issues per year: 6 ISSN 1069-7446
1806 Robert Fulton Drive
Reston, VA 20191 United States
http://www.menc.org/

TES: *Times Educational Supplement*
Issues per year: 52 ISSN 0040-7887
Admiral House
London E1 9XY United Kingdom
http://www.timeshighereducation.co.uk

Theat J: *Theatre Journal*
Issues per year: 4 ISSN 0192-2882
2715 N. Charles Street
Baltimore, MD 21218 United States
http://www.press.jhu.edu

Theol St: *Theological Studies*
Issues per year: 4 ISSN 0040-5639
2455 Teller Road
Thousand Oaks, CA 91320 United States
http://www.sagepub.com

Tikkun: *Tikkun*
Issues per year: 4 ISSN 0887-9982
905 W. Main St., Suite 18B
Durham, NC 27701 United States
http://dukeupress.edu/

TimHES: *Times Higher Education*
Issues per year: 52
Admiral House
London E1 9XY United Kingdom
http://www.timeshighereducation.co.uk

TLS: *TLS. Times Literary Supplement*
Issues per year: 52 ISSN 0307-661X
Admiral House
London E1 9XY United Kingdom
http://www.timeshighereducation.co.uk

TSWL: *Tulsa Studies in Women's Literature*
Issues per year: 2 ISSN 0732-7730
Tulsa Studies in Women's Literature
Tulsa, OK 74104-3189 United States

TT: *Theology Today*
Issues per year: 4 ISSN 0040-5736
Princeton Theological Seminary
Princeton, NJ 08542 United States

U

Under Nat: *Underwater Naturalist*
Issues per year: 1 ISSN 0041-6606
18 Hartshorne Drive, Suite 1
Highlands, NJ 07732 United States
http://littoralsociety.org/

UtneADi: *Utne Reader*
Issues per year: 4 ISSN 1544-2225
1503 SW 42nd Street
Topeka, KS 66609 United States

V

Veg J: *Vegetarian Journal*
Issues per year: 6 ISSN 0885-7636
P.O. Box 1463
Baltimore, MD 21203 United States
http://www.vrg.org

VOYA: *Voice of Youth Advocates*
Issues per year: 6 ISSN 0160-4201
P.O. Box 958
Bowie, MD 20718-0958 United States
http://www.kurdylapublishing.com/

VQR: *The Virginia Quarterly Review*
Issues per year: 4 ISSN 0042-675X
One West Range
Charlottesville, VA 22903 United States

VS: *Victorian Studies*
Issues per year: 4 ISSN 0042-5222
Office of Scholarly Publishing
Bloomington, IN 47405-3907 United States
http://www.iupress.indiana.edu

W

W&M Q: *The William and Mary Quarterly*
Issues per year: 4 ISSN 0043-5597
P.O. Box 8781
Williamsburg, VA 23187-8781 United States

WestFolk: *Western Folklore*
Issues per year: 4 ISSN 0043-373X
9420 Carrillo Avenue
Montclair, CA 91763-2412 United States

WHQ: *The Western Historical Quarterly*
Issues per year: 4 ISSN 0043-3810
Journals Customer Service Department
Oxford OX2 6DP United Kingdom

WLT: *World Literature Today*
Issues per year: 6 ISSN 0196-3570
630 Parrington Oval, Suite 110
Norman, OK 73019-4033 United States

Wom HR: *Women's History Review*
Issues per year: 4 ISSN 0961-2025
3 Park Square
Abingdon, Oxfordshire OX14 4RN United Kingdom
http://www.taylorandfrancis.com/

Wom R Bks: *The Women's Review of Books*
Issues per year: 11 ISSN 0738-1433
628 North 2nd St.
Philadelphia, PA 19123 United States
http://www.oldcitypublishing.com

World&I: *World and I*
Issues per year: 12 ISSN 0887-9346
3600 New York Avenue NE
Washington, DC 20002 United States

WSJEEd: *The Wall Street Journal Eastern Edition*
Issues per year: 260 ISSN 0099-9660
200 Burnett Rd.
Chicopee, MA 01020 United States

A

2. Dresdner Nachwuchskolloquium zur Geschlechterforschung
  HNet - July 2015 - pNA [501+]
2-Shirt, Charlie - *Vampire Jacques, the Last Templar*
  KR - Dec 1 2015 - pNA [501+]
3. Treffen des "Arbeitskreis Moulagen"
  HNet - March 2015 - pNA [501+]
4. Tagung des Zentralinstituts "Anthropologie der Religion(en)"
  HNet - May 2015 - pNA [501+]
4. ZeitgeschichtsTage Pragser Wildsee
  HNet - Sept 2015 - pNA [501+]
  HNet - Sept 2015 - pNA [501+]
5 Minute Bedtime Stories
  c HB Guide - v26 - i1 - Spring 2015 - p9(1) [51-500]
5 Minute Christmas Stories
  c HB Guide - v26 - i1 - Spring 2015 - p9(1) [51-500]
5 Seconds of Summer - *5 Seconds of Summer: Hey, Let's Make a Band!*
  c HB Guide - v26 - i1 - Spring 2015 - p192(1) [51-500]
25 Jahre Aufarbeitung der Geschichte der sowjetischen Speziallager
  HNet - Sept 2015 - pNA [501+]
28. Jahrestagung des Schwerter Arbeitskreises Katholizismusforschung
  HNet - Jan 2015 - pNA [501+]
39th Annual Conference on the Political Economy of the World-System: Global Inequalities: Hegemonic Shifts and Regional Differentiations
  HNet - April 2015 - pNA [501+]
68. Baltisches Historikertreffen
  HNet - August 2015 - pNA [501+]
100 Pablo Picassos (Illus. by Lemay, Violet)
  c PW - v262 - i17 - April 27 2015 - p74(1) [501+]
  c SLJ - v61 - i8 - August 2015 - p124(1) [51-500]
800 Jahre "Welscher Gast". Neue Fragen zu einer alten Verhaltenslehre in Wort und Bild
  HNet - August 2015 - pNA [501+]
817 - Die Urkundliche Ersterwahnung von Villingen und Schwenningen. Alemannien und das Reich in der Zeit Kaiser Ludwigs des Frommen
  HNet - June 2015 - pNA [501+]
1716 - Leibniz' Letztes Lebensjahr: Unbekanntes zu einem Bekannten Universalgenie
  HNet - March 2015 - pNA [501+]
1984
  Obs - Jan 18 2015 - p39 [501+]
2014 Official First Day Cover Collection
  Phil Lit R - v64 - i2 - Spring 2015 - p128(1) [501+]
The 2014 Postal Service Guide to U.S. Stamps
  Phil Lit R - v64 - i2 - Spring 2015 - p138(2) [501+]
A-Z of Embroidery Stitches 2
  LJ - v140 - i16 - Oct 1 2015 - p83(1) [51-500]
Aadland, Dan - *In Trace of TR: A Montana Hunter's Journey*
  Roundup M - v22 - i5 - June 2015 - p40(1) [501+]
Aamodt, Terrie Dopp - *Ellen Harmon White: American Prophet*
  JAH - v101 - i4 - March 2015 - p1267-1268 [501+]
Aanensen, Gayle Eggen - *Greater Than Gold*
  KR - June 15 2015 - pNA [501+]
Aaron, Jason - *Thor: The Goddess of Thunder (Illus. by Dauterman, Russell)*
  y BL - v111 - i22 - August 1 2015 - p47(1) [501+]
Aaslestad, Katherine B. - *Revisiting Napoleon's Continental System: Local, Regional and European Experiences*
  HNet - Sept 2015 - pNA(NA) [501+]

Abadzis, Nick - *The Tenth Doctor: Revolutions of Terror (Illus. by Casagrande, Elena)*
  y LJ - v140 - i9 - May 15 2015 - p61(3) [501+]
  y SLJ - v61 - i9 - Sept 2015 - p174(1) [51-500]
Abasiyanik, Sait Faik - *A Useless Man: Selected Stories*
  TLS - i5860 - July 24 2015 - p27(1) [501+]
Abate-Shen, Cory - *Mouse Models of Cancer: A Laboratory Manual*
  QRB - v90 - i1 - March 2015 - p108(2) [501+]
Abawi, Atia - *The Secret Sky: A Novel of Forbidden Love in Afghanistan (Read by Delwari, Ariana). Audiobook Review*
  y SLJ - v61 - i2 - Feb 2015 - p51(1) [51-500]
The Secret Sky: A Novel of Forbidden Love in Afghanistan
  c HB Guide - v26 - i1 - Spring 2015 - p98(1) [51-500]
Abbas, Sadia - *At Freedoms Limit: Islam and the Postcolonical Predicament*
  IJMES - v47 - i2 - May 2015 - p392-393 [501+]
Abbenhuis, Maartje - *An Age of Neutrals: Great Power Politics, 1815-1914*
  AHR - v120 - i4 - Oct 2015 - p1547-1548 [501+]
  CEH - v48 - i2 - June 2015 - p225-237 [501+]
  HNet - Jan 2015 - pNA [501+]
Abbey, Tina Landsman - *The Smart Palate: Delicious Recipes for a Healthy Lifestyle*
  LJ - v140 - i3 - Feb 15 2015 - p122(4) [501+]
Abbot, Judi - *Train (Illus. by Abbot, Judi)*
  c HB Guide - v26 - i1 - Spring 2015 - p5(1) [51-500]
  c SLJ - v61 - i7 - July 2015 - p54(1) [51-500]
Abbott, Christmas - *The Badass Body Diet: The Breakthrough Diet and Workout for a Tight Booty, Sexy Abs, and Lean Legs*
  PW - v262 - i11 - March 16 2015 - p79(2) [51-500]
Abbott, David R. - *Alliance and Landscape: On Perry Mesa in the Fourteenth Century*
  Am Ant - v80 - i1 - Jan 2015 - p208(2) [501+]
Abbott, E.F. - *John Lincoln Clem: Civil War Drummer Boy (Illus. by Noble, Steve)*
  c PW - v262 - i45 - Nov 9 2015 - p59(1) [51-500]
Abbott, Elizabeth - *Dogs and Underdogs: Finding Happiness at Both Ends of the Leash*
  Mac - v128 - i17 - May 4 2015 - p54(1) [51-500]
Abbott, Fanny - *Des comptes d'apothicaires: Les epices dans la comptabilite de la Maison de Savoie*
  Specu - v90 - i4 - Oct 2015 - p1076-1077 [501+]
Abbott, Jeff - *The First Order*
  KR - Dec 1 2015 - pNA [51-500]
  PW - v262 - i47 - Nov 23 2015 - p49(1) [51-500]
Abbott, Martin L. - *The Art of Scalability: Scalable Web Architecture, Processes, and Organizations for the Modern Enterprise*
  Bwatch - Oct 2015 - pNA [501+]
Abbott, Patricia - *Concrete Angel*
  BL - v111 - i21 - July 1 2015 - p35(1) [51-500]
  KR - May 1 2015 - pNA [51-500]
  LJ - v140 - i9 - May 15 2015 - p68(1) [51-500]
Abbott, Simon - *Meet the Ancient Egyptians*
  c CH Bwatch - Jan 2015 - pNA [51-500]
Meet the Incredible Romans
  c CH Bwatch - Feb 2015 - pNA [51-500]
Sensational Senses
  c CH Bwatch - Jan 2015 - pNA [51-500]
Abbott, Tony - *Becca and the Prisoner's Cross (Read by DeLisle, Arielle). Audiobook Review*
  c SLJ - v61 - i9 - Sept 2015 - p58(1) [51-500]
Abdelrazaq, Leila - *Baddawi (Illus. by Abdelrazaq, Leila)*
  y BL - v111 - i16 - April 15 2015 - p40(1) [51-500]
  PW - v262 - i18 - May 4 2015 - p104(1) [51-500]
  y SLJ - v61 - i5 - May 2015 - p143(1) [51-500]

Abdoh, Salar - *Tehran Noir*
  WLT - v89 - i2 - March-April 2015 - p65(2) [501+]
Abdou, Angie - *Between*
  Can Lit - i224 - Spring 2015 - p101 [501+]
Abdul-Jabbar, Kareem - *Mycroft Holmes*
  BL - v111 - i21 - July 1 2015 - p38(1) [51-500]
  KR - July 15 2015 - pNA [51-500]
  LJ - v140 - i14 - Sept 1 2015 - p89(1) [51-500]
  NYTBR - Nov 1 2015 - p10(L) [501+]
  PW - v262 - i26 - June 29 2015 - p44(1) [51-500]
Stealing the Game
  c CCB-B - v68 - i8 - April 2015 - p386(2) [51-500]
  c HB Guide - v26 - i2 - Fall 2015 - p73(1) [51-500]
Abdullah, Shaila - *A Manual for Marco (Illus. by Tejpar, Iman)*
  c HB Guide - v26 - i2 - Fall 2015 - p24(1) [51-500]
Rani in Search of a Rainbow: A Natural Disaster Survival Tale (Illus. by Samaddar, Bijan)
  c CH Bwatch - July 2015 - pNA [501+]
Abdur-Rahman, Aliyyah I. - *Against the Closet: Black Political Longing and the Erotics of Race*
  MFSF - v61 - i1 - Spring 2015 - p186-189 [501+]
Abel, James - *Protocol Zero*
  PW - v262 - i26 - June 29 2015 - p47(1) [51-500]
White Plague (Read by Porter, Ray). Audiobook Review
  BL - v111 - i17 - May 1 2015 - p60(1) [51-500]
Abel, Jessica - *Out on the Wire: The Storytelling Secrets of the New Masters of Radio (Illus. by Abel, Jessica)*
  BL - v111 - i22 - August 1 2015 - p46(1) [51-500]
  KR - June 1 2015 - pNA [51-500]
  PW - v262 - i20 - May 18 2015 - p72(1) [51-500]
Abel, Mary Bilderback - *Maddy Patti and the Great Curiosity: Helping Children Understand Diabetes (Illus. by Dey, Lorraine)*
  c CH Bwatch - August 2015 - pNA [501+]
Abela, Andrew V. - *A Catechism for Business: Tough Ethical Questions and Insights from Catholic Teaching*
  Theol St - v76 - i3 - Sept 2015 - p650(2) [501+]
Abelard, Peter - *The Letter Collection of Peter Abelard and Heloise*
  HER - v130 - i545 - August 2015 - p960(2) [501+]
Abeles, Vicki - *Beyond Measure: Rescuing an Overscheduled, Overtested, Underestimated Generation*
  LJ - v140 - i16 - Oct 1 2015 - p90(2) [51-500]
  NYTBR - Dec 20 2015 - p13(L) [501+]
Abend, Gabriel - *Life Interrupted: Trafficking into Forced Labor in the United States*
  AJS - v120 - i6 - May 2015 - p1871(3) [501+]
Abercrombie, Joe - *Half a King (Read by Keating, John). Audiobook Review*
  BL - v111 - i9-10 - Jan 1 2015 - p112(1) [51-500]
Half a War (Read by Keating, John). Audiobook Review
  LJ - v140 - i19 - Nov 15 2015 - p51(1) [51-500]
Half a War
  BL - v111 - i22 - August 1 2015 - p42(2) [51-500]
  KR - June 15 2015 - pNA [51-500]
  PW - v262 - i26 - June 29 2015 - p51(1) [51-500]
Half the World (Read by Keating, John). Audiobook Review
  LJ - v140 - i10 - June 1 2015 - p58(1) [51-500]
Half the World
  y BL - v111 - i9-10 - Jan 1 2015 - p60(1) [51-500]
Abernathy, Penelope Muse - *Saving Community Journalism: The Path to Profitability*
  NYRB - v62 - i10 - June 4 2015 - p43(3) [501+]
Abernathy, Steven - *Unspoken Valor*
  SPBW - March 2015 - pNA [51-500]
Abernethy, Graeme - *The Iconography of Malcolm X*
  Am St - v54 - i2 - Summer 2015 - p9-20 [501+]
  J Am St - v49 - i1 - Feb 2015 - p215-216 [501+]

Aberth, John - *An Environmental History of the Middle Ages: The Crucible of Nature*
    Specu - v90 - i1 - Jan 2015 - p195-196 [501+]
Plagues in World History
    Six Ct J - v46 - i2 - Summer 2015 - p531-532 [501+]
Abiodun, Rowland - *Yoruba Art and Language: Seeking the African in African Art*
    Africa T - v62 - i1 - Fall 2015 - p141(6) [501+]
Abirached, Zeina - *I Remember Beirut (Illus. by Abirached, Zeina)*
    y HB Guide - v26 - i1 - Spring 2015 - p190(1) [51-500]
Ableman, Paul - *As Near as I Can Get*
    TLS - i5849 - May 8 2015 - p19(2) [501+]
Abnett, Dan - *Everybody Wants to Rule the World (Read by Full cast). Audiobook Review*
    LJ - v140 - i12 - July 1 2015 - p42(1) [51-500]
Guardians of the Galaxy: Rocket Raccoon and Groot Steal the Galaxy! (Read by Full cast). Audiobook Review
    BL - v111 - i13 - March 1 2015 - p69(1) [51-500]
    LJ - v140 - i6 - April 1 2015 - p47(1) [51-500]
Aboff, Marcie - *Do You Really Want to Meet ... ? (Illus. by Fabbri, Daniele)*
    c HB Guide - v26 - i1 - Spring 2015 - p163(1) [51-500]
Abonji, Melinda Nadj - *Fly Away, Pigeon*
    WLT - v89 - i3-4 - May-August 2015 - p115(3) [501+]
Abood, Maureen - *Rose Water and Orange Blossoms: Fresh and Classic Recipes from My Lebanese Kitchen*
    LJ - v140 - i12 - July 1 2015 - p106(1) [51-500]
    PW - v262 - i14 - April 6 2015 - p53(1) [51-500]
Abott, Tony - *The Serpent's Curse (Illus. by Perkins, Bill)*
    c HB Guide - v26 - i1 - Spring 2015 - p67(1) [51-500]
Aboul-Enein, Youssef - *The Secret War for the Middle East: The Influence of Axis and Allied Intelligence Operations during World War II*
    HNet - Feb 2015 - pNA [501+]
Aboul-Enein, Youssef H. - *Reconstructing a Shattered Egyptian Army: War Minister Gen. Mohamed Fawzi's Memoirs, 1967-1971*
    NWCR - v68 - i1 - Wntr 2015 - p145(2) [501+]
    Parameters - v45 - i2 - Summer 2015 - p151(2) [501+]
Aboulafia, David I. - *Snapshots from My Uneventful Life*
    KR - July 15 2015 - pNA [501+]
Aboulela, Leila - *The Kindness of Enemies*
    y BL - v112 - i5 - Nov 1 2015 - p27(1) [51-500]
    KR - Oct 1 2015 - pNA [51-500]
    LJ - v140 - i20 - Dec 1 2015 - p88(1) [51-500]
Abraham, Antoine J. - *The Eternal War: A Psychological Perspective on the Arab-Israeli Conflict*
    JTWS - v32 - i1 - Spring 2015 - p361(3) [501+]
Abraham, Daniel - *A Shadow in Summer (Read by Shah, Neil). Audiobook Review*
    LJ - v140 - i2 - Feb 1 2015 - p44(1) [51-500]
Abraham, David S. - *The Element of Power: Gadgets, Guns, and the Struggle for a Sustainable Future in the Rare Metal Age*
    NH - v123 - i8 - Oct 2015 - p46(1) [501+]
Abraham, Itty - *How India Became Territorial: Foreign Policy, Diaspora, Geopolitics*
    JAS - v74 - i3 - August 2015 - p772-773 [501+]
Abrahamian, Atossa Araxia - *The Cosmopolites: The Coming of the Global Citizen*
    KR - Sept 15 2015 - pNA [501+]
    LJ - v140 - i17 - Oct 15 2015 - p103(2) [51-500]
    PW - v262 - i37 - Sept 14 2015 - p55(1) [51-500]
Abrahams, Fred C. - *Modern Albania: From Dictatorship to Democracy in Europe*
    Spec - v328 - i9744 - May 30 2015 - p39(1) [501+]
Abrajano, Marisa - *White Backlash*
    KR - Jan 15 2015 - pNA [501+]
Abramovich, Alex - *Bullies: A Friendship*
    KR - Dec 15 2015 - pNA [501+]
    PW - v262 - i48 - Nov 30 2015 - p48(1) [51-500]
Abramovitz, Melissa - *Amazing Feats of Biological Engineering*
    y HB Guide - v26 - i1 - Spring 2015 - p172(1) [51-500]
COPD
    y VOYA - v38 - i2 - June 2015 - p88(1) [51-500]
How Are Digital Devices Impacting Society?
    BL - v111 - i21 - July 1 2015 - p54(1) [51-500]
Privacy in the Online World: Online Privacy and Health Care
    y VOYA - v37 - i6 - Feb 2015 - p90(1) [501+]

Abramowitz, Andy - *Thank You, Goodnight*
    BL - v111 - i18 - May 15 2015 - p25(2) [51-500]
    KR - April 15 2015 - pNA [51-500]
Abrams, J.J. - *S.*
    PSQ - v89 - i1 - Spring 2015 - p161(3) [501+]
Abrams, Jeanne E. - *Revolutionary Medicine: The Founding Fathers and Mothers in Sickness and in Health*
    Historian - v77 - i3 - Fall 2015 - p542(2) [501+]
    J Am St - v49 - i1 - Feb 2015 - p191-194 [501+]
Abrams, Laura S. - *Compassionate Confinement: A Year in the Life of Unit C*
    CS - v44 - i4 - July 2015 - p476-477 [501+]
Abrams, M.J. - *Chubby Wubbles: A Ferret's Tale*
    c CH Bwatch - Feb 2015 - pNA [51-500]
Abrams, Nancy Ellen - *A God That Could Be Real: Spirituality, Science, and the Future of Our Planet*
    PW - v262 - i6 - Feb 9 2015 - p62(2) [51-500]
    RVBW - June 2015 - pNA [51-500]
Abrams, Scott - *Time Sailors of Pizzolungo*
    c PW - v262 - i21 - May 25 2015 - p59(1) [51-500]
Abramsky, Sasha - *The House of Twenty Thousand Books*
    KR - May 1 2015 - pNA [501+]
    PW - v262 - i20 - May 18 2015 - p74(2) [51-500]
Abramson, Michael - *Gotta Go, Gotta Flow: Life, Love, and Lust on Chicago's South Side from the Seventies*
    BL - v112 - i5 - Nov 1 2015 - p21(1) [51-500]
Abrego, Leisy J. - *Sacrificing Families: Navigating Laws, Labor, and Love Across Borders*
    AJS - v120 - i6 - May 2015 - p1862(3) [501+]
    HAHR - v95 - i1 - Feb 2015 - p192-193 [501+]
Sacrificing Families: Negotiating Laws, Labor, and Love Across Borders
    CS - v44 - i5 - Sept 2015 - p622-623 [501+]
Abschlusstagung des DFG-Netzwerks "ZeitenWelten. Zur Verschrankung von Weltdeutung und Zeitwahrnehmung im Fruhen und Hohen Mittelalter"
    HNet - June 2015 - pNA [501+]
Abse, Dannie - *Ask the Moon: New and Collected Poems 1948-2014*
    NS - v144 - i5245 - Jan 16 2015 - p47(1) [51-500]
    TLS - i5874 - Oct 30 2015 - p22(1) [51-500]
Absher, Amy - *The Black Musician and the White City: Race and Music in Chicago, 1900-1967*
    JAH - v102 - i1 - June 2015 - p280-280 [501+]
Abu-Jamal, Mumia - *Writing on the Wall*
    KR - March 15 2015 - pNA [501+]
Abu Saif, Atef - *The Drone Eats With Me: Diaries from a City Under Fire*
    NS - v144 - i5269 - July 3 2015 - p46(3) [501+]
Abulafia, David - *The Discovery of Mankind: Atlantic Encounters in the Age of Columbus*
    TimHES - i2211 - July 9 2015 - p47(1) [501+]
Abulhawa, Susan - *The Blue Between Sky and Water*
    BL - v112 - i1 - Sept 1 2015 - p40(1) [51-500]
    KR - July 1 2015 - pNA [501+]
    LJ - v140 - i15 - Sept 15 2015 - p65(1) [51-500]
    PW - v262 - i27 - July 6 2015 - p43(2) [51-500]
Acampora, Lauren - *The Wonder Garden*
    LJ - v140 - i6 - April 1 2015 - p87(1) [51-500]
    BL - v111 - i13 - March 1 2015 - p21(1) [51-500]
    KR - March 1 2015 - pNA [51-500]
    LJ - v140 - i10 - June 1 2015 - p139(1) [51-500]
    NYTBR - June 7 2015 - p19(L) [501+]
    PW - v262 - i11 - March 16 2015 - p58(1) [51-500]
Accardi, Maria T. - *Feminist Pedagogy for Library Instruction*
    R&USQ - v54 - i3 - Spring 2015 - p53(1) [501+]
Ace, Cathy - *The Case of the Dotty Dowager*
    BL - v111 - i21 - July 1 2015 - p35(1) [51-500]
    KR - May 15 2015 - pNA [51-500]
    PW - v262 - i21 - May 25 2015 - p38(1) [51-500]
The Case of the Missing Morris Dancer
    KR - Dec 1 2015 - pNA [51-500]
    PW - v262 - i50 - Dec 7 2015 - p72(1) [51-500]
Acevedo, Chantel - *The Distant Marvels*
    BL - v111 - i13 - March 1 2015 - p27(1) [51-500]
    BL - v111 - i16 - April 15 2015 - p34(1) [51-500]
    y Ent W - i1358 - April 10 2015 - p66(1) [51-500]
    KR - March 1 2015 - pNA [51-500]
    NYTBR - May 24 2015 - p20(L) [501+]
    WLT - v89 - i6 - Nov-Dec 2015 - p59(1) [51-500]
Acevedo, Silvia - *God Awful Loser*
    y SLJ - v61 - i7 - July 2015 - p85(1) [51-500]
Aceves, Maria Teresa Fernandez - *Mujeres en el cambio social en el siglo XX mexicano*
    HAHR - v95 - i2 - May 2015 - p365-366 [501+]
Acey, Denver - *The Quantum Deception*
    LJ - v140 - i6 - April 1 2015 - p66(4) [501+]
Acharya, Amitav - *The End of American World Order*
    For Aff - v94 - i1 - Jan-Feb 2015 - pNA [501+]

Acheson, Hugh - *The Broad Fork: Recipes for the Wide World of Vegetables and Fruits*
    Bwatch - August 2015 - pNA [501+]
Acheson, Katherine - *Visual Rhetoric and Early Modern English Literature*
    Ren Q - v68 - i3 - Fall 2015 - p1132-1134 [501+]
Acioli, Socorro - *The Head of the Saint*
    BL - v112 - i6 - Nov 15 2015 - p49(1) [51-500]
Acitelli, Tom - *American Wine: A Coming of Age Story*
    KR - July 1 2015 - pNA [501+]
    NYTBR - Dec 6 2015 - p86(L) [501+]
Ackam, Taner - *From Empire to Republic: Turkish Nationalism and the Armenian Genocide*
    HT - v65 - i7 - July 2015 - p56(2) [501+]
The Shameful Act: The Armenian Genocide and the Question of Turkish Responsibility
    HT - v65 - i7 - July 2015 - p56(2) [501+]
The Young Turks' Crime Against Humanity: The Armenian Genocide and the Ethnic Cleansing in the Ottoman Empire
    HT - v65 - i7 - July 2015 - p56(2) [501+]
Acker, Kathy - *I'm Very into You: Correspondence 1995-1996*
    PW - v262 - i4 - Jan 26 2015 - p160(2) [51-500]
Acker, Paul - *Revisiting the Poetic Edda: Essays on Old Norse Heroic Legend*
    JEGP - v114 - i1 - Jan 2015 - p117(5) [501+]
Ackerman, Bruce - *We the People, vol. 3: The Civil Rights Revolution*
    Ethics - v125 - i4 - July 2015 - p1178(7) [501+]
    JAH - v102 - i2 - Sept 2015 - p618-619 [501+]
    JIH - v46 - i1 - Summer 2015 - p90-104 [501+]
Ackerman, Diane - *The Human Age: The World Shaped By Us (Read by Caruso, Barbara). Audiobook Review*
    BL - v111 - i12 - Feb 15 2015 - p104(1) [51-500]
    BL - v112 - i7 - Dec 1 2015 - p71(1) [51-500]
The Human Age: The World Shaped By Us
    Bwatch - Nov 2015 - pNA [51-500]
    NYTBR - Oct 11 2015 - p28(L) [501+]
Ackerman, Elliot - *Green on Blue*
    CSM - March 27 2015 - pNA [501+]
    HM - v330 - i1977 - Feb 2015 - p77(3) [501+]
    Nat Post - v17 - i101 - Feb 28 2015 - pWP4(1) [501+]
    NYT - Feb 16 2015 - pC1(L) [501+]
    NYTBR - March 1 2015 - p13(L) [501+]
    TLS - i5854 - June 12 2015 - p19(2) [501+]
Ackerman-Lieberman, Phillip I. - *The Business of Identity: Jews, Muslims, and Economic Life in Medieval Egypt*
    AHR - v120 - i1 - Feb 2015 - p367-368 [501+]
    JEH - v75 - i2 - June 2015 - p610-611 [501+]
    JEH - v75 - i3 - Sept 2015 - p941-944 [501+]
Ackerman, Peter - *The Lonely Typewriter (Illus. by Dalton, Max)*
    c HB Guide - v26 - i1 - Spring 2015 - p20(1) [51-500]
Ackroyd, Peter - *Alfred Hitchcock*
    Lon R Bks - v37 - i11 - June 4 2015 - p19(4) [501+]
    NS - v144 - i5258 - April 17 2015 - p60(2) [501+]
    Si & So - v25 - i5 - May 2015 - p104(1) [501+]
    Spec - v327 - i9738 - April 18 2015 - p45(1) [501+]
Civil War
    TLS - i5860 - July 24 2015 - p24(1) [501+]
Rebellion: The History of England from James I to the Glorious Revolution (Read by Chafer, Clive). Audiobook Review
    LJ - v140 - i9 - May 15 2015 - p44(1) [51-500]
Rebellion: The History of England from James I to the Glorious Revolution
    NYTBR - Jan 25 2015 - p26(L) [501+]
Wilkie Collins: A Brief Life
    KR - Sept 15 2015 - pNA [501+]
    LJ - v140 - i11 - June 15 2015 - p90(1) [51-500]
    NYTBR - Nov 1 2015 - p15(L) [501+]
    PW - v262 - i20 - May 18 2015 - p73(1) [51-500]
Acosta-Hughes, Benjamin - *Callimachus in Context: From Plato to the Augustan Poets*
    AJP - v136 - i2 - Summer 2015 - p365-368 [501+]
Acosta, Katie L. - *Amigas y Amantes: Sexually Nonconforming Latinas Negotiate Family*
    CS - v44 - i6 - Nov 2015 - p870(1) [501+]
Acquista, Angelo - *The Mediterranean Family Table: 125 Simple, Everyday Recipes Made with the Most Delicious and Healthiest Food on Earth*
    PW - v262 - i38 - Sept 21 2015 - p67(2) [51-500]
Acton, Lesley - *Growing Space: A History of the Allotment Movement*
    TLS - i5861 - July 31 2015 - p12(1) [501+]

Acton, Sara - *As Big as You*
  c Magpies - v30 - i4 - Sept 2015 - p27(1) [501+]
Poppy Cat
  c Res Links - v21 - i1 - Oct 2015 - p1(1) [51-500]
Acuff, Jon - *Do Over: Rescue Monday, Reinvent Your Work, and Never Get Stuck*
  BL - v111 - i13 - March 1 2015 - p9(1) [51-500]
  LJ - v140 - i5 - March 15 2015 - p117(1) [501+]
  Par - v90 - i4 - April 2015 - p16(1) [501+]
  PW - v262 - i8 - Feb 23 2015 - p65(1) [51-500]
Acurio, Gatson - *Peru: The Cookbook*
  PW - v262 - i14 - April 6 2015 - p52(2) [51-500]
Aczel, Amir - *Finding Zero: A Mathematician's Odyssey to Uncover the Origins of Numbers*
  NYT - April 21 2015 - pD3(L) [501+]
Aczel, Amir D. - *Finding Zero: A Mathematician's Odyssey to Uncover the Origins of Numbers*
  Mac - v128 - i4 - Feb 2 2015 - p61(1) [51-500]
  Nature - v518 - i7537 - Feb 5 2015 - p33(1) [51-500]
Ada, Alma - *Island Treasures: Growing Up in Cuba (Illus. by Martorell, Antonio)*
  c KR - May 1 2015 - pNA [51-500]
Ada, Alma Flor - *Island Treasures: Growing Up in Cuba (Illus. by Martorell, Antonio)*
  c SLJ - v61 - i6 - June 2015 - p139(1) [51-500]
Adair, Marina - *Need You for Always*
  PW - v262 - i35 - August 31 2015 - p72(1) [51-500]
A Taste of Sugar
  PW - v262 - i29 - July 20 2015 - p177(1) [51-500]
Adam, Alfons - *"Die Arbeiterfrage soll mit Hilfe von KZ-Haftlingen Gelost Werden": Zwangsarbeit in KZ-Aussenlagern auf dem Gebiet der Heutigen Tschechischen Republik*
  HNet - March 2015 - pNA [501+]
Adam, Christopher S. - *Zambia: Building Prosperity from Resource Wealth*
  TLS - i5840 - March 6 2015 - p25(1) [501+]
Adam, David - *The Man Who Couldn't Stop: OCD and the True Story of a Life Lost in Thought*
  Mac - v128 - i3 - Jan 26 2015 - p57(1) [501+]
  BooChiTr - Feb 7 2015 - p10(1) [501+]
  NYTBR - Feb 1 2015 - p10(L) [501+]
Adam, Heribert - *Imagined Liberation: Xenophobia, Citizenship, and Identity in South Africa, Germany, and Canada*
  ERS - v38 - i8 - August 2015 - p1434(2) [501+]
Adam, Jens - *Formationen des Politischen: Anthropologie politischer Felder*
  HNet - Sept 2015 - pNA [501+]
Adam, Ryan - *New Orleans Mother Goose (Illus. by Gentry, Marita)*
  c HB Guide - v26 - i1 - Spring 2015 - p188(1) [51-500]
Adamo, Philip C. - *New Monks in Old Habits: The Formation of the Caulite Monastic Order, 1193-1267*
  CHR - v101 - i4 - Autumn 2015 - p916(2) [501+]
Adamov, Bob - *Missing*
  SPBW - May 2015 - pNA [51-500]
Adams, Alane - *The Red Sun*
  y SLJ - v61 - i9 - Sept 2015 - p156(1) [51-500]
Adams, Birch - *The Metaphor Deception*
  KR - Feb 15 2015 - pNA [51-500]
Adams, Bluford - *Old and New New Englanders: Immigration and Regional Identity in the Gilded Age*
  AHR - v120 - i1 - Feb 2015 - p256-257 [501+]
  J Am St - v49 - i1 - Feb 2015 - p197-198 [501+]
  JAH - v102 - i2 - Sept 2015 - p573-573 [501+]
Adams, C.T. - *The Exile*
  KR - Jan 15 2015 - pNA [51-500]
Adams, Carolyn Lee - *Ruthless*
  y KR - April 15 2015 - pNA [51-500]
  y SLJ - v61 - i5 - May 2015 - p116(2) [51-500]
  y VOYA - v38 - i2 - June 2015 - p52(1) [51-500]
Adams, Carolyn T. - *From the Outside In: Suburban Elites, Third-Sector Organizations, and the Reshaping of Philadelphia*
  HNet - May 2015 - pNA [501+]
From the Outside In: Suburban Elites, Third Sector Organizations, and the Reshaping of Philadelphia
  Soc Ser R - v89 - i3 - Sept 2015 - p564(5) [501+]
Adams, Cate - *Fireflies at Twilight: Letters from Pat Adams*
  SPBW - Feb 2015 - pNA [51-500]
Adams, Cheryll M. - *A Teacher's Guide to Using the Next Generation Science Standards with Gifted and Advanced Learners*
  Sci & Ch - v52 - i8 - April-May 2015 - p74 [501+]
  Sci Teach - v82 - i2 - Feb 2015 - p66 [51-500]

Adams, Christopher - *Metis in Canada: History, Identity, Law and Politics*
  Can Lit - i224 - Spring 2015 - p103 [501+]
Adams, Christopher Robin - *Spanish Cedar*
  KR - Oct 15 2015 - pNA [501+]
Adams, Clint - *Evangeline*
  KR - Oct 15 2015 - pNA [501+]
Adams, Colin - *Zombies and Calculus*
  WLT - v89 - i3-4 - May-August 2015 - p125(3) [501+]
Adams, Dennis - *Teaching Math, Science, and Technology in Schools Today: Guidelines for Engaging Both Eager and Reluctant Learners*
  TC Math - v21 - i9 - May 2015 - p567(1) [501+]
Adams, Edward - *The Earliest Christian Meeting Places: Almost Exclusively Houses?*
  BTB - v45 - i3 - August 2015 - p185(2) [501+]
Adams, Ellery - *Murder in the Paperback Parlor*
  BL - v111 - i22 - August 1 2015 - p35(1) [51-500]
Adams, Henry - *Thomas Hart Benton: Discoveries and Interpretations*
  LJ - v140 - i20 - Dec 1 2015 - p98(1) [51-500]
Adams, Jack - *Nequa, 3d ed.*
  SPBW - Oct 2015 - pNA [51-500]
Adams, Jad - *Women and the Vote: A World History*
  HNet - Oct 2015 - pNA [501+]
  HT - v65 - i2 - Feb 2015 - p61(1) [501+]
Adams, Jane A. - *Forgotten Voices*
  BL - v112 - i1 - Sept 1 2015 - p46(1) [51-500]
  PW - v262 - i33 - August 17 2015 - p54(1) [51-500]
A Murderous Mind
  KR - Jan 1 2016 - pNA [51-500]
Adams, Jocelyn Delk - *Grandbaby Cakes: Modern Recipes, Vintage Charm, Soulful Memories*
  LJ - v140 - i17 - Oct 15 2015 - p108(1) [51-500]
Adams, John Joseph - *Loosed upon the World*
  PW - v262 - i24 - June 15 2015 - p67(2) [51-500]
  Analog - v135 - i12 - Dec 2015 - p105(2) [51-500]
Adams, Jonathan - *Lessons in Contempt: Poul Raeff's Translation and Publication in 1516 of Johannes Pfefferkorn's The Confession of the Jews*
  JEGP - v114 - i1 - Jan 2015 - p130(3) [501+]
A Maritime Archaeology of Ships: Innovation and Social Change in Medieval and Early Modern Europe
  Med R - Sept 2015 - pNA [501+]
  Ren Q - v68 - i2 - Summer 2015 - p696-698 [501+]
Adams, Jonathan S. - *Nature's Fortune: How Business and Society Thrive by Investing in Nature*
  RVBW - Nov 2015 - pNA [501+]
Adams, Leigh - *Hostile Witness*
  KR - Dec 15 2015 - pNA [51-500]
  PW - v262 - i52 - Dec 21 2015 - p134(2) [51-500]
Adams, Louisa Catherine - *A Traveled First Lady: Writings of Louisa Catherine Adams*
  NEQ - v88 - i1 - March 2015 - p172-174 [501+]
Adams, Mack - *Missed Approach*
  PW - v262 - i15 - April 13 2015 - p60(1) [51-500]
Adams, Mark - *Bishops on the Border: Pastoral Responses to Immigration*
  Theol St - v76 - i4 - Dec 2015 - p899(2) [501+]
Meet Me in Atlantis: My Obsessive Quest to Find the Sunken City (Read by Garman, Andrew). Audiobook Review
  BL - v112 - i2 - Sept 15 2015 - p78(1) [51-500]
  LJ - v140 - i14 - Sept 1 2015 - p68(1) [51-500]
Meet Me in Atlantis: My Obsessive Quest to Find the Sunken City
  BL - v111 - i14 - March 15 2015 - p33(1) [51-500]
  Ent W - i1358 - April 10 2015 - p67(1) [501+]
  LJ - v140 - i2 - Feb 1 2015 - p93(1) [51-500]
  Mac - v128 - i9 - March 9 2015 - p54(2) [501+]
  NYTBR - May 31 2015 - p32(L) [501+]
  PW - v262 - i2 - Jan 12 2015 - p52(1) [51-500]
Adams, Max - *The Wisdom of Trees*
  TLS - i5844 - April 3 2015 - p30(1) [501+]
Adams, Michael C.C. - *Living Hell: The Dark Side of the Civil War*
  AHR - v120 - i2 - April 2015 - p628-629 [501+]
Adams, Nicholas - *Gunnar Aslund's Gothenburg: The Transformation of Public Architecture in Interwar Europe*
  TLS - i5847 - April 24 2015 - p26(1) [501+]
Adams, Noel - *Bright Lights in the Dark Ages: The Thaw Collection of Early Medieval Ornaments*
  Specu - v90 - i2 - April 2015 - p483-485 [501+]
Adams, Pete - *A Barrow Boy's Cadenza*
  KR - Dec 1 2015 - pNA [501+]
Adams, Peter - *Politics, Faith, and the Making of American Judaism*
  AHR - v120 - i2 - April 2015 - p623-624 [501+]

Adams, Rick A. - *Into the Night: Tales of Nocturnal Wildlife Expeditions*
  QRB - v90 - i2 - June 2015 - p241(2) [501+]
Adams, Robert - *Langland and the Rokele Family: The Gentry Background to Piers Plowman*
  JEGP - v114 - i3 - July 2015 - p456(3) [501+]
  MLR - v110 - i3 - July 2015 - p812-813 [501+]
Adams, Samuel L. - *Social and Economic Life in Second Temple Judea*
  CC - v132 - i7 - April 1 2015 - p39(3) [501+]
  Intpr - v69 - i4 - Oct 2015 - p473(3) [501+]
Adams, Sean Patrick - *Home Fires: How Americans Kept Warm in the 19th Century*
  NEQ - v88 - i1 - March 2015 - p177-179 [501+]
  T&C - v56 - i4 - Oct 2015 - p980-981 [501+]
Adams, Thomas J. - *Working in the Big Easy: The History and Politics of Labor in New Orleans*
  JAH - v102 - i2 - Sept 2015 - p522-523 [501+]
Adams, Tracy - *Christine de Pizan and the Fight for France*
  FS - v69 - i3 - July 2015 - p382(1) [501+]
Adams, Vincanne - *Markets of Sorrow, Labors of Faith: New Orleans in the Wake of Katrina*
  CS - v44 - i1 - Jan 2015 - p29-30 [501+]
Medicine between Science and Religion: Explorations on Tibetan Grounds
  MAQ - v29 - i1 - March 2015 - pB46-B48 [501+]
Adamson, Heather - *Ancient Egypt: An Interactive History Adventure*
  c Sch Lib - v63 - i3 - Autumn 2015 - p172(1) [51-500]
Adamson, Joni - *American Studies, Ecocriticism, and Citizenship: Thinking and Acting in the Local and Global Commons*
  Am Q - v67 - i1 - March 2015 - p267-276 [501+]
Adamson, Peter - *Philosophy in the Hellenistic and Roman Worlds*
  LJ - v140 - i15 - Sept 15 2015 - p80(1) [51-500]
Adamson, Thomas K. - *Learning about South America*
  c BL - v112 - i3 - Oct 1 2015 - p54(1) [51-500]
Tae Kwon Do
  c HB Guide - v26 - i2 - Fall 2015 - p196(1) [51-500]
  c SLJ - v61 - i6 - June 2015 - p139(1) [51-500]
World War II
  c Teach Lib - v42 - i4 - April 2015 - p9(1) [51-500]
Aday, Ronald H. - *Women Aging in Prison: A Neglected Population in the Correctional System*
  CS - v44 - i3 - May 2015 - p330-332 [501+]
Adcock, Fleur - *The Land Ballot*
  Sch Lib - v63 - i3 - Autumn 2015 - p177(1) [51-500]
  TLS - i5872 - Oct 16 2015 - p22(1) [501+]
Adcock, Phillip - *Master Your Brain: Training Your Mind for Success in Life*
  RVBW - Oct 2015 - pNA [51-500]
Addario, Lynsey - *It's What I Do: A Photographer's Life of Love and War*
  CJR - v53 - i5 - Jan-Feb 2015 - p55(5) [501+]
  CSM - Feb 19 2015 - pNA [501+]
  CSM - June 3 2015 - pNA [501+]
  Ent W - i1351 - Feb 20 2015 - p62(2) [501+]
  NYTBR - Feb 8 2015 - p11(L) [501+]
  UtneADi - i187 - Summer 2015 - p92(1) [501+]
Adderson, Caroline - *Eat, Leo! Eat! (Illus. by Bisaillon, Josee)*
  c HB Guide - v26 - i2 - Fall 2015 - p24(1) [51-500]
  c KR - Jan 15 2015 - pNA [51-500]
  c Res Links - v21 - i1 - Oct 2015 - p1(2) [51-500]
  c SLJ - v61 - i8 - August 2015 - p63(1) [51-500]
I Love You, One to Ten (Illus. by Leist, Christina)
  c KR - July 15 2015 - pNA [51-500]
  c SLJ - v61 - i10 - Oct 2015 - p70(1) [51-500]
Jasper John Dooley: Lost and Found (Illus. by Shiell, Mike)
  c Res Links - v21 - i1 - Oct 2015 - p12(1) [51-500]
Jasper John Dooley: You're in Trouble (Illus. by Clanton, Ben)
  c HB Guide - v26 - i2 - Fall 2015 - p63(1) [51-500]
  Nat Post - v17 - i153 - May 2 2015 - pWP6(1) [501+]
  c Res Links - v20 - i5 - June 2015 - p10(1) [51-500]
Norman, Speak! (Illus. by Leng, Qin)
  c Bkbird - v53 - i3 - Summer 2015 - p101(1) [501+]
A Simple Case of Angels
  c HB Guide - v26 - i1 - Spring 2015 - p67(1) [51-500]
Addis, Evelyn - *Monday Morning Leadership (Illus. by Loughmiller, Matt)*
  c CH Bwatch - July 2015 - pNA [51-500]

Addison, Corban - *The Tears of Dark Water*
    KR - August 15 2015 - pNA [501+]
    PW - v262 - i32 - August 10 2015 - p37(1) [51-500]
Addison, Paul - *Churchill on the Home Front, 1900-55*
    HT - v65 - i1 - Jan 2015 - p56(2) [501+]
Addyman, Thomas - *The Medieval Kirk, Cemetery and Hospice at Kirk Ness, North Berwick: The Scottish Seabird Centre Excavations 1999-2006*
    Specu - v90 - i4 - Oct 2015 - p1077-1078 [501+]
Adebanwi, Wale - *Yoruba Elites and Ethnics Politics in Nigeria: Obafemi Awolowo and Corporate Agency*
    IJAHS - v48 - i1 - Wntr 2015 - p126-128 [501+]
Adelman, Jeremy - *Worldly Philosopher: The Odyssey of Albert O. Hirschman*
    JEH - v75 - i1 - March 2015 - p267-268 [501+]
    JMH - v87 - i2 - June 2015 - p419(3) [501+]
    NYTBR - Feb 15 2015 - p28(L) [501+]
    TimHES - i2211 - July 9 2015 - p45(1) [501+]
Adelman, Michelle - *Piece of Mind*
    BL - v112 - i4 - Oct 15 2015 - p33(2) [51-500]
    KR - Nov 1 2015 - pNA [51-500]
    LJ - v140 - i19 - Nov 15 2015 - p74(1) [51-500]
    PW - v262 - i50 - Dec 7 2015 - p64(1) [51-500]
Aderin-Pocock, Maggie - *The Planets: The Definitive Visual Guide to Our Solar System*
    y VOYA - v37 - i6 - Feb 2015 - p86(1) [51-500]
Adesokan, Akin - *Postcolonial Artists and Global Aesthetics*
    Africa T - v61 - i4 - Summer 2015 - p110(2) [501+]
Adib-Moghaddam, Arshin - *On the Arab Revolts and the Iranian Revolution: Power and Resistance Today*
    IJMES - v47 - i4 - Nov 2015 - p849-850 [501+]
Adichie, Chimamanda Ngozi - *Half of a Yellow Sun: A Novel*
    CSM - Jan 29 2015 - pNA [51-500]
We Should All Be Feminists
    Prog - v79 - i4 - April 2015 - p41(3) [501+]
Adida, Claire - *Immigrant Exclusion and Insecurity in Africa: Coethnic Strangers*
    IJAHS - v48 - i1 - Wntr 2015 - p128-130 [501+]
Adler, Charles L. - *Wizards, Aliens, and Starships: Physics and Math in Science Fiction*
    SFS - v42 - i1 - March 2015 - p163-164 [501+]
Adler, Charlie - *Daredevil Duck (Illus. by Adler, Charlie)*
    c CH Bwatch - Feb 2015 - pNA [51-500]
Adler, Dahlia - *Just Visiting*
    y VOYA - v38 - i5 - Dec 2015 - p52(1) [51-500]
Under the Lights
    y BL - v111 - i22 - August 1 2015 - p60(2) [51-500]
    y SLJ - v61 - i8 - August 2015 - p100(1) [51-500]
Adler, David A. - *Colonel Theodore Roosevelt*
    c HB Guide - v26 - i1 - Spring 2015 - p190(1) [51-500]
Danny's Doodles: The Squirting Donuts
    c HB Guide - v26 - i1 - Spring 2015 - p56(1) [51-500]
Don't Throw It to Mo! (Illus. by Ricks, Sam)
    c BL - v111 - i18 - May 15 2015 - p57(1) [51-500]
    c KR - March 15 2015 - pNA [51-500]
    c SLJ - v61 - i4 - April 2015 - p139(1) [51-500]
Get a Hit, Mo! (Illus. by Ricks, Sam)
    c KR - Dec 1 2015 - pNA [51-500]
    c SLJ - v61 - i12 - Dec 2015 - p98(1) [51-500]
Hanukkah Cookies with Sprinkles (Illus. by Ebbeler, Jeffrey)
    c CH Bwatch - August 2015 - pNA [501+]
    c KR - Sept 1 2015 - pNA [51-500]
    c PW - v262 - i37 - Sept 14 2015 - p70(1) [51-500]
    c SLJ - v61 - i10 - Oct 2015 - p60(2) [51-500]
Place Value (Illus. by Miller, Edward)
    c KR - Dec 1 2015 - pNA [51-500]
Prices! Prices! Prices! Why They Go Up and Down (Illus. by Miller, Edward)
    c BL - v111 - i17 - May 1 2015 - p84(1) [51-500]
    c HB Guide - v26 - i2 - Fall 2015 - p152(1) [51-500]
Prices! Prices! Prices!: Why They Go Up and Down (Illus. by Miller, Edward)
    KR - Feb 1 2015 - pNA [51-500]
    SLJ - v61 - i3 - March 2015 - p168(1) [51-500]
Simple Machines: Wheels, Levers, and Pulleys (Illus. by Raff, Anna)
    c BL - v111 - i16 - April 15 2015 - p44(1) [51-500]
    c HB Guide - v26 - i2 - Fall 2015 - p165(1) [51-500]
    c KR - March 1 2015 - pNA [51-500]
    SLJ - v61 - i3 - March 2015 - p168(1) [51-500]
Triangles (Illus. by Miller, Edward)
    c BL - v111 - i9-10 - Jan 1 2015 - pS4(8) [501+]
    c HB - v91 - i1 - Jan-Feb 2015 - p106(2) [501+]
Adler, Elizabeth - *One Way or Another*
    BL - v111 - i19-20 - June 1 2015 - p56(2) [51-500]
    LJ - v140 - i2 - Feb 1 2015 - p54(5) [501+]
    PW - v262 - i20 - May 18 2015 - p64(2) [51-500]
Adler, Frederick R. - *Urban Ecosystems: Ecological Principles for the Built Environment*
    QRB - v90 - i1 - March 2015 - p83(1) [51-500]
Adler, Irene - *The Soprano's Last Song (Illus. by Bruno, Iacopo)*
    c HB Guide - v26 - i1 - Spring 2015 - p67(1) [51-500]
Adler, Jennifer - *Passionate Nutrition: A Guide to Using Food as Medicine from a Nutritionist Who Healed Herself from the Inside Out*
    Bwatch - March 2015 - pNA [51-500]
Adler, Karen - *BBQ Bistro: Simple, Sophisticated French Recipes for Your Grill*
    PW - v262 - i16 - April 20 2015 - p71(1) [51-500]
Adler-Olsen, Jussi - *The Alphabet House (Read by Malcolm, Graeme). Audiobook Review*
    BL - v111 - i17 - May 1 2015 - p57(1) [51-500]
    LJ - v140 - i10 - June 1 2015 - p58(1) [51-500]
The Hanging Girl
    BL - v112 - i1 - Sept 1 2015 - p47(1) [51-500]
    LJ - v140 - i6 - April 1 2015 - p58(4) [501+]
    PW - v262 - i27 - July 6 2015 - p46(1) [51-500]
The Marco Effect
    RVBW - May 2015 - pNA [51-500]
Adler, Renata - *After the Tall Timber: Collected Nonfiction*
    Nat Post - v17 - i169 - May 23 2015 - pWP4(1) [501+]
    Nation - v300 - i24 - June 15 2015 - p43(3) [501+]
    NYTBR - May 17 2015 - p18(L) [501+]
    Spec - v328 - i9749 - July 4 2015 - p40(2) [501+]
    BL - v111 - i13 - March 1 2015 - p4(1) [51-500]
    KR - Jan 15 2015 - pNA [501+]
    NYT - April 24 2015 - pC23(L) [501+]
    PW - v262 - i3 - Jan 19 2015 - p69(1) [51-500]
    New R - v246 - i5 - June 2015 - p78(2) [501+]
    TLS - i5854 - June 12 2015 - p26(1) [501+]
Adler, Warren - *Treadmill*
    PW - v262 - i23 - June 8 2015 - p41(1) [51-500]
Adler, William - *The Cambridge History of Religions in the Ancient World, vol. 2: From the Hellenistic Age to Late Antiquity*
    Class R - v65 - i2 - Oct 2015 - p489-492 [501+]
Adley, Angel - *Growing Up without My Daddy (Illus. by Shorter, Susan)*
    c CH Bwatch - July 2015 - pNA [501+]
Adlington, Lucy - *Stitches in Time: The Story of the Clothes We Wear*
    Spec - v329 - i9772 - Dec 12 2015 - p78(2) [501+]
Adluri, Vishwa - *The Nay Science: A History of German Indology*
    AHR - v120 - i3 - June 2015 - p1132-1133 [501+]
    CEH - v48 - i3 - Sept 2015 - p432-434 [501+]
Adogame, Afe - *Engaging the World: Christian Communities in Contemporary Global Societies*
    IBMR - v39 - i3 - July 2015 - p158(2) [501+]
Adornetto, Alexandra - *Ghost House*
    y HB Guide - v26 - i1 - Spring 2015 - p98(1) [51-500]
Adrian, Chris - *The New World*
    KR - April 15 2015 - pNA [501+]
    LJ - v140 - i9 - May 15 2015 - p68(1) [51-500]
    New Sci - v227 - i3032 - August 1 2015 - p44(2) [501+]
    NYT - May 28 2015 - pC6(L) [501+]
    NYTBR - June 7 2015 - p29(L) [501+]
Adrian, Emily - *Like It Never Happened*
    y BL - v111 - i17 - May 1 2015 - p91(2) [501+]
    y CCB-B - v69 - i2 - Oct 2015 - p74(1) [51-500]
    y HB Guide - v26 - i2 - Fall 2015 - p108(1) [51-500]
    y KR - March 15 2015 - pNA [51-500]
    c Nat Post - v17 - i200 - June 27 2015 - pWP5(1) [501+]
    y PW - v262 - i17 - April 27 2015 - p77(2) [51-500]
    y VOYA - v38 - i1 - April 2015 - p52(1) [51-500]
Adrian, Robert - *Target Citadel*
    SPBW - Oct 2015 - pNA [51-500]
Adrian, Susan - *Tunnel Vision*
    y CCB-B - v68 - i7 - March 2015 - p344(1) [51-500]
    y HB Guide - v26 - i2 - Fall 2015 - p108(1) [51-500]
    y VOYA - v37 - i6 - Feb 2015 - p71(1) [51-500]
Aebischer, Pascale - *Screening Early Modern Drama: Beyond Shakespeare*
    Ren Q - v68 - i1 - Spring 2015 - p404-406 [501+]
Afary, Janet - *Sexual Politics in Modern Iran*
    JWH - v27 - i2 - Summer 2015 - p182(12) [501+]
Affelt, Amy - *The Accidental Data Scientist*
    LR - v64 - i4-5 - April-May 2015 - p405-406 [501+]
    y VOYA - v38 - i1 - April 2015 - p90(1) [51-500]
Affield, Wendell - *Muddy Jungle Rivers: A River Assault Boat Cox'n's Memory Journey of His War in Vietnam and Return Home*
    PW - v262 - i13 - March 30 2015 - p72(1) [51-500]
Afsaruddin, Asma - *Striving in the Path of God: Jihad and Martyrdom in Islamic Thought*
    JAAR - v83 - i3 - Sept 2015 - p881-883 [501+]
Afsharirad, David - *The Year's Best Military SF and Space Opera*
    Analog - v135 - i11 - Nov 2015 - p105(1) [501+]
    PW - v262 - i15 - April 13 2015 - p61(1) [51-500]
Afzal, Rafique - *A History of the All-India Muslim League, 1906-1947*
    HER - v130 - i545 - August 2015 - p1048(3) [501+]
Agamben, Giorgio - *The Highest Poverty: Monastic Rules and Form-of-Life*
    JR - v95 - i4 - Oct 2015 - p539(2) [501+]
Agar, Nicholas - *The Sceptical Optimist: Why Technology Isn't the Answer to Everything*
    LJ - v140 - i14 - Sept 1 2015 - p134(1) [51-500]
Truly Human Enhancement: A Philosophical Defense of Limits
    QRB - v90 - i4 - Dec 2015 - p425(1) [501+]
Agard, John - *Book: My Autobiography (Illus. by Packer, Neil)*
    c BL - v112 - i4 - Oct 15 2015 - p38(1) [51-500]
    c KR - August 15 2015 - pNA [51-500]
    y SLJ - v61 - i9 - Sept 2015 - p156(1) [51-500]
    y VOYA - v38 - i5 - Dec 2015 - p76(1) [51-500]
Agarwala, Rina - *Informal Labor, Formal Politics, and Dignified Discontent in India*
    CS - v44 - i4 - July 2015 - p477-479 [501+]
Whatever Happened to Class? Reflections from South Asia
    JTWS - v32 - i1 - Spring 2015 - p320(4) [501+]
Agay, Denes - *More Classics to Moderns, Books 1-6, Second Series*
    Am MT - v65 - i3 - Dec 2015 - p50(2) [501+]
Agee, Christopher Lowen - *The Streets of San Francisco: Policing and the Creation of a Cosmopolitan Liberal Politics, 1950-1972*
    AHR - v120 - i4 - Oct 2015 - p1521-1522 [501+]
    JAH - v102 - i1 - June 2015 - p291-292 [501+]
    Reason - v47 - i2 - June 2015 - p61(4) [501+]
    WHQ - v46 - i2 - Summer 2015 - p255(1) [501+]
Agee, John - *Milo's Hat Trick (Read by Newbern, George). Audiobook Review*
    c SLJ - v61 - i2 - Feb 2015 - p47(1) [51-500]
Agee, Jon - *It's Only Stanley (Read by Newbern, George). Audiobook Review*
    c SLJ - v61 - i6 - June 2015 - p62(1) [51-500]
It's Only Stanley (Illus. by Agee, Jon)
    c CH Bwatch - June 2015 - pNA [501+]
    c HB - v91 - i3 - May-June 2015 - p77(2) [51-500]
    c KR - Jan 1 2015 - pNA [51-500]
    c NYTBR - May 10 2015 - p18(L) [51-500]
    c PW - v262 - i2 - Jan 12 2015 - p59(1) [51-500]
    c PW - v262 - i49 - Dec 2 2015 - p35(1) [51-500]
It's Only Stanley (Illus. by Newbern, George)
    c HB Guide - v26 - i2 - Fall 2015 - p5(1) [51-500]
Nothing (Read by Newbern, George). Audiobook Review
    c SLJ - v61 - i3 - March 2015 - p75(2) [51-500]
Terrific (Read by Heyborne, Kirby). Audiobook Review
    c SLJ - v61 - i4 - April 2015 - p60(1) [51-500]
Agee, Margaret Nelson - *Pacific Identities and Well-Being: Cross-Cultural Perspectives*
    Pac A - v88 - i2 - June 2015 - p377 [501+]
Ager, Deborah - *The Bloomsbury Anthology of Contemporary Jewish American Poetry*
    Tikkun - v30 - i1 - Wntr 2015 - p45(3) [501+]
Agger, Ben - *Texting toward Utopia: Kids, Writing, and Resistance*
    CS - v44 - i6 - Nov 2015 - p870-871 [501+]
Agier, Michel - *Un Monde de camps*
    TLS - i5870 - Oct 2 2015 - p11(1) [501+]
Agnew, Sheila - *Evie Brooks Is Marooned in Manhattan*
    c KR - Sept 1 2015 - pNA [51-500]
    c PW - v262 - i36 - Sept 7 2015 - p68(2) [51-500]
    c Res Links - v21 - i1 - Oct 2015 - p12(1) [51-500]
    c SLJ - v61 - i10 - Oct 2015 - p87(1) [51-500]
Agnone, Julie Vosburgh - *What in the World? Fantastic Photo Puzzles for Curious Minds*
    c HB Guide - v26 - i1 - Spring 2015 - p181(1) [51-500]
Ago, Renata - *Gusto for Things: A History of Objects in Seventeenth-Century Rome*
    JMH - v87 - i2 - June 2015 - p400(4) [501+]

Agosin, Marjorie - *Stitching Resistance: Women, Creativity, and Fiber Arts*
    WLT - v89 - i3-4 - May-August 2015 - p125(1) [51-500]
Agualusa, Jose Eduardo - *A General Theory of Oblivion*
    KR - Oct 15 2015 - pNA [51-500]
    TLS - i5862 - August 7 2015 - p20(1) [501+]
Aguilar, Mario I. - *Pope Francis: His Life and Thought*
    Theol St - v76 - i4 - Dec 2015 - p851(3) [501+]
    CHR - v101 - i2 - Spring 2015 - p389(2) [501+]
Aguilar, Raquel Gutierrez - *Rhythms of the Pachakuti: Indigenous Uprising and State Power in Bolivia*
    HAHR - v95 - i3 - August 2015 - p548-549 [501+]
Aguirre, Ann - *Mortal Danger*
    y HB Guide - v26 - i1 - Spring 2015 - p98(1) [51-500]
    Public Enemies
    y KR - June 1 2015 - pNA [51-500]
    y SLJ - v61 - i6 - June 2015 - p119(1) [51-500]
    y VOYA - v38 - i3 - August 2015 - p73(1) [51-500]
    The Queen of Bright and Shiny Things
    y HB Guide - v26 - i2 - Fall 2015 - p108(1) [51-500]
    c KR - Feb 1 2015 - pNA [51-500]
    y PW - v262 - i5 - Feb 2 2015 - p61(2) [51-500]
    y SLJ - v61 - i2 - Feb 2015 - p96(1) [51-500]
    y VOYA - v38 - i1 - April 2015 - p52(1) [51-500]
Aguirre, Forrest - *Heraclix and Pomp: A Novel of the Fabricated and the Fey*
    SPBW - Feb 2015 - pNA [51-500]
Aguirre, Jorge - *Dragons Beware!* (Illus. by Rosado, Rafael)
    c BL - v111 - i18 - May 15 2015 - p43(1) [51-500]
    c CH Bwatch - May 2015 - pNA [51-500]
    c SLJ - v61 - i4 - April 2015 - p150(1) [51-500]
Aguirre, Zurine - *Sardines of Love* (Illus. by Aguirre, Zurine)
    c KR - July 15 2015 - pNA [51-500]
Agus, David B. - *The Lucky Years*
    KR - Dec 1 2015 - pNA [501+]
Agyeman-Duah, Baffour - *My Ghanaian Odyssey*
    Africa T - v62 - i1 - Fall 2015 - p136(3) [501+]
Agyeman-Duah, Ivor - *Essays in Honour of Wole Soyinka at Eighty*
    WLT - v89 - i1 - Jan-Feb 2015 - p67(1) [501+]
Agyeman, Julian - *Sharing Cities: A Case for Truly Smart and Sustainable Cities*
    PW - v262 - i41 - Oct 12 2015 - p59(1) [51-500]
Ah-Sen, Jean Marc - *Grand Menteur*
    KR - August 15 2015 - pNA [501+]
Ahdieh, Renee - *The Wrath and the Dawn* (Read by Delawari, Ariana). Audiobook Review
    y SLJ - v61 - i8 - August 2015 - p52(1) [51-500]
    The Wrath and the Dawn
    PW - v262 - i14 - April 6 2015 - p62(1) [51-500]
    y BL - v111 - i16 - April 15 2015 - p48(1) [51-500]
    y CCB-B - v68 - i10 - June 2015 - p478(2) [51-500]
    CSM - June 8 2015 - pNA [501+]
    y HB Guide - v26 - i2 - Fall 2015 - p108(1) [51-500]
    y KR - March 15 2015 - pNA [51-500]
    SLJ - v61 - i4 - April 2015 - p158(2) [51-500]
    y VOYA - v38 - i1 - April 2015 - p73(1) [51-500]
Ahern, Carolyn L. - *Tino the Tortoise: Adventures in the Grand Canyon* (Illus. by Brooks, Erik)
    c CH Bwatch - August 2015 - pNA [51-500]
    c HB Guide - v26 - i2 - Fall 2015 - p24(1) [51-500]
Ahern, Shauna James - *American Classics Reinvented*
    PW - v262 - i29 - July 20 2015 - p184(1) [51-500]
Ahiborn, Ania - *Within These Walls*
    BL - v111 - i16 - April 15 2015 - p31(1) [51-500]
    NYTBR - May 31 2015 - p42(L) [501+]
Ahiers, Sarah - *Assassin's Heart*
    y BL - v112 - i7 - Dec 1 2015 - p53(1) [51-500]
    y KR - Nov 15 2015 - pNA [51-500]
    y PW - v262 - i47 - Nov 23 2015 - p69(1) [51-500]
    y SLJ - v61 - i12 - Dec 2015 - p112(1) [51-500]
Ahlberg, Jessica - *Fairytales for Mr. Barker* (Illus. by Ahlberg, Jessica)
    c KR - Dec 15 2015 - pNA [51-500]
Ahlborn, Ania - *Brother*
    PW - v262 - i35 - August 31 2015 - p65(1) [51-500]
    Within These Walls (Read by Bray, R.C.). Audiobook Review
    LJ - v140 - i12 - July 1 2015 - p42(1) [51-500]
Ahlqvist, Anders - *Celts and Their Cultures at Home and Abroad: A Festschrift for Malcolm Broun*
    Specu - v90 - i2 - April 2015 - p485-487 [501+]
Ahmad, Muhammad Idrees - *The Road to Iraq: The Making of a Neoconservative War*
    IJMES - v47 - i3 - August 2015 - p641-643 [501+]

Ahmed, Asad Q. - *The Religious Elite of the Early Islamic Hijaz: Five Prosopographical Case Studies*
    JNES - v74 - i1 - April 2015 - p167(3) [501+]
Ahmed, K. Anis - *Good Night, Mr. Kissinger and Other Stories*
    Nation - v300 - i11 - March 16 2015 - p42(3) [501+]
Ahmed, Shahab - *What Is Islam? The Importance of Being Islamic*
    PW - v262 - i41 - Oct 12 2015 - p63(2) [51-500]
Ahnert, Petra - *Beeswax Alchemy: How to Make Your Own Candles, Soap, Balms, Salves, and Home Decor from the Hive*
    LJ - v140 - i6 - April 1 2015 - p92(1) [51-500]
Aho, Kevin - *Existentialism: An Introduction*
    RM - v69 - i1 - Sept 2015 - p115(2) [501+]
Ahola, Robert Joseph - *Narcissus: The Last Days of Lord Byron*
    Clio - v44 - i2 - Spring 2015 - p217-237 [501+]
Ahrens, Prue - *Across the World with the Johnsons: Visual Culture and American Empire in the Twentieth Century*
    AHR - v120 - i1 - Feb 2015 - p280-281 [501+]
Ahrens, Ralf - *Jurgen Ponto: Bankier und Burger*
    HNet - Feb 2015 - pNA [501+]
Ahtisaari, Martti - *The United Nations at 70: Restoration and Renewal*
    LJ - v140 - i20 - Dec 1 2015 - p106(2) [501+]
Aicher, Linda - *Back in Play*
    PW - v262 - i11 - March 16 2015 - p71(1) [51-500]
Aicher, Peter J. - *Guide to the Aqueducts of Ancient Rome*
    TLS - i5854 - June 12 2015 - p11(1) [501+]
Aichner, Bernhard - *Woman of the Dead*
    KR - June 15 2015 - pNA [51-500]
    LJ - v140 - i12 - July 1 2015 - p72(1) [51-500]
    PW - v262 - i23 - June 8 2015 - p36(2) [51-500]
Aidi, Hisham D. - *Rebel Music: Race, Empire, and the New Muslim Youth Culture*
    NYTBR - Feb 1 2015 - p24(L) [501+]
Aidt, Naja Marie - *Rock, Paper, Scissors*
    KR - June 1 2015 - pNA [51-500]
Aiello, Vince - *Legion's Lawyers*
    SPBW - Jan 2015 - pNA [51-500]
Aikin, Judith P. - *A Ruler's Consort in Early Modern Germany: Aemilia Juliana of Schwarzburg-Rudolstadt*
    MLR - v110 - i2 - April 2015 - p583-585 [501+]
Aikin, Scott F. - *Evidentialism and the Will to Believe*
    RM - v68 - i4 - June 2015 - p833(2) [501+]
Aikman-Smith, Valerie - *Citrus: Sweet & Savory Sun-Kissed Recipes*
    LJ - v140 - i19 - Nov 15 2015 - p102(1) [51-500]
Aimee, Kayla - *Anchored: Finding Hope in the Unexpected*
    PW - v262 - i23 - June 8 2015 - p55(1) [51-500]
Ain, Beth - *Starring Jules (Third Grade Debut).* (Illus. by Higgins, Anne Keenan)
    c CH Bwatch - April 2015 - pNA [51-500]
    c HB Guide - v26 - i1 - Spring 2015 - p56(1) [51-500]
Ainslie, Ricardo C. - *The Fight to Save Juarez: Life in the Heart of Mexico's Drug War*
    CS - v44 - i3 - May 2015 - p332-333 [501+]
Ainsworth, Eve - *7 Days*
    c Sch Lib - v63 - i2 - Summer 2015 - p114(1) [51-500]
Aira, Cesar - *Dinner*
    KR - August 15 2015 - pNA [51-500]
    LJ - v140 - i20 - Dec 1 2015 - p88(1) [51-500]
    TLS - i5874 - Oct 30 2015 - p31(1) [51-500]
    The Musical Brain and Other Stories
    BL - v111 - i13 - March 1 2015 - p20(1) [51-500]
    KR - Jan 1 2015 - pNA [51-500]
    NYRB - v62 - i13 - August 13 2015 - p36(3) [501+]
    NYTBR - March 15 2015 - p10(L) [501+]
Aird, Catherine - *Dead Heading*
    RVBW - Jan 2015 - pNA [501+]
Airgood, Ellen - *The Education of Ivy Blake*
    c HB Guide - v26 - i2 - Fall 2015 - p73(1) [51-500]
    c KR - March 1 2015 - pNA [51-500]
    c SLJ - v61 - i4 - April 2015 - p143(1) [51-500]
    y VOYA - v38 - i2 - June 2015 - p52(1) [51-500]
Airhart, Phyllis D. - *A Church with the Soul of a Nation: Making and Remaking the United Church of Canada*
    CH - v84 - i2 - June 2015 - p487(3) [501+]
    CHR - v101 - i4 - Autumn 2015 - p956(2) [501+]
Airlie, Shiona - *Scottish Mandarin: The Life and Times of Sir Reginald Johnston*
    JAS - v74 - i2 - May 2015 - p453-455 [501+]
Aitken, Doug - *Station to Station*
    LJ - v140 - i20 - Dec 1 2015 - p98(1) [51-500]
Aitken, Martin - *Prophets of Eternal Fjord*
    LJ - v140 - i12 - July 1 2015 - p78(1) [51-500]

Aiyar, Pallavi - *The New Old World: An Indian Journalist Discovers the Changing Face of Europe*
    KR - July 1 2015 - pNA [501+]
    New Old World: An Indian Journalist Discovers the Changing Face of Europe
    LJ - v140 - i14 - Sept 1 2015 - p123(1) [51-500]
    PW - v262 - i27 - July 6 2015 - p58(2) [51-500]
Aiyer, Samita - *The Last Bargain*
    c KR - June 1 2015 - pNA [51-500]
Aizelwood, Robin - *Landmarks Revisited: The Vekhi Symposium 100 Years On*
    Slav R - v74 - i2 - Summer 2015 - p400-401 [501+]
Ajmera, Maya - *Every Breath We Take*
    c KR - Jan 1 2016 - pNA [51-500]
    Global Baby Boys
    c KR - Jan 1 2015 - pNA [51-500]
Ajzenstat, Janet - *Discovering Confederation: A Canadian's Story*
    Can Hist R - v96 - i2 - June 2015 - p289(2) [501+]
Akawa, Martha - *The Gender Politics of the Namibian Liberation Struggle*
    IJAHS - v48 - i1 - Wntr 2015 - p145-146 [501+]
Akbari, Suzanne Conklin - *The Ends of the Body: Identity and Community in Medieval Culture*
    JEGP - v114 - i3 - July 2015 - p438(4) [501+]
    A Sea of Languages: Rethinking the Arabic Role in Medieval Literary History
    Med R - March 2015 - pNA(NA) [501+]
Aker, Don - *Delusion Road*
    y Res Links - v21 - i1 - Oct 2015 - p28(1) [51-500]
Akerlof, George A. - *Phishing for Phools: The Economics of Manipulation and Deception*
    Fortune - v172 - i5 - Oct 1 2015 - p24(1) [501+]
    LJ - v140 - i17 - Oct 15 2015 - p96(1) [51-500]
    Nature - v526 - i7575 - Oct 29 2015 - p639(1) [51-500]
    NYRB - v62 - i16 - Oct 22 2015 - p40(3) [501+]
    TimHES - i2224 - Oct 8 2015 - p46(1) [51-500]
    What Have We Learned? Macroeconomic Policy After the Crisis
    For Aff - v94 - i2 - March-April 2015 - pNA [501+]
Akers, R.L. - *Prometheus Rebound*
    KR - March 1 2015 - pNA [51-500]
Akers, Tim - *The Pagan Night: Book One of the Hallowed War*
    PW - v262 - i41 - Oct 12 2015 - p51(1) [51-500]
Akers, William M. - *Ravenbach's Way*
    c KR - Dec 15 2015 - pNA [51-500]
Akerstrom, Malin - *Suspicious Gifts: Bribery, Morality, and Professional Ethics*
    AJS - v120 - i4 - Jan 2015 - p1278(3) [501+]
    CS - v44 - i4 - July 2015 - p479-481 [501+]
Akhavan, Niki - *Electronic Iran: The Cultural Politics of an Online Evolution*
    IJMES - v47 - i4 - Nov 2015 - p828-830 [501+]
Akhtar, Maha - *Footprints in the Desert*
    BL - v111 - i19-20 - June 1 2015 - p53(1) [51-500]
Akhtiorskaya, Yelena - *Panic in a Suitcase*
    ABR - v36 - i5 - July-August 2015 - p9(2) [501+]
Akhvlediani, Erlom - *Vano and Niko*
    TLS - i5856 - June 26 2015 - p20(2) [501+]
Akin, David W. - *Colonialism, Maasina Rule, and the Origins of Malaitan Kastom*
    Pac A - v88 - i2 - June 2015 - p383 [501+]
Akins, Karen - *Loop*
    y HB Guide - v26 - i2 - Fall 2015 - p108(1) [51-500]
    Twist
    y HB Guide - v26 - i2 - Fall 2015 - p108(1) [51-500]
    y SLJ - v61 - i4 - April 2015 - p158(1) [51-500]
    y VOYA - v38 - i2 - June 2015 - p70(1) [51-500]
Akinsha, Konstantin - *Russian Cross-Currents of German and Russian Art, 1907-1917*
    LJ - v140 - i14 - Sept 1 2015 - p110(1) [51-500]
    Russian Modernism: Cross-Currents of German and Russian Art, 1907-1917
    RVBW - August 2015 - pNA [51-500]
Akkerman, Nadine - *The Politics of Female Households: Ladies-in-Waiting across Early Modern Europe*
    Ren Q - v68 - i1 - Spring 2015 - p313-314 [501+]
Akpan, Uwem - *Say You're One of Them*
    ABR - v36 - i4 - May-June 2015 - p5(1) [501+]
Akteure Mittelalterlicher Aussenpolitik. Das Beispiel Ostmitteleuropas
    HNet - March 2015 - pNA [501+]
Akteure, Tiere, Dinge: Verfahrensweisen der Naturgeschichte
    HNet - August 2015 - pNA [501+]

Aktuelle Forschungen zu Postsozialistischen Stadten Ostmitteleuropas: Transformation Offentlicher Urbaner Raume nach 1989 - Akteure, Praxen und Strategien
   HNet - June 2015 - pNA [501+]

Akyeampong, Emmanuel - *The Culture of Mental Illness and Psychiatric Practice in Africa*
   Africa T - v62 - i1 - Fall 2015 - p146(3) [501+]

al-Arian, Abdullah - *Answering the Call: Popular Islamic Activism in Sadat's Egypt*
   IJMES - v47 - i3 - August 2015 - p646-647 [501+]

Al Aswany, Alaa - *The Automobile Club of Egypt*
   BL - v111 - i22 - August 1 2015 - p26(1) [51-500]
   CSM - August 20 2015 - pNA [501+]
   KR - June 15 2015 - pNA [501+]
   PW - v262 - i27 - July 6 2015 - p2(1) [51-500]

Al Crocevia della Storia: Poesia, Religione e Politica in Vittoria Colonna
   HNet - March 2015 - pNA [501+]

Al-Khalili, Jim - *Life on the Edge: The Coming of Age of Quantum Biology*
   PW - v262 - i21 - May 25 2015 - p47(2) [51-500]

Al Mansour, Haifaa - *The Green Bicycle*
   c BL - v112 - i1 - Sept 1 2015 - p115(2) [51-500]
   c KR - July 15 2015 - pNA [51-500]
   c SLJ - v61 - i8 - August 2015 - p82(1) [51-500]

Al-Mohaimeed, Yousef - *Where Pigeons Don't Fly*
   PW - v262 - i21 - May 25 2015 - p30(2) [51-500]

Al-Rawi, Rosina-Fawzia - *Divine Names: The 99 Healing Names of the One Love*
   LJ - v140 - i12 - July 1 2015 - p111(1) [51-500]

Al-Saleh, Asaad - *Voices of the Arab Spring: Personal Stories from the Arab Revolutions*
   NS - v144 - i5263 - May 22 2015 - p42(2) [501+]

Aladjai, Erni - *Kei*
   WLT - v89 - i2 - March-April 2015 - p55(1) [51-500]

Alaimo, Rino - *The Boy Who Loved the Moon (Illus. by Alaimo, Rino)*
   c CH Bwatch - March 2015 - pNA [51-500]
   c KR - March 1 2015 - pNA [51-500]

Alaina, Maria - *Counting Money*
   TC Math - v21 - i9 - May 2015 - p568(2) [501+]
Estimating
   TC Math - v21 - i9 - May 2015 - p568(2) [501+]
Fractions
   TC Math - v21 - i9 - May 2015 - p568(2) [501+]
Measuring
   TC Math - v21 - i9 - May 2015 - p568(2) [501+]

Alameda, Courtney - *Shutter*
   c HB Guide - v26 - i2 - Fall 2015 - p108(1) [51-500]

Alameddine, Rabih - *An Unnecessary Woman*
   NYTBR - June 21 2015 - p24(L) [51-500]

Alan Turing: Pioneer of the Information Age
   NYRB - v62 - i2 - Feb 5 2015 - p19(3) [501+]

Alarcon, Daniel - *At Night We Walk in Circles*
   For Aff - v94 - i1 - Jan-Feb 2015 - pNA [501+]
City of Clowns
   BL - v112 - i6 - Nov 15 2015 - p33(1) [51-500]
   KR - Sept 1 2015 - pNA [51-500]

Alarcon, Francisco X. - *Canto Hondo / Deep Song*
   BL - v111 - i11 - Feb 1 2015 - p15(1) [51-500]

Alard, Nelly - *Couple Mechanics*
   KR - Sept 15 2015 - pNA [501+]

Alaux, Jean-Pierre - *The Winemaker Detective*
   PW - v262 - i42 - Oct 19 2015 - p56(2) [51-500]

Alba, Ben - *Inventing Late Night: Steve Allen and the Original Tonight Show*
   BL - v111 - i19-20 - June 1 2015 - p30(2) [51-500]

Alba, Richard - *The Children of Immigrants at School: A Comparative Look at Integration in the United States and Western Europe*
   AJS - v120 - i4 - Jan 2015 - p1241(3) [501+]
   CS - v44 - i3 - May 2015 - p333-335 [501+]
Strangers No More: Immigration and the Challenges of Integration in North America and Western Europe
   CC - v132 - i22 - Oct 28 2015 - p42(2) [501+]

Albahari, David - *Learning Cyrillic*
   WLT - v89 - i5 - Sept-Oct 2015 - p57(1) [51-500]

Albahari, Maurizio - *Crimes of Peace: Mediterranean Migrations at the World's Deadliest Border*
   TLS - i5870 - Oct 2 2015 - p11(1) [501+]

Albanese, Giulia - *In the Society of Fascists: Acclimation, Acquiescence, and Agency in Mussolini's Italy*
   JMH - v87 - i2 - June 2015 - p467(6) [501+]

Albarran, Elena Jackson - *Seen and Heard in Mexico: Children and Revolutionary Cultural Nationalism*
   AHR - v120 - i4 - Oct 2015 - p1532-1533 [501+]

Albaugh, Ericka A. - *State-Building and Multilingual Education in Africa*
   For Aff - v94 - i1 - Jan-Feb 2015 - pNA [51-500]

Albee, Sarah - *Why'd They Wear That?*
   c BL - v111 - i12 - Feb 15 2015 - p72(1) [51-500]
   c CCB-B - v68 - i7 - March 2015 - p345(1) [51-500]
   y HB Guide - v26 - i2 - Fall 2015 - p156(1) [51-500]

Albers, Meike Michele - *Japanische Unternehmen in Deutschland. Ein Aufeinandertreffen verschiedener Kulturen*
   GSR - v38 - i3 - Oct 2015 - p675-677 [501+]

Albers, Susan - *50 More Ways to Soothe Yourself without Food: Mindfulness Strategies to Cope with Stress and End Emotional Eating*
   BL - v112 - i3 - Oct 1 2015 - p14(1) [51-500]

Albert, Annabeth - *Status Update*
   PW - v262 - i41 - Oct 12 2015 - p53(1) [51-500]

Albert, Elisa - *After Birth*
   NS - v144 - i5262 - May 15 2015 - p47(1) [501+]
   NYT - Feb 26 2015 - pC6(L) [501+]
   NYTBR - March 1 2015 - p21(L) [501+]
   TLS - i5855 - June 19 2015 - p20(1) [501+]

Albert, Susan Wittig - *Bittersweet*
   BL - v111 - i14 - March 15 2015 - p45(1) [51-500]
   KR - Feb 1 2015 - pNA [51-500]
   PW - v262 - i7 - Feb 16 2015 - p161(2) [51-500]
The Darling Dahlias and the Eleven O'Clock Lady
   PW - v262 - i31 - August 3 2015 - p36(2) [51-500]
Loving Eleanor
   KR - Jan 1 2016 - pNA [501+]
A Wilder Rose (Read by Kowal, Mary Robinette). Audiobook Review
   BL - v111 - i22 - August 1 2015 - p79(1) [51-500]

Albertalli, Becky - *Simon vs. the Homo Sapiens Agenda*
   y BL - v111 - i22 - August 1 2015 - p60(1) [51-500]
   y CCB-B - v68 - i9 - May 2015 - p436(2) [51-500]
   y Ent W - i1358 - April 10 2015 - p67(1) [501+]
   y HB Guide - v26 - i2 - Fall 2015 - p109(1) [51-500]
      KR - Feb 1 2015 - pNA [51-500]
   y Magpies - v30 - i2 - May 2015 - p40(1) [501+]
   c Nat Post - v119 - i17 - March 21 2015 - pWP5(1) [501+]
   y PW - v262 - i6 - Feb 9 2015 - p71(1) [51-500]
   y PW - v262 - i49 - Dec 2 2015 - p98(1) [51-500]

Alberti, John - *Masculinity in the Contemporary Romantic Comedy: Gender as Genre*
   SAH - v4 - i1 - Annual 2015 - p118-121 [501+]

Albertine, Viv - *Clothes, Clothes, Clothes. Music, Music, Music. Boys, Boys, Boys*
   TimHES - i2202 - May 7 2015 - p49(1) [501+]

Alberts, Heath D. - *Not on the List*
   KR - June 15 2015 - pNA [501+]

Alberts, Tara - *Conflict and Conversion: Catholicism in Southeast Asia, 1500-1700*
   AHR - v120 - i1 - Feb 2015 - p211-212 [501+]
   CHR - v101 - i1 - Wntr 2015 - p183(2) [501+]
   HER - v130 - i544 - June 2015 - p733(3) [501+]

Albertson, David - *Mathematical Theologies: Nicholas of Cusa and the Legacy of Thierry of Chartres*
   Med R - Jan 2015 - pNA [501+]
   CHR - v101 - i4 - Autumn 2015 - p921(2) [501+]
   Ren Q - v68 - i2 - Summer 2015 - p664-665 [501+]

Albin, Gennifer - *Unraveled*
   y HB Guide - v26 - i2 - Fall 2015 - p109(1) [51-500]

Albitz, Becky - *Rethinking Collection Development and Management*
   LRTS - v59 - i1 - Jan 2015 - p55(2) [501+]

Albom, Mitch - *The Magic Strings of Frankie Presto*
   KR - Sept 1 2015 - pNA [501+]

Alborough, Jez - *Albert and Little Henry*
   c Sch Lib - v63 - i4 - Winter 2015 - p217(1) [51-500]

Alborozo, Gabriel - *Good Night, Firefly (Illus. by Alborozo, Gabriel)*
   c KR - March 15 2015 - pNA [51-500]
   c SLJ - v61 - i6 - June 2015 - p76(1) [51-500]
Let's Play (Illus. by Alborozo, Gabriel)
   c Sch Lib - v63 - i3 - Autumn 2015 - p153(1) [51-500]

Albrecht, Don E. - *Rethinking Rural: Global Community and Economic Development in the Small Town West*
   WHQ - v46 - i2 - Summer 2015 - p234-235 [501+]

Albrecht, Donald - *Partners in Design: Alfred H. Barr Jr. and Philip Johnson*
   PW - v262 - i42 - Oct 19 2015 - p68(1) [51-500]

Albrecht, Sally K. - *Composer Songs: Meet 12 Famous Composers through Song*
   Teach Mus - v23 - i2 - Oct 2015 - p52(1) [501+]

Albrecht, Steve - *Library Security: Better Communication, Safer Facilities*
   LJ - v140 - i17 - Oct 15 2015 - p101(1) [51-500]
   RVBW - August 2015 - pNA [501+]
   VOYA - v38 - i5 - Dec 2015 - p81(1) [501+]

Albrechtsen, Nicky - *Vintage Fashion Complete*
   LJ - v140 - i5 - March 15 2015 - p102(3) [51-500]

Albright, Alex - *The Forgotten First: B-1 and the Integration of the Modern Navy*
   JSH - v81 - i2 - May 2015 - p505(2) [501+]

Albright, Ann Cooper - *Engaging Bodies: The Politics and Poetics of Corporeality*
   Dance RJ - v47 - i1 - April 2015 - p115-118 [501+]

Albright, Daniel - *Great Shakespeareans Set III, vol. II: Berlioz, Verdi, Wagner, Britten*
   Six Ct J - v46 - i1 - Spring 2015 - p180-182 [501+]

Albright, Emily - *The Heir and the Spare*
   y KR - Nov 15 2015 - pNA [51-500]
   y PW - v262 - i42 - Oct 19 2015 - p77(2) [51-500]
   y SLJ - v61 - i12 - Dec 2015 - p117(2) [51-500]

Albright, James M. - *Krazy Kodak Moments*
   KR - Jan 1 2016 - pNA [501+]

Alcala, Luisa Elena - *Painting in Latin America, 1550-1820*
   NYRB - v62 - i12 - July 9 2015 - p58(3) [501+]

Alciati, Andrea - *Contra vitam monasticam epistula: Andrea Alciato's Letter against Monastic Life*
   Sev Cent N - v73 - i3-4 - Fall-Winter 2015 - p193(3) [501+]

Alcott, Jessica - *Even When You Lie to Me*
   y BL - v111 - i17 - May 1 2015 - p90(1) [51-500]
   y CCB-B - v68 - i11 - July-August 2015 - p534(2) [51-500]
   y HB Guide - v26 - i2 - Fall 2015 - p109(1) [51-500]
   y KR - March 1 2015 - pNA [51-500]
   y VOYA - v38 - i2 - June 2015 - p52(1) [51-500]

Alcott, Kate - *A Touch of Stardust (Read by Campbell, Cassandra). Audiobook Review*
   BL - v111 - i19-20 - June 1 2015 - p138(1) [51-500]
   LJ - v140 - i10 - June 1 2015 - p58(1) [51-500]
A Touch of Stardust
   BL - v111 - i16 - April 15 2015 - p34(1) [51-500]
   LJ - v140 - i2 - Feb 1 2015 - p77(1) [51-500]
   NYTBR - March 29 2015 - p30(L) [501+]

Alcott, Kathleen - *Infinite Home (Read by Lewis, Christa). Audiobook Review*
   LJ - v140 - i20 - Dec 1 2015 - p58(1) [51-500]
Infinite Home
   BL - v111 - i19-20 - June 1 2015 - p42(1) [51-500]
   KR - June 1 2015 - pNA [51-500]
   NY - v91 - i25 - August 31 2015 - p89 [501+]
   NYT - August 27 2015 - pC4(L) [501+]
   PW - v262 - i21 - May 25 2015 - p28(1) [51-500]

Alcott, Louisa May - *The Annotated Little Women*
   LJ - v140 - i15 - Sept 15 2015 - p73(2) [51-500]
Little Women (Read by Berneis, Susie). Audiobook Review
   BL - v111 - i19-20 - June 1 2015 - p132(1) [51-500]
   LJ - v140 - i5 - March 15 2015 - p71(1) [51-500]
Louisa May Alcott: Work, Eight Cousins, Rose in Bloom, Stories and Other Writings
   HR - v67 - i4 - Wntr 2015 - p677-684 [501+]

Alda, Arlene - *Just Kids from the Bronx: Telling It the Way It Was: An Oral History (Read by Alda, Arlene). Audiobook Review*
   PW - v262 - i21 - May 25 2015 - p55(1) [51-500]
Just Kids from the Bronx: Telling It the Way It Was: An Oral History
   NYT - March 22 2015 - p2(L) [501+]
   NYTBR - May 31 2015 - p44(L) [501+]

Aldama, Frederick Luis - *Mex-Cine: Mexican Filmmaking, Production, and Consumption in the Twenty-First Century*
   Aztlan - v40 - i2 - Fall 2015 - p297-300 [501+]

Aldatz, Tina - *From Stilettos to the Stock Exchange: Inside the Life of a Serial Entrepreneur*
   SPBW - Sept 2015 - pNA [501+]

Aldcroft, Derek H. - *The European Economy Since 1914, 5th ed.*
   JEH - v75 - i1 - March 2015 - p264-266 [501+]

Alden, Elise - *Pitch Imperfect*
   KR - May 15 2015 - pNA [501+]

Alder, Charlie - *Daredevil Duck (Illus. by Adler, Charlie)*
   c CH Bwatch - July 2015 - pNA [51-500]
   c KR - March 1 2015 - pNA [51-500]
Daredevil Duck (Illus. by Alder, Charlie)
   c HB Guide - v26 - i2 - Fall 2015 - p5(1) [51-500]
   c SLJ - v61 - i11 - Nov 2015 - p77(1) [51-500]

Alder, Mark - *Son of the Morning*
   PW - v262 - i51 - Dec 14 2015 - p65(2) [51-500]

Alderman, Geoffrey - *British Jewry since Emancipation*
   TLS - i5841 - March 13 2015 - p24(1) [501+]

Aldersey-Williams, Hugh - *The Adventures of Sir Thomas Browne in the 21st Century*
    TLS - i5874 - Oct 30 2015 - p31(1) [501+]
    Econ - v416 - i8945 - July 4 2015 - p71(US) [501+]
    Nature - v521 - i7553 - May 28 2015 - p421(1) [51-500]
    Spec - v328 - i9747 - June 20 2015 - p39(2) [501+]
In Search of Sir Thomas Browne: The Life and Afterlife of the Seventeenth Century's Most Inquiring Mind (Read by Vance, Simon). Audiobook Review
    LJ - v140 - i14 - Sept 1 2015 - p68(1) [501+]
In Search of Sir Thomas Browne: The Life and Afterlife of the Seventeenth Century's Most Inquiring Mind
    BL - v111 - i19-20 - June 1 2015 - p29(1) [51-500]
    NYRB - v62 - i16 - Oct 22 2015 - p67(3) [501+]
    NYTBR - July 19 2015 - p1(L) [501+]
    KR - April 1 2015 - pNA [501+]
    LJ - v140 - i8 - May 1 2015 - p96(1) [51-500]
    PW - v262 - i15 - April 13 2015 - p68(1) [51-500]
Periodic Tales: A Cultural History of the Elements, from Arsenic to Zinc (Read by Ferguson, Antony). Audiobook Review
    LJ - v140 - i14 - Sept 1 2015 - p68(1) [501+]

Alderson, Sarah - *Out of Control*
    y KR - Feb 15 2015 - pNA [51-500]
    y Sch Lib - v63 - i1 - Spring 2015 - p50(1) [51-500]
    y VOYA - v38 - i1 - April 2015 - p52(1) [51-500]
The Sound
    y HB Guide - v26 - i1 - Spring 2015 - p98(1) [51-500]

Alderton, David - *Dinosaurs around the World*
    c HB Guide - v26 - i1 - Spring 2015 - p152(1) [51-500]
Jungle Animals around the World
    c HB Guide - v26 - i1 - Spring 2015 - p155(1) [51-500]
Mammals around the World
    c HB Guide - v26 - i1 - Spring 2015 - p165(1) [51-500]
Sharks and Sea Creatures around the World
    c HB Guide - v26 - i1 - Spring 2015 - p155(1) [51-500]
Snakes and Reptiles around the World
    c HB Guide - v26 - i1 - Spring 2015 - p161(1) [51-500]

Aldhouse-Green, Miranda - *Bog Bodies Uncovered: Solving Europe's Ancient Mystery*
    KR - July 1 2015 - pNA [501+]
    LJ - v140 - i14 - Sept 1 2015 - p133(1) [51-500]
The Celtic Myths: A Guide to the Ancient Gods and Legends
    BL - v111 - i9-10 - Jan 1 2015 - p28(1) [51-500]

Aldin, Lisa - *One of the Guys*
    SLJ - v61 - i3 - March 2015 - p148(1) [51-500]

Aldiss, Brian - *Jocasta*
    Spec - v327 - i9726 - Jan 24 2015 - p42(2) [501+]

Aldiss, Brian W. - *Finches of Mars*
    BL - v111 - i19-20 - June 1 2015 - p64(2) [51-500]
    PW - v262 - i22 - June 1 2015 - p44(1) [51-500]

Aldorozo, Gabriel - *Good Night, Firefly (Illus. by Alborozo, Gabriel)*
    c Teach Lib - v43 - i1 - Oct 2015 - p28(1) [51-500]

Aldrich, Daniel P. - *Building Resilience: Social Capital in Post-Disaster Recovery*
    CS - v44 - i1 - Jan 2015 - p30-31 [501+]

Aldrich, Margret - *The Little Free Library Book*
    LJ - v140 - i10 - June 1 2015 - p118(1) [51-500]

Aldridge, James - *The True Story of Spit MacPhee*
    y Magpies - v30 - i1 - March 2015 - p43(1) [51-500]

Aldridge, Susan - *Trailblazers in Medicine*
    y SLJ - v61 - i6 - June 2015 - p139(1) [51-500]

Aldrin, Buzz - *Welcome to Mars: Making a Home on the Red Planet*
    c BL - v112 - i3 - Oct 1 2015 - p39(1) [51-500]
    c CH Bwatch - Oct 2015 - pNA [51-500]
    c SLJ - v61 - i11 - Nov 2015 - p134(1) [51-500]

Alegre, Robert F. - *Railroad Radicals in Cold War Mexico: Gender, Class, and Memory*
    AHR - v120 - i2 - April 2015 - p681-682 [501+]

Alemagna, Beatrice - *The 5 Misfits (Illus. by Alemagna, Beatrice)*
    c Sch Lib - v63 - i4 - Winter 2015 - p217(1) [51-500]
Little Big Boubo (Illus. by Alemagna, Beatrice)
    c SLJ - v61 - i6 - June 2015 - p73(1) [51-500]
The Marvellous Fluffy Squishy Itty Bitty (Illus. by Alemagna, Beatrice)
    c Sch Lib - v63 - i4 - Winter 2015 - p217(1) [51-500]
The Wonderful Fluffy Little Squishy (Illus. by Alemagna, Beatrice)
    c KR - July 15 2015 - pNA [51-500]
    c SLJ - v61 - i10 - Oct 2015 - p71(2) [51-500]

Alender, Katie - *The Dead Girls of Hysteria Hall*
    y KR - June 1 2015 - pNA [51-500]
    y SLJ - v61 - i6 - June 2015 - p110(1) [51-500]
    y VOYA - v38 - i4 - Oct 2015 - p64(2) [51-500]
Famous Last Words
    y CCB-B - v68 - i5 - Jan 2015 - p246(2) [51-500]
    y HB Guide - v26 - i1 - Spring 2015 - p98(1) [51-500]
    y Teach Lib - v42 - i3 - Feb 2015 - p28(4) [51-500]

Alexande, Larry - *A Higher Call*
    APH - v62 - i1 - Spring 2015 - p53(2) [501+]

Alexander, Alyssa - *In Bed with a Spy*
    LJ - v140 - i3 - Feb 15 2015 - p133(1) [501+]

Alexander, Amir - *Infinitesimal: How a Dangerous Mathematical Theory Shaped the Modern World*
    HT - v65 - i3 - March 2015 - p65(1) [501+]
    NYTBR - June 21 2015 - p24(L) [501+]

Alexander, Audrey - *Witches and Wicca*
    c BL - v111 - i15 - April 1 2015 - p54(1) [51-500]

Alexander, Bob - *Bad Company and Burnt Powder: Justice and Injustice in the Old Southwest*
    Roundup M - v22 - i3 - Feb 2015 - p22(1) [501+]
    Roundup M - v22 - i6 - August 2015 - p33(1) [501+]
Six-Shooters and Shifting Sands
    Roundup M - v23 - i1 - Oct 2015 - p32(1) [501+]

Alexander, Bryan - *Gearing Up for Learning beyond K-12*
    RVBW - Nov 2015 - pNA [51-500]

Alexander, Carol - *Florence Nightingale*
    c BL - v112 - i4 - Oct 15 2015 - p43(1) [51-500]

Alexander, Claire - *Monkey and the Little One (Illus. by Alexander, Claire)*
    c KR - March 15 2015 - pNA [51-500]
    c PW - v262 - i13 - March 30 2015 - p73(1) [51-500]
    c SLJ - v61 - i5 - May 2015 - p80(2) [51-500]

Alexander, D.C. - *The Legend of Devil's Creek*
    RVBW - Jan 2015 - pNA [501+]

Alexander, Elizabeth - *The Light of the World*
    BL - v111 - i14 - March 15 2015 - p40(1) [51-500]
    Econ - v415 - i8933 - April 11 2015 - p77(US) [501+]
    Ent W - i1363 - May 15 2015 - p61(1) [501+]
    KR - Jan 1 2015 - pNA [501+]
    LJ - v140 - i1 - June 1 2015 - p120(2) [51-500]
    NYTBR - April 26 2015 - p16(L) [501+]
    PW - v262 - i12 - March 23 2015 - p67(1) [51-500]
    PW - v262 - i15 - April 13 2015 - p8(1) [51-500]

Alexander, Evam - *Condos and Condoms*
    SPBW - June 2015 - pNA [51-500]

Alexander, Goldie - *Hanna, My Holocaust Story*
    c Magpies - v30 - i2 - May 2015 - p34(1) [501+]

Alexander, Gregory - *The Holy Mark*
    New Or - v49 - i5 - Feb 2015 - p38(1) [501+]

Alexander, Heather - *Be a Star!*
    c KR - Feb 15 2015 - pNA [51-500]

Alexander, Jeffrey C. - *Interpreting Clifford Geertz: Cultural Investigation in the Social Sciences*
    CS - v44 - i4 - July 2015 - p481-482 [501+]

Alexander, Jeffrey W. - *Brewed in Japan: The Evolution of the Japanese Beer Industry*
    Pac A - v88 - i3 - Sept 2015 - p713 [501+]

Alexander, Kermit - *The Valley of the Shadow of Death: A Tale of Tragedy and Redemption*
    BL - v111 - i22 - August 1 2015 - p9(2) [51-500]
    KR - July 1 2015 - pNA [501+]
    PW - v262 - i25 - June 22 2015 - p130(1) [51-500]

Alexander, Kwame - *The Crossover*
    y Teach Lib - v42 - i3 - Feb 2015 - p28(4) [501+]
    y Teach Lib - v42 - i3 - Feb 2015 - p32(6) [501+]
The Crossover (Read by Allen, Corey). Audiobook Review
    c BL - v111 - i13 - March 1 2015 - p70(2) [51-500]
    c HB - v91 - i2 - March-April 2015 - p128(1) [51-500]
The Crossover
    y Teach Lib - v42 - i4 - April 2015 - p23(1) [51-500]
Surf's Up (Illus. by Miyares, Daniel)
    c KR - Nov 15 2015 - pNA [51-500]
    c PW - v262 - i45 - Nov 9 2015 - p59(1) [51-500]
    c SLJ - v61 - i12 - Dec 2015 - p86(1) [51-500]

Alexander, Lloyd - *The Book of Three*
    c HB Guide - v26 - i1 - Spring 2015 - p67(1) [51-500]

Alexander, Lori - *Backhoe Joe (Illus. by Cameron, Craig)*
    c HB Guide - v26 - i1 - Spring 2015 - p5(1) [51-500]

Alexander, Peter - *Class in Soweto*
    CS - v44 - i3 - May 2015 - p335-337 [501+]

Alexander, Rebecca - *The Secrets of Blood and Bone*
    KR - August 1 2015 - pNA [501+]
    PW - v262 - i30 - July 27 2015 - p46(2) [51-500]

Alexander, Rilla - *Her Idea (Illus. by Alexander, Rilla)*
    KR - Feb 1 2015 - pNA [51-500]
    c PW - v262 - i5 - Feb 2 2015 - p57(2) [51-500]
    c SLJ - v61 - i6 - June 2015 - p76(1) [51-500]

Alexander, S.L. - *The Times-Picayune in a Changing Media World: The Transformation of an American Newspaper*
    AM - v213 - i11 - Oct 19 2015 - p35(4) [501+]

Alexander, Sarah - *The Art of Not Breathing*
    y KR - Jan 1 2016 - pNA [51-500]

Alexander, Shannon Lee - *Love and Other Unknown Variables*
    KR - Jan 1 2015 - pNA [501+]

Alexander, Shelly - *It's in His Heart*
    PW - v262 - i24 - June 15 2015 - p71(1) [51-500]

Alexander, Tamera - *To Win Her Favor*
    PW - v262 - i10 - March 9 2015 - p60(1) [51-500]

Alexander, Tasha - *The Adventuress*
    BL - v112 - i2 - Sept 15 2015 - p29(1) [51-500]
    PW - v262 - i34 - August 24 2015 - p59(1) [51-500]
And Only to Deceive (Read by Reading, Kate). Audiobook Review
    LJ - v140 - i7 - April 15 2015 - p46(1) [51-500]

Alexander, Ted M. - *After and Before*
    KR - Dec 1 2015 - pNA [501+]

Alexander, Tyler - *Tyler Alexander: A Life and Times with McLaren*
    NYT - Sept 19 2015 - pNA(L) [501+]

Alexander, Victoria - *The Daring Exploits of a Runaway Heiress*
    BL - v111 - i17 - May 1 2015 - p80(1) [51-500]

Alexander, Victoria N. - *Locus Amoenus*
    KR - April 15 2015 - pNA [501+]

Alexander, William - *Ambassador*
    c HB Guide - v26 - i1 - Spring 2015 - p67(1) [51-500]
Nomad
    y KR - August 15 2015 - pNA [501+]

Alexandra, Belinda - *Golden Earrings*
    BL - v111 - i21 - July 1 2015 - p42(1) [51-500]
White Gardenia
    BL - v111 - i9-10 - Jan 1 2015 - p55(1) [51-500]

Alexandrakis, Jessica - *Get Started Quilting: The Complete Beginner Guide*
    LJ - v140 - i17 - Oct 15 2015 - p89(1) [51-500]

Alexandre, Sandrine - *Evaluation et contre-pouvoir: Portee ethique et politique du jugement de valeur dans le stoicisme romain*
    Class R - v65 - i2 - Oct 2015 - p397-399 [501+]

Alexeeva, Olga - *Ethnic Minorities of Central and Eastern Europe in the Internet Space: A Computer-Assisted Content Analysis*
    E-A St - v67 - i3 - May 2015 - p502(2) [501+]

Alexievich, Svetlana - *Second-Hand Time*
    Nation - v301 - i24 - Dec 14 2015 - p31(3) [501+]

Alexiou, Joseph - *Gowanus*
    KR - July 1 2015 - pNA [501+]

Alexis, Andre - *Fifteen Dogs*
    KR - March 1 2015 - pNA [51-500]
    Nat Post - v17 - i141 - April 18 2015 - pWP8(1) [501+]
    TLS - i5866 - Sept 4 2015 - p22(1) [501+]
    WLT - v89 - i5 - Sept-Oct 2015 - p56(1) [501+]

Aley, Ginette - *Union Heartland: The Midwestern Home Front during the Civil War*
    Historian - v77 - i3 - Fall 2015 - p543(2) [501+]

Alfani, Guido - *Calamities and the Economy in Renaissance Italy: The Grand Tour of the Horsemen of the Apocalypse*
    JMH - v87 - i1 - March 2015 - p204(2) [501+]

Alfano, Mark - *Character as Moral Fiction*
    RM - v68 - i4 - June 2015 - p834(3) [501+]

Alfarabi - *The Political Writings, vol. 2: The Political Regime and Summary of Plato's Laws*
    RM - v69 - i2 - Dec 2015 - p373(2) [501+]

Alfons, Bora - *Wissensregulierung und Regulierungswissen*
    HNet - Sept 2015 - pNA [501+]

Alfonso, Esperanza - *Patronage, Production, and Transmission of Texts in Medieval and Early Modern Jewish Cultures*
    Specu - v90 - i4 - Oct 2015 - p1188(1) [501+]

Alford, Jeffrey - *Chicken in the Mango Tree: Food and Life in a Thai-Khmer Village*
    PW - v262 - i35 - August 31 2015 - p76(1) [51-500]

Alford, Stephen - *Edward VI: The Last Boy King*
    NS - v144 - i5244 - Jan 9 2015 - p41(1) [51-500]
    TLS - i5841 - March 13 2015 - p10(2) [501+]

Alford, Terry - *Fortune's Fool: The Life of John Wilkes Booth*
    AM - v212 - i14 - April 27 2015 - p30(3) [501+]
    KR - Jan 15 2015 - pNA [51-500]
    LJ - v140 - i6 - April 1 2015 - p99(1) [51-500]
    For Aff - v94 - i3 - May-June 2015 - pNA [501+]
    HNet - August 2015 - pNA [501+]

Alford, Vanessa - *Fit Not Healthy: How One Woman's Obsession to Be the Best Nearly Killed Her*
    BL - v112 - i4 - Oct 15 2015 - p13(1) [51-500]
    PW - v262 - i36 - Sept 7 2015 - p62(1) [51-500]

Alfred Publishing - *Contest Winners for Three: Piano Trios from the Alfred, Belwin and Myklas Libraries, 5 vols.*
    Am MT - v64 - i5 - April-May 2015 - p47(1) [501+]

Algeo, Matthew - *Abe & Fido: Lincoln's Love of Animals and the Touching Story of His Favorite Canine Companion*
    KR - Jan 15 2015 - pNA [51-500]
    PW - v262 - i7 - Feb 16 2015 - p168(2) [51-500]

Alger, Cristina - *This Was Not the Plan*
    KR - Nov 1 2015 - pNA [51-500]
    PW - v262 - i46 - Nov 16 2015 - p48(2) [51-500]

Algonquin, Tim Johnston - *The Descent*
    NYTBR - Jan 18 2015 - p26(L) [501+]

Ali, Ayaan Hirsi - *Heretic: Why Islam Needs a Reformation Now*
    AM - v213 - i11 - Oct 19 2015 - p34(2) [501+]
    Nat Post - v17 - i165 - May 16 2015 - pA16(1) [501+]
    NYRB - v62 - i19 - Dec 3 2015 - p35(3) [501+]
    NYTBR - April 5 2015 - p10(L) [501+]

Ali, Cassius - *Black Poet*
    SPBW - August 2015 - pNA [51-500]

Ali, Kecia - *The Lives of Muhammad*
    JAAR - v83 - i4 - Dec 2015 - p1157-1160 [501+]
    Lon R Bks - v37 - i20 - Oct 22 2015 - p21(4) [501+]

Ali, Leyla - *Off Balance, the American Way of Health*
    KR - Feb 1 2015 - pNA [501+]

Ali, Monica - *Untold Story*
    VOYA - v38 - i3 - August 2015 - p10(2) [501+]

Ali, Naheed - *Understanding Chronic Fatigue Syndrome: An Introduction for Patients and Caregivers*
    BL - v112 - i1 - Sept 1 2015 - p22(1) [51-500]
Understanding Pain: An Introduction for Patients and Caregivers
    BL - v111 - i16 - April 15 2015 - p9(1) [51-500]

Alifirenka, Caitlin - *I Will Always Write Back: How One Letter Changed Two Lives*
    y HB Guide - v26 - i2 - Fall 2015 - p206(1) [51-500]
    y PW - v262 - i49 - Dec 2 2015 - p116(2) [51-500]
    y CCB-B - v68 - i11 - July-August 2015 - p535(1) [51-500]
    y NYTBR - May 10 2015 - p19(L) [501+]
    c KR - Feb 1 2015 - pNA [51-500]

Alink, Melissa - *Little House Living: The Make-Your-Own Guide to a Frugal, Simple, and Self-Sufficient Life*
    LJ - v140 - i17 - Oct 15 2015 - p107(1) [51-500]

Alisic, Adnan - *Arizona Dream: A True Story from a Real-Life "Ocean's Eleven"*
    SPBW - Jan 2015 - pNA [51-500]

Alison, Dana - *The Misadventures of the Family Fletcher (Read by Woren, Dan). Audiobook Review*
    c HB - v91 - i2 - March-April 2015 - p131(1) [51-500]

Alkan, Oktay - *Code of Disjointed Letters*
    KR - Jan 1 2015 - pNA [501+]

Alkebulan, Paul - *The African American Press in World War II: Toward Victory at Home and Abroad*
    AHR - v120 - i2 - April 2015 - p654-655 [501+]
    JSH - v81 - i3 - August 2015 - p768(2) [501+]

Alkemeyer, Thomas - *Selbst-Bildungen: Soziale und kulturelle Praktiken der Subjektivierung*
    HNet - April 2015 - pNA [501+]

AlKhayyat, Mithaa - *My Own Special Way (Illus. by Fidawi, Maya)*
    SLJ - v61 - i2 - Feb 2015 - p60(1) [51-500]

Alko, Selina - *The Case for Loving: The Fight for Interracial Marriage (Illus. by Alko, Selina)*
    c CCB-B - v68 - i7 - March 2015 - p345(1) [51-500]
The Case for Loving: The Fight for Interracial Marriage (Illus. by Qualls, Sean)
    c CH Bwatch - May 2015 - pNA [501+]
    c HB - v91 - i3 - May-June 2015 - p125(1) [51-500]
    c HB Guide - v26 - i2 - Fall 2015 - p152(1) [51-500]
    c NYTBR - Feb 8 2015 - p22(L) [501+]
    c PW - v262 - i49 - Dec 2 2015 - p44(1) [51-500]

Allabach, P.R. - *Dragon and Captain (Illus. by Turnbloom, Lucas)*
    c CH Bwatch - June 2015 - pNA [51-500]

Allaby, Michael - *The Dictionary of Science for Gardeners: 6000 Scientific Terms Explored and Explained*
    BL - v112 - i4 - Oct 15 2015 - p9(1) [51-500]
    LJ - v140 - i16 - Oct 1 2015 - p106(1) [51-500]
The Dictionary of Science for Gardens: 6000 Scientific Terms for Explored and Explained
    NYTBR - Dec 6 2015 - p66(L) [501+]
The Gardener's Guide to Weather and Climate: How to Understand the Weather and Make It Work for You
    BL - v111 - i19-20 - June 1 2015 - p18(1) [51-500]
    PW - v262 - i16 - April 20 2015 - p73(1) [51-500]

Allain, Rhett - *Geek Physics: Surprising Answers to the Planet's Most Interesting Questions, 2d ed.*
    LJ - v140 - i8 - May 1 2015 - p96(2) [51-500]

Allan, Barbara - *Antiques Swap*
    BL - v111 - i15 - April 1 2015 - p29(1) [51-500]
    PW - v262 - i11 - March 16 2015 - p65(1) [51-500]

Allan, Jay - *Shadow of Empire*
    PW - v262 - i31 - August 3 2015 - p39(1) [51-500]

Allan, Kathryn - *Accessing the Future*
    PW - v262 - i17 - April 27 2015 - p56(1) [51-500]

Allan, Tony - *Typewriter: The History, the Machine, the Writer*
    LJ - v140 - i20 - Dec 1 2015 - p104(1) [51-500]

Allan, William - *Classical Literature: A Very Short Introduction*
    Class R - v65 - i2 - Oct 2015 - p321-322 [501+]

Allawi, Ali A. - *Faisal I of Iraq*
    AHR - v120 - i3 - June 2015 - p1150-1151 [501+]

Allelopoiese - Konzepte zur Beschreibung Kulturellen Wandels. Jahrestagung 2014 des SFB 644 "Tranformationen der Antike"
    HNet - March 2015 - pNA [501+]

Allemann, Urs - *The Old Man and the Bench*
    TLS - i5869 - Sept 25 2015 - p27(1) [501+]

Allen, Barry - *Striking Beauty: A Philosophical Look at the Asian Martial Arts*
    PW - v262 - i25 - June 22 2015 - p133(1) [51-500]

Allen, Brooke - *Benazir Bhutto: Favored Daughter*
    KR - Oct 15 2015 - pNA [501+]
    LJ - v140 - i20 - Dec 1 2015 - p119(2) [51-500]

Allen, Charles - *The Prisoner of Kathmandu: Brian Hodgson in Nepal, 1820-43*
    Spec - v329 - i9772 - Dec 12 2015 - p74(2) [501+]

Allen, Crystal - *Spirit Week Showdown (Illus. by Kaban, Eda)*
    c KR - Oct 15 2015 - pNA [51-500]
    c SLJ - v61 - i11 - Nov 2015 - p93(1) [51-500]

Allen, Elaine - *Ann Olly Explores: 7 Wonders of the Chesapeake Bay*
    c HB Guide - v26 - i2 - Fall 2015 - p24(1) [51-500]

Allen, Elise - *Autumn's Secret Gift (Illus. by Pooler, Paige)*
    c HB Guide - v26 - i1 - Spring 2015 - p56(1) [51-500]
Gabby Duran and the Unsittables (Illus. by Conners, Daryle)
    c BL - v111 - i17 - May 1 2015 - p100(1) [51-500]
Gabby Duran and the Unsittables (Illus. by Connors, Daryle)
    c CCB-B - v69 - i1 - Sept 2015 - p4(1) [51-500]
    c KR - March 15 2015 - pNA [51-500]
Gabby Duran and the Unsittables
    c SLJ - v61 - i5 - May 2015 - p100(1) [51-500]
Spring's Sparkle Sleepover (Illus. by Pooler, Paige)
    c HB Guide - v26 - i2 - Fall 2015 - p63(1) [51-500]
Winter's Tlurry Adventure (Illus. by Pooler, Paige)
    c HB Guide - v26 - i1 - Spring 2015 - p56(1) [51-500]

Allen, Gemma - *The Cooke Sisters: Education, Piety and Politics in Early Modern England*
    HER - v130 - i542 - Feb 2015 - p186(2) [501+]

Allen, Gene - *Making National News: A History of Canadian Press*
    AHR - v120 - i1 - Feb 2015 - p225(1) [501+]

Allen, J.J. - *There's a Bug in the Tub and It Won't Get Out*
    KR - May 1 2015 - pNA [501+]

Allen, Jeffery Renard - *Song of the Shank*
    BL - v111 - i16 - April 15 2015 - p34(1) [501+]
    Comw - v142 - i13 - August 14 2015 - p34(4) [501+]

Allen, John - *Anime and Manga*
    c SLJ - v61 - i2 - Feb 2015 - p116(1) [51-500]
Legalizing Marijuana
    y SLJ - v61 - i2 - Feb 2015 - p116(1) [51-500]
The Russian Federation: Then and Now
    y VOYA - v37 - i6 - Feb 2015 - p89(1) [51-500]

Allen, John L., Jr. - *The Francis Miracle*
    People - v83 - i11 - March 16 2015 - p41(NA) [501+]

Allen, John S. - *Home*
    KR - Oct 1 2015 - pNA [501+]

Allen, Jonathan - *HRC: State Secrets and the Rebirth of Hillary Clinton*
    Lon R Bks - v37 - i3 - Feb 5 2015 - p8(3) [501+]
    NYTBR - March 22 2015 - p28(L) [501+]

Allen, Kathryn Madeline - *Show Me Happy (Illus. by Futran, Eric)*
    c SLJ - v61 - i2 - Feb 2015 - p60(1) [51-500]
    c BL - v111 - i17 - May 1 2015 - p74(1) [51-500]
    c PW - v262 - i8 - Feb 23 2015 - p76(1) [51-500]

Allen, Keegan - *life.love.beauty*
    Bwatch - August 2015 - pNA [51-500]

Allen, Laura - *The Water-Wise Home*
    y BL - v111 - i12 - Feb 15 2015 - p28(1) [51-500]
    Bwatch - April 2015 - pNA [51-500]

Allen, Liana-Melissa - *Donkey's Kite: A Horse Valley Adventure (Illus. by Allen, Liana-Melissa)*
    c CH Bwatch - April 2015 - pNA [501+]

Allen, Lisa Van - *The Night Garden (Read by Rubinate, Amy). Audiobook Review*
    PW - v262 - i5 - Feb 2 2015 - p54(1) [51-500]

Allen, Lori - *The Rise and Fall of Human Rights: Cynicism and Politics in Occupied Palestine*
    IJMES - v47 - i1 - Feb 2015 - p175-176 [501+]

Allen, Mardi - *Sons Without Fathers: What Every Mother Needs to Know*
    RVBW - May 2015 - pNA [501+]

Allen, Mark - *Tantra for the West: A Direct Path to Living the Life of Your Dreams*
    RVBW - July 2015 - pNA [51-500]

Allen, Mark W. - *Violence and Warfare among Hunter-Gatherers*
    Am Ant - v80 - i4 - Oct 2015 - p787(2) [501+]

Allen, Matthew G. - *Greed and Grievance: Ex-Militants' Perspectives on the Conflict in Solomon Islands, 1998-2003*
    Pac A - v88 - i4 - Dec 2015 - p971 [501+]

Allen, Nancy - *The Underground Railroad*
    c SLJ - v61 - i4 - April 2015 - p108(4) [501+]

Allen, Nancy Campbell - *My Fair Gentleman*
    BL - v112 - i7 - Dec 1 2015 - p37(1) [51-500]
    PW - v262 - i45 - Nov 9 2015 - p43(1) [51-500]

Allen, Pamela - *The Man with Messy Hair*
    c Magpies - v30 - i3 - July 2015 - p26(1) [51-500]

Allen, Rachael - *The Revenge Playbook*
    y BL - v111 - i18 - May 15 2015 - p54(1) [51-500]
    y KR - April 1 2015 - pNA [51-500]
    y SLJ - v61 - i4 - April 2015 - p158(2) [51-500]
    y VOYA - v38 - i2 - June 2015 - p52(2) [51-500]

Allen, Robert C. - *Global Economic History: A Very Short Introduction*
    JEH - v75 - i1 - March 2015 - p259-261 [501+]

Allen, Sally A. - *The Tail of the Christmas Cat (Illus. by Rodriguez, Raquel)*
    c CH Bwatch - Jan 2015 - pNA [51-500]

Allen, Sarah Addison - *First Frost (Read by Ericksen, Susan). Audiobook Review*
    BL - v111 - i21 - July 1 2015 - p78(1) [51-500]
    LJ - v140 - i7 - April 15 2015 - p46(1) [51-500]

Allen, Stephen - *The Chagos Islanders and International Law*
    Law Q Rev - v131 - Oct 2015 - p684-686 [501+]

Allen, Susan Jane - *The Crusades: A Reader*
    Specu - v90 - i2 - April 2015 - p487-487 [501+]

Allenby, Victoria - *Nat the Cat Can Sleep Like That (Illus. by Anderson, Tara)*
    c CH Bwatch - July 2015 - pNA [51-500]
    c CH Bwatch - August 2015 - pNA [51-500]
Timo's Garden (Illus. by Griffiths, Dean)
    c KR - Nov 1 2015 - pNA [51-500]
    c PW - v262 - i45 - Nov 9 2015 - p60(1) [51-500]

Allende, Isabel - *The Japanese Lover*
    BL - v112 - i3 - Oct 1 2015 - p30(1) [51-500]
The Japanese Lover (Illus. by Caistor, Nick)
    PW - v262 - i32 - August 10 2015 - p36(1) [51-500]

The Japanese Lover
    KR - Sept 15 2015 - pNA [501+]
    Nat Post - v18 - i4 - Oct 31 2015 - pWP5(1) [501+]
    NYTBR - Dec 13 2015 - p34(L) [501+]
Allert, Tilman - *Plessner in Wiesbaden*
    HNet - April 2015 - pNA [501+]
Allestree, Ann - *Barbara Pym: A Passionate Force*
    Spec - v328 - i9743 - May 23 2015 - p39(2) [501+]
Allewaert, Monique - *Ariel's Ecology: Plantations, Personhood, and Colonialism in the American Tropics*
    AL - v87 - i3 - Sept 2015 - p605-607 [501+]
    J Am St - v49 - i2 - May 2015 - p413-414 [501+]
Alley, R.W. - *Clark in the Deep Sea (Illus. by Alley, R.W.)*
    c KR - Jan 1 2016 - pNA [51-500]
    c PW - v262 - i52 - Dec 21 2015 - p152(1) [51-500]
Gretchen over the Beach
    c KR - Jan 1 2016 - pNA [51-500]
Allfrey, Ellah Wakatama - *Africa 39*
    NS - v144 - i5244 - Jan 9 2015 - p41(1) [51-500]
Allin, Lou - *The Woman Who Did*
    KR - Oct 15 2015 - pNA [51-500]
Allinson, Rayne - *A Monarchy of Letters: Royal Correspondence and English Diplomacy in the Reign of Elizabeth I*
    Six Ct J - v46 - i1 - Spring 2015 - p234-235 [501+]
Allis, Anniken - *Beaded Lace Knitting: Techniques and 25 Beaded Lace Designs for Shawls, Scarves, and More*
    LJ - v140 - i12 - July 1 2015 - p86(1) [51-500]
Allison, Anne - *Precarious Japan*
    Pac A - v88 - i2 - June 2015 - p308 [501+]
Allison, Jill - *Motherhood and Infertility in Ireland: Understanding the Presence of Absence*
    MAQ - v29 - i1 - March 2015 - pB33-B35 [501+]
Allison, John - *The Case of the Lonely One (Illus. by Allison, John)*
    y BL - v112 - i4 - Oct 15 2015 - p36(1) [51-500]
    y KR - Sept 1 2015 - pNA [51-500]
Allison, Raphael - *Bodies on the Line: Performance and the Sixties Poetry Reading*
    NEQ - v88 - i3 - Sept 2015 - p532-534 [501+]
Allison, Richard - *Operation Thunderclap and the Black March: Two World War II Stories from the Unstoppable 91st Bomb Group*
    APH - v62 - i2 - Summer 2015 - p50(1) [501+]
Allison, Robert - *The Letter Bearer*
    KR - Oct 15 2015 - pNA [501+]
    PW - v262 - i50 - Dec 7 2015 - p66(1) [51-500]
Allison, William T. - *American Military History: A Survey from Colonial Times to the Present*
    J Mil H - v79 - i3 - July 2015 - p783-802 [501+]
Allitt, Patrick - *A Climate of Crisis: America in the Age of Environmentalism*
    HNet - Sept 2015 - pNA(NA) [501+]
Allman, Keith A. - *Impact Investment*
    NYT - April 12 2015 - p14(L) [501+]
Allman, Toney - *The Enlightenment*
    y VOYA - v38 - i2 - June 2015 - p89(1) [501+]
Food in Schools
    c HB Guide - v26 - i1 - Spring 2015 - p175(1) [51-500]
Allmendinger, Blake - *The Melon Capital of the World*
    Roundup M - v23 - i1 - Oct 2015 - p32(1) [501+]
Allmendinger, David F., Jr. - *Nat Turner and the Rising in Southampton County*
    JAH - v102 - i2 - Sept 2015 - p555-556 [501+]
Alloway, Kit - *Dreamfever*
    y KR - Dec 15 2015 - pNA [51-500]
    y SLJ - v61 - i12 - Dec 2015 - p112(1) [51-500]
Dreamfire
    y CCB-B - v68 - i9 - May 2015 - p437(1) [51-500]
    y HB Guide - v26 - i2 - Fall 2015 - p109(1) [51-500]
    y VOYA - v38 - i1 - April 2015 - p73(1) [51-500]
Allport, Alan - *Browned Off Bloody-Minded: The British Soldier Goes to War 1939-1945*
    TimHES - i2199 - April 16 2015 - p58(2) [501+]
Allure, Kate - *Lawyer Up*
    PW - v262 - i25 - June 22 2015 - p126(2) [51-500]
Allwell-Brown, Kiru - *The Wishgranter's Babies Tucca and Tucco (Illus. by Winburn, Sean)*
    c CH Bwatch - August 2015 - pNA [51-500]
Almada, Ariel A. - *The Lighthouse of Souls*
    KR - April 1 2015 - pNA [501+]
Almagor, Eran - *Ancient Ethnography: New Approaches*
    Class R - v65 - i2 - Oct 2015 - p345-347 [501+]
Alman, Susan - *Crash Course in Marketing for Libraries 2d ed.*
    Teach Lib - v42 - i3 - Feb 2015 - p42(1) [51-500]

Almand, M. Nicholas - *Orphan Blade (Illus. by Myler, Jake)*
    y SLJ - v61 - i3 - March 2015 - p146(1) [51-500]
Almeida, Paul - *Mobilizing Democracy: Globalization and Citizenship Protest*
    AJS - v121 - i2 - Sept 2015 - p632(3) [501+]
Almeleh, Rachel - *A Legacy of Sephardic, Mediterranean and American Recipes*
    KR - Oct 15 2015 - pNA [501+]
Almereyda, Michael - *Experimenter*
    New York - Oct 5 2015 - pNA [501+]
    New York - Oct 5 2015 - pNA [501+]
Almog, Joseph - *Everything in Its Right Place: Spinoza and Life by the Light of Nature*
    RM - v68 - i4 - June 2015 - p836(3) [501+]
Almond, David - *The Great War: Stories Inspired by Items from the First World War (Illus. by Kay, Jim)*
    y BL - v111 - i16 - April 15 2015 - p56(1) [51-500]
    y CCB-B - v68 - i8 - April 2015 - p401(1) [51-500]
    y HB Guide - v26 - i2 - Fall 2015 - p202(1) [51-500]
    c PW - v262 - i6 - Feb 9 2015 - p68(2) [51-500]
    y PW - v262 - i49 - Dec 2 2015 - p80(1) [51-500]
    c VOYA - v37 - i6 - Feb 2015 - p86(1) [51-500]
Half a Creature from the Sea: A Life in Stories (Illus. by Taylor, Eleanor)
    y BL - v112 - i2 - Sept 15 2015 - p64(1) [51-500]
    y KR - July 1 2015 - pNA [51-500]
    y Magpies - v30 - i1 - March 2015 - p39(1) [501+]
    y PW - v262 - i26 - June 29 2015 - p70(1) [51-500]
    y PW - v262 - i49 - Dec 2 2015 - p92(1) [51-500]
    y SLJ - v61 - i8 - August 2015 - p96(1) [51-500]
A Song for Ella Grey
    y BL - v112 - i1 - Sept 1 2015 - p109(1) [51-500]
    y HB - v91 - i6 - Nov-Dec 2015 - p76(1) [51-500]
    y KR - August 15 2015 - pNA [51-500]
    y Magpies - v30 - i3 - July 2015 - p39(1) [501+]
    y PW - v262 - i30 - July 27 2015 - p68(2) [51-500]
    y PW - v262 - i49 - Dec 2 2015 - p108(1) [51-500]
    y Sch Lib - v63 - i1 - Spring 2015 - p50(1) [51-500]
    y SLJ - v61 - i9 - Sept 2015 - p163(1) [51-500]
    y VOYA - v38 - i4 - Oct 2015 - p65(1) [51-500]
The Tightrope Walkers
    y BL - v111 - i12 - Feb 15 2015 - p78(1) [501+]
    y CCB-B - v68 - i8 - April 2015 - p387(1) [51-500]
    y HB - v91 - i2 - March-April 2015 - p89(1) [51-500]
    y HB Guide - v26 - i2 - Fall 2015 - p109(1) [51-500]
    y NYTBR - May 31 2015 - p54(L) [501+]
    y PW - v262 - i4 - Jan 26 2015 - p174(1) [51-500]
    y PW - v262 - i49 - Dec 2 2015 - p98(2) [51-500]
    y VOYA - v37 - i6 - Feb 2015 - p52(1) [51-500]
Almond, Philip C. - *The Devil: A New Biography*
    CHR - v101 - i3 - Summer 2015 - p588(2) [501+]
    HNet - Jan 2015 - pNA [501+]
Almond, Steve - *Against Football: One Fan's Reluctant Manifesto*
    SLJ - v61 - i2 - Feb 2015 - p113(1) [501+]
Alon Confino - *A World without Jews: The Nazi Imagination from Persecution to Genocide*
    CEH - v48 - i1 - March 2015 - p132-134 [501+]
Alonso, Juan Carlos - *The Early Cretaceous: Notes, Drawings, and Observations from Prehistory (Illus. by Alonso, Juan Carlos)*
    c KR - Sept 15 2015 - pNA [501+]
    c SLJ - v61 - i11 - Nov 2015 - p128(1) [51-500]
Alonso Troncoso, Victor - *After Alexander: The Time of the Diadochi (323-281 BC).*
    Class R - v65 - i1 - April 2015 - p183-185 [501+]
Alperin, Mara - *Goldilocks and the Three Bears (Illus. by Daubney, Kate)*
    c HB Guide - v26 - i2 - Fall 2015 - p158(1) [51-500]
Jack and the Beanstalk (Illus. by Chambers, Mark)
    c HB Guide - v26 - i2 - Fall 2015 - p158(1) [51-500]
    c SLJ - v61 - i5 - May 2015 - p82(1) [51-500]
Little Red Riding Hood (Illus. by Schauer, Loretta)
    c HB Guide - v26 - i2 - Fall 2015 - p158(1) [51-500]
    c SLJ - v61 - i5 - May 2015 - p82(1) [51-500]
The Three Billy Goats Gruff (Illus. by Pankhurst, Kate)
    c HB Guide - v26 - i2 - Fall 2015 - p158(1) [51-500]
Alpern, Andrew - *The Dakota: A History of the World's Best-Known Apartment Building*
    LJ - v140 - i20 - Dec 1 2015 - p106(2) [501+]
Alpers, Edward A. - *The Indian Ocean in World History*
    HNet - June 2015 - pNA [501+]
Alpert, Mark - *The Orion Plan*
    KR - Dec 15 2015 - pNA [501+]
    PW - v262 - i50 - Dec 7 2015 - p69(1) [51-500]
The Six
    y BL - v111 - i18 - May 15 2015 - p64(1) [51-500]
    y SLJ - v61 - i5 - May 2015 - p117(1) [51-500]
    y VOYA - v38 - i2 - June 2015 - p70(1) [51-500]
    KR - April 1 2015 - pNA [501+]

Alpert, Michael - *The Republican Army in the Spanish Civil War, 1936-1939*
    JMH - v87 - i2 - June 2015 - p475(3) [501+]
Alpher, Yossi - *Periphery: Israel's Search for Middle East Allies*
    Lon R Bks - v37 - i21 - Nov 5 2015 - p21(4) [501+]
Alpine, Rachele - *Operation Pucker Up*
    c BL - v111 - i21 - July 1 2015 - p75(1) [51-500]
Alsaid, Adi - *Let's Get Lost*
    y HB Guide - v26 - i1 - Spring 2015 - p98(1) [51-500]
Never Always Sometimes
    y BL - v111 - i15 - April 1 2015 - p35(1) [501+]
    y BL - v111 - i18 - May 15 2015 - p53(2) [51-500]
    y KR - May 1 2015 - pNA [51-500]
    y SLJ - v61 - i7 - July 2015 - p89(2) [51-500]
Alsanousi, Saud - *The Bamboo Stalk*
    NY - v91 - i30 - Oct 5 2015 - p82 [51-500]
Alsenas, Linas - *Beyond Clueless*
    y HB - v91 - i4 - July-August 2015 - p128(1) [51-500]
    y KR - June 15 2015 - pNA [51-500]
    y Sch Lib - v63 - i4 - Winter 2015 - p242(1) [51-500]
    y SLJ - v61 - i7 - July 2015 - p89(1) [51-500]
    y VOYA - v38 - i3 - August 2015 - p52(1) [51-500]
Alston, Clair L. - *Case Studies in Bayesian Statistical Modelling and Analysis*
    QRB - v90 - i3 - Sept 2015 - p319(2) [501+]
Alston, Richard - *Rome's Revolution: Death of the Republic and Birth of the Empire*
    KR - April 1 2015 - pNA [501+]
    LJ - v140 - i9 - May 15 2015 - p90(2) [51-500]
Alt, Dirk - *"Der Farbfilm Marschiert!" Fruhe Farbfilmverfahren und NS-Propaganda 1933-1945*
    HNet - Feb 2015 - pNA [501+]
Altamirano-Jimenez, Isabel - *Indigenous Encounters with Neoliberalism: Place, Women, and the Environment in Canada and Mexico*
    Am Ind CRJ - v39 - i1 - Wntr 2015 - p127-129 [501+]
Altebrando, Tara - *The Battle of Darcy Lane*
    c HB Guide - v26 - i1 - Spring 2015 - p67(1) [51-500]
My Life in Dioramas (Illus. by Bonaddio, T.L.)
    c HB Guide - v26 - i2 - Fall 2015 - p73(1) [51-500]
    c KR - Feb 15 2015 - pNA [51-500]
    c PW - v262 - i9 - March 2 2015 - p83(1) [51-500]
    c SLJ - v61 - i3 - March 2015 - p131(1) [51-500]
Altein, Chani - *Wherever We Go! (Illus. by Lumer, Marc)*
    c HB Guide - v26 - i2 - Fall 2015 - p149(1) [51-500]
Alten, Steve - *Sharkman*
    y HB Guide - v26 - i1 - Spring 2015 - p99(1) [51-500]
Alter, Anna - *Five Stories*
    c HB Guide - v26 - i2 - Fall 2015 - p63(1) [51-500]
A New Arrival
    c KR - Nov 1 2015 - pNA [51-500]
Sprout Street Neighbors: Five Stories (Illus. by Alter, Anna)
    c BL - v111 - i14 - March 15 2015 - p80(1) [51-500]
    c KR - Feb 15 2015 - pNA [51-500]
Alter, Karen J. - *The New Terrain of International Law: Courts, Politics, Rights*
    HNet - Jan 2015 - pNA [501+]
Alter, Robert - *Ancient Israel: The Former Prophets Joshua, Judges, Samuel, and Kings: A Translation with Commentary*
    Historian - v77 - i1 - Spring 2015 - p155(2) [501+]
Strong as Death Is Love: The Song of Songs, Ruth, Esther, Jonah, Daniel
    NS - v144 - i5261 - May 7 2015 - p50(2) [501+]
    PW - v262 - i6 - Feb 9 2015 - p62(1) [51-500]
Alter, Stephen - *Becoming a Mountain*
    KR - Jan 15 2015 - pNA [501+]
The Rataban Betrayal
    KR - Nov 15 2015 - pNA [51-500]
The Alternative Jukebox: 500 Extraordinary Tracks That Tell a Story of Alternative Music
    LJ - v140 - i3 - Feb 15 2015 - p128(2) [51-500]
Altes, Marta - *The King Cat (Illus. by Altes, Marta)*
    c Sch Lib - v63 - i2 - Summer 2015 - p89(1) [51-500]
Althammer, Beate - *The Welfare State and the 'Deviant Poor' in Europe: 1870-1933*
    HNet - Feb 2015 - pNA [501+]

Alther, Lisa - *About Women: Conversations between a Writer and a Painter*
    KR - August 1 2015 - pNA [51-500]
    LJ - v140 - i16 - Oct 1 2015 - p99(1) [51-500]
    NYTBR - Dec 6 2015 - p61(L) [501+]
    PW - v262 - i31 - August 3 2015 - p45(1) [51-500]

Altman, Elissa - *Poor Man's Feast: Love Story of Comfort, Desire, and the Art of Simple Cooking*
    NYTBR - Oct 25 2015 - p32(L) [501+]

Altman, Jerald S. - *Don't Stick Sticks Up Your Nose! Don't Stuff Stuff In Your Ears!*
    c KR - March 15 2015 - pNA [51-500]

Altman, John - *Disposable Asset*
    BL - v112 - i1 - Sept 1 2015 - p46(1) [51-500]
    PW - v262 - i28 - July 13 2015 - p47(1) [51-500]

Altman, Josh - *It's Your Move: My Million Dollar Method for Taking Risks with Confidence and Succeeding at Work and Life*
    LJ - v140 - i16 - Oct 1 2015 - p89(1) [51-500]

Altman, Kathryn Reed - *Altman*
    LJ - v140 - i3 - Feb 15 2015 - p101(2) [51-500]
    Si & So - v25 - i3 - March 2015 - p107(1) [501+]

Altman, Linda Jacobs - *Hitler, Goebbels, Himmler: The Nazi Holocaust Masterminds*
    y HB Guide - v26 - i1 - Spring 2015 - p201(1) [51-500]

Warsaw, Lodz, Vilna: The Holocaust Ghettos
    y HB Guide - v26 - i1 - Spring 2015 - p201(1) [51-500]

Altman, Nancy J. - *Social Security Works! Why Social Security Isn't Going Broke and How Expanding It Will Help Us All*
    BL - v111 - i9-10 - Jan 1 2015 - p24(1) [51-500]
    NYRB - v62 - i4 - March 5 2015 - p48(3) [501+]

Altom, Laura Marie - *The Escort*
    PW - v262 - i27 - July 6 2015 - p54(1) [51-500]

Alton, William L. - *Flesh and Bone*
    y HB Guide - v26 - i2 - Fall 2015 - p109(1) [51-500]
    y SLJ - v61 - i5 - May 2015 - p117(1) [51-500]

Altrichter, Helmut - *Deutschland - Russland: Stationen gemeinsamer Geschichte, Orte der Erinnerung: Band 3: Das 20. Jahrhundert*
    HNet - April 2015 - pNA [501+]

Altshul, Victor - *Singing with Starlings*
    KR - Pac - v27 - i1 - Spring 2015 - pNA [51-500]

Alvandi, Roham - *Nixon, Kissinger, and the Shah: The United States and Iran in the Cold War*
    AHR - v120 - i4 - Oct 2015 - p1519-1520 [501+]
    HNet - June 2015 - pNA [501+]
    IJMES - v47 - i3 - August 2015 - p638-639 [501+]
    JAH - v102 - i2 - Sept 2015 - p627-628 [501+]
    JIH - v46 - i1 - Summer 2015 - p137-139 [501+]

Alvar, Mia - *In the Country: Stories*
    BL - v111 - i19-20 - June 1 2015 - p42(1) [51-500]
    NYT - June 25 2015 - pC4(L) [501+]
    NYTBR - June 21 2015 - p19(L) [501+]
    LJ - v140 - i7 - April 15 2015 - p82(1) [51-500]
    AM - v216 - i6 - Sept 14 2015 - p44(2) [501+]
    BooChiTr - July 11 2015 - p13(1) [501+]
    Ent W - i1369 - June 26 2015 - p66(1) [501+]
    KR - April 15 2015 - pNA [51-500]
    PW - v262 - i10 - March 9 2015 - p49(1) [51-500]

Alvarado, Anthony - *D.I.Y. Magic: A Strange and Whimsical Guide to Creativity*
    PW - v262 - i6 - Feb 9 2015 - p61(1) [51-500]

Alvarado, Rodolfo - *Perla Garcia and the Mystery of La Llorona, "The Weeping Woman" (Illus. by Nowakowski, Peter)*
    c CH Bwatch - July 2015 - pNA [51-500]

Alvarado Valdivia, Juan - *Cancerlandia!*
    KR - July 15 2015 - pNA [501+]

Alvarez, Jennifer Lynn - *Starfire*
    c HB Guide - v26 - i1 - Spring 2015 - p67(2) [51-500]

Stormbound
    c HB Guide - v26 - i2 - Fall 2015 - p73(1) [51-500]
    c KR - Feb 15 2015 - pNA [51-500]
    y VOYA - v38 - i1 - April 2015 - p73(1) [51-500]

Alvarez, Rene Luis - *Miles to Go before We Sleep: Well-Worn Paths and New Directions for Educational Historians*
    J Urban H - v41 - i3 - May 2015 - p534-540 [501+]

Alve, Maria Helena Moreira - *Living in the Crossfire: Favela Residents, Drug Dealers and Police Violence in Rio de Janeiro*
    SF - v93 - i3 - March 2015 - pe65 [501+]

Alvear, Michael - *Eat It Later: Mastering Self Control and the Slimming Power of Postponement*
    KR - August 1 2015 - pNA [501+]

Alward, Amy - *Madly*
    y KR - July 15 2015 - pNA [51-500]
    y VOYA - v38 - i4 - Oct 2015 - p65(1) [51-500]
    y BL - v112 - i2 - Sept 15 2015 - p74(1) [51-500]
    y SLJ - v61 - i9 - Sept 2015 - p156(1) [51-500]

The Potion Diaries
    c Sch Lib - v63 - i3 - Autumn 2015 - p178(1) [51-500]

Alworth, Jeff - *The Beer Bible*
    BL - v111 - i21 - July 1 2015 - p15(1) [51-500]
    LJ - v140 - i13 - August 1 2015 - p118(1) [51-500]

Aly, Gotz - *Die Belasteten: 'Euthanasie' 1939-1945: Eine Gesellschaftsgeschichte*
    HNet - June 2015 - pNA [501+]
    HNet - August 2015 - pNA [501+]

Why the Germans? Why the Jews? Envy, Race Hatred, and the Prehistory of the Holocaust
    NYRB - v62 - i1 - Jan 8 2015 - p44(2) [501+]

Alynn, Jess - *Christmas Is for Bad Girls*
    RVBW - July 2015 - pNA [51-500]

Alznauer, Mark - *Hegel's Theory of Responsibility*
    RM - v69 - i2 - Dec 2015 - p375(3) [501+]

Amadori, Arrigo - *Negociando la obediencia: Gestion y reforma de los virreinatos americanos en tiempos del conde-duque de Olivares*
    HAHR - v95 - i3 - August 2015 - p517-519 [501+]

Amako, Satoshi - *Regional Integration in East Asia: Theoretical and Historical Perspectives*
    Pac A - v88 - i1 - March 2015 - p151 [501+]

Amaldi, Ugo - *Particle Accelerators: From Big Bang Physics to Hadron Therapy*
    Phys Today - v68 - i10 - Oct 2015 - p50-50 [501+]

Amar, Akhil, Reed - *America's Unwritten Constitution: The Precendents and Principles We Live By*
    NYTBR - March 8 2015 - p32(L) [501+]

Amar, Akhil Reed - *The Law of the Land: A Grand Tour of Our Constitutional Republic*
    KR - Feb 1 2015 - pNA [501+]
    LJ - v140 - i3 - Feb 15 2015 - p115(2) [51-500]
    PW - v262 - i7 - Feb 16 2015 - p171(1) [51-500]

Amar, Paul - *The Security Archipelago: Human-Security States, Sexuality Politics and the End of Neoliberalism*
    Am Q - v67 - i1 - March 2015 - p219-229 [501+]

Amaru, Patrick Araia - *Nonahere Ori Tahiti: Pipiri Ma*
    Cont Pac - v27 - i1 - Spring 2015 - p302(3) [501+]

Amat-Piniella, Joaquim - *K.L. Reich*
    WLT - v89 - i5 - Sept-Oct 2015 - p57(1) [51-500]

Amateau, Gigi - *Dante of the Maury River (Read by Jackson, J.D.) Audiobook Review*
    c SLJ - v61 - i7 - July 2015 - p46(1) [51-500]

Dante of the Maury River
    c KR - Feb 15 2015 - pNA [51-500]
    c HB Guide - v26 - i2 - Fall 2015 - p73(1) [51-500]

Two for Joy (Illus. by Marble, Abigail)
    c BL - v111 - i19-20 - June 1 2015 - p107(2) [51-500]
    c CCB-B - v69 - i1 - Sept 2015 - p5(1) [51-500]
    c KR - March 15 2015 - pNA [51-500]
    c PW - v262 - i16 - April 20 2015 - p77(1) [51-500]
    c SLJ - v61 - i4 - April 2015 - p140(1) [51-500]
    c HB Guide - v26 - i2 - Fall 2015 - p63(1) [51-500]

Amato, Joe - *Samuel Taylor's Last Night*
    NYTBR - Feb 22 2015 - p34(L) [51-500]

Amato, Kimberly - *Steele Resolve*
    SPBW - May 2015 - pNA [51-500]

Amato, Mary - *Get Happy*
    y CCB-B - v68 - i6 - Feb 2015 - p296(2) [51-500]
    y HB Guide - v26 - i1 - Spring 2015 - p99(1) [51-500]
    y Sch Lib - v63 - i2 - Summer 2015 - p114(1) [51-500]

Sniff a Skunk! (Illus. by Marble, Abigail)
    c HB Guide - v26 - i2 - Fall 2015 - p63(1) [51-500]

Amato, Vic - *Incoming: Collected Stories*
    SPBW - August 2015 - pNA [51-500]

Amazing Robots Series: Robots in Industry
    c BL - v112 - i6 - Nov 15 2015 - p42(1) [501+]

Ambar, Saladin - *Malcolm X at Oxford Union: Racial Politics in a Global Era*
    AM - v212 - i2 - Jan 19 2015 - p34(3) [501+]

Amberson, Mary Margaret McAllen - *Maximilian and Carlota: Europe's Last Empire in Mexico*
    Ams - v72 - i1 - July 2015 - p169(3) [501+]
    HAHR - v95 - i1 - Feb 2015 - p159-160 [501+]

Ambiguitat und Gesellschaftliche Ordnung im Mittelalter. 21. Tagung des Brackweder Arbeitskreises fur Mittelalterforschung
    HNet - Jan 2015 - pNA [501+]

Ambros, Robert - *Griffith Stadium*
    PW - v262 - i23 - June 8 2015 - p41(1) [51-500]

Ambrose, Marylou - *Investigate Alcohol*
    y HB Guide - v26 - i1 - Spring 2015 - p141(1) [51-500]

Investigate Cocaine and Crack
    y HB Guide - v26 - i1 - Spring 2015 - p141(1) [51-500]

Investigate Methamphetamine
    y HB Guide - v26 - i1 - Spring 2015 - p141(1) [51-500]

Ambrose, Stephen - *Undaunted Courage*
    Esq - v163 - i6-7 - June-July 2015 - p26(2) [501+]
    BL - v111 - i9-10 - Jan 1 2015 - p120(1) [501+]

Ambrosini, Maurizio - *Irregular Migration and Invisible Welfare*
    CS - v44 - i5 - Sept 2015 - p623-625 [501+]

Ambroziak, K.P. - *The Journal of Vincent Du Maurier*
    PW - v262 - i15 - April 13 2015 - p62(1) [51-500]

Amdahl, Gary - *The Daredevils*
    KR - Dec 1 2015 - pNA [51-500]

Amelang, James S. - *Parallel Histories: Muslims and Jews in Inquisitorial Spain*
    AHR - v120 - i1 - Feb 2015 - p318-319 [501+]
    HER - v130 - i544 - June 2015 - p730(3) [501+]
    JMH - v87 - i2 - June 2015 - p472(2) [501+]
    Six Ct J - v46 - i3 - Fall 2015 - p756-757 [501+]

Amelang, Katrin - *Transplantierte Alltage: Zur Produktion von Normalitat nach einer Organtransplantation*
    HNet - April 2015 - pNA [501+]

Amendt, Linda J. - *Blue Ribbon Canning: Spreads, Sauces and More*
    LJ - v140 - i8 - May 1 2015 - p94(1) [51-500]

American Museum of Natural History - *ABC Insects*
    c KR - Jan 1 2015 - pNA [51-500]

American Psychiatric Association - *Understanding Mental Disorders*
    KR - May 15 2015 - pNA [501+]

American Psychological Association - *APA Dictionary of Psychology, 2d ed.*
    LJ - v140 - i10 - June 1 2015 - p133(1) [51-500]

America's Test Kitchen - *100 Recipes: The Absolute Best Ways to Make the True Essentials*
    LJ - v140 - i13 - August 1 2015 - p120(1) [51-500]
    PW - v262 - i36 - Sept 7 2015 - p61(1) [51-500]

Cook It in Cast Iron: Kitchen-Tested Recipes for the One Pan That Does it All
    PW - v262 - i50 - Dec 7 2015 - p81(2) [51-500]

Cook's Country Eats Local: 150 Regional Recipes You Should Be Making No Matter Where You Live
    LJ - v140 - i11 - June 15 2015 - p108(2) [51-500]

Amerini, Fabrizio - *A Companion to the Latin Medieval Commentaries on Aristotle's Metaphysics*
    Six Ct J - v46 - i1 - Spring 2015 - p159(3) [501+]

"In principio erat Verbum": Philosophy and Theology in the Commentaries on the Gospel of John
    Specu - v90 - i4 - Oct 2015 - p1188-1189 [501+]

Ames, Eric - *Ferocious Reality: Documentary according to Werner Herzog*
    GSR - v38 - i2 - May 2015 - p461-3 [501+]

Werner Herzog: Interviews
    FQ - v69 - i1 - Fall 2015 - p102(3) [501+]

Ames, Jonathan - *Wake Up, Sir!*
    NS - v144 - i5266 - June 12 2015 - p51(1) [51-500]
    Spec - v328 - i9750 - July 11 2015 - p35(2) [501+]

Ames, Phyllis - *Frozen in Amber*
    PW - v262 - i30 - July 27 2015 - p47(2) [51-500]

Amichai, Yehuda - *The Poetry of Yehuda Amichai*
    BL - v112 - i5 - Nov 1 2015 - p14(1) [51-500]
    PW - v262 - i46 - Nov 16 2015 - p52(1) [51-500]

Amici, Marco - *The Black Album: Il noir tra cronaca e romanzo*
    MLR - v110 - i2 - April 2015 - p569-572 [501+]

Amico, Stephen - *Roll Over Tchaikovsky! Russian Popular Music and Post-Soviet Homosexuality*
    Slav R - v74 - i2 - Summer 2015 - p366-369 [501+]

Amidon, Stephen - *The Real Justine*
    BL - v111 - i22 - August 1 2015 - p36(1) [51-500]
    KR - July 15 2015 - pNA [51-500]

Amidsen, Fred - *Portlandia*
    People - v83 - i2 - Jan 12 2015 - p29 [501+]
    People - v83 - i2 - Jan 12 2015 - p29 [501+]
    People - v83 - i2 - Jan 12 2015 - p29 [501+]
    People - v83 - i2 - Jan 12 2015 - p29 [501+]
    People - v83 - i2 - Jan 12 2015 - p29 [501+]

Amirahmadi, Hooshang - *The Political Economy of Iran under the Qajars: Society, Politics, Economics and Foreign Relations 1796-1936*
    IJMES - v47 - i4 - Nov 2015 - p818-820 [501+]

Amirsadeghl, Hossein - *Nordic Contemporary: Art from Denmark, Finland, Iceland, Norway and Sweden*
LJ - v140 - i7 - April 15 2015 - p83(1) [51-500]
Amiry, Suad - *Golda Slept Here*
PW - v262 - i18 - May 4 2015 - p109(1) [51-500]
Amis, Fedora - *Mayhem at Buffalo Bill's Wild West: A Jemmy McBustle Mystery*
PW - v262 - i52 - Dec 21 2015 - p136(1) [51-500]
Amis, Kingsley - *Lucky Jim*
TimHES - i2211 - July 9 2015 - p46(1) [501+]
Amis, Martin - *The Zone of Interest*
NYTBR - Sept 6 2015 - p24(L) [501+]
Amitai, Reuven - *Holy War and Rapprochement: Studies in the Relations between the Mamluk Sultanate and the Mongol Ilkhanate, 1260-1335*
TLS - i5872 - Oct 16 2015 - p27(1) [501+]
Nomads as Agents of Cultural Change: The Mongols and Their Eurasian Predecessors
HNet - Sept 2015 - pNA [501+]
Amling, Eric - *From the Author's Private Collection*
PW - v262 - i20 - May 18 2015 - p61(1) [51-500]
Ammerman, Dean - *Escape from Dorkville*
KR - Dec 1 2015 - pNA [501+]
Ammerman, Nancy Tatom - *Sacred Stories, Spiritual Tribes: Finding Religion in Everyday Life*
AJS - v120 - i4 - Jan 2015 - p1252(3) [501+]
CC - v132 - i3 - Feb 4 2015 - p30(2) [501+]
CS - v44 - i3 - May 2015 - p337-338 [501+]
Amnesty International UK - *Dreams of Freedom in Words and Pictures*
c Magpies - v30 - i1 - March 2015 - p24(1) [501+]
c PW - v262 - i8 - Feb 23 2015 - p76(1) [501+]
Dreams of Freedom: In Words and Pictures
c SLJ - v61 - i4 - April 2015 - p126(1) [51-500]
Dreams of Freedom in Words and Pictures
c KR - Feb 1 2015 - pNA [51-500]
Amodio, Mark C. - *The Anglo-Saxon Literature Handbook*
Med R - Sept 2015 - pNA [501+]
Amony, Evelyn - *I Am Evelyn Amony*
KR - August 15 2015 - pNA [51-500]
Amore, Anthony M. - *The Art of the Con: The Most Notorious Fakes, Frauds, and Forgeries in the Art World*
BooChiTr - August 1 2015 - p14(1) [501+]
KR - April 15 2015 - pNA [501+]
LJ - v140 - i11 - June 15 2015 - p92(1) [501+]
Mac - v128 - i29-30 - July 27 2015 - p70(1) [501+]
NYTBR - June 28 2015 - p22(L) [501+]
PW - v262 - i18 - May 4 2015 - p111(1) [51-500]
Amorose, Mark - *In the Saguaro Forest*
MA - v57 - i1 - Wntr 2015 - p49(8) [501+]
Amos, Clare - *Peace-ing Together Jerusalem*
RVBW - August 2015 - pNA [51-500]
Amos, Kim - *And Then He Kissed Me*
BL - v112 - i2 - Sept 15 2015 - p42(2) [501+]
PW - v262 - i26 - June 29 2015 - p53(2) [51-500]
Every Little Kiss
BL - v112 - i2 - Sept 15 2015 - p41(1) [51-500]
Amos, Martyn - *Beta-Life*
PW - v262 - i4 - Jan 26 2015 - p154(2) [51-500]
Amoss, Berthe - *Mischief and Malice*
c BL - v111 - i17 - May 1 2015 - p55(1) [51-500]
c PW - v262 - i9 - March 2 2015 - p85(1) [51-500]
c SLJ - v61 - i5 - May 2015 - p111(1) [51-500]
Amowitz, Lisa - *Until Beth*
y SLJ - v61 - i11 - Nov 2015 - p110(1) [51-500]
Amrith, Sunil S. - *Crossing the Bay of Bengal: The Furies of Nature and the Fortunes of Migrants*
JAS - v74 - i2 - May 2015 - p500-502 [501+]
Pac A - v88 - i3 - Sept 2015 - p729 [501+]
Amsden, Christine - *Madison's Song*
PW - v262 - i37 - Sept 14 2015 - p47(1) [51-500]
Amster, Ellen J. - *Medicine and the Saints: Science, Islam, and the Colonial Encounter in Morocco, 1877-1956*
JIH - v45 - i3 - Wntr 2015 - p452-454 [501+]
Amstutz, Lisa J. - *Awesome African Animals Series*
c HB Guide - v26 - i2 - Fall 2015 - p178(1) [51-500]
Amundsen, Lucie B. - *Locally Laid*
KR - Dec 1 2015 - pNA [501+]
Anagnostou, Sabine - *Missionspharmazie: Konzepte, Praxis, Organisation und wissenschaftliche Ausstrahlung*
Isis - v106 - i1 - March 2015 - p177(2) [501+]
Anand, Anita - *Sophia: Princess, Suffragette, Revolutionary*
NS - v144 - i5244 - Jan 9 2015 - p38(1) [501+]
NY - v90 - i44 - Jan 19 2015 - p75 [51-500]
NYTBR - Jan 25 2015 - p16(L) [501+]
Spec - v327 - i9726 - Jan 24 2015 - p44(1) [501+]
TLS - i5840 - March 6 2015 - p13(1) [501+]
Swing in the House and Other Stories
Nat Post - v17 - i165 - May 16 2015 - pWP4(1) [501+]
Anand, Mulk Raj - *Untouchable*
TLS - i5868 - Sept 18 2015 - p26(1) [501+]
Ananthaswamy, Anil - *The Man Who Wasn't There: Investigations into the Strange New Science of the Self*
KR - June 1 2015 - pNA [501+]
The Man Who Wasn't There: Investigations into the Strange New Science of the Self
Nature - v524 - i7563 - August 6 2015 - p32(2) [501+]
New Sci - v227 - i3036 - August 29 2015 - p42(2) [501+]
PW - v262 - i21 - May 25 2015 - p1(1) [51-500]
Anaries, Kathryn - *The Dream Doctor: A Lighthearted Journey to Help the Children in Your Life Discover Dreams Have Something to Teach Us (Illus. by Beening, Kathleen)*
c CH Bwatch - March 2015 - pNA [51-500]
Anasi, Robert - *The Last Bohemia: Scenes from the Life of Williamsburg, Brooklyn*
BL - v112 - i5 - Nov 1 2015 - p18(2) [501+]
Anastasiu, Heather - *Girl Last Seen*
y KR - Jan 1 2016 - pNA [51-500]
Anastasius the Librarian - *Gesta sanctae ac universalis octavae synodi quae Constantinopoli congregata est Anastasio bibliothecario interprete*
Specu - v90 - i2 - April 2015 - p487-489 [501+]
Anastasopoulos, Dimitri - *Farm for Mutes*
ABR - v36 - i3 - March-April 2015 - p10(2) [501+]
Anatolios, Khaled - *The Holy Trinity in the Life of the Church*
Theol St - v76 - i4 - Dec 2015 - p893(2) [501+]
Anaya, Rudolfo - *Poems from the Rio Grande*
BL - v111 - i22 - August 1 2015 - p18(1) [51-500]
Randy Lopez Goes Home
Roundup M - v22 - i6 - August 2015 - p25(1) [501+]
Rudolfo Anaya's The Farolitos of Christmas (Illus. by Cordova, Amy)
c KR - Sept 1 2015 - pNA [51-500]
c PW - v262 - i37 - Sept 14 2015 - p72(2) [501+]
c SLJ - v61 - i10 - Oct 2015 - p60(1) [51-500]
Ancelet, Barry Jean - *Qui est le plus fort? (Illus. by Boudreau, Joel)*
y Res Links - v20 - i3 - Feb 2015 - p42(1) [51-500]
Ancona, George - *Can We Help? Kids Volunteering to Help Their Communities (Illus. by Ancona, George)*
c KR - June 15 2015 - pNA [51-500]
c SLJ - v61 - i8 - August 2015 - p117(1) [51-500]
c BL - v111 - i21 - July 1 2015 - p52(1) [51-500]
Anctil, Michel - *Dawn of the Neuron: The Early Struggles to Trace the Origin of Nervous Systems*
BL - v112 - i2 - Sept 15 2015 - p7(1) [51-500]
LJ - v140 - i16 - Oct 1 2015 - p102(3) [51-500]
Andalibian, Rahimeh - *The Rose Hotel: A Memoir of Secrets, Loss, and Love from Iran to America*
BL - v111 - i16 - April 15 2015 - p5(2) [51-500]
LJ - v140 - i10 - June 1 2015 - p120(2) [501+]
KR - Feb 15 2015 - pNA [501+]
Andaya, Elise - *Conceiving Cuba: Reproduction, Women, and the State in the Post-Soviet Era*
MAQ - v29 - i2 - June 2015 - pb46-b48 [501+]
Andelman, Bob - *Will Eisner: A Spirited Life*
Bwatch - Oct 2015 - pNA [51-500]
Anders, Charlie Jane - *All the Birds in the Sky*
KR - Dec 15 2015 - pNA [501+]
PW - v262 - i45 - Nov 9 2015 - p40(2) [51-500]
Anders, Lou - *Frostborn (Read by Tassone, Fabio). Audiobook Review*
y BL - v111 - i13 - March 1 2015 - p71(1) [51-500]
Frostborn (Illus. by Gerard, Justin)
c HB Guide - v26 - i1 - Spring 2015 - p68(1) [51-500]
c SLJ - v61 - i6 - June 2015 - p46(6) [501+]
Nightborn (Illus. by Gerard, Justin)
c BL - v111 - i21 - July 1 2015 - p75(1) [51-500]
c SLJ - v61 - i9 - Sept 2015 - p137(1) [51-500]
Nightborn
c KR - June 1 2015 - pNA [51-500]
Andersen, Chris - *"Metis": Race, Recognition, and the Struggle for Indigenous Peoplehood*
Can Lit - i224 - Spring 2015 - p103 [501+]
Metis: Race, Recognition, and the Struggle for Indigenous Peoplehood
WHQ - v46 - i3 - Autumn 2015 - p366-367 [501+]
Andersen, Hans Christian - *The Snow Queen (Read by Kellgren, Katherine). Audiobook Review*
c BL - v111 - i9-10 - Jan 1 2015 - p118(1) [51-500]
The Snow Queen (Read by Yuen, Erin). Audiobook Review
c SLJ - v61 - i10 - Oct 2015 - p50(1) [51-500]
The Snow Queen (Illus. by Sedova, Yana)
c HB Guide - v26 - i2 - Fall 2015 - p25(1) [51-500]
Thumbelina (Illus. by Vivanco, Kelly)
c KR - August 15 2015 - pNA [51-500]
Andersen, Lisa M.F. - *The Politics of Prohibition: American Governance and the Prohibition Party, 1869-1933*
J Am St - v49 - i2 - May 2015 - p425-426 [501+]
Andersen, Steffen - *Inattention and Inertia in Household Finance: Evidence from the Danish Mortgage Market*
Econ - v415 - i8940 - May 30 2015 - p76(US) [501+]
Anderson, Aaron D. - *Builders of a New South: Merchants, Capital, and the Remaking of Natchez, 1865-1914*
JAH - v101 - i4 - March 2015 - p1289-1290 [501+]
Anderson, Alan B. - *Settling Saskatchewan*
Can Hist R - v96 - i1 - March 2015 - p130(4) [501+]
Anderson, Alex - *All Things Quilting with Alex Anderson: From First Step to Last Stitch*
LJ - v140 - i12 - July 1 2015 - p86(1) [51-500]
Anderson, Alison - *The Circle*
BL - v112 - i3 - Oct 1 2015 - p25(1) [51-500]
Anderson, Allan Heaton - *To the Ends of the Earth: Pentecostalism and the Transformation of World Christianity*
IBMR - v39 - i1 - Jan 2015 - p45(1) [501+]
Anderson, Benedict - *Imagined Communities: Reflections on the Origin and Spread of Nationalism*
TimHES - i2211 - July 9 2015 - p50(1) [501+]
Anderson, Benny - *Poetry for the Rest of Us (Read by Goldenman, Michael). Audiobook Review*
RVBW - April 2015 - pNA [51-500]
Anderson, Bonnie M. - *Pluto the Starfish: An Undersea Tale for Children 1 to 101 (Illus. by Raines, Malinda)*
c CH Bwatch - Jan 2015 - pNA [51-500]
Anderson, Catherine - *New Leaf*
PW - v262 - i48 - Nov 30 2015 - p46(1) [51-500]
Anderson, Clayton C. - *The Ordinary Spaceman: From Boyhood Dreams to Astronaut*
KR - April 15 2015 - pNA [501+]
LJ - v140 - i12 - July 1 2015 - p105(2) [51-500]
PW - v262 - i15 - April 13 2015 - p67(1) [51-500]
Anderson-Dargatz, Gail - *Playing With Fire*
y KR - August 15 2015 - pNA [51-500]
y SLJ - v61 - i9 - Sept 2015 - p151(4) [501+]
Anderson, Derek - *Ten Pigs: An Epic Bath Adventure*
c HB Guide - v26 - i2 - Fall 2015 - p5(1) [51-500]
c KR - Feb 1 2015 - pNA [51-500]
Anderson, Devery S. - *Emmett Till: The Murder That Shocked the World and Propelled the Civil Rights Movement*
BL - v112 - i2 - Sept 15 2015 - p5(1) [51-500]
Anderson, Emma - *The Death and Afterlife of the North American Martyrs*
Can Hist R - v96 - i3 - Sept 2015 - p429(3) [501+]
CH - v84 - i2 - June 2015 - p450(3) [501+]
JR - v95 - i3 - July 2015 - p417(2) [501+]
Anderson, Gary A. - *The Place of the Poor in the Biblical Tradition*
JR - Jan 2015 - p121(2) [501+]
Anderson, Gary Clayton - *Ethnic Cleansing and the Indian: The Crime That Should Haunt America*
AHR - v120 - i2 - April 2015 - p605-606 [501+]
Am Ind CRJ - v39 - i2 - Spring 2015 - p137-138 [501+]
J Mil H - v79 - i3 - July 2015 - p830-831 [501+]
PHR - v84 - i4 - Nov 2015 - p538(2) [501+]
WHQ - v46 - i1 - Spring 2015 - p101-102 [501+]
Anderson, Gerry - *Thunderbirds*
y Sch Lib - v63 - i1 - Spring 2015 - p50(1) [51-500]
Anderson, James - *I Can See in the Dark*
RVBW - April 2015 - pNA [501+]
The Never-Open Desert Diner
BL - v111 - i9-10 - Jan 1 2015 - p48(1) [51-500]
Anderson, Jameson - *Danica Patrick*
c HB Guide - v26 - i2 - Fall 2015 - p196(2) [51-500]
Anderson, Jeff - *Zack Delacruz: Me and My Big Mouth*
c KR - May 1 2015 - pNA [51-500]
c PW - v262 - i19 - May 11 2015 - p61(1) [51-500]
c SLJ - v61 - i5 - May 2015 - p100(1) [51-500]
Anderson, Jennifer Joline - *Albert Einstein: Revolutionary Physicist*
c HB Guide - v26 - i1 - Spring 2015 - p190(2) [51-500]
Miley Cyrus: Pop Princess
y HB Guide - v26 - i2 - Fall 2015 - p206(1) [51-500]
Writing Fantastic Fiction
c BL - v112 - i3 - Oct 1 2015 - p64(1) [51-500]
Anderson, Jerry - *The Money Trader*
KR - Sept 15 2015 - pNA [501+]

Anderson, Jodi Lynn - *My Diary from the Edge of the World*
- c BL - v112 - i5 - Nov 1 2015 - p61(1) [51-500]
- c KR - Sept 15 2015 - pNA [51-500]
- c PW - v262 - i37 - Sept 14 2015 - p78(1) [51-500]
- c PW - v262 - i49 - Dec 2 2015 - p78(1) [51-500]
- c SLJ - v61 - i8 - August 2015 - p82(1) [51-500]

The Vanishing Season
- y HB Guide - v26 - i1 - Spring 2015 - p99(1) [51-500]

Anderson, John David - *The Dungeoneers*
- c KR - April 1 2015 - pNA [51-500]
- SLJ - v61 - i2 - Feb 2015 - p82(1) [51-500]
- c PW - v262 - i49 - Dec 2 2015 - p77(1) [51-500]
- c BL - v111 - i18 - May 15 2015 - p65(1) [51-500]
- c CCB-B - v69 - i1 - Sept 2015 - p5(1) [51-500]
- c HB Guide - v26 - i2 - Fall 2015 - p73(1) [51-500]
- c PW - v262 - i16 - April 20 2015 - p75(2) [51-500]

Minion
- c HB Guide - v26 - i1 - Spring 2015 - p68(1) [51-500]

Anderson, Jonathan A. - *Renewing Christian Theology: Systematics for a Global Christianity*
- IBMR - v39 - i3 - July 2015 - p160(2) [501+]

Anderson, Joseph - *Debunking Darwin*
- KR - Oct 1 2015 - pNA [501+]

Anderson, Josh - *Backing Up the Beast*
- SLJ - v61 - i4 - April 2015 - p152(1) [51-500]

Anderson, Katie Elson - *Reinventing Reference: How Libraries Deliver Value in the Age of Google*
- VOYA - v38 - i5 - Dec 2015 - p81(1) [51-500]
- LJ - v140 - i5 - March 15 2015 - p119(1) [51-500]

Anderson, Kevin J. - *Blood of the Cosmos*
- BL - v111 - i19-20 - June 1 2015 - p64(1) [51-500]
- Bwatch - August 2015 - pNA [51-500]

Clockwork Lives
- PW - v262 - i31 - August 3 2015 - p39(2) [51-500]

Anderson, Laura Ellen - *Bunnies (Illus. by Anderson, Laura Ellen)*
- KR - July 1 2015 - pNA [51-500]
- c PW - v262 - i6 - Feb 9 2015 - p66(2) [501+]

Snow Babies
- c KR - Jan 1 2015 - pNA [51-500]

Anderson, Laura Lee - *The Army Surveys of Gold Rush California: Reports of the Topographical Engineers*
- Roundup M - v23 - i1 - Oct 2015 - p32(1) [501+]

Anderson, Laurie Halse - *The Impossible Knife of Memory (Read by Whelan, Julia). Audiobook Review*
- c BL - v111 - i14 - March 15 2015 - p24(2) [501+]

Anderson, Lena - *Willful Disregard*
- BL - v112 - i7 - Dec 1 2015 - p26(1) [51-500]

Anderson, Lin - *The Case of the Missing Madonna*
- BL - v112 - i5 - Nov 1 2015 - p30(1) [51-500]
- PW - v262 - i45 - Nov 9 2015 - p38(1) [51-500]

Anderson, M.T. - *The Astonishing Life of Octavian Nothing, Traitor to the Nation, vol. 1: The Pox Party*
- y BL - v111 - i9-10 - Jan 1 2015 - p66(1) [501+]

He Laughed with His Other Mouths
- c HB Guide - v26 - i1 - Spring 2015 - p68(1) [51-500]

Symphony for the City of the Dead: Dmitri Shostakovich and the Siege of Leningrad
- y BL - v111 - i21 - July 1 2015 - p49(2) [51-500]
- y CCB-B - v69 - i2 - Oct 2015 - p75(1) [51-500]
- y HB - v91 - i5 - Sept-Oct 2015 - p123(2) [51-500]
- y KR - July 1 2015 - pNA [51-500]
- NYTBR - Oct 11 2015 - p18(L) [501+]
- y PW - v262 - i26 - June 29 2015 - p71(1) [51-500]
- y SLJ - v61 - i9 - Sept 2015 - p186(1) [51-500]
- y VOYA - v38 - i4 - Oct 2015 - p80(1) [51-500]

Anderson, Mark D. - *Disaster Writing: The Cultural Politics of Catastrophe in Latin America*
- AL - v87 - i1 - March 2015 - p205-206 [501+]

Anderson, Martin - *Ronald Reagan: Decisions of Greatness*
- Nat R - v67 - i8 - May 4 2015 - p50 [501+]

Anderson, Michael Alan - *St. Anne in Renaissance Music: Devotion and Politics*
- CH - v84 - i4 - Dec 2015 - p873(3) [501+]
- Specu - v90 - i4 - Oct 2015 - p1079-1080 [501+]

Anderson, Michael L. - *After Phrenology: Neural Reuse and the Interactive Brain*
- TimHES - i2211 - July 9 2015 - p45(1) [501+]

Anderson, Misty G. - *Imagining Methodism in Eighteenth-Century Britain: Enthusiasm, Belief, and the Borders of the Self*
- MLR - v110 - i3 - July 2015 - p834-836 [501+]

Anderson, Nancy - *The Educated Eye: Visual Culture and Pedagogy in the Life Sciences*
- Isis - v106 - i1 - March 2015 - p208(2) [501+]

Anderson, Pam - *Three Many Cooks: One Mom, Two Daughters, Their Shared Stories of Food, Faith, and Family*
- KR - Feb 1 2015 - pNA [501+]
- PW - v262 - i11 - March 16 2015 - p78(1) [51-500]

Anderson, Peggy Perry - *I Can Help! (Illus. by Anderson, Peggy Perry)*
- c BL - v111 - i22 - August 1 2015 - p74(1) [51-500]
- c KR - August 1 2015 - pNA [51-500]

Anderson, Perry - *American Foreign Policy and Its Thinkers*
- NYRB - v62 - i18 - Nov 19 2015 - p29(2) [501+]

Anderson, R.J. - *A Pocket Full of Murder*
- c BL - v111 - i21 - July 1 2015 - p76(1) [51-500]
- c KR - June 15 2015 - pNA [51-500]
- c SLJ - v61 - i7 - July 2015 - p73(1) [51-500]

Anderson, Ray - *The Lotus Cross*
- PW - v262 - i31 - August 3 2015 - p38(1) [51-500]

Anderson, Richard Van - *The Organ Takers: A Novel of Surgical Suspense*
- PW - v262 - i2 - Jan 12 2015 - p39(2) [51-500]

Anderson, Robert L. - *Dreamland*
- y KR - June 15 2015 - pNA [51-500]
- y SLJ - v61 - i7 - July 2015 - p89(1) [51-500]
- y VOYA - v38 - i4 - Oct 2015 - p65(1) [51-500]

Anderson, Ryan T. - *Truth Overruled: The Future of Marriage and Religious Freedom*
- Nat R - v67 - i18 - Oct 5 2015 - p44(2) [501+]

Anderson, Samantha Wren - *Salsa with the Pope*
- KR - May 15 2015 - pNA [501+]

Anderson, Sara - *Verduras/Vegetables*
- c KR - Jan 1 2016 - pNA [501+]

Anderson, Shannon - *Penelope Perfect (Illus. by Kath, Katie)*
- c SLJ - v61 - i12 - Dec 2015 - p134(1) [51-500]

Anderson, Susan - *Running Wild*
- PW - v262 - i29 - July 20 2015 - p177(1) [51-500]

Anderson, T. Neill - *Massacre of the Miners*
- y BL - v111 - i16 - April 15 2015 - p56(1) [51-500]
- y HB Guide - v26 - i2 - Fall 2015 - p109(1) [51-500]
- y KR - March 1 2015 - pNA [51-500]
- y SLJ - v61 - i5 - May 2015 - p111(1) [51-500]
- y VOYA - v38 - i4 - Oct 2015 - p48(1) [51-500]

People of the Plague
- y HB Guide - v26 - i1 - Spring 2015 - p99(1) [51-500]

Anderson, Taylor - *Straits of Hell*
- Analog - v135 - i11 - Nov 2015 - p107(1) [501+]

Anderson, Thomas J. - *The Value of Debt in Retirement*
- NYT - April 12 2015 - p14(L) [501+]

Anderson, Tim - *The United States of Incarceration*
- KR - July 1 2015 - pNA [501+]

Anderson, Tory C. - *Joey and the Magic Map*
- y KR - June 15 2015 - pNA [501+]

Anderson, Zoe - *The Ballet Lover's Companion*
- BL - v111 - i21 - July 1 2015 - p15(1) [51-500]
- LJ - v140 - i10 - June 1 2015 - p105(1) [51-500]

Andersson, Lena - *Willful Disregard*
- KR - Dec 1 2015 - pNA [501+]
- PW - v262 - i52 - Dec 21 2015 - p126(1) [51-500]
- TLS - i5857 - July 3 2015 - p21(1) [501+]

Andersson, Ruben - *Illegality, Inc: Clandestine Migration and the Business of Bordering Europe*
- TimHES - i2211 - July 9 2015 - p51(1) [501+]

Anderst, Leah - *The Films of Eric Rohmer: French New Wave to Old Master*
- Si & So - v25 - i2 - Feb 2015 - p106(1) [501+]

Andes, Stephen J.C. - *The Vatican and Catholic Activism in Mexico and Chile: The Politics of Transnational Catholicism, 1920-1940*
- AHR - v120 - i3 - June 2015 - p1081-1082 [501+]
- CHR - v101 - i4 - Autumn 2015 - p963(2) [501+]
- HNet - May 2015 - pNA [501+]

Andic, Fuat - *Reforming Ottoman Governance: Success, Failure and the Path to Decline*
- JEH - v75 - i2 - June 2015 - p619-620 [501+]

Andonian, Michelle - *This Picture I Gift: An Armenian Memoir*
- RVBW - Nov 2015 - pNA [51-500]

Andrade, Nathanael J. - *Syrian Identity in the Greco-Roman World*
- Class R - v65 - i1 - April 2015 - p187-189 [501+]

Andrade, Susan Z. - *The Nation Writ Small: African Fictions and Feminisms 1958-1988*
- MFSF - v61 - i3 - Fall 2015 - p547-550 [501+]

Andrade, Tonio - *The Gunpowder Age*
- KR - Dec 1 2015 - pNA [501+]

Andraka, Jack - *Breakthrough: How One Teen Innovator Is Changing the World*
- y HB Guide - v26 - i2 - Fall 2015 - p206(2) [51-500]
- y VOYA - v38 - i2 - June 2015 - p86(1) [51-500]

Andre, Christophe - *Looking at Mindfulness: Twenty-Five Ways to Live in the Moment Through Art*
- LJ - v140 - i2 - Feb 1 2015 - p70(2) [501+]
- PW - v262 - i6 - Feb 9 2015 - p63(1) [51-500]

Andre-Driussi, Michael - *Handbook of Vance Space*
- Analog - v135 - i3 - March 2015 - p107(1) [501+]

Andre, Elizabeth - *The Time Slip Girl*
- PW - v262 - i29 - July 20 2015 - p175(1) [51-500]

Andreae, Giles - *Est-ce que les girafes dansent? (Illus. by Parker-Rees, Guy)*
- c Res Links - v21 - i1 - Oct 2015 - p47(1) [51-500]

I Love You, Baby (Illus. by Dodd, Emma)
- c KR - Oct 1 2015 - pNA [51-500]
- c PW - v262 - i41 - Oct 12 2015 - p66(2) [51-500]

Andreas, Peter - *Smuggler Nation: How Illicit Trade Made America*
- JAH - v102 - i1 - June 2015 - p213-213 [501+]

Andreo, Rogelio Bernal - *Hawai'i Nights*
- S&T - v129 - i3 - March 2015 - p67(1) [51-500]

Andresen, Knud - *Es gilt das Gesprochene Wort: Oral History und Zeitgeschichte Heute*
- HNet - July 2015 - pNA [501+]

Andress, David - *Experiencing the French Revolution*
- FS - v69 - i4 - Oct 2015 - p536-537 [501+]

Andretta, Elisa - *Roma medica: Anatomie d'un systeme medical au XVIe siecle*
- Isis - v106 - i1 - March 2015 - p179(2) [501+]

Andreu, Maria E. - *Secret Side of Empty*
- y CH Bwatch - Nov 2015 - pNA [51-500]

Andrew, Donna T. - *Aristocratic Vice: The Attack on Duelling, Suicide, Adultery, and Gambling in Eighteenth-Century England*
- HER - v130 - i545 - August 2015 - p1012(2) [501+]

Andrew, Dudley - *Andre Bazin's New Media*
- Si & So - v25 - i5 - May 2015 - p106(1) [501+]

Andrew, Joe - *Dostoevskii's Overcoat: Influence, Comparison, and Transposition*
- MLR - v110 - i2 - April 2015 - p621-623 [501+]

Andrew, Sally - *Recipes for Love and Murder*
- KR - Sept 1 2015 - pNA [501+]
- PW - v262 - i38 - Sept 21 2015 - p54(1) [51-500]

Andrews, Arin - *Some Assembly Required: The Not-So-Secret Life of a Transgender Teen*
- y CCB-B - v68 - i6 - Feb 2015 - p297(2) [51-500]
- y HB Guide - v26 - i2 - Fall 2015 - p207(1) [51-500]

Andrews, Bridie - *The Making of Modern Chinese Medicine, 1850-1960*
- Pac A - v88 - i3 - Sept 2015 - p700 [501+]

Andrews, Chris - *The Musical Brain - and Other Stories*
- PW - v262 - i1 - Jan 5 2015 - p49(1) [51-500]

Roberto Bolano's Fiction: An Expanding Universe
- TLS - i5842 - March 20 2015 - p3(2) [501+]

Andrews, Donna - *Lord of the Wings (Read by Dunne, Bernadette). Audiobook Review*
- BL - v112 - i6 - Nov 15 2015 - p60(1) [51-500]
- PW - v262 - i39 - Sept 28 2015 - p85(1) [51-500]

Lord of the Wings
- BL - v111 - i21 - July 1 2015 - p38(1) [51-500]
- PW - v262 - i25 - June 22 2015 - p121(2) [51-500]

Andrews, Eve-Marie - *Let Scholarships Pay the Way*
- SPBW - May 2015 - pNA [51-500]

Andrews, Frances - *Churchmen and Urban Government in Late Medieval Italy, c. 1200-c. 1450: Cases and Contexts*
- Med R - Jan 2015 - pNA [501+]

Andrews, Geoff - *The Shadow Man: At the Heart of the Cambridge Spy Circle*
- Spec - v329 - i9771 - Dec 5 2015 - p42(3) [501+]

Andrews, Ilona - *Magic Shifts*
- Bwatch - Nov 2015 - pNA [51-500]

Andrews, Jesse - *Me and Earl and the Dying Girl (Read by Various readers). Audiobook Review*
- y PW - v262 - i35 - August 31 2015 - p86(1) [51-500]

Me and Earl and the Dying Girl
- y Sch Lib - v63 - i3 - Autumn 2015 - p188(1) [51-500]

Andrews, Julie - *The Very Fairy Princess: A Spooky, Sparkly Halloween (Read by Cordaro, Alison). Audiobook Review*
- c SLJ - v61 - i3 - March 2015 - p76(1) [51-500]

The Very Fairy Princess: A Spooky, Sparkly Halloween (Illus. by Davenier, Christine)
- c KR - August 1 2015 - pNA [51-500]
- c SLJ - v61 - i9 - Sept 2015 - p105(1) [51-500]

Andrews, Maggie - *The Home Front in Britain: Images, Myths and Forgotten Experiences Since 1914*
- TimHES - i2191 - Feb 19 2015 - p49(1) [501+]

Andrews, Mary Kay - *Beach Town (Read by McInerney, Kathleen). Audiobook Review*
    LJ - v140 - i13 - August 1 2015 - p46(1) [51-500]
Beach Town
    KR - April 15 2015 - pNA [501+]
Andrews, Neil - *Andrews on Civil Processes, vol. 1: Court Proceedings and Principles*
    Law Q Rev - v131 - Jan 2015 - p162-164 [501+]
Andrews on Civil Processes, vol. 2: Arbitration and Mediation
    Law Q Rev - v131 - Jan 2015 - p162-164 [501+]
Andrews, Nin - *Why God Is a Woman*
    PW - v262 - i16 - April 20 2015 - p53(1) [51-500]
Andrews, Troy - *Trombone Shorty (Illus. by Collier, Bryan)*
    c CCB-B - v68 - i10 - June 2015 - p479(1) [51-500]
    c HB Guide - v26 - i2 - Fall 2015 - p207(1) [51-500]
    c KR - Feb 1 2015 - pNA [51-500]
    c Teach Mus - v23 - i1 - August 2015 - p60(1) [51-500]
    c BL - v111 - i14 - March 15 2015 - p62(1) [51-500]
    c HB - v91 - i3 - May-June 2015 - p125(2) [51-500]
    c PW - v262 - i6 - Feb 9 2015 - p71(1) [51-500]
    c PW - v262 - i49 - Dec 2 2015 - p51(1) [51-500]
Andreychuk, Ed - *Louis L'Amour on Film and Television*
    Roundup M - v22 - i6 - August 2015 - p33(1) [501+]
Andrian-Werburg Freiherr, Viktor Franz von - *"Osterreich wird meine Stimme erkennen lernen wie die Stimme Gottes in der Wuste": Tagebucher 1839-1858, hrsg. v. Franz Adlgasser*
    HNet - April 2015 - pNA [501+]
Andriopoulos, Stefan - *Ghostly Apparitions: German Idealism, the Gothic Novel, and Optical Media*
    MLN - v130 - i3 - April 2015 - p670-675 [501+]
Anedda, Antonella - *Archipelago*
    TLS - i5834 - Jan 23 2015 - p13(1) [501+]
Aneesh, A. - *Neutral Accent: How Language, Labor, and Life Became Global*
    TimHES - i2212 - July 16 2015 - p50-1 [501+]
Anemone, Anthony - *"I Am a Phenomenon Quite out of the Ordinary": The Notebooks, Diaries, and Letters of Daniil Kharms*
    NYRB - v62 - i8 - May 7 2015 - p36(3) [501+]
Anensen, Peer-Christian - *Norgeskatalogen Postal II*
    Phil Lit R - v64 - i1 - Wntr 2015 - p58(2) [501+]
Anesko, Michael - *Monopolizing the Master: Henry James and the Politics of Literary Scholarship*
    AL - v87 - i2 - June 2015 - p394-396 [501+]
Ang, Karen - *Collared Lizard*
    c SLJ - v61 - i4 - April 2015 - p89(4) [501+]
Ang, Li - *The Lost Garden*
    KR - Sept 15 2015 - pNA [501+]
Angel, Ann - *Things I'll Never Say: Stories About Our Secret Selves*
    y PW - v262 - i3 - Jan 19 2015 - p86(1) [51-500]
    y BL - v111 - i12 - Feb 15 2015 - p84(1) [51-500]
    c CCB-B - v68 - i9 - May 2015 - p437(2) [51-500]
    y HB - v91 - i2 - March-April 2015 - p89(2) [51-500]
    y HB Guide - v26 - i2 - Fall 2015 - p201(1) [51-500]
    y KR - Jan 1 2015 - pNA [51-500]
    y SLJ - v61 - i2 - Feb 2015 - p96(1) [51-500]
    y VOYA - v37 - i6 - Feb 2015 - p52(1) [51-500]
Angel, Marc D. - *The Rhythms of Jewish Living: A Sephardic Exploration of the Basic Teachings of Judaism*
    RVBW - Nov 2015 - pNA [501+]
Angel, Ronald J. - *Community Lost: The State, Civil Society, and Displaced Survivors of Hurricane Katrina*
    CS - v44 - i3 - May 2015 - p339-340 [501+]
Angel, Traci - *The Scars of Project 459: The Environmental Story of the Lake of the Ozarks*
    JSH - v81 - i3 - August 2015 - p785(2) [501+]
Angelini, Josephine - *Firewalker*
    y KR - July 15 2015 - pNA [51-500]
    y SLJ - v61 - i10 - Oct 2015 - p108(1) [51-500]
    y VOYA - v38 - i4 - Oct 2015 - p65(1) [51-500]
Trial by Fire
    y HB Guide - v26 - i1 - Spring 2015 - p99(1) [51-500]
Angell, Kate - *No One Like You*
    BL - v111 - i18 - May 15 2015 - p32(1) [51-500]
    PW - v262 - i12 - March 23 2015 - p54(1) [51-500]
Angell, Roger - *This Old Man: All in Pieces*
    BL - v112 - i6 - Nov 15 2015 - p9(1) [51-500]
    LJ - v140 - i17 - Oct 15 2015 - p86(1) [51-500]
    NYTBR - Dec 6 2015 - p42(L) [501+]
    KR - Sept 1 2015 - pNA [51-500]
    NYT - Dec 8 2015 - pC1(L) [501+]
    PW - v262 - i36 - Sept 7 2015 - p58(1) [51-500]
Angell, Tony - *The House of Owls*
    Am Sci - v103 - i4 - July-August 2015 - p297(2) [501+]
    KR - Feb 15 2015 - pNA [51-500]
    NYTBR - Dec 6 2015 - p66(L) [501+]
    TLS - i5863 - August 14 2015 - p29(1) [501+]
    Nature - v522 - i7544 - June 4 2015 - p33(1) [51-500]
Angelos, James - *The Full Catastrophe: Travels among the New Greek Ruins*
    BL - v111 - i19-20 - June 1 2015 - p25(1) [51-500]
    KR - April 15 2015 - pNA [51-500]
    Mac - v128 - i22 - June 8 2015 - p58(1) [501+]
    NYTBR - July 5 2015 - p19(L) [501+]
    PW - v262 - i17 - April 27 2015 - p65(1) [51-500]
Anger, Kenneth - *Hollywood Babylon*
    BL - v111 - i9-10 - Jan 1 2015 - p120(1) [501+]
Anggard, Adele - *A Humanitarian Past*
    KR - Feb 15 2015 - pNA [51-500]
Angleberger, Tom - *Beware the Power of the Dark Side (Illus. by McQuarrie, Ralph)*
    c SLJ - v61 - i11 - Nov 2015 - p98(1) [501+]
Emperor Pickletine Rides the Bus
    c HB Guide - v26 - i1 - Spring 2015 - p68(1) [51-500]
McToad Mows Tiny Island (Illus. by Hendrix, John)
    c BL - v112 - i1 - Sept 1 2015 - p120(1) [51-500]
    c KR - July 15 2015 - pNA [51-500]
    c PW - v262 - i23 - June 8 2015 - p57(2) [51-500]
    c PW - v262 - i49 - Dec 2 2015 - p36(1) [51-500]
    c SLJ - v61 - i9 - Sept 2015 - p112(1) [51-500]
Poop Fountain!
    c HB Guide - v26 - i1 - Spring 2015 - p68(1) [51-500]
The Rat with the Human Face (Read by Turetsky, Mark). Audiobook Review
    c SLJ - v61 - i10 - Oct 2015 - p50(2) [51-500]
The Rat with the Human Face (Illus. by Angleberger, Tom)
    c BL - v111 - i12 - Feb 15 2015 - p87(1) [51-500]
    c HB Guide - v26 - i2 - Fall 2015 - p73(2) [51-500]
    KR - Feb 1 2015 - pNA [51-500]
    SLJ - v61 - i2 - Feb 2015 - p82(1) [51-500]
Star Wars - Return of the Jedi: Beware the Power of the Dark Side! (Illus. by Johnston, Joe)
    c BL - v112 - i1 - Sept 1 2015 - p115(1) [51-500]
Stranded on Planet Stripmall!
    c KR - Dec 1 2015 - pNA [51-500]
Angles, Jeffrey - *Wild Grass on the Riverbank*
    PW - v262 - i3 - Jan 19 2015 - p60(1) [51-500]
Angliss, Michael - *This Spy in France*
    KR - Oct 15 2015 - pNA [501+]
Anglund, Joan Walsh - *A Treasury of Wintertime Tales (Illus. by Anglund, Joan Walsh)*
    c CH Bwatch - Jan 2015 - pNA [51-500]
Angrist, Joshua D. - *Mastering "Metrics": The Path from Cause to Effect*
    Per Psy - v68 - i4 - Wntr 2015 - p931(3) [501+]
Angsten, David - *The Assassin Lotus*
    KR - Sept 15 2015 - pNA [501+]
Angus, Emily - *The Fashion Encyclopedia: A Visual Resource for Terms, Techniques, and Styles*
    BL - v111 - i19-20 - June 1 2015 - p22(1) [51-500]
Angus, Sam - *Captain*
    y Sch Lib - v63 - i1 - Spring 2015 - p50(1) [51-500]
A Horse Called Hero
    c HB Guide - v26 - i1 - Spring 2015 - p68(1) [51-500]
Anidjar, Gil - *Blood: A Critique of Christianity*
    CH - v84 - i2 - June 2015 - p441(2) [501+]
Anievas, Alexander - *Capital, the State and War: Class Conflict and Geopolitics in the Thirty Years' Crisis, 1914-1945*
    J Mil H - v79 - i2 - April 2015 - p503-504 [501+]
Race and Racism in International Relations: Confronting the Global Colour Line
    RVBW - Feb 2015 - pNA [501+]
Animales: Descubre la fascinante diversidad de la naturaleza
    c PW - v262 - i31 - August 3 2015 - p21(1) [51-500]
Anjelais, M. - *Breaking Butterflies*
    y CH Bwatch - Feb 2015 - pNA [51-500]
    y HB Guide - v26 - i1 - Spring 2015 - p99(1) [51-500]
Ankowski, Amber - *Think Like a Baby: 33 Simple Research Experiments You Can Do at Home to Better Understand Your Child's Developing Mind*
    LJ - v140 - i9 - May 15 2015 - p66(2) [501+]
Ann, Brooklyn - *Bite at First Sight*
    PW - v262 - i5 - Feb 2 2015 - p42(1) [51-500]
Anna, Dawn - *Heaven's Flower*
    c BL - v112 - i3 - Oct 1 2015 - p32(2) [51-500]
Anne Rice, - *Beauty's Kingdom (Read by Campbell, Cassandra). Audiobook Review*
    PW - v262 - i35 - August 31 2015 - p84(1) [51-500]
Annear, Judy - *The Photograph and Australia*
    NYTBR - Dec 6 2015 - p38(L) [501+]
Anner, Zach - *If at Birth You Don't Succeed: My Adventures with Disaster and Destiny*
    KR - Dec 15 2015 - pNA [501+]
    PW - v262 - i45 - Nov 9 2015 - p47(1) [51-500]
Annibali, Joseph A. - *Reclaim Your Brain*
    KR - Oct 1 2015 - pNA [51-500]
Anniss, Matt - *The History of Modern Music*
    c BL - v112 - i3 - Oct 1 2015 - p54(1) [51-500]
    y SLJ - v61 - i12 - Dec 2015 - p142(1) [51-500]
The Impact of Technology in Sport
    y Sch Lib - v63 - i4 - Winter 2015 - p251(1) [51-500]
The Music Industry
    y SLJ - v61 - i12 - Dec 2015 - p142(1) [51-500]
Performing Live
    y SLJ - v61 - i12 - Dec 2015 - p142(1) [51-500]
Anolik, Lili - *Dark Rooms*
    KR - Jan 15 2015 - pNA [51-500]
    LJ - v140 - i3 - Feb 15 2015 - p84(1) [51-500]
    PW - v262 - i4 - Jan 26 2015 - p150(1) [51-500]
Anonymous - *Calling Maggie May*
    y HB Guide - v26 - i2 - Fall 2015 - p109(1) [51-500]
    y SLJ - v61 - i7 - July 2015 - p90(1) [51-500]
    y VOYA - v38 - i3 - August 2015 - p52(1) [51-500]
Mirage
    TLS - i5843 - March 27 2015 - p21(1) [501+]
Anonymous, Johnny - *NFL Confidential*
    KR - Dec 15 2015 - pNA [51-500]
Ansari, Ali - *Iran: A Very Short Introduction*
    TLS - i5847 - April 24 2015 - p27(1) [501+]
Ansari, Aziz - *Modern Romance: An Investigation (Read by Ansari, Aziz). Audiobook Review*
    y BL - v112 - i2 - Sept 15 2015 - p78(1) [51-500]
    LJ - v140 - i13 - August 1 2015 - p48(2) [51-500]
Modern Romance: An Investigation
    y BL - v111 - i19-20 - June 1 2015 - p14(1) [51-500]
    Econ - v416 - i8946 - July 11 2015 - p76(US) [501+]
    KR - June 1 2015 - pNA [51-500]
    NYT - July 7 2015 - pC4(L) [501+]
    NYTBR - Sept 13 2015 - p16(L) [501+]
Ansary, Nina - *Jewels of Allah: The Untold Story of Women in Iran*
    KR - June 1 2015 - pNA [501+]
    PW - v262 - i24 - June 15 2015 - p78(1) [51-500]
Anscome, Frederick F. - *State, Faith and Nation in Ottoman and Post-Ottoman Lands*
    IJMES - v47 - i2 - May 2015 - p384-386 [501+]
Anscutz, Philip F. - *Out Where the West Begins: Profiles, Vision & Strategies of Early Western Business Leaders*
    Roundup M - v23 - i1 - Oct 2015 - p32(1) [501+]
Ansell, Aaron - *Zero Hunger: Political Culture and Antipoverty Policy in Northeast Brazil*
    HAHR - v95 - i2 - May 2015 - p381-383 [501+]
Ansell, Neil - *Deer Island*
    KR - June 15 2015 - pNA [501+]
Anselm of Laon - *Glosae super Iohannem*
    Specu - v90 - i3 - July 2015 - p766-767 [501+]
Anselme, Daniel - *On Leave (Illus. by Bellos, David)*
    NYTBR - June 21 2015 - p24(L) [501+]
Anselmi, Andrew Eustace - *The Autumn Crush*
    PW - v262 - i12 - March 23 2015 - p35(5) [501+]
Anson, Edward M. - *Alexander's Heirs: The Age of the Successors*
    NYRB - v62 - i4 - March 5 2015 - p40(3) [501+]
Anstee, Ashlyn - *Are We There, Yeti? (Illus. by Anstee, Ashlyn)*
    c BL - v111 - i19-20 - June 1 2015 - p108(1) [51-500]
    c KR - April 15 2015 - pNA [51-500]
    c PW - v262 - i18 - May 4 2015 - p118(1) [51-500]
    c SLJ - v61 - i6 - June 2015 - p76(1) [51-500]
No, No, Gnome! (Illus. by Anstee, Ashlyn)
    c KR - Nov 15 2015 - pNA [51-500]
    c PW - v262 - i44 - Nov 2 2015 - p83(1) [51-500]
    c SLJ - v61 - i12 - Dec 2015 - p86(1) [51-500]
Antalek, Robin - *The Grown Ups*
    KR - Jan 1 2015 - pNA [51-500]
Anteby, Michel - *Manufacturing Morals: The Values of Silence in Business School Education*
    CS - v44 - i5 - Sept 2015 - p625-626 [501+]
Antenhofer, Christina - *Barbara Gonzaga: Die Briefe / Le Lettere*
    Ren Q - v68 - i1 - Spring 2015 - p229-231 [501+]

Anthony, Barry - *Murder, Mayhem and Music Hall: The Dark Side of Victorian London*
    TLS - i5855 - June 19 2015 - p31(1) [501+]
Anthony, Carl Sferrazza - *Ida McKinley: The Turn-of-the-Century First Lady through War, Assassination, and Secret Disability*
    HNet - May 2015 - pNA [501+]
Anthony, Joseph - *The Dandelion Seed's Big Dream (Illus. by Arbo, Cris)*
    c HB Guide - v26 - i1 - Spring 2015 - p20(1) [51-500]
Anthony, La La - *The Power Playbook: Rules for Independence, Money, and Success*
    BL - v111 - i17 - May 1 2015 - p65(1) [51-500]
Anthony, Lawrence - *Babylon's Ark: The Incredible Wartime Rescue of the Baghdad Zoo (Read by Vance, Simon). Audiobook Review*
    LJ - v140 - i7 - April 15 2015 - p48(1) [51-500]
Anthony, Michael - *V Is for Vegetables: Inspired Recipes and Techniques for Home Cooks from Artichokes to Zucchini*
    LJ - v140 - i13 - August 1 2015 - p118(1) [51-500]
    PW - v262 - i31 - August 3 2015 - p51(2) [51-500]
Antisemitischer Alltag und Holocaust - Rekonstruktion und Erinnerung
    HNet - May 2015 - pNA [501+]
Antisemitismus und Rassismus- Verflechtungen? 5. Tagung: Blickwinkel. Antisemitismuskritisches Forum fur Bildung und Wissenschaft
    HNet - Feb 2015 - pNA [501+]
Antoinette - *A Taste of Pleasure*
    PW - v262 - i28 - July 13 2015 - p51(1) [51-500]
Anton, Anatole - *Taking Socialism Seriously*
    S&S - v79 - i1 - Jan 2015 - p127-129 [501+]
Antoniak-Mitchell, Dawn - *Teach Your Herding Breed to Be a Great Companion Dog: From Obsessive to Outstanding*
    RVBW - August 2015 - pNA [51-500]
Antoniou, Laura - *Best Lesbian Erotica*
    RVBW - April 2015 - pNA [51-500]
Antonius, Carl - *Europabild - Kulturwissenschaften - Staatsbegriff: Die Revista de Occidente (1923-1936) und der deutsch-spanische Kulturtransfer der Zwischenkriegszeit*
    HNet - April 2015 - pNA [501+]
Antonova, Katherine Pickering - *An Ordinary Marriage: The World of a Gentry Family in Provincial Russia*
    Historian - v77 - i2 - Summer 2015 - p372(2) [501+]
    JMH - v87 - i1 - March 2015 - p242(2) [501+]
Antonucci, Vince - *God for the Rest of Us: Experience Unbelievable Love, Unlimited Hope, and Uncommon Grace*
    PW - v262 - i27 - July 6 2015 - p67(1) [51-500]
Antony, Steve - *Betty Goes Bananas in Her Pyjamas (Illus. by Antony, Steve)*
    c Sch Lib - v63 - i4 - Winter 2015 - p217(1) [51-500]
Betty Goes Bananas (Illus. by Antony, Steve)
    c CCB-B - v68 - i5 - Jan 2015 - p247(1) [51-500]
    c HB Guide - v26 - i1 - Spring 2015 - p5(1) [51-500]
Green Lizards vs. Red Rectangles (Illus. by Antony, Steve)
    c KR - August 15 2015 - pNA [51-500]
    c PW - v262 - i33 - August 17 2015 - p69(1) [51-500]
    c SLJ - v61 - i9 - Sept 2015 - p112(1) [51-500]
Please, Mr. Panda (Illus. by Antony, Steve)
    c BL - v111 - i9-10 - Jan 1 2015 - p108(1) [51-500]
    c CCB-B - v68 - i7 - March 2015 - p346(1) [51-500]
    c CH Bwatch - May 2015 - pNA [501+]
    c HB Guide - v26 - i2 - Fall 2015 - p5(1) [51-500]
    c Sch Lib - v63 - i2 - Summer 2015 - p89(1) [51-500]
The Queen's Hat (Illus. by Antony, Steve)
    c BL - v112 - i1 - Sept 1 2015 - p122(1) [51-500]
    c KR - June 15 2015 - pNA [51-500]
    c PW - v262 - i19 - May 11 2015 - p57(1) [51-500]
    c SLJ - v61 - i6 - June 2015 - p76(1) [51-500]
Antoon, Sinan - *The Corpse Washer*
    Prog - v79 - i2 - Feb 2015 - p44(4) [501+]
Antrim, Donald - *The Emerald Light in the Air*
    NYRB - v62 - i3 - Feb 19 2015 - p28(3) [501+]
Antrim, Taylor - *Immunity*
    KR - April 1 2015 - pNA [501+]
    LJ - v140 - i9 - May 15 2015 - p68(2) [51-500]
    NYTBR - July 12 2015 - p10(L) [501+]
Antrim, Zayde - *Routes and Realms: The Power of Place in the Early Islamic World*
    IJMES - v47 - i4 - Nov 2015 - p858-859 [501+]

Antunes, Catia - *Exploring the Dutch Empire: Agents, Networks and Institutions, 1600-2000*
    TimHES - i2211 - July 9 2015 - p48(1) [501+]
Antus, Marjorie - *My Daughter, Her Suicide, and God*
    KR - April 1 2015 - pNA [51-500]
Apatow, Judd - *Sick in the Head: Conversations About Life and Comedy*
    KR - June 1 2015 - pNA [501+]
    LJ - v140 - i12 - July 1 2015 - p88(1) [51-500]
    y BL - v111 - i19-20 - June 1 2015 - p21(2) [51-500]
Apel, Kathryn - *On Track*
    c Magpies - v30 - i3 - July 2015 - p32(1) [51-500]
Apel, Peter - *Fred Pinsocket Loves Bananas*
    KR - July 1 2015 - pNA [51-500]
Apollinaire, Guillaume - *Les Obus miaulaient: Six lettres a Albert Dupont avec dix dessins de Olivier Jung*
    TLS - i5859 - July 17 2015 - p25(1) [51-500]
Zone: Selected Poems
    PW - v262 - i52 - Dec 21 2015 - p128(1) [51-500]
Apollon, Susan Barbara - *Touched by the Extraordinary: Healing Stories of Love, Loss and Hope*
    SPBW - Jan 2015 - pNA [51-500]
Appel, Anne Milano - *The Prince*
    BL - v111 - i9-10 - Jan 1 2015 - p50(1) [51-500]
    PW - v262 - i3 - Jan 19 2015 - p62(1) [51-500]
Appel, Jacob M. - *Einstein's Beach House*
    KR - Feb 1 2015 - pNA [51-500]
    SPBW - Feb 2015 - pNA [51-500]
    CQ - v64 - i3 - Spring 2015 - p130(2) [51-500]
Miracles and Conundrums of the Secondary Planets
    KR - Sept 1 2015 - pNA [51-500]
Scouting for the Reaper
    WLT - v89 - i1 - Jan-Feb 2015 - p60(1) [501+]
Appel, Marty - *Pinstripe Pride: The Inside Story of the New York Yankees*
    c CCB-B - v68 - i7 - March 2015 - p346(1) [51-500]
    c HB Guide - v26 - i2 - Fall 2015 - p197(1) [51-500]
    y SLJ - v61 - i3 - March 2015 - p175(2) [51-500]
Appelbaum, Patricia - *St. Francis of America: How a Thirteenth-Century Friar Became America's Most Popular Saint*
    LJ - v140 - i13 - August 1 2015 - p102(2) [51-500]
Appelbaum, Peter C. - *Loyal Sons: Jews in the German Army in the Great War*
    NWCR - v68 - i3 - Summer 2015 - p158(3) [501+]
Loyalty Betrayed: Jewish Chaplains in the German Army during the First World War
    HNet - Jan 2015 - pNA [501+]
Appelfeld, Aharon - *Adam & Thomas (Illus. by Dumas, Philippe)*
    c KR - August 1 2015 - pNA [51-500]
    c PW - v262 - i32 - August 10 2015 - p59(1) [51-500]
    c SLJ - v61 - i7 - July 2015 - p73(1) [51-500]
Appelhans, Lenore - *Chasing Before*
    y HB Guide - v26 - i1 - Spring 2015 - p99(1) [51-500]
Appelt, Kathi - *Counting Crows (Illus. by Dunlavey, Rob)*
    c BL - v111 - i11 - Feb 1 2015 - p54(1) [51-500]
    c CH Bwatch - May 2015 - pNA [51-500]
    c HB Guide - v26 - i2 - Fall 2015 - p5(1) [51-500]
    c PW - v262 - i49 - Dec 2 2015 - p19(2) [51-500]
    c RVBW - May 2015 - pNA [51-500]
Maybe a Fox
    c KR - Dec 15 2015 - pNA [51-500]
    c PW - v262 - i51 - Dec 14 2015 - p85(2) [51-500]
When Otis Courted Mama (Illus. by McElmurry, Jill)
    c CCB-B - v68 - i8 - April 2015 - p387(2) [51-500]
    c CH Bwatch - Feb 2015 - pNA [51-500]
Appignanesi, Lisa - *Trials of Passion: Crimes Committed in the Name of Love and Madness*
    BL - v111 - i21 - July 1 2015 - p11(1) [51-500]
    KR - May 15 2015 - pNA [501+]
    LJ - v140 - i9 - May 15 2015 - p93(2) [51-500]
    PW - v262 - i20 - May 18 2015 - p78(2) [51-500]
Trials of Passion: Crimes in the Name of Love and Madness
    TLS - i5864-5865 - August 21 2015 - p7(3) [501+]
Appleby, John C. - *Women and English Piracy, 1540-1720: Partners and Victims of Crime*
    HER - v130 - i543 - April 2015 - p449(3) [501+]
Appleford, Amy - *Learning to Die in London, 1380-1540*
    HNet - July 2015 - pNA [501+]
    Six Ct J - v46 - i3 - Fall 2015 - p804-805 [501+]
    Specu - v90 - i4 - Oct 2015 - p1082-1083 [501+]

Applegate, Katherine - *Crenshaw*
    c BL - v112 - i1 - Sept 1 2015 - p112(1) [51-500]
    c HB - v91 - i5 - Sept-Oct 2015 - p91(1) [51-500]
    c KR - July 15 2015 - pNA [51-500]
    y NYTBR - Nov 8 2015 - p25(L) [501+]
    c PW - v262 - i25 - June 22 2015 - p140(1) [51-500]
    c PW - v262 - i49 - Dec 2 2015 - p76(1) [51-500]
    c SLJ - v61 - i8 - August 2015 - p82(1) [51-500]
Ivan: The Remarkable True Story of the Shopping Mall Gorilla (Illus. by Karas, G. Brian)
    c CCB-B - v68 - i5 - Jan 2015 - p247(2) [51-500]
    c HB Guide - v26 - i1 - Spring 2015 - p163(1) [51-500]
The One and Only Ivan (Read by Crupper, Adam). Audiobook Review
    c SLJ - v61 - i2 - Feb 2015 - p38(3) [501+]
Appy, Christian G. - *American Reckoning: The Vietnam War and Our National Identity*
    AM - v212 - i14 - April 27 2015 - p40(2) [501+]
    BL - v111 - i9-10 - Jan 1 2015 - p33(1) [51-500]
    Comw - v142 - i7 - April 10 2015 - p22(3) [501+]
    HNet - Sept 2015 - pNA [501+]
Arabi, Oussama - *Islamic Legal Thought: A Compendium of Muslim Jurists*
    JNES - v74 - i2 - Oct 2015 - p383(4) [501+]
Aragonia, Guillelmus de - *De nobilitate animi, ed. and trans*
    Specu - v90 - i2 - April 2015 - p548-549 [501+]
Araiza, Lauren - *To March for Others: The Black Freedom Struggle and the United Farm Workers*
    Aztlan - v40 - i1 - Spring 2015 - p271-275 [501+]
Araki, Hirohiko - *Jojo's Bizarre Adventure, Part 1: Phantom Blood, Vol. 1*
    PW - v262 - i11 - March 16 2015 - p72(1) [51-500]
Arand, Dustin - *Truth Evolves*
    KR - August 1 2015 - pNA [501+]
Aranda, Elizabeth M. - *Making a Life in Multiethnic Miami: Immigration and the Rise of a Global City*
    CS - v44 - i5 - Sept 2015 - p615-618 [501+]
    JAH - v101 - i4 - March 2015 - p1355-1356 [501+]
Arango, Sascha - *The Truth and Other Lies*
    BL - v111 - i17 - May 1 2015 - p47(1) [51-500]
    KR - April 15 2015 - pNA [51-500]
    NYTBR - July 5 2015 - p10(L) [501+]
    PW - v262 - i15 - April 13 2015 - p56(1) [51-500]
Arapostathis, Stathis - *Patently Contestable: Electrical Technologies and Inventor Identities on Trial in Britain*
    BHR - v89 - i1 - Spring 2015 - p184(3) [501+]
    Isis - v106 - i2 - June 2015 - p471(2) [501+]
Araujo, Ana Lucia - *Shadows of the Slave Past: Memory, Heritage, and Slavery*
    AHR - v120 - i3 - June 2015 - p971-972 [501+]
    Pub Hist - v37 - i1 - Feb 2015 - p124(4) [501+]
Arbeid, Barbara - *Piccoli Grandi Bronzi*
    NYRB - v62 - i13 - August 13 2015 - p12(3) [501+]
Arblaster, John - *A Companion to John of Ruusbroec*
    Six Ct J - v46 - i1 - Spring 2015 - p148-150 [501+]
Arbogast, Claire S. - *Leave the Dogs at Home*
    KR - May 15 2015 - pNA [51-500]
Arbor, Lynn - *Intentional*
    KR - March 1 2015 - pNA [501+]
Arbuckle, Benjamin S. - *Animals and Inequality in the Ancient World*
    Am Ant - v80 - i4 - Oct 2015 - p783(2) [501+]
Arcan, Nelly - *Breakneck*
    Nat Post - v17 - i182 - June 6 2015 - pWP4(1) [501+]
    TLS - i5857 - July 3 2015 - p21(1) [501+]
Burqa of Skin
    Nat Post - v17 - i92 - Feb 14 2015 - pWP11(1) [501+]
    TLS - i5857 - July 3 2015 - p21(1) [501+]
Exit
    Nat Post - v17 - i92 - Feb 14 2015 - pWP11(1) [501+]
Hysteric
    Nat Post - v17 - i92 - Feb 14 2015 - pWP11(1) [501+]
Whore
    Nat Post - v17 - i92 - Feb 14 2015 - pWP11(1) [501+]
Arcand, Kimberly - *Light: The Visible Spectrum and Beyond*
    LJ - v140 - i20 - Dec 1 2015 - p125(1) [51-500]
Arcangeli, Myriam - *Sherds of History: Domestic Life in Colonial Guadeloupe*
    Am Ant - v80 - i4 - Oct 2015 - p785(2) [501+]

Arcarazo, Diego Acosta - *Global Migration Issues: Old Assumptions, New Dynamics*
 TimHES - i2211 - July 9 2015 - p50(1) [501+]
Archaimbault, Sylvie - *Evgenij Polivanov (1891-1938): Penser le langage au temps de Staline*
 Slav R - v74 - i3 - Fall 2015 - p676-677 [501+]
Archambeau, Robert - *The Poet Resigns: Poetry in a Difficult World*
 MP - v112 - i3 - Feb 2015 - pE276(E279) [501+]
Archaologie und Krieg. Ein Neues Arbeitsfeld
 HNet - Jan 2015 - pNA [501+]
Archard, David - *Reading Onora O'Neill*
 Ethics - v125 - i4 - July 2015 - p1184(6) [501+]
Archer, Claire - *Big Cats Series*
 c HB Guide - v26 - i1 - Spring 2015 - p163(1) [51-500]
 Bird-Eating Spiders
 c HB Guide - v26 - i1 - Spring 2015 - p157(1) [51-500]
 Jumping Spiders
 c HB Guide - v26 - i1 - Spring 2015 - p157(1) [51-500]
 Tarantula Spiders
 c HB Guide - v26 - i1 - Spring 2015 - p157(1) [51-500]
 Wolf Spiders
 c HB Guide - v26 - i1 - Spring 2015 - p157(1) [51-500]
Archer, Dale - *The ADHD Advantage: What You Thought Was a Diagnosis May Be Your Greatest Strength*
 LJ - v140 - i9 - May 15 2015 - p97(1) [51-500]
Archer, Dosh - *Little Elephant's Blocked Trunk*
 c HB Guide - v26 - i1 - Spring 2015 - p51(1) [51-500]
Archer, Jeffrey - *Mightier Than the Sword*
 RVBW - Nov 2015 - pNA [51-500]
Archer, Micha - *Daniel Finds a Poem (Illus. by Archer, Micha)*
 c KR - Nov 15 2015 - pNA [51-500]
 c PW - v262 - i47 - Nov 23 2015 - p68(1) [51-500]
Archer, Michael A. - *Ripped Off: A Serviceman's Guide to Common Scams, Frauds, and Bad Deals*
 Mar Crp G - v99 - i9 - Sept 2015 - p94(2) [501+]
Archibald, Samuel - *Arvida*
 KR - Sept 1 2015 - pNA [51-500]
 PW - v262 - i44 - Nov 2 2015 - p59(2) [51-500]
Arco-Mastromichalis, Andrea N. - *Wally McBap Needs a Nap! (Illus. by Teets, Ashley)*
 c CH Bwatch - Jan 2015 - pNA [51-500]
Ard, Catherine - *Origami Bugs*
 SLJ - v61 - i4 - April 2015 - p101(3) [501+]
Ardagh, Philip - *The Unlikely Outlaws (Illus. by Jones, Tom Morgan)*
 c Sch Lib - v63 - i3 - Autumn 2015 - p162(1) [51-500]
Arden, Leon - *The Ice Child and Other Stories*
 KR - Dec 15 2015 - pNA [501+]
Arden, Sara - *Finding Glory*
 PW - v262 - i16 - April 20 2015 - p62(1) [501+]
Arditti, Michael - *Widows and Orphans*
 Spec - v327 - i9731 - Feb 28 2015 - p42(1) [501+]
Ardizzone, Sarah - *A Prince Without a Kingdom*
 y BL - v111 - i21 - July 1 2015 - p58(2) [51-500]
Ardizzone, Tony - *The Whale Chaser*
 RVBW - August 2015 - pNA [51-500]
Ardolino, Bill - *Fallujah Awakens: Marines, Sheikhs, and the Battle against Al-Qaeda*
 Parameters - v45 - i2 - Summer 2015 - p140(2) [501+]
Areford, David S. - *The Art of Empathy: The Mother of Sorrows in Northern Renaissance Art and Devotion*
 Specu - v90 - i1 - Jan 2015 - p196-198 [501+]
Aregui, Matthias - *Before After (Illus. by Ramstein, Anne-Margot)*
 c HB Guide - v26 - i1 - Spring 2015 - p42(1) [51-500]
Arena, John - *Driven from New Orleans: How Nonprofits Betray Public Housing and Promote Privatization*
 J Am St - v49 - i3 - August 2015 - p646-649 [501+]
Arendt, Hannah - *Between Past and Future: Eight Exercises in Political Thought*
 TimHES - i2211 - July 9 2015 - p46(1) [501+]
 Eichmann in Jerusalem: A Report on the Banality of Evil
 Nation - v300 - i22 - June 1 2015 - p12(12) [501+]
Aretha, David - *Bossing the Bronx Bombers at Yankee Stadium*
 c HB Guide - v26 - i1 - Spring 2015 - p68(1) [51-500]
 Foul Ball Frame-Up at Wrigley Field
 c HB Guide - v26 - i1 - Spring 2015 - p68(1) [51-500]

A Hall Lot of Trouble at Cooperstown
 c HB Guide - v26 - i1 - Spring 2015 - p68(1) [51-500]
 Malala Yousafzai and the Girls of Pakistan
 c HB Guide - v26 - i1 - Spring 2015 - p191(1) [51-500]
 Sabotage, Sedition and Sundry Acts of Rebellion
 HB Guide - v26 - i2 - Fall 2015 - p218(1) [51-500]
 The Treasure Hunt Stunt at Fenway Park
 c HB Guide - v26 - i1 - Spring 2015 - p68(1) [51-500]
Argersinger, Jana L. - *Toward A Female Genealogy of Transcendentalism*
 Am St - v54 - i2 - Summer 2015 - p139-140 [501+]
Argueta, Jorge - *Salsa: Un Poema Para Cocinar/A Cooking Poem (Illus. by Tonatiuh, Duncan)*
 c BL - v111 - i15 - April 1 2015 - p36(1) [51-500]
 c HB - v91 - i4 - July-August 2015 - p151(1) [51-500]
 c KR - Jan 15 2015 - pNA [51-500]
 c SLJ - v61 - i3 - March 2015 - p111(2) [51-500]
Ari, Waskar - *Earth Politics: Religion, Decolonization, and Bolivia's Indigenous Intellectuals*
 AHR - v120 - i3 - June 2015 - p1084-1085 [501+]
 Ams - v72 - i3 - July 2015 - p490(3) [501+]
Arias, Lisa - *Groovy Graphing: Quadrant One and Beyond*
 c Teach Lib - v43 - i1 - Oct 2015 - p17(1) [51-500]
Arias, Santas - *Coloniality, Religion, and the Law in the Early Iberian World*
 CHR - v101 - i4 - Autumn 2015 - p928(2) [501+]
Aridjis, Chloe - *Where You Are: A Book of Maps That Will Leave You Completely Lost*
 GR - v105 - i3 - July 2015 - p377(4) [501+]
Aridjis, Homero - *The Child Poet*
 KR - Dec 15 2015 - pNA [501+]
Arielle, Phenice - *Phoenix Rising*
 y KR - Sept 1 2015 - pNA [501+]
Ariely, Dan - *The Honest Truth about Dishonesty: How We Lie to Everyone--Especially Ourselves*
 APJ - v29 - i5 - Sept-Oct 2015 - p102(2) [501+]
Aris, Sabah - *The Baghdad Lawyer: Fighting for Justice in Saddam's Iraq*
 LJ - v140 - i10 - June 1 2015 - p121(2) [501+]
Ariyana - *Light Atonement*
 Bwatch - June 2015 - pNA [501+]
Arjakovsky, Antoine - *The Way: Religious Thinkers of the Russian Emigration in Paris and Their Journal 1925-1940*
 TLS - i5832 - Jan 9 2015 - p9(1) [501+]
Arjomand, Said Amir - *Social Theory and Regional Studies in the Global Age*
 HNet - March 2015 - pNA [501+]
Arkin, William M. - *Unmanned: Drones, Data, and the Illusion of Perfect Warfare*
 KR - May 15 2015 - pNA [501+]
 PW - v262 - i19 - May 11 2015 - p48(1) [51-500]
Arkinstall, Christine - *Spanish Female Writers and the Freethinking Press, 1879-1926*
 TSWL - v34 - i1 - Spring 2015 - p179-181 [501+]
Arko, Andre - *The Ruby Way, 3d ed.*
 Bwatch - Oct 2015 - pNA [501+]
Arlidge, Anthony - *Magna Carta Uncovered*
 HT - v65 - i6 - June 2015 - p56(2) [501+]
 Lon R Bks - v37 - i8 - April 23 2015 - p15(3) [501+]
 TLS - i5868 - Sept 18 2015 - p3(2) [501+]
Arlidge, M.J. - *Eeny Meeny*
 LJ - v140 - i11 - June 15 2015 - p71(1) [51-500]
 PW - v262 - i13 - March 30 2015 - p52(1) [51-500]
 Pop Goes the Weasel
 PW - v262 - i35 - August 31 2015 - p62(1) [51-500]
 PW - v262 - i52 - Dec 21 2015 - p132(1) [51-500]
Arlon, Penelope - *Animal Faces*
 c CH Bwatch - Nov 2015 - pNA [51-500]
 c HB Guide - v26 - i2 - Fall 2015 - p169(1) [51-500]
 Birds
 c HB Guide - v26 - i1 - Spring 2015 - p162(1) [51-500]
 Pajaros
 c HB Guide - v26 - i2 - Fall 2015 - p162(1) [51-500]
 The Ultimate Book of Randomly Awesome Facts
 c BL - v112 - i6 - Nov 15 2015 - p40(1) [51-500]
Armacost, Michael H. - *Ballots, Bullets, and Bargains: American Foreign Policy and Presidential Elections*
 LJ - v140 - i13 - August 1 2015 - p111(1) [51-500]
 PW - v262 - i23 - June 8 2015 - p50(2) [51-500]

Armaline, William T. - *Human Rights in Our Own Backyard: Injustice and Resistance in the United States*
 CS - v44 - i4 - July 2015 - p483-484 [501+]
Arman, Khurram - *Lost Hierarchy*
 RVBW - August 2015 - pNA [51-500]
Armand, Glenda - *Ira's Shakespeare Dream (Illus. by Cooper, Floyd)*
 c HB Guide - v26 - i2 - Fall 2015 - p207(1) [51-500]
 c BL - v111 - i19-20 - June 1 2015 - p88(1) [51-500]
 c KR - April 15 2015 - pNA [51-500]
 c PW - v262 - i18 - May 4 2015 - p123(1) [51-500]
 c SLJ - v61 - i6 - June 2015 - p133(2) [51-500]
Armantrout, Rae - *Itself*
 LJ - v140 - i5 - March 15 2015 - p109(1) [51-500]
 PW - v262 - i3 - Jan 19 2015 - p59(1) [51-500]
Armenteros, Jorge - *The Book of I*
 ABR - v36 - i4 - May-June 2015 - p20(1) [501+]
Armentrout, Jennifer L. - *Fall with Me*
 KR - Feb 1 2015 - pNA [501+]
 PW - v262 - i4 - Jan 26 2015 - p155(1) [51-500]
 Forever with You
 BL - v112 - i2 - Sept 15 2015 - p41(1) [51-500]
 PW - v262 - i36 - Sept 7 2015 - p51(1) [51-500]
Armistead, Caitlyn - *Crossing the Line*
 PW - v262 - i31 - August 3 2015 - p43(2) [51-500]
Armitage, Christopher M. - *Literary and Visual Ralegh*
 MLR - v110 - i3 - July 2015 - p820-822 [501+]
Armitage, Simon - *Walking Away: Further Travels with a Troubadour on the South West Coast Path*
 NS - v144 - i5277 - August 28 2015 - p38(2) [501+]
 Spec - v328 - i9744 - May 30 2015 - p37(2) [501+]
 TimHES - i2211 - July 9 2015 - p47(1) [501+]
 TLS - i5855 - June 19 2015 - p33(1) [501+]
Armour, Violetta - *I'll Always Be with You*
 KR - Nov 1 2015 - pNA [501+]
Armsden, Catherine - *Dream House*
 BL - v112 - i4 - Oct 15 2015 - p32(1) [51-500]
Armstrong, Adrian - *The Virtuoso Circle: Competition, Collaboration, and Complexity in Late Medieval French Poetry*
 FS - v69 - i2 - April 2015 - p235-236 [501+]
 Med R - March 2015 - pNA(NA) [501+]
Armstrong, Benjamin E. - *21st Century Sims: Innovation, Education, and Leadership for the Modern Era*
 NWCR - v68 - i4 - Autumn 2015 - p121(2) [501+]
Armstrong, Cathleen - *At Home in Last Chance*
 BL - v112 - i2 - Sept 15 2015 - p42(2) [51-500]
 Last Chance Hero
 BL - v112 - i2 - Sept 15 2015 - p44(1) [51-500]
Armstrong, Charles I. - *Reframing Yeats: Genre, Allusion and History*
 RES - v66 - i273 - Feb 2015 - p195-197 [501+]
Armstrong, Charles K. - *Tyranny of the Weak: North Korea and the World, 1950-1992*
 E-A St - v67 - i5 - July 2015 - p844(1) [501+]
Armstrong, Christopher - *Making Toronto Modern: Architecture and Design, 1895-1975*
 Can Hist R - v96 - i1 - March 2015 - p126(2) [501+]
 Wilderness and Waterpower: How Banff National Park Became a Hydro-Electric Storage Reservoir
 WHQ - v46 - i2 - Summer 2015 - p228-229 [501+]
Armstrong, Dorsey - *Magistra Doctissima: Essays in Honor of Bonnie Wheeler*
 JEGP - v114 - i3 - July 2015 - p435(4) [501+]
 Specu - v90 - i1 - Jan 2015 - p198-199 [501+]
 Mapping Malory: Regional Identities and National Geographies in Le Morte Darthur
 Med R - June 2015 - pNA [501+]
Armstrong-Ellis, Carey F. - *I Love You More Than Moldy Ham (Illus. by Armstrong-Ellis, Carey F.)*
 c CH Bwatch - Oct 2015 - pNA [51-500]
 c PW - v262 - i30 - July 27 2015 - p67(1) [51-500]
Armstrong, Erika - *A Chick in the Cockpit: My Life Up in the Air*
 BL - v112 - i5 - Nov 1 2015 - p6(1) [51-500]
Armstrong, Guyda - *The English Boccaccio: A History in Books*
 MLR - v110 - i1 - Jan 2015 - p269-271 [501+]
Armstrong, Jesse - *Love, Sex and Other Foreign Policy Goals*
 NS - v144 - i5260 - May 1 2015 - p51(1) [501+]
 Spec - v328 - i9742 - May 16 2015 - p49(1) [501+]
 TLS - i5856 - June 26 2015 - p21(1) [501+]
Armstrong, Joseph E. - *How the Earth Turned Green: A Brief 3.8-Billion-Year History of Plants*
 BioSci - v65 - i5 - May 2015 - p529(2) [501+]

How The Earth Turned Green: A Brief 3.8-Billion-Year History of Plants
QRB - v90 - i3 - Sept 2015 - p347(2) [501+]
Armstrong, Julie Buckner - *The Cambridge Companion to American Civil Rights Literature*
TLS - i5871 - Oct 9 2015 - p31(1) [501+]
Armstrong, Karen - *Fields of Blood: Religion and the History of Violence (Read by Armstrong, Karen). Audiobook Review*
LJ - v140 - i2 - Feb 1 2015 - p46(1) [51-500]
Fields of Blood: Religion and the History of Violence
CC - v132 - i7 - April 1 2015 - p28(4) [501+]
J Mil H - v79 - i1 - Jan 2015 - p193-194 [501+]
Nation - v300 - i20 - May 18 2015 - p27(5) [501+]
NY - v90 - i45 - Jan 26 2015 - p77 [501+]
Parabola - v40 - i2 - Summer 2015 - p118-122 [501+]
St. Paul: The Apostle We Love to Hate
LJ - v140 - i16 - Oct 1 2015 - p64(2) [501+]
NYRB - v62 - i17 - Nov 5 2015 - p21(3) [501+]
St Paul: The Misunderstood Apostle
NS - v144 - i5287 - Nov 6 2015 - p38(3) [501+]
Armstrong, Kelley - *Deceptions*
BL - v111 - i19-20 - June 1 2015 - p64(1) [51-500]
PW - v262 - i25 - June 22 2015 - p124(1) [51-500]
Driven
PW - v262 - i44 - Nov 2 2015 - p65(1) [51-500]
Empire of Night
y BL - v111 - i9-10 - Jan 1 2015 - p88(1) [51-500]
y HB Guide - v26 - i2 - Fall 2015 - p109(1) [51-500]
y KR - Jan 15 2015 - pNA [51-500]
SLJ - v61 - i2 - Feb 2015 - p96(1) [51-500]
The Masked Truth
y BL - v112 - i3 - Oct 1 2015 - p27(1) [51-500]
y KR - August 1 2015 - pNA [51-500]
y PW - v262 - i32 - August 10 2015 - p62(1) [51-500]
y PW - v262 - i49 - Dec 2 2015 - p113(1) [51-500]
y SLJ - v61 - i9 - Sept 2015 - p163(1) [51-500]
y VOYA - v38 - i4 - Oct 2015 - p48(1) [51-500]
The Unquiet Past
y KR - July 15 2015 - pNA [51-500]
y Res Links - v21 - i1 - Oct 2015 - p28(1) [501+]
y SLJ - v61 - i10 - Oct 2015 - p99(1) [51-500]
y VOYA - v38 - i4 - Oct 2015 - p65(2) [51-500]
Armstrong, Pamela - *Authority in Byzantium*
HER - v130 - i542 - Feb 2015 - p155(2) [501+]
Armstrong, Pat - *Thinking Women and Health Care Reform in Canada*
CWS - v30 - i2-3 - Fall-Winter 2015 - p147(2) [501+]
Armstrong, Paul B. - *How Literature Plays with the Brain: The Neuroscience of Reading and Art*
MFSF - v61 - i2 - Summer 2015 - p359-369 [501+]
Arnaldo, Monica - *Arto's Big Move (Illus. by Arnaldo, Monica)*
c HB Guide - v26 - i1 - Spring 2015 - p20(1) [51-500]
The Little Book of Big Fears (Illus. by Arnaldo, Monica)
c KR - July 1 2015 - pNA [51-500]
c PW - v262 - i23 - June 8 2015 - p60(1) [501+]
c SLJ - v61 - i9 - Sept 2015 - p112(1) [51-500]
Arnaquq-Baril, Alethea - *The Blind Boy & the Loon (Illus. by Arnaquq-Baril, Alethea)*
c Res Links - v20 - i4 - April 2015 - p1(1) [51-500]
Arnason, David - *There Can Never Be Enough*
Can Lit - i224 - Spring 2015 - p106 [501+]
Arnason, Eleanor - *Hidden Folk: Icelandic Fantasies*
MFSF - v128 - i5-6 - May-June 2015 - p65(6) [501+]
Arndt, Theresa S. - *Getting Started with Demand-Driven Acquisitions for E-books: A LITA Guide*
LJ - v140 - i12 - July 1 2015 - p99(1) [51-500]
Arner, Lynn - *Chaucer, Gower, and the Vernacular Rising: Poetry and the Problem of the Populace after 1381*
Med R - August 2015 - pNA [501+]
Arnett, Mindee - *Avalon*
c BL - v112 - i1 - Sept 1 2015 - p114(1) [501+]
The Nightmare Charade
y KR - June 15 2015 - pNA [51-500]
y SLJ - v61 - i7 - July 2015 - p85(1) [51-500]
Polaris
y CCB-B - v68 - i6 - Feb 2015 - p298(1) [51-500]
y HB Guide - v26 - i2 - Fall 2015 - p109(1) [51-500]
Arney, Kat - *Herding Hemingway's Cats: Understanding How Our Genes Work*
KR - Jan 1 2016 - pNA [51-500]
Arney, Liz - *Go Blended! A Handbook for Blending Technology in Schools*
RVBW - May 2015 - pNA [501+]
Arning, Bill - *Marilyn Minter: Pretty/Dirty*
NYTBR - June 28 2015 - p23(L) [501+]
Arno, Ronni - *Ruby Reinvented*
c BL - v112 - i5 - Nov 1 2015 - p52(1) [51-500]
c KR - Sept 1 2015 - pNA [51-500]
Arnold, Andrew B. - *Fueling the Gilded Age: Railroads, Miners, and Disorder in Pennsylvania Coal Country*
HNet - Jan 2015 - pNA [501+]
JAH - v101 - i4 - March 2015 - p1286(1) [501+]
JIH - v46 - i1 - Summer 2015 - p131-132 [501+]
Arnold, Caroline - *A Day and Night in the Desert (Illus. by Arnold, Caroline)*
c HB Guide - v26 - i2 - Fall 2015 - p169(1) [51-500]
A Day and Night in the Rain Forest (Illus. by Arnold, Caroline)
c BL - v111 - i15 - April 1 2015 - p62(1) [51-500]
c HB Guide - v26 - i2 - Fall 2015 - p169(1) [51-500]
Living Fossils: Clues to the Past (Illus. by Plant, Andrew)
c KR - Dec 1 2015 - pNA [51-500]
c PW - v262 - i46 - Nov 16 2015 - p75(1) [501+]
Arnold, Catharine - *Globe: Life in Shakespeare's London*
TLS - i5863 - August 14 2015 - p27(1) [501+]
Arnold, Daniel - *Elisha Forerunner of Jesus Christ*
KR - Sept 15 2015 - pNA [501+]
Snowblind
KR - Feb 1 2015 - pNA [51-500]
Arnold, Daniel Anderson - *Brains, Buddhas, and Believing: The Problem of Intentionality in Classical Buddhist and Cognitive-Scientific Philosophy of Mind*
JR - Jan 2015 - p143(4) [501+]
Arnold, Dave (b. 1971-) - *Liquid Intelligence: The Art and Science of the Perfect Cocktail*
Am Sci - v103 - i4 - July-August 2015 - p298(2) [501+]
Arnold, David (b. 1946-) - *Everyday Technology: Machines and the Making of India's Modernity*
HER - v130 - i543 - April 2015 - p503(2) [501+]
IJMES - v47 - i2 - May 2015 - p369-381 [501+]
Arnold, David (b. 1981-) - *Mosquitoland (Read by Strole, Phoebe). Audiobook Review*
BL - v111 - i21 - July 1 2015 - p80(1) [51-500]
y SLJ - v61 - i6 - June 2015 - p65(1) [51-500]
Mosquitoland
y BL - v111 - i11 - Feb 1 2015 - p48(1) [51-500]
y CCB-B - v68 - i9 - May 2015 - p438(1) [51-500]
y Ent W - i1352 - Feb 27 2015 - p60(1) [501+]
y HB - v91 - i2 - March-April 2015 - p90(1) [51-500]
y HB Guide - v26 - i2 - Fall 2015 - p110(1) [51-500]
y KR - Jan 1 2015 - pNA [51-500]
y PW - v262 - i4 - Jan 26 2015 - p172(1) [51-500]
y PW - v262 - i49 - Dec 2 2015 - p94(1) [51-500]
Arnold, Denise Y. - *The Andean Science of Weaving: Structures and Techniques of Warp-Faced Weaves*
LJ - v140 - i12 - July 1 2015 - p82(1) [51-500]
Arnold, Elana K. - *Far from Fair*
c BL - v112 - i7 - Dec 1 2015 - p62(1) [51-500]
c KR - Dec 15 2015 - pNA [51-500]
Infandous
y BL - v111 - i9-10 - Jan 1 2015 - p94(1) [51-500]
y CCB-B - v68 - i9 - May 2015 - p438(2) [51-500]
y HB Guide - v26 - i2 - Fall 2015 - p110(1) [51-500]
y KR - Jan 15 2015 - pNA [51-500]
y PW - v262 - i3 - Jan 19 2015 - p85(1) [51-500]
The Question of Miracles
c CCB-B - v68 - i6 - Feb 2015 - p298(2) [51-500]
c HB - v91 - i4 - July-August 2015 - p128(2) [51-500]
c PW - v262 - i49 - Dec 2 2015 - p73(1) [51-500]
Arnold, Ellen F. - *Negotiating the Landscape: Environment and Monastic Identity in the Medieval Ardennes*
CH - v84 - i1 - March 2015 - p231(3) [501+]
HNet - May 2015 - pNA [501+]
Specu - v90 - i1 - Jan 2015 - p199-201 [501+]
Arnold, Guy - *America and Britain: Was There Ever a Special Relationship?*
For Aff - v94 - i1 - Jan-Feb 2015 - pNA [51-500]
Arnold, James R. - *Health under Fire: Medical Care during America's Wars*
R&USQ - v54 - i4 - Summer 2015 - p82(1) [501+]
Arnold, Jason Ross - *Secrecy in the Sunshine Era: The Promise and Failures of U.S. Open Government Laws*
JAH - v102 - i2 - Sept 2015 - p628-629 [501+]
Arnold, Johann Christoph - *Their Name Is Today: Reclaiming Childhood in a Hostile World*
LJ - v140 - i3 - Feb 15 2015 - p81(3) [501+]
Arnold, Jonathan - *Sacred Music in Secular Society*
JR - v95 - i4 - Oct 2015 - p564(3) [501+]
Arnold, Jonathan J. - *Theoderic and the Roman Imperial Restoration*
Class R - v65 - i2 - Oct 2015 - p550-552 [501+]
Arnold, Jorg - *The Allied Air War and Urban Memory: The Legacy of Strategic Bombing in Germany*
APJ - v29 - i3 - May-June 2015 - p88(2) [501+]
GSR - v38 - i3 - Oct 2015 - p702-703 [501+]
Arnold, Kathleen A. - *Contemporary Immigration in America: A State-by-State Encyclopedia, 2 vols.*
y BL - v111 - i19-20 - June 1 2015 - p8(1) [51-500]
Arnold, Marsha Diane - *Lost. Found. (Illus. by Cordell, Matthew)*
c HB - v91 - i6 - Nov-Dec 2015 - p63(2) [51-500]
c KR - Sept 1 2015 - pNA [51-500]
c PW - v262 - i49 - Dec 2 2015 - p16(1) [51-500]
c SLJ - v61 - i11 - Nov 2015 - p77(2) [51-500]
Arnold, Shari - *Kate Triumph*
y VOYA - v38 - i1 - April 2015 - p74(1) [51-500]
Neverland
y PW - v262 - i39 - Sept 28 2015 - p93(2) [51-500]
y VOYA - v38 - i4 - Oct 2015 - p66(1) [51-500]
Arnold, Stanley Keith - *Building the Beloved Community: Philadelphia's Interracial Civil Rights Organizations and Race Relations, 1930-1970*
AHR - v120 - i4 - Oct 2015 - p1512-1514 [501+]
JAH - v102 - i2 - Sept 2015 - p615-615 [501+]
Arnold, Tedd - *Fly Guy Presents: Bats (Illus. by Arnold, Tedd)*
c SLJ - v61 - i10 - Oct 2015 - p124(1) [51-500]
Fly Guy Presents: Insects (Illus. by Arnold, Tedd)
c SLJ - v61 - i6 - June 2015 - p133(1) [51-500]
Fly Guy's Amazing Tricks
c CH Bwatch - March 2015 - pNA [501+]
c HB Guide - v26 - i1 - Spring 2015 - p51(1) [51-500]
Noodlehead Nightmares (Illus. by Arnold, Tedd)
c KR - Jan 1 2016 - pNA [51-500]
Prince Fly Guy (Illus. by Arnold, Tedd)
c BL - v111 - i22 - August 1 2015 - p75(1) [51-500]
c SLJ - v61 - i7 - July 2015 - p70(1) [51-500]
Vincent Paints His House (Illus. by Arnold, Tedd)
c KR - June 1 2015 - pNA [51-500]
c SLJ - v61 - i8 - August 2015 - p63(2) [51-500]
Zig Zag et Frankenmouche
c Res Links - v20 - i3 - Feb 2015 - p42(1) [51-500]
Zig Zag et Zazie (Illus. by Arnold, Tedd)
c Res Links - v20 - i5 - June 2015 - p36(1) [51-500]
Arnosky, Jim - *Frozen Wild: How Animals Survive in the Coldest Places on Earth (Illus. by Arnosky, Jim)*
c BL - v112 - i2 - Sept 15 2015 - p54(1) [51-500]
c PW - v262 - i35 - August 31 2015 - p90(2) [501+]
c SLJ - v61 - i9 - Sept 2015 - p178(1) [51-500]
c KR - July 1 2015 - pNA [51-500]
Jim Arnosky's Wild World
c HB Guide - v26 - i1 - Spring 2015 - p152(1) [51-500]
Arnott, Peter - *Moon Country*
TLS - i5871 - Oct 9 2015 - p23(1) [501+]
Arntson, Steven - *The Trap*
c PW - v262 - i8 - Feb 23 2015 - p77(1) [51-500]
c Teach Lib - v42 - i5 - June 2015 - p15(1) [51-500]
y VOYA - v37 - i6 - Feb 2015 - p71(2) [51-500]
c BL - v111 - i18 - May 15 2015 - p68(1) [51-500]
c CCB-B - v68 - i10 - June 2015 - p479(2) [51-500]
c PW - v262 - i49 - Dec 2 2015 - p68(2) [51-500]
c KR - Jan 15 2015 - pNA [51-500]
Arntzen, Mari Grinde - *Dress Code: The Naked Truth about Fashion*
TLS - i5847 - April 24 2015 - p27(1) [501+]
Arntzen, Sonja - *The Sarashina Diary: A Woman's Life in Eleventh-Century Japan*
Med R - May 2015 - pNA [501+]
Aronin, Miriam - *Florida's Burmese Pythons: Squeezing the Everglades*
c BL - v112 - i3 - Oct 1 2015 - p54(1) [51-500]
Oklahoma's Devasting May 2013 Tornado
c HB Guide - v26 - i1 - Spring 2015 - p202(1) [51-500]
Aronovitz, Michael - *Phantom Effect*
PW - v262 - i52 - Dec 21 2015 - p138(1) [51-500]
Aronowitz, Nona Willis - *The Essential Ellen Willis*
Wom R Bks - v32 - i3 - May-June 2015 - p14(2) [501+]
Aronson, Marc - *One Death, Nine Stories*
y HB Guide - v26 - i1 - Spring 2015 - p186(1) [51-500]
Aros, Joyce - *Murdered on the Streets of Tombstone*
Roundup M - v22 - i6 - August 2015 - p33(1) [501+]
Arpin, Mylene - *Curieux de nature: Les oiseaux*
c Res Links - v21 - i1 - Oct 2015 - p47(1) [51-500]
Arpin-Ricci, Jamie - *Vulnerable Faith: Missional Living in the Radical Way of St. Patrick*
PW - v262 - i10 - March 9 2015 - p68(1) [51-500]

Arredondo, Francisco - *Finding You In Fertility*
    SPBW - August 2015 - pNA [51-500]
Arredondo, Jaime Marroquin - *Open Borders to a Revolution: Culture, Politics, and Migration*
    HAHR - v95 - i3 - August 2015 - p554-555 [501+]
Arreola, Daniel D. - *Postcards from the Rio Bravo Border: Picturing the Place, Placing the Picture, 1900s-1950s*
    PHR - v84 - i4 - Nov 2015 - p533(2) [501+]
Arrighi, Robert S. - *Pursuit of Power: NASA's Propulsion Systems Laboratory No. 1 and 2*
    APJ - v29 - i5 - Sept-Oct 2015 - p111(1) [501+]
Revolutionary Atmosphere, NASA SP 2010-4319
    APJ - v29 - i4 - July-August 2015 - p91(2) [501+]
Arrow, Cameron - *Into Focus: An Exhibitionist's Show & Tell-All*
    KR - May 15 2015 - pNA [501+]
Arroyo, Raymond - *The Relic of Perilous Falls*
    c KR - Dec 1 2015 - pNA [51-500]
Arsan, Andrew - *Interlopers of Empire: The Lebanese Diaspora in Colonial French West Africa*
    AHR - v120 - i3 - June 2015 - p1152-1153 [501+]
    IJAHS - v48 - i1 - Wntr 2015 - p135-136 [501+]
Arsenault, Emily - *The Evening Spider*
    BL - v112 - i7 - Dec 1 2015 - p27(2) [51-500]
    KR - Nov 15 2015 - pNA [501+]
    PW - v262 - i47 - Nov 23 2015 - p51(1) [51-500]
Arsenault, Isabelle - *Alpha (Illus. by Arsenault, Isabelle)*
    c KR - May 1 2015 - pNA [51-500]
    c PW - v262 - i19 - May 11 2015 - p60(1) [51-500]
    c SLJ - v61 - i7 - July 2015 - p59(1) [51-500]
Arsenault, Raymond - *Dixie Redux: Essays in Honor of Sheldon Hackney*
    JAH - v101 - i4 - March 2015 - p1277-1279 [501+]
Arthur, A.M. - *Getting It Right*
    PW - v262 - i3 - Jan 19 2015 - p66(1) [51-500]
Arthur, Donald - *Malevolent Muse: The Life of Alma Mahler*
    Lon R Bks - v37 - i21 - Nov 5 2015 - p7(4) [501+]
Arthur, Peter - *The Fight for Immortality*
    PW - v262 - i3 - Jan 19 2015 - p65(1) [51-500]
Arthur, Richard T.W. - *Leibniz*
    TLS - i5840 - March 6 2015 - p32(1) [501+]
Natural Deduction: An Introduction to Logic with Real Arguments, a Little History, and Some Humour
    Dialogue - v54 - i1 - March 2015 - p190-192 [501+]
Artimsi, Tony - *Rhythm Makers: The Drumming Legends of Nashville in Their Own Words*
    LJ - v140 - i5 - March 15 2015 - p100(1) [501+]
Artstein, Zvi - *Mathematics and the Real World: The Remarkable Role of Evolution in the Making of Mathematics*
    Math T - v109 - i1 - August 2015 - p78-78 [501+]
Artuso, Kathryn Stelmach - *Transatlantic Renaissances: Literature of Ireland and the American South*
    HNet - August 2015 - pNA [501+]
Virginia Woolf & 20th Century Women Writers
    BL - v111 - i16 - April 15 2015 - p12(1) [51-500]
Arum, Richard - *Aspiring Adults Adrift: Tentative Transitions of College Graduates*
    AJE - v121 - i4 - August 2015 - p633(4) [501+]
    AJS - v121 - i2 - Sept 2015 - p621(3) [501+]
Arumugam, Nadia - *Women Chefs of New York*
    BL - v112 - i3 - Oct 1 2015 - p21(1) [51-500]
    LJ - v140 - i13 - August 1 2015 - p118(1) [51-500]
    NYTBR - Dec 6 2015 - p20(L) [501+]
    NYTBR - Dec 6 2015 - p20(L) [501+]
    PW - v262 - i36 - Sept 7 2015 - p61(1) [51-500]
Aryan, Stephen - *Battlemage*
    KR - August 1 2015 - pNA [51-500]
    PW - v262 - i28 - July 13 2015 - p49(1) [51-500]
Arzt-Grabner, Peter - *2. Korinther*
    JR - v95 - i2 - April 2015 - p257(1) [501+]
Arzy, Shahar - *Kabbalah: A Neurocognitive Approach to Mystical Experiences*
    New Sci - v227 - i3033 - August 8 2015 - p42(1) [501+]
Asaro, Catherine - *Nebula Awards Showcase 2013*
    Analog - v135 - i10 - Oct 2015 - p106(1) [501+]
Asbach, Olaf - *The Ashgate Research Companion to the Thirty Years' War*
    HNet - July 2015 - pNA [501+]
    Sev Cent N - v73 - i1-2 - Spring-Summer 2015 - p37(5) [501+]
    Six Ct J - v46 - i2 - Summer 2015 - p423-424 [501+]
Asbridge, Thomas - *The Greatest Knight: The Remarkable Life of William Marshall, the Power Behind Five English Thrones*
    Lon R Bks - v37 - i10 - May 21 2015 - p29(2) [501+]
    NYTBR - Jan 25 2015 - p26(L) [501+]
    Spec - v327 - i9725 - Jan 17 2015 - p35(2) [501+]
The Greatest Knight: The Remarkable Life of William Marshall, the Power Behind Five English Thrones
    HT - v65 - i6 - June 2015 - p56(2) [501+]
    TLS - i5854 - June 12 2015 - p9(1) [501+]
Asch, Frank - *I Can Roar! (Illus. by Asch, Frank)*
    c KR - Jan 1 2016 - pNA [51-500]
    c SLJ - v61 - i7 - July 2015 - p54(1) [51-500]
Asch, Michael - *On Being Here to Stay: Treaties and Aboriginal Rights in Canada*
    Can Hist R - v96 - i1 - March 2015 - p109(4) [501+]
Asch, Ronald G. - *Sacral Kingship between Disenchantment and Re-Enactment: The French and English Monarchies, 1587-1688*
    AHR - v120 - i3 - June 2015 - p1119-1120 [501+]
Ascher, Carol - *A Call from Spooner Street*
    RVBW - Nov 2015 - pNA [51-500]
    SPBW - Sept 2015 - pNA [51-500]
Ascheri, Mario - *The Laws of Late Medieval Italy (1000-1500): Foundations for a European Legal System*
    Specu - v90 - i1 - Jan 2015 - p202-204 [501+]
Aschmann, Birgit - *Preussens Ruhm Deutschlands Ehre: Zum nationalen Ehrdiskurs im Vorfeld der preussisch-franzosischen Kriege des 19. Jahrhunderts*
    JMH - v87 - i1 - March 2015 - p153(3) [501+]
Aschoff, Nicole - *The New Prophets of Capital*
    New R - v246 - i4 - May 2015 - p86(4) [501+]
Ascoli, Albert Russell - *A Local Habitation and a Name: Imagining Histories in the Italian Renaissance*
    Clio - v44 - i2 - Spring 2015 - p242-248 [501+]
Ash-Milby, Kathleen - *Kay WalkingStick: An American Artist*
    PW - v262 - i44 - Nov 2 2015 - p79(2) [51-500]
Ash, Rhiannon - *Tacitus*
    Class R - v65 - i1 - April 2015 - p153-155 [501+]
Ash, Stephen V. - *A Massacre in Memphis: The Race Riot That Shook the Nation One Year After the Civil War*
    HNet - Sept 2015 - pNA [51-500]
    JSH - v81 - i2 - May 2015 - p483(2) [501+]
    RAH - v43 - i3 - Sept 2015 - p512-521 [501+]
Ashbery, John - *Breezeway: New Poems*
    LJ - v140 - i6 - April 1 2015 - p97(1) [51-500]
    NY - v91 - i15 - June 1 2015 - p73 [501+]
    PW - v262 - i20 - May 18 2015 - p61(2) [51-500]
Ashburn, Boni - *I Had a Favorite Dress (Read by Turpin, Bahni). Audiobook Review*
    c SLJ - v61 - i8 - August 2015 - p47(1) [51-500]
I Had a Favorite Hat (Illus. by Ng, Robyn)
    c SLJ - v61 - i4 - April 2015 - p123(2) [51-500]
    c HB Guide - v26 - i2 - Fall 2015 - p25(1) [51-500]
Ashburne, Ara Lucia - *Reconstruction: First A Body, Then A Life*
    KR - Feb 15 2015 - pNA [51-500]
Ashdown, Rebecca - *Bob and Flo (Illus. by Ashdown, Rebecca)*
    c HB - v91 - i4 - July-August 2015 - p107(2) [51-500]
    c KR - June 1 2015 - pNA [51-500]
    c PW - v262 - i17 - April 27 2015 - p75(1) [51-500]
    c SLJ - v61 - i7 - July 2015 - p58(1) [51-500]
Ashe, Bert - *Twisted*
    KR - March 15 2015 - pNA [51-500]
    BL - v111 - i14 - March 15 2015 - p34(1) [51-500]
Ashe, Charlotte - *The Sidhe*
    PW - v262 - i20 - May 18 2015 - p68(1) [51-500]
Ashe, Jeffrey - *In Their Own Hands*
    Bwatch - April 2015 - pNA [51-500]
Ashe, Laura - *War and Literature*
    TLS - i5838 - Feb 20 2015 - p26(1) [501+]
Ashenden, Jackie - *Make You Mine*
    PW - v262 - i15 - April 13 2015 - p64(1) [51-500]
Asher, Bridget - *All of Us and Everything*
    BL - v112 - i6 - Nov 15 2015 - p20(1) [51-500]
    KR - Sept 15 2015 - pNA [501+]
Asher, David - *The Art of Natural Cheesemaking: Using Traditional, Non-Industrial Methods and Raw Ingredients to Make the World's Best Cheeses*
    PW - v262 - i24 - June 15 2015 - p79(1) [51-500]
Asher, Dylan Edward - *Damage Day*
    KR - Jan 1 2015 - pNA [501+]
Strike a Poser
    KR - Oct 15 2015 - pNA [501+]
Asher, John J. - *My Big Brother's Birthday (Illus. by Asher, John J.)*
    c CH Bwatch - Jan 2015 - pNA [51-500]
Asher, Neal - *Dark Intelligence*
    BL - v111 - i11 - Feb 1 2015 - p32(1) [51-500]

Ashfeldt, Lane - *SaltWater*
    WLT - v89 - i1 - Jan-Feb 2015 - p61(2) [51-500]
Ashford, Jane - *Heir to the Duke*
    BL - v112 - i7 - Dec 1 2015 - p36(1) [51-500]
    PW - v262 - i45 - Nov 9 2015 - p43(1) [51-500]
Married to a Perfect Stranger
    BL - v111 - i12 - Feb 15 2015 - p44(1) [51-500]
    PW - v262 - i1 - Jan 5 2015 - p58(1) [51-500]
Ashley, Amanda - *Night's Surrender*
    PW - v262 - i31 - August 3 2015 - p43(1) [51-500]
Ashley-Hollinger, Mika - *Precious Bones*
    c CH Bwatch - Nov 2015 - pNA [51-500]
Ashley, J. Matthew - *A Grammar of Justice: The Legacy of Ignacio Ellacuria*
    Theol St - v76 - i4 - Dec 2015 - p885(2) [501+]
Ashley, Jennifer - *Mate Bond*
    PW - v262 - i7 - Feb 16 2015 - p165(1) [51-500]
The Stolen Mackenzie Bride
    BL - v112 - i2 - Sept 15 2015 - p48(1) [51-500]
Ashley, Katie - *Redemption Road*
    PW - v262 - i34 - August 24 2015 - p68(1) [51-500]
Vicious Cycle
    BL - v111 - i17 - May 1 2015 - p81(1) [51-500]
    PW - v262 - i16 - April 20 2015 - p62(1) [51-500]
Ashley, Kristen - *Ride Steady*
    PW - v262 - i20 - May 18 2015 - p70(2) [51-500]
Ashman, Linda - *Henry Wants More! (Illus. by Hughes, Brooke Boynton)*
    c BL - v112 - i6 - Nov 15 2015 - p58(1) [51-500]
    c KR - Oct 1 2015 - pNA [51-500]
    c PW - v262 - i42 - Oct 19 2015 - p75(1) [51-500]
    c SLJ - v61 - i11 - Nov 2015 - p76(1) [51-500]
Little Baby Buttercup (Illus. by Byun, You)
    c HB Guide - v26 - i2 - Fall 2015 - p5(1) [51-500]
Over the River and through the Wood: A Holiday Adventure (Illus. by Smith, Kim)
    c BL - v112 - i4 - Oct 15 2015 - p49(1) [51-500]
    c PW - v262 - i37 - Sept 14 2015 - p68(1) [51-500]
    c PW - v262 - i49 - Dec 2 2015 - p62(2) [51-500]
    c SLJ - v61 - i11 - Nov 2015 - p78(1) [51-500]
Over the River and through the Wood (Illus. by Smith, Kim)
    c KR - August 1 2015 - pNA [51-500]
Rock-A-Bye Romp (Illus. by Mulazzani, Simona)
    c KR - Oct 1 2015 - pNA [51-500]
    c PW - v262 - i41 - Oct 12 2015 - p65(1) [51-500]
    c SLJ - v61 - i12 - Dec 2015 - p84(1) [51-500]
Ashmore, Carl - *The Time Hunters*
    y KR - Jan 15 2015 - pNA [501+]
Ashour, Monica - *Theology of the Body Series (Illus. by Kaminski, Karol)*
    c CH Bwatch - Jan 2015 - pNA [51-500]
Ashraf, Kazi K. - *The Hermit's Hut: Architecture and Asceticism in India*
    AHR - v120 - i1 - Feb 2015 - p209-210 [501+]
    JAS - v74 - i1 - Feb 2015 - p230-231 [501+]
Ashton, Brodi - *Evertrue: An Everneath Novel*
    y Teach Lib - v42 - i3 - Feb 2015 - p28(4) [501+]
Ashton, Dianne - *Hanukkah in America: A History*
    HNet - Feb 2015 - pNA [501+]
Ashton, Kevin - *How to Fly a Horse: The Secret History of Creation, Invention, and Discovery*
    BL - v111 - i9-10 - Jan 1 2015 - p27(1) [51-500]
    New Sci - v225 - i3003 - Jan 10 2015 - p42(2) [501+]
Ashton, Rosemary - *Victorian Bloomsbury*
    VS - v57 - i2 - Wntr 2015 - p314(3) [501+]
Ashwell, Ken - *Neurobiology of Monotremes: Brain Evolution in Our Distant Mammalian Cousins*
    QRB - v90 - i1 - March 2015 - p93(2) [501+]
Ashwin, Paul - *Reflective Teaching in Higher Education*
    TimHES - i2197 - April 2 2015 - p56(1) [501+]
Asibong, Andrew - *Marie NDiaye: Blankness and Recognition*
    MLR - v110 - i3 - July 2015 - p875-876 [501+]
Asim, Jabari - *Only the Strong*
    KR - March 15 2015 - pNA [501+]
    LJ - v140 - i7 - April 15 2015 - p73(1) [51-500]
Asimov, Isaac - *Psychology Today: An Introduction, 2d ed.*
    S&T - v129 - i6 - June 2015 - p18(1) [501+]
Askari, Kavesh - *Making Movies into Art: Picture Craft from the Magic Lantern to Early Hollywood*
    FQ - v68 - i4 - Summer 2015 - p99(3) [501+]
    FQ - v68 - i4 - Summer 2015 - p99(3) [501+]
Askey, Jennifer Drake - *Good Girls, Good Germans: Girls' Education and Emotional Nationalism in Wilhelmine Germany*
    MLR - v110 - i1 - Jan 2015 - p292-294 [501+]

Aslan, Austin - *The Girl at the Center of the World*
   y KR - June 1 2015 - pNA [51-500]
   y BL - v111 - i21 - July 1 2015 - p55(1) [51-500]
   y SLJ - v61 - i6 - June 2015 - p119(1) [51-500]
   y VOYA - v38 - i3 - August 2015 - p73(1) [51-500]
The Islands at the End of the World
   y HB Guide - v26 - i1 - Spring 2015 - p99(1) [51-500]
Aslund, Anders - *The Great Rebirth*
     RVBW - Jan 2015 - pNA [501+]
Asmus, James - *The Delinquents*
     PW - v262 - i1 - Jan 5 2015 - p59(1) [51-500]
Aso, Noriko - *Public Properties: Museums in Imperial Japan*
     AHR - v120 - i1 - Feb 2015 - p220-221 [501+]
Aspe, Pieter - *From Bruges with Love*
     KR - May 1 2015 - pNA [501+]
     PW - v262 - i18 - May 4 2015 - p98(2) [51-500]
Asphyxia - *The Grimstones: Hatched*
   c Sch Lib - v63 - i1 - Spring 2015 - p34(1) [51-500]
Aspinall, Peter - *Mixed Race Identities*
     CS - v44 - i3 - May 2015 - p341-342 [501+]
     ERS - v38 - i8 - August 2015 - p1462(3) [51-500]
Asquith, Ros - *Vanishing Trick (Illus. by Asquith, Ros)*
   c BL - v112 - i7 - Dec 1 2015 - p41(1) [51-500]
   c Sch Lib - v63 - i4 - Winter 2015 - p241(1) [51-500]
   c SLJ - v61 - i12 - Dec 2015 - p134(1) [51-500]
Assaf, Andrea - *Pope Francis' Little Book of Wisdom: The Essential Teachings*
     LJ - v140 - i16 - Oct 1 2015 - p64(2) [501+]
Assange, Julian - *When Google Met WikiLeaks*
     TLS - i5838 - Feb 20 2015 - p3(3) [501+]
Asselin, Pierre - *Hanoi's Road to the Vietnam War, 1954-1965*
     HNet - Feb 2015 - pNA [501+]
     JAH - v102 - i1 - June 2015 - p298-299 [501+]
Asserate, Asfa-Wossen - *King of Kings: The Triumph and Tragedy of Emperor Haile Selassie I of Ethiopia*
     Spec - v329 - i9766 - Oct 31 2015 - p42(2) [501+]
King of Kings: Triumph and Tragedy of Emperor Haile Selassie I of Ethiopia
     PW - v262 - i39 - Sept 28 2015 - p79(1) [51-500]
Assis, Arthur Alfaix - *What Is History For? Johann Gustav Droysen and the Functions of Historiography*
     HNet - May 2015 - pNA [501+]
Assiter, Alison - *Kierkegaard, Eve and Metaphors of Birth*
     TimHES - i2214 - July 30 2015 - p51-51 [501+]
Assmann, Aleida - *Rendezvous mit dem Realen: Die Spur des Traumas in den Kunsten*
     HNet - Feb 2015 - pNA [501+]
Assmann, Jan - *From Akhenaten to Moses*
     RVBW - Jan 2015 - pNA [501+]
Assor, Michelle B. - *Snaygill*
   y KR - March 1 2015 - pNA [501+]
   y VOYA - v38 - i1 - April 2015 - p74(1) [51-500]
Astbury, Katherine - *Narrative Responses to the Trauma of the French Revolution*
     MLR - v110 - i2 - April 2015 - p547-548 [501+]
Aste, Gerardo - *Dando razones de nuestra esperanza: La pregunta acerca del mal*
     Theol St - v76 - i2 - June 2015 - p389(1) [51-500]
Asterino, Brenda M. - *Celebrating Life*
     SPBW - March 2015 - pNA [51-500]
Asthana, Praveen - *The Woman in the Movies Star Dress*
     KR - March 15 2015 - pNA [501+]
Astley, Neil - *Funny Ha-Ha Funny Peculiar*
   y Sch Lib - v63 - i4 - Winter 2015 - p241(1) [51-500]
The Hundred Years' War: Modern War Poems
     HR - v67 - i4 - Wntr 2015 - p667-676 [51-500]
Aston, Dianna Hutts - *A Nest Is Noisy (Illus. by Long, Sylvia)*
   c BL - v111 - i18 - May 15 2015 - p48(1) [51-500]
   c CCB-B - v68 - i10 - June 2015 - p480(1) [51-500]
   c HB Guide - v26 - i2 - Fall 2015 - p169(1) [51-500]
   c SLJ - v61 - i5 - May 2015 - p129(1) [51-500]
Aston, Mick - *Interpreting the English Village: Landscape and Community at Shapwick, Somerset*
     Specu - v90 - i4 - Oct 2015 - p1083-1084 [501+]
Astorga, Christina A. - *Catholic Moral Theology and Social Ethics: A New Method*
     Theol St - v76 - i2 - June 2015 - p374(3) [501+]
Aswany, Alaa Al - *The Automobile Club of Egypt*
     LJ - v140 - i12 - July 1 2015 - p72(1) [51-500]
     NYT - August 27 2015 - pC4(L) [501+]
Atalay, Sonya - *Transforming Archaeology: Activist Practices and Prospects*
     Pub Hist - v37 - i1 - Feb 2015 - p146(3) [501+]
Atanasoski, Neda - *Humanitarian Violence: The US Deployment of Diversity*
     AL - v87 - i1 - March 2015 - p209-211 [501+]

Ataton, Hilaire - *Civil Rights*
   c Res Links - v20 - i5 - June 2015 - p34(1) [51-500]
Ateek, Mona - *A Roving Eye: Head to Toe in Egyptian Arabic Expressions*
     RVBW - March 2015 - pNA [51-500]
Ates, Sabri - *Ottoman-Iranian Borderlands: Making a Boundary, 1843-1914*
     IJMES - v47 - i4 - Nov 2015 - p820-821 [501+]
Atherton, Nancy - *Aunt Dimity and the Summer King*
     PW - v262 - i8 - Feb 23 2015 - p54(1) [51-500]
     BL - v111 - i16 - April 15 2015 - p27(1) [51-500]
     KR - Feb 15 2015 - pNA [501+]
Athill, Diana - *Alive, Alive Oh! And Other Things That Matter*
     PW - v262 - i48 - Nov 30 2015 - p53(1) [51-500]
     KR - Nov 1 2015 - pNA [501+]
Athyal, Jesudas M. - *Religion in Southeast Asia: An Encyclopedia of Faiths and Culture*
   y BL - v111 - i22 - August 1 2015 - p6(2) [501+]
Atici, Levent - *Current Research at Kultepe-Kanesh: An Interdisciplinary and Integrative Approach to Trade Networks, Internationalism, and Identity*
     JNES - v74 - i2 - Oct 2015 - p351(4) [501+]
Atinuke - *Double Trouble for Anna Hibiscus! (Illus. by Tobia, Lauren)*
   c HB - v91 - i5 - Sept-Oct 2015 - p73(2) [51-500]
   c KR - June 1 2015 - pNA [501+]
   c Magpies - v30 - i2 - May 2015 - p28(1) [51-500]
   c SLJ - v61 - i7 - July 2015 - p56(1) [51-500]
The No. 1 Car Spotter Goes to School (Illus. by Cadwell, Warwick Johnson)
   c Magpies - v30 - i1 - March 2015 - p31(1) [51-500]
Atkin, Tamara - *The Drama of Reform: Theology and Theatricality, 1461-1553*
     Med R - Sept 2015 - pNA [501+]
Atkins, Ace - *The Forsaken*
     RVBW - August 2015 - pNA [51-500]
The Redeemers
     NYTBR - Dec 6 2015 - p85(L) [501+]
     BL - v111 - i18 - May 15 2015 - p28(1) [51-500]
     KR - May 15 2015 - pNA [51-500]
     LJ - v140 - i2 - Feb 1 2015 - p54(5) [51-500]
     NYTBR - August 2 2015 - p25(L) [501+]
     PW - v262 - i19 - May 11 2015 - p37(1) [51-500]
Robert B. Parker's Cheap Shot
     RVBW - May 2015 - pNA [51-500]
Robert B. Parker's Kickback
     BL - v111 - i17 - May 1 2015 - p43(1) [51-500]
     KR - March 15 2015 - pNA [51-500]
     PW - v262 - i10 - March 9 2015 - p52(1) [51-500]
Atkins, Ann - *Golda Meir: True Grit*
     SPBW - Jan 2015 - pNA [51-500]
Atkins, Dani - *The Story of Us*
     LJ - v140 - i9 - May 15 2015 - p69(1) [51-500]
     PW - v262 - i11 - March 16 2015 - p69(1) [51-500]
Atkins, Jeannine - *Little Woman in Blue*
     LJ - v140 - i14 - Sept 1 2015 - p89(1) [51-500]
Atkins, Jed W. - *Cicero on Politics and the Limits of Reason: The Republic and Laws*
     Class R - v65 - i1 - April 2015 - p120-122 [501+]
Atkins, Raymond L. - *Sweetwater Blues*
     RVBW - May 2015 - pNA [51-500]
Atkinson, Anthony - *Inequality: What Can Be Done?*
     NYRB - v62 - i11 - June 25 2015 - p26(3) [501+]
Atkinson, Anthony B. - *Inequality: What Can Be Done?*
     Econ - v415 - i8941 - June 6 2015 - p74(US) [501+]
     NYT - May 29 2015 - pNA(L) [501+]
     TLS - i5869 - Sept 25 2015 - p3(2) [501+]
Atkinson, Cale - *To the Sea (Illus. by Atkinson, Cale)*
   c KR - March 15 2015 - pNA [51-500]
   c PW - v262 - i14 - April 6 2015 - p57(1) [51-500]
   c SLJ - v61 - i5 - May 2015 - p82(1) [51-500]
   c Teach Lib - v43 - i1 - Oct 2015 - p28(1) [51-500]
Atkinson, Elizabeth - *The Sugar Mountain Snow Ball*
   c KR - July 15 2015 - pNA [51-500]
   c SLJ - v61 - i10 - Oct 2015 - p87(1) [51-500]
   y VOYA - v38 - i4 - Oct 2015 - p48(1) [51-500]
Atkinson, Jay - *Massacre on the Merrimack: Hannah Duston's Captivity and Revenge in Colonial America*
     KR - June 1 2015 - pNA [501+]
     PW - v262 - i28 - July 13 2015 - p59(1) [51-500]
Atkinson, Kate - *A God in Ruins (Read by Jennings, Alex).*
Audiobook Review
     BL - v112 - i4 - Oct 15 2015 - p61(1) [51-500]
     LJ - v140 - i13 - August 1 2015 - p46(1) [51-500]

A God in Ruins
     BL - v111 - i14 - March 15 2015 - p43(2) [51-500]
     Bwatch - August 2015 - pNA [51-500]
     Comw - v142 - i15 - Sept 25 2015 - p30(2) [501+]
     CSM - May 27 2015 - pNA [501+]
     Ent W - i1362 - May 8 2015 - p55(1) [51-500]
     KR - March 1 2015 - pNA [501+]
     LJ - v140 - i9 - May 15 2015 - p69(1) [51-500]
     New Sci - v227 - i3032 - August 1 2015 - p44(2) [501+]
     NS - v144 - i5261 - May 7 2015 - p54(1) [501+]
     NY - v91 - i21 - July 27 2015 - p71 [501+]
     NYT - May 1 2015 - pC17(L) [501+]
     NYTBR - May 10 2015 - p1(L) [501+]
     PW - v262 - i6 - Feb 9 2015 - p42(1) [51-500]
     SEP - v287 - i3 - May-June 2015 - p24(1) [501+]
     TLS - i5852 - May 29 2015 - p19(1) [501+]
Atkinson, Paul - *Delete: A Design History of Computer Vapourware*
     T&C - v56 - i4 - Oct 2015 - p1013-1015 [501+]
Atkinson, Rick - *Battle of the Bulge*
   y BL - v111 - i19-20 - June 1 2015 - p72(1) [51-500]
   c HB Guide - v26 - i2 - Fall 2015 - p217(1) [51-500]
   y SLJ - v61 - i5 - May 2015 - p137(1) [51-500]
D-Day
   c HB Guide - v26 - i1 - Spring 2015 - p201(1) [51-500]
Atkinson, Sam - *The Sociology Book: Big Ideas Simply Explained*
   y VOYA - v38 - i4 - Oct 2015 - p80(2) [51-500]
Atkinson, Tania - *John Joe's Tune: How New Zealand Got its National Anthem (Illus. by Ross, Christine)*
   c Magpies - v30 - i4 - Sept 2015 - pS6(1) [51-500]
Atlas, Nava - *Plant Power*
     Veg J - v34 - i3 - July-Sept 2015 - p31(1) [51-500]
Attaleiates, Michael - *The History*
     Specu - v90 - i1 - Jan 2015 - p204-206 [501+]
Attardo, Salvatore - *Encyclopedia of Humor Studies*
     R&USQ - v54 - i3 - Spring 2015 - p61(1) [501+]
Atteberry, Kevan - *Bunnies!!! (Illus. by Atteberry, Kevan)*
   c CCB-B - v68 - i7 - March 2015 - p347(1) [51-500]
   c HB Guide - v26 - i2 - Fall 2015 - p6(1) [51-500]
Attebery, Brian - *Stories About Stories: Fantasy and the Remaking of Myth*
     SFS - v42 - i1 - March 2015 - p164-166 [501+]
Attenberg, Jami - *Saint Mazie*
     KR - March 1 2015 - pNA [51-500]
     Nat Post - v17 - i182 - June 6 2015 - pWP4(1) [501+]
     NYTBR - June 14 2015 - p11(L) [501+]
     PW - v262 - i14 - April 6 2015 - p36(1) [51-500]
     SEP - v287 - i3 - May-June 2015 - p24(1) [501+]
Attias, Bernardo Alexander - *DJ Culture in the Mix: Power, Technology, and Social Change in Electronic Dance Music*
     PMS - v38 - i3 - July 2015 - p389(3) [501+]
Attlee, James - *Station to Station: Searching for Stories on the Great Western Line*
     Spec - v328 - i9745 - June 6 2015 - p39(2) [501+]
Attwell, David - *J.M. Coetzee and the Life of Writing: Face-to-Face with Time*
     KR - August 1 2015 - pNA [501+]
     LJ - v140 - i13 - August 1 2015 - p92(1) [51-500]
     PW - v262 - i34 - August 24 2015 - p74(1) [51-500]
Atwan, Abdel Bari - *Islamic State: The Digital Caliphate*
     NYRB - v62 - i12 - July 9 2015 - p74(4) [501+]
Atwater-Rhodes, Amelia - *Bloodkin*
   y BL - v111 - i15 - April 1 2015 - p68(1) [51-500]
   y CH Bwatch - August 2015 - pNA [51-500]
   y HB Guide - v26 - i2 - Fall 2015 - p110(1) [51-500]
     SLJ - v61 - i2 - Feb 2015 - p96(2) [51-500]
   y VOYA - v38 - i1 - April 2015 - p74(1) [51-500]
Atwood, Margaret - *The Heart Goes Last*
     BL - v111 - i22 - August 1 2015 - p28(1) [51-500]
     KR - July 15 2015 - pNA [501+]
     Nature - v527 - i7576 - Nov 5 2015 - p37(1) [51-500]
     NS - v144 - i5280 - Sept 18 2015 - p67(1) [51-500]
     NY - v91 - i31 - Oct 12 2015 - p103 [51-500]
     NYT - Sept 30 2015 - pC1(L) [501+]
     NYTBR - Sept 27 2015 - p10(L) [501+]
     PW - v262 - i26 - June 29 2015 - p42(1) [51-500]
     Spec - v329 - i9760 - Sept 19 2015 - p47(2) [501+]
     TLS - i5870 - Oct 2 2015 - p19(1) [501+]
Measures of Astonishment: Poets on Poetry
     PW - v262 - i13 - March 30 2015 - p69(1) [51-500]

Atwood, Megan - *Beat the Odds*
  y KR - Nov 15 2015 - pNA [51-500]
Cailyn and Chloe Learn about Conjunctions (Illus. by Haus, Estudio)
  c HB Guide - v26 - i2 - Fall 2015 - p161(1) [51-500]
  c BL - v111 - i15 - April 1 2015 - p60(1) [51-500]
Raise the Stakes
  y KR - Nov 15 2015 - pNA [51-500]
Stay in the Game
  y KR - Nov 15 2015 - pNA [51-500]
Aubert, Albert - *Du spiritualisme et de quelques-unes de ses consequences*
    MLR - v110 - i3 - July 2015 - p868-869 [501+]
Aubert, Annette G. - *The German Roots of Nineteenth-Century American Theology*
    AHR - v120 - i2 - April 2015 - p622-623 [501+]
Aubrey, John - *'Brief Lives' with 'An Apparatus for the Lives of Our English Mathematical Writers'*
    Lon R Bks - v37 - i19 - Oct 8 2015 - p17(2) [501+]
Auch, Mary Jane - *The Buk Buk Buk Festival (Illus. by Auch, Mary Jane)*
  c BL - v111 - i18 - May 15 2015 - p57(1) [51-500]
  c KR - Feb 15 2015 - pNA [51-500]
Auchmutey, Jim - *The Class of '65: A Student, a Divided Town, and the Long Road to Forgiveness*
    CC - v132 - i15 - July 22 2015 - p34(2) [501+]
Auden, W.H. - *The Complete Works of W.H. Auden: Prose, vol. 5: 1963-1968*
    Lon R Bks - v37 - i14 - July 16 2015 - p36(2) [501+]
    NYRB - v62 - i16 - Oct 22 2015 - p47(2) [501+]
The Complete Works of W.H. Auden: Prose, vol. 6: 1969-1973
    Lon R Bks - v37 - i14 - July 16 2015 - p36(2) [501+]
    NYRB - v62 - i16 - Oct 22 2015 - p47(2) [501+]
The Complete Works of W.H. Auden: Prose, vols. 5-6
    HR - v68 - i3 - Autumn 2015 - p491-500 [501+]
Audi, Robert - *Moral Perception*
    Ethics - v125 - i4 - July 2015 - p1189(6) [501+]
Audissino, Emilio - *John Williams's Film Music: Jaws, Star Wars, Raiders of the Lost Ark, and the Return of the Classical Hollywood Music Style*
    Notes - v72 - i1 - Sept 2015 - p165(4) [501+]
Auer, Peter - *Language Variation: European Perspectives IV*
    Lang Soc - v44 - i5 - Nov 2015 - p750-751 [501+]
Auerbach, Adam - *Edda: A Little Valkyrie's First Day at School (Read by Berneis, Susie). Audiobook Review*
  c SLJ - v61 - i9 - Sept 2015 - p56(1) [51-500]
Edda: A Little Valkyrie's First Day of School (Illus. by Auerbach, Adam)
  c HB Guide - v26 - i1 - Spring 2015 - p20(1) [51-500]
Auerbach, Karen - *The House at Ujazdowskie 16: Jewish Families in Warsaw after the Holocaust*
    HNet - Jan 2015 - pNA [501+]
Auf dem Weg zu einer Geschichte der Sensibilitat. Empfindsamkeit und Sorge fur Katastrophenopfer
    HNet - April 2015 - pNA [501+]
Auf dem Weg zu einer transnationalen Erinnerungskultur? Konvergenzen, Interferenzen und Differenzen der Erinnerung an den Ersten Weltkrieg im Jubilaumsjahr 2014
    HNet - April 2015 - pNA [501+]
Auffenorde, Daco - *The Pisces Affair*
    PW - v262 - i23 - June 8 2015 - p44(1) [51-500]
Augoustakis, Antony - *A Companion to Terence*
    Class R - v65 - i2 - Oct 2015 - p428-430 [501+]
Flavian Poetry and its Greek Past
    Class R - v65 - i2 - Oct 2015 - p466-468 [501+]
August, Arnold - *Cuba and its Neighbors: Democracy in Motion*
    S&S - v79 - i1 - Jan 2015 - p140-143 [501+]
Auman, William T. - *Civil War in the North Carolina Quaker Belt: The Confederate Campaign against Peace Agitators, Deserters, and Draft Dodgers*
    JSH - v81 - i4 - Nov 2015 - p991(2) [501+]
Aumhammer, Achim - *Arthur Schnitzler und die Musik*
    Ger Q - v88 - i1 - Wntr 2015 - p115(3) [501+]
Aune, David E. - *Greco-Roman Culture and the New Testament: Studies Commemorating the Centennial of the Pontifical Biblical Institute*
    Theol St - v76 - i1 - March 2015 - p208(1) [501+]
Auping, Michael - *Frank Stella: A Retrospective*
    NYTBR - Dec 6 2015 - p56(L) [501+]
Aureliani, Franco - *Dino-Mike and the T. Rex Attack*
  c PW - v262 - i3 - Jan 19 2015 - p83(1) [501+]
Aurell, Jaume - *Authoring the Past: History, Autobiography and Politics in Medieval Catalonia*
    Med R - Jan 2015 - pNA [501+]

Aurell, Martin - *Les strategies matrimoniales, IXe-XIIIe siecle*
    HER - v130 - i544 - June 2015 - p696(2) [501+]
Auricchio, Laura - *American Hero: The Marquis Lafayette Reconsidered*
    AM - v213 - i2 - July 20 2015 - p34(3) [501+]
The Marquis
    NY - v90 - i43 - Jan 12 2015 - p71 [501+]
Aurini, Janice - *Out of the Shadows: The Global Intensification of Supplementary Education*
    Pac A - v88 - i4 - Dec 2015 - p896 [501+]
Aus den Giftschranken des Kommunismus. Methodische Fragen zum Umgang mit den Uberwachungsakten in Sudost- und Mitteleuropa
    HNet - June 2015 - pNA [501+]
Auschwitz as World Heritage: UNESCO, Poland, and History Politics
    HNet - Feb 2015 - pNA [501+]
Auslandische Zwangsarbeiterinnen und Zwangsarbeiter und die Berliner Justiz, 1939-1945
    HNet - March 2015 - pNA [501+]
Aust, Martin - *Osteuropaische Geschichte und Globalgeschichte*
    Slav R - v74 - i3 - Fall 2015 - p686-686 [501+]
Aust, Patricia H. - *Shelter*
  c HB Guide - v26 - i1 - Spring 2015 - p99(1) [51-500]
Austen, Amy - *Surprisingly Scary!*
  c SLJ - v61 - i12 - Dec 2015 - p134(2) [51-500]
Austen, Jane - *Love and Friendship and Other Youthful Writings*
    TLS - i5838 - Feb 20 2015 - p9(2) [501+]
Pride and Prejudice (Illus. by Deas, Robert)
  y BL - v111 - i18 - May 15 2015 - p43(1) [51-500]
Volume the First: In Her Own Hand
    TLS - i5838 - Feb 20 2015 - p9(2) [501+]
Volume the Second: In Her Own Hand
    TLS - i5838 - Feb 20 2015 - p9(2) [501+]
Volume the Third: In Her Own Hand
    TLS - i5838 - Feb 20 2015 - p9(2) [501+]
Austen, Katherine - *Book M: A London Widow's Life Writings*
    Six Ct J - v46 - i3 - Fall 2015 - p734-736 [501+]
Austermann, Frauke - *China and Europe in 21st Century Global Politics: Partnership, Competition or Co-Evolution*
    E-A St - v67 - i9 - Nov 2015 - p1503(2) [501+]
Austermuhl, Frank - *The Great American Scaffold: Intertextuality and Identity in American Presidential Discourse*
    Lang Soc - v44 - i3 - June 2015 - p443-444 [501+]
    Pres St Q - v45 - i1 - March 2015 - p206(2) [501+]
Austin, Alex - *Nakamura Reality*
    KR - Dec 15 2015 - pNA [51-500]
    PW - v262 - i48 - Nov 30 2015 - p40(1) [51-500]
Austin, Allan W. - *Quaker Brotherhood: Interracial Activism and the American Friends Service Committee, 1917-1950*
    JSH - v81 - i1 - Feb 2015 - p229(2) [501+]
Austin, Elisabeth L. - *Exemplary Ambivalence in Late Nineteenth-Century Spanish America: Narrating Creole Subjectivity*
    HAHR - v95 - i4 - Nov 2015 - p683-684 [501+]
Austin, John Langshaw - *How to Do Things with Words*
    Nat R - v67 - i21 - Nov 19 2015 - p73(1) [501+]
Austin, Lisa M. - *Private Law and the Rule of Law*
    Law Q Rev - v131 - Oct 2015 - p679-681 [501+]
Austin, Lynnette - *The Best Laid Wedding Plans*
    BL - v112 - i3 - Oct 1 2015 - p31(1) [51-500]
Austin, Mike - *Fire Engine No. 9 (Illus. by Austin, Mike)*
  c BL - v112 - i2 - Sept 15 2015 - p67(1) [51-500]
  c HB - v91 - i5 - Sept-Oct 2015 - p74(1) [51-500]
  c KR - July 15 2015 - pNA [51-500]
  c SLJ - v61 - i7 - July 2015 - p59(1) [51-500]
Monsters Love School
  c HB Guide - v26 - i1 - Spring 2015 - p21(1) [51-500]
Austin, Terri L. - *His Kind of Trouble*
    KR - Sept 1 2015 - pNA [51-500]
    PW - v262 - i37 - Sept 14 2015 - p48(1) [51-500]
Australian National University - *Australian Dictionary of Biography, 19 vols.*
    Quad - v59 - i7-8 - July-August 2015 - p127(3) [501+]
Austrian, J.J. - *Worm Loves Worm (Illus. by Curato, Mike)*
  c BL - v112 - i7 - Dec 1 2015 - p67(1) [51-500]
  c KR - Oct 1 2015 - pNA [51-500]
  c SLJ - v61 - i11 - Nov 2015 - p78(1) [51-500]
Authenticity and Victimhood in 20th Century History and Commemorative Culture
    HNet - April 2015 - pNA [501+]

Autoritat und Krise. der Verlust der Eindeutigkeit und Seine Folgen am Beispiel der Mittelalterlichen Gegenpapste
    HNet - July 2015 - pNA [501+]
Auvergne, William - *On Morals*
    CHR - v101 - i1 - Wntr 2015 - p154(2) [501+]
Auxier, Jonathan - *The Night Gardener (Read by Crick, Beverley A.). Audiobook Review*
  y HB - v91 - i4 - July-August 2015 - p163(1) [51-500]
  c SLJ - v61 - i6 - June 2015 - p63(1) [51-500]
The Night Gardener
  y Teach Lib - v42 - i3 - Feb 2015 - p28(4) [501+]
  y Teach Lib - v42 - i3 - Feb 2015 - p52(6) [501+]
Auyero, Javier - *Invisible in Austin: Life and Labor in an American City*
    BL - v112 - i1 - Sept 1 2015 - p30(1) [51-500]
    KR - June 1 2015 - pNA [501+]
    PW - v262 - i24 - June 15 2015 - p73(1) [51-500]
Avadian, Brenda - *Stuffology 101: Get Your Mind Out of the Clutter*
    PW - v262 - i6 - Feb 9 2015 - p60(2) [51-500]
Avalon, Frankie - *Frankie Avalon's Italian Family Cookbook: From Mom's Kitchen to Mine and Yours*
    PW - v262 - i29 - July 20 2015 - p183(1) [51-500]
Avant, George - *The Strange Side of the Tracks*
    RVBW - August 2015 - pNA [51-500]
Avcioglu, Nebahat - *Architecture, Art and Identity in Venice and Its Territories, 1450-1750: Essays in Honour of Deborah Howard*
    Six Ct J - v46 - i2 - Summer 2015 - p414-416 [501+]
Aveline-Dubach, Natacha - *Invisible Population: The Place of the Dead in East Asian Megacities*
    J Urban H - v41 - i1 - Jan 2015 - p165-6 [501+]
Averbeck, Jim - *A Hitch at the Fairmont (Illus. by Bertozzi, Nick)*
  c HB Guide - v26 - i1 - Spring 2015 - p68(1) [51-500]
One Word from Sophia (Illus. by Ismail, Yasmeen)
  c HB Guide - v26 - i2 - Fall 2015 - p25(1) [51-500]
  c KR - March 15 2015 - pNA [51-500]
Averis, Kate - *Exile and Nomadism in French and Hispanic Women's Writing*
    FS - v69 - i4 - Oct 2015 - p560-561 [501+]
Avery, Ellis - *The Family Tooth*
    KR - Dec 15 2015 - pNA [501+]
Avery, Lara - *A Million Miles Away*
  y BL - v111 - i17 - May 1 2015 - p92(1) [51-500]
  y KR - May 1 2015 - pNA [51-500]
    SLJ - v61 - i4 - April 2015 - p159(1) [51-500]
  y VOYA - v38 - i1 - April 2015 - p52(2) [51-500]
Avery, Mark - *Behind the Binoculars: Interviews with Acclaimed Birdwatchers*
    Nature - v524 - i7563 - August 6 2015 - p33(1) [51-500]
Avery, Nanette L. - *Orphan in America*
    SPBW - Nov 2015 - pNA [501+]
Avery, Tom - *My Brother's Shadow*
  y HB Guide - v26 - i1 - Spring 2015 - p99(1) [51-500]
Not As We Know It (Illus. by Grove, Kate)
  c Sch Lib - v63 - i2 - Summer 2015 - p100(1) [51-500]
Aveyard, Victoria - *Glass Sword*
  y KR - Nov 15 2015 - pNA [51-500]
  y SLJ - v61 - i12 - Dec 2015 - p118(1) [51-500]
Red Queen
  y BL - v111 - i9-10 - Jan 1 2015 - p100(1) [51-500]
  y CCB-B - v68 - i6 - Feb 2015 - p299(1) [51-500]
  y HB Guide - v26 - i2 - Fall 2015 - p110(1) [51-500]
  y VOYA - v37 - i6 - Feb 2015 - p72(1) [51-500]
Avi - *Catch You Later, Traitor (Read by Turetsky, Mark). Audiobook Review*
  c SLJ - v61 - i9 - Sept 2015 - p58(1) [51-500]
Catch You Later, Traitor
  c BL - v111 - i11 - Feb 1 2015 - p50(2) [51-500]
  c CCB-B - v68 - i9 - May 2015 - p439(1) [51-500]
  y HB - v91 - i2 - March-April 2015 - p90(2) [51-500]
  c HB Guide - v26 - i2 - Fall 2015 - p74(1) [51-500]
  c KR - Jan 15 2015 - pNA [51-500]
  c PW - v262 - i3 - Jan 19 2015 - p81(1) [51-500]
  c PW - v262 - i49 - Dec 2 2015 - p79(1) [51-500]
  y Res Links - v20 - i4 - April 2015 - p23(1) [501+]
  c SLJ - v61 - i3 - March 2015 - p131(1) [51-500]
  y VOYA - v38 - i1 - April 2015 - p53(1) [51-500]
Old Wolf (Read by Heyborne, Kirby). Audiobook Review
  c BL - v112 - i6 - Nov 15 2015 - p63(1) [51-500]
  c SLJ - v61 - i10 - Oct 2015 - p51(1) [51-500]
Old Wolf (Illus. by Floca, Brian)
  c SLJ - v61 - i6 - June 2015 - p97(1) [51-500]
  c BL - v111 - i19-20 - June 1 2015 - p106(1) [51-500]
  c HB - v91 - i5 - Sept-Oct 2015 - p92(1) [51-500]
  c KR - May 1 2015 - pNA [51-500]
Sophia's War: A Tale of Revolution
  y BL - v111 - i19-20 - June 1 2015 - p86(2) [501+]

Avila, Eric - *The Folklore of the Freeway: Race and Revolt in the Modernist City*
    AHR - v120 - i3 - June 2015 - p1070-1071 [501+]
    Am Q - v67 - i1 - March 2015 - p231-240 [501+]
    Am St - v54 - i1 - Spring 2015 - p171-172 [501+]
    JAH - v102 - i1 - June 2015 - p300-301 [501+]
    Pub Hist - v37 - i1 - Feb 2015 - p130(3) [501+]

Avineri, Shlomo - *Herzl's Vision: Theodor Herzl and the Foundation of the Jewish State*
    HNet - March 2015 - pNA [501+]
    Comw - v142 - i4 - Feb 20 2015 - p22(3) [501+]

Avise, John C. - *Conceptual Breakthroughs in Evolutionary Genetics: A Brief History of Shifting Paradigms*
    QRB - v90 - i1 - March 2015 - p88(1) [501+]

Avison, Brett - *Ducks to Water (Illus. by Dawson, Janine)*
    c Magpies - v30 - i1 - March 2015 - p28(2) [501+]

Avner, Yehuda - *The Ambassador*
    BL - v112 - i2 - Sept 15 2015 - p36(1) [51-500]

Avni, Gideon - *The Byzantine-Islamic Transition in Palestine: An Archeological Approach*
    AHR - v120 - i4 - Oct 2015 - p1574-1575 [501+]

Awad, Mona - *13 Ways of Looking at a Fat Girl*
    KR - Dec 1 2015 - pNA [51-500]
    PW - v262 - i46 - Nov 16 2015 - p48(1) [51-500]

Awad, Najib George - *Persons in Relation: An Essay on the Trinity and Ontology*
    Theol St - v76 - i2 - June 2015 - p361(2) [501+]

Awoonor, Kofi - *The Promise of Hope: New and Selected Poems, 1964-2013*
    Ant R - v73 - i2 - Spring 2015 - p372(9) [501+]

Axe, David - *Shadow Wars: Chasing Conflict in an Era of Peace*
    APJ - v29 - i6 - Nov-Dec 2015 - p96(2) [501+]

Axelrod, Alan - *Lost Destiny: Joe Kennedy Jr. and the Doomed WWII Mission to Save London*
    KR - Feb 15 2015 - pNA [501+]
    LJ - v140 - i5 - March 15 2015 - p117(2) [501+]

Axelrod, Amy - *The Bullet Catch*
    c BL - v111 - i17 - May 1 2015 - p49(1) [51-500]
    c HB Guide - v26 - i2 - Fall 2015 - p74(1) [51-500]
    c KR - Feb 15 2015 - pNA [51-500]
    y SLJ - v61 - i2 - Feb 2015 - p82(1) [51-500]

Axelrod, David - *Believer: My Forty Years in Politics (Read by Axelrod, David). Audiobook Review*
    BL - v111 - i19-20 - June 1 2015 - p136(1) [51-500]

Believer: My Forty Years in Politics
    CSM - March 26 2015 - pNA [51-500]
    Econ - v414 - i8925 - Feb 14 2015 - p30(US) [501+]
    KR - March 15 2015 - pNA [501+]
    NYRB - v62 - i7 - April 23 2015 - p8(2) [501+]
    NYT - Feb 9 2015 - pC1(L) [501+]
    NYTBR - Feb 15 2015 - p12(L) [501+]
    TLS - i5847 - April 24 2015 - p23(1) [501+]
    LJ - v140 - i7 - April 15 2015 - p104(1) [51-500]

Axelrod, Howard - *The Point of Vanishing: A Memoir of Two Years in Solitude*
    BL - v111 - i22 - August 1 2015 - p13(1) [51-500]
    KR - June 15 2015 - pNA [51-500]
    RVBW - Oct 2015 - pNA [51-500]

Axelrod, Kate - *The Law of Loving Others (Read by Cooper-Novack, Hallie). Audiobook Review*
    SLJ - v61 - i4 - April 2015 - p64(1) [51-500]

The Law of Loving Others
    y CCB-B - v68 - i6 - Feb 2015 - p299(2) [51-500]
    y HB Guide - v26 - i2 - Fall 2015 - p110(1) [51-500]

Axster, Felix - *Koloniales Spektakel in 9x14: Bildpostkarten im Deutschen Kaiserreich*
    HNet - March 2015 - pNA [501+]

Axtell, James - *Wisdom's Workshop*
    KR - Dec 1 2015 - pNA [501+]

Ayala, Francisco J. - *Essential Readings in Evolutionary Biology*
    QRB - v90 - i2 - June 2015 - p215(1) [501+]

Ayatsuji, Yukito - *The Decagon House Murders*
    PW - v262 - i18 - May 4 2015 - p98(1) [51-500]
    SLJ - v61 - i10 - Oct 2015 - p121(1) [51-500]

Ayaz, Huda - *Freeze-land: A New Beginning*
    c CH Bwatch - Nov 2015 - pNA [501+]

Ayer, Paula - *Foodprints: The Story of What We Eat (Illus. by Kinnaird, Ross)*
    c SLJ - v61 - i8 - August 2015 - p125(1) [51-500]

Foodprints: The Story of What We Eat (Illus. by Olenina, Ira)
    c KR - May 1 2015 - pNA [51-500]
    c VOYA - v38 - i2 - June 2015 - p86(1) [51-500]

Foodprints: The Story of What we Eat (Illus. by Kinnaird, Ross)
    c Res Links - v21 - i1 - Oct 2015 - p45(1) [51-500]

Ready, Set, Kindergarten! (Illus. by Arbour, Danielle)
    c KR - June 1 2015 - pNA [51-500]
    c Res Links - v21 - i1 - Oct 2015 - p2(1) [51-500]

Aykol, Esmahan - *Divorce Turkish Style: A Kati Hirschel Mystery*
    PW - v262 - i33 - August 17 2015 - p52(2) [51-500]

Aylen, Jonathan - *Ribbon of Fire: How Europe Adopted and Developed US Strip Mill Technology (1920-2000)*
    T&C - v56 - i2 - April 2015 - p556-558 [501+]

Aylesworth, Jim - *My Grandfather's Coat (Illus. by McClintock, Barbara)*
    c CH Bwatch - Feb 2015 - pNA [51-500]
    c HB Guide - v26 - i1 - Spring 2015 - p143(1) [51-500]

Aylett, Mary - *Country Wines*
    CI - v23 - i1 - Jan 2015 - p30(1) [501+]

Aylward, William - *Excavations at Zeugma: Conducted by Oxford Archaeology*
    Class R - v65 - i2 - Oct 2015 - p573-576 [501+]

Aymer, Margaret - *James: Diaspora Rhetoric of a Friend of God*
    CC - v132 - i21 - Oct 14 2015 - p32(2) [501+]

Ayoade, Richard - *Ayoade on Ayoade: A Cinematic Odyssey*
    TLS - i5836 - Feb 6 2015 - p26(2) [501+]

Ayres-Bennett, Wendy - *Bon usage et variation sociolinguistique: Perspectives diachroniques et traditions nationales*
    MLR - v110 - i2 - April 2015 - p510-511 [501+]

Ayres, D.D. - *Force of Attraction*
    PW - v262 - i5 - Feb 2 2015 - p42(2) [51-500]

Primal Force
    PW - v262 - i30 - July 27 2015 - p48(1) [51-500]

Ayres, Jennifer - *Good Food: Grounded Practical Theology*
    TT - v72 - i3 - Oct 2015 - p342-344 [501+]

Azad, Arezou - *Sacred Landscape in Medieval Afghanistan: Revisiting the Fada'il-i Balkh*
    AHR - v120 - i3 - June 2015 - p1152(1) [501+]
    JNES - v74 - i2 - Oct 2015 - p386(3) [501+]

Azaro, Victoria M. - *Sage: I am the Middle Sister*
    c Magpies - v30 - i1 - March 2015 - pS6(1) [501+]

Azimi, Nassrine - *Last Boat to Yokohama: The Life and Legacy of Beate Sirota Gordon*
    SPBW - June 2015 - pNA [51-500]

Azose, Elana - *Never Insult a Killer Zucchini (Illus. by Clark, David)*
    c KR - Dec 1 2015 - pNA [51-500]

Azoulay, Vincent - *Les Tyrannicides d'Athenes: Vie et mort de deux statues*
    Class R - v65 - i2 - Oct 2015 - p612-613 [501+]

Azuela, Mariano - *The Underdogs*
    TLS - i5848 - May 1 2015 - p24(1) [501+]

Azzam, Abed - *Nietzsche Versus Paul*
    NYRB - v62 - i17 - Nov 5 2015 - p21(3) [501+]

Azzarello, Robert - *Queer Environmentality: Ecology, Evolution, and Sexuality in American Literature*
    MLR - v110 - i1 - Jan 2015 - p247-249 [501+]

B

B., David - *Incidents in the Night, Book 2*
PW - v262 - i15 - April 13 2015 - p65(1) [51-500]
Ba, Gabriel - *Two Brothers*
PW - v262 - i42 - Oct 19 2015 - p64(1) [51-500]
Baader, Benjamin Maria - *Jewish Masculinities: German Jews, Gender, and History*
HNet - Feb 2015 - pNA [501+]
Baar, Monika - *Historians and Nationalism: East-Central Europe in the Nineteenth Century*
AHR - v120 - i1 - Feb 2015 - p351-352 [501+]
Babb, Kent - *Not a Game: The Incredible Rise and Unthinkable Fall of Allen Iverson*
LJ - v140 - i8 - May 1 2015 - p78(1) [51-500]
PW - v262 - i17 - April 27 2015 - p62(1) [51-500]
Babbitt, Natalie - *Tuck Everlasting*
c HB Guide - v26 - i2 - Fall 2015 - p74(1) [51-500]
Babe, Peter - *The Cut of the Whip/Bring Me Another Corpse/Time Enough to Die*
BL - v111 - i21 - July 1 2015 - p36(1) [51-500]
Babel, Isaac - *Red Cavalry*
KR - March 15 2015 - pNA [51-500]
Babel, Nathalie - *Red Cavalry*
PW - v262 - i9 - March 2 2015 - p60(1) [51-500]
TLS - i5841 - March 13 2015 - p28(1) [501+]
Babine, Karen - *Water and What We Know: Following the Roots of a Northern Life*
BL - v111 - i12 - Feb 15 2015 - p28(1) [51-500]
Babiracki, Patryk - *Cold War Crossings: International Travel and Exchange across the Soviet Bloc, 1940s-1960s*
Slav R - v74 - i3 - Fall 2015 - p660-662 [501+]
Babitz, Eve - *Eve's Hollywood*
New R - v246 - i11 - Fall 2015 - p70(2) [51-500]
Babka, Daniel - *No More Illusions*
SPBW - April 2015 - pNA [51-500]
Babones, Salvatore - *Sixteen for '16: A Progressive Agenda for a Better America*
LJ - v140 - i5 - March 15 2015 - p122(1) [51-500]
Babstock, Ken - *On Malice*
Can Lit - i224 - Spring 2015 - p107 [501+]
Babusiaux, Ulrike - *Das Recht der "Soldatenkaiser": Rechtliche Stabilitat in Zeiten Politischen Umbruchs?*
HNet - July 2015 - pNA [501+]
Baby, Andre K. - *The Chimera Sanction*
SPBW - Jan 2015 - pNA [51-500]
Baby Loves Sports: A High-Contrast Action Book (Illus. by Rojas, R.D.)
c SLJ - v61 - i7 - July 2015 - p54(1) [51-500]
Baca, Salena - *Crochet for Christmas: 29 Patterns for Handmade Holiday Decorations and Gifts*
Bwatch - Oct 2015 - pNA [51-500]
Baccalario, Pierdomenico - *Compass of Dreams (Illus. by Bruno, Iacopo)*
c HB Guide - v26 - i1 - Spring 2015 - p68(2) [51-500]
Bacchilega, Cristina - *Fairy Tales Transformed? Twenty-First-Century Adaptations and the Politics of Wonder*
WestFolk - v74 - i2 - Spring 2015 - p227-228 [501+]
Bacci, Michele - *The Many Faces of Christ: Portraying the Holy in the East and West, 300-1300*
CHR - v101 - i3 - Summer 2015 - p592(2) [501+]
Bach, Annie - *Monster Party! (Illus. by Bach, Annie)*
c HB Guide - v26 - i1 - Spring 2015 - p5(1) [51-500]
Bach, Mette - *Femme*
y SLJ - v61 - i9 - Sept 2015 - p151(4) [501+]
y BL - v111 - i22 - August 1 2015 - p58(1) [51-500]
y KR - July 15 2015 - pNA [51-500]
y Res Links - v20 - i5 - June 2015 - p23(1) [51-500]
Bach, Robbie - *Xbox Revisited: A Game Plan for Corporate and Civic Renewal*
PW - v262 - i30 - July 27 2015 - p57(2) [51-500]

Bach, Shelby - *Of Enemies and Endings*
c HB Guide - v26 - i2 - Fall 2015 - p74(1) [51-500]
c KR - April 15 2015 - pNA [51-500]
c SLJ - v61 - i6 - June 2015 - p108(1) [51-500]
Of Sorcery and Snow
c HB Guide - v26 - i1 - Spring 2015 - p69(1) [51-500]
Bachardy, Don - *Hollywood*
Lon R Bks - v37 - i7 - April 9 2015 - p43(2) [501+]
Bachelder, Cheryl - *Dare to Serve: How to Drive Superior Results by Serving Others*
LJ - v140 - i6 - April 1 2015 - p100(1) [51-500]
Bachelder, Chris - *The Throwback Special*
BL - v112 - i1 - Sept 1 2015 - p38(1) [51-500]
KR - Dec 15 2015 - pNA [51-500]
Bachman, Walt - *Northern Slave, Black Dakota: The Life and Times of Joseph Godfrey*
J Mil H - v79 - i1 - Jan 2015 - p212-213 [501+]
Bachmann, Stefan - *The Cabinet of Curiosities: 36 Tales Brief and Sinister (Illus. by Jansson, Alexander)*
c HB Guide - v26 - i1 - Spring 2015 - p186(1) [51-500]
A Drop of Night
y KR - Jan 1 2016 - pNA [51-500]
y PW - v262 - i51 - Dec 14 2015 - p86(1) [51-500]
Bachner, Andrea - *Beyond Sinology: Chinese Writing and Scripts of Culture*
JAS - v74 - i1 - Feb 2015 - p183-184 [501+]
Bachrach, Bernard - *Charlemagne's Early Campaigns (768-777): A Diplomatic and Military Analysis*
HNet - July 2015 - pNA [501+]
Bachrach, Bernard S. - *Widukind of Corvey: Deeds of the Saxons*
J Mil H - v79 - i3 - July 2015 - p808-809 [501+]
Bacigalupi, Paolo - *The Doubt Factory*
y HB Guide - v26 - i1 - Spring 2015 - p100(1) [51-500]
The Water Knife (Read by Guerra, Almarie). Audiobook Review
y BL - v112 - i5 - Nov 1 2015 - p70(2) [51-500]
LJ - v140 - i13 - August 1 2015 - p46(1) [51-500]
The Water Knife
y BL - v111 - i13 - March 1 2015 - p31(1) [51-500]
KR - March 1 2015 - pNA [51-500]
PW - v262 - i11 - March 16 2015 - p66(1) [51-500]
Bacik, James J. - *Humble Confidence: Spiritual and Pastoral Guidance from Karl Rahner*
Theol St - v76 - i3 - Sept 2015 - p652(2) [501+]
Back from Afghanistan: Workshop on the Experiences of Veterans from the War in Afghanistan in Tajikistan, Ukraine, Belarus, Russia, Lithuania and Germany
HNet - Sept 2015 - pNA(NA) [501+]
Backderf, Derf - *Trashed*
PW - v262 - i26 - June 29 2015 - p54(1) [51-500]
y BL - v112 - i6 - Nov 15 2015 - p35(1) [51-500]
LJ - v140 - i15 - Sept 15 2015 - p60(3) [501+]
Backman, Fredrik - *My Grandmother Asked Me to Tell You She's Sorry*
KR - May 1 2015 - pNA [51-500]
LJ - v140 - i11 - June 15 2015 - p71(1) [51-500]
PW - v262 - i16 - April 20 2015 - p48(1) [51-500]
Backscheider, Paula R. - *Elizabeth Singer Rowe and the Development of the English Novel*
MLR - v110 - i3 - July 2015 - p833-834 [501+]
Backshall, Steve - *Deadly Pole to Pole Diaries*
c Sch Lib - v63 - i2 - Summer 2015 - p110(2) [51-500]
Wilds of the Wolf
y Sch Lib - v63 - i1 - Spring 2015 - p50(1) [51-500]

Backstrom, Per - *Decentring the Avant-Garde*
MLR - v110 - i3 - July 2015 - p790-792 [501+]
Bacon, Anne Cooke - *The Letters of Lady Anne Bacon*
Six Ct J - v46 - i3 - Fall 2015 - p722-724 [501+]
Bacon, John U. - *The Rise, Fall, and Return of Michigan Football*
LJ - v140 - i19 - Nov 15 2015 - p89(1) [51-500]
Bacon, Tony - *The SG Guitar Book: 50 Years of Gibson's Stylish Solid Guitar*
RVBW - Oct 2015 - pNA [51-500]
Bacovia, George - *Complete Poetical Works and Selected Prose*
Ant R - v73 - i1 - Wntr 2015 - p178(8) [501+]
Bacque, Raphaelle - *Richie*
TLS - i5872 - Oct 16 2015 - p5(1) [501+]
Baddiel, David - *The Parent Agency*
c Sch Lib - v63 - i3 - Autumn 2015 - p162(1) [51-500]
Bade, Klaus J. - *The Encyclopedia of European Migration and Minorities: From the Seventeenth Century to the Present*
ERS - v38 - i3 - March 2015 - p530(2) [501+]
Badger, Hilary - *State of Grace*
y CCB-B - v69 - i2 - Oct 2015 - p75(2) [501+]
y KR - June 15 2015 - pNA [51-500]
c PW - v262 - i24 - June 15 2015 - p86(1) [51-500]
y SLJ - v61 - i7 - July 2015 - p90(1) [51-500]
Badgett, M.V. Lee - *The Public Professor: How to Use Your Research to Change the World*
LJ - v140 - i17 - Oct 15 2015 - p98(1) [51-500]
Badgett, Nan - *The Accidental Indexer*
Bwatch - August 2015 - pNA [51-500]
Badian, Ernst - *Collected Papers on Alexander the Great*
Class R - v65 - i1 - April 2015 - p181-183 [501+]
Badiey, Naseem - *The State of Post-conflict Reconstruction: Land, Urban Development and State-Building in Juba, Southern Sudan*
HNet - Sept 2015 - pNA [501+]
Badkhen, Anna - *Walking with Abel: Journeys with the Nomads of the African Savannah (Illus. by #)*
CSM - August 12 2015 - pNA [501+]
Walking with Abel: Journeys with the Nomads of the African Savannah
KR - May 15 2015 - pNA [51-500]
LJ - v140 - i10 - June 1 2015 - p109(1) [51-500]
BL - v111 - i21 - July 1 2015 - p17(1) [51-500]
PW - v262 - i24 - June 15 2015 - p77(1) [51-500]
Baehr, Peter - *Hannah Arendt, Totalitarianism, and the Social Sciences*
CS - v44 - i3 - May 2015 - p305-314 [501+]
Baer, Elizabeth R. - *The Golem Redux: From Prague to Post-Holocaust Fiction*
AL - v87 - i1 - March 2015 - p200-202 [501+]
Baer, Josette - *A Life Dedicated to the Republic: Vavro Srobar's Slovak Czechoslovakism*
Slav R - v74 - i3 - Fall 2015 - p615-617 [501+]
Baer, Marc - *The Rise and Fall of Radical Westminster, 1780-1890*
VS - v57 - i3 - Spring 2015 - p563(3) [501+]
Baer, Neal - *Kill Again*
PW - v262 - i20 - May 18 2015 - p64(1) [51-500]
Baer, Robert B. - *The Perfect Kill: 21 Laws for Assassins*
For Aff - v94 - i1 - Jan-Feb 2015 - pNA [51-500]
Baert, Barbara - *Nymph: Motif, Phantom, Affect: A Contribution to the Study of Aby Warburg*
Ren Q - v68 - i3 - Fall 2015 - p991-992 [501+]
Baggaley, Ann - *Are You What You Eat? A Guide to What's on Your Plate and Why*
c BL - v111 - i22 - August 1 2015 - p50(2) [51-500]
Bagge, Sverre - *Cross and Scepter: The Rise of the Scandinavian Kingdoms from the Vikings to the*

Reformation
    CH - v84 - i3 - Sept 2015 - p654(3) [501+]
    CHR - v101 - i3 - Summer 2015 - p609(2) [501+]
    HER - v130 - i545 - August 2015 - p953(2) [501+]

Baggen, Martin - *The Secret Rebellion*
    KR - August 1 2015 - pNA [51-500]

Baggini, Julian - *Freedom Regained: the Possibility of Free Will*
    NS - v144 - i5260 - May 1 2015 - p42(3) [501+]
The Virtues of the Table
    NS - v144 - i5257 - April 10 2015 - p61(1) [501+]

Baggott, Jim - *Origins: The Scientific Story of Creation*
    Nature - v526 - i7571 - Oct 1 2015 - p40(2) [501+]

Baggott, Julianna - *Harriet Wolf's Seventh Book of Wonders*
    NYTBR - August 30 2015 - p21(L) [501+]
    KR - June 15 2015 - pNA [51-500]
    LJ - v140 - i15 - Sept 15 2015 - p65(1) [51-500]

Baggott, Sally - *Matthew Boulton: Enterprising Industrialist of the Enlightenment*
    T&C - v56 - i1 - Jan 2015 - p271-272 [501+]

Bagieu, Penelope - *Exquisite Corpse (Illus. by Bagieu, Penelope)*
    BL - v111 - i16 - April 15 2015 - p39(1) [51-500]
  y LJ - v140 - i9 - May 15 2015 - p61(3) [501+]
    PW - v262 - i22 - June 1 2015 - p49(1) [51-500]
  y VOYA - v38 - i2 - June 2015 - p53(2) [51-500]

Bagley, Caitlin A. - *Makerspaces: Top Trailblazing Projects*
    R&USQ - v54 - i3 - Spring 2015 - p54(2) [501+]

Bagley, Jessixa - *Before I Leave (Illus. by Bagley, Jessixa)*
  c KR - Nov 15 2015 - pNA [51-500]
  c PW - v262 - i44 - Nov 2 2015 - p82(1) [51-500]
Boats for Papa (Illus. by Bagley, Jessixa)
  c BL - v111 - i17 - May 1 2015 - p101(1) [51-500]
  c HB Guide - v26 - i2 - Fall 2015 - p25(1) [51-500]
  c KR - April 15 2015 - pNA [51-500]
  c NYTBR - Sept 13 2015 - p21(L) [501+]
  c PW - v262 - i17 - April 27 2015 - p73(1) [51-500]
  c PW - v262 - i49 - Dec 2 2015 - p26(1) [51-500]
  c SLJ - v61 - i5 - May 2015 - p82(1) [51-500]

Bagley, Will - *South Pass: Gateway to a Continent*
    Roundup M - v22 - i5 - June 2015 - p35(1) [501+]
    Roundup M - v22 - i6 - August 2015 - p33(1) [501+]
    WHQ - v46 - i1 - Spring 2015 - p81-82 [501+]

Bagnoli, Carla - *Constructivism in Ethics*
    Dialogue - v54 - i2 - June 2015 - p394-396 [501+]

Baguley, Elizabeth - *Ready, Steady, Ghost! (Illus. by Lindsay, Marion)*
  c HB Guide - v26 - i1 - Spring 2015 - p21(1) [51-500]

Bahadur, Gaiutra - *Coolie Woman: The Odyssey of Indenture*
    Am St - v54 - i2 - Summer 2015 - p59-71 [501+]
    Bks & Cult - v21 - i6 - Nov-Dec 2015 - p30(1) [501+]
    ERS - v38 - i3 - March 2015 - p516(2) [501+]

Bahk, Jane - *Juna's Jar (Illus. by Hoshino, Felicia)*
  c BL - v111 - i11 - Feb 1 2015 - p46(1) [51-500]
  c CH Bwatch - April 2015 - pNA [51-500]
  c HB Guide - v26 - i2 - Fall 2015 - p25(1) [51-500]
  c NYTBR - Jan 18 2015 - p18(L) [501+]

Bahr, Arthur - *Fragments and Assemblages: Forming Compilations of Medieval London*
    JEGP - v114 - i1 - Jan 2015 - p97(18) [501+]

Bahr, Diana Meyers - *The Students of Sherman Indian School: Education and Native Identity since 1892*
    Am Ind CRJ - v39 - i2 - Spring 2015 - p163-165 [501+]
    PHR - v84 - i4 - Nov 2015 - p556(557) [501+]
    Roundup M - v22 - i6 - August 2015 - p34(1) [501+]
    WHQ - v46 - i1 - Spring 2015 - p106-106 [501+]

Bahr, Howard M. - *Four Classic Mormon Village Studies*
    WHQ - v46 - i1 - Spring 2015 - p94-95 [501+]
Saints Observed: Studies of Mormon Village Life, 1850-2005
    WHQ - v46 - i1 - Spring 2015 - p94-95 [501+]

Bahr, Stephen J. - *Returning Home: Reintegration after Prison or Jail*
    RVBW - Sept 2015 - pNA [501+]

Bai, Matt - *All the Truth Is Out: The Week Politics Went Tabloid*
    NYTBR - Oct 25 2015 - p32(L) [501+]

Bai, Xiao - *French Concession*
    KR - May 1 2015 - pNA [51-500]
    LJ - v140 - i11 - June 15 2015 - p78(2) [501+]
    PW - v262 - i18 - May 4 2015 - p97(1) [51-500]

Baig, Edward C. - *iPad for Dummies*
    Bwatch - Feb 2015 - pNA [51-500]

Baigell, Matthew - *Social Concern and Left Politics in Jewish American Art: 1880-1940*
    LJ - v140 - i8 - May 1 2015 - p69(1) [51-500]

Baigent, Michael - *Astrology in Ancient Mesopotamia*
    Bwatch - Sept 2015 - pNA [501+]

Baika, Gabriella I. - *The Rose and Geryon: The Poetics of Fraud and Violence in Jean De Meun and Dante*
    FS - v69 - i2 - April 2015 - p232(1) [501+]
    Specu - v90 - i3 - July 2015 - p770-771 [501+]

Bail, Mina Mauerstein - *Max and Voltaire: Getting to Know You (Illus. by Choquette, Gabriel)*
  c CH Bwatch - April 2015 - pNA [51-500]

Bailat-Jones, Michelle - *Fog Island Mountains (Read by Ikeda, Jennifer). Audiobook Review*
    BL - v111 - i13 - March 1 2015 - p68(1) [51-500]
    BooChiTr - Jan 3 2015 - p12(1) [501+]
    PW - v262 - i5 - Feb 2 2015 - p55(1) [51-500]

Bailer, Darice - *African-American Culture*
  c HB Guide - v26 - i1 - Spring 2015 - p202(1) [51-500]
What's Great about Montana?
  c HB Guide - v26 - i1 - Spring 2015 - p203(1) [51-500]

Bailey, Alan R. - *Building a Core Print Collection for Preschoolers*
    R&USQ - v54 - i3 - Spring 2015 - p52(1) [51-500]

Bailey, Blake - *The Splendid Things We Planned: A Family Portrait*
    NYTBR - March 15 2015 - p28(L) [501+]

Bailey, Bryan - *Embracing the Wild in Your Dog*
    KR - Dec 1 2015 - pNA [501+]

Bailey, Catherine - *Mind Your Monsters (Illus. by Vidal, Oriol)*
  c KR - June 15 2015 - pNA [51-500]

Bailey, Christian - *Between Yesterday and Tomorrow: German Visions of Europe, 1926-1950*
    HNet - Feb 2015 - pNA [501+]

Bailey, Craig - *Irish London: Middle-Class Migration in the Global Eighteenth Century*
    Historian - v77 - i2 - Summer 2015 - p373(2) [501+]
    JMH - v87 - i2 - June 2015 - p426(3) [501+]

Bailey, Diane - *Coal Power*
  y HB Guide - v26 - i1 - Spring 2015 - p172(1) [51-500]
Skydiving
  c BL - v112 - i3 - Oct 1 2015 - p64(1) [51-500]

Bailey, Elizabeth - *Fly the Wild Echoes*
    PW - v262 - i19 - May 11 2015 - p32(2) [51-500]

Bailey, Ella - *One Day on Our Blue Planetain the Savannah (Illus. by Bailey, Ella)*
  c KR - June 15 2015 - pNA [51-500]
  c SLJ - v61 - i8 - August 2015 - p64(1) [51-500]

Bailey, Frankie Y. - *What the Fly Saw*
    PW - v262 - i1 - Jan 5 2015 - p53(1) [51-500]
  y BL - v111 - i13 - March 1 2015 - p31(1) [51-500]
    KR - Jan 1 2015 - pNA [51-500]

Bailey, Gerry - *World Money (Illus. by Beech, Mark)*
  c BL - v112 - i3 - Oct 1 2015 - p64(1) [51-500]
Your Money: How You Spend Your Money and Why (Illus. by Beech, Mark)
  c CH Bwatch - Oct 2015 - pNA [51-500]

Bailey, Holly - *The Mercy of the Sky: The Story of a Tornado*
    Bwatch - July 2015 - pNA [51-500]
    KR - April 1 2015 - pNA [51-500]
    PW - v262 - i13 - March 30 2015 - p69(2) [51-500]

Bailey, J. Leigh - *Nobody's Hero*
    LJ - v140 - i5 - March 15 2015 - p5(1) [51-500]

Bailey, Janies P. - *Rethinking Poverty: Income, Assets, and the Catholic Social Justice Tradition*
    RM - v68 - i3 - March 2015 - p639(2) [501+]

Bailey, Jessica - *Van Gogh*
  y BL - v112 - i5 - Nov 1 2015 - p48(1) [51-500]

Bailey, Jim - *The End of Healing*
    SPBW - May 2015 - pNA [501+]

Bailey, Kevin M. - *The Western Flyer: Steinbeck's Boat, the Sea of Cortez, and the Saga of Pacific Fisheries*
    LJ - v140 - i8 - May 1 2015 - p97(1) [51-500]

Bailey, Kristin - *Shadow of the War Machine*
  y HB Guide - v26 - i2 - Fall 2015 - p110(1) [51-500]

Bailey, Linda - *If Kids Ruled the World (Illus. by Huyck, David)*
  c HB Guide - v26 - i1 - Spring 2015 - p21(1) [51-500]
  c Res Links - v20 - i3 - Feb 2015 - p1(1) [51-500]
Seven Dead Pirates
  c KR - June 1 2015 - pNA [51-500]
  c Res Links - v21 - i1 - Oct 2015 - p12(1) [51-500]
  c SLJ - v61 - i9 - Sept 2015 - p137(1) [51-500]
Stanley at School (Illus. by Slavin, Bill)
  c CH Bwatch - Oct 2015 - pNA [51-500]
  c KR - June 1 2015 - pNA [51-500]
  c SLJ - v61 - i8 - August 2015 - p58(1) [51-500]
When Santa Was a Baby (Illus. by Godbout, Genevieve)
  c HB - v91 - i6 - Nov-Dec 2015 - p53(1) [51-500]
  c KR - Sept 1 2015 - pNA [51-500]
  c NYTBR - Dec 6 2015 - p33(L) [51-500]
  c PW - v262 - i37 - Sept 14 2015 - p67(1) [51-500]
  c PW - v262 - i49 - Dec 2 2015 - p63(1) [51-500]
  c Res Links - v21 - i1 - Oct 2015 - p2(1) [51-500]
  c SLJ - v61 - i10 - Oct 2015 - p60(2) [51-500]

Bailey, Mark - *The Decline of Serfdom in Late Medieval England: From Bondage to Freedom*
    AHR - v120 - i3 - June 2015 - p1096-1097 [501+]
    HER - v130 - i545 - August 2015 - p971(3) [501+]
    Ren Q - v68 - i1 - Spring 2015 - p311-313 [501+]
Of All the Gin Joints: Stumbling through Hollywood History (Illus. by Hemingway, Edward)
    Bwatch - Jan 2015 - pNA [51-500]

Bailey, Martha J. - *Legacies of the War on Poverty*
    NYRB - v62 - i6 - April 2 2015 - p82(4) [501+]
    NYRB - v62 - i7 - April 23 2015 - p37(3) [501+]

Bailey, Martine - *A Taste for Nightshade*
    KR - Nov 1 2015 - pNA [501+]
    LJ - v140 - i19 - Nov 15 2015 - p74(1) [51-500]

Bailey, Michael D. - *Fearful Spirits, Reasoned Follies: The Boundaries of Superstition in Late Medieval Europe*
    CHR - v101 - i3 - Summer 2015 - p635(2) [501+]
    HER - v130 - i544 - June 2015 - p720(2) [501+]
    Isis - v106 - i2 - June 2015 - p429(2) [501+]
    Med R - Feb 2015 - pNA [501+]
    Six Ct J - v46 - i2 - Summer 2015 - p461-463 [501+]
    Specu - v90 - i1 - Jan 2015 - p206-207 [501+]

Bailey, Ronald - *The End of Doom: Environmental Renewal in the Twenty-First Century*
    LJ - v140 - i12 - July 1 2015 - p108(1) [51-500]

Bailey, Tanya A. - *The First American Grand Prix: The Savannah Auto Races, 1908-1911*
    JSH - v81 - i3 - August 2015 - p754(2) [501+]

Bailey, Tessa - *Chase Me*
    PW - v262 - i1 - Jan 5 2015 - p57(1) [51-500]
Risking It All
    KR - Feb 1 2015 - pNA [501+]

Baillargeon, Denyse - *A Brief History of Women in Quebec*
    Can Hist R - v96 - i2 - June 2015 - p315(2) [501+]

Baillie, Allan - *Dragonquest (Illus. by Harris, Wayne)*
  c SLJ - v61 - i6 - June 2015 - p46(6) [501+]

Baillie, Marilyn - *How to Save a Species*
  c HB Guide - v26 - i1 - Spring 2015 - p140(1) [51-500]

Bailly, Austen Barron - *American Epics: Thomas Hart Benton and Hollywood*
    LJ - v140 - i13 - August 1 2015 - p91(1) [51-500]
    NYTBR - May 31 2015 - p41(L) [501+]

Baily, Virginia - *Early One Morning*
    BL - v111 - i22 - August 1 2015 - p39(1) [51-500]
    KR - July 15 2015 - pNA [501+]
    LJ - v140 - i15 - Sept 15 2015 - p65(1) [51-500]

Bailyn, Bernard - *Sometimes an Art: Nine Essays on History*
    Bks & Cult - v21 - i6 - Nov-Dec 2015 - p24(2) [501+]
    HT - v65 - i11 - Nov 2015 - p60(1) [501+]

Bailyn, Charles D. - *What Does a Black Hole Look Like?*
    Phys Today - v68 - i6 - June 2015 - p56-57 [501+]

Bain, Henry - *The Constitution of the United States of America: Modern Edition*
    RVBW - August 2015 - pNA [501+]

Bain, Mervyn J. - *From Lenin to Castro, 1917-1939: Early Encounters between Moscow and Havana*
    Historian - v77 - i2 - Summer 2015 - p407(2) [501+]

Bainbridge, David - *Curvology: The Origins and Power of Female Body Shape*
    BL - v112 - i5 - Nov 1 2015 - p6(1) [51-500]
    Econ - v414 - i8927 - Feb 28 2015 - p75(US) [501+]
Curvology: The Origins and Power of the Female Body Shape
    KR - July 15 2015 - pNA [501+]

Bainbridge, David A. - *Gardening with Less Water: Low-Tech, Low-Cost Techniques: Use Up to 90 Percent Less Water in Your Garden*
 LJ - v140 - i20 - Dec 1 2015 - p124(1) [501+]
 PW - v262 - i38 - Sept 21 2015 - p69(2) [51-500]

Baines, Beverley - *Feminist Constitutionalism: Global Perspectives*
 CWS - v30 - i2-3 - Fall-Winter 2015 - p143(2) [501+]

Baiocchi, Gianpaolo - *Bootstrapping Democracy: Transforming Local Governance and Civil Society in Brazil*
 CS - v44 - i1 - Jan 2015 - p32-33 [501+]
The Civic Imagination: Making a Difference in American Political Life
 CS - v44 - i5 - Sept 2015 - p627-628 [501+]

Baiogh, Mary - *Only a Promise*
 BL - v111 - i19-20 - June 1 2015 - p62(1) [51-500]

Bair, Julene - *Ogallala Road*
 Roundup M - v22 - i3 - Feb 2015 - p22(1) [501+]
 Roundup M - v22 - i6 - August 2015 - p34(1) [501+]

Bair, Sheila - *The Bullies of Wall Street*
 BL - v111 - i14 - March 15 2015 - p57(1) [51-500]
 y CCB-B - v68 - i9 - May 2015 - p439(2) [51-500]
 y KR - Jan 15 2015 - pNA [51-500]
 y VOYA - v37 - i6 - Feb 2015 - p86(1) [51-500]

Baird, Heather - *Sea Salt Sweet: The Art of Using Salts for the Ultimate Dessert Experience*
 LJ - v140 - i20 - Dec 1 2015 - p126(1) [51-500]

Baird, Jon - *The Explorers Guild, vol. 1: A Passage to Shambhalla*
 PW - v262 - i36 - Sept 7 2015 - p53(2) [51-500]
 KR - Sept 1 2015 - pNA [501+]

Baird, Mimi - *He Wanted the Moon: The Madness and Medical Genius of Dr. Perry Baird, and His Daughter's Quest to Know Him*
 NYT - Feb 24 2015 - pD3(L) [501+]

Baird, Penny Drue - *Dreamhouse: Interiors by Penny Drue Baird*
 PW - v262 - i11 - March 16 2015 - p81(1) [51-500]

Baird, Zoe - *America's Moment: Creating Opportunity in the Connected Age*
 KR - May 1 2015 - pNA [501+]

Baizerman, Michael - *Dawn and Sunset: Insight into the Mystery of the Early Mesopotamian Civilization*
 KR - June 15 2015 - pNA [501+]

Bajlo, Natalija - *King Burue Changes the Rules (Illus. by Beheshti, Amene)*
 c CH Bwatch - March 2015 - pNA [51-500]

Bajwa, Farooq - *From Kutch to Tashkent: The Indo-Pakistan War of 1965*
 J Mil H - v79 - i1 - Jan 2015 - p260-262 [501+]

Bak, Janos M. - *Chronicon: Medieval Narrative Sources, A Chronological Guide with Introductory Essays*
 Med R - April 2015 - pNA [501+]

Baker, Amy J.L. - *Getting through My Parents' Divorce*
 c RVBW - Sept 2015 - pNA [51-500]

Baker, Andrea - *Each Thing Unblurred Is Broken*
 PW - v262 - i46 - Nov 16 2015 - p53(1) [51-500]

Baker, Brianna - *Little White Lies*
 y KR - Nov 1 2015 - pNA [51-500]
 y PW - v262 - i47 - Nov 23 2015 - p69(1) [51-500]
 y SLJ - v61 - i12 - Dec 2015 - p118(1) [51-500]

Baker, Bruce E. - *After Slavery: Race, Labor, and Citizenship in the Reconstruction South*
 JSH - v81 - i1 - Feb 2015 - p214(3) [501+]
 Historian - v77 - i3 - Fall 2015 - p544(2) [501+]
 J Am St - v49 - i3 - August 2015 - p633-634 [501+]

Baker, Brynn - *Life in America: Comparing Immigrant Experiences*
 c BL - v112 - i3 - Oct 1 2015 - p54(1) [51-500]

Baker, Calvin - *Grace*
 KR - May 1 2015 - pNA [51-500]

Baker, Caroline - *Developing Excellent Care for People Living with Dementia in Care Homes*
 Bwatch - April 2015 - pNA [501+]
 Bwatch - July 2015 - pNA [501+]

Baker, Chandler - *Alive*
 y KR - April 15 2015 - pNA [51-500]
 y SLJ - v61 - i6 - June 2015 - p119(2) [51-500]
 y VOYA - v38 - i2 - June 2015 - p70(1) [51-500]
 y CCB-B - v69 - i1 - Sept 2015 - p6(1) [51-500]
 y HB Guide - v26 - i2 - Fall 2015 - p110(1) [51-500]
Teen Frankenstein
 y BL - v112 - i6 - Nov 15 2015 - p51(1) [51-500]
 y KR - Oct 15 2015 - pNA [51-500]
 y SLJ - v61 - i11 - Nov 2015 - p110(2) [51-500]

Baker, Courtney R. - *Humane Insight: Looking at Images of African American Suffering and Death*
 RVBW - Oct 2015 - pNA [501+]

Baker, David - *Vintage*
 KR - July 15 2015 - pNA [51-500]
 LJ - v140 - i13 - August 1 2015 - p77(1) [51-500]

Baker, David P. - *The Schooled Society: The Educational Transformation of Global Culture*
 AJS - v121 - i2 - Sept 2015 - p625(3) [501+]

Baker, E.D. - *The Fairy-Tale Matchmaker*
 c HB Guide - v26 - i1 - Spring 2015 - p69(1) [51-500]
The Perfect Match
 c BL - v112 - i2 - Sept 15 2015 - p75(1) [51-500]
 c KR - July 15 2015 - pNA [51-500]
Princess in Disguise
 c HB Guide - v26 - i2 - Fall 2015 - p74(1) [51-500]

Baker, Emerson W. - *A Storm of Witchcraft: The Salem Trials and the American Experience*
 JAH - v102 - i2 - Sept 2015 - p535-535 [501+]
 JIH - v46 - i3 - Wntr 2016 - p451-453 [501+]
 NEQ - v88 - i2 - June 2015 - p335-338 [501+]

Baker, Evan - *From the Score to the Stage: An Illustrated History of Continental Opera Production and Staging*
 Notes - v71 - i4 - June 2015 - p699(3) [501+]
 ON - v80 - i3 - Sept 2015 - p86(1) [501+]

Baker, Geoffrey - *El Sistema: Orchestrating Venezuela's Youth*
 NYRB - v62 - i14 - Sept 24 2015 - p74(3) [501+]

Baker, J.A. - *The Peregrine*
 NS - v144 - i5278 - Sept 4 2015 - p37(1) [51-500]

Baker, Jeni - *Patchwork Essentials: The Half-Square Triangle: Foolproof Patterns and Simple Techniques from Basic Blocks*
 LJ - v140 - i20 - Dec 1 2015 - p102(1) [51-500]

Baker, Jennifer S. - *The Readers' Advisory Guide to Historical Fiction*
 LJ - v140 - i3 - Feb 15 2015 - p114(1) [51-500]
 VOYA - v38 - i2 - June 2015 - p90(1) [501+]

Baker, Jes - *Things No One Will Tell Fat Girls: A Handbook for Unapologetic Living*
 PW - v262 - i36 - Sept 7 2015 - p59(1) [51-500]

Baker, Jo - *The Mermaid's Child*
 y BL - v111 - i12 - Feb 15 2015 - p41(1) [51-500]
 KR - Jan 1 2015 - pNA [51-500]
Offcomer (Read by Barber, Nicola). Audiobook Review
 LJ - v140 - i5 - March 15 2015 - p71(1) [51-500]
 PW - v262 - i17 - April 27 2015 - p70(2) [51-500]
Offcomer
 NYTBR - Jan 25 2015 - p19(L) [51-500]
The Telling
 KR - May 1 2015 - pNA [51-500]
 LJ - v140 - i12 - July 1 2015 - p72(1) [51-500]

Baker, John Hamilton - *Collected Papers on English Legal History*
 HER - v130 - i544 - June 2015 - p737(4) [501+]

Baker, John Haydn - *The Art of Nick Cave: New Critical Essays*
 Notes - v71 - i3 - March 2015 - p489(4) [501+]

Baker, John Timothy - *Beyond the Burghal Hidage: Anglo-Saxon Civil Defence in the Viking Age*
 HER - v130 - i543 - April 2015 - p416(2) [501+]

Baker, Jonny - *The Pioneer Gift: Explorations in Mission*
 IBMR - v39 - i4 - Oct 2015 - p242(2) [501+]

Baker, Kage - *The Empress of Mars*
 LJ - v140 - i11 - June 15 2015 - p118(1) [501+]

Baker, Keith - *Gumballs (Illus. by Baker, Keith)*
 c HB Guide - v26 - i1 - Spring 2015 - p51(1) [51-500]
Little Green Peas: A Big Book of Colors (Illus. by Baker, Keith)
 c HB Guide - v26 - i1 - Spring 2015 - p5(1) [51-500]
No Two Alike (Illus. by Baker, Keith)
 c HB Guide - v26 - i1 - Spring 2015 - p5(1) [51-500]

Baker, Kelly J. - *Gospel According to the Klan: The KKK's Appeal to Protestant America, 1915-1930*
 JR - Jan 2015 - p151(2) [501+]

Baker, Ken - *Finding Forever*
 y KR - July 15 2015 - pNA [51-500]
 y SLJ - v61 - i10 - Oct 2015 - p108(1) [51-500]
Old MacDonald Had a Dragon (Illus. by Santoro, Christopher)
 c SLJ - v61 - i6 - June 2015 - p46(6) [51-500]

Baker, Kevin - *A Coney Island Reader: Through Dizzy Gates of Illusion*
 NYT - Jan 11 2015 - p3(L) [501+]

Baker, Lynne Rudder - *Naturalism and the First-Person Perspective*
 Phil R - v124 - i1 - Jan 2015 - p156(3) [501+]

Baker, Matthew - *If You Find This*
 c PW - v262 - i3 - Jan 19 2015 - p82(1) [51-500]
 c BL - v111 - i17 - May 1 2015 - p40(1) [51-500]
 c CCB-B - v68 - i10 - June 2015 - p480(1) [51-500]
 c HB Guide - v26 - i2 - Fall 2015 - p74(1) [51-500]
 c KR - Jan 1 2015 - pNA [51-500]

Baker, Nicholas Scott - *After Civic Humanism: Learning and Politics in Renaissance Italy*
 Sev Cent N - v73 - i3-4 - Fall-Winter 2015 - p203(3) [501+]
The Fruit of Liberty: Political Culture in the Florentine Renaissance, 1480-1550
 AHR - v120 - i2 - April 2015 - p731-732 [501+]
 HER - v130 - i545 - August 2015 - p981(3) [501+]
 JMH - v87 - i1 - March 2015 - p200(3) [501+]

Baker, Nick - *Bug Book*
 Bwatch - July 2015 - pNA [51-500]

Baker, Peter S. - *Honour, Exchange and Violence in Beowulf*
 JEGP - v114 - i3 - July 2015 - p444(4) [501+]
 MLR - v110 - i3 - July 2015 - p802-804 [501+]

Baker, Phil - *Lord of Strange Deaths: The Fiendish World of Sax Rohmer*
 Spec - v329 - i9769 - Nov 21 2015 - p57(1) [501+]

Baker, Ray Stannard - *The Boy's Book of Inventions*
 c Nation - v300 - i14 - April 6 2015 - p34(1) [501+]

Baker, Raymond William - *One Islam, Many Muslim Worlds: Spirituality, Identity, and Resistance across Islamic Lands*
 BL - v111 - i21 - July 1 2015 - p5(1) [51-500]

Baker, Rita - *Of Bonds and Bondage*
 SPBW - March 2015 - pNA [501+]

Baker, Sarah - *Redefining Mainstream Popular Music*
 Am Q - v67 - i1 - March 2015 - p253-265 [501+]

Baker, Scott - *America Is Not Broke: Four Multi-Trillion Dollar Paths to a Thriving America*
 SPBW - July 2015 - pNA [51-500]
 SPBW - July 2015 - pNA [51-500]

Baker, Shannon - *Tattered Legacy*
 KR - Jan 1 2015 - pNA [51-500]

Baker, Sharon - *Executing God: Rethinking Everything You've Been Taught about Salvation and the Cross*
 Intpr - v69 - i1 - Jan 2015 - p103(2) [501+]

Baker, Simon - *George Condo*
 Art N - v114 - i10 - Nov 2015 - p99(1) [501+]

Baker, Stephanie Alice - *Social Tragedy: The Power of Myth, Ritual, and Emotion in the New Media Ecology*
 AJS - v121 - i1 - July 2015 - p336(3) [501+]

Baker, Tihema - *Watched*
 y Magpies - v30 - i2 - May 2015 - pS7(1) [501+]

Baker, William (b. 1944-) - *Bernard Kops: Fantasist, London Jew, Apocalyptic Humorist*
 TLS - i5833 - Jan 16 2015 - p27(1) [501+]

Baker, William F. - *The World's Your Stage: How Performing Artists Can Make a Living While Still Doing What They Love*
 LJ - v140 - i20 - Dec 1 2015 - p112(1) [51-500]

Bakewell, Sarah - *At the Existentialist Cafe*
 KR - Dec 15 2015 - pNA [501+]

Bakhos, Carol - *The Family of Abraham: Jewish, Christian and Muslim Interpretations*
 RM - v68 - i4 - June 2015 - p838(3) [501+]

Bakken, Gordon Morris - *Quite Contrary: The Litigious Life of Mary Bennett Love*
 WHQ - v46 - i2 - Summer 2015 - p256(1) [501+]

Bakker, Arnold B. - *Advances in Positive Organizational Psychology*
 Per Psy - v68 - i3 - Autumn 2015 - p700(3) [501+]

Bakker, Gerbrand - *June*
 TLS - i5869 - Sept 25 2015 - p20(1) [501+]

Bakker, Janel Kragt - *Sister Churches: American Congregations and Their Partners Abroad*
 CH - v84 - i2 - June 2015 - p473(3) [501+]

Bakker, Maaike - *Cups and Saucers: Paper-Pieced Kitchen Designs*
 Bwatch - May 2015 - pNA [501+]

Bakopoulos, Dean - *Summerlong*
 BL - v111 - i17 - May 1 2015 - p77(1) [51-500]
 Ent W - i1369 - June 26 2015 - p66(1) [51-500]
 KR - March 15 2015 - pNA [501+]
 LJ - v140 - i11 - June 15 2015 - p71(1) [51-500]
 NYT - June 25 2015 - pC4(L) [501+]
 NYTBR - July 12 2015 - p15(L) [501+]
 PW - v262 - i16 - April 20 2015 - p48(1) [51-500]

Bakos, Lisa M. - *The Wrong Side of the Bed (Illus. by Raff, Anna)*
 c KR - Jan 1 2016 - pNA [51-500]
 c PW - v262 - i52 - Dec 21 2015 - p152(1) [51-500]

Bakrania, Falu - *Bhangra and Asian Underground: South Asian Music and the Politics of Belonging in Britain*
AJS - v120 - i5 - March 2015 - p1572(3) [501+]
PMS - v38 - i1 - Feb 2015 - p106(4) [501+]

Bakutis, T. Eric - *Glyphbinder*
KR - August 15 2015 - pNA [501+]

Bala, Arun - *Asia, Europe and the Emergence of Modern Science: Knowledge Crossing Boundaries*
Isis - v106 - i1 - March 2015 - p175(2) [501+]

Bala, Poonam - *Contesting Colonial Authority: Medicine and Indigenous Responses in Nineteenth- and Twentieth-Century India*
Isis - v106 - i1 - March 2015 - p193(2) [501+]

Balaev, Michelle - *The Nature of Trauma in American Novels*
AL - v87 - i1 - March 2015 - p203-205 [501+]

Balaguer, Jorge - *The Monster Book of Manga Steampunk*
LJ - v140 - i6 - April 1 2015 - p92(1) [51-500]

Balak - *The Stranger (Illus. by Balak)*
y CCB-B - v68 - i9 - May 2015 - p440(1) [51-500]

Balandier, Claire - *La Defense de la Syrie-Palestine des Achemenides aux Lagides: Histoire et Archeologie des Fortifications a l'Ouest du Jourdain de 532 a 199 Avant J.-C.*
HNet - July 2015 - pNA [501+]

Balard, Michel - *Genes et l'outre-mer: Actes notaries de Famagouste et d'autres localites du Proche-Orient, XIVe-XVe s.*
Med R - March 2015 - pNA(NA) [501+]

Balay, Anne - *Steel Closets: Voices of Gay, Lesbian, and Transgender Steelworkers*
Wom R Bks - v32 - i2 - March-April 2015 - p10(3) [501+]

Balberg, Mira - *Purity, Body, and Self in Early Rabbinic Literature*
AHR - v120 - i2 - April 2015 - p689-690 [501+]

Balcerzak, Scott - *Buffoon Men: Classic Hollywood Comedians and Queered Masculinity*
SAH - v4 - i1 - Annual 2015 - p115-117 [501+]

Balcom, Karen A. - *The Traffic in Babies: Cross-Border Adoption and Baby-Selling Between the United States and Canada, 1930-1972*
JWH - v27 - i1 - Spring 2015 - p168(10) [501+]

Bald, Vivek - *Bengali Harlem and the Lost Histories of South Asian America*
Am St - v54 - i2 - Summer 2015 - p59-71 [501+]
JSH - v81 - i4 - Nov 2015 - p1006(2) [501+]
The Sun Never Sets: South Asian Migrants in an Age of U.S. Power
ERS - v38 - i3 - March 2015 - p517(3) [501+]

Baldacchino, Christine - *Morris Micklewhite and the Tangerine Dress (Illus. by Malenfant, Isabelle)*
c HB Guide - v26 - i1 - Spring 2015 - p21(1) [51-500]

Baldacci, David - *The Escape (Read by McLarty, Ron). Audiobook Review*
BL - v111 - i17 - May 1 2015 - p58(1) [51-500]
The Escape
Bwatch - Jan 2015 - pNA [501+]
Faceoff
RVBW - May 2015 - pNA [501+]
The Keeper
c KR - June 15 2015 - pNA [51-500]
y VOYA - v38 - i3 - August 2015 - p73(1) [51-500]
Sch Lib - v63 - i4 - Winter 2015 - p242(1) [51-500]
Memory Man (Read by McLarty, Ron). Audiobook Review
Bwatch - August 2015 - pNA [51-500]
Memory Man
KR - April 1 2015 - pNA [51-500]

Baldez, Lisa - *Defying Convention: U.S. Resistance to the UN Treaty on Women's Rights*
HNet - July 2015 - pNA [501+]

Baldini, Alessio - *Dipingere coi colori adatti: 'I Malavoglia' e il romanzo moderno*
MLR - v110 - i3 - July 2015 - p882-883 [501+]

Balducci, Tiffany - *The Tween Scene: A Year of Programs for 10- to 14-Year Olds*
y SLJ - v61 - i11 - Nov 2015 - p142(1) [51-500]

Baldwin, C. Edward - *Rememberers*
PW - v262 - i12 - March 23 2015 - p52(2) [51-500]

Baldwin, James - *James Baldwin: The Last Interview: And Other Conversations*
TLS - i5877 - Nov 20 2015 - p5(1) [501+]
Jimmy's Blues and Other Poems
TLS - i5877 - Nov 20 2015 - p5(1) [501+]

Baldwin, Kathleen - *A School for Unusual Girls*
y BL - v111 - i15 - April 1 2015 - p70(1) [51-500]
y CCB-B - v69 - i1 - Sept 2015 - p6(1) [51-500]
y KR - Feb 15 2015 - pNA [51-500]
c NYTBR - May 10 2015 - p22(L) [501+]
y VOYA - v38 - i2 - June 2015 - p54(1) [51-500]

Baldwin, Melinda - *Making Nature: The History of a Scientific Journal*
LJ - v140 - i6 - April 1 2015 - p112(2) [51-500]
TimHES - i2227 - Oct 29 2015 - p49(1) [501+]

Baldwin, Peter - *The Copyright Wars: Three Centuries of Trans-Atlantic Battle*
HLR - v128 - i4 - Feb 2015 - p1328(1) [1-50]
HNet - April 2015 - pNA [501+]
TLS - i5853 - June 5 2015 - p28(1) [501+]

Baldwin, Philip B. - *Pope Gregory X and the Crusades*
CHR - v101 - i3 - Summer 2015 - p628(2) [501+]
J Mil H - v79 - i1 - Jan 2015 - p195(1) [51-500]
Med R - August 2015 - pNA [501+]

Baldwin, Richard E. - *The Future of the World Trading System: Asian Perspectives*
Pac A - v88 - i1 - March 2015 - p147 [501+]

Baldwin, Sy Margaret - *Signal Fires*
KR - August 1 2015 - pNA [501+]

Bale, Anthony - *The Book of Margery Kempe*
Med R - Sept 2015 - pNA [501+]

Bale, Tim - *Five Year Mission: the Labour Party under Ed Miliband*
NS - v144 - i5258 - April 17 2015 - p56(3) [501+]

Balentine, Samuel E. - *The Oxford Encyclopedia of the Bible and Theology, 2 vols.*
LJ - v140 - i10 - June 1 2015 - p133(1) [51-500]
BL - v111 - i21 - July 1 2015 - p4(1) [501+]

Bales, Kevin - *Blood and Earth: Modern Slavery, Ecocide, and the Secret to Saving the World*
KR - Dec 1 2015 - pNA [501+]
LJ - v140 - i20 - Dec 1 2015 - p121(1) [51-500]
PW - v262 - i47 - Nov 23 2015 - p62(2) [51-500]

Bales, Melanie - *Dance on Its Own Terms: Histories and Methodologies*
Theat J - v67 - i3 - Oct 2015 - p586-587 [501+]

Balfour, Michael - *Refugee Performance: Practical Encounters*
Theat J - v67 - i2 - May 2015 - p363-365 [501+]

Balfour-Paul, Jenny - *Deeper Than Indigo: Tracing Thomas Machell, Forgotten Explorer*
Spec - v328 - i9748 - June 27 2015 - p40(2) [501+]
TLS - i5857 - July 3 2015 - p27(1) [501+]

Balik, Shelby M. - *Rally the Scattered Believers: Northern New England's Religious Geography*
CH - v84 - i3 - Sept 2015 - p676(3) [501+]

Balizet, Ariane M. - *Blood and Home in Early Modern Drama: Domestic Identity on the Renaissance Stage*
Ren Q - v68 - i2 - Summer 2015 - p781-783 [501+]

Balkan, Gabrielle - *The 50 States: Explore the U.S.A with 50 Fact-Filled Maps! (Illus. by Linero, Sol)*
c KR - Sept 1 2015 - pNA [51-500]
The 50 States: Explore the U.S.A. with 50 Fact-Filled Maps! (Illus. by Linero, Sol)
c PW - v262 - i32 - August 10 2015 - p60(1) [51-500]
The 50 States: Explore the U.S.A with 50 Fact-Filled Maps! (Illus. by Linero, Sol)
c SLJ - v61 - i10 - Oct 2015 - p124(1) [51-500]

Balken, Debra Bricker - *Edna Andrade*
RVBW - August 2015 - pNA [51-500]

Ball, Donna - *Flash*
SPBW - June 2015 - pNA [51-500]

Ball, Erica L. - *To Live an Antislavery Life: Personal Politics and the Antebellum Black Middle Class*
AL - v87 - i1 - March 2015 - p192-194 [501+]

Ball, Jesse - *A Cure for Suicide*
BL - v111 - i19-20 - June 1 2015 - p38(2) [51-500]
BooChiTr - August 8 2015 - p13(1) [501+]
KR - May 15 2015 - pNA [51-500]
NY - v91 - i23 - August 10 2015 - p77 [501+]
NYTBR - July 26 2015 - p17(L) [501+]
PW - v262 - i21 - May 25 2015 - p28(2) [51-500]
Silence Once Begun
TLS - i5837 - Feb 13 2015 - p20(1) [501+]

Ball, Kirstie - *The Surveillance-Industrial Complex: A Political Economy of Surveillance*
CS - v44 - i4 - July 2015 - p484-486 [501+]

Ball, Larry D. - *Tom Horn in Life and Legend*
Roundup M - v22 - i6 - August 2015 - p34(1) [501+]
WHQ - v46 - i2 - Summer 2015 - p257(1) [501+]

Ball, Nate - *On Impact! (Illus. by Pamintuan, Macky)*
c HB Guide - v26 - i1 - Spring 2015 - p56(1) [51-500]
Radio Active (Illus. by Pamintuan, Macky)
c HB Guide - v26 - i1 - Spring 2015 - p56(1) [51-500]

Ball, Philip - *Invisible: The Dangerous Allure of the Unseen*
BL - v111 - i16 - April 15 2015 - p8(1) [51-500]
PW - v262 - i6 - Feb 9 2015 - p58(1) [51-500]
Serving the Reich: The Struggle for the Soul of Physics Under Hitler
Phys Today - v68 - i4 - April 2015 - p55-56 [501+]
RM - v68 - i3 - March 2015 - p640(3) [501+]

Ball, Ruth - *Rebellious Spirits: The Illicit History of Booze in Britain*
Spec - v329 - i9768 - Nov 14 2015 - p52(2) [501+]

Ball, Susan C. - *Voices in the Band: A Doctor, Her Patients, and How the Outlook on AIDS Care Changed from Doomed to Hopeful*
LJ - v140 - i3 - Feb 15 2015 - p120(1) [51-500]
NYT - March 31 2015 - pD4(L) [501+]

Ball, Toby - *Invisible Streets*
RVBW - March 2015 - pNA [51-500]
RVBW - August 2015 - pNA [51-500]

Balla, Nicolaus - *Bar Tartine: Techniques and Recipes*
Ent W - i1346 - Jan 16 2015 - p67(1) [501+]
LJ - v140 - i3 - Feb 15 2015 - p122(4) [51-500]

Balla, Trace - *Shine: A Story About Saying Goodbye (Illus. by Balla, Trace)*
c Magpies - v30 - i3 - July 2015 - p29(1) [501+]

Ballantyne, Lisa - *Everything She Forgot*
BL - v112 - i3 - Oct 1 2015 - p26(1) [51-500]
KR - August 1 2015 - pNA [51-500]
NYTBR - Nov 1 2015 - p29(L) [501+]
PW - v262 - i35 - August 31 2015 - p62(2) [51-500]

Ballard, Phil - *Sams Teach Yourself Javascript in 24 Hours, 6th ed.*
Bwatch - Oct 2015 - pNA [51-500]

Ballarini, Marco - *Verso il centenario del Boccaccio: Presenze classiche e tradizione biblica*
Ren Q - v68 - i1 - Spring 2015 - p371-372 [501+]

Balliett, Blue - *Pieces and Players (Read by Turpin, Bahni). Audiobook Review*
c BL - v111 - i22 - August 1 2015 - p80(1) [51-500]
c SLJ - v61 - i7 - July 2015 - p46(1) [51-500]
Pieces and Players
c BL - v111 - i12 - Feb 15 2015 - p87(1) [51-500]
y CCB-B - v68 - i10 - June 2015 - p481(1) [51-500]
c CH Bwatch - May 2015 - pNA [501+]
c HB Guide - v26 - i2 - Fall 2015 - p74(1) [51-500]
c PW - v262 - i3 - Jan 19 2015 - p82(1) [51-500]

Balmaceda, Margarita M. - *The Politics of Energy Dependency: Ukraine, Belarus, and Lithuania between Domestic Oligarchs and Russian Pressure*
E-A St - v67 - i3 - May 2015 - p509(2) [501+]

Balme, Christopher B. - *The Theatrical Public Sphere*
TLS - i5843 - March 27 2015 - p32(1) [501+]

Balmer, Randall - *Redeemer: The Life of Jimmy Carter*
AHR - v120 - i1 - Feb 2015 - p297-298 [501+]

Balmes, Santi - *I Will Fight Monsters for You (Illus. by Lyona)*
c HB Guide - v26 - i2 - Fall 2015 - p25(1) [51-500]
c KR - Jan 15 2015 - pNA [51-500]
c PW - v262 - i2 - Jan 12 2015 - p57(1) [51-500]

Balogh, Brian - *Recapturing the Oval Office: New Historical Approaches to the American Presidency*
CHE - v62 - i14 - Dec 4 2015 - pB17(1) [501+]

Balogh, Mary - *Beyond the Sunrise (Read by Landor, Rosalyn). Audiobook Review*
BL - v112 - i2 - Sept 15 2015 - p76(1) [51-500]
Only a Kiss
PW - v262 - i30 - July 27 2015 - p48(1) [51-500]
Only a Promise
KR - April 1 2015 - pNA [51-500]
PW - v262 - i16 - April 20 2015 - p62(2) [51-500]
Only Enchanting (Read by Landor, Rosalyn). Audiobook Review
LJ - v140 - i10 - June 1 2015 - p58(1) [51-500]

Balot, Ryan K. - *Courage in the Democratic Polis: Ideology and Critique in Classical Athens*
HNet - July 2015 - pNA [501+]

Balserak, Jon - *John Calvin as Sixteenth-Century Prophet*
AHR - v120 - i3 - June 2015 - p1122-1123 [501+]
CH - v84 - i4 - Dec 2015 - p881(1) [501+]
Six Ct J - v46 - i2 - Summer 2015 - p508-510 [501+]

Book Review Index 2016 Cumulation **BAPTISTE • 25**

Balsley, Tilda - *Shalom Everybodeee! (Illus. by Fischer, Ellen)*
c KR - Dec 15 2015 - pNA [51-500]
Balson, Ronald H. - *Saving Sophie*
KR - July 15 2015 - pNA [501+]
PW - v262 - i28 - July 13 2015 - p46(2) [51-500]
Baltazar, Art - *Tiny Titans: Return to the Treehouse (Illus. by Franco)*
c BL - v111 - i16 - April 15 2015 - p41(1) [51-500]
Baltussen, Han - *The Art of Veiled Speech: Self-Censorship from Aristophanes to Hobbes*
JHI - v76 - i4 - Oct 2015 - p667(1) [501+]
Baltzer, Rochelle - *Dolphins (Illus. by Keimig, Candice)*
c HB Guide - v26 - i1 - Spring 2015 - p163(1) [51-500]
I Like to Draw!
c HB Guide - v26 - i2 - Fall 2015 - p192(1) [51-500]
Balzaretti, Ross - *Dark Age Liguria: Regional Identity and Local Power, c. 400-1020*
Med R - March 2015 - pNA(NA) [501+]
Balzer, David - *Curationism: How Curating Took Over the Art World and Everything Else*
Lon R Bks - v37 - i11 - June 4 2015 - p13(2) [501+]
TLS - i5861 - July 31 2015 - p26(1) [501+]
Curationism: How Curating Took Over the Art World
Spec - v327 - i9738 - April 18 2015 - p36(2) [501+]
Bamberger, Joanne Cronrath - *Love Her, Love Her Not: The Hillary Paradox*
PW - v262 - i35 - August 31 2015 - p75(2) [51-500]
Bamberger, Michael - *Men in Green*
KR - April 1 2015 - pNA [51-500]
LJ - v140 - i6 - April 1 2015 - p94(1) [501+]
WSJEEd - v0 - i0 - March 28 2015 - pA10(NA) [501+]
Bamberger, Michelle - *The Real Cost of Fracking: How America's Shale Gas Boom Is Threatening Our Families, Pets, and Food*
AM - v212 - i6 - Feb 23 2015 - p34(2) [501+]
Bambrick-Santoyo, Paul - *Leverage Leadership*
TES - i5159 - August 14 2015 - p35(1) [501+]
Bamford, Andrew - *Sickness, Suffering and the Sword: The British Regiment on Campaign, 1808-1815*
HER - v130 - i542 - Feb 2015 - p123(14) [501+]
Bamji, Alexandra - *The Ashgate Research Companion to the Counter-Reformation*
HER - v130 - i542 - Feb 2015 - p187(2) [501+]
Banai, Noit - *Art in Time: A World History of Styles and Movements*
LJ - v140 - i3 - Feb 15 2015 - p96(1) [51-500]
Banash, Jennifer - *Silent Alarm*
y BL - v111 - i12 - Feb 15 2015 - p84(1) [51-500]
y CCB-B - v68 - i8 - April 2015 - p388(1) [51-500]
y HB Guide - v26 - i2 - Fall 2015 - p110(1) [51-500]
y VOYA - v37 - i6 - Feb 2015 - p52(1) [501+]
Banasky, Carmiel - *The Suicide of Claire Bishop*
BL - v112 - i1 - Sept 1 2015 - p44(1) [51-500]
KR - July 15 2015 - pNA [51-500]
PW - v262 - i27 - July 6 2015 - p44(1) [51-500]
Banci, Lucia - *Metallomics and the Cell*
QRB - v90 - i1 - March 2015 - p95(1) [501+]
Bancks, Tristan - *On the Run*
y HB - v91 - i6 - Nov-Dec 2015 - p76(2) [51-500]
c SLJ - v61 - i7 - July 2015 - p73(1) [51-500]
c KR - August 1 2015 - pNA [51-500]
c PW - v262 - i36 - Sept 7 2015 - p70(1) [51-500]
Bancroft, Jack Manning - *The Eagle Inside (Illus. by Bancroft, Bronwyn)*
c Magpies - v30 - i2 - May 2015 - p30(1) [501+]
Bandinelli, Angela - *Le origini chimiche della vita: Legami tra la rivoluzione di Lavoisier e la biologia di Lamarck*
Isis - v106 - i1 - March 2015 - p192(2) [501+]
Bandy, Michael S. - *Granddaddy's Turn: A Journey to the Ballot Box (Illus. by Ransome, James E.)*
c BL - v111 - i21 - July 1 2015 - p62(2) [51-500]
c CCB-B - v69 - i2 - Oct 2015 - p76(1) [51-500]
c HB - v91 - i4 - July-August 2015 - p108(2) [501+]
c KR - May 1 2015 - pNA [51-500]
c PW - v262 - i26 - June 29 2015 - p67(1) [501+]
c SLJ - v61 - i5 - May 2015 - p129(1) [51-500]
Banerjee, Anindita - *We Modern People: Science Fiction and the Making of Russian Modernity*
Isis - v106 - i2 - June 2015 - p474(2) [501+]
Banet-Weiser, Sarah - *Authentic: The Politics of Ambivalence in a Brand Culture*
CS - v44 - i1 - Jan 2015 - p34-35 [501+]
Banfield, Kelsey - *The Family Calendar Cookbook: From Birthdays to Bake Sales, Good Food to Carry You through the Year*
LJ - v140 - i7 - April 15 2015 - p110(1) [51-500]
Bang, Herman - *As Trains Pass By*
TLS - i5875 - Nov 6 2015 - p31(1) [501+]
Bang-Jensen, Valerie - *Books in Bloom: Discovering the Plant Biology in Great Children's Literature*
SLJ - v61 - i4 - April 2015 - p186(1) [51-500]
Bang, Mary Jo - *The Last Two Seconds*
LJ - v140 - i5 - March 15 2015 - p109(1) [51-500]
BL - v111 - i14 - March 15 2015 - p38(1) [51-500]
PW - v262 - i3 - Jan 19 2015 - p56(2) [51-500]
Bang, Molly - *Buried Sunlight: How Fossil Fuels Have Change the Earth (Illus. by Bang, Molly)*
c CH Bwatch - March 2015 - pNA [51-500]
c Sci & Ch - v52 - i8 - April-May 2015 - p75 [51-500]
Buried Sunlight: How Fossil Fuels Have Changed the Earth (Illus. by Bang, Molly)
c BL - v111 - i9-10 - Jan 1 2015 - pS4(8) [501+]
c BL - v111 - i12 - Feb 15 2015 - p76(1) [501+]
c CCB-B - v68 - i6 - Feb 2015 - p300(1) [51-500]
When Sophie's Feelings Are Really, Really Hurt (Illus. by Bang, Molly)
c BL - v111 - i21 - July 1 2015 - p65(1) [51-500]
c HB - v91 - i5 - Sept-Oct 2015 - p74(2) [51-500]
c KR - June 1 2015 - pNA [51-500]
c PW - v262 - i49 - Dec 2 2015 - p22(1) [51-500]
c SLJ - v61 - i8 - August 2015 - p64(1) [51-500]
Bange, Matthias - *Kreditgeld in der romischen Antike: Ursprunge, Entstehung, Ubertragung und Verbreitung*
HNet - April 2015 - pNA [501+]
Bangs, J.S. - *Storm Bride*
PW - v262 - i5 - Feb 2 2015 - p40(1) [51-500]
Bangstad, Sindre - *Anders Breivik and the Rise of Islamophobia*
NYRB - v62 - i4 - March 5 2015 - p55(3) [501+]
Bangura, Abdul Karim - *African-Centered Research Methodologies: From Ancient Times to the Present*
JTWS - v32 - i1 - Spring 2015 - p325(3) [501+]
Banham, Debby - *Anglo-Saxon Farms and Farming*
Med R - Sept 2015 - pNA [501+]
Banisadr, Masoud - *Destructive and Terrorist Cults: A New Kind Slavery*
TimHES - i2226 - Oct 22 2015 - p45(1) [501+]
Banister, Michael - *Stolen Identity*
KR - Sept 15 2015 - pNA [501+]
Banker, James R. - *Piero della Francesca: Artist and Man*
AHR - v120 - i4 - Oct 2015 - p1558-1559 [501+]
Bankes, Ariane - *The Art of David Jones: Vision and Memory*
Spec - v329 - i9761 - Sept 26 2015 - p39(1) [501+]
Bankes, Liz - *Undeniable*
VOYA - v38 - i5 - Dec 2015 - p52(1) [51-500]
Banks, Angelica - *Finding Serendipity (Illus. by Lewis, Stevie)*
c BL - v111 - i11 - Feb 1 2015 - p51(1) [51-500]
c CCB-B - v68 - i7 - March 2015 - p347(1) [51-500]
c HB Guide - v26 - i2 - Fall 2015 - p74(1) [51-500]
c NYTBR - April 12 2015 - p21(L) [501+]
c PW - v262 - i49 - Dec 2 2015 - p77(1) [51-500]
A Week without Tuesday (Illus. by Lewis, Stevie)
c BL - v112 - i7 - Dec 1 2015 - p64(1) [51-500]
c KR - Nov 15 2015 - pNA [51-500]
c Magpies - v30 - i3 - July 2015 - p32(2) [501+]
c SLJ - v61 - i11 - Nov 2015 - p93(1) [51-500]
Banks, Anna - *Joyride*
y BL - v111 - i15 - April 1 2015 - p66(2) [51-500]
y HB Guide - v26 - i2 - Fall 2015 - p110(1) [51-500]
y KR - April 1 2015 - pNA [51-500]
y VOYA - v38 - i3 - August 2015 - p52(2) [51-500]
Of Neptune
y HB Guide - v26 - i1 - Spring 2015 - p100(1) [51-500]
Banks, Antoine J. - *Anger and Racial Politics: The Emotional Foundation of Racial Attitudes in America*
Pub Op Q - v79 - i2 - Summer 2015 - p620(3) [501+]
Banks, Iain - *Raw Spirit: In Search of the Perfect Dram*
TimHES - i2226 - Oct 22 2015 - p45(1) [501+]
Banks, Kate - *Boy's Best Friend*
c HB - v91 - i4 - July-August 2015 - p129(1) [51-500]
c KR - May 1 2015 - pNA [51-500]
c SLJ - v61 - i4 - April 2015 - p143(1) [51-500]
y VOYA - v38 - i2 - June 2015 - p54(1) [51-500]
c BL - v111 - i21 - July 1 2015 - p67(1) [51-500]
Max's Math (Illus. by Kulikov, Boris)
c CCB-B - v68 - i8 - April 2015 - p388(2) [51-500]
c HB - v91 - i2 - March-April 2015 - p69(2) [51-500]
c HB Guide - v26 - i2 - Fall 2015 - p25(1) [51-500]
c PW - v262 - i49 - Dec 2 2015 - p20(1) [51-500]
Banks, Leigh - *The Life Negroni*
Spec - v329 - i9768 - Nov 14 2015 - p52(2) [501+]
Banks, Lynne Reid - *Uprooted*
c BL - v112 - i5 - Nov 1 2015 - p62(1) [51-500]
y HB - v91 - i6 - Nov-Dec 2015 - p77(1) [51-500]
c KR - August 15 2015 - pNA [51-500]
c SLJ - v61 - i10 - Oct 2015 - p87(1) [51-500]
Banks, Mark - *Theorizing Cultural Work: Labour, Continuity and Change in the Cultural and Creative Industries*
CS - v44 - i4 - July 2015 - p486-487 [501+]
Banks, Maya - *Darkest before Dawn*
PW - v262 - i36 - Sept 7 2015 - p51(1) [51-500]
Banks, Miranda J. - *The Writers: A History of American Screenwriters and Their Guild*
FQ - v69 - i1 - Fall 2015 - p101(2) [501+]
Bankston, John - *Environmental Protection*
c BL - v111 - i16 - April 15 2015 - p45(1) [501+]
Long Ben (Henry Every).
c BL - v112 - i7 - Dec 1 2015 - p43(1) [51-500]
Bannalec, Jean-Luc - *Death in Brittany*
KR - May 1 2015 - pNA [51-500]
NYTBR - August 2 2015 - p25(L) [501+]
PW - v262 - i14 - April 6 2015 - p40(1) [51-500]
Bannan, Sarah - *Weightless*
y BL - v111 - i19-20 - June 1 2015 - p46(2) [51-500]
KR - May 1 2015 - pNA [51-500]
Banner, Catherine - *The Heart at War*
y Res Links - v21 - i1 - Oct 2015 - p28(2) [501+]
Banner, James M., Jr. - *Being a Historian: An Introduction to the Professional World of History*
JAH - v101 - i4 - March 2015 - p1226-1227 [501+]
Banner, Michael - *The Ethics of Everyday Life: Moral Theology, Social Anthropology, and the Imagination of the Human*
Theol St - v76 - i3 - Sept 2015 - p624(2) [501+]
TLS - i5837 - Feb 13 2015 - p28(1) [501+]
Bannerman, Stacy - *Homefront 911: How Families of Veterans Are Wounded by Our Wars*
KR - August 1 2015 - pNA [51-500]
LJ - v140 - i15 - Sept 15 2015 - p95(1) [51-500]
Bannister, Andy - *The Atheist Who Didn't Exist*
RVBW - Nov 2015 - pNA [51-500]
Bannister, Jo - *Deadly Virtues*
RVBW - August 2015 - pNA [501+]
Desperate Measures
KR - Oct 1 2015 - pNA [51-500]
Perfect Sins
RVBW - Sept 2015 - pNA [501+]
Bannister, Roger - *Twin Tracks: The Autobiography*
TimHES - i2188 - Jan 29 2015 - p47(1) [501+]
Bantman, Constance - *The French Anarchists in London, 1880-1914: Exile and Transnationalism in the First Globalisation*
Historian - v77 - i3 - Fall 2015 - p595(2) [501+]
Banville, John - *The Blue Guitar*
KR - August 1 2015 - pNA [51-500]
Lon R Bks - v37 - i22 - Nov 19 2015 - p33(1) [501+]
NY - v91 - i34 - Nov 2 2015 - p89 [51-500]
NYTBR - Sept 27 2015 - p18(L) [501+]
Spec - v328 - i9759 - Sept 12 2015 - p42(1) [501+]
TLS - i5869 - Sept 25 2015 - p19(1) [501+]
Bao, Karen - *Dove Arising*
y HB Guide - v26 - i2 - Fall 2015 - p110(1) [51-500]
y Magpies - v30 - i4 - Sept 2015 - p38(1) [501+]
Dove Exiled
y KR - Dec 15 2015 - pNA [51-500]
y SLJ - v61 - i12 - Dec 2015 - p112(1) [51-500]
Baptist, Edward E. - *The Half Has Never Been Told: Slavery and the Making of American Capitalism*
AHR - v120 - i4 - Oct 2015 - p1434-1436 [501+]
CC - v132 - i2 - Jan 21 2015 - p34(2) [501+]
JEH - v75 - i3 - Sept 2015 - p919-919 [501+]
JEH - v75 - i3 - Sept 2015 - p919-923 [501+]
JEH - v75 - i3 - Sept 2015 - p923-927 [501+]
JEH - v75 - i3 - Sept 2015 - p928-929 [501+]
JEH - v75 - i3 - Sept 2015 - p929-931 [501+]
JSH - v81 - i2 - May 2015 - p405(17) [501+]
TLS - i5844 - April 3 2015 - p7(2) [501+]
Baptiste, Tracey - *The Jumbies (Read by Miles, Robin). Audiobook Review*
c SLJ - v61 - i8 - August 2015 - p48(1) [51-500]
The Jumbies
BL - v111 - i14 - March 15 2015 - p74(1) [51-500]
c KR - Feb 1 2015 - pNA [51-500]
c Nat Post - v17 - i205 - July 4 2015 - pWP5(1) [501+]
c PW - v262 - i6 - Feb 9 2015 - p68(1) [51-500]
y SLJ - v61 - i4 - April 2015 - p143(1) [51-500]

Bar-El, Dan - *Audrey (Cow): An Oral Account of a Most Faring Escape, Based More or Less on a True Story (Illus. by Mai-Wyss, Tatjana)*
   c CH Bwatch - Jan 2015 - pNA [51-500]
Not Your Typical Dragon (Illus. by Bowers, Tim)
   c SLJ - v61 - i6 - June 2015 - p46(6) [501+]

Bar, Niall - *Eisenhower's Armies*
   KR - Sept 15 2015 - pNA [501+]

Bar-Noi, Uri - *The Cold War and Soviet Distrust of Churchill's Pursuit of Detente, 1951-55*
   HT - v65 - i1 - Jan 2015 - p56(2) [501+]

Bar-Zohar, Michael - *No Mission Is Impossible: The Death-Defying Missions of the Israeli Special Forces*
   KR - Sept 15 2015 - pNA [501+]

Baradaran, Mehrsa - *How the Other Half Banks: Exclusion, Exploitation, and the Threat to Democracy*
   KR - August 1 2015 - pNA [501+]
How the Other Half Banks
   Mac - v128 - i43 - Nov 2 2015 - p76(1) [501+]

Barahona, Maria Teresa - *Fun and Fruit (Illus. by Pijpers, Edie)*
   KR - Feb 1 2015 - pNA [51-500]

Barak, On - *On Time: Technology and Temporality in Modern Egypt*
   IJMES - v47 - i2 - May 2015 - p369-381 [501+]

Baraka, Amiri - *If Elvis Presley Is King Who Is James Brown, God?*
   NYT - Nov 27 2015 - pC31(L) [501+]
SOS: Poems, 1961-2013
   NYT - Jan 28 2015 - pC1(L) [501+]
   NYTBR - Feb 15 2015 - p16(L) [501+]
   PW - v262 - i3 - Jan 19 2015 - p58(1) [501+]
The System of Dante's Hell
   KR - Nov 1 2015 - pNA [51-500]
Tales
   KR - Nov 1 2015 - pNA [51-500]

Barakiva, Michael - *One Man Guy*
   y HB Guide - v26 - i1 - Spring 2015 - p100(1) [51-500]

Baran, Emily B. - *Dissent on the Margins: How Soviet Jehovah's Witnesses Defied Communism and Lived to Preach about It*
   AHR - v120 - i3 - June 2015 - p1141-1142 [501+]
   E-A St - v67 - i6 - August 2015 - p999(2) [501+]

Barash, Chris - *Is It Hanukkah Yet? (Illus. by Psacharopulo, Alessandra)*
   c HB - v91 - i6 - Nov-Dec 2015 - p53(1) [51-500]
   c KR - Sept 1 2015 - pNA [51-500]
   c PW - v262 - i37 - Sept 14 2015 - p69(1) [51-500]
   c SLJ - v61 - i10 - Oct 2015 - p60(2) [51-500]
Is It Passover Yet? (Illus. by Psacharopulo, Alessandra)
   c HB Guide - v26 - i2 - Fall 2015 - p6(1) [51-500]
   c KR - Feb 1 2015 - pNA [51-500]
   c PW - v262 - i2 - Jan 12 2015 - p63(1) [51-500]

Barash, David P. - *Buddhist Biology: Ancient Eastern Wisdom Meets Modern Western Science*
   QRB - v90 - i3 - Sept 2015 - p318(2) [501+]

Baratz-Logsted, Lauren - *Falling for Prince Charles*
   PW - v262 - i51 - Dec 14 2015 - p69(1) [51-500]
Red Girl, Blue Boy
   y BL - v112 - i2 - Sept 15 2015 - p75(1) [51-500]
   y KR - August 1 2015 - pNA [51-500]
   y VOYA - v38 - i4 - Oct 2015 - p48(2) [51-500]

Barba, Andres - *August, October*
   KR - August 1 2015 - pNA [501+]

Barbagil, Marzio - *Farewell to the World: A History of Suicide*
   TimHES - i2220 - Sept 10 2015 - p46-47 [501+]

Barbassa, Juliana - *Dancing with the Devil in the City of God: Rio De Janeiro on the Brink*
   BL - v111 - i16 - April 15 2015 - p13(1) [51-500]
   KR - May 1 2015 - pNA [501+]
   LJ - v140 - i9 - May 15 2015 - p91(1) [51-500]
   PW - v262 - i13 - March 30 2015 - p64(1) [51-500]

Barbat, William N. - *Science Myths We Tell Ourselves*
   RVBW - June 2015 - pNA [51-500]

Barbeau, Edward - *More Fallacies, Flaws, and Flimflam*
   Math T - v108 - i7 - March 2015 - p558-559 [501+]

Barbeau, Jeffrey W. - *Sara Coleridge: Her Life and Thought*
   TLS - i5835 - Jan 30 2015 - p22(1) [501+]

Barbedette, Sarah - *Pierre Boulez*
   TLS - i5849 - May 8 2015 - p17(2) [501+]

Barbee, Matthew Mace - *Race and Masculinity in Southern Memory: History of Richmond, Virginia's Monument Avenue, 1948-1996*
   JSH - v81 - i2 - May 2015 - p509(2) [501+]

Barber, Dan - *The Third Plate: Field Notes on the Future of Food*
   NYTBR - May 17 2015 - p32(L) [501+]
   TLS - i5849 - May 8 2015 - p28(1) [501+]
The Third Plate
   CSM - May 29 2015 - pNA [501+]

Barber, Jon Warner - *Historical Collections*
   Bwatch - March 2015 - pNA [51-500]

Barber, Marilyn - *Invisible Immigrants: The English in Canada since 1945*
   RVBW - May 2015 - pNA [51-500]

Barber, Michael - *How to Run a Government So that Citizens Benefit and Taxpayers Don't Go Crazy*
   Econ - v414 - i8931 - March 28 2015 - p87(US) [501+]
   NS - v144 - i5260 - May 1 2015 - p48(1) [501+]
   PW - v262 - i33 - August 17 2015 - p62(1) [51-500]
   Spec - v327 - i9735 - March 28 2015 - p44(1) [501+]
   TLS - i5848 - May 1 2015 - p23(1) [501+]

Barber, Richard - *Edward III and the Triumph of England: The Battle of Crecy and the Company of the Garter*
   HER - v130 - i544 - June 2015 - p708(3) [501+]
   Med R - Jan 2015 - pNA [501+]
Henry II: A Prince among Princes
   TLS - i5859 - July 17 2015 - p23(1) [501+]

Barber, Ros - *Devotion*
   TLS - i5868 - Sept 18 2015 - p21(1) [501+]

Barber, Rose - *30-Second Shakespeare: 50 Key Aspects of His Works, Life and Legacy, Each Explained in Half a Minute*
   Spec - v329 - i9771 - Dec 5 2015 - p41(2) [501+]

Barber, William J., II - *The Third Reconstruction*
   KR - Oct 1 2015 - pNA [501+]

Barberie, Peter - *Paul Strand: Master of Modern Photography*
   LJ - v140 - i6 - April 1 2015 - p88(1) [51-500]

Barbery, Muriel - *The Life of Elves*
   KR - Dec 1 2015 - pNA [501+]

Barbey d'Aurevilly, Jules - *Diaboliques: Six Tales of Decadence*
   LJ - v140 - i14 - Sept 1 2015 - p100(1) [51-500]

Barbier, Edward B. - *Nature and Wealth: Overcoming Environmental Scarcity and Inequality*
   Nature - v525 - i7568 - Sept 10 2015 - p185(1) [51-500]

Barbier, Jean-Claude - *The Road to Social Europe: A Contemporary Approach to Political Cultures and Diversity in Europe*
   CS - v44 - i5 - Sept 2015 - p629-630 [501+]

Barbierato, Federico - *The Inquisitor in the Hat Shop: Inquisition, Forbidden Books and Unbelief in Early Modern Venice*
   HER - v130 - i542 - Feb 2015 - p208(2) [501+]

Barbieri, Maggie - *Lies That Bind*
   BL - v111 - i9-10 - Jan 1 2015 - p47(1) [51-500]

Barbieri, Patrizio - *Physics of Wind Instruments and Organ Pipes, 1100-2010: New and Extended Writings*
   Isis - v106 - i1 - March 2015 - p164(2) [501+]

Barbieri, Pierpaolo - *Hitler's Shadow Empire: Nazi Economics and the Spanish Civil War*
   Lon R Bks - v37 - i21 - Nov 5 2015 - p39(3) [501+]

Barbieri, William A., Jr. - *At the Limits of the Secular: Reflections on Faith and Public Life*
   J Ch St - v57 - i3 - Summer 2015 - p559-561 [501+]

Barbosa, Rubens - *The Washington Dissensus: A Privileged Observer's Perspective on US-Brazil Relations*
   For Aff - v94 - i1 - Jan-Feb 2015 - pNA [501+]
   HNet - March 2015 - pNA [501+]

Barbour, Alan G. - *Lyme Disease: Why It's Spreading, How It Makes You Sick, and What to Do about It*
   LJ - v140 - i6 - April 1 2015 - p110(1) [51-500]

Barbour, Karen - *Little Nino's Pizzaria*
   c CH Bwatch - August 2015 - pNA [51-500]

Barbour, Kathryn - *Who Died*
   KR - Dec 15 2015 - pNA [501+]

Barbour, Reid - *Sir Thomas Browne: A Life*
   Isis - v106 - i1 - March 2015 - p186(2) [501+]
   NYRB - v62 - i16 - Oct 22 2015 - p67(3) [501+]

Barbree, Jay - *Neil Armstrong: A Life of Flight (Read by Prichard, Michael). Audiobook Review*
   BL - v111 - i12 - Feb 15 2015 - p103(1) [51-500]

Barbuto, Richard - *The Canadian Theater 1813*
   J Mil H - v79 - i1 - Jan 2015 - p181-185 [501+]
The Canadian Theatre 1814
   J Mil H - v79 - i1 - Jan 2015 - p181-185 [501+]

Barca, Antonio Jimenez - *Unpaid Debts*
   KR - Sept 15 2015 - pNA [51-500]

Barca, Pedro Calderon de la - *La Semilla Y La Cizana*
   Ren Q - v68 - i2 - Summer 2015 - p745-746 [501+]

Barchers, Suzanne - *Energy in Action*
   c SLJ - v61 - i4 - April 2015 - p86(4) [501+]

Barchiesi, Alessandro - *Homeric Effects in Vergil's Narrative*
   TLS - i5874 - Oct 30 2015 - p31(1) [501+]

Barclay, Eric - *Counting Dogs (Illus. by Barclay, Eric)*
   c BL - v111 - i19-20 - June 1 2015 - p110(1) [51-500]
   c KR - July 1 2015 - pNA [51-500]
   c PW - v262 - i15 - April 13 2015 - p78(2) [501+]

Barclay, Linwood - *Broken Promise*
   BL - v111 - i21 - July 1 2015 - p35(1) [51-500]
   LJ - v140 - i12 - July 1 2015 - p72(1) [51-500]
   NYTBR - August 2 2015 - p25(L) [501+]
   PW - v262 - i21 - May 25 2015 - p35(1) [51-500]
No Safe House (Read by Winton, Graham). Audiobook Review
   BL - v111 - i14 - March 15 2015 - p83(1) [51-500]

Barcott, Bruce - *Weed the People: The Future of Legal Marijuana in America*
   KR - Feb 15 2015 - pNA [501+]
   LJ - v140 - i7 - April 15 2015 - p106(1) [51-500]
   NYTBR - May 17 2015 - p19(L) [501+]

Bard-Collins, J. - *Honor above All*
   SPBW - Feb 2015 - pNA [51-500]

Bard, Elizabeth - *Picnic in Provence: A Memoir with Recipes (Read by Bard, Elizabeth). Audiobook Review*
   LJ - v140 - i12 - July 1 2015 - p44(1) [51-500]
Picnic in Provence: A Memoir with Recipes
   Bwatch - June 2015 - pNA [51-500]
   KR - Jan 1 2015 - pNA [501+]
   BL - v111 - i14 - March 15 2015 - p36(1) [51-500]

Bard, Richard - *Everlast*
   KR - Feb 1 2015 - pNA [501+]

Bardhan-Quallen, Sudipta - *Duck Duck Moose (Illus. by Jones, Noah Z.)*
   c HB Guide - v26 - i1 - Spring 2015 - p6(1) [51-500]

Bardi, Nandor - *Otthon es haza: Tanulmanyok a romaniai magyar kisebbseg torteneterol*
   Slav R - v74 - i1 - Spring 2015 - p165-166 [501+]

Bardugo, Leigh - *Six of Crows*
   y BL - v111 - i21 - July 1 2015 - p49(1) [501+]
   y BL - v111 - i22 - August 1 2015 - p64(2) [51-500]
   y HB - v91 - i5 - Sept-Oct 2015 - p92(2) [51-500]
   y KR - July 15 2015 - pNA [51-500]
   y NYTBR - Oct 25 2015 - p34(L) [501+]
   y PW - v262 - i28 - July 13 2015 - p68(1) [51-500]
   y PW - v262 - i49 - Dec 2 2015 - p106(1) [51-500]
   c Sch Lib - v63 - i4 - Winter 2015 - p242(1) [51-500]
   y SLJ - v61 - i9 - Sept 2015 - p156(2) [51-500]
   y VOYA - v38 - i3 - August 2015 - p73(1) [51-500]

Bareilles, Sara - *Sounds Like Me: My Life (So Far) in Song*
   KR - Sept 1 2015 - pNA [501+]
   PW - v262 - i35 - August 31 2015 - p81(2) [51-500]

Baren, Wim - *The Crimson Emperor: A Tale of Imperial Byzantium*
   KR - Nov 1 2015 - pNA [501+]

Barenberg, Alan - *Gulag Town, Company Town: Forced Labor and Its Legacy in Vorkuta*
   HNet - March 2015 - pNA [501+]

Barendregt, Bart - *Recollecting Resonances: Indonesian-Dutch Musical Encounters*
   Pac A - v88 - i3 - Sept 2015 - p746 [501+]

Barfield, Raymond - *The Ancient Quarrel between Philosophy and Poetry*
   Class R - v65 - i1 - April 2015 - p58-59 [501+]
The Book of Colors
   BL - v111 - i17 - May 1 2015 - p74(1) [51-500]

Bargu, Banu - *Starve and Immolate: The Politics of Human Weapons*
   HNet - July 2015 - pNA [501+]

Barham, Lawrence - *From Hand to Handle: The First Industrial Revolution*
   Am Ant - v80 - i2 - April 2015 - p424(2) [501+]

Barish, Evelyn - *The Double Life of Paul de Man*
   Lon R Bks - v37 - i1 - Jan 8 2015 - p11(4) [501+]

Barker, Clive - *The Scarlet Gospels*
   BL - v111 - i18 - May 15 2015 - p40(1) [51-500]
   Ent W - i1364 - May 22 2015 - p64(1) [501+]
   KR - March 15 2015 - pNA [501+]
   NYTBR - May 31 2015 - p42(L) [501+]
   PW - v262 - i12 - March 23 2015 - p51(1) [51-500]

Barker, Geoff - *How Recycling Works*
   c Sch Lib - v63 - i3 - Autumn 2015 - p172(1) [51-500]

Barker, Gillian - *Beyond Biofatalism: Human Nature for an Evolving World*
LJ - v140 - i16 - Oct 1 2015 - p103(1) [51-500]

Barker, J.D. - *Forsaken*
PW - v262 - i12 - March 23 2015 - p52(1) [51-500]

Barker, Joshua - *Figures of Southeast Asian Modernity*
JAS - v74 - i2 - May 2015 - p519-521 [501+]

Barker, Juliet - *1381: The Year of the Peasants' Revolt*
Bks & Cult - v21 - i2 - March-April 2015 - p8(1) [501+]
Med R - June 2015 - pNA [501+]
NYRB - v62 - i12 - July 9 2015 - p49(3) [501+]

England, Arise: The People, the King and the Great Revolt of 1381
HT - v65 - i2 - Feb 2015 - p60(1) [501+]
TLS - i5837 - Feb 13 2015 - p26(1) [501+]

Barker, Kathryn - *In the Skin of a Monster*
y Magpies - v30 - i3 - July 2015 - p39(1) [501+]

Barker, M.P. - *Mending Horses*
y BL - v111 - i16 - April 15 2015 - p57(1) [501+]
y Teach Lib - v42 - i3 - Feb 2015 - p32(6) [501+]

Barker, Pat - *Liza's England*
TimHES - i2229 - Nov 12 2015 - p46(1) [501+]

Noonday
KR - Jan 1 2016 - pNA [501+]
NS - v144 - i5284 - Oct 16 2015 - p51(1) [501+]
Spec - v328 - i9757 - August 29 2015 - p34(1) [501+]
TLS - i5871 - Oct 9 2015 - p23(1) [501+]

Barker, Sebastian - *The Land of Gold*
TLS - i5861 - July 31 2015 - p23(1) [501+]

Barker, Susan - *The Incarnations*
BL - v111 - i21 - July 1 2015 - p31(1) [51-500]
HR - v68 - i3 - Autumn 2015 - p510-516 [501+]
KR - June 1 2015 - pNA [501+]
LJ - v140 - i9 - May 15 2015 - p69(1) [51-500]
NY - v91 - i34 - Nov 2 2015 - p89 [51-500]
NYT - August 17 2015 - pC1(L) [501+]
NYTBR - August 30 2015 - p11(L) [501+]
PW - v262 - i20 - May 18 2015 - p59(1) [51-500]

Barkham, Patrick - *Coastlines: The Story of Our Shore*
NS - v144 - i5277 - August 28 2015 - p38(2) [501+]
TLS - i5855 - June 19 2015 - p32(1) [501+]

Barkley, Callie - *Amy's Very Merry Christmas (Illus. by Riti, Marsha)*
c HB Guide - v26 - i1 - Spring 2015 - p56(1) [51-500]

Ellie and the Good-Luck Pig (Illus. by Riti, Marsha)
c HB Guide - v26 - i2 - Fall 2015 - p63(1) [51-500]

Barkley, Cathy - *Math Is a Verb: Activities and Lessons from Cultures around the World*
Math T - v109 - i1 - August 2015 - p77-77 [501+]

Barks, Carl - *Walt Disney's Uncle Scrooge: The Seven Cities of Gold*
BL - v111 - i13 - March 1 2015 - p40(1) [51-500]

Barlett, Wendy K. - *Floating Collections: A Collection Development Model for Long-Term Success*
LRTS - v59 - i1 - Jan 2015 - p55(1) [501+]

Barlis, Kalliope - *Play Golf Better Faster: The Classic Guide to Optimizing Your Performance and Building Your Best Fast*
RVBW - May 2015 - pNA [51-500]
SPBW - April 2015 - pNA [51-500]

Barlow, Maude - *Blue Future: Protecting Water for People and the Planet Forever*
CWS - v30 - i2-3 - Fall-Winter 2015 - p121(1) [501+]

Barlow, Steve - *Unite speciale (Illus. by Leong, Sonia)*
c Res Links - v20 - i3 - Feb 2015 - p42(1) [51-500]

Barman, Adrienne - *Creaturepedia: Welcome to the Greatest Show on Earth (Illus. by Barman, Adrienne)*
c PW - v262 - i28 - July 13 2015 - p67(1) [501+]
c Sch Lib - v63 - i2 - Summer 2015 - p111(1) [51-500]
c SLJ - v61 - i11 - Nov 2015 - p128(1) [51-500]

Barnaby, Hannah - *Some of the Parts*
c BL - v112 - i5 - Nov 1 2015 - p39(1) [51-500]
y BL - v112 - i6 - Nov 15 2015 - p51(1) [51-500]
y KR - Nov 15 2015 - pNA [51-500]
y PW - v262 - i48 - Nov 30 2015 - p63(1) [51-500]

Barnard, Stephanie - *Cards That Wow with Sizzix: Techniques and Ideas for Using Die-Cutting and Embossing Machines*
LJ - v140 - i15 - Sept 15 2015 - p76(1) [51-500]

Barnas, Jo-Ann - *Great Moments in Olympic Skating*
c HB Guide - v26 - i1 - Spring 2015 - p182(1) [51-500]

Barner, Bob - *Sea Bones (Illus. by Barner, Bob)*
c HB Guide - v26 - i2 - Fall 2015 - p169(1) [51-500]
c SLJ - v61 - i5 - May 2015 - p129(2) [51-500]

Barnes, David - *The Venice Myth: Culture, Literature, Politics, 1800 to the Present*
TimHES - i2186 - Jan 15 2015 - p52-53 [501+]

Barnes, David-Matthew - *Fifty Yards and Holding*
SLJ - v61 - i4 - April 2015 - p159(1) [51-500]

Barnes, Emily - *The Fine Art of Murder*
PW - v262 - i48 - Nov 30 2015 - p40(1) [51-500]

Barnes, Fred - *Jack Kemp: The Bleeding-Heart Conservative Who Changed America*
Nat R - v67 - i20 - Nov 2 2015 - p39(2) [501+]

Barnes, Geraldine - *The Bookish Riddarasogur: Writing Romance in Late Mediaeval Iceland*
JEGP - v114 - i3 - July 2015 - p419(2) [501+]
Med R - Sept 2015 - pNA [501+]

Barnes, Ian - *Restless Empire: A Historical Atlas of Russia*
CC - v132 - i13 - June 24 2015 - p43(1) [51-500]
NYTBR - Dec 6 2015 - p14(L) [501+]

Barnes, James J. - *The American Revolution through British Eyes: A Documentary Collection, 2 vols.*
JSH - v81 - i2 - May 2015 - p443(3) [501+]
RAH - v43 - i1 - March 2015 - p41-46 [501+]

Barnes, Jennifer Lynn - *The Fixer*
y VOYA - v38 - i3 - August 2015 - p53(1) [51-500]
y KR - May 1 2015 - pNA [501+]
SLJ - v61 - i4 - April 2015 - p159(1) [51-500]
y BL - v111 - i19-20 - June 1 2015 - p96(2) [51-500]

Killer Instinct
y HB Guide - v26 - i1 - Spring 2015 - p100(1) [51-500]

Barnes, Jessica - *Cultivating the Nile: The Everyday Politics of Water in Egypt*
For Aff - v94 - i3 - May-June 2015 - pNA [501+]

Barnes, Jonathan - *Cannonbridge*
TLS - i5847 - April 24 2015 - p19(1) [501+]

Barnes, Julian - *Arthur and George*
TimHES - i2201 - April 30 2015 - p51(1) [501+]

Innocence
Nation - v300 - i19 - May 11 2015 - p27(7) [501+]

Keeping an Eye Open: Essays on Art
Apo - v181 - i631 - May 2015 - p103(1) [501+]
BL - v112 - i4 - Oct 15 2015 - p12(1) [51-500]
KR - June 1 2015 - pNA [501+]
LJ - v140 - i20 - Dec 1 2015 - p98(1) [51-500]
NS - v144 - i5263 - May 22 2015 - p49(1) [501+]
NYTBR - Dec 6 2015 - p62(L) [501+]
PW - v262 - i25 - June 22 2015 - p129(1) [501+]
Spec - v328 - i9744 - May 30 2015 - p35(1) [501+]
TLS - i5874 - Oct 30 2015 - p30(1) [501+]

Through the Window: Seventeen Essays and a Short Story
Nation - v300 - i19 - May 11 2015 - p27(7) [501+]

Barnes, Keith - *Want to Wake Alive: Selected Poems/ K.B. Aussi petit que mon prochain*
WLT - v89 - i6 - Nov-Dec 2015 - p71(1) [501+]

Barnes, Liberty Walther - *Conceiving Masculinity: Male Infertility, Medicine, and Identity*
AJS - v120 - i6 - May 2015 - p1891(3) [501+]

Barnes, Natalie - *A Modern Twist: Create Quilts with a Colorful Spin*
Bwatch - May 2015 - pNA [501+]

Barnes, Nico - *Bulldogs*
c HB Guide - v26 - i1 - Spring 2015 - p167(1) [51-500]

Sharks Series
c HB Guide - v26 - i1 - Spring 2015 - p161(1) [51-500]

Barnes, Sandra L. - *Live Long and Prosper: How Black Megachurches Address HIV/AIDS and Poverty in the Age of Prosperity Theology*
ERS - v38 - i3 - March 2015 - p525(3) [501+]

Repositioning Race: Prophetic Research in a Postracial Obama Age
CS - v44 - i4 - July 2015 - p470-472 [501+]

Barnes, Simon - *Ten Million Aliens: A Journey through the Entire Animal Kingdom*
BL - v111 - i9-10 - Jan 1 2015 - p27(1) [501+]
CSM - Feb 26 2015 - pNA [501+]

Barnes, Sophie - *The Earl's Complete Surrender*
BL - v112 - i6 - Nov 15 2015 - p31(1) [51-500]
PW - v262 - i45 - Nov 9 2015 - p45(1) [501+]

Barnes-Svarney, Patricia - *The Handy Nutrition Answer Book*
BL - v111 - i19-20 - June 1 2015 - p20(1) [51-500]
Sci Teach - v82 - i5 - Summer 2015 - p72 [51-500]
SLJ - v61 - i6 - June 2015 - p69(2) [51-500]
VOYA - v37 - i6 - Feb 2015 - p90(1) [51-500]
LJ - v140 - i7 - April 1 2015 - p115(1) [501+]

Barnes, Timothy David - *The Funerary Speech for John Chrysostom*
Class R - v65 - i2 - Oct 2015 - p408-410 [501+]

Barnes, Vivi - *Paper or Plastic*
y CH Bwatch - May 2015 - pNA [51-500]

Barnes, Wiley - *C Is for Chickasaw (Illus. by Long, Aaron)*
c CH Bwatch - May 2015 - pNA [51-500]

Barnett, Cynthia - *Rain: A Natural and Cultural History*
BL - v111 - i15 - April 1 2015 - p9(1) [51-500]
KR - Feb 15 2015 - pNA [51-500]
LJ - v140 - i3 - Feb 15 2015 - p124(2) [51-500]
Nature - v520 - i7545 - April 2 2015 - p31(1) [51-500]
NYTBR - April 19 2015 - p20(L) [501+]
PW - v262 - i11 - March 16 2015 - p74(2) [51-500]

Barnett, David - *Gideon Smith and the Mask of the Ripper*
PW - v262 - i34 - August 24 2015 - p66(1) [51-500]

Barnett, LaShonda Katrice - *Jam on the Vine*
BL - v111 - i9-10 - Jan 1 2015 - p52(1) [51-500]
BooChiTr - Feb 14 2015 - p16(1) [501+]
KR - Jan 15 2015 - pNA [51-500]
LJ - v140 - i6 - April 1 2015 - p76(3) [501+]
LJ - v140 - i9 - May 15 2015 - p74(3) [501+]

Barnett, Laura - *The Versions of Us*
TLS - i5864-5865 - August 21 2015 - p23(1) [501+]

Barnett, Mac - *Battle Bunny (Illus. by Myers, Matthew, III)*
c Sch Lib - v63 - i2 - Summer 2015 - p109(1) [51-500]

Extra Yarn (Read by Barber, Nicole). Audiobook Review
SLJ - v61 - i2 - Feb 2015 - p47(1) [51-500]

Leo: A Ghost Story (Illus. by Robinson, Christian)
c KR - June 15 2015 - pNA [51-500]
c BL - v111 - i21 - July 1 2015 - p63(1) [51-500]
c HB - v91 - i6 - Nov-Dec 2015 - p64(1) [51-500]
c Nat Post - v18 - i4 - Oct 31 2015 - pWP5(1) [501+]
c NYTBR - Oct 11 2015 - p16(L) [501+]
c PW - v262 - i22 - June 1 2015 - p57(1) [51-500]
c PW - v262 - i49 - Dec 2 2015 - p28(1) [51-500]
c SLJ - v61 - i9 - Sept 2015 - p112(2) [51-500]

Sam and Dave Dig a Hole (Illus. by Klassen, Jon)
c HB Guide - v26 - i1 - Spring 2015 - p21(1) [51-500]

The Skunk (Illus. by McDonnell, Patrick)
c BL - v111 - i17 - May 1 2015 - p103(1) [51-500]
c CCB-B - v68 - i11 - July-August 2015 - p535(2) [51-500]
c HB - v91 - i4 - July-August 2015 - p109(1) [51-500]
c KR - March 15 2015 - pNA [51-500]
c NYTBR - May 10 2015 - p18(L) [501+]
c PW - v262 - i49 - Dec 2 2015 - p38(1) [51-500]
c SLJ - v61 - i3 - March 2015 - p112(1) [501+]

Telephone (Illus. by Corace, Jen)
c HB Guide - v26 - i1 - Spring 2015 - p6(2) [51-500]

The Terrible Two (Read by Verner, Adam). Audiobook Review
c BL - v111 - i19-20 - June 1 2015 - p141(1) [51-500]
SLJ - v61 - i4 - April 2015 - p62(1) [51-500]

The Terrible Two Get Worse (Illus. by Cornell, Kevin)
c KR - Oct 1 2015 - pNA [51-500]
c SLJ - v61 - i11 - Nov 2015 - p93(2) [51-500]

The Terrible Two (Illus. by Cornell, Kevin)
c BL - v111 - i9-10 - Jan 1 2015 - p103(2) [51-500]

Barnett, Michael N. - *The Star and the Stripes: A History of the Foreign Policies of American Jews*
KR - Jan 1 2016 - pNA [501+]

Barnett, Richard - *The Sick Rose or: Disease and the Art of Medical Illustration*
HT - v65 - i4 - April 2015 - p61(1) [501+]

Barnett, Scot - *Maxx Airborne and the Legends of Rucker Park*
c KR - Jan 1 2016 - pNA [501+]

Barnett, Teresa - *Sacred Relics: Pieces of the Past in Nineteenth-Century America*
RAH - v43 - i1 - March 2015 - p103-109 [501+]

Barnett, Vincent - *John Maynard Keynes*
Historian - v77 - i1 - Spring 2015 - p157(3) [501+]

Barney, Timothy - *Mapping the Cold War: Cartography and the Framing of America's International Power*
HNet - Sept 2015 - pNA(NA) [501+]

Barnham, Keith - *The Burning Answer: A User's Guide to the Solar Revolution*
KR - March 15 2015 - pNA [501+]

The Burning Answer: The Solar Revolution: A Quest for Sustainable Power
BL - v111 - i16 - April 15 2015 - p6(2) [51-500]
LJ - v140 - i7 - April 15 2015 - p116(1) [51-500]

Barnhart, Aaron - *Firebrand*
c SLJ - v61 - i9 - Sept 2015 - p137(1) [51-500]

Barnhart, Norm - *My First Guide to Magic Tricks (Illus. by Charney, Steve)*
    c HB Guide - v26 - i2 - Fall 2015 - p195(1) [51-500]
Barnhill, Kelly - *Iron Hearted Violet*
    c SLJ - v61 - i6 - June 2015 - p46(6) [501+]
The Witch's Boy
    c CCB-B - v68 - i5 - Jan 2015 - p248(1) [51-500]
    c HB Guide - v26 - i1 - Spring 2015 - p69(1) [51-500]
Barnholdt, Lauren - *From This Moment*
    y SLJ - v61 - i8 - August 2015 - p113(1) [51-500]
Heat of the Moment
    y SLJ - v61 - i2 - Feb 2015 - p97(1) [51-500]
    y VOYA - v38 - i1 - April 2015 - p53(2) [51-500]
One Moment in Time
    y SLJ - v61 - i8 - August 2015 - p113(1) [51-500]
Through to You
    y HB Guide - v26 - i1 - Spring 2015 - p100(1) [51-500]
Barnosky, Anthony D. - *Dodging Extinction: Power, Food, Money, and the Future of Life on Earth*
    BioSci - v65 - i6 - June 2015 - p624(2) [501+]
End Game: Tipping Point for Planet Earth
    TimHES - i2222 - Sept 24 2015 - p41(1) [501+]
Heatstroke: Nature in an Age of Global Warming
    RVBW - May 2015 - pNA [501+]
Barocke Baustellen in Bayern. Akteure, Ablaufe und Wirtschaftliche Bedeutung
    HNet - March 2015 - pNA [501+]
Barolini, Teodolinda - *Dante's Lyric Poetry: Poems of Youth and of the "Vita Nuova"*
    Med R - August 2015 - pNA [501+]
Baron, Beth - *The Orphan Scandal: Christian Missionaries and the Rise of the Muslim Brotherhood*
    IJMES - v47 - i2 - May 2015 - p383-384 [501+]
Baron, Chris - *The Nutcracker Comes to America: How Three Ballet-Loving Brothers Created a Holiday Tradition (Illus. by Gendron, Cathy)*
    c SLJ - v61 - i10 - Oct 2015 - p61(1) [51-500]
Baron, Naomi S. - *Words Onscreen: The Fate of Reading in a Digital World*
    AJPsy - v128 - i4 - Winter 2015 - p550(6) [501+]
    LJ - v140 - i2 - Feb 1 2015 - p105(1) [51-500]
    Nature - v518 - i7538 - Feb 12 2015 - p165(1) [51-500]
    TLS - i5857 - July 3 2015 - p13(1) [501+]
Barot, Rick - *Chord*
    PW - v262 - i24 - June 15 2015 - p60(2) [51-500]
Barr, Brady - *Crocodile Encounters! And More True Stories of Adventures with Animals*
    c SLJ - v61 - i2 - Feb 2015 - p47(2) [51-500]
Scrapes with Snakes! True Stories of Adventures with Animals
    c HB Guide - v26 - i2 - Fall 2015 - p175(1) [51-500]
Barr, Catherine - *Elliot's Arctic Surprise (Illus. by Chessa, Francesca)*
    c KR - Sept 1 2015 - pNA [51-500]
    c PW - v262 - i37 - Sept 14 2015 - p70(1) [51-500]
The Story of Life: A First Book about Evolution (Illus. by Husband, Amy)
    c KR - Feb 15 2015 - pNA [51-500]
    c Sch Lib - v63 - i2 - Summer 2015 - p111(1) [51-500]
    c SLJ - v61 - i5 - May 2015 - p130(1) [51-500]
Barr, Colin - *Nation/Nazione: Irish Nationalism and the Italian Risorgimento*
    ILS - v34 - i2 - Spring 2015 - p7(1) [501+]
Barr, Daniel P. - *A Colony Sprung from Hell: Pittsburgh and the Struggle for Authority on the Western Pennsylvania Frontier, 1744-1794*
    AHR - v120 - i3 - June 2015 - p1012-1013 [501+]
    Am St - v54 - i1 - Spring 2015 - p150-2 [501+]
Barr, Ellisa - *Outage (Read by Rudd, Kate). Audiobook Review*
    y SLJ - v61 - i8 - August 2015 - p52(1) [51-500]
Barr, Helen - *Transporting Chaucer*
    RES - v66 - i275 - June 2015 - p569-570 [501+]
Barr, John McKee - *Loathing Lincoln: An American Tradition from the Civil War to the Present*
    AHR - v120 - i2 - April 2015 - p631-632 [501+]
    JAH - v102 - i1 - June 2015 - p204-205 [501+]
    JSH - v81 - i4 - Nov 2015 - p987(3) [501+]
    Reason - v46 - i9 - Feb 2015 - p61(4) [501+]
Barr, Juliana - *Contested Spaces of Early America*
    JAH - v101 - i4 - March 2015 - p1252-1253 [501+]
    JSH - v81 - i3 - August 2015 - p691(3) [501+]
    WHQ - v46 - i1 - Spring 2015 - p98-99 [501+]
    W&M Q - v72 - i3 - July 2015 - p499-508 [501+]
    HAHR - v95 - i4 - Nov 2015 - p717-719 [501+]

Barr, Martyn - *The Lost Generation: The Young Person's Guide to World War I*
    c Sch Lib - v63 - i2 - Summer 2015 - p122(2) [51-500]
Barr, Mary - *Friends Disappear: The Battle for Racial Equality in Evanston*
    AJS - v121 - i2 - Sept 2015 - p604(3) [501+]
Barr, Nevada - *Destroyer Angel*
    RVBW - Feb 2015 - pNA [51-500]
Barr, Niall - *Yanks and Limeys: Alliance Warfare in the Second World War*
    TimHES - i2214 - July 30 2015 - p50-51 [501+]
Barragan, Philip C., III - *Fatizen 24602 (Illus. by Arrigo, Mason)*
    PW - v262 - i41 - Oct 12 2015 - p52(1) [51-500]
Barrah, Jessica - *What's the Time, Wilfred Wolf? (Illus. by Smallman, Steve)*
    c HB Guide - v26 - i2 - Fall 2015 - p25(1) [51-500]
    c KR - April 15 2015 - pNA [51-500]
Barraud, Ned - *Moonman (Illus. by Barraud, Ned)*
    c Magpies - v30 - i1 - March 2015 - pSS(2) [51-500]
Barre, Stephane La - *Outstanding Marine Molecules: Chemistry, Biology, Analysis*
    QRB - v90 - i2 - June 2015 - p227(2) [501+]
Barrell, Tony - *Born to Drum: The Truth about the World's Greatest Drummers--from John Bonham and Keith Moon to Sheila E. and Dave Grohl*
    LJ - v140 - i5 - March 15 2015 - p100(1) [501+]
    Spec - v328 - i9742 - May 16 2015 - p48(1) [501+]
Barrento, Pedro - *Marlene and Sofia: A Double Love Story*
    PW - v262 - i14 - April 6 2015 - p37(1) [51-500]
Barrera, Albino - *Biblical Economic Ethics: Sacred Scripture's Teachings on Economic Life*
    Intpr - v69 - i4 - Oct 2015 - p485(2) [501+]
Barrera, Noe C. - *Texas Seashells: A Field Guide*
    QRB - v90 - i2 - June 2015 - p218(1) [501+]
Barreto, Matt - *Latino America: How America's Most Dynamic Population Is Poised to Transform the Politics of the Nation*
    NYRB - v62 - i19 - Dec 3 2015 - p8(3) [501+]
Barrett, A. Igoni - *Blackass*
    KR - Jan 1 2016 - pNA [51-500]
    TLS - i5868 - Sept 18 2015 - p21(1) [501+]
Barrett, Carla J. - *Courting Kids: Inside an Experimental Youth Court*
    CS - v44 - i5 - Sept 2015 - p630-632 [501+]
Barrett, Chuck - *Breach of Power*
    SPBW - Jan 2015 - pNA [51-500]
Barrett, Colin - *Young Skins*
    KR - Jan 15 2015 - pNA [51-500]
    LJ - v140 - i10 - June 1 2015 - p139(1) [501+]
    NY - v91 - i11 - May 4 2015 - p70 [51-500]
    NYT - March 13 2015 - pC27(L) [501+]
    PW - v262 - i3 - Jan 19 2015 - p56(1) [51-500]
Barrett, Dawson - *Teenage Rebels: Successful High School Activists, from the Little Rock 9 to the Class of Tomorrow*
    c SLJ - v61 - i6 - June 2015 - p140(2) [51-500]
Barrett, Elisabeth - *The Best of Me*
    PW - v262 - i50 - Dec 7 2015 - p74(1) [51-500]
Barrett, Emma - *Extreme: Why Some People Thrive at the Limits*
    Nature - v523 - i7562 - July 30 2015 - pSB2(1) [51-500]
    NYT - May 12 2015 - pNA(L) [501+]
Barrett, Faith - *To Fight Aloud Is Very Brave: American Poetry and the Civil War*
    AL - v87 - i2 - June 2015 - p389-391 [501+]
Barrett, Janet R. - *The Musical Experience: Rethinking Music Teaching and Learning*
    Am MT - v64 - i5 - April-May 2015 - p45(2) [501+]
Barrett, Lorna - *A Fatal Chapter*
    BL - v111 - i19-20 - June 1 2015 - p50(1) [51-500]
    PW - v262 - i17 - April 27 2015 - p53(2) [51-500]
    y VOYA - v38 - i3 - August 2015 - p54(1) [51-500]
Barrett, Michael B. - *Prelude to Blitzkrieg: The 1916 Austro-German Campaign in Romania*
    GSR - v38 - i2 - May 2015 - p432-3 [501+]
    J Mil H - v79 - i4 - Oct 2015 - p1175-1176 [501+]
Barrett, Richard - *The Metrics of Human Consciousness*
    SPBW - August 2015 - pNA [51-500]
Barrett, Ron - *Cats Get Famous (Illus. by Barrett, Ron)*
    c KR - June 1 2015 - pNA [51-500]
    c SLJ - v61 - i6 - June 2015 - p76(2) [51-500]
Cats Got Talent
    c HB Guide - v26 - i1 - Spring 2015 - p21(1) [51-500]
Barrett, Ross - *Oil Culture*
    Am Q - v67 - i2 - June 2015 - p529-540 [501+]

Barrett, Tina - *Geometric Knitting Patterns: A Sourcebook of Classic to Contemporary Designs*
    LJ - v140 - i17 - Oct 15 2015 - p90(1) [51-500]
Barreyre, Nicolas - *Historians across Borders: Writing American History in a Global Age*
    JAH - v101 - i4 - March 2015 - p1230-1231 [501+]
Barrie, J.M. - *Peter Pan (Illus. by Flyman, Trina Schart)*
    c HB Guide - v26 - i1 - Spring 2015 - p69(1) [51-500]
Barrier, Michael - *Funnybooks: The Improbable Glories of the Best American Comic Books*
    TLS - i5844 - April 3 2015 - p27(1) [51-500]
Barringer, Tim - *Pastures Green and Dark Satanic Mills: The British Passion for Landscape*
    LJ - v140 - i10 - June 1 2015 - p100(1) [501+]
Barrios, Enrique - *Ami y Perlita (Illus. by Temperini, Eliana Judith)*
    c SLJ - v61 - i11 - Nov 2015 - p90(1) [51-500]
Barrios, Richard - *Dangerous Rhythm: Why Movie Musicals Matter*
    FQ - v68 - i4 - Summer 2015 - p94(3) [501+]
Barrish, Seth - *An Actor's Companion*
    Am Theat - v32 - i5 - May-June 2015 - p10(1) [51-500]
Barriteau, V. Eudine - *Love and Power: Caribbean Discourses on Gender*
    Signs - v40 - i2 - Wntr 2015 - p525(7) [501+]
Barron, Carrie - *The Creativity Cure: How to Build Happiness with Your Own Two hands*
    Am Craft - v75 - i1 - Feb-March 2015 - p26(1) [501+]
Barron, Stephanie - *Jane and the Waterloo Map*
    BL - v112 - i7 - Dec 1 2015 - p29(1) [51-500]
    KR - Dec 1 2015 - pNA [51-500]
    PW - v262 - i50 - Dec 7 2015 - p70(1) [51-500]
New Objectivity: Modern German Art in the Weimar Republic 1919-1933
    LJ - v140 - i19 - Nov 15 2015 - p81(1) [51-500]
    NYTBR - June 28 2015 - p14(L) [501+]
Barron, T.A. - *Atlantis in Peril*
    y BL - v111 - i13 - March 1 2015 - p47(1) [51-500]
    c BL - v111 - i15 - April 1 2015 - p76(2) [51-500]
    c HB Guide - v26 - i2 - Fall 2015 - p74(1) [51-500]
    c KR - March 15 2015 - pNA [51-500]
    c SLJ - v61 - i8 - August 2015 - p82(2) [51-500]
    y VOYA - v38 - i2 - June 2015 - p70(2) [51-500]
Wisdom of Merlin: 7 Magical Words for a Meaningful Life
    c HB Guide - v26 - i2 - Fall 2015 - p148(1) [51-500]
Barroux - *Where's the Elephant?*
    c Magpies - v30 - i2 - May 2015 - p26(2) [51-500]
Barrow, Cathy - *Mrs. Wheelbarrow's Practical Pantry: Recipes and Techniques for Year-Round Preserving*
    Bwatch - Feb 2015 - pNA [51-500]
Barrow, G.W.S. - *Robert Bruce and the Community of the Realm of Scotland*
    Six Ct J - v46 - i1 - Spring 2015 - p186(2) [501+]
Barrow, John D. - *100 Essential Things You Didn't Know You Didn't Know about Math and the Arts*
    LJ - v140 - i2 - Feb 1 2015 - p103(2) [501+]
Barrow, Jonathan - *On the Run with Mary*
    KR - Sept 1 2015 - pNA [51-500]
    PW - v262 - i37 - Sept 14 2015 - p37(1) [51-500]
Barrow, Will - *Buster: The Military Dog Who Saved a Thousand Lives*
    KR - August 1 2015 - pNA [51-500]
Barrows, Annie - *The Guernsey Literary and Potato Pie Society*
    LJ - v140 - i13 - August 1 2015 - p126(1) [501+]
Magic in the Mix
    c HB Guide - v26 - i1 - Spring 2015 - p69 [51-500]
The Truth According to Us (Read by Lee, Ann Marie). Audiobook Review
    LJ - v140 - i17 - Oct 15 2015 - p51(1) [51-500]
The Truth According to Us
    y BL - v111 - i17 - May 1 2015 - p79(1) [51-500]
    KR - April 15 2015 - pNA [501+]
    LJ - v140 - i7 - April 15 2015 - p73(1) [51-500]
    LJ - v140 - i9 - May 15 2015 - p74(3) [51-500]
Barrows, Frederick - *Solving for Y*
    SPBW - August 2015 - pNA [51-500]
Barry, Andrew - *Interdisciplinarity: Reconfigurations of the Social and Natural Sciences*
    CS - v44 - i5 - Sept 2015 - p632-634 [501+]
Barry, Dave - *Live Right and Find Happiness (Although Beer Is Much Faster): Life Lessons and Other Ravings from Dave Barry*
    KR - Feb 15 2015 - pNA [51-500]
    NYTBR - May 31 2015 - p22(L) [501+]

The Worst Class Trip Ever (Read by Haberkorn, Todd). Audiobook Review
c SLJ - v61 - i8 - August 2015 - p48(2) [51-500]
The Worst Class Trip Ever (Illus. by Cannell, Jon)
BL - v111 - i14 - March 15 2015 - p76(2) [51-500]
c CCB-B - v69 - i1 - Sept 2015 - p7(1) [51-500]
c HB Guide - v26 - i2 - Fall 2015 - p75(1) [51-500]
c KR - March 1 2015 - pNA [51-500]
c PW - v262 - i10 - March 9 2015 - p74(1) [51-500]
c PW - v262 - i49 - Dec 2 2015 - p69(1) [51-500]
c SLJ - v61 - i5 - May 2015 - p100(1) [51-500]
y VOYA - v38 - i2 - June 2015 - p54(1) [51-500]

Barry, Kevin - *Beatlebone*
BL - v112 - i4 - Oct 15 2015 - p25(1) [51-500]
KR - Sept 15 2015 - pNA [51-500]
LJ - v140 - i19 - Nov 15 2015 - p74(1) [51-500]
Mac - v128 - i50 - Dec 21 2015 - p63(1) [501+]
NS - v144 - i5287 - Nov 6 2015 - p45(1) [501+]
NYT - Nov 23 2015 - pC3(L) [501+]
NYTBR - Nov 29 2015 - p9(L) [501+]
PW - v262 - i37 - Sept 14 2015 - p38(1) [51-500]
Spec - v329 - i9765 - Oct 24 2015 - p42(1) [501+]

Barry, Lynda - *Syllabus: Notes from an Accidental Professor*
BL - v111 - i13 - March 1 2015 - p37(2) [51-500]
SLJ - v61 - i3 - March 2015 - p178(1) [51-500]

Barry, Quan - *Loose Strife*
BL - v111 - i12 - Feb 15 2015 - p21(1) [51-500]
PW - v262 - i3 - Jan 19 2015 - p59(1) [51-500]
She Weeps Each Time You're Born
NYTBR - Feb 8 2015 - p30(L) [501+]

Barry, Rebecca - *Recipes for a Beautiful Life: A Memoir in Stories*
BL - v111 - i14 - March 15 2015 - p40(1) [51-500]
KR - Feb 1 2015 - pNA [51-500]
LJ - v140 - i12 - July 1 2015 - p118(1) [501+]

Barry, Rick - *The Methuselah Project*
PW - v262 - i30 - July 27 2015 - p50(1) [51-500]

Barry, Sebastian - *The Temporary Gentleman (Read by Grimes, Frank). Audiobook Review*
LJ - v140 - i8 - May 1 2015 - p40(1) [51-500]

Barrymore, Drew - *Wildflower*
y BL - v112 - i3 - Oct 1 2015 - p10(1) [51-500]
KR - Oct 1 2015 - pNA [501+]
NYTBR - Dec 6 2015 - p70(L) [501+]
PW - v262 - i37 - Sept 14 2015 - p59(1) [51-500]
LJ - v140 - i16 - Oct 1 2015 - p79(1) [51-500]

Barshaw, Ruth McNally - *The Ellie McDoodle Diaries: Ellie for President*
c HB Guide - v26 - i1 - Spring 2015 - p69(1) [51-500]

Barshinger, David P. - *Jonathan Edwards and the Psalms: A Redemptive-Historical Vision of Scripture*
CH - v84 - i4 - Dec 2015 - p901(2) [501+]

Barslund, Charlotte - *The Son*
RVBW - Feb 2015 - pNA [51-500]

Bartas, Magnus - *All Monsters Must Die*
KR - Nov 1 2015 - pNA [51-500]

Barth, John - *Collected Stories of William Faulkner*
KR - August 15 2015 - pNA [501+]
Collected Stories
PW - v262 - i31 - August 3 2015 - p31(1) [51-500]

Bartha, Eszter - *Alienating Labour: Workers on the Road from Socialism to Capitalism in East Germany and Hungary*
HER - v130 - i545 - August 2015 - p1061(3) [501+]

Barthel, Urno - *Death by Arbitrage, or, Live Low Die High*
KR - August 15 2015 - pNA [501+]

Barthelemy, Dominique - *Moines et demons: Autobiographie et individualite au Moyen Age, VIIe-XIIIe siecle*
Med R - Sept 2015 - pNA [501+]

Barthes, Roland - *A Lover's Discourse: Fragments*
TimHES - i2211 - July 9 2015 - p51(1) [501+]

Bartholomew, Robert E. - *A Colorful History of Popular Delusions*
PW - v262 - i30 - July 27 2015 - p53(1) [51-500]

Bartholomew, Steve - *Black Bart Reborn*
Roundup M - v22 - i6 - August 2015 - p25(1) [501+]

Bartig, Kevin - *Composing for the Red Screen: Prokofiev and Soviet Film*
Notes - v71 - i3 - March 2015 - p481(3) [501+]

Bartlett, A. Jennie - *Elder Northfield's Home, or, Sacrificed on the Mormon Altar: A Story of the Blighting Curse of Polygamy*
RVBW - April 2015 - pNA [501+]

Bartlett, David L. - *Feasting on the Word: Guide to Children's Sermons*
CC - v132 - i6 - March 18 2015 - p43(1) [51-500]

Bartlett, Don - *I Refuse*
NYRB - v62 - i13 - August 13 2015 - p57(2) [501+]
WLT - v89 - i6 - Nov-Dec 2015 - p64(2) [501+]

Bartlett, Jamie - *The Dark Net: Inside the Digital Underworld*
Lon R Bks - v37 - i6 - March 19 2015 - p34(2) [501+]
Mac - v128 - i23 - June 15 2015 - p61(1) [51-500]
NYRB - v62 - i15 - Oct 8 2015 - p55(3) [501+]
TLS - i5838 - Feb 20 2015 - p3(3) [501+]

Bartlett, Neil - *The Disappearance Boy*
G&L Rev W - v22 - i4 - July-August 2015 - p36(2) [501+]

Bartlett, Robert - *Why Can the Dead Do Such Great Things? Saints and Worshippers from the Martyrs to the Reformation*
AHR - v120 - i1 - Feb 2015 - p174-176 [501+]
CHR - v101 - i4 - Autumn 2015 - p905(3) [501+]
HER - v130 - i543 - April 2015 - p400(6) [501+]
Lon R Bks - v37 - i9 - May 7 2015 - p20(2) [501+]

Bartlett, Rosamund - *Anna Karenina*
TLS - i5842 - March 20 2015 - p12(2) [501+]

Bartlett, Sarah - *The Secrets of the Universe in 100 Symbols*
BL - v111 - i18 - May 15 2015 - p5(1) [51-500]
LJ - v140 - i6 - April 1 2015 - p116(2) [51-500]
LJ - v140 - i9 - May 15 2015 - p94(2) [501+]

Bartlett, T.C. - *A Dog Named Zero and the Apple with No Name (Illus. by Bartlett, T.C.)*
c KR - Jan 15 2015 - pNA [51-500]
Eat, Eat, Eat! Cheese, Cheese, Cheese! (Illus. by Bartlett, T.C.)
c KR - April 15 2015 - pNA [51-500]
Never Was a Grump Grumpier (Illus. by Bartlett, T.C.)
c KR - March 15 2015 - pNA [501+]

Bartley, Christopher - *Every Secret Thing*
KR - Feb 1 2015 - pNA [501+]

Bartley, Niccole - *The Southwest*
c CH Bwatch - Jan 2015 - pNA [51-500]

Bartmanski, Dominik - *Vinyl: The Analogue Record in the Digital Age*
TimHES - i2191 - Feb 19 2015 - p50(1) [501+]

Barto, Terry John - *Gollywood Here I Come! (Illus. by Cerato, Mattia)*
c CH Bwatch - Jan 2015 - pNA [51-500]
Nickerbacher: The Funniest Dragon (Illus. by Sponaugle, Kim)
c BL - v112 - i7 - Dec 1 2015 - p34(2) [501+]
c KR - Feb 1 2015 - pNA [501+]

Bartol, Amy A. - *Under Different Stars (Read by Rudd, Kate). Audiobook Review*
y SLJ - v61 - i6 - June 2015 - p65(2) [51-500]

Bartoletti, Susan Campbell - *The Boy Who Dared*
y BL - v111 - i19-20 - June 1 2015 - p86(2) [501+]
Terrible Typhoid Mary: A True Story of the Deadliest Cook in America (Read by Postel, Donna). Audiobook Review
y BL - v112 - i5 - Nov 1 2015 - p72(1) [51-500]
c SLJ - v61 - i11 - Nov 2015 - p69(2) [51-500]
Terrible Typhoid Mary: A True Story of the Deadliest Cook in America
c CCB-B - v69 - i1 - Sept 2015 - p7(1) [51-500]
y HB - v91 - i4 - July-August 2015 - p152(2) [51-500]
c KR - June 15 2015 - pNA [51-500]
c PW - v262 - i22 - June 1 2015 - p62(1) [51-500]
c SLJ - v61 - i5 - May 2015 - p137(1) [51-500]
y VOYA - v38 - i3 - August 2015 - p86(1) [51-500]
y BL - v111 - i19-20 - June 1 2015 - p83(1) [51-500]

Barton, Benjamin H. - *Glass Half Full: The Decline and Rebirth of the Legal Profession*
LJ - v140 - i5 - March 15 2015 - p121(2) [51-500]

Barton, Bernadette - *Pray the Gay Away: The Extraordinary Lives of Bible Belt Gays*
CS - v44 - i2 - March 2015 - p171-172 [501+]

Barton, Bethany - *I'm Trying to Love Spiders (Illus. by Barton, Bethany)*
c BL - v111 - i21 - July 1 2015 - p53(1) [51-500]
c CCB-B - v69 - i2 - Oct 2015 - p76(2) [51-500]
c KR - April 1 2015 - pNA [51-500]
c PW - v262 - i17 - April 27 2015 - p79(1) [51-500]
c PW - v262 - i49 - Dec 2 2015 - p48(1) [51-500]
c SLJ - v61 - i6 - June 2015 - p133(2) [51-500]

Barton, Byron - *My Bike (Illus. by Barton, Byron)*
c BL - v111 - i12 - Feb 15 2015 - p88(1) [51-500]
c HB - v91 - i3 - May-June 2015 - p78(2) [501+]
c HB Guide - v26 - i2 - Fall 2015 - p6(1) [51-500]
My House (Illus. by Barton, Byron)
c KR - Jan 1 2016 - pNA [51-500]

Barton, Chris - *The Amazing Age of John Roy Lynch (Illus. by Tate, Don)*
c BL - v111 - i15 - April 1 2015 - p35(2) [51-500]
c CCB-B - v68 - i10 - June 2015 - p481(1) [51-500]
c KR - Feb 15 2015 - pNA [51-500]
c PW - v262 - i49 - Dec 2 2015 - p43(1) [51-500]
The Nutcracker Comes to America: How Three Ballet-Loving Brothers Created a Holiday Tradition (Illus. by Gendron, Cathy)
c BL - v112 - i2 - Sept 15 2015 - p56(1) [51-500]
c HB - v91 - i6 - Nov-Dec 2015 - p54(1) [51-500]
c KR - Sept 1 2015 - pNA [51-500]
c PW - v262 - i37 - Sept 14 2015 - p77(1) [51-500]
c PW - v262 - i49 - Dec 2 2015 - p62(1) [51-500]
That's Not Bunny! (Illus. by Jack, Colin)
c KR - Nov 15 2015 - pNA [51-500]
c SLJ - v61 - i11 - Nov 2015 - p78(2) [51-500]

Barton, Erin E. - *The Preschool Inclusion Toolbox*
Bwatch - Oct 2015 - pNA [51-500]

Barton, Jen - *Cub Reporter Meets Famous Americans Series (Illus. by Jones, Doug)*
c BL - v112 - i7 - Dec 1 2015 - p42(1) [51-500]

Barton, John - *Ethics in Ancient Israel*
TLS - i5857 - July 3 2015 - p27(1) [501+]

Barton, Julie - *Dog Medicine: How My Dog Saved Me from Myself*
SPBW - Nov 2015 - pNA [51-500]

Barton, Marlin - *Pasture Art*
KR - Jan 15 2015 - pNA [501+]
PW - v262 - i3 - Jan 19 2015 - p53(1) [51-500]

Barton, Ruth - *Rex Ingram: Visionary Director of the Silent Screen*
Si & So - v25 - i3 - March 2015 - p107(1) [501+]

Barton, Suzanne - *The Sleepy Songbird*
c KR - Nov 15 2015 - pNA [51-500]
c PW - v262 - i45 - Nov 9 2015 - p58(1) [51-500]

Bartosik-Velez, Elise - *The Legacy of Christopher Columbus in the Americas: New Nations and a Transatlantic Discourse of Empire*
HAHR - v95 - i2 - May 2015 - p386-387 [501+]
JIH - v46 - i1 - Summer 2015 - p121-123 [501+]

Bartram, Peter - *Headline Murder*
RVBW - Nov 2015 - pNA [51-500]

Bartrop, Paul R. - *Modern Genocide: The Definitive Resource and Document Collection*
BL - v111 - i16 - April 15 2015 - p5(1) [51-500]

Bartsch, Jeff - *Two Across*
y BL - v111 - i19-20 - June 1 2015 - p46(1) [51-500]
LJ - v140 - i13 - August 1 2015 - p77(1) [51-500]
NYTBR - August 16 2015 - p19(L) [501+]
PW - v262 - i24 - June 15 2015 - p59(1) [51-500]

Bartsch, William H. - *Victory Fever on Guadalcanal: Japan's First Land Defeat of WWII*
HNet - March 2015 - pNA [501+]
J Mil H - v79 - i2 - April 2015 - p529-530 [501+]

Bartusiak, Marcia - *Black Hole: How an Idea Abandoned by Newtonians, Hated by Einstein, and Gambled on by Hawking Became Loved*
Econ - v415 - i8943 - June 20 2015 - p82(US) [501+]
Spec - v328 - i9744 - May 30 2015 - p36(2) [501+]
KR - Feb 15 2015 - pNA [51-500]
TimHES - i2206 - June 4 2015 - p48(1) [501+]

Bartusiak, Paul J. - *Cool Jazz Spy*
PW - v262 - i19 - May 11 2015 - p39(1) [51-500]

Bartynski, Julie M. - *Margret and H.A. Rey's Curious George Goes to a Bookstore (Illus. by Young, Mary O'Keefe)*
c HB Guide - v26 - i2 - Fall 2015 - p25(1) [51-500]

Baru, Sanjaya - *The Accidental Prime Minister: The Making and Unmaking of Manmohan Singh*
TLS - i5842 - March 20 2015 - p25(1) [501+]

Baruzzi, Agnese - *Dining with ... Monsters!*
c KR - Dec 1 2015 - pNA [51-500]
Who's Hiding?
c PW - v262 - i27 - July 6 2015 - p70(2) [501+]

Barwin, Gary - *Moon Baboon Canoe*
Can Lit - i224 - Spring 2015 - p107 [501+]

Barzak, Christopher - *Wonders of the Invisible World*
y BL - v111 - i22 - August 1 2015 - p61(1) [51-500]
y KR - July 1 2015 - pNA [51-500]
y PW - v262 - i49 - Dec 2 2015 - p109(1) [51-500]
y SLJ - v61 - i7 - July 2015 - p90(1) [51-500]

Barzel, Tamar - *New York Noise: Radical Jewish Music and the Downtown Scene*
LJ - v140 - i2 - Feb 1 2015 - p84(2) [51-500]

Barzilai, Yaniv - *102 Days of War: How Osama Bin Laden, Al Qaeda & The Taliban Survived 2001*
APH - v62 - i1 - Spring 2015 - p50(1) [501+]

Basara, Svetislav - *Fata Morgana*
KR - Sept 15 2015 - pNA [501+]

Basch, Rachel - *The Listener*
    LJ - v140 - i3 - Feb 15 2015 - p84(1) [51-500]
    BL - v111 - i11 - Feb 1 2015 - p22(1) [51-500]
    KR - Jan 1 2015 - pNA [51-500]

Baschera, Luca - *Following Zwingli: Applying the Past in Reformation Zurich*
    Ger Q - v88 - i3 - Summer 2015 - p400(3) [501+]
    Ren Q - v68 - i3 - Fall 2015 - p1050-1051 [501+]

Bascom, Tim - *Running to the Fire: An American Missionary Comes of Age in Revolutionary Ethiopia*
    Bks & Cult - v21 - i5 - Sept-Oct 2015 - p13(2) [501+]
    CC - v132 - i12 - June 10 2015 - p42(1) [51-500]
    CC - v132 - i22 - Oct 28 2015 - p43(1) [501+]

Base, Graeme - *Eye to Eye (Illus. by Base, Graeme)*
    c Magpies - v30 - i5 - Nov 2015 - p28(2) [501+]
    The Last King of Angkor Wat
    c HB Guide - v26 - i2 - Fall 2015 - p25(1) [51-500]

Basevi, Abramo - *The Operas of Giuseppe Verdi*
    Notes - v72 - i2 - Dec 2015 - p358(3) [501+]

Basher, Simon - *The Periodic Table: Elements with Style*
    c HB Guide - v26 - i2 - Fall 2015 - p165(1) [51-500]

Bashford, Alison - *Global Population: History, Geopolitics, and Life on Earth*
    AHR - v120 - i1 - Feb 2015 - p192-193 [501+]

Bashkin, Orit - *New Babylonians: A History of Jews in Modern Iraq*
    IJMES - v47 - i1 - Feb 2015 - p198-200 [501+]

Basho, Midori - *The Homemade Cake Contest*
    c KR - Feb 1 2015 - pNA [51-500]

Basile, Elisabetta - *Capitalist Development in India's Informal Economy*
    S&S - v79 - i4 - Oct 2015 - p638-641 [501+]

Basile, Salvatore - *Cool: How Air Conditioning Changed Everything*
    Am Sci - v103 - i3 - May-June 2015 - p228(1) [501+]

Basilieres, Michel - *A Free Man*
    PW - v262 - i18 - May 4 2015 - p96(1) [51-500]

Baskette, Molly Phinney - *Standing Naked Before God: The Art of Public Confession*
    CC - v132 - i21 - Oct 14 2015 - p57(2) [501+]

Baskin, Nora Raleigh - *Ruby on the Outside*
    c BL - v111 - i18 - May 15 2015 - p56(1) [51-500]
    c CCB-B - v68 - i11 - July-August 2015 - p536(1) [51-500]
    c HB Guide - v26 - i2 - Fall 2015 - p75(1) [51-500]
    c KR - March 15 2015 - pNA [51-500]
    c SLJ - v61 - i4 - April 2015 - p143(2) [51-500]

Basnight, Gray - *Shadows in the Fire*
    LJ - v140 - i7 - April 15 2015 - p73(1) [51-500]
    Roundup M - v22 - i4 - April 2015 - p26(1) [501+]

Bass, Alexis - *Love and Other Theories*
    y HB Guide - v26 - i1 - Spring 2015 - p100(1) [51-500]
    What's Broken Between Us
    y KR - Oct 1 2015 - pNA [51-500]
    y PW - v262 - i38 - Sept 21 2015 - p76(1) [51-500]
    y SLJ - v61 - i11 - Nov 2015 - p111(2) [51-500]
    y VOYA - v38 - i5 - Dec 2015 - p52(1) [51-500]

Bass, Diana Butler - *Grounded: Finding God in the World: A Spiritual Revolution*
    LJ - v140 - i16 - Oct 1 2015 - p64(2) [501+]
    PW - v262 - i32 - August 10 2015 - p55(1) [51-500]

Bass, Henry - *Seeds of Freedom (Illus. by Lewis, E.B.)*
    c PW - v262 - i49 - Dec 2 2015 - p50(1) [51-500]

Bass, Hester - *The Secret World of Walter Anderson (Illus. by Lewis, E.B.)*
    c HB Guide - v26 - i1 - Spring 2015 - p178(1) [51-500]

Bass, Jefferson - *The Breaking Point*
    BL - v111 - i19-20 - June 1 2015 - p48(1) [51-500]
    PW - v262 - i17 - April 27 2015 - p51(1) [51-500]

Bass, Jennifer Vogel - *Edible Colors*
    c HB Guide - v26 - i1 - Spring 2015 - p174(1) [51-500]
    Edible Numbers
    c PW - v262 - i23 - June 8 2015 - p58(1) [51-500]
    c BL - v111 - i22 - August 1 2015 - p52(1) [51-500]
    c HB Guide - v26 - i2 - Fall 2015 - p164(1) [51-500]
    c KR - Feb 15 2015 - pNA [51-500]

Bass, Karen - *Uncertain Soldier*
    y KR - June 1 2015 - pNA [51-500]
    c Res Links - v20 - i5 - June 2015 - p23(1) [501+]
    y SLJ - v61 - i8 - August 2015 - p100(1) [51-500]
    y VOYA - v38 - i3 - August 2015 - p54(1) [51-500]

Bass, Len - *DevOps: A Software Architect's Perspective*
    Bwatch - Nov 2015 - pNA [51-500]

Bass, Patrik Henry - *The Zero Degree Zombie Zone (Illus. by Craft, Jerry)*
    c CH Bwatch - April 2015 - pNA [51-500]
    c HB Guide - v26 - i1 - Spring 2015 - p69(1) [51-500]

Bass, Richard F. - *Stochastic Processes*
    SIAM Rev - v57 - i2 - June 2015 - p317-318 [501+]

Bass, Rick - *For a Little While*
    KR - Jan 1 2016 - pNA [51-500]

Basselin, Timothy J. - *Flannery O'Connor: Writing a Theology of Disabled Humanity*
    Theol St - v76 - i2 - June 2015 - p398(2) [501+]

Bassett, Richard - *For God and Kaiser: The Imperial Austrian Army from 1619-1918*
    HT - v65 - i11 - Nov 2015 - p62(1) [501+]
    Spec - v328 - i9747 - June 20 2015 - p38(2) [501+]

Bassetti, Amanda - *Arm Knitting*
    BL - v112 - i5 - Nov 1 2015 - p7(2) [51-500]

Bassiouney, Reem - *Language and Identity in Modern Egypt*
    Lang Soc - v44 - i3 - June 2015 - p444-445 [501+]

Bassoff, Jon - *The Incurables*
    PW - v262 - i46 - Nov 16 2015 - p60(1) [51-500]

Bassons, Christophe - *A Clean Break: My Story*
    LJ - v140 - i2 - Feb 1 2015 - p88(1) [51-500]

Bastedo, Jamie - *Cut Off*
    y KR - August 15 2015 - pNA [51-500]
    y Res Links - v21 - i1 - Oct 2015 - p29(1) [501+]
    y SLJ - v61 - i9 - Sept 2015 - p157(1) [51-500]
    y VOYA - v38 - i5 - Dec 2015 - p52(2) [51-500]

Bastian, Alexander - *Repression, Haft und Geschlecht: Die Untersuchungshaftanstalt des Ministeriums fur Staatssicherheit Magdeburg-Neustadt 1958-1989*
    HNet - June 2015 - pNA [501+]

Bastian, Corina - *Das Geschlecht der Diplomatie: Geschlechterrollen in den Aussenbeziehungen vom Spatmittelalter bis zum 20. Jahrhundert*
    HNet - March 2015 - pNA [501+]

Bastianich, Joseph - *Healthy Pasta: The Sexy, Skinny, and Smart Way to Eat Your Favorite Food*
    LJ - v140 - i7 - April 15 2015 - p110(1) [51-500]
    PW - v262 - i14 - April 6 2015 - p53(2) [51-500]

Bastianich, Lidia - *Lidia's Egg-Citing Farm Adventure (Illus. by Graef, Renee)*
    c HB Guide - v26 - i2 - Fall 2015 - p25(2) [51-500]
    c SLJ - v61 - i3 - March 2015 - p112(1) [51-500]
    Nonna Tell Me a Story: Lidia's Egg-citing Farm Adventure (Illus. by Graef, Renee)
    c CH Bwatch - April 2015 - pNA [501+]

Bastianich, Lidia Matticchio - *Lidia's Mastering the Art of Italian Cuisine: Everything You Need to Know to Be a Great Italian Cook*
    PW - v262 - i33 - August 17 2015 - p65(2) [51-500]

Basu, Balaka - *Contemporary Dystopian Fiction for Young Adults: Brave New Teenagers*
    Bkbird - v53 - i3 - Summer 2015 - p87(1) [501+]

Batacan, F.H. - *Smaller and Smaller Circles*
    BL - v111 - i17 - May 1 2015 - p45(1) [51-500]
    PW - v262 - i26 - June 29 2015 - p46(1) [51-500]

Batalion, Judy - *White Walls: A Memoir about Motherhood, Daughterhood, and the Mess in Between*
    BL - v112 - i7 - Dec 1 2015 - p8(1) [51-500]

Batcheller, Lori - *Rosa Blooms (Illus. by Batcheller, Lori)*
    c CH Bwatch - Nov 2015 - pNA [51-500]

Batchelor, Paul - *The Love Darg*
    TLS - i5839 - Feb 27 2015 - p24(1) [51-500]

Batchelor, Robert K. - *London: The Selden Map and the Making of a Global City, 1549-1689*
    AHR - v120 - i2 - April 2015 - p573-575 [501+]
    Eight-C St - v49 - i1 - Fall 2015 - pNA [501+]

Batchelor, Stephen - *After Buddhism: Rethinking the Dharma for a Secular Age*
    PW - v262 - i37 - Sept 14 2015 - p61(1) [51-500]

Bate, Dana - *Too Many Cooks*
    BL - v112 - i5 - Nov 1 2015 - p29(1) [51-500]
    LJ - v140 - i17 - Oct 15 2015 - p73(1) [51-500]

Bate, Dick - *Soccer Speed*
    Bwatch - Jan 2015 - pNA [51-500]

Bate, Jonathan - *Ted Hughes: The Unauthorised Life*
    New Sci - v228 - i3045 - Oct 31 2015 - p45(1) [501+]
    NS - v144 - i5282 - Oct 2 2015 - p64(2) [501+]
    NYT - Oct 14 2015 - pC1(L) [501+]
    NYTBR - Dec 27 2015 - p10(L) [501+]
    Spec - v329 - i9762 - Oct 3 2015 - p38(2) [501+]

Bate, Simon T. - *The Design and Statistical Analysis of Animal Experiments*
    QRB - v90 - i4 - Dec 2015 - p426(2) [501+]

Bateman, Teresa - *Job Wanted (Illus. by Sheban, Chris)*
    c KR - August 1 2015 - pNA [51-500]
    c SLJ - v61 - i9 - Sept 2015 - p113(1) [51-500]

Bates, Catherine - *Masculinity and the Hunt: Wyatt to Spenser*
    Ren Q - v68 - i2 - Summer 2015 - p764-766 [501+]
    Six Ct J - v46 - i2 - Summer 2015 - p501-503 [501+]

Bates, David - *Anglo-Norman Studies, XXXVI: Proceedings of the Battle Conference 2013*
    Med R - August 2015 - pNA [501+]
    The Normans and Empire
    AHR - v120 - i1 - Feb 2015 - p310-311 [501+]
    HNet - April 2015 - pNA [501+]

Bates, Ivan - *The Hide-and-Scare Bear (Illus. by Bates, Ivan)*
    c KR - Dec 15 2015 - pNA [51-500]

Bates, Jeremy - *Black Canyon*
    PW - v262 - i22 - June 1 2015 - p46(1) [51-500]
    Suicide Forest
    KR - Feb 1 2015 - pNA [501+]
    PW - v262 - i5 - Feb 2 2015 - p38(1) [51-500]

Bates, Sonya Spreen - *Off the Rim*
    y SLJ - v61 - i9 - Sept 2015 - p151(4) [51-500]
    y Res Links - v20 - i3 - Feb 2015 - p26(1) [51-500]

Bathroom Readers Institute - *Uncle John's Robotica*
    RVBW - Jan 2015 - pNA [51-500]

Batra, Ravi - *End Unemployment Now: How to Eliminate Joblessness, Debt, and Poverty Despite Congress*
    BL - v111 - i18 - May 15 2015 - p6(1) [51-500]
    KR - March 1 2015 - pNA [501+]
    LJ - v140 - i7 - April 15 2015 - p95(1) [51-500]
    PW - v262 - i10 - March 9 2015 - p65(1) [51-500]

Batson, Jon - *In Search of a Legacy*
    PW - v262 - i18 - May 4 2015 - p102(1) [51-500]
    Starlost Child: Adventures of a Space Bum
    PW - v262 - i12 - March 23 2015 - p53(1) [51-500]

Batson, Stella Henson Griggs - *Memories of Thompson Orphanage: Charlotte, North Carolina*
    RVBW - Oct 2015 - pNA [51-500]

Battat, Erin Royston - *Ain't Got No Home: America's Great Migrations and the Making of an Interracial Left*
    AHR - v120 - i2 - April 2015 - p656-657 [501+]
    J Am St - v49 - i2 - May 2015 - p434-435 [501+]
    JAH - v102 - i1 - June 2015 - p281-282 [501+]

Battershill, Andrew - *Pillow*
    KR - July 15 2015 - pNA [51-500]

Battista, Maggie - *Food Gift Love: More Than 100 Recipes to Make, Wrap, and Share*
    LJ - v140 - i19 - Nov 15 2015 - p100(1) [51-500]

Battistella, Edwin L. - *Sorry about That: The Language of Public Apology*
    CC - v132 - i1 - Jan 7 2015 - p40(3) [501+]

Battles, Dominique - *Cultural Difference and Material Culture in Middle English Romance: Normans and Saxons*
    Specu - v90 - i2 - April 2015 - p494-496 [501+]

Battles, Matthew - *Palimpsest: A History of the Written Word*
    Bks & Cult - v21 - i6 - Nov-Dec 2015 - p18(2) [501+]
    Bwatch - Oct 2015 - pNA [51-500]
    KR - May 1 2015 - pNA [501+]
    LJ - v140 - i8 - May 1 2015 - p81(1) [51-500]
    Nature - v523 - i7562 - July 30 2015 - pSB2(1) [51-500]
    NYTBR - August 23 2015 - p17(L) [501+]
    PW - v262 - i16 - April 20 2015 - p64(1) [51-500]
    TLS - i5869 - Sept 25 2015 - p29(1) [501+]

Battles, Paul - *Sir Gawain and the Green Knight*
    Med R - May 2015 - pNA [501+]

Bauckham, Richard - *Old Testament Pseudepigrapha: More Noncanonical Scriptures, vol. 1*
    Intpr - v69 - i4 - Oct 2015 - p489(2) [501+]

Bauder, Julia - *The Reference Guide to Data Sources*
    R&USQ - v54 - i3 - Spring 2015 - p55(1) [501+]

Bauduin, Pierre - *L'Historiographie medievale normande et ses sources antiques (Xe-XIIe siecle): Actes du colloque de Cerisy-la-Salle et du Scriptorial d'Avranches*
    Med R - Sept 2015 - pNA [501+]

Bauer, Ann - *Forgiveness 4 You*
    BL - v111 - i12 - Feb 15 2015 - p30(1) [51-500]
    KR - Jan 15 2015 - pNA [51-500]

Bauer, Belinda - *Rubbernecker*
    NYTBR - Sept 20 2015 - p29(L) [501+]
    NYTBR - Dec 6 2015 - p85(L) [501+]
    The Shut Eye
    PW - v262 - i45 - Nov 9 2015 - p37(1) [51-500]

Bauer, Gerri - *At Home in Persimmon Hollow*
    PW - v262 - i23 - June 8 2015 - p47(1) [51-500]

Bauer, Grace - *Nowhere All at Once*
WLT - v89 - i1 - Jan-Feb 2015 - p72(2) [501+]
Bauer, Joan - *Soar*
c KR - Dec 1 2015 - pNA [51-500]
Tell Me
c HB Guide - v26 - i1 - Spring 2015 - p69(1) [51-500]
Bauer, Karen - *100 Things I Learned in Heaven*
RVBW - Nov 2015 - pNA [51-500]
Bauer, Marion Dane - *Celebrating North Carolina (Illus. by Canga, C.B.)*
c HB Guide - v26 - i2 - Fall 2015 - p218(2) [51-500]
Celebrating Washington State (Illus. by Canga, C.B.)
c HB Guide - v26 - i2 - Fall 2015 - p218(2) [51-500]
Crinkle, Crackle, Crack: It's Spring! (Illus. by Shelley, John)
c BL - v111 - i15 - April 1 2015 - p82(1) [51-500]
c HB Guide - v26 - i2 - Fall 2015 - p26(1) [51-500]
c SLJ - v61 - i3 - March 2015 - p112(1) [51-500]
Little Cat's Luck
c KR - Nov 1 2015 - pNA [51-500]
Toes, Ears, and Nose! (Illus. by Katz, Karen)
c SLJ - v61 - i7 - July 2015 - p54(1) [51-500]
Bauer, Michael Gerard - *Eric Vale, Epic Fail (Illus. by Bauer, Joe)*
c Res Links - v21 - i1 - Oct 2015 - p12(2) [501+]
Secret Agent Derek 'Danger' Dale: The Case of the Really, Really Scary Things (Illus. by Bauer, Joe)
c Magpies - v30 - i2 - May 2015 - p34(1) [501+]
Bauer, Michael J. - *Calvin Institute of Christian Worship Liturgical Series*
Intpr - v69 - i1 - Jan 2015 - p117(1) [501+]
Bauer, Nancy - *How to Do Things with Pornography*
TimHES - i2206 - June 4 2015 - p51(1) [501+]
Bauer, Robin - *Queer BDSM Intimacies: Critical Consent and Pushing Boundaries*
HNet - May 2015 - pNA [501+]
Bauer, Rudolph - *Kriege im 21. Jahrhundert: Neue Herausforderungen der Friedensbewegung*
HNet - June 2015 - pNA [501+]
Bauer, Susan Wise - *The Story of Science: From the Writings of Aristotle to the Big Bang Theory*
BL - v111 - i17 - May 1 2015 - p66(1) [51-500]
Bwatch - July 2015 - pNA [51-500]
KR - March 15 2015 - pNA [501+]
LJ - v140 - i6 - April 1 2015 - p113(1) [51-500]
TimHES - i2210 - July 2 2015 - p50-2 [501+]
The Well-Educated Mind
KR - Sept 1 2015 - pNA [501+]
Bauer, Volker - *Wurzel, Stamm, Krone: Furstliche Genealogie in Fruhneuzeitlichen Druckwerken*
HNet - Feb 2015 - pNA [501+]
Bauerkamper, Arnd - *Gesellschaft in der europaischen Integration seit den 1950er Jahren: Migration - Konsum - Sozialpolitik - Reprasentationen*
HNet - April 2015 - pNA [501+]
Sicherheitskulturen im Vergleich: Deutschland und Russland/UdSSR seit dem Spaten 19. Jahrhundert
HNet - March 2015 - pNA [501+]
Bauerlein, Mark - *The State of the American Mind: 16 Leading Critics on the New Anti-Intellectualism*
Nat R - v67 - i12 - July 6 2015 - p42 [501+]
Bauerleln, Mark - *The State of the American Mind: 16 Leading Critics on the New Anti-Intellectualism*
PW - v262 - i17 - April 27 2015 - p65(1) [51-500]
Baugh, Carolyn - *Quicksand*
BL - v112 - i1 - Sept 1 2015 - p48(1) [51-500]
PW - v262 - i28 - July 13 2015 - p43(1) [51-500]
Baugh, Daniel - *The Global Seven Years War, 1754-1763: Britain and France in a Great Power Contest*
AHR - v120 - i3 - June 2015 - p977-978 [501+]
JMH - v87 - i1 - March 2015 - p151(3) [501+]
Baugh, Helen - *Rudy's Windy Christmas (Illus. by Mantle, Ben)*
c KR - Sept 1 2015 - pNA [51-500]
c SLJ - v61 - i10 - Oct 2015 - p61(1) [51-500]
Baughan, Elizabeth P. - *Couched in Death: Klinai and Identity in Anatolia and Beyond*
Class R - v65 - i2 - Oct 2015 - p564-566 [501+]
Baughman, R. Wayne - *Wrestling On and Off the Mat*
Forbes - v196 - i6 - Nov 2 2015 - p42(1) [501+]
Baugus, Bruce P. - *China's Reforming Churches: Mission, Polity, and Ministry in the Next Christendom*
IBMR - v39 - i3 - July 2015 - p162(2) [501+]
Baum, Frank L - *Ozma of Oz (Read by Yuen, Erin). Audiobook Review*
SLJ - v61 - i4 - April 2015 - p62(1) [51-500]
Baum, G.D. - *Sleeping to Death*
c BL - v112 - i3 - Oct 1 2015 - p32(2) [501+]
Baum, Gregory - *Truth and Relevance: Catholic Theology in French Quebec Since the Quiet Revolution*
Theol St - v76 - i2 - June 2015 - p373(2) [501+]
Baum, L. Frank - *The Wizard of Oz (Illus. by Zwerger, Lisbeth)*
c BL - v112 - i5 - Nov 1 2015 - p40(1) [51-500]
Bauman, Bruce - *Broken Sleep*
BL - v112 - i2 - Sept 15 2015 - p26(1) [51-500]
KR - August 15 2015 - pNA [501+]
LJ - v140 - i19 - Nov 15 2015 - p74(1) [51-500]
Bauman, Chad M. - *Pentecostals, Proselytization, and Anti-Christian Violence in Contemporary India*
IBMR - v39 - i4 - Oct 2015 - p242(1) [501+]
Bauman, Zygmunt - *Moral Blindness: The Loss of Sensitivity in Liquid Modernity*
GSR - v38 - i2 - May 2015 - p478-3 [501+]
Baumann, Dan - *A Fresh Look at Fear: Encountering Jesus in Our Weakness*
SPBW - July 2015 - pNA [51-500]
Baumann, Nancy L. - *For the Love of Reading: Guide to K-8 Reading Promotions*
SLJ - v61 - i4 - April 2015 - p186(1) [501+]
Baumann, Tamra - *It Had to Be Him*
PW - v262 - i8 - Feb 23 2015 - p59(2) [51-500]
Baumbach, Noah - *Frances Ha: A Noah Baumbach Picture*
RVBW - Oct 2015 - pNA [51-500]
Baume, Sara - *Spill Simmer Falter Wither*
TimHES - i2221 - Sept 17 2015 - p45(1) [501+]
KR - Jan 1 2016 - pNA [51-500]
NS - v144 - i5251 - Feb 27 2015 - p48(1) [51-500]
TLS - i5840 - March 6 2015 - p21(1) [501+]
Baumgarten, Bret - *Beautiful Hands (Illus. by Otoshi, Kathryn)*
c PW - v262 - i30 - July 27 2015 - p1(1) [501+]
Baumgarten, Elisheva - *Practicing Piety in Medieval Ashkenaz: Men, Women, and Everyday Religious Observance*
Med R - Sept 2015 - pNA [501+]
Specu - v90 - i4 - Oct 2015 - p1085-1086 [501+]
Bausch, Richard - *Before, During, After (Read by Shah, Neil). Audiobook Review*
BL - v111 - i12 - Feb 15 2015 - p103(1) [51-500]
Bausch, Robert - *Far as the Eye Can See*
NYTBR - Jan 11 2015 - p9(L) [501+]
Bausum, Ann - *Stonewall: Breaking Out in the Fight for Gay Rights (Read by Federle, Tim). Audiobook Review*
y BL - v111 - i21 - July 1 2015 - p80(1) [51-500]
y SLJ - v61 - i7 - July 2015 - p48(2) [51-500]
Stonewall: Breaking Out in the Fight for Gay Rights
y BL - v111 - i15 - April 1 2015 - p35(1) [51-500]
y CCB-B - v68 - i11 - July-August 2015 - p536(2) [51-500]
y HB - v91 - i4 - July-August 2015 - p153(1) [51-500]
y KR - March 15 2015 - pNA [51-500]
y PW - v262 - i13 - March 30 2015 - p78(1) [51-500]
y PW - v262 - i49 - Dec 2 2015 - p117(1) [51-500]
y VOYA - v38 - i2 - June 2015 - p86(1) [51-500]
Bautch, Richard J. - *The Book of Isaiah: Enduring Questions Answered Anew: Essays Honoring Joseph Blenkinsopp and His Contribution to the Study of Isaiah*
Intpr - v69 - i1 - Jan 2015 - p124(1) [51-500]
Theol St - v76 - i3 - Sept 2015 - p633(1) [501+]
Bauval, Robert - *Black Genesis: The Prehistoric Origins of Ancient Egypt*
Am Ant - v80 - i3 - July 2015 - p621(2) [501+]
Baxter, Angus - *In Search of Your German Roots: A Complete Guide to Tracing Your Ancestors in the Germanic Areas of Europe, 5th ed.*
LJ - v140 - i8 - May 1 2015 - p99(1) [51-500]
Baxter, Charles - *There's Something I Want You to Do*
Comw - v142 - i8 - May 1 2015 - p37(2) [501+]
NYRB - v62 - i4 - March 5 2015 - p51(3) [501+]
NYTBR - March 8 2015 - p20(L) [501+]
Baxter, Greg - *Munich Airport*
Ent W - i1350 - Feb 13 2015 - p61(1) [501+]
NY - v91 - i7 - April 6 2015 - p81 [51-500]
NYTBR - Feb 15 2015 - p21(L) [501+]
Baxter, Jack - *Mike's Place: A True Story of Love, Blues, and Terror in Tel Aviv*
PW - v262 - i23 - June 8 2015 - p47(1) [51-500]
y VOYA - v38 - i3 - August 2015 - p54(1) [51-500]
Baxter, John - *Five Nights in Paris: After Dark in the City of Light*
TLS - i5858 - July 10 2015 - p27(1) [501+]
BL - v111 - i15 - April 1 2015 - p4(1) [501+]
KR - March 15 2015 - pNA [51-500]
LJ - v140 - i7 - April 15 2015 - p100(1) [51-500]
Baxter, Kate - *The Warrior Vampire*
PW - v262 - i41 - Oct 12 2015 - p53(2) [51-500]
Baxter, Lily - *The Shopkeeper's Daughter*
LJ - v140 - i7 - April 15 2015 - p5(1) [51-500]
Baxter, Mandy - *One Kiss More*
PW - v262 - i1 - Jan 5 2015 - p58(1) [51-500]
One Touch More
BL - v112 - i2 - Sept 15 2015 - p45(2) [51-500]
PW - v262 - i37 - Sept 14 2015 - p48(2) [51-500]
Baxter, Roberta - *Seismology: Our Violent Earth*
c HB Guide - v26 - i2 - Fall 2015 - p167(1) [51-500]
Baxter, Stephen - *The Long Utopia*
BL - v111 - i21 - July 1 2015 - p47(1) [51-500]
Proxima (Read by McCarley, Kyle). Audiobook Review
BL - v111 - i18 - May 15 2015 - p69(1) [51-500]
Ultima
BL - v111 - i22 - August 1 2015 - p44(1) [51-500]
Bwatch - Sept 2015 - pNA [51-500]
Bayani, Manijeh - *Persian Painting: The Arts of the Book and Portraiture*
LJ - v140 - i16 - Oct 1 2015 - p75(1) [51-500]
Bayard, Pierre - *How to Talk about Places You've Never Been: On the Importance of Armchair Travel*
KR - Oct 1 2015 - pNA [501+]
LJ - v140 - i20 - Dec 1 2015 - p132(2) [51-500]
Il existe d'autres mondes
FS - v69 - i2 - April 2015 - p277-278 [501+]
Bayat, Asef - *Post-Islamism: The Changing Faces of Political Islam*
J Ch St - v57 - i2 - Spring 2015 - p360-361 [501+]
Bayeh, Jumana - *The Literature of the Lebanese Diaspora: Representations of Place and Transnational Identity*
IJMES - v47 - i4 - Nov 2015 - p861-863 [501+]
Bayer, William - *The Luzern Photograph*
KR - Nov 15 2015 - pNA [51-500]
PW - v262 - i46 - Nov 16 2015 - p58(1) [51-500]
Bayerische Romer - Romische Bayern. Lebensgeschichten aus Vor- und Fruhmoderne
HNet - March 2015 - pNA [501+]
Bayles, Martha - *Through a Screen Darkly: Popular Culture, Public Diplomacy, and Americas Image Abroad*
NWCR - v68 - i3 - Summer 2015 - p161(3) [501+]
Bayless, Julie - *Roar! (Illus. by Bayless, Julie)*
c CH Bwatch - August 2015 - pNA [51-500]
c CH Bwatch - Oct 2015 - pNA [51-500]
c KR - August 1 2015 - pNA [51-500]
Bayless, Martha - *Sin and Filth in Medieval Culture: The Devil in the Latrine*
Med R - Sept 2015 - pNA [501+]
Bayless, Rick - *More Mexican Everyday: Simple, Seasonal, Celebratory*
BL - v111 - i17 - May 1 2015 - p68(1) [51-500]
LJ - v140 - i9 - May 15 2015 - p102(2) [501+]
Baylis, Jonathan - *So Buttons*
PW - v262 - i25 - June 22 2015 - p128(1) [51-500]
Bayly, Christopher Alan - *Recovering Liberties: Indian Thought in the Age of Liberalism and Empire*
JAS - v74 - i3 - August 2015 - p711-722 [501+]
Bayman, Anna - *Thomas Dekker and the Culture of Pamphleteering in Early Modern London*
AHR - v120 - i3 - June 2015 - p1110-1111 [501+]
Ren Q - v68 - i3 - Fall 2015 - p1153-1154 [501+]
Six Ct J - v46 - i1 - Spring 2015 - p128-2 [501+]
Bayme, Eytan - *High Holiday Porn*
KR - May 15 2015 - pNA [501+]
PW - v262 - i20 - May 18 2015 - p75(1) [51-500]
Bayne, Bijan C. - *Elgin Baylor: The Man Who Changed Basketball*
LJ - v140 - i13 - August 1 2015 - p104(1) [51-500]
PW - v262 - i26 - June 29 2015 - p61(1) [51-500]
Baynton-Williams, Ashley - *The Curious Map Book*
NYTBR - Dec 6 2015 - p14(L) [501+]
Bayoumi, Moustafa - *This Muslim American Life: Dispatches from the War on Terror*
KR - June 15 2015 - pNA [501+]
PW - v262 - i26 - June 29 2015 - p56(2) [51-500]
LJ - v140 - i14 - Sept 1 2015 - p123(2) [51-500]
Bayrasli, Elmira - *From the Other Side of the World: Extraordinary Entrepreneurs, Unlikely Places*
BL - v111 - i22 - August 1 2015 - p7(1) [51-500]
KR - June 15 2015 - pNA [501+]
LJ - v140 - i12 - July 1 2015 - p91(2) [51-500]
PW - v262 - i26 - June 29 2015 - p56(1) [51-500]
Baysden, E.T. - *The Rock Jaw Ladies Club: A Memoir of Vietnam, the Sick Crazy One!*
KR - Oct 15 2015 - pNA [501+]
Bazyler, Michael J. - *Forgotten Trials of the Holocaust*
NYRB - v62 - i12 - July 9 2015 - p52(3) [501+]
Beach, Derek - *Process-Tracing Methods: Foundations and Guidelines*
CS - v44 - i5 - Sept 2015 - p634-635 [501+]
Beachy, Robert - *Gay Berlin: Birthplace of a Modern Identity*
G&L Rev W - v22 - i5 - Sept-Oct 2015 - p47(1)

[501+]
    NY - v90 - i45 - Jan 26 2015 - p73 [501+]
Beacon, Eileen Pollack - *The Only Woman in the Room: Why Science is Still a Boys' Club*
    Nature - v525 - i7567 - Sept 3 2015 - p31(1) [51-500]
Beagin, Jen - *Pretend I'm Dead*
    BL - v112 - i4 - Oct 15 2015 - p34(1) [51-500]
    PW - v262 - i34 - August 24 2015 - p55(1) [51-500]
Beahm, George - *The Stephen King Companion: Four Decades of Fear from the Master of Horror, 3d ed. (Illus. by Whelan, Michael)*
    BL - v112 - i2 - Sept 15 2015 - p17(1) [51-500]
    LJ - v140 - i16 - Oct 1 2015 - p78(1) [51-500]
Beail, Linda - *Mad Men and Politics: Nostalgia and the Remaking of Modern America*
    TLS - i5863 - August 14 2015 - p27(1) [51-500]
Beaken, Robert - *Cosmo Lang: Archbishop in War and Crisis*
    HER - v130 - i542 - Feb 2015 - p241(2) [501+]
Beal, Jane - *Translating the Past: Essays on Medieval Literature in Honor of Marijane Osborn*
    Specu - v90 - i4 - Oct 2015 - p1189(1) [501+]
Beal, Rose M. - *Mystery of the Church, People of God: Yves Conger's Total Ecclesiology as a Path to Vatican II*
    Theol St - v76 - i4 - Dec 2015 - p868(2) [501+]
Beale, Fleur - *I am not Esther*
    Magpies - v30 - i3 - July 2015 - pS7(2) [501+]
Beale, G.K. - *Hidden But Now Revealed: A Biblical Theology of Mystery*
    Ch Today - v59 - i1 - Jan-Feb 2015 - p68(1) [501+]
Beales, Sally - *Thackeray's Angel: A Life of Jane Octavia Brookfield 1821-1896*
    TLS - i5861 - July 31 2015 - p9(1) [501+]
Beam, Alex - *American Crucifixion: The Murder of Joseph Smith and the Fate of the Mormon Church*
    CC - v132 - i14 - July 8 2015 - p32(2) [501+]
Beam, Cris - *To the End of June: The Intimate Life of American Foster Care*
    Wom R Bks - v32 - i1 - Jan-Feb 2015 - p10(2) [501+]
Beamer, Kamanamaikalani - *No Makou ka Mana: Liberating the Nation*
    Cont Pac - v27 - i2 - Fall 2015 - p591(3) [501+]
Bean, Jonathan - *This Is My Home, This Is My School (Illus. by Bean, Jonathan)*
    c BL - v112 - i3 - Oct 1 2015 - p84(1) [51-500]
    c HB - v91 - i5 - Sept-Oct 2015 - p75(2) [51-500]
    c KR - August 1 2015 - pNA [51-500]
    c PW - v262 - i29 - July 20 2015 - p188(1) [51-500]
    c SLJ - v61 - i8 - August 2015 - p58(2) [51-500]
Bean, Lydia - *The Politics of Evangelical Identity: Local Churches and Partisan Divides in the United States and Canada*
    J Ch St - v57 - i3 - Summer 2015 - p590-591 [501+]
    JAH - v102 - i2 - Sept 2015 - p632-633 [501+]
Bear, Elizabeth - *Karen Memory*
    MFSF - v128 - i3-4 - March-April 2015 - p73(8) [501+]
Bear, Greg - *Just over the Horizon*
    PW - v262 - i51 - Dec 14 2015 - p64(1) [501+]
    Killing Titan
    BL - v112 - i3 - Oct 1 2015 - p36(1) [51-500]
    Nebula Awards Showcase 2015
    KR - Sept 15 2015 - pNA [51-500]
    War Dogs
    Analog - v135 - i5 - May 2015 - p107(1) [501+]
Bearce, Stephanie - *The Cold War: Secrets, Special Missions, and Hidden Facts about the CIA, KGB, and MI6*
    c CH Bwatch - Oct 2015 - pNA [51-500]
    c KR - June 1 2015 - pNA [51-500]
    The Cold War: Secrets, Special Missions, and Hidden Facts about the CIA, KGB, and MI6
    c BL - v112 - i1 - Sept 1 2015 - p93(2) [51-500]
Beard, Henry - *Spinglish: The Definitive Dictionary of Deliberately Deceptive Language*
    LJ - v140 - i13 - August 1 2015 - p123(1) [51-500]
Beard, Mary - *Laughter in Ancient Rome: On Joking, Tickling, and Cracking Up*
    Class R - v65 - i2 - Oct 2015 - p456-457 [501+]
    JIH - v45 - i4 - Spring 2015 - p571-572 [501+]
    Lon R Bks - v37 - i14 - July 16 2015 - p33(3) [501+]
    SPQR: A History of Ancient Rome
    Atl - v316 - i5 - Dec 2015 - p34(3) [501+]
    CSM - Nov 25 2015 - pNA [501+]
    KR - Oct 1 2015 - pNA [501+]
    NS - v144 - i5286 - Oct 30 2015 - p36(3) [501+]
    NYRB - v62 - i20 - Dec 17 2015 - p26(3) [501+]
    NYT - Nov 18 2015 - pC1(L) [501+]
    NYTBR - Nov 22 2015 - p1(L) [501+]
    Spec - v329 - i9764 - Oct 17 2015 - p42(2) [501+]
    TimHES - i2229 - Nov 12 2015 - p49(1) [501+]
Beard, Philip - *Swing*
    SPBW - May 2015 - pNA [51-500]
Beardsley, David A. - *The Ideal in the West*
    KR - Sept 15 2015 - pNA [51-500]
Beardsley, Doug - *Swimming with Turtles: Travel Narratives, Spirit of Place*
    Can Lit - i224 - Spring 2015 - p108 [501+]
Beasley, Cassie - *Circus Mirandus (Read by Pinchot, Bronson). Audiobook Review*
    c PW - v262 - i30 - July 27 2015 - p62(1) [51-500]
    Circus Mirandus (Illus. by Sudyka, Diana)
    y PW - v262 - i49 - Dec 2 2015 - p74(2) [501+]
    c CCB-B - v69 - i1 - Sept 2015 - p8(1) [51-500]
    c CSM - July 22 2015 - pNA [501+]
    c HB - v91 - i5 - Sept-Oct 2015 - p93(1) [51-500]
    c KR - March 15 2015 - pNA [51-500]
    c NYTBR - June 21 2015 - p17(L) [501+]
    c PW - v262 - i16 - April 20 2015 - p76(1) [51-500]
    c Sch Lib - v63 - i4 - Winter 2015 - p225(1) [51-500]
    c SLJ - v61 - i4 - April 2015 - p144(2) [51-500]
    y VOYA - v38 - i1 - April 2015 - p74(1) [51-500]
Beasley, David - *Douglas MacAgy and the Foundations of Modern Art Curatorship*
    PW - v262 - i37 - Sept 14 2015 - p60(1) [51-500]
    A Life in Red
    KR - July 15 2015 - pNA [501+]
    Without Mercy: The Stunning True Story of Race, Crime, and Corruption in the Deep South
    JSH - v81 - i3 - August 2015 - p766(2) [501+]
Beasley, Edward - *The Victorian Reinvention of Race: New Racisms and the Problem of Grouping in the Human Sciences*
    VS - v57 - i2 - Wntr 2015 - p333(4) [501+]
Beasley, Maya A. - *Opting Out: Losing the Potential of America's Young Black Elite*
    SF - v93 - i3 - March 2015 - pe69 [501+]
Beasley, Sandra - *Count the Waves: Poems*
    PW - v262 - i24 - June 15 2015 - p61(1) [51-500]
Beaton, Kate - *The Princess and the Pony (Illus. by Beaton, Kate)*
    c BL - v111 - i17 - May 1 2015 - p102(1) [51-500]
    c CCB-B - v69 - i1 - Sept 2015 - p8(1) [51-500]
    KR - April 1 2015 - pNA [51-500]
    c Nat Post - v17 - i205 - July 4 2015 - pWP5(1) [501+]
    c PW - v262 - i49 - Dec 2 2015 - p36(2) [51-500]
    c SLJ - v61 - i4 - April 2015 - p188(1) [51-500]
    Step Aside, Pops: A Hark! A Vagrant Collection (Illus. by Beaton, Kate)
    y BL - v112 - i2 - Sept 15 2015 - p51(1) [51-500]
    LJ - v140 - i15 - Sept 15 2015 - p60(3) [51-500]
    NYTBR - Oct 18 2015 - p30(L) [501+]
    PW - v262 - i31 - August 3 2015 - p44(1) [51-500]
    y SLJ - v61 - i11 - Nov 2015 - p124(1) [51-500]
Beaton, Kathryn - *I See Rainbows*
    c SLJ - v61 - i4 - April 2015 - p82(4) [501+]
Beaton, M.C. - *Death of a Chimney Sweep (Read by Malcolm, Graeme). Audiobook Review*
    BL - v111 - i15 - April 1 2015 - p86(1) [51-500]
    Death of a Liar
    BL - v111 - i12 - Feb 15 2015 - p36(1) [51-500]
    RVBW - Oct 2015 - pNA [51-500]
    Death of a Nurse
    KR - Dec 15 2015 - pNA [51-500]
    PW - v262 - i50 - Dec 7 2015 - p70(1) [51-500]
    Death of a Policeman
    RVBW - Feb 2015 - pNA [51-500]
    Dishing the Dirt
    BL - v112 - i1 - Sept 1 2015 - p46(1) [51-500]
    KR - July 15 2015 - pNA [51-500]
    PW - v262 - i28 - July 13 2015 - p46(1) [51-500]
Beaton, Rhodora E. - *Embodied Words, Spoken Signs: Sacramentality and the Word in Rahner and Chauvet*
    Theol St - v76 - i4 - Dec 2015 - p888(2) [501+]
Beattie, Ann - *The State We're In: Maine Stories*
    KR - June 1 2015 - pNA [51-500]
    PW - v262 - i20 - May 18 2015 - p60(1) [51-500]
    BL - v111 - i19-20 - June 1 2015 - p45(1) [51-500]
    NYTBR - Sept 6 2015 - p7(L) [501+]
Beatty, Andrew - *After the Ancestors: An Anthropologist's Story*
    TimHES - i2201 - April 30 2015 - p52-53 [501+]
Beatty, Janna - *Quintessential Style*
    KR - June 1 2015 - pNA [501+]
Beatty, Paul - *The Sellout*
    Nation - v301 - i7-8 - August 17 2015 - p37(1) [501+]
    NY - v91 - i8 - April 13 2015 - p72 [51-500]
    NYTBR - April 12 2015 - p12(L) [501+]
    NYTBR - Dec 13 2015 - p12(L) [501+]
    TLS - i5852 - May 29 2015 - p20(1) [501+]
    KR - Jan 1 2015 - pNA [501+]
    NYT - Feb 27 2015 - pC19(L) [501+]
Beatty, Robert - *Serafina and the Black Cloak (Read by Campbell, Cassandra). Audiobook Review*
    c PW - v262 - i39 - Sept 28 2015 - p87(1) [51-500]
    c SLJ - v61 - i12 - Dec 2015 - p74(2) [51-500]
    Serafina and the Black Cloak
    c BL - v111 - i21 - July 1 2015 - p77(1) [51-500]
    c CCB-B - v69 - i1 - Sept 2015 - p9(1) [51-500]
    c KR - May 1 2015 - pNA [51-500]
    c SLJ - v61 - i6 - June 2015 - p97(1) [51-500]
Beaty, Andrea - *Happy Birthday, Madame Chapeau (Illus. by Roberts, David)*
    c HB Guide - v26 - i1 - Spring 2015 - p21(1) [51-500]
    The Schnoz of Doom (Illus. by Santat, Dan)
    c HB Guide - v26 - i2 - Fall 2015 - p75(1) [51-500]
    c KR - Jan 15 2015 - pNA [51-500]
Beaty, Daniel - *Knock Knock: My Dad's Dream for Me (Illus. by Collier, Bryan)*
    c HB - v91 - i1 - Jan-Feb 2015 - p32(1) [51-500]
Beauchamp, Christopher - *Invented by Law: Alexander Graham Bell and the Patent That Changed America*
    BHR - v89 - i3 - Autumn 2015 - p571(3) [501+]
Beauchamp, Guy - *Social Predation: How Group Living Benefits Predators and Prey*
    QRB - v90 - i2 - June 2015 - p221(1) [501+]
Beauchamp, Wade - *Skintight*
    KR - May 15 2015 - pNA [501+]
Beaudoin, Claire - *Les fabuleuses histoires de madame B.*
    c Res Links - v20 - i5 - June 2015 - p36(1) [51-500]
Beaudoin, Sean - *Welcome Thieves*
    KR - Jan 1 2016 - pNA [51-500]
Beaufrand, M.J. - *The Rise and Fall of the Gallivanters*
    y CCB-B - v68 - i10 - June 2015 - p482(1) [51-500]
    y HB Guide - v26 - i2 - Fall 2015 - p110(2) [51-500]
    y KR - Feb 15 2015 - pNA [51-500]
    y Sch Lib - v63 - i3 - Autumn 2015 - p188(2) [51-500]
    y SLJ - v61 - i2 - Feb 2015 - p97(1) [51-500]
    y VOYA - v37 - i6 - Feb 2015 - p52(2) [501+]
Beaulieu, Bradley P. - *Twelve Kings in Sharakhai*
    PW - v262 - i30 - July 27 2015 - p46(1) [51-500]
Beaulieu, Etienne - *Trop de lumiere pour Samuel Gaska*
    Can Lit - i224 - Spring 2015 - p109 [501+]
Beauman, Ned - *Glow*
    Ent W - i1348-1349 - Jan 30 2015 - p114(1) [51-500]
Beauman, Sally - *The Visitors*
    BL - v111 - i16 - April 15 2015 - p34(1) [501+]
Beaumont, Charles - *Perchance to Dream*
    KR - August 15 2015 - pNA [51-500]
    PW - v262 - i34 - August 24 2015 - p64(1) [51-500]
Beaumont, Holly - *Why Do Monkeys and Other Animals Have Fur?*
    c Sch Lib - v63 - i4 - Winter 2015 - p236(1) [51-500]
Beaumont, Karen - *Crybaby (Illus. by Yelchin, Eugene)*
    c BL - v111 - i22 - August 1 2015 - p71(1) [51-500]
    c HB - v91 - i4 - July-August 2015 - p109(2) [51-500]
    c KR - June 15 2015 - pNA [51-500]
    c SLJ - v61 - i5 - May 2015 - p78(1) [51-500]
    Wild about Us! (Illus. by Stevens, Janet)
    c BL - v111 - i14 - March 15 2015 - p82(1) [51-500]
    c CH Bwatch - May 2015 - pNA [51-500]
Beaumont, Maegan - *Promises to Keep*
    PW - v262 - i26 - June 29 2015 - p49(1) [51-500]
Beaumont, Mark - *Kanye West: God and Monster*
    y BL - v111 - i19-20 - June 1 2015 - p32(1) [51-500]
    LJ - v140 - i11 - June 15 2015 - p91(2) [51-500]
Beaumont, Matthew - *Nightwalking: A Nocturnal History of London*
    TimHES - i2192 - Feb 26 2015 - p48-49 [501+]
Beauregard, Isadora - *Tunnel Vision, A Focused Life*
    KR - May 15 2015 - pNA [501+]

Beauvais, Clementine - *Gargoyles Gone AWOL (Illus. by Horne, Sarah)*
c HB Guide - v26 - i2 - Fall 2015 - p75(1) [51-500]
c KR - March 1 2015 - pNA [51-500]
Sleuth on Skates (Illus. by Horne, Sarah)
c HB - v91 - i1 - Jan-Feb 2015 - p75(1) [51-500]
c HB Guide - v26 - i1 - Spring 2015 - p69(1) [51-500]
Beavan, Colin - *How to Be Alive: A Guide to the Kind of Happiness That Helps the World*
PW - v262 - i47 - Nov 23 2015 - p63(1) [51-500]
Beavis, Paul - *Hello World! (Illus. by Beavis, Paul)*
c KR - July 15 2015 - pNA [51-500]
c Magpies - v30 - i4 - Sept 2015 - pS6(1) [501+]
c SLJ - v61 - i8 - August 2015 - p64(1) [51-500]
Mrs. Mo's Monster
c HB Guide - v26 - i1 - Spring 2015 - p21(1) [51-500]
Bebbington, Anthony - *Subterranean Struggles: New Dynamics of Mining, Oil, and Gas in Latin America*
HAHR - v95 - i3 - August 2015 - p549-551 [501+]
Bebergal, Peter - *Season of the Witch: How the Occult Saved Rock and Roll*
TLS - i5831 - Jan 2 2015 - p25(1) [501+]
Bebris, Carrie - *The Suspicion at Sanditon*
y BL - v111 - i21 - July 1 2015 - p40(1) [51-500]
PW - v262 - i21 - May 25 2015 - p39(1) [51-500]
RVBW - August 2015 - pNA [51-500]
Becher, Debbie - *Private Property and Public Power: Eminent Domain in Philadelphia*
AJS - v121 - i2 - Sept 2015 - p643(3) [501+]
Bechtel, Greg - *Boundary Problems*
Can Lit - i224 - Spring 2015 - p106 [501+]
Bechtold, Lisze - *Buster the Very Shy Dog Finds a Kitten*
c HB Guide - v26 - i2 - Fall 2015 - p58(1) [51-500]
c KR - April 1 2015 - pNA [51-500]
Becirevic, Edina - *Genocide on the Drina River*
Slav R - v74 - i3 - Fall 2015 - p632-634 [501+]
Beck, Andrea Lynn - *Good Morning, Canada (Illus. by Beck, Andrea Lynn)*
c Res Links - v20 - i3 - Feb 2015 - p1(1) [51-500]
Beck, Barbara - *The Future Architect's Handbook*
c CH Bwatch - Jan 2015 - pNA [51-500]
Beck, Carolyn - *One Hungry Heron (Illus. by Patkau, Karen)*
c HB Guide - v26 - i2 - Fall 2015 - p26(1) [51-500]
c Res Links - v20 - i3 - Feb 2015 - p2(1) [51-500]
That Squeak (Illus. by Thisdale, Francois)
c CH Bwatch - Oct 2015 - pNA [51-500]
Beck, Derek W. - *Igniting the American Revolution: 1773-1775*
KR - July 15 2015 - pNA [51-500]
LJ - v140 - i14 - Sept 1 2015 - p116(1) [51-500]
Beck, Ian - *The Disappearance of Tom Pile*
c Sch Lib - v63 - i3 - Autumn 2015 - p162(1) [51-500]
Beck, Jamie - *Worth the Trouble*
PW - v262 - i52 - Dec 21 2015 - p138(2) [51-500]
Beck, Jane C. - *Daisy Turner's Kin: An African American Family Saga*
KR - April 15 2015 - pNA [501+]
BL - v111 - i21 - July 1 2015 - p18(1) [51-500]
PW - v262 - i17 - April 27 2015 - p61(1) [51-500]
Beck, Jennifer - *The Bantam and the Soldier (Illus. by Belton, Robyn)*
Magpies - v30 - i4 - Sept 2015 - pS4(1) [501+]
Beck, K.K. - *Tipping the Valet*
KR - July 1 2015 - pNA [51-500]
PW - v262 - i27 - July 6 2015 - p48(2) [51-500]
Beck, Paul N. - *Columns of Vengeance: Soldiers, Sioux, and the Punitive Expeditions, 1863-1864*
J Mil H - v79 - i1 - Jan 2015 - p216-218 [501+]
Beck, Richard - *We Believe the Children: A Moral Panic in the 1980s*
HM - v331 - i1986 - Nov 2015 - p89(6) [501+]
KR - June 1 2015 - pNA [501+]
LJ - v140 - i9 - May 15 2015 - p98(1) [51-500]
NYT - August 7 2015 - pC23(L) [501+]
NYTBR - August 23 2015 - p18(L) [501+]
PW - v262 - i23 - June 8 2015 - p52(1) [51-500]
Beck, W.H. - *Glow: Animals with Their Own Night-Lights (Illus. by Beck, W.H.)*
c BL - v112 - i7 - Dec 1 2015 - p51(1) [51-500]
Glow: Animals with Their Own Night-Lights
c KR - Oct 1 2015 - pNA [51-500]
Glow: Animals with Their Own Night-Lights (Illus. by Beck, W.H.)
c PW - v262 - i46 - Nov 16 2015 - p75(1) [501+]
Malcolm under the Stars (Illus. by Lies, Brian)
c CH Bwatch - Sept 2015 - pNA [51-500]
c KR - May 15 2015 - pNA [51-500]
c SLJ - v61 - i8 - August 2015 - p83(1) [51-500]
Becker, Aaron - *Quest (Illus. by Becker, Aaron)*
c HB Guide - v26 - i1 - Spring 2015 - p21(1) [51-500]
Becker, Adam H. - *Revival and Awakening: American Evangelical Missionaries in Iran and the Origins of Assyrian Nationalism*
JAAR - v83 - i2 - June 2015 - pNA [501+]
Becker, Anne - *9/11 als Bildereignis: Zur Visuellen Bewaltigung des Anschlags*
HNet - March 2015 - pNA [501+]
Becker, Bonny - *Cloud Country (Illus. by Klocek, Noah)*
c KR - July 15 2015 - pNA [51-500]
c PW - v262 - i34 - August 24 2015 - p78(1) [51-500]
c SLJ - v61 - i11 - Nov 2015 - p79(1) [51-500]
A Library Book for Bear (Illus. by Denton, Kady MacDonald)
c HB Guide - v26 - i1 - Spring 2015 - p21(1) [51-500]
Becker, Catherine - *Shifting Stones, Shaping the Past: Sculpture from the Buddhist Stupas of Andhra Pradesh*
HNet - August 2015 - pNA [501+]
Becker, Devin - *Shame - Shame: Poems*
BL - v111 - i15 - April 1 2015 - p22(1) [51-500]
Becker, Helaine - *Let Sleeping Dogs Lie*
c KR - Dec 1 2015 - pNA [51-500]
Becker, Howard S. - *What About Mozart? What About Murder? Reasoning from Cases*
CS - v44 - i4 - July 2015 - p472-475 [501+]
Becker, Jeffrey A. - *Roman Republican Villas: Architecture, Context, and Ideology*
Class R - v65 - i2 - Oct 2015 - p524-526 [501+]
Becker, Jo - *Forcing the Spring: Inside the Fight for Marriage Equality*
NYTBR - June 7 2015 - p36(L) [501+]
Becker, Jurgen - *Cultivating Chaos: How to Enrich Landscapes with Self-Seeding Plants*
PW - v262 - i27 - July 6 2015 - p64(1) [51-500]
Becker, Mary Louise - *The All-India Muslim League, 1906-1947: A Study of Leadership in the Evolution of a Nation*
HER - v130 - i545 - August 2015 - p1048(3) [501+]
HNet - April 2015 - pNA [501+]
Becker, Peggy Daniels - *Japanese-American Internment during World War II*
y VOYA - v38 - i3 - August 2015 - p88(2) [51-500]
Becker-Phelps, Leslie - *Love: The Psychology of Attraction*
PW - v262 - i51 - Dec 14 2015 - p76(2) [501+]
Becker, Shari - *The Stellow Project (Read by Rudd, Kate). Audiobook Review*
y SLJ - v61 - i11 - Nov 2015 - p72(1) [51-500]
The Stellow Project
y BL - v111 - i19-20 - June 1 2015 - p102(1) [51-500]
y HB Guide - v26 - i2 - Fall 2015 - p111(1) [51-500]
y KR - April 15 2015 - pNA [51-500]
y SLJ - v61 - i5 - May 2015 - p117(1) [51-500]
y VOYA - v38 - i2 - June 2015 - p54(1) [51-500]
Becker, Suzy - *Kate the Great: Except When She's Not (Illus. by Becker, Suzy)*
c HB Guide - v26 - i1 - Spring 2015 - p69(1) [51-500]
Becker, Wolfgang - *Die gregorianischen Gesange des Essener Liber ordinarius: Transkription und vergleichende Untersuchungen zu den Gesangen aus den Handschriften Essen Hs. 19 und Dusseldorf Ms. C 47*
HNet - April 2015 - pNA [501+]
Beckerman, Hannah - *The Dead Wife's Handbook*
BL - v111 - i9-10 - Jan 1 2015 - p36(1) [51-500]
Beckert, Sven - *Empire of Cotton: A Global History (Read by Frangione, Jim). Audiobook Review*
LJ - v140 - i5 - March 15 2015 - p72(2) [51-500]
Empire of Cotton: A Global History
NY - v91 - i7 - April 6 2015 - p81 [51-500]
Am St - v54 - i2 - Summer 2015 - p85-94 [501+]
Econ - v414 - i8919 - Jan 3 2015 - p68(US) [501+]
NYTBR - Jan 4 2015 - p15(L) [501+]
NYTBR - Dec 13 2015 - p12(L) [501+]
NYTBR - Dec 27 2015 - p24(L) [501+]
Empire of Cotton: A New History of Global Capitalism
HT - v65 - i5 - May 2015 - p60(2) [501+]
Spec - v327 - i9724 - Jan 10 2015 - p29(2) [501+]
TLS - i5845 - April 10 2015 - p3(2) [501+]
Beckett, Andy - *Promised You a Miracle: UK 80-82*
NS - v144 - i5279 - Sept 11 2015 - p38(3) [501+]
When the Lights Went Out: Britain in the Seventies
TimHES - i2222 - Sept 24 2015 - p41(1) [501+]
Beckett, Bernard - *Lullaby*
y Magpies - v30 - i3 - July 2015 - p39(1) [501+]
Beckett, Chris - *Mother of Eden*
KR - March 1 2015 - pNA [501+]
PW - v262 - i13 - March 30 2015 - p59(1) [51-500]
y SLJ - v61 - i12 - Dec 2015 - p131(1) [51-500]
Beckett, Francis - *Blair Inc.: The Man behind the Mask*
NS - v144 - i5254 - March 20 2015 - p47(1) [501+]
Beckett, Samuel - *The Collected Poems*
HR - v68 - i1 - Spring 2015 - p133-140 [501+]
Echo's Bones
HR - v67 - i4 - Wntr 2015 - p685-692 [501+]
The Letters of Samuel Beckett, vol. 3: 1957-1965
HR - v68 - i1 - Spring 2015 - p133-140 [501+]
Beckles, Hillary McD. - *Britain's Black Debt: Reparations for Caribbean Slavery and Genocide*
JTWS - v32 - i1 - Spring 2015 - p351(2) [501+]
Beckman, John - *American Fun: Four Centuries of Joyous Revolt*
SAH - v4 - i2 - Dec 15 2015 - p303-308 [501+]
Beckman, Robert - *Beyond Territorial Disputes in the South China Sea: Legal Frameworks for the Joint Development of Hydrocarbon Resources*
Pac A - v88 - i1 - March 2015 - p176 [501+]
Beckstrand, Jennifer - *Huckleberry Hearts*
BL - v112 - i6 - Nov 15 2015 - p17(1) [51-500]
Beckstrand, Karl - *Ma MacDonald Flees the Farm (Illus. by Mark, Alycia)*
c CH Bwatch - Feb 2015 - pNA [51-500]
Beckstrom, Matthew - *Protecting Patron Privacy: Safe Practices for Public Computers*
LJ - v140 - i17 - Oct 15 2015 - p101(1) [51-500]
Teach Lib - v43 - i1 - Oct 2015 - p41(3) [501+]
Beckwith, Christopher I. - *Warriors of the Cloisters: The Central Asian Origins of Science in the Medieval World*
Specu - v90 - i3 - July 2015 - p771-774 [501+]
Beckwith, Naomi - *Lynette Yiadom-Boakye*
NYTBR - June 28 2015 - p28(L) [501+]
Bedell, J.M. - *So, You Want to Work with the Ancient and Recent Dead? Unearthing Careers from Paleontology to Forensic Science*
c BL - v112 - i7 - Dec 1 2015 - p51(1) [51-500]
y SLJ - v61 - i12 - Dec 2015 - p142(1) [51-500]
Bedford, Martyn - *Never Ending*
y Teach Lib - v42 - i3 - Feb 2015 - p43(1) [51-500]
Bedier, Joseph - *The Romance of Tristan and Iseut*
Specu - v90 - i1 - Jan 2015 - p207-209 [501+]
Bednarek, Grazyna Anna - *Polish vs. American Courtroom Discourse: Inquisitorial and Adversarial Procedures of Witness Examination in Criminal Trials*
Lang Soc - v44 - i4 - Sept 2015 - p596-597 [501+]
Bedoyere, Camilla de la - *Creatures of the Night*
BL - v111 - i14 - March 15 2015 - p59(1) [51-500]
Bedrick, Claudia - *Mister Horizontal & Miss Vertical (Illus. by Zagnoli, Olimpia)*
c HB Guide - v26 - i1 - Spring 2015 - p43(1) [51-500]
BeDuhn, Jason David - *Augustine's Manichean Dilemma, vol. 2: Making a "Catholic" Self, 388-401 C.E.*
JR - v95 - i3 - July 2015 - p401(3) [501+]
Bee, Sarah - *The Yes (Illus. by Kitamura, Satoshi)*
c HB Guide - v26 - i2 - Fall 2015 - p26(1) [51-500]
Bee, William - *Migloo's Day (Illus. by Bee, William)*
c KR - Jan 15 2015 - pNA [51-500]
c Sch Lib - v63 - i3 - Autumn 2015 - p153(1) [51-500]
Stanley the Builder (Illus. by Bee, William)
c HB Guide - v26 - i1 - Spring 2015 - p6(1) [51-500]
c Sch Lib - v63 - i2 - Summer 2015 - p89(1) [51-500]
Stanley the Farmer (Illus. by Bee, William)
c CH Bwatch - April 2015 - pNA [51-500]
c HB Guide - v26 - i2 - Fall 2015 - p6(1) [51-500]
c Sch Lib - v63 - i2 - Summer 2015 - p89(1) [51-500]
SLJ - v61 - i2 - Feb 2015 - p61(1) [51-500]
Stanley's Cafe (Illus. by Bee, William)
c Sch Lib - v63 - i2 - Summer 2015 - p89(1) [51-500]
Stanley's Diner (Illus. by Bee, William)
c SLJ - v61 - i9 - Sept 2015 - p113(1) [51-500]
Stanley's Garage (Illus. by Bee, William)
c HB Guide - v26 - i1 - Spring 2015 - p6(1) [51-500]
c Sch Lib - v63 - i2 - Summer 2015 - p89(1) [51-500]
Worst in Show (Illus. by Hindley, Kate)
c CCB-B - v68 - i8 - April 2015 - p389(1) [51-500]
c HB Guide - v26 - i2 - Fall 2015 - p26(1) [51-500]
c Sch Lib - v63 - i1 - Spring 2015 - p25(1) [51-500]
Bee, Yann Le - *Danny (Illus. by Bee, Yann Le)*
c BL - v111 - i15 - April 1 2015 - p82(1) [51-500]

Beebe, Kathryne - *Pilgrim and Preacher: The Audiences and Observant Spirituality of Friar Felix Fabri, 1437/8-1502*
    Med R - June 2015 - pNA [501+]
Beebe, Rose Marie - *Junipero Serra: California, Indians, and the Transformation of a Missionary*
    AM - v213 - i5 - August 31 2015 - p34(3) [501+]
    Roundup M - v23 - i1 - Oct 2015 - p32(1) [501+]
Beebee, Thomas Oliver - *German Literature as World Literature*
    GSR - v38 - i3 - Oct 2015 - p654-657 [501+]
Beechum, Drew - *Experimental Homebrewing: Mad Science in the Pursuit of Great Beer*
    LJ - v140 - i2 - Feb 1 2015 - p103(1) [51-500]
Beecroft, Alex - *Blue-Eyed Stranger*
    PW - v262 - i9 - March 2 2015 - p71(1) [51-500]
Beecroft, Arthur - *Gallipoli: A Soldier's Story*
    Lon R Bks - v37 - i10 - May 21 2015 - p39(3) [501+]
Beeman, Richard - *Our Lives, Our Fortunes and Our Sacred Honor: The Forging of American Independence*
    Historian - v77 - i2 - Summer 2015 - p320(2) [501+]
Beene, Alex Anthony - *Letters from a Southern Mother (Illus. by Martin, Danny)*
    c CH Bwatch - March 2015 - pNA [501+]
Beer, Jeremy - *The Philanthropic Revolution: An Alternative History of American Charity*
    Soc - v52 - i5 - Oct 2015 - p498(1) [501+]
Beer, Julie - *5,000 Awesome Facts (about Everything!) 2*
    c HB Guide - v26 - i2 - Fall 2015 - p146(1) [51-500]
Beer, Nicky - *The Octopus Game*
    BL - v111 - i12 - Feb 15 2015 - p21(2) [51-500]
    PW - v262 - i3 - Jan 19 2015 - p59(2) [51-500]
Beerbohm, Max - *The Prince of Minor Writers: The Selected Essays of Max Beerbohm*
    KR - March 15 2015 - pNA [51-500]
    NYT - July 16 2015 - pC1(L) [501+]
    PW - v262 - i15 - April 13 2015 - p69(2) [51-500]
Beernink, Joe - *Nowhere Wild*
    y Res Links - v21 - i1 - Oct 2015 - p29(1) [501+]
Beers, Kurt - *100 Painters of Tomorrow*
    LJ - v140 - i2 - Feb 1 2015 - p79(1) [51-500]
Beers, Kylene - *Notice and Note: Strategies for Close Reading*
    RVBW - July 2015 - pNA [501+]
Beeson, Mark - *China's Regional Relations: Evolving Foreign Policy Dynamics*
    Pac A - v88 - i2 - June 2015 - p281 [501+]
Beestermoller, Gerhard - *Friedensethik im fruhen Mittalalter: Theologie zwischen Kritik und Legitimation von Gewalt*
    Theol St - v76 - i4 - Dec 2015 - p883(2) [501+]
Beetz, Michael - *Kraft der Symbole: Wie Wir Uns Von Der Gesellschaft Leiten Lassen und Dabei die Wirklichkeit Selbst Mitgestalten*
    HNet - July 2015 - pNA [501+]
Beevor, Antony - *Ardennes 1944: Hitler's Last Gamble*
    Spec - v328 - i9742 - May 16 2015 - p34(2) [501+]
    TimHES - i2207 - June 11 2015 - p53(1) [501+]
Ardennes 1944: The Battle of the Bulge
    CSM - Nov 3 2015 - pNA [501+]
    KR - Sept 15 2015 - pNA [501+]
    LJ - v140 - i16 - Oct 1 2015 - p91(2) [51-500]
    NYT - Dec 28 2015 - pC4(L) [501+]
    PW - v262 - i38 - Sept 21 2015 - p63(1) [51-500]
    TLS - i5858 - July 10 2015 - p24(1) [501+]
Ardenness 1944: The Battle of the Bulge
    NYTBR - Dec 13 2015 - p28(L) [501+]
Befeler, Mike - *Murder on the Switzerland Trail*
    KR - Sept 1 2015 - pNA [501+]
    PW - v262 - i38 - Sept 21 2015 - p56(1) [51-500]
Begbie, Jeremy - *Music, Modernity, and God: Essays in Listening*
    Bks & Cult - v21 - i1 - Jan-Feb 2015 - p27(2) [501+]
Begley, Adam - *Updike*
    Comw - v142 - i1 - Jan 9 2015 - p13(6) [501+]
    Sew R - v123 - i2 - Spring 2015 - pXXVII-XXIX [501+]
    Soc - v52 - i1 - Feb 2015 - p93(4) [501+]
    NYTBR - May 24 2015 - p28(L) [501+]
Begley, Louis - *Killer, Come Hither*
    BL - v111 - i9-10 - Jan 1 2015 - p47(1) [51-500]
    KR - Feb 1 2015 - pNA [51-500]
    PW - v262 - i7 - Feb 16 2015 - p159(2) [51-500]
    RVBW - May 2015 - pNA [501+]
Begot, Danielle - *Guide de la Recherche en Histoire Antillaise et Guyanaise*
    HNet - March 2015 - pNA [501+]

Begun, David R. - *The Real Planet of the Apes: A New Story of Human Origins*
    KR - Sept 1 2015 - pNA [501+]
    LJ - v140 - i19 - Nov 15 2015 - p104(1) [51-500]
    NYRB - v62 - i18 - Nov 19 2015 - p43(3) [501+]
    PW - v262 - i34 - August 24 2015 - p70(2) [51-500]
Begun, Gabrielle - *Freddy the Penny (Illus. by Genelza, Novella)*
    c CH Bwatch - Feb 2015 - pNA [51-500]
    c CH Bwatch - March 2015 - pNA [51-500]
Beha, Eileen - *The Secrets of Eastcliff-by-the-Sea*
    c HB Guide - v26 - i1 - Spring 2015 - p70(1) [51-500]
Behal, Rana Partap - *One Hundred Years of Servitude: Political Economy of Tea Plantations in Colonial Assam*
    HNet - July 2015 - pNA [501+]
Behdad, Ali - *Photography's Orientalisms: New Essays on Colonial Representation*
    HNet - May 2015 - pNA [501+]
Behen, Linda D. - *Recharge Your Library Programs with Pop Culture and Technology: Connect with Today's Teens*
    LQ - v85 - i2 - April 2015 - p206(3) [501+]
Behera, Navnita Chadha - *Political Science, vol. 4: India Engages the World*
    Pac A - v88 - i1 - March 2015 - p142 [501+]
Behnke, Alison Marie - *Up for Sale: Human Trafficking and Modern Slavery*
    y HB Guide - v26 - i1 - Spring 2015 - p140(1) [51-500]
Behr, John - *Irenaeus of Lyons: Identifying Christianity*
    CH - v84 - i1 - March 2015 - p225(3) [501+]
Behre, Mary - *Energized*
    PW - v262 - i26 - June 29 2015 - p53(1) [51-500]
Behrendt, Anja - *Mit Zitaten kommunizieren: Untersuchungen zur Zitierweise in der Korrespondenz des Marcus Tullius Cicero*
    Class R - v65 - i2 - Oct 2015 - p432-434 [501+]
Behrens, Peter - *Carry Me*
    KR - Dec 15 2015 - pNA [51-500]
    PW - v262 - i52 - Dec 21 2015 - p124(2) [51-500]
Behrman, Samuel Nathaniel - *Duveen: The Story of the Most Spectacular Art Dealer of All Time*
    TLS - i5838 - Feb 20 2015 - p23(1) [501+]
Beigel, Fernanda - *The Politics of Academic Autonomy in Latin America*
    CS - v44 - i3 - May 2015 - p305-314 [501+]
Beihammer, Alexander - *Court Ceremonies and Rituals of Power in Byzantium and the Medieval Mediterranean: Comparative Perspectives*
    Specu - v90 - i2 - April 2015 - p498-499 [501+]
Beikmann, Randy - *Physics for Gearheads: An Introduction to Vehicle Dynamics, Energy, and Power - with Examples from Motorsports*
    Sci Teach - v82 - i6 - Sept 2015 - p73 [51-500]
Beil, Michael D. - *Lantern Sam and the Blue Streak Bandits*
    c BL - v111 - i17 - May 1 2015 - p40(1) [51-500]
Beilein, Joseph M., Jr. - *The Civil War Guerilla: Unfolding the Black Flag in History, Memory, and Myth*
    J Mil H - v79 - i3 - July 2015 - p835-836 [501+]
Beilenson, Evelyn - *The Zoo Is Closed Today!: Until Further Notice (Illus. by Kennedy, Arme)*
    c HB Guide - v26 - i1 - Spring 2015 - p22(1) [51-500]
Beiser, Frederick - *Diotima's Children: German Aesthetic Rationalism from Leibniz to Lessing*
    HT - v65 - i10 - Oct 2015 - p56(2) [501+]
The Fate of Reason
    HT - v65 - i10 - Oct 2015 - p56(2) [501+]
Bekker-Nielsen, Tonnes - *Space, Place and Identity in Northern Anatolia*
    Class R - v65 - i2 - Oct 2015 - p529-531 [501+]
Bekoff, Marc - *Ignoring Nature No More: The Case for Compassionate Conservation*
    QRB - v90 - i1 - March 2015 - p86(2) [501+]
Belchem, John - *Before the Windrush: Race Relations in Twentieth-Century Liverpool*
    AHR - v120 - i2 - April 2015 - p721-722 [501+]
    HER - v130 - i545 - August 2015 - p1050(2) [501+]
Belcher, R.S. - *Nightwise*
    BL - v111 - i21 - July 1 2015 - p47(1) [51-500]
    KR - June 15 2015 - pNA [51-500]
    PW - v262 - i19 - May 11 2015 - p40(1) [51-500]
Belcher, W.B. - *Lay Down Your Weary Tune*
    BL - v112 - i4 - Oct 15 2015 - p33(1) [51-500]
    KR - Nov 1 2015 - pNA [51-500]
    LJ - v140 - i20 - Dec 1 2015 - p88(1) [51-500]
Belden, Chris - *Shriver*
    KR - July 15 2015 - pNA [51-500]

Belford, Bibi - *Canned and Crushed*
    c BL - v111 - i12 - Feb 15 2015 - p77(1) [51-500]
    c KR - Jan 15 2015 - pNA [51-500]
    c SLJ - v61 - i5 - May 2015 - p100(2) [51-500]
    y VOYA - v38 - i1 - April 2015 - p54(1) [51-500]
Belfoure, Charles - *House of Thieves*
    BL - v111 - i22 - August 1 2015 - p40(1) [51-500]
    KR - July 15 2015 - pNA [501+]
    LJ - v140 - i11 - June 15 2015 - p71(1) [51-500]
    PW - v262 - i22 - June 1 2015 - p38(1) [51-500]
Belgiojoso, Ricciarda - *Constructing Urban Space with Sounds and Music*
    GR - v105 - i1 - Jan 2015 - p126(2) [501+]
Belieu, Erin - *Slant Six*
    NYTBR - March 1 2015 - p30(L) [501+]
Belina-Johnson, Anastasia - *A Musician Divided: Andre Tchaikowsky in His Own Words*
    MT - v156 - i1930 - Spring 2015 - p111-114 [501+]
Bell, Adrian R. - *The Soldier in Later Medieval England*
    AHR - v120 - i1 - Feb 2015 - p315(1) [501+]
    HER - v130 - i542 - Feb 2015 - p171(2) [501+]
Bell, Alex - *Frozen Charlotte*
    y Sch Lib - v63 - i2 - Summer 2015 - p124(1) [51-500]
Bell, Anthea - *The Flying Classroom (Illus. by Trier, Walter)*
    SLJ - v61 - i4 - April 2015 - p146(2) [51-500]
Ice Cold
    PW - v262 - i16 - April 20 2015 - p55(1) [51-500]
Krabat & the Sorcerer's Mill
    y HB Guide - v26 - i1 - Spring 2015 - p90(1) [51-500]
The Pied Piper of Hamelin (Illus. by Zwerger, Lisbeth)
    c HB Guide - v26 - i1 - Spring 2015 - p145(1) [51-500]
Vasilisa the Beautiful (Illus. by Morgunova, Anna)
    c KR - Dec 15 2015 - pNA [51-500]
    c NYTBR - Nov 8 2015 - p24(L) [501+]
Bell, Cathleen Davitt - *I Remember You (Read by Rankin, Emily). Audiobook Review*
    y SLJ - v61 - i5 - May 2015 - p70(1) [51-500]
I Remember You
    y BL - v111 - i9-10 - Jan 1 2015 - p94(1) [51-500]
    y CCB-B - v68 - i8 - April 2015 - p389(2) [51-500]
    y CH Bwatch - April 2015 - pNA [51-500]
    y HB Guide - v26 - i2 - Fall 2015 - p111(1) [51-500]
Bell, Cece - *Chuck and Woodchuck (Illus. by Bell, Cece)*
    c KR - Dec 15 2015 - pNA [51-500]
El Deafo (Illus. by Bell, Cece)
    c HB Guide - v26 - i1 - Spring 2015 - p191(1) [51-500]
    c SLJ - v61 - i12 - Dec 2015 - p64(4) [51-500]
I Yam a Donkey! (Illus. by Bell, Cece)
    c CCB-B - v69 - i1 - Sept 2015 - p9(1) [51-500]
    c CH Bwatch - July 2015 - pNA [51-500]
    c HB - v91 - i3 - May-June 2015 - p79(1) [51-500]
    c HB Guide - v26 - i2 - Fall 2015 - p26(1) [51-500]
    c KR - April 1 2015 - pNA [51-500]
    c PW - v262 - i49 - Dec 2 2015 - p35(1) [51-500]
    c SLJ - v61 - i5 - May 2015 - p82(1) [51-500]
    c PW - v262 - i15 - April 13 2015 - p80(1) [51-500]
Bell, Daniel A. - *The China Model: Political Meritocracy and the Limits of Democracy*
    Nat R - v67 - i15 - August 24 2015 - p44 [501+]
    Soc - v52 - i5 - Oct 2015 - p498(1) [501+]
    TimHES - i2214 - July 30 2015 - p50-50 [501+]
Bell, David - *Somebody I Used to Know*
    PW - v262 - i21 - May 25 2015 - p36(1) [51-500]
Bell, Davina - *The Underwater Fancy Dress Parade (Illus. by Colpoys, Allison)*
    c Sch Lib - v63 - i2 - Summer 2015 - p89(1) [51-500]
Bell, Dawn M. - *Wife of the Deceased: A Memoir of Love, Loss, and Learning to Live Again*
    SPBW - June 2015 - pNA [51-500]
Bell, Gertrude - *A Woman in Arabia: The Writings of the Queen of the Desert*
    KR - June 1 2015 - pNA [51-500]
    LJ - v140 - i11 - June 15 2015 - p94(1) [51-500]
    PW - v262 - i22 - June 1 2015 - p54(1) [51-500]
Bell, James B. - *Empire, Religion and Revolution in Early Virginia, 1607-1786*
    HER - v130 - i544 - June 2015 - p751(3) [501+]
Bell, Jared - *Piri's Big All Black Dream (Illus. by Diaz, Jimmy)*
    y Magpies - v30 - i3 - July 2015 - pS5(1) [51-500]
Bell, Jeannine - *Hate Thy Neighbor: Move-In Violence and the Persistence of Racial Segregation in American Housing*
    AJS - v120 - i6 - May 2015 - p1859(3) [501+]

Bell, Jeremy - *Plato's Animals: Gadflies, Horses, Swans, and Other Philosophical Beasts*
J Phil - v112 - i5 - May 2015 - p282(1) [501+]

Bell, Jim - *The Interstellar Age: Inside the Forty-Year Voyager Mission.*
LJ - v140 - i2 - Feb 1 2015 - p104(2) [51-500]
PW - v262 - i3 - Jan 19 2015 - p71(1) [51-500]

Bell, Jonathan - *Making Sense of American Liberalism*
J Am St - v49 - i1 - Feb 2015 - p216-219 [501+]

Bell, Joshua A. - *Recreating First Contact: Expeditions, Anthropology, and Popular Culture*
Isis - v106 - i2 - June 2015 - p495(2) [501+]

Bell, Joyce M. - *The Black Power Movement and American Social Work*
AJS - v121 - i2 - Sept 2015 - p640(4) [501+]
CS - v44 - i6 - Nov 2015 - p774-775 [501+]

Bell, Julian - *Van Gogh: A Power Seething*
Lon R Bks - v37 - i15 - July 30 2015 - p7(2) [501+]
NYRB - v62 - i2 - Feb 5 2015 - p24(2) [501+]
NYTBR - Jan 25 2015 - p13(L) [501+]

Bell, Lisa - *Autumn: Leaves Fall From the Trees! (Illus. by Brooks, Emily)*
c CH Bwatch - Oct 2015 - pNA [51-500]

Bell, Lucy - *Do Your Ears Hang Low? (Illus. by Doss, Andrea)*
c CH Bwatch - April 2015 - pNA [51-500]
Miss Mary Mack
c KR - July 1 2015 - pNA [51-500]
A Sailor Went to Sea, Sea, Sea (Illus. by Pearse, Asha)
c CH Bwatch - June 2015 - pNA [51-500]

Bell, Marc - *Stroppy (Illus. by Bell, Marc)*
BL - v111 - i22 - August 1 2015 - p46(2) [51-500]

Bell, Mary Ann - *School Librarians and the Technology Department: A Practical Guide for Successful Collaboration*
LQ - v85 - i1 - Jan 2015 - p112(2) [501+]

Bell, Matt - *Scrapper*
BL - v112 - i1 - Sept 1 2015 - p49(1) [51-500]
LJ - v140 - i14 - Sept 1 2015 - p89(1) [51-500]
NYTBR - Sept 20 2015 - p23(L) [501+]
PW - v262 - i30 - July 27 2015 - p38(1) [51-500]

Bell, Nicholas R. - *A Measure of the Earth: The Cole-Ware Collection of American Baskets*
WestFolk - v74 - i2 - Spring 2015 - p215-218 [501+]
Nation Building: Craft and Contemporary American Culture
Am Craft - v75 - i6 - Dec 2015 - p26(1) [501+]

Bell, Reginald, Jr. - *Love: From the Big Screen to My Life Scene*
KR - June 1 2015 - pNA [501+]

Bell, Samantha - *Amazing Reptiles Series*
c HB Guide - v26 - i1 - Spring 2015 - p159(1) [51-500]

Bell, Samantha S. - *Ready for Military Action*
c HB Guide - v26 - i2 - Fall 2015 - p185(1) [51-500]

Bell-Scott, Patricia - *The Firebrand and the First Lady: Portrait of a Friendship: Pauli Murray, Eleanor Roosevelt, and the Struggle for Social Justice*
KR - Nov 15 2015 - pNA [501+]
PW - v262 - i50 - Dec 7 2015 - p80(1) [51-500]

Bell, Shannon Elizabeth - *Our Roots Run Deep as Ironweed: Appalachian Women and the Fight for Environmental Justice*
HNet - March 2015 - pNA [501+]
JSH - v81 - i2 - May 2015 - p529(2) [501+]

Bell, Suzanne S. - *Librarian's Guide to Online Searching: Cultivating Database Skills for Research and Instruction, 4th ed.*
LJ - v140 - i8 - May 1 2015 - p84(1) [501+]
VOYA - v38 - i2 - June 2015 - p90(1) [501+]

Bell, Taylor - *Dirty Rush*
y BL - v111 - i9-10 - Jan 1 2015 - p36(1) [51-500]

Bell, Ted - *The Patriot*
BL - v111 - i22 - August 1 2015 - p36(1) [51-500]
KR - August 1 2015 - pNA [51-500]
PW - v262 - i31 - August 3 2015 - p36(1) [51-500]

Bell, William - *Julian*
y Res Links - v20 - i4 - April 2015 - p23(1) [51-500]

Bellamy, David - *David Bellamy's Winter Landscapes in Watercolour*
BL - v111 - i9-10 - Jan 1 2015 - p30(1) [51-500]

Bellamy, Dodie - *When the Sick Rule the World*
PW - v262 - i31 - August 3 2015 - p49(1) [51-500]

Bellan, Monique - *Dismember Remember: Das Anatomische Theater von Lina Saneh und Rabih Mroue*
HNet - June 2015 - pNA [501+]

Bellany, Alistair - *The Murder of King James I*
Spec - v329 - i9771 - Dec 5 2015 - p49(2) [501+]

Belleau, Heidi - *Dead Ringer*
y BL - v112 - i2 - Sept 15 2015 - p40(1) [51-500]
PW - v262 - i34 - August 24 2015 - p67(1) [51-500]

Belles, Nita - *In Our Backyard: Human Trafficking in America and What We Can Do to Stop It (Read by Zanzarella, Nicol). Audiobook Review*
LJ - v140 - i16 - Oct 1 2015 - p44(1) [51-500]

Bellet, Annie - *Justice Calling*
MFSF - v128 - i3-4 - March-April 2015 - p62(3) [501+]
Murder of Crows
MFSF - v128 - i3-4 - March-April 2015 - p62(3) [501+]
Pack of Lies
MFSF - v128 - i3-4 - March-April 2015 - p62(3) [501+]

Belli, Meriam N. - *An Incurable Past: Nasser's Egypt Then and Now*
AHR - v120 - i1 - Feb 2015 - p369-370 [501+]

Bellin, Joshua David - *Survival Colony 9*
y HB Guide - v26 - i1 - Spring 2015 - p100(1) [51-500]

Bellinger, Vanya Eftimova - *Marie von Clausewitz: The Woman Behind the Making of On War*
LJ - v140 - i17 - Oct 15 2015 - p95(1) [51-500]

Bellingham, Brenda - *Les princesses ne portent pas de jeans (Illus. by Franson, Leanne)*
c Res Links - v21 - i1 - Oct 2015 - p48(1) [51-500]
Princesses Don't Wear Jeans (Illus. by Franson, Leanne)
c Res Links - v21 - i1 - Oct 2015 - p13(1) [51-500]

Belliveau, Elisabeth - *One Year in America*
BL - v111 - i9-10 - Jan 1 2015 - p62(1) [51-500]

Bellow, Saul - *Saul Bellow: Novels, 1944-1953*
HR - v68 - i1 - Spring 2015 - p158-166 [501+]
Saul Bellow: Novels, 1956-1964
HR - v68 - i1 - Spring 2015 - p158-166 [501+]
Saul Bellow: Novels, 1970-1982
HR - v68 - i1 - Spring 2015 - p158-166 [501+]
Saul Bellow: Novels, 1984-2000
HR - v68 - i1 - Spring 2015 - p158-166 [501+]
There Is Simply Too Much to Think About: Collected Nonfiction
AM - v212 - i20 - June 22 2015 - p31(3) [501+]
BL - v111 - i14 - March 15 2015 - p40(1) [51-500]
HM - v330 - i1980 - May 2015 - p85(6) [501+]
Nation - v301 - i13-14 - Sept 28 2015 - p39(3) [501+]
NYRB - v62 - i10 - June 4 2015 - p10(4) [501+]
NYT - March 25 2015 - pC1(L) [501+]
NYTBR - May 3 2015 - p1(L) [501+]
LJ - v140 - i3 - Feb 15 2015 - p98(1) [51-500]

Belmessous, Saliha - *Empire by Treaty: Negotiating European Expansion, 1600-1900*
HNet - May 2015 - pNA [501+]

Belmonte, David - *Creating Horror Comics*
c BL - v111 - i15 - April 1 2015 - p60(1) [51-500]

Belogolovsky, Vladimir - *Conversations with Architects: In the Age of Celebrity*
RVBW - August 2015 - pNA [501+]

Belsky, R.G. - *Shooting for the Stars*
BL - v111 - i19-20 - June 1 2015 - p57(1) [51-500]
KR - June 1 2015 - pNA [501+]
PW - v262 - i22 - June 1 2015 - p41(1) [51-500]

Belton, Blair - *Be a Zoologist*
c Teach Lib - v42 - i3 - Feb 2015 - p9(1) [51-500]

Belton, Robert - *The Crusade for Equality in the Workplace: The Griggs v. Duke Power Story*
JAH - v101 - i4 - March 2015 - p1334-1335 [501+]

Beltrame, Carlo - *Sveti Pavao Shipwreck: A 16th Century Venetian Merchantman from Mljet, Croatia, With Italian and Croatian Abstracts*
Specu - v90 - i4 - Oct 2015 - p1086-1087 [501+]

Bemelmans, Ludwig - *Madeline (Illus. by Bemelmans, Ludwig)*
c BL - v112 - i4 - Oct 15 2015 - p53(1) [51-500]

Bemis, John Claude - *The Wooden Prince*
c KR - Jan 1 2016 - pNA [51-500]

Bemonster, Ludworst - *Frankenstein's Fright before Christmas (Illus. by Walton, Rick)*
c HB Guide - v26 - i1 - Spring 2015 - p22(1) [51-500]

Ben-Atar, Doron S. - *Taming Lust: Crimes against Nature in the Early Republic*
AHR - v120 - i2 - April 2015 - p612-613 [501+]
JAH - v101 - i4 - March 2015 - p1257-1258 [501+]
NEQ - v88 - i2 - June 2015 - p343-345 [501+]
RAH - v43 - i3 - Sept 2015 - p462-467 [501+]

Ben-David, Mishka - *Duet in Beirut*
LJ - v140 - i6 - April 1 2015 - p72(1) [51-500]
PW - v262 - i8 - Feb 23 2015 - p51(1) [51-500]

Ben-Ghiat, Ruth - *Italian Fascism's Empire*
TimHES - i2205 - May 28 2015 - p48(1) [501+]

Ben-Moshe, Liat - *Disability Incarcerated: Imprisonment and Disability in the United States and Canada*
CS - v44 - i6 - Nov 2015 - p776-778 [501+]
HNet - April 2015 - pNA [501+]

Ben-Moshe, Tuvia - *Churchill, Strategy and History*
HT - v65 - i1 - Jan 2015 - p56(2) [501+]

Ben-Oni, Rosebud - *Solecism*
Poet - v205 - i5 - Feb 2015 - p499(3) [501+]

Ben-Porat, Guy - *Between State and Synagogue: The Secularization of Contemporary Israel*
J Ch St - v57 - i3 - Summer 2015 - p565-567 [501+]

Ben-Rafael, Eliezer - *The Communal Idea in the 21st Century*
CS - v44 - i3 - May 2015 - p342-344 [501+]

Benacre, John - *McCann*
KR - Sept 1 2015 - pNA [501+]

Benarde, Melvin A. - *Germs Are Us: Collaborating for Life*
KR - Sept 1 2015 - pNA [501+]

Benartzi, Shlomo - *The Smarter Screen: Surprising Ways to Influence and Improve Online Behavior*
LJ - v140 - i16 - Oct 1 2015 - p89(1) [51-500]

Benda, Julien - *The Treason of the Intellectuals*
Nat R - v67 - i9 - May 18 2015 - p52 [501+]

Benda, Vaclav - *Nocni kadrovy dotaznik a jine boje*
Soc - v52 - i1 - Feb 2015 - p87(6) [501+]

Bender, John - *Ends of Enlightenment*
Eight-C St - v48 - i2 - Wntr 2015 - p239-245 [501+]

Bender, Karen E. - *Refund*
BL - v111 - i9-10 - Jan 1 2015 - p38(1) [51-500]
NYTBR - March 22 2015 - p18(L) [501+]

Bender, Michael L. - *Paleoclimate*
QRB - v90 - i2 - June 2015 - p205(1) [51-500]

Bender, Mickey - *The StorySellers*
SPBW - May 2015 - pNA [51-500]

Bender, Rebecca - *Giraffe Meets Bird (Illus. by Bender, Rebecca)*
c KR - July 15 2015 - pNA [51-500]
c Res Links - v20 - i5 - June 2015 - p1(1) [51-500]
c SLJ - v61 - i8 - August 2015 - p64(1) [51-500]

Bender, Shawn - *Taiko Boom: Japanese Drumming in Place and Motion*
JAS - v74 - i3 - August 2015 - p749-750 [501+]

Bendet, Margaret - *Learning to Eat along the Way*
PW - v262 - i26 - June 29 2015 - p61(1) [51-500]

Bendick, Jeanne - *Archimedes and the Door of Science*
c CH Bwatch - Feb 2015 - pNA [51-500]

Bendis, Brian Michael - *Miles Morales: The Ultimate Spider-Man (Illus. by Marquez, David)*
c SLJ - v61 - i10 - Oct 2015 - p118(3) [501+]
Powers: Bureau, Vol 2 (Illus. by Oeming, Michael Avon)
BL - v111 - i13 - March 1 2015 - p36(1) [51-500]

Benditt, John - *The Boatmaker*
NYTBR - March 29 2015 - p18(L) [501+]

Bendix, Sebastian - *The Diorama*
PW - v262 - i13 - March 30 2015 - p61(1) [51-500]

Bendle, Mervyn F. - *Anzac and Its Enemies: The History War on Australia's National Identity*
Quad - v59 - i7-8 - July-August 2015 - p130(5) [501+]

Bendorf, Oliver - *The Spectral Wilderness*
Ant R - v73 - i2 - Spring 2015 - p383(1) [51-500]

Benedek, Gyora - *Hidato Fun 10*
KR - Sept 15 2015 - pNA [501+]

Benedict, Elizabeth - *Me, My Hair, and I: Twenty-Seven Women Untangle an Obsession*
y BL - v111 - i22 - August 1 2015 - p12(1) [51-500]
KR - June 15 2015 - pNA [501+]
LJ - v140 - i15 - Sept 15 2015 - p95(1) [51-500]
PW - v262 - i23 - June 8 2015 - p48(1) [51-500]

Benedict-Jones, Linda - *Storyteller: The Photographs of Duane Michals*
LJ - v140 - i5 - March 15 2015 - p99(1) [501+]

Benedict, Laura - *Charlotte's Story*
BL - v112 - i3 - Oct 1 2015 - p25(1) [51-500]
PW - v262 - i31 - August 3 2015 - p34(1) [51-500]

Benedis-Grab, Daphne - *The Angel Tree*
c HB Guide - v26 - i1 - Spring 2015 - p70(1) [51-500]
Clementine for Christmas
c PW - v262 - i37 - Sept 14 2015 - p75(1) [501+]

Benefield, James - *Carnivores (Illus. by Benefield, James)*
  c HB Guide - v26 - i2 - Fall 2015 - p170(1) [51-500]
Herbivores (Illus. by Benefield, James)
  c HB Guide - v26 - i2 - Fall 2015 - p170(1) [51-500]
Benenson, Joyce F. - *Warriors and Worriers: The Survival of the Sexes*
  QRB - v90 - i2 - June 2015 - p219(2) [501+]
Benesch, Oleg - *Inventing the Way of the Samurai: Nationalism, Internationalism, and Bushido in Modern Japan*
  J Mil H - v79 - i1 - Jan 2015 - p219-220 [501+]
Benfey, Philip N. - *Quickstart Molecular Biology: An Introduction for Mathematics, Physicists, and Computational Scientists*
  QRB - v90 - i4 - Dec 2015 - p444(1) [501+]
Benforado, Adam - *Unfair: The New Science of Criminal Injustice (Read by Barrett, Joe). Audiobook Review*
  LJ - v140 - i14 - Sept 1 2015 - p68(2) [51-500]
  PW - v262 - i35 - August 31 2015 - p85(1) [51-500]
Unfair: The New Science of Criminal Injustice
  LJ - v140 - i7 - April 15 2015 - p103(3) [51-500]
  New Sci - v226 - i3027 - June 27 2015 - p43(1) [501+]
  KR - April 1 2015 - pNA [501+]
Benford, Gregory - *The Best of Gregory Benford*
  PW - v262 - i23 - June 8 2015 - p42(1) [51-500]
Bengston, Vern L. - *Families and Faith: How Religion Is Passed Down across Generations*
  AJS - v120 - i4 - Jan 2015 - p1254(4) [501+]
  CS - v44 - i2 - March 2015 - p172-174 [501+]
Bengtsson, Jonas T. - *A Fairy Tale*
  WLT - v89 - i3-4 - May-August 2015 - p107(1) [51-500]
Benharrech, Sarah - *Marivaux et la science du caractere*
  MLR - v110 - i2 - April 2015 - p544-545 [501+]
Benincasa, Sara - *DC Trip*
  KR - Sept 1 2015 - pNA [51-500]
  LJ - v140 - i13 - August 1 2015 - p82(1) [51-500]
Benitez-Rojo, Antonio - *Woman in Battle Dress*
  BL - v111 - i22 - August 1 2015 - p25(1) [51-500]
  KR - July 1 2015 - pNA [51-500]
  WLT - v89 - i6 - Nov-Dec 2015 - p59(1) [51-500]
Benjamin, A.H. - *Wanted: Prince Charming (Illus. by Fiofin, Fabiano)*
  c CH Bwatch - April 2015 - pNA [51-500]
Benjamin, Ali - *The Thing About Jellyfish (Read by Franco, Sarah). Audiobook Review*
  c SLJ - v61 - i11 - Nov 2015 - p70(2) [51-500]
The Thing about Jellyfish
  y VOYA - v38 - i4 - Oct 2015 - p49(2) [501+]
  c BL - v111 - i22 - August 1 2015 - p70(1) [51-500]
  y KR - June 1 2015 - pNA [51-500]
  c NYTBR - Oct 11 2015 - p18(L) [51-500]
  c PW - v262 - i23 - June 8 2015 - p61(1) [51-500]
  c PW - v262 - i49 - Dec 2 2015 - p74(1) [51-500]
  c PW - v262 - i51 - Dec 14 2015 - p21(6) [51-500]
  c SLJ - v61 - i8 - August 2015 - p83(1) [51-500]
Benjamin, Arthur - *The Magic of Math: Solving for x and Figuring out Why*
  KR - July 15 2015 - pNA [501+]
  LJ - v140 - i14 - Sept 1 2015 - p133(1) [51-500]
  PW - v262 - i25 - June 22 2015 - p131(2) [51-500]
Benjamin, Melanie - *The Swans of Fifth Avenue*
  KR - Dec 1 2015 - pNA [501+]
  LJ - v140 - i14 - Sept 1 2015 - p89(1) [51-500]
Benjamin, Walter - *Illuminations*
  NS - v144 - i5284 - Oct 16 2015 - p44(3) [501+]
Radio Benjamin
  HM - v330 - i1977 - Feb 2015 - p89(6) [501+]
Benn, James R. - *The Rest Is Silence*
  RVBW - March 2015 - pNA [501+]
  RVBW - August 2015 - pNA [501+]
The White Ghost
  BL - v111 - i19-20 - June 1 2015 - p58(1) [51-500]
White Ghost
  PW - v262 - i29 - July 20 2015 - p170(1) [51-500]
The White Ghost
  RVBW - August 2015 - pNA [51-500]
Benn, Mitch - *Terra's World*
  KR - April 15 2015 - pNA [51-500]
  PW - v262 - i10 - March 9 2015 - p56(1) [51-500]
Bennema, Cornelis - *A Theory of Character in New Testament Narrative*
  Theol St - v76 - i2 - June 2015 - p348(2) [501+]
Bennett, Alexander C. - *Kendo: Culture of the Sword*
  LJ - v140 - i11 - June 15 2015 - p93(1) [51-500]
  Mac - v128 - i28 - July 20 2015 - p58(1) [51-500]
Bennett, Andrew - *This Thing Called Literature: Reading, Thinking, Writing*
  TLS - i5877 - Nov 20 2015 - p30(1) [501+]
William Wordsworth in Context
  TLS - i5875 - Nov 6 2015 - p3(2) [501+]
Bennett, Andy - *Music, Style, and Aging: Growing Old Disgracefully?*
  PMS - v38 - i2 - May 2015 - p263(3) [501+]
Bennett, Artie - *Belches, Burps, and Farts Oh My! (Illus. by Naujokaitis, Pranas T.)*
  c HB Guide - v26 - i2 - Fall 2015 - p170(1) [51-500]
Bennett, Chris - *Southeast Foraging: 120 Wild and Flavorful Edibles from Angelica to Wild Plums*
  LJ - v140 - i7 - April 15 2015 - p120(1) [51-500]
Bennett, Elizabeth - *Big and Small (Illus. by Chapman, Jane)*
  c HB Guide - v26 - i1 - Spring 2015 - p6(1) [51-500]
Bennett, Eric - *A Big Enough Lie*
  Ent W - i1370 - July 3 2015 - p63(1) [501+]
  HM - v331 - i1983 - August 2015 - p84(6) [501+]
  KR - May 1 2015 - pNA [501+]
  PW - v262 - i15 - April 13 2015 - p54(1) [51-500]
Workshops of Empire: Stegner, Engle, and American Creative Writing During the Cold War
  NYTBR - Nov 29 2015 - p11(L) [501+]
  PW - v262 - i31 - August 3 2015 - p49(1) [51-500]
Bennett, Evan P. - *When Tobacco Was King: Families, Farm Labor, and Federal Policy in the Piedmont*
  JSH - v81 - i4 - Nov 2015 - p975(4) [501+]
Bennett, Gill - *Six Moments of Crisis: Inside British Foreign Policy*
  Historian - v77 - i3 - Fall 2015 - p596(3) [501+]
Bennett, Janet M. - *The SAGE Encyclopedia of Intercultural Competence, 2 vols.*
  BL - v112 - i3 - Oct 1 2015 - p6(1) [51-500]
Bennett, Jeffrey - *Max Goes to the Space Station (Illus. by Carroll, Michael)*
  c Sci & Ch - v53 - i4 - Dec 2015 - p98 [501+]
Bennett, Jeffrey S. - *When the Sun Danced: Myth, Miracles, and Modernity in Early Twentieth-Century Portugal*
  JMH - v87 - i1 - March 2015 - p214(2) [501+]
Bennett, Jenn - *The Anatomical Shape of a Heart*
  y BL - v112 - i2 - Sept 15 2015 - p70(1) [51-500]
  y KR - August 15 2015 - pNA [51-500]
  y SLJ - v61 - i10 - Oct 2015 - p108(1) [51-500]
  y VOYA - v38 - i5 - Dec 2015 - p53(1) [51-500]
Grave Phantoms
  PW - v262 - i14 - April 6 2015 - p46(2) [51-500]
Night Owls
  y Sch Lib - v63 - i3 - Autumn 2015 - p189(1) [51-500]
Bennett, Judith M. - *The Oxford Handbook of Women and Gender in Medieval Europe*
  HER - v130 - i543 - April 2015 - p406(3) [501+]
  Specu - v90 - i2 - April 2015 - p500-502 [501+]
Bennett, Kyla - *No Worse Sin*
  c CH Bwatch - April 2015 - pNA [51-500]
  y SLJ - v61 - i6 - June 2015 - p120(1) [51-500]
Bennett, Maxwell R. - *History of Cognitive Neuroscience*
  QRB - v90 - i3 - Sept 2015 - p318(1) [51-500]
Bennett, Michael I. - *F*ck Feelings*
  KR - June 1 2015 - pNA [51-500]
Bennett, Owen - *Following Farage: On the Trail of the People's Army*
  NS - v144 - i5276 - August 21 2015 - p51(1) [501+]
Bennett, Robert Jackson - *City of Blades*
  BL - v112 - i7 - Dec 1 2015 - p38(1) [51-500]
  KR - Nov 15 2015 - pNA [51-500]
  PW - v262 - i46 - Nov 16 2015 - p59(1) [51-500]
Bennett, Scott H. - *Antiwar Dissent and Peace Activism in World War I America*
  J Mil H - v79 - i2 - April 2015 - p514-515 [501+]
Bennett, Susan - *Performing Environments: Site-Specificity in Medieval and Early Modern English Drama*
  Theat J - v67 - i3 - Oct 2015 - p571-572 [501+]
Bennett, Vanora - *Midnight in St. Petersburg*
  KR - Nov 15 2015 - pNA [501+]
  LJ - v140 - i20 - Dec 1 2015 - p88(1) [51-500]
Bennett, Veronica - *The Broomstick Bike*
  c SLJ - v61 - i11 - Nov 2015 - p94(1) [51-500]
Bennett, William J. - *Going to Pot: Why the Rush to Legalize Marijuana Is Harming America*
  Bwatch - April 2015 - pNA [51-500]
  Nat R - v67 - i4 - March 9 2015 - p37 [501+]
  Reason - v47 - i1 - May 2015 - p61(4) [501+]
Bennette, Rebecca Ayako - *Fighting for the Soul of Germany: The Catholic Struggle for Inclusion after Unification*
  JMH - v87 - i1 - March 2015 - p226(2) [501+]
Bennion, Janet - *Polygamy in Primetime: Media, Gender, and Politics in Mormon Fundamentalism*
  CS - v44 - i4 - July 2015 - p487-489 [501+]
Bennis, Phyllis - *Understanding ISIS and the New Global War on Terror: A Primer*
  LJ - v140 - i19 - Nov 15 2015 - p107(1) [51-500]
Benoit, Charles - *Snow Job*
  y KR - Dec 15 2015 - pNA [51-500]
Benoit, Peter - *Big Battles of World War II*
  c Teach Lib - v42 - i4 - April 2015 - p9(1) [51-500]
Benor, Sarah B. - *Becoming Frum: How Newcomers Learn the Language and Culture of Orthodox Judaism*
  Lang Soc - v44 - i1 - Feb 2015 - p113-116 [501+]
Bensaid, Daniel - *An Impatient Life: A Memoir*
  TLS - i5851 - May 22 2015 - p22(1) [501+]
Bensen, Clara - *No Baggage: A Minimalist Tale of Love and Wandering*
  KR - Sept 15 2015 - pNA [501+]
  LJ - v140 - i19 - Nov 15 2015 - p99(1) [51-500]
  BL - v112 - i2 - Sept 15 2015 - p20(2) [51-500]
Bensheimer Gespräche: Financiers und Staatsfinanzen (Teil 2).
  HNet - June 2015 - pNA [501+]
Benson, Amber - *The Last Dream Keeper*
  PW - v262 - i50 - Dec 7 2015 - p73(1) [51-500]
Benson, Bruce Ellis - *Liturgy as a Way of Life: Embodying the Arts in Christian Worship*
  Intpr - v69 - i1 - Jan 2015 - p117(2) [501+]
Benson, Bryan - *The Spy's Son: The True Story of the Highest-Ranking CIA Officer Ever Convicted of Espionage and the Son He Trained to Spy for Russia*
  CSM - May 14 2015 - pNA [501+]
Benson, Kathleen - *Draw What You See: The Life and Art of Benny Andrews (Illus. by Andrews, Benny)*
  c HB Guide - v26 - i2 - Fall 2015 - p192(1) [51-500]
  c CCB-B - v68 - i7 - March 2015 - p348(1) [51-500]
  c CH Bwatch - Feb 2015 - pNA [51-500]
  c HB - v91 - i1 - Jan-Feb 2015 - p93(1) [51-500]
  c Teach Lib - v42 - i5 - June 2015 - p44(1) [51-500]
Benson-Laboucane, Patti - *The Outside Circle (Illus. by Mellings, Kelly)*
  y SLJ - v61 - i10 - Oct 2015 - p119(2) [51-500]
Benson, Michael - *Cosmigraphics: Picturing Space through Time*
  Am Sci - v103 - i3 - May-June 2015 - p230(2) [501+]
  NYRB - v62 - i9 - May 21 2015 - p34(3) [501+]
  S&T - v129 - i2 - Feb 2015 - p71(1) [501+]
The Devil at Genesee Junction: The Murders of Kathy Bernhard and George-Ann Formicola, 6/66
  PW - v262 - i36 - Sept 7 2015 - p56(1) [51-500]
Benson, Nicky - *The Spirit of Christmas: A Giving Tradition (Illus. by Cockroft, Jason)*
  c HB Guide - v26 - i2 - Fall 2015 - p26(1) [51-500]
Benson, Pete - *Scratch*
  c BL - v112 - i7 - Dec 1 2015 - p42(1) [51-500]
Benson, Ray - *Comin' Right at Ya*
  KR - August 15 2015 - pNA [501+]
Benson, Rodney - *Shaping Immigration News: A French-American Comparison*
  AJS - v120 - i4 - Jan 2015 - p1247(4) [501+]
Bentham, Jeremy - *Unsinn auf Stelzen: Schriften zur Franzosischen Revolution*
  HNet - March 2015 - pNA [501+]
Bentley, Jonathan - *Little Big (Illus. by Bentley, Jonathan)*
  c HB - v91 - i6 - Nov-Dec 2015 - p64(2) [51-500]
  c KR - June 1 2015 - pNA [51-500]
  c PW - v262 - i28 - July 13 2015 - p63(1) [51-500]
  c SLJ - v61 - i10 - Oct 2015 - p70(1) [51-500]
Bentley, Paul - *Ted Hughes, Class and Violence*
  RES - v66 - i276 - Sept 2015 - p801-803 [501+]
Bentley, Tadgh - *Little Penguin Gets the Hiccups (Illus. by Bentley, Tadgh)*
  c BL - v112 - i2 - Sept 15 2015 - p67(1) [51-500]
  c KR - August 1 2015 - pNA [51-500]
  c SLJ - v61 - i12 - Dec 2015 - p86(1) [51-500]
Bently, Peter - *Captain Jack and the Pirates (Illus. by Oxenbury, Helen)*
  c KR - Jan 1 2016 - pNA [51-500]
Knightmare: Rotten Luck! (Illus. by Blunt, Fred)
  c Sch Lib - v63 - i2 - Summer 2015 - p100(1) [51-500]
The Prince and the Porker (Illus. by Roberts, David)
  c Sch Lib - v63 - i4 - Winter 2015 - p217(1) [51-500]
A Recipe for Bedtime (Illus. by Massini, Sarah)
  c KR - Oct 1 2015 - pNA [51-500]
Those Magnificent Sheep in Their Flying Machine (Illus. by Roberts, David)
  c HB Guide - v26 - i1 - Spring 2015 - p22(1) [51-500]
Train Is on Track
  c Sch Lib - v63 - i4 - Winter 2015 - p217(1) [51-500]

Book Review Index 2016 Cumulation **BERGER • 37**

Benton, Adia - *HIV Exceptionalism: Development through Disease in Sierra Leone*
CS - v44 - i5 - Sept 2015 - p591-603 [501+]
Benton, Gregory - *Smoke*
PW - v262 - i44 - Nov 2 2015 - p72(1) [51-500]
Benton, Jim - *Where's My Fnurgle?*
c KR - July 1 2015 - pNA [51-500]
Benton, Lauren - *Legal Pluralism and Empires, 1500-1850*
HER - v130 - i543 - April 2015 - p460(3) [501+]
Bentzinger, Rudolf - *Deutsch-Russische Arbeitsgesprache zu mittelalterlichen Handschriften und Drucken aus Halberstadt in russischen Bibliotheken*
Specu - v90 - i2 - April 2015 - p502-504 [501+]
Benulis, Sabrina - *Angelus*
PW - v262 - i52 - Dec 21 2015 - p138(1) [51-500]
Benveniste, Daniel - *The Interwoven Lives of Sigmund, Anna and W. Ernest Freud: Three Generations of Psychoanalysis*
TLS - i5854 - June 12 2015 - p7(1) [501+]
Benway, Robin - *Emmy & Oliver*
y BL - v111 - i18 - May 15 2015 - p53(1) [51-500]
y CCB-B - v69 - i1 - Sept 2015 - p9(2) [51-500]
y HB Guide - v26 - i2 - Fall 2015 - p111(1) [51-500]
y KR - April 15 2015 - pNA [51-500]
c Nat Post - v17 - i194 - June 20 2015 - pWP5(1) [501+]
y PW - v262 - i15 - April 13 2015 - p82(1) [51-500]
y PW - v262 - i49 - Dec 2 2015 - p90(1) [51-500]
y VOYA - v38 - i3 - August 2015 - p54(1) [501+]
Benwell, Sarah - *The Last Leaves Falling*
y BL - v111 - i12 - Feb 15 2015 - p82(1) [51-500]
y HB - v91 - i3 - May-June 2015 - p105(1) [501+]
y HB Guide - v26 - i2 - Fall 2015 - p111(1) [51-500]
y KR - March 1 2015 - pNA [51-500]
y Magpies - v30 - i1 - March 2015 - p39(1) [501+]
y PW - v262 - i17 - April 27 2015 - p77(1) [51-500]
y PW - v262 - i49 - Dec 2 2015 - p94(1) [51-500]
y Sch Lib - v63 - i2 - Summer 2015 - p124(1) [51-500]
y Teach Lib - v43 - i1 - Oct 2015 - p23(1) [51-500]
Benz, Angelika - *Handlanger der SS: Die Rolle der Trawniki-Manner im Holocaust*
HNet - July 2015 - pNA [501+]
Benz, Wolfgang - *Sinti und Roma: Die unerwunschte Minderheit - Uber das Vorurteil Antiziganismus*
HNet - May 2015 - pNA [501+]
Benza, A.J. - *'74 and Sunny*
y BL - v111 - i21 - July 1 2015 - p10(1) [51-500]
KR - June 1 2015 - pNA [51-500]
Benziman, Galia - *Narratives of Child Neglect in Romantic and Victorian Culture*
VS - v57 - i2 - Wntr 2015 - p302(4) [501+]
Beorn, Waitman W. - *Marching into Darkness: The Wehrmacht and the Holocaust in Belarus*
GSR - v38 - i3 - Oct 2015 - p686-688 [501+]
Beorn, Waitman Wade - *Marching into Darkness: The Wehrmacht and the Holocaust in Belarus*
AHR - v120 - i2 - April 2015 - p743-744 [501+]
HER - v130 - i545 - August 2015 - p1046(3) [501+]
Slav R - v74 - i1 - Spring 2015 - p194-195 [501+]
Beran, Michael Knox - *Murder by Candlelight: The Gruesome Crimes Behind Our Romance with the Macabre*
Nat R - v67 - i19 - Oct 19 2015 - p56(2) [501+]
NYTBR - August 30 2015 - p13(L) [501+]
Berber, Anne - *Wednesday (Illus. by Berber, Anne)*
c HB Guide - v26 - i1 - Spring 2015 - p6(1) [51-500]
Berberi, Carine - *30 Years After: Issues and Representations of the Falklands War*
J Mil H - v79 - i3 - July 2015 - p885-886 [501+]
Berberian, Charles - *Monsieur Jean: From Bachelor to Father*
PW - v262 - i1 - Jan 5 2015 - p59(1) [51-500]
Berberich, Christine - *The Bloomsbury Introduction to Popular Fiction*
TLS - i5849 - May 8 2015 - p24(1) [501+]
TimHES - i2212 - July 16 2015 - p=47-1 [501+]
Berbig, Roland - *Metropole, Provinz und Welt: Raum und Mobilitat in der Literatur des Realismus*
GSR - v38 - i1 - Feb 2015 - p175-177 [501+]
Berdiev, Neil - *The Little Silver Book - Interviewing*
KR - July 15 2015 - pNA [501+]
Berebitsky, Julie - *Sex and the Office: A History of Gender, Power, and Desire*
JWH - v27 - i3 - Fall 2015 - p176(11) [501+]
Berend, Ivan - *An Economic History of Nineteenth-Century Europe: Diversity and Industrialization*
JEH - v75 - i1 - March 2015 - p262-263 [501+]
An Economic History of Twentieth-Century Europe: Economic Regimes from Laissez-Faire to Globalization
JEH - v75 - i1 - March 2015 - p264-264 [501+]
Berend, Nora - *Central Europe in the High Middle Ages: Bohemia, Hungary and Poland, c. 900-c.1300*
AHR - v120 - i2 - April 2015 - p697-698 [501+]
Specu - v90 - i3 - July 2015 - p774-775 [501+]
Berenson, Alex - *Twelve Days (Read by Guidall, George). Audiobook Review*
LJ - v140 - i11 - June 15 2015 - p48(1) [51-500]
Twelve Days
BL - v111 - i9-10 - Jan 1 2015 - p51(1) [51-500]
KR - Jan 15 2015 - pNA [51-500]
Wolves
KR - Dec 1 2015 - pNA [51-500]
The Wolves
PW - v262 - i50 - Dec 7 2015 - p67(2) [51-500]
Berenson, Bernard - *My Dear BB: The Letters of Bernard Berensen and Kenneth Clark, 1925-1959*
TLS - i5873 - Oct 23 2015 - p11(2) [501+]
Berenson, Edward - *The French Republic: History, Values, Debates*
HER - v130 - i543 - April 2015 - p511(3) [501+]
Berenson, Laurien - *The Bark before Christmas*
BL - v112 - i2 - Sept 15 2015 - p29(1) [51-500]
PW - v262 - i35 - August 31 2015 - p63(1) [51-500]
Berenstain, Mike - *The Berenstain Bears' Please and Thank You Book (Illus. by Berenstain, Mike)*
c CH Bwatch - March 2015 - pNA [51-500]
The Berenstain Bears: The Biggest Brag (Illus. by Berenstain, Mike)
c CH Bwatch - July 2015 - pNA [51-500]
Beresford, James - *The Ancient Sailing Season*
Class R - v65 - i2 - Oct 2015 - p497-498 [501+]
Beresford, Lucy - *Invisible Threads*
Spec - v328 - i9746 - June 13 2015 - p39(2) [501+]
Beresin, Anna R. - *The Art of Play: Recess and the Practice of Invention*
WestFolk - v74 - i2 - Spring 2015 - p237-240 [501+]
Berest, Anne - *Sagan, Paris 1954*
TLS - i5870 - Oct 2 2015 - p25(1) [501+]
Beretta, Marco - *Fakes!? Hoaxes, Counterfeits, and Deceptions in Early Modern Science*
Isis - v106 - i2 - June 2015 - p434(2) [501+]
Berg, Alban - *Pro Mondo-Pro Domo: The Writings of Alban Berg*
ON - v79 - i9 - March 2015 - p59(2) [501+]
Berg, Bruce F. - *Healing Gotham: New York City's Public Health Policies for the Twenty-First Century*
Bwatch - August 2015 - pNA [51-500]
LJ - v140 - i7 - April 15 2015 - p108(1) [51-500]
Berg, Charles Ramirez - *The Classical Mexican Cinema: The Poetics of the Exceptional Golden Age Films*
LJ - v140 - i12 - July 1 2015 - p85(1) [51-500]
Si & So - v25 - i12 - Dec 2015 - p106(1) [501+]
Berg, Elizabeth - *The Dream Lover (Read by Sutton-Smith, Emily). Audiobook Review*
LJ - v140 - i11 - June 15 2015 - p48(1) [51-500]
The Dream Lover
BL - v111 - i12 - Feb 15 2015 - p40(1) [51-500]
KR - Feb 1 2015 - pNA [501+]
LJ - v140 - i6 - April 1 2015 - p72(1) [51-500]
NYTBR - June 14 2015 - p26(L) [501+]
PW - v262 - i7 - Feb 16 2015 - p152(2) [51-500]
Berg, Erika - *Forced to Flee: Visual Stories by Refugee Youth from Burma*
KR - July 15 2015 - pNA [501+]
PW - v262 - i44 - Nov 2 2015 - p79(1) [51-500]
Berg, James J. - *The American Isherwood*
TLS - i5854 - June 12 2015 - p11(1) [501+]
Berg, Jean Horton - *The Noisy Clock Shop (Illus. by Seiden, Art)*
c HB Guide - v26 - i2 - Fall 2015 - p6(1) [51-500]
Berg, Jesse - *Visual Leap: A Step-by-Step Guide to Visual Learning for Teachers and Students*
LJ - v140 - i15 - Sept 15 2015 - p86(1) [51-500]
Berg, Jon - *Rosie and Rolland in the Legendary Show-and-Tell (Illus. by Berg, Jon)*
c KR - Feb 15 2015 - pNA [51-500]
c Res Links - v20 - i5 - June 2015 - p1(2) [51-500]
Berg, Nicolas - *The Holocaust and the West German Historians: Historical Interpretations and Autobiographical Memory*
JIH - v46 - i3 - Wntr 2016 - p448-449 [501+]
Berg, Ryan - *No House to Call My Home: Love, Family, and Other Transgressions*
y BL - v111 - i22 - August 1 2015 - p22(1) [51-500]
Bwatch - Oct 2015 - pNA [51-500]
KR - June 15 2015 - pNA [501+]
LJ - v140 - i12 - July 1 2015 - p101(1) [51-500]
Bergant, Dianne - *Genesis: In the Beginning*
Intpr - v69 - i4 - Oct 2015 - p488(1) [501+]
Bergdolt, Klaus - *Armut in der Renaissance*
Six Ct J - v46 - i3 - Fall 2015 - p748-750 [501+]
Berge, Clark - *The Vows Book: Anglican Teaching on the Vows of Obedience, Poverty, and Chastity*
Theol St - v76 - i3 - Sept 2015 - p652(1) [501+]
Bergeaud, Emeric - *Stella: A Novel of the Haitian Revolution*
RVBW - Oct 2015 - pNA [501+]
Bergemann, Rosalind A. - *An Asperger's Guide to Entrepreneurship: Setting Up Your Own Business for Professionals with Autism Spectrum Disorder*
Bwatch - Feb 2015 - pNA [51-500]
Bwatch - July 2015 - pNA [51-500]
Bergen, Candice - *A Fine Romance (Read by Bergen, Candice). Audiobook Review*
BL - v112 - i1 - Sept 1 2015 - p138(2) [51-500]
LJ - v140 - i9 - May 15 2015 - p44(2) [51-500]
A Fine Romance
NYTBR - May 31 2015 - p34(L) [501+]
A Fine Romance (Read by Bergen, Candice). Audiobook Review
PW - v262 - i26 - June 29 2015 - p64(2) [51-500]
A Fine Romance
BL - v111 - i12 - Feb 15 2015 - p18(1) [51-500]
KR - Jan 1 2015 - pNA [501+]
LJ - v140 - i2 - Feb 1 2015 - p85(2) [51-500]
PW - v262 - i7 - Feb 16 2015 - p172(1) [51-500]
Bergen, Peter L. - *Drone Wars: Transforming Conflict, Law, and Policy*
HNet - August 2015 - pNA [501+]
Parameters - v45 - i2 - Summer 2015 - p128(3) [501+]
Berger, Carin - *Finding Spring (Illus. by Berger, Carin)*
c BL - v111 - i9-10 - Jan 1 2015 - p106(1) [51-500]
c CCB-B - v68 - i8 - April 2015 - p390(1) [51-500]
c HB - v91 - i1 - Jan-Feb 2015 - p59(2) [51-500]
c HB Guide - v26 - i2 - Fall 2015 - p6(1) [51-500]
c PW - v262 - i49 - Dec 2 2015 - p20(1) [51-500]
Berger, Edward - *Softly, with Feeling: Joe Wilder and the Breaking of Barriers in American Music*
Notes - v72 - i1 - Sept 2015 - p139(3) [501+]
Berger, Harry, Jr. - *A Fury in the Words: Love and Embarrassment in Shakespeare's Venice*
Ren Q - v68 - i2 - Summer 2015 - p784-785 [501+]
Berger, J.M. - *ISIS: The State of Terror*
NYTBR - April 5 2015 - p11(L) [501+]
Berger, John - *A Fortunate Man: The Story of a Country Doctor*
TLS - i5847 - April 24 2015 - p27(1) [501+]
Portraits: John Berger on Artists
KR - Sept 1 2015 - pNA [501+]
NYTBR - Dec 6 2015 - p77(L) [501+]
PW - v262 - i35 - August 31 2015 - p75(2) [51-500]
Why Look at Animals?
NYTBR - June 28 2015 - p16(L) [501+]
Berger, Jutta - *Referendariat Geschichte: Kompaktwissen fur Berufseinstieg und Examensvorbereitung*
HNet - April 2015 - pNA [501+]
Berger, Peter L. - *The Many Altars of Modernity: Toward a Paradigm for Religion in a Pluralist Age*
Soc - v52 - i3 - June 2015 - p283(1) [501+]
Berger, Rachel - *Ayurveda Made Modern: Political Histories of Indigenous Medicine in North India, 1900-1955*
AHR - v120 - i1 - Feb 2015 - p210-211 [501+]
Berger, Samantha - *Boo-La-La Witch Spa (Illus. by Roxas, Isabel)*
c KR - August 1 2015 - pNA [51-500]
c PW - v262 - i30 - July 27 2015 - p63(1) [51-500]
c SLJ - v61 - i9 - Sept 2015 - p105(1) [51-500]
Crankenstein (Illus. by Santat, Dan)
c HB Guide - v26 - i2 - Fall 2015 - p6(2) [51-500]
Grognonstein (Illus. by Santat, Dan)
c Res Links - v20 - i3 - Feb 2015 - p42(1) [51-500]
Snoozefest (Illus. by Litten, Kristyna)
c HB Guide - v26 - i2 - Fall 2015 - p26(1) [51-500]
Berger, Sandra L. - *The Best Summer Programs for Teens, 2016-2017*
y VOYA - v38 - i5 - Dec 2015 - p80(1) [501+]
Berger, Sara - *Experten der Vernichtung: Das T4-Reinhardt-Netzwerk in den Lagern Belzec, Sobibor und Treblinka*
HNet - August 2015 - pNA [501+]
Berger, Sidney E. - *Rare Books and Special Collections*
LR - v64 - i1-2 - Jan-Feb 2015 - p179-180 [501+]
LRTS - v59 - i2 - April 2015 - p96(2) [501+]
Berger, Thomas L. - *Paratexts in English Printed Drama to 1642, 2 vols.*
TLS - i5840 - March 6 2015 - p23(1) [501+]

Berger, Thomas U. - *War, Guilt, and World Politics after World War II*
    Pac A - v88 - i1 - March 2015 - p194 [501+]
Bergeron, Alain - *Do You Know the Rhinoceros? (Illus. by Sampar)*
    c Res Links - v20 - i5 - June 2015 - p12(1) [51-500]
Bergeron, Alain M. - *C'etait un 8 aout*
    y Res Links - v21 - i1 - Oct 2015 - p48(1) [501+]
Do You Know? Series (Illus. by Sampar)
    c BL - v111 - i18 - May 15 2015 - p50(1) [51-500]
Do You Know the Rhinoceros? (Illus. by Sampar)
    c SLJ - v61 - i7 - July 2015 - p101(1) [51-500]
Do You Know Tigers? (Illus. by Sampar)
    c Res Links - v20 - i5 - June 2015 - p12(1) [51-500]
Le Defi de Dominic (Illus. by Sampar)
    c Res Links - v20 - i5 - June 2015 - p36(1) [51-500]
Mission Ouaouaron (Illus. by Cormier, France)
    c Res Links - v20 - i3 - Feb 2015 - p43(1) [51-500]
Bergeron, Janith - *Complete Photo Guide to Sewing*
    c CH Bwatch - Oct 2015 - pNA [51-500]
Berghahn, Volker R. - *American Big Business in Britain and Germany: A Comparative History of Two "Special Relationships" in the 20th Century*
    AHR - v120 - i3 - June 2015 - p980-981 [501+]
    BHR - v89 - i2 - Summer 2015 - p345(3) [501+]
    GSR - v38 - i2 - May 2015 - p436-2 [501+]
    JEH - v75 - i2 - June 2015 - p592-594 [501+]
Berghaus, Benjamin - *The Management of Luxury: A Practitioner's Handbook*
    Bwatch - Feb 2015 - pNA [501+]
Bergheim, David - *Greenbeaux*
    KR - April 15 2015 - pNA [501+]
Berghoff, Hartmut - *Business in the Age of Extremes: Essays in Modern German and Austrian Economic History*
    HNet - Jan 2015 - pNA [501+]
Bergin, Joseph - *The Politics of Religion in Early Modern France*
    TLS - i5838 - Feb 20 2015 - p12(1) [501+]
Bergin, Mark - *Castle (Illus. by McCall, Henrietta)*
    c HB Guide - v26 - i2 - Fall 2015 - p215(1) [51-500]
Wonders of the World
    c HB Guide - v26 - i2 - Fall 2015 - p215(1) [51-500]
Bergin, Tiffany - *The Evidence Enigma: Correctional Boot Camps and Other Failures in Evidence-Based Policymaking*
    CS - v44 - i5 - Sept 2015 - p636-637 [501+]
Bergin, Virginia - *H2O*
    y HB Guide - v26 - i1 - Spring 2015 - p100(1) [51-500]
    y Teach Lib - v42 - i3 - Feb 2015 - p28(4) [501+]
Bergler, Thomas E. - *The Juvenilization of American Christianity*
    CH - v84 - i3 - Sept 2015 - p704(4) [501+]
    CHR - v101 - i4 - Autumn 2015 - p958(2) [501+]
Bergman, Jill - *The Motherless Child in the Novels of Pauline Hopkins*
    MFSF - v61 - i1 - Spring 2015 - p192-195 [501+]
    TSWL - v34 - i1 - Spring 2015 - p177-179 [501+]
Bergman, Megan Mayhew - *Almost Famous Women: Stories (Read by Lockford, Lesa). Audiobook Review*
    PW - v262 - i12 - March 23 2015 - p69(1) [51-500]
    LJ - v140 - i6 - April 1 2015 - p47(1) [51-500]
Almost Famous Women: Stories
    NYTBR - Feb 1 2015 - p26(L) [501+]
Bergmann, Daniel - *The Curse of the Baskervilles (Illus. by Breyer, Mark)*
    c KR - May 1 2015 - pNA [501+]
Sharkie and the Haunted Cat Box
    c KR - August 15 2015 - pNA [501+]
Bergren, Lisa T. - *Season of Fire*
    SLJ - v61 - i4 - April 2015 - p152(1) [51-500]
Bergstrom, Heather Brittain - *Steal the North*
    Roundup M - v22 - i6 - August 2015 - p25(2) [501+]
Bergung von Kulturgut im Nationalsozialismus. Mythen - Hintergrunde - Auswirkungen
    HNet - July 2015 - pNA [501+]
Bericht zur VII. Nachwuchstagung der Konferenz fur Geschichtsdidaktik
    HNet - Jan 2015 - pNA [501+]
Beriou, Nicole - *Entre stabilite et itinerance: Livres et Culture des Ordres Mendiants*
    Specu - v90 - i3 - July 2015 - p870(1) [501+]
Berk, Sheryl - *Let's Rock!*
    c HB Guide - v26 - i1 - Spring 2015 - p70(1) [51-500]
On Pointe
    c HB Guide - v26 - i2 - Fall 2015 - p75(1) [51-500]
Showstopper
    c HB Guide - v26 - i2 - Fall 2015 - p75(1) [51-500]

Berk, Steven L. - *Anatomy of a Kidnapping: A Doctor's Story*
    RVBW - July 2015 - pNA [51-500]
Berkel, Klaas van - *Isaac Beeckman on Matter and Motion: Mechanical Philosophy in the Making*
    Ren Q - v68 - i1 - Spring 2015 - p270-271 [501+]
Berkes, Marianne - *Over On a Mountain: Somewhere in the World (Illus. by Dubin, Jill)*
    c CH Bwatch - April 2015 - pNA [51-500]
    c HB Guide - v26 - i2 - Fall 2015 - p26(1) [51-500]
    c PW - v262 - i9 - March 2 2015 - p84(1) [501+]
Tortoise and Hare's Amazing Race (Illus. by Morrison, Cathy)
    c KR - July 15 2015 - pNA [501+]
Berkhout, Nina - *The Gallery of Lost Species*
    Nat Post - v17 - i80 - Jan 31 2015 - pWP8(1) [501+]
Berkin, Carol - *The Bill of Rights: James Madison and the Politics of the People's Parchment Barrier*
    KR - Jan 15 2015 - pNA [501+]
The Bill of Rights: The Fight To Secure America's Liberties
    LJ - v140 - i8 - May 1 2015 - p86(1) [501+]
    PW - v262 - i13 - March 30 2015 - p67(1) [51-500]
Berkoff, Nancy - *Vegan in Volume*
    Veg J - v34 - i2 - April-June 2015 - p33(1) [51-500]
Vegan Meals for One or Two--Your Own Personal Recipes
    Veg J - v34 - i2 - April-June 2015 - p33(1) [51-500]
Vegan Menu for People with Diabetes
    Veg J - v34 - i2 - April-June 2015 - p34(1) [51-500]
Vegan Microwave Cookbook
    Veg J - v34 - i2 - April-June 2015 - p34(1) [51-500]
Vegan Passover Recipes
    Veg J - v34 - i2 - April-June 2015 - p33(1) [51-500]
Vegans Know How to Party
    Veg J - v34 - i2 - April-June 2015 - p33(1) [51-500]
Berkow, Ira - *Giants among Men: Y.A., L.T., the Big Tuna, and Other New York Giants Stories*
    BL - v112 - i1 - Sept 1 2015 - p34(1) [51-500]
Berkowitz, Eric - *The Boundaries of Desire: A Century of Bad Laws, Good Sex, and Changing Identities*
    BL - v111 - i22 - August 1 2015 - p22(1) [51-500]
    KR - June 15 2015 - pNA [501+]
    PW - v262 - i26 - June 29 2015 - p58(2) [501+]
Berkowitz, Tracey - *Not My Buddy*
    KR - June 15 2015 - pNA [501+]
Berla, Kathryn - *Going Places*
    KR - Jan 1 2016 - pNA [501+]
Berlak, Ann - *Joelito's Big Decision/La gran decision de Joelito (Illus. by Camacho, Daniel)*
    c SLJ - v61 - i12 - Dec 2015 - p86(1) [51-500]
Berland, Kevin Joel - *The Dividing Line Histories of William Byrd II of Westover*
    JSH - v81 - i1 - Feb 2015 - p163(2) [501+]
    Eight-C St - v48 - i4 - Summer 2015 - p553-555 [501+]
Berlatsky, Noah - *Wonder Woman: Bondage and Feminism in the Marston/Peter Comics, 1941-1948*
    G&L Rev W - v22 - i4 - July-August 2015 - p38(1) [501+]
    Wom R Bks - v32 - i3 - May-June 2015 - p5(3) [501+]
Berlin, Ira - *The Long Emancipation: The Demise of Slavery in the United States*
    BL - v111 - i22 - August 1 2015 - p20(1) [51-500]
    NYTBR - Sept 13 2015 - p15(L) [501+]
    PW - v262 - i29 - July 20 2015 - p181(1) [51-500]
Berlin, Isaiah - *Affirming: Letters, 1975-1997*
    NS - v144 - i5285 - Oct 23 2015 - p49(1) [501+]
    TLS - i5872 - Oct 16 2015 - p3(2) [501+]
Building: Letters, 1960-1975
    TLS - i5872 - Oct 16 2015 - p3(2) [501+]
Berlin, Lucia - *A Manual for Cleaning Women: Selected Stories*
    PW - v262 - i14 - April 6 2015 - p36(1) [51-500]
    NYT - August 19 2015 - pC1(L) [501+]
    BooChiTr - Sept 12 2015 - p12(1) [501+]
    Ent W - i1376 - August 14 2015 - p60(2) [501+]
    KR - June 15 2015 - pNA [501+]
    NS - v144 - i5288 - Nov 13 2015 - p43(1) [501+]
    NY - v91 - i33 - Oct 26 2015 - p79 [501+]
    NYTBR - August 16 2015 - p15(L) [501+]

Berlina, Alexandra - *Brodsky Translating Brodsky: Poetry in Self-Translation*
    Slav R - v74 - i3 - Fall 2015 - p674-675 [501+]
Berlinski, Mischa - *Peacekeeping*
    KR - Dec 15 2015 - pNA [51-500]
Berlow, Ali - *The Food Activist Handbook*
    Bwatch - July 2015 - pNA [51-500]
Berman, Ari - *Give Us the Ballot: The Modern Struggle for Voting Rights in America*
    BL - v111 - i19-20 - June 1 2015 - p9(2) [51-500]
    CSM - August 14 2015 - pNA [501+]
    HM - v331 - i1983 - August 2015 - p89(6) [501+]
    KR - May 1 2015 - pNA [501+]
    LJ - v140 - i12 - July 1 2015 - p97(2) [51-500]
    NY - v91 - i34 - Nov 2 2015 - p90 [501+]
    NYTBR - August 30 2015 - p14(L) [501+]
    PW - v262 - i18 - May 4 2015 - p106(1) [51-500]
Misdirected
    y HB Guide - v26 - i1 - Spring 2015 - p100(1) [51-500]
Berman, Jacob Rama - *American Arabesque: Arabs, Islams, and the Nineteenth-Century Imaginary*
    Am Q - v67 - i2 - June 2015 - p491-503 [501+]
Berman, Lawrence M. - *The Priest, the Prince, and the Pasha: The Life and Afterlife of an Ancient Egyptian Sculpture*
    NYRB - v62 - i14 - Sept 24 2015 - p18(2) [501+]
Berman, Steve - *Daughters of Frankenstein: Lesbian Mad Scientists!*
    KR - Oct 15 2015 - pNA [501+]
    PW - v262 - i22 - June 1 2015 - p44(1) [51-500]
Wilde Stories
    PW - v262 - i18 - May 4 2015 - p101(1) [51-500]
Bermensolo, Nicole - *Kyotofu: Uniquely Delicious Japanese Desserts*
    LJ - v140 - i6 - April 1 2015 - p112(1) [51-500]
    PW - v262 - i11 - March 16 2015 - p78(1) [51-500]
Bernal, Victoria - *Theorizing NGOs: States, Feminisms, and Neoliberalism*
    Wom R Bks - v32 - i5 - Sept-Oct 2015 - p25(2) [501+]
Bernanke, Ben S. - *The Courage to Act: A Memoir of a Crisis and Its Aftermath*
    Nat R - v67 - i23 - Dec 21 2015 - p41(2) [501+]
    NYTBR - Oct 25 2015 - p1(L) [501+]
    PW - v262 - i42 - Oct 19 2015 - p13(1) [501+]
Bernard, Andreas - *Lifted: A Cultural History of the Elevator*
    AHR - v120 - i2 - April 2015 - p637-638 [501+]
Bernard, April - *Berryman's Sonnets*
    Atl - v315 - i2 - March 2015 - p51(3) [501+]
    NYRB - v62 - i10 - June 4 2015 - p40(4) [501+]
Bernard, Floris - *Writing and Reading Byzantine Secular Poetry, 1025-1081*
    Med R - June 2015 - pNA [501+]
Bernard, Jacques-Emmanuel - *La sociabilite epistolaire chez Ciceron*
    Class R - v65 - i2 - Oct 2015 - p434-435 [501+]
Bernard, Mary E. - *Objects of Culture in the Literature of Imperial Spain*
    Hisp R - v83 - i3 - Summer 2015 - p370-373 [501+]
Bernard, Romily - *Remember Me*
    y HB Guide - v26 - i1 - Spring 2015 - p100(1) [51-500]
Bernard, Sean - *Studies in the Hereafter*
    KR - June 15 2015 - pNA [501+]
Bernard, Warren - *Cartoons for Victory*
    BL - v112 - i6 - Nov 15 2015 - p33(1) [51-500]
Bernardin, Marc - *Genius, vol. 1: Siege (Illus. by Richardson, Afua)*
    PW - v262 - i27 - July 6 2015 - p55(1) [51-500]
Bernardini, Giovanni - *Nuova Germania, antichi timori: Stati Uniti, Ostpolitik e sicurezza europea*
    AHR - v120 - i3 - June 2015 - p982-983 [501+]
Bernasek, Anna - *All You Can Pay: How Companies Use Our Data to Empty Our Wallet*
    KR - March 15 2015 - pNA [501+]
Bernauer, James A. - *Integrating Pedagogy and Technology: Improving Teaching and Learning in Higher Education*
    VOYA - v38 - i5 - Dec 2015 - p81(2) [501+]
Bernauer, James W. - *"The Tragic Couple": Encounters between Jews and Jesuits*
    Six Ct J - v46 - i2 - Summer 2015 - p448-450 [501+]
Berndt, David - *Overcoming Anxiety: Self-Help Anxiety Relief*
    SPBW - Oct 2015 - pNA [51-500]

Berndt, Guido M. - *Arianism: Roman Heresy and Barbarian Creed*
  HNet - May 2015 - pNA [501+]
Berndt, Rainer - *Eure Namen sind im Buch des Lebens geschrieben: Antike und mittelalterliche Quellen als Grundlage moderner prosopographischer Forschung*
  Med R - May 2015 - pNA [501+]
  Glaubensheil: Wegweisung ins Christentum gemass der Lehre Hildegards von Bingen
  Specu - v90 - i2 - April 2015 - p504-505 [501+]
Berne, Emma Carlson - *Did Christopher Columbus Really Discover America?: And Other Questions about the New World*
  c HB Guide - v26 - i2 - Fall 2015 - p214(1) [51-500]
  Run Your Own Babysitting Business
  c Teach Lib - v42 - i3 - Feb 2015 - p9(1) [51-500]
  What Are Graphic Novels?
  c HB Guide - v26 - i1 - Spring 2015 - p186(1) [51-500]
Berne, Jennifer - *Calvin, Look Out!: A Bookworm Birdie Gets Glasses (Illus. by Bendis, Keith)*
  c HB Guide - v26 - i1 - Spring 2015 - p22(1) [51-500]
Berne, Suzanne - *The Dogs of Littlefield*
  y BL - v112 - i6 - Nov 15 2015 - p21(1) [51-500]
  KR - Oct 1 2015 - pNA [501+]
  PW - v262 - i48 - Nov 30 2015 - p36(3) [51-500]
Berneger, Marcia - *Buster the Little Garbage Truck (Illus. by Zimmer, Kevin)*
  c CH Bwatch - June 2015 - pNA [51-500]
  c HB Guide - v26 - i2 - Fall 2015 - p6(1) [51-500]
  c KR - Feb 15 2015 - pNA [51-500]
Berner, Alexander - *Kreuzzug und Regionale Herrschaft: Die Alteren Grafen von Berg 1147-1225*
  HNet - Feb 2015 - pNA [501+]
Berner, Boel - *Knowledge and Evidence: Investigating Technologies in Practice*
  T&C - v56 - i3 - July 2015 - p749-750 [501+]
Berney, Lou - *The Long and Faraway Gone*
  BL - v111 - i9-10 - Jan 1 2015 - p47(2) [51-500]
  WLT - v89 - i3-4 - May-August 2015 - p109(1) [51-500]
Bernhard, Durga Yael - *Just Like Me, Climbing a Tree: Exploring Trees around the World (Illus. by Bernhard, Durga Yael)*
  c SLJ - v61 - i9 - Sept 2015 - p178(1) [51-500]
  c CH Bwatch - May 2015 - pNA [501+]
  c CH Bwatch - June 2015 - pNA [51-500]
  c KR - Feb 15 2015 - pNA [51-500]
Bernhard, Michael H. - *Twenty Years After Communism: The Politics of Memory and Commemoration*
  E-A St - v67 - i3 - July 2015 - p1331(2) [501+]
Bernhard, Virginia - *The Hoggs of Texas: Letters and Memoirs of an Extraordinary Family, 1887-1906*
  SHQ - v118 - i3 - Jan 2015 - p329-330 [501+]
Bernick, Michael - *The Autism Job Club: The Neurodiverse Workforce in the New Normal of Employment*
  LJ - v140 - i6 - April 1 2015 - p101(1) [51-500]
Bernier, Celeste-Marie - *Suffering and Sunset: World War I in the Art and Life of Horace Pippin*
  KR - June 15 2015 - pNA [501+]
Bernier, Craig - *Your Life Idyllic*
  ABR - v36 - i2 - Jan-Feb 2015 - p30(4) [501+]
Bernieres, Louis de - *Birds without Wings*
  CC - v132 - i9 - April 29 2015 - p3(1) [51-500]
Bernofsky, Susan - *The End of Days*
  NY - v90 - i42 - Jan 5 2015 - p73 [51-500]
  NYRB - v62 - i6 - April 2 2015 - p70(3) [501+]
  The Metamorphosis
  WLT - v89 - i1 - Jan-Feb 2015 - p66(2) [501+]
Berns, Nancy - *Closure: The Rush to End Grief and What It Costs Us*
  SF - v93 - i3 - March 2015 - pe81 [501+]
  SF - v93 - i3 - March 2015 - pNA [501+]
Bernstein, David - *Goblins*
  BL - v111 - i22 - August 1 2015 - p42(1) [51-500]
Bernstein, Howard - *All Simple Things But Time*
  KR - May 15 2015 - pNA [51-500]
Bernstein, Jeremy - *Hitler's Uranium Club: The Secret Recordings at Farm Hall*
  TimHES - i2200 - April 23 2015 - p51(1) [501+]
Bernstein, Jonathan - *Bridget Wilder: Spy-in-Training*
  c KR - June 15 2015 - pNA [51-500]
  c SLJ - v61 - i6 - June 2015 - p97(1) [51-500]
Bernstein, Leonard - *On the Town*
  Theat J - v67 - i2 - May 2015 - p295-309 [501+]
  Theat J - v67 - i2 - May 2015 - p295-309 [501+]
Bernstein, Mary - *The Marrying Kind? Debating Same-Sex Marriage within the Lesbian and Gay Movement*
  CS - v44 - i1 - Jan 2015 - p35-37 [501+]

Bernstein, Nell - *Burning Down the House: The End of Youth Prison*
  SLJ - v61 - i2 - Feb 2015 - p113(1) [501+]
Bernstein, Richard - *China 1945: Mao's Revolution and America's Fateful Choice*
  J Mil H - v79 - i2 - April 2015 - p536-538 [501+]
  Nat R - v67 - i1 - Jan 26 2015 - p48 [501+]
  NYTBR - Jan 11 2015 - p17(L) [501+]
  NYTBR - Nov 22 2015 - p36(L) [501+]
Bernstein, William J. - *Rational Expectations: Asset Allocation for Investing Adults*
  Barron's - v95 - i27 - July 6 2015 - p35(1) [501+]
Berra, Tim M. - *Darwin and His Children: His Other Legacy*
  QRB - v90 - i1 - March 2015 - p72(1) [501+]
Berridge, W.J. - *Civil Uprisings in Modern Sudan: The 'Khartoum Springs' of 1964 and 1985*
  TLS - i5860 - July 24 2015 - p26(1) [501+]
Berrigan, Frida - *It Runs in the Family*
  AM - v212 - i3 - Feb 2 2015 - p14(1) [501+]
Berry, Amanda - *Animal Knits for Kids: 30 Cute Knitted Projects They'll Love*
  PW - v262 - i11 - March 16 2015 - p81(1) [501+]
Berry, Ciaran - *The Dead Zoo*
  ILS - v35 - i1 - Fall 2015 - p23(1) [501+]
Berry, D.H. - *Form and Function in Roman Oratory*
  Class R - v65 - i2 - Oct 2015 - p435-438 [501+]
Berry, David M. - *Understanding Digital Humanities*
  HNet - Jan 2015 - pNA [501+]
Berry, Ian - *Someday Is Now: The Art of Corita Kent*
  Stud Hum - v41 - i1-2 - March 2015 - p259(3) [501+]
Berry, Julie - *The Scandalous Sisterhood of Prickwillow Place (Read by Entwistle, Jayne). Audiobook Review*
  c BL - v111 - i14 - March 15 2015 - p24(2) [501+]
  y SLJ - v61 - i6 - June 2015 - p53(3) [501+]
  The Scandalous Sisterhood of Prickwillow Place
  y HB Guide - v26 - i1 - Spring 2015 - p70(1) [51-500]
  y Sch Lib - v63 - i2 - Summer 2015 - p114(1) [51-500]
Berry, Liz - *Black Country*
  NS - v144 - i5246 - Jan 23 2015 - p42(2) [501+]
Berry, Lynne - *Pig and Pug (Illus. by Correll, Gemma)*
  c CCB-B - v69 - i1 - Sept 2015 - p10(1) [51-500]
  c CH Bwatch - Sept 2015 - pNA [51-500]
  c HB Guide - v26 - i2 - Fall 2015 - p6(1) [51-500]
  c KR - April 1 2015 - pNA [51-500]
  c PW - v262 - i15 - April 13 2015 - p77(2) [51-500]
  c SLJ - v61 - i5 - May 2015 - p82(1) [51-500]
  c Teach Lib - v43 - i1 - Oct 2015 - p28(1) [51-500]
  Squid Kid the Magnificent (Illus. by LaMarca, Luke)
  c HB Guide - v26 - i2 - Fall 2015 - p6(1) [51-500]
  c KR - April 15 2015 - pNA [51-500]
  c SLJ - v61 - i6 - June 2015 - p78(1) [51-500]
Berry, Mark - *After Wagner: Histories of Modernist Music Drama from Parsifal to Nono*
  MT - v156 - i1930 - Spring 2015 - p117-120 [501+]
Berry, Mary Frances - *Five Dollars and a Pork Chop Sandwich*
  KR - Nov 1 2015 - pNA [501+]
Berry, Nina - *The Notorious Pagan Jones*
  PW - v262 - i14 - April 6 2015 - p63(1) [51-500]
  y BL - v111 - i16 - April 15 2015 - p56(1) [51-500]
  y HB Guide - v26 - i2 - Fall 2015 - p111(1) [51-500]
  y KR - March 15 2015 - pNA [51-500]
  y SLJ - v61 - i6 - June 2015 - p120(2) [51-500]
  y VOYA - v38 - i3 - August 2015 - p54(1) [51-500]
Berry, S.L. - *E.E. Cummings (Illus. by Eidrigevicius, Stasys)*
  c HB Guide - v26 - i1 - Spring 2015 - p191(1) [51-500]
  Emily Dickinson (Illus. by Stermer, Dugald)
  c HB Guide - v26 - i1 - Spring 2015 - p191(1) [51-500]
  Langston Hughes
  c HB Guide - v26 - i1 - Spring 2015 - p191(1) [51-500]
Berry, Stephen R. - *A Path in the Mighty Waters: Shipboard Life and Atlantic Crossings to the New World*
  CC - v132 - i21 - Oct 14 2015 - p33(2) [501+]
  W&M Q - v72 - i3 - July 2015 - p509-512 [501+]
Berry, Steve - *The Patriot Threat*
  BL - v111 - i9-10 - Jan 1 2015 - p50(1) [51-500]
  KR - Jan 15 2015 - pNA [51-500]
  LJ - v140 - i1 - Feb 1 2015 - p72(1) [51-500]
  PW - v262 - i4 - Jan 26 2015 - p148(1) [51-500]
Berry, Wendell - *Our Only World: Ten Essays*
  AM - v212 - i20 - June 22 2015 - p31(3) [51-500]
  CC - v132 - i15 - July 22 2015 - p43(1) [51-500]

This Day: Collected and New Sabbath Poems
  Sew R - v123 - i1 - Wntr 2015 - p182-191 [501+]
  WLT - v89 - i5 - Sept-Oct 2015 - p70(2) [501+]
Berryman, John - *77 Dream Songs*
  Lon R Bks - v37 - i13 - July 2 2015 - p9(4) [501+]
  NYRB - v62 - i10 - June 4 2015 - p40(4) [501+]
  TLS - i5836 - Feb 6 2015 - p8(2) [501+]
  Berryman's Sonnets
  Lon R Bks - v37 - i13 - July 2 2015 - p9(4) [501+]
  TLS - i5836 - Feb 6 2015 - p8(2) [501+]
  The Dream Songs
  Lon R Bks - v37 - i13 - July 2 2015 - p9(4) [501+]
  TLS - i5836 - Feb 6 2015 - p8(2) [501+]
  The Heart Is Strange: New Selected Poems
  Atl - v315 - i2 - March 2015 - p51(3) [501+]
  NYRB - v62 - i10 - June 4 2015 - p40(4) [501+]
  TLS - i5836 - Feb 6 2015 - p8(2) [501+]
  The Heart Is Strange
  Lon R Bks - v37 - i13 - July 2 2015 - p9(4) [501+]
Bersani, Leo - *Thoughts and Things*
  G&L Rev W - v22 - i5 - Sept-Oct 2015 - p37(1) [501+]
Berthard, Wayne - *The Valley of Two Moons*
  Roundup M - v22 - i6 - August 2015 - p26(1) [501+]
Berthinussen, Anna - *Bat Conservation: Global Evidence for the Effects of Interventions*
  QRB - v90 - i2 - June 2015 - p212(1) [501+]
Berthon, Guillaume - *L'Intention du poete: Clement Marot "autheur"*
  Ren Q - v68 - i3 - Fall 2015 - p1123-1124 [501+]
Bertino, Marie-Helene - *2 a.m. at the Cat's Pajamas (Read by Goethals, Angela). Audiobook Review*
  y BL - v111 - i11 - Feb 1 2015 - p58(1) [51-500]
Bertman, Jennifer Chambliss - *Book Scavenger (Illus. by Watts, Sarah)*
  c CCB-B - v69 - i1 - Sept 2015 - p10(2) [51-500]
  y HB - v91 - i5 - Sept-Oct 2015 - p93(2) [51-500]
  c KR - April 15 2015 - pNA [51-500]
  c PW - v262 - i15 - April 13 2015 - p80(2) [51-500]
  c PW - v262 - i49 - Dec 2 2015 - p74(1) [51-500]
  c SLJ - v61 - i5 - May 2015 - p101(2) [51-500]
  y VOYA - v38 - i2 - June 2015 - p54(2) [51-500]
Berto, Luigi Andrea - *In Search of the First Venetians: Prosopography of Early Medieval Venice*
  Med R - August 2015 - pNA [501+]
Bertrand, Cara - *Lost in Thought*
  y Teach Lib - v42 - i3 - Feb 2015 - p28(4) [51-500]
Bertrand-Dagenbach, Cecile - *Histoire Auguste, vol. 3, part 2: Vie d'Alexandre Severe*
  HNet - March 2015 - pNA [501+]
Bertrand, Diane Gonzales - *A Bean and Cheese Taco Birthday / Un Cumpleanos Con Tacos de Frijoles Con Queso (Illus. by Trujillo, Robert)*
  c KR - Sept 1 2015 - pNA [51-500]
  Cecilia and Miguel Are Best Friends (Illus. by Muraida, Thelma)
  c CH Bwatch - Jan 2015 - pNA [51-500]
  c HB Guide - v26 - i1 - Spring 2015 - p22(1) [51-500]
Bertrand, Neal - *Dad's War Photos: Adventures in the South Pacific*
  RVBW - June 2015 - pNA [51-500]
Bertsch, David Riley - *The River of No Return*
  RVBW - Feb 2015 - pNA [51-500]
Berube, Claude - *Syren's Song*
  PW - v262 - i39 - Sept 28 2015 - p67(1) [51-500]
Berube, Kristen - *Confessions of a Camo Queen: Living with an Outdoorsman*
  RVBW - Nov 2015 - pNA [51-500]
Berube, Michael - *The Humanities, Higher Education, and Academic Freedom: Three Necessary Arguments*
  TimHES - i2198 - April 9 2015 - p52-53 [501+]
  TLS - i5869 - Sept 25 2015 - p26(2) [501+]
  The Secret Life of Stories: From Don Quixote to Harry Potter, How Understanding Intellectual Disability Transforms the Way We Read
  KR - Nov 1 2015 - pNA [501+]
  LJ - v140 - i20 - Dec 1 2015 - p100(1) [51-500]
Berwald, Olaf - *A Companion to the Works of Max Frisch*
  MLR - v110 - i2 - April 2015 - p597-599 [501+]
Besant, Annie - *The Dragon's Toothache*
  c KR - Dec 1 2015 - pNA [51-500]
Besatzungskinder und Wehrmachtskinder - Auf der Suche nach Identitat und Resilienz
  HNet - July 2015 - pNA [501+]

Besel, Jen - *Custom Confections: Delicious Desserts You Can Create and Enjoy*
   c VOYA - v38 - i1 - April 2015 - p86(1) [51-500]

Besel, Richard D. - *Performance on Behalf of the Environment*
   Theat J - v67 - i3 - Oct 2015 - p568-569 [501+]

Besh, John - *Besh Big Easy*
   New Or - v50 - i2 - Nov 2015 - p50(1) [501+]

Beskow, Elsa - *The Tale of the Little, Little Old Woman*
   c CH Bwatch - Jan 2015 - pNA [51-500]

Besky, Sarah - *The Darjeeling Distinction: Labor and Justice on Fair-Trade Tea Plantations in India*
   Pac A - v88 - i2 - June 2015 - p341 [501+]

Besnier, Niko - *Gender on the Edge: Transgender, Gay, and Other Pacific Islanders*
   Pac A - v88 - i4 - Dec 2015 - p968 [501+]

Bess, Michael - *Our Grandchildren Redesigned: Life in the Bioengineered Society of the Near Future*
   KR - July 1 2015 - pNA [501+]

Bessel, Richard - *Violence: A Modern Obsession*
   NS - v144 - i5273 - July 31 2015 - p62(3) [501+]

Bessen, James - *Learning by Doing*
   Har Bus R - v93 - i3 - March 2015 - p126(2) [501+]

Bessenecker, Scott A. - *Overturning Tables: Freeing Missions from the Christian-Industrial Complex*
   IBMR - v39 - i2 - April 2015 - p98(2) [501+]

Bessire, Lucas - *Behold the Black Caiman: A Chronicle of Ayoreo Life*
   TLS - i5860 - July 24 2015 - p22(1) [501+]
   Radio Fields: Anthropology and Wireless Sound in the 21st Century
   JRAI - v21 - i1 - March 2015 - p214(2) [501+]

Bessler, John D. - *The Birth of American Law: An Italian Philosopher and the American Revolution*
   CrimJR - v40 - i1 - March 2015 - p107-109 [501+]
   JSH - v81 - i4 - Nov 2015 - p945(2) [501+]

Best, Cari - *My Three Best Friends and Me, Zulay (Illus. by Brantley-Newton, Vanessa)*
   c HB Guide - v26 - i2 - Fall 2015 - p26(1) [51-500]

Best, Clare - *Excisions*
   CWS - v30 - i2-3 - Fall-Winter 2015 - p122(2) [501+]

Best, Joel - *Everyone's a Winner: Life in Our Congratulatory Culture*
   SF - v93 - i3 - March 2015 - pe76 [501+]

Best, Shaun - *Zygmunt Bauman: Why Good People Do Bad Things*
   CS - v44 - i3 - May 2015 - p305-314 [501+]

Betancourt, Ingrid - *The Blue Line*
   BL - v112 - i6 - Nov 15 2015 - p20(1) [51-500]
   KR - Nov 15 2015 - pNA [501+]
   LJ - v140 - i20 - Dec 1 2015 - p89(1) [51-500]
   PW - v262 - i42 - Oct 19 2015 - p51(2) [51-500]

Betancur, John J. - *Reinventing Race, Reinventing Racism*
   CS - v44 - i3 - May 2015 - p435(1) [501+]

Bethencourt, Francisco - *Racism and Ethnic Relations in the Portuguese-Speaking World*
   HER - v130 - i543 - April 2015 - p509(3) [501+]

Bethke, Jefferson - *It's Not What You Think: Why Christianity Is so Much More Than Going to Heaven When You Die*
   LJ - v140 - i16 - Oct 1 2015 - p64(2) [501+]

Bettalli, Marco - *Mercenari: Il mestiere delle armi nel mondo greco antico*
   Class R - v65 - i2 - Oct 2015 - p499-500 [501+]

Bettencourt, Megan Feldman - *Triumph of the Heart: Forgiveness in an Unforgiving World*
   PW - v262 - i24 - June 15 2015 - p76(2) [51-500]

Betteridge, Thomas - *Writing Faith and Telling Tales: Literature, Politics, and Religion in the Work of Thomas More*
   CHR - v101 - i3 - Summer 2015 - p648(3) [501+]
   HER - v130 - i544 - June 2015 - p729(2) [501+]
   MLR - v110 - i3 - July 2015 - p817-819 [501+]
   Ren Q - v68 - i1 - Spring 2015 - p351-352 [501+]

Betts, A.J. - *Zac & Mia (Read by Mondelli, Nicholas, with Kristin Condon)*
   SLJ - v61 - i3 - March 2015 - p78(2) [51-500]
   Zac & Mia
   y HB Guide - v26 - i1 - Spring 2015 - p100(2) [51-500]

Betts, Kate - *My Paris Dream: An Education in Style, Slang, and Seduction in the Great City on the Seine*
   BL - v111 - i17 - May 1 2015 - p73(1) [51-500]
   KR - March 1 2015 - pNA [51-500]
   LJ - v140 - i7 - April 15 2015 - p100(1) [51-500]
   NYT - July 18 2015 - pNA(L) [501+]

Betts, Matt - *Indelible Ink*
   PW - v262 - i24 - June 15 2015 - p67(1) [51-500]

Betts, Reginald Dwayne - *Bastards of the Reagan Era*
   NYT - Oct 13 2015 - pC1(L) [501+]
   BL - v112 - i3 - Oct 1 2015 - p11(1) [51-500]
   PW - v262 - i33 - August 17 2015 - p47(1) [51-500]

Betts, Richard K. - *American Force: Dangers, Delusions, and Dilemmas in National Security*
   NWCR - v68 - i2 - Spring 2015 - p131(3) [501+]

Between Politics and Culture: New Perspectives on the History of the Bohemian Lands and the First Czechoslovak Republic
   HNet - Jan 2015 - pNA [501+]

Betz, Ann - *Integration: The Power of Being Co-Active in Work and Life*
   RVBW - Nov 2015 - pNA [501+]

Beudel, Saskia - *A Country in Mind*
   WLT - v89 - i1 - Jan-Feb 2015 - p63(1) [51-500]

Beukeboom, Leo W. - *The Evolution of Sex Determination*
   QRB - v90 - i3 - Sept 2015 - p333(2) [501+]

Beus, Bryan - *Westly: A Spider's Tale (Illus. by Beus, Bryan)*
   c BL - v112 - i1 - Sept 1 2015 - p118(2) [51-500]

Beveridge, Charles E. - *Frederick Law Olmsted: Plans and Views of Public Parks*
   NYRB - v62 - i17 - Nov 5 2015 - p12(3) [501+]
   Frederick Law Olmsted: Writings on Landscape, Culture, and Society
   NYRB - v62 - i17 - Nov 5 2015 - p12(3) [501+]

Beveridge, Jan - *Children into Swans: Fairy Tales and the Pagan Imagination*
   TLS - i5869 - Sept 25 2015 - p26(1) [501+]

Beveridge, Judith - *Devadatta's Poems*
   Meanjin - v74 - i1 - Autumn 2015 - p68(10) [501+]

Beverley, Jo - *Too Dangerous for a Lady*
   PW - v262 - i9 - March 2 2015 - p71(2) [51-500]

Beviglia, Jim - *Counting Down The Rolling Stones: Their 100 Finest Songs*
   BL - v112 - i3 - Oct 1 2015 - p8(1) [51-500]
   PW - v262 - i41 - Oct 12 2015 - p61(1) [51-500]

Bevine, Victor - *Certainty*
   G&L Rev W - v22 - i1 - Jan-Feb 2015 - p38(2) [501+]

Bew, John - *Castlereagh: A Life*
   CEH - v48 - i2 - June 2015 - p225-237 [501+]

Bew, Paul - *A Yankee in De Valera's Ireland: The Memoir of David Gray*
   ILS - v34 - i2 - Spring 2015 - p6(2) [501+]

Bewegung/en - 5. Jahrestagung der Fachgesellschaft Geschlechterstudien/Gender Studies Association
   HNet - April 2015 - pNA [501+]

Beyer, Kat - *The Halcyon Bird*
   c HB Guide - v26 - i1 - Spring 2015 - p101(1) [51-500]

Beylin, Marek - *Spokojnie, to tylko rewolucja*
   Nation - v300 - i1 - Jan 5 2015 - p27(10) [501+]

Beyond Modernity. Transepochal Perspectives on Spaces, Actors, and Structures
   HNet - March 2015 - pNA [501+]

Bezzant, Rhys S. - *Jonathan Edwards and the Church*
   CH - v84 - i2 - June 2015 - p452(3) [501+]
   JR - v95 - i4 - Oct 2015 - p540(3) [501+]

Bhadra, Sangeeta - *Sam's Pet Temper (Illus. by Arbona, Marion)*
   c HB Guide - v26 - i2 - Fall 2015 - p26(1) [51-500]
   c Res Links - v20 - i3 - Feb 2015 - p21(1) [501+]

Bhardwaj, Chandresh - *Break the Norms: Questioning Everything You Think You Know about God and Truth, Life and Death, Love and Sex*
   PW - v262 - i41 - Oct 12 2015 - p62(2) [51-500]

Bhaskar, Sita - *Product Details*
   KR - August 15 2015 - pNA [501+]

Bhattacharya, Shaoni - *Watch My Baby Grow: One Baby, One Year, One Extraordinary Project*
   LJ - v140 - i3 - Feb 15 2015 - p81(3) [501+]

Bhattacharyay, Biswa Nath - *Infrastructure for Asian Connectivity*
   Pac A - v88 - i1 - March 2015 - p149 [501+]

Bhreathnach, Edel - *Ireland in the Medieval World AD 400-1000: Landscape, Kingship, and Religion*
   Med R - May 2015 - pNA [501+]

Bhutto, Fatima - *The Shadow of the Crescent Moon*
   BL - v111 - i12 - Feb 15 2015 - p32(2) [51-500]
   KR - Feb 1 2015 - pNA [501+]
   NY - v91 - i12 - May 11 2015 - p77 [501+]
   NYTBR - April 19 2015 - p23(L) [501+]
   PW - v262 - i4 - Jan 26 2015 - p146(1) [51-500]

Bialosky, Jill - *The Players: Poems*
   BL - v111 - i12 - Feb 15 2015 - p22(1) [51-500]
   LJ - v140 - i6 - April 1 2015 - p97(1) [51-500]
   NY - v91 - i9 - April 20 2015 - p89 [501+]
   PW - v262 - i7 - Feb 16 2015 - p159(1) [51-500]

The Prize
   BL - v111 - i22 - August 1 2015 - p29(1) [51-500]
   KR - Sept 1 2015 - pNA [501+]
   NY - v91 - i29 - Sept 28 2015 - p72 [501+]
   NYTBR - Sept 27 2015 - p30(L) [501+]
   PW - v262 - i29 - July 20 2015 - p162(1) [51-500]

Bianca, Mari - *The Lost Girl*
   y KR - Oct 1 2015 - pNA [501+]

Biancotti, Deborah - *Zer0es (Read by Benson, Amber). Audiobook Review*
   y SLJ - v61 - i11 - Nov 2015 - p74(1) [51-500]
   Zer0es
   y HB - v91 - i6 - Nov-Dec 2015 - p93(2) [51-500]
   y Magpies - v30 - i4 - Sept 2015 - p17(1) [501+]
   y Sch Lib - v63 - i4 - Winter 2015 - p251(1) [51-500]
   c VOYA - v38 - i3 - August 2015 - p85(1) [51-500]

Bible, Michael - *Sophia*
   PW - v262 - i41 - Oct 12 2015 - p47(1) [51-500]
   KR - Oct 1 2015 - pNA [501+]

Bick, Ilsa J. - *The Dickens Mirror*
   y BL - v111 - i12 - Feb 15 2015 - p80(1) [51-500]
   y HB Guide - v26 - i2 - Fall 2015 - p111(1) [51-500]
   y KR - Jan 1 2015 - pNA [501+]
   y VOYA - v37 - i6 - Feb 2015 - p72(1) [51-500]
   White Space (Read by McInerney, Kathleen). Audiobook Review
   c BL - v111 - i14 - March 15 2015 - p24(2) [51-500]
   White Space
   y Teach Lib - v42 - i3 - Feb 2015 - p28(4) [501+]

Bickenbach, Matthias - *Die Geschwindigkeitsfabrik: Eine Fragmentarische Kulturgeschichte des Autounfalls*
   HNet - Feb 2015 - pNA [501+]

Bickerton, Derek - *More Than Nature Needs: Language, Mind, and Evolution*
   Lang Soc - v44 - i5 - Nov 2015 - p749-750 [501+]

Bickle, Laura - *Dark Alchemy*
   PW - v262 - i4 - Jan 26 2015 - p152(1) [51-500]
   Mercury Retrograde. E-book Review
   PW - v262 - i36 - Sept 7 2015 - p50(1) [51-500]

Bicknell, John - *America, 1844: Religious Fervor, Westward Expansion, and the Presidential Election That Transformed the Nation*
   Reason - v46 - i11 - April 2015 - p62(1) [51-500]

Bicudo, Edison - *Review of Pharmaceutical Research, Democracy and Conspiracy: International Clinical Trials in Local Medical Institutions*
   MAQ - v29 - i2 - June 2015 - pb1-b3 [501+]

Biddinger, Betty - *Small Enterprise*
   RVBW - Nov 2015 - pNA [501+]

Biddle, Buffie - *Pura Vida Mae!: An Original Story for Children*
   c KR - Oct 15 2015 - pNA [501+]

Biddlecombe, Steven - *The Historia Ierosolimitana of Baldric of Bourgueil*
   CHR - v101 - i3 - Summer 2015 - p619(2) [501+]
   Med R - Feb 2015 - pNA [501+]

Biddulph, Rob - *Blown Away (Illus. by Biddulph, Rob)*
   c CCB-B - v68 - i7 - March 2015 - p348(1) [51-500]
   c HB - v91 - i2 - March-April 2015 - p70(2) [51-500]
   c HB Guide - v26 - i2 - Fall 2015 - p27(1) [51-500]

Bidwell, John - *American Paper Mills, 1690-1832: A Directory of the Paper Trade with Notes on Products, Watermarks, Distribution Methods, and Manufacturing Techniques*
   RAH - v43 - i3 - Sept 2015 - p468-470 [501+]

Biederman, Edwin W., Jr. - *Improbable Future*
   SPBW - Nov 2015 - pNA [501+]

Biedrzycki, David - *Breaking News: Bear Alert*
   c HB Guide - v26 - i2 - Fall 2015 - p27(1) [51-500]
   Me and My Dragon: Christmas Spirit (Illus. by Biedrzycki, David)
   c PW - v262 - i37 - Sept 14 2015 - p71(1) [51-500]
   c SLJ - v61 - i10 - Oct 2015 - p61(1) [51-500]
   Me and My Dragon (Illus. by Biedrzycki, David)
   c KR - Sept 1 2015 - pNA [51-500]

Bieger, Laura - *Revisiting the Sixties: Interdisciplinary Perspectives on America's Longest Decade*
   JAH - v102 - i1 - June 2015 - p308-309 [501+]

Biehl, Janet - *Ecology or Catastrophe: The Life of Murray Bookchin*
   Nature - v527 - i7577 - Nov 12 2015 - p163(1) [51-500]

Biehler, Dawn Day - *Pests in the City: Flies, Bedbugs, Cockroaches, and Rats*
   RAH - v43 - i3 - Sept 2015 - p527-531 [501+]

Bien, David - *Interpreting the Ancien Regime*
   JMH - v87 - i2 - June 2015 - p448(3) [501+]

Bien, Peter A. - *Zorba the Greek*
   WLT - v89 - i2 - March-April 2015 - p65(1) [51-500]

Bienert, Maren - *Protestantische Selbstverortung: Die Rezensionen Ernst Troeltschs*
    Theol St - v76 - i2 - June 2015 - p352(2) [501+]

Bienvenu, Marcelle - *Cooking Up a Storm: Recipes Lost and Found from the Times-Picayune of New Orleans*
    New Or - v49 - i11 - August 2015 - p42(1) [501+]

Bier, Laura - *Revolutionary Womanhood: Feminism, Modernity, and the State in Nasser's Egpyt*
    CWS - v30 - i2-3 - Fall-Winter 2015 - p132(2) [501+]

  Revolutionary Womanhood: Feminisms, Modernity, and the State in Nasser's Egypt
    JWH - v27 - i2 - Summer 2015 - p182(12) [501+]

Biermann, Joel D. - *A Case for Character: Towards a Lutheran Virtue Ethics*
    Theol St - v76 - i3 - Sept 2015 - p648(2) [501+]

Biermann, Pieke - *"Wir sind Frauen wie andere auch!" Prostituierte und ihre Kampfe*
    Ger Q - v88 - i3 - Summer 2015 - p402(2) [501+]

Biers, Katherine - *Virtual Modernism: Writing and Technology in the Progressive Era*
    Am St - v54 - i2 - Summer 2015 - p99-101 [501+]

Bierschenk, Thomas - *50 Jahre Unabhangigkeit in Afrika: Kontinuitaten, Bruche, Perspektiven*
    HNet - July 2015 - pNA [501+]

  States at Work: Dynamics of African Bureaucracies
    For Aff - v94 - i3 - May-June 2015 - pNA [501+]

Bierut, Michael - *How to Use Graphic Design to Sell Things, Explain Things, Make Things Look Better, Make People Laugh, Make People Cry, and (Every Once in a While) Change the World*
    NYTBR - Dec 6 2015 - p30(L) [501+]

Biespiel, David - *A Long High Whistle: Selected Columns on Poetry*
    LJ - v140 - i11 - June 15 2015 - p85(2) [51-500]

Bieter, John P., Jr. - *Showdown in the Big Quiet: Land, Myth, and Government in the American West*
    Bwatch - August 2015 - pNA [51-500]
    Roundup M - v23 - i1 - Oct 2015 - p32(1) [51-500]

Big Data in a Transdisciplinary Perspective: Herrenhauser Konferenz
    HNet - July 2015 - pNA [501+]

Big Freedia - *Big Freedia: God Save the Queen Diva!*
    y BL - v111 - i22 - August 1 2015 - p22(1) [51-500]

The Big Trip: Your Ultimate Guide to Gap Years and Overseas Adventures, 3d ed.
    LJ - v140 - i13 - August 1 2015 - p115(1) [51-500]

Biggar, Nigel - *In Defence of War*
    NWCR - v68 - i3 - Summer 2015 - p155(3) [501+]
    Parameters - v45 - i2 - Summer 2015 - p125(2) [501+]
    TT - v72 - i2 - July 2015 - p244-245 [501+]

Biggs, Joanna - *All Day Long: A Portrait of Britain at Work*
    NS - v144 - i5258 - April 17 2015 - p59(1) [501+]
    Spec - v327 - i9739 - April 25 2015 - p43(2) [501+]
    TLS - i5875 - Nov 6 2015 - p30(1) [51-500]

Bigliazzi, Silvia - *Revisiting The Tempest: The Capacity to Signify*
    Ren Q - v68 - i2 - Summer 2015 - p790-791 [501+]

Bigs, Ward - *The Complete Poems of James Dickey*
    PSQ - v89 - i1 - Spring 2015 - p158(2) [501+]

Bijsterveld, Karin - *Sound and Safe: A History of Listening behind the Wheel*
    T&C - v56 - i2 - April 2015 - p555-556 [501+]

Bikont, Anna - *The Crime and the Silence: A Quest for the Truth of a Wartime Massacre*
    NS - v144 - i5281 - Sept 25 2015 - p72(2) [501+]

  The Crime and the Silence: Confronting the Massacre of Jews in Wartime Jedwabne
    LJ - v140 - i10 - June 1 2015 - p112(1) [51-500]
    NYRB - v62 - i18 - Nov 19 2015 - p31(3) [501+]
    NYTBR - Nov 8 2015 - p38(L) [501+]
    PW - v262 - i27 - July 6 2015 - p58(1) [501+]

  The Crime and the Silence
    KR - May 15 2015 - pNA [501+]

Bilal, Dania - *New Directions in Children's and Adolescents' Information Behavior Research*
    LR - v64 - i4-5 - April-May 2015 - p398-400 [501+]

Bilderback, Leslie - *No-Churn Ice Cream: Over 100 Simply Delicious No-Machine Frozen Treats*
    LJ - v140 - i7 - April 15 2015 - p110(1) [51-500]

  The Spiralized Kitchen: Transform Your Vegetables into Fresh and Surprising Meals
    BL - v111 - i14 - March 15 2015 - p36(1) [51-500]

Bildner, Phil - *Marvelous Cornelius: Hurricane Katrina and the Spirit of New Orleans (Illus. by Parra, John)*
    c KR - July 1 2015 - pNA [51-500]
    c SLJ - v61 - i10 - Oct 2015 - p72(1) [51-500]

  A Whole New Ballgame (Illus. by Probert, Tim)
    c KR - June 15 2015 - pNA [51-500]
    c PW - v262 - i20 - May 18 2015 - p86(1) [51-500]
    c SLJ - v61 - i3 - March 2015 - p131(2) [51-500]

Bilgrami, Akeel - *Who's Afraid of Academic Freedom?*
    HNet - Sept 2015 - pNA [501+]
    TLS - i5857 - July 3 2015 - p26(2) [501+]

Bilings, J. Todd - *Rejoicing in Lament: Wrestling with Incurable Cancer and Life in Christ*
    CC - v132 - i19 - Sept 16 2015 - p36(2) [501+]

Biller, Maxim - *Inside the Head of Bruno Schulz*
    NS - v144 - i5260 - May 1 2015 - p46(2) [51-500]
    TLS - i5852 - May 29 2015 - p21(1) [51-500]

Biller, Thomas - *Templerburgen*
    HNet - Jan 2015 - pNA [501+]

Billet, Marion - *Littleland: Around the World (Illus. by Billet, Marion)*
    c HB Guide - v26 - i2 - Fall 2015 - p6(1) [51-500]

Billett, Jesse D. - *The Divine Office in Anglo-Saxon England, 597-c. 1000*
    Med R - August 2015 - pNA [501+]

Billig, Michael - *Learn to Write Badly: How to Succeed in the Social Sciences*
    CS - v44 - i5 - Sept 2015 - p741-742 [501+]

Billingham, Mark - *From the Dead*
    RVBW - Feb 2015 - pNA [501+]

  Time of Death
    BL - v111 - i17 - May 1 2015 - p46(1) [51-500]
    KR - April 1 2015 - pNA [51-500]
    PW - v262 - i15 - April 13 2015 - p57(1) [51-500]

Billings, J. Todd - *Rejoicing in Lament: Wrestling with Incurable Cancer and Life in Christ*
    Ch Today - v59 - i1 - Jan-Feb 2015 - p63(1) [501+]
    PW - v262 - i3 - Jan 19 2015 - p78(1) [51-500]

Billings, Joshua - *Choruses, Ancient and Modern*
    Class R - v65 - i1 - April 2015 - p27-29 [501+]

  Genealogy of the Tragic: Greek Tragedy and German Philosophy
    TLS - i5874 - Oct 30 2015 - p9(2) [501+]

Bills, E.R. - *The 1910 Slocum Massacre: An Act of Genocide in East Texas*
    JSH - v81 - i3 - August 2015 - p756(2) [501+]

Bilton, Alan - *Silent Film Comedy and American Culture*
    J Am St - v49 - i3 - August 2015 - p637-639 [501+]
    SAH - v4 - i2 - Dec 15 2015 - p291-295 [501+]

Bilyeau, Nancy - *The Tapestry*
    KR - Jan 1 2015 - pNA [501+]

  The Tapestry (Read by Barber, Nicola). Audiobook Review
    LJ - v140 - i10 - June 1 2015 - p60(1) [51-500]

Binchy, Maeve - *Maeve's Times: In Her Own Words (Read by Binchy, Kate). Audiobook Review*
    LJ - v140 - i8 - May 1 2015 - p42(2) [51-500]

Binder, Amy J. - *Becoming Right: How Campuses Shape Young Conservatives*
    SF - v94 - i2 - Dec 2015 - pNA [501+]

Binder, Mike - *Keep Calm*
    BL - v112 - i7 - Dec 1 2015 - p29(1) [51-500]
    KR - Dec 1 2015 - pNA [51-500]
    PW - v262 - i51 - Dec 14 2015 - p60(1) [51-500]

Bindman, David - *The Image of the Black in Western Art, Vol. 5: The Twentieth Century: The Rise of Black Artists*
    LJ - v140 - i2 - Feb 1 2015 - p79(1) [51-500]

Bingham, Elizabeth - *Italian Survival Guide: The Language and Culture You Need to Travel with Confidence in Italy*
    SPBW - Nov 2015 - pNA [501+]

Bingham, Emily - *Irrepressible: The Jazz Age Life of Henrietta Bingham*
    BL - v111 - i16 - April 15 2015 - p5(1) [51-500]
    G&L Rev W - v22 - i5 - Sept-Oct 2015 - p45(1) [501+]
    KR - March 15 2015 - pNA [501+]
    LJ - v140 - i7 - April 15 2015 - p93(1) [51-500]
    NY - v91 - i18 - June 29 2015 - p71 [501+]
    NYT - June 7 2015 - p2(L) [51-500]
    NYTBR - July 5 2015 - p21(L) [501+]
    PW - v262 - i14 - April 6 2015 - p49(1) [51-500]
    Spec - v328 - i9748 - June 27 2015 - p36(2) [501+]
    TimHES - i2222 - Sept 24 2015 - p45(1) [501+]

Bingham, Harry - *The Strange Death of Fiona Griffiths*
    PW - v262 - i22 - June 1 2015 - p44(1) [51-500]

Bingham, Jane - *Neil Armstrong: First Man on the Moon (Fact Cat)*
    c Sch Lib - v63 - i3 - Autumn 2015 - p172(1) [51-500]

Bingham, Kelly - *Circle, Square, Moose (Illus. by Zelinsky, Paul O.)*
    c HB Guide - v26 - i1 - Spring 2015 - p22(1) [51-500]
    c Sch Lib - v63 - i1 - Spring 2015 - p25(1) [51-500]

Bingham, Lisa - *Desperado*
    PW - v262 - i16 - April 20 2015 - p61(1) [51-500]

Bingham, Sandra - *The Praetorian Guard: A History of Rome's Elite Special Forces*
    Historian - v77 - i2 - Summer 2015 - p374(2) [501+]

Bingmann, Melissa - *Prep School Cowboys: Ranch Schools in the American West*
    Roundup M - v22 - i5 - June 2015 - p35(1) [501+]
    Roundup M - v22 - i6 - August 2015 - p34(1) [501+]

Binkley, Sam - *Happiness as an Enterprise: An Essay on Neoliberal Life*
    CS - v44 - i2 - March 2015 - p288(1) [501+]

Binkow, Ana Howard - *Howard B. Wigglebottom Listens to a Friend (Illus. by Cutting, David A.)*
    c CH Bwatch - July 2015 - pNA [501+]

Binnema, Ted - *Enlightened Zeal: The Hudson's Bay Company and Scientific Networks, 1670-1870*
    AHR - v120 - i2 - April 2015 - p610-611 [501+]
    Beav - v95 - i2 - April-May 2015 - p52(2) [501+]
    Can Hist R - v96 - i1 - March 2015 - p114(3) [501+]
    HNet - July 2015 - pNA [501+]
    Isis - v106 - i2 - June 2015 - p449(2) [501+]
    WHQ - v46 - i4 - Winter 2015 - p504-505 [501+]

Binning, Sadhu - *Fauji Banta Singh and Other Stories*
    Can Lit - i224 - Spring 2015 - p111 [501+]

Binnington, Ian - *Confederate Visions: Nationalism, Symbolism, and the Imagined South in the Civil War*
    AHR - v120 - i2 - April 2015 - p626-627 [501+]
    JAH - v101 - i4 - March 2015 - p1275-1276 [501+]
    RAH - v43 - i3 - Sept 2015 - p490-497 [501+]

Binski, Paul - *Gothic Wonder: Art, Artifice and the Decorated Style, 1290-1350*
    HT - v65 - i8 - August 2015 - p60(2) [501+]
    TLS - i5845 - April 10 2015 - p10(3) [501+]

Bintley, Michael D.J. - *Trees and Timber in the Anglo-Saxon World*
    Med R - Feb 2015 - pNA [501+]

Biondi, Giuseppe Gilberto - *Il liber di Catullo: Tradizione, modelli e fortleben*
    Class R - v65 - i2 - Oct 2015 - p440-442 [501+]

Biow, Douglas - *On the Importance of Being an Individual in Renaissance Italy: Men, Their Professions, and Their Beards*
    Med R - August 2015 - pNA [501+]

Birch, Dinah - *The Small House at Allington*
    TLS - i5847 - April 24 2015 - p7(f2) [501+]

Birch, Kate Jarvik - *Perfected (Read by Durante, Emily). Audiobook Review*
    c SLJ - v61 - i6 - June 2015 - p66(1) [51-500]

Bird, Benjamin - *A Baby's Guide to Surviving Dad (Illus. by Americo, Tiago)*
    c KR - Dec 15 2015 - pNA [51-500]

  A Cat Is Chasing Me through This Book! (Illus. by Perez, Carmen)
    c Sch Lib - v63 - i2 - Summer 2015 - p89(1) [51-500]

  Don't Give This Book a Bowl of Milk! (Illus. by Perez, Carmen)
    c HB Guide - v26 - i2 - Fall 2015 - p27(1) [51-500]

  There's a Mouse Hiding in This Book (Illus. by Perez, Carmen)
    c HB Guide - v26 - i2 - Fall 2015 - p27(1) [51-500]

Bird, Betsy - *Wild Things! Acts of Mischief in Children's Literature*
    y HB Guide - v26 - i1 - Spring 2015 - p186(1) [51-500]

Bird, Faye - *My Second Life*
    y KR - Nov 15 2015 - pNA [51-500]
    y SLJ - v61 - i11 - Nov 2015 - p111(2) [51-500]
    y VOYA - v38 - i5 - Dec 2015 - p66(1) [51-500]

Bird, Fiona - *Seaweed in the Kitchen*
    TLS - i5872 - Oct 16 2015 - p30(1) [501+]

Bird, Gayle - *Freeform Wire Art Jewelry: Techniques for Designing with Wire, Beads and Gems*
    LJ - v140 - i10 - June 1 2015 - p104(2) [51-500]

Bird, Joan Carol - *The Holy Innocents and Other Stories*
    KR - Feb 1 2015 - pNA [501+]

Bird, Kai - *The Good Spy*
AM - v212 - i2 - Jan 19 2015 - p32(2) [501+]
Ent W - i1364 - May 22 2015 - p66(1) [501+]
NYTBR - June 7 2015 - p36(L) [501+]

Bird, Michael F. - *The Gospel of the Lord: How the Early Church Wrote the Story of Jesus*
Theol St - v76 - i4 - Dec 2015 - p836(2) [501+]

Bird, Susan Imhoff - *Howl: Of Woman and Wolf*
BL - v112 - i3 - Oct 1 2015 - p7(1) [501+]

Bird, William L., Jr. - *Souvenir Nation: Relics, Keepsakes, and Curios from the Smithsonian's National Museum of American History*
RAH - v43 - i1 - March 2015 - p103-109 [501+]

Birdsall, Bridget - *Double Exposure*
y CH Bwatch - Feb 2015 - pNA [51-500]

Birdsall, Jeanne - *The Penderwicks in Spring (Read by Denaker, Susan). Audiobook Review*
PW - v262 - i21 - May 25 2015 - p56(1) [51-500]
The Penderwicks in Spring
c HB Guide - v26 - i2 - Fall 2015 - p75(1) [51-500]
c BL - v111 - i11 - Feb 1 2015 - p53(1) [51-500]
c CCB-B - v68 - i8 - April 2015 - p390(1) [51-500]
y HB - v91 - i2 - March-April 2015 - p92(1) [51-500]
c KR - Jan 15 2015 - pNA [51-500]
c PW - v262 - i2 - Jan 12 2015 - p59(1) [51-500]
c PW - v262 - i49 - Dec 2 2015 - p72(2) [51-500]
c SLJ - v61 - i3 - March 2015 - p132(1) [51-500]
y VOYA - v37 - i6 - Feb 2015 - p53(2) [51-500]

Bireley, Robert - *Ferdinand II: Counter-Reformation Emperor, 1578-1637*
AM - v213 - i1 - Oct 26 2015 - p36(2) [501+]
CHR - v101 - i4 - Autumn 2015 - p939(2) [501+]

Birger, Jon - *Date-Onomics: How Dating Became a Lopsided Numbers Game*
KR - June 15 2015 - pNA [501+]
LJ - v140 - i2 - July 1 2015 - p101(2) [51-500]
NYTBR - Sept 13 2015 - p16(L) [501+]

Birk, Stine - *Using Images in Late Antiquity*
Med R - May 2015 - pNA [501+]

Birkerts, Sven - *Changing the Subject: Art and Attention in the Internet Age*
BL - v112 - i3 - Oct 1 2015 - p5(1) [51-500]
CHE - v62 - i4 - Sept 25 2015 - pB17(1) [501+]
KR - July 1 2015 - pNA [501+]
LJ - v140 - i14 - Sept 1 2015 - p136(1) [51-500]
NYTBR - Oct 4 2015 - p1(L) [501+]
PW - v262 - i32 - August 10 2015 - p52(1) [51-500]

Birkett, Georgie - *Teddy Bedtime (Illus. by Birkett, Georgie)*
c SLJ - v61 - i11 - Nov 2015 - p76(1) [51-500]

Birkett, Jennifer - *Undoing Time: The Life and Work of Samuel Beckett*
RVBW - Oct 2015 - pNA [501+]

Birkner, Thomas - *Mann des gedruckten Wortes: Helmut Schmidt und die Medien*
HNet - May 2015 - pNA [501+]

Birks, Peter - *The Roman Law of Obligations*
Law Q Rev - v131 - April 2015 - p338-340 [501+]

Birman, Lisa - *How to Walk Away*
ABR - v36 - i2 - Jan-Feb 2015 - p21(1) [501+]

Birmant, Julie - *Pablo (Illus. by Oubrerie, Clement)*
NS - v144 - i5262 - May 15 2015 - p43(1) [51-500]
BL - v111 - i18 - May 15 2015 - p41(1) [51-500]
PW - v262 - i17 - April 27 2015 - p60(1) [51-500]

Birmingham, John - *Ascendance*
PW - v262 - i16 - April 20 2015 - p60(1) [51-500]

Birmingham, Kevin - *The Most Dangerous Book: The Battle for James Joyce's Ulysses*
Ga R - v69 - i1 - Spring 2015 - p142-145 [501+]
NYRB - v62 - i7 - April 23 2015 - p50(3) [501+]

Birmingham, Maria - *A Beginner's Guide to Immortality: From Alchemy to Avatars (Illus. by Holinaty, Josh)*
c BL - v112 - i3 - Oct 1 2015 - p37(2) [51-500]
c KR - August 1 2015 - pNA [51-500]
c PW - v262 - i33 - August 17 2015 - p74(1) [501+]
c SLJ - v61 - i9 - Sept 2015 - p186(1) [51-500]
Tastes Like Music: 17 Quirks of the Brain and Body (Illus. by Melnychuk, Monika)
c CCB-B - v68 - i5 - Jan 2015 - p248(1) [51-500]
c HB Guide - v26 - i1 - Spring 2015 - p170(1) [51-500]

Birnbaum, Phyllis - *Manchu Princess, Japanese Spy: The Story of Kawashima Yoshiko, the Cross-Dressing Spy Who Commanded Her Own Army*
LJ - v140 - i5 - March 15 2015 - p113(1) [51-500]
NYTBR - May 3 2015 - p18(L) [501+]

Birnbaum, Pierre - *Leon Blum: Prime Minister, Socialist, Zionist*
Lon R Bks - v37 - i21 - Nov 5 2015 - p26(2) [501+]
NYRB - v62 - i13 - August 13 2015 - p76(2) [501+]
TLS - i5867 - Sept 11 2015 - p9(1) [501+]

Birney, Betty G. - *Humphrey Audio Collection, bks. 8-11. Audiobook Review*
c SLJ - v61 - i4 - April 2015 - p62(2) [51-500]
Humphrey's Creepy-Crawly Camping Adventure (Illus. by Burris, Priscilla)
c HB Guide - v26 - i2 - Fall 2015 - p64(1) [51-500]
c SLJ - v61 - i5 - May 2015 - p98(1) [51-500]
Humphrey's Playful Puppy Problem (Illus. by Burris, Priscilla)
c HB Guide - v26 - i1 - Spring 2015 - p57 [51-500]
Humphrey's Really Wheely Racing Day (Illus. by Burris, Priscilla)
c HB Guide - v26 - i1 - Spring 2015 - p57 [51-500]
Imagination According to Humphrey
c HB Guide - v26 - i2 - Fall 2015 - p75(1) [51-500]
c CH Bwatch - August 2015 - pNA [51-500]

Biro, Daniel Peter - *The String Quartets of Bela Bartok: Tradition and Legacy in Analytical Perspective*
MT - v156 - i1931 - Summer 2015 - p111-114 [501+]

Birstein, Yossel - *And So Is the Bus*
KR - Dec 15 2015 - pNA [51-500]

Birtcher, Baron R. - *Hard Latitudes*
KR - April 15 2015 - pNA [501+]
PW - v262 - i13 - March 30 2015 - p55(1) [51-500]

Birtolo, Dylan - *The Sheynan Trilogy*
PW - v262 - i27 - July 6 2015 - p50(1) [51-500]

Birzer, Bradley J. - *Russell Kirk: American Conservative*
Nat R - v67 - i22 - Dec 7 2015 - p42(2) [501+]

Bisanswa, Justin K. - *Dire le social dans le roman francophone contemporain*
Callaloo - v38 - i1 - Wntr 2015 - p206-208 [501+]

Bischof, Gunter - *The Life and Work of Gunther Anders: Emigre, Iconoclast, Philosopher, Man of Letters*
HNet - Feb 2015 - pNA [501+]
Relationships/Beziehungsgeschichten: Austria and the United States in the Twentieth Century
CEH - v48 - i3 - Sept 2015 - p446-447 [501+]
Relationships / Beziehungsgeschichten: Austria and the United States in the Twentieth Century
HNet - April 2015 - pNA [501+]

Bishir, Catherine W. - *Crafting Lives: African American Artisans in New Bern, North Carolina, 1770-1900*
JSH - v81 - i1 - Feb 2015 - p168(2) [501+]

Bishoff, Chad - *Surviving Puberty: Erecting Your Future and Making the Breast Decisions*
RVBW - August 2015 - pNA [51-500]

Bishop, Anne - *Vision in Silver*
BL - v111 - i13 - March 1 2015 - p31(1) [51-500]

Bishop, Cecile - *Postcolonial Criticism and Representations of African Dictatorship: The Aesthetics of Tyranny*
FS - v69 - i3 - July 2015 - p430-431 [501+]

Bishop, Claire - *Artificial Hells: Participatory Art and the Politics of Spectatorship*
PAJ - v37 - i2 - May 2015 - p103-110 [501+]

Bishop, Elizabeth - *The Collected Prose of Elizabeth Bishop*
TLS - i5868 - Sept 18 2015 - p16(1) [501+]

Bishop, Jeanne - *Change of Heart: Justice, Mercy, and Making Peace with My Sister's Killer*
CC - v132 - i9 - April 29 2015 - p40(2) [501+]
PW - v262 - i3 - Jan 19 2015 - p76(1) [51-500]

Bishop, Jeffrey P. - *The Anticipatory Corpse: Medicine, Power, and the Care of the Dying*
Pers PS - v44 - i4 - Oct-Dec 2015 - p261-265 [501+]

Bishop, Kay - *The Collection Program in Schools: Concepts and Practices, 5th ed.*
LQ - v85 - i1 - Jan 2015 - p114(3) [501+]

Bishop, Mary Harelkin - *Gina's Wheels (Illus. by Greenhorn, Diane L.)*
c Res Links - v20 - i3 - Feb 2015 - p2(2) [51-500]

Bishop, Nic - *Frogs*
c BL - v111 - i17 - May 1 2015 - p74(1) [51-500]

Bishop, Patrick - *The Hunt for Hitler's Warship*
Historian - v77 - i1 - Spring 2015 - p159(2) [501+]
The Reckoning: Death and Intrigue in the Promised Land: A True Detective Story
NYRB - v62 - i14 - Sept 24 2015 - p80(4) [501+]

Bishop, Sean - *The Night We're Not Sleeping In*
PSQ - v89 - i3 - Fall 2015 - p167(3) [501+]

Biskup, Agnieszka - *Super Cool Forces and Motion Activities with Max Axiom*
c HB Guide - v26 - i2 - Fall 2015 - p166(1) [51-500]
c Sch Lib - v63 - i1 - Autumn 2015 - p172(1) [51-500]

Bispinck, Henrik - *Fluchtlingslager im Nachkriegsdeutschland: Migration, Politik, Erinnerung*
HNet - March 2015 - pNA [501+]

Biss, Eula - *Notes From No Man's Land: American Essays*
Nation - v300 - i5 - Feb 2 2015 - p30(3) [501+]
On Immunity: An Inoculation (Read by Marston, Tamara). Audiobook Review
BL - v111 - i13 - March 1 2015 - p69(1) [51-500]
BL - v112 - i7 - Dec 1 2015 - p71(1) [501+]
On Immunity: An Inoculation
Am Sci - v103 - i3 - May-June 2015 - p229(2) [501+]
Bks & Cult - v21 - i1 - Jan-Feb 2015 - p33(1) [501+]
Nation - v300 - i5 - Feb 2 2015 - p30(3) [501+]
NS - v144 - i5249 - Feb 13 2015 - p54(2) [501+]
NYRB - v62 - i4 - March 5 2015 - p29(3) [501+]
NYTBR - Sept 20 2015 - p28(L) [501+]

Bissell, Tom - *Apostle: Travels among the Tombs of the Twelve*
LJ - v140 - i20 - Dec 1 2015 - p108(2) [501+]

Bissonette, Aimee - *North Woods Girl (Illus. by McGehee, Claudia)*
c KR - July 15 2015 - pNA [51-500]
c PW - v262 - i29 - July 20 2015 - p188(2) [51-500]
c SLJ - v61 - i10 - Oct 2015 - p72(1) [51-500]

Bissonnette, Zac - *Debt-Free U: How I Paid for an Outstanding College Education without Loans, Scholarships, or Mooching off My Parents*
BL - v111 - i21 - July 1 2015 - p22(2) [501+]
The Great Beanie Baby Bubble: Mass Delusion and the Dark Side of Cute
BL - v111 - i12 - Feb 15 2015 - p12(1) [501+]
NYTBR - March 22 2015 - p20(L) [501+]

Bittman, Mark - *A Bone to Pick. Audiobook Review*
y BL - v112 - i3 - Oct 1 2015 - p87(1) [501+]
A Bone to Pick (Read by Fass, Robert). Audiobook Review
LJ - v140 - i13 - August 1 2015 - p48(1) [51-500]
A Bone to Pick
BL - v111 - i17 - May 1 2015 - p64(1) [51-500]
KR - March 15 2015 - pNA [501+]
PW - v262 - i16 - April 20 2015 - p69(1) [51-500]
Mark Bittman's Kitchen Matrix
LJ - v140 - i15 - Sept 15 2015 - p100(1) [51-500]
PW - v262 - i38 - Sept 21 2015 - p68(1) [51-500]
Mark Bittman's Kitchen Matrix: Visual Recipes to Make Cooking Easier than Ever
NYTBR - Dec 6 2015 - p20(L) [501+]
NYTBR - Dec 6 2015 - p20(L) [501+]

Bittner, Kathleen - *Josette*
BL - v112 - i2 - Sept 15 2015 - p44(1) [51-500]

Bittner, Rosanne - *Do Not Forsake Me*
PW - v262 - i19 - May 11 2015 - p42(1) [51-500]
Thunder on the Plains
PW - v262 - i31 - August 3 2015 - p41(1) [51-500]

Bitton-Ashkelony, Brouria - *Between Personal and Institutional Religion: Self, Doctrine, and Practice in Late Antique Eastern Christianity*
Med R - June 2015 - pNA [501+]
Specu - v90 - i1 - Jan 2015 - p209-210 [501+]

Bivald, Katarina - *The Readers of Broken Wheel Recommend*
TimHES - i2222 - Sept 24 2015 - p41(1) [501+]
BL - v112 - i4 - Oct 15 2015 - p34(1) [501+]
KR - Nov 1 2015 - pNA [501+]
LJ - v140 - i13 - August 1 2015 - p77(1) [501+]

Bivins, Jason C. - *Spirits Rejoice! Jazz and American Religion*
BL - v111 - i13 - March 1 2015 - p13(1) [501+]
Dbt - v82 - i8 - August 2015 - p92(1) [501+]
LJ - v140 - i8 - May 1 2015 - p74(2) [51-500]

Bivins, Roberta - *Contagious Communities: Medicine, Migration, and the NHS in Post War Britain*
New Sci - v227 - i3039 - Sept 19 2015 - p43(1) [501+]

Bivolarov, Vasil - *Inquisitoren-Handbuher: Papsturkunden und juristische Gutachten aus dem 13. Jahrhundert mit Edition des Consilium von Guido Fulcodii*
Med R - June 2015 - pNA [501+]

Bivona, Michael - *Retiring? Beware!! Don't Run Out of Money and Don't Become Bored*
RVBW - June 2015 - pNA [51-500]

Bix, Amy Sue - *Girls Coming to Tech! A History of American Engineering Education for Women*
AHR - v120 - i3 - June 2015 - p1059-1061 [501+]
Isis - v106 - i1 - March 2015 - p207(2) [501+]
T&C - v56 - i4 - Oct 2015 - p995-996 [501+]
Wom R Bks - v32 - i2 - March-April 2015 - p8(3) [501+]

Bixley, Donovan - *Pussycat, Pussycat and More: Purrfect Nursery Rhymes (Illus. by Bixley, Donovan)*
   c Magpies - v30 - i5 - Nov 2015 - pS5(1) [501+]

Bizzle, Ben - *Start a Revolution: Stop Acting Like a Library*
   LJ - v140 - i7 - April 15 2015 - p107(1) [51-500]
   VOYA - v38 - i2 - June 2015 - p90(2) [501+]

Bjergso, Mikkel Borg - *Mikkeller's Book of Beer: Includes 25 Original Mikkeller Brewing Recipes*
   LJ - v140 - i9 - May 15 2015 - p99(2) [51-500]

Bjorge, Eirik - *The Evolutionary Interpretation of Treaties*
   Law Q Rev - v131 - July 2015 - p507-510 [501+]

Bjorgolfsson, Thor - *Billions to Bust--and Back: How I Made, Lost and Rebuilt a Fortune, and What I Learned on the Way*
   Econ - v414 - i8920 - Jan 10 2015 - p78(US) [501+]

Bjork, Robert E. - *The Old English Poems of Cynewulf*
   Med R - Feb 2015 - pNA [501+]
Old English Shorter Poems, vol. 2: Wisdom and Lyric
   Med R - Sept 2015 - pNA [501+]

Bjork, Samuel - *I'm Traveling Alone*
   BL - v112 - i7 - Dec 1 2015 - p29(1) [51-500]
   KR - Nov 15 2015 - pNA [51-500]
   PW - v262 - i48 - Nov 30 2015 - p38(1) [51-500]

Bjorklund, Ruth - *Jamaica*
   y VOYA - v38 - i5 - Dec 2015 - p79(1) [501+]

Bjorkman, Steve - *Look Out, Mouse!*
   c HB Guide - v26 - i2 - Fall 2015 - p58(1) [501+]
   c KR - March 1 2015 - pNA [51-500]
   SLJ - v61 - i3 - March 2015 - p112(1) [51-500]

Bjornlund, Lydia - *The History of Video Games*
   y VOYA - v38 - i4 - Oct 2015 - p86(1) [51-500]

Blaber, Donna - *Hide and Seek: Kiwi Critters (Illus. by Shaw, Rupert)*
   c Magpies - v30 - i1 - March 2015 - pS4(1) [501+]

Blabey, Aaron - *The Bad Guys Episode 1*
   c Magpies - v30 - i4 - Sept 2015 - p33(1) [501+]
Carlos le carlin
   c Res Links - v20 - i5 - June 2015 - p36(1) [51-500]
Pig the Fibber
   c Magpies - v30 - i3 - July 2015 - p28(1) [501+]
Pig the Pug
   c Res Links - v20 - i5 - June 2015 - p2(1) [51-500]
Thelma the Unicorn (Illus. by Blabey, Aaron)
   c Magpies - v30 - i1 - March 2015 - p28(1) [501+]

Black, Benjamin - *The Black-Eyed Blonde*
   NYTBR - April 12 2015 - p28(L) [501+]
   RVBW - March 2015 - pNA [51-500]
Even the Dead
   BL - v112 - i3 - Oct 1 2015 - p25(2) [51-500]
   KR - Oct 15 2015 - pNA [501+]
   PW - v262 - i45 - Nov 9 2015 - p35(1) [51-500]

Black, Brian C. - *Nature's Entrepot: Philadelphia's Urban Sphere and Its Environmental Thresholds*
   HNet - May 2015 - pNA [501+]

Black, C. Clifton - *The Disciples According to Mark: Markan Redaction in Current Debate*
   BTB - v45 - i2 - May 2015 - p121(3) [501+]

Black, Cara - *Murder in Pigalle*
   RVBW - March 2015 - pNA [51-500]
Murder on the Champ de Mars
   BL - v111 - i12 - Feb 15 2015 - p38(1) [51-500]
   KR - Jan 15 2015 - pNA [501+]
   PW - v262 - i4 - Jan 26 2015 - p149(2) [51-500]

Black, Conrad - *Rise to Greatness: The History of Canada from the Vikings to the Present*
   Beav - v95 - i3 - June-July 2015 - p55(1) [501+]
   Nat R - v67 - i4 - March 9 2015 - p45 [501+]

Black, Daniel - *The Death of Magic*
   KR - August 1 2015 - pNA [501+]
God War
   KR - July 15 2015 - pNA [501+]

Black, David - *Falling Off Broadway*
   PW - v262 - i7 - Feb 16 2015 - p173(1) [51-500]
   KR - March 1 2015 - pNA [501+]
Fast Shuffle
   BL - v111 - i18 - May 15 2015 - p27(1) [51-500]
   KR - May 1 2015 - pNA [51-500]
   PW - v262 - i19 - May 11 2015 - p37(2) [51-500]

Black, Donald - *Moral Time*
   SF - v93 - i3 - March 2015 - pe74 [501+]

Black, Holly - *The Copper Gauntlet (Illus. by Fischer, Scott)*
   c BL - v112 - i1 - Sept 1 2015 - p112(1) [51-500]
   c KR - July 15 2015 - pNA [51-500]
The Darkest Part of the Forest (Read by Fortgang, Lauren). Audiobook Review
   PW - v262 - i17 - April 27 2015 - p72(1) [51-500]
   y SLJ - v61 - i3 - March 2015 - p80(1) [51-500]
The Darkest Part of the Forest
   y CCB-B - v68 - i6 - Feb 2015 - p300(2) [51-500]
   y HB - v91 - i1 - Jan-Feb 2015 - p75(2) [51-500]
   y HB Guide - v26 - i2 - Fall 2015 - p111(1) [51-500]
   c Nat Post - v17 - i86 - Feb 7 2015 - pWP11(1) [501+]
   y NYTBR - Jan 18 2015 - p19(L) [501+]
   y Sch Lib - v63 - i1 - Spring 2015 - p61(1) [51-500]
The Iron Trial (Read by Boehmer, Paul). Audiobook Review
   BL - v111 - i13 - March 1 2015 - p71(1) [51-500]
The Iron Trial (Illus. by Fischer, Scott)
   y HB Guide - v26 - i1 - Spring 2015 - p70(1) [51-500]
   c Sch Lib - v63 - i1 - Spring 2015 - p34(1) [51-500]
   y Teach Lib - v42 - i3 - Feb 2015 - p39(1) [51-500]
L'Epreuve de fer (Illus. by Fisher, Scott)
   y Res Links - v20 - i5 - June 2015 - p36(2) [501+]

Black, Jenna - *Revolution*
   CH Bwatch - Feb 2015 - pNA [501+]

Black, Jeremy - *Contesting History: Narratives of Public History*
   AHR - v120 - i3 - June 2015 - p964-965 [501+]
Metropolis: Mapping the City
   LJ - v140 - i16 - Oct 1 2015 - p76(1) [501+]
Other Pasts, Different Presents, Alternative Futures
   HT - v65 - i11 - Nov 2015 - p64(1) [501+]
   KR - June 1 2015 - pNA [501+]
   PW - v262 - i21 - May 25 2015 - p48(1) [51-500]
Politics and Foreign Policy in the Age of George I, 1714-1727
   AHR - v120 - i3 - June 2015 - p1113(1) [501+]
The Power of Knowledge: How Information and Technology Made the Modern World
   AHR - v120 - i1 - Feb 2015 - p191-192 [501+]
   RAH - v43 - i3 - Sept 2015 - p420-426 [501+]
   Six Ct J - v46 - i2 - Summer 2015 - p532-534 [501+]

Black, Jonathan - *Abstraction and Reality: The Sculpture of Ivor Roberts-Jones*
   HT - v65 - i7 - July 2015 - p63(1) [501+]
Making the American Body: The Remarkable Saga of the Men and Women Whose Feats, Feuds, and Passions Shaped Fitness History
   Am St - v54 - i2 - Summer 2015 - p23-30 [501+]

Black, Kojo - *The Athletic Aesthetic*
   PW - v262 - i30 - July 27 2015 - p48(1) [51-500]
Wanderlust
   PW - v262 - i20 - May 18 2015 - p71(1) [51-500]

Black, Martha Jo - *Joe Black: More Than a Dodger*
   BL - v111 - i11 - Feb 1 2015 - p16(1) [51-500]

Black, Michael Ian - *Cock-a-Doodle-Doo-Bop! (Illus. by Myers, Matt)*
   c KR - August 1 2015 - pNA [51-500]
   c PW - v262 - i31 - August 3 2015 - p57(1) [51-500]
Navel Gazing: True Tales of Bodies, Mostly Mine (but Also My Mom's, Which I Know Sounds Weird)
   KR - Oct 15 2015 - pNA [51-500]
   PW - v262 - i48 - Nov 30 2015 - p53(1) [51-500]

Black, Peter Jay - *Blackout*
   c HB Guide - v26 - i2 - Fall 2015 - p75(1) [501+]
   c KR - March 15 2015 - pNA [51-500]

Black, Richard L. - *Maximus*
   RVBW - July 2015 - pNA [51-500]

Black, Robert - *Machiavelli*
   AHR - v120 - i4 - Oct 2015 - p1424-1426 [501+]
   JMH - v87 - i3 - Sept 2015 - p744(2) [501+]
Night of the Frightening Fractions
   y CH Bwatch - May 2015 - pNA [51-500]

Black, Robin - *Life Drawing*
   Wom R Bks - v32 - i2 - March-April 2015 - p17(2) [501+]

Black, Sarah - *One Dough, Ten Breads: Making Great Bread by Hand*
   BL - v112 - i3 - Oct 1 2015 - p20(1) [51-500]
   PW - v262 - i38 - Sept 21 2015 - p67(1) [51-500]

Black, Saul - *The Killing Lessons*
   BL - v111 - i22 - August 1 2015 - p34(2) [51-500]
   KR - July 15 2015 - pNA [51-500]
   LJ - v140 - i12 - July 1 2015 - p76(1) [51-500]
   NYTBR - Sept 20 2015 - p29(L) [501+]
   PW - v262 - i27 - July 6 2015 - p48(1) [51-500]

Black, Shayla - *His to Take*
   PW - v262 - i3 - Jan 19 2015 - p66(2) [51-500]

Black, William - *Inheritances: Stories*
   KR - Feb 15 2015 - pNA [51-500]

Blackaby, Susan - *The Twelve Days of Christmas in Oregon (Illus. by Conahan, Carolyn)*
   c HB Guide - v26 - i1 - Spring 2015 - p22(1) [51-500]

Blackadder, Jesse - *Dexter the Courageous Koala*
   c Magpies - v30 - i2 - May 2015 - p34(1) [501+]

Blackburn, Alexander - *The Door of the Sad People*
   Roundup M - v22 - i3 - Feb 2015 - p25(1) [501+]
   Roundup M - v22 - i6 - August 2015 - p26(1) [501+]

Blackburn, Julia - *The Emperor's Last Island: A Journey to St Helena*
   TLS - i5854 - June 12 2015 - p12(2) [501+]
Threads: The Delicate Life of John Craske
   Lon R Bks - v37 - i17 - Sept 10 2015 - p23(2) [501+]
   Spec - v327 - i9736 - April 4 2015 - p37(1) [501+]
   TLS - i5860 - July 24 2015 - p9(1) [501+]

Blackburne, Livia - *Daughter of Dusk (Read by Amato, Bianca). Audiobook Review*
   y SLJ - v61 - i12 - Dec 2015 - p78(1) [51-500]
Daughter of Dusk
   y VOYA - v38 - i4 - Oct 2015 - p66(1) [51-500]
Midnight Thief (Read by Amato, Bianca). Audiobook Review
   y SLJ - v61 - i6 - June 2015 - p66(1) [51-500]
Midnight Thief
   c HB Guide - v26 - i1 - Spring 2015 - p101(1) [51-500]

Blackehart, Stephen - *A Stranger to the Darklands*
   KR - Feb 1 2015 - pNA [501+]

Blacker, Terence - *The Twyning*
   c CCB-B - v68 - i5 - Jan 2015 - p249(1) [51-500]
   c HB Guide - v26 - i1 - Spring 2015 - p101(1) [51-500]
   y RVBW - March 2015 - pNA [501+]

Blackett, R.J.M. - *Making Freedom: The Underground Railroad and the Politics of Slavery*
   J Am St - v49 - i2 - May 2015 - p419-420 [501+]
   JSH - v81 - i1 - Feb 2015 - p188(2) [501+]

Blackford, Cheryl - *Hungry Coyote (Illus. by Caple, Laurie)*
   c HB Guide - v26 - i2 - Fall 2015 - p27(1) [51-500]
   c KR - April 1 2015 - pNA [501+]
   c SLJ - v65 - i7 - July 2015 - p59(1) [51-500]
Lizzie and the Lost Baby
   c BL - v112 - i4 - Oct 15 2015 - p58(2) [51-500]
   c KR - Oct 1 2015 - pNA [501+]
   y VOYA - v38 - i5 - Dec 2015 - p53(2) [51-500]
Powerful Muscle Cars
   c HB Guide - v26 - i2 - Fall 2015 - p185(1) [51-500]

Blackford, Harriet - *Let's Talk about Dinosaurs (Illus. by Teckentrup, Britta)*
   c KR - July 15 2015 - pNA [51-500]

Blackford, Mansel - *Making Seafood Sustainable: American Experiences in Global Perspective*
   BHR - v89 - i2 - Summer 2015 - p383(4) [501+]

Blackhawk, Terry - *To Light a Fire: 20 Years with the InsideOut Literary Arts Project*
   RVBW - Nov 2015 - pNA [501+]

Blacklock, Mark - *I'm Jack*
   NS - v144 - i5270 - July 10 2015 - p41(1) [501+]

Blackman, Andrew - *A Virtual Love*
   PW - v262 - i17 - April 27 2015 - p54(1) [51-500]

Blackman, Malorie - *Contact (Illus. by Fisher-Johnson, Paul)*
   c Sch Lib - v63 - i3 - Autumn 2015 - p162(1) [51-500]
Noughts and Crosses Graphic Novel (Illus. by Aggs, John)
   y Sch Lib - v63 - i4 - Winter 2015 - p242(1) [51-500]
Robot Girl
   c Sch Lib - v63 - i2 - Summer 2015 - p100(1) [51-500]

Blackman, W. Haden - *Elektra: Bloodlines (Illus. by Del Mundo, Michael)*
   BL - v111 - i13 - March 1 2015 - p33(1) [51-500]

Blackmon, Jimmy - *Pale Horse: Hunting Terrorists and Commanding Heroes with the 101st Airborne Division*
   KR - Dec 1 2015 - pNA [51-500]
   LJ - v140 - i20 - Dec 1 2015 - p110(1) [51-500]

Blackmon, Richard D. - *The Creek War 1813-1815*
   J Mil H - v79 - i1 - Jan 2015 - p181-185 [501+]

Black'Mor, Elian - *Black'Mor Chronicles: The Cursed; Welcome to the Park of Chimeras*
   PW - v262 - i48 - Nov 30 2015 - p47(1) [51-500]

Blackshaw, Gemma - *Journeys into Madness: Mapping Mental Illness in the Austro-Hungarian Empire*
GSR - v38 - i1 - Feb 2015 - p189-191 [501+]
CEH - v48 - i3 - Sept 2015 - p429-430 [501+]
Blackstone, Stella - *Baby Talk*
c KR - Jan 1 2016 - pNA [51-500]
Blackthorn, J.D. - *Crown of Three*
KR - April 1 2015 - pNA [51-500]
y SLJ - v61 - i3 - March 2015 - p132(1) [51-500]
Blackwelder, Julia Kirk - *Electric City: General Electric in Schenectady*
BHR - v89 - i2 - Summer 2015 - p369(3) [501+]
Blackwell, Elise - *The Lower Quarter*
BL - v111 - i21 - July 1 2015 - p38(1) [51-500]
KR - July 15 2015 - pNA [51-500]
PW - v262 - i29 - July 20 2015 - p164(1) [51-500]
Blackwell, Juliet - *The Paris Key (Read by Blackwell, Juliet). Audiobook Review*
LJ - v140 - i20 - Dec 1 2015 - p58(1) [51-500]
The Paris Key
LJ - v140 - i14 - Sept 1 2015 - p90(1) [51-500]
Blackwell, Wiley - *30 Great Myths about the Romantics*
TimHES - i2215 - August 6 2015 - p47-47 [501+]
Blackwood, Sage - *Jinx's Fire*
y HB - v91 - i2 - March-April 2015 - p92(2) [51-500]
c HB Guide - v26 - i2 - Fall 2015 - p75(1) [51-500]
Blackwood, Scott - *See How Small*
BooChiTr - Jan 31 2015 - p14(1) [501+]
NYTBR - Feb 1 2015 - p16(L) [501+]
NYTBR - Oct 25 2015 - p32(L) [501+]
Spec - v327 - i9726 - Jan 24 2015 - p45(1) [501+]
Blades, David M. - *A History of U.S. Nuclear Testing and Its Influence on Nuclear Thought, 1945-1963*
AHR - v120 - i3 - June 2015 - p1063(1) [501+]
JAH - v102 - i1 - June 2015 - p287-287 [501+]
Blaedel, Sara - *The Forgotten Girls*
RVBW - Nov 2015 - pNA [51-500]
The Killing Forest
BL - v112 - i7 - Dec 1 2015 - p29(1) [51-500]
PW - v262 - i45 - Nov 9 2015 - p34(1) [51-500]
Blagojevich, Robert - *Fundraiser A: My Fight for Freedom and Justice*
RVBW - Oct 2015 - pNA [501+]
Blaine, Victor - *My Bike*
c SLJ - v61 - i4 - April 2015 - p97(4) [501+]
Blair, Amy L. - *Reading Up: Middle-Class Readers and the Culture of Success in the Early Twentieth-Century United States*
AL - v87 - i2 - June 2015 - p394-396 [501+]
Blair, Gabrielle Stanley - *Design Mom: How to Live with Kids: A Room-by-Room Guide*
PW - v262 - i14 - April 6 2015 - p56(1) [51-500]
Blair, Kitty Hunter - *Poetry and Film: Artistic Kinship between Arsenii and Andrei Tarkovsky*
TLS - i5862 - August 7 2015 - p22(1) [501+]
Blair, Melissa Estes - *Revolutionizing Expectations: Women's Organizations, Feminism, and American Politics, 1965-1980*
JAH - v102 - i2 - Sept 2015 - p622-623 [501+]
Blair, Peggy - *Hungry Ghosts*
Nat Post - v17 - i205 - July 4 2015 - pWP4(1) [501+]
Blair, William - *With Malice toward Some: Treason and Loyalty in the Civil War Era*
JAH - v101 - i4 - March 2015 - p1223-1225 [501+]
Blair, William A. - *With Malice toward Some: Treason and Loyalty in the Civil War Era*
AHR - v120 - i2 - April 2015 - p627-628 [501+]
RAH - v43 - i3 - Sept 2015 - p490-497 [501+]
Blake, Deborah - *Everyday Witchcraft: Making Time for Spirit in a Too-Busy World*
Bwatch - May 2015 - pNA [501+]
Wickedly Powerful
PW - v262 - i52 - Dec 21 2015 - p140(1) [51-500]
Blake, Elizabeth A. - *Dostoevsky and the Catholic Underground*
Slav R - v74 - i3 - Fall 2015 - p669-670 [501+]
Blake, Heidi - *The Ugly Game: The Corruption of FIFA and the Qatari Plot to Buy the World Cup*
LJ - v140 - i16 - Oct 1 2015 - p87(1) [51-500]
Blake, James Carlos - *The House of Wolfe: A Border Noir (Read by DeSantos, David). Audiobook Review*
PW - v262 - i17 - April 27 2015 - p68(2) [51-500]
The House of Wolfe: A Border Noir
PW - v262 - i1 - Jan 5 2015 - p54(1) [51-500]
KR - Jan 1 2015 - pNA [51-500]
Blake, Kasi - *Crushed (AA) Novel*
y SLJ - v61 - i6 - June 2015 - p120(1) [51-500]
Blake, Kendare - *Mortal Gods*
y CH Bwatch - March 2015 - pNA [51-500]
c HB Guide - v26 - i1 - Spring 2015 - p101(1) [51-500]
Ungodly
y CH Bwatch - Nov 2015 - pNA [51-500]
y KR - July 15 2015 - pNA [51-500]
y SLJ - v61 - i9 - Sept 2015 - p157(1) [51-500]
Blake, Kevin - *Balto's Story*
SLJ - v61 - i2 - Feb 2015 - p114(1) [51-500]
Bodie: The Town That Belongs to Ghosts
c HB Guide - v26 - i2 - Fall 2015 - p219(1) [51-500]
c Teach Lib - v42 - i5 - June 2015 - p9(1) [51-500]
c BL - v111 - i15 - April 1 2015 - p60(1) [51-500]
Blake, Michael - *Maize for the Gods: Unearthing the 9,000-Year History of Corn*
NH - v123 - i8 - Oct 2015 - p47(1) [501+]
TLS - i5870 - Oct 2 2015 - p9(1) [501+]
Blake, Quentin - *The Five of Us (Illus. by Blake, Quentin)*
c HB - v91 - i4 - July-August 2015 - p111(2) [51-500]
c SLJ - v61 - i9 - Sept 2015 - p113(1) [51-500]
Tell Me a Picture
c Sch Lib - v63 - i2 - Summer 2015 - p111(1) [51-500]
Blake, Richard - *Religion in the British Navy, 1815-1879: Piety and Professionalism*
HER - v130 - i544 - June 2015 - p765(3) [501+]
Blake, Robin - *The Hidden Man*
KR - Jan 1 2015 - pNA [51-500]
PW - v262 - i3 - Jan 19 2015 - p61(1) [51-500]
BL - v111 - i12 - Feb 15 2015 - p37(1) [51-500]
LJ - v140 - i2 - Feb 1 2015 - p61(4) [501+]
Blake, Russell - *The Solomon Curse*
BL - v111 - i22 - August 1 2015 - p37(1) [51-500]
PW - v262 - i30 - July 27 2015 - p42(2) [51-500]
Blake, Sarah - *Mr. West*
NYTBR - April 26 2015 - p19(L) [501+]
Blake, Stephanie - *I Don't Want to Go to School!*
c Sch Lib - v63 - i1 - Spring 2015 - p25(1) [51-500]
Poop-di-doop! (Illus. by Blake, Stephanie)
c HB Guide - v26 - i2 - Fall 2015 - p7(1) [51-500]
SLJ - v61 - i4 - April 2015 - p122(1) [51-500]
c SLJ - v61 - i5 - May 2015 - p78(1) [51-500]
Super Bunny (Illus. by Blake, Stephanie)
c KR - August 15 2015 - pNA [51-500]
c SLJ - v61 - i9 - Sept 2015 - p113(1) [51-500]
Blake, Stephanie J. - *My Rotten Friend (Illus. by Epelbaum, Mariano)*
c KR - August 1 2015 - pNA [51-500]
c PW - v262 - i30 - July 27 2015 - p64(1) [51-500]
Blake, Stephen P. - *Time in Early Modern Islam: Calendar, Ceremony, and Chronology in the Safavid, Mughal, and Ottoman Empires*
AHR - v120 - i1 - Feb 2015 - p361-362 [501+]
Blake, Toni - *Love Me If You Dare*
BL - v112 - i2 - Sept 15 2015 - p42(2) [501+]
Take Me All the Way
BL - v112 - i4 - Oct 15 2015 - p27(2) [51-500]
Blake, William - *Poems*
NYRB - v62 - i19 - Dec 3 2015 - p71(3) [501+]
Blakemore, Megan Frazer - *The Friendship Riddle (Read by Rustin, Sandy). Audiobook Review*
c SLJ - v61 - i12 - Dec 2015 - p75(1) [51-500]
The Friendship Riddle
c CCB-B - v69 - i1 - Sept 2015 - p11(1) [51-500]
c HB - v91 - i3 - May-June 2015 - p105(2) [501+]
c HB Guide - v26 - i2 - Fall 2015 - p76(1) [51-500]
c KR - March 1 2015 - pNA [51-500]
c PW - v262 - i13 - March 30 2015 - p76(1) [51-500]
c SLJ - v61 - i4 - April 2015 - p144(2) [51-500]
Very in Pieces
y KR - June 15 2015 - pNA [51-500]
y PW - v262 - i24 - June 15 2015 - p84(1) [51-500]
y SLJ - v61 - i8 - August 2015 - p100(1) [51-500]
y VOYA - v38 - i3 - August 2015 - p55(1) [51-500]
Blakeney, Justina - *The New Bohemians: Cool and Collected Homes*
LJ - v140 - i10 - June 1 2015 - p104(1) [51-500]
Blakeslee, Vanessa - *Juventud*
KR - Sept 1 2015 - pNA [51-500]
LJ - v140 - i16 - Oct 1 2015 - p66(1) [51-500]
Blakiston, Georgiana - *Letters of Conrad Russell, 1897-1947*
NYRB - v62 - i10 - June 4 2015 - p33(3) [501+]
Blanch, Lesley - *On the Wilder Shores of Love: A Bohemian Life*
TLS - i5863 - August 14 2015 - p10(1) [501+]
Blanchard, Evonne - *Amelia, the Moochins and the Sapphire Palace (Illus. by Blanchard, Evonne)*
c KR - June 15 2015 - pNA [51-500]
Blanchard, Joel - *1511-2011: Philippe de Commynes. Droit, ecriture: Deux piliers de la souverainete*
HER - v130 - i545 - August 2015 - p973(3) [501+]
Blanchard, Ken - *Collaboration Begins with You*
Har Bus R - v93 - i9 - Sept 2015 - p122(2) [501+]
Refire! Don't Retire: Make the Rest of Your Life the Best of Your Life
Bwatch - May 2015 - pNA [51-500]
LJ - v140 - i2 - Feb 1 2015 - p70(2) [501+]
Blanchard, Richard - *Care Giver*
KR - March 15 2015 - pNA [501+]
Blanchet, M. Wylie - *The Curve of Time (Read by Henderson, Heather). Audiobook Review*
LJ - v140 - i8 - May 1 2015 - p42(1) [51-500]
Blanck, Emily - *Tyrannicide: Forging an American Law of Slavery in Revolutionary South Carolina and Massachusetts*
AHR - v120 - i4 - Oct 2015 - p1480-1481 [501+]
HNet - April 2015 - pNA [501+]
JAH - v102 - i2 - Sept 2015 - p538-539 [501+]
Blanckaert, Claude - *La Venus hottentote: Entre Barnum et Museum*
Isis - v106 - i1 - March 2015 - p195(2) [501+]
Blanckeman, Bruno - *Narrations d'un nouveau siecle: romans et ecrits francais*
MLR - v110 - i1 - Jan 2015 - p264-265 [501+]
Blanco, Fernando A. - *Neoliberal Bonds: Undoing Memory in Chilean Art and Literature*
RVBW - Nov 2015 - pNA [501+]
Blanco, Jodee - *Bullied Kids Speak Out: We Survived--How You Can Too*
y VOYA - v38 - i1 - April 2015 - p86(1) [51-500]
Blanco, Richard - *One Today (Illus. by Pilkey, Dav)*
c BL - v112 - i2 - Sept 15 2015 - p58(1) [51-500]
c KR - August 1 2015 - pNA [51-500]
c PW - v262 - i33 - August 17 2015 - p69(1) [51-500]
c PW - v262 - i49 - Dec 2 2015 - p31(1) [51-500]
c SLJ - v61 - i11 - Nov 2015 - p128(2) [51-500]
The Prince of los Cocuyos: A Miami Childhood
G&L Rev W - v22 - i2 - March-April 2015 - p32(2) [501+]
Bland, Christopher - *Ashes in the Wind*
TimHES - i2196 - March 26 2015 - p51(1) [501+]
Bland, Lucy - *Modern Women on Trial: Sexual Transgression in the Age of the Flapper*
Wom HR - v24 - i1 - Feb 2015 - p137-139 [501+]
Bland, Nick - *The Very Cranky Bear (Illus. by Bland, Nick)*
c HB Guide - v26 - i2 - Fall 2015 - p27(1) [51-500]
The Very Noisy Bear
c Magpies - v30 - i3 - July 2015 - p26(2) [501+]
Bland, Peter - *Remembering England: New and Selected Poems*
TLS - i5861 - July 31 2015 - p23(1) [501+]
Blandiana, Ana - *My Native Land A4*
WLT - v89 - i1 - Jan-Feb 2015 - p73(2) [501+]
Blanes, Ruy Llera - *A Prophetic Trajectory: Ideologies of Place, Time and Belonging in an Angolan Religious Movement*
IJAHS - v48 - i1 - Wntr 2015 - p117-118 [501+]
Blank, Trevor J. - *Folk Culture in the Digital Age: The Emergent Dynamics of Human Interaction*
WestFolk - v74 - i2 - Spring 2015 - p212-215 [501+]
The Last Laugh: Folk Humor, Celebrity Culture, and Mass-Mediated Disasters in the Digital Age
WestFolk - v74 - i1 - Wntr 2015 - p87-91 [501+]
Blankman, Anne - *Conspiracy of Blood and Smoke (Read by Wilds, Heather). Audiobook Review*
y SLJ - v61 - i8 - August 2015 - p52(1) [51-500]
Conspiracy of Blood and Smoke
y HB Guide - v26 - i2 - Fall 2015 - p111(1) [51-500]
y KR - Jan 15 2015 - pNA [51-500]
y SLJ - v61 - i3 - March 2015 - p149(1) [51-500]
y VOYA - v38 - i1 - April 2015 - p54(1) [51-500]
Blanning, Tim - *Frederick the Great: King of Prussia*
KR - Jan 1 2016 - pNA [501+]
Spec - v329 - i9762 - Oct 3 2015 - p40(2) [501+]
Blanton, Ward - *A Materialism for the Masses: Saint Paul and the Philosophy of Undying Life*
TLS - i5835 - Jan 30 2015 - p27(1) [501+]
Blasco, Elisabet - *Chocolate's Dream (Illus. by Coco, Cha)*
c KR - August 15 2015 - pNA [51-500]
Blaser, Martin J. - *Missing Microbes: How the Overuse of Antibiotics Is Fueling Our Modern Plagues (Read by Lawlor, Patrick G.). Audiobook Review*
LJ - v140 - i2 - Feb 1 2015 - p46(1) [51-500]
Missing Microbes: How the Overuse of Antibiotics Is Fueling Our Modern Plagues
Am Sci - v103 - i2 - March-April 2015 - p148(2) [501+]

Blashfield, Jean F. - *Argentina*
   y VOYA - v38 - i5 - Dec 2015 - p79(1) [501+]
Blasiman, Jayme - *Grandpa's Wisdom: Secrets to the Good Life*
   KR - May 15 2015 - pNA [501+]
Blastland, Michael - *The Norm Chronicles: Stories and Numbers about Danger and Death*
   Math T - v109 - i2 - Sept 2015 - p158-158 [501+]
Blatteis, Angela - *The Soup Cleanse: A Revolutionary Detox of Nourishing Soups and Healing Broths from the Founders of Soupure*
   PW - v262 - i46 - Nov 16 2015 - p73(1) [51-500]
Blau, Sara - *If I Went to the Moon (Illus. by Romanenko, Vasilisa)*
   c CH Bwatch - May 2015 - pNA [51-500]
   c HB Guide - v26 - i2 - Fall 2015 - p7(1) [51-500]
Blaufuss, Dietrich - *Wilhelm Lohe: Theologie und Geschichte*
   Ger Q - v88 - i1 - Wntr 2015 - p132(1) [501+]
Blauner, Andrew - *The Good Book: Writers Reflect on Favorite Bible Passages*
   BL - v112 - i6 - Nov 15 2015 - p14(1) [51-500]
   KR - Oct 1 2015 - pNA [501+]
   LJ - v140 - i13 - August 1 2015 - p103(1) [51-500]
Blay, Michel - *Dieu, la nature et l'homme: L'originalite de l'Occident*
   Isis - v106 - i2 - June 2015 - p413(3) [501+]
Blayney, Peter - *The Stationers' Company and the Printers of London: 1501-57*
   Lon R Bks - v37 - i16 - August 27 2015 - p37(3) [501+]
Blecha, Aaron - *Goodnight, Grizzle Grump! (Illus. by Blecha, Aaron)*
   c BL - v112 - i3 - Oct 1 2015 - p82(1) [51-500]
   c KR - August 15 2015 - pNA [501+]
   c SLJ - v61 - i9 - Sept 2015 - p113(1) [51-500]
Bleck, Linda - *What's In My Truck? (Illus. by Bleck, Linda)*
   c KR - Jan 1 2015 - pNA [51-500]
Bleck, Reinhard - *Entstehung des Nibelungenstoffes im 8: Jahrhundert*
   JEGP - v114 - i2 - April 2015 - p311(2) [501+]
Bledsoe, Alex - *Long Black Curl*
   BL - v111 - i18 - May 15 2015 - p38(1) [51-500]
   LJ - v140 - i9 - May 15 2015 - p57(4) [501+]
   PW - v262 - i13 - March 30 2015 - p60(1) [51-500]
Blee, Kathleen M. - *Democracy in the Making: How Activist Groups Form*
   CS - v44 - i3 - May 2015 - p344-346 [501+]
Blee, Lisa - *Framing Chief Leschi: Narratives and the Politics of Historical Justice*
   AHR - v120 - i1 - Feb 2015 - p247-248 [501+]
   JAH - v101 - i4 - March 2015 - p1228-1229 [501+]
   PHR - v84 - i4 - Nov 2015 - p547(2) [501+]
   WHQ - v46 - i1 - Spring 2015 - p105-105 [501+]
Blehm, Eric - *Legend: A Harrowing Story from the Vietnam War of One Green Beret's Heroic Mission to Rescue a Special Forces Team Caught Behind Enemy Lines*
   KR - April 1 2015 - pNA [501+]
   LJ - v140 - i8 - May 1 2015 - p88(3) [501+]
Bleicken, Jochen - *Augustus: The Biography*
   Spec - v328 - i9758 - Sept 5 2015 - p37(2) [501+]
Bleiman, Andrew - *1-2-3 ZooBorns!*
   c SLJ - v61 - i10 - Oct 2015 - p72(1) [51-500]
Blessing, Patricia - *Rebuilding Anatolia after the Mongol Conquest: Islamic Architecture in the Lands of Rum, 1240-1330*
   JNES - v74 - i2 - Oct 2015 - p388(3) [501+]
   Specu - v90 - i4 - Oct 2015 - p1089-1090 [501+]
Bletter, Diana - *A Remarkable Kindness*
   KR - June 1 2015 - pNA [51-500]
Bletter, Rosemarie Haag - *MAS: The Modern Architecture Symposia, 1962-1966*
   NYRB - v62 - i20 - Dec 17 2015 - p36(3) [501+]
Blevins, Amy - *Curriculum-Based Library Instruction: From Cultivating Faculty Relationships to Assessment*
   LJ - v140 - i3 - Feb 15 2015 - p114(1) [51-500]
   LR - v64 - i6-7 - June-July 2015 - p503-504 [501+]
Blevins, Wiley - *How to Deal with Bullies Superhero Style (Illus. by Palen, Debbie)*
   c SLJ - v61 - i9 - Sept 2015 - p133(1) [51-500]
I'm Not Moving (Illus. by Cerato, Mattia)
   c HB Guide - v26 - i2 - Fall 2015 - p27(1) [51-500]
Rice and Beans (Illus. by Cerato, Mattia)
   SLJ - v61 - i2 - Feb 2015 - p117(1) [51-500]
Blevins, Win - *The Darkness Rolling*
   PW - v262 - i17 - April 27 2015 - p51(1) [51-500]

Dictionary of the American West
   Roundup M - v22 - i5 - June 2015 - p14(1) [501+]
Give Your Heart to the Hawks: A Tribute to the Mountain Men
   Roundup M - v22 - i5 - June 2015 - p14(1) [501+]
Stone Song: A Novel of the Life of Crazy Horse
   Roundup M - v22 - i5 - June 2015 - p14(1) [501+]
Blewett, Ashlee Brown - *Brown Horse Escape Artist! and More True Stories of Animals*
   c HB Guide - v26 - i1 - Spring 2015 - p167(1) [51-500]
National Geographic Kids Mission
   c HB Guide - v26 - i2 - Fall 2015 - p178(1) [51-500]
Blichmann, Annika - *Erziehung als Wissenschaft: Ovide Decroly und sein Weg vom Arzt zum Pädagogen*
   HNet - Feb 2015 - pNA [51-500]
Blick, Andrew - *Beyond Magna Carta: A Constitution for the United Kingdom*
   TLS - i5868 - Sept 18 2015 - p3(2) [501+]
Blick, Sarah - *Push Me, Pull You, 2 vols.*
   Med R - Sept 2015 - pNA [501+]
Blincoe, Kate - *The No Nonsense Guide to Green Parenting: How to Raise Your Child, Help Save the Planet and Not Go Mad*
   RVBW - Nov 2015 - pNA [501+]
   RVBW - Nov 2015 - pNA [51-500]
Bliss, Bryan - *No Parking at the End Times*
   y CCB-B - v68 - i8 - April 2015 - p391(1) [51-500]
   y HB - v91 - i1 - Jan-Feb 2015 - p76(1) [51-500]
   y HB Guide - v26 - i2 - Fall 2015 - p111(1) [51-500]
   y VOYA - v37 - i6 - Feb 2015 - p54(1) [51-500]
Bliss, Catherine - *Race Decoded: The Genomic Fight for Social Justice*
   CS - v44 - i1 - Jan 2015 - p37-39 [501+]
Bliss, Eula - *On Immunity: An Inoculation*
   TLS - i5833 - Jan 16 2015 - p27(1) [501+]
Bliss, Jane - *La Vie d'Edouard le Confesseur, by a Nun of Barking Abbey*
   Med R - June 2015 - pNA [501+]
Bliss, Jeanne - *Chief Customer Officer 2.0: How to Build Your Customer-Driven Growth Engine*
   BL - v111 - i21 - July 1 2015 - p21(1) [501+]
Blobaum, Cindy - *Explore Honey Bees! With 25 Great Projects (Illus. by Stone, Bryan)*
   c SLJ - v61 - i7 - July 2015 - p101(1) [51-500]
Bloch, Alice - *Race, Multiculture and Social Policy*
   ERS - v38 - i3 - March 2015 - p503(2) [501+]
Bloch, Chana - *Swimming in the Rain: New and Selected Poems, 1980-2015*
   PSQ - v89 - i3 - Fall 2015 - p174(3) [501+]
   TLS - i5839 - Feb 27 2015 - p25(1) [501+]
   Wom R Bks - v32 - i4 - July-August 2015 - p17(3) [501+]
Bloch, Michael - *Closet Queens: Some 20th Century British Politicians*
   NS - v144 - i5265 - June 5 2015 - p49(1) [501+]
   TLS - i5862 - August 7 2015 - p26(1) [501+]
Jeremy Thorpe
   TLS - i5844 - April 3 2015 - p11(1) [501+]
Block, David - *Social Class in Applied Linguistics*
   Lang Soc - v44 - i4 - Sept 2015 - p581-4 [501+]
Block, Francesca Lia - *The Island of Excess Love*
   c HB Guide - v26 - i1 - Spring 2015 - p101(1) [51-500]
Block, Fred - *The Power of Market Fundamentalism: Karl Polanyi's Critique*
   JEH - v75 - i2 - June 2015 - p587-588 [501+]
   AJS - v121 - i1 - July 2015 - p318(3) [501+]
Block, Helen Martin - *The Shoemaker's Daughter*
   KR - May 1 2015 - pNA [501+]
Block, Kristen - *Ordinary Lives in the Early Caribbean: Religion, Colonial Competition, and the Politics of Profit*
   Historian - v77 - i1 - Spring 2015 - p106(3) [501+]
Block, Lawrence - *Borderline*
   RVBW - Jan 2015 - pNA [501+]
The Burglar Who Counted the Spoons
   PW - v262 - i6 - Feb 9 2015 - p47(1) [51-500]
Dark City Lights: New York Stories
   RVBW - June 2015 - pNA [51-500]
The Girl with the Deep Blue Eyes
   BL - v111 - i22 - August 1 2015 - p34(1) [51-500]
   PW - v262 - i27 - July 6 2015 - p48(1) [51-500]
Block, Sandra - *Little Black Lies*
   BL - v111 - i11 - Feb 1 2015 - p27(1) [51-500]
Blodgett, Peter J. - *Motoring West, vol. 1: Automobile Pioneers, 1900-1909*
   Roundup M - v23 - i1 - Oct 2015 - p33(1) [501+]

Blofield, Robert - *How to Make a Movie in 10 Easy Lessons*
   y BL - v111 - i19-20 - June 1 2015 - p70(1) [51-500]
   c KR - May 1 2015 - pNA [501+]
   c Sch Lib - v63 - i3 - Autumn 2015 - p172(1) [51-500]
Blohm, Craig E. - *Holocaust Resistance*
   y VOYA - v38 - i5 - Dec 2015 - p80(1) [51-500]
Blom, Philipp - *Fracture: Life and Culture in the West, 1918-1938*
   KR - Feb 1 2015 - pNA [501+]
   NY - v91 - i20 - July 20 2015 - p71 [501+]
   NYT - May 26 2015 - pC4(L) [501+]
Fracture: Life & Culture in the West, 1918-1938
   PW - v262 - i7 - Feb 16 2015 - p170(1) [51-500]
Blomberg, Craig L. - *Christians in an Age of Wealth: A Biblical Theology of Stewardship*
   BTB - v45 - i3 - August 2015 - p189(2) [501+]
Blomgren, Jennifer - *Where Do I Sleep? A Pacific Northwest Lullaby (Illus. by Gabriel, Andrea)*
   c SLJ - v61 - i7 - July 2015 - p54(1) [51-500]
Why Do I Sing? Animal Songs of the Pacific Northwest (Illus. by Gabriel, Andrea)
   c SLJ - v61 - i7 - July 2015 - p54(1) [51-500]
Blon, Maria - *Living Passionately*
   PW - v262 - i9 - March 2 2015 - p78(1) [51-500]
Blondel, Jean-Philippe - *The 6:41 to Paris*
   KR - Sept 1 2015 - pNA [501+]
   LJ - v140 - i14 - Sept 1 2015 - p90(1) [51-500]
   NYTBR - Dec 6 2015 - p76(L) [501+]
   PW - v262 - i38 - Sept 21 2015 - p46(1) [501+]
   WLT - v89 - i6 - Nov-Dec 2015 - p61(1) [501+]
Blondell, Ruby - *Ancient Sex: New Essays*
   RVBW - Sept 2015 - pNA [501+]
Blood, Peter - *Rise Again Songbook: Words and Chords to Nearly 1,200 Songs*
   BL - v112 - i5 - Nov 1 2015 - p23(1) [51-500]
Bloodworth, Jeffrey - *Losing the Center: The Decline of American Liberalism, 1968-1992*
   AHR - v120 - i2 - April 2015 - p670-671 [501+]
Bloom, Amy - *Lucky Us*
   TLS - i5834 - Jan 23 2015 - p19(2) [501+]
Bloom, C.P. - *The Monkey and the Bee (Illus. by Raymundo, Peter)*
   c CH Bwatch - June 2015 - pNA [51-500]
   c HB - v91 - i3 - May-June 2015 - p79(2) [51-500]
   c HB Guide - v26 - i2 - Fall 2015 - p7(1) [51-500]
Bloom, Harold - *The Daemon Knows: Literary Greatness and the American Sublime*
   ABR - v36 - i4 - May-June 2015 - p16(2) [501+]
   BL - v111 - i18 - May 15 2015 - p11(1) [51-500]
   KR - March 15 2015 - pNA [501+]
   LJ - v140 - i7 - April 15 2015 - p83(2) [501+]
   PW - v262 - i13 - March 30 2015 - p67(1) [51-500]
Bloom, Howard - *The God Problem: How a Godless Cosmos Creates*
   BL - v112 - i6 - Nov 15 2015 - p14(1) [51-500]
Bloom, J.P. - *Jupiter*
   c HB Guide - v26 - i2 - Fall 2015 - p164(1) [51-500]
Mars
   c HB Guide - v26 - i2 - Fall 2015 - p164(1) [51-500]
Neptune
   c HB Guide - v26 - i2 - Fall 2015 - p164(1) [51-500]
Venus
   c HB Guide - v26 - i2 - Fall 2015 - p164(1) [51-500]
Bloom, Jack - *Seeing through the Eyes of the Polish Revolution: Solidarity and the Struggle Against Communism in Poland*
   HNet - April 2015 - pNA [501+]
Bloom, Jeremy - *Fueled by Failure: Using Detours and Defeats to Power Progress*
   RVBW - July 2015 - pNA [51-500]
Bloom, M. Beth - *Don't Ever Change*
   y KR - April 15 2015 - pNA [501+]
   y PW - v262 - i18 - May 4 2015 - p122(1) [51-500]
   y SLJ - v61 - i5 - May 2015 - p117(1) [51-500]
   y VOYA - v38 - i3 - August 2015 - p55(1) [51-500]
Bloom, Patience - *Romance Is My Day Job: A Memoir of Finding Love at Last (Read by Bloom, Patience). Audiobook Review*
   LJ - v140 - i3 - Feb 15 2015 - p59(1) [51-500]
Bloom, Suzanne - *Alone Together (Illus. by Bloom, Suzanne)*
   c HB Guide - v26 - i2 - Fall 2015 - p7(1) [51-500]
Bear Can Dance! (Illus. by Bloom, Suzanne)
   c KR - July 1 2015 - pNA [51-500]
   c PW - v262 - i39 - Sept 28 2015 - p90(2) [501+]
   c SLJ - v61 - i9 - Sept 2015 - p113(2) [51-500]

Bloomfield, April - *A Girl and Her Greens: Hearty Meals from the Garden*
    Bwatch - June 2015 - pNA [51-500]
    LJ - v140 - i5 - March 15 2015 - p126(2) [501+]
    NYTBR - May 31 2015 - p24(L) [501+]
    PW - v262 - i11 - March 16 2015 - p78(2) [51-500]

Bloomsbury Publishing - *The Masters at Home: Recipes, Stories and Photographs*
    Bwatch - Nov 2015 - pNA [51-500]

Bloomson, Carrie - *The Little Spark: 30 Ways to Ignite Your Creativity*
    KR - Feb 15 2015 - pNA [501+]

Bloshteyn, Maria - *The Prank: The Best of Young Chekhov*
    PW - v262 - i11 - March 16 2015 - p57(1) [51-500]

Blouin, Katherine - *Triangular Landscapes: Environment, Society, and the State in the Nile Delta under Roman Rule*
    AJP - v136 - i3 - Fall 2015 - p528-532 [501+]

Blount, Patty - *Nothing Left to Burn*
    y KR - June 15 2015 - pNA [51-500]
    y SLJ - v61 - i8 - August 2015 - p100(2) [51-500]

Blow, Charles M. - *Fire Shut Up in My Bones: A Memoir*
    G&L Rev W - v22 - i3 - May-June 2015 - p36(2) [501+]
    NYTBR - Nov 1 2015 - p28(L) [501+]

Bloxham, Donald - *The Great Game of Genocide: Imperialism, Nationalism and the Destruction of the Ottoman Armenians*
    HT - v65 - i7 - July 2015 - p56(2) [501+]

Blue, Ally - *Down*
    PW - v262 - i3 - Jan 19 2015 - p65(1) [51-500]

Blue, Violet - *The Smart Girl's Guide to Privacy: Practical Tips for Staying Safe Online*
    y SLJ - v61 - i10 - Oct 2015 - p132(1) [51-500]
    y VOYA - v38 - i4 - Oct 2015 - p81(1) [51-500]

Bluhm, Lisa - *Creative Soldered Jewelry and Accessories: 20+ Earrings, Necklaces, Bracelets and More (Illus. by Bluhm, Lisa)*
    LJ - v140 - i3 - Feb 15 2015 - p101(1) [51-500]

Bluitt, Burnita - *Quiver of the Pure Heart*
    PW - v262 - i28 - July 13 2015 - p43(1) [51-500]

Blum, Art - *Code Name: Tracker*
    KR - August 15 2015 - pNA [501+]

Blum, Gabriella - *Laws, Outlaws, and Terrorists: Lessons from the War on Terrorism*
    Parameters - v45 - i1 - Spring 2015 - p159(2) [501+]

Blum, Jason - *The Blumhouse Book of Nightmares: The Haunted City*
    PW - v262 - i19 - May 11 2015 - p40(1) [51-500]

Blum, Linda M. - *Raising Generation Rx*
    KR - Jan 15 2015 - pNA [501+]

Blum, Raul Richard - *Giordano Bruno: An Introduction*
    Six Ct J - v46 - i1 - Spring 2015 - p242-243 [501+]

Blumberg, Arnold - *When Washington Burned: An Illustrated History of the War of 1812*
    J Mil H - v79 - i2 - April 2015 - p490-491 [501+]

Blumberg, Rhoda - *Shipwrecked! The True Adventures of a Japanese Boy*
    y BL - v111 - i19-20 - June 1 2015 - p86(2) [51-500]

Blume, Judy - *In the Unlikely Event (Read by McInerney, Kathleen). Audiobook Review*
    y BL - v112 - i4 - Oct 15 2015 - p62(1) [51-500]
    LJ - v140 - i13 - August 1 2015 - p46(2) [51-500]
    PW - v262 - i39 - Sept 28 2015 - p86(1) [51-500]
In the Unlikely Event
    BL - v111 - i16 - April 15 2015 - p36(1) [51-500]
    BooChiTr - June 27 2015 - p13(1) [501+]
    KR - April 1 2015 - pNA [501+]
    NS - v144 - i5264 - May 29 2015 - p82(1) [501+]
    NYTBR - May 31 2015 - p29(L) [501+]
    Par - v90 - i8 - August 2015 - p22(1) [51-500]
    PW - v262 - i9 - March 2 2015 - p60(1) [51-500]
    y SLJ - v61 - i11 - Nov 2015 - p126(2) [51-500]

Blume, Lesley M.M. - *Julia and the Art of Practical Travel (Illus. by Blume, Lesley M.M.)*
    c CCB-B - v68 - i7 - March 2015 - p349(1) [51-500]
    c HB Guide - v26 - i2 - Fall 2015 - p76(1) [51-500]
    c PW - v262 - i2 - Jan 12 2015 - p59(1) [51-500]

Blumenfeld, Robert - *All the Tricks of the Trade: Everything You Need to Know about Comedy*
    KR - June 1 2015 - pNA [501+]

Blumenthal, Deborah - *A Different Me*
    c HB Guide - v26 - i1 - Spring 2015 - p101(1) [51-500]

Blumenthal, Heston - *Historic Heston*
    TLS - i5831 - Jan 2 2015 - p11(1) [501+]

Blumenthal, Karen - *Hillary Rodham Clinton: A Woman Living History*
    c BL - v112 - i5 - Nov 1 2015 - p38(1) [501+]
    y KR - Oct 15 2015 - pNA [51-500]
    c PW - v262 - i42 - Oct 19 2015 - p78(1) [51-500]
    y SLJ - v61 - i12 - Dec 2015 - p142(1) [51-500]
Tommy: The Gun that Changed America
    y HB - v91 - i4 - July-August 2015 - p154(1) [51-500]
    y BL - v111 - i19-20 - June 1 2015 - p72(1) [51-500]
    y CCB-B - v68 - i11 - July-August 2015 - p537(1) [51-500]
    y KR - April 15 2015 - pNA [51-500]
    y PW - v262 - i49 - Dec 2 2015 - p117(1) [51-500]
    y SLJ - v61 - i6 - June 2015 - p140(2) [51-500]
    y VOYA - v38 - i2 - June 2015 - p86(2) [51-500]
    y PW - v262 - i16 - April 20 2015 - p79(1) [51-500]

Blumenthal, Max - *The 51 Day War: Ruin and Resistance in Gaza*
    AM - v213 - i16 - Nov 23 2015 - p34(2) [51-500]
    KR - June 1 2015 - pNA [51-500]
    PW - v262 - i21 - May 25 2015 - p49(1) [51-500]

Blumenthal, Uta-Renate - *Canon Law, Religion, and Politics: Liber Amicorum Robert Somerville*
    CHR - v101 - i2 - Spring 2015 - p356(2) [501+]

Blumi, Isa - *Ottoman Refugees, 1878-1939: Migration in a Post-Imperial World*
    AHR - v120 - i1 - Feb 2015 - p364-365 [501+]

Blunden, Edmund - *Undertones of War*
    TimHES - i2226 - Oct 22 2015 - p47(1) [501+]

Blyden, Edward W. - *Christianity, Islam, and the Negro Race*
    AJS - v120 - i4 - Jan 2015 - p1285(9) [501+]

Blythman, Joanna - *Swallow This: Serving Up the Food Industry's Darkest Secrets*
    New Sci - v225 - i3014 - March 28 2015 - p48(1) [501+]

Boak, Helen - *Women in the Weimar Republic*
    GSR - v38 - i3 - Oct 2015 - p685-686 [501+]

Boak, Rachel - *Sacred Stiches: Ecclesiastical Textiles in the Rothschild Collection at Waddesdon Manor*
    NYRB - v62 - i11 - June 25 2015 - p29(4) [501+]

Boantza, Victor D. - *Matter and Method in the Long Chemical Revolution: Laws of Another Order*
    Isis - v106 - i2 - June 2015 - p439(2) [501+]

Boardman, John - *The Greeks in Asia*
    LJ - v140 - i10 - June 1 2015 - p112(1) [51-500]

Boast, Will - *Epilogue*
    Spec - v327 - i9726 - Jan 24 2015 - p41(1) [501+]

Boatwright, Alice K. - *Under an English Heaven*
    KR - June 1 2015 - pNA [501+]

Bob, Clifford - *The Global Right Wing and the Clash of World Politics*
    J Ch St - v57 - i1 - Wntr 2015 - p166-168 [501+]

Bobbins, Alexandra - *The Nurses: A Year of Secrets, Drama, and Miracles with the Heroes of the Hospital*
    BL - v111 - i17 - May 1 2015 - p67(1) [51-500]

Bober, Melody - *Christian Hits for Teens, 3 vols.*
    Am MT - v64 - i4 - Feb-March 2015 - p61(1) [501+]

Bobet, Leah - *An Inheritance of Ashes*
    y BL - v112 - i3 - Oct 1 2015 - p70(1) [51-500]
    y KR - Sept 1 2015 - pNA [51-500]
    y PW - v262 - i34 - August 24 2015 - p81(1) [51-500]
    y PW - v262 - i49 - Dec 2 2015 - p103(1) [51-500]
    y VOYA - v38 - i5 - Dec 2015 - p66(1) [501+]

Bobrick, Benson - *The Caliph's Splendor*
    CSM - June 4 2015 - pNA [51-500]

Bobrow, Joseph - *Waking Up from War: A Better Way Home for Veterans and Nations*
    KR - Sept 15 2015 - pNA [501+]

Bobrow, Warren - *Whiskey Cocktails: Rediscovered Classics and Contemporary Craft Drinks Using the World's Most Popular Spirit*
    LJ - v140 - i2 - Feb 1 2015 - p103(1) [51-500]

Bobrowsky, Mathew - *Using Physical Science Gadgets and Gizmos, Grades 3-5: Phenomenon-Based Learning*
    Sci & Ch - v52 - i5 - Jan 2015 - p83 [501+]
    Sci & Ch - v52 - i9 - Summer 2015 - p29 [51-500]

Boccaccio, Giovanni - *Decameron*
    NYRB - v62 - i1 - Jan 8 2015 - p41(3) [501+]
Rime
    Specu - v90 - i1 - Jan 2015 - p210-213 [501+]

Bocci, Stefano - *Ammiano Marcellino XXVIII e XXIX: Problemi storici e storiografici*
    Class R - v65 - i2 - Oct 2015 - p479-481 [501+]

Bochet, Isabelle - *Augustin, philosophe et predicateur: Hommage a Goulven Madec; Actes du colloque international organise a Paris les 8 et 9 septembre 2011*
    JR - v95 - i3 - July 2015 - p391(3) [501+]

Bock, Joseph G. - *The Technology of Nonviolence: Social Media and Violence Prevention*
    CS - v44 - i2 - March 2015 - p174-176 [501+]

Bock, Kris - *The Dead Man's Treasure*
    PW - v262 - i16 - April 20 2015 - p63(1) [51-500]

Bock, Laszlo - *Work Rules! Insights from Inside Google that Will Transform How You Live and Lead (Read by Bock, Laszlo). Audiobook Review*
    LJ - v140 - i14 - Sept 1 2015 - p68(2) [51-500]
    PW - v262 - i21 - May 25 2015 - p55(1) [51-500]
Work Rules! Insights from Inside Google that Will Transform How You Live and Lead
    Econ - v415 - i8934 - April 18 2015 - p77(US) [501+]
    KR - Jan 15 2015 - pNA [501+]
    LJ - v140 - i3 - Feb 15 2015 - p109(1) [51-500]
    PW - v262 - i3 - Jan 19 2015 - p70(1) [51-500]

Bock, Raymond - *Atavisms*
    TLS - i5863 - August 14 2015 - p27(1) [501+]
    WLT - v89 - i6 - Nov-Dec 2015 - p61(1) [51-500]

Bockman, Johanna - *Markets in the Name of Socialism: The Left-Wing Origins of Neoliberalism*
    SF - v93 - i3 - March 2015 - pe63 [501+]

Bocuse, Paul - *Paul Bocuse: Simply Delicious*
    LJ - v140 - i12 - July 1 2015 - p106(1) [51-500]

Bod, Rens - *A New History of the Humanities: The Search for Principles and Patterns from Antiquity to the Present*
    AHR - v120 - i2 - April 2015 - p555-558 [501+]
    Ren Q - v68 - i3 - Fall 2015 - p1019-1021 [501+]

Bodach, Vijaya - *Ten Easter Eggs (Illus. by Logan, Laura)*
    c KR - July 1 2015 - pNA [51-500]

Bodden, James W. - *Coffin Riders*
    PW - v262 - i18 - May 4 2015 - p100(1) [51-500]

Bodden, Mary-Catherine - *Language as the Site of Revolt in Medieval and Early Modern England: Speaking as a Woman*
    Specu - v90 - i2 - April 2015 - p505-507 [501+]

Bodden, Valerie - *Analyze and Define the Assignment*
    SLJ - v61 - i4 - April 2015 - p76(4) [501+]
Apple
    c HB Guide - v26 - i1 - Spring 2015 - p157(1) [51-500]
Aztec Empire
    c HB Guide - v26 - i1 - Spring 2015 - p200(1) [51-500]
Aztec Warriors
    c CH Bwatch - April 2015 - pNA [501+]
Being Fit
    c HB Guide - v26 - i2 - Fall 2015 - p197(1) [51-500]
    c SLJ - v61 - i4 - April 2015 - p72(4) [501+]
Big Time Series
    c HB Guide - v26 - i2 - Fall 2015 - p207(1) [51-500]
Calvin Johnson
    c HB Guide - v26 - i2 - Fall 2015 - p197(1) [51-500]
China
    c HB Guide - v26 - i1 - Spring 2015 - p200(1) [51-500]
Club and Prescription Drug Abuse
    y HB Guide - v26 - i1 - Spring 2015 - p141(1) [51-500]
Dairy
    c HB Guide - v26 - i2 - Fall 2015 - p188(1) [51-500]
Eagle
    c HB Guide - v26 - i1 - Spring 2015 - p162(1) [51-500]
Egypt
    c HB Guide - v26 - i1 - Spring 2015 - p200(1) [51-500]
Giving a Presentation (Illus. by Williams, Nate)
    c HB Guide - v26 - i1 - Spring 2015 - p130(1) [51-500]
Greece
    c HB Guide - v26 - i1 - Spring 2015 - p200(1) [51-500]
Kevin Durant
    c HB Guide - v26 - i2 - Fall 2015 - p197(1) [51-500]
Kristen Stewart
    c BL - v111 - i19-20 - June 1 2015 - p90(1) [51-500]
LeBron James: Champion Basketball Star
    y HB Guide - v26 - i1 - Spring 2015 - p182(1) [51-500]
Man Walks on the Moon
    y BL - v112 - i3 - Oct 1 2015 - p40(1) [51-500]
Rome
    c HB Guide - v26 - i1 - Spring 2015 - p200(1) [51-500]
Snake
    c HB Guide - v26 - i1 - Spring 2015 - p159(1) [51-500]
Spider
    c HB Guide - v26 - i1 - Spring 2015 - p157(1) [51-500]

What Are Fiction Genres?
  c HB Guide - v26 - i1 - Spring 2015 - p186(1) [51-500]
What Are Nonfiction Genres?
  c HB Guide - v26 - i1 - Spring 2015 - p186(1) [51-500]
Bodeen, S.A. - *The Detour*
  y KR - August 1 2015 - pNA [51-500]
     PW - v262 - i31 - August 3 2015 - p62(1) [51-500]
  y SLJ - v61 - i9 - Sept 2015 - p157(1) [51-500]
Lost
  c BL - v111 - i19-20 - June 1 2015 - p96(1) [51-500]
  c KR - April 15 2015 - pNA [51-500]
  c SLJ - v61 - i4 - April 2015 - p144(1) [51-500]
Shipwreck Island (Read by Heyborne, Kirby). Audiobook Review
  c SLJ - v61 - i12 - Dec 2015 - p75(1) [51-500]
Shipwreck Island
  y HB Guide - v26 - i1 - Spring 2015 - p70(1) [51-500]
Boden, Diane - *Quilled Animals*
     LJ - v140 - i6 - April 1 2015 - p92(1) [51-500]
Boden, Petra - *So viel Wende war nie: Zur Geschichte des Projekts "Asthetische Grundbegriffe" - Stationen zwischen 1983 und 2000*
     HNet - May 2015 - pNA [501+]
Bodenheimer, George - *Every Town Is a Sports Town: Business Leadership at ESPN, from the Mailroom to the Boardroom (Read by Bodenheimer, George). Audiobook Review*
     Bwatch - July 2015 - pNA [501+]
Every Town Is a Sports Town: Business Leadership at ESPN, from the Mailroom to the Boardroom
     KR - April 1 2015 - pNA [51-500]
     PW - v262 - i12 - March 23 2015 - p61(2) [51-500]
Bodeus, Richard - *Oeuvres: Ethiques, Politique, Rhetoric, Poetique, Metaphysique*
     Dialogue - v54 - i1 - March 2015 - p193-195 [501+]
Bodger, Holly - *5 to 1*
  y BL - v111 - i15 - April 1 2015 - p64(1) [51-500]
  y HB Guide - v26 - i2 - Fall 2015 - p111(1) [51-500]
  y SLJ - v61 - i2 - Feb 2015 - p97(2) [51-500]
  y VOYA - v38 - i2 - June 2015 - p71(1) [51-500]
Bodies beyond Borders: The Circulation of Anatomical Knowledge, 1750-1950
     HNet - March 2015 - pNA [501+]
Bodin, Jean - *Method for the Easy Comprehension of History*
     Ren Q - v68 - i1 - Spring 2015 - p238-240 [501+]
Boecker, Virginia - *The Witch Hunter*
  y CCB-B - v69 - i1 - Sept 2015 - p11(2) [51-500]
  y HB Guide - v26 - i2 - Fall 2015 - p112(1) [51-500]
  y BL - v111 - i18 - May 15 2015 - p65(1) [51-500]
  y KR - April 1 2015 - pNA [51-500]
  y PW - v262 - i16 - April 20 2015 - p79(1) [51-500]
  y PW - v262 - i49 - Dec 2 2015 - p109(1) [51-500]
  y SLJ - v61 - i4 - April 2015 - p159(2) [51-500]
  y VOYA - v38 - i2 - June 2015 - p71(1) [51-500]
Boehlert, Bart - *How I Look: From Upstate New York to Downtown Manhattan, Adventures in American Style*
     PW - v262 - i39 - Sept 28 2015 - p84(1) [51-500]
Boehlert, Paul A. - *The Battle of Oriskany and General Nicholas Herkimer*
     J Mil H - v79 - i1 - Jan 2015 - p200-201 [501+]
Boehm, Katharina - *Bodies and Things in Nineteenth-Century Literature and Culture*
     MLR - v110 - i2 - April 2015 - p531-532 [501+]
Boehme, Jacob - *Aurora (Morgen Rote im Auffgang, 1612) and Fundamental Report (Grundlicher Bericht, Mysterium Pansophicum, 1620).*
     Six Ct J - v46 - i3 - Fall 2015 - p716-717 [501+]
Boehmer, Elleke - *The Shouting in the Dark*
     KR - Jan 1 2016 - pNA [51-500]
Boeholt, Veronica - *The Ship Captain's Tale (Illus. by Yesh, Jeff)*
  c CH Bwatch - August 2015 - pNA [501+]
Boelte, Kyle - *The Beautiful Unseen: Variations on Fog and Forgetting*
     BL - v111 - i11 - Feb 1 2015 - p10(1) [51-500]
Boeri, Miriam - *Women on Ice: Methamphetamine Use Among Suburban Women*
     Signs - v40 - i2 - Wntr 2015 - p531(2) [501+]
Boes, Maria R. - *Crime and Punishment in Early Modern Germany*
     CEH - v48 - i1 - March 2015 - p115-116 [501+]
Boes, Tobias - *Formative Fictions: Nationalism, Cosmopolitanism, and the Bildungsroman*
     MFSF - v61 - i3 - Fall 2015 - p541-544 [501+]

Boesak, Allan Aubrey - *Dare We Speak of Hope*
     J Ch St - v57 - i3 - Summer 2015 - p551-552 [501+]
Boeve, Eunice - *The Summer of the Crow*
     Roundup M - v22 - i6 - August 2015 - p26(1) [501+]
Boeve, Lieven - *Questioning the Human: Toward a Theological Anthropology for the Twenty-First Century*
     JRAI - v21 - i3 - Sept 2015 - p710(2) [501+]
     Theol St - v76 - i3 - Sept 2015 - p645(2) [501+]
Boff, Leonardo - *Holy Spirit: Inner Fire, Giver of Life and Comforter of the Poor*
     JAAR - v83 - i2 - June 2015 - pNA [501+]
Boffey, Julia - *A Companion to Fifteenth-Century English Poetry*
     Specu - v90 - i2 - April 2015 - p507-508 [501+]
Manuscript and Print in London c. 1475-1530
     JEGP - v114 - i1 - Jan 2015 - p97(18) [501+]
Bofkin, Lee - *Global Street Art: The Street Artists and Trends Taking Over the World*
     VOYA - v37 - i6 - Feb 2015 - p86(1) [51-500]
Bogan, Paulette - *Virgil & Owen (Illus. by Bogan, Paulette)*
  c HB Guide - v26 - i2 - Fall 2015 - p27(1) [51-500]
Virgil & Owen Stick Together (Illus. by Bogan, Paulette)
  c BL - v112 - i6 - Nov 15 2015 - p59(1) [51-500]
  c KR - Oct 1 2015 - pNA [51-500]
  c PW - v262 - i44 - Nov 2 2015 - p84(1) [501+]
  c SLJ - v61 - i11 - Nov 2015 - p79(1) [51-500]
Bogaski, George - *American Protestants and the Debate over the Vietnam War: Evil Was Loose in the World*
     JAH - v101 - i4 - March 2015 - p1346-1347 [501+]
Bogg, Alan - *Voices at Work: Continuity and Change in the Common Law World*
     Law Q Rev - v131 - April 2015 - p328-333 [501+]
Boggan, Steve - *Gold Fever*
     KR - June 1 2015 - pNA [51-500]
     Bus W - i4436 - July 27 2015 - p71(1) [501+]
     Spec - v327 - i9737 - April 11 2015 - p40(2) [501+]
Boggs, Johnny D. - *The Cane Creek Regulators*
     Roundup M - v22 - i6 - August 2015 - p27(1) [501+]
Lonely Trumpet
     Roundup M - v22 - i3 - Feb 2015 - p13(1) [501+]
Poison Spring
  y Roundup M - v22 - i5 - June 2015 - p37(1) [501+]
  c Roundup M - v22 - i6 - August 2015 - p24(1) [501+]
Bogle, Eric - *And the Band Played Waltzing Matilda (Illus. by Whatley, Bruce)*
  y Magpies - v30 - i1 - March 2015 - p32(1) [501+]
Bogosian, Eric - *Operation Nemesis: The Assassination Plot That Avenged the Armenian Genocide*
     KR - Feb 1 2015 - pNA [51-500]
     LJ - v140 - i5 - March 15 2015 - p118(1) [501+]
     NYTBR - April 19 2015 - p17(L) [501+]
     PW - v262 - i11 - March 16 2015 - p75(1) [51-500]
Operation Nemesis: The Assassination Plot to Avenge the Armenian Genocide
     Spec - v328 - i9748 - June 27 2015 - p43(1) [501+]
Boguslawski, Alexander - *A School for Fools*
     PW - v262 - i12 - March 23 2015 - p42(2) [51-500]
Bohince, Paula - *Swallows and Waves*
     LJ - v140 - i19 - Nov 15 2015 - p88(1) [51-500]
Bohjalian, Chris - *Close Your Eyes, Hold Hands (Read by Blewer, Grace). Audiobook Review*
  y BL - v111 - i12 - Feb 15 2015 - p103(1) [51-500]
The Guest Room
     BL - v112 - i5 - Nov 1 2015 - p30(1) [51-500]
     KR - Nov 1 2015 - pNA [501+]
     PW - v262 - i42 - Oct 19 2015 - p50(1) [51-500]
Bohler, Jochen - *Legacies of Violence: Eastern Europe's First World War*
     AHR - v120 - i3 - June 2015 - p1104-1106 [501+]
Bohm, Enrico - *Die Sicherheit des Westens: Entstehung und Funktion der G7-Gipfel*
     HNet - Jan 2015 - pNA [501+]
Bohn, Anna - *Denkmal Film, vol. 1: Der Film als Kulturerbe*
     HNet - July 2015 - pNA [501+]
Bohn, Thomas M. - *De-Stalinization Reconsidered: Persistence and Change in the Soviet Union*
     HNet - March 2015 - pNA [501+]
Bohnert, Suzy Beamer - *Game-Day Youth: Learning Football's Lingo*
  c CH Bwatch - July 2015 - pNA [51-500]

Bohnet, Iris - *What Works*
     KR - Jan 1 2016 - pNA [501+]
Bohr, Marianne C. - *Gap Year Girl: A Baby Boomer Adventure across 21 Countries*
     BL - v112 - i2 - Sept 15 2015 - p20(1) [51-500]
     PW - v262 - i24 - June 15 2015 - p73(1) [51-500]
Bohr, Roland - *Gifts from the Thunder Beings: Indigenous and European Firearms in the Northern Plains and the Central Subarctic, 1670-1870*
     JAH - v102 - i2 - Sept 2015 - p531-532 [501+]
Bohringer, Letha - *Labels and Libels: Naming Beguines in Northern Medieval Europe*
     Specu - v90 - i3 - July 2015 - p870-871 [501+]
Boiger, Alexandra - *Max and Marla (Illus. by Boiger, Alexandra)*
  c BL - v112 - i1 - Sept 1 2015 - p101(1) [51-500]
  c KR - July 15 2015 - pNA [51-500]
  c PW - v262 - i31 - August 3 2015 - p55(1) [51-500]
  c SLJ - v61 - i10 - Oct 2015 - p72(1) [51-500]
Boilard, Jon - *The Castaway Lounge*
     PW - v262 - i21 - May 25 2015 - p29(1) [51-500]
Boin, Douglas - *Coming Out Christian in the Roman World: How the Followers of Jesus Made a Place in Caesar's Empire*
     Bks & Cult - v21 - i6 - Nov-Dec 2015 - p17(1) [501+]
     CC - v132 - i9 - April 29 2015 - p46(2) [501+]
     LJ - v140 - i2 - Feb 1 2015 - p93(1) [51-500]
Ostia in Late Antiquity
     CJ - v110 - i4 - April-May 2015 - p505(3) [501+]
Bois, Marcel - *Kommunisten Gegen Hitler und Stalin: Die Linke Opposition der KPD in der Weimarer Republik. Eine Gesamtdarstellung*
     HNet - March 2015 - pNA [501+]
Bois, Yve-Alain - *Matisse in the Barnes Foundation*
     Art N - v114 - i10 - Nov 2015 - p99(1) [501+]
Boissevain, Jeremy - *Factions, Friends and Feasts: Anthropological Perspectives on the Mediterranean*
     JRAI - v21 - i2 - June 2015 - p492(2) [501+]
Bokich, Dom - *Your Dream Job: Use Dating Secrets to Get Hired and Build a Career You Love*
     PW - v262 - i21 - May 25 2015 - p52(1) [51-500]
Boland, Eavan - *A Poet's Dublin*
     TLS - i5844 - April 3 2015 - p22(1) [501+]
A Woman without a Country
     TLS - i5844 - April 3 2015 - p22(1) [501+]
     ILS - v35 - i1 - Fall 2015 - p18(1) [501+]
Boland, Ed - *The Battle for Room 314: My Year of Hope and Despair in a New York City High School*
     LJ - v140 - i19 - Nov 15 2015 - p94(1) [51-500]
     PW - v262 - i46 - Nov 16 2015 - p66(1) [51-500]
     KR - Nov 15 2015 - pNA [501+]
Boland, John C. - *The Spy Who Knew Nothing*
     BL - v111 - i21 - July 1 2015 - p40(1) [51-500]
Bolano, Roberto - *A Little Lumpen Novelita*
     TLS - i5842 - March 20 2015 - p3(2) [501+]
The Secret of Evil
     TLS - i5842 - March 20 2015 - p3(2) [501+]
Bolden, Tonya - *Beautiful Moon: A Child's Prayer (Illus. by Velasquez, Eric)*
  c CH Bwatch - Feb 2015 - pNA [51-500]
  c HB Guide - v26 - i1 - Spring 2015 - p22(1) [51-500]
Capital Days: Michael Shiner's Journal and the Growth of Our Nation's Capital
  c CCB-B - v68 - i6 - Feb 2015 - p301(1) [51-500]
  c CH Bwatch - Feb 2015 - pNA [51-500]
  c HB Guide - v26 - i2 - Fall 2015 - p222(1) [51-500]
  c SLJ - v61 - i2 - Feb 2015 - p126(1) [51-500]
Emancipation Proclamation
  y SE - v79 - i3 - May-June 2015 - p143(2) [501+]
Searching for Sarah Rector: The Richest Black Girl in America
  y SE - v79 - i3 - May-June 2015 - p145(1) [501+]
Bolder, David - *Think Like a Commoner: A Short Introduction to the Life of the Commons*
     Tikkun - v30 - i1 - Wntr 2015 - p49(3) [501+]
Boldt, Mike - *Colors versus Shapes*
  c HB Guide - v26 - i1 - Spring 2015 - p22(2) [51-500]
Boldyrev, Ivan - *Ernst Bloch and His Contemporaries: Locating Utopian Messianism*
     MLR - v110 - i3 - July 2015 - p906-908 [501+]
Bolger, Dermot - *Tanglewood*
     TLS - i5857 - July 3 2015 - p26(1) [501+]
Bolger, Kevin - *Fun with Ed and Fred (Illus. by Hodson, Ben)*
  c KR - Dec 15 2015 - pNA [51-500]
Gran on a Fan (Illus. by Hodson, Ben)
  c HB Guide - v26 - i2 - Fall 2015 - p27(1) [51-500]
Lazy Bear, Crazy Bear (Illus. by Hodson, Ben)
  c KR - April 15 2015 - pNA [51-500]

48 • BOLICK Book Review Index 2016 Cumulation

Bolick, Kate - *Spinster: Making a Life of One's Own (Read by Bolick, Kate). Audiobook Review*
BL - v112 - i4 - Oct 15 2015 - p64(1) [51-500]
LJ - v140 - i13 - August 1 2015 - p48(1) [51-500]
Spinster: Making a Life of One's Own
y BL - v111 - i14 - March 15 2015 - p42(1) [51-500]
KR - Jan 1 2015 - pNA [51-500]
Nat Post - v17 - i141 - April 18 2015 - pWP8(1) [501+]
PW - v262 - i7 - Feb 16 2015 - p172(2) [51-500]
Ent W - i1361 - May 1 2015 - p67(1) [501+]
LJ - v140 - i2 - Feb 1 2015 - p89(1) [51-500]
NYTBR - April 19 2015 - p11(L) [501+]
Bolitho, Mark - *The Origami Home: More Than 30 Projects to Craft, Fold, and Create*
LJ - v140 - i2 - Feb 1 2015 - p80(2) [51-500]
PW - v262 - i7 - Feb 16 2015 - p175(1) [51-500]
Bollas, Christopher - *When the Sun Bursts: The Enigma of Schizophrenia*
KR - Sept 15 2015 - pNA [501+]
PW - v262 - i39 - Sept 28 2015 - p82(2) [51-500]
Bollen, Christopher - *Orient*
KR - March 15 2015 - pNA [501+]
LJ - v140 - i6 - April 1 2015 - p72(1) [51-500]
PW - v262 - i12 - March 23 2015 - p45(1) [51-500]
Bolles, Richard N. - *What Color Is Your Parachute? 2015*
NACEJou - v75 - i3 - Feb 2015 - p15(1) [501+]
Bolling, Ruben - *Alien Invasion in My Backyard (Illus. by Boiling, Ruben)*
c BL - v111 - i17 - May 1 2015 - p54(1) [51-500]
c KR - Feb 15 2015 - pNA [51-500]
Alien Invasion in My Backyard
c HB Guide - v26 - i2 - Fall 2015 - p64(1) [51-500]
Ghostly Thief of Time
c KR - August 15 2015 - pNA [51-500]
Bolt, John - *Economic Shalom: A Reformed Primer on Faith, Work, and Human Flourishing*
Intpr - v69 - i4 - Oct 2015 - p505(1) [501+]
Bolt, Lisa M. - *Acrostic Poems (Illus. by Petelinsek, Kathleen)*
c CH Bwatch - March 2015 - pNA [51-500]
Boltanski, Luc - *Love and Justice as Competences: Three Essays on the Sociology of Action*
CS - v44 - i3 - May 2015 - p346-347 [501+]
Bolton, Jonathan - *Worlds of Dissent: Charter 77, the Plastic People of the Universe, and Czech Culture under Communism*
Soc - v52 - i1 - Feb 2015 - p87(6) [501+]
Bolton, Sharon - *A Dark and Twisted Tide*
RVBW - Feb 2015 - pNA [51-500]
RVBW - March 2015 - pNA [51-500]
Little Black Lies
BL - v111 - i15 - April 1 2015 - p30(1) [51-500]
KR - March 15 2015 - pNA [51-500]
LJ - v140 - i6 - April 1 2015 - p84(1) [501+]
NYTBR - May 17 2015 - p33(L) [501+]
PW - v262 - i10 - March 9 2015 - p53(2) [51-500]
Bolz-Weber, Nadia - *Accidental Saints: Finding God in All the Wrong People*
BL - v112 - i2 - Sept 15 2015 - p4(1) [51-500]
CC - v132 - i21 - Oct 14 2015 - p54(3) [501+]
PW - v262 - i27 - July 6 2015 - p65(1) [51-500]
Bomback, Mark - *Mapmaker (Read by Moon, Erin). Audiobook Review*
y SLJ - v61 - i9 - Sept 2015 - p60(1) [51-500]
Mapmaker
c BL - v111 - i17 - May 1 2015 - p51(1) [51-500]
y CCB-B - v68 - i11 - July-August 2015 - p537(2) [51-500]
y HB Guide - v26 - i2 - Fall 2015 - p112(1) [51-500]
y KR - Feb 15 2015 - pNA [51-500]
y PW - v262 - i8 - Feb 23 2015 - p78(1) [51-500]
y SLJ - v61 - i4 - April 2015 - p159(1) [51-500]
y VOYA - v38 - i2 - June 2015 - p55(1) [51-500]
Bommersbach, Jana - *Funeral Hotdish*
KR - Dec 1 2015 - pNA [51-500]
PW - v262 - i48 - Nov 30 2015 - p40(2) [51-500]
Boncens, Christophe - *Band Instruments*
c KR - July 1 2015 - pNA [51-500]
Bond, Alma H. - *Hillary Rodham Clinton: On the Couch: Inside the Mind and Life of Hillary Clinton*
BL - v111 - i19-20 - June 1 2015 - p28(1) [51-500]
Bond, Brian - *Britain's Two World Wars against Germany: Myth, Memory and the Distortions of Hindsight*
HNet - June 2015 - pNA [501+]
Bond, Cynthia - *Ruby (Read by Bond, Cynthia). Audiobook Review*
LJ - v140 - i9 - May 15 2015 - p42(1) [51-500]
Ruby
NYTBR - March 15 2015 - p28(L) [501+]
Bond, Gwenda - *Fallout*
BL - v111 - i17 - May 1 2015 - p50(2) [51-500]
y VOYA - v38 - i1 - April 2015 - p54(1) [51-500]
y CCB-B - v69 - i1 - Sept 2015 - p12(1) [51-500]
y HB Guide - v26 - i2 - Fall 2015 - p112(1) [51-500]
y KR - March 1 2015 - pNA [51-500]
y SLJ - v61 - i2 - Feb 2015 - p97(1) [51-500]
Bond, Heidi - *Who's the New Kid?*
BL - v111 - i16 - April 15 2015 - p10(1) [51-500]
Bond, Michael - *The Power of Others: Peer Pressure, Groupthink, and How the People Around Us Shape Everything We Do*
KR - Jan 1 2015 - pNA [501+]
LJ - v140 - i3 - Feb 15 2015 - p116(2) [51-500]
Bond, Michael (b. 1926-) - *A Bear Called Paddington (Read by Fry, Stephen). Audiobook Review*
c SLJ - v61 - i2 - Feb 2015 - p38(3) [501+]
Love from Paddington (Illus. by Fortnum, Peggy)
c HB Guide - v26 - i2 - Fall 2015 - p76(1) [51-500]
More about Paddington (Illus. by Fortnum, Peggy)
c HB Guide - v26 - i2 - Fall 2015 - p76(1) [51-500]
Paddington at the Beach (Illus. by Alley, R.W.)
c HB Guide - v26 - i2 - Fall 2015 - p27(1) [51-500]
Paddington in the Garden (Illus. by Alley, R.W.)
c HB Guide - v26 - i2 - Fall 2015 - p27(1) [51-500]
Paddington (Illus. by Alley, R.W.)
c HB Guide - v26 - i1 - Spring 2015 - p23(1) [51-500]
The Paddington Treasury: Six Classic Bedtime Stories about the Bear from Peru (Illus. by Alley, R.W.)
c HB Guide - v26 - i1 - Spring 2015 - p23(1) [51-500]
Bond, Mike - *Killing Maine*
KR - August 1 2015 - pNA [501+]
RVBW - July 2015 - pNA [51-500]
SPBW - August 2015 - pNA [51-500]
Bond, Rebecca - *Escape from Baxters' Barn (Illus. by Bond, Rebecca)*
c KR - April 15 2015 - pNA [51-500]
Escape from Baxter's Barn (Illus. by Bond, Rebecca)
SLJ - v61 - i2 - Feb 2015 - p61(1) [51-500]
Escape from Baxters' Barn (Illus. by Bond, Rebecca)
c BL - v111 - i17 - May 1 2015 - p98(1) [51-500]
c CH Bwatch - August 2015 - pNA [51-500]
c PW - v262 - i18 - May 4 2015 - p119(1) [51-500]
Out of the Woods: A True Story of an Unforgettable Event (Illus. by Bond, Rebecca)
c HB - v91 - i5 - Sept-Oct 2015 - p124(2) [51-500]
c KR - April 15 2015 - pNA [51-500]
c SLJ - v61 - i3 - March 2015 - p169(2) [51-500]
Out of the Woods (Illus. by Bond, Rebecca)
c BL - v111 - i17 - May 1 2015 - p74(1) [51-500]
c CCB-B - v69 - i1 - Sept 2015 - p3(2) [501+]
Bondor-Stone, Annabeth - *The Pirate Who's Back in Bunny Slippers (Illus. by Holden, Anthony)*
c SLJ - v61 - i12 - Dec 2015 - p99(1) [51-500]
Shivers! The Pirate Who's Afraid of Everything (Illus. by Holden, Anthony)
c HB Guide - v26 - i2 - Fall 2015 - p76(1) [51-500]
Bonds, Mark Evan - *Absolute Music: The History of an Idea*
MT - v156 - i1931 - Summer 2015 - p111-114 [501+]
Notes - v72 - i2 - Dec 2015 - p388(4) [501+]
Bondy, Filip - *The Pine Tar Game*
KR - March 15 2015 - pNA [501+]
The Pine Tar Game: The Kansas City Royals, the New York Yankees, and Baseball's Most Absurd and Entertaining Controversy
BL - v111 - i17 - May 1 2015 - p70(2) [51-500]
LJ - v140 - i7 - April 15 2015 - p91(2) [51-500]
PW - v262 - i19 - May 11 2015 - p51(1) [51-500]
Bondy, Halley - *Speak Up! A Guide to Having Your Say and Speaking Your Mind*
c CH Bwatch - Oct 2015 - pNA [51-500]
y VOYA - v38 - i5 - Dec 2015 - p76(1) [51-500]
Bone, Michael - *Steppes: The Plants and Ecology of the World's Semi-Arid Regions*
LJ - v140 - i12 - July 1 2015 - p111(1) [51-500]
Boneham, Sheila Webster - *Shepherd's Crook*
BL - v112 - i4 - Oct 15 2015 - p23(2) [51-500]
KR - August 1 2015 - pNA [51-500]
Bonfield, Chloe - *The Perfect Tree (Illus. by Bonfield, Chloe)*
c CH Bwatch - Nov 2015 - pNA [51-500]
c KR - Oct 15 2015 - pNA [51-500]
c PW - v262 - i41 - Oct 12 2015 - p65(1) [51-500]
c SLJ - v61 - i12 - Dec 2015 - p86(2) [51-500]
Bonfiglioli, Kyril - *The Great Mortdecai Moustache Mystery*
BL - v112 - i4 - Oct 15 2015 - p21(1) [51-500]
PW - v262 - i36 - Sept 7 2015 - p47(2) [51-500]
Bongino, Dan - *The Fight: A Secret Service Agent's Inside Account of Security Failings and the Political Machine*
KR - Nov 1 2015 - pNA [501+]
Boniface, William - *The Adventures of Max the Minnow (Illus. by Sullivan, Don)*
c CH Bwatch - March 2015 - pNA [51-500]
Bonin-Rodrigue, Paul - *Performing Policy: How Contem-Porary Politics and Cultural Programs Redefined U.S. Artists for the Twenty-First Century*
Theat J - v67 - i3 - Oct 2015 - p580-581 [501+]
Bonker, Dirk - *Militarism in a Global Age: Naval Ambitions in Germany and the United States before World War I*
HNet - July 2015 - pNA [501+]
Bonn 1314 - Kronung, Krieg und Kompromiss
HNet - Jan 2015 - pNA [501+]
Bonn, Maria - *Getting the Word Out: Academic Libraries as Scholarly Publishers*
LJ - v140 - i12 - July 1 2015 - p99(1) [51-500]
Bonnan, Matthew F. - *The Bare Bones: An Unconventional Evolutionary History of the Skeleton*
PW - v262 - i51 - Dec 14 2015 - p70(1) [51-500]
Bonnell, Jennifer - *Historical GIS Research in Canada*
Can Hist R - v96 - i2 - June 2015 - p308(3) [501+]
Pub Hist - v37 - i3 - August 2015 - p148(3) [501+]
T&C - v56 - i4 - Oct 2015 - p1006-1008 [501+]
Reclaiming the Don: An Environmental History of Toronto's Don River Valley
Can Hist R - v96 - i3 - Sept 2015 - p453(3) [501+]
Bonner, Fred A., III - *Black Faculty in the Academy: Narratives for Negotiating Identity and Achieving Career Success*
CHE - v61 - i41 - July 24 2015 - pA16(1) [51-500]
Bonner, Jeremy - *Empowering the People of God: Catholic Action before and after Vatican II*
CHR - v101 - i3 - Summer 2015 - p686(2) [501+]
CH - v84 - i1 - March 2015 - p274(3) [501+]
Bonner, Larry - *Soleil's Star*
KR - April 1 2015 - pNA [51-500]
Bonnett, Alastair - *Unruly Places: Lost Spaces, Secret Cities, and Other Inscrutable Geographies (Read by Perkins, Derek). Audiobook Review*
LJ - v140 - i3 - Feb 15 2015 - p59(1) [51-500]
Bonnin, Michel - *The Lost Generation: The Rustication of China's Educated Youth (1968-1980).*
Pac A - v88 - i2 - June 2015 - p287 [501+]
Bonoli, Fabrizio - *I pronostici di Domenico Maria da Novara*
Isis - v106 - i1 - March 2015 - p173(2) [501+]
Bonsall, Will - *Will Bonsall's Essential Guide to Radical, Self-Reliant Gardening*
PW - v262 - i18 - May 4 2015 - p115(1) [51-500]
Bontemps, Arna - *Boy of the Border*
Callaloo - v38 - i2 - Spring 2015 - p398-401 [501+]
Bonvicini, Mariella - *Il novus libellus di Catullo: Transmissione del testo, problematicita della grafia e dell'interpunzione*
Class R - v65 - i2 - Oct 2015 - p442-444 [501+]
Boobbyer, Philip - *The Spiritual Vision of Frank Buchman*
CH - v84 - i1 - March 2015 - p278(3) [501+]
Bookbinder, Lawrence J. - *Win Friends and Customers*
SPBW - March 2015 - pNA [51-500]
Booker, Carol McCabe - *Alone Atop the Hill: The Autobiography of Alice Dunnigan, Pioneer of the National Black Press*
Wom R Bks - v32 - i4 - July-August 2015 - p29(3) [501+]
Booker, Courtney M. - *Past Convictions: The Penance of Louis the Pious and the Decline of the Carolingians*
CHR - v101 - i2 - Spring 2015 - p352(3) [501+]
Booker, M. Keith - *Comics through Time: A History of Icons, Idols, and Ideas, 4 vols.*
BL - v111 - i13 - March 1 2015 - p32(1) [501+]
R&USQ - v54 - i4 - Summer 2015 - p80(1) [501+]
Booker, Stephen Todd - *The Reharkening*
WLT - v89 - i1 - Jan-Feb 2015 - p63(1) [51-500]
Boone and Crockett Club - *Big Trophies, Epic Hunts*
Bwatch - April 2015 - pNA [51-500]
Boone and Crockett Club Collection
RVBW - Feb 2015 - pNA [501+]
Boone, Joseph Allen - *The Homoerotics of Orientalism*
IJMES - v47 - i3 - August 2015 - p607-608 [501+]
Boone, Martina - *Compulsion*
c HB Guide - v26 - i1 - Spring 2015 - p101(1) [51-500]
Persuasion
y KR - August 15 2015 - pNA [51-500]
Persuasion: Heirs of Watson Island
y VOYA - v38 - i4 - Oct 2015 - p66(1) [51-500]

Boone, Rebecca Ard - *Mercurino di Gattinara and the Creation of the Spanish Empire*
    Ren Q - v68 - i2 - Summer 2015 - p685-686 [501+]
    Six Ct J - v46 - i3 - Fall 2015 - p770-771 [501+]

Boor, Jackie - *Logan: The Honorable Life and Scandalous Death of a Western Lawman*
    Roundup M - v22 - i4 - April 2015 - p28(1) [501+]
    Roundup M - v22 - i6 - August 2015 - p34(1) [501+]

Boorman, Kate A. - *Darkthaw*
    y KR - August 15 2015 - pNA [51-500]
    y VOYA - v38 - i4 - Oct 2015 - p66(1) [501+]
Winterkill
    c HB Guide - v26 - i1 - Spring 2015 - p101(1) [51-500]

Boorn, D.W. - *The Big Secret: The Whole and Honest Truth About Santa Claus (Illus. by Boorn, D.W.)*
    c CH Bwatch - Jan 2015 - pNA [51-500]

Boote, Julian - *Exit*
    KR - June 1 2015 - pNA [501+]

Booth, Anne - *Dog Ears*
    c Sch Lib - v63 - i3 - Autumn 2015 - p162(1) [51-500]

Booth, Coe - *Kinda Like Brothers*
    y HB Guide - v26 - i1 - Spring 2015 - p70(1) [51-500]

Booth, David - *Exploding the Reading: Building a World of Responses from One Small Story, 50 Interactive Strategies for Increasing Comprehension*
    Res Links - v20 - i4 - April 2015 - p35(1) [501+]

Booth, Heather - *The Whole Library Handbook: Teen Services*
    R&USQ - v54 - i3 - Spring 2015 - p56(1) [51-500]

Booth, Howard J. - *The Cambridge Companion to Rudyard Kipling*
    VS - v57 - i3 - Spring 2015 - p552(3) [501+]

Booth, James - *Philip Larkin: Life, Art and Love*
    Comw - v142 - i18 - Nov 13 2015 - p25(5) [501+]
    NY - v90 - i45 - Jan 26 2015 - p77 [51-500]

Booth, Lawrence - *Wisden Cricketers' Almanack 2015*
    NS - v144 - i5259 - April 24 2015 - p52(1) [501+]

Booth, Louise - *When Fraser Met Billy: An Autistic Boy, a Rescue Cat, and the Transformative Power of Animal Connections*
    LJ - v140 - i6 - April 1 2015 - p109(1) [51-500]

Booth-Lynch, Pat - *A Shocking Reunion*
    SPBW - March 2015 - pNA [51-500]

Booth, Michael - *The Almost Nearly Perfect People: Behind the Myth of the Scandinavian Utopia*
    Barron's - v95 - i40 - Oct 5 2015 - p34(1) [501+]
    BL - v111 - i9-10 - Jan 1 2015 - p33(1) [501+]
    LJ - v140 - i3 - Feb 15 2015 - p118(1) [51-500]
    Mac - v128 - i9 - March 9 2015 - p55(2) [501+]

Booth, Stephen - *The Corpse Bridge*
    RVBW - Feb 2015 - pNA [501+]
The Murder Road
    RVBW - Sept 2015 - pNA [501+]

Booth, Ted - *A Body Politic to Govern: The Political Humanism of Elizabeth I*
    Historian - v77 - i2 - Summer 2015 - p376(2) [501+]

Boothe, Joan N. - *The Storied Ice: Exploration, Discovery, and Adventure in Antarctica's Peninsula Region*
    RVBW - June 2015 - pNA [501+]

Boothroyd, Jennifer - *Animal Pollinators*
    c HB Guide - v26 - i2 - Fall 2015 - p172(1) [51-500]
    c SLJ - v61 - i4 - April 2015 - p86(4) [501+]
Endangered and Extinct Birds
    c HB Guide - v26 - i1 - Spring 2015 - p162(1) [51-500]
Endangered and Extinct Fish
    c HB Guide - v26 - i1 - Spring 2015 - p161(1) [51-500]
Endangered and Extinct Invertebrates
    c HB Guide - v26 - i1 - Spring 2015 - p158(1) [51-500]
Endangered and Extinct Mammals
    c HB Guide - v26 - i1 - Spring 2015 - p163(2) [51-500]
Endangered and Extinct Reptiles
    c HB Guide - v26 - i1 - Spring 2015 - p159(1) [51-500]
How Does Weather Change?
    c HB Guide - v26 - i2 - Fall 2015 - p167(1) [51-500]
Light Helps Me See
    c HB Guide - v26 - i1 - Spring 2015 - p170(1) [51-500]
Light Makes Colors
    c HB Guide - v26 - i1 - Spring 2015 - p150(1) [51-500]

Playing with Light and Shadows
    c HB Guide - v26 - i1 - Spring 2015 - p150(1) [51-500]
Vibrations Make Sound
    c HB Guide - v26 - i1 - Spring 2015 - p150(1) [51-500]

Boots, Cheryl C. - *Singing for Equality: Hymns in the American Antislavery and Indian Rights Movements*
    AHR - v120 - i1 - Feb 2015 - p251-252 [501+]

Boraine, Alex - *What's Gone Wrong? South Africa on the Brink of Failed Statehood*
    For Aff - v94 - i1 - Jan-Feb 2015 - pNA [51-500]

Boran, Pat - *If Ever You Go: A Map of Dublin in Poetry and Song*
    ILS - v34 - i2 - Spring 2015 - p18(2) [501+]

Borando, Silvia - *Black Cat, White Cat (Illus. by Borando, Silvia)*
    c KR - June 1 2015 - pNA [501+]
    c Magpies - v30 - i3 - July 2015 - p26(1) [501+]
    c SLJ - v61 - i8 - August 2015 - p66(2) [51-500]
The White Book (Illus. by Borando, Silvia)
    c KR - May 15 2015 - pNA [501+]
    c Sch Lib - v63 - i4 - Winter 2015 - p218(1) [51-500]
    c SLJ - v61 - i8 - August 2015 - p66(1) [51-500]

Borboroglu, Pablo Garcia - *Penguins: Natural History and Conservation*
    QRB - v90 - i1 - March 2015 - p105(2) [501+]

Borchardt, Karl - *Documents Concerning Cyprus from the Hospitallers' Rhodian Archives: 1409-1459*
    HER - v130 - i543 - April 2015 - p384(16) [501+]

Borchgrevink, Aage - *A Norwegian Tragedy: Anders Behring Breivik and the Massacre on Utoya*
    NYRB - v62 - i4 - March 5 2015 - p55(3) [501+]

Borcutzky, Daniel - *In the Murmurs of the Rotten Carcass Economy*
    PW - v262 - i24 - June 15 2015 - p61(2) [51-500]

Borden, Louise - *Kindergarten Luck (Illus. by Godbout, Genevieve)*
    c BL - v111 - i21 - July 1 2015 - p63(1) [51-500]
    c KR - June 1 2015 - pNA [51-500]
    c SLJ - v61 - i8 - August 2015 - p58(2) [51-500]

Border, Terry - *Happy Birthday, Cupcake!*
    c KR - April 15 2015 - pNA [501+]
Peanut Butter & Cupcake! (Illus. by Border, Terry)
    c HB Guide - v26 - i1 - Spring 2015 - p23(1) [51-500]

Bordewich, Fergus M. - *The First Congress: How James Madison, George Washington, and a Group of Extraordinary Men Invented the Government*
    KR - Oct 1 2015 - pNA [501+]
    LJ - v140 - i20 - Dec 1 2015 - p112(2) [51-500]
    PW - v262 - i51 - Dec 14 2015 - p70(2) [51-500]

Borel, Brooke - *Infested: How the Bed Bug Infiltrated Our Bedrooms and Took Over the World*
    LJ - v140 - i6 - April 1 2015 - p110(1) [51-500]
    Mac - v128 - i15 - April 20 2015 - p55(1) [501+]
    NYTBR - April 19 2015 - p21(L) [501+]
    Soc - v52 - i4 - August 2015 - p383(1) [501+]
    Spec - v327 - i9739 - April 25 2015 - p41(2) [501+]
    TLS - i5857 - July 3 2015 - p30(1) [51-500]

Boren, M. Scott - *Leading Small Groups in the Way of Jesus*
    RVBW - March 2015 - pNA [51-500]

Boret, Sebastien Penmellen - *Japanese Tree Burial: Ecology, Kinship and the Culture of Death*
    HNet - August 2015 - pNA [501+]

Borg, Emma - *Pursuing Meaning*
    Phil R - v124 - i3 - July 2015 - p437(4) [501+]

Borg, Mark B. - *Irrelationship: How We Use Dysfunctional Relationships to Hide From Intimacy*
    SPBW - Nov 2015 - pNA [501+]

Borg, Ruben - *Flann O'Brien: Contesting Legacies*
    TLS - i5853 - June 5 2015 - p9(2) [501+]

Borgenicht, David - *The Worst-Case Scenario Handbook (Illus. by Gonzales, Chuck)*
    c HB Guide - v26 - i1 - Spring 2015 - p176(1) [51-500]

Borger, Julian - *The Butcher's Trail: How the Search for Balkan War Criminals Became the World's Most Successful Manhunt*
    KR - Oct 1 2015 - pNA [501+]
    LJ - v140 - i20 - Dec 1 2015 - p120(1) [51-500]
    PW - v262 - i45 - Nov 9 2015 - p50(2) [51-500]

Borgert-Spaniol, Megan - *Baby Foxes*
    c SLJ - v61 - i9 - Sept 2015 - p175(1) [51-500]
Baby Giraffes
    c SLJ - v61 - i9 - Sept 2015 - p175(1) [51-500]
Baby Hedgehogs
    c SLJ - v61 - i9 - Sept 2015 - p175(1) [51-500]
Baby Hippos
    c SLJ - v61 - i9 - Sept 2015 - p175(1) [51-500]
Baby Koalas
    c SLJ - v61 - i9 - Sept 2015 - p175(1) [51-500]
Baby Squirrels
    c SLJ - v61 - i9 - Sept 2015 - p175(1) [51-500]
Black Bears
    c SLJ - v61 - i4 - April 2015 - p89(4) [501+]

Borges, Cassandra - *New Literary Papyri from the Michigan Collection: Mythographic Lyric and a Catalogue of Poetic First Lines*
    Class R - v65 - i1 - April 2015 - p70-72 [501+]

Borgman, Christine L. - *Big Data, Little Data, No Data: Scholarship in the Networked World*
    Nature - v518 - i7540 - Feb 26 2015 - p480(2) [501+]

Borgmann, Nils - *Matiere de France oder Matiere des Francs? Die germanische Heldenepik und die Anfange der Chanson de Geste*
    JEGP - v114 - i2 - April 2015 - p312(2) [501+]

Boris, Daniel - *Dozi the Alligator Finds a New Home (Illus. by Sammarco, Nicola)*
    c CH Bwatch - May 2015 - pNA [51-500]

Borman, Tracy - *Thomas Cromwell: The Untold Story of Henry VIII's Most Faithful Servant*
    AM - v213 - i4 - August 17 2015 - p42(2) [501+]
    NYTBR - Jan 25 2015 - p26(L) [501+]

Born, James O. - *Scent of Murder*
    KR - Feb 1 2015 - pNA [51-500]

Borneman, Walter R. - *American Spring: Lexington, Concord, and the Road to Revolution*
    NEQ - v88 - i2 - June 2015 - p348-350 [501+]

Borner, Katy - *Atlas of Knowledge: Anyone Can Map*
    LJ - v140 - i6 - April 1 2015 - p115(1) [51-500]

Bornholdt, Claudia - *Saintly Spouses: Chaste Marriage in Sacred and Secular Narrative from Medieval Germany (12th and 13th Centuries)*
    Specu - v90 - i3 - July 2015 - p777-778 [501+]

Bornstein, Bernard - *Blood of My Fathers*
    KR - Oct 1 2015 - pNA [501+]

Bornstein, Mitchell - *Last Chance Mustang: The Story of One Horse, One Horseman, and One Final Shot at Redemption*
    BL - v111 - i17 - May 1 2015 - p76(1) [51-500]
    KR - April 15 2015 - pNA [501+]
    LJ - v140 - i8 - May 1 2015 - p93(1) [51-500]

Borntrager, Mary Christner - *Reuben*
    c CH Bwatch - July 2015 - pNA [51-500]

Borodale, Sean - *Human Work*
    NS - v144 - i5262 - May 15 2015 - p46(2) [501+]

Boroughs, Allan - *Bloodstone: Legend of Ironheart (Illus. by van Deelan, Fred)*
    y Sch Lib - v63 - i2 - Summer 2015 - p114(1) [51-500]

Borrie, Cathie - *The Long Hello: Memory, My Mother and Me*
    Mac - v128 - i1 - Jan 12 2015 - p68(2) [501+]
    Nat Post - v17 - i56 - Jan 3 2015 - pWP10(1) [501+]

Borst, Hugo - *O. Louis: In Search of van Gaal*
    NS - v144 - i5251 - Feb 27 2015 - p44(2) [501+]

Borsuk, Richard - *Liem Sioe Liong's Salim Group: The Business Pillar of Suharto's Indonesia*
    For Aff - v94 - i1 - Jan-Feb 2015 - pNA [51-500]

Borth, Teddy - *Baseball: Great Moments, Records, and Facts*
    c SLJ - v61 - i4 - April 2015 - p97(4) [501+]
Blue Animals
    c SLJ - v61 - i4 - April 2015 - p89(4) [501+]
    c HB Guide - v26 - i2 - Fall 2015 - p170(1) [51-500]
Buildings on the Farm
    c HB Guide - v26 - i2 - Fall 2015 - p187(1) [51-500]
Football: Great Moments, Records, and Facts
    c HB Guide - v26 - i2 - Fall 2015 - p197(1) [51-500]
Green Animals
    c HB Guide - v26 - i2 - Fall 2015 - p170(1) [51-500]
Gymnastics: Great Moments, Records, and Facts
    c HB Guide - v26 - i2 - Fall 2015 - p197(1) [51-500]
Hockey: Great Moments, Records, and Facts
    c HB Guide - v26 - i2 - Fall 2015 - p197(1) [51-500]
Orange Animals
    c HB Guide - v26 - i2 - Fall 2015 - p170(1) [51-500]
Red Animals
    c HB Guide - v26 - i2 - Fall 2015 - p170(1) [51-500]
White Animals
    c HB Guide - v26 - i2 - Fall 2015 - p170(1) [51-500]
Yellow Animals
    c HB Guide - v26 - i2 - Fall 2015 - p170(1) [51-500]

Bortz, Lauri - *Kung Fu Kitty: Laying Down the Law (Illus. by Gentile, Michael)*
    c CH Bwatch - May 2015 - pNA [51-500]

Borum, Traci - *Finding the Rainbow*
    PW - v262 - i38 - Sept 21 2015 - p61(1) [51-500]
Painting the Moon
    PW - v262 - i9 - March 2 2015 - p72(1) [51-500]

Borwein, Peter B. - *Mathematicians on Creativity*
    SIAM Rev - v57 - i1 - March 2015 - p164-164 [501+]

Borys, Ann Marie - *Vincenzo Scamozzi and the Chorography of Early Modern Architecture*
    Ren Q - v68 - i1 - Spring 2015 - p255-256 [501+]
    Six Ct J - v46 - i2 - Summer 2015 - p425-426 [501+]

Bos, James M. - *Reconsidering the Date and Provenance of the Book of Hosea: The Case for Persian-Period Yehud*
    JR - v95 - i2 - April 2015 - p252(2) [501+]

Boscaljon, Daniel - *Vigilant Faith: Passionate Agnosticism in a Secular World*
    JAAR - v83 - i4 - Dec 2015 - p1189-1192 [501+]

Bosch, Pseudonymous - *Bad Luck*
    c KR - Dec 1 2015 - pNA [51-500]
    Bad Magic (Illus. by Ford, Gilbert)
    y HB Guide - v26 - i1 - Spring 2015 - p70(1) [51-500]

Bose, Bobby - *Reincarnation, Oblivion, or Heaven? An Exploration from a Christian Perspective*
    IBMR - v39 - i2 - April 2015 - p103(2) [501+]

Bosler, Denise - *Creative Anarchy*
    SPBW - March 2015 - pNA [51-500]

Bosma, Sam - *Fantasy Sports*
    c SLJ - v61 - i8 - August 2015 - p94(1) [51-500]
    Fantasy Sports No. 1 (Illus. by Bosma, Sam)
    c CCB-B - v69 - i1 - Sept 2015 - p13(1) [51-500]
    KR - April 1 2015 - pNA [51-500]
    PW - v262 - i14 - April 6 2015 - p47(1) [51-500]

Bosnak, Robert - *Red Sulphur*
    KR - July 15 2015 - pNA [51-500]
    PW - v262 - i21 - May 25 2015 - p42(1) [51-500]

Bossche, Chris R. Vanden - *Reform Acts: Chartism, Social Agency, and the Victorian Novel, 1832-1867*
    Nine-C Lit - v70 - i2 - Sept 2015 - p277(6) [501+]
    RES - v66 - i273 - Feb 2015 - p191-193 [501+]

Bossier, Beverly - *Courtesans, Concubines, and the Cult of Female Fidelity*
    Historian - v77 - i3 - Fall 2015 - p588(3) [501+]

Boster, Dea H. - *African American Slavery and Disability: Bodies, Property, and Power in the Antebellum South, 1800-1860*
    JAH - v102 - i1 - June 2015 - p249-249 [501+]
    JSH - v81 - i1 - Feb 2015 - p180(3) [501+]
    JWH - v27 - i1 - Spring 2015 - p178(9) [501+]

Boston, Maria - *I Love Grass* (Illus. by Boston, Maria)
    c CH Bwatch - Jan 2015 - pNA [51-500]

Bostridge, Ian - *Schubert's Winter Journey: Anatomy of an Obsession*
    ON - v79 - i12 - June 2015 - p65(1) [501+]
    TLS - i5848 - May 1 2015 - p3(3) [501+]
    BL - v111 - i9-10 - Jan 1 2015 - p30(1) [51-500]
    Econ - v414 - i8921 - Jan 17 2015 - p80(US) [501+]
    NY - v91 - i1 - Feb 16 2015 - p71 [51-500]
    NYRB - v62 - i10 - June 4 2015 - p28(2) [501+]
    NYT - Feb 19 2015 - pC6(L) [501+]
    Spec - v327 - i9724 - Jan 10 2015 - p32(1) [501+]

Bostridge, Mark - *Vera Brittain and the First World War: The Story of Testament of Youth*
    TimHES - i2198 - April 9 2015 - p49(1) [501+]

Bostwick, Marie - *The Second Sister*
    BL - v111 - i15 - April 1 2015 - p28(1) [51-500]

Boswell, Marshall - *David Foster Wallace and 'The Long Thing'*
    TLS - i5854 - June 12 2015 - p3(2) [501+]

Bosworth, David - *The Demise of Virtue in Virtual America: The Moral Origins of the Great Recession*
    Nation - v300 - i21 - May 25 2015 - p31(3) [501+]

Bosworth, Jennifer - *The Killing Jar*
    y BL - v112 - i6 - Nov 15 2015 - p51(1) [51-500]
    y KR - Oct 15 2015 - pNA [51-500]
    y SLJ - v61 - i11 - Nov 2015 - p112(1) [51-500]

Bosworth, R.J.B. - *Italian Venice: A History*
    HT - v65 - i4 - April 2015 - p64(1) [501+]

Bothe, Alina - *Geschlecht in der Geschichte: Integriert oder Separiert? Gender als Historische Forschungskategorie*
    HNet - July 2015 - pNA [501+]

Botman, Loes - *Hello Animals, What Makes You Special?* (Illus. by Botman, Loes)
    c KR - Jan 1 2016 - pNA [51-500]

Bottner, Barbara - *Feet, Go to Sleep* (Illus. by Smith, Maggie)
    c HB Guide - v26 - i2 - Fall 2015 - p27(1) [51-500]
    c KR - March 1 2015 - pNA [51-500]
    c SLJ - v61 - i3 - March 2015 - p112(2) [51-500]
    Miss Brooks' Story Nook (Where Tales Are Told and Ogres Are Welcome). (Illus. by Emberley, Michael)
    c HB Guide - v26 - i1 - Spring 2015 - p23(1) [51-500]

Bottura, Massimo - *Never Trust a Skinny Italian Chef*
    TLS - i5831 - Jan 2 2015 - p11(1) [501+]

Botwinick, Aryeh - *Emmanuel Levinas and the Limits to Ethics: A Critique and a Re-Appropriation*
    RM - v68 - i3 - March 2015 - p642(3) [501+]

Bouchard, Camille - *La forme floue ties fantomes*
    y Res Links - v20 - i3 - Feb 2015 - p43(1) [501+]

Bouchard, Constance Brittain - *Rewriting Saints and Ancestors: Memory and Forgetting in France, 500-1200*
    Med R - August 2015 - pNA [501+]

Bouchard, David - *The First Flute / Whowhoahyayzo Tohkohya* (Illus. by Oelze, Don)
    c CH Bwatch - July 2015 - pNA [501+]
    c CH Bwatch - July 2015 - pNA [501+]
    c KR - August 15 2015 - pNA [51-500]
    The First Flute / Whowhoahyayzo Tohkohya
    c CH Bwatch - July 2015 - pNA [501+]
    c CH Bwatch - July 2015 - pNA [501+]
    The Song within My Heart (Illus. by Sapp, Allen)
    c KR - August 1 2015 - pNA [51-500]
    c SLJ - v61 - i8 - August 2015 - p66(1) [51-500]

Bouchard, Patrice - *The Book of Beetles: A Life-Size Guide to Six Hundred of Nature's Gems*
    LJ - v140 - i2 - Feb 1 2015 - p104(1) [51-500]

Boucher, Ellen - *Empire's Children: Child Emigration, Welfare, and the Decline of the British World, 1869-1967*
    AHR - v120 - i2 - April 2015 - p716-717 [501+]

Boucher, Stanley - *Watcher in Black and Other Poems*
    PW - v262 - i52 - Dec 21 2015 - p129(2) [501+]

Boucheron, Patrick - *Leonardo da Vinci: Vorbild Natur - Zeichnungen und Modelle*
    Ren Q - v68 - i1 - Spring 2015 - p265-267 [501+]

Boudet, Jean-Patrice - *Medecine, astrologie et magie entre Moyen Age et Renaissance: Autour de Pietro d'Abano*
    Isis - v106 - i1 - March 2015 - p172(2) [501+]

Boudia, Soraya - *Powerless Science? Science and Politics in a Toxic World*
    MAQ - v29 - i1 - March 2015 - p22-25 [501+]

Boudon, Jacques-Olivier - *Monseigneur Darboy (1813-1871): Archeveque de Paris entre Pie IX et Napoleon III*
    CHR - v101 - i4 - Autumn 2015 - p945(2) [501+]

Boudreaux, Megan - *Miracle on Voodoo Mountain: A Young Woman's Remarkable Story of Pushing Back the Darkness for the Children of Haiti*
    Bks & Cult - v21 - i1 - Jan-Feb 2015 - p6(2) [501+]
    Ch Today - v59 - i2 - March 2015 - p65(1) [51-500]

Bouhassira, Eric E. - *The SAGE Encyclopedia of Stem Cell Research, 2d ed.*
    BL - v112 - i7 - Dec 1 2015 - p21(1) [51-500]

Bouk, Dan - *How Our Days Became Numbered: Risk and the Rise of the Statistical Individual*
    New Sci - v226 - i3027 - June 27 2015 - p42(1) [501+]

Boule, Jean-Pierre - *Existentialism and Contemporary Cinema: A Beauvoirian Perspective*
    FS - v69 - i2 - April 2015 - p283-284 [501+]

Boullata, Issa J. - *The Bells of Memory*
    WLT - v89 - i5 - Sept-Oct 2015 - p59(2) [51-500]

Boullosa, Carmen - *A Narco-History: How the United States and Mexico Jointly Created the "Mexican Drug War"*
    TLS - i5855 - June 19 2015 - p31(1) [501+]
    When Mexico Recaptures Texas: Essays
    PW - v262 - i35 - August 31 2015 - p80(1) [51-500]

Boulton, Mark - *Failing Our Veterans: The G.I. Bill and the Vietnam Generation*
    JAH - v102 - i1 - June 2015 - p310-310 [501+]

Boulton, Maureen B.M. - *Piety and Persecution in the French Texts of England*
    MLR - v110 - i1 - Jan 2015 - p257-258 [501+]

Boum, Aomar - *Memories of Absence: How Muslims Remember Jews in Morocco*
    AHR - v120 - i1 - Feb 2015 - p365-366 [501+]

Bouman, Mark - *The Tank Man's Son*
    KR - April 15 2015 - pNA [51-500]
    PW - v262 - i23 - June 8 2015 - p56(1) [51-500]

Bound, Samantha-Ellen - *Silver Shoes, Book 1: And All the Jazz* (Illus. by Bound, Samantha-Ellen)
    c Magpies - v30 - i1 - March 2015 - p31(1) [501+]
    Silver Shoes, Book 2: Hit the Streets (Illus. by Bound, Samantha-Ellen)
    c Magpies - v30 - i1 - March 2015 - p31(1) [501+]

Bourdaghs, Michael K. - *Sayonara Amerika, Sayonara Nippon: A Geopolitical Prehistory of J-Pop*
    PMS - v38 - i1 - Feb 2015 - p100(3) [501+]

Bourdieu, Jerome - *L'enquete TRA, histoire d'un outil, outil pour l'histoire. Tome 1: 1793-1902*
    JEH - v75 - i1 - March 2015 - p272-274 [501+]

Bourdieu, Pierre - *On the State*
    RVBW - March 2015 - pNA [501+]

Bourdon, Murielle - *Sami the Magic Bear: No to Bullying!* (Illus. by Bourdon, Murielle)
    c CH Bwatch - July 2015 - pNA [51-500]

Bourgeois, Pam - *Food and French*
    RVBW - Jan 2015 - pNA [501+]

Bourgeois, Paulette - *Li Jun and the Iron Road*
    y Res Links - v21 - i1 - Oct 2015 - p42(1) [501+]

Bourgeois, Suzanne - *Genesis of the Salk Institute: The Epic of Its Founders*
    QRB - v90 - i2 - June 2015 - p201(2) [501+]

Bourget, Edith - *Lili Tutti-Frutti* (Illus. by Richard, Serge V.)
    c Res Links - v20 - i4 - April 2015 - p36(1) [501+]

Bourguignon, Francois - *The Globalization of Inequality*
    LJ - v140 - i9 - May 15 2015 - p89(1) [51-500]
    PW - v262 - i13 - March 30 2015 - p68(1) [51-500]
    TimHES - i2202 - May 7 2015 - p52(1) [501+]

Bourin, Monique - *Dynamiques du monde rural dans la conjoncture de 1300: Echanges, prelevements et consommation en Mediterranee occidentale*
    Med R - June 2015 - pNA [501+]

Bourke, Joanna - *Deep Violence: Military Violence, War Play, and the Social Life of Weapons*
    KR - Jan 1 2015 - pNA [501+]
    LJ - v140 - i3 - Feb 15 2015 - p118(1) [51-500]
    PW - v262 - i4 - Jan 26 2015 - p159(1) [51-500]
    The Story of Pain: From Prayer to Painkillers
    HT - v65 - i4 - April 2015 - p59(2) [501+]

Bourne, Henry - *Arcadia Britannica: A Modern British Folklore Portrait*
    Art N - v114 - i6 - June 2015 - p77(1) [501+]
    LJ - v140 - i14 - Sept 1 2015 - p98(1) [51-500]
    NYT - June 9 2015 - p3(L) [501+]

Bourne, Holly - *Am I Normal Yet?*
    y Sch Lib - v63 - i4 - Winter 2015 - p252(1) [51-500]

Bourne, J.L. - *Tomorrow War*
    KR - May 1 2015 - pNA [501+]

Bourne, Joanna - *Rogue Spy*
    LJ - v140 - i3 - Feb 15 2015 - p133(1) [501+]

Bourne, Joel K., Jr. - *The End of Plenty: The Race to Feed a Crowded World*
    BL - v111 - i17 - May 1 2015 - p62(2) [51-500]
    KR - April 1 2015 - pNA [501+]
    NYTBR - July 26 2015 - p12(L) [501+]
    PW - v262 - i16 - April 20 2015 - p66(1) [51-500]

Bourne, Richard - *Nigeria: A New History of a Turbulent Century*
    Spec - v329 - i9764 - Oct 17 2015 - p43(1) [501+]

Bourque, Dominique - *Femmes et Exils: Forms et figures*
    CWS - v30 - i2-3 - Fall-Winter 2015 - p150(2) [501+]

Bourree, Katrin - *Dienst, Verdienst und Distinktion: Furstliche Selbstbehauptungsstrategien der Hohenzollern im 15. Jahrhundert*
    HNet - Feb 2015 - pNA [501+]

Boutwell, Bryant - *John P. McGovern: A Lifetime in Stories*
    SHQ - v118 - i3 - Jan 2015 - p336-337 [501+]

Boutwell, Clark - *Outland Exile*
    KR - Oct 15 2015 - pNA [501+]

Bouwmans, Thierry - *Background Modeling and Foreground Detection for Video Surveillance*
    Bwatch - June 2015 - pNA [51-500]

Bova, Ben - *Death Wave*
    KR - Sept 15 2015 - pNA [51-500]
    Moonrise
    Forbes - v196 - i6 - Nov 2 2015 - p42(1) [501+]
    Power Surge
    BL - v111 - i22 - August 1 2015 - p44(1) [51-500]
    KR - July 15 2015 - pNA [51-500]

Bove, Emmanuel - *Henri Duchemin and His Shadows*
    KR - June 1 2015 - pNA [51-500]
    PW - v262 - i23 - June 8 2015 - p35(1) [51-500]

Bow, Erin - *The Scorpion Rules*
    y BL - v111 - i22 - August 1 2015 - p64(1) [51-500]
    y HB - v91 - i5 - Sept-Oct 2015 - p94(1) [51-500]
    y KR - July 1 2015 - pNA [51-500]
    y PW - v262 - i24 - June 15 2015 - p86(1) [51-500]
    y PW - v262 - i49 - Dec 2 2015 - p111(1) [51-500]
    y SLJ - v61 - i8 - August 2015 - p101(1) [51-500]
    y VOYA - v38 - i4 - Oct 2015 - p66(1) [51-500]

Bow, Frankie - *The Musubi Murder*
    KR - May 15 2015 - pNA [51-500]
    PW - v262 - i23 - June 8 2015 - p40(1) [51-500]

Bow, James - *Ecosystems Inside Out Series*
   c BL - v111 - i18 - May 15 2015 - p50(1) [51-500]
   c Res Links - v20 - i4 - April 2015 - p14(3) [501+]
Forests Inside Out
   c CH Bwatch - May 2015 - pNA [51-500]
Straight Talk about ... Binge Drinking
   y Res Links - v21 - i1 - Oct 2015 - p45(1) [51-500]
Straight Talk about...Dealing with Loss
   y CH Bwatch - June 2015 - pNA [51-500]
Straight Talk about ... Dealing with Loss
   y Res Links - v21 - i1 - Oct 2015 - p45(1) [51-500]
Bowden, Hugh - *Alexander the Great: A Very Short Introduction*
   Class R - v65 - i2 - Oct 2015 - p508-510 [501+]
Bowden, Mark - *The Three Battles of Wanat and Other True Stories*
   BL - v112 - i7 - Dec 1 2015 - p6(1) [51-500]
   KR - Oct 1 2015 - pNA [501+]
   LJ - v140 - i19 - Nov 15 2015 - p98(1) [51-500]
Bowen, Alan C. - *Simplicius on the Planets and Their Motions: In Defense of a Heresy*
   Isis - v106 - i1 - March 2015 - p170(2) [501+]
Bowen, Anthony J. - *Aeschylus: Suppliant Women*
   Class R - v65 - i1 - April 2015 - p29-31 [501+]
Bowen, Brenda - *Enchanted August*
   BL - v111 - i17 - May 1 2015 - p74(2) [51-500]
   KR - April 1 2015 - pNA [51-500]
Bowen, Carl - *8-Bit Baseball (Illus. by Ferrara, Eduardo)*
   c HB Guide - v26 - i1 - Spring 2015 - p57(1) [51-500]
Dark Agent (Illus. by Tortosa, Wilson)
   y HB Guide - v26 - i1 - Spring 2015 - p70(1) [51-500]
Jules Verne's 20,000 Leagues under the Sea: A Graphic Novel (Illus. by Ruiz, Alfonso)
   y HB Guide - v26 - i1 - Spring 2015 - p72(2) [51-500]
Quarterback Rush (Illus. by Garcia, Eduardo)
   c HB Guide - v26 - i1 - Spring 2015 - p57(1) [51-500]
Sand Spider (Illus. by Fuentes, Benny)
   y HB Guide - v26 - i1 - Spring 2015 - p70(1) [51-500]
Bowen, Fred - *Double Reverse*
   c HB Guide - v26 - i2 - Fall 2015 - p76(1) [51-500]
Bowen, John - *Barchester Towers*
   TLS - i5847 - April 24 2015 - p7(f2) [501+]
Bowen, Kelly - *Good Rogue Is Hard to Find*
   PW - v262 - i11 - March 16 2015 - p71(2) [51-500]
You're the Earl That I Want
   BL - v111 - i22 - August 1 2015 - p42(1) [51-500]
   PW - v262 - i28 - July 13 2015 - p51(1) [51-500]
Bowen, Lila - *Wake of Vultures*
   KR - August 15 2015 - pNA [51-500]
   PW - v262 - i37 - Sept 14 2015 - p47(1) [51-500]
Bowen, Michael - *The Basics of Data Literacy: Helping Your Students (and You!) Make Sense of Data - PB343X*
   Sci Teach - v82 - i1 - Jan 2015 - p65 [51-500]
Bowen, Peter - *Bitter Creek*
   BL - v111 - i16 - April 15 2015 - p27(1) [51-500]
Bowen, Rhys - *Away in a Manger*
   BL - v112 - i6 - Nov 15 2015 - p24(1) [51-500]
   KR - Sept 15 2015 - pNA [51-500]
   PW - v262 - i39 - Sept 28 2015 - p67(1) [51-500]
City of Darkness and Light
   RVBW - Feb 2015 - pNA [51-500]
Death of Riley
   RVBW - August 2015 - pNA [51-500]
The Edge of Dreams
   PW - v262 - i2 - Jan 12 2015 - p37(1) [51-500]
   KR - Jan 1 2015 - pNA [51-500]
   RVBW - Oct 2015 - pNA [51-500]
Queen of Hearts
   RVBW - April 2015 - pNA [51-500]
   RVBW - August 2015 - pNA [51-500]
Time of Fog and Fire
   KR - Jan 1 2016 - pNA [51-500]
Bowen, William G. - *Locus of Authority: The Evolution of Faculty Roles in the Governance of Higher Education*
   TimHES - i2192 - Feb 26 2015 - p9(1) [501+]
Bowens, Natasha - *The Color of Food: Stories of Race, Resilience and Farming*
   LJ - v140 - i12 - July 1 2015 - p103(1) [51-500]
Bower, Chris - *Little Boy Needs Ride*
   SPBW - Oct 2015 - pNA [51-500]
Bower, Jody Gentian - *Jane Eyre's Sisters: How Women Live and Write the Heroine's Story*
   RVBW - Oct 2015 - pNA [51-500]
Bower, Shannon Stunden - *Wet Prairie: People, Land, and Water in Agricultural Manitoba*
   Can Hist R - v96 - i2 - June 2015 - p305(3) [501+]

Bowering, George - *Mirror on the Floor*
   Can Lit - i224 - Spring 2015 - p112 [501+]
Bowers Bahney, Jennifer - *Stealing Sisi's Star*
   KR - Oct 1 2015 - pNA [51-500]
Bowers, David - *A Guide Book of Mercury Dimes, Standing Liberty Quarters, and Liberty Walking Half Dollars*
   Bwatch - Oct 2015 - pNA [51-500]
Bowers, Kristy Wilson - *Plague and Public Health in Early Modern Seville*
   HER - v130 - i543 - April 2015 - p440(3) [501+]
Bowers, Mark - *8 Keys to Raising the Quirky Child: How to Help a Kid Who Doesn't Quite Fit In*
   Bwatch - August 2015 - pNA [51-500]
   PW - v262 - i27 - July 6 2015 - p62(1) [51-500]
Bowes, Lisa - *Lucy Tries Luge (Illus. by Hearne, James)*
   c BL - v112 - i1 - Sept 1 2015 - p101(1) [51-500]
   c KR - August 1 2015 - pNA [51-500]
   c Res Links - v21 - i1 - Oct 2015 - p2(2) [51-500]
Bowie, Andrew - *Adorno and the Ends of Philosophy*
   Dialogue - v54 - i2 - June 2015 - p387-389 [501+]
Bowie, Angus M. - *Homer: Odyssey Books XIII and XIV*
   Class R - v65 - i1 - April 2015 - p8-10 [501+]
Bowien, Danny - *The Mission Chinese Food Cookbook*
   LJ - v140 - i19 - Nov 15 2015 - p102(1) [51-500]
   PW - v262 - i46 - Nov 16 2015 - p68(1) [501+]
Bowker, Paul - *Playing Pro Football*
   c HB Guide - v26 - i1 - Spring 2015 - p182(1) [51-500]
   y VOYA - v38 - i1 - April 2015 - p89(2) [51-500]
Bowlby, Rachel - *A Child of One's Own: Parental Stories*
   VS - v57 - i2 - Wntr 2015 - p300(3) [501+]
Bowler, Peter J. - *Darwin Deleted: Imagining a World without Darwin*
   VS - v57 - i3 - Spring 2015 - p533(3) [501+]
Bowler, Tim - *Game Changer*
   y Sch Lib - v63 - i3 - Autumn 2015 - p178(1) [51-500]
Bowles, Anna - *Mind Muddlers: What You See Is Not What You Get!*
   c PW - v262 - i18 - May 4 2015 - p117(1) [501+]
   c CH Bwatch - April 2015 - pNA [51-500]
Bowles, David - *The Smoking Mirror*
   y Bkbird - v53 - i3 - Summer 2015 - p81(1) [501+]
Bowles, Paula - *Messy Jesse (Illus. by Bowles, Paula)*
   c HB Guide - v26 - i2 - Fall 2015 - p7(1) [51-500]
   c KR - Jan 1 2015 - pNA [51-500]
   c SLJ - v61 - i3 - March 2015 - p113(1) [51-500]
Bowling, Tim - *Selected Poems*
   Can Lit - i224 - Spring 2015 - p113 [501+]
Bowman, Alisa - *Outsmarting Alzheimer's: What You Can Do to Reduce Your Risk*
   PW - v262 - i50 - Dec 7 2015 - p82(1) [51-500]
Bowman, Brady - *Hegel and the Metaphysics of Absolute Negativity*
   Dialogue - v54 - i3 - Sept 2015 - p580-581 [501+]
Bowman, Crystal - *M Is for Manger (Illus. by Keay, Claire)*
   c PW - v262 - i37 - Sept 14 2015 - p64(1) [51-500]
Bowman, D.E. - *Lost Near Eternity*
   KR - July 15 2015 - pNA [501+]
Bowman, Dana - *Bottled: A Mom's Guide to Early Recovery*
   LJ - v140 - i17 - Oct 15 2015 - p104(1) [51-500]
Bowman, Erin - *Forged*
   y HB Guide - v26 - i2 - Fall 2015 - p112(1) [51-500]
   y KR - Feb 15 2015 - pNA [51-500]
Vengeance Road
   y BL - v112 - i1 - Sept 1 2015 - p110(1) [51-500]
   y KR - June 15 2015 - pNA [51-500]
   y PW - v262 - i26 - June 29 2015 - p70(1) [51-500]
   y PW - v262 - i49 - Dec 2 2015 - p116(1) [51-500]
   y SLJ - v61 - i6 - June 2015 - p120(1) [51-500]
   y VOYA - v38 - i3 - August 2015 - p55(1) [51-500]
Bowman, Glenn - *Sharing the Sacra: The Politics and Pragmatics of Inter-Communal Relations Around Holy Places*
   JRAI - v21 - i1 - March 2015 - p240(1) [51-500]
Bowman, Katy - *Don't Just Sit There*
   RVBW - Nov 2015 - pNA [51-500]
Bowman, Manoah - *Fellini: The Sixties*
   LJ - v140 - i20 - Dec 1 2015 - p103(1) [51-500]
Bowman, Patty - *The Amazing Hamweenie Escapes! (Illus. by Bowman, Patty)*
   c HB Guide - v26 - i2 - Fall 2015 - p28(1) [51-500]
   c KR - March 1 2015 - pNA [51-500]
Bowman, Rex - *Rot, Riot, and Rebellion: Mr. Jefferson's Struggle to Save the University That Changed America*
   JSH - v81 - i4 - Nov 2015 - p959(2) [51-500]
Bowman, Robert - *Aisle 17*
   y CH Bwatch - Feb 2015 - pNA [501+]

Bowman, Valerie - *The Irresistible Rogue*
   PW - v262 - i39 - Sept 28 2015 - p76(1) [51-500]
The Unlikely Lady
   KR - March 1 2015 - pNA [51-500]
   PW - v262 - i11 - March 16 2015 - p70(1) [51-500]
Bown, Stephen R. - *White Eskimo: Knud Rasmussen's Fearless Journey into the Heart of the Arctic*
   KR - July 1 2015 - pNA [501+]
   LJ - v140 - i15 - Sept 15 2015 - p84(1) [501+]
   BL - v112 - i2 - Sept 15 2015 - p25(1) [51-500]
   Nature - v582 - i7582 - Dec 17 2015 - p331(1) [501+]
Bowring, Bill - *Law, Rights and Ideology in Russia: Landmarks in the Destiny of a Great Power*
   E-A St - v67 - i3 - May 2015 - p496(2) [501+]
Bowser, Ken - *Homesick Penguin (Illus. by Palen, Debbie)*
   c HB Guide - v26 - i1 - Spring 2015 - p51(2) [51-500]
Bowskill, Sarah - *Gender, Nation and the Formation of the Twentieth-Century Mexican Literary Canon*
   MLR - v110 - i1 - Jan 2015 - p273-274 [501+]
Box, C.J. - *Badlands*
   BL - v111 - i17 - May 1 2015 - p20(2) [51-500]
   KR - May 15 2015 - pNA [51-500]
   PW - v262 - i20 - May 18 2015 - p65(1) [51-500]
Endangered (Read by Chandler, David). Audiobook Review
   PW - v262 - i21 - May 25 2015 - p53(1) [51-500]
Endangered
   BL - v111 - i11 - Feb 1 2015 - p26(1) [51-500]
   KR - Jan 15 2015 - pNA [51-500]
   LJ - v140 - i3 - Feb 15 2015 - p84(1) [51-500]
   RVBW - Nov 2015 - pNA [51-500]
Off the Grid
   KR - Jan 1 2016 - pNA [51-500]
Stone Cold
   Roundup M - v22 - i4 - April 2015 - p31(1) [501+]
   Roundup M - v22 - i6 - August 2015 - p27(1) [501+]
   RVBW - April 2015 - pNA [51-500]
Box, Harry - *Don't Throw the Book at Them: Communicating the Christian Message to People Who Don't Read*
   IBMR - v39 - i3 - July 2015 - p157(2) [501+]
Boxall, Ian - *Patmos in the Reception History of the Apocalypse*
   CH - v84 - i1 - March 2015 - p220(2) [501+]
Boxall, Peter - *Twenty-First-Century Fiction: A Critical Introduction*
   RES - v66 - i273 - Feb 2015 - p202-203 [501+]
Boxcar Children - *The Boxcar Children Guide to Adventure: A How-to for Mystery Solving, Make-It-Yourself Projects, and More*
   c HB Guide - v26 - i2 - Fall 2015 - p146(1) [51-500]
Boyadjian, Maral - *As the Poppies Bloomed*
   KR - Feb 1 2015 - pNA [51-500]
   SPBW - April 2015 - pNA [51-500]
Boyagoda, Randy - *Richard John Neuhaus: A Life in the Public Square*
   AM - v212 - i9 - March 16 2015 - p32(3) [501+]
   Comw - v142 - i14 - Sept 11 2015 - p30(2) [501+]
   MA - v57 - i4 - Fall 2015 - p65(5) [501+]
   Nat R - v67 - i4 - March 9 2015 - p38 [501+]
   NYTBR - March 29 2015 - p16(L) [501+]
Boyarin, Adrienne Williams - *The Siege of Jerusalem*
   TLS - i5855 - June 19 2015 - p22(2) [501+]
Boyarin, Daniel - *A Traveling Homeland: The Babylonian Talmud as Diaspora*
   RVBW - August 2015 - pNA [51-500]
Boyce, Brandon - *Here by the Bloods*
   Roundup M - v22 - i6 - August 2015 - p27(1) [501+]
Boyce, Charlotte - *Victorian Celebrity Culture and Tennyson's Circle*
   VS - v57 - i3 - Spring 2015 - p547(3) [501+]
Boyce, Christopher - *American Sons*
   KR - Oct 1 2015 - pNA [51-500]
Boyce, Frank Cottrell - *The Astounding Broccoli Boy*
   c BL - v111 - i21 - July 1 2015 - p67(1) [51-500]
   c HB - v91 - i5 - Sept-Oct 2015 - p94(2) [51-500]
   c KR - July 1 2015 - pNA [51-500]
   c PW - v262 - i23 - June 8 2015 - p59(1) [51-500]
   c SLJ - v61 - i7 - July 2015 - p73(2) [51-500]
Boyce, James - *Born Bad: Original Sin and the Making of the Western World*
   KR - April 1 2015 - pNA [501+]
   PW - v262 - i15 - April 13 2015 - p74(1) [51-500]
Boyce, Trudy Nan - *Out of the Blues*
   KR - Dec 1 2015 - pNA [51-500]
   PW - v262 - i51 - Dec 14 2015 - p59(1) [51-500]

Boyd, Daniel - *Carbon*
SPBW - Jan 2015 - pNA [51-500]
Boyd, David R. - *The Optimistic Environmentalist: Progressing Towards a Greener Future*
LJ - v140 - i13 - August 1 2015 - p119(3) [51-500]
Boyd, Herb - *Black Panthers for Beginners (Illus. by Tooks, Lance)*
RVBW - August 2015 - pNA [51-500]
Boyd, Lizi - *Big Bear Little Chair (Illus. by Boyd, Lizi)*
c KR - August 15 2015 - pNA [51-500]
c SLJ - v61 - i11 - Nov 2015 - p79(2) [51-500]
Flashlight (Illus. by Boyd, Lizi)
c HB Guide - v26 - i1 - Spring 2015 - p6(1) [51-500]
Boyd, Nika - *H Is for Holy (Illus. by Hayward, Heather)*
c CH Bwatch - June 2015 - pNA [51-500]
Boyd, Robert T. - *Chinookan Peoples of the Lower Columbia*
Am Ind CRJ - v39 - i2 - Spring 2015 - p131-132 [501+]
PHR - v84 - i3 - August 2015 - p386(3) [501+]
Boyd, Roger - *The Schizophrenic Society: Lost in a Make-Believe World While We Destroy the Real One*
KR - July 15 2015 - pNA [501+]
Boyd, Susan C. - *Killer Weed: Marijuana Grow Ops, Media, and Justice*
CS - v44 - i6 - Nov 2015 - p778-780 [501+]
Boyd, William - *Sweet Caress*
SEP - v287 - i5 - Sept-Oct 2015 - p24(1) [501+]
BL - v112 - i1 - Sept 1 2015 - p52(1) [51-500]
KR - July 1 2015 - pNA [51-500]
LJ - v140 - i13 - August 1 2015 - p77(2) [51-500]
NS - v144 - i5280 - Sept 18 2015 - p68(1) [501+]
NYTBR - Sept 20 2015 - p19(L) [501+]
PW - v262 - i29 - July 20 2015 - p162(1) [51-500]
Spec - v329 - i9761 - Sept 26 2015 - p43(1) [501+]
TLS - i5869 - Sept 25 2015 - p20(1) [501+]
Boyden, Joseph - *The Orenda*
Can Hist R - v96 - i3 - Sept 2015 - p426(4) [501+]
Boyer, Crispin - *That's Deadly*
c BL - v112 - i4 - Oct 15 2015 - p40(1) [51-500]
That's Sneaky!
c HB Guide - v26 - i2 - Fall 2015 - p146(1) [51-500]
Boyer, Dominic - *The Life Informatic: Newsmaking in the Digital Era*
JRAI - v21 - i4 - Dec 2015 - p928(2) [501+]
T&C - v56 - i1 - Jan 2015 - p298-299 [501+]
Boyer, G. Bruce - *True Style: The History and Principles of Classic Menswear*
Mac - v128 - i38 - Sept 28 2015 - p61(1) [501+]
NYTBR - Dec 6 2015 - p48(L) [501+]
Boyer, John W. - *The University of Chicago: A History*
TimHES - i2229 - Nov 12 2015 - p49(1) [501+]
Boyer, K.E. - *Ninelands*
c CH Bwatch - July 2015 - pNA [51-500]
Boyer, Michael - *Every Landlord's Guide to Managing Property: Best Practices, From Move-In to Move-Out*
RVBW - Nov 2015 - pNA [501+]
Boyers, Robert - *The Fate of Ideas: Seductions, Betrayals, Appraisals*
PW - v262 - i30 - July 27 2015 - p55(2) [51-500]
Boyes, Alice - *The Anxiety Toolkit: Strategies for Fine-Tuning Your Mind and Moving Past Your Stuck Points*
PW - v262 - i4 - Jan 26 2015 - p158(2) [51-500]
Boykin, Kim - *A Peach of a Pair*
LJ - v140 - i13 - August 1 2015 - p80(1) [51-500]
Boyle, Elizabeth - *Authorities and Adaptations: The Reworking and Transmission of Textual Sources in Medieval Ireland*
Specu - v90 - i4 - Oct 2015 - p1090-1092 [501+]
How I Met My Countess
LJ - v140 - i3 - Feb 15 2015 - p133(1) [501+]
Boyle, Gerry - *Once Burned*
BL - v111 - i17 - May 1 2015 - p42(1) [51-500]
PW - v262 - i9 - March 2 2015 - p66(1) [51-500]
SPBW - June 2015 - pNA [51-500]
Boyle, John - *Blood Ransom: Stories from the Front Line in the War against Somali Piracy*
KR - May 15 2015 - pNA [501+]
PW - v262 - i18 - May 4 2015 - p110(2) [51-500]
Boyle, John F. (b. 1958-) - *Master Thomas Aquinas and the Fullness of Life*
Theol St - v76 - i2 - June 2015 - p403(1) [51-500]
Boyle, Margaret E. - *Unruly Women: Performance, Penitence, and Punishment in Early Modern Spain*
MP - v112 - i4 - May 2015 - pE306(4) [501+]
Ren Q - v68 - i2 - Summer 2015 - p746-748 [501+]
Sev Cent N - v73 - i3-4 - Fall-Winter 2015 - p135(6) [501+]

Boyle, Max - *The Indrawn Heart: An Estonian Journey*
WLT - v89 - i3-4 - May-August 2015 - p109(1) [51-500]
Boyle, Michael J. - *Violence After War: Explaining Instability in Post-Conflict States*
Parameters - v45 - i2 - Summer 2015 - p133(3) [501+]
Boyle, Nicholas - *The Impact of Idealism: The Legacy of Post-Kantian German Thought*
TimHES - i2194 - March 12 2015 - p49(1) [501+]
Boyle, T.C. - *The Best American Short Stories 2015*
KR - Sept 1 2015 - pNA [501+]
The Harder They Come
BL - v111 - i11 - Feb 1 2015 - p19(1) [501+]
Ent W - i1357 - April 3 2015 - p66(1) [51-500]
KR - Jan 1 2015 - pNA [51-500]
NYT - March 24 2015 - pC1(L) [501+]
NYTBR - April 12 2015 - p10(L) [501+]
PW - v262 - i15 - April 13 2015 - p13(1) [51-500]
Boyle, T. Coraghessan - *Talk Talk*
CSM - Feb 24 2015 - pNA [51-500]
Boyle, Tish - *Flavorful: 150 Irresistible Desserts in All-Time Favorite Flavors*
LJ - v140 - i15 - Sept 15 2015 - p100(1) [51-500]
PW - v262 - i31 - August 3 2015 - p53(1) [51-500]
Boyne, John - *The Boy at the Top of the Mountain*
c Magpies - v30 - i4 - Sept 2015 - p38(2) [501+]
Sch Lib - v63 - i4 - Winter 2015 - p225(1) [51-500]
A History of Loneliness (Read by Doyle, Gerard). Audiobook Review
LJ - v140 - i9 - May 15 2015 - p42(1) [51-500]
A History of Loneliness
AM - v212 - i18 - May 25 2015 - p35(2) [501+]
NYT - Feb 26 2015 - pC6(L) [501+]
TLS - i5840 - March 6 2015 - p21(1) [501+]
Boynton, Robert S. - *The Invitation-Only Zone: The True Story of North Korea's Abduction Project*
KR - Sept 15 2015 - pNA [501+]
PW - v262 - i47 - Nov 23 2015 - p62(1) [501+]
Boynton, Sandra - *Spooky Pookie*
c KR - Jan 1 2016 - pNA [51-500]
c PW - v262 - i30 - July 27 2015 - p66(1) [51-500]
Boys, Mary C. - *Redeeming Our Sacred Story: The Death of Jesus and Relations between Jews and Christians*
CHR - v101 - i3 - Summer 2015 - p589(2) [501+]
Boyson, Rowan - *Wordsworth and the Enlightenment Idea of Pleasure*
MP - v113 - i1 - August 2015 - pE43(4) [501+]
Bozik, Chrissy - *The Ghosts Go Spooking (Illus. by Storms, Patricia)*
c Res Links - v21 - i1 - Oct 2015 - p3(1) [51-500]
Le defile des fantomes (Illus. by Storms, Patricia)
c Res Links - v21 - i1 - Oct 2015 - p4(1) [51-500]
Bozzo, Linda - *Serving in the Military Series*
c HB Guide - v26 - i1 - Spring 2015 - p138(1) [51-500]
Bracco, Lorraine - *To the Fullest: The Clean Up Your Act Plan to Lose Weight, Rejuvenate, and Be the Best You Can Be*
PW - v262 - i9 - March 2 2015 - p79(2) [51-500]
Bracewell, Patricia - *The Price of Blood*
BL - v111 - i9-10 - Jan 1 2015 - p53(1) [51-500]
Bracht, Johannes - *Geldlose Zeiten und Uberfullte Kassen: Sparen, Leihen und Vererben in der Landlichen Gesellschaft Westfalens (1830-1866).*
HNet - July 2015 - pNA [501+]
Bracke, Maud - *Women and the Reinvention of the Political: Feminism in Italy, 1968-1983*
AHR - v120 - i4 - Oct 2015 - p1563(1) [501+]
TimHES - i2229 - Nov 12 2015 - p46(1) [501+]
Bracken, Alexandra - *In the Afterlight*
c CH Bwatch - Feb 2015 - pNA [51-500]
y HB Guide - v26 - i2 - Fall 2015 - p112(1) [51-500]
y SLJ - v61 - i3 - March 2015 - p80(1) [51-500]
Passenger
y BL - v112 - i7 - Dec 1 2015 - p56(2) [51-500]
y KR - Nov 15 2015 - pNA [51-500]
y PW - v262 - i44 - Nov 2 2015 - p87(1) [51-500]
y SLJ - v61 - i12 - Dec 2015 - p118(1) [51-500]
Star Wars: A New Hope: The Princess, the Scoundrel, and the Farm Boy (Illus. by McQuarrie, Ralph)
c BL - v111 - i1 - Sept 1 2015 - p115(1) [501+]
c SLJ - v61 - i11 - Nov 2015 - p98(1) [501+]
Bracken, Beth - *Faerieground (Illus. by Sawyer, Odessa)*
c HB Guide - v26 - i1 - Spring 2015 - p70(1) [51-500]

The Hidden Things, vol. 9
y SLJ - v61 - i9 - Sept 2015 - p151(4) [501+]
Promise, vol. 12
y SLJ - v61 - i9 - Sept 2015 - p151(4) [501+]
Return to the Crows, vol. 11
y SLJ - v61 - i9 - Sept 2015 - p151(4) [501+]
The Seventh Kingdom, vol. 10
y SLJ - v61 - i9 - Sept 2015 - p151(4) [501+]
Too Shy for Show and Tell (Illus. by Bell, Jennifer)
c Sch Lib - v63 - i2 - Summer 2015 - p89(1) [51-500]
Brackett, Keith - *The Nutcracker's Night Before Christmas (Illus. by Cowman, Joseph)*
c PW - v262 - i37 - Sept 14 2015 - p77(1) [51-500]
Brackmann, Lisa - *Dragon Day*
BL - v111 - i21 - July 1 2015 - p36(1) [51-500]
PW - v262 - i22 - June 1 2015 - p41(1) [51-500]
Brackston, P.J. - *The Case of the Fickle Mermaid*
BL - v112 - i6 - Nov 15 2015 - p24(1) [51-500]
KR - Nov 15 2015 - pNA [501+]
PW - v262 - i45 - Nov 9 2015 - p35(2) [51-500]
Gretel and the Case of the Missing Frog Prints
BL - v111 - i12 - Feb 15 2015 - p37(1) [51-500]
LJ - v140 - i2 - Feb 1 2015 - p61(4) [501+]
Brackston, Paula - *Lamp Black, Wolf Grey*
KR - June 1 2015 - pNA [51-500]
PW - v262 - i26 - June 29 2015 - p51(1) [51-500]
Once upon a Crime
BL - v111 - i19-20 - June 1 2015 - p56(1) [51-500]
PW - v262 - i19 - May 11 2015 - p36(1) [51-500]
The Silver Witch
KR - Feb 15 2015 - pNA [501+]
LJ - v140 - i5 - March 15 2015 - p91(1) [51-500]
Bradatan, Costica - *Dying for Ideas: The Dangerous Lives of the Philosophers*
TimHES - i2200 - April 23 2015 - p52-53 [501+]
Bradbury, Dominic - *Waterside Modern*
LJ - v140 - i19 - Nov 15 2015 - p85(1) [51-500]
Bradbury, Jennifer - *River Runs Deep*
c BL - v111 - i16 - April 15 2015 - p60(1) [51-500]
c CCB-B - v69 - i1 - Sept 2015 - p13(1) [51-500]
c KR - April 15 2015 - pNA [51-500]
c SLJ - v61 - i5 - May 2015 - p101(1) [51-500]
y VOYA - v38 - i2 - June 2015 - p55(1) [51-500]
Bradbury, Ray - *The Martian Chronicles*
LJ - v140 - i11 - June 15 2015 - p118(1) [501+]
Braddock, Paige - *Stinky Cecil in Operation Pond Rescue*
c BL - v111 - i9-10 - Jan 1 2015 - p63(1) [51-500]
c SLJ - v61 - i2 - Feb 2015 - p82(1) [51-500]
Braddon, Maria Elizabeth - *The Face in the Glass: And Other Gothic Tales*
TLS - i5836 - Feb 6 2015 - p12(1) [501+]
Brademann, Jan - *Mit den Toten und fur die Toten: Zur Konfessionalisierung der Sepulkralkultur im Munsterland*
HNet - Jan 2015 - pNA [501+]
Braden, Linda Z. - *Mason Jar Crafts for Kids*
c BL - v111 - i19-20 - June 1 2015 - p79(1) [51-500]
Bradford. Anita Casavantes - *The Revolution Is for the Children: The Politics of Childhood in Havana and Miami, 1959-1962*
AHR - v120 - i3 - June 2015 - p1086-1087 [501+]
Bradford, Anita Casavantes - *The Revolution Is for the Children: The Politics of Childhood in Havana and Miami, 1959-1962*
JSH - v81 - i3 - August 2015 - p776(2) [501+]
Bradford, Anna - *Lily the Elf: The Elf Flute (Illus. by Coutts, Lisa)*
c Magpies - v30 - i4 - Sept 2015 - p32(1) [501+]
Lily the Elf: The Wishing Seed (Illus. by Coutts, Lisa)
c Magpies - v30 - i4 - Sept 2015 - p32(1) [501+]
Bradford, Arthur - *Turtleface and Beyond*
KR - Jan 1 2015 - pNA [51-500]
Bradford, Barbara Taylor - *The Cavendon Women*
BL - v111 - i11 - Feb 1 2015 - p30(1) [51-500]
KR - March 15 2015 - pNA [501+]
Bradford, Chris - *Bullet Catcher*
Sch Lib - v63 - i4 - Winter 2015 - p225(1) [51-500]
Bradford, Clare - *The Middle Ages in Children's Literature*
Bkbird - v53 - i4 - Fall 2015 - p67(2) [501+]
Bradford, Michael - *Button Hill*
y KR - Jan 1 2015 - pNA [51-500]
c Res Links - v20 - i3 - Feb 2015 - p11(1) [51-500]
c SLJ - v61 - i3 - March 2015 - p132(1) [51-500]
y VOYA - v38 - i2 - June 2015 - p71(1) [51-500]
Bradford, Richard - *The Importance of Elsewhere: Philip Larkin's Photographs*
Spec - v329 - i9772 - Dec 12 2015 - p91(1) [501+]

Literary Rivals: Feuds and Antagonisms in the World of Books
    HM - v330 - i1981 - June 2015 - p77(3) [501+]
    TLS - i5862 - August 7 2015 - p26(1) [501+]
Bradley, Alan - *As Chimney Sweepers Come to Dust (Read by Entwistle, Jayne). Audiobook Review*
    BL - v111 - i17 - May 1 2015 - p57(1) [51-500]
    LJ - v140 - i8 - May 1 2015 - p40(1) [51-500]
As Chimney Sweepers Come to Dust
  y BL - v111 - i9-10 - Jan 1 2015 - p44(1) [51-500]
    J Chem Ed - v92 - i7 - July 2015 - p1146-1148 [501+]
Bradley, Anna - *A Wicked Way to Win an Earl*
    BL - v112 - i3 - Oct 1 2015 - p34(1) [51-500]
Bradley, Barrie Scardino - *Houston's Hermann Park: A Century of Community*
    JSH - v81 - i2 - May 2015 - p498(2) [501+]
Bradley, Ed - *"We Never Retreat": Filibustering Expeditions into Spanish Texas, 1812-1822*
    HNet - July 2015 - pNA [501+]
Bradley, F.T. - *Double Vision*
  y HB Guide - v26 - i1 - Spring 2015 - p71(1) [51-500]
Bradley, Hadrian - *Seeking the Face of Love*
    SPBW - Feb 2015 - pNA [501+]
Bradley, Ian C. - *Lost Chords and Christian Soldiers: The Sacred Music of Sir Arthur Sullivan*
    Notes - v72 - i2 - Dec 2015 - p345(4) [501+]
Bradley, J.D. - *Surreality: Strange Tales of a Man Sitting Down the Bar from You*
    KR - June 1 2015 - pNA [501+]
Bradley, James - *The China Mirage: The Hidden History of American Disaster in Asia*
    CSM - June 24 2015 - pNA [501+]
    KR - Feb 15 2015 - pNA [51-500]
    LJ - v140 - i5 - March 15 2015 - p118(2) [51-500]
    PW - v262 - i10 - March 9 2015 - p62(1) [51-500]
Clade
    New Sci - v227 - i3032 - August 1 2015 - p44(2) [501+]
Bradley, Janice - *Designing Schools for Meaningful Professional Learning*
    Bwatch - May 2015 - pNA [501+]
Bradley, Jess - *I Know Sasquatch*
  c KR - June 15 2015 - pNA [51-500]
Bradley, Kimberly Brubaker - *The War That Saved My Life (Read by Entwistle, Jayne). Audiobook Review*
  y HB - v91 - i4 - July-August 2015 - p163(2) [51-500]
  y SLJ - v61 - i4 - April 2015 - p62(2) [51-500]
The War that Saved My Life
  c CCB-B - v68 - i7 - March 2015 - p343(2) [51-500]
  c HB - v91 - i1 - Jan-Feb 2015 - p76(2) [501+]
  c HB Guide - v26 - i2 - Fall 2015 - p76(2) [51-500]
  c PW - v262 - i49 - Dec 2 2015 - p81(1) [51-500]
Bradley, Mark A. - *A Very Principled Boy: The Life of Duncan Lee, Red Spy and Cold Warrior*
    HNet - June 2015 - pNA [501+]
    JAH - v102 - i1 - June 2015 - p293-293 [501+]
Bradley, Mark (b. 1977-) - *Rome, Pollution, and Propriety: Dirt, Disease and Hygiene in the Eternal City from Antiquity to Modernity*
    Isis - v106 - i2 - June 2015 - p411(2) [501+]
Bradley, Sandra - *Henry Holton Takes the Ice (Illus. by Palacios, Sara)*
  c CCB-B - v68 - i7 - March 2015 - p349(2) [51-500]
  c HB Guide - v26 - i1 - Spring 2015 - p23(1) [51-500]
  c Nat Post - v17 - i56 - Jan 3 2015 - pWP11(1) [501+]
  c Res Links - v20 - i4 - April 2015 - p1(2) [51-500]
Bradley, Simon - *Cambridgeshire*
    TLS - i5835 - Jan 30 2015 - p10(2) [501+]
The Railways: Nation, Network and People
    Spec - v329 - i9760 - Sept 19 2015 - p45(3) [501+]
    TLS - i5876 - Nov 13 2015 - p8(1) [501+]
Bradman, Tony - *Anzac Boys (Illus. by Cuthbertson, Ollie)*
  c Sch Lib - v63 - i2 - Summer 2015 - p100(1) [51-500]
Snow White and the Magic Mirror (Illus. by Warburton, Sarah)
  c HB Guide - v26 - i1 - Spring 2015 - p57(1) [51-500]
The Ugly Duckling Returns (Illus. by Warburton, Sarah)
  c HB Guide - v26 - i1 - Spring 2015 - p57(1) [51-500]
Bradnock, Marianne - *Picturebooks from 0 to 90: Riveting Reads*
    Sch Lib - v63 - i3 - Autumn 2015 - p191(1) [501+]

Bradshaw, David - *Prudes on the Prowl: Fiction and Obscenity in England, 1850 to the Present Day*
    RES - v66 - i273 - Feb 2015 - p193-195 [501+]
Bradt, Hale - *Wilber's War*
    RVBW - June 2015 - pNA [501+]
Brady, Bernard V. - *Be Good and Do Good: Thinking through Moral Theology*
    Theol St - v76 - i4 - Dec 2015 - p895(1) [501+]
Brady, Ciaran - *A Union Forever: The Irish Question and U.S. Foreign Relations in the Viphet*
    HER - v130 - i545 - August 2015 - p1023(2) [501+]
Brady, Conor - *A June of Ordinary Murders*
    BL - v111 - i14 - March 15 2015 - p46(1) [51-500]
    KR - Feb 15 2015 - pNA [51-500]
    LJ - v140 - i8 - May 1 2015 - p103(1) [51-500]
    PW - v262 - i6 - Feb 9 2015 - p45(1) [51-500]
Brady, Eileen - *Unleashed*
    KR - June 1 2015 - pNA [51-500]
    PW - v262 - i26 - June 29 2015 - p48(1) [51-500]
Brady, Joan - *America's Dreyfus: The Case Nixon Rigged*
    Spec - v329 - i9761 - Sept 26 2015 - p38(1) [501+]
Brady, John - *Frank & Ava: In Love and War*
    LJ - v140 - i15 - Sept 15 2015 - p74(1) [51-500]
    PW - v262 - i35 - August 31 2015 - p81(1) [51-500]
    Spec - v329 - i9767 - Nov 7 2015 - p46(2) [501+]
Brady, Michael - *Emotional Insight: The Epistemic Role of Emotional Experience*
    Ethics - v125 - i2 - Jan 2015 - p567(5) [501+]
Braestrup, Kate - *Anchor and Flares: A Memoir of Motherhood, Hope and Service*
    BL - v111 - i19-20 - June 1 2015 - p26(1) [51-500]
    KR - April 15 2015 - pNA [51-500]
Braff, Joshua - *The Daddy Diaries*
    BL - v111 - i17 - May 1 2015 - p74(1) [51-500]
Brafman, Michelle - *Washing the Dead*
    BL - v111 - i16 - April 15 2015 - p27(1) [51-500]
    KR - March 1 2015 - pNA [51-500]
Bragg, C.L. - *Crescent Moon over Carolina: William Moultrie and American Liberty*
    JSH - v81 - i1 - Feb 2015 - p169(3) [51-500]
Bragg, Clint - *Marriage on the Mend: Healing Your Relationship After Crisis, Separation, or Divorce*
    RVBW - August 2015 - pNA [501+]
Bragg, John - *The Broom of God*
    KR - Nov 1 2015 - pNA [501+]
Bragg, Melvyn - *Now Is the Time*
    Spec - v329 - i9766 - Oct 31 2015 - p39(2) [501+]
    TLS - i5876 - Nov 13 2015 - p20(1) [501+]
Bragg, Rick - *Jerry Lee Lewis: His Own Story*
    Bwatch - Jan 2015 - pNA [51-500]
Braggs, Rashida K. - *Jazz Diasporas*
    KR - Nov 15 2015 - pNA [501+]
Brahm, Ajahn - *Kindfulness Meditation*
    PW - v262 - i45 - Nov 9 2015 - p54(2) [501+]
Brahmachari, Sita - *Brace Mouth, False Teeth*
  y Sch Lib - v63 - i1 - Spring 2015 - p50(1) [51-500]
Jasmine Skies
  y HB Guide - v26 - i1 - Spring 2015 - p71(1) [51-500]
Red Leaves
  y Sch Lib - v63 - i1 - Spring 2015 - p34(1) [51-500]
Brain, Marshall - *The Engineering Book: From the Catapult to the Curiosity Rover, 250 Milestones in the History of Engineering*
    BL - v111 - i18 - May 15 2015 - p15(1) [51-500]
    LJ - v140 - i11 - June 15 2015 - p106(2) [51-500]
How "God" Works
    Hum - v75 - i3 - May-June 2015 - p40(2) [501+]
Brake, Mark - *How to Be a Space Explorer*
  c HB Guide - v26 - i1 - Spring 2015 - p174(1) [51-500]
  c Magpies - v30 - i1 - March 2015 - p23(1) [51-500]
Brallier, Max - *Cosmoe's Wiener Getaway (Read by Martella, Vincent). Audiobook Review*
  c SLJ - v61 - i7 - July 2015 - p46(1) [51-500]
Cosmoe's Wiener Getaway (Illus. by Maguire, Rachel)
  c HB Guide - v26 - i2 - Fall 2015 - p76(1) [51-500]
  c PW - v262 - i13 - March 30 2015 - p75(2) [51-500]
  c CCB-B - v69 - i1 - Sept 2015 - p14(1) [51-500]
  c KR - Feb 15 2015 - pNA [51-500]
  c SLJ - v61 - i5 - May 2015 - p101(2) [51-500]
The Last Kids on Earth (Illus. by Holgate, Douglas)
  c BL - v112 - i3 - Oct 1 2015 - p78(1) [51-500]
  c SLJ - v61 - i6 - June 2015 - p137(2) [51-500]
  c KR - August 15 2015 - pNA [51-500]
  c PW - v262 - i31 - August 3 2015 - p60(1) [51-500]
  c PW - v262 - i49 - Dec 2 2015 - p66(1) [51-500]

Bram, Elizabeth - *Rufus the Writer (Illus. by Groenink, Chuck)*
  c KR - April 15 2015 - pNA [51-500]
  c PW - v262 - i17 - April 27 2015 - p75(1) [51-500]
  c SLJ - v61 - i6 - June 2015 - p78(1) [51-500]
Bramble, Ben - *The Moral Complexities of Eating Meat*
    BL - v112 - i3 - Oct 1 2015 - p18(1) [51-500]
Brambles, Lindsay Francis - *Becoming Darkness*
    BL - v112 - i1 - Sept 1 2015 - p103(1) [51-500]
  y KR - July 15 2015 - pNA [501+]
  y PW - v262 - i33 - August 17 2015 - p72(2) [51-500]
  y SLJ - v61 - i7 - July 2015 - p90(2) [51-500]
Bramsen, Carin - *Just a Duck? (Illus. by Bramsen, Carin)*
  c HB Guide - v26 - i2 - Fall 2015 - p7(1) [51-500]
Bramwell, Lincoln - *Wilderburbs: Communities on Nature's Edge*
    JAH - v102 - i2 - Sept 2015 - p603-603 [501+]
    Roundup M - v22 - i5 - June 2015 - p35(1) [501+]
    Roundup M - v22 - i6 - August 2015 - p34(1) [501+]
Branan, Karen - *The Family Tree: A Kinship Lynching in Georgia, a Legacy of Secrets, and My Search for the Truth*
    KR - Nov 15 2015 - pNA [501+]
Branch, Miko - *Miss Jessie's: Creating a Successful Business from Scratch--Naturally*
    BL - v111 - i13 - March 1 2015 - p9(1) [51-500]
    LJ - v140 - i7 - April 15 2015 - p95(1) [51-500]
    PW - v262 - i6 - Feb 9 2015 - p57(2) [51-500]
Branch, Susan - *The Fairy Tale Girl*
    RVBW - Nov 2015 - pNA [501+]
Brand, Benjamin - *Holy Treasure and Sacred Song: Relic Cults and Their Liturgies in Medieval Tuscany*
    Med R - August 2015 - pNA [501+]
Brand, Jack - *Freddy Tangles: Champ or Chicken (Illus. by Jellett, Tom)*
  c Magpies - v30 - i5 - Nov 2015 - p33(1) [501+]
Freddy Tangles: Legend or Loser (Illus. by Jellett, Tom)
  c Magpies - v30 - i5 - Nov 2015 - p33(1) [501+]
Brand, Laurie A. - *Official Stories: Politics and National Narratives in Egypt and Algeria*
    IJMES - v47 - i4 - Nov 2015 - p845-846 [501+]
Brand, Max - *Rodeo Ranch*
    KR - May 1 2015 - pNA [501+]
Brand, Russell - *Russell Brand's Trickster Tales: The Pied Piper of Hamelin (Read by Brand, Russell). Audiobook Review*
    SLJ - v61 - i2 - Feb 2015 - p48(1) [51-500]
Russell Brand's Trickster Tales: The Pied Piper of Hamelin (Illus. by Riddell, Chris)
  c HB Guide - v26 - i2 - Fall 2015 - p158(1) [51-500]
Brandes, Roberta - *We're Still Here Ya Bastards: How the People of New Orleans Rebuilt Their City*
    BL - v111 - i19-20 - June 1 2015 - p12(1) [51-500]
Brandl, Felix - *Von der Entstehung des Geldes zur Sicherung der Wahrung: Die Theorien von Bernhard Laum und Wilhelm Gerloff zur Genese des Geldes*
    HNet - Sept 2015 - pNA(NA) [501+]
Brandlee, Ben, Jr. - *The Kid*
    NYTBR - Jan 25 2015 - p24(L) [501+]
Brandon, Diane - *Dream Interpretation for Beginners: Understand the Wisdom of Your Sleeping Mind*
    Bwatch - May 2015 - pNA [501+]
Brandon, Ivan - *Drifter*
    BL - v111 - i22 - August 1 2015 - p46(1) [51-500]
    LJ - v140 - i13 - August 1 2015 - p5(1) [51-500]
Brandon, Mark E. - *States of Union: Family and Change in the American Constitutional Order*
    AHR - v120 - i2 - April 2015 - p615-616 [501+]
Brandow, Michael - *New York's Poop Scoop Law*
    NY - v91 - i30 - Oct 5 2015 - p80 [501+]
Brands, H.W. - *Reagan: The Life*
    BL - v111 - i14 - March 15 2015 - p42(1) [51-500]
    CSM - May 26 2015 - pNA [501+]
    Econ - v415 - i8936 - May 2 2015 - p73(US) [501+]
    KR - April 1 2015 - pNA [501+]
    LJ - v140 - i7 - April 15 2015 - p93(1) [51-500]
    NY - v91 - i17 - June 22 2015 - p81 [51-500]
    NYTBR - June 7 2015 - p14(L) [501+]
    PW - v262 - i14 - April 6 2015 - p49(2) [51-500]
    SEP - v287 - i3 - May-June 2015 - p73(1) [501+]
Brands, Hal - *What Good Is Grand Strategy? Power and Purpose in American Statecraft from Harry S. Truman to George W. Bush*
    AHR - v120 - i2 - April 2015 - p658-659 [501+]
    J Am St - v49 - i3 - August 2015 - p653-654 [501+]
    JAH - v101 - i4 - March 2015 - p1321-1322

[501+]
    NWCR - v68 - i3 - Summer 2015 - p138(10) [501+]
    PHR - v84 - i4 - Nov 2015 - p544(2) [501+]

Brandt, Barbara - *Your Kids: Cooking! A Recipe for Turning Ordinary Kids into Extraordinary Cooks*
  y CH Bwatch - March 2015 - pNA [51-500]
  c KR - April 15 2015 - pNA [51-500]
    SPBW - May 2015 - pNA [501+]

Brandt, Harry - *The Whites*
    NYT - Feb 10 2015 - pC1(L) [501+]
    RVBW - Nov 2015 - pNA [51-500]

The Whites (Read by Fliakos, Ari). Audiobook Review
    BL - v111 - i21 - July 1 2015 - p79(1) [51-500]
    PW - v262 - i17 - April 27 2015 - p69(1) [51-500]

The Whites
    BL - v111 - i9-10 - Jan 1 2015 - p35(1) [501+]
    Esq - v164 - i5 - Dec 2015 - p52(1) [501+]

Brandt, Lois - *Maddi's Fridge (Illus. by Vogel, Vin)*
  c HB Guide - v26 - i1 - Spring 2015 - p23(1) [51-500]

Brandt, Michael Jason - *Plagued, with Guilt*
    KR - Nov 1 2015 - pNA [51-500]

Brandt, Richard L. - *The Google Guys: Inside the Brilliant Minds of Google Founders Larry Page and Sergey Brin*
    Forbes - v196 - i6 - Nov 2 2015 - p42(1) [501+]

Brandt, Robert - *Chameleon: The True Story of an Impostor's Remarkable Odyssey*
    KR - Sept 15 2015 - pNA [501+]

Brandvold, Peter - *Lonnie Gentry*
    Roundup M - v22 - i6 - August 2015 - p27(1) [501+]

Once More into the Breech
    Roundup M - v23 - i1 - Oct 2015 - p29(1) [501+]
    BL - v111 - i16 - April 15 2015 - p37(1) [51-500]

Thunder over the Superstitions
    BL - v112 - i1 - Sept 1 2015 - p52(2) [51-500]

Branford, Anna - *The Midnight Owl (Illus. by Coutts, Lisa)*
  c Magpies - v30 - i2 - May 2015 - p33(1) [501+]

The Precious Ring (Illus. by Coutts, Lisa)
  c Magpies - v30 - i2 - May 2015 - p33(1) [501+]

Violet Mackerel's Formal Occasion (Illus. by Davis, Sarah)
  c Magpies - v30 - i1 - March 2015 - p16(1) [501+]

Violet Mackerel's Pocket Protest
  c HB Guide - v26 - i1 - Spring 2015 - p57(1) [51-500]

Branley, Eden - *Dangerously Broken*
    PW - v262 - i34 - August 24 2015 - p66(3) [51-500]

Brannen, Sarah S. - *Madame Martine Breaks the Rules (Illus. by Brannen, Sarah S.)*
  c KR - June 15 2015 - pNA [51-500]
  c SLJ - v61 - i9 - Sept 2015 - p114(1) [51-500]

Madame Martine (Illus. by Brannen, Sarah S.)
  c CH Bwatch - April 2015 - pNA [51-500]
  c HB Guide - v26 - i1 - Spring 2015 - p23(1) [51-500]

Branscombe, Allison - *All about China: Stories, Songs, Crafts and More for Kids (Illus. by Wang, Lin)*
  c SLJ - v61 - i2 - Feb 2015 - p117(1) [51-500]

Branscome, David - *Textual Rivals: Self-Presentation in Herodotus' Histories*
    AHR - v120 - i3 - June 2015 - p1088-1089 [501+]
    Class R - v65 - i1 - April 2015 - p38-40 [501+]

Branson, Richard - *The Virgin Way: Everything I Know About Leadership*
    NYTBR - Oct 25 2015 - p35(L) [501+]

Brantly, Kent - *Called for Life: How Loving Our Neighbor Led Us into the Heart of the Ebola Epidemic*
    PW - v262 - i23 - June 8 2015 - p56(1) [51-500]

Brashares, Ann - *The Here and Now*
  c Sch Lib - v63 - i2 - Summer 2015 - p114(1) [501+]

Brasher, Cecil - *Turvytops: A Really Wild Island*
  c Sch Lib - v63 - i2 - Summer 2015 - p90(1) [51-500]

Brass, Marilyn - *Baking with the Brass Sisters: Over 125 Recipes for Classic Cakes, Pies, Cookies, Breads, Desserts, and Savories from America's Favorite Home Bakers (Illus. by Ryan, Andy)*
    LJ - v140 - i13 - August 1 2015 - p118(2) [51-500]

Brasset, Rose-Line - *Juliette a Barcelone*
  c Res Links - v20 - i3 - Feb 2015 - p43(1) [51-500]

Juliette a la Havane (Illus. by Charette, Geraldine)
  y Res Links - v21 - i1 - Oct 2015 - p48(1) [51-500]

Brasseux, Carl A. - *Ruined by this Miserable War: The Dispatches of Charles Prosper Fauconnet, a French Diplomat in New Orleans, 1863-1868*
    SHQ - v118 - i3 - Jan 2015 - p324-325 [501+]

Brassley, Paul - *War, Agriculture, and Food: Rural Europe from the 1930s to the 1950s*
    JEH - v75 - i2 - June 2015 - p590-592 [501+]

Braswell, Liz - *A Whole New World: A Twisted Tale*
  y SLJ - v61 - i10 - Oct 2015 - p99(1) [51-500]
  y VOYA - v38 - i4 - Oct 2015 - p67(1) [501+]

A Whole New World
  y KR - July 15 2015 - pNA [51-500]

Bratman, Michael E. - *Shared Agency: A Planned Theory of Acting Together*
    Dialogue - v54 - i1 - March 2015 - p188-189 [501+]

Bratt, James D. - *Abraham Kuyper: Modern Calvinist, Christian Democrat*
    Bks & Cult - v21 - i4 - July-August 2015 - p8(1) [501+]
    CH - v84 - i2 - June 2015 - p462(4) [501+]
    J Ch St - v57 - i2 - Spring 2015 - p378-379 [501+]

Bratton, William J. - *The NYPD's First Fifty Years: Politicians, Police Commissioners and Patrolmen*
    NYT - May 3 2015 - p5(L) [501+]

Braud, Alexis - *Parade*
  c KR - Dec 15 2015 - pNA [51-500]

Braude, Mark - *Making Monte Carlo: A History of Speculation and Spectacle*
    PW - v262 - i44 - Nov 2 2015 - p74(1) [51-500]

Brauer, Christoph - *Unter dem roten Wunderschirm: Lesarten klassischer Kinder- und Jugendliteratur*
    Bkbird - v53 - i3 - Summer 2015 - p91(1) [501+]

Braumoeller, Bear F. - *The Great Powers and the International System: Systemic Theory in Empirical Perspective*
    HER - v130 - i542 - Feb 2015 - p258(2) [501+]

Braun, Emily - *Cubism: The Leonard A. Lauder Collection*
    LJ - v140 - i3 - Feb 15 2015 - p96(1) [51-500]

Braun, Eric - *Fatal Faults: The Story of the Challenger Explosion*
  y SLJ - v61 - i9 - Sept 2015 - p151(4) [501+]

John Green: Star Author, Vlogbrother, and Nerdfighter
  c HB Guide - v26 - i2 - Fall 2015 - p207(1) [51-500]
  c BL - v111 - i14 - March 15 2015 - p59(1) [51-500]

Plan a Holiday Party. E-book Review
  c HB Guide - v26 - i1 - Spring 2015 - p142(1) [51-500]

Plan an Outdoor Party. E-book Review
  c HB Guide - v26 - i1 - Spring 2015 - p142(1) [51-500]

Super Baseball Infographics (Illus. by Westlund, Laura)
  c HB Guide - v26 - i2 - Fall 2015 - p197(1) [51-500]
  c SLJ - v61 - i2 - Feb 2015 - p114(1) [51-500]

Super Football Infographics (Illus. by Westlund, Laura)
  c HB Guide - v26 - i2 - Fall 2015 - p197(1) [51-500]

Braun, Erik - *The Birth of Insight: Meditation, Modern Buddhism, and the Burmese Monk Ledi Sayadaw*
    HNet - July 2015 - pNA [501+]

Braun, Karl-Heinz - *Das Konstanzer Konzil 1414-1418: Weltereignis des Mittelalters: Essays*
    HNet - Feb 2015 - pNA [501+]

Braun, Lundy - *Breathing Race into the Machine: The Surprising Career of the Spirometer from Plantation to Genetics*
    AHR - v120 - i3 - June 2015 - p972-973 [501+]
    JAH - v102 - i1 - June 2015 - p218-218 [501+]
    MAQ - v29 - i3 - Sept 2015 - pb-17-b-19 [501+]

Braun, Matt - *WesternLore*
    Roundup M - v22 - i6 - August 2015 - p27(1) [501+]

Braun, Melinda - *Stranded*
  y VOYA - v38 - i4 - Oct 2015 - p50(1) [51-500]
  y SLJ - v61 - i10 - Oct 2015 - p99(1) [51-500]

Braun, Sebastien - *Can You Say It, Too? Jingle! Jingle! (Illus. by Braun, Sebastian)*
  c PW - v262 - i37 - Sept 14 2015 - p72(2) [501+]

Can You Say It, Too? Jingle! Jingle! (Illus. by Braun, Sebastien)
  c KR - Sept 1 2015 - pNA [51-500]

Can You Say It, Too? Quack! Quack! (Illus. by Braun, Sebastien)
  c CH Bwatch - May 2015 - pNA [51-500]

Brauner, Barbara - *The Spell Bind (Illus. by Halpin, Abigail)*
  y HB Guide - v26 - i1 - Spring 2015 - p71(1) [51-500]

Brauning, Kate - *How We Fall*
  c HB Guide - v26 - i1 - Spring 2015 - p101(1) [51-500]

Brautigam, Deborah - *Will Africa Feed China?*
    Nature - v527 - i7576 - Nov 5 2015 - p37(1) [501+]

Braver, Lee - *Heidegger: Thinking of Being*
    RM - v68 - i3 - March 2015 - p644(3) [501+]

Braver, Vanita - *Madison and the New Neighbors (Illus. by Brown, Jonathan)*
  c HB Guide - v26 - i2 - Fall 2015 - p28(1) [51-500]

Braverman, Irus - *Wild Life: The Institution of Nature*
    NH - v123 - i6 - July-August 2015 - p46(2) [501+]
    TLS - i5867 - Sept 11 2015 - p24(1) [501+]

Bravo, Ellen - *Again and Again*
    SPBW - Oct 2015 - pNA [501+]

Brawer, Richard - *Love's Sweet Sorrow*
    SPBW - Jan 2015 - pNA [501+]

Brawley, Robert L. - *The Oxford Encyclopedia of the Bible and Ethics, 2 vols.*
    BL - v111 - i14 - March 15 2015 - p29(1) [501+]

Brawn, Dale - *Paths to the Bench: The Judicial Appointment Process in Manitoba, 1870-1950*
    Can Hist R - v96 - i3 - Sept 2015 - p441(5) [501+]

Bray, Alan - *The Puppet's Tattered Clothes*
    SPBW - Feb 2015 - pNA [501+]

Bray, Libba - *Beauty Queens (Read by Bray, Libba). Audiobook Review*
  c SLJ - v61 - i2 - Feb 2015 - p38(3) [501+]

Lair of Dreams
  y BL - v111 - i21 - July 1 2015 - p56(1) [51-500]
  y CCB-B - v69 - i2 - Oct 2015 - p77(1) [51-500]
  y HB - v91 - i5 - Sept-Oct 2015 - p95(1) [51-500]
  y KR - July 1 2015 - pNA [51-500]
  y Magpies - v30 - i4 - Sept 2015 - p39(1) [51-500]
  y PW - v262 - i49 - Dec 2 2015 - p104(1) [51-500]
  y Sch Lib - v63 - i4 - Winter 2015 - p242(1) [51-500]
  y SLJ - v61 - i8 - August 2015 - p101(1) [51-500]

Lair of Dreams (Read by LaVoy, January). Audiobook Review
  y SLJ - v61 - i11 - Nov 2015 - p72(1) [51-500]

Lair of Dreams
  y VOYA - v38 - i3 - August 2015 - p73(2) [501+]

Brazeau, Robert - *Eco-Joyce: The Environmental Imagination of James Joyce*
    ILS - v34 - i2 - Spring 2015 - p21(2) [501+]

Braziller, George - *Encounters: My Life in Publishing*
    NY - v91 - i23 - August 10 2015 - p77 [51-500]
    PW - v262 - i17 - April 27 2015 - p61(1) [51-500]

Brazzeal, David - *Pray Like a Gourmet: Creative Ways to Feed Your Soul*
    PW - v262 - i10 - March 9 2015 - p69(1) [51-500]

Brazzel, William - *The Seventh Holy Man*
    SPBW - June 2015 - pNA [501+]

Breakfield, Charles V. - *The Enigma Always*
    KR - Dec 1 2015 - pNA [501+]

Bream, Jon - *Dylan: Disc by Disc*
    BL - v112 - i5 - Nov 1 2015 - p16(1) [51-500]

Brears, Peter - *Cooking and Dining in Tudor and Early Stuart England*
    TLS - i5860 - July 24 2015 - p3(2) [501+]

Breathnach, Sarah Ban - *The Best Part of the Day (Illus. by Edelson, Wendy)*
  c CH Bwatch - Jan 2015 - pNA [51-500]

Breault, Donna Adair - *The Red Light in the Ivory Tower: Contexts and Implications of Entrepreneurial Education*
    CS - v44 - i2 - March 2015 - p176-178 [501+]

Breay, Claire - *Magna Carta: Law, Liberty, Legacy*
    HT - v65 - i6 - June 2015 - p56(2) [501+]
    TLS - i5842 - March 20 2015 - p17(2) [501+]

Breazeale, Daniel - *Fichte's Vocation of Man: New Interpretive and Critical Essays*
    RM - v68 - i3 - March 2015 - p646(2) [501+]

Brecher, Jeremy - *Climate Insurgency: A Strategy for Survival*
    HNet - Sept 2015 - pNA [501+]
    LJ - v140 - i7 - April 15 2015 - p116(1) [51-500]

Brecher, W. Puck - *The Aesthetics of Strangeness: Eccentricity and Madness in Early Modern Japan*
    JAS - v74 - i3 - August 2015 - p750-751 [501+]

Brecht, Bertolt - *Love Poems*
    TLS - i5856 - June 26 2015 - p9(2) [501+]

Breckenridge, Keith - *Biometrics State: The Global Politics of Identification and Surveillance in South Africa, 1850 to the Present*
    IJAHS - v48 - i1 - Wntr 2015 - p149-150 [501+]

Breckman, Warren - *Adventures of the Symbolic: Post-Marxism and Radical Democracy*
    AHR - v120 - i1 - Feb 2015 - p342-343 [501+]
    JMH - v87 - i3 - Sept 2015 - p721(3) [501+]

Brecon, Connah - *Frank!*
  c HB Guide - v26 - i1 - Spring 2015 - p23(1) [51-500]

There's This Thing (Illus. by Brecon, Connah)
  c HB Guide - v26 - i1 - Spring 2015 - p23(1) [51-500]
  c NYTBR - Feb 8 2015 - p24(L) [501+]

Breen, Christine - *Her Name Is Rose*
    BL - v111 - i14 - March 15 2015 - p53(1) [51-500]

Breen, Mike - *Pig and Sheep (Illus. by Berg, Blake)*
  c CH Bwatch - June 2015 - pNA [51-500]
Breen, Patrick H. - *The Land Shall Be Deluged in Blood: A New History of the Nat Turner Revolt*
  LJ - v140 - i17 - Oct 15 2015 - p99(1) [51-500]
  PW - v262 - i31 - August 3 2015 - p46(1) [51-500]
Breen, T.H. - *George Washington's Journey: The President Forges a New Nation*
  KR - Oct 1 2015 - pNA [501+]
Breen, U.M. - *The Guardian Dragon (Illus. by Lucas, Diane)*
  c CH Bwatch - April 2015 - pNA [51-500]
Bregman, Ahron - *Cursed Victory: A History of Israel and the Occupied Territories*
  KR - Feb 15 2015 - pNA [501+]
  LJ - v140 - i7 - April 15 2015 - p100(1) [51-500]
  PW - v262 - i8 - Feb 23 2015 - p62(1) [51-500]
  TLS - i5873 - Oct 23 2015 - p24(1) [501+]
Breiger, Marek - *The City and the Fields*
  KR - Oct 15 2015 - pNA [501+]
Breitenstein, Mirak - *Rules and Observance: Devising Forms of Communal Life*
  Six Ct J - v46 - i2 - Summer 2015 - p491-492 [501+]
Brekke, Jergen - *Dreamless*
  BL - v111 - i9-10 - Jan 1 2015 - p46(1) [51-500]
Brelinski, Val - *The Girl Who Slept with God*
  y BL - v111 - i21 - July 1 2015 - p30(2) [51-500]
  KR - June 1 2015 - pNA [501+]
  y LJ - v140 - i8 - May 1 2015 - p60(1) [51-500]
  y NYTBR - Oct 11 2015 - p30(L) [501+]
  PW - v262 - i22 - June 1 2015 - p38(1) [51-500]
Bremer, Jeff - *A Store Almost in Sight: The Economic Transformation of Missouri from the Louisiana Purchase to the Civil War*
  JAH - v101 - i4 - March 2015 - p1270-1271 [501+]
  JSH - v81 - i3 - August 2015 - p704(2) [501+]
  WHQ - v46 - i2 - Summer 2015 - p232-233 [501+]
Bremer, Thomas - *Cross and Kremlin: A Brief History of the Orthodox Church in Russia*
  CHR - v101 - i3 - Summer 2015 - p593(2) [501+]
Bremm, Klaus-Jurgen - *Propaganda im Ersten Weltkrieg*
  HNet - Jan 2015 - pNA [501+]
Bremmer, Ian - *Superpower: Three Choices for America's Role in the World*
  TLS - i5860 - July 24 2015 - p12(2) [501+]
Bremner, G.A. - *Imperial Gothic: Religious Architecture and High Anglican Culture in the British Empire, c. 1840-1870*
  VS - v57 - i2 - Wntr 2015 - p330(2) [501+]
Brence, Gerald - *Ox in the Culvert*
  Roundup M - v23 - i1 - Oct 2015 - p29(1) [51-500]
Brencher, Hannah - *If You Find This Letter: My Journey to Find Purpose through Hundreds of Letters to Strangers*
  CSM - March 24 2015 - pNA [501+]
Brendan, Lanctot - *Beyond Civilization and Barbarism: Culture and Politics in Postrevolutionary Argentina*
  Hisp R - v83 - i4 - Autumn 2015 - p488-491 [501+]
Brendan, Maggie - *The Trouble with Patience*
  BL - v111 - i12 - Feb 15 2015 - p44(2) [51-500]
Brendecke, Arndt - *Imperio e informacion: funciones del saber en el dominio colonial espanol*
  Hisp R - v83 - i2 - Spring 2015 - p237-241 [501+]
Brendler, Carol - *Not Very Scary (Illus. by Pizzoli, Greg)*
  c HB Guide - v26 - i1 - Spring 2015 - p6(1) [51-500]
Brennan, Allison - *Compulsion*
  BL - v111 - i13 - March 1 2015 - p22(1) [51-500]
  KR - Feb 1 2015 - pNA [501+]
  LJ - v140 - i3 - Feb 15 2015 - p84(1) [51-500]
  PW - v262 - i6 - Feb 9 2015 - p47(1) [51-500]
No Good Deed
  BL - v112 - i5 - Nov 1 2015 - p31(1) [51-500]
Brennan, Denis - *The Making of an Abolitionist*
  HNet - August 2015 - pNA [501+]
Brennan, Denise - *Life Interrupted: Trafficking into Forced Labor in the United States*
  AJS - v120 - i6 - May 2015 - p1868(4) [501+]
  CS - v44 - i6 - Nov 2015 - p780-782 [501+]
Brennan, Geoffrey - *Explaining Norms*
  Dialogue - v54 - i3 - Sept 2015 - p578-579 [501+]
Brennan, Janet K. - *A Dance in the Woods: A Mother's Insight*
  RVBW - April 2015 - pNA [51-500]
Brennan, Jason - *Why Not Capitalism?*
  IndRev - v20 - i2 - Fall 2015 - p304(5) [501+]

Brennan, Marie - *Voyage of the Basilisk*
  PW - v262 - i2 - Jan 12 2015 - p40(1) [51-500]
  Bwatch - Sept 2015 - pNA [51-500]
  KR - Jan 15 2015 - pNA [51-500]
Brennan-Nelson, Denise - *Leopold the Lion (Illus. by Barshaw, Ruth McNally)*
  c KR - July 15 2015 - pNA [51-500]
  c SLJ - v61 - i9 - Sept 2015 - p116(1) [51-500]
Tallulah: Mermaid of the Great Lakes (Illus. by Hartung, Susan Kathleen)
  c CH Bwatch - July 2015 - pNA [501+]
  c SLJ - v61 - i7 - July 2015 - p59(1) [51-500]
Teach Me to Love (Illus. by Brennan-Nelson, Denise)
  c HB Guide - v26 - i1 - Spring 2015 - p6(1) [51-500]
Brennan, Net - *Child Convicts*
  c KR - Oct 1 2015 - pNA [51-500]
Brennan, Sarah Rees - *Unmade*
  c CH Bwatch - Jan 2015 - pNA [51-500]
  y HB - v91 - i1 - Jan-Feb 2015 - p77(2) [51-500]
  c HB Guide - v26 - i1 - Spring 2015 - p101(1) [51-500]
Brennan, Summer - *The Oyster War: The True Story of a Small Farm, Big Politics, and the Future of Wilderness in America*
  KR - June 1 2015 - pNA [501+]
  PW - v262 - i25 - June 22 2015 - p134(1) [51-500]
  Reason - v47 - i4 - August-Sept 2015 - p66(3) [501+]
Brenneman, Todd M. - *Homespun Gospel: The Triumph of Sentimentality in Contemporary American Evangelicalism*
  CH - v84 - i1 - March 2015 - p281(3) [501+]
Brenner, Gail - *The End of Self Help: Discovering Peace and Happiness Right at the Heart of Your Messy, Scary Brilliant Life*
  SPBW - July 2015 - pNA [51-500]
Brenner, Tom - *And Then Comes Christmas (Illus. by Christy, Jana)*
  c HB Guide - v26 - i1 - Spring 2015 - p23(2) [51-500]
Brera, Matteo - *Lingua e identita a 150 anni dall'Unita d'Italia*
  MLR - v110 - i1 - Jan 2015 - p266-268 [501+]
Bresc, Henri - *Le livre de raison de Paul de Sade (Avignon, 1390-1394).*
  Specu - v90 - i1 - Jan 2015 - p213-214 [501+]
Breslaw, Elaine G. - *Lotions, Potions, Pills, and Magic: Health Care in Early America*
  J Am St - v49 - i1 - Feb 2015 - p191-194 [501+]
Breslin, Abigail - *This May Sound Crazy*
  y BL - v112 - i6 - Nov 15 2015 - p37(1) [51-500]
Breslin, Theresa - *The Dragon Stoorworm (Illus. by Land, Matthew)*
  c CCB-B - v68 - i7 - March 2015 - p350(1) [51-500]
  c SLJ - v61 - i6 - June 2015 - p46(6) [501+]
An Illustrated Treasury of Scottish Mythical Creatures (Illus. by Leiper, Kate)
  c BL - v112 - i5 - Nov 1 2015 - p40(2) [51-500]
  c KR - Sept 1 2015 - pNA [51-500]
  c PW - v262 - i35 - August 31 2015 - p93(1) [51-500]
  c Sch Lib - v63 - i4 - Winter 2015 - p225(1) [51-500]
Bretherton, Luke - *Resurrecting Democracy: Faith, Citizenship, and the Politics of a Common Life*
  TLS - i5856 - June 26 2015 - p24(1) [501+]
Brett, Flora - *First Facts: Your Body Systems*
  c HB Guide - v26 - i2 - Fall 2015 - p183(1) [501+]
Get to Know Chameleons
  c HB Guide - v26 - i2 - Fall 2015 - p175(1) [501+]
Get to Know Komodo Dragons
  c HB Guide - v26 - i2 - Fall 2015 - p175(1) [501+]
Get to Know Reptiles
  c SLJ - v61 - i6 - June 2015 - p134(1) [51-500]
Brett, Jan - *The Animals' Santa (Illus. by Brett, Jan)*
  c HB Guide - v26 - i1 - Spring 2015 - p6(1) [51-500]
The Turnip (Illus. by Brett, Jan)
  c CH Bwatch - Nov 2015 - pNA [51-500]
  c KR - Sept 1 2015 - pNA [51-500]
  c PW - v262 - i33 - August 17 2015 - p69(1) [51-500]
  c PW - v262 - i49 - Dec 2 2015 - p24(2) [51-500]
Brett, Jeannie - *Wild About Bears (Illus. by Brett, Jeannie)*
  c Sci & Ch - v53 - i1 - Sept 2015 - p95 [51-500]
Brett, Simon - *Mrs. Pargeter's Principle*
  BL - v111 - i19-20 - June 1 2015 - p55(2) [51-500]
  PW - v262 - i25 - June 22 2015 - p121(1) [51-500]
The Tomb in Turkey
  PW - v262 - i2 - Jan 12 2015 - p39(1) [51-500]
  BL - v111 - i11 - Feb 1 2015 - p28(1) [51-500]
  KR - Jan 15 2015 - pNA [51-500]
Brettschneider, Dean - *Bread*
  LJ - v140 - i2 - Feb 1 2015 - p102(1) [501+]

Breuilly, John - *The Oxford Handbook of the History of Nationalism*
  HER - v130 - i543 - April 2015 - p513(3) [501+]
Breul, Wolfgang - *Geschichtsbewusstsein und Zukunftserwartung in Pietismus und Erweckungsbewegung*
  HNet - June 2015 - pNA [501+]
Breunig, Werner - *Funf Monate in Berlin: Briefe von Edgar N. Johnson aus dem Jahre 1946*
  HNet - July 2015 - pNA [501+]
Brewer, Daniel - *The Cambridge Companion to the French Enlightment*
  FS - v69 - i4 - Oct 2015 - p532-532 [501+]
Brewer, Dominic J. - *Encyclopedia of Education Economics and Finance*
  BL - v111 - i15 - April 1 2015 - p6(2) [51-500]
Brewer, Heather - *The Cemetery Boys*
  y CCB-B - v68 - i8 - April 2015 - p391(1) [51-500]
  y HB Guide - v26 - i2 - Fall 2015 - p112(1) [51-500]
  y PW - v262 - i3 - Jan 19 2015 - p85(1) [51-500]
  y VOYA - v37 - i6 - Feb 2015 - p54(1) [51-500]
Brewer, John D. - *Ex-Combatants, Religion and Peace in Northern Ireland: The Role of Religion in Transitional Justice*
  CS - v44 - i2 - March 2015 - p178-180 [501+]
The Public Value of the Social Sciences
  CS - v44 - i6 - Nov 2015 - p782-784 [501+]
Brewer, Killian B. - *The Rules of Ever After*
  y SLJ - v61 - i6 - June 2015 - p120(1) [51-500]
Brewer, Richard - *Occupied Earth: Stories of Aliens, Resistance, and Survival at All Costs*
  PW - v262 - i28 - July 13 2015 - p48(1) [51-500]
Brewster, David - *India's Ocean: The Story of India's Bid for Regional Leadership*
  Pac A - v88 - i4 - Dec 2015 - p945 [501+]
Breyer, Stephen - *The Court and the World: American Law and the New Global Realities*
  BL - v112 - i1 - Sept 1 2015 - p17(2) [51-500]
  KR - August 15 2015 - pNA [501+]
  LJ - v140 - i14 - Sept 1 2015 - p122(1) [51-500]
  NYRB - v62 - i19 - Dec 3 2015 - p14(2) [501+]
  NYTBR - Sept 20 2015 - p1(L) [501+]
Brian, Janeen - *I'm a Dirty Dinosaur (Illus. by James, Ann)*
  c HB Guide - v26 - i1 - Spring 2015 - p6(1) [51-500]
I'm a Hungry Dinosaur (Illus. by James, Ann)
  c Magpies - v30 - i2 - May 2015 - p26(1) [51-500]
Silly Squid! Poems About the Sea (Illus. by Johns, Cheryll)
  c Magpies - v30 - i3 - July 2015 - p27(1) [51-500]
Brian, Kate - *Endless*
  c HB Guide - v26 - i1 - Spring 2015 - p102(1) [51-500]
Briant, Pierre - *Darius in the Shadow of Alexander*
  G&L Rev W - v22 - i5 - Sept-Oct 2015 - p43(1) [501+]
  HT - v65 - i11 - Nov 2015 - p58(1) [501+]
  Spec - v327 - i9729 - Feb 14 2015 - p38(2) [501+]
  TimHES - i2187 - Jan 22 2015 - p51(1) [501+]
Brickhouse, Anna - *The Unsettlement of America: Translation, Interpretation, and the Story of Don Luis de Velasco, 1560-1945*
  JAH - v102 - i2 - Sept 2015 - p512-513 [501+]
  Nine-C Lit - v70 - i2 - Sept 2015 - p267(4) [501+]
Brickhouse, Jamie - *Dangerous When Wet*
  BL - v111 - i14 - March 15 2015 - p32(1) [51-500]
  Ent W - i1363 - May 15 2015 - p62(1) [51-500]
  G&L Rev W - v22 - i4 - July-August 2015 - p42(2) [501+]
  KR - Feb 15 2015 - pNA [51-500]
Brideson, Cynthia - *Ziegfeld and His Follies: A Biography of Broadway's Greatest Producer*
  LJ - v140 - i12 - July 1 2015 - p85(1) [51-500]
Bridge, Kathleen - *Better Homes and Corpses*
  BL - v111 - i22 - August 1 2015 - p31(1) [51-500]
Bridge, Krista - *The Eliot Girls*
  BL - v111 - i9-10 - Jan 1 2015 - p36(1) [51-500]
Bridgen, Anne - *Reverse Genetics of RNA Viruses: Applications and Perspectives*
  QRB - v90 - i1 - March 2015 - p96(2) [51-500]
Bridger, Sarah - *Scientists at War: The Ethics of Cold War Weapons Research*
  Am Sci - v103 - i6 - Nov-Dec 2015 - p426(2) [501+]
Bridges, Anne - *Terra Incognita: An Annotated Bibliography of the Great Smoky Mountains, 1544-1934*
  JSH - v81 - i2 - May 2015 - p537(1) [51-500]
Bridges, Brian - *The Two Koreas and the Politics of Global Sport*
  Pac A - v88 - i2 - June 2015 - p333 [501+]

Bridges, Emma - *Imagining Xerxes: Ancient Perspectives on a Persian King*
  Spec - v327 - i9729 - Feb 14 2015 - p38(2) [501+]

Bridges, Karl - *Customer-Based Collection Development: An Overview*
  LR - v64 - i4-5 - April-May 2015 - p394-395 [501+]

Bridges, Margaret Park - *I Love You Forever (Illus. by McNicholas, Shelagh)*
  c HB Guide - v26 - i2 - Fall 2015 - p7(1) [51-500]
  c KR - April 1 2015 - pNA [51-500]

Bridges, Shirin Yim - *Call Me Athena: Greek Goddess of Wisdom*
  y HB Guide - v26 - i1 - Spring 2015 - p71(1) [51-500]

Bridges, Victor - *Trouble on the Thames*
  PW - v262 - i34 - August 24 2015 - p61(1) [51-500]

Bridgwater, Patrick - *The German Gothic Novel in Anglo-German Perspective*
  MLR - v110 - i2 - April 2015 - p588-590 [501+]

Bridwell, Norman - *Clifford Celebrates Hanukkah*
  c SLJ - v61 - i10 - Oct 2015 - p61(2) [51-500]

Briegel, Francoise - *Negocier la defense: Plaider pour les criminels au siecle des Lumieres a Geneve*
  JMH - v87 - i1 - March 2015 - p217(3) [501+]

Briere-Haquet, Alice - *Madam Eiffle: The Love Story of the Eiffel Tower (Illus. by Csil)*
  c KR - Sept 1 2015 - pNA [51-500]
  Madame Eiffel: The Love Story of the Eiffel Tower (Illus. by Csil)
  c PW - v262 - i35 - August 31 2015 - p88(1) [51-500]
  c SLJ - v61 - i12 - Dec 2015 - p87(1) [51-500]

Briesewitz, Gernot - *Raum und Nation in der polnischen Westforschung 1918-1948: Wissenschaftsdiskurse, Raumdeutungen und geopolitische Visionen im Kontext der deutsch-polnischen Beziehungsgeschichte*
  HNet - August 2015 - pNA [501+]

Briggle, Adam - *A Field Philosopher's Guide to Fracking: How One Texas Town Stood Up to Big Oil and Gas*
  BL - v112 - i3 - Oct 1 2015 - p5(1) [51-500]
  KR - June 15 2015 - pNA [51-500]
  NYTBR - Dec 13 2015 - p15(L) [501+]
  PW - v262 - i31 - August 3 2015 - p47(1) [51-500]

Briggs, Daniel - *Crack Cocaine Users: High Society and Low Life in South London*
  CS - v44 - i5 - Sept 2015 - p637-639 [501+]
  Deviance and Risk on Holiday: An Ethnography of British Tourists in Ibiza
  CS - v44 - i4 - July 2015 - p489-491 [501+]

Briggs, J.R. - *Eldership and the Mission of God: Equipping Teams for Faithful Church Leadership*
  Bwatch - May 2015 - pNA [51-500]

Briggs, Kevin - *Guardian of the Golden Gate*
  KR - August 15 2015 - pNA [501+]

Briggs, Laura - *Somebody's Children: The Politics of Transracial and Transnational Adoption*
  JWH - v27 - i1 - Spring 2015 - p168(10) [501+]

Briggs, Patricia - *Shifting Shadows (Read by King, Lorelei). Audiobook Review*
  BL - v111 - i16 - April 15 2015 - p61(1) [51-500]

Briggs, Raymond - *The Snowman and the Snowdog*
  c HB Guide - v26 - i1 - Spring 2015 - p24(1) [51-500]

Brighouse, Harry - *Family Values: The Ethics of Parent-Child Relationships*
  NS - v144 - i5250 - Feb 20 2015 - p50(2) [501+]

Bright, J.E. - *American Fun Facts (Illus. by Dewalle, Medhi)*
  c CH Bwatch - August 2015 - pNA [51-500]

Bright, Matthew - *The Myriad Carnival*
  PW - v262 - i51 - Dec 14 2015 - p66(1) [51-500]

Bright, Neil - *Rethinking Everything: Personal Growth through Transactional Analysis*
  RVBW - August 2015 - pNA [51-500]

Bright, Rachel - *The Lion Inside (Illus. by Field, Jim)*
  c Sch Lib - v63 - i4 - Winter 2015 - p218(1) [51-500]
  Love Monster and the Last Chocolate (Illus. by Bright, Rachel)
  c KR - Oct 1 2015 - pNA [51-500]
  c PW - v262 - i41 - Oct 12 2015 - p66(2) [51-500]
  c SLJ - v61 - i11 - Nov 2015 - p80(1) [51-500]
  Love Monster and the Perfect Present (Illus. by Bright, Rachel)
  c HB Guide - v26 - i2 - Fall 2015 - p7(1) [51-500]
  Side by Side (Illus. by Gliori, Debi)
  c BL - v111 - i18 - May 15 2015 - p59(1) [51-500]
  c HB Guide - v26 - i2 - Fall 2015 - p28(1) [51-500]
  c KR - Feb 15 2015 - pNA [51-500]
  c Sch Lib - v63 - i3 - Autumn 2015 - p153(1) [51-500]

Brighton, Paul - *Original Spin: Downing Street and the Press in Victorian Britain*
  Spec - v329 - i9771 - Dec 5 2015 - p51(1) [501+]

Brignall, Richard - *Real Justice: A Police Mr. Big Sting Goes Wrong: The Story of Kyle Unger*
  y KR - July 15 2015 - pNA [51-500]
  y Res Links - v20 - i5 - June 2015 - p30(1) [51-500]
  y SLJ - v61 - i9 - Sept 2015 - p151(4) [51-500]

Brill, Ariane - *Abgrenzung und Hoffnung: gt;gt:Europa<< in der deutschen, britischen und amerikanischen Presse 1945-1980*
  HNet - April 2015 - pNA [501+]

Brill, Steven - *America's Bitter Pill: Money, Politics, Backroom Deals, and the Fight to Fix Our Broken Healthcare System*
  Barron's - v95 - i22 - June 1 2015 - p37(1) [501+]
  CC - v132 - i8 - April 15 2015 - p34(2) [501+]
  Econ - v414 - i8921 - Jan 17 2015 - p79(US) [501+]
  NYRB - v62 - i7 - April 23 2015 - p44(3) [501+]
  NYT - Jan 27 2015 - pD3(L) [501+]
  NYTBR - Jan 11 2015 - p1(L) [501+]
  NYTBR - Sept 13 2015 - p32(L) [501+]
  Reason - v47 - i1 - May 2015 - p54(7) [501+]

Brillhart, Wayne L. - *The Deer with the Purple Nose (Illus. by Brillhart, Wayne L.)*
  c CH Bwatch - Oct 2015 - pNA [51-500]

Brim, Matt - *James Baldwin and the Queer Imagination*
  TLS - i5877 - Nov 20 2015 - p5(1) [501+]

Brimmer, Larry - *Strike! The Farm Workers' Fight for Their Rights*
  y HB Guide - v26 - i1 - Spring 2015 - p138(1) [51-500]

Brimner, Larry Dane - *The Rain Wizard: The Amazing, Mysterious, True Life of Charles Mallory Hatfield*
  y BL - v111 - i19-20 - June 1 2015 - p92(1) [51-500]
  c KR - June 15 2015 - pNA [51-500]
  y SLJ - v61 - i6 - June 2015 - p140(1) [51-500]
  c HB - v91 - i6 - Nov-Dec 2015 - p98(2) [51-500]
  Strike! The Farm Workers' Fight for Their Rights
  y Teach Lib - v42 - i3 - Feb 2015 - p28(4) [501+]

Bringhurst, Robert - *A Story as Sharp as a Knife: The Classical Haida Mythtellers and Their World*
  NS - v144 - i5282 - Oct 2 2015 - p54(3) [501+]

brinig, Margaret F. - *Lost Classroom, Lost Community: Catholic Schools' Importance in Urban America*
  AM - v213 - i1 - July 6 2015 - p42(2) [501+]

Brinkema, Eugenie - *The Forms of the Affects*
  Afterimage - v42 - i4 - Jan-Feb 2015 - p38(2) [501+]

Brinker-Gabler, Gisela - *Image in Outline: Reading Lou Andreas-Salome*
  GSR - v38 - i2 - May 2015 - p423-3 [501+]

Brinker, Walt - *Roadside Survival: Low-tech Solutions to Automobile Breakdowns*
  SPBW - June 2015 - pNA [51-500]

Brinkley, Douglas - *The Nixon Tapes: 1971-72*
  Lon R Bks - v37 - i21 - Nov 5 2015 - p33(2) [501+]
  The Nixon Tapes: 1973
  PW - v262 - i31 - August 3 2015 - p48(1) [51-500]
  KR - August 1 2015 - pNA [51-500]
  LJ - v140 - i15 - Sept 15 2015 - p104(1) [51-500]

Brinkmann, Martin - *Musik und Melancholie im Werk Heimito von Doderers*
  MLR - v110 - i3 - July 2015 - p905-906 [501+]

Brioist, Pascal - *Leonard de Vinci, l'homme de Guerre*
  Six Ct J - v46 - i1 - Spring 2015 - p125-126 [501+]

Brioso, Cesar - *Havana Hardball: Spring Training, Jackie Robinson, and The Cuban League*
  LJ - v140 - i14 - Sept 1 2015 - p110(1) [51-500]

Brisbin, Terri - *Raging Sea*
  BL - v112 - i3 - Oct 1 2015 - p36(1) [51-500]
  Rising Fire
  PW - v262 - i3 - Jan 19 2015 - p68(1) [51-500]

Briscione, James - *The Great Cook: Essential Techniques and Inspired Flavors to Make Every Dish Better*
  LJ - v140 - i9 - May 15 2015 - p102(2) [501+]

Brisick, Jamie - *Becoming Westerly: Surf Champion Peter Drouyn's Transformation into Westerly Windina*
  TLS - i5868 - Sept 18 2015 - p29(1) [501+]

Bristow, Jennie - *Baby Boomers and Generational Conflict*
  TimHES - i2212 - July 16 2015 - p52-1 [501+]

Bristow, Joseph - *Oscar Wilde's Chatterton: Literary History, Romanticism, and the Art of Forgery*
  LJ - v140 - i3 - Feb 15 2015 - p98(1) [51-500]

Britnell, Richard - *Durham Priory Manorial Accounts, 1277-1310*
  Med R - June 2015 - pNA [501+]

Britt, Chris - *Blabbering Bethann*
  c HB Guide - v26 - i1 - Spring 2015 - p24(1) [51-500]

Britt, Paige - *The Lost Track of Time (Read by Jiles, Jennifer). Audiobook Review*
  c SLJ - v61 - i7 - July 2015 - p46(1) [51-500]
  The Lost Track of Time (Illus. by White, Lee)
  c SLJ - v61 - i2 - Feb 2015 - p84(1) [51-500]
  c CCB-B - v68 - i11 - July-August 2015 - p538(1) [51-500]
  c CH Bwatch - June 2015 - pNA [501+]
  c HB Guide - v26 - i2 - Fall 2015 - p76(1) [51-500]
  c KR - Jan 1 2015 - pNA [51-500]
  c PW - v262 - i49 - Dec 2 2015 - p78(1) [51-500]

Britt, Ryan - *Luke Skywalker Can't Read: And Other Geeky Truths*
  LJ - v140 - i20 - Dec 1 2015 - p121(1) [51-500]

Brittain, David - *Eduardo Paolozzi at New Worlds: Science Fiction and Art in the Sixties*
  SFS - v42 - i1 - March 2015 - p166-170 [501+]

Brittain, Vera - *Testament of Youth*
  CSM - March 31 2015 - pNA [51-500]

Brittan, Jane - *The Edge of Me*
  y Sch Lib - v63 - i3 - Autumn 2015 - p189(1) [51-500]

Britten, Thomas A. - *The National Council on Indian Opportunity: Quiet Champion of Self-Determination*
  JAH - v102 - i2 - Sept 2015 - p625-626 [501+]
  JSH - v81 - i4 - Nov 2015 - p1046(3) [501+]
  WHQ - v46 - i3 - Autumn 2015 - p367-368 [501+]

Britton, Celia - *Language and Literary Form in French Caribbean Writing*
  MLR - v110 - i2 - April 2015 - p558-560 [501+]

Britton, Dennis Austin - *Becoming Christian: Race, Reformation, and Early Modern English Romance*
  Six Ct J - v46 - i2 - Summer 2015 - p510-512 [501+]

Britton, John A. - *Cables, Crises, and the Press: The Geopolitics of the New International Information System in the Americas, 1866-1903*
  AHR - v120 - i2 - April 2015 - p579-580 [501+]
  BHR - v89 - i3 - Autumn 2015 - p600(3) [501+]
  RAH - v43 - i2 - June 2015 - p288-293 [501+]

Brizeula, Natalia - *Fotografia e Imperio: paisagens para um Brasil moderno*
  Hisp R - v83 - i3 - Summer 2015 - p364-367 [501+]

Broach, Elise - *James to the Rescue (Illus. by Murphy, Kelly)*
  c KR - August 15 2015 - pNA [51-500]
  c HB - v91 - i5 - Sept-Oct 2015 - p96(1) [51-500]
  Revenge of Superstition Mountain (Illus. by Ivanov, Olga)
  y HB Guide - v26 - i1 - Spring 2015 - p71(1) [51-500]

Brobeck, Stephen - *Watchdogs and Whistleblowers: A Reference Guide to Consumer Activism*
  BL - v112 - i7 - Dec 1 2015 - p6(2) [51-500]

Brock-Broido, Lucie - *Stay, Illusion*
  NYRB - v62 - i2 - Feb 5 2015 - p40(4) [501+]

Brock, David - *Killing the Messenger*
  KR - Oct 1 2015 - pNA [51-500]
  NYTBR - Sept 27 2015 - p11(L) [501+]

Brock, Geoffrey - *Voices Bright Flags*
  HR - v68 - i2 - Summer 2015 - p327-335 [501+]

Brock, George - *Out of Print: Newspapers, Journalism and the Business of News in the Digital Age*
  NYRB - v62 - i10 - June 4 2015 - p43(3) [501+]

Brock, Jared - *A Year of Living Prayerfully: How a Curious Traveler Met the Pope, Walked on Coals, Danced with Rabbis, and Revived His Prayer Life (Read by Brock, Jared). Audiobook Review*
  BL - v111 - i19-20 - June 1 2015 - p138(1) [51-500]
  A Year of Living Prayerfully: How A Curious Traveler Met the Pope, Walked on Coals, Danced with Rabbis, and Revived His Prayer Life
  BL - v111 - i11 - Feb 1 2015 - p4(1) [51-500]
  PW - v262 - i6 - Feb 9 2015 - p62(1) [51-500]

Brock, Julia - *Beyond Rosie: A Documentary History of Women and World War II*
  HNet - August 2015 - pNA [501+]

Brock, Michael - *Margot Asquith's Great War Diary, 1914-16: The View from Downing Street*
  Lon R Bks - v37 - i1 - Jan 8 2015 - p17(4) [501+]

Brock, Richard M. - *Cross Dog Blues*
  KR - June 1 2015 - pNA [51-500]

Brock, Rita Nakashima - *Soul Repair: Recovering from Moral Injury After War*
  Intpr - v69 - i1 - Jan 2015 - p102(2) [501+]

Brockenbrough, Martha - *The Game of Love and Death*
  y BL - v111 - i16 - April 15 2015 - p47(1) [51-500]
  y CCB-B - v68 - i11 - July-August 2015 - p538(2) [51-500]
  y HB - v91 - i3 - May-June 2015 - p106(1) [501+]
  y HB Guide - v26 - i2 - Fall 2015 - p112(1) [51-500]
  y KR - Feb 15 2015 - pNA [51-500]
  y PW - v262 - i7 - Feb 16 2015 - p179(2) [51-500]
  y PW - v262 - i49 - Dec 2 2015 - p101(2) [51-500]
Brocket, Jane - *1 Cookie, 2 Chairs, 3 Pears: Numbers Everywhere*
  c HB - v91 - i1 - Jan-Feb 2015 - p106(2) [501+]
Rainy, Sunny, Blowy, Snowy: What Are Seasons?
  c HB Guide - v26 - i1 - Spring 2015 - p147(1) [51-500]
Stickiest, Fluffiest, Crunchiest: Super Superlatives (Illus. by Brocket, Jane)
  c SLJ - v61 - i10 - Oct 2015 - p124(2) [51-500]
  c BL - v112 - i4 - Oct 15 2015 - p41(1) [51-500]
Brockett, Keith - *The Nutcracker's Night Before Christmas (Illus. by Cowman, Joseph)*
  c KR - Sept 1 2015 - pNA [51-500]
  c SLJ - v61 - i10 - Oct 2015 - p61(1) [51-500]
Brockey, Liam Matthew - *The Visitor: Andre Palmeiro and the Jesuits in Asia*
    AHR - v120 - i4 - Oct 2015 - p1459-1460 [501+]
    AM - v212 - i6 - Feb 23 2015 - p37(2) [501+]
    CHR - v101 - i3 - Summer 2015 - p554(19) [501+]
    HNet - Sept 2015 - pNA [501+]
    Theol St - v76 - i4 - Dec 2015 - p842(2) [501+]
    TLS - i5859 - July 17 2015 - p28(1) [501+]
Brockman, John - *This Idea Must Die: Scientific Theories That Are Blocking Progress*
    J Chem Ed - v92 - i7 - July 2015 - p1146-1148 [501+]
    LJ - v140 - i2 - Feb 1 2015 - p104(1) [51-500]
    Nature - v518 - i7539 - Feb 19 2015 - p299(1) [51-500]
    New Sci - v225 - i3011 - March 7 2015 - p47(1) [501+]
The Universe: Leading Scientists Explore the Origin, Mysteries, and Future of the Cosmos (Read by Campbell, Danny). Audiobook Review
    LJ - v140 - i5 - March 15 2015 - p74(1) [51-500]
What to Think About Machines That Think: Today's Leading Thinkers on the Edge of Machine Intelligence
    KR - August 1 2015 - pNA [51-500]
    New Sci - v228 - i3044 - Oct 24 2015 - p43(1) [501+]
Brockmann, Suzanne - *Night Sky*
  c HB Guide - v26 - i1 - Spring 2015 - p102(1) [51-500]
Way of the Warrior
    PW - v262 - i10 - March 9 2015 - p57(2) [51-500]
Wild Sky
  y KR - Sept 1 2015 - pNA [51-500]
  y VOYA - v38 - i4 - Oct 2015 - p67(1) [51-500]
Brockmann, Thomas - *Die Konfessionalisierungparadigma: Leistungen, Probleme, Grenzen*
    CHR - v101 - i1 - Wntr 2015 - p161(2) [501+]
Brockopp, Jonathan E. - *The Cambridge Companion to Muhammad*
    HER - v130 - i542 - Feb 2015 - p142(2) [501+]
Brockway, Connie - *Highlander Undone*
    KR - July 15 2015 - pNA [501+]
    PW - v262 - i23 - June 8 2015 - p44(1) [51-500]
Brockway, Robert - *The Unnoticeables*
    KR - May 15 2015 - pNA [501+]
    PW - v262 - i20 - May 18 2015 - p67(2) [51-500]
Broday, Linda - *Forever His Texas Bride*
    PW - v262 - i42 - Oct 19 2015 - p62(2) [51-500]
Twice a Texas Bride
    BL - v111 - i16 - April 15 2015 - p31(1) [51-500]
Brodbeck, David - *Defining Deutschtum: Political Ideology, German Identity, and Music-Critical Discourse in Liberal Vienna*
    MT - v156 - i1932 - Autumn 2015 - p109-111 [501+]
    TLS - i5849 - May 8 2015 - p9(1) [501+]
Brode, Douglas - *Dream West: Politics and Religion in Cowboy Movies*
    WHQ - v46 - i1 - Spring 2015 - p96-97 [501+]
Fantastic Planets, Forbidden Zones, and Lost Continents: The 100 Greatest Science-Fiction Films
    LJ - v140 - i6 - Oct 1 2015 - p106(1) [51-500]
Broder, Melissa - *So Sad Today: Personal Essays*
    PW - v262 - i51 - Dec 14 2015 - p70(1) [51-500]
Broder, Mitch - *Discovering Vintage New York: A Guide to the City's Timeless Shops, Bars, Delis and More*
    NYT - Dec 27 2015 - p3(L) [501+]

Brodie, Ian - *A Vulgar Art: A New Approach to Stand-up Comedy*
    SAH - v4 - i2 - Dec 15 2015 - p279-281 [501+]
Brodsky, Alexandra - *The Feminist Utopia Project: Fifty-Seven Visions of a Wildly Better Future*
    KR - August 15 2015 - pNA [51-500]
    BL - v112 - i3 - Oct 1 2015 - p5(1) [51-500]
    LJ - v140 - i17 - Oct 15 2015 - p105(1) [51-500]
Brodsky, Jordanna Max - *The Immortals*
    KR - Dec 1 2015 - pNA [501+]
Brodsky, Stanley L. - *The Expert Expert Witness: More Maxims and Guidelines for Testifying in Court, 2d ed.*
    RVBW - Nov 2015 - pNA [51-500]
Brodwin, Martin G. - *Medical, Psychosocial and Vocational Aspects of Disability, 4th ed.*
    J Rehab - v81 - i3 - July-Sept 2015 - p58(2) [501+]
Brodwin, Paul - *Everyday Ethics: Voices from the Front Line of Community Psychiatry*
    MAQ - v29 - i1 - March 2015 - p26-29 [501+]
Brody, Douglas - *John Wayne's Way: Life Lessons from the Duke*
    Roundup M - v22 - i4 - April 2015 - p28(1) [501+]
    Roundup M - v22 - i6 - August 2015 - p34(1) [501+]
Brody, Frances - *Murder on a Summer's Day*
    KR - Dec 15 2015 - pNA [501+]
    PW - v262 - i51 - Dec 14 2015 - p62(1) [501+]
A Woman Unknown
    BL - v111 - i9-10 - Jan 1 2015 - p51(1) [51-500]
Brody, Mark - *Mosaic Garden Projects: Add Color to Your Garden with Tables, Fountains, Bird Baths, and More*
    PW - v262 - i1 - Jan 5 2015 - p69(1) [51-500]
Mosaic Garden Projects: Add Color to Your Garden with Tables, Fountains, Birdbaths, and More
    BL - v111 - i13 - March 1 2015 - p11(2) [51-500]
Broers, Michael - *Napoleon: Soldier of Destiny*
    BL - v112 - i2 - Sept 15 2015 - p18(1) [51-500]
    KR - June 15 2015 - pNA [501+]
    LJ - v140 - i11 - June 15 2015 - p94(1) [51-500]
    PW - v262 - i32 - August 10 2015 - p50(2) [51-500]
Brogaard, Berit - *On Romantic Love: Simple Truths about a Complex Emotion*
    CHE - v61 - i33 - May 1 2015 - pB16(1) [501+]
    TimHES - i2206 - June 4 2015 - p48-49 [501+]
    TLS - i5866 - Sept 4 2015 - p12(1) [501+]
The Superhuman Mind: Free the Genius in Your Brain
    LJ - v140 - i10 - June 1 2015 - p124(1) [51-500]
    PW - v262 - i24 - June 15 2015 - p76(1) [501+]
Brokaw, Tom - *A Lucky Life Interrupted (Read by Bramhall, Mark). Audiobook Review*
    BL - v112 - i1 - Sept 1 2015 - p142(1) [51-500]
A Lucky Life Interrupted
    BL - v111 - i19-20 - June 1 2015 - p33(1) [51-500]
    BL - v112 - i7 - Dec 1 2015 - p13(1) [501+]
    KR - April 1 2015 - pNA [501+]
Bromberg, K. - *Hard Beat*
    PW - v262 - i38 - Sept 21 2015 - p60(1) [51-500]
Bromell, Nick - *The Time Is Always Now: Black Thought and the Transformation of US Democracy*
    AL - v87 - i3 - Sept 2015 - p622-624 [501+]
Bromilow, Pollie - *Authority in European Book Culture 1400-1600*
    FS - v69 - i3 - July 2015 - p383-384 [501+]
Bromley, James M. - *Sex before Sex: Figuring the Act in Early Modern England*
    Shakes Q - v66 - i1 - Spring 2015 - p107-109 [501+]
Bromwich, David - *The Intellectual Life of Edmund Burke: From the Sublime and Beautiful to American Independence*
    For Aff - v94 - i1 - Jan-Feb 2015 - pNA [501+]
    HR - v68 - i2 - Summer 2015 - p247-255 [501+]
    NYRB - v62 - i4 - March 5 2015 - p35(3) [501+]
    RAH - v43 - i2 - June 2015 - p193-202 [501+]
    Eight-C St - v48 - i3 - Spring 2015 - p359-362 [501+]
    Soc - v52 - i2 - April 2015 - p189(4) [501+]
Moral Imagination
    NYRB - v62 - i5 - March 19 2015 - p37(3) [501+]
Bronfen, Elisabeth - *Hollywoods Kriege: Geschichte einer Heimsuchung*
    HNet - Sept 2015 - pNA [501+]
Bronfman, Edgar M. - *Why Be Jewish?*
    BL - Dec 1 2015 - pNA [501+]
Bronner, Stephen Eric - *Modernism at the Barricades: Aesthetics, Politics, Utopia*
    HNet - Jan 2015 - pNA [501+]

Bronsky, Alina - *Just Call Me Superhero*
    NYTBR - Jan 4 2015 - p26(L) [501+]
Bronson, Dan - *Confessions of a Hollywood Nobody*
    CSM - April 10 2015 - pNA [51-500]
Bronstein, Christine - *Stewie Boom! Boss of the Big Boy Bed (Illus. by Young, Karen)*
    KR - August 1 2015 - pNA [51-500]
Bronte, Charlotte - *Villette*
    TimHES - i2193 - March 5 2015 - p49(1) [501+]
Bronte, Emily - *The Annotated Wuthering Heights*
    Bks & Cult - v21 - i6 - Nov-Dec 2015 - p33(1) [501+]
Broodbank, Cyprian - *The Making of the Middle Sea: A History of the Mediterranean from the Beginning to the Emergency of the Classical World*
    JNES - v74 - i2 - Oct 2015 - p373(6) [501+]
Brook, David - *The Road to Character*
    Comw - v142 - i13 - August 14 2015 - p30(2) [501+]
Brook, LeeAnn - *Points of Inspiration: An Artist's Journey with Painting and Photography*
    PW - v262 - i31 - August 3 2015 - p50(2) [51-500]
    PW - v262 - i34 - August 24 2015 - p54(1) [51-500]
Brook, Madeleine - *Popular History and Fiction: The Myth of August the Strong in German Literature, Art and Media*
    MLR - v110 - i2 - April 2015 - p619-621 [501+]
Brook-Piper, Holly - *Animal Friends*
  c KR - July 1 2015 - pNA [51-500]
Brook, Timothy - *Mr. Selden's Map of China: Decoding the Secrets of a Vanished Cartographer*
    AHR - v120 - i2 - April 2015 - p573-575 [501+]
Brooke-Hitching, Edward - *Fox Tossing and Other Forgotten and Dangerous Sports, Pastimes, and Games*
    LJ - v140 - i17 - Oct 15 2015 - p93(2) [51-500]
Fox Tossing, Octopus Wrestling and Other Forgotten Sports
    Spec - v328 - i9751 - July 18 2015 - p37(2) [501+]
    TLS - i5860 - July 24 2015 - p26(1) [501+]
Brooke, John L. - *Climate Change and the Course of Global History: A Rough Journey*
    AHR - v120 - i3 - June 2015 - p965(1) [501+]
    JIH - v45 - i4 - Spring 2015 - p549-566 [501+]
    W&M Q - v72 - i1 - Jan 2015 - p159-167 [501+]
Brooke-Rose, Christine - *Life, End Of*
    NS - v144 - i5282 - Oct 2 2015 - p74(2) [501+]
Brookes, Adam - *Midnight Blind*
    LJ - v140 - i2 - Feb 1 2015 - p54(5) [51-500]
Spy Games
    LJ - v140 - i11 - June 15 2015 - p78(2) [51-500]
    PW - v262 - i20 - May 18 2015 - p64(1) [501+]
Brookfield, Tarah - *Cold War Comforts: Canadian Women, Child Safety, and Global Insecurity*
    CWS - v30 - i2-3 - Fall-Winter 2015 - p141(2) [501+]
Brookhiser, Richard - *Founder's Son: A Life of Abraham Lincoln*
    NYTBR - Feb 8 2015 - p1(L) [501+]
Brookhouse, Christopher - *Finn*
    KR - Jan 15 2015 - pNA [51-500]
Brookins, Carl - *The Case of the Yellow Diamond*
    KR - July 1 2015 - pNA [51-500]
Brookmyre, Christopher - *Dead Girl Walking*
    BL - v111 - i14 - March 15 2015 - p45(1) [51-500]
    KR - March 1 2015 - pNA [51-500]
    PW - v262 - i11 - March 16 2015 - p64(1) [51-500]
Brooks, Adrian - *The Right Side of History: 100 Years of LGBTQI Activism*
    RVBW - Oct 2015 - pNA [51-500]
  y VOYA - v38 - i4 - Oct 2015 - p81(1) [51-500]
Brooks, Amanda - *Always Pack a Party Dress*
    KR - April 1 2015 - pNA [501+]
    NYT - July 18 2015 - pNA(L) [501+]
Brooks, Andrew - *Clothing Poverty: The Hidden World of Fast Fashion and Second-Hand Clothes*
    TimHES - i2198 - April 9 2015 - p53(1) [501+]
Brooks, Arthur C. - *The Conservative Heart: How to Build a Fairer, Happier, and More Prosperous America*
    BL - v111 - i22 - August 1 2015 - p7(1) [51-500]
    Nat R - v67 - i15 - August 24 2015 - p38 [501+]
    NYTBR - August 2 2015 - p10(L) [501+]
    PW - v262 - i30 - July 27 2015 - p10(1) [51-500]
Brooks, Bill - *Go and Bury Your Dead*
    Roundup M - v22 - i6 - August 2015 - p27(1) [501+]
Men of Violence: A John Henry Cole Story
    Roundup M - v22 - i6 - August 2015 - p27(1) [501+]

The Righteous Revenge of Lucy Moon
    Roundup M - v22 - i4 - April 2015 - p31(2) [501+]
    Roundup M - v22 - i6 - August 2015 - p27(1) [501+]

Brooks, Carellin - *One Hundred Days of Rain*
    LJ - v140 - i6 - April 1 2015 - p76(3) [501+]
    Nat Post - v17 - i130 - April 4 2015 - pWP4(1) [501+]

Brooks, Charlotte - *Between Mao and McCarthy: Chinese American Politics in the Cold War Years*
    HNet - Sept 2015 - pNA [501+]

Brooks, Cheryl - *Cowboy Heaven*
    PW - v262 - i1 - Jan 5 2015 - p58(1) [51-500]

Brooks-Dalton, Lily - *Motorcycles I've Loved: A Memoir*
    PW - v262 - i3 - Jan 19 2015 - p69(1) [51-500]
    KR - Feb 1 2015 - pNA [501+]

Brooks, Danielle - *Good Decisions...Most of the Time: Because Life Is Too Short Not to Eat Chocolate*
    PW - v262 - i36 - Sept 7 2015 - p62(2) [51-500]

Brooks, David - *The Road to Character*
    BL - v111 - i16 - April 15 2015 - p4(1) [51-500]
    Econ - v415 - i8939 - May 23 2015 - p73(US) [501+]
    KR - March 1 2015 - pNA [501+]
    Nat R - v67 - i11 - June 22 2015 - p34 [501+]
    NYTBR - April 26 2015 - p12(L) [501+]
    TLS - i5862 - August 7 2015 - p9(1) [501+]

Brooks, Deborah Jordan - *He Runs, She Runs: Why Gender Stereotypes Do Not Harm Women Candidates*
    Pub Op Q - v79 - i2 - Summer 2015 - p622(4) [501+]

Brooks, Geraldine - *The Secret Chord*
    SEP - v287 - i5 - Sept-Oct 2015 - p24(1) [501+]
    BL - v111 - i22 - August 1 2015 - p40(1) [51-500]
    KR - August 15 2015 - pNA [501+]
    LJ - v140 - i13 - August 1 2015 - p80(1) [501+]
    NYTBR - Oct 25 2015 - p23(L) [501+]
    PW - v262 - i25 - June 22 2015 - p116(1) [51-500]

Brooks, Graham - *Fraud, Corruption and Sport*
    CS - v44 - i5 - Sept 2015 - p639-640 [501+]

Brooks, James F. - *Mesa of Sorrows: A History of the Awat'ovi Massacre*
    KR - Nov 1 2015 - pNA [501+]
    LJ - v140 - i19 - Nov 15 2015 - p94(1) [501+]
    PW - v262 - i51 - Dec 14 2015 - p72(2) [51-500]

Brooks, Jayde - *Daughter of Gods and Shadows*
    PW - v262 - i2 - Jan 12 2015 - p41(1) [51-500]

Brooks, Jen - *In a World Just Right*
    y CCB-B - v68 - i10 - June 2015 - p482(1) [51-500]
    y HB Guide - v26 - i2 - Fall 2015 - p112(1) [51-500]
    y KR - Feb 1 2015 - pNA [51-500]
    y PW - v262 - i6 - Feb 9 2015 - p70(1) [51-500]
    y SLJ - v61 - i2 - Feb 2015 - p97(2) [51-500]
    y VOYA - v37 - i6 - Feb 2015 - p72(1) [51-500]

Brooks, John - *The Girl behind the Door: A Father's Quest to Understand His Daughter's Suicide*
    KR - Dec 15 2015 - pNA [501+]

Brooks, Julian - *Andrea del Sarto: The Renaissance Workshop in Action*
    LJ - v140 - i12 - July 1 2015 - p82(1) [51-500]

Brooks, Kevin - *The Bunker Diary*
    y CCB-B - v68 - i10 - June 2015 - p483(1) [51-500]
    y HB Guide - v26 - i2 - Fall 2015 - p112(1) [51-500]
The Devil's Angel
    y Sch Lib - v63 - i2 - Summer 2015 - p115(1) [51-500]
Dumb Chocolate Eyes (Illus. by Shoard, Emma)
    y Sch Lib - v63 - i3 - Autumn 2015 - p178(2) [51-500]
The Snake Trap
    y Sch Lib - v63 - i4 - Winter 2015 - p242(1) [51-500]

Brooks, Leslie - *Soul Writer*
    SPBW - Nov 2015 - pNA [51-500]

Brooks, Maegan Parker - *A Voice That Could Stir an Army: Fannie Lou Hamer and the Rhetoric of the Black Freedom Movement*
    JAH - v102 - i1 - June 2015 - p304-304 [501+]
    JSH - v81 - i4 - Nov 2015 - p1037(2) [501+]

Brooks, Marla - *The Witch's Oracle*
    Bwatch - Oct 2015 - pNA [51-500]

Brooks, Martha - *Winter Moon Song (Illus. by Ruifernandez, Leticia)*
    c HB Guide - v26 - i1 - Spring 2015 - p24(1) [51-500]

Brooks, Mary D. - *Where Shadows Linger*
    PW - v262 - i26 - June 29 2015 - p54(1) [51-500]

Brooks, Michael - *At the Edge of Uncertainty: 11 Discoveries Taking Science by Surprise*
    Bwatch - April 2015 - pNA [51-500]

Brooks, Nicholas P. - *Charters of Christ Church Canterbury, 2 vols.*
    Med R - June 2015 - pNA [501+]

Brooks, Susie - *Get into Art Animals: Enjoy Great Art: Then Create Your Own! (Illus. by Brooks, Susie)*
    c BL - v112 - i5 - Nov 1 2015 - p50(1) [501+]
Get into Art Places: Discover Great Art and Create Your Own! (Illus. by Brooks, Susie)
    c HB Guide - v26 - i1 - Spring 2015 - p178(1) [51-500]
    c HB Guide - v26 - i2 - Fall 2015 - p192(1) [51-500]
Get into Art: Telling Stories (Illus. by Brooks, Susie)
    c BL - v111 - i19-20 - June 1 2015 - p78(1) [51-500]
    c CH Bwatch - April 2015 - pNA [51-500]
    c SLJ - v61 - i6 - June 2015 - p140(1) [51-500]

Brooks, Terry - *The Darkling Child*
    BL - v111 - i18 - May 15 2015 - p33(2) [51-500]
    KR - May 15 2015 - pNA [51-500]
    PW - v262 - i18 - May 4 2015 - p100(1) [51-500]

Brooks, Victor - *The Longest Year: America at War and at Home in 1944*
    BL - v111 - i22 - August 1 2015 - p20(1) [51-500]
    KR - June 1 2015 - pNA [51-500]

Brookshaw, David - *Confession of the Lioness*
    WLT - v89 - i6 - Nov-Dec 2015 - p58(2) [51-500]

Broom, Dave - *Gin: The Manual*
    BL - v112 - i7 - Dec 1 2015 - p8(2) [51-500]
    LJ - v140 - i6 - Oct 1 2015 - p101(1) [51-500]
The World Atlas of Whiskey
    Bwatch - Feb 2015 - pNA [51-500]
The World Atlas of Whisky
    BL - v111 - i9-10 - Jan 1 2015 - p28(1) [51-500]

Broom, Jenny - *Animalium (Illus. by Scott, Katie)*
    c HB Guide - v26 - i1 - Spring 2015 - p152(2) [51-500]
The Wonder Garden (Illus. by Williams, Kristjana S.)
    c PW - v262 - i49 - Dec 2 2015 - p84(2) [51-500]
    c SLJ - v61 - i11 - Nov 2015 - p129(1) [51-500]
    c BL - v112 - i5 - Nov 1 2015 - p44(1) [51-500]
    c NYTBR - Dec 6 2015 - p32(L) [501+]
    c PW - v262 - i32 - August 10 2015 - p60(1) [51-500]

Broome, John - *Rationality through Reasoning*
    Ethics - v125 - i4 - July 2015 - p1194(6) [501+]

Broomfield, Andrea L. - *Kansas City: A Food Biography*
    PW - v262 - i48 - Nov 30 2015 - p50(1) [51-500]

Bross, Lanie - *Chaos*
    y CH Bwatch - March 2015 - pNA [51-500]

Bross, Lee - *Tangled Webs*
    y CCB-B - v69 - i1 - Sept 2015 - p14(1) [51-500]
    y HB Guide - v26 - i2 - Fall 2015 - p112(1) [51-500]
    y SLJ - v61 - i5 - May 2015 - p111(1) [51-500]
    y VOYA - v38 - i3 - August 2015 - p55(1) [51-500]
    y KR - April 15 2015 - pNA [51-500]

Brosseder, Claudia - *The Power of Huacas: Change and Resistance in the Andean World of Colonial Peru*
    AHR - v120 - i3 - June 2015 - p1083(1) [501+]
    HAHR - v95 - i3 - August 2015 - p514-515 [501+]

Brotherlin, Wendy - *Freaks of Nature*
    y SLJ - v61 - i6 - June 2015 - p120(2) [51-500]

Brothers, Meagan - *Weird Girl and What's His Name*
    y BL - v111 - i22 - August 1 2015 - p61(1) [51-500]
    y KR - July 15 2015 - pNA [51-500]
    y PW - v262 - i30 - July 27 2015 - p71(1) [51-500]
    y SLJ - v61 - i10 - Oct 2015 - p99(2) [51-500]

Brothers, Michael - *Distance in Preaching: Room to Speak, Space to Listen*
    CC - v132 - i19 - Sept 16 2015 - p30(4) [501+]
    TT - v72 - i3 - Oct 2015 - p340-341 [501+]

Brothers, Thomas - *Louis Armstrong: Master of Modernism*
    Notes - v72 - i1 - Sept 2015 - p137(3) [501+]
Louis Armstrong's New Orleans
    BL - v112 - i5 - Nov 1 2015 - p18(2) [51-500]

Brotherton, Rob - *Suspicious Minds: Why We Believe Conspiracy Theories*
    KR - Sept 1 2015 - pNA [501+]
    LJ - v140 - i14 - Sept 1 2015 - p136(2) [51-500]
    PW - v262 - i36 - Sept 7 2015 - p56(1) [51-500]

Brott, Armin A. - *The Expectant Father: The Ultimate Guide for Dads-to-Be, 4th ed.*
    Bwatch - July 2015 - pNA [51-500]

Broun, Dauvit - *Scottish Independence and the Idea of Britain: From the Picts to Alexander III*
    Specu - v90 - i1 - Jan 2015 - p214-216 [501+]

Brouwer, Sigmund - *Rock the Boat*
    y KR - Jan 1 2015 - pNA [51-500]
Unleashed
    y SLJ - v61 - i9 - Sept 2015 - p151(4) [501+]
    y Res Links - v21 - i1 - Oct 2015 - p29(1) [51-500]
    y VOYA - v38 - i5 - Dec 2015 - p63(1) [51-500]

Brow, James - *Inside Out Series*
    c CH Bwatch - Sept 2015 - pNA [51-500]

Browder, Bill - *Red Notice: A True Story of High Finance, Murder, and One Man's Fight for Justice (Read by Grupper, Adam). Audiobook Review*
    LJ - v140 - i14 - Sept 1 2015 - p69(1) [51-500]
Red Notice: A True Story of High Finance, Murder, and One Man's Fight for Justice
    CSM - Feb 4 2015 - pNA [501+]
    Econ - v414 - i8923 - Jan 31 2015 - p73(US) [501+]
    For Aff - v94 - i3 - May-June 2015 - pNA [501+]
    Fortune - v171 - i2 - Feb 1 2015 - p96(1) [51-500]
    LJ - v140 - i2 - Feb 1 2015 - p89(1) [51-500]
    NYT - Feb 2 2015 - pC1(L) [501+]
    NYTBR - March 22 2015 - p20(L) [501+]
    BL - v111 - i9-10 - Jan 1 2015 - p24(1) [51-500]
Red Notice: How I Became Putin's No 1 Enemy
    Spec - v327 - i9728 - Feb 7 2015 - p44(1) [501+]

Brower, Kate Andersen - *The Residence: Inside the Private World of the White House*
    KR - March 15 2015 - pNA [501+]
    LJ - v140 - i6 - April 1 2015 - p102(1) [51-500]

Browman, David L. - *Cultural Negotiations: The Role of Women in the Founding of Americanist Archaeology*
    Isis - v106 - i1 - March 2015 - p162(2) [501+]

Brown, Alison - *Mighty Mo (Illus. by Brown, Alison)*
    c HB Guide - v26 - i2 - Fall 2015 - p28(1) [51-500]

Brown, Alison K. - *First Nations, Museums, Narrations: Stories of the 1929 Franklin Motor Expedition to the Canadian Prairies*
    Can Hist R - v96 - i2 - June 2015 - p300(3) [501+]

Brown, Andrew J. - *Opera Omnia VI.4*
    Six Ct J - v46 - i3 - Fall 2015 - p718(1) [501+]

Brown, Ashley M.L. - *Sexuality in Role-Playing Games*
    TimHES - i2214 - July 30 2015 - p48-49 [501+]

Brown, Ava - *Bamboo & Fern*
    SPBW - Jan 2015 - pNA [51-500]

Brown, Barry S. - *Mrs. Hudson In New York*
    RVBW - July 2015 - pNA [51-500]

Brown, Brandon R. - *Planck: Driven by Vision, Broken by War*
    HT - v65 - i10 - Oct 2015 - p58(2) [51-500]
    Nature - v523 - i7559 - July 9 2015 - p157(1) [51-500]
    NYRB - v62 - i16 - Oct 22 2015 - p33(2) [501+]
    Phys Today - v68 - i11 - Nov 2015 - pNA [501+]
    PW - v262 - i11 - March 16 2015 - p73(1) [51-500]

Brown, Brene - *Daring Greatly*
    RVBW - May 2015 - pNA [51-500]
Rising Strong
    KR - June 15 2015 - pNA [501+]

Brown, Calef - *Hypnotize a Tiger: Poems about Just about Everything (Illus. by Brown, Calef)*
    c BL - v111 - i14 - March 15 2015 - p60(1) [51-500]
    c HB - v91 - i2 - March-April 2015 - p116(1) [51-500]
    c HB Guide - v26 - i2 - Fall 2015 - p203(1) [51-500]
    c KR - Jan 1 2015 - pNA [51-500]
    c PW - v262 - i6 - Feb 9 2015 - p69(1) [51-500]

Brown, Carl - *Natural to Knockout Makeup, Beauty & You: Techniques for Straight Corrective Makeup*
    SPBW - May 2015 - pNA [51-500]

Brown, Carolyn - *Wild Cowboy Ways*
    PW - v262 - i46 - Nov 16 2015 - p64(1) [51-500]

Brown, Carrie (b. 1955-) - *The New Christmas Tree: 24 Dazzling Trees and Over 100 Handcrafted Projects for an Inspired Holiday*
    PW - v262 - i36 - Sept 7 2015 - p63(1) [51-500]

Brown, Carrie (b. 1959-) - *The Stargazer's Sister*
    KR - Nov 1 2015 - pNA [501+]
    PW - v262 - i46 - Nov 16 2015 - p50(1) [51-500]

Brown, Carron - *On the Construction Site (Illus. by Johnson, Bee)*
    c Sch Lib - v63 - i4 - Winter 2015 - p218(1) [51-500]
    c SLJ - v61 - i11 - Nov 2015 - p129(1) [51-500]
Secrets of the Rain Forest (Illus. by Nassner, Alyssa)
    c SLJ - v61 - i7 - July 2015 - p101(1) [51-500]
Secrets of the Rainforest: A Shine-a-Light Book (Illus. by Nassner, Alyssa)
    c HB - v91 - i4 - July-August 2015 - p154(2) [51-500]
Secrets of the Rainforest (Illus. by Nassner, Alyssa)
    c Sch Lib - v63 - i1 - Spring 2015 - p25(1) [51-500]
Secrets of the Seashore (Illus. by Nassner, Alyssa)
    c HB Guide - v26 - i1 - Spring 2015 - p153(1) [51-500]

Secrets of Winter (Illus. by Johnson, Bee)
 c PW - v262 - i41 - Oct 12 2015 - p69(1) [51-500]
Secrets of Winter (Illus. by Tee, Georgina)
 c KR - Dec 1 2015 - pNA [51-500]
 c SLJ - v61 - i11 - Nov 2015 - p129(1) [51-500]

Brown, Cynthia Light - *Explore Fossils! With 25 Great Projects* (Illus. by Stone, Bryan)
 c PW - v262 - i47 - Nov 23 2015 - p70(1) [501+]

Brown, Dale - *Iron Wolf*
 BL - v111 - i22 - August 1 2015 - p38(1) [51-500]
 KR - June 15 2015 - pNA [501+]

Brown, Daniel (b. 1961-) - *The Poetry of Victorian Scientists: Style, Science and Nonsense*
 VS - v57 - i3 - Spring 2015 - p529(5) [501+]

Brown, Daniel James - *The Boys in the Boat* (Read by Bramhall, Mark). Audiobook Review
 y SLJ - v61 - i12 - Dec 2015 - p78(1) [51-500]
The Boys in the Boat
 y BL - v111 - i19-20 - June 1 2015 - p70(1) [51-500]
 c BL - v112 - i1 - Sept 1 2015 - p99(1) [501+]
  CC - v132 - i9 - April 29 2015 - p3(1) [501+]
 c KR - July 1 2015 - pNA [51-500]
 y VOYA - v38 - i3 - August 2015 - p86(1) [51-500]
 c SLJ - v61 - i8 - August 2015 - p125(1) [51-500]

Brown, Daniel James (b. 1951-) - *The Boys in the Boat*
 y HB - v91 - i5 - Sept-Oct 2015 - p125(2) [51-500]

Brown, Daren W. - *Fusarium: Genomics, Molecular and Cellular Biology*
 QRB - v90 - i4 - Dec 2015 - p443(2) [501+]
 QRB - v90 - i4 - Dec 2015 - p443(2) [501+]

Brown, David (b. 1948-) - *Durham Cathedral: History, Fabric and Culture*
 TLS - i5864-5865 - August 21 2015 - p26(2) [501+]

Brown, David Blayney - *J.M.W. Turner: Painting Set Free*
 LJ - v140 - i3 - Feb 15 2015 - p97(1) [51-500]

Brown, Don - *Aaron and Alexander: The Most Famous Duel in American History* (Illus. by Brown, Don)
 c BL - v111 - i19-20 - June 1 2015 - p92(2) [51-500]
 c HB - v91 - i5 - Sept-Oct 2015 - p126(1) [51-500]
 c KR - August 15 2015 - pNA [51-500]
 c NYTBR - Nov 8 2015 - p28(L) [501+]
 c PW - v262 - i33 - August 17 2015 - p73(2) [51-500]
 c SLJ - v61 - i7 - July 2015 - p101(2) [51-500]
Drowned City: Hurricane Katrina and New Orleans (Illus. by Brown, Don)
 c NYTBR - August 9 2015 - p16(L) [501+]
 y PW - v262 - i21 - May 25 2015 - p62(1) [51-500]
 y SLJ - v61 - i8 - August 2015 - p131(2) [51-500]
 y BL - v111 - i22 - August 1 2015 - p47(1) [51-500]
 y CCB-B - v69 - i2 - Oct 2015 - p77(2) [51-500]
 y CH Bwatch - Sept 2015 - pNA [501+]
 y HB - v91 - i5 - Sept-Oct 2015 - p126(2) [51-500]
 y KR - May 1 2015 - pNA [51-500]
 y PW - v262 - i49 - Dec 2 2015 - p118(1) [51-500]

Brown, Eric - *Wings of the Navy: Testing British and U.S. Carrier Aircraft*
 APH - v62 - i2 - Summer 2015 - p54(1) [501+]

Brown, Erica - *Comedy and the Feminine Middlebrow Novel: Elizabeth Von Arnim and Elizabeth Taylor*
 TSWL - v34 - i1 - Spring 2015 - p181-184 [501+]

Brown, Floyd - *Universal Meaning: In Search of the Reason for Our Existence*
 KR - Dec 1 2015 - pNA [501+]

Brown, Gavin - *Josh Baxter Levels Up*
 c KR - Nov 15 2015 - pNA [51-500]
 c PW - v262 - i46 - Nov 16 2015 - p76(1) [51-500]

Brown, Gerry - *The Independent Director: The Non-Executive Director's Guide to Effective Board Presence*
 TimHES - i2200 - April 23 2015 - p51(1) [501+]

Brown, Harriet - *Body of Truth: How Science, History, and Culture Drive Our Obsession with Weight--and What We Can Do about It*
 Bwatch - May 2015 - pNA [51-500]
 LJ - v140 - i5 - March 15 2015 - p123(1) [51-500]
 RVBW - June 2015 - pNA [51-500]

Brown, Harry - *Golf Ball*
 CHE - v61 - i33 - May 1 2015 - pB10(4) [501+]

Brown, Haydn - *Advice to Single Women*
 TLS - i5856 - June 26 2015 - p26(2) [501+]

Brown, Herman - *A Cut Too Far*
 y PW - v262 - i31 - August 3 2015 - p61(1) [501+]
 y VOYA - v38 - i5 - Dec 2015 - p65(1) [51-500]
The Option
 y HB Guide - v26 - i2 - Fall 2015 - p113(1) [51-500]

Brown, Holly - *A Necessary End*
 KR - May 1 2015 - pNA [51-500]

Brown, Ian - *Burma's Economy in the Twentieth Century*
 AHR - v120 - i1 - Feb 2015 - p212-213 [501+]
 JEH - v75 - i1 - March 2015 - p299-300 [501+]

Brown, James - *Anzac's Long Shadow: The Cost of Our National Obsession*
 Quad - v59 - i5 - May 2015 - p104(3) [501+]
My New Zealand 123 Book
 c Magpies - v30 - i1 - March 2015 - pS4(1) [501+]
My New Zealand ABC Book
 c Magpies - v30 - i1 - March 2015 - pS4(1) [501+]
My New Zealand Colours Book
 c Magpies - v30 - i1 - March 2015 - pS4(1) [501+]

Brown, James Francis - *Ralph Vaughan Williams: Burley Heath - Study Score*
 Notes - v71 - i3 - March 2015 - p573(5) [501+]
Ralph Vaughan Williams: Harnham Down - Study Score
 Notes - v71 - i3 - March 2015 - p573(5) [501+]
Ralph Vaughan Williams: The Solent - Study Score
 Notes - v71 - i3 - March 2015 - p573(5) [501+]

Brown, Jane - *Both Sides of the Sunset: Photographing Los Angeles*
 NYTBR - Dec 6 2015 - p38(L) [501+]

Brown, Jane K. - *Goethe's Allegories of Identity*
 GSR - v38 - i3 - Oct 2015 - p657-659 [501+]
 Eight-C St - v49 - i1 - Fall 2015 - p109-110 [501+]

Brown, Jason I. - *Mathematics for the Liberal Arts*
 RVBW - Jan 2015 - pNA [51-500]

Brown, Jaye Robin - *No Place to Fall*
 y CCB-B - v68 - i6 - Feb 2015 - p301(2) [51-500]
 c HB Guide - v26 - i1 - Spring 2015 - p102(1) [51-500]

Brown, Jeff - *Escape to California* (Illus. by Pamintuan, Macky)
 c HB Guide - v26 - i1 - Spring 2015 - p57(1) [51-500]
Flat Stanley and the Very Big Cookie (Illus. by Pamintuan, Macky)
 c HB Guide - v26 - i2 - Fall 2015 - p58(1) [51-500]
Framed in France (Illus. by Pamintuan, Macky)
 c HB Guide - v26 - i1 - Spring 2015 - p57(1) [51-500]
Show-and-Tell, Flat Stanley! (Illus. by Pamintuan, Macky)
 c HB Guide - v26 - i1 - Spring 2015 - p52(1) [51-500]

Brown, Jeff (b. 1969-) - *Runner's World: The Runner's Brain: How to Think Smarter to Run Better*
 PW - v262 - i33 - August 17 2015 - p67(1) [51-500]

Brown, Jeffrey - *Darth Vader and Friends* (Illus. by Brown, Jeffrey)
 c HB Guide - v26 - i2 - Fall 2015 - p76(1) [51-500]
The Phantom Bully (Illus. by Brown, Jeffrey)
 c BL - v111 - i19-20 - June 1 2015 - p68(1) [51-500]
 c KR - April 15 2015 - pNA [51-500]
 c SLJ - v61 - i6 - June 2015 - p107(1) [51-500]
Star Wars: Jedi Academy: Return of the Padawan
 c CH Bwatch - March 2015 - pNA [501+]
 c HB Guide - v26 - i1 - Spring 2015 - p71(1) [51-500]
Star Wars--L'Academie Jedi--Le retour du Padawan
 c Res Links - v21 - i1 - Oct 2015 - p48(2) [501+]

Brown, Jeffrey (b. 1956-) - *The News: Poems*
 y BL - v111 - i17 - May 1 2015 - p72(1) [51-500]
 PW - v262 - i20 - May 18 2015 - p63(1) [51-500]

Brown, Jennifer - *How Lunchbox Jones Saved Me From Robots, Traitors, and Missy the Cruel*
 c CCB-B - v69 - i2 - Oct 2015 - p78(1) [51-500]
 c KR - June 15 2015 - pNA [51-500]
 c PW - v262 - i19 - May 11 2015 - p61(1) [51-500]
 c SLJ - v61 - i6 - June 2015 - p97(2) [51-500]
Life on Mars
 c CCB-B - v68 - i7 - March 2015 - p350(2) [51-500]
 c HB Guide - v26 - i2 - Fall 2015 - p77(1) [51-500]
Shade Me
 y BL - v112 - i7 - Dec 1 2015 - p57(1) [51-500]
 y KR - Oct 1 2015 - pNA [51-500]
 y PW - v262 - i41 - Oct 12 2015 - p71(1) [51-500]
 y SLJ - v61 - i11 - Nov 2015 - p112(1) [51-500]

Brown, Jeremy - *Anaconda Choke*
 BL - v111 - i15 - April 1 2015 - p28(1) [51-500]

Brown, Jeremy (b. 1976-) - *City versus Countryside in Mao's China: Negotiating the Divide*
 AHR - v120 - i1 - Feb 2015 - p217-218 [501+]

Brown, Jericho - *The New Testament*
 Ant R - v73 - i1 - Wntr 2015 - p189(2) [501+]

Brown, Joan L. - *Approaches to Teaching the Works of Carmen Martin Gaite*
 RVBW - Oct 2015 - pNA [501+]

Brown, John - *Why Not? Conquering The Road Less Traveled*
 SPBW - Jan 2015 - pNA [501+]

Brown, Jordan D. - *Science Stunts: Fun Feats of Physics* (Illus. by Owsley, Anthony)
 c KR - Nov 1 2015 - pNA [51-500]
 c PW - v262 - i47 - Nov 23 2015 - p70(1) [501+]

Brown, Judy - *This Is Not a Love Story*
 c KR - April 1 2015 - pNA [51-500]

Brown, Julie - *Schoenberg and Redemption*
 TLS - i5838 - Feb 20 2015 - p24(2) [501+]
 Notes - v72 - i2 - Dec 2015 - p348(4) [501+]
The Sounds of the Silents in Britain
 Notes - v72 - i2 - Dec 2015 - p372(3) [501+]

Brown, Karma - *Come Away with Me*
 BL - v111 - i14 - March 15 2015 - p51(1) [51-500]

Brown, Kate - *Vulnerability and Young People: Care and Social Control in Policy and Practice*
 TimHES - i2225 - Oct 15 2015 - p45-1 [501+]

Brown, Kate Lord - *The Perfume Garden*
 BL - v111 - i14 - March 15 2015 - p53(1) [51-500]
 KR - Feb 15 2015 - pNA [51-500]

Brown, Katherine A. - *Boccaccio's Fabliaux: Medieval Short Stories and the Function of Reversal*
 TLS - i5844 - April 3 2015 - p25(1) [501+]
 Med R - August 2015 - pNA [501+]
 MLR - v110 - i2 - April 2015 - p513-514 [501+]

Brown, Kathryn - *The Art Book Tradition in Twentieth-Century Europe*
 FS - v69 - i2 - April 2015 - p276-277 [501+]

Brown, Kathryn L. - *Dispatches from Dystopia: Histories of Places Not Yet Forgotten*
 LJ - v140 - i6 - April 1 2015 - p108(1) [51-500]
 NS - v144 - i5266 - June 12 2015 - p51(1) [51-500]
 TLS - i5872 - Oct 16 2015 - p7(1) [51-500]

Brown, Kathy - *Educate Your Brain: Use Mind-Body Balance to Learn Faster, Work Smarter and Move More Easily through Life*
 SPBW - June 2015 - pNA [51-500]

Brown, Kathy (b. 1955-) - *Take 5 Fat Quarters: 15 Easy Quilt Patterns*
 Bwatch - March 2015 - pNA [51-500]

Brown, Keith Ballard - *Sleeping in Trees*
 KR - Jan 15 2015 - pNA [51-500]

Brown, Keith M. - *Noble Power in Scotland from the Reformation to the Revolution*
 HER - v130 - i543 - April 2015 - p445(3) [501+]

Brown, Keith R. - *Buying into Fair Trade: Culture, Morality, and Consumption*
 CS - v44 - i3 - May 2015 - p348-349 [501+]

Brown, Kerry - *Lest We Forget* (Illus. by Knowles, Isobel)
 c Magpies - v30 - i1 - March 2015 - p27(1) [501+]

Brown, Leanne - *Good and Cheap: Eat Well on $4/Day*
 LJ - v140 - i9 - May 15 2015 - p102(2) [501+]

Brown, Leslie - *African American Voices: A Documentary Reader from Emancipation to the Present*
 JSH - v81 - i2 - May 2015 - p541(1) [501+]

Brown, Lester R. - *The Great Transition: Shifting from Fossil Fuels to Solar and Wind Energy*
 BL - v111 - i17 - May 1 2015 - p63(1) [51-500]
 LJ - v140 - i9 - May 15 2015 - p101(1) [51-500]
 Nature - v520 - i7545 - April 2 2015 - p31(1) [51-500]

Brown, Marc - *Monkey* (Illus. by Brown, Marc)
 c KR - June 1 2015 - pNA [51-500]
Monkey: Not Ready for Kindergarten (Illus. by Brown, Marc)
 c CCB-B - v69 - i1 - Sept 2015 - p14(2) [51-500]
 c PW - v262 - i49 - Dec 2 2015 - p16(1) [51-500]
 c SLJ - v61 - i8 - August 2015 - p58(1) [51-500]

Brown, Margaret Wise - *The Dead Bird* (Illus. by Robinson, Christian)
 c BL - v112 - i6 - Nov 15 2015 - p48(1) [51-500]
 c PW - v262 - i52 - Dec 21 2015 - p153(1) [51-500]
The Find It Book (Illus. by Sheehan, Lisa)
 c SLJ - v61 - i11 - Nov 2015 - p80(2) [51-500]
Goodnight Moon / Buenas Noches, Luna (Illus. by Hurd, Clement)
 c HB Guide - v26 - i1 - Spring 2015 - p6(1) [51-500]
Goodnight Songs: A Celebration of the Seasons (Illus. by Brown, Peter)
 c KR - June 1 2015 - pNA [51-500]
 c PW - v262 - i29 - July 20 2015 - p192(1) [51-500]
 c SLJ - v61 - i8 - August 2015 - p62(1) [51-500]
Margaret Wise Brown's The Golden Bunny: And 17 Other Stories and Poems (Illus. by Weisgard, Leonard)
 c HB Guide - v26 - i2 - Fall 2015 - p201(1) [51-500]

Brown, Mary Moss - *How to Innovate: The Essential Guide for Fearless School Leaders*
 HER - v85 - i2 - Summer 2015 - p294-296 [501+]

Brown, Meredith Mason - *Touching America's History: From the Pequot War through World War II*
 HNet - July 2015 - pNA [501+]

Brown, Michael - *Performing Medicine: Medical Culture and Identity in Provincial England, c.1760-1850*
    HER - v130 - i543 - April 2015 - p470(2) [501+]

Brown, Monica - *Lola Levine Is Not Mean! (Illus. by Dominguez, Angela)*
    c BL - v112 - i5 - Nov 1 2015 - p65(1) [51-500]
    c KR - Sept 1 2015 - pNA [51-500]
    c PW - v262 - i38 - Sept 21 2015 - p77(1) [501+]
    c SLJ - v61 - i7 - July 2015 - p71(1) [51-500]

Maya's Blanket / La Manta de Maya (Illus. by Diaz, David)
    c KR - July 1 2015 - pNA [51-500]
    c PW - v262 - i24 - June 15 2015 - p82(1) [501+]

Maya's Blanket/La manta de Maya (Illus. by Diaz, David)
    c SLJ - v61 - i10 - Oct 2015 - p72(1) [51-500]

Brown, Nancy Marie - *Ivory Vikings: The Mystery of the Most Famous Chessmen in the World and the Woman Who Made Them*
    BL - v112 - i1 - Sept 1 2015 - p36(1) [51-500]
    Econ - v416 - i8953 - August 29 2015 - p68(US) [501+]
    KR - June 15 2015 - pNA [51-500]
    LJ - v140 - i12 - July 1 2015 - p92(2) [51-500]
    NY - v91 - i34 - Nov 2 2015 - p89 [51-500]
    PW - v262 - i25 - June 22 2015 - p131(1) [51-500]

The Saga of Gudrid the Far-Traveler
    KR - April 1 2015 - pNA [51-500]
    y CCB-B - v69 - i2 - Oct 2015 - p78(2) [51-500]
    c HB - v91 - i4 - July-August 2015 - p129(2) [51-500]
    y PW - v262 - i19 - May 11 2015 - p63(1) [51-500]
    y SLJ - v61 - i6 - June 2015 - p121(1) [51-500]
    y VOYA - v38 - i3 - August 2015 - p74(1) [51-500]

Brown, Nic - *In Every Way*
    NYTBR - March 15 2015 - p20(L) [501+]

Brown, Nicholas A. - *Re-collecting Black Hawk: Landscape, Memory, and Power in the American Midwest*
    HNet - August 2015 - pNA [501+]

Brown, Nickole - *Fanny Says*
    ABR - v36 - i4 - May-June 2015 - p11(1) [501+]
    BL - v111 - i15 - April 1 2015 - p13(1) [51-500]
    LJ - v140 - i6 - April 1 2015 - p97(2) [51-500]

Brown, Nikki L.M. - *Jim Crow: A Historical Encyclopedia of the American Mosaic*
    BL - v111 - i11 - Feb 1 2015 - p15(1) [51-500]
    LJ - v140 - i9 - May 15 2015 - p105(1) [501+]

Brown, Paul B. - *Entrepreneurship for the Rest of Us: How to Create Innovation and Opportunity Everywhere*
    PW - v262 - i4 - Jan 26 2015 - p159(2) [51-500]

Brown, Peter (b. 1935-) - *The Ransom of the Soul: Afterlife and Wealth in Early Western Christianity*
    AM - v213 - i14 - Nov 9 2015 - p37(4) [501+]
    CHR - v101 - i4 - Autumn 2015 - p879(10) [501+]
    HT - v65 - i10 - Oct 2015 - p60(1) [501+]
    LJ - v140 - i6 - April 1 2015 - p98(1) [51-500]
    NS - v144 - i5262 - May 15 2015 - p42(2) [501+]
    NYRB - v62 - i9 - May 21 2015 - p28(3) [501+]
    PW - v262 - i10 - March 9 2015 - p69(1) [51-500]
    Spec - v327 - i9737 - April 11 2015 - p38(1) [501+]
    TLS - i5854 - June 12 2015 - p12(1) [501+]

The World of Late Antiquity: AD 150-170
    HT - v65 - i5 - May 2015 - p59(1) [501+]

Brown, Peter (b. 1948-) - *Reading Chaucer: Selected Essays*
    MLR - v110 - i3 - July 2015 - p807-808 [501+]

Brown, Peter (b. 1979-) - *Mr. Tiger Goes Wild*
    c HB - v91 - i1 - Jan-Feb 2015 - p34(5) [501+]

My Teacher Is a Monster! (No, I Am Not). (Illus. by Brown, Peter)
    c HB Guide - v26 - i1 - Spring 2015 - p24(1) [51-500]

Brown, Petra - *Old MacDonald*
    c KR - Jan 1 2016 - pNA [51-500]

Brown, Pierce - *Golden Son*
    Ent W - i1345 - Jan 9 2015 - p71(1) [501+]

Morning Star
    KR - Dec 15 2015 - pNA [51-500]

Red Rising
    LJ - v140 - i11 - June 15 2015 - p118(1) [501+]

Brown, Rachel Manija - *Stranger*
    y CCB-B - v68 - i6 - Feb 2015 - p302(1) [51-500]
    c HB Guide - v26 - i1 - Spring 2015 - p102(1) [51-500]

Brown, Ras Michael - *African-Atlantic Cultures and the South Carolina Lowcountry*
    JSH - v81 - i1 - Feb 2015 - p165(2) [501+]

Brown, Rebecca A. - *Monsters and Monstrosity from the Fin de Siecle to the Millennium*
    TLS - i5874 - Oct 30 2015 - p7(1) [501+]

Brown, Ricardo - *Until Darwin, Science, Human Variety and the Origins of Race*
    VS - v57 - i2 - Wntr 2015 - p333(4) [501+]

Brown, Richard D. - *Taming Lust: Crimes against Nature in the Early Republic*
    JIH - v46 - i3 - Wntr 2016 - p459-460 [501+]

Brown, Richard Danson - *A Concordance to the Rhymes of the Faerie Queene*
    TLS - i5861 - July 31 2015 - p25(1) [501+]

Brown, Richard H. - *Revolution*
    KR - June 15 2015 - pNA [501+]

Brown, Richard L. - *Fitness Running: 78 Workouts from the Mile to the Marathon*
    Bwatch - June 2015 - pNA [51-500]

Brown, Ron - *The Train Doesn't Stop Here Anymore: An Illustrated History of Railway Stations in Canada*
    Beav - v95 - i2 - April-May 2015 - p57(1) [501+]

Brown, Sandra - *The Devil's Own*
    BL - v112 - i4 - Oct 15 2015 - p26(1) [51-500]

Brown, Shirley Ann - *The Bayeux Tapestry, Bayeux MediathEque Municipale: MS 1 - A Sourcebook*
    Med R - March 2015 - pNA(NA) [501+]

Brown, Skila - *Slickety Quick: Poems About Sharks (Illus. by Kolar, Bob)*
    c KR - Dec 15 2015 - pNA [51-500]
    c PW - v262 - i52 - Dec 21 2015 - p156(2) [501+]

Brown, Stacia M. - *Accidents of Providence*
    CC - v132 - i3 - Feb 4 2015 - p31(3) [501+]

Brown, Stewart J. - *Religion, Identity and Conflict in Britain: From the Restoration to the Twentieth Century: Essays in Honour of Keith Robbins*
    HER - v130 - i545 - August 2015 - p1063(3) [501+]

Brown, T.G. - *O'Henry*
    PW - v262 - i39 - Sept 28 2015 - p71(1) [51-500]

Brown, Taylor - *Fallen Land*
    BL - v112 - i5 - Nov 1 2015 - p33(1) [51-500]
    KR - Nov 15 2015 - pNA [501+]
    LJ - v140 - i17 - Oct 15 2015 - p73(1) [51-500]

Brown, Terence - *The Irish Times: 150 Years of Influence*
    TLS - i5861 - July 31 2015 - p27(1) [501+]

Brown, Teri - *Velvet Undercover*
    y BL - v112 - i3 - Oct 1 2015 - p75(2) [51-500]
    y KR - August 1 2015 - pNA [51-500]
    y SLJ - v61 - i9 - Sept 2015 - p157(1) [51-500]
    y VOYA - v38 - i5 - Dec 2015 - p54(1) [51-500]

Brown, Theresa - *The Shift: One Nurse, Twelve Hours, Four Patients' Lives*
    BL - v112 - i1 - Sept 1 2015 - p22(1) [51-500]
    KR - July 15 2015 - pNA [51-500]
    LJ - v140 - i12 - July 1 2015 - p103(1) [51-500]
    PW - v262 - i30 - July 27 2015 - p54(1) [51-500]

Brown, Tracy (b. 1974-) - *White Lines III: All Falls Down*
    PW - v262 - i37 - Sept 14 2015 - p48(1) [51-500]

Brown, Tracy L. - *Pueblo Indians and Spanish Colonial Authority in Eighteenth-Century New Mexico*
    Am Ind CRJ - v39 - i1 - Wntr 2015 - p150-153 [501+]
    HAHR - v95 - i3 - August 2015 - p523-524 [501+]

Brown, Tricia - *Charlie and the Blanket Toss (Illus. by Martinsen, Sarah)*
    c HB Guide - v26 - i1 - Spring 2015 - p24(1) [51-500]

Brown, Valerie - *The Mindful School Leader: Practices to Transform Your Leadership and School*
    Bwatch - March 2015 - pNA [51-500]

Brown, Warren C. - *Documentary Culture and the Laity in the Early Middle Ages*
    HER - v130 - i542 - Feb 2015 - p148(2) [501+]

Brown, Wendy - *The Power of Tolerance: A Debate*
    Dialogue - v54 - i3 - Sept 2015 - p557-559 [501+]

Brown, William P. - *The Oxford Handbook of the "Psalms"*
    Theol St - v76 - i3 - Sept 2015 - p597(3) [501+]

Sacred Sense: Discovering the Wonder of God's Word and World
    CC - v132 - i21 - Oct 14 2015 - p32(2) [51-500]

Wisdom's Wonder: Character, Creation, and Crisis in the Bible's Wisdom Literature
    Intpr - v69 - i4 - Oct 2015 - p476(3) [501+]
    Theol St - v76 - i1 - March 2015 - p207(1) [501+]

Brown-Wood, JaNay - *Imani's Moon (Read by Boafo, MaameYaa). Audiobook Review*
    c BL - v112 - i6 - Nov 15 2015 - p63(1) [501+]

Imani's Moon (Illus. by Mitchell, Hazel)
    c HB Guide - v26 - i1 - Spring 2015 - p24(1) [51-500]

Browne, Anthony - *Frida and Bear*
    c Magpies - v30 - i1 - March 2015 - p30(1) [501+]
    c Sch Lib - v63 - i2 - Summer 2015 - p90(1) [51-500]

What if...? (Illus. by Browne, Anthony)
    c HB Guide - v26 - i1 - Spring 2015 - p24(1) [51-500]

Willy's Stories (Illus. by Browne, Anthony)
    c BL - v112 - i6 - Nov 15 2015 - p59(1) [51-500]
    c KR - Oct 1 2015 - pNA [51-500]
    c PW - v262 - i36 - Sept 7 2015 - p68(1) [51-500]
    c SLJ - v61 - i11 - Nov 2015 - p80(1) [51-500]

Browne, Arthur - *One Righteous Man: Samuel Battle and the Shattering of the Color Line in New York*
    KR - March 1 2015 - pNA [501+]
    LJ - v140 - i8 - May 1 2015 - p82(1) [51-500]
    NYT - July 12 2015 - p2(L) [501+]

Browne, David - *So Many Roads: The Life and Times of the Grateful Dead (Read by Runnette, Sean). Audiobook Review*
    LJ - v140 - i15 - Sept 15 2015 - p43(1) [501+]

So Many Roads: The Life and Times of the Grateful Dead
    KR - April 1 2015 - pNA [501+]
    LJ - v140 - i8 - May 1 2015 - p76(1) [51-500]

Browne, John - *Connect: How Companies Succeed by Engaging Radically with Society*
    KR - Jan 1 2016 - pNA [51-500]

Browne, Katherine E. - *Standing in the Need: Culture, Comfort, and Coming Home After Katrina*
    BL - v112 - i1 - Sept 1 2015 - p31(1) [51-500]
    LJ - v140 - i12 - July 1 2015 - p100(2) [501+]

Browne, S.G. - *Less Than Hero*
    BL - v111 - i13 - March 1 2015 - p30(1) [51-500]

Browne, Thomas - *Religio Medici and Urne-Buriall*
    NYRB - v62 - i16 - Oct 22 2015 - p67(3) [501+]

Brownell, Will - *The First Nazi*
    KR - Dec 1 2015 - pNA [501+]

Browner, Jesse - *How Did I Get Here?: Making Peace with the Road Not Taken*
    BL - v111 - i17 - May 1 2015 - p71(1) [51-500]
    KR - April 15 2015 - pNA [501+]
    PW - v262 - i11 - March 16 2015 - p73(1) [51-500]

Browning, Glenn F. - *Mollicutes: Molecular Biology and Pathogensis*
    QRB - v90 - i4 - Dec 2015 - p444(1) [501+]

Browning, Sherri - *An Affair Downstairs*
    BL - v111 - i9-10 - Jan 1 2015 - p55(1) [51-500]

The Great Estate
    KR - June 1 2015 - pNA [51-500]
    PW - v262 - i22 - June 1 2015 - p48(1) [51-500]

Brownjohn, John - *A Price to Pay*
    WLT - v89 - i2 - March-April 2015 - p55(1) [51-500]

Brownlee, George G. - *Fred Sanger: Double Nobel Laureate: A Biography*
    QRB - v90 - i4 - Dec 2015 - p419(2) [501+]

Brownlee, Jason - *Democracy Prevention: The Politics of the US-Egyptian Alliance*
    IJMES - v47 - i1 - Feb 2015 - p153-168 [501+]

Brownlie, Siobhan - *Memory and Myths of the Norman Conquest*
    Med R - Jan 2015 - pNA [501+]

Brownsey, Paul - *His Steadfast Love and Other Stories*
    PW - v262 - i24 - June 15 2015 - p70(1) [51-500]

Brownson, James V. - *Bible, Gender, Sexuality: Reframing the Church's Debate on Same-Sex Relationships*
    BTB - v45 - i2 - May 2015 - p119(2) [501+]
    Intpr - v69 - i1 - Jan 2015 - p118(2) [501+]

Brownstein, Carrie - *Hunger Makes Me a Modern Girl: A Memoir*
    BL - v112 - i2 - Sept 15 2015 - p14(2) [51-500]
    KR - August 15 2015 - pNA [51-500]
    LJ - v140 - i16 - Oct 1 2015 - p79(2) [51-500]
    NYTBR - Nov 22 2015 - p10(L) [501+]

Brownstein, Henry H. - *The Methamphetamine Industry in America: Transnational Cartels and Local Entrepreneurs*
    CS - v44 - i1 - Jan 2015 - p136(1) [501+]

The Methamphetamine Industry in America: Transnational Cartels and Local Entrepreneurs
    CrimJR - v40 - i2 - June 2015 - p240-241 [501+]

Brownworth, Lars - *The Sea Wolves: A History of the Vikings (Read by Barrett, Joe). Audiobook Review*
    LJ - v140 - i16 - Oct 1 2015 - p44(1) [51-500]

Broyles, Bill - *Among Unknown Tribes: Rediscovering the Photographs of Explorer Carl Lumholtz*
    TLS - i5833 - Jan 16 2015 - p28(1) [501+]

Brozek, Gary - *The Reaper: Autobiography of One of the Deadliest Special Ops Snipers*
    Bwatch - April 2015 - pNA [51-500]

Brozek, Jennifer - *Never Let Me Leave*
    PW - v262 - i47 - Nov 23 2015 - p53(2) [51-500]
Brozgal, Lia Nicole - *Against Autobiography: Albert Memmi and the Production of Theory*
    FS - v69 - i1 - Jan 2015 - p110-111 [501+]
Brremaud, Frederic - *The Fox (Illus. by Bertolucci, Federico)*
    c BL - v112 - i6 - Nov 15 2015 - p36(1) [51-500]
    Love (Illus. by Bertolucci, Federico)
    c KR - Sept 1 2015 - pNA [51-500]
Brubaker, Ed - *Coward (Illus. by Phillips, Sean)*
    PW - v262 - i10 - March 9 2015 - p60(1) [51-500]
    The Fade Out (Illus. by Phillips, Sean)
    BL - v111 - i18 - May 15 2015 - p41(1) [51-500]
    PW - v262 - i12 - March 23 2015 - p57(1) [51-500]
Brubaker, Leslie - *Approaches to the Byzantine Family*
    Class R - v65 - i1 - April 2015 - p189-191 [501+]
Bruce, Judy - *Death Steppe*
    KR - July 1 2015 - pNA [51-500]
Bruce, Valerie - *A Distant Dream*
    KR - April 15 2015 - pNA [501+]
Bruchac, Joseph - *Brothers of the Buffalo*
    y KR - Jan 1 2016 - pNA [51-500]
    The Hunter's Promise: An Abenaki Tale (Illus. by Farnsworth, Bill)
    c BL - v111 - i22 - August 1 2015 - p52(1) [51-500]
    c CH Bwatch - Oct 2015 - pNA [51-500]
    c CH Bwatch - Nov 2015 - pNA [51-500]
    c KR - June 15 2015 - pNA [51-500]
    c PW - v262 - i24 - June 15 2015 - p82(1) [51-500]
    c SLJ - v61 - i7 - July 2015 - p59(2) [51-500]
    Killer of Enemies
    c BL - v111 - i9-10 - Jan 1 2015 - p39(2) [501+]
    Trail of the Dead
    y HB - v91 - i6 - Nov-Dec 2015 - p77(2) [51-500]
    y KR - August 1 2015 - pNA [51-500]
    y SLJ - v61 - i10 - Oct 2015 - p100(1) [51-500]
    Walking Two Worlds
    y BL - v111 - i16 - April 15 2015 - p58(2) [51-500]
    c KR - March 1 2015 - pNA [51-500]
    c PW - v262 - i14 - April 6 2015 - p60(1) [501+]
    c SLJ - v61 - i5 - May 2015 - p111(2) [51-500]
    y VOYA - v38 - i2 - June 2015 - p55(1) [51-500]
Brucken, Rowland M. - *A Most Uncertain Crusade: The United States, the United Nations, and Human Rights, 1941-1953*
    JAH - v102 - i2 - Sept 2015 - p597-598 [501+]
Bruckner, Leslie - *Literarische Deutschlandreisen nach 1989*
    Ger Q - v88 - i1 - Wntr 2015 - p118(2) [501+]
Bruder, Edith - *The Black Jews of Africa: History, Religion, Identity*
    JR - Jan 2015 - p107(14) [501+]
Brueggemann, Walter - *The Collected Sermons of Walter Brueggemann, vol. 2*
    CC - v132 - i12 - June 10 2015 - p42(1) [51-500]
    Psalms
    CC - v132 - i10 - May 13 2015 - p37(2) [501+]
Bruel, Nick - *Bad Kitty Goes to the Vet (Illus. by Bruel, Nick)*
    c KR - Oct 15 2015 - pNA [51-500]
    c SLJ - v61 - i12 - Dec 2015 - p99(1) [51-500]
    Bad Kitty: Puppy's Big Day
    c HB Guide - v26 - i1 - Fall 2015 - p64(1) [51-500]
    Mechant Minou: Quelle journee!
    c Res Links - v21 - i1 - Oct 2015 - p49(1) [51-500]
    A Wonderful Year (Illus. by Bruel, Nick)
    c CCB-B - v68 - i6 - Feb 2015 - p302(2) [51-500]
    c HB - v91 - i1 - Jan-Feb 2015 - p60(1) [51-500]
    c HB Guide - v26 - i2 - Fall 2015 - p28(1) [51-500]
    c PW - v262 - i49 - Dec 2 2015 - p22(2) [51-500]
Bruell, Christopher - *Aristotle as Teacher: His Introduction to a Philosophic Science*
    RM - v69 - i1 - Sept 2015 - p118(3) [501+]
Bruen, Ken - *Green Hell*
    BL - v111 - i17 - May 1 2015 - p36(1) [51-500]
    KR - May 1 2015 - pNA [51-500]
    PW - v262 - i15 - April 13 2015 - p56(1) [51-500]
    Pimp
    KR - Jan 1 2016 - pNA [51-500]
Bruendel, Steffen - *Zeitenwende 1914: Kunstler, Dichter und Denker im Ersten Weltkrieg*
    HNet - July 2015 - pNA [501+]
Bruggemeier, Franz-Josef - *Weltmeister im Schatten Hitlers: Deutschland und die Fussball-Weltmeisterschaft 1954*
    Ger Q - v88 - i3 - Summer 2015 - p403(4) [501+]
Bruggisser-Lanker, Therese - *Musik und Tod im Mittelalter: Imaginationsraume der Transzendenz*
    HNet - July 2015 - pNA [501+]

Bruhwiler, Ingrid - *Finanzierung des Bildungswesens in der Helvetischen Republik: Vielfalt - Entwicklungen - Herausforderungen*
    HNet - March 2015 - pNA [501+]
Bruin, D.L. - *Ten Percent: Hollywood Can Be Murder*
    PW - v262 - i36 - Sept 7 2015 - p49(2) [51-500]
Bruisch, Katja - *Als das Dorf noch Zukunft war: Agrarismus und Expertise zwischen Zarenreich und Sowjetunion*
    HNet - May 2015 - pNA [501+]
Brukner, Lauren - *The Kids' Guide to Staying Awesome and in Control: Simple Stuff to Help Children Regulate Their Emotions and Sense (Illus. by Apsley)*
    c CH Bwatch - Jan 2015 - pNA [51-500]
Bruleigh, Nylora - *Fine Art Portrait Photography: Lighting, Posing & Postproduction from Concept to Completion*
    Bwatch - April 2015 - pNA [51-500]
Brulez, Nicolas - *The Tattoorialist: Tattoo Street Style*
    LJ - v140 - i16 - Oct 1 2015 - p78(1) [501+]
Brumbach, Andrew - *The Eye of Midnight*
    c KR - Dec 15 2015 - pNA [51-500]
Brumfield, William - *Architecture at the End of the Earth: Photographing the Russian North*
    LJ - v140 - i14 - Sept 1 2015 - p110(1) [501+]
    New Or - v49 - i12 - Sept 2015 - p42(1) [501+]
Brummett, Nancy Parker - *Take My Hand Again: A Faith-Based Guide for Helping Aging Parents*
    RVBW - Oct 2015 - pNA [51-500]
Brun-Lambert, David - *Unforgotten New York: Legendary Spaces of the Twentieth-Century Avant-Garde*
    LJ - v140 - i20 - Dec 1 2015 - p106(2) [501+]
Bruna, Denis - *Fashioning the Body: An Intimate History of the Silhouette*
    TLS - i5864-5865 - August 21 2015 - p12(2) [501+]
Brundage, Elizabeth - *All Things Cease to Appear*
    KR - Jan 1 2016 - pNA [501+]
    PW - v262 - i51 - Dec 14 2015 - p57(1) [51-500]
Brune, Jeffrey A. - *Disability and Passing: Blurring the Lines of Identity*
    TimHES - i2201 - April 30 2015 - p51(1) [501+]
Brunelle, Michael - *Paint Like the Masters: An Excellent Way to Learn from Those Who Have Much to Teach*
    LJ - v140 - i11 - June 15 2015 - p86(1) [51-500]
Brunet-Jailly, Emmanuel - *Border Disputes: A Global Encyclopedia*
    y BL - v112 - i7 - Dec 1 2015 - p6(1) [51-500]
Bruni, Frank - *Where You Go Is Not Who You'll Be: An Antidote to the College Admissions Mania*
    y BL - v111 - i12 - Feb 15 2015 - p14(1) [51-500]
    CHE - v62 - i5 - Oct 2 2015 - pA26(1) [51-500]
    Comw - v142 - i14 - Sept 11 2015 - p32(3) [501+]
    CSM - March 17 2015 - pNA [501+]
    KR - Jan 1 2015 - pNA [51-500]
    LJ - v140 - i2 - Feb 1 2015 - p92(1) [51-500]
    NYT - March 23 2015 - pC4(L) [501+]
    NYTBR - March 29 2015 - p13(L) [501+]
    PW - v262 - i4 - Jan 26 2015 - p166(2) [51-500]
Brunkhorst, Alex - *The Gilded Life of Matilda Duplaine*
    KR - July 15 2015 - pNA [501+]
    PW - v262 - i31 - August 3 2015 - p33(2) [51-500]
Brunnbauer, Ulf - *The Ambiguous Nation: Case Studies from Southeastern Europe in the 20th Century*
    Slav R - v74 - i3 - Fall 2015 - p630-631 [501+]
Brunner, Jose - *Die Politik des Traumas: Gewalterfahrungen und Psychisches Leid in den USA, in Deutschland und im Israel/Palastina-Konflikt*
    HNet - March 2015 - pNA [501+]
Bruno, Cat - *The Girl from the North*
    SPBW - April 2015 - pNA [51-500]
Bruno, Frank J. - *The Knute Rockne Kid*
    KR - Sept 15 2015 - pNA [51-500]
Bruno, Holly Elissa - *The Comfort of Little Things: An Educator's Guide to Second Chances*
    Bwatch - Sept 2015 - pNA [51-500]
Bruno, Tom - *Wearable Technology*
    VOYA - v38 - i5 - Dec 2015 - p83(1) [51-500]
Brunskill, Ian - *The Times Guide to the House of Commons 2015*
    TLS - i5869 - Sept 25 2015 - p9(2) [501+]
Brunsman, David L. - *Handbook of Sociology and Human Rights*
    CS - v44 - i2 - March 2015 - p180-182 [501+]
Brunsman, Denver - *The Evil Necessity: British Naval Impressment in the Eighteenth-Century Atlantic World*
    J Mil H - v79 - i2 - April 2015 - p481-482 [51-500]
Brunstetter, Wanda E. - *The Decision*
    LJ - v140 - i2 - Feb 1 2015 - p67(3) [501+]
    PW - v262 - i2 - Jan 12 2015 - p44(1) [51-500]

The Gift (Read by Gallagher, Rebecca). Audiobook Review
    BL - v112 - i6 - Nov 15 2015 - p61(1) [51-500]
Brury, Louis - *Exercises in Criticism: The Theory and Practice of Literary Constraint*
    RVBW - June 2015 - pNA [51-500]
Bruschini, Vito - *The Prince*
    KR - Jan 15 2015 - pNA [51-500]
Bruscoli, Francesco Guidi - *Bartolomeo Marchionni "Homem de grossa fazend" (ca. 1450-1530): Un mercante fiorentino a Lisbona e l'Impero portoghese*
    Ren Q - v68 - i3 - Fall 2015 - p1063-1065 [501+]
Brusilow, Anshel - *Shoot the Conductor*
    RVBW - Oct 2015 - pNA [501+]
Bruun, Christer - *The Oxford Handbook of Roman Epigraphy*
    HNet - June 2015 - pNA [501+]
Bruzzone, Catherine - *Mira donde vivo! / Look Where I Live! (Illus. by Comfort, Louise)*
    c BL - v111 - i11 - Feb 1 2015 - p42(1) [51-500]
Bryan, Ashley - *Ashley Bryan's Puppets: Making Something from Everything*
    c HB Guide - v26 - i1 - Spring 2015 - p188(1) [51-500]
    By Trolley Past Thimbledon Bridge (Illus. by Bileck, Marvin)
    c KR - March 1 2015 - pNA [51-500]
    c SLJ - v61 - i9 - Sept 2015 - p116(1) [51-500]
Bryan, Charles S. - *Asylum Doctor: James Woods Babcock and the Red Plague of Pellagra*
    JSH - v81 - i4 - Nov 2015 - p1019(2) [501+]
Bryan, Christopher - *Listening to the Bible: The Art of Faithful Biblical Interpretation*
    TT - v71 - i4 - Jan 2015 - p467-468 [501+]
Bryan, Daniel - *Yes! My Improbable Journey to the Main Event of WrestleMania*
    LJ - v140 - i10 - June 1 2015 - p108(1) [51-500]
Bryant, Anne - *The Fantasy Soccer Wall (Illus. by Kennedy, Kelly)*
    c CH Bwatch - Nov 2015 - pNA [51-500]
Bryant, Gerald James - *The Emergence of British Power in India, 1600-1784: A Grand Strategic Interpretation*
    Eight-C St - v49 - i1 - Fall 2015 - pNA [501+]
Bryant, Howard - *Legends: The Best Players, Games, and Teams in Baseball*
    c BL - v111 - i16 - April 15 2015 - p44(1) [51-500]
    c VOYA - v38 - i1 - April 2015 - p86(1) [51-500]
    c SLJ - v61 - i3 - March 2015 - p176(1) [51-500]
    Legends: The Best Players, Games, and Teams in Football
    c BL - v112 - i6 - Nov 15 2015 - p39(1) [51-500]
Bryant, Jen - *The Right Word: Roget and His Thesaurus (Illus. by Sweet, Melissa)*
    c BL - v111 - i9-10 - Jan 1 2015 - pS4(8) [501+]
    c HB Guide - v26 - i1 - Spring 2015 - p191(1) [51-500]
    c Magpies - v30 - i1 - March 2015 - p23(1) [51-500]
Bryant, Jonathan M. - *Dark Places of the Earth: The Voyage of the Slave Ship Antelope*
    BL - v111 - i19-20 - June 1 2015 - p25(1) [51-500]
    KR - April 15 2015 - pNA [51-500]
    LJ - v140 - i7 - April 15 2015 - p100(2) [51-500]
    PW - v262 - i18 - May 4 2015 - p107(2) [51-500]
Bryant, Sherwin K. - *Africans to Spanish America: Expanding the Diaspora*
    AHR - v120 - i3 - June 2015 - p1085-1086 [501+]
    Two Troubled Souls: An Eighteenth-Century Couple's Spiritual Journey in the Atlantic World
    Eight-C St - v49 - i1 - Fall 2015 - pNA [501+]
Bryant, Walter L. - *The Preacher's Legacy*
    RVBW - June 2015 - pNA [51-500]
Bryars, Tim - *Tom Harper's A History of the Twentieth Century in 100 Maps*
    LJ - v140 - i9 - May 15 2015 - p94(2) [51-500]
Bryce, Colette - *The Whole and Rain-Domed Universe*
    TLS - i5839 - Feb 27 2015 - p25(1) [501+]
Brye, Elaine Lowry - *Be Safe, Love Mom*
    KR - Feb 1 2015 - pNA [51-500]
    PW - v262 - i1 - Jan 5 2015 - p68(1) [51-500]
Bryen, Ari Z. - *Violence in Roman Egypt: A Study in Legal Interpretation*
    AHR - v120 - i3 - June 2015 - p1148-1149 [501+]
    Class R - v65 - i1 - April 2015 - p220-222 [501+]
Brykczynski, Jan - *The Gardener*
    NS - v144 - i5271 - July 17 2015 - p53(1) [51-500]
Brynjolfsson, Erik - *The Second Machine Age*
    Har Bus R - v93 - i3 - March 2015 - p126(2) [501+]

Bryson, Bill - *The Road to Little Dribbling: Adventures of an American in Britain*
BL - v112 - i7 - Dec 1 2015 - p11(1) [51-500]
KR - Nov 15 2015 - pNA [501+]
The Road to Little Dribbling: More Notes from a Small Island
NS - v144 - i5285 - Oct 23 2015 - p53(1) [501+]
Brzezinski, Mika - *Grow Your Value: Living and Working to Your Full Potential*
BL - v111 - i18 - May 15 2015 - p6(1) [51-500]
KR - April 1 2015 - pNA [501+]
Bsumek, Erika Marie - *Nation-States and the Global Environment: New Approaches to International Environmental History*
PHR - v84 - i1 - Feb 2015 - p105(3) [501+]
Bubalo, Djordje - *Pragmatic Literacy in Medieval Serbia*
Med R - April 2015 - pNA [501+]
Specu - v90 - i2 - April 2015 - p512-514 [501+]
Bubenheimer-Erhart, Friederike - *Die Etrusker*
HNet - July 2015 - pNA [501+]
Buc, Philippe - *Holy War, Martyrdom, and Terror: Christianity, Violence, and the West, ca. 70 C. E. to the Iraq War*
CHR - v101 - i4 - Autumn 2015 - p892(3) [501+]
Bucay, Jorge - *The King and the Magician (Illus. by Gusti)*
c HB Guide - v26 - i2 - Fall 2015 - p28(1) [51-500]
Bucciantini, Massimo - *Galileo's Telescope*
KR - Jan 15 2015 - pNA [501+]
LJ - v140 - i5 - March 15 2015 - p128(1) [51-500]
RM - v69 - i1 - Sept 2015 - p120(2) [501+]
Spec - v327 - i9737 - April 11 2015 - p37(1) [501+]
TimHES - i2195 - March 19 2015 - p50-51 [501+]
Bucerius, Sandra M. - *Unwanted: Muslim Immigrants, Dignity, and Drug Dealing*
AJS - v121 - i3 - Nov 2015 - p997(3) [501+]
Buchalter, Susan - *Raising Self-Esteem in Adults: An Eclectic Approach with Art Therapy, CBT and DBT Based Techniques*
Bwatch - May 2015 - pNA [51-500]
Buchan, John - *Greenmantle*
RVBW - Nov 2015 - pNA [51-500]
Memory Hold-the-Door: The Autobiography of John Buchan
TimHES - i2220 - Sept 10 2015 - p45-1 [501+]
Buchanan, Allen - *The Heart of Human Rights*
Ethics - v125 - i4 - July 2015 - p1199(6) [501+]
Buchanan, Andrew - *American Grand Strategy in the Mediterranean during World War II*
HNet - June 2015 - pNA [501+]
Buchanan, Shelly C. - *Animal Senses*
c BL - v112 - i2 - Sept 15 2015 - p60(2) [51-500]
Plant Reproduction
c BL - v112 - i2 - Sept 15 2015 - p60(2) [51-500]
Buchen, Tim - *Antisemitismus in Galizien: Agitation, Gewalt und Politik gegen Juden in der Habsburgermonarchie um 1900*
HNet - March 2015 - pNA [501+]
Buchenbacher, Hans - *Hans Buchenbacher: Erinnerungen 1933-1949 - Zugleich eine Studie zur Geschichte der Anthroposophie im Nationalsozialismus*
HNet - Feb 2015 - pNA [501+]
Bucher, Henry H. - *Two Women: Anyentyuwe and Ekakise*
IBMR - v39 - i1 - Jan 2015 - p47(1) [501+]
Buchhart, Dieter - *Basquiat: The Unknown Notebooks*
G&L Rev W - v22 - i6 - Nov-Dec 2015 - p45(2) [501+]
PW - v262 - i19 - May 11 2015 - p49(1) [51-500]
Jean-Michel Basquiat: Now's the Time
NYTBR - June 28 2015 - p27(L) [501+]
Buchholz, Frank - *The Great War Dawning: Germany and Its Army at the Start of World War I*
J Mil H - v79 - i1 - Jan 2015 - p228-229 [501+]
Buchholz, Jason - *A Paper Son*
BL - v112 - i7 - Dec 1 2015 - p22(2) [51-500]
PW - v262 - i44 - Nov 2 2015 - p57(2) [51-500]
Buchli, Victor - *An Anthropology of Architecture*
JRAI - v21 - i1 - March 2015 - p222(3) [501+]
Buchman, M.L. - *Bring On the Dusk*
PW - v262 - i2 - Jan 12 2015 - p43(1) [51-500]
Hot Point
BL - v111 - i21 - July 1 2015 - p44(1) [51-500]
PW - v262 - i24 - June 15 2015 - p71(1) [51-500]
Target Engaged
BL - v112 - i5 - Nov 1 2015 - p37(1) [51-500]
PW - v262 - i42 - Oct 19 2015 - p61(1) [51-500]
Buchmann, Jacinda - *Whispers from Eternity*
KR - Dec 15 2015 - pNA [51-500]
Buchmann, Stephen - *The Reason for Flowers: Their History, Culture, Biology, and How They Change Our Lives*
BL - v111 - i21 - July 1 2015 - p14(1) [51-500]
KR - May 15 2015 - pNA [51-500]
LJ - v140 - i11 - June 15 2015 - p107(1) [51-500]
PW - v262 - i26 - June 29 2015 - p57(2) [51-500]
Buchner, Bernd - *Wagners Welttheater: Die Geschichte der Bayreuther Festspiele zwischen Kunst und Politik*
HNet - Sept 2015 - pNA [501+]
Buchstaller, Isabelle - *Pidgins and Creoles Beyond Africa-Europe Encounters*
Lang Soc - v44 - i3 - June 2015 - p438-441 [501+]
Buchwald, Jed Z. - *Newton and the Origin of Civilization*
Ren Q - v68 - i2 - Summer 2015 - p662-664 [501+]
The Oxford Handbook of the History of Physics
Isis - v106 - i1 - March 2015 - p156(2) [501+]
Buck, Craig Faustus - *Go Down Hard*
BL - v84 - i4 - May 1 2015 - p36(1) [51-500]
Buck, Lawrence P. - *The Roman Monster: An Icon of the Papal Antichrist in Reformation Polemics*
CH - v84 - i4 - Dec 2015 - p878(3) [501+]
Six Ct J - v46 - i3 - Fall 2015 - p786-788 [501+]
Buck, Marny - *Quilts du Jour: Make it Your Own with a la Carte Blocks and Settings*
LJ - v140 - i14 - Sept 1 2015 - p105(2) [51-500]
Buck, Rinker - *The Oregon Trail: An American Journey (Read by Buck, Rinker). Audiobook Review*
LJ - v140 - i15 - Sept 15 2015 - p43(1) [51-500]
The Oregon Trail: An American Journey
PW - v262 - i16 - April 20 2015 - p65(1) [51-500]
BL - v111 - i21 - July 1 2015 - p19(1) [51-500]
LJ - v140 - i7 - April 15 2015 - p106(2) [51-500]
NYT - June 24 2015 - pC6(L) [501+]
KR - June 1 2015 - pNA [501+]
Buck, Thomas M. - *Das Konstanzer Konzil: Kirchenpolitik - Weltgeschehen - Alltagsleben*
HNet - Feb 2015 - pNA [501+]
Buckingham, Royce Scott - *Impasse*
BL - v111 - i12 - Feb 15 2015 - p38(1) [51-500]
LJ - v140 - i2 - Feb 1 2015 - p76(1) [501+]
The Terminals
y CCB-B - v68 - i5 - Jan 2015 - p249(1) [51-500]
c HB Guide - v26 - i1 - Spring 2015 - p102(1) [51-500]
Buckland, Adelene - *Novel Science: Fiction and the Invention of Nineteenth-Century Geology*
VS - v57 - i3 - Spring 2015 - p529(5) [501+]
Buckle, J.A. - *Half My Facebook Friends Are Ferrets*
c HB Guide - v26 - i1 - Spring 2015 - p102(1) [51-500]
My Smoky Bacon Crisp Obsession
y Sch Lib - v63 - i3 - Autumn 2015 - p179(1) [51-500]
Buckler, Rick - *That's Entertainment: My Life in the Jam*
NS - v144 - i5266 - June 12 2015 - p48(2) [501+]
Buckley, Ann - *Music, Dance and Society: Medieval and Renaissance Studies in Memory of Ingrid G. Brainard*
Ren Q - v68 - i2 - Summer 2015 - p731-733 [501+]
Buckley-Archer, Linda - *The Many Lives of John Stone*
y BL - v112 - i3 - Oct 1 2015 - p73(1) [51-500]
c KR - August 15 2015 - pNA [51-500]
y PW - v262 - i32 - August 10 2015 - p62(1) [51-500]
y PW - v262 - i49 - Dec 2 2015 - p110(1) [51-500]
y SLJ - v61 - i10 - Oct 2015 - p108(1) [51-500]
y VOYA - v38 - i5 - Dec 2015 - p54(1) [51-500]
Buckley, Carla - *The Good Goodbye*
BL - v112 - i7 - Dec 1 2015 - p28(2) [51-500]
PW - v262 - i44 - Nov 2 2015 - p59(1) [51-500]
Buckley, Christopher - *The Relic Master*
NYTBR - Dec 13 2015 - p17(L) [501+]
KR - Nov 15 2015 - pNA [51-500]
NYT - Dec 31 2015 - pC7(L) [501+]
Buckley, Cornelius Michael - *Stephen Larigaudelle Dubuisson, S.J. (1786-1864), and the Reform of the American Jesuits*
CHR - v101 - i4 - Autumn 2015 - p952(2) [501+]
Buckley, David - *Kraftwerk: Publikation*
LJ - v140 - i17 - Oct 15 2015 - p86(1) [51-500]
Buckley, Fiona - *A Perilous Alliance*
PW - v262 - i35 - August 31 2015 - p64(2) [51-500]
Buckley, Frank - *The Once and Future King: The Rise of Crown Government in America*
IndRev - v19 - i4 - Spring 2015 - p618(5) [501+]
Buckley, Gail Lumet - *The Black Calhouns: From Civil War to Civil Rights with One African American Family*
KR - Nov 1 2015 - pNA [501+]
LJ - v140 - i19 - Nov 15 2015 - p92(1) [51-500]
PW - v262 - i47 - Nov 23 2015 - p59(1) [51-500]
Buckley, James, Jr. - *Animals: A Visual Encyclopedia*
c BL - v112 - i7 - Dec 1 2015 - p48(2) [51-500]
Math
y BL - v111 - i17 - May 1 2015 - p88(1) [51-500]
Technology
y BL - v111 - i17 - May 1 2015 - p88(1) [51-500]
Buckley, James L. - *Saving Congress from Itself: Emancipating the States and Empowering Their People*
Nat R - v67 - i3 - Feb 23 2015 - p44 [501+]
Buckley, Jay H. - *Historical Dictionary of the American Frontier*
BL - v112 - i2 - Sept 15 2015 - p12(1) [51-500]
LJ - v140 - i14 - Sept 1 2015 - p144(1) [51-500]
Buckley, John - *Monty's Men: The British Army and the Liberation of Europe, 1944-5*
AHR - v120 - i1 - Feb 2015 - p335-336 [501+]
Buckley, Michael - *Raging Sea*
y KR - Dec 15 2015 - pNA [51-500]
Undertow (Read by Grace, Jennifer). Audiobook Review
y BL - v112 - i7 - Dec 1 2015 - p72(1) [51-500]
y SLJ - v61 - i9 - Sept 2015 - p60(1) [51-500]
Undertow
y CCB-B - v69 - i1 - Sept 2015 - p15(1) [51-500]
y HB Guide - v26 - i2 - Fall 2015 - p113(1) [51-500]
y PW - v262 - i13 - March 30 2015 - p77(1) [51-500]
y SLJ - v61 - i2 - Feb 2015 - p98(2) [51-500]
y BL - v111 - i13 - March 1 2015 - p60(1) [51-500]
y CH Bwatch - June 2015 - pNA [51-500]
y KR - March 1 2015 - pNA [51-500]
y VOYA - v37 - i6 - Feb 2015 - p72(1) [51-500]
Buckley, Thomas E. - *Establishing Religious Freedom: Jefferson's Statute in Virginia*
JSH - v81 - i4 - Nov 2015 - p956(3) [501+]
Buckley, William F., Jr. - *Did You Ever See a Dream Walking? American Conservative Thought in the Twentieth Century*
Nat R - v67 - i21 - Nov 19 2015 - p76(2) [501+]
Bucklow, Spike - *The Riddle of the Image: The Secret Science of Medieval Art*
Med R - June 2015 - pNA [501+]
Bucko, Adam - *Occupy Spirituality: A Radical Vision for a New Generation*
AM - v212 - i10 - March 23 2015 - p36(3) [501+]
Bucossi, Alessandra - *Andronicus Camaterus*
HNet - March 2015 - pNA [501+]
Med R - August 2015 - pNA [501+]
Budde, Nadia - *Bristly Hair and I Don't Care! (Illus. by Budde, Nadia)*
c HB Guide - v26 - i2 - Fall 2015 - p28(1) [51-500]
Bude, John - *The Sussex Downs Murder*
BL - v111 - i17 - May 1 2015 - p46(1) [51-500]
Budiansky, Stephen - *Mad Music: Charles Ives, the Nostalgic Rebel*
Notes - v72 - i2 - Dec 2015 - p351(3) [501+]
Budig, Bridget Hoolihan - *My World Is Over: The Day it All Went Dark*
y CH Bwatch - Feb 2015 - pNA [51-500]
Budzik, Mary - *Mythology: Oh My! Gods and Goddesses*
c HB Guide - v26 - i1 - Spring 2015 - p143(1) [51-500]
Buehner, Caralyn - *Merry Christmas, Mr. Mouse (Illus. by Buehner, Mark)*
c KR - Sept 1 2015 - pNA [51-500]
c PW - v262 - i37 - Sept 14 2015 - p64(1) [51-500]
c SLJ - v61 - i10 - Oct 2015 - p61(1) [51-500]
Buelens, Geert - *Everything to Nothing: The Poetry of the Great War, Revolution and the Transformation of Europe*
TimHES - i2229 - Nov 12 2015 - p44-45 [501+]
Buelens, Gert - *The Future of Trauma Theory: Contemporary Literary and Cultural Criticism*
Stud Hum - v41 - i1-2 - March 2015 - p255(3) [501+]
Buell, Lawrence - *The Dream of the Great American Novel*
JAH - v102 - i2 - Sept 2015 - p520-521 [501+]
Nine-C Lit - v69 - i4 - March 2015 - p539(5) [501+]
RAH - v43 - i2 - June 2015 - p294-299 [501+]
Sew R - v123 - i2 - Spring 2015 - pXVIII-XIX [501+]
Soc - v52 - i4 - August 2015 - p398(4) [501+]
Buelow, Beth L. - *The Introvert Entrepreneur: Amplify Your Strengths and Create Success On Your Own Terms*
BL - v112 - i4 - Oct 15 2015 - p8(1) [51-500]
PW - v262 - i36 - Sept 7 2015 - p59(1) [51-500]
Bueno, Carlos - *Lauren Ipsum: A Story about Computer Science and Other Improbable Things (Illus. by Lipovaca, Miran)*
c BL - v111 - i18 - May 15 2015 - p56(1) [51-500]
Buettner, Dan - *The Blue Zones Solution: Eating and Living Like the World's Healthiest People*
LJ - v140 - i6 - April 1 2015 - p110(2) [51-500]

Buffery, Helena - *Barcelona: Visual Culture, Space and Power*
   MLR - v110 - i1 - Jan 2015 - p278-281 [501+]

Buffington, Robert M. - *A Global History of Sexuality: The Modern Era*
   HNet - March 2015 - pNA [501+]

Buffon, Georges-Louis Leclerc de - *Oeuvres completes, vol. 5: Histoire naturelle, generale et particuliere, avec la description du Cabinet du Roi*
   Isis - v106 - i1 - March 2015 - p187(2) [501+]
Oeuvres completes, vol. 7: Histoire naturelle, generale et particuliere, avec la description du Cabinet du Roi
   Isis - v106 - i1 - March 2015 - p187(2) [501+]

Bugler, Beth - *My First Book of Football (Illus. by Hinds, Bill)*
   c CH Bwatch - Nov 2015 - pNA [51-500]
   c SLJ - v61 - i11 - Nov 2015 - p129(2) [51-500]

Buhl, Sarah - *Dear Elizabeth: A Play in Letters from Elizabeth Bishop to Robert Lowell and Back Again (Read by Williams, JoBeth). Audiobook Review*
   BL - v112 - i7 - Dec 1 2015 - p68(1) [51-500]

Buhler, Walter - *Musikalische Skalen bei Naturwissenschaftlern der fruhen Neuzeit: Eine elementarmathematische Analyse*
   Isis - v106 - i2 - June 2015 - p442(3) [501+]

Buhmann, Elizabeth - *Lay Death at Her Door*
   PW - v262 - i32 - August 10 2015 - p41(1) [51-500]
   PW - v262 - i34 - August 24 2015 - p53(1) [51-500]

Buitrago, Jairo - *El edificio (Illus. by Rabanal, Daniel)*
   c Bkbird - v53 - i4 - Fall 2015 - p77(1) [501+]
Two White Rabbits (Illus. by Yockteng, Rafael)
   c BL - v112 - i3 - Oct 1 2015 - p84(1) [51-500]
   c CH Bwatch - Nov 2015 - pNA [51-500]
   c KR - Sept 1 2015 - pNA [51-500]
   c PW - v262 - i35 - August 31 2015 - p89(2) [51-500]
   c PW - v262 - i49 - Dec 2 2015 - p22(1) [51-500]
   c Res Links - v21 - i1 - Oct 2015 - p3(1) [51-500]
   c SLJ - v61 - i7 - July 2015 - p60(1) [51-500]

Bujold, Lois McMaster - *Gentleman Jole and the Red Queen*
   PW - v262 - i52 - Dec 21 2015 - p137(1) [51-500]

Buk-Swienty, Tom - *1864: The Forgotten War That Shaped Modern Europe*
   TLS - i5851 - May 22 2015 - p30(1) [501+]

Bukowski, Charles - *The Bell Tolls for No One*
   KR - June 15 2015 - pNA [51-500]
   PW - v262 - i24 - June 15 2015 - p59(1) [51-500]
   TLS - i5867 - Sept 11 2015 - p26(1) [501+]
On Cats
   KR - June 15 2015 - pNA [51-500]
On Writing
   PW - v262 - i21 - May 25 2015 - p51(1) [51-500]
   KR - June 1 2015 - pNA [501+]
   LJ - v140 - i11 - June 15 2015 - p86(2) [51-500]
   NYT - August 10 2015 - pC4(L) [501+]

Bukuru, Zacharie - *We Are All Children of God: The Story of the Forty Young Martyrs of Buta-Burundi*
   AM - v213 - i18 - Dec 7 2015 - p41(4) [501+]

Bulatovic, Marija - *Fantastical: Tales of Bears, Beer and Hemophilia*
   RVBW - March 2015 - pNA [51-500]

Bulawayo, NoViolet - *We Need New Names*
   TimHES - i2216 - August 13 2015 - p43(1) [501+]

Bulhak-Paterson, Danuta - *I Am an Aspie Girl: A Book for Young Girls with Autism Spectrum Conditions (Illus. by Ferguson, Teresa)*
   c CH Bwatch - August 2015 - pNA [51-500]

Bulion, Leslie - *Random Body Parts: Gross Anatomy Riddles in Verse (Illus. by Lowery, Mike)*
   c HB Guide - v26 - i2 - Fall 2015 - p183(1) [51-500]
   c BL - v111 - i14 - March 15 2015 - p61(1) [51-500]
   c KR - Jan 15 2015 - pNA [51-500]
   c PW - v262 - i6 - Feb 9 2015 - p69(1) [51-500]
   c SLJ - v61 - i3 - March 2015 - p169(1) [51-500]
Where Is Fluffy? (Illus. by Ho, Jannie)
   c CH Bwatch - May 2015 - pNA [51-500]
   c KR - July 1 2015 - pNA [51-500]
   c PW - v262 - i15 - April 13 2015 - p78(2) [51-500]

Bull, Andy - *Speed Kings: The 1932 Winter Olympics and the Fastest Men in the World*
   KR - August 15 2015 - pNA [501+]
   LJ - v140 - i16 - Oct 1 2015 - p80(1) [51-500]
   NS - v144 - i5281 - Sept 25 2015 - p71(1) [501+]
   TLS - i5877 - Nov 20 2015 - p34(1) [501+]

Bull, Anna Cento - *Ending Terrorism in Italy*
   HNet - Feb 2015 - pNA [501+]

Bull, Marcus - *Writing the Early Crusades: Text, Transmission and Memory*
   AHR - v120 - i3 - June 2015 - p1090-1091 [501+]
   Med R - April 2015 - pNA [501+]

Bull, Martin - *This Is Not a Photo Opportunity: The Street Art of Banksy*
   LJ - v140 - i6 - April 1 2015 - p96(1) [501+]

Bull, Melissa - *Rue*
   Nat Post - v17 - i188 - June 13 2015 - pWP4(1) [501+]

Bullard, Alan - *Joining the Dots: A Fresh Approach to Piano Sight-Reading, vols. 6-8*
   Am MT - v64 - i5 - April-May 2015 - p48(1) [501+]

Bullard, Lisa - *I'm a Midnight Snacker! Meet a Vampire (Illus. by Buccheri, Chiara)*
   c HB Guide - v26 - i1 - Spring 2015 - p143(1) [51-500]
I'm Fearsome and Furry! Meet a Werewolf (Illus. by Moran, Mike)
   c HB Guide - v26 - i1 - Spring 2015 - p143(1) [51-500]
My Clothes, Your Clothes (Illus. by Kurilla, Renee)
   c SLJ - v61 - i4 - April 2015 - p72(4) [501+]
   c HB Guide - v26 - i2 - Fall 2015 - p156(1) [51-500]
My Family, Your Family (Illus. by Kurilla, Renee)
   c HB Guide - v26 - i2 - Fall 2015 - p151(1) [51-500]
My Food, Your Food (Illus. by Schneider, Christine M.)
   c HB Guide - v26 - i2 - Fall 2015 - p188(1) [51-500]
My Home, Your Home (Illus. by Becker, Paula)
   c HB Guide - v26 - i2 - Fall 2015 - p156(1) [51-500]
My Language, Your Language
   c HB Guide - v26 - i2 - Fall 2015 - p162(1) [51-500]
My Religion, Your Religion (Illus. by Conger, Holli)
   c HB Guide - v26 - i2 - Fall 2015 - p149(1) [51-500]

Buller, Jeffrey L. - *A Toolkit for Department Chairs*
   VOYA - v38 - i5 - Dec 2015 - p82(1) [51-500]

Bullivant, Stephen - *The Oxford Handbook of Atheism*
   Rel St - v51 - i4 - Dec 2015 - p583-586 [501+]

Bulloch, Jamie - *Raw Material*
   TLS - i5835 - Jan 30 2015 - p20(1) [51-500]

Bullock, David - *Coal Wars: Unions, Strikes, and Violence in Depression-Era Central Washington*
   RVBW - Jan 2015 - pNA [501+]
   WHQ - v46 - i3 - Autumn 2015 - p390-390 [501+]

Bullock, Joe S. - *Walking with Herb: A Spiritual Golfing Journey to the Masters*
   c BL - v112 - i7 - Dec 1 2015 - p34(2) [51-500]

Bulthuis, Kyle T. - *Four Steeples Over the City Streets: Religion and Society in New York's Early Republic Congregations*
   CH - v84 - i4 - Dec 2015 - p893(3) [501+]
   W&M Q - v72 - i3 - July 2015 - p523-526 [501+]

Bumgarner, Jeff - *Profiling and Criminal Justice in America, 2d ed.*
   BL - v111 - i16 - April 15 2015 - p12(1) [51-500]

Bumpus, Carole - *A Cup of Redemption*
   KR - Sept 15 2015 - pNA [51-500]

Bums and Tums (Illus. by Foot, Mandy)
   c Magpies - v30 - i2 - May 2015 - p27(1) [51-500]

Bundesrepublik. Politische und Intellektuelle Allianzen im Jahrhundert der Aufklarung
   HNet - March 2015 - pNA [501+]

Bundock, Michael - *The Fortunes of Francis Barber: The True Story of the Jamaican Slave Who Became Samuel Johnson's Heir*
   Lon R Bks - v37 - i14 - July 16 2015 - p21(3) [501+]
   NS - v144 - i5263 - May 22 2015 - p45(1) [501+]
   PW - v262 - i4 - Jan 26 2015 - p160(1) [51-500]
   TLS - i5861 - July 31 2015 - p8(2) [501+]
   Spec - v328 - i9743 - May 23 2015 - p42(2) [501+]

Bunjevac, Nina - *Fatherland: A Family History (Illus. by Bunjevac, Nina)*
   NYTBR - Feb 22 2015 - p12(L) [501+]
   WLT - v89 - i5 - Sept-Oct 2015 - p74(2) [501+]

Bunker, Jack - *True Grift*
   BL - v112 - i3 - Oct 1 2015 - p28(2) [51-500]
   PW - v262 - i39 - Sept 28 2015 - p68(2) [51-500]

Bunker, Nick - *An Empire on the Edge: How Britain Came to Fight America*
   TLS - i5852 - May 29 2015 - p8(1) [501+]

Bunker, Steven B. - *Creating Mexican Consumer Culture in the Age of Porfirio Diaz*
   BHR - v89 - i2 - Summer 2015 - p381(3) [501+]

Bunn, Austin - *The Brink*
   KR - Feb 15 2015 - pNA [51-500]
   PW - v262 - i8 - Feb 23 2015 - p47(2) [51-500]
   PW - v262 - i11 - March 16 2015 - p44(2) [51-500]
   BL - v111 - i13 - March 1 2015 - p17(1) [51-500]

Bunn, Bill - *Kill Shot*
   KR - Feb 1 2015 - pNA [51-500]

Bunn, Cullen - *Terrible Lizard (Illus. by Moss, Drew)*
   c SLJ - v61 - i9 - Sept 2015 - p148(1) [51-500]

Bunnell, Tim - *Cleavage, Connection and Conflict in Rural, Urban and Contemporary Asia*
   Pac A - v88 - i1 - March 2015 - p156 [501+]

Bunten, Alexis C. - *So, How Long Have You Been Native? Life as an Alaska Native Tour Guide*
   KR - Jan 1 2015 - pNA [501+]
   PW - v262 - i2 - Jan 12 2015 - p52(1) [51-500]

Bunting, Eve - *Forbidden*
   y BL - v112 - i6 - Nov 15 2015 - p50(1) [51-500]
   y KR - Oct 1 2015 - pNA [51-500]
   y PW - v262 - i39 - Sept 28 2015 - p93(1) [51-500]
   y SLJ - v61 - i9 - Sept 2015 - p157(2) [51-500]
   y VOYA - v38 - i5 - Dec 2015 - p66(2) [51-500]
Frog and Friends Celebrate Thanksgiving, Christmas, and New Year's Eve
   c KR - Sept 1 2015 - pNA [51-500]
Mr. Goat's Valentine (Illus. by Zimmer, Kevin)
   c KR - Nov 15 2015 - pNA [51-500]
   c PW - v262 - i41 - Oct 12 2015 - p66(2) [501+]
P Is for Pirate: A Pirate Alphabet (Illus. by Manders, John)
   c HB Guide - v26 - i1 - Spring 2015 - p200(1) [51-500]
Washday (Read by Cottle, Elizabeth). Audiobook Review
   SLJ - v61 - i4 - April 2015 - p60(1) [51-500]
Whose Shoe? (Illus. by Ruzzier, Sergio)
   c BL - v111 - i19-20 - June 1 2015 - p125(1) [51-500]
   c CH Bwatch - July 2015 - pNA [51-500]
   c HB Guide - v26 - i2 - Fall 2015 - p7(1) [51-500]
   KR - April 1 2015 - pNA [51-500]
   c SLJ - v61 - i5 - May 2015 - p78(1) [51-500]
Yard Sale (Illus. by Castillo, Lauren)
   c BL - v111 - i15 - April 1 2015 - p84(1) [51-500]
   c CCB-B - v68 - i11 - July-August 2015 - p539(1) [51-500]
   c HB - v91 - i2 - March-April 2015 - p71(1) [51-500]
   c HB Guide - v26 - i2 - Fall 2015 - p28(1) [51-500]
   c KR - Feb 1 2015 - pNA [51-500]
   c PW - v262 - i6 - Feb 9 2015 - p64(2) [51-500]

Bunyan, John - *Pilgrim's Progress*
   SPBW - March 2015 - pNA [51-500]

Burach, Ross - *There's a Giraffe in My Soup (Illus. by Burach, Ross)*
   c KR - Oct 15 2015 - pNA [51-500]

Burack, Emilie Christie - *The Runaway's Gold*
   c BL - v111 - i16 - April 15 2015 - p60(1) [51-500]
   c HB Guide - v26 - i2 - Fall 2015 - p77(1) [51-500]
   c KR - March 1 2015 - pNA [51-500]
   c SLJ - v61 - i2 - Feb 2015 - p84(1) [51-500]

Burack-Weiss, Ann - *The Lioness in Winter: Writing an Old Woman's Life*
   PW - v262 - i30 - July 27 2015 - p54(2) [51-500]

Burakov, Alexander - *The Beslan Massacre: Myths & Facts*
   KR - May 15 2015 - pNA [501+]

Burakowski, Ella - *Hidden Gold: A True Story of the Holocaust*
   y BL - v112 - i5 - Nov 1 2015 - p39(1) [51-500]
   y VOYA - v38 - i5 - Dec 2015 - p76(2) [501+]
   y KR - August 1 2015 - pNA [51-500]
   y PW - v262 - i32 - August 10 2015 - p63(1) [51-500]
   y SLJ - v61 - i10 - Oct 2015 - p100(1) [51-500]

Burbank, James - *The Oxbow Poems*
   KR - August 15 2015 - pNA [51-500]

Burbank, Lucille - *Secrets from Sesame Street's Pioneers: How They Produced a Successful Television Series*
   RVBW - July 2015 - pNA [51-500]

Burbridge, John - *Cause for Thought: An Essay in Metaphysics*
   RM - v69 - i1 - Sept 2015 - p122(2) [501+]

Burcaw, Shane - *Laughing at My Nightmare*
   y HB Guide - v26 - i1 - Spring 2015 - p191(1) [51-500]

Burcell, Robin - *The Last Good Place*
   PW - v262 - i37 - Sept 14 2015 - p45(1) [51-500]

Burch, Heather - *Along the Broken Road*
   PW - v262 - i15 - April 13 2015 - p63(2) [51-500]
Summer by Summer
   y SLJ - v61 - i6 - June 2015 - p110(1) [51-500]

Burch, Melissa - *My Journey through War and Peace: Explorations of a Young Filmmaker, Feminist and Spiritual Seeker*
   KR - Dec 1 2015 - pNA [501+]

Burch, Noel - *The Battle of the Sexes in French Cinema, 1930-1956*
AHR - v120 - i2 - April 2015 - p727-728 [501+]
Burchett, Dave - *Stay: Lessons My Dogs Taught Me About Life, Loss, and Grace*
PW - v262 - i3 - Jan 19 2015 - p77(2) [51-500]
Burchik, Steven - *Compass and a Camera*
KR - March 15 2015 - pNA [501+]
Burchill, John K. - *Bullets, Badges, and Bridles: Horse Thieves and the Societies That Pursued Them*
Roundup M - v22 - i6 - August 2015 - p34(2) [501+]
Burda-Stengel, Felix - *Andrea Pozzo and Video Art*
Six Ct J - v46 - i3 - Fall 2015 - p780-781 [501+]
Theol St - v76 - i1 - March 2015 - p228(1) [501+]
BurdaStyle, Inc. - *BurdaStyle Modern Sewing: Wardrobe Essentials*
LJ - v140 - i3 - Feb 15 2015 - p99(1) [51-500]
Burden, Robert - *Travel, Modernism and Modernity*
TLS - i5864-5865 - August 21 2015 - p35(1) [501+]
Burdett, John - *The Bangkok Asset*
BL - v111 - i22 - August 1 2015 - p31(1) [51-500]
PW - v262 - i26 - June 29 2015 - p46(1) [51-500]
Burdick, John - *The Color of Sound: Race, Religion, and Music in Brazil*
ERS - v38 - i3 - March 2015 - p531(2) [501+]
Bure, Candace Cameron - *Dancing through Life*
PW - v262 - i27 - July 6 2015 - p66(1) [51-500]
Burfoot, Ella - *How to Bake a Book (Illus. by Burfoot, Ella)*
c CH Bwatch - April 2015 - pNA [51-500]
Recipe for a Story
c Sch Lib - v63 - i3 - Autumn 2015 - p153(1) [51-500]
Burgan, Michael - *Shadow Catcher: How Edward S. Curtis Documented American Indian Dignity and Beauty*
c BL - v111 - i19-20 - June 1 2015 - p92(1) [51-500]
c HB Guide - v26 - i2 - Fall 2015 - p222(1) [51-500]
Sidney Crosby
c BL - v111 - i19-20 - June 1 2015 - p92(1) [51-500]
c HB Guide - v26 - i2 - Fall 2015 - p197(1) [51-500]
The Untold Story of the Battle of Saratoga: A Turning Point in the Revolutionary War
c HB Guide - v26 - i2 - Fall 2015 - p219(1) [51-500]
The Untold Story of the Black Regiment: Fighting in the Revolutionary War
c HB Guide - v26 - i2 - Fall 2015 - p219(1) [51-500]
The Voting Rights Act of 1965: An Interactive History Adventure
c HB Guide - v26 - i2 - Fall 2015 - p152(1) [51-500]
Burge, Kimberly - *The Born Frees: Writing with the Girls of Gugulethu*
y BL - v111 - i19-20 - June 1 2015 - p22(2) [51-500]
KR - June 15 2015 - pNA [501+]
LJ - v140 - i10 - June 1 2015 - p124(2) [51-500]
PW - v262 - i20 - May 18 2015 - p76(2) [51-500]
Burger, Deborah - *Complete Photo Guide to Crochet*
Bwatch - Sept 2015 - pNA [51-500]
c CH Bwatch - Oct 2015 - pNA [51-500]
Burger, Michael - *Bishops, Clerks, and Diocesan Governance in Thirteenth-Century England: Reward and Punishment*
Historian - v77 - i1 - Spring 2015 - p161(2) [501+]
Burgess, Anthony - *A Clockwork Orange*
NS - v144 - i5282 - Oct 2 2015 - p74(2) [501+]
Burgess, Gemma - *The Wild One*
PW - v262 - i37 - Sept 14 2015 - p49(1) [51-500]
Burgess, Matt - *Uncle Janice (Read by Fulginiti, Rachel). Audiobook Review*
PW - v262 - i5 - Feb 2 2015 - p52(1) [51-500]
Burgess, Matthew - *Enormous Smallness: A Story of E.E. Cummings (Illus. by Di Giacomo, Kris)*
c BL - v111 - i19-20 - June 1 2015 - p83(2) [51-500]
Enormous Smallness: A Story of E. E. Cummings (Illus. by Di Giacomo, Kris)
c CH Bwatch - May 2015 - pNA [51-500]
c SLJ - v61 - i5 - May 2015 - p130(1) [51-500]
Enormous Smallness: A Story of E.E. Cummings (Illus. by Di Giacomo, Kris)
c HB Guide - v26 - i2 - Fall 2015 - p207(1) [51-500]
c KR - March 1 2015 - pNA [501+]
Burgess, Melvin - *The Hit (Read by Roukin, Samuel). Audiobook Review*
y BL - v111 - i9-10 - Jan 1 2015 - p118(1) [51-500]
The Hit
y Teach Lib - v42 - i3 - Feb 2015 - p28(4) [501+]
Persist (Illus. by Brett, Cathy)
y Sch Lib - v63 - i3 - Autumn 2015 - p179(1) [51-500]

Burgess, Richard W. - *Roman Imperial Chronology and Early-Fourth-Century Historiography: The Regnal Durations of the So-Called "Chronica urbis Romae" of the "Chronograph of 354"*
HNet - March 2015 - pNA [501+]
Burgin, Michael - *Bram Stoker's Dracula: A Graphic Novel (Illus. by Alfonso, Jose)*
y HB Guide - v26 - i1 - Spring 2015 - p72(2) [51-500]
Burgis, Tom - *The Looting Machine*
For Aff - v94 - i4 - July-August 2015 - pNA [501+]
KR - Feb 1 2015 - pNA [501+]
NYTBR - March 22 2015 - p21(L) [501+]
The Looting Machine: Warlords, Tycoons, Smugglers and the Systematic Theft of Africa's Wealth
Econ - v415 - i8933 - April 11 2015 - p76(US) [501+]
Burgo, Joseph - *The Narcissist You Know: Defending Yourself against Extreme Narcissists in an All-about-Me Age*
KR - June 15 2015 - pNA [501+]
NYTBR - Sept 27 2015 - p13(L) [501+]
PW - v262 - i27 - July 6 2015 - p59(1) [51-500]
Burgraff, Roger - *Deacon's Winter*
KR - Jan 1 2015 - pNA [501+]
Burgschwenter, Joachim - *Other Fronts, Other Wars? First World War Studies on the Eve of the Centennial*
J Mil H - v79 - i4 - Oct 2015 - p1131-1133 [501+]
Burgundy, Rosalind - *Odyssey of an Etruscan Noblewoman*
KR - Feb 15 2015 - pNA [501+]
Burillo-Kirch, Christine - *Microbes: Discover an Unseen World with 25 Projects (Illus. by Casteel, Tom)*
c BL - v112 - i5 - Nov 1 2015 - p44(1) [51-500]
Burk, Graeme - *The Doctors Are In: The Essential and Unofficial Guide to Doctor Who's Greatest Time Lord*
LJ - v140 - i14 - Sept 1 2015 - p102(2) [51-500]
Burk, Robert F. - *Marvin Miller: Baseball Revolutionary*
LJ - v140 - i3 - Feb 15 2015 - p103(2) [501+]
Burkard, Dominik - *Der Jansenismus--eine "katholische Haresie"? Das Ringen um Gnade, Rechtfertigung und die Autoritat Augustins in der fruhen Neuzeit*
Theol St - v76 - i3 - Sept 2015 - p610(2) [501+]
Burke, Alafair - *All Day and a Night*
RVBW - Feb 2015 - pNA [501+]
RVBW - July 2015 - pNA [501+]
All Dressed in White
BL - v112 - i6 - Nov 15 2015 - p24(1) [51-500]
The Cinderella Murder
RVBW - Sept 2015 - pNA [501+]
The Ex
BL - v112 - i7 - Dec 1 2015 - p28(1) [51-500]
KR - Nov 1 2015 - pNA [501+]
Burke, Colin B. - *Information and Intrigue: From Index Cards to Dewey Decimals to Alger Hiss*
JAH - v102 - i1 - June 2015 - p276-277 [501+]
Burke, Declan - *The Lost and the Blind*
BL - v111 - i13 - March 1 2015 - p24(1) [51-500]
KR - March 1 2015 - pNA [501+]
PW - v262 - i13 - March 30 2015 - p56(1) [51-500]
Burke, Edmund - *Reflections on the Revolution in France*
Nat R - v67 - i21 - Nov 19 2015 - p76(1) [501+]
Burke, Glen Alan - *Jesse*
RVBW - Sept 2015 - pNA [501+]
Burke, James Lee - *House of the Rising Sun*
BL - v112 - i6 - Nov 15 2015 - p25(1) [51-500]
KR - Sept 15 2015 - pNA [501+]
LJ - v140 - i16 - Oct 1 2015 - p66(1) [51-500]
Wayfaring Stranger
AM - v212 - i13 - April 13 2015 - p35(3) [501+]
RVBW - May 2015 - pNA [501+]
Burke, Jason - *The New Threat from Islamic Militancy*
Econ - v416 - i8953 - August 29 2015 - p69(US) [501+]
The New Threat: The Past, Present, and Future of Islamic Militancy
KR - Sept 15 2015 - pNA [501+]
PW - v262 - i39 - Sept 28 2015 - p82(1) [51-500]
Burke, Monte - *Saban: The Making of a Coach*
KR - June 15 2015 - pNA [501+]
PW - v262 - i28 - July 13 2015 - p62(1) [51-500]
BL - v111 - i19-20 - June 1 2015 - p34(1) [51-500]
Burke, Peter - *Year-Round Indoor Salad Gardening: How to Grow Nutrient-Dense, Soil-Sprouted Greens in Less Than 10 Days*
LJ - v140 - i14 - Sept 1 2015 - p128(1) [51-500]
PW - v262 - i29 - July 20 2015 - p186(1) [51-500]

Burke, Roland - *Decolonization and the Evolution of International Human Rights*
ABR - v36 - i4 - May-June 2015 - p10(1) [501+]
Burke, Shannon - *Into the Savage Country*
NYTBR - August 16 2015 - p30(L) [501+]
Burke, Sue - *Prodigies*
KR - June 15 2015 - pNA [501+]
PW - v262 - i20 - May 18 2015 - p58(1) [51-500]
Burke, Zoe - *Charley Harper's Count the Birds (Illus. by Harper, Charley)*
c PW - v262 - i49 - Dec 2 2015 - p56(1) [51-500]
c PW - v262 - i31 - August 3 2015 - p58(2) [501+]
Charley Harper's What's in the Coral Reef?: A Nature Discovery Book (Illus. by Harper, Charley)
c HB Guide - v26 - i1 - Spring 2015 - p154(1) [51-500]
No Gun Intended
BL - v112 - i5 - Nov 1 2015 - p31(2) [51-500]
KR - Nov 1 2015 - pNA [51-500]
PW - v262 - i44 - Nov 2 2015 - p63(1) [51-500]
Burkett, Paul - *Marx and Nature: A Red and Green Perspective*
CS - v44 - i3 - May 2015 - p314-321 [501+]
Burkey, John M. - *The Hearing-Loss Guide: Useful Information and Advice for Patients and Families*
BL - v111 - i13 - March 1 2015 - p10(1) [51-500]
RVBW - June 2015 - pNA [501+]
Burkey, Roxanne E. - *The Enigma Stolen*
KR - August 1 2015 - pNA [501+]
Burkhardt, Frederick - *The Correspondence of Charles Darwin*
QRB - v90 - i3 - Sept 2015 - p318(1) [501+]
Burkhardt, Stefan - *Mediterranes Kaisertum und imperiale Ordnungen: Das lateinische Kaiserreich von Konstantinopel*
Med R - Sept 2015 - pNA [501+]
Burkhart, Jessica - *Bella's Birthday Unicorn (Illus. by Ying, Victoria)*
c HB Guide - v26 - i1 - Spring 2015 - p57(1) [51-500]
The Hidden Treasure (Illus. by Ying, Victoria)
c HB Guide - v26 - i2 - Fall 2015 - p64(1) [51-500]
Where's Glimmer? (Illus. by Ying, Victoria)
c HB Guide - v26 - i1 - Spring 2015 - p57(1) [51-500]
Wild Hearts
y HB Guide - v26 - i2 - Fall 2015 - p113(1) [51-500]
y KR - March 1 2015 - pNA [51-500]
Burkhart, Louise M. - *Aztecs on Stage: Religious Theater in Colonial Mexico*
CHR - v101 - i2 - Spring 2015 - p398(2) [501+]
Burkholder, Andy - *Qviet*
PW - v262 - i26 - June 29 2015 - p54(1) [51-500]
Burkinshaw, Paula - *Higher Education, Leadership and Women Vice Chancellors: Fitting in to Communities of Practice of Masculinities*
TimHES - i2215 - August 6 2015 - p49-49 [501+]
Burks, James - *Bird & Squirrel on the Edge! (Illus. by Burks, James)*
c BL - v112 - i4 - Oct 15 2015 - p37(1) [51-500]
c KR - August 15 2015 - pNA [51-500]
c SLJ - v61 - i9 - Sept 2015 - p148(1) [51-500]
Burleigh, Robert - *Edward Hopper Paints His World (Illus. by Minor, Wendell)*
c HB Guide - v26 - i1 - Spring 2015 - p178(1) [51-500]
Solving the Puzzle Under the Sea: Marie Tharp Maps the Ocean Floor (Illus. by Colon, Raul)
c BL - v112 - i7 - Dec 1 2015 - p51(1) [51-500]
c KR - Oct 1 2015 - pNA [51-500]
c PW - v262 - i51 - Dec 14 2015 - p82(2) [501+]
c SLJ - v61 - i12 - Dec 2015 - p135(2) [51-500]
Trapped! A Whale's Rescue (Illus. by Minor, Wendell)
c BL - v111 - i17 - May 1 2015 - p86(1) [51-500]
c CH Bwatch - July 2015 - pNA [51-500]
c HB Guide - v26 - i2 - Fall 2015 - p179(1) [51-500]
c KR - Feb 15 2015 - pNA [51-500]
Magpies - v30 - i3 - July 2015 - p24(1) [501+]
c SLJ - v61 - i3 - March 2015 - p169(2) [51-500]
Burlingame, Jeff - *50 Cent: Hip-Hop Mogul*
c HB Guide - v26 - i1 - Spring 2015 - p191(1) [51-500]
Eminem: Hip-Hop Mogul
c HB Guide - v26 - i1 - Spring 2015 - p191(1) [51-500]
How to Camp like a Pro
c HB Guide - v26 - i1 - Spring 2015 - p183(1) [51-500]
How to Freshwater Fish like a Pro
c HB Guide - v26 - i1 - Spring 2015 - p183(1) [51-500]

Kanye West: Hip-Hop Mogul
   c HB Guide - v26 - i1 - Spring 2015 - p191(1) [51-500]
Burlingame, Lloyd - *A Blessing Well Disguised: A Blinded Artist's Inner Journey out of the Dark*
   SPBW - Feb 2015 - pNA [51-500]
Burlingham, Abi - *Grub in Love (Illus. by Warburton, Sarah)*
   c KR - Nov 1 2015 - pNA [51-500]
   c PW - v262 - i41 - Oct 12 2015 - p66(2) [501+]
Ruby and Grub (Illus. by Warburton, Sarah)
   c KR - April 15 2015 - pNA [51-500]
   c SLJ - v61 - i9 - Sept 2015 - p116(1) [51-500]
Burnell, Cerrie - *Mermaid (Illus. by Anderson, Laura Ellen)*
   c Sch Lib - v63 - i3 - Autumn 2015 - p153(1) [51-500]
Burnett, Guy F. - *The Safeguard of Liberty and Property: The Supreme Court, Kelo v. New London, and the Takings Clause*
   Soc - v52 - i2 - April 2015 - p181(1) [501+]
Burnett, Jason Bige - *Graphic Clay: Ceramic Surfaces and Printed Image Transfer Techniques*
   LJ - v140 - i11 - June 15 2015 - p86(1) [51-500]
Burnett, W.R. - *Little Men, Big World / Vanity Row*
   BL - v111 - i17 - May 1 2015 - p40(1) [51-500]
Burnette, W.E. - *The Requiem Shark*
   KR - Dec 15 2015 - pNA [501+]
Burnham, Cathleen - *Doyli to the Rescue: Saving Baby Monkeys in the Amazon (Illus. by Burnham, Cathleen)*
   c SLJ - v61 - i7 - July 2015 - p102(1) [51-500]
Doyli to the Rescue: Saving Baby Monkeys in the Amazon
   c CH Bwatch - July 2015 - pNA [51-500]
Burnham, James - *Suicide of the West: An Essay on the Meaning and Destiny of Liberalism*
   Nat R - v67 - i5 - March 23 2015 - p41 [501+]
Burnham, Karen - *Greg Egan*
   SFS - v42 - i2 - July 2015 - p366-369 [501+]
Burnham, Molly B. - *Teddy Mars: Almost a World Record Breaker (Illus. by Spencer, Trevor)*
   c HB Guide - v26 - i2 - Fall 2015 - p77(1) [51-500]
   PW - v262 - i2 - Jan 12 2015 - p59(2) [501+]
Burnham, Philip - *Song of Dewey Beard*
   Roundup M - v22 - i4 - April 2015 - p28(1) [501+]
   Am St - v54 - i1 - Spring 2015 - p167-2 [501+]
   Roundup M - v22 - i6 - August 2015 - p35(1) [501+]
Burnham, Sophy - *Love, Alba*
   SPBW - Nov 2015 - pNA [51-500]
Burningham, John - *The Way to the Zoo (Illus. by Burningham, John)*
   c HB Guide - v26 - i1 - Spring 2015 - p7(1) [51-500]
Burns, Amy - *Breast Cancer at 35: A Memoir*
   LJ - v140 - i5 - March 15 2015 - p110(1) [501+]
   PW - v262 - i6 - Feb 9 2015 - p61(1) [51-500]
Burns, Andrea A. - *From Storefront to Monument: Tracing the Public History of the Black Museum Movement*
   JAH - v101 - i4 - March 2015 - p1330-1331 [501+]
   LQ - v85 - i2 - April 2015 - p208(4) [501+]
Burns, Carina Sue - *The Syrian Jewelry Box: A Daughter's Journey for Truth*
   RVBW - Nov 2015 - pNA [51-500]
Burns, Carole - *The Missing Woman and Other Stories*
   ABR - v36 - i5 - July-August 2015 - p16(1) [501+]
Burns, Catherine Lloyd - *The Good, the Bad, and the Beagle*
   y HB Guide - v26 - i1 - Spring 2015 - p71(1) [51-500]
Burns, Christa - *Google Search Secrets*
   LQ - v85 - i2 - April 2015 - p211(3) [501+]
Burns, Edward - *Independent Ed: Inside a Career of Big Dreams, Little Movies, and the Twelve Best Days of My Life*
   Bwatch - April 2015 - pNA [51-500]
   Ent W - i1347 - Jan 23 2015 - p65(1) [501+]
Burns, Eric - *1920: The Year That Made the Decade Roar*
   BL - v111 - i18 - May 15 2015 - p12(1) [51-500]
   Bwatch - July 2015 - pNA [51-500]
   CSM - May 19 2015 - pNA [501+]
   KR - Feb 1 2015 - pNA [51-500]
   LJ - v140 - i5 - March 15 2015 - p118(2) [51-500]
   NYTBR - July 5 2015 - p30(L) [51-500]
   PW - v262 - i9 - March 2 2015 - p74(1) [51-500]
The Golden Lad: The Haunting Story of Quentin and Theodore Roosevelt
   KR - Dec 15 2015 - pNA [51-500]
   PW - v262 - i51 - Dec 14 2015 - p71(1) [51-500]

Burns, J. Patout, Jr. - *Christianity in Roman Africa: The Development of Its Practices and Beliefs*
   Theol St - v76 - i4 - Dec 2015 - p840(3) [501+]
Burns, Jennifer - *Migrant Imaginaries: Figures in Italian Migration Literature*
   HNet - Sept 2015 - pNA(NA) [501+]
Burns, Jim - *Pass It On*
   RVBW - Nov 2015 - pNA [51-500]
Burns, Jimmy - *Francis: Pope of Good Promise*
   AM - v213 - i8 - Sept 28 2015 - p41(2) [501+]
   KR - July 15 2015 - pNA [51-500]
   LJ - v140 - i14 - Sept 1 2015 - p108(1) [51-500]
   NS - v144 - i5278 - Sept 4 2015 - p26(4) [501+]
Burns, K.S.R. - *Rules for the Perpetual Diet*
   KR - Jan 15 2015 - pNA [501+]
Burns, Kara M. - *Nutrition and Disease Management for Veterinary Technicians and Nurses*
   RVBW - July 2015 - pNA [501+]
Burns, Kelly - *Cultural Traditions in Kenya*
   Res Links - v21 - i1 - Oct 2015 - p22(1) [501+]
Burns, Laura J. - *Bewitched in Oz*
   c HB Guide - v26 - i1 - Spring 2015 - p72(1) [51-500]
Sanctuary Bay
   y KR - Nov 15 2015 - pNA [51-500]
   y PW - v262 - i44 - Nov 2 2015 - p87(1) [51-500]
   y SLJ - v61 - i12 - Dec 2015 - p118(1) [51-500]
Burns, Loree Griffin - *Beetle Busters: A Rogue Insect and the People Who Track It (Illus. by Harasimowicz, Ellen)*
   c BL - v111 - i9-10 - Jan 1 2015 - pS4(8) [501+]
   c BL - v111 - i12 - Feb 15 2015 - p76(1) [501+]
   c HB - v91 - i1 - Jan-Feb 2015 - p93(2) [51-500]
   c HB Guide - v26 - i1 - Spring 2015 - p158(1) [51-500]
Burns, Lucy Mae San Pablo - *Puro Arte: Filipinos on the Stages of Empire*
   J Am St - v49 - i2 - May 2015 - p446-447 [501+]
Burns, Richard D. - *The Challenges of Nuclear Non-Proliferation*
   Bwatch - Oct 2015 - pNA [51-500]
Burns, Robert P. - *Kafka's Law: The Trial and American Criminal Justice*
   HNet - August 2015 - pNA [501+]
Burns, Susan L. - *Gender and Law in the Japanese Imperium*
   AHR - v120 - i1 - Feb 2015 - p222-224 [501+]
   HNet - Sept 2015 - pNA(NA) [501+]
   Pac A - v88 - i2 - June 2015 - p315 [501+]
Burns, T.R. - *Watch Your Step*
   c HB Guide - v26 - i1 - Spring 2015 - p72(1) [51-500]
Burnside, John - *All One Breath*
   TLS - i5838 - Feb 20 2015 - p22(1) [501+]
Black Cat Bone: Poems
   BL - v111 - i21 - July 1 2015 - p17(1) [51-500]
   LJ - v140 - i12 - July 1 2015 - p87(2) [51-500]
   PW - v262 - i24 - June 15 2015 - p60(1) [51-500]
I Put a Spell on You
   TLS - i5838 - Feb 20 2015 - p22(1) [501+]
Burnsworth, David - *Burning Heat*
   BL - v112 - i2 - Sept 15 2015 - p30(1) [51-500]
   KR - Sept 1 2015 - pNA [51-500]
Buron, Stacy - *Travel Narrative and the Ends of Modernity*
   RES - v66 - i273 - Feb 2015 - p197-200 [501+]
Burr, Trish - *Miniature Needle Painting Embroidery: Vintage Portraits, Florals and Birds*
   LJ - v140 - i7 - April 15 2015 - p89(1) [51-500]
Burrell, Jennifer L. - *Maya after War: Conflict, Power and Politics in Guatemala*
   CS - v44 - i1 - Jan 2015 - p39-40 [501+]
Burrough, Bryan - *Days of Rage: America's Radical Underground, the FBI, and the Forgotten Age of Revolutionary Violence (Read by Porter, Ray). Audiobook Review*
   LJ - v140 - i12 - July 1 2015 - p44(2) [51-500]
Days of Rage: America's Radical Underground, the FBI, and the Forgotten Age of Revolutionary Violence
   NY - v91 - i16 - June 8 2015 - p109 [51-500]
   BL - v111 - i14 - March 15 2015 - p41(1) [51-500]
   CHE - v61 - i38 - June 12 2015 - pB5(1) [51-500]
   HM - v331 - i1985 - Oct 2015 - p90(5) [501+]
   KR - Feb 15 2015 - pNA [51-500]
   LJ - v140 - i5 - March 15 2015 - p119(2) [51-500]
   Nat R - v67 - i9 - May 18 2015 - p41 [501+]
   Nation - v300 - i27 - July 6 2015 - p27(5) [501+]
   NYTBR - May 3 2015 - p14(L) [501+]
   PW - v262 - i8 - Feb 23 2015 - p65(1) [51-500]
   Reason - v47 - i4 - August-Sept 2015 - p72(4) [501+]
Burroughs, Augusten - *Lust & Wonder*
   BL - v112 - i7 - Dec 1 2015 - p10(1) [51-500]
   KR - Dec 15 2015 - pNA [501+]

Burrow, Colin - *Shakespeare and Classical Antiquity*
   Lon R Bks - v37 - i6 - March 19 2015 - p41(4) [501+]
Burrow, John A. - *English Poets in the Late Middle Ages: Chaucer, Langland and Others*
   MLR - v110 - i3 - July 2015 - p808-810 [501+]
Burrow, Rufus, Jr. - *A Child Shall Lead Them: Martin Luther King Jr., Young People, and the Movement*
   JSH - v81 - i4 - Nov 2015 - p1036(2) [501+]
   Theol St - v76 - i3 - Sept 2015 - p631(2) [501+]
Extremist for Love: Martin Luther King Jr., Man of Ideas and Nonviolent Social Action
   CH - v84 - i3 - Sept 2015 - p701(1) [501+]
Burrowes, Grace - *Daniel's True Desire*
   BL - v112 - i4 - Oct 15 2015 - p26(1) [51-500]
   PW - v262 - i38 - Sept 21 2015 - p60(1) [51-500]
The Duke's Disaster
   BL - v111 - i14 - March 15 2015 - p49(1) [51-500]
   PW - v262 - i8 - Feb 23 2015 - p58(2) [51-500]
Kiss Me Hello
   KR - Jan 15 2015 - pNA [51-500]
   PW - v262 - i2 - Jan 12 2015 - p43(1) [51-500]
Tremaine's True Love
   KR - May 15 2015 - pNA [51-500]
   PW - v262 - i22 - June 1 2015 - p47(1) [51-500]
Burrows, Ailsa - *The Jar of Happiness (Illus. by Burrows, Ailsa)*
   c KR - Dec 1 2015 - pNA [51-500]
Burrows, Steve - *A Pitying of Doves*
   BL - v111 - i19-20 - June 1 2015 - p57(1) [51-500]
Bursa, Andrzej - *Killing Auntie*
   WLT - v89 - i6 - Nov-Dec 2015 - p63(1) [51-500]
Burschel, Peter - *Die Erfindung der Reinheit: Eine andere Geschichte der fruhen Neuzeit*
   Six Ct J - v46 - i3 - Fall 2015 - p825-826 [501+]
Burstein, Elizabeth - *Robert Elsmere*
   Bks & Cult - v21 - i1 - Jan-Feb 2015 - p9(2) [501+]
Burstein, Mark - *Alice's Adventures in Wonderland: 150th Anniversary ed.*
   LJ - v140 - i17 - Oct 15 2015 - p94(1) [51-500]
Burstein, Miriam Elizabeth - *Victorian Reformations: Historical Fiction and Religious Controversy, 1820-1900*
   CHR - v101 - i3 - Summer 2015 - p668(2) [501+]
Burstein, Nicole - *Other Girl*
   y Sch Lib - v63 - i3 - Autumn 2015 - p179(1) [51-500]
Burstein, Paul - *American Public Opinion, Advocacy, and Policy in Congress: What the Public Wants and What It Gets*
   AJS - v121 - i1 - July 2015 - p311(3) [501+]
   Pub Op Q - v79 - i1 - Spring 2015 - p204(206) [501+]
Burt, John - *Lincoln's Tragic Pragmatism: Lincoln, Douglas, and Moral Conflict*
   Historian - v77 - i3 - Fall 2015 - p546(2) [501+]
Burt, Marissa - *A Sliver of Stardust*
   c BL - v112 - i3 - Oct 1 2015 - p79(2) [51-500]
   c KR - July 1 2015 - pNA [51-500]
   c SLJ - v61 - i7 - July 2015 - p74(1) [51-500]
Burton, Antoinette - *The First Anglo-Afghan Wars: A Reader*
   HNet - Sept 2015 - pNA [501+]
Burton, David - *How to be Happy*
   y Magpies - v30 - i4 - Sept 2015 - p22(1) [51-500]
Burton, Donald N. - *By What Is Sure to Follow*
   KR - April 15 2015 - pNA [51-500]
Burton, Jaci - *Make Me Stay*
   PW - v262 - i45 - Nov 9 2015 - p45(1) [51-500]
Burton, Jeffrey - *The Itsy Bitsy Snowman (Illus. by Rescek, Sanja)*
   c KR - Jan 1 2016 - pNA [51-500]
   c PW - v262 - i31 - August 3 2015 - p58(2) [51-500]
Burton, Ryan - *Dark Engine, vol. 1: The Art of Destruction*
   PW - v262 - i4 - Jan 26 2015 - p157(1) [51-500]
Burton, Suzanne L. - *Engaging Musical Practices: A Sourcebook for Middle School General Music*
   M Ed J - v102 - i1 - Sept 2015 - p23(1) [501+]
Burton, Tom L. - *The Complete Poems of William Barnes, vol. 1: Poems in the Broad Form of the Dorset Dialect*
   TLS - i5845 - April 10 2015 - p23(1) [501+]
Burton, Virginia Lee - *Mike Mulligan and His Steam Shovel*
   c CH Bwatch - Jan 2015 - pNA [51-500]
Burtt, Edward H., Jr. - *Alexander Wilson: The Scot Who Founded American Ornithology*
   QRB - v90 - i1 - March 2015 - p74(1) [501+]
Buruma, Ian - *45: Die Welt am Wendepunkt*
   HNet - August 2015 - pNA [501+]

Their Promised Land: My Grandparents in Love and War
    BL - v112 - i6 - Nov 15 2015 - p10(1) [51-500]
    KR - Oct 15 2015 - pNA [501+]
    LJ - v140 - i19 - Nov 15 2015 - p92(1) [51-500]
    PW - v262 - i44 - Nov 2 2015 - p75(1) [51-500]
Year Zero: A History of 1945
    BL - v111 - i9-10 - Jan 1 2015 - p120(1) [501+]
    Historian - v77 - i2 - Summer 2015 - p377(2) [501+]

Burwell, Rex - *Capone, the Cobbs, and Me*
    ABR - v36 - i4 - May-June 2015 - p27(2) [501+]
    RVBW - Nov 2015 - pNA [501+]

Bury, Col - *My Kind of Justice*
    PW - v262 - i45 - Nov 9 2015 - p40(1) [51-500]

Bury, Harry J. - *An Invitation to Think and Feel Differently in the New Millennium*
    SPBW - August 2015 - pNA [51-500]

Bury, Helen - *Eisenhower and the Cold War Arms Race: "Open Skies" and the Military-Industrial Complex*
    AHR - v120 - i2 - April 2015 - p667-668 [501+]

Busbee, Jay - *Earnhardt Nation: The Full-Throttle Saga of NASCAR's First Family*
    KR - Dec 15 2015 - pNA [501+]
    PW - v262 - i46 - Nov 16 2015 - p66(1) [51-500]

Busby, Ailie - *Winter*
    c KR - Jan 1 2016 - pNA [51-500]

Busby, Cylin - *The Nine Lives of Jacob Tibbs (Illus. by Kelley, Gerald)*
    c PW - v262 - i48 - Nov 30 2015 - p60(2) [51-500]
    c KR - Nov 1 2015 - pNA [51-500]

Buscema, Sal - *The Kree/Skrull War*
    LJ - v140 - i9 - May 15 2015 - p110(1) [501+]

Busch, Miriam - *Lion, Lion (Illus. by Day, Larry)*
    c HB Guide - v26 - i1 - Spring 2015 - p24(1) [51-500]

Busch, Susan Ellison - *Yearning for Normal*
    KR - May 1 2015 - pNA [501+]

Buschak, Willy - *Die Vereinigten Staaten von Europa Sind Unser Ziel: Arbeiterbewegung und Europa im Fruhen 20. Jahrhundert*
    HNet - Jan 2015 - pNA [501+]

Buschenfeld, Jurgen - *Bielefeld und die Welt: Pragungen und Impulse*
    HNet - May 2015 - pNA [501+]

Buschmann, Rainer F. - *Navigating the Spanish Lake: The Pacific in the Iberian World, 1521-1898*
    AHR - v120 - i2 - April 2015 - p602-603 [501+]
    HNet - June 2015 - pNA [501+]

Buser, Mary E. - *Lockdown on Rikers: Shocking Stories of Abuse and Injustice at New York's Notorious Jail*
    BL - v112 - i4 - Oct 15 2015 - p7(1) [51-500]
    PW - v262 - i30 - July 27 2015 - p56(1) [51-500]

Bush, George W. - *41: A Portrait of My Father (Read by Bush, George W.). Audiobook Review*
    BL - v111 - i13 - March 1 2015 - p68(1) [51-500]
41: A Portrait of My Father
    CSM - Feb 2 2015 - pNA [51-500]

Bush, Jonathan - *"Papists" and Prejudice: Popular Anti-Catholicism and Anglo-Irish Conflict in the North East of England, 1845-70*
    CHR - v101 - i2 - Spring 2015 - p385(2) [501+]
    Historian - v77 - i2 - Summer 2015 - p378(3) [501+]

Bush, Richard C. - *Uncharted Strait: The Future of China-Taiwan Relations*
    E-A St - v67 - i4 - June 2015 - p687(2) [501+]

Bush, William J. - *Greenback Dollar: The Incredible Rise of the Kingston Trio*
    Notes - v71 - i3 - March 2015 - p483(4) [501+]

Bushell, Anthony - *Polemical Austria: The Rhetorics of National Identity - From Empire to the Second Republic*
    MLR - v110 - i2 - April 2015 - p615-617 [501+]

Bushkin, Henry - *Johnny Carson*
    BL - v111 - i19-20 - June 1 2015 - p30(2) [51-500]

Bushmiller, Ernie - *Nancy Loves Sluggo: Complete Dailies 1949-1951*
    BL - v111 - i9-10 - Jan 1 2015 - p61(2) [51-500]

Bushnaf, Mansour - *Chewing Gum*
    TLS - i5833 - Jan 16 2015 - p19(2) [501+]

Bushnell, Candace - *Killing Monica (Read by Plummer, Therese). Audiobook Review*
    BL - v112 - i7 - Dec 1 2015 - p68(1) [51-500]
    LJ - v140 - i19 - Nov 15 2015 - p51(1) [51-500]
Killing Monica
    BL - v111 - i18 - May 15 2015 - p23(1) [51-500]
    KR - May 1 2015 - pNA [501+]
    LJ - v140 - i9 - May 15 2015 - p69(1) [51-500]
    NYTBR - July 26 2015 - p26(L) [501+]

Bushnell, Karima Vargas - *The Life and Times of Halycon Sage: Or the Last Book Ever Published*
    KR - Nov 1 2015 - pNA [501+]

Busiek, Kurt - *The Autumnlands, vol. 1: Tooth and Claw*
    PW - v262 - i31 - August 3 2015 - p44(1) [51-500]

Busman, Debra - *Like a Woman*
    KR - Feb 15 2015 - pNA [501+]
    PW - v262 - i1 - Jan 5 2015 - p49(2) [51-500]

Buss, James Joseph - *The Victory with No Name: The Native American Defeat of the First American Army*
    AHR - v120 - i3 - June 2015 - p1017(1) [501+]
Winning the West with Words: Language and Conquest in the Lower Great Lakes
    AL - v87 - i1 - March 2015 - p194-197 [501+]

Bussard, Katherine A. - *The City Lost and Found: Capturing New York, Chicago, and Los Angeles, 1960-1980*
    LJ - v140 - i10 - June 1 2015 - p98(1) [51-500]

Bussey, Lewis E. - *United States Postal Card Catalog*
    Phil Lit R - v64 - i3 - Summer 2015 - p209(2) [501+]

Bussi, Michel - *After the Crash*
    BL - v112 - i7 - Dec 1 2015 - p26(1) [51-500]
    KR - Nov 1 2015 - pNA [51-500]
    PW - v262 - i46 - Nov 16 2015 - p56(1) [51-500]

Bustard, Anne - *Anywhere but Paradise*
    c HB Guide - v26 - i2 - Fall 2015 - p77(1) [51-500]
    c KR - Jan 15 2015 - pNA [51-500]
    c PW - v262 - i9 - March 2 2015 - p85(1) [51-500]

Butchart, Amber Jane - *Nautical Chic*
    TLS - i5863 - August 14 2015 - p27(1) [51-500]

Butchart, Pamela - *Never Tickle a Tiger (Illus. by Boutavant, Marc)*
    c Sch Lib - v63 - i2 - Summer 2015 - p90(1) [51-500]

Butcher, Amy - *Visiting Hours: A Memoir of Friendship and Murder*
    KR - Jan 1 2015 - pNA [501+]
    NYTBR - July 19 2015 - p26(L) [501+]

Butcher, Jim - *The Aeronaut's Windlass*
    y BL - v112 - i2 - Sept 15 2015 - p37(1) [51-500]
    PW - v262 - i35 - August 31 2015 - p66(1) [501+]
Working for Bigfoot: Stories from the Dresden Files
    PW - v262 - i18 - May 4 2015 - p101(1) [51-500]

Butcher, Kristin - *In Search of Sam*
    y Res Links - v20 - i4 - April 2015 - p23(1) [51-500]
    y SLJ - v61 - i6 - June 2015 - p110(1) [51-500]

Butcher, William - *Jules Verne inedit: les manuscrits dechiffres*
    SFS - v42 - i3 - Nov 2015 - p557-555 [501+]

Butera, Robert - *Yoga Therapy for Stress and Anxiety: Create a Personalized Holistic Plan to Balance Your Life*
    PW - v262 - i27 - July 6 2015 - p63(1) [51-500]

Butland, Stephanie - *The Secrets We Keep*
    LJ - v140 - i10 - June 1 2015 - p90(1) [51-500]

Butler, Alexandra - *Walking the Night Road: Coming of Age in Grief*
    RVBW - Nov 2015 - pNA [501+]

Butler, Andrew M. - *Eternal Sunshine of the Spotless Mind*
    TLS - i5850 - May 15 2015 - p27(1) [501+]

Butler-Bowdon, Tom - *50 Politics Classics*
    LJ - v140 - i14 - Sept 1 2015 - p144(1) [51-500]

Butler, Brin-Jonathan - *The Domino Diaries: My Decade Boxing with Olympic Champions and Chasing Hemingway's Ghost in the Last Days of Castro's Cuba*
    LJ - v140 - i8 - May 1 2015 - p78(2) [51-500]
    PW - v262 - i17 - April 27 2015 - p63(1) [51-500]
    BL - v111 - i17 - May 1 2015 - p70(1) [51-500]
    KR - April 1 2015 - pNA [501+]

Butler, Bryna - *Wrong Side of the Grave*
    KR - May 1 2015 - pNA [501+]

Butler, Dave (b. 1953-) - *Paradise Saved: The Remarkable Story of New Zealand's Wildlife Sanctuaries and How They are Stemming the Tide of Extinction*
    y Magpies - v30 - i1 - March 2015 - pS8(1) [51-500]

Butler, David - *Design to Grow: How Coca-Cola Learned to Combine Scale & Agility (and How You Can Too).*
    BL - v111 - i9-10 - Jan 1 2015 - p25(1) [51-500]

Butler, David (b. 1964-) - *City of Dis*
    KR - Sept 1 2015 - pNA [501+]

Butler, Dori Hillestad - *The Haunted Library (Illus. by Damant, Aurore)*
    c HB Guide - v26 - i1 - Spring 2015 - p57(1) [51-500]

Butler, Erin - *Chicago Blackhawks*
    c BL - v112 - i3 - Oct 1 2015 - p48(1) [51-500]

Butler, Heather - *The Milkshake Detectives*
    c Sch Lib - v63 - i3 - Autumn 2015 - p162(2) [51-500]

Butler, Hubert - *The Appleman and the Poet*
    ILS - v35 - i1 - Fall 2015 - p18(2) [51-500]

Butler, Judith - *Notes Toward a Performative Theory of Assembly*
    LJ - v140 - i17 - Oct 15 2015 - p88(1) [51-500]
    PW - v262 - i37 - Sept 14 2015 - p55(1) [51-500]
Senses of the Subject
    TimHES - i2212 - July 16 2015 - p48-1 [501+]

Butler, Kirker - *Pretty Ugly*
    BL - v111 - i11 - Feb 1 2015 - p24(1) [51-500]
    KR - Jan 15 2015 - pNA [501+]

Butler, Lorna Michael - *Tapping Philanthropy for Development: Lessons Learned from a Public-Private Partnership in Rural Uganda*
    RVBW - August 2015 - pNA [501+]

Butler, M. Christina - *One Snowy Rescue (Illus. by Macnaughton, Tina)*
    c KR - July 1 2015 - pNA [51-500]

Butler, Marcus - *Hello Life!*
    BL - v112 - i7 - Dec 1 2015 - p39(1) [51-500]

Butler, Nickolas - *Beneath the Bonfire*
    NYT - May 28 2015 - pC6(L) [501+]
    BL - v111 - i15 - April 1 2015 - p23(1) [51-500]
    LJ - v140 - i6 - April 1 2015 - p87(1) [51-500]
    PW - v262 - i13 - March 30 2015 - p46(1) [51-500]
Shotgun Lovesongs (Read by Sowers, Scott). Audiobook Review
    LJ - v140 - i5 - March 15 2015 - p134(1) [501+]
Shotgun Lovesongs
    NYTBR - March 8 2015 - p32(L) [501+]

Butler, Rebecca P. - *School Libraries 3.0: Principles and Practices for the Digital Age*
    y VOYA - v38 - i4 - Oct 2015 - p86(2) [51-500]

Butler, Sara M. - *Forensic Medicine and Death Investigation in Medieval England*
    Med R - August 2015 - pNA [501+]

Butler, Steve - *The Diary of Dennis the Menace: Bash Street Bandit!*
    c Sch Lib - v63 - i2 - Summer 2015 - p100(2) [51-500]

Butler, Steven - *The Wrong Pong (Illus. by Fisher, Chris)*
    c PW - v262 - i30 - July 27 2015 - p69(1) [51-500]

Butler, Susan - *Roosevelt and Stalin: Portrait of a Partnership*
    CSM - March 5 2015 - pNA [501+]
    LJ - v140 - i2 - Feb 1 2015 - p93(1) [51-500]
    NY - v91 - i7 - April 6 2015 - p81 [51-500]
    PW - v262 - i1 - Jan 5 2015 - p65(1) [51-500]
    BL - v111 - i11 - Feb 1 2015 - p13(1) [51-500]

Butler, Tom - *Overdevelopment, Overpopulation, Overshoot*
    LJ - v140 - i5 - March 15 2015 - p129(1) [51-500]
    SPBW - May 2015 - pNA [501+]

Buttar, Debbie - *Funky Little Monkey (Illus. by Davis, Christopher)*
    c CH Bwatch - Oct 2015 - pNA [51-500]

Butterfield, David J. - *The Early Textual History of Lucretius' De Rerum Natura*
    Class R - v65 - i1 - April 2015 - p112-113 [501+]

Butterfield, Jeremy - *Fowler's Dictionary of Modern English Usage, 4th ed.*
    TLS - i5868 - Sept 18 2015 - p29(1) [501+]

Butterfield, Moira - *Stardragon (Illus. by Serra, Adolfo)*
    c SLJ - v61 - i5 - May 2015 - p82(2) [51-500]
Superstats: Amazing Body
    c BL - v112 - i2 - Sept 15 2015 - p57(1) [51-500]
Superstats: Extreme Planet
    c SLJ - v61 - i11 - Nov 2015 - p130(1) [51-500]

Butterfield, Rosaria - *Openness Unhindered: Further Thoughts of an Unlikely Convert on Sexual Identity and Union with Christ*
    Ch Today - v59 - i7 - Sept 2015 - p80(1) [51-500]

Butterworth, Chris - *Where Did My Clothes Come From? (Illus. by Gaggiotti, Lucia)*
    c SLJ - v61 - i9 - Sept 2015 - p178(2) [51-500]
    c CCB-B - v69 - i2 - Oct 2015 - p79(1) [51-500]
    c KR - June 15 2015 - pNA [51-500]

Butterworth, Jon - *Most Wanted Particle: The Inside Story of the Hunt for the Higgs, the Heart of the Future of Physics*
    BL - v111 - i9-10 - Jan 1 2015 - p26(1) [51-500]
    Nature - v517 - i7536 - Jan 29 2015 - p551(1) [51-500]

Butterworth, Philip - *Staging Conventions in Medieval English Theatre*
    Specu - v90 - i4 - Oct 2015 - p1092-1093 [501+]

Butterworth, William E., III - *The Hunting Trip*
    BL - v112 - i7 - Dec 1 2015 - p29(1) [51-500]
    KR - Oct 15 2015 - pNA [501+]

Buttigieg, Emanuel - *Islands and the Military Orders, c. 1291-c. 1798*
    Med R - August 2015 - pNA [501+]
    Specu - v90 - i2 - April 2015 - p516-518 [501+]

Buttress, Derrick - *Welcome to the Bike Factory*
TLS - i5861 - July 31 2015 - p23(1) [501+]
Butts, Ed - *Behind the Badge: Crimefighters through History (Illus. by Williams, Gareth)*
c VOYA - v38 - i1 - April 2015 - p86(1) [51-500]
Butts, Mary - *The Complete Stories*
RVBW - Jan 2015 - pNA [501+]
TLS - i5863 - August 14 2015 - p7(1) [501+]
Buwalda, Peter - *Bonita Avenue*
NYTBR - Feb 15 2015 - p20(L) [501+]
WLT - v89 - i5 - Sept-Oct 2015 - p57(2) [501+]
Buxton, Jamie - *Temple Boys*
y BL - v111 - i16 - April 15 2015 - p58(1) [51-500]
y CCB-B - v68 - i8 - April 2015 - p391(2) [51-500]
y HB Guide - v26 - i2 - Fall 2015 - p113(1) [51-500]
y VOYA - v37 - i6 - Feb 2015 - p54(1) [51-500]
Buyandelger, Manduhai - *Tragic Spirits: Shamanism, Memory, and Gender in Contemporary Mongolia*
JAS - v74 - i3 - August 2015 - p747-748 [501+]
Buyea, Rob - *Saving Mr. Terupt*
c KR - May 1 2015 - pNA [51-500]
c SLJ - v61 - i5 - May 2015 - p102(1) [51-500]
y VOYA - v38 - i3 - August 2015 - p55(2) [51-500]
Buzbee, William W. - *Fighting Westway: Environmental Law, Citizen Activism, and the Regulatory War That Transformed New York City*
JAH - v101 - i4 - March 2015 - p1341-1342 [501+]
Buzo, Laura - *Love and Other Perishable Items*
y Sch Lib - v63 - i4 - Winter 2015 - p252(1) [51-500]
Buzzeo, Toni - *My Bibi Always Remembers (Illus. by Wohnoutka, Mike)*
c HB Guide - v26 - i1 - Spring 2015 - p24(1) [51-500]
One Cool Friend (Read by Dean, Robertson). Audiobook Review
BL - v111 - i13 - March 1 2015 - p70(1) [51-500]
A Passion for Elephants: The Real Life Adventure of Field Scientist Cynthia Moss (Illus. by Berry, Holly)
c BL - v111 - i21 - July 1 2015 - p52(2) [51-500]
c KR - June 15 2015 - pNA [51-500]
c PW - v262 - i29 - July 20 2015 - p190(2) [501+]
c SLJ - v61 - i8 - August 2015 - p117(1) [51-500]
The Twelve Days of Christmas in New England (Illus. by Woodruff, Liza)
c PW - v262 - i37 - Sept 14 2015 - p77(1) [51-500]
Whose Tools? (Illus. by Datz, Jim)
c PW - v262 - i49 - Dec 2 2015 - p58(1) [51-500]
c BL - v111 - i19-20 - June 1 2015 - p110(1) [51-500]
c CH Bwatch - May 2015 - pNA [51-500]
c KR - July 1 2015 - pNA [51-500]
Whose Truck? (Illus. by Datz, Jim)
c KR - Jan 1 2016 - pNA [51-500]
c PW - v262 - i31 - August 3 2015 - p58(2) [501+]
Byant, Ann - *Stinky (Illus. by Elkerton, Andy)*
c CH Bwatch - Feb 2015 - pNA [501+]
Byard, Olivia - *The Wilding Eye*
NS - v144 - i5266 - June 12 2015 - p51(1) [51-500]

Bybee, Catherine - *Seduced by Sunday*
PW - v262 - i6 - Feb 9 2015 - p50(1) [51-500]
Treasured by Thursday
KR - July 15 2015 - pNA [501+]
PW - v262 - i23 - June 8 2015 - p44(1) [51-500]
Bybee, Rodger W. - *The BSCS 5E Instructional Model*
Sci & Ch - v52 - i9 - Summer 2015 - p29 [51-500]
Sci Teach - v82 - i5 - Summer 2015 - p71 [51-500]
Byers, A. Martin - *From Cahokia to Larson to Moundville*
RVBW - March 2015 - pNA [51-500]
Byers, Ann - *Anti-Semitism and the "Final Solution": The Holocaust Overview*
y HB Guide - v26 - i1 - Spring 2015 - p201(1) [51-500]
Auschzvitz, Bergen-Belsen, Treblinka: The Holocaust Camps
y HB Guide - v26 - i1 - Spring 2015 - p201(1) [51-500]
Byers, Sam - *Idiopathy*
NYTBR - June 14 2015 - p24(L) [501+]
Byfield, Natalie P. - *Savage Portrayals: Race, Media, and the Central Park Jogger Story*
AJS - v121 - i2 - Sept 2015 - p611(3) [501+]
Byington, Mark E. - *The Han Commanderies in Early Korean History*
JAS - v74 - i1 - Feb 2015 - p223-225 [501+]
Byler, Linda - *Hester on the Run*
y BL - v112 - i6 - Nov 15 2015 - p17(1) [51-500]
Bylin, Victoria - *Together with You*
BL - v111 - i14 - March 15 2015 - p50(1) [51-500]
PW - v262 - i6 - Feb 9 2015 - p51(1) [51-500]
Byman, Daniel - *Al Qaeda, the Islamic State, and the Global Jihadist Movement: What Everyone Needs to Know*
LJ - v140 - i19 - Nov 15 2015 - p106(1) [51-500]
Byrd, James P. - *Sacred Scripture, Sacred War: The Bible and the American Revolution*
HNet - March 2015 - pNA [51-500]
Byrd, Robert - *Brave Chicken Little (Illus. by Byrd, Robert)*
c HB Guide - v26 - i1 - Spring 2015 - p143(2) [51-500]
Byrd, Tommy Lee - *Detroit Speed's How to Build a Pro Touring Car*
Bwatch - July 2015 - pNA [51-500]
Byrd, William, II - *The Dividing Line Histories of William Byrd II of Westover*
RAH - v43 - i2 - June 2015 - p210-215 [501+]
Byrkskog, Samuel - *The Identity of Jesus: Nordic Voices*
Theol St - v76 - i3 - Sept 2015 - p639(2) [501+]
Byrne, Angela - *Geographies of the Romantic North: Science, Antiquarianism, and Travel, 1790-1830*
Can Hist R - v96 - i2 - June 2015 - p294(3) [501+]
JMH - v87 - i2 - June 2015 - p432(3) [501+]
Byrne, Ben - *Fire Flowers*
BL - v111 - i11 - Feb 1 2015 - p30(1) [51-500]
KR - Jan 1 2015 - pNA [51-500]
TLS - i5845 - April 10 2015 - p20(1) [501+]

Byrne, Fergus - *More Lives than One: The Extraordinary Life of Felix Dennis*
Spec - v329 - i9765 - Oct 24 2015 - p41(2) [501+]
Byrne, James - *Everything Broken Up Dances*
LJ - v140 - i20 - Dec 1 2015 - p107(1) [51-500]
PW - v262 - i46 - Nov 16 2015 - p52(1) [501+]
Byrne, Katherine - *Tuberculosis and the Victorian Literary Imagination*
HNet - April 2015 - pNA [501+]
Byrne, Kerrigan - *The Highwayman*
PW - v262 - i32 - August 10 2015 - p43(1) [51-500]
Byrne, Malcolm - *Iran-Contra: Reagan's Scandal and the Unchecked Abuse of Presidential Power*
JAH - v102 - i2 - Sept 2015 - p629-630 [501+]
Byrne, Michael - *Lottery Boy*
y KR - Dec 15 2015 - pNA [51-500]
y PW - v262 - i52 - Dec 21 2015 - p154(2) [51-500]
y Sch Lib - v63 - i2 - Summer 2015 - p115(1) [51-500]
Byrne, Paula - *Belle: the True Story of Dido Belle*
TimHES - i2193 - March 5 2015 - p49(1) [501+]
Byrne, Richard - *Ce livre a mange mon chien!*
c Res Links - v20 - i4 - April 2015 - p36(1) [51-500]
This Book Just Ate My Dog! (Illus. by Byrne, Richard)
c HB - v91 - i1 - Jan-Feb 2015 - p60(2) [51-500]
c HB Guide - v26 - i1 - Spring 2015 - p24(1) [51-500]
c JE - v195 - i2 - Spring 2015 - p56-57 [501+]
Byrne, Ryan P. - *Help in Our Time and Manet's Genre Paintings of Everyday Light*
KR - April 1 2015 - pNA [501+]
Byrne, Skye - *The Power of Henry's Imagination (Illus. by George, Nic)*
c KR - July 15 2015 - pNA [51-500]
c PW - v262 - i32 - August 10 2015 - p58(1) [51-500]
Byrne, Susan - *Ficino in Spain*
Sev Cent N - v73 - i3-4 - Fall-Winter 2015 - p186(2) [501+]
Law and History in Cervantes'Don Quixote
Hisp R - v83 - i2 - Spring 2015 - p241-244 [501+]
Byrnes, Joseph F. - *Priests of the French Revolution: Saints and Renegades in a New Political Era*
CHR - v101 - i4 - Autumn 2015 - p943(2) [501+]
Byron, Ellen - *Plantation Shudders*
SPBW - August 2015 - pNA [51-500]
Plantation Shuddersy
PW - v262 - i25 - June 22 2015 - p121(1) [51-500]
Byron, Mark - *Ezra Pound's Eriugena*
J Am St - v49 - i2 - May 2015 - p430-431 [501+]
Byron, Tanya - *The Skeleton Cupboard*
BL - v111 - i11 - Feb 1 2015 - p8(1) [51-500]
KR - Jan 1 2015 - pNA [501+]
Byrum, Katie - *Burn It Down*
PW - v262 - i16 - April 20 2015 - p50(1) [51-500]
Bystander, Rescuer or Perpetrators? The Neutral Countries and the Shoah
HNet - Feb 2015 - pNA [501+]
Bysted, Ane L. - *The Crusade Indulgence: Spiritual Rewards and the Theology of Crusades, c. 1095-1216*
CHR - v101 - i4 - Autumn 2015 - p912(2) [501+]
Bywaters, Grant - *Red Storm Rising*
KR - Oct 1 2015 - pNA [51-500]

C

Ca, Nha - *Mourning Headband for Hue: An Account of the Battle for Hue, Vietnam 1968*
    HNet - Feb 2015 - pNA [501+]
    J Mil H - v79 - i2 - April 2015 - p549(1) [501+]

Cabanas, Kaira M. - *Off-Screen Cinema: Isidore Isou and the Lettrist Avant-Garde*
    FQ - v69 - i1 - Fall 2015 - p97(3) [501+]

Cabanes, Bruno - *The Great War and the Origins of Humanitarianism, 1918-1924*
    AHR - v120 - i3 - June 2015 - p960-962 [501+]
    JIH - v45 - i3 - Wntr 2015 - p415-416 [501+]

Cabatingan, Erin - *The World According to Musk Ox (Illus. by Myers, Matthew)*
    c HB Guide - v26 - i1 - Spring 2015 - p24(2) [51-500]

Cabej, Nelson R. - *Building the Most Complex Structure on Earth: An Epigenetic Narrative of Development and Evolution of Animals*
    QRB - v90 - i1 - March 2015 - p98(1) [501+]

Cabot, Amanda - *In Firefly Valley*
    RVBW - July 2015 - pNA [51-500]

Cabot, Meg - *From the Notebooks of a Middle School Princess (Read by McInerney, Kathleen). Audiobook Review*
    c BL - v112 - i2 - Sept 15 2015 - p80(1) [51-500]
    c CH Bwatch - June 2015 - pNA [51-500]
    c SLJ - v61 - i10 - Oct 2015 - p51(1) [51-500]
From the Notebooks of a Middle School Princess (Illus. by Cabot, Meg)
    c BL - v111 - i17 - May 1 2015 - p100(1) [51-500]
    c CCB-B - v68 - i11 - July-August 2015 - p539(2) [51-500]
    c HB Guide - v26 - i2 - Fall 2015 - p77(1) [51-500]
      KR - April 1 2015 - pNA [51-500]
    c PW - v262 - i10 - March 9 2015 - p71(1) [51-500]
    c SLJ - v61 - i6 - June 2015 - p98(1) [51-500]
Remembrance
    KR - Jan 1 2016 - pNA [51-500]
Royal Wedding
    y BL - v111 - i15 - April 1 2015 - p32(2) [51-500]
      KR - April 1 2015 - pNA [51-500]
      LJ - v140 - i8 - May 1 2015 - p60(1) [51-500]
      PW - v262 - i15 - April 13 2015 - p52(1) [51-500]

Cabranes, Amaya - *Franciscanos eminentes en territorios de fronteras*
    CHR - v101 - i3 - Summer 2015 - p694(2) [501+]

Cabrera, Jane - *Baa, Baa, Black Sheep (Illus. by Cabrera, Jane)*
    c KR - July 15 2015 - pNA [51-500]
    c SLJ - v61 - i8 - August 2015 - p62(1) [51-500]
Row, Row, Row Your Boat (Illus. by Cabrera, Jane)
    c CH Bwatch - May 2015 - pNA [51-500]
Row, Row, Row Your Boat
    c HB Guide - v26 - i1 - Spring 2015 - p180(1) [51-500]

Cabrita, Joel - *Text and Authority in the South African Nazaretha Church*
    AHR - v120 - i3 - June 2015 - p1157-1158 [501+]

Cacoyannis, Panayotis - *Bowl of Fruit (1907).*
    KR - Oct 15 2015 - pNA [501+]
The Dead of August
    KR - Sept 1 2015 - pNA [501+]

Cadava, Geraldo L. - *Standing on Common Ground*
    PHR - v84 - i3 - August 2015 - p377(2) [501+]

Cadbury, Deborah - *Princes at War: The Bitter Battle Inside Britain's Royal Family in the Darkest Days of WWII*
    KR - Jan 15 2015 - pNA [501+]
    LJ - v140 - i3 - Feb 15 2015 - p111(1) [51-500]
    Mac - v128 - i11 - March 23 2015 - p61(2) [501+]
    PW - v262 - i3 - Jan 19 2015 - p71(1) [51-500]

Cadden, Joan - *Nothing Natural Is Shameful: Sodomy and Science in Late Medieval Europe*
    Specu - v90 - i4 - Oct 2015 - p1093-1095 [501+]

Caddick-Adams, Peter - *Monte Cassino: Ten Armies in Hell*
    HNet - Jan 2015 - pNA [501+]
Snow and Steel: The Battle of the Bulge, 1944-45
    HNet - April 2015 - pNA [501+]
    J Mil H - v79 - i2 - April 2015 - p531-532 [501+]
    TLS - i5858 - July 10 2015 - p24(1) [501+]

Caddoo, Cara - *Envisioning Freedom: Cinema and the Building of Modern Black Life*
    AHR - v120 - i3 - June 2015 - p1046-1047 [501+]
    JSH - v81 - i4 - Nov 2015 - p1016(2) [501+]

Cadle, Nathaniel - *The Mediating Nation: Late American Realism, Globalization, and the Progressive State*
    JAH - v102 - i1 - June 2015 - p272-273 [501+]

Cadwallader, Robyn - *The Anchoress*
    Bks & Cult - v21 - i4 - July-August 2015 - p29(1) [501+]
    CC - v132 - i14 - July 8 2015 - p30(2) [501+]
    SLJ - v61 - i10 - Oct 2015 - p121(1) [51-500]
    Wom R Bks - v32 - i6 - Nov-Dec 2015 - p19(2) [501+]
    BL - v111 - i13 - March 1 2015 - p27(1) [51-500]
    KR - March 15 2015 - pNA [501+]
    LJ - v140 - i9 - May 15 2015 - p69(1) [51-500]
    y NYTBR - June 7 2015 - p29(L) [501+]

Caesar, Ed - *Two Hours: The Quest to Run the Impossible Marathon*
    y BL - v112 - i1 - Sept 1 2015 - p38(1) [51-500]
    Econ - v416 - i8946 - July 11 2015 - p76(US) [501+]
    KR - July 1 2015 - pNA [501+]
    LJ - v140 - i14 - Sept 1 2015 - p110(2) [51-500]
    NS - v144 - i5270 - July 10 2015 - p40(2) [501+]
    Spec - v328 - i9750 - July 11 2015 - p34(2) [501+]

Cafaro, Philip - *How Many Is Too Many? The Progressive Argument for Reducing Immigration into the United States*
    LJ - v140 - i2 - Feb 1 2015 - p97(2) [51-500]

Caffey, David L. - *Chasing the Santa Fe Ring: Power and Privilege in Territorial New Mexico*
    AHR - v120 - i1 - Feb 2015 - p245-246 [501+]
    JAH - v101 - i4 - March 2015 - p1291-1292 [501+]
    PHR - v84 - i4 - Nov 2015 - p539(3) [501+]
    Roundup M - v22 - i6 - August 2015 - p35(1) [501+]
    SHQ - v118 - i4 - April 2015 - p434-435 [501+]
    WHQ - v46 - i3 - Autumn 2015 - p382-383 [501+]

Cafiero, Giuseppe - *Edgar Allan Poe*
    KR - Nov 1 2015 - pNA [501+]

Cagan, Andrea - *Memoirs of a Ghost: One Sheet Away*
    KR - Oct 1 2015 - pNA [501+]
    SPBW - Sept 2015 - pNA [51-500]

Cagaptay, Soner - *The Rise of Turkey: The Twenty-First Century's First Muslim Power*
    Parameters - v45 - i2 - Summer 2015 - p120(3) [501+]

Cage, E. Claire - *Unnatural Frenchmen: The Politics of Priestly Celibacy and Marriage*
    JAAR - v83 - i2 - June 2015 - pNA [501+]

Cahalan, Kathleen A. - *Opening the Field of Practical Theology: An Introduction*
    CC - v132 - i21 - Oct 14 2015 - p34(2) [501+]
    TT - v72 - i1 - April 2015 - p114-116 [501+]

Cahan, Susan E. - *Mounting Frustration: The Art Museum in the Age of Black Power*
    BL - v112 - i7 - Dec 1 2015 - p9(1) [51-500]
    PW - v262 - i52 - Dec 21 2015 - p143(3) [51-500]

Cahill, Edward - *Liberty of the Imagination: Aesthetic Theory, Literary Form, and Politics in the Early United States*
    AL - v87 - i1 - March 2015 - p187-189 [501+]

Cahill, Ellie - *When Joss Met Matt*
    BL - v111 - i11 - Feb 1 2015 - p31(1) [51-500]
    PW - v262 - i3 - Jan 19 2015 - p67(1) [51-500]

Cahill, John M. - *Primitive Passions*
    SPBW - March 2015 - pNA [51-500]

Cahn, Steven M. - *Freedom and the Self: Essays on the Philosophy of David Foster Wallace*
    RVBW - Nov 2015 - pNA [501+]
    LJ - v140 - i6 - April 1 2015 - p97(1) [51-500]
Happiness and Goodness: Philosophical Reflections on Living Well
    LJ - v140 - i8 - May 1 2015 - p77(1) [51-500]

Cai, Liang - *Witchcraft and the Rise of the First Confucian Empire*
    AHR - v120 - i3 - June 2015 - p988-989 [501+]

Cailler, Mathieu - *Loss Angeles: Stories*
    SPBW - May 2015 - pNA [51-500]

Caillois, Roger - *A Little Guide to the 15th Arrondissement for the Use of Phantoms*
    TLS - i5873 - Oct 23 2015 - p30(1) [501+]

Caillot, Marc-Antoine - *A Company Man: The Remarkable French-Atlantic Voyage of a Clerk for the Company of the Indies*
    JSH - v81 - i3 - August 2015 - p694(2) [501+]

Cain, Barbara - *Go Big, Go Bold--Large-Scale Modern Quilts: 10 Projects, Quick to Cut, Fast to Sew*
    LJ - v140 - i19 - Nov 15 2015 - p84(1) [51-500]

Cain, Chelsea - *Kick-Back*
    BL - v112 - i3 - Oct 1 2015 - p4(1) [51-500]
One Kick (Read by Lind, Heather). Audiobook Review
    BL - v111 - i14 - March 15 2015 - p83(2) [51-500]
One Kick
    RVBW - April 2015 - pNA [501+]
    RVBW - June 2015 - pNA [501+]
Sweetheart
    PW - v262 - i2 - Jan 12 2015 - p64(1) [51-500]

Cain, Michael L. - *Ecology*
    QRB - v90 - i3 - Sept 2015 - p323(2) [501+]

Cain, Sarah - *The 8th Circle*
    BL - v112 - i7 - Dec 1 2015 - p26(1) [51-500]
    KR - Nov 1 2015 - pNA [51-500]
    PW - v262 - i45 - Nov 9 2015 - p39(1) [51-500]

Cain, Susan - *Quiet: The Power of Introverts in a World That Can't Stop Talking*
    BL - v111 - i9-10 - Jan 1 2015 - p120(1) [501+]

Cain, Tom - *The Complete Poetry of Robert Herrick. 2 vols.*
    TLS - i5833 - Jan 16 2015 - p3(3) [501+]

Caine, Rachel - *Ink and Bone*
    y BL - v112 - i1 - Sept 1 2015 - p104(1) [51-500]
    y CSM - August 5 2015 - pNA [501+]
    y PW - v262 - i49 - Dec 7 2015 - p103(2) [51-500]
    y SLJ - v61 - i10 - Oct 2015 - p108(2) [51-500]
    y VOYA - v38 - i3 - August 2015 - p74(1) [51-500]

Caines, Michael - *Shakespeare and the Eighteenth Century*
    Six Ct J - v46 - i2 - Summer 2015 - p507-508 [501+]

Cairns, Douglas L. - *Defining Greek Narrative*
    Class R - v65 - i2 - Oct 2015 - p329-330 [501+]
Tragedy and Archaic Greek Thought
    Class R - v65 - i2 - Oct 2015 - p349-351 [501+]

Cairns, Kathleen A. - *Proof of Guilt: Barbara Graham and the Politics of Executing Women in America*
    PHR - v84 - i3 - August 2015 - p390(2) [501+]

Cairns, Scott - *Slow Pilgrim: The Collected Poems*
    Bks & Cult - v21 - i6 - Nov-Dec 2015 - p36(2) [501+]

Cairo, Elias - *Olympia Provisions: Cured Meats and Tales from an American Charcuterie*
    LJ - v140 - i16 - Oct 1 2015 - p101(1) [51-500]
    PW - v262 - i31 - August 3 2015 - p52(1) [51-500]

Caisley, Raewyn - *Uncle Vic's Farm (Illus. by Allen, Lisa)*
    c Magpies - v30 - i5 - Nov 2015 - pS6(1) [501+]

Caistor, Nick - *Fidel Castro*
    Historian - v77 - i3 - Fall 2015 - p547(2) [501+]

Calabrese, Michael - *Yee? Baw for Bokes: Essays on Medieval Manuscripts and Poetics in Honor of Hoyt N. Duggan*
    Med R - August 2015 - pNA [501+]

Calabrese, Rosalie - *Remembering Chris*
    ABR - v36 - i5 - July-August 2015 - p19(2) [501+]

Calaprice, Alice - *An Einstein Encyclopedia*
    BL - v112 - i7 - Dec 1 2015 - p12(2) [51-500]

Calasso, Roberto - *Ardor*
    NYRB - v62 - i1 - Jan 8 2015 - p49(3) [501+]
The Art of the Publisher
    KR - Sept 1 2015 - pNA [501+]
    LJ - v140 - i14 - Sept 1 2015 - p114(1) [51-500]
    PW - v262 - i26 - June 29 2015 - p55(1) [51-500]

Caldecott, Elen - *The Marsh Road Mysteries: Diamonds and Daggers (Illus. by Reed, Nathan)*
    c Sch Lib - v63 - i2 - Summer 2015 - p101(1) [51-500]

Calderhead, Christopher - *Illuminating the Word: The Making of the Saint John's Bible*
    RVBW - June 2015 - pNA [51-500]

Caldesi, Katie - *Venice: Recipes Lost and Found*
    TLS - i5841 - March 13 2015 - p30(1) [501+]

Caldwell, Charlotte - *The Cow's Girl: The Making of a Real Cowgirl*
    c CH Bwatch - May 2015 - pNA [501+]
Kirby's Journal: Backyard Butterfly Magic
    c SLJ - v61 - i6 - June 2015 - p140(2) [51-500]
    c KR - April 15 2015 - pNA [51-500]

Caldwell, Dorigen - *Continuing Encounters between Past and Present*
    J Urban H - v41 - i1 - Jan 2015 - p152-5 [501+]

Caldwell, Ian - *The Fifth Gospel (Read by Davenport, Jack). Audiobook Review*
    BL - v111 - i17 - May 1 2015 - p58(1) [51-500]
The Fifth Gospel
    Nat Post - v17 - i107 - March 7 2015 - pWP4(1) [501+]
    BL - v111 - i9-10 - Jan 1 2015 - p52(1) [51-500]
    KR - Jan 15 2015 - pNA [501+]
    PW - v262 - i2 - Jan 12 2015 - p38(1) [51-500]

Caldwell, Shawn - *Sheila*
    KR - June 1 2015 - pNA [501+]

Caletti, Deb - *The Last Forever*
    c BL - v111 - i12 - Feb 15 2015 - p76(1) [501+]
    y Teach Lib - v42 - i3 - Feb 2015 - p43(1) [51-500]
The Secrets She Keeps
    BL - v111 - i21 - July 1 2015 - p43(1) [51-500]

Calhoun, Ada - *St. Marks Is Dead: The Many Lives of America's Hippest Street*
    BL - v112 - i5 - Nov 1 2015 - p25(1) [51-500]
    KR - Sept 1 2015 - pNA [501+]
    LJ - v140 - i17 - Oct 15 2015 - p99(2) [51-500]
    NYTBR - Dec 6 2015 - p40(L) [501+]
    PW - v262 - i34 - August 24 2015 - p72(1) [51-500]

Calhoun, Anne - *The List*
    PW - v262 - i2 - Jan 12 2015 - p42(1) [51-500]

Calhoun, Bonnie S. - *Lightning*
    y SLJ - v61 - i10 - Oct 2015 - p108(2) [51-500]

Calhoun, Craig - *Habermas and Religion*
    AJS - v120 - i4 - Jan 2015 - p1257(3) [501+]

Calhoun, Laurie - *We Kill Because We Can: From Soldiering to Assassination in the Drone Age*
    PW - v262 - i37 - Sept 14 2015 - p53(2) [51-500]

Cali, Davide - *A Funny Thing Happened on the Way to School ... (Illus. by Chaud, Benjamin)*
    c HB Guide - v26 - i2 - Fall 2015 - p28(1) [51-500]
    c KR - Jan 15 2015 - pNA [51-500]
    c SLJ - v61 - i3 - March 2015 - p113(1) [51-500]
I Didn't Do My Homework Because ... (Illus. by Chaud, Benjamin)
    c HB Guide - v26 - i1 - Spring 2015 - p25(1) [51-500]
Snow White and the 77 Dwarfs (Illus. by Barbanegre, Raphaelle)
    c HB Guide - v26 - i2 - Fall 2015 - p28(1) [51-500]
    c Nat Post - v17 - i165 - May 16 2015 - pWP5(1) [501+]
    c Res Links - v20 - i4 - April 2015 - p2(1) [501+]
    c SLJ - v61 - i5 - May 2015 - p83(1) [51-500]
Snow White and the 77 Dwarves (Illus. by Barbanegre, Raphaelle)
    c KR - Feb 15 2015 - pNA [51-500]

Calico, Joy H. - *Arnold Schoenberg's A Survivor from Warsaw in Postwar Europe*
    CEH - v48 - i2 - June 2015 - p275-276 [501+]
    TLS - i5838 - Feb 20 2015 - p24(2) [501+]

Califano, Joseph A. - *The Triumph & Tragedy of Lyndon Johnson: The White House Years*
    SEP - v287 - i1 - Jan-Feb 2015 - p20(1) [51-500]

Califra, Michael - *No Man's Land*
    PW - v262 - i18 - May 4 2015 - p96(1) [51-500]

Calin, William - *The Lily and the Thistle: The French Tradition and the Older Literature of Scotland*
    Specu - v90 - i2 - April 2015 - p518-519 [501+]

Calkins, Kaijsa - *The Embedded Librarian's Cookbook*
    R&USQ - v54 - i3 - Spring 2015 - p52(2) [501+]

Calkins, Susanna - *The Masque of a Murderer*
    y BL - v111 - i14 - March 15 2015 - p46(1) [51-500]
    PW - v262 - i7 - Feb 16 2015 - p161(1) [51-500]

Call, Lewis - *BDSM in American Science Fiction and Fantasy*
    SFS - v42 - i1 - March 2015 - p158-162 [501+]

Callaghan, Cindy - *Lost in London*
    c HB Guide - v26 - i2 - Fall 2015 - p77(1) [51-500]
Lost in Paris
    c HB Guide - v26 - i2 - Fall 2015 - p77(1) [51-500]

Callaghan, Tom - *A Killing Winter*
    KR - August 1 2015 - pNA [51-500]

Callahan, Daniel - *In Search of the Good: A Life in Bioethics*
    QRB - v90 - i1 - March 2015 - p76(2) [51-500]

Callahan, Rebecca M. - *Coming of Political Age: American Schools and the Civic Development of Immigrant Youth*
    CS - v44 - i4 - July 2015 - p491-493 [501+]

Calle, Juan - *Good Dream, Bad Dream: The World's Heroes Save the Night!*
    c HB Guide - v26 - i1 - Spring 2015 - p25(1) [51-500]

Calle, Sophie - *Suite Venitienne*
    HM - v330 - i1980 - May 2015 - p79(3) [501+]

Callen, Gayle - *The Wrong Bride*
    PW - v262 - i39 - Sept 28 2015 - p74(2) [51-500]

Callen, Paulette - *Fervent Charity*
    Roundup M - v22 - i6 - August 2015 - p27(1) [501+]

Callender, Wayne A. - *Using RTI in Secondary Schools: A Training Manual for Successful Implementation*
    Bwatch - Jan 2015 - pNA [51-500]

Callery, Sean - *Scholastic Discover More: Hurricane Katrina*
    c CCB-B - v69 - i1 - Sept 2015 - p15(2) [51-500]

Callihan, Kristen - *Soulbound*
    PW - v262 - i3 - Jan 19 2015 - p66(1) [51-500]

Callison, Daniel - *The Evolution of Inquiry: Controlled, Guided, Modeled, and Free*
    Teach Lib - v43 - i1 - Oct 2015 - p41(3) [501+]

Callow, Simon - *At Freddie's*
    Nation - v300 - i19 - May 11 2015 - p27(7) [501+]
Orson Welles: One-Man Band
    NS - v144 - i5289 - Nov 20 2015 - p54(2) [51-500]
    Spec - v329 - i9772 - Dec 12 2015 - p82(1) [501+]

Calloway, Colin G. - *Pen and Ink Witchcraft: Treaties and Treaty-Making in American Indian History*
    J Am St - v49 - i1 - Feb 2015 - p190-191 [501+]

Calmenson, Stephanie - *Ollie's Class Trip: A Yes-and-No Book (Illus. by Carter, Abby)*
    c CCB-B - v69 - i2 - Oct 2015 - p79(2) [51-500]
    c KR - June 1 2015 - pNA [51-500]
Teacher's Pets (Illus. by Ross, Heather)
    c HB Guide - v26 - i1 - Spring 2015 - p57(2) [51-500]

Calo, Ambra - *Trails of Bronze Drums Across Early Southeast Asia: Exchange Routes and Connected Cultural Spheres*
    Pac A - v88 - i2 - June 2015 - p371 [501+]

Calomiris, Charles W. - *Fragile by Design: The Political Origins of Banking Crises and Scarce Credit*
    IndRev - v19 - i4 - Spring 2015 - p612(7) [51-500]

Calonita, Jen - *Flunked (Read by Condon, Kristin). Audiobook Review*
    c SLJ - v61 - i6 - June 2015 - p63(1) [51-500]
Flunked
    c BL - v111 - i12 - Feb 15 2015 - p86(1) [51-500]
    c CCB-B - v68 - i10 - June 2015 - p483(1) [51-500]
    c KR - Jan 1 2015 - pNA [51-500]
    c PW - v262 - i4 - Jan 26 2015 - p170(1) [51-500]
    c SLJ - v61 - i3 - March 2015 - p132(2) [51-500]
VIP: I'm with the Band (Illus. by Gudsnuk, Kristen)
    c PW - v262 - i39 - Sept 28 2015 - p89(1) [51-500]
    c SLJ - v61 - i9 - Sept 2015 - p138(1) [51-500]
    c BL - v112 - i5 - Nov 1 2015 - p52(1) [51-500]

Caloyeras, Jennifer - *Strays*
    c KR - March 15 2015 - pNA [51-500]

Calton, Jayson - *The Micronutrient Miracle: The 28-Day Plan to Lose Weight, Increase Your Energy, and Reduce Disease*
    PW - v262 - i20 - May 18 2015 - p80(1) [51-500]

Calverley, Julian - *iPhoneOnly*
    NS - v144 - i5260 - May 1 2015 - p51(1) [51-500]

Calvert, Candace - *By Your Side*
    BL - v111 - i12 - Feb 15 2015 - p43(2) [51-500]

Calvino, Italo - *Collection of Sand: Essays*
    WLT - v89 - i5 - Sept-Oct 2015 - p75(2) [501+]

Calvo, Carlos E. - *Curious George: Gymnastics Fun*
    c HB Guide - v26 - i2 - Fall 2015 - p59(1) [51-500]
Jorge el Curioso: Se Divierte Haciendo Gimnasia / Curious George: Gymnastics Fun
    c HB Guide - v26 - i2 - Fall 2015 - p59(1) [51-500]

Calvo, Ignacio Lopez - *Critical Insights: Magical Realism*
    BL - v111 - i11 - Feb 1 2015 - p10(1) [51-500]

Camalliere, Pat - *The Mystery at Sag Bridge*
    KR - June 1 2015 - pNA [501+]

Camara, Mohamed Saliou - *Political History of Guinea since World War Two*
    AHR - v120 - i2 - April 2015 - p758-759 [501+]

Camarata, Stephen - *The Intuitive Parent: Why the Best Thing for Your Child Is You*
    PW - v262 - i27 - July 6 2015 - p63(1) [51-500]

Cambanis, Thanassis - *Once upon a Revolution: An Egyptian Story*
    For Aff - v94 - i3 - May-June 2015 - pNA [501+]
    NYTBR - Feb 15 2015 - p19(L) [501+]

Cambias, James L. - *Corsair*
    KR - March 15 2015 - pNA [501+]
    PW - v262 - i11 - March 16 2015 - p68(1) [51-500]
A Darkling Sea (Read by Lowlor, Patrick). Audiobook Review
    BL - v111 - i19-20 - June 1 2015 - p126(1) [51-500]

Camcam, Princesse - *Fox's Garden*
    c HB Guide - v26 - i1 - Spring 2015 - p25(1) [51-500]

Camden, Elizabeth - *Until the Dawn*
    BL - v112 - i6 - Nov 15 2015 - p19(1) [51-500]

Camden, Steven - *It's about Love*
    y Sch Lib - v63 - i3 - Autumn 2015 - p179(1) [51-500]
    y SLJ - v61 - i7 - July 2015 - p91(1) [51-500]
    y VOYA - v38 - i3 - August 2015 - p56(1) [51-500]

Camel, West - *Best European Fiction 2015*
    TLS - i5839 - Feb 27 2015 - p27(1) [501+]

Cameli, Christina - *Step-by-Step Free-Motion Quilting: Turn 9 Simple Shapes into 80+ Distinctive Designs*
    LJ - v140 - i2 - Feb 1 2015 - p82(1) [51-500]

Cameron, Alan - *The Last Pagans of Rome*
    Class R - v65 - i1 - April 2015 - p230-233 [501+]

Cameron, Anne - *The Lightning Catcher (Illus. by Jamieson, Victoria)*
    c Teach Lib - v42 - i4 - April 2015 - p37(1) [51-500]
The Secrets of the Storm Vortex (Illus. by Jamieson, Victoria)
    c BL - v111 - i15 - April 1 2015 - p68(1) [51-500]
    c HB Guide - v26 - i2 - Fall 2015 - p77(1) [51-500]
    c KR - March 1 2015 - pNA [51-500]
The Secrets of the Storm Vortex: The Lightning Catcher, Book 3 (Illus. by Jamieson, Victoria)
    y VOYA - v38 - i2 - June 2015 - p71(1) [51-500]

Cameron, Ardis - *Unbuttoning America: A Biography of Peyton Place*
    LJ - v140 - i10 - June 1 2015 - p100(2) [51-500]
    Mac - v128 - i21 - June 1 2015 - p56(1) [501+]

Cameron, Averil - *Byzantine Matters*
    Med R - August 2015 - pNA [501+]
    JIH - v45 - i4 - Spring 2015 - p573-574 [501+]
    Six Ct J - v46 - i2 - Summer 2015 - p522-523 [501+]
    Specu - v90 - i1 - Jan 2015 - p218-220 [501+]
Dialog und Debatte in der Spatantike
    Class R - v65 - i2 - Oct 2015 - p417-419 [501+]

Cameron, Cate - *Just a Summer Fling*
    KR - June 1 2015 - pNA [51-500]
    PW - v262 - i23 - June 8 2015 - p44(1) [51-500]

Cameron, Christopher - *To Plead Our Own Cause: African Americans in Massachusetts and the Making of the Antislavery Movement*
    AHR - v120 - i3 - June 2015 - p1008(1) [501+]
    Am St - v54 - i1 - Spring 2015 - p176-2 [501+]
    JAH - v102 - i2 - Sept 2015 - p553-554 [501+]
    JSH - v81 - i4 - Nov 2015 - p948(2) [501+]

Cameron, Deborah - *Working with Written Discourse*
    Lang Soc - v44 - i4 - Sept 2015 - p597-598 [501+]

Cameron, Don - *Marked Off*
PW - v262 - i37 - Sept 14 2015 - p45(1) [51-500]
Cameron, Eileen - *Rupert's Parchment: Story of Magna Carta (Illus. by Ettlinger, Doris)*
c CH Bwatch - April 2015 - pNA [51-500]
Cameron, Graeme - *Normal*
BL - v111 - i13 - March 1 2015 - p25(1) [51-500]
KR - Feb 1 2015 - pNA [51-500]
LJ - v140 - i2 - Feb 1 2015 - p72(1) [51-500]
PW - v262 - i2 - Jan 12 2015 - p38(1) [51-500]
Cameron, Michael - *Christ Meets Me Everywhere: Augustine's Early Figurative Exegesis*
JR - v95 - i3 - July 2015 - p393(2) [501+]
Cameron, Sharon - *Rook*
y CCB-B - v68 - i11 - July-August 2015 - p540(1) [51-500]
y HB Guide - v26 - i2 - Fall 2015 - p113(1) [51-500]
y PW - v262 - i5 - Feb 2 2015 - p62(1) [51-500]
y VOYA - v38 - i1 - April 2015 - p74(1) [51-500]
y KR - Feb 15 2015 - pNA [51-500]
y VOYA - v38 - i2 - June 2015 - p71(2) [51-500]
Cameron, Stella - *Folly*
BL - v111 - i14 - March 15 2015 - p45(2) [51-500]
PW - v262 - i10 - March 9 2015 - p55(1) [51-500]
Out Comes the Evil
BL - v112 - i7 - Dec 1 2015 - p30(1) [51-500]
KR - Oct 15 2015 - pNA [51-500]
PW - v262 - i42 - Oct 19 2015 - p57(1) [51-500]
Cameron, W. Bruce - *The Dog Master*
KR - June 1 2015 - pNA [51-500]
PW - v262 - i22 - June 1 2015 - p39(1) [51-500]
Ellie's Story (Illus. by Cowdrey, Richard)
c CH Bwatch - July 2015 - pNA [51-500]
c KR - Feb 1 2015 - pNA [51-500]
c SLJ - v61 - i3 - March 2015 - p133(1) [51-500]
y VOYA - v38 - i1 - April 2015 - p54(1) [51-500]
Camerota, Michele - *Galileo's Telescope: A European Story*
TimHES - i2211 - July 9 2015 - p44(1) [501+]
Camia, Shirley - *The Significance of Moths*
SPBW - August 2015 - pNA [51-500]
Camilleri, Andrea - *Angelica's Smile*
RVBW - Jan 2015 - pNA [51-500]
A Beam of Light
BL - v112 - i2 - Sept 15 2015 - p29(1) [51-500]
KR - July 15 2015 - pNA [51-500]
PW - v262 - i27 - July 6 2015 - p48(1) [51-500]
Game of Mirrors
BL - v111 - i13 - March 1 2015 - p23(1) [51-500]
KR - Feb 1 2015 - pNA [51-500]
PW - v262 - i2 - Jan 12 2015 - p35(1) [51-500]
Montalbano's First Case and Other Stories
KR - Dec 15 2015 - pNA [51-500]
PW - v262 - i51 - Dec 14 2015 - p2(1) [51-500]
Camilletti, Fabio A. - *Leopardi's Nymphs: Grace, Melancholy, and the Uncanny*
MLR - v110 - i3 - July 2015 - p881-882 [501+]
Camin, Hector Aguilar - *Death in Veracruz*
KR - August 1 2015 - pNA [51-500]
PW - v262 - i34 - August 24 2015 - p62(1) [51-500]
Camming, Robert - *My Dear BB: The Letters of Bernard Berenson and Kenneth Clark, 1925-1959*
Spec - v327 - i9739 - April 25 2015 - p45(1) [501+]
Cammuso, Frank - *The Misadventures of Salem Hyde: Cookie Catastrophe (Illus. by Cammuso, Frank)*
c HB Guide - v26 - i1 - Spring 2015 - p58(1) [51-500]
The Misadventures of Salem Hyde: Dinosaur Dilemma (Illus. by Cammuso, Frank)
c HB Guide - v26 - i2 - Fall 2015 - p64(1) [51-500]
c SLJ - v61 - i5 - May 2015 - p98(1) [51-500]
Camos, Rosanna Gorris - *Les Muses secretes: Kabbale, alchimie et litterature a la Renaissance*
Six Ct J - v46 - i2 - Summer 2015 - p469-471 [501+]
Camosy, Charles C. - *Beyond the Abortion Wars: A Way Forward for a New Generation*
AM - v213 - i7 - Sept 21 2015 - p38(3) [501+]
Comw - v142 - i9 - May 15 2015 - p23(2) [501+]
LJ - v140 - i6 - April 1 2015 - p96(2) [501+]
Nat R - v67 - i6 - April 6 2015 - p43 [501+]
For Love of Animals: Christian Ethics, Consistent Action
Theol St - v76 - i3 - Sept 2015 - p625(2) [501+]
Camp, Francesca - *Do I Need It? (And What If I Do?): Answers to All Your Questions about Plastic Surgery*
c BL - v112 - i7 - Dec 1 2015 - p34(2) [51-500]
Camp, Greg - *The Willing Spirit*
Roundup M - v22 - i6 - August 2015 - p27(1) [501+]

Campa, Laurence - *Guillaume Apollinaire*
TLS - i5836 - Feb 6 2015 - p3(3) [501+]
Campagne, Herve-Thomas - *Le Cinquiesme Tome des 'Histoires tragiques'*
FS - v69 - i2 - April 2015 - p238-239 [501+]
Campagnol, Isabella - *Forbidden Fashions: Invisible Luxuries in Early Venetian*
Eight-C St - v48 - i2 - Wntr 2015 - p246-248 [501+]
Campanale, Joe - *Downtown Italian: Recipes Inspired by Italy, Created in New York's West Village*
Bwatch - Feb 2015 - pNA [51-500]
Campanella, Richard - *Bourbon Street: A History*
JIH - v45 - i3 - Wntr 2015 - p439-441 [501+]
JSH - v81 - i4 - Nov 2015 - p960(2) [501+]
Campbell, Alastair - *Winners and How They Succeed*
BL - v111 - i22 - August 1 2015 - p10(2) [51-500]
NS - v144 - i5253 - March 13 2015 - p47(1) [501+]
PW - v262 - i35 - August 31 2015 - p80(2) [51-500]
Campbell, Alex - *Cloud 9*
y Sch Lib - v63 - i4 - Winter 2015 - p243(1) [51-500]
Campbell, Anna - *A Scoundrel by Moonlight*
PW - v262 - i12 - March 23 2015 - p54(1) [51-500]
BL - v111 - i16 - April 15 2015 - p31(1) [51-500]
Campbell, Bonnie Jo - *Mothers, Tell Your Daughters (Read by Delaine, Christina). Audiobook Review*
LJ - v140 - i20 - Dec 1 2015 - p58(1) [51-500]
Mothers, Tell Your Daughters
KR - August 1 2015 - pNA [501+]
PW - v262 - i31 - August 3 2015 - p31(2) [51-500]
BL - v111 - i22 - August 1 2015 - p29(1) [51-500]
LJ - v140 - i13 - August 1 2015 - p90(1) [51-500]
NYTBR - Oct 11 2015 - p10(L) [501+]
Campbell, Catherine - *Letting Them Die: Why AIDS Prevention Programmes Fail*
CS - v44 - i5 - Sept 2015 - p591-603 [501+]
Campbell, Christy - *Dogs of Courage: When Britain's Pets Went to War*
Spec - v329 - i9761 - Sept 26 2015 - p44(1) [501+]
Campbell, Colin - *Snake Pass*
KR - Feb 1 2015 - pNA [51-500]
Campbell, David E. - *Seeking the Promised Land: Mormons and American Politics*
J Ch St - v57 - i3 - Summer 2015 - p594-596 [501+]
Campbell, Eddie - *Bacchus (Illus. by Campbell, Eddie)*
BL - v112 - i6 - Nov 15 2015 - p33(1) [51-500]
Campbell, Ellie - *How to Survive Your Sisters*
PW - v262 - i37 - Sept 14 2015 - p40(1) [51-500]
Campbell, Erin J. - *The Early Modern Italian Domestic Interior, 1400-1700: Objects, Spaces, Domesticities*
Six Ct J - v46 - i2 - Summer 2015 - p412-414 [501+]
Campbell, Ian - *Renaissance Humanism and Ethnicity before Race: The Irish and the English in the Seventeenth Century*
HER - v130 - i545 - August 2015 - p994(3) [501+]
Campbell, Isaiah - *The Struggles of Johnny Cannon*
c BL - v112 - i3 - Oct 1 2015 - p80(1) [51-500]
c KR - July 15 2015 - pNA [51-500]
The Troubles of Johnny Cannon
y HB Guide - v26 - i1 - Spring 2015 - p72(1) [51-500]
Campbell, Jack - *Imperfect Sword*
Bwatch - Feb 2015 - pNA [51-500]
Leviathan
PW - v262 - i14 - April 6 2015 - p44(1) [51-500]
Campbell, John (b. 1956-) - *Berkeley's Puzzle: What Does Experience Teach Us?*
TLS - i5837 - Feb 13 2015 - p24(1) [501+]
Campbell, John L. - *The National Origins of Policy Ideas: Knowledge Regimes in the United States, France, Germany, and Denmark*
AJS - v121 - i1 - July 2015 - p338(3) [501+]
Campbell, Joseph - *Romance of the Grail: The Magic and Mystery of Arthurian Myth*
LJ - v140 - i15 - Sept 15 2015 - p74(1) [51-500]
Campbell, K.G. - *Dylan the Villain (Illus. by Campbell, K.G.)*
c KR - Dec 1 2015 - pNA [51-500]
c PW - v262 - i45 - Nov 9 2015 - p58(1) [51-500]
Campbell, Karen - *Rise*
KR - April 1 2015 - pNA [51-500]
NYTBR - July 19 2015 - p10(L) [501+]

Campbell, Karlyn Kohrs - *The Great Silent Majority: Nixon's 1969 Speech on Vietnamization*
Pres St Q - v45 - i3 - Sept 2015 - p619(2) [501+]
Campbell, L.A. - *Cartboy Goes to Camp*
c HB Guide - v26 - i1 - Spring 2015 - p72(1) [51-500]
Campbell, Marissa - *Avelynn*
PW - v262 - i30 - July 27 2015 - p49(1) [51-500]
Campbell, Melodie - *The Goddaughter Caper*
KR - Nov 15 2015 - pNA [51-500]
Campbell, Neil - *Post-Westerns: Cinema, Region, West*
J Am St - v49 - i1 - Feb 2015 - p219-220 [501+]
PHR - v84 - i2 - May 2015 - p273(3) [501+]
Campbell, Patricia Shehan - *The Oxford Handbook of Children's Musical Cultures*
Notes - v72 - i1 - Sept 2015 - p154(4) [501+]
Campbell, Patty - *Spirituality in Young Adult Literature: The Last Taboo*
y BL - v112 - i6 - Nov 15 2015 - p44(1) [51-500]
Campbell, Rick - *Empire Rising*
BL - v111 - i9-10 - Jan 1 2015 - p50(1) [51-500]
Campbell, Scott - *Great Showdowns: The Revenge (Illus. by Campbell, Scott)*
y SLJ - v61 - i8 - August 2015 - p111(1) [51-500]
Hug Machine (Illus. by Campbell, Scott)
c HB Guide - v26 - i1 - Spring 2015 - p7(1) [51-500]
Campbell, Stacey R. - *Sock Monster (Illus. by Thieme, Elizabeth)*
c KR - Dec 15 2015 - pNA [501+]
Campbell, W. Joseph - *1995: The Year the Future Began*
Mac - v128 - i4 - Feb 2 2015 - p60(2) [501+]
Campe, Rudiger - *The Game of Probability: Literature and Calculation from Pascal to Kleist*
AHR - v120 - i3 - June 2015 - p1131-1132 [501+]
Camper, Cathy - *Lowriders in Space (Illus. by Raul the Third)*
c CCB-B - v68 - i5 - Jan 2015 - p249(2) [51-500]
c HB Guide - v26 - i1 - Spring 2015 - p72(1) [51-500]
y VOYA - v37 - i6 - Feb 2015 - p72(2) [51-500]
Camporeale, Salvatore I. - *Christianity, Latinity, and Culture: Two Studies on Lorenzo Valla*
Ren Q - v68 - i3 - Fall 2015 - p971-972 [501+]
Campos, Elmer Hernan Rodriguez - *Under the Sour Sun: Hunger through the Eyes of a Child*
PW - v262 - i45 - Nov 9 2015 - p54(1) [51-500]
Campos, Luis A. - *Radium and the Secret of Life*
TimHES - i2203 - May 14 2015 - p51(1) [501+]
Campoy, F. Isabel - *Maybe Something Beautiful: How Art Transformed a Neighborhood (Illus. by Lopez, Rafael)*
c BL - v112 - i5 - Nov 1 2015 - p53(1) [51-500]
Camprubi, Lino - *Engineers and the Making of the Francoist Regime*
Isis - v106 - i2 - June 2015 - p490(2) [501+]
T&C - v56 - i3 - July 2015 - p767-768 [501+]
Canaday, Margot - *The Straight State: Sexuality and Citizenship in Twentieth-Century America*
JWH - v27 - i1 - Spring 2015 - p161(7) [501+]
Canadeo, Anne - *The Postman Always Purls Twice*
BL - v111 - i16 - April 15 2015 - p29(1) [51-500]
Canales, Jimena - *The Physicist and the Philosopher: Einstein, Bergson, and the Debate That Changed Our Understanding of Time*
BL - v111 - i17 - May 1 2015 - p61(1) [51-500]
CHE - v61 - i38 - June 12 2015 - pB17(1) [501+]
KR - March 15 2015 - pNA [501+]
LJ - v140 - i6 - April 1 2015 - p114(1) [501+]
PW - v262 - i16 - April 20 2015 - p67(1) [51-500]
Canatsey, Kenneth - *Silk Road: The Journey*
KR - Dec 1 2015 - pNA [51-500]
Canavan, Trudi - *Angel of Storms*
PW - v262 - i39 - Sept 28 2015 - p73(2) [51-500]
Canby, Kelly - *All the Lost Things (Illus. by Canby, Kelly)*
c KR - May 15 2015 - pNA [51-500]
c PW - v262 - i19 - May 11 2015 - p60(1) [51-500]
Candela, Tony - *EFI Conversions: How to Swap Your Carb for Electronic Fuel Injection*
Bwatch - July 2015 - pNA [51-500]
Candelaria, Mario - *Ashes: A Firefighter's Tale*
PW - v262 - i42 - Oct 19 2015 - p64(1) [51-500]
Cander, Chris - *Whisper Hollow*
BL - v111 - i12 - Feb 15 2015 - p34(1) [51-500]
KR - Jan 1 2015 - pNA [51-500]
PW - v262 - i2 - Jan 12 2015 - p33(1) [51-500]
Candiani, Vera - *Dreaming of Dry Land: Environmental Transformation in Colonial Mexico City*
Ams - v72 - i3 - July 2015 - p489(2) [501+]
HNet - April 2015 - pNA [501+]
Candido, Igor - *Boccaccio umanista: Studi su Boccaccio e Apuleio*
Med R - Jan 2015 - pNA [501+]
Ren Q - v68 - i1 - Spring 2015 - p369-371 [501+]

Candido, Mariana P. - *An African Slaving Port and the Atlantic World: Benguela and Its Hinterland*
    AHR - v120 - i4 - Oct 2015 - p1579-1580 [501+]

Candlewick Press - *Peppa Pig and the Day at Snowy Mountain*
    c HB Guide - v26 - i2 - Fall 2015 - p16(1) [51-500]

Candlin, Kit - *The Last Caribbean Frontier, 1795-1815*
    HAHR - v95 - i2 - May 2015 - p358-359 [501+]

Cane, Ella - *The U.S. Presidency*
    c HB Guide - v26 - i1 - Spring 2015 - p138(1) [51-500]

The U.S. Supreme Court
    c HB Guide - v26 - i1 - Spring 2015 - p138(1) [51-500]

Canessa, Andrew - *Intimate Indigeneities: Race, Sex, and History in the Small Spaces of Andean Life*
    ERS - v38 - i3 - March 2015 - p481(3) [501+]

Canessa, Roberto - *I Had to Survive*
    KR - Dec 15 2015 - pNA [501+]

Canfield, Jack - *The 30-Day Sobriety Solution: How to Cut Back or Quit Drinking in the Privacy of Your Own Home*
    PW - v262 - i36 - Sept 7 2015 - p61(2) [51-500]
    PW - v262 - i42 - Oct 19 2015 - p39(1) [501+]

The 30-Day Sobriety Solution: How to Quit or Cut Back Drinking in the Privacy of Your Own Home
    BL - v111 - i22 - August 1 2015 - p11(1) [51-500]

Cangany, Catherine - *Frontier Seaport: Detroit's Transformation into an Atlantic Entrepot*
    AHR - v120 - i1 - Feb 2015 - p230-231 [501+]
    JAH - v101 - i4 - March 2015 - p1260-1261 [501+]
    W&M Q - v72 - i3 - July 2015 - p527-531 [501+]

Canguilhem, Georges - *Writings on Medicine*
    MAQ - v29 - i1 - March 2015 - pB58-B60 [501+]

Canguilhem, Philippe - *Chanter sur le livre a la Renaissance: Les traites de contrepoint de Vicente Lusitano*
    Notes - v71 - i4 - June 2015 - p716(4) [501+]

Canin, Ethan - *A Doubter's Almanac*
    BL - v112 - i3 - Oct 1 2015 - p4(1) [51-500]
    BL - v112 - i5 - Nov 1 2015 - p27(1) [51-500]
    KR - Nov 15 2015 - pNA [51-500]
    PW - v262 - i35 - August 31 2015 - p59(1) [51-500]

Cann, John P. - *Flight Plan Africa: Portuguese Airpower in Counterinsurgency, 1961-1974*
    J Mil H - v79 - i2 - April 2015 - p546-547 [501+]

Cannadine, David - *George V: The Unexpected King*
    TLS - i5841 - March 13 2015 - p10(2) [501+]

Cannady, Laurie Jean - *Crave*
    KR - Sept 1 2015 - pNA [51-500]

Cannell, Dorothy - *Death at Dovecote Hatch*
    BL - v111 - i17 - May 1 2015 - p28(1) [51-500]
    KR - May 15 2015 - pNA [51-500]
    PW - v262 - i20 - May 18 2015 - p66(1) [51-500]

Cannell, John - *Autism Causes, Prevention and Treatment*
    SPBW - May 2015 - pNA [501+]

Canning, Joseph - *Ideas of Power in the Late Middle Ages, 1296-1417*
    Specu - v90 - i3 - July 2015 - p782-783 [501+]

Cannon, Aubrey - *Structured Worlds: The Archaeology of Hunter-Gatherer Thought and Action*
    JRAI - v21 - i1 - March 2015 - p224(2) [501+]

Cannon, Dolores - *The Search For Hidden Sacred Knowledge*
    RVBW - Feb 2015 - pNA [501+]

Cannon, Eoin F. - *The Saloon and the Mission: Addiction, Conversion and the Politics of Redemption in American Culture*
    JAH - v101 - i4 - March 2015 - p1293-1294 [501+]

Cannon, Geonn - *The Virtuous Feats of the Indomitable Miss Trafalgar and the Erudite Lady Boone*
    KR - August 15 2015 - pNA [51-500]

Cannon, Joanna - *Religious Poverty, Visual Riches: Art in the Dominican Churches of Central Italy in the Thirteenth and Fourteenth Centuries*
    Ren Q - v68 - i1 - Spring 2015 - p244-246 [501+]
    Six Ct J - v46 - i3 - Fall 2015 - p833-834 [501+]

Cannon, John - *The Oxford Companion to British History*
    TimHES - i2228 - Nov 5 2015 - p47(1) [501+]

Cannon, Julie - *Countdown*
    PW - v262 - i37 - Sept 14 2015 - p50(1) [51-500]

Cannon, Katy - *Secrets, Schemes and Sewing Machines*
    y Sch Lib - v63 - i2 - Summer 2015 - p115(1) [51-500]

Cannon, Nick - *Neon Aliens Ate My Homework and Other Poems*
    c HB Guide - v26 - i2 - Fall 2015 - p203(1) [51-500]
    c PW - v262 - i6 - Feb 9 2015 - p69(1) [51-500]

Roc and Roe's Twelve Days of Christmas (Illus. by Ford, A.G.)
    c HB Guide - v26 - i1 - Spring 2015 - p25(1) [51-500]

Cannon, Sherrill S. - *Mice and Spider and Webs...Oh My! (Illus. by KJ of Kalpart)*
    c CH Bwatch - August 2015 - pNA [51-500]

Cannon, Zander - *Kaijumax: Terror and Respect*
    PW - v262 - i50 - Dec 7 2015 - p75(1) [51-500]

Cano, Felipe - *Bonjour Camille (Illus. by Aguilar, Laia)*
    c HB Guide - v26 - i1 - Spring 2015 - p25(1) [51-500]

Cano, Lesley M. - *3D Printing: A Powerful New Curriculum Tool for Your School Library*
    RVBW - Oct 2015 - pNA [51-500]
    Teach Lib - v43 - i1 - Oct 2015 - p41(3) [501+]

Canova-Green, Marie-Claude - *Writing Royal Entries in Early Modern Europe*
    Ren Q - v68 - i1 - Spring 2015 - p291-293 [501+]

Cantavella, Rosanna - *El "Facet," una "ars amandi" medieval: Edicio i estudi*
    Specu - v90 - i4 - Oct 2015 - p1095-1096 [501+]

Cantello, Matthew - *Communing with Music: Practicing the Art of Conscious Listening*
    RVBW - March 2015 - pNA [501+]

Cantle, Ted - *Interculturalism: The New Era of Cohesion and Diversity*
    ERS - v38 - i3 - March 2015 - p464(3) [501+]

Cantor, Geoffrey - *The Great Exhibition: A Documentary History, 4 vols.*
    Isis - v106 - i1 - March 2015 - p199(2) [501+]

Cantor, Jillian - *The Hours Count*
    BL - v112 - i1 - Sept 1 2015 - p52(1) [51-500]
    KR - August 15 2015 - pNA [51-500]
    LJ - v140 - i13 - August 1 2015 - p80(1) [51-500]
    NYTBR - Nov 22 2015 - p38(L) [501+]
    PW - v262 - i32 - August 10 2015 - p35(1) [51-500]

Cantor, Rachel - *Good on Paper*
    BL - v112 - i6 - Nov 15 2015 - p21(1) [51-500]
    KR - Oct 1 2015 - pNA [501+]
    LJ - v140 - i16 - Oct 1 2015 - p66(1) [51-500]
    PW - v262 - i42 - Oct 19 2015 - p50(1) [51-500]

Cantore, Janice - *Drawing Fire: Cold Case Justice*
    BL - v111 - i19-20 - June 1 2015 - p52(1) [51-500]

Cantrell, Christian - *Equinox*
    PW - v262 - i2 - Jan 12 2015 - p41(1) [51-500]

Cantrell, Kat - *From Fake to Forever*
    RVBW - June 2015 - pNA [51-500]

Cantwell, Laureen P. - *Memphis Noir*
    PW - v262 - i38 - Sept 21 2015 - p55(2) [51-500]

Cantwell, Michael - *Rosa's Gift and Other Stories*
    KR - May 1 2015 - pNA [51-500]

Canuel, Mark - *Justice, Dissent, and the Sublime*
    MLR - v110 - i1 - Jan 2015 - p229-230 [501+]

Canzano, Joe - *Magno Girl*
    SPBW - June 2015 - pNA [51-500]

Cao, Qing - *Discourse, Politics and Media in Contemporary China*
    Lang Soc - v44 - i4 - Sept 2015 - p595-596 [501+]

Capek, Michael - *The Battle over Slavery: Causes and Effects of the U.S. Civil War*
    c HB Guide - v26 - i2 - Fall 2015 - p219(1) [51-500]

Capelo, Joaquin - *Sociologica de Lima*
    AJS - v121 - i2 - Sept 2015 - p662(12) [51-500]

Capetanos, Leon - *The Time Box*
    y SLJ - v61 - i11 - Nov 2015 - p106(1) [51-500]

Capetta, Amy Rose - *Entangled*
    c BL - v112 - i1 - Sept 1 2015 - p114(1) [501+]
    y CH Bwatch - Jan 2015 - pNA [51-500]

Unmade
    y CCB-B - v68 - i9 - May 2015 - p440(2) [51-500]

Caple, Kathy - *A Night at the Zoo (Illus. by Caple, Kathy)*
    c HB Guide - v26 - i1 - Spring 2015 - p52(1) [51-500]

Caples, Garrett - *The Collected Poems of Philip Lamantia*
    Poet - v205 - i5 - Feb 2015 - p475(9) [501+]

Capote, Truman - *Brooklyn: A Personal Memoir: With the Lost Photographs of David Attie (Illus. by Attie, David)*
    NYT - Sept 20 2015 - p4(L) [501+]
    PW - v262 - i41 - Oct 12 2015 - p61(1) [501+]

The Early Stories of Truman Capote
    KR - August 15 2015 - pNA [501+]
    NS - v144 - i5287 - Nov 6 2015 - p42(2) [51-500]
    NYTBR - Dec 20 2015 - p26(L) [501+]
    PW - v262 - i31 - August 3 2015 - p31(1) [51-500]

Cappelli, Peter - *Will College Pay Off? A Guide to the Most Important Financial Decision You'll Ever Make (Read by Perkins, Tom). Audiobook Review*
    PW - v262 - i35 - August 31 2015 - p84(1) [51-500]

Will College Pay Off? A Guide to the Most Important Financial Decision You'll Ever Make
    Barron's - v95 - i49 - Dec 7 2015 - p48(1) [501+]
    BL - v111 - i18 - May 15 2015 - p7(1) [51-500]
    BL - v111 - i21 - July 1 2015 - p22(2) [501+]
    KR - April 15 2015 - pNA [501+]
    LJ - v140 - i9 - May 15 2015 - p90(1) [51-500]

Cappelorn, Niels Jorgen - *Kierkegaard's Journals and Notebooks, vol. 7*
    RM - v68 - i4 - June 2015 - p857(3) [501+]

Cappiello, Katie - *Slut: A Play and Guidebook for Combating Sexism and Sexual Violence*
    Bwatch - May 2015 - pNA [51-500]

Capponi, Niccolo - *The Day the Renaissance Was Saved: The Battle of Anghiari and da Vinci's Lost Masterpiece*
    KR - Oct 1 2015 - pNA [51-500]
    LJ - v140 - i19 - Nov 15 2015 - p81(1) [51-500]

Cappucilli, Alyssa Satin - *Not This Bear: A First Day of School Story (Illus. by Hussey, Lorna)*
    c SLJ - v61 - i8 - August 2015 - p57(1) [51-500]

Caprio, Chiara De - *Scrivere la storia a Napoli tra Medioevo e prima et a moderna*
    Ren Q - v68 - i1 - Spring 2015 - p231-232 [501+]

Capriolo, Paola - *Mi ricordo*
    TLS - i5870 - Oct 2 2015 - p21(1) [501+]

Capucilli, Alyssa Satin - *Hannah Is a Big Sister (Illus. by Stott, Dorothy)*
    c HB Guide - v26 - i1 - Spring 2015 - p7(1) [51-500]

Henry Is a Big Brother (Illus. by Stott, Dorothy)
    c HB Guide - v26 - i1 - Spring 2015 - p7(1) [51-500]

Katy Duck's Happy Halloween (Illus. by Cole, Henry)
    c HB Guide - v26 - i2 - Fall 2015 - p59(1) [51-500]

Not This Bear: A First Day of School Story (Illus. by Hussey, Lorna)
    c HB Guide - v26 - i2 - Fall 2015 - p7(1) [51-500]
    c KR - June 1 2015 - pNA [51-500]

Tulip and Rex Write a Story (Illus. by Massini, Sarah)
    c KR - June 15 2015 - pNA [51-500]

Caputo, John D. - *The Insistence of God: A Theology of Perhaps*
    JR - v95 - i4 - Oct 2015 - p542(2) [501+]

Caraballo, Samuel - *Estas manos: Manitas de mi familia/These Hands: My Family's Hands (Illus. by Costello, Shawn)*
    c CH Bwatch - Jan 2015 - pNA [51-500]
    c HB Guide - v26 - i1 - Spring 2015 - p25(1) [51-500]
    SLJ - v61 - i3 - March 2015 - p113(1) [51-500]

Carafano, James Jay - *Wiki at War: Conflict in a Socially Networked World*
    APJ - v29 - i6 - Nov-Dec 2015 - p97(3) [501+]

Carapico, Sheila - *Political Aid and Arab Activism: Democracy Promotion, Justice, and Representation*
    IJMES - v47 - i3 - August 2015 - p648-649 [501+]

Carassai, Sebastian - *The Argentine Silent Majority: Middle Classes, Politics, Violence, and Memory in the Seventies*
    AHR - v120 - i4 - Oct 2015 - p1536-1537 [501+]
    CS - v44 - i6 - Nov 2015 - p784-786 [501+]
    HAHR - v95 - i4 - Nov 2015 - p701-702 [501+]

Carasso, Lucienne - *Growing Up Jewish in Alexandria: The Story of a Sephardic Family's Exodus from Egypt*
    KR - Jan 1 2015 - pNA [501+]

Caravale, Giorgio - *Intellettuali in esilio: Dall'inquisizione romana al fascismo*
    Six Ct J - v46 - i2 - Summer 2015 - p473-474 [501+]

Storia di una doppia censura: Gli Strategemmi di Satana di Giacomo Aconcio nell'Europa del Seicento
    Six Ct J - v46 - i1 - Spring 2015 - p213-215 [501+]

Caravante, Peggy - *Marooned in the Arctic: The True Story of Ada Blackjack, the "Female Robinson Crusoe"*
    c PW - v262 - i48 - Nov 30 2015 - p62(1) [501+]

Caravantes, Peggy - *The Many Faces of Josephine Baker: Dancer, Activist, Spy*
    VOYA - v38 - i2 - June 2015 - p87(1) [51-500]

Carawan, Edwin, - *The Athenian Amnesty and Reconstructing the Law*
    Class R - v65 - i2 - Oct 2015 - p504-506 [501+]

Caraza, Xanath - *Silabas De Viento/Syllables Of Wind*
    Am St - v54 - i2 - Summer 2015 - p131-132 [501+]

Carbado, Devon W. - *Acting White?: Rethinking Race in "Post-Racial" America*
    CS - v44 - i3 - May 2015 - p349-351 [501+]

Carbia, Mylo - *The Raping of Ava DeSantis*
    RVBW - Nov 2015 - pNA [51-500]

Carbo, Christine - *The Wild Inside*
    PW - v262 - i14 - April 6 2015 - p38(1) [51-500]
    BL - v111 - i19-20 - June 1 2015 - p58(2) [51-500]
    KR - April 15 2015 - pNA [501+]

Carbone, June - *Marriage Markets: How Inequality Is Remaking the American Family*
    Bks & Cult - v21 - i3 - May-June 2015 - p19(2) [501+]

Card, David - *Immigration, Poverty, and Socioeconomic Inequality*
    CS - v44 - i6 - Nov 2015 - p786-788 [501+]

Card, Orson Scott - *Visitors*
  y HB - v91 - i2 - March-April 2015 - p93(1) [51-500]
  y HB Guide - v26 - i2 - Fall 2015 - p113(1) [51-500]

Cardello, Ruth - *Tycoon Takedown*
    PW - v262 - i2 - Jan 12 2015 - p42(1) [51-500]

Carden, Allen - *Freedom's Delay: America's Struggle for Emancipation, 1776-1865*
    JSH - v81 - i4 - Nov 2015 - p950(2) [501+]

Carden-Coyne, Ana - *The Politics of Wounds: Military Patients and Medical Power in the First World War*
    HNet - July 2015 - pNA [501+]

Cardi, Annie - *The Chance You Won't Return*
  c HB Guide - v26 - i1 - Spring 2015 - p102(1) [51-500]

Cardillo, Joseph - *Body Intelligence: Harness Your Body's Energies for Your Best Life*
    BL - v112 - i4 - Oct 15 2015 - p5(1) [51-500]
    PW - v262 - i36 - Sept 7 2015 - p59(2) [51-500]

Cardim, Pedro - *Polycentric Monarchies: How Did Early Modern Spain and Portugal Achieve and Maintain a Global Hegemony?*
    JMH - v87 - i2 - June 2015 - p403(7) [501+]

Cardin, Matt - *Mummies around the World: An Encyclopedia of Mummies in History, Religion, and Popular Culture*
    BL - v111 - i13 - March 1 2015 - p8(1) [51-500]
    LJ - v140 - i3 - Feb 15 2015 - p130(2) [51-500]

Cardoza-Orlandi, Carlos F. - *To All Nations from All Nations: A History of the Christian Missionary Movement*
    IBMR - v39 - i3 - July 2015 - p154(2) [501+]

Cardozo, Christopher - *Edward S. Curtis: One Hundred Masterworks*
    LJ - v140 - i15 - Sept 15 2015 - p81(3) [501+]

Carducci, Bernardo J. - *Shyness: The Ultimate Teen Guide*
    VOYA - v38 - i2 - June 2015 - p87(1) [51-500]

Carducci, Tad - *The Tippling Bros: A Lime and a Shaker: Discovering Mexican-Inspired Cocktails*
    LJ - v140 - i3 - Feb 15 2015 - p122(1) [51-500]

Cardullo, Bert - *Bazin on Global Cinema 1948-1958*
    Si & So - v25 - i5 - May 2015 - p106(1) [51-500]

Carens, Joseph H. - *The Ethics of Immigration*
    Ethics - v125 - i2 - Jan 2015 - p571(6) [501+]

Carew, Michael G. - *The Impact of the First World War on U.S. Policymakers: American Strategic and Foreign Policy Formulation, 1938-1942*
    J Mil H - v79 - i1 - Jan 2015 - p246-247 [501+]
    J Mil H - v79 - i4 - Oct 2015 - p1166-1167 [501+]

Carey, Anna - *Blackbird*
  c HB Guide - v26 - i1 - Spring 2015 - p102(1) [51-500]
    Deadfall
  y HB Guide - v26 - i2 - Fall 2015 - p113(1) [51-500]
  y SLJ - v61 - i5 - May 2015 - p112(1) [51-500]
  y VOYA - v38 - i2 - June 2015 - p72(1) [51-500]
    KR - April 1 2015 - pNA [51-500]

Carey, Brycchan - *Quakers and Abolition*
    JAH - v101 - i4 - March 2015 - p1266-1267 [501+]

Carey, Daniel - *Money and Political Economy in the Enlightenment*
    FS - v69 - i1 - Jan 2015 - p98-98 [501+]
    Richard Hakluyt and Travel Writing in Early Modern Europe
    HER - v130 - i543 - April 2015 - p442(2) [501+]

Carey, Edward - *Foulsham*
  y KR - April 15 2015 - pNA [51-500]
  y Sch Lib - v63 - i1 - Spring 2015 - p50(1) [51-500]
  y SLJ - v61 - i6 - June 2015 - p110(1) [51-500]
    Heap House
  y HB Guide - v26 - i1 - Spring 2015 - p72(1) [51-500]
  y Sch Lib - v63 - i1 - Spring 2015 - p50(1) [501+]
    Lungdon (Illus. by Carey, Edward)
  y SLJ - v61 - i12 - Dec 2015 - p112(2) [51-500]

Carey, Janet Lee - *In the Time of Dragon Moon*
  y CCB-B - v68 - i9 - May 2015 - p441(1) [51-500]
  y HB Guide - v26 - i2 - Fall 2015 - p113(1) [51-500]
  y VOYA - v37 - i6 - Feb 2015 - p73(1) [51-500]

Carey, Juliet - *Theatres of Life: Drawings from the Rothschild Collection at Waddesdon Manor*
    NYRB - v62 - i11 - June 25 2015 - p29(4) [501+]

Carey, Kevin - *The End of College: Creating the Future of Learning and the University of Everywhere*
  y BL - v111 - i12 - Feb 15 2015 - p12(1) [51-500]
    CSM - March 17 2015 - pNA [51-500]
    KR - Jan 1 2015 - pNA [501+]
    LJ - v140 - i3 - Feb 15 2015 - p110(2) [51-500]
    NYTBR - March 29 2015 - p13(L) [501+]
    PW - v262 - i4 - Jan 26 2015 - p164(1) [501+]

Carey, Lorraine - *Cinderella's Stepsister and the Big Bad Wolf (Illus. by Blanco, Migy)*
  c KR - July 15 2015 - pNA [51-500]
  c PW - v262 - i28 - July 13 2015 - p64(1) [501+]
  c SLJ - v61 - i10 - Oct 2015 - p72(1) [501+]

Carey, Mariah - *All I Want For Christmas Is You (Illus. by Madden, Colleen)*
  c KR - Oct 15 2015 - pNA [51-500]
  c PW - v262 - i37 - Sept 14 2015 - p66(1) [51-500]

Carey, Mike - *The Girl with All the Gifts*
  y Teach Lib - v42 - i3 - Feb 2015 - p28(4) [51-500]

Carey, Nessa - *Junk DNA: A Jouney through the Dark Matter of the Genome*
    LJ - v140 - i3 - Feb 15 2015 - p124(1) [51-500]
    PW - v262 - i6 - Feb 9 2015 - p56(2) [51-500]
    QRB - v90 - i4 - Dec 2015 - p444(2) [501+]
    Junk DNA: A Journey through the Dark Matter of the Genome
    New Sci - v225 - i3007 - Feb 7 2015 - p44(1) [501+]

Carey, Peter - *Amnesia*
    LJ - v140 - i3 - Feb 15 2015 - p84(2) [51-500]
    Mac - v128 - i4 - Feb 2 2015 - p60(2) [501+]
    Nat Post - v17 - i68 - Jan 17 2015 - pWP8(1) [501+]
    NY - v90 - i47 - Feb 9 2015 - p69 [51-500]
    NYRB - v62 - i8 - May 7 2015 - p51(3) [501+]
    NYT - Jan 22 2015 - pC7(L) [501+]
    NYTBR - Feb 22 2015 - p17(L) [501+]
    NYTBR - Dec 13 2015 - p44(L) [501+]
    TLS - i5837 - Feb 13 2015 - p20(1) [501+]
    Jack Maggs
    TimHES - i2228 - Nov 5 2015 - p46(1) [501+]

Carey, Richard Adams - *In the Evil Day: Violence Comes to One Small Town*
    BL - v112 - i2 - Sept 15 2015 - p6(1) [51-500]

Carey, Tanith - *Taming the Tiger Parent*
    NS - v144 - i5250 - Feb 20 2015 - p50(2) [501+]

Carl, Anna Watson - *The Yellow Table: A Celebration of Everyday Gatherings (Illus. by Birck, Signe)*
    LJ - v140 - i13 - August 1 2015 - p119(1) [51-500]

Carl, JoAnna - *The Chocolate Clown Corpse*
    Bwatch - April 2015 - pNA [51-500]

Carl, Scott - *Verbum Domini and the Complementarity of Exegesis and Theology*
    Theol St - v76 - i4 - Dec 2015 - p881(1) [501+]

Carl, William D. - *Out of the Woods*
    PW - v262 - i8 - Feb 23 2015 - p57(1) [51-500]

Carla, Heidi - *The Tiny Portrait (Illus. by Cinquanta, Karla)*
    RVBW - Jan 2015 - pNA [51-500]

Carlberg, Ingrid - *Raoul Wallenberg: The Heroic Life and Mysterious Disappearance of the Man Who Saved Thousands of Hungarian Jews from the Holocaust*
    KR - Dec 15 2015 - pNA [501+]

Carle, Eric - *A House for Hermit Crab*
  c HB Guide - v26 - i1 - Spring 2015 - p52(1) [51-500]
    My First Busy Book
  c KR - Jan 1 2016 - pNA [51-500]
    The Nonsense Show (Illus. by Carle, Eric)
  c BL - v111 - i21 - July 1 2015 - p64(2) [51-500]
  c HB - v91 - i5 - Sept-Oct 2015 - p76(2) [51-500]
  c KR - August 15 2015 - pNA [51-500]
  c PW - v262 - i29 - July 20 2015 - p188(1) [51-500]
  c SLJ - v61 - i8 - August 2015 - p66(2) [51-500]
    Walter the Baker
  c HB Guide - v26 - i1 - Spring 2015 - p52(1) [51-500]
    What's Your Favorite Animal? (Illus. by Carle, Eric)
  c SLJ - v61 - i7 - July 2015 - p54(1) [51-500]

Carles, Philippe - *Free Jazz/Black Power*
    NYRB - v62 - i12 - July 9 2015 - p55(3) [501+]

Carleson, J.C. - *Placebo Junkies*
  y BL - v112 - i4 - Oct 15 2015 - p45(2) [51-500]
  y KR - July 15 2015 - pNA [51-500]
  y PW - v262 - i34 - August 24 2015 - p83(1) [51-500]
  y SLJ - v61 - i10 - Oct 2015 - p109(1) [51-500]

Carlin, John - *Chase Your Shadow: The Trials of Oscar Pistorius*
    TLS - i5840 - March 6 2015 - p34(1) [501+]

Carlin, Kelly - *A Carlin Home Companion: Growing Up with George*
    BL - v111 - i22 - August 1 2015 - p14(1) [51-500]
    KR - July 1 2015 - pNA [51-500]
    NYTBR - Dec 6 2015 - p58(L) [501+]
    PW - v262 - i19 - May 11 2015 - p45(1) [51-500]

Carlisle, Emma - *Lion Practice*
  c Sch Lib - v63 - i4 - Winter 2015 - p218(1) [51-500]

Carlisle, J.M. - *The Cowboy and the Canal: How Theodore Roosevelt Cheated Colombia, Stole Panama, and Bamboozled America*
    HNet - Sept 2015 - pNA(NA) [501+]

Carlisle, Kate - *Ripped from the Pages (Read by Berneis, Susie). Audiobook Review*
    BL - v112 - i6 - Nov 15 2015 - p62(1) [51-500]
    Ripped from the Pages
    BL - v111 - i19-20 - June 1 2015 - p50(1) [51-500]

Carlon, Mick - *Girl Singer*
  y BL - v112 - i6 - Nov 15 2015 - p50(1) [51-500]
    KR - Sept 1 2015 - pNA [51-500]

Carlos, John - *Ireland's Western Islands: Inishbofin, the Aran Islands, Inishturk, Inishark, Clare and Turbot Islands*
    ILS - v35 - i1 - Fall 2015 - p25(2) [501+]

Carlsen, Spike - *Cabin Lessons: A Nail-by-Nail Tale: Building Our Dream Cottage from 2x4s, Blisters, and Love*
    RVBW - July 2015 - pNA [51-500]

Carlson, Amanda B. - *Africa in Florida: Five Hundred Years of African Presence in the Sunshine State*
    JSH - v81 - i4 - Nov 2015 - p935(2) [501+]

Carlson, Angela Doll - *Nearly Orthodox: On Being a Modern Woman in an Ancient Tradition*
    PW - v262 - i8 - Feb 23 2015 - p69(1) [51-500]

Carlson, Brady - *Dead Presidents: An American Adventure into the Strange Deaths and Surprising Afterlives of Our Nation's Leaders*
    KR - Nov 1 2015 - pNA [501+]
    LJ - v140 - i19 - Nov 15 2015 - p94(1) [51-500]

Carlson, Caroline - *The Terror of the Southlands (Illus. by Phillips, Dave)*
  y HB Guide - v26 - i1 - Spring 2015 - p72(1) [51-500]

Carlson, David R. - *John Gower, Poetry and Propaganda in Fourteenth-Century England*
    MLR - v110 - i3 - July 2015 - p810-811 [501+]
    Specu - v90 - i4 - Oct 2015 - p1097-1098 [501+]

Carlson, Dean - *Field & Feast: Sublime Food from a Brave New Farm*
    PW - v262 - i46 - Nov 16 2015 - p71(1) [51-500]

Carlson, Gretchen - *Getting Real*
    KR - April 15 2015 - pNA [51-500]
    LJ - v140 - i8 - May 1 2015 - p80(1) [51-500]

Carlson, Melody - *Prom Date*
  y VOYA - v38 - i2 - June 2015 - p55(1) [51-500]

Carlson, N.O. - *Broken Vows*
    SPBW - July 2015 - pNA [51-500]

Carlson, Nancy - *Sometimes You Barf (Illus. by Carlson, Nancy)*
  c HB Guide - v26 - i1 - Spring 2015 - p25(1) [51-500]

Carlson, Nicholas - *Marissa Mayer and the Fight to Save Yahoo!*
    Econ - v414 - i8920 - Jan 10 2015 - p79(US) [501+]
    Har Bus R - v93 - i5 - May 2015 - p118(2) [501+]
    LJ - v140 - i2 - Feb 1 2015 - p89(1) [51-500]
    Mac - v128 - i2 - Jan 19 2015 - p58(1) [501+]
    NYT - Jan 27 2015 - pC1(L) [501+]
    NYTBR - Jan 25 2015 - p7(L) [501+]

Carlson, Paul H. - *Dancin' in Anson*
    Roundup M - v22 - i5 - June 2015 - p35(1) [501+]
    Roundup M - v22 - i6 - August 2015 - p35(1) [501+]
    West Texas: A History of the Giant Side of the State
    SHQ - v118 - i4 - April 2015 - p424-425 [501+]
    Roundup M - v22 - i6 - August 2015 - p35(1) [501+]
    WHQ - v46 - i1 - Spring 2015 - p85-86 [501+]

Carlson, Toby - *An Observer's Guide to Clouds and Weather: A Northeastern Primer on Prediction*
    Phys Today - v68 - i5 - May 2015 - p50-52 [501+]

Carlson, W. Bernard - *Tesla: Inventor of the Electrical Age*
    Historian - v77 - i2 - Summer 2015 - p409(3) [501+]
    Isis - v106 - i2 - June 2015 - p406(4) [501+]
    Lon R Bks - v37 - i3 - Feb 5 2015 - p32(3) [501+]

Carlston, Erin G. - *Double Agents: Espionage, Literature, and Liminal Citizens*
    Clio - v44 - i2 - Spring 2015 - p293-298 [501+]

Carlton, Bree - *Women Exiting Prison: Critical Essays on Gender, Post-Release Support and Survival*
    CS - v44 - i5 - Sept 2015 - p640-642 [501+]

Carlton, Kat - *Sealed with a Lie*
    c HB Guide - v26 - i1 - Spring 2015 - p102(1) [51-500]

Carluccio, Antonio - *Pasta: The Essential New Collection from the Master of Italian Cookery*
    PW - v262 - i46 - Nov 16 2015 - p71(2) [51-500]

Carman, Charles H. - *Leon Battista Alberti and Nicholas Cusanus: Towards an Epistemology of Vision for Italian Renaissance Art and Culture*
    Ren Q - v68 - i3 - Fall 2015 - p989-900 [501+]

Carman, Emily - *Independent Stardom: Freelance Women in the Hollywood Studio System*
    LJ - v140 - i20 - Dec 1 2015 - p103(2) [51-500]

Carman, Patrick - *Quake*
    y HB Guide - v26 - i2 - Fall 2015 - p113(1) [51-500]
    y BL - v111 - i9-10 - Jan 1 2015 - p100(1) [51-500]
    y VOYA - v37 - i6 - Feb 2015 - p73(1) [51-500]
The Trouble with Fuzzwonker Fizz
    c KR - Dec 1 2015 - pNA [51-500]

Carmel, Claudine - *Lucy Lick-Me-Not and the Greedy Gubbins*
    c KR - Oct 1 2015 - pNA [51-500]

Carmichael, L.E. - *Forensic Science: In Pursuit of Justice*
    y HB Guide - v26 - i2 - Fall 2015 - p154(1) [51-500]
Fox Talk
    c Res Links - v20 - i5 - June 2015 - p12(1) [51-500]
Fuzzy Forensics: DNA Fingerprinting Gets Wild
    y Res Links - v20 - i5 - June 2015 - p30(1) [51-500]

Carmichael, Robert - *When Clouds Fell from the Sky*
    CSM - Oct 13 2015 - pNA [501+]

Carmody, Carolyn - *The Nantucket Lightship Basket Mystery (Illus. by Bell, Samantha)*
    c CH Bwatch - April 2015 - pNA [51-500]

Carmody, Isobelle - *Evermore (Illus. by Reed, Daniel)*
    c Magpies - v30 - i5 - Nov 2015 - p40(1) [501+]

Carmon, Irin - *Notorious RBG: The Life and Times of Ruth Bader Ginsburg*
    LJ - v140 - i19 - Nov 15 2015 - p95(3) [501+]
    NYTBR - Dec 6 2015 - p57(L) [501+]
    NYT - Oct 26 2015 - pC1(L) [501+]

Carnavas, Peter - *Blue Whale Blues (Illus. by Carnavas, Peter)*
    c Magpies - v30 - i5 - Nov 2015 - p29(1) [501+]
The Boy on the Page (Illus. by Carnavas, Peter)
    c CH Bwatch - March 2015 - pNA [51-500]
    c HB Guide - v26 - i1 - Spring 2015 - p25(1) [51-500]
Jessica's Box (Illus. by Carnavas, Peter)
    c HB - v91 - i3 - May-June 2015 - p80(2) [51-500]
    c HB Guide - v26 - i2 - Fall 2015 - p28(1) [51-500]
    c KR - Jan 15 2015 - pNA [51-500]
    c PW - v262 - i24 - June 15 2015 - p81(2) [51-500]
    c SLJ - v61 - i5 - May 2015 - p83(1) [51-500]

Carnegie, Dale - *How to Win Friends and Influence People*
    Forbes - v196 - i6 - Nov 2 2015 - p42(1) [51-500]

Carner, Talia - *Hotel Moscow*
    KR - April 15 2015 - pNA [501+]

Carnes, Matthew E. - *Continuity despite Change: The Politics of Labor Regulation in Latin America*
    HAHR - v95 - i2 - May 2015 - p366-368 [501+]

Carnesi, Monica - *Sleepover with Beatrice and Bear (Illus. by Carnesi, Monica)*
    c HB Guide - v26 - i1 - Spring 2015 - p7(1) [51-500]

Carney, Elizabeth - *Mars*
    c HB Guide - v26 - i1 - Spring 2015 - p149(1) [51-500]

Carney, Elizabeth Donnelly - *Arsinoe of Egypt and Macedon: A Royal Life*
    CJ - v110 - i3 - Feb-March 2015 - p376(7) [501+]

Carney, Scott - *A Death on Diamond Mountain: A True Story of Obsession, Madness, and the Path to Enlightenment*
    BL - v111 - i11 - Feb 1 2015 - p4(1) [51-500]
    KR - Jan 15 2015 - pNA [51-500]
    Mac - v128 - i13-14 - April 6 2015 - p76(1) [501+]

Carney, Sean - *The Politics and Poetics of Contemporary English Tragedy*
    Theat J - v67 - i1 - March 2015 - p155-156 [501+]

Caro, Jane - *Just a Queen*
    y Magpies - v30 - i2 - May 2015 - p40(1) [501+]

Caro, Robert - *The Power Broker: Robert Moses and the Fall of New York*
    Spec - v328 - i9749 - July 4 2015 - p32(2) [501+]

Carolan, Michael - *Reclaiming Food Security*
    CS - v44 - i2 - March 2015 - p182-184 [501+]

Carole, Bonnie - *Black and White in Winter*
    c BL - v111 - i17 - May 1 2015 - p87(1) [51-500]
Blue and Yellow in Summer
    c BL - v111 - i17 - May 1 2015 - p87(1) [51-500]
Brown and Orange in Fall
    c BL - v111 - i17 - May 1 2015 - p87(1) [51-500]
Junk Food, Yes or No
    c BL - v112 - i6 - Nov 15 2015 - p43(1) [51-500]
Red and Green in Spring
    c BL - v111 - i17 - May 1 2015 - p87(1) [51-500]
School Uniforms, Yes or No
    c BL - v112 - i6 - Nov 15 2015 - p43(1) [51-500]

Carole Haber - *The Trials of Laura Lair: Sex, Murder, and Insanity in the Victorian West*
    Historian - v77 - i2 - Summer 2015 - p334(2) [501+]

Caroli, Betty Boyd - *Lady Bird and Lyndon: The Hidden Story of a Marriage That Made a President*
    KR - August 1 2015 - pNA [501+]
    LJ - v140 - i14 - Sept 1 2015 - p120(2) [51-500]

Caroline Jayne Church - *Sweet Child of Mine (Illus. by Church, Caroline Jayne)*
    c CH Bwatch - Feb 2015 - pNA [51-500]

Caroll, Robin - *Samantha Sanderson: Off the Record*
    c BL - v111 - i17 - May 1 2015 - p52(1) [51-500]

Caron, David - *The Nearness of Others: Searching for Tact and Contact in the Age of HIV*
    FS - v69 - i2 - April 2015 - p284(1) [501+]

Caron, Francois - *Dynamics of Innovation: The Expansion of Technology in Modern Times*
    Historian - v77 - i2 - Summer 2015 - p411(3) [501+]

Carp, E. Wayne - *Jean Paton and the Struggle to Reform American Adoption*
    AHR - v120 - i2 - April 2015 - p666(1) [501+]

Carpenter, Amber - *Indian Buddhist Philosophy*
    HNet - July 2015 - pNA [51-500]

Carpenter, Ben - *The Bigs: The Secrets Nobody Tells Students and Young Professionals About How to Find a Great Job*
    NACEJou - v75 - i3 - Feb 2015 - p15(1) [501+]

Carpenter, C.J. - *Hidden Vices*
    KR - May 1 2015 - pNA [501+]

Carpenter, Dana Chamblee - *Bohemian Gospel*
    KR - Sept 15 2015 - pNA [501+]
    LJ - v140 - i17 - Oct 15 2015 - p73(1) [501+]
    PW - v262 - i36 - Sept 7 2015 - p42(2) [501+]

Carpenter, David - *Magna Carta*
    TLS - i5842 - March 20 2015 - p17(2) [501+]
    HT - v65 - i6 - June 2015 - p56(2) [501+]
    Lon R Bks - v37 - i8 - April 23 2015 - p15(3) [501+]

Carpenter, Jeff - *The Organic Medicinal Herb Farmer: The Ultimate Guide to Producing High-Quality Herbs on a Market Scale*
    LJ - v140 - i7 - April 15 2015 - p108(1) [51-500]

Carpenter, Joel - *Christian Higher Education: A Global Reconnaissance*
    CC - v132 - i21 - Oct 14 2015 - p33(2) [501+]

Carpenter, Nancy E. - *Chemistry of Sustainable Energy*
    J Chem Ed - v92 - i4 - April 2015 - p601-602 [501+]

Carpenter, Tad - *Arctic Animals*
    c KR - Jan 1 2016 - pNA [51-500]
On the Go
    c PW - v262 - i20 - May 18 2015 - p82(2) [51-500]

Carpenter, Thomas H. - *The Italic People of Ancient Apulia: New Evidence from Pottery for Workshops, Markets and Customs*
    Class R - v65 - i2 - Oct 2015 - p570-572 [501+]

Carpernter, Bruce W. - *Lempad of Bali: The Illuminating Line*
    Apo - v181 - i629 - March 2015 - p212(2) [501+]

Carr, Aaron - *Migrants and Refugees*
    c Res Links - v20 - i4 - April 2015 - p18(1) [501+]

Carr, Forrest - *The Dark*
    PW - v262 - i37 - Sept 14 2015 - p47(2) [51-500]

Carr, Julie - *Think Tank*
    PW - v262 - i11 - March 16 2015 - p62(1) [51-500]

Carr, Karen - *My Hot Air Balloon (Illus. by Drzycimski, Leigh)*
    c CH Bwatch - Feb 2015 - pNA [51-500]

Carr, Matthew - *Sherman's Ghosts: Soldiers, Civilians, and the American Way of War*
    AS - v84 - i2 - Spring 2015 - p124(3) [501+]
    HNet - June 2015 - pNA [501+]
    KR - Jan 1 2015 - pNA [501+]
    LJ - v140 - i2 - Feb 1 2015 - p93(1) [51-500]
    NYTBR - March 29 2015 - p12(L) [501+]
    Pub Hist - v37 - i3 - August 2015 - p141(2) [501+]

Carr, Nicholas - *The Glass Cage: Automation and Us*
    Bwatch - Feb 2015 - pNA [51-500]
    NYRB - v62 - i6 - April 2 2015 - p24(3) [501+]
The Glass Cage: Where Automation Is Taking Us
    NS - v144 - i5245 - Jan 16 2015 - p44(3) [501+]
    Spec - v327 - i9731 - Feb 28 2015 - p45(1) [501+]
    TLS - i5857 - July 3 2015 - p28(1) [501+]

Carr, Robyn - *A New Hope*
    RVBW - July 2015 - pNA [501+]
    BL - v112 - i2 - Sept 15 2015 - p42(2) [501+]
    KR - May 15 2015 - pNA [501+]
    PW - v262 - i16 - April 20 2015 - p62(1) [501+]
One Wish
    PW - v262 - i4 - Jan 26 2015 - p156(1) [51-500]
Wildest Dreams
    BL - v112 - i2 - Sept 15 2015 - p48(1) [51-500]
    PW - v262 - i28 - July 13 2015 - p51(2) [501+]

Carr, Toni - *Geek Knits: Over 30 Projects for Fantasy Fanatics, Science Fiction Fiends, and Knitting Nerds*
    LJ - v140 - i10 - June 1 2015 - p103(3) [51-500]

Carrasco, Jesus - *Out in the Open*
    NS - v144 - i5263 - May 22 2015 - p53(1) [501+]
    TLS - i5860 - July 24 2015 - p20(1) [501+]

Carrere, Emmanuel - *Limonov: The Outrageous Adventures of the Radical Soviet Poet Who Became a Bum in New York, a Sensation in France and a Political Antihero in Russia*
    NYRB - v62 - i9 - May 21 2015 - p45(3) [501+]

Carrick, Carol - *The Great Big Dinosaur Treasury: Tales of Adventure and Discovery*
    c HB Guide - v26 - i2 - Fall 2015 - p36(1) [51-500]

Carriel, Jonathan - *Exquisite Folly*
    KR - Sept 15 2015 - pNA [501+]

Carrier, Henry - *Ripeness Is All: A Boomer's Mirthful, Spiritual Journey*
    KR - Dec 15 2015 - pNA [501+]

Carrier, Roch - *Montcalm & Wolfe: Two Men Who Forever Changed the Course of Canadian History*
    Beav - v95 - i5 - Oct-Nov 2015 - p59(2) [501+]

Carriere, Marie - *Regenerations: Canadian Women's Writing*
    Can Lit - i224 - Spring 2015 - p141 [501+]

Carrigan, William D. - *Forgotten Dead: Mob Violence against Mexicans in the United States, 1848-1928*
    JSH - v81 - i3 - August 2015 - p716(3) [501+]
Swift to Wrath: Lynching in Global Historical Perspective
    JSH - v81 - i1 - Feb 2015 - p218(3) [501+]

Carriger, Gail - *Curtsies and Conspiracies (Read by Quick, Moira). Audiobook Review*
    c BL - v111 - i14 - March 15 2015 - p24(2) [501+]
Prudence (Read by Quirk, Moira). Audiobook Review
    LJ - v140 - i11 - June 15 2015 - p48(1) [51-500]
    PW - v262 - i21 - May 25 2015 - p54(1) [501+]
Prudence
    y BL - v111 - i15 - April 1 2015 - p34(1) [501+]
    PW - v262 - i2 - Jan 12 2015 - p41(1) [501+]
Waistcoats and Weaponry
    y HB - v91 - i2 - March-April 2015 - p93(2) [51-500]
    y HB Guide - v26 - i2 - Fall 2015 - p113(2) [51-500]

Carroll, Carleton W. - *The Medieval Shepherd: Jean de Brie's Le Bon Berger, 1379*
    Med R - May 2015 - pNA [501+]
    MLR - v110 - i2 - April 2015 - p542-543 [501+]
    Specu - v90 - i4 - Oct 2015 - p1098-1099 [501+]

Carroll, Charlie - *Peaks on the Horizon: Two Journeys in Tibet*
    BL - v111 - i13 - March 1 2015 - p15(1) [51-500]
    LJ - v140 - i3 - Feb 15 2015 - p118(2) [51-500]

Carroll, Emily - *Through the Woods*
    c HB Guide - v26 - i1 - Spring 2015 - p102(1) [51-500]

Carroll, Emma - *In Darkling Wood*
    c Sch Lib - v63 - i3 - Autumn 2015 - p164(1) [51-500]

Carroll, James - *Warburg in Rome (Read by Doersch, David). Audiobook Review*
    BL - v111 - i13 - March 1 2015 - p69(1) [51-500]

Carroll, James Christopher - *Papa's Backpack: A Tribute to the Bond Between a Child and Military Parent (Illus. by Carroll, James Christopher)*
   c BL - v111 - i21 - July 1 2015 - p65(1) [51-500]
   c CH Bwatch - Nov 2015 - pNA [51-500]
   c KR - May 15 2015 - pNA [51-500]
   c PW - v262 - i18 - May 4 2015 - p116(1) [51-500]
   c SLJ - v61 - i7 - July 2015 - p60(1) [51-500]

Carroll, Jim - *Marriage Boot Camp: Defeat the Top Ten Marriage Killers and Build a Rock-Solid Relationship*
   PW - v262 - i51 - Dec 14 2015 - p76(2) [51-500]

Carroll, Joe - *Feeding the Fire: Recipes and Strategies for Better Barbecue and Grilling*
   LJ - v140 - i9 - May 15 2015 - p102(2) [51-500]

Carroll, John Millar - *The Neighborhood in the Internet: Design Research Projects in Community Informatics*
   CS - v44 - i4 - July 2015 - p493-494 [501+]

Carroll, Jonathan - *Teaching the Dog to Read*
   PW - v262 - i17 - April 27 2015 - p55(2) [51-500]

Carroll, Lewis - *Alice in Wonderland: Down the Rabbit Hole (Illus. by Puybaret, Eric)*
   SLJ - v61 - i3 - March 2015 - p113(2) [51-500]
Alice in Wonderland
   Forbes - v195 - i8 - June 15 2015 - p22(1) [51-500]
Alice in Wonderland (Illus. by Ferran, Daniel)
   y HB Guide - v26 - i1 - Spring 2015 - p72(2) [51-500]
Alice in Wonderland: With Three Dimensional Pop-Up Scenes (Illus. by Taylor, Maria)
   c KR - Dec 1 2015 - pNA [51-500]
   c PW - v262 - i21 - May 25 2015 - p58(1) [501+]
The Annotated Alice: 150th Anniversary Deluxe ed.
   LJ - v140 - i17 - Oct 15 2015 - p94(1) [501+]
Through the Looking-Glass and What Alice Found There
   New R - v246 - i11 - Fall 2015 - p76(4) [501+]

Carroll, Peter N. - *From Guernica to Human Rights: Essays on the Spanish Civil War*
   J Mil H - v79 - i3 - July 2015 - p869-871 [501+]

Carroll, Quincy - *Up to the Mountains and Down to the Countryside*
   KR - Dec 15 2015 - pNA [501+]

Carroll, Sean B. - *The Serengeti Rules: The Quest to Discover How Life Works and Why It Matters*
   KR - Dec 15 2015 - pNA [501+]

Carroll, William - *Galileo: Science and Faith*
   Sev Cent N - v73 - i1-2 - Spring-Summer 2015 - p41(4) [501+]

Carruth, Allison - *Global Appetites: American Power and the Literature of Food*
   MFSF - v61 - i1 - Spring 2015 - p168-176 [501+]

Carson, Ann Elizabeth - *We All Become Stories*
   CWS - v30 - i2-3 - Fall-Winter 2015 - p126(1) [501+]

Carson, Anne - *Short Talks*
   Can Lit - i224 - Spring 2015 - p115 [501+]

Carson, Ben - *Gifted Hands: The Ben Carson Story*
   NYRB - v62 - i17 - Nov 5 2015 - p18(3) [501+]
One Nation: What We Can All Do to Save America's Future
   NS - v144 - i5278 - Sept 4 2015 - p40(4) [501+]
   Reason - v47 - i4 - August-Sept 2015 - p58(8) [501+]

Carson, Candace D. - *Diary of a Deadhead: A Wild Magical Ride into the World of Sound and Vibration*
   KR - Nov 15 2015 - pNA [501+]

Carson, Candy - *One Nation: What We Can All Do to Save America's Future*
   NYRB - v62 - i5 - March 19 2015 - p18(3) [501+]

Carson, Ciaran - *From Elsewhere*
   TLS - i5868 - Sept 18 2015 - p23(1) [501+]

Carson, David A. - *Grit, Noise and Revolution: The Birth of Detroit Rock 'n' Roll*
   BL - v112 - i5 - Nov 1 2015 - p18(2) [501+]

Carson, Mary Kay - *How Strong Is an Ant?: And Other Questions about Bugs and Insects*
   c HB Guide - v26 - i1 - Spring 2015 - p158(1) [51-500]
Inside Biosphere 2: Earth Science under Glass (Illus. by Uhlman, Tom)
   c BL - v112 - i4 - Oct 15 2015 - p38(2) [51-500]
   y HB - v91 - i6 - Nov-Dec 2015 - p99(2) [51-500]
   y KR - August 15 2015 - pNA [51-500]
   c SLJ - v61 - i10 - Oct 2015 - p132(1) [51-500]
What Makes a Tornado Twist?: And Other Questions about Weather
   c HB Guide - v26 - i1 - Spring 2015 - p150(1) [51-500]

Which Way to Freedom? And Other Questions about the Underground Railroad
   c HB Guide - v26 - i2 - Fall 2015 - p219(1) [51-500]
Why Couldn't Susan B. Anthony Vote? And Other Questions about Women's Suffrage
   c HB Guide - v26 - i2 - Fall 2015 - p153(1) [51-500]

Carson, Mina - *Ava Helen Pauling: Partner, Activist, Visionary*
   PHR - v84 - i1 - Feb 2015 - p100(3) [501+]

Carson, Penelope - *The East India Company and Religion, 1698-1858*
   Historian - v77 - i1 - Spring 2015 - p162(2) [501+]

Carson, Rachel - *Silent Spring*
   TimHES - i2211 - July 9 2015 - p47(1) [501+]

Carson, Rae - *Walk on Earth a Stranger*
   y BL - v111 - i22 - August 1 2015 - p67(1) [51-500]
   y HB - v91 - i5 - Sept-Oct 2015 - p96(2) [51-500]
   y KR - June 15 2015 - pNA [51-500]
   y PW - v262 - i25 - June 22 2015 - p142(2) [51-500]
   y PW - v262 - i49 - Dec 2 2015 - p108(2) [51-500]
   y SLJ - v61 - i8 - August 2015 - p96(1) [51-500]
   y VOYA - v38 - i4 - Oct 2015 - p67(1) [51-500]

Carson, Thomas L. - *Lincoln's Ethics*
   CHE - v62 - i15 - Dec 11 2015 - pB16(1) [501+]

Carstairs, Sue - *Saving Turtles: A Kid's Guide to Helping Endangered Creatures*
   Am Bio T - v77 - i4 - April 2015 - p302(1) [501+]
   c Sch Lib - v63 - i1 - Spring 2015 - p46(1) [51-500]

Cart, Michael - *Taking Aim: Power and Pain, Teens and Guns*
   y VOYA - v38 - i4 - Oct 2015 - p50(1) [51-500]
   y BL - v111 - i21 - July 1 2015 - p60(1) [51-500]
   y KR - June 15 2015 - pNA [51-500]
   y SLJ - v61 - i6 - June 2015 - p121(2) [51-500]
Top 250 LGBTQ Books for Teens: Coming Out, Being Out, and the Search for Community
   y BL - v111 - i22 - August 1 2015 - p60(1) [51-500]
   y CCB-B - v68 - i7 - March 2015 - p380(1) [51-500]
   y SLJ - v61 - i6 - June 2015 - p147(1) [51-500]

Carte, Tim - *Orpheus in the Marketplace: Jacopo Peri and the Economy of Late Renaissance Florence*
   Ren Q - v68 - i2 - Summer 2015 - p675-677 [501+]

Carter, Aimee - *Captive*
   c HB Guide - v26 - i1 - Spring 2015 - p103(1) [51-500]
Simon Thorn and the Wolf's Den
   c KR - Dec 1 2015 - pNA [51-500]
   c SLJ - v61 - i12 - Dec 2015 - p100(1) [51-500]

Carter, Ally - *All Fall Down (Read by Stevens, Eileen). Audiobook Review*
   y SLJ - v61 - i6 - June 2015 - p66(1) [51-500]
All Fall Down
   y HB Guide - v26 - i2 - Fall 2015 - p114(1) [51-500]
   y VOYA - v37 - i6 - Feb 2015 - p54(1) [51-500]
Embassy Row
   c Sch Lib - v63 - i2 - Summer 2015 - p101(1) [51-500]

Carter, Alton - *The Boy Who Carried Bricks: A True Story*
   VOYA - v38 - i2 - June 2015 - p87(1) [51-500]

Carter, Angela - *The Bloody Chamber and Other Stories*
   Ent W - i1364 - May 22 2015 - p66(1) [501+]
Love
   TimHES - i2228 - Nov 5 2015 - p46(1) [501+]

Carter, Betsy - *Swim to Me*
   LJ - v140 - i17 - Oct 15 2015 - p118(1) [501+]

Carter, Caela - *My Life with Liars*
   c KR - Dec 15 2015 - pNA [51-500]

Carter, Chris - *An Evil Mind*
   BL - v112 - i4 - Oct 15 2015 - p20(2) [51-500]
   KR - Oct 1 2015 - pNA [51-500]

Carter, David A. - *B Is for Box: The Happy Little Yellow Box (Illus. by Carter, David A.)*
   c HB Guide - v26 - i1 - Spring 2015 - p7(1) [51-500]
Bitsy Bee Goes to School
   c HB Guide - v26 - i1 - Spring 2015 - p52(1) [51-500]
If You're a Robot and You Know It (Illus. by Musical Robot)
   c KR - Dec 1 2015 - pNA [51-500]
   c PW - v262 - i27 - July 6 2015 - p70(2) [51-500]
   c PW - v262 - i49 - Dec 2 2015 - p59(1) [51-500]
Merry Christmas, Bugs!
   c HB Guide - v26 - i1 - Spring 2015 - p52(1) [51-500]
Winter
   c KR - Dec 1 2015 - pNA [51-500]
   c PW - v262 - i27 - July 6 2015 - p70(2) [501+]

Carter, Graydon - *Bohemians, Bootleggers, Flappers, and Swells*
   NY - v90 - i42 - Jan 5 2015 - p73 [51-500]

Bohemians, Bootleggers, Flappers and Swells: The Best of Early Vanity Fair
   TLS - i5859 - July 17 2015 - p26(1) [51-500]

Carter, Heath W. - *Union Made: Working People and the Rise of Social Christianity in Chicago*
   CC - v132 - i22 - Oct 28 2015 - p38(2) [501+]

Carter, Hilary H. - *New Life Stories: Journeys of Recovery in a Mindful Community*
   Bwatch - April 2015 - pNA [51-500]

Carter, Jimmy - *A Full Life: Reflections at Ninety (Illus. by Carter, Jimmy) (Read by Carter, Jimmy). Audiobook Review*
   BL - v112 - i3 - Oct 1 2015 - p85(1) [51-500]
A Full Life: Reflections at Ninety
   CSM - July 7 2015 - pNA [51-500]
   Har Bus R - v93 - i12 - Dec 2015 - p124(2) [501+]
   LJ - v140 - i11 - June 15 2015 - p94(1) [51-500]
   Prog - v79 - i11 - Nov 2015 - p43(3) [501+]
   BL - v111 - i21 - July 1 2015 - p18(2) [51-500]
   KR - June 1 2015 - pNA [51-500]
   PW - v262 - i20 - May 18 2015 - p77(1) [51-500]

Carter, Lisa - *Vines of Entanglemento*
   RVBW - May 2015 - pNA [51-500]

Carter, M.J. - *The Infidel Stain*
   HT - v65 - i11 - Nov 2015 - p56(2) [51-500]
   Spec - v327 - i9738 - April 18 2015 - p38(1) [501+]
The Strangler Vine
   KR - Feb 1 2015 - pNA [51-500]
   LJ - v140 - i8 - May 1 2015 - p103(1) [51-500]
   PW - v262 - i1 - Jan 5 2015 - p51(1) [51-500]

Carter, Maureen - *Next of Kin*
   KR - Jan 1 2016 - pNA [51-500]

Carter, Meg - *The Lies We Tell*
   y Sch Lib - v63 - i4 - Winter 2015 - p210(1) [51-500]

Carter, Miranda J. - *The Infidel Stain*
   TLS - i5854 - June 12 2015 - p13(1) [51-500]
The Strangler Vine
   TLS - i5854 - June 12 2015 - p13(1) [501+]

Carter, Monika - *The Defenders: Bully Patrol (Illus. by Butler, Tad)*
   c CH Bwatch - May 2015 - pNA [501+]

Carter, Stephen L. - *Back Channel (Read by Turpin, Bahni). Audiobook Review*
   BL - v111 - i13 - March 1 2015 - p68(1) [51-500]

Carter, Steven D. - *The Columbia Antology of Japanese Essays: "Zuihitsu" from the Tenth to the Twenty-First Century*
   TLS - i5847 - April 24 2015 - p26(1) [501+]

Carter, Thomas F. - *In Foreign Fields: The Politics and Experiences of Transnational Sport Migration*
   SSJ - v32 - i1 - March 2015 - p112-114 [501+]

Carter, Tim - *Orpheus in the Marketplace: Jacopo Peri and the Economy of Late Renaissance Florence*
   Historian - v77 - i3 - Fall 2015 - p598(2) [501+]
   JMH - v87 - i2 - June 2015 - p463(3) [501+]

Carthage, Lynn - *Haunted*
   y BL - v111 - i15 - April 1 2015 - p65(1) [51-500]
   y VOYA - v38 - i1 - April 2015 - p74(2) [51-500]

Carthew, Natasha - *The Light That Gets Lost*
   y Sch Lib - v63 - i4 - Winter 2015 - p243(1) [51-500]

Carthy, Ita Mac - *Renaissance Keywords*
   MP - v112 - i3 - Feb 2015 - pE231(E233) [501+]

Cartier, Jennifer - *5 Practices for Orchestrating Task-Based Discussions in Science*
   Math T - v108 - i6 - Feb 2015 - p475(1) [501+]

Cartier, Marie - *Baby, You Are My Religion: Women, Gay Bars, and Theology Before Stonewall*
   JR - v95 - i3 - July 2015 - p403(2) [501+]

Cartwright, Jane - *Mary Magdalene and Her Sister Martha: An Edition and Translation of the Medieval Welsh Lives*
   Specu - v90 - i1 - Jan 2015 - p220-221 [501+]

Cartwright, Justin - *Up Against the Night*
   BL - v112 - i3 - Oct 1 2015 - p23(1) [51-500]
   KR - Oct 15 2015 - pNA [501+]
   LJ - v140 - i12 - July 1 2015 - p72(2) [51-500]

Caruso, Carlo - *Adonis: The Myth of the Dying God in the Italian Renaissance*
   Class R - v65 - i1 - April 2015 - p277-279 [501+]

Caruthers, Yancy - *Northwest of Eden*
   SPBW - Sept 2015 - pNA [501+]

Carvajal y Mendoza, Luisa de - *The Life and Writings of Luisa de Carvajal y Mendoza*
   Six Ct J - v46 - i3 - Fall 2015 - p730-731 [501+]

Carvalhaes, Claudio - *Liturgy in Postcolonial Perspectives: Only One Is Holy*
   CC - v132 - i21 - Oct 14 2015 - p34(2) [501+]

Carvalho, Adelia - *There Once Was A Dog (Illus. by Vaz de Carvalho, Joao)*
  c HB Guide - v26 - i1 - Spring 2015 - p25(1) [51-500]

Carvalho, Bruno - *Porous City: A Cultural History of Rio de Janeiro*
  HAHR - v95 - i1 - Feb 2015 - p167-168 [501+]

Carvaljo, Edward J. - *Acknowledged Legislator: Critical Essays on the Poetry of Martin Espada*
  NAR - v300 - i3 - Summer 2015 - p48(2) [501+]

Carvell, Tim - *Return to Planet Tad (Illus. by Holgate, Douglas)*
  y HB Guide - v26 - i1 - Spring 2015 - p73(1) [51-500]

Carver, Lin - *Reading Basics for All Teachers: Supporting the Common Core*
  VOYA - v38 - i5 - Dec 2015 - p82(1) [51-500]

Caryl, Christian - *Strange Rebels: 1979 and the Birth of the 21st Century*
  Historian - v77 - i1 - Spring 2015 - p200(2) [501+]

Casale, Alexia - *House of Windows*
  y Sch Lib - v63 - i3 - Autumn 2015 - p179(1) [51-500]
  y Sch Lib - v63 - i4 - Winter 2015 - p243(1) [51-500]

Casanova, Giacomo - *Memoirs of Casanova*
  FS - v69 - i2 - April 2015 - p248(1) [501+]

Casanova, Helena - *Public Space Acupuncture*
  RVBW - July 2015 - pNA [51-500]

Casanova, Julian - *Twentieth-Century Spain: A History*
  TLS - i5855 - June 19 2015 - p7(2) [501+]

Casanova, Mary - *Wake Up, Island (Illus. by Wroblewski, Nick)*
  c KR - Jan 1 2016 - pNA [51-500]

Casarett, David - *A Doctor's Case for Medical Marijuana*
  NYT - Sept 8 2015 - pD3(L) [501+]
Shocked: Adventures in Bringing Back the Recently Dead
  Am Sci - v103 - i1 - Jan-Feb 2015 - p66(3) [501+]
Stoned: A Doctor's Case for Medical Marijuana
  BL - v111 - i21 - July 1 2015 - p13(1) [51-500]
  Bus W - i4436 - July 27 2015 - p71(1) [501+]

Casden, Mahra - *Survival*
  SPBW - June 2015 - pNA [501+]

Case, Alison - *Nelly Dean: A Return to Wuthering Heights*
  BL - v112 - i7 - Dec 1 2015 - p33(2) [51-500]
  KR - Nov 15 2015 - pNA [501+]
  LJ - v140 - i16 - Oct 1 2015 - p66(1) [51-500]
  PW - v262 - i45 - Nov 9 2015 - p32(2) [51-500]

Case, Andrew - *The Big Fear*
  PW - v262 - i51 - Dec 14 2015 - p62(1) [51-500]

Casella, Jean - *Hell Is a Very Small Place: Voices from Solitary Confinement*
  KR - Dec 1 2015 - pNA [501+]
  LJ - v140 - i20 - Dec 1 2015 - p118(1) [51-500]

Casey, Bart - *The Double Life of Laurence Oliphant*
  KR - Dec 1 2015 - pNA [51-500]

Casey, Betty Selakovich - *That Is a Hat (Illus. by Casey, Betty Selakovich)*
  c Roundup M - v22 - i4 - April 2015 - p27(1) [501+]
  c Roundup M - v22 - i6 - August 2015 - p24(1) [501+]

Casey, Brycchan - *Quakers and Abolition*
  JSH - v81 - i3 - August 2015 - p723(3) [501+]

Casey, Caroline - *Cat Is Art Spelled Wrong*
  KR - August 1 2015 - pNA [501+]
  PW - v262 - i30 - July 27 2015 - p59(1) [51-500]

Casey, Dawn - *A Lullaby for Little One (Illus. by Fuge, Charles)*
  c CH Bwatch - April 2015 - pNA [51-500]
  c HB Guide - v26 - i2 - Fall 2015 - p7(2) [51-500]

Casey, Donis - *All Men Fear Me*
  KR - Sept 1 2015 - pNA [51-500]
  PW - v262 - i35 - August 31 2015 - p60(1) [51-500]

Casey, Jane - *Bet Your Life*
  y HB Guide - v26 - i2 - Fall 2015 - p114(1) [51-500]
  y VOYA - v38 - i1 - April 2015 - p54(2) [51-500]
Hide and Seek
  y SLJ - v61 - i8 - August 2015 - p113(1) [51-500]
  y VOYA - v38 - i3 - August 2015 - p56(1) [51-500]
How to Fall
  c HB Guide - v26 - i1 - Spring 2015 - p103(1) [51-500]
The Kill
  BL - v111 - i17 - May 1 2015 - p39(2) [51-500]
  KR - April 1 2015 - pNA [51-500]
  PW - v262 - i17 - April 27 2015 - p51(1) [51-500]

Casey, Joe - *The Bounce, Vol. 1*
  PW - v262 - i2 - Jan 12 2015 - p45(1) [51-500]

Casey, Maud - *The Man Who Walked Away*
  NYTBR - Feb 22 2015 - p32(L) [501+]

Casey, Steven - *When Soldiers Fall: How Americans Have Confronted Combat Losses from World War I to Afghanistan*
  AHR - v120 - i1 - Feb 2015 - p276-277 [501+]

Casey, Susan - *Voices in the Ocean: A Journey into the Wild and Haunting World of Dolphins (Read by Campbell, Cassandra). Audiobook Review*
  LJ - v140 - i20 - Dec 1 2015 - p61(2) [51-500]
  PW - v262 - i39 - Sept 28 2015 - p86(2) [51-500]
Voices in the Ocean: A Journey into the Wild and Haunting World of Dolphins
  KR - August 1 2015 - pNA [501+]
  LJ - v140 - i13 - August 1 2015 - p120(1) [51-500]
  Mac - v128 - i32-33 - August 17 2015 - p68(1) [501+]
  NYTBR - August 30 2015 - p16(L) [501+]
  PW - v262 - i28 - July 13 2015 - p61(2) [51-500]
Women Heroes of the American Revolution: 20 Stories of Espionage, Sabotage, Defiance, and Rescue
  BL - v111 - i12 - Feb 15 2015 - p70(1) [51-500]
  y KR - Jan 15 2015 - pNA [51-500]

Cash, Megan Montague - *Bow-Wow's Nightmare Neighbors (Illus. by Newgarden, Mark)*
  c HB Guide - v26 - i1 - Spring 2015 - p13(1) [51-500]

Cash, Michael Phillip - *The Battle for Darracia*
  RVBW - July 2015 - pNA [51-500]
Monsterland
  KR - Jan 1 2016 - pNA [501+]
Pokergeist
  KR - Oct 1 2015 - pNA [501+]
  SPBW - Sept 2015 - pNA [51-500]
Stillwell: A Haunting on Long Island
  PW - v262 - i26 - June 29 2015 - p49(1) [51-500]
Witches Protection Program
  KR - August 15 2015 - pNA [501+]
  PW - v262 - i38 - Sept 21 2015 - p59(1) [51-500]

Cash, Wiley - *The Dark Road to Mercy (Read by Bergmann, Erik). Audiobook Review*
  LJ - v140 - i5 - March 15 2015 - p134(1) [51-500]

Cashion, Matt - *Last Words of the Holy Ghost*
  KR - Sept 1 2015 - pNA [51-500]

Casiday, Augustine - *Reconstructing the Theology of Evagrius Ponticus: Beyond Heresy*
  JR - Jan 2015 - p136(3) [501+]

Casper, Andrew R. - *Art and Religious Image in El Greco's Italy*
  Six Ct J - v46 - i3 - Fall 2015 - p769-770 [501+]

Cass, Kiera - *The Heir*
  y BL - v111 - i18 - May 15 2015 - p53(1) [51-500]
  y HB Guide - v26 - i2 - Fall 2015 - p114(1) [51-500]
  y SLJ - v61 - i5 - May 2015 - p117(2) [51-500]

Cassam, Quassim - *Self-Knowledge for Humans*
  TLS - i5858 - July 10 2015 - p28(1) [501+]

Cassanello, Robert - *To Render Invisible: Jim Crow and Public Space in New South Jacksonville*
  Historian - v77 - i1 - Spring 2015 - p108(2) [501+]

Cassar, George H. - *Trial by Gas: The British Army at the Second Battle of Ypres*
  J Mil H - v79 - i3 - July 2015 - p856-857 [501+]

Cassedy, Steven - *Connected: How Trains, Genes, Pineapples, Piano Keys, and a Few Disasters Transformed Americans at the Dawn of the Twentieth Century*
  AHR - v120 - i1 - Feb 2015 - p265-266 [501+]
  RAH - v43 - i2 - June 2015 - p288-293 [501+]

Cassel, Par Kristoffer - *Grounds of Judgment: Extraterritoriality and Imperial Power in Nineteenth-Century China and Japan*
  JAS - v74 - i2 - May 2015 - p459-460 [501+]
  RAH - v43 - i2 - June 2015 - p268-273 [501+]

Cassell, Dewey - *The Incredible Herb Trimpe*
  Bwatch - Nov 2015 - pNA [51-500]

Cassese, Frank - *Ocean Beach*
  KR - Feb 1 2015 - pNA [501+]

Cassidy, Bonny - *Final Theory*
  Meanjin - v74 - i1 - Autumn 2015 - p68(10) [501+]

Cassidy, Cathy - *Looking Glass Girl*
  c Sch Lib - v63 - i2 - Summer 2015 - p101(1) [501+]

Cassidy, D.K. - *Spilt Milk: A Collection of Stories*
  KR - July 15 2015 - pNA [501+]

Cassidy, Sara - *Not for Sale (Illus. by Flook, Helen)*
  c BL - v111 - i21 - July 1 2015 - p75(1) [51-500]
  c KR - March 1 2015 - pNA [51-500]
  c Res Links - v20 - i3 - Feb 2015 - p11(1) [51-500]
  c SLJ - v61 - i5 - May 2015 - p95(1) [51-500]

Cassin, Barbara - *Dictionary of Untranslatables: A Philosophical Lexicon*
  Lon R Bks - v37 - i17 - Sept 10 2015 - p35(3) [501+]
  TLS - i5835 - Jan 30 2015 - p8(2) [501+]

Cassuto, Leonard - *The Graduate School Mess: What Caused It and How We Can Fix It*
  BL - v112 - i2 - Sept 15 2015 - p5(2) [51-500]
  LJ - v140 - i14 - Sept 1 2015 - p116(1) [51-500]

Cast, David J. - *The Ashgate Research Companion to Giorgio Vasari*
  Ren Q - v68 - i1 - Spring 2015 - p240-241 [501+]

Cast, Kristin - *Amber Smoke*
  PW - v262 - i15 - April 13 2015 - p63(1) [51-500]
  y VOYA - v38 - i3 - August 2015 - p74(1) [51-500]

Cast, P.C. - *Redeemed*
  c HB Guide - v26 - i1 - Spring 2015 - p103(1) [51-500]

Castagna, Luca - *A Bridge across the Ocean: The United States and the Holy See between the Two World Wars*
  CHR - v101 - i3 - Summer 2015 - p685(2) [501+]
  JAH - v102 - i2 - Sept 2015 - p594-595 [501+]
  Theol St - v76 - i4 - Dec 2015 - p847(2) [501+]

Castaldo, Chris - *Talking with Catholics About the Gospel: A Guide for Evangelicals*
  Ch Today - v59 - i5 - June 2015 - p76(1) [51-500]

Castaldo, Nancy F. - *Sniffer Dogs: How Dogs (and Their Noses) Save the World*
  c HB Guide - v26 - i1 - Spring 2015 - p167(1) [51-500]
  y Teach Lib - v42 - i3 - Feb 2015 - p28(4) [501+]
The Story of Seeds
  y KR - Nov 15 2015 - pNA [51-500]

Castaneda, Jorge - *Amarres Perros*
  Econ - v415 - i8932 - April 4 2015 - p34(US) [501+]

Castaneda, Luis M. - *Spectacular Mexico: Design, Propaganda, and the 1968 Olympics*
  HAHR - v95 - i4 - Nov 2015 - p698-699 [501+]

Castanet, Herve - *Pierre Klossowski: The Pantomime of Spirits*
  FS - v69 - i4 - Oct 2015 - p553-554 [501+]

Casteel, Seth - *Underwater Babies*
  People - v83 - i15 - April 13 2015 - p41(NA) [501+]

Castelain, Louis - *Jean-Marie Leclair: Concertos pour violon et orchestre op. VII*
  Notes - v71 - i4 - June 2015 - p750(3) [501+]

Castellani, Christopher - *The Art of Perspective*
  KR - Oct 1 2015 - pNA [501+]

Castellano, Katey - *The Ecology of British Romantic Conservatism, 1790-1837*
  RES - v66 - i273 - Feb 2015 - p185-187 [501+]

Castellucci, Cecil - *Stone in the Sky*
  y CCB-B - v68 - i9 - May 2015 - p441(2) [51-500]
  y HB - v91 - i2 - March-April 2015 - p94(1) [51-500]
  y HB Guide - v26 - i2 - Fall 2015 - p114(1) [51-500]
  y VOYA - v37 - i6 - Feb 2015 - p73(1) [51-500]

Castiglia, Christopher - *If Memory Serves: Gay Men, AIDS, and the Promise of the Queer Past*
  AL - v87 - i3 - Sept 2015 - p614-616 [501+]

Castille, Sarah - *Full Contact*
  PW - v262 - i8 - Feb 23 2015 - p60(1) [51-500]
Rough Justice
  BL - v111 - i12 - Feb 15 2015 - p44(1) [51-500]
Sinner's Steel
  PW - v262 - i37 - Sept 14 2015 - p49(2) [51-500]

Castillo Fernandez, Simon - *El Rio Mapocho y sus riberas: Espacio public e intervencion urbana en Santiago de Chile (1855-1918).*
  HAHR - v95 - i4 - Nov 2015 - p684-686 [501+]

Castillo, Julie - *Eat Local for Less: The Ultimate Guide to Opting Out of Our Broken Industrial Food System*
  BL - v111 - i15 - April 1 2015 - p10(1) [51-500]
  LJ - v140 - i2 - Feb 1 2015 - p103(1) [51-500]

Castillo, Lauren - *Nana in the City (Read by Gebauer, Christopher). Audiobook Review*
  c SLJ - v61 - i5 - May 2015 - p68(1) [51-500]
Nana in the City (Illus. by Castillo, Lauren)
  c HB Guide - v26 - i1 - Spring 2015 - p7(1) [51-500]

Castillo, Linda - *After the Storm (Read by McInerney, Kathleen). Audiobook Review*
  BL - v112 - i5 - Nov 1 2015 - p69(1) [51-500]
  PW - v262 - i35 - August 31 2015 - p83(1) [51-500]
After the Storm
  BL - v111 - i21 - July 1 2015 - p34(1) [51-500]
  KR - May 15 2015 - pNA [51-500]
  LJ - v140 - i11 - June 15 2015 - p71(2) [51-500]
  PW - v262 - i18 - May 4 2015 - p47(1) [51-500]
The Dead Will Tell (Read by McInerney, Kathleen). Audiobook Review
  LJ - v140 - i5 - March 15 2015 - p71(1) [51-500]

Castle, Anna - *Black and White and Dead All Over*
SPBW - Nov 2015 - pNA [51-500]

Castle, Jayne - *The Hot Zone (Read by Rosenblat, Barbara)*. Audiobook Review
BL - v111 - i13 - March 1 2015 - p68(1) [51-500]
Siren's Call
PW - v262 - i22 - June 1 2015 - p48(1) [51-500]
BL - v111 - i21 - July 1 2015 - p45(1) [51-500]

Castle, Jill - *Eat Like a Champion*
y VOYA - v38 - i3 - August 2015 - p90(2) [51-500]

Castle, Kendra Leigh - *Every Little Kiss*
PW - v262 - i5 - Feb 2 2015 - p44(1) [51-500]
One of These Nights
PW - v262 - i32 - August 10 2015 - p43(2) [51-500]

Castledine, Jacqueline - *Cold War Progressives: Women's Interracial Organizing for Peace and Freedom*
JWH - v27 - i3 - Fall 2015 - p204(7) [501+]
Wom HR - v24 - i1 - Feb 2015 - p135-137 [501+]

Castleman, Virginia - *Sara Lost and Found*
c KR - Nov 1 2015 - pNA [51-500]

Castner, Brian - *All the Ways We Kill and Die*
KR - Jan 1 2016 - pNA [51-500]

Castor, Helen - *Joan of Arc: A History (Read by Flosnik, Anne)*. Audiobook Review
LJ - v140 - i17 - Oct 15 2015 - p52(2) [51-500]
Joan of Arc: A History
BL - v111 - i17 - May 1 2015 - p73(1) [51-500]
KR - Feb 15 2015 - pNA [501+]
LJ - v140 - i6 - April 1 2015 - p102(1) [51-500]
NY - v91 - i22 - August 3 2015 - p73 [51-500]
NYTBR - July 5 2015 - p15(L) [501+]
PW - v262 - i9 - March 2 2015 - p75(1) [51-500]

Castro, Fidel - *Cuba & Angola: Fighting for Africa's Freedom and Our Own*
JTWS - v32 - i1 - Spring 2015 - p352(4) [501+]

Castroman, Nicole - *Blackhearts*
y KR - Oct 15 2015 - pNA [51-500]

Castronova, Edward - *Wildcat Currency: How the Virtual Money Revolution Is Transforming the Economy*
Reason - v46 - i10 - March 2015 - p67(3) [501+]

Castronovo, Russ - *The Oxford Handbook of Nineteenth-Century American Literature*
MLR - v110 - i3 - July 2015 - p839-840 [501+]

Caswell, Deanna - *The Beach House (Illus. by Bates, Amy June)*
c HB Guide - v26 - i2 - Fall 2015 - p8(1) [51-500]
c SLJ - v61 - i7 - July 2015 - p60(1) [51-500]
Guess Who, Haiku (Illus. by Shea, Bob)
c PW - v262 - i52 - Dec 21 2015 - p156(2) [501+]

Caswell, Kurt - *Getting to Grey Owl*
WLT - v89 - i6 - Nov-Dec 2015 - p63(1) [51-500]

Caswell, Michelle - *Archiving the Unspeakable: Silence, Memory, and the Photographic Record in Cambodia*
AHR - v120 - i4 - Oct 2015 - p1443-1444 [501+]
Pac A - v88 - i4 - Dec 2015 - p960 [501+]

Catalano, Nick - *Tales of a Hamptons Sailor*
RVBW - June 2015 - pNA [51-500]

Catalanotto, Peter - *The Newbies (Illus. by Catalanotto, Peter)*
c KR - May 1 2015 - pNA [51-500]
c SLJ - v61 - i5 - May 2015 - p83(1) [51-500]

Catanese, P.W. - *Donny's Inferno*
c KR - Dec 15 2015 - pNA [51-500]

Catani, Damian - *Evil: A History in Modern French Literature and Thought*
MLR - v110 - i1 - Jan 2015 - p263-264 [501+]

Catapano, Peter - *The Stone Reader: Modern Philosophy in 133 Arguments*
BL - v112 - i5 - Nov 1 2015 - p4(1) [51-500]
KR - Sept 1 2015 - pNA [501+]

Caterer, Claire M. - *The Wand and the Sea*
c BL - v111 - i18 - May 15 2015 - p66(1) [51-500]
c CH Bwatch - Sept 2015 - pNA [51-500]
c HB Guide - v26 - i2 - Fall 2015 - p77(1) [51-500]
c KR - April 15 2015 - pNA [51-500]
c SLJ - v61 - i6 - June 2015 - p98(2) [51-500]

Cathcart, Brian - *The News from Waterloo: The Race to Tell Britain of Wellington's Victory*
TLS - i5871 - Oct 9 2015 - p29(1) [51-500]
The News From Waterloo: The Race to Tell Britain of Willington's Victory
TimHES - i2210 - July 2 2015 - p48-1 [501+]

Catino, Maurizio - *Organizational Myopia: Problems of Rationality and Foresight in Organizations*
AJS - v120 - i5 - March 2015 - p1588(3) [501+]
CS - v44 - i6 - Nov 2015 - p788-789 [501+]

Catlin, Christine - *Spectaccolo: A Tale of Darkness and Light*
y VOYA - v38 - i5 - Dec 2015 - p67(1) [51-500]

Catling, B. - *The Vorrh*
BL - v111 - i14 - March 15 2015 - p50(1) [51-500]
KR - March 1 2015 - pNA [51-500]
PW - v262 - i6 - Feb 9 2015 - p49(2) [51-500]
TLS - i5853 - June 5 2015 - p19(1) [501+]

Catlos, Brian A. - *Infidel Kings and Unholy Warriors: Faith, Power, and Violence in the Age of Crusade and Jihad*
Med R - August 2015 - pNA [501+]
Muslims of Medieval Latin Christendom, c. 1050-1614
Med R - June 2015 - pNA [501+]

Catmull, Katherine - *The Radiant Road*
y KR - Nov 1 2015 - pNA [51-500]
y PW - v262 - i41 - Oct 12 2015 - p70(1) [51-500]
y SLJ - v61 - i12 - Dec 2015 - p113(2) [51-500]

Cato, Beth - *The Clockwork Crown*
KR - April 15 2015 - pNA [501+]
PW - v262 - i10 - March 9 2015 - p56(1) [51-500]
The Clockwork Dagger
LJ - v140 - i2 - Feb 1 2015 - p111(1) [501+]

Catrow, David - *Fun in the Sun (Illus. by Catrow, David)*
c CCB-B - v69 - i1 - Sept 2015 - p16(1) [51-500]
c HB - v91 - i3 - May-June 2015 - p81(2) [51-500]
c HB Guide - v26 - i2 - Fall 2015 - p8(1) [51-500]
c KR - March 1 2015 - pNA [51-500]
c PW - v262 - i14 - April 6 2015 - p57(1) [51-500]

Cattani, Adriano - *I Tasso e le Poste d'Europa - The Tassis Family and the European Postal Service - First International Symposium*
Phil Lit R - v64 - i3 - Summer 2015 - p210(2) [501+]

Cattell, James McKeen - *University Control*
TimHES - i2211 - July 9 2015 - p49(1) [501+]

Catterick, Maria - *Understanding Fetal Alcohol Spectrum Disorder: A Guide to FASD for Parents, Carers and Professionals*
Bwatch - Feb 2015 - pNA [51-500]

Catullus - *Carmina*
TLS - i5848 - May 1 2015 - p12(1) [501+]

Caudill, Edward - *Intelligently Designed: How Creationists Built the Campaign against Evolution*
JSH - v81 - i2 - May 2015 - p500(3) [501+]
Inventing Custer: The Making of an American Legend
PW - v262 - i35 - August 31 2015 - p77(1) [51-500]

Caudle, Melissa - *Alphabet Al's ABC Book of Words and Rhymes*
c CH Bwatch - June 2015 - pNA [51-500]
Colors, Shapes & Counting: A Point & Name Book of Rhymes
c CH Bwatch - June 2015 - pNA [51-500]

Caughey, Melissa - *A Kid's Guide to Keeping Chickens*
c BL - v111 - i19-20 - June 1 2015 - p78(2) [51-500]

Caulfield, Timothy - *Is Gwyneth Paltrow Wrong about Everything?: How the Famous Sell Us Exilers of Health, Beauty & Happiness*
KR - March 1 2015 - pNA [501+]

Cavaiani, Jay - *Altar'd: Faith Building Evidence Leading to New Life*
SPBW - Nov 2015 - pNA [51-500]

Cavaliero, Roderick - *Genius, Power and Magic: A Cultural History of Germany from Goethe to Wagner*
GSR - v38 - i1 - Feb 2015 - p168-170 [501+]

Cavallaro, Brittany - *A Study in Charlotte*
y KR - Dec 15 2015 - pNA [51-500]
y PW - v262 - i50 - Dec 7 2015 - p87(1) [51-500]
y SLJ - v61 - i12 - Dec 2015 - p118(2) [51-500]

Cavallini, Nadia Yacoub - *The Proactive Health Solution*
KR - Sept 1 2015 - pNA [51-500]

Cavallo, Jo Ann - *The World beyond Europe in the Romance Epics of Boiardo and Ariosto*
Six Ct J - v46 - i3 - Fall 2015 - p818-820 [501+]

Cavanagh, David - *Straddle*
WLT - v89 - i6 - Nov-Dec 2015 - p72(2) [51-500]

Cavanaugh, Alex J. - *Dragon of the Stars*
PW - v262 - i5 - Feb 2 2015 - p39(2) [51-500]

Cavanaugh, Nancy J. - *Always, Abigail*
y HB Guide - v26 - i1 - Spring 2015 - p73(1) [51-500]

Cavazos, Xavier - *Diamond Grove Slave Tree*
NAR - v300 - i3 - Summer 2015 - p49(1) [501+]

Cave, Carolyn - *Beautiful Designs with SuperDuos and Twin Beads*
Bwatch - March 2015 - pNA [51-500]

Cave, George - *Just Be a Dad: Things My Father Never Told Me*
SPBW - Jan 2015 - pNA [501+]

Cave, Roderick - *The History of the Book in 100 Books*
WLT - v89 - i3-4 - May-August 2015 - p111(1) [51-500]
LJ - v140 - i9 - May 15 2015 - p94(2) [51-500]

Cave, Terence - *Reading Literature Cognitively*
FS - v69 - i2 - April 2015 - p280-281 [501+]

Cavell, Richard - *Marinetti Dines with the High Command*
Can Lit - i224 - Spring 2015 - p116 [501+]

Cavender, Cathy - *Country Living Porches and Outdoor Spaces*
LJ - v140 - i9 - May 15 2015 - p83(1) [51-500]

Cavendish, Philip - *The Men with the Movie Camera: The Poetics of Visual Style in Soviet Avant-Garde Cinema of the 1920s*
Slav R - v74 - i2 - Summer 2015 - p426-427 [501+]

Caver, Joseph - *The Tuskegee Airmen: An Illustrated History, 1939-1949*
JSH - v81 - i4 - Nov 2015 - p1058(2) [501+]

Caviness, Madeline H. - *The Ancestors of Christ Windows at Canterbury Cathedral*
Med R - May 2015 - pNA [501+]

Caviness, Ylonda Gault - *Child, Please: How Mama's Old-School Lessons Helped Me Check Myself before I Wreck Myself*
KR - March 1 2015 - pNA [51-500]
Child, Please: How Mama's Old-School Lessons Helped Me Check Myself before I Wrecked Myself
LJ - v140 - i9 - May 15 2015 - p66(2) [501+]

Cawood, Ian - *The Liberal Unionist Party: A History*
VS - v57 - i2 - Wntr 2015 - p292(3) [501+]

Caxton, William - *The Booke of Ovyde Named Methamorphose*
Med R - May 2015 - pNA [501+]

Cayley, Emma - *Manuscripts and Printed Books in Europe 1350-1550*
HER - v130 - i545 - August 2015 - p977(3) [501+]

Cayley, Kate - *How You Were Born*
Can Lit - i224 - Spring 2015 - p118 [501+]

Cayne, Pamela - *The Fighter and the Fallen Woman*
PW - v262 - i4 - Jan 26 2015 - p155(1) [51-500]

Cayton, Andrew - *Love in the Time of Revolution: Transatlantic Literary Radicalism and Historical Change, 1793-1818*
JMH - v87 - i1 - March 2015 - p177(3) [501+]
JWH - v27 - i3 - Fall 2015 - p194(10) [501+]

Cazzuffi, Elena - *Decimi Magni Ausonii: Ludus septem sapientum*
Class R - v65 - i2 - Oct 2015 - p478-479 [501+]

Ceballos, Gerardo - *The Annihilation of Nature: Human Extinction of Birds and Mammals*
LJ - v140 - i17 - Oct 15 2015 - p107(2) [51-500]

Ceccarelli, Leah - *On the Frontier of Science: An American Rhetoric of Exploration and Exploitation*
Isis - v106 - i1 - March 2015 - p215(2) [501+]
QRB - v90 - i1 - March 2015 - p78(2) [501+]

Cece, Adam - *Wesley Booth Super Sleuth (Illus. by Streich, Michel)*
c Magpies - v30 - i3 - July 2015 - p33(1) [501+]

Ceceri, Kathy - *Video Games: Design and Code Your Own Adventure (Illus. by Crosier, Mike)*
c BL - v112 - i6 - Nov 15 2015 - p40(1) [51-500]
c PW - v262 - i30 - July 27 2015 - p70(1) [51-500]

Cecil, Hugh - *Rex Whistler: Inspirations, 2 vols.*
Apo - v181 - i631 - May 2015 - p103(1) [51-500]
Rex Whistler: Inspirations: Family, Friendships, Landscapes
Spec - v329 - i9768 - Nov 14 2015 - p60(2) [501+]
Rex Whistler: Inspirations: Love and War
Spec - v329 - i9768 - Nov 14 2015 - p60(2) [501+]

Cecillon, Jack D. - *Prayers, Petitions, and Protests: The Catholic Church and the Ontario Schools Crisis in the Windsor Border Region, 1910-1928*
Can Hist R - v96 - i2 - June 2015 - p317(3) [501+]
CHR - v101 - i2 - Spring 2015 - p393(3) [501+]

Cederstrom, Carl - *The Wellness Syndrome*
TLS - i5873 - Oct 23 2015 - p28(1) [501+]

Celan, Paul - *Breathturn into Timestead*
WLT - v89 - i2 - March-April 2015 - p57(1) [51-500]

Celenza, Anna Harwell - *Music as Cultural Mission: Explorations of Jesuit Practices in Italy and North America*
Theol St - v76 - i3 - Sept 2015 - p651(1) [501+]

Celenza, Christopher A. - *Machiavelli: A Portrait*
BL - v111 - i11 - Feb 1 2015 - p6(1) [51-500]

Celenza, Harwell Anna - *Explorations of Jesuit Practices in Italy and North America*
Ren Q - v68 - i2 - Summer 2015 - p736-737 [501+]

Celestin, Ray - *The Axeman*
LJ - v140 - i14 - Sept 1 2015 - p90(1) [51-500]
NYTBR - Sept 6 2015 - p25(L) [501+]
PW - v262 - i30 - July 27 2015 - p44(1) [51-500]

Celine, Marie - *Lights, Camera, Murder!*
    KR - Nov 1 2015 - pNA [51-500]
    PW - v262 - i47 - Nov 23 2015 - p52(1) [51-500]

Cell Phones and Society Series
    c BL - v111 - i15 - April 1 2015 - p58(1) [501+]

Celt, Adrienne - *The Daughters*
    BL - v111 - i21 - July 1 2015 - p29(1) [51-500]
    KR - June 1 2015 - pNA [51-500]
    LJ - v140 - i11 - June 15 2015 - p74(1) [51-500]
    PW - v262 - i25 - June 22 2015 - p116(1) [51-500]

Centamore, Adam - *Tasting Wine and Cheese: An Insider's Guide to Mastering the Principles of Pairing*
    BL - v112 - i3 - Oct 1 2015 - p20(2) [51-500]

Centeno, Miguel A. - *State and Nation Making in Latin America and Spain: Republics of the Possible*
    CS - v44 - i5 - Sept 2015 - p642-644 [501+]

Center, Katherine - *Happiness for Beginners*
    BL - v111 - i13 - March 1 2015 - p18(1) [51-500]

Centore, Michael - *Japan*
    c BL - v112 - i3 - Oct 1 2015 - p54(1) [51-500]

Central Intelligence Agency - *CIA's June 2013 Response to the SSCI Study on the Former Detention and Interrogation Program*
    For Aff - v94 - i3 - May-June 2015 - pNA [501+]
Overview of CIA-Congress Interactions Concerning the Agency's Rendition-Detention-Interrogation Program
    For Aff - v94 - i3 - May-June 2015 - pNA [501+]

A Century of War, a Century of Debate: Historians Debate German History
    HNet - Jan 2015 - pNA [501+]

Cerasani, Richard - *Love Letters from Mount Rushmore: The Story of a Marriage, a Monument, and a Moment in History*
    Roundup M - v22 - i6 - August 2015 - p35(1) [501+]

Cerato, Mattia - *Drew the Screw (Illus. by Cerato, Mattia)*
    c KR - Nov 15 2015 - pNA [51-500]
Sheep in the Closet (Illus. by Cerato, Mattia)
    c CH Bwatch - Jan 2015 - pNA [51-500]

Cercas, Javier - *Outlaws*
    NYTBR - Jan 4 2015 - p26(L) [501+]

Cerda, Roxane - *75 Fun Fat-Quarter Quilts: 13 Quilts + 62 Innovative Variations*
    LJ - v140 - i19 - Nov 15 2015 - p84(1) [51-500]

Cerf, Christopher - *Spinglish: The Definitive Dictionary of Deliberately Deceptive Language*
    NYTBR - May 31 2015 - p22(L) [501+]

Ceroni, Andrew - *Snow Men*
    KR - June 15 2015 - pNA [501+]

Cerquiglini-Toulet, Jacqueline - *A New History of Medieval French Literature*
    Specu - v90 - i1 - Jan 2015 - p222-223 [501+]

Cerra, Kerry O'Malley - *Just a Drop of Water*
    y HB Guide - v26 - i1 - Spring 2015 - p73(1) [51-500]

Cerrito, Angela - *The Safest Lie*
    c BL - v112 - i2 - Sept 15 2015 - p66(1) [51-500]
    c SLJ - v61 - i8 - August 2015 - p83(1) [51-500]
    c KR - June 1 2015 - pNA [51-500]

Cervantes, Angela - *Allie, First at Last*
    c KR - Dec 15 2015 - pNA [51-500]
    c PW - v262 - i50 - Dec 7 2015 - p85(1) [51-500]

Cervantes, Fernando - *Angels, Demons and the New World*
    CH - v84 - i1 - March 2015 - p240(3) [501+]
    Ren Q - v68 - i1 - Spring 2015 - p325-326 [501+]

Cervantes, Jorge - *The Cannabis Encyclopedia: The Definitive Guide to Cultivation and Consumption of Medical Marijuana*
    BL - v111 - i18 - May 15 2015 - p15(1) [51-500]
    LJ - v140 - i8 - May 1 2015 - p99(1) [51-500]

Cervenak, Sarah Jane - *Wandering: Philosophical Performances of Racial and Sexual Freedom*
    JAH - v102 - i2 - Sept 2015 - p509-510 [501+]
    JSH - v81 - i4 - Nov 2015 - p1060(5) [501+]

Cervone, Barbara - *In Our Village: San Francisco's Tenderloin through the Eyes of Its Youth*
    y SLJ - v61 - i8 - August 2015 - p125(1) [51-500]

Cervone, Cristina Maria - *Poetics of the Incarnation: Middle English Writing and the Leap of Love*
    JEGP - v114 - i2 - April 2015 - p297(4) [501+]
    MLR - v110 - i3 - July 2015 - p806-807 [501+]
    Specu - v90 - i2 - April 2015 - p522-523 [501+]

Cesari, Jocelyne - *Why the West Fears Islam: An Exploration of Muslims in Liberal Democracies*
    IJMES - v47 - i4 - Nov 2015 - p837-839 [501+]

Cevellos, Santiago - *El Barroco, marco de agua de la narrativa hispanoamericana*
    Hisp R - v83 - i2 - Spring 2015 - p234-237 [501+]

Cha, Grace - *From Korea to California: Our Journey to America (Illus. by Kim, Arnold)*
    c KR - Nov 15 2015 - pNA [51-500]

Cha, Steph - *Dead Soon Enough*
    BL - v111 - i19-20 - June 1 2015 - p52(1) [51-500]
    KR - June 1 2015 - pNA [51-500]
    PW - v262 - i25 - June 22 2015 - p120(1) [51-500]

Chabert, Jack - *The Locker Ate Lucy! (Illus. by Ricks, Sam)*
    c HB Guide - v26 - i1 - Spring 2015 - p58(1) [51-500]
    c CH Bwatch - March 2015 - pNA [501+]
Mystery of the Map
    c KR - Dec 15 2015 - pNA [51-500]

Chace, Teri Dunn - *Seeing Seeds: A Journey Into the World of Seedheads, Pods, and Fruit*
    NYTBR - Dec 6 2015 - p66(L) [501+]

Chachavalpongpun, Pavin - *Entering Uncharted Waters? ASEAN and the South China Sea*
    Pac A - v88 - i2 - June 2015 - p350 [501+]

Chaconas, Dori - *Cork and Fuzz: Merry Merry Holly Holly (Illus. by McCue, Lisa)*
    c HB - v91 - i6 - Nov-Dec 2015 - p54(1) [51-500]
    c KR - Sept 1 2015 - pNA [51-500]
    c PW - v262 - i37 - Sept 14 2015 - p64(2) [51-500]
    c SLJ - v61 - i10 - Oct 2015 - p61(2) [51-500]
Cork and Fuzz: Spring Cleaning (Illus. by McCue, Lisa)
    c HB Guide - v26 - i2 - Fall 2015 - p59(1) [51-500]

Chadwick, David - *Liberty Bazaar*
    KR - May 1 2015 - pNA [501+]

Chadwick, Frank - *Come the Revolution*
    PW - v262 - i42 - Oct 19 2015 - p59(1) [51-500]

Chafe, Eric - *J.S. Bach's Johannine Theology: The St. John Passion and the Cantatas for Spring 1725*
    MT - v156 - i1930 - Spring 2015 - p101-104 [501+]

Chafets, Zev - *The Bridge Builder: The Life and Continuing Legacy of Rabbi Yechiel Eckstein*
    KR - June 15 2015 - pNA [501+]
    PW - v262 - i27 - July 6 2015 - p66(1) [51-500]

Chainani, Soman - *The Last Ever After*
    y SLJ - v61 - i10 - Oct 2015 - p100(1) [51-500]

Chakkalakal, Silvy - *Die Welt in Bildern: Erfahrung und Evidenz in Friedrich J. Bertuchs "Bilderbuch fur Kinder"*
    HNet - Jan 2015 - pNA [501+]

Chakrabarti, Pratik - *Bacteriology in British India: Laboratory Medicine and the Tropics*
    HER - v130 - i542 - Feb 2015 - p228(229) [501+]

Chaline, Eric - *The Temple of Perfection: A History of the Gym*
    HT - v65 - i4 - April 2015 - p58(1) [501+]
    Spec - v327 - i9732 - March 7 2015 - p41(1) [501+]

Chalker-Scott, Linda - *How Plants Work: The Science behind the Amazing Things Plants Do*
    NYTBR - May 31 2015 - p36(L) [501+]

Challen, Paul - *Learning about World War I and World War II with Arts and Crafts*
    c Teach Lib - v42 - i4 - April 2015 - p9(1) [51-500]

Challies, Tim - *The Next Story: Faith, Friends, Family, and the Digital World*
    RVBW - June 2015 - pNA [51-500]

Challinor, C.S. - *Murder Comes Calling*
    BL - v111 - i21 - July 1 2015 - p38(1) [51-500]
    KR - June 1 2015 - pNA [51-500]
    PW - v262 - i24 - June 15 2015 - p66(1) [51-500]

Challinor, Deborah - *My Australian Story: Vietnam*
    c Magpies - v30 - i3 - July 2015 - p33(2) [51-500]

Challoner, Jack - *The Elements: The New Guide to the Building Blocks of Our Universe*
    BL - v111 - i12 - Feb 15 2015 - p21(1) [51-500]

Chalmers, Aaron - *Interpreting the Prophets: Reading, Understanding, and Preaching from the Worlds of the Prophets*
    LJ - v140 - i9 - May 15 2015 - p64(2) [501+]

Chalmers, Claudine - *Cronicling the West of Harper's: Coast to Coast with Frenzeny and Tavernier in 1873-1874*
    SHQ - v118 - i3 - Jan 2015 - p325-327 [501+]

Chalmers, David J. - *Constructing the World*
    Phil R - v124 - i3 - July 2015 - p430(8) [501+]

Chaltain, Sam - *Our School: Searching for Community in the Era of Choice*
    HER - v85 - i1 - Spring 2015 - p132-134 [501+]

Chamanara, Sohrab - *2020: The Fall of Islamic States*
    KR - May 15 2015 - pNA [501+]

Chamayou, Gregoire - *Drone Theory*
    NS - v144 - i5267 - June 19 2015 - p48(1) [501+]
    TLS - i5854 - June 12 2015 - p28(1) [501+]
A Theory of the Drone
    NYTBR - Feb 1 2015 - p19(L) [501+]

Chamberet, Georgia de - *Lesley Blanch: On the Wilder Shores of Love*
    Spec - v327 - i9735 - March 28 2015 - p42(2) [501+]

Chamberlain, Diane - *Pretending to Dance*
    y BL - v112 - i4 - Oct 15 2015 - p17(1) [51-500]
    KR - August 1 2015 - pNA [501+]
    SLJ - v61 - i12 - Dec 2015 - p131(1) [51-500]
The Silent Sister (Read by Bennett, Susan). Audiobook Review
    BL - v111 - i16 - April 15 2015 - p61(2) [51-500]

Chamberlain, Mary - *The Dressmaker's War*
    KR - Oct 15 2015 - pNA [501+]
    PW - v262 - i46 - Nov 16 2015 - p51(1) [51-500]

Chamberlain, Penny - *Shack Island Summer*
    c Res Links - v20 - i4 - April 2015 - p10(1) [51-500]

Chamberland, Marc - *Single Digits: In Praise of Small Numbers*
    BL - v111 - i18 - May 15 2015 - p8(2) [51-500]
    PW - v262 - i17 - April 27 2015 - p64(1) [51-500]

Chamberlin, Holly - *Summer with My Sisters*
    LJ - v140 - i11 - June 15 2015 - p74(1) [51-500]

Chamberlin, Paul Thomas - *The Global Offensive: The United States, the Palestine Liberation Organization, and the Making of the Post-Cold War Order*
    HNet - Jan 2015 - pNA [501+]

Chambers, Aidan - *Blindside*
    y Sch Lib - v63 - i2 - Summer 2015 - p115(1) [51-500]
This Is All: The Pillow Book of Cordelia Kenn
    y BL - v111 - i9-10 - Jan 1 2015 - p66(1) [501+]

Chambers, Alan - *My Exodus: Leaving the Slavery of Religion, Loving the Image of God in Everyone*
    PW - v262 - i27 - July 6 2015 - p64(2) [51-500]

Chambers, Catherine - *Are Humans Damaging the Atmosphere?*
    c HB Guide - v26 - i2 - Fall 2015 - p155(1) [51-500]
How Effective Is Recycling?
    c HB Guide - v26 - i2 - Fall 2015 - p155(1) [51-500]
The Loch Ness Monster (Illus. by Billau, Lois)
    c Sch Lib - v63 - i4 - Winter 2015 - p236(1) [51-500]
Silent Soldiers (Illus. by Juta, Jason)
    c KR - Jan 1 2016 - pNA [51-500]
Under Pressure
    y HB Guide - v26 - i1 - Spring 2015 - p131(2) [51-500]

Chambers, Claire Maria - *Performing Religion in Public*
    Theat J - v67 - i3 - Oct 2015 - p577-579 [501+]

The Chambers Dictionary, 13th ed.
    TLS - i5835 - Jan 30 2015 - p25(1) [501+]

Chambers, Emily - *The Cheese Lover's Cookbook*
    Bwatch - August 2015 - pNA [51-500]

Chambers, Helen - *Fontane-Studien: Gesammelte Aufsatze zu Romanen, Gedichten und Reportagen*
    MLR - v110 - i3 - July 2015 - p895-896 [501+]

Chambers, Iain - *The Postcolonial Museum: The Arts of Memory and the Pressures of History*
    LQ - v85 - i3 - July 2015 - p328(3) [501+]

Chambers, John - *From Dust to Life: The Origin and Evolution of Our Solar System*
    Phys Today - v68 - i2 - Feb 2015 - p50(1) [501+]

Chambers-Letson, Joshua Takano - *Joshua Takano Chambers-Letson, a Race So Different: Performance and Law in Asian America*
    J Am St - v49 - i1 - Feb 2015 - p208-210 [501+]

Chambers, M. Scott - *Future Imperfect*
    KR - Oct 15 2015 - pNA [501+]

Chambers, Roland - *Nelly and the Quest for Captain Peabody*
    Sch Lib - v63 - i4 - Winter 2015 - p225(1) [51-500]

Chambers, Stephen - *No God But Gain: The Untold Story of Cuban Slavery, the Monroe Doctrine, and the Making of the United States*
    PW - v262 - i26 - June 29 2015 - p56(1) [51-500]

Chambliss, Daniel F. - *How College Works*
    CS - v44 - i5 - Sept 2015 - p644-645 [501+]

Chan, Arlene - *The Chinese Head Tax and Anti-Chinese Immigration Policies in the Twentieth Century*
    y Res Links - v20 - i3 - Feb 2015 - p37(2) [51-500]

Chan, Daniel L. - *Nutritional Management of Hospitalized Small Animals*
    RVBW - Oct 2015 - pNA [51-500]

Chan, Darcie - *The Promise of Home*
    KR - July 15 2015 - pNA [501+]

Chan, Gillian - *Defend or Die: The Siege of Hong Kong*
    y Res Links - v20 - i5 - June 2015 - p23(2) [51-500]

Chan, Marty - *Infinity Coil*
    c Res Links - v20 - i4 - April 2015 - p26(1) [51-500]
    c SLJ - v61 - i6 - June 2015 - p108(1) [51-500]
    y VOYA - v38 - i1 - April 2015 - p76(1) [51-500]

Chan, Simon - *Grassroots Asian Theology: Thinking the Faith from the Ground Up*
    IBMR - v39 - i1 - Jan 2015 - p46(1) [501+]
    Theol St - v76 - i2 - June 2015 - p394(2) [501+]

Chan, Steve - *Looking for Balance: China, the United States, and Power Balancing in East Asia*
    J Am St - v49 - i1 - May 2015 - p449-451 [501+]

Chance, Jane - *Medieval Mythography, vol. 3: The Emergence of Italian Humanism, 1321-1475*
    Med R - August 2015 - pNA [501+]

Chance, Karen - *Reap the Wind*
    PW - v262 - i39 - Sept 28 2015 - p73(1) [51-500]

Chance, Maia - *Come Hell or Highball*
    BL - v112 - i1 - Sept 1 2015 - p45(1) [51-500]
    KR - July 15 2015 - pNA [51-500]
    PW - v262 - i27 - July 6 2015 - p47(1) [51-500]

Joy to the Worlds: Mysterious Speculative Fiction for the Holidays
    PW - v262 - i45 - Nov 9 2015 - p41(1) [51-500]

Chance, Megan - *The Shadows (Read by Peakes, Karen). Audiobook Review*
    c BL - v111 - i14 - March 15 2015 - p24(2) [501+]

The Web (Read by Peakes, Karen). Audiobook Review
    y SLJ - v61 - i8 - August 2015 - p52(1) [51-500]

Chancellor, Deborah - *Spymaster*
    c Sch Lib - v63 - i1 - Spring 2015 - p34(1) [51-500]

Chancey, Mark A. - *The Bible in the Public Square: Its Enduring Influence in American Life*
    Intpr - v69 - i4 - Oct 2015 - p508(1) [501+]

Chancy, Myriam J.A. - *From Sugar to Revolution: Women's Visions of Haiti, Cuba, and the Dominican Republic*
    AL - v87 - i3 - Sept 2015 - p616-618 [501+]

Chandler, A.K. - *Lord of War*
    SPBW - Sept 2015 - pNA [51-500]

Chandler, Andrea - *Democracy, Gender and Social Policy in Russia: A Wayward Society*
    E-A St - v67 - i1 - Jan 2015 - p143(2) [501+]

Chandler, Deborah - *Traditional Weavers of Guatemala: Their Stories, Their Lives*
    LJ - v140 - i13 - August 1 2015 - p91(1) [51-500]
    RVBW - Nov 2015 - pNA [51-500]

Chandler, Hannah - *I Don't Like Cheese (Illus. by Merrick, Lauren)*
    c Sch Lib - v63 - i2 - Summer 2015 - p90(1) [51-500]
    c SLJ - v61 - i9 - Sept 2015 - p116(1) [51-500]

Chandler, John - *Faith-Based Policy: A Litmus Test for Understanding Contemporary America*
    J Ch St - v57 - i3 - Summer 2015 - p581-583 [501+]

Chandler, Matt - *The Trojan War: A Graphic Retelling (Illus. by Haus, Estudio)*
    c HB Guide - v26 - i2 - Fall 2015 - p158(1) [51-500]

Chandler, Robert - *The Penguin Book of Russian Poetry*
    NS - v144 - i5267 - June 19 2015 - p49(1) [501+]
    TLS - i5864-5865 - August 21 2015 - p30(2) [501+]

Chandler, Susan - *The Greedy Rainbow*
    c KR - May 1 2015 - pNA [51-500]

Chandra, Shefali - *The Sexual Life of English: Languages of Caste and Desire in Colonial India*
    JAS - v74 - i2 - May 2015 - p502-504 [501+]

Chandra, Vikram - *Geek Sublime: The Beauty of Code, the Code of Beauty (Read by Shah, Neil). Audiobook Review*
    LJ - v140 - i9 - May 15 2015 - p45(1) [51-500]

Chandrasekaran, Rajiv - *For Love of Country: What Our Veterans Can Teach Us about Citizenship, Heroism, and Sacrifice (Read by Chandrasekaran, Rajiv). Audiobook Review*
    LJ - v140 - i6 - April 1 2015 - p52(1) [51-500]

Chaney, Celeste - *In Absence of Fear*
    KR - Dec 15 2015 - pNA [501+]

Chaney, Jen - *As If! The Oral History of "Clueless" as Told by Amy Heckerling and the Cast and Crew (Read by Marie, Jorjeana). Audiobook Review*
    LJ - v140 - i19 - Nov 15 2015 - p54(1) [51-500]

As If! The Oral History of "Clueless" as Told by Amy Heckerling and the Cast and Crew
    KR - June 15 2015 - pNA [501+]
    LJ - v140 - i13 - August 1 2015 - p96(1) [51-500]

Chang, Danielle - *Lucky Rice*
    PW - v262 - i46 - Nov 16 2015 - p68(1) [51-500]

Chang, Eileen - *Chi di zhi lian*
    y BL - v111 - i17 - May 1 2015 - p77(1) [51-500]
    PW - v262 - i4 - Jan 26 2015 - p144(1) [51-500]

Half a Lifelong Romance
    KR - Jan 1 2016 - pNA [501+]
    TLS - i5832 - Jan 9 2015 - p18(1) [501+]

Naked Earth
    KR - Jan 15 2015 - pNA [51-500]

Chang, Gordon H. - *Fateful Ties: A History of America's Preoccupation with China*
    KR - Feb 1 2015 - pNA [51-500]
    PW - v262 - i8 - Feb 23 2015 - p66(1) [51-500]
    TimHES - i2212 - July 16 2015 - p48-2 [501+]

Chang, Hee-jung - *"Could You Lift Up Your Bottom?" (Illus. by Chung, Sung-hwa)*
    c KR - March 15 2015 - pNA [51-500]

Chang, Henry - *Death Money*
    RVBW - April 2015 - pNA [51-500]

Chang, Jeff - *Who We Be: The Colorization of America*
    Nat Post - v17 - i62 - Jan 10 2015 - pWP8(1) [501+]

Chang, Juliana - *Inhuman Citizenship: Traumatic Enjoyment and Asian American Literature*
    AL - v87 - i1 - March 2015 - p203-205 [501+]

Chang, Jung - *Empress Dowager Cixi: The Concubine Who Launched Modern China*
    JTWS - v32 - i1 - Spring 2015 - p318(2) [501+]

Chang, Rayond - *Physical Chemistry for the Chemical Sciences*
    J Chem Ed - v92 - i9 - Sept 2015 - p1435-1436 [501+]

Chang, Ting - *Travel, Collecting, and Museums of Asian Art in Nineteenth-Century Paris*
    FS - v69 - i1 - Jan 2015 - p105-105 [501+]

Chang, Victoria - *Is Mommy? (Illus. by Frazee, Marla)*
    c BL - v112 - i5 - Nov 1 2015 - p65(1) [51-500]
    c KR - Sept 15 2015 - pNA [51-500]
    c NYTBR - Nov 8 2015 - p20(L) [501+]
    c PW - v262 - i35 - August 31 2015 - p88(1) [51-500]
    c SLJ - v61 - i12 - Dec 2015 - p84(1) [51-500]

The Changing Nature of Citizenship
    HNet - July 2015 - pNA [501+]

Chanin, Natalie - *Alabama Studio Sewing Patterns: A Guide to Customizing a HandStitched Alabama Chanin Wardrobe*
    LJ - v140 - i10 - June 1 2015 - p105(1) [51-500]

Chaniotis, Angelos - *Unveiling Emotions II: Emotions in Greece and Rome - Texts, Images, Material Culture*
    HNet - Jan 2015 - pNA [501+]

Channer, Colin - *Providential*
    y BL - v112 - i1 - Sept 1 2015 - p30(1) [501+]
    PW - v262 - i29 - July 20 2015 - p166(1) [51-500]

Channing, Margot - *Amazing Animals (Illus. by Channing, Margot)*
    c HB Guide - v26 - i2 - Fall 2015 - p170(1) [51-500]

Dinosaurs and Other Prehistoric Creatures (Illus. by Scrace, Carolyn)
    c HB Guide - v26 - i2 - Fall 2015 - p168(1) [51-500]

Incredible Creatures (Illus. by Scrace, Carolyn)
    c HB Guide - v26 - i2 - Fall 2015 - p170(1) [51-500]

Planet Earth (Illus. by Wood, Gerald)
    c HB Guide - v26 - i1 - Spring 2015 - p150(1) [51-500]

Rain Forest (Illus. by Scrace, Carolyn)
    c HB Guide - v26 - i1 - Spring 2015 - p153(1) [51-500]

Seas and Oceans (Illus. by Scrace, Carolyn)
    c HB Guide - v26 - i1 - Spring 2015 - p153(1) [51-500]

Space and Other Flying Machines
    c HB Guide - v26 - i2 - Fall 2015 - p187(1) [51-500]

Stars and Planets (Illus. by Donohoe, Bill)
    c HB Guide - v26 - i1 - Spring 2015 - p149(1) [51-500]

The Teddy Potty Book
    c KR - Jan 1 2015 - pNA [51-500]

Chanter, Catherine - *The Well*
    BL - v111 - i15 - April 1 2015 - p28(1) [51-500]
    KR - March 15 2015 - pNA [51-500]
    LJ - v140 - i3 - Feb 15 2015 - p85(1) [51-500]
    PW - v262 - i9 - March 2 2015 - p64(1) [51-500]

Chantler, Scott - *The Dark Island*
    c KR - Jan 1 2016 - pNA [51-500]

Les pirates de la cote d'argent
    c Res Links - v20 - i3 - Feb 2015 - p55(1) [1-50]

Pirates of the Silver Coast (Illus. by Chantler, Scott)
    c HB Guide - v26 - i1 - Spring 2015 - p73(1) [51-500]

Chany, Kalman A. - *Paying for College Without Going Broke*
    Bwatch - Jan 2015 - pNA [51-500]

Chaoui, Maren - *Seelsorge, Frommigkeit und Kriegserfahrungen im Ersten Weltkrieg: Feldpost an den Pfarrer zu Brochterbeck*
    HNet - Feb 2015 - pNA [501+]

Chapin, Andrea - *The Tutor*
    Ent W - i1351 - Feb 20 2015 - p63(1) [501+]
    BL - v111 - i9-10 - Jan 1 2015 - p55(1) [51-500]
    NYTBR - April 12 2015 - p30(L) [501+]

Chapin, David - *Freshwater Passages: The Trade and Travels of Peter Pond*
    WHQ - v46 - i2 - Summer 2015 - p227-228 [501+]

Chapin, Tom - *The Backwards Birthday Party (Illus. by Groenink, Chuck)*
    RVBW - July 2015 - pNA [51-500]
    c CH Bwatch - April 2015 - pNA [51-500]
    c HB Guide - v26 - i2 - Fall 2015 - p194(1) [51-500]

Chapleau, Heather - *Alison's Little Brother (Illus. by Patterson, Josh)*
    c Res Links - v20 - i5 - June 2015 - p2(1) [51-500]

Chaplin, Lisa - *The Tide Watchers*
    BL - v111 - i19-20 - June 1 2015 - p60(1) [51-500]

Chapman, Alice - *Sacred Authority and Temporal Power in the Writings of Bernard of Clairvaux*
    AHR - v120 - i3 - June 2015 - p1091-1092 [501+]
    Med R - June 2015 - pNA [501+]
    Specu - v90 - i3 - July 2015 - p785-786 [501+]

Chapman, Allan Westcott - *Adventures with Mr. Wugidgem*
    c CH Bwatch - June 2015 - pNA [501+]

Mr. Wugidgem and the Dark Journey
    c CH Bwatch - June 2015 - pNA [501+]

Mr. Wugidgem and the Faces of Freedom
    c CH Bwatch - June 2015 - pNA [501+]

Mr. Wugidgem and the Phoenix Journey
    c CH Bwatch - June 2015 - pNA [501+]

Mr. Wugidgem and the Snow Queen
    c CH Bwatch - June 2015 - pNA [501+]

Chapman, Ann - *Women in My Rose Garden: The History, Romance and Adventure of Old Roses*
    LJ - v140 - i3 - Feb 15 2015 - p120(1) [51-500]

Chapman, Bob - *Everybody Matters: The Extraordinary Power of Caring for Your People Like Family*
    LJ - v140 - i16 - Oct 1 2015 - p89(1) [51-500]

Chapman, Brenda - *Butterfly Kills*
    Nat Post - v17 - i80 - Jan 31 2015 - pWP8(1) [501+]
    RVBW - March 2015 - pNA [501+]

Chapman, Danielle - *Delinquent Palaces*
    BL - v111 - i16 - April 15 2015 - p13(1) [51-500]

Chapman, Drew - *The King of Fear*
    KR - Jan 1 2016 - pNA [501+]
    PW - v262 - i51 - Dec 14 2015 - p60(1) [51-500]

Chapman, Elsie - *Divided*
    c HB Guide - v26 - i1 - Spring 2015 - p103(1) [51-500]

Chapman, Gary - *Chad*
    KR - Jan 15 2015 - pNA [51-500]

Chapman, James - *Projecting Tomorrow: Science Fiction and Popular Cinema*
    SFS - v42 - i2 - July 2015 - p369-371 [501+]

Chapman, Jane - *No More Cuddles!*
    c KR - May 15 2015 - pNA [51-500]

Chapman, Jared - *Pirate, Viking and Scientist (Illus. by Chapman, Jared)*
    c HB Guide - v26 - i1 - Spring 2015 - p25(1) [51-500]

Steve, Raised by Wolves (Illus. by Chapman, Jared)
    c BL - v112 - i1 - Sept 1 2015 - p122(2) [51-500]
    c CCB-B - v69 - i2 - Oct 2015 - p80(1) [51-500]
    c KR - June 1 2015 - pNA [51-500]
    c SLJ - v61 - i8 - August 2015 - p58(1) [51-500]

Vegetables in Underwear (Illus. by Chapman, Jared)
    c BL - v111 - i15 - April 1 2015 - p84(1) [51-500]
    c HB - v91 - i3 - May-June 2015 - p82(2) [51-500]
    c HB Guide - v26 - i2 - Fall 2015 - p8(1) [51-500]
    c KR - Feb 15 2015 - pNA [51-500]

Chapman, Jessica M. - *Cauldron of Resistance: Ngo Dinh Diem, the United States, and 1950s Southern Vietnam*
    Pac A - v88 - i1 - March 2015 - p222 [501+]
    PHR - v84 - i1 - Feb 2015 - p109(2) [501+]

Chapman, Lara - *Accidentally Evil*
    c HB Guide - v26 - i2 - Fall 2015 - p77(1) [51-500]

The XYZs of Being Wicked
    c HB Guide - v26 - i2 - Fall 2015 - p77(1) [51-500]

Chapman, Mark D. - *Theology and Society in Three Cities: Berlin, Oxford, and Chicago, 1800-1914*
    Theol St - v76 - i3 - Sept 2015 - p638(1) [501+]

Chapman, Martin - *The Salon Dore from the Hotel de la Tremoille*
    NYRB - v62 - i11 - June 25 2015 - p29(4) [501+]

Chapman, Patricia Luce - *Tea on the Great Wall: An American Girl in War-Torn China*
    BL - v112 - i2 - Sept 15 2015 - p25(1) [51-500]

Chapman, Rob - *Psychedelia and Other Colours*
    NS - v144 - i5278 - Sept 4 2015 - p44(2) [501+]
    Spec - v328 - i9759 - Sept 12 2015 - p41(1) [501+]

Chapman, Susan Margaret - *The Old Ways: Inspired by a True Story (Illus. by Mantha, John)*
   c Res Links - v20 - i3 - Feb 2015 - p3(1) [51-500]
Chapman, Vannetta - *Murder Freshly Baked (Read by Ertl, Renee). Audiobook Review*
   BL - v112 - i6 - Nov 15 2015 - p61(1) [51-500]
Murder Freshly Baked
   BL - v111 - i17 - May 1 2015 - p41(1) [51-500]
Chappell, David A. - *The Kanak Awakening: The Rise of Nationalism in New Caledonia*
   Pac A - v88 - i2 - June 2015 - p381 [501+]
Chappell, David L. - *Waking from the Dream: The Struggle for Civil Rights in the Shadow of Martin Luther King, Jr.*
   JSH - v81 - i2 - May 2015 - p520(2) [501+]
Chappey, Jean-Luc - *Pour Quoi Faire la Revolution*
   HNet - July 2015 - pNA [501+]
Chaput, Erik J. - *The People's Martyr: Thomas Wilson Dorr and His 1842 Rhode Island Rebellion*
   Historian - v77 - i3 - Fall 2015 - p548(2) [501+]
Char, Rene - *Hypnos: Notes from the French Resistance, 1943-44*
   TLS - i5839 - Feb 27 2015 - p22(1) [501+]
Charaipotra, Sona - *Tiny Pretty Things*
   y CCB-B - v69 - i1 - Sept 2015 - p16(2) [51-500]
      SLJ - v61 - i4 - April 2015 - p160(1) [51-500]
   y VOYA - v38 - i1 - April 2015 - p55(1) [51-500]
Charalabopoulos, Nikos G. - *Platonic Drama and its Ancient Reception*
   Class R - v65 - i1 - April 2015 - p55-57 [501+]
Charbonneau, Joel - *Need*
   y BL - v112 - i1 - Sept 1 2015 - p105(2) [51-500]
Charbonneau, Joelle - *Graduation Day*
   c HB Guide - v26 - i1 - Spring 2015 - p103(1) [51-500]
Independent Study
   y Teach Lib - v42 - i3 - Feb 2015 - p28(4) [501+]
Need
   y PW - v262 - i37 - Sept 14 2015 - p79(1) [51-500]
   y SLJ - v61 - i10 - Oct 2015 - p100(2) [51-500]
   y VOYA - v38 - i5 - Dec 2015 - p54(1) [51-500]
   y KR - August 15 2015 - pNA [51-500]
Charbonneau, Louis - *"Fievres d'Afrique", suivi de trois recits inedits: "La Recluse", "La Duchesse" et "Minne Water: Lac d'Amour"*
   MLR - v110 - i2 - April 2015 - p551-553 [501+]
Mambu et son amour
   MLR - v110 - i2 - April 2015 - p551-553 [501+]
Charbonnier, Stephane - *Open Letter*
   KR - Dec 1 2015 - pNA [501+]
Chari, Sangita - *Accomplishing NAGPRA: Perspectives on the Intent, Impact, and Future of the Native American Graves Protection and Repatriation Act*
   Am Ind CRJ - v39 - i1 - Wntr 2015 - p113-115 [501+]
Charles, Casey - *The Trials of Christopher Mann*
   KR - May 1 2015 - pNA [501+]
Charles, Dora - *A Real Southern Cook in Her Savannah Kitchen*
   LJ - v140 - i19 - Nov 15 2015 - p102(1) [51-500]
   PW - v262 - i24 - June 15 2015 - p79(1) [51-500]
Charles, Edward - *The House of Medici: Inheritance of Power*
   BL - v111 - i16 - April 15 2015 - p36(1) [51-500]
Charles, K.J. - *A Fashionable Indulgence*
   PW - v262 - i28 - July 13 2015 - p52(2) [51-500]
Charles, Kate - *False Tongues*
   KR - Feb 1 2015 - pNA [51-500]
   PW - v262 - i5 - Feb 2 2015 - p38(1) [51-500]
Charlesworth, Liza - *Belles baleines*
   c Res Links - v21 - i1 - Oct 2015 - p49(1) [51-500]
La chasse aux bestioles
   c Res Links - v21 - i1 - Oct 2015 - p49(1) [51-500]
Les abeilles
   c Res Links - v21 - i1 - Oct 2015 - p49(1) [51-500]
Les cochons
   c Res Links - v21 - i1 - Oct 2015 - p49(1) [51-500]
Les crabes
   c Res Links - v21 - i1 - Oct 2015 - p49(1) [51-500]
Les escargots
   c Res Links - v21 - i1 - Oct 2015 - p49(1) [51-500]
Les grenouilles
   c Res Links - v21 - i1 - Oct 2015 - p49(1) [51-500]
Les oeufs de la poule
   c Res Links - v21 - i1 - Oct 2015 - p49(1) [51-500]
Les phoques
   c Res Links - v21 - i1 - Oct 2015 - p49(1) [51-500]
Les sauterelles
   c Res Links - v21 - i1 - Oct 2015 - p49(1) [51-500]
Les serpents
   c Res Links - v21 - i1 - Oct 2015 - p49(1) [51-500]
Mes premiers petits livres series C, 20 vols.
   c Res Links - v20 - i4 - April 2015 - p36(2) [51-500]

Charlet, Izabella - *Tobby's Day at the Beach*
   c CH Bwatch - August 2015 - pNA [51-500]
Charleyboy, Lisa - *Dreaming in Indian: Contemporary Native American Voices*
   y HB - v91 - i1 - Jan-Feb 2015 - p94(1) [51-500]
   c HB Guide - v26 - i1 - Spring 2015 - p205(1) [51-500]
   y Res Links - v20 - i3 - Feb 2015 - p38(1) [51-500]
Urban Tribes: Native Americans in the City
   BL - v112 - i7 - Dec 1 2015 - p39(1) [51-500]
   y KR - Sept 15 2015 - pNA [51-500]
   y SLJ - v61 - i12 - Dec 2015 - p142(2) [51-500]
Charlier, Marj - *Hacienda*
   KR - March 1 2015 - pNA [501+]
Charlton, David - *Opera in the Age of Rousseau: Music, Confrontation, Realism*
   Notes - v71 - i4 - June 2015 - p701(3) [501+]
Charlton, James - *Non-Dualism in Echart, Julian of Norwich and Traherne: A Theopoetic Reflection*
   JR - v95 - i3 - July 2015 - p404(3) [501+]
Charlton-Jones, Kate - *Dismembering the American Dream: The Life and Fiction of Richard Yates*
   TLS - i5832 - Jan 9 2015 - p22(1) [501+]
Charlton, William - *Metaphysics and Grammar*
   RM - v68 - i4 - June 2015 - p840(3) [501+]
Charmley, John - *Duff Cooper: The Authorized Biography*
   NYRB - v62 - i10 - June 4 2015 - p33(3) [501+]
Charney, Noah - *The Art of Forgery: The Minds, Motives and Methods of the Master Forgers*
   Bwatch - August 2015 - pNA [51-500]
   Spec - v328 - i9742 - May 16 2015 - p45(2) [501+]
   TimHES - i2209 - June 25 2015 - p48(1) [51-500]
Charnock, Anne - *Sleeping Embers of an Ordinary Mind*
   PW - v262 - i45 - Nov 9 2015 - p42(1) [51-500]
Charters, Erica - *Disease, War, and the Imperial State: The Welfare of the British Armed Forces during the Seven Years' War*
   J Mil H - v79 - i2 - April 2015 - p484-485 [501+]
Chartier, Brent - *Collateral Damage*
   y SLJ - v61 - i9 - Sept 2015 - p151(4) [501+]
Chartier, Roger - *The Author's Hand and the Printer's Mind*
   HER - v130 - i542 - Feb 2015 - p260(2) [501+]
Chartier, Tim - *Math Bytes: Google Bombs, Chocolate-Covered Pi, and Other Cool Bits in Computing*
   Math T - v109 - i3 - Oct 2015 - p239-239 [501+]
Charyn, Jerome - *Bitter Bronx*
   PW - v262 - i14 - April 6 2015 - p35(1) [51-500]
Bitter Bronx: Thirteen Stories
   KR - April 15 2015 - pNA [501+]
   BL - v111 - i19-20 - June 1 2015 - p38(1) [51-500]
   NYRB - v62 - i14 - Sept 24 2015 - p58(3) [501+]
   NYTBR - May 31 2015 - p44(L) [501+]
A Loaded Gun: Emily Dickinson for the 21st Century
   KR - Nov 15 2015 - pNA [501+]
   PW - v262 - i50 - Dec 7 2015 - p76(1) [51-500]
Chase, Bethany - *The One That Got Away*
   KR - March 1 2015 - pNA [501+]
Chase, Dale - *Hot Copy: Classic Gay Erotica from the Magazine Era*
   PW - v262 - i11 - March 16 2015 - p71(1) [51-500]
Chase, Eve - *Black Rabbit Hall*
   KR - Dec 1 2015 - pNA [501+]
   PW - v262 - i52 - Dec 21 2015 - p124(1) [51-500]
Chase, Kit - *Lulu's Party (Illus. by Chase, Kit)*
   c KR - June 1 2015 - pNA [501+]
   c SLJ - v61 - i6 - June 2015 - p73(1) [51-500]
Chase, L.C. - *A Fortunate Blizzard*
   BL - v112 - i4 - Oct 15 2015 - p26(2) [51-500]
Chase, Lil - *The Boys School Girls: Abby's Shadow*
   y Sch Lib - v63 - i2 - Summer 2015 - p115(1) [51-500]
Chase, Loretta - *Dukes Prefer Blondes*
   BL - v112 - i6 - Nov 15 2015 - p31(1) [51-500]
   KR - Oct 15 2015 - pNA [501+]
   PW - v262 - i41 - Oct 12 2015 - p52(2) [51-500]
Lord of Scoundrels (Read by Reading, Kate). Audiobook Review
   BL - v111 - i14 - March 15 2015 - p23(2) [51-500]
Chase, Malcolm - *1820: Disorder and Stability in the United Kingdom*
   HER - v130 - i544 - June 2015 - p764(2) [501+]
Chase, Martin - *Eddic, Skaldic, and Beyond: Poetic Variety in Medieval Iceland and Norway*
   JEGP - v114 - i3 - July 2015 - p420(4) [501+]
Chase, Robin - *Peers Inc: How People and Platforms Are Inventing the Collaborative Economy and Reinventing Capitalism*
   KR - April 15 2015 - pNA [501+]
   LJ - v140 - i8 - May 1 2015 - p81(2) [51-500]
Chase, Samantha - *I'll Be There*
   BL - v112 - i5 - Nov 1 2015 - p36(1) [51-500]
   PW - v262 - i44 - Nov 2 2015 - p70(1) [51-500]
Made for Us
   PW - v262 - i21 - May 25 2015 - p43(1) [51-500]
Meant for You
   BL - v111 - i15 - April 1 2015 - p32(1) [51-500]
   PW - v262 - i8 - Feb 23 2015 - p59(1) [51-500]
Return to You
   BL - v111 - i13 - March 1 2015 - p29(1) [51-500]
   PW - v262 - i1 - Jan 5 2015 - p57(1) [51-500]
Chase, Sarah Leah - *New England Open-House Cookbook: 300 Recipes Inspired by the Bounty of New England*
   LJ - v140 - i7 - April 15 2015 - p110(1) [51-500]
   PW - v262 - i16 - April 20 2015 - p70(1) [51-500]
Chase, Simon - *Zero Footprint*
   KR - Dec 1 2015 - pNA [501+]
Chast, Roz - *Around the Clock*
   c HB Guide - v26 - i2 - Fall 2015 - p29(1) [51-500]
Can't We Talk about Something More Pleasant?
   LJ - v140 - i12 - July 1 2015 - p118(1) [501+]
Chasteen, John Charles - *Getting High: Marijuana Through the Ages*
   PW - v262 - i51 - Dec 14 2015 - p75(1) [51-500]
Chateauvert, Melinda - *Sex Workers Unite: A History of the Movement from Stonewall to SlutWalk*
   JAH - v102 - i1 - June 2015 - p311-312 [501+]
Chatelain, Marcia - *South Side Girls: Growing Up in the Great Migration*
   Wom R Bks - v32 - i6 - Nov-Dec 2015 - p6(3) [501+]
Chatfield, Graeme R. - *Balthasar Hubmaier and the Clarity of Scripture: A Critical Response Issue*
   Six Ct J - v46 - i3 - Fall 2015 - p828-829 [501+]
Chatterjee, Deen K. - *The Ethics of Preventive War*
   Dialogue - v54 - i3 - Sept 2015 - p565-566 [501+]
Chatterjee, Paroma - *The Living Icon in Byzantium and Italy: The Vita Image, Eleventh to Thirteenth Centuries*
   Med R - Feb 2015 - pNA [501+]
Chatterjee, Piya - *The Imperial University: Academic Repression and Scholarly Dissent*
   Am St - v54 - i2 - Summer 2015 - p120-122 [501+]
   Col Lit - v42 - i2 - Spring 2015 - p337(11) [501+]
Chattman, Lauren - *Maangchi's Real Korean Cooking: Authentic Dishes for the Home Cook*
   BL - v111 - i19-20 - June 1 2015 - p20(1) [51-500]
Chattopadhyay, Bhaskar - *Fourteen Stories That Inspired Satyajit Ray*
   WLT - v89 - i1 - Jan-Feb 2015 - p78(2) [501+]
Chau, Donovan C. - *Exploiting Africa: The Influence of Maoist China in Algeria, Ghana, and Tanzania*
   HNet - April 2015 - pNA [501+]
Chaucer, Geoffrey - *Troilus and Criseyde in Modern Verse*
   TLS - i5855 - June 19 2015 - p22(2) [501+]
   Med R - August 2015 - pNA [501+]
A Variorum Edition of the Works of Geoffrey Chaucer, vol. 2: The Canterbury Tales: The Wife of Bath's Prologue and Tale, Parts 5A and 5B
   Specu - v90 - i1 - Jan 2015 - p224-226 [501+]
Chaud, Benjamin - *The Bear's Sea Escape (Illus. by Chaud, Benjamin)*
   c HB Guide - v26 - i1 - Spring 2015 - p26(1) [51-500]
The Bear's Surprise (Illus. by Chaud, Benjamin)
   c KR - July 15 2015 - pNA [501+]
   c SLJ - v61 - i10 - Oct 2015 - p72(2) [51-500]
The Bear's Surprise
   c PW - v262 - i39 - Sept 28 2015 - p90(2) [501+]
   c PW - v262 - i49 - Dec 2 2015 - p12(1) [51-500]
Farewell Floppy (Illus. by Chaud, Benjamin)
   c BooChiTr - June 27 2015 - p14(1) [501+]
   c HB Guide - v26 - i2 - Fall 2015 - p29(1) [51-500]
   c SLJ - v61 - i9 - Sept 2015 - p116(2) [51-500]
Chaudhry, Ayesha S. - *Islam Is a Foreign Country*
   JAAR - v83 - i2 - June 2015 - p575-577 [501+]
Chaudhry, T.S. - *The Queen of Sparta*
   SPBW - March 2015 - pNA [51-500]
Chaudhry, Tariq - *A Queen of Sparta*
   HT - v65 - i8 - August 2015 - p56(2) [501+]
Chaudhuri, Amit - *Odysseus Abroad (Read by Wyndham, Alex). Audiobook Review*
   BL - v112 - i2 - Sept 15 2015 - p78(1) [51-500]
   LJ - v140 - i11 - June 15 2015 - p48(1) [51-500]

Odysseus Abroad
    BL - v111 - i15 - April 1 2015 - p26(1) [51-500]
    CSM - April 14 2015 - pNA [501+]
    HR - v68 - i2 - Summer 2015 - p343-351 [501+]
    KR - Feb 1 2015 - pNA [501+]
    LJ - v140 - i6 - April 1 2015 - p72(1) [51-500]
    Lon R Bks - v37 - i13 - July 2 2015 - p33(2) [501+]
    NYT - April 30 2015 - pC6(L) [501+]
    NYTBR - May 17 2015 - p21(L) [501+]
    PW - v262 - i6 - Feb 9 2015 - p43(1) [51-500]

Chaudhuri, Pramit - *The War with God: Theomachy in Roman Imperial Poetry*
    Class R - v65 - i2 - Oct 2015 - p464-466 [501+]

Chaudhuri, Rosinka - *The Literary Thing: History, Poetry and the Making of Modern Cultural Sphere*
    TLS - i5836 - Feb 6 2015 - p27(1) [501+]

Chaudhuri, Soma - *Witches, Tea Plantations, and Lives of Migrant Laborers in India: Tempest in a Teapot*
    AJS - v121 - i2 - Sept 2015 - p656(2) [501+]
    CS - v44 - i6 - Nov 2015 - p789-791 [501+]

Chaudhuri, Una - *Animal Acts: Performing Species Today*
    Theat J - v67 - i1 - March 2015 - p162-163 [501+]
    Theat J - v67 - i1 - March 2015 - p162-163 [501+]
Research Theatre, Climate Change, and the Ecocide Project: A Casebook
    Theat J - v67 - i3 - Oct 2015 - p567-568 [501+]

Chauran, Alexandra - *365 Ways to Develop Your Psychic Ability: Simple Tools to Increase Your Intuition and Clairvoyance*
    Bwatch - May 2015 - pNA [501+]

Chavals, Mark - *Women in the Ancient Near East: A Sourcebook*
    JNES - v74 - i2 - Oct 2015 - p378(3) [501+]

Chavez-Garcia, Miroslava - *States of Delinquency: Race and Science in the Making of California's Juvenile Justice System*
    JAH - v102 - i1 - June 2015 - p284-285 [501+]

Chavez, Karma R. - *Queer Migration Politics: Activist Rhetoric and Coalitional Possibilities*
    NWSA Jnl - v27 - i1 - Spring 2015 - p192-196 [501+]

Chavez, Maria - *Living the Dream: New Immigration Policies and the Lives of Undocumented Latino Youth*
    CS - v44 - i5 - Sept 2015 - p742(1) [501+]
    J Hi E - v86 - i6 - Nov-Dec 2015 - p955(5) [501+]

Chavez, Nicolasa - *The Spirit of Flamenco: From Spain to New Mexico*
    RVBW - Nov 2015 - pNA [51-500]

Chavtik, Ivan - *Jan Patocka and the Heritage of Phenomenology*
    Soc - v52 - i1 - Feb 2015 - p87(6) [501+]

Chawla, Devika - *Home, Uprooted: Oral Histories of India's Partition*
    HNet - April 2015 - pNA [501+]

Chayes, Sarah - *Thieves of State: Why Corruption Threatens Global Security*
    For Aff - v94 - i3 - May-June 2015 - pNA [501+]
    NYTBR - Feb 22 2015 - p20(L) [501+]
    BL - v111 - i9-10 - Jan 1 2015 - p24(2) [51-500]

Chayut, Noam - *The Girl Who Stole My Holocaust*
    Tikkun - v30 - i1 - March 2015 - pNA [51-500]

Chazin, Suzanne - *A Blossom of Bright Light*
    KR - August 15 2015 - pNA [51-500]
    PW - v262 - i37 - Sept 14 2015 - p44(1) [51-500]

Cheallaigh, Gillian Ni - *'Quand la folie parle': The Dialectic Effect of Madness in French Literature since the Nineteenth Century*
    FS - v69 - i1 - Jan 2015 - p130-131 [501+]

Cheaney, J.B. - *I Don't Know How the Story Ends*
    c KR - Sept 1 2015 - pNA [51-500]
    c PW - v262 - i31 - August 3 2015 - p62(1) [51-500]
    c SLJ - v61 - i8 - August 2015 - p83(1) [51-500]
Somebody on This Bus Is Going to Be Famous
    y HB Guide - v26 - i1 - Spring 2015 - p73(1) [51-500]

Cheathem, Mark R. - *Andrew Jackson, Southerner*
    JSH - v81 - i1 - Feb 2015 - p183(2) [501+]

Chebankova, Elena - *Civil Society in Putin's Russia*
    E-A St - v67 - i4 - June 2015 - p673(3) [501+]

Checkoway, Julie - *The Three-Year Swim Club: The Untold Story of Maui's Sugar Ditch Kids and Their Quest for Olympic Glory*
    y BL - v112 - i4 - Oct 15 2015 - p14(1) [51-500]
    KR - Sept 15 2015 - pNA [51-500]
    LJ - v140 - i16 - Oct 1 2015 - p80(1) [51-500]

Chee, Alexander - *Queen of the Night*
    KR - Oct 1 2015 - pNA [51-500]

Cheeseman, Nic - *Routledge Handbook of African Politics*
    Africa T - v61 - i4 - Summer 2015 - p106(4) [501+]

Cheesman, Nick - *Debating Democratization in Myanmar*
    Pac A - v88 - i4 - Dec 2015 - p964 [501+]

Cheetham, David - *Understanding Interreligious Relations*
    Theol St - v76 - i1 - March 2015 - p219(2) [501+]

Cheetham, Stephen - *Off to the Park!*
    c Sch Lib - v63 - i1 - Spring 2015 - p25(1) [51-500]

Cheever, John - *The Collected Stories of John Cheever*
    BL - v111 - i9-10 - Jan 1 2015 - p120(1) [51-500]

Cheever, Susan - *Drinking in America: Our Secret History*
    BL - v112 - i3 - Oct 1 2015 - p5(1) [51-500]
    KR - July 15 2015 - pNA [501+]
    LJ - v140 - i16 - Oct 1 2015 - p101(2) [51-500]
    PW - v262 - i32 - August 10 2015 - p53(2) [51-500]

Cheevers, William - *In Every Way That Matters*
    KR - April 15 2015 - pNA [501+]

Chef Gorji - *Zing! By Gorji*
    SPBW - March 2015 - pNA [51-500]

Chehak, Susan Taylor - *It's Not about the Dog*
    KR - Feb 15 2015 - pNA [51-500]

Cheit, Ross E. - *The Witch-Hunt Narrative: Politics, Psychology, and the Sexual Abuse of Children*
    HLR - v128 - i3 - Jan 2015 - p1063(1) [51-500]

Chekhov, Anton - *The Prank: The Best of Young Chekhov*
    NS - v144 - i5281 - Sept 25 2015 - p76(2) [501+]

Chema, Boona - *Boombin and Lama: A Story of Friendship, Investigation and Adventure! (Illus. by Guthrie, Damon)*
    c CH Bwatch - Feb 2015 - pNA [51-500]

Chemerinsky, Erwin - *The Case Against the Supreme Court*
    HLR - v128 - i4 - Feb 2015 - p1328(2) [1-50]

Chemi, Tatiana - *The Art of Arts Integration: Theoretical Perspectives and Practical Guidelines*
    RVBW - March 2015 - pNA [51-500]

Chen, David - *The ALTA Project*
    SPBW - August 2015 - pNA [51-500]

Chen, G.X. - *The Fatal Sin of Love*
    SPBW - July 2015 - pNA [51-500]

Chen, Justina - *A Blind Spot for Boys*
    y HB Guide - v26 - i2 - Fall 2015 - p114(1) [51-500]

Chen, Kai - *Comparative Study of Child Soldiering on Myanmar-China Border: Evolutions, Challenges and Countermeasures*
    HNet - July 2015 - pNA [501+]

Chen, Taylor - *Bone Deep Broth: Healing Recipes with Bone Broth*
    PW - v262 - i52 - Dec 21 2015 - p148(1) [51-500]

Chen, Yong - *Chop Suey, USA: The Story of Chinese Food in America*
    HNet - Feb 2015 - pNA [501+]

Cheney-Coker, Syl - *Sacred River*
    WLT - v89 - i2 - March-April 2015 - p57(1) [51-500]

Cheney, Dick - *Exceptional: Why the World Needs a Powerful America*
    NYT - Sept 10 2015 - pC1(L) [501+]

Cheney, J. Kathleen - *The Shores of Spain*
    PW - v262 - i22 - June 1 2015 - p45(1) [51-500]

Cheney, Lynne - *James Madison: A Life Reconsidered*
    JAH - v102 - i1 - June 2015 - p238-239 [501+]

Cheng, Andrea - *The Year of the Three Sisters (Illus. by Barton, Patrice)*
    c CH Bwatch - July 2015 - pNA [51-500]
    c HB Guide - v26 - i2 - Fall 2015 - p77(2) [51-500]
    c KR - Feb 15 2015 - pNA [51-500]

Cheng, Cindy I-Fen - *Citizens of Asian America: Democracy and Race during the Cold War*
    ERS - v38 - i3 - March 2015 - p462(3) [501+]
    PHR - v84 - i1 - Feb 2015 - p112(3) [501+]

Cheng, Eugenia - *How to Bake Pi: An Edible Exploration of the Mathematics of Mathematics (Read by Gilbert, Tavia). Audiobook Review*
    BL - v112 - i4 - Oct 15 2015 - p61(2) [51-500]
    BL - v112 - i7 - Dec 1 2015 - p71(1) [51-500]
How to Bake Pi: An Edible Exploration of the Mathematics of Mathematics
    AS - v84 - i2 - Spring 2015 - p119(3) [501+]
    BL - v111 - i18 - May 15 2015 - p8(1) [51-500]
    BL - v112 - i7 - Dec 1 2015 - p13(1) [51-500]
    KR - March 15 2015 - pNA [51-500]
    NYTBR - June 14 2015 - p14(L) [501+]
    PW - v262 - i9 - March 2 2015 - p75(1) [51-500]

Cheng, Sealing - *On the Move for Love: Migrant Entertainers and the U.S. Military in South Korea*
    JWH - v27 - i3 - Fall 2015 - p187(7) [501+]

Cheng, Wendy - *The Changs Next Door to the Diazes: Remapping Race in Suburban California*
    CS - v44 - i5 - Sept 2015 - p645-647 [501+]
    PHR - v84 - i3 - August 2015 - p381(2) [501+]

Cheng, William - *Sound Play: Video Games and the Musical Imagination*
    Notes - v72 - i1 - Sept 2015 - p162(4) [501+]

Chercover, Sean - *The Devil's Game*
    BL - v111 - i17 - May 1 2015 - p30(2) [51-500]
    PW - v262 - i17 - April 27 2015 - p52(1) [51-500]

Chernesky, Felicia Sanzari - *From Apple Trees to Cider, Please! (Illus. by Patton, Julia)*
    c KR - July 15 2015 - pNA [51-500]
    c PW - v262 - i31 - August 3 2015 - p56(1) [51-500]
    c SLJ - v61 - i9 - Sept 2015 - p117(1) [51-500]
Sugar White Snow and Evergreens: A Winter Wonderland of Color (Illus. by Swan, Susan)
    c HB Guide - v26 - i1 - Spring 2015 - p7(1) [51-500]
Sun Above and Blooms Below: A Springtime of Opposites (Illus. by Swan, Susan)
    c KR - Jan 15 2015 - pNA [51-500]
    c PW - v262 - i5 - Feb 2 2015 - p58(1) [51-500]
Sun Above and Blooms Below: A Springtime of Opposties (Illus. by Swan, Susan)
    c HB Guide - v26 - i2 - Fall 2015 - p8(1) [51-500]

Chernila, Alana - *The Homemade Kitchen: Recipes for Cooking with Pleasure*
    LJ - v140 - i13 - August 1 2015 - p119(1) [51-500]
    PW - v262 - i31 - August 3 2015 - p52(2) [51-500]

Chernow, Ron - *Alexander Hamilton*
    Forbes - v196 - i6 - Nov 2 2015 - pNA [501+]

Chernyshova, Natalya - *Soviet Consumer Culture in the Brezhnev Era*
    Slav R - v74 - i1 - Spring 2015 - p198-199 [501+]

Cherry, Alison - *The Classy Crooks Club*
    y KR - Jan 1 2016 - pNA [51-500]
For Real
    y CCB-B - v68 - i6 - Feb 2015 - p303(2) [51-500]
    c HB Guide - v26 - i1 - Spring 2015 - p103(1) [51-500]

Cherry, Dave - *Sweep Rowing*
    KR - Sept 15 2015 - pNA [51-500]

Cherry, Georgia - *City Atlas*
    c Sch Lib - v63 - i4 - Winter 2015 - p236(1) [51-500]

Cherry, Stephen M. - *Faith, Family, and Filipino American Community Life*
    AJS - v120 - i4 - Jan 2015 - p1250(3) [501+]
    CS - v44 - i5 - Sept 2015 - p647-649 [501+]

Chesire, Scott - *High as the Horses' Bridles*
    NYTBR - Nov 1 2015 - p28(L) [501+]

Chesler, Phyllis - *Living History: On the Front Lines for Israel and the Jews 2003-2015*
    RVBW - June 2015 - pNA [51-500]
The New Anti-Semitism
    RVBW - Jan 2015 - pNA [51-500]

Chesman, Andrea - *The Backyard Homestead Book of Kitchen Know-How*
    Bwatch - Nov 2015 - pNA [51-500]

Chesshyre, Tom - *Gatecrashing Paradise: Misadventures in the Real Maldives*
    TLS - i5845 - April 10 2015 - p30(1) [51-500]

Chester, Eric Thomas - *The Wobblies in Their Heyday: The Rise and Destruction of the Industrial Workers of the World During the World War I Era*
    JAH - v102 - i2 - Sept 2015 - p584-585 [501+]

Chesterton, Bridget Maria - *The Grandchildren of Solano Lopez: Frontier and Nation in Paraguay*
    HAHR - v95 - i1 - Feb 2015 - p165-167 [501+]

Chet, Guy - *The Ocean Is a Wilderness: Atlantic Piracy and the Limits of State Authority, 1688-1856*
    AHR - v120 - i3 - June 2015 - p969(1) [501+]
    JAH - v102 - i1 - June 2015 - p224-224 [501+]
    JEH - v75 - i3 - Sept 2015 - p933-936 [501+]

Cheung, Roderick - *Kings of Fortune*
    KR - August 1 2015 - pNA [51-500]

Chevalier, Tracy - *At the Edge of the Orchard*
    KR - Dec 15 2015 - pNA [51-500]

Cheverton, Mark - *Battle for the Nether*
    c Sch Lib - v63 - i1 - Spring 2015 - p34(1) [51-500]
Invasion of the Overworld
    c CH Bwatch - July 2015 - pNA [51-500]
    c Sch Lib - v63 - i1 - Spring 2015 - p34(1) [51-500]

Chew, J.W. - *The Green Eyed Girl*
    KR - April 15 2015 - pNA [51-500]

Chew, Ruth - *The Witch at the Window*
    c HB Guide - v26 - i1 - Spring 2015 - p58(1) [51-500]
The Would-Be Witch
    c HB Guide - v26 - i1 - Spring 2015 - p58(1) [51-500]

Cheyette, Bryan - *Diasporas of the Mind: Jewish and Postcolonial Writing and the Nightmare of History*
    Col Lit - v42 - i3 - Summer 2015 - p528(4) [501+]

Chezar, Ariella - *The Flower Workshop: Lessons in Arranging Blooms, Branches, Fruit, and Foraged Materials*
    PW - v262 - i52 - Dec 21 2015 - p149(1) [51-500]

Chhabra, Ashvin B. - *The Aspirational Investor: Taming the Markets to Achieve Your Life's Goals*
    LJ - v140 - i9 - May 15 2015 - p89(1) [51-500]
    PW - v262 - i14 - April 6 2015 - p48(1) [51-500]

Chiabo, Myriam - *Egidio da Viterbo: Cardinale Agostiniano tra Roma e l'Europa del Rinascimento - Atti del Convegno, Viterbo, 22-23 setiembre 2012--Roma, 26-28 setiembre 2012*
    CHR - v101 - i1 - Wntr 2015 - p165(2) [501+]

Chiang, Howard - *Transgender China*
    Signs - v40 - i3 - Spring 2015 - p773(7) [501+]

Chiang, Ted - *The Lifecyle of Software Objects*
    J Chem Ed - v92 - i7 - July 2015 - p1143-1145 [501+]

Chiaramonte, Jose Carlos - *Usos politicos de la historia: Lenguaje de clases y revisionismo historico*
    HAHR - v95 - i3 - August 2015 - p507-509 [501+]

Chiarella, Jessica - *And Again*
    BL - v112 - i4 - Oct 15 2015 - p30(1) [51-500]
    KR - Oct 15 2015 - pNA [51-500]
    PW - v262 - i42 - Oct 19 2015 - p50(2) [51-500]

Chiarello, Michael - *Wild Gourmet*
    Bwatch - April 2015 - pNA [51-500]

Chiaverini, Jennifer - *Christmas Bells*
    BL - v112 - i3 - Oct 1 2015 - p22(1) [51-500]
    KR - August 15 2015 - pNA [501+]
    Mrs. Grant and Madame Jule
    KR - Jan 1 2015 - pNA [501+]
    LJ - v140 - i3 - Feb 15 2015 - p85(1) [51-500]

Chibbaro, Julie - *Into the Dangerous World (Illus. by Sovak, Jean-Marc Superville)*
    y BL - v111 - i21 - July 1 2015 - p55(2) [51-500]
    y HB - v91 - i5 - Sept-Oct 2015 - p97(1) [51-500]
    y KR - May 15 2015 - pNA [51-500]
    y PW - v262 - i21 - May 25 2015 - p61(1) [51-500]
    y SLJ - v61 - i7 - July 2015 - p91(2) [51-500]
    y VOYA - v38 - i3 - August 2015 - p56(1) [51-500]

Chicago Tribune Staff - *Summer Cooking: Kitchen-Tested Recipes for Picnics, Patios, Grilling and More*
    Bwatch - Nov 2015 - pNA [51-500]

Chichester Clark, Emma - *Bears Don't Read! (Illus. by Chichester Clark, Emma)*
    c BL - v111 - i14 - March 15 2015 - p77(1) [51-500]
    c CH Bwatch - Nov 2015 - pNA [501+]
    c HB Guide - v26 - i2 - Fall 2015 - p29(1) [51-500]
    c KR - Jan 1 2015 - pNA [51-500]
    SLJ - v61 - i4 - April 2015 - p125(1) [51-500]
    Love Is My Favorite Thing (Illus. by Chichester Clark, Emma)
    c KR - Oct 1 2015 - pNA [51-500]
    c PW - v262 - i41 - Oct 12 2015 - p66(2) [51-500]
    c SLJ - v61 - i9 - Sept 2015 - p117(2) [51-500]

Chickering, V.C. - *Nookietown*
    KR - Dec 15 2015 - pNA [51-500]

Chidester, David - *Empire of Religion: Imperialism and Comparative Religion*
    JR - v95 - i4 - Oct 2015 - p543(3) [501+]
    Wild Religion: Tracking the Sacred in South Africa
    JR - v95 - i2 - April 2015 - p282(3) [501+]

Chideya, Farai - *The Episodic Career: How to Thrive at Work in the Age of Disruption*
    PW - v262 - i46 - Nov 16 2015 - p70(1) [51-500]

Chiew, Elaine - *Cooked Up: Food Fiction from around the World*
    TLS - i5851 - May 22 2015 - p26(1) [501+]

Chiew, Suzanne - *When You Need a Friend (Illus. by Pedler, Caroline)*
    SLJ - v61 - i2 - Feb 2015 - p62(1) [51-500]

Chikwanine, Michel - *Child Soldier: When Boys and Girls Are Used in War (Illus. by Davila, Claudia)*
    c BL - v111 - i22 - August 1 2015 - p47(1) [51-500]
    c SLJ - v61 - i7 - July 2015 - p111(1) [51-500]

Chiladze, Tamaz - *The Brueghel Moon*
    TLS - i5856 - June 26 2015 - p20(2) [51-500]

Child, Emily - *Jeff and George and the Totem Pole (Illus. by Anastasopoulos, Julia)*
    c Bkbird - v53 - i3 - Summer 2015 - p92(1) [501+]

The Child Garden
    NYTBR - Oct 4 2015 - p29(L) [501+]

Child, Laura - *Parchment and Old Lace*
    Bwatch - Nov 2015 - pNA [51-500]

Child, Lauren - *Absolutely One Thing*
    KR - Jan 1 2016 - pNA [51-500]

Catch Your Death
    y VOYA - v38 - i1 - April 2015 - p55(1) [51-500]
The New Small Person (Illus. by Child, Lauren)
    c CCB-B - v68 - i8 - April 2015 - p392(1) [51-500]
    c CH Bwatch - March 2015 - pNA [51-500]
    c HB - v91 - i1 - Jan-Feb 2015 - p61(2) [51-500]
    c HB Guide - v26 - i2 - Fall 2015 - p8(1) [51-500]
    c NYTBR - March 15 2015 - p18(L) [501+]
    c NYTBR - March 15 2015 - p18(L) [501+]
    c Sch Lib - v63 - i1 - Spring 2015 - p25(1) [51-500]
Ruby Redfort: Catch Your Death
    c HB Guide - v26 - i2 - Fall 2015 - p78(1) [51-500]
Ruby Redfort: Look into My Eyes (Read by Stirling, Rachel). Audiobook Review
    c SLJ - v61 - i8 - August 2015 - p49(1) [51-500]
Take Your Last Breath (Read by Stirling, Rachael). Audiobook Review
    c SLJ - v61 - i9 - Sept 2015 - p58(1) [51-500]

Child, Lee - *Killer Year: Stories to Die For (Read by Devries, David). Audiobook Review*
    LJ - v140 - i15 - Sept 15 2015 - p41(1) [51-500]
Make Me
    y BL - v111 - i22 - August 1 2015 - p35(1) [51-500]
    Esq - v164 - i5 - Dec 2015 - p52(1) [501+]
    KR - August 2015 - pNA [501+]
    LJ - v140 - i6 - April 1 2015 - p58(4) [501+]
    NYT - Sept 1 2015 - pC4(L) [501+]
    NYTBR - Sept 20 2015 - p29(L) [501+]
    PW - v262 - i30 - July 27 2015 - p42(1) [51-500]
    RVBW - Oct 2015 - pNA [501+]
Personal
    RVBW - April 2015 - pNA [501+]
    RVBW - May 2015 - pNA [501+]

Child, Lincoln - *Crimson Shore*
    PW - v262 - i36 - Sept 7 2015 - p45(2) [51-500]
The Forgotten Room (Read by McClain, Johnathan). Audiobook Review
    BL - v112 - i1 - Sept 1 2015 - p139(1) [51-500]
The Forgotten Room
    BL - v111 - i17 - May 1 2015 - p38(1) [51-500]
    PW - v262 - i12 - March 23 2015 - p46(1) [51-500]

Child, Lydia Maria - *Over the River and through the Wood: A Thanksgiving Poem (Illus. by Manson, Christopher)*
    c HB Guide - v26 - i1 - Spring 2015 - p180(1) [51-500]

Childers, Carr Leisl - *Imagining Hoover Dam: The Making of a Cultural Icon*
    Pub Hist - v37 - i2 - May 2015 - p143(2) [501+]

Childers, Jay P. - *The Evolving Citizen: American Youth and the Changing Norms of Democratic Engagement*
    CS - v44 - i1 - Jan 2015 - p40-42 [501+]

Children of Wild Dance Farm - *Saving Annie's Mountain*
    c CH Bwatch - Nov 2015 - pNA [51-500]

Childress, Ron - *And West Is West*
    BL - v112 - i3 - Oct 1 2015 - p22(1) [51-500]
    KR - August 1 2015 - pNA [51-500]
    LJ - v140 - i13 - August 1 2015 - p80(2) [51-500]
    y NYTBR - Oct 11 2015 - p30(L) [501+]
    PW - v262 - i32 - August 10 2015 - p32(1) [51-500]

Childs, Donald J. - *The Birth of New Criticism: Conflict and Conciliation in the Early Works of William Empson, I.A. Richards, Robert Graves and Laura Riding*
    TLS - i5841 - March 13 2015 - p13(1) [501+]

Childs, Jessie - *God's Traitors: Terror and Faith in Elizabethan England*
    AM - v212 - i3 - Feb 2 2015 - p40(2) [501+]

Childs, John - *General Percy Kirke and the Later Stuart Army*
    HER - v130 - i545 - August 2015 - p1001(3) [501+]

Childs, Laura - *Ming Tea Murder*
    BL - v111 - i17 - May 1 2015 - p31(1) [51-500]
    Bwatch - July 2015 - pNA [51-500]
    PW - v262 - i11 - March 16 2015 - p66(1) [51-500]
Parchment and Old Lace
    PW - v262 - i35 - August 31 2015 - p63(2) [51-500]

Child's Play - *Choo Choo*
    c KR - Jan 1 2016 - pNA [51-500]

Childs, Tera Lynn - *Powerless*
    y HB Guide - v26 - i2 - Fall 2015 - p114(1) [51-500]
    KR - April 1 2015 - pNA [51-500]

Childs, Wendy R. - *Trade and Shipping in the Medieval West: Portugal, Castile and England*
    Specu - v90 - i3 - July 2015 - p786-787 [501+]

Chilton, Andrew S. - *The Goblin's Puzzle: Being the Adventures of a Boy with No Name and Two Girls Called Alice (Illus. by Eckwall, Jensine)*
    c KR - Oct 15 2015 - pNA [51-500]
    c PW - v262 - i44 - Nov 2 2015 - p85(1) [51-500]
    c SLJ - v61 - i11 - Nov 2015 - p94(2) [51-500]

Chilton, Bruce - *Visions of the Apocalypse: Receptions of John's Revelation in Western Imagination*
    Intpr - v69 - i4 - Oct 2015 - p495(1) [501+]

Chima, Cinda - *Williams the Sorcerer Heir*
    y HB Guide - v26 - i2 - Fall 2015 - p114(1) [51-500]

Chin, Angelina - *Bound to Emancipate: Working Women and Urban Citizenship in Early Twentieth-Century China and Hong Kong*
    JAS - v74 - i2 - May 2015 - p460-462 [501+]

Chin, Frank - *The Confessions of a Number One Son: The Great Chinese American Novel*
    WLT - v89 - i5 - Sept-Oct 2015 - p58(1) [501+]

Chin, Oliver - *The Year of the Sheep: Tales from the Chinese Zodiac (Illus. by Chau, Alina)*
    c HB Guide - v26 - i2 - Fall 2015 - p29(1) [51-500]

Chin, Peter - *Blindsided by God: Disappointment, Suffering, and the Untamable Goodness of God*
    Bwatch - May 2015 - pNA [51-500]

Ching, Erik - *Authoritarian El Salvador: Politics and the Origins of the Military Regimes, 1880-1940*
    AHR - v120 - i1 - Feb 2015 - p301-302 [501+]
    Ams - v72 - i3 - July 2015 - p508(3) [501+]

Chinitz, David E. - *Which Sin to Bear? Authenticity and Compromise in Langston Hughes*
    J Am St - v49 - i1 - Feb 2015 - p173-179 [501+]

Chinoy, Helen Krich - *The Group Theater: Passion, Politics, and Performance in the Depression Era*
    Theat J - v67 - i1 - March 2015 - p151-152 [501+]

Chiofalo, Rosanna - *Stella Mia*
    BL - v111 - i9-10 - Jan 1 2015 - p42(1) [51-500]

Chippendale, Brian - *Puke Force*
    PW - v262 - i44 - Nov 2 2015 - p72(1) [51-500]

Chirbes, Rafael - *On the Edge*
    KR - Nov 1 2015 - pNA [501+]
    LJ - v140 - i19 - Nov 15 2015 - p75(1) [51-500]
    PW - v262 - i46 - Nov 16 2015 - p49(1) [51-500]

Chirimuuta, Mazviita - *Outside Color: Perceptual Science and the Puzzle of Color in Philosophy*
    New R - v246 - i5 - June 2015 - p80(2) [501+]

Chirot, Daniel - *Confronting Memories of World War II: European and Asian Legacies*
    Pac A - v88 - i2 - June 2015 - p270 [501+]
    JIH - v46 - i2 - Autumn 2015 - p271-272 [501+]

Chisholm, P.F. - *A Chorus of Innocents*
    KR - June 1 2015 - pNA [51-500]
    PW - v262 - i25 - June 22 2015 - p122(1) [51-500]

Chisholm, Penny - *Buried Sunlight: How Fossil Fuels Have Changed the Earth (Illus. by Bang, Molly)*
    c HB Guide - v26 - i1 - Spring 2015 - p150(1) [51-500]
    c Magpies - v30 - i1 - March 2015 - p24(1) [501+]
My Light (Illus. by Bang, Molly)
    c Magpies - v30 - i1 - March 2015 - p24(1) [501+]
Ocean Sunlight: How Tiny Plants Feed the Seas (Illus. by Bang, Molly)
    c Magpies - v30 - i1 - March 2015 - p24(1) [501+]

Chittister, Joan - *Between the Dark and the Daylight: Embracing the Contradictions of Life*
    PW - v262 - i6 - Feb 9 2015 - p62(1) [51-500]

Chitty, Antonia - *Sleep and Your Special Needs Child*
    LJ - v140 - i3 - Feb 15 2015 - p81(3) [51-500]

Chiu, Kwong Chiu - *In the Forbidden City*
    c Magpies - v30 - i1 - March 2015 - p24(1) [501+]

Chiu, Melissa - *Shirin Neshat: Facing History*
    BL - v112 - i1 - Sept 1 2015 - p26(1) [51-500]

Chmakova, Svetlana - *Awkward (Illus. by Chmakova, Svetlana)*
    c SLJ - v61 - i7 - July 2015 - p99(2) [51-500]

Cho, Joy - *Oh Joy! 60 Ways to Create and Give Joy*
    LJ - v140 - i10 - June 1 2015 - p102(1) [51-500]

Cho, Mun Young - *The Specter of "The People": Urban Poverty in Northeast China*
    Pac A - v88 - i1 - March 2015 - p183 [501+]

Cho, Yeol Je - *Stability of Functional Equations in Random Normed Spaces*
    SIAM Rev - v57 - i1 - March 2015 - p157-159 [501+]

Cho, Zen - *Sorcerer to the Crown*
    KR - August 1 2015 - pNA [51-500]
    PW - v262 - i33 - August 17 2015 - p56(1) [51-500]

Chochinov, Allan - *Designing Here/Now: A Global Selection of Objects, Concepts and Spaces for the Future*
    Bwatch - Feb 2015 - pNA [51-500]

Chodron, Pema - *Fail, Fail Again, Fail Better: Wise Advice for Leaning into the Unknown*
PW - v262 - i27 - July 6 2015 - p65(1) [51-500]

Choe, In-hun - *The Square*
TLS - i5840 - March 6 2015 - p31(1) [501+]

Choi, Eric - *Carbide Tipped Pens*
Analog - v135 - i5 - May 2015 - p106(1) [501+]

Choi, Jeonglm - *Who's Coming Tonight? (Illus. by Gang, Minjeong)*
c HB Guide - v26 - i1 - Spring 2015 - p26(1) [51-500]

Choi, Suhi - *Embattled Memories: Contested Meanings in Korean War Memorials*
HNet - June 2015 - pNA [501+]
Pub Hist - v37 - i2 - May 2015 - p152(3) [501+]

Choldenko, Gennifer - *Chasing Secrets (Read by Vacker, Karissa). Audiobook Review*
c BL - v112 - i7 - Dec 1 2015 - p70(1) [51-500]
c SLJ - v61 - i12 - Dec 2015 - p75(2) [51-500]
Chasing Secrets
c BL - v111 - i19-20 - June 1 2015 - p103(2) [51-500]
c CCB-B - v69 - i2 - Oct 2015 - p81(1) [51-500]
c CH Bwatch - Sept 2015 - pNA [51-500]
c HB - v91 - i5 - Sept-Oct 2015 - p97(2) [51-500]
c KR - May 1 2015 - pNA [51-500]
c PW - v262 - i20 - May 18 2015 - p86(1) [51-500]
c SLJ - v61 - i6 - June 2015 - p99(1) [51-500]
y VOYA - v38 - i3 - August 2015 - p56(1) [51-500]
The Monkey's Secret
c Magpies - v30 - i5 - Nov 2015 - p33(1) [501+]
Sch Lib - v63 - i4 - Winter 2015 - p226(1) [51-500]
Putting the Monkeys to Bed (Illus. by Davis, Jack E.)
c CCB-B - v69 - i1 - Sept 2015 - p17(1) [51-500]
c HB - v91 - i4 - July-August 2015 - p111(1) [51-500]
c KR - March 1 2015 - pNA [51-500]
c PW - v262 - i17 - April 27 2015 - p73(1) [51-500]
c SLJ - v61 - i6 - June 2015 - p78(1) [51-500]

Chomsky, Noah - *Because We Say So*
KR - June 1 2015 - pNA [501+]

Chomsky, Noam - *The Science of Language: Interviews with James McGilvray*
MLR - v110 - i1 - Jan 2015 - p222-224 [501+]
What Kind of Creatures are We?
KR - Sept 15 2015 - pNA [501+]

Chong, Denise - *Lives of the Family: Stories of Fate and Circumstances*
Beav - v95 - i3 - June-July 2015 - p58(1) [501+]

Choo, Andrew L-T - *The Privilege Against Self-Incrimination*
Law&PolBR - v25 - i3 - March 2015 - p40(3) [501+]

Chopel, Gendun - *Grains of Gold: Tales of a Cosmopolitan Traveler*
JAS - v74 - i2 - May 2015 - p489-490 [501+]

Chopra, Deepak - *Super Genes: Unlock the Astonishing Power of Your DNA for Optimum Health and Well-Being*
BL - v112 - i4 - Oct 15 2015 - p10(2) [51-500]

Chopra, Mallika - *Living with Intent: My Somewhat Messy Journey to Purpose, Peace, and Joy*
PW - v262 - i7 - Feb 16 2015 - p171(1) [51-500]
KR - Feb 1 2015 - pNA [51-500]

Chopra, Shweta - *The Diwali Gift (Illus. by Koan, Anna)*
c PW - v262 - i46 - Nov 16 2015 - p78(1) [51-500]

Choquet-Bruhat, Yvonne - *Introduction to General Relativity, Black Holes, and Cosmology*
Phys Today - v68 - i11 - Nov 2015 - p51-53 [501+]

Chorzempa, Rosemary A. - *Polish Roots, 2d ed.*
BL - v111 - i12 - Feb 15 2015 - p21(1) [51-500]

Chou, Rosalind S. - *Asian American Sexual Politics: The Construction of Race, Gender and Sexuality*
CS - v44 - i1 - Jan 2015 - p42-44 [501+]

Chourchoulis, Dionysios - *The Southern Flank of NATO, 1951-1959: Military Strategy or Political Stabilization*
J Mil H - v79 - i3 - July 2015 - p880-881 [501+]

Chow, Alexander - *Theosis, Sino-Christian Theology, and the Second Chinese Enlightenment: Heaven and Humanity in Unity*
IBMR - v39 - i2 - April 2015 - p102(2) [501+]

Chow, Jennifer J. - *The 228 Legacy*
PW - v262 - i29 - July 20 2015 - p165(1) [51-500]

Chowdhury, G.G. - *Sustainability of Scholarly Information*
LR - v64 - i1-2 - Jan-Feb 2015 - p182-183 [501+]

Choy, Catherine Ceniza - *Global Families: A History of Asian International Adoption in America*
CS - v44 - i5 - Sept 2015 - p649-650 [501+]

Choyce, Lesley - *Into the Wasteland*
y Res Links - v20 - i3 - Feb 2015 - p26(1) [51-500]
y VOYA - v38 - i3 - August 2015 - p56(1) [51-500]
Off the Grid
y Res Links - v20 - i4 - April 2015 - p26(1) [51-500]
y SLJ - v61 - i9 - Sept 2015 - p151(4) [501+]

Chrastil, Rachel - *The Siege of Strasbourg*
AHR - v120 - i2 - April 2015 - p726-727 [501+]

Chris, Jerry - *Brain Launch & Other Perfectly Awesome Stories*
c CH Bwatch - Nov 2015 - pNA [51-500]

Chriscoe, Sharon - *The Sparrow and the Trees (Illus. by Detwiler, Susan)*
c KR - July 15 2015 - pNA [51-500]

Chrisman-Campbell, Kimberly - *Fashion Victims: Dress at the Court of Louis XVI and Marie-Antoinette*
LJ - v140 - i7 - April 15 2015 - p83(1) [51-500]
TLS - i5864-5865 - August 21 2015 - p12(2) [501+]

Chrisp, Peter - *Explore 360: Pompeii (Illus. by Vongprachanh, Somchith)*
c HB Guide - v26 - i2 - Fall 2015 - p216(1) [51-500]
Explore 360: Pompeii
c BL - v111 - i19-20 - June 1 2015 - p76(1) [51-500]
Explore 360: Pompeii (Illus. by Vongprachanh, Somchith)
c SLJ - v61 - i5 - May 2015 - p137(2) [51-500]

Christ, Mark K. - *I Do Wish This Cruel War Was Over: First-Person Accounts of Civil War Arkansas from the Arkansas Historical Quarterly*
JSH - v81 - i4 - Nov 2015 - p1055(2) [501+]

Christ-Von Wedel, Christine - *Erasmus of Rotterdam: Advocate of a New Christianity*
AHR - v120 - i1 - Feb 2015 - p348-349 [501+]

Christakis, Erika - *The Importance of Being Little: What Preschoolers Really Need from Grownups*
KR - Dec 15 2015 - pNA [501+]
PW - v262 - i50 - Dec 7 2015 - p82(2) [51-500]

Christensen, Bonnie - *Elvis: The Story of the Rock and Roll King (Illus. by Christensen, Bonnie)*
c CCB-B - v68 - i11 - July-August 2015 - p541(1) [51-500]
c KR - Jan 15 2015 - pNA [51-500]
c SLJ - v61 - i3 - March 2015 - p169(2) [51-500]
c HB Guide - v26 - i2 - Fall 2015 - p207(1) [51-500]
c PW - v262 - i49 - Dec 2 2015 - p46(1) [51-500]
c HB - v91 - i2 - March-April 2015 - p118(2) [51-500]

Christensen, Bryce - *'The Portals of Sheol' and Other Poems*
MA - v57 - i1 - Wntr 2015 - p49(8) [501+]

Christensen, Dorthe Refslund - *Taming Time, Timing Death: Social Technologies and Ritual*
JRAI - v21 - i1 - March 2015 - p225(2) [501+]

Christensen, Jo Ippolito - *The Needlepoint Book: New, Revised, and Updated Third Edition*
LJ - v140 - i3 - Feb 15 2015 - p99(3) [501+]

Christensen, Kate - *How to Cook a Moose: A Culinary Memoir*
KR - June 15 2015 - pNA [501+]
LJ - v140 - i12 - July 1 2015 - p104(2) [51-500]
BL - v112 - i2 - Sept 15 2015 - p8(2) [51-500]

Christensen, Lisbeth Bredholt - *The Handbook of Religions in Ancient Europe*
Class R - v65 - i1 - April 2015 - p167-168 [501+]

Christensen, Mark Z. - *Nahua and Maya Catholicisms: Texts and Religion in Colonial Central Mexico and Yucatan*
HNet - August 2015 - pNA [501+]
Translated Christianities: Nahuatl and Maya Religious Texts
CHR - v101 - i3 - Summer 2015 - p692(2) [501+]
Theol St - v76 - i2 - June 2015 - p384(2) [501+]
HAHR - v95 - i4 - Nov 2015 - p675-676 [501+]
IBMR - v39 - i4 - Oct 2015 - p241(2) [501+]

Christensen, Thomas J. - *The China Challenge: Shaping the Choices of a Rising Power*
BL - v111 - i19-20 - June 1 2015 - p8(1) [51-500]
KR - April 1 2015 - pNA [51-500]
LJ - v140 - i8 - May 1 2015 - p90(1) [51-500]
NYTBR - July 26 2015 - p14(L) [501+]

Christgau, John - *Incident at the Otterville Station: A Civil War Story of Slavery and Rescue*
JSH - v81 - i3 - August 2015 - p743(2) [501+]

Christgau, Robert - *Going into the City: Portrait of a Critic as a Young Man*
Ent W - i1355-1356 - March 20 2015 - p105(1) [501+]
NYT - Feb 25 2015 - pC1(L) [501+]
NYTBR - March 8 2015 - p26(L) [501+]
PW - v262 - i5 - Feb 2 2015 - p49(1) [51-500]
BL - v111 - i13 - March 1 2015 - p13(1) [51-500]
KR - Jan 1 2015 - pNA [501+]
LJ - v140 - i5 - March 15 2015 - p107(2) [51-500]

Christian, Garna L. - *El Paso's Muckraker: The Life of Owen Payne White*
Roundup M - v23 - i1 - Oct 2015 - p33(1) [501+]

Christian, Kathleen W. - *The Muses and Their Afterlife in Post-Classical Europe*
Ren Q - v68 - i3 - Fall 2015 - p981-983 [501+]

Christian, M. - *Skin Effect: More Science Fiction and Fantasy Erotica*
PW - v262 - i51 - Dec 14 2015 - p64(1) [51-500]

Christian Prophecies as a Reflex to Competing Concepts of Order
HNet - July 2015 - pNA [501+]

Christianse, Yvette - *Toni Morrison: An Ethical Poetics*
MFSF - v61 - i3 - Fall 2015 - p553-555 [501+]

Christiansen, Nancy L. - *Figuring Style: The Legacy of Renaissance Rhetoric*
Six Ct J - v46 - i3 - Fall 2015 - p809-810 [501+]

Christiansen, Richard - *A Theater of Our Own: A History and a Memoir of 1,001 Nights in Chicago*
BL - v112 - i5 - Nov 1 2015 - p18(2) [501+]

Christie, Agatha - *The Secret Adversary (Read by Larkin, Alison). Audiobook Review*
PW - v262 - i48 - Nov 30 2015 - p54(1) [51-500]

Christie, Alix - *Gutenberg's Apprentice*
LJ - v140 - i2 - Feb 1 2015 - p111(1) [51-500]

Christie, Heather - *Heliopause*
PW - v262 - i7 - Feb 16 2015 - p157(1) [51-500]

Christie, Michael - *If I Fall, If I Die*
Nat Post - v17 - i80 - Jan 31 2015 - pWP6(1) [501+]
NYTBR - Jan 25 2015 - p8(L) [501+]
NYTBR - Nov 29 2015 - p24(L) [501+]
TLS - i5848 - May 1 2015 - p19(2) [501+]

Christie, Niall - *Muslims and Crusaders: Christianity's Wars in the Middle East, 1095-1382, from the Islamic Sources*
Med R - June 2015 - pNA [501+]

Christie, R. Gregory - *Mousetropolis (Illus. by Christie, R. Gregory)*
c BL - v111 - i21 - July 1 2015 - p64(1) [51-500]
c KR - June 15 2015 - pNA [51-500]
c NYTBR - Oct 11 2015 - p17(L) [501+]
c PW - v262 - i25 - June 22 2015 - p136(1) [51-500]
c SLJ - v61 - i8 - August 2015 - p66(1) [51-500]

Christin, Pierre - *Robert Moses: The Master Builder of New York City (Illus. by Balez, Olivier)*
SLJ - v61 - i3 - March 2015 - p178(2) [51-500]

Christina, Dominique - *This Is Woman's Work: Calling Forth Your Inner Council of Wise, Brave, Crazy, Rebellious, Loving, Luminous Selves*
LJ - v140 - i13 - August 1 2015 - p112(1) [51-500]

Christman, Robert J. - *Doctrinal Controversy and Lay Religiosity in Late Reformation Germany: The Case of Mansfeld*
Six Ct J - v46 - i2 - Summer 2015 - p440-442 [501+]

Christoff, Peter - *Four Degrees of Global Warming: Australia in a Hot World*
QRB - v90 - i3 - Sept 2015 - p331(2) [501+]

Christofora, Kevin - *Nick's Very First Day of Baseball (Illus. by Tangeman, Dale)*
c CH Bwatch - August 2015 - pNA [51-500]
c KR - March 15 2015 - pNA [501+]

Christopher, Adam - *The Machine Awakes*
BL - v111 - i13 - March 1 2015 - p30(2) [51-500]
KR - Feb 15 2015 - pNA [51-500]
PW - v262 - i8 - Feb 23 2015 - p55(2) [51-500]
Made to Kill
BL - v112 - i6 - Nov 15 2015 - p32(1) [51-500]
KR - Sept 15 2015 - pNA [51-500]
PW - v262 - i39 - Sept 28 2015 - p73(1) [51-500]

Christopher, Brandon - *The Job Pirate: An Entertaining Tale of My Job-Hopping Journey in America*
KR - Feb 15 2015 - pNA [51-500]

Christopher, Lauren - *The Kiss on Castle Road*
PW - v262 - i48 - Nov 30 2015 - p46(1) [51-500]
Ten Good Reasons
KR - Feb 15 2015 - pNA [51-500]

Christopher, Lucy - *The Killing Woods (Read by Hardingham, Fiona). Audiobook Review*
c BL - v111 - i14 - March 15 2015 - p24(2) [501+]

Christopher, Neil - *The Dreaded Ogress of the Tundra (Illus. by MacDougall, Larry)*
   c CCB-B - v69 - i2 - Oct 2015 - p81(1) [51-500]
   c KR - May 1 2015 - pNA [51-500]
   c Res Links - v21 - i1 - Oct 2015 - p13(1) [51-500]
The Hidden
      MFSF - v128 - i3-4 - March-April 2015 - p64(2) [501+]
On the Shoulder of a Giant (Illus. by Nelson, James)
   c CCB-B - v69 - i2 - Oct 2015 - p82(1) [51-500]
   c KR - June 1 2015 - pNA [51-500]
   c PW - v262 - i24 - June 15 2015 - p82(1) [501+]
   c PW - v262 - i49 - Dec 2 2015 - p24(1) [51-500]
   c Res Links - v21 - i1 - Oct 2015 - p3(2) [51-500]
   c SLJ - v61 - i10 - Oct 2015 - p125(1) [51-500]
Way Back Then (Illus. by Arnaktauyok, Germaine)
   c KR - Oct 15 2015 - pNA [51-500]

Christopher, Valerie - *I Am Not a Minority! I'm Part of the Majority!*
   c CH Bwatch - Nov 2015 - pNA [51-500]

Chrustowski, Rick - *Bee Dance (Illus. by Chrustowski, Rick)*
   c BL - v111 - i19-20 - June 1 2015 - p79(1) [51-500]
   c HB Guide - v26 - i2 - Fall 2015 - p173(1) [51-500]
   c KR - March 15 2015 - pNA [51-500]
   c SLJ - v61 - i3 - March 2015 - p169(1) [51-500]

Chryssavgis, John - *Saint Anthony the Great (Illus. by Brent, Isabelle)*
   c BL - v112 - i6 - Nov 15 2015 - p45(2) [51-500]
   c KR - Oct 1 2015 - pNA [51-500]
Toward an Ecology of Transfiguration: Orthodox Christian Perspectives on Environment, Nature, and Creation
      Intpr - v69 - i4 - Oct 2015 - p503(1) [501+]

Chrystal, Paul - *Women in Ancient Rome*
      Class R - v65 - i1 - April 2015 - p193-195 [501+]

Chu, Judy Y. - *When Boys Become Boys: Development, Relationships and Masculinity*
      JGS - v24 - i3 - June 2015 - p372-373 [501+]

Chu, Wesley - *Time Salvager*
      PW - v262 - i20 - May 18 2015 - p68(1) [51-500]

Chu, Yiu-Wai - *Lost in Transition: Hong Kong Culture in the Age of China*
      Pac A - v88 - i1 - March 2015 - p190 [501+]

Chuang, Angie - *The Four Words For Home*
      Wom R Bks - v32 - i2 - March-April 2015 - p24(2) [501+]

Chubb, Danielle L. - *Contentious Activism and Inter-Korean Relations*
      Pac A - v88 - i3 - Sept 2015 - p715 [501+]

Chubb, Taryn E.L. - *Mendicants and Merchants in the Medieval Mediterranean*
      Specu - v90 - i2 - April 2015 - p525-526 [501+]

Chuguna, Jukuna Mona - *The Girl from the Great Sandy Desert (Illus. by Street, Mervyn)*
   c Magpies - v30 - i1 - March 2015 - p23(1) [501+]

Chun, Pam - *The Perfect Tea Thief*
      PW - v262 - i7 - Feb 16 2015 - p156(1) [51-500]

Chung, A.S. - *A Brand New Day: A Banana Split Story (Illus. by Bossio, Paula). E-book Review*
   c PW - v262 - i8 - Feb 23 2015 - p74(1) [51-500]

Chung, Arree - *Ninja! (Illus. by Chung, Arree)*
   c HB Guide - v26 - i1 - Spring 2015 - p26(1) [51-500]

Chung, Steven - *Split Screen Korea: Shin Sang-ok and Postwar Cinema*
      Pac A - v88 - i3 - Sept 2015 - p723 [501+]

Chung, Thomas - *Younger-Generation Korean Experiences in the United States: Personal Narratives on Ethnic and Racial Identities*
      CS - v44 - i6 - Nov 2015 - p829-830 [501+]

Chupeco, Rin - *The Suffering*
   y KR - July 15 2015 - pNA [51-500]
   y SLJ - v61 - i8 - August 2015 - p101(1) [51-500]
   y VOYA - v38 - i4 - Oct 2015 - p67(1) [51-500]

Church, Caroline Jayne - *Dix petits orteils (Illus. by Church, Caroline Jayne)*
   c Res Links - v20 - i4 - April 2015 - p38(1) [51-500]
I Am a Big Brother
   c KR - July 1 2015 - pNA [51-500]
I Love My Puppy
   c KR - Jan 1 2016 - pNA [51-500]
I Love My Robot
   c KR - Jan 1 2016 - pNA [51-500]
Sweet Child of Mine (Illus. by Church, Caroline Jayne)
   c KR - Jan 1 2015 - pNA [51-500]

Church, Jennifer - *Possibilities of Perception*
      Dialogue - v54 - i3 - Sept 2015 - p553-555 [501+]

Church, Michael - *The Other Classical Musics: Fifteen Great Traditions*
      Spec - v329 - i9764 - Oct 17 2015 - p38(2) [501+]

Church, Stephen - *King John: And the Road to Magna Carta*
      KR - Jan 15 2015 - pNA [51-500]
      PW - v262 - i8 - Feb 23 2015 - p67(1) [51-500]
King John: England, Magna Carta and the Making of a Tyrant
      Spec - v327 - i9737 - April 11 2015 - p47(1) [501+]
      HT - v65 - i6 - June 2015 - p56(2) [501+]
      TLS - i5854 - June 12 2015 - p9(1) [501+]

Church, Steven - *Ultrasonic: Essays*
      ABR - v36 - i2 - Jan-Feb 2015 - p24(2) [501+]

Churchill, Frederick B. - *August Weismann: Development, Heredity, and Evolution*
      QRB - v90 - i4 - Dec 2015 - p421(2) [501+]
      Nature - v522 - i7544 - June 4 2015 - p31(2) [501+]

Churchill, Larry R. - *Patients Teach: The Everyday Ethics of Health Care*
      Hast Cen R - v45 - i1 - Jan-Feb 2015 - p46(2) [501+]

Churchill, Lindsey - *Becoming the Tupamaros: Solidarity and Transnational Revolutionaries in Uruguay and the United States*
      AHR - v120 - i2 - April 2015 - p688-689 [501+]
      Ams - v72 - i3 - July 2015 - p510(2) [501+]

Churchill, Steven - *Jean-Paul Sartre: Key Concepts*
      FS - v69 - i1 - Jan 2015 - p108-109 [501+]

Churchwell, Sarah - *Careless People: Murder, Mayhem, and the Invention of The Great Gatsby*
      NYTBR - March 8 2015 - p32(L) [501+]

Churnin, Nancy - *The William Hoy Story: How a Deaf Baseball Player Changed the Game (Illus. by Tuya, Jez)*
   c PW - v262 - i51 - Dec 14 2015 - p82(2) [501+]

Churton, Tobias - *Gnostic Mysteries of Sex: Sophia the Wild One and Erotic Christianity*
      RVBW - Nov 2015 - pNA [501+]

Chute, Hillary L. - *Disaster Drawn: Visual Witness, Comics, and Documentary Form*
      KR - Nov 15 2015 - pNA [51-500]

Chutkan, Robynne - *The Microbiome Solution: A Radical New Way to Heal Your Body from the Inside Out*
      PW - v262 - i24 - June 15 2015 - p80(1) [51-500]

Chwast, Seymour - *Doctor Dolittle (Illus. by Chwast, Seymour)*
   c BL - v112 - i4 - Oct 15 2015 - p37(1) [51-500]
   c KR - July 15 2015 - pNA [51-500]

Ciabattoni, Francesco - *The Decameron Third Day in Perspective*
      Ren Q - v68 - i3 - Fall 2015 - p1110-1111 [501+]

Ciccariello-Maher, George - *We Created Chavez: A People's History of the Venezuelan Revolution*
      CS - v44 - i5 - Sept 2015 - p650-652 [501+]
      Historian - v77 - i1 - Spring 2015 - p109(2) [501+]

Cicek, M. Talha - *War and State Formation in Syria: Cemal Pasha's Governorate during World War I, 1914-1917*
      IJMES - v47 - i3 - August 2015 - p616-618 [501+]

Cieradkowski, Gary Joseph - *The League of Outsider Baseball: An Illustrated History of Baseball's Forgotten Heores (Illus. by Cieradkowski, Gary Joseph)*
      KR - Feb 1 2015 - pNA [51-500]
The League of Outsider Baseball: An Illustrated History of Baseball's Forgotten Heroes (Illus. by Cieradkowski, Gary Joseph)
      LJ - v140 - i3 - Feb 15 2015 - p103(2) [501+]

Cifichiello, Tom - *Of Darkest Valor*
      RVBW - May 2015 - pNA [51-500]

Ciment, Jill - *Act of God*
      BL - v111 - i11 - Feb 1 2015 - p20(1) [51-500]
      NYTBR - April 5 2015 - p17(L) [501+]
      PW - v262 - i3 - Jan 19 2015 - p55(1) [51-500]

Cimino, Richard - *Mystical Science and Practical Religion: Muslim, Hindu, and Sikh Discourse on Science and Technology*
      AJS - v121 - i2 - Sept 2015 - p658(3) [501+]

Cinotto, Simone - *The Italian American Table: Food, Family, and Community in New York City*
      JAH - v101 - i4 - March 2015 - p1308(1) [501+]
      WestFolk - v74 - i2 - Spring 2015 - p234-237 [501+]

Ciocca, Gina - *Last Year's Mistake*
   y BL - v111 - i19-20 - June 1 2015 - p98(1) [51-500]
   y HB Guide - v26 - i2 - Fall 2015 - p114(1) [51-500]
      KR - April 1 2015 - pNA [51-500]
      SLJ - v61 - i4 - April 2015 - p160(1) [51-500]

Ciocchi, Catherine - *This Land Is Your Land (Illus. by Morrison, Cathy)*
   c CH Bwatch - June 2015 - pNA [51-500]

Ciocia, Stefania - *Vietnam and Beyond: Tim O'Brien and the Power of Storytelling*
      MFSF - v61 - i1 - Spring 2015 - p195-197 [501+]

Ciociltan, Virgil - *The Mongols and the Black Sea Trade in the Thirteenth and Fourteenth Centuries*
      Specu - v90 - i3 - July 2015 - p788(1) [501+]

Cioffari, Philip - *Dark Road, Dead End*
      RVBW - July 2015 - pNA [51-500]

Cioffi, Frank L. - *Day in the Life of the English Language: A Microcosmic Usage Handbook*
      LJ - v140 - i2 - Feb 1 2015 - p106(1) [51-500]

Cipriani, Curzio - *Le collezioni mineralogiche del Museo di Storia Naturale dell'Universita di Firenze dalle origini a oggi*
      Isis - v106 - i1 - March 2015 - p163(2) [501+]

Cipriani, Nicola Luciano - *Il Servizio Prioritario: storia, francobolli, tariffe ed aspetti collezionistici*
      Phil Lit R - v64 - i3 - Summer 2015 - p215(3) [501+]

Ciraolo, Simona - *Whatever Happened to My Sister? (Illus. by Ciraolo, Simona)*
   c BL - v112 - i6 - Nov 15 2015 - p59(1) [51-500]
   c NYTBR - Dec 20 2015 - p15(L) [501+]
   c SLJ - v61 - i11 - Nov 2015 - p80(1) [51-500]
Whatever Happened to My Sister?
   c KR - August 1 2015 - pNA [51-500]
   c PW - v262 - i34 - August 24 2015 - p79(1) [51-500]

The Circulation of (Post)Colonial Knowledge: A Transpacific History, 1800-1980
      HNet - May 2015 - pNA [501+]

Cisneros, Sandra - *Hairs / Pelitos (Illus. by Ybanez, Terry)*
   c BL - v111 - i9-10 - Jan 1 2015 - pS18(5) [501+]
A House of My Own: Stories from My Life
   y BL - v112 - i2 - Sept 15 2015 - p16(2) [51-500]
      BooChiTr - Oct 17 2015 - p12(1) [501+]
      KR - August 1 2015 - pNA [501+]
      LJ - v140 - i14 - Sept 1 2015 - p101(2) [51-500]
      PW - v262 - i36 - Sept 7 2015 - p60(1) [51-500]

Cistaro, Melissa - *Pieces of My Mother*
      BL - v111 - i14 - March 15 2015 - p33(1) [51-500]
      KR - Feb 15 2015 - pNA [501+]
      PW - v262 - i8 - Feb 23 2015 - p64(1) [51-500]

Cities and River Environments: A Versatile Relationship: Conflicts between Local, National and Transnational Patterns of Governance in East Central Europe and Beyond
      HNet - March 2015 - pNA [501+]

Cities and Science: Urban History and the History of Science in the Study of Early Modern and Modern Europe
      HNet - Sept 2015 - pNA [501+]

Citrin, Jack - *American Identity and the Politics of Multiculturalism*
      Pub Op Q - v79 - i3 - Fall 2015 - p820(24) [501+]

Citroen, Lida D. - *Your Next Mission: A Personal Branding Guide for the Military-to-Civilian Transition*
      NACEJou - v75 - i3 - Feb 2015 - p14(1) [501+]

Citron, Danielle Keats - *Hate Crimes in Cyberspace*
      HLR - v128 - i7 - May 2015 - p2106(1) [1-50]

Claburn, Thomas - *Oversight*
      PW - v262 - i23 - June 8 2015 - p42(1) [51-500]
The Oversight
      KR - June 1 2015 - pNA [501+]

Claerbaut, A. Alyce - *Strayhorn: An Illustrated Life*
      LJ - v140 - i19 - Nov 15 2015 - p87(2) [51-500]
      BL - v112 - i5 - Nov 1 2015 - p25(1) [51-500]

Claflin, Willy - *The Little Moose Who Couldn't Go to Sleep (Illus. by Stimson, James)*
   c HB Guide - v26 - i1 - Spring 2015 - p26(1) [51-500]

Clamp, Cathy - *Forbidden*
      PW - v262 - i24 - June 15 2015 - p68(2) [51-500]

CLAMP (Mangaka writing/artist group) - *Legal Drug: A Drugstore with Medicine and a Danger*
   y VOYA - v38 - i2 - June 2015 - p50(2) [501+]

Clampitt, Cynthia - *Midwest Maize: How Corn Shaped the U.S. Heartland*
      Bwatch - June 2015 - pNA [51-500]

Clancey, Lee - *A Bale of Turtles (Illus. by Rothermel, Mary)*
   c PW - v262 - i47 - Nov 23 2015 - p67(2) [51-500]

Clanchy, Kate - *Meeting the English*
      BL - v111 - i11 - Feb 1 2015 - p23(1) [51-500]
      KR - Jan 1 2015 - pNA [501+]
      NYTBR - April 5 2015 - p18(L) [501+]

Clancy, Judith - *Kyoto Gardens: Masterworks of the Japanese Gardener's Art*
      Bwatch - July 2015 - pNA [51-500]
      LJ - v140 - i6 - April 1 2015 - p109(1) [51-500]

Clanton, Ben - *Rex Wrecks It! (Illus. by Clanton, Ben)*
   c HB Guide - v26 - i1 - Spring 2015 - p7(1) [51-500]
Something Extraordinary (Illus. by Clanton, Ben)
     KR - March 15 2015 - pNA [51-500]
   c PW - v262 - i15 - April 13 2015 - p80(1) [51-500]
Something Extraordinary
   c HB Guide - v26 - i2 - Fall 2015 - p29(1) [51-500]

Clapper, Nikki Bruno - *High Speed Trains*
     Sch Lib - v63 - i4 - Winter 2015 - p218(1) [51-500]
Learning about Plagiarism
   c SLJ - v61 - i9 - Sept 2015 - p175(1) [51-500]
Learning about Primary Sources
     Sch Lib - v63 - i4 - Winter 2015 - p236(1) [51-500]
   c SLJ - v61 - i9 - Sept 2015 - p175(1) [51-500]

Clare, Alys - *A Shadowed Evil*
     BL - v112 - i2 - Sept 15 2015 - p35(1) [51-500]
     KR - August 15 2015 - pNA [51-500]
     PW - v262 - i35 - August 31 2015 - p64(1) [51-500]

Clare, Cassandra - *The Bane Chronicles*
   c HB Guide - v26 - i1 - Spring 2015 - p103(1) [51-500]
The Copper Gauntlet (Illus. by Fischer, Scott)
   c SLJ - v61 - i10 - Oct 2015 - p87(2) [51-500]

Clare, Janet - *Shakespeare's Stage Traffic: Imitation, Borrowing and Competition in Renaissance Theatre*
     RES - v66 - i274 - April 2015 - p374-376 [501+]
     Six Ct J - v46 - i2 - Summer 2015 - p453-455 [501+]

Clare, Pamela - *Seduction Game*
     PW - v262 - i36 - Sept 7 2015 - p52(1) [51-500]

Clare, Ralph - *Fictions Inc.: The Corporation in Postmodern Fiction, Film and Popular Culture*
     Am St - v54 - i2 - Summer 2015 - p116-117 [501+]

Claridge, Laura - *The Lady with the Borzoi: Blanche Knopf, Literary Tastemaker Extraordinaire*
     KR - Dec 15 2015 - pNA [501+]
     PW - v262 - i52 - Dec 21 2015 - p142(1) [51-500]

Clark, Adrian - *Queer Saint: The Cultured Life of Peter Watson, Who Shook Twentieth-Century Art and Shocked High Society*
     Spec - v328 - i9743 - May 23 2015 - p37(1) [501+]
     TLS - i5858 - July 10 2015 - p11(1) [501+]

Clark, Andy - *Surfing Uncertainty: Prediction, Action, and the Embodied Mind*
     LJ - v140 - i17 - Oct 15 2015 - p89(1) [51-500]

Clark, Anthony - *The Last Campaign: How Presidents Rewrite History, Run for Posterity & Enshrine Their Legacies*
     Pub Hist - v37 - i3 - August 2015 - p142(3) [501+]

Clark, Anthony E. - *China's Saints: Catholic Martyrdom during the Qing (1644-1911)*
     CHR - v101 - i1 - Wntr 2015 - p184(2) [501+]
Heaven in Conflict: Franciscans and the Boxer Uprising in Shanxi
     CHR - v101 - i4 - Autumn 2015 - p968(2) [501+]

Clark, Audrey Wu - *The Asian American Avant-Garde: Universalist Aspirations in Modernist Literature and Art*
     PW - v29 - i29 - July 20 2015 - p178(2) [51-500]

Clark, Beverly Lyon - *The Afterlife of 'Little Women'*
     TLS - i5836 - Feb 6 2015 - p22(1) [501+]

Clark, C.A. - *The Oath*
     KR - Sept 15 2015 - pNA [501+]

Clark, Cassandra - *The Dragon of Handale*
     KR - Jan 1 2015 - pNA [51-500]
     PW - v262 - i3 - Jan 19 2015 - p62(1) [51-500]

Clark, Catherine - *The Headmaster's Darlings*
     KR - June 15 2015 - pNA [51-500]

Clark, Christopher - *The Sleepwalkers: How Europe Went to War in 1914*
     J Mil H - v79 - i4 - Oct 2015 - p1142-1144 [501+]

Clark, Clare - *We That Are Left*
     BL - v112 - i2 - Sept 15 2015 - p37(1) [51-500]
     KR - August 1 2015 - pNA [51-500]
     LJ - v140 - i13 - August 1 2015 - p81(1) [51-500]
     NYTBR - Nov 15 2015 - p10(L) [501+]

Clark, David - *Voices from Labour's Past*
     NS - v144 - i5253 - March 13 2015 - p53(1) [51-500]

Clark-Deces, Isabelle - *The Right Spouse: Preferential Marriages in Tamil Nadu*
     Pac A - v88 - i4 - Dec 2015 - p950 [501+]

Clark, Dorie - *Stand Out: How to Find Your Breakthrough Idea and Build a Following around It*
     BL - v111 - i15 - April 1 2015 - p8(1) [51-500]
     LJ - v140 - i5 - March 15 2015 - p114(1) [501+]

Clark, Elizabeth A. - *Founding the Fathers: Early Church History and Protestant Professors in Nineteenth Century America*
     CHR - v101 - i3 - Summer 2015 - p680(2) [501+]

Clark, Emily - *The Strange History of the American Quadroon: Free Women of Color in the Revolutionary Atlantic World*
     JAH - v102 - i1 - June 2015 - p233-234 [501+]
     RAH - v43 - i2 - June 2015 - p223-230 [501+]
Women and Religion in the Atlantic Age, 1550-1900
     Six Ct J - v46 - i3 - Fall 2015 - p842-845 [501+]

Clark, Gregory - *The Son Also Rises: Surnames and the History of Social Mobility*
     JEH - v75 - i1 - March 2015 - p301-302 [501+]

Clark, Henry - *The Book That Proves Time Travel Happens*
   c BL - v111 - i15 - April 1 2015 - p78(1) [51-500]
The Book That Proves Time Travel Happens (Illus. by Holmes, Jeremy)
   c HB Guide - v26 - i2 - Fall 2015 - p78(1) [51-500]
   y VOYA - v38 - i1 - April 2015 - p76(1) [51-500]
The Book That Proves Time Travel Happens
   c KR - Feb 1 2015 - pNA [51-500]

Clark, Jay - *Finding Mr. Brightside*
   y BL - v111 - i12 - Feb 15 2015 - p80(1) [51-500]
   y CCB-B - v68 - i9 - May 2015 - p442(1) [51-500]
   y HB Guide - v26 - i2 - Fall 2015 - p114(1) [51-500]
   y KR - Jan 1 2015 - pNA [51-500]
     PW - v262 - i2 - Jan 12 2015 - p61(1) [51-500]
   y SLJ - v61 - i5 - May 2015 - p112(1) [51-500]
   y VOYA - v37 - i6 - Feb 2015 - p54(2) [51-500]

Clark, Jennifer - *The American Idea of England, 1776-1840: Transatlantic Writing*
     J Am St - v49 - i2 - May 2015 - p414-416 [501+]

Clark, Jerry - *A History of Heists: Bank Robbery in America*
     PW - v262 - i21 - May 25 2015 - p50(1) [51-500]

Clark, Jessica Homan - *Triumph in Defeat: Military Loss and the Roman Republic*
     Class R - v65 - i2 - Oct 2015 - p523-524 [501+]

Clark, Joan - *The Birthday Lunch*
     Nat Post - v17 - i188 - June 13 2015 - pWP4(1) [501+]
The Dream Carvers
   y Res Links - v20 - i3 - Feb 2015 - p26(1) [501+]

Clark, John H. - *Hazelet's Journal*
     SPBW - May 2015 - pNA [51-500]

Clark, John Lee - *Where I Stand: On the Signing Community and My DeafBlind Experience*
     HNet - Oct 2015 - pNA [51-500]

Clark, Kathleen Ann - *Georgia Women: Their Lives and Times, vol. 2*
     JSH - v81 - i4 - Nov 2015 - p1013(3) [501+]

Clark, Kathy - *The Choice*
   c CH Bwatch - May 2015 - pNA [51-500]
   c Res Links - v20 - i4 - April 2015 - p10(1) [51-500]
   y VOYA - v38 - i3 - August 2015 - p56(2) [51-500]
   y VOYA - v38 - i4 - Oct 2015 - p81(2) [51-500]

Clark, Larry - *14 Characteristic Pieces for the Intermediate Pianist*
     Am MT - v65 - i3 - Dec 2015 - p45(1) [51-500]
Festival Classics for Alto Saxophone: 21 Solo Pieces with Piano Accompaniment
     Am MT - v64 - i5 - April-May 2015 - p53(1) [501+]
Festival Classics for Violin: 13 Solo Pieces with Piano Accompaniment
     Am MT - v64 - i5 - April-May 2015 - p52(2) [51-500]

Clark, Linda - *Society in an Age of Plague*
     Specu - v90 - i2 - April 2015 - p526-528 [501+]

Clark, Lorna - *The Court Journals and Letters of Frances Burney, vols. 3 and 4: 1788*
     Lon R Bks - v37 - i16 - August 27 2015 - p40(2) [501+]

Clark, Lorna J. - *The Court Journals and Letters of Frances Burney, vols. 3 and 4: 1788*
     TLS - i5867 - Sept 11 2015 - p8(2) [501+]

Clark, Lynn Schofield - *The Parent App: Understanding Families in the Digital Age*
     TLS - i5838 - Feb 20 2015 - p5(1) [501+]

Clark, M.H. - *The Man Made of Stars*
   c SLJ - v61 - i9 - Sept 2015 - p117(2) [51-500]

Clark, Marcia - *The Competition: A Rachel Knight Novel*
     RVBW - March 2015 - pNA [51-500]
The Competition
     RVBW - March 2015 - pNA [51-500]

Clark, Mark - *Stars Wars FAQ: Everything Left to Know about the Trilogy That Changed the Movies*
     Bwatch - Nov 2015 - pNA [51-500]

Clark, Martin - *The Jezebel Remedy*
     PW - v262 - i14 - April 6 2015 - p37(1) [51-500]
     BL - v111 - i16 - April 15 2015 - p24(1) [51-500]
     KR - May 15 2015 - pNA [51-500]
     LJ - v140 - i8 - May 1 2015 - p60(2) [51-500]

Clark, Mary Higgins - *All Dressed in White*
     KR - Nov 1 2015 - pNA [51-500]
The Cinderella Murder
     RVBW - August 2015 - pNA [51-500]
Death Wears a Beauty Mask and Other Stories (Read by Maxwell, Jan, with Robert Petkoff). Audiobook Review
     PW - v262 - i30 - July 27 2015 - p60(2) [51-500]
I've Got You Under My Skin
     RVBW - April 2015 - pNA [51-500]
Manhattan Mayhem: New Crime Stories from Mystery Writers of America
     RVBW - June 2015 - pNA [51-500]
   y SLJ - v61 - i11 - Nov 2015 - p126(2) [501+]
     TLS - i5866 - Sept 4 2015 - p26(1) [501+]

Clark, Mindy Starns - *The Amish Clockmaker*
     LJ - v140 - i2 - Feb 1 2015 - p67(3) [501+]

Clark, Neil - *Stranger than Fiction: The Life of Edgar Wallace, the Man Who Created King Kong*
     Spec - v327 - i9727 - Jan 31 2015 - p36(1) [501+]

Clark, Paul W. - *George Owen Squier: U.S. Army Major General, Inventor, Aviation Pioneer, Founder of Muzak*
     APH - v62 - i2 - Summer 2015 - p57(2) [501+]

Clark, Platte F. - *Fluff Dragon*
   c SLJ - v61 - i6 - June 2015 - p46(6) [501+]
Good Ogre
   c HB Guide - v26 - i2 - Fall 2015 - p78(1) [51-500]

Clark, Roy Peter - *The Art of X-Ray Reading*
     KR - Oct 15 2015 - pNA [501+]

Clark, Sherryl - *1915: Do You Dare? Jimmy's War*
   y Magpies - v30 - i1 - March 2015 - p34(1) [51-500]

Clark, Simon - *The Mammoth Book of Sherlock Holmes Abroad*
     PW - v262 - i21 - May 25 2015 - p39(1) [51-500]

Clark, Simon (b. 1958-) - *Inspector Abberline and the Gods of Rome*
     PW - v262 - i37 - Sept 14 2015 - p45(1) [51-500]
Rage Master
     PW - v262 - i36 - Sept 7 2015 - p50(1) [51-500]

Clark, Simon P. - *Eren*
   y Sch Lib - v63 - i1 - Spring 2015 - p51(1) [51-500]
Tell the Story to Its End
   c KR - August 15 2015 - pNA [51-500]
   y PW - v262 - i34 - August 24 2015 - p83(1) [51-500]
   y SLJ - v61 - i11 - Nov 2015 - p106(1) [51-500]
   y VOYA - v38 - i4 - Oct 2015 - p67(2) [51-500]

Clark, Stacy - *When the Wind Blows (Illus. by Sneed, Brad)*
   c BL - v111 - i18 - May 15 2015 - p46(1) [51-500]
   c KR - Feb 15 2015 - pNA [51-500]

Clark, Steve - *Justice Is for the Lonely*
     RVBW - August 2015 - pNA [51-500]
     RVBW - Nov 2015 - pNA [51-500]

Clark, Stuart - *The Unknown Universe: What We Don't Know About Time and Space in Ten Chapters*
     Nature - v526 - i7574 - Oct 22 2015 - p503(1) [51-500]

Clark, Susan G. - *Large Carnivore Conservation: Integrating Science and Policy in the North American West*
     QRB - v90 - i3 - Sept 2015 - p333(1) [501+]

Clark, Terence N. - *Rewriting Marpole: The Path to Cultural Complexity in the Gulf of Georgia*
     Am Ant - v80 - i1 - Jan 2015 - p211(2) [501+]

Clark, Thomas A. - *Yellow and Blue*
     TLS - i5844 - April 3 2015 - p23(1) [501+]

Clark, Tom - *Hard Times: Inequality, Recession, Aftermath*
     TLS - i5853 - June 5 2015 - p27(1) [501+]

Clark, Tracy - *Deviate*
   y KR - Jan 15 2015 - pNA [51-500]

Clark, Travis - *Guy's Guide*
   y HB Guide - v26 - i1 - Spring 2015 - p132(1) [51-500]

Clarke, A.W. - *Jaspar Tristram*
     TLS - i5874 - Oct 30 2015 - p30(1) [501+]

Clarke, Ardy Sixkiller - *Sky People: Untold Stories of Alien Encounters in Mesoamerica*
     RVBW - Jan 2015 - pNA [51-500]

Clarke, Austin - *In Your Crib*
     Can Lit - i224 - Spring 2015 - p144 [51-500]

Clarke, Brock - *The Happiest People in the World*
     NYTBR - Jan 4 2015 - p16(L) [501+]

Clarke, Bruce - *Neocybernetics and Narrative*
     SFS - v42 - i2 - July 2015 - p371-373 [501+]

Clarke, Cassandra Rose - *Our Lady of the Ice*
     KR - August 15 2015 - pNA [501+]
     PW - v262 - i26 - June 29 2015 - p49(1) [51-500]

Clarke, Christopher - *The Sleepwalkers: How Europe Went to War in 1914*
AHR - v120 - i3 - June 2015 - p951-953 [501+]

clarke, Clare - *Late Victorian Crime Fiction in the Shadow of Sherlock*
TimHES - i2185 - Jan 8 2015 - p48-49 [501+]

Clarke, David - *How UFOs Conquered the World: The History of a Modern Myth*
TLS - i5863 - August 14 2015 - p27(1) [501+]

Clarke, Erskine - *By the Rivers of Water: A Nineteenth-Century Atlantic Odyssey*
JSH - v81 - i3 - August 2015 - p710(3) [501+]

Clarke, Frances M. - *War Stories: Suffering and Sacrifice in the Civil War North*
HNet - Jan 2015 - pNA [501+]

Clarke, Frank - *The Unaccountable & Ungovernable Corporation: Companies' Use-By Dates Close In*
AR - v90 - i3 - May 2015 - p1241(4) [501+]

Clarke, Ginjer L. - *What's Up in the Amazon Rainforest*
c PW - v262 - i28 - July 13 2015 - p67(1) [501+]

Clarke, Jaime - *World Gone Water*
KR - Feb 15 2015 - pNA [51-500]

Clarke, Jane - *Dr. KittyCat Is Ready to Rescue Posy the Puppy*
c Sch Lib - v63 - i2 - Summer 2015 - p90(1) [51-500]
Posy the Puppy
c KR - Dec 15 2015 - pNA [51-500]
Who Woke the Baby? (Illus. by Fuge, Charles)
c KR - Jan 1 2016 - pNA [51-500]

Clarke, Jeremy - *The Virgin Mary and Catholic Identities in Chinese History*
AHR - v120 - i1 - Feb 2015 - p204(1) [501+]
Theol St - v76 - i3 - Sept 2015 - p638(2) [501+]

Clarke, John - *Middle Waters*
PW - v262 - i27 - July 6 2015 - p51(2) [51-500]

Clarke, Kevin - *Oscar Romero: Love Must Win Out*
AM - v213 - i16 - Nov 23 2015 - p35(4) [501+]

Clarke, Laura - *Decline of the Animal Kingdom*
PW - v262 - i38 - Sept 21 2015 - p49(2) [51-500]

Clarke, Lucy - *The Blue*
KR - June 1 2015 - pNA [501+]
LJ - v140 - i11 - June 15 2015 - p74(1) [51-500]
PW - v262 - i24 - June 15 2015 - p64(1) [51-500]

Clarke, Neil - *Upgraded*
Analog - v135 - i5 - May 2015 - p106(2) [501+]

Clarke, Peter - *Mr Churchill's Profession: Statesman, Orator, Writer*
HT - v65 - i1 - Jan 2015 - p56(2) [501+]

Clarke, Richard A. - *Pinnacle Event*
BL - v111 - i16 - April 15 2015 - p29(1) [51-500]
KR - April 1 2015 - pNA [501+]
LJ - v140 - i11 - June 15 2015 - p78(2) [51-500]
PW - v262 - i9 - March 2 2015 - p64(1) [51-500]

Clarke, Susanna - *Jonathan Strange & Mr. Norrell*
Bwatch - July 2015 - pNA [51-500]

Clarkson, Stephanie - *Sleeping Cinderella and Other Princess Mix-Ups (Illus. by Barrager, Brigette)*
c CCB-B - v68 - i8 - April 2015 - p392(2) [51-500]
c HB Guide - v26 - i2 - Fall 2015 - p29(1) [51-500]

Clary, Julian - *The Bolds (Illus. by Roberts, David)*
c KR - Dec 15 2015 - pNA [51-500]
c PW - v262 - i52 - Dec 21 2015 - p154(1) [51-500]

Class Stories Series
c CH Bwatch - March 2015 - pNA [51-500]

Classen, Albrecht - *Early History of the Southwest through the Eyes of German-Speaking Jesuit Missionaries: A Transcultural Experience in the Eighteenth Century*
CHR - v101 - i3 - Summer 2015 - p677(2) [501+]
Handbook of Medieval Studies: Terms-Methods-Trends, 3 vols
Specu - v90 - i1 - Jan 2015 - p226-229 [501+]

Classen, Constance - *A Cultural History of the Senses, 6 vols.*
TLS - i5846 - April 17 2015 - p9(1) [501+]

Claudel, Philippe - *Parfums: A Catalogue of Remembered Smells*
TLS - i5860 - July 24 2015 - p29(1) [501+]

Clausen, Jan - *Veiled Spill: A Sequence*
APR - v44 - i1 - Jan-Feb 2015 - p9(3) [501+]

Clavell, James - *Shogun (Read by Lister, Ralph). Audiobook Review*
BL - v111 - i16 - April 15 2015 - p63(1) [51-500]

Claverie, Pierre-Vincent - *La conquete du Roussillon par Pierre le Ceremonieux*
Specu - v90 - i1 - Jan 2015 - p229-230 [501+]

Clavier, Mark F.M. - *Eloquent Wisdom: Rhetoric, Cosmology and Delight in the Theology of Augustine of Hippo*
TLS - i5874 - Oct 30 2015 - p30(2) [501+]

Clavin, Patricia - *Securing the World Economy: The Reinvention of the League of Nations, 1920-1946*
JMH - v87 - i3 - Sept 2015 - p716(3) [501+]

Clawson, Dan - *Unequal Time: Gender, Class, and Family in Employment Schedules*
AJS - v121 - i3 - Nov 2015 - p985(3) [501+]

Claxton, Guy - *Intelligence in the Flesh: Why Your Mind Needs Your Body Much More Than it Thinks*
KR - July 1 2015 - pNA [501+]
LJ - v140 - i15 - Sept 15 2015 - p97(3) [51-500]
TimHES - i2221 - Sept 17 2015 - p44-45 [501+]

Clay, Alexa - *The Misfit Economy: Lessons in Creativity from Pirates, Hackers, Gangsters and Other Informal Entrepreneurs*
Econ - v416 - i8945 - July 4 2015 - p74(US) [501+]
The Misfit Economy: Lessons in Creativity from Pirates, Hackers, Gangsters, and Other Informal Entrepreneurs
LJ - v140 - i11 - June 15 2015 - p95(1) [51-500]
The Misfit Economy
NS - v144 - i5272 - July 24 2015 - p14(1) [501+]
RVBW - July 2015 - pNA [51-500]

Clay, James - *Reverend Colt*
Roundup M - v22 - i6 - August 2015 - p27(1) [501+]
Wild West Detective
Roundup M - v22 - i4 - April 2015 - p32(1) [501+]
Roundup M - v22 - i6 - August 2015 - p27(1) [501+]

Clay, Kathryn - *Battling for Victory: The Coolest Robot Competitions*
c HB Guide - v26 - i1 - Spring 2015 - p172(1) [51-500]
Robots in Risky Jobs: On the Battlefield and Beyond
c HB Guide - v26 - i1 - Spring 2015 - p172(1) [51-500]
Wild About Wheels
c HB Guide - v26 - i2 - Fall 2015 - p184(2) [51-500]

Clay, Lauren R. - *Stagestruck: The Business of Theater in Eighteenth-Century France and Its Colonies*
JMH - v87 - i3 - Sept 2015 - p734(3) [501+]

Claybourne, Anna - *Disgusting & Dreadful Science Series*
c CH Bwatch - Feb 2015 - pNA [51-500]
The Human Body in 30 Seconds (Illus. by Robins, Wesley)
c Sch Lib - v63 - i1 - Spring 2015 - p46(1) [51-500]
I Love This Tree: Discover the Life, Beauty and Importance of Trees
c Sch Lib - v63 - i3 - Autumn 2015 - p172(1) [51-500]
Killer Plants and Other Green Gunk
c Res Links - v20 - i3 - Feb 2015 - p18(2) [51-500]
Smelly Farts and Other Body Horrors
c CH Bwatch - Nov 2015 - pNA [51-500]
c Res Links - v20 - i3 - Feb 2015 - p18(2) [51-500]

Clayman, Dee L. - *Berenice II and the Golden Age of Ptolemaic Egypt*
CJ - v110 - i3 - Feb-March 2015 - p376(7) [501+]
Class R - v65 - i2 - Oct 2015 - p517-519 [501+]

Claypool, Mark K. - *We're in this Together: Public-Private Partnerships in Special and At-Risk Education*
VOYA - v38 - i5 - Dec 2015 - p82(1) [51-500]

Clayton, Blake C. - *Market Madness: A Century of Oil Panics, Crises, and Crashes*
For Aff - v94 - i3 - May-June 2015 - pNA [501+]

Clayton, Dhonielle - *Tiny Pretty Things*
y KR - March 1 2015 - pNA [51-500]

Clayton, Emma - *The Whisper*
y Sch Lib - v63 - i2 - Summer 2015 - p115(2) [51-500]

Clayton, Jamie - *George (Read by Clayton, Jamie). Audiobook Review*
c SLJ - v61 - i11 - Nov 2015 - p70(1) [51-500]

Clayton, Mary - *Two Aelfric Texts: The Twelve Abuses and the Vices and Virtues*
Specu - v90 - i4 - Oct 2015 - p1101-1102 [501+]

Clayton, Meg Waite - *The Race for Paris*
BL - v111 - i16 - April 15 2015 - p37(2) [51-500]
Mac - v128 - i32-33 - August 17 2015 - p69(2) [501+]

Clayton, Mega Waite - *The Race for Paris*
KR - June 1 2015 - pNA [51-500]

Clayton, Tim - *Waterloo: Four Days That Changed Europe's Destiny*
Econ - v415 - i8939 - May 23 2015 - p71(US) [501+]
HT - v65 - i7 - July 2015 - p58(2) [501+]

Cleall, Esme - *Missionary Discourses of Difference: Negotiating Otherness in the British Empire, 1840-1900*
JMH - v87 - i2 - June 2015 - p435(3) [501+]

Cleantis, Tracey - *The Next Happy: Let Go of the Life You Planned and Find a New Way Forward*
PW - v262 - i4 - Jan 26 2015 - p163(1) [51-500]

Clear, Todd R. - *The Punishment Imperative: The Rise and Failure of Mass Incarceration in America*
Am St - v54 - i1 - Spring 2015 - p138-4 [501+]

Cleary, Beverly - *Ramona the Pest (Read by Channing, Stockard). Audiobook Review*
y SLJ - v61 - i6 - June 2015 - p53(3) [501+]

Cleary, Brian P. - *A Bat Cannot Bat, a Stair Cannot Stare: More about Homonyms and Homophones (Illus. by Goneau, Martin)*
c HB Guide - v26 - i1 - Spring 2015 - p146(1) [51-500]
Bow-Tie Pasta: Acrostic Poems (Illus. by Rowland, Andy)
c BL - v112 - i4 - Oct 15 2015 - p38(1) [51-500]
c KR - Sept 15 2015 - pNA [51-500]
c PW - v262 - i38 - Sept 21 2015 - p75(1) [501+]
c SLJ - v61 - i11 - Nov 2015 - p130(1) [51-500]
Chips and Cheese and Nana's Knees: What Is Alliteration? (Illus. by Goneau, Martin)
c HB Guide - v26 - i2 - Fall 2015 - p161(1) [51-500]
Madam and Nun and 1001 (Illus. by Gable, Brian)
c CH Bwatch - Jan 2015 - pNA [51-500]
Ode to a Commode: Concrete Poems (Illus. by Rowland, Andy)
BL - v111 - i14 - March 15 2015 - p61(1) [51-500]
c HB Guide - v26 - i1 - Spring 2015 - p188(1) [51-500]
Something Sure Smells Around Here: Limericks (Illus. by Rowland, Andy)
c HB Guide - v26 - i2 - Fall 2015 - p203(1) [51-500]
Something Sure Smells Around Here (Illus. by Rowland, Andy)
BL - v111 - i14 - March 15 2015 - p61(1) [51-500]
c KR - Feb 1 2015 - pNA [51-500]
They're There on Their Vacation (Illus. by Paillot, Jim)
c KR - Sept 1 2015 - pNA [51-500]
c SLJ - v61 - i11 - Nov 2015 - p130(2) [51-500]

Cleary, Jon - *GoGo Juice*
New Or - v49 - i11 - August 2015 - p42(1) [501+]

Cleave, Paul - *Trust No One*
BL - v111 - i19-20 - June 1 2015 - p57(2) [51-500]
KR - June 1 2015 - pNA [51-500]
LJ - v140 - i12 - July 1 2015 - p73(1) [51-500]
PW - v262 - i22 - June 1 2015 - p43(1) [51-500]

Cleaver, Thomas McKelvey - *Fabled Fifteen, The Pacific War Saga of Carrier Air Group 15*
APH - v62 - i1 - Spring 2015 - p50(1) [501+]

Cleeland, Anne - *Murder in Hindsight*
BL - v111 - i16 - April 15 2015 - p29(1) [51-500]
PW - v262 - i5 - Feb 2 2015 - p38(1) [51-500]

Cleeves, Ann - *Harbour Street*
BL - v112 - i5 - Nov 1 2015 - p31(1) [51-500]
KR - Oct 1 2015 - pNA [51-500]
PW - v262 - i41 - Oct 12 2015 - p50(1) [51-500]
Thin Air
BL - v111 - i17 - May 1 2015 - p46(1) [51-500]

Cleeves, Anne - *Thin Air: A Shetland Mystery*
PW - v262 - i12 - March 23 2015 - p49(1) [51-500]

Clegg, Bill - *Did You Ever Have a Family*
BL - v111 - i21 - July 1 2015 - p29(2) [51-500]
Ent W - i1380 - Sept 11 2015 - p67(1) [501+]
KR - July 1 2015 - pNA [51-500]
LJ - v140 - i12 - July 1 2015 - p73(3) [51-500]
Lon R Bks - v37 - i21 - Nov 5 2015 - p19(2) [501+]
NS - v144 - i5279 - Sept 11 2015 - p49(1) [501+]
NY - v91 - i35 - Nov 9 2015 - p81 [501+]
NYT - Sept 9 2015 - pC1(L) [501+]
NYTBR - Sept 6 2015 - p8(L) [501+]
Spec - v329 - i9760 - Sept 19 2015 - p45(1) [501+]
Trial by Fire
PW - v262 - i26 - June 29 2015 - p2(1) [51-500]

Clegg, Brian - *Ten Billion Tomorrows: How Science Fiction Technology Became a Reality and Shapes the Future*
PW - v262 - i27 - July 6 2015 - p56(1) [51-500]
Ten Billion Tomorrows: How Science Fiction Technology Became Reality and Shapes the Future
BL - v112 - i5 - Nov 1 2015 - p12(1) [51-500]
KR - Nov 1 2015 - pNA [51-500]

Cleland, Jane K. - *Ornaments of Death*
BL - v112 - i5 - Nov 1 2015 - p32(1) [51-500]
KR - Oct 1 2015 - pNA [51-500]
PW - v262 - i42 - Oct 19 2015 - p56(1) [51-500]

Clemans, Ernest G. - *Notes to the Nations*
KR - March 15 2015 - pNA [501+]

Clemence, Jessie - *If I Plug My Ears, God Can't Tell Me What to Do: And Other Ways We Miss Out on God's Adventures*
PW - v262 - i10 - March 9 2015 - p67(1) [51-500]

Clemens, Gabriele B. - *Zensur im Vormarz: Pressefreiheit und Informationskontrolle in Europa*
JMH - v87 - i2 - June 2015 - p414(3) [501+]

Clemens Wischermann - *Tiere und Geschichte: Konturen einer "Animate History"*
HNet - Sept 2015 - pNA(NA) [501+]

Clement, Blaize - *The Cat Sitter's Whiskers*
BL - v111 - i12 - Feb 15 2015 - p34(2) [51-500]

Clement, Gary - *Swimming, Swimming (Illus. by Clement, Gary)*
c CH Bwatch - March 2015 - pNA [51-500]
c KR - March 15 2015 - pNA [51-500]
c NYTBR - May 31 2015 - p45(L) [501+]
c Res Links - v20 - i5 - June 2015 - p2(2) [51-500]
c SLJ - v61 - i5 - May 2015 - p93(1) [51-500]
Swimming, Swimming
c HB Guide - v26 - i2 - Fall 2015 - p29(1) [51-500]

Clement, Jeff - *The Lieutenant Don't Know: One Marine's Story of Warfare and Combat Logistics in Afghanistan*
Mar Crp G - v99 - i1 - Jan 2015 - p84(2) [501+]

Clement, John - *The Cat Sitter's Whiskers*
PW - v262 - i3 - Jan 19 2015 - p63(1) [51-500]

Clement, Nathan - *Big Tractor (Illus. by Clement, Nathan)*
SLJ - v61 - i2 - Feb 2015 - p62(1) [51-500]
c HB Guide - v26 - i2 - Fall 2015 - p8(1) [51-500]

Clemente, Deirdre - *Dress Casual: How College Students Redefined American Style*
AHR - v120 - i3 - June 2015 - p1052-1053 [501+]
CS - v44 - i6 - Nov 2015 - p791-793 [501+]
JAH - v102 - i1 - June 2015 - p273-274 [501+]

Clementi, Federica K. - *Holocaust Mothers and Daughters: Family, History, and Trauma*
Wom R Bks - v32 - i2 - March-April 2015 - p14(3) [501+]

Clements, Andrew - *Because Your Grandparents Love You (Illus. by Alley, R.W.)*
c PW - v262 - i26 - June 29 2015 - p67(1) [501+]
The Map Trap
y HB Guide - v26 - i1 - Spring 2015 - p73(1) [51-500]

Clements, David L. - *Infrared Astronomy--Seeing the Heat: From William Herschel to the Herschel Space Observatory*
Bwatch - March 2015 - pNA [51-500]

Clements, Jonathan - *The Anime Encyclopedia: A Century of Japanese Animation, 3rd ed.*
BL - v112 - i2 - Sept 15 2015 - p12(1) [51-500]
Dirty Rotten Vikings: Three Centuries of Longships, Looting, and Bad Behavior (Illus. by Mazzara, Mauro)
c SLJ - v61 - i7 - July 2015 - p102(1) [51-500]

Clements, William M. - *Imagining Geronimo: An Apache Icon in Popular Culture*
Roundup M - v22 - i4 - April 2015 - p29(1) [501+]
PHR - v84 - i2 - May 2015 - p265(2) [501+]
Roundup M - v22 - i6 - August 2015 - p35(1) [501+]

Clemmons, Linda M. - *Conflicted Mission: Faith, Disputes, and Deception on the Dakota Frontier*
AHR - v120 - i2 - April 2015 - p619-620 [501+]
JAH - v101 - i4 - March 2015 - p1268-1269 [501+]
WHQ - v46 - i3 - Autumn 2015 - p368-369 [501+]

Clerge, Nesly - *When the Serpent Bites*
KR - Nov 15 2015 - pNA [51-500]

Cleveland, David A. - *Balancing on a Planet: The Future of Food and Agriculture*
BioSci - v65 - i3 - March 2015 - p331(2) [501+]

Cleveland, Susannah - *Careers in Music Librarianship III: Reality and Reinvention*
Notes - v72 - i1 - Sept 2015 - p135(3) [501+]

Cleveland, Todd - *Stones of Contention: A History of Africa's Diamonds*
AHR - v120 - i2 - April 2015 - p759(1) [501+]
BHR - v89 - i1 - Spring 2015 - p200(3) [501+]
For Aff - v94 - i3 - May-June 2015 - pNA [501+]

Cleverly, Barbara - *Enter Pale Death (Read by Brenher, Matthew). Audiobook Review*
BL - v111 - i17 - May 1 2015 - p57(2) [501+]

Cleves, Rachel Hope - *Charity & Sylvia: A Same-Sex Marriage in Early America*
AHR - v120 - i2 - April 2015 - p614-615 [501+]
JIH - v45 - i4 - Spring 2015 - p588-589 [501+]
NEQ - v88 - i1 - March 2015 - p162-164 [501+]
W&M Q - v72 - i1 - Jan 2015 - p168-170 [501+]
Wom R Bks - v32 - i2 - March-April 2015 - p31(2) [501+]
HNet - August 2015 - pNA [501+]
JAH - v102 - i2 - Sept 2015 - p546-547 [501+]

Clewes, Rosemary - *Paper Wings*
CWS - v30 - i2-3 - Fall-Winter 2015 - p123(2) [501+]

Clifford, Catherine E. - *Decoding Vatican II: Interpretation and Ongoing Reception*
Theol St - v76 - i3 - Sept 2015 - p654(1) [501+]

Clifford, James - *Returns: Becoming Indigenous in the Twenty-First Century*
HNet - June 2015 - pNA [501+]
JIH - v45 - i3 - Wntr 2015 - p421-423 [501+]

Clifford, Mark - *The Greening of Asia: The Business Case for Solving Asia's Environmental Emergency*
Econ - v415 - i8935 - April 25 2015 - p77(US) [501+]

Clifford, Stephanie - *Everybody Rise (Read by Kellgren, Katherine). Audiobook Review*
BL - v112 - i6 - Nov 15 2015 - p60(1) [51-500]
Everybody Rise
KR - June 15 2015 - pNA [501+]
LJ - v140 - i7 - April 15 2015 - p73(1) [51-500]
Mac - v128 - i32-33 - August 17 2015 - p65(1) [501+]
NYT - August 20 2015 - pC6(L) [501+]
NYTBR - August 23 2015 - p10(L) [501+]
PW - v262 - i25 - June 22 2015 - p118(2) [51-500]
PW - v262 - i35 - August 31 2015 - p11(1) [51-500]

Clift, A. Denis - *A Death In Geneva*
RVBW - Jan 2015 - pNA [501+]

Clifton, James - *Imago Exegetica: Visual Images as Exegetical Instruments, 1400-1700*
Six Ct J - v46 - i2 - Summer 2015 - p442-444 [501+]

Clifton, Lu - *Scalp Dance*
KR - Sept 15 2015 - pNA [501+]

Clifton, Lutricia - *Immortal Max*
y HB Guide - v26 - i1 - Spring 2015 - p73(1) [51-500]

Clifton, Ted - *The Bootlegger's Legacy*
KR - Dec 15 2015 - pNA [501+]

Climo, Liz - *Rory the Dinosaur: Me and My Dad (Illus. by Climo, Liz)*
c HB Guide - v26 - i2 - Fall 2015 - p8(1) [51-500]
c KR - April 1 2015 - pNA [51-500]
c PW - v262 - i15 - April 13 2015 - p81(1) [501+]
Rory the Dinosaur: Me and My Dad
c Nat Post - v17 - i194 - June 20 2015 - pWP5(1) [501+]

Cline, Dale K. - *Banking on Confidence: A Guidebook to Financial Literacy*
Bwatch - July 2015 - pNA [51-500]

Cline, Eric H. - *1177 B.C.: The Year Civilization Collapsed*
AHR - v120 - i2 - April 2015 - p693-694 [501+]
Class R - v65 - i2 - Oct 2015 - p611-612 [501+]

Cline, Ernest - *Armada (Read by Wheaton, Wil). Audiobook Review*
y BL - v112 - i4 - Oct 15 2015 - p60(1) [51-500]
LJ - v140 - i15 - Sept 15 2015 - p41(1) [51-500]
PW - v262 - i35 - August 31 2015 - p83(1) [51-500]
Armada
y BL - v111 - i21 - July 1 2015 - p45(2) [51-500]
KR - June 15 2015 - pNA [51-500]
PW - v262 - i25 - June 22 2015 - p125(1) [51-500]
y SLJ - v61 - i11 - Nov 2015 - p126(2) [501+]

Cline-Ransome, Lesa - *Freedom's School (Illus. by Ransome, James E.)*
c HB Guide - v26 - i2 - Fall 2015 - p29(1) [51-500]
c SLJ - v61 - i4 - April 2015 - p126(1) [51-500]
My Story, My Dance: Robert Battle's Journey to Alvin Ailey (Illus. by Ransome, James E.)
c BL - v112 - i5 - Nov 1 2015 - p49(1) [51-500]
My Story, My Dance: Robert Battle's Journey to Alvin Ailey
c KR - Sept 1 2015 - pNA [51-500]
Whale Trails: Before and Now (Illus. by Karas, G. Brian)
c CCB-B - v68 - i8 - April 2015 - p393(1) [51-500]
c HB Guide - v26 - i2 - Fall 2015 - p219(1) [51-500]

Cline-Ranson, Lesa - *My Story, My Dance: Robert Battle's Journey to Alvin Ailey (Illus. by Ransome, James E.)*
c SLJ - v61 - i10 - Oct 2015 - p125(2) [51-500]

Clines, Peter - *The Fold*
BL - v111 - i17 - May 1 2015 - p36(1) [51-500]
KR - April 1 2015 - pNA [51-500]
PW - v262 - i14 - April 6 2015 - p43(2) [51-500]

Clinton, Amanda B. - *Assessing Bilingual Children in Context: An Integrated Approach*
Lang Soc - v44 - i3 - June 2015 - p447-448 [501+]

Clinton, Chelsea - *It's Your World: Get Informed, Get Inspired, and Get Going!*
c BL - v112 - i1 - Sept 1 2015 - p94(1) [51-500]
It's Your World: Get Informed, Get Inspired and Get Going!
c VOYA - v38 - i5 - Dec 2015 - p77(1) [51-500]
c KR - Sept 1 2015 - pNA [51-500]
It's Your World: Get Informed, Get Inspired & Get Going! (Read by Clinton, Chelsea). Audiobook Review
c PW - v262 - i48 - Nov 30 2015 - p56(1) [51-500]
It's Your World: Get Informed, Get Inspired & Get Going!
c SLJ - v61 - i10 - Oct 2015 - p132(1) [51-500]

Clinton, Greg - *Willa Cather and Westward Expansion*
y BL - v111 - i9-10 - Jan 1 2015 - p85(1) [501+]

Clinton, Hillary Rodham - *Hard Choices (Read by Chalfant, Kathleen). Audiobook Review*
BL - v111 - i9-10 - Jan 1 2015 - p112(1) [501+]
Hard Choices
Lon R Bks - v37 - i3 - Feb 5 2015 - p8(3) [501+]
Reason - v47 - i4 - August-Sept 2015 - p58(8) [501+]

Clipston, Amy - *The Forgotten Recipe*
y BL - v112 - i6 - Nov 15 2015 - p17(1) [51-500]
PW - v262 - i41 - Oct 12 2015 - p54(1) [51-500]
Miles from Nowhere
y SLJ - v61 - i2 - Feb 2015 - p98(1) [51-500]

Cloonan, Becky - *Gotham Academy: Welcome to Gotham Academy*
y SLJ - v61 - i6 - June 2015 - p131(1) [51-500]

Clooney, Francis X. - *His Hiding Place Is Darkness: A Hindu-Catholic Theopoetics of Divine Absence*
JR - v95 - i2 - April 2015 - p266(2) [501+]

Close, Frank - *Half-Life: The Divided Life of Bruno Pontecorvo, Physicist or Spy*
Econ - v414 - i8924 - Feb 7 2015 - p80(US) [501+]
Nature - v518 - i7537 - Feb 5 2015 - p32(2) [51-500]
NYRB - v62 - i4 - March 5 2015 - p18(2) [501+]
Phys Today - v68 - i3 - March 2015 - p48-48 [501+]
TimHES - i2194 - March 12 2015 - p48-49 [501+]
Half Life: The Divided Life of Bruno Pontecorvo, Physicist or Spy
TLS - i5873 - Oct 23 2015 - p5(2) [501+]

Close, Jessie - *Resilience: Two Sisters and a Story of Mental Illness (Read by Close, Jessie). Audiobook Review*
LJ - v140 - i6 - April 1 2015 - p48(2) [51-500]
Resilience: Two Sisters and a Story of Mental Illness
LJ - v140 - i2 - Feb 1 2015 - p98(2) [51-500]
Mac - v128 - i2 - Jan 19 2015 - p57(1) [501+]
SEP - v287 - i1 - Jan-Feb 2015 - p20(1) [501+]

Clostermann, Pierre - *The Big Show: The Greatest Pilot's Story of World War II*
APH - v62 - i2 - Summer 2015 - p22(6) [501+]

Clough, Arthur Hugh - *Mari Magno, Dipsychus and Other Poems*
TLS - i5845 - April 10 2015 - p23(1) [501+]

Clough, Lisa - *Petal and Poppy and the Mystery Valentine (Illus. by Briant, Ed)*
c BL - v111 - i22 - August 1 2015 - p75(1) [51-500]
c KR - Oct 1 2015 - pNA [51-500]
Petal and Poppy and the Spooky Halloween! (Illus. by Briant, Ed)
c HB Guide - v26 - i1 - Spring 2015 - p52(1) [51-500]

Cloughley, Brian - *A History of the Pakistan Army: Wars and Insurrection*
TLS - i5832 - Jan 9 2015 - p19(1) [501+]

Cloutier, David - *The Vice of Luxury: Economic Excess in a Consumer Age*
AM - v213 - i14 - Nov 9 2015 - p42(2) [501+]

Clow, Barbara Hand - *Revelations of the Ruby Crystal*
PW - v262 - i28 - July 13 2015 - p53(1) [51-500]

Clulow, Adam - *The Company and the Shogun: The Dutch Encounter with Tokugawa Japan*
AHR - v120 - i2 - Feb 2015 - p218(1) [501+]
HNet - May 2015 - pNA [501+]

Clune, Michael W. - *Gamelife: A Memoir*
BL - v111 - i22 - August 1 2015 - p15(1) [51-500]
KR - June 1 2015 - pNA [501+]
LJ - v140 - i11 - June 15 2015 - p98(2) [51-500]
New R - v246 - i12 - Nov 2015 - p76(3) [51-500]
NS - v144 - i5290 - Nov 27 2015 - p46(3) [501+]
NYTBR - Oct 18 2015 - p22(L) [501+]

Clydesdale, Tim - *The Purposeful Graduate: Why Colleges Must Talk to Students About Vocation*
LJ - v140 - i5 - March 15 2015 - p117(1) [501+]

Clymer, Jeffory A. - *Family Money: Property, Race, and Literature in the Nineteenth Century*
    AHR - v120 - i1 - Feb 2015 - p249-251 [501+]
    AL - v87 - i1 - March 2015 - p192-194 [501+]
    Callaloo - v38 - i2 - Spring 2015 - p408-409 [501+]

Clynes, Tom - *The Boy Who Played with Fusion: Extreme Science, Extreme Parenting, and How to Make a Star*
    KR - May 1 2015 - pNA [501+]
    LJ - v140 - i8 - May 1 2015 - p97(1) [51-500]
    y BL - v111 - i19-20 - June 1 2015 - p14(1) [51-500]
    Spec - v328 - i9749 - July 4 2015 - p34(1) [501+]
    TLS - i5867 - Sept 11 2015 - p26(2) [501+]

Coakley, Lena - *Worlds of Ink and Shadow*
    y BL - v112 - i6 - Nov 15 2015 - p52(1) [51-500]
    y KR - Oct 1 2015 - pNA [51-500]
    y SLJ - v61 - i11 - Nov 2015 - p106(1) [51-500]

Coakley, Rachael - *When Your Child Hurts: Effective Strategies to Increase Comfort, Reduce Stress, and Break the Cycle of Chronic Pain*
    PW - v262 - i50 - Dec 7 2015 - p83(1) [51-500]

Coat, Janik - *Rhymoceros*
    c PW - v262 - i49 - Dec 2 2015 - p58(1) [51-500]
Rhymoceros (Illus. by Coat, Janik)
    c CCB-B - v68 - i9 - May 2015 - p442(2) [51-500]
    c KR - July 1 2015 - pNA [51-500]
    c PW - v262 - i6 - Feb 9 2015 - p66(2) [501+]

Coates, Jennifer - *Women, Men and Everyday Talk*
    Lang Soc - v44 - i3 - June 2015 - p448-449 [501+]

Coates, Peter - *A Story of Six Rivers: History, Culture and Ecology*
    PHR - v84 - i2 - May 2015 - p227(5) [501+]

Coates, Ta-Nehisi - *Between the World and Me (Read by Coates, Ta-Nehisi). Audiobook Review*
    PW - v262 - i30 - July 27 2015 - p61(1) [51-500]
Between the World and Me
    y BL - v111 - i22 - August 1 2015 - p7(1) [51-500]
    CC - v132 - i20 - Sept 30 2015 - p37(3) [501+]
    CSM - August 13 2015 - pNA [501+]
    Econ - v416 - i8945 - July 4 2015 - p69(US) [501+]
    Ent W - i1374 - July 31 2015 - p63(1) [501+]
    KR - July 1 2015 - pNA [501+]
    LJ - v140 - i13 - August 1 2015 - p106(1) [51-500]
Between the World and Me (Read by Coates, Ta-Nehisi). Audiobook Review
    LJ - v140 - i15 - Sept 15 2015 - p43(2) [51-500]
Between the World and Me
    Nat Post - v17 - i220 - July 25 2015 - pWP4(1) [501+]
    Nation - v301 - i23 - Dec 7 2015 - p14(8) [501+]
    New R - v246 - i9-10 - Sept-Oct 2015 - p78(4) [501+]
    New York - July 13 2015 - pNA [501+]
    NYT - July 10 2015 - pC1(L) [501+]
    NYTBR - Sept 6 2015 - p10(L) [501+]
    NYTBR - Dec 13 2015 - p12(L) [501+]
    Mac - v128 - i29-30 - July 27 2015 - p68(1) [501+]

Coats, Lucy - *Beast Keeper (Illus. by Bean, Brett)*
    c PW - v262 - i49 - Dec 2 2015 - p64(1) [51-500]
Beasts of Olympus: Beast Keeper (Illus. by Roberts, David)
    c Sch Lib - v63 - i2 - Summer 2015 - p101(1) [51-500]
Captain Beastlie's Pirate Party (Illus. by Mould, Chris)
    c HB Guide - v26 - i1 - Spring 2015 - p26(1) [51-500]

Cobb, Allan B. - *How the US Security Agencies Work*
    c HB Guide - v26 - i2 - Fall 2015 - p153(1) [51-500]

Cobb, Amy - *Dude, Where's My Saxophone? (Illus. by Cattish, Anna)*
    c HB Guide - v26 - i2 - Fall 2015 - p78(1) [51-500]
Notes from a Pro (Illus. by Cattish, Anna)
    c HB Guide - v26 - i2 - Fall 2015 - p78(1) [51-500]
Shredding with the Geeks (Illus. by Cattish, Anna)
    c HB Guide - v26 - i2 - Fall 2015 - p78(1) [51-500]

Cobb, Cathy - *The Chemistry of Alchemy: From Dragon's Blood to Donkey Dung: How Chemistry Was Forged*
    J Chem Ed - v92 - i6 - June 2015 - p969-970 [501+]

Cobb, Charles E. - *We Will Shoot Back: Armed Resistance in the Mississippi Freedom Movement*
    HNet - August 2015 - pNA [501+]

Cobb, Charles E., Jr. - *This Nonviolent Stuff'll Get You Killed: How Guns Made the Civil Rights Cumvement Possible*
    AHR - v120 - i2 - April 2015 - p672-673 [501+]
    JSH - v81 - i3 - August 2015 - p774(2) [501+]

Cobb, Laurel K. - *Mark & Empire: Feminist Reflections*
    CC - v132 - i21 - Oct 14 2015 - p34(2) [501+]
    Theol St - v76 - i3 - Sept 2015 - p634(1) [501+]

Cobb, Matthew - *Life's Greatest Secret*
    KR - May 1 2015 - pNA [51-500]
Life's Greatest Secret: The Race to Crack the Genetic Code
    LJ - v140 - i9 - May 15 2015 - p101(1) [51-500]
    PW - v262 - i19 - May 11 2015 - p47(1) [51-500]
    TimHES - i2209 - June 25 2015 - p50-51 [501+]
Life's Greatest Secret: The Story of the Race to Crack the Genetic Code
    Econ - v416 - i8950 - August 8 2015 - p71(US) [501+]

Cobb, Michael - *Single: Arguments for the Uncoupled*
    AL - v87 - i2 - June 2015 - p415-417 [501+]

Cobb, Thomas - *Darkness the Color of Snow*
    BL - v111 - i21 - July 1 2015 - p36(1) [51-500]
    KR - June 15 2015 - pNA [51-500]
    PW - v262 - i30 - July 27 2015 - p40(1) [51-500]

Cobbs Hoffman, Elizabeth - *American Umpire*
    HNet - July 2015 - pNA [501+]

Coben, Harlan - *Found (Read by Podehl, Nick). Audiobook Review*
    y BL - v111 - i17 - May 1 2015 - p60(1) [51-500]

Coben, Harlan - *Found*
    y HB Guide - v26 - i2 - Fall 2015 - p114(1) [51-500]
The Magical Fantastical Fridge (Illus. by Tinari, Leah)
    c KR - Dec 15 2015 - pNA [51-500]
    c PW - v262 - i44 - Nov 2 2015 - p82(2) [51-500]
Missing You
    RVBW - Feb 2015 - pNA [51-500]
The Stranger
    BL - v111 - i13 - March 1 2015 - p26(1) [51-500]
    NYTBR - May 31 2015 - p16(L) [501+]
    KR - Feb 15 2015 - pNA [51-500]

Cobham, Catherine - *The Iraqi Novel: Key Writers, Key Texts*
    IJMES - v47 - i1 - Feb 2015 - p188-189 [501+]

Coble, Colleen - *The Inn at Ocean's Edge*
    PW - v262 - i6 - Feb 9 2015 - p51(1) [51-500]
Mermaid Moon
    PW - v262 - i47 - Nov 23 2015 - p57(1) [51-500]

Cobley, Michael - *Ancestral Machines*
    PW - v262 - i46 - Nov 16 2015 - p59(1) [51-500]

Coburn, Noah - *Derailing Democracy in Afghanistan: Elections in an Unstable Political Landscape*
    MEQ - v22 - i1 - Wntr 2015 - pNA [501+]

Cocca-Leffler, Maryann - *A Homemade Together Christmas (Illus. by Cocca-Leffler, Maryann)*
    c KR - Sept 1 2015 - pNA [51-500]
    c PW - v262 - i37 - Sept 14 2015 - p69(1) [51-500]
    c SLJ - v61 - i10 - Oct 2015 - p62(2) [51-500]
Janine (Illus. by Cocca-Leffler, Maryann)
    c BL - v111 - i14 - March 15 2015 - p78(1) [51-500]
    c HB Guide - v26 - i2 - Fall 2015 - p29(1) [51-500]
    c KR - Jan 15 2015 - pNA [51-500]
    c PW - v262 - i3 - Jan 19 2015 - p81(1) [51-500]
Voici l'automne
    c Res Links - v20 - i3 - Feb 2015 - p43(2) [51-500]
Voici le printemps
    c Res Links - v20 - i5 - June 2015 - p37(1) [51-500]
Voici l'hiver
    c Res Links - v20 - i5 - June 2015 - p37(1) [51-500]

Cochran, Molly - *Seduction*
    c HB Guide - v26 - i1 - Spring 2015 - p103(1) [51-500]

Cochran, Peter - *Byron's Romantic Politics: The Problem of Metahistory*
    Clio - v44 - i2 - Spring 2015 - p217-237 [501+]

Cochrane, Charlie - *Lessons for Survivors*
    BL - v111 - i9-10 - Jan 1 2015 - p47(1) [51-500]

Cochrane, Susan - *Living Art in Papua New Guinea*
    Cont Pac - v27 - i2 - Fall 2015 - p586(2) [501+]

Cock-Starkey, Claire - *How to Skin a Lion: A Treasury of Outmoded Advice*
    Spec - v328 - i9742 - May 16 2015 - p39(1) [501+]

Cockburn, Andrew - *Kill Chain: The Rise of High-Tech Assassins*
    KR - Jan 1 2015 - pNA [501+]
    New Sci - v227 - i3038 - Sept 12 2015 - p41(1) [501+]
Kill Chain: The Rise of the High-Tech Assassins
    BL - v111 - i11 - Feb 1 2015 - p6(1) [51-500]
    Comw - v142 - i10 - June 1 2015 - p21(2) [501+]
    NYRB - v62 - i13 - August 13 2015 - p18(3)

Cockburn, Patrick - *The Jihadis Return: ISIS and the New Sunni Uprising*
    TLS - i5834 - Jan 23 2015 - p24(1) [501+]

The Rise of Islamic State: ISIS and the New Sunni Revolution
    Lon R Bks - v37 - i14 - July 16 2015 - p5(6) [501+]
    NS - v144 - i5267 - June 19 2015 - p42(3) [501+]
    NYTBR - April 5 2015 - p11(L) [501+]
    Spec - v327 - i9727 - Jan 31 2015 - p38(2) [501+]

Cockerill, Sara - *Eleanor of Castille: The Shadow Queen*
    TLS - i5832 - Jan 9 2015 - p20(1) [51-500]

Cockrill, Kate - *Untold Stories: Life, Love, and Reproduction*
    KR - August 1 2015 - pNA [501+]

Cocks, Catherine - *Tropical Whites: The Rise of the Tourist South in the Americas*
    AHR - v120 - i2 - April 2015 - p639-640 [501+]
    HAHR - v95 - i2 - May 2015 - p387-389 [501+]
    JSH - v81 - i2 - May 2015 - p492(2) [501+]
    RAH - v43 - i1 - March 2015 - p116-125 [501+]

Cocks, Heather - *The Royal We*
    Ent W - i1358 - April 10 2015 - p63(1) [501+]
    KR - Feb 15 2015 - pNA [51-500]

Coco, Nancy - *Oh Say Can You Fudge*
    KR - Feb 15 2015 - pNA [51-500]

Cocroft, Reginald B. - *Studying Vibrational Communication*
    QRB - v90 - i3 - Sept 2015 - p337(2) [501+]

Cody, Matthew - *The Peddler's Road*
    c PW - v262 - i34 - August 24 2015 - p79(2) [51-500]
    c KR - July 15 2015 - pNA [51-500]
    c SLJ - v61 - i10 - Oct 2015 - p88(1) [501+]
Villainous
    SLJ - v61 - i4 - April 2015 - p144(1) [51-500]
    c HB Guide - v26 - i2 - Fall 2015 - p78(1) [51-500]

Coe, Alexia - *Alice + Freda Forever: A Murder in Memphis (Illus. by Klann, Sally)*
    Wom R Bks - v32 - i3 - May-June 2015 - p29(3) [501+]

Coe, Amanda - *The Love She Left Behind*
    BL - v111 - i21 - July 1 2015 - p32(1) [51-500]
    Bwatch - Sept 2015 - pNA [51-500]
    NYT - July 30 2015 - pC6(L) [501+]
    NYTBR - August 2 2015 - p16(L) [501+]

Coe, David B. - *His Father's Eyes*
    PW - v262 - i27 - July 6 2015 - p50(2) [51-500]

Coe, Jonathan - *Expo 58 (Read by Rvan, Nannlenn). Audiobook Review*
    BL - v111 - i16 - April 15 2015 - p64(1) [51-500]
Number 11
    NS - v144 - i5290 - Nov 27 2015 - p53(1) [501+]
    Spec - v329 - i9768 - Nov 14 2015 - p53(2) [501+]

Coe, Victoria J. - *Fenway and Hattie*
    c KR - Nov 15 2015 - pNA [51-500]
    c PW - v262 - i48 - Nov 30 2015 - p60(1) [51-500]

Coel, Margaret - *The Man Who Fell from the Sky*
    BL - v112 - i2 - Sept 15 2015 - p32(1) [51-500]
    Bwatch - Oct 2015 - pNA [51-500]
    PW - v262 - i29 - July 20 2015 - p169(1) [51-500]
Night of the White Buffalo
    RVBW - May 2015 - pNA [51-500]
    RVBW - Sept 2015 - pNA [51-500]

Coen, Ross - *Fu-Go: The Curious History of Japan's Balloon Bomb Attack on America*
    JAH - v102 - i2 - Sept 2015 - p596-596 [501+]

Coen, Ross Allen - *Fu-go: The Curious History of Japan's Balloon Bomb Attack on America*
    HNet - Feb 2015 - pNA [501+]

Coes, Ben - *Independence Day*
    PW - v262 - i13 - March 30 2015 - p52(1) [51-500]
    BL - v111 - i17 - May 1 2015 - p38(1) [51-500]

Coetzee, J.M. - *The Expedition to the Baobab Tree*
    TLS - i5847 - April 24 2015 - p20(1) [501+]
The Good Story: Exchanges on Truth, Fiction and Psychotherapy
    KR - July 15 2015 - pNA [501+]
    LJ - v140 - i14 - Sept 1 2015 - p124(1) [51-500]
    NS - v144 - i5263 - May 22 2015 - p46(2) [501+]
    PW - v262 - i34 - August 24 2015 - p74(1) [501+]

Coey, Julia - *Animal Hospital: Rescuing Urban Wildlife*
    c BL - v112 - i7 - Dec 1 2015 - p48(1) [51-500]
    c KR - Oct 1 2015 - pNA [51-500]
    c SLJ - v61 - i12 - Dec 2015 - p135(1) [51-500]

Coffee, John C., Jr. - *Entrepreneurial Litigation: It's Rise, Fall, and Future*
    NYRB - v62 - i18 - Nov 19 2015 - p38(3) [501+]

Coffee, Tea and Chocolate: Fueling Modernity: Athenaeum Lecture and Workshop
    HNet - July 2015 - pNA [501+]

Coffey, Billy - *The Curse of Crow Hollow*
    KR - June 1 2015 - pNA [501+]

Coffey, John - *Exodus and Liberation: Deliverance Politics from John Calvin to Martin Luther King Jr.*
  AHR - v120 - i1 - Feb 2015 - p226-227 [501+]
Coffey, Laura T. - *My Old Dog: Rescued Pets with Remarkable Second Acts (Illus. by Fusaro, Lori)*
  PW - v262 - i31 - August 3 2015 - p47(1) [501+]
  My Old Dog: Rescued Pets with Remarkable Second Acts
  LJ - v140 - i14 - Sept 1 2015 - p128(1) [51-500]
Coffey, Patrick - *American Arsenal: A Century of Waging War*
  J Mil H - v79 - i1 - Jan 2015 - p225-226 [501+]
Coffey, Tom - *Bright Morning Star*
  PW - v262 - i38 - Sept 21 2015 - p49(1) [51-500]
Coffman, Christopher K. - *William T. Vollmann: A Critical Companion*
  Col Lit - v42 - i4 - Fall 2015 - p728(3) [501+]
Coffman, Elesha J. - *The Christian Century and the Rise of the Protestant Mainline*
  JR - Jan 2015 - p157(2) [501+]
Coffman, Elisha J. - *The Christian Century and the Rise of the Protestant Mainline*
  CH - v84 - i2 - June 2015 - p468(3) [501+]
Cogan, Neil H. - *Union and States' Rights: A History and Interpretation of Interposition, Nullification, and Secession 150 Years After Sumter*
  JSH - v81 - i1 - Feb 2015 - p209(3) [501+]
Cogburn, Brett - *Two-Dollar Pistol*
  BL - v111 - i12 - Feb 15 2015 - p42(1) [501+]
  Roundup M - v22 - i4 - April 2015 - p32(1) [501+]
  Roundup M - v22 - i6 - August 2015 - p27(1) [501+]
Cogburn, Emily Beck - *Louisiana Saves the Library*
  BL - v112 - i6 - Nov 15 2015 - p22(1) [51-500]
Coggin, Linda - *The Dog, Ray*
  c Magpies - v30 - i5 - Nov 2015 - p33(1) [501+]
Coggins, Bridget - *Power Politics and State Formation in the Twentieth Century: The Dynamics of Recognition*
  HNet - Jan 2015 - pNA [501+]
Coghlan, David - *The SAGE Encyclopedia of Action Research*
  R&USQ - v54 - i3 - Spring 2015 - p66(1) [501+]
Cogliano, Francis D. - *Emperor of Liberty: Thomas Jefferson's Foreign Policy*
  JSH - v81 - i3 - August 2015 - p702(2) [501+]
  W&M Q - v72 - i4 - Oct 2015 - p693-696 [501+]
Cohan, William D. - *The Price of Silence: The Duke Lacrosse Scandal, The Power Elite, and the Corruption of Our Great Universities*
  Wom R Bks - v32 - i2 - March-April 2015 - p27(3) [501+]
  The Price of Silence: The Duke Lacrosse Scandal, the Power of the Elite, and the Corruption of Our Great Universities
  NYTBR - May 17 2015 - p32(L) [501+]
Cohen, Adam - *Imbeciles: The Supreme Court, American Eugenics, and the Sterilization of Carrie Buck*
  KR - Nov 15 2015 - pNA [501+]
  LJ - v140 - i20 - Dec 1 2015 - p118(1) [51-500]
Cohen, Alice Eve - *The Year My Mother Came Back*
  PW - v262 - i4 - Jan 26 2015 - p167(1) [51-500]
Cohen, Andrew Wender - *Contraband: Smuggling and the Birth of the American Century*
  KR - May 15 2015 - pNA [501+]
  LJ - v140 - i12 - July 1 2015 - p94(1) [51-500]
  PW - v262 - i20 - May 18 2015 - p75(1) [51-500]
  Reason - v47 - i5 - Oct 2015 - p65(2) [501+]
Cohen, Brigid - *Stefan Wolpe and the Avant-Garde Diaspora*
  GSR - v38 - i3 - Oct 2015 - p692-694 [501+]
Cohen, Claire - *Male Rape Is a Feminist Issue: Feminism, Governmentality and Male Rape*
  CS - v44 - i5 - Sept 2015 - p742-743 [501+]
Cohen, Cole - *Head Case: My Brain and Other Wonders*
  KR - Feb 15 2015 - pNA [51-500]
  BL - v111 - i17 - May 1 2015 - p67(1) [51-500]
  SLJ - v61 - i12 - Dec 2015 - p133(1) [51-500]
Cohen-Cole, Jamie - *The Open Mind: Cold War Politics and the Sciences of Human Nature*
  AHR - v120 - i1 - Feb 2015 - p287-289 [501+]
  T&C - v56 - i3 - July 2015 - p775-777 [501+]
Cohen-Cole, Jamie Nace - *The Open Mind: Cold War Politics and the Sciences of Human Nature*
  HNet - June 2015 - pNA [501+]
Cohen, David S. - *Living in the Crosshairs: The Untold Stories of Anti-Abortion Terrorism*
  Ms - v25 - i2 - Spring 2015 - p42(1) [501+]
Cohen, Deborah Bodin - *Engineer Ari and the Passover Rush (Illus. by Kober, Shahar)*
  c HB Guide - v26 - i2 - Fall 2015 - p29(1) [51-500]
  c KR - Feb 1 2015 - pNA [51-500]
  SLJ - v61 - i4 - April 2015 - p126(1) [51-500]

Cohen-First, Rena - *The Authentic Sale: A Goddess's Guide to Business*
  PW - v262 - i31 - August 3 2015 - p51(1) [51-500]
Cohen, Gary B. - *Understanding Multiculturalism: The Habsburg Central European Experience*
  AHR - v120 - i4 - Oct 2015 - p1568-1569 [501+]
Cohen, Gerald A. - *Lectures on the History of Moral and Political Philosophy*
  S&S - v79 - i4 - Oct 2015 - p633-635 [501+]
Cohen, Harlan - *The Stranger (Read by Newbern, George). Audiobook Review*
  BL - v111 - i22 - August 1 2015 - p78(1) [51-500]
Cohen, Herman J. - *The Mind of the African Strongman: Conversations with Dictators, Statesmen, and Father Figures*
  KR - August 15 2015 - pNA [501+]
Cohen-Janca, Irene - *Janusz Korczak and the Orphans of the Warsaw Ghetto*
  c Res Links - v21 - i1 - Oct 2015 - p22(1) [51-500]
  Mister Doctor: Janusz Korczak and the Orphans of the Warsaw (Illus. by Quarello, Maurizio)
  y KR - May 1 2015 - pNA [51-500]
Cohen, Jeff - *Eva and Sadie and the Best Classroom Ever! (Illus. by Allen, Elanna)*
  c HB Guide - v26 - i2 - Fall 2015 - p30(1) [51-500]
  c KR - June 1 2015 - pNA [51-500]
  c SLJ - v61 - i8 - August 2015 - p58(2) [51-500]
Cohen, Jeffrey Jerome - *Inhuman Nature*
  Med R - August 2015 - pNA [501+]
Cohen, Jessica - *Falling out of Time*
  NYTBR - Jan 4 2015 - p24(L) [501+]
Cohen, Josh - *The Private Life: Why We Remain in the Dark*
  TLS - i5840 - March 6 2015 - p30(1) [501+]
Cohen, Joshua - *Book of Numbers*
  Econ - v416 - i8950 - August 8 2015 - p71(US) [501+]
  Esq - v163 - i6-7 - June-July 2015 - p26(2) [501+]
  KR - April 15 2015 - pNA [501+]
  LJ - v140 - i9 - May 15 2015 - p69(2) [51-500]
  Lon R Bks - v37 - i18 - Sept 24 2015 - p29(3) [501+]
  NS - v144 - i5276 - August 21 2015 - p46(2) [501+]
  NYRB - v62 - i15 - Oct 8 2015 - p10(2) [501+]
  NYT - June 8 2015 - pC1(L) [501+]
  NYTBR - July 5 2015 - p13(L) [501+]
  PW - v262 - i13 - March 30 2015 - p2(1) [51-500]
  TLS - i5859 - July 17 2015 - p19(2) [501+]
Cohen, Joshua G. - *A Field Guide to the Natural Communities of Michigan*
  RVBW - Jan 2015 - pNA [501+]
Cohen, Julia Phillips - *Becoming Ottomans: Sephardi Jews and Imperial Citizenship in the Modern Era*
  AHR - v120 - i4 - Oct 2015 - p1575-1576 [501+]
  HNet - Feb 2015 - pNA [501+]
  IJMES - v47 - i1 - Feb 2015 - p196-198 [501+]
  Sephardi Lives: A Documentary History, 1700-1950
  HNet - Jan 2015 - pNA [501+]
Cohen, Laurie - *A White Butterfly (Illus. by Ortelli, Barbara)*
  c PW - v262 - i15 - April 13 2015 - p78(2) [501+]
Cohen, Laurie (b. 1988-) - *A White Butterfly (Illus. by Ortelli, Barbara)*
  c BL - v111 - i19-20 - June 1 2015 - p110(1) [51-500]
  c KR - July 1 2015 - pNA [51-500]
  c SLJ - v61 - i7 - July 2015 - p54(1) [51-500]
Cohen, Laurie R. - *Smolensk under the Nazis: Everyday Life in Occupied Russia*
  CEH - v48 - i3 - Sept 2015 - p441-442 [501+]
  HNet - Feb 2015 - pNA [501+]
  JIH - v45 - i3 - Wntr 2015 - p435-436 [501+]
  Slav R - v74 - i2 - Summer 2015 - p409-410 [501+]
Cohen, Leah Hager - *No Book but the World*
  NYTBR - June 14 2015 - p24(L) [501+]
Cohen, Leonardo - *The Missionary Strategies of the Jesuits in Ethiopia, 1555-1632*
  CHR - v101 - i2 - Spring 2015 - p373(2) [501+]
Cohen, Marina - *The Inn Between*
  c KR - Jan 1 2016 - pNA [51-500]
Cohen, Matt - *Colonial Mediascapes: Sensory Worlds of the Early Americas*
  JAH - v102 - i1 - June 2015 - p225-226 [501+]
  HAHR - v95 - i1 - Feb 2015 - p185-187 [501+]
Cohen, Meredith - *Space in the Medieval West: Places, Territories, and Imagined Geographies*
  FS - v69 - i3 - July 2015 - p380-381 [501+]
  Med R - August 2015 - pNA [501+]
  Specu - v90 - i2 - April 2015 - p530-531 [501+]

Cohen, Miriam - *Jacob's Little Sister*
  c KR - Jan 1 2015 - pNA [51-500]
Cohen, Morton - *Lewis Carroll*
  Lon R Bks - v37 - i14 - July 16 2015 - p17(3) [501+]
  The Selected Letters of Lewis Carroll
  Lon R Bks - v37 - i14 - July 16 2015 - p17(3) [501+]
Cohen, Nancy J. - *Peril by Ponytail*
  KR - August 1 2015 - pNA [51-500]
  PW - v262 - i34 - August 24 2015 - p62(1) [51-500]
Cohen, Nancy L. - *Breakthrough: The Making of America's First Woman President*
  KR - Nov 15 2015 - pNA [501+]
  PW - v262 - i51 - Dec 14 2015 - p72(1) [51-500]
Cohen, Paul A. - *History and Popular Memory: The Power of Story in Moments of Crisis*
  AHR - v120 - i4 - Oct 2015 - p1442-1443 [501+]
Cohen, Richard I. - *Jewish Culture in Early Modern Europe: Essays in Honor of David B. Ruderman*
  Six Ct J - v46 - i3 - Fall 2015 - p805-807 [501+]
Cohen, Roger - *The Girl from Human Street: Ghosts of Memory in a Jewish Family*
  NYRB - v62 - i13 - August 13 2015 - p72(2) [501+]
  The Girl from Human's Street: Ghosts of Memory in a Jewish Family
  NYTBR - Feb 1 2015 - p15(L) [501+]
Cohen, Ronald D. - *Folk City: New York and the American Folk Music Revival*
  NYTBR - August 9 2015 - p24(L) [501+]
  Folk City: New York and the American Folk Musical Revival
  Mac - v128 - i31 - August 10 2015 - p56(2) [501+]
  The Pete Seeger Reader
  J Am St - v49 - i2 - May 2015 - p444-445 [501+]
  Roots of the Revival: American and British Folk Music in the 1950s
  Notes - v72 - i2 - Dec 2015 - p376(3) [501+]
Cohen, Samuel - *The Legacy of David Foster Wallace*
  MLR - v110 - i1 - Jan 2015 - p253-255 [501+]
Cohen, Santiago - *The Yiddish Fish*
  SLJ - v61 - i3 - March 2015 - p114(1) [51-500]
Cohen, Simona - *Transformations of Time and Temporality in Medieval and Renaissance Art*
  Ren Q - v68 - i2 - Summer 2015 - p629-631 [501+]
Cohen-Solal, Annie - *Mark Rothko*
  KR - Jan 1 2015 - pNA [501+]
  Mark Rothko: Toward the Light in the Chapel
  BL - v111 - i14 - March 15 2015 - p37(1) [51-500]
  NYTBR - June 28 2015 - p25(L) [501+]
  PW - v262 - i1 - Jan 5 2015 - p64(2) [51-500]
  Spec - v327 - i9732 - March 7 2015 - p38(2) [501+]
  TimHES - i2197 - April 2 2015 - p52-53 [501+]
  TLS - i5851 - May 22 2015 - p5(3) [501+]
  Mark Rothko: Towards the Light in the Chapel
  Lon R Bks - v37 - i10 - May 21 2015 - p35(2) [501+]
Cohen, Stuart Archer - *This Is How It Really Sounds*
  BL - v111 - i15 - April 1 2015 - p28(1) [51-500]
  KR - Feb 15 2015 - pNA [51-500]
  PW - v262 - i8 - Feb 23 2015 - p48(1) [51-500]
Cohen, Tamar - *War of the Wives*
  BL - v111 - i9-10 - Jan 1 2015 - p43(1) [51-500]
Cohen, William A. - *Applying the Wisdom of the World's Greatest Management Thinker*
  Per Psy - v68 - i3 - Autumn 2015 - p706(4) [501+]
Cohen, William S. - *Collision*
  BL - v111 - i17 - May 1 2015 - p26(1) [51-500]
  KR - April 1 2015 - pNA [51-500]
  PW - v262 - i15 - April 13 2015 - p58(1) [51-500]
Cohn, Diana - *Crane Boy (Illus. by Landowne, Youme)*
  c CH Bwatch - Nov 2015 - pNA [51-500]
  c KR - Sept 15 2015 - pNA [51-500]
  c SLJ - v61 - i11 - Nov 2015 - p80(1) [51-500]
Cohn, Edith - *Spirit's Key*
  y HB Guide - v26 - i1 - Spring 2015 - p73(1) [51-500]
Cohn, Edward - *High Title of a Communist: Postwar Party Discipline and the Values of the Soviet Regime*
  HNet - Sept 2015 - pNA(NA) [501+]
Cohn, Marjorie - *Drones and Targeted Killing: Legal, Moral and Geopolitical Issues*
  AM - v212 - i4 - Feb 9 2015 - p12(1) [501+]
  NS - v144 - i5267 - June 19 2015 - p48(1) [501+]
  TLS - i5854 - June 12 2015 - p28(1) [501+]

Cohn, Rachel - *Emergent*
   c HB Guide - v26 - i1 - Spring 2015 - p103(1) [51-500]
Cohn, Samuel, Jr. - *Late Medieval and Early Modern Ritual: Studies in Italian Urban Culture*
   AHR - v120 - i2 - April 2015 - p730-731 [501+]
   Specu - v90 - i3 - July 2015 - p789-791 [501+]
Cohn, Scott M. - *Daddy Said a Word I Never Heard*
   c KR - Sept 15 2015 - pNA [51-500]
Daddy Sat on a Duck (Illus. by Cohn, Scott M.)
   c BL - v111 - i18 - May 15 2015 - p57(1) [51-500]
Daddy Sat on a Duck
   c HB Guide - v26 - i2 - Fall 2015 - p30(1) [51-500]
   KR - April 1 2015 - pNA [51-500]
   SLJ - v61 - i3 - March 2015 - p114(1) [51-500]
Cohn, Scotti - *Animal Partners (Illus. by Bersani, Shennen)*
   c CH Bwatch - April 2015 - pNA [51-500]
   c HB Guide - v26 - i1 - Spring 2015 - p153(1) [51-500]
Coissard, Francoise - *Incendies*
   FS - v69 - i2 - April 2015 - p267(1) [501+]
Coker, Christopher - *Future War: The Re-Enchantment of War in the Twenty-First Century*
   Lon R Bks - v37 - i18 - Sept 24 2015 - p31(1) [501+]
The Improbable War: China, the United States, and the Logic of Great Power Conflict
   For Aff - v94 - i3 - May-June 2015 - pNA [501+]
Coker, Mark - *The Smashwords Style Guide*
   LJ - v140 - i11 - June 15 2015 - p46(1) [501+]
Colan, Cameron - *Please Listen Up Parents*
   SPBW - July 2015 - pNA [51-500]
Colandro, Lucille - *There Was an Old Lady Who Swallowed a Frog! (Illus. by Lee, Jared)*
   c SLJ - v61 - i7 - July 2015 - p60(1) [51-500]
Colantuono, Anthony - *Critical Perspectives on Roman Baroque Sculpture*
   Ren Q - v68 - i3 - Fall 2015 - p1012-1013 [501+]
Colaresi, Michael P. - *Democracy Declassified: Oversight and the Secrecy Dilemma in Liberal States*
   HNet - June 2015 - pNA [51-500]
Colasanti, Susane - *City Love*
   y HB Guide - v26 - i2 - Fall 2015 - p114(1) [51-500]
   y KR - Feb 15 2015 - pNA [51-500]
   y PW - v262 - i6 - Feb 9 2015 - p70(1) [51-500]
   y VOYA - v38 - i1 - April 2015 - p55(1) [51-500]
Colato Lainez, Rene - *Vamonos! Let's Go! (Illus. by Cepeda, Joe)*
   c KR - June 1 2015 - pNA [51-500]
Colby, Laura - *Road to Power: How GM's Mary Barra Shattered the Glass Ceiling*
   Har Bus R - v93 - i5 - May 2015 - p118(2) [501+]
Colby, Rebecca - *It's Raining Bats and Frogs (Illus. by Henry, Steven)*
   c PW - v262 - i30 - July 27 2015 - p63(1) [51-500]
It's Raining Bats & Frogs (Illus. by Henry, Steven)
   c KR - August 1 2015 - pNA [51-500]
   c SLJ - v61 - i9 - Sept 2015 - p105(2) [51-500]
Colclough, David - *The Oxford Edition of the Sermons of John Donne, vol. 3: Sermons Preached at the Court of Charles I*
   Six Ct J - v46 - i1 - Spring 2015 - p225-226 [501+]
Cole, Alyssa - *Mixed Signals. E-book Review*
   PW - v262 - i37 - Sept 14 2015 - p49(1) [51-500]
Signal Boost
   PW - v262 - i14 - April 6 2015 - p46(1) [51-500]
Cole, Andrew - *The Birth of Theory*
   ABR - v36 - i2 - Jan-Feb 2015 - p28(2) [501+]
   Col Lit - v42 - i1 - Wntr 2015 - p167(4) [501+]
   MP - v113 - i2 - Nov 2015 - pE76(3) [501+]
   RM - v69 - i2 - Dec 2015 - p377(3) [501+]
Cole, Bernard D. - *Asian Maritime Strategies: Navigating Troubled Waters*
   APJ - v29 - i4 - July-August 2015 - p90(2) [501+]
   Parameters - v45 - i1 - Spring 2015 - p150(3) [501+]
Cole, Frank L. - *The Afterlife Academy*
   c KR - July 15 2015 - pNA [51-500]
   c SLJ - v61 - i7 - July 2015 - p74(1) [51-500]
Cole, Henri - *77 Dream Songs*
   Atl - v315 - i2 - March 2015 - p51(3) [501+]
Nothing to Declare
   G&L Rev W - v22 - i4 - July-August 2015 - p39(2) [501+]
Cole, Henry - *Brambleheart: A Story about Finding Treasure and the Unexpected Magic of Friendship (Illus. by Cole, Henry)*
   c SLJ - v61 - i11 - Nov 2015 - p94(1) [51-500]
Brambleheart (Illus. by Cole, Henry)
   c BL - v112 - i7 - Dec 1 2015 - p59(1) [51-500]
Brambleheart
   c KR - Oct 15 2015 - pNA [51-500]
Spot, the Cat (Illus. by Cole, Henry)
   c PW - v262 - i51 - Dec 14 2015 - p84(2) [51-500]

Cole, Isabel Fargo - *The Sleep of the Righteous*
   PW - v262 - i35 - August 31 2015 - p58(2) [51-500]
Cole, Jonathan R. - *Toward a More Perfect University*
   KR - Nov 15 2015 - pNA [501+]
   LJ - v140 - i20 - Dec 1 2015 - p112(1) [51-500]
Who's Afraid of Academic Freedom?
   TimHES - i2194 - March 12 2015 - p52(1) [51-500]
Cole, Juan - *The New Arabs: How the Millennial Generation Is Changing the Middle East*
   NYTBR - Dec 13 2015 - p44(L) [501+]
Cole, Kathryn - *Fifteen Dollars and Thirty-five Cents: A Story about Choices (Illus. by Cole, Kathryn)*
   c KR - July 15 2015 - pNA [51-500]
Fifteen Dollars and Thirty-five Cents: A Story about Choices (Illus. by Leng, Qin)
   c CH Bwatch - Nov 2015 - pNA [51-500]
   c Res Links - v21 - i1 - Oct 2015 - p4(1) [51-500]
Never Give Up: A Story about Self-Esteem (Illus. by Leng, Qin)
   c HB Guide - v26 - i2 - Fall 2015 - p30(1) [51-500]
   c PW - v262 - i8 - Feb 23 2015 - p76(1) [51-500]
   c Res Links - v21 - i1 - Oct 2015 - p4(1) [501+]
Reptile Flu: A Story about Communication (Illus. by Leng, Qin)
   c Res Links - v21 - i1 - Oct 2015 - p4(1) [51-500]
Cole, Kresley - *Dead of Winter: The Arcana Chronicles*
   y VOYA - v38 - i1 - April 2015 - p76(1) [51-500]
Cole, Laurence - *Military Culture and Popular Patriotism in Late Imperial Austria*
   J Mil H - v79 - i1 - Jan 2015 - p209-210 [501+]
Cole, Lincoln - *Graveyard of Empires*
   PW - v262 - i45 - Nov 9 2015 - p43(1) [51-500]
Cole, Michael W. - *Leonardo, Michelangelo, and the Art of the Figure*
   Apo - v181 - i630 - April 2015 - p108(2) [501+]
   Ren Q - v68 - i3 - Fall 2015 - p1005-1006 [501+]
Cole, Peter - *The Libyan Revolution and Its Aftermath*
   TLS - i5849 - May 8 2015 - p5(1) [501+]
   NYRB - v62 - i3 - Feb 19 2015 - p38(3) [501+]
Cole, Rachel Elizabeth - *The Rabbit Ate My Homework (Illus. by Dionne, Deanna)*
   y CH Bwatch - Feb 2015 - pNA [51-500]
Cole, Regina - *Sex Becomes Her*
   PW - v262 - i17 - April 27 2015 - p57(2) [51-500]
Cole, Steve - *Shoot to Kill*
   y Sch Lib - v63 - i1 - Spring 2015 - p51(1) [51-500]
Stop Those Monsters
   Sch Lib - v63 - i3 - Autumn 2015 - p164(1) [51-500]
Cole, Teju - *Every Day Is for the Thief*
   NYTBR - April 5 2015 - p28(L) [501+]
Cole, Timothy W. - *XML for Catalogers and Metadata Librarians*
   LQ - v85 - i3 - July 2015 - p331(3) [501+]
Cole, Tom Clohosy - *Wall (Illus. by Cole, Tom Clohosy)*
   c CH Bwatch - Jan 2015 - pNA [51-500]
   c HB Guide - v26 - i1 - Spring 2015 - p26(1) [51-500]
Cole, Trevor - *Hope Makes Love*
   Nat Post - v18 - i4 - Oct 31 2015 - pWP5(1) [501+]
Cole, Welcome - *The Burden of Memory*
   KR - Feb 15 2015 - pNA [501+]
Coleborne, Catharine - *Exhibiting Madness in Museums: Remembering Psychiatry through Collection and Display*
   HNet - Jan 2015 - pNA [501+]
Colella, Joseph - *The Appetite Solution: Lose Weight Effortlessly and Never be Hungry Again*
   PW - v262 - i11 - March 16 2015 - p79(1) [51-500]
Coleman, Arica L. - *That the Blood Stay Pure: African Americans, Native Americans, and the Predicament of Race and Identity in Virginia*
   AHR - v120 - i3 - June 2015 - p1010-1011 [501+]
   HNet - Jan 2015 - pNA [501+]
   JIH - v46 - i1 - Summer 2015 - p126-127 [501+]
Coleman, C. Craig - *The Dragon Ring*
   RVBW - Feb 2015 - pNA [50-500]
Coleman, Charly - *The Virtues of Abandon: An Anti-Individualist History of the French Enlightenment*
   AHR - v120 - i2 - April 2015 - p723-724 [501+]
Coleman, David - *The Presidential Recordings*
   KR - Dec 1 2015 - pNA [501+]
Region, Religion and English Renaissance Literature
   Sev Cent N - v73 - i3-4 - Fall-Winter 2015 - p124(4) [501+]
Coleman, Derrick, Jr. - *No Excuses: Growing Up Deaf and Achieving My Super Bowl Dreams*
   PW - v262 - i25 - June 22 2015 - p134(1) [51-500]

Coleman, Gabriella - *Hacker, Hoaxer, Whistleblower, Spy: The Many Faces of Anonymous*
   TimHES - i2185 - Jan 8 2015 - p53-53 [501+]
   TLS - i5838 - Feb 20 2015 - p3(3) [501+]
Coleman, Heather J. - *Orthodox Christianity in Imperial Russia: A Source Book on Lived Religion*
   RM - v68 - i4 - June 2015 - p842(3) [501+]
Coleman, Jeffrey Lamar - *Words of Protest, Words of Freedom: Poetry of the American Civil Rights Movement and Era*
   JSH - v81 - i2 - May 2015 - p540(1) [501+]
Coleman, Kathleen - *Le jardin dans l'Antiquite: Introduction et huit exposes suivis de discussions*
   Class R - v65 - i2 - Oct 2015 - p578-580 [501+]
Coleman, Reed Farrel - *The Boardwalk*
   y VOYA - v38 - i1 - April 2015 - p67(2) [51-500]
The Hollow Girl
   RVBW - Feb 2015 - pNA [51-500]
Robert B. Parker's Blind Spot
   RVBW - Sept 2015 - pNA [51-500]
Robert B. Parker's The Devil Wins
   BL - v111 - i22 - August 1 2015 - p36(2) [51-500]
   KR - July 1 2015 - pNA [51-500]
   PW - v262 - i28 - July 13 2015 - p44(1) [51-500]
Where It Hurts
   BL - v112 - i4 - Oct 15 2015 - p24(1) [51-500]
   KR - Oct 1 2015 - pNA [51-500]
   PW - v262 - i44 - Nov 2 2015 - p60(1) [51-500]
Coleman, Rowan - *The Day We Met*
   KR - Jan 15 2015 - pNA [51-500]
Coleman, Sue - *Breaking Up Is Hard to Do*
   SPBW - July 2015 - pNA [51-500]
Coleman, Terry - *The Old Vic: The Story of a Great Theatre from Kean to Olivier to Spacey*
   TLS - i5849 - May 8 2015 - p26(1) [501+]
Coleman, Wim - *Away She Goes Riding into Women's History (Illus. by Belloni, Valentina)*
   c CH Bwatch - Jan 2015 - pNA [51-500]
Follow the Drinking Gourd: Come Along the Underground Railroad (Illus. by Martin, Courtney A.)
   c HB Guide - v26 - i2 - Fall 2015 - p201(2) [51-500]
Runaway Train: Saved by Belle of the Mines and Mountains (Illus. by Renaud, Joanne)
   SLJ - v61 - i3 - March 2015 - p169(1) [501+]
Sequoyah and His Talking Leaves: A Play about the Cherokee Syllabary (Illus. by Feeney, Siri Weber)
   c HB Guide - v26 - i2 - Fall 2015 - p201(2) [51-500]
Coleridge, Samuel Taylor - *Biographia Literaria: Or, Biographical Sketches of My Literary Life and Opinions*
   Bks & Cult - v21 - i3 - May-June 2015 - p31(3) [501+]
   TLS - i5851 - May 22 2015 - p11(2) [501+]
Coles, Anthony - *John Heartfield: Ein politisches Leben*
   HNet - August 2015 - pNA [501+]
Zerrissene Loyalitaten. Politische und kulturelle Orientierungen im Ersten Weltkrieg: Bukowina, Galizien, Bessarabien
   HNet - August 2015 - pNA [501+]
Coles, Don - *A Serious Call*
   Can Lit - i224 - Spring 2015 - p115 [501+]
Coles, Tom - *Spirit Talker: The Legend of Nakosis*
   PW - v262 - i32 - August 10 2015 - p35(1) [51-500]
Colfer, Chris - *Beyond the Kingdoms (Read by Colfer, Chris). Audiobook Review*
   c SLJ - v61 - i10 - Oct 2015 - p51(1) [51-500]
The Curvy Tree (Illus. by Dorman, Brandon)
   c KR - Sept 15 2015 - pNA [51-500]
Colfer, Eoin - *Artemis Fowl: The Opal Deception: The Graphic Novel (Illus. by Rigano, Giovanni)*
   y HB Guide - v26 - i1 - Spring 2015 - p73(2) [51-500]
The Fish in the Bathtub: Little Gems (Illus. by Bailey, Peter)
   c Sch Lib - v63 - i1 - Spring 2015 - p34(2) [51-500]
Imaginary Fred (Illus. by Jeffers, Oliver)
   c BL - v111 - i22 - August 1 2015 - p72(1) [51-500]
   c KR - August 1 2015 - pNA [51-500]
   c NYTBR - Nov 8 2015 - p34(L) [501+]
   c PW - v262 - i27 - July 6 2015 - p72(1) [51-500]
   c PW - v262 - i49 - Dec 2 2015 - p14(2) [51-500]
   c SLJ - v61 - i9 - Sept 2015 - p118(1) [51-500]
Colgan, Jenny - *Little Beach Street Bakery*
   BL - v111 - i14 - March 15 2015 - p53(1) [51-500]
Colgrove, James - *Epidemic City: The Politics of Public Health in New York*
   SF - v93 - i3 - March 2015 - pNA [501+]
Colhoun, Jack - *Gangsterismo: The United States, Cuba, and the Mafia: 1933 to 1966*
   JAH - v102 - i1 - June 2015 - p295-296 [501+]

Colich, Abby - *Drawing Ocean Animals (Illus. by Calle, Juan)*
   c HB Guide - v26 - i2 - Fall 2015 - p192(1) [51-500]
Drawing Wild Animals (Illus. by Juta, Jason)
   c HB Guide - v26 - i2 - Fall 2015 - p192(1) [51-500]

Colins, Luke - *Mae Jemison*
   c HB Guide - v26 - i1 - Spring 2015 - p192(1) [51-500]

Colish, Marcia L. - *Faith, Fiction, and Force in Medieval Baptism Debates*
   CHR - v101 - i4 - Autumn 2015 - p904(2) [501+]

Coll, Susan - *The Stager*
   NYTBR - Sept 13 2015 - p32(L) [501+]

Collar, Anna - *Religious Networks in the Roman Empire: The Spread of New Ideas*
   Class R - v65 - i1 - April 2015 - p224-226 [501+]

Collard, Sneed B., III - *Fire Birds: Valuing Natural Wildfires and Burned Forests (Illus. by Collard, Braden G.)*
   c BL - v111 - i12 - Feb 15 2015 - p75(1) [51-500]
   c CCB-B - v68 - i8 - April 2015 - p393(2) [51-500]
   c CH Bwatch - Jan 2015 - pNA [51-500]
   c CH Bwatch - Nov 2015 - pNA [51-500]
Snakes, Alligators, and Broken Hearts: Journeys of a Biologist's Son
   c BL - v112 - i6 - Nov 15 2015 - p39(1) [51-500]

Collected Stories of William Faulkner
   TLS - i5854 - June 12 2015 - p11(1) [501+]

Collection Canada 2014
   Phil Lit R - v64 - i2 - Spring 2015 - p128(2) [501+]

Collen, Alanna - *10 Percent Human: How Your Body's Microbes Hold the Key to Health and Happiness*
   KR - April 1 2015 - pNA [51-500]
   LJ - v140 - i7 - April 15 2015 - p109(1) [51-500]

Collen, Ben - *Biodiversity Monitoring and Conservation: Bridging the Gap between Global Commitment and Local Action*
   QRB - v90 - i3 - Sept 2015 - p330(2) [501+]

Collet, Geraldine - *Ah! (Illus. by Spagnol, Estelle Billon)*
   c HB Guide - v26 - i1 - Fall 2015 - p8(1) [51-500]
   c KR - March 1 2015 - pNA [51-500]

Collett, Alice - *Women in Early Indian Buddhism: Comparative Textual Studies*
   JAS - v74 - i2 - May 2015 - p504-505 [501+]

Collette, Carolyn P. - *Rethinking Chaucer's Legend of Good Women*
   Med R - Jan 2015 - pNA [501+]
   TLS - i5833 - Jan 16 2015 - p25(1) [501+]

Colletti, Maria - *Terrariums: Gardens under Glass: Designing, Creating, and Planting Modern Indoor Gardens*
   PW - v262 - i38 - Sept 21 2015 - p70(1) [51-500]

Colley, Ann C. - *Wild Animal Skins in Victorian Britain: Zoos, Collections, Portraits, and Maps*
   TLS - i5875 - Nov 6 2015 - p31(1) [501+]

Collier, Grant - *Collier's Guide to Night Photography in the Great Outdoors*
   SPBW - June 2015 - pNA [501+]
Moab, Utah by Day & Night (Illus. by Collier, Grant)
   SPBW - Nov 2015 - pNA [51-500]

Collier, Peter - *Choosing Courage: Inspiring Stories of What It Means to Be a Hero*
   y BL - v111 - i16 - April 15 2015 - p42(1) [51-500]
   c PW - v262 - i10 - March 9 2015 - p75(1) [51-500]
   y VOYA - v38 - i4 - Oct 2015 - p82(1) [51-500]

Collin, Ellard - *Places of the Heart: The Psychogeography of Everyday Life*
   Nature - v525 - i7568 - Sept 10 2015 - p185(1) [51-500]

Collin, Matthew - *Pop Grenade: From Public Enemy to Pussy Riot, Despatches from Musical Frontlines*
   NS - v144 - i5281 - Sept 25 2015 - p75(1) [51-500]

Collinge, Alan Michael - *The Student Loan Scam: The Most Oppressive Debt in U.S. History--and How We Can Fight Back*
   BL - v111 - i21 - July 1 2015 - p22(2) [501+]

Collingridge, Richard - *Lionheart (Illus. by Collingridge, Richard)*
   c KR - Nov 15 2015 - pNA [51-500]
   c SLJ - v61 - i12 - Dec 2015 - p87(1) [51-500]

Collings, Austin - *The Myth of Brilliant Summers*
   NS - v144 - i5249 - Feb 13 2015 - p55(1) [51-500]

Collins, Andrew - *Gobekli Tepe: Genesis of the Gods: The Temple of the Watchers and the Discovery of Eden*
   Am Ant - v80 - i3 - July 2015 - p620(2) [501+]

Collins, Billy - *Aimless Love*
   AM - v212 - i5 - Feb 16 2015 - p25(3) [501+]
Voyage (Illus. by Romagna, Karen)
   BL - v111 - i14 - March 15 2015 - p61(1) [51-500]

Collins, Clifton, Jr. - *Prison Ramen: Recipes and Stories From Behind Bars*
   NYTBR - Nov 1 2015 - p30(L) [501+]

Collins, Dennis - *Alessandro Grandi: Il primo libro de motetti a due, tre, quattro, cinque, and otto voci, con una Messa a Quattro*
   Notes - v71 - i4 - June 2015 - p743(3) [501+]

Collins, Gary H. - *The Last Election*
   SPBW - Jan 2015 - pNA [51-500]

Collins, Gregor - *The Accidental Caregiver*
   PW - v262 - i6 - Feb 9 2015 - p61(1) [51-500]

Collins, Harry - *Are We All Scientific Experts Now?*
   Phys Today - v68 - i5 - May 2015 - p52-53 [501+]
Gravity's Ghost and Big Dog: Scientific Discovery and Social Analysis in the Twenty-Firt Century
   Isis - v106 - i1 - March 2015 - p218(2) [501+]

Collins, Jackie - *The Santangelos*
   BL - v111 - i18 - May 15 2015 - p25(1) [51-500]
   KR - May 1 2015 - pNA [501+]

Collins, John N. - *Diakonia Studies: Critical Issues in Ministry*
   Theol St - v76 - i2 - June 2015 - p401(1) [501+]

Collins, Judith - *Eduardo Paolozzi*
   TLS - i5860 - July 24 2015 - p26(1) [501+]

Collins, Katana - *Wicked Release*
   LJ - v140 - i16 - Oct 1 2015 - p62(2) [51-500]

Collins, L.K. - *Every Soul*
   PW - v262 - i44 - Nov 2 2015 - p71(2) [51-500]

Collins, Manda - *Good Earl Gone Bad*
   PW - v262 - i33 - August 17 2015 - p57(1) [51-500]
A Good Rake Is Hard to Find
   BL - v111 - i13 - March 1 2015 - p29(1) [51-500]
   PW - v262 - i3 - Jan 19 2015 - p68(1) [51-500]

Collins, Max Allan - *Quarry's Choice*
   RVBW - Sept 2015 - pNA [51-500]

Collins, Michael J. - *Reading What's There: Essays on Shakespeare in Honor of Stephen Booth*
   Six Ct J - v46 - i3 - Fall 2015 - p793-794 [501+]

Collins, Michael Patrick - *Psalmandala*
   KR - Feb 1 2015 - pNA [501+]
   SPBW - Feb 2015 - pNA [51-500]

Collins, Myfanwy - *The Book of Laney*
   y SLJ - v61 - i6 - June 2015 - p122(1) [51-500]

Collins, Patricia Hill - *On Intellectual Activism*
   CS - v44 - i1 - Jan 2015 - p44-45 [501+]

Collins, Paul - *The Burning Sea*
   y Magpies - v30 - i1 - March 2015 - p34(1) [501+]
Rich and Rare: A Collection of Australian Stories, Poetry and Artwork
   y Magpies - v30 - i5 - Nov 2015 - p33(2) [501+]

Collins, Renee - *Until We Meet Again*
   y BL - v112 - i2 - Sept 15 2015 - p75(1) [51-500]
   y SLJ - v61 - i9 - Sept 2015 - p163(2) [51-500]
   y KR - August 1 2015 - pNA [51-500]

Collins, Ross - *The Elephantom (Illus. by Collins, Ross)*
   c CH Bwatch - June 2015 - pNA [501+]
   c HB Guide - v26 - i2 - Fall 2015 - p30(1) [51-500]
   c KR - Feb 15 2015 - pNA [51-500]

Collins, Ross F. - *Children, War and Propaganda*
   AHR - v120 - i2 - April 2015 - p646-647 [501+]

Collins, Samuel W. - *The Carolingian Debate over Sacred Space*
   Specu - v90 - i4 - Oct 2015 - p1102-1104 [501+]

Collins, Steven - *Self and Society: Essays on Pali Literature and Social Theory, 1988-2010*
   JR - v95 - i4 - Oct 2015 - p545(3) [501+]

Collins, Terry - *Scooby-Doo! Unmasking Monsters Series (Illus. by Neely, Scott)*
   c HB Guide - v26 - i2 - Fall 2015 - p148(1) [51-500]

Collins, Tim - *Fangs a Lot: Final Notes from a Totally Lame Vampire (Illus. by Pinder, Andrew)*
   c HB Guide - v26 - i1 - Spring 2015 - p103(1) [51-500]

Collins, Timothy - *Dick Dowling: Galway's Hero of Confederate Texas*
   JSH - v81 - i1 - Feb 2015 - p205(2) [501+]

Collins, Tony - *The Oval World: A Global History of Rugby*
   TLS - i5869 - Sept 25 2015 - p30(1) [501+]

Collins, Wilkie - *The Moonstone (Read by Pickup, Ronald). Audiobook Review*
   BL - v111 - i14 - March 15 2015 - p23(2) [51-500]

Collinson, Clare - *British Mammals*
   c Sch Lib - v63 - i3 - Autumn 2015 - p172(2) [51-500]

Collis, Kathryn - *Ivan's Legacy*
   KR - July 15 2015 - pNA [501+]

Collison, Elizabeth - *Some Other Town*
   BL - v111 - i12 - Feb 15 2015 - p33(1) [51-500]

Collison, Linda - *Looking for Redfeather*
   y PW - v262 - i23 - June 8 2015 - p62(1) [51-500]
Water Ghosts
   y KR - July 15 2015 - pNA [51-500]

Collodi, Carlo - *The Patua Pinocchio (Illus. by Chitrakar, Swarna)*
   y HB - v91 - i4 - July-August 2015 - p130(1) [51-500]
   c KR - Feb 15 2015 - pNA [51-500]
   y Sch Lib - v63 - i1 - Spring 2015 - p36(1) [51-500]
   y SLJ - v61 - i6 - June 2015 - p104(1) [51-500]

Collom, Ed - *Equal Time, Equal Value: Community Currencies and Time Banking in the US*
   CS - v44 - i2 - March 2015 - p184-186 [501+]

Collum, Karen - *Small and Big (Illus. by Wood, Ben)*
   c Magpies - v30 - i5 - Nov 2015 - p27(1) [501+]

Collyer, Michael - *Emigration Nations: Policies and Ideologies of Emigrant Engagement*
   ERS - v38 - i8 - August 2015 - p1468(4) [501+]

Colombo, Enzo - *Children of Immigrants in a Globalized World: A Generational Experience*
   CS - v44 - i2 - March 2015 - p186-187 [501+]

Colon, Raul - *Draw! (Illus. by Colon, Raul)*
   c HB Guide - v26 - i1 - Spring 2015 - p26(1) [51-500]

Colon, Susan E. - *Victorian Parables*
   VS - v57 - i2 - Wntr 2015 - p325(4) [501+]

Colonna, Jill - *Teatime in Paris! A Walk through Easy French Patisserie Recipes*
   LJ - v140 - i12 - July 1 2015 - p105(1) [51-500]

Colonna, Sarah - *Has Anyone Seen My Pants?*
   PW - v262 - i1 - Jan 5 2015 - p64(1) [51-500]

Colorado, Carlos D. - *Aspiring to Fullness in a Secular Age: Essays on Religion and Theology in the Work of Charles Taylor*
   Theol St - v76 - i2 - June 2015 - p391(2) [501+]

Colossal, Eric - *Rutabaga: The Adventure Chef (Illus. by Colossal, Eric)*
   BL - v111 - i9-10 - Jan 1 2015 - p63(1) [51-500]
   c CCB-B - v68 - i9 - May 2015 - p443(1) [51-500]
   c HB Guide - v26 - i2 - Fall 2015 - p78(1) [51-500]
   c PW - v262 - i3 - Jan 19 2015 - p87(1) [51-500]

Colpitts, George - *North America's Indian Trade in European Commerce and Imagination, 1580-1850*
   JSH - v81 - i2 - May 2015 - p422(2) [501+]
Pemmican Empire: Food, Trade, and the Last Bison Hunts in the North American Plains, 1780-1882
   WHQ - v46 - i4 - Winter 2015 - p505-506 [501+]

Colson, Bruno - *Napoleon on War*
   KR - April 15 2015 - pNA [501+]

Colson, Mary - *Consumer Nation Series, 4 vols.*
   y Res Links - v20 - i4 - April 2015 - p34(1) [51-500]

Colson, Rob - *Bone Collection: Dinosaurs and Other Prehistoric Animals*
   c Sch Lib - v63 - i3 - Autumn 2015 - p173(1) [51-500]

Colt, Margaretta Barton - *Martial Bliss: The Story of The Military Bookman*
   NYT - July 31 2015 - pC19(L) [501+]
   KR - Sept 15 2015 - pNA [501+]
   PW - v262 - i39 - Sept 28 2015 - p84(1) [51-500]

Colt, Paul - *A Question of Bounty: The Shadow of Doubt*
   Roundup M - v22 - i6 - August 2015 - p27(1) [501+]
Wanted Sam Bass
   Roundup M - v22 - i4 - April 2015 - p32(1) [501+]
   Roundup M - v22 - i6 - August 2015 - p28(1) [501+]

Colten, Craig E. - *North American Odyssey: Historical Geographies for the Twenty-First Century*
   JSH - v81 - i4 - Nov 2015 - p931(2) [501+]
   GR - v105 - i2 - April 2015 - p249(3) [501+]

Columbus, Chris - *House of Secrets: Battle of the Beasts (Illus. by Call, Greg)*
   y CH Bwatch - Feb 2015 - pNA [51-500]
   y HB Guide - v26 - i1 - Spring 2015 - p74(1) [51-500]

Colvin, Geoff - *Managing the Cycle of Acting-Out Behavior in the Classroom*
   Bwatch - April 2015 - pNA [501+]

Colvin, Sarah - *The Routledge Handbook of German Politics and Culture*
   TLS - i5857 - July 3 2015 - p12(2) [501+]

Colwell, Guy - *Inner City Romance*
   PW - v262 - i7 - Feb 16 2015 - p166(1) [51-500]

Colwill, Simone - *What Does Super Jonny Do When Mum Gets Sick? (Illus. by Ting, Jasmine)*
   c Magpies - v30 - i1 - March 2015 - pS5(1) [501+]

Comber, Philippa - *Ariadne's Thread: In Memory of W.G. Sebald*
   TLS - i5838 - Feb 20 2015 - p27(1) [501+]

Combi, Chloe - *Generation Z: Their Voices, Their Lives*
TES - i5146 - May 15 2015 - p17(1) [501+]

Combs, Barbara Harris - *From Selma to Montgomery: The Long March to Freedom*
JSH - v81 - i2 - May 2015 - p542(1) [51-500]

Combs, Sarah - *Breakfast Served Anytime*
y Teach Lib - v42 - i3 - Feb 2015 - p28(4) [501+]

Comeau, Marie-France - *Le Pit a Papa (Illus. by Trudel, Jean-Luc)*
c Res Links - v21 - i1 - Oct 2015 - p47(1) [501+]

Comeaux, Jennifer - *Crossing the Ice*
PW - v262 - i10 - March 9 2015 - p59(1) [51-500]

Comentale, Edward P. - *The Year's Work at the Zombie Research Center*
TLS - i5840 - March 6 2015 - p30(1) [501+]

Comer, Greg - *Winner Take None*
KR - Sept 15 2015 - pNA [501+]

Comer, John Mark - *Garden City: Work, Rest, and the Art of Being Human*
PW - v262 - i32 - August 10 2015 - p56(2) [51-500]

Comes, Michael F. - *Adventures in Muniland: A Guide to Municipal Bond Investing in the Post-Crisis Era*
Barron's - v95 - i49 - Dec 7 2015 - p48(1) [501+]

Comis, Anna - *Casada: A History of an Italian Village and Its People*
RVBW - Nov 2015 - pNA [51-500]

Comisford, Sue - *Ranger Creek Guest Ranch*
Roundup M - v22 - i5 - June 2015 - p35(1) [501+]
Roundup M - v22 - i6 - August 2015 - p35(1) [501+]

Community Helpers Series
c BL - v111 - i15 - April 1 2015 - p58(1) [501+]

Comolli, Virginia - *Boko Haram: Nigeria's Islamist Insurgency*
Bks & Cult - v21 - i4 - July-August 2015 - p31(1) [501+]

Compton-Engle, Gwendolyn - *Costume in the Comedies of Aristophanes*
TLS - i5877 - Nov 20 2015 - p31(1) [501+]

Compton, John W. - *The Evangelical Origins of the Living Constitution*
AHR - v120 - i1 - Feb 2015 - p279-280 [501+]
Bks & Cult - v21 - i5 - Sept-Oct 2015 - p15(1) [501+]
JAH - v102 - i2 - Sept 2015 - p574-575 [501+]
JIH - v45 - i4 - Spring 2015 - p593-594 [501+]

Comstock, Eric - *Charlie Piechart and the Case of the Missing Pizza Slice (Illus. by Comstock, Eric)*
c PW - v262 - i23 - June 8 2015 - p58(1) [501+]
c SLJ - v61 - i6 - June 2015 - p78(1) [51-500]

Comyns, Barbara - *Our Spoons Came from Woolworths*
KR - August 15 2015 - pNA [501+]

Conant, Sean - *The Gettysburg Address: Perspectives on Lincoln's Greatest Speech*
PW - v262 - i13 - March 30 2015 - p68(1) [51-500]
y BL - v111 - i18 - May 15 2015 - p13(1) [51-500]

Conard, Jonathan - *Kansas Trail Guide: The Best Hiking, Biking, and Riding in the Sunflower State*
RVBW - Oct 2015 - pNA [501+]

The Concept of the World Economy: Intellectual Histories
HNet - Jan 2015 - pNA [501+]

Condie, Ally - *Atlantia*
y CCB-B - v68 - i5 - Jan 2015 - p250(2) [51-500]
c HB Guide - v26 - i1 - Spring 2015 - p104(1) [51-500]
Summerlost
c KR - Dec 15 2015 - pNA [51-500]
c PW - v262 - i50 - Dec 7 2015 - p86(2) [51-500]
c SLJ - v61 - i12 - Dec 2015 - p100(1) [51-500]

Condren, Conal - *Hobbes, the Scriblerians and the History of Philosophy*
HER - v130 - i543 - April 2015 - p455(3) [501+]

Condry, Ian - *The Soul of Anime: Collaborative Creativity and Japan's Media Success Story*
JAS - v74 - i2 - May 2015 - p433-436 [501+]

Cone, Daniel - *Last to Join the Fight: The 66th Georgia Infantry*
JSH - v81 - i3 - August 2015 - p744(2) [501+]

Cone, William - *Dead Ringer*
KR - Oct 1 2015 - pNA [501+]

Conefrey, Mick - *The Ghosts of K2*
KR - Sept 1 2015 - pNA [501+]
LJ - v140 - i15 - Sept 15 2015 - p84(1) [501+]
Spec - v329 - i9770 - Nov 28 2015 - p48(2) [501+]

Coney, Michael G. - *Michael G. Coney: SF Gateway Omnibus*
PW - v262 - i13 - March 30 2015 - p59(1) [51-500]

Mirror Image, Charisma, Brontomek!
BL - v111 - i18 - May 15 2015 - p38(1) [51-500]

Confalone, Nick - *Helicopters*
c HB Guide - v26 - i2 - Fall 2015 - p185(1) [51-500]

Confino, Alon - *A World without Jews: The Nazi Imagination from Persecution to Genocide*
HNet - Jan 2015 - pNA [501+]
JIH - v45 - i4 - Spring 2015 - p584-585 [501+]
Lon R Bks - v37 - i2 - Jan 22 2015 - p17(3) [501+]

Conforti, Joseph A. - *Lizzie Borden on Trial: Murder, Ethnicity, and Gender*
JIH - v46 - i3 - Wntr 2016 - p466-468 [501+]

Conger, Trace - *The Shadow Broker*
RVBW - April 2015 - pNA [51-500]

Conkle, Gina - *The Lady Meets Her Match*
BL - v111 - i14 - March 15 2015 - p50(1) [51-500]
KR - Feb 1 2015 - pNA [51-500]
PW - v262 - i6 - Feb 9 2015 - p50(2) [51-500]

Conklin, Alice L. - *In the Museum of Man: Race, Anthropology, and Empire in France, 1850-1950*
AHR - v120 - i1 - Feb 2015 - p176-179 [501+]
JMH - v87 - i3 - Sept 2015 - p736(3) [501+]

Conkling, Winifred - *Passenger on the Pearl: The True Story of Emily Edmonson's Flight from Slavery*
y HB - v91 - i1 - Jan-Feb 2015 - p95(2) [51-500]
y HB Guide - v26 - i2 - Fall 2015 - p207(1) [51-500]
y VOYA - v37 - i6 - Feb 2015 - p86(1) [51-500]
Radioactive! How Irene Curie and Lise Meitner Revolutionized Science and Changed the World
y BL - v112 - i7 - Dec 1 2015 - p45(2) [51-500]
y KR - Oct 1 2015 - pNA [51-500]
y SLJ - v61 - i11 - Nov 2015 - p134(1) [51-500]
Sylvia and Aki
c SLJ - v61 - i12 - Dec 2015 - p64(4) [51-500]

Conley, Ellen Alexander - *Queen Lear*
KR - July 1 2015 - pNA [501+]

Conley, Nicholas - *Pale Highway*
PW - v262 - i42 - Oct 19 2015 - p59(2) [51-500]

Conley, Robert J. - *Wil Usdi: Thoughts from the Asylum*
Roundup M - v22 - i5 - June 2015 - p38(1) [501+]
Roundup M - v22 - i6 - August 2015 - p28(1) [501+]

Conlogue, Bill - *Here and There: Reading Pennsylvania's Working Landscapes*
HNet - August 2015 - pNA [501+]
T&C - v56 - i2 - April 2015 - p542-543 [501+]

Conlon, Christopher - *Savaging the Dark*
BL - v111 - i18 - May 15 2015 - p34(1) [51-500]

Conn, Andrew Lewis - *O, Africa!*
G&L Rev W - v22 - i1 - Jan-Feb 2015 - p39(1) [51-500]

Conn, Kathe Crowley - *Juliette Kinzie: Frontier Storyteller*
c CH Bwatch - April 2015 - pNA [51-500]

Conn, P. Michael - *Animal Models for the Study of Human Disease*
QRB - v90 - i2 - June 2015 - p241(1) [501+]

Conn, Steven - *Americans against the City: Anti-urbanism in the Twentieth Century*
JAH - v102 - i2 - Sept 2015 - p505-506 [501+]

Connell, Carol M. - *Reforming the World Monetary System: Fritz Machlup and the Bellagio Group*
BHR - v89 - i3 - Autumn 2015 - p620(4) [501+]

Connell, Catherine - *School's Out: Gay and Lesbian Teachers in the Classroom*
Wom R Bks - v32 - i4 - July-August 2015 - p21(2) [501+]

Connell, John A. - *Ruins of War*
PW - v262 - i12 - March 23 2015 - p49(1) [51-500]
Spoils of Victory
PW - v262 - i52 - Dec 21 2015 - p132(1) [51-500]

Connell, John (b. 1946-) - *Islands at Risk? Environments, Economies and Contemporary Change*
Cont Pac - v27 - i2 - Fall 2015 - p593(4) [501+]

Connell, Monica - *Gathering Carrageen: A Return to Donegal*
TLS - i5853 - June 5 2015 - p27(1) [501+]

Connelly, Charlie - *Gilbert: The Last Years of W.G. Grace*
NS - v144 - i5285 - Oct 23 2015 - p50(2) [501+]
Spec - v329 - i9763 - Oct 10 2015 - p42(1) [501+]
TLS - i5876 - Nov 13 2015 - p10(1) [501+]

Connelly, Michael - *The Burning Room (Read by Welliver, Titus). Audiobook Review*
BL - v111 - i17 - May 1 2015 - p57(1) [51-500]
BooChiTr - Jan 3 2015 - p12(1) [51-500]
PW - v262 - i8 - Feb 23 2015 - p70(1) [51-500]
The Burning Room
Bwatch - Jan 2015 - pNA [501+]
NYTBR - May 10 2015 - p36(L) [501+]
RVBW - April 2015 - pNA [51-500]

The Crossing
BL - v112 - i4 - Oct 15 2015 - p18(1) [51-500]
CSM - Dec 17 2015 - pNA [501+]
KR - Oct 15 2015 - pNA [51-500]
NYTBR - Nov 1 2015 - p29(L) [501+]
PW - v262 - i39 - Sept 28 2015 - p65(1) [51-500]

Conner, Cindy - *Seed Libraries and Other Means of Keeping Seeds in the Hands of the People*
Bwatch - June 2015 - pNA [51-500]

Conner, Lester - *Weight of Chains*
LJ - v140 - i16 - Oct 1 2015 - p111(1) [501+]

Conner, Marisa - *The Power of Play: Designing Early Learning Spaces*
SLJ - v61 - i4 - April 2015 - p187(2) [51-500]

Conner, Robert C. - *General Gordon Granger: The Savior of Chickamauga and the Man behind "Juneteenth"*
JSH - v81 - i2 - May 2015 - p473(2) [501+]

Conner, Tom - *The Dreyfus Affair and the Rise of the French Public Intellectual*
FS - v69 - i3 - July 2015 - p410(1) [501+]

Conner, William D. - *Iron Age America before Columbus*
Am Ant - v80 - i3 - July 2015 - p627(2) [501+]

Conners, Bernard F. - *Cruising with Kate: A Parvenu in Xanadu*
RVBW - July 2015 - pNA [51-500]

Connington, Bill - *Physical Expression on Stage and Screen: Using the Alexander Technique to Create Unforgettable Performances*
Am Theat - v32 - i1 - Jan 2015 - p92(2) [501+]

Connolly, Annaliese - *Essex: The Cultural Impact of an Elizabethan Courtier*
Ren Q - v68 - i2 - Summer 2015 - p693-695 [501+]

Connolly, Brian - *Domestic Intimacies: Incest and the Liberal Subject in Nineteenth-Century America*
AHR - v120 - i3 - June 2015 - p1021-1022 [501+]
JAH - v102 - i2 - Sept 2015 - p557-558 [501+]

Connolly, Harry - *The Way into Chaos*
PW - v262 - i6 - Feb 9 2015 - p49(1) [51-500]
The Way Into Darkness
PW - v262 - i16 - April 20 2015 - p60(2) [51-500]
The Way into Magic
PW - v262 - i11 - March 16 2015 - p68(2) [51-500]

Connolly, John - *Empire*
KR - Jan 1 2015 - pNA [501+]
RVBW - Nov 2015 - pNA [501+]
Night Music: Nocturnes, vol. 2
PW - v262 - i35 - August 31 2015 - p62(1) [501+]
A Song of Shadows
BL - v111 - i22 - August 1 2015 - p37(1) [51-500]
PW - v262 - i30 - July 27 2015 - p42(1) [51-500]
RVBW - July 2015 - pNA [501+]
RVBW - Oct 2015 - pNA [501+]
The Wolf in Winter
MFSF - v128 - i5-6 - May-June 2015 - p65(6) [501+]
RVBW - June 2015 - pNA [51-500]

Connolly, John M. - *Living without a Why: Meister Eckhart's Critique of the Medieval Concept of Will*
RM - v68 - i4 - June 2015 - p844(2) [501+]

Connolly, John R. - *Newman and Life in the Spirit: Theological Reflections on Spirituality for Today*
Theol St - v76 - i2 - June 2015 - p398(1) [501+]

Connolly, Joy - *The Life of Roman Republicanism*
AJP - v136 - i2 - Summer 2015 - p372-375 [501+]

Connolly, MarcyKate - *Monstrous (Illus. by Young, Skottie)*
c BL - v111 - i9-10 - Jan 1 2015 - p101(1) [51-500]
Monstrous
c HB Guide - v26 - i2 - Fall 2015 - p78(1) [51-500]
Monstrous (Illus. by Young, Skottie)
c CCB-B - v68 - i8 - April 2015 - p394(1) [51-500]
Ravenous
c KR - Nov 15 2015 - pNA [51-500]

Connolly, Mary Beth Fraser - *Women of Faith: The Chicago Sisters of Mercy and the Evolution of a Religious Community*
AM - v212 - i2 - Jan 19 2015 - p33(2) [501+]

Connolly, Michael P. - *Young Enough to Change the World: Stories of Kids and Teens Who Turned Their Dreams into Actions*
c PW - v262 - i34 - August 24 2015 - p82(1) [501+]

Connolly, N.D.B. - *A World More Concrete: Real Estate and the Remaking of Jim Crow South Florida*
AHR - v120 - i4 - Oct 2015 - p1510-1511 [501+]
Am St - v54 - i2 - Summer 2015 - p101-102 [501+]
JSH - v81 - i4 - Nov 2015 - p1010(3) [501+]

Connolly, Paula T. - *Slavery in American Children's Literature, 1790-2010*
AL - v87 - i2 - June 2015 - p403-405 [501+]
Connolly, Tina - *Seriously Wicked*
y CH Bwatch - August 2015 - pNA [51-500]
y HB Guide - v26 - i2 - Fall 2015 - p115(1) [51-500]
y SLJ - v61 - i5 - May 2015 - p112(2) [51-500]
y VOYA - v38 - i2 - June 2015 - p72(1) [51-500]
Connor, Francis X. - *Literary Folios and Ideas of the Book in Early Modern England*
RES - v66 - i276 - Sept 2015 - p771-773 [501+]
Connor, James - *The Superyogi Scenario*
KR - June 1 2015 - pNA [501+]
Connor, Leslie - *All Rise for the Honorable Perry T. Cook*
c KR - Dec 15 2015 - pNA [51-500]
c SLJ - v61 - i12 - Dec 2015 - p100(1) [51-500]
The Things You Kiss Goodbye
y HB Guide - v26 - i1 - Spring 2015 - p104(1) [51-500]
Connor, Sara Witter - *Wisconsin's Flying Trees in World War II: A Victory for American Forest Products and Allied Aviation*
HNet - Sept 2015 - pNA(NA) [501+]
Connors, Anthony J. - *Ingenious Machinists: Two Inventive Lives from the American Industrial Revolution*
JEH - v75 - i1 - March 2015 - p288-290 [501+]
Connors, Bernard - *Cruising with Kate: A Parvenu in Xanadu*
SPBW - July 2015 - pNA [51-500]
Connors, Joanna - *I Will Find You: A Reporter Investigates the Life of the Man Who Raped Her*
KR - Jan 1 2016 - pNA [501+]
Connors, Joseph - *Bernard Berenson: Formation and Heritage*
Ren Q - v68 - i2 - Summer 2015 - p658-659 [501+]
Connors, Philip - *All The Wrong Places: A Life Lost and Found (Read by Verner, Adam). Audiobook Review*
LJ - v140 - i7 - April 15 2015 - p48(1) [51-500]
All the Wrong Places: A Life Lost and Found
BL - v111 - i12 - Feb 15 2015 - p4(1) [51-500]
Conquergood, Dwight - *Cultural Struggles: Performance, Ethnography, Praxis*
TDR - v59 - i1 - Spring 2015 - p181(3) [501+]
Conrad, Christoph - *Wohnen und die Okonomie des Raums - L'habitat et l'economie de l'espace*
HNet - April 2015 - pNA [501+]
Conrad, Gary D. - *Murder on Easter Island*
SPBW - March 2015 - pNA [51-500]
Conrad, Hy - *Dearly Departed*
PW - v262 - i52 - Dec 21 2015 - p133(1) [51-500]
Toured to Death
BL - v111 - i11 - Feb 1 2015 - p29(1) [51-500]
Conrad, Joseph - *Lord Jim (Read by Jerrom, Ric). Audiobook Review*
PW - v262 - i39 - Sept 28 2015 - p86(1) [51-500]
Victory
NS - v144 - i5283 - Oct 9 2015 - p52(2) [501+]
Conrad, Margaret - *Canadians and Their Pasts*
Beav - v95 - i3 - June-July 2015 - p56(2) [501+]
Conrad, Peter - *How the World Was Won: The Americanization of Everywhere*
TLS - i5848 - May 1 2015 - p11(1) [501+]
Conrad, Ryan - *Against Equality: Queer Revolution, Not Mere Inclusion*
G&L Rev W - v22 - i2 - March-April 2015 - p33(1) [51-500]
Conradie, Ernst M. - *Christian Faith and the Earth: Current Paths and Emerging Horizons in Ecotheology*
Intpr - v69 - i4 - Oct 2015 - p506(1) [501+]
Conran, Terence - *Conran on Color*
BL - v111 - i17 - May 1 2015 - p69(1) [51-500]
LJ - v140 - i8 - May 1 2015 - p74(1) [51-500]
Conroy, Christopher - *Anzard*
c CH Bwatch - March 2015 - pNA [51-500]
Conroy, Robert - *1882: Custer in Chains*
Analog - v135 - i11 - Nov 2015 - p106(1) [501+]
Germanica
PW - v262 - i31 - August 3 2015 - p40(1) [51-500]
Constable, Kate - *New Guinea Moon*
y Sch Lib - v63 - i1 - Spring 2015 - p61(1) [51-500]
Constable, Marianne - *Our Word Is Our Bond: How Legal Speech Acts*
HLR - v128 - i4 - Feb 2015 - p1329(1) [1-50]
Constantine, Alysia - *Sweet*
PW - v262 - i52 - Dec 21 2015 - p139(1) [51-500]
Constantine, David - *In Another Country: Selected Stories*
KR - April 15 2015 - pNA [501+]
NYTBR - August 16 2015 - p23(L) [501+]
PW - v262 - i19 - May 11 2015 - p32(1) [51-500]
New Selected Poems
TLS - i5875 - Nov 6 2015 - p7(1) [501+]
Constantine, Helen - *Copenhagen Tales*
TLS - i5842 - March 20 2015 - p26(1) [51-500]
Vienna Tales
TLS - i5832 - Jan 9 2015 - p23(1) [501+]
Constantine, Robin - *The Promise of Amazing*
c HB Guide - v26 - i1 - Spring 2015 - p104(1) [51-500]
The Secrets of Attraction
y CCB-B - v68 - i11 - July-August 2015 - p541(1) [51-500]
y HB Guide - v26 - i2 - Fall 2015 - p115(1) [51-500]
y KR - Jan 15 2015 - pNA [501+]
y PW - v262 - i5 - Feb 2 2015 - p63(1) [51-500]
y SLJ - v61 - i2 - Feb 2015 - p68(1) [51-500]
y VOYA - v38 - i1 - April 2015 - p55(1) [51-500]
Consumer Engineering: Mid-Century Mass Consumption between Planning Euphoria and the Limits of Growth, 1930s-1970s
HNet - Sept 2015 - pNA [501+]
Conte, Christopher - *Crossroads: Women Coming of Age in Today's Uganda*
KR - Oct 15 2015 - pNA [501+]
Conte, Louis - *Vaccine Injuries: Documented Adverse Reactions to Vaccines*
BL - v111 - i12 - Feb 15 2015 - p21(1) [51-500]
Contemporary Environmental History of the Soviet Union and the Successor States, 1970-2000: Ecological Globalization and Regional Dynamics (EcoGlobReg) - Arbeitstreffen
HNet - May 2015 - pNA [501+]
Conti, Brooke - *Confessions of Faith in Early Modern England*
CHR - v101 - i3 - Summer 2015 - p646(2) [501+]
MP - v112 - i4 - May 2015 - pE301(2) [501+]
Ren Q - v68 - i1 - Spring 2015 - p349-351 [501+]
Conti-Brown, Peter - *The Power and Independence of the Federal Reserve*
KR - Dec 1 2015 - pNA [501+]
Contouris, Nicola - *Resocialising Europe in a Time of Crisis*
Law Q Rev - v131 - April 2015 - p328-333 [501+]
Contreras, Randol - *The Stickup Kids: Race Drugs, Violence and the American Dream*
Am Q - v67 - i2 - June 2015 - p505-515 [501+]
The Stickup Kids: Race, Drugs, Violence and the American Dream
CrimJR - v40 - i2 - June 2015 - p235-237 [501+]
Conway, Anne-Marie - *Tangled Secrets*
y Sch Lib - v63 - i3 - Autumn 2015 - p180(1) [51-500]
Conway, Celeste - *Unlovely*
c HB Guide - v26 - i1 - Spring 2015 - p104(1) [51-500]
Conway, David - *With Friends Like These ... Why Britain Should Leave the EU-and How*
Soc - v52 - i1 - Feb 2015 - p86(1) [501+]
Conway, Ed - *The Summit: Bretton Woods, 1944: J.M. Keynes and the Reshaping of the Global Economy*
LJ - v140 - i2 - Feb 1 2015 - p89(2) [51-500]
NYRB - v62 - i19 - Dec 3 2015 - p66(3) [501+]
NYTBR - March 22 2015 - p11(L) [501+]
Conway, Kieran - *Southside Provisional*
KR - June 1 2015 - pNA [501+]
Conway, Martha - *Thieving Forest*
PW - v262 - i10 - March 9 2015 - p52(1) [51-500]
Conwill, William L. - *Spirit Training: A Book of Ethics for Black Teens*
y CH Bwatch - Oct 2015 - pNA [51-500]
SPBW - August 2015 - pNA [51-500]
Coodley, Lauren - *Upton Sinclair: California Socialist, Celebrity Intellectual*
JAH - v102 - i2 - Sept 2015 - p585-586 [501+]
PHR - v84 - i2 - May 2015 - p243(2) [501+]
Coogan, Michael - *The Ten Commandments: A Short History of an Ancient Text*
AM - v212 - i3 - Feb 2 2015 - p41(3) [501+]
J Ch St - v57 - i3 - Summer 2015 - p578-580 [501+]
Coogan, Steve - *Easily Distracted*
Spec - v329 - i9768 - Nov 14 2015 - p63(1) [501+]
Cook, Alexander C. - *Mao's Little Red Book: A Global History*
JAS - v74 - i3 - August 2015 - p723-724 [501+]
Cook, Angela V. - *Into a Million Pieces*
y PW - v262 - i28 - July 13 2015 - p70(1) [51-500]
Cook, Bruce - *Trumbo: A Biography of the Oscar-Winning Screenwriter Who Broke the Hollywood Blacklist (Read by Daniels, Luke). Audiobook Review*
LJ - v140 - i20 - Dec 1 2015 - p61(1) [51-500]
Cook, David C. - *The Action Bible 1: The Battle Begins: The Story of Creation (Illus. by Cariello, Sergio)*
c CH Bwatch - May 2015 - pNA [51-500]
Cook, Deanna F - *Cooking Class: 50 Fun Recipes Kids Will Love to Make (and Eat)! (Illus. by Bidwell, Julie)*
y SLJ - v61 - i2 - Feb 2015 - p118(1) [51-500]
Cook, Deanna F. - *Cooking Class: 50 Fun Recipes Kids Will Love to Make (and Eat)! (Illus. by Bidwell, Julie)*
c Sch Lib - v63 - i4 - Winter 2015 - p236(2) [51-500]
Teddy Bear Doctor: Be a Vet and Fix the Boo-Boos of Your Favorite Stuffed Animals
c SLJ - v61 - i7 - July 2015 - p102(1) [51-500]
Cook, Diane - *Man v. Nature: Stories*
NS - v144 - i5275 - August 14 2015 - p45(1) [51-500]
NYTBR - Dec 20 2015 - p24(L) [501+]
Cook, Eileen - *Remember*
y CCB-B - v68 - i7 - March 2015 - p351(1) [51-500]
Cook, Fred - *Improvise: Unconventional Career Advice from an Unlikely CEO*
Bwatch - March 2015 - pNA [51-500]
Cook, Gareth - *The Best American Infographics 2015*
Nature - v527 - i7579 - Nov 26 2015 - p445(1) [51-500]
Cook, Isham - *The Exact Unknown and Other Tales of Modern China*
KR - March 15 2015 - pNA [501+]
Cook, Jane Hampton - *American Phoenix: John Quincy and Louisa Adams, the War of 1812, and the Exile That Saved American Independence*
Historian - v77 - i2 - Summer 2015 - p324(2) [501+]
Cook, Jonathan (b. 1970-) - *Beer Terrain: From Field to Glass*
SPBW - March 2015 - pNA [501+]
Cook, Josh - *An Exaggerated Murder*
KR - Feb 1 2015 - pNA [501+]
Cook, Julia - *But It's Not My Fault (Illus. by DuFalla, Anita)*
c CH Bwatch - July 2015 - pNA [51-500]
I Can't Believe You Said That!: My Story about Using My Social Filter...or Not! (Illus. by DuFalla, Anita)
c CH Bwatch - May 2015 - pNA [51-500]
Cook, Katie - *Gronk: A Monster's Story (Illus. by Cook, Katie)*
c SLJ - v61 - i5 - May 2015 - p107(1) [51-500]
Cook, Kevin - *The Dad Report: Fathers, Sons, and Baseball Families*
BL - v111 - i17 - May 1 2015 - p70(1) [51-500]
KR - April 1 2015 - pNA [501+]
LJ - v140 - i7 - April 15 2015 - p92(1) [51-500]
Nat Post - v17 - i194 - June 20 2015 - pWP4(1) [501+]
PW - v262 - i18 - May 4 2015 - p112(1) [51-500]
Kitty Genovese: The Murder, the Bystanders, the Crime That Changed America
NYTBR - May 3 2015 - p28(L) [501+]
Cook, Kristi - *Magnolia*
c HB Guide - v26 - i1 - Spring 2015 - p104(1) [51-500]
Cook-Lynn, Elizabeth - *The Guy Wolf Dancing*
Am Ind CRJ - v39 - i2 - Spring 2015 - p167-169 [501+]
Cook, Marguerite Van - *The Late Child and Other Animals*
PW - v262 - i1 - Jan 5 2015 - p59(1) [51-500]
Cook-Martin, David - *The Scramble for Citizens: Dual Nationality and State Competition for Immigrants*
SF - v94 - i2 - Dec 2015 - pNA [51-500]
Cook, Matt - *Queer Domesticities: Homosexuality and Home Life in Twentieth-Century London*
HNet - April 2015 - pNA [51-500]
TimHES - i2193 - March 5 2015 - p49(1) [501+]
Cook, Michele - *Outrage*
y SLJ - v61 - i8 - August 2015 - p114(1) [51-500]
Uncaged
y HB Guide - v26 - i1 - Spring 2015 - p121(1) [51-500]
Cook, Michelle Schoffro - *The Probiotic Promise: Simple Steps to Heal Your Body from the Inside Out*
Bwatch - June 2015 - pNA [51-500]
Cook, Miki - *Green Home Building: Money-Saving Strategies for an Affordable, Healthy, High-Performance Home*
Bwatch - Feb 2015 - pNA [51-500]
Cook, Rebecca J. - *Abortion Law in Transnational Perspective: Cases and Controversies*
Cons - v36 - i1 - Spring 2015 - p40(2) [501+]
Cook, Robert - *Pulse: A National Security Thriller*
PW - v262 - i45 - Nov 9 2015 - p39(2) [51-500]

Cook, Robert J. - *Secession Winter: When the Union Fell Apart*
    Historian - v77 - i1 - Spring 2015 - p111(2) [501+]

Cook, Robin - *Coma (Read by LaVoy, January). Audiobook Review*
    BL - v111 - i12 - Feb 15 2015 - p103(1) [51-500]
Host
    BL - v112 - i2 - Sept 15 2015 - p31(2) [51-500]
    KR - Sept 15 2015 - pNA [501+]
    PW - v262 - i32 - August 10 2015 - p36(2) [51-500]

Cook, Scott - *Land, Livelihood, and Civility in Southern Mexico: Oaxaca Valley Communities in History*
    HAHR - v95 - i2 - May 2015 - p363-365 [501+]

Cook, Tim - *The Necessary War, vol. 1: Canadians Fighting the Second World War, 1939-1943*
    Beav - v95 - i2 - April-May 2015 - p54(2) [501+]

Cooke, Charles C.W. - *The Conservatarian Manifesto: Libertarians, Conservatives, and the Fight for the Right's Future*
    Nat R - v67 - i8 - May 4 2015 - p41 [501+]

Cooke, Miriam - *Nazira Zeineddine: A Pioneer of Islamic Feminism*
    IJMES - v47 - i2 - May 2015 - p388-390 [501+]
Tribal Modern: Branding New Nations in the Arab Gulf
    GR - v105 - i4 - Oct 2015 - p622(4) [501+]

Cooke, Philip E. - *European Resistance in the Second World War*
    J Mil H - v79 - i2 - April 2015 - p525-527 [501+]

Cooke, Phillip A. - *The Music of Herbert Howells*
    Notes - v71 - i4 - June 2015 - p708(3) [501+]

Cooke, Tim - *The Ancient Egyptians*
    c HB Guide - v26 - i2 - Fall 2015 - p216(1) [51-500]
At Home With...Series
    c BL - v111 - i19-20 - June 1 2015 - p80(1) [51-500]
Life in the War
    c BL - v112 - i3 - Oct 1 2015 - p54(1) [51-500]
Magic and Illusions
    c Res Links - v20 - i5 - June 2015 - p14(2) [51-500]
The Victorians
    c HB Guide - v26 - i2 - Fall 2015 - p215(1) [51-500]

Cooke, Trish - *Look Back! (Illus. by Binch, Caroline)*
    c BL - v111 - i11 - Feb 1 2015 - p46(1) [51-500]
    c HB Guide - v26 - i2 - Fall 2015 - p30(1) [51-500]
    SLJ - v61 - i3 - March 2015 - p114(2) [51-500]

The Cookers: Time and Time Again
    CSM - Jan 16 2015 - pNA [501+]

Cookson, Paul - *Crazy Classrooms (Illus. by Wells, Steve)*
    c Sch Lib - v63 - i3 - Autumn 2015 - p177(1) [51-500]

Cool, Michel - *Francis: A New World Pope*
    Theol St - v76 - i1 - March 2015 - p178(2) [501+]

Cooley, Aaron - *Four Seats*
    KR - July 15 2015 - pNA [501+]

Cooley, Angela Jill - *To Live and Dine in Dixie: The Evolution of Urban Food Culture in the Jim Crow South*
    HNet - Sept 2015 - pNA [501+]

Cooley, M.P. - *Flame Out*
    BL - v111 - i17 - May 1 2015 - p34(2) [51-500]
    PW - v262 - i13 - March 30 2015 - p54(1) [51-500]

Cooley, Peter - *Night Bus to the Afterlife*
    Ga R - v69 - i1 - Spring 2015 - p146-147 [501+]

Cooley, Timothy J. - *Surfing about Music*
    Notes - v72 - i2 - Dec 2015 - p367(3) [501+]

Coolidge, Grace E. - *The Formation of the Child in Early Modern Spain*
    Ren Q - v68 - i2 - Summer 2015 - p689-690 [501+]

Cooling, Benjamin Franklin, III - *Jubal Early: Robert E. Lee's "Bad Old Man"*
    J Mil H - v79 - i2 - April 2015 - p496-497 [501+]

Coombs, Benjamin - *British Tank Production and the War Economy, 1934-1945*
    AHR - v120 - i1 - Feb 2015 - p334-335 [501+]

Coombs, Kate - *The Tooth Fairy Wars (Illus. by Parker, Jake)*
    c HB Guide - v26 - i1 - Spring 2015 - p26(1) [51-500]

Coombs, Laurie A. - *Letters from My Father's Murderer: A Journey of Forgiveness*
    PW - v262 - i19 - May 11 2015 - p56(1) [51-500]

Coomes, David A. - *Forests and Global Change*
    QRB - v90 - i3 - Sept 2015 - p328(2) [501+]

Cooner, Donna - *Can't Look Away*
    y HB Guide - v26 - i1 - Spring 2015 - p104(1) [51-500]

Cooney, Caroline B. - *No Such Person (Read by Spencer, Erin). Audiobook Review*
    y BL - v112 - i4 - Oct 15 2015 - p64(1) [51-500]
    y SLJ - v61 - i10 - Oct 2015 - p53(2) [51-500]
No Such Person
    c BL - v111 - i17 - May 1 2015 - p51(2) [51-500]
    y CCB-B - v69 - i1 - Sept 2015 - p17(2) [51-500]
    y KR - April 1 2015 - pNA [51-500]
    y PW - v262 - i18 - May 4 2015 - p121(1) [51-500]
    y PW - v262 - i49 - Dec 2 2015 - p113(1) [51-500]
    y SLJ - v61 - i4 - April 2015 - p152(1) [51-500]
    y VOYA - v38 - i2 - June 2015 - p55(2) [51-500]

Cooney, Claire S.E. - *Bone Swans*
    PW - v262 - i21 - May 25 2015 - p41(1) [51-500]

Cooney, Kara - *The Woman Who Would Be King: Hatshepsut's Rise to Power in Ancient Egypt (Read by Cooney, Kara). Audiobook Review*
    LJ - v140 - i3 - Feb 15 2015 - p59(1) [51-500]
The Woman Who Would Be King: Hatshepsut's Rise to Power in Ancient Egypt
    TLS - i5853 - June 5 2015 - p21(1) [51-500]

Cooney, Robert - *Remembering Inez: The Last Campaign of Inez Milholland, Suffrage Martyr*
    SLJ - v61 - i2 - Feb 2015 - p126(2) [51-500]

Coonts, Stephen - *The Art of War*
    BL - v112 - i7 - Dec 1 2015 - p27(1) [51-500]
    PW - v262 - i46 - Nov 16 2015 - p54(1) [51-500]

Cooper, Alanna E. - *Bukharan Jews and the Dynamics of Global Judaism*
    JRAI - v21 - i1 - March 2015 - p233(2) [501+]

Cooper, Alex - *Saving Alex*
    KR - Jan 1 2016 - pNA [51-500]

Cooper, Andrew M. - *William Blake and the Productions of Time*
    RES - v66 - i273 - Feb 2015 - p182-183 [501+]

Cooper, Andrew Scott - *The Oil Kings: How the U.S., Iran, and Saudi Arabia Changed the Balance of Power in the Middle East*
    IJMES - v47 - i1 - Feb 2015 - p169-174 [501+]

Cooper, Artemis - *A Durable Fire: The Letters of Duff and Diana Cooper, 1913-1950*
    NYRB - v62 - i10 - June 4 2015 - p33(3) [501+]
The Letters of Evelyn Waugh and Diana Cooper
    NYRB - v62 - i10 - June 4 2015 - p33(3) [501+]

Cooper, Bernard - *My Avant-Garde Education*
    BL - v111 - i9-10 - Jan 1 2015 - p32(1) [51-500]

Cooper, Brenda - *Cracking the Sky*
    PW - v262 - i25 - June 22 2015 - p124(2) [51-500]
Edge of Dark
    PW - v262 - i1 - Jan 5 2015 - p56(1) [51-500]
    Analog - v135 - i6 - June 2015 - p108(1) [501+]

Cooper, Christopher - *The Truth About Tesla: The Myth of the Lone Genius in the History of Innovation*
    LJ - v140 - i20 - Dec 1 2015 - p125(1) [51-500]

Cooper, Constance - *Guile*
    y KR - Dec 15 2015 - pNA [51-500]

Cooper, Craig - *Your New Prime: 30 Days to Better Sex, Eternal Strength, and a Kick-Ass Life After 40*
    LJ - v140 - i14 - Sept 1 2015 - p128(2) [51-500]

Cooper, David - *Bela Bartok*
    Econ - v415 - i8935 - April 25 2015 - p79(US) [501+]
    LJ - v140 - i11 - June 15 2015 - p91(1) [51-500]
    Spec - v328 - i9745 - June 6 2015 - p42(2) [51-500]

Cooper, Dennis - *Horror Hospital Unplugged*
    ABR - v36 - i2 - Jan-Feb 2015 - p4(1) [501+]

Cooper, Diana - *Autobiography: The Rainbow Comes and Goes, The Light of Common Day, Trumpets from the Steep*
    NYRB - v62 - i10 - June 4 2015 - p33(3) [501+]

Cooper, Donal - *The Making of Assisi: The Pope, the Franciscans and the Painting of the Basilica*
    Ren Q - v68 - i3 - Fall 2015 - p998-1000 [501+]

Cooper, Duff - *Old Men Forget*
    NYRB - v62 - i10 - June 4 2015 - p33(3) [501+]

Cooper, E.E. - *Vanished*
    y CCB-B - v69 - i2 - Oct 2015 - p82(1) [51-500]
    y KR - Feb 15 2015 - pNA [51-500]
    y Res Links - v21 - i1 - Oct 2015 - p29(2) [51-500]
    c Nat Post - v17 - i165 - May 16 2015 - pWP5(1) [501+]
    y VOYA - v38 - i2 - June 2015 - p56(1) [51-500]

Cooper, Elisha - *8: An Animal Alphabet (Illus. by Cooper, Elisha)*
    c BL - v111 - i18 - May 15 2015 - p57(1) [51-500]
    c KR - April 15 2015 - pNA [51-500]
    c PW - v262 - i23 - June 8 2015 - p60(1) [51-500]
    c PW - v262 - i49 - Dec 2 2015 - p19(1) [51-500]
    c SLJ - v61 - i5 - May 2015 - p83(1) [51-500]

Cooper, Floyd - *Juneteenth for Mazie (Illus. by Cooper, Floyd)*
    c BL - v111 - i11 - Feb 1 2015 - p46(1) [51-500]
    c HB Guide - v26 - i2 - Fall 2015 - p30(1) [51-500]

Cooper, Frederick - *Africa in the World: Capitalism, Empire, Nation-State*
    Africa T - v61 - i3 - Spring 2015 - p84(4) [501+]
Citizenship between Empire and Nation: Remaking France and French Africa, 1945-1960
    Dis - v62 - i1 - Wntr 2015 - p145(7) [501+]

Cooper, Gemma - *A Day with Cinderella*
    c KR - Jan 1 2016 - pNA [51-500]

Cooper, Glenn - *The Devil Will Come*
    PW - v262 - i16 - April 20 2015 - p58(1) [51-500]
Near Death
    PW - v262 - i19 - May 11 2015 - p39(1) [51-500]
The Resurrection Maker
    PW - v262 - i14 - April 6 2015 - p42(1) [51-500]

Cooper, Ilene - *Little Lucy Goes to School (Illus. by Kanzler, John)*
    c HB Guide - v26 - i1 - Spring 2015 - p52(1) [51-500]
Lucy's Holiday Surprise (Illus. by Fitzgerald, Royce)
    c BL - v112 - i2 - Sept 15 2015 - p68(1) [51-500]
A Woman in the House (and Senate): How Women Came to the United States Congress, Broke Down Barriers, and Changed the Country (Illus. by Baddeley, Elizabeth)
    c BL - v111 - i9-10 - Jan 1 2015 - pS4(8) [501+]

Cooper, Isabel - *Night of the Highland Dragon*
    PW - v262 - i11 - March 16 2015 - p69(1) [51-500]

Cooper, Lisa H. - *The Arma Christi in Medieval and Early Modern Material Culture*
    Six Ct J - v46 - i2 - Summer 2015 - p405-407 [501+]

Cooper, Mariana M. - *The Aha! Factor: The Intuitive Guide to Getting What You Desire and Deserve*
    PW - v262 - i34 - August 24 2015 - p69(1) [51-500]

Cooper, Matthew J. - *Duke Ellington as Pianist: A Study of Styles*
    Notes - v71 - i4 - June 2015 - p723(4) [501+]

Cooper, Melinda - *Clinical Labor: Tissue Donors and Research Subjects in the Global Bioeconomy*
    AJS - v120 - i6 - May 2015 - p1893(3) [501+]
    CS - v44 - i5 - Sept 2015 - p652-653 [501+]

Cooper, Nate - *Build Your Own Website: A Comic Guide to HTML, CSS, and WordPress (Illus. by Gee, Kim)*
    y VOYA - v37 - i6 - Feb 2015 - p87(1) [51-500]

Cooper, Paul M.M. - *River of Ink*
    BL - v112 - i4 - Oct 15 2015 - p34(1) [51-500]
    KR - Nov 1 2015 - pNA [501+]

Cooper, Richard - *Roman Antiquities in Renaissance France, 1515-65*
    FS - v69 - i1 - Jan 2015 - p93-2 [501+]
    Ren Q - v68 - i1 - Spring 2015 - p261-262 [501+]

Cooper, Ron - *The Gospel of the Twin*
    PW - v262 - i17 - April 27 2015 - p59(1) [501+]

Cooper, Rose - *I Text Dead People*
    c HB Guide - v26 - i2 - Fall 2015 - p78(1) [51-500]
    c KR - March 1 2015 - pNA [51-500]
    SLJ - v61 - i4 - April 2015 - p144(2) [51-500]
    y VOYA - v38 - i2 - June 2015 - p72(1) [51-500]

Cooper, Sharon Katz - *When Butterflies Cross the Sky: The Monarch Butterfly Migration (Illus. by Brunet, Joshua S.)*
    c HB Guide - v26 - i2 - Fall 2015 - p173(1) [51-500]
When Whales Cross the Sea: The Grey Whale Migration (Illus. by Leonard, Tom)
    c Sch Lib - v63 - i3 - Autumn 2015 - p173(1) [51-500]
    c HB Guide - v26 - i2 - Fall 2015 - p179(1) [51-500]

Cooper, Susan Rogers - *Dead to the World*
    BL - v111 - i12 - Feb 15 2015 - p36(1) [51-500]
    KR - Jan 15 2015 - pNA [51-500]
    PW - v262 - i3 - Jan 19 2015 - p62(2) [51-500]

Cooper, T. - *Drew*
    y KR - Feb 15 2015 - pNA [51-500]
Oryon
    y SLJ - v61 - i6 - June 2015 - p111(1) [51-500]

Cooper, Tom - *The Marauders*
    y NYTBR - Feb 1 2015 - p25(L) [501+]

Cooper-White, Pamela - *The Cry of Tamar: Violence Against Women and the Church's Response*
    Intpr - v69 - i1 - Jan 2015 - p123(1) [51-500]
Exploring Practices of Ministry
    CC - v132 - i21 - Oct 14 2015 - p34(2) [501+]

Coopersmith, Jonathan - *Faxed: The Rise and Fall of the Fax Machine*
    TLS - i5868 - Sept 18 2015 - p12(2) [501+]

Cooray, Vernon - *An Introduction to Lightning*
    Phys Today - v68 - i6 - June 2015 - p54-56 [501+]

Cooter, Roger - *Writing History in the Age of Biomedicine*
  JMH - v87 - i1 - March 2015 - p137(3) [501+]
Copan, Paul - *Did God Really Command Genocide?*
  RVBW - Jan 2015 - pNA [501+]
Cope, J.T., IV - *Countryside: The Book of the Wise*
  c CH Bwatch - Jan 2015 - pNA [51-500]
  y KR - Feb 15 2015 - pNA [501+]
     KR - Sept 1 2015 - pNA [501+]
Copeland, B. Jack - *Turing: Pioneer of the Information Age*
  NYRB - v62 - i2 - Feb 5 2015 - p19(3) [501+]
  T&C - v56 - i3 - July 2015 - p772-773 [501+]
Copeland, Clare - *Angels of Light?: Sanctity and the Discernment of Spirits in the Early Modern Period*
  Ren Q - v68 - i1 - Spring 2015 - p345-346 [501+]
Copeland, Cyrus M. - *Off the Radar: A Father's Secret, a Mother's Heroism, and a Son's Quest*
  BL - v111 - i12 - Feb 15 2015 - p14(1) [51-500]
  KR - Jan 15 2015 - pNA [501+]
  LJ - v140 - i7 - April 15 2015 - p102(1) [51-500]
Copeland, Edward - *The Silver Fork Novel: Fashionable Fiction in the Age of Reform*
  VS - v57 - i2 - Wntr 2015 - p312(3) [501+]
Copeland, Misty - *Firebird: Ballerina Misty Copeland Shows a Young Girl How to Dance Like the Firebird (Illus. by Myers, Christopher)*
  c HB Guide - v26 - i1 - Spring 2015 - p27(1) [51-500]
Copeland, Mychal - *Struggling in Good Faith: LGBTQI Inclusion from 13 American Religious Perspectives*
  BL - v112 - i6 - Nov 15 2015 - p16(1) [51-500]
Copenhaver, Brian - *The Book of Magic: From Antiquity to the Enlightenment*
  Spec - v329 - i9772 - Dec 12 2015 - p80(1) [501+]
Coping with Immeasurable Losses: Population of the European Cities and World War I
  HNet - Feb 2015 - pNA [501+]
Coplan, Amy - *Empathy: Philosophical and Psychological Perspectives*
  TLS - i5872 - Oct 16 2015 - p11(2) [501+]
Copleton, Jackie - *A Dictionary of Mutual Understanding*
  KR - Sept 15 2015 - pNA [501+]
  LJ - v140 - i20 - Dec 1 2015 - p89(1) [51-500]
  NYT - Dec 31 2015 - pC7(L) [501+]
  PW - v262 - i41 - Oct 12 2015 - p46(1) [51-500]
Copnall, James - *A Poisonous Thorn in Our Hearts: Sudan and South Sudan's Bitter and Incomplete Divorce*
  For Aff - v94 - i1 - Jan-Feb 2015 - pNA [51-500]
Coppa, Frank J. - *The Life and Pontificate of Pope Pius XII: Between History and Controversy*
  J Ch St - v57 - i1 - Wntr 2015 - p185-188 [501+]
  The Papacy in the Modern World: A Political History
  CHR - v101 - i4 - Autumn 2015 - p901(2) [501+]
Coppenbarger, Brent - *Music Theory Secrets: 94 Strategies for the Starting Musician*
  Am MT - v64 - i5 - April-May 2015 - p45(1) [501+]
Coppens, Philip - *The Ancient Alien Question: A New Inquiry into the Existence, Evidence, and Influence of Ancient Visitors*
  Am Ant - v80 - i3 - July 2015 - p618(3) [501+]
Copperman, E.J. - *The Question of the Unfamiliar Husband*
  KR - August 1 2015 - pNA [51-500]
  PW - v262 - i35 - August 31 2015 - p64(1) [51-500]
  RVBW - Nov 2015 - pNA [501+]
Coppins, McKay - *The Wilderness: Deep Inside the Republican Party's Combative, Contentious, Chaotic Quest to Take Back the White House*
  KR - Dec 15 2015 - pNA [501+]
Coppola, Anne Turner - *Fly Away Free*
  SPBW - March 2015 - pNA [51-500]
Coppolani, Antoine - *Richard Nixon*
  Pres St Q - v45 - i3 - Sept 2015 - p620(3) [501+]
Coppula, Christopher A. - *Jimmy Van Heusen: Swinging on a Star*
  SPBW - May 2015 - pNA [51-500]
Copsey, Sue - *The Ghosts of Tarawera*
  c Magpies - v30 - i4 - Sept 2015 - pS7(1) [501+]
Cora, Cat - *Cooking as Fast as I Can: A Chef's Story of Family, Food, and Forgiveness*
  KR - June 15 2015 - pNA [501+]
  LJ - v140 - i9 - May 15 2015 - p100(2) [51-500]
  PW - v262 - i16 - April 20 2015 - p64(1) [51-500]
  y BL - v111 - i22 - August 1 2015 - p13(1) [51-500]
Corballis, Michael - *The Wandering Mind: What the Brain Does When You're Not Looking*
  LJ - v140 - i7 - April 15 2015 - p112(2) [51-500]
  NS - v144 - i5266 - June 12 2015 - p46(2) [51-500]
  TimHES - i2202 - May 7 2015 - p48-49 [501+]

Corbeau-Parsons, Caroline - *Prometheus in the Nineteenth Century: From Myth to Symbol*
  MLR - v110 - i3 - July 2015 - p788-789 [501+]
Corbellini, Sabrina - *Cultures of Religious Reading in the Late Middle Ages: Instructing the Soul, Feeding the Spirit, and Awakening the Passion*
  Specu - v90 - i1 - Jan 2015 - p230-233 [501+]
Corbett, David - *The Mercy of the Night*
  BL - v111 - i15 - April 1 2015 - p30(1) [51-500]
  KR - Feb 1 2015 - pNA [51-500]
  PW - v262 - i7 - Feb 16 2015 - p162(1) [51-500]
Corbett, Gavin - *Green Glowing Skull*
  NS - v144 - i5264 - May 29 2015 - p81(1) [501+]
  TLS - i5870 - Oct 2 2015 - p21(1) [501+]
Corbett, Ken - *A Murder over a Girl: Justice, Gender, Junior High*
  PW - v262 - i45 - Nov 9 2015 - p47(1) [51-500]
Corbett, Steve - *When Helping Hurts: How to Alleviate Poverty without Hurting Poor...and Yourself*
  Ch Today - v59 - i5 - June 2015 - p71(3) [501+]
Corbey, Raymond - *The Politics of Species: Reshaping Our Relationships with Other Animals*
  QRB - v90 - i2 - June 2015 - p209(2) [501+]
Corby, Gary - *Death Ex Machina*
  BL - v111 - i17 - May 1 2015 - p28(2) [51-500]
  PW - v262 - i13 - March 30 2015 - p54(1) [51-500]
Corcino, Kate - *Spark Rising*
  PW - v262 - i25 - June 22 2015 - p125(1) [51-500]
Cordell, Evie - *Two Girls Want a Puppy (Illus. by Lam, Maple)*
  c BL - v111 - i19-20 - June 1 2015 - p125(1) [51-500]
Cordell, Matthew - *Wish (Illus. by Cordell, Matthew)*
  c CH Bwatch - April 2015 - pNA [51-500]
  c HB Guide - v26 - i2 - Fall 2015 - p30(1) [51-500]
  c KR - Jan 15 2015 - pNA [51-500]
Cordell, Ryan - *Two Girls Want a Puppy (Illus. by Lam, Maple)*
  KR - April 1 2015 - pNA [51-500]
  c SLJ - v61 - i6 - June 2015 - p79(1) [51-500]
Corderoy, Tracey - *I Can Do It! (Illus. by Pedler, Caroline)*
  c HB Guide - v26 - i1 - Spring 2015 - p7(1) [51-500]
  I Want My Daddy! (Illus. by Edgson, Alison)
  c HB Guide - v26 - i2 - Fall 2015 - p8(1) [51-500]
     KR - April 1 2015 - pNA [51-500]
  c PW - v262 - i15 - April 13 2015 - p81(1) [51-500]
  Just Right for Two (Illus. by Beardshaw, Rosalind)
  c HB Guide - v26 - i1 - Spring 2015 - p27(1) [51-500]
  The Magical Snow Garden (Illus. by Chapman, Jane)
  c HB Guide - v26 - i1 - Spring 2015 - p27(1) [51-500]
  More! (Illus. by Warnes, Tim)
  c KR - May 1 2015 - pNA [51-500]
  No! (Illus. by Warnes, Tim)
  c SLJ - v61 - i7 - July 2015 - p54(2) [51-500]
  Why? (Illus. by Warnes, Tim)
  c HB Guide - v26 - i1 - Spring 2015 - p8(1) [51-500]
Cordova, James M. - *The Art of Professing in Bourbon Mexico: Crowned-Nun Portraits and Reform in the Convent*
  CHR - v101 - i2 - Spring 2015 - p399(3) [501+]
  HAHR - v95 - i3 - August 2015 - p529-531 [501+]
Cordova, Zoraida - *The Vast and Brutal Sea*
  c HB Guide - v26 - i1 - Spring 2015 - p104(1) [51-500]
Corea, Roger - *The Duesenberg Caper*
  PW - v262 - i28 - July 13 2015 - p48(1) [51-500]
  Scarback
  KR - April 15 2015 - pNA [51-500]
Corera, Gordon - *Intercept: The Secret History of Computers and Spies*
  Econ - v416 - i8947 - July 18 2015 - p70(US) [501+]
  Spec - v328 - i9752 - July 25 2015 - p31(2) [501+]
Corey, James S.A. - *Nemesis Games (Read by Mays, Jefferson). Audiobook Review*
  LJ - v140 - i13 - August 1 2015 - p47(1) [51-500]
  Nemesis Games
  PW - v262 - i20 - May 18 2015 - p69(1) [51-500]
  PW - v262 - i24 - June 15 2015 - p16(1) [51-500]
Corey, Shana - *The Secret Subway*
  c KR - Jan 1 2016 - pNA [51-500]
Corgiat, Sylviane - *The Swords of Glass (Illus. by Zuccheri, Laura)*
  c PW - v262 - i13 - March 30 2015 - p63(1) [51-500]
Cork, Richard - *Face to Face: Interviews with Artists*
  Spec - v328 - i9742 - May 16 2015 - p40(2) [501+]

Corkin, Stanley - *Starring New York: Filming the Grime and the Glamour of the Long 1970s*
  Am St - v54 - i2 - Summer 2015 - p45-55 [501+]
Corleone, Douglas - *Gone Cold*
  BL - v111 - i19-20 - June 1 2015 - p53(2) [51-500]
  KR - June 15 2015 - pNA [51-500]
  PW - v262 - i24 - June 15 2015 - p64(1) [51-500]
  Robert Ludlum's The Janson Equation
  BL - v111 - i17 - May 1 2015 - p38(1) [51-500]
Corlett, Richard T. - *The Ecology of Tropical East Asia*
  QRB - v90 - i4 - Dec 2015 - p433(1) [501+]
Corman, Richard - *Misty Copeland: Power and Grace*
  c BL - v111 - i5 - Nov 1 2015 - p48(1) [51-500]
Cormier, Zoe - *Sex, Drugs and Rock 'n' Roll: The Science of Hedonism and the Hedonism of Science*
  Nat Post - v17 - i125 - March 28 2015 - pWP10(1) [501+]
Corn, Alfred - *Miranda's Book*
  G&L Rev W - v22 - i3 - May-June 2015 - p39(2) [501+]
  Unions
  G&L Rev W - v22 - i4 - July-August 2015 - p39(2) [501+]
Cornebise, Alfred Emile - *The United States Army in China 1900-1938: A History of the 9th, 14th, 15th and 31st Regiments in the East*
  RVBW - August 2015 - pNA [51-500]
Cornelius, James Bryan - *The Masters Workshop Collection*
  KR - Feb 1 2015 - pNA [501+]
Cornell, Deirdre - *Jesus Was a Migrant*
  CC - v132 - i3 - Feb 4 2015 - p33(3) [501+]
Cornell, Drucilla - *Law and Revolution in South Africa: uBuntu, Dignity, and the Struggle for Constitutional Transformation*
  HNet - June 2015 - pNA [501+]
Cornell, Kari - *The Nitty-Gritty Gardening Book: Fun Projects for All Seasons (Illus. by Larson, Jennifer S.)*
  c HB Guide - v26 - i2 - Fall 2015 - p187(1) [51-500]
  Nitty-Gritty Gardening Book: Fun Projects for All Seasons (Illus. by Larson, Jennifer S.)
  c SLJ - v61 - i7 - July 2015 - p102(1) [51-500]
  The Nitty-Gritty Gardening Book
  c KR - Jan 1 2015 - pNA [51-500]
  The Nitty-Gritty Gardening Book (Illus. by Larson, Jennifer S.)
  Sci & Ch - v53 - i2 - Oct 2015 - p99 [501+]
Cornell, Paul - *Witches of Lychford*
  PW - v262 - i33 - August 17 2015 - p56(1) [51-500]
Cornell, Svante - *Conflict, Crime, and the State in Postcommunist Eurasia*
  Slav R - v74 - i3 - Fall 2015 - p611-613 [501+]
Cornelles, Jeronimo - *Mariama: Different But Just the Same (Illus. by Uya, Nivola)*
  PW - v262 - i2 - Jan 12 2015 - p56(1) [501+]
Corner, James - *The Landscape of Imagination: Collected Essays of James Corner 1990-2010*
  TLS - i5847 - April 24 2015 - p28(1) [501+]
Corner, Paul - *The Fascist Party and Popular Opinion in Mussolini's Italy*
  Historian - v77 - i1 - Spring 2015 - p163(2) [501+]
  Il fascismo in provincia: Articolazioni e gestione del potere tra centro e periferia
  HNet - August 2015 - pNA [501+]
Corner, T.E. - *List for Santa, List for Life*
  c CH Bwatch - July 2015 - pNA [51-500]
Cornia, Christian - *Scooby-Doo! and the Truth Behind Ghosts*
  c SLJ - v61 - i4 - April 2015 - p70(3) [501+]
Cornille, Didier - *Who Built That? Modern Houses: An Introduction to Modern Houses and Their Architects*
  c HB Guide - v26 - i1 - Spring 2015 - p179(1) [51-500]
  Who Built That? Skyscrapers: An Introduction to Skyscrapers and Their Architects
  c HB Guide - v26 - i1 - Spring 2015 - p179(1) [51-500]
Cornish, Graham P. - *Copyright: Interpreting the Law for Libraries, Archives and Information Services, 6th ed.*
  RVBW - August 2015 - pNA [501+]
  VOYA - v38 - i5 - Dec 2015 - p82(2) [51-500]
Cornwall, Deborah J. - *Things I Wish I'd Known: Cancer and Kids*
  SPBW - June 2015 - pNA [51-500]
Cornwell, Bernard - *Warriors of the Storm*
  KR - Nov 1 2015 - pNA [501+]
  Waterloo: The History of Four Days, Three Armies and Three Battles
  Bwatch - July 2015 - pNA [51-500]
  Econ - v415 - i8939 - May 23 2015 - p71(US)

[501+]
    KR - March 1 2015 - pNA [501+]
    LJ - v140 - i5 - March 15 2015 - p118(1) [501+]
    PW - v262 - i12 - March 23 2015 - p62(2) [501+]
    TLS - i5833 - Jan 16 2015 - p12(2) [501+]

Cornwell, Betsy - *Mechanica*
  y CH Bwatch - Oct 2015 - pNA [51-500]
  y KR - May 15 2015 - pNA [51-500]
  y PW - v262 - i21 - May 25 2015 - p60(1) [51-500]
  y SLJ - v61 - i6 - June 2015 - p111(1) [51-500]
  y VOYA - v38 - i2 - June 2015 - p72(1) [51-500]

Cornwell, Patricia - *Depraved Heart*
    BL - v112 - i4 - Oct 15 2015 - p20(1) [51-500]
    KR - Oct 1 2015 - pNA [51-500]
    NYTBR - Nov 15 2015 - p29(L) [501+]

Coronado, Raul - *A World Not to Come: A History of Latino Writing and Print Culture*
    AL - v87 - i3 - Sept 2015 - p624-627 [501+]

Coronado, Shawna - *Grow a Living Wall: Create Vertical Gardens with Purpose*
    LJ - v140 - i5 - March 15 2015 - p125(1) [51-500]

Corp, Carey - *Shades of Doon*
  y SLJ - v61 - i8 - August 2015 - p101(2) [51-500]

Corra, Bruno - *Sam Dunn Is Dead*
    TLS - i5875 - Nov 6 2015 - p25(1) [501+]

Corral, Will H. - *Bolano traducido: Nueva literatura mundial*
    MLN - v130 - i2 - March 2015 - p390-395 [501+]

Correll, Gemma - *The Worrier's Guide to Life*
  y BL - v111 - i22 - August 1 2015 - p47(1) [501+]

Correll, Mark R. - *Shepherds of the Empire: Germany's Conservative Protestant Leadership, 1888-1919*
    CH - v84 - i2 - June 2015 - p459(3) [501+]

Corrigan, Jim - *World War II*
  y BL - v112 - i6 - Nov 15 2015 - p43(1) [51-500]

Corrigan, John - *Emptiness: Feeling Christian in America*
    JAAR - v83 - i2 - June 2015 - p569(3) [501+]

Corrigan, Kevin - *Reason, Faith, and Otherness in Neoplatonic and Early Christian Thought*
    JR - v95 - i2 - April 2015 - p261(2) [501+]

Corrigan, Maya - *Scam Chowder*
    KR - April 15 2015 - pNA [51-500]

Corrin, Jay P. - *Catholic Progressives in England After Vatican II*
    CH - v84 - i1 - March 2015 - p271(3) [501+]
    J Ch St - v57 - i2 - Spring 2015 - p382-384 [501+]

Cortazar, Julio - *Fantomas versus the Multinational Vampires: An Attainable Utopia*
    WLT - v89 - i3-4 - May-August 2015 - p106(2) [501+]

Corteguera, Luis R. - *Death by Effigy: A Case from the Mexican Inquisition*
    CHR - v101 - i3 - Summer 2015 - p689(2) [501+]

Cortez, Brenda E. - *My Mom Is Having Surgery: A Kidney Story (Illus. by Contento, Dindo)*
  c CH Bwatch - Nov 2015 - pNA [501+]

Cortis, James - *illiam Cameron Menzies: The Shape of Films to Come*
    BL - v112 - i5 - Nov 1 2015 - p26(1) [51-500]

Corton, Christine L. - *London Fog: The Biography*
    KR - July 15 2015 - pNA [501+]
    Lon R Bks - v37 - i19 - Oct 8 2015 - p5(3) [501+]
    Nature - v527 - i7579 - Nov 26 2015 - p445(1) [51-500]
    NS - v144 - i5288 - Nov 13 2015 - p40(2) [501+]
    NYTBR - Nov 1 2015 - p17(L) [501+]
    PW - v262 - i35 - August 31 2015 - p75(1) [51-500]
    Spec - v329 - i9767 - Nov 7 2015 - p41(1) [501+]
    TimHES - i2227 - Oct 29 2015 - p50(1) [501+]

Corum, James S. - *The Second World War and the Baltic States*
    J Mil H - v79 - i2 - April 2015 - p524-525 [501+]

Corwin, Marc - *The Optical Lasso*
    KR - Dec 15 2015 - pNA [501+]

Cory, Steve - *Building Outdoor Kitchens for Every Budget*
    RVBW - April 2015 - pNA [51-500]

Cosgrove, Mary - *Born under Auschwitz: Melancholy Traditions in Postwar German Literature*
    MLR - v110 - i2 - April 2015 - p605-607 [501+]

Cosimano, Elle - *Nearly Found*
  c BL - v111 - i17 - May 1 2015 - p51(1) [51-500]
  y HB - v91 - i4 - July-August 2015 - p130(2) [51-500]
  y KR - March 15 2015 - pNA [51-500]
  y SLJ - v61 - i4 - April 2015 - p160(1) [51-500]
  y VOYA - v38 - i2 - June 2015 - p56(1) [51-500]

Coss, Edward J. - *All for the King's Shilling: The British Soldier under Wellington, 1808-1814*
    HER - v130 - i542 - Feb 2015 - p123(14) [501+]

Coss, Melinda - *Handmade Soap Book: Easy Soapmaking with Natural Ingredients, 2d ed.*
    LJ - v140 - i20 - Dec 1 2015 - p101(2) [51-500]

Coss, Stephen - *The Fever of 1721: The Epidemic That Revolutionized Medicine and American Politics*
    KR - Dec 1 2015 - pNA [501+]
    LJ - v140 - i20 - Dec 1 2015 - p113(1) [51-500]

Cossanteli, Veronica - *The Extincts (Illus. by Muradov, Roman)*
  c KR - Dec 1 2015 - pNA [51-500]
  c PW - v262 - i47 - Nov 23 2015 - p68(1) [51-500]
  c SLJ - v61 - i10 - Oct 2015 - p88(1) [51-500]

Cossey, Mark - *Trying: Love, Loose Pants & the Quest for a Baby*
    LJ - v140 - i2 - Feb 1 2015 - p101(2) [51-500]

Cost, Jay - *A Republic No More: Big Government and the Rise of American Political Corruption*
    MA - v57 - i4 - Fall 2015 - p76(4) [501+]
    Nat R - v67 - i7 - April 20 2015 - p42 [501+]

Cost, Matthew - *Joshua Chamberlain and the Civil War: At Every Hazard*
    KR - August 1 2015 - pNA [501+]

Costa, Catie - *Love on the Rocks*
    KR - Oct 1 2015 - pNA [501+]

Costa, Gustavo - *Celestino Galiani e la Sacra Scrittura: Alle radici del pensiero napoletano del Settecento*
    Ren Q - v68 - i2 - Summer 2015 - p717-719 [501+]

Costa, James T. - *On the Organic Law of Change*
    QRB - v90 - i1 - March 2015 - p74(3) [501+]
Wallace, Darwin, and the Origin of Species
    Nature - v523 - i7562 - July 30 2015 - p528(1) [51-500]
    QRB - v90 - i3 - Sept 2015 - p316(2) [501+]

Costa, Margaret Jull - *Skylight*
    NYTBR - Nov 22 2015 - p36(L) [501+]

Costa, Nicoletta - *The Little Tree That Would Not Share (Illus. by Costa, Nicoletta)*
  c KR - Nov 15 2015 - pNA [51-500]
  c PW - v262 - i47 - Nov 23 2015 - p65(1) [51-500]
Olga the Cloud
  c HB Guide - v26 - i2 - Fall 2015 - p30(1) [51-500]

Costa, Shelley - *Practical Sins for Cold Climates*
    PW - v262 - i47 - Nov 23 2015 - p52(1) [51-500]

Costain, Keith M. - *The Opera Singer*
    KR - March 1 2015 - pNA [501+]

Costamagna, Beatrice - *Shark Bite! (Illus. by Costamagna, Beatrice)*
  c BL - v112 - i6 - Nov 15 2015 - p57(1) [51-500]
Shark Bite!
  c KR - July 1 2015 - pNA [501+]

Costanza-chock, Sasha - *Out of the Shadows, Into the Streets! Transmedia Organizing and the Immigrant Rights Movement*
    J Hi E - v86 - i6 - Nov-Dec 2015 - p955(5) [501+]

Coste, Robin - *Voyage of the Sable Venus and Other Poems*
    NY - v91 - i32 - Oct 19 2015 - p91 [501+]

Costello, Elvis - *Unfaithful Music & Disappearing Ink (Read by Costello, Elvis). Audiobook Review*
    LJ - v140 - i20 - Dec 1 2015 - p59(1) [51-500]
    NYTBR - Nov 22 2015 - p20(L) [501+]
Unfaithful Music & Disappearing Ink
    AM - v213 - i14 - Nov 9 2015 - p44(1) [501+]
    BL - v112 - i3 - Oct 1 2015 - p9(1) [51-500]
    BooChiTr - Oct 31 2015 - p13(1) [501+]
    KR - Oct 1 2015 - pNA [501+]
    NS - v144 - i5286 - Oct 30 2015 - p44(2) [501+]
    NYT - Oct 9 2015 - pC21(L) [501+]
    PW - v262 - i38 - Sept 21 2015 - p66(1) [501+]

Costello, Kathleen - *Navigating Life with Multiple Sclerosis*
    BL - v112 - i2 - Sept 15 2015 - p8(1) [51-500]

Costello, Mary - *Academy Street*
    KR - Feb 1 2015 - pNA [501+]
    NY - v91 - i24 - August 24 2015 - p73 [51-500]
    NYT - May 28 2015 - pC6(L) [501+]
    NYTBR - May 3 2015 - p12(L) [501+]
    PW - v262 - i6 - Feb 9 2015 - p44(1) [501+]

Costelloe, Sarah - *Forecast*
  y Magpies - v30 - i1 - March 2015 - pS7(1) [501+]

Costelloe, Timothy M. - *The British Aesthetic Tradition: From Shaftesbury to Wittgenstein*
    MP - v112 - i4 - May 2015 - pE284(4) [501+]

Coster, Patience - *My Life in France*
  c BL - v111 - i16 - April 15 2015 - p45(2) [501+]
My Life in Jamaica
  c BL - v111 - i16 - April 15 2015 - p45(2) [501+]

Coster, Simon - *My Dinosaur is More Awesome! (Illus. by Coster, Simon)*
  c SLJ - v61 - i7 - July 2015 - p60(1) [51-500]

Costigan, Suzanne - *Empty Cup*
  y Res Links - v20 - i4 - April 2015 - p26(1) [501+]

Costolo, Raebeth - *The 3 W Boys: A Children's Book of Short Stories (Illus. by Ouano, Lucent)*
  c CH Bwatch - Jan 2015 - pNA [501+]

Cote, Denis - *Dessine-moi un Martien (Illus. by Lamontagne, Jacques)*
  c Res Links - v20 - i5 - June 2015 - p37(1) [51-500]

Cote, Genevieve - *Goodnight, You (Illus. by Cote, Genevieve)*
  c HB Guide - v26 - i2 - Fall 2015 - p8(1) [51-500]
  c Res Links - v20 - i3 - Feb 2015 - p3(1) [51-500]

Cote, Lynne Kathryn - *Strawberry Pie*
    KR - June 15 2015 - pNA [501+]

Cothran, Boyd - *Remembering the Modoc War: Redemptive Violence and the Making of American Innocence*
    Am St - v54 - i1 - Spring 2015 - p166-2 [501+]
    PHR - v84 - i4 - Nov 2015 - p559(2) [501+]
    Pub Hist - v37 - i1 - Feb 2015 - p121(3) [501+]

Cotler, Steve - *Cheesie Mack Is Sort of Freaked Out (Illus. by Holgate, Douglas)*
  y HB Guide - v26 - i1 - Spring 2015 - p74(1) [51-500]

Cotten, Sonia - *Marcher dans le ciel (Illus. by Boulanger, Annie)*
  c Res Links - v21 - i1 - Oct 2015 - p49(2) [501+]

Cotter, Charis - *The Swallow: A Ghost Story*
  y Teach Lib - v42 - i3 - Feb 2015 - p32(6) [501+]

Cotter, Sacha - *Keys (Illus. by Morgan, Josh)*
  c Magpies - v30 - i2 - May 2015 - pS5(1) [51-500]

Cotter, Tom - *Barn Find Road Trip*
    BL - v112 - i3 - Oct 1 2015 - p7(2) [51-500]

Cotterill, Colin - *Six and a Half Deadly Sins*
    BL - v111 - i17 - May 1 2015 - p45(1) [51-500]
    CSM - July 1 2015 - pNA [51-500]
    NYTBR - May 17 2015 - p33(L) [501+]
    PW - v262 - i13 - March 30 2015 - p55(1) [51-500]

Cottingham, John - *Philosophy of Religion: Towards a More Humane Approach*
    Rel St - v51 - i1 - March 2015 - p135-139 [501+]
    TLS - i5846 - April 17 2015 - p28(1) [501+]

Cottom, Daniel - *International Bohemia: Scenes of Nineteenth-Century Life*
    MP - v112 - i3 - Feb 2015 - pE261(E265) [501+]

Cotton, Anne K. - *Platonic Dialogue and the Education of the Reader*
    Class R - v65 - i1 - April 2015 - p49-51 [501+]

Cotton, Katie - *And the Cow Said (Illus. by Gausden, Vicki)*
  c KR - Dec 1 2015 - pNA [51-500]
  c PW - v262 - i27 - July 6 2015 - p70(2) [51-500]
Counting Lions: Portraits from the Wild (Illus. by Walton, Stephen)
  c BL - v112 - i3 - Oct 1 2015 - p81(2) [51-500]
  c KR - August 1 2015 - pNA [51-500]
  c Magpies - v30 - i5 - Nov 2015 - p22(1) [51-500]
  c PW - v262 - i32 - August 10 2015 - p60(1) [51-500]
  c PW - v262 - i49 - Dec 2 2015 - p44(1) [51-500]
  c RVBW - Oct 2015 - pNA [501+]
  c SLJ - v61 - i10 - Oct 2015 - p74(1) [51-500]
Dear Bunny
  c KR - Jan 1 2016 - pNA [51-500]
Ten Monsters in the Bed (Illus. by Blecha, Aaron)
  c KR - Dec 1 2015 - pNA [51-500]

Cotton, Peter B. - *When Fred the Snake Got Squished and Mended (Illus. by Lemaire, Bonnie)*
  c CH Bwatch - May 2015 - pNA [51-500]

Cottrell Boyce, Frank - *The Astounding Broccoli Boy*
  c Sch Lib - v63 - i2 - Summer 2015 - p102(1) [51-500]
Ted Rules the World (Illus. by Riddell, Chris)
  c Sch Lib - v63 - i4 - Winter 2015 - p226(1) [51-500]

Cottrell, Brett - *The End of the World Is Rye*
    PW - v262 - i18 - May 4 2015 - p101(1) [51-500]

Cottrell, Stephen - *Walking Backwards to Christmas*
    CC - v132 - i23 - Nov 11 2015 - p42(1) [51-500]

Cotugno, Katie - *99 Days*
    BL - v111 - i14 - March 15 2015 - p65(1) [51-500]
    y CCB-B - v68 - i10 - June 2015 - p484(1) [51-500]
    y HB Guide - v26 - i2 - Fall 2015 - p115(1) [51-500]
    y KR - Jan 15 2015 - pNA [51-500]
    y PW - v262 - i6 - Feb 9 2015 - p70(1) [51-500]
    SLJ - v61 - i2 - Feb 2015 - p98(1) [51-500]
    y VOYA - v38 - i1 - April 2015 - p55(2) [51-500]

Couch, Dick - *Navy SEALs: Their Untold Story*
    SLJ - v61 - i3 - March 2015 - p74(1) [51-500]

Tom Clancy's Op-Center: Into the Fire
    BL - v111 - i16 - April 15 2015 - p29(2) [51-500]

Coudray, Philippe - *Benjamin Bear in Brain Storms! (Illus. by Coudray, Philippe)*
    c BL - v111 - i16 - April 15 2015 - p41(1) [51-500]
    c HB - v91 - i3 - May-June 2015 - p106(2) [51-500]
    c HB Guide - v26 - i2 - Fall 2015 - p59(1) [51-500]
    c SLJ - v61 - i8 - August 2015 - p79(1) [51-500]

Couelle, Jennifer - *Kiss, Kiss (Illus. by Laplante, Jacques)*
    c KR - Nov 15 2015 - pNA [51-500]
    c PW - v262 - i41 - Oct 12 2015 - p66(2) [501+]

Couenhoven, Jesse - *Stricken by Sin, Cured by Christ: Agency, Necessity, and Culpability in Augustinian Theology*
    Bks & Cult - v21 - i3 - May-June 2015 - p11(2) [501+]

Coughlin, Jack - *The Night of the Cobra*
    BL - v111 - i22 - August 1 2015 - p36(1) [51-500]
    KR - June 15 2015 - pNA [51-500]
    PW - v262 - i25 - June 22 2015 - p120(1) [51-500]

Cougnon, Louise-Amelie - *SMS communication: A Linguistic Approach*
    Lang Soc - v44 - i4 - Sept 2015 - p588-4 [501+]

Coulon, Gerard - *Les Voies romaines en Gaule*
    TLS - i5854 - June 12 2015 - p11(1) [501+]

Coulson, Richard - *A Corkscrew Life*
    KR - April 1 2015 - pNA [51-500]

Coulter, Ann - *Adios, America! The Left's Plan to Turn Our Country into a Third World Hellhole*
    Nat R - v67 - i12 - July 6 2015 - p39 [501+]
    PW - v262 - i24 - June 15 2015 - p16(1) [51-500]

Coulter, Benedict - *It's Alright to Look Different (Illus. by Ferrando, Salva)*
    c CH Bwatch - March 2015 - pNA [51-500]
    RVBW - Jan 2015 - pNA [51-500]

Coulter, Catherine - *The End Game*
    BL - v111 - i22 - August 1 2015 - p33(1) [51-500]
    KR - July 15 2015 - pNA [51-500]
    LJ - v140 - i6 - April 1 2015 - p58(4) [501+]
    PW - v262 - i31 - August 3 2015 - p35(2) [51-500]

Nemesis
    BL - v111 - i19-20 - June 1 2015 - p56(1) [51-500]
    LJ - v140 - i11 - June 15 2015 - p74(2) [51-500]
    PW - v262 - i22 - June 1 2015 - p42(1) [51-500]

Coulthard, Glen Sean - *Red Skin, White Masks: Rejecting the Colonial Politics of Recognition*
    Am St - v54 - i2 - Summer 2015 - p130-131 [501+]

Coulthard, Sally - *Shed Decor: How to Decorate and Furnish Your Favorite Garden Room*
    LJ - v140 - i7 - April 15 2015 - p91(1) [51-500]

Country Bumpkin - *A-Z of Heirloom Sewing*
    LJ - v140 - i15 - Sept 15 2015 - p77(1) [51-500]
    RVBW - July 2015 - pNA [51-500]

Country Living Magazine - *Country Living American Style: Decorate, Create, Celebrate*
    LJ - v140 - i16 - Oct 1 2015 - p84(1) [51-500]

Couper, Alastair - *Fishers and Plunderers: Theft, Slavery and Violence at Sea*
    TLS - i5872 - Oct 16 2015 - p27(1) [501+]

Couperus, Louis - *Old People and the Things That Pass*
    TimHES - i2211 - July 9 2015 - p48(1) [501+]

Coupland, Douglas - *The Age of Earthquakes: A Guide to the Extreme Present*
    KR - Jan 15 2015 - pNA [501+]

Courage, Nick - *The Loudness*
    y SLJ - v61 - i6 - June 2015 - p111(1) [51-500]
    y VOYA - v38 - i2 - June 2015 - p72(1) [51-500]

Coureas, Nicholas - *The Latin Church in Cyprus, 1313-1378*
    HER - v130 - i543 - April 2015 - p384(16) [501+]

Court, Jurgen - *Deutsche Sportwissenschaft in der Weimarer Republik und im Nationalsozialismus, vol. 2: Die Geschichte der Deutschen Hochschule fur Leibesubungen 1919-1925*
    Ger Q - v88 - i3 - Summer 2015 - p406(2) [501+]

Courtauld, Sarah - *Buckle and Squash: The Perilous Princess Plot (Illus. by Courtauld, Sarah)*
    c BL - v111 - i18 - May 15 2015 - p65(1) [51-500]
    c PW - v262 - i14 - April 6 2015 - p59(1) [51-500]
    c CCB-B - v68 - i10 - June 2015 - p484(1) [51-500]
    c HB Guide - v26 - i2 - Fall 2015 - p64(1) [51-500]
    c KR - March 1 2015 - pNA [51-500]
    SLJ - v61 - i3 - March 2015 - p115(1) [51-500]

Courtley, Cade - *SEAL Survival Guide: A Navy SEAL'S Secrets to Surviving Any Disaster (Read by Bray, R.C.). Audiobook Review*
    LJ - v140 - i8 - May 1 2015 - p42(1) [51-500]

Courts, Marion - *The Iceberg*
    PW - v262 - i41 - Oct 12 2015 - p55(1) [51-500]

Cousins, Lucy - *Count with Maisy, Cheep, Cheep, Cheep! (Illus. by Cousins, Lucy)*
    c HB - v91 - i1 - Jan-Feb 2015 - p62(2) [51-500]
    c HB Guide - v26 - i2 - Fall 2015 - p8(2) [51-500]
    c Sch Lib - v63 - i3 - Autumn 2015 - p153(1) [51-500]

Maisy Goes on a Plane
    c SLJ - v61 - i9 - Sept 2015 - p110(1) [51-500]

Maisy Goes to London
    c KR - Jan 1 2016 - pNA [51-500]

Maisy's Christmas Tree (Illus. by Cousins, Lucy)
    c KR - Jan 1 2015 - pNA [51-500]

Maisy's Digger
    c KR - Jan 1 2016 - pNA [51-500]

Maisy's Pirate Ship
    c KR - Dec 1 2015 - pNA [51-500]

Maisy's Tractor (Illus. by Cousins, Lucy)
    c KR - July 1 2015 - pNA [51-500]

Couto, Mia - *Confession of the Lioness*
    Econ - v416 - i8950 - August 8 2015 - p72(US) [501+]
    KR - June 1 2015 - pNA [51-500]
    LJ - v140 - i7 - April 15 2015 - p74(2) [51-500]
    PW - v262 - i20 - May 18 2015 - p58(1) [51-500]
    TLS - i5860 - July 24 2015 - p20(1) [51-500]

Coutts, Alexandra - *Young Widows Club*
    y BL - v112 - i5 - Nov 1 2015 - p59(1) [51-500]
    y KR - Sept 1 2015 - pNA [51-500]
    y SLJ - v61 - i11 - Nov 2015 - p112(1) [51-500]
    y VOYA - v38 - i5 - Dec 2015 - p54(1) [51-500]

Coutts, Marion - *The Iceberg*
    BL - v112 - i6 - Nov 15 2015 - p5(1) [51-500]
    KR - Nov 1 2015 - pNA [51-500]

Couzens, Dominic - *Tales of Remarkable Birds*
    y BL - v111 - i18 - May 15 2015 - p9(1) [51-500]
    Bwatch - July 2015 - pNA [51-500]
    LJ - v140 - i9 - May 15 2015 - p101(2) [51-500]

Coval, Kevin - *The BreakBeat Poets: New American Poetry in the Age of Hip-Hop*
    BL - v111 - i14 - March 15 2015 - p38(1) [51-500]

Covell, Ann - *Jane Means Appleton Pierce: U.S. First Lady, 1853-1857: Her Family, Life, and Times*
    Historian - v77 - i3 - Fall 2015 - p550(2) [501+]

Covello, Paul - *Toronto ABC*
    c Res Links - v20 - i3 - Feb 2015 - p3(1) [51-500]

Coven, Wanda - *Heidi Heckelbeck and the Tie-Dyed Bunny*
    c HB Guide - v26 - i1 - Spring 2015 - p58(1) [51-500]

Heidi Heckelbeck Gets the Sniffles (Illus. by Burris, Priscilla)
    c HB Guide - v26 - i1 - Spring 2015 - p58(1) [51-500]

Heidi Heckelbeck Is a Flower Girl (Illus. by Burris, Priscilla)
    c HB Guide - v26 - i1 - Spring 2015 - p58(1) [51-500]

Heidi Heckelbeck Is Not a Thief! (Illus. by Burris, Priscilla)
    c HB Guide - v26 - i2 - Fall 2015 - p64(1) [51-500]

Coveney, Michael - *Maggie Smith: A Biography*
    BL - v112 - i5 - Nov 1 2015 - p22(1) [51-500]
    KR - Oct 1 2015 - pNA [51-500]
    LJ - v140 - i19 - Nov 15 2015 - p87(1) [51-500]
    PW - v262 - i42 - Oct 19 2015 - p68(1) [51-500]

Coverdale, Linda - *Queen's Caprice*
    PW - v262 - i7 - Feb 16 2015 - p151(1) [51-500]

Coverly, Dave - *Dogs Are People, Too: A Collection of Cartoons to Make Your Tail Wag (Illus. by Coverly, Dave)*
    c SLJ - v61 - i5 - May 2015 - p107(2) [51-500]

Night of the Living Worms: A Speed Bump and Slingshot Misadventure (Illus. by Coverly, Dave)
    c KR - July 1 2015 - pNA [51-500]

Night of the Living Worms (Illus. by Coverly, Dave)
    c BL - v112 - i3 - Oct 1 2015 - p79(1) [51-500]
    c PW - v262 - i30 - July 27 2015 - p69(1) [51-500]
    c SLJ - v61 - i7 - July 2015 - p71(1) [51-500]

Coviello, Peter - *Tomorrow's Parties: Sex and the Untimely in Nineteenth-Century America*
    AL - v87 - i3 - Sept 2015 - p614-616 [501+]
    J Am St - v49 - i1 - Feb 2015 - p198-200 [501+]
    Nine-C Lit - v69 - i4 - March 2015 - p547(5) [501+]

Coville, Bruce - *Amber Brown Is Tickled Pink (Read by Lubotsky, Dana). Audiobook Review*
    c BL - v112 - i7 - Dec 1 2015 - p70(1) [51-500]

Diary of a Mad Brownie (Read by Full cast). Audiobook Review
    c BL - v112 - i5 - Nov 1 2015 - p71(2) [51-500]
    c SLJ - v61 - i10 - Oct 2015 - p51(2) [51-500]

Diary of a Mad Brownie (Illus. by Kidby, Paul)
    c BL - v111 - i17 - May 1 2015 - p94(2) [51-500]
    c KR - April 15 2015 - pNA [51-500]
    c PW - v262 - i16 - April 20 2015 - p78(1) [51-500]
    c SLJ - v61 - i6 - June 2015 - p99(2) [51-500]
    c HB Guide - v26 - i2 - Fall 2015 - p78(1) [51-500]

Goblins on the Prowl
    c BL - v111 - i18 - May 15 2015 - p65(1) [51-500]
    c HB Guide - v26 - i2 - Fall 2015 - p79(1) [51-500]
    c KR - March 1 2015 - pNA [51-500]
    c PW - v262 - i16 - April 20 2015 - p78(1) [51-500]
    c SLJ - v61 - i4 - April 2015 - p145(2) [51-500]

My Teacher Flunked the Planet
    y HB Guide - v26 - i1 - Spring 2015 - p74(1) [51-500]

My Teacher Glows in the Dark
    y HB Guide - v26 - i1 - Spring 2015 - p74(1) [51-500]

Coville, Katherine - *The Cottage in the Woods*
    c CCB-B - v68 - i8 - April 2015 - p394(1) [51-500]
    y HB - v91 - i1 - Jan-Feb 2015 - p78(1) [51-500]
    c HB Guide - v26 - i2 - Fall 2015 - p79(1) [51-500]

Covington, Dennis - *Revelation*
    KR - Jan 1 2016 - pNA [51-500]

Cowan, Geoffrey - *Let the People Rule: Theodore Roosevelt and the Birth of the Presidential Primary*
    KR - Oct 1 2015 - pNA [501+]
    PW - v262 - i47 - Nov 23 2015 - p60(1) [501+]

Cowan, Mairi - *Death, Life, and Religious Change in Scottish Towns, c. 1350-1560*
    AHR - v120 - i1 - Feb 2015 - p316-317 [501+]

Cowan, Nancy - *Peregrine Spring: A Master Falconer's Extraordinary Life with Birds*
    KR - Dec 15 2015 - pNA [51-500]

Cowdell, Scott - *Rene Girard and Secular Modernity: Christ, Culture, and Crisis*
    Dialogue - v54 - i2 - June 2015 - p384-387 [501+]

Cowell, Cressida - *How to Train Your Dragon (Read by Tennant, David). Audiobook Review*
    y SLJ - v61 - i6 - June 2015 - p53(3) [501+]

How to Train Your Dragon
    c HB Guide - v26 - i1 - Spring 2015 - p74(1) [51-500]

Cowen, Rob - *Common Ground*
    Mac - v128 - i32-33 - August 17 2015 - p69(1) [501+]
    TLS - i5871 - Oct 9 2015 - p32(1) [501+]

Cowen, Tyler - *Average Is Over: Powering America beyond the Age of the Great Stagnation*
    Lon R Bks - v37 - i5 - March 5 2015 - p3(5) [501+]

Cowie, Helen - *Exhibiting Animals in Nineteenth-Century Britain: Empathy, Education, Entertainment*
    AHR - v120 - i3 - June 2015 - p1113-1114 [501+]

Cowin, Dana - *Chefs' Easy Weeknight Dinners*
    Ent W - i1346 - Jan 16 2015 - p67(1) [501+]

Cowley, Joy - *The Bakehouse*
    y Magpies - v30 - i3 - July 2015 - pS5(2) [501+]

Buzzy Bee's Birthday Party (Illus. by Holt, Richard)
    c Magpies - v30 - i2 - May 2015 - pS4(1) [501+]

Buzzy Bee's Food Shapes (Illus. by Holt, Richard)
    c Magpies - v30 - i2 - May 2015 - pS4(1) [501+]

Hush : A Kiwi Lullaby (Illus. by Burdan, Andrew)
    c Magpies - v30 - i2 - May 2015 - pS4(1) [501+]

Cowley, Philip - *Sex, Lies and the Ballot Box*
    NS - v144 - i5245 - Jan 16 2015 - p47(1) [51-500]

Cowling, Camillia - *Conceiving Freedom: Women of Color, Gender, and the Abolition of Slavery in Havana and Rio De Janeiro*
    Ams - v72 - i3 - July 2015 - p482(3) [501+]
    HAHR - v95 - i1 - Feb 2015 - p162-163 [501+]

Cox, David - *Good Enough for a Sheep Station*
    c Magpies - v30 - i4 - Sept 2015 - p22(2) [501+]

Cox, Devon - *The Street of Wonderful Possibilities: Whistler, Wilde and Sargent in Tite Street*
    Apo - v181 - i631 - May 2015 - p103(1) [51-500]
    TLS - i5873 - Oct 23 2015 - p12(1) [501+]

Cox, Harvey - *How to Read the Bible*
LJ - v140 - i5 - March 15 2015 - p110(2) [51-500]
PW - v262 - i10 - March 9 2015 - p67(2) [51-500]
BL - v111 - i15 - April 1 2015 - p5(1) [51-500]
CC - v132 - i20 - Sept 30 2015 - p41(2) [501+]
Cox, Howard - *Revolutions from Grub Street: A History of Magzine Publishing in Britain*
TimHES - i2229 - Nov 12 2015 - p47(1) [501+]
Cox, James H. - *The Oxford Handbook of Indigenous American Literature*
TLS - i5877 - Nov 20 2015 - p27(1) [501+]
The Red Land to the South: American Indian Writers and Indigenous Mexico
AL - v87 - i1 - March 2015 - p194-197 [501+]
Cox, Jeffrey N. - *Romanticism in the Shadow of War: Literary Culture in the Napoleonic War Years*
TLS - i5831 - Jan 2 2015 - p22(1) [501+]
Cox, Judy - *Cinco de Mouse-O! (Read by Heybome, Kirby). Audiobook Review*
c SLJ - v61 - i7 - July 2015 - p45(2) [51-500]
Go to Sleep, Groundhog! (Read by Berneis, Susie). Audiobook Review
c SLJ - v61 - i4 - April 2015 - p54(1) [51-500]
One Is a Feast for Mouse: A Thanksgiving Tale (Read by Heyborne, Kirby). Audiobook Review
c BL - v111 - i14 - March 15 2015 - p88(1) [51-500]
Cox, Karen L. - *Destination Dixie: Tourism and Southern History*
Historian - v77 - i1 - Spring 2015 - p112(4) [501+]
RAH - v43 - i1 - March 2015 - p116-125 [501+]
Cox, Karen M. - *At the Edge of the Sea*
PW - v262 - i16 - April 20 2015 - p63(1) [51-500]
Undeceived
PW - v262 - i52 - Dec 21 2015 - p141(1) [51-500]
Cox, Katherine - *Katie Fry, Private Eye: The Lost Kitten (Illus. by Newton, Vanessa Brantley)*
c BL - v111 - i22 - August 1 2015 - p74(1) [51-500]
Cox, Madison - *The Gardener's Garden*
TLS - i5845 - April 10 2015 - p30(2) [501+]
Cox, Paul - *Separado*
Roundup M - v22 - i3 - Feb 2015 - p25(1) [501+]
Roundup M - v22 - i6 - August 2015 - p28(1) [501+]
Cox, Rory - *John Wyclif on War and Peace*
CH - v84 - i4 - Dec 2015 - p871(2) [501+]
CHR - v101 - i3 - Summer 2015 - p632(2) [501+]
Cox, Russ - *Faraway Friends (Illus. by Cox, Russ)*
c PW - v262 - i13 - March 30 2015 - p73(1) [51-500]
c SLJ - v61 - i8 - August 2015 - p66(1) [51-500]
Cox, Stephen - *American Christianity: The Continuing Revolution*
CH - v84 - i2 - June 2015 - p478(2) [501+]
Cox, Steve - *If You Love Me, Take Me Now*
SPBW - Sept 2015 - pNA [51-500]
Cox, Tom - *The Good, the Bad, and the Furry: Life With the World's Most Melancholy Cat*
PW - v262 - i11 - March 16 2015 - p77(1) [51-500]
Coxe, Molly - *Wet Hen: A Short Vowel Adventure (Illus. by Coxe, Molly)*
c SLJ - v61 - i7 - July 2015 - p70(1) [51-500]
Coy, John - *Game Changer: John McLendon and the Secret Game (Illus. by DuBurke, Randy)*
c BL - v112 - i1 - Sept 1 2015 - p98(1) [51-500]
c HB - v91 - i6 - Nov-Dec 2015 - p100(1) [51-500]
c KR - July 15 2015 - pNA [51-500]
c NYTBR - Nov 8 2015 - p28(L) [501+]
c PW - v262 - i33 - August 17 2015 - p75(1) [51-500]
c PW - v262 - i49 - Dec 2 2015 - p46(2) [51-500]
c SLJ - v61 - i8 - August 2015 - p117(2) [51-500]
Their Great Gift: Courage, Sacrifice, and Hope in a New Land (Illus. by Huie, Wing Young)
c PW - v262 - i50 - Dec 7 2015 - p88(1) [51-500]
Coyle, Katie - *Vivian Apple at the End of the World (Read by Whelan, Julia). Audiobook Review*
y BL - v111 - i22 - August 1 2015 - p80(1) [51-500]
SLJ - v61 - i4 - April 2015 - p64(1) [51-500]
Vivian Apple at the End of the World
y CCB-B - v68 - i8 - April 2015 - p395(1) [51-500]
y CH Bwatch - Jan 2015 - pNA [51-500]
y HB - v91 - i1 - Jan-Feb 2015 - p78(2) [51-500]
y HB Guide - v26 - i2 - Fall 2015 - p115(1) [51-500]
y PW - v262 - i49 - Dec 2 2015 - p111(1) [51-500]
Vivian Apple Needs a Miracle
y BL - v112 - i2 - Sept 15 2015 - p64(2) [51-500]
y CCB-B - v69 - i2 - Oct 2015 - p83(1) [51-500]
y HB - v91 - i5 - Sept-Oct 2015 - p98(1) [51-500]
y KR - July 1 2015 - pNA [51-500]
y PW - v262 - i49 - Dec 2 2015 - p111(1) [51-500]
y SLJ - v61 - i7 - July 2015 - p91(2) [51-500]
y VOYA - v38 - i3 - August 2015 - p74(1) [501+]
Coyle, Matt - *Night Tremors*
BL - v111 - i17 - May 1 2015 - p38(1) [51-500]
LJ - v140 - i9 - May 15 2015 - p69(2) [51-500]
PW - v262 - i17 - April 27 2015 - p53(1) [51-500]
Coyle, Michael J. - *Taking Criminal Justice: Language and the Just Society*
CS - v44 - i3 - May 2015 - p351-352 [501+]
Coyle, Suzanne M. - *Uncovering Spiritual Narratives: Using Story in Pastoral Care and Ministry*
CC - v132 - i21 - Oct 14 2015 - p34(2) [501+]
Coyne, Jerry A. - *Faith vs. Fact: Why Science and Religion Are Incompatible*
BL - v111 - i17 - May 1 2015 - p61(2) [51-500]
CHE - v61 - i38 - June 12 2015 - pB5(1) [501+]
KR - March 15 2015 - pNA [501+]
PW - v262 - i12 - March 23 2015 - p62(1) [51-500]
Coyote, Peter - *The Rainman's Third Cure: An Irregular Education*
LJ - v140 - i10 - June 1 2015 - p120(2) [501+]
PW - v262 - i9 - March 2 2015 - p77(1) [51-500]
KR - Feb 1 2015 - pNA [501+]
Coysh, Louise - *Labyrinth: A Journey through London's Underground*
TLS - i5842 - March 20 2015 - p27(1) [501+]
Cozolino, Louis - *Why Therapy Works: Using Our Minds to Change Our Brains*
BL - v112 - i5 - Nov 1 2015 - p7(1) [51-500]
PW - v262 - i37 - Sept 14 2015 - p56(1) [51-500]
Cozzo, Karole - *How to Say I Love You Out Loud*
y SLJ - v61 - i5 - May 2015 - p112(1) [51-500]
Cozzolino, Robert - *David Lynch: The Unified Field*
LJ - v140 - i2 - Feb 1 2015 - p84(1) [501+]
Craats, Rennay - *The Cherokee*
c BL - v112 - i1 - Sept 1 2015 - p96(1) [51-500]
The Navajo
c BL - v112 - i1 - Sept 1 2015 - p96(1) [51-500]
Crabapple, Molly - *Drawing Blood: A Memoir*
BL - v112 - i7 - Dec 1 2015 - p9(1) [51-500]
KR - Oct 15 2015 - pNA [501+]
NYTBR - Dec 6 2015 - p60(L) [501+]
PW - v262 - i44 - Nov 2 2015 - p77(2) [51-500]
Crabb, David - *Bad Kid: A Memoir*
y BL - v111 - i17 - May 1 2015 - p71(1) [51-500]
KR - April 1 2015 - pNA [51-500]
PW - v262 - i15 - April 13 2015 - p73(1) [51-500]
Crabbe, Tony - *Busy: How to Thrive in a World of Too Much*
BL - v111 - i21 - July 1 2015 - p21(1) [51-500]
Nat Post - v17 - i225 - August 1 2015 - pWP4(1) [501+]
PW - v262 - i18 - May 4 2015 - p111(1) [51-500]
Crable, Bryan - *Ralph Ellison and Kenneth Burke: At the Roots of the Racial Divide*
Callaloo - v38 - i1 - Wntr 2015 - p216-219 [501+]
Crabtree, Sarah - *Holy Nation: The Transatlantic Quaker Ministry in an Age of Revolution*
JAAR - v83 - i2 - June 2015 - pNA [501+]
Craciun, Magdalena - *Material Culture and Authenticity: Fake Branded Fashion in Europe*
HNet - Sept 2015 - pNA(NA) [501+]
Craft, Kathryn - *The Far End of Happy*
LJ - v140 - i6 - April 1 2015 - p73(1) [51-500]
Craft, Tonya - *Accused: My Fight for Truth, Justice, and the Strength to Forgive*
RVBW - Oct 2015 - pNA [501+]
Crafton, Lisa Plummer - *Transgressive Theatricality, Romanticism, and Mary Wollstonecraft*
MLR - v110 - i3 - July 2015 - p836-837 [501+]
Crafts, Nicholas - *The Great Depression of the 1930s: Lessons for Today*
J Am St - v49 - i3 - August 2015 - p639-640 [501+]
Crago, Martha - *Applied Psycholinguistics*
Lang Soc - v44 - i4 - Sept 2015 - p607(1) [501+]
Cragwall, Jasper - *Lake Methodism: Polite Literature and Popular Religion in England, 1780-1830*
Bks & Cult - v21 - i4 - July-August 2015 - p32(2) [501+]
Nine-C Lit - v70 - i2 - Sept 2015 - p270(5) [501+]
Craig, Alan - *International Legitimacy and the Politics of Security: The Strategic Deployment of Lawmakers in the Israeli Military*
IJMES - v47 - i1 - Feb 2015 - p179-180 [501+]
Craig, Berry - *Kentucky Confederates: Secession, Civil War, and the Jackson Purchase*
JSH - v81 - i4 - Nov 2015 - p990(2) [501+]
Craig, David - *Languages of Politics in Nineteenth Century Britain*
HER - v130 - i544 - June 2015 - p767(3) [501+]
Petey & Wolf
KR - Sept 15 2015 - pNA [501+]
Craig, David M. - *Health Care as a Social Good: Religious Values and American Democracy*
AM - v212 - i7 - March 2 2015 - p42(2) [501+]
Craig, Douglas B. - *Progressives at War: William G. McAdoo and Newton D. Baker, 1863-1941*
Historian - v77 - i3 - Fall 2015 - p551(2) [501+]
Craig, Elizabeth - *The History of Nursing*
y VOYA - v38 - i3 - August 2015 - p90(1) [501+]
Craig, George - *The Letters of Samuel Beckett: 1957-1965*
Lon R Bks - v37 - i6 - March 19 2015 - p19(5) [501+]
NYRB - v62 - i6 - April 2 2015 - p54(3) [501+]
TLS - i5834 - Jan 23 2015 - p7(1) [501+]
Craig, Gerald M. - *Upper Canada: The Formative Years, 1784-1841*
Can Hist R - v96 - i1 - March 2015 - p118(3) [501+]
Craig, Lee A. - *Josephus Daniels: His Life and Times*
Historian - v77 - i1 - Spring 2015 - p115(2) [501+]
JAH - v102 - i2 - Sept 2015 - p571-572 [501+]
Pres St Q - v45 - i2 - June 2015 - p407(2) [501+]
Craig, Lizabeth - *Meningitis*
y VOYA - v38 - i2 - June 2015 - p88(1) [51-500]
Craig-Martin, Michael - *On Being an Artist*
NS - v144 - i5263 - May 22 2015 - p49(1) [501+]
TLS - i5867 - Sept 11 2015 - p26(1) [501+]
Craig, Maxine Leeds - *Sorry I Don't Dance: Why Men Refuse to Move*
AJS - v120 - i6 - May 2015 - p1889(2) [501+]
CS - v44 - i4 - July 2015 - p577-577 [501+]
Craig, Monique - *A Modern Look at the Hoof*
SPBW - March 2015 - pNA [51-500]
Craig, Ryan - *College Disrupted: The Great Unbundling of Higher Education*
BL - v111 - i21 - July 1 2015 - p22(2) [501+]
PW - v262 - i4 - Jan 26 2015 - p164(1) [501+]
Craig, Sherryn - *Midnight Madness at the Zoo (Illus. by Jones, Karen)*
c KR - Dec 15 2015 - pNA [51-500]
Craigo-Snell, Shannon - *The Empty Church: Theater, Theology, and Bodily Hope*
TT - v72 - i1 - April 2015 - p118-119 [501+]
Craik, Katharine A. - *Shakespearean Sensations: Experiencing Literature in Early Modern England*
MP - v113 - i1 - August 2015 - pE20(3) [501+]
Crais, Robert - *The Promise*
BL - v112 - i5 - Nov 1 2015 - p32(2) [51-500]
KR - Oct 1 2015 - pNA [51-500]
NYTBR - Nov 15 2015 - p29(L) [501+]
PW - v262 - i38 - Sept 21 2015 - p53(1) [51-500]
Cramby, Jonas - *Tex-Mex from Scratch*
LJ - v140 - i11 - June 15 2015 - p108(2) [501+]
Texas BBQ: Meat, Smoke, and Love
LJ - v140 - i11 - June 15 2015 - p108(2) [501+]
Cramer, Deborah - *The Narrow Edge: A Tiny Bird, an Ancient Crab, and an Epic Journey*
Nature - v521 - i7550 - May 7 2015 - p31(1) [501+]
New Sci - v226 - i3027 - June 27 2015 - p44(1) [501+]
NH - v123 - i2 - March 2015 - p46(1) [501+]
Cramp, Rosemary - *The Hirsel Excavations*
Specu - v90 - i1 - Jan 2015 - p233-235 [501+]
Cranach-Werke am Ort Ihrer Bestimmung
HNet - Jan 2015 - pNA [501+]
Crandall, Russell - *America's Dirty Wars: Irregular Warfare from 1776 to the War on Terror*
JAH - v101 - i4 - March 2015 - p1234-1235 [501+]
Crandall, Susan - *The Flying Circus*
BL - v111 - i19-20 - June 1 2015 - p59(1) [51-500]
KR - June 15 2015 - pNA [501+]
LJ - v140 - i12 - July 1 2015 - p75(1) [51-500]
PW - v262 - i21 - May 25 2015 - p29(2) [51-500]
Crane, Beverly E. - *How to Teach: A Practical Guide for Librarians*
LQ - v85 - i2 - April 2015 - p213(2) [501+]
Crane, David - *Went the Day Well? Witnessing Waterloo*
HT - v65 - i7 - July 2015 - p58(2) [501+]
KR - March 1 2015 - pNA [51-500]
LJ - v140 - i5 - March 15 2015 - p118(1) [501+]
PW - v262 - i12 - March 23 2015 - p62(2) [501+]
Spec - v327 - i9728 - Feb 7 2015 - p42(2) [501+]
Crane, Jakob - *Lies in the Dust: A Tale of Remorse from the Salem Witch Trials (Illus. by Decker, Timothy)*
y VOYA - v37 - i6 - Feb 2015 - p55(1) [51-500]
Crane, Joanna Tayloe - *Scrambling for Africa: AIDS, Expertise, and the Rise of American Global Health*

Science
    CS - v44 - i5 - Sept 2015 - p591-603 [501+]
Crane, Megan - *Make You Burn*
    PW - v262 - i27 - July 6 2015 - p53(1) [51-500]
Crane, Stuart - *Farmer David: The Dunster Show (Illus. by McLoughlin, Zack)*
    c CH Bwatch - Sept 2015 - pNA [51-500]
Crane, Tim - *Aspects of Psychologism*
    RM - v68 - i4 - June 2015 - p845(3) [501+]
Craney, Christopher M. - *Setting Aside All Authority: Giovanni Battista Riccioli and the Science against Copernicus in the Age of Galileo*
    S&T - v130 - i4 - Oct 2015 - p65(1) [501+]
Crangle, Richard - *Temptations Behind Stained Glass*
    RVBW - Oct 2015 - pNA [51-500]
Cranse, Pratima - *All the Major Constellations*
    y BL - v112 - i6 - Nov 15 2015 - p48(2) [51-500]
    y KR - Sept 1 2015 - pNA [51-500]
    y PW - v262 - i35 - August 31 2015 - p94(2) [51-500]
    y PW - v262 - i49 - Dec 2 2015 - p88(1) [51-500]
    y SLJ - v61 - i11 - Nov 2015 - p112(2) [51-500]
    y VOYA - v38 - i5 - Dec 2015 - p54(2) [51-500]
Crapanzano, Vincent - *Recapitulations*
    KR - Jan 15 2015 - pNA [51-500]
    NYTBR - July 19 2015 - p26(L) [501+]
    PW - v262 - i5 - Feb 2 2015 - p49(1) [51-500]
    TLS - i5848 - May 1 2015 - p9(1) [501+]
Crary, Jonathan - *24/7: Schlaflos im Spatkapitalismus*
    HNet - Jan 2015 - pNA [501+]
Crashaw, Richard - *The English Poems of Richard Crashaw*
    Ren Q - v68 - i1 - Spring 2015 - p411-412 [501+]
    Sev Cent N - v73 - i1-2 - Spring-Summer 2015 - p1(4) [501+]
Craven, Mike - *Born in a Burial Gown*
    KR - Nov 1 2015 - pNA [51-500]
    PW - v262 - i46 - Nov 16 2015 - p57(2) [51-500]
Cravens, Hamilton - *Cold War Social Science: Knowledge Production, Liberal Democracy, and Human Nature*
    T&C - v56 - i1 - Jan 2015 - p284-286 [501+]
Craw, Gloria - *Atlantis Rising*
    KR - Feb 1 2015 - pNA [501+]
Craw, Rachael - *Stray*
    y Magpies - v30 - i4 - Sept 2015 - p39(1) [501+]
Crawford, Alice - *The Meaning of the Library: A Cultural History*
    KR - April 15 2015 - pNA [501+]
    Mac - v128 - i31 - August 10 2015 - p57(2) [501+]
    BL - v111 - i19-20 - June 1 2015 - p5(1) [51-500]
    PW - v262 - i20 - May 18 2015 - p78(1) [51-500]
    Nature - v525 - i7567 - Sept 3 2015 - p31(1) [51-500]
Crawford, Brent - *Carter Finally Gets It (Read by Podehl, Nick). Audiobook Review*
    c SLJ - v61 - i2 - Feb 2015 - p38(3) [501+]
Crawford, C.F. - *Tales of Mr. Snuggywhiskers: The Autumn Tales (Illus. by Crawford, L.H.)*
    c CH Bwatch - Oct 2015 - pNA [51-500]
Crawford, Cassandra S. - *Phantom Limb: Amputation, Embodiment, and Prosthetic Technology*
    MAQ - v29 - i1 - March 2015 - pB49-B51 [501+]
Crawford, Dorothy H. - *Cancer Virus: The Story of Epstein-Barr Virus*
    Am Bio T - v77 - i1 - Jan 2015 - p79(2) [501+]
Crawford, Harriet - *Ur: The City of the Moon God*
    TLS - i5862 - August 7 2015 - p28(1) [501+]
Crawford, Isis - *A Catered Mother's Day*
    PW - v262 - i12 - March 23 2015 - p49(1) [51-500]
Crawford, James - *Fallen Glory: The Lives and Deaths of Twenty Lost Buildings from the Tower of Babel to the Twin Towers*
    Spec - v329 - i9768 - Nov 14 2015 - p56(1) [501+]
Crawford, Julie - *Mediatrix: Women, Politics, & Literary Production in Early Modern England*
    Ren Q - v68 - i3 - Fall 2015 - p1131-1132 [501+]
    RES - v66 - i274 - April 2015 - p369-370 [501+]
    TLS - i5850 - May 15 2015 - p27(1) [501+]
Crawford, Matthew B. - *The World beyond Your Head: How to Flourish in an Age of Distraction*
    NS - v144 - i5266 - June 12 2015 - p46(2) [501+]
The World beyond Your Head: On Becoming an Individual in an Age of Distraction
    BL - v111 - i4 - March 15 2015 - p28(2) [51-500]
    Comw - v142 - i8 - May 1 2015 - p43(3) [501+]
    LJ - v140 - i3 - Feb 15 2015 - p105(2) [51-500]
    Nature - v520 - i7547 - April 16 2015 - p293(1) [51-500]
    Soc - v52 - i3 - June 2015 - p283(1) [501+]
    TimHES - i2200 - April 23 2015 - p54(1) [501+]
Crawford, Michael J. - *The Fight for Status and Privilege in Late Medieval and Early Modern Castile, 1465-1598*
    AHR - v120 - i4 - Oct 2015 - p1565(1) [501+]
    JEH - v75 - i1 - March 2015 - p278-279 [501+]
    Ren Q - v68 - i2 - Summer 2015 - p683-685 [501+]
    Six Ct J - v46 - i1 - Spring 2015 - p237-239 [501+]
Crawford, Raymond - *Plague and Pestilence in Literature and Art*
    Nature - v517 - i7532 - Jan 1 2015 - p28(1) [51-500]
Crawford, Robert - *Young Eliot: From St. Louis to The Waste Land*
    BL - v111 - i12 - Feb 15 2015 - p20(2) [51-500]
    Econ - v414 - i8925 - Feb 14 2015 - p74(US) [501+]
    LJ - v140 - i3 - Feb 15 2015 - p99(1) [51-500]
    Nat R - v67 - i4 - August 10 2015 - p45 [501+]
    NS - v144 - i5247 - Jan 30 2015 - p40(3) [501+]
    NY - v91 - i13 - May 18 2015 - p97 [501+]
    NYTBR - August 23 2015 - p16(L) [501+]
    PW - v262 - i4 - Jan 26 2015 - p158(1) [51-500]
    Spec - v327 - i9727 - Jan 31 2015 - p34(2) [501+]
    TLS - i5863 - August 14 2015 - p3(3) [501+]
Crawford, Robert (b. 1959-) - *Young Eliot: From St. Louis to The Waste Land*
    KR - Jan 1 2015 - pNA [501+]
Crawford, Stanley - *The Canyon*
    Roundup M - v23 - i1 - Oct 2015 - p29(1) [501+]
Seed
    KR - Jan 15 2015 - pNA [51-500]
Crawford, Susan - *The Pocket Wife*
    BL - v111 - i11 - Feb 1 2015 - p28(1) [51-500]
    KR - Feb 1 2015 - pNA [51-500]
    LJ - v140 - i3 - Feb 15 2015 - p85(1) [51-500]
    PW - v262 - i4 - Jan 26 2015 - p147(2) [51-500]
Crawford, Tom - *Caging the Robin*
    KR - May 1 2015 - pNA [501+]
Crawford, Walt - *The Librarian's Guide to Micropublishing: Helping Patrons and Communities Use Free and Low-Cost Publishing Tools To Tell Their Stories*
    LJ - v140 - i11 - June 15 2015 - p46(1) [501+]
Crawforth, Hannah - *Etymology and the Invention of English in Early-Modern Literature*
    MP - v113 - i1 - August 2015 - pE17(3) [501+]
    Ren Q - v68 - i2 - Summer 2015 - p755-757 [501+]
    TLS - i5857 - July 3 2015 - p11(1) [501+]
Shakespeare in London
    HT - v65 - i8 - August 2015 - p63(1) [501+]
Cray, Robert E. - *Lovewell's Fight: War, Death, and Memory in Borderland New England*
    HNet - Feb 2015 - pNA [501+]
    J Mil H - v79 - i2 - April 2015 - p482-483 [501+]
    NEQ - v88 - i2 - June 2015 - p325-327 [501+]
Cready, Gwyn - *First Time with a Highlander*
    PW - v262 - i31 - August 3 2015 - p41(1) [51-500]
Just in Time for a Highlander
    BL - v111 - i9-10 - Jan 1 2015 - p56(1) [51-500]
Creager, Angela N.H. - *Life Atomic: A History of Radioisotopes in Science and Medicine*
    Isis - v106 - i1 - March 2015 - p221(2) [501+]
Creagh, Kelly - *Oblivion*
    y KR - May 1 2015 - pNA [501+]
    y BL - v111 - i19-20 - June 1 2015 - p100(1) [51-500]
    y SLJ - v61 - i6 - June 2015 - p122(1) [51-500]
Crease, Robert P. - *The Quantum Moment: How Planck, Bohr, Einstein, and Heisenberg Taught Us to Love Uncertainty*
    NYT - Feb 17 2015 - pD3(L) [501+]
    Phys Today - v68 - i2 - Feb 2015 - p50-51 [501+]
Creegan, Nicola Hoggard - *Animal Suffering and the Problem of Evil*
    Theol St - v76 - i2 - June 2015 - p395(2) [501+]
Creek, Dave - *The Human Equations*
    Analog - v135 - i5 - May 2015 - p105(2) [501+]
Cregan, Lisa - *House Beautiful Pink*
    LJ - v140 - i15 - Sept 15 2015 - p78(1) [51-500]
Creighton, Scott - *The Secret Chamber of Osiris: Lost Knowledge of the Sixteen Pyramids*
    RVBW - Feb 2015 - pNA [51-500]
Creighton, Susan Janssen - *Bringing Math Students into the Formative Assessment Equation: Tools and Strategies for the Middle Grades*
    Bwatch - May 2015 - pNA [501+]
Cremer, Andrea - *The Conjurer's Riddle*
    y KR - Sept 1 2015 - pNA [51-500]
    y VOYA - v38 - i5 - Dec 2015 - p67(1) [51-500]
Cremonesi, Kathleen - *Love in the Elephant Tent: How Running Away with the Circus Brought Me Home*
    BL - v111 - i18 - May 15 2015 - p10(1) [51-500]
    PW - v262 - i11 - March 16 2015 - p77(1) [51-500]
Crenn, Dominique - *Atelier Crenn: Metamorphosis of Taste (Illus. by Anderson, Ed)*
    BL - v112 - i4 - Oct 15 2015 - p11(1) [51-500]
    LJ - v140 - i13 - August 1 2015 - p118(1) [51-500]
Crespino, Joseph - *Strom Thurmond's America*
    RAH - v43 - i2 - June 2015 - p361-368 [501+]
Crespo, Ana - *J.P. and the Bossy Dinosaur (Illus. by Sirotich, Erica)*
    c KR - Dec 15 2015 - pNA [51-500]
J.P. and the Giant Octopus (Illus. by Sirotich, Erica)
    c KR - July 1 2015 - pNA [51-500]
    c PW - v262 - i22 - June 1 2015 - p58(1) [501+]
The Sock Thief (Illus. by Gonzalez, Nana)
    c CCB-B - v68 - i10 - June 2015 - p484(2) [501+]
    c HB Guide - v26 - i2 - Fall 2015 - p30(1) [501+]
Crespo, Hiram - *Tending the Epicurean Garden*
    Hum - v75 - i1 - Jan-Feb 2015 - p43(2) [501+]
Cresswell, Lisa T. - *Vessel*
    y SLJ - v61 - i10 - Oct 2015 - p109(1) [501+]
Cressy, David - *Charles I and the People of England*
    Bks & Cult - v21 - i6 - Nov-Dec 2015 - p22(2) [501+]
    TimHES - i2211 - July 9 2015 - p49(1) [501+]
    TLS - i5868 - Sept 18 2015 - p7(1) [501+]
Saltpeter: The Mother of Gunpowder
    Ren Q - v68 - i2 - Summer 2015 - p695-696 [501+]
Creswell, Helen - *The Return of the Psammead*
    c Magpies - v30 - i1 - March 2015 - p14(2) [501+]
Crew, Hilary Susan - *Experiencing America's Story through Fiction: Historical Novels for Grades 7-12*
    R&USQ - v54 - i4 - Summer 2015 - p71(1) [501+]
    CCB-B - v68 - i6 - Feb 2015 - p337(1) [501+]
    y VOYA - v38 - i1 - April 2015 - p90(1) [501+]
Crew, Joseph - *Fall In, Fall Out: The Dogface Years*
    SPBW - March 2015 - pNA [51-500]
Crewe, Don - *Becoming Criminal: The Socio-Cultural Origins of Law, Transgression, and Deviance*
    CS - v44 - i2 - March 2015 - p188-189 [501+]
Crewe, Emma - *The House of Commons: An Anthropology of Mps at Work*
    TimHES - i2199 - April 16 2015 - p60(1) [501+]
Crewe, Megan - *Earth and Sky (Read by Dykhouse, Whitney). Audiobook Review*
    SLJ - v61 - i2 - Feb 2015 - p51(1) [51-500]
    y SLJ - v61 - i12 - Dec 2015 - p78(1) [51-500]
Earth & Sky
    y Res Links - v20 - i3 - Feb 2015 - p26(2) [51-500]
Crewe, Sabrina - *Canadian Coins*
    c HB Guide - v26 - i2 - Fall 2015 - p219(2) [51-500]
Canadian Mounties
    c HB Guide - v26 - i2 - Fall 2015 - p219(2) [51-500]
Crews, C. Daniel - *Records of the Moravians Among the Cherokees, vol. 5: The Anna Rosina Years, Part 3: Farewell to Sister Gambold, 1817-1821*
    JSH - v81 - i4 - Nov 2015 - p967(2) [501+]
Crews, Donald - *Freight Train (Illus. by Crews, Donald)*
    c BL - v112 - i4 - Oct 15 2015 - p53(1) [51-500]
Crews, Robert D. - *Afghan Modern*
    KR - July 15 2015 - pNA [501+]
Criado-Perez, Caroline - *Do It Like a Woman*
    NS - v144 - i5264 - May 29 2015 - p83(1) [501+]
Cribb, Robert - *Wild Man from Borneo: A Cultural History of the Orangutan*
    AHR - v120 - i2 - April 2015 - p601-602 [501+]
Cribiore, Raffaella - *Libanius the Sophist: Rhetoric, Reality, and Religion in the Fourth Century*
    AJP - v136 - i3 - Fall 2015 - p537-540 [501+]
    Class R - v65 - i1 - April 2015 - p99-101 [501+]
Criblez, Adam - *Parading Patriotism: Independence Day Celebrations in the Urban Midwest, 1826-1876*
    JAH - v101 - i4 - March 2015 - p1273-1274 [501+]
Crichton, Michael - *Jurassic Park (Read by Brick, Scott). Audiobook Review*
    BL - v111 - i22 - August 1 2015 - p80(1) [51-500]
Jurassic Park
    Forbes - v195 - i8 - June 15 2015 - p22(1) [501+]
Crider, Bill - *Between the Living and the Dead*
    BL - v111 - i19-20 - June 1 2015 - p47(1) [51-

500]
    KR - June 1 2015 - pNA [51-500]
    PW - v262 - i21 - May 25 2015 - p33(2) [51-500]
Crilley, Mark - *The Realism Challenge: Drawing and Painting Secrets from a Modern Master of Hyperrealism*
    LJ - v140 - i5 - March 15 2015 - p106(1) [51-500]
Crimi, Frank - *Divine Roosters and Angry Clowns*
    SPBW - Feb 2015 - p20(1) [51-500]
Criminal Law and Emotions in European Legal Cultures: From the 16th Century to the Present
    HNet - July 2015 - pNA [501+]
Criniti, Nicola - *Mantissa Veleiate*
    Class R - v65 - i2 - Oct 2015 - p617-617 [501+]
Crisantino, Amelia - *Studii su la storia di Sicilia dalla meta del XVIII secolo al 1820 di Michele Amari*
    HER - v130 - i542 - Feb 2015 - p223(2) [501+]
Crises in Early Modern Times: Scenarios - Experiences - Management - Coping
    HNet - March 2015 - pNA [501+]
Crislip, Andrew - *Thorns in the Flesh: Illness and Sanctity in Late Ancient Christianity*
    Theol St - v76 - i1 - March 2015 - p170(2) [501+]
Crispin, Darla - *Artistic Experimentation in Music: An Anthology*
    Am MT - v65 - i3 - Dec 2015 - p44(1) [501+]
Crispin, Jessa - *The Creative Tarot: A Modern Guide to an Inspired Life*
    PW - v262 - i51 - Dec 14 2015 - p78(2) [51-500]
The Dead Ladies Project: Exiles, Expats, and Ex-Countries
    LJ - v140 - i12 - July 1 2015 - p102(1) [51-500]
    KR - August 1 2015 - pNA [501+]
    PW - v262 - i25 - June 22 2015 - p129(1) [51-500]
Crist, James J - *The Survival Guide for Making and Being Friends*
    c SLJ - v61 - i2 - Feb 2015 - p118(1) [51-500]
Cristofono, Peter - *Rockhounding New England: A Guide to 100 of the Region's Best Rockhounding Sites*
    RocksMiner - v90 - i2 - March-April 2015 - p189(2) [501+]
Critchley, Simon - *Memory Theater*
    KR - Sept 15 2015 - pNA [51-500]
    NYTBR - Dec 20 2015 - p11(L) [501+]
    PW - v262 - i27 - July 6 2015 - p43(1) [51-500]
    PW - v262 - i44 - Nov 2 2015 - p54(2) [501+]
Memory Theatre
    TLS - i5833 - Jan 16 2015 - p20(1) [501+]
Suicide
    KR - Sept 15 2015 - pNA [51-500]
Crites, Terry - *Putting Essential Understanding into Practice: Statistics, 9-12*
    Math T - v109 - i3 - Oct 2015 - p236-1 [501+]
Crivellari, Daniele - *Marcas autoriales de segmentacion en las comedias autografas de Lope de Vega: Estudio y analisis*
    Ren Q - v68 - i1 - Spring 2015 - p377-378 [501+]
Crivelli, Paolo - *Plato's Account of Falsehood: A Study of the Sophist*
    Class R - v65 - i1 - April 2015 - p53-55 [501+]
Croce, Marcella - *The Chivalric Folk Tradition in Sicily: A History of Storytelling, Puppetry, Painted Carts and Other Arts*
    TLS - i5838 - Feb 20 2015 - p27(1) [501+]
Crocker, Chester A. - *Managing Conflict in a World Adrift*
    HNet - Sept 2015 - pNA [501+]
Crocker, Terri Blom - *The Christmas Truce: Myth, Memory, and the First World War*
    KR - Sept 15 2015 - pNA [501+]
Crockett, Bryan - *Love's Alchemy*
    KR - Feb 1 2015 - pNA [51-500]
Crockett, Clayton - *Radical Political Theology: Religion and Politics after Liberalism*
    JR - v95 - i2 - April 2015 - p264(2) [501+]
Croft, Roger - *The Maghreb Conspiracy: The Third Spy Story in Croft's*
    PW - v262 - i2 - Jan 12 2015 - p40(1) [51-500]
Croft, Stuart - *Securitizing Islam: Identity and the Search for Security*
    J Ch St - v57 - i1 - Wntr 2015 - p158-160 [501+]
Croft, Susan - *The Sixth Form MBA*
    Sch Lib - v63 - i1 - Spring 2015 - p63(1) [51-500]
Crofts, Freeman Wills - *Antidote to Venom*
    BL - v111 - i19-20 - June 1 2015 - p47(1) [51-500]
The Hog's Back Mystery
    BL - v111 - i19-20 - June 1 2015 - p54(1) [51-500]
Croggon, Allison - *The River and the Book*
    y Magpies - v30 - i4 - Sept 2015 - p39(1) [501+]

Croizy-Naquet, Catherine - *Faire court: L'esthetique de la brievete dans la litterature du Moyen Age*
    Specu - v90 - i4 - Oct 2015 - p1104-1106 [501+]
Crombie, Deborah - *To Dwell in Darkness*
    RVBW - June 2015 - pNA [501+]
    RVBW - July 2015 - pNA [51-500]
Crompton, Laurie Boyle - *Adrenaline Crush*
    c HB Guide - v26 - i1 - Spring 2015 - p104(1) [51-500]
Crompton, Richard - *Hell's Gate*
    BL - v111 - i17 - May 1 2015 - p36(2) [51-500]
    KR - April 1 2015 - pNA [51-500]
    PW - v262 - i16 - April 20 2015 - p53(1) [51-500]
Crompton, Samuel Willard - *The Handy Military Answer Book*
    y VOYA - v38 - i1 - April 2015 - p90(1) [51-500]
Cromwell, Mare - *The Great Mother Bible*
    KR - Jan 1 2016 - pNA [51-500]
Cromwell, Rue L. - *Being Human: Human Being, Manifesto for a New Psychology*
    AJPsy - v128 - i1 - Spring 2015 - p128(5) [501+]
Cron, Lisa - *Wired for Story*
    J Chem Ed - v92 - i7 - July 2015 - p1140-1142 [501+]
Cronenberg, David - *Consumed*
    BL - v111 - i18 - May 15 2015 - p34(1) [501+]
    Lon R Bks - v37 - i12 - June 18 2015 - p36(3) [501+]
    NYTBR - Oct 18 2015 - p28(L) [501+]
Consumed (Read by Hurt, William). Audiobook Review
    LJ - v140 - i2 - Feb 1 2015 - p44(1) [51-500]
Cronin, Blaise - *Scholarly Metrics Under the Microscope*
    Bwatch - March 2015 - pNA [51-500]
Cronin, Doreen - *Bloom (Illus. by Small, David)*
    c BL - v112 - i7 - Dec 1 2015 - p64(2) [51-500]
    c KR - Nov 1 2015 - pNA [51-500]
Boom Snot Twitty (Read by Gilbert, Tavia). Audiobook Review
    c BL - v112 - i6 - Nov 15 2015 - p63(1) [51-500]
Boom Snot Twitty This Way That Way (Illus. by Liwska, Renata)
    c BL - v111 - i18 - May 15 2015 - p57(1) [51-500]
Boom Snot Twitty: This Way That Way (Illus. by Liwska, Renata)
    c HB - v91 - i4 - July-August 2015 - p112(1) [51-500]
Boom Snot Twitty This Way That Way (Illus. by Liwska, Renata)
    c KR - April 1 2015 - pNA [51-500]
    c SLJ - v61 - i5 - May 2015 - p83(1) [51-500]
The Case of the Weird Blue Chicken: The Next Misadventure (Read by Crupper, Adam). Audiobook Review
    c SLJ - v61 - i3 - March 2015 - p76(1) [51-500]
The Case of the Weird Blue Chicken: The Next Misadventure (Illus. by Cornell, Kevin)
    c HB Guide - v26 - i1 - Spring 2015 - p58(1) [51-500]
The Chicken Squad: The First Misadventure (Read by Grupper, Adam). Audiobook Review
    c SLJ - v61 - i4 - April 2015 - p52(2) [501+]
Click, Clack, Ho! Ho! Ho! (Illus. by Lewin, Betsy)
    c BL - v112 - i4 - Oct 15 2015 - p48(1) [51-500]
    c HB - v91 - i6 - Nov-Dec 2015 - p54(2) [51-500]
    c PW - v262 - i37 - Sept 14 2015 - p74(1) [51-500]
    c PW - v262 - i49 - Dec 2 2015 - p60(1) [51-500]
    c SLJ - v61 - i10 - Oct 2015 - p62(1) [51-500]
Click, Clack, Peep! (Illus. by Lewin, Betsy)
    c HB Guide - v26 - i2 - Fall 2015 - p9(1) [51-500]
Smick! (Illus. by Medina, Juana)
    c CCB-B - v68 - i7 - March 2015 - p351(2) [51-500]
    c HB - v91 - i1 - Jan-Feb 2015 - p63(1) [51-500]
    c HB Guide - v26 - i2 - Fall 2015 - p9(1) [51-500]
    SLJ - v61 - i2 - Feb 2015 - p64(2) [51-500]
Thump, Quack, Moo (Read by England, Maurice). Audiobook Review
    c SLJ - v61 - i12 - Dec 2015 - p74(1) [51-500]
Cronin, James E. - *Global Rules: America, Britain and a Disordered World*
    For Aff - v94 - i1 - Jan-Feb 2015 - pNA [51-500]
    HNet - May 2015 - pNA [501+]
Cronin, Paul - *Be Sand, Not Oil: The Life and Work of Amos Vogel*
    Si & So - v25 - i1 - Jan 2015 - p105(1) [501+]
The Guide for the Perplexed
    Si & So - v25 - i1 - Feb 2015 - p104(2) [501+]
Werner Herzog: A Guide for the for the Perplexed
    FQ - v69 - i1 - Fall 2015 - p102(3) [501+]

Cronn-Mills, Kirstin - *Transgender Lives: Complex Stories, Complex Voices*
    y CCB-B - v68 - i5 - Jan 2015 - p251(1) [51-500]
    y HB Guide - v26 - i2 - Fall 2015 - p151(1) [51-500]
Cronon, William - *Wilderburbs: Communities on Nature's Edge*
    WHQ - v46 - i3 - Autumn 2015 - p387-388 [501+]
Cronshagen, Jessica - *Einfach Vornehm: Die Hausleute der Nordwestwestdeutschen Kustenmarsch in der Fruhen Neuzeit*
    HNet - March 2015 - pNA [501+]
Crook, Elizabeth - *Monday, Monday*
    Roundup M - v22 - i4 - April 2015 - p32(1) [501+]
    Roundup M - v22 - i6 - August 2015 - p28(1) [501+]
Crook, Jeff - *The Covenant: A Jackie Lyons Mystery*
    PW - v262 - i47 - Nov 23 2015 - p47(2) [51-500]
Crooke, Robert - *The Chastened Heart*
    KR - Jan 15 2015 - pNA [501+]
Cropper, Susan - *Vintage Crochet: 30 Specially Commissioned Patterns (Illus. by Perers, Kristin)*
    LJ - v140 - i3 - Feb 15 2015 - p100(1) [51-500]
Crosbie, Lynn - *Where Did You Sleep Last Night?*
    Mac - v128 - i18 - May 11 2015 - p61(1) [501+]
Crosby, Christina - *A Body, Undone*
    KR - Dec 15 2015 - pNA [51-500]
Crosby, Ellen - *Ghost Image*
    BL - v111 - i13 - March 1 2015 - p23(1) [51-500]
    KR - Feb 15 2015 - pNA [51-500]
    PW - v262 - i3 - Jan 19 2015 - p61(1) [51-500]
Crosby, Heather - *YumUniverse: Infinite Possibilities for a Gluten-Free, Plant-Powerful, Whole-Food Lifestyle*
    LJ - v140 - i2 - Feb 1 2015 - p103(1) [51-500]
Crosby, John F. - *The Personalism of John Henry Newman*
    Theol St - v76 - i2 - June 2015 - p355(2) [501+]
Crosley, Sloane - *The Clasp*
    BL - v112 - i2 - Sept 15 2015 - p26(1) [51-500]
    NYT - Dec 7 2015 - pNA(L) [51-500]
    NYTBR - Oct 4 2015 - p10(L) [51-500]
    KR - August 1 2015 - pNA [501+]
    PW - v262 - i27 - July 6 2015 - p42(1) [51-500]
Cross, Craig - *London: A Visitor's Guide*
    KR - Oct 15 2015 - pNA [51-500]
Cross, Gillian - *The Iliad (Illus. by Packer, Neil)*
    c BL - v112 - i3 - Oct 1 2015 - p39(1) [51-500]
    y SLJ - v61 - i10 - Oct 2015 - p134(1) [51-500]
Shadow Cat
    c Sch Lib - v63 - i2 - Summer 2015 - p102(1) [51-500]
Cross, Graham - *The Diplomatic Education of Franklin D. Roosevelt, 1882-1933*
    Pres St Q - v45 - i1 - March 2015 - p208(2) [501+]
Cross, H.S. - *Wilberforce*
    y BL - v112 - i1 - Sept 1 2015 - p53(1) [501+]
    KR - July 15 2015 - pNA [501+]
    LJ - v140 - i12 - July 1 2015 - p75(1) [51-500]
    PW - v262 - i30 - July 27 2015 - p41(1) [51-500]
Cross, Julie - *Halfway Perfect*
    y KR - March 1 2015 - pNA [51-500]
    y KR - March 1 2015 - pNA [51-500]
    y VOYA - v38 - i1 - April 2015 - p56(1) [51-500]
Cross, Kady - *Sisters of Blood and Spirit*
    y BL - v111 - i16 - April 15 2015 - p48(1) [51-500]
    y HB Guide - v26 - i2 - Fall 2015 - p115(1) [51-500]
Cross, Keef - *DayBlack*
    PW - v262 - i25 - June 22 2015 - p128(1) [51-500]
Cross, Kim - *What Stands in a Storm: Three Days in the Worst Superstorm to Hit the South's Tornado Valley*
    KR - Jan 15 2015 - pNA [51-500]
    PW - v262 - i2 - Jan 12 2015 - p53(1) [51-500]
Cross, Mason - *The Samaritan*
    BL - v112 - i6 - Nov 15 2015 - p28(2) [51-500]
    KR - Dec 1 2015 - pNA [51-500]
    PW - v262 - i51 - Dec 14 2015 - p59(2) [51-500]
Cross, Mimi - *Before Goodbye*
    y VOYA - v38 - i5 - Dec 2015 - p55(1) [501+]
Cross, Sarah - *Tear You Apart*
    y HB Guide - v26 - i2 - Fall 2015 - p115(1) [51-500]
Cross, Stephen - *Schopenhauer's Encounter with Indian Thought: Representation and Will and Their Indian Parallels*
    JAS - v74 - i2 - May 2015 - p506-508 [501+]
Cross, Tim - *The Architecture of Freedom: How to Free Your Soul*
    KR - July 1 2015 - pNA [501+]
    SPBW - July 2015 - pNA [51-500]

Crossan, Jeff - *I Ate a Cicada Today (Illus. by Crossan, Jeff)*
  c   CH Bwatch - Jan 2015 - pNA [51-500]
  c   CH Bwatch - Jan 2015 - pNA [51-500]
I Ate a Cicada Today
  c   CH Bwatch - Jan 2015 - pNA [51-500]
  c   CH Bwatch - Jan 2015 - pNA [51-500]
Crossan, John Dominic - *How to Read the Bible and Still Be a Christian: Struggling with Divine Violence from Genesis through Revelation*
     BL - v111 - i14 - March 15 2015 - p29(1) [51-500]
Crossan, Sarah - *Apple and Rain*
  y   BL - v111 - i13 - March 1 2015 - p47(1) [501+]
  y   BL - v111 - i15 - April 1 2015 - p64(1) [51-500]
  y   CCB-B - v68 - i10 - June 2015 - p485(1) [51-500]
  y   HB Guide - v26 - i2 - Fall 2015 - p115(1) [51-500]
  y   KR - March 1 2015 - pNA [51-500]
     PW - v262 - i14 - April 6 2015 - p62(1) [51-500]
     SLJ - v61 - i4 - April 2015 - p152(2) [51-500]
  y   VOYA - v38 - i1 - April 2015 - p56(1) [51-500]
One
  y   Magpies - v30 - i4 - Sept 2015 - p40(1) [501+]
  y   PW - v262 - i49 - Dec 2 2015 - p96(1) [51-500]
  y   SLJ - v61 - i10 - Oct 2015 - p109(1) [51-500]
  y   HB - v91 - i5 - Sept-Oct 2015 - p98(2) [51-500]
  y   KR - July 1 2015 - pNA [51-500]
  y   Sch Lib - v63 - i3 - Autumn 2015 - p180(1) [501+]
  y   VOYA - v38 - i3 - August 2015 - p57(1) [51-500]
  y   BL - v111 - i21 - July 1 2015 - p58(1) [51-500]
  y   PW - v262 - i28 - July 13 2015 - p69(1) [51-500]
Crossingham, John - *Turn Off That Light!*
  c   KR - August 1 2015 - pNA [51-500]
Crossley-Holland, Kevin - *The Breaking Hour*
     Sch Lib - v63 - i4 - Winter 2015 - p241(1) [51-500]
Crossman, Virginia - *Poverty and the Poor Law in Ireland, 1850-1914*
     HER - v130 - i544 - June 2015 - p770(3) [501+]
Crouch, Christian A. - *Nobility Lost: French and Canadian Martial Cultures, Indians, and the End of New France*
     Six Ct J - v46 - i3 - Fall 2015 - p738-740 [501+]
Crouch, Christian Ayne - *Nobility Lost: French and Canadian Martial Cultures, Indians, and the End of New France*
     AHR - v120 - i4 - Oct 2015 - p1476-1477 [501+]
     HNet - August 2015 - pNA [501+]
     JAH - v102 - i1 - June 2015 - p222-223 [501+]
     NEQ - v88 - i1 - March 2015 - p164-166 [501+]
     W&M Q - v72 - i3 - July 2015 - p532-535 [501+]
Crouch, Hubert - *The Word*
     SPBW - June 2015 - pNA [51-500]
     KR - Feb 15 2015 - pNA [51-500]
Crouch, Katie - *Abroad*
     NYTBR - Sept 20 2015 - p28(L) [501+]
Crousaz, Karine - *Pierre Viret et la diffusion de la Reforme: Pense'e, action, contextes religieux*
     CHR - v101 - i3 - Summer 2015 - p651(2) [501+]
Crouse, Eric R. - *American Christian Support for Israel: Standing with the Chosen People, 1948-1975*
     CHR - v101 - i4 - Autumn 2015 - p971(1) [501+]
Crouwel, Joost H. - *Chariots and Other Wheeled Vehicles in Italy before the Roman Empire*
     Class R - v65 - i2 - Oct 2015 - p520-522 [501+]
Crouzet-Pavan, Elisabeth - *Cites humanistes, cites politiques, 1400-1600*
     Six Ct J - v46 - i3 - Fall 2015 - p773-775 [501+]
Crow, Donna Fletcher - *A Newly Crimsoned Reliquary*
     SPBW - May 2015 - pNA [51-500]
Crow, Joanna - *The Mapuche in Modern Chile: A Cultural History*
     Ams - v72 - i3 - July 2015 - p494(2) [501+]
Crow, Kristyn - *Zombelina Dances The Nutcracker (Illus. by Idle, Molly)*
  c   HB - v91 - i6 - Nov-Dec 2015 - p55(1) [51-500]
  c   KR - Sept 1 2015 - pNA [51-500]
     PW - v262 - i37 - Sept 14 2015 - p76(1) [51-500]
  c   SLJ - v61 - i10 - Oct 2015 - p62(1) [51-500]
Crow, Matthew - *The Brilliant Light of Amber Sunrise*
  y   BL - v111 - i12 - Feb 15 2015 - p79(1) [51-500]
  y   CCB-B - v68 - i8 - April 2015 - p395(2) [51-500]
  y   HB Guide - v26 - i2 - Fall 2015 - p115(1) [51-500]
  y   KR - Jan 1 2015 - pNA [51-500]
Crow, Michael M. - *Designing the New American University*
     CHE - v61 - i37 - May 29 2015 - pA18(1) [51-500]
     LJ - v140 - i7 - April 15 2015 - p98(3) [51-500]
     Nature - v523 - i7562 - July 30 2015 - p529(1) [51-500]
     TimHES - i2197 - April 2 2015 - p57(1) [501+]
Crow, Nosy - *Cutie Pie Looks for the Easter Bunny: A Tiny Tab Book (Illus. by Ho, Jannie)*
  c   KR - July 1 2015 - pNA [51-500]
Pookie Pop Plays Hide-and-Seek: A Tiny Tab Book (Illus. by Ho, Jannie)
  c   KR - July 1 2015 - pNA [51-500]
Crow, Thomas - *The Long March of Pop: Art, Music, and Design, 1930-1995*
     Apo - v181 - i631 - May 2015 - p104(2) [501+]
     TLS - i5874 - Oct 30 2015 - p17(1) [501+]
Crowder, Drew - *Kaya's Journey Begins, 2 vols. (Illus. by Myers, Morgan Rae)*
  c   SLJ - v61 - i12 - Dec 2015 - p109(2) [51-500]
Crowder, Melanie - *Audacity*
  y   CCB-B - v68 - i7 - March 2015 - p352(1) [51-500]
  y   Teach Lib - v42 - i5 - June 2015 - p18(1) [51-500]
A Nearer Moon
  c   KR - June 15 2015 - pNA [51-500]
  c   PW - v262 - i25 - June 22 2015 - p137(1) [51-500]
  c   PW - v262 - i49 - Dec 2 2015 - p78(1) [51-500]
  c   SLJ - v61 - i7 - July 2015 - p74(2) [51-500]
Crowe, Caroline - *Pirates in Pajamas (Illus. by Knight, Tom)*
  c   KR - July 1 2015 - pNA [51-500]
Crowe, Chris - *Death Coming up the Hill*
  y   CCB-B - v68 - i5 - Jan 2015 - p251(2) [51-500]
  y   HB Guide - v26 - i1 - Spring 2015 - p104(1) [51-500]
Crowe, Nicholas J. - *Jeremias Drexel's 'Christian Zodiac*
     Sev Cent N - v73 - i1-2 - Spring-Summer 2015 - p12(3) [501+]
Crowl, M. Tara - *Eden's Wish*
  c   KR - July 15 2015 - pNA [51-500]
  c   SLJ - v61 - i9 - Sept 2015 - p138(2) [51-500]
Crowley, Ashley - *Officer Panda: Fingerprint Detective (Illus. by Crowley, Ashley)*
  c   KR - August 1 2015 - pNA [51-500]
  c   SLJ - v61 - i6 - June 2015 - p79(1) [51-500]
Crowley, Jason - *The Psychology of the Athenian Hoplite: The Culture of Combat in Classical Athens*
     AHR - v120 - i2 - April 2015 - p691-692 [501+]
Crowley, Paul - *From Vatican II to Pope Francis*
     Theol St - v76 - i3 - Sept 2015 - p618(2) [501+]
Crowley, Roger - *Conquerors: How Portugal Forged the First Global Empire*
     CSM - Dec 7 2015 - pNA [501+]
     KR - Sept 1 2015 - pNA [51-500]
     LJ - v140 - i17 - Oct 15 2015 - p100(1) [51-500]
     PW - v262 - i41 - Oct 12 2015 - p58(1) [51-500]
Conquerors: How Portugal Seized the Indian Ocean and Forged the First Global Empire
     HT - v65 - i11 - Nov 2015 - p61(2) [501+]
Crown, Carol - *The New Encyclopedia of Southern Culture, Volume 23: Folk Art*
     WestFolk - v74 - i1 - Wntr 2015 - p100-101 [501+]
Crownover, James D. - *Wild Ran the Rivers*
     Roundup M - v22 - i5 - June 2015 - p38(1) [501+]
     Roundup M - v22 - i6 - August 2015 - p28(1) [501+]
Crownover, Jay - *Asa*
     BL - v111 - i15 - April 1 2015 - p30(1) [51-500]
     PW - v262 - i10 - March 9 2015 - p59(1) [51-500]
Better When He's Bold
     BL - v111 - i12 - Feb 15 2015 - p43(1) [51-500]
Better When He's Brave
     PW - v262 - i23 - June 8 2015 - p45(1) [51-500]
Built: Saints of Denver
     PW - v262 - i46 - Nov 16 2015 - p63(1) [51-500]
Crowston, Catherine - *Misled by Nature: Contemporary Art and the Baroque*
     PAJ - v37 - i3 - Sept 2015 - p134-135 [501+]
Crowston, Clare Haru - *Credit, Fashion, Sex: Economies of Regard in Old Regime France*
     FS - v69 - i4 - Oct 2015 - p532-533 [501+]
     JEH - v75 - i1 - March 2015 - p276-277 [501+]
Crowther, Gillian - *Eating Culture: An Anthropological Guide to Food*
     JRAI - v21 - i2 - June 2015 - p484(2) [501+]
Crowther, Kitty - *Scritch Scratch Scraww Plop (Illus. by Crowther, Kitty)*
  c   KR - Sept 15 2015 - pNA [51-500]
  c   PW - v262 - i49 - Dec 2 2015 - p17(1) [51-500]
Crowther, Robert - *Robert Crowther's Pop-Up Dinosaur ABC (Illus. by Crowther, Robert)*
  c   BL - v111 - i16 - April 15 2015 - p52(1) [51-500]
  c   KR - Dec 1 2015 - pNA [51-500]

Croxton, Derek - *Westphalia: The Last Christian Peace*
     AHR - v120 - i3 - June 2015 - p1130-1131 [501+]
Croxton, Randolph R. - *A Convergence of Two Minds*
     KR - August 15 2015 - pNA [501+]
Croy, Anita - *Myths and Legends of Australia, New Zealand, and Pacific Islands*
  c   BL - v112 - i6 - Nov 15 2015 - p42(2) [501+]
Crozier, Lorna - *Lots of Kisses*
  c   KR - Jan 1 2015 - pNA [51-500]
So Many Babies (Illus. by Watson, Laura)
  c   KR - Jan 1 2016 - pNA [51-500]
  c   Res Links - v20 - i5 - June 2015 - p3(1) [51-500]
Crozon, Alain - *All Shook Up!*
  c   KR - Jan 1 2016 - pNA [51-500]
Who's There?
  c   PW - v262 - i27 - July 6 2015 - p70(2) [501+]
Crucet, Jennine Capo - *Make Your Home Among Strangers*
  y   BL - v111 - i21 - July 1 2015 - p32(2) [51-500]
     Ent W - i1376 - August 14 2015 - p61(1) [501+]
     KR - June 1 2015 - pNA [51-500]
     LJ - v140 - i10 - June 1 2015 - p85(1) [51-500]
     NYT - August 27 2015 - pC4(L) [501+]
     NYTBR - August 16 2015 - p12(L) [501+]
     SLJ - v61 - i12 - Dec 2015 - p131(1) [51-500]
Cruden, Aaron - *The Beginner's Guide to Rugby*
  c   Magpies - v30 - i2 - May 2015 - pS8(1) [51-500]
Cruickshank, Dan - *A History of Architecture in 100 Buildings*
     LJ - v140 - i20 - Dec 1 2015 - p98(2) [51-500]
Cruickshank, Ruth - *Writing, Reading, Grieving: Essays in Memory of Suzanne Dow*
     MLR - v110 - i2 - April 2015 - p560-561 [501+]
Crul, Maurice - *The Changing Face of World Cities: Young Adult Children of Immigrants in Europe and the United States*
     CS - v44 - i1 - Jan 2015 - p46-47 [501+]
Crum, Shutta - *Uh-Oh! (Illus. by Barton, Patrice)*
  c   BL - v111 - i14 - March 15 2015 - p82(1) [51-500]
  c   HB Guide - v26 - i2 - Fall 2015 - p9(1) [51-500]
Crumey, Andrew - *Mobius Dick*
     KR - Feb 1 2015 - pNA [501+]
Crummey, Michael - *Sweetland (Read by Lee, John). Audiobook Review*
     LJ - v140 - i6 - April 1 2015 - p47(1) [51-500]
Sweetland
     NYTBR - March 22 2015 - p30(L) [501+]
     TLS - i5848 - May 1 2015 - p20(1) [501+]
Crump, David - *Encountering Jesus, Encountering Scripture*
     Intpr - v69 - i1 - Jan 2015 - p105(2) [501+]
Crump, Marty - *Eye of Newt and Toe of Frog, Adder's Fork and Lizard's Leg: The Lore and Mythology of Amphibians and Reptiles*
     BL - v112 - i4 - Oct 15 2015 - p9(1) [51-500]
     PW - v262 - i35 - August 31 2015 - p73(2) [51-500]
Cruney, Andrew - *The Secret Knowledge*
     PW - v262 - i4 - Jan 26 2015 - p146(2) [51-500]
Crusafont, Miquel - *Medieval European Coinage, vol. 6: The Iberian Peninsula*
     Specu - v90 - i3 - July 2015 - p792-794 [501+]
Cruschiform - *Full Speed Ahead! How Fast Things Go (Illus. by Cruschiform)*
  c   CCB-B - v68 - i5 - Jan 2015 - p252(1) [51-500]
  c   HB Guide - v26 - i1 - Spring 2015 - p147(1) [51-500]
Crutchfield, James A. - *Revolt at Taos: The New Mexican and Indian Insurrection of 1847*
     LJ - v140 - i7 - April 15 2015 - p101(1) [51-500]
     PW - v262 - i13 - March 30 2015 - p70(1) [51-500]
Crutchley, Edward B. - *The Black Carriage*
     KR - April 15 2015 - pNA [501+]
Crutchley, Lee - *How to Be Happy (or at Least Less Sad)*
     PW - v262 - i12 - March 23 2015 - p63(1) [51-500]
Crute, Jennifer - *Jennifer's Journal: The Life of a Suburban Girl, vol. 1*
     PW - v262 - i18 - May 4 2015 - p104(1) [51-500]
Cruvellier, Thierry - *The Master of Confessions: The Making of a Khmer Rouge Torturer (Illus. by Gilly, Alex)*
     NYTBR - June 21 2015 - p24(L) [501+]
Cruz, Anne J. - *Early Modern Habsburg Women: Transnational Contexts, Cultural Conflicts, Dynastic Continuities*
     JMH - v87 - i3 - Sept 2015 - p706(2) [501+]
     Ren Q - v68 - i2 - Summer 2015 - p687-689 [501+]

The Life and Writings of Luisa De Carvajal y Mendoza
    Ren Q - v68 - i1 - Spring 2015 - p327-328 [501+]
Cruz, Denise - *Transpacific Femininities: The Making of the Modern Filipina*
    AL - v87 - i2 - June 2015 - p410-413 [501+]
Cruz, Ed - *Kirin Rise: The Cast of Shadows*
  y VOYA - v37 - i6 - Feb 2015 - p73(1) [51-500]
Cruz, Ted - *A Time for Truth: Reigniting the Promise of America*
    NS - v144 - i5278 - Sept 4 2015 - p40(4) [501+]
Crysdale, Cynthia - *Creator God, Evolving World*
    TT - v72 - i3 - Oct 2015 - p337-338 [501+]
Crystal, David - *Making a Point: The Persnickety Story of English Punctuation*
    LJ - v140 - i16 - Oct 1 2015 - p88(1) [51-500]
    PW - v262 - i35 - August 31 2015 - p78(2) [51-500]
Oxford Illustrated Shakespeare Dictionary (Illus. by Bellamy, Kate)
    BL - v112 - i4 - Oct 15 2015 - p8(1) [51-500]
    LJ - v140 - i15 - Sept 15 2015 - p107(1) [51-500]
    Magpies - v30 - i3 - July 2015 - p24(1) [501+]
Oxford Illustrated Shakespeare Dictionary
  y Sch Lib - v63 - i3 - Autumn 2015 - p187(1) [51-500]
Tyndale's Bible: Saint Matthew's Gospel (Read by Crystal, David). Audiobook Review
    Med R - August 2015 - pNA [501+]
Csombor, Marton Szepsi - *Europica varietas*
    TLS - i5840 - March 6 2015 - p29(1) [501+]
Ctein - *Saturn Run*
    BL - v112 - i2 - Sept 15 2015 - p38(1) [51-500]
    LJ - v140 - i16 - Oct 1 2015 - p74(1) [51-500]
Cubbison, Douglas R. - *All Canada in the Hands of the British: General Jeffery Amherst and the 1760 Campaign to Conquer New France*
    Roundup M - v22 - i3 - Feb 2015 - p22(1) [501+]
    Roundup M - v22 - i6 - August 2015 - p35(1) [501+]
Cucchiara, Maia Bloomfield - *Marketing Schools, Marketing Cities: Who Wins and Who Loses When Schools Become Urban Amenities*
    CS - v44 - i4 - July 2015 - p495-496 [501+]
Cucchiarelli, Andrea - *Le Bucoliche*
    Class R - v65 - i1 - April 2015 - p129-130 [501+]
Cuccia, Phillip R. - *Napoleon in Italy: The Sieges of Mantua, 1796-1799*
    J Mil H - v79 - i1 - Jan 2015 - p201-203 [501+]
Cuddy-Keane, Melba - *Modernism: Keywords*
    TLS - i5839 - Feb 27 2015 - p27(1) [501+]
Cudmore, Libby - *The Big Rewind*
    KR - Oct 15 2015 - pNA [51-500]
Cuesta, Lee - *Seven Viking Days (Illus. by Hocking, Mia)*
  c PW - v262 - i31 - August 3 2015 - p60(1) [51-500]
Cueva, Edmund P. - *A Companion to the Ancient Novel*
    Class R - v65 - i2 - Oct 2015 - p472-474 [501+]
Cuevas, Michelle - *Beyond the Laughing Sky (Illus. by Morstad, Julie)*
  c HB Guide - v26 - i1 - Spring 2015 - p74(1) [51-500]
Confessions of an Imaginary Friend: A Memoir by Jacques Papier (Illus. by Cuevas, Michelle)
  c PW - v262 - i49 - Dec 2 2015 - p76(1) [51-500]
  c KR - June 15 2015 - pNA [51-500]
  c PW - v262 - i22 - June 1 2015 - p60(1) [51-500]
  c SLJ - v61 - i7 - July 2015 - p74(1) [51-500]
Culbertson, Kim - *The Possibility of Now*
  y KR - Oct 15 2015 - pNA [51-500]
  y BL - v112 - i6 - Nov 15 2015 - p51(1) [51-500]
  y PW - v262 - i44 - Nov 2 2015 - p86(1) [51-500]
Cull, Marisa R. - *Shakespeare's Princes of Wales: English Identity and the Welsh Connection*
    TLS - i5839 - Feb 27 2015 - p28(1) [501+]
Cull, Mark E. - *The King of the Sea Monkeys*
    ABR - v36 - i5 - July-August 2015 - p20(2) [51-500]
Cullen, David O'Donald - *The Texas Right: The Radical Roots of Lone Star Conservatism*
    JSH - v81 - i2 - May 2015 - p524(2) [501+]
    SHQ - v118 - i4 - April 2015 - p437-438 [501+]
Cullen, John - *The Meursault Investigation*
    NYRB - v62 - i16 - Oct 22 2015 - p56(2) [501+]
Cullen, Lynn - *Dear Mr. Washington (Illus. by Carpenter, Nancy)*
  c CCB-B - v68 - i8 - April 2015 - p396(1) [51-500]
  c HB Guide - v26 - i2 - Fall 2015 - p30(1) [51-500]
Twain's End
    BL - v112 - i2 - Sept 15 2015 - p37(1) [51-500]
    KR - August 1 2015 - p38(L) [501+]
    NYTBR - Nov 22 2015 - p38(L) [501+]
    PW - v262 - i31 - August 3 2015 - p32(1) [51-500]

Cullen, Sharon - *The Reluctant Duchess*
    PW - v262 - i39 - Sept 28 2015 - p75(1) [51-500]
Cullen, Tom - *The Man Who Was Norris: The Life of Gerald Hamilton*
    PW - v262 - i17 - April 27 2015 - p64(1) [51-500]
Culley, Amy - *British Women's Life Writing: 1760-1840*
    TLS - i5836 - Feb 6 2015 - p11(2) [501+]
Culley, Travis Hugh - *A Comedy and a Tragedy: A Memoir of Learning How to Read and Write*
  y BL - v111 - i21 - July 1 2015 - p16(1) [51-500]
    KR - May 15 2015 - pNA [51-500]
    PW - v262 - i24 - June 15 2015 - p78(1) [51-500]
Cullum, Patricia H. - *Religious Men and Masculine Identity in the Middle Ages*
    HER - v130 - i545 - August 2015 - p945(3) [501+]
Cullup, Michael - *W.H. Davies: Man and Poet: A Reassessment*
    TLS - i5843 - March 27 2015 - p22(1) [501+]
Cultural Mediation: Creativity, Performance, Display
    HNet - June 2015 - pNA [501+]
Cultural Traditions in My World Series
  c CH Bwatch - August 2015 - pNA [51-500]
Cuming, Pamela - *The Stranger Box*
  c BL - v112 - i3 - Oct 1 2015 - p32(2) [51-500]
Cummer, Don - *A Hanging Offence*
    Res Links - v20 - i5 - June 2015 - p24(1) [51-500]
Cumming, Alan - *Not My Father's Son*
    Ent W - i1364 - May 22 2015 - p66(1) [501+]
    G&L Rev W - v22 - i2 - March-April 2015 - p37(2) [501+]
    RVBW - June 2015 - pNA [501+]
Cumming, Charles - *The Hidden Man*
    BL - v112 - i5 - Nov 1 2015 - p31(1) [51-500]
    PW - v262 - i39 - Sept 28 2015 - p65(2) [51-500]
Cumming, Laura - *The Vanishing Velazquez*
    KR - Dec 15 2015 - pNA [51-500]
Cumming, Robert - *Art: A Visual History*
    LJ - v140 - i15 - Sept 15 2015 - p104(1) [51-500]
Cummings, Alex Sayf - *Democracy of Sound: Music Piracy and the Remaking of American Copyright in the Twentieth Century*
    J Am St - v49 - i1 - Feb 2015 - p221-222 [501+]
Cummings, Brian - *Mortal Thoughts: Religion, Secularity and Identity in Shakespeare and Early Modern Culture*
    TLS - i5860 - July 24 2015 - p10(2) [501+]
    Ren Q - v68 - i1 - Spring 2015 - p395-396 [501+]
    Six Ct J - v46 - i2 - Summer 2015 - p500-501 [501+]
Cummings, E.E. - *E.E. Cummings: Complete Poems, 1904-1962*
    CC - v132 - i15 - July 22 2015 - p43(1) [501+]
I Carry Your Heart with Me
  c CH Bwatch - March 2015 - pNA [51-500]
Maggie and Milly and Molly and May (Illus. by Perry, Marcia)
  c HB Guide - v26 - i2 - Fall 2015 - p203(1) [51-500]
Cummings, Laura L. - *Pachucas and Pachucos in Tucson: Situated Border Lives*
    CS - v44 - i6 - Nov 2015 - p871-872 [501+]
Cummings, Lindsay - *The Death Code*
  y SLJ - v61 - i8 - August 2015 - p113(1) [51-500]
The Fires of Calderon
  y HB Guide - v26 - i1 - Spring 2015 - p74(1) [51-500]
The Murder Complex
  y HB Guide - v26 - i1 - Spring 2015 - p104(1) [51-500]
The Pillars of Ponderay
  c KR - June 15 2015 - pNA [51-500]
Cummings, Phil - *Newspaper Hats (Illus. by Swan, Owen)*
  c Magpies - v30 - i3 - July 2015 - p28(1) [501+]
Ride, Ricardo, Ride! (Illus. by Devries, Shane)
  y Magpies - v30 - i1 - March 2015 - p32(2) [501+]
Cummings, Priscilla - *Cheating for the Chicken Man*
  c KR - May 1 2015 - pNA [51-500]
  y VOYA - v38 - i2 - June 2015 - p56(1) [51-500]
Cummings, Troy - *Pop of the Bumpy Mummy (Illus. by Cummings, Troy)*
  c HB Guide - v26 - i2 - Fall 2015 - p64(1) [51-500]
Whack of the P-Rex (Illus. by Cummings, Troy)
  c HB Guide - v26 - i1 - Spring 2015 - p58(1) [51-500]
  c CH Bwatch - March 2015 - pNA [501+]
Cummins, Lucy - *A Hungry Lion, or A Dwindling Assortment of Animals (Illus. by Cummins, Lucy)*
  c KR - Dec 15 2015 - pNA [51-500]
Cummins, Lucy Ruth - *A Hungry Lion, or a Dwindling Assortment of Animals (Illus. by Cummins, Lucy Ruth)*
  c PW - v262 - i51 - Dec 14 2015 - p84(1) [51-500]

Cummins, Paul F. - *Confessions of a Headmaster*
    KR - July 1 2015 - pNA [501+]
Cumo, Christoper - *The Ongoing Columbian Exchange: Stories of Biological and Economic Transfer in World History*
  y BL - v111 - i18 - May 15 2015 - p16(1) [51-500]
Cumo, Christopher - *Foods That Changed History: How Foods Shaped Civilization from the Ancient World to the Present*
    BL - v112 - i3 - Oct 1 2015 - p15(2) [51-500]
Cumper, Peter - *Religion, Rights and Secular Society: European Perspectives*
    J Ch St - v57 - i1 - Wntr 2015 - p171-173 [501+]
Cumpiano, Ina - *Quinito, Day and Night / Quinito, dia y noche (Illus. by Ramirez, Jose)*
  c BL - v111 - i9-10 - Jan 1 2015 - pS18(5) [51-500]
Cumyn, Alan - *Hot Pterodactyl Boyfriend*
  y KR - Jan 1 2016 - pNA [51-500]
  y PW - v262 - i52 - Dec 21 2015 - p158(1) [51-500]
Cuneo, Pia F. - *Animals and Early Modern Identity*
    HNet - Sept 2015 - pNA [501+]
    TLS - i5835 - Jan 30 2015 - p28(1) [501+]
Cunliffe, Ian - *I Want to Be a Witch (Illus. by Cunliffe, Ian)*
  c HB Guide - v26 - i1 - Spring 2015 - p27(1) [51-500]
  c Sch Lib - v63 - i1 - Spring 2015 - p25(2) [51-500]
Cunningham, Chet - *Double Cross Trail Drive*
    RVBW - July 2015 - pNA [51-500]
Cunningham, Darryl - *The Age of Selfishness: Ayn Rand, Morality, and the Financial Crisis (Illus. by Cunningham, Darryl)*
    BL - v111 - i16 - April 15 2015 - p39(1) [51-500]
    PW - v262 - i8 - Feb 23 2015 - p60(1) [51-500]
Cunningham, Laine - *He Drinks Poison*
    PW - v262 - i12 - March 23 2015 - p50(1) [51-500]
Cunningham, Lawrence A. - *Berkshire beyond Buffett: The Enduring Value of Values*
    Econ - v414 - i8920 - Jan 10 2015 - p78(US) [501+]
Cunningham, Liz - *Ocean Country: One Woman's Voyage from Peril to Hope in Her Quest to Save the Seas*
    BL - v112 - i1 - Sept 1 2015 - p19(1) [51-500]
    KR - June 15 2015 - pNA [51-500]
    PW - v262 - i29 - July 20 2015 - p182(1) [51-500]
Cunningham, Michael - *The Snow Queen*
    NYTBR - June 7 2015 - p36(L) [501+]
A Wild Swan and Other Tales (Illus. by Shimizu, Yuko)
    KR - Sept 1 2015 - pNA [501+]
  y BL - v112 - i4 - Oct 15 2015 - p17(1) [51-500]
    LJ - v140 - i17 - Oct 15 2015 - p84(1) [51-500]
  y NYT - Nov 9 2015 - pC4(L) [501+]
    NYTBR - Nov 1 2015 - p13(L) [501+]
    PW - v262 - i36 - Sept 7 2015 - p42(1) [51-500]
Cunningham, Valentine - *Victorian Poets: A Critical Reader*
    TLS - i5858 - July 10 2015 - p12(2) [501+]
Cunnington, Graham - *Total State Machine*
    TimHES - i2206 - June 4 2015 - p47(1) [501+]
Cuoco, Al - *Learning Modern Algebra: From Early Attempts to Prove Fermat's Last Theorem*
    Math T - v108 - i6 - Feb 2015 - p477(1) [501+]
Cuomo, Andrew M. - *All Things Possible: Setbacks and Success in Politics and Life*
    NYRB - v62 - i13 - August 13 2015 - p42(4) [501+]
Cupit, Margaret Caslisle - *Why, God? Suffering through Cancer into Faith*
    RVBW - Nov 2015 - pNA [501+]
Cupperi, Walter - *Multiples in Pre-Modern Art*
    Ren Q - v68 - i3 - Fall 2015 - p996-997 [501+]
Curato, Mike - *Little Elliot, Big City (Illus. by Curato, Mike)*
  c HB Guide - v26 - i1 - Spring 2015 - p8(1) [51-500]
Little Elliot, Big Family (Illus. by Curato, Mike)
  c HB - v91 - i5 - Sept-Oct 2015 - p77(1) [51-500]
  c KR - August 1 2015 - pNA [51-500]
  c Magpies - v30 - i5 - Nov 2015 - p27(1) [51-500]
  c PW - v262 - i28 - July 13 2015 - p65(1) [51-500]
  c PW - v262 - i49 - Dec 2 2015 - p30(1) [51-500]
  c SLJ - v61 - i7 - July 2015 - p60(2) [51-500]
Curcio, Vincent - *Henry Ford*
    T&C - v56 - i1 - Jan 2015 - p274-276 [501+]
Curl, James Stevens - *The Oxford Dictionary of Architecture, 3d ed.*
    LJ - v140 - i14 - Sept 1 2015 - p138(1) [501+]
Curley, Marianne - *Broken*
  y HB Guide - v26 - i2 - Fall 2015 - p115(1) [51-500]
Curnow, Rohan Michael - *The Preferential Option for the Poor: A Short History and a Reading Based on the*

Thought of Bernard Lonergan
    Theol St - v76 - i1 - March 2015 - p212(1) [501+]
Curnutt, Kirk - *A Historical Guide to F. Scott Fitzgerald*
    TLS - i5859 - July 17 2015 - p16(1) [501+]
Raising Aphrodite
    KR - May 15 2015 - pNA [51-500]
Curran, Abbey - *The Courage to Compete: Living with Cerebral Palsy and Following My Dreams*
    c BL - v111 - i22 - August 1 2015 - p52(1) [51-500]
    y KR - June 15 2015 - pNA [51-500]
    y SLJ - v61 - i7 - July 2015 - p106(1) [51-500]
    y VOYA - v38 - i4 - Oct 2015 - p82(1) [51-500]
Curran, Charles E. - *Ethics and Spirituality*
    Theol St - v76 - i3 - Sept 2015 - p653(2) [501+]
Curran, James - *Unholy Fury: Whitlam and Nixon at War*
    Quad - v59 - i7-8 - July-August 2015 - p137(4) [501+]
Curran, John E., Jr. - *Character and the Individual Personality in English Renaissance Drama: Tragedy, History and Tragicomedy*
    Six Ct J - v46 - i3 - Fall 2015 - p791-793 [501+]
Curran, Robert Emmett - *Papist Devils: Catholics in British America, 1574-1783*
    AHR - v120 - i1 - Feb 2015 - p228-229 [501+]
    AM - v212 - i4 - Feb 9 2015 - p30(3) [501+]
    CHR - v101 - i3 - Summer 2015 - p674(2) [501+]
    JAH - v102 - i1 - June 2015 - p226-227 [501+]
    JSH - v81 - i3 - August 2015 - p693(2) [501+]
    Six Ct J - v46 - i3 - Fall 2015 - p728-730 [501+]
Currie, James Alexander - *When Eagles Roar: The Amazing Journey of an African Wildlife Adventurer*
    RVBW - July 2015 - pNA [501+]
Currie, Lindsay - *Hardwired*
    y PW - v262 - i35 - August 31 2015 - p94(1) [51-500]
    y SLJ - v61 - i8 - August 2015 - p105(2) [51-500]
    y VOYA - v38 - i4 - Oct 2015 - p74(1) [51-500]
Sweet Madness
    y SLJ - v61 - i8 - August 2015 - p106(1) [51-500]
Currie-McGhee, Leanne - *Teens and Marijuana*
    y VOYA - v38 - i5 - Dec 2015 - p79(2) [501+]
What Are Sleep Disorders?
    y VOYA - v38 - i5 - Dec 2015 - p80(1) [51-500]
Currie, Robin - *1,000 Facts about the Bible*
    c HB Guide - v26 - i2 - Fall 2015 - p149(1) [51-500]
Currie, Stephen - *Thinking Critically: Cyberbullying*
    y BL - v112 - i2 - Sept 15 2015 - p60(1) [51-500]
Currier, Jameson - *Until My Heart Stops*
    KR - Dec 15 2015 - pNA [51-500]
Curry, Alexandra - *The Courtesan*
    BL - v111 - i22 - August 1 2015 - p39(1) [51-500]
    PW - v262 - i33 - August 17 2015 - p7(1) [51-500]
    KR - July 1 2015 - pNA [51-500]
    LJ - v140 - i11 - June 15 2015 - p76(1) [51-500]
Curry, Carolyn Newton - *Suffer and Grow Strong: The Life of Ella Gertrude Clanton Thomas, 1834-1907*
    JSH - v81 - i3 - August 2015 - p712(2) [51-500]
    RVBW - June 2015 - pNA [501+]
Curry, Dale - *Gumbo*
    New Or - v49 - i5 - Feb 2015 - p38(1) [501+]
Curry, Peggy Simson - *So Far from Spring*
    Roundup M - v23 - i1 - Oct 2015 - p29(1) [501+]
Curtin, Ann - *Dreamcatcher*
    c KR - Nov 15 2015 - pNA [501+]
Curtin, Charles G. - *The Science of Open Spaces: Theory and Practice for Conserving Large Complex Systems*
    New Sci - v227 - i3034 - August 15 2015 - p43(1) [501+]
Curtin, Michael - *Distribution Revolution: Conversations about the Digital Future of Film and Television*
    Nation - v300 - i20 - May 18 2015 - p37(1) [501+]
    FQ - v68 - i3 - Spring 2015 - p98(2) [501+]
Curtis, Andrea - *What's for Lunch?*
    Sci & Ch - v52 - i9 - Summer 2015 - p92 [501+]
Curtis, Cathy - *Restless Ambition: Grace Hartigan, Painter*
    BL - v111 - i12 - Feb 15 2015 - p18(1) [51-500]
    PW - v262 - i3 - Jan 19 2015 - p71(2) [51-500]
Curtis, Christopher Paul - *The Madman of Piney Woods (Read by Heyborne, Kirby, with J.D. Jackson). Audiobook Review*
    c BL - v111 - i15 - April 1 2015 - p87(1) [51-500]
The Madman of Piney Woods
    c BL - v111 - i9-10 - Jan 1 2015 - pS4(8) [51-500]
    y BL - v111 - i16 - April 15 2015 - p57(1) [501+]
    c CH Bwatch - April 2015 - pNA [51-500]
    y HB Guide - v26 - i1 - Spring 2015 - p74(1) [51-500]
    y Res Links - v20 - i4 - April 2015 - p27(1) [51-500]

Curtis, Craig M. - *Return of the Outlaw*
    Roundup M - v22 - i3 - Feb 2015 - p25(1) [51-500]
    Roundup M - v22 - i6 - August 2015 - p28(1) [501+]
Curtis, Daniel R. - *Coping with Crisis: The Resilience and Vulnerability of Pre-Industrial Settlements*
    Six Ct J - v46 - i3 - Fall 2015 - p674-676 [501+]
Curtis, Edward E. - *The Call of Bilal: Islam in the African Diaspora*
    Am St - v54 - i1 - Spring 2015 - p170-2 [501+]
Curtis, Ian - *So This Is Permanence: Joy Division Lyrics and Notebooks*
    Lon R Bks - v37 - i8 - April 23 2015 - p29(2) [501+]
    TimHES - i2201 - April 30 2015 - p51(1) [501+]
Curtis, James - *William Cameron Menzies: The Shape of Films to Come*
    KR - Sept 1 2015 - pNA [501+]
    LJ - v140 - i16 - Oct 1 2015 - p80(2) [51-500]
    PW - v262 - i37 - Sept 14 2015 - p56(1) [51-500]
Curtis, Jennifer Keats - *Animal Helpers: Raptor Centers*
    c CH Bwatch - March 2015 - pNA [51-500]
    c HB Guide - v26 - i1 - Spring 2015 - p162(1) [51-500]
The Lucky Litter
    c KR - July 15 2015 - pNA [51-500]
Salamander Season (Illus. by Bersani, Shennen)
    c CH Bwatch - March 2015 - pNA [51-500]
    c HB Guide - v26 - i2 - Fall 2015 - p175(1) [51-500]
Curtis, Kent A. - *Gambling on Ore: The Nature of Metal Mining in the United States, 1860-1910*
    PHR - v84 - i1 - Feb 2015 - p94(3) [501+]
    WHQ - v46 - i1 - Spring 2015 - p80-81 [501+]
Curtis, Marci Lyn - *The One Thing*
    y KR - August 1 2015 - pNA [51-500]
    y SLJ - v61 - i10 - Oct 2015 - p100(1) [51-500]
    y VOYA - v38 - i4 - Oct 2015 - p65(1) [51-500]
Curtis, Richard - *It's Snow Day (Illus. by Cobb, Rebecca)*
    c Sch Lib - v63 - i1 - Spring 2015 - p26(1) [51-500]
Curtis, Robert F. - *Surprised at Being Alive: An Accidental Helicopter Pilot in Vietnam and Beyond*
    APH - v62 - i2 - Summer 2015 - p54(2) [501+]
Curtis, Valerie - *Don't Look, Don't Touch, Don't Eat: The Science behind Revulsion*
    QRB - v90 - i3 - Sept 2015 - p338(339) [501+]
Curtis, Vanessa - *The Baking Life of Amelie Day*
    c Sch Lib - v63 - i1 - Spring 2015 - p36(1) [51-500]
The Earth is Singing
    y Sch Lib - v63 - i2 - Summer 2015 - p116(1) [51-500]
Curtright, Eileen - *The Burned Bridges of Ward, Nebraska*
    BL - v112 - i4 - Oct 15 2015 - p16(1) [51-500]
    KR - Oct 1 2015 - pNA [501+]
    PW - v262 - i39 - Sept 28 2015 - p62(1) [51-500]
Curvin, Robert - *Inside Newark: Decline, Rebellion, and the Search for Transformation*
    JAH - v102 - i2 - Sept 2015 - p620-621 [501+]
Curzer, Howard - *Aristotle and the Virtues*
    Phil R - v124 - i2 - April 2015 - p258(3) [501+]
Cushing, Dana - *"De itinere navali": A German Third Crusader's Chronicle of His Voyage and the Siege of Almohad Silves, 1189 AD/Muwahid Xelb, 585 AH*
    Specu - v90 - i1 - Jan 2015 - p235-236 [501+]
Cushing, Nicole - *Mr. Suicide*
    PW - v262 - i19 - May 11 2015 - p40(1) [51-500]
Cushing, Steve - *Pioneers of the Blues Revival*
    JSH - v81 - i3 - August 2015 - p779(2) [51-500]
Cushman, Gregory T. - *Guano and the Opening of the Pacific World: A Global Ecological History*
    JMH - v87 - i2 - June 2015 - p416(2) [501+]
    PHR - v84 - i2 - May 2015 - p259(3) [501+]
Cushman, Kathryn - *Finding Me*
    BL - v111 - i14 - March 15 2015 - p51(1) [51-500]
Cushman, Stephen - *Belligerent Muse: Five Northern Writers and How They Shaped Our Understanding of the Civil War*
    JSH - v81 - i4 - Nov 2015 - p998(2) [501+]
    NEQ - v88 - i3 - Sept 2015 - p527-529 [501+]
Cusick, Dawn - *Animals That Make Me Say Ewww!*
    c KR - Jan 1 2016 - pNA [51-500]
Animals That Make Me Say Ouch!
    c HB Guide - v26 - i1 - Spring 2015 - p153(1) [51-500]
Animals That Make Me Say Wow!
    c HB Guide - v26 - i1 - Spring 2015 - p153(1) [51-500]
Get the Scoop on Animal Puke! From Zombie Ants to Vampire Bats, 251 Cool Facts about Vomit, Regurgitation, & More! (Illus. by Cusick, Dawn)
    c HB Guide - v26 - i2 - Fall 2015 - p170(1) [51-500]

Cusk, Rachel - *Outline (Read by Reading, Kate). Audiobook Review*
    BL - v111 - i19-20 - June 1 2015 - p136(2) [51-500]
Outline
    Ent W - i1346 - Jan 16 2015 - p66(1) [501+]
    HR - v68 - i2 - Summer 2015 - p343-351 [501+]
    Nation - v300 - i29 - July 20 2015 - p35(4) [501+]
    New R - v246 - i1 - Feb 2015 - p58(2) [501+]
    NYRB - v62 - i7 - April 23 2015 - p28(3) [501+]
    NYT - Jan 7 2015 - pC1(L) [501+]
    NYTBR - Jan 11 2015 - p10(L) [501+]
Cussler, Clive - *The Assassin*
    KR - Jan 1 2015 - pNA [51-500]
Piranha
    KR - March 15 2015 - pNA [51-500]
    PW - v262 - i12 - March 23 2015 - p46(2) [51-500]
The Solomon Curse
    KR - July 1 2015 - pNA [501+]
    LJ - v140 - i12 - July 1 2015 - p75(1) [51-500]
Custodis, Michael - *Netzwerke der Entnazifizierung: Kontinuitaten im Deutschen Musikleben am Beispiel von Werner Egk, Hilde und Heinrich Strobel*
    HNet - Jan 2015 - pNA [501+]
Cusumano, Nicola - *Memory and Religious Experience in the Greco-Roman World*
    Class R - v65 - i2 - Oct 2015 - p514-517 [501+]
Cuthbert, Michael Scott - *City, Chant, and the Topography of Early Music: In Honor of Thomas Forrest Kelly*
    Notes - v71 - i3 - March 2015 - p525(3) [501+]
Cuthbertson, Ken - *A Complex Fate: William L. Shirer and the American Century*
    LJ - v140 - i6 - April 1 2015 - p99(2) [51-500]
    NYTBR - June 14 2015 - p16(L) [51-500]
Cutler, Alan - *Leadership Psychology: How the Best Leaders Inspire Their People*
    Per Psy - v68 - i4 - Wntr 2015 - p941(4) [501+]
Cutler, E.P. - *Art + Fashion: Collaborations and Connections between Icons*
    NYT - Nov 1 2015 - p3(L) [51-500]
Cutler, Judith - *Green and Pleasant Land*
    BL - v111 - i14 - March 15 2015 - p46(1) [51-500]
    KR - Feb 1 2015 - pNA [51-500]
    PW - v262 - i6 - Feb 9 2015 - p48(1) [51-500]
Guilty as Sin
    BL - v112 - i6 - Nov 15 2015 - p29(1) [51-500]
    KR - Oct 15 2015 - pNA [51-500]
    PW - v262 - i41 - Oct 12 2015 - p50(1) [51-500]
Cut'n Paste the Body. Korper und Geschlecht in Zeiten Ihrer Technologischen (Re)Produzierbarkeit
    HNet - March 2015 - pNA [501+]
Cutrofello, Andrew - *All for Nothing: Hamlet's Negativity*
    RM - v69 - i1 - Sept 2015 - p123(3) [501+]
Cutter, Charles - *The Pink Pony*
    KR - Sept 1 2015 - pNA [51-500]
Cutter, Nick - *The Acolyte*
    LJ - v140 - i9 - May 15 2015 - p57(4) [51-500]
The Deep
    Nat Post - v17 - i80 - Jan 31 2015 - pWP8(1) [501+]
Cutter, Susan L. - *Hurricane Katrina and the Forgotten Coast of Mississippi*
    GR - v105 - i4 - Oct 2015 - p628(3) [501+]
    JSH - v81 - i3 - August 2015 - p786(3) [51-500]
Cuttica, Cesare - *Sir Robert Filmer (1588-1653) and the Patriotic Monarch: Patriarchalism in Seventeenth-Century Political Thought*
    AHR - v120 - i1 - Feb 2015 - p323-324 [501+]
    JMH - v87 - i3 - Sept 2015 - p723(3) [501+]
Cutts, Lisa - *Remember, Remember*
    KR - Nov 1 2015 - pNA [51-500]
    PW - v262 - i47 - Nov 23 2015 - p52(1) [51-500]
Cvetkovski, Roland - *An Empire of Others: Creating Ethnographic Knowledge in Imperial Russia and the USSR*
    HNet - Sept 2015 - pNA [501+]
Cvitanic, Jaksa - *Contract Theory in Continuous-Time Models*
    SIAM Rev - v57 - i2 - June 2015 - p315-317 [501+]
Cvoro, Uros - *Turbo-Folk Music and Cultural Representations of National Identity in Former Yugoslavia*
    Slav R - v74 - i3 - Fall 2015 - p642-643 [501+]
Cvorovic, Jelena - *The Roma: A Balkan Underclass*
    TimHES - i2192 - Feb 26 2015 - p52-53 [501+]
Cybriwsky, Roman Adrian - *Kyiv, Ukraine: The City of Domes and Demons from the Collapse of Socialism to the*

Mass Uprising of 2013-2014
    For Aff - v94 - i3 - May-June 2015 - pNA [501+]
Cygan, Donna Skeels - *The Joy of Financial Security*
    SPBW - Jan 2015 - pNA [501+]
Cypess, Leah - *Death Marked*
    y KR - Jan 15 2015 - pNA [51-500]
    y VOYA - v37 - i6 - Feb 2015 - p73(2) [51-500]
Cyrus, Miley - *Miley Cyrus and Her Dead Petz*
    New York - Sept 7 2015 - pNA [501+]
    New York - Sept 7 2015 - pNA [501+]
    New York - Sept 7 2015 - pNA [501+]
Czajak, Paul - *Monster Needs a Christmas Tree (Illus. by Grieb, Wendy)*
    c HB Guide - v26 - i1 - Spring 2015 - p27(1) [51-500]
Monster Needs a Party (Illus. by Grieb, Wendy)
    c CH Bwatch - July 2015 - pNA [51-500]
    c SLJ - v61 - i8 - August 2015 - p66(2) [51-500]
Monster Needs Your Vote (Illus. by Grieb, Wendy)
    c CH Bwatch - Oct 2015 - pNA [51-500]
    c SLJ - v61 - i11 - Nov 2015 - p80(1) [51-500]
Seaver the Weaver (Illus. by The Brothers Hilts)
    c CH Bwatch - April 2015 - pNA [51-500]
    c HB Guide - v26 - i2 - Fall 2015 - p31(1) [51-500]
    c KR - Jan 15 2015 - pNA [51-500]
    c SLJ - v61 - i7 - July 2015 - p61(1) [51-500]
Czech, Brian - *Supply Shock: Economic Growth at the Crossroads and the Steady State Solution*
    BioSci - v65 - i3 - March 2015 - p329(3) [501+]

Czech-Jewish and Polish-Jewish Studies: (Dis) Similarities
    HNet - April 2015 - pNA [501+]
Czekaj, Jef - *Austin, Lost in America (Illus. by Czekaj, Jef)*
    c KR - July 1 2015 - pNA [51-500]
    c SLJ - v61 - i6 - June 2015 - p79(1) [51-500]
Czerwiec, MK - *Graphic Medicine Manifesto*
    LJ - v140 - i12 - July 1 2015 - p103(2) [51-500]
Czukas, Liz - *Top Ten Clues You're Clueless*
    y CSM - Jan 1 2015 - pNA [501+]
Czyzniejewski, Michael - *I Will Love You For the Rest of My Life: Breakup Stories*
    KR - Feb 1 2015 - pNA [51-500]

D

D' Arcens, Louise - *Comic Medievalism: Laughing at the Middle Ages*
    TLS - i5849 - May 8 2015 - p25(1) [501+]
da Bologna, Guizzardo - *Recollecte super Poetria magistri Gualfredi*
    Ren Q - v68 - i2 - Summer 2015 - p617-619 [501+]
da Capua, Raimondo - *Legenda maior sive Legenda admirabilis virginis Catherine de Senis*
    Specu - v90 - i4 - Oct 2015 - p1160-1161 [501+]
Da Costa, Pippa - *City of Fae. E-book Review*
    Sch Lib - v63 - i3 - Autumn 2015 - p147(1) [51-500]
    Sch Lib - v63 - i3 - Autumn 2015 - p147(1) [51-500]
Da Costa, Portia - *How to Seduce a Billionaire*
    PW - v262 - i38 - Sept 21 2015 - p59(2) [51-500]
Suite Seventeen
    PW - v262 - i15 - April 13 2015 - p63(1) [51-500]
da Eboli, Pietro - *Book in Honor of Augustus (Liber ad Honorem Augusti).*
    Specu - v90 - i4 - Oct 2015 - p1157-1158 [501+]
Da, Laura - *Tributaries*
    Roundup M - v23 - i1 - Oct 2015 - p28(1) [501+]
    BL - v111 - i14 - March 15 2015 - p39(1) [51-500]
da Settimello, Arrigo - *Elegia*
    Specu - v90 - i3 - July 2015 - p767-768 [501+]
Dabakis, Melissa - *A Sisterhood of Sculptors: American Artists in Nineteenth-Century Rome*
    G&L Rev W - v22 - i6 - Nov-Dec 2015 - p36(2) [501+]
Dabashi, Hamid - *The World of Persian Literary Humanism*
    Six Ct J - v46 - i3 - Fall 2015 - p752-753 [501+]
d'Abbadie, Joelle - *Ishmael: The Shepherd Boy of Bethlehem*
    c CH Bwatch - April 2015 - pNA [51-500]
Dabbs, Reggie - *Just Keep Breathing: A Shocking Expose of Letters You Never Imagined a Generation Would Write*
    PW - v262 - i45 - Nov 9 2015 - p56(1) [51-500]
D'Abo, Christine - *30 Days*
    PW - v262 - i23 - June 8 2015 - p45(1) [51-500]
d'Abo, Christine - *Rebound Remedy*
    BL - v112 - i5 - Nov 1 2015 - p36(1) [51-500]
Dacey, Linda - *Well Played: Building Mathematical Thinking through Number Games and Puzzles Grades 3-5*
    Bwatch - Oct 2015 - pNA [51-500]
Dacey, Patrick - *We've Already Gone This Far*
    KR - Nov 15 2015 - pNA [51-500]
    PW - v262 - i48 - Nov 30 2015 - p35(1) [51-500]
Dacey, Philip - *Church of the Adagio*
    WLT - v89 - i5 - Sept-Oct 2015 - p71(2) [501+]
D'Acunto, Matteo - *Il mondo del vaso Chigi: Pittura, guerra e societa a Corinto alla meta del VII secolo a.C*
    Class R - v65 - i1 - April 2015 - p256-258 [501+]
Dadey, Debbie - *A Royal Tea (Illus. by Avakyan, Tatevik)*
    c HB Guide - v26 - i1 - Spring 2015 - p58(1) [51-500]
A Tale of Two Sisters (Illus. by Avakyan, Tatevik)
    c HB Guide - v26 - i2 - Fall 2015 - p64(1) [51-500]
Treasure in Trident City (Illus. by Avakyan, Tatevik)
    c HB Guide - v26 - i1 - Spring 2015 - p58(1) [51-500]
Dadoyan, Seta B. - *The Armenians in the Medieval Islamic World: Paradigms of Interaction, Seventh to Fourteenth Centuries, vol. 3: Medieval Cosmopolitanism and the Images of Islam, Thirteenth to Fourteenth Centuries*
    AHR - v120 - i3 - June 2015 - p1144-1145 [501+]
Dadrian, Vahakn N. - *Judgment at Istanbul: The Armenian Genocide Trials*
    HT - v65 - i7 - July 2015 - p56(2) [501+]

Dadsetan, Mehdi - *La danse des ombres*
    WLT - v89 - i1 - Jan-Feb 2015 - p62(2) [501+]
Dadson, Trevor J. - *Tolerance and Coexistence in Early Modern Spain: Old Christians and Moriscos in the Campo de Calatrava*
    CH - v84 - i4 - Dec 2015 - p889(3) [501+]
    Ren Q - v68 - i1 - Spring 2015 - p329-330 [501+]
Daehner, Jens M. - *Power and Pathos: Bronze Sculpture of the Hellenistic World*
    NYRB - v62 - i13 - August 13 2015 - p12(3) [501+]
D'Agata, John - *The Making of the American Essay*
    KR - Dec 1 2015 - pNA [501+]
Dagerman, Stig - *A Burnt Child*
    NYRB - v62 - i12 - July 9 2015 - p42(2) [501+]
German Autumn
    NYRB - v62 - i12 - July 9 2015 - p42(2) [501+]
Sleet: Selected Stories
    NYRB - v62 - i12 - July 9 2015 - p42(2) [501+]
Dagg, Anne Innis - *Giraffe: Biology, Behaviour and Conservation*
    QRB - v90 - i2 - June 2015 - p237(2) [501+]
Dagg, Carole Estby - *Sweet Home Alaska*
    c KR - Nov 15 2015 - pNA [51-500]
D'Agincourt, Maryann - *Glimpses of Gauguin*
    KR - April 1 2015 - pNA [501+]
D'Agostino, Ryan - *The Eat Like a Man Guide to Feeding a Crowd: How to Cook for Family, Friends, and Spontaneous Parties*
    PW - v262 - i20 - May 18 2015 - p79(1) [51-500]
The Rising
    Esq - v164 - i4 - Nov 2015 - p38(1) [51-500]
The Rising: Murder, Heartbreak, and the Power of Human Resilience in an American Town
    BL - v112 - i3 - Oct 1 2015 - p6(1) [51-500]
    LJ - v140 - i14 - Sept 1 2015 - p122(1) [51-500]
    PW - v262 - i29 - July 20 2015 - p180(1) [51-500]
The Rising
    KR - July 15 2015 - pNA [501+]
Dahar, Anita - *Wonder Horse*
    c Res Links - v21 - i1 - Oct 2015 - p30(1) [501+]
Daheim, Mary - *The Alpine Zen*
    PW - v262 - i8 - Feb 23 2015 - p51(2) [51-500]
    LJ - v140 - i6 - April 1 2015 - p63(3) [51-500]
Dahl, Julia - *Invisible City*
    NYTBR - July 19 2015 - p25(L) [501+]
Run You Down (Read by Arndt, Andi). Audiobook Review
    LJ - v140 - i19 - Nov 15 2015 - p51(1) [51-500]
Run You Down
    BL - v111 - i19-20 - June 1 2015 - p57(1) [51-500]
    PW - v262 - i17 - April 27 2015 - p51(2) [51-500]
Dahl, Linda - *Loving Our Addicted Daughters Back to Life: A Guidebook for Parents*
    LJ - v140 - i11 - June 15 2015 - p103(1) [51-500]
Dahl, Michael - *Christmas (Illus. by Ho, Jannie)*
    c KR - Sept 1 2015 - pNA [51-500]
Goodnight Football (Illus. by Forshay, Christina)
    c HB Guide - v26 - i1 - Spring 2015 - p8(1) [51-500]
No More Pacifier, Duck (Illus. by Vidal, Oriol)
    c KR - July 1 2015 - pNA [51-500]
Dahl, Roger - *Comic Japan: Best of Zero Gravity Cartoons from The Japan Times*
    PW - v262 - i2 - Jan 12 2015 - p45(1) [51-500]
Dahl, Victoria - *Taking the Heat*
    PW - v262 - i27 - July 6 2015 - p53(2) [51-500]
Dahle, Margunn Serigstad - *The Lausanne Movement: A Range of Perspectives*
    IBMR - v39 - i4 - Oct 2015 - p245(1) [501+]

Dahlseng, Lesley - *My Kiss Won't Miss! (Illus. by Tufan, Mirela)*
    c CH Bwatch - Oct 2015 - pNA [51-500]
My Kiss Won't Miss (Illus. by Tufan, Mirela)
    c CH Bwatch - Nov 2015 - pNA [51-500]
Daif, Rashid al- - *Who's Afraid of Meryl Streep?*
    TLS - i5843 - March 27 2015 - p20(1) [501+]
    WLT - v89 - i2 - March-April 2015 - p55(2) [501+]
Daigle, Megan - *From Cuba with Love: Sex and Money in the Twenty-First Century*
    TLS - i5851 - May 22 2015 - p26(1) [501+]
Daigle, Tawni - *DIY Succulents: From Placecards to Wreaths, 35+ Ideas for Creative Projects with Succulents*
    LJ - v140 - i19 - Nov 15 2015 - p83(1) [51-500]
Dailey, Alice - *The English Martyr from Reformation to Revolution*
    MLR - v110 - i2 - April 2015 - p519-520 [501+]
Dailey, Patricia - *Promised Bodies: Time, Language, and Corporeality in Medieval Women's Mystical Texts*
    CH - v84 - i3 - Sept 2015 - p656(3) [501+]
Daily, Christopher A. - *Robert Morrison and the Protestant Plan for China*
    AHR - v120 - i2 - April 2015 - p594(1) [501+]
Daily Street, The - *Icons of Style: T-Shirts*
    Bwatch - Sept 2015 - pNA [51-500]
Daines, Ellie - *Shine Izzy Shine*
    c Sch Lib - v63 - i2 - Summer 2015 - p102(1) [51-500]
Dairman, Tara - *All Four Stars*
    y HB Guide - v26 - i1 - Spring 2015 - p74(1) [51-500]
The Stars of Summer
    c BL - v111 - i18 - May 15 2015 - p56(1) [51-500]
    c HB Guide - v26 - i2 - Fall 2015 - p79(1) [51-500]
    c KR - March 15 2015 - pNA [51-500]
    SLJ - v61 - i4 - April 2015 - p145(2) [51-500]
    y VOYA - v38 - i1 - April 2015 - p56(1) [51-500]
Dais, Dawn - *The Sh!t No One Tells You About Toddlers: A Guide to Surviving the Toddler Years*
    PW - v262 - i31 - August 3 2015 - p54(1) [51-500]
D'Aiuto, Francesco - *Guida ai Fondi Manoscritti, Numismatici, a Stampa della Biblioteca Vaticana, vol. 1: Dipartimento Manoscritti*
    CHR - v101 - i2 - Spring 2015 - p348(2) [501+]
Guida ai Fondi Manoscritti, Numismatici, a Stampa della Biblioteca Vaticana, vol 2: Dipartimento Stampati--Dipartimento del Gabinetto Numismatico--Ufficio della Prefettura
    CHR - v101 - i2 - Spring 2015 - p348(2) [501+]
Dakers, Diane - *Albert Einstein: Forging the Path of Modern Physics*
    y Teach Lib - v42 - i4 - April 2015 - p10(1) [51-500]
Bad Business
    y Res Links - v21 - i1 - Oct 2015 - p30(1) [501+]
The Carbon Cycle
    c Res Links - v20 - i5 - June 2015 - p12(2) [501+]
Earth's Cycles in Action Series
    c CH Bwatch - Feb 2015 - pNA [51-500]
    c CH Bwatch - March 2015 - pNA [501+]
Earth's Cycles
    c Res Links - v20 - i5 - June 2015 - p12(2) [501+]
    c Sci & Ch - v52 - i8 - April-May 2015 - p75 [51-500]
Earth's Water Cycle
    c Res Links - v20 - i5 - June 2015 - p12(2) [501+]
The Nitrogen Cycle
    c Res Links - v20 - i5 - June 2015 - p12(2) [501+]

Daks, Nongkran - *Nong's Thai Kitchen: 84 Classic Recipes That are Quick, Healthy and Delicious*
    BL - v111 - i14 - March 15 2015 - p36(1) [51-500]
    Bwatch - July 2015 - pNA [51-500]

Dal Lago, Enrico - *William Lloyd Garrison and Giuseppe Mazzini: Abolition, Democracy, and Radical Reform*
    JSH - v81 - i2 - May 2015 - p459(2) [501+]
    JMH - v87 - i3 - Sept 2015 - p713(3) [501+]

Dalai Lama XIV - *Caring Economics: Conversations on Altruism and Compassion Between Scientists, Economists, and the Dalai Lama*
    Prog - v79 - i6 - June 2015 - p44(2) [501+]

Dalal, Krishna - *Found All Around: A Show-and-Tell of Found Poetry (Illus. by Heathwood, Karen)*
    c CH Bwatch - Feb 2015 - pNA [51-500]

Dalarun, Jacques - *Vie et miracles de Berard, eveque de Marses*
    CHR - v101 - i3 - Summer 2015 - p612(2) [501+]
Vie et miracles de Berard eveque des Marses
    Specu - v90 - i1 - Jan 2015 - p236-237 [501+]

Daldin, Tom - *Under the Radar Michigan: The First 50*
    LJ - v140 - i2 - Feb 1 2015 - p100(2) [51-500]

Dale, Cyndi - *Llewellyn's Complete Book of Chakras: Your Definitive Source of Energy Center Knowledge for Health, Happiness, and Spiritual Evolution*
    PW - v262 - i37 - Sept 14 2015 - p62(1) [51-500]

Dale, Eric M. - *Hegel, the End of History, and the Future*
    RM - v68 - i4 - June 2015 - p847(3) [501+]

Dale, Eric Michael - *Hegel, the End of History, and the Future*
    Dialogue - v54 - i3 - Sept 2015 - p550-553 [501+]

Dale, Katie - *Little White Lies*
    y CCB-B - v68 - i6 - Feb 2015 - p305(2) [51-500]
    y HB Guide - v26 - i1 - Spring 2015 - p105(1) [51-500]
    y Res Links - v20 - i3 - Feb 2015 - p27(1) [51-500]

Dale, Penny - *Dinosaur Rocket! (Illus. by Dale, Penny)*
    c KR - Sept 1 2015 - pNA [51-500]

Dalembert, Louis-Philippe - *The Other Side of the Sea*
    WLT - v89 - i6 - Nov-Dec 2015 - p65(1) [51-500]

Daley, Lashon - *Mr. Okra Sells Fresh Fruits and Vegetables (Illus. by Henriquez, Emile)*
    c KR - Dec 15 2015 - pNA [51-500]

Dalglish, David - *Skyborn*
    KR - Oct 1 2015 - pNA [501+]
    PW - v262 - i39 - Sept 28 2015 - p71(2) [51-500]

Dalin, Karen - *Here and There*
    KR - April 15 2015 - pNA [501+]

Dallaire, Eric - *Shades: The Gehenna Dilemma*
    KR - Oct 1 2015 - pNA [51-500]
    PW - v262 - i24 - June 15 2015 - p69(1) [51-500]

Dallas, Sandra - *The Last Midwife*
    BL - v111 - i22 - August 1 2015 - p40(1) [51-500]
    KR - July 15 2015 - pNA [51-500]
A Quilt for Christmas
    Roundup M - v22 - i5 - June 2015 - p38(1) [501+]
    Roundup M - v22 - i6 - August 2015 - p28(1) [501+]
Red Berries, White Clouds, Blue Sky (Read by Ikeda, Jennifer). Audiobook Review
    c SLJ - v61 - i6 - June 2015 - p63(1) [51-500]
Red Berries, White Clouds, Blue Sky
    y HB Guide - v26 - i1 - Spring 2015 - p74(1) [51-500]
    y Roundup M - v22 - i3 - Feb 2015 - p22(1) [501+]
    y Roundup M - v22 - i6 - August 2015 - p24(2) [501+]

Dallek, Robert - *Camelot's Court: Inside the Kennedy White House*
    RAH - v43 - i2 - June 2015 - p355-360 [501+]
    NYTBR - Jan 25 2015 - p24(L) [501+]

Dalley, Lana L. - *Economic Women: Essays on Desire and Dispossession in Nineteenth-Century British Culture*
    VS - v57 - i3 - Spring 2015 - p542(3) [501+]

d'Almeida, Luis Duarte - *Allowing for Exceptions: A Theory of Defences and Defeasibility*
    Law Q Rev - v131 - Oct 2015 - p681-684 [501+]

Dalrymple, Theodore - *Admirable Evasions: How Psychology Undermines Morality*
    MA - v57 - i4 - Fall 2015 - p69(4) [501+]
    Nat R - v67 - i7 - April 20 2015 - p44 [501+]

Dalton, Annie - *The White Shepherd*
    BL - v112 - i2 - Sept 15 2015 - p35(1) [51-500]
    KR - August 1 2015 - pNA [51-500]
    PW - v262 - i35 - August 31 2015 - p63(1) [51-500]

Dalton, Lily Brooks - *Motorcycles I've Loved: A Memoir*
    BL - v111 - i13 - March 1 2015 - p14(2) [51-500]

Dalton, Michelle - *Sixteenth Summer*
    y KR - March 15 2015 - pNA [51-500]
Swept Away: A Sixteenth Summer Novel
    y HB Guide - v26 - i2 - Fall 2015 - p115(1) [51-500]
    y VOYA - v38 - i2 - June 2015 - p56(1) [51-500]
Swept Away
    y BL - v111 - i18 - May 15 2015 - p54(1) [51-500]
    SLJ - v61 - i4 - April 2015 - p154(1) [51-500]

Daly, Gavin - *The British Soldier in the Peninsular War*
    HER - v130 - i542 - Feb 2015 - p123(14) [501+]

Daly, Gerry - *Cycling the Mekong*
    KR - Dec 15 2015 - pNA [501+]

Daly, Jonathan W. - *Historians Debate the Rise of the West*
    HNet - August 2015 - pNA [501+]

Daly, Jude - *Thank You, Jackson: How One Little Boy Makes a Big Difference*
    c CH Bwatch - June 2015 - pNA [51-500]

Daly, Mary E. - *Gladstone: Ireland and Beyond*
    VS - v57 - i3 - Spring 2015 - p561(3) [501+]

Daly, Niki - *Thank you, Jackson: How One Little Boy Makes a Big Difference (Illus. by Daly, Jude)*
    c Sch Lib - v63 - i3 - Autumn 2015 - p153(2) [51-500]
    SLJ - v61 - i4 - April 2015 - p126(1) [51-500]
Thank You, Jackson: How One Little Boy Makes a Big Difference
    c PW - v262 - i4 - Jan 26 2015 - p168(2) [51-500]

Daly, Paula - *Keep Your Friends Close*
    RVBW - May 2015 - pNA [51-500]
    RVBW - Oct 2015 - pNA [51-500]
The Mistake I Made
    BL - v111 - i22 - August 1 2015 - p29(1) [51-500]
    KR - July 1 2015 - pNA [51-500]
    PW - v262 - i28 - July 13 2015 - p44(2) [51-500]

Daly, Ruth - *The Natural World of North America*
    c Res Links - v20 - i3 - Feb 2015 - p18(1) [51-500]

D'Ambrosio, Charles - *Loitering: New and Collected Essays*
    NYTBR - Jan 4 2015 - p8(L) [501+]

Damico, Gina - *Hellhole*
    y BL - v111 - i9-10 - Jan 1 2015 - p94(1) [51-500]
    y HB Guide - v26 - i2 - Fall 2015 - p115(2) [51-500]
    y VOYA - v37 - i6 - Feb 2015 - p74(1) [51-500]

D'Amico, Giuliano - *Domesticating Ibsen for Italy: Enrico and Icilio Polese's Ibsen Campaign*
    Scan St - v87 - i2 - Summer 2015 - p295(5) [501+]

D'Amico, Stefano - *Spanish Milan: A City within the Empire, 1535-1706*
    JMH - v87 - i2 - June 2015 - p403(7) [501+]

Damle, Amaleena - *The Becoming of the Body: Contemporary Women's Writing in French*
    FS - v69 - i4 - Oct 2015 - p558-558 [501+]
    MLR - v110 - i3 - July 2015 - p874-875 [501+]

Damm, Sigrid - *Goethes Freunde in Gotha und Weimar*
    Ger Q - v88 - i2 - Spring 2015 - p245(3) [501+]

Dammann, April - *Corita Kent: Art and Soul: The Biography*
    AM - v213 - i12 - Oct 26 2015 - p33(3) [501+]

Damour, Lisa - *Untangled: Guiding Teenage Girls through the Seven Transitions into Adulthood*
    KR - Nov 15 2015 - pNA [501+]
    PW - v262 - i52 - Dec 21 2015 - p150(1) [51-500]

Damrosch, Leo - *At Eternity's Sunrise: The Imaginative World of William Blake*
    PW - v262 - i34 - August 24 2015 - p76(1) [51-500]
Eternity's Sunrise: The Imaginative World of William Blake
    KR - August 15 2015 - pNA [501+]
    NYRB - v62 - i19 - Dec 3 2015 - p71(3) [501+]
    NYTBR - Nov 1 2015 - p24(L) [501+]
Jonathan Swift: His Life and His World
    ILS - v34 - i2 - Spring 2015 - p25(3) [501+]

Dams, Jeanne M. - *Blood Will Tell*
    KR - Dec 1 2015 - pNA [51-500]
    PW - v262 - i52 - Dec 21 2015 - p134(1) [51-500]
The Gentle Art of Murder: A Dorothy Martin Mystery
    PW - v262 - i17 - April 27 2015 - p53(1) [51-500]
The Gentle Art of Murder
    BL - v111 - i17 - May 1 2015 - p36(1) [51-500]

Dana, Jill - *Her Pink Hair (Illus. by Dana, Jill)*
    c CH Bwatch - March 2015 - pNA [51-500]

Danach - Der Holocaust als Erfahrungsgeschichte 1945 - 1949. 5. Internationale Konferenz zur Holocaustforschung
    HNet - April 2015 - pNA [501+]

Danaldson, Greg - *The Ville: Cops and Kids in Urban America*
    RVBW - July 2015 - pNA [501+]

Danbom, David - *Sod Busting: How Families Made Farms on the 19th-Century Plains*
    T&C - v56 - i4 - Oct 2015 - p982-983 [501+]

Danbom, David B. - *Sod Busting: How Families Made Farms on the 19th-Century Plains*
    JEH - v75 - i2 - June 2015 - p606-608 [501+]
    WHQ - v46 - i3 - Autumn 2015 - p391-391 [501+]

Dancy, J. Ross - *The Myth of the Press Gang: Volunteers, Impressment and the Naval Manpower Problem in the Late Eighteenth Century*
    TLS - i5859 - July 17 2015 - p22(1) [501+]

Dandelet, Thomas James - *The Renaissance of Empire in Early Modern Europe*
    AHR - v120 - i2 - April 2015 - p703-704 [501+]
    Ren Q - v68 - i3 - Fall 2015 - p1073-1074 [501+]
    Six Ct J - v46 - i1 - Spring 2015 - p113-118 [501+]

Dane, Jeffrey - *Creating Texas: A Brief History of the Revolution*
    Roundup M - v22 - i6 - August 2015 - p35(1) [501+]

Daneberg, Julie - *John Muir Wrestles a Waterfall (Illus. by Hogan, Jamie)*
    c PW - v262 - i3 - Jan 19 2015 - p80(1) [501+]

Danell, Rickard - *Social Science in Context: Historical, Sociological, and Global Perspectives*
    CS - v44 - i3 - May 2015 - p305-314 [501+]

Danely, Jason - *Aging and Loss: Mourning and Maturity in Contemporary Japan*
    MAQ - v29 - i3 - Sept 2015 - pb-24-b-26 [501+]

Daneshvari, Gitty - *The League of Unexceptional Children (Illus. by Lancett, James)*
    NYTBR - Nov 8 2015 - p32(L) [501+]
The League of Unexceptional Children
    c BL - v112 - i3 - Oct 1 2015 - p78(2) [51-500]
    c KR - August 1 2015 - pNA [51-500]
    c PW - v262 - i29 - July 20 2015 - p193(1) [51-500]
    c SLJ - v61 - i7 - July 2015 - p75(2) [51-500]

Danforth, John - *The Relevance of Religion: How Faithful People Can Change Politics*
    BL - v112 - i6 - Nov 15 2015 - p16(1) [51-500]
    KR - Oct 1 2015 - pNA [501+]

D'Angelo, Edoardo - *Auctor et Auctoritas in Latinis Medii Aevi Litteris*
    Specu - v90 - i3 - July 2015 - p871-873 [501+]

D'Angelo, Paul - *Stories I Tell*
    KR - May 15 2015 - pNA [51-500]

Daniel, Black - *Listen to the Lambs*
    KR - Dec 15 2015 - pNA [51-500]

Daniel, Danielle - *Sometimes I Feel Like a Fox (Illus. by Daniel, Danielle)*
    c KR - July 1 2015 - pNA [51-500]

Daniel, John - *The Trail Home*
    NAR - v300 - i3 - Summer 2015 - p52(1) [51-500]

Daniel, P.K. - *The Best Golfers of All Time*
    c HB Guide - v26 - i2 - Fall 2015 - p197(2) [51-500]
Indy Car Racing
    c HB Guide - v26 - i1 - Spring 2015 - p183(1) [51-500]
Magic vs. Bird in the NCAA Final
    c BL - v111 - i15 - April 1 2015 - p62(1) [51-500]

Daniel, Ray - *Corrupted Memory*
    KR - April 1 2015 - pNA [51-500]
    PW - v262 - i16 - April 20 2015 - p58(1) [51-500]

Daniel Torday - *The Last Flight of Poxl West*
    BL - v111 - i9-10 - Jan 1 2015 - p53(1) [51-500]

Danielewski, Mark - *The Familiar: One Rainy Day in May*
    TLS - i5854 - June 12 2015 - p10(1) [501+]

Danielewski, Mark Z. - *The Familiar: One Rainy Day in May*
    LJ - v140 - i6 - April 1 2015 - p73(1) [51-500]
The Familiar, vol. 1: One Rainy Day in May
    NYTBR - May 24 2015 - p23(L) [501+]
    PW - v262 - i6 - Feb 9 2015 - p42(1) [51-500]
The Familiar, vol. 2: Into the Forest
    LJ - v140 - i15 - Sept 15 2015 - p65(2) [51-500]
Into the Forest
    KR - August 15 2015 - pNA [51-500]
One Rainy Day in May
    KR - March 1 2015 - pNA [51-500]

Daniels, B.J. - *Lone Rider*
    PW - v262 - i22 - June 1 2015 - p47(1) [51-500]
Lucky Shot
    PW - v262 - i41 - Oct 12 2015 - p53(1) [51-500]
Wild Horses
    PW - v262 - i3 - Jan 19 2015 - p67(1) [51-500]

Daniels, Maurice C. - *Saving the Soul of Georgia: Donald L. Hollowell and the Struggle for Civil Rights*
    AHR - v120 - i1 - Feb 2015 - p291-292 [501+]
    JAH - v101 - i4 - March 2015 - p1327-1328 [501+]
    JSH - v81 - i3 - August 2015 - p773(2) [501+]

Daniels, Paul Raimond - *Nietzsche and The Birth of Tragedy*
    Class R - v65 - i1 - April 2015 - p288-289 [501+]
Daniels, Robert - *Once Shadows Fall*
    BL - v112 - i5 - Nov 1 2015 - p32(1) [51-500]
    KR - Oct 1 2015 - pNA [51-500]
Daniels, Roger - *Franklin D. Roosevelt: Road to the New Deal, 1882-1939*
    PW - v262 - i30 - July 27 2015 - p54(1) [51-500]
    KR - June 15 2015 - pNA [501+]
The Japanese American Cases: The Rule of Law in Time of War
    HNet - March 2015 - pNA [501+]
The Japanese-American Cases: The Rule of Law in Time of War
    PHR - v84 - i3 - August 2015 - p395(396) [501+]
Daniels, Smokey - *Teaching the Social Skills of Academic Interaction: Step-by-Step Lessons for Respect, Responsibility, and Results*
    Bwatch - April 2015 - pNA [501+]
Daniels, Tobias - *La Congiura dei Pazzi: I Documenti del Conflitto fra Lorenzo de' Medici e Sisto IV: Le Bolle di Scomunica, la "Florentina synodus," e la "Dissentio" Insoria tra la Santita del Papa e i Fiorentini*
    CHR - v101 - i1 - Wntr 2015 - p159(2) [501+]
La congiura dei Pazzi: I documenti del conflitto fra Lorenzo de' Medici e Sisto IV - Le bolle di scomunica, la "Florentina synodus," e la "Dissentio" insorta tra la Santita del Papa e i Fiorentini. Edizione critica e comment
    Six Ct J - v46 - i1 - Spring 2015 - p185-186 [501+]
Danielson, Leilah - *American Gandhi: A.J. Muste and the History of Radicalism in the Twentieth Century*
    AHR - v120 - i4 - Oct 2015 - p1508-1509 [501+]
    JAH - v102 - i2 - Sept 2015 - p613-614 [501+]
    JR - v95 - i4 - Oct 2015 - p547(3) [501+]
    Am St - v54 - i2 - Summer 2015 - p103-104 [501+]
Danielson, Sigrid - *Envisioning the Bishop: Images and the Episcopacy in the Middle Ages*
    HNet - Feb 2015 - pNA [501+]
Danielsson, Sarah K. - *The Explorer's Roadmap to National-Socialism: Sven Hedin, Geography and the Path to Genocide*
    CEH - v48 - i1 - March 2015 - p100-113 [501+]
Danker-Dake, Joshua - *The Retail*
    PW - v262 - i4 - Jan 26 2015 - p147(1) [51-500]
Danler, Stephanie - *Sweetbitter*
    PW - v262 - i50 - Dec 7 2015 - p66(1) [51-500]
Danley, Mark H. - *The Seven Years' War: Global Views*
    HNet - July 2015 - pNA [501+]
Danneberg, Julie - *Field-Trip Fiasco (Illus. by Love, Judy)*
    c HB Guide - v26 - i2 - Fall 2015 - p31(1) [51-500]
John Muir Wrestles a Waterfall (Illus. by Hogan, Jamie)
    c HB Guide - v26 - i2 - Fall 2015 - p207(2) [51-500]
    c Sci & Ch - v52 - i9 - Summer 2015 - p90 [501+]
    c BL - v111 - i12 - Feb 15 2015 - p75(1) [51-500]
    c KR - Jan 15 2015 - pNA [51-500]
    c SLJ - v61 - i2 - Feb 2015 - p118(1) [51-500]
Dannemiller, Scott - *The Year Without a Purchase: One Family's Quest to Stop Shopping and Start Connecting*
    CC - v132 - i25 - Dec 9 2015 - p38(2) [501+]
Dannenbring, Cheryl - *My Puppy Gave to Me (Illus. by Rremsner, Cynthia)*
    c HB Guide - v26 - i1 - Spring 2015 - p27(1) [51-500]
Danner, Matt - *Sock Monkey into the Deep Woods*
    BL - v111 - i9-10 - Jan 1 2015 - p62(1) [51-500]
Danova, Nadia - *Deportiraneto na evreite ot Vardarska Makedoniia, Belomorska Trakiia i Pirot, mart 1943 g. Dokumenti ot b'lgarskite arkhivi*
    Slav R - v74 - i3 - Fall 2015 - p618-620 [501+]
Dante, Joe - *Burying the Ex*
    NYT - June 19 2015 - pC6(L) [51-500]
Danticat, Edwidge - *Brother, I'm Dying*
    ABR - v36 - i4 - May-June 2015 - p4(1) [501+]
Mama's Nightingale: A Story of Immigration and Separation (Illus. by Staub, Leslie)
    c KR - July 1 2015 - pNA [51-500]
    c NYTBR - August 23 2015 - p24(L) [501+]
    c PW - v262 - i24 - June 15 2015 - p82(1) [51-500]
    c SLJ - v61 - i9 - Sept 2015 - p118(1) [51-500]
Mama's Nightingale (Illus. by Staub, Leslie)
    c HB - v91 - i5 - Sept-Oct 2015 - p77(2) [51-500]
Untwine
    y KR - June 15 2015 - pNA [51-500]
    y PW - v262 - i25 - June 22 2015 - p61(2) [51-500]
    y PW - v262 - i49 - Dec 2 2015 - p100(1) [51-500]
    y SLJ - v61 - i7 - July 2015 - p85(1) [51-500]
    y VOYA - v38 - i3 - August 2015 - p57(1) [51-500]

D'Antonio, Michael - *Never Enough: Donald Trump and the Pursuit of Success*
    Lon R Bks - v37 - i20 - Oct 22 2015 - p19(2) [501+]
    NYTBR - Sept 27 2015 - p12(L) [501+]
D'Antonio, William V. - *American Catholics in Transition*
    CS - v44 - i4 - July 2015 - p496-498 [501+]
Religion, Politics, and Polarization: How Religiopolitical Conflict Is Changing Congress and American Democracy
    J Ch St - v57 - i2 - Spring 2015 - p394-396 [501+]
Dantzig, Stephen - *The Essential Photographer Workbook: The Beginner's Guide to Creating Impressive Digital Photos*
    Bwatch - Oct 2015 - pNA [501+]
Danvers, Dennis - *Bad Angels*
    PW - v262 - i28 - July 13 2015 - p48(1) [51-500]
Danylyshyn, Greg - *A Crash of Rhinos (Illus. by Lomp, Stephan)*
    c KR - Oct 15 2015 - pNA [51-500]
Daoud, Hassan - *The Penguin's Song*
    WLT - v89 - i5 - Sept-Oct 2015 - p58(2) [501+]
Daoud, Kamel - *The Mersault Investigation*
    NYTBR - June 14 2015 - p1(L) [501+]
Meursault, Contre-Enquete
    TLS - i5831 - Jan 2 2015 - p23(1) [501+]
    WLT - v89 - i2 - March-April 2015 - p56(2) [501+]
The Meursault Investigation
    Comw - v142 - i14 - Sept 11 2015 - p35(3) [501+]
    CSM - June 2 2015 - pNA [501+]
    Econ - v415 - i8940 - May 30 2015 - p83(US) [501+]
    HR - v68 - i3 - Autumn 2015 - p510-516 [501+]
    KR - May 15 2015 - pNA [51-500]
    LJ - v140 - i10 - June 1 2015 - p92(3) [501+]
    Nat Post - v17 - i205 - July 4 2015 - pWP4(1) [501+]
    NS - v144 - i5276 - August 21 2015 - p47(1) [51-500]
    NYT - May 29 2015 - pC21(L) [501+]
    PW - v262 - i16 - April 20 2015 - p48(1) [51-500]
    Spec - v328 - i9750 - July 11 2015 - p35(1) [501+]
Darby, Peter - *Bede and the Future*
    Specu - v90 - i3 - July 2015 - p794-795 [501+]
Darby, Robert - *A Surgical Temptation: The Demonization of the Foreskin and the Rise of Circumcision in Britain*
    Historian - v77 - i3 - Fall 2015 - p599(2) [501+]
Darden, Joe T. - *Detroit: Race Riots, Racial Conflicts, and Efforts to Bridge the Racial Divide*
    JAH - v102 - i1 - June 2015 - p305-306 [501+]
Darden, Robert - *Nothing but Love in God's Water: Black Sacred Music from the Civil War to the Civil Rights Movement*
    Ch Today - v59 - i2 - March 2015 - p65(1) [51-500]
Nothing But Love in God's Water, vol. 1: Black Sacred Music from the Civil War to the Civil Rights Movement
    AM - v213 - i2 - July 20 2015 - p32(2) [501+]
Dardess, John W. - *A Political Life in Ming China: A Grand Secretary and His Times*
    JAS - v74 - i2 - May 2015 - p462-463 [501+]
Dare, Tessa - *When a Scot Ties the Knot*
    KR - June 15 2015 - pNA [51-500]
    PW - v262 - i29 - July 20 2015 - p175(1) [51-500]
Dargavel, John - *Science and Hope: A Forest History*
    HNet - Jan 2015 - pNA [501+]
Darien, Andrew T. - *Becoming New York's Finest: Race, Gender, and the Integration of the NYPD, 1935-1980*
    AHR - v120 - i2 - April 2015 - p651(1) [501+]
Dark, David - *Life's Too Short to Pretend You're Not Religious*
    PW - v262 - i51 - Dec 14 2015 - p79(2) [51-500]
Darke, Brian Allan - *Loving Nature, Fearing the State: Environmentalism and Antigovernment Politics before Reagan*
    PHR - v84 - i2 - May 2015 - p241(2) [501+]
Darke, J.A. - *The Grin in the Dark (Illus. by Evergreen, Nelson)*
    y Sch Lib - v63 - i4 - Winter 2015 - p243(1) [51-500]
Darke, John B. - *Climate Modeling for Scientists and Engineers*
    SIAM Rev - v57 - i2 - June 2015 - p307-308 [501+]
Darko, Daniel K. - *First the Kingdom of God: Global Voices on Global Mission*
    IBMR - v39 - i3 - July 2015 - p161(2) [501+]
Darling, Daniel - *The Original Jesus: Trading the Myths We Create for the Savior Who Is*
    Ch Today - v59 - i8 - Oct 2015 - p71(3) [501+]
Darling, Janet Kay - *The Timeless Love of Twin Souls*
    RVBW - May 2015 - pNA [501+]

Darling, Lynn - *Out of the Woods: A Memoir of Wayfinding*
    NYTBR - Feb 15 2015 - p28(L) [501+]
Darling, Nadine - *She Came from Beyond!*
    KR - August 1 2015 - pNA [51-500]
    LJ - v140 - i14 - Sept 1 2015 - p90(1) [51-500]
    PW - v262 - i34 - August 24 2015 - p55(2) [51-500]
Darling, Rosalyn Benjamin - *Disability and Identity: Negotiating Self in a Changing Society*
    CS - v44 - i2 - March 2015 - p189-191 [501+]
Darlinson, Aleesah - *Awesome Animal Stories for Kids (Illus. by Hart, James)*
    c Magpies - v30 - i5 - Nov 2015 - p34(1) [501+]
Laugh Your Head Off: Funny Stories for All Kinds of Kids (Illus. by Hart, James)
    c Magpies - v30 - i5 - Nov 2015 - p34(1) [501+]
Darned Sock Productions - *Loose Strands. E-book Review*
    c Teach Lib - v42 - i3 - Feb 2015 - p49(1) [501+]
Darnell, Rezneat Milton - *The American Sea: A Natural History of the Gulf of Mexico*
    Bwatch - Nov 2015 - pNA [51-500]
Darnielle, John - *Wolf in White Van*
    NYTBR - Oct 4 2015 - p28(L) [501+]
Darnton, Kate - *Chloe in India*
    c KR - Oct 15 2015 - pNA [51-500]
    c SLJ - v61 - i11 - Nov 2015 - p94(2) [51-500]
Darnton, Nina - *The Perfect Mother*
    NYTBR - Jan 18 2015 - p26(L) [501+]
Darnton, Robert - *Censors at Work: How States Shaped Literature*
    AHR - v120 - i2 - April 2015 - p578-579 [501+]
    TLS - i5852 - May 29 2015 - p25(1) [501+]
Darr, Orna Alyagon - *Marks of an Absolute Witch: Evidentiary Dilemmas in Early Modern England*
    Ren Q - v68 - i1 - Spring 2015 - p323-325 [501+]
Darrin, John - *The Rockets' Red Glare*
    PW - v262 - i35 - August 31 2015 - p65(1) [51-500]
Darroch, Gordon - *The Dawn of Canada's Century: Hidden Histories*
    Can Hist R - v96 - i2 - June 2015 - p310(3) [501+]
Darrows, Eva - *The Awesome*
    y KR - March 1 2015 - pNA [51-500]
    y PW - v262 - i13 - March 30 2015 - p78(1) [51-500]
    y PW - v262 - i49 - Dec 2 2015 - p100(1) [51-500]
Darvasi, Laszlo - *Ez egy ilyen csucs: A nagy Sziv Erno fuzet*
    WLT - v89 - i1 - Jan-Feb 2015 - p63(2) [501+]
Darwall, Stephen - *Honor, History, and Relationship: Essays in Second-Personal Ethics, vol. 2*
    RM - v68 - i3 - March 2015 - p648(2) [501+]
Darwin, John - *After Tamerlane: The Global History of Empire Since 1405*
    HNet - July 2015 - pNA [501+]
Darwish, Najwan - *Nothing More to Lose*
    WLT - v89 - i2 - March-April 2015 - p66(2) [501+]
Das Deutsche Volk und die Politik
    HNet - June 2015 - pNA [501+]
Das, Satyajit - *The Age of Stagnation: Why Perpetual Growth Is Unattainable and the Global Economy is in Peril*
    PW - v262 - i50 - Dec 7 2015 - p79(2) [51-500]
Das, Udaibir S. - *China's Road to Greater Financial Stability: Some Policy Perspectives*
    Pac A - v88 - i1 - March 2015 - p167 [501+]
Dasen, Veronique - *Les savoirs magiques et leur transmission de l'antiquite a la Renaissance*
    Specu - v90 - i3 - July 2015 - p873-874 [501+]
Dasgupta, Subrata - *It Began with Babbage: The Genesis of Computer Science*
    T&C - v56 - i2 - April 2015 - p537-538 [501+]
Dash, Meredith - *Calico Cats*
    c HB Guide - v26 - i1 - Spring 2015 - p167(2) [51-500]
Columbus Day
    c HB Guide - v26 - i1 - Spring 2015 - p142(1) [51-500]
Labor Day
    c HB Guide - v26 - i1 - Spring 2015 - p142(1) [51-500]
Martin Luther King, Jr. Day
    c HB Guide - v26 - i1 - Spring 2015 - p142(1) [51-500]
Thanksgiving
    c HB Guide - v26 - i1 - Spring 2015 - p142(1) [51-500]

Book Review Index 2016 Cumulation **DAVIES • 107**

Dashner, James - *The Game of Lives*
y BL - v112 - i5 - Nov 1 2015 - p54(1) [51-500]
VOYA - v38 - i5 - Dec 2015 - p67(2) [51-500]
The Games of Lives
y KR - Oct 15 2015 - pNA [51-500]
The Maze Runner Collector's Edition: The Scorch Trials
CH Bwatch - July 2015 - pNA [51-500]
The Rule of Thoughts
y HB Guide - v26 - i1 - Spring 2015 - p105(1) [51-500]
y Sch Lib - v63 - i1 - Spring 2015 - p51(1) [51-500]
Date, Sachin - *An Illustrated Guide to Mobile Technology*
KR - Sept 1 2015 - pNA [501+]
Datla, Kavita Saraswathi - *The Language of Secular Islam: Urdu Nationalism and Colonial India*
JR - v95 - i2 - April 2015 - p278(3) [501+]
Datlow, Ellen - *The Best Horror of the Year, vol. 7*
PW - v262 - i23 - June 8 2015 - p43(1) [51-500]
The Doll Collection
PW - v262 - i5 - Feb 2 2015 - p40(1) [51-500]
The Monstrous
PW - v262 - i36 - Sept 7 2015 - p48(1) [51-500]
Some of the Best from Tor.com: 2014
PW - v262 - i10 - March 9 2015 - p57(1) [51-500]
Datta, Pradip Kumar - *Political Science, vol. 3: India Political Thought*
Pac A - v88 - i1 - March 2015 - p141 [501+]
Dauber, Michele Landis - *The Sympathetic State: Disaster Relief and the Origins of the American Welfare State*
Historian - v77 - i1 - Spring 2015 - p116(3) [501+]
Daude, Cecile - *Scholies a Pindare*
Class R - v65 - i2 - Oct 2015 - p341-343 [501+]
Daugherty, C.J. - *The Secret Fire*
y Sch Lib - v63 - i4 - Winter 2015 - p243(1) [51-500]
Daugherty, Paul - *An Uncomplicated Life: A Father's Memoir of His Exceptional Daughter*
BL - v111 - i14 - March 15 2015 - p36(1) [51-500]
KR - Jan 1 2015 - pNA [51-500]
Daugherty, Tracy - *The Last Love Song: A Biography of Joan Didion*
BooChiTr - Sept 12 2015 - p13(1) [501+]
CSM - August 25 2015 - pNA [501+]
Ent W - i1377 - August 21 2015 - p105(1) [501+]
LJ - v140 - i8 - May 1 2015 - p70(1) [51-500]
NYT - August 18 2015 - pC1(L) [501+]
NYTBR - Sept 13 2015 - p14(L) [501+]
PW - v262 - i14 - April 6 2015 - p52(1) [51-500]
The Last Love Song
KR - June 1 2015 - pNA [501+]
The Last Love Song: The Biography of Joan Didion
BL - v111 - i19-20 - June 1 2015 - p32(1) [51-500]
Daughrity, Dyron B. - *To Whom Does Christianity Belong? Critical Issues in World Christianity*
CC - v132 - i21 - Oct 14 2015 - p33(2) [501+]
d'Aulaire, Ingri - *Leif the Lucky*
c HB Guide - v26 - i2 - Fall 2015 - p214(1) [51-500]
Daulatzai, Sohail - *Black Star, Crescent Moon: The Muslim International and Black Freedom beyond America*
Am Q - v67 - i2 - June 2015 - p491-503 [501+]
Am St - v54 - i2 - Summer 2015 - p9-20 [501+]
Daum, Meghan - *Selfish, Shallow, and Self-Absorbed*
KR - Jan 1 2015 - pNA [501+]
Selfish, Shallow, and Self-Absorbed: Sixteen Writers on the Decision Not to Have Kids
LJ - v140 - i2 - Feb 1 2015 - p100(1) [51-500]
Lon R Bks - v37 - i16 - August 27 2015 - p35(3) [501+]
Mac - v128 - i15 - April 20 2015 - p55(2) [501+]
Selfish, Shallow and Self-Absorbed: Sixteen Writers on the Decision Not to Have Kids
NS - v144 - i5258 - April 17 2015 - p54(2) [501+]
Selfish, Shallow, and Self-Absorbed: Sixteen Writers on the Decision Not to Have Kids
NYTBR - April 12 2015 - p21(L) [501+]
TLS - i5873 - Oct 23 2015 - p25(1) [501+]
PW - v262 - i2 - Jan 12 2015 - p52(1) [51-500]
The Unspeakable: And Other Subjects of Discussion (Read by Daum, Meghan). Audiobook Review
PW - v262 - i5 - Feb 2 2015 - p56(1) [51-500]
Daunais, Isabelle - *Le Roman sans aventure*
Can Lit - i224 - Spring 2015 - p118 [501+]
D'Aurevilly, Jules Barbey - *The Chevalier of Touches*
FS - v69 - i3 - July 2015 - p402(402) [501+]
D'Auria, Don - *Childhood Fears. E-book Review*
PW - v262 - i36 - Sept 7 2015 - p49(1) [51-500]
Daussy, Hugues - *Le parti huguenot: Chronique d'une desillusion, 1557-1572*
AHR - v120 - i3 - June 2015 - p1123-1124 [501+]
Dauverd, Celine - *Imperial Ambition in the Early Modern Mediterranean: Genoese Merchants and the Spanish Crown*
HER - v130 - i545 - August 2015 - p979(3) [501+]
Dauvergne, Peter - *Eco-Business: A Big-Brand Takeover of Sustainability*
CS - v44 - i3 - May 2015 - p353-354 [501+]
Dauvois, Sophie - *How Things Work: Facts and Fun, Questions and Answers, Things to Make and Do*
c CH Bwatch - May 2015 - pNA [51-500]
c SLJ - v61 - i7 - July 2015 - p103(1) [51-500]
c PW - v262 - i18 - May 4 2015 - p117(1) [501+]
Dave, Laura - *Eight Hundred Grapes*
BL - v111 - i17 - May 1 2015 - p74(1) [51-500]
KR - April 1 2015 - pNA [51-500]
LJ - v140 - i9 - May 15 2015 - p78(1) [501+]
Dave, Naisargi N. - *Queer Activism in India: A Story in the Anthropology of Ethics*
JRAI - v21 - i1 - March 2015 - p235(2) [501+]
Davenport, Bea - *In Too Deep*
PW - v262 - i14 - April 6 2015 - p41(2) [51-500]
This Little Piggy
PW - v262 - i17 - April 27 2015 - p55(1) [51-500]
Davenport, Caillan - *Fronto: Selected Letters*
Class R - v65 - i1 - April 2015 - p157-159 [501+]
Davenport-Hines, Richard - *Universal Man: The Lives of John Maynard Keynes*
BL - v111 - i15 - April 1 2015 - p8(1) [51-500]
Econ - v415 - i8937 - May 9 2015 - p80(US) [501+]
G&L Rev W - v22 - i6 - Nov-Dec 2015 - p35(2) [501+]
KR - March 1 2015 - pNA [501+]
LJ - v140 - i8 - May 1 2015 - p82(1) [51-500]
PW - v262 - i10 - March 9 2015 - p64(1) [51-500]
HNet - Sept 2015 - pNA [501+]
HNet - Sept 2015 - pNA [501+]
Universal Man: The Seven Lives of John Maynard Keynes
Spec - v327 - i9735 - March 28 2015 - p44(2) [501+]
TLS - i5852 - May 29 2015 - p3(2) [501+]
NS - v144 - i5257 - April 10 2015 - p50(2) [501+]
The Universal Man: The Seven Lives of John Maynard Keynes
TimHES - i2205 - May 28 2015 - p47(1) [501+]
Davenport, Matthew J. - *First Over There: The Attack on Cantigny, America's First Battle of World War I*
J Mil H - v79 - i4 - Oct 2015 - p1185-1186 [501+]
LJ - v140 - i8 - May 1 2015 - p88(3) [501+]
Davenport, Maxine - *Animal Sounds*
c KR - July 1 2015 - pNA [51-500]
Baby's First ABC
c KR - Jan 1 2016 - pNA [51-500]
Davey, Douglas - *Switch*
y Res Links - v20 - i3 - Feb 2015 - p27(1) [51-500]
y SLJ - v61 - i6 - June 2015 - p122(1) [51-500]
Davey, Janet - *Another Mother's Son*
Lon R Bks - v37 - i19 - Oct 8 2015 - p27(2) [501+]
Davey, Owen - *Mad about Monkeys (Illus. by Davey, Owen)*
c BL - v111 - i21 - July 1 2015 - p52(1) [51-500]
c CH Bwatch - Oct 2015 - pNA [51-500]
c KR - June 15 2015 - pNA [51-500]
c PW - v262 - i20 - May 18 2015 - p85(1) [501+]
c SLJ - v61 - i8 - August 2015 - p118(1) [51-500]
Daviau, Mo - *Every Anxious Wave*
KR - Dec 1 2015 - pNA [51-500]
Davick, Linda - *Say Hello! (Illus. by Davick, Linda)*
c CH Bwatch - Nov 2015 - pNA [51-500]
c KR - June 1 2015 - pNA [51-500]
David, Alison Matthews - *Fashion Victims: The Dangers of Dress Past and Present*
LJ - v140 - i16 - Oct 1 2015 - p75(1) [51-500]
NYT - Oct 31 2015 - pNA(L) [501+]
Spec - v329 - i9772 - Dec 12 2015 - p78(2) [501+]
TimHES - i2222 - Sept 24 2015 - p40-41 [501+]
David, Anthony - *An Improbable Friendship: The Remarkable Lives of Israeli Ruth Dayan and Palestinian Raymonda Tawil and Their Forty-Year Peace Mission*
LJ - v140 - i16 - Oct 1 2015 - p96(1) [51-500]
PW - v262 - i30 - July 27 2015 - p57(1) [51-500]
David, Butterfield - *The Early Textual History of Lucretius' De rerum natura*
AJP - v136 - i2 - Summer 2015 - p369-372 [501+]
David, Deborah Schoeberlein - *Living Mindfully: At Home, at Work, and in the World*
PW - v262 - i37 - Sept 14 2015 - p62(1) [51-500]
David, Deirdre - *Olivia Manning: A Woman at War*
MLR - v110 - i1 - Jan 2015 - p250-251 [501+]
Nation - v301 - i11-12 - Sept 14 2015 - p31(4) [501+]
David, Filip - *Kuca secanja i zaborava*
WLT - v89 - i3-4 - May-August 2015 - p107(2) [501+]
David-Fox, Michael - *The Holocaust in the East: Local Perpetrators and Soviet Responses*
Slav R - v74 - i2 - Summer 2015 - p373-375 [501+]
David, Gary A. - *Star Shrines and Earthworks of the Desert Southwest*
Am Ant - v80 - i3 - July 2015 - p622(3) [501+]
David, James Corbett - *Dunmore's New World: The Extraordinary Life of a Royal Governor in Revolutionary America--with Jacobites, Counterfeiters, Land Schemes, Shipwrecks, Scalping, Indian Politics, Runaway Slaves, and Two Illegal Royal Weddings*
HNet - August 2015 - pNA [501+]
David, James E. - *Spies and Shuttles: NASA's Secret Relationships with the DOD and CIA*
HNet - April 2015 - pNA [501+]
David, Juliet - *The Midnight Visitors (Illus. by Parry, Jo)*
c PW - v262 - i37 - Sept 14 2015 - p64(1) [51-500]
David, Massimiliano - *Eternal Ravenna: From the Etruscans to the Venetians*
Class R - v65 - i1 - April 2015 - p238-240 [501+]
Specu - v90 - i2 - April 2015 - p533-535 [501+]
David, Nicetas - *The Life of Patriarch Ignatius*
Theol St - v76 - i1 - March 2015 - p211(1) [501+]
David, Saul - *All the King's Men: The British Redcoat in the Era of Sword and Musket*
HER - v130 - i542 - Feb 2015 - p123(14) [501+]
All the King's Men: The British Soldier from the Restoration to Waterloo
HT - v65 - i7 - July 2015 - p58(2) [501+]
Operation Thunderbolt: Flight 139 and the Raid on Entebbe Airport
KR - Oct 1 2015 - pNA [501+]
Spec - v328 - i9751 - July 18 2015 - p36(1) [501+]
TimHES - i2217 - August 20 2015 - p47-47 [501+]
TLS - i5873 - Oct 23 2015 - p24(1) [501+]
David, Stuart - *In the All-Night Cafe: A Memoir of Belle and Sebastian's Formative Year*
NS - v144 - i5266 - June 12 2015 - p48(2) [501+]
TLS - i5848 - May 1 2015 - p21(2) [501+]
Jackdaw and the Randoms
c Magpies - v30 - i5 - Nov 2015 - p40(1) [501+]
David, Susan - *Beyond Goals: Effective Strategies for Coaching and Mentoring*
Per Psy - v68 - i3 - Autumn 2015 - p711(4) [501+]
David-Weill, Michel - *A Taste for Happiness*
KR - Jan 1 2016 - pNA [501+]
Davidds, Yasmin - *Your Own Terms: A Woman's Guide to Taking Charge of Any Negotiation*
PW - v262 - i24 - June 15 2015 - p77(1) [51-500]
Davidman, Lynn - *Becoming Un-Orthodox: Stories of Ex-Hasidic Jews*
CHE - v61 - i29 - March 30 2015 - pNA [501+]
Davidson, Alan - *The Oxford Companion to Food, 3d ed.*
BL - v111 - i12 - Feb 15 2015 - p21(1) [51-500]
Davidson, Anya - *School Spirits*
ABR - v36 - i2 - Jan-Feb 2015 - p5(1) [501+]
Davidson, James D. - *Ranking Faiths: Religious Stratification in America*
SF - v93 - i3 - March 2015 - pe66 [501+]
Davidson, James West - *A Little History of the United States*
BL - v111 - i22 - August 1 2015 - p20(1) [51-500]
KR - August 1 2015 - pNA [501+]
LJ - v140 - i17 - Oct 15 2015 - p100(1) [51-500]
PW - v262 - i29 - July 20 2015 - p181(1) [51-500]
Davidson, Mary Janice - *Undead and Unforgiven*
BL - v112 - i2 - Sept 15 2015 - p48(1) [51-500]
Davidson, MaryJanice - *Undead and Unforgiven*
PW - v262 - i33 - August 17 2015 - p55(2) [51-500]
Davidson, Peter - *The Last of the Light: About Twilight*
Nature - v527 - i7579 - Nov 26 2015 - p445(1) [51-500]
Davies, Benji - *Bizzy Bear's Big Building Book (Illus. by Davies, Benji)*
c KR - Jan 1 2015 - pNA [51-500]
Grandad's Island (Illus. by Davies, Benji)
c Sch Lib - v63 - i4 - Winter 2015 - p218(1) [51-500]
The Storm Whale (Illus. by Davies, Benji)
c HB - v91 - i1 - Jan-Feb 2015 - p63(2) [51-500]
c HB Guide - v26 - i1 - Spring 2015 - p27(1) [51-500]
Davies, Caitlin - *Down Stream: A History and Celebration of Swimming the River Thames*
TLS - i5864-5865 - August 21 2015 - p38(1) [501+]

Davies, Damian Walford - *Judas*
  NS - v144 - i5262 - May 15 2015 - p43(1) [51-500]
Davies, H. 'Tomi - *The African Project Manager*
  KR - Jan 15 2015 - pNA [501+]
Davies, Helen - *Gender and Ventriloquism in Victorian and Neo-Victorian Fiction: Passionate Puppets*
  VS - v57 - i2 - Wntr 2015 - p310(3) [501+]
Davies, Howard - *Can Financial Markets be Controlled*
  TimHES - i2196 - March 26 2015 - p54(1) [501+]
Davies, Huw J. - *Wellington's War: The Making of a Military Genius*
  HT - v65 - i7 - July 2015 - p58(2) [501+]
Davies, J.Q. - *Romantic Anatomies of Performance*
  TLS - i5844 - April 3 2015 - p9(1) [501+]
Davies, Jamie A. - *Life Unfolding: How the Human Body Creates Itself*
  TLS - i5847 - April 24 2015 - p25(1) [501+]
  Mechanisms of Morphogenesis
  QRB - v90 - i2 - June 2015 - p227(1) [501+]
Davies, Jeremy M. - *Fancy*
  TLS - i5838 - Feb 20 2015 - p20(1) [501+]
Davies, Jonathan - *Aspects of Violence in Renaissance Europe*
  AHR - v120 - i1 - Feb 2015 - p321-322 [501+]
Davies, Katie Quinn - *What Katie Ate on the Weekend*
  LJ - v140 - i5 - March 15 2015 - p126(2) [501+]
Davies, Linda - *Longbow Girl*
  y KR - Dec 15 2015 - pNA [51-500]
  y PW - v262 - i48 - Nov 30 2015 - p61(1) [51-500]
Davies, Luke - *God of Speed*
  WLT - v89 - i2 - March-April 2015 - p59(1) [51-500]
Davies, Matt - *Ben Draws Trouble*
  BL - v111 - i14 - March 15 2015 - p77(1) [51-500]
  c HB Guide - v26 - i2 - Fall 2015 - p31(1) [51-500]
  c KR - Feb 15 2015 - pNA [51-500]
Davies, Nick - *Cuckoo: Cheating by Nature*
  BL - v111 - i13 - March 1 2015 - p9(1) [51-500]
  KR - Jan 15 2015 - pNA [51-500]
  Nature - v519 - i7544 - March 26 2015 - p413(1) [51-500]
  NH - v123 - i9 - Nov 2015 - p46(2) [501+]
  PW - v262 - i6 - Feb 9 2015 - p54(1) [51-500]
  TLS - i5858 - July 10 2015 - p30(1) [51-500]
  Hack Attack: The Inside Story of How the Truth Caught Up with Rupert Murdoch
  NYRB - v62 - i1 - Jan 8 2015 - p31(3) [501+]
Davies, Nicola - *Heroes of the Wild: The Whale Who Saved (Illus. by Wright, Annabel)*
  c Sch Lib - v63 - i2 - Summer 2015 - p102(1) [51-500]
  I (Don't) Like Snakes (Illus. by Lozano, Luciano)
  c BL - v112 - i1 - Sept 1 2015 - p119(2) [51-500]
  c HB - v91 - i5 - Sept-Oct 2015 - p127(2) [51-500]
  c KR - July 1 2015 - pNA [51-500]
  c Magpies - v30 - i4 - Sept 2015 - p24(1) [501+]
  c PW - v262 - i35 - August 31 2015 - p90(2) [501+]
  c PW - v262 - i49 - Dec 2 2015 - p47(2) [51-500]
  c Sch Lib - v63 - i4 - Winter 2015 - p237(1) [51-500]
  c SLJ - v61 - i8 - August 2015 - p118(1) [51-500]
  The Leopard's Tail
  y Sch Lib - v63 - i4 - Winter 2015 - p226(1) [51-500]
  Manatee Rescue (Illus. by Wright, Annabel)
  c KR - Oct 1 2015 - pNA [51-500]
  c SLJ - v61 - i9 - Sept 2015 - p134(1) [51-500]
  The Promise (Illus. by Carlin, Laura)
  c BL - v111 - i12 - Feb 15 2015 - p76(1) [501+]
  Tiny Creatures: The World of Microbes (Illus. by Sutton, Emily)
  c BL - v111 - i9-10 - Jan 1 2015 - pS4(8) [501+]
  c HB Guide - v26 - i1 - Spring 2015 - p153(1) [51-500]
  c BL - v111 - i9-10 - Jan 1 2015 - p92(1) [501+]
Davies, Norman - *Trail of Hope: The Anders Army, an Odyssey Across Three Continents*
  Spec - v329 - i9771 - Dec 5 2015 - p39(1) [501+]
Davies, Paul - *The Paper Museum of Cassiano del Pozzo, Series A: Renaissance and Later Architecture and Ornament, part 10*
  Six Ct J - v46 - i3 - Fall 2015 - p700-702 [501+]
Davies, Richard O. - *The Main Event: Boxing in Nevada from the Mining Camps to the Las Vegas Strip*
  PHR - v84 - i4 - Nov 2015 - p570(2) [501+]
  WHQ - v46 - i2 - Summer 2015 - p258-259 [501+]
Davies, Sarah - *Stalin's World: Dictating the Soviet Order*
  AHR - v120 - i4 - Oct 2015 - p1570-1571 [501+]
  E-A St - v67 - i7 - Sept 2015 - p1130(15) [501+]
  HNet - Sept 2015 - pNA [501+]
  TimHES - i2195 - March 19 2015 - p52-53 [501+]

Davies, Simon - *India and Europe in the Global Eighteenth Century*
  MLR - v110 - i2 - April 2015 - p514-516 [501+]
  FS - v69 - i3 - July 2015 - p395-396 [501+]
Davies, Tod - *The Lizard Princess*
  y KR - August 15 2015 - pNA [51-500]
Davies, William - *The Happiness Industry: How the Government and Big Business Sold Us Well-Being*
  BL - v111 - i13 - March 1 2015 - p9(1) [51-500]
  Har Bus R - v93 - i7-8 - July-August 2015 - p130(2) [501+]
  HM - v331 - i1982 - July 2015 - p90(5) [501+]
  Lon R Bks - v37 - i20 - Oct 22 2015 - p31(2) [501+]
  TimHES - i2202 - May 7 2015 - p54(1) [501+]
  The Happiness Industry
  KR - March 1 2015 - pNA [501+]
Davieson, Adrian A. - *Ebola: Stigma and Western Conspiracy*
  LJ - v140 - i13 - August 1 2015 - p116(1) [51-500]
Davila, Claudia - *Super Red Riding Hood (Illus. by Davila, Claudia)*
  c HB Guide - v26 - i1 - Spring 2015 - p27(1) [51-500]
Davila, Jose Camilo - *Business Goals and Social Commitment: Shaping Organizational Capabilities--Colombia's Fundacion Social, 1984-2011*
  BHR - v89 - i2 - Summer 2015 - p379(2) [501+]
Davioliute, Violeta - *The Making and Breaking of Soviet Lithuania: Memory and Modernity in the Wake of War*
  Slav R - v74 - i2 - Summer 2015 - p384-385 [501+]
Davis, Angela Y. - *The Meaning of Freedom: And Other Difficult Dialogues*
  S&S - v79 - i4 - Oct 2015 - p622-624 [501+]
Davis, Aric - *Weavers*
  BL - v111 - i21 - July 1 2015 - p41(1) [51-500]
  PW - v262 - i18 - May 4 2015 - p99(1) [51-500]
Davis, Ben - *Return of the Geek: The Private Blog of Joe Cowley*
  y Sch Lib - v63 - i3 - Autumn 2015 - p180(1) [51-500]
Davis, Benjie - *Bizzy Bear: Knights' Castle (Illus. by Davis, Benjie)*
  c KR - July 1 2015 - pNA [51-500]
Davis, Blayne - *Wild Game*
  SPBW - Feb 2015 - pNA [51-500]
Davis, Brenda - *Becoming Vegan: The Complete Reference to Plant-Based Nutrition*
  Veg J - v34 - i4 - Oct-Dec 2015 - p31(1) [51-500]
Davis, Brooke - *Lost and Found (Read by Carrington, Nigel). Audiobook Review*
  BL - v111 - i19-20 - June 1 2015 - p126(2) [51-500]
Davis, Clark - *It Starts with Trouble*
  KR - Feb 15 2015 - pNA [51-500]
  Starts with Trouble: William Goyen and the Life of Writing
  PW - v262 - i11 - March 16 2015 - p76(1) [51-500]
Davis, Colin - *Postwar Renoir: Film and the Memory of Violence*
  FS - v69 - i1 - Jan 2015 - p135-136 [501+]
Davis, Cooper - *A King Undone*
  LJ - v140 - i2 - Feb 1 2015 - p5(1) [51-500]
Davis, Cornelia E. - *Searching for Sitala Mata*
  KR - August 15 2015 - pNA [501+]
Davis, Courtney - *Unhealthy Pharmaceutical Regulation: Innovation, Politics, and Promissory Science*
  AJS - v120 - i5 - March 2015 - p1585(3) [501+]
Davis, Daniel M. - *The Compatibility Gene: How Our Bodies Fight Disease, Attract Others, and Define Our Selves*
  QRB - v90 - i3 - Sept 2015 - p343(1) [501+]
Davis, David A. - *Writing in the Kitchen: Essays on Southern Literature and Foodways*
  JSH - v81 - i4 - Nov 2015 - p1050(3) [501+]
Davis, David Brion - *The Problem of Slavery in the Age of Emancipation*
  NYTBR - Feb 22 2015 - p32(L) [501+]
  RAH - v43 - i2 - June 2015 - p254-261 [501+]
Davis, Eleanor - *Flop to the Top! (Illus. by Davis, Eleanor)*
  c BL - v112 - i2 - Sept 15 2015 - p53(1) [51-500]
  c HB - v91 - i6 - Nov-Dec 2015 - p78(1) [51-500]
  c KR - July 15 2015 - pNA [51-500]
  c NYTBR - August 23 2015 - p26(L) [501+]
  Flop to the Top! (Illus. by Weing, Drew)
  c PW - v262 - i24 - June 15 2015 - p87(1) [51-500]
  c SLJ - v61 - i9 - Sept 2015 - p135(3) [51-500]

Davis, Elizabeth Anne - *Bad Souls, Madness and Responsibility in Modern Greece*
  MAQ - v29 - i2 - June 2015 - pb9-b12 [501+]
Davis, Ellen F. - *Biblical Prophecy: Perspectives for Christian Theology, Discipleship, and Ministry*
  CC - v132 - i17 - August 19 2015 - p39(3) [501+]
Davis, Forest Walker - *Duct Tape: 101 Adventurous Ideas for Art, Jewelry, Flowers, Wallets and More*
  LJ - v140 - i9 - May 15 2015 - p82(1) [51-500]
Davis, Fred E. - *U.S. Mica Industry Pioneers: The Ruggles and Bowers Families*
  RocksMiner - v90 - i2 - March-April 2015 - p187(2) [501+]
Davis, G Gordon - *Letters from the Road*
  KR - April 15 2015 - pNA [501+]
Davis, Garth - *Proteinaholic: How Our Obsession with Meat is Killing Us and What We Can Do about It*
  BL - v112 - i4 - Oct 15 2015 - p10(1) [51-500]
  LJ - v140 - i16 - Oct 1 2015 - p100(2) [51-500]
  PW - v262 - i36 - Sept 7 2015 - p62(1) [51-500]
Davis, Gerald - *Algerian Diary*
  KR - Dec 15 2015 - pNA [501+]
Davis, Ivor - *The Beatles and Me on Tour*
  PW - v262 - i10 - March 9 2015 - p66(1) [51-500]
Davis, Jacky - *Ladybug Girl and the Best Ever Playdate (Illus. by Soman, David)*
  c KR - June 15 2015 - pNA [51-500]
  c SLJ - v61 - i9 - Sept 2015 - p118(1) [51-500]
Davis, James A. - *Music along the Rapidan: Civil War Soldiers, Music, and Community during Winter Quarters*
  Am St - v54 - i1 - Spring 2015 - p165-2 [501+]
  Music along the Rapidan
  Roundup M - v22 - i4 - April 2015 - p26(1) [501+]
Davis, James C. - *Eric Walrond: A Life in the Harlem Renaissance and the Transatlantic Caribbean*
  TLS - i5855 - June 19 2015 - p31(1) [501+]
Davis, Joe S. - *The Kidnapping of Jamaica's Homeland Security: The Adventures of the Expeditor*
  PW - v262 - i12 - March 23 2015 - p35(5) [501+]
Davis, John M. Jr. - *Parole, Pardon, Pass and Amnesty Documents of the Civil War: An Illustrated History*
  SHQ - v118 - i4 - April 2015 - p432-433 [501+]
Davis, Jon - *Small Blue and the Deep Dark Night*
  c HB Guide - v26 - i1 - Spring 2015 - p27(1) [51-500]
Davis, Joshua - *Spare Parts: Four Undocumented Teenagers, One Ugly Robot, and the Battle for the American Dream*
  For Aff - v94 - i3 - May-June 2015 - pNA [501+]
  New Sci - v225 - i3003 - Jan 10 2015 - p42(2) [501+]
Davis, Julie L. - *Survival Schools: The American Indian Movement and Community Education in the Twin Cities*
  WHQ - v46 - i2 - Summer 2015 - p246-247 [501+]
Davis-Kahl, Stephanie - *Common Ground at the Nexus of Information Literacy and Scholarly Communication*
  LQ - v85 - i2 - April 2015 - p215(4) [501+]
Davis, Kaitlyn - *Gathering Frost*
  y PW - v262 - i41 - Oct 12 2015 - p71(1) [51-500]
Davis, Kathryn Gibbs - *Mr. Ferris and His Wheel (Illus. by Ford, Gilbert)*
  c HB Guide - v26 - i1 - Spring 2015 - p192(1) [51-500]
Davis, Kathy - *Dancing Tango, Passionate Encounters in a Globalizing World*
  Dance RJ - v47 - i2 - August 2015 - p89-3 [501+]
  Dancing Tango: Passionate Encounters in a Globalizing World
  TimHES - i2196 - March 26 2015 - p51(1) [501+]
  TLS - i5860 - July 24 2015 - p22(1) [501+]
  Wom R Bks - v32 - i6 - Nov-Dec 2015 - p23(2) [501+]
Davis, Kenneth C. - *The Hidden History of America at War: Untold Tales from Yorktown to Fallujah*
  KR - April 1 2015 - pNA [501+]
  LJ - v140 - i8 - May 1 2015 - p88(3) [501+]
  PW - v262 - i10 - March 9 2015 - p63(1) [51-500]
Davis, Kent - *A Riddle in Ruby*
  c BL - v111 - i21 - July 1 2015 - p76(1) [51-500]
  c KR - June 1 2015 - pNA [51-500]
  c PW - v262 - i26 - June 29 2015 - p68(2) [51-500]
  c SLJ - v61 - i6 - June 2015 - p100(1) [51-500]
Davis, Lennard J. - *Enabling Acts: The Hidden Story of How the Americans with Disabilities Act Gave the Largest U.S. Minority Its Rights*
  PW - v262 - i13 - March 30 2015 - p64(2) [51-500]
  Enabling Acts: The Hidden Story of How the Americans with Disabilities Act Gave the Largest US Minority Its

Rights
   BL - v111 - i21 - July 1 2015 - p10(1) [51-500]
   KR - April 15 2015 - pNA [501+]
   LJ - v140 - i9 - May 15 2015 - p93(1) [51-500]

Davis, Lindsey - *Deadly Election*
   BL - v111 - i19-20 - June 1 2015 - p52(1) [51-500]
   HT - v65 - i11 - Nov 2015 - p56(2) [501+]
   PW - v262 - i19 - May 11 2015 - p38(1) [51-500]

Davis, Lydia - *Alfred Ollivant's Bob, Son of Battle: The Last Gray Dog of Kenmuir (Illus. by Kirmse, Marguerite)*
  c HB Guide - v26 - i2 - Fall 2015 - p79(1) [51-500]

Davis, Nancy J. - *Claiming Society for God: Religious Movements & Social Welfare*
   SF - v94 - i2 - Dec 2015 - pNA [501+]

Davis, Nick - *Early Modern Writing and the Privatisation of Experience*
   Six Ct J - v46 - i1 - Spring 2015 - p141-143 [501+]

Davis, Rebecca L. - *More Perfect Unions: The American Search for Marital Bliss*
   JWH - v27 - i2 - Summer 2015 - p175(7) [501+]

Davis, Ren - *Landscapes for the People: George Alexander Grant, First Chief Photographer of the National Park Service*
   BL - v112 - i1 - Sept 1 2015 - p26(1) [51-500]
   LJ - v140 - i15 - Sept 15 2015 - p81(3) [501+]

Davis, Richard - *Covering the United States Supreme Court in the Digital Age*
   HLR - v128 - i7 - May 2015 - p2106(1) [1-50]
Last Indian Summer
   BL - v111 - i18 - May 15 2015 - p29(2) [51-500]
   Roundup M - v23 - i1 - Oct 2015 - p29(1) [501+]

Davis, Sarah - *My First Trucks*
  c BL - v111 - i19-20 - June 1 2015 - p110(1) [51-500]

Davis, Sean - *The Wax Bullet War: Chronicles of a Soldier and Artist*
   WLT - v89 - i2 - March-April 2015 - p59(1) [51-500]

Davis, Stephen J. - *Christ Child: Cultural Memories of a Young Jesus*
   CH - v84 - i3 - Sept 2015 - p646(3) [501+]
   Theol St - v76 - i1 - March 2015 - p209(2) [501+]

Davis, Steve - *Interesting: My Autobiography*
   Spec - v327 - i9739 - April 25 2015 - p39(1) [501+]

Davis, Sue - *The Political Thought of Elizabeth Cady Stanton*
   JWH - v27 - i2 - Summer 2015 - p159(10) [501+]

Davis, Tanita S. - *Peas and Carrots*
  y KR - Nov 15 2015 - pNA [51-500]
  y PW - v262 - i47 - Nov 23 2015 - p69(1) [51-500]
  y SLJ - v61 - i12 - Dec 2015 - p120(1) [51-500]

Davis, Wes - *The Ariadne Objective: The Underground War to Rescue Crete from the Nazis*
   CSM - April 3 2015 - pNA [51-500]

Davis, William - *Wheat Belly: 10-Day Grain Detox: Reprogram Your Body for Rapid Weight Loss and Amazing Health*
   LJ - v140 - i16 - Oct 1 2015 - p101(1) [51-500]

Davis, William C. - *Crucible of Command: Ulysses S. Grant and Robert E. Lee: The War They Fought, the Peace They Forged (Read by Burns, Traber). Audiobook Review*
   BL - v111 - i21 - July 1 2015 - p78(1) [51-500]
Crucible of Command: Ulysses S. Grant and Robert E. Lee--the War They Fought, the Peace They Forged
   BL - v111 - i9-10 - Jan 1 2015 - p33(1) [51-500]
Crucible of Command: Ulysses S. Grant and Robert E. Lee - the War They Fought, the Peace They Forged
   KR - Jan 1 2015 - pNA [501+]

Davison, Anita - *Murder on the Minneapolis*
   PW - v262 - i39 - Sept 28 2015 - p71(1) [51-500]

Davison, Claire - *Translation as Collaboration: Virginia Woolf, Katherine Mansfield and S.S. Koteliansky*
   RES - v66 - i274 - April 2015 - p396-398 [501+]

Davison, Michael H. - *Eshen: An American Colony*
   SPBW - June 2015 - pNA [51-500]

Davodeau, Etienne - *Lulu Anew (Illus. by Davodeau, Etienne)*
   BL - v111 - i16 - April 15 2015 - p39(1) [51-500]
  y VOYA - v38 - i3 - August 2015 - p57(2) [51-500]
Lulu Anew
   PW - v262 - i11 - March 16 2015 - p72(1) [51-500]

Davy, V.T. - *The Hystery App*
   KR - April 15 2015 - pNA [501+]

Davydov, Marina - *Baby Lady's Scary Night: A Ladybug Story (Illus. by Triplett, Ginger)*
  c CH Bwatch - July 2015 - pNA [51-500]

Dawes, Helena - *Catholic Women's Movements in Liberal and Fascist Italy*
   HNet - March 2015 - pNA [501+]

Dawes, James - *Evil Men*
   ABR - v36 - i4 - May-June 2015 - p9(1) [501+]

Dawes, Kwame - *Seven New Generation African Poets*
   Ant R - v73 - i2 - Spring 2015 - p372(9) [501+]

Dawes, Laura - *Childhood Obesity in America: Biography of an Epidemic*
   AHR - v120 - i3 - June 2015 - p1039-1040 [501+]

Dawisha, Karea - *Putin's Kleptocracy: Who Owns Russia?*
   TLS - i5836 - Feb 6 2015 - p25(1) [501+]

Dawisha, Karen - *Putin's Kleptocracy: Who Owns Russia?*
   For Aff - v94 - i1 - Jan-Feb 2015 - pNA [51-500]
   Lon R Bks - v37 - i3 - Feb 5 2015 - p13(3) [501+]

Dawkins, Richard - *Brief Candle in the Dark: My Life in Science*
   Har Bus R - v93 - i12 - Dec 2015 - p124(2) [501+]
   KR - June 15 2015 - pNA [501+]
   LJ - v140 - i11 - June 15 2015 - p107(1) [51-500]
   NYT - Oct 7 2015 - pC1(L) [501+]
   NYTBR - Nov 29 2015 - p8(L) [501+]
   PW - v262 - i31 - August 3 2015 - p46(1) [51-500]
   BL - v111 - i22 - August 1 2015 - p11(1) [51-500]

Dawkins, Redux: Nathaniel Comfort Takes Issue with the Second Instalment of the Evolutionary Biologist's Autobiography
   Nature - v525 - i7568 - Sept 10 2015 - p184(2) [501+]

Dawn, Amber - *Where the Words End and My Body Begins*
   Nat Post - v17 - i188 - June 13 2015 - pWP4(1) [501+]

Dawn, Tessa - *Blood Father*
   KR - June 15 2015 - pNA [501+]
Blood Vengeance
   SPBW - June 2015 - pNA [51-500]

Dawnay, Gabby - *A Possum's Tail (Illus. by Barrow, Alex)*
  c BL - v111 - i9-10 - Jan 1 2015 - p108(1) [51-500]

Dawson-Bowling, Paul - *The Wagner Experience and Its Meaning to Us*
   MT - v156 - i1930 - Spring 2015 - p114-117 [501+]

Dawson, Delilah S. - *Hit*
  y CCB-B - v68 - i10 - June 2015 - p485(2) [51-500]
  y HB Guide - v26 - i2 - Fall 2015 - p116(1) [51-500]
  y VOYA - v38 - i1 - April 2015 - p76(1) [51-500]
  y KR - Feb 1 2015 - pNA [51-500]
Servants of the Storm
  y HB Guide - v26 - i1 - Spring 2015 - p105(1) [51-500]

Dawson, James - *All of the Above*
  y Magpies - v30 - i4 - Sept 2015 - p40(1) [501+]
  y Sch Lib - v63 - i4 - Winter 2015 - p243(2) [51-500]
This Book Is Gay (Illus. by Gerrell, Spike)
  y BL - v111 - i18 - May 15 2015 - p44(1) [51-500]
  y PW - v262 - i25 - June 22 2015 - p141(1) [51-500]
  y SLJ - v61 - i6 - June 2015 - p141(1) [51-500]
This Book Is Gay
  y KR - April 15 2015 - pNA [51-500]
Under My Skin
  y Magpies - v30 - i1 - March 2015 - p39(1) [501+]
  y Sch Lib - v63 - i3 - Autumn 2015 - p180(1) [51-500]

Dawson, Jane - *John Knox*
   Spec - v327 - i9740 - May 2 2015 - p43(2) [501+]
   TimHES - i2206 - June 4 2015 - p52-53 [501+]

Dawson, Janet - *Cold Trail*
   KR - Feb 1 2015 - pNA [51-500]
   PW - v262 - i8 - Feb 23 2015 - p54(1) [51-500]

Dawson, Jennifer - *The Name of the Game*
   BL - v112 - i2 - Sept 15 2015 - p45(1) [51-500]
   PW - v262 - i32 - August 10 2015 - p43(1) [51-500]

Dawson, Jill - *The Tell-Tale Heart*
   BL - v111 - i12 - Feb 15 2015 - p33(1) [51-500]
   NYTBR - March 15 2015 - p12(L) [501+]

Dawson, M. Joan - *Paul Lauterbur and the Invention of MRI*
   T&C - v56 - i1 - Jan 2015 - p300-301 [501+]

Dawson, Willow - *The Wolf-Birds (Illus. by Dawson, Willow)*
  c HB - v91 - i6 - Nov-Dec 2015 - p65(2) [501+]
  c KR - June 1 2015 - pNA [501+]
  c PW - v262 - i25 - June 22 2015 - p143(1) [51-500]
  c SLJ - v61 - i8 - August 2015 - p118(1) [51-500]

Day, Alexandra - *Carl's Halloween (Illus. by Day, Alexandra)*
  c BL - v112 - i4 - Oct 15 2015 - p48(1) [51-500]
  c HB - v91 - i5 - Sept-Oct 2015 - p67(1) [51-500]
  c KR - August 1 2015 - pNA [51-500]
  c PW - v262 - i30 - July 27 2015 - p64(1) [51-500]
  c SLJ - v61 - i9 - Sept 2015 - p106(1) [51-500]

Day, Angela - *Red Light to Starboard: Recalling the Exxon Valdez Disaster*
   Roundup M - v22 - i5 - June 2015 - p36(1) [51-500]
   Roundup M - v22 - i6 - August 2015 - p35(2) [501+]

Day, Barry - *The World of Raymond Chandler: In His Own Words*
   NYTBR - Jan 11 2015 - p26(L) [501+]
   Bks & Cult - v21 - i4 - July-August 2015 - p33(2) [501+]

Day, David - *Alice's Adventures in Wonderland Decoded: The Full Text of Lewis Carroll's Novel with Its Many Hidden Meanings Revealed*
   LJ - v140 - i17 - Oct 15 2015 - p94(1) [501+]

Day, Elizabeth - *Paradise City*
   Spec - v328 - i9744 - May 30 2015 - p38(1) [501+]
   BL - v112 - i1 - Sept 1 2015 - p42(1) [51-500]
   KR - Sept 15 2015 - pNA [501+]

Day, Felicia - *You're Never Weird on the Internet (Almost). (Read by Day, Felicia). Audiobook Review*
   BL - v112 - i5 - Nov 1 2015 - p71(1) [51-500]
   LJ - v140 - i16 - Oct 1 2015 - p44(1) [51-500]
You're Never Weird on the Internet
   KR - June 1 2015 - pNA [501+]
You're Never Weird on the Internet (Almost).
   TLS - i5871 - Oct 9 2015 - p30(1) [501+]
You're Never Weird on the Internet
  y BL - v111 - i19-20 - June 1 2015 - p36(1) [51-500]

Day, James Sanders - *Diamonds in the Rough: A History of Alabama's Cahaba Coal Field*
   AHR - v120 - i1 - Feb 2015 - p252(1) [501+]
   JAH - v102 - i1 - June 2015 - p258-258 [501+]
   JSH - v81 - i1 - Feb 2015 - p220(2) [501+]

Day, Jennifer - *Thread Stories: A Visual Guide to Creating Stunning Stitched Portrait Quilts*
   LJ - v140 - i13 - August 1 2015 - p95(1) [51-500]

Day, John Kyle - *The Southern Manifesto: Massive Resistance and the Fight to Preserve Segregation*
   JAH - v102 - i2 - Sept 2015 - p619-620 [501+]
   JSH - v81 - i4 - Nov 2015 - p1034(2) [501+]

Day, Katie - *Faith on the Avenue: Religion on a City Street*
   AJS - v120 - i4 - Jan 2015 - p1262(3) [501+]

Day, Maddie - *Flipped for Murder*
   KR - August 15 2015 - pNA [51-500]

Day, Michael - *Being Berlusconi: The Rise and Fall from Cosa Nostra to Bunga Bunga*
   KR - April 15 2015 - pNA [501+]
   LJ - v140 - i11 - June 15 2015 - p102(1) [51-500]
   Mac - v128 - i31 - August 10 2015 - p56(1) [501+]
   PW - v262 - i18 - May 4 2015 - p110(1) [51-500]

Day, Nancy Raines - *Way Down Below Deep (Illus. by Sheldon, David)*
  c HB Guide - v26 - i1 - Spring 2015 - p153(1) [51-500]
What in the World? Numbers in Nature (Illus. by Cyrus, Kurt)
  c SLJ - v61 - i6 - June 2015 - p79(1) [51-500]
  c KR - July 15 2015 - pNA [51-500]
  c PW - v262 - i28 - July 13 2015 - p70(1) [51-500]

Day, Richard B. - *Discovering Imperialism: Social Democracy to World War I*
   S&S - v79 - i4 - Oct 2015 - p625-627 [501+]

Day, Sara K. - *Female Rebellion in Young Adult Dystopian Fiction*
   Bkbird - v53 - i2 - Spring 2015 - p82(2) [501+]
Reading Like a Girl: Narrative Intimacy in Contemporary American Young Adult Literature
   AL - v87 - i2 - June 2015 - p403-405 [501+]

Day, Susan - *Carpets of the Art Deco Era*
   LJ - v140 - i10 - June 1 2015 - p98(1) [51-500]

Dayan, Colin - *With Dogs at the Edge of Life*
   KR - Oct 1 2015 - pNA [501+]

Dayan, Peter - *TaTa Dada: The Real Life and Celestial Adventures of Tristan Tzara*
   FS - v69 - i4 - Oct 2015 - p552-552 [501+]

Daykin, Rosie - *Butter Baked Goods: Nostalgic Recipes from a Little Neighborhood Bakery*
   LJ - v140 - i5 - March 15 2015 - p126(2) [501+]

Dayton, Arwen Elys - *Seeker (Read by McEwan, Katharine). Audiobook Review*
- y BL - v111 - i21 - July 1 2015 - p80(1) [51-500]
- y SLJ - v61 - i7 - July 2015 - p48(2) [51-500]

Seeker
- y CCB-B - v68 - i8 - April 2015 - p396(2) [51-500]
- y HB Guide - v26 - i2 - Fall 2015 - p116(1) [51-500]
- y VOYA - v38 - i3 - August 2015 - p76(1) [51-500]
- y BL - v111 - i11 - Feb 1 2015 - p49(1) [51-500]

Dayton, Cornelia H. - *Robert Love's Warnings: Searching for Strangers in Colonial Boston*
- AHR - v120 - i1 - Feb 2015 - p234-235 [501+]
- JAH - v101 - i4 - March 2015 - p1254-1255 [501+]
- JIH - v45 - i4 - Spring 2015 - p586(588) [501+]
- W&M Q - v72 - i3 - July 2015 - p536-539 [501+]

Daywalt, Drew - *The Day the Crayons Came Home (Illus. by Jeffers, Oliver)*
- c CCB-B - v69 - i2 - Oct 2015 - p83(1) [51-500]

The Day the Crayons Came Home
- c CH Bwatch - Oct 2015 - pNA [51-500]

The Day the Crayons Came Home (Illus. by Jeffers, Oliver)
- c BL - v111 - i22 - August 1 2015 - p71(1) [51-500]
- c HB - v91 - i6 - Nov-Dec 2015 - p66(1) [51-500]
- c KR - July 15 2015 - pNA [51-500]
- c PW - v262 - i49 - Dec 2 2015 - p34(1) [51-500]
- c SLJ - v61 - i8 - August 2015 - p67(1) [51-500]

D'Costa, Gavin - *Vatican II: Catholic Doctrines on Jews and Muslims*
- Theol St - v76 - i2 - June 2015 - p368(3) [501+]

De Amicis, Edmondo - *Memories of London*
- TLS - i5831 - Jan 2 2015 - p23(1) [501+]

de Andrade, Carlos Drummond - *Multitudinous Heart: Selected Poems: A Bilingual Edition*
- PW - v262 - i24 - June 15 2015 - p61(1) [51-500]

de Assis, Machado - *Lord Taciturn*
- Spec - v328 - i9755 - August 15 2015 - p34(2) [501+]

De Baecque, Antoine - *Eric Rohmer: Biographie*
- Lon R Bks - v37 - i6 - March 19 2015 - p28(3) [501+]

De Barros, Juanita - *Reproducing the British Caribbean: Sex, Gender, and Population Politics after Slavery*
- AHR - v120 - i4 - Oct 2015 - p1534-1535 [501+]
- JIH - v46 - i2 - Autumn 2015 - p276-279 [501+]

De Bary, William Theodore - *The Great Civilized Conversation: Education for a World Community*
- JAS - v74 - i2 - May 2015 - p455-456 [501+]

de Beauvoir, Jeannette - *Asylum*
- BL - v111 - i12 - Feb 15 2015 - p34(1) [51-500]
- NYTBR - April 5 2015 - p29(L) [501+]
- PW - v262 - i2 - Jan 12 2015 - p37(2) [51-500]
- KR - Jan 1 2015 - pNA [51-500]

de Beer, Hans - *Nugget on Top of the World (Illus. by de Beer, Hans)*
- c KR - Nov 1 2015 - pNA [51-500]

De Benedetti, Augusto - *Lo sviluppo sospeso: Il Mezzogiorno e l'impresa pubblica, 1948-1973*
- BHR - v89 - i1 - Spring 2015 - p192(3) [501+]

de Bernieres, Louis - *The Dust That Falls from Dreams (Read by Jay, Avita). Audiobook Review*
- BL - v112 - i6 - Nov 15 2015 - p60(1) [51-500]

The Dust That Falls from Dreams
- BL - v111 - i21 - July 1 2015 - p42(1) [51-500]
- Ent W - i1377 - August 21 2015 - p108(1) [51-500]
- KR - July 1 2015 - pNA [501+]
- NS - v144 - i5271 - July 17 2015 - p48(1) [501+]
- NYTBR - August 16 2015 - p19(L) [501+]

De Blois, Helene - *L'autruche et l'ours polaire (Illus. by Perreault, Guillaume)*
- c Res Links - v20 - i5 - June 2015 - p37(2) [51-500]

de Bodard, Aliette - *The House of Shattered Wings*
- PW - v262 - i28 - July 13 2015 - p49(1) [51-500]

De Boeck, Filip - *Kinshasa: Tales of the Invisible City*
- HNet - August 2015 - pNA [501+]

de Bolla, Peter - *The Architecture of Concepts: The Historical Formation of Human Rights*
- ABR - v36 - i4 - May-June 2015 - p8(1) [501+]

De Bonte, Austina - *Scenario-Focused Engineering: A Toolbox for Innovation and Customer-Centricity*
- RVBW - March 2015 - pNA [501+]

De Bruyn, Wolfgang - *Der Schatten des grossen Konigs: Friedrich II und die Literatur*
- Ger Q - v88 - i2 - Spring 2015 - p242(4) [501+]

de Calan, Ronan - *The Ghost of Karl Marx (Illus. by Mary, Donatien)*
- y KR - July 15 2015 - pNA [51-500]

de Cambrai, Gui - *Barlaam and Josaphat: A Christian Tale of the Buddha*
- Bks & Cult - v21 - i2 - March-April 2015 - p28(1) [501+]

De Castrique, Mark - *A Specter of Justice*
- BL - v112 - i4 - Oct 15 2015 - p24(1) [51-500]
- KR - Sept 1 2015 - pNA [51-500]
- PW - v262 - i39 - Sept 28 2015 - p69(1) [51-500]

De Certeau, Michel - *The Practice of Everyday Life*
- TimHES - i2211 - July 9 2015 - p51(1) [501+]

de Cock, Nicole - *Nut and Bolt (Illus. by de Cock, Nicole)*
- c CH Bwatch - Nov 2015 - pNA [51-500]
- c HB Guide - v26 - i2 - Fall 2015 - p9(1) [51-500]
- c Res Links - v21 - i1 - Oct 2015 - p5(1) [51-500]
- c SLJ - v61 - i12 - Dec 2015 - p87(1) [51-500]

Nut and Bolt
- c KR - July 15 2015 - pNA [51-500]

de Courcy, Anne - *The Fishing Fleet: Husband-Hunting in the Raj*
- NYTBR - April 26 2015 - p28(L) [501+]

Margot at War: Love and Betrayal in Downing Street, 1912-16
- Lon R Bks - v37 - i1 - Jan 8 2015 - p17(4) [501+]

De Danaan, Llyn - *Katie Gale: A Coast Salish Woman's Life on Oyster Bay*
- Historian - v77 - i2 - Summer 2015 - p325(3) [501+]
- PHR - v84 - i2 - May 2015 - p264(2) [501+]

De Daran, Valerie - *Eclats d'Autriche: vingt etudes sur l'image de la culture autrichienne aux XXe et XXIe siecles*
- MLR - v110 - i3 - July 2015 - p915-917 [501+]

de Fombelle, Timothee - *A Prince without a Kingdom (Illus. by Ardizzone, Sarah)*
- VOYA - v38 - i4 - Oct 2015 - p68(1) [51-500]

A Prince without a Kingdom
- y HB - v91 - i5 - Sept-Oct 2015 - p99(1) [51-500]
- y KR - May 1 2015 - pNA [51-500]

De Fombelle, Timothee - *A Prince without a Kingdom*
- y SLJ - v61 - i7 - July 2015 - p85(2) [51-500]

de Fombelle, Timothee - *Vango: Between Sky and Earth*
- SLJ - v61 - i2 - Feb 2015 - p48(2) [51-500]

De Fombelle, Timothee - *Vango: Between Sky and Earth*
- y BL - v111 - i16 - April 15 2015 - p57(1) [501+]

de Fombelle, Timothee Vango - *Vango: Between Sky and Earth*
- y HB Guide - v26 - i1 - Spring 2015 - p105(2) [51-500]

De Francesco, A. - *The Antiquity of the Italian Nation: The Cultural Origins of a Political Myth in Modern Italy*
- Class R - v65 - i1 - April 2015 - p279-281 [501+]

de Gemeaux, Christine - *L'Europe Coloniale et le Grand Tournant de la Conference de Berlin*
- HNet - March 2015 - pNA [501+]

de Giovanni, Maurizio - *The Bottom of Your Heart: The Inferno for Commissario Ricciardi*
- KR - Oct 1 2015 - pNA [51-500]
- PW - v262 - i37 - Sept 14 2015 - p40(1) [51-500]

de Gramont, Nina - *The Boy I Love*
- y CCB-B - v68 - i5 - Jan 2015 - p252(2) [51-500]
- y HB Guide - v26 - i1 - Spring 2015 - p105(1) [51-500]

The Last September
- BL - v111 - i21 - July 1 2015 - p38(1) [51-500]
- y KR - July 1 2015 - pNA [51-500]

De Gramont, Nina - *The Last September*
- LJ - v140 - i15 - Sept 15 2015 - p66(1) [51-500]

De Groot, Jean - *Aristotle's Empiricism: Experience and Mechanics in the 4th Century BC*
- RM - v69 - i2 - Dec 2015 - p379(3) [501+]

Aristotle's Empiricism
- RVBW - Jan 2015 - pNA [501+]

De Heer, Margareet - *Religion: A Discovery in Comics*
- y SLJ - v61 - i11 - Nov 2015 - p140(2) [51-500]

De Heer, Margreet - *Religion: A Discovery in Comics*
- BL - v111 - i6 - Nov 15 2015 - p16(1) [51-500]

de Heer, Margreet - *Religion: A Discovery in Comics*
- PW - v262 - i42 - Oct 19 2015 - p64(1) [51-500]
- RVBW - Nov 2015 - pNA [51-500]

De Jesus, Pedro - *Vital Signs*
- WLT - v89 - i3-4 - May-August 2015 - p115(1) [51-500]

de Jong, Cees W. - *Piet Mondrian: Life and Work*
- LJ - v140 - i16 - Oct 1 2015 - p76(2) [51-500]

de Jong, I.J.F. - *Homer: Iliad Book XXII*
- Class R - v65 - i1 - April 2015 - p7-8 [501+]

De Jong, Irene J.F. - *Narratology and Classics: A Practical Guide*
- Class R - v65 - i2 - Oct 2015 - p327-329 [501+]

de Kerangal, Maylis - *Birth of a Bridge*
- TLS - i5874 - Oct 30 2015 - p21(1) [501+]

The Heart
- BL - v112 - i7 - Dec 1 2015 - p22(1) [51-500]
- KR - Dec 1 2015 - pNA [501+]
- PW - v262 - i39 - Sept 28 2015 - p64(1) [51-500]

De Kinder, Jan - *Red (Illus. by De Kinder, Jan)*
- c HB - v91 - i3 - May-June 2015 - p83(1) [51-500]
- c KR - Jan 15 2015 - pNA [51-500]
- SLJ - v61 - i3 - March 2015 - p115(2) [51-500]
- c BL - v111 - i17 - May 1 2015 - p102(1) [51-500]
- c PW - v262 - i2 - Jan 12 2015 - p57(2) [51-500]
- c RVBW - May 2015 - pNA [51-500]

Red
- c HB Guide - v26 - i2 - Fall 2015 - p31(1) [51-500]

De Kockere, Geert - *Piglet Bo Is Not Scared! (Illus. by Van Hemeldonck, Tineke)*
- c KR - Sept 1 2015 - pNA [51-500]

de la Bedoyere, Camilla - *Amazing Animals: A Collection of Creatures Great and Small*
- c HB Guide - v26 - i2 - Fall 2015 - p169(1) [51-500]

Animals
- c Sch Lib - v63 - i2 - Summer 2015 - p111(1) [51-500]

Beautiful Beasts: A Collection of Creatures Past and Present
- c HB Guide - v26 - i2 - Fall 2015 - p168(1) [51-500]

Bone Collection: Skulls (Illus. by Doyle, Sandra)
- c CH Bwatch - Feb 2015 - pNA [51-500]

Could a Penguin Ride a Bike? ... and Other Questions (Illus. by Bitskoff, Aleksei)
- c BL - v111 - i16 - April 15 2015 - p46(1) [51-500]
- c HB Guide - v26 - i2 - Fall 2015 - p177(1) [51-500]

Could a Shark Do Gymnastics? (Illus. by Bitskoff, Aleksei)
- c BL - v112 - i4 - Oct 15 2015 - p43(1) [51-500]
- c Sch Lib - v63 - i4 - Winter 2015 - p237(1) [51-500]

Could a Whale Swim to the Moon? (Illus. by Bitskoff, Aleksei)
- c BL - v112 - i4 - Oct 15 2015 - p43(1) [51-500]

Could an Octopus Climb a Skyscraper? ... and Other Questions (Illus. by Bitskoff, Aleksei)
- c BL - v111 - i16 - April 15 2015 - p46(1) [51-500]
- c HB Guide - v26 - i2 - Fall 2015 - p173(1) [51-500]

Creatures of the Deep
- c Sch Lib - v63 - i1 - Spring 2015 - p46(1) [51-500]

I Love Hugs
- c HB Guide - v26 - i2 - Fall 2015 - p171(1) [51-500]

I Love Kisses
- c HB Guide - v26 - i2 - Fall 2015 - p171(1) [51-500]
- c KR - March 15 2015 - pNA [51-500]

J'adore les calins
- c Res Links - v20 - i5 - June 2015 - p38(1) [51-500]

My Little Book of Sharks
- c SLJ - v61 - i11 - Nov 2015 - p131(1) [51-500]
- c Sch Lib - v63 - i2 - Summer 2015 - p111(1) [51-500]

Snow Babies
- c Sch Lib - v63 - i1 - Spring 2015 - p26(1) [51-500]

The Wild Life of Bears
- c BL - v111 - i17 - May 1 2015 - p88(1) [51-500]

The Wild Life of Lizards
- c BL - v111 - i17 - May 1 2015 - p88(1) [51-500]

The Wild Life of Owls
- c BL - v111 - i17 - May 1 2015 - p88(1) [51-500]

The Wild Life of Sharks
- c BL - v111 - i17 - May 1 2015 - p88(1) [51-500]

Would You Rather...Dine with a Dung Beetle or Lunch with a Maggot? (Illus. by Howells, Mel)
- c BL - v112 - i3 - Oct 1 2015 - p66(1) [51-500]

de la Bedoyere, Guy - *The Real Lives of Roman Britain*
- HT - v65 - i11 - Nov 2015 - p58(2) [501+]
- Lon R Bks - v37 - i22 - Nov 19 2015 - p26(3) [501+]

de la Cruz, Melissa - *Birthday Vicious*
- c HB Guide - v26 - i2 - Fall 2015 - p79(1) [51-500]

The Isle of the Lost (Read by Carson, Sofia). Audiobook Review
- y BL - v112 - i6 - Nov 15 2015 - p63(1) [51-500]
- y SLJ - v61 - i8 - August 2015 - p49(1) [51-500]

The Isle of the Lost
- y BL - v111 - i18 - May 15 2015 - p67(1) [51-500]
- c HB Guide - v26 - i2 - Fall 2015 - p79(1) [51-500]
- y KR - April 15 2015 - pNA [51-500]
- c SLJ - v61 - i7 - July 2015 - p75(1) [51-500]

Popularity Takeover
- c HB Guide - v26 - i2 - Fall 2015 - p79(1) [51-500]

Stolen
- y HB Guide - v26 - i1 - Spring 2015 - p105(1) [51-500]

Triple Moon
- y BL - v112 - i4 - Oct 15 2015 - p46(1) [51-500]
- y KR - Sept 15 2015 - pNA [51-500]
- y SLJ - v61 - i11 - Nov 2015 - p113(1) [51-500]
- y VOYA - v38 - i5 - Dec 2015 - p68(1) [501+]

De la Falaise, Daniel - *Nature's Larder: Cooking with the Senses*
  Spec - v329 - i9768 - Nov 14 2015 - p58(1) [501+]

De La Garza, Phyllis - *Death for Dinner: The Benders of (Old) Kansas: The Biography of a Family of Mass Killers*
  Roundup M - v22 - i6 - August 2015 - p36(1) [501+]

de la Hoz, Cindy - *Bogie and Bacall: Love Lessons from a Legendary Romance*
  PW - v262 - i51 - Dec 14 2015 - p76(2) [501+]

de la Mare, Walter - *The Ride-by-Nights (Illus. by Rabei, Carolina)*
  c Sch Lib - v63 - i4 - Winter 2015 - p219(1) [51-500]
  Snow (Illus. by Rabei, Carolina)
  c Sch Lib - v63 - i1 - Spring 2015 - p26(1) [51-500]
  Told Again: Old Tales Told Again
  TLS - i5841 - March 13 2015 - p3(3) [501+]

de la Motte, Anders - *MemoRandom*
  BL - v112 - i4 - Oct 15 2015 - p22(1) [51-500]
  KR - Nov 1 2015 - pNA [51-500]
  PW - v262 - i41 - Oct 12 2015 - p47(2) [51-500]

De la O, Marsha - *Antidote for Night*
  LJ - v140 - i13 - August 1 2015 - p99(2) [51-500]

de la Pena, Matt - *Eternity*
  y HB Guide - v26 - i1 - Spring 2015 - p75(1) [51-500]
  The Hunted
  y BL - v111 - i15 - April 1 2015 - p66(1) [51-500]
  y VOYA - v38 - i1 - April 2015 - p76(2) [51-500]
  y HB Guide - v26 - i2 - Fall 2015 - p116(1) [51-500]
  SLJ - v61 - i2 - Feb 2015 - p98(2) [51-500]

De la Pena, Matt - *Last Stop on Market Street (Read by Mitchell, Lizan). Audiobook Review*
  c SLJ - v61 - i8 - August 2015 - p47(2) [51-500]

de la Pena, Matt - *Last Stop on Market Street (Illus. by Robinson, Christian)*
  c BL - v111 - i11 - Feb 1 2015 - p46(1) [51-500]
  c HB - v91 - i2 - March-April 2015 - p71(2) [51-500]
  c HB Guide - v26 - i2 - Fall 2015 - p31(1) [51-500]
  c NYTBR - Jan 18 2015 - p18(L) [501+]
  c PW - v262 - i49 - Dec 2 2015 - p27(1) [51-500]

de La Sale, Antoine - *"Jean de Saintre": A Late Medieval Education in Love and Chivalry*
  MLR - v110 - i3 - July 2015 - p859-860 [501+]

de la Torre Curiel, Jose Refugio - *The Twilight of the Mission Frontier: Shifting Interethnic Alliances and Social Organization in Sonora, 1768-1855*
  CH - v84 - i1 - March 2015 - p256(3) [501+]

De La Torre, Miguel A. - *Liberation Theology for Armchair Theologians*
  Intpr - v69 - i4 - Oct 2015 - p497(2) [501+]
  The Quest for the Historical Satan
  JR - Jan 2015 - p131(2) [501+]

de las Cases, Zoe - *Secret Paris: Colour Your Way to Calm*
  Nat Post - v17 - i188 - June 13 2015 - pWP5(1) [501+]

De Laurentiis, Giada - *Rio de Janeiro! (Illus. by Gambatesa, Francesca)*
  c HB Guide - v26 - i2 - Fall 2015 - p79(1) [51-500]

de Leon, Charles L. Ponce - *That's the Way It Is: A History of Television News in America*
  BL - v111 - i15 - April 1 2015 - p5(1) [51-500]

De L'Hospital, Michel - *La Plume et la tribune, II: Discours et correspondance*
  FS - v69 - i1 - Jan 2015 - p90(2) [501+]

de Libero, Loretana - *Rache und Triumph: Krieg, Gefuhle und Gedenken in der Moderne*
  HNet - April 2015 - pNA [501+]

De Lint, Charles - *Out of This World*
  y Res Links - v20 - i4 - April 2015 - p27(2) [501+]

De Lisle, Sandy - *Hens for Friends (Illus. by Hansen, Amelia)*
  c KR - March 1 2015 - pNA [51-500]
  SLJ - v61 - i4 - April 2015 - p178(1) [51-500]

De los Angeles Torres, Maria - *Citizens in the Present: Youth Civic Engagement in the Americas*
  CS - v44 - i4 - July 2015 - p564-565 [501+]

De Los Angeles Torres, Maria - *Citizens in the Present: Youth Civic Engagement in the Americas*
  CS - v44 - i5 - Sept 2015 - p723-724 [501+]

de los Santos, Marisa - *Connect the Stars*
  c BL - v111 - i22 - August 1 2015 - p67(1) [51-500]
  c KR - June 15 2015 - pNA [51-500]
  The Precious One
  KR - Jan 15 2015 - pNA [51-500]
  LJ - v140 - i2 - Feb 1 2015 - p72(1) [51-500]

De Lucca, Denis - *Jesuits and Fortifications: The Contribution of the Jesuits to Military Architecture in the Baroque Age*
  CHR - v101 - i3 - Summer 2015 - p661(2) [501+]

De Marco, Clare - *The Mad Scientist Next Door (Illus. by Walker, Rory)*
  c CH Bwatch - Feb 2015 - pNA [501+]
  c Res Links - v20 - i3 - Feb 2015 - p14(2) [501+]

De Marco, Vittorio - *Il Beato P. Gabriele M. Allegra: Dall'Italia alla Cina*
  CHR - v101 - i4 - Autumn 2015 - p969(2) [501+]

de Mariaffi, Elisabeth - *The Devil You Know. Audiobook Review*
  LJ - v140 - i6 - April 1 2015 - p47(1) [51-500]
  The Devil You Know
  Nat Post - v17 - i62 - Jan 10 2015 - pWP9(1) [501+]
  y NYTBR - Feb 1 2015 - p25(L) [501+]

de Medeiros, Michael - *The North: From the Arctic Lowlands to Polar Deserts*
  c Res Links - v20 - i4 - April 2015 - p14(1) [501+]

de Mesa, Eduardo - *The Irish in the Spanish Armies in the Seventeenth Century*
  J Mil H - v79 - i3 - July 2015 - p813-814 [501+]

de Mille, Agnes - *Dance to the Piper*
  HM - v331 - i1986 - Nov 2015 - p77(3) [501+]

de Monfreid, Dorothee - *The Cake (Illus. by de Monfreid, Dorothee)*
  c HB Guide - v26 - i1 - Spring 2015 - p8(1) [51-500]

de Monzon, Francisco - *Libro segundo del Espejo del perfecto principe cristiano*
  Ren Q - v68 - i2 - Summer 2015 - p614-616 [501+]

de Mouy, Iris - *Naptime (Illus. by de Mouy, Iris)*
  c HB Guide - v26 - i1 - Spring 2015 - p8(1) [51-500]

De Munck, Viktor C. - *Macedonia: The Political, Social, Economic and Cultural Foundations of a Balkan State*
  E-A St - v67 - i1 - Jan 2015 - p157(2) [501+]

De Orive, Aaron - *Blade Singer*
  y KR - Jan 1 2016 - pNA [501+]

De Paola, Tomie - *Look and Be Grateful (Illus. by De Paola, Tomie)*
  c HB - v91 - i5 - Sept-Oct 2015 - p78(1) [51-500]

de Ranitz, Ariane - *Louis Raemaekers 'Armed with Pen and Pencil': How a Dutch Cartoonist Became World Famous during the First World War*
  HNet - July 2015 - pNA [501+]

De Robertis, Carolina - *The Gods of Tango*
  Wom R Bks - v32 - i6 - Nov-Dec 2015 - p23(2) [501+]
  BL - v111 - i16 - April 15 2015 - p35(1) [51-500]
  KR - May 1 2015 - pNA [51-500]
  LJ - v140 - i10 - June 1 2015 - p85(1) [51-500]
  PW - v262 - i16 - April 20 2015 - p46(1) [51-500]

De Roberto, Federico - *The Viceroys*
  PW - v262 - i47 - Nov 23 2015 - p45(1) [51-500]

de Rosnay, Tatiana - *A Paris Affair*
  KR - May 1 2015 - pNA [51-500]

De Roux, Paul - *Au Jour le jour 5*
  TLS - i5834 - Jan 23 2015 - p12(2) [501+]
  Entrevoir suivi de Le front contre la vitre et de La halte obscure
  TLS - i5834 - Jan 23 2015 - p12(2) [501+]

De Roy, Tui - *Penguins: The Ultimate Guide*
  Am Bio T - v77 - i6 - August 2015 - p469(2) [501+]
  R&USQ - v54 - i3 - Spring 2015 - p64(2) [501+]

De Sade, D.A.F. - *Justine et autres romans*
  Lon R Bks - v37 - i4 - Feb 19 2015 - p35(3r) [501+]

de Sagarra, Josep Maria - *Private Life*
  KR - July 15 2015 - pNA [501+]

de Saint Phalle, Niki - *Niki de Saint Phalle*
  LJ - v140 - i20 - Dec 1 2015 - p99(1) [51-500]

de Salcedo, Anastada Marx - *Combat-Ready Kitchen*
  KR - June 1 2015 - pNA [51-500]
  Mac - v128 - i32-33 - August 17 2015 - p70(1) [501+]

de Saulles, Martin - *Information 2.0: New Models of Information Production, Distribution and Consumption*
  RVBW - July 2015 - pNA [501+]

de Silva, Mark - *Square Wave*
  KR - Dec 15 2015 - pNA [51-500]
  PW - v262 - i52 - Dec 21 2015 - p122(1) [51-500]

de Smet, Ingrid A.R. - *La Fauconnerie a la Renaissance: Le "Hieracosophion" (1582-1584) de Jacques Auguste de Thou*
  MLR - v110 - i2 - April 2015 - p543-544 [501+]

de Sola, David - *Alice in Chains*
  KR - May 15 2015 - pNA [501+]

de Solier, Isabelle - *Food and the Self: Consumption, Production and Material Culture*
  JRAI - v21 - i2 - June 2015 - p484(2) [501+]

de Sousa Santos, Boaventura - *Epistemologies of the South: Justice against Epistemicide*
  CS - v44 - i6 - Nov 2015 - p843-845 [501+]

de Villiers, Gerard - *Lord of the Swallows*
  KR - Dec 1 2015 - pNA [501+]

de Vise, Daniel - *Andy & Don: The Making of a Friendship and a Classic American TV Show*
  KR - Sept 1 2015 - pNA [501+]
  LJ - v140 - i14 - Sept 1 2015 - p103(1) [51-500]
  PW - v262 - i30 - July 27 2015 - p52(2) [51-500]
  BL - v112 - i2 - Sept 15 2015 - p14(1) [51-500]

De Vise, Jean Donneau - *Les costeaux, ou, Les marquis frians*
  FS - v69 - i4 - Oct 2015 - p527-527 [501+]

De Visscher, Eva - *Reading the Rabbis: Christian Hebraism in the Works of Herbert of Bosham*
  AHR - v120 - i3 - June 2015 - p1092-1093 [501+]
  Specu - v90 - i1 - Jan 2015 - p239-240 [501+]

De Vries, Ardeth - *Old Dog Haven*
  CSM - June 2 2015 - pNA [51-500]

de Waal, Edmund - *The White Road: A Pilgrimage of Sorts*
  TLS - i5873 - Oct 23 2015 - p8(3) [501+]
  NS - v144 - i5280 - Sept 18 2015 - p62(2) [501+]
  Spec - v329 - i9760 - Sept 19 2015 - p38(2) [501+]
  The White Road: Journey into an Obsession
  BL - v112 - i4 - Oct 15 2015 - p12(2) [501+]
  CSM - Nov 11 2015 - pNA [51-500]
  LJ - v140 - i15 - Sept 15 2015 - p73(1) [51-500]
  Mac - v128 - i42 - Oct 26 2015 - p56(1) [501+]
  NYTBR - Dec 13 2015 - p30(L) [501+]
  PW - v262 - i37 - Sept 14 2015 - p56(1) [51-500]
  The White Road
  KR - August 1 2015 - pNA [501+]

de Waal, Thomas - *Great Catastrophe: Armenians and Turks in the Shadow of Genocide*
  Econ - v415 - i8934 - April 18 2015 - p75(US) [501+]
  Spec - v327 - i9738 - April 18 2015 - p34(2) [501+]

Deacon, Alexis - *I Am Henry Finch (Illus. by Schwarz, Viviane)*
  c KR - August 15 2015 - pNA [51-500]
  c Magpies - v30 - i2 - May 2015 - p31(1) [501+]
  c Sch Lib - v63 - i2 - Summer 2015 - p90(1) [51-500]
  c SLJ - v61 - i10 - Oct 2015 - p74(1) [51-500]

Deak, Erzsi - *Pumpkin Time! (Illus. by Cushman, Doug)*
  c HB Guide - v26 - i1 - Spring 2015 - p27(2) [51-500]

Deak, Gloria - *Passage to America: Celebrated European Visitors in Search of the American Adventure*
  RAH - v43 - i1 - March 2015 - p47-53 [501+]

Deak, Istvan - *Europe on Trial: The Story of Collaboration, Resistance, and Retribution During World War II*
  NYRB - v62 - i13 - August 13 2015 - p64(2) [501+]

Deakin, Ellen - *Beautiful Paper Cutting: 30 Creative Projects For Cards, Gifts, Decor, and Jewelry*
  LJ - v140 - i12 - July 1 2015 - p84(1) [51-500]

Deakin, Kathleen - *John Green: Teen Whisperer: Studies in Young Adult Literature*
  y VOYA - v38 - i5 - Dec 2015 - p80(2) [501+]

Deakin, Roger - *Waterlog*
  NS - v144 - i5278 - Sept 4 2015 - p37(1) [51-500]

Dean, Adam Wesley - *An Agrarian Republic: Farming, Antislavery Politics, and Nature Parks in the Civil War Era*
  HNet - July 2015 - pNA [501+]

Dean, Averil - *The Undoing*
  KR - Oct 15 2015 - pNA [51-500]
  PW - v262 - i45 - Nov 9 2015 - p36(2) [51-500]

Dean, Erik - *Garbageman*
  KR - Sept 15 2015 - pNA [501+]

Dean, Erika Lucke - *Splintered Soul*
  PW - v262 - i44 - Nov 2 2015 - p70(1) [51-500]

Dean, James - *Pat Au Baseball*
  c Res Links - v20 - i4 - April 2015 - p38(1) [51-500]
  Pete the Cat and the Bad Banana (Illus. by Dean, James)
  c HB Guide - v26 - i1 - Spring 2015 - p52(1) [51-500]
  Pete the Cat: And the Bedtime Blues (Illus. by Dean, Kimberly)
  c KR - August 15 2015 - pNA [51-500]
  c SLJ - v61 - i6 - June 2015 - p79(2) [51-500]

Dean, James Joseph - *Straights: Heterosexuality in Post-Closeted Culture*
  AJS - v121 - i1 - July 2015 - p332(3) [501+]
  JGS - v24 - i2 - April 2015 - p239-240 [501+]

Dean, Janice - *Freddy the Frogcaster and the Big Blizzard*
KR - April 1 2015 - pNA [501+]
Freddy the Frogcaster and the Huge Hurricane
c KR - May 1 2015 - pNA [51-500]

Dean, John W. - *The Nixon Defence: What He Knew and When He Knew It*
Lon R Bks - v37 - i21 - Nov 5 2015 - p33(2) [501+]

Dean, Kimberly - *Je porte mes lunettes magiques*
c Res Links - v20 - i4 - April 2015 - p38(2) [501+]
Pete the Cat and the New Guy (Illus. by Dean, James)
c HB Guide - v26 - i1 - Spring 2015 - p28(1) [51-500]
Pete the Cat's Groovy Guide to Life: Tips from a Cool Cat for Living an Awesome Life
c HB Guide - v26 - i2 - Fall 2015 - p190(1) [51-500]

Dean, Lou - *On My Ass*
Roundup M - v22 - i3 - Feb 2015 - p22(2) [501+]
Roundup M - v22 - i6 - August 2015 - p36(1) [501+]

Dean, Margaret Lazarus - *Leaving Orbit*
NY - v91 - i25 - August 31 2015 - p89 [51-500]
Leaving Orbit: Notes from the Last Days of American Spaceflight
BL - v111 - i16 - April 15 2015 - p5(1) [51-500]
KR - March 15 2015 - pNA [501+]

Dean, Margaret Lazarus. - *Leaving Orbit: Notes from the Last Days of American Spaceflight*
LJ - v140 - i6 - April 1 2015 - p113(1) [51-500]

Dean, Margaret Lazarus - *Leaving Orbit: Notes from the Last Days of American Spaceflight*
NYT - May 21 2015 - pC1(L) [501+]
NYTBR - Oct 11 2015 - p21(L) [501+]
PW - v262 - i12 - March 23 2015 - p64(1) [51-500]

Dean, Pamela - *Points of Departure*
PW - v262 - i16 - April 20 2015 - p60(1) [51-500]

Deane, Bradley - *Masculinity and the New Imperialism: Rewriting Manhood in British Popular Literature, 1870-1914*
Nine-C Lit - v69 - i4 - March 2015 - p560(3) [501+]

Deane-Drummond, Celia - *The Wisdom of the Liminal: Evolution and Other Animals in Human Becoming*
Theol St - v76 - i4 - Dec 2015 - p860(3) [501+]

DeAngelis, Camille - *Bones and All*
BL - v111 - i11 - Feb 1 2015 - p20(1) [51-500]
KR - Jan 1 2015 - pNA [51-500]
PW - v262 - i3 - Jan 19 2015 - p2(1) [51-500]

DeAngelis, Michael - *Reading the Bromance: Homosocial Relationships in Film and Television*
JGS - v24 - i3 - June 2015 - p368-370 [501+]
SAH - v4 - i1 - Annual 2015 - p118-121 [501+]

Deans, Karen - *Swing Sisters: The Story of the International Sweethearts of Rhythm* (Illus. by Cepeda, Joe)
c HB Guide - v26 - i2 - Fall 2015 - p194(1) [51-500]
c BL - v111 - i11 - Feb 1 2015 - p44(1) [51-500]

Dear, Michael - *Why Walls Won't Work: Repairing the US-Mexico Divide*
HAHR - v95 - i3 - August 2015 - p556-557 [501+]

Dearden, R.J. - *The Realignment Case*
RVBW - June 2015 - pNA [51-500]

Deardroff, David - *What's Wrong with My Houseplant?*
PW - v262 - i44 - Nov 2 2015 - p81(1) [51-500]

Dearen, Patrick - *The Big Drift*
Roundup M - v22 - i3 - Feb 2015 - p25(1) [501+]
Roundup M - v22 - i6 - August 2015 - p28(1) [501+]

Dearmon, Mary Beth - *Cadence to Glory*
KR - Feb 15 2015 - pNA [501+]

Dearstyne, Bruce W. - *The Spirit of New York: Defining Events in the Empire State's History*
LJ - v140 - i13 - August 1 2015 - p108(2) [51-500]

Deary, Vincent - *How We Are, How We Break, and How We Mend*
SEP - v287 - i1 - Jan-Feb 2015 - p20(1) [501+]

Deas, Stephen - *Dragon Queen*
PW - v262 - i24 - June 15 2015 - p68(1) [51-500]

Deason, Jude - *Tin Cup*
KR - Sept 1 2015 - pNA [51-500]

Deats, Sara Munson - *Christopher Marlowe at 450*
TLS - i5856 - June 26 2015 - p23(1) [501+]

Deaver, Jeffery - *The Skin Collector*
RVBW - May 2015 - pNA [51-500]
Solitude Creek
BL - v111 - i17 - May 1 2015 - p38(1) [51-500]
KR - March 15 2015 - pNA [51-500]
NYTBR - May 3 2015 - p29(L) [51-500]
NYTBR - Dec 6 2015 - p85(L) [501+]
PW - v262 - i12 - March 23 2015 - p48(1) [51-500]
The Starling Project (Read by Molina, Alfred). Audiobook Review
BL - v111 - i17 - May 1 2015 - p60(1) [51-500]
BooChiTr - Jan 3 2015 - p12(1) [501+]

DeBarbieri, Lili - *Location Filming in Arizona: The Screen Legacy of the Grand Canyon State*
Roundup M - v22 - i6 - August 2015 - p36(1) [501+]

Debax, Helene - *La Seigneurie collective: Pairs, pariers, paratge: les coseigneurs du XIe au XIIIe siecle*
HER - v130 - i542 - Feb 2015 - p159(2) [501+]

Debby, Ben-Aryeh Nirit - *The Cult of St. Clare of Assisi in Early Modern Italy*
Ren Q - v68 - i2 - Summer 2015 - p708-710 [501+]

Debby, Nirti Ben-Aryeh - *The Cult of St. Clare of Assisi in Early Modern Italy*
Six Ct J - v46 - i3 - Fall 2015 - p694-695 [501+]

Debeljak, Alex - *Smugglers*
PW - v262 - i20 - May 18 2015 - p61(1) [51-500]

DeBiase, Johanna - *Mama and the Hungry HOle*
PW - v262 - i16 - April 20 2015 - p59(1) [51-500]

deBoer, Robin - *The Amazing C on Science*
y KR - Oct 1 2015 - pNA [501+]

DeBoer, Stephanie - *Coproducing Asia: Locating Japanese-Chinese Regional Film and Media*
Pac A - v88 - i2 - June 2015 - p272 [501+]

DeBrabander, Firmin - *Do Guns Make Us Free? Democracy and the Armed Society*
CC - v132 - i16 - August 5 2015 - p36(2) [501+]

Debrot, Franklin - *Journey to Colonus*
KR - April 1 2015 - pNA [501+]

deBuys, William - *A Great Aridness: Climate Change and the Future of the American Southwest*
WHQ - v46 - i1 - Spring 2015 - p75-76 [501+]
The Last Unicorn: A Search for One of Earth's Fairest Creatures
PW - v262 - i1 - Jan 5 2015 - p64(1) [51-500]
The Last Unicorn: A Search for One of Earth's Rarest Creatures
BL - v111 - i12 - Feb 15 2015 - p16(1) [51-500]

DeBuys, William - *The Last Unicorn: A Search for One of Earth's Rarest Creatures*
Bwatch - May 2015 - pNA [51-500]

deBuys, William - *The Last Unicorn: A Search for One of Earth's Rarest Creatures*
CSM - March 26 2015 - pNA [501+]
Mac - v128 - i13-14 - April 6 2015 - p75(2) [501+]
Nature - v518 - i7540 - Feb 26 2015 - p481(1) [51-500]
NYT - March 24 2015 - pD5(L) [501+]

DeBuys, William - *The Last Unicorn*
KR - Jan 1 2015 - pNA [501+]

DeCamp, Alison - *My Near-Death Adventures*
c BL - v111 - i16 - April 15 2015 - p60(1) [51-500]
c CCB-B - v68 - i7 - March 2015 - p352(2) [51-500]
y CH Bwatch - April 2015 - pNA [51-500]

DeCarlo, Melissa - *The Art of Crash Landing*
BL - v111 - i22 - August 1 2015 - p26(1) [51-500]
KR - July 1 2015 - pNA [51-500]
LJ - v140 - i14 - Sept 1 2015 - p90(1) [51-500]
PW - v262 - i27 - July 6 2015 - p42(2) [51-500]
RVBW - Oct 2015 - pNA [51-500]

Decena, Carlos Ulises - *Tacit Subjects: Belonging and Same-Sex Desire among Dominican Immigrant Men*
Critm - v57 - i1 - Wntr 2015 - pNA [501+]

Dechaud, Jean-Marc - *Bibliographie critique des ouvrages et traductions de Gabriel Chappuys*
Ren Q - v68 - i3 - Fall 2015 - p1099-1100 [501+]

Decision Taking, Confidence and Risk Management in Banks in the 19th and 20th Century
HNet - April 2015 - pNA [501+]

Deck, Julia - *Le Triangle d'hiver*
WLT - v89 - i2 - March-April 2015 - p57(1) [501+]

Decker, Peter R. - *Red, White and Army Blue*
Roundup M - v23 - i1 - Oct 2015 - p29(1) [501+]

Decker, Tod - *Who Should Sing Ol' Man River: The Lives of an American Song*
Dbt - v82 - i3 - March 2015 - p68(1) [501+]

deClaisse-Walford, Nancy L. - *The Shape and Shaping of the Book of Psalms: The Current State of Scholarship*
Intpr - v69 - i4 - Oct 2015 - p507(1) [501+]

Decolonizing Knowledge: Figures, Narratives, and Practices
HNet - March 2015 - pNA [501+]

DeConnick, Kelly Sue - *Bitch Planet, bk.1: Extraordinary Machine* (Illus. by De Landro, Valentine)
NYTBR - Oct 18 2015 - p30(L) [501+]
Bitch Planet, vol. 1
PW - v262 - i22 - June 1 2015 - p49(1) [501+]

Deconnick, Kelly Sue - *Captain Marvel: Higher, Further, Faster, More* (Illus. by Lopez, David)
y SLJ - v61 - i5 - May 2015 - p126(2) [51-500]
Captain Marvel: Stay Fly (Illus. by Lopez, David)
y BL - v111 - i19-20 - June 1 2015 - p66(1) [51-500]
y SLJ - v61 - i10 - Oct 2015 - p119(1) [51-500]

Decosimo, David - *Ethics as a Work of Charity: Thomas Aquinas and Pagan Virtue*
Comw - v142 - i3 - Feb 6 2015 - p30(3) [501+]

Decoteau, Claire Laurier - *Ancestors and Antiretrovirals: The Biopolitics of HIV/AIDS in Post-Apartheid South Africa*
CS - v44 - i5 - Sept 2015 - p591-603 [501+]
CS - v44 - i5 - Sept 2015 - p654-655 [501+]
Ancestors and Antiretrovirals: The Biopolitics of HIV/AIDS in Postapartheid South Africa
AJS - v120 - i4 - Jan 2015 - p1232(3) [501+]

DeDonato, Rick - *Pipsie, Nature Detective: The Disappearing Caterpillar* (Illus. by Bishop, Tracy)
c HB Guide - v26 - i2 - Fall 2015 - p31(1) [51-500]

Dedonato, Rick - *Pipsie, Nature Detective: The Disappearing Caterpillar* (Illus. by Bishop, Tracy)
c SLJ - v61 - i6 - June 2015 - p80(1) [51-500]

Dee, Tim - *Four Fields*
BL - v111 - i9-10 - Jan 1 2015 - p25(2) [51-500]
HR - v68 - i3 - Autumn 2015 - p517-527 [501+]

Deeb, Lara - *Leisurely Islam: Negotiating Geography and Morality in Shi'ite South Beirut*
JRAI - v21 - i3 - Sept 2015 - p690(2) [501+]

Deeb-Sossa, Natalia - *Doing Good: Racial Tensions and Workplace Inequalities at a Community Clinic in El Nuevo South*
CS - v44 - i1 - Jan 2015 - p47-50 [501+]

Deebs, Tracy - *Powerless*
y CCB-B - v69 - i2 - Oct 2015 - p80(1) [51-500]
y SLJ - v61 - i6 - June 2015 - p110(2) [51-500]

Deedman, Heidi - *Too Many Toys* (Illus. by Deedman, Heidi)
c BL - v112 - i4 - Oct 15 2015 - p54(1) [51-500]
c KR - Sept 1 2015 - pNA [51-500]
c PW - v262 - i29 - July 20 2015 - p189(1) [51-500]
c PW - v262 - i49 - Dec 7 2015 - p32(2) [51-500]
c SLJ - v61 - i10 - Oct 2015 - p74(1) [51-500]

Deely, John - *Tractatus de Signis: The Semiotic of John Poinsot*, 2 ed.
RM - v69 - i2 - Dec 2015 - p381(3) [501+]

Deem, James M. - *The Prisoners of Breendonk*
y KR - May 1 2015 - pNA [51-500]
The Prisoners of Breendonk: Personal Histories from a World War II Concentration Camp
y BL - v111 - i15 - April 1 2015 - p35(1) [51-500]
y HB - v91 - i4 - July-August 2015 - p155(1) [51-500]
y SLJ - v61 - i10 - Oct 2015 - p132(2) [51-500]
y VOYA - v38 - i3 - August 2015 - p86(2) [51-500]

Deen, Natasha - *Burned*
y Res Links - v21 - i1 - Oct 2015 - p30(2) [501+]
y SLJ - v61 - i9 - Sept 2015 - p151(4) [501+]
y VOYA - v38 - i5 - Dec 2015 - p63(1) [51-500]
Guardian
y SLJ - v61 - i2 - Feb 2015 - p99(1) [51-500]
Sleight of Hand
c KR - Sept 15 2015 - pNA [51-500]
y Res Links - v21 - i1 - Oct 2015 - p34(1) [501+]
y SLJ - v61 - i9 - Sept 2015 - p151(4) [501+]
y VOYA - v38 - i4 - Oct 2015 - p58(1) [51-500]

Deen, Shulem - *All Who Go Do Not Return*
BL - v111 - i12 - Feb 15 2015 - p4(1) [51-500]
LJ - v140 - i3 - Feb 15 2015 - p107(1) [51-500]
Mac - v128 - i15 - April 20 2015 - p54(1) [501+]
KR - Jan 1 2015 - pNA [51-500]

Deener, Andrew - *Venice: A Contested Bohemia in Los Angeles*
CS - v44 - i3 - May 2015 - p354-356 [501+]

Deer, Sarah - *The Beginning and End of Rape: Confronting Sexual Violence in Native America*
KR - Sept 1 2015 - pNA [51-500]

Deery, Phillip - *Red Apple: Communism and McCarthyism in Cold War New York*
AHR - v120 - i1 - Feb 2015 - p286-287 [501+]
JAH - v102 - i2 - Sept 2015 - p606-607 [501+]
S&S - v79 - i1 - Jan 2015 - p132-135 [501+]

DeFarr, Ellie - *Melancholy Manor*
SPBW - June 2015 - pNA [51-500]

DeFelice, Cynthia - *Fort*
   c CCB-B - v68 - i11 - July-August 2015 - p542(1) [51-500]
   c HB Guide - v26 - i2 - Fall 2015 - p79(1) [51-500]
   c PW - v262 - i10 - March 9 2015 - p71(2) [51-500]
   y VOYA - v38 - i1 - April 2015 - p56(1) [51-500]
   y BL - v111 - i15 - April 1 2015 - p78(2) [51-500]
The Fort
   c NYTBR - July 12 2015 - p19(L) [501+]
Fort
   c SLJ - v61 - i3 - March 2015 - p133(1) [51-500]
Defining Documents in American History: American West, 1836-1900
   y BL - v111 - i18 - May 15 2015 - p15(1) [51-500]
Defizitare Souverane? Fruhneuzeitliche Rechtfertigungsnarrative im Konflikt/Deficient Monarchs? Legitimation in Conflict
   HNet - April 2015 - pNA [501+]
Defler, Thomas R. - *The Woolly Monkey: Behavior, Ecology, Systematics, and Captive Research*
   QRB - v90 - i2 - June 2015 - p239(2) [501+]
Defoe, Daniel - *Robinson Crusoe*
   World&I - v30 - i5 - May 2015 - pNA [501+]
Robinson Crusoe (Illus. by Wyeth, N.C.)
   c HB Guide - v26 - i2 - Fall 2015 - p79(1) [51-500]
DeForge, Michael - *Dressing (Illus. by DeForge, Michael)*
   BL - v112 - i4 - Oct 15 2015 - p35(1) [51-500]
First Year Healthy
   PW - v262 - i7 - Feb 16 2015 - p166(1) [51-500]
DeFrantz, Thomas F. - *Black Performance Theory*
   Dance RJ - v47 - i2 - August 2015 - p91-3 [501+]
DeFranza, Megan K. - *Sex Difference in Christian Theology: Male, Female and Intersex in the Image of God*
   PW - v262 - i15 - April 13 2015 - p75(2) [51-500]
Degelman, Charles - *A Bowl Full of Nails*
   RVBW - Jan 2015 - pNA [51-500]
Degen, A. - *Mighty Star and the Castle of the Cancatervater*
   PW - v262 - i19 - May 11 2015 - p44(1) [51-500]
Degen, Bruce - *Nate Likes to Skate*
   c KR - Nov 15 2015 - pNA [51-500]
Snow Joke
   c HB Guide - v26 - i1 - Spring 2015 - p52(1) [51-500]
Degiorgis, Nicolo - *Hidden Islam*
   NS - v144 - i5244 - Jan 9 2015 - p40(1) [51-500]
DeGirolami, Marc O. - *The Tragedy of Religious Freedom*
   J Ch St - v57 - i1 - Wntr 2015 - p173-175 [501+]
Degnen, Cathrine - *Ageing Selves and Everyday Life in the North of England: Years in the Making*
   JRAI - v21 - i1 - March 2015 - p211(33) [501+]
Degner, Virginia R. - *Without Consent*
   PW - v262 - i24 - June 15 2015 - p67(1) [51-500]
DeHaan, Heather D. - *Stalinist City Planning: Professionals, Performance, and Power*
   E-A St - v67 - i8 - Oct 2015 - p1329(3) [501+]
   JMH - v87 - i1 - March 2015 - p245(2) [501+]
DeHaven-Smith, Lance - *Conspiracy Theory in America*
   CS - v44 - i2 - March 2015 - p191-193 [501+]
Dehler, Gregory J. - *The Most Defiant Devil: William Temple Hornaday and His Controversial Crusade to Save American Wildlife*
   WHQ - v46 - i1 - Spring 2015 - p80-80 [501+]
Deigh, John - *On Emotions: Philosophical Essays*
   Ethics - v125 - i2 - Jan 2015 - p576(6) [501+]
Deighan, Helen - *Beautiful Braiding Made Easy: Using Kumihimo Disks and Plates, rev. ed.*
   BL - v111 - i11 - Feb 1 2015 - p9(2) [51-500]
   LJ - v140 - i5 - March 15 2015 - p106(2) [51-500]
Deitche, Scott M. - *Cocktail Noir: From Gangsters and Gin Joints to Gumshoes and Gimlets*
   BL - v112 - i4 - Oct 15 2015 - p11(1) [51-500]
   NYTBR - Nov 1 2015 - p30(L) [501+]
Deitsch, Chaya - *Here and There: Leaving Hasidism, Keeping My Family*
   y BL - v112 - i6 - Nov 15 2015 - p14(2) [51-500]
   LJ - v140 - i16 - Oct 1 2015 - p85(2) [51-500]
   PW - v262 - i32 - August 10 2015 - p56(1) [51-500]
   NYT - Dec 7 2015 - pC1(L) [501+]
Deitz, Dan - *The Complete Book of 1950s Broadway Musicals*
   R&USQ - v54 - i3 - Spring 2015 - p60(1) [501+]
Deitz, Luc - *Neo-Latin and the Humanities: Essays in Honour of Charles E. Fantazzi*
   HNet - May 2015 - pNA [501+]
   Sev Cent N - v73 - i3-4 - Fall-Winter 2015 - p211(3) [501+]
Deitz, William C. - *Andromeda's War*
   Bwatch - Feb 2015 - pNA [51-500]

Deiwiks, Shu-Jyuan - *Europe Meets China: China Meets Europe: The Beginnings of European-Chinese Scientific Exchange in the Seventeenth Century*
   IBMR - v39 - i4 - Oct 2015 - p237(2) [501+]
DeJean, Joan - *How Paris Became Paris: The Invention of the Modern City*
   TLS - i5839 - Feb 27 2015 - p9(2) [501+]
DeJesus, Gina - *Hope: A Memoir of Survival in Cleveland*
   y SLJ - v61 - i8 - August 2015 - p115(1) [51-500]
Dejung, Christof - *Auf der Suche nach der Okonomie: Historische Annaherungen*
   HNet - April 2015 - pNA [501+]
DeKay, Larry - *Book Fairs For Authors*
   SPBW - Jan 2015 - pNA [51-500]
DeKeyser, Stacy - *One Witch at a Time*
   c CCB-B - v68 - i8 - April 2015 - p397(1) [51-500]
One Witch At a Time (Illus. by Chaghatzbanian, Sonia)
   c CH Bwatch - August 2015 - pNA [51-500]
   c HB - v91 - i3 - May-June 2015 - p107(1) [51-500]
   c HB Guide - v26 - i2 - Fall 2015 - p79(1) [51-500]
Dekker, Elly - *Illustrating the Phaenomena: Celestial Cartography in Antiquity and the Middle Ages*
   Isis - v106 - i1 - March 2015 - p166(2) [501+]
Dekker, Laura - *One Girl, One Dream*
   y Magpies - v30 - i1 - March 2015 - pS8(1) [51-500]
Dekker, Rachelle - *The Choosing*
   PW - v262 - i12 - March 23 2015 - p56(1) [51-500]
del Mara, K.M. - *Whitebeam*
   y PW - v262 - i42 - Oct 19 2015 - p79(1) [51-500]
Del Mazo, Margarita - *Lucy's Light (Illus. by Alvarez, Silvia)*
   c PW - v262 - i36 - Sept 7 2015 - p68(1) [51-500]
Del Noce, Augusto - *The Crisis of Modernity*
   RM - v69 - i1 - Sept 2015 - p125(2) [501+]
del Rio, Tania - *Warren the 13th and the All-Seeing Eye (Illus. by Staehle, Will)*
   c BL - v112 - i5 - Nov 1 2015 - p62(2) [51-500]
   y KR - Sept 15 2015 - pNA [51-500]
   c PW - v262 - i37 - Sept 14 2015 - p78(1) [51-500]
Del Roscio, Nicola - *The Essential Cy Twombly*
   TLS - i5845 - April 10 2015 - p12(1) [501+]
Del Toro, Guillermo - *Troll Hunters (Illus. by Murray, Sean)*
   y SLJ - v61 - i8 - August 2015 - p96(1) [51-500]
del Toro, Guillermo - *Trollhunters (Read by Heyborne, Kirby). Audiobook Review*
   y BL - v112 - i7 - Dec 1 2015 - p72(1) [51-500]
Trollhunters (Illus. by Murray, Sean)
   c Sch Lib - v63 - i3 - Autumn 2015 - p164(1) [51-500]
Del Vecchio, Gene - *BetterNot! And the Tale of Bratsville: Teaching Morals and Manners (Illus. by Fong, Roderick)*
   c CH Bwatch - Oct 2015 - pNA [51-500]
Dela - *The 52nd*
   KR - June 15 2015 - pNA [51-500]
   y PW - v262 - i9 - March 2 2015 - p87(1) [51-500]
Delacre, Lulu - *Olinguito, de la A a la Z!/Olinguito, from A to Z!*
   c KR - Dec 1 2015 - pNA [51-500]
Delacroix, Sibylle - *Blanche Hates the Night (Illus. by Delacroix, Sibylle)*
   c KR - Jan 1 2016 - pNA [51-500]
   c PW - v262 - i51 - Dec 14 2015 - p81(1) [51-500]
Prickly Jenny (Illus. by Delacroix, Sibylle)
   c CCB-B - v68 - i10 - June 2015 - p486(1) [51-500]
   c HB Guide - v26 - i2 - Fall 2015 - p9(1) [51-500]
   c KR - Jan 1 2015 - pNA [51-500]
   c PW - v262 - i49 - Dec 2 2015 - p21(2) [51-500]
   c SLJ - v61 - i5 - May 2015 - p78(2) [51-500]
Prickly Jenny (Illus. by Prickly Jenny (Picture story))
   c Res Links - v21 - i1 - Oct 2015 - p5(1) [51-500]
Prickly Jenny
   c PW - v262 - i3 - Jan 19 2015 - p79(2) [51-500]
Delacruz, Nikki - *Shield of God (Illus. by Delacruz, Nikki)*
   c CH Bwatch - July 2015 - pNA [51-500]
Delage, Christian - *Caught on Camera: Film in the Courtroom from the Nuremberg Trials to the Trials of the Khmer Rouge*
   AHR - v120 - i2 - April 2015 - p571(1) [501+]
   Law&PolBR - v25 - i4 - April 2015 - p68(3) [501+]
DeLand, M. Maitland - *Baby Santa and the Gift of Giving (Illus. by Wilson, Phil)*
   c KR - May 1 2015 - pNA [501+]
Delaney, Joseph - *Arena 13*
   y Sch Lib - v63 - i4 - Winter 2015 - p244(1) [51-500]
A New Darkness
   y HB Guide - v26 - i1 - Spring 2015 - p105(1) [51-500]

Delaney, Kathleen - *Purebred Dead*
   BL - v111 - i22 - August 1 2015 - p38(1) [51-500]
   KR - June 1 2015 - pNA [51-500]
   PW - v262 - i25 - June 22 2015 - p123(1) [51-500]
Delaney, Norman C. - *The Maltby Brothers' Civil War*
   JSH - v81 - i2 - May 2015 - p468(2) [501+]
   SHQ - v118 - i3 - Jan 2015 - p323-324 [501+]
Delaney, Paul - *Sean O'Faolain: Literature, Inheritance and the 1930s*
   TLS - i5843 - March 27 2015 - p23(2) [501+]
Delaney, Sam - *Mad Men and Bad Men: What Happened When British Politics Met Advertising*
   NS - v144 - i5249 - Feb 13 2015 - p52(1) [501+]
   Spec - v327 - i9729 - Feb 14 2015 - p41(2) [501+]
Delano, Marfe - *Frogs*
   c HB Guide - v26 - i1 - Spring 2015 - p159(2) [51-500]
Delano, Marfe Ferguson - *Butterflies*
   c HB Guide - v26 - i1 - Spring 2015 - p158(1) [51-500]
Clouds
   c HB Guide - v26 - i2 - Fall 2015 - p167(1) [51-500]
Delany, Paul - *Fatal Glamour: The Life of Rupert Brooke*
   BL - v111 - i16 - April 15 2015 - p11(2) [51-500]
   G&L Rev W - v22 - i6 - Nov-Dec 2015 - p39(2) [501+]
Delany, Samuel R. - *A, B, C: Three Short Novels*
   PW - v262 - i22 - June 1 2015 - p44(2) [51-500]
Delany, Shannon - *Beware the Little White Rabbit: An Alice in Wonderland-Inspired Anthology*
   y SLJ - v61 - i11 - Nov 2015 - p106(2) [51-500]
Delany, Vicki - *Haitian Graves*
   KR - June 15 2015 - pNA [51-500]
Rest Ye Murdered Gentlemen
   BL - v112 - i6 - Nov 15 2015 - p28(1) [51-500]
Unreasonable Doubt
   BL - v112 - i5 - Nov 1 2015 - p33(1) [51-500]
   KR - Oct 15 2015 - pNA [51-500]
   PW - v262 - i50 - Dec 7 2015 - p71(1) [51-500]
Delaperriere, Maria - *Milosz et la France*
   Slav R - v74 - i3 - Fall 2015 - p634-635 [501+]
Delaporte, Berengere - *Superfab Saves the Day (Illus. by Delaporte, Berengere)*
   c HB Guide - v26 - i2 - Fall 2015 - p31(1) [51-500]
Delargy, Marlaine - *Hostage*
   PW - v262 - i36 - Sept 7 2015 - p47(1) [51-500]
Delaunois, Angele - *Magic Little Words (Illus. by Gauthier, Manon)*
   c KR - Feb 15 2015 - pNA [51-500]
   SLJ - v61 - i4 - April 2015 - p126(1) [51-500]
Magic Little Words ... to Help You through Your Day (Illus. by Gauthier, Manon)
   c HB Guide - v26 - i2 - Fall 2015 - p31(1) [51-500]
   c Res Links - v21 - i1 - Oct 2015 - p5(1) [51-500]
Un Papillon (Illus. by Dechassey, Laurence)
   c Res Links - v20 - i4 - April 2015 - p39(1) [51-500]
Delbanco, Andrew - *The Abolitionist Imagination*
   RAH - v43 - i1 - March 2015 - p60-69 [501+]
Delbanco, Elena - *The Silver Swan*
   BL - v111 - i14 - March 15 2015 - p56(1) [51-500]
Delbanco, Nicholas - *The Years*
   BL - v111 - i9-10 - Jan 1 2015 - p43(1) [51-500]
Delblanco, Elena - *The Silver Swan*
   PW - v262 - i13 - March 30 2015 - p50(2) [51-500]
DeLeeuw, Brian - *The Dismantling*
   KR - Feb 15 2015 - pNA [51-500]
   PW - v262 - i8 - Feb 23 2015 - p49(1) [51-500]
Delehanty, Ann T. - *Literary Knowing in Neoclassical France: From Poetics to Aesthetics*
   FS - v69 - i2 - April 2015 - p243-244 [501+]
Delessert, Etienne - *Night Circus (Illus. by Delessert, Etienne)*
   c KR - Jan 15 2015 - pNA [51-500]
   c PW - v262 - i6 - Feb 9 2015 - p65(1) [51-500]
Night Circus
   c HB Guide - v26 - i2 - Fall 2015 - p31(2) [51-500]
DeLillo, Don - *Zero K*
   PW - v262 - i52 - Dec 21 2015 - p124(1) [51-500]
Delinsky, Barbara - *Blueprints*
   BL - v111 - i13 - March 1 2015 - p17(1) [51-500]
   KR - May 1 2015 - pNA [501+]
Cardinal Rules
   BL - v111 - i14 - March 15 2015 - p49(1) [51-500]
Through My Eyes
   BL - v112 - i6 - Nov 15 2015 - p31(1) [51-500]
Delio, Ilia - *From Teilhard to Omega: Co-creating an Unfinished Universe*
   Theol St - v76 - i1 - March 2015 - p217(2) [501+]
Delisle, Dennis R. - *Executing Lean Improvements: A Practical Guide with Real-World Healthcare Case Studies*
   RVBW - July 2015 - pNA [51-500]

Dell, Pamela - *Apache Resistance: Causes and Effects of Geronimo's Campaign*
  c SLJ - v61 - i9 - Sept 2015 - p175(1) [51-500]
Last Battle: Causes and Effects of the Massacre at Wounded Knee
  c SLJ - v61 - i9 - Sept 2015 - p175(1) [51-500]

Della Pietra, Cheryl - *Gonzo Girl*
  PW - v262 - i18 - May 4 2015 - p92(1) [51-500]

Della Porta, Donatella - *Can Democracy Be Saved? Participation, Deliberation and Social Movements*
  CS - v44 - i1 - Jan 2015 - p50-52 [501+]

della Quercia, Jacopo - *License to Quill*
  BL - v112 - i7 - Dec 1 2015 - p30(1) [51-500]
  KR - Oct 15 2015 - pNA [501+]
  PW - v262 - i41 - Oct 12 2015 - p48(2) [51-500]

Dellaira, Ava - *Love Letters to the Dead (Read by Whelan, Julia). Audiobook Review*
  c BL - v111 - i14 - March 15 2015 - p24(2) [501+]

Dellamonica, A.M. - *A Daughter of No Nation*
  KR - Oct 1 2015 - pNA [51-500]
  PW - v262 - i45 - Nov 9 2015 - p41(1) [51-500]

Dellape, Kevin J. - *America's First Chaplain: The Life and Times of Reverend Jacob Duche*
  JAH - v101 - i4 - March 2015 - p1255-1256 [501+]

Dellevoet, Alexandra - *Rafa Was My Robot (Illus. by Turner, Ken)*
  c Res Links - v20 - i3 - Feb 2015 - p3(2) [51-500]

Dellosso, Mike - *Centralia*
  PW - v262 - i15 - April 13 2015 - p65(1) [51-500]

Delmolino, Lara - *Solve Common Teaching Challenges in Children with Autism: 8 Essential Strategies for Professionals and Parents*
  RVBW - August 2015 - pNA [51-500]

Delonge, Tom - *Poet Anderson ... of Nightmares*
  y SLJ - v61 - i12 - Dec 2015 - p120(1) [51-500]

Delpha, John - *Grilled Pizza the Right Way: The Best Technique for Cooking Incredible Tasting Pizza Flatbread on Your Barbecue Page Street*
  LJ - v140 - i11 - June 15 2015 - p108(2) [501+]

Delsaux, Olivier - *Manuscrits et pratiques autographes chez les ecrivains francais de la fin du Moyen Age: L'exemple de Christine de Pizan*
  Specu - v90 - i1 - Jan 2015 - p38-39 [501+]

Delsert, Bernard - *L'Artillerie de Campagne de l'Armee Imperiale Allemande, 5 vols.*
  J Mil H - v79 - i4 - Oct 2015 - p1186-1187 [501+]

Delvaux, Martine - *Bitter Rose*
  Nat Post - v17 - i147 - April 25 2015 - pWP4(1) [501+]

Dely, Renaud - *Les Annees 40 sont de retour: petite lecon d'histoire pour comprendre les crises du present*
  TLS - i5852 - May 29 2015 - p10(2) [501+]

Demacopoulos, George E. - *The Invention of Peter: Apostolic Discourse and Papal Authority in Late Antiquity*
  CH - v84 - i2 - June 2015 - p426(3) [501+]
  JR - v95 - i2 - April 2015 - p258(2) [501+]
Orthodox Constructions of the West
  CH - v84 - i1 - March 2015 - p236(3) [501+]

DeMarinis, Rick - *El Paso Twilight*
  BL - v112 - i2 - Sept 15 2015 - p31(1) [51-500]

DeMarino, Rebecca - *To Capture Her Heart*
  PW - v262 - i19 - May 11 2015 - p43(1) [51-500]

Dembeck, Till - *Philologie und Mehrsprachigkeit ed*
  GSR - v38 - i3 - Oct 2015 - p711-713 [501+]

Demcak, Andrew - *A Little Bit Langston*
  y KR - Sept 15 2015 - pNA [51-500]

Demers, Guillaume - *Hipster le chat: Chroniques de la faune urbaine*
  c Res Links - v20 - i4 - April 2015 - p39(1) [501+]

Demetrios, Heather - *Blood Passage*
  y KR - Nov 1 2015 - pNA [51-500]
Exquisite Captive
  y HB Guide - v26 - i1 - Spring 2015 - p105(1) [51-500]
  y Sch Lib - v63 - i1 - Spring 2015 - p61(2) [51-500]
I'll Meet You There
  y BL - v111 - i9-10 - Jan 1 2015 - p94(1) [51-500]
  y CCB-B - v68 - i6 - Feb 2015 - p307(1) [51-500]
  y HB Guide - v26 - i2 - Fall 2015 - p116(1) [51-500]
  y VOYA - v38 - i2 - June 2015 - p56(2) [51-500]

Demi - *President Lincoln (Illus. by Demi)*
  c KR - Dec 1 2015 - pNA [51-500]

DeMille, Nelson - *Radiant Angel (Read by Brick, Scott). Audiobook Review*
  Bwatch - August 2015 - pNA [51-500]
Radiant Angel
  KR - May 1 2015 - pNA [501+]

DeMillo, Richard A. - *Revolution in Higher Education: How a Small Band of Innovators Will Make College Accessible and Affordable*
  LJ - v140 - i16 - Oct 1 2015 - p91(1) [51-500]

DeMillo, Rivhard A. - *Revolution in Higher Education: How a Small Band of Innovators Will Make College Accessible and Affordable*
  TimHES - i2224 - Oct 8 2015 - p46-47 [501+]

Demmer, Klaus - *Selbstaufklarung theologischer Ethik: Themen-Thesen-Perspektiven*
  Theol St - v76 - i3 - Sept 2015 - p626(3) [501+]

Demokratie in der Geschichte - Herausforderungen in der Gegenwart
  HNet - May 2015 - pNA [501+]

Demos, John - *The Heathen School: A Story of Hope and Betrayal in the Age of the Early Republic*
  AHR - v120 - i1 - Feb 2015 - p239-240 [501+]
  Bks & Cult - v21 - i3 - May-June 2015 - p18(1) [501+]
  NEQ - v88 - i3 - Sept 2015 p537-540 [501+]
  RAH - v43 - i2 - June 2015 - p231-236 [501+]

Dempsey, Deborah Blake - *The Hoppernots*
  c KR - July 1 2015 - pNA [51-500]

Dempsey, James - *The Tortured Life of Scofield Thayer*
  Lon R Bks - v37 - i7 - April 9 2015 - p25(2) [501+]

Dempsey, Lorcan - *The Network Reshapes the Library: Lorcan Dempsey on Libraries, Services, and Networks*
  LR - v64 - i1-2 - Jan-Feb 2015 - p184-185 [501+]
The Network Reshapes the Library
  VOYA - v37 - i6 - Feb 2015 - p91(1) [51-500]

Dempsey, Sheena - *Bruno and Titch: A Tale of a Boy and His Guinea Pig*
  c HB Guide - v26 - i2 - Fall 2015 - p32(1) [51-500]

Demuth, Patricia Brennan - *Where Is the Great Wall? (Illus. by Hoare, Jerry)*
  c SLJ - v61 - i8 - August 2015 - p118(1) [51-500]

Den Boeft, Jan - *Philological and Historical Commentary on Ammianus Marcellinus XXVIII*
  Class R - v65 - i1 - April 2015 - p159-161 [501+]

Den Hollander, William - *Josephus, the Emperors, and the City of Rome: From Hostage to Historian*
  Class R - v65 - i1 - April 2015 - p222-224 [501+]

Den Krieg Denken: Kriegswahrnehmung und Kriegsdeutung in Mitteleuropa in der Ersten Halfte des 17. Jahrhunderts
  HNet - March 2015 - pNA [501+]

Den Protest Regieren. Staatliches Handeln, Neue Soziale Bewegungen und Linke Organisationen in den 1970er- und 1980er-Jahren
  HNet - March 2015 - pNA [501+]

DeNardis, Laura - *The Global War for Internet Governance*
  Isis - v106 - i2 - June 2015 - p507(2) [501+]
  T&C - v56 - i3 - July 2015 - p784-785 [501+]

Denaux, Adelbert - *The Ecumenical Legacy of Johannes Cardinal Willebrands*
  CHR - v101 - i2 - Spring 2015 - p387(3) [501+]

Denbow, James - *The Archaeology and Ethnography of Central Africa*
  IJAHS - v48 - i1 - Wntr 2015 - p175-176 [501+]

Denby, David - *Lit Up: One Reporter, Three Schools, and Twenty-Four Books That Can Change Lives*
  KR - Oct 15 2015 - pNA [501+]
  LJ - v140 - i20 - Dec 1 2015 - p112(1) [51-500]
  PW - v262 - i45 - Nov 9 2015 - p48(1) [51-500]

Dencer, Christine - *Misty (Illus. by Meserve, Jessica)*
  c HB Guide - v26 - i2 - Fall 2015 - p59(1) [51-500]
  c HB - v91 - i3 - May-June 2015 - p108(1) [51-500]

Deneire, Tom - *Dynamics of Neo-Latin and the Vernacular: Language and Poetics, Translation and Transfer*
  Sev Cent N - v73 - i1-2 - Spring-Summer 2015 - p80(3) [501+]

Denenberg, Barry - *Ali: An American Champion*
  c CH Bwatch - Feb 2015 - pNA [51-500]
  c HB Guide - v26 - i2 - Fall 2015 - p198(1) [51-500]

Denery, Dallas G. - *The Devil Wins: A History of Lying from the Garden of Eden to the Enlightenment*
  CHE - v61 - i18 - Jan 16 2015 - pNA [501+]
  TimHES - i2192 - Feb 26 2015 - p50-51 [501+]

Denery, Dallas G., II - *The Devil Wins: A History of Lying from the Garden of Eden to the Enlightenment*
  CHR - v101 - i4 - Autumn 2015 - p889(2) [501+]
The Devil Wins: A History of Lying from the Garden of Eden to the Enlightenment
  Six Ct J - v46 - i3 - Fall 2015 - p772-773 [501+]
Uncertain Knowledge: Scepticism, Relativism and Doubt in the Middle Ages
  Six Ct J - v46 - i3 - Fall 2015 - p702-704 [501+]

Denery II, Dallas G. - *Uncertain Knowledge: Scepticism, Relativism, and Doubt in the Middle Ages*
  Ren Q - v68 - i2 - Summer 2015 - p665-667 [501+]

Deneux, Xavier - *Vehicles (Illus. by Deneux, Xavier)*
  BL - v112 - i6 - Nov 15 2015 - p57(1) [51-500]
  c KR - Jan 1 2016 - pNA [51-500]

Denial, Catherine J. - *Making Marriage: Husbands, Wives and the American State in Dakota and Ojibwe Country*
  Am Ind CRJ - v39 - i1 - Wntr 2015 - p134-137 [501+]

Denis, Nelson A. - *War Against All Puerto Ricans*
  KR - Feb 1 2015 - pNA [501+]
War Against All Puerto Ricans: Revolution and Terror in America's Colony
  LJ - v140 - i6 - April 1 2015 - p102(1) [51-500]
  NYT - August 23 2015 - p3(L) [501+]

Denise, Anika - *Baking Day at Grandma's (Illus. by Denise, Christopher)*
  c HB Guide - v26 - i1 - Spring 2015 - p8(1) [51-500]

Denker, Joel S. - *The Carrot Purple and Other Curious Stories of the Food We Eat*
  LJ - v140 - i15 - Sept 15 2015 - p96(1) [51-500]
  PW - v262 - i36 - Sept 7 2015 - p60(1) [51-500]

Denman, Melanie - *Visiting the Sins*
  RVBW - June 2015 - pNA [51-500]

Dennard, Susan - *Truthwitch*
  y BL - v112 - i6 - Nov 15 2015 - p51(2) [51-500]
  y KR - Oct 1 2015 - pNA [51-500]
  y PW - v262 - i42 - Oct 19 2015 - p79(1) [51-500]
  y SLJ - v61 - i11 - Nov 2015 - p113(1) [51-500]

Denning, Andrew - *Skiing into Modernity: A Cultural and Environmental History*
  JIH - v46 - i3 - Wntr 2016 - p435-436 [501+]

Dennis, Andrew - *1635: A Parcel of Rogues*
  PW - v262 - i47 - Nov 23 2015 - p54(1) [51-500]

Dennis, H.L. - *Circle of Fire*
  y Sch Lib - v63 - i1 - Spring 2015 - p51(1) [51-500]

Dennis, Sarah - *Cinderella: A Paper-Cut Book (Illus. by Dennis, Sarah)*
  c KR - May 1 2015 - pNA [51-500]

Dennison, Hannah - *Deadly Desires at Honeychurch Hall*
  KR - March 1 2015 - pNA [501+]
  PW - v262 - i9 - March 2 2015 - p66(1) [51-500]

Dennison, James T., Jr. - *Reformed Confessions of the 16th and 17th Centuries in English Translation, vol. 4, 1600-1693*
  Six Ct J - v46 - i2 - Summer 2015 - p525-527 [501+]

Dennison, Matthew - *Behind the Mask: The Life of Vita Sackville-West*
  BL - v111 - i19-20 - June 1 2015 - p26(1) [51-500]
  KR - March 1 2015 - pNA [501+]
  LJ - v140 - i8 - May 1 2015 - p70(1) [51-500]
  PW - v262 - i13 - March 30 2015 - p65(1) [51-500]
  TLS - i5844 - April 3 2015 - p12(2) [501+]

Denny, Frederick M. - *The Norton Anthology of World Religions*
  JAAR - v83 - i2 - June 2015 - p596-598 [501+]

Denny, Walter B. - *How to Read Islamic Carpets*
  LJ - v140 - i3 - Feb 15 2015 - p96(1) [51-500]

Denos, Julia - *Swatch: The Girl Who Loved Color*
  c BL - v112 - i5 - Nov 1 2015 - p53(1) [51-500]

Denson, Abby - *Cool Japan Guide: Fun in the Land of Manga, Lucky Cats and Ramen*
  LJ - v140 - i5 - March 15 2015 - p124(1) [51-500]
  PW - v262 - i2 - Jan 12 2015 - p49(2) [51-500]
  SLJ - v61 - i3 - March 2015 - p179(1) [51-500]

Denson, Bryan - *The Spy's Son*
  KR - Feb 15 2015 - pNA [501+]

Dent, Julian - *Technology Distribution Channels: Understanding and Managing Channels to Market*
  Bwatch - Feb 2015 - pNA [501+]

Dentith, Simon - *Doctor Thorne*
  TLS - i5847 - April 24 2015 - p7(f2) [501+]
Nineteenth-Century British Literature Then and Now: Reading with Hindsight
  RES - v275 - June 2015 - p589-591 [501+]

Denton, Bradley - *Buddy Holly: Is Alive and Well on Ganymede (Read by Heyborne, Kirby). Audiobook Review*
  PW - v262 - i17 - April 27 2015 - p69(1) [51-500]

Denton, Kirk A. - *Exhibiting the Past: Historical Memory and the Politics of Museums in Postsocialist China*
  Pac A - v88 - i3 - Sept 2015 - p694 [501+]

Denton, Robert E., Jr. - *Studies of Communication in the 2012 Presidential Campaign*
  Pres St Q - v45 - i4 - Dec 2015 - p812(3) [501+]

Denton, Sally - *The Profiteers: Bechtel and the Men Who Built the World*
  KR - Dec 1 2015 - pNA [501+]
  LJ - v140 - i20 - Dec 1 2015 - p113(2) [51-500]
  PW - v262 - i50 - Dec 7 2015 - p77(2) [51-500]

Denzel, Jason - *Mystic*
   KR - Sept 1 2015 - pNA [51-500]
Deoden, Matt - *The Final Four: The Pursuit of College Basketball Glory*
   y KR - Dec 15 2015 - pNA [51-500]
Deon, Michel - *The Foundling's War*
   NYTBR - March 8 2015 - p34(L) [501+]
   RVBW - Jan 2015 - pNA [51-500]
   TLS - i5836 - Feb 6 2015 - p20(1) [501+]
dePaola, Tomie - *Jack (Illus. by dePaola, Tomie)*
   c HB Guide - v26 - i1 - Spring 2015 - p8(1) [51-500]
Look and Be Grateful (Illus. by dePaola, Tomie)
   c BL - v112 - i1 - Sept 1 2015 - p120(1) [51-500]
   c KR - August 1 2015 - pNA [51-500]
   PW - v262 - i29 - July 20 2015 - p188(1) [51-500]
Depaola, Tomie - *Look and Be Grateful (Illus. by dePaola, Tomie)*
   c SLJ - v61 - i12 - Dec 2015 - p85(1) [51-500]
dePaola, Tomie - *Michael Bird-Boy (Illus. by dePaola, Tomie)*
   c HB - v91 - i6 - Nov-Dec 2015 - p115(2) [501+]
When Andy Met Sandy (Illus. by dePaola, Tomie)
   c PW - v262 - i50 - Dec 7 2015 - p85(1) [51-500]
DePaoli, Tom - *Sydney the Monster Stops Bullies (Illus. by Barrows, Laurie)*
   c CH Bwatch - Sept 2015 - pNA [51-500]
DePaul, Virna - *Filthy Rich*
   PW - v262 - i39 - Sept 28 2015 - p74(1) [51-500]
DePaulo, Bella - *How We Live Now: Redefining Home and Family in the 21st Century*
   BL - v111 - i22 - August 1 2015 - p7(2) [51-500]
   KR - June 1 2015 - pNA [51-500]
   PW - v262 - i18 - May 4 2015 - p106(1) [51-500]
DePew, Alfred - *A Wedding Song for Poorer People*
   KR - May 1 2015 - pNA [501+]
DePoy, Phillip - *A Prisoner in Malta*
   BL - v112 - i6 - Nov 15 2015 - p28(1) [51-500]
   KR - Nov 15 2015 - pNA [51-500]
   PW - v262 - i44 - Nov 2 2015 - p62(2) [51-500]
DePrince, Michaela - *Hope in a Ballet Shoe*
   y Sch Lib - v63 - i2 - Summer 2015 - p116(1) [51-500]
Taking Flight: From War Orphan to Star Ballerina
   y HB Guide - v26 - i2 - Fall 2015 - p208(1) [51-500]
Der Antikommunismus in seiner Epoche. Weltanschauung, Bewegung, Regierende Partei
   HNet - Jan 2015 - pNA [501+]
Der Arbeitende Korper im Spannungsfeld von Krankheit und Gesundheit. Neue Perspektiven auf die Gewerkschaftsgeschichte V
   HNet - March 2015 - pNA [501+]
Der Aufbruch zur Demokratie in Ostmitteleuropa zwischen den Kriegen. Notwendige Bausteine fur ein Gesamtbild Europaischer Demokratiegeschichte
   HNet - July 2015 - pNA [501+]
Der Ausstellungsraum im Kunstmarkt
   HNet - Jan 2015 - pNA [501+]
Der Krieg ist vorbei. Heimkehr - Trauma - Weiterleben
   HNet - August 2015 - pNA [501+]
Der Matossian, Bedross - *Shattered Dreams of Revolution: From Liberty to Violence in the Late Ottoman Empire*
   HNet - Feb 2015 - pNA [501+]
Der Militarisch-Medizinische Komplex in der Fruhen Neuzeit: Zum Verhaltnis von Militar, Medizin, Gesellschaft und Staat
   HNet - March 2015 - pNA [501+]
Der "Unterricht der Visitatoren" und die Durchsetzung der Reformation in Kursachsen
   HNet - May 2015 - pNA [501+]
Der Zweite Weltkrieg. Kulturtourismus und Politik
   HNet - May 2015 - pNA [501+]
Derby, Sally - *Jump Back, Paul: The Life and Poems of Paul Laurence Dunbar*
   c KR - July 1 2015 - pNA [51-500]
Jump Back, Paul: The Life and Poems of Paul Laurence Dunbar (Illus. by Qualls, Sean)
   c BL - v111 - i19-20 - June 1 2015 - p88(1) [51-500]
   c SLJ - v61 - i7 - July 2015 - p106(1) [51-500]
Sunday Shopping (Illus. by Strickland, Shadra)
   c CCB-B - v68 - i11 - July-August 2015 - p542(1) [51-500]
   c CH Bwatch - August 2015 - pNA [51-500]
   c HB - v91 - i3 - May-June 2015 - p84(1) [501+]
   c HB Guide - v26 - i2 - Fall 2015 - p32(1) [51-500]
   c SLJ - v61 - i5 - May 2015 - p83(2) [51-500]
Sunday Shopping (Illus. by Strickland, Shandra)
   c KR - March 15 2015 - pNA [51-500]
Derechin, Michael - *Anna: A Doctor's Quest into the Unknown*
   KR - March 15 2015 - pNA [501+]
Deresiewicz, William - *Excellent Sheep: The Miseducation of the American Elite and the Way to a Meaningful Life (Read by Foster, Mel). Audiobook Review*
   LJ - v140 - i3 - Feb 15 2015 - p59(1) [51-500]
Excellent Sheep: The Miseducation of the American Elite and the Way to a Meaningful Life
   Bks & Cult - v21 - i3 - May-June 2015 - p24(2) [501+]
   Comw - v142 - i8 - May 1 2015 - p14(6) [501+]
   For Aff - v94 - i2 - March-April 2015 - pNA [501+]
Derges, Jane - *Ritual and Recovery in Post-Conflict Sri Lanka*
   JRAI - v21 - i1 - March 2015 - p240(2) [501+]
Derickson, Alan - *Dangerously Sleepy: Overworked Americans and the Cult of Manly Wakefulness*
   BHR - v89 - i1 - Spring 2015 - p168(3) [501+]
   JIH - v45 - i3 - Wntr 2015 - p443-445 [501+]
Derks, Scott - *This Is Who We Were: 1880-1899*
   y BL - v111 - i18 - May 15 2015 - p16(2) [51-500]
   LJ - v140 - i9 - May 15 2015 - p105(1) [51-500]
Derman, Joshua - *Max Weber in Politics and Social Thought: From Charisma to Canonization*
   CS - v44 - i4 - July 2015 - p577-578 [501+]
Dernavich, Drew - *It's Not Easy Being Number Three (Illus. by Dernavich, Drew)*
   c KR - Oct 15 2015 - pNA [51-500]
Derogatis, Amy - *Saving Sex: Sexuality and Salvation in American Evangelism*
   Bks & Cult - v21 - i1 - Jan-Feb 2015 - p15(2) [501+]
DeRossi, Ravi - *Cuban Cocktails: 100 Classic and Modern Drinks*
   LJ - v140 - i20 - Dec 1 2015 - p124(1) [51-500]
Derovan, David - *William Kidd*
   c BL - v112 - i7 - Dec 1 2015 - p43(1) [51-500]
Derr, Megan - *The High King's Golden Tongue*
   PW - v262 - i38 - Sept 21 2015 - p60(2) [51-500]
Derrick, David G., Jr. - *Play with Your Food*
   c HB Guide - v26 - i2 - Fall 2015 - p32(1) [51-500]
Derrida, Jacques - *The Death Penalty, vol. 1*
   TT - v72 - i1 - April 2015 - p100-108 [501+]
Dershowitz, Alan M. - *Abraham: The World's First (But Certainly Not Last) Jewish Lawyer*
   LJ - v140 - i16 - Oct 15 2015 - p64(2) [501+]
   BL - v112 - i4 - Oct 15 2015 - p5(1) [51-500]
   KR - August 1 2015 - pNA [51-500]
Derting, Kimberly - *The Replaced*
   y HB Guide - v26 - i2 - Fall 2015 - p116(1) [51-500]
   y KR - Feb 15 2015 - pNA [51-500]
   SLJ - v61 - i4 - April 2015 - p160(1) [51-500]
DeRubertis, Barbaara - *Let's Celebrate Constitution Day*
   c BL - v112 - i7 - Dec 1 2015 - p42(1) [51-500]
deRubertis, Barbara - *Let's Celebrate Columbus Day*
   c HB Guide - v26 - i1 - Spring 2015 - p142(1) [51-500]
Let's Celebrate Earth Day
   c CH Bwatch - March 2015 - pNA [51-500]
DeRubertis, Barbara - *Let's Celebrate Earth Day*
   c HB Guide - v26 - i2 - Fall 2015 - p156(1) [51-500]
Let's Celebrate Labor Day
   c BL - v112 - i7 - Dec 1 2015 - p42(1) [51-500]
deRubertis, Barbara - *Let's Celebrate Presidents' Day*
   c HB Guide - v26 - i1 - Spring 2015 - p142(1) [51-500]
Let's Celebrate Veterans Day
   c HB Guide - v26 - i1 - Spring 2015 - p142(1) [51-500]
Des Roches, Roger - *Boitamemoire*
   y Res Links - v20 - i3 - Feb 2015 - p44(1) [51-500]
Desai, Gaurav - *Commerce with the Universe: Africa, India, and the Afrasian Imagination*
   Pac A - v88 - i2 - June 2015 - p339 [501+]
Desai, Meghnad - *Hubris: Why Economists Failed to Predict the Crisis and How to Avoid the Next One*
   TimHES - i2205 - May 28 2015 - p50-51 [501+]
Desai, Radhika - *Geopolitical Economy: After U.S. Hegemony, Globalization and Empire*
   S&S - v79 - i4 - Oct 2015 - p630-633 [501+]
DeSalle, Rob - *Welcome to the Microbiome: Getting to Know the Trillions of Bacteria and Other Microbes in, on, and Around You*
   PW - v262 - i39 - Sept 28 2015 - p80(1) [51-500]
DeSalvo, Louise - *Chasing Ghosts: A Memoir of a Father, Gone to War*
   PW - v262 - i35 - August 31 2015 - p81(1) [51-500]
Desan, Christine - *Making Money: Coin, Currency and the Coming of Capitalism*
   Econ - v414 - i8925 - Feb 14 2015 - p74(US) [501+]
Desbordes, Astrid - *Edmond, the Moonlit Party (Illus. by Boutavant, Marc)*
   c BL - v111 - i21 - July 1 2015 - p61(2) [51-500]
   c CH Bwatch - July 2015 - pNA [51-500]
Edmond: The Moonlit Party (Illus. by Boutavant, Marc)
   c NYTBR - June 21 2015 - p16(L) [501+]
Edmond, the Moonlit Party (Illus. by Boutavant, Marc)
   c PW - v262 - i18 - May 4 2015 - p118(1) [51-500]
   c SLJ - v61 - i6 - June 2015 - p80(1) [51-500]
The Moonlit Party (Illus. by Boutavant, Marc)
   c KR - May 1 2015 - pNA [51-500]
Travels of an Extraordinary Hamster (Illus. by Martin, Pauline)
   c BL - v112 - i2 - Sept 15 2015 - p53(1) [51-500]
   Sch Lib - v63 - i4 - Winter 2015 - p226(1) [51-500]
   c KR - July 1 2015 - pNA [51-500]
   c PW - v262 - i24 - June 15 2015 - p87(1) [51-500]
   c SLJ - v61 - i8 - August 2015 - p80(1) [51-500]
Deschenes, Amy - *Free Technology for Libraries*
   VOYA - v38 - i5 - Dec 2015 - p83(1) [51-500]
The Design Museum - *Fifty Fashion Designers That Changed the World*
   Bwatch - August 2015 - pNA [51-500]
DeSilva, Bruce - *A Scourge of Vipers*
   KR - Feb 1 2015 - pNA [51-500]
   PW - v262 - i5 - Feb 2 2015 - p36(1) [51-500]
deSilva, David - *The Apocrypha: Core Biblical Studies*
   Intpr - v69 - i1 - Jan 2015 - p104(2) [51-500]
DeSimone, Erika - *Voices Beyond Bondage: An Anthology of Verse by African Americans of the 19th Century*
   JSH - v81 - i4 - Nov 2015 - p1054(1) [501+]
Desind, Jay - *Touching the Hem of Heaven*
   KR - Oct 1 2015 - pNA [501+]
DeSipio, Louis - *U.S. Immigration in the Twenty-First Century: Making Americans, Remaking America*
   RVBW - March 2015 - pNA [501+]
Desir, Christa - *Bleed Like Me*
   y HB Guide - v26 - i1 - Spring 2015 - p105(1) [51-500]
Other Broken Things
   y BL - v112 - i6 - Nov 15 2015 - p51(1) [51-500]
   KR - Nov 1 2015 - pNA [51-500]
   y SLJ - v61 - i11 - Nov 2015 - p113(2) [51-500]
Desjardins, India - *Marguerite's Christmas (Illus. by Blanchet, Pascal)*
   c KR - Oct 15 2015 - pNA [51-500]
   c PW - v262 - i37 - Sept 14 2015 - p77(2) [51-500]
Desjardins-Kelly, Irma - *It's My Life: My Struggle with Mental Illness*
   RVBW - Nov 2015 - pNA [51-500]
Deslauriers, Marguerite - *The Cambridge Companion to Aristotle's Politics*
   Class R - v65 - i1 - April 2015 - p61-63 [501+]
Desmond, Jenni - *The Blue Whale (Illus. by Desmond, Jenni)*
   c SLJ - v61 - i5 - May 2015 - p130(1) [51-500]
   c BL - v111 - i18 - May 15 2015 - p48(1) [51-500]
   c CH Bwatch - June 2015 - pNA [51-500]
   c PW - v262 - i49 - Dec 2 2015 - p43(1) [51-500]
The Blue Whale
   c HB Guide - v26 - i2 - Fall 2015 - p179(1) [51-500]
   c KR - March 15 2015 - pNA [51-500]
Desmond, Matthew - *Evicted*
   KR - Dec 15 2015 - pNA [501+]
Desmond, Richard - *The Real Deal: the Autobiography of Britain's Most Controversial Media Mogul*
   NS - v144 - i5269 - July 3 2015 - p52(1) [501+]
Desmond, Tara Mataraza - *Full Belly: Good Eats for a Healthy Pregnancy*
   LJ - v140 - i7 - April 15 2015 - p109(1) [51-500]
Despain, Bree - *The Eternity Key: Into the Dark, Book 2*
   y VOYA - v37 - i6 - Feb 2015 - p74(1) [51-500]
The Eternity Key
   y SLJ - v61 - i8 - August 2015 - p113(1) [51-500]
Despentes, Virginie - *Apocalypse Baby*
   KR - Feb 15 2015 - pNA [51-500]
Despommier, Dickson D. - *People, Parasites, and Plowshares: Learning from Our Body's Most Terrifying Invaders*
   QRB - v90 - i1 - March 2015 - p98(2) [501+]
Desrochers, Pierre - *Pepe Camisole: un hiver pas comme les autres (Illus. by Pare-Sorel, Julien)*
   c Res Links - v20 - i5 - June 2015 - p38(1) [501+]
Dessen, Sarah - *Saint Anything (Read by Meskimen, Taylor). Audiobook Review*
   y BL - v112 - i1 - Sept 1 2015 - p143(1) [51-500]
Saint Anything (Read by Meskimen, Taylor)
   y PW - v262 - i35 - August 31 2015 - p86(1) [51-500]

116 • DESTEFANO
Book Review Index 2016 Cumulation

Saint Anything (Read by Meskimen, Taylor). Audiobook Review
y SLJ - v61 - i10 - Oct 2015 - p54(1) [51-500]
Saint Anything
y BL - v111 - i15 - April 1 2015 - p70(1) [51-500]
y CCB-B - v68 - i11 - July-August 2015 - p543(1) [51-500]
y HB Guide - v26 - i2 - Fall 2015 - p116(1) [51-500]
y KR - March 15 2015 - pNA [51-500]
PW - v262 - i8 - Feb 23 2015 - p3(1) [1-50]
y PW - v262 - i49 - Dec 2 2015 - p96(1) [51-500]
SLJ - v61 - i4 - April 2015 - p160(2) [51-500]
y Teach Lib - v42 - i5 - June 2015 - p18(1) [51-500]
y VOYA - v38 - i1 - April 2015 - p56(2) [51-500]
DeStefano, Lauren - *Broken Crowns*
y KR - Dec 15 2015 - pNA [51-500]
Burning Kingdoms
y BL - v111 - i12 - Feb 15 2015 - p79(1) [51-500]
y CCB-B - v68 - i10 - June 2015 - p486(2) [51-500]
y HB Guide - v26 - i2 - Fall 2015 - p116(1) [51-500]
y KR - Jan 1 2015 - pNA [51-500]
y VOYA - v37 - i6 - Feb 2015 - p74(1) [51-500]
A Curious Tale of the In-Between
c BL - v111 - i21 - July 1 2015 - p69(1) [51-500]
The Curious Tale of the In-Between
c CCB-B - v69 - i2 - Oct 2015 - p84(1) [51-500]
A Curious Tale of the In-Between
y HB - v91 - i5 - Sept-Oct 2015 - p99(2) [51-500]
c KR - July 1 2015 - pNA [51-500]
c PW - v262 - i28 - July 13 2015 - p66(1) [51-500]
Destefano, Lauren - *A Curious Tale of the In-Between*
c SLJ - v61 - i8 - August 2015 - p83(2) [51-500]
Destiny, A. - *Love Is in the Air*
SLJ - v61 - i4 - April 2015 - p154(2) [51-500]
Sunset Ranch
y HB Guide - v26 - i1 - Spring 2015 - p105(1) [51-500]
y VOYA - v38 - i5 - Dec 2015 - p55(1) [51-500]
Determann, Jorg Matthias - *Historiography in Saudi Arabia: Globalization and the State in the Middle East*
AHR - v120 - i2 - April 2015 - p752-753 [501+]
IJMES - v47 - i1 - Feb 2015 - p184-185 [501+]
Detlefsen, Lisl - *Time for Cranberries (Illus. by Henry, Jed)*
c SLJ - v61 - i7 - July 2015 - p61(1) [51-500]
Detlefsen, Lisl H. - *Time for Cranberries (Illus. by Henry, Jed)*
c HB - v91 - i6 - Nov-Dec 2015 - p55(2) [51-500]
c KR - July 1 2015 - pNA [51-500]
c PW - v262 - i31 - August 3 2015 - p56(1) [501+]
Detter, Dag - *The Public Wealth of Nations*
Econ - v415 - i8942 - June 13 2015 - p70(US) [501+]
Detweiler, Katelyn - *Immaculate*
y CCB-B - v69 - i1 - Sept 2015 - p18(1) [51-500]
y KR - March 1 2015 - pNA [51-500]
SLJ - v61 - i4 - April 2015 - p162(1) [51-500]
y VOYA - v38 - i2 - June 2015 - p57(1) [501+]
Detweiler, Tim - *The Big Book of Wooden Locks: Complete Plans for Nine Working Wooden Locks*
LJ - v140 - i12 - July 1 2015 - p85(2) [51-500]
RVBW - May 2015 - pNA [51-500]
Deurper, Christian - *Theologe, Erbauungsschriftsteller, Hofprediger: Joachim Lutkemann in Rostock und Wolfenbuttel*
Ger Q - v88 - i3 - Summer 2015 - p407(4) [501+]
Deutermann, Allison K. - *Formal Matters: Reading the Materials of English Renaissance Literature*
Six Ct J - v46 - i2 - Summer 2015 - p493-495 [501+]
Sev Cent N - v73 - i3-4 - Fall-Winter 2015 - p121(4) [501+]
Deutermann, P.T. - *Cold Frame*
PW - v262 - i22 - June 1 2015 - p42(1) [51-500]
RVBW - July 2015 - pNA [51-500]
Deutsch, Barry - *Hereville: How Mirka Caught a Fish (Illus. by Deutsch, Barry)*
c HB - v91 - i6 - Nov-Dec 2015 - p79(1) [51-500]
How Mirka Caught a Fish
c KR - Oct 1 2015 - pNA [51-500]
Deutsch, Celia M. - *Toward the Future: Essays on Catholic-Jewish Relations in Memory of Rabbi Leon Klenicki*
Theol St - v76 - i1 - March 2015 - p213(2) [501+]
Deutsch-Israelische Fussballfreundschaft. 8. Sporthistorische Konferenz Irsee
HNet - May 2015 - pNA [501+]
Deutsch-Polnische-Ukrainische Sommerakademie
HNet - Jan 2015 - pNA [501+]
Deutsch, Sandra McGee - *Crossing Borders, Claiming a Nation: A History of Argentine Jewish Women, 1880-1955*
Ams - v72 - i3 - July 2015 - p481(2) [501+]
Deutscher, Thomas B. - *Punishment and Penance: Two Phases in the History of the Bishop's Tribunal of Novara*
CH - v84 - i2 - June 2015 - p434(2) [501+]
Six Ct J - v46 - i3 - Fall 2015 - p848-850 [501+]
Dev, Sonali - *The Bollywood Bride*
KR - August 15 2015 - pNA [51-500]
LJ - v140 - i16 - Oct 1 2015 - p68(2) [51-500]
PW - v262 - i31 - August 3 2015 - p43(1) [51-500]
Deva, Mukul - *Assassins*
PW - v262 - i22 - June 1 2015 - p43(1) [51-500]
Deval, Patrick - *American Indian Women*
BL - v112 - i3 - Oct 1 2015 - p4(1) [51-500]
Devaney, Julie - *My Leaky Body: Tales from the Gurney*
CWS - v30 - i2-3 - Fall-Winter 2015 - p146(2) [501+]
Deveney, Sean - *Fun City: John Lindsay, Joe Namath, and How Sports Saved New York in the 1960s*
BL - v112 - i1 - Sept 1 2015 - p33(2) [51-500]
LJ - v140 - i16 - Oct 1 2015 - p87(1) [51-500]
NYT - Oct 4 2015 - p2(L) [501+]
PW - v262 - i35 - August 31 2015 - p81(1) [51-500]
Devenney, Wing Mun - *The Complete Guide to Making Wire Jewelry: Techniques, Projects, and Jig Patterns from Beginner to Advanced*
RVBW - Nov 2015 - pNA [501+]
Dever, Zsu - *Everyday Vegan Eats*
Veg J - v34 - i1 - Jan-March 2015 - p31(1) [51-500]
Deveraux, Jude - *Ever After*
KR - April 15 2015 - pNA [501+]
PW - v262 - i10 - March 9 2015 - p59(1) [51-500]
Ever After (Read by Potter, Kirsten). Audiobook Review
BL - v112 - i1 - Sept 1 2015 - p138(1) [51-500]
LJ - v140 - i15 - Sept 15 2015 - p41(1) [51-500]
Ever After
BL - v111 - i17 - May 1 2015 - p80(1) [51-500]
Deverell, William - *Sing a Worried Song*
PW - v262 - i8 - Feb 23 2015 - p54(2) [51-500]
DeVine, Christine - *Nineteenth-Century British Travelers in the New World*
VS - v57 - i2 - Wntr 2015 - p357(4) [501+]
Devine, Eric - *Press Play*
c BL - v112 - i1 - Sept 1 2015 - p99(1) [501+]
y CCB-B - v68 - i5 - Jan 2015 - p253(1) [51-500]
RVBW - Feb 2015 - pNA [51-500]
Devine, Jenny Barker - *On Behalf of the Family Farm: Iowa Farm Women's Activism since 1945*
AHR - v120 - i3 - June 2015 - p1061-1062 [501+]
Devine, Shauna - *Learning from the Wounded: The Civil War and the Rise of American Medical Science*
AHR - v120 - i1 - Feb 2015 - p252-253 [501+]
JSH - v81 - i3 - August 2015 - p735(2) [501+]
DeVita, James - *A Winsome Murder*
PW - v262 - i17 - April 27 2015 - p53(1) [51-500]
DeVita, Vincent T. - *The Death of Cancer: After Fifty Years on the Front Lines of Medicine, a Pioneering Oncologist Reveals Why the War on Cancer is Winnable-and How We Can Get There*
BL - v112 - i4 - Oct 15 2015 - p10(1) [51-500]
The Death of Cancer: After Fifty Years on the Front Lines of Medicine, a Pioneering Oncologist Reveals Why the War on Cancer Is Winnable - and How We Can Get There
LJ - v140 - i15 - Sept 15 2015 - p97(1) [501+]
NYTBR - Dec 13 2015 - p14(L) [501+]
The Death of Cancer: After Fifty Years on the Front Lines of Medicine, a Pioneering Oncologist Reveals Why the War on Cancer is Winnable and How We Can Get There
PW - v262 - i35 - August 31 2015 - p73(1) [51-500]
An Unbowed Warrior
NYT - Dec 1 2015 - pD3(L) [501+]
DeVita, Vincent T., Jr. - *The Death of Cancer: After Fifty Years on the Front Lines of Medicine, a Pioneering Oncologist Reveals Why the War on Cancer Is Winnable--and How We Can Get There*
KR - Sept 1 2015 - pNA [501+]
DeVito, Carlo - *Mrs. Lee's Rose Garden: The True Story of the Founding of Arlington National Cemetery*
SPBW - May 2015 - pNA [501+]
Devji, Faisal - *Muslim Zion: Pakistan as a Political Idea*
Historian - v77 - i2 - Summer 2015 - p316(2) [501+]
HNet - Jan 2015 - pNA [501+]
Devlin, Judith - *War of Words: Culture and the Mass Media in the Making of the Cold War in Europe*
CEH - v48 - i1 - March 2015 - p143-144 [501+]
Devlin, Tom - *Drawn and Quarterly: Twenty-Five Years of Contemporary Cartooning, Comics and Graphic Novels*
BL - v111 - i19-20 - June 1 2015 - p66(1) [51-500]
NS - v144 - i5275 - August 14 2015 - p45(1) [51-500]
PW - v262 - i20 - May 18 2015 - p72(1) [51-500]
Devolder, Katrien - *The Ethics of Embryonic Stem Cell Research*
TimHES - i2199 - April 16 2015 - p59(1) [501+]
Devon, Natasha - *The Self Esteem Team's Guide to Sex, Drugs and WTFs?!!*
TES - i5165 - Sept 25 2015 - p15(1) [501+]
DeVor, Danielle - *Sorrow's Point*
PW - v262 - i44 - Nov 2 2015 - p66(1) [51-500]
Devraj, Rajesh - *From Darkness into Light: Perspectives on Film Preservation and Restoration*
Si & So - v25 - i9 - Sept 2015 - p106(1) [501+]
Devroey, Henri - *Histoire de l'Europe editee d'apres les carnets de captivite, 1916-1918*
Med R - August 2015 - pNA [501+]
Dewar, Kenneth C. - *Frank Underhill and the Politics of Ideas*
Nat Post - v17 - i176 - May 30 2015 - pWP4(1) [501+]
Dewar, Laura - *Women and Casualisation: Women's Experiences of Job Insecurity*
TimHES - i2211 - July 9 2015 - p47(1) [501+]
Dewar, Michael - *Leisured Resistance: Villas, Literature and Politics in the Roman World*
Class R - v65 - i1 - April 2015 - p210-212 [501+]
Dewdney, Anna - *Llama Llama Gram and Grandpa (Illus. by Dewdney, Anna)*
c KR - July 15 2015 - pNA [51-500]
Llama Llama Gram and Grandpa
c SLJ - v61 - i9 - Sept 2015 - p110(1) [51-500]
Llama Llama Sand and Sun (Illus. by Dewdney, Anna)
c PW - v262 - i15 - April 13 2015 - p78(2) [501+]
Llama Llama Trick or Treat
c KR - Jan 1 2015 - pNA [51-500]
DeWeese, Christopher - *The Father of the Arrow is the Thought*
PW - v262 - i38 - Sept 21 2015 - p52(1) [51-500]
Dewey, Alicia M. - *Pesos and Dollars: Entrepreneurs in the Texas-Mexico Borderlands, 1880-1940*
JAH - v102 - i2 - Sept 2015 - p576-577 [501+]
WHQ - v46 - i3 - Autumn 2015 - p380-381 [501+]
Pesos and Dollars
RVBW - Jan 2015 - pNA [51-500]
Dewey, Clive - *Steamboats on the Indus: The Limits of Western Technological Superiority in South Asia*
TLS - i5851 - May 22 2015 - p25(1) [501+]
Dewey, Joseph - *Understanding Michael Chabon*
J Am St - v49 - i2 - May 2015 - p453-454 [501+]
Dewey, Richard Lloyd - *Joseph Smith and The Latter-day Saints*
SPBW - Jan 2015 - pNA [51-500]
Dewhurst, Peter - *The Science of the Perfect Swing*
LJ - v140 - i17 - Oct 15 2015 - p109(2) [51-500]
Dewhurst, Richard J. - *The Ancient Giants Who Ruled America: The Missing Skeletons and the Great Smithsonian Cover-Up*
Am Ant - v80 - i3 - July 2015 - p628(2) [501+]
Dewing, Henry B. - *The Wars of Justinian*
Med R - August 2015 - pNA [501+]
DeWitt, Anne - *Moral Authority, Men of Science, and the Victorian Novel*
VS - v57 - i3 - Spring 2015 - p529(5) [501+]
DeWitt, Dave - *The Field Guide to Peppers*
LJ - v140 - i19 - Nov 15 2015 - p105(1) [501+]
Dewitt, Dave - *Microfarming for Profit: From Garden to Glory*
LJ - v140 - i2 - Feb 1 2015 - p101(1) [51-500]
DeWitt, David J. - *Handwriting Analysis: Discover Your Own Vocational/Career Potential*
SPBW - Jan 2015 - pNA [51-500]
SPBW - Feb 2015 - pNA [51-500]
DeWitt, Fowler - *The Amazing Wilmer Dooley: A Mumpley Middle School Mystery (Illus. by Montalvo, Rodolfo)*
c HB Guide - v26 - i1 - Spring 2015 - p75(1) [51-500]
deWitt, Patrick - *Undermajordomo Minor (Read by Prebble, Simon). Audiobook Review*
BL - v112 - i7 - Dec 1 2015 - p69(1) [51-500]
Undermajordomo Minor
y BL - v112 - i2 - Sept 15 2015 - p29(1) [51-500]
Esq - v164 - i2 - Sept 2015 - p56(1) [51-500]
KR - July 15 2015 - pNA [501+]
LJ - v140 - i12 - July 1 2015 - p75(1) [51-500]
NYT - Sept 24 2015 - pC6(L) [501+]
NYTBR - Sept 20 2015 - p17(L) [501+]
PW - v262 - i23 - June 8 2015 - p36(1) [51-500]
Spec - v329 - i9762 - Oct 3 2015 - p44(1) [501+]

DeWoskin, Rachel - *Blind*
    y HB Guide - v26 - i1 - Spring 2015 - p106(1) [51-500]

Deyo, Bentz - *The Undelightened*
    KR - Feb 15 2015 - pNA [501+]

Deyo, Frederic C. - *Reforming Asian Labor Systems: Economic Tensions and Worker Dissent*
    CS - v44 - i4 - July 2015 - p498-499 [501+]

Deyoe, Aaron - *Biggest, Baddest Book of Ghosts*
    c BL - v111 - i16 - April 15 2015 - p45(1) [501+]
    c Teach Lib - v42 - i5 - June 2015 - p9(1) [51-500]
    c HB Guide - v26 - i2 - Fall 2015 - p148(1) [51-500]

DeYoung, Kevin - *The Biggest Story: How the Snake Crusher Brings Us Back to the Garden (Illus. by Clark, Don)*
    c PW - v262 - i49 - Dec 2 2015 - p81(2) [51-500]
What Does the Bible Really Teach about Homosexuality?
    Ch Today - v59 - i6 - July-August 2015 - p91(1) [51-500]

DeYoung, Rebecca Konyndyk - *Vainglory: The Forgotten Vice*
    CC - v132 - i9 - April 29 2015 - p44(2) [501+]

Dezso, Andrea - *The Original Folk and Fairy Tales of the Brothers Grimm: The Complete First Edition*
    TLS - i5841 - March 13 2015 - p3(3) [501+]

Dhami, Narinder - *13 Hours*
    y Sch Lib - v63 - i3 - Autumn 2015 - p180(2) [51-500]

Dhanoa, Belinder - *Echoes in the Well*
    WLT - v89 - i5 - Sept-Oct 2015 - p61(1) [51-500]

Dharker, Imtiaz - *Over the Moon*
    c Sch Lib - v63 - i1 - Spring 2015 - p49(1) [501+]

Dharma - *The Power and Intelligence of Karma and Reincarnation*
    KR - Jan 1 2016 - pNA [501+]

Dhingra, Philip - *Dear Hannah: A Geek's Life in Self-Improvement*
    PW - v262 - i22 - June 1 2015 - p55(1) [51-500]

Dhooge, Bavo - *Styx*
    BL - v112 - i4 - Oct 15 2015 - p24(1) [51-500]
    KR - Sept 1 2015 - pNA [51-500]
    PW - v262 - i39 - Sept 28 2015 - p66(2) [51-500]

D'Hulst, Lieven - *Essais d'histoire de la traduction: avatars de Janus*
    FS - v69 - i3 - July 2015 - p429(1) [501+]

Di Bacco, Giuliano - *Citation, Intertextuality and Memory in the Middle Ages and Renaissance, vol. 2: Cross-Disciplinary Perspectives on Medieval Cultures*
    Ren Q - v68 - i2 - Summer 2015 - p728-730 [501+]

Di Bacco, Guiliano - *Citation, Intertextuality and Memory in the Middle Ages and Renaissance, vol. 2: Cross-Disciplinary Perspectives on Medieval Culture*
    Med R - April 2015 - pNA [501+]

Di Berardino, Angelo - *Historical Atlas of Ancient Christianity*
    SPBW - May 2015 - pNA [51-500]

Di Certo, Joseph J. - *The Saga of the Pony Express*
    RVBW - July 2015 - pNA [51-500]
The Wall People: In Search of a Home
    c CH Bwatch - July 2015 - pNA [51-500]

Di Filippo, Paul - *A Palazzo in the Stars: Science Fiction Stories*
    PW - v262 - i44 - Nov 2 2015 - p65(2) [51-500]

Di Fiore, Mariangela - *Elephant Man (Illus. by Hodnefjeld, Hilde)*
    c KR - June 1 2015 - pNA [51-500]
    c SLJ - v61 - i7 - July 2015 - p102(2) [51-500]

Di Giovanni, Janine - *Eve Arnold*
    LJ - v140 - i15 - Sept 15 2015 - p81(3) [501+]
    NYT - April 19 2015 - p2(L) [501+]

Di Grado, Viola - *Hollow Heart*
    TLS - i5870 - Oct 2 2015 - p21(1) [501+]

Di Leo, Jeffrey - *Corporate Humanities in Higher Education: Moving Beyond the Neoliberal Academy*
    Col Lit - v42 - i2 - Spring 2015 - p337(11) [501+]

Di Paola, Pietro - *The Knights Errant of Anarchy: London and the Italian Anarchist Diaspora*
    HNet - August 2015 - pNA [501+]

Di Paolo, David - *The Artemis Connection*
    KR - Nov 1 2015 - pNA [501+]
    SPBW - Nov 2015 - pNA [51-500]

Di Stefano, Diana L. - *Encounters in Avalanche Country: A History of Survival in the Mountain West, 1820-1920*
    PHR - v84 - i4 - Nov 2015 - p528(3) [501+]
    WHQ - v46 - i3 - Autumn 2015 - p385-386 [501+]

Di Tullio, Matteo - *The Wealth of Communities: War, Resources and Cooperation in Renaissance Lombardy*
    Six Ct J - v46 - i3 - Fall 2015 - p681-683 [501+]

Diagne, Souleymane Bachir - *African Art as Philosophy: Senghor, Bergson and the Idea of Negritude*
    NYTBR - June 28 2015 - p16(L) [501+]

Diamandis, Peter H. - *Bold*
    Har Bus R - v93 - i3 - March 2015 - p126(2) [501+]
Bold: How to Go Big, Create Wealth, and Impact the World (Read by Kotler, Steven). Audiobook Review
    BL - v111 - i21 - July 1 2015 - p79(1) [51-500]

Diamant, Anita - *The Boston Girl (Read by Lavin, Linda). Audiobook Review*
    BL - v111 - i14 - March 15 2015 - p85(1) [51-500]
    LJ - v140 - i10 - June 1 2015 - p60(1) [51-500]
The Boston Girl
    PW - v262 - i8 - Feb 23 2015 - p70(1) [51-500]

Diamant, Jeff - *Heist: The Oddball Crew behind the $17 Million Loomis Fargo Theft*
    BL - v111 - i22 - August 1 2015 - p7(1) [51-500]
    LJ - v140 - i11 - June 15 2015 - p100(2) [51-500]

Diamond, Becky Libourel - *The Thousand Dollar Dinner: America's First Great Cookery Challenge*
    BL - v112 - i3 - Oct 1 2015 - p21(1) [51-500]
    LJ - v140 - i20 - Dec 1 2015 - p124(1) [51-500]
    PW - v262 - i35 - August 31 2015 - p82(1) [51-500]

Diamond, Jared - *The Third Chimpanzee for Young People: On the Evolution and Future of the Human Animal*
    y Sci Teach - v82 - i1 - Jan 2015 - p65 [51-500]

Diamond, Larry - *Democratization and Authoritarianism in the Arab World*
    For Aff - v94 - i1 - Jan-Feb 2015 - pNA [501+]
New Challenges for Maturing Democracies in Korea and Taiwan
    Pac A - v88 - i4 - Dec 2015 - p893 [501+]

Diamond, Seymour - *The Headache Godfather: The Story of Dr. Seymour Diamond and How He Revolutionized the Treatment of Headaches*
    BL - v111 - i9-10 - Jan 1 2015 - p28(1) [51-500]

Diane, Marsha - *Lost. Found. (Illus. by Cordell, Matthew)*
    c PW - v262 - i34 - August 24 2015 - p78(1) [51-500]

Diaz, David R. - *Latino Urbanism: The Politics of Planning, Policy, and Redevelopment*
    Am Q - v67 - i1 - March 2015 - p231-240 [501+]

Diaz, Eva - *The Experimenters: Chance and Design at Black Mountain College*
    Nature - v518 - i7537 - Feb 5 2015 - p33(1) [51-500]

Diaz, Jonathan - *True Heroes: A Treasury of Modern-Day Fairy Tales Written by Best-Selling Authors (Illus. by Diaz, Jonathan)*
    c PW - v262 - i35 - August 31 2015 - p93(1) [501+]
    c SLJ - v61 - i9 - Sept 2015 - p147(1) [51-500]
    c BL - v112 - i1 - Sept 1 2015 - p118(1) [51-500]
True Heroes
    c KR - July 15 2015 - pNA [51-500]

Diaz, Lena - *Exit Strategy*
    PW - v262 - i21 - May 25 2015 - p44(1) [51-500]

Diaz, Linda - *The Wounded Yellow Butterfly*
    KR - March 1 2015 - pNA [501+]

Diaz, Natalia - *A Ticket around the World (Illus. by Owens, Melissa)*
    c KR - Jan 15 2015 - pNA [51-500]
A Ticket around the World (Illus. by Smith, Kim)
    c BL - v111 - i15 - April 1 2015 - p38(1) [51-500]
    c CH Bwatch - August 2015 - pNA [51-500]
    c HB Guide - v26 - i2 - Fall 2015 - p156(1) [51-500]
    c PW - v262 - i9 - March 2 2015 - p84(1) [51-500]
A Ticket around the World (Illus. by Smith, Kim (b. 1986-))
    c Res Links - v20 - i5 - June 2015 - p13(1) [51-500]

Diaz, Stephanie - *Extraction*
    y HB Guide - v26 - i2 - Fall 2015 - p116(1) [1-50]
Rebellion
    y HB Guide - v26 - i2 - Fall 2015 - p116(1) [51-500]

DiBattista, Maria - *Modernism and Autobiography*
    RES - v66 - i276 - Sept 2015 - p795-797 [501+]
    TLS - i5837 - Feb 13 2015 - p26(1) [501+]

Dibb, Carolyn - *Natalie and the Night Sky (Illus. by McAllister, Kent)*
    c KR - Oct 15 2015 - pNA [51-500]

Dibbell, Carola - *The Only Ones*
    PW - v262 - i2 - Jan 12 2015 - p32(1) [51-500]

DiBenedetto, David - *Southerner's Cookbook: Recipes, Wisdom, and Stories*
    NYTBR - Dec 6 2015 - p20(L) [501+]
    NYTBR - Dec 6 2015 - p20(L) [501+]

DiCamillo, Kate - *Francine Poulet Meets the Ghost Raccoon (Read by McInerney, Kathleen). Audiobook Review*
    c BL - v112 - i7 - Dec 1 2015 - p70(2) [51-500]
Francine Poulet Meets the Ghost Raccoon (Read by McInerney, Kathleen). Audiobook Review
    c SLJ - v61 - i11 - Nov 2015 - p69(2) [51-500]
Francine Poulet Meets the Ghost Raccoon (Illus. by Van Dusen, Chris)
    c BL - v111 - i21 - July 1 2015 - p72(1) [51-500]
    c HB - v91 - i5 - Sept-Oct 2015 - p100(1) [51-500]
    c PW - v262 - i24 - June 15 2015 - p85(1) [501+]
    c SLJ - v61 - i7 - July 2015 - p71(1) [51-500]
Francine Poulet Meets the Ghost Raccoon: Tales from Deckawoo Drive, vol. 2 (Illus. by Van Dusen, Chris)
    c KR - June 15 2015 - pNA [51-500]
Leroy Ninker Saddles Up (Read by Morey, Arthur). Audiobook Review
    c BL - v111 - i14 - March 15 2015 - p88(1) [51-500]
Leroy Ninker Saddles Up (Illus. by Van Dusen, Chris)
    c HB Guide - v26 - i1 - Spring 2015 - p59(1) [51-500]

Dicharry, Cate - *The Fine Art of Fucking Up*
    KR - Feb 1 2015 - pNA [501+]

Dichter, Heather L. - *Diplomatic Games: Sport, Statecraft, and International Relations since 1945*
    HNet - July 2015 - pNA [501+]

Dick, Gary L. - *Social Work Practice with Veterans*
    RVBW - Jan 2015 - pNA [51-500]

Dickens, Charles - *A Christmas Carol*
    c KR - Sept 1 2015 - pNA [51-500]
    c SLJ - v61 - i10 - Oct 2015 - p62(1) [51-500]
    World&I - v30 - i12 - Dec 2015 - pNA [501+]
A Christmas Carol (Illus. by Kelley, Gerald)
    c PW - v262 - i37 - Sept 14 2015 - p70(1) [51-500]
    c SLJ - v61 - i10 - Oct 2015 - p62(1) [51-500]
Great Expectations: Manga Classics (Illus. by Poon, Nokman)
    y VOYA - v38 - i4 - Oct 2015 - p54(1) [51-500]
Great Expectations (Illus. by Poon, Nokman)
    Nat R - v67 - i21 - Nov 19 2015 - p83(1) [501+]

Dickenson, Victoria - *Rabbit*
    Am Bio T - v77 - i4 - April 2015 - p301(2) [501+]

Dicker, Katie - *Missing!*
    c SLJ - v61 - i4 - April 2015 - p70(3) [51-500]
    c HB Guide - v26 - i2 - Fall 2015 - p215(1) [51-500]
Mysterious Creatures
    c HB Guide - v26 - i2 - Fall 2015 - p148(1) [51-500]
Mysterious Places
    c HB Guide - v26 - i2 - Fall 2015 - p215(1) [51-500]
Unsolved Crimes
    c HB Guide - v26 - i2 - Fall 2015 - p154(1) [51-500]

Dickerman, Leah - *Jacob Lawrence: The Migration Series*
    NYTBR - June 28 2015 - p11(L) [501+]

Dickerman, Sara - *Bon Appetit: The Food Lover's Cleanse: 140 Delicious, Nourishing Recipes That Will Tempt You Back into Healthful Eating*
    PW - v262 - i52 - Dec 21 2015 - p148(1) [51-500]

Dickerson, James L. - *Mojo Triangle: Birthplace of Country, Blues, Jazz and Rock 'n' Roll*
    RVBW - May 2015 - pNA [51-500]

Dickerson, Melanie - *The Golden Braid*
    y SLJ - v61 - i10 - Oct 2015 - p109(2) [51-500]

Dickerson, William - *Detour: Hollywood*
    KR - April 1 2015 - pNA [51-500]

Dickey, Christopher - *Our Man in Charleston*
    KR - May 1 2015 - pNA [501+]
Our Man in Charleston: Britain's Secret Agent in the Civil War South
    BL - v111 - i19-20 - June 1 2015 - p33(1) [51-500]
    CSM - July 21 2015 - pNA [501+]
    LJ - v140 - i9 - May 15 2015 - p91(1) [51-500]
    NYTBR - July 19 2015 - p13(L) [501+]
    PW - v262 - i20 - May 18 2015 - p76(1) [501+]

Dickey, Eric Jerome - *Naughtier Than Nice*
    BL - v112 - i2 - Sept 15 2015 - p45(1) [51-500]
    KR - August 15 2015 - pNA [51-500]
One Night
    BL - v111 - i13 - March 1 2015 - p29(1) [51-500]
    KR - Feb 15 2015 - pNA [51-500]
    PW - v262 - i5 - Feb 2 2015 - p42(1) [51-500]

Dickey, Jennifer W. - *A Tough Little Patch of History: Gone with the Wind and the Politics of Memory*
    AHR - v120 - i3 - June 2015 - p1067-1068 [501+]
A Tough Little Patch of History: "Gone with the Wind" and the Politics of Memory
    JAH - v101 - i4 - March 2015 - p1330(1) [501+]
A Tough Little Patch of History: Gone with the Wind and the Politics of Memory
    JSH - v81 - i4 - Nov 2015 - p1026(2) [501+]

Dickey, Lisa - *Then Comes Marriage: United States v. Windsor and the Defeat of DOMA*
    BL - v111 - i22 - August 1 2015 - p23(1) [51-500]

Dickey, Page - *Outstanding American Gardens: A Celebration*
    NYTBR - Dec 6 2015 - p66(L) [501+]

Dickie, Lloyd M. - *Awakening Higher Consciousness: Guidance from Ancient Egypt and Sumer*
    Bwatch - July 2015 - pNA [51-500]
    Parabola - v40 - i3 - Fall 2015 - p112-117 [501+]

Dickie, William - *A Window to the Soul*
    KR - Jan 1 2016 - pNA [501+]

Dickinson, Edward Ross - *Sex, Freedom, and Power in Imperial Germany, 1880-1914*
    AHR - v120 - i4 - Oct 2015 - p1569-1570 [501+]
    CEH - v48 - i2 - June 2015 - p262-263 [501+]

Dickinson, Emily - *Complete Poems of Emily Dickinson*
    NYT - August 21 2015 - pC24(L) [501+]

Dickinson, Frederick R. - *World War I and the Triumph of a New Japan, 1919-1930*
    Pac A - v88 - i2 - June 2015 - p319 [501+]

Dickinson, Gail K. - *School Library Management, 7th ed.*
    VOYA - v38 - i2 - June 2015 - p92(1) [51-500]

Dickinson, Gary - *First Day Covers of Canada's 1976 Olympic Games Issues*
    Phil Lit R - v64 - i2 - Spring 2015 - p129(2) [501+]
Seasons of the Maple on First Day Covers
    Phil Lit R - v64 - i2 - Spring 2015 - p131(2) [501+]

Dickinson, Seth - *The Traitor Baru Cormorant*
    KR - July 15 2015 - pNA [501+]
    PW - v262 - i29 - July 20 2015 - p173(1) [51-500]

Dickinson, Tommy - *Curing Queers: Mental Nurses and Their Patients, 1935-74*
    TimHES - i2196 - March 26 2015 - p50-51 [501+]
    TLS - i5841 - March 13 2015 - p9(1) [501+]

Dickmann, Nancy - *Rachel Carson: Environmental Crusader*
    c BL - v112 - i3 - Oct 1 2015 - p62(1) [51-500]

Dicks, Matthew - *The Perfect Comeback of Caroline Jacobs*
    y BL - v112 - i2 - Sept 15 2015 - p28(1) [51-500]
    KR - August 1 2015 - pNA [501+]
    LJ - v140 - i14 - Sept 1 2015 - p90(2) [51-500]

Dickson, Allison, M. - *The Last Supper*
    y VOYA - v37 - i6 - Feb 2015 - p74(1) [51-500]

Dickson, Andrew - *Worlds Elsewhere: Journeys Around Shakespeare's Globe*
    KR - Jan 1 2016 - pNA [501+]
    NS - v144 - i5284 - Oct 16 2015 - p46(2) [501+]

Dickson, David - *Dublin: The Making of a Capital City*
    JIH - v46 - i2 - Autumn 2015 - p280-281 [501+]
Irish Classrooms and British Empire: Imperial Contexts in the Origins of Modern Education
    VS - v57 - i2 - Wntr 2015 - p350(3) [501+]

Dickson, Gordon R. - *Wolf and Iron*
    RVBW - April 2015 - pNA [501+]

Dickson, H. Leighton - *To Journey in the Year of the Tiger*
    PW - v262 - i42 - Oct 19 2015 - p61(1) [51-500]

Dickstein, Morris - *Why Not Say What Happened: A Sentimental Education*
    CHE - v61 - i25 - March 6 2015 - pNA [501+]
    NY - v91 - i3 - March 9 2015 - p95 [51-500]
    NYTBR - March 1 2015 - p18(L) [501+]
    TLS - i5857 - July 3 2015 - p24(1) [501+]

Dicmas, Courtney - *Bathtime (Illus. by Dicmas, Courtney)*
    c KR - July 1 2015 - pNA [51-500]
The Great Googly Moogly
    c HB Guide - v26 - i1 - Spring 2015 - p28(1) [51-500]
Home Tweet Home
    c CH Bwatch - June 2015 - pNA [51-500]
    c HB Guide - v26 - i2 - Fall 2015 - p32(1) [51-500]

Did You Know That I Love You? (Illus. by Pierce, Christa)
    c HB Guide - v26 - i1 - Spring 2015 - p14(1) [51-500]

Diderot, Denis - *Rameau's Nephew: A Multi-Media Edition*
    FS - v69 - i2 - April 2015 - p246-247 [501+]

Didi-Huberman, Georges - *Remontagen der Erlittenen Zeit: Das Auge der Geschichte 2*
    HNet - Jan 2015 - pNA [501+]

Didion, Joan - *Where I Was From*
    TimHES - i2211 - July 9 2015 - p45(1) [501+]

Didriksen, Erik - *Pop Sonnets: Shakespearean Spins on Your Favorite Songs*
    LJ - v140 - i16 - Oct 1 2015 - p78(1) [51-500]

Die "Cantiones Sacrae" (1625) von Heinrich Schutz - Entstehungsbedingungen im konfessionellen Kontext des fruhen 17. Jahrhunderts
    HNet - May 2015 - pNA [501+]

Die Darstellung des Inkommensurablen in der Geschichtskultur des 19. Jahrhunderts
    HNet - May 2015 - pNA [501+]

Die Deutschen Dominikaner und Dominikanerinnen 1221-1515
    HNet - Feb 2015 - pNA [501+]

Die Externsteine. Ein Denkmal als Objekt wissenschaftlicher Forschung und Projektionsflache volkischer Vorstellungen
    HNet - May 2015 - pNA [501+]

Die Herausforderungen des "Kurzen Jahrhunderts": Die Deutsche und Italienische Geschichte und Geschichtswissenschaft zwischen Krieg, Diktatur und Demokratie
    HNet - Jan 2015 - pNA [501+]

Die Interaktion von Herrschern und Eliten in imperialen Ordnungen
    HNet - Sept 2015 - pNA [501+]

Die Klage des Kunstlers
    HNet - Feb 2015 - pNA [501+]

Die Konsumentenstadt - Konsumenten in der Stadt des Mittelalters
    HNet - June 2015 - pNA [501+]

Die Napoleonischen Kriege als Europaischer Erinnerungsort?
    HNet - July 2015 - pNA [501+]

Die Papste und die Einheit der Lateinischen Welt
    HNet - Feb 2015 - pNA [501+]

Die Tondi mit Kaiserbildern in Venedig und Washington, D.C.
    HNet - April 2015 - pNA [501+]

"Die Unsichtbaren": Hilfsberufe in der Medizin und den Naturwissenschaften
    HNet - May 2015 - pNA [501+]

Diederich, Phillippe - *Sofrito*
    RVBW - Nov 2015 - pNA [51-500]

Diedricksen, Derek - *Microshelters: 59 Creative Cabins, Tiny Houses, Tree Houses, and Other Small Structures*
    LJ - v140 - i16 - Oct 1 2015 - p69(1) [51-500]

Diehn, Andi - *Explore Poetry! With 25 Great Projects (Illus. by Stone, Bryan)*
    c PW - v262 - i18 - May 4 2015 - p117(1) [501+]
    SLJ - v61 - i8 - August 2015 - p125(2) [501+]
Technology: Cool Women Who Code (Illus. by Chandhok, Lena)
    c BL - v111 - i22 - August 1 2015 - p54(1) [51-500]

Diekmann, Odo - *Mathematical Tools for Understanding Infectious Disease Dynamics*
    QRB - v90 - i1 - March 2015 - p108(2) [501+]

Dienberg, Thomas - *Heavenward and Worldly: Church and Religious Orders in (Post) Secular Society*
    Theol St - v76 - i2 - June 2015 - p401(2) [501+]

Diepeveen, Leonard - *Mock Modernism: An Anthology of Parodies, Travesties, Frauds, 1910-1935*
    Clio - v44 - i2 - Spring 2015 - p282-288 [501+]

Dierksheide, Christa - *Amelioration and Empire: Progress and Slavery in the Plantation Americas*
    W&M Q - v72 - i4 - Oct 2015 - p697-699 [501+]

Diesen, Deborah - *Kiss, Kiss, Pout-Pout Fish (Illus. by Hanna, Dan)*
    c KR - Jan 1 2016 - pNA [51-500]
The Not Very Merry Pout-Pout Fish (Illus. by Flanna, Dan)
    c SLJ - v61 - i10 - Oct 2015 - p62(1) [51-500]
The Not Very Merry Pout-Pout Fish (Illus. by Hanna, Dan)
    c KR - Sept 1 2015 - pNA [51-500]
    c PW - v262 - i37 - Sept 14 2015 - p64(1) [51-500]

Diesenberger, Maximilian - *Sermo doctorum: Compilers, Preachers, and Their Audiences in the Early Medieval West*
    Med R - Jan 2015 - pNA [501+]

Dieterle, David A. - *Government and the Economy*
    BL - v111 - i11 - Feb 1 2015 - p5(2) [501+]

Dietl, Ralph L. - *Equal Security: Europe and the SALT Process, 1969-1976*
    AHR - v120 - i4 - Oct 2015 - p1548-1549 [501+]
    JAH - v102 - i1 - June 2015 - p299-299 [501+]

Dietrich, Tamara - *The Hummingbird's Cage*
    LJ - v140 - i10 - June 1 2015 - p85(1) [51-500]

Dietz, Dan - *The Complete Book of 1940s Broadway Musicals*
    BL - v112 - i1 - Sept 1 2015 - p24(1) [51-500]
    LJ - v140 - i14 - Sept 1 2015 - p144(1) [51-500]

Dietz, Feike - *Illustrated Religious Texts in the North of Europe, 1500-1800*
    Sev Cent N - v73 - i3-4 - Fall-Winter 2015 - p159(6) [501+]

Dietz, William C. - *Redzone*
    BL - v111 - i21 - July 1 2015 - p47(1) [51-500]
    PW - v262 - i19 - May 11 2015 - p40(1) [51-500]

Dietzel, Chris - *The Theta Prophecy*
    KR - Oct 15 2015 - pNA [51-500]

Diffee, Matthew - *Hand Drawn Jokes for Smart, Attractive People*
    NYTBR - May 31 2015 - p22(L) [501+]

Diffenbaugh, Vanessa - *We Never Asked for Wings (Read by Bering, Emma). Audiobook Review*
    LJ - v140 - i16 - Oct 1 2015 - p42(1) [51-500]
We Never Asked for Wings
    KR - June 15 2015 - pNA [501+]
    LJ - v140 - i13 - August 1 2015 - p81(2) [51-500]

Digantan-Dack, Mine - *Artistic Practice as Research in Music: Theory, Criticism, Practice*
    TimHES - i2211 - July 9 2015 - p48(1) [501+]

Digby Nelson, Joyce - *Mama Used to Say: Change Your Thinking, Change Your Life*
    KR - Jan 1 2016 - pNA [501+]

Digby, Tom - *Love and War: How Militarism Shapes Sexuality and Romance*
    HNet - April 2015 - pNA [501+]

Diggs, Taye - *Mixed Me! (Illus. by Evans, Shane)*
    c BL - v112 - i3 - Oct 1 2015 - p82(2) [501+]
Mixed Me! (Illus. by Evans, Shane W.)
    c KR - August 1 2015 - pNA [51-500]
    c NYTBR - Dec 20 2015 - p15(L) [501+]
    c PW - v262 - i39 - Sept 28 2015 - p90(2) [501+]
    c PW - v262 - i49 - Dec 2 2015 - p31(1) [51-500]
    c SLJ - v61 - i8 - August 2015 - p67(2) [51-500]

Digiacomo, Christine - *Morning Briefings*
    SPBW - April 2015 - pNA [501+]

Dijkhuizen, Jan Frans van - *Pain and Compassion in Early Modern Literature and Culture*
    MLR - v110 - i2 - April 2015 - p512-513 [501+]

Diliberto, Gioia - *Diane von Furstenberg: A Life Unwrapped*
    BL - v111 - i21 - July 1 2015 - p14(1) [501+]
    NYTBR - Nov 8 2015 - p50(L) [501+]

Dilks, David - *The Great Dominion: Winston Churchill in Canada, 1900-1954*
    HT - v65 - i1 - Jan 2015 - p56(2) [501+]

Dill-Shackleford, Karen E. - *Mad Men Unzipped: Fans on Sex, Love, and the Sixties on TV*
    LJ - v140 - i15 - Sept 15 2015 - p75(1) [51-500]

Dillard, Annie - *The Abundance: Narrative Essays Old and New*
    LJ - v140 - i20 - Dec 1 2015 - p100(2) [51-500]
    PW - v262 - i45 - Nov 9 2015 - p48(1) [51-500]

Dillard, Sarah - *Extraordinary Warren Saves the Day (Illus. by Dillard, Sarah)*
    c HB Guide - v26 - i1 - Spring 2015 - p59(1) [51-500]
First Day at Zoo School
    c HB Guide - v26 - i2 - Fall 2015 - p32(1) [51-500]
Mouse Scouts: Make a Difference (Illus. by Dillard, Sarah)
    c SLJ - v61 - i11 - Nov 2015 - p90(1) [51-500]
Mouse Scouts (Illus. by Dillard, Sarah)
    c KR - Oct 1 2015 - pNA [51-500]
    c PW - v262 - i45 - Nov 9 2015 - p60(1) [501+]

Dillard, Sherrie - *Develop Your Medical Intuition: Activate Your Natural Wisdom for Optimum Health and Well-being*
    Bwatch - July 2015 - pNA [51-500]

Dillehay, Tom D. - *The Telescopic Polity: Andean Patriarchy and Materiality*
    Lat Ant - v26 - i3 - Sept 2015 - p424(2) [501+]

Dillemuth, Julie - *Lucy in the City: A Story about Developing Spatial Thinking Skills (Illus. by Wood, Laura)*
    c CH Bwatch - Oct 2015 - pNA [51-500]
    c PW - v262 - i23 - June 8 2015 - p58(1) [501+]

Dilling, Emily - *My Paris Market Cookbook: A Culinary Tour of French Flavors and Seasonal Recipes*
    LJ - v140 - i17 - Oct 15 2015 - p107(1) [51-500]

Dillon, Brian - *The Great Explosion: Gunpowder, the Great War, and a Disaster on the Kent Marshes*
    TimHES - i2209 - June 25 2015 - p49(1) [501+]
    TLS - i5859 - July 17 2015 - p13(1) [501+]

Dillon, Christopher - *Dachau and the SS: A Schooling in Violence*
    TimHES - i2197 - April 2 2015 - p53(1) [501+]

Dillon, Elizabeth Maddock - *New World Drama: The Performative Commons in the Atlantic World, 1649-1849*
    W&M Q - v72 - i3 - July 2015 - p513-516 [501+]
    AHR - v120 - i4 - Oct 2015 - p1450-1451 [501+]

Dillon, Leo - *If Kids Ran the World (Illus. by Dillon, Diane)*
    c CH Bwatch - Jan 2015 - pNA [51-500]
    c HB Guide - v26 - i1 - Spring 2015 - p28(1) [51-500]

Dillon, Mark C. - *The Montana Vigilantes, 1863-1870: Gold, Guns, and Gallows*
 WHQ - v46 - i2 - Summer 2015 - p257-258 [501+]
The Montana Vigilantes, 1863-1870: Golds, Guns, and Gallows
 Roundup M - v22 - i6 - August 2015 - p36(1) [501+]

Dillon, Roxy - *Bio-Young: Get Younger at a Cellular and Hormonal Level*
 BL - v112 - i7 - Dec 1 2015 - p12(1) [51-500]

Dillon, Wilton S. - *Smithsonian Stories: Chronicle of a Golden Age, 1964-1984*
 Soc - v52 - i2 - April 2015 - p181(1) [501+]

Dilloway, Margaret - *Sisters of Heart and Snow (Read by Cronyn, Tandy). Audiobook Review*
 LJ - v140 - i11 - June 15 2015 - p48(2) [51-500]
Sisters of Heart and Snow
 BL - v111 - i14 - March 15 2015 - p56(1) [51-500]
 KR - Feb 1 2015 - pNA [501+]
 LJ - v140 - i6 - April 1 2015 - p82(1) [51-500]

Dilts, Catherine - *Stone Cold Case*
 KR - August 1 2015 - pNA [51-500]

Dilworth, Craig - *Simplicity: A Meta-Metaphysics*
 RM - v68 - i3 - March 2015 - p649(3) [501+]

Dimant, Devorah - *History, Ideology, and Bible Interpretation in the Dead Sea Scrolls: Collected Studies*
 Theol St - v76 - i1 - March 2015 - p167(3) [501+]

Dimbleby, Jonathan - *The Battle of the Atlantic: How the Allies Won the War*
 KR - Jan 1 2016 - pNA [501+]

Dimechkie, Karim - *Lifted by the Great Nothing*
 BL - v111 - i13 - March 1 2015 - p20(1) [51-500]
 KR - March 15 2015 - pNA [51-500]
 PW - v262 - i13 - March 30 2015 - p50(1) [51-500]

DiMeo, Philip F. - *Binoculars: Masquerading as a Sighted Person*
 RVBW - June 2015 - pNA [501+]

DiMicco, Dan - *American Made: Why Making Things Will Return Us to Greatness*
 BL - v111 - i11 - Feb 1 2015 - p6(1) [51-500]

Dimier, Veronique - *The Invention of a European Development Aid Bureaucracy: Recycling Empire*
 HNet - March 2015 - pNA [501+]

Dimitrov, Martin K. - *Why Communism Did Not Collapse: Understanding Authoritarian Regime Resilience in Asia and Europe*
 Pac A - v88 - i1 - March 2015 - p159 [501+]

Dimmock, Matthew - *Mythologies of the Prophet Muhammad in Early Modern English Culture*
 MP - v112 - i4 - May 2015 - pE298(3) [501+]

Dimodica, Steve - *The Einstein Proxy*
 KR - July 1 2015 - pNA [501+]

Dimon, HelenKay - *Facing Fire*
 BL - v112 - i4 - Oct 15 2015 - p26(1) [51-500]
 PW - v262 - i27 - July 6 2015 - p53(1) [51-500]
Falling Hard
 BL - v111 - i18 - May 15 2015 - p31(1) [51-500]
Mine
 PW - v262 - i33 - August 17 2015 - p56(1) [51-500]

Dimopoulos, Elaine - *Material Girls*
 y HB Guide - v26 - i2 - Fall 2015 - p116(1) [51-500]
 y KR - March 1 2015 - pNA [51-500]
 y SLJ - v61 - i5 - May 2015 - p118(1) [51-500]
 y VOYA - v38 - i1 - April 2015 - p77(1) [51-500]

Dimou, Nikos - *Unhappiness of Being Greek*
 TimHES - i2218 - August 27 2015 - p43(1) [501+]

Din, Gilbert C. - *Populating the Barrera: Spanish Immigration Efforts in Colonial Louisiana*
 JSH - v81 - i3 - August 2015 - p695(2) [501+]

Dinardo, Jeff - *The Sunrise Band (Illus. by Palen, Debbie)*
 c HB Guide - v26 - i1 - Spring 2015 - p51(2) [51-500]

Diner, Hasia R. - *1929: Mapping the Jewish World*
 AHR - v120 - i1 - Feb 2015 - p193-194 [501+]
Roads Taken: The Great Jewish Migrations to the New World and the Peddlers Who Forged the Way
 CHE - v61 - i24 - Feb 27 2015 - pNA [501+]
 HT - v65 - i1 - Jan 2015 - p65(1) [501+]
 TimHES - i2196 - March 26 2015 - p52(1) [501+]

Dinerstein, Rebecca - *Finding Inspiration at the Top of the World*
 PW - v262 - i2 - Jan 12 2015 - p27(5) [501+]
The Sunlit Night
 KR - April 1 2015 - pNA [51-500]
 BL - v111 - i14 - March 15 2015 - p56(1) [51-500]
 LJ - v140 - i7 - April 15 2015 - p75(1) [51-500]
 NY - v91 - i27 - Sept 14 2015 - p91 [501+]
 NYTBR - Sept 13 2015 - p34(L) [501+]
 PW - v262 - i2 - Jan 12 2015 - p33(1) [51-500]

Dinets, Vladimir - *Peterson Field Guide to Finding Mammals in North America*
 LJ - v140 - i12 - July 1 2015 - p111(3) [51-500]

Dingeldein, Noelle - *Walter's Wheels*
 c KR - Jan 1 2016 - pNA [51-500]

Dingle, Hughp - *Migration: The Biology of Life on the Move by Hugh Dingle*
 QRB - v90 - i2 - June 2015 - p223(1) [501+]

Dini, Paul - *Bloodspell*
 LJ - v140 - i15 - Sept 15 2015 - p60(3) [501+]

Dini, Pietro U. - *Prelude to Baltic Linguistics: Earliest Theories about Baltic Languages*
 Slav R - v74 - i2 - Summer 2015 - p387-388 [501+]

Dinkelspiel, Frances - *Tangled Vines: Greed, Murder, Obsession, and an Arsonist in the Vineyards of California*
 KR - Sept 15 2015 - pNA [501+]
 LJ - v140 - i16 - Oct 1 2015 - p92(2) [51-500]
 NYTBR - Dec 6 2015 - p86(L) [501+]

Dinkova-Bruun, Greti - *Catalogus Translationum et Commentariorum: Medieval and Renaissance Latin Translations and Commentaries*
 Sev Cent N - v73 - i3-4 - Fall-Winter 2015 - p208(4) [501+]

Dinnison, Kris - *You and Me and Him*
 y BL - v111 - i18 - May 15 2015 - p54(2) [51-500]
 y CCB-B - v69 - i2 - Oct 2015 - p84(2) [51-500]
 y HB - v91 - i4 - July-August 2015 - p131(1) [51-500]
 y KR - April 15 2015 - pNA [51-500]
 y PW - v262 - i18 - May 4 2015 - p123(1) [51-500]
 y SLJ - v61 - i4 - April 2015 - p162(1) [51-500]
 y VOYA - v38 - i2 - June 2015 - p57(2) [51-500]

Dinshah, H. Jay - *Powerful Vegan Messages*
 Veg J - v34 - i1 - Jan-March 2015 - p31(1) [51-500]

Dinshaw, Carolyn - *How Soon Is Now? Medieval Texts, Amateur Readers, and the Queerness of Time*
 Specu - v90 - i4 - Oct 2015 - p1106-1108 [501+]

Dinsmoor, Rob - *You Can Leave Anytime*
 KR - Oct 1 2015 - pNA [501+]

Dionne, Erin - *Ollie and the Science of Treasure Hunting: A 14-Day Mystery*
 c HB Guide - v26 - i2 - Fall 2015 - p80(1) [51-500]

Dionne Jr., E.J. - *Why the Right Went Wrong: Conservatism--from Goldwater to the Tea Party and Beyond*
 KR - Dec 15 2015 - pNA [501+]

DiOrio, Rana - *What Does It Mean to Be Kind? (Illus. by Jorisch, Stephane)*
 c CH Bwatch - Oct 2015 - pNA [51-500]

Diouf, Sylviane A. - *Slavery's Exiles: The Story of the American Maroons*
 J Am St - v49 - i1 - Feb 2015 - p195-197 [501+]
 JAH - v102 - i2 - Sept 2015 - p552-553 [501+]
 JSH - v81 - i3 - August 2015 - p697(2) [501+]

DiPiazza, Francesca Davis - *Remaking the John: The Invention and Reinvention of the Toilet*
 y HB Guide - v26 - i2 - Fall 2015 - p185(1) [51-500]

DiPrete, Thomas A. - *The Rise of Women: The Growing Gender Gap in Education and What It Means for American Schools*
 CS - v44 - i1 - Jan 2015 - p52-54 [501+]

Diprimio, Pete - *Neil deGrasse Tyson*
 c SLJ - v61 - i10 - Oct 2015 - p125(1) [51-500]

DiPucchio, Kelly - *Everyone Loves Bacon (Illus. by Wight, Eric)*
 c KR - June 15 2015 - pNA [51-500]
 c PW - v262 - i25 - June 22 2015 - p136(1) [51-500]

Dipucchio, Kelly - *Everyone Loves Bacon (Illus. by Wright, Eric)*
 c SLJ - v61 - i7 - July 2015 - p61(2) [51-500]

DiPucchio, Kelly - *Zombie in Love 2 + 1 (Illus. by Campbell, Scott)*
 c HB Guide - v26 - i2 - Fall 2015 - p32(1) [51-500]

Dirck, Brian R. - *Abraham Lincoln and White America*
 RVBW - August 2015 - pNA [501+]

Dirda, Michael - *Browsings: A Year of Reading, Collecting, and Living with Books (Read by Lescault, John). Audiobook Review*
 BL - v112 - i6 - Nov 15 2015 - p60(1) [51-500]
Browsings: A Year of Reading, Collecting, and Living with Books
 BL - v111 - i21 - July 1 2015 - p4(1) [51-500]
 KR - June 1 2015 - pNA [51-500]
 LJ - v140 - i10 - June 15 2015 - p88(2) [51-500]
 NYTBR - August 23 2015 - p38(L) [501+]
 PW - v262 - i25 - June 22 2015 - p133(1) [51-500]
 TLS - i5872 - Oct 16 2015 - p26(1) [51-500]

Disabato, Catie - *The Ghost Network*
 KR - March 15 2015 - pNA [51-500]
 LJ - v140 - i6 - April 1 2015 - p76(3) [501+]
 LJ - v140 - i8 - May 1 2015 - p61(1) [51-500]
 NYTBR - June 21 2015 - p14(L) [501+]
 PW - v262 - i11 - March 16 2015 - p64(1) [51-500]
 TLS - i5854 - June 12 2015 - p11(2) [501+]

DiSalvo, Daniel - *Government against Itself: Public Union Power and its Consequences*
 Dis - v62 - i4 - Fall 2015 - p166(4) [501+]
 Nat R - v67 - i3 - Feb 23 2015 - p37 [501+]
 Soc - v52 - i4 - August 2015 - p387(3) [501+]

Disaster Science Series
 c BL - v111 - i15 - April 1 2015 - p58(1) [501+]

The Disasters of Violence, War and Extremism
 HNet - August 2015 - pNA [501+]

Disher, Garry - *Hell to Pay*
 RVBW - Feb 2015 - pNA [51-500]

DiSiena, Laura Lyn - *Dinosaurs Live On! And Other Fun Facts (Illus. by Spurgeon, Aaron)*
 c HB Guide - v26 - i2 - Fall 2015 - p168(1) [51-500]

Disiena, Laura Lyn - *Dinosaurs Live On! And Other Fun Facts (Illus. by Spurgeon, Aaron)*
 c SLJ - v61 - i6 - June 2015 - p134(1) [51-500]

DiSiena, Laura Lyn - *Frogs Play Cellos: And Other Fun Facts (Illus. by Oswald, Pete)*
 c HB Guide - v26 - i1 - Spring 2015 - p180(1) [51-500]
Rainbows Never End: And Other Fun Facts (Illus. by Oswald, Pete)
 c HB Guide - v26 - i1 - Spring 2015 - p151(1) [51-500]
Saturn Could Sail: And Other Fun Facts (Illus. by Oswald, Pete)
 c HB Guide - v26 - i2 - Fall 2015 - p164(1) [51-500]
Trains Can Float: And Other Fun Facts (Illus. by Oswald, Pete)
 c HB Guide - v26 - i1 - Spring 2015 - p172(1) [51-500]

DiSilverio, Laura - *The Readaholics and the Poirot Puzzle*
 BL - v112 - i7 - Dec 1 2015 - p31(1) [51-500]
The Reckoning Stones
 PW - v262 - i30 - July 27 2015 - p45(1) [51-500]

Dismondy, Maria - *Chocolate Milk, Por Favor: Celebrating Diversity with Empathy (Illus. by Farrell, Donna)*
 c CH Bwatch - May 2015 - pNA [51-500]

Dispenza, Mary - *Split*
 KR - Sept 15 2015 - pNA [51-500]

Dispossession: The Plundering of German Jewry, 1933-1945 and Beyond
 HNet - Feb 2015 - pNA [501+]

Distler, Dixie - *The Life and Times of Bob Cratchit*
 KR - Oct 1 2015 - pNA [51-500]

DiTerlizzi Angela - *Baby Love (Illus. by Hughes, Brooke Boynton)*
 c HB Guide - v26 - i2 - Fall 2015 - p9(1) [51-500]

DiTerlizzi, Tony - *Star Wars: The Adventures of Luke Skywalker, Jedi Knight (Illus. by McQuarrie, Ralph)*
 c HB Guide - v26 - i1 - Spring 2015 - p28(1) [51-500]

DiTomaso, Nancy - *The American Non-Dilemma: Racial Inequality Without Racism*
 CS - v44 - i3 - May 2015 - p356-358 [501+]

Dittmar, Kelly - *Navigating Gendered Terrain: Stereotypes and Strategy in Political Campaigns*
 CS - v44 - i5 - Sept 2015 - p743(1) [501+]

Dittmer, Jason - *Comic Book Geographies*
 GR - v105 - i3 - July 2015 - p380(4) [501+]

Diver, Lucas - *Austin Mahone: Famous Pop Singer and Songwriter*
 c HB Guide - v26 - i2 - Fall 2015 - p208(1) [51-500]
Katy Perry: Famous Pop Singer and Songwriter
 c HB Guide - v26 - i2 - Fall 2015 - p208(1) [51-500]
One Direction: Popular Boy Band
 c HB Guide - v26 - i2 - Fall 2015 - p208(1) [51-500]
Ross Lynch: Disney Channel Actor
 c HB Guide - v26 - i2 - Fall 2015 - p208(1) [51-500]
Rowan Blanchard: Star of Girl Meets World
 c HB Guide - v26 - i2 - Fall 2015 - p208(1) [51-500]
Zendaya: Disney Channel Actress
 c HB Guide - v26 - i2 - Fall 2015 - p208(1) [51-500]

The Divine
 NYTBR - Oct 18 2015 - p30(L) [501+]

Diwan, Ishac - *Understanding the Political Economy of the Arab Uprisings*
 For Aff - v94 - i1 - Jan-Feb 2015 - pNA [501+]

Dixie, Quinton Hosford - *Witness: Two Hundred Years of African-American Faith and Practice at the Abyssinian Baptist Church of Harlem, New York*
 CH - v84 - i4 - Dec 2015 - p908(3) [501+]

Dixon, Amy - *Sophie's Animal Parade (Illus. by Wish, Katia)*
   c PW - v262 - i10 - March 9 2015 - p70(1) [51-500]
   c SLJ - v61 - i7 - July 2015 - p62(1) [51-500]
Dixon, Franklin W. - *The Battle of Bayport*
   c HB Guide - v26 - i1 - Spring 2015 - p75(1) [51-500]
Deception on the Set
   c HB Guide - v26 - i2 - Fall 2015 - p80(1) [51-500]
Shadows at Predator Reef
   c HB Guide - v26 - i2 - Fall 2015 - p80(1) [51-500]
Dixon, Heather - *Illusionarium*
   y HB - v91 - i3 - May-June 2015 - p108(1) [501+]
   y HB Guide - v26 - i2 - Fall 2015 - p116(1) [51-500]
   y PW - v262 - i49 - Dec 2 2015 - p102(2) [51-500]
   y SLJ - v61 - i2 - Feb 2015 - p99(2) [51-500]
   y VOYA - v38 - i1 - April 2015 - p77(1) [51-500]
Dixon, John - *Devil's Pocket*
     PW - v262 - i25 - June 22 2015 - p120(2) [51-500]
   y SLJ - v61 - i8 - August 2015 - p113(1) [51-500]
Dixon, Juli K. - *Beyond the Common Core: A Handbook for Mathematics in a PLC at Work, Grades K-5*
     TC Math - v22 - i2 - Sept 2015 - p115(1) [501+]
Dixon, Leif - *Practical Predestinarians in England, c. 1590-1640*
     Sev Cent N - v73 - i3-4 - Fall-Winter 2015 - p179(5) [501+]
Dixon, Thomas - *Weeping Britannia: Portrait of a Nation in Tears*
     Spec - v329 - i9763 - Oct 10 2015 - p41(1) [501+]
     TimHES - i2223 - Oct 1 2015 - p52(1) [501+]
Dixon, Wheeler Winston - *Black & White Cinema: A Short History*
     LJ - v140 - i19 - Nov 15 2015 - p86(1) [51-500]
Dizon, Louella - *The Underground Labyrinth*
   c CH Bwatch - Feb 2015 - pNA [51-500]
DJ Ross One - *Rap Tees: A Collection of Hip-Hop T-Shirts 1980-1999*
     NYT - Nov 17 2015 - pC1(L) [501+]
d'Jeranian, Olivier - *Epictete: Sentences et fragments*
     Class R - v65 - i2 - Oct 2015 - p609-610 [501+]
Djerassi, Carl - *In Retrospect: From the Pill to the Pen*
     J Chem Ed - v92 - i5 - May 2015 - p785-787 [501+]
Djuric-Milovanovic, Aleksandra - *Dvostruke manjine u Srbiji: O posebnostima u religiji i etnicitetu Rumuna u Vojvodini*
     HNet - Oct 2015 - pNA [501+]
DK - *Careers: The Graphic Guide to Finding the Perfect Job for You*
   y BL - v111 - i18 - May 15 2015 - p44(1) [51-500]
   y SLJ - v61 - i6 - June 2015 - p70(2) [51-500]
   y VOYA - v38 - i3 - August 2015 - p92(1) [501+]
World War II: The Definitive Visual History
   y BL - v111 - i18 - May 15 2015 - p17(1) [501+]
DK Publishing - *Are You What You Eat? A Guide to What's on Your Plate and Why!*
   c SLJ - v61 - i6 - June 2015 - p139(2) [51-500]
Musicals: The Definitive Illustrated Story
     LJ - v140 - i20 - Dec 1 2015 - p99(1) [501+]
Paper Craft
     LJ - v140 - i19 - Nov 15 2015 - p82(1) [51-500]
SENSEational Illusions
   c KR - Dec 1 2015 - pNA [51-500]
Sophie's Big Noisy Day Book
   c KR - Dec 1 2015 - pNA [51-500]
DK Publishing, Inc. - *Handmade Interiors: Create Your Own Soft Furnishings from Cushions to Curtains*
     LJ - v140 - i14 - Sept 1 2015 - p106(2) [51-500]
History of the World in 1,000 Objects
     LJ - v140 - i9 - May 15 2015 - p94(2) [501+]
Dlabacova, Anna - *Literatuur en observantie: De "Spieghel der volcomenheit" van Hendrik Herp en de dynamiek van laatmiddeleeuwse tekstverspreiding*
     Specu - v90 - i3 - July 2015 - p796-797 [501+]
D'Lacey, Chris - *Alexander's Army (Read by Corkhill, Raphael). Audiobook Review*
   c SLJ - v61 - i9 - Sept 2015 - p58(2) [51-500]
d'Lacey, Chris - *Alexander's Army*
   c BL - v111 - i15 - April 1 2015 - p76(1) [51-500]
D'Lacey, Chris - *Alexander's Army*
   c HB Guide - v26 - i2 - Fall 2015 - p80(1) [51-500]
   y KR - Feb 15 2015 - pNA [51-500]
   c SLJ - v61 - i7 - July 2015 - p74(2) [51-500]
Do Nice. Be Kind. Spread Happy
   c PW - v262 - i30 - July 27 2015 - p70(1) [501+]
Do You Know? Tigers
   c SLJ - v61 - i7 - July 2015 - p101(1) [51-500]
Doak, Robin S. - *Malala Yousafzai*
   c BL - v111 - i19-20 - June 1 2015 - p90(1) [51-500]
A True Book: Biographies
   c SLJ - v61 - i12 - Dec 2015 - p135(1) [51-500]

Doak, Tom - *The Confidential Guide to Golf Courses*
     Esq - v163 - i4 - April 2015 - p40(1) [501+]
Doan, Laura - *Disturbing Practices: History, Sexuality, and Women's Experience of Modern War*
     Clio - v44 - i2 - Spring 2015 - p266-271 [501+]
Doan, Lisa - *Jack and the Wild Life (Illus. by Stevanovic, Ivica)*
   c HB Guide - v26 - i2 - Fall 2015 - p80(1) [51-500]
Jack at the Helm (Illus. by Stevanovic, Ivica)
   c HB Guide - v26 - i2 - Fall 2015 - p80(1) [51-500]
Dobbernack, Jan - *Tolerance, Intolerance and Respect: Hard to Accept?*
     ERS - v38 - i8 - August 2015 - p1447(3) [501+]
Dobbs, Maisie - *A Dangerous Place*
     NYTBR - March 22 2015 - p29(L) [501+]
Dobbs, Richard - *No Ordinary Disruption: The Four Global Forces Breaking All the Trends*
     KR - April 1 2015 - pNA [51-500]
     LJ - v140 - i6 - April 1 2015 - p100(2) [51-500]
Doblin, Alfred - *The Three Leaps of Wang-lun*
     TLS - i5871 - Oct 9 2015 - p25(1) [501+]
Dobransky, Kerry Michael - *Managing Madness in the Community: The Challenge of Contemporary Mental Health Care*
     AJS - v121 - i3 - Nov 2015 - p990(3) [501+]
Dobrow, Larry - *Derek Jeter's Ultimate Baseball Guide 2015 (Illus. by Jones, Damien)*
   c SLJ - v61 - i5 - May 2015 - p130(1) [51-500]
Dobski, Bernard J. - *Shakespeare and the Body Politic*
     Six Ct J - v46 - i1 - Spring 2015 - p207-208 [501+]
Dobson, Melanie - *Shadows of Ladenbrooke Manor*
     PW - v262 - i12 - March 23 2015 - p56(1) [51-500]
Dobson, Michael Singer - *How To Get into a Military Service Academy: A Step-by-Step Guide to Getting Qualified, Nominated, and Appointed*
     LJ - v140 - i17 - Oct 15 2015 - p98(2) [51-500]
Dobson, Wendy - *Partners and Rivals: The Uneasy Future of China's Relationship with the United States*
     Pac A - v88 - i2 - June 2015 - p289 [501+]
Dobyns, Stephen - *Is Fat Bob Dead Yet?*
     BL - v112 - i2 - Sept 15 2015 - p32(1) [51-500]
     KR - July 1 2015 - pNA [51-500]
     LJ - v140 - i13 - August 1 2015 - p82(1) [51-500]
     PW - v262 - i30 - July 27 2015 - p42(1) [51-500]
Docherty, Helen - *Abracazebra (Illus. by Docherty, Thomas)*
   c Sch Lib - v63 - i2 - Summer 2015 - p91(1) [51-500]
Docherty, Thomas - *Universities at War*
     TimHES - i2190 - Feb 12 2015 - p50(1) [501+]
Dochuk, Darren - *American Evangelicalism: George Marsden and the State of American Religious History*
     CH - v84 - i4 - Dec 2015 - p928(3) [501+]
     PHR - v84 - i4 - Nov 2015 - pNA [501+]
Dockrill, Laura - *Lorali*
   y Magpies - v30 - i4 - Sept 2015 - p40(1) [51-500]
Dockter, Debra - *Deadly Design*
   y BL - v111 - i18 - May 15 2015 - p61(1) [51-500]
   y CCB-B - v69 - i1 - Sept 2015 - p18(2) [51-500]
   y HB Guide - v26 - i2 - Fall 2015 - p117(1) [51-500]
     KR - April 1 2015 - pNA [51-500]
     SLJ - v61 - i4 - April 2015 - p162(1) [51-500]
   y VOYA - v38 - i2 - June 2015 - p73(2) [51-500]
Dockter, Warren - *Churchill and the Islamic World: Orientalism, Empire and Diplomacy in the Middle East*
     HT - v65 - i11 - Nov 2015 - p63(2) [501+]
     TimHES - i2203 - May 14 2015 - p48(1) [501+]
     TLS - i5864-5865 - August 21 2015 - p29(1) [501+]
Winston Churchill and the Islamic World: Orientalism, Empire and Diplomacy in the Middle East
     HT - v65 - i1 - Jan 2015 - p56(2) [501+]
Doctor Dread - *The Half That's Never Been Told: The Real-Life Reggae Adventures of Doctor Dread*
   y BL - v111 - i12 - Feb 15 2015 - p18(1) [501+]
Dodd, Christina - *Obsession Falls*
     BL - v112 - i1 - Sept 1 2015 - p54(1) [51-500]
     KR - July 1 2015 - pNA [51-500]
     PW - v262 - i28 - July 13 2015 - p52(1) [51-500]
Virtue Falls (Read by Soler, Rebecca). Audiobook Review
     BL - v111 - i12 - Feb 15 2015 - p104(1) [51-500]

Dodd, Emma - *Always (Illus. by Dodd, Emma)*
   c HB Guide - v26 - i1 - Spring 2015 - p8(1) [51-500]
The Entertainer (Illus. by Dodd, Emma)
   c HB Guide - v26 - i2 - Fall 2015 - p32(1) [51-500]
   c KR - April 15 2015 - pNA [51-500]
   c SLJ - v61 - i8 - August 2015 - p68(1) [51-500]
Everything (Illus. by Dodd, Emma)
   c SLJ - v61 - i5 - May 2015 - p79(1) [51-500]
Everything
   c HB Guide - v26 - i2 - Fall 2015 - p9(1) [51-500]
Happy! (Illus. by Dodd, Emma)
   c SLJ - v61 - i12 - Dec 2015 - p84(2) [51-500]
More and More (Illus. by Dodd, Emma)
   c HB Guide - v26 - i1 - Spring 2015 - p8(1) [51-500]
When I Grow Up (Illus. by Dodd, Emma)
   c SLJ - v61 - i11 - Nov 2015 - p76(1) [51-500]
When You Were Born (Illus. by Dodd, Emma)
   c SLJ - v61 - i5 - May 2015 - p79(1) [51-500]
When You Were Born
   c HB Guide - v26 - i2 - Fall 2015 - p9(1) [51-500]
Wish
   c KR - Oct 15 2015 - pNA [51-500]
Dodd, Nigel - *The Social Life of Money*
     Soc - v52 - i1 - Feb 2015 - p86(1) [501+]
Dodd, Philip - *Englishness: Politics and Culture, 1880-1920, 2d ed.*
     HT - v65 - i3 - March 2015 - p60(2) [501+]
Dodge, Trevor - *The Laws of Average*
     ABR - v36 - i2 - Jan-Feb 2015 - p20(2) [501+]
Dodgen, Charles E. - *Simple Lessons for a Better Life*
     BL - v111 - i17 - May 1 2015 - p64(1) [51-500]
Simple Lessons for a Better Life: Unexpected Inspiration from Inside the Nursing Home
     PW - v262 - i12 - March 23 2015 - p65(1) [51-500]
Dodier, Sylvain - *Un Arbre (Illus. by Pallegoix, Luc)*
   c Res Links - v20 - i4 - April 2015 - p39(2) [501+]
Dodson, Scott - *The Legacy of Ruth Bader Ginsburg*
     LJ - v140 - i7 - April 15 2015 - p104(1) [51-500]
Dodson, Zachary Thomas - *Bats of the Republic*
     BL - v112 - i4 - Oct 15 2015 - p30(2) [51-500]
     KR - August 1 2015 - pNA [501+]
     PW - v262 - i33 - August 17 2015 - p46(1) [51-500]
Doe, Sue - *Generation Vet: Composition, Student Veterans, and the Post-9/11 University*
     HNet - May 2015 - pNA [501+]
Doeden, Matt - *All about Baseball*
   c SLJ - v61 - i4 - April 2015 - p97(4) [501+]
All about Football
   c HB Guide - v26 - i2 - Fall 2015 - p198(1) [51-500]
All about Hockey
   c HB Guide - v26 - i2 - Fall 2015 - p198(1) [51-500]
At Battle in World War II: An Interactive Battlefield Adventure
   c HB Guide - v26 - i2 - Fall 2015 - p217(1) [51-500]
The College Football Championship: The Fight for the Top Spot
   c BL - v112 - i1 - Sept 1 2015 - p98(1) [51-500]
   c KR - August 15 2015 - pNA [51-500]
   c SLJ - v61 - i10 - Oct 2015 - p133(1) [51-500]
GoPro Inventor Nick Woodman
   c HB Guide - v26 - i2 - Fall 2015 - p208(1) [51-500]
Impact: The Story of the September 11 Terrorist Attacks
   y SLJ - v61 - i9 - Sept 2015 - p151(4) [501+]
Malala Yousafzai: Shot by the Taliban, Still Fighting for Equal Education
   c HB Guide - v26 - i1 - Spring 2015 - p192(1) [51-500]
Nelson Mandela: World Leader for Human Rights
   c HB Guide - v26 - i1 - Spring 2015 - p192(1) [51-500]
Outrageous Football Rivalries
   c HB Guide - v26 - i2 - Fall 2015 - p198(1) [51-500]
Searchlight Books: What Are Energy Sources? Series
   c HB Guide - v26 - i1 - Spring 2015 - p172(2) [51-500]
SpaceX and Tesla Motors Engineer Elon Musk
     BL - v111 - i14 - March 15 2015 - p63(1) [51-500]
   c HB Guide - v26 - i2 - Fall 2015 - p208(1) [51-500]
Theoretical Physicist Brian Greene
   c HB Guide - v26 - i2 - Fall 2015 - p208(1) [51-500]
Whistle-Blowers: Exposing Crime and Corruption
   y KR - Jan 15 2015 - pNA [51-500]
Doeden, Matt Whistle-Blowers - *Exposing Crime and Corruption*
   y HB Guide - v26 - i2 - Fall 2015 - p154(1) [51-500]
Doellinger, David - *Turning Prayers into Protests: Religious-Based Activism and Its Challenge to State Power in Socialist Slovakia and East Germany*
     AHR - v120 - i1 - Feb 2015 - p354(1) [501+]
     CEH - v48 - i3 - Sept 2015 - p447-448 [501+]

Doerr, Anthony - *All the Light We Cannot See*
    BL - v111 - i16 - April 15 2015 - p34(1) [501+]
    CC - v132 - i9 - April 29 2015 - p3(1) [501+]
    CSM - April 16 2015 - pNA [51-500]
    c PW - v262 - i52 - Dec 21 2015 - p152(2) [51-500]

Doerrfeld, Cori - *Maggie and Wendel: Imagine Everything!* (Illus. by Doerrfeld, Cori)
    c KR - Dec 15 2015 - pNA [51-500]
    c PW - v262 - i52 - Dec 21 2015 - p152(2) [51-500]

Doerries, Bryan - *All That You've Seen Here Is God*
    LJ - v140 - i13 - August 1 2015 - p92(1) [51-500]
    Bks & Cult - v21 - i6 - Nov-Dec 2015 - p11(2) [501+]
The Theater of War: What Ancient Greek Tragedies Can Teach Us Today
    KR - June 15 2015 - pNA [501+]
    Bks & Cult - v21 - i6 - Nov-Dec 2015 - p11(2) [501+]
    BL - v111 - i22 - August 1 2015 - p18(1) [51-500]
    NYT - Sept 29 2015 - pD3(L) [501+]
    NYTBR - Oct 4 2015 - p21(L) [501+]
    PW - v262 - i21 - May 25 2015 - p46(1) [51-500]
The Theatre of War: What Ancient Greek Tragedies Can Teach Us Today
    NS - v144 - i5290 - Nov 27 2015 - p51(1) [51-500]

Doescher, Ian - *William Shakespeare's Star Wars Collection* (Read by Various readers). Audiobook Review
    c BL - v111 - i14 - March 15 2015 - p24(2) [501+]
    LJ - v140 - i5 - March 15 2015 - p134(1) [501+]
William Shakespeare's Star Wars: William Shakespeare's Star Wars, William Shakespeare's The Empire Striketh Back, and William Shakespeare's The Jedi Doth Return (Read by Davis, Daniel). Audiobook Review
    BL - v111 - i18 - May 15 2015 - p71(1) [51-500]
William Shakespeare's Tragedy of the Sith's Revenge: Star Wars Part the Third
    NYT - Dec 25 2015 - pC29(L) [501+]

Dog, Tieraona Low - *Fortify Your Life: Your Guide to Vitamins, Minerals, and More*
    PW - v262 - i44 - Nov 2 2015 - p80(1) [51-500]

Doggett, Peter - *Electric Shock: From the Gramophone to the iPhone: 125 Years of Pop Music*
    Spec - v328 - i9756 - August 22 2015 - p37(1) [501+]

Doh, Jenny - *More Creative Lettering: Techniques and Tips from Top Artists*
    LJ - v140 - i14 - Sept 1 2015 - p104(1) [51-500]

Doherty, Berlie - *Far from Home: The Sisters of Street Child*
    c Sch Lib - v63 - i2 - Summer 2015 - p102(1) [51-500]

Doherty, Gabriel - *The Home Rule Crisis, 1912-14*
    ILS - v35 - i1 - Fall 2015 - p9(2) [501+]

Doherty, Paul - *The Herald of Hell*
    KR - Nov 15 2015 - pNA [51-500]
    PW - v262 - i44 - Nov 2 2015 - p63(2) [51-500]

Doherty, Peter - *The Shaolin Cowboy: Shemp Buffet*
    PW - v262 - i14 - April 6 2015 - p47(1) [51-500]

Doherty, Simon - *The Indian Corps on the Western Front: A Handbook and Battlefield Guide*
    J Mil H - v79 - i2 - April 2015 - p509-510 [501+]

Doherty, Thomas - *Hollywood and Hitler, 1933-1939*
    HNet - March 2015 - pNA [501+]
    JMH - v87 - i3 - Sept 2015 - p718(4) [501+]
    RAH - v43 - i1 - March 2015 - p143-148 [501+]

Dohna, Jesko Graf zu - *Erinnerungen: Emma Furstin zu Castell-Rudenhausen*
    HNet - May 2015 - pNA [501+]

Dohrmann, Natalie B. - *Jews, Christians, and the Roman Empire: The Poetics of Power in Late Antiquity*
    Class R - v65 - i1 - April 2015 - p233-236 [501+]

Doidge, Norman - *The Brain's Way of Healing*
    SEP - v287 - i1 - Jan-Feb 2015 - p20(1) [501+]
The Brain's Way of Healing: Remarkable Discoveries and Recoveries from the Frontiers of Neuroplasticity (Read by Newbern, George). Audiobook Review
    LJ - v140 - i8 - May 1 2015 - p42(1) [51-500]
The Brain's Way of Healing: Remarkable Discoveries and Recoveries from the Frontiers of Neuroplasticity
    LJ - v140 - i5 - March 15 2015 - p128(2) [51-500]

Doig, Ivan - *Last Bus to Wisdom*
    BL - v111 - i19-20 - June 1 2015 - p59(2) [51-500]
    BooChiTr - August 29 2015 - p13(1) [501+]
    CSM - August 19 2015 - pNA [501+]
    KR - June 1 2015 - pNA [501+]
    LJ - v140 - i12 - July 1 2015 - p75(1) [51-500]
    NYTBR - August 16 2015 - p12(L) [501+]
    PW - v262 - i23 - June 8 2015 - p32(1) [51-500]
    PW - v262 - i35 - August 31 2015 - p11(1) [51-500]

Doiron, Paul - *The Bone Orchard*
    RVBW - March 2015 - pNA [501+]
    RVBW - July 2015 - pNA [501+]
The Precipice (Read by Leyva, Henry). Audiobook Review
    BL - v112 - i6 - Nov 15 2015 - p61(2) [51-500]
    PW - v262 - i35 - August 31 2015 - p83(2) [51-500]
The Precipice
    BL - v111 - i17 - May 1 2015 - p42(2) [51-500]
    KR - April 15 2015 - pNA [501+]
    LJ - v140 - i9 - May 15 2015 - p79(1) [51-500]
    PW - v262 - i17 - April 27 2015 - p50(1) [51-500]

Dojc, Yuri - *Last Folio*
    LJ - v140 - i15 - Sept 15 2015 - p81(3) [501+]

Dojny, Brooke - *Chowderland: Hearty Soups and Stews with Sides and Salads to Match*
    Bwatch - July 2015 - pNA [501+]

Doktoranden-Kolloquium *"FUER Geschichtsbewusstsein"*
    HNet - Jan 2015 - pNA [501+]

Doktorski, Jennifer Salvato - *The Summer After You and Me*
    y KR - March 15 2015 - pNA [51-500]
The Summer after You + Me
    y BL - v111 - i18 - May 15 2015 - p54(1) [51-500]
    y VOYA - v38 - i2 - June 2015 - p58(1) [51-500]

Dolan, Alex - *The Euthanist*
    y VOYA - v38 - i2 - June 2015 - p58(1) [51-500]

Dolan, Chris - *Potter's Field*
    KR - May 1 2015 - pNA [51-500]
    PW - v262 - i20 - May 18 2015 - p66(1) [51-500]

Dolan, Elys - *Nuts in Space* (Illus. by Dolan, Elys)
    c BL - v111 - i17 - May 1 2015 - p101(1) [51-500]
    c HB Guide - v26 - i2 - Fall 2015 - p32(1) [51-500]
    c KR - March 15 2015 - pNA [51-500]
    c SLJ - v61 - i5 - May 2015 - p84(1) [51-500]

Dolan, Frances E. - *True Relations: Reading, Literature, and Evidence in Seventeenth-Century England*
    MLR - v110 - i3 - July 2015 - p825-826 [501+]
    MP - v112 - i3 - Feb 2015 - pE252(E254) [501+]

Dolan, Hugh - *Gallipoli: The Landing* (Illus. by Gardiner, Mal)
    y Magpies - v30 - i1 - March 2015 - p22(1) [501+]
Reg Saunders: An Indigenous War Hero (Illus. by Barbu, Adrian)
    c Magpies - v30 - i2 - May 2015 - p22(1) [501+]

Dolan, John - *George the Dog, John the Artist: A Rescue Story*
    LJ - v140 - i11 - June 15 2015 - p106(1) [51-500]
George the Dog, John the Artist
    KR - April 15 2015 - pNA [501+]
John and George: The Dog Who Saved My Life
    PW - v262 - i15 - April 13 2015 - p69(1) [51-500]

Dolan, John R. - *The Biology and Ecology of Tintinnid Ciliates: Models for Marine Plankton*
    QRB - v90 - i3 - Sept 2015 - p341(2) [501+]

Dolan, Penny - *The Egyptian Cat Mystery* (Illus. by Elkerton, Andy)
    c CH Bwatch - Nov 2015 - pNA [501+]

Dolan, Richard M. - *Project Disclosure: Revealing Government Secrets and Breaking the Truth Embargo*
    y Teach Lib - v42 - i5 - June 2015 - p10(1) [51-500]

Dolan, Wendy - *Layer, Paint and Stitch*
    RVBW - Sept 2015 - pNA [501+]

Dole, Christopher - *Healing Secular Life: Loss and Devotion in Modern Turkey*
    MAQ - v29 - i1 - March 2015 - pB55-B57 [501+]

Dolenec, Danijela - *Democratic Institutions and Authoritarian Rule in Southeast Europe*
    E-A St - v67 - i1 - Jan 2015 - p154(2) [501+]

Dolezalova, Lucie - *Obscurity and Memory in Late Medieval Latin Manuscript Culture: The Case of the Summarium Biblie*
    Med R - Sept 2015 - pNA [501+]
Obscurity in Medieval Texts
    Med R - May 2015 - pNA [501+]

Dolinskiy, Irina Gonikberg - *Parts of Speech Parade: New York City* (Illus. by Adams, Mark Wayne)
    c CH Bwatch - Feb 2015 - pNA [51-500]

Doll, Martin - *Falschung und Fake: Zur diskurskritischen Dimension des Tauschens*
    HNet - August 2015 - pNA [501+]

Dollahite, Derek - *WYW*
    y KR - April 15 2015 - pNA [501+]

Dollar, Trish - *The Devil You Know*
    c BL - v111 - i17 - May 1 2015 - p49(1) [51-500]

Doller, Trish - *The Devil You Know*
    y HB Guide - v26 - i2 - Fall 2015 - p117(1) [501+]
    y KR - March 15 2015 - pNA [51-500]
      SLJ - v61 - i4 - April 2015 - p162(2) [51-500]
    y VOYA - v38 - i2 - June 2015 - p58(1) [51-500]

Dolley, Chris - *The Unpleasantness at Baskerville Hall*
    PW - v262 - i52 - Dec 21 2015 - p137(1) [51-500]

Dolnick, Ben - *At The Bottom of the Everything*
    NYTBR - Feb 8 2015 - p28(L) [501+]

Dolski, Michael - *D-Day in History and Memory: The Normandy Landings in International Remembrance and Commemoration*
    JAH - v101 - i4 - March 2015 - p1351-1352 [501+]

Dolzer, Krista Van - *The Sound of Life and Everything*
    c BL - v111 - i18 - May 15 2015 - p68(1) [51-500]

Doman, Mary Kate - *Tragedy at the Triangle*
    c KR - Jan 15 2015 - pNA [501+]

Domanick, Joe - *Blue*
    KR - July 15 2015 - pNA [501+]
Blue: The LAPD and the Battle to Redeem American Policing
    NYTBR - August 9 2015 - p14(L) [501+]

Domanski, Walerian - *The Dog Called Hitler Lena*
    KR - July 15 2015 - pNA [501+]

Dombrink, John - *The Twilight of Social Conservatism: American Culture Wars in the Obama Era*
    Soc - v52 - i5 - Oct 2015 - p498(1) [501+]

Dombrowski, Peter - *The Indian Ocean and US Grand Strategy: Ensuring Access and Promoting Security*
    Parameters - v45 - i1 - Spring 2015 - p147(3) [501+]

Domeny, Lisa - *Winnie and the Red Winniebago*
    c CH Bwatch - Oct 2015 - pNA [51-500]

Domhoff, G. William - *The Myth of Liberal Ascendancy: Corporate Dominance from the Great Depression to the Great Recession*
    CS - v44 - i5 - Sept 2015 - p655-657 [501+]

Domingo, Jose - *Jose Pablo & Jane and the Hot Air Contraption* (Illus. by Domingo, Jose)
    c KR - Sept 1 2015 - pNA [501+]
Pablo & Jane and the Hot Air Contraption (Illus. by Domingo, Jose)
    c BL - v112 - i4 - Oct 15 2015 - p37(1) [51-500]
    c PW - v262 - i49 - Dec 2 2015 - p59(1) [51-500]
    c SLJ - v61 - i12 - Dec 2015 - p109(2) [51-500]

Domingos, Pedro - *The Master Algorithm: How the Quest for the Ultimate Learning Machine Will Remake Our World*
    BL - v111 - i22 - August 1 2015 - p11(1) [51-500]
    New Sci - v228 - i3045 - Oct 31 2015 - p44(2) [501+]
    TimHES - i2221 - Sept 17 2015 - p48(1) [501+]
The Master Algorithm
    KR - July 1 2015 - pNA [501+]

Dominguez, Angela - *Knit Together* (Illus. by Dominguez, Angela)
    c CCB-B - v68 - i10 - June 2015 - p487(1) [51-500]
    c HB - v91 - i2 - March-April 2015 - p72(2) [51-500]
    c HB Guide - v26 - i2 - Fall 2015 - p9(1) [51-500]

Dominguez Michael, Christopher - *Octavio Paz en su siglo*
    TLS - i5863 - August 14 2015 - p22(1) [501+]

Dominiguez, Pablo - *Concise Pun-ishing Dictionary for English Speakers*
    TimHES - i2188 - Jan 29 2015 - p47(1) [501+]

Dominy, Amy Fellner - *A Matter of Heart*
    y BL - v111 - i15 - April 1 2015 - p67(2) [501+]
    c BL - v112 - i1 - Sept 1 2015 - p99(1) [501+]
    c CCB-B - v69 - i1 - Sept 2015 - p19(1) [51-500]
    y HB Guide - v26 - i2 - Fall 2015 - p117(1) [501+]
    y KR - Feb 15 2015 - pNA [51-500]
    y VOYA - v38 - i1 - April 2015 - p57(1) [51-500]

Dommen, Edward - *A Peaceable Economy*
    RVBW - April 2015 - pNA [501+]

Don, Katherine - *Nujood Ali and the Fight against Child Marriage*
    c BL - v111 - i19-20 - June 1 2015 - p90(1) [51-500]
Out in Front: Nujood Ali and the Fight Against Child Marriage
    y CH Bwatch - Nov 2015 - pNA [501+]
Out in Front Series
    y SLJ - v61 - i6 - June 2015 - p141(1) [51-500]

Don, Lari - *The Tale of Tam Linn* (Illus. by Longson, Philip)
    c CCB-B - v68 - i7 - March 2015 - p350(1) [51-500]

Donaghey, Reese - *The History of Independence Day*
    c BL - v111 - i16 - April 15 2015 - p46(1) [501+]
Pocahontas and the Powhatans
    c BL - v111 - i16 - April 15 2015 - p46(1) [501+]

Donaghue, Chris - *Sex Outside the Lines: Authentic Sexuality in a Sexually Dysfunctional Culture*
    LJ - v140 - i12 - July 1 2015 - p99(2) [51-500]

Donaghy, Greg - *Grit: The Life and Politics of Paul Martin Sr*
    Beav - v95 - i4 - August-Sept 2015 - p68(1) [501+]

Donahue, John R. - *Seek Justice That You May Live: Reflections and Resources on the Bible and Social Justice*
    Theol St - v76 - i3 - Sept 2015 - p596(2) [501+]

Donahue, Katherine C. - *Steaming to the North: The First Summer Cruise of the US Revenue Cutter Bear, Alaska and Chukotka, Siberia, 1886*
    RVBW - March 2015 - pNA [501+]

Donahue, William Collins - *Nexus: Essays in German Jewish Studies, vol. 2*
    TLS - i5841 - March 13 2015 - p27(1) [501+]

Donald, Diana - *The Art of Thomas Bewick*
    NYRB - v62 - i16 - Oct 22 2015 - p12(3) [501+]

Donald, Rhonda Lucas - *Dino Treasures (Illus. by Morrison, Cathy)*
    c HB Guide - v26 - i2 - Fall 2015 - p168(1) [51-500]
    c CH Bwatch - March 2015 - pNA [51-500]
    c Sci & Ch - v52 - i5 - Jan 2015 - p84 [501+]

Donaldson, Greg - *The Ville*
    Bwatch - Oct 2015 - pNA [51-500]

Donaldson, Julia - *Princess Mirror Belle and the Dragon Pox (Illus. by Monks, Lydia)*
    c Sch Lib - v63 - i1 - Spring 2015 - p26(1) [51-500]
The Scarecrows' Wedding (Illus. by Scheffler, Axel)
    c CH Bwatch - Feb 2015 - pNA [51-500]
    c HB Guide - v26 - i1 - Spring 2015 - p28(1) [51-500]
What the Jackdaw Saw (Illus. by Sharratt, Nick)
    c Magpies - v30 - i5 - Nov 2015 - p27(2) [501+]
    c Sch Lib - v63 - i3 - Autumn 2015 - p154(1) [51-500]
What the Ladybird Heard Next (Illus. by Monks, Lydia)
    c Magpies - v30 - i4 - Sept 2015 - p27(1) [501+]
What the Ladybird Heard (Illus. by Monks, Lydia)
    c Magpies - v30 - i4 - Sept 2015 - p27(1) [501+]
Whit the Clockleddy Heard: What the Ladybird Heard in Scots
    c Sch Lib - v63 - i4 - Winter 2015 - p219(1) [51-500]

Donaldson, Rachel Clare - *"I Hear America Singing": Folk Music and National Identity*
    JAH - v102 - i2 - Sept 2015 - p610-611 [501+]

Donaldson, Scott - *The Impossible Craft: Literary Biography*
    Comw - v142 - i18 - Nov 13 2015 - p23(2) [501+]

Donaldson, Stephen R. - *The King's Justice: Two Novellas*
    PW - v262 - i36 - Sept 7 2015 - p50(1) [51-500]

Donati, Sara - *The Gilded Hour*
    BL - v111 - i22 - August 1 2015 - p39(1) [51-500]
    KR - July 15 2015 - pNA [51-500]

Donato, Clorinda - *Jesuit Accounts of the Colonial Americas: Intercultural Transfers, Intellectual Transfers, intellectual Disutes, and Textualities*
    FS - v69 - i4 - Oct 2015 - p525-526 [501+]

Donato, Maria Pia - *Medecine et religion: Collaborations, competitions, conflits (XIIe-Xxe siecle).*
    CHR - v101 - i4 - Autumn 2015 - p898(2) [501+]
Medecine et religion: Competitions, collaborations, conflits - XII-XX siecles
    Isis - v106 - i1 - March 2015 - p165(2) [501+]

Donaugrenzen in Literatur und Film. Internationale Tagung
    HNet - Jan 2015 - pNA [501+]

Donavin, Georgiana - *Scribit Mater: Mary and the Language Arts in the Literature of Medieval England*
    JEGP - v114 - i1 - Jan 2015 - p147(3) [501+]

Donbavand, Tommy - *Teen Reads: Home*
    y Sch Lib - v63 - i2 - Summer 2015 - p116(1) [51-500]

Donegan, Kathleen - *Seasons of Misery: Catastrophe and Colonial Settlement in Early America*
    AHR - v120 - i2 - April 2015 - p606-607 [501+]
    JSH - v81 - i1 - Feb 2015 - p157(2) [501+]
    RAH - v43 - i3 - Sept 2015 - p434-440 [501+]

Donenfeld, Jill - *Better on Toast: Happiness on a Slice of Bread*
    LJ - v140 - i5 - March 15 2015 - p126(2) [51-500]

Donenfeld, Maya Pagan - *Hope, Make, Heal: 20 Crafts to Mend the Heart*
    LJ - v140 - i20 - Dec 1 2015 - p100(2) [51-500]

Doney, Meryl - *The Very Worried Sparrow (Illus. by Hansen, Gaby)*
    c CH Bwatch - August 2015 - pNA [51-500]

Donges, Alexander - *Die Vereinigte Stahlwerke AG im Nationalsozialismus: Konzernpolitik zwischen Marktwirtschaft und Staatsinterventionismus*
    HNet - August 2015 - pNA [501+]

Donia, Robert J. - *Radovan Karadzic: Architect of the Bosnian Genocide*
    TLS - i5834 - Jan 23 2015 - p9(2) [501+]
    For Aff - v94 - i3 - May-June 2015 - pNA [501+]
    Slav R - v74 - i3 - Fall 2015 - p631-632 [501+]

Doniger, Wendy - *On Hinduism*
    Rel St - v51 - i2 - June 2015 - p275-279 [501+]
    TLS - i5849 - May 8 2015 - p8(1) [501+]

Donlay, Philip - *Aftershock*
    BL - v111 - i13 - March 1 2015 - p21(1) [51-500]
    PW - v262 - i3 - Jan 19 2015 - p63(2) [51-500]

Donlea, Charlie - *Summit Lake*
    BL - v112 - i7 - Dec 1 2015 - p31(2) [51-500]
    PW - v262 - i48 - Nov 30 2015 - p40(1) [51-500]

Donne, John - *The Oxford Edition of the Sermons of John Donne. Volume 3: Sermons Preached at the Court of Charles I*
    Ren Q - v68 - i1 - Spring 2015 - p355-357 [501+]

Donnelly, Jennifer - *Rogue Wave*
    y CH Bwatch - March 2015 - pNA [51-500]
    y HB Guide - v26 - i2 - Fall 2015 - p177(1) [501+]
    SLJ - v61 - i2 - Feb 2015 - p84(1) [51-500]
These Shallow Graves
    BL - v112 - i1 - Sept 1 2015 - p102(1) [501+]
    y HB - v91 - i5 - Sept-Oct 2015 - p101(1) [51-500]
    y KR - August 1 2015 - pNA [51-500]
    y Magpies - v30 - i5 - Nov 2015 - p40(1) [51-500]
    y PW - v262 - i33 - August 17 2015 - p72(1) [51-500]
    y PW - v262 - i49 - Dec 2 2015 - p115(1) [51-500]
    y SLJ - v61 - i8 - August 2015 - p102(1) [51-500]
    y VOYA - v38 - i4 - Oct 2015 - p50(1) [51-500]

Donnelly, Liza - *The End of the Rainbow (Illus. by Donnelly, Liza)*
    c HB Guide - v26 - i2 - Fall 2015 - p59(1) [51-500]
    c KR - Feb 15 2015 - pNA [51-500]
The End of the Rainbow
    SLJ - v61 - i4 - April 2015 - p139(1) [51-500]
A Hippo in Our Yard (Illus. by Donnelly, Liza)
    c KR - Dec 1 2015 - pNA [51-500]

Donnelly, Patrick - *The Best NBA Centers of All Time*
    c HB Guide - v26 - i1 - Spring 2015 - p183(1) [51-500]
The Best NBA Forwards of All Time
    c HB Guide - v26 - i1 - Spring 2015 - p183(1) [51-500]

Donofrio, Jeanine - *The Love and Lemons Cookbook: An Apple-to-Zucchini Celebration of Impromptu Cooking*
    PW - v262 - i50 - Dec 7 2015 - p81(1) [51-500]

Donoghue, Clare - *No Place to Die*
    BL - v111 - i17 - May 1 2015 - p42(1) [51-500]
    KR - April 1 2015 - pNA [51-500]
    PW - v262 - i14 - April 6 2015 - p41(1) [51-500]

Donoghue, Denis - *Metaphor*
    Lon R Bks - v37 - i8 - April 23 2015 - p27(2) [501+]

Donoghue, Emma - *Frog Music*
    NYTBR - Sept 6 2015 - p24(L) [501+]

Donoghue, Frank - *The Last Professors: The Corporate University and the Fate of the Humanities*
    J Hi E - v86 - i1 - Jan-Feb 2015 - p156(15) [501+]

Donoghue, John - *The Death's Head Chess Club*
    BL - v111 - i14 - March 15 2015 - p43(1) [51-500]
    KR - March 1 2015 - pNA [501+]
    LJ - v140 - i8 - May 1 2015 - p61(1) [51-500]

Donoghue, Michael E. - *Borderland on the Isthmus: Race, Culture, and the Struggle for the Canal Zone*
    AHR - v120 - i4 - Oct 2015 - p1535-1536 [501+]

Donohue, Meg - *Dog Crazy: A Novel of Love Lost and Found*
    LJ - v140 - i3 - Feb 15 2015 - p90(1) [51-500]

Donohue, Moira Rose - *Parrot Genius!: And More True Stories of Amazing Animal Talents*
    c HB Guide - v26 - i1 - Spring 2015 - p153(1) [51-500]

Donovan, Kemper - *The Decent Proposal*
    KR - Jan 1 2016 - pNA [51-500]

Donovan, Lois - *The Journal*
    y Res Links - v20 - i4 - April 2015 - p28(1) [501+]

Donovan, Nancy - *Wild Dolphin Rider (Illus. by Spellman, Susan)*
    c CH Bwatch - June 2015 - pNA [51-500]

Donovan, Sandy - *Movies and TV Top Tens*
    c HB Guide - v26 - i2 - Fall 2015 - p194(1) [51-500]
Music and Theater Top Tens
    c HB Guide - v26 - i2 - Fall 2015 - p194(1) [51-500]
Sports Top Tens
    c HB Guide - v26 - i2 - Fall 2015 - p198(1) [51-500]
Technology Top Tens
    c HB Guide - v26 - i2 - Fall 2015 - p185(1) [51-500]

Donovan, Susan - *Moondance Beach*
    PW - v262 - i31 - August 3 2015 - p43(1) [51-500]

Donovan, Tristan - *Feral Cities: Adventures with Animals in the Urban Jungle*
    BL - v111 - i15 - April 1 2015 - p8(1) [51-500]
    KR - Feb 1 2015 - pNA [51-500]
    PW - v262 - i6 - Feb 9 2015 - p55(1) [51-500]

Don't Throw It to Mo! - *Don't Throw It to Mo! (Illus. by Ricks, Sam)*
    c HB Guide - v26 - i2 - Fall 2015 - p58(1) [51-500]

Dontchev, Asen L. - *Implicit Functions and Solution Mappings: A View from Variational Analysis, 2d ed.*
    SIAM Rev - v57 - i2 - June 2015 - p308-310 [501+]

Donvan, John - *In a Different Key: The Story of Autism*
    BL - v112 - i7 - Dec 1 2015 - p14(1) [51-500]
    KR - Oct 15 2015 - pNA [51-500]
    PW - v262 - i45 - Nov 9 2015 - p53(1) [51-500]

Donze, Pierre-Yves - *A Business History of the Swatch Group: The Rebirth of Swiss Watchmaking and the Globalization of the Luxury Industry*
    BHR - v89 - i2 - Summer 2015 - p367(2) [501+]
"Rattraper et depasser la Suisse": Histoire de l'industrie horlogere japonaise de 1850 a nos jours
    BHR - v89 - i1 - Spring 2015 - p194(4) [501+]

Doodler, Todd H. - *Super Fly: The World's Smallest Superhero!*
    KR - Feb 1 2015 - pNA [51-500]
    c PW - v262 - i16 - April 20 2015 - p77(1) [51-500]
    SLJ - v61 - i4 - April 2015 - p140(1) [51-500]
Super Fly: The World's Smallest Superhero! (Illus. by Doodler, Todd H.)
    c BL - v111 - i16 - April 15 2015 - p55(1) [51-500]
    c HB Guide - v26 - i2 - Fall 2015 - p64(1) [51-500]
    c NYTBR - June 21 2015 - p18(L) [501+]

Doody, John - *Augustine and Apocalyptic*
    Theol St - v76 - i1 - March 2015 - p210(2) [501+]

Doody, Margaret - *Jane Austen's Names: Riddles, Persons, Places*
    TLS - i5870 - Oct 2 2015 - p22(1) [501+]

Dooley, Ann - *Constructing Gender in Medieval Ireland*
    Med R - August 2015 - pNA [501+]

Dooley, Brendan - *A Companion to Astrology in the Renaissance*
    Six Ct J - v46 - i2 - Summer 2015 - p435-436 [501+]
    Ren Q - v68 - i2 - Summer 2015 - p659-661 [501+]
A Mattress Maker's Daughter: The Renaissance Romance of Don Giovanni de' Medici and Livia Vernazza
    JMH - v87 - i3 - Sept 2015 - p747(3) [501+]

Dooley, Rhonda Nell - *Heaven's Consciousness: A Near-Death Experience with Relevant Poetry*
    SPBW - Nov 2015 - pNA [501+]

Dooley, Sarah - *Free Verse*
    c KR - Dec 15 2015 - pNA [51-500]

Dooley, Terence - *The Decline and Fall of the Dukes of Leinster, 1872-1948: Love, War, Debt and Madness*
    ILS - v35 - i1 - Fall 2015 - p7(2) [501+]

Dopress Books - *Sketch City: Tips and Inspiration for Drawing on Location*
    LJ - v140 - i15 - Sept 15 2015 - p76(1) [51-500]

Dor, George Worlasi Kwasi - *West African Drumming and Dance in North American Universities: An Ethnomusicological Perspective*
    Notes - v72 - i1 - Sept 2015 - p148(4) [501+]

Dorado-Otero, Angela - *Dialogic Aspects of the Cuban Novel of the 1990s*
    MP - v113 - i1 - August 2015 - pE56(3) [501+]

Doran, John - *Jolly Lad*
    TimHES - i2216 - August 13 2015 - p43(1) [501+]

Doran, Susan - *Elizabeth I and Her Circle*
    LJ - v140 - i6 - April 1 2015 - p102(1) [51-500]

Dore, Garance - *Love Style Life*
    PW - v262 - i36 - Sept 7 2015 - p64(1) [51-500]

Dorff, Elliot N. - *Jews and Genes: The Genetic Future in Contemporary Jewish Thought*
    RVBW - August 2015 - pNA [501+]

Doring, Jorg - *Alfred Andersch Desertiert: Fahnenflucht und Literatur (1944-1952).*
    HNet - June 2015 - pNA [501+]

Dorison, Xavier - *The Mongoose: XIII Mystery, vol. 1 (Illus. by Meyer, Ralph)*
    y Sch Lib - v63 - i3 - Autumn 2015 - p190(1) [51-500]

Dorling, Danny - *Inequality and the 1 Per Cent*
    Lon R Bks - v37 - i8 - April 23 2015 - p19(2) [501+]
Injustice: Why Social Inequality Still Persists
    TimHES - i2209 - June 25 2015 - p47(1) [501+]

Dorling Kindersley Publishing, Inc - *Tractor: The Definitive Visual History*
    BL - v111 - i18 - May 15 2015 - p17(1) [51-500]

Dorman, Andrew M. - *Providing for National Security: A Comparative Analysis*
    HNet - Feb 2015 - pNA [501+]

Dorn, A. Walter - *Air Power in UN Operations: Wings for Peace*
    J Mil H - v79 - i2 - April 2015 - p545(1) [501+]

Dorn, T. Felder - *Challenges on the Emmaus Road: Episcopal Bishops Confront Slavery, Civil War, and Emancipation*
    CH - v84 - i2 - June 2015 - p465(2) [501+]

Dorner, Daniel G. - *Information Needs Analysis: Principles and Practice in Information Organizations*
    LR - v64 - i4-5 - April-May 2015 - p402-403 [501+]

Dorner-Horig, Christian - *Habitus und Politik in Karnten: Soziogenetische und Psychogenetische Grundlagen des Systems Jorg Haider*
    HNet - June 2015 - pNA [501+]

Doron, Assa - *The Great Indian Phone Book: How Cheap Mobile Phones Change Business, Politics and Daily Life*
    JRAI - v21 - i1 - March 2015 - p215(2) [51-500]
    The Great Indian Phone Book: How the Cheap Cell Phone Changes Business, Politics, and Daily Life
    T&C - v56 - i2 - April 2015 - p563-565 [501+]

Dorondo, David R. - *Riders of the Apocalypse: German Cavalry and Modern Warfare, 1870-1945*
    HNet - June 2015 - pNA [501+]

Dorosz, Beata - *Nowojorski pasjans: Polski Instytut Naukowy w Ameryce, Jan Lechon, Kazimierz Wierzynski. Studia o wybranych zagadnieniach dzialalnosci 1939-1969*
    Slav R - v74 - i1 - Spring 2015 - p179-181 [501+]

Dorren, Gaston - *Lingo: Around Europe in Sixty Languages*
    BL - v112 - i5 - Nov 1 2015 - p5(1) [51-500]
    PW - v262 - i41 - Oct 12 2015 - p57(2) [51-500]
    Lingo
    KR - Sept 1 2015 - pNA [501+]

Dorrestein, Renate - *The Darkness That Divides Us*
    ABR - v36 - i2 - Jan-Feb 2015 - p22(1) [501+]

Dorris, Joseph - *Salmon River Kid*
    c BL - v112 - i3 - Oct 1 2015 - p32(2) [501+]
    KR - April 15 2015 - pNA [51-500]
    y Roundup M - v22 - i4 - April 2015 - p32(1) [501+]
    Roundup M - v22 - i6 - August 2015 - p28(1) [501+]

Dorros, Arthur - *Abuela (Illus. by Kleven, Elisa)*
    c BL - v111 - i9-10 - Jan 1 2015 - pS18(5) [501+]

Dorsette, Chelsea - *Legally Tied*
    RVBW - Feb 2015 - pNA [51-500]

Dorsey, C. Michele - *No Virgin Island*
    BL - v111 - i22 - August 1 2015 - p36(1) [51-500]
    PW - v262 - i23 - June 8 2015 - p40(1) [51-500]

Dorsey, Kurkpatrick - *Whales and Nations: Environmental Diplomacy on the High Seas*
    AHR - v120 - i1 - Feb 2015 - p196-197 [501+]
    JAH - v101 - i4 - March 2015 - p1339-1340 [501+]
    JIH - v45 - i3 - Wntr 2015 - p416-418 [501+]

Dorsey, Tim - *Coconut Cowboy*
    KR - Nov 15 2015 - pNA [501+]
    PW - v262 - i46 - Nov 16 2015 - p54(1) [51-500]
    Shark Skin Suite
    RVBW - Oct 2015 - pNA [501+]
    RVBW - Nov 2015 - pNA [501+]

Doshi, Neel - *Primed to Perform: How to Build the Highest Performing Cultures Through the Science of Total Motivation*
    LJ - v140 - i13 - August 1 2015 - p107(1) [51-500]

Dostoevsky, Fyodor - *Notes from a Dead House*
    HM - v330 - i1978 - March 2015 - p79(3) [501+]
    KR - Jan 15 2015 - pNA [501+]
    PW - v262 - i1 - Jan 5 2015 - p49(1) [51-500]

Dotan, Yoav - *Lawyering for the Rule of Law: Government Lawyers and the Rise of Judicial Power in Israel*
    Law&PolBR - v25 - i3 - March 2015 - p43(3) [501+]

Doten, Mark - *The Infernal*
    HM - v330 - i1977 - Feb 2015 - p77(3) [501+]
    KR - Jan 15 2015 - pNA [51-500]
    Mac - v128 - i10 - March 16 2015 - p58(1) [501+]
    NYTBR - Feb 22 2015 - p34(L) [501+]

Dotlich, Rebecca Kai - *All Aboard! (Illus. by Lowery, Mike)*
    c HB Guide - v26 - i1 - Spring 2015 - p8(1) [51-500]
    The Knowing Book (Illus. by Cordell, Matthew)
    c KR - Dec 15 2015 - pNA [51-500]
    c PW - v262 - i46 - Nov 16 2015 - p74(2) [51-500]
    One Day, the End: Short, Very Short, Shorter-than-Ever Stories (Illus. by Koehler, Fred)
    c BL - v112 - i3 - Oct 1 2015 - p83(1) [51-500]
    c HB - v91 - i5 - Sept-Oct 2015 - p79(1) [51-500]
    c KR - July 15 2015 - pNA [51-500]
    c PW - v262 - i29 - July 20 2015 - p189(1) [51-500]
    c SLJ - v61 - i8 - August 2015 - p68(1) [51-500]
    Race Car Count
    c KR - August 1 2015 - pNA [51-500]
    Race Car Count (Illus. by Slack, Michael)
    c SLJ - v61 - i9 - Sept 2015 - p118(2) [51-500]

Dotta, Jessica - *Price of Privilege*
    BL - v111 - i9-10 - Jan 1 2015 - p56(2) [51-500]

Doty, James R. - *Into the Magic Shop: A Neurosurgeon's Quest to Discover the Mysteries of the Brain and the Secrets of the Heart*
    PW - v262 - i51 - Dec 14 2015 - p71(2) [51-500]
    KR - Dec 1 2015 - pNA [51-500]

Doty, Mark - *Deep Lane*
    BL - v111 - i16 - April 15 2015 - p13(1) [51-500]
    Deep Lane: Poems
    PW - v262 - i11 - March 16 2015 - p61(1) [51-500]
    Deep Lane
    G&L Rev W - v22 - i5 - Sept-Oct 2015 - p44(2) [501+]

Doubinsky, Seb - *The Song of Synth*
    PW - v262 - i24 - June 15 2015 - p67(1) [51-500]

Doubleday, Simon R. - *The Wise King: A Christian Prince, Muslim Spain, and the Birth of the Renaissance*
    KR - Sept 15 2015 - pNA [501+]
    LJ - v140 - i17 - Oct 15 2015 - p100(1) [51-500]

Doucett, Elisabeth - *New Routes to Library Success: 100+ Ideas from Outside the Stacks*
    LJ - v140 - i14 - Sept 1 2015 - p126(1) [501+]
    VOYA - v38 - i5 - Dec 2015 - p83(1) [51-500]

Doudna, Kelly - *The Kids' Book of Simple Machines: Cool Projects and Activities That Make Science Fun!*
    c BL - v112 - i7 - Dec 1 2015 - p50(1) [51-500]

Dougherty, Barbara J. - *Developing Essential Understanding of Geometry and Measurement, Grades 3-5*
    TC Math - v22 - i1 - August 2015 - p51(2) [51-500]
    Putting Essential Understanding of Addition and Subtraction into Practice, Pre-K-Grade 2
    TC Math - v22 - i2 - Sept 2015 - p116(1) [501+]

Dougherty, Kerrie - *History of Rocketry and Astronautics: AAS History Series, vol. 41*
    APH - v62 - i2 - Summer 2015 - p55(1) [501+]

Dougherty, Trent - *The Problem of Animal Pain: A Theodicy for All Creatures Great and Small*
    Rel St - v51 - i4 - Dec 2015 - p593-597 [501+]

Doughty, Becky - *Juliette and the Monday ManDates*
    PW - v262 - i41 - Oct 12 2015 - p54(1) [51-500]

Doughty, Caitlin - *Smoke Gets in Your Eyes: And Other Lessons from the Crematorium*
    New Sci - v226 - i3021 - May 16 2015 - p46(1) [501+]
    Smoke Gets in Your Eyes: And Other Lessons from the Crematory
    CC - v132 - i10 - May 13 2015 - p34(2) [501+]
    Smoke Gets in Your Eyes: And Other Lessons from the Crematory. Audiobook Review
    LJ - v140 - i7 - April 15 2015 - p48(1) [501+]

Douglas, Anne - *Nothing Ventured*
    BL - v112 - i6 - Nov 15 2015 - p31(1) [51-500]
    PW - v262 - i41 - Oct 12 2015 - p54(1) [51-500]

Douglas, Carole Nelson - *Cat in a Zebra Zoot Suit: A Midnight Louie Mystery*
    PW - v262 - i34 - August 24 2015 - p62(1) [51-500]

Douglas, Daniel P. - *Truth Insurrected: The Saint Mary Project*
    KR - Jan 15 2015 - pNA [501+]
    PW - v262 - i11 - March 16 2015 - p68(1) [51-500]

Douglas-Fairhurst, Robert - *The Story of Alice: Lewis Carroll and the Secret History of Wonderland*
    KR - March 15 2015 - pNA [501+]
    NS - v144 - i5255 - March 27 2015 - p68(3) [501+]
    NYTBR - June 14 2015 - p15(L) [501+]
    Spec - v327 - i9735 - March 28 2015 - p36(2) [501+]
    TLS - i5850 - May 15 2015 - p22(2) [501+]
    BL - v111 - i17 - May 1 2015 - p72(1) [51-500]
    LJ - v140 - i10 - June 1 2015 - p102(2) [51-500]

Douglas, Illeana - *I Blame Dennis Hopper: And Other Stories from a Life Lived in and out of the Movies*
    BL - v112 - i5 - Nov 1 2015 - p21(1) [51-500]
    KR - Sept 1 2015 - pNA [51-500]
    LJ - v140 - i16 - Oct 1 2015 - p80(1) [51-500]

Douglas, Kate - *Intimate*
    PW - v262 - i42 - Oct 19 2015 - p61(1) [51-500]

Douglas, Kelly Brown - *Stand Your Ground: Black Bodies and the Justice of God*
    CC - v132 - i20 - Sept 30 2015 - p36(2) [501+]
    JAAR - v83 - i2 - June 2015 - pNA [501+]
    PW - v262 - i15 - April 13 2015 - p74(2) [501+]

Douglas, Lady Margaret - *The Devonshire Manuscript: A Women's Book of Courtly Poetry*
    MLR - v110 - i3 - July 2015 - p819-820 [501+]

Douglas, Lawrence - *The Right Wrong Man*
    KR - Oct 15 2015 - pNA [501+]

Douglas, Mary - *Purity and Danger: An Analysis of Concepts of Pollution and Taboo*
    TimHES - i2211 - July 9 2015 - p50-51 [501+]

Douglas, R.M. - *Orderly and Humane: The Expulsion of the Germans after the Second World War*
    CEH - v48 - i1 - March 2015 - p136-137 [501+]

Douglas, Rhonda - *Welcome to the Circus*
    PW - v262 - i7 - Feb 16 2015 - p151(1) [51-500]

Douglas, Ronnie - *Undaunted*
    PW - v262 - i28 - July 13 2015 - p51(1) [51-500]

Douglas, Ryke Leigh - *The Tale of Tumeleng*
    c BL - v112 - i3 - Oct 1 2015 - p32(2) [51-500]

Douglas, Stuart - *The Albino's Treasure*
    PW - v262 - i11 - March 16 2015 - p66(1) [51-500]

Douglas, Yellowlees - *The Reader's Brain: How Neuroscience Can Make You a Better Writer*
    LJ - v140 - i13 - August 1 2015 - p106(2) [51-500]

Douglass, Frederick - *The Life and Times of Frederick Douglass (Read by Allen, Richard). Audiobook Review*
    CSM - April 23 2015 - pNA [51-500]

Doumani, Narissa - *A Spacious Life: Memoir of a Meditator*
    KR - March 1 2015 - pNA [501+]

Doussard, Marc - *Degraded Work: The Struggle at the Bottom of the Labor Market*
    AJS - v120 - i4 - Jan 2015 - p1243(3) [501+]
    CS - v44 - i4 - July 2015 - p499-501 [501+]

Douthwaite, Julia V. - *The Frankenstein of 1790 and Other Lost Chapters from Revolutionary France*
    JMH - v87 - i1 - March 2015 - p189(3) [501+]
    MLR - v110 - i1 - Jan 2015 - p262-263 [501+]

Dove, Emily - *Wendell the Narwhal (Illus. by Dove, Emily)*
    c KR - July 15 2015 - pNA [51-500]

Dovey, Ceridwen - *Only the Animals*
    KR - July 15 2015 - pNA [51-500]
    LJ - v140 - i12 - July 1 2015 - p81(1) [51-500]
    NYTBR - Sept 20 2015 - p18(L) [501+]
    PW - v262 - i28 - July 13 2015 - p41(2) [51-500]

D'Ovidio, Francesco Lefebvre - *I Documenti diplomatici italiani. Terza Serie: 1896-1907. Vol. IX: 29 marzo 1905-28 maggio 1906*
    HER - v130 - i545 - August 2015 - p1029(3) [501+]

Dovlatov, Sergei - *Pushkin Hills*
    Lon R Bks - v37 - i10 - May 21 2015 - p37(2) [501+]
    The Zone: A Prison Camp Guard's Story
    Lon R Bks - v37 - i10 - May 21 2015 - p37(2) [501+]

Dow, Bonnie J. - *Watching Women's Liberation, 1970: Feminism's Pivotal Year on the Network News*
    HNet - May 2015 - pNA [501+]

Dow, Douglas N. - *Apostolic Iconography and Florentine Confraternities in the Age of Reform*
    Ren Q - v68 - i3 - Fall 2015 - p1001-1003 [501+]

Dow, Mirah J. - *School Libraries Matter: Views from the Research*
    LQ - v85 - i1 - Jan 2015 - p116(3) [501+]

Dowd, Nancy E. - *A New Juvenile Justice System: Total Reform for a Broken System*
    y VOYA - v38 - i3 - August 2015 - p92(1) [51-500]

Dowd, Susan - *Beyond Book Sales: The Complete Guide to Raising Real Money for Your Library*
    LQ - v85 - i2 - April 2015 - p218(3) [501+]

Dowdall, Courtney Marie - *Pesticides and Global Health: Understanding Agrochemical Dependence and Investing in Sustainable Solutions*
    MAQ - v29 - i2 - June 2015 - pb31-b33 [501+]

Dowding, Philippa - *Myles and the Monster Outside*
  c KR - July 15 2015 - pNA [51-500]
  c Res Links - v21 - i1 - Oct 2015 - p13(1) [51-500]

Dowell, Frances O'Roark - *Anybody Shining*
  c HB Guide - v26 - i1 - Spring 2015 - p75(1) [51-500]
  Phineas L. MacGuire ... Gets Cooking! (Illus. by McDaniels, Preston)
  c CCB-B - v68 - i5 - Jan 2015 - p253(2) [51-500]
  c HB Guide - v26 - i1 - Spring 2015 - p59(1) [51-500]

Dowell, Frances O'Rourke - *Anybody Shining (Read by Jackson, Suzy). Audiobook Review*
  c SLJ - v61 - i2 - Feb 2015 - p48(2) [51-500]

Dowell, Kristin L. - *Sovereign Screens: Aboriginal Media on the Canadian West Coast*
  PHR - v84 - i4 - Nov 2015 - p565(3) [501+]

Dower, Laura - *101 Things to Do before You Grow Up: Fun Activities for You to Check off Your List (Illus. by Bramall, Dan)*
  c SLJ - v61 - i7 - July 2015 - p106(1) [51-500]

Dowling, Julie A. - *Mexican Americans and the Question of Race*
  AJS - v120 - i5 - March 2015 - p1550(3) [501+]
  Aztlan - v40 - i2 - Fall 2015 - p281-285 [501+]

Dowling, Robert M. - *Eugene O'Neill: A Life in Four Acts*
  AM - v213 - i4 - August 17 2015 - p41(2) [501+]
  Lon R Bks - v37 - i3 - Feb 5 2015 - p21(2) [501+]
  TLS - i5849 - May 8 2015 - p13(1) [501+]

Dowling, Terry - *Grand Crusades: The Early Jack Vance, vol. 5*
  PW - v262 - i3 - Jan 19 2015 - p65(1) [51-500]

Dowling, Tim - *How to Be a Husband*
  LJ - v140 - i2 - Feb 1 2015 - p80(1) [51-500]
  NYTBR - Feb 15 2015 - p30(L) [501+]

Dowling, Timothy C. - *Russia at War: From the Mongol Conquest to Afghanistan, Chechnya, and Beyond*
  R&USQ - v54 - i4 - Summer 2015 - p83(2) [501+]

Down, Reg - *The Alphabet*
  c CH Bwatch - Nov 2015 - pNA [51-500]
  King Red and the White Snow: And Other Tales for Children (Illus. by Down, Reg)
  c CH Bwatch - Oct 2015 - pNA [51-500]
  The Nine Lives of Pinrut the Turnip Boy
  c CH Bwatch - May 2015 - pNA [51-500]

Down, Therese - *Only in Blood*
  PW - v262 - i20 - May 18 2015 - p38(1) [51-500]

Downer, Ann - *Smart and Spineless: Exploring Invertebrate Intelligence*
  y BL - v112 - i1 - Sept 1 2015 - p92(1) [51-500]
  y KR - June 15 2015 - pNA [51-500]
      Sci & Ch - v53 - i4 - Dec 2015 - p97 [501+]
  y Sci Teach - v82 - i9 - Dec 2015 - p74 [51-500]
  y SLJ - v61 - i8 - August 2015 - p126(2) [51-500]

Downes, Patrick - *Fell of Dark*
  y BL - v111 - i17 - May 1 2015 - p90(2) [51-500]
  y CCB-B - v68 - i11 - July-August 2015 - p543(1) [51-500]
  y HB Guide - v26 - i2 - Fall 2015 - p117(1) [501+]
  y KR - March 15 2015 - pNA [51-500]
  y PW - v262 - i10 - March 9 2015 - p75(1) [51-500]
  y PW - v262 - i49 - Dec 2 2015 - p91(1) [51-500]
      SLJ - v61 - i4 - April 2015 - p163(1) [51-500]
  y VOYA - v38 - i1 - April 2015 - p57(1) [51-500]

Downes, Stephen - *After Mahler: Britten, Weill, Henze, and Romantic Redemption*
  Notes - v71 - i4 - June 2015 - p694(3) [501+]

Downey, Anthony - *Uncommon Grounds: New Media and Critical Practices in the Middle East and North Africa*
  HNet - May 2015 - pNA [501+]

Downham, Jenny - *Unbecoming*
  y KR - Nov 15 2015 - pNA [51-500]
  y Magpies - v30 - i4 - Sept 2015 - p18(1) [501+]
      PW - v262 - i47 - Nov 23 2015 - p71(1) [51-500]
      Sch Lib - v63 - i4 - Winter 2015 - p252(2) [501+]
  y SLJ - v61 - i12 - Dec 2015 - p120(1) [51-500]

Downie, David - *A Passion for Paris: Romanticism and Romance in the City of Light*
  BL - v111 - i15 - April 1 2015 - p4(1) [501+]
  KR - Feb 15 2015 - pNA [51-500]
  LJ - v140 - i7 - April 15 2015 - p100(1) [51-500]

Downing, David - *Jack of Spies*
  RVBW - August 2015 - pNA [501+]
  One Man's Flag
  BL - v112 - i4 - Oct 15 2015 - p22(1) [51-500]
  KR - Sept 1 2015 - pNA [51-500]
  LJ - v140 - i16 - Oct 1 2015 - p68(1) [51-500]
  PW - v262 - i39 - Sept 28 2015 - p66(1) [51-500]

Downing, Erin - *For Soccer-Crazy Girls Only*
  c HB Guide - v26 - i1 - Spring 2015 - p183(1) [51-500]

Downing, Johnette - *The Fifolet (Illus. by Lindsley, Jennifer)*
  c HB Guide - v26 - i2 - Fall 2015 - p158(2) [51-500]
  Louisiana, the Jewel of the Deep South (Illus. by Marshall, Julia)
  c SLJ - v61 - i11 - Nov 2015 - p131(1) [51-500]
  Macarooned on a Dessert Island (Illus. by Wald, Christina)
  c CH Bwatch - Feb 2015 - pNA [51-500]
  c HB Guide - v26 - i1 - Spring 2015 - p28(1) [51-500]

Downing, Lisa - *Fuckology: Critical Essays on John Money's Diagnostic Concepts*
  JGS - v24 - i3 - June 2015 - p361-362 [501+]

Downing, Michael - *The Chapel*
  BL - v111 - i13 - March 1 2015 - p17(1) [51-500]
  KR - Feb 1 2015 - pNA [51-500]
  PW - v262 - i8 - Feb 23 2015 - p49(1) [51-500]

Downing, Taylor - *Secret Warriors: Key Scientists, Code Breakers and Propagandists of the Great War*
  HT - v65 - i6 - June 2015 - p63(1) [501+]
  Secret Warriors: The Spies, Scientists and Code Breakers of World War I
  KR - Jan 1 2015 - pNA [501+]
  LJ - v140 - i3 - Feb 15 2015 - p111(1) [51-500]
  PW - v262 - i6 - Feb 9 2015 - p59(1) [51-500]

Downs, Gregory P. - *After Appomattox: Military Occupation and the Ends of War*
  CHE - v61 - i34 - May 8 2015 - pB16(1) [501+]
  J Mil H - v79 - i3 - July 2015 - p847-848 [501+]
  LJ - v140 - i8 - May 1 2015 - p88(3) [501+]

Downs, Jim - *Sick from Freedom: African-American Illness and Suffering during the Civil War and Reconstruction*
  HNet - May 2015 - pNA [501+]
  Stand By Me
  KR - Jan 1 2016 - pNA [501+]

Downs, Matthew L. - *Transforming the South: Federal Development in the Tennessee Valley 1915-1960*
  JEH - v75 - i2 - June 2015 - p603-604 [501+]

Downs, Paul - *Boss Life: Surviving My Own Small Business*
  KR - June 1 2015 - pNA [51-500]
  LJ - v140 - i12 - July 1 2015 - p91(1) [51-500]
  BL - v111 - i21 - July 1 2015 - p21(1) [51-500]
  PW - v262 - i26 - June 29 2015 - p59(1) [51-500]
  SEP - v287 - i5 - Sept-Oct 2015 - p24(1) [501+]

Downum, Amanda - *Dreams of Shreds & Tatters*
  KR - March 1 2015 - pNA [51-500]
  NYTBR - Oct 18 2015 - p18(L) [501+]
  PW - v262 - i13 - March 30 2015 - p60(1) [51-500]

Dowson, Jeff - *Closing the Distance*
  RVBW - July 2015 - pNA [51-500]

Dowswell, Paul - *Bomber*
  y Magpies - v30 - i3 - July 2015 - p40(1) [501+]

Doxey, Heidi Jo - *Liam Darcy, I Loathe You*
  y SLJ - v61 - i8 - August 2015 - p96(2) [51-500]

Doyal, Lesley - *Living with HIV and Dying with AIDS: Diversity, Inequality and Human Rights in the Global Pandemic*
  CS - v44 - i5 - Sept 2015 - p657-659 [501+]

Doyle, Arthur Conan - *The Hound of the Baskervilles (Read by Klinger, Leslie). Audiobook Review*
  LJ - v140 - i3 - Feb 15 2015 - p57(1) [51-500]
  The Hound of the Baskervilles (Illus. by Ferran, Daniel)
  y HB Guide - v26 - i1 - Spring 2015 - p72(2) [51-500]
  Sherlock Holmes in a Study in Scarlet
  y HB Guide - v26 - i2 - Fall 2015 - p117(1) [51-500]

Doyle, Brian - *Martin Marten*
  y BL - v111 - i15 - April 1 2015 - p26(1) [51-500]
      LJ - v140 - i5 - March 15 2015 - p91(1) [51-500]
  Martin Marten (Illus. by van Dusen, Katrina)
  y SLJ - v61 - i12 - Dec 2015 - p131(2) [51-500]
  Martin Marten
  y VOYA - v38 - i2 - June 2015 - p58(1) [51-500]

Doyle, Catherine - *Vendetta (Read by Bouvard, Laurence). Audiobook Review*
  y SLJ - v61 - i9 - Sept 2015 - p60(2) [51-500]
  The Vendetta
  y HB Guide - v26 - i2 - Fall 2015 - p117(1) [51-500]
  Vendetta
  y VOYA - v37 - i6 - Feb 2015 - p55(1) [51-500]

Doyle, Don H. - *The Cause of All Nations: An International History of the American Civil War*
  BooChiTr - Jan 10 2015 - p14(1) [501+]
  Econ - v414 - i8922 - Jan 24 2015 - p73(US) [501+]
  For Aff - v94 - i3 - May-June 2015 - pNA [501+]
  HT - v65 - i7 - July 2015 - p64(1) [501+]
  J Mil H - v79 - i3 - July 2015 - p831-833 [501+]
  TLS - i5852 - May 29 2015 - p9(2) [501+]

Doyle, Elizabeth - *ABSee (Illus. by Doyle, Elizabeth)*
  c SLJ - v61 - i7 - July 2015 - p55(2) [51-500]
  A B See
  c KR - Jan 1 2016 - pNA [51-500]

Doyle, Laura - *First, Kill All the Marriage Counselors: Modern-Day Secrets to Being Desired, Cherished, and Adored for Life*
  PW - v262 - i18 - May 4 2015 - p114(1) [51-500]

Doyle, Lisa - *Milked*
  KR - May 1 2015 - pNA [501+]

Doyle, Peter - *The Big Whatever*
  BL - v111 - i21 - July 1 2015 - p35(1) [51-500]
  The First World War in 100 Objects
  LJ - v140 - i9 - May 15 2015 - p94(2) [51-500]

Doyle, Rob - *Here Are the Young Men*
  KR - May 1 2015 - pNA [501+]
  LJ - v140 - i10 - June 1 2015 - p85(1) [51-500]
  PW - v262 - i15 - April 13 2015 - p54(2) [51-500]

Doyle, Roddy - *Brilliant (Illus. by Hughes, Emily)*
  c KR - July 1 2015 - pNA [51-500]
  c PW - v262 - i23 - June 8 2015 - p59(2) [51-500]
  c SLJ - v61 - i7 - July 2015 - p75(2) [51-500]
      TES - i5141 - April 10 2015 - p39(1) [501+]
  The Guts
  ILS - v34 - i2 - Spring 2015 - p16(1) [501+]
  NYTBR - Jan 25 2015 - p24(L) [501+]

Doyle, Tom - *The Left-Hand Way*
  BL - v111 - i21 - July 1 2015 - p47(1) [51-500]
  PW - v262 - i18 - May 4 2015 - p100(1) [51-500]

Doyle, Trinity - *Pieces of Sky*
  y Magpies - v30 - i2 - May 2015 - p40(1) [501+]

Doyle, William - *France and the Age of Revolution: Regimes Old and New from Louis XIV to Napoleon Bonaparte*
  HER - v130 - i542 - Feb 2015 - p217(2) [501+]
  PT 109: An American Epic of War, Survival, and the Destiny of John F. Kennedy
  KR - Sept 15 2015 - pNA [501+]
  LJ - v140 - i17 - Oct 15 2015 - p100(1) [51-500]

Dozier, Graham T. - *A Gunner in Lee's Army: The Civil War Letters of Thomas Henry Carter*
  J Mil H - v79 - i1 - Jan 2015 - p213-215 [501+]

Dozois, Gardner - *Old Venus*
  BL - v111 - i12 - Feb 15 2015 - p45(1) [51-500]
  The Year's Best Science Fiction, 2015
  BL - v111 - i18 - May 15 2015 - p40(1) [51-500]

Dr. Seuss - *One Fish, Two Fish, Red Fish, Blue Fish (Illus. by Dr. Seuss)*
  NYT - Nov 27 2015 - pC31(L) [501+]
  What Pet Should I Get? and One Fish Two Fish Red Fish Blue Fish (Read by Wilson, Rainn, with David Hyde Pierce). Audiobook Review
  c PW - v262 - i48 - Nov 30 2015 - p56(1) [51-500]
  c SLJ - v61 - i10 - Oct 2015 - p50(1) [51-500]
  What Pet Should I Get? (Illus. by Dr. Seuss)
  c BL - v111 - i22 - August 1 2015 - p76(1) [51-500]
  c CH Bwatch - Oct 2015 - pNA [51-500]
  c SLJ - v61 - i9 - Sept 2015 - p128(1) [51-500]
  What Pet Should I Get?
  c KR - August 1 2015 - pNA [501+]
      NYT - July 20 2015 - pC1(L) [501+]
  c NYTBR - July 26 2015 - p1(L) [501+]

Drager, Lindsey - *The Sorrow Proper*
  LJ - v140 - i7 - April 15 2015 - p75(1) [51-500]

Drago, Thomas - *Queensboro*
  KR - July 1 2015 - pNA [501+]

The Dragon Lantern: A League of Seven
  y CH Bwatch - Sept 2015 - pNA [51-500]

Dragoon, Leigh - *Legend: The Graphic Novel (Illus. by Kaari)*
  y SLJ - v61 - i5 - May 2015 - p127(2) [51-500]

Dragt, Tonke - *The Letter for the King*
  c HB - v91 - i5 - Sept-Oct 2015 - p101(2) [51-500]
  c KR - June 15 2015 - pNA [51-500]
  y PW - v262 - i21 - May 25 2015 - p60(1) [51-500]
  y PW - v262 - i49 - Dec 2 2015 - p104(1) [51-500]
  y SLJ - v61 - i8 - August 2015 - p102(1) [51-500]
  y VOYA - v38 - i3 - August 2015 - p58(1) [51-500]
  The Secrets of the Wild Wood
  TLS - i5876 - Nov 13 2015 - p31(1) [501+]

Draheim, Megan - *Human Wildlife Conflict: Complexity in the Marine Environment*
  TimHES - i2220 - Sept 10 2015 - p47(1) [501+]

Drake, Annette - *Bone Girl*
  CH Bwatch - April 2015 - pNA [51-500]

Drake, Brian Allen - *Loving Nature, Fearing the State: Environmentalism and Antigovernment Politics before Reagan*
  JAH - v101 - i4 - March 2015 - p1343-1344 [501+]

Drake, David - *Air and Darkness*
    KR - Sept 1 2015 - pNA [51-500]
    PW - v262 - i39 - Sept 28 2015 - p74(1) [51-500]
Into the Maelstrom
    Analog - v135 - i11 - Nov 2015 - p105(1) [501+]
    PW - v262 - i4 - Jan 26 2015 - p153(2) [51-500]
Paris at War
    KR - July 15 2015 - pNA [51-500]
Drake, Susanna - *Slandering the Jew: Sexuality and Difference in Early Christian Texts*
    HNet - Feb 2015 - pNA [501+]
Drakeford, Lisa - *The Baby*
    y Sch Lib - v63 - i4 - Winter 2015 - p253(1) [51-500]
Dralyuk, Boris - *Red Cavalry*
    Bks & Cult - v21 - i5 - Sept-Oct 2015 - p44(2) [501+]
Dransart, Penelope - *Living Beings: Perspectives on Interspecies Engagements*
    JRAI - v21 - i1 - March 2015 - p216(2) [501+]
Draper, Sharon - *Stella By Starlight*
    c Magpies - v30 - i2 - May 2015 - p34(2) [501+]
Draper, Sharon M. - *Stella By Starlight*
    SLJ - v61 - i4 - April 2015 - p62(2) [51-500]
    c HB - v91 - i1 - Jan-Feb 2015 - p79(2) [501+]
    c HB Guide - v26 - i2 - Fall 2015 - p80(1) [51-500]
    c NYTBR - Feb 8 2015 - p23(L) [501+]
    c PW - v262 - i49 - Dec 2 2015 - p80(2) [51-500]
    RVBW - Feb 2015 - pNA [501+]
    y VOYA - v37 - i6 - Feb 2015 - p55(1) [501+]
Drawing with Mark: Let's Go to the Zoo!/Zoo Stories
    SLJ - v61 - i2 - Feb 2015 - p41(1) [51-500]
Dray, Stephanie - *America's First Daughter*
    KR - Jan 1 2016 - pNA [51-500]
Dreby, Joanna - *Everyday Illegal: When Policies Undermine Immigrant Families*
    HER - v85 - i3 - Fall 2015 - p514-517 [501+]
Dreger, Alice - *Galileo's Middle Finger: Heretics, Activists, and the Search for Justice in Science*
    BL - v111 - i11 - Feb 1 2015 - p4(1) [51-500]
    Comw - v142 - i15 - Sept 25 2015 - p28(2) [501+]
    KR - Jan 1 2015 - pNA [51-500]
    LJ - v140 - i3 - Feb 15 2015 - p124(2) [51-500]
    Nature - v519 - i7543 - March 19 2015 - p290(1) [501+]
    NY - v91 - i15 - June 1 2015 - p75 [51-500]
    NYTBR - April 19 2015 - p14(L) [501+]
Dreher, Rod - *How Dante Can Save Your Life: The Life-Changing Wisdom of History's Greatest Poem*
    KR - March 15 2015 - pNA [501+]
    Ch Today - v59 - i5 - June 2015 - p67(3) [501+]
    Nat R - v67 - i15 - August 24 2015 - p42 [501+]
Dreidemy, Lucile - *Der Dollfuss-Mythos: Eine Biographie des Posthumen*
    HNet - March 2015 - pNA [501+]
Dreier, Daniel - *Grace Kelly: Film Stills*
    RVBW - Jan 2015 - pNA [501+]
Dreier, Mary Sue Dehmlow - *Created and Led by the Spirit: Planting Missional Congregations*
    Intpr - v69 - i4 - Oct 2015 - p501(2) [501+]
Dreisbach, Daniel L. - *Faith and the Founders of the American Republic*
    JAH - v102 - i2 - Sept 2015 - p543-544 [501+]
    JR - v95 - i4 - Oct 2015 - p549(3) [501+]
Dreise, Gregg - *Kookoo Kookaburra (Illus. by Dreise, Gregg)*
    c Magpies - v30 - i3 - July 2015 - p28(1) [501+]
Dreisinger, Baz - *Incarceration Nations: A Journey to Justice in Prisons around the World*
    KR - Nov 15 2015 - pNA [501+]
    PW - v262 - i41 - Oct 12 2015 - p55(1) [51-500]
Drelichman, Mauricio - *Lending to the Borrower from Hell: Debt, Taxes, and Default in the Age of Philip II*
    BHR - v89 - i3 - Autumn 2015 - p586(3) [501+]
    HER - v130 - i545 - August 2015 - p988(3) [501+]
    JEH - v75 - i2 - June 2015 - p594-595 [501+]
    Ren Q - v68 - i1 - Spring 2015 - p286-287 [501+]
Drescher, Daniela - *Pippa and Pelle in the Winter Snow (Illus. by Drescher, Daniela)*
    c KR - Jan 1 2016 - pNA [51-500]
Dressen, Angela - *The Library of the Badia Fiesolana: Intellectual History and Education under the Medici*
    Specu - v90 - i3 - July 2015 - p797-799 [501+]
Drever, Matthew - *Image, Identity, and the Forming of the Augustinian Soul*
    JR - v95 - i3 - July 2015 - p406(3) [501+]
Drew, Elizabeth - *Washington Journal: Reporting Watergate and Richard Nixon's Downfall*
    Lon R Bks - v37 - i21 - Nov 5 2015 - p33(2) [501+]

Drexler, Michael J. - *The Traumatic Colonel: The Founding Fathers, Slavery, and the Phantasmatic Aaron Burr*
    JSH - v81 - i4 - Nov 2015 - p951(2) [501+]
The Traumatic Colonel: The Founding Fathers, Slavery, and the Phantasmic Aaron Burr
    AHR - v120 - i3 - June 2015 - p1022-1023 [501+]
Dreyer, Boris - *Orte der Varuskatastrophe und der romischen Okkupation in Germanien: Der historisch-archaologische Fuhrer*
    HNet - April 2015 - pNA [501+]
Dreyfus, Hubert - *Retrieving Realism*
    RM - v69 - i2 - Dec 2015 - p383(2) [501+]
Drezner, Daniel W. - *The System Worked: How the World Stopped Another Great Depression*
    For Aff - v94 - i1 - Jan-Feb 2015 - pNA [51-500]
Drieu, Cloe - *Fictions nationales: Cinema, empire et nation en Ouzbekistan*
    Slav R - v74 - i2 - Summer 2015 - p393-394 [501+]
Driggers, James - *Lovesick*
    BL - v111 - i16 - April 15 2015 - p28(2) [51-500]
    PW - v262 - i7 - Feb 16 2015 - p161(1) [51-500]
Driggs, Shad - *The Midwife of Bethlehem (Illus. by Lucas, Diane)*
    c SPBW - Nov 2015 - pNA [51-500]
Drinan, Patrick - *The 12 Drop Rule: Getting the Most out of Wine and Life*
    KR - July 15 2015 - pNA [51-500]
Driscoll, Amanda - *Duncan the Story Dragon (Illus. by Driscoll, Amanda)*
    c HB Guide - v26 - i2 - Fall 2015 - p32(1) [51-500]
    c KR - March 1 2015 - pNA [51-500]
    c SLJ - v61 - i10 - Oct 2015 - p74(1) [51-500]
Driscoll, Laura - *A Mousy Mess (Illus. by Melmon, Deborah)*
    c HB Guide - v26 - i1 - Spring 2015 - p28(1) [51-500]
Dritter Workshop zur Jugendbewegungsforschung
    HNet - Sept 2015 - pNA [501+]
Driver, Dave - *Supermom and the Big Baby (Illus. by Laird, Guy)*
    c Res Links - v20 - i4 - April 2015 - p2(2) [51-500]
Drixler, Fabian - *Mabiki: Infanticide and Population Growth in Eastern Japan, 1660-1950*
    Historian - v77 - i1 - Spring 2015 - p150(2) [51-500]
    Pac A - v88 - i4 - Dec 2015 - p939 [501+]
Drndic, Dasa - *Trieste*
    NYTBR - May 24 2015 - p28(L) [501+]
Drogula, Fred K. - *Commanders and Command in the Roman Republic and Early Empire*
    J Mil H - v79 - i3 - July 2015 - p807-808 [501+]
Drohojowska-Philp, Hunter - *Rebels in Paradise: The Los Angeles Art Scene and the 1960s*
    BL - v112 - i5 - Nov 1 2015 - p18(2) [501+]
Droit, Emmanuel - *Vorwarts zum neuen Menschen? Die sozialistische Erziehung in der DDR 1949-1989*
    HNet - May 2015 - pNA [501+]
Drouin, Jean-Marc - *Philosophie de l'insecte*
    Isis - v106 - i2 - June 2015 - p416(2) [501+]
Drout, Michael D.C. - *Singers and Tales: Oral Tradition and the Roots of Literature (Read by Drout, Michael D.C.) Audiobook Review*
    LJ - v140 - i8 - May 1 2015 - p42(1) [51-500]
Tradition and Influence in Anglo-Saxon Literature: An Evolutionary, Cognitivist Approach
    Specu - v90 - i4 - Oct 2015 - p1108-1110 [501+]
Druchunas, Donna - *How to Knit Socks That Fit: Techniques for Toe-Up and Cuff-Down Styles*
    BL - v112 - i5 - Nov 1 2015 - p12(1) [51-500]
    LJ - v140 - i19 - Nov 15 2015 - p84(2) [51-500]
Drucker, Donna J. - *The Classification of Sex: Alfred Kinsey and the Organization of Knowledge*
    HNet - Jan 2015 - pNA [501+]
    TimHES - i2199 - April 16 2015 - p57-1 [501+]
    TLS - i5842 - March 20 2015 - p23(1) [51-500]
Drucker, Lance - *How to Avoid Bag Lady Syndrome*
    SPBW - Feb 2015 - pNA [51-500]
Druick, Zoe - *The Grierson Effect: Tracing Documentary's International Movement*
    Si & So - v25 - i3 - March 2015 - p106(1) [501+]
Druillet, Philippe - *The 6 Voyages of Lone Sloane (Illus. by Druillet, Philippe)*
    BL - v112 - i4 - Oct 15 2015 - p35(1) [51-500]
    y SLJ - v61 - i10 - Oct 2015 - p119(1) [51-500]
Druke, Luise - *Innovations in Refugee Protection: A Compendium of UNHCR's 60 Years. Including Case Studies on IT Communities, Vietnamese Boatpeople, Chilean Exile and Namibian Repatriation*
    HNet - Feb 2015 - pNA [501+]

Drummond, Allan - *Banjo Paterson (Illus. by Lumsden, Glen)*
    y Magpies - v30 - i4 - Sept 2015 - p22(1) [501+]
Drummond, Carlos - *Multitudinous Heart: Selected Poems: A Bilingual Edition*
    BL - v111 - i19-20 - June 1 2015 - p24(2) [51-500]
Drummond, Ree - *Charlie and the New Baby (Illus. by deGroat, Diane)*
    c HB Guide - v26 - i1 - Spring 2015 - p28(1) [51-500]
Charlie le chien du ranch (Illus. by de Groat, Diane)
    c Res Links - v20 - i3 - Feb 2015 - p44(1) [501+]
Charlie Plays Ball (Illus. by deGroat, Diane)
    c HB Guide - v26 - i2 - Fall 2015 - p32(1) [51-500]
Charlie the Ranch Dog (Illus. by deGroat, Diane)
    SLJ - v61 - i2 - Feb 2015 - p66(1) [51-500]
The Pioneer Woman Cooks: Dinnertime: Comfort Classics...
    PW - v262 - i44 - Nov 2 2015 - p18(1) [51-500]
Drury, Allen - *Advise and Consent*
    Nat R - v67 - i2 - Feb 9 2015 - p24 [501+]
Drury, Amanda Hontz - *Saying Is Believing: The Necessity of Testimony in Adolescent Spiritual Development*
    Ch Today - April 2015 - p82(1) [51-500]
Drury, Bob - *A Dog's Gift*
    KR - April 1 2015 - pNA [51-500]
A Dog's Gift: The Inspirational Story of Veterans and Children Healed by Man's Best Friend
    LJ - v140 - i11 - June 15 2015 - p106(1) [501+]
Red Cloud: The Greatest Warrior Chief of the American West
    TLS - i5837 - Feb 13 2015 - p7(2) [501+]
Drury, Frank - *Random Shootings*
    SPBW - July 2015 - pNA [51-500]
Drury, John - *Music at Midnight: The Life and Poetry of George Herbert*
    AM - v213 - i7 - Sept 21 2015 - p40(2) [501+]
    JR - v95 - i3 - July 2015 - p424(2) [501+]
Drury, Tom - *Pacific*
    NYTBR - Jan 25 2015 - p24(L) [501+]
Druse, Ken - *The New Shade Garden: Creating a Lush Oasis in the Age of Climate Change*
    NYTBR - May 31 2015 - p36(L) [501+]
    PW - v262 - i16 - April 20 2015 - p73(1) [51-500]
Dry, Sarah - *The Newton Papers*
    Archiv - i79 - Spring 2015 - p179(5) [501+]
Drye, Willie - *For Sale--American Paradise: How Our Nation Was Sold an Impossible Dream in Florida*
    BL - v112 - i1 - Sept 1 2015 - p30(1) [51-500]
    LJ - v140 - i16 - Oct 1 2015 - p93(1) [51-500]
Drysdale, Rosemary - *Entrelac 2: New Techniques for Interlace Knitting*
    LJ - v140 - i2 - Feb 1 2015 - p82(1) [51-500]
D'Souza, Dinesh - *Stealing America: What My Experience with Criminal Gangs Taught Me About Obama, Hillary, and the Democratic Party*
    KR - Oct 1 2015 - pNA [51-500]
    Nat R - v67 - i23 - Dec 21 2015 - p39(2) [501+]
du Bouchet, Andre - *Openwork: Poetry and Prose*
    TLS - i5856 - June 26 2015 - p22(1) [501+]
Du Bouchet, Andre - *Openwork: Poetry and Prose*
    Bks & Cult - v21 - i1 - Jan-Feb 2015 - p36(1) [501+]
Du Brul, Jack - *The Lightning Stones*
    PW - v262 - i26 - June 29 2015 - p47(1) [51-500]
Du Plessis, Paul J. - *Letting and Hiring in Roman Legal Thought: 27 BCE-284 CE*
    Class R - v65 - i1 - April 2015 - p214-216 [501+]
Du Quesnay, Ian M. - *Catullus: Poems, Books, Readers*
    Class R - v65 - i2 - Oct 2015 - p438-440 [501+]
Duane, Diane - *Games Wizards Play*
    y KR - Dec 1 2015 - pNA [51-500]
    c SLJ - v61 - i12 - Dec 2015 - p113(1) [51-500]
Dubber, Geoff - *Riveting Reads: World War I*
    Sch Lib - v63 - i2 - Summer 2015 - p118(1) [51-500]
World War I
    Sch Lib - v63 - i1 - Spring 2015 - p63(1) [51-500]
Dubberley, Emily - *Blue Mondays: The Complete Series*
    LJ - v140 - i6 - April 1 2015 - p70(2) [501+]
Dubbs, Chris - *America's U-boats: Terror Trophies of World War I*
    NWCR - v68 - i4 - Autumn 2015 - p135(3) [51-500]
Dube, Peter - *Beginning with the Mirror: Ten Stories about Love, Desire and Moving between Worlds*
    G&L Rev W - v22 - i2 - March-April 2015 - p42(1) [501+]

Dubin, Amanda S. - *Assassin's Wall. E-book Review*
PW - v262 - i32 - August 10 2015 - p42(2) [51-500]

Dubinsky, Karen - *Babies without Borders: Adoption and Migration across the Americas*
JWH - v27 - i1 - Spring 2015 - p168(10) [501+]

Duble, Kathleen Benner - *Madame Tussaud's Apprentice*
y HB Guide - v26 - i1 - Spring 2015 - p106(1) [51-500]
y Sch Lib - v63 - i4 - Winter 2015 - p244(1) [51-500]

Dubler, Joshua - *Down in the Chapel: Religious Life in American Prison*
Comw - v142 - i4 - Feb 20 2015 - p27(4) [501+]
Down in the Chapel: Religious Life in an American Prison
Am St - v54 - i1 - Spring 2015 - p138-4 [501+]

Dublin, Anne - *44 Hours or Strike!*
y KR - August 1 2015 - pNA [51-500]

Dubnau, Josh - *Behavioral Genetics of the Fly*
QRB - v90 - i3 - Sept 2015 - p344(1) [501+]

Dubner, Stephen J. - *When to Rob a Bank and 131 More Warped Suggestions and Well-Intended Rants*
y SLJ - v61 - i11 - Nov 2015 - p126(2) [501+]

DuBois, Brendan - *Blood Foam*
PW - v262 - i14 - April 6 2015 - p41(1) [51-500]
BL - v111 - i17 - May 1 2015 - p20(2) [51-500]
Dark Victory
PW - v262 - i42 - Oct 19 2015 - p59(1) [51-500]

Dubois, Vincent - *The Sociology of Wind Bands: Amateur Music Between Cultural Domination and Autonomy*
CS - v44 - i3 - May 2015 - p358-360 [501+]

Dubosarsky, Ursula - *The Red Shoe*
Sch Lib - v63 - i4 - Winter 2015 - p226(1) [51-500]
Reindeer's Christmas Surprise (Illus. by deGennaro, Sue)
c Magpies - v30 - i5 - Nov 2015 - p29(1) [501+]
Tim and Ed (Illus. by Joyner, Andrew)
c Magpies - v30 - i1 - March 2015 - p26(1) [501+]

Dubow, Charles - *Girl in the Moonlight*
BL - v111 - i17 - May 1 2015 - p75(1) [51-500]
KR - March 15 2015 - pNA [51-500]
LJ - v140 - i5 - March 15 2015 - p91(1) [51-500]
PW - v262 - i11 - March 16 2015 - p58(1) [51-500]

Dubreuil, Annie - *Les tranches de vie de Felix Tome 4: Un ninja sous le soleil*
c Res Links - v20 - i5 - June 2015 - p38(2) [51-500]

Dubrow, Jehanne - *"Tell Me Why I Shouldn't Kill You": On Johanna Dubrow's The Arranged Marriage*
Ken R - v37 - i6 - Nov-Dec 2015 - p111(5) [501+]

Dubuc, Marianne - *The Bus Ride (Illus. by Dubuc, Marianne)*
c CCB-B - v68 - i10 - June 2015 - p487(2) [51-500]
c HB - v91 - i3 - May-June 2015 - p84(2) [51-500]
c HB Guide - v26 - i2 - Fall 2015 - p33(1) [51-500]
c NYTBR - May 10 2015 - p21(L) [501+]
c PW - v262 - i3 - Jan 19 2015 - p79(1) [51-500]
SLJ - v61 - i4 - April 2015 - p126(1) [51-500]
The Bus Ride
c Res Links - v20 - i5 - June 2015 - p3(1) [501+]
The Lion and the Bird (Illus. by Dubuc, Marianne)
c BL - v111 - i9-10 - Jan 1 2015 - pS4(8) [501+]
c BL - v112 - i4 - Oct 15 2015 - p53(1) [51-500]
c HB Guide - v26 - i1 - Spring 2015 - p28(1) [51-500]
c Magpies - v30 - i5 - Nov 2015 - p28(1) [501+]
Mr. Postmouse's Rounds (Illus. by Dubuc, Marianne)
c BL - v112 - i1 - Sept 1 2015 - p122(1) [51-500]
c CCB-B - v69 - i2 - Oct 2015 - p85(1) [51-500]
c NYTBR - Oct 11 2015 - p17(L) [501+]
c PW - v262 - i22 - June 1 2015 - p57(2) [51-500]
c SLJ - v61 - i9 - Sept 2015 - p119(1) [51-500]
Mr. Postmouse's Rounds
c KR - May 15 2015 - pNA [51-500]

Ducarre, Claude Julien - *Contes a Cristaux: Memoires d'un Cristallier Savoisien*
RocksMiner - v90 - i1 - Jan-Feb 2015 - p93(2) [501+]

Ducharme, Michel - *The Idea of Liberty in Canada during the Age of Atlantic Revolutions, 1776-1838*
AHR - v120 - i4 - Oct 2015 - p1482-1483 [501+]

Duchhardt, Heinz - *Der Wiener Kongress: Die Neugestaltung Europas 1814/15*
HNet - August 2015 - pNA [501+]
Der Wiener Kongress: Die neugestaltung Europas 1814-1815
CEH - v48 - i2 - June 2015 - p225-237 [501+]

Ducie, Joe - *Crystal Force*
y Sch Lib - v63 - i3 - Autumn 2015 - p182(1) [51-500]
The Rig
y BL - v111 - i18 - May 15 2015 - p63(2) [51-500]
y KR - August 1 2015 - pNA [51-500]
y SLJ - v61 - i11 - Nov 2015 - p107(2) [51-500]
y VOYA - v38 - i3 - August 2015 - p58(1) [501+]

Duckworth, Carolee - *Shifting Gears to Your Life and Work After Retirement*
RVBW - May 2015 - pNA [51-500]

Duckworth, Jessicah Krey - *Wide Welcome: How the Unsettling Presence of Newcomers Can Save the Church*
Intpr - v69 - i1 - Jan 2015 - p119(2) [501+]

Duddle, Jonny - *Gigantosaurus (Illus. by Duddle, Jonny)*
c HB Guide - v26 - i2 - Fall 2015 - p33(1) [51-500]

Duder, Tessa - *Out on the Water: Twelve Tales of the Sea (Illus. by Potter, Bruce)*
y Magpies - v30 - i1 - March 2015 - pS6(2) [51-500]

Dudley, Kathryn Marie - *Guitar Makers: The Endurance of Artisanal Values in North America*
TLS - i5836 - Feb 6 2015 - p27(1) [501+]

Dudley, Rebecca - *Hank Has a Dream*
c HB Guide - v26 - i1 - Spring 2015 - p28(2) [51-500]

Dudley, Robert - *The Drunken Monkey: Why We Drink and Abuse Alcohol*
MAQ - v29 - i2 - June 2015 - pb34-b36 [501+]
QRB - v90 - i2 - June 2015 - p218(2) [501+]

Dudley, William - *Thinking Critically: Biofuels*
y BL - v112 - i2 - Sept 15 2015 - p60(1) [51-500]

Dudziak, Mary L. - *War Time: An Idea, Its History, Its Consequences*
HNet - July 2015 - pNA [501+]

Due, Tananarive - *Ghost Summer: Stories*
PW - v262 - i29 - July 20 2015 - p174(1) [51-500]

Dueck, Colin - *The Obama Doctrine: American Grand Strategy Today*
LJ - v140 - i8 - May 1 2015 - p90(2) [51-500]
Nat R - v67 - i10 - June 1 2015 - p42 [501+]
TLS - i5860 - July 24 2015 - p12(2) [51-500]
The Obama Doctrine
KR - Feb 15 2015 - pNA [501+]

Duey, Kathleen - *Blizzard: Colorado, 1886*
c HB Guide - v26 - i2 - Fall 2015 - p80(1) [51-500]
Earthquake: San Francisco, 1906
c HB Guide - v26 - i1 - Spring 2015 - p75(1) [51-500]

Dufek, Holly - *Big Tractors (Illus. by Nunn, Paul E.)*
c CH Bwatch - August 2015 - pNA [51-500]

Duff, Sue - *Fade to Black*
PW - v262 - i5 - Feb 2 2015 - p41(2) [51-500]

Duffett, Mark - *Understanding Fandom: An Introduction to the Study of Media Fan Culture*
PMS - v38 - i1 - Feb 2015 - p109(3) [501+]

Duffield, Katy S. - *Loud Lula (Illus. by Boldt, Mike)*
c SLJ - v61 - i12 - Dec 2015 - p87(1) [51-500]

Duffin, Jacalyn - *Medical Saints: Cosmas and Damian in a Postmodern World*
Isis - v106 - i2 - June 2015 - p505(2) [501+]
JR - v95 - i2 - April 2015 - p259(3) [501+]

Duffin, Ross W. - *The Music Treatises of Thomas Ravenscroft: 'Treatise of Practicall Musick' and A Briefe Discourse*
Sev Cent N - v73 - i3-4 - Fall-Winter 2015 - p153(7) [501+]

Duffy, Brendan - *House of Echoes*
BL - v111 - i11 - Feb 1 2015 - p27(1) [51-500]
KR - Feb 1 2015 - pNA [51-500]
LJ - v140 - i3 - Feb 15 2015 - p85(1) [51-500]
PW - v262 - i5 - Feb 2 2015 - p36(1) [51-500]

Duffy, Carol Ann - *Collected Poems*
Spec - v329 - i9771 - Dec 5 2015 - p51(2) [501+]

Duffy, Chris - *Above the Dreamless Dead: World War I in Poetry and Comics*
y HB Guide - v26 - i1 - Spring 2015 - p187(1) [51-500]
Fable Comics
c KR - July 1 2015 - pNA [51-500]
PW - v262 - i25 - June 22 2015 - p143(1) [51-500]
c SLJ - v61 - i7 - July 2015 - p111(1) [51-500]
c BL - v112 - i2 - Sept 15 2015 - p52(2) [51-500]
c PW - v262 - i49 - Dec 2 2015 - p85(1) [51-500]

Duffy, James P. - *War at the End of the World: Douglas MacArthur and the Forgotten Fight for New Guinea, 1942-1945*
KR - Dec 15 2015 - pNA [51-500]
LJ - v140 - i20 - Dec 1 2015 - p114(1) [51-500]
PW - v262 - i47 - Nov 23 2015 - p62(1) [51-500]

Duffy, Jennifer Nugent - *Who's Your Paddy? Racial Expectations and the Struggle for Irish American Identity*
ERS - v38 - i8 - August 2015 - p1440(2) [501+]

Duffy, John J. - *Inventing Ethan Allen*
JAH - v102 - i1 - June 2015 - p232-232 [501+]

Duffy, Margaret - *Ashes to Ashes*
BL - v111 - i17 - May 1 2015 - p20(1) [51-500]
PW - v262 - i15 - April 13 2015 - p60(1) [51-500]

Duffy, Owen - *The Artichoke Queen*
BL - v112 - i1 - Sept 1 2015 - p38(1) [51-500]
KR - Dec 15 2015 - pNA [51-500]

Duffy, Sean - *Brian Boru and the Battle of Clontarf*
ILS - v34 - i2 - Spring 2015 - p3(2) [501+]

Dufour, Alain - *Correspondance de Theodore de Beze, vol. 38*
Six Ct J - v46 - i2 - Summer 2015 - p468-469 [501+]

Dugan, Ellen - *The Natural Psychic: Ellen Dugan's Personal Guide to the Psychic Realm*
PW - v262 - i19 - May 11 2015 - p56(1) [51-500]

Dugan, Emily - *Finding Home: Real Stories of Migrant Britain*
TimHES - i2221 - Sept 17 2015 - p45(1) [501+]

Dugan, Polly - *Sweetheart Deal*
BL - v111 - i16 - April 15 2015 - p27(1) [501+]
The Sweetheart Deal
KR - March 15 2015 - pNA [51-500]
LJ - v140 - i7 - April 15 2015 - p75(1) [51-500]
PW - v262 - i12 - March 23 2015 - p44(2) [51-500]

Dugard, Martin - *Killing Jesus*
JTWS - v32 - i1 - Spring 2015 - p346(2) [501+]
Killing Patton: The Strange Death of World War II's Most Audacious General
APH - v62 - i1 - Spring 2015 - p55(2) [501+]

Duggan, Anne E. - *Queer Enchantments: Gender, Sexuality, and Class in the Fairy-Tale Cinema of Jacques Demy*
WestFolk - v74 - i2 - Spring 2015 - p224-226 [501+]

Duggan, Christopher - *The Emperor of Ice-Cream*
TLS - i5844 - April 3 2015 - p20(1) [501+]
Fascist Voices: An Intimate History of Mussolini's Italy
JMH - v87 - i2 - June 2015 - p467(6) [501+]

Duggan, Lawrence C. - *Armsbearing and the Clergy in the History and Canon Law of Western Christianity*
HER - v130 - i543 - April 2015 - p410(3) [501+]

Duggan, M. - *Lawless Guns*
RVBW - May 2015 - pNA [51-500]

Dugoni, Robert - *Her Final Breath*
BL - v111 - i22 - August 1 2015 - p34(1) [51-500]
KR - July 15 2015 - pNA [51-500]
PW - v262 - i29 - July 20 2015 - p172(1) [51-500]

Duguay, Joanie - *Maya et Mitaine: De Saint-Jean a Paris (Illus. by Roy, Rejean)*
c Res Links - v20 - i5 - June 2015 - p39(1) [51-500]

Duin, Steve - *The Less We Touch*
KR - July 1 2015 - pNA [501+]

Duits, Rembrandt - *Images of the Pagan Gods: Papers of a Conference in Memory of Jean Seznec*
Six Ct J - v46 - i1 - Spring 2015 - p258-259 [501+]

Duke, Kate - *In the Rainforest (Illus. by Duke, Kate)*
c BL - v111 - i12 - Feb 15 2015 - p76(1) [51-500]
c HB Guide - v26 - i1 - Spring 2015 - p153(2) [51-500]
c BL - v111 - i9-10 - Jan 1 2015 - pS4(8) [501+]

Duke, Robert Harold - *LBJ and Grassroots Federalism: Congressman Bob Poage, Race, and Change in Texas*
AHR - v120 - i3 - June 2015 - p1054-1055 [501+]
Pres St Q - v45 - i4 - Dec 2015 - p814(2) [501+]

Duke, Shirley - *Cells*
c HB Guide - v26 - i1 - Spring 2015 - p154(1) [51-500]

Duley, Margaret - *Cold Pastoral*
Can Lit - i224 - Spring 2015 - p120 [501+]

Dumas, Marti - *Jala and the Wolves*
c PW - v262 - i27 - July 6 2015 - p72(2) [51-500]
The Quest for Screen Time (Illus. by Muravski, Mari)
c PW - v262 - i38 - Sept 21 2015 - p77(1) [51-500]

Dumit, Joseph - *Drugs for Life: How Pharmaceutical Companies Define Our Health*
JRAI - v21 - i3 - Sept 2015 - p700(2) [501+]

Dumitrescu, Theodor - *Early Music Editing: Principles, Historiography, Future Directions*
Specu - v90 - i4 - Oct 2015 - p1110-1112 [501+]

Dummett, Jeremy - *Palermo, City of Kings: The Heart of Sicily*
Spec - v328 - i9745 - June 6 2015 - p44(2) [501+]
TLS - i5862 - August 7 2015 - p30(1) [501+]

Dumon Tak, Bibi - *Mikis and the Donkey (Illus. by Hopman, Philip)*
   c HB Guide - v26 - i1 - Spring 2015 - p75(1) [51-500]

DuMont, Brianna - *Famous Phonies: Legends, Fakes, and Frauds Who Changed History*
   c HB Guide - v26 - i1 - Spring 2015 - p197(1) [51-500]
Fantastic Fugitives
   c KR - Nov 1 2015 - pNA [51-500]

Dumont, Jean-Francois - *I Am a Bear (Illus. by Dumont, Jean-Francois)*
   c HB - v91 - i5 - Sept-Oct 2015 - p79(2) [51-500]
   c KR - July 1 2015 - pNA [51-500]
   c RVBW - Nov 2015 - pNA [51-500]
I Am a Bear
   c PW - v262 - i24 - June 15 2015 - p81(1) [51-500]
The Sheep Go On Strike (Illus. by Dumont, Jean-Francois)
   c CH Bwatch - Feb 2015 - pNA [51-500]
The Sheep Go on Strike
   c HB Guide - v26 - i1 - Spring 2015 - p29(1) [51-500]

Dumpelmann, Sonja - *Flights of Imagination: Aviation, Landscape, Design*
     TLS - i5847 - April 24 2015 - p28(1) [501+]

Dunagan, Ted M. - *The Salvation of Miss Lucretia*
   y HB Guide - v26 - i2 - Fall 2015 - p80(1) [51-500]

Dunak, Karen M. - *As Long as We Both Shall Love: The White Wedding in Postwar America*
     J Am St - v49 - i2 - May 2015 - p440-441 [501+]

Dunaway, Dennis - *Snakes! Guillotines! Electric Chairs! My Adventures in the Alice Cooper Group*
     LJ - v140 - i12 - July 1 2015 - p85(2) [51-500]
     NS - v144 - i5266 - June 12 2015 - p48(2) [51-500]

Dunaway, Finis - *Seeing Green: The Use and Abuse of American Environmental Images*
     HNet - June 2015 - pNA [501+]
     New Sci - v226 - i3015 - April 4 2015 - p45(1) [501+]

Dunaway, Wilma A. - *Gendered Commodity Chains: Seeing Women's Work and Households in Global Production*
     AJS - v120 - i5 - March 2015 - p1578(3) [501+]
     CS - v44 - i6 - Nov 2015 - p793-794 [501+]

Dunbar, Eve - *Black Regions of the Imagination: African American Writers between the Nation and the World*
     AL - v87 - i2 - June 2015 - p398-400 [501+]

Dunbar, Helene - *What Remains*
   y KR - March 1 2015 - pNA [51-500]
   y VOYA - v38 - i1 - April 2015 - p57(2) [51-500]

Dunbar, Joyce - *Pat-a-Cake Baby (Illus. by Dunbar, Polly)*
   c HB Guide - v26 - i2 - Fall 2015 - p9(1) [51-500]
     KR - April 1 2015 - pNA [51-500]
   c PW - v262 - i16 - April 20 2015 - p74(1) [51-500]
   c Sch Lib - v63 - i3 - Autumn 2015 - p154(1) [51-500]
   c SLJ - v61 - i8 - August 2015 - p62(2) [51-500]

Dunbar-Ortiz, Roxanne - *An Indigenous Peoples' History of the United States (Read by Merlington, Laural). Audiobook Review*
     LJ - v140 - i11 - June 15 2015 - p51(1) [51-500]
An Indigenous Peoples' History of the United States
     Wom R Bks - v32 - i5 - Sept-Oct 2015 - p19(3) [501+]
Outlaw Woman: A Memoir of the War Years, 1960-1975
     WLT - v89 - i2 - March-April 2015 - p72(3) [501+]

Duncan, Alexandra - *Sound*
   y KR - July 15 2015 - pNA [51-500]
   y SLJ - v61 - i6 - June 2015 - p111(2) [51-500]
Sound: Salvage, Book 2
   y VOYA - v38 - i4 - Oct 2015 - p68(1) [51-500]

Duncan, Alice - *Thanksgiving Angels*
   y BL - v111 - i15 - April 1 2015 - p30(1) [51-500]
     KR - March 1 2015 - pNA [51-500]

Duncan, Charles M. - *Eat, Drink, and be Wary: How Unsafe Is Our Food?*
     BL - v111 - i11 - Feb 1 2015 - p5(1) [51-500]

Duncan, Dave - *Irona 700*
   y BL - v111 - i21 - July 1 2015 - p46(2) [51-500]
     PW - v262 - i17 - April 27 2015 - p56(1) [51-500]

Duncan, Elizabeth J. - *Slated for Death (Read by Flosnik, Anne). Audiobook Review*
     BL - v112 - i1 - Sept 1 2015 - p142(1) [51-500]
Slated for Death
     BL - v111 - i13 - March 1 2015 - p26(1) [51-500]
     KR - Feb 1 2015 - pNA [51-500]
     LJ - v140 - i6 - April 1 2015 - p63(3) [501+]
     PW - v262 - i6 - Feb 9 2015 - p47(1) [51-500]

Untimely Death
     BL - v112 - i2 - Sept 15 2015 - p35(1) [51-500]
     KR - Sept 1 2015 - pNA [51-500]
     PW - v262 - i36 - Sept 7 2015 - p48(2) [51-500]
     RVBW - Nov 2015 - pNA [51-500]

Duncan, Lois - *One to the Wolves: On the Trail of a Killer*
     LJ - v140 - i13 - August 1 2015 - p110(2) [51-500]

Duncan, Paul - *The Charlie Chaplin Archives*
     Si & So - v25 - i12 - Dec 2015 - p104(2) [501+]

Duncan, S.L. - *The Salvation of Gabriel Adam*
   y KR - May 1 2015 - pNA [51-500]
   y SLJ - v61 - i8 - August 2015 - p113(1) [51-500]
   y VOYA - v38 - i3 - August 2015 - p76(1) [51-500]

Duncan, Steven - *How Free Will Works: A Dualist Theory of Human Action*
     RM - v69 - i2 - Dec 2015 - p384(3) [501+]

Duncanson, Ian - *Historiography, Empire and the Rule of Law: Imagined Constitutions, Remembered Legalities*
     VS - v57 - i2 - Wntr 2015 - p287(2) [501+]

Duncker, Patricia - *Sophie and the Sibyl: A Victorian Romance*
     LJ - v140 - i7 - April 15 2015 - p75(1) [51-500]
     NYTBR - August 16 2015 - p20(L) [501+]
Sophie and the Sibyl
     BL - v111 - i17 - May 1 2015 - p79(1) [51-500]
     KR - June 15 2015 - pNA [51-500]
     TLS - i5857 - July 3 2015 - p19(2) [501+]

Duncklee, John - *Tales from Corral Fences*
     Roundup M - v22 - i6 - August 2015 - p28(2) [501+]
To the Harvest
     Roundup M - v23 - i1 - Oct 2015 - p29(2) [501+]

Dunckley, Victoria L. - *Reset Your Child's Brain: A Four-Week Plan to End Meltdowns, Raise Grades, and Boost Social Skills by Reversing the Effects of Electronic Screen Time*
     PW - v262 - i27 - July 6 2015 - p63(1) [51-500]

Dundas, Zach - *The Great Detective*
     KR - March 15 2015 - pNA [51-500]
The Great Detective: The Amazing Rise and Immortal Life of Sherlock Holmes
     LJ - v140 - i11 - June 15 2015 - p90(1) [501+]
     BL - v111 - i16 - April 15 2015 - p12(1) [51-500]
     PW - v262 - i13 - March 30 2015 - p66(2) [51-500]

Dungan, Myles - *If You Want to Know Who We Are: The Rathmines and Rathgar Musical Society 1913-2013*
     ILS - v35 - i1 - Fall 2015 - p13(3) [501+]

Dungy, Tony - *Here Comes the Parade! (Illus. by Newton, Vanessa Brantley)*
   c HB Guide - v26 - i1 - Spring 2015 - p52(2) [51-500]

Dunham, Lena - *Not That Kind of Girl: A Young Woman Tells You What She's "Learned"*
     Prog - v79 - i3 - March 2015 - p41(3) [501+]

Dunham, Wendy - *My Name Is River*
   c BL - v112 - i6 - Nov 15 2015 - p49(1) [51-500]
   c KR - Sept 1 2015 - pNA [51-500]

Dunham's, Jeffrey S. - *The Low Glycal Diet*
     PW - v262 - i1 - Jan 5 2015 - p71(1) [51-500]

Dunkerly, Robert M. - *To the Bitter End: Appomattox, Bennett Place, and the Surrenders of the Confederacy*
     RVBW - June 2015 - pNA [501+]

Dunkle, Elena - *Elena Vanishing: A Memoir*
   y HB Guide - v26 - i2 - Fall 2015 - p208(1) [51-500]
   y KR - March 1 2015 - pNA [51-500]
   y PW - v262 - i14 - April 6 2015 - p63(1) [51-500]
     SLJ - v61 - i4 - April 2015 - p183(2) [51-500]
   y VOYA - v38 - i1 - April 2015 - p86(2) [51-500]
Elena Vanishing
     RVBW - June 2015 - pNA [51-500]

Dunklee, Annika - *Me, Too! (Illus. by Smith, Lori Joy)*
   c BL - v111 - i15 - April 1 2015 - p83(1) [51-500]
   c HB Guide - v26 - i2 - Fall 2015 - p33(1) [51-500]
   c KR - Jan 1 2015 - pNA [51-500]
   c Res Links - v21 - i1 - Oct 2015 - p5(1) [51-500]

Dunlap, Jan - *The Kiskadee of Death*
     KR - July 1 2015 - pNA [51-500]
     PW - v262 - i28 - July 13 2015 - p47(2) [51-500]

Dunlap, Phil - *Cotton's Inferno*
     Roundup M - v22 - i6 - August 2015 - p29(1) [501+]

Dunlap, Susan - *Switchback*
     BL - v112 - i2 - Sept 15 2015 - p34(1) [51-500]
     PW - v262 - i32 - August 10 2015 - p40(1) [51-500]

Dunlop, Andrea - *Losing the Light*
     KR - Dec 15 2015 - pNA [51-500]

Dunlop, Susan - *Style and Swing: 12 Structured Handbags for Beginners and Beyond*
     Bwatch - Oct 2015 - pNA [51-500]

Dunlop, Tessa - *The Bletchley Girls*
     NS - v144 - i5260 - May 1 2015 - p49(1) [501+]

Dunmore, Tom - *Encyclopedia of the FIFA World Cup*
     BL - v112 - i1 - Sept 1 2015 - p32(2) [51-500]

Dunn, Andrew - *Rethinking Unemployment and the Work Ethic: Beyond the 'Quasi-Titmuss' Paradigm*
     TimHES - i2185 - Jan 8 2015 - p50-50 [501+]

Dunn, Carola - *Superfluous Women*
     BL - v111 - i17 - May 1 2015 - p46(1) [51-500]
     KR - April 1 2015 - pNA [51-500]
     PW - v262 - i15 - April 13 2015 - p59(1) [51-500]

Dunn, Durwood - *The Civil War in Southern Appalachian Methodism*
     JSH - v81 - i1 - Feb 2015 - p206(2) [501+]

Dunn, Herb - *Jackie Robinson (Illus. by Henderson, Meryl)*
   c HB Guide - v26 - i1 - Spring 2015 - p183(1) [51-500]

Dunn, John - *Breaking Democracy's Spell*
     Nation - v300 - i12 - March 23 2015 - p27(5) [501+]

Dunn, John M. - *The Birth of Modern India*
   y VOYA - v38 - i3 - August 2015 - p90(1) [51-500]

Dunn, Ken - *The Greatest Prospector in the World*
     PW - v262 - i28 - July 13 2015 - p40(1) [51-500]

Dunn, Larry A. - *Discovering Forgiveness*
     RVBW - Jan 2015 - pNA [51-500]

Dunn, Leslie C. - *Gender and Song in Early Modern England*
     Sev Cent N - v73 - i3-4 - Fall-Winter 2015 - p101(7) [501+]

Dunn, Mark - *We Five*
     KR - Sept 1 2015 - pNA [51-500]

Dunn, Mary - *From Mother to Son: The Selected Letters of Marie de l'Incarnation to Claude Martin*
     Can Hist R - v96 - i3 - Sept 2015 - p431(3) [501+]

Dunn, Mary R. - *Pebble Plus: Birds of Prey*
   c HB Guide - v26 - i2 - Fall 2015 - p177(1) [51-500]

Dunn, Matthew - *Dark Spies (Read by Orlow, Rich). Audiobook Review*
     PW - v262 - i26 - June 29 2015 - p62(1) [51-500]
The Spy House
     BL - v112 - i3 - Oct 1 2015 - p26(1) [51-500]
     PW - v262 - i35 - August 31 2015 - p62(1) [51-500]

Dunn, Pintip - *Forget Tomorrow*
   y SLJ - v61 - i10 - Oct 2015 - p100(2) [51-500]

Dunn, Richard S. - *A Tale of Two Plantations: Slave Life and Labor in Jamaica and Virginia*
     AHR - v120 - i4 - Oct 2015 - p1431-1434 [501+]
     JAH - v102 - i2 - Sept 2015 - p550-551 [501+]
     JSH - v81 - i4 - Nov 2015 - p961(3) [501+]
     NYTBR - Jan 4 2015 - p14(L) [501+]
     W&M Q - v72 - i4 - Oct 2015 - p659-664 [501+]
     W&M Q - v72 - i4 - Oct 2015 - p665-670 [501+]
     W&M Q - v72 - i4 - Oct 2015 - p671-675 [501+]
     W&M Q - v72 - i4 - Oct 2015 - p676-679 [501+]
     W&M Q - v72 - i4 - Oct 2015 - p680-685 [501+]

Dunn, Rob - *The Man Who Touched His Own Heart: True Tales of Science, Surgery, and Mystery*
     Nature - v518 - i7539 - Feb 19 2015 - p299(1) [51-500]

Dunn, Robin Wyatt - *Julia, Skydaughter*
     PW - v262 - i34 - August 24 2015 - p66(1) [51-500]

Dunn, Scarlett - *Finding Promise*
   y BL - v112 - i6 - Nov 15 2015 - p16(2) [51-500]
     PW - v262 - i45 - Nov 9 2015 - p43(2) [51-500]

Dunn, Suzannah - *The Lady of Misrule*
     BL - v112 - i7 - Dec 1 2015 - p33(1) [51-500]
     KR - Nov 1 2015 - pNA [51-500]

Dunnage, Jonathan - *Mussolini's Policemen: Behaviour, Ideology and Institutional Culture in Representation and Practice*
     HER - v130 - i542 - Feb 2015 - p248(2) [501+]
Mussolini's Policemen: Behaviour, Ideology, and Institutional Culture in Representation and Practice
     JMH - v87 - i1 - March 2015 - p209(2) [501+]

Dunnavant, Keith - *Montana: The Biography of Football's Joe Cool*
     BL - v112 - i4 - Oct 15 2015 - p13(2) [51-500]
     LJ - v140 - i17 - Oct 15 2015 - p92(2) [501+]

Dunne, John S. - *Dark Light of Love*
     Theol St - v76 - i4 - Dec 2015 - p897(2) [501+]

Dunne, Matthew W. - *A Cold War State of Mind: Brainwashing and Postwar American Society*
    AHR - v120 - i2 - April 2015 - p660-661 [501+]
    JAH - v101 - i4 - March 2015 - p1318(1) [501+]
    PHR - v84 - i3 - August 2015 - p396(398) [501+]

Dunnett, Kaitlyn - *The Scottie Barked at Midnight*
    BL - v112 - i3 - Oct 1 2015 - p28(1) [51-500]
    KR - August 15 2015 - pNA [51-500]
    PW - v262 - i39 - Sept 28 2015 - p67(1) [51-500]

Dunnigan, Alice - *Alone atop the Hill: The Autobiography of Alice Dunnigan, Pioneer of the National Black Press*
    BL - v111 - i11 - Feb 1 2015 - p14(1) [501+]
    LJ - v140 - i2 - Feb 1 2015 - p90(1) [501+]

Dunrea, Olivier - *Gemma & Gus (Illus. by Dunrea, Olivier)*
    c HB - v91 - i2 - March-April 2015 - p73(1) [51-500]
    c HB Guide - v26 - i2 - Fall 2015 - p9(2) [51-500]
    c KR - Jan 15 2015 - pNA [51-500]
Gus
    c KR - Jan 15 2015 - pNA [51-500]
Gus (Illus. by Dunrea, Olivier)
    c HB Guide - v26 - i2 - Fall 2015 - p9(2) [51-500]

Dunstan, Kylie - *Puddles Are for Jumping (Illus. by Dunstan, Kylie)*
    c Magpies - v30 - i5 - Nov 2015 - p28(1) [51-500]

Dunwoody, Ann - *A Higher Standard: Leadership Strategies from America's First Female Four-Star General*
    J Mil H - v79 - i3 - July 2015 - p883-884 [501+]
    RVBW - August 2015 - pNA [501+]

Duong, Lan P. - *Treacherous Subjects: Gender, Culture, and Trans-Vietnamese Feminism*
    AL - v87 - i2 - June 2015 - p410-413 [501+]

Duong, Lan P - *Treacherous Subjects: Gender, Culture, and Trans-Vietnamese Feminism*
    Amerasia J - v41 - i1 - Wntr 2015 - p128-131 [501+]

Duplaine, Matilda - *The Gilded Life of Matilda Duplaine*
    y BL - v112 - i1 - Sept 1 2015 - p40(1) [51-500]

Duplass, Mark - *Togetherness*
    People - v83 - i3 - Jan 19 2015 - p29 [501+]
    People - v83 - i3 - Jan 19 2015 - p29 [501+]
    People - v83 - i3 - Jan 19 2015 - p29 [501+]
    People - v83 - i3 - Jan 19 2015 - p29 [501+]
    People - v83 - i3 - Jan 19 2015 - p29 [501+]

Dupon, Olivier - *The New Artisans II*
    Am Craft - v75 - i3 - June-July 2015 - p20(1) [501+]

Dupont, Carolyn Renee - *Mississippi Praying: Southern White Evangelicals and the Civil Rights Movement, 1945-1975*
    Historian - v77 - i3 - Fall 2015 - p553(2) [501+]

Duppe, Till - *Finding Equilibrium: Arrow, Debreu, McKenzie, and the Problem of Scientific Credit*
    BHR - v89 - i2 - Summer 2015 - p350(3) [501+]

Dupre, Louise - *L'Album multicolore*
    Can Lit - i224 - Spring 2015 - p121 [501+]

DuPre, Mark - *How to Act Like a Grown-Up*
    PW - v262 - i15 - April 13 2015 - p74(1) [51-500]

Dupret, Baudouin - *Adjudication in Action: An Ethnomethodology of Law, Morality and Justice*
    CS - v44 - i3 - May 2015 - p360-362 [501+]

DuPuis, E. Melanie - *Dangerous Digestion: The Politics of American Dietary Advice*
    CHE - v62 - i16 - Dec 18 2015 - pB13(1) [501+]

Duran, Angelica - *King James Bible across Borders and Centuries*
    Six Ct J - v46 - i3 - Fall 2015 - p742-743 [501+]

Duran, Jane - *American Sampler*
    TLS - i5844 - April 3 2015 - p23(1) [501+]

Duran, Leslie - *JoJo and the Big Day (Illus. by Duran, Leslie)*
    c CH Bwatch - Nov 2015 - pNA [51-500]

Duran, Meredith - *Lady Be Good*
    PW - v262 - i25 - June 22 2015 - p126(1) [51-500]
Luck Be a Lady
    PW - v262 - i29 - July 20 2015 - p176(1) [51-500]

Duran, Mike - *The Ghost Box*
    PW - v262 - i18 - May 4 2015 - p102(1) [51-500]

Duran, Robert J. - *Gang Life in Two Cities: An Insider's Journey*
    CS - v44 - i4 - July 2015 - p501-503 [501+]

Durand, Jean-Dominique - *Christian Democrat Internationalism: Its Action in Europe and Worldwide from post World War II until the 1990s*
    HNet - April 2015 - pNA [501+]

Durand-Ruel, Paul-Louis - *Paul Durand-Ruel: Memoirs of the First Impressionist Art Dealer*
    NYRB - v62 - i19 - Dec 3 2015 - p62(3) [501+]

Durango, Julia - *The Leveller*
    y BL - v111 - i18 - May 15 2015 - p63(1) [51-500]
    y CCB-B - v69 - i1 - Sept 2015 - p19(2) [51-500]
    y HB Guide - v26 - i2 - Fall 2015 - p117(1) [51-500]
    SLJ - v61 - i4 - April 2015 - p155(1) [51-500]
    y VOYA - v38 - i2 - June 2015 - p73(1) [51-500]

Durant, Judith - *Increase, Decrease: 99 Step-by-Step Methods: Find the Perfect Technique for Shaping Every Knitting Project*
    Bwatch - July 2015 - pNA [51-500]
One-Skein Wonders for Babies: 101 Knitting Projects for Infants and Toddlers
    Bwatch - Nov 2015 - pNA [51-500]
    LJ - v140 - i15 - Sept 15 2015 - p77(2) [51-500]

Durant, Sabine - *Under Your Skin*
    RVBW - May 2015 - pNA [501+]

Durant, Will - *Fallen Leaves: Last Words on Life, Love, War and God*
    AM - v212 - i17 - May 18 2015 - p43(3) [501+]

Durbin, Andrew - *Mature Themes*
    NYTBR - June 28 2015 - p16(L) [501+]

Durden, Robert F. - *The Life of Carter G. Woodson: Father of African-American History*
    y HB Guide - v26 - i1 - Spring 2015 - p192(1) [51-500]

Duret, Jay - *Nine Digits*
    y KR - April 15 2015 - pNA [501+]

Durga Lai Shrestha - *The Blossoms of Sixty-Four Sunsets*
    WLT - v89 - i5 - Sept-Oct 2015 - p75(1) [51-500]

Durham, Janis Heaphy - *The Hand on the Mirror: A True Story of Life Beyond Death*
    LJ - v140 - i6 - April 1 2015 - p106(1) [51-500]
The Hand on the Mirror
    KR - Feb 15 2015 - pNA [501+]
    PW - v262 - i10 - March 9 2015 - p69(1) [51-500]

Durham, Mercedes - *The Acquisition of Sociolinguistic Competence in a Lingua Franca Context*
    Lang Soc - v44 - i4 - Sept 2015 - p603-604 [501+]

Durham, Paul - *Fork-Tongue Charmers*
    c KR - Jan 15 2015 - pNA [51-500]
    y VOYA - v38 - i1 - April 2015 - p77(1) [51-500]
The Luck Uglies: Fork-Tongue Charmers (Illus. by Antonsson, Petur)
    SLJ - v61 - i2 - Feb 2015 - p84(1) [51-500]
    c HB Guide - v26 - i2 - Fall 2015 - p80(1) [51-500]
The Luck Uglies: Fork-Tongue Charmers
    c BL - v111 - i11 - Feb 1 2015 - p52(1) [51-500]
Rise of the Ragged Clover
    c KR - Jan 1 2016 - pNA [51-500]

Duriez, Colin - *Bedeviled: Lewis, Tolkien and the Shadow of Evil*
    LJ - v140 - i7 - April 15 2015 - p91(1) [51-500]

Durkop, Martina - *Das Archiv fur Religionswissenschaft in den Jahren 1919 bis 1939: Dargestellt auf der Grundlage des Briefwechsels zwischen Otto Weinrich und Martin P:n Nilsson*
    HNet - Jan 2015 - pNA [501+]

Durkota, Michael D. - *Once in a Blue Year*
    KR - May 15 2015 - pNA [501+]

Durnovo, Marina - *Moi Muzh Daniil Kharms*
    NYRB - v62 - i8 - May 7 2015 - p36(3) [501+]

Durrant, Sabine - *Remember Me This Way*
    BL - v111 - i15 - April 1 2015 - p30(1) [51-500]
    KR - March 15 2015 - pNA [501+]
    LJ - v140 - i8 - May 1 2015 - p68(1) [51-500]

Durst, Sarah Beth - *Chasing Power*
    y HB Guide - v26 - i1 - Spring 2015 - p106(1) [51-500]
The Girl Who Could Not Dream
    c BL - v112 - i5 - Nov 1 2015 - p60(1) [51-500]
    y HB - v91 - i6 - Nov-Dec 2015 - p79(2) [51-500]
    c KR - August 1 2015 - pNA [51-500]
    c PW - v262 - i38 - Sept 21 2015 - p74(1) [51-500]
    c SLJ - v61 - i7 - July 2015 - p76(1) [51-500]

Dussere, Erik - *America is Elsewhere: The Noir Tradition in the Age of Consumer Culture*
    Film Cr - v39 - i3 - Spring 2015 - p84(4) [501+]
    MP - v112 - i4 - May 2015 - pE336(3) [501+]

Dussinger, John A. - *Correspondence with Sarah Wescomb, Frances Grainger and Laetitia Pilkington*
    RES - v66 - i276 - Sept 2015 - p784-786 [501+]

Dutcher, Jamie - *A Friend for Lakota: The Incredible True Story of a Wolf Who Braved Bullying (Illus. by Dutcher, Jim)*
    c CH Bwatch - Oct 2015 - pNA [51-500]

Dutcher, Jim - *A Friend for Lakota: The Incredible True Story of a Wolf Who Braved Bullying (Illus. by Dutcher, Jim)*
    c SLJ - v61 - i10 - Oct 2015 - p125(1) [51-500]

Duthu, N. Bruce - *Shadow Nations: Tribal Sovereignty and the Limits of Legal Pluralism*
    Am Ind CRJ - v39 - i1 - Wntr 2015 - p158-161 [501+]

Dutil, Patrice - *Macdonald at 200: New Reflections and Legacies*
    Can Hist R - v96 - i2 - June 2015 - p286(3) [501+]

Dutra, Janice J. - *The Fisherman's Ball*
    PW - v262 - i48 - Nov 30 2015 - p42(2) [51-500]

Dutt, Carsten - *Zwischen Sprache und Geschichte: Zum Werk Reinhart Kosellecks*
    HER - v130 - i544 - June 2015 - p793(3) [501+]

Dutta, Sourav - *Ganesha: The Curse on the Moon (Illus. by Nagulakonda, Rajesh)*
    c KR - July 15 2015 - pNA [51-500]
    c KR - Nov 1 2015 - pNA [51-500]
    c PW - v262 - i39 - Sept 28 2015 - p90(2) [51-500]

Dutton, Erin - *For the Love of Cake*
    PW - v262 - i4 - Jan 26 2015 - p156(1) [51-500]

Dutton, Hugh - *Supposed to Die*
    BL - v111 - i9-10 - Jan 1 2015 - p51(1) [51-500]

Dutton, J.B. - *Silent Symmetry*
    y Res Links - v20 - i5 - June 2015 - p24(1) [51-500]
Starley's Rust
    y Res Links - v20 - i5 - June 2015 - p24(1) [51-500]

DuVal, Kathleen - *Independence Lost: Lives on the Edge of the American Revolution*
    BL - v111 - i19-20 - June 1 2015 - p29(2) [51-500]
    KR - May 1 2015 - pNA [51-500]
    LJ - v140 - i8 - May 1 2015 - p88(3) [51-500]
    NY - v91 - i21 - July 27 2015 - p71 [51-500]
    PW - v262 - i18 - May 4 2015 - p109(2) [51-500]

Duval, Kathy - *A Bear's Year (Illus. by Turley, Gerry)*
    c KR - August 1 2015 - pNA [51-500]
    c NYTBR - Nov 8 2015 - p33(L) [51-500]
    c PW - v262 - i29 - July 20 2015 - p192(1) [51-500]
    c SLJ - v61 - i10 - Oct 2015 - p70(1) [51-500]

DuVernay, Ava - *Selma*
    Pub Hist - v37 - i3 - August 2015 - p128(9) [501+]

Duyvis, Corinne - *Otherbound*
    y Teach Lib - v42 - i3 - Feb 2015 - p39(1) [51-500]

Dvorak, John - *The Last Volcano: A Man, a Romance, and the Quest to Understand Nature's Most Magnificent Fury*
    BL - v112 - i7 - Dec 1 2015 - p14(2) [51-500]
    CSM - Dec 31 2015 - pNA [501+]
The Last Volcano
    KR - Oct 15 2015 - pNA [501+]

Dwar, Andrew - *Origami Toy Monsters: Easy-to-Assemble Paper Toys That Shudder, Shake, Lurch and Amaze*
    Bwatch - July 2015 - pNA [51-500]

Dweck, Nicole - *The Debt of Tamar*
    KR - July 1 2015 - pNA [51-500]

Dworkin, Mark J. - *American Mythmaker: Walter Noble Burns and the Legends of Billy the Kid, Wyatt Earp, and Joaquin Murrieta*
    Roundup M - v22 - i5 - June 2015 - p36(1) [501+]
    Roundup M - v22 - i6 - August 2015 - p36(1) [501+]

Dwyer, Jim - *More Awesome Than Money: Four Boys and Their Heroic Quest to Save Your Privacy from Facebook*
    AM - v212 - i19 - June 8 2015 - p34(3) [501+]
More Awesome Than Money: Four Boys, Three Years, and a Chronicle of Ideals and Ambition in Silicon Valley
    NYTBR - Dec 13 2015 - p44(L) [501+]

Dwyer, Johnny - *American Warlord: A True Story*
    CSM - April 16 2015 - pNA [501+]
    KR - Jan 15 2015 - pNA [501+]
    LJ - v140 - i3 - Feb 15 2015 - p112(1) [51-500]
    Mac - v128 - i15 - April 20 2015 - p54(2) [501+]
    NYTBR - April 19 2015 - p18(L) [501+]
    BL - v111 - i12 - Feb 15 2015 - p23(1) [51-500]
    Nation - v301 - i7-8 - August 17 2015 - p35(2) [501+]

Dwyer, Kate - *Reindeer Dust (Illus. by Lew-Vriethoff, Joanne)*
    c CH Bwatch - Jan 2015 - pNA [51-500]

Dwyer-McNulty, Sally - *Common Threads: A Cultural History of Clothing in American Catholicism*
    AHR - v120 - i3 - June 2015 - p1020-1021 [501+]
    CHR - v101 - i1 - Wntr 2015 - p179(2) [501+]
    JAH - v102 - i1 - June 2015 - p214-215 [501+]

Dwyer, Mindy - *Alaska's Snow White and Her Seven Sled Dogs*
    PW - v262 - i4 - Jan 26 2015 - p171(1) [51-500]

Dyal, Donald H. - *The Fleet Book of the Alaska Packers Association, 1893-1945: An Historical Overview and List*
    KR - July 1 2015 - pNA [501+]

Dyck, Corey W. - *Kant and Rational Psychology*
    RM - v68 - i3 - March 2015 - p651(3) [501+]

Dyck, Erika - *Facing Eugenics: Reproduction, Sterilization, and the Politics of Choice*
    Can Hist R - v96 - i1 - March 2015 - p135(3) [501+]
    Isis - v106 - i2 - June 2015 - p478(2) [501+]

Dyckman, Ame - *Wolfie the Bunny (Illus. by OHora, Zachariah)*
  c CCB-B - v68 - i8 - April 2015 - p397(2) [51-500]
  c HB Guide - v26 - i2 - Fall 2015 - p10(1) [51-500]
  c NYTBR - March 15 2015 - p18(L) [501+]
  c NYTBR - March 15 2015 - p18(L) [501+]
  c PW - v262 - i49 - Dec 2 2015 - p39(2) [51-500]

Dyckman, Anne - *Wolfie the Bunny (Illus. by OHora, Zachariah)*
  c HB - v91 - i2 - March-April 2015 - p73(2) [51-500]

Dyckman, Arne - *Wolfie the Bunny (Illus. by OHora, Zachariah)*
  c BL - v111 - i11 - Feb 1 2015 - p57(1) [51-500]
  c Teach Lib - v42 - i4 - April 2015 - p32(1) [51-500]

Dyer, Andy - *Chasing the Red Queen: The Evolutionary Race between Agricultural Pests and Poisons*
    QRB - v90 - i4 - Dec 2015 - p431(1) [501+]

Dyer, Gwynne - *Canada in the Great Power Game, 1914-2014*
    Beav - v95 - i2 - April-May 2015 - p53(1) [501+]

Dyja, Thomas - *The Third Coast: When Chicago Built the American Dream*
    BL - v112 - i5 - Nov 1 2015 - p18(2) [501+]

Dyke, Noel - *Fields of Play: An Ethnography of Children's Sports*
    SSJ - v32 - i1 - March 2015 - p110-111 [501+]

Dykeman, Arne - *Wolfie the Bunny (Illus. by OHora, Zachariah)*
  c BL - v112 - i4 - Oct 15 2015 - p53(1) [501+]

Dyllin, D.T. - *Starblind*
    PW - v262 - i17 - April 27 2015 - p58(2) [51-500]

Dynin, George - *Aryan Papers*
    SPBW - June 2015 - pNA [51-500]

Dynner, Glenn - *Yankel's Tavern: Jews, Liquor, and Life in the Kingdom of Poland*
    HNet - June 2015 - pNA [501+]

Dyson, Freeman - *Dreams of Earth and Sky*
    KR - Jan 15 2015 - pNA [501+]
    PW - v262 - i10 - March 9 2015 - p63(1) [51-500]
    Nature - v521 - i7553 - May 28 2015 - p421(1) [51-500]
    Phys Today - v68 - i8 - August 2015 - p54-55 [501+]

Dyson, Freeman J. - *Birds and Frogs: Selected Papers, 1990-2014*
    Phys Today - v68 - i8 - August 2015 - p54-55 [501+]

Birds and Frogs: Selected Papers, 1990-2014
    TimHES - i2207 - June 11 2015 - p56(1) [501+]

Dyson, Kenneth - *States, Debt, and Power: "Saints" and "Sinners" in European History and Integration*
    For Aff - v94 - i3 - May-June 2015 - pNA [501+]

Dyson, Michael Eric - *The Black Presidency*
    KR - Dec 15 2015 - pNA [501+]

Dzaldov, Brenda Stein - *Ready, Set, Learn: Integrating Powerful Learning Skills and Strategies into Daily Instruction*
    Res Links - v21 - i1 - Oct 2015 - p46(1) [501+]

Dzielska, Maria - *Divine Men and Women in the History and Society of Late Hellenism*
    HNet - June 2015 - pNA [501+]

Dzon, Mary - *The Christ Child in Medieval Culture: Alpha es et O!*
    CHR - v101 - i3 - Summer 2015 - p605(2) [501+]

E

Eaddy, Susan - *Best Paper*
 c KR - April 15 2015 - pNA [51-500]
Eade, James - *The Chess Player's Bible: Illustrated Strategies for Staying Ahead of the Game, 2d ed.*
  LJ - v140 - i10 - June 1 2015 - p106(1) [51-500]
Eads, Sean - *Lord Byron's Prophecy*
  KR - Oct 15 2015 - pNA [501+]
  PW - v262 - i26 - June 29 2015 - p49(2) [51-500]
Eager, Edward - *Half Magic (Illus. by Bodecker, N.M.)*
 c Magpies - v30 - i1 - March 2015 - p14(2) [501+]
Eager, Lindsay - *Hour of the Bees*
 c PW - v262 - i50 - Dec 7 2015 - p86(1) [51-500]
Eagland, Jane - *The World Within: A Novel of Emily Bronte*
 y CCB-B - v68 - i9 - May 2015 - p443(1) [51-500]
 y VOYA - v37 - i6 - Feb 2015 - p55(1) [51-500]
The World Within
 y BL - v111 - i19-20 - June 1 2015 - p86(2) [501+]
 y CH Bwatch - August 2015 - pNA [51-500]
 y HB Guide - v26 - i2 - Fall 2015 - p117(1) [501+]
Eagle, Adam Fortunate - *Scalping Columbus and Other Damn Indian Stories: Truths, Half-Truths and Outright Lies*
  Roundup M - v22 - i3 - Feb 2015 - p26(1) [501+]
Scalping Columbus and Other Damn Indian Stories: Truths, Half-Truths, and Outright Lies
  Roundup M - v22 - i6 - August 2015 - p29(1) [501+]
Eagleman, David - *The Brain: The Story of You*
  LJ - v140 - i19 - Nov 15 2015 - p101(2) [51-500]
Eagleton, Terry - *Culture and the Death of God*
  CC - v132 - i24 - Nov 25 2015 - p39(2) [501+]
Eakes, Laurie Alice - *The Mountain Midwife*
  BL - v112 - i6 - Nov 15 2015 - p18(2) [51-500]
  PW - v262 - i41 - Oct 12 2015 - p54(1) [51-500]
Eakin, Lenden - *Showdown: The Looming Crisis over Gun Control*
  SPBW - Nov 2015 - pNA [51-500]
Eames, Charles - *An Eames Anthology*
  Apo - v181 - i631 - May 2015 - p103(1) [51-500]
Eamon, Tom - *The Making of a Southern Democracy: North Carolina Politics from Kerr Scott to Pat McCrory*
  JAH - v101 - i4 - March 2015 - p1326-1327 [501+]
  JSH - v81 - i2 - May 2015 - p508(2) [501+]
Earenfight, Theresa - *Queenship in Medieval Europe*
  Historian - v77 - i2 - Summer 2015 - p381(2) [501+]
Earhart, Kristin - *Rain Forest Relay*
 c SLJ - v61 - i5 - May 2015 - p95(1) [51-500]
Welcome Home!
  KR - April 1 2015 - pNA [51-500]
 c SLJ - v61 - i5 - May 2015 - p98(1) [51-500]
Welcome Home! (Illus. by Geddes, Serena)
 c HB Guide - v26 - i2 - Fall 2015 - p65(1) [51-500]
Earl, Jennifer - *Digitally Enabled Social Change: Activism in the Internet Age*
  SF - v93 - i3 - March 2015 - pe88 [501+]
  SF - v93 - i3 - March 2015 - pNA [501+]
Earle, Jonathan - *Bleeding Kansas, Bleeding Missouri: The Long Civil War on the Border*
  JSH - v81 - i1 - Feb 2015 - p197(2) [501+]
Earle, Phil - *The Bubble Wrap Boy*
 c BL - v112 - i3 - Oct 1 2015 - p78(1) [51-500]
 c KR - August 1 2015 - pNA [51-500]
 c SLJ - v61 - i9 - Sept 2015 - p139(1) [501+]
 y VOYA - v68 - i5 - Dec 2015 - p55(1) [51-500]
Demolition Dad (Illus. by Ogilvie, Sara)
 c Sch Lib - v63 - i2 - Summer 2015 - p102(2) [51-500]

Demolition Dad
 c Sch Lib - v63 - i4 - Winter 2015 - p226(1) [51-500]
Earley, Chris - *Weird Birds*
  Am Bio T - v77 - i6 - August 2015 - p470(2) [501+]
 c Res Links - v20 - i3 - Feb 2015 - p19(1) [51-500]
Weird Frogs
  Am Bio T - v77 - i6 - August 2015 - p470(2) [501+]
 c Res Links - v20 - i3 - Feb 2015 - p19(1) [51-500]
Earley, Pete - *Resilience: Two Sisters and a Story of Mental Illness (Read by Close, Jessie). Audiobook Review*
  Bwatch - May 2015 - pNA [51-500]
Earlstone, Allen J. - *Worlds Apart*
  SPBW - Jan 2015 - pNA [501+]
Early, Chris - *Weird Frogs*
 c Sch Lib - v63 - i1 - Spring 2015 - p46(1) [51-500]
Early Medieval Monasticism in the North Sea Zone: A Conference Examining New Research and Fresh Perspectives
  HNet - August 2015 - pNA [501+]
Easley, Warren C. - *Never Look Down*
 y BL - v112 - i1 - Sept 1 2015 - p48(1) [51-500]
  KR - July 1 2015 - pNA [51-500]
  PW - v262 - i28 - July 13 2015 - p47(1) [51-500]
East, Genevieve - *Derapages*
 y Res Links - v20 - i4 - April 2015 - p40(1) [51-500]
Eastberg, John C. - *Pabst Farms: The History of a Model Farm*
  Bwatch - March 2015 - pNA [51-500]
Easter-Clutter, Melody - *Ready, Set, Rhythm! Sequential Lessons to Develop Rhythmic Reading*
 c Teach Mus - v22 - i3 - Jan 2015 - p60(1) [51-500]
Easterbrook, Gregg - *The Game's Not Over: In Defense of Football*
  KR - Oct 1 2015 - pNA [501+]
  LJ - v140 - i17 - Oct 15 2015 - p92(2) [501+]
  PW - v262 - i44 - Nov 2 2015 - p78(1) [51-500]
Easterly, William - *The Tyranny of Experts: Economists, Dictators, and the Forgotten Rights of the Poor*
  AM - v212 - i9 - March 16 2015 - p34(3) [501+]
  TLS - i5855 - June 19 2015 - p30(2) [501+]
Easting, Robert - *Peter of Cornwall's "Book of Revelations": British Writers, 5*
  Med R - Feb 2015 - pNA [501+]
Eastland, Sam - *Red Icon*
  BL - v112 - i7 - Dec 1 2015 - p31(1) [51-500]
  KR - Oct 15 2015 - pNA [501+]
  LJ - v140 - i16 - Oct 1 2015 - p68(1) [51-500]
Eastland, Sue - *A Very Top Secret Mission*
 c Sch Lib - v63 - i4 - Winter 2015 - p219(1) [51-500]
Eastman, P.D. - *Aaron Has a Lazy Day*
 c HB Guide - v26 - i2 - Fall 2015 - p59(1) [51-500]
Aaron Loves Apples and Pumpkins (Illus. by Eastman, P.D.)
 c SLJ - v61 - i9 - Sept 2015 - p106(1) [51-500]
Easton, Brandon - *Andre the Giant: Closer to Heaven*
  KR - Sept 15 2015 - pNA [51-500]
  PW - v262 - i51 - Dec 14 2015 - p69(1) [51-500]
Easton, Don - *Art and Murder*
  BL - v112 - i6 - Nov 15 2015 - p29(1) [51-500]
  PW - v262 - i36 - Sept 7 2015 - p49(1) [51-500]
Easton, Richard D. - *GPS Declassified: From Smart Bombs to Smartphones*
  HNet - Feb 2015 - pNA [501+]
Easton, T.S. - *Boys Don't Knit (in Public).*
 y CCB-B - v68 - i9 - May 2015 - p444(1) [51-500]
 y HB Guide - v26 - i2 - Fall 2015 - p117(1) [501+]
  SLJ - v61 - i2 - Feb 2015 - p100(1) [51-500]
 y VOYA - v37 - i6 - Feb 2015 - p55(2) [51-500]

Easton, Tom - *Boys Don't Knit*
 y KR - Jan 1 2015 - pNA [51-500]
Seven Second Delay
 y BL - v111 - i15 - April 1 2015 - p70(1) [51-500]
 y CCB-B - v69 - i1 - Sept 2015 - p20(1) [51-500]
 y KR - Feb 15 2015 - pNA [51-500]
  SLJ - v61 - i2 - Feb 2015 - p100(1) [51-500]
Eastwood, David - *Government and Community in the English Provinces, 1700-1870*
  TimHES - i2221 - Sept 17 2015 - p45(1) [501+]
Eatherley, Dan - *Bushmaster: Raymond Ditmars and the Hunt for the World's Largest Viper*
  PW - v262 - i17 - April 27 2015 - p63(1) [51-500]
  LJ - v140 - i20 - Dec 1 2015 - p125(2) [51-500]
Eaton, Barry - *No Goodbyes: Life-Changing Insights from the Other Side*
  LJ - v140 - i10 - June 1 2015 - p119(2) [51-500]
Eaton, Gale - *A History of Civilization in 50 Disasters*
 c KR - Sept 15 2015 - pNA [51-500]
Eaton, Hannah - *Naming Monsters*
  KR - Oct 1 2015 - pNA [51-500]
Eaton, Heather - *The Intellectual Journey of Thomas Berry: Imagining the Earth Community*
  Theol St - v76 - i3 - Sept 2015 - p655(1) [501+]
Eaton, Linda - *Printed Textiles: British and American Cottons and Linens, 1700-1850 (Illus. by Schneck, Jim)*
  Mag Antiq - v182 - i1 - Jan-Feb 2015 - p104(1) [501+]
Eaton, Maxwell, III - *Andy, Also (Illus. by Eaton, Maxwell, III)*
 c HB Guide - v26 - i2 - Fall 2015 - p65(1) [51-500]
The Flying Beaver Brothers and the Crazy Critter Race (Illus. by Eaton, Maxwell, III)
 c HB Guide - v26 - i2 - Fall 2015 - p65(1) [51-500]
The Flying Beaver Brothers and the Hot-Air Baboons
 c HB Guide - v26 - i1 - Spring 2015 - p59(1) [51-500]
Eaton, Susan E. - *Integration Nation: Immigrants, Refugees, and America at Its Best*
  KR - Nov 15 2015 - pNA [501+]
  LJ - v140 - i19 - Nov 15 2015 - p98(1) [51-500]
  PW - v262 - i47 - Nov 23 2015 - p61(1) [51-500]
Eatwell, Piu Marie - *The Dead Duke, His Secret Wife, and the Missing Corpse: An Extraordinary Edwardian Case of Deception and Intrigue*
  LJ - v140 - i15 - Sept 15 2015 - p90(1) [51-500]
The Dead Duke, His Secret Wife and the Missing Corpse
  KR - June 15 2015 - pNA [51-500]
  PW - v262 - i1 - Jan 5 2015 - p66(1) [51-500]
They Eat Horses, Don't They? The Truth About the French
  NYTBR - Feb 1 2015 - p14(L) [501+]
Eaverly, M. A. - *Tan Men/Pale Women: Color and Gender in Archaic Greece and Egypt. A Comparative Approach*
  Class R - v65 - i1 - April 2015 - p252-254 [501+]
Ebadi, Shirin - *Until We Are Free*
  KR - Dec 15 2015 - pNA [51-500]
Ebbeier, Jeffrey - *Click! (Illus. by Ebbeier, Jeffrey)*
 c BL - v111 - i17 - May 1 2015 - p101(1) [51-500]
Ebbeler, Jeffrey - *Click! (Illus. by Ebbeler, Jeffrey)*
 c CCB-B - v69 - i1 - Sept 2015 - p20(2) [51-500]
 c HB Guide - v26 - i2 - Fall 2015 - p10(1) [51-500]
 c HB - v91 - i3 - May-June 2015 - p85(2) [51-500]
 c KR - March 1 2015 - pNA [51-500]
 c PW - v262 - i13 - March 30 2015 - p73(1) [51-500]
Ebenstein, Lanny - *Chicagonomics: The Evolution of Chicago Free Market Economics*
  KR - August 15 2015 - pNA [501+]
  NYTBR - Nov 22 2015 - p25(L) [501+]
Eberhard, Geisler - *El dinero en la obra de Quevedo: la crisis de identidad en la sociedad feudal espanola a*

principios del siglo XVII
    Hisp R - v83 - i1 - Wntr 2015 - p99-102 [501+]

Eberhart, Dikkon - *The Time Mom Met Hitler, Frost Came to Dinner, and I Heard the Greatest Story Ever Told*
    PW - v262 - i19 - May 11 2015 - p53(2) [51-500]
    KR - June 15 2015 - pNA [501+]

Ebert, David A. - *A Pocket Guide to Sharks of the World (Illus. by Dando, Marc)*
    LJ - v140 - i11 - June 15 2015 - p112(1) [51-500]

Ebisch, Glen - *The Bad Actor*
    KR - May 15 2015 - pNA [51-500]

Eboch, Chris - *Chaco Canyon*
  y HB Guide - v26 - i1 - Spring 2015 - p200(2) [51-500]

Eboch, M.M. - *A History of Film*
  c BL - v111 - i15 - April 1 2015 - p61(1) [51-500]

Ebode, Eugene - *Souveraine Magnifique*
    WLT - v89 - i3-4 - May-August 2015 - p108(2) [501+]

Ebrahimnejad, Hormoz - *Medicine in Iran: Profession, Practice, and Politics, 1800-1925*
    AHR - v120 - i1 - Feb 2015 - p372-373 [501+]

Ebrey, Patricia Buckley - *Emperor Huizong*
    AHR - v120 - i2 - April 2015 - p592-593 [501+]
    HNet - May 2015 - pNA [501+]
    JAS - v74 - i1 - Feb 2015 - p188-189 [501+]

Ebright, Malcolm - *Four Square Leagues: Pueblo Indian Land in New Mexico*
    AHR - v120 - i3 - June 2015 - p1015-1016 [501+]
    SHQ - v118 - i4 - April 2015 - p429-430 [501+]

EBSCO Publishing - *Arab World Research Source*
    LJ - v140 - i2 - Feb 1 2015 - p108(2) [501+]

Ebury, Katherine - *Modernism and Cosmology: Absurd Lights*
    TLS - i5843 - March 27 2015 - p30(1) [501+]

Eby, Clare Virginia - *Until Choice Do Us Part: Marriage Reform in the Progressive Era*
    AHR - v120 - i2 - April 2015 - p638-639 [501+]

Eby, Jan - *The Grammie Guide: Activities and Answers for Grandparenting Today*
    SPBW - May 2015 - pNA [51-500]

Eby, Margaret - *South toward Home: Travels in Southern Literature*
    BL - v111 - i19-20 - June 1 2015 - p5(1) [501+]
    KR - June 1 2015 - pNA [501+]
    LJ - v140 - i10 - June 1 2015 - p103(1) [51-500]
    NYTBR - Oct 4 2015 - p16(L) [501+]
    PW - v262 - i19 - May 11 2015 - p45(2) [51-500]

The EC Archives: The Haunt of Fear, vol. 2
    NYT - Oct 30 2015 - pC35(L) [501+]

Eccles, Marjorie - *Heirs and Assigns*
    BL - v112 - i2 - Sept 15 2015 - p31(1) [501+]
    KR - Sept 15 2015 - pNA [51-500]
    PW - v262 - i39 - Sept 28 2015 - p70(1) [51-500]

Echenoz, Jean - *The Queen's Caprice*
    KR - Feb 15 2015 - pNA [51-500]

Echevarria, Antulio J., II - *Reconsidering the American Way of War: US Military Practice from the Revolution to Afghanistan*
    J Mil H - v79 - i1 - Jan 2015 - p187-188 [501+]
    J Mil H - v79 - i1 - Jan 2015 - p189-190 [501+]

Echevarria, Antulio J., III - *Reconsidering the American Way of War: US Military Practice from the Revolution to Afghanistan*
    APJ - v29 - i6 - Nov-Dec 2015 - p91(1) [501+]

Echevarria, Roberto Gonzalez - *Cervantes' "Don Quixote"*
    TLS - i5874 - Oct 30 2015 - p8(1) [501+]

Echeverria Bender, Christine - *Aboard Cabrillo's Galleon*
    Roundup M - v22 - i6 - August 2015 - p25(1) [501+]

Echeverria, Darius V. - *Aztlan Arizona: Mexican American Educational Empowerment, 1968-1978*
    JAH - v102 - i1 - June 2015 - p309-309 [501+]
    PHR - v84 - i4 - Nov 2015 - p548(2) [501+]

Echols, Jennifer - *Most Likely to Succeed*
  y KR - June 15 2015 - pNA [51-500]
  y SLJ - v61 - i6 - June 2015 - p122(1) [51-500]
  y VOYA - v38 - i2 - June 2015 - p58(1) [51-500]
Perfect Couple
  y HB Guide - v26 - i2 - Fall 2015 - p118(1) [51-500]
Perfect Couple: The Superlatives
  y VOYA - v37 - i6 - Feb 2015 - p56(1) [51-500]

Echterholter, Anna - *Schattengefechte: Genealogische Praktiken in Nachrufen auf Naturwissenschaftler*
    HNet - Jan 2015 - pNA [501+]
Schattengefechte: Genealogische Praktiken in Nachrufen auf Naturwissenschaftler, 1710-1860
    Isis - v106 - i1 - March 2015 - p191(2) [501+]

Eck, Werner - *Offentlichkeit - Monument - Text: XIV Congressus Internationalis Epigraphiae Graecae et Latinae. 27.-31. Augusti MMXII - Akten*
    HNet - Feb 2015 - pNA [501+]

Eckardt, Hella - *Objects and Identities: Roman Britain and the North-Western Provinces*
    Class R - v65 - i2 - Oct 2015 - p585-586 [501+]

Eckel, Jan - *Die Ambivalenz des Guten: Menschenrechte in der Internationalen Politik seit den 1940ern*
    HNet - Jan 2015 - pNA [501+]

Eckel, Wendy Sand - *Murder at Barclay Meadow*
    PW - v262 - i20 - May 18 2015 - p65(2) [51-500]

Eckerele, Julie A. - *Romancing the Self in Early Modern Englishwomen's Life Writing*
    Six Ct J - v46 - i2 - Summer 2015 - p409-411 [501+]

Eckerle, Julie A. - *Romancing the Self in Early Modern Englishwomen's Life Writing*
    Wom HR - v24 - i1 - Feb 2015 - p144-3 [501+]

Eckes, Christopher - *Les groupes de Lie dans l'oeuvre de Hermann Weyl*
    Isis - v106 - i2 - June 2015 - p487(2) [501+]

Eckhardt, Joseph P. - *Living Large: Wilna Hervey and Nan Mason*
    SPBW - June 2015 - pNA [501+]
    G&L Rev W - v22 - i6 - Nov-Dec 2015 - p44(1) [501+]

Eckhardt, Joshua - *Manuscript Miscellanies in Early Modern England*
    TLS - i5867 - Sept 11 2015 - p27(1) [501+]

Eckstein, Nicholas A. - *Painted Glories: The Brancacci Chapel in Renaissance Florence*
    Spec - v327 - i9724 - Jan 10 2015 - p30(2) [501+]

Eckstein, Susan Eva - *How Immigrants Impact Their Homelands*
    CS - v44 - i4 - July 2015 - p503-504 [501+]

Eco, Umberto - *How to Write a Thesis*
    TimHES - i2195 - March 19 2015 - p48-49 [501+]
    PW - v262 - i2 - Jan 12 2015 - p48(1) [51-500]
    TLS - i5858 - July 10 2015 - p27(1) [501+]
Numero Zero
    BL - v112 - i3 - Oct 1 2015 - p27(1) [51-500]
Numero Zero (Illus. by Dixon, Richard)
    NYTBR - Nov 22 2015 - p12(L) [501+]
Numero Zero
    KR - Sept 1 2015 - pNA [501+]
    NYT - Nov 26 2015 - pC6(L) [501+]
    PW - v262 - i32 - August 10 2015 - p32(1) [51-500]
    Spec - v329 - i9767 - Nov 7 2015 - p42(2) [501+]

The Economists
    TimHES - i2225 - Oct 15 2015 - p43-1 [501+]

Economy, Elizabeth - *By All Means Necessary: How China's Resource Quest Is Changing the World*
    E-A St - v67 - i5 - July 2015 - p842(2) [501+]

Edde, Dominique - *Kamal Jann*
    WLT - v89 - i2 - March-April 2015 - p57(3) [501+]

Eddie, Sean A. - *Freedom's Price: Serfdom, Subjection, and Reform in Prussia, 1648-1848*
    AHR - v120 - i4 - Oct 2015 - p1566-1567 [501+]

Eddleman, Peggy - *The Forbidden Flats*
  c HB Guide - v26 - i1 - Spring 2015 - p75(1) [51-500]

Eddy, Carson - *Beaded Jewelry: Wirework Techniques*
    LJ - v140 - i5 - March 15 2015 - p107(1) [51-500]

Ede, Piers Moore - *Kaleidoscope City: A Year in Varanasi*
    KR - Jan 15 2015 - pNA [501+]
    LJ - v140 - i5 - March 15 2015 - p124(1) [51-500]
    TLS - i5847 - April 24 2015 - p27(1) [501+]

Edel, Charles N. - *Nation Builder: John Quincy Adams and the Grand Strategy of the Republic*
    JAH - v102 - i2 - Sept 2015 - p542-543 [501+]
    AHR - v120 - i3 - June 2015 - p1018-1019 [501+]
    For Aff - v94 - i3 - May-June 2015 - pNA [501+]

Edelman, Diana V. - *Deuteronomy-Kings as Emerging Authoritative Books: A Conversation*
    Intpr - v69 - i1 - Jan 2015 - p123(1) [501+]

Edelman, Hope - *I'll Tell You Mine: Thirty Years of Essays from the Iowa Nonfiction Writing Program*
    PW - v262 - i38 - Sept 21 2015 - p65(1) [51-500]

Edelmann, Jonathan B. - *Hindu Theology and Biology: the Bhagavata Purana and Contemporary Theory*
    JAAR - v83 - i3 - Sept 2015 - p861-866 [501+]

Edelstein, Melvin - *The French Revolution and the Birth of Electoral Democracy*
    FS - v69 - i2 - April 2015 - p251-2 [501+]
    HER - v130 - i544 - June 2015 - p759(2) [501+]

Eden, Anise - *All the Broken Places*
    PW - v262 - i50 - Dec 7 2015 - p74(1) [501+]

Eden, Bradford L. - *Enhancing Teaching and Learning in the 21st-Century Academic Library*
  y VOYA - v38 - i4 - Oct 2015 - p88(1) [51-500]

Eden, Dawn - *Remembering God's Mercy: Redeem the Past and Free Yourself from Painful Memories*
    PW - v262 - i51 - Dec 14 2015 - p79(1) [51-500]

Edgar, Gordon - *Cheddar: A Journey to the Heart of America's Most Iconic Cheese*
    LJ - v140 - i15 - Sept 15 2015 - p96(2) [51-500]

Edgar, Sherra G. - *Large Animal Veterinarian*
    SLJ - v61 - i4 - April 2015 - p76(4) [501+]

Edgar, Walter - *Conversations with the Conroys: Interviews with Pat Conroy and His Family*
    PW - v262 - i34 - August 24 2015 - p76(1) [51-500]

Edge, Christopher - *The Black Crow Conspiracy*
  c HB Guide - v26 - i2 - Fall 2015 - p80(1) [51-500]
    SLJ - v61 - i3 - March 2015 - p133(2) [501+]
  y VOYA - v38 - i1 - April 2015 - p58(1) [51-500]
How to Write Your Best Story Ever!
  c Sch Lib - v63 - i3 - Autumn 2015 - p173(1) [51-500]
Shadows of the Silver Screen
  c HB Guide - v26 - i1 - Spring 2015 - p75(1) [51-500]

Edge, John T. - *The Larder: Food Studies Methods from the American South*
    JAH - v101 - i4 - March 2015 - p1231-1232 [501+]

Edgecombe, James - *The Art of Kozu*
    WLT - v89 - i5 - Sept-Oct 2015 - p61(1) [501+]

Edghill, India - *Game of Queens*
  y BL - v112 - i1 - Sept 1 2015 - p51(1) [51-500]

Edghill, Rosemary - *Victories*
  y HB Guide - v26 - i1 - Spring 2015 - p113(1) [51-500]

Edgington, Ryan H. - *Range Wars: The Environmental Contest for White Sands Missile Range*
    AHR - v120 - i3 - June 2015 - p1057-1058 [501+]
    J Mil H - v79 - i1 - Jan 2015 - p254-256 [501+]

Edgington, Susan B. - *Deeds Done beyond the Sea: Essays on William of Tyre, Cyprus and the Military Orders Presented to Peter Edbury*
    Specu - v90 - i3 - July 2015 - p874(1) [501+]

Edgren-Henrichson, Nina - *Dolce Far Niente in Arabia: Georg August Wallin and His Travels in the 1840s*
    HNet - May 2015 - pNA [501+]

Edin, Kathryn J. - *$2.00 a Day: Living on Almost Nothing in America (Read by Johnson, Allyson). Audiobook Review*
    PW - v262 - i48 - Nov 30 2015 - p55(1) [51-500]
$2.00 a Day: Living on Almost Nothing in America
    BL - v111 - i21 - July 1 2015 - p5(1) [501+]
    BooChiTr - Oct 24 2015 - p13(1) [501+]
    KR - June 15 2015 - pNA [501+]
    LJ - v140 - i13 - August 1 2015 - p114(1) [51-500]
    NYTBR - Sept 6 2015 - p14(L) [501+]
    PW - v262 - i25 - June 22 2015 - p130(1) [51-500]

Edison, Erin - *Marie Curie*
  c HB Guide - v26 - i1 - Spring 2015 - p192(1) [51-500]
Sally Ride
  c HB Guide - v26 - i1 - Spring 2015 - p192(1) [51-500]

Editionen! Wozu? Wie? Und wie Viele? Zum Stand der Historischen 'Edition' in der Schweiz im Digitalen Zeitalter
    HNet - March 2015 - pNA [501+]

Editors of Sixth&Springs Books - *Noro Lace: 30 Exquisite Knits*
    LJ - v140 - i5 - March 15 2015 - p108(2) [51-500]

Edkins, Rita - *When All the Saints Come Marching In*
    KR - Sept 15 2015 - pNA [501+]

Edlich-Muth, Miriam - *Malory and His European Contemporaries: Adapting Late Arthurian Romance*
    Ren Q - v68 - i1 - Spring 2015 - p381-382 [501+]

Edling, Max M. - *A Hercules in the Cradle: War, Money, and the American State, 1783-1867*
    NEQ - v88 - i3 - Sept 2015 - p548-550 [501+]

Edlitz, Mark - *How to Be a Superhero*
    KR - May 1 2015 - pNA [501+]

Edlund, Alexander - *Keelic and the Space Pirates*
    KR - June 15 2015 - pNA [501+]

Edmond, Jacob - *A Common Strangeness: Contemporary Poetry, Cross-Cultural Encounter, Comparative Literature*
    AL - v87 - i3 - Sept 2015 - p618-622 [501+]

Edmonds, Antony - *Oscar Wilde's Scandalous Summer: The 1894 Worthing Holiday and the Aftermath*
    TLS - i5849 - May 8 2015 - p27(1) [501+]

Edmonds, Bill Russell - *God Is Not Here: A Soldier's Struggle with Torture, Trauma, and the Moral Injuries of War*
    KR - March 15 2015 - pNA [501+]
    PW - v262 - i10 - March 9 2015 - p63(1) [51-500]
    NYTBR - May 24 2015 - p21(L) [501+]

Edmonds, Michael - *Risking Everything: A Freedom Summer Reade*
JSH - v81 - i2 - May 2015 - p541(2) [501+]

Edmonds, Radcliffe G., III - *Redefining Ancient Orphism: A Study in Greek Religion*
Class R - v65 - i2 - Oct 2015 - p494-496 [501+]

Edmondson, Paul - *Shakespeare*
LJ - v140 - i14 - Sept 1 2015 - p101(1) [51-500]
The Shakespeare Circle: An Alternative Biography
Spec - v329 - i9771 - Dec 5 2015 - p41(2) [501+]
Shakespeare
Spec - v328 - i9742 - May 16 2015 - p38(2) [501+]
TimHES - i2211 - July 9 2015 - p50-51 [501+]

Edmundson, Mark - *Self and Soul: A Defense of Ideals*
KR - July 15 2015 - pNA [501+]
LJ - v140 - i14 - Sept 1 2015 - p109(1) [51-500]

Edric, Robert - *Sanctuary: A Novel*
NS - v144 - i5248 - Feb 6 2015 - p43(1) [501+]

Edwards, Andrew V. - *Digital Is Destroying Everything: What the Tech Giants Won't Tell You about How Robots, Big Data and Algorithms Are Radically Remaking Your Future*
PW - v262 - i14 - April 6 2015 - p49(1) [51-500]

Edwards, Anthony Stockwell Garfield - *A Companion to Fifteenth-Century English Poetry*
MLR - v110 - i3 - July 2015 - p815-816 [501+]

Edwards, Cyril - *German Romance V: Hartmann von Aue, Erec*
Med R - June 2015 - pNA [501+]

Edwards, David W. - *Nightscape: Cynopolis*
KR - Nov 15 2015 - pNA [501+]

Edwards, Denis - *Partaking of God: Trinity, Evolution, and Ecology*
Theol St - v76 - i1 - March 2015 - p181(2) [501+]

Edwards, Douglas - *Properties*
RM - v69 - i1 - Sept 2015 - p130(3) [501+]

Edwards, Frederick - *Angel in Aisle 3: The True Story of a Mysterious Vagrant, a Convicted Banker, and the Unlikely Friendship That Saved Both Their Lives*
BL - v112 - i6 - Nov 15 2015 - p11(1) [51-500]

Edwards, Gareth - *The Littlest Bird (Illus. by Ellis, Elina)*
c SLJ - v61 - i8 - August 2015 - p68(1) [51-500]
Never Ask a Dinosaur to Dinner (Illus. by Parker-Rees, Guy)
c CCB-B - v68 - i10 - June 2015 - p488(1) [51-500]
c HB Guide - v26 - i2 - Fall 2015 - p10(1) [51-500]
c KR - Feb 15 2015 - pNA [51-500]
SLJ - v61 - i4 - April 2015 - p126(2) [51-500]

Edwards, H.J. - *Gallic War*
TLS - i5854 - June 12 2015 - p11(1) [501+]

Edwards, Janet - *Earth Flight*
Bwatch - Nov 2015 - pNA [501+]
c KR - June 1 2015 - pNA [501+]
y SLJ - v61 - i8 - August 2015 - p113(1) [51-500]
y VOYA - v38 - i3 - August 2015 - p76(1) [501+]

Edwards, Judith - *The Journey of Lewis and Clark in United States History*
y HB Guide - v26 - i1 - Spring 2015 - p199(1) [51-500]

Edwards, Karl - *Newsom, Fly!*
c HB Guide - v26 - i2 - Fall 2015 - p10(1) [51-500]

Edwards, Karl Newsom - *Fly! (Illus. by Edwards, Karl Newsom)*
c CCB-B - v68 - i8 - April 2015 - p398(1) [51-500]
Fly!
PW - v262 - i3 - Jan 19 2015 - p79(1) [51-500]
KR - Jan 1 2015 - pNA [51-500]

Edwards, Laura F. - *A Legal History of the Civil War and Reconstruction: A Nation of Rights*
HNet - August 2015 - pNA [501+]

Edwards, Lisa - *Please Don't Bite the Baby: Keeping Your Kids and Your Dogs Safe and Happy Together*
PW - v262 - i36 - Sept 7 2015 - p64(1) [51-500]

Edwards, Martin - *The Dungeon House*
BL - v112 - i2 - Sept 15 2015 - p31(1) [51-500]
KR - July 15 2015 - pNA [501+]
PW - v262 - i29 - July 20 2015 - p171(1) [51-500]
The Golden Age of Murder: The Mystery of the Writers Who Invented the Modern Detective Story
KR - April 1 2015 - pNA [501+]
LJ - v140 - i11 - June 15 2015 - p90(1) [501+]
PW - v262 - i13 - March 30 2015 - p68(2) [51-500]
Spec - v328 - i9742 - May 16 2015 - p41(1) [501+]
Murder at the Manor: Country House Mysteries
BL - v112 - i7 - Dec 1 2015 - p30(1) [51-500]
KR - Dec 1 2015 - pNA [501+]
PW - v262 - i52 - Dec 21 2015 - p135(1) [51-500]
Resorting to Murder
KR - April 1 2015 - pNA [501+]

Serpents in Paradise
KR - Dec 15 2015 - pNA [51-500]
Silent Nights: Christmas Mysteries
PW - v262 - i39 - Sept 28 2015 - p70(1) [51-500]

Edwards, Michael - *Time and the Science of the Soul in Early Modern Philosophy*
Sev Cent N - v73 - i3-4 - Fall-Winter 2015 - p131(5) [501+]

Edwards, Natalie - *The Contemporary Francophone African Intellectual*
FS - v69 - i3 - July 2015 - p431-432 [501+]

Edwards, Nina - *Dressed for War: Uniform, Civilian Clothing and Trappings, 1914 to 1918*
TLS - i5836 - Feb 6 2015 - p21(1) [501+]

Edwards, Paul - *The Concise Guide to Hip-Hop Music: A Fresh Look at the Art of Hip Hop, from Old School Beats to Freestyle Rap*
LJ - v140 - i3 - Feb 15 2015 - p102(1) [51-500]

Edwards, Sebastian - *Toxic Aid: Economic Collapse and Recovery in Tanzania*
BHR - v89 - i3 - Autumn 2015 - p623(4) [501+]
For Aff - v94 - i1 - Jan-Feb 2015 - pNA [51-500]

Edwards, Sue - *Ancient Maya*
y HB Guide - v26 - i2 - Fall 2015 - p216(1) [51-500]

Edwards, Tanille - *Broken*
SPBW - April 2015 - pNA [51-500]

Edwards, Wallace - *Once Upon a Line (Illus. by Edwards, Wallace)*
c Res Links - v21 - i1 - Oct 2015 - p5(1) [51-500]
c SLJ - v61 - i12 - Dec 2015 - p87(1) [51-500]
Once Upon a Line
c KR - July 15 2015 - pNA [51-500]
Unnatural Selections
c HB Guide - v26 - i1 - Spring 2015 - p29(1) [51-500]

Ee, Susan - *End of Days*
y VOYA - v38 - i2 - June 2015 - p73(1) [51-500]

Eekhout, Greg van - *California Bones*
BL - v111 - i18 - May 15 2015 - p35(1) [501+]

Eff, Elaine - *The Painted Screen of Baltimore: An Urban Folk Art Revealed*
WestFolk - v74 - i2 - Spring 2015 - p218-220 [501+]

Effa, Gaston-Paul - *Rendez-vous avec l'heure qui blesse*
WLT - v89 - i5 - Sept-Oct 2015 - p59(1) [501+]

Efford, Alison Clark - *German Immigrants, Race, and Citizenship in the Civil War Era*
JSH - v81 - i1 - Feb 2015 - p191(2) [501+]

Effros, Bonnie - *Uncovering the Germanic Past: Merovingian Archaeology in France, 1830-1914*
Specu - v90 - i1 - Jan 2015 - p240-242 [501+]

Efrati, Noga - *Women in Iraq: Past Meets Present*
JWH - v27 - i2 - Summer 2015 - p182(12) [501+]

Efthymiadis, Stephanos - *The Ashgate Research Companion to Byzantine Hagiography, vol. 2: Genres and Contexts*
Med R - August 2015 - pNA [501+]
Specu - v90 - i3 - July 2015 - p799-801 [501+]

Egan, Catherine - *Bone, Fog, Ash & Star*
y Res Links - v20 - i3 - Feb 2015 - p27(2) [501+]

Egan, Elisabeth - *A Window Opens*
y BL - v111 - i21 - July 1 2015 - p34(1) [51-500]
KR - June 15 2015 - pNA [501+]
PW - v262 - i24 - June 15 2015 - p59(1) [51-500]

Egan, Elizabeth - *A Window Opens*
NYTBR - August 23 2015 - p8(L) [501+]

Egan, Gabriel - *Electronic Publishing : Politics and Pragmatics*
BSA-P - v109 - i2 - June 2015 - p265-268 [501+]

Egan, Greg - *The Arrows of Time*
Analog - v135 - i1-2 - Jan-Feb 2015 - p181(2) [501+]

Egan, Jennifer - *The Keep*
c LJ - v140 - i7 - April 15 2015 - p126(1) [51-500]

Egan, Kate - *The Great Escape (Illus. by Wight, Eric)*
c HB Guide - v26 - i2 - Fall 2015 - p81(1) [51-500]
The Incredible Twisting Arm (Illus. by Wight, Eric)
c HB Guide - v26 - i1 - Spring 2015 - p75(1) [51-500]
The Vanishing Coin (Illus. by Wight, Eric)
c HB Guide - v26 - i1 - Spring 2015 - p75(1) [51-500]

Egan, Kevin - *The Missing Piece*
PW - v262 - i8 - Feb 23 2015 - p52(1) [51-500]
KR - Feb 1 2015 - pNA [501+]

Egan, Sean - *Bowie on Bowie: Interviews and Encounters with David Bowie*
y BL - v111 - i17 - May 1 2015 - p59(1) [51-500]
LJ - v140 - i6 - April 1 2015 - p90(1) [51-500]

Egan, Timothy - *The Immortal Irishman: The Irish Revolutionary Who Became an American Hero*
KR - Dec 1 2015 - pNA [501+]
PW - v262 - i51 - Dec 14 2015 - p70(1) [501+]

Egeler, Matthias - *Celtic Influences in Germanic Religion: A Survey*
JEGP - v114 - i1 - Jan 2015 - p123(3) [501+]

Egenolf, Susan B. - *British Family Life, 1780-1914, vol. 3: Wives and Mothers*
HER - v130 - i545 - August 2015 - p1015(3) [501+]
British Family Life, 1780-1914, vol. 4: Extended Families
HER - v130 - i545 - August 2015 - p1015(3) [501+]

Egerton, Douglas R. - *The Wars of Reconstruction: The Brief, Violent History of America's Most Progressive Era*
RAH - v43 - i3 - Sept 2015 - p512-521 [501+]

Eggemeier, Matthew T. - *A Sacramental-Prophetic Vision: Christian Spirituality in a Suffering World*
Theol St - v76 - i1 - March 2015 - p200(2) [501+]

Egger, Josef - *"Ein Wunderwerk der Technik": Fruhe Computernutzung in der Schweiz*
HNet - Jan 2015 - pNA [501+]

Egger, Matthias - *Other Fronts, Other Wars? First World War Studies on the Eve of the Centennial*
J Mil H - v79 - i3 - July 2015 - p862-864 [501+]

Eggers, Dave - *The Circle*
ABR - v36 - i5 - July-August 2015 - p11(2) [501+]
This Bridge Will Not Be Gray (Illus. by Nichols, Tucker)
c BL - v112 - i6 - Nov 15 2015 - p39(1) [51-500]
c KR - August 1 2015 - pNA [51-500]
c PW - v262 - i38 - Sept 21 2015 - p76(2) [51-500]
c PW - v262 - i49 - Dec 2 2015 - p51(1) [51-500]
c SLJ - v61 - i12 - Dec 2015 - p87(1) [51-500]

Eggert, James - *Meadowlark Economics*
KR - Dec 1 2015 - pNA [501+]

Eggert, Katherine - *Disknowledge: Literature, Alchemy, and the End of Humanism in Renaissance England*
JHI - v76 - i4 - Oct 2015 - p666(1) [501+]

Eggington, Tim - *The Advancement of Music in Enlightenment England: Benjamin Cooke and the Academy of Ancient Music*
MT - v156 - i1931 - Summer 2015 - p115-117 [501+]

Egginton, William - *The Man Who Invented Fiction: How Cervantes Ushered in the Modern World*
BL - v112 - i7 - Dec 1 2015 - p10(1) [51-500]
KR - Oct 15 2015 - pNA [501+]

Eggleton, Jill - *Brachio (Illus. by Fitzgibbon, Terry)*
c Magpies - v30 - i5 - Nov 2015 - pS5(1) [501+]
Oh Me, Oh My! (Illus. by Holt, Richard)
c Magpies - v30 - i5 - Nov 2015 - pS5(1) [501+]
Wobbling Whiskers (Illus. by Rumsey, Ricky)
c Magpies - v30 - i5 - Nov 2015 - pS5(1) [501+]

Egremont, Max - *Some Desperate Glory: The First World War the Poets Knew*
G&L Rev W - v22 - i5 - Sept-Oct 2015 - p42(1) [51-500]

Egyedi, Tineke M. - *Inverse Infrastructures: Disrupting Networks from Below*
T&C - v56 - i2 - April 2015 - p570-572 [501+]

Ehin, Kristiina - *Walker on Water*
WLT - v89 - i1 - Jan-Feb 2015 - p65(1) [501+]

Ehle, John - *The Land Breakers*
Spec - v327 - i9735 - March 28 2015 - p39(2) [501+]

Ehler, Lois - *Holey Moley (Illus. by Ehler, Lois)*
c KR - July 15 2015 - pNA [51-500]

Ehlers, Jr., Robert S. - *The Mediterranean Air War: Airpower and Allied Victory in World War II*
HNet - August 2015 - pNA [501+]

Ehlers, Nadine - *Racial Imperatives: Discipline, Performativity, and Struggles against Subjection*
JAH - v102 - i1 - June 2015 - p216-217 [501+]

Ehlert, Hans - *The Schlieffen Plan: International Perspectives on the German Strategy for World War I*
J Mil H - v79 - i2 - April 2015 - p467-471 [501+]

Ehlert, Lois - *Holey Moley (Illus. by Ehlert, Lois)*
c SLJ - v61 - i10 - Oct 2015 - p74(1) [51-500]

Ehmer, Kerstin - *The School of Sophisticated Drinking: An Intoxicating History of Seven Spirits*
BL - v112 - i1 - Sept 1 2015 - p24(1) [51-500]

Ehrgott, Roberts - *Mr. Wrigley's Ball Club: Chicago and the Cubs during the Jazz Age*
Historian - v77 - i1 - Spring 2015 - p118(2) [501+]

Ehrhart, Mark G. - *Organizational Climate and Culture: An Introduction to Theory, Research, and Practice*
Per Psy - v68 - i3 - Autumn 2015 - p703(4) [501+]

Ehrlich, David - *Who Will Die Last*
WLT - v89 - i1 - Jan-Feb 2015 - p65(1) [51-500]

Ehrlich, Esther - *Nest* (Read by Lamia, Jenna). Audiobook Review
   c BL - v111 - i21 - July 1 2015 - p80(1) [51-500]
   c SLJ - v61 - i6 - June 2015 - p63(1) [51-500]
Nest
   c CH Bwatch - Jan 2015 - pNA [501+]
   c HB Guide - v26 - i1 - Spring 2015 - p76(1) [51-500]

Ehrlich, Fred - *You Can't Build a House If You're a Hippo!: A Book about All Kinds of Houses* (Illus. by Haley, Amanda)
   c HB Guide - v26 - i1 - Spring 2015 - p154(1) [51-500]
You Can't Take Your Body to a Car Mechanic! A Book About What Makes You Sick (Illus. by Haley, Amanda)
   c HB Guide - v26 - i1 - Spring 2015 - p170(1) [51-500]

Ehrlich, J. Shoshanna - *Regulating Desire: From the Virtuous Maiden to the Purity Princess*
   Wom R Bks - v32 - i5 - Sept-Oct 2015 - p10(2) [501+]

Ehrlich, Paul R. - *Hope on Earth: A Conversation*
   QRB - v90 - i4 - Dec 2015 - p429(2) [501+]

Ehrlin, Carl-Johan Forssen - *The Rabbit Who Wants to Fall Asleep: A New Way of Getting Children to Sleep* (Illus. by Maununen, Irina)
   c KR - Oct 15 2015 - pNA [51-500]
   c SLJ - v61 - i12 - Dec 2015 - p88(1) [51-500]

Ehrman, Bart D. - *How Jesus Became God: The Exaltation of a Jewish Preacher from Galilee*
   Comw - v142 - i3 - Feb 6 2015 - p24(3) [501+]

Eich-Krohm, Astrid - *German Professionals in the United States: A Gendered Analysis of the Migration Decision of Highly Skilled Families*
   CS - v44 - i3 - May 2015 - p435-436 [501+]

Eich, Raymond - *A Bodyguard of Lies*
   Analog - v135 - i7-8 - July-August 2015 - p186(2) [501+]

Eichengreen, Barry - *Hall of Mirrors: The Great Depression, the Great Recession, and the Uses--and Misuses--of History*
   Atl - v315 - i1 - Jan-Feb 2015 - p41(3) [501+]
   BHR - v89 - i3 - Autumn 2015 - p557(13) [501+]
   Econ - v414 - i8921 - Jan 17 2015 - p80(US) [501+]
   TLS - i5867 - Sept 11 2015 - p3(2) [501+]

Eichenstein, Rita - *Not What I Expected: Help and Hope for Parents of Atypical Children*
   KR - Jan 15 2015 - pNA [501+]
   PW - v262 - i7 - Feb 16 2015 - p173(2) [51-500]

Eicher, Jerry S. - *A Heart Once Broken*
   PW - v262 - i52 - Dec 21 2015 - p141(1) [51-500]

Eichhorn, Kate - *The Archival Turn in Feminism: Outrage in Order*
   Signs - v40 - i2 - Wntr 2015 - p515(7) [501+]

Eickhoff, Diane - *Speaking Up for Women: Clarina Nichols and the World's First Women's Rights Campaign*
   c PW - v262 - i48 - Nov 30 2015 - p62(1) [501+]

Eig, Jonathan - *The Birth of the Pill: How Four Crusaders Reinvented Sex and Launched a Revolution*
   NYTBR - Dec 20 2015 - p24(L) [501+]
   Wom R Bks - v32 - i2 - March-April 2015 - p13(1) [501+]

Eijffinger, Sylvester C.W. - *Interactions of Monetary Policy and Central Bank Governance: Modern Monetary Policy and Central Bank Governance*
   IJCM - v25 - i2 - Summer 2015 - p257(3) [501+]

Eiland, Howard - *Walter Benjamin: A Critical Life*
   AHR - v120 - i2 - April 2015 - p569-570 [501+]
   Nation - v301 - i23 - Dec 7 2015 - p30(7) [501+]
   NS - v144 - i5284 - Oct 16 2015 - p44(3) [501+]
   TLS - i5839 - Feb 27 2015 - p5(1) [501+]
   CEH - v48 - i2 - June 2015 - p270-271 [501+]
   JMH - v87 - i3 - Sept 2015 - p754(3) [501+]

Eilberg, Amy - *From Enemy to Friend: Jewish Wisdom and the Pursuit of Peace*
   TT - v71 - i4 - Jan 2015 - p464-465 [501+]

Eilbert, Natalie - *Swan Feast*
   PW - v262 - i16 - April 20 2015 - p52(1) [51-500]

Einstein, Albert - *The Collected Papers of Albert Einstein, vol. 12: The Berlin Years: Correspondence, January-December 1921*
   Isis - v106 - i1 - March 2015 - p209(3) [501+]
The Collected Papers of Albert Einstein: vol. 13: The Berlin Years: Writings and Correspondence, January 1922-March 1923
   Isis - v106 - i1 - March 2015 - p209(3) [501+]
Relativity: The Special and the General Theory
   Phys Today - v68 - i11 - Nov 2015 - p51-51 [501+]

Eisen, Benjy - *Deal: My Three Decades of Drumming, Dreams, and Drugs with the Grateful Dead*
   Bwatch - July 2015 - pNA [51-500]

Eisenberg, Christine - *The Rise of Market Society in England 1066-1800*
   JEH - v75 - i3 - Sept 2015 - p931-933 [501+]

Eisenberg, Jefferey - *Suckered: The History of Sugar, Our Toxic Addiction, Our Power to Change*
   RVBW - Oct 2015 - pNA [51-500]

Eisenberg, Jeffrey - *Suckered: The History of Sugar, Our Toxic Addiction, Our Power to Change*
   KR - Jan 1 2016 - pNA [501+]

Eisenberg, Jesse - *Bream Gives Me Hiccups and Other Stories*
   y BL - v111 - i22 - August 1 2015 - p26(2) [51-500]
   KR - July 1 2015 - pNA [51-500]
   PW - v262 - i27 - July 6 2015 - p42(1) [51-500]

Eisenberg, Lee - *The Point Is*
   KR - Jan 1 2016 - pNA [501+]

Eisenberg, Ronald L. - *850 Intriguing Questions about Judaism: True, False, or in Between*
   BL - v112 - i3 - Oct 1 2015 - p11(1) [51-500]

Eisenbichler, Konrad - *The Sword and the Pen: Women, Politics, and Poetry in Sixteenth-Century Siena*
   Historian - v77 - i1 - Spring 2015 - p164(3) [501+]

Eisenhower, John S.D. - *Teddy Roosevelt and Leonard Wood: Partners in Command*
   J Mil H - v79 - i1 - Jan 2015 - p232-234 [501+]

Eisentraut, Jochen - *The Accessibility of Music: Participation, Reception, and Contact*
   PMS - v38 - i3 - July 2015 - p395(4) [501+]

Eisler, Barry - *The God's Eye View*
   BL - v112 - i7 - Dec 1 2015 - p28(1) [51-500]
   PW - v262 - i48 - Nov 30 2015 - p41(1) [51-500]

Eisler, Cornelia - *Verwaltete Erinnerung - Symbolische Politik: Die Heimatsammlungen der Deutschen Flüchtlinge, Vertriebenen und Aussiedler*
   HNet - June 2015 - pNA [51-500]

Eisler, Hanns - *Alternative Filmmusik zu einem Ausschnitt aus The Grapes of Wrath*
   Notes - v72 - i2 - Dec 2015 - p422(4) [501+]

Eisner, Will - *The Spirit: A Celebration of 75 Years*
   LJ - v140 - i15 - Sept 15 2015 - p5(1) [51-500]

Ejaz, Khadija - *My Friend Is Hindu*
   c SLJ - v61 - i8 - August 2015 - p126(1) [51-500]

Ekback, Cecilia - *Wolf Winter: A Novel*
   ABR - v36 - i4 - May-June 2015 - p19(1) [501+]
Wolf Winter
   LJ - v140 - i8 - May 1 2015 - p103(1) [51-500]
   Nat Post - v17 - i80 - Jan 31 2015 - pWP8(1) [501+]

Ekemar, Kim - *The Lost Identity Casualties*
   KR - Feb 15 2015 - pNA [501+]
Where the Bones of a Buried Rat Lie
   KR - May 15 2015 - pNA [501+]

Ekholst, Christine - *A Punishment for Each Criminal: Gender and Crime in Swedish Medieval Law*
   AHR - v120 - i4 - Oct 2015 - p1544-1545 [501+]

Ekin, Des - *The Last Armada: Queen Elizabeth, Juan del Aguila, and the 100-Day Spanish Invasion of England*
   KR - Oct 1 2015 - pNA [501+]
   PW - v262 - i45 - Nov 9 2015 - p51(1) [51-500]

Ekrem, Erica - *Bound: Over 20 Artful Handmade Books*
   BL - v111 - i15 - April 1 2015 - p11(2) [51-500]
   LJ - v140 - i5 - March 15 2015 - p107(1) [51-500]

Ekster, Carol Gordon - *Before I Sleep I Say Thank You* (Illus. by Rojas, Mary)
   c CH Bwatch - March 2015 - pNA [51-500]

El-Ariss, Tarek - *Trials of Arab Modernity: Literary Affects and the New Political*
   Col Lit - v42 - i1 - Wntr 2015 - p174(4) [501+]

El-Erian, Mohamed A. - *The Only Game in Town: Central Banks, Instability, and Avoiding the Next Collapse*
   KR - Dec 15 2015 - pNA [501+]

El Kouri, Zahie - *Don't Tell Her to Relax: 22 Ways to Support Your Infertile Loved One*
   SPBW - August 2015 - pNA [51-500]

El Kourl, Zahie - *Don't Tell Her to Relax: 22 Ways to Support Your Infertile Loved One through Diagnosis, Treatment, and Beyond*
   PW - v262 - i33 - August 17 2015 - p67(2) [51-500]

el Moncef, Salah - *The Offering*
   KR - August 15 2015 - pNA [501+]

El-Rayess, Miranda - *Henry James and the Culture of Consumption*
   RES - v66 - i276 - Sept 2015 - p792-793 [501+]

Elam, Michele - *The Cambridge Companion to James Baldwin*
   TLS - i5877 - Nov 20 2015 - p5(1) [51-500]

Eldarova, Sofia - *Builder Mouse*
   c KR - Nov 1 2015 - pNA [51-500]

Elden, Stuart - *The Birth of Territory*
   AHR - v120 - i1 - Feb 2015 - p188-189 [501+]

Elder, Charlie - *Few and Far Between: On the Trail of Britain's Rarest Animals*
   TLS - i5861 - July 31 2015 - p13(1) [501+]

Elder, Josh - *Reading with Pictures: Comics That Make Kids Smarter* (Illus. by McMeel, Andrews)
   c BL - v111 - i9-10 - Jan 1 2015 - pS4(8) [501+]
Scribblenauts Unmasked: A DC Comics Adventure (Illus. by Archer, Adam)
   c SLJ - v61 - i6 - June 2015 - p107(1) [51-500]

Eldredge, Niles - *Concrete Jungle: New York City and Our Last Best Hope for a Sustainable Future*
   TLS - i5837 - Feb 13 2015 - p22(1) [501+]
Eternal Ephemera: Adaptation and the Origin of Species from the Nineteenth Century through Punctuated Equilibria and Beyond
   BL - v111 - i16 - April 15 2015 - p7(1) [51-500]
   QRB - v90 - i4 - Dec 2015 - p417(2) [501+]
   TimHES - i2194 - March 12 2015 - p50-51 [501+]
Extinction and Evolution: What Fossils Reveal about the History of Life
   LJ - v140 - i2 - Feb 1 2015 - p104(1) [51-500]
   Nature - v523 - i7562 - July 30 2015 - p529(1) [51-500]

Eldridge, Alison - *Investigate Club Drugs*
   y HB Guide - v26 - i1 - Spring 2015 - p141(1) [51-500]

Eldridge, Arthur A. - *First Aid in the Laboratory and Workshop*
   Nature - v528 - i7581 - Dec 10 2015 - p203(1) [51-500]

Eldridge, Jim - *I Was There: 1066* (Illus. by Garton, Michael)
   c Sch Lib - v63 - i2 - Summer 2015 - p104(1) [51-500]

Eldridge, Richard - *An Introduction to the Philosophy of Art*
   Dialogue - v54 - i3 - Sept 2015 - p555-557 [501+]

Elena, Rodriguez-Guridi - *Exegesis del "error": una reinterpretacion de la praxis de escritura en Libro de la vida, Novelas ejemplares y Desenganos amorosos*
   Hisp R - v83 - i1 - Wntr 2015 - p102-104 [501+]

Elenbogen, Dina - *Drawn from Water: An American Poet, An Ethiopian Family, an Israeli Story*
   KR - Feb 15 2015 - pNA [501+]
   RVBW - June 2015 - pNA [51-500]

Eleveld, Kerry - *Don't Tell Me to Wait: How the Fight for Gay Rights Changed America and Transformed Obama's Presidency*
   LJ - v140 - i17 - Oct 15 2015 - p104(1) [51-500]
   NYTBR - Oct 25 2015 - p15(L) [501+]
   Reason - v47 - i7 - Dec 2015 - p52(4) [501+]
Don't Tell Me to Wait
   KR - Sept 1 2015 - pNA [501+]

Elfgren, Sara B. - *The Key*
   y HB - v91 - i5 - Sept-Oct 2015 - p102(1) [51-500]
   y KR - May 1 2015 - pNA [51-500]

Elfman, Eric - *Edison's Alley*
   c CCB-B - v68 - i9 - May 2015 - p468(1) [51-500]
   y CH Bwatch - April 2015 - pNA [51-500]
   c CH Bwatch - May 2015 - pNA [51-500]
   c HB Guide - v26 - i2 - Fall 2015 - p101(1) [51-500]
   c VOYA - v38 - i1 - April 2015 - p83(1) [71-500]

Elgar, Edward - *Critical Reflections on Ownership*
   TimHES - i2215 - August 6 2015 - p44-45 [501+]

Elgort, Arthur - *Arthur Elgort: The Big Picture*
   RVBW - August 2015 - pNA [51-500]

Eliason, Eric A. - *Latter-Day Lore: Mormon Folklore Studies*
   WestFolk - v74 - i1 - Wntr 2015 - p94 [501+]

Eliezrie, David - *The Secret Of Chabad*
   RVBW - Nov 2015 - pNA [51-500]

Eliot, Hannah - *Carrots Like Peas: And Other Fun Facts* (Illus. by Spurgeon, Aaron)
   c SLJ - v61 - i12 - Dec 2015 - p135(1) [51-500]
Glasses to Go
   c KR - Jan 1 2015 - pNA [51-500]
If Everything Were Pink (Illus. by Lalalimola)
   c PW - v262 - i20 - May 18 2015 - p82(2) [501+]

Eliot, T.S. - *The Letters of T. S. Eliot, vol. 5: 1930-1931*
   AM - v213 - i14 - Nov 9 2015 - p30(3) [501+]
Mr. Mistoffelees (Illus. by Robins, Arthur)
   c Sch Lib - v63 - i3 - Autumn 2015 - p154(1) [51-500]
The Poems of T.S. Eliot, 2 vols.
   NS - v144 - i5289 - Nov 20 2015 - p52(2) [501+]
The Poems of T.S. Eliot, vol. 2: Practical Cats and Further Verses
   Spec - v329 - i9772 - Dec 12 2015 - p72(2) [501+]

Elizabeth, Anne - *A SEAL Forever*
BL - v112 - i7 - Dec 1 2015 - p37(1) [51-500]
PW - v262 - i42 - Oct 19 2015 - p63(1) [51-500]

Elizabeth D. Samet - *No Man's Land: Preparing for War and Peace in Post-9/11 America*
Comw - v142 - i5 - March 6 2015 - p26(3) [501+]

Elizabeth M. Aranda, - *Making a Life in Multiethnic Miami: Immigration and the Rise of a Global City*
ERS - v38 - i3 - March 2015 - p458(3) [501+]

Elizarov, Mikhail - *The Librarian*
TLS - i5859 - July 17 2015 - p21(1) [501+]

Elkins, Ansel - *Blue Yodel*
BL - v111 - i15 - April 1 2015 - p13(1) [51-500]
PW - v262 - i11 - March 16 2015 - p60(2) [51-500]

Ell, Paul S. - *Troubled Geographies: A Spatial History of Religion and Society in Ireland*
JIH - v46 - i3 - Wntr 2016 - pNA [501+]

Ella and Penguin Stick Together
c KR - Oct 1 2015 - pNA [501+]

Elleman, Bruce A. - *Taiwan Straits: Crisis in Asia and the Role of the U.S. Navy*
J Mil H - v79 - i3 - July 2015 - p803-805 [501+]

Ellenberg, Jordan - *How Not to Be Wrong: The Hidden Maths of Everyday Life*
Nature - v523 - i7562 - July 30 2015 - p529(1) [51-500]
How Not to Be Wrong: The Power of Mathematical Thinking
Har Bus R - v93 - i10 - Oct 2015 - p130(2) [501+]
J Chem Ed - v92 - i7 - July 2015 - p1146-1148 [501+]

Ellenbogen, Josh - *Reasoned and Unreasoned Images: The Photography of Bertillon, Galton, and Marey*
Isis - v106 - i2 - June 2015 - p469(3) [501+]

Eller, Jonathan R. - *Ray Bradbury Unbound*
SFS - v42 - i3 - Nov 2015 - p583-584 [501+]

Elliot, David - *Henry's Stars (Illus. by Elliot, David)*
c KR - March 1 2015 - pNA [51-500]
Magpies - v30 - i3 - July 2015 - pS5(1) [501+]
SLJ - v61 - i4 - April 2015 - p127(1) [51-500]

Elliot, Graham - *Cooking Like a Master Chef: 100 Recipes to Make the Everyday Extraordinary*
LJ - v140 - i15 - Sept 15 2015 - p100(1) [51-500]
PW - v262 - i31 - August 3 2015 - p51(1) [51-500]

Elliot, Rachel - *The Adventurers*
c KR - Dec 1 2015 - pNA [51-500]
Marguerite's Fountain
c KR - Dec 1 2015 - pNA [51-500]

Elliot, Will - *The Pilo Traveling Show*
PW - v262 - i30 - July 27 2015 - p46(1) [51-500]

Elliott, Cara - *Passionately Yours*
PW - v262 - i14 - April 6 2015 - p45(1) [51-500]

Elliott, Christopher L. - *High Command: British Military Leadership in the Iraq and Afghanistan Wars*
J Mil H - v79 - i2 - April 2015 - p553-556 [501+]
Spec - v327 - i9726 - Jan 24 2015 - p47(2) [501+]

Elliott, Clark - *The Ghost in My Brain: How a Concussion Stole My Life and How the New Science of Brain Plasticity Helped Me Get It Back*
PW - v262 - i15 - April 13 2015 - p66(1) [51-500]
BL - v111 - i19-20 - June 1 2015 - p18(1) [51-500]
KR - April 1 2015 - pNA [51-500]

Elliott, David - *Nobody's Perfect (Illus. by Zuppardi, Sam)*
c BL - v111 - i9-10 - Jan 1 2015 - p108(1) [51-500]
c CH Bwatch - March 2015 - pNA [51-500]
c HB Guide - v26 - i2 - Fall 2015 - p33(1) [51-500]
On the Wing (Illus. by Stadtlander, Becca)
c HB Guide - v26 - i1 - Spring 2015 - p188(2) [51-500]
c SLJ - v61 - i4 - April 2015 - p42(4) [501+]
c Teach Lib - v42 - i3 - Feb 2015 - p52(1) [51-500]
This Orq. (He Cave Boy.). (Illus. by Nichols, Lori)
c CH Bwatch - Jan 2015 - pNA [51-500]
This Orq (He Cave Boy.). (Illus. by Nichols, Lori)
c HB Guide - v26 - i1 - Spring 2015 - p8(1) [51-500]
This Orq. (Illus. by Nichols, Lori)
c KR - June 15 2015 - pNA [51-500]
This Orq: He Say "Ugh!". (Illus. by Nichols, Lori)
c SLJ - v61 - i9 - Sept 2015 - p119(1) [51-500]

Elliott, Devlin - *Naughty Mabel (Illus. by Krall, Dan)*
c NYTBR - Dec 20 2015 - p14(L) [501+]

Elliott, Dyan - *The Bride of Christ Goes to Hell: Metaphor and Embodiment in the Lives of Pious Women, 200-1500*
Specu - v90 - i3 - July 2015 - p801-802 [501+]

Elliott, J. - *Ennius and the Architecture of the Annales*
Class R - v65 - i2 - Oct 2015 - p423-425 [501+]

Elliott, Jenny - *Save Me*
y CCB-B - v68 - i6 - Feb 2015 - p308(2) [51-500]
y VOYA - v37 - i6 - Feb 2015 - p74(2) [51-500]

Elliott, Julia - *The New and Improved Romie Futch*
KR - August 1 2015 - pNA [51-500]
PW - v262 - i32 - August 10 2015 - p34(2) [51-500]
The Wilds
ABR - v36 - i3 - March-April 2015 - p11(1) [501+]

Elliott, Kate - *Black Wolves*
BL - v112 - i6 - Nov 15 2015 - p32(1) [51-500]
KR - August 15 2015 - pNA [51-500]
PW - v262 - i39 - Sept 28 2015 - p74(1) [51-500]
Court of Fives
y BL - v111 - i18 - May 15 2015 - p60(1) [51-500]
y CCB-B - v69 - i2 - Oct 2015 - p85(2) [51-500]
y KR - May 1 2015 - pNA [51-500]
y PW - v262 - i21 - May 25 2015 - p60(1) [51-500]
y SLJ - v61 - i5 - May 2015 - p112(3) [51-500]
y VOYA - v38 - i3 - August 2015 - p76(1) [51-500]
The Very Best of Kate Elliott
MFSF - v128 - i3-4 - March-April 2015 - p71(2) [51-500]

Elliott, Kevin D., Sr. - *I'm a Different Type of Apple*
SPBW - April 2015 - pNA [51-500]

Elliott, Laura - *Da Vinci's Tiger*
y PW - v262 - i34 - August 24 2015 - p83(1) [51-500]

Elliott, Laura Malone - *Da Vinci's Tiger*
y BL - v112 - i5 - Nov 1 2015 - p49(2) [51-500]
y KR - Sept 1 2015 - pNA [51-500]
y PW - v262 - i49 - Dec 2 2015 - p114(1) [51-500]
y SLJ - v61 - i10 - Oct 2015 - p110(1) [51-500]
y VOYA - v38 - i5 - Dec 2015 - p55(1) [51-500]

Elliott, Mark W. - *The Heart of Biblical Theology: Providence Experienced*
JR - v95 - i2 - April 2015 - p255(2) [501+]

Elliott, Martha - *The Man in the Monster: An Intimate Portrait of a Serial Killer*
LJ - v140 - i13 - August 1 2015 - p111(1) [51-500]
BL - v111 - i22 - August 1 2015 - p8(2) [51-500]
PW - v262 - i23 - June 8 2015 - p51(2) [51-500]
The Man in the Monster
KR - June 1 2015 - pNA [501+]

Elliott, Ned - *F is for Football (Illus. by Somerville, Charles C.)*
c Sch Lib - v63 - i1 - Spring 2015 - p46(2) [51-500]

Elliott, Okla - *The Doors You Mark Are Your Own*
PW - v262 - i2 - Jan 12 2015 - p40(1) [51-500]
BL - v111 - i13 - March 1 2015 - p30(1) [51-500]

Elliott, Patricia - *The House of Eyes*
Sch Lib - v63 - i4 - Winter 2015 - p228(1) [51-500]

Elliott, Rebecca - *Eva Sees a Ghost (Illus. by Elliott, Rebecca)*
c HB Guide - v26 - i2 - Fall 2015 - p65(1) [51-500]
Eva's Treetop Festival (Illus. by Elliott, Rebecca)
c HB Guide - v26 - i2 - Fall 2015 - p65(1) [51-500]
Naked Trevor
c HB Guide - v26 - i2 - Fall 2015 - p10(1) [51-500]
Owl Diaries: Eva Sees a Ghost
c SLJ - v61 - i5 - May 2015 - p98(1) [51-500]

Ellis, Carson - *Home (Illus. by Ellis, Carson)*
c BL - v111 - i9-10 - Jan 1 2015 - p106(1) [51-500]
c HB - v91 - i1 - Jan-Feb 2015 - p64(2) [51-500]
c NYTBR - March 15 2015 - p16(L) [50+]
c Res Links - v20 - i5 - June 2015 - p3(2) [51-500]
c SLJ - v61 - i6 - June 2015 - p80(1) [51-500]
Home
c HB Guide - v26 - i2 - Fall 2015 - p10(1) [51-500]
c PW - v262 - i49 - Dec 2 2015 - p27(1) [51-500]

Ellis, Charles D. - *Falling Short: The Coming Retirement Crisis and What to Do about It*
NYRB - v62 - i4 - March 5 2015 - p48(3) [501+]

Ellis, David - *Byron in Geneva: That Summer of 1816*
Clio - v44 - i2 - Spring 2015 - p217-237 [501+]
Frank Cioffi: The Philosopher in Shirt-Sleeves
TimHES - i2213 - July 23 2015 - p45(1) [501+]

Ellis, Deborah - *The Cat at the Wall*
c HB Guide - v26 - i1 - Spring 2015 - p76(1) [51-500]
Looks Like Daylight
c SLJ - v61 - i12 - Dec 2015 - p64(4) [501+]
Moon at Nine
y Magpies - v30 - i1 - March 2015 - p39(2) [501+]
No Ordinary Day
c SLJ - v61 - i12 - Dec 2015 - p64(4) [501+]

Ellis, Elina - *The Big Adventure*
c Sch Lib - v63 - i4 - Winter 2015 - p219(1) [51-500]
c SLJ - v61 - i10 - Oct 2015 - p75(1) [51-500]

Ellis, Fiona - *God, Value, and Nature*
TimHES - i2220 - Sept 10 2015 - p45-1 [501+]

Ellis, Garfield - *The Angel's Share*
KR - Oct 15 2015 - pNA [51-500]

Ellis, Hannah - *Dylan Thomas: A Centenary Celebration*
AM - v212 - i5 - Feb 16 2015 - p25(3) [501+]

Ellis, Heather - *Generational Conflict and University Reform: Oxford in the Age of Revolution*
HER - i543 - April 2015 - p471(2) [501+]

Ellis, Helen - *American Housewife*
BL - v112 - i6 - Nov 15 2015 - p20(1) [51-500]
KR - Oct 1 2015 - pNA [51-500]
LJ - v140 - i20 - Dec 1 2015 - p97(1) [51-500]
PW - v262 - i41 - Oct 12 2015 - p44(1) [51-500]

Ellis, Jay - *Critical Insights: American Creative Nonfiction*
BL - v111 - i21 - July 1 2015 - p15(1) [51-500]

Ellis, Joseph J. - *The Quartet*
KR - Jan 1 2015 - pNA [51-500]
The Quartet: Orchestrating the Second American Revolution, 1783-1789 (Read by Dean, Robertson). Audiobook Review
PW - v262 - i35 - August 31 2015 - p85(1) [51-500]
The Quartet: Orchestrating the Second American Revolution, 1783-1789
Econ - v415 - i8937 - May 9 2015 - p79(US) [501+]
LJ - v140 - i5 - March 15 2015 - p120(1) [501+]
NYT - June 30 2015 - pC4(L) [501+]
NYTBR - May 10 2015 - p12(L) [501+]
PW - v262 - i8 - Feb 23 2015 - p64(1) [51-500]

Ellis, Kate - *Walking by Night*
BL - v111 - i17 - May 1 2015 - p48(1) [51-500]
PW - v262 - i21 - May 25 2015 - p39(1) [51-500]

Ellis, Mark - *Race Harmony and Black Progress: Jack Woofter and the Interracial Cooperation Movement*
AHR - v120 - i3 - June 2015 - p1050(1) [501+]
JSH - v81 - i3 - August 2015 - p761(2) [501+]

Ellis, Markman - *Empire of Tea: The Asian Leaf That Conquered the World*
Lon R Bks - v37 - i15 - July 30 2015 - p17(2) [501+]
Nature - v522 - i7544 - June 4 2015 - p33(1) [51-500]

Ellis Nilsson, Sara E. - *Creating Holy People and Places on the Periphery: A Study on the Emergence of Cults of Native Saints in the Ecclesiastical Provinces of Lund and Uppsala from the Eleventh to the Thirteenth Centuries*
HNet - April 2015 - pNA [501+]

Ellis, Richard J. - *Judging the Boy Scouts of America: Gay Rights, Freedom of Association, and the Dale Case*
HLR - v128 - i3 - Jan 2015 - p1063(2) [51-500]

Ellis, Robert - *City of Echoes*
BL - v111 - i19-20 - June 1 2015 - p48(1) [51-500]
PW - v262 - i28 - July 13 2015 - p47(1) [51-500]
RVBW - Nov 2015 - pNA [51-500]

Ellis, Samantha - *How to Be a Heroine, or, What I've Learned from Reading Too Much*
LJ - v140 - i2 - Feb 1 2015 - p80(3) [51-500]

Ellis, Sarah - *A+ for Big Ben (Illus. by LaFave, Kim)*
c KR - Jan 1 2016 - pNA [51-500]
c PW - v262 - i20 - May 18 2015 - p82(2) [501+]
c Res Links - v20 - i4 - April 2015 - p3(1) [51-500]
c SLJ - v61 - i8 - August 2015 - p57(1) [51-500]
Ben Says Goodbye (Illus. by LaFave, Kim)
c KR - Dec 15 2015 - pNA [51-500]
c Res Links - v21 - i1 - Oct 2015 - p5(2) [51-500]

Ellis, Sherry - *Ten Zany Birds (Illus. by Jain, Charu)*
c CH Bwatch - August 2015 - pNA [51-500]

Ellis, Sylvia - *Freedom's Pragmatist: Lyndon Johnson and Civil Rights*
JSH - v81 - i1 - Feb 2015 - p244(2) [501+]

Ellis, Warren - *Trees, vol. 1: In Shadow*
PW - v262 - i15 - April 13 2015 - p65(1) [51-500]

Ellison, Betty Boles - *The Early Laps of Stock Car Racing: A History of the Sport and Business Through 1974*
JSH - v81 - i4 - Nov 2015 - p1020(2) [501+]

Ellison, Harlan - *Can and Can'tankerous*
PW - v262 - i41 - Oct 12 2015 - p52(1) [51-500]

Ellison, J.T. - *No One Knows*
PW - v262 - i50 - Dec 7 2015 - p66(2) [51-500]
What Lies Behind
BL - v111 - i19-20 - June 1 2015 - p58(1) [51-500]
PW - v262 - i15 - April 13 2015 - p58(1) [51-500]

Ellison, James A. - *John Wesley and Universalism*
KR - March 15 2015 - pNA [501+]

Ellison, Katherine - *Topographies of the Imagination: New Approaches to Daniel Defoe*
RES - v66 - i274 - April 2015 - p382-384 [501+]

Ellisor, John T. - *The Second Creek War: Interethnic Conflict and Collusion on a Collapsing Frontier*
HNet - Feb 2015 - pNA [501+]

Ellman, Barat - *Memory and Covenant: The Role of Israel's and God's Memory in Sustaining the Deuteronomic and Priestly Covenants*
    Intpr - v69 - i4 - Oct 2015 - p490(2) [501+]

Ellory, R.J. - *Ghostheart*
    BL - v111 - i17 - May 1 2015 - p36(1) [51-500]
    PW - v262 - i15 - April 13 2015 - p56(2) [51-500]
Saints of New York
    RVBW - Feb 2015 - pNA [51-500]

Ellory, Roger Jon - *Saints of New York*
    RVBW - Nov 2015 - pNA [51-500]

Ellroy, James - *LAPD '53*
    NS - v144 - i5263 - May 22 2015 - p50(2) [501+]

Ellsworth, Scott - *The Secret Game: A Basketball Story in Black and White*
    y BL - v111 - i12 - Feb 15 2015 - p20(1) [51-500]
The Secret Game
    KR - Jan 15 2015 - pNA [501+]

Ellul, Jacques - *On Being Rich and Poor: Christianity in a Time of Economic Globalization*
    Bks & Cult - v21 - i6 - Nov-Dec 2015 - p14(2) [501+]
On Freedom, Love and Power
    Bks & Cult - v21 - i6 - Nov-Dec 2015 - p14(2) [501+]

Ellwood, David W. - *The Shock of America: Europe and the Challenge of the Century*
    AHR - v120 - i2 - April 2015 - p584(1) [501+]

Elm, Michael - *The Horrors of Trauma in Cinema: Violence Void Visualization*
    HNet - July 2015 - pNA [501+]

Elmer, Peter - *The Miraculous Conformist: Valentine Greatrakes, the Body Politic and the Politics of Healing in Restoration Britain*
    Isis - v106 - i1 - March 2015 - p184(2) [501+]
The Miraculous Conformist: Valentine Greatrakes, the Body Politic, and the Politics of Healing in Restoration Britain
    JMH - v87 - i1 - March 2015 - p172(3) [501+]

Elmore, Bartow J. - *Citizen Coke: The Making of Coca-Cola Capitalism*
    NS - v144 - i5248 - Feb 6 2015 - p43(1) [51-500]
    NYTBR - Jan 4 2015 - p11(L) [501+]
    TimHES - i2190 - Feb 12 2015 - p48-2 [501+]

Elovic, Barbara - *Other People's Stories*
    ABR - v36 - i5 - July-August 2015 - p19(2) [501+]

Elrod, P.N. - *The Hanged Man*
    BL - v111 - i15 - April 1 2015 - p34(1) [51-500]
    KR - March 15 2015 - pNA [51-500]
    PW - v262 - i6 - Feb 9 2015 - p49(1) [51-500]

Elschner, Geraldine - *Like A Wolf (Illus. by Guilloppe, Antoine)*
    c KR - August 1 2015 - pNA [51-500]
    c PW - v262 - i28 - July 13 2015 - p65(1) [51-500]
    c SLJ - v61 - i12 - Dec 2015 - p88(1) [51-500]
The Little Hippo: A Children's Book Inspired by Egyptian Art (Illus. by Klauss, Anja)
    c HB Guide - v26 - i1 - Spring 2015 - p29(1) [51-500]
    c SLJ - v61 - i10 - Oct 2015 - p75(1) [51-500]
The Nativity (Illus. by di Bondone, Giotto)
    c KR - Sept 1 2015 - pNA [51-500]
The Nativity (Illus. by Giotto)
    c PW - v262 - i37 - Sept 14 2015 - p68(1) [51-500]
    c SLJ - v61 - i10 - Oct 2015 - p62(2) [51-500]

Else, Barbara - *The Volume of Possible Endings (Illus. by Broad, Sam)*
    SLJ - v61 - i2 - Feb 2015 - p84(2) [51-500]
    c HB Guide - v26 - i2 - Fall 2015 - p81(1) [51-500]

Elsesser, Kim - *Sex and the Office: Women, Men, and the Sex Partition That's Dividing the Workplace*
    PW - v262 - i20 - May 18 2015 - p74(1) [51-500]

Elshakry, Marwa - *Reading Darwin in Arabic, 1860-1950*
    HNet - May 2015 - pNA [501+]
    IJMES - v47 - i1 - Feb 2015 - p180-182 [501+]
    NYRB - v62 - i10 - June 4 2015 - p77(2) [501+]
    QRB - v90 - i1 - March 2015 - p72(2) [501+]

Elsir, Amir Tag - *Ebola '76*
    Spec - v327 - i9737 - April 11 2015 - p44(1) [501+]

Elson, Bryan - *Canada's Bastions of Empire: Haliflax, Victoria and the Royal Navy 1749-1918*
    Beav - v95 - i4 - August-Sept 2015 - p70(2) [501+]

Elson, Jane - *How to Fly with Broken Wings*
    c Sch Lib - v63 - i3 - Autumn 2015 - p164(1) [51-500]

Elswit, Kate - *Watching Weimar Dance*
    TLS - i5838 - Feb 20 2015 - p29(1) [501+]

Eltahawy, Mona - *Headscarves and Hymens: Why The Midde East Needs a Sexual Revolution*
    KR - Feb 15 2015 - pNA [501+]

Headscarves and Hymens: Why the Middle East Needs a Sexual Revolution
    BL - v111 - i13 - March 1 2015 - p7(1) [51-500]
    Ms - v25 - i2 - Spring 2015 - p43(1) [501+]
    NS - v144 - i5267 - June 19 2015 - p50(1) [51-500]
    PW - v262 - i6 - Feb 9 2015 - p60(1) [51-500]

Elton, Ben - *Time and Time Again*
    BL - v112 - i7 - Dec 1 2015 - p38(1) [51-500]

Elves, The - *Letters to Santa Claus*
    LJ - v140 - i16 - Oct 1 2015 - p99(1) [51-500]

Elvgren, Jennifer - *The Whispering Town (Read by Cottle, Elizabeth). Audiobook Review*
    c SLJ - v61 - i7 - July 2015 - p45(2) [51-500]

Elwood, Tessa - *Inherit the Stars*
    y BL - v112 - i6 - Nov 15 2015 - p50(2) [51-500]
    y KR - Sept 1 2015 - pNA [51-500]
    y SLJ - v61 - i11 - Nov 2015 - p107(2) [51-500]
    y VOYA - v38 - i5 - Dec 2015 - p68(1) [501+]

Ely, Mark C. - *Dictionary of Music Education*
    M Ed J - v101 - i3 - March 2015 - p17(2) [501+]

Elya, Susan Middleton - *Bebe Goes Shopping (Illus. by Salerno, Steven)*
    c BL - v111 - i9-10 - Jan 1 2015 - pS18(5) [501+]
Oh No, Gotta Go! (Illus. by Karas, G. Brian)
    c BL - v111 - i9-10 - Jan 1 2015 - pS18(5) [501+]

Elyot, Justine - *Diamond*
    PW - v262 - i14 - April 6 2015 - p45(2) [51-500]

Emanuel, Lynn - *The Nerve of It: Poems New and Selected*
    PW - v262 - i29 - July 20 2015 - p167(1) [51-500]

Emberley, Barbara - *The Story of Paul Bunyan (Illus. by Emberley, Ed)*
    c HB - v91 - i6 - Nov-Dec 2015 - p115(2) [501+]

Emberley, Ed - *Itsy Bitsy Spider*
    c CH Bwatch - Jan 2015 - pNA [501+]
Spare Parts (Illus. by Emberley, Ed)
    c PW - v262 - i34 - August 24 2015 - p78(2) [51-500]

Emberley, Rebecca - *Spare Parts (Illus. by Emberley, Ed)*
    c BL - v112 - i5 - Nov 1 2015 - p68(1) [51-500]
    c KR - August 15 2015 - pNA [51-500]
    c SLJ - v61 - i10 - Oct 2015 - p75(1) [51-500]

Emberton, Carole - *Beyond Redemption: Race, Violence, and the American South after the Civil War*
    J Am St - v49 - i1 - Feb 2015 - p181-185 [501+]
    Historian - v77 - i2 - Summer 2015 - p327(2) [501+]
    RAH - v43 - i3 - Sept 2015 - p512-521 [501+]

Embree, Dan - *Short Scottish Prose Chronicles*
    Med R - Jan 2015 - pNA [501+]

Embrey, Jenelle R. - *Dangerous Jeeps and Me*
    KR - August 1 2015 - pNA [501+]

Embry, Jessie - *Oral History, Community, and Work in the American West*
    WestFolk - v74 - i2 - Spring 2015 - p221-224 [501+]

Embry, Jessie L. - *Oral History, Community, and Work in the American West*
    PHR - v84 - i3 - August 2015 - p376(2) [501+]

Emdin, Christopher - *For White Folks Who Teach in the Hood ... and the Rest of Y'all Too*
    KR - Dec 15 2015 - pNA [501+]

Emerging German-Language Novelists of the Twenty-First Century
    HNet - Sept 2015 - pNA [501+]

Emerson, Allan J. - *Death of a Bride and Groom*
    KR - March 15 2015 - pNA [51-500]
    PW - v262 - i16 - April 20 2015 - p58(1) [51-500]

Emerson, Claudia - *Impossible Bottle: Poems*
    LJ - v140 - i13 - August 1 2015 - p101(1) [51-500]
    PW - v262 - i33 - August 17 2015 - p48(2) [51-500]
The Opposite House
    PW - v262 - i7 - Feb 16 2015 - p158(1) [51-500]

Emerson, Clint - *100 Deadly Skills: The SEAL Operative's Guide to Eluding Pursuers, Evading Capture, and Surviving Any Dangerous Situation*
    NYTBR - Oct 25 2015 - p35(L) [501+]

Emerson, Jim - *Futures Past: 1926: The Birth of Modern Science Fiction*
    Analog - v135 - i3 - March 2015 - p106(1) [501+]

Emerson, Kathy Lynn - *Murder in the Merchant's Hall*
    PW - v262 - i41 - Oct 12 2015 - p49(2) [51-500]
Murder in the Queen's Wardrobe
    BL - v111 - i12 - Feb 15 2015 - p38(1) [51-500]
    KR - Jan 1 2015 - pNA [51-500]
    PW - v262 - i4 - Jan 26 2015 - p151(1) [51-500]

Emerson, Kevin - *Breakout (Read by Berman, Fred). Audiobook Review*
    BL - v111 - i21 - July 1 2015 - p80(1) [51-500]
    y SLJ - v61 - i6 - June 2015 - p66(1) [51-500]
Breakout
    c BL - v112 - i5 - Nov 1 2015 - p52(1) [501+]
    y CCB-B - v68 - i8 - April 2015 - p398(2) [51-500]
    y SLJ - v61 - i3 - March 2015 - p134(1) [51-500]
Encore to an Empty Room
    y BL - v111 - i15 - April 1 2015 - p64(2) [51-500]
    y HB Guide - v26 - i2 - Fall 2015 - p118(1) [501+]
    y KR - Feb 15 2015 - pNA [501+]
    y VOYA - v38 - i1 - April 2015 - p58(1) [51-500]

Emerson, Lori - *Reading Writing Interfaces: From the Digital to the Bookbound*
    AL - v87 - i3 - Sept 2015 - p630-632 [501+]

Emerson, Melinda F. - *Become Your Own Boss in 12 Months: A Month-by-Month Guide to a Business That Works*
    PW - v262 - i32 - August 10 2015 - p54(2) [51-500]

Emerson, Michael - *Britain's Future in Europe: Reform, Renegotiation, Repatriation or Secession?*
    Econ - v415 - i8932 - April 4 2015 - p78(US) [501+]

Emerson, Ralph Waldo - *English Traits*
    TimHES - i2204 - May 21 2015 - p49(1) [501+]

Emerson, Roger L. - *An Enlightened Duke: The Life of Archibald Campbell, 1682-1761, Earl of Ilay, 3rd Duke of Argyll*
    JMH - v87 - i3 - Sept 2015 - p729(3) [501+]

Emerson, Stephen - *A Manual for Cleaning Women: Selected Stories*
    Bks & Cult - v21 - i6 - Nov-Dec 2015 - p30(2) [501+]
    BL - v111 - i22 - August 1 2015 - p29(1) [51-500]
    NYTBR - Dec 13 2015 - p12(L) [501+]

Emerson, Stephen A. - *The Battle for Mozambique: The Frelimo-Renamo Struggle, 1977-1992*
    HNet - Jan 2015 - pNA [501+]
    NWCR - v68 - i4 - Autumn 2015 - p126(2) [501+]

Emery, Anne - *Ruined Abbey*
    BL - v111 - i17 - May 1 2015 - p43(1) [51-500]
    PW - v262 - i12 - March 23 2015 - p50(1) [51-500]

Emery, Christian - *US Foreign Policy and the Iranian Revolution: The Cold War Dynamics of Engagement and Strategic Alliance*
    AHR - v120 - i3 - June 2015 - p1076-1077 [501+]

Emery, Elizabeth - *Medievalism: Key Critical Terms*
    Med R - Sept 2015 - pNA [501+]
    Specu - v90 - i4 - Oct 2015 - p1190(1) [501+]
Photojournalism and the Origins of the French Writer House Museum (1881-1914)
    FS - v69 - i2 - April 2015 - p270-271 [501+]

Emery, Jennifer - *Lighting Design for Commercial Portrait Photography*
    Bwatch - Oct 2015 - pNA [501+]

Eming, Jutta - *Visuality and Materiality in the Story of Tristan and Isolde*
    Specu - v90 - i3 - July 2015 - p803-804 [501+]

Emiralioglu, Pinar - *Geographical Knowledge and Imperial Culture in the Early Modern Ottoman Empire*
    AHR - v120 - i2 - April 2015 - p748-749 [501+]
    IJMES - v47 - i2 - May 2015 - p386-388 [501+]
    Six Ct J - v46 - i2 - Summer 2015 - p402-403 [501+]

Emlen, Douglas J. - *Animal Weapons: The Evolution of Battle*
    BioSci - v65 - i7 - July 2015 - p730(2) [501+]

Emma - *Emma (Illus. by Tse, Po)*
    y SLJ - v61 - i11 - Nov 2015 - p123(2) [51-500]

Emmerich, Michael - *The Book of Tokyo: A City in Short Fiction*
    WLT - v89 - i6 - Nov-Dec 2015 - p23(1) [501+]
The Book of Tokyo
    NS - v144 - i5287 - Nov 6 2015 - p47(1) [51-500]
The Tale of Genji: Translation, Canonization, and World Literature by
    MP - v112 - i3 - Feb 2015 - pE212(E216) [501+]

Emmert, Scott D. - *World War I in American Fiction: An Anthology of Short Stories*
    Am St - v54 - i1 - Spring 2015 - p179-2 [501+]

Emmett, Brian - *Get Your Bake On: Sweet and Savory Recipes from My Home to Yours*
    BL - v111 - i19-20 - June 1 2015 - p20(1) [51-500]

Emmett, Jonathan - *Fast and Furry Racers: The Silver Serpent Cup*
    c Sch Lib - v63 - i3 - Autumn 2015 - p154(1) [51-500]
A Spot of Bother (Illus. by Cabban, Vanesa)
    c Sch Lib - v63 - i2 - Summer 2015 - p91(1) [51-500]

Emmons, Henry - *Staying Sharp: 9 Keys for a Youthful Brain through Modern Science and Ageless Wisdom*
    PW - v262 - i24 - June 15 2015 - p76(1) [501+]

Emond, Stephen - *Bright Lights, Dark Nights (Illus. by Emond, Stephen)*
    y BL - v111 - i21 - July 1 2015 - p55(1) [51-500]
    y CCB-B - v69 - i2 - Oct 2015 - p86(1) [51-500]
    y KR - June 1 2015 - pNA [51-500]
    y PW - v262 - i22 - June 1 2015 - p60(1) [51-500]
    y SLJ - v61 - i5 - May 2015 - p113(2) [51-500]
    y VOYA - v38 - i3 - August 2015 - p58(1) [51-500]

Emory, T.W. - *Trouble in Rooster Paradise*
    PW - v262 - i20 - May 18 2015 - p67(1) [51-500]

Emsley, Clive - *Soldier, Sailor, Beggarman, Thief: Crime and the British Armed Services since 1914*
    JMH - v87 - i1 - March 2015 - p181(2) [501+]

Enard, Mathias - *Street of Thieves*
    CSM - Feb 6 2015 - pNA [501+]
    NS - v144 - i5277 - August 28 2015 - p45(1) [501+]
    NYTBR - Feb 22 2015 - p21(L) [501+]

Enayati, Amanda - *Seeking Serenity: The 10 New Rules for Health and Happiness in the Age of Anxiety*
    BL - v111 - i14 - March 15 2015 - p28(1) [51-500]

Encarnacioon, Omar G. - *Democracy without Justice in Spain: The Politics of Forgetting*
    HNet - May 2015 - pNA [501+]

The End of Days
    VQR - v91 - i1 - Wntr 2015 - p193-196 [501+]

Endelman, Todd M. - *Leaving the Jewish Fold: Conversion and Radical Assimilation in Modern Jewish History*
    TLS - i5868 - Sept 18 2015 - p8(1) [501+]

Enders, Giulia - *Gut: The Inside Story of Our Body's Most Underrated Organ*
    LJ - v140 - i8 - May 1 2015 - p96(1) [51-500]
    Nat Post - v17 - i165 - May 16 2015 - pWP4(1) [501+]
    New Sci - v226 - i3024 - June 6 2015 - p45(1) [501+]
    Spec - v328 - i9742 - May 16 2015 - p37(1) [501+]

Endicott, Marina - *Close to Hugh*
    Mac - v128 - i22 - June 8 2015 - p57(2) [501+]

Endo, Shusaku - *White Man, Yellow Man: Two Novellas*
    AM - v212 - i14 - April 27 2015 - p38(2) [501+]

Enduring Mysteries Series
    c BL - v111 - i15 - April 1 2015 - p58(1) [501+]

Enenkel, Karl - *Neo-Latin Commentaries and the Management of Knowledge in the Late Middle Ages and the Early Modern Period (1400-1700).*
    Sev Cent N - v73 - i1-2 - Spring-Summer 2015 - p84(3) [501+]

Enenkel, Karl A.E. - *Transformations of the Classics via Early Modern Commentaries*
    Six Ct J - v46 - i2 - Summer 2015 - p430-431 [501+]

Enersen, Adele - *Vincent and the Night (Illus. by Enersen, Adele)*
    c BL - v111 - i16 - April 15 2015 - p55(1) [51-500]
Vincent and the Night
    c HB Guide - v26 - i2 - Fall 2015 - p10(1) [51-500]

Enfield, Nick J. - *Relationship Thinking: Agency, Enchrony, and Human Sociality*
    Lang Soc - v44 - i4 - Sept 2015 - p584-587 [501+]

Eng-Beng Lim - *Brown Boys and Rice Queens: Spell-Binding Performance in the Asias*
    Theat J - v67 - i1 - March 2015 - p159-160 [501+]

Eng-Beng, Lim - *Brown Boys and Rice Queens: Spellbinding Performance in the Asias*
    JAS - v74 - i1 - Feb 2015 - p178-180 [501+]
    Signs - v40 - i3 - Spring 2015 - p773(7) [501+]

Engammare, Max - *Soixante-trois: La peur de la grande annee climacterique a la Renaissance*
    Ren Q - v68 - i2 - Summer 2015 - p661-662 [501+]

Engard, Nicole C. - *More Library Mashups: Exploring New Ways to Deliver Library Data*
    LR - v64 - i4-5 - April-May 2015 - p395-396 [501+]
    VOYA - v37 - i6 - Feb 2015 - p91(1) [51-500]

Engberg-Pedersen, Anders - *Empire of Chance: The Napoleonic Wars and the Disorder of Things*
    J Mil H - v79 - i3 - July 2015 - p822-824 [501+]

Engel, Amy - *The Book of Ivy*
    SLJ - v61 - i2 - Feb 2015 - p100(1) [51-500]
The Revolution of Ivy
    y KR - Sept 15 2015 - pNA [51-500]
    y VOYA - v38 - i4 - Oct 2015 - p68(1) [51-500]

Engel, Barbara Alpern - *Breaking the Ties that Bound: The Politics of Marital Strife in Late Imperial Russia*
    JWH - v27 - i2 - Summer 2015 - p175(7) [501+]

Engel, Elisabeth - *The U.S. South in the Black Atlantic: Transnational Histories of the Jim Crow South Since 1865*
    HNet - August 2015 - pNA [501+]

Engel, Matthew - *Engel's England: Thirty-Nine Counties, One Capital and One Man*
    TLS - i5831 - Jan 2 2015 - p22(1) [501+]

Engel, Monroe - *The Middle of the Journey*
    New R - v246 - i9-10 - Sept-Oct 2015 - p68(5) [501+]

Engel, Susan - *The End of the Rainbow: How Educating for Happiness - Not Money - Would Transform Our Schools*
    RVBW - March 2015 - pNA [501+]
The Hungry Mind: The Origins of Curiosity in Childhood
    LJ - v140 - i5 - March 15 2015 - p123(1) [51-500]

Engelbreit, Mary - *The Blessings of Friendship Treasury (Illus. by Engelbreit, Mary)*
    c HB Guide - v26 - i1 - Spring 2015 - p187(1) [51-500]

Engelhardt, Elizabeth - *The Larder: Food Studies Methods from the American South*
    JSH - v81 - i1 - Feb 2015 - p258(3) [501+]

Engels, David - *Religion and Competition in Antiquity*
    HNet - June 2015 - pNA [501+]

Enger, Lin - *The High Divide*
    Roundup M - v22 - i3 - Feb 2015 - p25(2) [51-500]
    Roundup M - v22 - i6 - August 2015 - p29(1) [501+]

Engh, Line Cecilie - *Gendered Identities in Bernard of Clairvaux's Sermons on The Song of Songs: Performing the Bride*
    Med R - June 2015 - pNA [501+]
    Specu - v90 - i4 - Oct 2015 - p1112-1113 [501+]

Englade, Kenneth F. - *Meltdown in Haditha: The Killing of 24 Iraqi Civilians by US Marines and the Failure of Military Justice*
    Parameters - v45 - i2 - Summer 2015 - p138(3) [501+]

Engle, Debra Landwehr - *The Only Little Prayer You Need: The Shortest Route to a Life of Joy, Abundance, and Peace of Mind*
    Bwatch - Feb 2015 - pNA [51-500]

Engle, Margarita - *Drum Dream Girl: How One Girl's Courage Changed Music (Illus. by Lopez, Rafael)*
    c BL - v111 - i11 - Feb 1 2015 - p46(1) [51-500]
    c CCB-B - v68 - i9 - May 2015 - p444(1) [51-500]
    c CH Bwatch - May 2015 - pNA [501+]
    c HB - v91 - i3 - May-June 2015 - p86(1) [51-500]
    c HB Guide - v26 - i2 - Fall 2015 - p33(1) [51-500]
    c PW - v262 - i3 - Jan 19 2015 - p86(1) [51-500]
Enchanted Air: Two Cultures, Two Wings: A Memoir (Illus. by Rodriguez, Edel)
    c BL - v111 - i18 - May 15 2015 - p46(1) [51-500]
    y HB - v91 - i4 - July-August 2015 - p156(1) [51-500]
    y SLJ - v61 - i5 - May 2015 - p138(2) [51-500]
       VOYA - v38 - i2 - June 2015 - p87(1) [51-500]
    y KR - May 1 2015 - pNA [51-500]
Orangutanka: A Story in Poems (Illus. by Kurilla, Renee)
    c HB Guide - v26 - i2 - Fall 2015 - p203(1) [51-500]
    c PW - v262 - i2 - Jan 12 2015 - p58(1) [51-500]
Orangutanka (Illus. by Kurilla, Renee)
    c BL - v111 - i16 - April 15 2015 - p55(1) [51-500]
Silver People
    c SLJ - v61 - i12 - Dec 2015 - p64(4) [501+]
The Sky Painter: Louis Fuertes, Bird Artist (Illus. by Bereghici, Aliona)
    c HB Guide - v26 - i2 - Fall 2015 - p192(1) [51-500]
    c PW - v262 - i17 - April 27 2015 - p74(1) [501+]
    c SLJ - v61 - i5 - May 2015 - p132(2) [51-500]

Engler, Mark - *This Is an Uprising*
    KR - Dec 1 2015 - pNA [501+]

Engler, Michael - *Elephantastic! (Illus. by Tourlonias, Joelle)*
    c HB Guide - v26 - i2 - Fall 2015 - p33(1) [51-500]

English, Alex - *Pirates Don't Drive Diggers (Illus. by Beedie, Duncan)*
    c Sch Lib - v63 - i4 - Winter 2015 - p219(1) [51-500]
Yuck! Said the Yak (Illus. by Levey, Emma)
    c Sch Lib - v63 - i1 - Spring 2015 - p26(1) [51-500]

English, Christy - *How to Seduce a Scot*
    PW - v262 - i42 - Oct 19 2015 - p61(2) [51-500]
How to Wed a Warrior
    PW - v262 - i51 - Dec 14 2015 - p67(1) [51-500]

English, John - *Harvest Your Own Lumber: How to Fell, Saw, Dry and Mill Wood*
    LJ - v140 - i13 - August 1 2015 - p95(1) [51-500]
    RVBW - June 2015 - pNA [501+]

English, Karen - *Don't Feed the Geckos!*
    c KR - Oct 1 2015 - pNA [51-500]
Skateboard Party (Illus. by Freeman, Laura)
    c HB Guide - v26 - i1 - Spring 2015 - p59(1) [51-500]

English, Linda - *By All Accounts: General Stores and Community Life in Texas and Indian Territory*
    RAH - v43 - i1 - March 2015 - p98-102 [501+]

English, T.J. - *Where the Bodies Were Buried: Whitey Bulger and the World That Made Him*
    KR - July 15 2015 - pNA [51-500]
    LJ - v140 - i14 - Sept 1 2015 - p122(1) [51-500]
    PW - v262 - i29 - July 20 2015 - p179(2) [51-500]

English, Timothy - *Popology*
    KR - June 1 2015 - pNA [501+]

Enke, Anne - *Transfeminist Perspectives: In and Beyond Transgender and Gender Studies*
    NWSA Jnl - v27 - i1 - Spring 2015 - p196-200 [501+]

Enlightened World Appropriations. Imperial Actors and Scenarios of Change
    HNet - July 2015 - pNA [501+]

Ennaji, Mohammed - *Slavery, the State, and Islam*
    AHR - v120 - i2 - April 2015 - p746-747 [501+]

Ennals, Peter - *Opening a Window to the West: The Foreign Concession at Kobe, Japan, 1868-1899*
    Pac A - v88 - i2 - June 2015 - p321 [501+]

Ennis, John - *Travel Every Day*
    KR - June 1 2015 - pNA [501+]

Enniss, Stephen - *After the Titanic: A Life of Derek Mahon*
    LJ - v140 - i11 - June 15 2015 - p89(1) [51-500]
    TLS - i5836 - Feb 6 2015 - p10(1) [501+]
Red Sails: Prose
    TLS - i5836 - Feb 6 2015 - p10(1) [501+]

Enoch, Suzanne - *Some Like It Scot*
    PW - v262 - i28 - July 13 2015 - p50(2) [51-500]

Enquist, Per Olov - *The Wandering Pine*
    TLS - i5853 - June 5 2015 - p20(1) [501+]

Enric, Bou - *Invention of Space: City Travel Literature*
    Hisp R - v83 - i4 - Autumn 2015 - p485-488 [501+]

Enright, Anne - *The Green Road*
    BL - v111 - i14 - March 15 2015 - p52(2) [51-500]
    Comw - v142 - i12 - July 10 2015 - p27(2) [501+]
    CSM - May 29 2015 - pNA [501+]
    Econ - v415 - i8937 - May 9 2015 - p80(US) [501+]
    ILS - v35 - i1 - Fall 2015 - p24(2) [501+]
    KR - March 1 2015 - pNA [501+]
    LJ - v140 - i6 - April 1 2015 - p73(2) [51-500]
    Lon R Bks - v37 - i11 - June 4 2015 - p3(2) [501+]
    Mac - v128 - i19-20 - May 18 2015 - p78(1) [501+]
    NS - v144 - i5265 - June 5 2015 - p52(1) [501+]
    NY - v91 - i14 - May 25 2015 - p71 [501+]
    PW - v262 - i9 - March 2 2015 - p62(1) [51-500]
    TLS - i5850 - May 15 2015 - p19(1) [501+]
The Green Room
    BL - v111 - i1 - Feb 1 2015 - p4(1) [51-500]

Enright, Michael J. - *Prophecy and Kingship in Adomnan's "Life of Saint Columba"*
    Specu - v90 - i1 - Jan 2015 - p242-244 [501+]

Enrigue, Alvaro - *Sudden Death*
    KR - Dec 15 2015 - pNA [501+]

Enrique, Alvaro - *Sudden Death*
    LJ - v140 - i20 - Dec 1 2015 - p89(2) [51-500]

Enss, Chris - *Mochi's War: The Tragedy of Sand Creek*
    LJ - v140 - i9 - May 15 2015 - p91(2) [51-500]

Entrekin, Alison - *Near to the Wild Heart*
    Nation - v301 - i21-22 - Nov 23 2015 - p31(4) [501+]

Entwistle, Vaughn - *The Dead Assassin*
    BL - v111 - i17 - May 1 2015 - p38(1) [51-500]
The Dead Assassin: The Paranormal Casebooks of Sir Arthur Conan Doyle
    PW - v262 - i14 - April 6 2015 - p42(1) [51-500]

Enz, Tammy - *Super Cool Mechanical Activities with Max Axiom*
    c HB Guide - v26 - i2 - Fall 2015 - p166(1) [51-500]

Enzerink, Mirjam - *The Day the Sun Did Not Rise and Shine (Illus. by Rauwerda, Peter-Paul)*
    c CH Bwatch - July 2015 - pNA [51-500]
    c KR - Feb 15 2015 - pNA [51-500]
    c SLJ - v61 - i5 - May 2015 - p84(1) [51-500]

Ephron, Dan - *Killing a King: The Assassination of Yitzhak Rabin and the Remaking of Israel*
KR - August 15 2015 - pNA [51-500]
LJ - v140 - i15 - Sept 15 2015 - p87(1) [51-500]
Mac - v128 - i45 - Nov 16 2015 - p56(1) [501+]
NY - v91 - i33 - Oct 26 2015 - p75 [501+]
NYTBR - Nov 15 2015 - p14(L) [501+]
PW - v262 - i32 - August 10 2015 - p50(1) [51-500]
Ephron, Delia - *Do I Have to Say Hello? Aunt Delia's Manners Quiz (Illus. by Koren, Edward)*
BL - v112 - i7 - Dec 1 2015 - p40(1) [51-500]
Ephron, Hallie - *Night Night, Sleep Tight (Read by Lee, Ann Marie). Audiobook Review*
PW - v262 - i26 - June 29 2015 - p63(1) [51-500]
Night Night, Sleep Tight
BL - v111 - i9-10 - Jan 1 2015 - p48(1) [51-500]
KR - Jan 1 2015 - pNA [51-500]
PW - v262 - i7 - Feb 16 2015 - p159(1) [51-500]
Epistemologies of In-Betweenness: East Central Europe and the World History of Social Science, 1890-1945
HNet - August 2015 - pNA [501+]
Epp, Charles R. - *Pulled Over: How Police Stops Define Race and Citizenship*
AJS - v120 - i5 - March 2015 - p1555(3) [501+]
Epperson, Bruce D. - *More Important than the Music: A History of Jazz Discography*
Notes - v71 - i4 - June 2015 - p721(3) [501+]
Epps, Garrett - *American Justice 2014: Nine Clashing Visions on the Supreme Court*
HLR - v128 - i7 - May 2015 - p2106(2) [1-50]
Epstein, Adam - *Starbounders*
c Teach Lib - v42 - i4 - April 2015 - p37(1) [51-500]
Epstein, Alex - *The Moral Case for Fossil Fuels*
Barron's - v95 - i1 - Jan 5 2015 - p18(1) [501+]
Epstein, Edward Z. - *Audrey and Bill: A Romantic Biography of Audrey Hepburn & William Holden*
LJ - v140 - i6 - April 1 2015 - p90(2) [51-500]
Epstein, Katherine - *Torpedo: Inventing the Military-Industrial Complex in the United States and Great Britain*
NWCR - v68 - i4 - Autumn 2015 - p127(3) [501+]
Epstein, Katherine C. - *Torpedo: Inventing the Military Industrial Complex in the United States and Great Britain*
AHR - v120 - i2 - April 2015 - p588-589 [501+]
Torpedo: Inventing the Military-Industrial Complex in the United States and Great Britain
RAH - v43 - i2 - June 2015 - p300-306 [501+]
Epstein, Lawrence J. - *Converts to Judaism: Stories from Biblical Times to Today*
BL - v111 - i9-10 - Jan 1 2015 - p20(1) [51-500]
Epstein, Richard A. - *The Classical Liberal Constitution: The Uncertain Quest for Limited Government*
Historian - v77 - i3 - Fall 2015 - p554(2) [501+]
HLR - v128 - i5 - March 2015 - p1452(23) [501+]
IndRev - v19 - i4 - Spring 2015 - p609(4) [501+]
TLS - i5841 - March 13 2015 - p23(1) [501+]
Epstein, Robin - *H.E.A.R.*
y BL - v112 - i5 - Nov 1 2015 - p55(1) [51-500]
y SLJ - v61 - i11 - Nov 2015 - p114(1) [51-500]
Hear
y KR - Oct 1 2015 - pNA [51-500]
Equi, Elaine - *Sentences and Rain*
LJ - v140 - i16 - Oct 1 2015 - p85(1) [51-500]
PW - v262 - i38 - Sept 21 2015 - p52(1) [51-500]
Erasmus, Desiderius - *Vie de saint Jerome*
Sev Cent N - v73 - i3-4 - Fall-Winter 2015 - p189(5) [501+]
Eraso, Yolanda - *Representing Argentinian Mothers: Medicine, Ideas and Culture in the Modern Era, 1900-1946*
JIH - v45 - i4 - Spring 2015 - p602-603 [501+]
Erdelac, Edward M. - *Andersonville*
PW - v262 - i25 - June 22 2015 - p124(1) [51-500]
Erdi, Peter - *Stochastic Chemical Kinetics: Theory and (Mostly) Systems Biology Applications*
SIAM Rev - v57 - i3 - Sept 2015 - p475-477 [501+]
Erdinast-Vulcan, Daphna - *Between Philosophy and Literature: Bakhtin and the Question of the Subject*
Comp L - v67 - i2 - June 2015 - p234-238 [501+]
Erelle, Anna - *In the Skin of a Jihadist: A Young Journalist Enters the ISIS Recruitment Network*
LJ - v140 - i12 - July 1 2015 - p98(1) [51-500]
Eremeeva, Jennifer - *Lenin Lives Next Door: Marriage, Martinis, and Mayhem in Moscow*
KR - Sept 1 2015 - pNA [501+]
Erfourth, Jill - *Interacting with Informational Text for Close and Critical Reading*
RVBW - July 2015 - pNA [51-500]
Ericksen, Robert P. - *Complicity in the Holocaust: Churches and Universities in Nazi Germany*
CHR - v101 - i4 - Autumn 2015 - p949(2) [501+]
Erickson, Alex - *Death by Tea*
BL - v112 - i7 - Dec 1 2015 - p27(1) [51-500]
Erickson, Edward J. - *Ottomans and Armenians: A Study in Counterinsurgency*
HNet - Sept 2015 - pNA [501+]
Erickson, J.M. - *Future Promotheus II: Revolution, Successions & Resurrections*
KR - Jan 15 2015 - pNA [501+]
Erickson, Jay - *Blood Wizard Chronicles*
KR - Nov 1 2015 - pNA [501+]
Erickson, Karla A. - *How We Die Now: Intimacy and the Work of Dying*
CS - v44 - i1 - Jan 2015 - p54-55 [501+]
Erickson, Laura - *Into the Nest: Intimate Views of the Courting, Parenting, and Family Lives of Familiar Birds*
BL - v111 - i13 - March 1 2015 - p10(1) [51-500]
SLJ - v61 - i3 - March 2015 - p176(1) [51-500]
Erickson, Megan - *Focus on Me*
PW - v262 - i23 - June 8 2015 - p46(1) [51-500]
Erickson, Mike C. - *Pianist in a Bordello*
KR - July 1 2015 - pNA [501+]
Erickson, Paul - *How Reason Almost Lost Its Mind: The Strange Career of Cold War Rationality*
AHR - v120 - i1 - Feb 2015 - p287-289 [501+]
Isis - v106 - i2 - June 2015 - p501(2) [501+]
The Pier at the End of the World
c Sci & Ch - v53 - i1 - Sept 2015 - p94 [501+]
Erickson, Paul (b. 1952-) - *The Pier at the End of the World (Illus. by Martinez, Andrew)*
c CH Bwatch - April 2015 - pNA [51-500]
c HB Guide - v26 - i1 - Spring 2015 - p154(1) [51-500]
Erickson, Teresa - *The Master Communicator's Handbook*
SPBW - Oct 2015 - pNA [51-500]
Ericson, Nora - *Dill & Bizzy: An Odd Duck and a Strange Bird (Illus. by Ericson, Lisa)*
c KR - Oct 1 2015 - pNA [51-500]
Ericson, P.J. - *Diary of an Airdale*
SPBW - May 2015 - pNA [51-500]
Ericsson, Gustav - *My Christian Journey with Zen*
PW - v262 - i32 - August 10 2015 - p57(1) [51-500]
Eriksen, Anne - *From Antiquities to Heritage: Transformations of Cultural Memory*
AHR - v120 - i4 - Oct 2015 - p1444-1445 [501+]
Eriksen, Stefka Georgieva - *Writing and Reading in Medieval Manuscript Culture: The Translation and Transmission of the Story of Elye in Old French and Old Norse Literary Texts*
JEGP - v114 - i2 - April 2015 - p313(4) [501+]
Erikson, Emily - *Between Monopoly and Free Trade: The English East India Company, 1600-1757*
CS - v44 - i6 - Nov 2015 - p794-795 [501+]
Eriksson, Hazel - *Boho Crochet: 30 Hip and Happy Projects*
Bwatch - July 2015 - pNA [51-500]
Eriksson, Kjell - *Open Grave*
BL - v111 - i19-20 - June 1 2015 - p50(1) [51-500]
NYTBR - July 19 2015 - p25(L) [501+]
PW - v262 - i19 - May 11 2015 - p36(2) [51-500]
Erisman, Porter - *Alibaba's World: How a Remarkable Chinese Company Is Changing the Face of Global Business*
PW - v262 - i8 - Feb 23 2015 - p62(1) [51-500]
Erla, Gudrun - *Learn to Quilt-as-You-Go: 14 Projects You Can Finish Fast*
Bwatch - Sept 2015 - pNA [51-500]
Strip Your Stash: Dynamic Quilts Made from Strips: 12 Projects in Multiple Sizes from GE Designs
LJ - v140 - i16 - Oct 1 2015 - p83(1) [51-500]
Erlbruch, Wolf - *Duck, Death and the Tulip (Illus. by Erlbruch, Wolf)*
c BL - v112 - i6 - Nov 15 2015 - p48(1) [501+]
Erler, Mary C. - *Reading and Writing during the Dissolution: Monks, Friars, and Nuns 1530-1558*
CHR - v101 - i4 - Autumn 2015 - p937(2) [501+]
Six Ct J - v46 - i3 - Fall 2015 - p724-725 [501+]
Erlich, Reese - *Inside Syria*
Tikkun - v30 - i1 - Wntr 2015 - pNA [51-500]
Erlinger, Amanda - *Sinatra*
Spec - v329 - i9767 - Nov 7 2015 - p46(2) [501+]
Ernaux, Annie - *A Woman's Story*
TLS - i5841 - March 13 2015 - p26(1) [501+]
Ernst, Daniel R. - *Tocqueville's Nightmare: The Administrative State Emerges in America, 1900-1940*
HLR - v128 - i4 - Feb 2015 - p1329(2) [1-50]
JAH - v102 - i2 - Sept 2015 - p581-582 [501+]
Nation - v300 - i12 - March 23 2015 - p27(5) [501+]
RAH - v43 - i3 - Sept 2015 - p544-549 [501+]
Ernst, Edzard - *A Scientist in Wonderland: A Memoir of Searching for Truth and Finding Trouble*
Nature - v518 - i7537 - Feb 5 2015 - p33(1) [51-500]
TimHES - i2188 - Jan 29 2015 - p46-47 [501+]
Ernst, Kathleen - *Death on the Prairie*
BL - v112 - i1 - Sept 1 2015 - p46(1) [51-500]
KR - August 1 2015 - pNA [51-500]
Ernst, Linda L. - *The Essential Lapsit Guide: A Multimedia How-To-Do-It Manual and Programming Guide for Stimulating Literacy Development from 12 to 24 Months*
R&USQ - v54 - i4 - Summer 2015 - p71(1) [501+]
SLJ - v61 - i6 - June 2015 - p147(1) [501+]
Ernst, Lyle - *Wisdom from Our First Nations*
y Res Links - v20 - i5 - June 2015 - p31(2) [51-500]
Ernst, Wolfgang - *Digital Memory and the Archive*
T&C - v56 - i2 - April 2015 - p560-562 [501+]
Erpenbeck, Jenny - *The End of Days*
NS - v144 - i5254 - March 20 2015 - p51(1) [501+]
TLS - i5835 - Jan 30 2015 - p20(1) [501+]
Erskine, Gizzi - *Gizzi's Healthy Appetite: Food to Nourish the Body and Feed the Soul*
PW - v262 - i52 - Dec 21 2015 - p148(1) [51-500]
Erskine, Kathryn - *The Badger Knight (Read by Halstead, Graham). Audiobook Review*
SLJ - v61 - i2 - Feb 2015 - p49(1) [51-500]
The Badger Knight
c HB Guide - v26 - i1 - Spring 2015 - p76(1) [51-500]
Ersoy, Ahmet - *Cosmopolitan Attachment: Pluralism and Civic Identity in Late Ottoman Cities*
J Urban H - v41 - i3 - May 2015 - p521-525 [501+]
Erspamer, Lisa - *A Letter to My Mom*
KR - Jan 1 2015 - pNA [501+]
Ervin, Andrew - *Burning Down George Orwell's House*
BL - v111 - i15 - April 1 2015 - p23(1) [51-500]
KR - March 1 2015 - pNA [51-500]
LJ - v140 - i6 - April 1 2015 - p74(1) [51-500]
PW - v262 - i9 - March 2 2015 - p63(1) [51-500]
Ervin, Phil - *Maya Moore: WNBA Champion*
c BL - v112 - i4 - Oct 15 2015 - p43(1) [51-500]
Ervine, Jonathan - *Cinema and the Republic: Filming on the Margins in Comtemporary France*
FS - v69 - i1 - Jan 2015 - p134-135 [501+]
Erway, Cathy - *The Food of Taiwan: Recipes from the Beautiful Island*
LJ - v140 - i8 - May 1 2015 - p94(1) [51-500]
PW - v262 - i5 - Feb 2 2015 - p50(2) [51-500]
Erwin, Douglas H. - *The Cambrian Explosion: The Construction of Animal Biodiversity*
QRB - v90 - i2 - June 2015 - p204(2) [501+]
Erwin, Scott R. - *The Theological Vision of Reinhold Niebuhr's The Irony of American History: "In the Battle and Above It"*
JAAR - v83 - i3 - Sept 2015 - p878-880 [501+]
Es, Evelien van - *Atlas of the Functional City: CIAM 4 and Comparative Urban Analysis*
HNet - Oct 2015 - pNA [501+]
Es gilt das gesprochene Wort. Oral History und Zeitgeschichte heute. Tagung zu Ehren von Dorothee Wierling
HNet - May 2015 - pNA [501+]
Esack, Farid - *Domestic Violence and the Islamic Tradition*
JAAR - v83 - i2 - June 2015 - p585-587 [501+]
Esarey, Ashley - *The Internet in China: Cultural, Political, and Social Dimensions, 1980s-2000s*
RVBW - Sept 2015 - pNA [51-500]
Esbaum, Jill - *Elwood Bigfoot (Illus. by Wragg, Nate)*
c KR - July 1 2015 - pNA [51-500]
Explore My World: Penguins
c HB Guide - v26 - i1 - Spring 2015 - p162(1) [51-500]
Koalas
c HB Guide - v26 - i2 - Fall 2015 - p179(1) [51-500]
Little Kids First Big Book of How
c KR - Jan 1 2016 - pNA [51-500]
Little Kids First Big Book of Who
c BL - v111 - i18 - May 15 2015 - p48(1) [51-500]
c HB Guide - v26 - i2 - Fall 2015 - p213(1) [51-500]
Snow Leopards
c HB Guide - v26 - i1 - Spring 2015 - p164(1) [51-500]
Esberger, Trudi - *The Boy Who Lost His Bumble (Illus. by Esberger, Trudi)*
c HB Guide - v26 - i2 - Fall 2015 - p10(1) [51-500]
c KR - Jan 15 2015 - pNA [51-500]
c SLJ - v61 - i6 - June 2015 - p80(1) [51-500]

Escalona, Julio - *Scale and Scale Change in the Early Middle Ages: Exploring Landscape, Local Society, and the World Beyond*
    Specu - v90 - i3 - July 2015 - p874-875 [501+]

Eschliman, Dwight - *Ingredients: A Visual Exploration of 75 Additives and 25 Food Products*
    NYTBR - Dec 6 2015 - pNA(L) [501+]

Escobar, Mary Chris - *Neverending Beginnings*
    PW - v262 - i28 - July 13 2015 - p53(1) [51-500]

Escobar-Vargas, M. Carolina - *Law's Dominion: Medieval Studies for Paul Hyams*
    Med R - June 2015 - pNA [501+]

Escoffier, Michael - *Take Away the A: An Alphabeast of a Book (Illus. by Di Giacomo, Kris)*
    c CCB-B - v68 - i5 - Jan 2015 - p254(1) [51-500]
  Take Away the A (Illus. by Di Giacomo, Kris)
    c HB Guide - v26 - i1 - Spring 2015 - p29(1) [51-500]
  Where's the Baboon? (Illus. by Di Giacomo, Kris)
    c BL - v112 - i3 - Oct 1 2015 - p84(1) [51-500]
    c KR - Sept 15 2015 - pNA [51-500]
    c PW - v262 - i39 - Sept 28 2015 - p90(2) [501+]
  Where's the Baboon? (Illus. by Giacomo, Kris Di)
    c SLJ - v61 - i12 - Dec 2015 - p88(1) [51-500]

Escolme, Bridget - *Emotional Excess on the Shakespearean Stage: Passion's Slaves*
    Ren Q - v68 - i2 - Summer 2015 - p785-787 [501+]

Escott, Paul D. - *Uncommonly Savage: Civil War and Remembrance in Spain and the United States*
    AHR - v120 - i2 - April 2015 - p581-582 [501+]
    JAH - v101 - i4 - March 2015 - p1279(1) [51-500]
    JSH - v81 - i4 - Nov 2015 - p999(2) [501+]

Esdaile, Charles J. - *Women in the Peninsular War*
    J Mil H - v79 - i1 - Jan 2015 - p203-204 [501+]

Eshelman, Kendra - *The Social World of Intellectuals in the Roman Empire: Sophists, Philosophers, and Christians*
    CH - v84 - i4 - Dec 2015 - p864(3) [51-500]

Eskens, Allen - *The Guise of Another*
    BL - v112 - i1 - Sept 1 2015 - p46(2) [51-500]
    KR - August 1 2015 - pNA [51-500]
    NYTBR - Nov 1 2015 - p29(L) [51-500]
    PW - v262 - i32 - August 10 2015 - p39(1) [51-500]

Eskew, Glenn T. - *Johnny Mercer: Southern Songwriter for the World*
    JSH - v81 - i1 - Feb 2015 - p238(3) [501+]

Esola, Louise - *American Boys: The True Story of the Lost 74 of the Vietnam War*
    LJ - v140 - i16 - Oct 1 2015 - p92(1) [501+]

Espada, Martin - *Vivas to Those Who Have Failed*
    BL - v112 - i6 - Nov 15 2015 - p9(1) [51-500]

Espedal, Tomas - *Against Nature*
    WLT - v89 - i6 - Nov-Dec 2015 - p65(1) [51-500]

Espina, Eduardo - *The Milli Vanilli Condition: Essays on Culture in the New Millennium*
    RVBW - August 2015 - pNA [51-500]

Espinosa, David - *Jesuit Student Groups, the Universidad Iberoamericana, and Political Resistance in Mexico, 1913-1979*
    CHR - v101 - i2 - Spring 2015 - p401(2) [501+]

Espinosa, Gaston - *Latino Pentecostals in America: Faith and Politics in Action*
    CC - v132 - i6 - March 18 2015 - p42(2) [501+]
    Comw - v142 - i4 - Feb 20 2015 - p25(2) [501+]
    JAH - v102 - i2 - Sept 2015 - p578-579 [501+]
    Theol St - v76 - i4 - Dec 2015 - p845(3) [501+]
    WHQ - v46 - i3 - Autumn 2015 - p377-378 [501+]

Espinosa, Rod - *Steampunk Fables*
    y VOYA - v38 - i2 - June 2015 - p50(2) [501+]

Espinosa, Ruben - *Shakespeare and Immigration*
    Ren Q - v68 - i1 - Spring 2015 - p390-392 [501+]

Espinosa, Victor M. - *Martin Ramirez: Framing His Life and Art*
    BL - v112 - i5 - Nov 1 2015 - p22(2) [51-500]
    PW - v262 - i31 - August 3 2015 - p46(2) [51-500]

Espinoza, G. Antonio - *Education and the State in Modern Peru: Primary Schooling in Lima, 1821-c. 1921*
    AHR - v120 - i1 - Feb 2015 - p305-306 [501+]

Espiritu, Yen Le - *Body Counts: The Vietnam War and Militarized Refugees*
    Am St - v54 - i2 - Summer 2015 - p108-109 [501+]
    Amerasia J - v41 - i1 - Wntr 2015 - p121-123 [501+]

Esposito, Anna - *Donne del Rinascimento a Roma e dintorni*
    Ren Q - v68 - i2 - Summer 2015 - p680-681 [501+]

Esposito, Joey - *Pawn Shop*
    PW - v262 - i51 - Dec 14 2015 - p69(1) [51-500]

Esposito, Shannon - *Faux Pas*
    KR - Oct 15 2015 - pNA [51-500]
    PW - v262 - i42 - Oct 19 2015 - p58(1) [51-500]

Essamuah, Casely B. - *Communities of Faith in Africa and the African Diaspora: In Honor of Dr. Tite Tienou, with Additional Essays on World Christianity*
    IBMR - v39 - i2 - April 2015 - p99(1) [51-500]

Essbaum, Jill Alexander - *Exploring the Dilemma of Domesticity*
    PW - v262 - i2 - Jan 12 2015 - p27(5) [501+]
  Hausfrau (Read by Marno, Mozhan). Audiobook Review
    LJ - v140 - i9 - May 15 2015 - p42(1) [51-500]
  Hausfrau
    BL - v111 - i12 - Feb 15 2015 - p31(1) [51-500]
    Ent W - i1355-1356 - March 20 2015 - p105(1) [501+]
    KR - Feb 1 2015 - pNA [51-500]
    NYT - March 20 2015 - pC21(L) [501+]
    NYTBR - March 29 2015 - p10(L) [501+]
    NYTBR - Sept 6 2015 - p24(L) [501+]
    PW - v262 - i1 - Jan 5 2015 - p50(1) [51-500]

Essen, Marty - *Endangered Edens: Exploring the Arctic National Wildlife Refuge, Costa Rica, the Everglades, and Puerto Rico*
    SPBW - Nov 2015 - pNA [51-500]

Essif, Les - *American "Unculture" in French Drama: Homo Americanus and the Post-1960 French Resistance*
    FS - v69 - i1 - Jan 2015 - p117-118 [501+]

Essig, Mark - *Lesser Beasts: A Snout-to-Tail History of the Humble Pig*
    Econ - v415 - i8936 - May 2 2015 - p75(US) [501+]
    KR - March 1 2015 - pNA [501+]
  Lesser Beasts: A Snout-to-Tail-History of the Humble Pig
    LJ - v140 - i6 - April 1 2015 - p113(1) [51-500]
  Lesser Beasts: A Snout-to-Tail History of the Humble Pig
    Mac - v128 - i18 - May 11 2015 - p60(2) [501+]
    New Sci - v226 - i3023 - May 30 2015 - p47(1) [501+]
    Spec - v328 - i9746 - June 13 2015 - p35(1) [501+]

Essin, Christin - *Stage Designers in Early Twentieth-Century America: Artists, Activists, Cultural Critics*
    Theat J - v67 - i3 - Oct 2015 - p587-589 [501+]

Estabrook, Barry - *Pig Tales: An Omnivore's Quest for Sustainable Meat*
    Bwatch - July 2015 - pNA [51-500]
    KR - Feb 15 2015 - pNA [51-500]
    LJ - v140 - i12 - July 1 2015 - p103(1) [51-500]
    PW - v262 - i15 - April 13 2015 - p70(1) [51-500]

Estella, Lucy - *Suri's Wall (Illus. by Ottley, Matt)*
    Magpies - v30 - i4 - Sept 2015 - p32(1) [51-500]

Estep, Jennifer - *Bitter Bite*
    KR - Dec 15 2015 - pNA [51-500]
  Cold Burn of Magic
    y BL - v111 - i19-20 - June 1 2015 - p95(1) [51-500]
    y SLJ - v61 - i6 - June 2015 - p111(2) [51-500]
    y VOYA - v38 - i2 - June 2015 - p73(1) [51-500]
  Spider's Trap
    PW - v262 - i25 - June 22 2015 - p124(1) [51-500]

Esterly, David - *The Lost Carving: A Journey to the Heart of Making*
    TLS - i5845 - April 10 2015 - p8(2) [501+]

Estes, Allison - *Izzy & Oscar (Illus. by Dockray, Tracy)*
    c KR - Feb 15 2015 - pNA [51-500]
    c SLJ - v61 - i5 - May 2015 - p84(1) [51-500]

Estes, Kelli - *The Girl Who Wrote in Silk (Read by Zeller, Emily Woo). Audiobook Review*
    LJ - v140 - i20 - Dec 1 2015 - p58(1) [51-500]
  The Girl Who Wrote in Silk
    BL - v111 - i19-20 - June 1 2015 - p40(1) [51-500]

Estes, Steve - *Charleston in Black and White: Race and Power in the South after the Civil Rights Movement*
    LJ - v140 - i13 - August 1 2015 - p108(1) [51-500]

Esteve, Cesc - *Las razones del censor: Control ideologico y censura de libros en la primera Edad Moderna*
    Six Ct J - v46 - i1 - Spring 2015 - p245-247 [501+]

Estill, Lyle - *Backyard Biodiesel: How to Brew Your Own Fuel*
    RVBW - July 2015 - pNA [51-500]

Estlack, Russell W. - *The Aleut Internments of World War II: Islanders Removed from Their Homes by Japan and the United States*
    HNet - July 2015 - pNA [501+]

Estleman, Loren - *Detroit Is Our Beat: Tales of the Four Horsemen*
    PW - v262 - i9 - March 2 2015 - p66(1) [51-500]

Estleman, Loren D. - *The Adventure of the Plated Spoon and Other Tales of Sherlock Holmes*
    RVBW - August 2015 - pNA [51-500]
  Detroit Is Our Beat: Tales of the Four Horsemen
    BL - v111 - i17 - May 1 2015 - p30(1) [51-500]
    LJ - v140 - i8 - May 1 2015 - p68(1) [51-500]
  The Long High Noon
    BL - v111 - i16 - April 15 2015 - p36(2) [51-500]
    RVBW - June 2015 - pNA [51-500]
  Ragtime Cowboys
    Roundup M - v22 - i6 - August 2015 - p29(1) [501+]
  Shoot
    KR - Dec 15 2015 - pNA [51-500]
    PW - v262 - i50 - Dec 7 2015 - p71(1) [51-500]
  The Sundown Speech
    BL - v112 - i3 - Oct 1 2015 - p28(1) [51-500]
    KR - Sept 1 2015 - pNA [51-500]
    PW - v262 - i38 - Sept 21 2015 - p53(1) [51-500]
  The Wister Trace: Assaying Classic Western Fiction, 2d ed.
    Roundup M - v22 - i3 - Feb 2015 - p23(1) [501+]
  The Wister Trace: Assaying Classic Western Fiction
    Roundup M - v22 - i6 - August 2015 - p36(1) [501+]
  You Know Who Killed Me
    RVBW - August 2015 - pNA [51-500]

Estraikh, Gennady - *Uncovering the Hidden: The Works and Life of Der Nister*
    Slav R - v74 - i2 - Summer 2015 - p423-424 [501+]

Eszterhas, Suzi - *Koala Hospital*
    c PW - v262 - i35 - August 31 2015 - p90(2) [501+]
    c BL - v112 - i4 - Oct 15 2015 - p40(1) [51-500]
    c KR - August 1 2015 - pNA [51-500]
  Tiger
    c Sch Lib - v63 - i1 - Spring 2015 - p47(1) [51-500]

Etchison, Dennis - *It Only Comes Out at Night and Other Stories*
    NYT - Oct 30 2015 - pC35(L) [501+]

Etherton, Tameri - *The Stones of Kaldaar*
    KR - Jan 1 2016 - pNA [51-500]

Etingoff, Kim - *Women in Medicine*
    y Teach Lib - v42 - i3 - Feb 2015 - p10(1) [51-500]
    y Teach Lib - v42 - i4 - April 2015 - p10(1) [51-500]

Etkind, Alexander - *Internal Colonization: Russia's Imperial Experience*
    HER - v130 - i543 - April 2015 - p477(3) [501+]

Etulain, Richard W. - *The Life and Legends of Calamity Jane*
    Roundup M - v22 - i4 - April 2015 - p29(1) [501+]
    Roundup M - v22 - i6 - August 2015 - p36(1) [501+]
    WHQ - v46 - i4 - Winter 2015 - p531-532 [501+]
  Lincoln and Oregon Country Politics in the Civil War Era
    WHQ - v46 - i1 - Spring 2015 - p86-87 [501+]

Eugenia Cheng - *Cakes, Custard and Category Theory: Easy Recipes for Understanding Complex Maths*
    TimHES - i2206 - June 4 2015 - p46-47 [501+]

Eugster, David - *Das Imaginare des Kalten Krieges: Beitrage zu einer Kulturgeschichte des Ost-West-Konfliktes in Europa*
    HNet - July 2015 - pNA [501+]

Eulberg, Elizabeth - *We Can Work It Out*
    y HB Guide - v26 - i2 - Fall 2015 - p118(1) [501+]
    y VOYA - v37 - i6 - Feb 2015 - p56(1) [51-500]

Eungie Joo - *Yin Xiuzhen*
    RVBW - April 2015 - pNA [51-500]

Eunsun Kim - *A Thousand Miles to Freedom: My Escape from North Korea*
    KR - April 15 2015 - pNA [501+]

Europa, das Meer und die Welt. Akteure, Agenten, Abenteurer
    HNet - Jan 2015 - pNA [501+]
    HNet - Feb 2015 - pNA [501+]

Europa der Regionen - Nordrhein-Westfalen und seine Grenzraume
    HNet - June 2015 - pNA [501+]

A Europe of Courts, a Europe of Factions
    HNet - March 2015 - pNA [501+]

The European Retail Trade and the Clothing Industry in Historical Perspective
    HNet - July 2015 - pNA [501+]

Europeanization of Foreign Policies: International Socialization in Intergovernmental Policy Fields and the Example of the EPC/CSFP
    HNet - August 2015 - pNA [501+]

Eusden, J. Dykstra - *The Geology of New Hampshire's White Mountains*
RocksMiner - v90 - i2 - March-April 2015 - p189(1) [501+]

Evain, Aurore - *Theatre de femmes de l'Ancien Regime*
MLR - v110 - i3 - July 2015 - p863-864 [501+]

Evangelista, Matthew - *The American Way of Bombing: Changing Ethical and Legal Norms, From Flying Fortresses to Drones*
JAH - v102 - i2 - Sept 2015 - p597-597 [501+]

Evangeliste, Mary - *Letting Go of Legacy Services: Library Case Studies*
R&USQ - v54 - i4 - Summer 2015 - p72(2) [501+]

Evanier, David - *Woody*
BL - v112 - i5 - Nov 1 2015 - p26(1) [501+]
KR - Oct 1 2015 - pNA [501+]
Woody: The Biography
LJ - v140 - i19 - Nov 15 2015 - p86(1) [51-500]

Evanoff, Douglas D. - *The Role of Central Banks in Financial Stability: How Has It Changed?*
BHR - v89 - i1 - Spring 2015 - p178(2) [501+]

Evanovich, Janet - *The Job*
KR - Jan 1 2015 - pNA [51-500]
The Job (Read by Brick, Scott). Audiobook Review
PW - v262 - i5 - Feb 2 2015 - p53(1) [51-500]

Evans, Adrienne - *Technologies of Sexiness: Sex, Identity and Consumer Culture*
TimHES - i2184 - Jan 1 2015 - p66-67 [501+]

Evans, Ann Anderson - *Daring to Date Again*
KR - April 15 2015 - pNA [501+]

Evans, Anne M. - *Beating Autism: How Alternative Medicine Cured My Child*
SPBW - Oct 2015 - pNA [501+]

Evans, Arthur B. - *Vintage Visions: Essays on Early Science Fiction*
SFS - v42 - i1 - March 2015 - p170-172 [501+]

Evans, Arthur V. - *Beetles of Eastern North America*
QRB - v90 - i2 - June 2015 - p233(2) [501+]

Evans, Brad - *Resilient Life: The Art of Living Dangerously*
JRAI - v21 - i2 - June 2015 - p473(2) [501+]
Return to the Land of the Head Hunters: Edward S. Curtis, the Kwakwaka'wakw and the Making of Modern Cinema
Am Ind CRJ - v39 - i2 - Spring 2015 - p155-158 [501+]
Return to the Land of the Head Hunters: Edward S. Curtis, the Kwakwaka'wakw, and the Making of the Modern Cinema
Beav - v95 - i2 - April-May 2015 - p53(2) [501+]

Evans, Charles - *Boats and Harbours in Acrylic*
LJ - v140 - i9 - May 15 2015 - p82(1) [51-500]

Evans, Claude - *L'abbaye cistercienne de Begard des origines a 1476: Histoire et chartes*
Specu - v90 - i1 - Jan 2015 - p244-246 [501+]

Evans, Craig A. - *God Speaks: What He Says, What He Means*
RVBW - Nov 2015 - pNA [51-500]

Evans, Dylan - *The Utopia Experiment*
Spec - v327 - i9729 - Feb 14 2015 - p40(1) [501+]

Evans, Elizabeth - *As Good as Dead*
BL - v111 - i11 - Feb 1 2015 - p20(1) [51-500]
KR - Jan 1 2015 - pNA [501+]
LJ - v140 - i3 - Feb 15 2015 - p85(1) [51-500]

Evans, G. Edward - *Library Programs and Services: The Fundamentals. 8th ed.*
LJ - v140 - i20 - Dec 1 2015 - p116(1) [51-500]
Teach Lib - v43 - i1 - Oct 2015 - p41(3) [501+]

Evans, Gareth - *The Edge is Where the Centre Is: David Rudkin and Penda's Fen - A Conversation*
Si & So - v25 - i9 - Sept 2015 - p106(1) [501+]

Evans, Harriet - *A Place for Us*
KR - April 15 2015 - pNA [501+]
LJ - v140 - i8 - May 1 2015 - p61(1) [51-500]

Evans, James Allan - *Daily Life in the Hellenistic Age: From Alexander to Cleopatra*
HNet - Jan 2015 - pNA [501+]

Evans, Jane DeRose - *A Companion to the Archaeology of the Roman Republic*
Class R - v65 - i2 - Oct 2015 - p576-578 [501+]

Evans, Jennifer - *Aphrodisiacs, Fertility and Medicine in Early Modern England*
HT - v65 - i5 - May 2015 - p59(2) [501+]
Six Ct J - v46 - i3 - Fall 2015 - p778-780 [501+]
TimHES - i2205 - May 28 2015 - p47(1) [501+]

Evans, Jeremy - *The Battle for Paradise*
KR - August 1 2015 - pNA [501+]

Evans, Julian - *Transit of Venus: Travels in the Pacific*
BL - v111 - i18 - May 15 2015 - p12(1) [51-500]

Evans, Lissa - *Crooked Heart*
CSM - Sept 2 2015 - pNA [501+]
KR - May 15 2015 - pNA [51-500]
LJ - v140 - i9 - May 15 2015 - p70(1) [51-500]
Nat Post - v17 - i225 - August 1 2015 - pWP5(1) [501+]
NYTBR - August 9 2015 - p23(L) [501+]
PW - v262 - i19 - May 11 2015 - p28(1) [51-500]
Wom R Bks - v32 - i6 - Nov-Dec 2015 - p19(2) [501+]

Evans, Marilyn Grohoske - *Spit and Sticks: A Chimney Full of Swifts (Illus. by Gsell, Nicole)*
c BL - v112 - i1 - Sept 1 2015 - p95(1) [51-500]
CH Bwatch - Nov 2015 - pNA [51-500]
c KR - July 1 2015 - pNA [51-500]
c PW - v262 - i35 - August 31 2015 - p90(2) [501+]

Evans, Martin - *France since 1815*
FS - v69 - i2 - April 2015 - p269-270 [501+]

Evans, Mary Anna - *Isolation*
BL - v111 - i17 - May 1 2015 - p39(1) [501+]
KR - June 15 2015 - pNA [51-500]
PW - v262 - i23 - June 8 2015 - p40(1) [51-500]

Evans, Max - *Goin' Crazy with Sam Peckinpah and All Our Friends*
Roundup M - v22 - i3 - Feb 2015 - p23(1) [501+]
Roundup M - v22 - i6 - August 2015 - p36(2) [501+]

Evans, Mel - *Artwash: Big Oil and the Arts*
TLS - i5848 - May 1 2015 - p26(1) [501+]

Evans, Michael R. - *Inventing Eleanor: The Medieval and Post-Medieval Image of Eleanor of Aquitaine*
HT - v65 - i3 - March 2015 - p57(1) [501+]

Evans, Michelle - *X-15 Rocket Plane: Plying the First Wings into Space*
Historian - v77 - i2 - Summer 2015 - p329(2) [501+]

Evans, Paul M. - *Engaging China: Myth, Aspiration, and Strategy in Canadian Policy from Trudeau to Harper*
Pac A - v88 - i3 - Sept 2015 - p692 [501+]

Evans, Rachel Held - *Searching for Sunday: Loving, Leaving and Finding the Church*
LJ - v140 - i9 - May 15 2015 - p64(2) [51-500]

Evans, Richard J. - *The Third Reich in History and Memoryq*
TimHES - i2195 - March 19 2015 - p54(1) [501+]

Evans, Richard Paul - *Michael Vey: Hunt for Jade Dragon*
y HB Guide - v26 - i1 - Spring 2015 - p106(1) [51-500]

Evans, Sterling D. - *Working Women into the Borderlands*
WHQ - v46 - i2 - Summer 2015 - p236-237 [501+]

Evans, Walker - *Let Us Now Praise Famous Men*
TimHES - i2211 - July 9 2015 - p45(1) [501+]

Eve, Helen - *Boarding School Girls*
y HB Guide - v26 - i2 - Fall 2015 - p118(1) [501+]
y VOYA - v38 - i1 - April 2015 - p58(1) [51-500]

Eve, Martin Paul - *Open Access and the Humanities: Contexts, Controversies and the Future*
TimHES - i2192 - Feb 26 2015 - p47(1) [501+]

Evenden, Matthew - *Allied Power: Mobilizing Hydro-electricity during Canada's Second World War*
HNet - Sept 2015 - pNA [501+]

Evening, Martin - *The Adobe Photoshop Lightroom CC / Lightroom 6 Book: The Complete Guide for Photographers*
RVBW - June 2015 - pNA [501+]

Evenson, Brian - *A Collapse of Horses: Stories*
KR - Nov 1 2015 - pNA [501+]
PW - v262 - i42 - Oct 19 2015 - p48(1) [51-500]

Everard, Mark - *Breathing Space: The Natural and Unnatural History of Air*
Nature - v521 - i7553 - May 28 2015 - p421(1) [501+]

Everest, D.D. - *Archie Greene and the Magician's Secret*
BL - v111 - i14 - March 15 2015 - p72(1) [501+]
c HB Guide - v26 - i2 - Fall 2015 - p81(1) [501+]
c PW - v262 - i9 - March 2 2015 - p83(1) [51-500]
SLJ - v61 - i4 - April 2015 - p146(1) [51-500]

Everett, Alyssa - *The Marriage Act*
PW - v262 - i18 - May 4 2015 - p102(1) [51-500]

Everett, Derek R. - *Creating the American West: Boundaries and Borderlands*
AHR - v120 - i3 - June 2015 - p1038(1) [501+]
PHR - v84 - i4 - Nov 2015 - p534(2) [501+]
Roundup M - v22 - i3 - Feb 2015 - p23(1) [501+]
Roundup M - v22 - i6 - August 2015 - p37(1) [501+]
SHQ - v118 - i4 - April 2015 - p425-426 [501+]

Everett, Hugh, III - *The Everett Interpretation of Quantum Mechanics: Collected Works, 1955-1980, with Commentary*
Isis - v106 - i1 - March 2015 - p220(2) [501+]

Everett, Lily - *Three Promises*
PW - v262 - i51 - Dec 14 2015 - p69(1) [51-500]

Everett, Melissa - *If You're Happy and You Know It (Illus. by Krummer, Mark)*
c CH Bwatch - May 2015 - pNA [51-500]

Everett, Mikaela - *The Unquiet*
y KR - June 15 2015 - pNA [51-500]
The Unquiet
y PW - v262 - i24 - June 15 2015 - p86(1) [51-500]
y SLJ - v61 - i7 - July 2015 - p92(1) [51-500]

Everett, Nigel - *The Woods of Ireland: A History, 700-1800*
ILS - v35 - i1 - Fall 2015 - p9(1) [501+]
Specu - v90 - i3 - July 2015 - p804-805 [501+]

Everett, Percival - *Half an Inch of Water: Stories*
KR - July 15 2015 - pNA [501+]
PW - v262 - i29 - July 20 2015 - p162(1) [51-500]
BL - v111 - i22 - August 1 2015 - p28(1) [51-500]
HM - v331 - i1986 - Nov 2015 - p82(7) [501+]
NYTBR - Oct 4 2015 - p30(L) [501+]

Everhart, Cherie H. - *The Complete Guide to Growing Tomatoes: Everything You Need to Know Explained Simply: Including Heirloom Tomatoes*
Bwatch - Sept 2015 - pNA [51-500]

Evers, Stuart - *Your Father Sends His Love*
y BL - v112 - i6 - Nov 15 2015 - p24(1) [51-500]
KR - Nov 1 2015 - pNA [51-500]
Spec - v328 - i9744 - May 30 2015 - p34(2) [501+]

Eversberg, Gerd - *"Der Schimmelreiter": Novelle von Theodor Storm. Historisch-kritische Edition*
MLR - v110 - i2 - April 2015 - p592-593 [501+]

Everson, Eva Marie - *Five Brides*
PW - v262 - i17 - April 27 2015 - p59(1) [51-500]

Everson, Katie - *Drop*
y Sch Lib - v63 - i2 - Summer 2015 - p116(1) [51-500]
y Sch Lib - v63 - i4 - Winter 2015 - p253(1) [51-500]

Everson, Seven - *Ashes of Eden*
KR - June 15 2015 - pNA [51-500]

Evert, Lori - *The Reindeer Wish (Illus. by Breiehagen, Per)*
c CH Bwatch - Nov 2015 - pNA [51-500]
c PW - v262 - i37 - Sept 14 2015 - p66(2) [501+]
c SLJ - v61 - i10 - Oct 2015 - p63(1) [51-500]
The Reindeer Wish
c KR - Sept 1 2015 - pNA [51-500]
The Tiny Wish (Illus. by Breiehagen, Per)
c HB Guide - v26 - i2 - Fall 2015 - p33(1) [51-500]

Everyday Heroism in the United States, Britain, and Germany from the 19th to the 21st Century
HNet - May 2015 - pNA [501+]

Evison, Jonathan - *This Is Your Life, Harriet Chance!*
BL - v111 - i21 - July 1 2015 - p33(2) [51-500]
KR - July 1 2015 - pNA [51-500]
NYTBR - Sept 27 2015 - p20(L) [501+]
PW - v262 - i30 - July 27 2015 - p39(2) [51-500]

Evrard, Amy Young - *The Moroccan Women's Rights Movement*
IJMES - v47 - i4 - Nov 2015 - p856-858 [501+]

Ewald, Johannes - *Johann Adolph Scheibe: Passions-Cantata "Vor Harpe er bleven til Sorrig"*
Notes - v71 - i3 - March 2015 - p569(5) [501+]

Ewald, Wiliam - *Hilbert's Lectures on the Foundations of Arithmetic and Logic, 1917-1933*
Isis - v106 - i2 - June 2015 - p481(3) [501+]

Ewan, Chris - *Dark Tides*
KR - Oct 1 2015 - pNA [51-500]
PW - v262 - i41 - Oct 12 2015 - p48(1) [51-500]

Ewazen, Eric - *Trio for Horn, Violin, and Piano*
Am MT - v64 - i4 - Feb-March 2015 - p59(2) [501+]

Ewens, Tracy - *Candidate*
KR - August 1 2015 - pNA [51-500]

Ewert, Marcus - *Mummy Cat (Illus. by Brown, Lisa)*
c BL - v111 - i17 - May 1 2015 - p101(1) [51-500]
c CH Bwatch - Sept 2015 - pNA [51-500]
c HB - v91 - i4 - July-August 2015 - p112(2) [51-500]
c KR - August 1 2015 - pNA [51-500]
c NYTBR - Oct 11 2015 - p17(L) [501+]
c PW - v262 - i18 - May 4 2015 - p118(2) [51-500]
c SLJ - v61 - i5 - May 2015 - p84(1) [51-500]

Ewing, Al - *The Eleventh Doctor: After Life (Illus. by Fraser, Simon)*
y SLJ - v61 - i9 - Sept 2015 - p174(1) [51-500]

Ewing, Amy - *The Jewel*
 y HB Guide - v26 - i1 - Spring 2015 - p106(1) [51-500]
 y VOYA - v38 - i5 - Dec 2015 - p68(1) [51-500]
The White Rose
 y KR - July 1 2015 - pNA [51-500]
 y SLJ - v61 - i7 - July 2015 - p92(1) [51-500]
The White Rose: Jewel, Book 2
 y VOYA - v38 - i4 - Oct 2015 - p68(1) [51-500]
Ewing, Lynne - *The Lure*
 y VOYA - v38 - i3 - August 2015 - p58(1) [51-500]
Ewing, Tabetha Leigh - *Rumor, Diplomacy and War in Enlightment Paris*
 FS - v69 - i2 - April 2015 - p250-251 [501+]
Exley, William - *Golemchik (Illus. by Exley, William)*
 c SLJ - v61 - i6 - June 2015 - p107(1) [51-500]
 c KR - May 1 2015 - pNA [51-500]
Eyal, Nir - *Hooked: How to Build Habit-Forming Products*
 Econ - v414 - i8919 - Jan 3 2015 - p53(US) [501+]
Eye, Lelia - *Thorny*
 y PW - v262 - i5 - Feb 2 2015 - p62(1) [51-500]

Eyerman, Ann - *Mediterranean Journey*
 KR - Jan 15 2015 - pNA [501+]
Eyerman, Ron - *Is This America? Katrina as Cultural Trauma*
 NYTBR - August 9 2015 - p34(L) [501+]
Eyers, Jonathan - *The Thieves of Pudding Lane*
 y Sch Lib - v63 - i1 - Spring 2015 - p36(1) [51-500]
Eyma, Xavier - *Les Peaux noires: scenes de la vie des esclaves*
 MLR - v110 - i3 - July 2015 - p867-868 [501+]
Eyman, Scott - *John Wayne*
 NYTBR - May 31 2015 - p52(L) [501+]
John Wayne: The Life and Legend
 Roundup M - v22 - i6 - August 2015 - p37(1) [501+]
Eyre, Banning - *Lion Songs*
 KR - March 1 2015 - pNA [501+]
Eyre, Hermione - *Viper Wine*
 KR - Feb 1 2015 - pNA [501+]
 LJ - v140 - i3 - Feb 15 2015 - p85(2) [51-500]
 NYTBR - June 28 2015 - p38(L) [501+]
 PW - v262 - i7 - Feb 16 2015 - p151(2) [51-500]
 WLT - v89 - i5 - Sept-Oct 2015 - p63(1) [51-500]

Eyre, Lindsay - *The Best Friend Battle (Illus. by Santoso, Charles)*
 c BL - v111 - i12 - Feb 15 2015 - p85(1) [51-500]
 c PW - v262 - i3 - Jan 19 2015 - p81(1) [51-500]
 c CH Bwatch - August 2015 - pNA [51-500]
 c HB Guide - v26 - i2 - Fall 2015 - p65(1) [51-500]
The Mean Girl Meltdown (Illus. by Hanson, Sydney)
 c BL - v111 - i21 - July 1 2015 - p74(1) [51-500]
The Mean Girl Meltdown
 c KR - June 15 2015 - pNA [51-500]
Eyre, Richard - *What Do I Know? People, Politics and the Arts*
 Am Theat - v32 - i7 - Sept 2015 - p54(2) [501+]
Eyton, Christopher - *The Balloon Is Doomed (Illus. by Mundt, A.M.)*
 c KR - Jan 1 2015 - pNA [51-500]
Ezzell, Tim - *Chattanooga, 1865-1900: A City Set Down in Dixie*
 JSH - v81 - i2 - May 2015 - p480(2) [501+]

F

Faas, Daniel - *Negotiating Political Identities: Multiethnic Schools and Youth in Europe*
 CS - v44 - i1 - Jan 2015 - p55-57 [501+]

Faber, Eberhard L. - *Building the Land of Dreams: New Orleans and the Transformation of Early America*
 LJ - v140 - i16 - Oct 1 2015 - p93(1) [51-500]
 PW - v262 - i39 - Sept 28 2015 - p78(1) [51-500]

Faber, Eike - *Von Ulfila bis Rekkared: Die Goten und Ihr Christentum*
 HNet - June 2015 - pNA [501+]

Faber, Michel - *The Book of Strange New Things* (Read by Cohen, Josh). Audiobook Review
 LJ - v140 - i6 - April 1 2015 - p48(1) [51-500]
The Book of Strange New Things
 AM - v213 - i1 - July 6 2015 - p43(2) [501+]
 y HR - v68 - i1 - Spring 2015 - p151-157 [501+]
 WLT - v89 - i2 - March-April 2015 - p58(2) [501+]
The Crimson Petal and the White
 HT - v65 - i11 - Nov 2015 - p56(2) [501+]

Faber, Polly - *Mango and Bambang, the Not-a-Pig*
 c Sch Lib - v63 - i4 - Winter 2015 - p228(1) [51-500]

Faber, Richard - *Totale Erziehung in Europaischer und Amerikanischer Literatur*
 HNet - June 2015 - pNA [501+]

Fabinyi, Michael - *Fishing for Fairness: Poverty, Morality and Marine Resource Regulation in the Philippines*
 JRAI - v21 - i1 - March 2015 - p218(2) [501+]

Fabre, Cedric - *Marseille Noir*
 KR - Oct 15 2015 - pNA [51-500]

Fabre, Dominique - *Guys Like Me*
 NYTBR - March 8 2015 - p34(L) [501+]

Fabricant, Michael - *The Changing Politics of Education: Privatization and the Dispossessed Lives Left Behind*
 CS - v44 - i2 - March 2015 - p193-195 [501+]
 Soc Ser R - v89 - i1 - March 2015 - p218(5) [501+]

Fabry, Chris - *War Room*
 PW - v262 - i23 - June 8 2015 - p46(1) [51-500]

Fabry-Tehranchi, Irene - *L'Humain et l'animal dans la France Medievale*
 FS - v69 - i3 - July 2015 - p376-2 [501+]

Facas, Charles - *The Cooks*
 PW - v262 - i25 - June 22 2015 - p119(1) [51-500]

Faccone, Gregory - *Tethered Worlds: Unwelcome Star*
 RVBW - May 2015 - pNA [51-500]

Facio, Elisa - *Fleshing the Spirit: Spirituality and Activism in Chicana, Latina, and Indigenous Women's Lives*
 NWSA Jnl - v27 - i2 - Summer 2015 - p196-199 [501+]
 Theol St - v76 - i4 - Dec 2015 - p900(2) [501+]
 Aztlan - v40 - i1 - Spring 2015 - p231-235 [501+]

Faciolince, Hector Abad - *La Oculta*
 Econ - v415 - i8936 - May 2 2015 - p31(US) [501+]

Fadal, Tamsen - *The New Single: Finding, Fixing and Falling Back in Love with Yourself*
 PW - v262 - i16 - April 20 2015 - p71(2) [51-500]

Fadda-Conrey, Carol - *Contemporary Arab-American Literature: Transnational Reconfigurations of Citizenship and Belonging*
 IJMES - v47 - i2 - May 2015 - p390-392 [501+]

Fader Jamie J. - *Falling Back: Incarceration and Transitions to Adulthood among Urban Youth*
 CS - v44 - i1 - Jan 2015 - p57-59 [501+]

Faderman, Lillian - *The Gay Revolution: The Story of the Struggle*
 BL - v111 - i22 - August 1 2015 - p22(1) [51-500]
 KR - July 15 2015 - pNA [501+]
 LJ - v140 - i12 - July 1 2015 - p94(1) [51-500]
 NYTBR - Oct 4 2015 - p15(L) [501+]
 PW - v262 - i27 - July 6 2015 - p57(1) [51-500]

Fagan, Brian - *The Great Archaeologists*
 NH - v123 - i1 - Feb 2015 - p46(2) [501+]
The Intimate Bond: How Animals Shaped Human History
 KR - Feb 1 2015 - pNA [501+]
 LJ - v140 - i3 - Feb 15 2015 - p112(1) [51-500]
 PW - v262 - i7 - Feb 16 2015 - p171(1) [51-500]

Fagan, Cary - *I Wish I Could Draw*
 c HB Guide - v26 - i1 - Spring 2015 - p29(1) [51-500]

Fagans, Michael - *The iPhone Photographer: How to Take Professional Photographs with Your iPhone*
 Bwatch - June 2015 - pNA [51-500]

Faggioli, Massimo - *A Council for the Global Church: Receiving Vatican II in History*
 AM - v213 - i12 - Oct 26 2015 - p32(3) [501+]
John XXIII: The Medicine of Mercy
 Theol St - v76 - i2 - June 2015 - p386(2) [501+]
Pope Francis: Tradition in Transition
 RVBW - Oct 2015 - pNA [51-500]
Sorting Out Catholicism: A Brief History of the New Ecclesial Movements
 Theol St - v76 - i4 - Dec 2015 - p898(2) [501+]

Fagin, Betsy - *All Is Not Yet Lost*
 PW - v262 - i24 - June 15 2015 - p61(1) [501+]

Fagin, Dan - *Tom's River: A Story of Science and Salvation*
 NYTBR - May 10 2015 - p36(L) [501+]

Fahey, Joseph E. - *James K. McGuire: Boy Mayor and Irish Nationalist*
 ILS - v34 - i2 - Spring 2015 - p3(1) [501+]

Fahy, Thomas - *Understanding Truman Capote*
 G&L Rev W - v22 - i1 - Jan-Feb 2015 - p36(2) [501+]

FAILE: Works on Wood: Process, Paintings and Sculpture
 RVBW - Feb 2015 - pNA [51-500]

Fairbanks, Daniel J. - *Everyone Is African: How Science Explodes the Myth of Race*
 BL - v111 - i13 - March 1 2015 - p10(1) [51-500]

Fairbanks, Robert B. - *Making Sense of the City: Local Government, Civic Culture, and Community Life in Urban America*
 J Urban H - v41 - i1 - Jan 2015 - p143-9 [501+]
The War on Slums in the Southwest: Public Housing and Slum Clearance in Texas, Arizona, and New Mexico, 1935-1965
 AHR - v120 - i3 - June 2015 - p1054(1) [501+]
 JAH - v102 - i2 - Sept 2015 - p600-601 [501+]
 JSH - v81 - i4 - Nov 2015 - p1029(2) [501+]
 SHQ - v118 - i4 - April 2015 - p438-439 [501+]

Fairbanks, Robert P., II - *How It Works: Recovering Citizens in Post-Welfare Philadelphia*
 J Urban H - v41 - i1 - Jan 2015 - p143-9 [501+]

Fairey, Wendy - *Bookmarked: Reading My Way from Hollywood to Brooklyn*
 LJ - v140 - i3 - Feb 15 2015 - p99(2) [51-500]

Fairfield, John D. - *The Public and Its Possibilities: Triumphs and Tragedies in the American City*
 J Urban H - v41 - i1 - Jan 2015 - p143-9 [501+]

Fairgray, Richard - *Gorillas in Our Midst* (Illus. by Fairgray, Richard)
 c SLJ - v61 - i10 - Oct 2015 - p75(2) [51-500]

Fairhead, James - *The Captain and "The Cannibal": An Epic Story of Exploration, Kidnapping, and the Broadway Stage*
 NH - v123 - i1 - Feb 2015 - p46(2) [501+]

Fairstein, Linda - *Devil's Bridge*
 BL - v111 - i19-20 - June 1 2015 - p52(1) [51-500]
 PW - v262 - i23 - June 8 2015 - p36(1) [51-500]

Terminal City
 RVBW - Jan 2015 - pNA [51-500]
 RVBW - Sept 2015 - pNA [51-500]

Fairweather, Jack - *The Good War: Why We Couldn't Win the War or the Peace in Afghanistan*
 J Mil H - v79 - i2 - April 2015 - p557-558 [501+]
 NS - v144 - i5265 - June 5 2015 - p42(3) [501+]

Faith, Nicholas - *The World the Railways Made*
 TLS - i5845 - April 10 2015 - p32(1) [501+]

Faith, Thomas I. - *Behind the Gas Mask: The U.S. Chemical Warfare Service in War and Peace*
 HNet - August 2015 - pNA [501+]
 J Mil H - v79 - i2 - April 2015 - p518-519 [501+]

Faithful, George - *Mothering the Fatherland: A Protestant Sisterhood Repents for the Holocaust*
 AHR - v120 - i1 - Feb 2015 - p350-351 [501+]
 CH - v84 - i3 - Sept 2015 - p686(1) [501+]

Faktorovich, Anna - *Gender Bias in Mystery and Romance Novel Publishing: Mimicking Masculinity and Femininity*
 SPBW - June 2015 - pNA [501+]

Falatko, Julie - *Snappsy the Alligator (Did Not Ask to Be in This Book).* (Illus. by Miller, Tim)
 c KR - Dec 1 2015 - pNA [51-500]

Falcon, Andrea - *Aristotelianism in the First Century B.C.E.: Xenarchus of Seleucia*
 Isis - v106 - i1 - March 2015 - p169(2) [501+]

Falcon, Jeremy - *The Book of Wisdom*
 c KR - Oct 1 2015 - pNA [51-500]

Falcone, L.M. - *The Dirty Trick* (Illus. by Smith, Kim)
 c Res Links - v21 - i1 - Oct 2015 - p13(2) [51-500]
The Magic Box (Illus. by Smith, Kim)
 c HB Guide - v26 - i1 - Spring 2015 - p59(1) [51-500]
The Missing Zucchini
 c KR - Feb 1 2015 - pNA [51-500]
The Missing Zucchini (Illus. by Smith, Kim)
 c SLJ - v61 - i2 - Feb 2015 - p58(1) [51-500]
 c HB Guide - v26 - i2 - Fall 2015 - p65(1) [51-500]
 c Res Links - v20 - i5 - June 2015 - p10(1) [51-500]

Falconer, Morgan - *Painting Beyond Pollock*
 LJ - v140 - i7 - April 15 2015 - p92(1) [51-500]

Faletra, Michael A. - *Wales and the Medieval Colonial Imagination: The Matters of Britain in the Twelfth Century*
 Med R - Jan 2015 - pNA [501+]

Falk, Marcia - *The Days Between*
 Tikkun - v30 - i1 - Wntr 2015 - pNA [51-500]

Falken, Linda - *Noah's Ark: Adapted from Genesis, Chapters 6-9*
 c HB Guide - v26 - i2 - Fall 2015 - p149(1) [51-500]
Noah's Ark
 c CH Bwatch - June 2015 - pNA [51-500]
 c KR - Jan 15 2015 - pNA [51-500]
 c PW - v262 - i8 - Feb 23 2015 - p79(1) [51-500]
 c SLJ - v61 - i8 - August 2015 - p123(2) [51-500]
Puzzling Cats
 c PW - v262 - i5 - Feb 2 2015 - p60(1) [501+]
Puzzling Dogs
 c KR - Dec 1 2015 - pNA [51-500]

Falkin, Mark - *Contract City*
 y CH Bwatch - July 2015 - pNA [501+]
 y HB Guide - v26 - i2 - Fall 2015 - p118(1) [501+]
 y VOYA - v38 - i3 - August 2015 - p76(1) [51-500]

Falkner, Brian - *Battlesaurus: Rampage at Waterloo*
 y KR - April 1 2015 - pNA [501+]
 y BL - v111 - i19-20 - June 1 2015 - p95(1) [51-500]
 y VOYA - v38 - i2 - June 2015 - p73(2) [501+]
Ice War
 y HB Guide - v26 - i2 - Fall 2015 - p118(1) [501+]
Maddy West and the Tongue Taker (Illus. by Bixley, Donovan)
 c HB Guide - v26 - i1 - Spring 2015 - p76(1) [51-500]

Falkoff, Michelle - *Playlist for the Dead*
  y CCB-B - v68 - i7 - March 2015 - p353(1) [51-500]
  y Sch Lib - v63 - i3 - Autumn 2015 - p182(1) [51-500]

Falkowski, Paul G. - *Life's Engines: How Microbes Made Earth Habitable*
  LJ - v140 - i7 - April 15 2015 - p109(1) [51-500]
  Mac - v128 - i21 - June 1 2015 - p57(1) [501+]
  NYRB - v62 - i12 - July 9 2015 - p30(1) [501+]

Fallada, Hans - *A Small Circus*
  BL - v111 - i9-10 - Jan 1 2015 - p54(1) [51-500]
  KR - Jan 1 2015 - pNA [51-500]

A Stranger in My Own Country: The 1944 Prison Diary
  Econ - v414 - i8919 - Jan 3 2015 - p70(US) [501+]

Fallaw, Ben - *Religion and State Formation in Postrevolutionary Mexico*
  Historian - v77 - i1 - Spring 2015 - p119(2) [501+]

Falletti, Sebastien - *A Thousand Miles to Freedom: My Escape from North Korea*
  NYTBR - Nov 29 2015 - p26(L) [501+]

Fallon, Jimmy - *Your Baby's First Word Will be Dada (Illus. by Ordonez, Miguel)*
  c KR - May 1 2015 - pNA [51-500]
  c PW - v262 - i17 - April 27 2015 - p73(1) [51-500]

Fallon, Michael - *Creating the Future: Art and Los Angeles in the 1970s*
  BL - v112 - i5 - Nov 1 2015 - p18(2) [51-500]

Fallon, Peter - *Strong, My Love*
  ILS - v35 - i1 - Fall 2015 - p22(2) [501+]

Fallows, David - *Facsimile of the Henry VIII Book*
  Notes - v72 - i2 - Dec 2015 - p407(4) [501+]

The Henry VIII Book
  Ren Q - v68 - i3 - Fall 2015 - p1089-1090 [501+]

Fallwell, Lynne - *Modern German Midwifery, 1885-1960*
  Isis - v106 - i2 - June 2015 - p472(3) [501+]

Falola, Toyin - *Eshu: Yoruba God, Powers, and the Imaginative Frontiers*
  IJAHS - v48 - i1 - Wntr 2015 - p165-166 [501+]

Nigeria
  BL - v111 - i19-20 - June 1 2015 - p22(1) [51-500]

Faltum, Andrew - *The Supercarriers: The Forrestal and Kitty Hawk Classes*
  APH - v62 - i2 - Summer 2015 - p55(2) [501+]

Falwell, Cathryn - *The Nesting Quilt (Illus. by Falwell, Cathryn)*
  c CH Bwatch - Oct 2015 - pNA [501+]
  c KR - March 15 2015 - pNA [51-500]
  c SLJ - v61 - i10 - Oct 2015 - p76(1) [51-500]

Familiensache Kirche? Die Fugger und die Konfessionalisierung
  HNet - July 2015 - pNA [501+]

Famines during the 'Little Ice Age,' 1300-1800: Socio-Natural Entanglements in Premodern Societies
  HNet - April 2015 - pNA [501+]

Fan, Mary - *Artificial Absolutes*
  PW - v262 - i17 - April 27 2015 - p57(1) [51-500]

Fan, Terry - *The Night Gardener (Illus. by Fan, Eric)*
  c KR - Dec 15 2015 - pNA [51-500]
  c PW - v262 - i46 - Nov 16 2015 - p74(1) [51-500]

Fancy, Emillie - *Science and Religion in Mamluk Egypt: Ibn al-Nafis, Pulmonary Transit and Bodily Resurrection*
  JNES - v74 - i2 - Oct 2015 - p390(3) [501+]

Fandel, Jennifer - *William Shakespeare (Illus. by Imsand, Marcel)*
  c HB Guide - v26 - i1 - Spring 2015 - p191(1) [51-500]

Fang, Lizhi - *The Most Wanted Man in China: My Journey from Scientist to Enemy of the State*
  KR - Nov 15 2015 - pNA [501+]

Fang, Suzhen - *Grandma Lives in a Perfume Village (Illus. by Danowski, Sonja)*
  c CH Bwatch - August 2015 - pNA [51-500]
  c HB Guide - v26 - i2 - Fall 2015 - p53(1) [51-500]
  c NYTBR - Sept 13 2015 - p21(L) [501+]

Fang, Xiaoping - *Barefoot Doctors and Western Medicine in China*
  T&C - v56 - i3 - July 2015 - p780-782 [501+]

Fanning, Bryan - *The Books That Define Ireland*
  ILS - v35 - i1 - Fall 2015 - p13(2) [501+]

Fanning, Jim - *The Disney Book: A Celebration of the World of Disney*
  c SLJ - v61 - i12 - Dec 2015 - p143(1) [51-500]

Fanning, Kieran - *The Black Lotus*
  y Sch Lib - v63 - i4 - Winter 2015 - p244(1) [51-500]

Fanning, Ronan - *Eamon de Valera: A Will to Power*
  Spec - v329 - i9768 - Nov 14 2015 - p59(2) [501+]

Fanning, Rory - *Worth Fighting For*
  RVBW - Jan 2015 - pNA [51-500]

Fantaskey, Beth - *Buzz Kill (Read by Moon, Erin). Audiobook Review*
  BL - v111 - i13 - March 1 2015 - p70(1) [51-500]

Isabel Feeney: Star Reporter
  c KR - Jan 1 2016 - pNA [51-500]
  c PW - v262 - i52 - Dec 21 2015 - p154(1) [51-500]
  c SLJ - v61 - i10 - Oct 2015 - p88(2) [51-500]

Fantham, Elaine - *Cicero's Pro L. Murena Oratio*
  Class R - v65 - i1 - April 2015 - p118-120 [501+]

Fara, Giovanni Maria - *Albrecht Durer nelle fonti Italiane antiche, 1508-1686*
  Ren Q - v68 - i1 - Spring 2015 - p246-247 [501+]

Faraday, Jess - *Death and a Cup of Tea*
  SPBW - May 2015 - pNA [51-500]

Faragher, John Mack - *Eternity Street: Violence and Justice in Frontier Los Angeles*
  KR - Sept 15 2015 - pNA [501+]
  PW - v262 - i45 - Nov 9 2015 - p50(1) [51-500]

Farah, Alain - *Pourquoi Bologne*
  Can Lit - i224 - Spring 2015 - p122 [501+]

Ravenscrag
  Mac - v128 - i5-6 - Feb 9 2015 - p75(1) [51-500]

Farah, Nuruddin - *Hiding in Plain Sight (Read by Miles, Robin). Audiobook Review*
  LJ - v140 - i2 - Feb 1 2015 - p44(1) [51-500]

Hiding in Plain Sight
  NYTBR - Oct 11 2015 - p28(L) [501+]

Farber, David - *Thai Stick: Surfers, Scammers, and the Untold Story of the Marijuana Trade*
  PHR - v84 - i3 - August 2015 - p400(401) [501+]

Farber, Walter - *Lamastu: An Edition of the Canonical Series of Lamastu Incantations and Rituals and Related Texts from the Second and First Millennia B.C*
  JNES - v74 - i2 - Oct 2015 - p354(2) [501+]

Fares, Roy - *United States of Cakes: Tasty Traditional American Cakes, Cookies, Pies, and Baked Goods*
  Bwatch - June 2015 - pNA [51-500]

Farfan, Penny - *Contemporary Women Playwrights: Into the Twenty-First Century*
  Theat J - v67 - i2 - May 2015 - p367-369 [501+]

Farge, Arlette - *The Allure of the Archives*
  Archiv - i79 - Spring 2015 - p183(5) [501+]
  Signs - v40 - i2 - Wntr 2015 - p515(7) [501+]

Fargo, Ford - *Night of the Assassins. E-book Review*
  Roundup M - v22 - i4 - April 2015 - p32(2) [501+]

Wolf Creek
  Roundup M - v22 - i6 - August 2015 - p29(1) [501+]

Farhadian, Charles E. - *Introducing World Religions: A Christian Engagement*
  LJ - v140 - i2 - Feb 1 2015 - p106(1) [51-500]

Farina, Laura - *Some Talk of Being Human*
  Nat Post - v17 - i68 - Jan 17 2015 - pWP10(1) [501+]

Faris, Stephanie - *25 Roses*
  c HB Guide - v26 - i2 - Fall 2015 - p81(1) [51-500]

Farish, Terry - *Either the Beginning or the End of the World*
  y BL - v112 - i2 - Sept 15 2015 - p71(1) [51-500]
  y HB - v91 - i6 - Nov-Dec 2015 - p80(1) [51-500]
  y KR - Sept 1 2015 - pNA [51-500]
  y SLJ - v61 - i9 - Sept 2015 - p164(1) [51-500]
  y VOYA - v38 - i5 - Dec 2015 - p55(2) [501+]

Farizan, Sara - *If You Could Be Mine*
  c SLJ - v61 - i12 - Dec 2015 - p64(4) [501+]

Tell Me Again How a Crush Should Feel (Read by Farsad, Negin). Audiobook Review
  y BL - v111 - i11 - Feb 1 2015 - p62(1) [51-500]

Tell Me Again How a Crush Should Feel
  y HB Guide - v26 - i1 - Spring 2015 - p106(1) [51-500]

Farjeon, J. Jefferson - *Thirteen Guests*
  PW - v262 - i30 - July 27 2015 - p45(1) [51-500]

Farkas, Beata - *The Aftermath of the Global Crisis in the European Union*
  E-A St - v67 - i1 - Jan 2015 - p160(3) [501+]

Farley, Margaret A. - *Changing the Questions: Explorations in Christian Ethics*
  AM - v216 - i6 - Sept 14 2015 - p41(2) [501+]

Farley, Terri - *Wild at Heart: Mustangs and the Young People Fighting to Save Them (Illus. by Farlow, Melissa)*
  c KR - July 1 2015 - pNA [51-500]
  c SLJ - v61 - i6 - June 2015 - p141(3) [51-500]
  c BL - v112 - i1 - Sept 1 2015 - p92(2) [51-500]

Farley, Tom - *Saving Gotham: A Billionaire Mayor, Activist Doctors, and the Fight for Eight Million Lives*
  BL - v112 - i3 - Oct 1 2015 - p8(1) [51-500]
  KR - August 15 2015 - pNA [501+]
  NYTBR - Nov 22 2015 - p15(L) [501+]
  PW - v262 - i34 - August 24 2015 - p75(1) [51-500]

Farmelo, Graham - *Churchill's Bomb: How the United States Overtook Britain in the First Nuclear Arms Race*
  HNet - July 2015 - pNA [501+]
  JMH - v87 - i2 - June 2015 - p441(3) [501+]

Farmer, Bonnie - *Oscar Lives Next Door: A Story Inspired by Oscar Peterson's Childhood (Illus. by Lafrance, Marie)*
  c KR - July 1 2015 - pNA [51-500]
  c SLJ - v61 - i8 - August 2015 - p68(1) [51-500]

Farmer, Jared - *Trees in Paradise: A California History*
  PHR - v84 - i3 - August 2015 - p369(1) [501+]
  WHQ - v46 - i1 - Spring 2015 - p76-77 [501+]

Farmer, Kenneth - *Real Lawyers*
  KR - Feb 15 2015 - pNA [501+]

Farmer, T.L. - *Project Nephili*
  PW - v262 - i21 - May 25 2015 - p39(2) [501+]

Farndon, John - *Megafast Trucks*
  c KR - Dec 15 2015 - pNA [51-500]

Stickmen's Guide to Watercraft
  c KR - Jan 1 2016 - pNA [51-500]

Stuff You Need to Know!
  c SLJ - v61 - i12 - Dec 2015 - p135(1) [51-500]

Farnham, Andrew High - *Playing The Canterbury Tales: The Continuations and Additions*
  JEGP - v114 - i1 - Jan 2015 - p152(3) [501+]

Farnham, K.J. - *Don't Call Me Kit Kat*
  y KR - August 1 2015 - pNA [51-500]

Farnsworth, Christopher - *The Eternal World*
  KR - June 1 2015 - pNA [501+]
  PW - v262 - i25 - June 22 2015 - p122(1) [51-500]

Farnsworth, Stephen J. - *The Global President: International Media and the US Government*
  Pres St Q - v45 - i3 - Sept 2015 - p622(3) [501+]

Farnsworth, Ward - *Restitution: Civil Liability for Unjust Enrichment*
  HLR - v128 - i7 - May 2015 - p2107(1) [1-50]

Farooq, Jennifer - *Preaching in Eighteenth-Century London*
  AHR - v120 - i1 - Feb 2015 - p327-328 [501+]
  HER - v130 - i545 - August 2015 - p1009(2) [501+]

Farouky, Naila - *I Will Not (Illus. by Eitan, Ora)*
  c KR - July 1 2015 - pNA [51-500]

Faroult, Guillaume - *Delicious Decadence: The Rediscovery of French Eighteenth-Century Painting in the Nineteenth Century*
  FS - v69 - i4 - Oct 2015 - p537-538 [501+]

Farquhar, Michael - *Bad Days in History*
  KR - Feb 1 2015 - pNA [51-500]

Farr, Cecilia Konchar - *Wizard of Their Age: Critical Essays from the Harry Potter Generation*
  HNet - Sept 2015 - pNA [501+]

Farr, David - *Major-General Thomas Harrison: Millenarianism, Fifth Monarchism and the English Revolution 1616-1660*
  AHR - v120 - i4 - Oct 2015 - p1550(1) [501+]

Farrall, Melissa Lee - *Wrightslaw: All about Tests and Assessments*
  SPBW - July 2015 - pNA [501+]

Farrar-Myers, Victoria A. - *Controlling the Message: New Media in American Political Campaigns.*
  LJ - v140 - i6 - April 1 2015 - p106(1) [51-500]

Farred, Grant - *In Motion, at Rest: The Event of the Athletic Body*
  TDR - v59 - i1 - Spring 2015 - p193(1) [501+]

Farrell, Elaine - *'She Said She Was in the Family Way': Pregnancy and Infancy in Modern Ireland*
  HER - v130 - i542 - Feb 2015 - p235(2) [501+]

Farrell, Holly - *Plants from Pips: Pots of Plants for the Whole Family to Enjoy*
  PW - v262 - i31 - August 3 2015 - p53(1) [51-500]

Farrelly, Lorrie - *Terms of Surrender*
  PW - v262 - i7 - Feb 16 2015 - p165(2) [51-500]

Timelapse
  PW - v262 - i31 - August 3 2015 - p40(2) [51-500]

Farrer, Maria - *Broken Strings*
  y Sch Lib - v63 - i1 - Spring 2015 - p51(2) [51-500]

A Flash of Blue
  y Sch Lib - v63 - i3 - Autumn 2015 - p182(1) [51-500]

Farrey, Brian - *The Grimjinx Rebellion (Illus. by Helquist, Brett)*
  c HB Guide - v26 - i1 - Spring 2015 - p76(1) [51-500]

Farrin, Raymond - *Abundance from the Desert: Classical Arabic Poetry*
  JNES - v74 - i1 - April 2015 - p184(4) [501+]

Farrington, Ian - *Cusco: Urbanism and Archaeology in the Inka World*
Historian - v77 - i2 - Summer 2015 - p330(2) [501+]

Farris, Frank A. - *Creating Symmetry: The Artful Mathematics of Wallpaper Patterns*
Am Sci - v103 - i5 - Sept-Oct 2015 - p360(3) [501+]

Farris, Sara R. - *Max Weber's Theory of Personality: Individuation, Politics and Orientalism in the Sociology of Religion*
CS - v44 - i4 - July 2015 - p505-505 [501+]
Theol St - v76 - i4 - Dec 2015 - p865(2) [501+]

Farrow Bruns, Prudence - *Dear Prudence*
KR - Oct 1 2015 - pNA [501+]

Farrow, John - *The Storm Murders*
BL - v111 - i17 - May 1 2015 - p45(1) [51-500]
KR - March 15 2015 - pNA [51-500]
LJ - v140 - i6 - April 1 2015 - p74(1) [51-500]
PW - v262 - i9 - March 2 2015 - p65(1) [51-500]

Farthing, Linda C. - *Evo's Bolivia: Continuity and Change*
Ams - v72 - i3 - July 2015 - p496(2) [501+]

Faruqi, Reem - *Lailah's Lunchbox (Illus. by Lyon, Lea)*
c BL - v111 - i21 - July 1 2015 - p63(1) [51-500]
c CH Bwatch - July 2015 - pNA [51-500]
c SLJ - v61 - i8 - August 2015 - p68(1) [51-500]

Faruqi, Sonia - *Project Animal Farm: An Accidental Journey into the Secret World of Farming and the Truth about Our Food*
BL - v111 - i21 - July 1 2015 - p13(1) [51-500]
KR - April 15 2015 - pNA [501+]
LJ - v140 - i12 - July 1 2015 - p102(1) [51-500]

Fasano, Donna - *Following His Heart*
PW - v262 - i18 - May 4 2015 - p103(1) [51-500]
The Merry-Go-Round
PW - v262 - i25 - June 22 2015 - p127(1) [51-500]

Fasick, Adele M. - *Managing Children's Services in Libraries, 4th ed.*
LQ - v85 - i1 - Jan 2015 - p119(3) [501+]

Fassin, Didier - *Enforcing Order: An Ethnography of Urban Policing*
CS - v44 - i6 - Nov 2015 - p770-772 [501+]

Fassnacht, Erik - *A Good Family*
KR - June 15 2015 - pNA [51-500]

Fast, Jonathan - *Beyond Bullying: Breaking the Cycle of Shame, Bullying, and Violence*
LJ - v140 - i19 - Nov 15 2015 - p96(1) [51-500]

Fathi, Nazila - *The Lonely War: One Woman's Account of the Struggle for Modern Iran*
NYT - Jan 1 2015 - pC9(L) [501+]

Fatio, Louise - *A Doll for Marie (Illus. by Duvoisin, Roger)*
c HB Guide - v26 - i2 - Fall 2015 - p33(1) [51-500]

Fatovic, Clement - *America's Founding and the Struggle Over Economic Inequality*
NYTBR - Dec 20 2015 - p27(L) [501+]

Fattori, MariaTeresa - *Le fatiche di Benedetto XIV: Origine ed evoluzione dei trattati di Prospero Lambertini*
CHR - v101 - i2 - Spring 2015 - p377(3) [501+]

Fatus, Sophie - *My Big Barefoot Book of Wonderful Words*
c Sch Lib - v63 - i1 - Spring 2015 - p26(2) [51-500]
My Big, Wonderful Barefoot Book of Words
c HB Guide - v26 - i2 - Fall 2015 - p10(1) [51-500]

Fauche, Xavier - *The Daltons' Amnesia (Illus. by Morris)*
c Sch Lib - v63 - i2 - Summer 2015 - p106(2) [51-500]

Faugerolas, Marie-Ange - *Angels: The Definitive Guide to Angels from around the World*
BL - v112 - i6 - Nov 15 2015 - p11(1) [51-500]

Faulk, Richard - *The Next Big Thing: A History of the Boom-or-Bust Moments that Shaped the Modern World (Illus. by Beyer, Ramsey)*
y SLJ - v61 - i12 - Dec 2015 - p143(2) [51-500]
y VOYA - v38 - i4 - Oct 2015 - p82(1) [51-500]

Faulkes, Anthony - *The Uppsala Edda: DG 11 4T0*
JEGP - v114 - i1 - Jan 2015 - p121(3) [501+]

Faulkner, Carol - *Interconnections: Gender and Race in American History*
RAH - v43 - i2 - June 2015 - p223-230 [501+]
Lucretia Mott's Heresy: Abolition and Women's Rights in Nineteenth-Century America
JWH - v27 - i2 - Summer 2015 - p159(10) [501+]

Faulks, Sebastian - *Jeeves and the Wedding Bells (Read by Rhind-Tutt, Julian). Audiobook Review*
LJ - v140 - i5 - March 15 2015 - p134(1) [501+]
Where My Heart Used to Beat
KR - Nov 15 2015 - pNA [51-500]
Spec - v328 - i9759 - Sept 12 2015 - p41(1) [501+]

Fause, Avraham - *Judah in the Neo-Babylonian Period: The Archaeology of Desolation*
JR - Jan 2015 - p122(3) [501+]

Fauser, Annegret - *Sounds of War: Music in the United States during World War II*
Notes - v72 - i1 - Sept 2015 - p157(6) [501+]

Fauser, Margit - *Migrants and Cities: The Accommodation of Migrant Organizations in Europe*
CS - v44 - i4 - July 2015 - p578-579 [501+]

Faust, Avraham - *The Archaeology of Israelite Society in Iron Age II*
HNet - Feb 2015 - pNA [501+]

Faust, Joan - *Andrew Marvell's Liminal Lyrics: The Space Between*
MLR - v110 - i3 - July 2015 - p830-831 [501+]

Fauzia, Amelia - *Faith and the State: A History of Islamic Philanthropy in Indonesia*
Pac A - v88 - i1 - March 2015 - p231 [501+]

Favazza, Paddy C. - *The Making Friends Program: Supporting Acceptance in Your K-2 Classroom*
RVBW - Nov 2015 - pNA [51-500]

Favret-Saada, Jeanne - *The Anti-Witch*
TLS - i5870 - Oct 2 2015 - p8(1) [51-500]
Deadly Words: Witchcraft in the Bocage
TLS - i5870 - Oct 2 2015 - p16(1) [51-500]

Fawaz, Leila Tarazi - *A Land of Aching Hearts: The Middle East in the Great War*
JIH - v46 - i3 - Wntr 2016 - p475-476 [501+]
Nation - v300 - i7 - Feb 16 2015 - p34(3) [501+]

Fawaz, Ramzi - *The New Mutants: Superheroes and the Radical Imagination of American Comics*
LJ - v140 - i19 - Nov 15 2015 - p98(1) [51-500]
PW - v262 - i41 - Oct 12 2015 - p57(1) [51-500]

Fawcett, Edmund - *Liberalism: The Life of an Idea*
Nation - v300 - i2-3 - Jan 12 2015 - p32(4) [501+]

Fawcett, Katherine - *The Little Washer of Sorrows*
Can Lit - i224 - Spring 2015 - p120 [501+]

Fawkes, Ray - *Junction True*
PW - v262 - i38 - Sept 21 2015 - p62(1) [51-500]

Fawn, Rick - *International Organizations and Internal Conditionality: Making Norms Matter*
E-A St - v67 - i8 - Oct 2015 - p1336(2) [501+]

Fay, Emma - *Elevator*
KR - May 1 2015 - pNA [51-500]

Faye, Lyndsay - *The Fatal Flame*
BL - v111 - i17 - May 1 2015 - p34(1) [51-500]
KR - April 1 2015 - pNA [51-500]
LJ - v140 - i7 - April 15 2015 - p75(1) [51-500]
NYTBR - May 17 2015 - p33(L) [51-500]
NYTBR - Dec 6 2015 - p85(L) [51-500]
PW - v262 - i13 - March 30 2015 - p56(1) [51-500]

Faye, Sanderia - *Mourner's Bench*
y BL - v112 - i2 - Sept 15 2015 - p37(1) [51-500]
KR - July 15 2015 - pNA [51-500]

Fayet, Jean-Francois - *VOKS: Le laboratoire helvetique. Histoire de la diplomatie culturelle sovietique durant l'entre-deux-guerres*
Slav R - v74 - i3 - Fall 2015 - p654-655 [501+]

Fayman, Corey Lynn - *Desert City Diva*
KR - Nov 1 2015 - pNA [51-500]
PW - v262 - i47 - Nov 23 2015 - p51(1) [51-500]

Fazio, John C. - *Decapitating the Union: Jefferson Davis, Judah Benjamin and the Plot to Assassinate Lincoln*
RVBW - May 2015 - pNA [51-500]
RVBW - July 2015 - pNA [51-500]

Fazl, Abu'l - *The History of Akbar, vol. 1*
NYRB - v62 - i14 - Sept 24 2015 - p64(3) [501+]

Feagin, Joe R. - *Latinos Facing Racism: Discrimination, Resistance, and Endurance*
CS - v44 - i6 - Nov 2015 - p872(1) [501+]
ERS - v38 - i8 - August 2015 - p1453(3) [501+]

Fearing, Mark - *Dilly Dally Daisy*
c BL - v111 - May 1 2015 - pNA [51-500]
The Great Thanksgiving Escape
c HB Guide - v26 - i1 - Spring 2015 - p29(1) [51-500]

Fearon, H. Dana - *Straining at the Oars: Case Studies in Pastoral Leadership*
Intpr - v69 - i1 - Jan 2015 - p120(1) [501+]

Feather, Jane - *Trapped at the Altar (Read by Tanner, Jill). Audiobook Review*
BL - v111 - i16 - April 15 2015 - p63(1) [51-500]
Trapped by Scandal
BL - v111 - i19-20 - June 1 2015 - p64(1) [51-500]

Feather, Jennifer - *Violent Masculinities: Male Aggression in Early Modern Texts and Culture*
Ren Q - v68 - i1 - Spring 2015 - p322-323 [501+]

Fechtor, Jessica - *Stir: My Broken Brain and the Meals That Brought Me Home*
LJ - v140 - i9 - May 15 2015 - p100(1) [51-500]
KR - May 1 2015 - pNA [51-500]
PW - v262 - i18 - May 4 2015 - p108(1) [51-500]

Feddema, Anne - *De triennen fan cheetah: 27 Fryske ferhalen*
WLT - v89 - i6 - Nov-Dec 2015 - p59(2) [501+]

Fedele, Clemente - *Europa Postale: L'opera di Ottavio Codogno luogotenente del Tasso nella Milano Seicentesca*
Phil Lit R - v64 - i3 - Summer 2015 - p217(4) [501+]

Federbusch, Serge - *La Marche des lemmings: la deuxieme mort de Charlie Hebdo*
TLS - i5864-5865 - August 21 2015 - p28(2) [501+]

Federici, Silvia - *Revolution at Point Zero: Housework, Reproduction, and Feminist Struggle*
S&S - v79 - i3 - July 2015 - p475-477 [501+]

Federle, Tim - *Better Nate Than Ever*
c Sch Lib - v63 - i3 - Autumn 2015 - p164(1) [51-500]
Five, Six, Seven, Nate! (Read by Federle, Tim). Audiobook Review
c BL - v111 - i14 - March 15 2015 - p24(2) [501+]
The Great American Whatever
y BL - v112 - i7 - Dec 1 2015 - p56(1) [51-500]
y KR - Dec 15 2015 - pNA [51-500]
y PW - v262 - i50 - Dec 7 2015 - p87(1) [51-500]
Tommy Can't Stop! (Illus. by Fearing, Mark)
c BL - v111 - i14 - March 15 2015 - p82(1) [51-500]
c HB Guide - v26 - i2 - Fall 2015 - p33(1) [51-500]
c KR - Feb 15 2015 - pNA [51-500]
c PW - v262 - i6 - Feb 9 2015 - p64(1) [51-500]
c SLJ - v61 - i4 - April 2015 - p127(1) [51-500]

Fedolfi, Laura - *Revealing Hannah*
KR - Jan 1 2016 - pNA [501+]

Fedosov, Dmitry - *Diary of General Patrick Gordon of Auchleuchries, 1635-99, vol. 3-5*
J Mil H - v79 - i4 - Oct 2015 - p1127-1129 [501+]

Fedou, Michel - *Les theologiens jesuites: Un courant uniforme?*
Theol St - v76 - i3 - Sept 2015 - p641(1) [501+]

Feeley, Kathleen A. - *When Private Talk Goes Public: Gossip in American History*
JAH - v102 - i2 - Sept 2015 - p519-520 [501+]

Feely, Caro - *Saving Our Skins: Building a Vineyard Dream in France*
NYTBR - Dec 6 2015 - p86(L) [501+]

Feeney, F.X. - *Orson Welles: Power, Heart & Soul*
Si & So - v25 - i9 - Sept 2015 - p107(1) [501+]

Feeney, Tatyana - *Small Elephant's Bathtime*
c HB Guide - v26 - i2 - Fall 2015 - p10(1) [51-500]
c KR - Jan 15 2015 - pNA [51-500]
c Sch Lib - v63 - i2 - Summer 2015 - p91(1) [51-500]

Feerick, Jean E. - *The Indistinct Human in Renaissance Literature*
Ren Q - v68 - i1 - Spring 2015 - p398-400 [501+]

Feeser, Andrea - *Red, White, and Black Make Blue: Indigo in the Fabric of Colonial South Carolina Life*
BHR - v89 - i3 - Autumn 2015 - p590(4) [501+]

Feet, Amanda - *Dear Santa, Love, Rachel Rosenstein (Illus. by Davenier, Christine)*
c BL - v112 - i4 - Oct 15 2015 - p48(1) [51-500]

Fehervary, Krisztina - *Politics in Color and Concrete: Socialist Materialities and the Middle Class in Hungary*
AHR - v120 - i2 - April 2015 - p741-743 [501+]

Fehler, Timothy G. - *Religious Diaspora in Early Modern Europe: Strategies of Exile*
AHR - v120 - i1 - Feb 2015 - p322-323 [501+]

Fehrenbach, T.R. - *Lone Star: A History of Texas and the Texans*
Roundup M - v22 - i5 - June 2015 - p5(1) [501+]

Fehribach, Paul - *The Big Jones Cookbook: Recipes for Savoring the Heritage of Regional Southern Cooking*
BL - v111 - i19-20 - June 1 2015 - p20(1) [51-500]

Fei, Deanna - *Girl in Glass: How My "Distressed Baby" Defied the Odds, Shamed a CEO, and Taught Me the Essence of Love, Heartbreak, and Miracles*
BL - v111 - i21 - July 1 2015 - p10(1) [51-500]
KR - May 15 2015 - pNA [51-500]
NYT - Dec 14 2015 - pC1(L) [501+]

Feierabend, John M. - *Jennie Jenkins (Illus. by Ashley, Maurer)*
c CH Bwatch - Oct 2015 - pNA [51-500]

Feiertag, Olivier - *Les Banques centrales a l'echelle du monde*
BHR - v89 - i1 - Spring 2015 - p179(3) [501+]

Feiffer, Jules - *Kill My Mother*
NS - v144 - i5282 - Oct 2 2015 - p79(1) [501+]
Rupert Can Dance (Illus. by Feiffer, Jules)
c HB Guide - v26 - i1 - Spring 2015 - p29(1) [51-500]

Feiffer, Kate - *The Problem with the Puddles (Read by Feiffer, Halley). Audiobook Review*
y SLJ - v61 - i6 - June 2015 - p53(3) [501+]

Feigenbaum, Gail - *Display of Art in the Roman Palace, 1550-1750*
TLS - i5876 - Nov 13 2015 - p24(1) [501+]

Feiman-Nemser, Sharon - *Inspiring Teaching: Preparing Teachers to Succeed in Mission-Driven Schools*
HER - v85 - i2 - Summer 2015 - p296-299 [501+]

Fein, Ronnie - *The Modern Kosher Kitchen: More Than 125 Inspired Recipes for a New Generation of Kosher Cooks*
LJ - v140 - i7 - April 15 2015 - p109(2) [51-500]

Fein, Susanna - *Robert Thornton and His Books: Essays on the Lincoln and London Thornton Manuscripts*
Med R - March 2015 - pNA(NA) [501+]
Ren Q - v68 - i1 - Spring 2015 - p365-366 [501+]
RES - v66 - i275 - June 2015 - p570-571 [501+]
Specu - v90 - i4 - Oct 2015 - p1114-1115 [501+]

Feinde, Freunde, Fremde? Deutsche Perspektiven auf die USA
HNet - July 2015 - pNA [501+]

Feinland, Stephen - *King of the Lions and other Animal Stories*
KR - April 1 2015 - pNA [501+]

Feinman, Ronald L. - *Assassinations, Threats, and the American Presidency: From Andrew Jackson to Barack Obama*
PW - v262 - i19 - May 11 2015 - p48(1) [501+]

Feinstein, Dianne - *Senate Intelligence Committee Report on Torture: Committee Study of the Central Intelligence Agency's Detention and Interrogation Program*
HM - v330 - i1979 - April 2015 - p84(5) [501+]
VQR - v91 - i2 - Spring 2015 - p211-217 [501+]

Feinstein, John - *The Sixth Man*
y KR - July 15 2015 - pNA [501+]
The Walk On
c HB Guide - v26 - i1 - Spring 2015 - p76(1) [51-500]

Feinstein, Marc - *Catch Us If You Can*
y CH Bwatch - Feb 2015 - pNA [51-500]

Feist, Ulrike - *Sonne, Mond und Venus: Visualisierungen astronomischen Wissens im fruhneuzeitlichen Rom*
Isis - v106 - i2 - June 2015 - p444(1) [501+]

Feiveson, Harold A. - *Unmaking the Bomb: A Fissile Material Approach to Nuclear Disarmament and Nonproliferation*
Phys Today - v68 - i5 - May 2015 - p50-50 [501+]

Feld, Barry C. - *Kids, Cops, and Confessions: Inside the Interrogation Room*
CS - v44 - i2 - March 2015 - p195-196 [501+]

Feld, Marjorie N. - *Nations Divided: American Jews and the Struggle over Apartheid*
JAH - v102 - i2 - Sept 2015 - p623-624 [501+]

Feldman, Glenn - *Nation within a Nation: The American South and the Federal Government*
JAH - v101 - i4 - March 2015 - p1242-1243 [501+]

Feldman, Hannah - *From a Nation Torn: Decolonizing Art and Representation in France, 1945-1962*
FS - v69 - i2 - April 2015 - p273-274 [501+]
HNet - May 2015 - pNA [501+]

Feldman, Jody - *The Gollywhopper Games: Friend of Foe (Illus. by Jamieson, Victoria)*
c KR - Feb 1 2015 - pNA [51-500]
The Gollywhopper Games: Friend or Foe (Illus. by Jamieson, Victoria)
c HB Guide - v26 - i2 - Fall 2015 - p81(1) [51-500]
c SLJ - v61 - i6 - June 2015 - p108(1) [51-500]

Feldman, Llewellyn - *In the Rainforest*
c HB Guide - v26 - i1 - Spring 2015 - p154(1) [51-500]
Rivers
c HB Guide - v26 - i1 - Spring 2015 - p156(1) [51-500]

Feldman, Martha - *The Castrato: Reflections on Natures and Kinds*
HNet - June 2015 - pNA [501+]
Lon R Bks - v37 - i19 - Oct 8 2015 - p13(4) [501+]

Feldman, Matthew - *Broadcasting in the Modernist Era*
RES - v66 - i275 - June 2015 - p593-595 [501+]

Feldman, Sabrina - *Thomas Sackville and the Shakespearean Glass Slipper*
KR - Dec 1 2015 - pNA [501+]

Feldman, Thea - *Animal Colors*
c HB Guide - v26 - i1 - Spring 2015 - p154(1) [51-500]
Gabe: The Dog Who Sniffs Out Danger
c HB Guide - v26 - i1 - Spring 2015 - p168(1) [51-500]
Rudolph the Red-Nosed Reindeer: The Classic Story (Illus. by Madrid, Erwin)
c HB Guide - v26 - i2 - Fall 2015 - p33(1) [51-500]
Sadie: The Dog Who Finds the Evidence
c HB Guide - v26 - i1 - Spring 2015 - p168(1) [51-500]
Time
c HB Guide - v26 - i2 - Fall 2015 - p166(1) [51-500]

Feldstein, Al - *Spawn of Mars (Illus. by Wood, Wallace)*
BL - v111 - i13 - March 1 2015 - p37(1) [51-500]

Feldstein, Ruth - *How It Feels to Be Free: Black Women Entertainers and the Civil Rights Movement*
Am Q - v67 - i1 - March 2015 - p241-252 [501+]

Felicitas Fischer von Weikersthal - *The Russian Revolution of 1905 in Transcultural Perspective: Identities, Peripheries, and the Flow of Ideas*
Slav R - v74 - i3 - Fall 2015 - p648-650 [501+]

Felix, Rebecca - *12 Things to Know about Fracking*
c BL - v111 - i15 - April 1 2015 - p54(1) [51-500]
Are You a Ewe?
c HB Guide - v26 - i2 - Fall 2015 - p161(1) [51-500]
Big, Bigger, Biggest
c HB Guide - v26 - i2 - Fall 2015 - p161(1) [51-500]
Eating Ethically
c BL - v112 - i3 - Oct 1 2015 - p52(1) [51-500]
What's Great about Oregon?
c HB Guide - v26 - i2 - Fall 2015 - p220(1) [51-500]

Felix, Stanford - *The Complete Idiot's Guide Music Dictionary*
M Ed J - v102 - i1 - Sept 2015 - p23(2) [51-500]

Fellner, Astrid M. - *Gender Uberall!? Beitrage zur Interdisziplinaren Geschlechterforschung*
HNet - March 2015 - pNA [501+]

Felony, Miles - *Beg For Mercy*
SPBW - Feb 2015 - pNA [51-500]

Felsch, Philipp - *Der Lange Sommer der Theorie: Geschichte einer Revolte 1960-1990*
HNet - June 2015 - pNA [501+]
TLS - i5852 - May 29 2015 - p12(1) [501+]

Felsenstein, Frank - *What Middletown Read: Print Culture in an American Small City*
TimHES - i2208 - June 18 2015 - p50-51 [501+]

Felton, Mark - *Zero Night*
KR - June 15 2015 - pNA [501+]

Fenady, Andrew J. - *The Range Wolf*
Roundup M - v22 - i6 - August 2015 - p29(1) [501+]

Fenby, Jonathan - *The History of Modern France: From the Revolution to the Present Day*
Econ - v416 - i8948 - July 25 2015 - p68(US) [501+]
Spec - v328 - i9751 - July 18 2015 - p36(2) [501+]
TLS - i5871 - Oct 9 2015 - p29(1) [501+]

Feng, Anita M. - *Sid*
PW - v262 - i25 - June 22 2015 - p127(1) [51-500]

Fenn, Elizabeth A. - *Encounters at the Heart of the World: A History of the Mandan People*
AHR - v120 - i3 - June 2015 - p1003-1004 [501+]
HNet - Sept 2015 - pNA [501+]
JAH - v101 - i4 - March 2015 - p1222-1223 [501+]

Fenske, Tawna - *About That Fling*
PW - v262 - i22 - June 1 2015 - p46(2) [501+]

Fenton, Corinne - *Bob the Railway Dog (Illus. by McLean, Andrew)*
Magpies - v30 - i3 - July 2015 - p30(1) [51-500]

Fenton, Laurence - *Frederick Douglass in Ireland: The Black O'Connell*
ILS - v34 - i2 - Spring 2015 - p2(1) [501+]
Palmerston and The Times: Foreign Policy, the Press and Public Opinion in Mid-Victorian Britain
HER - v130 - i544 - June 2015 - p769(2) [501+]

Fenton, Liz - *The Status of All Things*
KR - April 1 2015 - pNA [501+]
LJ - v140 - i11 - June 15 2015 - p80(1) [51-500]

Feola, Maryann - *Geography of Shame*
KR - Sept 1 2015 - pNA [501+]

Ferber, Bruce - *Cascade Falls*
KR - Jan 1 2015 - pNA [51-500]

Ferejohn, Michael T. - *Formal Causes: Definition, Explanation, and Primacy in Socratic and Aristotelian Thought*
RM - v69 - i1 - Sept 2015 - p132(3) [501+]

Ferentinos, Susan - *Interpreting LGBT History at Museums and Historic Sites*
Pub Hist - v37 - i3 - August 2015 - p154(2) [501+]

Fergus, Claudius - *Revolutionary Emancipation: Slavery and Abolitionism in the British West Indies*
Historian - v77 - i2 - Summer 2015 - p382(3) [501+]

Fergus, Maureen - *And What If I Won't? (Illus. by Davila, Claudia)*
c CH Bwatch - July 2015 - pNA [51-500]
And What If I Won't? (Illus. by Leng, Qin)
c CH Bwatch - July 2015 - pNA [51-500]
c HB Guide - v26 - i2 - Fall 2015 - p34(1) [51-500]
c Nat Post - v17 - i130 - April 4 2015 - pWP5(1) [501+]
c SLJ - v61 - i9 - Sept 2015 - p119(2) [51-500]
Buddy and Earl Go Exploring (Illus. by Sookocheff, Carey)
c KR - Dec 1 2015 - pNA [51-500]
Buddy and Earl (Illus. by Sookocheff, Carey)
c BL - v111 - i22 - August 1 2015 - p71(1) [51-500]
c HB - v91 - i5 - Sept-Oct 2015 - p80(1) [51-500]
c KR - July 15 2015 - pNA [51-500]
c PW - v262 - i49 - Dec 2 2015 - p12(1) [51-500]
c Res Links - v21 - i1 - Oct 2015 - p6(1) [51-500]
c SLJ - v61 - i7 - July 2015 - p62(1) [51-500]
A Dog Day for Susan
c KR - Jan 1 2016 - pNA [51-500]
InvisiBill (Illus. by Petricic, Dusan)
c CH Bwatch - August 2015 - pNA [51-500]
c CH Bwatch - Sept 2015 - pNA [51-500]
c Nat Post - v17 - i220 - July 25 2015 - pWP5(1) [501+]
c Res Links - v21 - i1 - Oct 2015 - p6(1) [51-500]

Ferguson, Cheryl Caldwell - *Highland Park and River Oaks: The Origins of Garden Suburban Community Planning in Texas*
JSH - v81 - i4 - Nov 2015 - p1012(2) [501+]

Ferguson, Christine - *Determined Spirits: Eugenics, Heredity and Racial Regeneration in Anglo-American Spiritualist Writing, 1848-1930*
VS - v57 - i2 - Wntr 2015 - p331(3) [501+]

Ferguson, Eliza Earle - *Gender and Justice: Violence, Intimacy, and Community in Fin-de-Siecle Paris*
JWH - v27 - i2 - Summer 2015 - p175(7) [501+]

Ferguson, Giana - *Gubbeen: The Story of a Working Farm and Its Foods*
Bwatch - Nov 2015 - pNA [501+]
RVBW - Nov 2015 - pNA [501+]

Ferguson, Kathryn - *The Haunting of the Mexican Border*
KR - June 15 2015 - pNA [51-500]

Ferguson, Mark Andrew - *The Lost Boys Symphony*
BL - v111 - i11 - Feb 1 2015 - p22(2) [51-500]
KR - Jan 15 2015 - pNA [51-500]
PW - v262 - i1 - Jan 5 2015 - p50(1) [51-500]

Ferguson, Niall - *Kissinger: The Idealist, 1923-1968*
BL - v112 - i1 - Sept 1 2015 - p30(2) [51-500]
CSM - Oct 2 2015 - pNA [51-500]
KR - July 15 2015 - pNA [51-500]
LJ - v140 - i14 - Sept 1 2015 - p120(2) [51-500]
Nat R - v67 - i19 - Oct 19 2015 - p51(2) [501+]
NS - v144 - i5287 - Nov 6 2015 - p40(2) [501+]
PW - v262 - i32 - August 10 2015 - p50(1) [51-500]
Spec - v329 - i9760 - Sept 19 2015 - p41(1) [501+]

Ferguson Publishing - *Encyclopedia of Careers and Vocational Guidance, 16th ed., 5 vols.*
y SLJ - v61 - i6 - June 2015 - p70(1) [51-500]

Ferguson, Richard - *Richard: Blue's Point*
KR - Sept 15 2015 - pNA [501+]

Ferguson, Robert A. - *Inferno: An Anatomy of American Punishment*
AM - v212 - i8 - March 9 2015 - p31(3) [501+]

Ferguson, Robert G. - *NASA's First A: Aeronautics from 1958 to 2008. E-book Review*
APJ - v29 - i6 - Nov-Dec 2015 - p95(1) [501+]

Ferguson, Trish - *Victorian Time: Technologies, Standardizations, Catastrophes*
VS - v57 - i2 - Wntr 2015 - p316(3) [501+]

Fergusson, Bruce - *Pass on the Cup of Dreams*
PW - v262 - i13 - March 30 2015 - p61(1) [51-500]

Fergusson, David - *Creation*
Theol St - v76 - i4 - Dec 2015 - p889(2) [501+]

Ferk, Janko - *Der Kaiser schickt Soldaten aus: Ein Sarajevo-Roman*
WLT - v89 - i1 - Jan-Feb 2015 - p64(2) [501+]

Ferling, John - *Whirlwind: The American Revolution and the War That Won It*
KR - Jan 15 2015 - pNA [501+]
LJ - v140 - i5 - March 15 2015 - p120(1) [501+]
PW - v262 - i12 - March 23 2015 - p66(1) [51-500]

Ferlinghetti, Lawrence - *I Greet You at the Beginning of a Great Career: The Selected Correspondence of Lawrence Ferlinghetti and Allen Ginsberg, 1955-1997*
   HM - v330 - i1981 - June 2015 - p77(3) [501+]
   LJ - v140 - i10 - June 1 2015 - p103(1) [51-500]
   KR - April 15 2015 - pNA [501+]
Writing Across the Landscape: Travel Journals, 1960-2010
   KR - June 15 2015 - pNA [51-500]
   LJ - v140 - i13 - August 1 2015 - p92(2) [51-500]
   PW - v262 - i26 - June 29 2015 - p59(2) [51-500]
   BL - v112 - i2 - Sept 15 2015 - p25(1) [51-500]
   NYT - Sept 20 2015 - p4(L) [501+]
Fermor, Patrick Leigh - *Abducting a General*
   KR - Sept 15 2015 - pNA [501+]
The Broken Road: From the Iron Gates to Mount Athos
   NYTBR - Jan 11 2015 - p24(L) [501+]
Fern, Tracey - *W Is for Webster: Noah Webster and His American Dictionary (Illus. by Kulikov, Boris)*
   c BL - v111 - i19-20 - June 1 2015 - p93(1) [501+]
   c KR - Sept 1 2015 - pNA [51-500]
   c HB - v91 - i6 - Nov-Dec 2015 - p100(2) [51-500]
W Is for Webster (Illus. by Kulikov, Boris)
   c SLJ - v61 - i7 - July 2015 - p103(2) [51-500]
Fernandes, Wilson Geraldo - *Neotropical Insect Galls*
   QRB - v90 - i2 - June 2015 - p210(2) [501+]
Fernandez-Armesto, Felipe - *A Foot in the River: Why Our Lives Change--and the Limits of Evolution*
   Nature - v526 - i7574 - Oct 22 2015 - p503(1) [51-500]
   PW - v262 - i41 - Oct 12 2015 - p58(1) [51-500]
Our America: A Hispanic History of the United States
   NYTBR - Jan 11 2015 - p24(L) [501+]
   SHQ - v118 - i3 - Jan 2015 - p317-318 [501+]
Fernandez, Eleazar S. - *Teaching for a Culturally Diverse and Racially Just World*
   CC - v132 - i21 - Oct 14 2015 - p34(2) [501+]
Fernandez, Jorge - *Rustic: Simple Food and Drink, from Morning to Night*
   NYTBR - Dec 6 2015 - pNA(L) [501+]
Fernandez l'Hoeste, Hector D. - *Cumbia!: Scenes of a Migrant Latin American Music Genre*
   Notes - v71 - i3 - March 2015 - p502(3) [501+]
Fernandez, Maria - *Cosmopolitanism in Mexican Visual Culture*
   HAHR - v95 - i1 - Feb 2015 - p144-146 [501+]
Fernandez, Nadine T. - *Revolutionizing Romance: Interracial Couples in Contemporary Cuba*
   Signs - v40 - i2 - Wntr 2015 - p525(7) [501+]
Fernandez-Pintado, Mylene - *A Corner of the World*
   WLT - v89 - i3-4 - May-August 2015 - p109(2) [501+]
Fernando, Ajith - *Sharing the Truth in Love*
   RVBW - Feb 2015 - pNA [51-500]
Fernando, Chantal - *Arrow's Hell*
   BL - v111 - i19-20 - June 1 2015 - p61(1) [51-500]
Tracker's End
   PW - v262 - i26 - June 29 2015 - p52(2) [501+]
Ferngren, Gary B. - *Medicine and Religion: A Historical Introduction*
   CC - v132 - i5 - March 4 2015 - p35(3) [501+]
   Isis - v106 - i2 - June 2015 - p410(2) [501+]
   Theol St - v76 - i3 - Sept 2015 - p640(1) [501+]
Fernie, Eric - *Romanesque Architecture: The First Style of the European Age*
   Specu - v90 - i1 - Jan 2015 - p246-248 [501+]
Fernstrom, Madelyn Hirsch - *Don't Eat This If You're Taking That: The Hidden Risks of Mixing Food and Medicine*
   BL - v112 - i3 - Oct 1 2015 - p14(1) [51-500]
   PW - v262 - i36 - Sept 7 2015 - p62(1) [51-500]
Ferrall, Victor E., Jr. - *Liberal Arts at the Brink*
   J Hi E - v86 - i1 - Jan-Feb 2015 - p156(15) [501+]
Ferrante, Anthony - *Archie vs. Sharknado*
   Bus W - i4436 - July 27 2015 - p71(1) [501+]
Ferrante, Elena - *My Brilliant Friend*
   BL - v111 - i9-10 - Jan 1 2015 - p120(1) [501+]
   TLS - i5854 - June 12 2015 - p13(1) [501+]
The Story of the Lost Child
   NYT - Sept 4 2015 - pC19(L) [501+]
   BL - v111 - i21 - July 1 2015 - p33(1) [51-500]
   Econ - v416 - i8953 - August 29 2015 - p66(US) [501+]
   Ent W - i1380 - Sept 11 2015 - p62(1) [501+]
   KR - June 15 2015 - pNA [501+]
   Lon R Bks - v37 - i17 - Sept 10 2015 - p11(2) [501+]
   Mac - v128 - i36 - Sept 14 2015 - p75(2) [501+]
   NS - v144 - i5279 - Sept 11 2015 - p44(2) [501+]
   NY - v91 - i28 - Sept 21 2015 - p105 [501+]
   NYTBR - August 30 2015 - p1(L) [501+]
   NYTBR - Dec 13 2015 - p12(L) [501+]
   PW - v262 - i24 - June 15 2015 - p57(1) [51-500]
   Spec - v329 - i9762 - Oct 3 2015 - p45(1) [501+]
   TLS - i5867 - Sept 11 2015 - p20(2) [501+]
Those Who Leave and Those Who Stay
   Lon R Bks - v37 - i1 - Jan 8 2015 - p25(2) [501+]
Ferrara, Silvia - *Cypro-Minoan Inscriptions, vol. 2: The Corpus*
   Class R - v65 - i2 - Oct 2015 - p558-560 [501+]
Ferrari, Emiliano - *Montaigne: une anthropologie des passions*
   FS - v69 - i4 - Oct 2015 - p523-524 [501+]
Ferrari, Rossella - *Pop Goes the Avant-Garde: Experimental Theater in Contemporary China*
   Theat J - v67 - i3 - Oct 2015 - p584-586 [501+]
Ferrari, Silvio - *Religion in Public Spaces: A European Perspective*
   J Ch St - v57 - i1 - Wntr 2015 - p181-183 [501+]
Ferraris, Zoe - *The Galaxy Pirates: Hunt for the Pyxis*
   c BL - v111 - i21 - July 1 2015 - p72(1) [51-500]
   c SLJ - v61 - i7 - July 2015 - p76(1) [51-500]
   c KR - June 1 2015 - pNA [51-500]
Ferraro, Gene - *Ordinary Evil*
   KR - Oct 15 2015 - pNA [501+]
Ferraro, Vincent A. - *Immigrants and Crime in the New Destinations*
   CS - v44 - i2 - March 2015 - p288-289 [501+]
Ferraro, William M. - *Papers of George Washington: Revolutionary War Series, vol. 21: 1 June-31 July 1779*
   JSH - v81 - i1 - Feb 2015 - p171(2) [501+]
Ferrebe, Alice - *Teaching Gender*
   MLR - v110 - i3 - July 2015 - p797-799 [501+]
Ferreira, Roquinaldo - *Cross-Cultural Exchange in the Atlantic World: Angola and Brazil during the Era of the Slave Trade*
   AHR - v120 - i3 - June 2015 - p970(1) [501+]
Ferreira, Stacey - *2 Billion under 20: How Millennial Are Breaking Down Age Barriers and Changing the World*
   y BL - v111 - i21 - July 1 2015 - p5(2) [51-500]
Ferrell, Nancy - *The Battle of Little Bighorn in United States History*
   y HB Guide - v26 - i1 - Spring 2015 - p203(1) [51-500]
Ferrell, Sean - *I Don't Like Koala (Illus. by Santoso, Charles)*
   c BL - v111 - i14 - March 15 2015 - p78(1) [51-500]
   c CH Bwatch - June 2015 - pNA [51-500]
   c HB - v91 - i2 - March-April 2015 - p74(2) [51-500]
   c HB Guide - v26 - i2 - Fall 2015 - p11(1) [51-500]
   c KR - Feb 1 2015 - pNA [51-500]
   c PW - v262 - i5 - Feb 2 2015 - p59(1) [51-500]
Ferrer, Ada - *Freedom's Mirror: Cuba and Haiti in the Age of Revolution*
   W&M Q - v72 - i3 - July 2015 - p540-543 [501+]
Ferrer, Barbara - *Between Here and Gone*
   PW - v262 - i50 - Dec 7 2015 - p74(1) [501+]
Ferrer, Charley - *Shhh: It's a Secret BDSM*
   LJ - v140 - i16 - Oct 1 2015 - p62(2) [51-500]
Ferret, Olivier - *Biographie and Politique: Vie publique, vie privee, de l'Ancien Regime a la Restauration*
   Biomag - v38 - i3 - Summer 2015 - p450(3) [501+]
Ferretti, Tony - *The Love Fight*
   SPBW - March 2015 - pNA [51-500]
Ferri, Giuliano - *Luke and the Little Seed (Illus. by Ferri, Giuliano)*
   c KR - March 1 2015 - pNA [51-500]
   c SLJ - v61 - i6 - June 2015 - p82(1) [51-500]
Peekaboo! (Illus. by Ferri, Giuliano)
   c KR - July 1 2015 - pNA [51-500]
   c PW - v262 - i15 - April 13 2015 - p78(2) [501+]
Peekaboo!
   c PW - v262 - i49 - Dec 2 2015 - p58(1) [51-500]
Ferrier, Katherine - *Hotel Strange: Wake Up, Spring (Illus. by Ferrier, Katherine)*
   c PW - v262 - i38 - Sept 21 2015 - p78(1) [501+]
   c BL - v112 - i6 - Nov 15 2015 - p36(1) [51-500]
On the Sapphire's Trail
   c KR - Dec 15 2015 - pNA [501+]
Wake Up, Spring
   c KR - August 15 2015 - pNA [501+]
Ferris, Amy - *Shades of Blue: Writers on Depression, Suicide, and Feeling Blue*
   PW - v262 - i30 - July 27 2015 - p55(1) [51-500]
Ferris, Fleur - *Risk*
   y Magpies - v30 - i4 - Sept 2015 - p40(1) [501+]

Ferris, Gloria - *Shroud of Roses*
   PW - v262 - i22 - June 1 2015 - p41(2) [51-500]
Ferris, Joshua - *To Rise Again at a Decent Hour*
   y NYTBR - April 19 2015 - p28(L) [501+]
Ferris, Marc - *Star-Spangled Banner: The Unlikely Story of America's National Anthem*
   M Ed J - v102 - i1 - Sept 2015 - p22(2) [501+]
Ferris, Marcie Cohen - *The Edible South: The Power of Food and the Making of an American Region*
   AHR - v120 - i3 - June 2015 - p1004-1005 [501+]
   JSH - v81 - i4 - Nov 2015 - p1048(2) [501+]
   Pub Hist - v37 - i2 - May 2015 - p148(3) [501+]
Ferriter, Diarmaid - *A Nation and Not a Rabble: The Irish Revolution, 1913-1923*
   Spec - v327 - i9739 - April 25 2015 - p36(2) [501+]
Ferrone, Vincenzo - *The Enlightenment: History of an Idea*
   New R - v246 - i5 - June 2015 - p74(4) [501+]
   TimHES - i2204 - May 21 2015 - p52(1) [501+]
Ferry, Beth - *Land Shark (Illus. by Mantle, Ben)*
   c SLJ - v61 - i10 - Oct 2015 - p76(1) [51-500]
Stick and Stone (Illus. by Lichtenheld, Tom)
   c CH Bwatch - May 2015 - pNA [501+]
   c HB - v91 - i2 - March-April 2015 - p75(1) [51-500]
   c HB Guide - v26 - i2 - Fall 2015 - p11(1) [51-500]
   c KR - Feb 1 2015 - pNA [51-500]
   c Magpies - v30 - i4 - Sept 2015 - p27(1) [501+]
   c PW - v262 - i5 - Feb 2 2015 - p59(2) [51-500]
Ferster, Bill - *Teaching Machines: Learning from the Intersection of Education and Technology*
   TimHES - i2194 - March 12 2015 - p51(1) [501+]
Fertel, Randy - *A Taste for Chaos: The Art of Literary Improvisation*
   KR - Jan 15 2015 - pNA [501+]
   RVBW - May 2015 - pNA [501+]
   RVBW - June 2015 - pNA [501+]
Fertig, Judith - *Bake Happy: 100 Playful Desserts with Rainbow Layers, Hidden Fillings, Billowy Frostings, and More*
   LJ - v140 - i12 - July 1 2015 - p106(1) [51-500]
   PW - v262 - i22 - June 1 2015 - p55(1) [51-500]
The Cake Therapist
   BL - v111 - i19-20 - June 1 2015 - p38(1) [51-500]
   KR - April 15 2015 - pNA [501+]
Ferullo, Donna L. - *Managing Copyright in Higher Education: A Guidebook*
   LJ - v140 - i3 - Feb 15 2015 - p114(1) [51-500]
Fery, Suzanne - *Aventures de l'analyse de Fermat a Borel: Melanges en l'honneur de Christian Gilain*
   Isis - v106 - i1 - March 2015 - p160(2) [501+]
Feser, Edward - *Scholastic Metaphysics: A Contemporary Introduction*
   RM - v68 - i3 - March 2015 - p653(2) [501+]
Fetch! With Ruff Ruffman: Ruff Ruffman's 44 Favorite Science Activities (Illus. by WGBH Educational Foundation)
   c BL - v111 - i15 - April 1 2015 - p36(1) [51-500]
Feterl, Amanda - *Affordable Art Projects for Kids*
   c CH Bwatch - August 2015 - pNA [51-500]
Fetter-Vorm, Jonathan - *Battle Lines: A Graphic History of the Civil War (Illus. by Fetter-Vorm, Jonathan)*
   y BL - v111 - i18 - May 15 2015 - p42(1) [51-500]
Battle Lines: A Graphic History of the Civil War (Illus. by Kelman, Ari)
   y HNet - May 2015 - pNA [501+]
Battle Lines: A Graphic History of the Civil War (Illus. by Fetter-Vorm, Jonathan)
   y KR - Feb 15 2015 - pNA [501+]
   PW - v262 - i7 - Feb 16 2015 - p166(1) [51-500]
Feuer, Rhoda - *The Growing Up of Princess Eva (Illus. by Rangala, Gopinath)*
   c CH Bwatch - July 2015 - pNA [51-500]
Feuerman, Ruchama King - *The Mountain Jews and the Mirror (Illus. by Kosec, Polona)*
   c BL - v112 - i6 - Nov 15 2015 - p49(1) [51-500]
   c KR - August 15 2015 - pNA [501+]
Feuerman, Ruchama Kinger - *The Mountain Jews and the Mirror (Illus. by Calderon, Polona)*
   c PW - v262 - i32 - August 10 2015 - p63(1) [51-500]
Feusi, Rene - *The Beautiful Way Of Life*
   RVBW - March 2015 - pNA [51-500]
Fevre, Ralph - *Trouble at Work*
   CS - v44 - i5 - Sept 2015 - p659-661 [501+]
Few, Martha - *Centering Animals in Latin American History*
   HAHR - v95 - i4 - Nov 2015 - p671-673 [501+]
Fey, Tina - *Bossypants*
   BL - v111 - i9-10 - Jan 1 2015 - p120(1) [501+]

Feynman, Richard P. - *The Quotable Feynman*
  LJ - v140 - i15 - Sept 15 2015 - p101(1) [51-500]
Fforde, Jasper - *The Eye of Zoltar*
  y HB - v91 - i1 - Jan-Feb 2015 - p80(1) [51-500]
  y HB Guide - v26 - i1 - Spring 2015 - p106(1) [51-500]
  y Sch Lib - v63 - i4 - Winter 2015 - p244(1) [51-500]
Fialka, John J. - *Car Wars: The Rise, the Fall, and the Resurgence of the Electric Car*
  BL - v111 - i21 - July 1 2015 - p21(1) [51-500]
  KR - June 15 2015 - pNA [501+]
Fiarman, Sarah E. - *Becoming a School Principal: Learning to Lead, Leading to Learn*
  LJ - v140 - i15 - Sept 15 2015 - p86(2) [51-500]
Fichte, Byjoerg O. - *From Camelot to Obamalot: Essays on Medieval and Modern Arthurian Literature*
  JEGP - v114 - i3 - July 2015 - p453(4) [501+]
Fichtner, Paula Sutter - *The Habsburgs: Dynasty, Culture and Politics*
  HNet - August 2015 - pNA [501+]
Fickle, James E. - *Green Gold: Alabama's Forests and Forest Industries*
  JSH - v81 - i3 - August 2015 - p784(2) [501+]
Ficklin, Sherry D. - *Prodigal*
  PW - v262 - i9 - March 2 2015 - p67(1) [51-500]
  Queen of Tomorrow
  y SLJ - v61 - i5 - May 2015 - p118(1) [51-500]
  Riven
  PW - v262 - i14 - April 6 2015 - p45(1) [51-500]
Ficuciello, Laura - *Lemnos: Cultura, storia, archeologia, topografia di un'isola del nord-Egeo*
  Class R - v65 - i2 - Oct 2015 - p562-564 [501+]
Fiddes, Paul S. - *Seeing the World and Knowing God: Hebrew Wisdom and Christian Doctrine in a Late-Modern Context*
  TLS - i5837 - Feb 13 2015 - p28(1) [501+]
Fiddian-Qasmiyeh, Elena - *The Ideal Refugees: Gender, Islam, and the Sahrawi Politics of Survival, Gender, Culture, and Politics in the Middle East (Gender, Culture, and Politics in the Middle East)*
  IJAHS - v48 - i1 - Wntr 2015 - p140-142 [501+]
  IJMES - v47 - i1 - Feb 2015 - p191-193 [501+]
Fidler, David P. - *The Snowden Reader*
  PW - v262 - i13 - March 30 2015 - p70(1) [51-500]
  BL - v111 - i16 - April 15 2015 - p6(1) [51-500]
  KR - Feb 15 2015 - pNA [501+]
Fidora, Alexander - *Latin-into-Hebrew: Texts and Studies, vol. 2: Texts in Context*
  Six Ct J - v46 - i2 - Summer 2015 - p436-437 [501+]
Fidyk, Steve - *Big Band Drumming Fill-osophy*
  Teach Mus - v22 - i3 - Jan 2015 - p60(1) [51-500]
Fiebrandt, Maria - *Auslese fur die Siedlergesellschaft: Die Einbeziehung Volksdeutscher in die NS-Erbgesundheitspolitik im Kontext der Umsiedlungen 1939-1945*
  HNet - Feb 2015 - pNA [501+]
Fiedler, Lisa - *Hopper's Destiny (Illus. by To, Vivienne)*
  c HB Guide - v26 - i1 - Spring 2015 - p76(1) [51-500]
  c HB Guide - v26 - i2 - Fall 2015 - p81(1) [51-500]
  c KR - Jan 1 2015 - pNA [51-500]
  Return of the Forgotten (Illus. by To, Vivienne)
  c KR - August 15 2015 - pNA [51-500]
  c SLJ - v61 - i10 - Oct 2015 - p88(2) [51-500]
  Stagestruck: Curtain Up
  c BL - v111 - i19-20 - June 1 2015 - p106(2) [51-500]
  c SLJ - v61 - i5 - May 2015 - p102(1) [51-500]
Field, Andrew David - *Mu Shiying: China's Lost Modernist*
  HNet - Feb 2015 - pNA [501+]
Field, Corinne T. - *The Struggle for Equal Adulthood: Gender, Race, Age, and the Fight for Citizenship in Antebellum America*
  AHR - v120 - i4 - Oct 2015 - p1490-1491 [501+]
  JAH - v102 - i1 - June 2015 - p251-251 [501+]
Field, Dawn - *Biocode: The New Age of Genomics*
  LJ - v140 - i6 - April 1 2015 - p113(1) [51-500]
  PW - v262 - i12 - March 23 2015 - p58(1) [51-500]
Field, Douglas - *All Those Strangers: The Art and Lives of James Baldwin*
  G&L Rev W - v22 - i6 - Nov-Dec 2015 - p41(2) [501+]
  TLS - i5877 - Nov 20 2015 - p5(1) [501+]
Field, John - *Working Men's Bodies: Work Camps in Britain, 1880-1940*
  HER - v130 - i543 - April 2015 - p493(3) [501+]

Field, L.L. - *The Marriage of True Minds*
  KR - Jan 1 2015 - pNA [501+]
Field, Larry F. - *The Sanctity of Louis IX: Early Lives of Saint Louis by Geoffrey of Beaulieu and William of Chartres*
  CHR - v101 - i3 - Summer 2015 - p627(2) [501+]
  Med R - Feb 2015 - pNA [501+]
Field-Lewis, Jane - *My Cool Kitchen: A Style Guide to Unique and Inspirational Kitchens (Illus. by Maxted, Richard)*
  LJ - v140 - i8 - May 1 2015 - p74(1) [51-500]
Field, Marjorie N. - *Nations Divided: American Jews and the Struggle over Apartheid*
  AHR - v120 - i3 - June 2015 - p1065-1066 [501+]
Field, P.J.C. - *Sir Thomas Malory: Le Morte Darthur, 2 vols.*
  RES - v66 - i274 - April 2015 - p367-369 [501+]
  Med R - Feb 2015 - pNA [501+]
Field, Sean - *Oral History, Community, and Displacement: Imagining Memories in Post-Apartheid South Africa*
  JTWS - v32 - i1 - Spring 2015 - p361(3) [501+]
Field, Sean L. - *The Rules of Isabelle of France: An English Translation with Introductory Study*
  Med R - August 2015 - pNA [501+]
Field, Simon Quellen - *Electronics for Artists: Adding Light, Motion, and Sound to Your Artwork*
  LJ - v140 - i3 - Feb 15 2015 - p98(1) [51-500]
Field, Thomas C., Jr. - *From Development to Dictatorship: Bolivia and the Alliance for Progress in the Kennedy Era*
  JAH - v102 - i1 - June 2015 - p296-297 [501+]
Fielding, Joy - *She's Not There*
  KR - Dec 15 2015 - pNA [501+]
  Someone Is Watching (Read by Traister, Christina). Audiobook Review
  BL - v112 - i3 - Oct 1 2015 - p85(2) [51-500]
  Someone Is Watching
  BL - v111 - i13 - March 1 2015 - p26(1) [51-500]
  KR - Jan 15 2015 - pNA [501+]
  PW - v262 - i4 - Jan 26 2015 - p147(1) [51-500]
Fielding, Steven - *A State of Play: British Politics on Screen, Stage and Page, from Anthony Trollope to the Thick of It*
  HT - v65 - i1 - Jan 2015 - p58(1) [501+]
Fields, Hilary - *Last Chance Llama Ranch*
  KR - May 15 2015 - pNA [501+]
Fields, J.L. - *Vegan Pressure Cooking: Delicious Beans, Grains, and One-Pot Meals in Minutes*
  LJ - v140 - i5 - March 15 2015 - p126(3) [51-500]
Fields, Jan - *The Emerald Dragon (Illus. by McMorris, Kelly)*
  c CH Bwatch - Jan 2015 - pNA [51-500]
  Facing a Frenemy (Illus. by Bishop, Tracy)
  c HB Guide - v26 - i1 - Spring 2015 - p59(1) [51-500]
  Ghost Light Burning (Illus. by Fabbretti, Valerio)
  c HB Guide - v26 - i1 - Fall 2015 - p65(1) [51-500]
  Monster Hunters (Illus. by Brundage, Scott)
  c HB Guide - v26 - i1 - Spring 2015 - p76(1) [51-500]
Fields, Jeffrey R. - *State Behavior and the Nuclear Nonproliferation Regime*
  HNet - May 2015 - pNA [501+]
Fields, Michael - *Twin River II*
  KR - April 15 2015 - pNA [501+]
Fields, R. Douglas - *Why We Snap: Understanding the Rage Circuit in Your Brain*
  BL - v112 - i7 - Dec 1 2015 - p21(1) [51-500]
  KR - Nov 1 2015 - pNA [501+]
Fields, Terri - *One Good Deed (Illus. by Melmon, Deborah)*
  c KR - June 15 2015 - pNA [51-500]
  c PW - v262 - i21 - May 25 2015 - p62(1) [51-500]
  c SLJ - v61 - i8 - August 2015 - p68(2) [51-500]
Fields, Tricia - *Firebreak*
  PW - v262 - i1 - Jan 5 2015 - p52(1) [51-500]
Fields, Ylleya - *Princess Cupcake Jones Won't Go to School (Illus. by LaDuca, Michael)*
  c CH Bwatch - July 2015 - pNA [51-500]
Fieldston, Sara - *Raising the World: Child Welfare in the American Century*
  HNet - Sept 2015 - pNA [501+]
Fiennes, Ranulph - *Agincourt: The Fight for France*
  BL - v112 - i7 - Dec 1 2015 - p11(1) [51-500]
  KR - Oct 1 2015 - pNA [501+]
Fierstein, Ronald - *A Triumph of Genius: Edwin Land, Polaroid, and the Kodak Patent War*
  Econ - v414 - i8931 - March 28 2015 - p86(US) [501+]
Fievet, Paddy - *The Making Of A Mystic*
  SPBW - March 2015 - pNA [51-500]

Fife, D. M - *Light & Dark: The Awakening of the Magekniht*
  y KR - Dec 15 2015 - pNA [501+]
Fiffe, Michael - *All-New Ultimates Vol. 1: Power for Power (Illus. by Pinna, Amilcar)*
  y SLJ - v61 - i2 - Feb 2015 - p111(1) [51-500]
Fifield, Adam - *A Mighty Purpose: How Jim Grant Sold the World on Saving its Children*
  BL - v111 - i19-20 - June 1 2015 - p33(1) [51-500]
  KR - July 1 2015 - pNA [501+]
  NYRB - v62 - i17 - Nov 5 2015 - p62(3) [501+]
Fifield, Richard - *The Flood Girls*
  KR - Nov 15 2015 - pNA [501+]
  PW - v262 - i52 - Dec 21 2015 - p123(2) [51-500]
Figueroa, Victor - *Prophetic Visions of the Past: Pan-Caribbean Representations of the Haitian Revolution*
  RVBW - June 2015 - pNA [501+]
Filanci, Franco - *Il Novellario - Enciclatalogo della Posta in Italia, vol. II: Una Posta Belle Epoque 1889-1921*
  Phil Lit R - v64 - i1 - Wntr 2015 - p55(4) [501+]
Filby, Eliza - *God & Mrs Thatcher: The Battle for Britain's Soul*
  Spec - v327 - i9737 - April 11 2015 - p38(2) [501+]
Filichia, Peter - *The Great Parade: Broadway's Astonishing, Never-to-Be-Forgotten 1963-1964 Season*
  LJ - v140 - i6 - April 1 2015 - p92(3) [51-500]
  PW - v262 - i13 - March 30 2015 - p72(1) [51-500]
  KR - Jan 15 2015 - pNA [501+]
Filipacchi, Amanda - *The Unfortunate Importance of Beauty (Read by Delaine, Christina). Audiobook Review*
  LJ - v140 - i8 - May 1 2015 - p40(1) [51-500]
  NYTBR - May 17 2015 - p17(L) [501+]
  The Unfortunate Importance of Beauty
  y BL - v111 - i9-10 - Jan 1 2015 - p42(1) [51-500]
  NY - v91 - i3 - March 9 2015 - p95 [51-500]
Filiu, Jean-Pierre - *From Deep State to Islamic State: The Arab Counter-Revolution and its Jihadi Legacy*
  Econ - v416 - i8950 - August 8 2015 - p70(US) [501+]
  Lon R Bks - v37 - i14 - July 16 2015 - p5(6) [501+]
  TLS - i5869 - Sept 25 2015 - p7(2) [501+]
  Gaza: A History
  HT - v65 - i6 - June 2015 - p65(1) [501+]
Filloy, Juan - *Caterva*
  KR - June 15 2015 - pNA [501+]
Finch, Alison - *Selected Essays of Malcolm Bowie*
  TimHES - i2184 - Jan 1 2015 - p63(1) [501+]
Finch, Ava - *Fishing with RayAnne*
  BL - v112 - i1 - Sept 1 2015 - p38(1) [51-500]
  LJ - v140 - i19 - Nov 15 2015 - p75(1) [51-500]
Finch, Charles - *Home by Nightfall*
  NYTBR - Nov 15 2015 - p29(L) [501+]
  PW - v262 - i39 - Sept 28 2015 - p67(1) [51-500]
  The Laws of Murder (Read by Langton, James). Audiobook Review
  BL - v111 - i15 - April 1 2015 - p85(1) [51-500]
Finch, David - *Forever Evil*
  LJ - v140 - i9 - May 15 2015 - p110(1) [51-500]
Finch, Dawn - *Skara Brae*
  c Sch Lib - v63 - i4 - Winter 2015 - p237(1) [51-500]
Finch, Michael - *Finding Home*
  KR - Nov 1 2015 - pNA [501+]
Findell, Martin - *Runes*
  BL - v112 - i1 - Sept 1 2015 - p31(1) [51-500]
Finder, Harry - *The 50s: The Story of a Decade*
  KR - August 1 2015 - pNA [501+]
Finder, Joseph - *The Fixer (Read by Kearney, Steven). Audiobook Review*
  PW - v262 - i30 - July 27 2015 - p60(1) [51-500]
  The Fixer
  NYTBR - June 14 2015 - p12(L) [501+]
  PW - v262 - i17 - April 27 2015 - p49(1) [51-500]
  The Fixer (Read by Kearney, Steven). Audiobook Review
  BL - v112 - i4 - Oct 15 2015 - p60(1) [51-500]
  The Fixer
  KR - April 1 2015 - pNA [51-500]
  BL - v111 - i17 - May 1 2015 - p34(1) [51-500]
  The Fixer (Read by Kearny, Steven). Audiobook Review
  LJ - v140 - i15 - Sept 15 2015 - p41(1) [51-500]
  Suspicion
  RVBW - May 2015 - pNA [51-500]
  RVBW - Jan 2015 - pNA [51-500]

Findlay, Jean - *Chasing Lost Time: The Life of C.K. Scott Moncrieff: Soldier, Spy, and Translator*
    AS - v84 - i2 - Spring 2015 - p126(3) [501+]
    HR - v68 - i2 - Summer 2015 - p336-342 [501+]
    NY - v91 - i29 - Sept 28 2015 - p72 [51-500]
    NYRB - v62 - i10 - June 4 2015 - p54(3) [501+]
    PW - v262 - i2 - Jan 12 2015 - p49(1) [51-500]

Findlen, Paula - *Early Modern Things: Objects and Their Histories, 1500-1800*
    JMH - v87 - i2 - June 2015 - p400(4) [501+]

Findon, Joanne - *Seeking Our Eden: The Dreams and Migrations of Sarah Jameson Craig*
    TLS - i5876 - Nov 13 2015 - p30(1) [501+]

Fine, Gary Alan - *Players and Pawns: How Chess Builds Community and Culture*
    PW - v262 - i19 - May 11 2015 - p46(2) [51-500]
    TimHES - i2223 - Oct 1 2015 - p50(1) [501+]

Fine, Jon - *Your Band Sucks: What I Saw at Indie Rock's Failed Revolution (But Can No Longer Hear).*
    KR - March 15 2015 - pNA [51-500]

Your Band Sucks: What I Saw at Indie Rock's Failed Revolution (but Can No Longer Hear). (Read by Fine, Jon). Audiobook Review
    LJ - v140 - i15 - Sept 15 2015 - p43(1) [51-500]

Fine, Sarah - *The Impostor Queen*
    y KR - Oct 1 2015 - pNA [51-500]
    y SLJ - v61 - i11 - Nov 2015 - p114(1) [51-500]

Of Dreams and Rust
    y VOYA - v38 - i4 - Oct 2015 - p68(2) [51-500]
    y KR - June 15 2015 - pNA [51-500]
    y SLJ - v61 - i6 - June 2015 - p122(2) [51-500]

Of Metal and Wishes
    y HB Guide - v26 - i2 - Fall 2015 - p118(1) [501+]

Fingeroth, Daniel J. - *101 Outstanding Graphic Novels, 4th ed.*
    LJ - v140 - i12 - July 1 2015 - p110(2) [51-500]

Fink, Dennis L. - *The Battle of Marathon in Scholarship: Research, Theories and Controversies since 1850*
    HNet - April 2015 - pNA [501+]

Fink, Joseph - *Welcome to Night Vale*
    BL - v112 - i1 - Sept 1 2015 - p56(1) [51-500]
    KR - August 15 2015 - pNA [51-500]
    LJ - v140 - i14 - Sept 1 2015 - p91(1) [51-500]
    LJ - v140 - i16 - Oct 1 2015 - p111(1) [51-500]
    PW - v262 - i17 - April 27 2015 - p55(1) [51-500]

Fink, Leon - *Workers in Hard Times: A Long View of Economic Crises*
    Can Hist R - v96 - i1 - March 2015 - p148(3) [501+]

Fink, Megan P. - *Teen Services 101: A Practical Guide for Busy Library Staff*
    y SLJ - v61 - i11 - Nov 2015 - p142(1) [51-500]

Finkel, Irving - *Cuneiform*
    BL - v112 - i1 - Sept 1 2015 - p31(1) [51-500]

Finkelstein, Gabriel - *Emil du Bois-Reymond: Neuroscience, Self, and Society in Nineteenth-Century Germany*
    Isis - v106 - i2 - June 2015 - p467(2) [501+]
    CEH - v48 - i3 - Sept 2015 - p430-432 [501+]

Finlay, Graeme - *Human Evolution: Genes, Genealogies and Phylogenies*
    BioSci - v65 - i1 - Jan 2015 - p101(2) [501+]

Finlay, Victoria - *The Brilliant History of Color in Art*
    y HB Guide - v26 - i1 - Spring 2015 - p179(1) [51-500]

Finley, Guy - *The Secret of Your Immortal Self: Key Lessons for Realizing the Divinity Within*
    Bwatch - March 2015 - pNA [51-500]

Finn, Chester E., Jr. - *Failing Our Brightest Kids: The Global Challenge of Educating High-Ability Students*
    LJ - v140 - i16 - Oct 1 2015 - p91(1) [51-500]

Finn, Daniel K. - *Christian Economic Ethics: History and Implications*
    Intpr - v69 - i4 - Oct 2015 - p486(2) [501+]

Distant Markets, Distant Harms: Economic Complicity and Christian Ethics
    Theol St - v76 - i3 - Sept 2015 - p649(2) [501+]

Finn, Declan - *A Pius Man: A Holy Thriller*
    SPBW - Jan 2015 - pNA [51-500]

Finn, Ed - *Hieroglyph: Stories & Visions for a Better Future*
    Analog - v135 - i3 - March 2015 - p108(1) [501+]

Finn, Katie - *Revenge, Ice Cream, and Other Things Best Served Cold*
    y HB Guide - v26 - i2 - Fall 2015 - p118(1) [501+]
    y VOYA - v38 - i1 - April 2015 - p58(1) [51-500]

Finn, Peter - *The Zhivago Affair: The Kremlin, the CIA, and the Battle Over a Forbidden Book*
    MLR - v110 - i3 - July 2015 - p921-922 [501+]

Finne, Stephanie - *American Curl Cats*
    c HB Guide - v26 - i1 - Spring 2015 - p168(1) [51-500]

Beagles
    c HB Guide - v26 - i2 - Fall 2015 - p181(1) [51-500]

Finnegan, Amy - *Not in the Script*
    y HB Guide - v26 - i1 - Spring 2015 - p106(1) [51-500]

Finnegan, Ruth - *Black Inked Pearl*
    KR - Dec 1 2015 - pNA [51-500]

Finnegan, William - *Barbarian Days: A Surfing Life*
    Ent W - i1373 - July 24 2015 - p62(1) [501+]
    KR - May 15 2015 - pNA [501+]
    LJ - v140 - i9 - May 15 2015 - p88(1) [51-500]
    Mac - v128 - i29-30 - July 27 2015 - p68(2) [501+]
    NS - v144 - i5273 - July 31 2015 - p64(2) [501+]
    NYRB - v62 - i13 - August 13 2015 - p30(2) [501+]
    NYT - July 22 2015 - pC1(L) [501+]
    PW - v262 - i17 - April 27 2015 - p62(1) [501+]

Finocchiaro, Maurice A. - *The Routledge Guidebook to Galileo's "Dialogue"*
    Isis - v106 - i1 - March 2015 - p182(2) [501+]

The Trial of Galileo: Essential Documents
    RM - v68 - i3 - March 2015 - p655(2) [501+]

Fiorato, Marina - *Beatrice and Benedick*
    BL - v112 - i7 - Dec 1 2015 - p33(1) [501+]
    KR - Oct 1 2015 - pNA [51-500]
    LJ - v140 - i17 - Oct 15 2015 - p76(1) [51-500]

Fiore, Kelly - *Just Like the Movies*
    y HB Guide - v26 - i1 - Spring 2015 - p106(1) [51-500]

Thicker Than Water
    y SLJ - v61 - i11 - Nov 2015 - p114(1) [51-500]

Fiorina, Carly - *Rising to the Challenge: My Leadership Journey*
    NYRB - v62 - i17 - Nov 5 2015 - p18(3) [501+]
    Reason - v47 - i4 - August-Sept 2015 - p58(8) [501+]

Firestein, Stuart - *Failure: Why Science Is So Successful*
    LJ - v140 - i17 - Oct 15 2015 - p110(1) [51-500]
    Nature - v527 - i7576 - Nov 5 2015 - p37(1) [51-500]

Firnhaber-Baker, Justine - *Violence and the State in Languedoc, 1250-1400*
    Specu - v90 - i3 - July 2015 - p806-808 [501+]

Firpo, Massimo - *La presa di potere dell'Inquizitione romana, 1550-1553*
    AHR - v120 - i3 - June 2015 - p1138-1139 [501+]

Firschein, Warren - *Out of Synch*
    y CH Bwatch - Feb 2015 - pNA [51-500]

Firsov, Fridrikh I. - *Secret Cables of the Comintern, 1933-1943*
    AHR - v120 - i4 - Oct 2015 - p1457-1458 [501+]

First Global Humanitarianism Research Academy (GHRA) 2015
    HNet - Sept 2015 - pNA(NA) [501+]

First Ladies: NPR American Chronicles (Read by Roberts, Cokie). Audiobook Review
    BL - v111 - i19-20 - June 1 2015 - p138(1) [51-500]

Firstbrook, Peter - *A Man Most Driven: Captain John Smith, Pocahontas and the Founding of America*
    TLS - i5845 - April 10 2015 - p25(1) [501+]

Fisch, Sholly - *Happy Birthday, Superman! (Illus. by Bone, J.)*
    c HB Guide - v26 - i1 - Spring 2015 - p59(1) [51-500]

Scooby-Doo Team-Up (Illus. by Brizuela, Dario)
    c BL - v111 - i16 - April 15 2015 - p41(1) [51-500]

Teen Titans Go! Party, Party! (Illus. by Hernandez, Lea)
    c BL - v111 - i16 - April 15 2015 - p41(1) [51-500]

Fischel, Emma - *Witchworld (Illus. by Riddell, Chris)*
    c Sch Lib - v63 - i1 - Spring 2015 - p36(1) [51-500]

Fischer, Bernd - *Heinrich von Kleist and Modernity*
    MLR - v110 - i1 - Jan 2015 - p284-285 [501+]

Fischer, Brodwyn - *Cities from Scratch: Poverty and Informality in Urban Latin America*
    HAHR - v95 - i2 - May 2015 - p374-376 [501+]

Fischer, Chris - *The Beetlebung Farm Cookbook*
    PW - v262 - i18 - May 4 2015 - p113(1) [51-500]

Fischer, Ellen - *If An Elephant Went to School (Illus. by Wood, Laura)*
    c CH Bwatch - Nov 2015 - pNA [51-500]
    c SLJ - v61 - i9 - Sept 2015 - p110(2) [51-500]

Latke, the Lucky Dog (Illus. by Beeke, Tiphanie)
    c HB Guide - v26 - i1 - Spring 2015 - p29(1) [51-500]

Fischer, Jens - *The Art of the Burger: More Than 50 Recipes to Elevate the Burger to Perfection*
    BL - v111 - i19-20 - June 1 2015 - p20(1) [51-500]
    PW - v262 - i22 - June 1 2015 - p55(2) [51-500]

Fischer, Jeremie - *The Night Watchman*
    y KR - August 1 2015 - pNA [51-500]

Wild About Shapes
    c PW - v262 - i49 - Dec 2 2015 - p60(1) [51-500]
    c PW - v262 - i5 - Feb 2 2015 - p60(1) [501+]

Fischer, Joschka - *Scheitert Europa?*
    GSR - v38 - i2 - May 2015 - p472-3 [501+]

Fischer-Lichte, Erika - *Dionysus Resurrected: Perfrmances of Euripides' The Bacchae in a Globalizing World*
    AJP - v136 - i1 - Spring 2015 - p162-166 [501+]

Fischer, Luke - *The Blue Forest (Illus. by Young, Stephanie)*
    c SLJ - v61 - i9 - Sept 2015 - p120(1) [51-500]

Fischer, Michael - *Musik in neuzeitlichen Konfessionskulturen (16. bis 19. Jahrhundert): Raume - Medien - Funktionen*
    Ren Q - v68 - i3 - Fall 2015 - p1090-1091 [501+]

Religion, Nation, Krieg: Der Lutherchoral zwischen Befreiungskriegen und Erstem Weltkrieg
    HNet - Feb 2015 - pNA [501+]

Fischer, Normandie - *Heavy Weather*
    KR - August 1 2015 - pNA [501+]

Fischer, P.J. - *Grandma and Her Chocolate Labrador (Illus. by Nguyen, Cindy)*
    c CH Bwatch - Jan 2015 - pNA [51-500]

Fischer, Paul - *A Kim Jong-Il Production: The Extraordinary True Story of a Kidnapped Filmmaker, His Star Actress, and a Young Dictator's Rise to Power (Read by Park, Stephen). Audiobook Review*
    PW - v262 - i17 - April 27 2015 - p71(1) [51-500]

A Kim Jong-Il Production: The Extraordinary True Story of a Kidnapped Filmmaker, His Star Actress, and a Young Dictator's Rise to Power
    BL - v111 - i11 - Feb 1 2015 - p9(1) [51-500]
    LJ - v140 - i3 - Feb 15 2015 - p112(1) [51-500]
    Mac - v128 - i4 - Feb 2 2015 - p59(1) [51-500]
    NYT - Feb 17 2015 - pC1(L) [51-500]
    Spec - v327 - i9732 - March 7 2015 - p45(1) [501+]

Fischer, Peter S. - *Expendable*
    KR - Nov 15 2015 - pNA [51-500]

Fischer, Rusty - *The Vampire Book of the Month Club*
    y KR - Dec 15 2015 - pNA [51-500]

Fischer-Tine, Harald - *Pidgin-Knowledge: Wissen und Kolonialismus*
    HNet - Feb 2015 - pNA [501+]

Fischler, Stan - *The Handy Hockey Answer Book*
    RVBW - Oct 2015 - pNA [51-500]

Fish, Stanley - *Surprised by Sin: The Reader in Paradise Lost*
    New R - v246 - i11 - Fall 2015 - p66(5) [501+]

Think Again: Contrarian Reflections on Life, Culture, Politics, Religion, Law, and Education
    CHE - v62 - i10 - Nov 6 2015 - pB17(1) [501+]
    KR - Sept 1 2015 - pNA [501+]

Versions of Academic Freedom: From Professionalism to Revolution
    Dis - v62 - i1 - Wntr 2015 - p151(5) [501+]
    TimHES - i2192 - Feb 26 2015 - p47(1) [501+]

Fishbane, Joel - *The Thunder of Giants*
    BL - v111 - i12 - Feb 15 2015 - p42(1) [51-500]
    LJ - v140 - i6 - April 1 2015 - p74(1) [51-500]
    NYTBR - May 3 2015 - p23(1) [51-500]

Fishbaugh, Angela Schmidt - *Angela's Decision: Outsmarting My Cancer Genes and Determining My Fate*
    LJ - v140 - i6 - April 1 2015 - p111(1) [51-500]

Fishel, Anne K. - *Home for Dinner: Mixing Food, Fun, and Conversation for a Happier Family and Healthier Kids*
    LJ - v140 - i3 - Feb 15 2015 - p81(3) [501+]

Fisher, Alexander J. - *Music, Piety, and Propaganda: The Soundscapes of Counter-Reformation Bavaria*
    CEH - v48 - i2 - June 2015 - p252-253 [501+]
    Ren Q - v68 - i1 - Spring 2015 - p360-361 [501+]
    Six Ct J - v46 - i1 - Spring 2015 - p218-219 [501+]

Fisher, Catherine - *At the World's End*
    y Sch Lib - v63 - i4 - Winter 2015 - p244(1) [51-500]

Circle of Stones
    y HB Guide - v26 - i1 - Spring 2015 - p106(1) [51-500]

The Door in the Moon
    y BL - v111 - i9-10 - Jan 1 2015 - p64(1) [51-500]
    y BL - v111 - i11 - Feb 1 2015 - p47(1) [51-500]
    y CCB-B - v68 - i9 - May 2015 - p445(1) [51-500]
    y KR - Jan 15 2015 - pNA [51-500]
        SLJ - v61 - i4 - April 2015 - p174(1) [51-500]
    y VOYA - v37 - i6 - Feb 2015 - p75(1) [51-500]

Fisher, David - *Cool Jump-Rope Tricks You Can Do!*
  c CH Bwatch - Feb 2015 - pNA [51-500]
Morality and War: Can War Be Just in the Twenty-First Century?
  NWCR - v68 - i4 - Autumn 2015 - p124(3) [501+]
Fisher, Donatella - *The Tradition of the Actor-Author in Italian Theatre*
  MLR - v110 - i3 - July 2015 - p885-887 [501+]
Fisher, Helen - *Anatomy of Love: A Natural History of Mating, Marriage, and Why We Stray*
  LJ - v140 - i20 - Dec 1 2015 - p120(1) [51-500]
  PW - v262 - i42 - Oct 19 2015 - p73(1) [51-500]
Fisher, Jaimey - *Generic Histories of German Cinema: Genre and Its Deviations*
  GSR - v38 - i3 - Oct 2015 - p682-684 [501+]
Fisher, James - *Historical Dictionary of American Theater: Beginnings*
  BL - v112 - i5 - Nov 1 2015 - p26(1) [51-500]
  LJ - v140 - i12 - July 1 2015 - p110(1) [51-500]
Fisher, James T. - *The Catholic Studies Reader*
  CHR - v101 - i2 - Spring 2015 - p390(2) [501+]
Fisher, Jessica - *Good Cheap Eats: Dinner in 30 Minutes (or Less!).*
  BL - v112 - i3 - Oct 1 2015 - p16(1) [51-500]
  LJ - v140 - i17 - Oct 15 2015 - p108(1) [51-500]
Good Cheap Eats: Everyday Dinners and Fantastic Feasts for $10 (or Less).
  Bwatch - Jan 2015 - pNA [51-500]
Fisher, Julie A. - *Ninigret, Sachem of the Niantics and Narragansetts: Diplomacy, War, and the Balance of Power in Seventeenth-Century New England and Indian Country*
  AHR - v120 - i2 - April 2015 - p608-609 [501+]
  JAH - v102 - i1 - June 2015 - p223-224 [501+]
Fisher, M.F.K. - *The Theoretical Foot*
  KR - Dec 15 2015 - pNA [51-500]
Fisher, Mark - *Ghosts of My Life: Writings on Depression, Hauntology and Lost Futures*
  TimHES - i2216 - August 13 2015 - p43(1) [501+]
Fisher, Melissa - *Wall Street Women*
  JWH - v27 - i3 - Fall 2015 - p176(11) [501+]
Fisher, Sam - *Scare Scape (Illus. by Bosma, Sam)*
  c Res Links - v20 - i5 - June 2015 - p10(1) [51-500]
Scare Scape: The Midnight Door
  y HB Guide - v26 - i2 - Fall 2015 - p81(1) [51-500]
Fisher, Suzanne Woods - *Anna's Crossing*
  BL - v111 - i14 - March 15 2015 - p49(1) [51-500]
  PW - v262 - i2 - Jan 12 2015 - p44(1) [51-500]
  VOYA - v38 - i1 - April 2015 - p59(1) [51-500]
Fisher, Teri Lyn - *The Perfect Egg: A Fresh Take on Recipes for Morning, Noon, and Night.*
  PW - v262 - i1 - Jan 5 2015 - p66(2) [51-500]
Fisher, Valorie - *I Can Do It Myself (Illus. by Fisher, Valorie)*
  c HB Guide - v26 - i1 - Spring 2015 - p9(1) [51-500]
Fishkin, Shelley Fisher - *Writing America: Literary Landmarks from Walden Pond to Wounded Knee*
  PW - v262 - i32 - August 10 2015 - p47(1) [51-500]
  RVBW - Oct 2015 - pNA [501+]
Fishman, Boris - *Don't Let My Baby Do Rodeo*
  KR - Jan 1 2016 - pNA [501+]
  LJ - v140 - i20 - Dec 1 2015 - p90(1) [51-500]
A Replacement Life
  NYTBR - Feb 1 2015 - p24(L) [501+]
Fishman, Charles - *A Curious Mind: The Secret to a Bigger Life*
  BL - v111 - i14 - March 15 2015 - p28(1) [51-500]
Fishman, Lisa - *24 Pages and Other Poems*
  PW - v262 - i11 - March 16 2015 - p60(1) [51-500]
Fishman, Loren M. - *Trust: The Spiritual Impulse After Darwin*
  KR - Feb 1 2015 - pNA [501+]
Fishman, Seth - *The Dark Water*
  KR - Jan 15 2015 - pNA [51-500]
  y BL - v111 - i15 - April 1 2015 - p64(1) [51-500]
  y HB Guide - v26 - i2 - Fall 2015 - p118(1) [51-500]
  y VOYA - v38 - i1 - April 2015 - p77(1) [51-500]
Fishwick, Duncan - *Cult Places and Cult Personnel in the Roman Empire*
  Class R - v65 - i2 - Oct 2015 - p583-584 [501+]
Fiske, Alan Page - *Virtuous Violence: Hurting and Killing To Create, Sustain, End, and Honor Social Relationships*
  LJ - v140 - i1 - July 1 2015 - p99(1) [51-500]
  TimHES - i2184 - Jan 1 2015 - p64(1) [501+]
Fiske, Susan T. - *Envy Up, Scorn Down: How Status Divides Us*
  CS - v44 - i2 - March 2015 - p196-197 [501+]

Fisman, Karen - *Nonna's Hanukkah Surprise (Illus. by Aviles, Martha)*
  c BL - v112 - i4 - Oct 15 2015 - p49(1) [51 500]
  c KR - Sept 1 2015 - pNA [51-500]
  c PW - v262 - i37 - Sept 14 2015 - p68(1) [51-500]
  c SLJ - v61 - i10 - Oct 2015 - p63(1) [51-500]
Fiss, Owen - *A War Like No Other: The Constitution in a Time of Terror*
  LJ - v140 - i10 - June 1 2015 - p117(1) [51-500]
  NYRB - v62 - i13 - August 13 2015 - p18(3) [501+]
  KR - March 15 2015 - pNA [51-500]
Fitter, Chris - *Radical Shakespeare: Politics and Stagecraft in the Early Career*
  MP - v113 - i1 - August 2015 - pE26(4) [501+]
Fitts, Robert K. - *Mashi: The Unfulfilled Baseball Dreams of Masanori Murakami, the First Japanese Major Leaguer*
  LJ - v140 - i5 - March 15 2015 - p111(1) [501+]
Fitts, Ruth - *Australia to Zimbabwe: A Rhyming Romp around the World to 24 Countries*
  c CH Bwatch - Oct 2015 - pNA [51-500]
  c SLJ - v61 - i12 - Dec 2015 - p144(1) [51-500]
  y VOYA - v38 - i5 - Dec 2015 - p81(1) [51-500]
Fitzell, Philip - *On the Brink: A Trio of Genres*
  PW - v262 - i29 - July 20 2015 - p173(1) [51-500]
Fitzgerald, Adam - *The Late Parade: Poems*
  NYTBR - Feb 15 2015 - p28(L) [501+]
FitzGerald, David Scott - *Culling the Masses: The Democratic Origins of Racist Immigration Policy in the Americas*
  AHR - v120 - i3 - June 2015 - p984-985 [501+]
  AJS - v121 - i2 - Sept 2015 - p627(3) [501+]
  CS - v44 - i6 - Nov 2015 - p764-766 [501+]
  HAHR - v95 - i4 - Nov 2015 - p719-721 [501+]
Fitzgerald, F. Scott - *The Cambridge Edition of the Works of F. Scott Fitzgerald, 14 vols.*
  TLS - i5859 - July 17 2015 - p10(2) [501+]
Fitzgerald, Isaac - *Pen and Ink: Tattoos and the Stories Behind Them*
  Bwatch - Feb 2015 - pNA [51-500]
FitzGerald, Jennifer - *Helen Waddell and Maude Clarke: Irishwomen, Friends, and Scholars*
  Med R - Jan 2015 - pNA [501+]
Helen Waddell Reassessed: New Readings
  Med R - Jan 2015 - pNA [501+]
Fitzgerald, John M. - *Favorite Bedtime Stories*
  WLT - v89 - i1 - Jan-Feb 2015 - p74(1) [501+]
Fitzgerald, Laura Marx - *Under the Egg (Read by Almasy, Jessica). Audiobook Review*
  c BL - v112 - i1 - Sept 1 2015 - p143(1) [51-500]
  c PW - v262 - i35 - August 31 2015 - p85(2) [51-500]
  c SLJ - v61 - i8 - August 2015 - p49(1) [51-500]
Fitzgerald, Michael J. - *Fracking Justice*
  KR - Oct 1 2015 - pNA [51-500]
Fitzgerald, Robert - *The Odyssey. Audiobook Review*
  LJ - v140 - i2 - Feb 1 2015 - p45(1) [51-500]
Fitzgerald, Ruth - *Emily Sparkes and the Friendship Fiasco*
  y Sch Lib - v63 - i1 - Spring 2015 - p36(1) [51-500]
Fitzgerald, Theresa R. - *Dictionary for Kids: The Essential Guide to Math Terms, 4th ed.*
  c SLJ - v61 - i6 - June 2015 - p70(2) [51-500]
Fitzgerald, William - *How to Read a Latin Poem: If You Can't Read Latin Yet*
  Sew R - v123 - i2 - Spring 2015 - p350-357 [501+]
FitzGibbon, Brian - *Butterflies in November*
  NY - v91 - i5 - March 23 2015 - p91 [501+]
FitzHenry, Amy - *Cold Feet*
  LJ - v140 - i15 - Sept 15 2015 - p67(1) [51-500]
Fitzjerrell, Karen Casey - *Forgiving Effie Beck*
  KR - August 15 2015 - pNA [51-500]
Fitzpatrick, Becca - *Black Ice*
  y HB Guide - v26 - i1 - Spring 2015 - p107(1) [51-500]
Dangerous Lies
  y BL - v112 - i2 - Sept 15 2015 - p70(1) [51-500]
  y KR - Sept 1 2015 - pNA [51-500]
  y PW - v262 - i35 - August 31 2015 - p95(1) [51-500]
  y SLJ - v61 - i9 - Sept 2015 - p164(1) [51-500]
  y VOYA - v38 - i5 - Dec 2015 - p56(1) [51-500]
Fitzpatrick, Coeli - *Muhammad in History, Thought, and Culture: An Encyclopedia of the Prophet of God*
  R&USQ - v54 - i4 - Summer 2015 - p82(2) [501+]

Fitzpatrick, Huntley - *The Boy Most Likely To (Read by Andrews, MacLeod). Audiobook Review*
  y SLJ - v61 - i12 - Dec 2015 - p78(1) [51-500]
The Boy Most Likely To
  y VOYA - v38 - i4 - Oct 2015 - p50(2) [51-500]
  y SLJ - v61 - i10 - Oct 2015 - p110(1) [51-500]
What I Thought was True (Read by Spencer, Erin). Audiobook Review
  y SLJ - v61 - i7 - July 2015 - p49(1) [51-500]
Fitzpatrick, Kevin C. - *The Algonquin Round Table New York: A Historical Guide*
  NYT - Feb 8 2015 - p7(L) [501+]
FitzPatrick, Kristin - *My Pulse is an Earthquake*
  KR - July 1 2015 - pNA [51-500]
Fitzpatrick, Matthew P. - *Purging the Empire: Mass Expulsions in Germany, 1871-1914*
  TLS - i5869 - Sept 25 2015 - p25(1) [501+]
Fitzpatrick, Melody - *On a Slippery Slope*
  c KR - Dec 15 2015 - pNA [51-500]
Operation Josh Taylor
  c KR - August 15 2015 - pNA [51-500]
  c Res Links - v21 - i1 - Oct 2015 - p14(1) [51-500]
Fitzpatrick, Richard - *Plasma Physics: An Introduction*
  Phys Today - v68 - i7 - July 2015 - p48-1 [501+]
Fitzpatrick, Sheila - *On Stalin's Team: The Years of Living Dangerously in Soviet Politics*
  KR - August 1 2015 - pNA [501+]
  LJ - v140 - i14 - Sept 1 2015 - p116(2) [51-500]
  NYRB - v62 - i19 - Dec 3 2015 - p69(2) [501+]
  TimHES - i2227 - Oct 29 2015 - p46-47 [501+]
A Spy in the Archive: A Memoir of Cold War Russia
  Slav R - v74 - i1 - Spring 2015 - p195-196 [501+]
Fitzpatrick, Tony - *Dime Stories*
  BL - v112 - i1 - Sept 1 2015 - p26(1) [51-500]
FitzRoy, Charles - *The Rape of Europa: The Intriguing History of Titian's Masterpiece*
  KR - April 1 2015 - pNA [51-500]
  NS - v144 - i5279 - Sept 11 2015 - p40(2) [501+]
FitzSimmons, David - *Curious Critters: Marine (Illus. by FitzSimmons, David)*
  c SLJ - v61 - i4 - April 2015 - p178(1) [51-500]
  c BL - v111 - i17 - May 1 2015 - p82(1) [51-500]
  c PW - v262 - i49 - Dec 2 2015 - p44(2) [51-500]
Curious Critters: Michigan (Illus. by FitzSimmons, David)
  c PW - v262 - i31 - August 3 2015 - p58(2) [51-500]
Fitzsimmons, Jim - *The Snowbirds*
  c Sch Lib - v63 - i2 - Summer 2015 - p104(1) [51-500]
FitzSimmons, Matthew - *The Short Drop*
  KR - Oct 1 2015 - pNA [51-500]
Fitzsimons, Eleanor - *Wilde's Women: How Oscar Wilde Was Shaped by the Women of His Life*
  KR - Oct 1 2015 - pNA [51-500]
  LJ - v140 - i19 - Nov 15 2015 - p84(1) [51-500]
FitzSimons, Peter - *Gallipoli*
  NS - v144 - i5255 - March 27 2015 - p64(3) [501+]
Fixico, Donald L. - *Call for Change: The Medicine Way of American Indian History, Ethos, and Reality*
  HNet - Jan 2015 - pNA [501+]
  PHR - v84 - i1 - Feb 2015 - p122(2) [501+]
Indian Resilience and Rebuilding: Indigenous Nations in the Modern American West
  AHR - v120 - i2 - April 2015 - p647-648 [501+]
  Am Ind CRJ - v39 - i1 - Wntr 2015 - p122-125 [501+]
Fixmer, Elizabeth - *Down from the Mountain*
  y HB Guide - v26 - i2 - Fall 2015 - p118(1) [51-500]
  y KR - Jan 15 2015 - pNA [51-500]
  y PW - v262 - i4 - Jan 26 2015 - p173(1) [51-500]
  y SLJ - v61 - i2 - Feb 2015 - p100(1) [51-500]
  y VOYA - v38 - i1 - April 2015 - p59(1) [51-500]
Fjestad, S.P. - *Blue Book of Gun Values, 36th ed.*
  Bwatch - Sept 2015 - pNA [51-500]
Flacker, Marilyn - *Diaspo/Renga*
  WLT - v89 - i2 - March-April 2015 - p63(1) [51-500]
Fladmark, C.R. - *The Gatekeeper's Son*
  KR - March 1 2015 - pNA [51-500]
Flaherty, Michael G. - *The Textures of Time: Agency and Temporal Experience*
  SF - v94 - i2 - Dec 2015 - pNA [501+]
Flake, Emily - *Mama Tried*
  KR - July 15 2015 - pNA [501+]
Flake, Sharon G. - *Unstoppable Octobia May (Read by Turpin, Bahni). Audiobook Review*
  c BL - v111 - i14 - March 15 2015 - p88(1) [51-500]
  c HB - v91 - i2 - March-April 2015 - p128(2) [51-500]

Unstoppable Octobia May
   c HB Guide - v26 - i1 - Spring 2015 - p76(1) [51-500]

Flammarion, Michel Houllebecq - *Soumission*
   Nat Post - v17 - i86 - Feb 7 2015 - pWP11(1) [501+]

Flammer, Lawrence - *Science Surprises: Exploring the Nature of Science*
   y Sci Teach - v82 - i5 - Summer 2015 - p71 [51-500]

Flanagan, Constance A. - *Teenage Citizens: The Political Theories of the Young*
   CS - v44 - i1 - Jan 2015 - p59-61 [501+]

Flanagan, Damian - *The Tower of London*
   TLS - i5855 - June 19 2015 - p16(1) [501+]
Yukio Mishima
   G&L Rev W - v22 - i4 - July-August 2015 - p32(2) [501+]
   TLS - i5864-5865 - August 21 2015 - p35(1) [501+]

Flanagan, Joe - *Lesser Evils*
   KR - Dec 15 2015 - pNA [51-500]

Flanagan, John - *Ranger's Apprentice: The Early Years*
   c SLJ - v61 - i9 - Sept 2015 - p157(2) [51-500]
Scorpion Mountain
   y HB Guide - v26 - i2 - Fall 2015 - p81(1) [51-500]
The Tournament at Gorlan
   c BL - v112 - i3 - Oct 1 2015 - p80(1) [51-500]
   c KR - August 15 2015 - pNA [51-500]
   y VOYA - v38 - i4 - Oct 2015 - p69(1) [51-500]

Flanagan, Richard - *The Narrow Road to the Deep North*
   NYTBR - May 10 2015 - p36(L) [501+]

Flanagan, Victoria - *Technology and Identity in Young Adult Fiction: The Posthuman Subject*
   Bkbird - v53 - i2 - Spring 2015 - p84(2) [501+]

Flanders, Jefferson - *The Boston Trader*
   KR - June 1 2015 - pNA [501+]
The Republic of Virtue
   KR - April 1 2015 - pNA [501+]

Flanders, Judith - *A Bed of Scorpions*
   KR - Jan 1 2016 - pNA [51-500]
The Making of Home: The 500-Year Story of How Our Houses Became Our Homes
   BL - v112 - i1 - Sept 1 2015 - p18(2) [51-500]
   CSM - Sept 9 2015 - pNA [501+]
   HT - v65 - i2 - Feb 2015 - p65(1) [501+]
   KR - June 1 2015 - pNA [501+]
   LJ - v140 - i11 - June 15 2015 - p97(1) [51-500]
   NYTBR - Sept 13 2015 - p25(L) [501+]
   PW - v262 - i26 - June 29 2015 - p55(2) [51-500]
A Murder of Magpies (Read by Duerden, Susan). Audiobook Review
   BL - v111 - i17 - May 1 2015 - p59(1) [51-500]
   PW - v262 - i17 - April 27 2015 - p70(1) [51-500]
A Murder of Magpies
   BL - v111 - i9-10 - Jan 1 2015 - p48(1) [51-500]
   KR - Jan 1 2015 - pNA [51-500]

Flango, Victor E. - *Reimagining Courts: A Design for the Twenty-First Century*
   Law&PolBR - v25 - i3 - March 2015 - p36(4) [501+]

Flannery, Mary C. - *The Culture of Inquisition in Medieval England*
   Specu - v90 - i2 - April 2015 - p535-537 [501+]

Flannery, Tim - *Atmosphere of Hope: Searching for Solutions to the Climate Crisis*
   BL - v112 - i2 - Sept 15 2015 - p4(2) [51-500]
   KR - August 1 2015 - pNA [501+]
   LJ - v140 - i16 - Oct 1 2015 - p103(2) [51-500]
The Mystery of the Venus Island Fetish
   KR - Dec 1 2015 - pNA [501+]
   PW - v262 - i52 - Dec 21 2015 - p132(1) [51-500]

Flasar, Milena Michiko - *I Called Him Necktie*
   TLS - i5839 - Feb 27 2015 - p20(1) [501+]

Flassbeck, Heiner - *Against the Troika: Crisis and Austerity in the Eurozone*
   TimHES - i2193 - March 5 2015 - p50(1) [501+]

Flatt, Lizann - *How to Write Realistic Fiction*
   c CH Bwatch - April 2015 - pNA [51-500]
Immigration
   c BL - v111 - i15 - April 1 2015 - p61(1) [51-500]
   c Res Links - v20 - i5 - June 2015 - p34(1) [501+]

Flavin, Susan - *Consumption and Culture in Sixteenth-Century Ireland: Saffron, Stockings and Silk*
   Six Ct J - v46 - i3 - Fall 2015 - p699-700 [501+]

Flavin, Teresa - *Jet Black Heart*
   y Sch Lib - v63 - i1 - Spring 2015 - p52(1) [51-500]
The Shadow Lantern
   c HB Guide - v26 - i1 - Spring 2015 - p77(1) [51-500]

Flax, Mike - *A Better Place*
   Roundup M - v22 - i6 - August 2015 - p29(1) [501+]

Flay, Bobby - *Brunch at Bobby's: 140 Recipes for the Best Part of the Weekend*
   BL - v112 - i1 - Sept 1 2015 - p22(2) [51-500]
   PW - v262 - i24 - June 15 2015 - p79(1) [51-500]

Fleagle, John G. - *Primate Adaptation and Evolution*
   QRB - v90 - i3 - Sept 2015 - p335(2) [51-500]

Fleck, Christian - *Etablierung in der Fremde: Vertriebene Wissenschaftler in den USA nach 1933*
   HNet - Sept 2015 - pNA [501+]
A Transatlantic History of the Social Sciences: Robber Barons, the Third Reich and the Invention of Empirical Social Research
   CS - v44 - i3 - May 2015 - p305-314 [501+]

Fleckenstein, Peter - *Anatomy in Diagnostic Imaging, 3d ed.*
   Bwatch - Feb 2015 - pNA [51-500]

Fleegler, Robert L. - *Ellis Island Nation: Immigration Policy and American Identity in the Twentieth Century*
   Historian - v77 - i3 - Fall 2015 - p555(2) [501+]

Fleischer-Camp, Dean - *Marcel the Shell: The Most Surprised I've Ever Been (Illus. by Lind, Amy)*
   c HB Guide - v26 - i1 - Spring 2015 - p29(1) [51-500]

Fleischer, Jeff - *Rockin' the Boat: 50 Iconic Rebels and Revolutionaries-from Joan of Arc to Malcolm X*
   y BL - v111 - i19-20 - June 1 2015 - p70(1) [51-500]
   y SLJ - v61 - i3 - March 2015 - p176(1) [51-500]
Rockin' the Boat
   c KR - Jan 1 2015 - pNA [51-500]

Fleischman, Carol Chiodo - *Nadine, My Funny and Trusty Guide Dog (Illus. by Ford, Stephanie)*
   c CH Bwatch - July 2015 - pNA [51-500]
   c HB Guide - v26 - i2 - Fall 2015 - p34(1) [51-500]

Fleischman, Paul - *Eyes Wide Open: Going behind the Environmental Headlines (Read by Parks, Tom). Audiobook Review*
   y SLJ - v61 - i2 - Feb 2015 - p51(1) [51-500]
Eyes Wide Open: Going behind the Environmental Headlines
   c BL - v111 - i12 - Feb 15 2015 - p76(1) [501+]
   y HB Guide - v26 - i1 - Spring 2015 - p140(1) [51-500]

Fleisher, Mark S. - *Living Black: Social Life in an African American Neighborhood*
   KR - Sept 1 2015 - pNA [501+]

Fleming, Bryn - *Jasper and Willie: Wildfire*
   c CH Bwatch - Nov 2015 - pNA [51-500]

Fleming, Candace - *Bulldozer's Big Day (Illus. by Rohmann, Eric)*
   c BL - v111 - i14 - March 15 2015 - p77(1) [51-500]
   c CCB-B - v69 - i1 - Sept 2015 - p21(1) [51-500]
   c CH Bwatch - July 2015 - pNA [51-500]
   c HB - v91 - i3 - May-June 2015 - p87(1) [51-500]
   c HB Guide - v26 - i2 - Fall 2015 - p11(1) [51-500]
   c KR - March 15 2015 - pNA [51-500]
   c PW - v262 - i13 - March 30 2015 - p73(2) [51-500]
   SLJ - v61 - i3 - March 2015 - p116(1) [51-500]
The Family Romanov: Murder, Rebellion, and the Fall of Imperial Russia
   y BL - v111 - i19-20 - June 1 2015 - p86(2) [51-500]
   c BL - v111 - i9-10 - Jan 1 2015 - pS4(8) [501+]
   y HB Guide - v26 - i1 - Spring 2015 - p202(1) [51-500]
Muncha! Muncha! Muncha! (Illus. by Karas, G. Brian)
   c BL - v112 - i4 - Oct 15 2015 - p53(1) [51-500]

Fleming, Colin M. - *Clausewitz's Timeless Trinity: A Framework for Modern War*
   APJ - v29 - i3 - May-June 2015 - p89(2) [501+]

Fleming, Denise - *Go, Shapes, Go! (Illus. by Fleming, Denise)*
   c HB Guide - v26 - i1 - Spring 2015 - p9(1) [51-500]

Fleming, Fergus - *The Man with the Golden Typewriter: Ian Fleming's James Bond Letters*
   KR - Oct 15 2015 - pNA [501+]
   LJ - v140 - i20 - Dec 1 2015 - p101(1) [51-500]

Fleming, Ian - *Chitty-Chitty Bang-Bang: The Magical Car (Illus. by Burningham, John)*
   c HB Guide - v26 - i1 - Spring 2015 - p77(1) [51-500]
The Man with the Golden Typewriter: Ian Fleming's James Bond Letters
   NYT - Nov 24 2015 - pC1(L) [501+]
Moonraker (Read by Nighy, Bill). Audiobook Review
   BL - v111 - i9-10 - Jan 1 2015 - p116(1) [51-500]
   BL - v111 - i14 - March 15 2015 - p23(2) [51-500]

Fleming, John V. - *The Dark Side of the Enlightenment: Wizards, Alchemists, and Spiritual Seekers in the Age of Reason*
   Historian - v77 - i2 - Summer 2015 - p384(2) [501+]

Fleming, Michael - *Communism, Nationalism and Ethnicity in Poland, 1944-1950*
   HNet - May 2015 - pNA [501+]

Fleming, Peter - *The Mythology of Work: How Capitalism Persists Despite Itself*
   TimHES - i2218 - August 27 2015 - p44(1) [501+]
Resisting Work: The Corporatization of Life and Its Discontents
   CS - v44 - i1 - Jan 2015 - p136-137 [501+]
Would I Like Jesus? A Casual Walk through the Life of Jesus
   RVBW - August 2015 - pNA [51-500]

Fleming, Thomas - *A Disease in the Public Mind: A New Understanding of Why We Fought the Civil War*
   Historian - v77 - i1 - Spring 2015 - p121(2) [501+]
The Great Divide: The Conflict between Washington and Jefferson That Defined a Nation
   BL - v111 - i14 - March 15 2015 - p41(1) [51-500]
   Bwatch - May 2015 - pNA [51-500]

Flemming, Gregory N. - *At the Point of a Cutlass: The Pirate Capture, Bold Escape, and Lonely Exile of Philip Ashton*
   HNet - Sept 2015 - pNA(NA) [501+]

Flemming, LeRoy - *Soul Splitting, vol. 1*
   SPBW - Feb 2015 - pNA [51-500]

Fletcer, Susan - *Alphabet of Dreams*
   y BL - v111 - i16 - April 15 2015 - p58(1) [501+]

Fletcher, Alan J. - *The Presence of Medieval English Literature: Studies at the Interface of History, Author, and Text in a Selection of Middle English Literary Landmarks*
   MLR - v110 - i3 - July 2015 - p804-806 [501+]

Fletcher, Brenden - *The Batgirl of Burnside (Illus. by Tarr, Babs)*
   y BL - v111 - i22 - August 1 2015 - p47(1) [51-500]
   y SLJ - v61 - i6 - June 2015 - p131(1) [51-500]

Fletcher, Charlie - *Dragon Shield*
   c Sch Lib - v63 - i3 - Autumn 2015 - p165(1) [501+]
The Oversight
   BL - v111 - i18 - May 15 2015 - p35(1) [51-500]
Paradox
   PW - v262 - i24 - June 15 2015 - p67(1) [51-500]

Fletcher, Corina - *Small Smaller Smallest (Illus. by Marshall, Natalie)*
   c SLJ - v61 - i7 - July 2015 - p55(1) [51-500]
Up Down Across (Illus. by Marshall, Natalie)
   c KR - July 1 2015 - pNA [51-500]

Fletcher, Jared - *Teen Titans (Illus. by Dodson, Terry)*
   y VOYA - v38 - i2 - June 2015 - p50(2) [501+]

Fletcher, Jennifer - *Teaching Arguments: Rhetorical Comprehension, Critique, and Response*
   Bwatch - August 2015 - pNA [51-500]

Fletcher, John - *Deer*
   Am Bio T - v77 - i4 - April 2015 - p301(2) [501+]
Preaching to Convert: Evangelical Outreach and Performance Activism in a Secular Age
   Theat J - v67 - i1 - March 2015 - p160-162 [501+]

Fletcher, Martin - *The War Reporter*
   KR - August 15 2015 - pNA [501+]

Fletcher, Michael R. - *Beyond Redemption*
   BL - v111 - i18 - May 15 2015 - p33(1) [51-500]
   PW - v262 - i14 - April 6 2015 - p43(1) [501+]

Fletcher, Richard - *Apuleius' Platonism: The Impersonation of Philosophy*
   Class R - v65 - i2 - Oct 2015 - p476-478 [501+]

Fletcher, Robert - *Romancing the Wild: Cultural Dimensions of Ecotourism*
   AJS - v120 - i4 - Jan 2015 - p1280(3) [501+]

Fletcher-Spear, Kristen - *Intellectual Freedom for Teens: A Practical Guide for Young Adult and School Librarians*
   SLJ - v61 - i2 - Feb 2015 - p131(1) [51-500]
   VOYA - v38 - i3 - August 2015 - p92(1) [51-500]

Fletcher, Susan - *A Little in Love*
   y BL - v112 - i2 - Sept 15 2015 - p74(1) [51-500]
   y KR - June 1 2015 - pNA [51-500]
   y SLJ - v61 - i6 - June 2015 - p112(1) [51-500]
   y VOYA - v38 - i3 - August 2015 - p58(2) [51-500]

Fletcher, Willard Allen - *Defiant Diplomat: George Platt Waller, American Consul in Nazi-Occupied Luxembourg, 1939-1941*
   J Mil H - v79 - i2 - April 2015 - p522-524 [501+]

Flett-Giordano, Anne - *Marry, Kiss, Kill*
   BL - v111 - i17 - May 1 2015 - p40(2) [51-500]
   KR - April 15 2015 - pNA [51-500]
   PW - v262 - i16 - April 20 2015 - p57(1) [51-500]
   y SLJ - v61 - i10 - Oct 2015 - p121(1) [51-500]

Fleury-Steiner, Benjamin - *Disposable Heroes: The Betrayal of African American Veterans*
   CS - v44 - i2 - March 2015 - p198-199 [501+]

Flicker, Siggy - *Write Your Own Fairy Tale: The New Rules for Dating, Relationships, and Finding Love on*

Your Terms
    PW - v262 - i31 - August 3 2015 - p54(1) [51-500]
Fliess, Sue - *Books for Me! (Illus. by Laughead, Mike)*
  c HB Guide - v26 - i2 - Fall 2015 - p34(1) [51-500]
Calling All Cars (Illus. by Beise, Sarah)
  c KR - Dec 15 2015 - pNA [51-500]
Flinders, Tim - *Henry David Thoreau: Spiritual and Prophetic Writings*
    Bwatch - August 2015 - pNA [51-500]
Flinn, Alex - *Mirrored*
  y KR - May 15 2015 - pNA [51-500]
  y SLJ - v61 - i6 - June 2015 - p123(1) [51-500]
  y VOYA - v38 - i4 - Oct 2015 - p69(1) [51-500]
Flinn, Kathleen - *Burnt Toast Makes You Sing Good (Read by Campbell, Cassandra). Audiobook Review*
    LJ - v140 - i2 - Feb 1 2015 - p46(1) [51-500]
Flinn, Margaret C. - *The Social Architecture of French Cinema: 1929-1939*
    FS - v69 - i3 - July 2015 - p423-424 [501+]
Flint, Anthony - *Modern Man*
    NY - v90 - i46 - Feb 2 2015 - p65 [51-500]
Flint, Eric - *Castaway Planet: A Crash Course in Survival*
    Bwatch - May 2015 - pNA [51-500]
Grantville Gazette VII
    Bwatch - June 2015 - pNA [51-500]
Flint, Shamini - *Diary of a Basketball Hero (Illus. by Heinrich, Sally)*
  y Magpies - v30 - i1 - March 2015 - p34(1) [501+]
Diary of a Golf Pro (Illus. by Heinrich, Sally)
  y Magpies - v30 - i1 - March 2015 - p34(1) [501+]
Ten
  c Magpies - v30 - i3 - July 2015 - p34(1) [501+]
Flitcroft, Ian - *The Reluctant Cannibals*
    BL - v111 - i18 - May 15 2015 - p24(2) [51-500]
    LJ - v140 - i11 - June 15 2015 - p76(1) [51-500]
Flohr, Miko - *The World of the Fullo: Work, Economy, and Society in Roman Italy*
    Class R - v65 - i2 - Oct 2015 - p531-532 [501+]
Flood, Charles Bracelen - *First to Fly: The Story of the Lafayette Escadrille: The American Heroes Who Flew for France in World War I*
    KR - March 1 2015 - pNA [501+]
Flood, David - *Early Commentaries on the Rule of the Friars Minor, vol. 1: The 1242 Commentary, Hugh of Digne, David of Augsburg, John of Wales*
    Med R - Sept 2015 - pNA [501+]
Flood, Gavin - *The Truth Within: A History of Inwardness in Christianity, Hinduism, and Buddhism*
    IBMR - v39 - i2 - April 2015 - p109(2) [501+]
Florand, Laura - *All for You*
    PW - v262 - i23 - June 8 2015 - p46(1) [51-500]
Florczyk, Piotr - *Los Angeles Sketchbook*
    WLT - v89 - i6 - Nov-Dec 2015 - p67(1) [51-500]
Flore, Jeanne - *Tales and Trials of Love, Concerning Venus's Punishment of Those Who Scorn True Love and Denounce Cupid's Sovereignty: A Bilingual Edition and Study*
    Six Ct J - v46 - i3 - Fall 2015 - p731-733 [501+]
Floreani, Tracy - *Fifties Ethnicities: The Ethnic Novel and Mass Culture at Midcentury*
    JAH - v102 - i2 - Sept 2015 - p609-609 [501+]
Floreen, Tim - *Willful Machines*
  y BL - v111 - i22 - August 1 2015 - p61(1) [51-500]
  y KR - August 1 2015 - pNA [51-500]
  y PW - v262 - i30 - July 27 2015 - p71(1) [51-500]
  y SLJ - v61 - i9 - Sept 2015 - p164(2) [51-500]
Flores, Carlos Nicolas - *Sex as a Political Condition*
    BL - v111 - i19-20 - June 1 2015 - p45(1) [51-500]
Flores, David - *Gift: The Art of David Flores*
    Bwatch - March 2015 - pNA [51-500]
Flores, Edward Orozco - *God's Gangs: Barrio Ministry, Masculinity, and Gang Recovery*
    CS - v44 - i4 - July 2015 - p506-507 [501+]
Flores-Gonzalez, Nilda - *Immigrant Women Workers in the Neoliberal Age*
    CS - v44 - i4 - July 2015 - p507-509 [501+]
Flores, John W. - *Marine Sergeant Freddy Gonzalez, Vietnam War Hero*
    HNet - August 2015 - pNA [501+]
Flores, Ruben - *Backroads Pragmatists: Mexico's Melting Pot and Civil Rights in the United States*
    AHR - v120 - i4 - Oct 2015 - p1503-1504 [501+]
    HAHR - v95 - i2 - May 2015 - p391-392 [501+]
    JAH - v102 - i2 - Sept 2015 - p577-578 [501+]
    WHQ - v46 - i3 - Autumn 2015 - p379-380 [501+]

Florian, Douglas - *How to Draw a Dragon (Illus. by Florian, Douglas)*
  c BL - v111 - i14 - March 15 2015 - p77(1) [51-500]
  c CCB-B - v68 - i10 - June 2015 - p488(2) [51-500]
  c HB - v91 - i2 - March-April 2015 - p76(1) [51-500]
  c HB Guide - v26 - i2 - Fall 2015 - p11(1) [51-500]
  c PW - v262 - i6 - Feb 9 2015 - p65(1) [51-500]
  c SLJ - v61 - i5 - May 2015 - p84(1) [51-500]
Pig Is Big on Books (Illus. by Florian, Douglas)
  c KR - July 15 2015 - pNA [51-500]
  c NYTBR - August 23 2015 - p26(L) [501+]
  c SLJ - v61 - i12 - Dec 2015 - p98(1) [51-500]
The Wonderful Habits of Rabbits (Illus. by Sanchez, Sonia)
  c KR - Dec 1 2015 - pNA [51-500]
  c PW - v262 - i47 - Nov 23 2015 - p67(1) [51-500]
  c SLJ - v61 - i12 - Dec 2015 - p88(2) [51-500]
Floridi, Luciano - *The Ethics of Information*
    Dialogue - v54 - i2 - June 2015 - p402-404 [501+]
The Onlife Manifesto: Being Human in a Hyperconnected Era
    LR - v64 - i4-5 - April-May 2015 - p403-404 [501+]
Florio, Gwen - *Disgraced*
    KR - Dec 15 2015 - pNA [501+]
Flory, Jane - *The Too Little Fire Engine*
  c HB Guide - v26 - i2 - Fall 2015 - p11(1) [51-500]
Flournoy, Angela - *Summoning the Ghosts of Detroit*
    PW - v262 - i2 - Jan 12 2015 - p27(5) [501+]
The Turner House
    PW - v262 - i1 - Jan 5 2015 - p51(1) [51-500]
    BL - v111 - i12 - Feb 15 2015 - p33(1) [51-500]
    CSM - April 30 2015 - pNA [501+]
    Ent W - i1363 - May 15 2015 - p61(1) [501+]
    KR - Feb 15 2015 - pNA [51-500]
    Nation - v301 - i9-10 - August 31 2015 - p43(1) [501+]
    NYTBR - May 3 2015 - p23(L) [501+]
Flower, Amanda - *The Final Reveille*
    BL - v111 - i16 - April 15 2015 - p28(1) [51-500]
    KR - March 1 2015 - pNA [51-500]
    LJ - v140 - i6 - April 1 2015 - p63(3) [51-500]
Flowers, Arthur - *I See the Promised Land: A Life of Martin Luther King Jr. (Illus. by Chitrakar, Manu)*
  c SLJ - v61 - i12 - Dec 2015 - p64(4) [51-500]
Flowers, Graham J. - *Shadow Trails*
    Roundup M - v22 - i3 - Feb 2015 - p26(1) [51-500]
    Roundup M - v22 - i6 - August 2015 - p29(1) [501+]
Flowers, Tamsin - *The Forbidden Fruit*
    PW - v262 - i46 - Nov 16 2015 - p63(1) [51-500]
Floyd, Barbara L. - *The Glass City: Toledo and the Industry That Built It*
    JEH - v75 - i2 - June 2015 - p608-609 [501+]
Floyd, Harry - *Panic: One Man's Struggle with Anxiety*
    PW - v262 - i8 - Feb 23 2015 - p69(1) [51-500]
Fluck, Jason Squire - *Jon Fixx*
    KR - June 1 2015 - pNA [51-500]
Flueckiger, Joyce Burkhalter - *When the World Becomes Female: Guises of a South Indian Goddess*
    HNet - April 2015 - pNA [501+]
Fluhman, J. Spencer - *A Peculiar People: Anti-Mormonism and the Making of Religion in Nineteenth-Century America*
    HNet - April 2015 - pNA [501+]
Fluke, Joanne - *Double Fudge Brownie Murder (Read by Toren, Susan). Audiobook Review*
    PW - v262 - i17 - April 27 2015 - p70(1) [501+]
Double Fudge Brownie Murder
    KR - Jan 15 2015 - pNA [51-500]
    PW - v262 - i4 - Jan 26 2015 - p150(1) [51-500]
Wedding Cake Murder
    KR - Dec 15 2015 - pNA [51-500]
    PW - v262 - i52 - Dec 21 2015 - p130(1) [51-500]
Flusfeder, David - *John the Pupil*
    BL - v111 - i9-10 - Jan 1 2015 - p53(1) [51-500]
    KR - Jan 1 2015 - pNA [51-500]
    NYT - March 26 2015 - pC6(L) [501+]
    PW - v262 - i4 - Jan 26 2015 - p145(1) [51-500]
Flynn, Alex - *The Misshapes: Annihilation Day*
  y SLJ - v61 - i12 - Dec 2015 - p113(1) [51-500]
Flynn, Brendan - *Miguel Cabrera: MVP and Triple Crown Winner*
  c BL - v111 - i19-20 - June 1 2015 - p90(1) [51-500]
Flynn, Gillian - *Gone Girl*
    Lon R Bks - v37 - i17 - Sept 10 2015 - p25(2) [501+]
Flynn, Hazel - *Missions Impossible: Extraordinary Stories of Daring and Courage*
  y VOYA - v37 - i6 - Feb 2015 - p87(1) [51-500]

Flynn, Kevin - *American Sweepstakes: How One Small State Bucked the Church, the Feds, and the Mob to Usher in the Lottery Age*
    LJ - v140 - i16 - Oct 1 2015 - p93(1) [51-500]
Flynn, Laurie Elizabeth - *Firsts*
  y BL - v112 - i6 - Nov 15 2015 - p50(1) [51-500]
  y KR - Oct 15 2015 - pNA [51-500]
  y PW - v262 - i41 - Oct 12 2015 - p70(1) [51-500]
  y SLJ - v61 - i11 - Nov 2015 - p114(1) [51-500]
Flynn, Leontia - *Reading Medbh McGuckian*
    ILS - v35 - i1 - Fall 2015 - p19(2) [51-500]
Flynn, Nick - *My Feelings: Poems*
    BL - v111 - i19-20 - June 1 2015 - p25(1) [51-500]
    NYT - July 9 2015 - pC6(L) [501+]
    PW - v262 - i24 - June 15 2015 - p62(1) [51-500]
Flynn, Riley - *Bessie Coleman*
  c HB Guide - v26 - i1 - Spring 2015 - p192(1) [51-500]
Flynn, Sarah Wassner - *Weird But True! Food: 300 Bite-Sized Facts About Incredible Edibles!*
  c HB Guide - v26 - i2 - Fall 2015 - p190(1) [51-500]
Flynn, Simon - *Sciku: The Wonder of Science - In Haiku!*
  c Sch Lib - v63 - i2 - Summer 2015 - p113(1) [51-500]
Flynn, Thomas R. - *Sartre: A Philosophical Biography*
    Econ - v414 - i8926 - Feb 21 2015 - p82(US) [501+]
    Spec - v327 - i9732 - March 7 2015 - p47(1) [501+]
    TimHES - i2189 - Feb 5 2015 - p57-57 [501+]
Flynn, Vince - *The Survivor*
    PW - v262 - i42 - Oct 19 2015 - p13(1) [51-500]
Fo, Dario - *The Pope's Daughter*
    CSM - August 6 2015 - pNA [501+]
    KR - June 1 2015 - pNA [51-500]
    NYTBR - August 16 2015 - p17(L) [501+]
    TLS - i5868 - Sept 18 2015 - p20(1) [501+]
Foa, Michelle - *Georges Seurat: The Art of Vision*
    LJ - v140 - i17 - Oct 15 2015 - p85(1) [51-500]
Foard, Glenn - *Bosworth 1485: A Battlefield Rediscovered*
    Specu - v90 - i2 - April 2015 - p537-538 [501+]
Fobes, Tracy - *Hard Charger*
    KR - Feb 1 2015 - pNA [501+]
Stowaway: Curse of the Red Pearl
    SPBW - August 2015 - pNA [51-500]
Focht, Eric - *For the Record*
    SPBW - Feb 2015 - pNA [51-500]
Foerster, Thomas - *Norman Tradition and Transcultural Heritage: Exchange of Cultures in the "Norman" Peripheries of Medieval Europe*
    Historian - v77 - i3 - Fall 2015 - p600(3) [501+]
Foertsch, Jacqueline - *Reckoning Day: Race, Place, and the Atom Bomb in Postwar America*
    JSH - v81 - i1 - Feb 2015 - p240(2) [501+]
Fogel, Joshua A. - *Japanese Historiography and the Gold Seal of 57 C.E.: Relic, Text, Object, Fake*
    AHR - v120 - i1 - Feb 2015 - p218-219 [501+]
Maiden Voyage: The Senzaimaru and the Creation of Modern Sino-Japanese Relations
    HNet - Feb 2015 - pNA [501+]
Fogelin, Adrian - *Some Kind of Magic*
  y CH Bwatch - May 2015 - pNA [51-500]
  y HB Guide - v26 - i2 - Fall 2015 - p81(1) [51-500]
  c KR - Feb 15 2015 - pNA [51-500]
  y SLJ - v61 - i3 - March 2015 - p134(2) [51-500]
The Sorta Sisters
  c Teach Lib - v42 - i5 - June 2015 - p47(1) [51-500]
Fogelson, Robert M. - *The Great Rent Wars: New York, 1917-1929*
    BHR - v89 - i2 - Summer 2015 - p386(3) [501+]
Fogerty, John - *Fortunate Son*
    KR - Oct 15 2015 - pNA [51-500]
Fogg, Marnie - *The Dress: 100 Ideas That Changed Fashion Forever*
    LJ - v140 - i5 - March 15 2015 - p102(3) [501+]
Fogle, Bruce - *Barefoot at the Lake: A Boyhood Summer in Cottage Country*
    BL - v111 - i16 - April 15 2015 - p4(1) [51-500]
Barefoot at the Lake: A Memoir of Summer People and Water Creatures
    TLS - i5875 - Nov 6 2015 - p30(2) [501+]
Fogleman, Aaron Spencer - *Two Troubled Souls: An Eighteenth-Century Couple's Spiritual Journey in the Atlantic World*
    AHR - v120 - i2 - April 2015 - p577-578 [501+]
    JSH - v81 - i1 - Feb 2015 - p166(2) [501+]
Fogliano, Julie - *When Green Becomes Tomatoes: Poems for All Seasons (Illus. by Morstad, Julie)*
  c PW - v262 - i52 - Dec 21 2015 - p156(2) [501+]
Foias, Antonia E. - *Ancient Maya Political Dynamics*
    Historian - v77 - i3 - Fall 2015 - p557(2) [501+]

Fojas, Camilla - *Islands of Empire: Pop Culture and U.S. Power*
J Am St - v49 - i2 - May 2015 - p445-446 [501+]
Transnational Crossroads: Remapping the Americas and the Pacific
PHR - v84 - i1 - Feb 2015 - p127(2) [501+]
Fokus Handwerk: Aktuelle Perspektiven einer Interdisziplinaren Handwerksforschung. Themen, Fragestellungen, Quellen und Methoden
HNet - July 2015 - pNA [501+]
Folau, Israel - *Chance of a Lifetime*
c Magpies - v30 - i3 - July 2015 - p36(1) [501+]
Folbre, Nancy - *For Love and Money: Care Provision in the United States*
CS - v44 - i2 - March 2015 - p199-201 [501+]
Foley, Bridget - *Hugo & Rose*
BL - v111 - i16 - April 15 2015 - p24(1) [501+]
KR - March 15 2015 - pNA [501+]
Foley, Catherine E. - *Step Dancing in Ireland: Culture and History*
Dance RJ - v47 - i2 - August 2015 - p94-3 [501+]
Foley, Edward - *Theological Reflection Across Religious Traditions: The Turn to Reflective Believing*
CC - v132 - i21 - Oct 14 2015 - p34(2) [501+]
Foley, Elizabeth - *Shakespeare Basics for Grown-Ups: Everything You Need to Know About the Bard*
LJ - v140 - i7 - April 15 2015 - p84(2) [51-500]
Foley, Janice R. - *Unions, Equity and the Path to Renewal*
CWS - v30 - i2-3 - Fall-Winter 2015 - p133(2) [501+]
Foley, Jessie Ann - *The Carnival at Bray (Read by Moon, Erin).* Audiobook Review
y SLJ - v61 - i11 - Nov 2015 - p72(1) [51-500]
The Carnival at Bray
y Teach Lib - v42 - i4 - April 2015 - p23(1) [51-500]
Foley, Lucy - *The Book of Lost and Found*
BL - v111 - i21 - July 1 2015 - p29(1) [51-500]
Foley, Michael P. - *Drinking with the Saints: The Sinner's Guide to a Holy Happy Hour*
RVBW - August 2015 - pNA [51-500]
Foley, Michael Stewart - *Front Porch Politics: The Forgotten Heyday of American Activism in the 1970s and 1980s*
RAH - v43 - i1 - March 2015 - p134-142 [501+]
Foley, Neil - *Mexicans in the Making of America*
Am St - v54 - i1 - Spring 2015 - p164-2 [501+]
NYRB - v62 - i19 - Dec 3 2015 - p8(3) [501+]
Foley, Patrick - *Missionary Bishop: Jean-Marie Odin in Galveston and New Orleans*
CHR - v101 - i2 - Spring 2015 - p391(2) [501+]
Foley, Patrick C. - *Tillie and P-Trap the Plumber (Illus. by Chamness, Julia)*
c KR - March 1 2015 - pNA [51-500]
Folger, Robert - *Writing as Poaching: Interpellation and Self-Fashioning in Colonial Relaciones de meritos y servicios*
Six Ct J - v46 - i1 - Spring 2015 - p166-167 [501+]
Foligno, Angela of - *Memoriale: Edizione critica*
Specu - v90 - i4 - Oct 2015 - p1080-1082 [501+]
Follett, Ross C. - *Beebear Board (Illus. by Sievers, Lee)*
c SLJ - v61 - i7 - July 2015 - p55(1) [51-500]
Follis, Edward - *The Dark Art: My Undercover Life in Global Narco-Terrorism*
NS - v144 - i5246 - Jan 23 2015 - p40(1) [501+]
NY - v91 - i13 - May 18 2015 - p93 [501+]
Follis, Karolina S. - *Building Fortress Europe: The Polish-Ukrainian Frontier*
JRAI - v21 - i3 - Sept 2015 - p703(2) [501+]
Follmer, Moritz - *Individuality and Modernity in Berlin: Self and Society from Weimar to the Wall*
JMH - v87 - i1 - March 2015 - p228(2) [501+]
Folman, Ari - *The Congress*
MFSF - v128 - i1-2 - Jan-Feb 2015 - p150(6) [501+]
Folsom, Raphael Brewster - *The Yaquis and the Empire: Violence, Spanish Imperial Power, and Native Resilience in Colonial Mexico*
Ams - v72 - i3 - July 2015 - p492(3) [501+]
HAHR - v95 - i4 - Nov 2015 - p676-678 [501+]
Fonclare, Guillaume de - *Inside My Own Skin*
WLT - v89 - i2 - March-April 2015 - p61(1) [51-500]
Fonder, Mark - *Patrick Conway and His Famous Band*
M Ed J - v102 - i1 - Sept 2015 - p22(1) [501+]
Fondin, Michelle S. - *The Wheel of Healing with Ayurveda: An Easy Guide to a Healthy Lifestyle*
BL - v111 - i18 - May 15 2015 - p9(1) [51-500]
RVBW - July 2015 - pNA [501+]
Fondren, Kristi M. - *Walking on the Wild Side: Long-Distance Hiking on the Appalachian Trail*
LJ - v140 - i19 - Nov 15 2015 - p89(1) [51-500]

Foner, Eric - *Gateway to Freedom: The Hidden History of the Underground Railroad (Read by Jackson, J.D.).* Audiobook Review
BL - v111 - i16 - April 15 2015 - p61(1) [51-500]
PW - v262 - i12 - March 23 2015 - p72(1) [51-500]
Gateway to Freedom: The Hidden History of the Underground Railroad
AHR - v120 - i4 - Oct 2015 - p1436-1439 [501+]
AS - v84 - i1 - Wntr 2015 - p114(3) [501+]
Atl - v315 - i2 - March 2015 - p48(3) [501+]
BL - v111 - i9-10 - Jan 1 2015 - p34(1) [51-500]
Bwatch - May 2015 - pNA [51-500]
CC - v132 - i9 - April 29 2015 - p57(1) [501+]
CSM - Jan 19 2015 - pNA [51-500]
Nation - v300 - i19 - May 11 2015 - p33(1) [501+]
NYRB - v62 - i10 - June 4 2015 - p69(2) [501+]
NYT - Jan 15 2015 - pC1(L) [501+]
NYT - Jan 25 2015 - p3(L) [501+]
NYT - April 19 2015 - p2(L) [501+]
NYTBR - Feb 1 2015 - p11(L) [501+]
Foner, Nancy - *New York and Amsterdam: Immigration and the New Urban Landscape*
CS - v44 - i5 - Sept 2015 - p661-662 [501+]
ERS - v38 - i8 - August 2015 - p1449(3) [501+]
One Out of Three: Immigrant New York in the Twenty-First Century
CS - v44 - i4 - July 2015 - p509-510 [501+]
ERS - v38 - i3 - March 2015 - p485(3) [501+]
Fong, Kevin - *Extreme Medicine: How Exploration Transformed Medicine in the Twentieth Century*
NYTBR - May 24 2015 - p28(L) [501+]
Fong, Mei - *One Child*
KR - Dec 15 2015 - pNA [501+]
Fontaine, Laurence - *The Moral Economy: Poverty, Credit, and Trust in Early Modern Europe*
AHR - v120 - i3 - June 2015 - p1103-1104 [501+]
Six Ct J - v46 - i3 - Fall 2015 - p720-722 [501+]
Fontaine, Michael - *The Oxford Handbook of Greek and Roman Comedy*
Col Lit - v42 - i3 - Summer 2015 - p525(3) [501+]
Class R - v65 - i2 - Oct 2015 - p361-362 [501+]
Fontana, Johannes - *"Liber instrumentorum iconographicus": Ein illustriertes Maschinenbuch*
Specu - v90 - i1 - Jan 2015 - p248-249 [501+]
Fontana, Paolo - *Riti proibiti: Liturgia e inquisizione nella Francia del Settecento*
HER - v130 - i543 - April 2015 - p459(2) [501+]
Fontane, Theodor - *Die Reisetagebucher*
MLR - v110 - i1 - Jan 2015 - p291-292 [501+]
Fontani, Marco - *The Lost Elements: The Periodic Table's Shadow Side*
TimHES - i2191 - Feb 19 2015 - p52(1) [501+]
Fontes, Lisa Aronson - *Invisible Chains: Overcoming Coercive Control in Your Intimate Relationship*
LJ - v140 - i6 - April 1 2015 - p107(1) [51-500]
Fontichiaro, Kristin - *Hacking Fashion: Fleece*
c BL - v112 - i7 - Dec 1 2015 - p42(1) [51-500]
Fontinel-Gibran, R.J. - *Poetic License*
KR - Jan 1 2015 - pNA [501+]
Foose, Martha - *Oh Gussie! Cooking and Visiting in Kimberly's Southern Kitchen*
BL - v111 - i21 - July 1 2015 - p14(1) [501+]
Foot, John - *The Man Who Closed the Asylums: Franco Basaglia and the Revolution in Mental Health Care*
Nature - v524 - i7565 - August 20 2015 - p290(1) [501+]
NS - v144 - i5281 - Sept 25 2015 - p70(1) [501+]
TimHES - i2218 - August 27 2015 - p42-2 [501+]
Foote, Mary Q. - *Implementing the Common Core State Standards through Mathematical Problem Solving, Grades 3-5*
TC Math - v21 - i8 - April 2015 - p508(1) [501+]
Foote, Nicola - *Immigration and National Identities in Latin America*
HNet - July 2015 - pNA [501+]
Foran, Racquel - *Robotics: From Automatons to the Roomba*
y HB Guide - v26 - i2 - Fall 2015 - p185(1) [51-500]
Forbes, Anne L. - *Trials and Triumphs: The Gordons of Huntly in Sixteenth-Century Scotland*
Historian - v77 - i1 - Spring 2015 - p166(2) [501+]
Forbes, Bruce David - *America's Favorite Holidays: Candid Histories*
TLS - i5877 - Nov 20 2015 - p30(1) [501+]
Forbes, Carrie - *Rethinking Reference for Academic Libraries: Innovative Developments and Future Trends*
LJ - v140 - i3 - March 15 2015 - p119(1) [51-500]
Forbes, Elena - *Jigsaw Man*
Nat Post - v17 - i176 - May 30 2015 - pWP5(1) [501+]

Forbes, Helen Foxhall - *Heaven and Earth in Anglo-Saxon England: Theology and Society in an Age of Faith*
CH - v84 - i1 - March 2015 - p234(3) [501+]
Six Ct J - v46 - i2 - Summer 2015 - p418-419 [501+]
Forbes, Nancy - *Faraday, Maxwell, and the Electromagnetic Field: How Two Men Revolutionized Physics*
Isis - v106 - i2 - June 2015 - p462(2) [501+]
Forbes, Peter - *A Man Apart: Bill Coperthwaite's Radical Experiment in Living*
BL - v111 - i12 - Feb 15 2015 - p27(1) [51-500]
Forbes, Rob - *See for Yourself: A Visual Guide to Beauty*
PW - v262 - i13 - March 30 2015 - p71(3) [51-500]
Forbes, Scott - *You Rule! A Practical Guide to Creating Your Own Kingdom*
c PW - v262 - i34 - August 24 2015 - p82(1) [501+]
Forbringer, Linda L. - *RtI in Math: Evidence-Based Interventions for Struggling Students*
TC Math - v22 - i4 - Nov 2015 - p262(1) [501+]
Force, Marie - *And I Love Her*
PW - v262 - i4 - Jan 26 2015 - p155(1) [51-500]
It's Only Love
BL - v112 - i4 - Oct 15 2015 - p27(1) [51-500]
Forche, Carolyn - *Poetry of Witness: The Tradition in English 1500-001*
Ken R - v37 - i5 - Sept-Oct 2015 - p94(14) [501+]
Forclaz, Bertrand - *Catholiques au defi de la Reforme: La coexistence confessionnelle a Utrecht au XVIIe siecle*
Six Ct J - v46 - i2 - Summer 2015 - p489-491 [501+]
Ford, April L. - *The Poor Children*
KR - Feb 1 2015 - pNA [51-500]
Ford, Arielle - *Turn Your Mate into Your Soulmate: A Practical Guide to Happily Ever After*
PW - v262 - i42 - Oct 19 2015 - p73(1) [51-500]
Ford, Christine - *The Navy's Night Before Christmas (Illus. by Manders, John)*
c HB Guide - v26 - i2 - Fall 2015 - p37(1) [51-500]
Ford, David - *The Drama of Living: Becoming Wise in the Spirit*
TLS - i5861 - July 31 2015 - p11(1) [501+]
Ford, Emily - *Ten Playful Penguins*
c KR - Jan 1 2016 - pNA [51-500]
Ford, G.M. - *Threshold*
KR - Feb 15 2015 - pNA [501+]
PW - v262 - i6 - Feb 9 2015 - p47(2) [51-500]
Ford, Gina - *Good Mother, Bad Mother*
LJ - v140 - i3 - Feb 15 2015 - p81(3) [51-500]
Ford, Joan - *When Bad Things Happen to Good Quilters: Survival Guide for Fixing and Finishing Any Quilting Project*
LJ - v140 - i12 - July 1 2015 - p86(2) [51-500]
Ford, John C. - *The Cipher*
y BL - v111 - i9-10 - Jan 1 2015 - p87(1) [501+]
y CCB-B - v68 - i7 - March 2015 - p353(2) [501+]
y HB Guide - v26 - i2 - Fall 2015 - p119(1) [51-500]
Ford, Katie - *Blood Lyrics*
NYTBR - March 1 2015 - p30(L) [501+]
Ford, Kenneth W. - *Building the H Bomb: A Personal History*
Phys Today - v68 - i7 - July 2015 - p46-1 [501+]
Ford, Mark - *This Dialogue of One: Essays on Poets from John Dunne to Joan Murray*
TLS - i5863 - August 14 2015 - p26(1) [501+]
Ford, Martin - *Rise of the Robots: Technology and the Threat of a Jobless Future*
BL - v111 - i16 - April 15 2015 - p7(1) [51-500]
KR - March 15 2015 - pNA [501+]
Nature - v526 - i7573 - Oct 15 2015 - p320(2) [501+]
New Sci - v225 - i3008 - Feb 14 2015 - p46(2) [501+]
NYTBR - May 17 2015 - p1(L) [501+]
Reason - v46 - i11 - April 2015 - p60(4) [501+]
TimHES - i2211 - July 9 2015 - p45(1) [501+]
Ford, Martyn - *The Imagination Box*
c Sch Lib - v63 - i3 - Autumn 2015 - p165(1) [51-500]
Ford, Pamela - *To Ride a White Horse*
SPBW - August 2015 - pNA [51-500]
Ford, Philip - *Brill's Encyclopaedia of the Neo-Latin World*
Sev Cent N - v73 - i3-4 - Fall-Winter 2015 - p199(5) [501+]
Six Ct J - v46 - i2 - Summer 2015 - p444-446 [501+]
TLS - i5837 - Feb 13 2015 - p25(1) [501+]
La Librairie de Montaigne: Proceedings of the Tenth Cambridge French Renaissance Colloquium 1-4

September 2008
 FS - v69 - i2 - April 2015 - p239-240 [501+]
Ford, Richard - *Let Me Be Frank with You*
 HR - v68 - i2 - Summer 2015 - p343-351 [501+]
 NYTBR - Nov 1 2015 - p28(L) [501+]
Ford, Tanisha C. - *Liberated Threads: Black Women, Style, and the Global Politics of Soul*
 LJ - v140 - i17 - Oct 15 2015 - p105(2) [51-500]
Ford, William - *Numerical Linear Algebra with Application: Using MATLAB*
 SIAM Rev - v57 - i3 - Sept 2015 - p473-474 [501+]
Forde, Cathy - *The Blitz Next Door*
 c KR - Nov 1 2015 - pNA [51-500]
Forde, Patricia - *The Wordsmith*
 y Sch Lib - v63 - i4 - Winter 2015 - p246(1) [501+]
Fordham, Demetrius - *What They Didn't Teach You in Photo School: What You Actually Need to Know to Succeed in the Industry*
 Bwatch - Oct 2015 - pNA [51-500]
Forecki, Piotr - *Reconstructing Memory: The Holocaust in Polish Public Debates*
 Slav R - v74 - i1 - Spring 2015 - p172-173 [501+]
Foreign Rule in Western Europe: Towards a Comparative History of Military Occupations 1940-1949
 HNet - April 2015 - pNA [501+]
Foreman, Michael - *Cat & Dog*
 c HB Guide - v26 - i1 - Spring 2015 - p30(1) [51-500]
The Little Bookshop and the Origami Army
 c Sch Lib - v63 - i3 - Autumn 2015 - p154(1) [51-500]
The Seeds of Friendship (Illus. by Foreman, Michael)
 c CH Bwatch - Sept 2015 - pNA [51-500]
 c KR - May 15 2015 - pNA [51-500]
 c NYTBR - August 23 2015 - p24(L) [501+]
 c PW - v262 - i20 - May 18 2015 - p84(1) [51-500]
 c Sch Lib - v63 - i3 - Autumn 2015 - p154(2) [51-500]
 c SLJ - v61 - i8 - August 2015 - p69(1) [51-500]
The Tortoise and the Soldier: A Story of Courage and Friendship in World War I (Illus. by Foreman, Michael)
 c BL - v112 - i6 - Nov 15 2015 - p56(1) [51-500]
 c KR - Sept 15 2015 - pNA [51-500]
 c PW - v262 - i35 - August 31 2015 - p92(1) [51-500]
 c SLJ - v61 - i10 - Oct 2015 - p88(2) [51-500]
Foreman, Tom - *My Year of Running Dangerously: A Dad, a Daughter, and a Ridiculous Plan*
 PW - v262 - i34 - August 24 2015 - p77(1) [51-500]
 KR - July 15 2015 - pNA [501+]
Forest, Christopher - *What You Need to Know About Cancer*
 c Sch Lib - v63 - i4 - Winter 2015 - p237(1) [51-500]
Forest, Jim - *Loving Our Enemies: Reflections on the Hardest Commandment*
 AM - v213 - i1 - July 6 2015 - p40(3) [501+]
Foresta, Merry A. - *Artists Unframed: Snapshots from the Smithsonian's Archives of American Art*
 LJ - v140 - i15 - Sept 15 2015 - p81(3) [501+]
Forester, Amanda - *The Highlander's Bride*
 PW - v262 - i30 - July 27 2015 - p48(1) [51-500]
Forester, Thad - *My Brother in Arms*
 KR - Oct 15 2015 - pNA [501+]
Forester, Victoria - *The Boy Who Knew Everything*
 c KR - July 1 2015 - pNA [51-500]
 c SLJ - v61 - i8 - August 2015 - p84(1) [51-500]
Forg, Nicola - *Tod auf der Piste*
 TimHES - i2195 - March 19 2015 - p49(1) [501+]
Forgacs, David - *Italy's Margins: Social Exclusion and Nation Formation since 1861*
 AHR - v120 - i4 - Oct 2015 - p1559-1560 [501+]
 HNet - Feb 2015 - pNA [501+]
Forgan, James W. - *The Impulsive, Disorganized Child: Solutions for Parenting Kids with Executive Functioning Difficulties*
 LJ - v140 - i9 - May 15 2015 - p66(2) [501+]
 RVBW - June 2015 - pNA [501+]
Forister, J. Glenn - *Introduction to Research and Medical Literature, 4th ed.*
 Bwatch - Sept 2015 - pNA [501+]
Forkner, Andrew - *A-Z of Bird Portraits: An Illustrated Guide to Painting Beautiful Birds in Acrylics*
 LJ - v140 - i3 - Feb 15 2015 - p98(1) [51-500]
Forman, Deborah - *Color Lab for Mixed-Media Artists: 52 Exercises for Exploring Color Concepts through Paint, Collage, Paper, and More*
 LJ - v140 - i20 - Dec 1 2015 - p100(1) [51-500]

Forman, Gayle - *I Was Here (Read by Marie, Jorjeana). Audiobook Review*
 y HB - v91 - i4 - July-August 2015 - p164(1) [51-500]
 y SLJ - v61 - i4 - April 2015 - p64(2) [51-500]
I Was Here
 y CH Bwatch - April 2015 - pNA [51-500]
 y HB - v91 - i1 - Jan-Feb 2015 - p81(2) [51-500]
 y HB Guide - v26 - i2 - Fall 2015 - p119(1) [501+]
 y NYTBR - Feb 8 2015 - p24(L) [501+]
 y PW - v262 - i49 - Dec 2 2015 - p92(2) [51-500]
Formenti, Laura - *Embodied Narratives: Connecting Stories, Bodies, Cultures and Ecologies*
 Biomag - v38 - i3 - Summer 2015 - p438(4) [501+]
Formichi, Chiara - *Islam and the Making of the Nation: Kartosuwiryo and Political Islam in 20th Century Indonesia*
 Pac A - v88 - i1 - March 2015 - p234 [501+]
Formicola, Crescenzo - *Tacito: Il libro quarto degli Annales*
 Class R - v65 - i1 - April 2015 - p155-156 [501+]
Forna, Aminatta - *The Hired Man*
 RVBW - Feb 2015 - pNA [51-500]
 Wom R Bks - v32 - i2 - March-April 2015 - p17(2) [501+]
Forner, Sean A. - *German Intellectuals and the Challenge of Democratic Renewal: Culture and Politics after 1945*
 HNet - April 2015 - pNA [501+]
Foroutan, Parnaz - *The Girl from the Garden*
 BL - v111 - i19-20 - June 1 2015 - p39(1) [51-500]
 KR - June 15 2015 - pNA [51-500]
 LJ - v140 - i12 - July 1 2015 - p76(1) [51-500]
Forrest, Alan - *Waterloo*
 KR - Jan 15 2015 - pNA [51-500]
Forrest, Allan - *Waterloo*
 HT - v65 - i7 - July 2015 - p58(2) [501+]
Forrest, Lisa - *Inheritance*
 y SLJ - v61 - i9 - Sept 2015 - p158(1) [51-500]
Forrester, James - *The Heart Healers: The Misfits, Mavericks, and Rebels Who Created the Greatest Medical Breakthrough of Our Lives*
 BL - v112 - i1 - Sept 1 2015 - p22(1) [51-500]
 KR - June 15 2015 - pNA [51-500]
 LJ - v140 - i12 - July 1 2015 - p104(1) [51-500]
 PW - v262 - i27 - July 6 2015 - p58(1) [51-500]
Forrester, Viviane - *Virginia Woolf: A Portrait*
 KR - March 15 2015 - pNA [501+]
 RVBW - August 2015 - pNA [51-500]
 TLS - i5863 - August 14 2015 - p5(1) [501+]
 LJ - v140 - i6 - April 1 2015 - p88(1) [51-500]
 PW - v262 - i13 - March 30 2015 - p70(2) [51-500]
Forsey, Jane - *The Aesthetics of Design*
 RM - v68 - i3 - March 2015 - p657(2) [501+]
Forsgren, Todd - *Ornithological Photographs*
 Nature - v526 - i7573 - Oct 15 2015 - p321(1) [51-500]
Forshaw, Barry - *Sex and Film: The Erotic in British, American and World Cinema*
 NS - v144 - i5254 - March 20 2015 - p44(3) [501+]
Forss, Amy Helene - *Black Print with a White Carnation: Mildred Brown and the Omaha Star Newspaper, 1938-1989*
 AHR - v120 - i2 - April 2015 - p653-654 [501+]
Forss, George - *The Way We Were*
 KR - May 1 2015 - pNA [501+]
Forst, Rainer - *Toleration in Conflict: Past and Present*
 HER - v130 - i543 - April 2015 - p515(4) [501+]
Forstchen, William R. - *One Year After*
 KR - July 15 2015 - pNA [501+]
 PW - v262 - i30 - July 27 2015 - p43(2) [51-500]
Forster, Carolyn - *Hexagon Happenings*
 LJ - v140 - i3 - Feb 15 2015 - p100(1) [51-500]
Little Quilts and Gifts from Jelly Roll Scraps: 30 Gorgeous Projects for Using up Your Left-Over Fabric
 LJ - v140 - i9 - May 15 2015 - p82(1) [51-500]
Forster, Gabriele - *Quellen zur Nationalen und Internationalen Schulgesundheitspflege Wahrend der Weimarer Republik*
 HNet - Feb 2015 - pNA [501+]
Forster, Horst - *Umweltgeschichte(n): Ostmitteleuropa von der Industrialisierung bis zum Postsozialismus*
 HNet - July 2015 - pNA [501+]
Forster, Margaret - *My Life in Houses*
 NS - v144 - i5245 - Jan 16 2015 - p48(1) [501+]
Forster, Miriam - *Empire of Shadows*
 y HB Guide - v26 - i1 - Spring 2015 - p107(1) [51-500]

Forsyth, Alison - *Testimonial Plays in Contemporary American Theater*
 Theat J - v67 - i1 - March 2015 - p135-146 [501+]
Forsyth, Frederick - *The Outsider: My Life in Intrigue*
 BL - v112 - i2 - Sept 15 2015 - p17(1) [51-500]
 LJ - v140 - i15 - Sept 15 2015 - p75(1) [51-500]
 NYTBR - Nov 1 2015 - p18(L) [501+]
 KR - August 15 2015 - pNA [501+]
 PW - v262 - i33 - August 17 2015 - p64(1) [51-500]
Forsyth, James - *The Caucasus: A History*
 E-A St - v67 - i4 - June 2015 - p685(3) [501+]
Forsyth, Kate - *The Impossible Quest: The Beast of Blackmoor Bog*
 c Magpies - v30 - i2 - May 2015 - p35(1) [51-500]
The Impossible Quest: Wolves of the Witchwood
 c Magpies - v30 - i2 - May 2015 - p35(1) [51-500]
The Wild Girl
 LJ - v140 - i10 - June 1 2015 - p86(1) [51-500]
Forsyth, Mark - *Collins English Dictionary, 12th ed.*
 TLS - i5835 - Jan 30 2015 - p25(1) [501+]
The Elements of Eloquence: How to Turn the Perfect English Phrase
 TimHES - i2211 - July 9 2015 - p45(1) [501+]
Forsythe, Mark - *From the West Coast to the Western Front: British Columbians and the Great War*
 Beav - v95 - i4 - August-Sept 2015 - p73(1) [501+]
Fort, Bailey - *The Bewundering World of Bewilderbeests (Illus. by Fort, Bailey)*
 c PW - v262 - i19 - May 11 2015 - p57(2) [51-500]
Fort, Tom - *Channel Shore: From the White Cliffs to Land's End*
 TLS - i5858 - July 10 2015 - p27(1) [501+]
Forte, Hugh - *The Sprouted Kitchen Bowl and Spoon: Simple and Inspired Whole Foods Recipes to Savor and Share*
 PW - v262 - i3 - Jan 19 2015 - p74(1) [51-500]
Forte, Sara - *The Sprouted Kitchen Bowl and Spoon: Simple and Inspired Whole Foods Recipes to Savor and Share*
 NYTBR - May 31 2015 - p24(L) [501+]
Fortin, Bill - *Redeye Fulda Cold*
 SPBW - Nov 2015 - pNA [51-500]
Fortini, Franco - *The Dogs of the Sinai*
 TLS - i5839 - Feb 27 2015 - p23(1) [501+]
Fortino, Lauri - *The Peddler's Bed (Illus. by Redila, Bong)*
 c CH Bwatch - Nov 2015 - pNA [51-500]
 c KR - July 1 2015 - pNA [51-500]
Fortmann, Patrick - *Commitment and Compassion: Essays on Georg Buchner. Festschrift for Gerhard P. Knapp*
 MLR - v110 - i1 - Jan 2015 - p289-290 [501+]
Fortner, Michael Javen - *Black Silent Majority: The Rockefeller Drug Laws and the Politics of Punishment*
 NYTBR - Sept 27 2015 - p14(L) [501+]
 Reason - v47 - i8 - Jan 2016 - p55(5) [501+]
Fortunato, John - *Dark Reservations*
 BL - v112 - i2 - Sept 15 2015 - p30(1) [51-500]
 KR - August 15 2015 - pNA [51-500]
 PW - v262 - i26 - June 29 2015 - p43(2) [51-500]
Fortune, Brandon - *Elaine de Kooning: Portraits*
 LJ - v140 - i11 - June 15 2015 - p84(1) [51-500]
Fortune, Margaret - *Nova*
 y BL - v111 - i21 - July 1 2015 - p47(1) [51-500]
 LJ - v140 - i9 - May 15 2015 - p57(4) [51-500]
 PW - v262 - i19 - May 11 2015 - p41(1) [51-500]
 y VOYA - v38 - i2 - June 2015 - p74(1) [51-500]
Forty, Adrian - *Concrete and Culture: A Material History*
 T&C - v56 - i1 - Jan 2015 - p279-281 [501+]
Forward, Toby - *Doubleborn*
 y HB Guide - v26 - i2 - Fall 2015 - p81(1) [51-500]
The Quayside Cat (Illus. by Brown, Ruth)
 c Sch Lib - v63 - i1 - Spring 2015 - p27(1) [51-500]
Foss, Peter J. - *The Conquering Worm: Llewelyn Powys: A Consumptive's Diary, 1910*
 TLS - i5863 - August 14 2015 - p8(1) [501+]
Fosse, Jon - *An Angel Walks through the Stage and Other Essays*
 TLS - i5877 - Nov 20 2015 - p19(1) [501+]
Best European Fiction 2016
 KR - Sept 1 2015 - pNA [501+]
Melancholy II
 TLS - i5877 - Nov 20 2015 - p19(1) [501+]
Morning and Evening
 KR - July 1 2015 - pNA [51-500]
 PW - v262 - i30 - July 27 2015 - p38(2) [51-500]
 TLS - i5877 - Nov 20 2015 - p19(1) [501+]
Fossum, Karin - *The Drowned Boy*
 BL - v111 - i21 - July 1 2015 - p37(1) [51-500]
 KR - June 1 2015 - pNA [51-500]
 NYTBR - August 16 2015 - p29(L) [501+]
 PW - v262 - i23 - June 8 2015 - p36(1) [51-500]

The Murder of Harriet Krohn
  RVBW - Nov 2015 - pNA [501+]
Foster, Alan Dean - *The Deavys*
  c PW - v262 - i45 - Nov 9 2015 - p61(1) [51-500]
Foster, Elizabeth - *Faith in Empire: Religion, Politics, and Colonial Rule in French Senegal, 1880-1940*
  Historian - v77 - i1 - Spring 2015 - p102(2) [501+]
  JMH - v87 - i1 - March 2015 - p193(2) [501+]
Foster, Emily - *The Drowning Eyes*
  PW - v262 - i48 - Nov 30 2015 - p44(1) [51-500]
Foster, Evelyn - *The Elves and the Trendy Shoes*
  c CH Bwatch - July 2015 - pNA [501+]
Foster, Hal - *Bad New Days: Art, Criticism, Emergency*
  Art N - v114 - i8 - Sept 2015 - p20(3) [501+]
Foster, Jane - *Jane Foster's 123 (Illus. by Foster, Jane)*
  c PW - v262 - i49 - Dec 2 2015 - p56(2) [51-500]
  c KR - Jan 1 2016 - pNA [51-500]
  c PW - v262 - i20 - May 18 2015 - p82(2) [51-500]
  c SLJ - v61 - i7 - July 2015 - p55(1) [51-500]
  Jane Foster's ABC (Illus. by Foster, Jane)
  c SLJ - v61 - i7 - July 2015 - p55(1) [51-500]
Foster, John - *Cambrian Ocean World: Ancient Sea Life of North America*
  QRB - v90 - i3 - Sept 2015 - p321(2) [501+]
Foster, John Burt, Jr. - *Transnational Tolstoy: Between the West and the World*
  Slav R - v74 - i1 - Spring 2015 - p207-208 [501+]
Foster, John C. - *Dead Men*
  PW - v262 - i23 - June 8 2015 - p41(2) [51-500]
Foster, John D. - *White Race Discourse: Preserving Racial Privilege in a Post-Racial Society*
  ERS - v38 - i3 - March 2015 - p493(3) [501+]
Foster, John Wilson - *Pilgrims of the Air*
  TLS - i5834 - Jan 23 2015 - p26(1) [501+]
Foster, Lori - *Tough Love*
  PW - v262 - i26 - June 29 2015 - p51(2) [51-500]
Foster, Michael Dylan - *The Book of Yokai: Mysterious Creatures of Japanese Folklore*
  TLS - i5850 - May 15 2015 - p27(1) [501+]
Foster, Pamela - *Ridgeline*
  Roundup M - v22 - i4 - April 2015 - p33(1) [501+]
  Roundup M - v22 - i6 - August 2015 - p29(1) [501+]
Foster, Peter - *Why We Bite the Invisible Hand*
  KR - March 1 2015 - pNA [501+]
Foster, R.F. - *Vivid Faces: The Revolutionary Generation in Ireland, 1890-1923*
  AHR - v120 - i4 - Oct 2015 - p1551-1552 [501+]
  AS - v84 - i2 - Spring 2015 - p116(4) [501+]
  ILS - v35 - i1 - Fall 2015 - p5(1) [501+]
  Lon R Bks - v37 - i14 - July 16 2015 - p11(3) [501+]
  NY - v91 - i6 - March 30 2015 - p74 [51-500]
Foster, Ruscombe - *Wellington and Waterloo: The Duke, the Battle and Posterity, 1815-2015*
  HER - v130 - i542 - Feb 2015 - p123(14) [501+]
Foster, Sara - *Foster's Market Favorites: 25th Anniversary Collection*
  LJ - v140 - i19 - Nov 15 2015 - p102(1) [51-500]
Foster, Stephen - *British North America in the Seventeenth and Eighteenth Centuries*
  HER - v130 - i545 - August 2015 - p1003(3) [501+]
  AHR - v120 - i3 - June 2015 - p1005-1007 [501+]
Foster, Thomas A. - *Sex and the Founding Fathers: The American Quest for a Relatable Past*
  JAH - v101 - i4 - March 2015 - p1256-1257 [501+]
  Women in Early America
  TLS - i5864-5865 - August 21 2015 - p34(1) [501+]
Foster, Tonya M. - *A Swarm of Bees in High Court*
  PW - v262 - i33 - August 17 2015 - p48(1) [51-500]
Foteva, Ana - *Do the Balkans Begin in Vienna? The Geopolitical and Imaginary Borders between the Balkans and Europe*
  Slav R - v74 - i3 - Fall 2015 - p644-646 [501+]
Fothergill, Alice - *Children of Katrina*
  PW - v262 - i25 - June 22 2015 - p130(2) [51-500]
Fotheringham, William - *The Badger: The Life of Bernard Hinault and the Legacy of French Cycling*
  KR - July 1 2015 - pNA [501+]
  LJ - v140 - i13 - August 1 2015 - p104(1) [51-500]
Fotografie im Dienst der Wissenschaft
  HNet - March 2015 - pNA [501+]
Foucault, Michel - *Language, Madness, and Desire: On Literature*
  TimHES - i2223 - Oct 1 2015 - p52-53 [501+]

The Order of Things: An Archaeology of the Human Sciences
  TimHES - i2211 - July 9 2015 - p44(1) [501+]
Fouce, Paula - *Not In God's Name: Making Sense of Religious Conflict*
  SPBW - August 2015 - pNA [51-500]
Fougner, Dave - *The Manly Art of Knitting*
  Am Craft - v75 - i2 - April-May 2015 - p18(1) [501+]
Fountain, Charles - *The Betrayal: The 1919 World Series and the Birth of Modern Baseball*
  BL - v112 - i1 - Sept 1 2015 - p32(1) [51-500]
  KR - July 15 2015 - pNA [51-500]
  LJ - v140 - i12 - July 1 2015 - p89(1) [51-500]
  Mac - v128 - i47 - Nov 30 2015 - p59(1) [501+]
FourEagles, Russell - *The Making of a Healer: Teachings of My Oneida Grandmother*
  Bwatch - April 2015 - pNA [51-500]
Fourest, Caroline - *Eloge du blaspheme*
  TLS - i5864-5865 - August 21 2015 - p28(2) [501+]
Fournel, Paul - *Dear Reader*
  TLS - i5836 - Feb 6 2015 - p26(1) [501+]
Fournier, Alain - *Le Grand Meaulnes*
  Bks & Cult - v21 - i2 - March-April 2015 - p36(1) [501+]
Fournier, Lanzoni Remi - *French Comedy on Screen: A Cinematic History*
  FS - v69 - i4 - Oct 2015 - p573-574 [501+]
Fournier, Martin - *The Adventures of Radisson 2: Back to the New World*
  y Res Links - v20 - i4 - April 2015 - p28(1) [501+]
Foust, Graham - *Time Down to Mind*
  PW - v262 - i52 - Dec 21 2015 - p129(1) [51-500]
Foust, Rebecca - *Paradise Drive*
  HR - v68 - i1 - Spring 2015 - p141-150 [501+]
Fowden, Garth - *Before and after Muhammad: The First Millennium Refocused*
  IBMR - v39 - i4 - Oct 2015 - p239(2) [501+]
Fowler, A.A. - *Organs of Greed*
  SPBW - May 2015 - pNA [51-500]
Fowler, Christopher - *Bryant & May and the Burning Man*
  KR - Oct 1 2015 - pNA [51-500]
  LJ - v140 - i19 - Nov 15 2015 - p80(1) [51-500]
  PW - v262 - i38 - Sept 21 2015 - p52(2) [51-500]
  The Sand Men
  BL - v112 - i2 - Sept 15 2015 - p34(1) [51-500]
Fowler, David - *Going to the Palais: A Social and Cultural History of Dancing and Dance Halls in Britain, 1918-1960*
  TimHES - i2224 - Oct 8 2015 - p45(1) [501+]
Fowler, Doreen - *Drawing the Line: The Father Reimagined in Faulkner, Wright, O'Connor, and Morrison*
  MFSF - v61 - i3 - Fall 2015 - p562-564 [501+]
Fowler, Gloria - *Come with Me to Paris (Illus. by Heo, Min)*
  c HB Guide - v26 - i2 - Fall 2015 - p34(1) [501+]
Fowler, James - *Richardson and the Philosophes*
  FS - v69 - i2 - April 2015 - p245(1) [501+]
  MLR - v110 - i3 - July 2015 - p785-786 [501+]
Fowler, Karen Joy - *Black Glass*
  Nat Post - v17 - i210 - July 11 2015 - pWP4(1) [501+]
  We Are All Completely Beside Ourselves
  TimHES - i2188 - Jan 29 2015 - p47(1) [501+]
Fowler, Katie - *An Artist's Journey through Wonderland*
  KR - Sept 15 2015 - pNA [501+]
Fowler, Robert Booth - *Religion and Politics in America: Faith, Culture, and Strategic Choices*
  J Ch St - v57 - i2 - Spring 2015 - p386-388 [501+]
Fowler, Robert L. - *Early Greek Mythography, vol. 1: Text and Introduction*
  Class R - v65 - i2 - Oct 2015 - p335-338 [501+]
  Early Greek Mythography, vol. 2: Commentary
  Class R - v65 - i2 - Oct 2015 - p335-338 [501+]
Fowler, Susan - *Why Motivating People Doesn't Work...and What Does: The New Science of Leading, Energizing and Engaging*
  Bwatch - Jan 2015 - pNA [51-500]
Fowley-Doyle, Moira - *The Accident Season (Read by Minifie, Colby). Audiobook Review*
  y BL - v112 - i7 - Dec 1 2015 - p70(1) [51-500]
  The Accident Season
  y CCB-B - v69 - i2 - Oct 2015 - p86(2) [501+]
  y KR - May 1 2015 - pNA [51-500]
  y Magpies - v30 - i3 - July 2015 - p40(1) [501+]
  y PW - v262 - i19 - May 11 2015 - p63(1) [51-500]
  y Sch Lib - v63 - i2 - Summer 2015 - p124(1) [51-500]
  y Sch Lib - v63 - i4 - Winter 2015 - p246(1) [51-500]
  y SLJ - v61 - i8 - August 2015 - p102(2) [51-500]
  y VOYA - v38 - i3 - August 2015 - p60(1) [51-500]

Fox, Benjamin - *The Great and the Grand (Illus. by Robbins, Elizabeth)*
  c KR - August 1 2015 - pNA [51-500]
  c PW - v262 - i26 - June 29 2015 - p67(1) [51-500]
Fox, Calista - *Burned Deep*
  PW - v262 - i28 - July 13 2015 - p52(1) [51-500]
Fox, Candice - *Eden*
  LJ - v140 - i13 - August 1 2015 - p82(2) [51-500]
  PW - v262 - i31 - August 3 2015 - p37(1) [51-500]
Fox, Christyan - *Dinosaur Poo! (Illus. by Fox, Diane)*
  c Sch Lib - v63 - i2 - Summer 2015 - p91(1) [51-500]
Fox, Diane - *The Cat, the Dog, Little Red, the Exploding Eggs, the Wolf, and Grandma (Illus. by Fox, Christyan)*
  c CH Bwatch - Feb 2015 - pNA [51-500]
  c HB Guide - v26 - i2 - Fall 2015 - p34(1) [501+]
  The Cat, the Dog, Little Red, the Exploding Eggs, the Wolf and Grandma's Wardrobe (Illus. by Fox, Christyan)
  c Sch Lib - v63 - i1 - Spring 2015 - p27(1) [51-500]
Fox, Everett - *The Early Prophets: Joshua, Judges, Samuel and Kings*
  CC - v132 - i6 - March 18 2015 - p38(2) [501+]
Fox, Georgia L. - *The Archaeology of Smoking and Tobacco*
  Am Ant - v80 - i4 - Oct 2015 - p784(2) [501+]
Fox, Gordon A. - *Ecological Statistics: Contemporary Theory and Application*
  BioSci - v65 - i10 - Oct 2015 - p1021(5) [501+]
Fox, Janet - *The Charmed Children of Rookskill Castle*
  c KR - Dec 15 2015 - pNA [51-500]
  y SLJ - v61 - i12 - Dec 2015 - p100(2) [51-500]
Fox, Joel - *The Mark on Eve*
  KR - June 1 2015 - pNA [501+]
Fox, Lauren - *Days of Awe*
  BL - v111 - i19-20 - June 1 2015 - p39(1) [51-500]
  Ent W - i1375 - August 7 2015 - p66(1) [501+]
  KR - June 15 2015 - pNA [51-500]
  NYTBR - August 9 2015 - p17(L) [501+]
  PW - v262 - i24 - June 15 2015 - p57(3) [501+]
Fox, Mae - *Pattern of Betrayal*
  KR - March 1 2015 - pNA [51-500]
  Threads of Deceit
  KR - Feb 1 2015 - pNA [51-500]
Fox, Mem - *Baby Bedtime (Illus. by Quay, Emma)*
  c HB Guide - v26 - i1 - Spring 2015 - p9(1) [51-500]
  Nellie Belle (Illus. by Austin, Mike)
  c KR - Nov 15 2015 - pNA [51-500]
  c PW - v262 - i39 - Sept 28 2015 - p88(2) [51-500]
  This and That (Illus. by Horacek, Judy)
  c Magpies - v30 - i4 - Sept 2015 - p26(1) [51-500]
Fox, Michael - *Old English Literature and the Old Testament*
  Specu - v90 - i3 - July 2015 - p808-2 [501+]
Fox, Paula - *Desperate Characters*
  y Ent W - i1358 - April 10 2015 - p66(1) [501+]
Fox, Renee C. - *Doctors without Borders: Humanitarian Quests, Impossible Dreams of Medecins Sans Frontieres*
  AM - v213 - i15 - Nov 16 2015 - p34(3) [501+]
Fox, Richard Wightman - *Lincoln's Body: A Cultural History (Read by Larkin, Pete). Audiobook Review*
  LJ - v140 - i9 - May 15 2015 - p45(1) [51-500]
  PW - v262 - i12 - March 23 2015 - p72(1) [51-500]
  Lincoln's Body: A Cultural History
  CC - v132 - i11 - May 27 2015 - p36(2) [501+]
  HNet - August 2015 - pNA [51-500]
  NYTBR - Feb 8 2015 - p1(L) [501+]
  NYTBR - Feb 8 2015 - p1(L) [501+]
  TLS - i5858 - July 10 2015 - p24(2) [501+]
Fox, Robert - *Thomas Harriot and His World: Mathematics, Exploration, and Natural Philosophy in Early Modern England*
  Ren Q - v68 - i1 - Spring 2015 - p271-273 [501+]
Fox, Robin Lane - *Augustine: Conversions to Confessions*
  BL - v112 - i4 - Oct 15 2015 - p5(1) [51-500]
  KR - Sept 1 2015 - pNA [51-500]
  LJ - v140 - i17 - Oct 15 2015 - p95(1) [51-500]
  Nat R - v67 - i24 - Dec 31 2015 - p37(2) [501+]
  NS - v144 - i5287 - Nov 6 2015 - p38(3) [501+]
  NYTBR - Nov 22 2015 - p1(L) [501+]
Fox, Sarah - *Dead Ringer*
  BL - v111 - i19-20 - June 1 2015 - p50(1) [51-500]
Fox, Sarah Alisabeth - *Downwind: A People's History of the Nuclear West*
  JAH - v102 - i2 - Sept 2015 - p603-604 [501+]
Fox, Stuart - *Exile at Dawn*
  KR - Sept 15 2015 - pNA [501+]

Fox, Susan - *Love Somebody Like You*
PW - v262 - i33 - August 17 2015 - p57(1) [51-500]

Foxlee, Karen - *Ophelia and the Marvelous Boy (Read by Entwistle, Jayne). Audiobook Review*
c SLJ - v61 - i2 - Feb 2015 - p38(3) [501+]

Foxlee, Neil - *Albert Cammu's 'The New Mediterranean Culture': A Text and its Contexts*
FS - v69 - i2 - April 2015 - p260-261 [501+]

Foxley, Rachel - *The Levellers: Radical Political Thought in the English Revolution*
JMH - v87 - i1 - March 2015 - p170(3) [501+]

Foxwood, Orion - *The Flame In The Cauldron*
RVBW - March 2015 - pNA [51-500]

Fozy, Istvan - *Fossils of the Carpathian Region*
QRB - v90 - i3 - Sept 2015 - p322(1) [501+]

Fraction, Matt - *Casanova*
PW - v262 - i50 - Dec 7 2015 - p75(1) [51-500]
The Hawkeye (Illus. by Pulido, Javier)
BL - v111 - i9-10 - Jan 1 2015 - p62(1) [51-500]
Off to Far Ithicaa
LJ - v140 - i15 - Sept 15 2015 - p60(3) [51-500]
Sex Criminals: Two Worlds, One Cop
LJ - v140 - i5 - March 15 2015 - p88(3) [51-500]
Sex Criminals, vol. 2: Two Worlds, One Cop (Illus. by Zdarsky, Chip)
BL - v111 - i18 - May 15 2015 - p42(1) [51-500]

Fradera, Josep M. - *Slavery and Antislavery in Spain's Atlantic Empire*
HAHR - v95 - i3 - August 2015 - p534-536 [501+]

Fradkin, Barbara - *The Night Thief*
BL - v111 - i12 - Feb 15 2015 - p38(2) [51-500]
KR - Jan 15 2015 - pNA [51-500]
y VOYA - v38 - i1 - April 2015 - p67(1) [51-500]

Fraenkel, Carlos - *Philosophical Religions from Plato to Spinoza*
JMH - v87 - i2 - June 2015 - p397(3) [501+]
Teaching Plato in Palestine: Philosophy in a Divided World
KR - March 1 2015 - pNA [501+]
LJ - v140 - i7 - April 15 2015 - p90(1) [51-500]

Fraeters, Veerle - *Mulieres Religiosae: Shaping Female Spiritual Authority in the Medieval and Early Modern Periods*
Specu - v90 - i3 - July 2015 - p875(1) [501+]

Fragoulaki, Maria - *Kinship in Thucydides: Intercommunal Ties and Historical Narrative*
Class R - v65 - i1 - April 2015 - p42-44 [501+]
JRAI - v21 - i1 - March 2015 - p220(2) [501+]

Frahmann, Dennis - *The Finnish Girl*
PW - v262 - i9 - March 2 2015 - p63(2) [51-500]

Fraistat, Neil - *A Cambridge Companion to Textual Scholarship*
Poetics T - v36 - i1-2 - June 2015 - p127-129 [501+]

Frakes, Colleen - *Prison Island: A Graphic Memoir (Illus. by Frakes, Colleen)*
y BL - v112 - i2 - Sept 15 2015 - p52(1) [51-500]

Frakes, Jerold J. - *Early Yiddish Epic*
Specu - v90 - i2 - April 2015 - p540-541 [501+]

Frame, Ronald - *Havisham*
NYTBR - March 1 2015 - p28(L) [501+]

Framing Floors, Walls and Ceilings
LJ - v140 - i15 - Sept 15 2015 - p76(1) [51-500]

Frampton, Megan - *Put Up Your Duke*
BL - v111 - i21 - July 1 2015 - p44(2) [51-500]
PW - v262 - i21 - May 25 2015 - p42(1) [51-500]

Frampton, Otis - *Oddly Normal (Illus. by Frampton, Otis)*
c SLJ - v61 - i5 - May 2015 - p108(1) [51-500]

Francavilla, Francesco - *Afterlife with Archie*
MFSF - v128 - i1-2 - Jan-Feb 2015 - p40(3) [501+]

France, Alan - *A Political Ecology of Youth and Crime*
CS - v44 - i6 - Nov 2015 - p873(1) [501+]

France, Sue - *The Definitive Personal Assistant and Secretarial Handbook*
RVBW - Sept 2015 - pNA [51-500]

Frances, Bryan - *Disagreement*
Dialogue - v54 - i3 - Sept 2015 - p563-564 [501+]

Franceschelli, Christopher - *Countablock (Illus. by Peskimo)*
c HB Guide - v26 - i1 - Spring 2015 - p9(1) [51-500]
c KR - Jan 1 2015 - pNA [51-500]
Dinoblock (Illus. by Peskimo)
c BL - v112 - i6 - Nov 15 2015 - p57(1) [51-500]
c KR - July 1 2015 - pNA [51-500]
c PW - v262 - i20 - May 18 2015 - p82(2) [51-500]
c PW - v262 - i49 - Dec 2 2015 - p56(1) [51-500]
c SLJ - v61 - i10 - Oct 2015 - p76(1) [51-500]
Mix It Up! (Illus. by Tullet, Herve)
c HB Guide - v26 - i1 - Spring 2015 - p17(1) [51-500]

Franchino, Vicky - *Animal Brainiacs*
c BL - v112 - i3 - Oct 1 2015 - p42(1) [501+]
Black Mambas
c BL - v112 - i7 - Dec 1 2015 - p42(2) [51-500]

Francia, Giada - *Aladdin (Illus. by Rossi, Francesca)*
c BL - v111 - i17 - May 1 2015 - p87(1) [51-500]
Fairy Tale Adventures (Illus. by Rossi, Francesca)
c HB Guide - v26 - i2 - Fall 2015 - p160(1) [51-500]
Little Red Riding Hood (Illus. by Rossi, Francesca)
c BL - v111 - i17 - May 1 2015 - p87(1) [51-500]
Rapunzel (Illus. by Rossi, Francesca)
c BL - v111 - i17 - May 1 2015 - p87(1) [51-500]
Snow White (Illus. by Rossi, Francesca)
c BL - v111 - i17 - May 1 2015 - p87(1) [51-500]

Francis, Barbara - *Are You Misusing Other People's Words? What Plagiarism Is and How to Avoid It*
y HB Guide - v26 - i1 - Spring 2015 - p140(1) [51-500]

Francis, Daniel - *Closing Time: Prohibition, Rum-Runners, and Border Wars*
Beav - v95 - i5 - Oct-Nov 2015 - p63(2) [501+]
BL - v111 - i16 - April 15 2015 - p4(1) [51-500]

Francis, Felix - *Dick Francis's Damage*
RVBW - August 2015 - pNA [51-500]
Front Runner
BL - v112 - i3 - Oct 1 2015 - p26(1) [51-500]
PW - v262 - i35 - August 31 2015 - p61(1) [51-500]

Francis, Gavin - *The Adventure of Being Human: Lessons on Soulful Living from the Heart of the Urantia Revelation*
Econ - v415 - i8942 - June 13 2015 - p80(US) [501+]
Adventures in Human Being: A Grand Tour from the Cranium to the Calcaneum
KR - August 1 2015 - pNA [501+]
PW - v262 - i33 - August 17 2015 - p63(1) [51-500]
NS - v144 - i5289 - Nov 20 2015 - p55(1) [501+]
NYRB - v62 - i17 - Nov 5 2015 - p48(2) [501+]

Francis I, Pope - *Encyclical on Climate Change and Inequality: On Care for Our Common Home*
LJ - v140 - i17 - Oct 15 2015 - p110(2) [501+]
Family and Life: Pastoral Reflections
RVBW - July 2015 - pNA [51-500]
Laudato Si': On Care for Our Common Home
NYRB - v62 - i13 - August 13 2015 - p40(3) [501+]

Francis, June - *Love Letters in the Sand*
BL - v111 - i22 - August 1 2015 - p41(1) [51-500]
LJ - v140 - i12 - July 1 2015 - p76(1) [51-500]

Francis, Keith A. - *Oxford Handbook of the British Sermon, 1689-1901*
CH - v84 - i1 - March 2015 - p245(3) [501+]

Francis, Leah Gunning - *Ferguson and Faith: Sparking Leadership and Awakening Community*
CC - v132 - i21 - Oct 14 2015 - p34(2) [501+]

Francis, Lee DeCora - *Kunu's Basket: A Story From Indian Island (Illus. by Drucker, Susan)*
c CH Bwatch - Sept 2015 - pNA [51-500]

Francis, Lesley Lee - *You Come Too*
KR - Sept 15 2015 - pNA [51-500]

Francis, Megan Ming - *Civil Rights and the Making of the Modern American State*
AHR - v120 - i3 - June 2015 - p1044-1046 [501+]
HLR - v128 - i3 - Jan 2015 - p1064(1) [51-500]
JAH - v102 - i1 - June 2015 - p268-269 [501+]

Francis, Norbert - *Bilingual Development and Literacy Learning: East Asian and International Perspectives*
Lang Soc - v44 - i1 - Feb 2015 - p123-124 [501+]

Francis, Pope - *The Spirit of Saint Francis: Inspiring Words from Pope Francis*
LJ - v140 - i2 - Feb 1 2015 - p86(1) [51-500]

Francis, Raymond - *The Great American Health Hoax*
RVBW - March 2015 - pNA [51-500]

Francis, Richard C. - *Domesticated: Evolution in a Man-Made World*
BL - v111 - i17 - May 1 2015 - p67(1) [51-500]
KR - April 1 2015 - pNA [501+]
LJ - v140 - i6 - April 1 2015 - p113(3) [51-500]
Nature - v522 - i7555 - June 11 2015 - p155(1) [51-500]
PW - v262 - i9 - March 2 2015 - p74(1) [51-500]

Francis-Sharma, Lauren - *Til the Well Runs Dry*
NYTBR - Nov 29 2015 - p24(L) [51-500]

Francis, Wendy - *The Summer of Good Intentions*
BL - v111 - i19-20 - June 1 2015 - p46(1) [51-500]
KR - May 15 2015 - pNA [51-500]

Francisco X - *The Memory of Light*
y PW - v262 - i41 - Oct 12 2015 - p70(1) [51-500]

Franck, Julia - *West*
TLS - i5841 - March 13 2015 - p20(1) [501+]

Franco, Betsy - *A Spectacular Selection of Sea Critters: Concrete Poems (Illus. by Wertz, Michael)*
c BL - v112 - i1 - Sept 1 2015 - p95(1) [51-500]
c KR - August 1 2015 - pNA [51-500]
c PW - v262 - i38 - Sept 21 2015 - p75(1) [501+]
c SLJ - v61 - i8 - August 2015 - p118(2) [51-500]

Franco, Cristiana - *Shameless: The Canine and the Feminine in Ancient Greece*
TLS - i5839 - Feb 27 2015 - p10(1) [501+]

Franco, Jean - *Cruel Modernity*
Am Q - v67 - i2 - June 2015 - p505-515 [501+]

Franco, Jorge - *El mundo de afuera*
WLT - v89 - i1 - Jan-Feb 2015 - p65(2) [501+]

Francombe, Leona - *The Sage of Waterloo*
KR - April 1 2015 - pNA [501+]
LJ - v140 - i8 - May 1 2015 - p61(3) [51-500]
NYTBR - July 12 2015 - p14(L) [501+]
PW - v262 - i15 - April 13 2015 - p55(1) [51-500]

Francombe, Colin - *Unsafe Abortion and Women's Health: Change and Liberation*
Cons - v36 - i2 - Summer 2015 - p44(1) [51-500]

Frank, Alan - *Intimacies: A New World of Relational Life*
CS - v44 - i4 - July 2015 - p510-512 [501+]

Frank, Barney - *Frank: A Life in Politics from the Great Society to Same-Sex Marriage (Read by Frank, Barney). Audiobook Review*
BL - v111 - i19-20 - June 1 2015 - p138(1) [51-500]
PW - v262 - i17 - April 27 2015 - p71(1) [51-500]
Frank: A Life in Politics from the Great Society to Same-Sex Marriage
Barron's - v95 - i44 - Nov 2 2015 - p36(1) [501+]
BL - v111 - i13 - March 1 2015 - p6(2) [51-500]
Comw - v142 - i12 - July 10 2015 - p30(3) [501+]
G&L Rev W - v22 - i5 - Sept-Oct 2015 - p34(2) [501+]
KR - Feb 1 2015 - pNA [501+]
LJ - v140 - i5 - March 15 2015 - p122(2) [51-500]
NYRB - v62 - i10 - June 4 2015 - p6(2) [501+]
NYT - March 12 2015 - pC1(L) [501+]
NYTBR - March 15 2015 - p13(L) [501+]
Pers PS - v44 - i4 - Oct-Dec 2015 - p266-267 [501+]
PW - v262 - i4 - Jan 26 2015 - p160(1) [51-500]

Frank, E.R. - *Dime*
y BL - v111 - i16 - April 15 2015 - p47(1) [51-500]
y CCB-B - v69 - i1 - Sept 2015 - p21(2) [51-500]
y HB - v91 - i4 - July-August 2015 - p131(1) [51-500]
y KR - March 1 2015 - pNA [501+]
PW - v262 - i12 - March 23 2015 - p78(1) [51-500]
y PW - v262 - i49 - Dec 2 2015 - p90(1) [51-500]
y Teach Lib - v42 - i4 - April 2015 - p28(1) [51-500]
y VOYA - v38 - i2 - June 2015 - p59(1) [51-500]

Frank, Jacquelyn - *Bound by Sin*
PW - v262 - i31 - August 3 2015 - p41(2) [51-500]
Cursed by Fire
PW - v262 - i3 - Jan 19 2015 - p68(1) [51-500]
Cursed by Ice
PW - v262 - i7 - Feb 16 2015 - p165(1) [51-500]

Frank, Jerry J. - *Making Rocky Mountain National Park: The Environmental History of an American Treasure*
JAH - v102 - i1 - June 2015 - p269-270 [501+]
JIH - v45 - i3 - Wntr 2015 - p445-447 [501+]
PHR - v84 - i2 - May 2015 - p233(4) [501+]
RAH - v43 - i2 - June 2015 - p346-354 [501+]

Frank, John - *Lend a Hand: Poems about Giving (Illus. by Ladd, London)*
c HB Guide - v26 - i1 - Spring 2015 - p188(1) [51-500]
c SLJ - v61 - i4 - April 2015 - p42(4) [501+]

Frank, Lucy - *Two Girls: Staring at the Ceiling*
y HB Guide - v26 - i1 - Spring 2015 - p107(1) [51-500]

Frank, Marc - *Cuban Revelations: Behind the Scenes in Havana*
AM - v212 - i5 - Feb 16 2015 - pNA [501+]
NYRB - v62 - i5 - March 19 2015 - p24(3) [501+]

Frank, Matthew - *If I Should Die*
TimHES - i2216 - August 13 2015 - p43(1) [501+]
The Mad Feast
KR - August 15 2015 - pNA [501+]

Frank, Matthew Gavin - *The Mad Feast: An Ecstatic Tour through America's Food*
PW - v262 - i35 - August 31 2015 - p76(1) [51-500]
LJ - v140 - i19 - Nov 15 2015 - p100(2) [51-500]

Frank, Miriam - *Out in the Union: A Labor History of Queer America*
    AHR - v120 - i3 - June 2015 - p1068-1069 [501+]
    JAH - v102 - i1 - June 2015 - p310-311 [501+]
    Wom R Bks - v32 - i2 - March-April 2015 - p10(3) [501+]

Frank, Robin Jaffee - *Coney Island: Visions of an American Dreamland, 1861-2008*
    NYT - March 8 2015 - p3(L) [501+]

Frank, Scott - *Shaker*
    PW - v262 - i46 - Nov 16 2015 - p54(2) [51-500]

Frank, Walter - *Law and the Gay Rights Story: The Long Search for Equal Justice in a Divided Democracy*
    G&L Rev W - v22 - i1 - Jan-Feb 2015 - p41(2) [501+]
    HLR - v128 - i6 - April 2015 - p1894(1) [1-50]

Frank, Wayne - *Tavern Tales 2004-2014*
    RVBW - May 2015 - pNA [51-500]

Frankel, Bethenny - *Cookie Meets Peanut (Illus. by Roode, Daniel)*
    c HB Guide - v26 - i1 - Spring 2015 - p30(1) [51-500]
I Suck at Relationships So You Don't Have To
    PW - v262 - i9 - March 2 2015 - p80(2) [51-500]

Frankel, Erin - *Nobody! A Story about Overcoming Bullying in Schools (Illus. by Heaphy, Paula)*
    c CH Bwatch - Sept 2015 - pNA [51-500]
    c SLJ - v61 - i5 - May 2015 - p132(1) [51-500]

Frankel, Jordana - *The Isle*
    y KR - Nov 1 2015 - pNA [51-500]

Frankel, Lauren - *Hyacinth Girls (Read by Hamilton, Laura. with Emily Sutton-Smith). Audiobook Review*
    LJ - v140 - i12 - July 1 2015 - p42(1) [51-500]
Hyacinth Girls
    y BL - v111 - i18 - May 15 2015 - p23(1) [51-500]
    KR - March 1 2015 - pNA [501+]
    LJ - v140 - i10 - June 1 2015 - p86(1) [51-500]
    PW - v262 - i13 - March 30 2015 - p49(1) [51-500]
    y SLJ - v61 - i10 - Oct 2015 - p121(2) [51-500]

Franketienne - *Ready to Burst*
    TLS - i5838 - Feb 20 2015 - p27(1) [501+]

Frankfurt, Harry G. - *On Inequality*
    CSM - Sept 28 2015 - pNA [501+]
    LJ - v140 - i15 - Sept 15 2015 - p80(1) [501+]
    Nation - v301 - i24 - Dec 14 2015 - p37(1) [501+]
    NYTBR - Dec 20 2015 - p27(L) [501+]
    Spec - v329 - i9764 - Oct 17 2015 - p43(2) [501+]

Franklin, Aaron - *Franklin Barbecue: A Meat-Smoking Manifesto*
    PW - v262 - i5 - Feb 2 2015 - p50(1) [51-500]

Franklin, Allan - *Shifting Standards: Experiments in Particle Physics in the Twentieth Century*
    Isis - v106 - i2 - June 2015 - p502(2) [501+]

Franklin, Ariana - *The Siege Winter*
    BL - v111 - i9-10 - Jan 1 2015 - p54(1) [51-500]
    NYTBR - March 22 2015 - p29(L) [501+]

Franklin, Arnold E. - *Jews, Christians and Muslims in Medieval and Early Modern Times: A Festschrift in Honor of Mark R. Cohen*
    Ren Q - v68 - i2 - Summer 2015 - p706-708 [501+]

Franklin, Carolyn - *Gorilla Journal*
    c HB Guide - v26 - i1 - Spring 2015 - p164(1) [51-500]

Franklin, Cory - *Cook County ICU: 30 Years of Unforgettable Patients and Odd Cases*
    BL - v112 - i1 - Sept 1 2015 - p21(1) [51-500]
    PW - v262 - i28 - July 13 2015 - p58(1) [51-500]

Franklin, Emily - *Last Night at the Circle Cinema*
    y KR - June 1 2015 - pNA [51-500]
    y SLJ - v61 - i8 - August 2015 - p103(1) [51-500]

Franklin, James - *An Aristotelian Realist Philosophy of Mathematics: Mathematics as the Science of Quantity and Structure*
    RM - v68 - i3 - March 2015 - p658(3) [501+]

Franklin, Jo - *I'm an Alien and I Want to Go Home! (Illus. by Kelley, Marty)*
    c KR - Sept 1 2015 - pNA [501+]
    c PW - v262 - i35 - August 31 2015 - p92(2) [51-500]

Franklin, Joey - *My Wife Wants You to Know I'm Happily Married*
    KR - Sept 15 2015 - pNA [501+]

Franklin, Jonathan - *438 Days: An Extraordinary True Story of Survival at Sea*
    BL - v112 - i1 - Nov 1 2015 - p14(1) [51-500]
    KR - Oct 1 2015 - pNA [501+]

Franklin, Keara A. - *Temperature and Plant Development*
    QRB - v90 - i1 - March 2015 - p99(2) [501+]

Franklin, Miriam Spitzer - *Extraordinary*
    c BL - v111 - i19-20 - June 1 2015 - p104(1) [51-500]
    c SLJ - v61 - i8 - August 2015 - p84(1) [51-500]

Franklin, Peter - *Reclaiming Late-Romantic Music: Singing Devils and Distant Sounds*
    Notes - v72 - i1 - Sept 2015 - p181(3) [501+]

Franklin, Sarah - *Biological Relatives: IVF, Stem Cells, and the Future of Kinship*
    AJS - v120 - i5 - March 2015 - p1581(3) [501+]
    MAQ - v29 - i2 - June 2015 - pb17-b20 [501+]
    T&C - v56 - i1 - Jan 2015 - p303-305 [501+]

Franklin, Sarah L. - *Women and Slavery in Nineteenth-Century Colonial Cuba*
    Ams - v72 - i3 - July 2015 - p484(2) [501+]

Frankopan, Peter - *The Silk Roads: A New History of the World*
    Econ - v416 - i8952 - August 22 2015 - p71(US) [501+]
    HT - v65 - i11 - Nov 2015 - p57(1) [501+]
    KR - Nov 15 2015 - pNA [501+]
    PW - v262 - i52 - Dec 21 2015 - p144(1) [51-500]

Franks, Lane - *The Adventures and Life Lessons of Wolfy (Illus. by Escalona, Earlene Gayle)*
    c CH Bwatch - Jan 2015 - pNA [51-500]

Franks, Lucinda - *Timeless: Love, Morgenthau, and Me*
    Bks & Cult - v21 - i1 - Jan-Feb 2015 - p15(1) [501+]

Fransman, Karrie - *Death of the Artist*
    TLS - i5854 - June 12 2015 - p27(1) [501+]

Franta, Connor - *A Work in Progress*
    G&L Rev W - v22 - i5 - Sept-Oct 2015 - p41(2) [501+]

Frantz, Laura - *The Mistress of Tall Acre*
    BL - v112 - i1 - Sept 1 2015 - p54(1) [51-500]

Frantz, Timothy - *Hearing Loss: Facts and Fiction*
    KR - April 1 2015 - pNA [501+]

Frantzen, Allen J. - *Anglo-Saxon Keywords*
    JEGP - v114 - i2 - April 2015 - p292(3) [501+]
    Med R - Feb 2015 - pNA [501+]
    Specu - v90 - i1 - Jan 2015 - p249-251 [501+]
Food, Eating and Identity in Early Medieval England
    AHR - v120 - i3 - June 2015 - p1095-1096 [501+]
    JIH - v46 - i1 - Summer 2015 - p114-115 [501+]
    Med R - May 2015 - pNA [501+]

Franz, Albrecht - *Kooperation statt Klassenkampf? Zur Bedeutung kooperativer wirtschaftlicher Leitbilder fur die Arbeitszeitsenkung in Kaiserreich und Bundesrepublik*
    HNet - May 2015 - pNA [501+]

Franzblau, Robert - *So You Want to Be a Music Major: A Guide for High School Students, Their Parents, Guidance Counselors, and Music Teachers*
    Am MT - v64 - i6 - June-July 2015 - p66(2) [501+]

Franzen, Jonathan - *Purity*
    BL - v111 - i21 - July 1 2015 - p33(1) [501+]
    Comw - v142 - i17 - Oct 23 2015 - p35(2) [501+]
    CSM - Sept 1 2015 - pNA [501+]
    Esq - v164 - i2 - Sept 2015 - p56(2) [501+]
    HM - v331 - i1984 - Sept 2015 - p84(5) [501+]
    KR - June 1 2015 - pNA [501+]
    LJ - v140 - i12 - July 1 2015 - p76(1) [51-500]
    Lon R Bks - v37 - i18 - Sept 24 2015 - p25(3) [501+]
    Mac - v128 - i36 - Sept 14 2015 - p75(1) [51-500]
    Nat R - v67 - i20 - Nov 2 2015 - p45(2) [501+]
    Nation - v301 - i11 - Oct 26 2015 - p31(5) [501+]
    NS - v144 - i5276 - August 21 2015 - p44(2) [501+]
    NYRB - v62 - i16 - Oct 22 2015 - p24(3) [501+]
    NYTBR - August 30 2015 - p12(L) [501+]
    PW - v262 - i21 - May 25 2015 - p28(1) [501+]
    SEP - v287 - i5 - Sept-Oct 2015 - p24(1) [501+]
    Spec - v328 - i9757 - August 29 2015 - p35(2) [501+]
    TLS - i5874 - Oct 30 2015 - p19(2) [501+]
    NYT - August 25 2015 - pC1(L) [501+]

Franzen, Trisha - *Anna Howard Shaw: The Work of Woman Suffrage*
    AHR - v120 - i2 - April 2015 - p620-621 [501+]
    J Am St - v49 - i3 - August 2015 - p635-636 [501+]
    JAH - v102 - i1 - June 2015 - p270-271 [501+]
    Wom R Bks - v32 - i1 - Jan-Feb 2015 - p18(3) [501+]

Franzius, Claudio - *Recht und Politik in der Transnationalen Konstellation*
    HNet - Feb 2015 - pNA [501+]

Frare, Gail - *Painkillers and Gummi Bears*
    KR - July 1 2015 - pNA [501+]

Frary, Lucien J. - *Russia and the Making of Modern Greek Identity, 1821-1844*
    TLS - i5868 - Sept 18 2015 - p10(1) [501+]

Fraser, Anthea - *A Tangled Thread*
    KR - Nov 1 2015 - pNA [51-500]
    PW - v262 - i46 - Nov 16 2015 - p57(1) [51-500]

Fraser, Antonia - *My History: A Memoir of Growing Up*
    BL - v111 - i22 - August 1 2015 - p17(1) [51-500]
    LJ - v140 - i13 - August 1 2015 - p94(1) [51-500]
    NS - v144 - i5247 - Jan 30 2015 - p46(2) [501+]
    NYTBR - Dec 6 2015 - p68(L) [501+]
    PW - v262 - i23 - June 8 2015 - p48(2) [51-500]
    Spec - v327 - i9724 - Jan 10 2015 - p31(1) [501+]
    TLS - i5858 - July 10 2015 - p21(1) [501+]
    TimHES - i2224 - Oct 8 2015 - p43(1) [501+]
The Pleasure of Reading: 43 Writers on the Discovery of Reading and the Books that Inspired Them
    TLS - i5858 - July 10 2015 - p21(1) [501+]
    BL - v112 - i1 - Sept 1 2015 - p29(1) [51-500]
    KR - June 1 2015 - pNA [501+]
    LJ - v140 - i14 - Sept 1 2015 - p101(2) [51-500]

Fraser, Diane - *Growing Up Superheroes: The Extraordinary Adventures of Deihlia Nye*
    RVBW - Oct 2015 - pNA [51-500]

Fraser, Flora - *George & Martha Washington: A Revolutionary Marriage*
    Spec - v329 - i9771 - Dec 5 2015 - p34(2) [501+]
The Washingtons: George and Martha, Join'd by Friendship, Crown'd by Love
    LJ - v140 - i14 - Sept 1 2015 - p120(2) [501+]
    BL - v111 - i19-20 - June 1 2015 - p36(1) [51-500]
    KR - July 15 2015 - pNA [501+]
    NYTBR - Dec 6 2015 - p36(L) [501+]

Fraser, George MacDonald - *Captain in Calico*
    BL - v111 - i22 - August 1 2015 - p31(2) [51-500]
    KR - July 1 2015 - pNA [51-500]
    PW - v262 - i28 - July 13 2015 - p45(1) [51-500]

Fraser, L.E. - *Skully: Perdition Games*
    KR - August 15 2015 - pNA [501+]

Fraser, Mary Ann - *No Yeti Yet (Illus. by Fraser, Mary Ann)*
    c PW - v262 - i23 - June 8 2015 - p59(1) [51-500]
    c SLJ - v61 - i9 - Sept 2015 - p120(1) [51-500]

Fraser, Mary Beth - *Women of Faith: The Chicago Sisters of Mercy and the Evolution of a Religious Community*
    CHR - v101 - i2 - Spring 2015 - p392(2) [501+]

Fraser, Melissa - *Welcome to PlanitDo!*
    KR - August 1 2015 - pNA [501+]

Fraser, Sara - *The Devil's Monk*
    PW - v262 - i24 - June 15 2015 - p65(1) [51-500]

Fraser, Stephen - *The Spoonflower Handbook: A DIY Guide to Designing Fabric, Wallpaper and Gift Wrap*
    LJ - v140 - i16 - Oct 1 2015 - p82(1) [51-500]

Fraser, Steve - *The Age of Acquiescence: The Life and Death of American Resistance to Organised Wealth and Power*
    Lon R Bks - v37 - i14 - July 16 2015 - p28(3) [501+]
The Age of Acquiescence: The Life and Death of American Resistance to Organized Wealth and Power
    CC - v132 - i9 - April 29 2015 - p53(2) [501+]
    HM - v331 - i1985 - Oct 2015 - p90(5) [501+]
    Nation - v300 - i21 - May 25 2015 - p31(3) [501+]
    NYRB - v62 - i17 - Nov 5 2015 - p55(4) [501+]
    NYTBR - March 22 2015 - p12(L) [501+]
Spinoza's Metaphysics: Substance and Thought
    Dis - v62 - i3 - Summer 2015 - p140(145) [501+]

Fraser, Susan M. - *Flora Illustrata: Great Works from the LuEsther T. Mertz Library of the New York Botanical Garden*
    NYRB - v62 - i1 - Jan 8 2015 - p52(3) [501+]

Fratantoro, Christa - *Selected Letters of Langston Hughes*
    NYT - Feb 4 2015 - pC1(L) [501+]

Frater, Adrienne M. - *Flying Free: Stories and Where They Come From: A Book for Curious Children*
    c Magpies - v30 - i3 - July 2015 - pS5(1) [501+]

Frater, Rhiannon - *Dead Spots*
    BL - v111 - i9-10 - Jan 1 2015 - p58(2) [51-500]

Frawley, Ashley - *Semiotics of Happiness: Rhetorical Beginnings of a Public Problem*
    TimHES - i2185 - Jan 8 2015 - p47-47 [501+]

Frayling, Christopher - *Inside the Bloody Chamber: Aspects of Angela Carter*
    TLS - i5854 - June 12 2015 - p13(1) [501+]
The Yellow Peril: Dr. Fu Manchu and the Rise of Chinaphobia
    Lon R Bks - v37 - i5 - March 5 2015 - p34(2) [501+]
    TLS - i5832 - Jan 9 2015 - p3(2) [501+]

Frayn, Michael - *Matchbox Theatre: Thirty Short Entertainments*
    NYTBR - May 31 2015 - p22(L) [501+]

Frazee, Marla - *The Farmer and the Clown*
    c   HB Guide - v26 - i1 - Spring 2015 - p30(1) [51-500]

Frazier, Harriet C. - *Lynchings in Kansas, 1850s-1932*
    HNet - July 2015 - pNA [501+]

Frazier, Kathleen - *Sleepwalker: The Mysterious Makings and Recovery of a Somnambulist*
    BL - v112 - i1 - Sept 1 2015 - p22(1) [51-500]

Frazier, Kathy - *Power Up Your Creative Mind*
    RVBW - August 2015 - pNA [51-500]

Frazier, Sundee T. - *Cleo Edison Oliver, Playground Millionaire (Illus. by Meyer, Jennifer L.)*
    c   BL - v112 - i6 - Nov 15 2015 - p53(1) [51-500]
    c   KR - Nov 1 2015 - pNA [51-500]

Freadman, Anne - *The Livres-Souvenirs of Colette: Genre and the Telling of Time*
    Biomag - v38 - i3 - Summer 2015 - p453(5) [501+]

Frebel, Anna - *Searching for the Oldest Stars: Ancient Relics from the Early Universe*
    LJ - v140 - i16 - Oct 1 2015 - p104(1) [51-500]
    Mac - v128 - i45 - Nov 16 2015 - p56(2) [501+]
    NH - v123 - i8 - Oct 2015 - p46(2) [501+]

Frechette, Christopher G. - *Biblical Essays in Honor of Daniel J. Harrington, SJ, and Richard J. Clifford, SJ: Opportunity for No Little Instruction*
    Theol St - v76 - i4 - Dec 2015 - p882(1) [501+]

Fred - *Cast Away on the Letter A (Illus. by Fred)*
    c   CH Bwatch - Jan 2015 - pNA [51-500]
    c   HB Guide - v26 - i1 - Spring 2015 - p77(1) [51-500]
The Suspended Castle (Illus. by Kutner, Richard)
    c   BL - v112 - i2 - Sept 15 2015 - p51(1) [51-500]
    c   KR - July 15 2015 - pNA [51-500]
The Wild Piano (Illus. by Kutner, Richard)
    c   SLJ - v61 - i4 - April 2015 - p150(2) [51-500]
    y   HB Guide - v26 - i2 - Fall 2015 - p82(1) [51-500]
    c   KR - March 1 2015 - pNA [51-500]
    c   BL - v111 - i18 - May 15 2015 - p43(1) [51-500]

Frederick, Heather Vogel - *Absolutely Truly (Read by Rubinate, Amy). Audiobook Review*
    c   SLJ - v61 - i12 - Dec 2015 - p76(1) [51-500]
Absolutely Truly
    c   CCB-B - v68 - i5 - Jan 2015 - p254(2) [51-500]
    c   CH Bwatch - Jan 2015 - pNA [51-500]
    c   HB Guide - v26 - i1 - Spring 2015 - p77(1) [51-500]
A Little Women Christmas (Illus. by Ibatoulline, Bagram)
    c   HB Guide - v26 - i1 - Spring 2015 - p30(1) [51-500]

Frederick, Jen - *Revealed to Him*
    PW - v262 - i38 - Sept 21 2015 - p61(1) [51-500]

Frederick, Shane - *Alexander Ovechkin*
    c   HB Guide - v26 - i2 - Fall 2015 - p197(1) [51-500]
The Story of the Miami Heat
    c   HB Guide - v26 - i2 - Fall 2015 - p198(1) [51-500]
The Story of the San Antonio Spurs
    c   HB Guide - v26 - i2 - Fall 2015 - p198(1) [51-500]

Frederickson, Kari A. - *Cold War Dixie: Militarization and Modernization in the American South*
    JSH - v81 - i1 - Feb 2015 - p241(2) [501+]

Frederickson, Mary E. - *Gendered Resistance: Women, Slavery, and the Legacy of Margaret Garner*
    JAH - v102 - i1 - June 2015 - p250-250 [501+]

Frederik, Laurie - *Trumpets in the Mountains: Theater and the Politics of National Culture in Cuba*
    Ams - v72 - i3 - July 2015 - p485(3) [501+]

Frederiksen, Martin Demant - *Young Men, Time, and Boredom in the Republic of Georgia*
    CS - v44 - i4 - July 2015 - p512-513 [501+]

Fredrickson, Caroline - *Under the Bus: How Working Women Are Being Run Over*
    BL - v111 - i15 - April 1 2015 - p8(1) [51-500]
    KR - Feb 15 2015 - pNA [501+]
    LJ - v140 - i6 - April 1 2015 - p106(1) [51-500]

Fredrickson, Jack - *The Confessors' Club*
    BL - v111 - i19-20 - June 1 2015 - p50(1) [51-500]
    KR - May 1 2015 - pNA [51-500]
    PW - v262 - i18 - May 4 2015 - p99(1) [51-500]

Fredrickson, John M. - *Warbird Factory: North American Aviation in World War II*
    LJ - v140 - i20 - Dec 1 2015 - p129(1) [51-500]

Fredrickson, Lane - *Monster Trouble! (Illus. by Robertson, Michael)*
    c   KR - July 1 2015 - pNA [51-500]
    c   PW - v262 - i30 - July 27 2015 - p66(1) [51-500]
    c   SLJ - v61 - i10 - Oct 2015 - p76(1) [51-500]

Freeberg, Ernest - *The Age of Edison: Electric Light and the Invention of Modern America*
    JAH - v101 - i4 - March 2015 - p1285(1) [501+]

Freed, David - *The Three-Nine Line*
    BL - v111 - i22 - August 1 2015 - p38(1) [51-500]
    KR - July 1 2015 - pNA [51-500]
    PW - v262 - i23 - June 8 2015 - p40(1) [51-500]

Freed, Jenn - *The Last Encampment: A Novel*
    y   VOYA - v38 - i2 - June 2015 - p59(1) [51-500]

Freedland, Jonathan - *The 3rd Woman*
    PW - v262 - i26 - June 29 2015 - p47(2) [51-500]

Freedman, Adam - *A Less Perfect Union: The Case for States' Rights*
    BL - v111 - i19-20 - June 1 2015 - p11(1) [51-500]

Freedman, Claire - *Dragon Jelly (Illus. by Hendra, Sue)*
    c   KR - August 1 2015 - pNA [51-500]
    c   Sch Lib - v63 - i1 - Spring 2015 - p27(1) [51-500]
Oliver and Patch (Illus. by Hindley, Kate)
    c   Sch Lib - v63 - i2 - Summer 2015 - p91(1) [51-500]
Spider Sandwiches (Illus. by Hendra, Sue)
    c   HB Guide - v26 - i1 - Spring 2015 - p30(1) [51-500]

Freedman, Deborah - *By Mouse & Frog (Illus. by Freedman, Deborah)*
    c   CCB-B - v68 - i10 - June 2015 - p489(1) [51-500]
    c   HB Guide - v26 - i2 - Fall 2015 - p34(1) [51-500]
    c   KR - Feb 15 2015 - pNA [51-500]
    c   PW - v262 - i49 - Dec 2 2015 - p12(2) [51-500]

Freedman, Estelle B. - *Redefining Rape: Sexual Violence in the Era of Suffrage and Segregation*
    RAH - v43 - i2 - June 2015 - p262-267 [501+]

Freedman, Harry - *The Talmud: A Biography*
    TLS - i5838 - Feb 20 2015 - p28(1) [501+]

Freedman, John - *Real and Phantom Pains: An Anthology of New Russian Drama*
    TLS - i5850 - May 15 2015 - p12(2) [501+]

Freedman, Lew - *Knuckleball: The History of the Unhittable Pitch*
    LJ - v140 - i3 - Feb 15 2015 - p103(2) [501+]

Freedman, Paul - *Food in Time and Place: The American Historical Association Companion to Food History*
    TLS - i5861 - July 31 2015 - p27(1) [501+]

Freedman, Russell - *Angel Island: Gateway to Gold Mountain*
    c   BL - v111 - i9-10 - Jan 1 2015 - pS4(8) [501+]
    c   SLJ - v61 - i12 - Dec 2015 - p64(4) [501+]
Because They Marched: The People's Campaign for Voting Rights That Changed America
    c   BL - v111 - i9-10 - Jan 1 2015 - pS4(8) [501+]
    c   CCB-B - v68 - i5 - Jan 2015 - p255(1) [51-500]
    c   CH Bwatch - Feb 2015 - pNA [51-500]
    y   HB Guide - v26 - i1 - Spring 2015 - p138(1) [51-500]
The Voice That Challenged a Nation: Marion Anderson and the Struggle for Equal Rights
    c   JE - v195 - i1 - Wntr 2015 - p53-54 [501+]

Freedman, Stuart - *The Palaces of Memory*
    NS - v144 - i5281 - Sept 25 2015 - p70(1) [51-500]

Freedson, Bette J. - *Soul Mothers' Wisdom*
    SPBW - May 2015 - pNA [51-500]

Freeland, Claire A.B. - *What to Do When Mistakes Make You Quake: A Kid's Guide to Accepting Imperfection*
    c   CH Bwatch - Oct 2015 - pNA [51-500]

Freely, John - *A Travel Guide to Homer: On the Trail of Odysseus through Turkey and the Mediterranean*
    TLS - i5836 - Feb 6 2015 - p30(1) [51-500]

Freeman, Anna - *The Fair Fight*
    KR - March 1 2015 - pNA [51-500]
    NYTBR - May 3 2015 - p12(L) [51-500]

Freeman, Arthur - *Bibliotheca Fictiva: A Collection of Books and Manuscripts Relating to Literary Forgery*
    TLS - i5866 - Sept 4 2015 - p7(2) [501+]

Freeman, Barbara Claire - *Every Day but Tuesday*
    PW - v262 - i42 - Oct 19 2015 - p52(1) [51-500]

Freeman, Brian - *Goodbye to the Dead*
    KR - Jan 1 2016 - pNA [51-500]
Season of Fear
    RVBW - Oct 2015 - pNA [51-500]

Freeman, Brian James - *Dark Screams, vol. 1 (Read by Daniels, Luke). Audiobook Review*
    PW - v262 - i17 - April 27 2015 - p69(1) [51-500]
Dark Screams, vol. 4
    PW - v262 - i23 - June 8 2015 - p42(1) [51-500]
Dark Screams, vol. 5
    PW - v262 - i34 - August 24 2015 - p64(2) [51-500]

Freeman, Carla - *Entrepreneurial Selves: Neoliberal Respectability and the Making of a Caribbean Middle Class*
    HAHR - v95 - i4 - Nov 2015 - p714-716 [501+]

Freeman, Castle - *The Devil in the Valley*
    BL - v112 - i4 - Oct 15 2015 - p28(1) [51-500]

Freeman, Curtis W. - *Contesting Catholicity: Theology for Other Baptists*
    CC - v132 - i4 - Feb 18 2015 - p34(4) [501+]
    Comw - v142 - i16 - Oct 9 2015 - p40(5) [501+]
    JR - v95 - i4 - Oct 2015 - p551(3) [501+]

Freeman, Damien - *Figuring Out Figurative Art*
    TLS - i5875 - Nov 6 2015 - p20(1) [501+]

Freeman, Deborah - *By Mouse & Frog (Illus. by Freeman, Deborah)*
    c   CH Bwatch - June 2015 - pNA [501+]

Freeman, Hadley - *Life Moves Pretty Fast: The Lessons We Learned from 1980s Movies (and Why We Don't Learn Them from Movies Any More).*
    NS - v144 - i5275 - August 14 2015 - p42(2) [501+]

Freeman, Hilary - *When I Was Me*
    y   Sch Lib - v63 - i4 - Winter 2015 - p246(1) [51-500]

Freeman, Jane Ellen - *Jeremiah Lucky and the Guardian Angel (Illus. by Hammond, Eric)*
    c   CH Bwatch - March 2015 - pNA [51-500]

Freeman, Jean - *Do Trees Sneeze? (Illus. by Lawton, Val)*
    c   Res Links - v20 - i4 - April 2015 - p3(1) [51-500]

Freeman, John - *Freeman's: The Best New Writing on Arrival*
    KR - August 15 2015 - pNA [51-500]

Freeman, Kimberley - *Evergreen Falls*
    LJ - v140 - i12 - July 1 2015 - p76(2) [51-500]

Freeman, Lindsey A. - *Longing for the Bomb: Oak Ridge and Atomic Nostalgia*
    New Sci - v226 - i3015 - April 4 2015 - p45(1) [501+]

Freeman, Lisa - *Honey Girl*
    y   BL - v111 - i16 - April 15 2015 - p56(1) [51-500]
    y   VOYA - v38 - i1 - April 2015 - p59(1) [51-500]

Freeman, Martha - *The Orphan and the Mouse (Illus. by McPhail, David)*
    c   CCB-B - v68 - i6 - Feb 2015 - p310(2) [51-500]
    c   HB Guide - v26 - i1 - Spring 2015 - p77(1) [51-500]
    c   CH Bwatch - Jan 2015 - pNA [51-500]
The Secret Cookie Club
    c   CCB-B - v69 - i1 - Sept 2015 - p22(1) [51-500]
    y   HB Guide - v26 - i2 - Fall 2015 - p82(1) [51-500]
    c   SLJ - v61 - i6 - June 2015 - p100(1) [51-500]
Who Stole Uncle Sam?
    c   Teach Lib - v42 - i4 - April 2015 - p43(1) [51-500]

Freeman, Philip - *Burgos in the Peninsular War, 1808-1814: Occupation, Siege, Aftermath*
    J Mil H - v79 - i3 - July 2015 - p824-825 [501+]
Sacrifice
    BL - v112 - i2 - Sept 15 2015 - p34(1) [51-500]
    KR - August 15 2015 - pNA [501+]
Searching for Sappho: The Lost Songs and World of the First Woman Poet
    KR - Nov 15 2015 - pNA [501+]
    PW - v262 - i51 - Dec 14 2015 - p72(1) [51-500]

Freeman, Ru - *Extraordinary Rendition*
    KR - Oct 1 2015 - pNA [501+]

Freeman, Shannon - *The Accident*
    y   BL - v111 - i9-10 - Jan 1 2015 - p87(1) [51-500]
Listed
    y   BL - v111 - i17 - May 1 2015 - p98(1) [51-500]
The Most Beautiful Bully
    y   BL - v111 - i17 - May 1 2015 - p92(1) [51-500]
    y   PW - v262 - i14 - April 6 2015 - p60(1) [501+]
    y   VOYA - v38 - i1 - April 2015 - p59(1) [51-500]

Freeman, Tor - *Olive and the Embarrassing Gift*
    c   HB Guide - v26 - i1 - Spring 2015 - p30(1) [51-500]

Freemantle, Brian - *The Cloud Collector*
    BL - v112 - i3 - Oct 1 2015 - p25(1) [51-500]
    PW - v262 - i36 - Sept 7 2015 - p46(1) [51-500]

Freese, Gene Scott - *Hollywood Stunt Performers, 1910s-1970s: A Biographical Dictionary*
    Roundup M - v22 - i6 - August 2015 - p37(1) [501+]

Freidenreich, David - *Foreigners and Their Food: Constructing Otherness in Jewish, Christian, and Islamic Law*
    Specu - v90 - i3 - July 2015 - p810-811 [501+]

Freiermuth, Harry - *Lo! Jacaranda: A Spanish Gypsy's Cante Jondo*
    SPBW - May 2015 - pNA [51-500]

Freiheit, Menschenwurde, Solidaritat. Das Erbe der Revolutionen von 1989
    HNet - Feb 2015 - pNA [501+]

Freitag, Florian - *The Farm Novel in North America: Genre and Nation in the United States, English Canada,*

and *French Canada, 1845-1945*
    Dal R - v95 - i1 - Spring 2015 - p133(3) [501+]
Freitas, Bethany V. - *Curious George Discovers the Ocean*
  c HB Guide - v26 - i2 - Fall 2015 - p31(1) [51-500]
Freitas, Donna - *The Tenderness of Thieves*
  y BL - v111 - i17 - May 1 2015 - p53(1) [51-500]
  y CCB-B - v68 - i10 - June 2015 - p489(2) [51-500]
    HB Guide - v26 - i2 - Fall 2015 - p119(1) [501+]
  c KR - March 1 2015 - pNA [501+]
  y PW - v262 - i13 - March 30 2015 - p78(1) [51-500]
    SLJ - v61 - i4 - April 2015 - p163(1) [51-500]
  y VOYA - v38 - i2 - June 2015 - p59(1) [51-500]
Freitas, Roger - *Portrait of a Castrato: Politics, Patronage and Music in the Life of Atto Melani*
    Lon R Bks - v37 - i19 - Oct 8 2015 - p13(4) [501+]
Freitus, Joe - *Virginia in the War Years, 1938-1945: Military Bases, the U-Boat War and Daily Life*
    HNet - May 2015 - pNA [501+]
Fremantle, Elizabeth - *Watch the Lady*
    LJ - v140 - i11 - June 15 2015 - p76(2) [51-500]
Frembgen, Jurgen Wasim - *Wrestlers, Pigeon Fanciers and Kite Flyers: Traditional Sports and Pastimes in Lahore*
    TLS - i5841 - March 13 2015 - p27(1) [501+]
Fremon, David K. - *Schindler, Wallenberg, Miep Gies: The Holocaust Heroes*
  y HB Guide - v26 - i1 - Spring 2015 - p201(1) [51-500]
French, Aaron J. - *The Gods of H.P. Lovecraft*
    PW - v262 - i45 - Nov 9 2015 - p42(1) [51-500]
French, Deborah - *The Cookbook for Children with Special Needs: Learning a Life Skill with Fun, Tasty, Healthy Recipes*
    RVBW - Oct 2015 - pNA [51-500]
French, Henry - *Walter Wink: Collected Readings*
    Theol St - v76 - i1 - March 2015 - p212(2) [51-500]
French, Howard - *China's Second Continent: How a Million Migrants Are Building a New Empire in Africa*
    NS - v144 - i5267 - June 19 2015 - p42(3) [501+]
    NYTBR - March 1 2015 - p28(L) [501+]
French, Howard A. - *China's Second Continent: How a Million Migrants Are Building a New Empire in Africa*
    Lon R Bks - v37 - i6 - March 19 2015 - p15(3) [501+]
French, Jack - *Radio Rides the Range: A Reference Guide to Western Drama on the Air, 1929-1967*
    Roundup M - v22 - i6 - August 2015 - p37(1) [501+]
French, Jackie - *Birrung: The Secret Friend*
    Magpies - v30 - i1 - March 2015 - p34(2) [501+]
Ophelia: Queen of Denmark
  y Magpies - v30 - i4 - Sept 2015 - p40(2) [501+]
Wombat Wins (Illus. by Whatley, Bruce)
  c Magpies - v30 - i5 - Nov 2015 - p27(1) [501+]
French, Simon - *My Cousin's Keeper*
  c HB Guide - v26 - i1 - Spring 2015 - p77(1) [51-500]
French, Tana - *Faithful Place (Read by Reynolds, Tim Gerard). Audiobook Review*
    BL - v111 - i15 - April 1 2015 - p86(1) [501+]
The Secret Place
    RVBW - June 2015 - pNA [51-500]
    RVBW - August 2015 - pNA [51-500]
French, Tom - *Midnightstown*
    ILS - v35 - i1 - Fall 2015 - p22(2) [501+]
French, Vivian - *Blood and Guts and Rats' Tail Pizza (Illus. by Fisher, Chris)*
  c SLJ - v61 - i5 - May 2015 - p95(1) [51-500]
Dragons Can't Swim (Illus. by Melling, David)
  c Sch Lib - v63 - i3 - Autumn 2015 - p165(1) [51-500]
The Most Powerful Thing in the World (Illus. by Barrett, Angela)
  c NYTBR - Nov 8 2015 - p24(L) [501+]
The Most Wonderful Thing in the World (Illus. by Barrett, Angela)
  c BL - v112 - i6 - Nov 15 2015 - p59(1) [51-500]
  c KR - Sept 1 2015 - pNA [51-500]
    Magpies - v30 - i3 - July 2015 - p30(1) [501+]
  c PW - v262 - i39 - Sept 28 2015 - p89(1) [51-500]
  c PW - v262 - i49 - Dec 2 2015 - p24(1) [51-500]
  c Sch Lib - v63 - i3 - Autumn 2015 - p165(1) [51-500]
  c SLJ - v61 - i11 - Nov 2015 - p81(1) [51-500]
Pig in Love (Illus. by Archbold, Tim)
  c SLJ - v61 - i6 - June 2015 - p96(1) [51-500]
Frenee-Hutchins, Samantha - *Boudica's Odyssey in Early Modern England*
    Ren Q - v68 - i3 - Fall 2015 - p1128-1129 [501+]

Frenkel, Edward - *Love and Math: The Heart of Hidden Reality*
    Math T - v108 - i6 - Feb 2015 - p478(1) [501+]
    NYTBR - Feb 8 2015 - p28(L) [501+]
Frenz, Barbara - *Music to Silence to Music: A Biography of Henry Grimes*
    BL - v112 - i6 - Nov 15 2015 - p8(1) [501+]
Fresina, Jayne - *How to Rescue a Rake*
    BL - v112 - i7 - Dec 1 2015 - p36(2) [51-500]
    PW - v262 - i46 - Nov 16 2015 - p62(1) [51-500]
Fretheim, Terence E. - *Reading Hosea-Micah: A Literary and Theological Commentary*
    Intpr - v69 - i4 - Oct 2015 - p488(2) [501+]
Freud, Esther - *Mr. Mac and Me*
    NYTBR - Jan 25 2015 - p12(L) [501+]
    TLS - i5835 - Jan 30 2015 - p21(1) [501+]
Freund, Gisle - *Frida Kahlo: The Gisle Freund Photographs*
    NYTBR - Dec 6 2015 - p38(L) [501+]
Freund, Nancy - *Mailbox*
  y KR - Dec 15 2015 - pNA [501+]
Frevert, Ute - *Learning How to Feel: Children's Literature and Emotional Socialization, 1870-1970*
    JGS - v24 - i2 - April 2015 - p241-242 [501+]
Frey, Hugo - *Nationalism and the Cinema in France: Political Mythologies and Film Events, 1945-1995*
    FS - v69 - i2 - April 2015 - p285(1) [501+]
    Si & So - v25 - i1 - Jan 2015 - p106(1) [501+]
Frey, James - *Endgame: The Complete Training Diaries, vols. 1-3*
  y VOYA - v38 - i3 - August 2015 - p77(1) [51-500]
Sky Key
  y KR - Sept 15 2015 - pNA [501+]
  y VOYA - v38 - i5 - Dec 2015 - p68(2) [51-500]
Frey, Valerie J. - *Preserving Family Recipes: How to Save and Celebrate Your Food Traditions*
    LJ - v140 - i17 - Oct 15 2015 - p111(1) [51-500]
Freyne, Sean - *The Jesus Movement and Its Expansion: Meaning and Mission*
    Theol St - v76 - i3 - Sept 2015 - p600(3) [501+]
Freytag, Lorna - *My Humongous Hamster Goes to School (Illus. by Freytag, Lorna)*
  c BL - v111 - i16 - April 15 2015 - p54(1) [51-500]
  c HB Guide - v26 - i2 - Fall 2015 - p34(1) [51-500]
  c KR - June 1 2015 - pNA [51-500]
  c SLJ - v61 - i8 - August 2015 - p59(1) [51-500]
Frick, David - *Kith, Kin, and Neighbors: Communities and Confessions in Seventeenth-Century Wilno*
    CHR - v101 - i3 - Summer 2015 - p662(2) [501+]
    HNet - Sept 2015 - pNA [501+]
    JMH - v87 - i2 - June 2015 - p477(3) [501+]
Fridenson, Patrick - *Reimagining Business History*
    T&C - v56 - i1 - Jan 2015 - p263-265 [501+]
Fridolfs, Derek - *Study Hall of Justice*
  c KR - Dec 1 2015 - pNA [501+]
Fridriksdottir, Johanna Katrin - *Women in Old Norse Literature: Bodies, Words, and Power*
    Specu - v90 - i1 - Jan 2015 - p263-265 [501+]
Fried, Gabriel - *Heart of the Order: Baseball Poems*
    ABR - v36 - i3 - March-April 2015 - p17(1) [501+]
Fried, Johannes - *Karl der Grosse: Gewalt und Glaube*
    HNet - Jan 2015 - pNA [501+]
The Middle Ages
    HT - v65 - i6 - June 2015 - p57(2) [501+]
    NYRB - v62 - i12 - July 9 2015 - p49(3) [501+]
    Spec - v327 - i9726 - Jan 24 2015 - p38(2) [501+]
Fried, Marvin Benjamin - *Austro-Hungarian War Aims in the Balkans during World War I*
    AHR - v120 - i3 - June 2015 - p1137-1138 [501+]
Friedberg, Aaron L. - *Beyond Air-Sea Battle: The Debate over US Military Strategy in Asia*
    Parameters - v45 - i2 - Summer 2015 - p97(11) [501+]
Friedberg, Errol C. - *A Biography of Paul Berg: The Recombinant DNA: Controversy Revisited*
    QRB - v90 - i4 - Dec 2015 - p420(2) [501+]
Frieden, Lisa - *Dialysis*
    KR - April 15 2015 - pNA [501+]
Friedensordnungen in Geschichtswissenschaftlicher und Geschichtsdidaktischer Perspektive
    HNet - March 2015 - pNA [501+]
Friedewald, Boris - *A Butterfly Journey: Maria Sibylla Merian, Artist and Scientist*
    LJ - v140 - i17 - Oct 15 2015 - p110(1) [51-500]
Friedland, Elyssa - *Love and Miss Communication*
    BL - v111 - i17 - May 1 2015 - p76(1) [51-500]
    KR - March 15 2015 - pNA [501+]
Friedlander, Judah - *If the Raindrops United: Drawings and Cartoons*
    NYTBR - Dec 6 2015 - p58(L) [501+]
    KR - Sept 1 2015 - pNA [51-500]

Friedlander, Saul - *Franz Kafka: The Poet of Shame and Guilt*
    Tikkun - v30 - i2 - Spring 2015 - p49(11) [501+]
Friedman, Andrea - *Citizenship in Cold War America: The National Security State and the Possibilities of Dissent*
    AHR - v120 - i3 - June 2015 - p1074-1075 [501+]
    HNet - March 2015 - pNA [501+]
    JAH - v102 - i2 - Sept 2015 - p611-612 [501+]
Friedman, Asia - *Blind to Sameness: Sexpectations and the Social Construction of Male and Female Bodies*
    CS - v44 - i6 - Nov 2015 - p796-798 [501+]
Friedman, Avi - *A View from the Porch: Rethinking Home and Community Design*
    RVBW - Oct 2015 - pNA [51-500]
Friedman, Bill - *30 Illegal Years to the Strip: The Untold Stories of the Gangsters Who Built the Early Las Vegas Strip*
    KR - June 1 2015 - pNA [501+]
    SPBW - May 2015 - pNA [501+]
Friedman, Brent A. - *21st Century Ellis: Operational Art and Strategic Prophecy for the Modern Era*
    NWCR - v68 - i4 - Autumn 2015 - p129(2) [51-500]
Friedman, Bruce Jay - *The Peace Process*
    KR - August 1 2015 - pNA [51-500]
Friedman, Daniel - *Don't Ever Look Back*
    RVBW - April 2015 - pNA [501+]
Riot Most Uncouth
    BL - v112 - i4 - Oct 15 2015 - p23(1) [51-500]
    KR - Oct 1 2015 - pNA [51-500]
Friedman, David M. - *Wilde in America: Oscar Wilde and the Invention of Modern Celebrity*
    NS - v144 - i5264 - May 29 2015 - p78(2) [501+]
Friedman, Dayle A. - *Jewish Wisdom for Growing Older*
    RVBW - May 2015 - pNA [501+]
Friedman, Debbie - *Lullaby (Illus. by Bubar, Lorraine)*
  c CH Bwatch - Feb 2015 - pNA [51-500]
Friedman, Eli - *The Insurgency Trap: Labor Politics in Postsocialist China*
    AJS - v121 - i1 - July 2015 - p343(4) [501+]
Friedman, Elias Weiss - *The Dogist: Photographic Encounters with 1,000 Dogs*
    PW - v262 - i34 - August 24 2015 - p77(2) [51-500]
    LJ - v140 - i17 - Oct 15 2015 - p107(1) [51-500]
Friedman, Ellis - *A Valediction*
    PW - v262 - i5 - Feb 2 2015 - p35(1) [51-500]
Friedman, George - *Flashpoints: The Emerging Crisis in Europe (Read by Turk, Bruce). Audiobook Review*
    Bwatch - April 2015 - pNA [51-500]
Friedman, Hilary Levey - *Playing to Win: Raising Children in a Competitive Culture*
    AJS - v121 - i2 - Sept 2015 - p618(3) [501+]
    SSJ - v32 - i3 - Sept 2015 - p349-352 [501+]
Friedman, Isaiah - *British Miscalculations: The Rise of Muslim Nationalism, 1918-1925*
    HNet - May 2015 - pNA [501+]
Friedman, Laurie - *Game Time, Mallory! (Illus. by Kalis, Jennifer)*
  y HB Guide - v26 - i2 - Fall 2015 - p82(1) [51-500]
Love or Something Like It
  c SLJ - v61 - i6 - June 2015 - p108(1) [51-500]
Mallory McDonald, Baby Expert (Illus. by Kalis, Jennifer)
  c HB Guide - v26 - i1 - Spring 2015 - p77(1) [51-500]
Ruby Valentine and the Sweet Surprise (Illus. by Avril, Lynne)
  c HB Guide - v26 - i1 - Spring 2015 - p30(1) [51-500]
Friedman, Laurie B. - *Love or Something Like It*
  y HB Guide - v26 - i2 - Fall 2015 - p119(1) [51-500]
  y VOYA - v38 - i1 - April 2015 - p59(1) [51-500]
Not What I Expected: The Mostly Miserable Life of April Sinclair, Bk. 5
  y VOYA - v38 - i5 - Dec 2015 - p56(1) [51-500]
Truth and Kisses
  y HB Guide - v26 - i2 - Fall 2015 - p119(1) [51-500]
Friedman, Lawrence J. - *The Lives of Erich Fromm: Love's Prophet*
    Soc - v52 - i3 - June 2015 - p298(9) [501+]
Friedman, Maya - *3 Falafels in My Pita (Illus. by Mack, Steve)*
  c KR - July 1 2015 - pNA [51-500]
Friedman, Norman - *Fighting the Great War at Sea: Strategy, Tactics and Technology*
    J Mil H - v79 - i2 - April 2015 - p507-508 [501+]
    J Mil H - v79 - i4 - Oct 2015 - p1177-1178 [501+]
    NWCR - v68 - i4 - Autumn 2015 - p130(3) [51-500]

Friedman, Russell L. - *Intellectual Traditions at the Medieval University: The Use of Philosophical Psychology in Trinitarian Theology among the Franciscans and Dominicans, 1250-1350, 2 vols.*
RM - v68 - i4 - June 2015 - p849(4) [501+]

Friedman, Samantha - *Matisse's Garden (Illus. by Amodeo, Cristina)*
c HB Guide - v26 - i1 - Spring 2015 - p179(1) [51-500]

Friedman, Sanford - *Conversations with Beethoven*
NS - v144 - i5244 - Jan 9 2015 - p36(2) [501+]

Friedman, Sara L. - *Wives, Husbands, and Lovers: Marriage and Sexuality in Hong Kong, Taiwan, and Urban China*
Pac A - v88 - i3 - Sept 2015 - p706 [501+]

Friedman, Walter A. - *Fortune Tellers: The Story of America's First Economic Forecasters*
T&C - v56 - i2 - April 2015 - p547-549 [501+]

Friedrich, Jorg - *14/18: Der Weg nach Versailles*
HNet - July 2015 - pNA [501+]

Friedrich Max Muller and His Asian Interlocutors: Academic Knowledge about 'Oriental Religions' in Late Nineteenth-Century Europe
HNet - Feb 2015 - pNA [501+]

Friedrich, Thomas - *Hitler's Berlin: Abused City*
HER - v130 - i544 - June 2015 - p780(3) [501+]

Friedrichs, Jorg - *The Future Is Not What It Used To Be: Climate Change and Energy Scarcity*
QRB - v90 - i1 - March 2015 - p84(1) [501+]

Frieman, Richie - *Reply All...and Other Ways to Tank Your Career*
NACEJou - v75 - i4 - April 2015 - p12(1) [501+]

Friend, Alison - *Bramble and Maggie: Spooky Season*
c HB Guide - v26 - i1 - Spring 2015 - p60(1) [51-500]
Freddy and Frito and the Clubhouse Rules (Illus. by Friend, Alison)
c KR - Feb 1 2015 - pNA [51-500]
Freddy and Frito and the Clubhouse Rules
SLJ - v61 - i3 - March 2015 - p116(1) [51-500]

Friend, Natasha - *Where You'll Find Me*
y SLJ - v61 - i12 - Dec 2015 - p113(1) [51-500]

Friends, Patrons, Clients. Final Conference of the PhD Research Group Graduiertenkolleg 1288
HNet - Sept 2015 - pNA(NA) [501+]

Frierson, Cathy A. - *Silence was Salvation: Child Survivors of Stalin's Terror and World War II in the Soviet Union*
TimHES - i2195 - March 19 2015 - p51(1) [501+]

Friesen, Helen Lepp - *Chimpanzees*
c BL - v112 - i6 - Nov 15 2015 - p42(1) [51-500]

Friesen, Jonathan - *Both of Me*
SPBW - Feb 2015 - pNA [51-500]

Friesen, Melinda - *Enslavement*
y Res Links - v20 - i4 - April 2015 - p28(2) [501+]

Friesner, Esther - *Deception's Pawn*
y KR - Jan 1 2015 - pNA [51-500]
y CH Bwatch - June 2015 - pNA [51-500]
y HB Guide - v26 - i2 - Fall 2015 - p119(1) [501+]
y SLJ - v61 - i2 - Feb 2015 - p100(2) [51-500]
y VOYA - v38 - i1 - April 2015 - p59(2) [51-500]

Friester, Paul - *Owl Howl (Illus. by Goossens, Philippe)*
c HB Guide - v26 - i1 - Spring 2015 - p30(1) [51-500]

Frigeri, Flavia - *The World Goes Pop*
TLS - i5874 - Oct 30 2015 - p17(1) [501+]

Friis, Agnete - *Death of a Nightingale*
RVBW - Feb 2015 - pNA [51-500]

Friman, Alice - *The View from Saturn*
ABR - v36 - i2 - Jan-Feb 2015 - p29(2) [501+]

Friot, Bernard - *Worms (Illus. by Guillerey, Aurelie)*
c KR - June 1 2015 - pNA [51-500]
c PW - v262 - i28 - July 13 2015 - p65(2) [51-500]
c SLJ - v61 - i9 - Sept 2015 - p120(1) [51-500]

Frisch, Aaron - *Bees*
c HB Guide - v26 - i1 - Spring 2015 - p158(1) [51-500]
Edgar Allan Poe (Illus. by Kelley, Gary)
c HB Guide - v26 - i1 - Spring 2015 - p191(1) [51-500]
Frogs
c HB Guide - v26 - i1 - Spring 2015 - p160(1) [51-500]

Frisch, Belinda - *Fatal Reaction*
PW - v262 - i30 - July 27 2015 - p46(1) [51-500]

Frisch, Nate - *The Story of the Indiana Pacers*
c HB Guide - v26 - i2 - Fall 2015 - p198(1) [51-500]

Frisch-Schmoll, Joy - *Pebble Plus: Ice Age Animals*
c HB Guide - v26 - i1 - Spring 2015 - p168(1) [51-500]

Frische, M.M. - *Moon Tears*
y PW - v262 - i24 - June 15 2015 - p84(1) [51-500]

Frischlin, Nicodemus - *Samtliche Werke, vol. 3: Dramen, part. 3: Kommentar zu Prisciamus Vapulans und Iulius Redivivus*
Sev Cent N - v73 - i1-2 - Spring-Summer 2015 - p74(3) [501+]

Friss, Evan - *The Cycling City: Bicycles & Urban America in the 1890s*
NY - v91 - i30 - Oct 5 2015 - p80 [501+]

Frith, Alex - *My Very First Dinosaurs Book (Illus. by Frith, Alex)*
c KR - Nov 15 2015 - pNA [51-500]

Frith, Nicholas John - *Hector and Hummingbird (Illus. by Frith, Nicholas John)*
c KR - Jan 1 2016 - pNA [51-500]

Frith, Nicola - *The French Colonial Imagination: Writing the Indian Uprisings, 1857-1858, from Second Empire to Third Republic*
FS - v69 - i3 - July 2015 - p404-405 [501+]

Fritsche, Maria - *Homemade Men in Postwar Austrian Cinema: Nationhood, Genre and Masculinity*
HNet - May 2015 - pNA [501+]

Fritz, Jean - *Bunny Hopwell's First Spring (Illus. by Dixon, Rachel)*
c HB Guide - v26 - i2 - Fall 2015 - p11(1) [51-500]

Fritz, Marianne - *The Weight of Things*
KR - August 1 2015 - pNA [51-500]
NYTBR - Dec 13 2015 - p46(L) [51-500]
PW - v262 - i35 - August 31 2015 - p58(1) [51-500]

Fritz, Peter Joseph - *Karl Rahner's Theological Aesthetics*
Theol St - v76 - i1 - March 2015 - p188(3) [501+]

Fritz, Randy - *Hail of Fire: A Man and His Family Face Natural Disaster*
BL - v111 - i19-20 - June 1 2015 - p10(1) [51-500]
KR - April 1 2015 - pNA [51-500]

Fritz, Stephen G. - *Ostkrieg: Hitler's War of Extermination in the East*
HNet - June 2015 - pNA [501+]

Fritzman, Hegel J.M. - *Hegel*
Dialogue - v54 - i3 - Sept 2015 - p561-562 [501+]

Fritzsche, Sonja - *The Liverpool Companion to World Science Fiction Film*
SFS - v42 - i1 - March 2015 - p173-176 [501+]

Frizzell, D.L. - *The Narrow Path to War*
PW - v262 - i2 - Jan 12 2015 - p42(1) [51-500]

Froehlich, Karlfried - *Sensing the Scriptures: Aminadab's Chariot and the Predicament of Biblical Interpretation*
CH - v84 - i4 - Dec 2015 - p876(3) [501+]

Froese, Deborah - *Mr. Jacobson's Window*
c Res Links - v20 - i5 - June 2015 - p4(1) [51-500]

Froese, Paul - *On Purpose: How We Create the Meaning of Life*
PW - v262 - i41 - Oct 12 2015 - p63(1) [51-500]

Frohman, Jesse - *Kurt Cobain: The Last Session*
LJ - v140 - i3 - Feb 15 2015 - p102(1) [501+]

Frohn, Julia - *Literaturaustausch im Geteilten Deutschland 1945-1972*
HNet - July 2015 - pNA [501+]

Froiland, Paul - *Accidental Brownie: A Childhood Memoir*
SPBW - Feb 2015 - pNA [51-500]

Froley, Margaux - *Hero Complex*
y HB Guide - v26 - i1 - Spring 2015 - p107(1) [51-500]

From Command to Consent: The Representation and Interpretation of Power in the Late Medieval Eurasian World
HNet - Jan 2015 - pNA [501+]

From Middle Class Society to an Age of Inequality? Social Change and Changing Concepts of Inequality in Germany and Great Britain after 1945
HNet - June 2015 - pNA [501+]

From War to Post-War. Reflections on the End of the Second World War
HNet - Sept 2015 - pNA(NA) [501+]

Fromm, Jeff - *Millennials with Kids: Marketing to This Powerful and Surprisingly Different Generation of Parents*
LJ - v140 - i13 - August 1 2015 - p107(2) [51-500]
PW - v262 - i22 - June 1 2015 - p53(2) [51-500]

Fromm, Megan - *Accuracy in Media*
c BL - v111 - i15 - April 1 2015 - p59(1) [51-500]

Frommer, Harvey - *When It Was Just a Game: Remembering the First Super Bowl*
PW - v262 - i34 - August 24 2015 - p77(1) [51-500]

Frommer, Myrna katz - *It Happened on Broadway: An Oral History of the Great White Way*
Am Theat - v32 - i2 - Feb 2015 - p58(2) [501+]

Fromont, Cecile - *The Art of Conversion*
Ch Today - v59 - i2 - March 2015 - p62(1) [51-500]

Froning, Alan - *The First Days of August*
KR - Dec 1 2015 - pNA [51-500]

Fronis, Aly - *Kisses and Cuddles (Illus. by Galloway, Fhiona)*
c KR - Jan 1 2016 - pNA [51-500]
c PW - v262 - i41 - Oct 12 2015 - p66(2) [51-500]

Frontz, Leslie - *The Watercolor Course You've Always Wanted: Guided Lessons for Beginners and Experienced Artists*
LJ - v140 - i16 - Oct 1 2015 - p82(1) [51-500]

Frost, Adam - *A Brush with Danger*
Sch Lib - v63 - i4 - Winter 2015 - p228(1) [51-500]

Frost, Allen - *Roosevelt (Illus. by Sodt, Fred)*
y KR - Sept 1 2015 - pNA [51-500]

Frost, Helen - *Among a Thousand Fireflies (Illus. by Lieder, Rick)*
c KR - Dec 15 2015 - pNA [51-500]
Salt: A Story of Friendship in a Time of War
SLJ - v61 - i2 - Feb 2015 - p49(1) [51-500]
Sweep Up the Sun (Illus. by Lieder, Rick)
c PW - v262 - i5 - Feb 2 2015 - p58(1) [501+]
c PW - v262 - i49 - Dec 2 2015 - p50(1) [51-500]
c SLJ - v61 - i2 - Feb 2015 - p68(2) [51-500]

Frost, Michael - *Surprise the World*
PW - v262 - i45 - Nov 9 2015 - p56(1) [51-500]

Froud, Brian - *Brian Froud's Faeries' Tales*
SLJ - v61 - i2 - Feb 2015 - p127(2) [51-500]
BL - v111 - i11 - Feb 1 2015 - p33(1) [51-500]

Frozen: The Junior Novelization (Read by Arndt, Andi). Audiobook Review
y SLJ - v61 - i6 - June 2015 - p53(3) [51-500]

Frucht, Abby - *A Well-Made Bed*
KR - Jan 1 2016 - pNA [51-500]

Fruhneuzeitliche Bildungssysteme im Interkonfessionellen Vergleich. Inhalte - Infrastrukturen - Netzwerke
HNet - Feb 2015 - pNA [501+]

Frumkin, Peter - *Building for the Arts: The Strategic Design of Cultural Facilities*
AJS - v120 - i6 - May 2015 - p1879(3) [501+]

Fry, Andy - *Paris Blues: African American Music and French Popular Culture, 1920-1960*
AHR - v120 - i3 - June 2015 - p1128-1129 [501+]

Fry, Jason - *Curse of the Iris*
c HB Guide - v26 - i1 - Spring 2015 - p77(1) [51-500]
Hunt for the Hydra
c BL - v112 - i1 - Sept 1 2015 - p114(1) [501+]

Fry, Michael - *The Naughty List (Illus. by Fry, Michael)*
c SLJ - v61 - i10 - Oct 2015 - p63(2) [51-500]
c PW - v262 - i37 - Sept 14 2015 - p75(1) [501+]
The Naughty List
c KR - June 15 2015 - pNA [51-500]
The Odd Squad: King Karl
c HB Guide - v26 - i1 - Spring 2015 - p77(1) [51-500]

Fry, Sonali - *Where Are You, Blue? (Illus. by Clifton-Brown, Holly)*
c BL - v112 - i6 - Nov 15 2015 - p57(1) [51-500]
c KR - Jan 1 2016 - pNA [51-500]

Fry, Stephen - *More Fool Me: A Memoir*
KR - April 15 2015 - pNA [501+]
PW - v262 - i16 - April 20 2015 - p69(1) [51-500]
More Fool Me
BL - v111 - i19-20 - June 1 2015 - p33(1) [51-500]

Frydenborg, Kay - *Chocolate: Sweet Science and Dark Secrets of the World's Favorite Treat*
y BL - v111 - i12 - Feb 15 2015 - p75(1) [51-500]
Bwatch - June 2015 - pNA [51-500]
y CCB-B - v68 - i11 - July-August 2015 - p543(2) [51-500]
y HB Guide - v26 - i2 - Fall 2015 - p188(1) [51-500]
y KR - Feb 15 2015 - pNA [51-500]
y PW - v262 - i9 - March 2 2015 - p87(1) [51-500]
Chocolate: Sweet Science & Dark Secrets of the World's Favorite Treat
SLJ - v61 - i3 - March 2015 - p176(2) [51-500]

Frye, David - *Simone*
NYT - Nov 26 2015 - pC6(L) [501+]
PW - v262 - i34 - August 24 2015 - p56(1) [51-500]

Frye, Northrop - *Northrop Frye's Uncollected Prose*
Nat Post - v17 - i205 - July 4 2015 - pWP5(1) [501+]

Fu, Kim - *For Today I Am a Boy*
NYTBR - May 17 2015 - p32(L) [501+]

Fuchs, Barbara - *The Poetics of Piracy: Emulating in English Literature*
    Hisp R - v83 - i3 - Summer 2015 - p357-364 [501+]

Fudge, Thomas A. - *The Trial of Jan Hus: Medieval Heresy and Criminal Procedure*
    HNet - Feb 2015 - pNA [501+]

Fuechtner, Veronika - *Imagining Germany Imagining Asia: Essays in Asian-German Studies*
    MLR - v110 - i2 - April 2015 - p599-601 [501+]

Fuentes, Laura - *The Best Homemade Kids' Snacks on the Planet: More Than 200 Healthy Homemade Snacks You and Your Kids Will Love*
    LJ - v140 - i14 - Sept 1 2015 - p129(1) [51-500]

Fugelso, Karl - *Studies in Medievalism XXIII: Ethics and Medievalism*
    TLS - i5843 - March 27 2015 - p30(1) [501+]

Fuhrer, Margaret - *American Dance: The Complete Illustrated History*
    LJ - v140 - i3 - Feb 15 2015 - p102(2) [51-500]

Fuhrer, Mary Babson - *A Crisis of Community: The Trials and Transformation of a New England Town, 1815-1848*
    AHR - v120 - i2 - April 2015 - p618-619 [501+]

Fuji, Hideaki - *New Dawn Raisers*
    c SLJ - v61 - i2 - Feb 2015 - p95(2) [51-500]

Fujii, Taiyo - *Gene Mapper*
    PW - v262 - i20 - May 18 2015 - p69(2) [51-500]

Fujikane, Candace - *Restoring Independence and Abundance on the Kulaiwi and Aina Momona*
    Am Q - v67 - i3 - Sept 2015 - p969-985 [501+]

Fujitani, Takashi - *Race for Empire: Koreans as Japanese and Japanese as Americans during World War II*
    HNet - June 2015 - pNA [501+]
    Pac A - v88 - i2 - June 2015 - p328 [501+]

Fujiwara, Hiro - *Maid-Sama!, 2 vols. (Illus. by Fujiwara, Hiro)*
    y SLJ - v61 - i11 - Nov 2015 - p124(1) [51-500]

Fukuyama, Francis - *Political Order and Political Decay: From the Industrial Revolution to the Globalisation of Democracy*
    TLS - i5842 - March 20 2015 - p28(1) [501+]
Political Order and Political Decay: From the Industrial Revolution to the Globalization of Democracy
    For Aff - v94 - i1 - Jan-Feb 2015 - pNA [501+]
    Nation - v300 - i12 - March 23 2015 - p27(5) [501+]

Fulford, Kenneth William Musgrave - *The Oxford Handbook of Philosophy and Psychiatry*
    TimHES - i2211 - July 9 2015 - p51(1) [501+]

Fulford, Tim - *The Late Poetry of the Lake Poets: Romanticism Revised*
    RES - v66 - i273 - Feb 2015 - p187-189 [501+]

Fulk, David - *Raising Rufus*
    c CCB-B - v69 - i2 - Oct 2015 - p87(1) [51-500]
    y HB Guide - v26 - i2 - Fall 2015 - p82(1) [51-500]
        PW - v262 - i17 - April 27 2015 - p76(1) [51-500]
    c VOYA - v38 - i2 - June 2015 - p74(1) [51-500]

Fulkerson, Gregory M. - *Studies in Urbanormativity: Rural Communities in Urban Society*
    AJS - v121 - i1 - July 2015 - p295(3) [501+]

Fuller, A. James - *The Election of 1860 Reconsidered*
    Historian - v77 - i2 - Summer 2015 - p332(2) [501+]

Fuller, Alexandra - *Leaving before the Rains Come (Read by Fuller, Alexandra). Audiobook Review*
    LJ - v140 - i11 - June 15 2015 - p51(1) [51-500]
Leaving before the Rains Come
    CSM - Jan 15 2015 - pNA [501+]
    Econ - v414 - i8923 - Jan 31 2015 - p74(US) [501+]
    Ent W - i1347 - Jan 23 2015 - p65(1) [501+]
    NYT - Feb 3 2015 - pC1(L) [501+]
    NYTBR - Jan 18 2015 - p11(L) [501+]
    SEP - v287 - i1 - Jan-Feb 2015 - p20(1) [501+]
    Spec - v327 - i9730 - Feb 21 2015 - p49(1) [501+]

Fuller, Claire - *Our Endless Numbered Days*
    y BL - v111 - i12 - Feb 15 2015 - p32(1) [51-500]
        KR - Jan 1 2015 - pNA [51-500]
        LJ - v140 - i3 - Feb 15 2015 - p86(2) [51-500]
        PW - v262 - i4 - Jan 26 2015 - p142(1) [51-500]
    y VOYA - v38 - i1 - April 2015 - p60(1) [51-500]

Fuller, David - *Sundance*
    Roundup M - v22 - i6 - August 2015 - p29(2) [501+]

Fuller, Errol - *Lost Animals: Extinction and the Photographic Record*
    QRB - v90 - i2 - June 2015 - p240(2) [501+]
The Passenger Pigeon
    QRB - v90 - i2 - June 2015 - p237(1) [501+]

Fuller, Howard J. - *Empire, Technology and Seapower: Royal Navy Crisis in the Age of Palmerston*
    J Mil H - v79 - i2 - April 2015 - p494-495 [501+]

Fuller, Janet M. - *Spanish in the USA*
    Lang Soc - v44 - i1 - Feb 2015 - p121-122 [501+]

Fuller, John - *The Dice Cup*
    TLS - i5839 - Feb 27 2015 - p24(1) [501+]
Sketches from the Sierra De Tejada
    TLS - i5839 - Feb 27 2015 - p24(1) [501+]

Fuller, Kathleen - *A Reluctant Bride*
    BL - v112 - i2 - Sept 15 2015 - p46(2) [51-500]

Fuller, Michael A. - *Drifting among Rivers and Lakes: Southern Song Dynasty Poetry and the Problem of Literary History*
    JAS - v74 - i1 - Feb 2015 - p189-191 [501+]

Fuller, Randall - *From Battlefields Rising: How the Civil War Transformed American Literature*
    HNet - Sept 2015 - pNA [501+]

Fuller, Robert C. - *The Body of Faith: A Biological History of Religion in America*
    Historian - v77 - i2 - Summer 2015 - p331(2) [501+]
    JR - Jan 2015 - p154(2) [501+]

Fuller, Ryan - *The Evil of Oz*
    KR - July 15 2015 - pNA [501+]

Fullerton, Alma - *In a Cloud of Dust (Illus. by Deines, Brian)*
    c KR - July 1 2015 - pNA [51-500]
    c PW - v262 - i26 - June 29 2015 - p66(2) [51-500]
    c Res Links - v20 - i4 - April 2015 - p3(1) [51-500]
    c SLJ - v61 - i8 - August 2015 - p69(1) [51-500]

Fulton, Alice - *Barely Composed*
    HR - v68 - i3 - Autumn 2015 - p481-491 [501+]
    NYTBR - March 1 2015 - p30(L) [501+]

Fulton, Henry L. - *Dr. John Moore, 1792-1802: A Life in Medicine, Travel, and Revolution*
    TLS - i5871 - Oct 9 2015 - p10(2) [501+]

Fulton, Julie - *Daniel O'Dowd Was Ever So Loud, Ever So Loud (Illus. by Ellis, Elina)*
    c Sch Lib - v63 - i2 - Summer 2015 - p91(1) [51-500]

Fulton, Richard D.L. - *The Last to Fall: The 1922 March, Battles, and Deaths of U.S. Marines at Gettysburg*
    SPBW - July 2015 - pNA [501+]

Fumaroli, Marc - *La Republique des lettres*
    NYRB - v62 - i12 - July 9 2015 - p61(3) [501+]
    TLS - i5875 - Nov 6 2015 - p27(1) [501+]

Fumerton, Patricia - *Broadside Ballads from the Pepys Collection: A Selection of Texts, Approaches, and Recordings*
    Ren Q - v68 - i3 - Fall 2015 - p1158-1160 [501+]

Funaro, Gregory - *Alistair Grim's Odditorium (Illus. by To, Vivienne)*
    c CCB-B - v68 - i8 - April 2015 - p399(1) [51-500]
    y HB Guide - v26 - i2 - Fall 2015 - p82(1) [51-500]
    c KR - Oct 1 2015 - pNA [51-500]
    c SLJ - v61 - i2 - Feb 2015 - p86(1) [51-500]

Funchion, John - *Novel Nostalgias: The Aesthetics of Antagonism in Nineteenth-Century U.S. Literature*
    RVBW - Oct 2015 - pNA [501+]

Funk, Josh - *Lady Pancake & Sir French Toast (Illus. by Kearney, Brendan)*
    c KR - June 15 2015 - pNA [51-500]
    c PW - v262 - i25 - June 22 2015 - p137(1) [51-500]

Funk, Robert W. - *A Beginning-Intermediate Grammar of Hellenistic Greek*
    BTB - v45 - i3 - August 2015 - p186(2) [501+]

Funke, Cornelia - *Emma and the Blue Genie (Illus. by Meyer, Kerstin)*
    c HB Guide - v26 - i1 - Spring 2015 - p60(1) [51-500]
Monster Busters
    Sch Lib - v63 - i4 - Winter 2015 - p228(1) [51-500]
The Pirate Pig (Illus. by Meyer, Kerstin)
    c CCB-B - v68 - i11 - July-August 2015 - p544(1) [51-500]
    c HB Guide - v26 - i2 - Fall 2015 - p65(1) [51-500]
Ruffleclaw (Illus. by Funke, Cornelia)
    c SLJ - v61 - i11 - Nov 2015 - p90(1) [51-500]
Ruffleclaw
    c KR - Sept 1 2015 - pNA [51-500]
Ruffleclaw (Illus. by Funke, Cornelia)
    c BL - v112 - i2 - Sept 15 2015 - p66(1) [51-500]

Funnell, Lisa - *Warrior Women: Gender, Race, and the Transnational Chinese Action Star*
    HNet - April 2015 - pNA [501+]

Fuqua, J. Scott - *The Secrets of the Greaser Hotel*
    c HB Guide - v26 - i1 - Spring 2015 - p77(2) [51-500]

Furani, Khaled - *Silencing the Sea: Secular Rhythms in Palestinian Poetry*
    JRAI - v21 - i2 - June 2015 - p486(2) [501+]

Furchtgott-Roth, Diana - *Disinherited: How Washington Is Betraying America's Young*
    Nat R - v67 - i11 - June 22 2015 - p37 [501+]

Fure-Slocum, Eric - *Contesting the Postwar City: Working-Class and Growth in 1940s Milwaukee*
    RAH - v43 - i1 - March 2015 - p161-167 [501+]

Furey, Hester - *Issues That Concern You*
    y VOYA - v38 - i4 - Oct 2015 - p85(2) [51-500]

Furlong, Dayle - *Saltwater Cowboys*
    Nat Post - v17 - i97 - Feb 21 2015 - pWP5(1) [501+]

Furman, Laura - *The O. Henry Prize Stories 2015*
    KR - July 15 2015 - pNA [501+]

Furniss, Clare. - *The Year of the Rat. Audiobook Review*
    SLJ - v61 - i2 - Feb 2015 - p51(1) [51-500]

Furniss, Clare - *The Year of the Rat*
    y CCB-B - v68 - i5 - Jan 2015 - p255(2) [51-500]
    y HB Guide - v26 - i1 - Spring 2015 - p107(1) [51-500]

Furnivall, Kate - *An Italian Wife*
    BL - v112 - i4 - Oct 15 2015 - p25(1) [51-500]

Furrow, Dwight - *American Foodie: Taste, Art and the Cultural Revolution*
    PW - v262 - i47 - Nov 23 2015 - p64(1) [51-500]

Furry, Timothy J. - *Allegorizing History: The Venerable Bede, Figural Exegesis, and Historical Theory*
    Specu - v90 - i3 - July 2015 - p811-3 [501+]

Furse, Margaret Lewis - *The Hawkins Ranch in Texas: From Plantation Times to the Present*
    JSH - v81 - i3 - August 2015 - p722(2) [501+]
    SHQ - v118 - i3 - Jan 2015 - p321-322 [501+]

Furst und Furstin als Kunstler. Herrschaftliches Kunstlertum zwischen Habitus, Norm und Neigung
    HNet - Jan 2015 - pNA [501+]

Furstenberg, Francois - *When the United States Spoke French: Five Refugees Who Shaped a Nation*
    JAH - v102 - i1 - June 2015 - p241-242 [501+]

Furstinger, Nancy - *Dogs*
    c HB Guide - v26 - i1 - Spring 2015 - p168(1) [51-500]

Furth, Yvonne James - *From the Yoga Mat to the Corner Office*
    SPBW - Feb 2015 - pNA [51-500]

Furuhata, Yuriko - *Cinema of Actuality: Japanese Avant-Garde Filmmaking in the Season of Image Politics*
    Pac A - v88 - i1 - March 2015 - p205 [501+]

Fury, Dalton - *One Killer Force*
    BL - v112 - i3 - Oct 1 2015 - p26(1) [51-500]

Fury, Shawn - *Rise and Fire: The Origins, Science, and Evolution of the Jump Shot--and How It Transformed Basketball Forever*
    BL - v112 - i5 - Nov 1 2015 - p12(1) [51-500]
    KR - Dec 15 2015 - pNA [501+]
    LJ - v140 - i19 - Nov 15 2015 - p89(1) [51-500]

Fusaro, Maria - *Political Economies of Empire in Early Modern Mediterranean: The Decline of Venice and the Rise of England, 1450-1700*
    HT - v65 - i10 - Oct 2015 - p61(1) [501+]

Fuss, Diana - *Dying Modern: A Meditation on Elegy*
    AL - v87 - i1 - March 2015 - p200-202 [501+]
    MP - v112 - i3 - Feb 2015 - pE266(E271) [501+]

Fussell, Mark L. - *The Slums of Palo Alto*
    KR - Feb 1 2015 - pNA [501+]

Fussell, Sandy - *Sad, the Dog*
    c KR - Sept 1 2015 - pNA [51-500]
Sad, the Dog (Illus. by Suwannakit, Tull)
    c NYTBR - Dec 20 2015 - p14(L) [501+]
    c SLJ - v61 - i10 - Oct 2015 - p76(2) [51-500]

Futamura, Madoka - *War Crimes Tribunals and Transitional Justice: The Tokyo Trial and the Nuremburg Legacy*
    HNet - Jan 2015 - pNA [501+]

G

G., Ashley - *Critter Colors*
    c   KR - Jan 1 2016 - pNA [51-500]
Out of Shapes
    c   KR - Jan 1 2016 - pNA [51-500]
Gabaccia, Donna R. - *Foreign Relations: American Immigration in Global Perspective*
    PHR - v84 - i1 - Feb 2015 - p125(3) [501+]
Gabaldon, Diana - *Written in My Own Heart's Blood*
    BL - v111 - i18 - May 15 2015 - p35(1) [501+]
Gabbler, G.B. - *The Automation*
    PW - v262 - i27 - July 6 2015 - p51(1) [51-500]
Gabel, Claudia - *Etherworld*
    y   HB Guide - v26 - i2 - Fall 2015 - p119(1) [501+]
    y   VOYA - v38 - i1 - April 2015 - p77(2) [51-500]
Gabhart, Ann H. - *The Innocent*
    RVBW - August 2015 - pNA [51-500]
Gabis, Rita - *A Guest at the Shooters' Banquet: My Grandfather's SS Past, My Jewish Family, a Search for the Truth*
    BL - v111 - i22 - August 1 2015 - p18(2) [51-500]
    KR - July 1 2015 - pNA [51-500]
    LJ - v140 - i11 - June 15 2015 - p96(1) [51-500]
    NY - v91 - i30 - Oct 5 2015 - p82 [51-500]
    PW - v262 - i28 - July 13 2015 - p57(1) [51-500]
Gable, Michelle - *I'll See You in Paris*
    KR - Dec 1 2015 - pNA [501+]
    LJ - v140 - i19 - Nov 15 2015 - p75(2) [51-500]
Gabowitsch, Mischa - *Putin kaputt!? Russlands neue Protestkultur*
    Slav R - v74 - i2 - Summer 2015 - p431-432 [501+]
Gabriel, Andrea - *Wandering Woolly (Illus. by Gabriel, Andrea)*
    c   CH Bwatch - Oct 2015 - pNA [501+]
Gabriel, Joseph M. - *Medical Monopoly: Intellectual Property Rights and the Origins of the Modern Pharmaceutical Industry*
    JAH - v102 - i2 - Sept 2015 - p548-549 [501+]
Gabriel, Louise - *Unsingle: The Art and Science of Finding True Love*
    PW - v262 - i51 - Dec 14 2015 - p76(2) [51-500]
Gabriel, Markus - *Why the World Does Not Exist*
    CHE - v62 - i7 - Oct 16 2015 - pB16(1) [501+]
Gabriel, Richard - *Between Flesh and Steel: A History of Military Medicine from the Middle Ages to the War in Afghanistan*
    Arm F&S - v41 - i3 - July 2015 - p582-584 [501+]
Gabriele, Matthew - *An Empire of Memory: The Legend of Charlemagne, the Franks, and Jerusalem Before the First Crusade*
    HER - v130 - i542 - Feb 2015 - p150(3) [501+]
Gaby, Nina - *Dumped: Stories of Women Unfriending Women*
    BL - v111 - i13 - March 1 2015 - p6(1) [51-500]
Gachagua, Clifton - *Madman at Kilifi*
    Ant R - v73 - i2 - Spring 2015 - p372(9) [501+]
Gadd, Ian - *The History of Oxford University Press*
    LR - v64 - i1-2 - Jan-Feb 2015 - p188-190 [501+]
Gadzikowski, Ann - *Creating a Beautiful Mess: Ten Essential Play Experiences for a Joyous Childhood*
    RVBW - Nov 2015 - pNA [51-500]
Gaetz, Dayle Campbell - *Disappearing Act*
    y   VOYA - v38 - i1 - April 2015 - p67(2) [51-500]
Gaffield, Nancy - *Continental Drift*
    TLS - i5839 - Feb 27 2015 - p25(1) [501+]
Gaffigan, Jim - *Food: A Love Story (Read by Gaffigan, Jim). Audiobook Review*
    LJ - v140 - i2 - Feb 1 2015 - p46(1) [51-500]
    PW - v262 - i5 - Feb 2 2015 - p56(1) [51-500]

Gage, Eleni N. - *The Ladies of Managua*
    y   BL - v111 - i18 - May 15 2015 - p23(1) [51-500]
    KR - March 15 2015 - pNA [501+]
    PW - v262 - i13 - March 30 2015 - p50(1) [51-500]
Gage, Leighton - *The Ways of Evil Men*
    RVBW - Feb 2015 - pNA [501+]
Gage, Randy - *Mad Genius: A Manifesto for Entrepreneurs*
    LJ - v140 - i19 - Nov 15 2015 - p93(1) [51-500]
Gage, Ruth - *Lion of Rora (Illus. by Lewis, Jackie)*
    PW - v262 - i33 - August 17 2015 - p58(1) [51-500]
Gage, Susy - *Not Easy Being Green*
    PW - v262 - i4 - Jan 26 2015 - p154(1) [51-500]
Gager, John G. - *Who Made Early Christianity? The Jewish Lives of the Apostle Paul*
    LJ - v140 - i9 - May 15 2015 - p86(1) [51-500]
    NYRB - v62 - i17 - Nov 5 2015 - p21(3) [501+]
Gagne, Natacha - *Being Maori in the City: Indigenous Everyday Life in Auckland*
    Cont Pac - v27 - i1 - Spring 2015 - p300(3) [501+]
Gagne, Renaud - *Ancestral Fault in Ancient Greece*
    Class R - v65 - i2 - Oct 2015 - p419-421 [501+]
Choral Mediations in Greek Tragedy
    Class R - v65 - i1 - April 2015 - p25-27 [501+]
Gagne, Tammy - *African Dance Trends*
    BL - v111 - i9-10 - Jan 1 2015 - p84(1) [51-500]
Blackbeard
    c   BL - v112 - i7 - Dec 1 2015 - p43(1) [51-500]
Eliot Ness
    c   BL - v112 - i1 - Sept 1 2015 - p96(2) [51-500]
The Most Adorable Animals in the World
    SLJ - v61 - i4 - April 2015 - p92(4) [501+]
The Most Endangered Animals in the World
    c   HB Guide - v26 - i2 - Fall 2015 - p170(1) [51-500]
Robin Hood
    c   BL - v112 - i1 - Sept 1 2015 - p96(2) [51-500]
Smartest Animals Series
    c   HB Guide - v26 - i1 - Spring 2015 - p164(1) [51-500]
The Strangest Animals in the World
    c   HB Guide - v26 - i2 - Fall 2015 - p170(1) [51-500]
The Tuskegee Airmen
    c   BL - v112 - i1 - Sept 1 2015 - p96(2) [51-500]
Gagnon, Cecile - *Qui EsTu? (Illus. by Perreault, Guillaume)*
    c   Res Links - v20 - i4 - April 2015 - p40(1) [51-500]
Gagnon, Michael J. - *Transition to an Industrial South: Athens, Georgia, 1830-1870*
    JAH - v101 - i4 - March 2015 - p1271-1272 [501+]
    RAH - v43 - i1 - March 2015 - p83-91 [501+]
Gagnon, Michelle - *Don't Let Go*
    y   HB Guide - v26 - i1 - Spring 2015 - p107(1) [51-500]
    MFSF - v128 - i5-6 - May-June 2015 - p57(2) [501+]
Don't Look Now
    MFSF - v128 - i5-6 - May-June 2015 - p57(2) [501+]
Gagnon, Sarah - *Date with a Rockstar*
    y   SLJ - v61 - i8 - August 2015 - p97(1) [51-500]
Gailey, Andrew - *The Lost Imperialist: Lord Dufferin, Memory and Myth-Making in an Age of Celebrity*
    TLS - i5846 - April 17 2015 - p25(1) [501+]
The Lost Imperialist: Lord Dufferin, Memory and Mythmaking in an Age of Celebrity
    Spec - v327 - i9731 - Feb 28 2015 - p43(1) [501+]
Gaillard, Mary K. - *A Singularly Unfeminine Profession: One Woman's Journey in Physics*
    TimHES - i2220 - Sept 10 2015 - p46-1 [501+]

Gaiman, Neil - *Chu's Day at the Beach (Illus. by Rex, Adam)*
    y   BL - v111 - i9-10 - Jan 1 2015 - p64(1) [51-500]
    c   BL - v111 - i12 - Feb 15 2015 - p87(1) [51-500]
    c   HB Guide - v26 - i2 - Fall 2015 - p11(1) [51-500]
    KR - Feb 15 2015 - pNA [51-500]
    c   SLJ - v61 - i2 - Feb 2015 - p69(1) [51-500]
Chu's First Day of School (Illus. by Rex, Adam)
    c   HB Guide - v26 - i1 - Spring 2015 - p9(1) [51-500]
    c   Sch Lib - v63 - i1 - Spring 2015 - p27(1) [51-500]
    c   SLJ - v61 - i7 - July 2015 - p55(1) [51-500]
Eternity's Wheel
    y   HB Guide - v26 - i2 - Fall 2015 - p119(1) [501+]
    y   BL - v111 - i15 - April 1 2015 - p68(1) [51-500]
    KR - March 1 2015 - pNA [51-500]
    SLJ - v61 - i2 - Feb 2015 - p101(1) [51-500]
    y   VOYA - v38 - i1 - April 2015 - p78(1) [51-500]
The Graveyard Book (Read by Jacobi, Derek). Audiobook Review
    y   SLJ - v61 - i6 - June 2015 - p53(3) [501+]
The Graveyard Book Graphic Novel, vol. 1 (Illus. by Scott, Steve)
    y   HB Guide - v26 - i1 - Spring 2015 - p78(1) [51-500]
The Graveyard Book Graphic Novel, vol. 2 (Illus. by LaFuente, David)
    y   HB Guide - v26 - i1 - Spring 2015 - p78(1) [51-500]
The Graveyard Book Graphic Novel, vol. 2 (Illus. by Russell, P. Craig)
    y   VOYA - v37 - i6 - Feb 2015 - p75(1) [51-500]
Hansel and Gretel (Illus. by Mattotti, Lorenzo)
    c   Sch Lib - v63 - i2 - Summer 2015 - p104(1) [51-500]
Hansel & Gretel (Illus. by Mattotti, Lorenzo)
    c   HB Guide - v26 - i1 - Spring 2015 - p144(1) [51-500]
    c   Magpies - v30 - i1 - March 2015 - p35(1) [501+]
The Sandman: Overture
    BL - v112 - i6 - Nov 15 2015 - p34(2) [51-500]
The Sleeper and the Spindle (Read by Rhind-Tutt, Julian). Audiobook Review
    y   BL - v112 - i7 - Dec 1 2015 - p72(1) [51-500]
    y   SLJ - v61 - i11 - Nov 2015 - p72(2) [51-500]
The Sleeper and the Spindle (Illus. by Riddell, Chris)
    y   PW - v262 - i23 - June 8 2015 - p62(1) [51-500]
    y   PW - v262 - i49 - Dec 2 2015 - p106(2) [51-500]
    y   SLJ - v61 - i8 - August 2015 - p97(2) [51-500]
    y   VOYA - v38 - i4 - Oct 2015 - p69(2) [51-500]
The Sleeper and the Spindle
    y   KR - July 15 2015 - pNA [51-500]
The Sleeper and the Spindle (Illus. by Riddell, Chris)
    y   BL - v111 - i21 - July 1 2015 - p49(1) [501+]
    y   BL - v111 - i22 - August 1 2015 - p66(1) [51-500]
    y   NYTBR - Nov 8 2015 - p24(L) [501+]
    c   Sch Lib - v63 - i1 - Spring 2015 - p36(2) [51-500]
Trigger Warning: Short Fictions and Disturbances (Read by Gaiman, Neil). Audiobook Review
    LJ - v140 - i12 - July 1 2015 - p42(1) [51-500]
Trigger Warning: Short Fictions and Disturbances
    y   BL - v111 - i13 - March 1 2015 - p31(1) [51-500]
    BooChiTr - Feb 21 2015 - p12(1) [501+]
    KR - Feb 1 2015 - pNA [51-500]
    NS - v144 - i5250 - Feb 20 2015 - p48(1) [501+]
    NYTBR - March 8 2015 - p18(L) [501+]
    NYTBR - Dec 27 2015 - p24(L) [501+]
Gaines, Caseen - *We Don't Need Roads: The Making of the Back to the Future Trilogy (Read by Butler, Ron). Audiobook Review*
    LJ - v140 - i17 - Oct 15 2015 - p53(1) [51-500]

We Don't Need Roads: The Making of the Back to the Future Trilogy
    BL - v111 - i18 - May 15 2015 - p9(2) [51-500]
    LJ - v140 - i9 - May 15 2015 - p84(2) [51-500]

Gaither, Stefanie - *Falls the Shadow*
    y HB Guide - v26 - i1 - Spring 2015 - p107(1) [51-500]

Gaitskill, Mary - *The Mare*
    New R - v246 - i12 - Nov 2015 - p69(3) [501+]
    y BL - v112 - i1 - Sept 1 2015 - p42(1) [501+]
    BooChiTr - Nov 14 2015 - p12(1) [501+]
    KR - Sept 1 2015 - pNA [501+]
    LJ - v140 - i16 - Oct 1 2015 - p68(1) [51-500]
    NY - v91 - i35 - Nov 9 2015 - p77 [501+]
    NYRB - v62 - i17 - Nov 5 2015 - p26(2) [501+]
    PW - v262 - i34 - August 24 2015 - p55(1) [51-500]

Gajano, Boesch Sofia - *Da santa Chiara a suor Francesca Farnese: Il francescanesimo femminile e il monastero di Fara in Sabina*
    Ren Q - v68 - i2 - Summer 2015 - p708-710 [501+]

Gal, Hans - *Music behind Barbed Wire: A Diary of Summer 1940*
    MT - v156 - i1931 - Summer 2015 - p117-118 [501+]
    TLS - i5852 - May 29 2015 - p17(2) [501+]

Gal, Ofer - *Baroque Science*
    RM - v68 - i3 - March 2015 - p660(3) [501+]
    T&C - v56 - i2 - April 2015 - p533-535 [501+]

Galan, Nely - *Self-Made: How to Become Self-Reliant, Self-Realized, and Rich in Every Way*
    PW - v262 - i51 - Dec 14 2015 - p30(3) [501+]

Galante, Cecilia - *Be Not Afraid*
    y CCB-B - v68 - i9 - May 2015 - p445(2) [51-500]
    y HB Guide - v26 - i2 - Fall 2015 - p119(1) [501+]
    y KR - Jan 15 2015 - pNA [51-500]
    y PW - v262 - i8 - Feb 23 2015 - p77(1) [51-500]
    y VOYA - v38 - i1 - April 2015 - p78(1) [51-500]
The Invisibles
    y BL - v111 - i21 - July 1 2015 - p31(1) [51-500]
    LJ - v140 - i11 - June 15 2015 - p77(1) [51-500]

Galassi, Jonathan - *Muse: A Novel*
    Nat Post - v17 - i176 - May 30 2015 - pWP4(1) [501+]
Muse
    Nat Post - v17 - i200 - June 27 2015 - pWP5(1) [501+]
    TLS - i5859 - July 17 2015 - p20(1) [501+]
    BL - v111 - i18 - May 15 2015 - p24(1) [51-500]
    KR - April 1 2015 - pNA [51-500]
    NYRB - v62 - i12 - July 9 2015 - p18(2) [501+]
    NYT - June 9 2015 - pC1(L) [501+]
    NYTBR - June 21 2015 - p10(L) [501+]
    PW - v262 - i11 - March 16 2015 - p57(1) [51-500]
    Spec - v328 - i9755 - August 15 2015 - p32(2) [501+]

Galavotti, Enrico - *Il Professorino: Giuseppe Dossetti tra Crisi del Fascismo e Costruzione della Democrazia, 1940-1948*
    CHR - v101 - i1 - Wntr 2015 - p177(3) [501+]

Galaxy Craze - *Mapmaker*
    CSM - May 1 2015 - pNA [501+]

Galbert of Bruges - *The Murder, Betrayal, and Slaughter of the Glorious Charles, Count of Flanders*
    Specu - v90 - i3 - July 2015 - p813-814 [501+]

Galbraith, James K. - *The End of Normal: The Great Crisis and the Future of Growth*
    For Aff - v94 - i1 - Jan-Feb 2015 - pNA [51-500]

Galbraith, Kathryn O. - *Planting the Wild Garden (Illus. by Halperin, Wendy Anderson)*
    c CH Bwatch - April 2015 - pNA [51-500]

Galbraith, Robert - *Career of Evil*
    KR - Nov 1 2015 - pNA [51-500]
    Mac - v128 - i43 - Nov 2 2015 - p76(2) [51-500]
    NYT - Oct 20 2015 - pC1(L) [501+]
    NYTBR - Nov 1 2015 - p9(L) [501+]
    TLS - i5876 - Nov 13 2015 - p20(1) [501+]
The Silkworm (Read by Glenister, Robert). Audiobook Review
    BL - v111 - i14 - March 15 2015 - p23(2) [51-500]

Galdos, Benito Perez - *Tristana*
    TLS - i5843 - March 27 2015 - p31(1) [501+]

Gale, Emily - *My Super-Spy Diary (Illus. by Dreidemy, Joelle)*
    c HB Guide - v26 - i1 - Spring 2015 - p60(1) [51-500]

Gale, Eric Kahn - *The Zoo at the Edge of the World (Read by Elfer, Julian). Audiobook Review*
    c BL - v112 - i5 - Nov 1 2015 - p72(1) [51-500]
    c SLJ - v61 - i8 - August 2015 - p49(1) [51-500]
The Zoo at the Edge of the World (Illus. by Nielson, Sam)
    c HB Guide - v26 - i1 - Spring 2015 - p78(1) [51-500]

Gale, Laurel - *Dead Boy*
    c KR - July 1 2015 - pNA [51-500]
    c SLJ - v61 - i7 - July 2015 - p76(2) [51-500]

Gale, Patrick - *A Place Called Winter*
    Mac - v128 - i28 - July 20 2015 - p54(1) [501+]

Galen, Shana - *Earls Just Want to Have Fun*
    BL - v111 - i9-10 - Jan 1 2015 - p56(1) [51-500]
The Rogue You Know
    BL - v112 - i1 - Sept 1 2015 - p54(1) [51-500]
    PW - v262 - i25 - June 22 2015 - p126(1) [51-500]

Galenorn, Yasmine - *Flight from Death*
    PW - v262 - i21 - May 25 2015 - p44(1) [51-500]

Galera, Daniel - *Blood-Drenched Beard*
    NYT - Jan 20 2015 - pC1(L) [501+]
    WLT - v89 - i3-4 - May-August 2015 - p113(1) [51-500]

Galfard, Christophe - *The Universe in Your Hand: A Journey Through Space, Time and Beyond*
    Spec - v328 - i9756 - August 22 2015 - p34(2) [501+]

Galgut, Damon - *Arctic Summer*
    BL - v111 - i16 - April 15 2015 - p34(1) [501+]
    G&L Rev W - v22 - i4 - July-August 2015 - p33(2) [501+]
    WLT - v89 - i3-4 - May-August 2015 - p110(1) [501+]

Galindo, Renata - *The Cherry Thief*
    c HB Guide - v26 - i1 - Spring 2015 - p30(1) [51-500]

Galinsky, Adam - *Friend and Foe: When to Cooperate, When to Compete, and How to Succeed at Both*
    NYT - Sept 26 2015 - pNA(L) [501+]
Friend & Foe
    Har Bus R - v93 - i9 - Sept 2015 - p122(2) [501+]

Galinsky, Karl - *Memoria Romana: Memory in Rome and Rome in Memory*
    Class R - v65 - i2 - Oct 2015 - p526-528 [501+]

Gall, Carlotta - *The Wrong Enemy: America in Afghanistan, 2001-2014*
    CC - v132 - i25 - Dec 9 2015 - p34(3) [501+]
    NYTBR - May 3 2015 - p28(L) [501+]

Gall, Chris - *Dinotrux Dig the Beach (Illus. by Gall, Chris)*
    c HB Guide - v26 - i2 - Fall 2015 - p34(1) [51-500]
    c KR - March 15 2015 - pNA [51-500]
    c SLJ - v61 - i5 - May 2015 - p84(2) [51-500]

Gall, Griff - *Ring, Dance, Play: First Experiences with Choirchimes and Orff Schulwerk*
    Teach Mus - v23 - i1 - August 2015 - p60(1) [51-500]

Gallagher, Brian - *Friend or Foe: Which Side Are You On?*
    y KR - Sept 15 2015 - pNA [51-500]
    y VOYA - v38 - i5 - Dec 2015 - p56(1) [51-500]

Gallagher, Charles A. - *Race and Racism in the United States: An Encyclopedia of the American Mosaic*
    R&USQ - v54 - i3 - Spring 2015 - p65(2) [51-500]

Gallagher, Gary W. - *Becoming Confederates: Paths to a New National Loyalty*
    RAH - v43 - i3 - Sept 2015 - p490-497 [501+]

Gallagher, Jim - *US-Led Wars in Iraq: 1991-Present*
    y BL - v112 - i6 - Nov 15 2015 - p43(1) [51-500]

Gallagher, John - *Yamasaki in Detroit*
    RVBW - Oct 2015 - pNA [501+]

Gallagher, Julie A. - *Black Women and Politics in New York City*
    Callaloo - v38 - i2 - Spring 2015 - p416-418 [501+]

Gallagher, Kevin P. - *The China Triangle: Latin America's China Boom and the Fate of the Washington Consensus*
    LJ - v140 - i19 - Nov 15 2015 - p96(1) [51-500]

Gallagher, Matt - *Fire and Forget: Short Stories from the Long War*
    HM - v331 - i1983 - August 2015 - p84(6) [501+]
Youngblood
    KR - Nov 1 2015 - pNA [51-500]

Gallagher, Monica - *Part-Time Princesses (Illus. by Galagher, Monica)*
    y BL - v111 - i19-20 - June 1 2015 - p67(1) [51-500]
Part-Time Princesses (Illus. by Gallagher, Monica)
    y VOYA - v37 - i6 - Feb 2015 - p50(2) [51-500]
    y SLJ - v61 - i5 - May 2015 - p127(1) [51-500]

Gallagher, Peter - *Requiem for Rosco*
    PW - v262 - i33 - August 17 2015 - p55(1) [51-500]

Gallagher, Sally K. - *Making Do in Damascus: Navigating a Generation of Change in Family and Work, Contemporary Issues in the Middle East*
    IJMES - v47 - i1 - Feb 2015 - p194-196 [501+]

Gallagher, Toni - *The Popularity Spell*
    c KR - July 15 2015 - pNA [501+]
Twist My Charm: The Popularity Spell
    c BL - v112 - i1 - Sept 1 2015 - p118(1) [51-500]

Gallaher, Bill - *High Rider*
    BL - v111 - i16 - April 15 2015 - p35(1) [51-500]

Gallamore, Robert E. - *American Railroads: Decline and Renaissance in the Twentieth Century*
    BHR - v89 - i1 - Spring 2015 - p170(4) [501+]
    JAH - v102 - i1 - June 2015 - p289-290 [501+]
    T&C - v56 - i2 - April 2015 - p551-553 [501+]

Galland, Nicole - *Stepdog*
    BL - v111 - i22 - August 1 2015 - p30(1) [51-500]

Gallardo, Raymond - *The Java Tutorial: A Short Course on the Basics, 6th ed.*
    Bwatch - May 2015 - pNA [51-500]

Gallman, J. Matthew - *Lens of War: Exploring Iconic Photographs of the Civil War*
    BL - v111 - i14 - March 15 2015 - p37(1) [51-500]
    KR - Jan 15 2015 - pNA [501+]

Gallo, Carmine - *The Storyteller's Secret: From TED Speakers to Business Legends, Why Some Ideas Catch On and Others Don't*
    KR - Dec 15 2015 - pNA [501+]
    PW - v262 - i52 - Dec 21 2015 - p146(1) [51-500]

Gallo, Marcia M. - *"No One Helped": Kitty Genovese, New York City, and the Myth of Urban Apathy*
    LJ - v140 - i8 - May 1 2015 - p86(2) [51-500]

Gallo, Ruben - *Proust's Latin Americans*
    TLS - i5845 - April 10 2015 - p22(1) [501+]

Gallouet, Catherine - *Marivaudage: theories et pratiques d'un discours*
    MLR - v110 - i3 - July 2015 - p862-863 [501+]

Galloway, Fhiona - *Hickory, Dickory, Dock (Illus. by Galloway, Fhiona)*
    c KR - July 1 2015 - pNA [501+]
Twinkle, Twinkle, Little Star: A Collection of Bedtime Rhymes (Illus. by Galloway, Fhiona)
    c PW - v262 - i6 - Feb 9 2015 - p66(2) [501+]

Galloway, Janice - *Jellyfish*
    Spec - v328 - i9756 - August 22 2015 - p36(1) [501+]

Galm, Ruth - *Into the Valley*
    BL - v111 - i22 - August 1 2015 - p28(1) [51-500]
    PW - v262 - i24 - June 15 2015 - p60(1) [51-500]

Galpern, Steven G. - *Money, Oil and Empire in the Middle East: Sterling amd Postwar Imperialism, 1944-1971*
    IJMES - v47 - i1 - Feb 2015 - p169-174 [501+]

Galveston, Louise - *In Todd We Trust*
    c CCB-B - v68 - i11 - July-August 2015 - p544(2) [51-500]
    c HB Guide - v26 - i2 - Fall 2015 - p82(1) [51-500]
    c KR - Jan 15 2015 - pNA [51-500]
    y VOYA - v37 - i6 - Feb 2015 - p75(1) [501+]

Galvin, Anthony - *Old Sparky: The Electric Chair and the History of the Death Penalty*
    BL - v111 - i19-20 - June 1 2015 - p11(2) [51-500]
    LJ - v140 - i12 - July 1 2015 - p97(1) [51-500]

Galvin, John R. - *Fighting the Cold War: A Soldier's Memoir*
    Parameters - v45 - i2 - Summer 2015 - p145(3) [501+]

Galvin, Michael M.B. - *Rebels of the Lamp*
    y HB Guide - v26 - i2 - Fall 2015 - p82(1) [51-500]
    c KR - March 1 2015 - pNA [51-500]
    c SLJ - v61 - i5 - May 2015 - p102(1) [51-500]
    c VOYA - v38 - i2 - June 2015 - p74(1) [51-500]

Gamache, Dan - *Arthur's Men*
    KR - July 1 2015 - pNA [501+]

Gambaccini, Paul - *Love, Paul Gambaccini: My Year under the Yewtree*
    Spec - v329 - i9768 - Nov 14 2015 - p63(1) [501+]

Gamber, John Blair - *Positive Pollutions and Cultural Toxins: Waste and Contamination in US Ethnic Literatures*
    AL - v87 - i2 - June 2015 - p413-415 [501+]

Gamble, John - *No Bull Information: A Humorous Practical Guide to Help Americans Adapt to the Information Age*
    RVBW - August 2015 - pNA [51-500]

Gamble, Miriam - *Pirate Music*
    WLT - v89 - i3-4 - May-August 2015 - p113(1) [51-500]

Gambles, Robert - *Espen Ash Lad: Folk Tales from Norway*
    TLS - i5864-5865 - August 21 2015 - p31(1) [501+]

Gambrell, Jamey - *The Blizzard*
  BL - v112 - i6 - Nov 15 2015 - p20(1) [51-500]
  PW - v262 - i39 - Sept 28 2015 - p62(1) [51-500]
Gamburd, Michele Ruth - *The Golden Wave: Culture and Politics after Sri Lanka's Tsunami Disaster*
  JAS - v74 - i2 - May 2015 - p508-509 [501+]
  Pac A - v88 - i2 - June 2015 - p343 [501+]
Gameau, Damon - *That Sugar Film*
  NYT - July 31 2015 - pC9(L) [51-500]
Gamer, Helen - *This House of Grief: The Story of a Murder Trial*
  PW - v262 - i8 - Feb 23 2015 - p68(1) [51-500]
Gamerro, Carlos - *The Adventure of the Busts of Eva Peron*
  KR - Jan 15 2015 - pNA [501+]
  TLS - i5846 - April 17 2015 - p20(1) [501+]
  WLT - v89 - i5 - Sept-Oct 2015 - p60(1) [501+]
Gamier, Pascal - *Boxes*
  PW - v262 - i33 - August 17 2015 - p54(1) [51-500]
  The Islanders
  PW - v262 - i16 - April 20 2015 - p57(1) [51-500]
Gamliel, Tovah - *Aesthetics of Sorrow: The Wailing Culture of Yemenite Jewish Women*
  HNet - July 2015 - pNA [501+]
Gammeltoft, Tine M. - *Haunting Images: A Cultural Account of Selective Reproduction in Vietnam*
  MAQ - v29 - i3 - Sept 2015 - pb-20-b-23 [501+]
Gamow, George - *A Star Called the Sun*
  Nature - v524 - i7565 - August 20 2015 - p299(1) [51-500]
Gamson, Joshua - *Modern Families: Stories of Extraordinary Journeys to Kinship*
  BL - v111 - i21 - July 1 2015 - p11(1) [51-500]
Ganahl, Pat - *Hot Rod Gallery: A Nostalgic Look at Hot Rodding's Golden Years: 1930-1960*
  Bwatch - July 2015 - pNA [51-500]
Gander, Forrest - *The Trace*
  ABR - v36 - i3 - March-April 2015 - p9(2) [501+]
Ganderton, Lucinda - *Embroidery: A Step-by-Step Guide to More Than 200 Stitches*
  LJ - v140 - i13 - August 1 2015 - p95(2) [51-500]
Gandhi, Leela - *The Common Cause: Postcolonial Ethics and the Practice of Democracy, 1900-1955*
  AHR - v120 - i4 - Oct 2015 - p1456-1457 [501+]
Gandlevsky, Sergey - *Trepanation of the Skull*
  WLT - v89 - i3-4 - May-August 2015 - p126(1) [501+]
Gandy, Matthew - *Fabric of Space: Water, Modernity, and the Urban Imagination*
  HNet - August 2015 - pNA [501+]
  The Fabric of Space: Water, Modernity, and the Urban Imagination
  NYRB - v62 - i16 - Oct 22 2015 - p45(2) [501+]
Ganeri, Anita - *Around the World: A Colorful Atlas for Kids (Illus. by Corr, Christopher)*
  c PW - v262 - i9 - March 2 2015 - p84(1) [501+]
  Astonishing Animals (Illus. by Dogi, Fiammetta)
  c PW - v262 - i13 - March 30 2015 - p74(1) [51-500]
  c KR - Dec 1 2015 - pNA [51-500]
  Cultures and Customs Series
  c BL - v112 - i5 - Nov 1 2015 - p46(1) [51-500]
  Endurance
  c Sch Lib - v63 - i3 - Autumn 2015 - p173(1) [51-500]
  Heroes of History (Illus. by Stanton, Joe Todd)
  c BL - v112 - i7 - Dec 1 2015 - p41(1) [51-500]
  How to Live Like a Roman Gladiator (Illus. by Epelbaum, Mariano)
  c PW - v262 - i33 - August 17 2015 - p74(1) [501+]
  How to Live Like a Viking Warrior (Illus. by Epelbaum, Mariano)
  c KR - July 15 2015 - pNA [51-500]
  Le gout
  c Res Links - v20 - i3 - Feb 2015 - p44(1) [51-500]
  Lifesize Ocean (Illus. by Jackson-Carter, Stuart)
  c HB Guide - v26 - i1 - Spring 2015 - p154(1) [51-500]
  Lifesize Rainforest (Illus. by Jackson-Carter, Stuart)
  c HB Guide - v26 - i1 - Spring 2015 - p154(1) [51-500]
  United States of America
  c Sch Lib - v63 - i3 - Autumn 2015 - p173(1) [51-500]
Ganeshram, Ramin - *A Birthday Cake for George Washington (Illus. by Brantley-Newton, Vanessa)*
  c KR - Dec 1 2015 - pNA [51-500]
  c SLJ - v61 - i12 - Dec 2015 - p135(2) [51-500]
Ganger, Stefanie - *Relics of the Past: The Collecting and Studying of Pre-Columbian Antiquities in Peru and Chile, 1837-1911*
  HNet - May 2015 - pNA [501+]
Gangloff, Sylvaine - *Ping and Pong the Penguins (Illus. by Gangloff, Sylvaine)*
  c PW - v262 - i28 - July 13 2015 - p63(1) [51-500]
Gangloff, Sylviane - *Ping and Pong the Penguins*
  c SLJ - v61 - i12 - Dec 2015 - p88(1) [51-500]
Gangloff, Tammy - *The Ultimate Dehydrator Cookbook: The Complete Guide to Drying Food, Plus 398 Recipes, Including Making Jerky, Fruit Leather and Just-Add Water Meals*
  BL - v111 - i9-10 - Jan 1 2015 - p29(2) [51-500]
Gangsei, Jan - *Zero Day*
  y KR - Oct 1 2015 - pNA [51-500]
  y BL - v112 - i7 - Dec 1 2015 - p59(1) [51-500]
  y SLJ - v61 - i2 - Dec 2015 - p113(2) [51-500]
Ganieva, Alisa - *The Mountain and the Wall*
  WLT - v89 - i5 - Sept-Oct 2015 - p13(1) [51-500]
Gannon, Charles E. - *Raising Caine*
  PW - v262 - i35 - August 31 2015 - p65(1) [51-500]
Gannon, Joe - *The Last Dawn*
  PW - v262 - i44 - Nov 2 2015 - p61(1) [51-500]
  Night of the Jaguar
  RVBW - June 2015 - pNA [51-500]
Gannon, Nicholas - *The Doldrums (Illus. by Gannon, Nicholas)*
  c BL - v111 - i21 - July 1 2015 - p69(1) [51-500]
  c KR - June 1 2015 - pNA [51-500]
  c Magpies - v30 - i5 - Nov 2015 - p34(1) [501+]
  c NYTBR - Nov 8 2015 - p29(L) [501+]
  c PW - v262 - i49 - Dec 2 2015 - p65(1) [51-500]
  c PW - v262 - i51 - Dec 14 2015 - p21(6) [501+]
  c SLJ - v61 - i8 - August 2015 - p84(2) [51-500]
  c PW - v262 - i24 - June 15 2015 - p83(1) [51-500]
Ganson, Barbara - *Texas Takes Wing: A Century of Flight in the Lone Star State*
  JSH - v81 - i2 - May 2015 - p497(2) [501+]
  T&C - v56 - i2 - April 2015 - p553-554 [501+]
Ganson, Barbara Anne - *Texas Takes Wing: A Century of Flight in the Lone Star State*
  SHQ - v118 - i3 - Jan 2015 - p337-338 [501+]
Gansworth, Eric - *If I Ever Get Out of Here (Read by Gansworth, Eric). Audiobook Review*
  y HB - v91 - i2 - March-April 2015 - p129(1) [51-500]
Gant, Andrew - *O Sing Unto the Lord: A History of English Church Music*
  Spec - v329 - i9772 - Dec 12 2015 - p83(2) [501+]
Gantner, Clemens - *Freunde Roms und Volker der Finsternis: Die papstliche Konstruktion von Anderen im 8. und 9. Jahrhundert*
  HNet - April 2015 - pNA [501+]
  Med R - August 2015 - pNA [501+]
Gantos, Jack - *The Key That Swallowed Joey Pigza (Read by Gantos, Jack). Audiobook Review*
  c BL - v111 - i16 - April 15 2015 - p63(2) [51-500]
  c HB - v91 - i2 - March-April 2015 - p129(1) [51-500]
  The Key that Swallowed Joey Pigza. Audiobook Review
  c SLJ - v61 - i2 - Feb 2015 - p49(1) [51-500]
  The Key That Swallowed Joey Pigza
  c HB Guide - v26 - i1 - Spring 2015 - p78(1) [51-500]
  The Key That Swallowed Joey Pigza (Illus. by Tazzyman, David)
  c Sch Lib - v63 - i3 - Autumn 2015 - p165(1) [51-500]
  Rotten Ralph's Rotten Family (Illus. by Rubel, Nicole)
  c HB Guide - v26 - i1 - Spring 2015 - p53(1) [51-500]
  The Trouble in Me (Read by Gantos, Jack). Audiobook Review
  y PW - v262 - i48 - Nov 30 2015 - p56(1) [51-500]
  y SLJ - v61 - i12 - Dec 2015 - p78(1) [51-500]
  The Trouble in Me
  y BL - v111 - i22 - August 1 2015 - p60(1) [51-500]
  y CCB-B - v69 - i2 - Oct 2015 - p87(2) [501+]
  c HB - v91 - i5 - Sept-Oct 2015 - p128(2) [51-500]
  c KR - June 1 2015 - pNA [51-500]
  y PW - v262 - i25 - June 22 2015 - p142(1) [51-500]
  y SLJ - v61 - i10 - Oct 2015 - p102(1) [51-500]
Gantz, Carroll - *Refrigeration: A History*
  BL - v112 - i4 - Oct 15 2015 - p9(1) [51-500]
Ganz, James A. - *Jewel City: Art from San Francisco's Panama-Pacific International Exposition*
  LJ - v140 - i19 - Nov 15 2015 - p81(1) [51-500]
Ganz-Schmitt, Sue - *Planet Kindergarten (Illus. by Prigmore, Shane)*
  c HB Guide - v26 - i1 - Spring 2015 - p30(1) [51-500]

Gao, Bei - *Shanghai Sanctuary: Chinese and Japanese Policy toward European Jewish Refugees during World War II*
  JMH - v87 - i1 - March 2015 - p159(3) [501+]
Gao, Yunxiang - *Sporting Gender: Women Athletes and Celebrity-Making during China's National Crisis, 1931-45*
  AHR - v120 - i4 - Oct 2015 - p1466-1467 [501+]
Gaponenko, Marjana - *Who Is Martha?*
  WLT - v89 - i5 - Sept-Oct 2015 - p60(2) [501+]
Gappah, Petina - *The Book of Memory*
  BL - v112 - i6 - Nov 15 2015 - p21(1) [51-500]
  KR - Oct 1 2015 - pNA [51-500]
  PW - v262 - i52 - Dec 21 2015 - p125(2) [51-500]
Gaquin, Deirdre A. - *The Almanac of American Education, 2014-2015*
  BL - v112 - i2 - Sept 15 2015 - p12(1) [51-500]
  County and City Extra: Special Historical Edition
  BL - v112 - i2 - Sept 15 2015 - p12(1) [51-500]
Garan, Ron - *The Orbital Perspective: Lessons in Seeing the big Picture from a Journey of 71 Million Miles*
  Bwatch - May 2015 - pNA [51-500]
Garb, Margaret - *Freedom's Ballot: African American Political Struggles in Chicago from Abolition to the Great Migration*
  AHR - v120 - i3 - June 2015 - p1029-1030 [501+]
  JAH - v101 - i4 - March 2015 - p1274-1275 [501+]
Garbarino, James - *Listening to Killers: Lessons Learned from My Twenty Years as a Psychological Expert Witness in Murder Cases*
  LJ - v140 - i3 - Feb 15 2015 - p117(1) [51-500]
Garbett, Lee - *Loki, Agent of Asgard, vol. 2*
  BL - v112 - i6 - Nov 15 2015 - p36(1) [51-500]
Garcia-Arenal, Mercedes - *The Expulsion of the Moriscos from Spain: A Mediterranean Diaspora*
  Six Ct J - v46 - i2 - Summer 2015 - p431-433 [501+]
  The Orient in Spain: Converted Muslims, the Forged Lead Books of Granada, and the Rise of Orientalism
  Six Ct J - v46 - i2 - Summer 2015 - p450-451 [501+]
Garcia, Belinda Vasquez - *Alicia's Misadventures in Computer Land*
  c KR - March 1 2015 - pNA [501+]
Garcia, Bobbito - *Where'd You Get Those? New York City's Sneaker Culture, 1960-1987*
  HM - v331 - i1984 - Sept 2015 - p89(6) [501+]
Garcia, Cindy - *Salsa Crossings: Dancing Latinidad in Los Angeles*
  Aztlan - v40 - i1 - Spring 2015 - p237-241 [501+]
Garcia, Encarnacion Sanchez - *Lingua Spagnola e cultura Ispanica a Napoli fra rinascimento e barocco: Testimonianze a stampa*
  Ren Q - v68 - i3 - Fall 2015 - p1113-1114 [501+]
Garcia, Hector A. - *Alpha God: The Psychology of Religious Violence and Oppression*
  Hum - v75 - i4 - July-August 2015 - p44(2) [501+]
Garcia Hernan, Enrique - *Ignacio de Loyola*
  CHR - v101 - i3 - Summer 2015 - p636(2) [501+]
Garcia, Ignacio M. - *When Mexicans Could Play Ball: Basketball, Race, and Identity in San Antonio, 1928-1945*
  JSH - v81 - i2 - May 2015 - p503(2) [501+]
  SHQ - v118 - i3 - Jan 2015 - p333-334 [501+]
Garcia, Jay - *Psychology Comes to Harlem: Rethinking the Race Question in Twentieth-Century America*
  AL - v87 - i2 - June 2015 - p398-400 [501+]
Garcia, Jerry - *Looking Like the Enemy: Japanese Mexicans, the Mexican State, and US Hegemony, 1897-1945*
  AHR - v120 - i1 - Feb 2015 - p300-301 [501+]
  WHQ - v46 - i1 - Spring 2015 - p90-91 [501+]
Garcia, Juan Carlos Moreno - *Ancient Egyptian Administration*
  JNES - v74 - i2 - Oct 2015 - p364(7) [501+]
Garcia, Kami - *Unbreakable*
  y Teach Lib - v42 - i3 - Feb 2015 - p28(4) [501+]
  Unmarked
  y HB Guide - v26 - i2 - Fall 2015 - p119(1) [501+]
Garcia, Lorena - *Lorena Garcia's New Taco Classics*
  PW - v262 - i33 - August 17 2015 - p66(1) [51-500]
  Respect Yourself, Protect Yourself: Latina Girls and Sexual Identity
  CS - v44 - i1 - Jan 2015 - p61-63 [501+]
  SF - v94 - i2 - Dec 2015 - pNA [501+]
Garcia, Mario T. - *The Chicano Movement: Perspectives from the Twenty-First Century*
  WHQ - v46 - i2 - Summer 2015 - p238(1) [501+]
  The Latino Generation: Voices of the New America
  NYRB - v62 - i19 - Dec 3 2015 - p8(3) [501+]
  SHQ - v118 - i4 - April 2015 - p445-446 [501+]

Garcia, Michael Nieto - *Autobiography in Black and Brown: Ethnic Identity in Richard Wright and Richard Rodriguez*
    Afr Am R - v48 - i1-2 - Spring-Summer 2015 - p218(3) [501+]
    Biomag - v38 - i3 - Summer 2015 - p444(6) [501+]

Garcia, Nasario - *Hoe, Heaven & Hell*
    Roundup M - v23 - i1 - Oct 2015 - p34(1) [501+]

Garcia-Robles, Jorge - *The Stray Bullet: William S. Burroughs in Mexico*
    ABR - v36 - i3 - March-April 2015 - p13(2) [501+]

Garcia-Sanchez, Inmaculada Ma - *Language and Muslim Immigrant Childhoods: The Politics of Belonging*
    ERS - v38 - i8 - August 2015 - p1457(3) [501+]

Garcia, Stephanie - *My Mommy, M.S. and Me (Illus. by Jakosalem, Lyle)*
    c CH Bwatch - Oct 2015 - pNA [51-500]

Garcia, Vanessa - *White Light*
    KR - July 15 2015 - pNA [51-500]

Gardam, Jane - *The Hollow Land*
    NYTBR - Jan 4 2015 - p9(L) [501+]

Garde, Francois - *What Became of the White Savage*
    TLS - i5874 - Oct 30 2015 - p21(1) [501+]

Garde, Murray - *Culture, Interaction and Person Reference in an Australian Language*
    Lang Soc - v44 - i1 - Feb 2015 - p130-131 [501+]

Gardella, Peter - *American Civil Religion: What Americans Hold Sacred*
    JR - v95 - i3 - July 2015 - p425(3) [501+]

Garden, Kenneth - *The First Islamic Reviver: Abu Hamid al-Ghazali and His Revival of the Religious Sciences*
    HNet - August 2015 - pNA [501+]

Gardes, Jean-Claude - *La Guerre Apres la Guerre: L'Echo de la Grande Guerre dans la Caricature*
    HNet - July 2015 - pNA [501+]

Gardiner, John Eliot - *Bach: Music in the Castle of Heaven*
    Sew R - v123 - i1 - Wntr 2015 - pVI-VIII [501+]

Gardiner, Kelly - *Goddess*
    NYTBR - Nov 15 2015 - p20(L) [501+]
    y LJ - v140 - i14 - Sept 1 2015 - p91(1) [51-500]

Gardini, Nicola - *Lost Words*
    KR - Nov 15 2015 - pNA [51-500]
    PW - v262 - i45 - Nov 9 2015 - p33(2) [51-500]

Gardner, Faith - *Perdita*
    y KR - May 15 2015 - pNA [51-500]
    y SLJ - v61 - i7 - July 2015 - p92(1) [51-500]
    y VOYA - v38 - i3 - August 2015 - p60(1) [51-500]

Gardner, Felicity - *The Complete Guide to a Dog's Best Friend (Illus. by West, David)*
    c Magpies - v30 - i1 - March 2015 - p28(1) [501+]

Gardner, Hall - *The Failure to Prevent World War I: The Unexpected Armageddon*
    J Mil H - v79 - i4 - Oct 2015 - p1156-1158 [501+]

Gardner, Howard - *The App Generation: How Today's Youth Navigate Identity, Intimacy, and Imagination in the Digital World*
    TLS - i5838 - Feb 20 2015 - p5(1) [501+]

Gardner, Hunter H. - *Odyssean Identities in Modern Cultures: Journey Home*
    Class R - v65 - i2 - Oct 2015 - p586-588 [501+]

Gardner, James - *Buenos Aires*
    KR - Oct 1 2015 - pNA [501+]

Gardner, Julian - *The Roman Crucible: The Artistic Patronage of the Papacy, 1198-1304*
    CHR - v101 - i3 - Summer 2015 - p624(2) [501+]

Gardner, Leigh A. - *Taxing Colonial Africa: The Political Economy of British Imperialism*
    BHR - v89 - i1 - Spring 2015 - p202(3) [501+]

Gardner, Lisa - *Find Her*
    KR - Dec 1 2015 - pNA [51-500]
    PW - v262 - i48 - Nov 30 2015 - p38(1) [51-500]

Gardner, Lloyd C. - *The War on Leakers*
    KR - Dec 15 2015 - pNA [51-500]

Gardner, Lyn - *The Ghastly McNastys: The Lost Treasure of Little Snoring (Illus. by Asquith, Ros)*
    BL - v111 - i14 - March 15 2015 - p74(1) [51-500]
    c HB Guide - v26 - i2 - Fall 2015 - p66(1) [51-500]
    c Res Links - v20 - i5 - June 2015 - p10(2) [51-500]
Raiders of the Lost Shark
    c KR - June 15 2015 - pNA [51-500]

Gardner, Martin - *The Ambidextrous Universe*
    TimHES - i2211 - July 9 2015 - p45(1) [501+]
Undiluted Hocus-Pocus: The Autobiography of Martin Gardner
    Math T - v108 - i6 - Feb 2015 - p478(1) [501+]

Gardner, Matt - *Alabaster Shadows (Illus. by Doucet, Rashad)*
    c BL - v112 - i6 - Nov 15 2015 - p36(1) [51-500]
    c KR - Sept 15 2015 - pNA [51-500]

Gardner, Nikolas - *The Siege of Kut-al-Amara: At War in Mesopotamia 1915-1916*
    J Mil H - v79 - i1 - Jan 2015 - p235-236 [501+]
The Siege of Kut-al-Amara: At War in Mesopotamia, 1915-1916
    J Mil H - v79 - i4 - Oct 2015 - p1158-1159 [501+]

Gardner, Richard - *Righteous Release*
    SPBW - August 2015 - pNA [51-500]

Gardner, Robert - *Last Minute Science Projects with Biomes (Illus. by LaBaff, Tom)*
    c HB Guide - v26 - i1 - Spring 2015 - p147(2) [51-500]

Gardner, Sally - *The Door That Lead to Where*
    y Magpies - v30 - i1 - March 2015 - p40(1) [501+]
The Door That Led to Where
    y Sch Lib - v63 - i2 - Summer 2015 - p116(1) [51-500]
    y Spec - v327 - i9725 - Jan 17 2015 - p38(1) [51-500]
Three Pickled Herrings (Illus. by Roberts, David)
    c HB Guide - v26 - i1 - Spring 2015 - p78(1) [51-500]

Gardner, Scot - *The Dead I Know*
    y CCB-B - v68 - i8 - April 2015 - p399(2) [51-500]
    y HB Guide - v26 - i2 - Fall 2015 - p119(2) [51-500]
    y KR - Jan 1 2015 - pNA [51-500]
    y PW - v262 - i3 - Jan 19 2015 - p85(2) [51-500]
    y PW - v262 - i49 - Dec 2 2015 - p89(1) [51-500]

Gardner, Scott - *The Dead I Know*
    y HB - v91 - i2 - March-April 2015 - p94(2) [51-500]

Gardner, Susan - *Lifted to the Wind*
    KR - Nov 15 2015 - pNA [501+]

Gareau, Colleen - *Sam(uel)*.
    KR - Jan 1 2015 - pNA [501+]

Garelick, Rhonda K. - *Mademoiselle: Coco Chanel and the Pulse of History (Read by Gilbert, Tavia). Audiobook Review*
    BL - v111 - i14 - March 15 2015 - p83(1) [51-500]
    LJ - v140 - i6 - April 1 2015 - p50(1) [51-500]
Mademoiselle: Coco Chanel and the Pulse of History
    NYTBR - Oct 4 2015 - p28(L) [501+]
    TLS - i5873 - Oct 23 2015 - p26(1) [501+]

Garey, Anita Ilta - *Open to Disruption: Time and Craft in the Practice of Slow Sociology*
    CS - v44 - i6 - Nov 2015 - p798-800 [501+]

Garfield, Leon - *The Complete Bostock and Harris*
    y HB Guide - v26 - i2 - Fall 2015 - p82(1) [51-500]

Garfield, Robert - *Breaking the Male Code: Unlocking the Power of Friendship*
    KR - Feb 15 2015 - pNA [501+]
    LJ - v140 - i6 - April 1 2015 - p107(1) [51-500]
    PW - v262 - i12 - March 23 2015 - p58(2) [51-500]

Garfield, Seth - *In Search of the Amazon: Brazil, the United States, and the Nature of a Region*
    HNet - Jan 2015 - pNA [501+]

Garfield, Simon - *To the Letter: A Celebration of the Lost Art of Letter Writing*
    NYTBR - Jan 4 2015 - p24(L) [501+]

Garfinkel, Harold - *Ethnomethodology's Program: Working out Durkheim's Aphorism*
    CS - v44 - i5 - Sept 2015 - p604-614 [501+]

Gargash, Maha - *That Other Me*
    KR - Nov 15 2015 - pNA [51-500]
    PW - v262 - i47 - Nov 23 2015 - p47(1) [51-500]

Garipzanov, Ildar - *Conversion and Identity in the Viking Age*
    Med R - May 2015 - pNA [501+]

Garland, Lance - *Second-Class Sailors*
    KR - August 1 2015 - pNA [501+]

Garland, Libby - *After They Closed the Gates: Jewish Illegal Immigration to the United States, 1921-1965*
    AHR - v120 - i2 - April 2015 - p649-650 [501+]
    J Am St - v49 - i2 - May 2015 - p437-440 [501+]
    JAH - v101 - i4 - March 2015 - p1307-1308 [501+]

Garland, Michael - *Lost Dog (Illus. by Garland, Michael)*
    c SLJ - v61 - i9 - Sept 2015 - p120(1) [51-500]
Lost Dog
    KR - July 1 2015 - pNA [51-500]

Garland, Robert - *Wandering Greeks: The Ancient Greek Diaspora from the Age of Homer to the Death of Alexander the Great*
    AHR - v120 - i3 - June 2015 - p1100(1) [501+]

Garland, Sally - *Tig and Tog's Dinosaur Discovery (Illus. by Garland, Sally)*
    c SLJ - v61 - i12 - Dec 2015 - p88(1) [51-500]

Garland, Sarah - *Azzi in Between (Illus. by Garland, Sarah)*
    c SLJ - v61 - i12 - Dec 2015 - p64(4) [501+]
Eddie's Tent and How to Go Camping
    c Sch Lib - v63 - i3 - Autumn 2015 - p155(1) [51-500]

Garland, Sherry - *Voices of the Western Frontier (Illus. by Buckner, Julie)*
    c KR - Dec 15 2015 - pNA [51-500]

Garlick, Jacqueline E. - *Lumiere*
    y SLJ - v61 - i11 - Nov 2015 - p114(2) [51-500]
Noir
    y SLJ - v61 - i12 - Dec 2015 - p120(1) [51-500]

Garlock, Dorothy - *Twice in a Lifetime*
    KR - May 1 2015 - pNA [51-500]
    PW - v262 - i17 - April 27 2015 - p57(1) [51-500]

Garmestani, Ahjond S. - *Social-Ecological Resilience and Law*
    QRB - v90 - i3 - Sept 2015 - p329(1) [501+]

Garner, Em - *Mercy Mode*
    y HB Guide - v26 - i1 - Spring 2015 - p107(1) [51-500]

Garner, Helen - *This House of Grief: The Story of a Murder Trial*
    Atl - v315 - i3 - April 2015 - p46(1) [501+]
    Spec - v327 - i9732 - March 7 2015 - p44(1) [501+]

Garner, Lynna - *The Best Sweater (Illus. by Gill, Sarah)*
    c BL - v112 - i6 - Nov 15 2015 - p56(1) [51-500]

Garnier, Pascal - *The A26*
    WLT - v89 - i5 - Sept-Oct 2015 - p63(1) [51-500]
The Front Seat Passenger
    RVBW - March 2015 - pNA [501+]
Moon in a Dead Eye
    RVBW - March 2015 - pNA [501+]

Garoche, Camille - *The Snow Rabbit (Illus. by Garoche, Camille)*
    c KR - Oct 15 2015 - pNA [51-500]
    c NYTBR - Nov 8 2015 - p31(L) [501+]
    c PW - v262 - i38 - Sept 21 2015 - p71(1) [51-500]

Garofalo, Joseph - *Chicago Law: A Trial Lawyer's Journey*
    KR - April 1 2015 - pNA [501+]

Garrard-Burnett, Virginia - *Beyond the Eagle's Shadow: New Histories of Latin America's Cold War*
    HAHR - v95 - i1 - Feb 2015 - p172-173 [501+]
    AHR - v120 - i3 - June 2015 - p1077-1078 [501+]

Garrard, Greg - *The Oxford Handbook of Ecocriticism*
    TLS - i5866 - Sept 4 2015 - p28(1) [501+]

Garrels, Anne - *Putin Country: A Journey into the Real Russia*
    KR - Nov 1 2015 - pNA [501+]
    LJ - v140 - i20 - Dec 1 2015 - p114(2) [51-500]

Garrelts, Colby - *Made in America: A Modern Collection of Classic Recipes*
    LJ - v140 - i9 - May 15 2015 - p102(2) [501+]

Garreta, Anne - *Sphinx*
    Lon R Bks - v37 - i15 - July 30 2015 - p9(4) [501+]
    TLS - i5872 - Oct 16 2015 - p27(1) [501+]
    WLT - v89 - i6 - Nov-Dec 2015 - p67(1) [51-500]

Garrett, A.D. - *Believe No One*
    KR - May 15 2015 - pNA [501+]
    LJ - v140 - i11 - June 15 2015 - p77(1) [51-500]
    PW - v262 - i19 - May 11 2015 - p34(1) [51-500]

Garrett, Brad - *When the Balls Drop*
    KR - March 15 2015 - pNA [51-500]
When The Balls Drop: How I Learned to Get Real and Embrace Life's Second Half
    NYTBR - May 31 2015 - p22(L) [501+]

Garrett, Brandon L. - *Too Big to Jail: How Prosecutors Compromise with Corporations*
    NYRB - v62 - i3 - Feb 19 2015 - p8(2) [501+]

Garrett, Charles Hiroshi - *The Grove Dictionary of American Music, 2d ed., 8 vols.*
    TLS - i5852 - May 29 2015 - p22(1) [501+]

Garrett, Greg - *Entertaining Judgement: The Afterlife in Popular Imagination*
    NS - v144 - i5250 - Feb 20 2015 - p44(3) [501+]
Entertaining Judgment: The Afterlife in Popular Imagination
    Ch Today - v59 - i2 - March 2015 - p60(3) [501+]

Garrett, Matthew - *Episodic Poetics: Politics and Literary Form after the Constitution*
    NEQ - v88 - i1 - March 2015 - p169-172 [501+]

Garrison, Gene K. - *Artists of Sedona, 1930-1999*
    Roundup M - v22 - i4 - April 2015 - p29(1) [501+]
    Roundup M - v22 - i6 - August 2015 - p37(1) [501+]

Garrison, Justin D. - "An Empire of Ideals": The Chimeric Imagination of Ronald Reagan
    Pres St Q - v45 - i1 - March 2015 - p209(3) [501+]

Garritano, Carmela - African Video Movies and Global Desires: A Ghanaian History
    HNet - June 2015 - pNA [501+]

Garro, Amy - Paper Pieced Modern: 13 Stunning Quilts - Step-by-Step Visual Guide
    LJ - v140 - i7 - April 15 2015 - p89(2) [51-500]

Garstecki, Julia - Life during the Industrial Revolution
    c HB Guide - v26 - i2 - Fall 2015 - p220(1) [51-500]

Garth, John - Tolkien und der Erste Weltkrieg: Das Tor zu Mittelerde
    HNet - Jan 2015 - pNA [501+]

Gartman, Eric - Return to Zion
    KR - Sept 1 2015 - pNA [51-500]
Return to Zion: The History of Modern Israel
    LJ - v140 - i17 - Oct 15 2015 - p100(1) [51-500]

Gartner, Kurt - Mittelhochdeutsches Worterbuch, Band 2, Doppellieferung 1/2: Lieferung 1: evuegerin - gemeilic; Lieferung 2: gemeinde-gevaerlich
    Med R - August 2015 - pNA [501+]

Garton, Christie - U Chic: College Girls' Real Advice for Your First Year
    LJ - v140 - i7 - April 15 2015 - p99(1) [51-500]

Garton, Sam - Otter in Space (Illus. by Garton, Sam)
    c CCB-B - v68 - i11 - July-August 2015 - p545(1) [51-500]
    c HB Guide - v26 - i2 - Fall 2015 - p34(1) [51-500]
    c KR - March 1 2015 - pNA [51-500]
    c SLJ - v61 - i2 - Feb 2015 - p69(1) [51-500]
Otter Loves Halloween! (Illus. by Garton, Sam)
    c KR - August 1 2015 - pNA [51-500]
    c PW - v262 - i30 - July 27 2015 - p67(1) [51-500]
Otter Loves Halloween (Illus. by Garton, Sam)
    c SLJ - v61 - i9 - Sept 2015 - p106(2) [51-500]

Garvey Berger, Jennifer - Simple Habits for Complex Times
    KR - May 15 2015 - pNA [501+]

Garvin, Jeff - Symptoms of Being Human
    y BL - v112 - i5 - Nov 1 2015 - p56(2) [51-500]
    y KR - Nov 1 2015 - pNA [51-500]
    y PW - v262 - i46 - Nov 16 2015 - p78(1) [51-500]
    y SLJ - v61 - i12 - Dec 2015 - p120(3) [51-500]

Garyash, Maha - The Other Me
    BL - v112 - i7 - Dec 1 2015 - p24(1) [51-500]

Garza, Xavier - The Donkey Lady Fights La Llorona and Other Stories / La Senora Asno Se Enfrenta a La Llorona Y Otros Cuentos
    c KR - Sept 15 2015 - pNA [51-500]
The Donkey Lady Fights La Llorona and Other Stories/La Senora Asno se enfrenta a La Llorona y otros cuentos
    c SLJ - v61 - i11 - Nov 2015 - p95(1) [51-500]
The Great and Mighty Nikko! A Bilingual Counting Book (Illus. by Garza, Xavier)
    c CH Bwatch - Oct 2015 - pNA [51-500]
    c SLJ - v61 - i6 - June 2015 - p82(1) [51-500]
The Great and Mighty Nikko! (Illus. by Garza, Xavier)
    c KR - May 1 2015 - pNA [51-500]
    c PW - v262 - i19 - May 11 2015 - p57(1) [51-500]

Garzilli, Enrica - L'Esploratore del Duce: Le avventure di Giuseppe Tucci e la politica Italiana in Oriente da Mussolini a Andreotti: con il carteggio di Giulio Andreotti
    JAS - v74 - i1 - Feb 2015 - p213-215 [501+]

Gasaway, Brantley W. - Progressive Evangelicals and the Pursuit of Social Justice
    CC - v132 - i8 - April 15 2015 - p40(2) [501+]

Gasch, Stefan - Senfl-Studien I
    Six Ct J - v46 - i1 - Spring 2015 - p192-193 [501+]

Gascoigne, John - Encountering the Pacific in the Age of the Enlightenment
    Isis - v106 - i2 - June 2015 - p454(2) [501+]

Gash, Jim - Divine Collision: An African Boy, an American Lawyer, and Their Remarkable Battle for Freedom
    PW - v262 - i41 - Oct 12 2015 - p62(1) [51-500]

Gasior, Agnieszka - Post-Panslavismus: Slavizitat, Slavische Idee und Antislavismus im 20. und 21. Jahrhundert
    Slav R - v74 - i3 - Fall 2015 - p686-686 [501+]

Gaskill, Malcolm - Between Two Worlds: How the English Became Americans
    HT - v65 - i3 - March 2015 - p58(2) [501+]
    NEQ - v88 - i2 - June 2015 - p330-332 [501+]
    NY - v90 - i44 - Jan 19 2015 - p75 [51-500]
    TimHES - i2190 - Feb 13 2015 - p51(1) [501+]
    TLS - i5845 - April 10 2015 - p24(2) [501+]

Gaskin, Richard - Horace and Housman
    Class R - v65 - i1 - April 2015 - p141-143 [501+]

Gaspard, Terry - Daughters of Divorce: Overcome the Legacy of Your Parents' Breakup and Enjoy a Happy, Long-Lasting Relationship
    PW - v262 - i51 - Dec 14 2015 - p76(2) [501+]

Gasper, Giles E.M. - Ambition & Anxiety: Courts and Courtly Discourse, c. 700-1600
    Med R - August 2015 - pNA [501+]

Gass, William H. - Eyes
    BL - v112 - i3 - Oct 1 2015 - p22(1) [51-500]
    LJ - v140 - i15 - Sept 15 2015 - p72(1) [51-500]
Eyes: Novellas & Stories
    KR - August 15 2015 - pNA [51-500]
    PW - v262 - i28 - July 13 2015 - p40(1) [51-500]

Gasser, Georg - Personal Identity: Complex or Simple?
    Phil R - v124 - i3 - July 2015 - p425(6) [501+]

Gast, Holger - Katholische Missionsschulen in Deutschland 1887-1940
    HNet - Jan 2015 - pNA [501+]

Gaston, Rozsa - Black Is Not a Color
    SPBW - March 2015 - pNA [51-500]
Budapest Romance
    PW - v262 - i25 - June 22 2015 - p127(1) [51-500]

Gatalica, Aleksandar - The Great War
    TLS - i5841 - March 13 2015 - p20(1) [501+]

Gately, Iain - Rush Hour: How 500 Million Commuters Survive the Daily Journey to Work
    Econ - v414 - i8919 - Jan 3 2015 - p69(US) [501+]
    Mac - v128 - i40 - Oct 12 2015 - p56(1) [51-500]
    TLS - i5860 - July 24 2015 - p27(1) [501+]

Gately, Ian - Rush Hour: How 500 Million Commuters Survive the Daily Journey to Work
    TimHES - i2188 - Jan 29 2015 - p47(1) [501+]

Gates, David - A Hand Reached Down to Guide Me: Stories and a Novella
    BL - v111 - i17 - May 1 2015 - p75(1) [51-500]
    KR - March 1 2015 - pNA [51-500]
    LJ - v140 - i6 - April 1 2015 - p87(1) [51-500]
    NY - v91 - i17 - June 22 2015 - p81 [51-500]
    NYT - May 11 2015 - pC4(L) [501+]
    NYTBR - July 26 2015 - p7(L) [501+]
    Lon R Bks - v37 - i16 - August 27 2015 - p16(3) [501+]
Jernigan
    Lon R Bks - v37 - i16 - August 27 2015 - p16(3) [501+]

Gates, Emma - Private Lines
    PW - v262 - i35 - August 31 2015 - p60(1) [51-500]

Gates, Henry Louis, Jr. - And Still I Rise: Black America since MLK
    BL - v112 - i2 - Sept 15 2015 - p4(1) [51-500]
    KR - Sept 15 2015 - pNA [501+]
    LJ - v140 - i16 - Oct 1 2015 - p93(1) [51-500]
    NYTBR - Dec 6 2015 - p73(L) [501+]

Gates, Jay Paul - Capital and Corporal Punishment in Anglo-Saxon England
    JIH - v46 - i2 - Autumn 2015 - p272-273 [501+]

Gates, Mariam - Good Night Yoga: A Pose-by-Pose Bedtime Story (Illus. by Hinder, Sarah Jane)
    c CH Bwatch - May 2015 - pNA [51-500]
    c PW - v262 - i18 - May 4 2015 - p117(1) [51-500]

Gates, Robert M. - Duty
    CSM - March 30 2015 - pNA [51-500]
A Passion for Leadership: Lessons on Change and Reform from Fifty Years in Public Service
    KR - Oct 1 2015 - pNA [51-500]
    LJ - v140 - i20 - Dec 1 2015 - p111(1) [51-500]
    PW - v262 - i42 - Oct 19 2015 - p66(1) [51-500]

Gates, Valerie - The Alphabet of Bugs: An ABC Book (Illus. by Cutting, Ann)
    c PW - v262 - i23 - June 8 2015 - p60(1) [51-500]
    c SLJ - v61 - i8 - August 2015 - p102(1) [51-500]

Gatrell, Peter - The Making of the Modern Refugee
    HER - v130 - i542 - Feb 2015 - p255(2) [501+]

Gatrell, Vic - The First Bohemians: Life and Art in London's Golden Age
    BL - v112 - i3 - Oct 1 2015 - p13(1) [51-500]
    BL - v112 - i5 - Nov 1 2015 - p18(2) [51-500]

Gatta, Mary - All I Want Is a Job: Unemployed Women Navigating the Public Workforce System
    Soc Ser R - v89 - i3 - Sept 2015 - p582(5) [501+]

Gatti, Alessandro - The Story of Snowflake and Inkdrop (Illus. by Mulazzani, Simona)
    c PW - v262 - i39 - Sept 28 2015 - p89(1) [51-500]
The Story of Snowflake and Inkdrop (Illus. by Mulazzini, Simona)
    c KR - Oct 15 2015 - pNA [51-500]

Gatti, Hilary - Ideas of Liberty in Early Modern Europe: From Machiavelli to Milton
    TimHES - i2215 - August 6 2015 - p46-46 [501+]
    TLS - i5866 - Sept 4 2015 - p9(2) [501+]

Gattis, Ryan - All Involved
    KR - Feb 15 2015 - pNA [51-500]
    LJ - v140 - i3 - Feb 15 2015 - p87(1) [51-500]
    NS - v144 - i5268 - June 26 2015 - p47(1) [51-500]
    NY - v91 - i12 - May 11 2015 - p77 [51-500]
    NYT - April 30 2015 - pC1(L) [501+]
    NYTBR - June 21 2015 - p19(L) [501+]
    PW - v262 - i7 - Feb 16 2015 - p155(1) [51-500]
    TLS - i5854 - June 12 2015 - p10(1) [501+]

Gauch, Sarah - The Tomb Robber and King Tu (Illus. by Garns, Allen)
    c KR - April 15 2015 - pNA [51-500]
The Tomb Robber and King Tut (Illus. by Garns, Allen)
    c BL - v111 - i21 - July 1 2015 - p65(1) [51-500]
    c CCB-B - v69 - i1 - Sept 2015 - p22(2) [51-500]

Gauci, Perry - William Beckford: First Prime Minister of the London Empire
    HER - v130 - i545 - August 2015 - p1010(3) [501+]
    Historian - v77 - i2 - Summer 2015 - p385(2) [501+]

Gaudreault, Andre - The End of Cinema? A Medium in Crisis in the Digital Age
    TimHES - i2210 - July 2 2015 - p48-2 [501+]

Gaughan, Joan Mickelson - The "Incumberances": British Women in India 1615-1856
    AHR - v120 - i3 - June 2015 - p1111-1112 [501+]

Gaughen, A.C. - Lion Heart: A Scarlet Novel
    y HB Guide - v26 - i2 - Fall 2015 - p120(1) [51-500]
Lion Heart
    y KR - March 1 2015 - pNA [51-500]
    SLJ - v61 - i4 - April 2015 - p163(2) [51-500]
    y VOYA - v38 - i3 - August 2015 - p60(1) [51-500]

Gaul, Gilbert M. - Billion-Dollar Ball: A Journey through the Big-Money Culture of College Football
    BL - v111 - i21 - July 1 2015 - p16(1) [51-500]
    KR - June 15 2015 - pNA [501+]
    PW - v262 - i23 - June 8 2015 - p52(1) [51-500]
A Journey Through the Big-Money Culture of College Football
    NYT - August 26 2015 - pC4(L) [501+]

Gaul, Theresa Strouth - Cherokee Sister: The Collected Writings of Catharine Brown, 1818-1823
    JSH - v81 - i2 - May 2015 - p452(2) [501+]

Gaus, Paul L. - Whiskers of the Lion
    BL - v111 - i12 - Feb 15 2015 - p39(1) [51-500]
    KR - Feb 1 2015 - pNA [51-500]
    PW - v262 - i1 - Jan 5 2015 - p53(2) [51-500]

Gautier, Ana Maria Ochoa - Aurality: Listening and Knowledge in Nineteenth-Century Colombia
    HAHR - v95 - i4 - Nov 2015 - p681-683 [501+]

Gauvin, Mitchell - Vandal Confession
    Mac - v128 - i41 - Oct 19 2015 - p62(2) [501+]

Gavalda, Anna - Billie
    NYT - April 30 2015 - pC6(L) [501+]
Life, Only Better
    NYT - Nov 26 2015 - pC6(L) [501+]

Gavaler, Chris - On the Origin of Superheroes
    KR - Sept 1 2015 - pNA [51-500]

Gavian Rivers, Virginia - Prelude to Genocide
    KR - Jan 1 2016 - pNA [501+]

Gavilan Sanchez, Lurgio - When Rains Became Floods: A Child Soldier's Story
    HAHR - v95 - i4 - Nov 2015 - p703-704 [501+]
    WLT - v89 - i5 - Sept-Oct 2015 - p65(1) [501+]

Gavin, Ciara - Bear Is Not Tired
    c KR - Oct 1 2015 - pNA [51-500]
    c PW - v262 - i44 - Nov 2 2015 - p84(1) [51-500]
Room for Bear (Illus. by Gavin, Ciara)
    c BL - v111 - i15 - April 1 2015 - p84(1) [51-500]
    c CCB-B - v68 - i8 - April 2015 - p400(1) [51-500]
Room for Bear
    c KR - Jan 1 2015 - pNA [51-500]

Gavin, Francis J. - Beyond the Cold War: Lyndon Johnson and the New Global Challenges of the 1960s
    JAH - v102 - i2 - Sept 2015 - p612-613 [501+]

Gavin, James - Is That All There Is?: The Strange Life of Peggy Lee
    Dbt - v82 - i1 - Jan 2015 - p74(1) [501+]

Gavin, Rohan - Knightley and Son: K-9
    y HB Guide - v26 - i2 - Fall 2015 - p82(1) [51-500]

Gavrilyuk, Paul L. - Georges Florovsky and the Russian Religious Renaissance
    Slav R - v74 - i3 - Fall 2015 - p662-663 [501+]
    TLS - i5832 - Jan 9 2015 - p9(1) [501+]

Gavron, Assaf - The Hilltop (Read by Fass, Robert).
Audiobook Review
    BL - v111 - i16 - April 15 2015 - p60(1) [51-500]
The Hilltop
    TLS - i5831 - Jan 2 2015 - p17(2) [501+]

Gawande, Atul - *Being Mortal: Illness, Medicine and What Matters in the End*
    TLS - i5848 - May 1 2015 - p7(2) [501+]
Being Mortal: Medicine and What Matters in the End (Read by Petkoff, Robert). Audiobook Review
    BL - v111 - i15 - April 1 2015 - p85(1) [51-500]
Being Mortal: Medicine and What Matters in the End
    CC - v132 - i4 - Feb 18 2015 - p32(2) [501+]
    Nation - v300 - i18 - May 4 2015 - p42(3) [501+]
    NYRB - v62 - i1 - Jan 8 2015 - p20(3) [501+]
    Reason - v46 - i10 - March 2015 - p56(6) [501+]
    TimHES - i2185 - Jan 8 2015 - p48-48 [501+]
    WLT - v89 - i5 - Sept-Oct 2015 - p76(1) [501+]
Gawrych, George W. - *The Young Ataturk: From Ottoman Soldier to Statesman of Turkey*
    J Mil H - v79 - i4 - Oct 2015 - p1159-1161 [501+]
Gay, Jason - *Little Victories*
    KR - Sept 1 2015 - pNA [501+]
Little Victories: Perfect Rules for Imperfect Living
    BL - v112 - i5 - Nov 1 2015 - p5(1) [51-500]
    PW - v262 - i38 - Sept 21 2015 - p64(1) [51-500]
Gay, Kathlyn - *Are You Fat? The Obesity Issue for Teens*
    y HB Guide - v26 - i1 - Spring 2015 - p170(2) [51-500]
Gay, Malcolm - *The Brain Electric: The Dramatic High-Tech Race to Merge Minds and Machines*
    BL - v112 - i3 - Oct 1 2015 - p8(1) [51-500]
    LJ - v140 - i15 - Sept 15 2015 - p101(1) [51-500]
    PW - v262 - i33 - August 17 2015 - p59(1) [51-500]
Gay, Marie-Louise - *Any Questions? (Illus. by Gay, Marie-Louise)*
    c CCB-B - v68 - i5 - Jan 2015 - p256(1) [51-500]
    c HB Guide - v26 - i2 - Fall 2015 - p34(1) [51-500]
    c Magpies - v30 - i2 - May 2015 - p31(1) [501+]
Princess Pistachio and the Pest (Illus. by Gay, Marie-Louise)
    c KR - June 15 2015 - pNA [51-500]
    c Res Links - v20 - i4 - April 2015 - p10(1) [51-500]
    c SLJ - v61 - i7 - July 2015 - p71(1) [51-500]
Princess Pistachio
    SLJ - v61 - i4 - April 2015 - p139(1) [51-500]
The Traveling Circus (Illus. by Gay, Marie-Louise)
    c BL - v111 - i17 - May 1 2015 - p98(1) [51-500]
    c HB - v91 - i4 - July-August 2015 - p132(1) [51-500]
The Traveling Circus
    c KR - Feb 15 2015 - pNA [51-500]
    SLJ - v61 - i4 - April 2015 - p140(1) [51-500]
The Traveling Circus (Illus. by Gay, marie-Louise)
    c Res Links - v20 - i4 - April 2015 - p10(2) [51-500]
Gay, Mary-Louise - *Princess Pistachio and the Pest (Illus. by Gay, Mary-Louise)*
    c BL - v111 - i22 - August 1 2015 - p75(1) [51-500]
Gay, Peter - *Weimar Culture: The Outsider as Insider*
    HT - v65 - i10 - Oct 2015 - p56(2) [51-500]
Why the Romantics Matter
    Comw - v142 - i11 - June 12 2015 - p29(2) [501+]
Gay, Robert - *Conversations with a Brazilian Drug Dealer*
    TimHES - i2200 - April 23 2015 - p54-55 [501+]
Gay, Roxane - *An Untamed State (Read by Miles, Robin). Audiobook Review*
    BL - v111 - i17 - May 1 2015 - p60(1) [51-500]
    LJ - v140 - i3 - Feb 15 2015 - p57(1) [51-500]
An Untamed State
    NS - v144 - i5253 - March 13 2015 - p53(1) [51-500]
Gay, William - *Little Sister Death*
    KR - July 15 2015 - pNA [501+]
    PW - v262 - i30 - July 27 2015 - p40(1) [51-500]
Gaye, Jan - *After the Dance: My Life with Marvin Gaye*
    BL - v111 - i18 - May 15 2015 - p9(1) [51-500]
    KR - April 1 2015 - pNA [501+]
    LJ - v140 - i7 - April 15 2015 - p88(1) [51-500]
Gayer, Laurent - *Karachi: Ordered Disorder and the Struggle for the City*
    JAS - v74 - i3 - August 2015 - p773-775 [501+]
Gayle, Stephanie - *Idyll Threats*
    BL - v111 - i22 - August 1 2015 - p25(1) [51-500]
    PW - v262 - i29 - July 20 2015 - p170(1) [51-500]
Gaylin, Alison - *What Remains of Me*
    KR - Dec 15 2015 - pNA [501+]
    PW - v262 - i52 - Dec 21 2015 - p130(1) [51-500]
Gaylord, Joshua - *When We Were Animals*
    y BL - v111 - i14 - March 15 2015 - p44(2) [51-500]
    KR - Feb 15 2015 - pNA [501+]
    LJ - v140 - i6 - April 1 2015 - p74(2) [501+]
    PW - v262 - i7 - Feb 16 2015 - p160(2) [51-500]
Gaynor, Hazel - *A Memory of Violets*
    BL - v111 - i9-10 - Jan 1 2015 - p53(1) [51-500]

Gaytan, Marie Sarita - *Tequila! Distilling the Spirit of Mexico*
    TLS - i5850 - May 15 2015 - p26(1) [501+]
Gayton, Sam - *The Adventures of Lettie Peppercorn (Illus. by Bernatene, Poly)*
    c KR - Nov 1 2015 - pNA [51-500]
    c SLJ - v61 - i12 - Dec 2015 - p101(1) [51-500]
Hercufleas (Illus. by Cottrill, Peter)
    c Sch Lib - v63 - i3 - Autumn 2015 - p166(1) [51-500]
Lilliput
    c KR - June 1 2015 - pNA [51-500]
Lilliput (Illus. by Ratterree, Alice)
    c BL - v111 - i21 - July 1 2015 - p73(2) [51-500]
    RVBW - Sept 2015 - pNA [501+]
    c SLJ - v61 - i8 - August 2015 - p84(1) [51-500]
Gazan, Sissel-Jo - *The Arc of the Swallow*
    KR - April 1 2015 - pNA [51-500]
    BL - v111 - i17 - May 1 2015 - p18(1) [51-500]
Gazotti, Bruno - *The Vanishing*
    y Sch Lib - v63 - i1 - Spring 2015 - p52(1) [51-500]
Gazzaniga, Michael S. - *Tales from Both Sides of the Brain: A Life in Neuroscience*
    Ent W - i1352 - Feb 27 2015 - p61(1) [501+]
    New Sci - v225 - i3011 - March 7 2015 - p46(2) [501+]
    TimHES - i2211 - July 9 2015 - p45(1) [501+]
Gazzanign, Michael S. - *The Cognitive Neurosciences*
    QRB - v90 - i4 - Dec 2015 - p441(2) [501+]
Gazzetta, Katherine Cutchin - *Love from a Star (Illus. by Gazzeta, Katherine Cutchin)*
    c CH Bwatch - Nov 2015 - pNA [501+]
Gazzinga, Michael S. - *Tales from Both Sides of the Brain: A Life in Neuroscience*
    Nature - v518 - i7539 - Feb 19 2015 - p298(2) [501+]
Gear, W. Michael - *People of the Songtrail*
    BL - v111 - i16 - April 15 2015 - p37(1) [51-500]
    KR - March 15 2015 - pNA [51-500]
Geary, Ian - *Blue Labour: Forging a New Politics*
    NS - v144 - i5259 - April 24 2015 - p55(1) [501+]
Geary, Patrick J. - *Manufacturing Middle Ages: Entangled History of Medievalism in Nineteenth-Century Europe*
    Specu - v90 - i3 - July 2015 - p814-816 [501+]
Geary, Rick - *Louise Brooks: Detective*
    PW - v262 - i22 - June 1 2015 - p49(1) [51-500]
A Treasury of Victorian Murder Compendium II
    SLJ - v61 - i2 - Feb 2015 - p129(2) [51-500]
    y VOYA - v38 - i1 - April 2015 - p87(1) [51-500]
Gebo, Daniel L. - *Primate Comparative Anatomy*
    QRB - v90 - i3 - Sept 2015 - p339(1) [501+]
Gebo, Erika - *Looking beyond Suppression: Community Strategies to Reduce Gang Violence*
    CS - v44 - i2 - March 2015 - p201-202 [501+]
Gecser, Otto - *The Feast and the Pulpit: Sermons and the Cult of St. Elizabeth of Hungary, 1235-ca. 1500*
    Specu - v90 - i1 - Jan 2015 - p253-254 [501+]
Gedenken und (k)ein Ende - Was bleibt vom Jahr 2014? Das Gedenkjahr 1914/2014 und sein historiografisches Vermachtnis
    HNet - April 2015 - pNA [501+]
Gee, Allen - *My Chinese America*
    PW - v262 - i2 - Jan 12 2015 - p46(1) [51-500]
Gee, Brain - *Francis Watkins and the Dollond Telescope Patent Controversy*
    Isis - v106 - i2 - June 2015 - p453(2) [501+]
Gee, Emma - *Aratus and the Astronomical Tradition*
    Class R - v65 - i1 - April 2015 - p76-78 [501+]
    Isis - v106 - i1 - March 2015 - p168(2) [501+]
Gee, Graham - *The Politics of Judicial Independence in the UK's Changing Constitution*
    Law Q Rev - v131 - i7 - July 2015 - p496-499 [501+]
Geesman, Robin - *Under Lock and Key*
    KR - August 1 2015 - pNA [501+]
Gefter, Philip - *Wagstaff: Before and After Mapplethorpe: A Biography*
    G&L Rev W - v22 - i3 - May-June 2015 - p30(3) [501+]
Geggus, David - *The Haitian Revolution: A Documentary History*
    HNet - June 2015 - pNA [501+]
Geheimdienste: Netzwerke, Seilschaften und Patronage in Nachrichtendienstlichen Institutionen
    HNet - Jan 2015 - pNA [501+]
Gehl, Laura - *And Then Another Sheep Turned Up (Illus. by Adele, Amy)*
    c HB Guide - v26 - i2 - Fall 2015 - p34(2) [51-500]
    c KR - Feb 1 2015 - pNA [51-500]
    PW - v262 - i2 - Jan 12 2015 - p63(1) [51-500]

Hare and Tortoise Race across Israel (Illus. by Goodreau, Sarah)
    c HB Guide - v26 - i2 - Fall 2015 - p159(1) [51-500]
    SLJ - v61 - i3 - March 2015 - p116(1) [51-500]
I'm Not Hatching
    c KR - Nov 1 2015 - pNA [51-500]
One Big Pair of Underwear (Illus. by Lichtenheld, Tom)
    c HB Guide - v26 - i1 - Spring 2015 - p9(1) [51-500]
Peep and Egg: I'm Not Hatching (Illus. by Wan, Joyce)
    c PW - v262 - i47 - Nov 23 2015 - p65(1) [51-500]
Gehrig, Astrid - *Im Dienste der nationalsozialistischen Volkstumspolitik in Lothringen: Auf den Spuren meines Gro[sz&rqsb:vaters*
    HNet - August 2015 - pNA [501+]
Gehring, David Scott - *Anglo-German Relations and the Protestant Cause: Elizabethan Foreign Policy and Pan-Protestantism*
    HER - v130 - i542 - Feb 2015 - p184(2) [501+]
Gehring, Dietrich - *The Hop Grower's Handbook: The Essential Guide for Sustainable, Small-Scale Production for Home and Market*
    PW - v262 - i33 - August 17 2015 - p68(1) [51-500]
Gehring, John - *The Francis Effect: A Radical Pope's Challenge to the American Catholic Church*
    LJ - v140 - i16 - Oct 1 2015 - p64(2) [501+]
Geier, Clarence R. - *From These Honored Dead: Historical Archaeology of the American Civil War*
    JSH - v81 - i3 - August 2015 - p733(3) [501+]
Geiger, Chris - *The Cancer Survivors Club: A Collection of Inspirational and Uplifting Survival Stories*
    PW - v262 - i22 - June 1 2015 - p56(1) [51-500]
    LJ - v140 - i11 - June 15 2015 - p110(1) [501+]
Geiger, Roger L. - *The History of American Higher Education: Learning and Culture from the Founding to World War II*
    HNet - Jan 2015 - pNA [501+]
Geis, Lioba - *Hofkapelle und Kaplane im Konigreich Sizilien (1130-1266).*
    HNet - March 2015 - pNA [501+]
Geisinger, Kurt F. - *Psychological Testing of Hispanics: Clinical and Intellectual Assessment*
    RVBW - July 2015 - pNA [501+]
Geismar, Haidy - *Treasured Possessions: Indigenous Interventions into Cultural and Intellectual Property*
    Pac A - v88 - i1 - March 2015 - p236 [501+]
    PHR - v84 - i2 - May 2015 - p253(2) [501+]
Geiss, Peter - *Die Presse in der Julikrise 1914: Die Internationale Berichterstattung und der Weg in den Ersten Weltkrieg*
    Ger Q - v88 - i2 - Spring 2015 - p256(2) [501+]
Geissinger, J.T. - *Sweet as Sin*
    PW - v262 - i20 - May 18 2015 - p71(1) [51-500]
Geisst, Charles R. - *Beggar Thy Neighbor: A History of Usury and Debt*
    Historian - v77 - i1 - Spring 2015 - p201(3) [501+]
Geisthardt, Johannes - *Zwischen Princeps und Res Publica: Tacitus, Plinius und die senatorische Selbstdarstellung in der Hohen Kaiserzeit*
    HNet - Sept 2015 - pNA(NA) [501+]
Geithner, Timothy F. - *Stress Test: Reflections on Financial Crises*
    NYTBR - May 10 2015 - p36(L) [501+]
Gelder, Alex Van - *Mumbling Reality Louise Bourgeois*
    Art N - v114 - i10 - Nov 2015 - p99(1) [51-500]
Gelderblom, Oscar - *Cities of Commerce: The Institutional Foundations of International Trade in the Low Countries, 1250-1650*
    BHR - v89 - i2 - Summer 2015 - p360(3) [501+]
    Historian - v77 - i3 - Fall 2015 - p602(2) [501+]
GelEman, Vladimir - *Iz ognia da v polymia: Rossiiskaia politika posle*
    Slav R - v74 - i2 - Summer 2015 - p430-431 [501+]
Gelernter, David - *The Tides of Mind: Uncovering the Spectrum of Consciousness*
    KR - Dec 15 2015 - pNA [501+]
    PW - v262 - i52 - Dec 21 2015 - p145(2) [51-500]
Gelinas, Luc - *La LNH, un reve impossible*
    y Res Links - v20 - i3 - Feb 2015 - p44(2) [501+]
Gellately, Robert - *Stalin's Curse: Battling for Communism in War and Cold War*
    HER - v130 - i542 - Feb 2015 - p250(2) [501+]
Gelles, David - *Mindful Work: How Meditation Is Changing Business from the Inside Out*
    BL - v111 - i11 - Feb 1 2015 - p6(2) [51-500]
    New R - v246 - i2-3 - March-April 2015 - p57(3) [501+]

Gellman, Ellie B. - *Tamar's Sukkah (Illus. by Kahn, Katherine)*
   c KR - June 15 2015 - pNA [51-500]
   Tamar's Sukkah (Illus. by Kahn, Katherine Janus)
   c SLJ - v61 - i8 - August 2015 - p70(1) [51-500]

Gellman, Irwin F. - *The President and the Apprentice: Eisenhower and Nixon, 1952-1961*
    BL - v111 - i21 - July 1 2015 - p20(1) [51-500]
    NYTBR - Sept 13 2015 - p26(L) [501+]
    PW - v262 - i23 - June 8 2015 - p50(1) [51-500]

Gellner, David N. - *Borderland Lives in Northern South Asia*
    Pac A - v88 - i3 - Sept 2015 - p727 [501+]

Gelman, Rita Golden - *Tales of a Female Nomad: Living at Large in the World (Read by Gelman, Rita Golden). Audiobook Review*
    LJ - v140 - i5 - March 15 2015 - p73(1) [51-500]

Geltner, Guy - *The Making of Medieval Antifraternalism: Polemic, Violence, Deviance, and Remembrance*
    JR - v95 - i4 - Oct 2015 - p553(2) [501+]

Geltzer, Jeremy - *Dirty Words and Filthy Pictures*
    KR - Nov 1 2015 - pNA [501+]

Gelvin, James L. - *Global Muslims in the Age of Steam and Print*
    AHR - v120 - i1 - Feb 2015 - p360-361 [501+]
    IJMES - v47 - i2 - May 2015 - p369-381 [501+]

Gemeinhart, Dan - *The Honest Truth*
   c CCB-B - v68 - i9 - May 2015 - p446(1) [51-500]
   c CSM - April 6 2015 - pNA [501+]
   y HB Guide - v26 - i2 - Fall 2015 - p82(1) [51-500]
   y Magpies - v30 - i3 - July 2015 - p34(1) [501+]
   c NYTBR - March 15 2015 - p17(L) [501+]
   c PW - v262 - i49 - Dec 2 2015 - p71(2) [51-500]
   y Sch Lib - v63 - i2 - Summer 2015 - p104(1) [51-500]
   Some Kind of Courage
   c BL - v112 - i6 - Nov 15 2015 - p55(2) [51-500]
   c KR - Oct 15 2015 - pNA [51-500]
   c PW - v262 - i44 - Nov 2 2015 - p85(1) [51-500]
   c SLJ - v61 - i11 - Nov 2015 - p95(1) [51-500]

Gemmill, R.L. - *The Demon Conspiracy*
   y KR - Nov 15 2015 - pNA [501+]

Gems, Gerald R. - *Sport and the Shaping of Italian-American Identity*
    AHR - v120 - i1 - Feb 2015 - p257-258 [501+]
   Sport and the Shaping of Italian American Identity
    CS - v44 - i4 - July 2015 - p513-514 [501+]

Gemunden, Gerd - *Continental Strangers: German Exile Cinema, 1933-1951*
    Ger Q - v88 - i2 - Spring 2015 - p248(2) [501+]
    AHR - v120 - i3 - June 2015 - p981-982 [501+]
    GSR - v38 - i3 - Oct 2015 - p694-697 [501+]
    JAH - v101 - i4 - March 2015 - p1314-1315 [501+]

Gench, Frances Taylor - *Encountering God in Tyrannical Texts: Reflections on Paul, Women, and the Authority of Scripture*
    CC - v132 - i21 - Oct 14 2015 - p32(2) [501+]
    CC - v132 - i24 - Nov 25 2015 - p34(2) [501+]

Gender and Authority in Medieval Society
    HNet - Sept 2015 - pNA [501+]
    HNet - Sept 2015 - pNA [501+]

Gender in Geschichtsdidaktik und Geschichtsunterricht. Einig in der Kontroverse
    HNet - April 2015 - pNA [501+]

Gender - Nation - Emancipation. Women and Families in the 'Long' Nineteenth Century in Italy and Germany
    HNet - June 2015 - pNA [501+]

"Gendered Voices" - Neue Perspektiven auf Digitale Zeitzeug_Innen-Archive
    HNet - March 2015 - pNA [501+]

Gendler, Robert - *Breakthrough! 100 Astronomical Images That Changed the World*
    S&T - v130 - i6 - Dec 2015 - p60(1) [51-500]

Gendzier, Irene L. - *Dying to Forget*
    KR - Sept 15 2015 - pNA [501+]

Genelin, Michael - *For the Dignified Dead*
    BL - v112 - i4 - Oct 15 2015 - p21(1) [51-500]
    PW - v262 - i39 - Sept 28 2015 - p69(1) [51-500]

Genequand, Philippe - *Une politique pontificale en temps de crise: Clement VII d'Avignon et les premieres annees du grand Schisme d'Occident*
    AHR - v120 - i1 - Feb 2015 - p311-312 [501+]

Generation und Medizin. Generationen in der Sozialgeschichte der Medizin
    HNet - June 2015 - pNA [501+]

Genetin-Pilawa, C. Joseph - *Crooked Paths to Allotment: The Fight over Federal Indian Policy after the Civil War*
    JEH - v75 - i2 - June 2015 - p601-602 [501+]

Genette, Gerard - *Paratexts: Thresholds of Interpretation*
    TimHES - i2211 - July 9 2015 - p48(1) [501+]

Genetti, Carol - *How Languages Work: Art Introduction to Language Linguistics.*
    Lang Soc - v44 - i4 - Sept 2015 - p606-1 [501+]

Geni, Abby - *The Lightkeepers*
    BL - v112 - i6 - Nov 15 2015 - p22(1) [51-500]
    KR - Nov 1 2015 - pNA [51-500]
    PW - v262 - i48 - Nov 30 2015 - p36(1) [51-500]

Genoux, Nicole - *Entre la Renaissance et Les Lumieres, le 'Theophrastus redivivus' (1659).*
    Sev Cent N - v73 - i3-4 - Fall-Winter 2015 - p195(3) [501+]

Genova, Lisa - *Inside the O'Briens (Read by Sudduth, Skipp). Audiobook Review*
    LJ - v140 - i10 - June 1 2015 - p60(2) [51-500]
   Inside the O'Briens
    BL - v111 - i13 - March 1 2015 - p18(2) [51-500]
    KR - Feb 15 2015 - pNA [501+]
    LJ - v140 - i5 - March 15 2015 - p91(2) [51-500]
    People - v83 - i15 - April 13 2015 - p41(NA) [501+]

Genovesi, Fabio - *Live Bait*
    WLT - v89 - i1 - Jan-Feb 2015 - p66(1) [501+]

Genoways, Ted - *The Chain: Farm, Factory, and the Fate of Our Food*
    VQR - v91 - i2 - Spring 2015 - p218-222 [501+]

Genscher, Hans-Dietrich - *Zundfunke aus Prag: Wie 1989 der Mut zur Freiheit die Geschichte Veranderte*
    HNet - March 2015 - pNA [501+]

Gensler, Sonia - *Ghostlight*
   c CCB-B - v69 - i1 - Sept 2015 - p23(1) [51-500]
   c KR - June 1 2015 - pNA [501+]
   c SLJ - v61 - i7 - July 2015 - p76(1) [51-500]

Gentry, Caron E. - *Beyond Mothers, Monsters, Whores: Thinking about Women's Violence in Global Politics*
    TimHES - i2229 - Nov 12 2015 - p49(1) [501+]
    TLS - i5869 - Sept 25 2015 - p27(1) [501+]

Geoghegan, Thomas - *Only One Thing Can Save Us: Why America Needs a New Kind of Labor Movement*
    AM - v212 - i16 - May 11 2015 - p42(3) [501+]
Geoghegan,Thomas - *Only One Thing Can Save Us: Why America Needs a New Kind of Labor Movement*
    Dis - v62 - i3 - Summer 2015 - p145(6) [501+]
Geoghegan, Thomas - *Only One Thing Can Save Us: Why Our Country Needs a New Kind of Labor Movement*
    NYTBR - Feb 1 2015 - p14(L) [501+]

George, Adrian - *The Curator's Handbook*
    LJ - v140 - i10 - June 1 2015 - p119(1) [51-500]

George, Aleta - *Ina Coolbrith: The Bittersweet Song of California's First Poet Laureate*
    PW - v262 - i37 - Sept 14 2015 - p59(2) [51-500]

George, Bobby - *Montessori Map Work (Illus. by Nassner, Alyssa)*
   c KR - Jan 1 2015 - pNA [51-500]

George, C.B. - *The Death of Rex Nhongo*
    Spec - v328 - i9754 - August 8 2015 - p30(1) [501+]

George, Carol V.R. - *One Mississippi, Two Mississippi*
    NY - v91 - i34 - Nov 2 2015 - p90 [501+]

George, David - *Sergi Belbel and Catalan Theatre: Text, Performance and Identity*
    MLR - v110 - i1 - Jan 2015 - p276-278 [501+]

George, Don - *Better Than Fiction 2: More True Travel Tales From Great Fiction Writers*
    BL - v112 - i2 - Sept 15 2015 - p19(1) [51-500]
    KR - Oct 1 2015 - pNA [501+]
    LJ - v140 - i17 - Oct 15 2015 - p106(1) [51-500]

George, Edward - *Murder at San Quentin*
    KR - Oct 1 2015 - pNA [51-500]

George, Elizabeth - *A Banquet of Consequences*
    BL - v111 - i22 - August 1 2015 - p31(1) [51-500]
    KR - Sept 1 2015 - pNA [501+]
    PW - v262 - i32 - August 10 2015 - p36(1) [51-500]
   The Edge of the Shadows
   y VOYA - v38 - i2 - June 2015 - p74(1) [51-500]
   c BL - v111 - i17 - May 1 2015 - p49(1) [501+]
   y SLJ - v61 - i6 - June 2015 - p123(2) [51-500]

George, Jean Craighead - *The Eagles are Back (Read by Minor, Wendell). Audiobook Review*
   c SLJ - v61 - i5 - May 2015 - p68(1) [51-500]

George, Jessica Day - *Silver in the Blood*
   y BL - v111 - i15 - April 1 2015 - p35(1) [501+]
   y BL - v111 - i18 - May 15 2015 - p64(1) [501+]
   y CCB-B - v69 - i2 - Oct 2015 - p88(1) [51-500]
   y KR - April 15 2015 - pNA [51-500]
   y PW - v262 - i18 - May 4 2015 - p122(1) [51-500]
   y SLJ - v61 - i5 - May 2015 - p113(1) [51-500]
   y VOYA - v38 - i3 - August 2015 - p77(1) [51-500]
   Thursdays with the Crown (Read by Jackson, Suzy). Audiobook Review
    SLJ - v61 - i2 - Feb 2015 - p49(1) [51-500]
   Thursdays with the Crown
   c HB Guide - v26 - i1 - Spring 2015 - p78(1) [51-500]

George, Kallie - *Clover's Luck (Illus. by Boiger, Alexandra)*
   c CCB-B - v68 - i9 - May 2015 - p446(1) [51-500]
   y HB Guide - v26 - i2 - Fall 2015 - p83(1) [51-500]
   c PW - v262 - i3 - Jan 19 2015 - p83(1) [501+]
   c Res Links - v20 - i3 - Feb 2015 - p11(1) [501+]
   c SLJ - v61 - i2 - Feb 2015 - p69(1) [51-500]
   Duck, Duck, Dinosaur (Illus. by Vidal, Oriol)
   c KR - Dec 1 2015 - pNA [51-500]
   The Enchanted Egg
   c KR - Sept 15 2015 - pNA [501+]

George, Martha Sibley - *Goodbye, Miss Emily*
    KR - August 1 2015 - pNA [501+]

George, Michael D. - *To Kill the Valko Kid*
    RVBW - July 2015 - pNA [51-500]

George, Nina - *The Little Paris Bookshop (Read by West, Steve). Audiobook Review*
    BL - v112 - i4 - Oct 15 2015 - p62(2) [51-500]
    LJ - v140 - i16 - Oct 1 2015 - p42(1) [51-500]
   The Little Paris Bookshop
    KR - April 15 2015 - pNA [501+]
    LJ - v140 - i11 - June 15 2015 - p5(1) [51-500]
    PW - v262 - i17 - April 27 2015 - p44(1) [51-500]

George, Patrick - *Animal Rescue*
   c Sch Lib - v63 - i2 - Summer 2015 - p97(1) [51-500]

George, Robert P. - *Conscience and Its Enemies: Confronting the Dogmas of Liberal Secularism*
    IndRev - v20 - i2 - Fall 2015 - p291(4) [501+]

George, Rosemary Marangoly - *Indian English and the Fiction of Natural Literature*
    TLS - i5868 - Sept 18 2015 - p26(1) [501+]

George, Susan A. - *Gendering Science Fiction Films: Invaders from the Suburbs*
    Film Cr - v39 - i3 - Spring 2015 - p82(3) [501+]

George W. Bush Presidential Center - *We Are Afghan Women*
    KR - Jan 1 2016 - pNA [501+]

Georgievska-Shine, Aneta - *Rubens, Velazquez, and the King of Spain*
    Ren Q - v68 - i2 - Summer 2015 - p638-641 [501+]
    Sev Cent N - v73 - i3-4 - Fall-Winter 2015 - p164(4) [501+]

Georgy, R.F. - *Absolution: A Palestinian Israeli Love Story*
    Tikkun - v30 - i1 - Wntr 2015 - pNA [51-500]

Gephart, Donna - *Death by Toilet Paper*
   y HB Guide - v26 - i2 - Fall 2015 - p83(1) [51-500]

Geppert, Dominik - *The Wars Before the Great War: Conflict and International Politics before the Outbreak of the First World War*
    HT - v65 - i11 - Nov 2015 - p62(1) [501+]

Gerald, Michael C - *The Biology Book: From the Origin of Life to Epigenetics, 250 Milestones in the History of Biology*
    LJ - v140 - i2 - Feb 1 2015 - p104(2) [51-500]

Gerald N. Callahan - *Lousy Sex: Creating Self in an Infectious World*
    QRB - v90 - i2 - June 2015 - p200(2) [501+]

Gerard, Cindy - *Taking Fire*
    KR - Dec 15 2015 - pNA [51-500]

Gerard, Emmanuel - *Death in the Congo: Murdering Patrice Lumumba*
    Bks & Cult - v21 - i6 - Nov-Dec 2015 - p25(2) [501+]
    Ch Today - v59 - i2 - March 2015 - p62(1) [51-500]
    Spec - v327 - i9732 - March 7 2015 - p42(2) [501+]
    TimHES - i2192 - Feb 26 2015 - p53(1) [501+]

Gerard, Philip - *The Patron Saint of Dreams*
    South CR - v47 - i2 - Spring 2015 - p164-167 [501+]

Gerard, Sarah - *Binary Star*
    CQ - v64 - i3 - Spring 2015 - p132(3) [501+]
    NYTBR - Feb 22 2015 - p34(L) [501+]
    PW - v262 - i2 - Jan 12 2015 - p3(1) [51-500]

Gerard, William Blake - *The Florida Edition of the World of Laurence Sterne, vol. 9: The Miscellaneous Writings and Sterne's Subscribers, an Identification List*
    TLS - i5850 - May 15 2015 - p24(1) [501+]

Gerber, Carole - *Stingrays! Underwater Fliers (Illus. by Mones, Isidre)*
   c HB Guide - v26 - i2 - Fall 2015 - p176(1) [51-500]
   Tuck-in Time (Illus. by Pearson, Tracey Campbell)
   c HB Guide - v26 - i1 - Spring 2015 - p9(1) [51-500]
   The Twelve Days of Christmas in Ohio (Illus. by Ebbeler, Jeffrey)
    HB Guide - v26 - i1 - Spring 2015 - p22(1) [51-500]

Gerber, Larry G. - *The Rise and Decline of Faculty Governance*
    Am St - v54 - i1 - Spring 2015 - p175-2 [501+]
    TimHES - i2200 - April 23 2015 - p55(1) [501+]
The Rise and Decline of Faculty Governance: Professionalization and the Modern American University
    JAH - v102 - i2 - Sept 2015 - p573-574 [501+]
Gerber, Richie - *Jazz: America's Gift: From Its Birth to George Gershwin's Rhapsody in Blue and Beyond*
    PW - v262 - i42 - Oct 19 2015 - p70(1) [51-500]
    RVBW - Oct 2015 - pNA [501+]
    SPBW - Sept 2015 - pNA [501+]
Jazz: America's Gift
    KR - Sept 1 2015 - pNA [501+]
Gerber, Sophie - *Kuche, Kuhlschrank, Kilowatt: Zur Geschichte des Privaten Energiekonsums in Deutschland 1945-1990*
    HNet - July 2015 - pNA [501+]
Gerbino, Giuseppe - *Music and the Myth of Arcadia in Renaissance Italy*
    Ren Q - v68 - i2 - Summer 2015 - p733-734 [501+]
Gere, Richard - *Time Out of Mind*
    New York - Sept 7 2015 - pNA [501+]
    New York - Sept 7 2015 - pNA [501+]
    New York - Sept 7 2015 - pNA [501+]
Gerhard, Jane F. - *The Dinner Party: Judy Chicago and the Power of Popular Feminism, 1970-2007*
    Signs - v40 - i2 - Wntr 2015 - p521(4) [501+]
Gerhard Martin - *Easiest if I Had a Gun*
    KR - Nov 15 2015 - pNA [501+]
Gerhardsen, Carin - *Cinderella Girl*
    KR - Oct 1 2015 - pNA [501+]
Gerhardt, Christine - *A Place for Humility: Whitman, Dickinson, and the Natural World*
    NEQ - v88 - i2 - June 2015 - p345-348 [501+]
Gerhardt, Michael J. - *The Forgotten Presidents: Their Untold Constitutional Legacy*
    Historian - v77 - i1 - Spring 2015 - p122(2) [501+]
    HNet - May 2015 - pNA [501+]
Gericke, Shane - *The Fury (Read by Dean, Robertson). Audiobook Review*
    LJ - v140 - i20 - Dec 1 2015 - p58(2) [51-500]
The Fury
    PW - v262 - i29 - July 20 2015 - p172(1) [51-500]
Gerlach, Henry - *Augenzeuge des Konstanzer Konzils: Die Chronik des Ulrich Richental*
    HNet - Feb 2015 - pNA [501+]
Germana, Monica - *Apocalyptic Discourse in Contemporary Culture: Post-Millennial Perspectives on the End of the World*
    SFS - v42 - i2 - July 2015 - p373-376 [501+]
Germein, Katrina - *Thunderstorm Dancing (Illus. by Watson, Judy)*
    c Magpies - v30 - i2 - May 2015 - p28(1) [501+]
Germeten, Nicole von - *Violent Delights, Violent Ends: Sex, Race, and Honor in Colonial Cartagena de Indias*
    AHR - v120 - i1 - Feb 2015 - p302-303 [501+]
    HAHR - v95 - i1 - Feb 2015 - p152-154 [501+]
Gerrard, K.A. - *My Family Is a Zoo*
    c KR - Jan 1 2016 - pNA [51-500]
Gerritsen, Anne - *Writing Material Culture History*
    HNet - May 2015 - pNA [501+]
Gerritsen, Reinier - *The Last Book*
    TLS - i5857 - July 3 2015 - p13(1) [501+]
Gerritsen, Tess - *Never Say Die*
    BL - v111 - i19-20 - June 1 2015 - p62(1) [51-500]
Playing With Fire
    KR - Sept 1 2015 - pNA [51-500]
    LJ - v140 - i13 - August 1 2015 - p83(1) [51-500]
    PW - v262 - i31 - August 3 2015 - p34(1) [51-500]
    BL - v112 - i5 - Nov 1 2015 - p32(1) [51-500]
Whistleblower
    BL - v112 - i6 - Nov 15 2015 - p31(1) [51-500]
Gerry, Lisa M. - *Puppy Love: True Stories of Doggie Devotion*
    c HB Guide - v26 - i2 - Fall 2015 - p182(1) [51-500]
Puppy Love: True Stories of Doggy Devotion
    c SLJ - v61 - i2 - Feb 2015 - p127(1) [51-500]
Gersh, David L. - *Desperate Shop Girls*
    KR - August 1 2015 - pNA [501+]
Gersh, Stephen - *Interpreting Proclus: From Antiquity to the Renaissance*
    HNet - August 2015 - pNA [501+]
Gershator, Phillis - *Time for a Bath (Illus. by Walker, David)*
    c HB Guide - v26 - i2 - Fall 2015 - p11(1) [51-500]
Gershoni, Israel - *Arab Responses to Fascism and Nazism: Attraction and Repulsion*
    AHR - v120 - i4 - Oct 2015 - p1577-1579 [501+]

Gerson, Lloyd P. - *From Plato to Platonism*
    Class R - v65 - i1 - April 2015 - p60-61 [501+]
    RM - v69 - i2 - Dec 2015 - p386(2) [501+]
Gerstein, Mordicai - *The Night World*
    c CCB-B - v69 - i1 - Sept 2015 - p23(2) [51-500]
The Night World (Illus. by Gerstein, Mordicai)
    c BL - v111 - i14 - March 15 2015 - p80(1) [51-500]
    c HB - v91 - i3 - May-June 2015 - p87(2) [51-500]
    c NYTBR - June 21 2015 - p16(L) [501+]
    PW - v262 - i16 - April 20 2015 - p75(1) [51-500]
    SLJ - v61 - i3 - March 2015 - p116(1) [51-500]
The Night World
    c HB Guide - v26 - i2 - Fall 2015 - p35(1) [51-500]
    c PW - v262 - i49 - Dec 2 2015 - p40(1) [51-500]
Gerstenberger, Katharina - *German Literature in a New Century: Trends, Traditions, Transitions, Transformations*
    MLR - v110 - i1 - Jan 2015 - p301-303 [501+]
Gerstler, Amy - *Scattered at Sea*
    LJ - v140 - i8 - May 1 2015 - p77(1) [51-500]
    PW - v262 - i24 - June 15 2015 - p62(1) [51-500]
Gerth, Holley - *You're Loved No Matter What: Freeing Your Heart from the Need to Be Perfect*
    PW - v262 - i6 - Feb 9 2015 - p63(1) [51-500]
Gertz, Genelle - *Heresy Trials and English Women Writers, 1400-1670*
    Six Ct J - v46 - i1 - Spring 2015 - p167-169 [501+]
Gerund, Katharina - *Die amerikanische Reeducation-Politik nach 1945: Interdisziplinare Perspektiven auf "America's Germany"*
    HNet - April 2015 - pNA [501+]
Gerver, Robert - *Write On! Math*
    Math T - v108 - i8 - April 2015 - p639(1) [501+]
Gerwarth, Robert - *Empires at War, 1911-1923*
    HNet - Feb 2015 - pNA [501+]
Geschichtsmythen in Europa - Chancen und Herausforderungen im Geschichtsunterricht
    HNet - April 2015 - pNA [501+]
Geschlecht und Gewaltgemeinschaften
    HNet - March 2015 - pNA [501+]
Geselbracht, Raymond H. - *Foreign Aid and the Legacy of Harry S. Truman*
    RVBW - April 2015 - pNA [501+]
Gess, Nicola - *Wissens-Ordnungen: Zu einer historischen Epistemologie der Literatur*
    MLN - v130 - i3 - April 2015 - p675-679 [501+]
Gessen, Keith - *City by City: Dispatches from the American Metropolis*
    KR - March 1 2015 - pNA [501+]
    LJ - v140 - i7 - April 15 2015 - p106(1) [51-500]
    PW - v262 - i11 - March 16 2015 - p76(1) [51-500]
Gessen, Masha - *The Brothers*
    KR - April 15 2015 - pNA [51-500]
The Brothers: The Road to an American Tragedy
    AM - v213 - i5 - August 31 2015 - p36(3) [501+]
    LJ - v140 - i11 - June 15 2015 - p102(1) [51-500]
    Lon R Bks - v37 - i17 - Sept 10 2015 - p13(3) [501+]
    Nat Post - v17 - i220 - July 25 2015 - pWP5(1) [501+]
    NYRB - v62 - i11 - June 25 2015 - p33(3) [501+]
    NYT - March 31 2015 - pC1(L) [501+]
    NYTBR - April 12 2015 - p1(L) [501+]
The Man Without A Face: The Unlikely Rise of Vladimir Putin
    Lon R Bks - v37 - i3 - Feb 5 2015 - p13(3) [501+]
The Tsarnaev Brothers: The Road to a Modern Tragedy
    NS - v144 - i5265 - June 5 2015 - p51(1) [501+]
    Spec - v328 - i9747 - June 20 2015 - p34(2) [501+]
    TLS - i5852 - May 29 2015 - p26(1) [501+]
Gessner, David - *All the Wild That Remains: Edward Abbey, Wallace Stegner, and the American West*
    BL - v111 - i12 - Feb 15 2015 - p8(1) [51-500]
    CSM - April 21 2015 - pNA [501+]
    PW - v262 - i5 - Feb 2 2015 - p2(1) [51-500]
All the Wild That Remains
    AM - v213 - i9 - Oct 5 2015 - p32(3) [501+]
    KR - Jan 1 2015 - pNA [501+]
Gessner, Marina - *The Distance from Me to You*
    y BL - v112 - i2 - Sept 15 2015 - p70(1) [51-500]
    y KR - August 1 2015 - pNA [51-500]
    y PW - v262 - i29 - July 20 2015 - p193(1) [51-500]
    y SLJ - v61 - i9 - Sept 2015 - p165(1) [51-500]
    y VOYA - v38 - i3 - August 2015 - p60(2) [51-500]
Getty, J. Arch - *Practicing Stalinism. Bolsheviks, Boyars, and the Persistence of Tradition*
    E-A St - v67 - i8 - Oct 2015 - p1328(2) [501+]

Getz, Gin - *Last of the Living Blue: A Year of Living and Dying Among the Trees*
    Roundup M - v22 - i3 - Feb 2015 - p23(1) [501+]
    Roundup M - v22 - i6 - August 2015 - p37(1) [501+]
Geuss, Raymond - *Politics and the Imagination*
    TimHES - i2211 - July 9 2015 - p47-48 [501+]
Gewaltkulturen von den Kolonialkriegen bis zur Gegenwart
    HNet - July 2015 - pNA [501+]
Gewerkschaftspolitik in den Langen 1970er Jahren. Ein Workshop zur Edition "Quellen zur Geschichte der Deutschen Gewerkschaftsbewegung im 20. Jahrhundert"
    HNet - Jan 2015 - pNA [501+]
Geyer, Kim - *Go to Sleep, Monty! (Illus. by Geyer, Kim)*
    c KR - August 15 2015 - pNA [51-500]
    c SLJ - v61 - i10 - Oct 2015 - p77(1) [51-500]
Geyken, Frauke - *Wirstanden nicht Abseits: Frauen im Widerstandgegen Hitler*
    Ger Q - v88 - i1 - Wntr 2015 - p133(3) [501+]
Ghannam, Farha - *Live and Die Like a Man: Gender Dynamics in Urban Egypt*
    IJMES - v47 - i2 - May 2015 - p406-407 [501+]
Ghayour, Sabrina - *Persiana: Recipes from the Middle East and Beyond*
    BL - v111 - i9-10 - Jan 1 2015 - p29(1) [51-500]
Ghaziani, Amin - *There Goes the Gayborhood?*
    AJS - v121 - i3 - Nov 2015 - p992(3) [501+]
    G&L Rev W - v22 - i2 - March-April 2015 - p35(2) [501+]
Ghent, Natale - *Dark Company*
    y Res Links - v20 - i5 - June 2015 - p24(2) [51-500]
Gherghel, Daniela - *Who Handles Retruns? And, Maybe Repayment? (Illus. by Scratchmann, Max)*
    c CH Bwatch - Sept 2015 - pNA [51-500]
Ghermandi, Gabriella - *Queen of Flowers and Pearls*
    KR - Jan 1 2015 - pNA [51-500]
    WLT - v89 - i6 - Nov-Dec 2015 - p69(1) [51-500]
Gherovici, Patricia - *Lacan on Madness: Madness, Yes You Can't*
    ABR - v36 - i4 - May-June 2015 - p28(2) [501+]
Ghesquiere, Rita - *Een land van waan en wijs: Geschiedens van de Nederlandse jeugdliteratuur*
    Bkbird - v53 - i3 - Summer 2015 - p89(2) [501+]
Ghez, Didier - *They Drew as They Pleased: The Hidden Art of Disney's Golden Age: The 1930s*
    LJ - v140 - i19 - Nov 15 2015 - p86(1) [51-500]
    TLS - i5873 - Oct 23 2015 - pNA [501+]
Ghigna, Charles - *A Carnival of Cats (Illus. by Bridgeman, Kristi)*
    c KR - Jan 1 2016 - pNA [51-500]
    c PW - v262 - i31 - August 3 2015 - p58(2) [51-500]
    c Res Links - v20 - i5 - June 2015 - p4(1) [51-500]
Numbers at the Park
    c TC Math - v22 - i1 - August 2015 - p54(1) [501+]
Raindrops Fall All Around (Illus. by Watson, Laura)
    c HB Guide - v26 - i2 - Fall 2015 - p35(1) [51-500]
    c KR - July 1 2015 - pNA [51-500]
    c Sch Lib - v63 - i3 - Autumn 2015 - p155(1) [51-500]
Shapes are Everywhere!
    c TC Math - v22 - i1 - August 2015 - p54(1) [501+]
Ghilarducci, Teresa - *How to Retire with Enough Money: And How to Know What Enough Is*
    LJ - v140 - i20 - Dec 1 2015 - p118(1) [501+]
Ghobrial, John-Paul A. - *The Whispers of Cities: Information Flows in Istanbul, London, and Paris in the Age of William Trumbull*
    AHR - v120 - i2 - April 2015 - p576-577 [501+]
    HNet - Feb 2015 - pNA [501+]
    HNet - April 2015 - pNA [501+]
Ghodrati, Esfandiar - *Land of the Legend*
    c KR - Oct 15 2015 - pNA [501+]
Ghodsee, Kristen Rogheh - *The Left Side of History: World War II and the Unfulfilled Promise of Communism in Eastern Europe*
    HNet - Sept 2015 - pNA(NA) [501+]
Ghoneim, Hadil - *Sana fi Qina (Illus. by Gueissa, Yasser)*
    c Bkbird - v53 - i3 - Summer 2015 - p100(1) [501+]
Ghosh, Amitav - *Flood of Fire*
    BL - v111 - i21 - July 1 2015 - p42(1) [51-500]
    BooChiTr - August 15 2015 - p13(1) [51-500]
    CSM - August 4 2015 - pNA [51-500]
    Econ - v415 - i8938 - May 16 2015 - p75(US) [501+]
    KR - June 1 2015 - pNA [51-500]
    LJ - v140 - i6 - April 1 2015 - p74(2) [51-500]
    NS - v144 - i5265 - June 5 2015 - p53(1) [501+]
    NY - v91 - i33 - Oct 26 2015 - p77(1) [51-500]
    NYTBR - August 30 2015 - p23(L) [501+]
    PW - v262 - i22 - June 1 2015 - p37(1) [51-500]
    Spec - v328 - i9743 - May 23 2015 - p43(1)

[501+]
    TLS - i5854 - June 12 2015 - p10(1) [501+]
    WLT - v89 - i6 - Nov-Dec 2015 - p60(1) [501+]
Ghosh, Peter - *Max Weber and 'The Protestant Ethic': Twin Histories*
    HNet - Sept 2015 - pNA [501+]
Max Weber and the Protestant Ethic: Twin Histories
    TLS - i5837 - Feb 13 2015 - p3(3) [501+]
Ghuman, Nalini - *Resonances of the Raj: India in the English Musical Imagination, 1897-1947*
    Notes - v72 - i2 - Dec 2015 - p369(4) [501+]
Ghuman, Paul - *British Untouchables: A Study of Dalit Identity and Education*
    CS - v44 - i2 - March 2015 - p289(1) [501+]
    CS - v44 - i2 - March 2015 - p289-1 [501+]
Giacometti, Eric - *Shadow Ritual*
    KR - Feb 1 2015 - pNA [51-500]
Giacomotto-Charra, Violaine - *Lire, choisir, ecrire: La vulgarisation des savoirs du Moyen Age a la Renaissance*
    Isis - v106 - i2 - June 2015 - p433(2) [501+]
Gianferrari, Maria - *Penny & Jelly: The School Show (Illus. by Heder, Thyra)*
    c BL - v111 - i21 - July 1 2015 - p65(1) [51-500]
    c CH Bwatch - August 2015 - pNA [501+]
The School Show (Illus. by Heder, Thyra)
    c KR - June 1 2015 - pNA [51-500]
Gianighian, Raphael - *Khodorchur 100 Years Later*
    KR - May 1 2015 - pNA [51-500]
Giannini, Massimo Carlo - *Papacy, Religious Orders, and International Politics in the Sixteenth and Seventeenth Centuries*
    Six Ct J - v46 - i3 - Fall 2015 - p823-825 [501+]
    Ren Q - v68 - i1 - Spring 2015 - p332-334 [501+]
Gianquitto, Tina - *America's Darwin: Darwinian Theory and U.S. Literary Culture*
    Am St - v54 - i1 - Spring 2015 - p153-2 [501+]
Giarratano, Kimberly G. - *Grunge Gods and Graveyards*
    y PW - v262 - i17 - April 27 2015 - p78(1) [51-500]
Gibaldi, Lauren - *The Night We Said Yes*
    c HB Guide - v26 - i2 - Fall 2015 - p120(1) [51-500]
    y KR - March 15 2015 - pNA [51-500]
    y PW - v262 - i17 - April 27 2015 - p78(1) [51-500]
    SLJ - v61 - i4 - April 2015 - p164(1) [51-500]
    y VOYA - v38 - i3 - August 2015 - p61(1) [51-500]
Gibb, Camilla - *This is Happy: A Memoir*
    Mac - v128 - i34-35 - August 31 2015 - p78(2) [501+]
Gibb, Robert - *The Empty Loom*
    PSQ - v89 - i2 - Summer 2015 - p173(3) [501+]
Gibb, Sarah - *Sleeping Beauty (Illus. by Gibb, Sarah)*
    c BL - v112 - i5 - Nov 1 2015 - p66(2) [51-500]
    c SLJ - v61 - i10 - Oct 2015 - p77(1) [51-500]
Gibbins, David - *Total War Rome: The Sword of Attila*
    KR - Jan 15 2015 - pNA [51-500]
Gibbon, Maureen - *Paris Red*
    y BL - v111 - i14 - March 15 2015 - p48(2) [51-500]
    KR - Feb 1 2015 - pNA [51-500]
    NY - v91 - i20 - July 20 2015 - p71 [501+]
    NYTBR - June 28 2015 - p38(L) [501+]
    PW - v262 - i6 - Feb 9 2015 - p44(1) [51-500]
Gibbons, Brittany - *Fat Girl Walking: Sex, Food, Love, and Being Comfortable in Your Skin ... Every Inch of It*
    LJ - v140 - i12 - July 1 2015 - p92(1) [51-500]
Gibbons, Eric - *If Picasso Went to the Zoo: An Illustrated Introduction to Art History for Children by Art Teachers*
    c CH Bwatch - Nov 2015 - pNA [501+]
Gibbons, Faye - *Halley*
    y HB Guide - v26 - i1 - Spring 2015 - p107(1) [51-500]
Gibbons, Gail - *The Fruits We Eat (Illus. by Gibbons, Gail)*
    c CH Bwatch - June 2015 - pNA [51-500]
    c HB Guide - v26 - i2 - Fall 2015 - p187(1) [51-500]
    c KR - March 15 2015 - pNA [51-500]
The Fruits We Eat
    SLJ - v61 - i3 - March 2015 - p169(2) [51-500]
Sun Up, Sun Down
    Sci & Ch - v53 - i4 - Dec 2015 - p16 [501+]
Gibbons, John - *The Norm of Belief*
    Phil R - v124 - i2 - April 2015 - p272(4) [501+]
Gibbons, Katy - *English Catholic Exiles in Late Sixteenth-Century Paris*
    Ren Q - v68 - i2 - Summer 2015 - p719-721 [501+]
Gibbons, Luke - *Charles O'Conor of Ballinagare: Life and Works*
    ILS - v35 - i1 - Fall 2015 - p8(1) [51-500]
Gibbs, Camille - *A Sky of Diamonds*
    c CH Bwatch - May 2015 - pNA [51-500]
Gibbs, Christopher H. - *Franz Schubert and His World*
    ON - v79 - i8 - Feb 2015 - p60(1) [501+]

Gibbs, Jenna M. - *Performing the Temple of Liberty: Slavery, Theater, and Popular Culture in London and Philadelphia, 1760-1850*
    JAH - v102 - i2 - Sept 2015 - p551-552 [501+]
    W&M Q - v72 - i3 - July 2015 - p513-516 [501+]
    AHR - v120 - i4 - Oct 2015 - p1451-1452 [501+]
Gibbs, Matt - *Themes in Roman Society and Culture: An Introduction to Ancient Rome*
    Class R - v65 - i1 - April 2015 - p191-193 [501+]
Gibbs, Stuart - *Belly Up*
    c Teach Lib - v42 - i3 - Feb 2015 - p57(1) [51-500]
Big Game
    c KR - July 15 2015 - pNA [51-500]
Double Cross
    c Teach Lib - v42 - i4 - April 2015 - p37(1) [51-500]
Evil Spy School (Read by Frazier, Gibson). Audiobook Review
    c SLJ - v61 - i7 - July 2015 - p46(1) [51-500]
Evil Spy School
    c BL - v111 - i22 - August 1 2015 - p79(1) [51-500]
    y HB Guide - v26 - i1 - Fall 2015 - p83(1) [51-500]
    c Teach Lib - v43 - i1 - Oct 2015 - p48(1) [51-500]
The Last Musketeer
    c Teach Lib - v42 - i4 - April 2015 - p37(1) [51-500]
Poached
    c Teach Lib - v42 - i3 - Feb 2015 - p57(1) [51-500]
Space Case
    c HB Guide - v26 - i1 - Spring 2015 - p78(1) [51-500]
    c Teach Lib - v42 - i3 - Feb 2015 - p57(1) [51-500]
Spaced Out
    c KR - Jan 1 2016 - pNA [51-500]
Spy Camp
    c Teach Lib - v42 - i4 - April 2015 - p43(1) [51-500]
Spy School
    c Teach Lib - v42 - i3 - Feb 2015 - p57(1) [51-500]
Traitor's Chase
    c Teach Lib - v42 - i4 - April 2015 - p37(1) [51-500]
Gibbs, Susan - *Modern Country Knits: 30 Designs from Juniper Moon Farm*
    Bwatch - Feb 2015 - pNA [51-500]
    LJ - v140 - i2 - Feb 1 2015 - p82(1) [51-500]
Gibbs, Timothy - *Mandela's Kinsmen: Nationalist Elites and Apartheid's First Bantustan*
    AHR - v120 - i1 - Feb 2015 - p377-378 [501+]
    JIH - v45 - i4 - Spring 2015 - p607-609 [501+]
Giberson, Karl W. - *Saving the Original Sinner: How Christians Have Used the Bible's First Man to Oppress, Inspire, and Make Sense of the World*
    CC - v132 - i17 - August 19 2015 - p38(2) [501+]
Saving the Original Sinner
    KR - March 15 2015 - pNA [51-500]
Gibney, John - *The Shadow of a Year: The 1641 Rebellion in Irish History and Memory*
    Ren Q - v68 - i1 - Spring 2015 - p299-301 [501+]
Gibney, Michael - *The Brotherhood and the Shield: The Three Thorns*
    y VOYA - v38 - i1 - April 2015 - p78(1) [51-500]
Sous Chef: 24 Hous on the Line
    NYTBR - June 14 2015 - p24(L) [501+]
Gibney, Shannon - *See No Color*
    y BL - v112 - i4 - Oct 15 2015 - p46(1) [51-500]
    y KR - Sept 15 2015 - pNA [51-500]
    y PW - v262 - i49 - Dec 2 2015 - p96(1) [51-500]
    y SLJ - v61 - i10 - Oct 2015 - p110(1) [51-500]
Gibsen, Cole - *Life Unaware*
    y KR - Feb 15 2015 - pNA [51-500]
    y SLJ - v61 - i7 - July 2015 - p92(1) [51-500]
    y VOYA - v38 - i2 - June 2015 - p59(1) [51-500]
Gibson, Amy - *By Day, By Night (Illus. by So, Meilo)*
    c HB Guide - v26 - i2 - Fall 2015 - p111(1) [51-500]
For Keeps: Meaningful Patchwork for Everyday Living
    LJ - v140 - i14 - Sept 1 2015 - p106(1) [51-500]
Gibson, Andrew - *The Strong Spirit: History, Politics, and Aesthetics in the Writings of James Joyce, 1898-1915*
    MFSF - v61 - i3 - Fall 2015 - p550-553 [501+]
Gibson, Bob - *Pitch by Pitch: My View of One Unforgettable Game*
    BL - v112 - i1 - Sept 1 2015 - p36(1) [51-500]
    KR - August 1 2015 - pNA [51-500]
    LJ - v140 - i14 - Sept 1 2015 - p111(2) [51-500]
    PW - v262 - i35 - August 31 2015 - p81(1) [51-500]
Gibson, Carrie - *Empire's Crossroads: A History of the Caribbean from Columbus to the Present Day*
    CSM - Feb 23 2015 - pNA [501+]
    NYTBR - Jan 4 2015 - p19(L) [501+]
Gibson, Cay - *Cajun 'Ti Beau and the Cocodries (Illus. by D'Antoni, Colleen)*
    c HB Guide - v26 - i2 - Fall 2015 - p35(1) [51-500]

Gibson, Craig - *Behind the Front: British Soldiers and French Civilians, 1914-1918*
    AHR - v120 - i4 - Oct 2015 - p1552-1553 [501+]
    J Mil H - v79 - i2 - April 2015 - p511-512 [501+]
Gibson, D.W. - *The Edge Becomes the Center: An Oral History of Gentrification in the Twenty-First Century*
    HM - v331 - i1985 - Oct 2015 - p90(5) [501+]
    KR - March 15 2015 - pNA [501+]
    NYT - May 15 2015 - pC26(L) [501+]
    PW - v262 - i12 - March 23 2015 - p61(1) [51-500]
Gibson, David R. - *Talk at the Brink: Deliberation and Decision during the Cuban Missile Crisis*
    CS - v44 - i2 - March 2015 - p202-204 [501+]
Gibson, David William - *The Edge Becomes the Center: An Oral History of Gentrification in the Twenty-First Century*
    Nation - v300 - i22 - June 1 2015 - p34(1) [501+]
Gibson, Dawn-Marie - *Women of the Nation: Between Black Protest and Sunni Islam*
    JAH - v102 - i2 - Sept 2015 - p621-621 [501+]
    Wom R Bks - v32 - i4 - July-August 2015 - p7(3) [501+]
Gibson, Jasper - *A Bright Moon for Fools*
    BL - v112 - i1 - Sept 1 2015 - p40(1) [51-500]
    KR - July 1 2015 - pNA [51-500]
Gibson, John - *The Philosophy of Poetry*
    TLS - i5873 - Oct 23 2015 - p22(1) [501+]
Gibson, Julia Mary - *Copper Magic*
    c HB Guide - v26 - i1 - Spring 2015 - p78(1) [51-500]
Gibson, Marion - *Shakespeare's Demonology: A Dictionary*
    Ren Q - v68 - i1 - Spring 2015 - p393-395 [501+]
Gibson, Miles - *Dancing with Mermaids*
    TLS - i5849 - May 8 2015 - p19(2) [501+]
Gibson, Neil - *Twisted Dark, vol. 1*
    PW - v262 - i37 - Sept 14 2015 - p51(1) [51-500]
Gibson, Sarah Katherine - *Canada Transformed: The Speeches of Sir John A. Macdonald: A Bicentennial Celebration*
    Can Hist R - v96 - i2 - June 2015 - p286(3) [501+]
Gibson, Susannah - *Animal, Vegetable, Mineral? How Eighteenth-Century Science Disrupted the Natural Order*
    Nature - v523 - i7562 - July 30 2015 - p530(1) [51-500]
    TLS - i5877 - Nov 20 2015 - p32(1) [501+]
Gibson, Thomas - *Anarchic Solidarity: Autonomy, Equality, and Fellowship in Southeast Asia*
    JAS - v74 - i1 - Feb 2015 - p239-241 [501+]
Gibson, William - *Distrust That Particular Flavor*
    TLS - i5832 - Jan 9 2015 - p17(2) [501+]
Neuromancer
    TLS - i5832 - Jan 9 2015 - p14(1) [501+]
The Peripheral (Read by King, Lorelei). Audiobook Review
    PW - v262 - i5 - Feb 2 2015 - p53(1) [51-500]
The Peripheral
    ABR - v36 - i5 - July-August 2015 - p12(2) [501+]
    NYRB - v62 - i6 - April 2 2015 - p49(2) [501+]
    Reason - v46 - i9 - Feb 2015 - p58(1) [51-500]
    TLS - i5832 - Jan 9 2015 - p17(2) [501+]
Gidwitz, Adam - *Star Wars: The Empire Strikes Back: So You Want to Be a Jedi? (Illus. by McQuarrie, Ralph)*
    c BL - v112 - i1 - Sept 1 2015 - p115(1) [501+]
    c SLJ - v61 - i11 - Nov 2015 - p98(1) [501+]
Gielan, Michelle - *Broadcasting Happiness: The Science of Igniting and Sustaining Positive Change*
    PW - v262 - i25 - June 22 2015 - p133(1) [51-500]
Gienny, Misha - *Nemesis*
    Mac - v128 - i45 - Nov 16 2015 - p57(2) [501+]
Gier, Kerstin - *Dream a Little Dream*
    y BL - v111 - i9-10 - Jan 1 2015 - p88(1) [51-500]
    y VOYA - v38 - i2 - June 2015 - p74(2) [51-500]
Gierstberg, Frits - *European Portrait Photography since 1990*
    LJ - v140 - i11 - June 15 2015 - p84(1) [51-500]
Gies, Miep - *Anne Frank Remembered: The Story of the Woman Who Helped to Hide the Frank Family (Read by Rosenblat, Barbara). Audiobook Review*
    BL - v111 - i15 - April 1 2015 - p86(1) [51-500]
Giesecke, Joan - *Navigating the Future with Scenario Planning: A Guidebook for Librarians*
    LJ - v140 - i17 - Oct 15 2015 - p101(1) [51-500]
Giesser, Mark R. - *A Cheese of Some Importance*
    KR - June 1 2015 - pNA [501+]
Giessmann, Ursula - *Der letzte Gegenpapst: Felix V. Studien zu Herrschaftspraxis und Legitimationsstrategien, 1434-1451*
    Med R - June 2015 - pNA [501+]

Giff, Patricia Reilly - *The Garden Monster (Illus. by Palmisciano, Diane)*
   c HB Guide - v26 - i1 - Spring 2015 - p53(1) [51-500]
Hunter Moran Digs Deep
   c HB Guide - v26 - i1 - Spring 2015 - p78(1) [51-500]
Until I Find Julian
   c HB - v91 - i5 - Sept-Oct 2015 - p102(2) [51-500]
   c KR - July 15 2015 - pNA [51-500]
   c SLJ - v61 - i7 - July 2015 - p76(2) [51-500]
Giffford, Clive - *Computer Networks*
   c CH Bwatch - Nov 2015 - pNA [51-500]
Gifford, Behan - *Voyaging with Kids: A Guide to Family Life Afloat*
   SPBW - Oct 2015 - pNA [51-500]
Gifford, Bill - *Spring Chicken*
   KR - Jan 1 2015 - pNA [501+]
Spring Chicken: Stay Young Forever (or Die Trying)
   LJ - v140 - i3 - Feb 15 2015 - p120(2) [51-500]
   PW - v262 - i1 - Jan 5 2015 - p68(1) [51-500]
   PW - v262 - i11 - March 16 2015 - p15(1) [51-500]
Gifford, Clive - *Amazing Applications and Perfect Programs*
   c CH Bwatch - Nov 2015 - pNA [51-500]
Awesome Algorithms and Creative Coding
   c CH Bwatch - Nov 2015 - pNA [51-500]
   c Sch Lib - v63 - i3 - Autumn 2015 - p173(2) [51-500]
Dead or Alive? Discover the Most Amazing Animal Survivors (Illus. by Horne, Sarah)
   c Sch Lib - v63 - i1 - Spring 2015 - p47(1) [51-500]
The Kingfisher Soccer Encyclopedia
   c HB Guide - v26 - i1 - Spring 2015 - p183(1) [51-500]
The Science of Computers
   c CH Bwatch - Nov 2015 - pNA [51-500]
Gifford, Elisabeth - *The Sea House*
   LJ - v140 - i17 - Oct 15 2015 - p118(1) [501+]
Gifford, James - *Personal Modernisms: Anarchist Networks and the Later Avant-Gardes*
   TLS - i5844 - April 3 2015 - p27(1) [501+]
Gifford, Justin - *Street Poison: The Biography of Iceberg Slim (Read by Jackson, J.D.). Audiobook Review*
   LJ - v140 - i16 - Oct 1 2015 - p44(1) [51-500]
   PW - v262 - i39 - Sept 28 2015 - p87(1) [51-500]
Street Poison: The Biography of Iceberg Slim
   BL - v111 - i19-20 - June 1 2015 - p34(2) [51-500]
   NYT - August 5 2015 - pC1(L) [501+]
   PW - v262 - i18 - May 4 2015 - p106(1) [51-500]
   KR - May 15 2015 - pNA [501+]
   LJ - v140 - i9 - May 15 2015 - p83(2) [51-500]
Gift, Patricia Reilly - *Until I Find Julian*
   c BL - v112 - i1 - Sept 1 2015 - p118(1) [51-500]
   c PW - v262 - i25 - June 22 2015 - p137(2) [51-500]
Gigantino, James J., II - *The Ragged Road to Abolition: Slavery and Freedom in New Jersey, 1775-1865*
   AHR - v120 - i4 - Oct 2015 - p1485-1486 [501+]
   JSH - v81 - i4 - Nov 2015 - p949(2) [501+]
Gigantino, James J., III - *The Ragged Road to Abolition: Slavery and Freedom in New Jersey, 1775-1865*
   JAH - v102 - i2 - Sept 2015 - p554-555 [501+]
Gigase, Marc - *Le Tourisme Comme Facteur de Transformations Economiques, Techniques et Sociales (XIXe-Xxe Siecles): Tourism as a Factor of Economic, Technical and Social Transformations (XIXth-XXth Centuries).*
   HNet - March 2015 - pNA [501+]
Giglio, Shannon - *Short Bus Hero*
   PW - v262 - i22 - June 1 2015 - p39(2) [51-500]
Gigliotti, Jim - *Science*
   y BL - v111 - i17 - May 1 2015 - p88(1) [51-500]
Gigot, Jami - *Mae and the Moon (Illus. by Gigot, Jami)*
   c CH Bwatch - July 2015 - pNA [51-500]
   c KR - July 15 2015 - pNA [51-500]
   c PW - v262 - i24 - June 15 2015 - p81(1) [51-500]
   c SLJ - v61 - i9 - Sept 2015 - p120(2) [51-500]
Giguere, Joy M. - *Characteristically American: Memorial Architecture, National Identity, and the Egyptian Revival*
   AHR - v120 - i4 - Oct 2015 - p1487-1488 [501+]
Giirth, Per-Henrik - *First Hockey Words*
   c HB Guide - v26 - i1 - Spring 2015 - p184(1) [51-500]
Gil, Daniel Juan - *Shakespeare's Anti-Politics: Sovereign Power and the Life of the Flesh*
   Shakes Q - v66 - i1 - Spring 2015 - p97-99 [501+]
Gilardi, Therese - *Narvla's Celtic New Year*
   SPBW - May 2015 - pNA [51-500]
Gilbert, Christopher - *Turning Into Dwelling: Poems*
   NYTBR - Dec 27 2015 - p16(L) [501+]
Turning into Dwelling
   PW - v262 - i24 - June 15 2015 - p62(1) [51-500]
Gilbert, Elizabeth - *Big Magic: Creative Living beyond Fear (Read by Gilbert, Elizabeth). Audiobook Review*
   LJ - v140 - i19 - Nov 15 2015 - p54(1) [51-500]
   PW - v262 - i48 - Nov 30 2015 - p54(1) [51-500]
Big Magic: Creative Living beyond Fear
   BL - v111 - i21 - July 1 2015 - p4(1) [51-500]
   BooChiTr - Oct 10 2015 - p14(1) [501+]
   KR - June 15 2015 - pNA [501+]
   NYTBR - Sept 20 2015 - p13(L) [501+]
   PW - v262 - i24 - June 15 2015 - p74(1) [51-500]
   SEP - v287 - i5 - Sept-Oct 2015 - p24(1) [501+]
Gilbert, Elizabeth T. - *Learn to Draw Forest Animals: Step-by-Step Instructions for MoreThan 25 Woodland Creatures (Illus. by Cuddy, Robbin)*
   c SLJ - v61 - i8 - August 2015 - p120(1) [51-500]
Gilbert, Faye Alison - *Fiddle Dee Dee (Illus. by Berndt, Jackie)*
   c CH Bwatch - March 2015 - pNA [51-500]
Gilbert, Kellie Coates - *Where Rivers Part*
   BL - v111 - i12 - Feb 15 2015 - p33(1) [51-500]
Gilbert, Kelly Loy - *Conviction*
   y BL - v111 - i18 - May 15 2015 - p53(1) [51-500]
   c BL - v112 - i1 - Sept 1 2015 - p99(1) [501+]
   y CCB-B - v68 - i11 - July-August 2015 - p545(2) [51-500]
   y KR - March 15 2015 - pNA [51-500]
   PW - v262 - i14 - April 6 2015 - p62(1) [51-500]
   y SLJ - v61 - i5 - May 2015 - p118(1) [51-500]
   y Teach Lib - v43 - i1 - Oct 2015 - p22(1) [51-500]
   y VOYA - v38 - i2 - June 2015 - p59(2) [51-500]
   c HB Guide - v26 - i2 - Fall 2015 - p120(1) [51-500]
Gilbert, Martin - *Churchill and America*
   HT - v65 - i1 - Jan 2015 - p56(2) [501+]
Churchill and the Jews: A Lifelong Friendship
   HT - v65 - i1 - Jan 2015 - p56(2) [501+]
Gilbert, Paul D. - *Sherlock Holmes and the Unholy Trinity*
   PW - v262 - i48 - Nov 30 2015 - p42(1) [51-500]
Gilbert, Ronnie - *Ronnie Gilbert: A Radical Life in Song*
   BL - v112 - i5 - Nov 1 2015 - p23(1) [51-500]
Gilbert, Sandra M. - *The Culinary Imagination*
   Hum - v75 - i3 - May-June 2015 - p42(2) [501+]
Eating Words: A Norton Anthology of Food Writing
   KR - June 15 2015 - pNA [501+]
   LJ - v140 - i11 - June 15 2015 - p105(2) [51-500]
   BL - v111 - i22 - August 1 2015 - p14(1) [51-500]
Gilbert, Sara - *American Food*
   SLJ - v61 - i4 - April 2015 - p101(3) [501+]
Cooking School
   c HB Guide - v26 - i2 - Fall 2015 - p188(1) [51-500]
French Food
   c BL - v111 - i15 - April 1 2015 - p62(1) [51-500]
The Story of MTV
   c HB Guide - v26 - i1 - Spring 2015 - p173(1) [51-500]
Gilbert, Scott F. - *Developmental Biology*
   QRB - v90 - i2 - June 2015 - p227(1) [501+]
Gilboa, Amos - *Israel's Silent Defender: An Inside Look at Sixty Years of Israeli Intelligence*
   J Mil H - v79 - i3 - July 2015 - p881-883 [501+]
Gilby, Nancy Benovich - *First Robotics*
   c BL - v112 - i7 - Dec 1 2015 - p42(1) [51-500]
Gilchrist, Kelvin K. - *Inventions and Discoveries of People of Color: Prehistoric to Today*
   LJ - v140 - i16 - Oct 1 2015 - p106(1) [51-500]
   y VOYA - v38 - i4 - Oct 2015 - p82(1) [51-500]
Gilcris, Eric - *Bear Hugging and Cancer Crushing (Illus. by Hogan, Steve)*
   c CH Bwatch - April 2015 - pNA [51-500]
Gildea, Robert - *Fighters in the Shadows: A New History of the French Resistance*
   Econ - v416 - i8953 - August 29 2015 - p68(US) [501+]
   KR - Sept 15 2015 - pNA [501+]
   Spec - v328 - i9757 - August 29 2015 - p32(2) [501+]
   TimHES - i2228 - Nov 5 2015 - p46(1) [501+]
Gilder, Ginny - *Course Correction: A Story of Rowing and Resilience in the Wake of Title IX*
   BL - v111 - i15 - April 1 2015 - p12(1) [51-500]
Course Correction
   KR - Jan 15 2015 - pNA [501+]
Gilens, Martin - *Affluence and Influence: Economic Inequality and Political Power in America*
   CS - v44 - i4 - July 2015 - p449-462 [501+]
   Pub Op Q - v79 - i1 - Spring 2015 - p207(209) [501+]
Giles, Laini - *The Forgotten Flapper*
   KR - Dec 1 2015 - pNA [501+]

Giles, Lamar - *Endangered*
   y CCB-B - v68 - i10 - June 2015 - p490(1) [51-500]
   y HB - v91 - i2 - March-April 2015 - p95(1) [51-500]
   c HB Guide - v26 - i2 - Fall 2015 - p120(1) [51-500]
   y KR - Jan 15 2015 - pNA [51-500]
   y PW - v262 - i8 - Feb 23 2015 - p78(1) [51-500]
   y VOYA - v38 - i1 - April 2015 - p60(1) [51-500]
Fake ID
   y HB Guide - v26 - i1 - Spring 2015 - p107(1) [51-500]
Giles, Paul - *Antipodean America: Australasia and the Constitution of U.S. Literature*
   ABR - v36 - i5 - July-August 2015 - p7(2) [501+]
   AL - v87 - i2 - June 2015 - p408-410 [501+]
   J Am St - v49 - i3 - August 2015 - p631-633 [501+]
   JAH - v102 - i1 - June 2015 - p202-204 [501+]
Gilfillan, Kathy - *Sons + Fathers: An Anthology of Words and Images*
   BL - v112 - i4 - Oct 15 2015 - p7(2) [501+]
Gilgen, Peter - *Lekturen der Erinnerung: Lessing, Kant, Hegel*
   Eight-C St - v48 - i4 - Summer 2015 - p551-553 [501+]
Gilham, Jamie - *Loyal Enemies: British Converts to Islam, 1850-1950*
   Bks & Cult - v21 - i5 - Sept-Oct 2015 - p8(2) [501+]
Giliomee, Hermann - *The Last Afrikaner Leaders: A Supreme Test of Power*
   JIH - v45 - i3 - Wntr 2015 - p454-456 [501+]
Giliotti, Laurence - *Gambrelli and the Prosecutor*
   KR - June 1 2015 - pNA [501+]
Gill, Adrian A. - *Pour Me: A Life*
   NS - v144 - i5287 - Nov 6 2015 - p46(2) [501+]
   Spec - v329 - i9772 - Dec 12 2015 - p86(2) [501+]
Gill, Amyrose McCue - *Friendship and Sociability in Premodern Europe: Contexts, Concepts and Expressions*
   Six Ct J - v46 - i3 - Fall 2015 - p736-738 [501+]
Friendship and Sociability in Premodern Europe: Contexts, Concepts, and Expressions
   FS - v69 - i3 - July 2015 - p389-390 [501+]
Gill, David James - *Britain and the Bomb: Nuclear Diplomacy, 1964-1970*
   AHR - v120 - i3 - June 2015 - p1118-1119 [501+]
Gill, Deirdre - *Outside (Illus. by Gill, Deirdre)*
   c HB Guide - v26 - i1 - Spring 2015 - p9(1) [51-500]
   c NYTBR - Jan 18 2015 - p20(L) [501+]
Gill, Jonathan - *Harlem: The Four Hundred Year History from Dutch Village to Capital of Black America*
   BL - v112 - i5 - Nov 1 2015 - p18(2) [501+]
Gill, Malcolm - *Knowing Who You Are: Eight Surprising Images of Christian Identity*
   Ch Today - v59 - i7 - Sept 2015 - p80(1) [51-500]
Gill, Penny - *What in the World Is Going On? Wisdom Teachings for Our Time*
   SPBW - July 2015 - pNA [51-500]
Gillan, Kieron - *The Wicked + The Divine, vol. 1: The Faust Act*
   PW - v262 - i9 - March 2 2015 - p73(1) [51-500]
Gillard, Julia - *My Story*
   TLS - i5833 - Jan 16 2015 - p21(1) [501+]
Gilleland, Diane - *All Points Patchwork: English Paper Piecing beyond the Hexagon for Quilts & Small Projects*
   LJ - v140 - i11 - June 15 2015 - p88(2) [51-500]
Gillespie, Gerald - *The Nightwatches of Bonaventura*
   Spec - v327 - i9727 - Jan 31 2015 - p36(2) [501+]
Gillespie, Hollis - *We Will Be Crashing Shortly*
   c HB Guide - v26 - i2 - Fall 2015 - p120(1) [51-500]
   y KR - April 15 2015 - pNA [51-500]
   y SLJ - v61 - i5 - May 2015 - p118(1) [51-500]
   y VOYA - v38 - i2 - June 2015 - p60(1) [51-500]
Gillespie, Kevin - *Pure Pork Awesomeness: Totally Cookable Recipes from Around the World*
   Bwatch - June 2015 - pNA [51-500]
Gillespie, Michele - *North Carolina Women: Their Lives and Times, vol. 1*
   JSH - v81 - i3 - August 2015 - p713(3) [501+]
Gillespie, Vincent - *After Arundel: Religious Writing in Fifteenth-Century England*
   Specu - v90 - i1 - Jan 2015 - p255-256 [501+]
A Companion to the Early Modern Printed Book in Britain, 1476-1558
   HER - v130 - i545 - August 2015 - p977(3) [501+]
A Companion to the Early Printed Book in Britain, 1476-1558
   Med R - Feb 2015 - pNA [501+]
Probable Truth: Editing Medieval Texts from Britain in the Twenty-First Century
   Med R - June 2015 - pNA [501+]

Gillett, J.T. - *Orphans, Assassins and the Existential Eggplant*
KR - Dec 15 2015 - pNA [501+]

Gillett, Robert - *"Aber eines lugt er nicht: Echtheit" - Perspektiven auf Hubert Fichte*
MLR - v110 - i2 - April 2015 - p602-605 [501+]

Gilley, Bruce - *The Nature of Asian Politics*
For Aff - v94 - i3 - May-June 2015 - pNA [501+]

Gilliam, Bryan - *Rounding Wagner's Mountain: Richard Strauss and Modern German Opera*
ON - v80 - i6 - Dec 2015 - p66(1) [501+]

Gilliam, Terry - *Gilliamesque: A Pre-posthumous Memoir*
NYTBR - Dec 6 2015 - p58(L) [501+]
Gilliamesque
KR - Oct 1 2015 - pNA [501+]

Gillies, Andrea - *The Enlightenment of Nina Findlay*
BL - v111 - i16 - April 15 2015 - p23(1) [51-500]
KR - March 1 2015 - pNA [51-500]
LJ - v140 - i6 - April 1 2015 - p75(2) [51-500]
NYTBR - May 17 2015 - p22(L) [501+]
PW - v262 - i13 - March 30 2015 - p48(1) [51-500]

Gillies, Isabel - *Starry Night*
y HB Guide - v26 - i1 - Spring 2015 - p108(1) [51-500]

Gilliland, Ben - *Rocket Science for the Rest of Us*
y BL - v111 - i19-20 - June 1 2015 - p70(1) [51-500]
y SLJ - v61 - i5 - May 2015 - p138(2) [51-500]

Gillin, Kate Cote - *Shrill Hurrahs: Women, Gender, and Racial Violence in South Carolina, 1865-1900*
AHR - v120 - i1 - Feb 2015 - p254-255 [501+]
JAH - v101 - i4 - March 2015 - p1281-1282 [501+]
JSH - v81 - i4 - Nov 2015 - p1002(2) [501+]

Gillingham, John - *1215: The Year of Magna Carta*
HT - v65 - i6 - June 2015 - p56(2) [501+]

Gillingham, Paul - *Dictablanda: Politics, Work, and Culture in Mexico, 1938-1968*
Ams - v72 - i2 - April 2015 - p349(2) [501+]
JIH - v46 - i1 - Summer 2015 - p147-149 [501+]
Dictablanda: Politics, Work, and Culture in Mexico
HAHR - v95 - i4 - Nov 2015 - p692-694 [501+]

Gillingham, Sara - *Busy Baby: Friends (Illus. by Gillingham, Sara)*
c PW - v262 - i31 - August 3 2015 - p58(2) [501+]
How to Mend a Heart (Illus. by Gillingham, Sara)
c KR - Oct 1 2015 - pNA [51-500]
c PW - v262 - i41 - Oct 12 2015 - p66(2) [501+]
c SLJ - v61 - i12 - Dec 2015 - p88(2) [501+]
On My Beach (Illus. by Siminovich, Lorena)
c SLJ - v61 - i7 - July 2015 - p55(1) [51-500]
Trucks
c KR - Jan 1 2016 - pNA [51-500]

Gillis, Alan - *Scapegoat*
ILS - v35 - i1 - Fall 2015 - p23(1) [501+]
TLS - i5853 - June 5 2015 - p25(1) [501+]

Gillis, Bryan - *Sexual Content in Young Adult Literature: Reading Between the Sheets*
y SLJ - v61 - i11 - Nov 2015 - p142(1) [51-500]
y VOYA - v38 - i4 - Oct 2015 - p88(1) [51-500]

Gillis, Steven - *Benchere in Wonderland*
KR - July 15 2015 - pNA [51-500]

Gillmor, Don - *Long Change*
Nat Post - v17 - i240 - August 22 2015 - pWP5(1) [501+]

Gillock, William - *Accent on Two Pianos: Intermediate to Advanced Level*
Am MT - v65 - i3 - Dec 2015 - p45(2) [501+]

Gillota, David - *Ethnic Humor in Multiethnic America*
ERS - v38 - i3 - March 2015 - p514(2) [501+]

Gillson, Lindsey - *Biodiversity Conservation and Environmental Change*
TimHES - i2220 - Sept 10 2015 - p47(1) [501+]

Gilly, Alex - *Devil's Harbor*
BL - v111 - i17 - May 1 2015 - p32(1) [51-500]
KR - April 15 2015 - pNA [51-500]

Gilman, Carolyn Ives - *Dark Orbit*
Analog - v135 - i9 - Sept 2015 - p106(2) [501+]
KR - May 15 2015 - pNA [51-500]
PW - v262 - i18 - May 4 2015 - p100(1) [51-500]

Gilman, Grace - *Dixie and the Best Day Ever (Illus. by Rogers, Jacqueline)*
c HB Guide - v26 - i1 - Spring 2015 - p53 [51-500]

Gilman, Laura Anne - *Silver on the Road*
PW - v262 - i35 - August 31 2015 - p66(1) [51-500]

Gilmore, Bob - *Claude Vivier: A Composer's Life*
MT - v156 - i1930 - Spring 2015 - p111-114 [501+]

Gilmore, Glenda Elizabeth - *These United States: A Nation in the Making, 1890 to the Present*
LJ - v140 - i15 - Sept 15 2015 - p87(1) [51-500]
NYTBR - Nov 22 2015 - p27(L) [501+]
PW - v262 - i30 - July 27 2015 - p54(1) [51-500]
These United States
KR - August 1 2015 - pNA [51-500]

Gilmore, Grace - *Logan Pryce Makes a Mess (Illus. by Brown, Petra)*
c SLJ - v61 - i7 - July 2015 - p71(2) [51-500]
c HB Guide - v26 - i2 - Fall 2015 - p66(1) [51-500]
The Lucky Wheel, Book 2 (Illus. by Brown, Petra)
c SLJ - v61 - i7 - July 2015 - p71(2) [51-500]
The Lucky Wheel (Illus. by Brown, Petra)
c HB Guide - v26 - i2 - Fall 2015 - p66(1) [51-500]

Gilmore, Susan E. - *The Peace Seeker: One Woman's Battle in the Church's War on Homosexuality*
SPBW - August 2015 - pNA [501+]

Gilmour, Rachelle - *Juxtaposition and the Elisha Cycle*
JR - v95 - i4 - Oct 2015 - p554(3) [501+]

Gilovich, Thomas - *The Wisest One in the Room*
KR - Oct 1 2015 - pNA [501+]

Giloy-Hirtz, Petra - *David Lynch: The Factory Photographs*
LJ - v140 - i2 - Feb 1 2015 - p84(1) [501+]

Gilpin, Caroline Crosson - *National Geographic Readers: Barack Obama*
c HB Guide - v26 - i1 - Spring 2015 - p192(1) [51-500]

Gilsdorf, Sean - *The Favor of Friends: Intercession and Aristocratic Politics in Carolingian and Ottonian Europe*
Specu - v90 - i4 - Oct 2015 - p1116-1118 [501+]

Gilson, Jamie - *My Teacher Is an Idiom*
c KR - May 15 2015 - pNA [51-500]
My Teacher Is an Idiom (Illus. by Meisel, Paul)
c BL - v111 - i21 - July 1 2015 - p75(1) [51-500]

Gilstrap, Beth - *I Am Barbarella: Stories*
KR - July 15 2015 - pNA [51-500]

Gimbel, Steven - *Einstein: His Space and Times*
BL - v111 - i16 - April 15 2015 - p7(1) [51-500]
KR - Feb 15 2015 - pNA [501+]
LJ - v140 - i6 - April 1 2015 - p114(1) [501+]
NYRB - v62 - i8 - May 7 2015 - p14(3) [501+]
PW - v262 - i13 - March 30 2015 - p68(2) [501+]

Gimlette, John - *Elephant Complex: Travels in Sri Lanka*
KR - Dec 15 2015 - pNA [501+]
PW - v262 - i52 - Dec 21 2015 - p143(1) [501+]
Spec - v329 - i9766 - Oct 31 2015 - p37(2) [501+]

Gimpel, Diane Marczely - *Pompeii*
y Teach Lib - v42 - i5 - June 2015 - p10(1) [501+]
A Timeline History of Early American Indian Peoples
c HB Guide - v26 - i2 - Fall 2015 - p222(1) [51-500]

Gindlesperger, James - *So You Think You Know Gettysburg? The Stories Behind the Monuments and the Men Who Fought One of America's Most Epic Battles, vol. 2*
JSH - v81 - i4 - Nov 2015 - p1057(1) [501+]

Ginell, Cary - *The Evolution of Mann: Herbie Mann and the Flute in Jazz*
Notes - v72 - i1 - Sept 2015 - p141(3) [501+]

Giner, Gonzalo - *The Horse Healer: A Novel*
KR - Feb 1 2015 - pNA [51-500]

Ginger Foglesong Guy - *Fiesta! (Illus. by Moreno, Rene King)*
c BL - v111 - i9-10 - Jan 1 2015 - pS18(5) [501+]

Gingeras, Ryan - *Heroin, Organized Crime, and the Making of Modern Turkey*
AHR - v120 - i4 - Oct 2015 - p1576-1577 [501+]
IJMES - v47 - i3 - August 2015 - p620-623 [501+]

Gingerich, Owen - *God's Planet*
CC - v132 - i4 - Feb 18 2015 - p37(6) [501+]

Gingrich, Callista - *From Sea to Shining Sea (Illus. by Arciero, Susan)*
c HB Guide - v26 - i1 - Spring 2015 - p203(1) [51-500]

Gingrich, Heather Davediuk - *Restoring the Shattered Self: A Christian Counselor's Guide to Complex Trauma*
Intpr - v69 - i1 - Jan 2015 - p122(1) [51-500]

Gino, Alex - *George*
c BL - v111 - i22 - August 1 2015 - p61(1) [51-500]
c CCB-B - v69 - i2 - Oct 2015 - p88(2) [51-500]
c HB - v91 - i5 - Sept-Oct 2015 - p103(1) [51-500]
c KR - June 1 2015 - pNA [51-500]
c NYTBR - Sept 13 2015 - p23(L) [51-500]
c PW - v262 - i19 - May 11 2015 - p61(1) [51-500]
c PW - v262 - i51 - Dec 14 2015 - p21(6) [501+]
c SLJ - v61 - i7 - July 2015 - p77(2) [51-500]

Ginsberg, Al - *Mrs. Valentine's Revenge*
KR - Oct 1 2015 - pNA [501+]

Ginsberg, Allen - *The Essential Ginsberg*
BL - v111 - i18 - May 15 2015 - p11(1) [51-500]
KR - Feb 15 2015 - pNA [501+]

Ginsberg, Benjamin - *The Fall of the Faculty: The Rise of the All-Administrative University and Why It Matters*
CS - v44 - i1 - Jan 2015 - p137-138 [501+]
The Worth of War
Bwatch - Jan 2015 - pNA [51-500]

Ginsberg, Margery B. - *Excited to Learn: Motivation and Culturally Responsive Teaching*
Bwatch - August 2015 - pNA [501+]
Bwatch - Sept 2015 - pNA [51-500]

Ginsborg, Paul - *Family Politics: Domestic Life, Devastation and Survival, 1900-1950*
Econ - v414 - i8922 - Jan 24 2015 - p75(US) [501+]
HNet - June 2015 - pNA [501+]
HT - v65 - i3 - March 2015 - p62(1) [501+]

Ginzburg, Carlo - *The Cheese and the Worms: The Cosmos of a Sixteenth-Century Miller*
TimHES - i2208 - June 18 2015 - p47(1) [501+]

Ginzburg, Natalia - *The Manzoni Family*
TimHES - i2192 - Feb 26 2015 - p47(1) [501+]

Gioeli, Anthony - *International Business Expansion: A Step-by-Step Guide to Launch Your Company into Other Countries*
PW - v262 - i17 - April 27 2015 - p67(1) [501+]

Gioia, Ted - *Love Songs: The Hidden History*
Atl - v315 - i2 - March 2015 - p40(2) [501+]
BL - v111 - i11 - Feb 1 2015 - p9(1) [51-500]
Econ - v414 - i8925 - Feb 14 2015 - p76(US) [501+]

Gioielli, Robert - *The City and American Environmentalism*
J Urban H - v41 - i3 - May 2015 - p526-533 [501+]

Gioielli, Robert R. - *Environmental Activism and the Urban Crisis: Baltimore, St. Louis, Chicago*
AHR - v120 - i4 - Oct 2015 - p1525-1526 [501+]
JAH - v102 - i1 - June 2015 - p307-308 [501+]

Giordano, Cristiana - *Migrants in Translation: Caring and the Logics of Difference in Contemporary Italy*
HNet - Feb 2015 - pNA [501+]
MAQ - v29 - i3 - Sept 2015 - pb-14-b-16 [501+]

Giordano, Fausto - *Lo studio dell' antichita: Giorgio Pasquali e i filologi classici*
Class R - v65 - i2 - Oct 2015 - p603-605 [501+]

Giordano, Paolo - *Like Family*
KR - Oct 1 2015 - pNA [501+]
NYT - Nov 30 2015 - pC6(L) [501+]
PW - v262 - i39 - Sept 28 2015 - p63(1) [51-500]

Gipe, Robert - *Trampoline: An Illustrated Novel (Illus. by Gipe, Robert)*
y SLJ - v61 - i10 - Oct 2015 - p122(2) [51-500]

Gipouloux, Francois - *The Asian Mediterranean: Port Cities and Trading Networks in China, Japan and Southeast Asia, 13th-21st Century*
J Urban H - v41 - i1 - Jan 2015 - p165-6 [501+]

Gippert, Wolfgang - *Bildungsreisende und Arbeitsmigrantinnen: Auslandserfahrungen Deutscher Lehrerinnen zwischen Nationaler und Internationaler Orientierung*
HNet - July 2015 - pNA [501+]

Girard, Anne - *Madame Picasso. Audiobook Review*
LJ - v140 - i2 - Feb 1 2015 - p44(2) [501+]

Girard, Edith - *Miss Solitude*
y Res Links - v20 - i3 - Feb 2015 - p45(1) [501+]

Girard, Rene - *The One by Whom Scandal Comes*
JR - v95 - i4 - Oct 2015 - p556(4) [501+]
Sacrifice
Dialogue - v54 - i2 - June 2015 - p384-387 [501+]
When These Things Begin: Conversation with Michel Treguer
JR - v95 - i4 - Oct 2015 - p556(4) [501+]

Girardot, Norman - *Envisioning Howard Finster: The Religion and Art of a Stranger from Another World*
LJ - v140 - i13 - August 1 2015 - p91(1) [51-500]

Giraud, Cedric - *Notre-Dame de Paris, 1163-2013: Actes du colloque scientifique tenu au College des Bernardins, a Paris, du 12 au 15 decembre 2012*
CHR - v101 - i.- Autumn 2015 - p894(2) [501+]

Giraud, Robert - *The Snow Girl (Illus. by Muller, Hlne)*
c NYTBR - Jan 18 2015 - p20(L) [501+]

Giribone, Pietro - *Le Armate Francesi in Italia, 1792-1814: Storia Postale e Catalogazione*
Phil Lit R - v64 - i3 - Summer 2015 - p213(3) [501+]

Giridharadas, Anand - *The True American: Murder and Mystery in Texas*
NYTBR - April 26 2015 - p28(L) [501+]

Girl Power 5-Minute Stories
c HB Guide - v26 - i2 - Fall 2015 - p35(1) [51-500]

Girot, Jean-Eudes - *Marc-Antoine Muret: Des "Isles Fortunees" au Rivage Romain*
    Six Ct J - v46 - i1 - Spring 2015 - p183-185 [501+]

Giroud, Vincent - *Nicolas Nabokov: A Life in Freedom and Music*
    NY - v91 - i24 - August 24 2015 - p73 [51-500]
    NYRB - v62 - i14 - Sept 24 2015 - p46(3) [501+]

Gischler, Victor - *Stay*
    KR - April 15 2015 - pNA [51-500]
    BL - v111 - i19-20 - June 1 2015 - p57(1) [51-500]
    PW - v262 - i17 - April 27 2015 - p52(2) [51-500]

Gish, Melissa - *Beavers*
    c HB Guide - v26 - i1 - Spring 2015 - p164(1) [51-500]
Living Wild Series
    c SLJ - v61 - i9 - Sept 2015 - p176(1) [51-500]

Gish, Robert F. - *River of Ghosts: A Cedar Valley Odyssey*
    Roundup M - v22 - i3 - Feb 2015 - p26(1) [501+]
River of Ghosts
    Roundup M - v22 - i6 - August 2015 - p30(1) [501+]

Gist, Deeanne - *Tiffany Girl (Read by Botchan, Rachael). Audiobook Review*
    BL - v112 - i6 - Nov 15 2015 - p61(1) [51-500]
Tiffany Girl
    y BL - v111 - i17 - May 1 2015 - p81(1) [51-500]

Gitelman, Lisa - *Paper Knowledge*
    T&C - v56 - i4 - Oct 2015 - p957-964 [501+]
Paper Knowledge: Toward a Media History of Documents
    TLS - i5846 - April 17 2015 - p22(2) [501+]

Gitelman, Zvi - *Jewish Identities in Postcommunist Russia and Ukraine: An Uncertain Ethnicity*
    Slav R - v74 - i1 - Spring 2015 - p217-218 [501+]

Gitlin, Martin - *Cyber Attack*
    y HB Guide - v26 - i2 - Fall 2015 - p154(1) [51-500]
World War II U.S. Homefront: A History Perspectives Book
    c Teach Lib - v42 - i4 - April 2015 - p9(1) [51-500]

Gitlin, Marty - *The Best Tennis Players of All Time*
    c HB Guide - v26 - i2 - Fall 2015 - p197(2) [51-500]
Playing Pro Basketball
    c HB Guide - v26 - i1 - Spring 2015 - p182(1) [51-500]

Gittins, Rob - *The Secret Shelter*
    PW - v262 - i42 - Oct 19 2015 - p58(1) [51-500]

Giuffre, Kathy - *The Drunken Spelunker's Guide to Plato*
    KR - July 1 2015 - pNA [51-500]
    LJ - v140 - i15 - Sept 15 2015 - p67(1) [51-500]
    PW - v262 - i30 - July 27 2015 - p40(1) [51-500]

Giuseppetti, M. - *L'isola esile: Studi sull'Inno a Delo di Callimaco*
    Class R - v65 - i1 - April 2015 - p79-81 [501+]

Givel, Michael S. - *Heartland Tobacco War*
    CS - v44 - i6 - Nov 2015 - p873(1) [501+]

Givhan, Robin - *The Battle of Versailles: The Night American Fashion Stumbled into the Spotlight and Made History*
    BL - v111 - i14 - March 15 2015 - p37(1) [51-500]
    LJ - v140 - i5 - March 15 2015 - p102(3) [501+]
    NYT - March 12 2015 - pD2(L) [501+]
    NYTBR - May 3 2015 - p18(L) [501+]

Gjelten, Tom - *A Nation of Nations: A Great American Immigration Story*
    KR - August 1 2015 - pNA [501+]
    LJ - v140 - i14 - Sept 1 2015 - p117(1) [51-500]
    NYRB - v62 - i19 - Dec 3 2015 - p8(3) [501+]
    NYTBR - Sept 13 2015 - p17(L) [501+]

Gladstone, Max - *Last First Snow*
    PW - v262 - i15 - April 13 2015 - p60(1) [51-500]

Gladstone, Wayne - *Agents of the Internet Apocalypse*
    BL - v111 - i22 - August 1 2015 - p26(1) [51-500]

Glancey, Jonathan - *Concorde: The Rise and Fall of the Supersonic Airliner*
    Spec - v329 - i9768 - Nov 14 2015 - p55(2) [501+]

Glancy, Diane - *Fort Marion Prisoners and the Trauma of Native Education*
    Am St - v54 - i2 - Summer 2015 - p118-119 [501+]
Uprising of Goats
    Ch Today - v59 - i4 - May 2015 - p60(1) [51-500]

Glancy, Gabrielle - *I'm Already Disturbed Please Come In: Parasites, Social Media and Other Planetary Disturbances (a Memoir, of Sorts)*
    G&L Rev W - v22 - i3 - May-June 2015 - p35(2) [501+]

Glantz, David M. - *The Stalingrad Trilogy, vol. 3: Endgame at Stalingrad, Book One: November 1942*
    J Mil H - v79 - i1 - Jan 2015 - p249-250 [501+]

The Stalingrad Trilogy, vol. 3: Endgame at Stalingrad, Book Two: December 1942-February 1943
    J Mil H - v79 - i1 - Jan 2015 - p249-250 [501+]

Glanzman, Sam - *A Sailor's Story (Illus. by Glanzman, Sam)*
    RVBW - June 2015 - pNA [51-500]

Glasberg, Beth A. - *Functional Behavior Assessment for People with Autism: Making Sense of Seemingly Senseless Behavior, 2d ed.*
    LJ - v140 - i2 - Feb 1 2015 - p99(1) [51-500]

Glasbrook, Kirsten - *Tapestry Weaving*
    LJ - v140 - i20 - Dec 1 2015 - p102(1) [51-500]

Glaser, Chaya - *Icy Comets Sometimes Have Tails*
    c HB Guide - v26 - i2 - Fall 2015 - p164(2) [51-500]
    c SLJ - v61 - i4 - April 2015 - p82(4) [501+]
Pluto: The Icy Dwarf Planet
    c HB Guide - v26 - i2 - Fall 2015 - p164(2) [51-500]
Saturn: Amazing Rings
    c BL - v111 - i17 - May 1 2015 - p87(2) [51-500]
The Sun: A Super Star
    c BL - v111 - i17 - May 1 2015 - p87(2) [51-500]
    c HB Guide - v26 - i2 - Fall 2015 - p164(2) [51-500]
Uranus: Cold and Blue
    c BL - v111 - i17 - May 1 2015 - p87(2) [51-500]

Glaser, J.D. - *Secure Development for Mobile Apps: How to Design and Code Secure Mobile Applications with PHP and JavaScript*
    Bwatch - June 2015 - pNA [501+]

Glaser, Rachel B. - *Paulina and Fran*
    KR - July 1 2015 - pNA [501+]
Paulina & Fran
    y NYTBR - Oct 11 2015 - p30(L) [501+]

Glaskin, Katie - *Sleep Around the World: Anthropological Perspectives*
    JRAI - v21 - i2 - June 2015 - p478(2) [501+]

Glaspey, Terry - *75 Masterpieces Every Christian Should Know: The Fascinating Stories behind Great Works of Art, Literature, Music, and Film*
    Ch Today - v59 - i9 - Nov 2015 - p76(1) [501+]

Glasrud, Bruce A. - *Discovering Texas History*
    Roundup M - v22 - i3 - Feb 2015 - p23(1) [501+]
    Roundup M - v22 - i6 - August 2015 - p37(1) [501+]

Glass, Andrew - *Flying Cars: The True Story*
    c BL - v111 - i19-20 - June 1 2015 - p76(2) [51-500]
    c CCB-B - v69 - i2 - Oct 2015 - p89(1) [51-500]
    c CH Bwatch - Nov 2015 - pNA [51-500]
    c KR - June 15 2015 - pNA [51-500]
    c SLJ - v61 - i4 - April 2015 - p183(1) [51-500]

Glass, Brent D. - *50 Great American Places*
    KR - Dec 15 2015 - pNA [501+]

Glass, Calliope - *Do You Want to Build a Snowman? (Illus. by Mosqueda, Olga T.)*
    c HB Guide - v26 - i2 - Fall 2015 - p11(1) [51-500]

Glass, Charles - *Syria Burning: ISIS and the Death of the Arab Spring*
    Econ - v416 - i8946 - July 11 2015 - p73(US) [501+]
    LJ - v140 - i12 - July 1 2015 - p98(1) [51-500]
    TLS - i5869 - Sept 25 2015 - p7(2) [501+]

Glass, George S. - *The Overparenting Epidemic: Why Helicopter Parenting Is Bad for Your Kids ... and Dangerous for You, Too!*
    Bwatch - Sept 2015 - pNA [51-500]

Glass, Jefferson - *Reshaw: The Life and Times of John Baptiste Richard*
    Roundup M - v22 - i6 - August 2015 - p37(1) [501+]

Glass, Julia - *And the Dark Sacred Night*
    NYTBR - Feb 1 2015 - p24(L) [501+]

Glass, Lisa - *Blue*
    y Sch Lib - v63 - i4 - Winter 2015 - p253(1) [51-500]

Glass, Philip - *Word Without Music*
    KR - Jan 15 2015 - pNA [501+]
Words Without Music: A Memoir
    HR - v68 - i2 - Summer 2015 - p309-317 [501+]
    Lon R Bks - v37 - i9 - May 7 2015 - p36(2) [501+]
    Nation - v300 - i18 - May 4 2015 - p39(3) [501+]
    NY - v91 - i16 - June 8 2015 - p109 [51-500]
    NYTBR - June 7 2015 - p18(L) [501+]
    TLS - i5862 - August 7 2015 - p3(3) [501+]
Words Without Music
    y BL - v111 - i12 - Feb 15 2015 - p20(1) [51-500]
    Econ - v414 - i8931 - March 28 2015 - p88(US) [501+]
    LJ - v140 - i6 - April 1 2015 - p95(1) [51-500]
    NYT - April 6 2015 - pC1(L) [501+]
    ON - v79 - i11 - May 2015 - p71(1) [501+]
    PW - v262 - i10 - March 9 2015 - p65(1) [51-500]
    Spec - v327 - i9737 - April 11 2015 - p34(2) [501+]
    Mac - v128 - i16 - April 27 2015 - p55(1) [501+]

Glassenberg, Abby - *Sew & Play Puzzle Ball Animals: 6 Little Pets with Big Personalities*
    RVBW - Oct 2015 - pNA [51-500]

Glassgold, Peter - *The Collected Poems of James Laughlin*
    TLS - i5840 - March 6 2015 - p24(1) [501+]

Glatt, John - *Live at the Fillmore East and West: Getting Backstage and Personal with Rock's Greatest Hits (Read by Berkrot, Peter). Audiobook Review*
    LJ - v140 - i5 - March 15 2015 - p73(1) [51-500]
The Lost Girls
    KR - March 1 2015 - pNA [501+]
The Lost Girls: The True Story of the Cleveland Abductions and the Incredible Rescue of Michelle Knight, Amanda Berry, and Gina DeJesus
    BL - v111 - i16 - April 15 2015 - p5(1) [51-500]
    LJ - v140 - i6 - April 1 2015 - p105(1) [51-500]

Glatt, Lisa - *The Nakeds*
    y BL - v111 - i17 - May 1 2015 - p78(2) [51-500]
    KR - April 15 2015 - pNA [51-500]
    LJ - v140 - i9 - May 15 2015 - p70(1) [51-500]
    PW - v262 - i17 - April 27 2015 - p46(1) [51-500]

Glaude, Eddie S., Jr. - *Democracy in Black: How Race Still Enslaves the American Soul*
    BL - v112 - i6 - Nov 15 2015 - p5(1) [51-500]
    KR - Nov 1 2015 - pNA [501+]
    LJ - v140 - i19 - Nov 15 2015 - p98(2) [51-500]

Glauser, Jurg - *Rittersagas: Ubersetzung, Uberlieferung, Transmission*
    JEGP - v114 - i3 - July 2015 - p427(4) [501+]

Glavovic, Bruce C. - *Adapting to Climate Change: Lessons from Natural Hazards Planning*
    QRB - v90 - i3 - Sept 2015 - p330(1) [501+]

Glaze, Florence Eliza - *Between Text and Patient: The Medical Enterprise in Medieval and Early Modern Europe*
    Specu - v90 - i2 - April 2015 - p544-545 [501+]

Gleason, Carrie - *Everything Insects*
    c HB Guide - v26 - i2 - Fall 2015 - p173(1) [51-500]

Gleason, Colleen - *The Chess Queen Enigma*
    y KR - August 15 2015 - pNA [51-500]
    y SLJ - v61 - i7 - July 2015 - p86(1) [51-500]
    y VOYA - v38 - i5 - Dec 2015 - p69(1) [51-500]
The Spiritglass Charade
    y HB Guide - v26 - i1 - Spring 2015 - p108(1) [51-500]

Gleave, Robert - *Islam and Literalism: Literal Meaning and Interpretation in Islamic Legal Theory*
    JNES - v74 - i1 - April 2015 - p179(4) [501+]

Gleeson, David T. - *Ambiguous Anniversary: The Bicentennial of the International Slave Trade Bans*
    JAH - v101 - i4 - March 2015 - p1237-1238 [501+]
The Civil War as Global Conflict: Transnational Meanings of the American Civil War
    JAH - v102 - i1 - June 2015 - p254-255 [501+]
    JSH - v81 - i3 - August 2015 - p747(3) [501+]
The Green and the Gray: The Irish in the Confederate States of America
    Historian - v77 - i3 - Fall 2015 - p558(2) [501+]
    HNet - March 2015 - pNA [501+]
    J Am St - v49 - i2 - May 2015 - p421-422 [501+]
    RAH - v43 - i1 - March 2015 - p70-76 [501+]

Gleeson, Libby - *Mum Goes to Work (Illus. by Rudge, Leila)*
    c Magpies - v30 - i2 - May 2015 - p27(1) [501+]

Gleiberman, Owen - *Movie Freak: My Life Watching Movies*
    KR - Nov 15 2015 - pNA [501+]
    LJ - v140 - i20 - Dec 1 2015 - p104(1) [51-500]
    PW - v262 - i46 - Nov 16 2015 - p67(1) [51-500]

Gleiner, Kelli - *A Day with Monster*
    c KR - Jan 1 2015 - pNA [51-500]

Gleiser, Marcelo - *The Island of Knowledge: The Limits of Science and the Search for Meaning*
    Phys Today - v68 - i2 - Feb 2015 - p49-50 [501+]
    TimHES - i2195 - March 19 2015 - p49(1) [501+]

Gleisner, Jenna Lee - *My Body Needs Exercise*
    c HB Guide - v26 - i1 - Spring 2015 - p171(1) [51-500]

Gleitzman, Morris - *Soon*
    y Magpies - v30 - i3 - July 2015 - p40(1) [501+]

Glencross, Michael - *The Officer's Prey*
    LJ - v140 - i8 - May 1 2015 - p103(1) [501+]

Glennon, Michael J. - *National Security and Double Government*
    Reason - v46 - i10 - March 2015 - p62(5) [501+]

Glenny, Misha - *Nemesis: One Man and the Battle for Rio*
    KR - Dec 15 2015 - pNA [501+]
    PW - v262 - i51 - Dec 14 2015 - p73(1) [51-500]
    Spec - v329 - i9760 - Sept 19 2015 - p50(2) [501+]

Glete, Jan - *Swedish Naval Administration, 1521-1721: Resource Flows and Organisational Capabilities*
    Six Ct J - v46 - i1 - Spring 2015 - p164-166 [501+]

Glewwe, Eleanor - *Sparkers*
    c HB Guide - v26 - i1 - Spring 2015 - p78(1) [51-500]

Glickman, Mark - *Stolen Words*
    KR - Nov 15 2015 - pNA [501+]

Glickman, Mary - *An Undisturbed Peace*
    BL - v112 - i6 - Nov 15 2015 - p30(1) [51-500]

Glickman, Susan - *Safe as Houses*
    Nat Post - v17 - i176 - May 30 2015 - pWP5(1) [501+]

Glickstein, Don - *After Yorktown: The Final Struggle for American Independence*
    PW - v262 - i39 - Sept 28 2015 - p78(1) [51-500]

Glickstein, Mitchell - *Neuroscience: A Historical Introduction*
    QRB - v90 - i4 - Dec 2015 - p439(1) [501+]

Gliksman, Sam - *iPad in Education for Dummies*
    y VOYA - v38 - i1 - April 2015 - p90(2) [51-500]

Glines, Abbi - *Bad for You*
    c HB Guide - v26 - i2 - Fall 2015 - p120(1) [51-500]
Hold on Tight
    y SLJ - v61 - i8 - August 2015 - p114(1) [51-500]
    y VOYA - v38 - i2 - June 2015 - p60(1) [51-500]
Misbehaving
    c HB Guide - v26 - i2 - Fall 2015 - p120(1) [51-500]
Until Friday Night
    y SLJ - v61 - i8 - August 2015 - p103(1) [51-500]
    y VOYA - v38 - i3 - August 2015 - p61(1) [51-500]
Until the End
    y KR - Sept 15 2015 - pNA [51-500]

Glinski, Robert - *The Friendship of Criminals*
    PW - v262 - i1 - Jan 5 2015 - p52(1) [51-500]
    BL - v111 - i9-10 - Jan 1 2015 - p46(2) [51-500]

Gliori, Debi - *Alfie in the Garden (Illus. by Gliori, Debi)*
    c Sch Lib - v63 - i1 - Spring 2015 - p27(1) [51-500]
Dragon's Extraordinary Egg (Illus. by Gliori, Debi)
    c SLJ - v61 - i6 - June 2015 - p46(6) [501+]
Dragon's Extraordinary Egg
    c HB Guide - v26 - i1 - Spring 2015 - p31(1) [51-500]

Gloag, Kenneth - *The Cambridge Companion to Michael Tippett*
    Notes - v71 - i4 - June 2015 - p710(5) [501+]

Global Diasporas in the Age of High Imperialism
    HNet - April 2015 - pNA [501+]

Global Fund for Children - *Global Baby Bedtimes*
    c KR - Jan 1 2016 - pNA [51-500]

Global Fund For Children - *Global Baby Bedtimes*
    c SLJ - v61 - i7 - July 2015 - p55(1) [51-500]

Glocal Affairs: Art Biennials in Context
    HNet - July 2015 - pNA [501+]

Gloege, Timothy E.W. - *Guaranteed Pure: The Moody Bible Institute, Business, and the Making of Modern Evangelicalism*
    Bks & Cult - v21 - i5 - Sept-Oct 2015 - p26(1) [501+]

Glosserman, Brad - *The Japan-South Korea Identity Clash: East Asian Security and the United States*
    RVBW - July 2015 - pNA [501+]

Glover, Gareth - *The Waterloo Archive, vol. 5: German Sources*
    J Mil H - v79 - i1 - Jan 2015 - p206-207 [501+]

Glover, Jeffrey - *Paper Sovereigns: Anglo-Native Treaties and the Law of Nations, 1604-1664*
    AHR - v120 - i2 - April 2015 - p607-608 [501+]
    JAH - v102 - i2 - Sept 2015 - p530-530 [501+]
    NEQ - v88 - i2 - June 2015 - p333-335 [501+]

Glover, Lorri - *Founders as Fathers: The Private Lives and Politics of the American Revolutionaries*
    AHR - v120 - i4 - Oct 2015 - p1481-1482 [501+]
    JAH - v102 - i2 - Sept 2015 - p541-542 [501+]

Gluck, Helmut - *Mehrsprachigkeit in der Fruhen Neuzeit*
    Six Ct J - v46 - i3 - Fall 2015 - p836-837 [501+]

Gluck, Louise - *Faithful and Virtuous Night*
    WLT - v89 - i2 - March-April 2015 - p67(3) [501+]

Glucker, John - *Greek into Latin from Antiquity until the Nineteenth Century*
    Class R - v65 - i1 - April 2015 - p274-275 [501+]

Glynn, Ruth - *Women, Terrorism, and Trauma in Italian Culture*
    HNet - March 2015 - pNA [501+]
    Wom HR - v24 - i1 - Feb 2015 - p146-3 [501+]

Glynn, Tom - *Reading Publics: New York City's Public Libraries, 1754-1911*
    NYT - July 12 2015 - p2(L) [501+]

Glynne, Andy - *Navid's Story (Illus. by Topf, Jonathan)*
    c Sch Lib - v63 - i3 - Autumn 2015 - p174(1) [51-500]

Gnarr, Jon - *The Indian*
    WLT - v89 - i5 - Sept-Oct 2015 - p65(1) [51-500]

Gneuss, Helmut - *Anglo-Saxon Manuscripts: A Bibliographical Handlist of Manuscripts and Manuscript Fragments Written or Owned in England up to 1100*
    Med R - August 2015 - pNA [501+]

Gobbell, Phyllis - *Pursuit in Provence*
    BL - v111 - i14 - March 15 2015 - p46(2) [51-500]
    KR - Jan 1 2015 - pNA [51-500]
    PW - v262 - i8 - Feb 23 2015 - p54(1) [51-500]

Gobel, David - *Commemoration in America: Essays on Monuments, Memorialization, and Memory*
    Pub Hist - v37 - i1 - Feb 2015 - p138(3) [501+]

Gobert, R. Darren - *The Mind-Body Stage: Passion and Interaction In the Cartesian Theater*
    Theat J - v67 - i2 - May 2015 - p361-362 [501+]

Gobetti, Ada - *Partisan Diary: A Woman's Life in the Italian Resistance*
    TLS - i5850 - May 15 2015 - p30(1) [501+]

Goble, Paul - *Horse Raid: The Making of a Warrior (Illus. by Goble, Paul)*
    c HB Guide - v26 - i1 - Spring 2015 - p31(1) [51-500]
Red Cloud's War: Brave Eagle's Account of the Fetterman Fight December 21, 1866
    c CH Bwatch - Sept 2015 - pNA [51-500]
Red Cloud's War: Brave Eagle's Account of the Fetterman Fight (Illus. by Goble, Paul)
    c CH Bwatch - July 2015 - pNA [51-500]
Red Cloud's War
    c KR - April 15 2015 - pNA [51-500]

Gobo, Giampietro - *Constructing Survey Data: An Interactional Approach*
    Pub Op Q - v79 - i3 - Fall 2015 - p823(3) [501+]

Gocek, Fatma Muge - *Denial of Violence: Ottoman Past, Turkish Present, and Collective Violence against the Armenians, 1789-2009*
    HT - v65 - i7 - July 2015 - p56(2) [501+]

Goda, Norman J.W. - *To the Gates of Jerusalem: The Diaries and Papers of James G. McDonald, 1945-1947*
    HNet - Sept 2015 - pNA(NA) [501+]

Godard, Jean-Luc - *Introduction to a True History of Cinema and Television*
    Nation - v300 - i11 - March 16 2015 - p35(4) [501+]

Godbeer, Richard - *The Overflowing of Friendship: Love Between Men and the Creation of the American Republic*
    JWH - v27 - i3 - Fall 2015 - p194(10) [501+]

Goddard, Robert - *The Ways of the World: A James Maxted Thriller*
    PW - v262 - i10 - March 9 2015 - p52(1) [51-500]
The Ways of the World (Read by Perkins, Derek).
Audiobook Review
    BL - v112 - i3 - Oct 1 2015 - p86(1) [51-500]
The Ways of the World
    BL - v111 - i17 - May 1 2015 - p48(1) [51-500]
    KR - April 1 2015 - pNA [51-500]
    NYTBR - June 7 2015 - p37(L) [501+]

Godden, Rumer - *An Episode of Sparrows*
    NS - v144 - i5282 - Oct 2 2015 - p74(2) [501+]

Goddu, Krystyna Poray - *A Primary Source History of U.S. Independence*
    c HB Guide - v26 - i2 - Fall 2015 - p220(1) [51-500]
    c SLJ - v61 - i4 - April 2015 - p108(4) [51-500]

Godenberg, E. Paul - *Developing Essential Understanding of Geometry and Measurement, Pre-K-Grade 2*
    TC Math - v22 - i4 - Nov 2015 - p261(1) [501+]

Godfrey, Barry - *Policing the Factory: Theft, Private Policing and the Law in Modern England*
    Historian - v77 - i2 - Summer 2015 - p386(2) [501+]

Godfrey, Emelyne - *Femininity, Crime and Self-Defence in Victorian Literature and Society: From Dagger-Fans to Suffragettes*
    VS - v57 - i2 - Wntr 2015 - p308(3) [501+]

Godfrey, Joseph J. - *Trust of People, Words, and God: A Route for Philosophy of Religion*
    JR - v95 - i3 - July 2015 - p412(2) [501+]

Godfrey, Mark - *Kings, Lords, and Men in Scotland and Britain, 1300-1625: Essays in Honour of Jenny Wormald*
    Med R - August 2015 - pNA [501+]

Godfrey, Martyn - *Mystery in the Frozen Lands*
    y Res Links - v20 - i5 - June 2015 - p25(1) [51-500]

Godfrey-Smith, Peter - *Philosophy of Biology*
    BioSci - v65 - i2 - Feb 2015 - p213(3) [501+]

Godin, Thelma Lynne - *How to Dress a Dragon (Illus. by Barclay, Eric)*
    c KR - Oct 15 2015 - pNA [51-500]
The Hula-Hoopin' Queen (Illus. by Brantley-Newton, Vanessa)
    c HB Guide - v26 - i1 - Spring 2015 - p31(1) [51-500]

Godwin, Gail - *Publishing: A Writer's Memoir*
    NYTBR - July 19 2015 - p26(L) [501+]
Publishing
    Ent W - i1346 - Jan 16 2015 - p66(1) [501+]

Godwin, Jane - *What Do You Wish For? (Illus. by Walker, Anna)*
    c Magpies - v30 - i5 - Nov 2015 - p14(1) [501+]

Godwin, Joscelyn - *The John Michell Reader: Writings and Rants of a Radical Traditionalist*
    Bwatch - Sept 2015 - pNA [501+]
The Starlight Years: Love and War at Kelmscott Manor, 1940-1948
    Spec - v327 - i9740 - May 2 2015 - p42(1) [501+]

Godwin, Richard - *The Spirits: A Guide to Modern Cocktailing*
    Spec - v329 - i9768 - Nov 14 2015 - p52(2) [501+]

Goebel, Jenny - *Fortune Falls*
    c BL - v112 - i7 - Dec 1 2015 - p62(1) [51-500]
    c KR - Oct 1 2015 - pNA [51-500]
    c SLJ - v61 - i10 - Oct 2015 - p89(1) [51-500]

Goeglein, T. M. - *Embers & Ash*
    y HB Guide - v26 - i1 - Spring 2015 - p108(1) [51-500]

Goeman, Mishuana - *Mark My Words: Native Women Mapping Our Nations*
    AL - v87 - i1 - March 2015 - p194-197 [501+]

Goerdt, Sonja L. - *Fostering Algebraic Thinking with Casio Technology: Investigations for the PRISM Graphing Calculator*
    Math T - v108 - i7 - March 2015 - p558(1) [501+]

Goessel, Tracey - *The First King of Hollywood*
    KR - July 15 2015 - pNA [501+]
The First King of Hollywood: The Life of Douglas Fairbanks
    LJ - v140 - i15 - Sept 15 2015 - p74(1) [51-500]
    NYTBR - Dec 6 2015 - p70(L) [501+]

Goethe, Johann Wolfgang von - *The Essential Goethe*
    PW - v262 - i34 - August 24 2015 - p69(2) [51-500]

Goetz, Edward G. - *New Deal Ruins: Race, Economic Justice, and Public Housing Policy*
    CS - v44 - i4 - July 2015 - p515-516 [501+]

Goetz, Stewart - *A Philosophical Walking Tour with C.S. Lewis: Why It Did Not Include Rome*
    CC - v132 - i19 - Sept 16 2015 - p38(2) [501+]

Goetzinger, Annie - *Girl in Dior (Illus. by Goetzinger, Annie)*
    y BL - v111 - i16 - April 15 2015 - p39(1) [51-500]
    LJ - v140 - i5 - March 15 2015 - p88(3) [501+]
Girl in Dior
    SLJ - v61 - i3 - March 2015 - p179(1) [501+]

Goff, Chris - *Dark Waters*
    BL - v111 - i22 - August 1 2015 - p38(1) [51-500]
    KR - July 15 2015 - pNA [501+]
    PW - v262 - i25 - June 22 2015 - p123(1) [51-500]

Goff, Jacques Le - *Must We Divide History into Periods?*
    TimHES - i2225 - Oct 15 2015 - p44-1 [501+]

Goff, Jennifer - *Eileen Gray: Her Work and Her World*
    Apo - v181 - i630 - April 2015 - p106(2) [501+]

Goff, Sara - *I Always Cry at Weddings*
    PW - v262 - i27 - July 6 2015 - p55(1) [51-500]

Goffart, Walter - *The Narrators of Barbarian History*
    HT - v65 - i5 - May 2015 - p56(2) [501+]

Goffman, Alice - *On the Run: Fugitive Life in an American City*
    AJS - v121 - i1 - July 2015 - p306(3) [501+]
    NYTBR - May 10 2015 - p36(L) [501+]
    Soc Ser R - v89 - i2 - June 2015 - p407(6) [501+]

Goh, Daniel P.S. - *Race and Multiculturalism in Malaysia and Singapore*
    JAS - v74 - i1 - Feb 2015 - p241-244 [501+]

Goh, Jaymee - *The SEA Is Ours: Tales from Steampunk Southeast Asia*
    PW - v262 - i39 - Sept 28 2015 - p72(1) [51-500]

Goheen, Michael W. - *Introducing Christian Mission Today: Scripture, History, and Issues*
    IBMR - v39 - i3 - July 2015 - p156(2) [501+]

Going, K.L. - *Pieces of Why*
    c BL - v111 - i21 - July 1 2015 - p76(1) [51-500]
    c KR - June 15 2015 - pNA [51-500]
    c PW - v262 - i27 - July 6 2015 - p74(1) [51-500]
    c SLJ - v61 - i7 - July 2015 - p77(2) [51-500]
    y VOYA - v38 - i4 - Oct 2015 - p51(1) [501+]

Golash-Boza, Tanya - *Yo Soy Negro: Blackness in Peru*
    SF - v93 - i3 - March 2015 - pe78 [501+]

Golburt, Luba - *The First Epoch: The Eighteenth Century and the Russian Cultural Imagination*
    Slav R - v74 - i2 - Summer 2015 - p354-357 [501+]

Gold, Alan - *The Pretender's Lady*
    KR - May 15 2015 - pNA [51-500]

Gold, Marv - *Ghostly Adventures of Sherlock Holmes*
    SPBW - April 2015 - pNA [51-500]

Gold, Matthew K. - *Debates in the Digital Humanities*
    HNet - Jan 2015 - pNA [51-500]

Gold, Roberta - *When Tenants Claimed the City: The Struggle for Citizenship in New York City Housing*
    AHR - v120 - i2 - April 2015 - p661-663 [501+]

Gold, Tammy - *Secrets of the Nanny Whisperer: A Practical Guide for Finding and Achieving the Gold Standard of Care for Your Child*
    LJ - v140 - i3 - Feb 15 2015 - p81(3) [501+]

Gold, Thomas - *Taking the Back Off the Watch: A Personal Memoir*
    Isis - v106 - i2 - June 2015 - p500(2) [501+]

Goldbarth, Albert - *Selfish*
    BL - v111 - i18 - May 15 2015 - p12(1) [51-500]
    LJ - v140 - i10 - June 1 2015 - p107(1) [51-500]
    PW - v262 - i16 - April 20 2015 - p51(1) [51-500]

Goldberg, Barbara - *Kingdom of Speculation*
    KR - August 1 2015 - pNA [501+]

Goldberg, Daniel - *The State of Play: Creators and Critics on Video Game Culture*
    NYTBR - Oct 18 2015 - p10(L) [501+]
The State of Play: Sixteen Voices on Video Games
    LJ - v140 - i11 - June 15 2015 - p98(2) [51-500]
    KR - August 1 2015 - pNA [501+]

Goldberg, Holly - *I'll Be There*
    y Magpies - v30 - i2 - May 2015 - p44(1) [501+]

Goldberg, Jessica L. - *Trade and Institutions in the Medieval Mediterranean: The Geniza Merchants and Their Business World*
    BHR - v89 - i3 - Autumn 2015 - p583(4) [501+]

Goldberg, Michelle - *The Goddess Pose*
    NY - v91 - i18 - June 29 2015 - p71 [51-500]
The Goddess Pose: The Audacious Life of Indra Devi, the Woman Who Helped Bring Yoga to the West
    BL - v111 - i19-20 - June 1 2015 - p28(1) [51-500]
    KR - April 15 2015 - pNA [501+]
    LJ - v140 - i7 - April 15 2015 - p93(1) [51-500]
    NYTBR - July 19 2015 - p7(L) [501+]
    PW - v262 - i17 - April 27 2015 - p66(1) [51-500]

Goldberg, Paul - *The Yid*
    BL - v112 - i4 - Oct 15 2015 - p29(1) [501+]
    KR - Nov 15 2015 - pNA [501+]
    LJ - v140 - i14 - Sept 1 2015 - p91(2) [51-500]

Goldberg, Rita - *Motherland: Growing Up with the Holocaust*
    y BL - v111 - i16 - April 15 2015 - p14(1) [51-500]
    KR - Jan 15 2015 - pNA [501+]

Goldberg, Tod - *Gangsterland (Read by Heller, Johnny). Audiobook Review*
    BL - v111 - i21 - July 1 2015 - p78(1) [51-500]
Gangsterland
    RVBW - May 2015 - pNA [51-500]
    RVBW - Sept 2015 - pNA [51-500]

Goldberger, Paul - *Building Art: The Life and Work of Frank Gehry*
    BL - v112 - i2 - Sept 15 2015 - p14(1) [51-500]
    KR - July 15 2015 - pNA [501+]
    LJ - v140 - i16 - Oct 1 2015 - p75(1) [51-500]
    NYTBR - Oct 25 2015 - p22(L) [501+]
    PW - v262 - i28 - July 13 2015 - p57(1) [51-500]

Goldblatt, Howard - *Frog*
    NYT - Feb 26 2015 - pC1(L) [501+]

Goldblatt, Mark - *Finding the Worm (Read by Plew, Everette). Audiobook Review*
    c SLJ - v61 - i6 - June 2015 - p63(2) [51-500]
Finding the Worm
    c BL - v111 - i12 - Feb 15 2015 - p85(1) [51-500]
    c CH Bwatch - May 2015 - pNA [51-500]
    y HB Guide - v26 - i2 - Fall 2015 - p83(1) [51-500]
    c SLJ - v61 - i2 - Feb 2015 - p86(1) [51-500]
    y VOYA - v38 - i1 - April 2015 - p60(1) [51-500]

Golden Age
    NYTBR - Dec 20 2015 - p26(L) [501+]

Golden, Che - *The Unicorn Hunter*
    y HB Guide - v26 - i2 - Fall 2015 - p83(1) [51-500]

Golden, Christopher - *Seize the Night: New Tales of Vampiric Terror*
    PW - v262 - i30 - July 27 2015 - p47(1) [51-500]
Tin Men
    KR - April 15 2015 - pNA [51-500]
    PW - v262 - i6 - Feb 9 2015 - p49(1) [51-500]
The Tin Men
    BL - v111 - i16 - April 15 2015 - p31(1) [51-500]

Golden, Frank - *The Night Game*
    PW - v262 - i34 - August 24 2015 - p61(2) [51-500]
    RVBW - Oct 2015 - pNA [51-500]

Golden, Peter - *Wherever There Is Light*
    BL - v112 - i3 - Oct 1 2015 - p31(1) [51-500]
    KR - Sept 1 2015 - pNA [51-500]
    LJ - v140 - i16 - Oct 1 2015 - p68(2) [51-500]

Golden Son
    BL - v111 - i18 - May 15 2015 - p35(1) [501+]

Goldenbaum, Sally - *A Finely Knit Murder*
    Bwatch - July 2015 - pNA [51-500]

Goldenberg, Gideon - *Semitic Languages: Features, Structures, Relations, Processes*
    JNES - v74 - i2 - Oct 2015 - p358(4) [501+]

Goldfarb, Ronald - *After Snowden: Privacy, Secrecy, and Security in the Information Age*
    LJ - v140 - i11 - June 15 2015 - p100(1) [51-500]

Goldhagen, Daniel Jonah - *The Devil That Never Dies: The Rise and Threat of Global Antisemitism*
    JTWS - v32 - i1 - Spring 2015 - p347(2) [501+]

Goldhagen, Shari - *In Some Other World, Maybe*
    Ent W - i1347 - Jan 23 2015 - p65(1) [501+]

Goldin, Kat - *Crochet the Perfect Gift: Designs Just Right for Giving and Ideas for Every Occasion*
    LJ - v140 - i5 - March 15 2015 - p108(1) [51-500]

Golding, Michael - *A Poet of the Invisible World*
    BL - v112 - i3 - Oct 1 2015 - p30(2) [51-500]
    KR - August 1 2015 - pNA [501+]
    LJ - v140 - i13 - August 1 2015 - p83(1) [51-500]

Golding, William - *The Inheritors*
    NS - v144 - i5282 - Oct 2 2015 - p74(2) [501+]
Lord of the Flies
    Nat R - v67 - i21 - Nov 19 2015 - p83(1) [51-500]

Goldish, Meish - *Brave Hearts*
    c HB Guide - v26 - i2 - Fall 2015 - p182(1) [51-500]
City Firefighters
    c HB Guide - v26 - i1 - Spring 2015 - p137(1) [51-500]
Hotshots
    c HB Guide - v26 - i1 - Spring 2015 - p137(1) [51-500]
Marine Firefighters
    c HB Guide - v26 - i1 - Spring 2015 - p137(1) [51-500]
R.E.A.D. Dogs
    SLJ - v61 - i2 - Feb 2015 - p114(1) [51-500]
Skydiving Dogs
    c HB Guide - v26 - i1 - Spring 2015 - p168(1) [51-500]
Smokejumpers
    c HB Guide - v26 - i1 - Spring 2015 - p137(1) [51-500]

Goldman, Andrea S. - *Opera and the City: The Politics of Culture in Beijing, 1770-1900*
    JAS - v74 - i3 - August 2015 - p732-734 [501+]

Goldman, Brian - *The Secret Language of Doctors: Cracking the Code*
    BL - v111 - i15 - April 1 2015 - p10(1) [51-500]

Goldman, Charles R. - *Climate Change and Global Warming of Inland Waters: Impacts and Mitigation for Ecosystems and Societies*
    QRB - v90 - i1 - March 2015 - p85(1) [501+]

Goldman, Duff - *Duff Bakes: Think and Bake Like a Pro at Home*
    LJ - v140 - i19 - Nov 15 2015 - p101(1) [51-500]
    PW - v262 - i36 - Sept 7 2015 - p60(2) [51-500]

Goldman, Eric A. - *The American Jewish Story through Cinema*
    J Am St - v49 - i3 - August 2015 - p621-624 [501+]

Goldman, Ivan G. - *The Debtor Class*
    BL - v111 - i14 - March 15 2015 - p45(1) [51-500]
    PW - v262 - i7 - Feb 16 2015 - p154(1) [51-500]

Goldman, Lawrence - *The Life of R. H. Tawney: Socialism and History*
    AHR - v120 - i1 - Feb 2015 - p333-334 [501+]
    TimHES - i2190 - Feb 12 2015 - p49(1) [501+]

Goldman, Lee - *Too Much of a Good Thing: How Four Key Survival Traits Are Now Killing Us*
    KR - Oct 1 2015 - pNA [501+]

Goldman, Marcia - *Lola and the Tattletale Zeke*
    c KR - Feb 1 2015 - pNA [51-500]

Goldmann, Renate - *Moderne. Weltkrieg. Irrenhaus. 1900-1930*
    Ger Q - v88 - i3 - Summer 2015 - p384(9) [501+]

Goldner, Rita - *Orangutan: A Day in the Rainforest Canopy*
    c CH Bwatch - Nov 2015 - pNA [51-500]

Goldreich, Gloria - *The Bridal Chair*
    BL - v111 - i13 - March 1 2015 - p27(1) [51-500]

Goldrick, James - *Before Jutland: The Naval War in Northern European Waters, August 1914-February 1915*
    Parameters - v45 - i2 - Summer 2015 - p155(2) [501+]

Goldring, Elizabeth - *John Nichols's The Progresses and Public Processions of Queen Elizabeth I: A New Edition of the Early Modern Sources*
    HER - v130 - i545 - August 2015 - p985(3) [501+]
    Ren Q - v68 - i2 - Summer 2015 - p775-779 [501+]
    RES - v66 - i273 - Feb 2015 - p168-170 [501+]

Goldring, Luin - *Producing and Negotiating Non-Citizenship: Precarious Legal Status in Canada*
    CS - v44 - i5 - Sept 2015 - p662-664 [501+]
    ERS - v38 - i3 - March 2015 - p489(3) [501+]

Goldschmidt, Nora - *Shaggy Crowns: Ennius' Annales and Virgil's Aeneid*
    Class R - v65 - i2 - Oct 2015 - p426-427 [501+]

Goldsmith, Becky - *The Quilter's Practical Guide to Color*
    PW - v262 - i3 - Jan 19 2015 - p75(1) [51-500]
The Quitter's Practical Guide to Color
    LJ - v140 - i6 - April 1 2015 - p93(1) [51-500]

Goldsmith, Connie - *Dietary Supplements: Harmless, Helpful, or Hurtful?*
    c KR - June 1 2015 - pNA [51-500]
    y SLJ - v61 - i6 - June 2015 - p142(2) [51-500]
The Ebola Epidemic: The Fight, the Future
    y BL - v112 - i7 - Dec 1 2015 - p44(1) [51-500]
    y KR - Nov 1 2015 - pNA [51-500]

Goldsmith, Francisca - *Libraries and the Affordable Care ACT: Helping the Community Understand Health-Care Options*
    LJ - v140 - i2 - Feb 1 2015 - p97(1) [51-500]

Goldsmith, Kenneth - *Capital: New York, Capital of the 20th Century*
    KR - August 15 2015 - pNA [501+]

Goldsmith, Leon - *Cycle of Fear: Syria's Alawites in War and Peace*
    Econ - v416 - i8946 - July 11 2015 - p74(US) [501+]

Goldsmith, Mike - *Eureka! The Most Amazing Scientific Discoveries of All Time*
    c HB Guide - v26 - i1 - Spring 2015 - p148(1) [51-500]
Under the Sea (Illus. by Daubney, Kate)
    c KR - July 1 2015 - pNA [51-500]

Goldsmith, William - *The Bind*
    NS - v144 - i5282 - Oct 2 2015 - p79(1) [501+]

Goldstein, Ann - *The Complete Works of Primo Levi*
    NYTBR - Nov 29 2015 - p1(L) [501+]

Goldstein, Dana - *The Teacher Wars: A History of America's Most Embattled Profession*
    Dis - v62 - i2 - Spring 2015 - p140(6) [501+]
    NYTBR - Sept 6 2015 - p24(L) [501+]

Goldstein, Daniel M. - *Outlawed: Between Security and Rights in a Bolivian City*
    Ams - v72 - i3 - July 2015 - p511(3) [501+]
    JRAI - v21 - i2 - June 2015 - p480(2) [501+]

Goldstein, Darra - *Fire + Ice: Classic Nordic Cooking*
    LJ - v140 - i20 - Dec 1 2015 - p126(1) [51-500]
The Oxford Companion to Sugar and Sweets
    Spec - v328 - i9746 - June 13 2015 - p32(2) [501+]
    BL - v112 - i3 - Oct 1 2015 - p20(1) [51-500]
    LJ - v140 - i11 - June 15 2015 - p114(2) [51-500]
    TLS - i5854 - June 12 2015 - p13(1) [501+]
    TLS - i5864-5865 - August 21 2015 - p10(2) [501+]

Goldstein, Leah - *No Limits: The Powerful True Story of Leah Goldstein: World Kickboxing Champion, Israeli Undercover Police and Cycling Champion*
    SPBW - August 2015 - pNA [51-500]

Goldstein, Lisa - *Weighing Shadows*
    KR - Sept 15 2015 - pNA [51-500]

Goldstein, Lori - *Becoming Jinn*
    y CCB-B - v69 - i1 - Sept 2015 - p24(1) [51-500]
    c HB Guide - v26 - i2 - Fall 2015 - p120(1) [51-500]
    y KR - Feb 15 2015 - pNA [51-500]
    y VOYA - v38 - i1 - April 2015 - p78(1) [51-500]

Goldstein, Lyle J. - *Meeting China Halfway: How to Defuse the Emerging US-China Rivalry*
    HNet - Sept 2015 - pNA(NA) [501+]

Goldstein, Margaret J. - *Fuel under Fire*
    y KR - May 1 2015 - pNA [51-500]
Fuel under Fire: Petroleum and Its Perils
    BL - v111 - i21 - July 1 2015 - p49(1) [51-500]
    y SLJ - v61 - i5 - May 2015 - p138(1) [51-500]

Goldstein, Martin B. - *What to Do to Retire Successfully: Navigating Psychological, Financial, and Lifestyle*

Hurdles New Horizon
LJ - v140 - i2 - Feb 1 2015 - p70(2) [501+]
What to Do to Retire Successfully: Navigating Psychological, Financial, and Lifestyle Hurdles
BL - v111 - i12 - Feb 15 2015 - p14(2) [51-500]
RVBW - April 2015 - pNA [501+]

Goldstein, Melvyn C. - *A History of Modern Tibet, Volume 3: The Storm Clouds Descend, 1955-1957*
JAS - v74 - i2 - May 2015 - p491-492 [501+]

Goldstein, Neal - *Fishtown: A Jack Regan/Izzy Ichowitz Novel*
SPBW - July 2015 - pNA [501+]

Goldstein, Rebecca Newberger - *Plato at the Googleplex: Why Philosophy Won't Go Away*
NYTBR - Jan 25 2015 - p24(L) [501+]

Goldstein, Richard - *Another Little Piece of My Heart: My Life of Rock and Revolution in the '60s*
y BL - v111 - i15 - April 1 2015 - p11(1) [51-500]
CSM - April 29 2015 - pNA [501+]

Goldstein, Robert Justin - *Little "Red Scares": Anti-Communism and Political Repression in the United States, 1921-1946*
JAH - v102 - i1 - June 2015 - p292-293 [501+]

Goldstene, Claire - *The Struggle for America's Promise: Equal Opportunity at the Dawn of Corporate Capital*
AHR - v120 - i3 - June 2015 - p1036-1037 [501+]
JAH - v102 - i1 - June 2015 - p263-264 [501+]

Goldstone, Bruce - *I See a Pattern Here (Illus. by Goldstone, Bruce)*
c PW - v262 - i8 - Feb 23 2015 - p76(1) [501+]
c CCB-B - v68 - i9 - May 2015 - p447(1) [51-500]
c HB Guide - v26 - i1 - Spring 2015 - p148(1) [51-500]
c KR - Jan 1 2015 - pNA [51-500]

Goldstone, Genevieve Okada - *Urban Jewish Transformations*
J Urban H - v41 - i3 - May 2015 - p501-507 [501+]

Goldstone, Jack A. - *Revolutions: A Very Short Introduction*
HNet - July 2015 - pNA [501+]

Goldstone, Lawrence - *Birdmen: The Wright Brothers, Glenn Curtiss, and the Battle to Control the Skies*
BHR - v89 - i2 - Summer 2015 - p339(5) [501+]

Goldstone, Nancy - *The Rival Queen: Catherine de' Medici, Her Daughter Marguerite of Valois, and the Betrayal That Ignited a Kingdom*
NYRB - v62 - i13 - August 13 2015 - p24(3) [501+]
The Rival Queens: Catherine de' Medici, Her Daugher Marguerite de Valois, and the Betrayal That Ignited a Kingdom
LJ - v140 - i7 - April 15 2015 - p101(1) [51-500]
The Rival Queens: Catherine de' Medici, Her Daughter Marguerite de Valois, and the Betrayal That Ignited a Kingdom
BL - v111 - i19-20 - June 1 2015 - p34(1) [51-500]
Mac - v128 - i28 - July 20 2015 - p56(2) [501+]
PW - v262 - i18 - May 4 2015 - p110(1) [501+]
The Rival Queens
KR - March 15 2015 - pNA [501+]

Goldstone, Patricia - *Interlock: Art, Conspiracy, and the Shadow Worlds of Mark Lombardi*
KR - August 1 2015 - pNA [501+]
PW - v262 - i34 - August 24 2015 - p76(2) [51-500]

Goldsworthy, Adrian - *Antony and Cleopatra (Read by Crossley, Steven). Audiobook Review*
LJ - v140 - i15 - Sept 15 2015 - p43(2) [51-500]
Augustus: First Emperor of Rome
Sew R - v123 - i2 - Spring 2015 - p350-357 [501+]
How Rome Fell (Read by Perkins, Derek). Audiobook Review
LJ - v140 - i8 - May 1 2015 - p42(2) [51-500]
Roman Warfare
TLS - i5854 - June 12 2015 - p11(1) [501+]

Goldsworthy, Sandy - *Aftermath*
y SLJ - v61 - i3 - March 2015 - p154(2) [51-500]

Goldsworthy, Vesna - *Gorsky*
NYTBR - Dec 20 2015 - p19(L) [501+]
Spec - v327 - i9738 - April 18 2015 - p44(1) [501+]
TLS - i5876 - Nov 13 2015 - p20(1) [501+]

Goldthwaite, Carmen - *Texas Ranch Women: Three Centuries of Mettle and Moxie*
Roundup M - v22 - i4 - April 2015 - p29(1) [501+]
Roundup M - v22 - i6 - August 2015 - p37(1) [501+]

Goldthwaite, Melissa A. - *Books That Cook: The Making of a Literary Meal*
Am St - v54 - i2 - Summer 2015 - p109-110 [501+]
TLS - i5836 - Feb 6 2015 - p26(1) [501+]

Goldthwaite, Richard A. - *Orpheus in the Marketplace: Jacopo Peri and the Economy of Late Renaissance Florence*
Six Ct J - v46 - i1 - Spring 2015 - p194-195 [501+]

Gole, Henry G. - *Exposing the Third Reich: Colonel Truman Smith in Hitler's Germany*
Historian - v77 - i2 - Summer 2015 - p388(2) [501+]

Gole, Nilufer - *Islam and Public Controversy in Europe*
ERS - v38 - i8 - August 2015 - p1437(4) [501+]

Golec, Janusz - *Literatur und Zeitgeschichte: Zwischen Historisierung und Musealisierung*
MLR - v110 - i3 - July 2015 - p917-918 [501+]

Goleman, Daniel - *A Force for Good: The Dalai Lama's Vision for Our World*
BL - v111 - i19-20 - June 1 2015 - p6(1) [51-500]
LJ - v140 - i11 - June 15 2015 - p85(2) [51-500]

Golinkin, Lev - *A Backpack, a Bear, and Eight Crates of Vodka*
Comw - v142 - i7 - April 10 2015 - p28(3) [501+]

Golinski, Jan - *British Weather and the Climate of Enlightenment*
HNet - May 2015 - pNA [501+]

Golio, Gary - *Bird & Diz (Illus. by Young, Ed)*
c CCB-B - v68 - i11 - July-August 2015 - p546(1) [51-500]
c HB - v91 - i2 - March-April 2015 - p76(2) [51-500]
c HB Guide - v26 - i2 - Fall 2015 - p35(1) [51-500]
c KR - Jan 1 2015 - pNA [51-500]
c PW - v262 - i49 - Dec 2 2015 - p43(1) [501+]

Golombok, Susan - *Modern Families: Parents and Children in New Family Forms*
LJ - v140 - i8 - May 1 2015 - p91(3) [51-500]

Golos, Veronica - *Rootwork*
ABR - v36 - i4 - May-June 2015 - p13(2) [501+]

Golpalkrishna, Sara Lynn - *How to Study Math: 80 Ways to Make the Grade*
TC Math - v22 - i2 - Sept 2015 - p115(2) [501+]

Golper, Zachary - *Bien Cuit: The Art of Bread*
NYTBR - Dec 6 2015 - pNA(L) [501+]

Golub, Alex - *Leviathans at the Gold Mine: Creating Indigenous and Corporate Actors in Papua New Guinea*
Pac C - v88 - i3 - Sept 2015 - p753 [501+]

Golubev, Alexey - *The Search for a Socialist El Dorado: Finnish Immigration to Soviet Karelia from the United States and Canada in the 1930s*
HNet - May 2015 - pNA [501+]

Golway, Terry - *Machine Made: Tammany Hall and the Creation of Modern American Politics*
AM - v212 - i6 - Feb 23 2015 - p33(2) [501+]

Golze, Rolfe - *Siegerwald und Westerwald: Bergbaugschichte - Mineralienschatze - Fundorte*
RocksMiner - v90 - i1 - Jan-Feb 2015 - p94(2) [501+]

Gomel, Elana - *Science Fiction, Alien Encounters, and the Ethics of Posthumanism: Beyond the Golden Rule*
SFS - v42 - i2 - July 2015 - p376-378 [501+]

Gomes, Laurentino - *1808: The Flight of the Emperor*
Historian - v77 - i3 - Fall 2015 - p603(2) [501+]

Gomez, Art - *New Mexico: A History*
Roundup M - v22 - i6 - August 2015 - p40(1) [501+]

Gomez-Bravo, Ana M. - *Textual Agency: Writing Culture and Social Networks in Fifteenth-Century Spain*
Ren Q - v68 - i3 - Fall 2015 - p1114-1116 [501+]

Gomez-Davila, Nicolas - *Scholia to an Implicit Text*
MA - v57 - i1 - Wntr 2015 - p77(7) [501+]

Gomez, Laura - *Mapping "Race": Critical Approaches to Health Disparities Research*
CS - v44 - i4 - July 2015 - p516-517 [501+]

Gomez, Laura E. - *Mapping Race: Critical Approaches to Health Disparities Research*
AJS - v120 - i4 - Jan 2015 - p1234(3) [501+]

Gomez-Lobo, Alfonso - *Bioethics and the Human Goods: An Introduction to Natural Law Bioethics*
LJ - v140 - i19 - Nov 15 2015 - p87(2) [501+]

Gomez, Mar - *The Best Natural Homemade Skin and Hair Care Products*
RVBW - August 2015 - pNA [501+]

Gomez-Quinones, Juan - *Making Aztlan: Ideology and Culture of the Chicana and Chicano Movement, 1966-1977*
SHQ - v118 - i4 - April 2015 - p440-442 [501+]
WHQ - v46 - i2 - Summer 2015 - p237(1) [501+]

Gomez-Rivas, Camilo - *Law and Islamization of Morocco under the Almoravids: The Fatwas of Ibn Rushd al-Jadd to the Far Maghrib*
Med R - Sept 2015 - pNA [501+]

Gompert, David C. - *Blinders, Blunders, and Wars: What America and China Can Learn*
For Aff - v94 - i3 - May-June 2015 - pNA [501+]

Gonick, Larry - *The Cartoon Guide to Algebra (Illus. by Gonick, Larry)*
y SLJ - v61 - i6 - June 2015 - p142(1) [51-500]

Gonsalves, Rob - *Imagine a World*
c KR - July 15 2015 - pNA [51-500]
Imagine a World (Illus. by Sonsalves, Rob)
c SLJ - v61 - i10 - Oct 2015 - p77(1) [51-500]

Gonser, Simon - *Der Kapitalismus Entdeckt das Volk: Wie die Deutschen Grossbanken in den 1950er und 1960er Jahren zu Ihrer Privaten Kundschaft Kamen*
HNet - Jan 2015 - pNA [501+]

Gonzales, Doreen - *Silly Cat Jokes to Tickle Your Funny Bone*
c HB Guide - v26 - i1 - Spring 2015 - p181(1) [51-500]

Gonzales, Laurence - *Flight 232: A Story of Disaster and Survival*
Bwatch - Sept 2015 - pNA [51-500]

Gonzales, Mike - *The Last Drop: The Politics of Water*
New Sci - v228 - i3041 - Oct 3 2015 - p46(2) [501+]

Gonzalez, Christina Diaz - *Moving Target*
c SLJ - v61 - i8 - August 2015 - p84(3) [51-500]
y BL - v111 - i21 - July 1 2015 - p57(1) [51-500]
c KR - June 1 2015 - pNA [51-500]
c PW - v262 - i22 - June 1 2015 - p59(2) [51-500]

Gonzalez, Maya Christina - *Call Me Tree / Llamame Arbol*
c CH Bwatch - Feb 2015 - pNA [51-500]
c HB Guide - v26 - i2 - Fall 2015 - p35(1) [51-500]
My Colors, My World / Mis colores, mi mundo (Illus. by Gonzalez, Maya Christina)
c BL - v111 - i9-10 - Jan 1 2015 - pS18(5) [501+]

Gonzalez, Mike - *The Last Drop: The Politics of Water*
TimHES - i2229 - Nov 12 2015 - p49(1) [501+]
TLS - i5870 - Oct 2 2015 - p9(2) [501+]

Gonzalez, Ondina E. - *Nuestra Fe: A Latin American Church History Sourcebook*
IBMR - v39 - i1 - Jan 2015 - p49(2) [501+]

Gonzalez, Ray - *Beautiful Wall*
BL - v112 - i4 - Oct 15 2015 - p14(1) [51-500]
LJ - v140 - i15 - Sept 15 2015 - p80(1) [51-500]

Gonzalez, Rigoberto - *Mariposa U*
y SLJ - v61 - i5 - May 2015 - p118(2) [51-500]
Unpeopled Eden
Poet - v205 - i5 - Feb 2015 - p497(3) [501+]

Gonzalez, Sara - *The Musical Iconography of Power in Seventeenth-Century Spain and Her Territories*
HER - v130 - i543 - April 2015 - p451(3) [501+]

Gonzalez, Vernadette Vicuna - *Securing Paradise: Tourism and Militarism in Hawai'i and the Philippines*
PHR - v84 - i2 - May 2015 - p250(3) [501+]

Gooch, Brad - *Smash Cut: A Memoir of Howard & Art & the '70s & the '80s*
NYTBR - August 2 2015 - p26(L) [501+]
BL - v111 - i13 - March 1 2015 - p13(1) [51-500]
Smash Cut
G&L Rev W - v22 - i6 - Nov-Dec 2015 - p44(1) [51-500]

Gooch, John - *The Italian Army and the First World War*
HT - v65 - i2 - Feb 2015 - p62(2) [501+]

Good, David - *The Way Around: Finding My Mother and Myself among the Yanomami*
y BL - v112 - i5 - Nov 1 2015 - p14(1) [501+]

Good Housekeeping Grilling
BL - v111 - i15 - April 1 2015 - p10(1) [51-500]

Good, Jason - *Must. Push. Buttons (Illus. by Krosoczka, Jarrett J.)*
c HB Guide - v26 - i2 - Fall 2015 - p12(1) [51-500]
Rock, Meet Window: A Father-Son Story
Par - v90 - i6 - June 2015 - p18(1) [501+]

The Good Years! Historical Trajectories 1980-2010
HNet - August 2015 - pNA [501+]

Goodall, Alex - *Loyalty and Liberty: American Countersubversion from World War I to the McCarthy Era*
AHR - v120 - i1 - Feb 2015 - p275-276 [501+]
J Am St - v49 - i1 - Feb 2015 - p210-211 [501+]
JAH - v102 - i2 - Sept 2015 - p584-584 [501+]

Goodall, Jane - *The Chimpanzee Children of Gombe: 50 Years with Jane Goodall at Gombe National Park (Illus. by Neugebauer, Michael)*
c CCB-B - v68 - i5 - Jan 2015 - p256(1) [51-500]
c HB Guide - v26 - i1 - Spring 2015 - p164(1) [51-500]

A Prayer for World Peace (Illus. by Golmohammadi, Feeroozeh)
 c BL - v112 - i6 - Nov 15 2015 - p45(1) [51-500]
With Love (Illus. by Marks, Alan)
 c HB Guide - v26 - i1 - Spring 2015 - p164(1) [51-500]
Goodare, Julian - *Scottish Witches and Witch-Hunters*
 HER - v130 - i543 - April 2015 - p447(3) [501+]
Gooday, Graeme - *Patently Contestable: Electrical Technologies and Inventor Identities on Trial in Britain*
 T&C - v56 - i1 - Jan 2015 - p276-277 [501+]
Goodbody, Axel - *Ecocritical Theory: New European Approaches*
 GSR - v38 - i3 - Oct 2015 - p635-652 [501+]
Goodchild, Harriet - *After the Ruin*
 PW - v262 - i1 - Jan 5 2015 - p56(1) [51-500]
Goodchild, Lester F. - *Higher Education in the American West: Regional History and State Contexts*
 WHQ - v46 - i3 - Autumn 2015 - p383-383 [501+]
Goodden, Angelica - *Rousseau's Hand: The Crafting of a Writer*
 MLR - v110 - i1 - Jan 2015 - p260-261 [501+]
 FS - v69 - i1 - Jan 2015 - p96-97 [501+]
Goode, Angelina - *The Average Girl*
 KR - Nov 1 2015 - pNA [51-500]
Goodfellow, Richard - *Collector of Secrets*
 BL - v111 - i21 - July 1 2015 - p35(1) [51-500]
 KR - July 1 2015 - pNA [51-500]
 PW - v262 - i23 - June 8 2015 - p39(1) [51-500]
Goodhart, Pippa - *Just Imagine (Illus. by Sharratt, Nick)*
 c HB Guide - v26 - i1 - Spring 2015 - p31(1) [51-500]
Goodin, Robert - *The Kurdles (Illus. by Goodin, Robert)*
 c BL - v111 - i18 - May 15 2015 - p43(1) [51-500]
Goodley, Heloise - *An Officer and a Gentlewoman: The Making of a Female British Army Officer*
 RVBW - April 2015 - pNA [51-500]
Goodman, Alison - *The Dark Days Club*
 y KR - Oct 15 2015 - pNA [51-500]
 y PW - v262 - i42 - Oct 19 2015 - p79(1) [51-500]
 y SLJ - v61 - i12 - Dec 2015 - p121(1) [51-500]
Goodman, Allan H. - *Father, Son, Stone*
 SPBW - July 2015 - pNA [51-500]
Goodman, Carol - *Hawthorn*
 y KR - Sept 15 2015 - pNA [51-500]
 y VOYA - v38 - i5 - Dec 2015 - p69(1) [51-500]
Ravencliffe
 y HB Guide - v26 - i1 - Spring 2015 - p108(1) [51-500]
River Road
 KR - Nov 1 2015 - pNA [51-500]
 BL - v112 - i5 - Nov 1 2015 - p33(1) [51-500]
 PW - v262 - i47 - Nov 23 2015 - p48(1) [51-500]
Goodman, David A. - *The Autobiography of James T. Kirk*
 KR - Sept 1 2015 - pNA [501+]
Goodman, Dena - *Becoming a Woman in the Age of Letters*
 Eight-C St - v48 - i4 - Summer 2015 - p546-547 [501+]
Goodman, Dennis - *The Thrill of the Krill: What You Should Know About Krill Oil*
 Bwatch - Sept 2015 - pNA [51-500]
Goodman, Fielder - *Edmonds Beginner's Cookbook*
 c Magpies - v30 - i4 - Sept 2015 - pS8(1) [501+]
Goodman, Fred - *Allen Klein: The Man Who Bailed Out the Beatles, Made the Stones, and Transformed Rock and Roll*
 BL - v111 - i19-20 - June 1 2015 - p26(1) [51-500]
 KR - May 1 2015 - pNA [501+]
 Mac - v128 - i28 - July 20 2015 - p57(1) [501+]
Goodman, Jo - *This Gun for Hire*
 KR - Feb 15 2015 - pNA [51-500]
 PW - v262 - i8 - Feb 23 2015 - p58(1) [51-500]
Goodman, Jordan - *Paul Robeson: A Watched Man*
 Historian - v77 - i3 - Fall 2015 - p559(2) [501+]
Goodman, Katie - *The Night Our Parents Went Out (Illus. by Bui, Cat Tuong)*
 c KR - Nov 1 2015 - pNA [51-500]
 c PW - v262 - i39 - Sept 28 2015 - p88(1) [51-500]
Goodman, Lee - *Injustice*
 PW - v262 - i22 - June 1 2015 - p40(1) [51-500]
 BL - v112 - i1 - Sept 1 2015 - p48(1) [51-500]
Goodman, Marc - *Future Crimes: Everything is Connected, Everyone is Vulnerable and What We Can Do About It*
 Har Bus R - v93 - i11 - Nov 2015 - p150(2) [501+]
Future Crimes: Everything is Connected, Everyone is Vulnerable and What We Can Do About It (Read by Dean, Robertson). Audiobook Review
 NYTBR - May 17 2015 - p14(L) [501+]

Future Crimes: Everything is Connected, Everyone is Vulnerable and What We Can Do About It
 Econ - v414 - i8926 - Feb 21 2015 - p81(US) [501+]
 KR - Jan 1 2015 - pNA [501+]
 PW - v262 - i3 - Jan 19 2015 - p72(1) [501+]
Goodman, Michael E. - *Cold War Spies*
 c BL - v112 - i3 - Oct 1 2015 - p48(1) [51-500]
Goodman, Rachel - *From Scratch. E-book Review*
 PW - v262 - i15 - April 13 2015 - p62(2) [51-500]
Goodman, Ruth - *How to Be a Tudor: A Dawn-to-Dusk Guide to Tudor Life*
 KR - Dec 15 2015 - pNA [51-500]
Goodman, Simon - *The Orpheus Clock: The Search for My Family's Art Treasures Stolen by the Nazis*
 BL - v111 - i21 - July 1 2015 - p20(1) [51-500]
 CSM - August 18 2015 - pNA [501+]
 KR - June 15 2015 - pNA [501+]
 PW - v262 - i23 - June 8 2015 - p51(1) [51-500]
Goodman, Susan E. - *The First Step: How One Girl Put Segregation on Trial (Illus. by Lewis, E.B.)*
 c BL - v112 - i5 - Nov 1 2015 - p39(1) [51-500]
 c KR - Nov 1 2015 - pNA [51-500]
 c PW - v262 - i41 - Oct 12 2015 - p71(1) [51-500]
Goodman, Timothy - *Sharpie Art Workshop: Techniques and Ideas for Transforming Your World*
 LJ - v140 - i14 - Sept 1 2015 - p104(1) [51-500]
 PW - v262 - i22 - June 1 2015 - p64(2) [51-500]
Goodrich, Carter - *We Forgot Brock! (Illus. by Goodrich, Carter)*
 c BL - v111 - i22 - August 1 2015 - p73(1) [51-500]
 c CH Bwatch - Oct 2015 - pNA [51-500]
 c KR - June 15 2015 - pNA [51-500]
 c NYTBR - Nov 8 2015 - p34(L) [501+]
 c PW - v262 - i20 - May 18 2015 - p84(1) [51-500]
 c PW - v262 - i49 - Dec 2 2015 - p39(1) [51-500]
 c SLJ - v61 - i8 - August 2015 - p70(1) [51-500]
Goodrich, Jaime - *Faithful Translators: Authorship, Gender, and Religion in Early Modern England*
 TLS - i5873 - Oct 23 2015 - p26(1) [501+]
 Ren Q - v68 - i2 - Summer 2015 - p763-764 [501+]
Goodridge, Sehon S. - *Facing the Challenge of Emancipation: A Study of the Ministry of William Hart Coleridge, First Bishop of Barbados, 1824-1842*
 HNet - March 2015 - pNA [501+]
Goodwin, Craufurd D. - *Walter Lippmann: Public Economist*
 AM - v212 - i16 - May 11 2015 - p41(1) [501+]
 BHR - v89 - i2 - Summer 2015 - p352(3) [501+]
 HNet - March 2015 - pNA [501+]
 JEH - v75 - i1 - March 2015 - p294-295 [501+]
 For Aff - v94 - i1 - Jan-Feb 2015 - pNA [501+]
Goodwin, Doris Kearns - *The Bully Pulpit: Theodore Roosevelt, William Howard Taft, and the Golden Age of Journalism*
 RAH - v43 - i1 - March 2015 - p110-115 [501+]
Goodwin, George - *Benjamin Franklin in London*
 KR - Dec 1 2015 - pNA [501+]
Fatal Rivalry, Flodden 1513: Henry VIII, James IV and the Battle for Renaissance Britain
 Historian - v77 - i3 - Fall 2015 - p604(3) [501+]
Goodwin, Joanne L. - *Changing the Game: Women at Work in Las Vegas, 1940-1990*
 JAH - v102 - i2 - Sept 2015 - p602-602 [501+]
 WHQ - v46 - i4 - Winter 2015 - p530-531 [501+]
Goodwin, R.C. - *The Stephen Hawking Death Row Fan Club*
 KR - Sept 15 2015 - pNA [501+]
Goodwin, Robert - *Spain: The Center of the World, 1519-1682*
 KR - June 1 2015 - pNA [501+]
 PW - v262 - i19 - May 11 2015 - p51(1) [501+]
Spain: The Centre of the World 1519-1682
 Econ - v416 - i8948 - July 25 2015 - p67(US) [501+]
Spain: The Centre of the World, 1519-1682
 LJ - v140 - i9 - May 15 2015 - p91(1) [501+]
 Spec - v328 - i9751 - July 18 2015 - p38(1) [501+]
Spain: The Centre of the World, 1519-1862
 TLS - i5876 - Nov 13 2015 - p29(1) [501+]
Goodwin, Rosie - *Splendid Cities: Colour Your Way to Calm (Illus. by Chadwick, Alice)*
 Nat Post - v17 - i188 - June 13 2015 - pWP5(1) [501+]
Goody, Jack - *Metals, Culture, and Capitalism: An Essay on the Origins of the Modern World*
 JMH - v87 - i1 - March 2015 - p139(2) [501+]
Goodyear-Ka'opua, Noelani - *A Nation Rising: Hawaiian Movements for Life, Land, and Sovereignty*
 Am Ind CRJ - v39 - i2 - Spring 2015 - p151-3 [501+]

 JAH - v102 - i2 - Sept 2015 - p511-511 [501+]
Gooley, Tristan - *The Lost Art of Reading Nature's Signs: Use Outdoor Clues to Find Your Way, Predict the Weather, Locate Water, Track Animals - and Other Forgotten Skills*
 PW - v262 - i26 - June 29 2015 - p57(1) [51-500]
Goolrick, Robert - *The Fall of Princes*
 SEP - v287 - i5 - Sept-Oct 2015 - p24(1) [51-500]
 BL - v111 - i19-20 - June 1 2015 - p39(1) [51-500]
 KR - June 15 2015 - pNA [501+]
 PW - v262 - i22 - June 1 2015 - p39(1) [51-500]
Goolsby, Jesse - *I'd Walk with My Friends if I Could Find Them*
 BL - v111 - i17 - May 1 2015 - p75(2) [51-500]
 KR - April 1 2015 - pNA [51-500]
 PW - v262 - i15 - April 13 2015 - p52(1) [51-500]
Goossen, Ted - *Hear the Wind Sing*
 Econ - v416 - i8949 - August 1 2015 - p74(US) [501+]
Pinball, 1973
 Econ - v416 - i8949 - August 1 2015 - p74(US) [501+]
Gopal, Anand - *No Good Men Among the Living: America, the Taliban, and the War through Afghan Eyes*
 CC - v132 - i25 - Dec 9 2015 - p34(3) [501+]
Gopalkrishna, Sara Lynn - *How to Study Math: 80 Ways to Make the Grade*
 Math T - v109 - i2 - Sept 2015 - p158-158 [501+]
Goral, Pawel - *Cold War Rivalry and the Perception of the American West*
 WHQ - v46 - i2 - Summer 2015 - p253-254 [501+]
Goransson, Johannes - *The Sugar Book*
 PW - v262 - i16 - April 20 2015 - p52(1) [51-500]
Gorbachev, Valeri - *Cats Are Cats*
 c CH Bwatch - Feb 2015 - pNA [51-500]
 c HB Guide - v26 - i1 - Spring 2015 - p31(1) [51-500]
Doctor Nice (Illus. by Gorbachev, Valeri)
 c KR - July 1 2015 - pNA [51-500]
 c SLJ - v61 - i9 - Sept 2015 - p121(1) [51-500]
Goldilocks and the Three Bears
 c HB Guide - v26 - i2 - Fall 2015 - p159(1) [51-500]
Not Me! (Illus. by Gorbachev, Valeri)
 c KR - Dec 15 2015 - pNA [51-500]
Gordin, Michael - *Scientific Babel: The Language of Science from the Fall of Latin to the Rise of English*
 Nature - v519 - i7542 - March 12 2015 - p154(2) [501+]
Gordin, Michael D. - *Scientific Babel: The Language of Science from the Fall of Latin to the Rise of English*
 New Sci - v226 - i3019 - May 2 2015 - p45(1) [501+]
 TimHES - i2198 - April 9 2015 - p50(1) [501+]
Gordon, Bruce - *The Spirit of Attack: Fighter Pilot Stories*
 APJ - v29 - i6 - Nov-Dec 2015 - p93(1) [501+]
Gordon, Charlotte - *Romantic Outlaws: The Extraordinary Lives of Mary Wollstonecraft and Her Daughter Mary Shelley*
 BL - v111 - i17 - May 1 2015 - p72(1) [51-500]
 KR - Feb 1 2015 - pNA [501+]
 LJ - v140 - i5 - March 15 2015 - p100(1) [501+]
 Nat Post - v17 - i159 - May 9 2015 - pWP5(1) [501+]
 NY - v91 - i17 - June 22 2015 - p81 [51-500]
 NYTBR - May 10 2015 - p29(L) [501+]
 PW - v262 - i12 - March 23 2015 - p65(1) [51-500]
 Reason - v47 - i2 - June 2015 - p54(7) [501+]
 TLS - i5860 - July 24 2015 - p7(1) [501+]
 Wom R Bks - v32 - i6 - Nov-Dec 2015 - p27(3) [501+]
 Lon R Bks - v37 - i19 - Oct 8 2015 - p35(2) [501+]
 TimHES - i2213 - July 23 2015 - p51(1) [501+]
Romantic Outlaws: The Extraordinary Lives of Mary Wollstonecraft and Mary Shelley
 NS - v144 - i5265 - June 5 2015 - p50(1) [501+]
 Spec - v327 - i9739 - April 25 2015 - p44(2) [501+]
Gordon, Colin Douglas - *The Age of Attila: Fifth-Century Byzantium and the Barbarians*
 Med R - August 2015 - pNA [501+]
Gordon, Edwin E. - *Discovering Music from the Inside: An Autobiography*
 Teach Mus - v23 - i2 - Oct 2015 - p52(1) [51-500]
Gordon, Eleo - *Dearest Margarita: An Edwardian Love Story in Postcards*
 NS - v144 - i5284 - Oct 16 2015 - p50(1) [51-500]

Gordon, Eliza - *Must Love Otters (Read by Nordlinger, Romy). Audiobook Review*
    LJ - v140 - i10 - June 1 2015 - p60(1) [51-500]
Gordon, Elsbeth "Buff" - *Walking St. Augustine: An Illustrated Guide and Pocket History to America's Oldest City*
    Pub Hist - v37 - i3 - August 2015 - p152(3) [501+]
Gordon, G.B. - *When to Hold Them*
    PW - v262 - i24 - June 15 2015 - p70(1) [51-500]
Gordon, Gina - *Rush*
    PW - v262 - i14 - April 6 2015 - p46(1) [51-500]
Gordon, Greg - *When Money Grew on Trees: A. B. Hammond and the Age of the Timber Baron*
    JAH - v101 - i4 - March 2015 - p1287-1288 [501+]
  When Money Grew on Trees: A.B. Hammond and the Age of the Timber Baron
    AHR - v120 - i3 - June 2015 - p1031-1032 [501+]
    WHQ - v46 - i2 - Summer 2015 - p229-230 [501+]
  When Money Grew on Trees: A.B. Hammond and the Age of Timber Baron
    Roundup M - v22 - i6 - August 2015 - p37(1) [501+]
Gordon, John Steele - *Washington's Monument: And the Fascinating History of the Obelisk*
    KR - Nov 15 2015 - pNA [51-500]
Gordon, Kim - *Girl in a Band: A Memoir (Read by Gordon, Kim). Audiobook Review*
    LJ - v140 - i6 - April 1 2015 - p50(1) [51-500]
  Girl in a Band: A Memoir
    BooChiTr - March 7 2015 - p12(1) [501+]
    TLS - i5848 - May 1 2015 - p21(2) [501+]
    Art N - v114 - i2 - Feb 2015 - p20(2) [501+]
    BL - v111 - i12 - Feb 15 2015 - p18(1) [51-500]
    LJ - v140 - i2 - Feb 1 2015 - p86(1) [51-500]
    Nat Post - v17 - i97 - Feb 21 2015 - pWP6(1) [501+]
    New R - v246 - i1 - Feb 2015 - p52(4) [501+]
    NS - v144 - i5251 - Feb 27 2015 - p43(1) [501+]
    NYT - March 26 2015 - pNA(L) [51-500]
    NYTBR - March 15 2015 - p11(L) [501+]
    Spec - v327 - i9731 - Feb 28 2015 - p39(1) [501+]
  Girl in a Band
    Lon R Bks - v37 - i6 - March 19 2015 - p47(3) [501+]
    PW - v262 - i2 - Jan 12 2015 - p54(1) [51-500]
  Is It My Body? Selected Texts
    Dis - v62 - i1 - Wntr 2015 - p155(5) [501+]
Gordon, Mary - *The Liar's Wife. (Read by Podehl, Nick). Audiobook Review*
    BL - v111 - i9-10 - Jan 1 2015 - p114(1) [51-500]
  The Liar's Wife: Four Novellas
    AM - v212 - i7 - March 2 2015 - p43(3) [501+]
Gordon McMullan, - *Women Making Shakespeare: Text, Reception and Performance*
    Ren Q - v68 - i3 - Fall 2015 - p1150-1151 [501+]
Gordon-Nesbitt, Rebecca - *To Defend the Revolution Is to Defend Culture: The Cultural Policy of the Cuban Revolution*
    PW - v262 - i41 - Oct 12 2015 - p59(1) [51-500]
Gordon, Noah Eli - *The Word Kingdom*
    PW - v262 - i11 - March 16 2015 - p63(1) [51-500]
Gordon, Peter E. - *Weimar Thought: A Contested Legacy*
    CEH - v48 - i1 - March 2015 - p126-127 [501+]
    JMH - v87 - i3 - Sept 2015 - p756(3) [501+]
Gordon, Rebecca - *Mainstreaming Torture: Ethical Approaches in the Post-9/11 United States*
    CC - v132 - i7 - April 1 2015 - p34(2) [501+]
Gordon, Robert - *Respect Yourself: Stax Records and the Soul Explosion*
    NYTBR - March 15 2015 - p28(L) [501+]
    PMS - v38 - i3 - May 2015 - p267(4) [501+]
Gordon, Robert J. - *The Rise and Fall of American Growth: The U.S. Standard of Living since the Civil War*
    KR - Nov 15 2015 - pNA [501+]
    LJ - v140 - i20 - Dec 1 2015 - p111(1) [51-500]
Gordon, Sam - *Arab Jazz*
    TLS - i5838 - Feb 20 2015 - p21(1) [501+]
Gordon, Sherri Mabry - *Are You at Risk for Food Allergies? Peanut Butter, Milk, and Other Deadly Threats*
    y HB Guide - v26 - i1 - Spring 2015 - p170(2) [51-500]
  Are You Downloading Copyrighted Stuff? Stealing or Fair Use
    y HB Guide - v26 - i1 - Spring 2015 - p140(1) [51-500]
    VOYA - v38 - i2 - June 2015 - p88(2) [51-500]
  Be Smart about Money: Money Management and Budgeting
    y HB Guide - v26 - i1 - Spring 2015 - p138(1) [51-500]

Gordon-Smith, Dolores - *The Chessman*
    BL - v112 - i7 - Dec 1 2015 - p27(1) [51-500]
Gordon, Stan - *Whitewash*
    KR - Feb 1 2015 - pNA [501+]
Gordon, Steve - *The Future of the Music Business: How to Succeed with the New Digital Technologies*
    RVBW - Sept 2015 - pNA [51-500]
  Let's Talk about Death: Asking the Questions That Profoundly Change the Way We Live and Die
    LJ - v140 - i16 - Oct 1 2015 - p97(2) [51-500]
    PW - v262 - i38 - Sept 21 2015 - p66(1) [51-500]
Gordon, Tammy S. - *The Spirit of 1976: Commerce, Community, and the Politics of Commemoration*
    JAH - v101 - i4 - March 2015 - p1350-1351 [501+]
    Pub Hist - v37 - i1 - Feb 2015 - p140(3) [501+]
Gordon, Virginia N. - *The Undecided College Student: An Academic and Career Advising Challenge, 4th ed.*
    RVBW - August 2015 - pNA [51-500]
Gordonm, J.S. - *Esoteric Egypt: The Sacred Science of the Land of Khem*
    RVBW - March 2015 - pNA [51-500]
Gore, Emily - *And Nick (Illus. by Gore, Leonid)*
    c CH Bwatch - Oct 2015 - pNA [51-500]
    c HB Guide - v26 - i2 - Fall 2015 - p35(1) [51-500]
    c KR - March 15 2015 - pNA [51-500]
    c PW - v262 - i17 - April 27 2015 - p75(1) [51-500]
    c SLJ - v61 - i4 - April 2015 - p127(2) [51-500]
Gore, Steven - *Night Is the Hunter*
    BL - v111 - i9-10 - Jan 1 2015 - p48(1) [51-500]
Goreau, Thomas J. - *Innovative Methods of Marine Ecosystem Restoration*
    QRB - v90 - i1 - March 2015 - p85(2) [501+]
Goren, Yitzhak Gormezano - *Alexandrian Summer*
    TLS - i5877 - Nov 20 2015 - p30(2) [501+]
Gorenberg, Steve - *The Rock House Method: The Only Chord Book You Will Ever Need!*
    Am MT - v64 - i5 - April-May 2015 - p50(3) [501+]
Gorham, Michael S. - *After Newspeak: Language Culture and Politics in Russia from Gorbachev to Putin*
    E-A St - v67 - i4 - June 2015 - p671(2) [501+]
    MLR - v110 - i3 - July 2015 - p922-924 [501+]
Gorham, Sarah - *Study in Perfect*
    Ant R - v73 - i2 - Spring 2015 - p381(1) [501+]
Gorissen, Stefan - *Geschichte des Bergischen Landes: Band 1: Bis zum Ende des Herzogtums 1806*
    HNet - May 2015 - pNA [501+]
Gorman, Chris - *Indi Surfs*
    c PW - v262 - i17 - April 27 2015 - p73(1) [51-500]
Gorman, Ed - *The Autumn Dead / The Night Remembers*
    RVBW - March 2015 - pNA [51-500]
  Elimination
    BL - v111 - i17 - May 1 2015 - p34(1) [51-500]
    KR - May 15 2015 - pNA [51-500]
    PW - v262 - i19 - May 11 2015 - p38(1) [51-500]
  Graves' Retreat / Night of Shadows
    RVBW - August 2015 - pNA [51-500]
Gorman , Hugh S. - *The Story of N: A Social History of the Nitrogen Cycle and the Challenge of Sustainability*
    T&C - v56 - i4 - Oct 2015 - p970-971 [501+]
Gorman, Jane - *Blind Eye*
    KR - Sept 15 2015 - pNA [501+]
Gorman, Karyn - *Betty Q Investigates (Illus. by McClellan, Maddy)*
    c CH Bwatch - Nov 2015 - pNA [51-500]
  Rapunzel and the Prince of Pop
    c CH Bwatch - July 2015 - pNA [51-500]
Gorman, Michael (b. 1941-) - *Our Enduring Values Revisited: Librarianship in an Ever-Changing World*
    LJ - v140 - i11 - June 15 2015 - p101(1) [51-500]
    RVBW - May 2015 - pNA [51-500]
    VOYA - v38 - i3 - August 2015 - p92(1) [51-500]
Gorman, Michael J. (b. 1955-) - *The Death of the Messiah and the Birth of the New Covenant: A (Not So) New Model of the Atonement*
    CC - v132 - i6 - March 18 2015 - p40(2) [501+]
Gormezano Goren, Yitzhak - *Alexandrian Summer*
    LJ - v140 - i10 - June 1 2015 - p92(3) [501+]
Gormley, Amelia C. - *Juggernaut*
    PW - v262 - i25 - June 22 2015 - p124(1) [51-500]
Gormley, Beatrice - *Nelson Mandela: South African Revolutionary*
    c BL - v111 - i12 - Feb 15 2015 - p70(1) [51-500]
    c HB Guide - v26 - i2 - Fall 2015 - p208(1) [51-500]
    c KR - Feb 1 2015 - pNA [51-500]
  Poisoned Honey: A Story of Mary Magdalene
    y BL - v111 - i16 - April 15 2015 - p58(1) [51-500]
  Salome
    y BL - v111 - i16 - April 15 2015 - p58(1) [51-500]
Gormley, Dennis M. - *A Low-Visibility Force Multiplier: Assessing China's Cruise Missile Ambitions. E-book Review*
    APJ - v29 - i6 - Nov-Dec 2015 - p99(2) [501+]
Gornick, Lisa - *Louisa Meets Bear*
    BL - v111 - i17 - May 1 2015 - p76(1) [51-500]
    Ent W - i1374 - July 31 2015 - p66(1) [501+]
    PW - v262 - i17 - April 27 2015 - p44(1) [51-500]
    KR - April 1 2015 - pNA [51-500]
Gornick, Vivian - *The Odd Woman and the City: A Memoir*
    CHE - v61 - i39 - June 26 2015 - pB16(1) [501+]
    NYT - May 18 2015 - pC1(L) [501+]
    NYTBR - June 21 2015 - p8(L) [501+]
    PW - v262 - i15 - April 13 2015 - p72(1) [51-500]
  The Odd Woman and the City
    KR - Feb 15 2015 - pNA [51-500]
    New R - v246 - i4 - May 2015 - p90(4) [501+]
    NY - v91 - i19 - July 6 2015 - p87 [51-500]
  The Old Woman and the City: A Memoir
    Ent W - i1364 - May 22 2015 - p66(1) [501+]
Gorodetsky, Gabriel - *The Maisky Diaries: Red Ambassador to the Court of Sir Jame's, 1932-1943*
    Mac - v128 - i44 - Nov 9 2015 - p124(2) [501+]
  The Maisky Diaries: Red Ambassador to the Court of St. James's, 1932-1943
    Spec - v328 - i9759 - Sept 12 2015 - p44(3) [501+]
    TLS - i5875 - Nov 6 2015 - p12(1) [501+]
Gorokhova, Elena - *Russian Tattoo*
    Ent W - i1350 - Feb 13 2015 - p61(1) [501+]
    Wom R Bks - v32 - i4 - July-August 2015 - p25(2) [501+]
Gorry, Jonathan - *Cold War Christians and the Spectre of Nuclear Deterrence, 1945-1959*
    AHR - v120 - i2 - April 2015 - p585(1) [501+]
Gorter, Durk - *Minority Languages in the Linguistic Landscape*
    Lang Soc - v44 - i1 - Feb 2015 - p122-123 [501+]
Gortner, C.W. - *Mademoiselle Chanel*
    BL - v111 - i12 - Feb 15 2015 - p41(1) [51-500]
    KR - Jan 1 2015 - pNA [501+]
    PW - v262 - i2 - Jan 12 2015 - p34(1) [501+]
  The Vatican Princess
    KR - Dec 15 2015 - pNA [501+]
    PW - v262 - i52 - Dec 21 2015 - p124(1) [501+]
Gorton, Henry E. - *The Implacable Absence: A Non-Idiomatic Improvisational Duet*
    SPBW - Feb 2015 - pNA [51-500]
Gorup, Radmila Jovanovic - *After Yugoslavia: The Cultural Spaces of a Vanished Land*
    E-A St - v67 - i9 - Nov 2015 - p1502(2) [501+]
Gorzelanczyk, Melissa - *Arrows*
    y KR - Nov 1 2015 - pNA [51-500]
    y SLJ - v61 - i11 - Nov 2015 - p115(1) [51-500]
    y VOYA - v38 - i5 - Dec 2015 - p69(1) [51-500]
Gosewinkel, Dieter - *Anti-Liberal Europe: A Neglected Story of Europeanization*
    HNet - August 2015 - pNA [501+]
Goska, Danusha V. - *Bieganski: The Brute Polak Stereotype in Polish-Jewish Relations and American Popular Culture*
    HNet - March 2015 - pNA [501+]
Gosling, Sharon - *The Diamond Thief*
    y CCB-B - v68 - i5 - Jan 2015 - p257(1) [51-500]
    y HB Guide - v26 - i1 - Spring 2015 - p108(1) [51-500]
  The Ruby Airship
    c HB Guide - v26 - i2 - Fall 2015 - p120(1) [51-500]
Gospodinov, Georgi - *The Physics of Sorrow*
    LJ - v140 - i10 - June 1 2015 - p92(3) [501+]
Goss, Jared - *French Art Deco*
    Mag Antiq - v182 - i1 - Jan-Feb 2015 - p102(1) [501+]
Goss, Mini - *Too Hot For Spots*
    c Sch Lib - v63 - i3 - Autumn 2015 - p155(1) [51-500]
Gossai, Hemchand - *The Hebrew Prophets after the Shoah: A Mandate for Change*
    Intpr - v69 - i1 - Jan 2015 - p121(1) [51-500]
Gossett, GiGi - *The Midwife Factor*
    SPBW - May 2015 - pNA [51-500]
Goswami, Amit - *Quantum Economics: Unleashing the Power of an Economics of Consciousness*
    Bwatch - Sept 2015 - pNA [51-500]
Gotham, Kevin Fox - *Crisis Cities: Disaster and Redevelopment in New York and New Orleans*
    AJS - v120 - i5 - March 2015 - p1560(3) [501+]
Gott, J. Richard - *The Cosmic Web: Mysterious Architecture of the Universe*
    PW - v262 - i52 - Dec 21 2015 - p142(1) [51-500]

Gottfred, B.T. - *Forever for a Year*
   y HB - v91 - i4 - July-August 2015 - p133(1) [51-500]
   y KR - May 1 2015 - pNA [51-500]
   y PW - v262 - i18 - May 4 2015 - p122(1) [51-500]
   y PW - v262 - i49 - Dec 2 2015 - p91(2) [51-500]
   y SLJ - v61 - i4 - April 2015 - p164(1) [51-500]
   y VOYA - v38 - i2 - June 2015 - p60(1) [51-500]

Gottfried, Sara - *The Hormone Reset Diet: Heal Your Metabolism to Lose Up to 15 Pounds in 21 Days*
    PW - v262 - i7 - Feb 16 2015 - p174(1) [51-500]

Gotthard, Axel - *Der liebe und werthe Fried: Kriegskonzepte und Neutralitatsvorstellungen in der Fruhen Neuzeit*
    HER - v130 - i545 - August 2015 - p990(3) [501+]

Gottlieb, Amy - *The Beautiful Possible*
    KR - Dec 1 2015 - pNA [51-500]

Gottlieb, Eli - *Best Boy (Read by Pinchot, Bronson). Audiobook Review*
    BL - v112 - i6 - Nov 15 2015 - p60(1) [51-500]
    LJ - v140 - i20 - Dec 1 2015 - p59(1) [51-500]
Best Boy
    BL - v111 - i21 - July 1 2015 - p27(1) [51-500]
    KR - June 15 2015 - pNA [501+]
    LJ - v140 - i9 - May 15 2015 - p70(2) [51-500]
    NY - v91 - i29 - Sept 28 2015 - p72 [51-500]
    NYTBR - August 30 2015 - p15(L) [501+]
    PW - v262 - i22 - June 1 2015 - p37(2) [51-500]
    RVBW - Oct 2015 - pNA [51-500]

Gottman, John - *The Man's Guide to Women: Scientifically Proven Secrets from the "Love Lab" about What Women Really Want*
    PW - v262 - i51 - Dec 14 2015 - p76(2) [501+]

Gottschalk, Marie - *Caught: The Prison State and the Lockdown of American Politics*
    AM - v213 - i3 - August 3 2015 - p30(2) [501+]
    CC - v132 - i9 - April 29 2015 - p54(2) [501+]
    TimHES - i2188 - Jan 29 2015 - p48-49 [501+]

Gottschall, Jonathan - *The Professor in the Cage: Why Men Fight and Why We Like To Watch (Read by Dunn-Baker, Quincy)*
    LJ - v140 - i11 - June 15 2015 - p51(2) [51-500]
The Professor in the Cage: Why Men Fight and Why We Like to Watch
    PW - v262 - i2 - Jan 12 2015 - p47(1) [51-500]
    KR - Jan 1 2015 - pNA [51-500]
    BL - v111 - i13 - March 1 2015 - p5(1) [51-500]
The Storytelling Animal: How Stories Make Us Human
    J Chem Ed - v92 - i7 - July 2015 - p1140-1142 [501+]

Gottsche, Dirk - *Realism and Romanticism in German Literature*
    GSR - v38 - i1 - Feb 2015 - p172-175 [501+]
Remembering Africa: The Rediscovery of Colonialism in Contemporary German Literature
    MLR - v110 - i2 - April 2015 - p610-612 [501+]

Goudge, Elizabeth - *Linnets and Valerians*
    RVBW - Oct 2015 - pNA [51-500]

Goudie, Joshua - *Jack and the Hurricane (Illus. by Goudie, Craig)*
   c Res Links - v20 - i3 - Feb 2015 - p4(1) [501+]

Goudsouzian, Aram - *Down to the Crossroads: Civil Rights, Black Power, and the Meredith March against Fear*
    HNet - Sept 2015 - pNA [501+]
    JAH - v101 - i4 - March 2015 - p1328-1329 [501+]
    JSH - v81 - i4 - Nov 2015 - p1043(2) [501+]

Gough, Barry - *From Classroom to Battlefield: Victoria High School and the First World War*
    Beav - v95 - i4 - August-Sept 2015 - p73(1) [501+]

Gough, Erin - *The Flywheel*
   y Magpies - v30 - i1 - March 2015 - p40(1) [501+]

Gough, Kathleen M. - *Kinship and Performance in the Black and Green Atlantic*
    J Am St - v49 - i2 - May 2015 - p427-428 [501+]

Gough, Kerry - *Dear Jeff*
    KR - August 15 2015 - pNA [501+]

Gould, David - *BSAVA Manual of Canine and Feline Ophthalmology, 3d ed.*
    Bwatch - June 2015 - pNA [51-500]

Gould, Emily - *Friendship*
    NYTBR - Oct 11 2015 - p28(L) [501+]

Gould, Georgia - *Wasted: How Misunderstanding Young Britain Threatens Our Future*
    NS - v144 - i5254 - March 20 2015 - p46(2) [501+]
    TLS - i5847 - April 24 2015 - p21(1) [501+]

Gould, Lewis L. - *Chief Executive to Chief Justice: Taft betwixt the White House and Supreme Court*
    Pres St Q - v45 - i4 - Dec 2015 - p815(2) [501+]
Edith Kermit Roosevelt: Creating the Modern First Lady
    Pres St Q - v45 - i3 - Sept 2015 - p624(2) [501+]

Gould, Marilyn Amster - *Son of a Son*
    SPBW - Feb 2015 - pNA [51-500]

Gould, Philip - *Writing the Rebellion: Loyalists and the Literature of Politics in British America*
    W&M Q - v72 - i3 - July 2015 - p549-552 [501+]

Gould, Steven - *Exo*
    Analog - v135 - i1-2 - Jan-Feb 2015 - p183(1) [501+]

Goulden, John - *Michael Costa: England's First Conductor: The Revolution in Musical Performance in England, 1830-1880*
    MT - v156 - i1932 - Autumn 2015 - p107-109 [501+]

Goulding, Matt - *Rice, Noodle, Fish: Deep Travels Through Japan's Food Culture*
    KR - July 15 2015 - pNA [501+]
    LJ - v140 - i13 - August 1 2015 - p114(1) [51-500]
    PW - v262 - i29 - July 20 2015 - p179(1) [51-500]

Gouldthorpe, Peter - *The White Mouse: The Story of Nancy Wake*
    Magpies - v30 - i3 - July 2015 - p22(1) [51-500]

Goulson, Dave - *A Buzz in the Meadow: The Natural History of a French Farm*
    BL - v111 - i12 - Feb 15 2015 - p25(1) [51-500]
    KR - Feb 1 2015 - pNA [501+]
    LJ - v140 - i7 - April 15 2015 - p113(2) [51-500]
    NYTBR - May 31 2015 - p36(L) [501+]
    PW - v262 - i12 - March 23 2015 - p60(1) [51-500]

Gounev, Georgy - *The Dark Side of the Crescent Moon*
    Bwatch - July 2015 - pNA [51-500]

Gourevitch, Alex - *From Slavery to the Cooperative Common Wealth: Labor and Republican Liberty in the Nineteenth Century*
    Dis - v62 - i4 - Fall 2015 - p161(5) [501+]

Gourgey, Bill - *Gene.sys: Magigate Returns*
    PW - v262 - i22 - June 1 2015 - p46(1) [501+]

Gourley, Robbin - *Talkin' Guitar: A Story of Young Doc Watson (Illus. by Gourley, Robbin)*
   c HB Guide - v26 - i2 - Fall 2015 - p208(1) [51-500]
Talkin' Guitar: A Story of Young Doc Watson
   c CH Bwatch - May 2015 - pNA [501+]
Talkin' Guitar: A Story of Young Doc Watson (Illus. by Gourley, Robbin)
   c HB - v91 - i2 - March-April 2015 - p119(2) [51-500]
   c PW - v262 - i3 - Jan 19 2015 - p80(1) [51-500]

Goutor, David - *Taking Liberties: A History of Human Rights in Canada*
    HER - v130 - i545 - August 2015 - p1056(2) [501+]

Gouveia, Georgette - *Water Music*
    G&L Rev W - v22 - i1 - Jan-Feb 2015 - p39(1) [51-500]

Govaere, Devin - *Girrrl*
    PW - v262 - i20 - May 18 2015 - p68(2) [51-500]

Govinden, Niven - *All The Days and Nights*
    KR - Jan 1 2015 - pNA [501+]

Govrin, David - *The Journey to the Arab Spring: The Ideological Roots of the Middle East Upheaval in Arab Liberal Thought*
    IJMES - v47 - i4 - Nov 2015 - p846-849 [501+]

Gow, James - *Security, Democracy and War Crimes: Security Sector Transformation in Serbia*
    Slav R - v74 - i3 - Fall 2015 - p647-648 [501+]

Gow, Lawson - *Silly Shoes: Poems to Make You Smile (Illus. by Guillory, Mike)*
   c CH Bwatch - Feb 2015 - pNA [51-500]

Gowans, Jacob - *Secrets of Neverak*
   y SLJ - v61 - i8 - August 2015 - p114(1) [51-500]
A Tale of Light and Shadow
    RVBW - August 2015 - pNA [51-500]

Gowda, Shilpi Somaya - *The Golden Son*
    PW - v262 - i36 - Sept 7 2015 - p42(1) [51-500]

Gowland, Rebecca - *Human Identity and Identification*
    QRB - v90 - i2 - June 2015 - p241(1) [501+]

Goyal, Nikhil - *Schools on Trial*
    KR - Dec 15 2015 - pNA [501+]

Goyer, David S. - *Heaven's Fall*
    Analog - v135 - i11 - Nov 2015 - p106(1) [51-500]

Goyer, Tricia - *Prayers That Changed History*
   c BL - v112 - i3 - Oct 1 2015 - p39(1) [51-500]

Grabenstein, Chris - *Escape from Mr. Lemoncello's Library (Read by Bernstein, Jesse). Audiobook Review*
   c SLJ - v61 - i2 - Feb 2015 - p38(3) [51-500]
The Island of Dr. Libris (Read by Heyborne, Kirby). Audiobook Review
    PW - v262 - i26 - June 29 2015 - p65(1) [51-500]
The Island of Dr. Libris
   c CCB-B - v68 - i10 - June 2015 - p490(2) [51-500]
   c CH Bwatch - May 2015 - pNA [51-500]
   c HB Guide - v26 - i2 - Fall 2015 - p83(1) [51-500]
   c NYTBR - April 12 2015 - p21(L) [501+]
Mr. Lemoncello's Library Olympics
   c BL - v112 - i4 - Oct 15 2015 - p51(1) [51-500]
   c KR - Oct 1 2015 - pNA [51-500]
   c SLJ - v61 - i12 - Dec 2015 - p101(2) [51-500]

Grabmayr, Susanna - *Franz Ferdinand: Der eigensinnige Thronfolger*
    JMH - v87 - i2 - June 2015 - p488(3) [501+]

Grabski, Jozef - *Art in Sixteenth-Century Venice: Context, Practices, Developments*
    Ren Q - v68 - i3 - Fall 2015 - p1006-1007 [501+]

Grace, Christine - *Rising from the Mire*
    KR - Nov 1 2015 - pNA [501+]

Grace, Dominick - *The Science Fiction of Phyllis Gotlieb*
    SFS - v42 - i3 - Nov 2015 - p585-587 [501+]

Grace, Margaret - *Manhattan in Miniature*
    KR - Feb 1 2015 - pNA [501+]
    PW - v262 - i7 - Feb 16 2015 - p163(1) [51-500]

Grace, Richard J. - *Opium and Empire: The Lives and Careers of William Jardine and James Matheson*
    BHR - v89 - i2 - Summer 2015 - p391(3) [501+]

Grace, Samantha - *The Best of Both Rogues*
    PW - v262 - i23 - June 8 2015 - p46(1) [51-500]

Grace, Sherrill - *Landscapes of War and Memory: The Two World Wars in Canadian Literature and the Arts, 1977-2007*
    Beav - v95 - i3 - June-July 2015 - p55(2) [501+]

Grace, Sina - *Penny Dora and the Wishing Box (Illus. by Bonvillain, Tamra)*
   c BL - v112 - i4 - Oct 15 2015 - p37(1) [51-500]

Grace, Stephen - *The Great Divide*
    PW - v262 - i21 - May 25 2015 - p46(1) [51-500]

Gracen, Jennifer - *More Than You Know*
    PW - v262 - i44 - Nov 2 2015 - p68(1) [51-500]

Gracia Armendariz, Juan - *The Plimsoll Line*
    KR - Oct 1 2015 - pNA [51-500]

Gracian, Alex - *The Harvest Man*
    KR - March 15 2015 - pNA [51-500]

Gracie, Anne - *The Spring Bride*
    KR - April 15 2015 - pNA [51-500]

Grada, Cormac O. - *Eating People Is Wrong, and Other Essays on Famine, Its Past, and Its Future*
    NS - v144 - i5288 - Nov 13 2015 - p38(3) [501+]
    TimHES - i2202 - May 7 2015 - p50(1) [501+]

Grade, Anne - *The Spring Bride*
    PW - v262 - i17 - April 27 2015 - p58(1) [51-500]

Graden, Dale T. - *Disease, Resistance, and Lies: The Demise of the Transatlantic Slave Trade to Brazil and Cuba*
    JIH - v46 - i1 - Summer 2015 - p144-146 [501+]

Grady, Frank - *Answerable Style: The Idea of the Literary in Medieval England*
    JEGP - v114 - i1 - Jan 2015 - p145(3) [501+]
    MP - v112 - i4 - May 2015 - pE292(3) [501+]

Grady, Hugh - *Shakespeare and Impure Aesthetics*
    Shakes Q - v66 - i1 - Spring 2015 - p102-104 [501+]

Grady, James - *Last Days of the Condor*
    BL - v111 - i11 - Feb 1 2015 - p27(1) [51-500]

Grady, John - *Matthew Fontaine Maury, Father of Oceanography: A Biography, 1806-1873*
    J Mil H - v79 - i3 - July 2015 - p828-830 [501+]

Grady, Timothy P. - *Recovering the Piedmont Past: Unexplored Moments in Nineteenth-Century Upcountry South Carolina History*
    JSH - v81 - i2 - May 2015 - p453(3) [501+]

Graeber, David - *Debt: The First 5,000 Years*
    S&S - v79 - i2 - April 2015 - p318-325 [501+]
The Utopia of Rules: On Technology, Stupidity, and the Secret Joys of Bureaucracy
    CHE - v61 - i37 - May 29 2015 - pB16(1) [51-500]
    KR - Jan 1 2015 - pNA [51-500]
The Utopia of Rules: On Technology, Stupidity, and the Secret Joys of Bureaucracy
    Mac - v128 - i11 - March 23 2015 - p61(1) [51-500]
    NS - v144 - i5261 - May 7 2015 - p49(1) [51-500]
The Utopia of Rules: On Technology, Stupidity, and the Secret Joys of Bureaucracy
    TimHES - i2203 - May 14 2015 - p50-1 [501+]
The Utopia of Rules: On Technology, Stupidity, and the Secret Joys of Bureaucracy
    TimHES - i2211 - July 9 2015 - p48-49 [501+]

Graeff, Alexander - *Kandinsky als Padagoge*
    HNet - March 2015 - pNA [501+]

Graeme-Evans, Posie - *Wild Wood*
    KR - March 1 2015 - pNA [501+]

Graevenitz, Gerhart von - *Theodor Fontane: Angstliche Moderne - Uber das Imagindre*
Ger Q - v88 - i1 - Wntr 2015 - p104(2) [501+]

Graf, Erich - *Erich Graf--Musician, Flutist, Advocate*
KR - Oct 1 2015 - pNA [501+]

Graf, Friedrich Wilhelm - *Ernst Troeltsch: Kritische Gesamtausgabe, vol. 2*
Theol St - v76 - i4 - Dec 2015 - p844(2) [501+]

Graff, Harvey J. - *Undisciplining Knowledge: Interdisciplinary in the Twentieth Century*
TimHES - i2211 - July 9 2015 - p45(1) [501+]

Graff, Laurence - *Graff*
NYT - Nov 23 2015 - pNA(L) [501+]

Graff, Lisa - *Lost in the Sun (Read by De Ocampo, Ramon). Audiobook Review*
  c BL - v112 - i1 - Sept 1 2015 - p143(1) [51-500]
  c HB - v91 - i6 - Nov-Dec 2015 - p109(1) [51-500]
  c SLJ - v61 - i8 - August 2015 - p49(1) [51-500]
Lost in the Sun
  c BL - v111 - i14 - March 15 2015 - p74(1) [51-500]
  c BL - v112 - i1 - Sept 1 2015 - p99(1) [501+]
  c CCB-B - v69 - i1 - Sept 2015 - p24(2) [51-500]
  c HB - v91 - i3 - May-June 2015 - p109(1) [51-500]
  c HB Guide - v26 - i2 - Fall 2015 - p83(1) [51-500]
  c KR - March 1 2015 - pNA [51-500]
  c NYTBR - May 10 2015 - p21(L) [51-500]
  c PW - v262 - i11 - March 16 2015 - p85(1) [51-500]
  c PW - v262 - i49 - Dec 2 2015 - p72(1) [51-500]
  c SLJ - v61 - i4 - April 2015 - p146(1) [501+]

Graffin, Greg - *Population Wars*
KR - July 15 2015 - pNA [501+]

Grafton, Anthony T. - *Henricus Glareanus's (1488-1563) Chronologia of the Ancient World: A Facsimile Edition of a Heavily Annotated Copy Held in Princeton University Library*
Six Ct J - v46 - i1 - Spring 2015 - p152-153 [501+]

Grafton, Sue - *X*
KR - June 15 2015 - pNA [51-500]
NYTBR - Sept 6 2015 - p25(L) [501+]
PW - v262 - i26 - June 29 2015 - p46(1) [51-500]

Gragnolati, Manuele - *Amor che move: linguaggio del corpo e forma del desiderio in Dante, Pasolini e Morante*
MLR - v110 - i2 - April 2015 - p567-568 [501+]

Graham, Amy - *Be Smart about Your Career: College, Income, and Careers*
  y HB Guide - v26 - i1 - Spring 2015 - p138(1) [51-500]
Be Smart about Your Future: Risk Management and Insurance
  y HB Guide - v26 - i1 - Spring 2015 - p138(1) [51-500]

Graham, Barbara - *Murder by Kindness: The Gift Quilt*
BL - v112 - i4 - Oct 15 2015 - p23(1) [51-500]

Graham, Bob - *How the Sun Got to Coco's House (Illus. by Graham, Bob)*
  c CCB-B - v69 - i2 - Oct 2015 - p89(1) [51-500]
  c HB - v91 - i6 - Nov-Dec 2015 - p66(2) [51-500]
  c KR - July 15 2015 - pNA [51-500]
  c Magpies - v30 - i4 - Sept 2015 - p29(1) [501+]
  c NYTBR - Nov 8 2015 - p29(L) [51-500]
  c PW - v262 - i28 - July 13 2015 - p63(1) [51-500]
Vanilla Ice Cream
  c HB Guide - v26 - i1 - Spring 2015 - p31(1) [51-500]

Graham, Chris. - *The Chicken Keeper's Problem Solver: 100 Common Problems Explored and Explained*
LJ - v140 - i6 - April 1 2015 - p112(1) [51-500]

Graham, Daniel W. - *Science before Socrates: Parmenides, Anaxagoras and the New Astronomy*
Isis - v106 - i1 - March 2015 - p167(2) [501+]

Graham, Georgia - *Cub's Journey Home (Illus. by Graham, Georgia)*
  c KR - July 1 2015 - pNA [51-500]
  c Res Links - v21 - i1 - Oct 2015 - p6(1) [51-500]

Graham, Ian - *Asteroids and Comets*
  c HB Guide - v26 - i2 - Fall 2015 - p165(1) [51-500]
Galaxies and Stars
  c HB Guide - v26 - i2 - Fall 2015 - p165(1) [51-500]
Great Building Designs, 1900-Today
  c BL - v112 - i6 - Nov 15 2015 - p54(1) [51-500]
Great Electronic Gadget Designs 1900-Today
  c Sch Lib - v63 - i4 - Winter 2015 - p238(1) [51-500]

Our Moon
  c HB Guide - v26 - i2 - Fall 2015 - p165(1) [51-500]
Our Sun
  c HB Guide - v26 - i2 - Fall 2015 - p165(1) [51-500]
Planets Far from Earth
  c HB Guide - v26 - i2 - Fall 2015 - p165(1) [51-500]
Planets Near Earth
  c HB Guide - v26 - i2 - Fall 2015 - p165(1) [51-500]
Scarlet Women: The Scandalous Lives of Courtesans, Concubines, and Royal Mistresses
BL - v112 - i7 - Dec 1 2015 - p6(1) [51-500]
LJ - v140 - i19 - Nov 15 2015 - p94(1) [51-500]

Graham, Joan Bransfield - *The Poem That Will Not End: Fun with Poetic Forms and Voices*
  c SLJ - v61 - i4 - April 2015 - p42(4) [501+]

Graham-Jones, Jean - *Evita, Inevitably: Performing Argentina's Female Icons before and after Eva Peron*
TimHES - i2227 - Oct 29 2015 - p47(1) [501+]

Graham, Jorie - *From the New World: Poems 1976-2014*
Nation - v301 - i20 - Nov 16 2015 - p27(3) [501+]
NY - v91 - i6 - March 30 2015 - p77 [501+]
NYT - Feb 11 2015 - pC1(L) [501+]
NYTBR - March 1 2015 - p16(L) [501+]
PW - v262 - i3 - Jan 19 2015 - p60(1) [501+]

Graham, Judith S. - *Diary and Autobiographical Writings of Louisa Catherine Adams, 2 vols.*
RAH - v43 - i3 - Sept 2015 - p477-483 [501+]

Graham, Julie-Anne - *The Perfect Percival Priggs (Illus. by Graham, Julie-Anne)*
  c HB Guide - v26 - i2 - Fall 2015 - p35(1) [51-500]
  c KR - March 1 2015 - pNA [51-500]
  c PW - v262 - i14 - April 6 2015 - p59(1) [51-500]

Graham, Scott - *Mountain Rampage*
KR - April 1 2015 - pNA [51-500]

Graham, Thomas (b. 1943-) - *Mr. Flagler's St. Augustine*
JSH - v81 - i3 - August 2015 - p753(2) [501+]

Graham, Thomas, Jr. (b. 1933-) - *Sapphire: A Tale of the Cold War*
KR - June 1 2015 - pNA [501+]

Graham, Toni - *The Suicide Club*
PW - v262 - i29 - July 20 2015 - p165(1) [51-500]

Graham, Wade - *Dream Cities: Seven Urban Ideas That Shape the World*
KR - Oct 15 2015 - pNA [501+]
PW - v262 - i44 - Nov 2 2015 - p75(1) [51-500]

Grahame-Smith, Seth - *The Last American Vampire (Read by Andrews, MacLeod). Audiobook Review*
BL - v111 - i18 - May 15 2015 - p69(1) [51-500]
Bwatch - April 2015 - pNA [51-500]
LJ - v140 - i11 - June 15 2015 - p50(1) [51-500]

Grainger, A.J. - *Captive*
  y KR - Sept 1 2015 - pNA [51-500]
  y Sch Lib - v63 - i2 - Summer 2015 - p117(1) [51-500]
  y SLJ - v61 - i10 - Oct 2015 - p110(2) [51-500]
Sundberg
  y BL - v112 - i4 - Oct 15 2015 - p56(1) [51-500]

Graire, Virginie - *Colors*
  c KR - Jan 1 2016 - pNA [51-500]

Grais, Jennifer - *Christa's Luck*
  y KR - June 15 2015 - pNA [51-500]

Grambling, Lois G. - *Can I Bring Saber to New York City, Ms. Mayor? (Illus. by Love, Judy)*
  c HB Guide - v26 - i2 - Fall 2015 - p35(1) [51-500]

Gramling, Michael - *The Great Disconnect in Early Childhood Education*
Bwatch - August 2015 - pNA [51-500]

Gramm, Jeff - *Dear Chairman: Boardroom Battles and the Rise of Shareholder Activism*
KR - Dec 15 2015 - pNA [501+]
LJ - v140 - i19 - Nov 15 2015 - p93(1) [51-500]
PW - v262 - i45 - Nov 9 2015 - p48(2) [51-500]

Granada, Miguel Angel - *Novas y cometas entre 1572 y 1618: Revolucion cosmologica y renovacion politica y religiosa*
Isis - v106 - i1 - March 2015 - p181(2) [501+]

Granade, S. Andrew - *Harry Partch: Hobo Composer*
Notes - v72 - i2 - Dec 2015 - p353(3) [501+]

Granatstein, J.L. - *The Greatest Victory: Canada's One Hundred Days, 1918*
Beav - v95 - i3 - June-July 2015 - p57(1) [501+]
TLS - i5841 - March 13 2015 - p27(1) [51-500]

Grand, David - *Mount Terminus*
NYTBR - May 17 2015 - p32(L) [501+]

Grandbois, Peter - *The Girl on the Swing and At Night in Crumbling Voices*
PW - v262 - i2 - Jan 12 2015 - p41(1) [501+]

Grande, James - *William Cobbett, the Press and Rural England: Radicalism and the Fourth Estate, 1792-1835*
TLS - i5832 - Jan 9 2015 - p23(1) [501+]

Grandin, Greg - *The Empire of Necessity: Slavery, Freedom, and Deception in the New World*
NYTBR - Feb 15 2015 - p28(L) [501+]
The Empire of Necessity: The Untold History of a Slave Rebellion in the Age of Liberty
Lon R Bks - v37 - i6 - March 19 2015 - p36(3) [501+]
Kissinger's Shadow: The Long Reach of America's Most Controversial Statesman
BL - v111 - i21 - July 1 2015 - p19(1) [51-500]
CSM - August 27 2015 - pNA [501+]
KR - June 1 2015 - pNA [501+]
LJ - v140 - i14 - Sept 1 2015 - p120(2) [51-500]
NYTBR - Oct 4 2015 - p13(L) [501+]
PW - v262 - i23 - June 8 2015 - p49(1) [51-500]

Grandin, Temple - *Emergence: Labeled Autistic*
TimHES - i2212 - July 16 2015 - p47-1 [501+]
Thinking in Pictures
TimHES - i2212 - July 16 2015 - p47-1 [501+]

Grandits, Hannes - *Jugoslawien in den 1960er Jahren: Auf dem Weg zu einem (a)Normalen Staat?*
HNet - July 2015 - pNA [501+]
Slav R - v74 - i1 - Spring 2015 - p175-176 [501+]

Grandjean, Katherine - *American Passage: The Communications Frontier in Early New England*
JIH - v46 - i3 - Wntr 2016 - p450-451 [501+]

Grandolini, Albert - *Fall of the Flying Dragon: South Vietnamese Air Force 1973-75*
APH - v62 - i2 - Summer 2015 - p56(1) [501+]

Granstrom, Brita - *Wild Adventures (Illus. by Manning, Mick)*
  c BL - v111 - i15 - April 1 2015 - p36(2) [51-500]

Grant, Adam - *Originals: How Non-Conformists Move the World*
KR - Dec 1 2015 - pNA [501+]
PW - v262 - i51 - Dec 14 2015 - p74(1) [51-500]

Grant, Adrian - *Irish Socialist Republicanism, 1906-36*
HER - v130 - i543 - April 2015 - p488(2) [501+]

Grant, Andrew - *False Positive*
BL - v112 - i7 - Dec 1 2015 - p28(1) [51-500]
KR - Sept 15 2015 - pNA [51-500]
PW - v262 - i44 - Nov 2 2015 - p60(1) [51-500]

Grant, Callie - *To the Sea (Illus. by Tugeau, Jeremy)*
  c PW - v262 - i15 - April 13 2015 - p78(2) [501+]

Grant , Cathryn - *Faceless*
KR - Sept 15 2015 - pNA [51-500]

Grant, H. Roger - *The Louisville, Cincinnati and Charleston Rail Road: Dreams of Linking North and South*
JSH - v81 - i4 - Nov 2015 - p970(2) [501+]

Grant, Helen - *Urban Legends*
  y Sch Lib - v63 - i3 - Autumn 2015 - p189(1) [51-500]

Grant, Holly - *The Dastardly Deed (Illus. by Portillo, Josie)*
  c SLJ - v61 - i12 - Dec 2015 - p101(1) [501+]
  c KR - Oct 15 2015 - pNA [51-500]
The League of Beastly Dreadfuls (Read by Landor, Rosalyn). Audiobook Review
  c BL - v112 - i3 - Oct 1 2015 - p87(1) [51-500]
  c SLJ - v61 - i8 - August 2015 - p49(1) [51-500]
The League of Beastly Dreadfuls, book 1 (Illus. by Portillo, Josie)
  c CCB-B - v68 - i8 - April 2015 - p400(1) [51-500]
The League of Beastly Dreadfuls (Illus. by Portillo, Josie)
  c PW - v262 - i4 - Jan 26 2015 - p169(1) [51-500]
  c BL - v111 - i11 - Feb 1 2015 - p52(1) [51-500]
  c HB Guide - v26 - i2 - Fall 2015 - p83(1) [51-500]

Grant, Jacob - *Little Bird's Bad Word (Illus. by Grant, Jacob)*
  c CCB-B - v69 - i2 - Oct 2015 - p90(1) [51-500]
  c HB - v91 - i4 - July-August 2015 - p113(2) [51-500]
  c PW - v262 - i18 - May 4 2015 - p118(1) [51-500]
  c SLJ - v61 - i5 - May 2015 - p79(1) [51-500]

Grant, James - *The Forgotten Depression, 1921: The Crash That Cured Itself*
NYTBR - Jan 25 2015 - p18(L) [501+]

Grant, Jamie - *Glass on the Chimney and Other Poems*
Quad - v59 - i1-2 - Jan-Feb 2015 - p108(2) [501+]

Grant, John - *Debunk It!: How to Stay Sane in a World of Misinformation*
  y BL - v111 - i19-20 - June 1 2015 - p70(1) [51-500]
  y CH Bwatch - April 2015 - pNA [51-500]
  y SLJ - v61 - i3 - March 2015 - p176(2) [51-500]
Divine Sex: A Compelling Vision for Christian Relationships in a Hypersexualized Age
Ch Today - v59 - i7 - Sept 2015 - p71(3) [501+]
PW - v262 - i23 - June 8 2015 - p56(1) [51-500]

Grant, Julia - *The Boy Problem: Educating Boys in Urban America, 1870-1970*
 AHR - v120 - i1 - Feb 2015 - p258-259 [501+]
 JAH - v101 - i4 - March 2015 - p1249-1250 [501+]
Grant, Katharine - *The Marriage Recital*
 NYTBR - Dec 13 2015 - p44(L) [501+]
Grant, Katherine - *Sedition*
 Wom R Bks - v32 - i4 - July-August 2015 - p15(2) [501+]
Grant, Kelley - *Desert Rising*
 PW - v262 - i8 - Feb 23 2015 - p56(2) [51-500]
Grant, Maria C. - *Reading and Writing in Science: Tools to Develop Disciplinary Literacy*
 Bwatch - July 2015 - pNA [501+]
Grant, Michael - *BZRK Apocalypse (Read by Evers-Swindell, Nico). Audiobook Review*
 y SLJ - v61 - i3 - March 2015 - p80(1) [51-500]
 BZRK Apocalypse
 y HB Guide - v26 - i1 - Spring 2015 - p108(1) [51-500]
 y Teach Lib - v42 - i3 - Feb 2015 - p28(4) [501+]
 Front Lines
 y BL - v112 - i4 - Oct 15 2015 - p44(1) [51-500]
 y KR - Oct 15 2015 - pNA [51-500]
 y PW - v262 - i44 - Nov 2 2015 - p87(1) [51-500]
 y SLJ - v61 - i11 - Nov 2015 - p115(1) [51-500]
 y VOYA - v38 - i5 - Dec 2015 - p69(1) [51-500]
 Messenger of Fear
 y Sch Lib - v63 - i1 - Spring 2015 - p52(1) [51-500]
 Messenger: The Legend of Joan of Arc (Illus. by Hart, Sam)
 c HB Guide - v26 - i2 - Fall 2015 - p120(1) [51-500]
 The Tattooed Heart: A Messenger of Fear
 y BL - v111 - i21 - July 1 2015 - p60(1) [51-500]
 y KR - June 15 2015 - pNA [51-500]
 The Tattooed Heart: A Messenger of Fear Novel
 y SLJ - v61 - i7 - July 2015 - p92(3) [51-500]
Grant, Mira - *Chimera*
 KR - Sept 15 2015 - pNA [51-500]
 PW - v262 - i39 - Sept 28 2015 - p73(1) [51-500]
 Rolling in the Deep
 LJ - v140 - i17 - Oct 15 2015 - p118(1) [501+]
 PW - v262 - i5 - Feb 2 2015 - p39(1) [51-500]
Grant, Patrick - *Original Man: The Tautz Compendium of Less Ordinary Gentlemen*
 RVBW - Feb 2015 - pNA [51-500]
Grant, Peter - *Philanthropy and Voluntary Action in the First World War*
 AHR - v120 - i2 - April 2015 - p718-719 [501+]
Grant, Richard - *Dispatches from Pluto: Lost and Found in the Mississippi Delta*
 KR - August 15 2015 - pNA [501+]
 NYTBR - Dec 6 2015 - p46(L) [501+]
 LJ - v140 - i16 - Oct 1 2015 - p99(1) [51-500]
Grant, Scott - *The Lebensborn Experiment*
 KR - Oct 15 2015 - pNA [51-500]
Grant, Stephen H. - *Collecting Shakespeare: The Story of Henry and Emily Folger*
 AHR - v120 - i4 - Oct 2015 - p1497-1498 [501+]
 Ren Q - v68 - i1 - Spring 2015 - p406-408 [501+]
 Six Ct J - v46 - i1 - Spring 2015 - p204-205 [501+]
 TLS - i5836 - Feb 6 2015 - p13(1) [501+]
Grant, Thomas - *Jeremy Hutchinson's Case Histories: From Lady Chatterley's Lover to Howard Marks*
 Spec - v328 - i9748 - June 27 2015 - p44(1) [501+]
 TLS - i5876 - Nov 13 2015 - p26(1) [501+]
Grant, Vicki - *Small Bones*
 y BL - v112 - i3 - Oct 1 2015 - p74(2) [51-500]
 y KR - July 15 2015 - pNA [51-500]
 y Res Links - v21 - i1 - Oct 2015 - p34(1) [501+]
 y SLJ - v61 - i11 - Nov 2015 - p116(1) [51-500]
 y VOYA - v38 - i4 - Oct 2015 - p51(1) [51-500]
Grant, Virginia - *Australia's Greatest Landmarks and Locations*
 y SLJ - v61 - i8 - August 2015 - p126(2) [51-500]
Grasshopper Jungle (Read by Smith, Andrew)
 y Teach Lib - v42 - i3 - Feb 2015 - p28(4) [501+]
Gratch, Alon - *The Israeli Mind: How the Israeli National Character Shapes Our World*
 KR - June 1 2015 - pNA [501+]
 PW - v262 - i19 - May 11 2015 - p45(1) [51-500]
Gratz, Alan - *Code of Honor*
 y KR - May 15 2015 - pNA [51-500]
 y SLJ - v61 - i7 - July 2015 - p93(1) [51-500]
 y VOYA - v38 - i3 - August 2015 - p61(1) [51-500]
 The Dragon Lantern: A League of Seven (Illus. by Helquist, Brett)
 c BL - v111 - i19-20 - June 1 2015 - p96(1) [51-500]
 y KR - April 15 2015 - pNA [51-500]
 The Dragon Lantern: A League of Seven Novel (Illus. by Helquist, Brett)
 c HB Guide - v26 - i2 - Fall 2015 - p83(1) [51-500]
 The League of Seven (Illus. by Helquist, Brett)
 y HB Guide - v26 - i1 - Spring 2015 - p78(2) [51-500]

Gratz, Roberta Brandes - *We're Still Here Ya Bastards: How the People of New Orleans Rebuilt Their City*
 LJ - v140 - i8 - May 1 2015 - p92(1) [51-500]
 NYTBR - August 9 2015 - p10(L) [51-500]
 PW - v262 - i15 - April 13 2015 - p71(1) [51-500]
Grau, Donatien - *Neron en Occident: Une figure de l'histoire*
 NYRB - v62 - i20 - Dec 17 2015 - p26(3) [501+]
Grau, Sheila - *Dr. Critchlore's School for Minions (Illus. by Sutphin, Joe)*
 c BL - v111 - i15 - April 1 2015 - p78(1) [51-500]
 c CCB-B - v68 - i10 - June 2015 - p491(1) [51-500]
 c HB Guide - v26 - i2 - Fall 2015 - p83(1) [51-500]
 Gorilla Tactics
 y KR - Dec 15 2015 - pNA [51-500]
Grau, T.E. - *The Nameless Dark: A Collection*
 PW - v262 - i25 - June 22 2015 - p123(2) [51-500]
Graudin, Ryan - *The Walled City*
 y CCB-B - v68 - i5 - Jan 2015 - p257(1) [51-500]
 y HB - v91 - i1 - Jan-Feb 2015 - p81(1) [51-500]
 y HB Guide - v26 - i1 - Spring 2015 - p108(1) [51-500]
 y Sch Lib - v63 - i1 - Spring 2015 - p62(1) [51-500]
 Wolf by Wolf
 y VOYA - v38 - i4 - Oct 2015 - p70(1) [51-500]
 y BL - v112 - i1 - Sept 1 2015 - p110(2) [51-500]
 y KR - July 15 2015 - pNA [51-500]
 y PW - v262 - i31 - August 3 2015 - p63(1) [51-500]
 y PW - v262 - i49 - Dec 2 2015 - p113(2) [51-500]
 y Sch Lib - v63 - i4 - Winter 2015 - p246(1) [51-500]
 y SLJ - v61 - i8 - August 2015 - p103(1) [51-500]
Graulich, Michel - *Moctezuma. Apogeo y caida del imperio azteca*
 Lat Ant - v26 - i1 - March 2015 - p138(2) [501+]
Graun, Eric - *Super Baseball Infographics (Illus. by Westlund, Laura)*
 c BL - v112 - i1 - Sept 1 2015 - p98(1) [51-500]
Gravel, Elise - *Head Lice (Illus. by Gravel, Elise)*
 c Res Links - v20 - i4 - April 2015 - p18(1) [51-500]
 c CCB-B - v68 - i9 - May 2015 - p447(1) [51-500]
 c HB Guide - v26 - i2 - Fall 2015 - p173(1) [51-500]
 c Nat Post - v17 - i86 - Feb 7 2015 - pWP11(1) [501+]
 c SLJ - v61 - i4 - April 2015 - p178(1) [51-500]
 I Want a Monster!
 c KR - Jan 1 2016 - pNA [51-500]
 Jessie Elliot Is a Big Chicken
 c HB Guide - v26 - i1 - Spring 2015 - p79(1) [51-500]
 The Rat
 c HB Guide - v26 - i1 - Spring 2015 - p164(1) [51-500]
 The Slug
 c HB Guide - v26 - i1 - Spring 2015 - p158(1) [51-500]
 The Spider (Illus. by Gravel, Elise)
 c Res Links - v20 - i4 - April 2015 - p18(1) [51-500]
 c CCB-B - v68 - i9 - May 2015 - p447(1) [51-500]
 c Nat Post - v17 - i86 - Feb 7 2015 - pWP11(1) [501+]
 c HB Guide - v26 - i2 - Fall 2015 - p173(1) [51-500]
Gravel, Ryan - *Where We Want to Live: Reclaiming Infrastructure for a New Generation of Cities*
 KR - Jan 1 2016 - pNA [501+]
Gravell, Kim - *Child of the Covenant*
 RVBW - August 2015 - pNA [501+]
Graves, Alice - *The Small Library Manager's Handbook*
 LR - v64 - i6-7 - June-July 2015 - p509-510 [501+]
Graves, Annie - *A Dog's Breakfast (Illus. by McElhinney, Glenn)*
 c PW - v262 - i3 - Jan 19 2015 - p83(1) [501+]
 c BL - v111 - i18 - May 15 2015 - p68(1) [51-500]
 c HB Guide - v26 - i2 - Fall 2015 - p66(1) [51-500]
 Guinea Pig Killer (Illus. by McElhinney, Glenn)
 c HB Guide - v26 - i2 - Fall 2015 - p66(1) [51-500]
 Help! My Brother's a Zombie (Illus. by McElhinney, Glenn)
 c HB Guide - v26 - i2 - Fall 2015 - p66(1) [51-500]
 Mirrored (Illus. by McElhinney, Glenn)
 c HB Guide - v26 - i2 - Fall 2015 - p66(1) [51-500]
Graves, Diana - *Fatal Retribution*
 RVBW - Oct 2015 - pNA [51-500]
Graves, Emily - *How to Be a Good Mommy When You're Sick: A Guide to Motherhood with Chronic Illness*
 LJ - v140 - i3 - Feb 15 2015 - p81(3) [501+]
Graves, Judith - *Exposed*
 y Res Links - v21 - i1 - Oct 2015 - p34(2) [51-500]
 y SLJ - v61 - i9 - Sept 2015 - p151(4) [501+]
 y VOYA - v38 - i5 - Dec 2015 - p63(1) [51-500]

Graves, Judith Canty - *Parents Have the Power to Make Special Education Work: An Insider Guide*
 KR - Feb 15 2015 - pNA [501+]
Graves, Keith - *The Monsterator*
 c HB Guide - v26 - i1 - Spring 2015 - p31(1) [51-500]
 Puppy! (Illus. by Graves, Keith)
 c KR - Jan 1 2016 - pNA [51-500]
 Second Banana
 c HB Guide - v26 - i2 - Fall 2015 - p36(1) [51-500]
Graves, Melissa - *Tainted Heart*
 BL - v112 - i5 - Nov 1 2015 - p37(1) [51-500]
 LJ - v140 - i16 - Oct 1 2015 - p62(2) [51-500]
Graves, Michael - *The Inspiration and Interpretation of Scripture: What the Early Church Can Teach Us*
 Theol St - v76 - i1 - March 2015 - p166(2) [501+]
Graves, Sarah - *The Girls She Left Behind*
 KR - Nov 15 2015 - pNA [51-500]
 PW - v262 - i46 - Nov 16 2015 - p57(1) [51-500]
 Winter at the Door
 BL - v111 - i9-10 - Jan 1 2015 - p51(1) [51-500]
Graves, Will - *The Best Hockey Players of All Time*
 c HB Guide - v26 - i2 - Fall 2015 - p197(2) [51-500]
 The Best NBA Guards of All Time
 c HB Guide - v26 - i1 - Spring 2015 - p183(1) [51-500]
Gravett, Emily - *Bear & Hare Go Fishing (Illus. by Gravett, Emily)*
 c HB - v91 - i4 - July-August 2015 - p114(1) [51-500]
 c KR - May 1 2015 - pNA [51-500]
 c SLJ - v61 - i6 - June 2015 - p82(1) [51-500]
 Bear & Hare: Snow! (Illus. by Gravett, Emily)
 c BL - v112 - i5 - Nov 1 2015 - p64(1) [51-500]
 c KR - Sept 15 2015 - pNA [51-500]
 c SLJ - v61 - i11 - Nov 2015 - p81(1) [51-500]
Gravett, Paul - *Comics Art*
 S&S - v79 - i4 - Oct 2015 - p628-630 [501+]
Gravil, Richard - *The Oxford Handbook on William Wordsworth*
 TLS - i5875 - Nov 6 2015 - p3(2) [501+]
Grawitch, Matthew J. - *The Psychologically Healthy Workplace: Building a Win-Win Environment for Organizations and Employees*
 RVBW - Sept 2015 - pNA [501+]
Gray, Allegra - *Entrusted*
 y VOYA - v38 - i5 - Dec 2015 - p56(2) [501+]
Gray, Amelia - *Gutshot: Stories*
 BL - v111 - i16 - April 15 2015 - p23(2) [51-500]
 KR - Feb 15 2015 - pNA [51-500]
 NYTBR - May 24 2015 - p20(L) [501+]
 PW - v262 - i8 - Feb 23 2015 - p48(1) [51-500]
Gray, C. Raymond - *The FunGkins: The Battle for Halladon*
 c CH Bwatch - April 2015 - pNA [51-500]
Gray, Casey - *Discount*
 BL - v111 - i14 - March 15 2015 - p43(1) [51-500]
 KR - Feb 15 2015 - pNA [51-500]
Gray, Claudia - *Sorceress*
 y HB Guide - v26 - i2 - Fall 2015 - p120(1) [51-500]
 y SLJ - v61 - i4 - April 2015 - p174(1) [51-500]
 y VOYA - v37 - i6 - Feb 2015 - p75(1) [51-500]
 Ten Thousand Skies above You
 y KR - Sept 1 2015 - pNA [51-500]
 y SLJ - v61 - i10 - Oct 2015 - p111(1) [51-500]
 y VOYA - v38 - i5 - Dec 2015 - p69(2) [51-500]
 A Thousand Pieces of You
 y CCB-B v68 - i5 - Jan 2015 - p257(2) [51-500]
 y HB Guide - v26 - i1 - Spring 2015 - p108(1) [51-500]
Gray, Colin S. - *Perspectives on Strategy*
 Parameters - v45 - i1 - Spring 2015 - p137(2) [501+]
 Strategy and Defence Planning: Meeting the Challenge of Uncertainty
 Parameters - v45 - i1 - Spring 2015 - p137(2) [501+]
 The Strategy Bridge: Theory for Practice
 Parameters - v45 - i1 - Spring 2015 - p137(2) [501+]
Gray, Edward G. - *The Oxford Handbook of the American Revolution*
 RAH - v43 - i1 - March 2015 - p32-40 [501+]
Gray, Emily - *Blue Stars*
 BL - v111 - i9-10 - Jan 1 2015 - p35(1) [51-500]
Gray, Floyd - *Montaigne et les livres*
 Ren Q - v68 - i1 - Spring 2015 - p378-380 [501+]

Gray, John - *The Soul of the Marionette: A Short Inquiry into Human Freedom*
    BL - v111 - i4 - March 15 2015 - p28(1) [51-500]
    KR - Feb 1 2015 - pNA [501+]
    LJ - v140 - i3 - Feb 15 2015 - p105(1) [51-500]
    NS - v144 - i5260 - May 1 2015 - p42(3) [501+]
    NY - v91 - i27 - Sept 14 2015 - p91 [51-500]
    NYRB - v62 - i17 - Nov 5 2015 - p55(4) [501+]
    PW - v262 - i6 - Feb 9 2015 - p53(2) [501+]
    Soc - v52 - i4 - August 2015 - p383(1) [501+]
    Spec - v327 - i9732 - March 7 2015 - p46(2) [501+]
    TLS - i5861 - July 31 2015 - p28(1) [501+]
Gray, Jonathan W. - *Civil Rights in the White Literary Imagination: Innocence by Association*
    AL - v87 - i2 - June 2015 - p400-402 [501+]
Gray, Keith - *The Last Soldier*
  c Sch Lib - v63 - i4 - Winter 2015 - p246(1) [51-500]
Gray, Kes - *Frog on a Log? (Illus. by Field, Jim)*
  c BL - v112 - i4 - Oct 15 2015 - p51(2) [51-500]
    KR - July 15 2015 - pNA [51-500]
  c SLJ - v61 - i9 - Sept 2015 - p121(1) [51-500]
How Many Legs? (Illus. by Field, Jim)
  c Sch Lib - v63 - i2 - Summer 2015 - p91(2) [51-500]
Gray, LaGuana - *We Just Keep Running the Line: Black Southern Women and the Poultry Processing Industry*
    JAH - v102 - i2 - Sept 2015 - p601-602 [501+]
    JSH - v81 - i4 - Nov 2015 - p1033(2) [501+]
Gray, Leon - *Amazing Animal Communications*
  c Sch Lib - v63 - i4 - Winter 2015 - p238(1) [51-500]
Deserts
  c BL - v112 - i1 - Sept 1 2015 - p96(1) [51-500]
Oceans
  c BL - v112 - i1 - Sept 1 2015 - p96(1) [51-500]
Polar Lands
  c BL - v112 - i1 - Sept 1 2015 - p96(1) [51-500]
Tropical Rain Forests
  c BL - v112 - i1 - Sept 1 2015 - p96(1) [51-500]
Gray, Lila Ellen - *Fado Resounding: Affective Politics and Urban Life*
    JRAI - v21 - i2 - June 2015 - p488(2) [501+]
    Notes - v71 - i4 - June 2015 - p719(3) [501+]
Gray, Mila - *Come Back to Me*
  y BL - v112 - i5 - Nov 1 2015 - p54(1) [51-500]
  y KR - Oct 1 2015 - pNA [51-500]
Gray, Nick - *Escape from Tibet: A True Story*
  y HB Guide - v26 - i2 - Fall 2015 - p209(1) [51-500]
  y Res Links - v20 - i3 - Feb 2015 - p39(1) [501+]
  y Sch Lib - v63 - i1 - Spring 2015 - p60(1) [51-500]
Gray, Nigel - *Aunty Edna of Duck Creek Pond (Illus. by Allen, Lisa)*
  c Magpies - v30 - i4 - Sept 2015 - pS5(1) [501+]
Gray, Rita - *Flowers Are Calling (Illus. by Pak, Kenard)*
  c CH Bwatch - April 2015 - pNA [51-500]
  c HB Guide - v26 - i2 - Fall 2015 - p170(1) [51-500]
  c KR - Jan 15 2015 - pNA [51-500]
  c PW - v262 - i5 - Feb 2 2015 - p58(1) [501+]
Have You Heard the Nesting Bird? (Illus. by Pak, Kenard)
  c Teach Lib - v42 - i3 - Feb 2015 - p52(1) [51-500]
Gray, Shelley - *Whispers in the Reading Room*
    KR - Sept 15 2015 - pNA [51-500]
Gray, Susan E. - *Contingent Maps: Rethinking Western Women's History and the North American West*
    JAH - v102 - i2 - Sept 2015 - p590-590 [501+]
Gray, Susan H. - *Animals Helping to Detect Diseases*
  c BL - v111 - i15 - April 1 2015 - p59(1) [51-500]
Discover Jellyfish
  c BL - v112 - i3 - Oct 1 2015 - p66(1) [51-500]
Gray, Theodore - *Molecules: The Elements and Architecture of Everything*
    Am Sci - v103 - i1 - Jan-Feb 2015 - p70(2) [501+]
Gray, Virginia Butler - *My Magic Glasses*
  c CH Bwatch - May 2015 - pNA [501+]
Gray-Wilburn, Renee - *Floods: Be Aware and Prepare*
  c HB Guide - v26 - i1 - Spring 2015 - p151(1) [51-500]
Gray, William - *Little Sister Death*
    NYTBR - Nov 1 2015 - p22(L) [501+]
Graybill, Andrew R. - *The Red and the White: A Family Saga of the American West*
    PHR - v84 - i3 - August 2015 - p385(2) [501+]
Graydon, Shari - *In Your Face: The Culture of Beauty and You (Illus. by Klassen, Karen)*
  y Res Links - v20 - i3 - Feb 2015 - p39(1) [501+]
Graykin, Justine - *Awake Chimera*
    Analog - v135 - i12 - Dec 2015 - p104(2) [501+]
Grayling, A.C - *The Age of Genius*
    KR - Dec 1 2015 - pNA [501+]

Grayling, A.C. - *The Challenge of Things: Thinking through Troubled Times*
    BL - v112 - i1 - Sept 1 2015 - p16(1) [51-500]
    KR - Oct 1 2015 - pNA [501+]
    PW - v262 - i20 - May 18 2015 - p73(1) [51-500]
    LJ - v140 - i13 - August 1 2015 - p99(1) [51-500]
Grayson, Patti - *Ghost Most Foul*
  c BL - v111 - i18 - May 15 2015 - p65(1) [51-500]
  y Res Links - v21 - i1 - Oct 2015 - p35(1) [501+]
  y VOYA - v38 - i2 - June 2015 - p76(1) [51-500]
Grayson, Robert - *The US Air Force*
  y HB Guide - v26 - i1 - Spring 2015 - p138(2) [51-500]
Grazer, Brian - *A Curious Mind: The Secret to a Bigger Life (Read by Butz, Norbert Leo). Audiobook Review*
    LJ - v140 - i14 - Sept 1 2015 - p69(1) [51-500]
A Curious Mind: The Secret to a Bigger Life
    KR - Feb 1 2015 - pNA [501+]
    LJ - v140 - i3 - Feb 15 2015 - p109(2) [51-500]
    PW - v262 - i7 - Feb 16 2015 - p169(2) [51-500]
Grazian, David - *American Zoo: A Sociological Safari*
    LJ - v140 - i14 - Sept 1 2015 - p125(2) [51-500]
    Nature - v526 - i7575 - Oct 29 2015 - p639(1) [51-500]
Graziani, E. - *War in My Town*
  y Res Links - v20 - i4 - April 2015 - p34(1) [51-500]
Graziosi, Andrea - *After the Holodomor: The Enduring Impact of the Great Famine on Ukraine*
    Slav R - v74 - i2 - Summer 2015 - p379-381 [501+]
Greaney, Mark - *Back Blast*
    PW - v262 - i50 - Dec 7 2015 - p67(1) [51-500]
Full Force and Effect (Read by Brick, Scott). Audiobook Review
    Bwatch - Feb 2015 - pNA [51-500]
Full Force and Effect
    KR - Jan 15 2015 - pNA [51-500]
Great American Railroad Stories
    Bwatch - Jan 2015 - pNA [51-500]
Great Britain: Parliament: House of Commons - *Trade Union Bill*
    Lon R Bks - v37 - i20 - Oct 22 2015 - p25(4) [501+]
The Great Reformer: Francis and the Making of a Radical Pope
    NYRB - v62 - i3 - Feb 19 2015 - p11(3) [501+]
The Great War: Stories Inspired by Items from the First World War. Audiobook Review
  c SLJ - v61 - i7 - July 2015 - p46(2) [51-500]
The Greatest Books You'll Never Read
    NYTBR - July 26 2015 - p4(L) [501+]
Greathead, Helen - *My T-Shirt and Other Clothes: Well Made, Fair Trade*
    Sch Lib - v63 - i3 - Autumn 2015 - p187(1) [51-500]
Greathouse, Mark L. - *Dancing for Fun*
    KR - March 1 2015 - pNA [501+]
Greaves, C. Joseph - *Tom and Lucky (and George and Cokey Flo).*
    KR - Sept 1 2015 - pNA [501+]
Tom and Lucky and George and Cokey Flo
    LJ - v140 - i16 - Oct 1 2015 - p69(1) [51-500]
    PW - v262 - i38 - Sept 21 2015 - p47(2) [51-500]
Greci, Paul - *Surviving Bear Island*
  c KR - Jan 15 2015 - pNA [51-500]
Grecian, Alex - *The Harvest Man: a Novel of Scotland Yard's Murder Squad*
    BL - v111 - i15 - April 1 2015 - p29(1) [51-500]
    LJ - v140 - i6 - April 1 2015 - p78(2) [51-500]
    PW - v262 - i10 - March 9 2015 - p53(1) [51-500]
The Road to the Winter Palace
    LJ - v140 - i15 - Sept 15 2015 - p60(3) [51-500]
The Road to the Winter Palace (Illus. by Rossmo, Riley)
    BL - v112 - i2 - Sept 15 2015 - p51(1) [51-500]
Green, Abigail - *Religious Internationals in the Modern World: Globalization and Faith Communities Since 1750*
    J Ch St - v57 - i1 - Wntr 2015 - p168-170 [501+]
Green, Adam Isaiah - *Sexual Fields: Towards a Sociology of Collective Social Life*
    AJS - v120 - i4 - Jan 2015 - p1272(3) [501+]
Green, Allison - *The Ghosts Who Travel with Me: A Literary Pilgrimage Through Brautigan's America*
    LJ - v140 - i11 - June 15 2015 - p104(1) [51-500]
Green, B. - *Father Ghost*
    KR - Nov 1 2015 - pNA [51-500]
Green, D.L. - *Zeke Meeks vs. the Annoying Princess Sing-Along (Illus. by Alves, Josh)*
  c HB Guide - v26 - i1 - Spring 2015 - p79(1) [51-500]

Zeke Meeks vs. the Crummy Class Play (Illus. by Alves, Josh)
  c HB Guide - v26 - i1 - Spring 2015 - p79(1) [51-500]
Green, Dan - *Basher History: States and Capitals: United We Stand!*
  c HB Guide - v26 - i1 - Spring 2015 - p203(1) [51-500]
Climate Change (Illus. by Basher, Simon)
  y BL - v111 - i17 - May 1 2015 - p82(1) [51-500]
  y CH Bwatch - Jan 2015 - pNA [51-500]
Green, Daniel R. - *Fallujah Redux: The Anbar Awakening and the Struggle with Al-Qaeda*
    Mar Crp G - v99 - i2 - Feb 2015 - p93(2) [501+]
    Parameters - v45 - i2 - Summer 2015 - p140(2) [501+]
Green, David - *The Hundred Years War: A People's History*
    HT - v65 - i6 - June 2015 - p58(1) [501+]
    Med R - August 2015 - pNA [501+]
Green, Dawn - *When Kacey Left*
  y KR - July 15 2015 - pNA [51-500]
  y Res Links - v20 - i5 - June 2015 - p25(1) [51-500]
  y SLJ - v61 - i8 - August 2015 - p103(2) [51-500]
  y VOYA - v38 - i3 - August 2015 - p61(2) [501+]
Green, Donovan - *No Excuses Fitness: The 30-Day Plan to Tone Your Body and Supercharge Your Health*
    PW - v262 - i9 - March 2 2015 - p79(1) [51-500]
Green, Elizabeth - *Building a Better Teacher: How Teaching Works (and How to Teach it to Everyone).*
    JE - v195 - i2 - Spring 2015 - p49-53 [501+]
    NYTBR - Oct 25 2015 - p32(L) [501+]
Green, Fiona - *Writing for the "New Yorker": Critical Essays on an American Periodical*
    TLS - i5855 - June 19 2015 - p26(1) [501+]
Green, Gene L. - *Jesus without Borders: Christology in the Majority World*
    Theol St - v76 - i4 - Dec 2015 - p890(2) [501+]
Green, Georgina - *The Majesty of the People: Popular Sovereignty and the Role of the Writer in the 1790s*
    RES - v66 - i275 - June 2015 - p587-589 [501+]
Green, James - *The Devil Is Here in These Hills: West Virginia's Coal Miners and Their Battle for Freedom*
    BL - v111 - i1 - Feb 1 2015 - p5(1) [51-500]
    NYT - Jan 30 2015 - pC27(L) [501+]
Green, Jane - *Saving Grace (Read by Green, Jane). Audiobook Review*
    BL - v111 - i14 - March 15 2015 - p84(1) [51-500]
Summer Secrets
    BL - v111 - i16 - April 15 2015 - p27(1) [51-500]
    KR - April 15 2015 - pNA [51-500]
    LJ - v140 - i8 - May 1 2015 - p62(1) [51-500]
Green, Jen - *Mapping a Village*
  c Sch Lib - v63 - i3 - Autumn 2015 - p155(1) [51-500]
Oceans in 30 Seconds (Illus. by Robins, Wesley)
  c Sch Lib - v63 - i3 - Autumn 2015 - p174(1) [51-500]
    Magpies - v30 - i2 - May 2015 - p24(1) [501+]
The Planets and the Solar System (Read by Sillers, Ruth). Audiobook Review
  c BL - v111 - i14 - March 15 2015 - p88(1) [51-500]
Green, Joel B. - *The World of the New Testament: Cultural, Social, and Historical Contexts*
    Intpr - v69 - i4 - Oct 2015 - p479(3) [501+]
Green, John - *The Fault in Our Stars*
  y BL - v111 - i9-10 - Jan 1 2015 - p66(1) [501+]
Indy Writes Books: A Book Lovers Anthology
    SPBW - August 2015 - pNA [51-500]
Green, Jonathan - *The Strange and Terrible Visions of Wilhelm Friess: The Paths of Prophecy in Reformation Europe*
    Ren Q - v68 - i3 - Fall 2015 - p1047-1048 [501+]
Green, Jonathon - *Language! 500 Years of the Vulgar Tongue*
    TLS - i5852 - May 29 2015 - p23(1) [501+]
Odd Job Man: Some Confessions of a Slang Lexicographer
    TLS - i5852 - May 29 2015 - p23(1) [501+]
Green, K.C. - *Graveyard Quest*
  y PW - v262 - i50 - Dec 7 2015 - p88(1) [51-500]
Green, Karen - *Bough Down*
    Wom R Bks - v32 - i1 - Jan-Feb 2015 - p25(2) [501+]
Green, Katie May - *Seen and Not Heard (Illus. by Green, Katie May)*
  c KR - August 1 2015 - pNA [51-500]
  c Sch Lib - v63 - i1 - Spring 2015 - p27(1) [51-500]
  c SLJ - v61 - i9 - Sept 2015 - p121(1) [51-500]
Green, Kristen - *Something Must Be Done about Prince Edward County: A Family, a Virginia Town, a Civil*

Rights Battle
    CSM - June 1 2015 - pNA [501+]
    Ent W - i1369 - June 26 2015 - p64(1) [501+]
    S Liv - v50 - i6 - June 2015 - pMW2(1) [501+]
    BL - v111 - i16 - April 15 2015 - p6(1) [51-500]
    KR - April 1 2015 - pNA [501+]
    LJ - v140 - i7 - April 15 2015 - p101(1) [51-500]
    NYT - July 28 2015 - pC1(L) [501+]
    NYTBR - July 5 2015 - p14(L) [501+]
    PW - v262 - i11 - March 16 2015 - p73(2) [51-500]

Green, Laurie B. - *Precarious Prescriptions: Contested Histories of Race and Health in North America*
    JAH - v102 - i1 - June 2015 - p217-218 [501+]
    WHQ - v46 - i3 - Autumn 2015 - p378-379 [501+]
    PHR - v84 - i4 - Nov 2015 - p557(558) [501+]
    SHQ - v118 - i4 - April 2015 - p446-447 [501+]

Green, Lisa - *On Your Case: A Comprehensive, Compassionate (and Only Slightly Bossy) Legal Guide for Every Stage of a Woman's Life*
    LJ - v140 - i2 - Feb 1 2015 - p96(1) [51-500]

Green, Louisa Oakley - *Sightseeing in the Undiscovered Country*
    KR - Dec 15 2015 - pNA [501+]

Green, Matthew - *Aftershock: The Untold Story of Surviving Peace*
    Spec - v329 - i9760 - Sept 19 2015 - p52(1) [501+]

Green, Michelle - *Jebel Marra*
    TLS - i5854 - June 12 2015 - p20(1) [501+]

Green, Nancy L. - *The Other Americans in Paris: Businessmen, Countesses, Wayward Youth, 1880-1941*
    AHR - v120 - i3 - June 2015 - p976-977 [501+]
    JAH - v102 - i1 - June 2015 - p273-273 [501+]

Green, Nile - *Writing Travel in Central Asian History*
    AHR - v120 - i4 - Oct 2015 - p1458-1459 [501+]

Green, Peter - *The Iliad: A New Translation*
    Lon R Bks - v37 - i12 - June 18 2015 - p5(3) [501+]
    Spec - v328 - i9754 - August 8 2015 - p32(1) [501+]
    TLS - i5854 - June 12 2015 - p10(1) [501+]

Green, Philip - *Taking Sides: A Memoir in Stories*
    Nation - v301 - i21-22 - Nov 23 2015 - p37(1) [501+]

Green, Poppy - *The Emerald Berries (Illus. by Bell, Jennifer A.)*
    c HB Guide - v26 - i2 - Fall 2015 - p66(1) [51-500]
    c SLJ - v61 - i5 - May 2015 - p98(1) [51-500]
A New Friend (Illus. by Bell, Jennifer A.)
    c HB Guide - v26 - i2 - Fall 2015 - p66(1) [51-500]

Green, R.M. - *Stone Blood*
    KR - Jan 15 2015 - pNA [51-500]

Green, Robert - *Cause and Effect: The French Revolution*
    y BL - v112 - i3 - Oct 1 2015 - p40(1) [51-500]

Green, Rod - *Emergency Vehicles (Illus. by Biesty, Stephen)*
    c BL - v112 - i1 - Sept 1 2015 - p94(1) [51-500]
    c KR - Dec 1 2015 - pNA [51-500]
    c PW - v262 - i21 - May 25 2015 - p58(1) [51-500]
Giant Vehicles (Illus. by Biesty, Stephen)
    c HB Guide - v26 - i1 - Spring 2015 - p173(1) [51-500]

Green, Ruth - *Stanley's Plan: The Birthday Surprise (Illus. by Green, Ruth)*
    c Sch Lib - v63 - i2 - Summer 2015 - p92(1) [51-500]
    c SLJ - v61 - i11 - Nov 2015 - p81(1) [51-500]

Green, S.E. - *Killer Within*
    c BL - v111 - i17 - May 1 2015 - p51(1) [51-500]
    c HB Guide - v26 - i2 - Fall 2015 - p121(1) [51-500]
    y KR - Feb 15 2015 - pNA [501+]

Green, Sally - *Half Bad (Read by Prekopp, Carl). Audiobook Review*
    c BL - v111 - i14 - March 15 2015 - p24(2) [51-500]
    y HB - v91 - i2 - March-April 2015 - p129(2) [51-500]
Half Lost
    y KR - Jan 1 2016 - pNA [51-500]
    y PW - v262 - i51 - Dec 14 2015 - p86(1) [51-500]
Half Wild
    y KR - Jan 15 2015 - pNA [51-500]
    y BL - v111 - i9-10 - Jan 1 2015 - p64(1) [51-500]
    y BL - v111 - i11 - Feb 1 2015 - p47(2) [51-500]
    y HB Guide - v26 - i2 - Fall 2015 - p121(1) [51-500]
    y PW - v262 - i2 - Jan 12 2015 - p60(1) [51-500]
    y PW - v262 - i49 - Dec 2 2015 - p102(1) [51-500]
    y SLJ - v61 - i2 - Feb 2015 - p101(1) [51-500]
    y VOYA - v38 - i1 - April 2015 - p78(2) [51-500]

Green, Sara - *Apple*
    c SLJ - v61 - i9 - Sept 2015 - p176(1) [51-500]

Green, Simon R. - *The Dark Side of the Road*
    BL - v111 - i16 - April 15 2015 - p28(1) [51-500]
    PW - v262 - i10 - March 9 2015 - p54(1) [51-500]
From a Drood to a Kill
    BL - v111 - i18 - May 15 2015 - p35(1) [51-500]
Ghost Finders: Ghost of a Chance. Audiobook Review
    LJ - v140 - i8 - May 1 2015 - p40(2) [51-500]

Green, Stanley - *American Musicals: The Complete Books and Lyrics of 16 Broadway Classics, 1927-1969*
    Am Theat - v32 - i2 - Feb 2015 - p58(2) [501+]
Broadway Musicals Show by Show, 8th ed.
    Am Theat - v32 - i2 - Feb 2015 - p58(2) [501+]

Green, Stephen - *Reluctant Meister: How Germany's Past in Shaping Its European Future*
    TLS - i5835 - Jan 30 2015 - p27(1) [501+]

Green, Steven K. - *Inventing a Christian America: The Myth of the Religious Founding*
    JAAR - v83 - i4 - Dec 2015 - p1183-1186 [501+]
    LJ - v140 - i9 - May 15 2015 - p86(2) [51-500]

Green, Surya - *Once Upon a Yugoslavia: When the American Way Met Tito's Third Way*
    BL - v112 - i6 - Nov 15 2015 - p10(1) [51-500]

Green, Susan - *Verity Sparks and the Scarlet Hand*
    c Magpies - v30 - i3 - July 2015 - p34(2) [51-500]

Green, Tim - *First Team*
    c HB Guide - v26 - i1 - Spring 2015 - p79(1) [51-500]
Home Run
    c KR - Dec 15 2015 - pNA [51-500]
Kid Owner
    c BL - v112 - i1 - Sept 1 2015 - p100(2) [51-500]
    c KR - July 1 2015 - pNA [51-500]
    c SLJ - v61 - i8 - August 2015 - p86(1) [51-500]
Lost Boy
    c BL - v111 - i12 - Feb 15 2015 - p86(1) [51-500]
    c HB Guide - v26 - i2 - Fall 2015 - p84(1) [51-500]
    c KR - Jan 1 2015 - pNA [51-500]

Green, Todd H. - *The Fear of Islam*
    RVBW - August 2015 - pNA [501+]

Green, William D. - *Degrees of Freedom: The Origins of Civil Rights in Minnesota, 1865-1912*
    HNet - Sept 2015 - pNA(NA) [501+]

Greenan, Russell H. - *It Happened in Boston? (Read by Fass, Robert). Audiobook Review*
    PW - v262 - i8 - Feb 23 2015 - p71(1) [51-500]

Greenberg, David - *Republic of Spin: An Inside History of the American Presidency*
    KR - Oct 15 2015 - pNA [501+]
    LJ - v140 - i19 - Nov 15 2015 - p94(2) [51-500]
    PW - v262 - i47 - Nov 23 2015 - p60(1) [51-500]

Greenberg, Gary - *The Secrets of Sand: A Journey into the Amazing Microscopic World of Sand*
    Nature - v527 - i7579 - Nov 26 2015 - p445(1) [501+]

Greenberg, Jessica - *After the Revolution: Youth, Democracy, and the Politics of Disappointment in Serbia*
    HNet - May 2015 - pNA [501+]
    JRAI - v21 - i3 - Sept 2015 - p688(2) [501+]
    Slav R - v74 - i3 - Fall 2015 - p597-600 [501+]

Greenberg, Joel - *A Feathered River across the Sky: The Passenger Pigeon's Flight to Extinction*
    IndRev - v19 - i3 - Wntr 2015 - p443(4) [501+]

Greenberg, Karin-Lin - *Faulty Predictions*
    Ant R - v73 - i1 - Wntr 2015 - p186(1) [501+]

Greenberg, Keith Elliot - *Too Fast to Live, Too Young to Die: James Dean's Final Hours*
    BL - v112 - i2 - Sept 15 2015 - p16(1) [51-500]
    RVBW - Nov 2015 - pNA [501+]

Greenberg, Mike - *My Father's Wives*
    BL - v111 - i9-10 - Jan 1 2015 - p38(1) [51-500]

Greenberg, Nicki - *The Naughtiest Reindeer at the Zoo (Illus. by Greenberg, Nicki)*
    c Magpies - v30 - i5 - Nov 2015 - p29(1) [501+]
Teddy Took the Train (Illus. by Greenberg, Nicki)
    c Magpies - v30 - i3 - July 2015 - p28(1) [51-500]

Greenberg, Paul - *American Catch: The Fight for Our Local Seafood*
    NYTBR - Nov 1 2015 - p28(L) [501+]

Greenberg, Stanley B. - *America Ascendant: A Revolutionary Nation's Path to Addressing Its Deepest Problems and Leading the 21st Century*
    KR - Sept 1 2015 - pNA [501+]
    LJ - v140 - i17 - Oct 15 2015 - p104(1) [51-500]

Greenberg, Uri - *The Weimar Century*
    HT - v65 - i10 - Oct 2015 - p56(2) [501+]

Greenblatt, Rachel L. - *To Tell Their Children: Jewish Communal Memory in Early Modern Prague*
    Slav R - v74 - i1 - Spring 2015 - p161-162 [501+]

Greene, Ann Norton - *Horses at Work: Harnessing Power in Industrial America*
    T&C - v56 - i1 - Jan 2015 - p252-260 [501+]

Greene, David - *Midnight in Siberia: A Train Journey into the Heart of Russia (Read by Greene, David). Audiobook Review*
    LJ - v140 - i3 - Feb 15 2015 - p59(2) [51-500]
Midnight in Siberia: A Train Journey into the Heart of Russia
    TLS - i5850 - May 15 2015 - p26(1) [501+]

Greene, Graham - *Dr Fischer of Geneva*
    TimHES - i2223 - Oct 1 2015 - p49(1) [501+]
The Quiet American
    CSM - April 30 2015 - pNA [51-500]

Greene, Jack P. - *Creating the British Atlantic: Essays on Transportation, Adaptation, and Continuity*
    Historian - v77 - i2 - Summer 2015 - p389(2) [501+]
Evaluating Empire and Confronting Colonialism in Eighteenth-Century Britain
    HNet - Feb 2015 - pNA [501+]

Greene, Jerome A. - *American Carnage: Wounded Knee, 1890*
    Am Ind CRJ - v39 - i2 - Spring 2015 - p129-131 [501+]
    J Mil H - v79 - i1 - Jan 2015 - p221-222 [501+]
    JAH - v101 - i4 - March 2015 - p1301-1302 [501+]
    Roundup M - v22 - i5 - June 2015 - p36(1) [501+]
    Roundup M - v22 - i6 - August 2015 - p37(1) [501+]

Greene, Joshua M. - *The Littlest Giant: The Story of Vamana (Illus. by Moore, Emma V.)*
    c HB Guide - v26 - i1 - Spring 2015 - p144(1) [51-500]

Greene, Karen - *Art Deco Mailboxes: An Illustrated Design History*
    Bwatch - March 2015 - pNA [501+]

Greene, Roland - *Five Words: Critical Semantics in the Age of Shakespeare and Cervantes*
    MP - v112 - i3 - Feb 2015 - pE234(E237) [501+]

Greene, Ronnie - *Shots on the Bridge: Police Violence and Cover-Up in the Wake of Katrina*
    CJR - v54 - i3 - Sept-Oct 2015 - p26(4) [501+]
    KR - June 15 2015 - pNA [501+]
    LJ - v140 - i12 - July 1 2015 - p100(2) [51-500]
    NYTBR - August 9 2015 - p34(L) [501+]

Greene, Samuel A. - *Moscow in Movement: Power and Opposition in Putin's Russia*
    For Aff - v94 - i1 - Jan-Feb 2015 - pNA [51-500]

Greene, Stephanie - *Princess Posey and the First Grade Boys (Read by Nielson, Stina). Audiobook Review*
    c SLJ - v61 - i3 - March 2015 - p76(1) [51-500]

Greene, Vanessa - *The Seafront Tearoom*
    LJ - v140 - i20 - Dec 1 2015 - p90(1) [51-500]

Greenfield, Karl Taro - *The Subprimes*
    BL - v111 - i18 - May 15 2015 - p25(1) [51-500]
    KR - March 1 2015 - pNA [501+]
    NYTBR - May 17 2015 - p25(L) [501+]
    PW - v262 - i11 - March 16 2015 - p59(1) [51-500]

Greenfield, Amy Butler - *Chantress Fury*
    y BL - v111 - i18 - May 15 2015 - p66(1) [51-500]
    y KR - March 15 2015 - pNA [51-500]
    y SLJ - v61 - i8 - August 2015 - p114(1) [51-500]
    y VOYA - v38 - i3 - August 2015 - p77(1) [51-500]

Greenfield, Edward A. - *Antibodies: A Laboratory Manual*
    QRB - v90 - i2 - June 2015 - p228(1) [51-500]

Greenfield, Karl Taro - *The Subprimes*
    HM - v330 - i1981 - June 2015 - p82(6) [501+]

Greenfield, Martin - *Measure of a Man: From Auschwitz Survivor to Presidents' Tailor*
    Bwatch - Jan 2015 - pNA [501+]

Greenfield, Richard P.H. - *Niketas Stethatos: The Life of Saint Symeon the New Theologian*
    Med R - March 2015 - pNA(NA) [501+]

Greenfield, Rob - *Dude Making a Difference*
    KR - Oct 15 2015 - pNA [501+]

Greengard, Samuel - *The Internet of Things*
    TimHES - i2199 - April 16 2015 - p58-59 [501+]

Greengrass, Jessie - *An Account of the Decline of the Great Auk, According to One Who Saw It*
    TLS - i5873 - Oct 23 2015 - p20(1) [501+]

Greenhalgh, Michael - *The Military and Colonial Destruction of the Roman Landscape of North Africa, 1830-1900*
    J Mil H - v79 - i1 - Jan 2015 - p207-208 [501+]

Greenidge, Kaitlyn - *We Love You, Charlie Freeman*
    KR - Jan 1 2016 - pNA [51-500]

Greenland, Seth - *I Regret Everything*
    NYT - Feb 26 2015 - pC6(L) [501+]

Greenlaw, Lavinia - *A Double Sorrow: A Version of Troilus and Criseyde*
    BL - v112 - i2 - Sept 15 2015 - p17(2) [51-500]

Greenlaw, M. Jean - *Flood*
  c HB Guide - v26 - i1 - Spring 2015 - p151(1) [51-500]
  Inundacion
  c SLJ - v61 - i5 - May 2015 - p132(1) [51-500]

Greenlee, David - *Longing for Community: Church, Ummah, or Somewhere in Between?*
  IBMR - v39 - i1 - Jan 2015 - p39(2) [501+]

Greenlee, Jill S. - *The Political Consequences of Motherhood*
  JAH - v101 - i4 - March 2015 - p1247-1248 [501+]

Greenough, Sarah - *The Memory of Time: Contemporary Photographs at the National Gallery of Art*
  LJ - v140 - i15 - Sept 15 2015 - p81(3) [501+]

Greensdale, Jesse - *First Week Blues (Illus. by Evans, Anna)*
  Magpies - v30 - i3 - July 2015 - pS4(1) [501+]

Greenspan, Dorie - *Baking Chez Moi: Recipes From My Paris Home to Your Home Anywhere*
  Bwatch - Jan 2015 - pNA [51-500]
  Ent W - i1346 - Jan 16 2015 - p67(1) [501+]

Greenspan, Elizabeth - *Battle for Ground Zero: Inside the Political Struggle to Rebuild the World Trade Center*
  JAH - v101 - i4 - March 2015 - p1354-1355 [501+]

Greenspan, Ezra - *William Wells Brown: An African American Life*
  Sew R - v123 - i2 - Spring 2015 - pXXV-XXVII [501+]

Greenstein, Shane - *How the Internet Became Commercial*
  KR - Sept 15 2015 - pNA [501+]

Greenwald, Glenn - *No Place to Hide: Edward Snowden, the NSA, and the U.S. Surveillance State*
  Barron's - v95 - i1 - Jan 5 2015 - p17(2) [501+]
  IndRev - v19 - i4 - Spring 2015 - p605(5) [501+]
  NYTBR - May 24 2015 - p28(L) [501+]

Greenwald, Helen M. - *The Oxford Handbook of Opera*
  MT - v156 - i1932 - Autumn 2015 - p105-107 [501+]

Greenwald, Lisa - *Dog Beach Unleashed*
  y HB Guide - v26 - i2 - Fall 2015 - p84(1) [51-500]
  y SLJ - v61 - i6 - June 2015 - p108(1) [51-500]
  Pink and Green Is the New Black
  y HB Guide - v26 - i1 - Spring 2015 - p108(1) [51-500]

Greenwald, Tommy - *Charlie Joe Jackson's Guide to Making Money (Illus. by Coovert, J.P.)*
  c HB Guide - v26 - i1 - Spring 2015 - p79(1) [51-500]
  Charlie Joe Jackson's Guide to Planet Girl (Read by Andrews, MacLeod). Audiobook Review
  c SLJ - v61 - i12 - Dec 2015 - p76(1) [51-500]
  Charlie Joe Jackson's Guide to Planet Girl (Illus. by Coovert, J.P.)
  c SLJ - v61 - i7 - July 2015 - p78(1) [51-500]
  Katie Friedman Gives Up Texting! (Illus. by Coovert, J.P.)
  y CCB-B - v68 - i7 - March 2015 - p354(1) [51-500]
  Katie Friedman Gives Up Texting! (and Lives to Tell about It). (Illus. by Coovert, J.P.)
  y HB Guide - v26 - i2 - Fall 2015 - p84(1) [51-500]
  My Dog Is Better Than Your Dog (Illus. by Stower, Adam)
  c KR - July 1 2015 - pNA [51-500]
  Pete Milano's Guide to Being a Movie Star
  c KR - Nov 1 2015 - pNA [51-500]

Greenwell, Garth - *What Belongs to You*
  BL - v111 - i22 - August 1 2015 - p25(1) [51-500]
  KR - Oct 15 2015 - pNA [51-500]

Greenwell, Jessica - *1,000 Animals (Illus. by Dyson, Nikki)*
  c CH Bwatch - June 2015 - pNA [51-500]

Greenwood, Ed - *The Iron Assassin*
  Analog - v135 - i7-8 - July-August 2015 - p186(1) [501+]
  PW - v262 - i14 - April 6 2015 - p44(1) [51-500]
  BL - v111 - i18 - May 15 2015 - p36(1) [51-500]
  LJ - v140 - i9 - May 15 2015 - p57(4) [501+]

Greenwood, Emily - *The Beautiful One*
  KR - April 1 2015 - pNA [51-500]
  PW - v262 - i13 - March 30 2015 - p61(1) [51-500]

Greenwood, Jo - *Siren Song*
  KR - Feb 1 2015 - pNA [51-500]

Greenwood, Kerry - *Murder and Mendelssohn*
  RVBW - Jan 2015 - pNA [51-500]
  Unnatural Habits (Read by Daniel, Stephanie). Audiobook Review
  BL - v111 - i15 - April 1 2015 - p86(1) [501+]

Greenwood, Lee - *Proud to Be an American (Illus. by Sekulow, Amanda)*
  c CH Bwatch - July 2015 - pNA [51-500]

Greenwood, Mark - *The Mayflower (Illus. by Lessac, Frane)*
  c HB Guide - v26 - i1 - Spring 2015 - p203(1) [51-500]
  Midnight: A True Story of Loyalty in World War I (Illus. by Lessac, Frane)
  c CCB-B - v69 - i1 - Sept 2015 - p25(1) [51-500]
  c HB Guide - v26 - i2 - Fall 2015 - p217(1) [51-500]
  c SLJ - v61 - i5 - May 2015 - p132(1) [51-500]

Greenwood, T. - *Where I Lost Her*
  PW - v262 - i46 - Nov 16 2015 - p48(1) [51-500]

Greer, Christina M. - *Black Ethnics: Race, Immigration, and the Pursuit of the American Dream*
  Am St - v54 - i1 - Spring 2015 - p135-3 [501+]

Greer, Germaine - *Ten Bedtime Poems, vol. 2*
  NS - v144 - i5267 - June 19 2015 - p50(1) [51-500]

Greer, Neville - *Grumpmuffin across the Pond*
  KR - Jan 1 2016 - pNA [51-500]

Greer, Peter - *40/40 Vision: Clarifying Your Mission in Midlife*
  Ch Today - v59 - i10 - Dec 2015 - p70(1) [501+]
  PW - v262 - i37 - Sept 14 2015 - p61(1) [51-500]

Greetings from Frank L.L.C. - *From Frank: Desk Notes to Make Humans Smile*
  Bwatch - August 2015 - pNA [51-500]

Greg van Eekhout - *Dragon Coast*
  PW - v262 - i28 - July 13 2015 - p48(2) [51-500]

Gregario, I.W. - *None of the Above*
  c BL - v112 - i1 - Sept 1 2015 - p99(1) [501+]

Gregerson, Linda - *Prodigal: New and Selected Poems, 1976-2014*
  BL - v112 - i1 - Sept 1 2015 - p30(1) [51-500]
  NYTBR - Dec 27 2015 - p12(L) [501+]
  PW - v262 - i33 - August 17 2015 - p49(1) [51-500]

Gregg, Donald P. - *Pot Shards: Fragments of a Life Lived in CIA, the White House, and the Two Koreas*
  For Aff - v94 - i3 - May-June 2015 - pNA [51-500]

Gregg, Justin - *Are Dolphins Really Smart?*
  QRB - v90 - i1 - March 2015 - p106(2) [501+]

Gregg, Robert C. - *Shared Stories, Rival Tellings: Early Encounters of Jews, Christians, and Muslims*
  PW - v262 - i27 - July 6 2015 - p65(1) [51-500]
  CC - v132 - i17 - August 19 2015 - p36(2) [501+]

Gregg, Stacy - *The Girl Who Rode the Wind*
  c Magpies - v30 - i4 - Sept 2015 - pS7(1) [501+]
  The Princess and the Foal
  c HB Guide - v26 - i1 - Spring 2015 - p79(1) [51-500]

Greggs, Tom - *Theology against religion: Constructive Dialouges with Bonhoeffer and Barth*
  TT - v71 - i4 - Jan 2015 - p470-471 [501+]

Gregor, A. James - *Marxism and the Making of China: A Doctrinal History*
  AHR - v120 - i3 - June 2015 - p993-994 [501+]

Gregorio, I.W. - *None of the Above*
  y BL - v111 - i13 - March 1 2015 - p59(1) [51-500]
  y CCB-B - v68 - i9 - May 2015 - p448(1) [51-500]
  y HB Guide - v26 - i2 - Fall 2015 - p121(1) [51-500]
  y KR - Jan 15 2015 - pNA [51-500]
  c Nat Post - v17 - i147 - April 25 2015 - pWP4(1) [501+]
  y PW - v262 - i49 - Dec 2 2015 - p94(2) [51-500]
  y VOYA - v37 - i6 - Feb 2015 - p56(1) [51-500]

Gregorio, Michael - *Cry Wolf*
  BL - v111 - i13 - March 1 2015 - p22(1) [51-500]
  KR - Feb 1 2015 - pNA [51-500]
  PW - v262 - i5 - Feb 2 2015 - p38(1) [51-500]

Gregory, Brad - *The Unintended Reformation: How a Religious Revolution Secularized Society*
  Intpr - v69 - i1 - Jan 2015 - p97(4) [501+]

Gregory, Danny - *Art before Breakfast: A Zillion Ways to Be More Creative No Matter How Busy You Are*
  LJ - v140 - i7 - April 15 2015 - p88(1) [51-500]

Gregory, Daryl - *Harrison Squared*
  BL - v111 - i12 - Feb 15 2015 - p45(1) [51-500]
  KR - Jan 15 2015 - pNA [51-500]
  PW - v262 - i4 - Jan 26 2015 - p153(1) [51-500]
  VOYA - v38 - i1 - April 2015 - p79(1) [51-500]

Gregory, David - *How's Your Faith? An Unlikely Spiritual Journey*
  LJ - v140 - i15 - Sept 15 2015 - p80(1) [51-500]
  KR - July 1 2015 - pNA [51-500]

Gregory, Ian N. - *Toward Spatial Humanities: Historical GIS & Spatial History*
  JIH - v46 - i2 - Autumn 2015 - p266-267 [501+]

Gregory, Josh - *Abraham Lincoln: The 16th President*
  c HB Guide - v26 - i2 - Fall 2015 - p209(1) [51-500]
  Andrew Luck
  c HB Guide - v26 - i1 - Spring 2015 - p183(1) [51-500]
  Apps: From Concept to Consumer
  y BL - v111 - i14 - March 15 2015 - p63(1) [51-500]
  y VOYA - v38 - i5 - Dec 2015 - p78(2) [51-500]
  Blake Griffin
  c HB Guide - v26 - i1 - Spring 2015 - p183(2) [51-500]
  Brachiosaurus
  c BL - v112 - i2 - Sept 15 2015 - p59(1) [501+]
  Franklin D. Roosevelt: The 32nd President
  c BL - v111 - i19-20 - June 1 2015 - p84(1) [51-500]
  Hedgehogs
  c BL - v112 - i7 - Dec 1 2015 - p42(2) [51-500]
  Lebron James
  c HB Guide - v26 - i1 - Spring 2015 - p183(2) [51-500]
  Sloths
  c BL - v112 - i7 - Dec 1 2015 - p42(2) [51-500]

Gregory, Mollie - *Stuntwomen: The Untold Hollywood Story*
  LJ - v140 - i15 - Sept 15 2015 - p75(2) [51-500]
  NYTBR - Dec 6 2015 - p70(L) [501+]

Gregory, Philippa - *Fool's Gold*
  y HB Guide - v26 - i1 - Spring 2015 - p108(1) [51-500]
  The Taming of the Queen (Read by Amato, Bianca). Audiobook Review
  BL - v112 - i6 - Nov 15 2015 - p63(1) [51-500]
  The Taming of the Queen
  BL - v111 - i21 - July 1 2015 - p43(1) [51-500]
  KR - June 15 2015 - pNA [51-500]
  LJ - v140 - i12 - July 1 2015 - p77(1) [51-500]

Gregory, Robin - *The Improbable Wonders of Moojie Littleman*
  y KR - Nov 1 2015 - pNA [501+]

Gregson, J.M. - *Backhand Smash*
  KR - Jan 1 2016 - pNA [51-500]
  Skeleton Plot
  BL - v111 - i22 - August 1 2015 - p37(1) [51-500]
  PW - v262 - i29 - July 20 2015 - p170(2) [51-500]

Gregson, Sally - *The Plant Lover's Guide to Epidemiums*
  NYTBR - May 31 2015 - p36(L) [501+]

Grehan, Helena - *"We're People Who Do Shows": Back to Back Theatre: Performance, Politics, Visibility*
  TDR - v59 - i1 - Spring 2015 - p190(3) [501+]

Grehan, James - *Twilight of the Saints: Everyday Religion in Ottoman Syria and Palestine*
  HNet - March 2015 - pNA [501+]

Greif, Mark - *The Age of the Crisis of Man: Thought and Fiction in America, 1933-1973*
  Bks & Cult - v21 - i4 - July-August 2015 - p19(3) [501+]
  Comw - v142 - i11 - June 12 2015 - p27(3) [501+]
  Dis - v62 - i2 - Spring 2015 - p154(4) [501+]
  HM - v330 - i1981 - June 2015 - p88(6) [501+]
  Lon R Bks - v37 - i16 - August 27 2015 - p13(2) [501+]
  NYRB - v62 - i11 - June 25 2015 - p53(3) [501+]

Greig, Christopher J. - *Ontario Boys: Masculinity and the Idea of Boyhood in Postwar Ontario, 1945-1960*
  Can Hist R - v96 - i1 - March 2015 - p139(5) [501+]

Greig, Hannah - *The Beau Monde: Fashionable Society in Georgian London*
  HER - v130 - i542 - Feb 2015 - p210(2) [501+]

Greiner, Bettina - *Suppressed Terror: History and Perception of Soviet Special Camps in Germany*
  Ger Q - v88 - i3 - Summer 2015 - p410(3) [501+]
  Slav R - v74 - i3 - Fall 2015 - p659-660 [501+]

Greiner, Linda - *Sashi Adopts a Brother (Illus. by Spicer, Morgan)*
  c KR - July 15 2015 - pNA [51-500]
  c PW - v262 - i50 - Dec 7 2015 - p85(1) [51-500]

Greitens, Eric - *Resilience: Hard-Won Wisdom for Living a Better Life*
  KR - Jan 1 2015 - pNA [51-500]

Grell, Chantal - *La lune aux XVIIe et XVIIIe siecles*
  Isis - v106 - i1 - March 2015 - p183(2) [501+]

Gremillon, Helene - *The Case of Lisandra P.*
  BL - v112 - i5 - Nov 1 2015 - p30(1) [51-500]
  KR - Oct 15 2015 - pNA [51-500]
  PW - v262 - i46 - Nov 16 2015 - p57(1) [51-500]

Grenier, Robert L. - *88 Days to Kandahar: A CIA Diary*
  For Aff - v94 - i3 - May-June 2015 - pNA [501+]
  NYTBR - Feb 15 2015 - p18(L) [501+]
  Econ - v414 - i8927 - Feb 28 2015 - p76(US) [501+]

Grenzen der Pluralisierung? Zur Konflikthaftigkeit Religioser Identitatsbildung und Erinnerungskultur in Europa seit der Fruhen Neuzeit
    HNet - Jan 2015 - pNA [501+]

Grenzraume - Raumgrenzen: Landliche Lebenswelten aus Kulturwissenschaftlicher Sicht
    HNet - July 2015 - pNA [501+]

Greschat, Martin - *Der Erste Weltkrieg und die Christenheit: Ein Globaler Uberblick*
    HNet - Feb 2015 - pNA [501+]

Gresham, Charlene - *The Monster Under My Web (Illus. by Gresham, Charlene)*
    c CH Bwatch - April 2015 - pNA [51-500]

Greteman, Blaine - *The Poetics and Politics of Youth in Milton's England*
    RES - v66 - i276 - Sept 2015 - p782-784 [501+]

Grethlein, Jonas - *Experience and Teleology in Ancient Historiography: "Futures Past" from Herodotus to Augustine*
    AHR - v120 - i3 - June 2015 - p1089-1090 [501+]
    Class R - v65 - i2 - Oct 2015 - p343-345 [501+]

Grewal, Zareena - *Islam Is a Foreign Country: American Muslims and the Global Crisis of Authority*
    Am St - v54 - i1 - Spring 2015 - p161-162 [501+]
    IJMES - v47 - i3 - August 2015 - p643-646 [501+]

Grewing, Farouk - *The Door Ajar: False Closure in Greek and Roman Literature and Art*
    Class R - v65 - i1 - April 2015 - p105-107 [501+]

Grey, Amelia - *The Earl Claims a Bride*
    BL - v111 - i21 - July 1 2015 - p44(1) [51-500]
    PW - v262 - i22 - June 1 2015 - p47(1) [51-500]
Wedding Night with the Earl
    KR - Jan 1 2016 - pNA [51-500]

Grey, C.R. - *Flight of the King*
    c KR - August 1 2015 - pNA [51-500]
Legacy of the Claw
    y HB Guide - v26 - i2 - Fall 2015 - p84(1) [51-500]

Grey House Publishing - *Educators Resource Directory, 11th ed.*
    BL - v112 - i6 - Nov 15 2015 - p6(1) [51-500]

Grey, Iona - *Letters to the Lost*
    BL - v111 - i17 - May 1 2015 - p78(1) [51-500]
    LJ - v140 - i7 - April 15 2015 - p75(2) [51-500]

Grey, Jacob - *Ferals*
    y BL - v111 - i14 - March 15 2015 - p74(1) [51-500]
    y CCB-B - v68 - i10 - June 2015 - p491(2) [51-500]
    y HB Guide - v26 - i2 - Fall 2015 - p84(1) [51-500]
    y KR - Feb 1 2015 - pNA [51-500]
    y Sch Lib - v63 - i3 - Autumn 2015 - p166(1) [51-500]
    y SLJ - v61 - i3 - March 2015 - p135(1) [51-500]
    y VOYA - v38 - i1 - April 2015 - p79(1) [51-500]

Grey, Jeanette - *Seven Nights to Surrender*
    LJ - v140 - i16 - Oct 1 2015 - p62(2) [501+]

Grey, Melissa - *The Girl at Midnight (Read by Whelan, Julia). Audiobook Review*
    y BL - v111 - i22 - August 1 2015 - p80(1) [51-500]
    y SLJ - v61 - i7 - July 2015 - p49(2) [51-500]
The Girl at Midnight
    y BL - v111 - i14 - March 15 2015 - p65(1) [51-500]
    y CCB-B - v68 - i10 - June 2015 - p492(1) [51-500]
    y HB Guide - v26 - i2 - Fall 2015 - p121(1) [51-500]
    y KR - Jan 15 2015 - pNA [51-500]
    y Sch Lib - v63 - i2 - Summer 2015 - p117(1) [51-500]
    y Sch Lib - v63 - i3 - Autumn 2015 - p182(1) [51-500]
    y SLJ - v61 - i3 - March 2015 - p155(1) [51-500]
    y VOYA - v38 - i1 - April 2015 - p79(1) [51-500]

Grey, Mini - *Hermelin the Detective Mouse (Illus. by Grey, Mini)*
    c BL - v111 - i17 - May 1 2015 - p40(1) [51-500]
    c BL - v111 - i9-10 - Jan 1 2015 - p92(1) [501+]
    c HB Guide - v26 - i1 - Spring 2015 - p31(1) [51-500]
Space Dog (Illus. by Grey, Mini)
    c Magpies - v30 - i4 - Sept 2015 - p30(2) [501+]
    c Sch Lib - v63 - i3 - Autumn 2015 - p155(1) [51-500]
    c SLJ - v61 - i12 - Dec 2015 - p89(1) [51-500]

Grey, Stephen - *The New Spymasters: Inside Espionage from the Cold War to Global Terror*
    KR - June 1 2015 - pNA [51-500]
    Spec - v328 - i9745 - June 6 2015 - p47(1) [501+]

Grey, Zane - *Riders of Purple Sage (Read by Lackey, Michael). Audiobook Review*
    LJ - v140 - i5 - March 15 2015 - p71(1) [51-500]

Greygoose, David - *Brunt Boggart: A Tapestry of Tales*
    y Sch Lib - v63 - i2 - Summer 2015 - p117(1) [51-500]

Greyson, Maeve - *My Highland Bride*
    PW - v262 - i26 - June 29 2015 - p53(1) [51-500]

Greystone, Andrew Nikiforuk - *Slick Water: Fracking and One Insider's Stand against the World's Most Powerful Industry*
    Nature - v582 - i7582 - Dec 17 2015 - p331(1) [501+]

Gribbin, John - *Computing with Quantum Cats: From Colossus to Qubits*
    Phys Today - v68 - i1 - Jan 2015 - p46-47 [501+]

Gribble, Francis Henry - *The Love Affairs of Lord Byron*
    Clio - v44 - i2 - Spring 2015 - p217-237 [501+]

Gribble, J.L. - *Steel Victory*
    PW - v262 - i21 - May 25 2015 - p42(1) [51-500]

Gribble, Richard - *Navy Priest: The Life of Captain Jake Laboon, S.J.*
    AM - v213 - i17 - Nov 30 2015 - p35(3) [501+]

Grice, Elizabeth - *Norman Janes: Wood Engravings and the Man*
    TLS - i5858 - July 10 2015 - p9(1) [501+]

Grice, Gordon - *Collecting and Understanding the Wonders of the Natural World*
    c NYTBR - Dec 6 2015 - p32(L) [501+]

Grice, Scott - *Decks Complete: Expert Advice from Start to Finish*
    LJ - v140 - i14 - Sept 1 2015 - p104(2) [51-500]

Grieco, Viviana L. - *The Politics of Giving in the Viceroyalty of Rio de la Plata: Donors, Lenders, Subjects, and Citizens*
    AHR - v120 - i2 - April 2015 - p687-688 [501+]
    HAHR - v95 - i2 - May 2015 - p353-355 [501+]
The Politics of Giving in the Viceroyalty of the Rio de la Plata: Donors, Lenders, Subjects, and Citizens
    JIH - v45 - i4 - Spring 2015 - p598-600 [501+]

Griemert, Andre - *Judische Klagen Gegen Reichsadelige: Prozesse am Reichshofrat in den Herrschaftsjahren Rudolfs II. und Franz I. Stephans*
    HNet - July 2015 - pNA [501+]

Griep, Camielle - *Letters to Zell*
    y BL - v111 - i18 - May 15 2015 - p36(2) [51-500]

Griep, Camille - *Letters to Zell*
    PW - v262 - i11 - March 16 2015 - p68(1) [51-500]

Grierson, Tim - *Public Enemy: Inside the Terrordome*
    LJ - v140 - i8 - May 1 2015 - p76(1) [51-500]

Griesel, Dian - *Engage*
    KR - Feb 15 2015 - pNA [501+]

Griesinger, Alan - *A Comic Vision of Great Constancy: Stories about Unlocking the Wisdom of Everyman*
    SPBW - April 2015 - pNA [501+]

Griesse, Malte - *From Mutual Observation to Propaganda War: Premodern Revolts in Their Transnational Representations*
    Ren Q - v68 - i3 - Fall 2015 - p1062-1063 [501+]
    Six Ct J - v46 - i2 - Summer 2015 - p458-459

Griessner, Florika - *150 Jahre Italien: Themen, Wege, offene Fragen*
    HNet - April 2015 - pNA [501+]

Griffin, Adele - *Agnes and Clarabelle (Illus. by Palacios, Sara)*
    c SLJ - v61 - i9 - Sept 2015 - p134(1) [51-500]
Oona Finds an Egg (Illus. by Wu, Mike)
    c BL - v112 - i7 - Dec 1 2015 - p62(2) [51-500]
    c KR - Oct 15 2015 - pNA [51-500]
    c PW - v262 - i41 - Oct 12 2015 - p68(1) [51-500]
The Unfinished Life of Addison Stone
    c BL - v111 - i17 - May 1 2015 - p40(1) [51-500]
    y HB Guide - v26 - i1 - Spring 2015 - p108(2) [51-500]

Griffin, Bethany - *The Fall*
    y HB Guide - v26 - i1 - Spring 2015 - p109(1) [51-500]
    y Sch Lib - v63 - i1 - Spring 2015 - p62(1) [51-500]

Griffin, Donna - *The Twelve Days of Christmas of Indiana (Illus. by Cummings, Troy)*
    c HB Guide - v26 - i1 - Spring 2015 - p22(1) [51-500]

Griffin, Dustin - *Authorship in the Long Eighteenth Century*
    RES - v66 - i273 - Feb 2015 - p178-182 [501+]

Griffin, Emma - *Liberty's Dawn: A People's History of the Industrial Revolution*
    JEH - v75 - i2 - June 2015 - p589-590 [501+]
    JMH - v87 - i2 - June 2015 - p430(2) [501+]

Griffin, Farah Jasmine - *Harlem Nocturne: Women Artists and Progressive Politics during World War II*
    Am Q - v67 - i1 - March 2015 - p241-252 [501+]

Griffin, H. Terrell - *Chasing Justice*
    PW - v262 - i29 - July 20 2015 - p172(1) [51-500]

Griffin, James J. - *A Ranger to Fight With*
    c Roundup M - v22 - i5 - June 2015 - p38(1) [501+]
    c Roundup M - v22 - i6 - August 2015 - p25(1) [501+]
A Ranger to Reckon With
    c Roundup M - v22 - i6 - August 2015 - p25(1) [501+]
A Ranger to Ride With
    c Roundup M - v22 - i6 - August 2015 - p25(1) [501+]
A Ranger to Stand With
    c Roundup M - v23 - i1 - Oct 2015 - p28(1) [501+]
A Ranger's Christmas
    c Roundup M - v22 - i4 - April 2015 - p27(1) [501+]
    c Roundup M - v22 - i6 - August 2015 - p25(1) [501+]
West of the Big River: The Ranger
    c Roundup M - v22 - i6 - August 2015 - p30(1) [501+]

Griffin, John Michael - *This'll Be the Day That I Die*
    KR - Jan 1 2015 - pNA [501+]

Griffin, Kevin - *Recovering Joy: A Mindful Life After Addiction*
    RVBW - Nov 2015 - pNA [51-500]

Griffin, Lynne - *Girl Sent Away*
    KR - Sept 1 2015 - pNA [51-500]

Griffin, Matt - *A Cage of Rotos*
    c Sch Lib - v63 - i2 - Summer 2015 - p117(1) [501+]

Griffin, Matthew - *Hide*
    KR - Oct 1 2015 - pNA [501+]
    PW - v262 - i50 - Dec 7 2015 - p64(2) [51-500]

Griffin, Molly Beth - *Rhoda's Rock Hunt (Illus. by Bell, Jennifer A.)*
    c HB Guide - v26 - i1 - Spring 2015 - p31(1) [51-500]

Griffin, N. - *Smashie McPerter and the Mystery of Room 11 (Illus. by Hindley, Kate)*
    c CCB-B - v68 - i8 - April 2015 - p401(2) [51-500]
    c CH Bwatch - March 2015 - pNA [51-500]
    c HB - v91 - i2 - March-April 2015 - p95(2) [51-500]

Griffin, N. Smashie - *Smashie McPerter and the Mystery of Room 11 (Illus. by Hindley, Kate)*
    y HB Guide - v26 - i2 - Fall 2015 - p84(1) [51-500]

Griffin, Neal - *Benefit of the Doubt*
    BL - v111 - i17 - May 1 2015 - p20(1) [51-500]
    KR - March 15 2015 - pNA [501+]
    LJ - v140 - i7 - April 15 2015 - p76(1) [51-500]
    PW - v262 - i10 - March 9 2015 - p52(2) [51-500]
A Voice from the Field
    PW - v262 - i52 - Dec 21 2015 - p133(2) [51-500]

Griffin, Nicholas - *Ping-Pong Diplomacy: Ivor Montagu and the Astonishing Story Behind the Game that Changed the World*
    TLS - i5852 - May 29 2015 - p27(1) [501+]

Griffin, Paul - *Adrift*
    y CCB-B - v69 - i2 - Oct 2015 - p90(1) [51-500]
    y HB - v91 - i4 - July-August 2015 - p133(2) [51-500]
    y Magpies - v30 - i4 - Sept 2015 - p41(1) [501+]
    y PW - v262 - i18 - May 4 2015 - p121(1) [51-500]
    y PW - v262 - i49 - Dec 2 2015 - p111(2) [51-500]
    y VOYA - v38 - i3 - August 2015 - p62(1) [51-500]
    y KR - April 15 2015 - pNA [51-500]
    y SLJ - v61 - i4 - April 2015 - p164(1) [51-500]

Griffin, Rachel - *The Twelve Days of Christmas (Illus. by Griffin, Rachel)*
    c BL - v112 - i4 - Oct 15 2015 - p49(1) [51-500]
    c SLJ - v61 - i10 - Oct 2015 - p64(1) [51-500]

Griffin, Stephen M. - *Long Wars and the Constitution*
    NWCR - v68 - i2 - Spring 2015 - p128(3) [501+]

Griffin, Tren - *Charlie Munger: The Complete Investor*
    PW - v262 - i28 - July 13 2015 - p61(1) [51-500]

Griffin, W.E.B. - *Deadly Assets*
    PW - v262 - i26 - June 29 2015 - p47(1) [51-500]

Griffith, Bill - *Invisible Ink: My Mother's Secret Love Affair with a Famous Cartoonist*
    PW - v262 - i38 - Sept 21 2015 - p62(1) [51-500]
    BL - v112 - i6 - Nov 15 2015 - p34(1) [51-500]

Griffith, Clay - *The Geomancer*
    PW - v262 - i31 - August 3 2015 - p39(1) [51-500]

Griffith-Jones, John - *The Postage Due Stamps of Zanzibar 1875-1964: The Stamps, the Covers and Their Story*
    Phil Lit R - v64 - i1 - Wntr 2015 - p60(3) [501+]

Griffith, Mark - *Aristophanes' Frogs*
    CJ - v110 - i4 - April-May 2015 - p508(3) [501+]

Griffith, Nicola - *Slow River*
    TimHES - i2191 - Feb 19 2015 - p49(1) [501+]

Griffiths, Andy - *The 13-Storey Treehouse (Read by Wemyss, Stig). Audiobook Review*
  c CH Bwatch - Jan 2015 - pNA [51-500]
The 13-Storey Treehouse (Illus. by Denton, Terry)
  c Sch Lib - v63 - i2 - Summer 2015 - p104(1) [51-500]
The 26-Storey Treehouse (Read by Wemyss, Stig). Audiobook Review
  c CH Bwatch - March 2015 - pNA [51-500]
  c SLJ - v61 - i5 - May 2015 - p68(1) [51-500]
The 39-Storey Treehouse (Read by Wemyss, Stig). Audiobook Review
  c SLJ - v61 - i12 - Dec 2015 - p74(1) [51-500]
The 65-Storey Treehouse (Illus. by Denton, Terry)
  c Magpies - v30 - i4 - Sept 2015 - p33(1) [501+]
Griffiths, Elly - *The Ghost Fields: A Ruth Galloway Mystery*
  PW - v262 - i13 - March 30 2015 - p54(2) [51-500]
The Zig Zag Girl (Read by Langton, James). Audiobook Review
  BL - v112 - i7 - Dec 1 2015 - p69(1) [51-500]
The Zig Zag Girl
  BL - v111 - i22 - August 1 2015 - p38(2) [51-500]
  KR - July 15 2015 - pNA [51-500]
  PW - v262 - i28 - July 13 2015 - p45(1) [51-500]
Griffiths, Fiona J. - *Partners in Spirit: Women, Men, and Religious Life in Germany, 1100-1500*
  AHR - v120 - i4 - Oct 2015 - p1539-1540 [501+]
  Med R - Feb 2015 - pNA [501+]
  HNet - Sept 2015 - pNA [501+]
  Specu - v90 - i3 - July 2015 - p875(1) [501+]
Griffiths, G.J. - *So What's Next!*
  SPBW - Feb 2015 - pNA [51-500]
Griffiths, Jay - *A Country Called Childhood: Children and the Exuberant World*
  Par - v90 - i1 - Jan 2015 - p9(1) [501+]
Griffiths, K. - *Myrrh*
  RVBW - Feb 2015 - pNA [51-500]
Griffiths, Neil - *The Jolly Dodgers! Pirates Who Pretended (Illus. by Louden, Janette)*
  c Sch Lib - v63 - i2 - Summer 2015 - p92(1) [51-500]
Griffiths, Paul - *Genetics and Philosophy: An Introduction*
  BioSci - v65 - i2 - Feb 2015 - p212(2) [501+]
  Isis - v106 - i2 - June 2015 - p419(2) [501+]
Griffiths Paul J. - *Decreation: The Last Things of All Creatures*
  Theol St - v76 - i4 - Dec 2015 - p863(3) [501+]
Grigor, Talinn - *Contemporary Iranian Art: From the Street to the Studio*
  HNet - Sept 2015 - pNA [501+]
Grigorescu, Alexandra - *Cauchemar*
  Nat Post - v17 - i113 - March 14 2015 - pWP5(1) [501+]
Grigoriu, Brindusa - *'Amor' sans 'desonor': une pragmatique pour Tristan et Yseult*
  FS - v69 - i2 - April 2015 - p228(1) [501+]
Grill, Joyce - *Choo-Choo Boogie*
  c Am MT - v64 - i6 - June-July 2015 - p67(2) [501+]
Grillo, Ioan - *Gangster Warlords: Drug Dollars, Killing Fields, and the New Politics of Latin America*
  KR - Oct 1 2015 - pNA [501+]
  LJ - v140 - i17 - Oct 15 2015 - p103(1) [51-500]
Grillo, Luca - *Cicero's De Provinciis Consularibus Oratio: Introduction and Commentary*
  HNet - August 2015 - pNA [501+]
Grillo, Paolo - *Milano guelfa, 1302-1310*
  HER - v130 - i545 - August 2015 - p969(3) [501+]
Grillot, Thomas - *Apres la Grande Guerre: Comment les Amerindiens des Etats-Unis sont devenus patriotes*
  JAH - v102 - i2 - Sept 2015 - p587-588 [501+]
Grim, Alastair - *Odditorium*
  y CH Bwatch - March 2015 - pNA [51-500]
Grimaldi, Judith D. - *5@55: The 5 Essential Legal Documents You Need by Age 55*
  Bwatch - Oct 2015 - pNA [51-500]
  LJ - v140 - i12 - July 1 2015 - p97(1) [51-500]
Grimes, Linda - *The Big Fix*
  BL - v111 - i8 - May 15 2015 - p33(1) [51-500]
  PW - v262 - i13 - March 30 2015 - p60(1) [51-500]
Grimes, Martha - *Vertigo 42*
  RVBW - May 2015 - pNA [51-500]
Grimes, Michelle - *Where Is Pidge? (Illus. by DeOre, Bill)*
  y KR - July 15 2015 - pNA [51-500]

Grimes, Nikki - *Chasing Freedom: The Life Journeys of Harriet Tubman and Susan B. Anthony, Inspired by Historical Facts (Read by Mitchell, Lizan). Audiobook Review*
  c SLJ - v61 - i11 - Nov 2015 - p70(1) [51-500]
Chasing Freedom: The Life Journeys of Harriet Tubman and Susan B. Anthony, Inspired by Historical Facts (Illus. by Wood, Michele)
  c CCB-B - v68 - i7 - March 2015 - p355(1) [51-500]
  c CH Bwatch - March 2015 - pNA [51-500]
  c CH Bwatch - July 2015 - pNA [51-500]
  c HB Guide - v26 - i2 - Fall 2015 - p36(1) [51-500]
  c NYTBR - Feb 8 2015 - p22(L) [501+]
Poems in the Attic (Illus. by Zunon, Elizabeth)
  c BL - v111 - i16 - April 15 2015 - p50(1) [51-500]
Poems in the Attic (Illus. by Zunon, Elizabeth)
  c HB - v91 - i3 - May-June 2015 - p124(1) [501+]
  c HB Guide - v26 - i2 - Fall 2015 - p203(1) [51-500]
  c KR - March 15 2015 - pNA [51-500]
     SLJ - v61 - i4 - April 2015 - p178(1) [51-500]
  c CH Bwatch - Nov 2015 - pNA [51-500]
Grimm, Friedrich Melchior - *Correspondance litteraire*
  MLR - v110 - i2 - April 2015 - p546(1) [501+]
Grimm, Hans Herbert - *Schlump*
  TLS - i5856 - June 26 2015 - p26(1) [501+]
Grimm, Jacob - *The Complete First Edition: The Original Folk and Fairy Tales of the Brothers Grimm*
  c NYRB - v62 - i12 - July 9 2015 - p65(3) [501+]
King Thrushbeard (Illus. by Dobrescu, Irina)
  c HB Guide - v26 - i2 - Fall 2015 - p159(1) [51-500]
Little Red Riding Hood (Illus. by Schenker, Sybille)
  c HB Guide - v26 - i2 - Fall 2015 - p159(1) [51-500]
Tales from the Brothers Grimm (Illus. by Leupin, Herbert)
  c BL - v112 - i7 - Dec 1 2015 - p41(1) [51-500]
Grimm, Wilhelm - *Fairy Tales from the Brothers Grimm*
  c NYRB - v62 - i12 - July 9 2015 - p65(3) [501+]
The Six Swans (Illus. by Raidt, Gerda)
  c CH Bwatch - April 2015 - pNA [51-500]
Grimsley, Jim - *How I Shed My Skin: Unlearning the Racist Lessons of a Southern Childhood (Read by Leyva, Henry). Audiobook Review*
  PW - v262 - i26 - June 29 2015 - p64(2) [51-500]
How I Shed My Skin: Unlearning the Racist Lessons of a Southern Childhood
  BL - v111 - i12 - Feb 15 2015 - p12(1) [51-500]
  KR - Jan 15 2015 - pNA [51-500]
  NYTBR - June 7 2015 - p26(L) [501+]
Grimstad, Paul - *Experience and Experimental Writing: Literary Pragmatism from Emerson to the Jameses*
  AL - v87 - i3 - Sept 2015 - p611-613 [501+]
Grinapol, Corinne - *Harvey Milk: Pioneering Gay Politician*
  y BL - v111 - i22 - August 1 2015 - p55(1) [51-500]
Racial Profiling and Discrimination: Your Legal Rights
  y BL - v111 - i3 - Oct 1 2015 - p25(1) [51-500]
Griner, Paul - *Hurry Please I Want to Know: Stories*
  KR - March 15 2015 - pNA [51-500]
  NYTBR - July 12 2015 - p30(L) [501+]
  PW - v262 - i9 - March 2 2015 - p62(1) [51-500]
Grinmaldi, Mark A. - *The Money Compass: Where Your Money Went and How to Get It Back*
  Bwatch - Feb 2015 - pNA [51-500]
Grinnell, Dustin - *Without Limits*
  SPBW - Nov 2015 - pNA [51-500]
Grinspoon, Peter - *Free Refills*
  KR - Dec 1 2015 - pNA [51-500]
Grippando, James - *Cane and Abe*
  RVBW - Sept 2015 - pNA [51-500]
  RVBW - Nov 2015 - pNA [51-500]
Cash Landing
  BL - v111 - i17 - May 1 2015 - p24(2) [51-500]
  KR - April 1 2015 - pNA [51-500]
  PW - v262 - i16 - April 20 2015 - p55(1) [51-500]
Grise, Virginia - *The Panza Monologues*
  Aztlan - v40 - i2 - Fall 2015 - p309-312 [501+]
Grisham, John - *The Fugitive (Read by Thomas, Richard). Audiobook Review*
  c SLJ - v61 - i9 - Sept 2015 - p59(1) [51-500]
Rogue Lawyer
  BL - v112 - i2 - Sept 15 2015 - p34(1) [51-500]
  KR - August 15 2015 - pNA [51-500]
  LJ - v140 - i14 - Sept 1 2015 - p96(1) [501+]
  PW - v262 - i33 - August 17 2015 - p52(1) [51-500]
Theodore Boone
  y SLJ - v61 - i8 - August 2015 - pS1(35) [501+]
Grisinger, Joanna L. - *The Unwieldy American State: Administrative Politics since the New Deal*
  RAH - v43 - i2 - June 2015 - p327-332 [501+]
Grisone, Federico - *The Rules of Riding: An Edited Translation of the First Renaissance Treatise on Classical Horsemanship*
  Ren Q - v68 - i3 - Fall 2015 - p1033-1035 [501+]
Grissom, Eric - *Dead Birds*
  PW - v262 - i44 - Nov 2 2015 - p72(1) [51-500]
Planet Gigantic: New World Home (Illus. by Halverson, David)
  c SLJ - v61 - i5 - May 2015 - p108(1) [51-500]
Grissom, James - *Follies of God: Tennessee Williams and the Women of the Fog*
  Am Theat - v32 - i3 - March 2015 - p54(2) [501+]
  BL - v111 - i11 - Feb 1 2015 - p10(1) [51-500]
  LJ - v140 - i2 - Feb 1 2015 - p82(1) [51-500]
Grist, Hilary - *Tomorrow Is a Chance to Start Over*
  c CH Bwatch - April 2015 - pNA [51-500]
Gristwood, Sarah - *Blood Sisters: The Women behind the Wars of the Roses*
  Historian - v77 - i1 - Spring 2015 - p167(2) [501+]
Griswell, Kim T. - *Rufus Goes to Sea (Illus. by Gorbachev, Valeri)*
  c BL - v111 - i16 - April 15 2015 - p55(1) [51-500]
  c HB Guide - v26 - i2 - Fall 2015 - p36(1) [51-500]
  c SLJ - v61 - i4 - April 2015 - p128(1) [51-500]
Griswold, Cliff - *Dressing Up for Halloween*
  SLJ - v61 - i4 - April 2015 - p101(3) [51-500]
Gritsch, Eric W. - *Martin Luther's Anti-Semitism: Against His Better Judgment*
  CHR - v101 - i4 - Autumn 2015 - p929(5) [501+]
Gritter, Elizabeth - *River of Hope: Black Politics and the Memphis Freedom Movement, 1865-1954*
  AHR - v120 - i2 - April 2015 - p633-634 [501+]
  JAH - v102 - i1 - June 2015 - p301-302 [501+]
  JSH - v81 - i2 - May 2015 - p481(2) [501+]
Gritter, Matthew - *Mexican Inclusion: The Origins of Anti-Discrimination Policy in Texas and the Southwest*
  Aztlan - v40 - i2 - Fall 2015 - p305-308 [501+]
Grivno, Cody - *DCC Projects and Applications*
  Bwatch - April 2015 - pNA [51-500]
Groarke, Vona - *X*
  NS - v144 - i5246 - Jan 23 2015 - p42(2) [501+]
Grobman, Svetlana - *The Education of a Traitor*
  KR - April 1 2015 - pNA [501+]
Grocock, Christopher - *The Abbots of Wearmouth and Jarrow*
  Med R - Jan 2015 - pNA [501+]
Grode, Eric - *The Book of Broadway: The 150 Definitive Plays and Musicals*
  BL - v112 - i5 - Nov 1 2015 - p26(1) [51-500]
  LJ - v140 - i16 - Oct 1 2015 - p80(2) [51-500]
Groen, Jos M.H. - *Junior Leadership in Afghanistan, 2006-2010*
  Arm F&S - v41 - i3 - July 2015 - p584-586 [501+]
Groff, Lauren - *Fates and Furies (Read by Damron, Will, with Julia Whelan). Audiobook Review*
  LJ - v140 - i19 - Nov 15 2015 - p51(2) [51-500]
Fates and Furies (Read by Damron, Will, with Julia Whelan)
  BL - v112 - i5 - Nov 1 2015 - p71(1) [51-500]
Fates and Furies
  BL - v112 - i21 - July 1 2015 - p30(1) [51-500]
  BooChiTr - Sept 26 2015 - p13(1) [501+]
  Esq - v164 - i1 - August 2015 - p32(1) [51-500]
  KR - July 15 2015 - pNA [51-500]
  LJ - v140 - i10 - June 1 2015 - p86(2) [51-500]
  Mac - v128 - i37 - Sept 21 2015 - p57(1) [51-500]
  NY - v91 - i34 - Nov 2 2015 - p83 [501+]
  NYT - Sept 7 2015 - pC1(L) [501+]
  NYTBR - Sept 13 2015 - p1(L) [501+]
  PW - v262 - i22 - June 1 2015 - p2(1) [51-500]
Grogan, Shannon - *From Where I Watch You*
  y SLJ - v61 - i8 - August 2015 - p104(1) [51-500]
  y VOYA - v38 - i4 - Oct 2015 - p51(1) [501+]
Groh, Jennifer M. - *Making Space: How the Brain Knows Where Things Are*
  TimHES - i2189 - Feb 5 2015 - p58-58 [501+]
Gronkowski, Rob - *It's Good to Be Gronk*
  PW - v262 - i30 - July 27 2015 - p10(1) [51-500]
Groody, Daniel G. - *The Preferential Option for the Poor Beyond Theology*
  Theol St - v76 - i1 - March 2015 - p221(1) [501+]
Groom, Winston - *The Aviators: Eddie Rickenbacker, Jimmy Doolittle, Charles Lindbergh, and the Epic Age of Flight*
  CSM - April 29 2015 - pNA [51-500]
The Generals: Patton, MacArthur, Marshall, and the Winning of World War II
  KR - Oct 1 2015 - pNA [501+]
  LJ - v140 - i15 - Sept 15 2015 - p87(1) [51-500]
Groome, Harry - *Celebrity Cast*
  KR - Sept 1 2015 - pNA [501+]
Groot, Jerone de - *Remaking history: The Past in Contemporary Historical Fictions*
  TimHES - i2226 - Oct 22 2015 - p49-1 [501+]

Groot, Tracy - *Maggie Bright: A Novel of Dunkirk*
PW - v262 - i10 - March 9 2015 - p59(2) [51-500]

Grootaers, Jan-Lodewijk - *Visions from the Forests: The Art of Liberia and Sierra Leone*
HNet - Feb 2015 - pNA [501+]

Groppe, Alison M. - *Sinophone Malaysian Literature: Not Made in China*
JAS - v74 - i3 - August 2015 - p724-726 [501+]

Groschner, Annett - *City Spaces: Filling in Berlin's Gaps*
TLS - i5873 - Oct 23 2015 - p30(1) [501+]

Grose, Peter - *A Good Place to Hide: How One French Village Saved Thousands of Lives during World War II*.
BL - v111 - i11 - Feb 1 2015 - p12(1) [51-500]

Gross, Alan G. - *Science from Sight to Insight: How Scientists Illustrate Meaning*
Isis - v106 - i2 - June 2015 - p420(2) [501+]

Gross, Andrew - *One Mile Under*
KR - March 15 2015 - pNA [51-500]
PW - v262 - i8 - Feb 23 2015 - p50(1) [51-500]

Gross, Daniel - *Plenus litteris Lucanus: Zur Rezeption der horazischen Oden und Epoden in Lucans Bellum Civile*
Class R - v65 - i1 - April 2015 - p145-147 [501+]

Gross, David R. - *Animals Don't Blush*
KR - Dec 1 2015 - pNA [51-500]

Gross, Irena Grudzinska - *The Trouble with History: Morality, Revolution, and Counterrevolution*
Slav R - v74 - i3 - Fall 2015 - p625-627 [501+]

Gross, Jan T. - *Neighbors: The Destruction of the Jewish Community in Jedwabne, Poland*
Nation - v300 - i1 - Jan 5 2015 - p27(10) [501+]

Gross, Jan Tomasz - *Collected Essays on War, Holocaust and the Crisis of Communism*
Slav R - v74 - i3 - Fall 2015 - p621-622 [501+]

Gross, Kali Nicole - *Hannah Mary Tabbs and the Disembodied Torso*
KR - Nov 1 2015 - pNA [501+]

Gross, Kate - *Late Fragments*
NS - v144 - i5246 - Jan 23 2015 - p39(1) [501+]

Gross, Michael L. - *The Ethics of Insurgency: A Critical Guide to Just Guerrilla Warfare*
HNet - May 2015 - pNA [501+]

Gross, Milt - *Milt Gross' New York (Illus. by Gross, Milt)*
BL - v111 - i19-20 - June 1 2015 - p66(2) [51-500]

Gross, Neil - *Professors and Their Politics*
CS - v44 - i6 - Nov 2015 - p803-804 [501+]
AJS - v121 - i3 - Nov 2015 - p983(3) [501+]
Why Are Professors Liberal and Why Do Conservatives Care?
CS - v44 - i1 - Jan 2015 - p63-65 [501+]
J Hi E - v86 - i5 - Sept-Oct 2015 - p804(3) [501+]

Gross, Peter - *101 Ways to Amaze & Entertain: Amazing Magic and Hilarious Jokes to Try on Your Friends and Family*
c BL - v112 - i6 - Nov 15 2015 - p37(1) [51-500]

Grossberg, Benjamin S. - *Space Traveler*
G&L Rev W - v22 - i4 - July-August 2015 - p39(2) [501+]

Grossberg, Blythe - *Asperger's Teens: Understanding High School for Students on the Autism Spectrum*
BL - v111 - i14 - March 15 2015 - p57(1) [51-500]

Grossbolting, Thomas - *Der verlorene Himmel: Glaube in Deutschland seit 1945*
JMH - v87 - i2 - June 2015 - p492(2) [501+]

Grosse, Judith - *Biopolitik und Sittlichkeitsreform: Kampagnen Gegen Alkohol, Drogen und Prostitution 1880-1950*
HNet - July 2015 - pNA [501+]

Grosseteste, Robert - *The Dimension of Color: Robert Grosseteste's "De colore"*
Specu - v90 - i3 - July 2015 - p816-2 [501+]

Grossman, Austin - *Crooked*
KR - May 15 2015 - pNA [51-500]
LJ - v140 - i7 - April 15 2015 - p76(2) [51-500]
PW - v262 - i18 - May 4 2015 - p97(1) [51-500]

Grossman, Edith - *In the Night of Time*
Lon R Bks - v37 - i12 - June 18 2015 - p11(3) [501+]
Sor Juana Ines De La Cruz: Selected Works
Wom R Bks - v32 - i2 - March-April 2015 - p18(3) [501+]

Grossman, Lev - *The Magician's Land (Read by Bramhall, Mark). Audiobook Review*
BL - v111 - i9-10 - Jan 1 2015 - p114(1) [51-500]
The Magician's Land
BL - v111 - i18 - May 15 2015 - p35(1) [51-500]

Grossman, Richard S. - *Wrong: Nine Economic Policy Disasters and What We Can Learn from Them*
JIH - v45 - i3 - Wntr 2015 - p414-415 [501+]

Grossmann, Johannes - *Die Internationale der Konservativen: Transnationale Elitenzirkel und private Aussenpolitik in Westeuropa seit 1945*
HNet - May 2015 - pNA [501+]

Grossnickle, Mary - *A Place in my Heart (Illus. by Relyea-Parr, Alison)*
c Sch Lib - v63 - i2 - Summer 2015 - p92(1) [51-500]

Grosso, Chris - *Everything Mind*
PW - v262 - i32 - August 10 2015 - p55(1) [51-500]

Grosso, Mike - *I Am Drums*
y VOYA - v38 - i4 - Oct 2015 - p51(2) [51-500]

Grosz-Ngate, Maria - *Africa, 4th ed.*
Africa T - v61 - i3 - Spring 2015 - p91(2) [501+]

Groth, Darren - *Are You Seeing Me?*
y KR - June 1 2015 - pNA [51-500]
y PW - v262 - i19 - May 11 2015 - p62(1) [51-500]
y Res Links - v20 - i5 - June 2015 - p25(2) [501+]
y VOYA - v38 - i3 - August 2015 - p62(1) [51-500]

Groth, Helen - *Moving Images: Nineteenth-Century Reading and Screen Practices*
VS - v57 - i2 - Wntr 2015 - p322(2) [501+]

Grothe, Ewald - *Carl Schmitt - Ernst Rudolf Huber: Briefwechsel 1926-1981*
HNet - Jan 2015 - pNA [501+]

Grotta, Marit - *Baudelaire's Media Aesthetics: The Gaze of the Flaneur and 19th-Century Media*
TLS - i5868 - Sept 18 2015 - p28(1) [501+]

Group Majoongmul - *Math at the Art Museum (Illus. by Kim, Yun-ju)*
c KR - Feb 15 2015 - pNA [51-500]
c SLJ - v61 - i8 - August 2015 - p120(1) [51-500]

Grove, David C. - *Discovering the Olmecs: An Unconventional History*
HAHR - v95 - i4 - Nov 2015 - p667-668 [501+]

Grove, S.E. - *The Glass Sentence*
y Teach Lib - v42 - i3 - Feb 2015 - p39(1) [51-500]
The Golden Specific (Read by Campbell, Cassandra). Audiobook Review
y SLJ - v61 - i10 - Oct 2015 - p52(1) [51-500]
The Golden Specific
y BL - v111 - i19-20 - June 1 2015 - p98(1) [51-500]
y CCB-B - v69 - i2 - Oct 2015 - p90(2) [51-500]
y SLJ - v61 - i6 - June 2015 - p100(1) [51-500]
y VOYA - v38 - i4 - Oct 2015 - p70(1) [51-500]

Grove, Tara - *The World is Waiting for You*
KR - Feb 1 2015 - pNA [51-500]

Grove, Tim - *First Flight around the World: The Adventures of the American Fliers Who Won the Race*
c BL - v111 - i17 - May 1 2015 - p82(2) [51-500]
c CCB-B - v68 - i9 - May 2015 - p448(2) [51-500]
c HB Guide - v26 - i2 - Fall 2015 - p217(1) [51-500]
c KR - Feb 15 2015 - pNA [51-500]
c PW - v262 - i7 - Feb 16 2015 - p182(1) [51-500]
c SLJ - v61 - i3 - March 2015 - p177(1) [51-500]
A Grizzly in the Mail and Other Adventures in American History
Roundup M - v22 - i6 - August 2015 - p37(1) [501+]

Grover, Linda LeGarde - *The Road Back to Sweetgrass*
WLT - v89 - i5 - Sept-Oct 2015 - p67(1) [51-500]

Grover, Sean - *When Kids Call the Shots: How to Seize Control from Your Darling Bully--and Enjoy Being a Parent Again*
PW - v262 - i14 - April 6 2015 - p55(1) [51-500]

Groves, David - *The Digital Apocalypse*
Quad - v59 - i5 - May 2015 - p108(3) [501+]

Groves, Melody - *Butterfield's Byway: America's First Overland Mail Route across the West*
Roundup M - v22 - i3 - Feb 2015 - p23(2) [501+]
Roundup M - v22 - i6 - August 2015 - p37(1) [501+]

Grow, Jen - *My Life as a Mermaid and Other Stories*
ABR - v36 - i4 - May-June 2015 - p24(1) [51-500]
KR - May 1 2015 - pNA [51-500]

Growing Up in 20th Century European Borderlands/Kindheit in europaischen Grenzregionen im 20. Jahrhundert
HNet - April 2015 - pNA [501+]

Grua, David W. - *Surviving Wounded Knee: The Lakotas and the Politics of Memory*
LJ - v140 - i19 - Nov 15 2015 - p95(1) [51-500]
PW - v262 - i41 - Oct 12 2015 - p56(1) [51-500]

Grubb, Michelle - *Keep Hold*
PW - v262 - i37 - Sept 14 2015 - p50(1) [51-500]

Grubb, Valerie M. - *Planes, Canes, and Automobiles: Connecting with Your Aging Parents through Travel*
LJ - v140 - i15 - Sept 15 2015 - p95(1) [51-500]
RVBW - July 2015 - pNA [51-500]

Grubbs, David - *Records Ruin the Landscape: John Cage, the Sixties, and Sound Recording*
Notes - v72 - i1 - Sept 2015 - p176(3) [501+]
PMS - v38 - i3 - July 2015 - p398(3) [501+]

Grubbs, Morris Allen - *Every Leaf a Mirror: A Jim Wayne Miller Reader*
JSH - v81 - i2 - May 2015 - p543(1) [51-500]

Grube, Dennis - *At the Margins of Victorian Britain: Politics, Immorality and Britishness in the Nineteenth Century*
Historian - v77 - i3 - Fall 2015 - p606(2) [501+]

Gruber, Allison - *You're Not Edith*
BL - v111 - i9-10 - Jan 1 2015 - p32(1) [51-500]

Gruber, Christiane - *Visual Culture in the Modern Middle East: Rhetoric of the Image*
HNet - May 2015 - pNA [501+]

Gruber, Fiona - *Strange Country: Why Australian Painting Matters*
TLS - i5856 - June 26 2015 - p19(1) [501+]

Gruber, John - *Railroaders: Jack Delano's Homefront Photography*
LJ - v140 - i16 - Oct 1 2015 - p76(2) [51-500]

Grubiak, Margaret M. - *White Elephants on Campus: The Decline of the University Chapel in America, 1920-1960*
CH - v84 - i3 - Sept 2015 - p688(3) [501+]

Grudem, Wayne - *The Poverty of Nations: A Sustainable Solution*
IndRev - v20 - i1 - Summer 2015 - p141(4) [501+]
J Ch St - v57 - i3 - Summer 2015 - p553-554 [501+]

Gruen, J. Philip - *Manifest Destinations: Cities and Tourists in the Nineteenth-Century American West*
WHQ - v46 - i3 - Autumn 2015 - p388-389 [501+]

Gruen, Sara - *At the Water's Edge (Read by Eyre, Justine). Audiobook Review*
BL - v111 - i19-20 - June 1 2015 - p126(1) [51-500]
LJ - v140 - i11 - June 15 2015 - p50(1) [51-500]
At the Water's Edge
BL - v111 - i12 - Feb 15 2015 - p40(1) [51-500]
KR - Jan 15 2015 - pNA [51-500]

Gruenbaum, Michael - *Somewhere There Is Still a Sun: A Memoir of the Holocaust*
c BL - v111 - i19-20 - June 1 2015 - p92(1) [51-500]
y NYTBR - Sept 13 2015 - p22(L) [51-500]
c PW - v262 - i21 - May 25 2015 - p61(1) [51-500]
c PW - v262 - i49 - Dec 2 2015 - p84(1) [51-500]
c SLJ - v61 - i7 - July 2015 - p106(2) [51-500]
c KR - June 1 2015 - pNA [51-500]

Gruesser, John Cullen - *The Empire Abroad and the Empire at Home: African American Literature and the Era of Overseas Expansion*
MFSF - v61 - i1 - Spring 2015 - p183-186 [501+]
Race, Gender and Empire in American Detective Fiction
Sew R - v123 - i2 - Spring 2015 - pXXI-XXIII [501+]

Grumbach, Didier - *History of International Fashion*
LJ - v140 - i5 - March 15 2015 - p102(3) [51-500]

Grumberg, Jean-Claude - *Jean-Claude Grumberg: Three Plays*
TLS - i5857 - July 3 2015 - p18(1) [501+]

Grumet, Robert S. - *Manhattan to Minisink: American Indian Place Names in Greater New York and Vicinity*
Am Ind CRJ - v39 - i1 - Wntr 2015 - p137-139 [501+]

Grun, Anselm - *The Legend of Saint Nicholas (Illus. by Ferri, Giuliano)*
c HB Guide - v26 - i1 - Spring 2015 - p134(2) [51-500]

Grundman, Reiner - *The Power of Scientific Knowledge: From Research to Public Policy*
CS - v44 - i2 - March 2015 - p204-206 [501+]

Grunert, Robert - *Der Europagedanke westeuropaischer faschistischer Bewegungen 1940-1945*
HER - v130 - i545 - August 2015 - p1040(2) [501+]

Grunes, Dorothy T. - *What Shakespeare Teaches Us about Psychoanalysis: A Local Habitation and a Name*
Ren Q - v68 - i2 - Summer 2015 - p787-788 [501+]

Grunfelder, Anna Maria - *Von der Shoa eingeholt: Auslandische judische Fluchtlinge im ehemaligen Jugoslawien 1933-1945*
Slav R - v74 - i1 - Spring 2015 - p171-172 [501+]

Grunwald, Henning - *Courtroom to Revolutionary Stage: Performance and Ideology in Weimar Political Trials*
JMH - v87 - i1 - March 2015 - p229(3) [501+]

Grushcow, Rabbi Lisa J. - *The Sacred Encounter: Jewish Perspectives on Sexuality*
Bwatch - Jan 2015 - pNA [51-500]

Grushin, Olga - *Forty Rooms*
KR - Dec 1 2015 - pNA [51-500]
PW - v262 - i50 - Dec 7 2015 - p62(2) [51-500]

Gruss, Karin - *One Red Shoe (Illus. by Krejtschi, Tobias)*
c SLJ - v61 - i8 - August 2015 - p70(1) [51-500]

Gruyaert, Harry - *Harry Gruyaert*
    NYTBR - Dec 6 2015 - p38(L) [501+]

Gruzinski, Serge - *The Eagle and the Dragon: Globalization and European Dreams of Conquest in China and America in the Sixteenth Century*
    HNet - June 2015 - pNA [501+]

Grygiel, Jakub J. - *The Unquiet Frontier: Rising Rivals, Vulnerable Allies, and the Crisis of American Power*
    KR - Dec 15 2015 - pNA [501+]
    PW - v262 - i50 - Dec 7 2015 - p76(1) [51-500]

Grygiel, Stanislaw - *Discovering the Human Person: In Conversation with John Paul II*
    RM - v68 - i4 - June 2015 - p852(3) [501+]

Grylls, Bear - *True Grit*
    c Sch Lib - v63 - i1 - Spring 2015 - p47(1) [51-500]

Grynaviski, Eric - *Constructive Illusions: Misperceiving the Origins of International Cooperation*
    For Aff - v94 - i1 - Jan-Feb 2015 - pNA [51-500]

Grzymala-Busse, Anna - *Nations under God: How Churches Use Moral Authority to Influence Policy*
    JAAR - v83 - i2 - June 2015 - pNA [501+]

Gu, Raquel - *Dragonario: Un catalogo de dragonas y dragones (Illus. by Gu, Raquel)*
    c SLJ - v61 - i12 - Dec 2015 - p89(2) [51-500]

Guangcheng, Chen - *The Barefoot Lawyer: A Blind Man's Fight for Justice and Freedom in China*
    Ch Today - v59 - i2 - March 2015 - p61(1) [501+]
    Comw - v142 - i14 - Sept 11 2015 - p37(2) [501+]
    Econ - v414 - i8929 - March 14 2015 - p83(US) [501+]
    KR - Jan 15 2015 - pNA [51-500]
    NYRB - v62 - i12 - July 9 2015 - p45(2) [501+]
    NYTBR - May 10 2015 - p38(L) [501+]
    PW - v262 - i4 - Jan 26 2015 - p159(2) [501+]
    BL - v111 - i12 - Feb 15 2015 - p8(1) [501+]
    Nat R - v67 - i9 - May 18 2015 - p45 [501+]

Guard, Candy - *Jelly Has a Wobble*
    c Sch Lib - v63 - i3 - Autumn 2015 - p166(1) [51-500]

Guas, David - *Grill Nation: 200 Surefire Recipes, Tips, and Techniques to Grill Like a Pro*
    New Or - v49 - i9 - June 2015 - p38(1) [501+]

Guasco, Michael - *Slaves and Englishmen: Human Bondage in the Early Modern Atlantic World*
    AHR - v120 - i2 - April 2015 - p712-713 [501+]
    JAH - v102 - i1 - June 2015 - p219-219 [501+]

Guasco, Michael - *Slaves and Englishmen: Human Bondage in the Early Modern Atlantic World*
    JIH - v45 - i4 - Spring 2015 - p574-576 [501+]

Guasco, Michael - *Slaves and Englishmen: Human Bondage in the Early Modern Atlantic World*
    JSH - v81 - i2 - May 2015 - p423(3) [501+]
    Six Ct J - v46 - i3 - Fall 2015 - p800-801 [501+]

Gubar, Justine - *Fanaticus: Mischief and Madness in the Modern Sports Fan*
    PW - v262 - i21 - May 25 2015 - p52(1) [501+]

Gubin, Steve - *Chicagoland: Illusions of the Literal*
    PW - v262 - i16 - April 20 2015 - p69(2) [51-500]

Gubser, Michael - *The Far Reaches: Phenomenology, Ethics, and Social Renewal in Central Europe*
    AHR - v120 - i3 - June 2015 - p1106-1107 [501+]

Gude, Paul - *A Surprise for Giraffe and Elephant (Illus. by Gude, Paul)*
    c CH Bwatch - April 2015 - pNA [51-500]
    c HB Guide - v26 - i2 - Fall 2015 - p12(1) [51-500]
    c SLJ - v61 - i2 - Feb 2015 - p69(1) [51-500]

Gudenkauf, Heather - *Missing Pieces*
    BL - v112 - i7 - Dec 1 2015 - p30(1) [51-500]
    KR - Dec 1 2015 - pNA [51-500]
    PW - v262 - i52 - Dec 21 2015 - p131(1) [51-500]

Gudeon, Adam - *Ping Wants to Play*
    c HB Guide - v26 - i1 - Spring 2015 - p53(1) [51-500]

Gudlat, Ted - *Funny-Hahas*
    PW - v262 - i36 - Sept 7 2015 - p54(1) [51-500]

Guelzo, Allen C. - *Gettysburg*
    JAH - v101 - i4 - March 2015 - p1272-1273 [501+]

Redeeming the Great Emancipator
    KR - Dec 1 2015 - pNA [501+]
    PW - v262 - i50 - Dec 7 2015 - p78(1) [51-500]

Gueniffey, Patrice - *Bonaparte: 1769-1802*
    J Mil H - v79 - i3 - July 2015 - p820-822 [501+]
    KR - Jan 15 2015 - pNA [501+]
    Nation - v300 - i24 - June 15 2015 - p35(5) [501+]
    Spec - v328 - i9742 - May 16 2015 - p42(2) [501+]
    TLS - i5854 - June 12 2015 - p12(2) [501+]

Guerra, Lillian - *Visions of Power in Cuba: Revolution, Redemption, and Resistance, 1959-1971*
    NYRB - v62 - i6 - April 2 2015 - p51(3) [501+]
    RAH - v43 - i1 - March 2015 - p184-191 [501+]

Guerra, Stephanie - *Out of Aces (Read by Podehl, Nick). Audiobook Review*
    y SLJ - v61 - i8 - August 2015 - p52(1) [51-500]

Guerre et deplacements de populations. Regards croises sur l'Europe aux XIXe et XXe siecles
    HNet - May 2015 - pNA [501+]

Guerrero, Joanne Michel - *A Sign Catalog: Glyphs in Selected Text-Like Layouts at Teotihuacan*
    Lat Ant - v26 - i2 - June 2015 - p283(2) [501+]

Guertin, Chantel - *Leading Lines: A Pippa Greene Novel*
    y KR - July 15 2015 - pNA [51-500]
    y VOYA - v38 - i4 - Oct 2015 - p52(1) [51-500]

Guesnet, Francois - *Antisemitism in an Era of Transition: Continuities and Impact in Post-Communist Poland and Hungary*
    Slav R - v74 - i3 - Fall 2015 - p624-625 [501+]

Guess, George M. - *Government Budgeting: A Practical Guidebook*
    RVBW - Sept 2015 - pNA [51-500]

Guest, Harriet - *Unbounded Attachment: Sentiment and Politics in the Age of the French Revolution*
    RES - v66 - i273 - Feb 2015 - p183-185 [501+]

Guest, Jacqueline - *Fire Fight*
    y KR - August 15 2015 - pNA [501+]

Guest, Mathew - *Religion and Knowledge: Sociological Perspectives*
    CS - v44 - i1 - Jan 2015 - p65-66 [501+]

Guest, Patrick - *That's What Wings Are For (Illus. by Germain, Daniella)*
    c Magpies - v30 - i2 - May 2015 - p30(1) [51-500]

Guettel, Jens-Uwe - *German Expansionism, Imperial Liberalism and the United States, 1776-1945*
    JMH - v87 - i1 - March 2015 - p221(4) [501+]

Guettier, Benedicte - *The Chicken Who Had a Toothache (Illus. by Guettier, Benedicte)*
    c CCB-B - v69 - i1 - Sept 2015 - p25(1) [51-500]

The Dad with 10 Children (Illus. by Guettier, Benedicte)
    c HB Guide - v26 - i2 - Fall 2015 - p12(1) [51-500]
    KR - April 1 2015 - pNA [51-500]
    PW - v262 - i14 - April 6 2015 - p57(1) [51-500]

I Am the Wolf ... and Here I Come! (Illus. by Guettier, Benedicte)
    c KR - July 1 2015 - pNA [51-500]
    c PW - v262 - i6 - Feb 9 2015 - p66(2) [51-500]
    c PW - v262 - i49 - Dec 2 2015 - p56(1) [51-500]

Guez, Jeremie - *Eyes Full of Empty*
    PW - v262 - i38 - Sept 21 2015 - p55(1) [51-500]

Gugglberger, Martina - *Reguliertes Abenteuer: Missionarinnen in Sudafrika nach 1945*
    HNet - Jan 2015 - pNA [501+]

Guha, Ramachandra - *Gandhi before India*
    NYTBR - March 15 2015 - p28(L) [501+]

Guha, Sumit - *Beyond Caste: Identity and Power in South Asia, Past and Present*
    JAS - v74 - i2 - May 2015 - p510-511 [501+]

Guhrke, Laura Lee - *Catch a Falling Heiress*
    BL - v111 - i9-10 - Jan 1 2015 - p55(2) [51-500]

Guibernau, Montserrat - *Belonging: Solidarity and Division in Modern Societies*
    ERS - v38 - i3 - March 2015 - p507(4) [501+]

Guiberson, Brenda Z. - *Feathered Dinosaurs (Illus. by Low, William)*
    c KR - Dec 1 2015 - pNA [51-500]

The Most Amazing Creature in the Sea (Illus. by Spirin, Gennady)
    SLJ - v61 - i4 - April 2015 - p178(3) [51-500]
    c BL - v111 - i16 - April 15 2015 - p44(1) [51-500]
    c CCB-B - v69 - i1 - Sept 2015 - p26(1) [51-500]
    c HB Guide - v26 - i2 - Fall 2015 - p170(1) [51-500]
    c PW - v262 - i20 - May 18 2015 - p85(1) [51-500]
    c PW - v262 - i49 - Dec 2 2015 - p48(1) [51-500]

Guild, Elizabeth - *Unsettling Montaigne*
    FS - v69 - i3 - July 2015 - p386(1) [501+]
    MP - v113 - i2 - Nov 2015 - pE79(2) [501+]
    Ren Q - v68 - i2 - Summer 2015 - p751-752 [501+]

Guild, Nicholas - *Blood Ties*
    PW - v262 - i13 - March 30 2015 - p56(1) [51-500]

Guilding, Ruth - *Owning the Past: Why the English Collected Antique Sculpture, 1640-1840*
    TLS - i5837 - Feb 13 2015 - p10(2) [501+]

Guillain, Adam - *The Pirate Pie Ship (Illus. by Van Wyk, Rupert)*
    c Res Links - v20 - i3 - Feb 2015 - p14(2) [501+]

Pirates Are Stealing Our Cows
    c Res Links - v20 - i3 - Feb 2015 - p14(2) [501+]

Zak's King Arthur Adventure (Illus. by Alder, Charlie)
    c CH Bwatch - April 2015 - pNA [51-500]
    c Res Links - v20 - i3 - Feb 2015 - p14(2) [501+]

Guillain, Charlotte - *Cat and the Beanstalk (Illus. by Beacon, Dawn)*
    c HB Guide - v26 - i1 - Spring 2015 - p144(1) [51-500]

Connect with Text
    c BL - v111 - i19-20 - June 1 2015 - p80(1) [51-500]

The Emperor Penguin's New Clothes (Illus. by Beacon, Dawn)
    c HB Guide - v26 - i1 - Spring 2015 - p31(1) [51-500]

The Pirate Pie Ship
    c CH Bwatch - Feb 2015 - pNA [501+]

The Pirates on Holiday (Illus. by Alder, Charlie)
    c Res Links - v20 - i3 - Feb 2015 - p14(2) [501+]

The Pirates on Holiday
    c CH Bwatch - Feb 2015 - pNA [501+]

Rumpelstiltskin Returns
    c Res Links - v20 - i3 - Feb 2015 - p14(2) [501+]

Stinky! (Illus. by Elkerton, Andy)
    c Res Links - v20 - i3 - Feb 2015 - p14(2) [501+]

Stories of Women's Suffrage: Votes for Women!
    c HB Guide - v26 - i2 - Fall 2015 - p213(1) [51-500]

The Three Frilly Goats Fluff
    c CH Bwatch - July 2015 - pNA [501+]

What Is a Graphic Novel?
    c HB Guide - v26 - i2 - Fall 2015 - p202(1) [51-500]
    c SLJ - v61 - i4 - April 2015 - p106(3) [51-500]

What Is a Poem?
    c HB Guide - v26 - i2 - Fall 2015 - p203(1) [51-500]

What Is Literary Non-Fiction?
    c Sch Lib - v63 - i4 - Winter 2015 - p238(1) [51-500]

Guillaume, Laurent - *White Leopard*
    BL - v112 - i5 - Nov 1 2015 - p33(1) [51-500]
    PW - v262 - i38 - Sept 21 2015 - p55(1) [51-500]

Guillen, Nalleli - *The Costs and Consequences of Living in a World Shaped by Leisure Culture: New Literature on Tourism and Urban Recreation in America*
    J Urban H - v41 - i3 - May 2015 - p495-500 [501+]

Guillermo, Jorge - *Sibyls: Prophecy and Power in the Ancient World*
    Class R - v65 - i2 - Oct 2015 - p533-534 [501+]

Guillot, Rene - *Le Blanc qui s'etait fait negre*
    MLR - v110 - i2 - April 2015 - p554-555 [501+]

Guilluy, Christophe - *La France peripherique*
    TLS - i5852 - May 29 2015 - p10(2) [501+]

Guinier, Arnaud - *L'honneur du soldat: ethique martiale et discipline guerriere dans la France des Lumieres*
    J Mil H - v79 - i3 - July 2015 - p816-817 [501+]

Guinier, Lani - *The Tyranny of the Meritocracy: Democratizing Higher Education in America*
    NYTBR - April 19 2015 - p30(L) [501+]
    RVBW - April 2015 - pNA [501+]
    Soc - v52 - i5 - Oct 2015 - p498(1) [51-500]

Guinn, Jeff - *Buffalo Trail*
    BL - v112 - i1 - Sept 1 2015 - p51(1) [51-500]
    KR - August 1 2015 - pNA [501+]
    LJ - v140 - i14 - Sept 1 2015 - p92(1) [51-500]
    PW - v262 - i34 - August 24 2015 - p57(1) [51-500]

Glorious: A Novel of the American West
    Roundup M - v22 - i6 - August 2015 - p30(1) [501+]

Guinn, Matthew - *The Scribe*
    BL - v111 - i19-20 - June 1 2015 - p57(1) [51-500]
    KR - July 1 2015 - pNA [501+]
    LJ - v140 - i15 - Sept 15 2015 - p67(1) [51-500]
    PW - v262 - i30 - July 27 2015 - p43(1) [51-500]

Guinness, Bunny - *Highgrove: An English Country Garden*
    NYTBR - May 31 2015 - p36(L) [501+]

Guinness, Os - *Fool's Talk: Recovering the Art of Christian Persuasion*
    Ch Today - v59 - i6 - July-August 2015 - p86(1) [501+]
    PW - v262 - i19 - May 11 2015 - p53(1) [51-500]

Guirao, Fernando - *Alan S. Milward and a Century of European Change*
    HNet - March 2015 - pNA [501+]

Guiteau, Leif - *Religion and Man: Our Story*
    PW - v262 - i4 - Jan 26 2015 - p143(1) [51-500]

Guittar, Nicholas A. - *Coming Out: The New Dynamics*
    AJS - v120 - i4 - Jan 2015 - p1274(3) [501+]

Guittard, Amy - *Guittard Chocolate Cookbook: Decadent Recipes from San Francisco's Premium Bean-to-Bar Chocolate Company*
    NYTBR - Dec 6 2015 - pNA(L) [501+]

Book Review Index 2016 Cumulation GUTKIND • 187

Guldi, Jo - *The History Manifesto*
JEH - v75 - i2 - June 2015 - p584-587 [501+]
JIH - v46 - i2 - Autumn 2015 - p265-266 [501+]
Nation - v300 - i6 - Feb 9 2015 - p27(5) [501+]
NS - v144 - i5246 - Jan 23 2015 - p36(3) [501+]
Gumbert, Heather - *Envisioning Socialism: Television and the Cold War in the German Democratic Republic*
AHR - v120 - i3 - June 2015 - p1136-1137 [501+]
GSR - v38 - i3 - Oct 2015 - p699-701 [501+]
Gumbert, Heather L. - *Envisioning Socialism: Television and the Cold War in the German Democratic Republic*
CEH - v48 - i2 - June 2015 - p278-280 [501+]
HNet - March 2015 - pNA [501+]
Gumnut, I.B. - *Mad Dogs*
c CH Bwatch - August 2015 - pNA [51-500]
Gunaratnam, Tracy - *Preposterous Rhinoceros (Illus. by Costa, Marta)*
c Sch Lib - v63 - i2 - Summer 2015 - p92(1) [501+]
Gundar-Goshen, Ayelet - *One Night, Markovitch*
TLS - i5838 - Feb 20 2015 - p21(1) [501+]
Gundermann, Christine - *Die versohnten Burger: Der Zweite Weltkrieg in deutsch-niederlandischen Begegnungen 1945-2000*
HNet - April 2015 - pNA [501+]
Gunderson, Erik - *The Sublime Seneca: Ethics, Literature, Metaphysics*
TLS - i5867 - Sept 11 2015 - p12(1) [501+]
Gunderson, Jessica - *Impressionism*
y BL - v112 - i5 - Nov 1 2015 - p48(1) [51-500]
A Rebel among Redcoats
c HB Guide - v26 - i2 - Fall 2015 - p84(1) [51-500]
The Songs of Stones River: A Civil War Novel
c HB Guide - v26 - i2 - Fall 2015 - p84(1) [51-500]
The Wound Is Mortal: The Story of the Assassination of Abraham Lincoln
y SLJ - v61 - i9 - Sept 2015 - p151(4) [501+]
Gundlach, Bradley J. - *Process and Providence: The Evolution Question at Princeton, 1845-1929*
CH - v84 - i1 - March 2015 - p261(3) [501+]
JAH - v101 - i4 - March 2015 - p1297(1) [501+]
Gundle, Stephen - *The Cult of the Duce: Mussolini and the Italians*
JMH - v87 - i2 - June 2015 - p467(6) [501+]
Gunesekera, Romesh - *Noontide Toll*
WLT - v89 - i2 - March-April 2015 - p61(1) [51-500]
NYRB - v62 - i4 - March 5 2015 - p31(3) [501+]
NYTBR - Jan 4 2015 - p7(L) [501+]
Gunn, Drewey Wayne - *Gay Novels of Britain, Ireland and the Commonwealth, 1881-1981: A Reader's Guide*
G&L Rev W - v22 - i2 - March-April 2015 - p40(2) [501+]
Gunn, Elizabeth - *Noontime Follies*
BL - v111 - i18 - May 15 2015 - p28(1) [51-500]
PW - v262 - i19 - May 11 2015 - p38(2) [51-500]
Gunn, Tim - *Tim Gunn: The Natty Professor: A Master Class on Mentoring, Motivating, and Making It Work! (Read by Gunn, Tim). Audiobook Review*
BL - v112 - i1 - Sept 1 2015 - p142(1) [51-500]
Tim Gunn: The Natty Professor: A Master Class on Mentoring, Motivating and Making It Work (Read by Gunn, Tim). Audiobook Review
LJ - v140 - i13 - August 1 2015 - p48(2) [51-500]
Gunnell, John - *Social Inquiry after Wittgenstein and Kuhn: Leaving Everything As It Is*
RM - v68 - i4 - June 2015 - p854(3) [501+]
Gunnell, Kristine Ashton - *Daughters of Charity: Women, Religious Mission, and Hospital Care in Los Angeles, 1856-1927*
CH - v84 - i3 - Sept 2015 - p683(3) [501+]
CHR - v101 - i3 - Summer 2015 - p679(2) [501+]
PHR - v84 - i3 - August 2015 - p392(3) [501+]
Gunnell, Terry - *The Nordic Apocalypse: Approaches to Voluspa and Nordic Days of Judgement*
JEGP - v114 - i3 - July 2015 - p423(4) [501+]
Gunning, Tom - *Fantasia of Color in Early Cinema*
Si & So - v25 - i10 - Oct 2015 - p113(1) [501+]
Gunter, Michael M. - *Out of Nowhere: The Kurds of Syria in Peace and War*
NYRB - v62 - i19 - Dec 3 2015 - p24(4) [501+]
Gunzel, Stephan - *Bild: Ein Interdisziplinares Handbuch*
HNet - July 2015 - pNA [501+]
Guo, Jun - *Chan Heart, Chan Mind: A Meditation on Serenity and Growth*
PW - v262 - i41 - Oct 12 2015 - p62(1) [51-500]
Guojing - *The Only Child (Illus. by Guojing)*
c PW - v262 - i39 - Sept 28 2015 - p95(1) [51-500]
c PW - v262 - i49 - Dec 2 2015 - p31(1) [51-500]
c BL - v112 - i6 - Nov 15 2015 - p36(1) [51-500]
c KR - Sept 15 2015 - pNA [51-500]
c NYTBR - Nov 8 2015 - p20(L) [501+]
c PW - v262 - i51 - Dec 14 2015 - p21(6) [501+]
c SLJ - v61 - i8 - August 2015 - p70(1) [51-500]
Gupta, Akhil - *Red Tape: Bureaucracy, Structural Violence, and Poverty in India*
CS - v44 - i3 - May 2015 - p362-364 [501+]
Gura, Judith - *Interior Landmarks: Treasures of New York*
LJ - v140 - i20 - Dec 1 2015 - p106(2) [501+]
Gura, Philip E. - *Truth's Ragged Edge: The Rise of the American Novel*
JAH - v102 - i1 - June 2015 - p245-245 [501+]
Gura, Philip F. - *The Life of William Apess, Pequot*
BL - v111 - i11 - Feb 1 2015 - p17(1) [51-500]
PW - v262 - i4 - Jan 26 2015 - p161(2) [51-500]
Guralnick, Peter - *Sam Phillips: The Man Who Invented Rock 'n' Roll*
BL - v112 - i5 - Nov 1 2015 - p24(1) [51-500]
Dbt - v82 - i12 - Dec 2015 - p80(1) [501+]
KR - Sept 1 2015 - pNA [501+]
LJ - v140 - i15 - Sept 15 2015 - p78(2) [51-500]
Mac - v128 - i46 - Nov 23 2015 - p56(1) [501+]
NYT - Nov 6 2015 - pC23(L) [501+]
NYTBR - Dec 6 2015 - p16(L) [501+]
PW - v262 - i41 - Oct 12 2015 - p60(1) [51-500]
Guran, Paula - *Blood Sisters: Vampire Stories*
LJ - v140 - i9 - May 15 2015 - p57(4) [501+]
New Cthulhu 2: More Recent Weird
PW - v262 - i14 - April 6 2015 - p44(2) [51-500]
Warrior Women
PW - v262 - i44 - Nov 2 2015 - p66(1) [51-500]
Guran, Paula - *The Year's Best Science Fiction and Fantasy Novellas 2015*
PW - v262 - i29 - July 20 2015 - p174(1) [51-500]
Gurevich, Margaret - *Balancing Act: Chloe by Design (Illus. by Hagel, Brooke)*
y VOYA - v38 - i3 - August 2015 - p62(1) [51-500]
Balancing Act
c KR - May 15 2015 - pNA [51-500]
Design Diva (Illus. by Hagel, Brooke)
y HB Guide - v26 - i2 - Fall 2015 - p84(1) [51-500]
Unraveling (Illus. by Hagel, Brooke)
y HB Guide - v26 - i2 - Fall 2015 - p84(1) [51-500]
Gurian, Michael - *Lessons of Lifelong Intimacy: Building a Stronger Marriage Without Losing Yourself - The 9 Principles of a Balanced and Happy Relationship*
LJ - v140 - i9 - May 15 2015 - p97(2) [51-500]
Lessons of Lifelong Intimacy: Building a Stronger Marriage Without Losing Yourself; The 9 Principles of a Balanced and Happy Relationship
PW - v262 - i11 - March 16 2015 - p80(1) [51-500]
Guriel, Jason - *Satisfying Clicking Sound*
Can Lit - i224 - Spring 2015 - p123 [501+]
Gurley, Jason - *Eleanor*
BL - v112 - i3 - Oct 1 2015 - p4(1) [51-500]
BL - v112 - i7 - Dec 1 2015 - p38(1) [51-500]
KR - Nov 1 2015 - pNA [501+]
Gurney, Chris - *The Three Cattle Dogs Gruff (Illus. by Lawford, Myles)*
c Magpies - v30 - i3 - July 2015 - pS5(1) [501+]
Gurney, George - *No Saddle for the Cowboy*
Roundup M - v22 - i6 - August 2015 - p30(1) [501+]
Gurney, John - *Gerrard Winstanley: The Digger's Life and Legacy*
Historian - v77 - i3 - Fall 2015 - p607(2) [501+]
Gurnow, Michael - *Nature's Housekeeper*
SPBW - Nov 2015 - pNA [501+]
Gurock, Jeffrey - *The Holocaust Averted: An Alternate History of American Jewry, 1938-1967*
TimHES - i2203 - May 14 2015 - p48-1 [501+]
Gurpinar, Dogan - *Ottoman Imperial Diplomacy: A Political, Social, and Cultural History*
AHR - v120 - i1 - Feb 2015 - p363-364 [501+]
Ottoman/Turkish Visions of the Nation, 1860-1950
AHR - v120 - i1 - Feb 2015 - p363(1) [501+]
Gurr, Barbara - *Reproductive Justice: The Politics of Health Care for Native American Women*
Wom R Bks - v32 - i5 - Sept-Oct 2015 - p12(2) [501+]
Gurses, Mehmet - *Conflict, Democratization, and the Kurds in the Middle East: Turkey, Iran, Iraq, and Syria*
IJMES - v47 - i4 - Nov 2015 - p850-852 [501+]
Gurth, Per-Henrik - *Canada en une journee*
c Res Links - v20 - i5 - June 2015 - p39(1) [51-500]
A Day in Canada (Illus. by Gurth, Per-Henrik)
KR - Jan 15 2015 - pNA [51-500]
c Res Links - v20 - i5 - June 2015 - p4(1) [51-500]
Gurtler, Janet - *Secrets Beneath the Sea (Illus. by Wood, Katie)*
c HB Guide - v26 - i2 - Fall 2015 - p85(1) [51-500]
c KR - Jan 1 2015 - pNA [51-500]
The Truth about Us
y BL - v111 - i19-20 - June 1 2015 - p102(1) [51-500]
y SLJ - v61 - i4 - April 2015 - p164(1) [51-500]
y VOYA - v38 - i1 - April 2015 - p60(1) [51-500]
Gurunanda - *Gurunanda's Happy Breath Yoga: Wall Street Yoga*
SPBW - June 2015 - pNA [501+]
Guseva, Alya - *Plastic Money: Constructing Markets for Credit Cards in Eight Postcommunist Countries*
E-A St - v67 - i4 - June 2015 - p679(3) [501+]
Gusinde, Martin - *The Lost Tribes of Tierra del Fuego: Selk'nam, Yamana, Kawsqar*
NYTBR - Dec 6 2015 - p38(L) [501+]
Guskin, Sharon - *The Forgetting Time*
KR - Dec 1 2015 - pNA [501+]
Gussow, Adam - *Busker's Holiday*
KR - Nov 15 2015 - pNA [501+]
Gustafson, Bruce - *Paris, Bibliotheque nationale de France, Res. Vm7 674-675: The Bauyn Manuscript - Part I, Works by Jacques Champion de Chambonnieres*
Notes - v72 - i1 - Sept 2015 - p216(6) [501+]
Paris, Bibliotheque nationale de France, Res. Vm7 674-675: The Bauyn Manuscript - Part II, Works by Louis Couperin
Notes - v72 - i1 - Sept 2015 - p216(6) [501+]
Paris, Bibliotheque nationale de France, Res. Vm7 674-675: The Bauyn Manuscript - Part III, Works by Various Composers
Notes - v72 - i1 - Sept 2015 - p216(6) [501+]
Paris, Bibliotheque nationale de France, Res. Vm7 674-675: The Bauyn Manuscript - Part IV, Commentary
Notes - v72 - i1 - Sept 2015 - p216(6) [501+]
Gustafson, Thane - *Wheel of Fortune: The Battle for Oil and Power in Russia*
En Jnl - v36 - i3 - July 2015 - p363(2) [501+]
Gustafsson, Lars - *Smile of a Midsummer Night: A Picture of Sweden*
TLS - i5857 - July 3 2015 - p25(1) [501+]
Gustavson, Adam - *Dirty Rats?*
BL - v111 - i9-10 - Jan 1 2015 - p78(1) [51-500]
Gustine, Amy - *You Should Pity Us Instead*
KR - Oct 15 2015 - pNA [51-500]
Guterl, Matthew Pratt - *Josephine Baker and the Rainbow Tribe*
AHR - v120 - i4 - Oct 2015 - p1518-1519 [501+]
Seeing Race in Modern America
JSH - v81 - i1 - Feb 2015 - p255(3) [501+]
Guterman, Gad - *Performance, Identity, and Immigration Law: A Theatre of Undocumentedness*
Theat J - v67 - i3 - Oct 2015 - p582-583 [501+]
Gutermann, Sven - *Die Stuhlbruder des Speyerer Domstifts: Betbruder, Kirchendiener und Almosener des Reichs*
HNet - March 2015 - pNA [501+]
Gutfeld, Arnon - *Treasure State Justice: Judge George M. Bourquin, Defender of the Rule of Law*
PHR - v84 - i4 - Nov 2015 - p541(2) [501+]
Guth, Christine M.E. - *Hokusai's Great Wave: A Global Icon*
TLS - i5857 - July 3 2015 - p26(1) [501+]
Guthman, Julie - *Weighing In: Obesity, Food Justice, and the Limits of Capitalism*
CS - v44 - i3 - May 2015 - p364-365 [501+]
Guthrie, Thomas H. - *Recognizing Heritage: The Politics of Multiculturalism in New Mexico*
PHR - v84 - i3 - August 2015 - p379(2) [501+]
WHQ - v46 - i2 - Summer 2015 - p239(1) [501+]
Guthrie, Woody - *Honeyky Hanukah (Illus. by Horowitz, Dave)*
c HB Guide - v26 - i1 - Spring 2015 - p9(1) [51-500]
Gutierrez, Avelino - *The Archaeology of Medieval Spain, 1100-1500*
Med R - May 2015 - pNA [501+]
Gutierrez, Edward A. - *Doughboys on the Great War: How American Soldiers Viewed Their Military Experience*
J Mil H - v79 - i2 - April 2015 - p516-517 [501+]
J Mil H - v79 - i4 - Oct 2015 - p1167-1168 [501+]
Parameters - v45 - i1 - Spring 2015 - p166(2) [501+]
Gutierrez, Gabriel - *Latinos and Latinas at Risk: Issues in Education, Health, Community, and Justice, 2 vols.*
BL - v111 - i19-20 - June 1 2015 - p10(2) [501+]
Gutierrez, Gustavo - *On the Side of the Poor: The Theology of Liberation*
JAAR - v83 - i2 - June 2015 - pNA [501+]
Gutierrez, Michael Keenan - *The Trench Angel*
KR - August 1 2015 - pNA [501+]
Gutierrez , Sylvia M. - *Mortgage Matters*
KR - Sept 1 2015 - pNA [501+]
Gutierrez y Muhs, Gabriella - *Presumed Incompetent: The Intersections of Race and Class for Women in Academia*
Signs - v40 - i2 - Wntr 2015 - p513(2) [501+]
Gutkind, Lee - *Oh, Baby! True Stories About Conception, Adoption, Surrogacy, Pregnancy, Labor, and Love*
PW - v262 - i36 - Sept 7 2015 - p64(1) [51-500]

Same Time Next Week: True Stories of Working through Mental Illness
    BL - v111 - i13 - March 1 2015 - p11(1) [51-500]

Gutknecht, Allison - *Never Wear Red Lipstick on Picture Day: And Other Lessons I've Learned (Illus. by Lewis, Stevie)*
    c HB Guide - v26 - i2 - Fall 2015 - p66(1) [51-500]
Pizza Is the Best Breakfast: And Other Lessons I've Learned (Illus. by Lewis, Stevie)
    c HB Guide - v26 - i2 - Fall 2015 - p66(1) [51-500]

Gutman, Dan - *Flashback Four: The Lincoln Project*
    c BL - v112 - i6 - Nov 15 2015 - p54(1) [51-500]
    c KR - Nov 1 2015 - pNA [51-500]
    c SLJ - v61 - i10 - Oct 2015 - p89(2) [51-500]
License to Thrill
    c HB Guide - v26 - i2 - Fall 2015 - p85(1) [51-500]
Miss Suki Is Kooky! (Read by Goldsmith, Jared). Audiobook Review
    c SLJ - v61 - i6 - June 2015 - p62(1) [51-500]
Mrs. Yonkers is Bonkers! (Read by Goldsmith, Jared). Audiobook Review
    c SLJ - v61 - i7 - July 2015 - p45(1) [51-500]
Ms. Coco Is Loco (Read by Goldsmith, Jared). Audiobook Review
    c SLJ - v61 - i2 - Feb 2015 - p47(1) [51-500]
Rappy the Raptor (Illus. by Bowers, Tim)
    c HB Guide - v26 - i2 - Fall 2015 - p36(1) [51-500]
    c KR - Feb 1 2015 - pNA [51-500]
    c SLJ - v61 - i2 - Feb 2015 - p69(2) [51-500]
Willie & Me: A Baseball Card Adventure (Read by Heller, Johnny). Audiobook Review
    c BL - v112 - i1 - Sept 1 2015 - p142(1) [51-500]
    c SLJ - v61 - i9 - Sept 2015 - p59(1) [51-500]
Willie & Me: A Baseball Card Adventure
    c HB Guide - v26 - i2 - Fall 2015 - p85(1) [51-500]

Gutman, Marta - *A City for Children: Women, Architecture, and the Charitable Landscapes of Oakland, 1850-1950*
    JAH - v102 - i2 - Sept 2015 - p570-571 [501+]

Guttenplan, D.D. - *The Nation: A Biography: The First 150 Years*
    TLS - i5866 - Sept 4 2015 - p27(1) [501+]

Gutting, Gary - *What Philosophy Can Do*
    LJ - v140 - i13 - August 1 2015 - p99(1) [51-500]
    BL - v111 - i22 - August 1 2015 - p6(1) [51-500]
    KR - July 15 2015 - pNA [501+]

Guttler, Nils - *Das Kosmoskop: Karten und ihre Benutzer in der Pflanzengeographie des 19. Jahrhunderts*
    HNet - May 2015 - pNA [501+]
    Isis - v106 - i2 - June 2015 - p459(2) [501+]

Guttman, Jon - *Reconnaissance and Bomber Aces of World War 1*
    APH - v62 - i2 - Summer 2015 - p56(2) [501+]

Guttner-Sporzynski, Darius von - *Poland, Holy War, and the Piast Monarchy, 1100-1230*
    Med R - June 2015 - pNA [501+]

Guttormsson, Hjorleifur - *I Spor Jons Laerda*
    JEGP - v114 - i3 - July 2015 - p426(2) [501+]

Guy, Christine Fischer - *The Umbrella Mender*
    SPBW - March 2015 - pNA [51-500]

Guy, David - *Do Not Disturb the Dragon (Illus. by Schoenmaker, Patrick)*
    c Sch Lib - v63 - i1 - Spring 2015 - p27(1) [51-500]

Guy, John - *The Children of Henry VIII*
    JMH - v87 - i1 - March 2015 - p166(2) [501+]
Henry VIII: The Quest for Fame
    TLS - i5841 - March 13 2015 - p10(2) [501+]

Guyer, Paul - *A History of Modern Aesthetics, 3 vols.*
    TLS - i5839 - Feb 27 2015 - p12(2) [501+]

Guynn, Noah D. - *Violence and the Writing of History in the Medieval Francophone World*
    MLR - v110 - i2 - April 2015 - p541-542 [501+]

Guyot, Alain - *Analogie et recit de voyage: voir, mesurer, interpreter le monde*
    MLR - v110 - i2 - April 2015 - p537-538 [501+]

Gwendolen
    NYTBR - April 12 2015 - p30(L) [501+]

Gwinn, Dylan - *Bias in the Booth: An Insider Exposes How Sports Media Distort the News*
    CJR - v53 - i6 - March-April 2015 - p58(2) [501+]

Gwynn, R.S. - *Dogwatch: Poems*
    HR - v68 - i2 - Summer 2015 - p327-335 [501+]

Gwynn, Robin - *The Huguenots in Later Stuart Britain, Volume I*
    TimHES - i2224 - Oct 8 2015 - p43(1) [501+]

Gwynne, Paul - *Poets and Princes: The Panegyric Poetry of Johannes Michael Nagonius*
    Sev Cent N - v73 - i1-2 - Spring-Summer 2015 - p64(3) [501+]

Gwynne, Phillip - *Catch the Volt*
    c KR - June 1 2015 - pNA [51-500]

Gwynne, S.C. - *Rebel Yell: The Violence, Passion, and Redemption of Stonewall Jackson. Audiobook Review*
    LJ - v140 - i7 - April 15 2015 - p48(1) [51-500]
Rebel Yell: The Violence, Passion, and Redemption of Stonewall Jackson
    Roundup M - v22 - i4 - April 2015 - p26(1) [501+]

Gyling, Gemma - *CP Cats: A Complete Guide to Drawing Cats in Colored Pencil*
    SPBW - May 2015 - pNA [501+]

Gyorffy, Dora - *Institutional Trust and Economic Policy: Lessons from the History of the Euro*
    E-A St - v67 - i8 - Oct 2015 - p1337(2) [501+]

H

Ha Jin - *A Map of Betrayal*. Audiobook Review
LJ - v140 - i5 - March 15 2015 - p71(2) [51-500]
A Map of Betrayal
NY - v90 - i43 - Jan 12 2015 - p71 [51-500]
Ha, Marie-Paul - *French Women and the Empire: The Case of Indochina*
FS - v69 - i2 - April 2015 - p256-257 [501+]
Haab, Sherri - *Charm Love Friendship Bracelets: 35 Unique Designs with Polymer Clay, Macrame, Knotting, and Braiding*
Bwatch - Sept 2015 - pNA [51-500]
LJ - v140 - i14 - Sept 1 2015 - p104(1) [51-500]
Haan, Francisca de - *The 'Problem of Women' in Post-War Europe Women's Activism: Global Perspectives from the 1890s to the Present*
HER - v130 - i545 - August 2015 - p934(11) [501+]
Haarmann, Anke - *Shanghai (Urban Public) Space*
HNet - June 2015 - pNA [501+]
Haas, Derek - *A Different Lie*
BL - v112 - i1 - Sept 1 2015 - p46(1) [51-500]
KR - Sept 15 2015 - pNA [51-500]
PW - v262 - i33 - August 17 2015 - p50(1) [51-500]
Haas, Ernst - *Ernst Haas: On Set*
RVBW - August 2015 - pNA [51-500]
Haas, Frans A.J. de - *Interpreting AristotleEs Posterior Analytics in Late Antiquity and Beyond*
Class R - v65 - i2 - Oct 2015 - p380-382 [501+]
Haas, Lisbeth - *Saints and Citizens: Indigenous Histories of Colonial Missions and Mexican California*
AHR - v120 - i1 - Feb 2015 - p231-232 [501+]
JAH - v102 - i2 - Sept 2015 - p549-549 [501+]
Haas, Michael - *Asian and Pacific Regional Cooperation: Turning Zones of Conflict into Arenas of Peace*
JAS - v74 - i1 - Feb 2015 - p175-176 [501+]
Haas, Stefan - *Die Wirklichkeit der Geschichte: Wissenschaftstheoretische, Mediale und Lebensweltliche Aspekte eines (Post-)Konstruktivistischen Wirklichkeitsbegriffes in den Kulturwissenschaften*
HNet - July 2015 - pNA [501+]
Haas, Timothy C. - *Introduction to Probability and Statistics for Ecosystem Managers: Simulation and Resampling*
QRB - v90 - i4 - Dec 2015 - p432(2) [501+]
Haase, Tom - *Secret of the Thorns*
RVBW - April 2015 - pNA [501+]
Habegger, Alfred - *Masked: The Life of Anna Leonowens, Schoolmistress at the Court of Siam*
JAS - v74 - i3 - August 2015 - p780-782 [501+]
Habel, Dorothy Metzger - *"When All of Rome Was Under Construction": The Building Process in Baroque Rome*
J Urban H - v41 - i1 - Jan 2015 - p152-5 [501+]
Haber, Carole - *The Trials of Laura Fair: Sex, Murder, and Insanity in the Victorian West*
PHR - v84 - i1 - Feb 2015 - p90(2) [501+]
Haber, Peter - *Historyblogosphere: Bloggen in den Geschichtswissenschaften*
HNet - July 2015 - pNA [501+]
Haberfeld, M.R. - *Introduction to Policing: The Pillar of Democracy*
CrimJR - v40 - i2 - June 2015 - p233-235 [501+]
Haberman, David L. - *People Trees: Worship of Trees in Northern India*
JR - v95 - i4 - Oct 2015 - p559(2) [501+]
Habermas, Jurgen - *The Lure of Technocracy*
NYRB - v62 - i16 - Oct 22 2015 - p70(3) [501+]
Habermas, Rebekka - *Von Kafern, Markten und Menschen: Kolonialismus und Wissen in der Moderne*
HNet - Feb 2015 - pNA [501+]

Habets, Myk - *Ecumenical Perspectives on the Filioque for the Twenty-First Century*
Theol St - v76 - i3 - Sept 2015 - p642(2) [501+]
Habito, Ruben L.F. - *Zen and the Spiritual Exercises: Paths of Awakening and Transformation*
TT - v72 - i2 - July 2015 - p245-247 [501+]
Hachisu, Nancy Singleton - *Preserving the Japanese Way: Traditions of Salting, Fermenting, and Pickling for the Modern Kitchen*
LJ - v140 - i14 - Sept 1 2015 - p129(2) [51-500]
Hachmeister, Lutz - *Heideggers Testament: Der Philosoph, der Spiegel und die SS*
HNet - Jan 2015 - pNA [501+]
Hachtmann, Rudiger - *Berlin im Nationalsozialismus: Politik und Gesellschaft, 1933-1945*
HER - v130 - i544 - June 2015 - p780(3) [501+]
Hachtroudi, Fariba - *The Man Who Snapped His Fingers*
KR - Nov 15 2015 - pNA [51-500]
Hackel, Steven W. - *Junipero Serra: California's Founding Father*
RAH - v43 - i3 - Sept 2015 - p447-455 [501+]
Hackenberg, Rachel G. - *Sacred Pause: A Creative Retreat for the Word-Weary Christian*
RVBW - March 2015 - pNA [51-500]
Hacker, Andrew - *The Math Myth*
KR - Dec 1 2015 - pNA [51-500]
Hacker, Marilyn - *A Stranger's Mirror: New and Selected Poems, 1994-2014*
BL - v111 - i9-10 - Jan 1 2015 - p32(2) [51-500]
LJ - v140 - i3 - Feb 15 2015 - p105(2) [51-500]
PW - v262 - i3 - Jan 19 2015 - p60(1) [51-500]
Wom R Bks - v32 - i4 - July-August 2015 - p17(3) [501+]
Hackett, David G. - *That Religion in Which All Men Agree: Freemasonry in American Culture*
AHR - v120 - i3 - June 2015 - p1008-1009 [501+]
CH - v84 - i3 - Sept 2015 - p695(4) [501+]
JAH - v102 - i1 - June 2015 - p240-241 [501+]
JIH - v46 - i1 - Summer 2015 - p129-130 [501+]
Hacking, Juliet - *Lives of the Great Photographers*
BL - v111 - i5 - Nov 1 2015 - p22(1) [51-500]
Hackman, William - *Out of Sight: The Los Angeles Art Scene of the Sixties*
LJ - v140 - i3 - Feb 15 2015 - p96(2) [51-500]
PW - v262 - i5 - Feb 2 2015 - p48(1) [51-500]
Hacohen, Dean - *Who's Hungry? (Illus. by Scharschmidt, Sherry)*
c KR - June 1 2015 - pNA [51-500]
c PW - v262 - i21 - May 25 2015 - p58(1) [501+]
c SLJ - v61 - i8 - August 2015 - p63(1) [51-500]
Haddad, Qassim - *Chronicles of Majnun Layla and Selected Poems*
WLT - v89 - i5 - Sept-Oct 2015 - p67(1) [51-500]
Haddad, Saleem - *Guapa*
KR - Jan 1 2016 - pNA [51-500]
Haddam, Jane - *Fighting Chance (Read by Colacci, David)*. Audiobook Review
BL - v111 - i15 - April 1 2015 - p85(1) [51-500]
Haddick, Robert - *Fire on the Water: China, America, and the Future of the Pacific*
For Aff - v94 - i1 - Jan-Feb 2015 - pNA [51-500]
Mar Crp G - v99 - i3 - March 2015 - p86(2) [501+]
NWCR - v68 - i3 - Summer 2015 - p165(2) [501+]
Parameters - v45 - i2 - Summer 2015 - p97(11) [501+]
Haddix, Margaret - *Revealed*
c HB Guide - v26 - i1 - Spring 2015 - p79(1) [51-500]

Haddix, Margaret Peterson - *Palace of Lies*
y BL - v111 - i9-10 - Jan 1 2015 - p103(1) [51-500]
y HB Guide - v26 - i2 - Fall 2015 - p121(1) [51-500]
y KR - Feb 1 2015 - pNA [51-500]
y SLJ - v61 - i6 - June 2015 - p108(1) [51-500]
y VOYA - v38 - i1 - April 2015 - p79(1) [51-500]
Redeemed
c KR - July 1 2015 - pNA [51-500]
Revealed (Read by Sorensen, Chris). Audiobook Review
c SLJ - v61 - i3 - March 2015 - p80(1) [51-500]
Under Their Skin
c BL - v112 - i7 - Dec 1 2015 - p64(1) [51-500]
c PW - v262 - i41 - Oct 12 2015 - p68(1) [51-500]
c SLJ - v61 - i11 - Nov 2015 - p95(2) [51-500]
Haddon, Karen - *How to Juggle without Balls*
SPBW - Oct 2015 - pNA [51-500]
Hadfield, Andrfew - *The Ashgate Research Companion in Popular Culture in Early Modern England*
Six Ct J - v46 - i3 - Fall 2015 - p692-693 [501+]
Hadfield, Andrew - *The Oxford Handbook of English Prose, 1500u-1640*
MP - v112 - i4 - May 2015 - pE295(3) [501+]
Hadfield, Chris - *You Are Here: Around the World in 92 Minutes - Photographs from the International Space Station*
NYRB - v62 - i9 - May 21 2015 - p34(3) [501+]
Hadfield, Dorothy A. - *Shaw and Feminisms: On Stage and Off*
ILS - v34 - i2 - Spring 2015 - p15(1) [51-500]
Hadland, Tony - *Bicycle Design: An Illustrated History*
T&C - v56 - i4 - Oct 2015 - p983-984 [501+]
Isis - v106 - i2 - June 2015 - p480(2) [501+]
Hadler, Susan Johnson - *The Beauty of What Remains: Family Lost, Family Found*
BL - v112 - i2 - Sept 15 2015 - p18(1) [51-500]
Hadley, Dawn M. - *Everyday Life in Viking-Age Towns: Social Approaches to Towns in England and Ireland, c. 800-1100*
Med R - Jan 2015 - pNA [501+]
Medieval Childhood: Archaeological Approaches
Specu - v90 - i4 - Oct 2015 - p1190-1191 [501+]
Hadley, Tessa - *The Past*
BL - v112 - i6 - Nov 15 2015 - p22(1) [51-500]
KR - Nov 1 2015 - pNA [51-500]
LJ - v140 - i16 - Oct 1 2015 - p69(1) [51-500]
Spec - v329 - i9761 - Sept 26 2015 - p44(1) [501+]
TLS - i5868 - Sept 18 2015 - p19(1) [501+]
Hadlow, Janice - *A Royal Experiment: The Private Life of King George III*
BL - v111 - i19-20 - June 1 2015 - p27(1) [501+]
Haecker, Theodor - *Virgil, Father of the West*
AM - v213 - i14 - Nov 9 2015 - p23(3) [501+]
Haedrich, Ken - *Dinner Pies: From Shepherd's Pies and Pot Pies to Turnovers, Quiches, Hand Pies, and More*
LJ - v140 - i20 - Dec 1 2015 - p126(1) [51-500]
Haefeli, Evan - *New Netherland and the Dutch Origins of American Toleration*
HER - v130 - i542 - Feb 2015 - p192(2) [501+]
Haeg, Larry - *Harriman vs. Hill: Wall Street's Great Railroad War*
BHR - v89 - i3 - Autumn 2015 - p605(3) [501+]
JEH - v75 - i1 - March 2015 - p295-297 [501+]
Haffner, Ernst - *Blood Brothers*
TLS - i5851 - May 22 2015 - p20(1) [501+]
Haffner, Jeanne - *The View from Above: The Science of Social Space*
JMH - v87 - i1 - March 2015 - p199(2) [501+]
Hafter, Daryl M. - *Women and Work in Eighteenth-Century France*
T&C - v56 - i4 - Oct 2015 - p978-980 [501+]

Hagar, Amit - *Discrete or Continuous?: The Quest for Fundamental Length in Modern Physics*
    Phys Today - v68 - i1 - Jan 2015 - p44-44 [501+]
Hagar, Erin - *Julia Child: An Extraordinary Life in Words and Pictures (Illus. by Gorham, Joanna)*
    c SLJ - v61 - i7 - July 2015 - p107(1) [51-500]
Hagar, Sammy - *Are We Having Fun Yet? The Cooking and Partying Handbook*
    PW - v262 - i33 - August 17 2015 - p66(1) [51-500]
Hagberg, David - *The Fourth Horseman*
    PW - v262 - i51 - Dec 14 2015 - p62(1) [51-500]
Hagedorn, Anselm C. - *Law and Religion in the Eastern Mediterranean: From Antiquity to Early Islam*
    JNES - v74 - i2 - Oct 2015 - p380(4) [501+]
Hagemann, Jorg - *Pragmatischer Standard*
    MLR - v110 - i2 - April 2015 - p580-581 [501+]
Hagemann, Karen - *Gender and the Long Postwar: The United States and the Two Germanys, 1945-1989*
    J Mil H - v79 - i2 - April 2015 - p540-541 [501+]
Hagen, Bethany - *Jubilee Manor*
    y VOYA - v38 - i3 - August 2015 - p77(2) [51-500]
    y BL - v111 - i21 - July 1 2015 - p56(1) [51-500]
    y KR - June 15 2015 - pNA [51-500]
    y SLJ - v61 - i8 - August 2015 - p114(1) [51-500]
Hagen, George - *Gabriel Finley and the Raven's Riddle (Read by Goldstrom, Michael). Audiobook Review*
    c HB - v91 - i2 - March-April 2015 - p130(1) [51-500]
Gabriel Finley and the Raven's Riddle (Illus. by Bakal, Scott)
    c BL - v111 - i9-10 - Jan 1 2015 - pS4(8) [501+]
Gabriel Finley and the Raven's Riddle
    c CH Bwatch - Jan 2015 - pNA [501+]
    c HB Guide - v26 - i1 - Spring 2015 - p79(1) [51-500]
Hagendorf, Colin Atrophy - *Slice Harvester: A Memoir in Pizza*
    PW - v262 - i22 - June 1 2015 - p54(1) [51-500]
Hager, Mandy - *Resurrection*
    y HB Guide - v26 - i1 - Spring 2015 - p109(1) [51-500]
Hagerty, Barbara Bradley - *Life Reimagined*
    KR - Dec 15 2015 - pNA [501+]
Hagerud, Angelique - *No Billionaire Left Behind: Satirical Activism in America*
    SAH - v4 - i2 - Dec 15 2015 - p299-303 [501+]
Hageseth, Christian - *Big Weed: An Entrepreneur's High-Stakes Adventures in Budding Legal Marijuana Business*
    KR - Feb 15 2015 - pNA [501+]
Big Weed: An Entrepreneur's High-Stakes Adventures in the Budding Legal Marijuana Business
    PW - v262 - i5 - Feb 2 2015 - p45(1) [51-500]
Hagiwara, Sakutaro - *Cat Town*
    TLS - i5843 - March 27 2015 - p30(1) [501+]
Hagler, Kaye - *Take 5! for Science: 150 Prompts That Build Writing and Critical-Thinking Skills*
    Teach Lib - v43 - i1 - Oct 2015 - p41(3) [501+]
Hagopian, Patrick - *American Immunity: War Crimes and the Limits of International Law*
    JAH - v101 - i4 - March 2015 - p1320-1321 [501+]
Hague, Harlan - *The People*
    Roundup M - v22 - i6 - August 2015 - p30(1) [501+]
Hahn, Beth - *The Singing Bone*
    KR - Jan 1 2016 - pNA [51-500]
Hahn, Daniel - *The Oxford Companion to Children's Literature, 2d ed.*
    c LJ - v140 - i16 - Oct 1 2015 - p106(2) [51-500]
    c Sch Lib - v63 - i2 - Summer 2015 - p123(1) [51-500]
    c TLS - i5850 - May 15 2015 - p20(1) [501+]
The Oxford Companion to Children's Literature
    Spec - v327 - i9737 - April 11 2015 - p42(3) [501+]
Hahn, Hans-Joachim - *Beschreibungsversuche der Judenfeindschaft: Zur Geschichte der Antisemitismusforschung vor 1944*
    HNet - July 2015 - pNA [501+]
Hahn, Jan - *A Peculiar Connection*
    PW - v262 - i33 - August 17 2015 - p58(1) [51-500]
Hahn, Linda J. - *Rock That Quilt Block: Weathervane*
    Bwatch - Nov 2015 - pNA [51-500]
Hahn, Mary - *Where I Belong*
    c HB Guide - v26 - i1 - Spring 2015 - p79(1) [51-500]

Hahn, Mary Downing - *Took: A Ghost Story*
    c KR - July 1 2015 - pNA [51-500]
    c PW - v262 - i28 - July 13 2015 - p66(1) [51-500]
    c SLJ - v61 - i7 - July 2015 - p78(1) [51-500]
    c VOYA - v38 - i3 - August 2015 - p78(1) [51-500]
Took
    c HB - v91 - i5 - Sept-Oct 2015 - p103(2) [51-500]
Hahn, Rebecca - *A Creature of Moonlight*
    c SLJ - v61 - i6 - June 2015 - p46(6) [51-500]
The Shadow Behind the Stars
    y BL - v112 - i1 - Sept 1 2015 - p109(1) [51-500]
    KR - June 1 2015 - pNA [51-500]
    y PW - v262 - i49 - Dec 2 2015 - p105(1) [51-500]
    y SLJ - v61 - i7 - July 2015 - p86(2) [51-500]
    y VOYA - v38 - i4 - Oct 2015 - p70(1) [51-500]
Hahnemann, Trine - *Scandinavian Baking*
    NYT - Dec 2 2015 - pD6(L) [501+]
Hahnenberg, Edward P. - *Theology for Ministry: An Introduction for Lay Ministers*
    Theol St - v76 - i2 - June 2015 - p400(1) [501+]
Haid, Karen - *Calabria: The Other Italy*
    PW - v262 - i17 - April 27 2015 - p67(1) [51-500]
Haig, Francesca - *The Fire Sermon*
    BL - v111 - i11 - Feb 1 2015 - p32(1) [51-500]
    BL - v111 - i18 - May 15 2015 - p35(1) [501+]
    KR - Jan 15 2015 - pNA [51-500]
    LJ - v140 - i3 - Feb 15 2015 - p88(1) [51-500]
    PW - v262 - i1 - Jan 5 2015 - p56(1) [51-500]
    y SLJ - v61 - i10 - Oct 2015 - p122(2) [51-500]
Haig, Matt - *Reasons to Stay Alive*
    KR - Nov 15 2015 - pNA [501+]
Haigaz, Aram - *Four Years in the Mountains of Kurdistan: An Armenian Boy's Memoir of Survival*
    BL - v111 - i11 - Feb 1 2015 - p12(1) [51-500]
    KR - Jan 1 2015 - pNA [51-500]
Four Years in the Mountains of Kurdistan: An Armenian Boy's Memoir of Survival (Read by Chekenian, Iris Haigaz.)
    PW - v262 - i7 - Feb 16 2015 - p173(1) [51-500]
Four Years in the Mountains of Kurdistan: An Armenian Boy's Memoir of Survival
    TLS - i5870 - Oct 2 2015 - p26(1) [501+]
Haight, Jessica - *The Secret Files of Fairday Morrow (Illus. by Muradov, Roman)*
    c BL - v112 - i6 - Nov 15 2015 - p55(1) [51-500]
    c KR - Sept 15 2015 - pNA [51-500]
    c PW - v262 - i38 - Sept 21 2015 - p74(1) [51-500]
    c SLJ - v61 - i10 - Oct 2015 - p90(1) [501+]
Haight, Roger - *Spirituality Seeking Theology*
    Theol St - v76 - i2 - June 2015 - p399(2) [501+]
Hailwood, Mark - *Alehouses and Good Fellowship in Early Modern England*
    AHR - v120 - i4 - Oct 2015 - p1549(1) [501+]
    HNet - Sept 2015 - pNA [501+]
    HT - v65 - i4 - April 2015 - p58(2) [501+]
    TLS - i5860 - July 24 2015 - p25(1) [501+]
Hain, Peter - *Back to the Future of Socialism*
    NS - v144 - i5250 - Feb 20 2015 - p49(1) [501+]
Haines, Amber C. - *Wild in the Hollow*
    PW - v262 - i23 - June 8 2015 - p54(2) [51-500]
Haines, Brigid - *Herta Muller*
    MLR - v110 - i2 - April 2015 - p609-610 [501+]
Haines, Carolyn - *Bone to be Wild*
    BL - v111 - i17 - May 1 2015 - p22(1) [51-500]
    PW - v262 - i13 - March 30 2015 - p52(2) [51-500]
Haines, David W. - *Wind Over Water: Migration in an East Asian Context*
    JRAI - v21 - i3 - Sept 2015 - p704(2) [501+]
Hainnu, Rebecca - *The Spirit of the Sea (Illus. by Lim, Hwei)*
    c CH Bwatch - Sept 2015 - pNA [51-500]
    c KR - Jan 15 2015 - pNA [51-500]
    c Res Links - v20 - i4 - April 2015 - p4(1) [51-500]
Hainsworth, Emily - *Take the Fall*
    y KR - Nov 15 2015 - pNA [51-500]
Hainsworth, Peter - *Dante: A Very Short Introduction*
    TLS - i5843 - March 27 2015 - p31(1) [501+]
Hair, David - *Mage's Blood (Read by Podehl, Nick). Audiobook Review*
    BL - v111 - i18 - May 15 2015 - p69(1) [51-500]
Hairston, Julia L. - *The Poems and Letters of Tullia d'Aragona and Others*
    Ren Q - v68 - i1 - Spring 2015 - p372-374 [501+]
Hajari, Nisid - *Midnight's Furies: The Deadly Legacy of India's Partition*
    BL - v111 - i16 - April 15 2015 - p14(1) [51-500]
    Econ - v416 - i8945 - July 4 2015 - p70(US) [501+]

    KR - Feb 15 2015 - pNA [501+]
    LJ - v140 - i7 - April 15 2015 - p101(1) [51-500]
    NYRB - v62 - i6 - April 2 2015 - p46(3) [501+]
    NYTBR - July 12 2015 - p13(L) [501+]
    PW - v262 - i16 - April 20 2015 - p67(1) [51-500]
Hajdu, Laszlo - *Baghdad Blues*
    KR - August 15 2015 - pNA [501+]
Hajimu, Masuda - *Cold War Crucible: The Korean Conflict and the Postwar World*
    HNet - May 2015 - pNA [501+]
Hajin, Seo - *A Good Family*
    KR - Oct 1 2015 - pNA [501+]
Hake, Sabine - *Screen Nazis: Cinema, History, and Democracy*
    GSR - v38 - i1 - Feb 2015 - p213-215 [501+]
Turkish German Cinema in the New Millennium: Sites, Sounds, and Screens
    GSR - v38 - i2 - May 2015 - p463-5 [501+]
Hake, Terrence - *Operation Greylord: The True Story of an Untrained Undercover Agent and America's Biggest Corruption Bust*
    PW - v262 - i15 - April 13 2015 - p66(2) [51-500]
    LJ - v140 - i10 - June 1 2015 - p117(2) [51-500]
Hakim, Joy - *Reading Science Stories: Narrative Tales of Science Adventurers*
    c Sci & Ch - v53 - i3 - Nov 2015 - p89 [501+]
    Sci Teach - v82 - i8 - Nov 2015 - p70 [501+]
Hal Leonard Publishing Corporation - *Anthology of Easier Classical Piano: 174 Favorite Piano Pieces by 44 Composers*
    Am MT - v64 - i4 - Feb-March 2015 - p62(2) [51-500]
Halaban, Eytan - *The Vermeer Conspiracy*
    KR - Oct 15 2015 - pNA [501+]
Halabi, Abbas - *The Druze: A New Cultural and Historical Appreciation*
    RVBW - August 2015 - pNA [501+]
Haladjian, Haroutioun - *Consciousness, Attention, and Conscious Attention*
    RM - v69 - i1 - Sept 2015 - p134(2) [501+]
Halberstam, J. Jack - *Gaga Feminism: Sex, Gender, and the End of Normal*
    CWS - v30 - i2-3 - Fall-Winter 2015 - p140(2) [501+]
Halbrook, Kristin - *Every Last Promise*
    y BL - v111 - i14 - March 15 2015 - p65(1) [51-500]
    y CCB-B - v68 - i10 - June 2015 - p492(1) [51-500]
    y KR - Feb 1 2015 - pNA [51-500]
    y VOYA - v38 - i1 - April 2015 - p60(2) [51-500]
Haldane, Sean - *The Devil's Making*
    KR - March 1 2015 - pNA [51-500]
    PW - v262 - i11 - March 16 2015 - p65(1) [51-500]
Hale, Bruce - *Big Bad Detective Agency (Illus. by Hale, Bruce)*
    c CCB-B - v68 - i6 - Feb 2015 - p311(2) [51-500]
    c HB Guide - v26 - i2 - Fall 2015 - p66(1) [51-500]
Clark the Shark Takes Heart (Illus. by Francis, Guy)
    c HB Guide - v26 - i2 - Fall 2015 - p46(3) [51-500]
Clark the Shark: Tooth Trouble (Illus. by Francis, Guy)
    c HB Guide - v26 - i1 - Spring 2015 - p53(1) [51-500]
Danny and the Dinosaur and the New Puppy
    c KR - July 1 2015 - pNA [51-500]
Ends of the Earth (Illus. by Dorman, Brandon)
    c CCB-B - v69 - i2 - Oct 2015 - p91(1) [51-500]
Trouble Is My Beeswax
    c Teach Lib - v42 - i4 - April 2015 - p43(1) [51-500]
Hale, Dean - *The Princess in Black (Illus. by Pham, LeUyen)*
    c HB Guide - v26 - i1 - Spring 2015 - p60(1) [51-500]
    RVBW - Jan 2015 - pNA [51-500]
Hale, Elizabeth - *Readers Writing: Strategy Lessons for Responding to Narrative and Informational Text*
    VOYA - v38 - i2 - June 2015 - p92(1) [51-500]
Hale, Ginn - *Champion of the Scarlet Wolf, Book 1*
    PW - v262 - i32 - August 10 2015 - p42(1) [51-500]
Champion of the Scarlet Wolf, Book 2
    PW - v262 - i34 - August 24 2015 - p65(2) [51-500]
Hale, Kathleen - *Nothing Bad Is Going to Happen*
    y KR - Oct 15 2015 - pNA [51-500]
    y SLJ - v61 - i11 - Nov 2015 - p116(1) [51-500]
Hale, Mimsy - *100 Days*
    PW - v262 - i8 - Feb 23 2015 - p59(1) [51-500]
Hale, Nathan - *Nathan Hale's Hazardous Tales: The Underground Abductor (Illus. by Hale, Nathan)*
    c SLJ - v61 - i5 - May 2015 - p143(1) [51-500]

Hale, Piers J. - *Political Descent: Malthus, Mutualism, and the Politics of Evolution in Victorian England*
    QRB - v90 - i4 - Dec 2015 - p419(1) [501+]
    TLS - i5857 - July 3 2015 - p3(2) [501+]
Hale, Shannon - *Fire and Ice*
    c HB Guide - v26 - i1 - Spring 2015 - p79(2) [51-500]
  The Forgotten Sisters
    c CCB-B - v68 - i10 - June 2015 - p493(1) [51-500]
    c HB - v91 - i2 - March-April 2015 - p96(1) [51-500]
    c HB Guide - v26 - i2 - Fall 2015 - p85(1) [51-500]
    c SLJ - v61 - i6 - June 2015 - p108(1) [51-500]
    c Teach Lib - v43 - i1 - Oct 2015 - p42(1) [51-500]
  Palace of Stone
    c Teach Lib - v43 - i1 - Oct 2015 - p42(1) [51-500]
  The Princess in Black and the Hungry Bunny Horde
    c KR - Nov 15 2015 - pNA [51-500]
  The Princess in Black and the Perfect Princess Party (Illus. by Pham, LeUyen)
    c KR - July 15 2015 - pNA [51-500]
    c SLJ - v61 - i8 - August 2015 - p80(1) [51-500]
    c BL - v112 - i1 - Sept 1 2015 - p122(1) [51-500]
Hales, Peter B. - *Outside the Gates of Eden: The Dream of America from Hiroshima to Now*
    AHR - v120 - i2 - April 2015 - p663-664 [501+]
    JAH - v102 - i1 - June 2015 - p288-289 [501+]
Haley, Guy - *Sci-Fi Chronicles*
    Analog - v135 - i4 - April 2015 - p105(1) [501+]
    MFSF - v128 - i3-4 - March-April 2015 - p65(3) [501+]
Halfmann, Janet - *Animal Teachers (Illus. by Hudson, Katy)*
    c HB Guide - v26 - i1 - Spring 2015 - p154(1) [51-500]
  Grandma Is a Slowpoke (Illus. by Coxon, Michele)
    c KR - Dec 15 2015 - pNA [51-500]
    c PW - v262 - i47 - Nov 23 2015 - p66(1) [501+]
Halik, Thomas - *Night of the Confessor: Christian Faith in an Age of Uncertainty*
    Bks & Cult - v21 - i1 - Jan-Feb 2015 - p22(2) [501+]
  Patience with God: The Story of Zacchaeus
    Bks & Cult - v21 - i1 - Jan-Feb 2015 - p22(2) [501+]
Halim, Hala - *Alexandrian Cosmopolitanism: An Archive*
    IJMES - v47 - i1 - Feb 2015 - p186-189 [501+]
Hall, Alexis - *For Real*
    PW - v262 - i17 - April 27 2015 - p58(1) [51-500]
  Liberty and Other Stories. E-book Review
    PW - v262 - i9 - March 2 2015 - p67(2) [51-500]
Hall, Algy Craig - *The Deep Dark Wood (Illus. by Pye, Ali)*
    c Sch Lib - v63 - i2 - Summer 2015 - p92(2) [51-500]
Hall, Billy - *Duel of Shadows*
    RVBW - Jan 2015 - pNA [51-500]
Hall, Brian - *Quantum Theory for Mathematics*
    SIAM Rev - v57 - i3 - Sept 2015 - p478-479 [501+]
Hall, Catherine - *Macaulay and Son: Architects of Imperial Britain*
    VS - v57 - i2 - Wntr 2015 - p298(3) [501+]
Hall, Christopher - *Analysing Social Work Communication: Discourse in Practice*
    Lang Soc - v44 - i4 - Sept 2015 - p599-600 [501+]
Hall, Crystal - *Galileo's Reading*
    Ren Q - v68 - i1 - Spring 2015 - p268-270 [501+]
    Six Ct J - v46 - i2 - Summer 2015 - p455-457 [501+]
Hall, Darla - *Go Packers Activity Book*
    c CH Bwatch - Jan 2015 - pNA [51-500]
Hall, David - *The Open Fields of England*
    Med R - June 2015 - pNA [501+]
Hall, David Locke - *Crack99: The Takedown of a $100 Million Chinese Software Pirate*
    BL - v112 - i1 - Sept 1 2015 - p18(1) [51-500]
    KR - August 1 2015 - pNA [501+]
    PW - v262 - i24 - June 15 2015 - p73(1) [51-500]
Hall, Deirdre Riordan - *Sugar*
    y KR - April 15 2015 - pNA [51-500]
  Sugar (Read by Sands, Tara). Audiobook Review
    y SLJ - v61 - i10 - Oct 2015 - p54(1) [51-500]
  Sugar
    y PW - v262 - i17 - April 27 2015 - p77(1) [51-500]
Hall, Dewey W. - *Romantic Naturalists, Early Environmentalists: An Ecocritical Study, 1789-1912*
    RES - v66 - i276 - Sept 2015 - p790-792 [501+]
Hall, Donald - *Essays after Eighty*
    NYT - Jan 20 2015 - pD3(L) [501+]
    NYTBR - May 24 2015 - p30(L) [501+]
    Sew R - v123 - i1 - Wntr 2015 - pIII-IV [501+]
  The Selected Poems of Donald Hall
    PW - v262 - i46 - Nov 16 2015 - p52(1) [51-500]
  Unpacking the Boxes: A Memoir of a Life in Poetry
    Sew R - v123 - i1 - Wntr 2015 - pIII-IV [501+]
Hall, Edith - *Introducing the Ancient Greeks: From Bronze Age Seafarers to Navigators of the Western Mind*
    HT - v65 - i8 - August 2015 - p57(1) [51-500]
    NYRB - v62 - i19 - Dec 3 2015 - p59(2) [501+]
Hall, Eric Allen - *Arthur Ashe: Tennis and Justice in the Civil Rights Era*
    AHR - v120 - i4 - Oct 2015 - p1514-1515 [501+]
    HNet - July 2015 - pNA [501+]
    JAH - v102 - i2 - Sept 2015 - p616-617 [501+]
    JSH - v81 - i4 - Nov 2015 - p1044(2) [501+]
    TLS - i5835 - Jan 30 2015 - p30(1) [501+]
Hall, John A. - *The Importance of Being Civil: The Struggle for Political Decency*
    Soc - v52 - i1 - Feb 2015 - p102(3) [501+]
  Nationalism and War
    CS - v44 - i6 - Nov 2015 - p805-806 [501+]
Hall, Jonathan M. - *Artifact & Artifice: Classical Archaeology and the Ancient Historian*
    Class R - v65 - i2 - Oct 2015 - p554-556 [501+]
Hall, Katharine - *Amphibians and Reptiles: A Compare and Contrast Book*
    c CH Bwatch - Sept 2015 - pNA [51-500]
  Amphibians and Reptiles
    c KR - July 15 2015 - pNA [51-500]
  Clouds: A Compare and Contrast Book
    c CH Bwatch - April 2015 - pNA [51-500]
    c HB Guide - v26 - i1 - Spring 2015 - p151(1) [51-500]
  Trees: A Compare and Contrast Book
    c SLJ - v61 - i6 - June 2015 - p134(1) [51-500]
    c CH Bwatch - March 2015 - pNA [51-500]
    c HB Guide - v26 - i1 - Spring 2015 - p157(1) [51-500]
Hall, Kenneth R. - *The Growth of Non-Western Cities: Primary and Secondary Urban Networking, c. 900-1900*
    J Urban H - v41 - i1 - Jan 2015 - p165-6 [501+]
Hall, Kirsten - *The Jacket (Illus. by Tolstikova, Dasha)*
    c HB Guide - v26 - i1 - Spring 2015 - p32(1) [51-500]
Hall, Leanne - *Queen of the Night*
    y KR - Sept 15 2015 - pNA [51-500]
Hall, Louisa - *Speak*
    BL - v111 - i18 - May 15 2015 - p40(1) [51-500]
    LJ - v140 - i11 - June 15 2015 - p77(2) [51-500]
    NYT - July 30 2015 - pC6(L) [501+]
    NYTBR - August 30 2015 - p18(L) [501+]
    PW - v262 - i21 - May 25 2015 - p33(1) [51-500]
    Ent W - i1374 - July 31 2015 - p66(1) [501+]
Hall, Maggie - *The Conspiracy of Us (Read by Whelan, Julia). Audiobook Review*
    y BL - v111 - i19-20 - June 1 2015 - p140(1) [51-500]
    SLJ - v61 - i4 - April 2015 - p65(1) [51-500]
  The Conspiracy of Us
    y CCB-B - v68 - i7 - March 2015 - p355(2) [501+]
  Map of Fates
    y KR - Jan 1 2016 - pNA [51-500]
Hall, Mary Jane - *Colorful Crochet Lace: 22 Chic Garments and Accessories*
    LJ - v140 - i16 - Oct 1 2015 - p83(1) [51-500]
Hall, Michael - *Frankencrayon (Illus. by Hall, Michael)*
    c KR - Oct 15 2015 - pNA [51-500]
    c PW - v262 - i41 - Oct 12 2015 - p68(1) [51-500]
    c SLJ - v61 - i12 - Dec 2015 - p90(1) [51-500]
  George Frederick Bodley: And the Later Gothic Revival in Britain and America
    TLS - i5845 - April 10 2015 - p10(3) [501+]
  It's an Orange Aardvark
    c Sch Lib - v63 - i1 - Spring 2015 - p28(1) [51-500]
  Red: A Crayon's Story (Illus. by Hall, Michael)
    c BL - v111 - i11 - Feb 1 2015 - p57(1) [51-500]
    c HB - v91 - i1 - Jan-Feb 2015 - p65(1) [51-500]
    c HB Guide - v26 - i2 - Fall 2015 - p12(1) [51-500]
  Red, A Crayon's Story (Illus. by Hall, Michael)
    c Magpies - v30 - i2 - May 2015 - p32(1) [51-500]
  Red: A Crayon's Story (Illus. by Hall, Michael)
    c SLJ - v61 - i2 - Feb 2015 - p70(1) [51-500]
Hall, Parnell - *A Fool for a Client*
    BL - v112 - i1 - Sept 1 2015 - p46(1) [51-500]
    PW - v262 - i32 - August 10 2015 - p38(2) [51-500]
  Presumed Puzzled
    KR - Nov 15 2015 - pNA [51-500]
    PW - v262 - i45 - Nov 9 2015 - p38(1) [51-500]
  Puzzled Indemnity
    RVBW - Sept 2015 - pNA [51-500]

Hall, Peter A. - *Teach, Reflect, Learn: Building Your Capacity for Success in the Classroom*
    RVBW - June 2015 - pNA [501+]
Hall, Peter Geoffrey - *Cities in Civilization*
    TimHES - i2211 - July 9 2015 - p51(1) [501+]
Hall, Rachel Howzell - *Skies of Ash*
    KR - March 15 2015 - pNA [51-500]
    NYTBR - June 21 2015 - p25(L) [501+]
    PW - v262 - i6 - Feb 9 2015 - p45(1) [51-500]
Hall, Russ - *Three-Legged Horse*
    y BL - v112 - i1 - Sept 1 2015 - p52(1) [51-500]
Hall, Sandy - *Signs Point to Yes*
    y BL - v112 - i2 - Sept 15 2015 - p75(1) [51-500]
    y SLJ - v61 - i9 - Sept 2015 - p165(1) [51-500]
    y VOYA - v38 - i5 - Dec 2015 - p57(1) [51-500]
Hall, Sarah - *The Wolf Border*
    BL - v111 - i18 - May 15 2015 - p26(1) [51-500]
    CSM - August 7 2015 - pNA [501+]
    Econ - v415 - i8933 - April 11 2015 - p78(US) [501+]
    KR - April 1 2015 - pNA [501+]
    NS - v144 - i5259 - April 24 2015 - p49(1) [501+]
    NYT - June 25 2015 - pC4(L) [501+]
    NYTBR - July 19 2015 - p11(L) [501+]
    PW - v262 - i17 - April 27 2015 - p46(1) [51-500]
    Spec - v327 - i9735 - March 28 2015 - p38(2) [501+]
    TLS - i5845 - April 10 2015 - p19(2) [501+]
Hall, Tiffany - *Maxi and the Magical Money Tree*
    c Magpies - v30 - i4 - Sept 2015 - p33(1) [501+]
Hall, Tim - *Shadow of the Wolf*
    y CCB-B - v68 - i10 - June 2015 - p493(1) [51-500]
    y BL - v111 - i18 - May 15 2015 - p64(1) [51-500]
    y HB - v91 - i4 - July-August 2015 - p134(1) [51-500]
    y KR - March 1 2015 - pNA [51-500]
    y SLJ - v61 - i5 - May 2015 - p119(1) [51-500]
    y VOYA - v38 - i2 - June 2015 - p76(1) [51-500]
Hall, William J. - *The Bridgeport Poltergeist: True Tales of a Haunted House*
    y Teach Lib - v43 - i1 - Oct 2015 - p14(1) [51-500]
  The Haunted House Diaries: The True Story of a Quiet Connecticut Town in the Center of a Paranormal Mystery
    Bwatch - Oct 2015 - pNA [51-500]
Hallberg, Garth Risk - *City on Fire*
    BL - v111 - i22 - August 1 2015 - p39(1) [51-500]
    Esq - v164 - i4 - Nov 2015 - p38(1) [51-500]
    KR - July 15 2015 - pNA [501+]
    LJ - v140 - i13 - August 1 2015 - p83(1) [51-500]
    Mac - v128 - i42 - Oct 26 2015 - p57(1) [51-500]
    Nat Post - v17 - i277 - Oct 10 2015 - pWP4(1) [501+]
    New York - Oct 5 2015 - pNA [501+]
    NS - v144 - i5285 - Oct 23 2015 - p55(1) [501+]
    NY - v91 - i31 - Oct 12 2015 - p100 [501+]
    NYT - Oct 6 2015 - pC1(L) [501+]
    NYTBR - Oct 11 2015 - p1(L) [501+]
    PW - v262 - i22 - June 1 2015 - p37(1) [51-500]
    SEP - v287 - i5 - Sept-Oct 2015 - p24(1) [501+]
    Spec - v329 - i9764 - Oct 17 2015 - p41(2) [501+]
    TLS - i5872 - Oct 16 2015 - p19(1) [501+]
Halldenius, Lena - *Mary Wollstonecraft and Feminist Republicanism*
    TLS - i5871 - Oct 9 2015 - p12(1) [501+]
Halle, David - *New York and Los Angeles: The Uncertain Future*
    CS - v44 - i3 - May 2015 - p365-367 [501+]
Halleck, Mindy - *Return to Sender*
    KR - Jan 15 2015 - pNA [51-500]
Hallett, Christine E. - *Veiled Warriors: Allied Nurses of the First World War*
    AHR - v120 - i3 - June 2015 - p953-955 [501+]
Hallett, Hilary A. - *Dolores del Rio: Beauty in Light and Shade*
    PHR - v84 - i4 - Nov 2015 - p564(2) [501+]
Hallevy, Gabriel - *When Robots Kill: Artificial Intelligence Under Criminal Law*
    Reason - v46 - i11 - April 2015 - p70(2) [501+]
Halliday, Stephen - *Princes at War: The British Royal Family's Private Battle in the Second World War*
    TimHES - i2203 - May 14 2015 - p47-1 [501+]
Halliday, Sylvia - *My Lady Gloriana*
    PW - v262 - i41 - Oct 12 2015 - p54(1) [51-500]
Hallinan, P.K. - *A Love Letter from God (Illus. by Watson, Laura)*
    c CH Bwatch - Jan 2015 - pNA [51-500]
Hallinan, Timothy - *For the Dead*
    RVBW - July 2015 - pNA [51-500]
    RVBW - Sept 2015 - pNA [51-500]
  Herbie's Game
    RVBW - March 2015 - pNA [51-500]

The Hot Countries
    BL - v112 - i3 - Oct 1 2015 - p27(1) [51-500]
    PW - v262 - i32 - August 10 2015 - p38(1) [51-500]
    RVBW - Oct 2015 - pNA [51-500]

Hallisey, Charles - *Therigatha: Poems of the First Buddhist Women*
    NYRB - v62 - i14 - Sept 24 2015 - p64(3) [501+]

Halliwell, Martin - *Therapeutic Revolutions: Medicine, Psychiatry, and American Culture, 1945-1970*
    AHR - v120 - i2 - April 2015 - p659-660 [501+]

William James and the Transatlantic Conversation: Pragmatism, Pluralism, and Philosophy of Religion
    JAH - v102 - i1 - June 2015 - p267-267 [501+]

Hallman, J.C. - *B & Me: A True Story of Literary Arousal*
    WLT - v89 - i2 - March-April 2015 - p76(2) [501+]

Hallmundsson, Hallberg - *A Potpourri of Icelandic Poetry through Eleven Centuries*
    WLT - v89 - i5 - Sept-Oct 2015 - p71(1) [51-500]

Halloran, Bob - *White Devil: The True Story of the First White Asian Crime Boss*
    PW - v262 - i47 - Nov 23 2015 - p61(1) [51-500]

Halloran, Fiona Deans - *Thomas Nast: The Father of Modern Political Cartoons*
    SAH - v4 - i1 - Annual 2015 - p126-128 [501+]

Hallowell, Gerald - *The August Gales: The Tragic Loss of Fishing Schooners in the North Atlantic, 1926 and 1927*
    Beav - v95 - i2 - April-May 2015 - p57(1) [501+]

Halls, Kelly Milner - *Blazing Courage*
    c BL - v112 - i6 - Nov 15 2015 - p53(1) [51-500]
    c KR - Sept 15 2015 - pNA [51-500]

Ghostly Evidence: Exploring the Paranormal
    y HB Guide - v26 - i1 - Spring 2015 - p133(1) [51-500]
    y Teach Lib - v43 - i1 - Oct 2015 - p14(1) [51-500]

Halpern, Faye - *Sentimental Readers: The Rise, Fall, and Revival of a Disparaged Rhetoric*
    AL - v87 - i1 - March 2015 - p207-209 [501+]

Halpern, Jake - *Nightfall*
    y KR - July 15 2015 - pNA [51-500]
    y SLJ - v61 - i8 - August 2015 - p97(1) [51-500]
    y VOYA - v38 - i4 - Oct 2015 - p70(1) [51-500]
    y BL - v112 - i2 - Sept 15 2015 - p64(1) [51-500]

Halpern, Julie - *Maternity Leave*
    LJ - v140 - i13 - August 1 2015 - p83(1) [51-500]

Halpern, Monda - *Alice in Shandehland: Scandal and Scorn in the Edelsonj-Horowitz Murder Case*
    BL - v111 - i19-20 - June 1 2015 - p8(1) [51-500]

Halpern, Orit - *Beautiful Data: A History of Vision and Reason since 1945*
    HNet - Sept 2015 - pNA [501+]

Halpern, Paul - *Einstein's Dice and Schrodinger's Cat: How Two Great Minds Battled Quantum Randomness to Create a Unified Theory of Physics*
    BL - v111 - i13 - March 1 2015 - p10(1) [51-500]
    KR - Jan 15 2015 - pNA [501+]
    LJ - v140 - i3 - Feb 15 2015 - p125(1) [51-500]
    Mac - v128 - i17 - May 4 2015 - p55(1) [501+]
    Nature - v520 - i7547 - April 16 2015 - p293(1) [51-500]
    NYTBR - May 3 2015 - p10(L) [501+]
    PW - v262 - i5 - Feb 2 2015 - p46(1) [51-500]

Halpern, Shari - *Dinosaur Parade (Illus. by Halpern, Shari)*
    c HB Guide - v26 - i1 - Spring 2015 - p10(1) [51-500]

Halsey, Stephen R. - *Queen For Power: European Imperialism and the Making of Chinese Statecraft*
    TimHES - i2225 - Oct 15 2015 - p47(1) [501+]

Halsted, Deborah D. - *Library as Safe Haven: Disaster Planning, Response, and Recovery*
    R&USQ - v54 - i4 - Summer 2015 - p73(1) [501+]
    VOYA - v37 - i6 - Feb 2015 - p91(1) [501+]

Halston, Sidney - *Fighting Dirty*
    PW - v262 - i47 - Nov 23 2015 - p56(1) [51-500]

Halter, Paul - *Death Invites You*
    PW - v262 - i48 - Nov 30 2015 - p41(2) [51-500]

The Phantom Passage
    PW - v262 - i24 - June 15 2015 - p64(1) [51-500]

Haltom, E.A. - *Gwendolyn's Sword*
    KR - May 15 2015 - pNA [501+]
    PW - v262 - i25 - June 22 2015 - p125(1) [51-500]

Halton, David - *Despatches from the Front: Matthew Halton, Canada's Voice at War*
    TLS - i5845 - April 10 2015 - p31(1) [501+]

Halverson, Cathryn - *Playing House in the American West: Western Women's Life Narratives, 1839-1987*
    TSWL - v34 - i1 - Spring 2015 - p172-174 [501+]

Halverson, Sere Prince - *All the Winters After*
    BL - v112 - i4 - Oct 15 2015 - p16(1) [51-500]
    LJ - v140 - i20 - Dec 1 2015 - p90(1) [51-500]

Ham, Mary Katharine - *End of Discussion: How the Left's Outrage Industry Shuts Down Debate, Manipulates Voters, and Makes America Less Free and Fun*
    LJ - v140 - i12 - July 1 2015 - p98(2) [51-500]

Ham, Rosalie - *The Dressmaker*
    BL - v111 - i22 - August 1 2015 - p39(1) [51-500]
    NYTBR - August 16 2015 - p20(L) [501+]

Hama, Larry - *The Death of Captain America (Read by Rohan, Richard). Audiobook Review*
    LJ - v140 - i10 - June 1 2015 - p60(1) [51-500]

The Death of Captain America. Audiobook Review
    PW - v262 - i17 - April 27 2015 - p69(1) [51-500]

Hamann, Julian - *Die Bildung der Geisteswissenschaften: Zur Genese einer Sozialen Konstruktion zwischen Diskurs und Feld*
    HNet - Jan 2015 - pNA [501+]

Hamann, Matthias - *Der Liber Ordinarius Hallensis 1532 (Staatsbibliothek Bamberg, Msc. Lit. 119): Liturgische Reformen am Neuen Stift in Halle an der Saale unter Albrecht Kardinal von Brandenburg*
    HNet - April 2015 - pNA [501+]

Hamantaschen, J.R. - *With a Voice That Is Often Still Confused But Is Becoming Ever Louder and Clearer*
    KR - Dec 15 2015 - pNA [501+]

Hamblin, Joseph Darwin - *Arming Mother Nature: The Birth of Catastrophic Environmentalism*
    T&C - v56 - i1 - Jan 2015 - p293-295 [501+]

Hambly, Barbara - *Darkness on His Bones*
    BL - v112 - i2 - Sept 15 2015 - p38(1) [51-500]
    PW - v262 - i34 - August 24 2015 - p63(2) [51-500]

Hamburg, Jennifer - *Monkey and Duck Quack Up! (Illus. by Fotheringham, Edwin)*
    c BL - v111 - i12 - Feb 15 2015 - p88(1) [51-500]
    c CH Bwatch - May 2015 - pNA [501+]
    c HB Guide - v26 - i2 - Fall 2015 - p36(1) [51-500]

Hamburger, Jeffrey F. - *Catherine of Siena: The Creation of a Cult*
    Specu - v90 - i2 - April 2015 - p549-551 [501+]

Hamby, Alonzo L. - *Man of Destiny: FDR and the Making of the American Century*
    BL - v111 - i22 - August 1 2015 - p20(1) [51-500]
    KR - June 1 2015 - pNA [501+]
    LJ - v140 - i11 - June 15 2015 - p94(2) [51-500]
    PW - v262 - i28 - July 13 2015 - p59(1) [51-500]

Hamby, Barbara - *On The Street of Divine Love: New and Selected Poems*
    Wom R Bks - v32 - i3 - May-June 2015 - p20(1) [501+]

Hamel, Chouki el - *Black Morocco: A History of Slavery, Race, and Islam*
    AHR - v120 - i3 - June 2015 - p1142-1143 [501+]

Hamer, Kate - *The Girl in the Red Coat*
    y BL - v112 - i6 - Nov 15 2015 - p21(1) [51-500]
    KR - Dec 15 2015 - pNA [501+]

Hamer, Mary - *Kipling and Trix*
    PW - v262 - i45 - Nov 9 2015 - p34(1) [51-500]

Hamid, Mohsin - *Discontent and Its Civilizations: Dispatches from Lahore, New York, and London*
    CSM - Feb 25 2015 - pNA [501+]
    LJ - v140 - i3 - Feb 15 2015 - p100(1) [51-500]
    Mac - v128 - i8 - March 2 2015 - p62(1) [51-500]
    NYRB - v62 - i6 - April 2 2015 - p46(3) [51-500]
    NYT - March 10 2015 - pC1(L) [501+]
    TLS - i5839 - Feb 27 2015 - p26(2) [51-500]
    NYTBR - May 24 2015 - p30(L) [501+]
    WLT - v89 - i5 - Sept-Oct 2015 - p77(2) [501+]

Hamid, Omar Shahid - *The Prisoner of Zenda*
    BL - v111 - i12 - Feb 15 2015 - p39(1) [51-500]
    PW - v262 - i4 - Jan 26 2015 - p152(1) [51-500]

Hamilton, Alissa - *Got Milked? The Great Dairy Deception and Why You'll Thrive without Milk*
    LJ - v140 - i6 - April 1 2015 - p111(1) [51-500]
    PW - v262 - i11 - March 16 2015 - p79(1) [51-500]

Hamilton, Alwyn - *Rebel of the Sands*
    y KR - Dec 15 2015 - pNA [501+]

Hamilton, Amy T. - *Before the West Was West: Critical Essays on Pre-1800 Literature of the American Frontiers*
    Roundup M - v23 - i1 - Oct 2015 - p33(1) [501+]

Hamilton, Edmond - *The Universe Wreckers*
    Analog - v135 - i11 - Nov 2015 - p108(1) [501+]

Hamilton, Emma Walton - *The Very Fairy Princess: A Spooky, Sparkly Halloween (Illus. by Davenier, Christine)*
    c PW - v262 - i30 - July 27 2015 - p63(2) [51-500]

Hamilton, Gabrielle - *Prune*
    TLS - i5831 - Jan 2 2015 - p11(1) [501+]

Hamilton, Glen Erik - *Past Crimes*
    BL - v111 - i9-10 - Jan 1 2015 - p48(2) [51-500]
    PW - v262 - i1 - Jan 5 2015 - p52(1) [51-500]

Hamilton, James - *A Strange Business: A Revolution in Art, Culture, and Commerce in Nineteenth Century London*
    BL - v112 - i1 - Sept 1 2015 - p27(1) [51-500]
    KR - June 1 2015 - pNA [501+]
    LJ - v140 - i12 - July 1 2015 - p82(1) [51-500]

Hamilton, Jed - *Large Us the Smallest We've Got: A Jigsaw Puzzle*
    SPBW - May 2015 - pNA [501+]

Hamilton, John - *Battle of Little Bighorn*
    c Roundup M - v22 - i5 - June 2015 - p37(1) [501+]
    c Roundup M - v22 - i6 - August 2015 - p25(1) [501+]

BMX
    c HB Guide - v26 - i1 - Spring 2015 - p184(1) [51-500]

Go-Kart Racing
    c HB Guide - v26 - i1 - Spring 2015 - p184(1) [51-500]

Inline Skating
    c HB Guide - v26 - i1 - Spring 2015 - p184(1) [51-500]

Motocross
    c HB Guide - v26 - i1 - Spring 2015 - p184(1) [51-500]

Hamilton, Kersten - *The Ire of Iron Claw (Illus. by Hamilton, James)*
    c BL - v111 - i18 - May 15 2015 - p66(1) [51-500]
    c KR - April 15 2015 - pNA [51-500]

Yellow Copter (Illus. by Petrone, Valeria)
    c HB Guide - v26 - i2 - Fall 2015 - p12(1) [51-500]
    c KR - March 1 2015 - pNA [51-500]
    c SLJ - v61 - i5 - May 2015 - p79(1) [51-500]

Hamilton, Kiki - *The Midnight Spy*
    KR - Sept 1 2015 - pNA [501+]

Hamilton, Libby - *The Fairy-Tale Handbook (Illus. by Tomic, Tomislav)*
    c CH Bwatch - Jan 2015 - pNA [51-500]

How to Find Magical Creatures
    c Sch Lib - v63 - i4 - Winter 2015 - p238(1) [51-500]

The Ultimate Pirate Handbook (Illus. by Leyssenne, Matheiu)
    c KR - Dec 1 2015 - pNA [51-500]
    c PW - v262 - i27 - July 6 2015 - p70(2) [501+]
    c PW - v262 - i49 - Dec 2 2015 - p59(1) [51-500]

Hamilton, Liller - *Shoo, Fly! You Can't Eat Here! (Illus. by Switzer, Bobbi)*
    c CH Bwatch - Sept 2015 - pNA [51-500]

Hamilton, Margaret - *B Is for Bedtime (Illus. by Pignataro, Anna)*
    c KR - June 1 2015 - pNA [51-500]
    c SLJ - v61 - i6 - June 2015 - p72(2) [51-500]

Hamilton, Martha - *40 Fun Fables: Tales That Trick, Tickle and Teach (Illus. by Hoffmire, F. Baird)*
    c CH Bwatch - August 2015 - pNA [51-500]

40 Fun Fables: Tales That Trick, Tickle and Teach (Illus. by Hoffmeier, F. Baird)
    c CH Bwatch - July 2015 - pNA [51-500]

Hamilton, Matthew - *Make It Here: Inciting Creativity and Innovation in Your Library*
    c SLJ - v61 - i4 - April 2015 - p186(1) [51-500]
    c VOYA - v38 - i2 - June 2015 - p92(1) [51-500]

Hamilton, Maurice - *Alain Prost*
    NYT - Sept 19 2015 - pNA(L) [501+]

Grand Prix Circuits
    NYT - Sept 26 2015 - pNA(L) [501+]

Hamilton, Nigel - *The Mantle of Command: FDR at War, 1941-1942*
    AHR - v120 - i4 - Oct 2015 - p1505-1506 [501+]

Hamilton, Peter F. - *Great North Road*
    LJ - v140 - i19 - Nov 15 2015 - p110(1) [501+]

The Secret Throne
    c Sch Lib - v63 - i4 - Winter 2015 - p228(1) [51-500]

Hamilton, S.L. - *Fly Fishing*
    c HB Guide - v26 - i2 - Fall 2015 - p198(1) [51-500]

Ghost Hunting
    y Teach Lib - v43 - i1 - Oct 2015 - p14(1) [51-500]

Ice Fishing
    c HB Guide - v26 - i2 - Fall 2015 - p198(1) [51-500]

Spearfishing
    c HB Guide - v26 - i2 - Fall 2015 - p198(1) [51-500]

Xtreme Fish Series
    c HB Guide - v26 - i1 - Spring 2015 - p161(1) [51-500]

Xtreme Insects
    c HB Guide - v26 - i2 - Fall 2015 - p174(1) [51-500]

Hamilton, Sheila - *All the Things We Never Knew: Chasing the Chaos of Mental Illness*
    BL - v112 - i5 - Nov 1 2015 - p6(2) [51-500]
    KR - August 1 2015 - pNA [501+]
    LJ - v140 - i17 - Oct 15 2015 - p104(2) [51-500]

Hamilton, Steve - *A Stolen Season*
 RVBW - Jan 2015 - pNA [51-500]
Hamilton, Tim - *But!*
 c HB Guide - v26 - i2 - Fall 2015 - p36(1) [51-500]
Is That a Cat? (Illus. by Hamilton, Tim)
 c KR - July 1 2015 - pNA [51-500]
 c PW - v262 - i23 - June 8 2015 - p57(1) [51-500]
 c SLJ - v61 - i9 - Sept 2015 - p122(1) [51-500]
Hamilton, Virginia - *The Planet of Junior Brown*
 c HB - v91 - i1 - Jan-Feb 2015 - p47(4) [501+]
Hamlin, Christopher - *More Than Hot: A Short History of Fever*
 TLS - i5847 - April 24 2015 - p25(1) [501+]
Hamlin, Edward - *Night in Erg Chebbi*
 PW - v262 - i33 - August 17 2015 - p45(2) [51-500]
Hamlin, Hannibal - *The Bible in Shakespeare*
 TLS - i5860 - July 24 2015 - p10(2) [501+]
 MP - v112 - i3 - Feb 2015 - pE241(E243) [501+]
Hamlin, Kimberly A. - *From Eve to Evolution: Darwin, Science, and Women's Rights in Gilded Age America*
 Am St - v54 - i1 - Spring 2015 - p157-3 [501+]
 JAH - v102 - i1 - June 2015 - p266-266 [501+]
 Wom R Bks - v32 - i1 - Jan-Feb 2015 - p3(2) [501+]
Hamlin, William M. - *Montaigne's English Journey: Reading the Essays in Shakespeare's Day*
 Six Ct J - v46 - i1 - Spring 2015 - p226-228 [501+]
 Ren Q - v68 - i1 - Spring 2015 - p380-381 [501+]
Hamlyn - *Ella's Kitchen: The First Foods Book: The Purple One*
 CH Bwatch - June 2015 - pNA [51-500]
Hamm, Berndt - *The Early Luther: Stages in a Reformation Reorientation*
 TT - v72 - i1 - April 2015 - p111-112 [501+]
Hamm, Mark S. - *The Spectacular Few: Prisoner Radicalization and the Evolving Terrorist Threat*
 CS - v44 - i2 - March 2015 - p206-207 [501+]
 SF - v94 - i2 - Dec 2015 - pNA [501+]
Hammack, David C. - *A Versatile American Institution: The Changing Ideals and Realities of Philanthropic Foundations*
 JIH - v46 - i3 - Wntr 2016 - p456-458 [501+]
Hammann, Konrad - *Rudolf Bultmann: A Biography*
 Intpr - v69 - i1 - Jan 2015 - p113(1) [501+]
Hammelef, Danielle S - *Awesome Special Effects*
 c HB Guide - v26 - i2 - Fall 2015 - p192(2) [51-500]
Hammelef, Danielle S. - *Epic Stunts*
 c HB Guide - v26 - i2 - Fall 2015 - p199(1) [51-500]
Hammer, Langdon - *James Merrill: Life and Art*
 Comw - v142 - i12 - July 10 2015 - p35(3) [501+]
 Econ - v415 - i8934 - April 18 2015 - p75(US) [501+]
 G&L Rev W - v22 - i5 - Sept-Oct 2015 - p38(2) [501+]
 HR - v68 - i2 - Summer 2015 - p318-326 [501+]
 LJ - v140 - i12 - July 1 2015 - p83(1) [51-500]
 Nation - v301 - i23 - Dec 7 2015 - p23(4) [501+]
 NYT - April 15 2015 - pC1(L) [501+]
 NYTBR - May 17 2015 - p23(L) [501+]
 TimHES - i2211 - July 9 2015 - p47(1) [501+]
 TimHES - i2211 - July 9 2015 - p49(1) [501+]
Hammer, Lotte - *The Girl in the Ice*
 KR - Sept 1 2015 - pNA [51-500]
 PW - v262 - i37 - Sept 14 2015 - p42(1) [51-500]
Hammermann, Gabriele - *Sanierung - Rekonstruktion - Neugestaltung: Zum Umgang mit historischen Bauten in Gedenkstatten*
 HNet - April 2015 - pNA [501+]
Hammerstein, Peter - *Evolution and the Mechanisms of Decision Making*
 QRB - v90 - i1 - March 2015 - p67(4) [501+]
Hammill, Elizabeth - *Over the Hills and Far Away: A Treasury of Nursery Rhymes*
 c BL - v111 - i16 - April 15 2015 - p44(1) [51-500]
Over the Hills and Far Away: A Treasury of Nursery Rhymes (Illus. by Bryan, Ashley)
 PW - v262 - i4 - Jan 26 2015 - p171(1) [501+]
Over the Hills and Far Away: A Treasury of Nursery Rhymes
 c HB Guide - v26 - i2 - Fall 2015 - p160(1) [51-500]
 c KR - Jan 1 2015 - pNA [51-500]
 c NYTBR - April 12 2015 - p18(L) [501+]
 c PW - v262 - i49 - Dec 2 2015 - p55(1) [51-500]
 c Sch Lib - v63 - i1 - Spring 2015 - p28(1) [51-500]
Hammill, Faye - *Magazines, Travel, and Middlebrow Culture: Canadian Periodicals in English and French, 1925-1960*
 RVBW - Nov 2015 - pNA [51-500]
Hammilton, Alwyn - *Rebel of the Sands*
 y PW - v262 - i52 - Dec 21 2015 - p155(1) [51-500]

Hammond, Cally - *The Sound of the Liturgy: How Words Work in Worship*
 TLS - i5862 - August 7 2015 - p26(2) [501+]
Hammond, Geordan - *John Wesley in America: Restoring Primitive Christianity*
 JSH - v81 - i4 - Nov 2015 - p942(1) [501+]
Hammond, Heidi K. - *Reading the Art in Caldecott Award Books: A Guide to the Illustrations*
 CCB-B - v68 - i10 - June 2015 - p527(1) [51-500]
Hammond, Jay M. - *A Companion to Bonaventure*
 Theol St - v76 - i1 - March 2015 - p216(2) [501+]
 Six Ct J - v46 - i1 - Spring 2015 - p154-155 [501+]
Hammond, Kristie - *The Moment*
 y Res Links - v20 - i4 - April 2015 - p30(1) [51-500]
Hammond, Martin - *Arrian: Alexander the Great*
 Class R - v65 - i2 - Oct 2015 - p610-611 [501+]
Homer: The Odyssey
 Class R - v65 - i2 - Oct 2015 - p606-606 [501+]
Hammond, Mary - *Charles Dickens's Great Expectations: A Cultural Life, 1860-2012*
 TLS - i5862 - August 7 2015 - p27(1) [501+]
Hammond, Paul - *Milton and the People*
 RES - v66 - i275 - June 2015 - p581-583 [501+]
 TLS - i5831 - Jan 2 2015 - p21(1) [501+]
 HER - v130 - i545 - August 2015 - p998(2) [501+]
 Ren Q - v68 - i3 - Fall 2015 - p1156-1157 [501+]
Hammontree, Marie - *Walt Disney (Illus. by Irvin, Frank)*
 c HB Guide - v26 - i1 - Spring 2015 - p193(1) [51-500]
Hamnett, Stephen - *Planning Asian Cities: Risks and Resilience*
 J Urban H - v41 - i1 - Jan 2015 - p165-6 [501+]
Hamoudi, Haider Ala - *Negotiating in Civil Conflict: Constitutional Construction and Imperfect Bargaining in Iraq*
 IJMES - v47 - i1 - Feb 2015 - p177-178 [501+]
Hampf, M. Michaela - *Global Communication Electric: Business, News, and Politics in the World of Telegraphy*
 T&C - v56 - i3 - July 2015 - p756-757 [501+]
Hampson, Daphne - *Kierkegaard: Exposition and Critique*
 JR - v95 - i3 - July 2015 - p394(2) [501+]
Hampton, Dan - *The Hunter Killers: The Extraordinary Story of the First Wild Weasels, the Band of Maverick Aviators Who Flew the Most Dangerous Missions of the Vietnam War*
 KR - April 15 2015 - pNA [501+]
 LJ - v140 - i8 - May 1 2015 - p88(3) [501+]
 PW - v262 - i15 - April 13 2015 - p68(1) [51-500]
Hampton, Elaine - *Anay's Will to Learn: A Woman's Education in the Shadow of the Maquiladoras*
 Aztlan - v40 - i2 - Fall 2015 - p301-304 [501+]
Hampton, Isaac - *The Black Officer Corps: A History of Black Military Advancement from Integration through Vietnam*
 Arm F&S - v41 - i4 - Oct 2015 - p756-760 [501+]
Hamshaw, Gena - *Food52 Vegan: 60 Vegetable-Driven Recipes for Any Kitchen*
 LJ - v140 - i16 - Oct 1 2015 - p102(2) [51-500]
Hamstead, Katie - *Kiya: Hope of the Pharaoh*
 PW - v262 - i18 - May 4 2015 - p104(1) [51-500]
Hamza, Aziz - *Eterlimus*
 KR - Nov 1 2015 - pNA [501+]
Han, Enze - *Contestation and Adaptation: The Politics of National Identity in China*
 Pac A - v88 - i1 - March 2015 - p180 [501+]
Han, Eric C. - *Rise of a Japanese Chinatown: Yokohama, 1894-1972*
 Pac A - v88 - i3 - Sept 2015 - p709 [501+]
Han, Eun-sun - *The Flying Birds (Illus. by Kim, Ju-kyoung)*
 c BL - v111 - i19-20 - June 1 2015 - p79(1) [51-500]
 c PW - v262 - i23 - June 8 2015 - p58(1) [51-500]
 c SLJ - v61 - i8 - August 2015 - p120(1) [51-500]
Han, Jenny - *Ashes to Ashes*
 c HB Guide - v26 - i2 - Fall 2015 - p121(1) [51-500]
P.S. I Still Love You (Read by Keating, Laura Knight). Audiobook Review
 y SLJ - v61 - i11 - Nov 2015 - p72(2) [51-500]
P.S. I Still Love You
 y SLJ - v61 - i6 - June 2015 - p124(1) [51-500]
Han, Kang - *The Vegetarian*
 KR - Nov 1 2015 - pNA [501+]
 NS - v144 - i5250 - Feb 20 2015 - p51(1) [501+]
 TLS - i5839 - Feb 27 2015 - p20(1) [501+]
Hancock, Angela Dienhart - *Karl Barth's Emergency Homiletic, 1932-1933: A Summons to Prophetic Witness at the Dawn of the Third Reich*
 Intpr - v69 - i1 - Jan 2015 - p116(2) [501+]
Hancock, Graham - *Fingerprints of the Gods: The Evidence of Earth's Lost Civilization*
 Am Ant - v80 - i3 - July 2015 - p617(2) [501+]

Magicians of the Gods
 KR - Sept 15 2015 - pNA [501+]
Hancock, Herbie - *Herbie Hancock: Possibilities (Read by Hancock, Herbie). Audiobook Review*
 LJ - v140 - i3 - Feb 15 2015 - p60(1) [51-500]
Herbie Hancock: Possibilities
 TLS - i5862 - August 7 2015 - p3(3) [501+]
Hancock, Larry - *Surprise Attack: From Pearl Harbor to 9/11 to Benghazi*
 KR - July 1 2015 - pNA [501+]
 LJ - v140 - i15 - Sept 15 2015 - p92(2) [501+]
 PW - v262 - i28 - July 13 2015 - p60(1) [51-500]
Hancock, Sheila - *Miss Carter's War*
 KR - Feb 15 2015 - pNA [51-500]
Hancocks, Helen - *William & the Missing Masterpiece (Illus. by Hancocks, Helen)*
 c CH Bwatch - July 2015 - pNA [51-500]
 c HB Guide - v26 - i2 - Fall 2015 - p36(1) [51-500]
 KR - Feb 1 2015 - pNA [51-500]
 c SLJ - v61 - i7 - July 2015 - p62(1) [51-500]
Hand, Carol - *Dead Zones: Why Earth's Waters Are Losing Oxygen*
 y BL - v112 - i7 - Dec 1 2015 - p44(1) [51-500]
 y KR - Nov 1 2015 - pNA [51-500]
 y SLJ - v61 - i12 - Dec 2015 - p144(1) [51-500]
Epidemiology: The Fight against Ebola and Other Diseases
 y BL - v111 - i15 - April 1 2015 - p54(1) [51-500]
Hand, Cynthia - *The Last Time We Say Goodbye*
 y BL - v111 - i11 - Feb 1 2015 - p48(1) [51-500]
 y CCB-B - v68 - i9 - May 2015 - p449(1) [51-500]
 y NYTBR - Feb 8 2015 - p24(L) [501+]
 y VOYA - v37 - i6 - Feb 2015 - p56(1) [51-500]
Hand, Elizabeth - *Wylding Hall*
 PW - v262 - i15 - April 13 2015 - p60(2) [51-500]
Hand, Joni M. - *Women, Manuscripts and Identity in Northern Europe, 1350-1550*
 HER - v130 - i544 - June 2015 - p715(6) [501+]
Handel, Nick - *Calling the Shots! Using Film Techniques to Inspire Brilliant Creative Writing*
 Sch Lib - v63 - i3 - Autumn 2015 - p191(1) [51-500]
Handeland, Lori - *In the Air Tonight*
 PW - v262 - i14 - April 6 2015 - p46(1) [51-500]
Handerland, Lori - *Heat of the Moment*
 PW - v262 - i21 - May 25 2015 - p44(1) [51-500]
Handford, Jennifer - *The Light of Hidden Flowers*
 LJ - v140 - i17 - Oct 15 2015 - p82(2) [51-500]
Handler, Daniel - *Hurry Up and Wait (Illus. by Kalman, Maira)*
 c PW - v262 - i6 - Feb 9 2015 - p65(1) [51-500]
We Are Pirates
 NYTBR - March 1 2015 - p17(L) [501+]
 NYTBR - Nov 29 2015 - p24(L) [501+]
Handler, David - *The Lavender Lane Lothario*
 PW - v262 - i51 - Dec 14 2015 - p63(1) [51-500]
Phantom Angel
 BL - v111 - i9-10 - Jan 1 2015 - p50(1) [51-500]
Handler, Jerome S. - *Enacting Power: The Criminalization of Obeah in the Anglophone Caribbean 1760-2011*
 JRAI - v21 - i2 - June 2015 - p496(2) [501+]
Handler, Richard - *Excluded Ancestors, Inventible Traditions: Essays Toward a More Inclusive History of Anthropology*
 Bwatch - Nov 2015 - pNA [51-500]
Handlin, Amy - *Dirty Deals? An Encyclopedia of Lobbying, Political Influence, and Corruption*
 BL - v111 - i17 - May 1 2015 - p62(1) [51-500]
 R&USQ - v54 - i3 - Spring 2015 - p60(2) [501+]
Hands, Africa S. - *Successfully Serving the College Bound*
 LJ - v140 - i6 - April 1 2015 - p103(1) [51-500]
Hands, John - *Cosmosapiens: How We Are Evolving from the Origin of the Universe*
 KR - Oct 1 2015 - pNA [501+]
 LJ - v140 - i19 - Nov 15 2015 - p104(1) [501+]
 PW - v262 - i48 - Nov 30 2015 - p51(1) [501+]
Hanel, Marnie - *The Picnic: Recipes and Inspiration from Blanket to Basket*
 LJ - v140 - i5 - March 15 2015 - p126(2) [501+]
 PW - v262 - i24 - June 15 2015 - p79(2) [501+]
Hanel, Tilmann - *Die Bombe als Option: Motive fur den Aufbau einer atomtechnischen Infrastruktur in der Bundesrepublik bis 1963*
 HNet - May 2015 - pNA [501+]
Haney, Jill - *Area 51*
 y SLJ - v61 - i9 - Sept 2015 - p151(4) [501+]
Hanh, Thich Nhat - *Silence: The Power of Quiet in a World Full of Noise*
 Bwatch - April 2015 - pNA [51-500]
 LJ - v140 - i9 - May 15 2015 - p64(2) [501+]
Hanh, Tich Nhat - *How to Relax*
 LJ - v140 - i16 - Oct 1 2015 - p86(1) [51-500]

Hanhardt, Christina B. - *Safe Space: Gay Neighborhood History and the Politics of Violence*
  AHR - v120 - i4 - Oct 2015 - p1520-1521 [501+]
  CS - v44 - i5 - Sept 2015 - p664-665 [501+]
  J Am St - v49 - i3 - August 2015 - p645-646 [501+]
  JAH - v102 - i2 - Sept 2015 - p630-631 [501+]
  PHR - v84 - i3 - August 2015 - p398(400) [501+]

Hanick, Riley - *Three Kinds of Motion: Kerouac, Pollock, and the Making of American Highways*
  BL - v111 - i15 - April 1 2015 - p13(1) [51-500]
  KR - Feb 1 2015 - pNA [51-500]
  PW - v262 - i9 - March 2 2015 - p77(1) [51-500]

Hanink, Johanna - *Lycurgan Athens and the Making of Classical Tragedy*
  Class R - v65 - i2 - Oct 2015 - p385-387 [501+]

Hankela, Elina - *Ubuntu, Migration, and Ministry: Being Human in a Johannesburg Church*
  IBMR - v39 - i3 - July 2015 - p163(2) [501+]

Hankiewicz, John - *Education*
  ABR - v36 - i2 - Jan-Feb 2015 - p9(1) [501+]

Hankins, Dena - *Heart of the Liliko'i*
  PW - v262 - i36 - Sept 7 2015 - p53(1) [51-500]

Hankins, James - *Shady Cross*
  KR - Jan 1 2015 - pNA [51-500]

Hanks, Thomas D. - *Malory and Christianity: Essay on Sir Thomas Malory's " Morte Darthur"*
  Specu - v90 - i3 - July 2015 - p818-2 [501+]

Hanley, Jason - *Music Lab: We Rock!: A Fun Family Guide for Exploring Rock Music History*
  SLJ - v61 - i3 - March 2015 - p177(1) [51-500]

Hanley, Steve - *The Big Midweek: Life Inside the Fall*
  NS - v144 - i5248 - Feb 6 2015 - p41(1) [501+]

Hanlon, Abby - *Dory and the Real True Friend (Illus. by Hanlon, Abby)*
  c BL - v111 - i19-20 - June 1 2015 - p112(1) [51-500]
  c CCB-B - v69 - i2 - Oct 2015 - p91(2) [51-500]
  c KR - April 15 2015 - pNA [51-500]
  c PW - v262 - i24 - June 15 2015 - p85(1) [501+]
  c PW - v262 - i49 - Dec 2 2015 - p64(1) [51-500]
  Dory and the Real True Friend
  c SLJ - v61 - i4 - April 2015 - p140(2) [51-500]
  Dory Fantasmagory (Read by Jackson, Suzy). Audiobook Review
  c SLJ - v61 - i7 - July 2015 - p45(1) [51-500]
  Dory Fantasmagory
  c HB Guide - v26 - i1 - Spring 2015 - p60(1) [51-500]

Hanlon, Christopher - *America's England: Antebellum Literature and Atlantic Sectionalism*
  AL - v87 - i2 - June 2015 - p389-391 [501+]

Hanlon, David - *Making Micronesia: A Political Biography of Tosiwo Nakayama*
  AHR - v120 - i4 - Oct 2015 - p1471-1472 [501+]
  Amerasia J - v41 - i1 - Wntr 2015 - p123-126 [501+]

Hanlon, Gregory - *The Hero of Italy: Odoardo Farnese, Duke of Parma, His Soldiers and His Subjects in the Thirty Years' War*
  HNet - April 2015 - pNA [501+]
  HNet - Sept 2015 - pNA [501+]

Hanmin Kim - *Tiptoe Tapirs (Illus. by Hanmin Kim)*
  c HB - v91 - i6 - Nov-Dec 2015 - p70(2) [51-500]

Hanna, Earle W., Sr. - *My Reincarnations: Time Traveler*
  SPBW - Nov 2015 - pNA [51-500]

Hanna, Erika - *Modern Dublin: Urban Change and the Irish Past, 1957-1973*
  AHR - v120 - i2 - April 2015 - p711-712 [501+]
  HER - v130 - i544 - June 2015 - p790(2) [501+]

Hanna, Ralph - *Introducing English Medieval Book History: Manuscripts, their Producers and their Readers*
  Med R - Sept 2015 - pNA [501+]
  Richard Morris's Prick of Conscience: A Corrected and Amplified Reading Text
  Med R - Jan 2015 - pNA [501+]

Hanna, Virginia - *Shelby the Flying Snail (Illus. by Piu, Amandine)*
  c CH Bwatch - July 2015 - pNA [51-500]

Hannah, Kristin - *The Nightingale (Read by Stone, Polly). Audiobook Review*
  LJ - v140 - i9 - May 15 2015 - p42(2) [51-500]
  PW - v262 - i17 - April 27 2015 - p68(1) [51-500]

Hannah, Sophie - *Woman with a Secret*
  BL - v111 - i17 - May 1 2015 - p48(1) [51-500]
  KR - May 15 2015 - pNA [51-500]
  LJ - v140 - i9 - May 15 2015 - p79(1) [51-500]
  NYT - August 14 2015 - pC21(L) [501+]
  PW - v262 - i20 - May 18 2015 - p63(2) [51-500]

Hannaham, James - *Delicious Foods (Read by Hannaham, James). Audiobook Review*
  BL - v112 - i1 - Sept 1 2015 - p138(1) [51-500]
  LJ - v140 - i12 - July 1 2015 - p43(1) [51-500]
  PW - v262 - i30 - July 27 2015 - p61(1) [51-500]
  Delicious Foods
  BL - v111 - i15 - April 1 2015 - p23(1) [51-500]
  Ent W - i1357 - April 3 2015 - p63(1) [51-500]
  KR - Jan 15 2015 - pNA [51-500]
  Mac - v128 - i12 - March 30 2015 - p54(2) [501+]
  Nat Post - v119 - i17 - March 21 2015 - pWP5(1) [501+]
  NY - v91 - i11 - May 4 2015 - p70 [51-500]
  NYTBR - April 5 2015 - p19(L) [501+]
  PW - v262 - i4 - Jan 26 2015 - p1(1) [51-500]

Hannan, Peter - *Petlandia (Illus. by Hannan, Peter)*
  c BL - v111 - i16 - April 15 2015 - p50(1) [51-500]
  c HB Guide - v26 - i2 - Fall 2015 - p66(1) [51-500]
  c KR - Jan 15 2015 - pNA [51-500]
  c SLJ - v61 - i3 - March 2015 - p116(2) [51-500]

Hannas, William C. - *Chinese Industrial Espionage: Technology Acquisition and Military Modernization*
  Pac A - v88 - i1 - March 2015 - p178 [501+]

Hannickel, Erica - *Empire of Vines: Wine Culture in America*
  AHR - v120 - i4 - Oct 2015 - p1488-1489 [501+]
  JAH - v101 - i4 - March 2015 - p1261-1262 [501+]
  JIH - v45 - i3 - Wntr 2015 - p442-443 [501+]

Hannigan, Jessica Djabrayan - *The PBIS Tier One Handbook: A Practical Approach to Implementing the Champion Model*
  Bwatch - Sept 2015 - pNA [501+]

Hannigan, Kate - *The Detective's Assistant*
  c BL - v111 - i17 - May 1 2015 - p55(1) [51-500]
  c CCB-B - v68 - i11 - July-August 2015 - p546(2) [51-500]
  c HB Guide - v26 - i2 - Fall 2015 - p85(1) [51-500]
  c KR - Feb 1 2015 - pNA [51-500]
  c PW - v262 - i6 - Feb 9 2015 - p65(2) [51-500]
  c SLJ - v61 - i2 - Feb 2015 - p86(1) [51-500]

Hannigan, Katherine - *Gwendolyn Grace (Illus. by Hannigan, Katherine)*
  c HB Guide - v26 - i2 - Fall 2015 - p36(1) [51-500]
  c KR - Feb 15 2015 - pNA [51-500]
  c SLJ - v61 - i2 - Feb 2015 - p70(1) [51-500]

Hannon, Irene - *Buried Secrets*
  BL - v111 - i15 - April 1 2015 - p32(1) [51-500]
  PW - v262 - i9 - March 2 2015 - p72(1) [51-500]
  Hope Harbor (Read by Plummer, Therese). Audiobook Review
  BL - v112 - i6 - Nov 15 2015 - p61(1) [51-500]
  Hope Harbor
  BL - v111 - i21 - July 1 2015 - p44(1) [51-500]

Hannon, Kerry - *Love Your Job: The New Rules of Career Happiness*
  LJ - v140 - i6 - April 1 2015 - p101(1) [51-500]

Hanqing, Wu - *Web Security: A WhiteHat Perspective*
  Bwatch - Oct 2015 - pNA [51-500]

Hanrahan, Mairead - *Cixous's Semi-Fictions: Thinking at the Borders of Fiction*
  FS - v69 - i4 - Oct 2015 - p556-557 [501+]

Hanrahan, Rosemary - *When Dreams Touch*
  SPBW - August 2015 - pNA [501+]

Hans Sigrist Symposium: Women and Precarity: Historical Perspectives
  HNet - August 2015 - pNA [501+]

Hanscom, Christopher P. - *Imperatives of Culture: Selected Essays on Korean History, Literature, and Society from the Japanese Colonial Era*
  JAS - v74 - i3 - August 2015 - p760-761 [501+]

Hansen, Aliena - *Chomp, Chomp, Chomp*
  PW - v262 - i50 - Dec 7 2015 - p81(1) [51-500]

Hansen, Gitte - *Everyday Products in the Middle Ages: Crafts, Consumption and the Individual in Northern Europe c. AD 800-1600*
  Specu - v90 - i4 - Oct 2015 - p1191(1) [501+]

Hansen, Grace - *Ants*
  c HB Guide - v26 - i1 - Spring 2015 - p158(1) [51-500]
  Dolphins: Ocean Life
  c HB Guide - v26 - i2 - Fall 2015 - p179(1) [51-500]
  Jackie Robinson: Baseball Legend
  c HB Guide - v26 - i2 - Fall 2015 - p199(1) [51-500]
  Jane Goodall: Chimpanzee Expert & Activist
  c HB Guide - v26 - i2 - Fall 2015 - p209(1) [51-500]
  Jellyfish
  c HB Guide - v26 - i2 - Fall 2015 - p174(1) [51-500]
  Octopuses
  c HB Guide - v26 - i2 - Fall 2015 - p174(1) [51-500]
  Reptiles Series
  c HB Guide - v26 - i1 - Spring 2015 - p160(1) [51-500]
  Seahorses
  c HB Guide - v26 - i2 - Fall 2015 - p176(1) [51-500]
  Thunder and Lightning
  c BL - v112 - i3 - Oct 1 2015 - p66(1) [51-500]
  Tropical Fish
  c HB Guide - v26 - i2 - Fall 2015 - p176(1) [51-500]
  Walt Disney: Animator & Founder
  c SLJ - v61 - i4 - April 2015 - p118(4) [51-500]
  Whales: Ocean Life
  c HB Guide - v26 - i2 - Fall 2015 - p179(1) [51-500]

Hansen, Hans V. - *Riel's Defence: Perspectives on His Speeches*
  Can Hist R - v96 - i2 - June 2015 - p298(3) [501+]

Hansen, Imke - *"Nie Wieder Auschwitz!": Die Entstehung eines Symbols und der Alltag einer Gedenkstatte 1945-1955*
  HNet - June 2015 - pNA [501+]

Hansen, Karen V. - *Encounter on the Great Plains: Scandinavian Settlers and the Dispossession of Dakota Indians, 1890-1930*
  AJS - v120 - i6 - May 2015 - p1900(3) [501+]

Hansen, Lulu Anne - *Bunkers: Atlantvoldens perspektiver i Danmark*
  HNet - May 2015 - pNA [501+]

Hansen, Peter H. - *The Summits of Modern Man: Mountaineering after the Enlightenment*
  JMH - v87 - i3 - Sept 2015 - p710(2) [501+]

Hansen, Stig Jarle - *Al-Shabaab in Somalia: The History and Ideology of a Militant Islamist Group, 2005-2012*
  J Mil H - v79 - i1 - Jan 2015 - p267-268 [501+]

Hanshaw, Julian - *Tim Ginger (Illus. by Hanshaw, Julian)*
  BL - v112 - i4 - Oct 15 2015 - p36(1) [51-500]

Hanshew, Karrin - *Terror and Democracy in West Germany*
  JMH - v87 - i2 - June 2015 - p495(3) [501+]

Hansische Identitaten
  HNet - May 2015 - pNA [501+]

Hanson, Anders - *Do Something for Others: The Kids' Book of Citizenship*
  c HB Guide - v26 - i1 - Spring 2015 - p139(1) [51-500]
  Everyone Is Equal: The Kids' Book of Tolerance
  c HB Guide - v26 - i1 - Spring 2015 - p132(1) [51-500]
  Keeping the Peace: The Kids' Book of Peacemaking
  c HB Guide - v26 - i1 - Spring 2015 - p132(1) [51-500]
  Land of the Free: The Kids' Book of Freedom
  c HB Guide - v26 - i1 - Spring 2015 - p139(1) [51-500]

Hanson, Faye - *The Wonder (Illus. by Hanson, Faye)*
  c KR - June 15 2015 - pNA [51-500]
  c BL - v111 - i22 - August 1 2015 - p76(1) [51-500]
  c PW - v262 - i27 - July 6 2015 - p68(1) [51-500]

Hanson, Holly - *The LGBT and Modern Family Money Manual: Financial Strategies for You and Your Loved Ones*
  RVBW - June 2015 - pNA [51-500]

Hanson, Jason - *Spy Secrets That Can Save Your Life: A Former CIA Officer Reveals Safety and Survival Techniques To Keep You and Your Family Protected*
  LJ - v140 - i14 - Sept 1 2015 - p144(1) [51-500]

Hanson, Molly - *Free-Motion Quilting for Beginners: And Those Who Think They Can't*
  Bwatch - Feb 2015 - pNA [51-500]

Hanson, Thor - *The Triumph of Seeds: How Grains, Nuts, Kernels, Pulses, and Pips Conquered the Plant Kingdom and Shaped Human History*
  BioSci - v65 - i6 - June 2015 - p626(2) [501+]
  BL - v111 - i12 - Feb 15 2015 - p28(1) [51-500]
  KR - Feb 1 2015 - pNA [51-500]
  Mac - v128 - i13-14 - April 6 2015 - p74(2) [501+]
  Nature - v519 - i7543 - March 19 2015 - p288(2) [501+]
  NH - v123 - i3 - April 2015 - p47(1) [501+]
  NYTBR - April 19 2015 - p21(L) [501+]

Hansson, Lars-Anders - *Animal Movement across Scales*
  QRB - v90 - i4 - Dec 2015 - p437(2) [501+]

Hanstedt, Constance - *Don't Leave Yet: How My Mother's Alzheimer's Opened My Heart*
  BL - v111 - i15 - April 1 2015 - p9(2) [51-500]

Hanway, Donald - *Her Appearing*
  KR - May 1 2015 - pNA [501+]

Hapka, Catherine - *Blue Ribbon Summer*
  c HB Guide - v26 - i1 - Spring 2015 - p80(1) [51-500]
  Chasing Gold
  c HB Guide - v26 - i2 - Fall 2015 - p85(1) [51-500]
  Jingle Bells (Illus. by Sanderson, Ruth)
  c HB Guide - v26 - i1 - Spring 2015 - p60(1) [51-500]

Maddie's Dream
   c HB Guide - v26 - i1 - Spring 2015 - p80(1) [51-500]

Happe, Kelley E. - *The Material Gene: Gender, Race, and Heredity After the Human Genome Project*
   CS - v44 - i2 - March 2015 - p207-209 [501+]

Happe, Peter - *The Tide Tarrieth No Man*
   BSA-P - v109 - i2 - June 2015 - p268-269 [501+]

Haramija, Dragica - *Poetika slikanice*
   Bkbird - v53 - i3 - Summer 2015 - p90(2) [501+]

Harari, Yuval Noah - *Sapiens: A Brief History of Humankind*
   BL - v111 - i12 - Feb 15 2015 - p16(1) [51-500]
   CHE - v61 - i30 - April 10 2015 - pNA [501+]
   CSM - Feb 18 2015 - pNA [501+]
   J Chem Ed - v92 - i7 - July 2015 - p1143-1145 [501+]
   Nation - v300 - i29 - July 20 2015 - p42(3) [501+]

Harazin, S.A. - *Painless*
   y BL - v111 - i12 - Feb 15 2015 - p83(1) [51-500]
   y CCB-B - v68 - i7 - March 2015 - p356(1) [51-500]
   y HB Guide - v26 - i2 - Fall 2015 - p121(1) [51-500]
   y KR - Jan 15 2015 - pNA [51-500]
   y SLJ - v61 - i5 - May 2015 - p119(2) [51-500]
   y VOYA - v38 - i1 - April 2015 - p61(1) [51-500]

Harber, Cristin - *Black Dawn*
   PW - v262 - i47 - Nov 23 2015 - p56(2) [51-500]

Harbison, Beth - *Driving with the Top Down (Read by Cassidy, Orlagh). Audiobook Review*
   y BL - v111 - i14 - March 15 2015 - p85(1) [51-500]
If I Could Turn Back Time (Read by Cassidy, Orlagh). Audiobook Review
   LJ - v140 - i19 - Nov 15 2015 - p52(1) [51-500]
If I Could Turn Back Time
   y BL - v111 - i21 - July 1 2015 - p31(1) [51-500]
   LJ - v140 - i11 - June 15 2015 - p80(1) [501+]

Harbison, Lawrence - *25 10-Minute Plays for Teens*
   y CH Bwatch - Feb 2015 - pNA [51-500]

Harbison, Robert - *Ruins and Fragments: Tales of Loss and Rediscovery*
   Spec - v329 - i9768 - Nov 14 2015 - p56(1) [501+]

Harbo, Christopher - *Humpty Dumpty (Illus. by Chatzikonstantinou, Danny)*
   c HB Guide - v26 - i2 - Fall 2015 - p160(1) [51-500]
My First Guide to Paper Airplanes
   c HB Guide - v26 - i2 - Fall 2015 - p191(1) [51-500]
Origami Palooza: Dragons, Turtles, Birds, and More!
   c HB Guide - v26 - i2 - Fall 2015 - p191(1) [51-500]
Origami Papertainment: Samurai, Owls, Ninja Stars, and More!
   c HB Guide - v26 - i2 - Fall 2015 - p191(1) [51-500]

Harbo, Christopher L. - *Bill Gates*
   c HB Guide - v26 - i1 - Spring 2015 - p193(1) [51-500]
The Wizard of Oz Shapes
   TC Math - v21 - i9 - May 2015 - p567(2) [501+]

Harbour, Katherine - *Briar Queen*
   y BL - v111 - i18 - May 15 2015 - p33(1) [51-500]
   KR - April 1 2015 - pNA [51-500]
   LJ - v140 - i9 - May 15 2015 - p57(4) [501+]
   PW - v262 - i12 - March 23 2015 - p51(1) [51-500]
Nettle King
   PW - v262 - i52 - Dec 21 2015 - p136(1) [51-500]

Harbus, Antonina - *Cognitive Approaches to Old English Poetry*
   JEGP - v114 - i1 - Jan 2015 - p137(4) [501+]

Harbutt, Juliet - *World Cheese Book*
   LJ - v140 - i15 - Sept 15 2015 - p106(3) [51-500]
   BL - v112 - i1 - Sept 1 2015 - p24(1) [51-500]

Harcourt, Alexander H. - *Humankind: How Biology and Geography Shape Human Diversity*
   BL - v111 - i19-20 - June 1 2015 - p10(1) [51-500]
   Bwatch - Oct 2015 - pNA [51-500]
   KR - April 15 2015 - pNA [501+]
   LJ - v140 - i9 - May 15 2015 - p101(2) [51-500]
   PW - v262 - i16 - April 20 2015 - p67(1) [51-500]

Harcourt, Bernard E. - *Exposed: Desire and Disobedience in the Digital Age*
   TLS - i5877 - Nov 20 2015 - p24(2) [501+]

Harcourt, Maggie - *The Last Summer of Us*
   y Sch Lib - v63 - i3 - Autumn 2015 - p189(1) [51-500]

Hardeastle, Kevin - *Debris*
   BL - v112 - i6 - Nov 15 2015 - p25(1) [51-500]

Harden, Alastair - *Animals in the Classical World: Ethical Perspectives from Greek and Roman Texts*
   Class R - v65 - i2 - Oct 2015 - p370-372 [501+]

Harden, Blaine - *The Great Leader and the Fighter Pilot: The True Story of the Tyrant Who Created North Korea and the Young Lieutenant Who Stole His Way to Freedom*
   BL - v111 - i11 - Feb 1 2015 - p12(1) [51-500]
   CSM - March 19 2015 - pNA [501+]
   KR - Jan 1 2015 - pNA [51-500]
   Econ - v415 - i8938 - May 16 2015 - p78(US) [501+]
   LJ - v140 - i6 - April 1 2015 - p102(2) [51-500]
   NYTBR - March 29 2015 - p20(L) [51-500]
   PW - v262 - i5 - Feb 2 2015 - p46(2) [51-500]

Harder, Clara - *Pseudoisidor und das Papsttum: Funktion und Bedeutung des apostolischen Stuhls in den pseudoisidorischen Falschungen*
   Med R - August 2015 - pNA [501+]

Harder, Myra - *Urban and Amish: Classic Quilts and Modern Updates*
   Bwatch - Feb 2015 - pNA [51-500]

Harders, Levke - *American Studies: Disziplingeschichte und Geschlecht*
   AHR - v120 - i1 - Feb 2015 - p270(1) [501+]

Hardie, Philip - *The Last Trojan Hero: A Cultural History of Virgil's "Aeneid"*
   TLS - i5832 - Jan 9 2015 - p24(1) [501+]

Harding, Christopher - *Religion and Psychotherapy in Modern Japan*
   HNet - August 2015 - pNA [501+]

Harding, David - *Reality Check*
   c Magpies - v30 - i3 - July 2015 - p36(1) [501+]

Harding, Gunnar - *Guarding the Air*
   WLT - v89 - i2 - March-April 2015 - p63(1) [51-500]

Harding, James M. - *The Ghosts of the Avant-Garde(s): Exorcising Experimental Theater and Performance*
   TDR - v59 - i1 - Spring 2015 - p187(2) [501+]
   Theat J - v67 - i1 - March 2015 - p156-157 [501+]

Harding, John - *The Girl Who Couldn't Read (Read by Roberts, William). Audiobook Review*
   LJ - v140 - i17 - Oct 15 2015 - p51(1) [51-500]

Harding, Kate - *Asking for It: The Alarming Rise of Rape Culture--and What We Can Do about It*
   LJ - v140 - i14 - Sept 1 2015 - p126(2) [51-500]

Harding, Rachel Elizabeth - *Remnants: A Memoir of Spirit, Activism, and Mothering*
   PW - v262 - i10 - March 9 2015 - p67(1) [51-500]

Harding, Richard - *The Contractor State and its Implications, 1659-1815*
   JEH - v75 - i1 - March 2015 - p279-281 [501+]

Harding, Rosemarie Freeney - *Remnants: A Memoir of Spirit, Activism, and Mothering*
   KR - March 1 2015 - pNA [501+]

Harding, Stephen - *The Last Battle: When U.S. and German Soldiers Joined Forces in the Waning Hours of World War II in Europe*
   HNet - Jan 2015 - pNA [501+]
Last to Die: A Defeated Empire, a Forgotten Mission, and the Last American Killed in World War II
   BL - v111 - i19-20 - June 1 2015 - p32(1) [51-500]
   KR - June 15 2015 - pNA [501+]
   PW - v262 - i25 - June 22 2015 - p134(1) [51-500]

Harding, Thomas - *The House by the Lake: A Story of Germany*
   NS - v144 - i5283 - Oct 9 2015 - p46(2) [501+]
   Spec - v329 - i9760 - Sept 19 2015 - p53(2) [501+]

Harding, Wendy - *The Myth of Emptiness and the New American Literature of Place*
   NEQ - v88 - i3 - Sept 2015 - p540-542 [501+]

Hardinge, Frances - *Cuckoo Song*
   y BL - v111 - i15 - April 1 2015 - p64(1) [51-500]
   y CCB-B - v68 - i10 - June 2015 - p494(1) [51-500]
   y HB - v91 - i3 - May-June 2015 - p109(2) [51-500]
   y HB Guide - v26 - i2 - Fall 2015 - p85(1) [51-500]
   y KR - Feb 15 2015 - pNA [51-500]
   y PW - v262 - i13 - March 30 2015 - p77(1) [51-500]
   y PW - v262 - i49 - Dec 2 2015 - p101(1) [51-500]
   y VOYA - v37 - i6 - Feb 2015 - p76(1) [501+]
The Lie Tree
   y Sch Lib - v63 - i2 - Summer 2015 - p117(2) [51-500]

Hardisty, Paul E. - *The Abrupt Physics of Dying*
   TimHES - i2223 - Oct 1 2015 - p49(1) [501+]

Hardman, Gabriel - *Kinski*
   BL - v111 - i9-10 - Jan 1 2015 - p61(1) [51-500]

Hardstaff, Jane - *The Executioner's Daughter*
   y CCB-B - v69 - i1 - Sept 2015 - p26(1) [51-500]
   y VOYA - v38 - i2 - June 2015 - p76(1) [51-500]

Hardt, Marah J. - *Sex in the Sea: Our Intimate Connection with Sex-Changing Fish, Romantic Lobsters, Kinky Squid, and Other Salty Erotica of the Deep*
   KR - Dec 15 2015 - pNA [51-500]
   PW - v262 - i52 - Dec 21 2015 - p145(1) [51-500]

Hardwig, Bill - *Upon Provincialism: Southern Literature and National Periodical Culture, 1870-1900*
   AL - v87 - i2 - June 2015 - p391-393 [501+]

Hardy, Jorg - *Plato: Laches*
   Class R - v65 - i2 - Oct 2015 - p376-378 [501+]

Hardy, Ross C. - *Cafe Noir*
   KR - March 1 2015 - pNA [501+]

Hardy, Shawnee Thornton - *Asanas for Autism and Special Needs*
   Bwatch - April 2015 - pNA [501+]

Hardy, Thomas - *Return of the Native*
   Forbes - v196 - i6 - Nov 2 2015 - p42(1) [51-500]

Hare, Brendan - *From Working to Wisdom: The Adventures and Dreams of Older Americans*
   SPBW - April 2015 - pNA [51-500]

Hare, David - *The Blue Touch Paper: A Memoir*
   BL - v112 - i1 - Sept 1 2015 - p24(1) [51-500]
   KR - July 15 2015 - pNA [501+]
   NS - v144 - i5279 - Sept 11 2015 - p43(1) [51-500]
   NYT - Nov 20 2015 - pC23(L) [501+]
   NYTBR - Nov 22 2015 - p14(L) [501+]

Hareven, Gail - *Lies, First Person*
   LJ - v140 - i10 - June 1 2015 - p92(3) [501+]
   NYTBR - Feb 22 2015 - p27(L) [501+]

Hargittai, Istvan - *Buried Glory: Portraits of Soviet Scientists*
   Historian - v77 - i3 - Fall 2015 - p608(3) [501+]

Hargrave, John - *Mind Hacking: How to Change Your Mind for Good in 21 Days*
   PW - v262 - i42 - Oct 19 2015 - p65(2) [51-500]

Hargreaves, Paul - *Libra Road*
   KR - March 1 2015 - pNA [501+]

Hargreaves, Roger - *The Mr. Men Collection, vol. 1 (Read by Dale, Jim). Audiobook Review*
   c SLJ - v61 - i5 - May 2015 - p68(1) [51-500]

Hargrove, John - *Beneath the Surface: Killer Whales, SeaWorld, and the Truth beyond Blackfish*
   BL - v111 - i14 - March 15 2015 - p34(1) [51-500]
   KR - Jan 15 2015 - pNA [501+]

Hari, Johann - *Chasing the Scream: The First and Last Days of the War on Drugs*
   BL - v111 - i11 - Feb 1 2015 - p5(1) [51-500]
   CSM - Jan 27 2015 - pNA [501+]
   Hum - v75 - i3 - May-June 2015 - p38(2) [501+]
   LJ - v140 - i2 - Feb 1 2015 - p96(2) [51-500]
   Mac - v128 - i5-6 - Feb 9 2015 - p74(1) [501+]
   NS - v144 - i5246 - Jan 23 2015 - p40(1) [501+]
   NYTBR - Feb 15 2015 - p14(L) [501+]
   Spec - v327 - i9725 - Jan 17 2015 - p34(1) [501+]

Hari, Vani - *The Food Babe Way: Break Free from the Hidden Toxins in Your Food and Lose Weight, Look Years Younger, and Get Healthy in Just 21 Days!*
   Bwatch - May 2015 - pNA [51-500]
   LJ - v140 - i3 - Feb 15 2015 - p121(1) [51-500]

Harjo, Joy - *Conflict Resolution for Holy Beings: Poems*
   BL - v112 - i1 - Sept 1 2015 - p30(1) [51-500]
   LJ - v140 - i13 - August 1 2015 - p101(1) [51-500]
   PW - v262 - i42 - Oct 19 2015 - p54(1) [51-500]

Harkaway, Mick - *Tigerman (Read by Bates, Matt). Audiobook Review*
   BL - v111 - i15 - April 1 2015 - p86(2) [51-500]

Harkaway, Nick - *Gone-Away World*
   BL - v111 - i9-10 - Jan 1 2015 - p120(1) [51-500]

Harker, Jaime - *Middlebrow Queer: Christopher Isherwood in America*
   AL - v87 - i2 - June 2015 - p415-417 [501+]

Harker, Kevin M. - *Awaken from the Darkness*
   KR - Feb 1 2015 - pNA [501+]

Harkey, Faith - *Genuine Sweet*
   y BL - v111 - i19-20 - June 1 2015 - p104(2) [51-500]
   y CCB-B - v68 - i10 - June 2015 - p494(1) [51-500]
   y HB Guide - v26 - i2 - Fall 2015 - p85(1) [51-500]
   y VOYA - v37 - i6 - Feb 2015 - p76(1) [51-500]

Harkness, Deborah - *The Book of Life*
   Ent W - i1364 - May 22 2015 - p66(1) [501+]

Harkness, Geoff - *Chicago Hustle and Flow: Gangs, Gangsta Rap, and Social Class*
   CrimJR - v40 - i2 - June 2015 - p242-243 [501+]

Harkness, Geoffrey - *Chicago Hustle and Flow: Gangs, Gangsta Rap, and Social Class*
   AJS - v121 - i3 - Nov 2015 - p999(3) [501+]

Harkness, Nicholas - *Songs of Seoul: An Ethnography of Voice and Voicing in Christian South Korea*
   JAS - v74 - i3 - August 2015 - p761-763 [501+]

Harkup, Kathryn - *A Is for Arsenic: The Poisons of Agatha Christie*
BL - v112 - i1 - Sept 1 2015 - p28(1) [51-500]
KR - June 15 2015 - pNA [501+]
LJ - v140 - i14 - Sept 1 2015 - p136(2) [51-500]
NYTBR - Nov 1 2015 - p30(L) [501+]
PW - v262 - i28 - July 13 2015 - p58(1) [51-500]

Harlan Coben - *The Magical Fantastical Fridge (Illus. by Tinari, Leah)*
c BL - v112 - i5 - Nov 1 2015 - p39(1) [501+]

Harland, Jessie - *Steve Jobs: Insanely Great (Illus. by Harland, Jessie)*
PW - v262 - i18 - May 4 2015 - p104(1) [51-500]

Harland, Philip A. - *Travel and Religion in Antiquity*
BTB - v45 - i1 - Feb 2015 - p62(2) [501+]

Harlen, Wynne - *Teaching Science for Understanding in Elementary and Middle Schools*
Sci & Ch - v52 - i9 - Summer 2015 - p91 [501+]

Harley, Bill - *Charlie Bumpers vs. The Perfect Little Turkey (Read by Harley, Bill). Audiobook Review*
c CH Bwatch - Sept 2015 - pNA [51-500]
Charlie Bumpers vs. the Perfect Little Turkey (Illus. by Gustavson, Adam)
c PW - v262 - i34 - August 24 2015 - p80(1) [501+]
Charlie Bumpers vs. the Squeaking Skull (Illus. by Gustavson, Adam)
c HB Guide - v26 - i1 - Spring 2015 - p80(1) [51-500]

Harlick, R.J. - *A Cold White Fear*
PW - v262 - i44 - Nov 2 2015 - p64(2) [51-500]

Harline, Paula Kelly - *The Polygamous Wives Writing Club: From the Diaries of Mormon Pioneer Women*
CH - v84 - i4 - Dec 2015 - p910(4) [501+]
WHQ - v46 - i3 - Autumn 2015 - p384-384 [501+]

Harloe, Katherine - *Winckelmann and the Invention of Antiquity*
Class R - v65 - i2 - Oct 2015 - p595-597 [501+]

Harlow, George E. - *Gems & Crystals: From One of the World's Great Collections, rev. ed.*
LJ - v140 - i19 - Nov 15 2015 - p106(2) [51-500]

Harlow, Jennifer - *Witch upon a Star*
KR - Jan 1 2015 - pNA [51-500]

Harlow, Joan - *The Watcher*
y HB Guide - v26 - i1 - Spring 2015 - p80(1) [51-500]

Harlow, Luke E. - *Religion, Race, and the Making of Confederate Kentucky, 1830-1880*
AHR - v120 - i3 - June 2015 - p1027-1028 [501+]
JAH - v101 - i4 - March 2015 - p1269-1270 [501+]
JSH - v81 - i3 - August 2015 - p709(2) [501+]

Harlum, Raewyn - *I Was Only Nineteen: A Memoir*
SPBW - Nov 2015 - pNA [51-500]

Harman, Jay - *The Shark's Paintbrush: Biomimicry and How Nature is Inspiring Innovation*
BioSci - v65 - i4 - April 2015 - p440(2) [501+]

Harman, Oren - *Outsider Scientists: Routes to Innovation in Biology*
Isis - v106 - i2 - June 2015 - p492(3) [501+]

Harman, Patricia - *The Reluctant Midwife*
BL - v111 - i12 - Feb 15 2015 - p41(1) [51-500]

Harmening, Marcia - *Flip and Fuse Quilts: 12 Fun Projects: Easy Foolproof Technique: Transform Your Applique*
LJ - v140 - i20 - Dec 1 2015 - p102(2) [51-500]

Harmer, David - *There's a Monster in the Garden*
c Sch Lib - v63 - i3 - Autumn 2015 - p177(1) [51-500]

Harmon, Charles - *Best Practices: Mobile Library Services*
LQ - v85 - i1 - Jan 2015 - p121(3) [501+]

Harmon, Daniel - *Plotted: A Literary Atlas*
y BL - v112 - i4 - Oct 15 2015 - p12(1) [51-500]
Powering Up a Career in Software Development and Programming
y BL - v112 - i7 - Dec 1 2015 - p45(1) [51-500]

Harmon, Michael - *Stick*
y CCB-B - v69 - i1 - Sept 2015 - p27(1) [51-500]
y PW - v262 - i22 - June 1 2015 - p61(1) [51-500]
y SLJ - v61 - i7 - July 2015 - p93(1) [51-500]
y VOYA - v38 - i4 - Oct 2015 - p70(2) [51-500]
y BL - v111 - i21 - July 1 2015 - p59(2) [51-500]
y KR - May 15 2015 - pNA [51-500]

Harmony, Cassey Ho. - *Cassey Ho's Hot Body Year-Round: The Pop Pilates to Get Slim, Eat Clean, and Live Happy through Every Season*
PW - v262 - i1 - Jan 5 2015 - p67(2) [51-500]

Harms, Erik - *Saigon's Edge*
JAS - v74 - i2 - May 2015 - p521-523 [501+]

Harms, Wolfgang - *Friedrich Ohly: Vergegenwärtigung eines grossen Philologen*
Ger Q - v88 - i1 - Wntr 2015 - p135(3) [501+]

Harmsen, Peter - *Shanghai, 1937: Stalingrad on the Yangtze*
J Mil H - v79 - i3 - July 2015 - p873-874 [501+]

Harner, Michael - *Cave and Cosmos*
KR - Jan 1 2016 - pNA [501+]

Harness, Cheryl - *Flags over America: A Star-Spangled Story (Illus. by Harness, Cheryl)*
c CH Bwatch - March 2015 - pNA [501+]
c HB Guide - v26 - i1 - Spring 2015 - p203(1) [51-500]

Harney, Marion - *Place-Making for the Imagination*
TLS - i5846 - April 17 2015 - p27(1) [501+]

Harnisch, Jonathan - *Lover in the Nobody*
KR - March 15 2015 - pNA [501+]

Harnon, Kerry - *Love Your Job: The New Rules for Career Happiness*
BL - v111 - i17 - May 1 2015 - p65(1) [51-500]

Harold, Franklin M. - *In Search of Cell History: The Evolution of Life's Building Blocks*
Am Bio T - v77 - i6 - August 2015 - p471(1) [501+]

Harp, Stephen L. - *Au Naturel: Naturism, Nudism, and Tourism in Twentieth-Century France*
AHR - v120 - i2 - April 2015 - p728-729 [501+]
FS - v69 - i2 - April 2015 - p282-283 [501+]

Harper, Annie - *Summer Love: An LGBTQ Collection*
y SLJ - v61 - i6 - June 2015 - p124(1) [51-500]

Harper, Ben - *Ben and Ellen Harper: A House Is a Home*
CSM - May 29 2015 - pNA [501+]

Harper, Bob - *Skinny Habits: The Six Secrets of Thin People*
PW - v262 - i9 - March 2 2015 - p80(1) [51-500]

Harper, Charise Mericle - *A Big Surprise for Little Card (Illus. by Raff, Anna)*
c KR - Dec 1 2015 - pNA [51-500]
c PW - v262 - i42 - Oct 19 2015 - p76(1) [51-500]
Go! Go! Go! Stop! (Illus. by Harper, Charise Mericle)
c SLJ - v61 - i7 - July 2015 - p55(1) [51-500]
Just Grace Gets Crafty
c HB Guide - v26 - i1 - Spring 2015 - p60(1) [51-500]
Princess Patty Meets Her Match
c HB Guide - v26 - i1 - Spring 2015 - p32(1) [51-500]
Super Sasquatch Showdown (Illus. by Harper, Charise Mericle)
c SLJ - v61 - i2 - Feb 2015 - p86(1) [51-500]
c HB Guide - v26 - i2 - Fall 2015 - p85(1) [51-500]
Superlove (Illus. by Chambers, Mark)
c HB Guide - v26 - i2 - Fall 2015 - p37(1) [51-500]

Harper, Gayle - *Roadtrip with a Raindrop*
SPBW - Jan 2015 - pNA [51-500]

Harper, Glyn - *Rolly the Anzac Donkey (Illus. by Cooper, Jenny)*
c Magpies - v30 - i2 - May 2015 - pS5(2) [501+]

Harper, Graeme - *The Future for Creative Writing*
TLS - i5849 - May 8 2015 - p23(1) [501+]

Harper, Jamie - *Bella's Best of All (Illus. by Harper, Jamie)*
c KR - Nov 15 2015 - pNA [501+]

Harper, Janis - *Emails from India*
CSM - March 27 2015 - pNA [501+]

Harper, Jennifer - *Classroom Routines for Real Learning: Daily Management Exercises That Empower and Engage Students*
Res Links - v20 - i5 - June 2015 - p35(1) [501+]

Harper, Jonathan - *Daydreamers*
KR - June 15 2015 - pNA [501+]

Harper, Jordan - *Love and Other Wounds*
KR - May 1 2015 - pNA [501+]
BL - v111 - i19-20 - June 1 2015 - p55(1) [51-500]
PW - v262 - i18 - May 4 2015 - p92(1) [51-500]

Harper, Josephine - *Whistling Willie from Amarillo, Texas (Illus. by Harrington, David)*
c PW - v262 - i32 - August 10 2015 - p59(1) [51-500]

Harper, Julia - *Once and Always*
BL - v111 - i13 - March 1 2015 - p29(1) [51-500]
PW - v262 - i3 - Jan 19 2015 - p66(1) [51-500]

Harper, Kyle - *From Shame to Sin: The Christian Transformation of Sexual Morality in Late Antiquity*
AHR - v120 - i1 - Feb 2015 - p172-174 [501+]
CH - v84 - i1 - March 2015 - p228(3) [501+]
Historian - v77 - i1 - Spring 2015 - p168(2) [501+]
JR - v95 - i3 - July 2015 - p396(3) [501+]

Harper, Molly - *The Single Undead Moms Club*
BL - v112 - i4 - Oct 15 2015 - p27(1) [51-500]
PW - v262 - i39 - Sept 28 2015 - p75(2) [51-500]

Harper, Tom - *Zodiac Station*
BL - v111 - i17 - May 1 2015 - p48(1) [51-500]
PW - v262 - i13 - March 30 2015 - p54(1) [51-500]

Harrell, Rob - *Life of Zarf: The Trouble with Weasels. Audiobook Review*
c SLJ - v61 - i2 - Feb 2015 - p49(2) [51-500]
Life of Zarf: The Trouble with Weasels
c HB Guide - v26 - i1 - Spring 2015 - p80(1) [51-500]
Monster on the Hill (Illus. by Harrell, Rob)
c SLJ - v61 - i6 - June 2015 - p46(6) [51-500]
The Troll Who Cried Wolf
c KR - July 1 2015 - pNA [51-500]

Harrell-Sesniak, Mary - *Dear Santa: Children's Christmas Letters and Wish Lists, 1870-1920*
NYT - Nov 27 2015 - pC28(L) [501+]

Harries, Jill - *Imperial Rome AD 284 to 363: The New Empire*
Class R - v65 - i2 - Oct 2015 - p544-545 [501+]

Harriet Harriss, Daisy - *Radical Pedagogies: Architectural Education and the British Tradition*
TimHES - i2213 - July 23 2015 - p45(1) [51-500]

Harrigan, Stephen - *A Friend of Mr. Lincoln*
KR - Nov 15 2015 - pNA [501+]
PW - v262 - i46 - Nov 16 2015 - p50(1) [51-500]
The Gates of the Alamo
Roundup M - v22 - i5 - June 2015 - p35(1) [501+]

Harrington, Anna - *Dukes Are Forever*
BL - v112 - i5 - Nov 1 2015 - p33(2) [51-500]
PW - v262 - i44 - Nov 2 2015 - p70(1) [51-500]

Harrington, Claudia - *My Military Mom (Illus. by Persico, Zoe)*
c SLJ - v61 - i11 - Nov 2015 - p81(1) [51-500]
My Two Homes (Illus. by Persico, Zoe)
c SLJ - v61 - i11 - Nov 2015 - p81(1) [51-500]

Harrington, Emily - *Second Person Singular: Late Victorian Poets and the Bonds of Verse*
TLS - i5870 - Oct 2 2015 - p23(1) [501+]

Harrington, Jenna - *Katie Mcginty Wants a Pet (Illus. by Simpson, Finn)*
c KR - May 1 2015 - pNA [51-500]

Harrington, Joel F. - *The Faithful Executioner: Life and Death, Honor and Shame in the Turbulent Sixteenth Century*
JMH - v87 - i1 - March 2015 - p215(3) [501+]

Harrington, Karen - *Courage for Beginners*
c HB Guide - v26 - i1 - Spring 2015 - p80(1) [51-500]

Harrington, Kim - *Forget Me*
y HB Guide - v26 - i1 - Spring 2015 - p109(1) [51-500]

Harrington, Lisa - *Twisted*
y Res Links - v20 - i3 - Feb 2015 - p30(1) [51-500]

Harrington, Rebecca - *I'll Have What She's Having: My Adventures in Celebrity Dieting*
People - v83 - i2 - Jan 12 2015 - p29 [501+]

Harrington, Sue - *The Early Anglo-Saxon Kingdoms of Southern Britain AD 450-650: Beneath the Tribal Hidage*
Med R - August 2015 - pNA [501+]
Specu - v90 - i3 - July 2015 - p819-820 [501+]

Harrington, Tim - *Nose to Toes, You Are Yummy! (Illus. by Harrington, Tim)*
c HB Guide - v26 - i2 - Fall 2015 - p12(1) [51-500]
c KR - March 1 2015 - pNA [501+]
c SLJ - v61 - i5 - May 2015 - p79(1) [51-500]

Harrington, Wilfrid - *Reading "Matthew" for the First Time*
Theol St - v76 - i3 - Sept 2015 - p634(2) [501+]

Harris, Alexandra - *Weatherland: Writers and Artists Under English Skies*
Lon R Bks - v37 - i21 - Nov 5 2015 - p37(2) [501+]
Nature - v525 - i7567 - Sept 3 2015 - p31(1) [51-500]
NS - v144 - i5288 - Nov 13 2015 - p40(2) [501+]
PW - v262 - i47 - Nov 23 2015 - p60(3) [51-500]
Spec - v328 - i9759 - Sept 12 2015 - p44(1) [501+]

Harris, Amber - *Wisteria Jane (Illus. by Hoyt, Ard)*
c KR - August 15 2015 - pNA [51-500]
c SLJ - v61 - i10 - Oct 2015 - p77(1) [51-500]

Harris, Brayton - *The Age of the Battleship, 1890-1922*
RVBW - July 25 2015 - pNA [51-500]

Harris, C.S. - *When Falcons Fall*
KR - Jan 1 2016 - pNA [501+]
Who Buries the Dead
New Or - v49 - i6 - March 2015 - p40(1) [501+]
BL - v111 - i11 - Feb 1 2015 - p29(2) [51-500]
KR - Jan 1 2015 - pNA [51-500]
PW - v262 - i3 - Jan 19 2015 - p63(1) [51-500]

Harris, Carolyn - *Magna Carta and Its Gifts to Canada*
   y Res Links - v21 - i1 - Oct 2015 - p45(1) [501+]
Harris, Carrie - *Demon Derby*
   c HB Guide - v26 - i2 - Fall 2015 - p121(1) [51-500]
Harris, Charlaine - *Day Shift*
   PW - v262 - i12 - March 23 2015 - p52(1) [51-500]
Harris, Charles H., III - *The Plan de San Diego: Tejano Rebellion, Mexican Intrigue*
   AHR - v120 - i2 - April 2015 - p644-645 [501+]
Harris, Dianne - *Second Suburb: Levittown, Pennsylvania*
   J Urban H - v41 - i1 - Jan 2015 - p171-10 [501+]
Harris, Edward Monroe - *The Rule of Law in Action in Democratic Athens*
   Class R - v65 - i1 - April 2015 - p175-176 [501+]
Harris, Elizabeth - *Tristano Dies*
   NYRB - v62 - i10 - June 4 2015 - p63(3) [501+]
Harris, Ellen T. - *George Frideric Handel: A Life with Friends*
   Bwatch - Feb 2015 - pNA [51-500]
Harris, Eugene E. - *Ancestors in Our Genome: The New Science of Human Evolution*
   BioSci - v65 - i7 - July 2015 - p729(2) [501+]
Harris, Fredrick - *Beyond Discrimination: Racial Inequality in a Postracist Era*
   CS - v44 - i4 - July 2015 - p470-472 [501+]
Harris, Gregory - *The Connicle Curse: A Colin Pendragon Mystery*
   PW - v262 - i4 - Jan 26 2015 - p151(2) [51-500]
Harris, Ian - *Buddhism in a Dark Age: Cambodian Monks under Pol Pot*
   Pac A - v88 - i2 - June 2015 - p360 [501+]
Harris, James - *The Anatomy of Terror: Political Violence under Stalin*
   E-A St - v67 - i5 - July 2015 - p832(2) [501+]
   HNet - Jan 2015 - pNA [501+]
Harris, James A. - *Hume: An Intellectual Biography*
   TimHES - i2224 - Oct 8 2015 - p42-43 [501+]
Harris, Joanne M. - *The Gospel of Loki (Read by Corduner, Allan). Audiobook Review*
   LJ - v140 - i12 - July 1 2015 - p43(1) [51-500]
The Gospel of Loki
   PW - v262 - i14 - April 6 2015 - p44(1) [51-500]
   BL - v111 - i18 - May 15 2015 - p35(2) [51-500]
   KR - April 15 2015 - pNA [51-500]
Harris, Joseph - *Inventing the Spectator: Subjectivity and the Theatrical Experience in Early Modern France*
   FS - v69 - i2 - April 2015 - p241-242 [501+]
Harris, Julie Mahler - *The Wish of the Well-Witcher*
   c CH Bwatch - May 2015 - pNA [51-500]
Harris, Leslie J. - *State of the Marital Union: Rhetoric, Identity, and Nineteenth-Century Marriage Controversies*
   J Am St - v49 - i3 - August 2015 - p629-631 [501+]
Harris, Leslie M. - *Slavery and Freedom in Savannah*
   JSH - v81 - i3 - August 2015 - p718(2) [501+]
Harris, Lionel, Jr. - *The Word Window: Black History and the Bible Reference Book, vol. 2*
   LJ - v140 - i7 - April 15 2015 - p118(1) [501+]
Harris, Lisa - *Vendetta*
   BL - v112 - i3 - Oct 1 2015 - p34(1) [51-500]
Harris, M.G. - *Black Horizon*
   c Sch Lib - v63 - i2 - Summer 2015 - p105(1) [51-500]
Harris, M. Keith - *Across the Bloody Chasm: The Culture of Commemoration among Civil War Veterans*
   HNet - Feb 2015 - pNA [501+]
   JAH - v102 - i2 - Sept 2015 - p568-568 [501+]
Harris, Mark - *Five Came Back: A Story of Hollywood and the Second World War*
   TLS - i5846 - April 17 2015 - p26(2) [501+]
   NYTBR - April 12 2015 - p28(L) [501+]
Harris, Maury - *Inside the Crystal Ball: How to Make and Use Forecasts*
   Barron's - v95 - i40 - Oct 5 2015 - p35(1) [501+]
Harris, Melissa - *99 Keys to a Creative Life: Spiritual, Intuitive and Awareness Practices for Personal Fulfillment*
   PW - v262 - i15 - April 13 2015 - p76(1) [51-500]
Harris, Michael - *The End of Absence: Reclaiming What We've Lost in a World of Constant Connection*
   Can Lit - i224 - Spring 2015 - p124 [501+]
Mathematics without Apologies: Porteait of a Problematic vocation
   TimHES - i2190 - Feb 12 2015 - p50-51 [501+]
Mathematics without Apologies: Portrait of a Problematic Vocation
   Nature - v519 - i7541 - March 5 2015 - p31(2) [501+]
   Nature - v519 - i7541 - March 5 2015 - p31(2) [501+]
   NYRB - v62 - i19 - Dec 3 2015 - p50(3) [501+]

Harris, Neil - *Capital Culture: J. Carter Brown, the National Gallery of Art, and the Reinvention of the Museum Experience*
   RAH - v43 - i2 - June 2015 - p384-389 [501+]
   NEQ - v88 - i1 - March 2015 - p159-162 [501+]
Harris, Rachael Lee - *My Autistic Awakening: Unlocking the Potential for a Life Well Lived*
   BL - v111 - i16 - April 15 2015 - p9(1) [51-500]
Harris, Rachel - *Gender in Chinese Music*
   JAS - v74 - i1 - Feb 2015 - p193-194 [501+]
Harris, Rachel S. - *An Ideological Death: Suicide in Israeli Literature*
   HNet - July 2015 - pNA [501+]
Harris, Robbie H. - *It's Perfectly Normal: Changing Bodies, Growing Up, Sex, and Sexual Health (Illus. by Emberley, Michael)*
   c HB Guide - v26 - i1 - Spring 2015 - p136(1) [51-500]
Harris, Robert - *Dictator*
   KR - Dec 1 2015 - pNA [501+]
   NS - v144 - i5289 - Nov 20 2015 - p57(1) [501+]
   PW - v262 - i48 - Nov 30 2015 - p36(1) [51-500]
   Spec - v329 - i9762 - Oct 3 2015 - p43(1) [501+]
   TLS - i5873 - Oct 23 2015 - p20(1) [501+]
Harris, Robert J. (b. 1955-) - *Thor Is Locked in My Garage*
   c Sch Lib - v63 - i1 - Spring 2015 - p37(1) [51-500]
Harris, Robie H. - *It's So Amazing!: A Book about Eggs, Sperm, Birth, Babies, and Families (Illus. by Emberley, Michael)*
   c HB Guide - v26 - i1 - Spring 2015 - p136(1) [51-500]
Turtle and Me (Illus. by Freeman, Tor)
   c KR - Feb 15 2015 - pNA [51-500]
   c PW - v262 - i6 - Feb 9 2015 - p65(1) [51-500]
   c PW - v262 - i49 - Dec 2 2015 - p33(1) [51-500]
   c SLJ - v61 - i4 - April 2015 - p128(1) [51-500]
What's So Yummy? All About Eating Well and Feeling Good (Illus. by Westcott, Nadine Bernard)
   c HB Guide - v26 - i2 - Fall 2015 - p188(1) [51-500]
Who We Are!: All About Being the Same and Being Different (Illus. by Westcott, Nadine Bernard)
   c KR - Jan 1 2016 - pNA [51-500]
Harris, Rosie - *The Mixture as Before*
   BL - v112 - i5 - Nov 1 2015 - p27(1) [51-500]
Harris, Sam - *Islam and the Future of Tolerance: A Dialogue*
   BL - v112 - i1 - Sept 1 2015 - p17(1) [51-500]
   KR - July 1 2015 - pNA [51-500]
Waking Up: A Guide to Spirituality Without Religion
   TLS - i5869 - Sept 25 2015 - p28(1) [501+]
Harris, Sherry Lynn - *Adapting to Alzheimer's: Support for When Your Parent Becomes Your Child*
   RVBW - Sept 2015 - pNA [51-500]
   SPBW - August 2015 - pNA [51-500]
Harris, Steven E. - *Communism on Tomorrow Street: Mass Housing and Everyday Life after Stalin*
   JMH - v87 - i2 - June 2015 - p500(3) [501+]
Harris, Teresa E. - *The Perfect Place*
   c CCB-B - v68 - i5 - Jan 2015 - p258(2) [501+]
   c HB Guide - v26 - i1 - Spring 2015 - p80(1) [51-500]
Harris, Tessa - *Shadow of the Raven (Read by Vance, Simon). Audiobook Review*
   LJ - v140 - i11 - June 15 2015 - p50(1) [51-500]
Harris, Thomas - *The Silence of the Lambs*
   TimHES - i2211 - July 9 2015 - p51(1) [501+]
Harris, Tim - *Africa*
   y HB Guide - v26 - i2 - Fall 2015 - p169(1) [51-500]
Australia and Southeast Asia
   y BL - v111 - i15 - April 1 2015 - p54(1) [51-500]
Europe
   y HB Guide - v26 - i2 - Fall 2015 - p169(1) [51-500]
The Final Crisis of the Stuart Monarchy: The Revolutions of 1688-91 in their British, Atlantic and European Contexts
   HNet - March 2015 - pNA [501+]
North and South America
   y HB Guide - v26 - i2 - Fall 2015 - p169(1) [51-500]
South and Central Asia
   y HB Guide - v26 - i2 - Fall 2015 - p169(1) [51-500]
The World of Endangered Animals: South and Central Asia
   c Sci Teach - v82 - i5 - Summer 2015 - p70 [51-500]
Harris, Trudier - *Martin Luther King Jr., Heroism, and African American Literature*
   Am St - v54 - i2 - Summer 2015 - p123-124 [501+]
Harris, William V. - *The Ancient Mediterranean Environment between Science and History*
   Class R - v65 - i1 - April 2015 - p245-247 [501+]

Moses Finley and Politics
   HNet - May 2015 - pNA [501+]
Harrison, Carol - *The Art of Listening in the Early Church*
   CH - v84 - i2 - June 2015 - p421(3) [501+]
   JAAR - v83 - i3 - Sept 2015 - p876-878 [501+]
Being Christian in Late Antiquity: A Festschrift for Gillian Clark
   CH - v84 - i3 - Sept 2015 - p649(3) [501+]
Harrison, Carol E. - *Romantic Catholics: France's Postrevolutionary Generation in Search of a Modern Faith*
   AHR - v120 - i2 - April 2015 - p725-726 [501+]
   CHR - v101 - i3 - Summer 2015 - p666(3) [501+]
   FS - v69 - i1 - Jan 2015 - p104-105 [501+]
Harrison, Charles Yale - *Generals Die in Bed*
   y VOYA - v37 - i6 - Feb 2015 - p56(2) [51-500]
Harrison, Chris - *The Perfect Letter (Read by Eby, Tanya). Audiobook Review*
   LJ - v140 - i14 - Sept 1 2015 - p66(1) [51-500]
Harrison, Cora - *Condemned to Death*
   LJ - v140 - i2 - Feb 1 2015 - p61(4) [501+]
A Shameful Murder
   BL - v111 - i22 - August 1 2015 - p37(1) [51-500]
   PW - v262 - i30 - July 27 2015 - p45(1) [51-500]
Harrison, Craig - *The Longest Kill: The Story of Maverick 41, One of the World's Greatest Snipers*
   KR - Dec 1 2015 - pNA [501+]
   LJ - v140 - i19 - Nov 15 2015 - p92(1) [51-500]
   PW - v262 - i50 - Dec 7 2015 - p77(1) [51-500]
Harrison, D.M. - *The Comanche Fights Again*
   RVBW - June 2015 - pNA [51-500]
Harrison, David - *Now You See Them, Now You Don't: Poems About Creatures That Hide (Illus. by Laroche, Giles)*
   c KR - Dec 1 2015 - pNA [51-500]
   c PW - v262 - i52 - Dec 21 2015 - p156(2) [51-500]
Harrison, Emma - *Escaping Perfect*
   y KR - Dec 15 2015 - pNA [51-500]
Harrison, Guy P. - *Good Thinking: What You Need to Know to Be Smarter, Safer, Wealthier, and Wiser*
   LJ - v140 - i15 - Sept 15 2015 - p101(2) [51-500]
   PW - v262 - i31 - August 3 2015 - p49(1) [51-500]
Harrison, Hannah E. - *Bernice Gets Carried Away (Illus. by Harrison, Hannah E.)*
   c BL - v111 - i21 - July 1 2015 - p61(1) [51-500]
   c CCB-B - v69 - i2 - Oct 2015 - p92(1) [51-500]
   c KR - April 15 2015 - pNA [51-500]
   c PW - v262 - i18 - May 4 2015 - p116(1) [51-500]
   c PW - v262 - i49 - Dec 2 2015 - p12(1) [51-500]
   c SLJ - v61 - i6 - June 2015 - p82(1) [51-500]
Harrison, Harry - *Harry Harrison, Harry Harrison*
   Analog - v135 - i3 - March 2015 - p106(1) [501+]
West of Eden
   TLS - i5832 - Jan 9 2015 - p14(1) [501+]
Harrison, Hazel - *The Encyclopedia of Drawing Techniques*
   LJ - v140 - i2 - Feb 1 2015 - p80(1) [51-500]
Harrison, Henrietta - *The Missionary's Curse and Other Tales from a Chinese Catholic Village*
   JAS - v74 - i3 - August 2015 - p734-735 [501+]
Harrison, Jeffrey - *Into Daylight*
   Ga R - v69 - i1 - Spring 2015 - p122-129 [501+]
Harrison, Jim - *The Big Seven*
   BL - v111 - i9-10 - Jan 1 2015 - p44(1) [51-500]
   KR - Jan 1 2015 - pNA [51-500]
   NYTBR - March 1 2015 - p14(L) [501+]
Dead Man's Float
   BL - v112 - i3 - Oct 1 2015 - p11(1) [51-500]
Harrison, Joel - *Distilled: From Absinthe and Brandy to Vodka and Whiskey, the World's Finest Artisan Spirits Unearthed, Explained and Enjoyed*
   Bwatch - June 2015 - pNA [51-500]
Harrison, Kathryn - *Joan of Arc: A Life Transfigured*
   NYTBR - Nov 1 2015 - p28(L) [501+]
True Crimes
   KR - Dec 1 2015 - pNA [51-500]
Harrison, Kenny - *Hide and Seek Harry at the Playground (Illus. by Harrison, Kenny)*
   c KR - July 1 2015 - pNA [51-500]
   c PW - v262 - i6 - Feb 9 2015 - p66(2) [51-500]
Harrison, Kim - *The Drafter*
   KR - July 1 2015 - pNA [51-500]
   PW - v262 - i30 - July 27 2015 - p43(1) [51-500]
Harrison, Lisi - *License to Spill: A Pretenders Novel*
   y HB Guide - v26 - i1 - Spring 2015 - p109(1) [51-500]
Harrison, Mark - *Jazz-Rock Piano Chops: Firing Up Your Technique*
   Am MT - v64 - i4 - Feb-March 2015 - p63(2) [501+]

Play Like Elton John: The Ultimate Piano Lesson
    Am MT - v65 - i3 - Dec 2015 - p51(1) [501+]
Harrison, Martin - *Saul Leiter: Early Color*
    NYRB - v62 - i12 - July 9 2015 - p10(3) [501+]
    NYRB - v62 - i12 - July 9 2015 - p10(3) [501+]
Harrison, Melissa - *At Hawthorn Time*
    HR - v68 - i3 - Autumn 2015 - p510-516 [501+]
    KR - May 1 2015 - pNA [51-500]
    LJ - v140 - i10 - June 1 2015 - p86(2) [51-500]
    PW - v262 - i20 - May 18 2015 - p58(1) [51-500]
    Spec - v327 - i9738 - April 18 2015 - p38(1) [501+]
    TLS - i5857 - July 3 2015 - p20(1) [501+]
Harrison, Mette Ivie - *The Bishop's Wife (Read by Potter, Kirsten). Audiobook Review*
    BL - v111 - i17 - May 1 2015 - p57(1) [51-500]
  y PW - v262 - i17 - April 27 2015 - p70(1) [51-500]
His Right Hand
    BL - v112 - i4 - Oct 15 2015 - p21(1) [51-500]
    KR - Sept 15 2015 - pNA [51-500]
    PW - v262 - i41 - Oct 12 2015 - p48(1) [51-500]
Harrison, Olivia C. - *Decolonising the Intellectual: Politics, Culture, and Humanism at the End of the French Empire*
    FS - v69 - i4 - Oct 2015 - p558-559 [501+]
Harrison, Paul - *Extreme Supercars*
  c HB Guide - v26 - i2 - Fall 2015 - p185(1) [51-500]
Harrison, Peter - *The Territories of Science and Religion*
    TLS - i5866 - Sept 4 2015 - p25(1) [501+]
Harrison, Randolph Carter - *West from Yesterday*
    Roundup M - v22 - i6 - August 2015 - p30(1) [501+]
Harrison, Regina - *Sin and Confession in Colonial Peru: Spanish-Quechua Penitential Texts, 1560-1650*
    Ams - v72 - i3 - July 2015 - p518(2) [501+]
    CHR - v101 - i2 - Spring 2015 - p397(2) [501+]
    HAHR - v95 - i3 - August 2015 - p512-514 [501+]
    Six Ct J - v46 - i3 - Fall 2015 - p812-814 [501+]
Harrison, Ross - *Strategic Thinking in 3D: A Guide for National Security, Foreign Policy, and Business Professionals*
    APJ - v29 - i2 - March-April 2015 - p185(4) [501+]
Harrison, S. - *Infinity Lost*
  y BL - v112 - i6 - Nov 15 2015 - p50(1) [51-500]
  y KR - Sept 1 2015 - pNA [51-500]
  y PW - v262 - i37 - Sept 14 2015 - p79(1) [51-500]
  y SLJ - v61 - i10 - Oct 2015 - p111(1) [51-500]
  y VOYA - v38 - i5 - Dec 2015 - p70(1) [51-500]
Harrison, Sheri-Marie - *Jamaica's Difficult Subjects*
    RVBW - Jan 2015 - pNA [501+]
Harrisville, Roy A. - *Pandora's Box Opened: An Examination and Defense of Historical-Critical Method and Its Master Practitioners*
    Bks & Cult - v21 - i1 - Jan-Feb 2015 - p24(2) [501+]
Harrod-Eagles, Cynthia - *One Under*
    KR - Dec 1 2015 - pNA [51-500]
    PW - v262 - i48 - Nov 30 2015 - p41(1) [51-500]
Star Fall
    BL - v111 - i9-10 - Jan 1 2015 - p51(1) [51-500]
    KR - Jan 1 2015 - pNA [51-500]
    PW - v262 - i1 - Jan 5 2015 - p54(1) [51-500]
    RVBW - May 2015 - pNA [501+]
    RVBW - Sept 2015 - pNA [501+]
Harrod, Mary - *From France with Love: Gender and Identity in French Romantic Comedy*
    TimHES - i2221 - Sept 17 2015 - p47(1) [501+]
Harrod, Tanya - *The Real Thing: Essays on Making in the Modern World*
    Am Craft - v75 - i4 - August-Sept 2015 - p20(1) [501+]
Harrold, A.F. - *Fizzlebert Stump: The Boy Who Cried Fish (Illus. by Horne, Sarah)*
  c Sch Lib - v63 - i1 - Spring 2015 - p37(1) [51-500]
The Imaginary (Illus. by Gravett, Emily)
  c BL - v111 - i11 - Feb 1 2015 - p51(2) [51-500]
  c CCB-B - v68 - i11 - July-August 2015 - p547(1) [51-500]
  c HB - v91 - i2 - March-April 2015 - p96(2) [51-500]
  c HB Guide - v26 - i2 - Fall 2015 - p85(1) [51-500]
  c KR - Jan 15 2015 - pNA [51-500]
  c PW - v262 - i3 - Jan 19 2015 - p82(1) [51-500]
  c Sch Lib - v63 - i1 - Spring 2015 - p37(1) [51-500]
  c SLJ - v61 - i2 - Feb 2015 - p86(2) [51-500]
Harrop, Isobel - *The Isobel Journal: Just a Girl from Where Nothing Really Happens*
  c HB Guide - v26 - i2 - Fall 2015 - p121(1) [51-500]
Harrower, Elizabeth - *The Catherine Wheel*
    KR - May 15 2015 - pNA [51-500]
    PW - v262 - i17 - April 27 2015 - p43(1) [51-500]

In Certain Circles
    TLS - i5838 - Feb 20 2015 - p19(2) [501+]
Harry, Pip - *Head of the River*
  y CH Bwatch - Oct 2015 - pNA [51-500]
Harry, Rebecca - *Snow Bunny's Christmas Gift (Illus. by Harry, Rebecca)*
  c KR - Sept 1 2015 - pNA [51-500]
  c PW - v262 - i37 - Sept 14 2015 - p71(1) [51-500]
  c SLJ - v61 - i10 - Oct 2015 - p64(1) [51-500]
Harsent, David - *Fire Songs*
    TLS - i5839 - Feb 27 2015 - p25(1) [501+]
Harshman, Marc - *One Big Family (Illus. by Palacios, Sara)*
  c KR - Dec 15 2015 - pNA [51-500]
  c PW - v262 - i47 - Nov 23 2015 - p67(1) [51-500]
Harst, Joachim - *Heilstheater: Figur des barocken Trauerspiels zwischen Gryphius und Kleist*
    MLN - v130 - i3 - April 2015 - p667-670 [501+]
Hart, Adrian - *That's Racist!: How the Regulation of Speech and Thought Divides Us All*
    TimHES - i2194 - March 12 2015 - p49(1) [501+]
Hart, Aidan - *Beauty, Spirit, Matter: Icons in the Modern World*
    Theol St - v76 - i4 - Dec 2015 - p874(2) [501+]
Hart, Alison - *Finder, Coal Mine Dog*
  c KR - August 1 2015 - pNA [51-500]
Gold Rush Dog (Illus. by Montgomery, Michael G.)
  c HB Guide - v26 - i1 - Spring 2015 - p80(1) [51-500]
Hart, Amber - *After Us*
  y VOYA - v37 - i6 - Feb 2015 - p57(1) [51-500]
Hart, Amy - *RDA Made Simple: A Practical Guide to the New Cataloging Rules*
  y VOYA - v38 - i4 - Oct 2015 - p88(1) [51-500]
Hart, Bobby - *Psychedelic Bubble Gum: Boyce and Hart, the Monkees, and Turning Mayhem into Miracles*
    LJ - v140 - i8 - May 1 2015 - p76(1) [51-500]
    KR - June 1 2015 - pNA [51-500]
Hart, Brian - *The Bully of Order*
    NYTBR - Jan 4 2015 - p18(L) [501+]
Hart, C.J. - *The Hunted*
  y SLJ - v61 - i3 - March 2015 - p155(1) [51-500]
Hart, Carolyn - *Don't Go Home (Read by Reading, Kate). Audiobook Review*
    BL - v112 - i2 - Sept 15 2015 - p76(1) [51-500]
Don't Go Home
    BL - v111 - i18 - May 15 2015 - p27(1) [51-500]
    Bwatch - July 2015 - pNA [51-500]
    PW - v262 - i13 - March 30 2015 - p54(1) [51-500]
Ghost Wanted
    Bwatch - Feb 2015 - pNA [51-500]
Hart, Caryl - *The Princess and the Giant (Illus. by Warburton, Sarah)*
  c KR - August 1 2015 - pNA [51-500]
  c SLJ - v61 - i10 - Oct 2015 - p77(2) [51-500]
The Princess and the Presents (Illus. by Warburton, Sarah)
  c HB Guide - v26 - i1 - Spring 2015 - p32(1) [51-500]
Whiffy Wilson The Wolf Who Wouldn't Go to School (Illus. by Lord, Leonie)
  c CH Bwatch - Sept 2015 - pNA [51-500]
  c SLJ - v61 - i8 - August 2015 - p59(1) [51-500]
Hart, Christopher - *Cartoon Faces: How to Draw Faces, Features & Expressions*
    LJ - v140 - i2 - Feb 1 2015 - p80(1) [51-500]
Hart, Darryl G. - *Calvinism: A History*
    Historian - v77 - i2 - Summer 2015 - p390(2) [501+]
Hart, David Bentley - *The Experience of God: Being, Consciousness, Bliss*
    Theol St - v76 - i1 - March 2015 - p182(3) [501+]
Hart-Davis, Duff - *Our Land at War: A Portrait of Rural Britain, 1939-45*
    Spec - v328 - i9748 - June 27 2015 - p42(1) [501+]
Hart, Deborah - *Guarding Eden: Champions of Climate Action*
    Magpies - v30 - i3 - July 2015 - p22(1) [501+]
Hart, Drew G.I. - *Trouble I've Seen*
    PW - v262 - i45 - Nov 9 2015 - p55(1) [51-500]
Hart, Ellen - *The Grave Soul*
    KR - August 1 2015 - pNA [51-500]
    PW - v262 - i32 - August 10 2015 - p39(1) [51-500]
Hart, Elsa - *Jade Dragon Mountain (Read by Shih, David). Audiobook Review*
    PW - v262 - i48 - Nov 30 2015 - p54(1) [51-500]

Jade Dragon Mountain
    BL - v111 - i22 - August 1 2015 - p34(1) [51-500]
    CSM - Sept 21 2015 - pNA [501+]
    KR - July 1 2015 - pNA [51-500]
    PW - v262 - i29 - July 20 2015 - p168(1) [51-500]
Hart, Gary - *The Republic of Conscience*
    BL - v111 - i17 - May 1 2015 - p64(1) [51-500]
    KR - April 15 2015 - pNA [51-500]
    LJ - v140 - i10 - June 1 2015 - p122(1) [51-500]
    PW - v262 - i18 - May 4 2015 - p111(1) [51-500]
Hart, Kevin - *Kingdoms of God*
    RM - v69 - i2 - Dec 2015 - p388(2) [501+]
Hart, Mamrie - *You Deserve a Drink: Boozy Misadventures and Tales of Debauchery*
    NYTBR - May 31 2015 - p22(L) [501+]
Hart, Megan - *Hold Me Close*
    BL - v112 - i7 - Dec 1 2015 - p36(1) [51-500]
    PW - v262 - i42 - Oct 19 2015 - p62(1) [51-500]
Hart, Rob - *City of Rose*
    KR - Dec 1 2015 - pNA [51-500]
    PW - v262 - i51 - Dec 14 2015 - p62(1) [51-500]
New Yorked
    BL - v111 - i17 - May 1 2015 - p41(1) [51-500]
    KR - April 15 2015 - pNA [51-500]
    PW - v262 - i15 - April 13 2015 - p59(2) [51-500]
Hart, Stephen M. - *Essays on Alfredo Bryce Echenique, Peruvian Literature and Culture*
    MLR - v110 - i1 - Jan 2015 - p274-276 [501+]
Latin American Cinema
    TLS - i5860 - July 24 2015 - p27(1) [501+]
Hart, Tom - *Rosalie Lightning: A Graphic Memoir (Illus. by Hart, Tom)*
    BL - v112 - i6 - Nov 15 2015 - p34(1) [51-500]
    LJ - v140 - i17 - Oct 15 2015 - p5(1) [51-500]
    PW - v262 - i46 - Nov 16 2015 - p64(1) [51-500]
    KR - Nov 1 2015 - pNA [51-500]
She's Not into Poetry: Mini Comics 1991-1996
    PW - v262 - i48 - Nov 30 2015 - p47(1) [51-500]
Hartan, Davida - *The Growing Up Book for Boys: What Boys on the Autism Spectrum Need to Know! (Illus. by Suggs, Margaret Anne)*
  c CH Bwatch - July 2015 - pNA [51-500]
The Growing Up Guide for Girls: What Girls on the Autism Spectrum Need to Know! (Illus. by Suggs, Margaret Anne)
  c CH Bwatch - July 2015 - pNA [51-500]
Hartas, Dimitra - *Parenting, Family Policy, and Children's Well-Being in an Unequal Society: A New Culture War for Parents*
    CS - v44 - i6 - Nov 2015 - p807-808 [501+]
Hartch, Todd - *The Prophet of Cuernavaca: Ivan Illich and the Crisis of the West*
    AM - v213 - i13 - Nov 2 2015 - p34(2) [501+]
The Rebirth of Latin American Christianity
    CHR - v101 - i4 - Autumn 2015 - p964(2) [501+]
    Theol St - v76 - i2 - June 2015 - p358(3) [501+]
Harten, Hans-Christian - *Himmlers Lehrer: Die Weltanschauliche Schulung in der SS 1933-1945*
    HNet - March 2015 - pNA [501+]
Hartford, Paul - *Waiter to the Rich and Shameless*
    PW - v262 - i25 - June 22 2015 - p135(1) [51-500]
Hartl, Michael - *Ruby on Rails Tutorial, 3d ed.*
    Bwatch - Nov 2015 - pNA [51-500]
Hartland, Jessie - *Steve Jobs: A Biography*
    KR - April 15 2015 - pNA [51-500]
Steve Jobs: Insanely Great (Illus. by Hartland, Jessie)
  y BL - v111 - i19-20 - June 1 2015 - p68(1) [51-500]
  y Magpies - v30 - i5 - Nov 2015 - p23(2) [501+]
  y SLJ - v61 - i6 - June 2015 - p145(2) [51-500]
Hartley, Janet M. - *Siberia: A History of the People*
    For Aff - v94 - i1 - Jan-Feb 2015 - pNA [501+]
Hartley, Julie - *The Finding Place*
  y KR - Nov 1 2015 - pNA [51-500]
Hartling, Julia - *Pluck This*
    KR - Jan 1 2016 - pNA [501+]
Hartman, Andrew - *A War for the Soul of America: A History of the Culture Wars*
    BL - v111 - i16 - April 15 2015 - p6(1) [51-500]
    CC - v132 - i24 - Nov 25 2015 - p30(3) [501+]
    HNet - August 2015 - pNA [501+]
    PW - v262 - i12 - March 23 2015 - p66(1) [51-500]
    TimHES - i2204 - May 21 2015 - p53(1) [501+]
Hartman, Ben - *The Lean Farm: How to Minimize Waste, Increase Efficiency, and Maximize Value and Profits with Less Work*
    BL - v112 - i1 - Sept 1 2015 - p20(1) [51-500]
Hartman, Donniel - *Putting God Second: How to Save Religion from Itself*
    KR - Dec 1 2015 - pNA [501+]
    PW - v262 - i51 - Dec 14 2015 - p79(1) [51-500]

Hartman, Michele - *Other Lives*
    TLS - i5843 - March 27 2015 - p20(1) [501+]
Hartman, Michelle - *Native Tongue Stranger Talk: The Arabic and French Literary Landscapes of Lebanon*
    IJMES - v47 - i4 - Nov 2015 - p859-861 [501+]
Hartman, Rachel - *Seraphina*
    y Res Links - v20 - i3 - Feb 2015 - p55(1) [1-50]
Shadow Scale (Read by Williams, Mandy). Audiobook Review
    y HB - v91 - i4 - July-August 2015 - p164(1) [51-500]
    y SLJ - v61 - i6 - June 2015 - p66(2) [51-500]
Shadow Scale
    y HB - v91 - i2 - March-April 2015 - p97(1) [51-500]
    y HB Guide - v26 - i2 - Fall 2015 - p121(1) [51-500]
    y KR - Jan 1 2015 - pNA [51-500]
    y PW - v262 - i4 - Jan 26 2015 - p172(2) [51-500]
    y PW - v262 - i49 - Dec 2 2015 - p105(1) [51-500]
    y Res Links - v20 - i5 - June 2015 - p26(1) [51-500]
    y Sch Lib - v63 - i3 - Autumn 2015 - p182(1) [51-500]
    c SLJ - v61 - i6 - June 2015 - p46(6) [501+]
    y VOYA - v37 - i6 - Feb 2015 - p76(1) [51-500]
Hartmann, Florian - *Ars Dictaminis: Briefsteller und verbale Kommunikation in den italienischen Stadtkommunen des 11. Bis 13. Jahrhunderts*
    HER - v130 - i545 - August 2015 - p968(2) [501+]
Hartmann, Kat - *Hot Knots: Fresh Macrame Ideas for Jewelry, Home, and Fashion*
    LJ - v140 - i9 - May 15 2015 - p82(1) [51-500]
Hartmann, Martina - *Das Briefbuch Abt Wibalds von Stablo und Corvey, 3 vols.*
    Med R - August 2015 - pNA [501+]
Hartmann, Thom - *Death in the Pines*
    RVBW - March 2015 - pNA [51-500]
Hartmann, Wilfried - *Die Konzilien der karolingischen Teilreiche 875-911/Concilia aevi Karolini DCCCLXXV-DCCCCXI*
    Specu - v90 - i4 - Oct 2015 - p1118-1119 [501+]
Hartmann, William K. - *Searching for Golden Empires: Epic Cultural Collisions in Sixteenth-Century America*
    Roundup M - v22 - i4 - April 2015 - p29(1) [501+]
    Roundup M - v22 - i6 - August 2015 - p37(1) [501+]
    WHQ - v46 - i4 - Winter 2015 - p506-507 [501+]
Hartnett, Kimberly Marlowe - *Carolina Israelite: How Harry Golden Made Us Care about Jews, the South, and Civil Rights*
    KR - March 1 2015 - pNA [501+]
    LJ - v140 - i7 - April 15 2015 - p93(2) [51-500]
Hartnett, Lynne Ann - *The Defiant Life of Vera Figner: Surviving the Russian Revolution*
    AHR - v120 - i1 - Feb 2015 - p357-358 [501+]
    Slav R - v74 - i3 - Fall 2015 - p653-654 [501+]
Hartsell-Gundy, Arianne - *Digital Humanities in the Library: Challenges and Opportunities for Subject Specialists*
    LJ - v140 - i11 - June 15 2015 - p101(1) [51-500]
Hartvigsen, Gregg - *A Primer in Biological Data Analysis and Visualization Using R*
    QRB - v90 - i2 - June 2015 - p203(1) [501+]
Hartwell, Sadie - *Yarned and Dangerous*
    PW - v262 - i42 - Oct 19 2015 - p57(1) [51-500]
Hartzler, Aaron - *What We Saw*
    y BL - v112 - i1 - Sept 1 2015 - p110(1) [51-500]
    y KR - June 15 2015 - pNA [51-500]
    y SLJ - v61 - i8 - August 2015 - p104(1) [51-500]
    y VOYA - v38 - i4 - Oct 2015 - p52(1) [51-500]
Haruf, Kent - *Our Souls at Night (Read by Bramhall, Mark). Audiobook Review*
    BL - v112 - i1 - Sept 1 2015 - p142(1) [51-500]
Our Souls at Night
    Atl - v315 - i4 - May 2015 - p52(1) [51-500]
    BL - v111 - i16 - April 15 2015 - p26(2) [51-500]
    Esq - v163 - i6-7 - June-July 2015 - p26(2) [501+]
    KR - March 15 2015 - pNA [51-500]
    LJ - v140 - i6 - April 1 2015 - p79(1) [51-500]
    NY - v91 - i16 - June 8 2015 - p109 [51-500]
    NYTBR - June 7 2015 - p11(L) [501+]
    PW - v262 - i9 - March 2 2015 - p63(1) [51-500]
Harvey, Alyxandra - *Whisper the Dead*
    y HB Guide - v26 - i1 - Spring 2015 - p109(1) [51-500]
Harvey, Brian - *Beethoven's Tenth*
    y KR - Jan 15 2015 - pNA [51-500]
    y VOYA - v38 - i1 - April 2015 - p67(1) [51-500]
Harvey, Bruce G. - *World's Fairs in a Southern Accent: Atlanta, Nashville, and Charleston, 1895-1902*
    JSH - v81 - i4 - Nov 2015 - p1009(2) [501+]

Harvey, Cameron - *The Evidence Room*
    PW - v262 - i14 - April 6 2015 - p38(2) [51-500]
    KR - April 1 2015 - pNA [51-500]
Harvey, Caroline - *Contemporary Challenges to the Laws of War: Essays in Honour of Professor Peter Rowe*
    HNet - April 2015 - pNA [501+]
Harvey, David - *The Ways of the World*
    KR - Jan 1 2016 - pNA [51-500]
Harvey, Derek - *Super Shark Encyclopedia and Other Creatures of the Deep*
    c CH Bwatch - July 2015 - pNA [51-500]
    c SLJ - v61 - i10 - Oct 2015 - p57(1) [51-500]
Harvey, Eleanor J. - *The Civil War and American Art*
    South CR - v47 - i2 - Spring 2015 - p162-164 [501+]
Harvey, J.M. - *Justice for None*
    KR - July 1 2015 - pNA [501+]
Harvey, Jacky Colliss - *Red: A History of the Redhead*
    BL - v111 - i19-20 - June 1 2015 - p12(1) [51-500]
    LJ - v140 - i9 - May 15 2015 - p91(2) [51-500]
Red: A Natural History of the Redhead
    Spec - v328 - i9757 - August 29 2015 - p34(2) [501+]
Harvey, Jacqueline - *Alice-Miranda in Paris*
    c Sch Lib - v63 - i1 - Spring 2015 - p37(1) [51-500]
Harvey, Jennifer - *Dear White Christians: For Those Still Longing for Racial Reconciliation*
    Theol St - v76 - i4 - Dec 2015 - p886(2) [501+]
Harvey, John - *Darkness, Darkness*
    RVBW - Jan 2015 - pNA [51-500]
Harvey, Katherine - *Episcopal Appointments in England, c.1214-1344: From Episcopal Election to Papal Provision*
    HER - v130 - i544 - June 2015 - p704(3) [501+]
Harvey, Kenneth J. - *The Town That Forgot How to Breathe*
    CSM - Jan 20 2015 - pNA [51-500]
Harvey, Kevin - *Investigating Adolescent Health Communication: A Corpus Linguistics Approach*
    Lang Soc - v44 - i3 - June 2015 - p445-447 [501+]
Harvey, Matthea - *If the Tabloids Are True What Are You?*
    Bks & Cult - v21 - i5 - Sept-Oct 2015 - p35(1) [501+]
Harvey, Michael - *The Governor's Wife (Read by Hoye, Stephen). Audiobook Review*
    BL - v112 - i2 - Sept 15 2015 - p76(1) [51-500]
The Governor's Wife
    PW - v262 - i14 - April 6 2015 - p39(1) [51-500]
    KR - April 1 2015 - pNA [51-500]
Harvey, Polly Jean - *The Hollow of the Hand*
    NS - v144 - i5283 - Oct 9 2015 - p47(1) [51-500]
Harvey, Ross - *The Preservation Management Handbook: A 21st-Century Guide for Libraries, Archives, and Museums*
    LRTS - v59 - i2 - April 2015 - p95(2) [501+]
Harvey, Sally - *Domesday: Book of Judgement*
    HER - v130 - i544 - June 2015 - p694(2) [501+]
    Med R - June 2015 - pNA [501+]
    TLS - i5857 - July 3 2015 - p10(1) [501+]
Harvey, Samantha - *Dear Thief*
    TLS - i5854 - June 12 2015 - p12(1) [501+]
Harvey, Sarah N. - *Spirit Level*
    y KR - Nov 15 2015 - pNA [51-500]
Harvey, Tamsin - *Constantinople Quilts: 8 Stunning Applique Projects Inspired by Turkish Iznik Tiles*
    LJ - v140 - i9 - May 15 2015 - p82(2) [51-500]
    PW - v262 - i9 - March 2 2015 - p81(1) [51-500]
Harwell, Andrew - *The Spider Ring*
    c CCB-B - v68 - i6 - Feb 2015 - p312(2) [51-500]
    c CH Bwatch - June 2015 - pNA [501+]
    c HB Guide - v26 - i2 - Fall 2015 - p86(1) [51-500]
Harwell, Debbie Z. - *Wednesdays in Mississippi: Proper Ladies Working for Radical Change, Freedom Summer 1964*
    JAH - v102 - i2 - Sept 2015 - p616-616 [501+]
    JSH - v81 - i4 - Nov 2015 - p1040(2) [501+]
Harwood, B. Thomas - *Eternidad*
    KR - May 1 2015 - pNA [501+]
Harwood, Elaine - *Space, Hope and Brutalism: English Architecture, 1945-1975*
    Spec - v329 - i9763 - Oct 10 2015 - p36(2) [501+]
Harwood, Jonathan - *Europe's Green Revolution and Others Since: The Rise and Fall of Peasant-Friendly Plant Breeding*
    HNet - Sept 2015 - pNA [501+]
Harwood, Lee - *The Orchid Boat*
    Lon R Bks - v37 - i7 - April 9 2015 - p42(1) [501+]

Hasak-Lowy, Todd - *Me Being Me Is Exactly as Insane as You Being You*
    y BL - v111 - i12 - Feb 15 2015 - p82(1) [51-500]
    y CCB-B - v68 - i10 - June 2015 - p495(1) [51-500]
    y HB Guide - v26 - i2 - Fall 2015 - p122(1) [51-500]
    y KR - Jan 1 2015 - pNA [51-500]
    y VOYA - v37 - i6 - Feb 2015 - p57(1) [51-500]
Hasan, Mushirul - *Between Worlds: The Travels of Yusuf Khan Kambalposh*
    TLS - i5848 - May 1 2015 - p26(2) [501+]
Hasan-Rokem, Galit - *Louis Ginzberg's "Legends of the Jews": Ancient Jewish Folk Literature Reconsidered*
    TLS - i5858 - July 10 2015 - p26(2) [501+]
Hasebe, Yasuharu - *Massacre Gun*
    LJ - v140 - i13 - August 2015 - p50(1) [51-500]
    LJ - v140 - i13 - August 2015 - p50(1) [51-500]
Haselby, Sam - *The Origins of American Religious Nationalism*
    HNet - August 2015 - pNA [501+]
    NYRB - v62 - i12 - July 9 2015 - p27(3) [501+]
    W&M Q - v72 - i4 - Oct 2015 - p700-703 [501+]
Hasen, Richard L. - *Plutocrats United*
    KR - Nov 1 2015 - pNA [501+]
The Voting Wars: From Florida 2000 to the Next Election Meltdown
    NYRB - v62 - i9 - May 21 2015 - p20(3) [501+]
Hashimi, Nadia - *When the Moon Is Low*
    y BL - v111 - i21 - July 1 2015 - p34(1) [51-500]
    LJ - v140 - i12 - July 1 2015 - p77(1) [51-500]
Hashimoto, Daniel - *Action Movie Kid (Illus. by Fabbretti, Valerio)*
    c CH Bwatch - June 2015 - pNA [51-500]
    c Sch Lib - v63 - i3 - Autumn 2015 - p155(1) [51-500]
    c SLJ - v61 - i12 - Dec 2015 - p90(1) [51-500]
Hashimoto, Shinobu - *Akira Kurosawa and I*
    Si & So - v25 - i7 - July 2015 - p105(1) [501+]
Hasinoff, Amy Adele - *Sexting Panic: Rethinking Criminalization, Privacy, and Consent*
    Reason - v47 - i1 - May 2015 - p68(2) [501+]
Hasiuk, Brenda - *Boy Lost in Wild*
    Can Lit - i224 - Spring 2015 - p118 [501+]
Haskel, Peter - *Sword of Zen: Master Takuan and His Writings on Immovable Wisdom and the Sword Tale*
    Historian - v77 - i2 - Summer 2015 - p369(2) [501+]
Haskell, Marrie - *The Princess Curse*
    c Teach Lib - v43 - i1 - Oct 2015 - p42(1) [51-500]
Haskell, Merrie - *Handbook For Dragon Slayers*
    c SLJ - v61 - i6 - June 2015 - p46(6) [501+]
Hasker, William - *Metaphysics and the Tri-Personal God*
    JR - v95 - i3 - July 2015 - p408(2) [501+]
Haskins, Lori - *Spooky & Spookier: Four American Ghost Stories (Illus. by Diaz, Viviana)*
    c SLJ - v61 - i9 - Sept 2015 - p106(1) [51-500]
Haslam, Dave - *Life after Dark: A History of British Nightclubs and Music Venues*
    TLS - i5876 - Nov 13 2015 - p34(1) [501+]
Haslam, Gerald W. - *Leon Patterson*
    KR - August 15 2015 - pNA [501+]
Haslam, Jonathan - *Near and Distant Neighbors: A New History of Soviet Intelligence*
    BL - v111 - i21 - July 1 2015 - p11(1) [51-500]
    KR - June 1 2015 - pNA [501+]
    LJ - v140 - i9 - May 15 2015 - p92(1) [51-500]
    PW - v262 - i24 - June 15 2015 - p75(1) [51-500]
Hasler, Nikol - *Sex: An Uncensored Introduction (Illus. by Capozzola, Michael)*
    y SLJ - v61 - i10 - Oct 2015 - p133(2) [51-500]
Sex: An Uncensored Introduction
    y RVBW - June 2015 - pNA [51-500]
Haspiel, Dean - *Beef with Tomato*
    PW - v262 - i42 - Oct 19 2015 - p64(1) [51-500]
Hass, Kristin Ann - *Sacrificing Soldiers on the National Mall*
    HNet - April 2015 - pNA [501+]
    Pub Hist - v37 - i1 - Feb 2015 - p138(3) [501+]
Hassan, Amina - *Loren Miller: Civil Rights Attorney and Journalist*
    LJ - v140 - i15 - Sept 15 2015 - p85(1) [51-500]
Hassan, Wail S. - *Immigrant Narratives: Orientalism and Cultural Translation in Arab American and Arab British Literature*
    Am Q - v67 - i2 - June 2015 - p491-503 [501+]
Hassed, Craig - *The Mindful Home: The Secrets to Making Your Home a Place of Harmony, Beauty, Wisdom and True Happiness*
    LJ - v140 - i20 - Dec 1 2015 - p103(1) [51-500]
Hasselhorn, Benjamin - *Johannes Haller (1865-1947): Briefe eines Historikers*
    HNet - Feb 2015 - pNA [501+]

Hasselius, Michelle M. - *Richard M. Nixon*
c HB Guide - v26 - i1 - Spring 2015 - p193(1) [51-500]
Hassib, Rajia - *In the Language of Miracles*
BL - v111 - i22 - August 1 2015 - p28(1) [51-500]
KR - June 1 2015 - pNA [501+]
NYTBR - August 16 2015 - p13(L) [501+]
PW - v262 - i23 - June 8 2015 - p34(2) [51-500]
Hassing, Arne - *Church Resistance to Nazism in Norway: 1940-1945*
J Ch St - v57 - i3 - Summer 2015 - p571-572 [501+]
Hasso, Frances S. - *Consuming Desires: Family Crisis and the State in the Middle East*
JWH - v27 - i2 - Summer 2015 - p182(12) [501+]
Hasson, Mary Rice - *Promise and Challenge: Catholic Women Reflect on Feminism, Complementarity, and the Church*
Comw - v142 - i16 - Oct 9 2015 - p30(3) [501+]
Haste, Cate - *Craigie Aitchison: A Life in Colour*
TLS - i5834 - Jan 23 2015 - p26(1) [501+]
Hastings, Avery - *Torn*
y SLJ - v61 - i6 - June 2015 - p124(1) [51-500]
y HB Guide - v26 - i1 - Spring 2015 - p109(1) [51-500]
y KR - May 1 2015 - pNA [51-500]
y VOYA - v38 - i3 - August 2015 - p78(1) [51-500]
Hastings, Max - *Catastrophe 1914: Europe Goes to War*
J Mil H - v79 - i4 - Oct 2015 - p1144(1) [501+]
The Secret War: Spies, Codes and Guerillas, 1939-1945
Spec - v329 - i9767 - Nov 7 2015 - p50(1) [501+]
TLS - i5876 - Nov 13 2015 - p28(1) [501+]
Hastings, Michael - *The Last Magazine*
Ent W - i1364 - May 22 2015 - p66(1) [501+]
Hastings, Philip A. - *Fishes: A Guide to Their Diversity*
TLS - i5852 - May 29 2015 - p24(1) [501+]
Hastings, Samantha K. - *Annual Review of Cultural Heritage Informatics 2012-2013*
LR - v64 - i3 - March 2015 - p266-267 [501+]
Hastings, Selina - *The Red Earl*
TLS - i5835 - Jan 30 2015 - p26(1) [501+]
Hastings, William - *Stray Dogs: Writing from the Other America*
ABR - v36 - i3 - March-April 2015 - p21(2) [501+]
Haston, Meg - *Paperweight*
y PW - v262 - i49 - Dec 2 2015 - p96(1) [51-500]
y Sch Lib - v63 - i4 - Winter 2015 - p247(1) [51-500]
y HB - v91 - i4 - July-August 2015 - p134(2) [51-500]
y KR - May 1 2015 - pNA [51-500]
y PW - v262 - i18 - May 4 2015 - p122(2) [51-500]
y SLJ - v61 - i5 - May 2015 - p120(1) [51-500]
y VOYA - v38 - i3 - August 2015 - p62(1) [51-500]
Hatanaka, Kellen - *Drive: A Look at Roadside Opposites (Illus. by Hatanaka, Kellen)*
c CH Bwatch - August 2015 - pNA [51-500]
c HB Guide - v26 - i2 - Fall 2015 - p12(1) [51-500]
c Res Links - v20 - i5 - June 2015 - p4(1) [51-500]
c SLJ - v61 - i5 - May 2015 - p85(1) [51-500]
Drive: A Look at Roadside Opposites
c PW - v262 - i14 - April 6 2015 - p58(1) [51-500]
Drive: A Look Roadside Opposites
Nat Post - v17 - i153 - May 2 2015 - pWP6(1) [501+]
Work: An Occupational ABC
c HB Guide - v26 - i1 - Spring 2015 - p32(1) [51-500]
Hatch, Molly - *A Teacup Collection: Paintings of Porcelain Treasures*
Am Craft - v75 - i3 - June-July 2015 - p20(1) [501+]
Hatch, Steven - *Snowball in a Blizzard*
KR - Dec 1 2015 - pNA [501+]
Hatch, Tylor - *Fargo's Legacy*
RVBW - Feb 2015 - pNA [51-500]
Hatch, Warren A. - *In One Yard: Close to Nature*
LJ - v140 - i16 - Oct 1 2015 - p104(1) [51-500]
Hatcher, Robin Lee - *Whenever You Come Around*
BL - v111 - i18 - May 15 2015 - p32(1) [51-500]
Hatdane, Sean - *The Devil's Making*
BL - v111 - i17 - May 1 2015 - p32(1) [51-500]
Hatfield, Ruth - *The Book of Storms*
c CCB-B - v68 - i6 - Feb 2015 - p313(1) [51-500]
c HB Guide - v26 - i2 - Fall 2015 - p86(1) [51-500]
Hatfield, Shanna - *Aundy*
PW - v262 - i29 - July 20 2015 - p177(1) [51-500]
Hatfield, Thomas M. - *Rudder: From Leader to Legend*
APJ - v29 - i2 - March-April 2015 - p172(3) [501+]
Hatherley, Owen - *Landscapes of Communism: A History through Buildings*
KR - Dec 15 2015 - pNA [501+]
Lon R Bks - v37 - i15 - July 30 2015 - p5(2) [501+]
NS - v144 - i5275 - August 14 2015 - p44(2) [501+]
TLS - i5866 - Sept 4 2015 - p3(3) [501+]
Hathorn, Libby - *Eventual Poppy Day*
y Magpies - v30 - i2 - May 2015 - p40(2) [501+]
Hatje, Frank - *Die Tagebucher I (1792-1801), vols. 1-5*
JMH - v87 - i1 - March 2015 - p224(3) [501+]
Hatke, Ben - *Julia's House for Lost Creatures (Illus. by Hatke, Ben)*
c CCB-B - v68 - i5 - Jan 2015 - p259(1) [51-500]
Little Robot (Illus. by Hatke, Ben)
c KR - June 15 2015 - pNA [51-500]
c PW - v262 - i22 - June 1 2015 - p62(1) [51-500]
c SLJ - v61 - i8 - August 2015 - p94(2) [51-500]
c BL - v111 - i22 - August 1 2015 - p49(1) [51-500]
c HB - v91 - i5 - Sept-Oct 2015 - p104(2) [51-500]
Hattemer, Kate - *The Vigilante Poets of Selwyn Academy*
y Teach Lib - v42 - i3 - Feb 2015 - p28(4) [501+]
Hatton, Erin - *The Temp Economy: From Kelly Girls to Permatemps in Postwar America*
CS - v44 - i4 - July 2015 - p463-469 [501+]
Hatton, Jackie - *Flesh and Wires*
PW - v262 - i38 - Sept 21 2015 - p56(2) [51-500]
Hatton, L.J. - *Sing Down the Stars*
y SLJ - v61 - i11 - Nov 2015 - p107(2) [51-500]
Hatzimichali, M. - *Potamo of Alexandria and the Emergence of Eclecticism in Late Hellenistic Philosophy*
Class R - v65 - i1 - April 2015 - p81-83 [501+]
Hauben, Hans - *The Age of the Successors and the Creation of the Hellenistic Kingdoms*
NYRB - v62 - i4 - March 5 2015 - p40(3) [501+]
Haubold, Johannes - *Greece and Mesopotamia. Dialogues in Literature*
Class R - v65 - i1 - April 2015 - p5-6 [501+]
Hauck, Rachel - *How to Catch a Prince*
BL - v111 - i9-10 - Jan 1 2015 - p56(1) [51-500]
The Wedding Chapel
BL - v112 - i3 - Oct 1 2015 - p34(1) [51-500]
Hauerwas, Stanley - *Approaching the End: Eschatological Reflections on Church, Politics, and Life*
Theol St - v76 - i3 - Sept 2015 - p644(1) [51-500]
The Work of Theology
Bks & Cult - v21 - i6 - Nov-Dec 2015 - p8(2) [501+]
CC - v132 - i21 - Oct 14 2015 - p48(3) [501+]
Haugen, Hayley - *Mitchell Video Games*
c HB Guide - v26 - i1 - Spring 2015 - p140(1) [51-500]
Haughey, John - *A Biography of the Spirit*
AM - v213 - i17 - Nov 30 2015 - p33(3) [501+]
RVBW - April 2015 - pNA [51-500]
Haught, Brandon - *Going Ape: Florida's Battles over Evolution in the Classroom*
JSH - v81 - i4 - Nov 2015 - p1045(2) [501+]
Haught, John F. - *Science and Faith: A New Introduction*
TT - v72 - i2 - July 2015 - p236-237 [501+]
Haughton, Chris - *Shh! We Have a Plan (Illus. by Haughton, Chris)*
c HB Guide - v26 - i1 - Spring 2015 - p10(1) [51-500]
Haughton, Emma - *Better Left Buried*
y Sch Lib - v63 - i3 - Autumn 2015 - p189(2) [51-500]
Haulman, Kate - *The Politics of Fashion in Eighteenth-Century America*
HER - v130 - i543 - April 2015 - p466(2) [501+]
Hault, Derrick - *Experiencing Globalization: Religion in Contemporary Contexts*
J Ch St - v57 - i1 - Wntr 2015 - p170-171 [501+]
Hauptman, Laurence Marc - *In the Shadow of Kinzua: The Seneca Nation of Indians since World War II*
AHR - v120 - i1 - Feb 2015 - p282(1) [501+]
Hauser, Thomas - *The Baker's Tale*
KR - Oct 15 2015 - pNA [501+]
The Baker's Tale: Ruby Spriggs and the Legacy of Charles Dickens
PW - v262 - i41 - Oct 12 2015 - p46(2) [51-500]
The Final Recollections of Charles Dickens
NYTBR - April 12 2015 - p30(L) [501+]
A Hurting Sport: Another Year inside the Sweet Science
BL - v112 - i1 - Sept 1 2015 - p36(1) [51-500]
Hausmann, Klaus - *Cilia and Flagella-Ciliates and Flagellates: Ultrastructure and Cell Biology, Function and Systematics, Symbiosis and Biodiversity*
QRB - v90 - i3 - Sept 2015 - p342(1) [501+]
Haustein, Katja - *Regarding Lost Time: Photography, Identity, and Affect in Proust, Benjamin, and Barthes*
MLR - v110 - i1 - Jan 2015 - p228-229 [501+]
Hautala, Beth - *Waiting for Unicorns*
c CCB-B - v68 - i6 - Feb 2015 - p313(2) [51-500]
c HB Guide - v26 - i2 - Fall 2015 - p86(1) [51-500]
Hautman, Pete - *Eden West (Read by Haberkorn, Todd). Audiobook Review*
y SLJ - v61 - i8 - August 2015 - p54(1) [51-500]
Eden West
y BL - v111 - i11 - Feb 1 2015 - p47(1) [51-500]
y CCB-B - v68 - i10 - June 2015 - p495(1) [51-500]
y HB - v91 - i3 - May-June 2015 - p110(1) [51-500]
y HB Guide - v26 - i2 - Fall 2015 - p122(1) [51-500]
KR - Feb 1 2015 - pNA [51-500]
y PW - v262 - i5 - Feb 2 2015 - p62(1) [51-500]
SLJ - v61 - i2 - Feb 2015 - p101(2) [51-500]
y VOYA - v38 - i1 - April 2015 - p61(1) [51-500]
The Flinkwater Factor
c BL - v111 - i21 - July 1 2015 - p72(1) [51-500]
c KR - June 15 2015 - pNA [51-500]
c SLJ - v61 - i7 - July 2015 - p78(2) [51-500]
c PW - v262 - i27 - July 6 2015 - p73(2) [51-500]
Havea, Jione - *Bible, Borders, Belonging(s): Engaging Readings from Oceania*
Intpr - v69 - i1 - Jan 2015 - p123(1) [51-500]
Havel, Geoff - *Dropping In*
y CH Bwatch - Oct 2015 - pNA [51-500]
y Magpies - v30 - i2 - May 2015 - p35(1) [501+]
Havemeyer, Janie - *Call Me Ixchel: Mayan Goddess of the Moon (Illus. by Bridges, Shirin Yim)*
y HB Guide - v26 - i1 - Spring 2015 - p71(1) [51-500]
Haven, Kendall - *Writing Workouts to Develop Common Core Writing Skills: Step by Step Exercises, Activities, and Tips for Student Success, Grades 2-6*
Teach Lib - v42 - i3 - Feb 2015 - p43(1) [51-500]
Writing Workouts to Develop Common Core Writing Skills: Step by Step Exercises, Activities, and Tips for Student Success, Grades 7-12
Teach Lib - v42 - i3 - Feb 2015 - p42(1) [51-500]
Havens, John C. - *Heartificial Intelligence*
KR - Dec 15 2015 - pNA [51-500]
Haverkamp, Heidi - *Advent in Narnia: Reflections for the Season*
CC - v132 - i23 - Nov 11 2015 - p42(1) [51-500]
Havers, Grant N. - *Leo Strauss and Anglo-American Democracy: A Conservative Critique*
Dialogue - v54 - i2 - June 2015 - p400-402 [501+]
Haviland, Sara Rzeszutek - *James and Esther Cooper Jackson: Love and Courage in the Black Freedom Movement*
LJ - v140 - i16 - Oct 1 2015 - p88(1) [51-500]
Haviland, William A. - *Tikal Report 20A: Excavations in Residential Areas of Tikal: Non-elite Groups without Shrines: The Excavations*
Lat Ant - v26 - i3 - Sept 2015 - p423(2) [501+]
Tikal Report 20B: Excavations in Residential Areas of Tikal: Non-elite Groups without Shrines: Analysis and Conclusions
Lat Ant - v26 - i3 - Sept 2015 - p423(2) [501+]
Havill, Steven F. - *Blood Sweep*
PW - v262 - i7 - Feb 16 2015 - p163(1) [51-500]
BL - v111 - i15 - April 1 2015 - p29(1) [51-500]
KR - Feb 1 2015 - pNA [51-500]
Haw, Chris - *From Willow Creek to Sacred Heart: Rekindling My Love for Catholicism*
AM - v212 - i10 - March 23 2015 - p36(3) [501+]
Hawcock, David - *0-20 (Illus. by Hawcock, David)*
c KR - Dec 1 2015 - pNA [51-500]
Aa-Zz: A Pop-Up Alphabet (Illus. by Hawcock, David)
c KR - Dec 1 2015 - pNA [51-500]
c PW - v262 - i27 - July 6 2015 - p70(2) [501+]
Dinosaurs! Pop-Up Paper Designs
c PW - v262 - i27 - July 6 2015 - p70(2) [501+]
Hawdon, James - *The Causes and Consequences of Group Violence: From Bullies to Terrorists*
CS - v44 - i5 - Sept 2015 - p743-744 [501+]
Hawke, Ethan - *Rules for a Knight*
y BL - v112 - i4 - Oct 15 2015 - p25(1) [51-500]
KR - Sept 1 2015 - pNA [51-500]
PW - v262 - i37 - Sept 14 2015 - p38(1) [51-500]
Hawke, Rosanne - *Kerenza: A New Australian*
c Magpies - v30 - i3 - July 2015 - p36(1) [501+]
The Truth about Peacock Blue
y Magpies - v30 - i4 - Sept 2015 - p41(1) [501+]
Hawken, Sam - *Missing*
BL - v111 - i16 - April 15 2015 - p29(1) [51-500]
The Night Charter
BL - v112 - i4 - Oct 15 2015 - p22(1) [51-500]
KR - Sept 15 2015 - pNA [51-500]
PW - v262 - i36 - Sept 7 2015 - p45(1) [51-500]

Hawkes, Kevin - *Remy and Lulu (Illus. by Harrison, Hannah E.)*
   c   HB Guide - v26 - i1 - Spring 2015 - p32(1) [51-500]

Hawkins, Alexandra - *A Duke But No Gentleman*
   KR - May 1 2015 - pNA [51-500]
   PW - v262 - i19 - May 11 2015 - p42(1) [51-500]

Hawkins, Ann R. - *Women Writers and the Artifacts of Celebrity in the Long Nineteenth Century*
   VS - v57 - i2 - Wntr 2015 - p305(4) [501+]

Hawkins, Deborah - *Ride Your Heart 'Til It Breaks*
   KR - July 1 2015 - pNA [501+]

Hawkins, Donald T. - *Personal Archiving: Preserving Our Digital Heritage*
   Archiv - i79 - Spring 2015 - p187(5) [501+]
   LRTS - v59 - i2 - April 2015 - p94(2) [501+]

Hawkins, Gordon - *The de cosmos enigma*
   Beav - v95 - i5 - Oct-Nov 2015 - p64(1) [501+]

Hawkins, Jeff - *Playing Pro Hockey*
   c   HB Guide - v26 - i1 - Spring 2015 - p182(1) [51-500]

Hawkins, Jeremy - *The Last Days of Video*
   BL - v111 - i12 - Feb 15 2015 - p31(1) [51-500]
   KR - Jan 15 2015 - pNA [51-500]

Hawkins, Joan - *Downtown Film and TV Culture: 1975-2001*
   HM - v331 - i1982 - July 2015 - p85(3) [501+]

Hawkins, Michael C. - *Making Moros: Imperial Historism and American Military Rule in the Philippines' Muslim South*
   PHR - v84 - i2 - May 2015 - p249(2) [501+]

Hawkins, Paula - *The Girl on the Train (Read by Corbett, Clare). Audiobook Review*
   BL - v111 - i14 - March 15 2015 - p83(1) [51-500]
   Bwatch - April 2015 - pNA [51-500]
   LJ - v140 - i5 - March 15 2015 - p72(1) [51-500]
   PW - v262 - i12 - March 23 2015 - p71(1) [51-500]
The Girl on the Train
   Ent W - i1346 - Jan 16 2015 - p64(1) [501+]
   Esq - v164 - i1 - August 2015 - p32(1) [501+]
   Lon R Bks - v37 - i17 - Sept 10 2015 - p25(2) [501+]
   NYT - Jan 5 2015 - pC1(L) [501+]
   NYTBR - Feb 1 2015 - p12(L) [501+]
   People - v83 - i3 - Jan 19 2015 - p29 [501+]
   People - v83 - i3 - Jan 19 2015 - p29 [501+]
   People - v83 - i3 - Jan 19 2015 - p29 [501+]
   People - v83 - i3 - Jan 19 2015 - p29 [501+]
   People - v83 - i3 - Jan 19 2015 - p29 [501+]
   TLS - i5861 - July 31 2015 - p20(1) [501+]

Hawkins, Rachel - *Miss Mayhem*
   y   BL - v111 - i9-10 - Jan 1 2015 - p94(1) [51-500]
   y   CCB-B - v68 - i10 - June 2015 - p495(2) [51-500]
   y   HB Guide - v26 - i2 - Fall 2015 - p122(1) [51-500]
   y   SLJ - v61 - i3 - March 2015 - p155(1) [51-500]
   y   VOYA - v37 - i6 - Feb 2015 - p76(1) [51-500]
Rebel Belle (Read by Rubinate, Amy). Audiobook Review
   c   BL - v111 - i14 - March 15 2015 - p24(2) [51-500]

Hawkins, Ralph K. - *How Israel Became a People*
   Intpr - v69 - i4 - Oct 2015 - p507(1) [501+]

Hawkins, Scott - *The Library at Mount Char*
   LJ - v140 - i9 - May 15 2015 - p57(4) [51-500]
The Library at Mount Char (Read by Huber, Hillary). Audiobook Review
   y   BL - v112 - i5 - Nov 1 2015 - p69(2) [51-500]
The Library at Mount Char
   BL - v111 - i18 - May 15 2015 - p38(1) [51-500]
   KR - April 15 2015 - pNA [51-500]
   LJ - v140 - i16 - Oct 1 2015 - p111(1) [51-500]
   PW - v262 - i15 - April 13 2015 - p61(1) [51-500]

Hawkins, Tim - *Diary of a Jackwagon*
   PW - v262 - i27 - July 6 2015 - p65(1) [51-500]

Hawks, John Twelve - *Spark (Read by Brick, Scott). Audiobook Review*
   BL - v111 - i17 - May 1 2015 - p59(2) [51-500]

Hawks, Lyn Fairchild - *How Wendy Redbird Dancing Survived the Dark Ages of Nought*
   y   PW - v262 - i18 - May 4 2015 - p123(1) [51-500]

Hawks, Melanie - *Designing Training*
   LQ - v85 - i2 - April 2015 - p220(4) [501+]

Hawksley, Lucinda - *Charles Dickens' Favorite Daughter: The Life, Loves, And Art Of Katey Dickens Perugini*
   TimHES - i2199 - April 16 2015 - p57-1 [501+]
Queen Victoria's Mysterious Daughter: A Biography of Princess Louise
   KR - Sept 15 2015 - pNA [501+]
   LJ - v140 - i17 - Oct 15 2015 - p95(1) [51-500]
   PW - v262 - i31 - August 3 2015 - p45(1) [51-500]

Hawley, Richard - *Singing from the Floor: A History of British Folk Clubs*
   TimHES - i2220 - Sept 10 2015 - p45-1 [501+]

Haworth, Katie - *Around the World (Illus. by Shuttlewood, Craig)*
   c   BL - v111 - i19-20 - June 1 2015 - p110(1) [51-500]
   c   SLJ - v61 - i7 - July 2015 - p55(2) [51-500]
Through the Town (Illus. by Shuttlewood, Craig)
   c   BL - v111 - i19-20 - June 1 2015 - p110(1) [51-500]
   c   KR - July 1 2015 - pNA [51-500]

Haworth, Kelly - *Y Negative*
   KR - Sept 15 2015 - pNA [51-500]

Hawthorn, Geoffrey - *Thucydides on Politics: Back to the Present*
   Class R - v65 - i1 - April 2015 - p40-42 [501+]

Hawthorne, Nathaniel - *The Scarlet Letter: Manga Classics (Illus. by Lee, SunNeko)*
   y   BL - v111 - i19-20 - June 1 2015 - p67(2) [51-500]
   y   SLJ - v61 - i6 - June 2015 - p131(1) [51-500]
   y   VOYA - v38 - i2 - June 2015 - p60(1) [51-500]

Hawthorne, Rachel - *Trouble from the Start*
   y   VOYA - v38 - i1 - April 2015 - p61(1) [51-500]

Hay, Daisy - *Mr. and Mrs. Disraeli: A Strange Romance*
   Atl - v315 - i1 - Jan-Feb 2015 - p43(3) [501+]
   BL - v111 - i11 - Feb 1 2015 - p13(1) [51-500]
   CSM - Feb 11 2015 - pNA [501+]
   Econ - v414 - i8928 - March 7 2015 - p87(US) [501+]
   NY - v91 - i4 - March 16 2015 - p83 [51-500]
   Spec - v327 - i9725 - Jan 17 2015 - p34(2) [501+]
   TLS - i5842 - March 20 2015 - p30(1) [501+]
   Lon R Bks - v37 - i14 - July 16 2015 - p24(1) [501+]

Hay, Elizabeth - *His Whole Life*
   Mac - v128 - i32-33 - August 17 2015 - p68(2) [501+]

Hay, Gay - *Go, Green Gecko! (Illus. by Tolland, Margaret)*
   Magpies - v30 - i3 - July 2015 - pS4(1) [501+]

Hay, Mavis Doriel - *The Santa Klaus Murder*
   BL - v112 - i1 - Sept 1 2015 - p48(2) [51-500]
   PW - v262 - i33 - August 17 2015 - p54(1) [51-500]

Hay, Sam - *Knit-Knotters: A Branches Book (Illus. by Tran, Turine)*
   c   KR - Dec 15 2015 - pNA [51-500]

Hayden, David Alastair - *The Storm Dragon's Heart*
   RVBW - Oct 2015 - pNA [51-500]

Hayden, J. Michael - *The Catholicisms of Coutances: Varieties of Religion in Early Modern France, 1350-1789*
   CHR - v101 - i1 - Wntr 2015 - p158(2) [501+]

Hayden, Jennifer - *The Story of My Tits (Illus. by Hayden, Jennifer)*
   BL - v111 - i22 - August 1 2015 - p46(1) [51-500]
   PW - v262 - i33 - August 17 2015 - p58(1) [51-500]
   LJ - v140 - i14 - Sept 1 2015 - p130(2) [51-500]

Hayden, Michael J. - *Crutched Friars and Croisiers: The Canons Regular of the Holy Cross in England and France*
   CHR - v101 - i3 - Summer 2015 - p594(2) [501+]

Hayden-Smith, Rose - *Sowing the Seeds of Victory: American Gardening Programs of World War I*
   HNet - May 2015 - pNA [501+]
   Pub Hist - v37 - i1 - Feb 2015 - p134(2) [501+]

Hayder, Mo - *Wolf*
   RVBW - May 2015 - pNA [51-500]

Haydock, Nickolas - *Beowulf on Film: Adaptations and Variations*
   Specu - v90 - i4 - Oct 2015 - p1119-1121 [501+]

Haydon, Elizabeth - *The Hollow Queen*
   BL - v111 - i18 - May 15 2015 - p36(1) [51-500]
   KR - May 1 2015 - pNA [51-500]
   PW - v262 - i14 - April 6 2015 - p44(1) [51-500]
The Tree of Water
   y   HB Guide - v26 - i2 - Fall 2015 - p86(1) [51-500]
   y   CH Bwatch - Jan 2015 - pNA [51-500]

Haydu, Corey Ann - *Making Pretty*
   y   BL - v111 - i16 - April 15 2015 - p48(1) [51-500]
   y   CCB-B - v68 - i11 - July-August 2015 - p547(2) [51-500]
   y   HB Guide - v26 - i2 - Fall 2015 - p122(1) [51-500]
   y   KR - Feb 15 2015 - pNA [51-500]
   y   PW - v262 - i10 - March 9 2015 - p75(2) [51-500]
   y   VOYA - v38 - i1 - April 2015 - p61(1) [51-500]
Rules for Stealing Stars
   c   BL - v112 - i1 - Sept 1 2015 - p118(1) [51-500]
   c   HB - v91 - i5 - Sept-Oct 2015 - p105(1) [51-500]
   c   KR - June 15 2015 - pNA [51-500]
   c   PW - v262 - i24 - June 15 2015 - p83(1) [51-500]
   c   SLJ - v61 - i7 - July 2015 - p78(2) [51-500]
   c   VOYA - v38 - i5 - Dec 2015 - p70(1) [51-500]

Hayek, Friedrich - *Hayek on Mill: The Mill-Taylor Friendship and Other Writings*
   NYRB - v62 - i6 - April 2 2015 - p67(3) [501+]
Hayek on Mill: The Mill-Taylor Friendship and Related Writings
   NS - v144 - i5263 - May 22 2015 - p40(3) [501+]

Hayes, Charles D. - *A Mile North of Good and Evil*
   SPBW - August 2015 - pNA [51-500]

Hayes, Christine - *Mothman's Curse (Illus. by Hindle, James K.)*
   c   HB - v91 - i5 - Sept-Oct 2015 - p105(2) [51-500]
   c   BL - v111 - i19-20 - June 1 2015 - p105(2) [51-500]
   c   PW - v262 - i17 - April 27 2015 - p75(2) [51-500]
   c   SLJ - v61 - i5 - May 2015 - p102(2) [51-500]

Hayes, Denis - *Cowed: The Hidden Impact of 93 Million Cows on America's Health, Economy, Politics, Culture, and Environment*
   BL - v111 - i11 - Feb 1 2015 - p7(2) [51-500]
   Bwatch - May 2015 - pNA [51-500]
   Nature - v520 - i7546 - April 9 2015 - p155(1) [51-500]
   NH - v123 - i4 - May 2015 - p46(1) [501+]
   PW - v262 - i8 - Feb 23 2015 - p67(1) [501+]

Hayes, Frank - *Death at the Black Bull*
   RVBW - July 2015 - pNA [501+]
Death on the High Lonesome
   PW - v262 - i32 - August 10 2015 - p40(1) [51-500]

Hayes, Geoffrey - *Benny and Penny in Lost and Found!*
   c   HB Guide - v26 - i1 - Spring 2015 - p53(1) [51-500]

Hayes, Jack Patrick - *A Change in Worlds on the Sino-Tibetan Borderlands: Politics, Economics, and Environments in Northern Sichuan*
   AHR - v120 - i1 - Feb 2015 - p216-217 [501+]

Hayes, Joe - *My Pet Rattlesnake (Illus. by Castro L., Antonio)*
   c   HB Guide - v26 - i1 - Spring 2015 - p32(1) [51-500]

Hayes, John P. - *12 Amazing Franchise Opportunities for 2015*
   RVBW - Feb 2015 - pNA [51-500]

Hayes, Leah - *Not Funny Ha-Ha (Illus. by Hayes, Leah)*
   y   BL - v112 - i2 - Sept 15 2015 - p50(2) [51-500]
   y   PW - v262 - i32 - August 10 2015 - p45(1) [51-500]

Hayes, Nicole - *One True Thing*
   y   Magpies - v30 - i2 - May 2015 - p41(1) [501+]

Hayes, Paddy - *Queen of Spies: Daphne Park, Britain's Cold War Spy Master*
   KR - Oct 1 2015 - pNA [501+]
   LJ - v140 - i19 - Nov 15 2015 - p92(2) [51-500]
   PW - v262 - i48 - Nov 30 2015 - p52(1) [51-500]
   Spec - v329 - i9767 - Nov 7 2015 - p50(1) [501+]

Hayes, Patrick - *Philip Roth: Fiction and Power*
   RES - v66 - i275 - June 2015 - p599-600 [501+]
   J Am St - v49 - i3 - August 2015 - p641-642 [501+]

Hayes, Samantha - *What You Left Behind (Read by Bentinck, Anna). Audiobook Review*
   LJ - v140 - i11 - June 15 2015 - p50(1) [51-500]
What You Left Behind
   BL - v111 - i12 - Feb 15 2015 - p39(1) [51-500]
   KR - Feb 1 2015 - pNA [51-500]
   PW - v262 - i5 - Feb 2 2015 - p37(2) [51-500]

Hayes, Shane - *The Last Dreamgirl*
   SPBW - August 2015 - pNA [51-500]

Hayes, Terrance - *How to Be Drawn*
   BL - v111 - i14 - March 15 2015 - p38(1) [51-500]
   LJ - v140 - i9 - May 15 2015 - p86(1) [51-500]
   NY - v91 - i12 - May 11 2015 - p78 [501+]
   PW - v262 - i7 - Feb 16 2015 - p158(1) [51-500]

Hayes, Tim - *Riding Home: The Power of Horses to Heal*
   BL - v111 - i13 - March 1 2015 - p11(1) [51-500]

Hayes, Tom - *Secret of the Warlock's Crypt*
   KR - Feb 1 2015 - pNA [501+]

Haygood, Wil - *Showdown: Thurgood Marshall and the Supreme Court Nomination That Changed America*
   LJ - v140 - i11 - June 15 2015 - p95(1) [51-500]
   BL - v112 - i3 - Oct 1 2015 - p6(2) [51-500]
   KR - June 15 2015 - pNA [51-500]
   NYTBR - Sept 20 2015 - p1(L) [501+]
   PW - v262 - i20 - May 18 2015 - p73(2) [51-500]

Hayley, Elizabeth - *Just Say Yes*
   PW - v262 - i45 - Nov 9 2015 - p44(2) [51-500]

Haymore, Sheri Wren - *A Deeper Cut*
   PW - v262 - i12 - March 23 2015 - p50(1) [51-500]

Hayner, Steve - *Joy in the Journey: Finding Abundance in the Shadow of Death*
   PW - v262 - i23 - June 8 2015 - p55(2) [51-500]

Haynes, April R. - *Riotous Flesh: Women, Physiology, and the Solitary Vice in Nineteenth-Century America*
　　TimHES - i2220 - Sept 10 2015 - p481(1) [501+]
Haynes, Elizabeth - *Behind Closed Doors*
　y　BL - v111 - i12 - Feb 15 2015 - p34(1) [51-500]
　y　LJ - v140 - i3 - Feb 15 2015 - p87(1) [51-500]
　y　PW - v262 - i6 - Feb 9 2015 - p46(2) [51-500]
　y　SLJ - v61 - i6 - June 2015 - p132(1) [501+]
Unlocking the Mysteries of Cataloging: A Workbook of Examples
　　RVBW - April 2015 - pNA [501+]
Haynes, Jane - *Doctors Dissected*
　　NS - v144 - i5253 - March 13 2015 - p53(1) [51-500]
Haynes, Rose M. - *The Ore Knob Mine Murders: The Crimes, the Investigation and the Trials*
　　JSH - v81 - i2 - May 2015 - p530(3) [501+]
Haynes, Sarah F. - *Wading into the Stream of Wisdom: Essays in Honor of Leslie Kawamura*
　　HNet - May 2015 - pNA [501+]
Haynie, Rachel - *First, You Explore: The Story of the Young Charles Townes (Illus. by Cook, Trahem)*
　c　HB Guide - v26 - i1 - Spring 2015 - p193(1) [51-500]
First, You Explore: The Story of Young Charles Townes (Illus. by Cook, Trahem)
　c　Sci & Ch - v53 - i3 - Nov 2015 - p90 [51-500]
Hays, Avery - *The Sixth*
　　PW - v262 - i16 - April 20 2015 - p50(1) [51-500]
Hays, J.E.S. - *Devon Day and the Sweetwater Kid: Down the Owlhoot Trail*
　y　Roundup M - v22 - i3 - Feb 2015 - p22(1) [501+]
　y　Roundup M - v22 - i6 - August 2015 - p25(1) [501+]
Hays, Richard B. - *Reading Backwards: Figural Christology and the Fourfold Gospel Witness*
　　Bks & Cult - v21 - i3 - May-June 2015 - p22(2) [501+]
　　CC - v132 - i9 - April 29 2015 - p49(2) [501+]
Hays, Tony - *Shakespeare No More*
　　KR - July 1 2015 - pNA [51-500]
Haythornthwaite, Philip - *Redcoats: The British Soldiers of the Napoleonic Wars*
　　HER - v130 - i542 - Feb 2015 - p123(14) [501+]
Hayton, Bill - *The South China Sea: The Struggle for Power in Asia*
　　For Aff - v94 - i1 - Jan-Feb 2015 - pNA [501+]
　　HNet - June 2015 - pNA [501+]
　　TLS - i5843 - March 27 2015 - p29(1) [501+]
Hayton, Katherine - *Found, Near Water*
　　KR - Jan 1 2015 - pNA [501+]
Skeletal
　　KR - May 1 2015 - pNA [501+]
Hayward, Bill - *Chasing Dragons: An Uncommon Memoir in Photographs*
　　PW - v262 - i30 - July 27 2015 - p58(1) [51-500]
Hayward, Clarissa Rile - *How Americans Make Race: Stories, Institutions, Spaces*
　　CS - v44 - i6 - Nov 2015 - p808-810 [501+]
Hayward, Richard - *Ulster and the City of Belfast*
　　TLS - i5855 - June 19 2015 - p30(1) [501+]
Haywood, Wil - *Showdown: Thurgood Marshall and the Supreme Court Nomination that Changed America*
　　CSM - Oct 29 2015 - pNA [501+]
Hazan, Eric - *A People's History of the French Revolution*
　　NS - v144 - i5276 - August 21 2015 - p50(2) [501+]
　　TLS - i5856 - June 26 2015 - p5(2) [501+]
Hazareesingh, Sudhir - *How the French Think: An Affectionate Portrait of an Intellectual People*
　　Econ - v415 - i8942 - June 13 2015 - p79(US) [501+]
　　KR - July 1 2015 - pNA [501+]
　　NS - v144 - i5272 - July 24 2015 - p46(2) [501+]
　　NYRB - v62 - i16 - Oct 22 2015 - p50(3) [501+]
　　PW - v262 - i29 - July 20 2015 - p178(1) [51-500]
　　Spec - v328 - i9747 - June 20 2015 - p32(2) [501+]
　　TimHES - i2210 - July 2 2015 - p51-1 [501+]
　　TLS - i5859 - July 17 2015 - p4(2) [501+]
Hazelgrove, William - *Jack Pine*
　　BL - v111 - i16 - April 15 2015 - p28(1) [51-500]
Hazen, John - *Journey of an American Son*
　　SPBW - April 2015 - pNA [51-500]
Hazlet, Allan - *A Luxury of the Understanding: On the Value of the True Belief*
　　Dialogue - v54 - i1 - March 2015 - p202-204 [501+]
Hazzard-Donald, Katrina - *Mojo Workin': The Old African American Hoodoo System*
　　Am St - v54 - i1 - Spring 2015 - p147-2 [501+]
　　CS - v44 - i1 - Jan 2015 - p67-68 [501+]

Hazzard, Kevin - *A Thousand Naked Strangers: A Paramedic's Wild Ride to the Edge and Back*
　　KR - Oct 15 2015 - pNA [501+]
　　PW - v262 - i46 - Nov 16 2015 - p69(1) [51-500]
　　BL - v112 - i7 - Dec 1 2015 - p21(1) [51-500]
Hazzard, Shirley - *We Need Silence to Find Out What We Think: Selected Essays*
　　KR - Oct 1 2015 - pNA [501+]
　　LJ - v140 - i19 - Nov 15 2015 - p84(2) [51-500]
　　PW - v262 - i41 - Oct 12 2015 - p56(1) [51-500]
He, Wenkai - *Paths toward the Modern Fiscal State: England, Japan, and China*
　　BHR - v89 - i3 - Autumn 2015 - p615(3) [501+]
　　JMH - v87 - i1 - March 2015 - p148(2) [501+]
Heaberlin, Julia - *Black Eyed Susans (Read by Dykhouse, Whitney). Audiobook Review*
　　BL - v112 - i5 - Nov 1 2015 - p69(1) [51-500]
Black-Eyed Susans
　　KR - May 15 2015 - pNA [51-500]
　　NYTBR - Sept 6 2015 - p25(L) [501+]
　　PW - v262 - i19 - May 11 2015 - p33(2) [51-500]
Heacox, Kim - *Jimmy Bluefeather*
　　BL - v112 - i1 - Sept 1 2015 - p40(1) [51-500]
　　KR - July 1 2015 - pNA [51-500]
　　LJ - v140 - i13 - August 1 2015 - p83(1) [51-500]
Rhythm of the Wild: A Life Inspired by Alaska's Denali National Park
　　BL - v111 - i18 - May 15 2015 - p13(1) [51-500]
　　KR - Feb 15 2015 - pNA [51-500]
Head, Elaine - *Back to Vietnam*
　　KR - Sept 1 2015 - pNA [501+]
Head, Glenn - *Chicago: A Comix Memoir*
　　PW - v262 - i37 - Sept 14 2015 - p51(1) [51-500]
Head, Honor - *The Dog Lover's Guide*
　c　Sch Lib - v63 - i2 - Summer 2015 - p111(2) [51-500]
My Little Book of Big Trucks
　c　Sch Lib - v63 - i3 - Autumn 2015 - p155(2) [51-500]
Head, Matthew - *Sovereign Feminine: Music and Gender in Eighteenth-Century Germany*
　　JMH - v87 - i2 - June 2015 - p483(2) [501+]
Head, Vernon R.L. - *The Rarest Bird in the World: The Search for the Nechisar Nightjar*
　　BL - v112 - i5 - Nov 1 2015 - p6(1) [51-500]
　　KR - Dec 15 2015 - pNA [51-500]
Head, William P. - *Night Hunters: The AC-130s and Their Role in U.S. Airpower*
　　APH - v62 - i1 - Spring 2015 - p50(2) [501+]
Headley, Maria Dahvana - *Magonia*
　y　CCB-B - v68 - i9 - May 2015 - p449(1) [51-500]
　y　HB Guide - v26 - i2 - Fall 2015 - p122(1) [51-500]
　y　KR - Feb 15 2015 - pNA [51-500]
　y　PW - v262 - i5 - Feb 2 2015 - p62(1) [51-500]
　y　PW - v262 - i49 - Dec 2 2015 - p104(1) [51-500]
　y　SLJ - v61 - i4 - April 2015 - p164(2) [51-500]
　y　VOYA - v38 - i4 - Oct 2015 - p72(1) [51-500]
Heads, Michael - *Biogeography of Australasia: A Molecular Analysis*
　　QRB - v90 - i3 - Sept 2015 - p327(2) [501+]
Heagerty Marton - *Unholy Innocents*
　　KR - Nov 15 2015 - pNA [501+]
Heal, Felicity - *The Power of Gifts: Gift-Exchange in Early Modern England*
　　JIH - v46 - i3 - Wntr 2016 - p438-439 [501+]
　　TLS - i5859 - July 17 2015 - p13(1) [501+]
Heald, Paul - *Death in Eden*
　　RVBW - April 2015 - pNA [501+]
Heale, Martin - *The Prelate in England and Europe, 1300-1560*
　　Med R - Sept 2015 - pNA [501+]
Healey, Emma - *Elizabeth Is Missing*
　　RVBW - Feb 2015 - pNA [501+]
　　RVBW - July 2015 - pNA [501+]
Healey, Paul D. - *Legal Reference for Librarians: How and Where to Find the Answers*
　　R&USQ - v54 - i3 - Spring 2015 - p54(1) [501+]
Healey, Tim - *Mortimer Keene: Dino Danger (Illus. by Mould, Chris)*
　c　Sch Lib - v63 - i2 - Summer 2015 - p105(1) [51-500]
Healy, Christopher - *The Hero's Guide to Being an Outlaw*
　c　Teach Lib - v43 - i1 - Oct 2015 - p48(1) [51-500]
Healy-Clancy, Meghan - *A World of Their Own: A History of South Africa Women's Education*
　　IJAHS - v48 - i1 - Wntr 2015 - p125-126 [501+]
Healy, Dermot - *The Collected Short Stories*
　　LJ - v140 - i19 - Nov 15 2015 - p97(1) [51-500]
Healy, Nicholas M. - *Hauerwas: A (Very) Critical Introduction*
　　TLS - i5831 - Jan 2 2015 - p24(1) [51-500]

Healy, Nick - *Love and Profanity: A Collection of True, Tortured, Wild, Hilarious, Concise, and Intense Tales of Teenage Life*
　y　BL - v111 - i12 - Feb 15 2015 - p70(1) [51-500]
　y　PW - v262 - i3 - Jan 19 2015 - p87(1) [51-500]
　y　VOYA - v37 - i6 - Feb 2015 - p87(1) [501+]
　y　CCB-B - v68 - i9 - May 2015 - p450(1) [51-500]
Love and Profanity.
　y　HB Guide - v26 - i2 - Fall 2015 - p202(1) [51-500]
Healy, Roisin - *The Shadow of Colonialism on Europe's Modern Past*
　　HNet - June 2015 - pNA [501+]
Heaney, Katie - *Dear Emma*
　　KR - Dec 15 2015 - pNA [501+]
Heaney, Michael T. - *Party in the Street: The Antiwar Movement and the Democratic Party after 9/11*
　　Reason - v47 - i7 - Dec 2015 - p46(6) [501+]
Heaney, Seamus - *New Selected Poems 1988-2013*
　　Lon R Bks - v37 - i11 - June 4 2015 - p9(2) [501+]
Selected Poems, 1988-2013
　　WLT - v89 - i6 - Nov-Dec 2015 - p73(1) [501+]
Heap, Sue - *Mine! (Illus. by Heap, Sue)*
　c　HB Guide - v26 - i1 - Spring 2015 - p10(1) [51-500]
Heapy, Teresa - *Very Little Cinderella (Illus. by Heap, Sue)*
　c　KR - August 15 2015 - pNA [51-500]
　c　PW - v262 - i28 - July 13 2015 - p64(1) [501+]
　c　PW - v262 - i49 - Dec 2 2015 - p25(1) [51-500]
　c　Sch Lib - v63 - i3 - Autumn 2015 - p156(1) [51-500]
Very Little Red Riding Hood (Illus. by Heap, Sue)
　c　HB Guide - v26 - i1 - Spring 2015 - p10(1) [51-500]
Heard, Edith - *Epigenetics and Development*
　　QRB - v90 - i2 - June 2015 - p229(2) [501+]
Hearn, Jeff - *Rethinking Transnational Men: Beyond, Between, and Within Nations*
　　CS - v44 - i2 - March 2015 - p209-211 [501+]
Hearn, Sam - *Christmas at Last! (Illus. by Dann, Penny)*
　c　KR - Sept 1 2015 - pNA [51-500]
Hearne, Joanna - *Native Recognition: Indigenous Cinema and the Western*
　　Am Ind CRJ - v39 - i1 - Wntr 2015 - p145-148 [501+]
Hearne, Kevin - *A Fantasy Medley 3*
　　PW - v262 - i42 - Oct 19 2015 - p59(1) [51-500]
Heir to the Jedi: Star Wars (Read by Thompson, Marc). Audiobook Review
　y　PW - v262 - i21 - May 25 2015 - p54(1) [51-500]
Hearst, Alice - *Children and the Politics of Cultural Belonging*
　　CS - v44 - i1 - Jan 2015 - p68-70 [501+]
Hearst, Michael - *Extraordinary People: A Semi-Comprehensive Guide to Some of the World's Most Fascinating Individuals (Illus. by Scamihorn, Aaron)*
　y　SLJ - v61 - i4 - April 2015 - p183(3) [51-500]
　y　BL - v111 - i19-20 - June 1 2015 - p76(1) [51-500]
　y　HB Guide - v26 - i2 - Fall 2015 - p213(1) [51-500]
　y　PW - v262 - i18 - May 4 2015 - p120(1) [51-500]
Hearth, Amy Hill - *Miss Dreamsville and the Lost Heiress of Collier County*
　　BL - v112 - i1 - Sept 1 2015 - p42(1) [51-500]
　　KR - July 1 2015 - pNA [501+]
Heath, Anna - *Beings: Contemporary Peruvian Short Stories*
　　WLT - v89 - i1 - Jan-Feb 2015 - p62(1) [501+]
Heath, Christian - *The Dynamics of Auction: Social Interaction and the Sale of Fine Art and Antiques*
　　CS - v44 - i2 - March 2015 - p211-213 [501+]
Heath, Gordon L. - *Canadian Churches and the First World War*
　　Can Hist R - v96 - i2 - June 2015 - p319(2) [501+]
Heath, Jack - *300 Minutes of Danger*
　c　Magpies - v30 - i4 - Sept 2015 - p33(1) [51-500]
The Cut Out
　y　Magpies - v30 - i4 - Sept 2015 - p33(2) [51-500]
Heath, Lorraine - *The Duke and the Lady in Red*
　　KR - Feb 15 2015 - pNA [51-500]
　　PW - v262 - i6 - Feb 9 2015 - p50(1) [51-500]
Falling into Bed with a Duke
　　BL - v112 - i4 - Oct 15 2015 - p26(1) [51-500]
　　PW - v262 - i24 - June 15 2015 - p69(1) [51-500]
Heath, Melanie - *One Marriage under God: The Campaign to Promote Marriage in America*
　　SF - v94 - i2 - Dec 2015 - pNA [501+]
Heath, Robert - *The Judas Dilemma*
　　PW - v262 - i52 - Dec 21 2015 - p136(1) [51-500]
Heath, Russell - *Broken Angels*
　　KR - Sept 15 2015 - pNA [51-500]

Heath, William - *The Children Bob Moses Led: A Novel of Freedom Summer*
    ABR - v36 - i2 - Jan-Feb 2015 - p15(1) [501+]

Heathcote, Owen - *From Bad Boys to New Men? Masculinity, Sexuality, and Violence in the Work of Eric Jourdan*
    MLR - v110 - i3 - July 2015 - p873-874 [501+]

Heathfield, Lisa - *Seed*
  y BL - v111 - i12 - Feb 15 2015 - p84(1) [51-500]
  y SLJ - v61 - i2 - Feb 2015 - p102(1) [51-500]
  y VOYA - v37 - i6 - Feb 2015 - p57(1) [51-500]
  y HB Guide - v26 - i2 - Fall 2015 - p122(1) [51-500]

Heaton, Matthew M. - *Black Skin, White Coats: Nigerian Psychiatrists, Decolonization, and the Globalization of Psychiatry*
    HNet - June 2015 - pNA [501+]

Hebel, Francois - *Harry Gruyaert*
    LJ - v140 - i15 - Sept 15 2015 - p81(3) [501+]
Harry Gruyaert (Illus. by Gruyaert, Harry)
    NS - v144 - i5272 - July 24 2015 - p46(1) [51-500]

Hebert-Collins, Sheila - *Petite Rouge: A Cajun Twist to an Old Tale (Illus. by Lyne, Alison Davis)*
  c HB Guide - v26 - i2 - Fall 2015 - p159(1) [51-500]

Hebert, Jill M. - *Morgan le Fay, Shapeshifter*
    Specu - v90 - i1 - Jan 2015 - p256-257 [501+]

Hebert, Michel - *Parlementer: Assemblees representatives et echange politique en Europe occidentale a la fin du Moyen Age*
    HER - v130 - i544 - June 2015 - p710(2) [501+]

Heble, Ajay - *People Get Ready: The Future of Jazz Is Now!*
    J Am St - v49 - i2 - May 2015 - p405-412 [501+]

Hebrew Congregation - *Washington's Rebuke to Bigotry: Reflections on Our First President's Famous 1790 Letter to the Hebrew Congregation in Newport, Rhode Island*
    SPBW - August 2015 - pNA [501+]

Hecht, Gabrielle - *Being Nuclear: Africans and the Global Uranium Trade*
    JMH - v87 - i1 - March 2015 - p164(2) [501+]

Hecht, Susanna B. - *The Social Lives of Forests: Past, Present, and Future of Woodland Resurgence*
    JRAI - v21 - i1 - March 2015 - p219(2) [501+]

Hechter, Michael - *Alien Rule*
    HNet - March 2015 - pNA [501+]

Hector, Andy - *The New Statistics with R: An Introduction for Biologists*
    BioSci - v65 - i10 - Oct 2015 - p1021(5) [501+]

Heder, Thyra - *The Bear Report (Illus. by Heder, Thyra)*
  c BL - v112 - i3 - Oct 1 2015 - p81(1) [51-500]
  c KR - August 1 2015 - pNA [51-500]
  c NYTBR - Nov 8 2015 - p33(L) [501+]
  c SLJ - v61 - i10 - Oct 2015 - p78(1) [51-500]

Hedge Coke, Allison Adelle - *Streaming*
    WLT - v89 - i5 - Sept-Oct 2015 - p72(2) [501+]

Hedges, Chris - *Wages of Rebellion*
    Hum - v75 - i5 - Sept-Oct 2015 - p42(2) [501+]
    KR - March 15 2015 - pNA [501+]
    LJ - v140 - i7 - April 15 2015 - p106(1) [51-500]
    NYTBR - July 5 2015 - p1(L) [501+]
    PW - v262 - i12 - March 23 2015 - p65(2) [51-500]

Hedin, Benjamin - *In Search of the Movement*
    KR - April 1 2015 - pNA [501+]

Hedlund, Jody - *Hearts Made Whole*
    BL - v111 - i19-20 - June 1 2015 - p61(2) [51-500]
    PW - v262 - i17 - April 27 2015 - p59(1) [51-500]
An Uncertain Choice
    SLJ - v61 - i4 - April 2015 - p165(1) [51-500]
Undaunted Hope
    BL - v112 - i7 - Dec 1 2015 - p37(1) [51-500]

Hedstrom, Matthew - *The Rise of Liberal Religion: Book Culture and American Spirituality in the Twentieth Century*
    Bks & Cult - v21 - i2 - March-April 2015 - p19(2) [501+]

Heer, Jeet - *Sweet Lechery*
    Nat Post - v17 - i56 - Jan 3 2015 - pWP11(1) [501+]

Heern, Zackery - *The Emergence of Modern Shiism: Islamic Reform in Iraq and Iran*
    Econ - v416 - i8948 - July 25 2015 - p69(US) [501+]

Heese, Thorsten - *Justus Moser 1720-1794*
    Ger Q - v88 - i3 - Summer 2015 - p378(2) [501+]

Heffernan, John - *Naveed: Through My Eyes*
  y Sch Lib - v63 - i2 - Summer 2015 - p118(1) [51-500]

Heffernan, Valerie - *Transitions: Emerging Women Writers in German-Language Literature*
    MLR - v110 - i2 - April 2015 - p612-613 [501+]

Heffron, Margery M. - *Louisa Catherine: The Other Mrs. Adams*
    Bks & Cult - v21 - i2 - March-April 2015 - p9(2) [501+]
    CSM - June 26 2015 - pNA [51-500]
    NEQ - v88 - i1 - March 2015 - p172-174 [501+]
    RAH - v43 - i3 - Sept 2015 - p477-483 [501+]

Hefner, Robert - *Religions in Movement: The Local and the Global in Contemporary Faith Traditions*
    J Ch St - v57 - i2 - Spring 2015 - p366-367 [501+]

Hefti, Matthew J. - *A Hard and Heavy Thing*
    BL - v112 - i7 - Dec 1 2015 - p22(1) [51-500]

Hegarty, Dan - *Buried Treasure: Overlooked, Forgotten and Uncrowned Classic Albums*
    RVBW - Oct 2015 - pNA [51-500]

Hegarty, Neil - *Frost: That Was the Life That Was: The Authorised Biography*
    Spec - v329 - i9766 - Oct 31 2015 - p38(2) [501+]

Hegarty, Patricia - *Bear's Truck Is Stuck! (Illus. by Truong, Tom)*
  c KR - Dec 1 2015 - pNA [51-500]
Please (Illus. by Galloway, Fhiona)
  c KR - July 1 2015 - pNA [51-500]
Who's There? Beware! (Illus. by Truong, Tom)
  c KR - Dec 1 2015 - pNA [51-500]
Zip It: A First Book of Fasteners (Illus. by Galloway, Fhiona)
  c KR - July 1 2015 - pNA [51-500]
  c PW - v262 - i6 - Feb 2 2015 - p60(1) [51-500]

Hegarty, Shane - *Darkmouth*
  y Magpies - v30 - i1 - March 2015 - p35(1) [51-500]
Darkmouth: The Legends Begin (Illus. by de la Rue, James)
  c PW - v262 - i8 - Feb 23 2015 - p75(1) [51-500]
Darkmouth: The Legends Begin (Illus. by Rue, James de la)
    BL - v111 - i14 - March 15 2015 - p73(1) [51-500]
The Legends Begin (Illus. by de la Rue, James)
  c CCB-B - v68 - i11 - July-August 2015 - p548(1) [51-500]
  c HB Guide - v26 - i2 - Fall 2015 - p86(1) [51-500]
The Legends Begin
    KR - Feb 1 2015 - pNA [51-500]

Hegedus, Anna Molnar - *As the Lilacs Bloomed*
  y Res Links - v20 - i5 - June 2015 - p30(2) [51-500]

Hegel, Georg Wilhelm Friedrich - *Lectures on the Philosophy of Art: The Hotho Transcript of the 1823 Berlin Lectures*
    RM - v69 - i1 - Sept 2015 - p137(5) [501+]

Heggarty, Paul - *Archaeology and Language in the Andes: A Cross-Disciplinary Exploration of Prehistory*
    Lat Ant - v26 - i3 - Sept 2015 - p421(2) [501+]

Hegger, Sarah - *Nobody's Angel*
    PW - v262 - i7 - Feb 16 2015 - p165(1) [51-500]
Nobody's Fool
    PW - v262 - i31 - August 3 2015 - p42(2) [51-500]

Hegland, Jean - *Still Time*
    BL - v111 - i22 - August 1 2015 - p30(1) [51-500]
    RVBW - Nov 2015 - pNA [51-500]

Hegland, Mary Elaine - *Days of Revolution: Political Unrest in an Iranian Village*
    IJMES - v47 - i3 - August 2015 - p649-651 [501+]
    JRAI - v21 - i1 - March 2015 - p236(2) [501+]

Heibel, Tara - *Rooted in Design: Sprout Home's Guide to Creative Indoor Planting*
    PW - v262 - i9 - March 2 2015 - p81(1) [51-500]

Heiberger, Frank - *The Seventh Seal*
    KR - Sept 15 2015 - pNA [51-500]

Heidbreder, Robert - *Crocs at Work (Illus. by Mate, Rae)*
  c KR - Nov 1 2015 - pNA [51-500]
  c SLJ - v61 - i12 - Dec 2015 - p90(1) [51-500]
Song for a Summer Night: A Lullaby (Illus. by Leng, Qin)
  c HB Guide - v26 - i2 - Fall 2015 - p12(1) [51-500]
  c Res Links - v20 - i5 - June 2015 - p4(2) [51-500]
  c SLJ - v61 - i7 - July 2015 - p62(1) [51-500]
Song for a Summer Night (Illus. by Leng, Qin)
  c KR - March 15 2015 - pNA [51-500]

Heidegger, Martin - *Hegel*
    J Phil - v112 - i5 - May 2015 - p281(1) [501+]
Holderlin's Hymns: "Germania" and "The Rhine"
    RM - v69 - i1 - Sept 2015 - p135(3) [501+]

Heideking, Jurgen - *The Constitution Before the Judgment Seat: The Prehistory and Ratification of the American Constitution, 1787-1791*
    Historian - v77 - i1 - Spring 2015 - p123(4) [501+]

Heidler, David S. - *Washington's Circle: The Creation of the President*
    PW - v262 - i7 - Feb 16 2015 - p172(1) [51-500]
    KR - Jan 15 2015 - pNA [501+]
    LJ - v140 - i2 - Feb 1 2015 - p94(1) [501+]

Heiduschke, Sebastian - *East German Cinema: DEFA and Film History*
    GSR - v38 - i2 - May 2015 - p449-3 [501+]

Heijens, Janet - *Wrongful Conviction*
    KR - July 1 2015 - pNA [51-500]

Heikaus, Ulrike - *Krieg! Juden zwischen den Fronten 1914-1918*
    Ger Q - v88 - i3 - Summer 2015 - p384(9) [501+]

Heilbron, Hilary - *Rose Heilbron: The Story of England's First Woman Queen's Counsel and Judge*
    TimHES - i2192 - Feb 26 2015 - p47(1) [501+]

Heilbron, John L. - *Physics: A Short History from Quintessence to Quarks*
    BL - v112 - i7 - Dec 1 2015 - p20(1) [51-500]
    KR - Oct 1 2015 - pNA [501+]
    Nature - v526 - i7571 - Oct 1 2015 - p37(2) [501+]

Heilbrunn, John R. - *Oil, Democracy, and Development in Africa*
    HNet - Feb 2015 - pNA [501+]

Heilig, Heidi - *The Girl from Everywhere*
  y KR - Dec 1 2015 - pNA [51-500]
  y SLJ - v61 - i12 - Dec 2015 - p121(1) [51-500]

Heilig, Markus - *The Thirteenth Step: Addiction in the Age of Brain Science*
    KR - March 15 2015 - pNA [501+]
    LJ - v140 - i6 - April 1 2015 - p114(1) [51-500]
    TLS - i5877 - Nov 20 2015 - p26(1) [51-500]

Heilige und geheiligte Dinge. Formen und Funktionen
    HNet - Sept 2015 - pNA [501+]

Heiligman, Deborah - *The Boy Who Loved Math: The Improbable Life of Paul Erdos (Illus. by LeUyen, Pham)*
  c TC Math - v22 - i1 - August 2015 - p53(2) [501+]

Heim, Maria - *Theravada Buddhism: Continuity, Diversity, and Identity*
    JAAR - v83 - i2 - June 2015 - pNA [501+]

Heiman, Rachel - *Driving after Class: Anxious Times in an American Suburb*
    TimHES - i2208 - June 18 2015 - p48(1) [501+]

Heimbold, Dick - *Dream Wrecks*
    KR - Dec 15 2015 - pNA [51-500]

Heimmermann, Daniel - *Work, Regulation, and Identity in Provincial France: The Bordeaux Leather Trades, 1740-1815*
    AHR - v120 - i4 - Oct 2015 - p1553-1554 [501+]

Hein, John - *Fast Food Maniac*
    PW - v262 - i52 - Dec 21 2015 - p147(1) [51-500]

Hein, Jurgen - *Ferdinand Raimund: Samtliche Werke - Historisch-kritische Ausgabe, vol. i: Der Barometermacher auf der Zauberinsel; Der Diamant des Geisterkonigs*
    MLR - v110 - i2 - April 2015 - p585-587 [501+]

Heine, Florian - *13 Architects Children Should Know*
  c BL - v111 - i18 - May 15 2015 - p44(1) [51-500]
  c HB Guide - v26 - i2 - Fall 2015 - p193(1) [51-500]
  c SLJ - v61 - i7 - July 2015 - p107(1) [51-500]
Impressionism: 13 Artists Children Should Know
  c SLJ - v61 - i7 - July 2015 - p107(1) [51-500]

Heine, Steven - *Zen Koans*
    HNet - May 2015 - pNA [501+]

Heinecke, Liz - *Kitchen Science Lab for Kids*
  c Sci & Ch - v52 - i9 - Summer 2015 - p91 [51-500]

Heineman, David S. - *Thinking about Video Games: Interviews with the Experts*
    LJ - v140 - i11 - June 15 2015 - p98(2) [501+]

Heineman, Kenneth J. - *Civil War Dynasty: The Ewing Family of Ohio*
    JAH - v102 - i1 - June 2015 - p252-253 [501+]

Heinemann, Meenoo Rami - *Thrive: 5 Ways to (Re)Invigorate Your Teaching*
    RVBW - Jan 2015 - pNA [51-500]

Heines, Matthew D. - *Another Year in Oman*
    SPBW - Jan 2015 - pNA [51-500]
Killing Time in Saudi Araba
    SPBW - Jan 2015 - pNA [51-500]
My Year in Oman
    SPBW - Jan 2015 - pNA [51-500]

Heinlein, Michael - *Futures of Modernity: Challenges for Cosmopolitical Thought and Practice*
    T&C - v56 - i4 - Oct 2015 - p973-975 [501+]

Heinlein, Robert A. - *The Rolling Stones*
    LJ - v140 - i11 - June 15 2015 - p118(1) [51-500]

Heinlein, Sabine - *Among Murderers: Life after Prison*
    Comw - v142 - i4 - Feb 20 2015 - p27(4) [501+]

Heinrich, Ari Larissa - *Last Words from Montmartre*
    WLT - v89 - i5 - Sept-Oct 2015 - p66(1) [501+]

Heinrich, Bernd - *The Homing Instinct: Meaning and Mystery in Animal Migration*
    QRB - v90 - i1 - March 2015 - p91(2) [501+]
The Homing Instinct
  y Ent W - i1358 - April 10 2015 - p66(1) [501+]
One Wild Bird at a Time
    KR - Jan 1 2016 - pNA [501+]
Heiny, Katherine - *Single, Carefree, Mellow: Stories*
    BL - v111 - i9-10 - Jan 1 2015 - p42(1) [51-500]
    Ent W - i1350 - Feb 13 2015 - p60(1) [51-500]
    LJ - v140 - i10 - June 1 2015 - p139(1) [51-500]
    NYT - Feb 12 2015 - pC1(L) [51-500]
    NYTBR - Feb 1 2015 - p26(L) [51-500]
    TLS - i5864-5865 - August 21 2015 - p23(1) [501+]
Heinz, Brian - *Mocha Dick: The Legend and Fury (Illus. by Enos, Randall)*
  c HB Guide - v26 - i1 - Spring 2015 - p32(1) [51-500]
Heinzle, Joachim - *"Das Nibelungenlied" und "Die Klage", nach der Handschrift 857 der Stiftsbibliothek St. Gallen*
    MLR - v110 - i2 - April 2015 - p581-583 [501+]
Heise, Ursula K. - *Nach der Natur. Das Artensterben und die modern Kulter*
    GSR - v38 - i3 - Oct 2015 - p635-652 [501+]
Heisey, Daniel J. - *Yet All Shall Be Well*
    MA - v57 - i1 - Wntr 2015 - p49(8) [501+]
Heiss, Anita - *Harry's Secret*
  c Magpies - v30 - i4 - Sept 2015 - p32(1) [501+]
Heist, Christopher T. - *What I've Learned*
    SPBW - Jan 2015 - pNA [501+]
Heisterberg, Rodney - *Creating Business Agility: How Convergence of Cloud, Social, Mobile, Video, and Big Data Enables Competitive Advantage*
    Bwatch - Feb 2015 - pNA [51-500]
Heitman, Carrie C. - *Choco Revisited: New Research on the Prehistory of Chaco Canyon, New Mexico*
    Roundup M - v23 - i1 - Oct 2015 - p33(1) [501+]
Heitmann, John A. - *Stealing Cars: Technology and Society from the Model T to the Gran Torino*
    AHR - v120 - i2 - April 2015 - p642-643 [501+]
    JAH - v102 - i1 - June 2015 - p275-276 [501+]
Heitzer, Enrico - *Die Kampfgruppe Gegen Unmenschlichkeit (KgU): Widerstand und Spionage im Kalten Krieg 1948-1959*
    HNet - July 2015 - pNA [501+]
Heivig, Kristi - *Strange Skies*
  y BL - v111 - i18 - May 15 2015 - p66(1) [51-500]
Heker, Liliana - *Please Talk to Me*
    TLS - i5869 - Sept 25 2015 - p21(1) [501+]
Helas, Alexander - *Societe*
    RVBW - Oct 2015 - pNA [51-500]
Helbert, Sharon - *Sassy Gal's How to Lose the Last Damn 10 Pounds or 15, 20, 25....*
    SPBW - August 2015 - pNA [51-500]
Helbig, Grace - *Grace and Style: The Art of Pretending You Have It*
    KR - Dec 15 2015 - pNA [51-500]
Helbling, Marc - *Islamophobia in the West: Measuring and Explaining Individual Attitudes*
    CS - v44 - i2 - March 2015 - p213-215 [501+]
Held, George - *Culling: New and Selected Nature Poems*
    ABR - v36 - i3 - March-April 2015 - p26(1) [501+]
Neighbors: The Water Critters (Illus. by Kim, Joung un)
  c PW - v262 - i2 - Jan 12 2015 - p58(1) [501+]
Neighbors: The Water Critters (Illus. by Kim, Joung un)
  c CH Bwatch - Feb 2015 - pNA [51-500]
Held, Shai - *Abraham Joshua Heschel: The Call of Transcendence*
    JR - v95 - i2 - April 2015 - p272(3) [501+]
Helder, William - *How the Beowulf Poet Employs Biblical Typology: His Christian Portrayal of Heroism*
    Med R - Sept 2015 - pNA [501+]
Heldt, Guido - *Music and Levels of Narration in Film: Steps across the Border*
    Notes - v72 - i2 - Dec 2015 - p374(3) [501+]
Heley, Veronica - *False Impression*
    BL - v111 - i13 - March 1 2015 - p23(1) [501+]
    KR - Jan 15 2015 - pNA [51-500]
    PW - v262 - i1 - Jan 5 2015 - p54(1) [51-500]
Murder by Suspicion
    PW - v262 - i34 - August 24 2015 - p60(2) [51-500]
    BL - v112 - i3 - Oct 1 2015 - p27(1) [51-500]
    KR - August 1 2015 - pNA [51-500]
Helfer, Rebecca - *Spenser's Ruins and the Art of Recollection*
    MLR - v110 - i2 - April 2015 - p523-525 [501+]

Helfferich, Tryntje - *The Iron Princess: Amalia Elisabeth and the Thirty Years War*
    CEH - v48 - i1 - March 2015 - p116-118 [501+]
    JMH - v87 - i2 - June 2015 - p479(3) [501+]
Helgesen, Leif Magne - *The Ice is Melting: Ethics in the Arctic*
    RVBW - August 2015 - pNA [51-500]
Helgeson, Jeffrey - *Crucibles of Black Empowerment: Chicago's Neighborhood Politics from the New Deal to Harold Washington*
    AHR - v120 - i4 - Oct 2015 - p1511-1512 [501+]
    JAH - v101 - i4 - March 2015 - p1332-1333 [501+]
Helget, Nicole - *Wonder at the Edge of the World*
  c BL - v111 - i16 - April 15 2015 - p60(1) [51-500]
  c HB Guide - v26 - i2 - Fall 2015 - p86(1) [51-500]
  c KR - Feb 1 2015 - pNA [51-500]
  c VOYA - v37 - i6 - Feb 2015 - p76(2) [51-500]
Heling, Kathryn - *Clothesline Clues to Sports People Play (Illus. by Davies, Andy Robert)*
  c KR - June 15 2015 - pNA [51-500]
  c SLJ - v61 - i11 - Nov 2015 - p82(1) [51-500]
Hell, Richard - *Massive Pissed Love*
    KR - August 15 2015 - pNA [51-500]
Helland, Jenna - *The August 5*
  y BL - v112 - i5 - Nov 1 2015 - p54(1) [51-500]
  y KR - August 15 2015 - pNA [51-500]
  y SLJ - v61 - i10 - Oct 2015 - p102(1) [51-500]
  y VOYA - v38 - i5 - Dec 2015 - p70(1) [51-500]
Helle, Helle - *This Should Be Written in the Present Tense*
    BL - v112 - i7 - Dec 1 2015 - p26(1) [51-500]
    KR - Oct 15 2015 - pNA [51-500]
    PW - v262 - i46 - Nov 16 2015 - p49(2) [51-500]
Helleiner, Eric - *Forgotten Foundations of Bretton Woods: International Development and the Making of the Postwar Order*
    JIH - v45 - i3 - Wntr 2015 - p419-420 [501+]
Heller, Anne C. - *Hannah Arendt: A Life in Dark Times*
    KR - June 1 2015 - pNA [501+]
    LJ - v140 - i12 - July 1 2015 - p87(1) [51-500]
    PW - v262 - i22 - June 1 2015 - p53(1) [51-500]
Heller, Caroline - *Reading Claudius: A Memoir in Two Parts*
    NYTBR - Nov 15 2015 - p30(L) [501+]
Heller, Chaia - *Food, Farms, and Solidarity: French Farmers Challenge Industrial Agriculture and Genetically Modified Crops*
    CS - v44 - i2 - March 2015 - p215-216 [501+]
Heller, Gregory L. - *Ed Bacon: Planning, Politics, and the Building of Modern Philadelphia*
    RAH - v43 - i1 - March 2015 - p161-167 [501+]
Heller, Janet Ruth - *The Passover Surprise (Illus. by Kauffman, Ronald)*
  c CH Bwatch - Oct 2015 - pNA [51-500]
Heller, Jean - *The Someday File: Deuce Mora Series, vol. 1*
    KR - August 15 2015 - pNA [501+]
    PW - v262 - i22 - June 1 2015 - p44(1) [51-500]
Heller, Marielle - *The Diary of a Teenage Girl*
    Ent W - i1376 - August 14 2015 - p46(1) [51-500]
Heller, Peter - *The Painter*
  y NYTBR - April 19 2015 - p28(L) [501+]
    RVBW - Jan 2015 - pNA [51-500]
    RVBW - March 2015 - pNA [51-500]
Heller, Rebecca - *Falling Rock (Illus. by Robertson, Joyce)*
  c CH Bwatch - Feb 2015 - pNA [51-500]
Heller, Steven - *Edward Gorey: His Book Cover Art and Design*
    BL - v112 - i1 - Sept 1 2015 - p26(1) [51-500]
Heller, Wendy - *Music in the Baroque*
    Notes - v72 - i2 - Dec 2015 - p356(3) [501+]
Heller, Yoseph - *Israel and the Cold War from the War of Independence to the Six Days War: The United States, the Soviet Union, the Arab-Israeli Conflict, and the Question of Soviet Jewry*
    JAH - v102 - i1 - June 2015 - p297-298 [501+]
Hellier, Jennifer L. - *The Brain, the Nervous System, and Their Diseases*
    R&USQ - v54 - i4 - Summer 2015 - p79(2) [501+]
Hellinga, Lotte - *Texts in Transit: Manuscript to Proof and Print in the Fifteenth Century*
    TLS - i5848 - May 1 2015 - p29(1) [501+]
    Ren Q - v68 - i3 - Fall 2015 - p1096-1097 [501+]
Hellisen, Cat - *Beastkeeper*
  y CCB-B - v68 - i7 - March 2015 - p356(1) [51-500]
  y HB Guide - v26 - i2 - Fall 2015 - p122(1) [51-500]
  y PW - v262 - i49 - Dec 2 2015 - p100(2) [51-500]
  y VOYA - v37 - i6 - Feb 2015 - p77(1) [51-500]
Hellman, Ben - *Fairy Tales and True Stories: The History of Russian Literature for Children and Young People*
    Slav R - v74 - i1 - Spring 2015 - p211-212 [501+]

Hellmann, Libby Fischer - *Jump Cut*
    KR - Jan 1 2016 - pNA [51-500]
Nobody's Child
    RVBW - May 2015 - pNA [51-500]
Hello, Ocean Friends: A High-Contrast Book (Illus. by Lemay, Violet)
  c PW - v262 - i15 - April 13 2015 - p78(2) [51-500]
  c SLJ - v61 - i7 - July 2015 - p54(1) [51-500]
Helm, Dieter - *Natural Capital: Valuing the Planet*
    Lon R Bks - v37 - i18 - Sept 24 2015 - p34(3) [501+]
Helm, Nicole - *Rebel Cowboy*
    PW - v262 - i46 - Nov 16 2015 - p62(1) [51-500]
Helm, Sarah - *Ravensbruck: Life and Death in Hitler's Concentration Camp for Women*
    KR - Jan 1 2015 - pNA [501+]
    NYRB - v62 - i12 - July 9 2015 - p52(3) [501+]
    PW - v262 - i5 - Feb 2 2015 - p46(1) [51-500]
Helman, Scott - *Long Mile Home: Boston under Attack, the City's Courageous Recovery, and the Epic Hunt for Justice*
    NYRB - v62 - i11 - June 25 2015 - p33(3) [501+]
Helmer, Christine - *Theology and the End of Doctrine*
    Theol St - v76 - i4 - Dec 2015 - p862(2) [501+]
Helmers, Helmer J. - *The Royalist Republic: Literature, Politics and Religion in the Anglo-Dutch Public Sphere, 1639-1660*
    HNet - June 2015 - pNA [501+]
Helmick, Raymond G. - *The Crisis of Confidence in the Catholic Church*
    Theol St - v76 - i4 - Dec 2015 - p853(2) [501+]
Helmreich, William B. - *The New York Nobody Knows: Walking 6,000 Miles in the City*
    GR - v105 - i1 - Jan 2015 - p120(4) [501+]
Helms, Rhonda - *Break Your Heart*
    BL - v111 - i22 - August 1 2015 - p41(1) [51-500]
    PW - v262 - i22 - June 1 2015 - p47(1) [51-500]
Promposal
  y BL - v111 - i9-10 - Jan 1 2015 - p96(1) [51-500]
  y HB Guide - v26 - i2 - Fall 2015 - p122(1) [51-500]
  y SLJ - v61 - i3 - March 2015 - p155(2) [51-500]
  y VOYA - v37 - i6 - Feb 2015 - p57(1) [51-500]
Helmstutler Di Dio, Kelley - *Sculpture Collections in Early Modern Spain*
    Ren Q - v68 - i2 - Summer 2015 - p644-646 [501+]
Helo, Ari - *Thomas Jefferson's Ethics and the Politics of Human Progress: The Morality of a Slaveholder*
    AHR - v120 - i3 - June 2015 - p1017-1018 [501+]
    JAH - v102 - i1 - June 2015 - p236-236 [501+]
Helping the Community Series
  c CH Bwatch - Nov 2015 - pNA [51-500]
Helton, Peter - *A Good Way to Go*
    BL - v111 - i13 - March 1 2015 - p23(2) [51-500]
    KR - March 1 2015 - pNA [51-500]
    PW - v262 - i9 - March 2 2015 - p66(1) [51-500]
Heltzel, Anne - *Charlie, Presumed Dead*
  y CCB-B - v69 - i1 - Sept 2015 - p27(1) [51-500]
  y HB Guide - v26 - i2 - Fall 2015 - p122(1) [51-500]
    KR - April 15 2015 - pNA [51-500]
  y PW - v262 - i16 - April 20 2015 - p79(1) [51-500]
  y SLJ - v61 - i5 - May 2015 - p120(2) [51-500]
  y VOYA - v38 - i2 - June 2015 - p60(2) [51-500]
Helvig, Kristi - *Strange Skies*
  y HB Guide - v26 - i2 - Fall 2015 - p122(1) [51-500]
  y KR - March 15 2015 - pNA [51-500]
  y VOYA - v37 - i6 - Feb 2015 - p77(1) [51-500]
Helwig, Jenna - *Real Baby Food: Easy, All-Natural Recipes for Your Baby and Toddler*
    LJ - v140 - i12 - July 1 2015 - p105(2) [51-500]
Hemelrijk, Emily A. - *Women and the Roman City in the Latin West*
    Class R - v65 - i1 - April 2015 - p195-197 [501+]
Hemenway, Toby - *The Permaculture City: Regenerative Design for Urban, Suburban, and Town Resilience*
    LJ - v140 - i15 - Sept 15 2015 - p102(2) [51-500]
Hemingway, Collins - *The Marriage of Miss Jane Austen*
  c BL - v112 - i7 - Dec 1 2015 - p34(2) [51-500]
Hemingway, Edward - *Bad Apple's Perfect Day*
  c HB Guide - v26 - i1 - Spring 2015 - p32(1) [51-500]
Hemingway, Ernest - *Green Hills of Africa*
    KR - June 1 2015 - pNA [51-500]
The Letters of Ernest Hemingway, vol. 3: 1926-1929
    BL - v112 - i3 - Oct 1 2015 - p11(1) [51-500]
    KR - July 15 2015 - pNA [501+]

Hemingway, Mariel - *Invisible Girl*
  y BL - v111 - i19-20 - June 1 2015 - p84(2) [51-500]
  y VOYA - v38 - i3 - August 2015 - p87(1) [51-500]
Out Came the Sun: Overcoming the Legacy of Mental Illness, Addiction, and Suicide in My Family
  BL - v111 - i16 - April 15 2015 - p9(1) [51-500]
  KR - Feb 15 2015 - pNA [51-500]
Hemler, Steven R. - *The Reality of God: The Layman's Guide to Scientific Evidence for the Creator*
  RVBW - July 2015 - pNA [51-500]
Hemming, Henry - *The Ingenious Mr. Pyke: Inventor, Fugitive, Spy*
  BL - v111 - i11 - Feb 1 2015 - p13(1) [51-500]
  CSM - May 7 2015 - pNA [51-500]
  KR - April 1 2015 - pNA [501+]
  LJ - v140 - i6 - April 1 2015 - p99(1) [51-500]
  PW - v262 - i11 - March 16 2015 - p74(1) [51-500]
Hemming, John - *Naturalists in Paradise: Wallace, Bates and Spruce in the Amazon*
  Nature - v520 - i7545 - April 2 2015 - p31(1) [51-500]
  TLS - i5860 - July 24 2015 - p23(1) [501+]
Hemmings, Kaui Hart - *Juniors*
  y KR - July 1 2015 - pNA [51-500]
  y PW - v262 - i28 - July 13 2015 - p69(2) [51-500]
  y SLJ - v61 - i8 - August 2015 - p104(2) [51-500]
The Possibilities
  NYTBR - April 5 2015 - p28(L) [501+]
Hemmungs, Eva - *Making Marie Curie: Intellectual Property and Celebrity Culture in an Age of Information*
  Nature - v519 - i7544 - March 26 2015 - p413(1) [51-500]
Hemon, Aleksandar - *The Making of Zombie Wars*
  KR - Feb 1 2015 - pNA [501+]
  BL - v111 - i15 - April 1 2015 - p26(1) [51-500]
  Ent W - i1365-1366 - May 29 2015 - p109(1) [501+]
  LJ - v140 - i6 - April 1 2015 - p79(1) [51-500]
  Mac - v128 - i24 - June 22 2015 - p57(1) [501+]
  NYTBR - June 7 2015 - p16(L) [501+]
  PW - v262 - i6 - Feb 9 2015 - p42(1) [51-500]
  Spec - v328 - i9759 - Sept 12 2015 - p42(2) [501+]
Hemphill, Paul - *The Nashville Sound: Bright Lights and Country Music*
  Bwatch - June 2015 - pNA [51-500]
Hempleman-Adams, David - *No Such Thing As Failure: My Life in Adventure, Exploration, and Survival*
  KR - Feb 1 2015 - pNA [501+]
  LJ - v140 - i6 - April 1 2015 - p108(1) [51-500]
Hemstreet, Keith - *Travels with Gannon and Wyatt: Ireland*
  y CH Bwatch - April 2015 - pNA [501+]
Henchman, Anna - *The Starry Sky Within: Astronomy and the Reach of the Mind in Victorian Literature*
  RES - v66 - i273 - Feb 2015 - p189-191 [501+]
Hendee, Barb - *The Night Voice*
  PW - v262 - i50 - Dec 7 2015 - p73(1) [51-500]
Henderickson, Jon K. - *The Moral Economy: Poverty, Credit, and Trust in Early Modern Europe*
  AHR - v120 - i3 - June 2015 - p1104(1) [501+]
Henderson, Artis - *Unremarried Widow: A Memoir*
  NYTBR - March 1 2015 - p28(L) [501+]
Henderson, Bill - *The Pushcart Prize XL: Best of the Small Presses*
  BL - v112 - i6 - Nov 15 2015 - p9(1) [51-500]
  KR - Sept 1 2015 - pNA [51-500]
  PW - v262 - i48 - Nov 30 2015 - p37(1) [51-500]
Henderson, Bruce - *Rescue at Los Banos: The Most Daring Prison Camp Raid of World War II*
  LJ - v140 - i5 - March 15 2015 - p120(1) [51-500]
Henderson, David W. - *Tranquility: Cultivating a Quiet Soul in a Busy World*
  Ch Today - v59 - i8 - Oct 2015 - p76(1) [51-500]
Henderson, Dee - *Taken*
  BL - v111 - i16 - April 15 2015 - p31(1) [51-500]
Henderson, Ella - *Chapter One*
  People - v83 - i3 - Jan 19 2015 - p29 [501+]
  People - v83 - i3 - Jan 19 2015 - p29 [501+]
  People - v83 - i3 - Jan 19 2015 - p29 [501+]
  People - v83 - i3 - Jan 19 2015 - p29 [501+]
  People - v83 - i3 - Jan 19 2015 - p29 [501+]
Henderson, Geri - *Healing from Incest: Intimate Conversations with My Therapist*
  RVBW - July 2015 - pNA [51-500]
Henderson, Gretchen E. - *Ugliness: A Cultural History*
  Mac - v128 - i47 - Nov 30 2015 - p58(1) [501+]
  NS - v144 - i5290 - Nov 27 2015 - p51(1) [51-500]

Henderson, Harry - *Privacy in the Online World: Online Privacy and Government*
  y VOYA - v37 - i6 - Feb 2015 - p90(1) [51-500]
Henderson, Keith - *The Roof Walkers*
  KR - Jan 1 2015 - pNA [501+]
Henderson, Paul - *GQ Drinks: The Cocktail Collection for Discerning Drinkers*
  Bwatch - Feb 2015 - pNA [51-500]
Henderson, Randy - *Finn Fancy Necromancy (Read by Haberkorn, Todd). Audiobook Review*
  y SLJ - v61 - i6 - June 2015 - p67(1) [51-500]
Finn Fancy Necromancy
  CH Bwatch - May 2015 - pNA [51-500]
Henderson, Robert - *Emotion and Healing in the Energy Body: A Handbook of Subtle Energies in Massage and Yoga*
  Bwatch - Sept 2015 - pNA [501+]
Henderson, Smith - *Fourth of July Creek*
  y Ent W - i1358 - April 10 2015 - p66(1) [501+]
Henderson, Suzanne Watts - *Christ and Community: The Gospel Witness to Jesus*
  CC - v132 - i21 - Oct 14 2015 - p32(2) [501+]
Hendon, Julia A. - *Material Relations: The Marriage Figurines of Prehispanic Honduras*
  Lat Ant - v26 - i1 - March 2015 - p137(2) [501+]
Hendrick, Dave - *Granuaile: Queen of Storms (Illus. by Pizzari, Luca)*
  c SLJ - v61 - i9 - Sept 2015 - p190(1) [51-500]
Hendricks, Barbara - *Lifting My Voice*
  ON - v79 - i9 - March 2015 - p60(1) [51-500]
Hendricks, John Allen - *Presidential Campaigning and Social Media: An Analysis of the 2012 Campaign*
  Pres St Q - v45 - i2 - June 2015 - p410(3) [501+]
Hendricks, Wanda A. - *Fannie Barrier Williams: Crossing the Borders of Region and Race*
  AHR - v120 - i8 - Feb 2015 - p263(1) [51-500]
  JAH - v101 - i4 - March 2015 - p1299-1300 [501+]
  JSH - v81 - i2 - May 2015 - p485(2) [501+]
Hendrickson, Jon K. - *Crisis in the Mediterranean: Naval Competition and Great Power Politics, 1904-1914*
  J Mil H - v79 - i4 - Oct 2015 - p1145-1146 [501+]
Hendrickson, Kenneth E., III - *The Encyclopedia of the Industrial Revolution in World History*
  BL - v112 - i6 - Nov 15 2015 - p6(1) [51-500]
  LJ - v140 - i15 - Sept 15 2015 - p104(1) [51-500]
Hendrickson, Mark - *American Labor and Economic Citizenship: New Capitalism from World War I to the Great Depression*
  JEH - v75 - i2 - June 2015 - p599-601 [501+]
  JIH - v46 - i2 - Autumn 2015 - p299-300 [501+]
Hendrix, John - *Shooting at the Stars (Illus. by Hendrix, John)*
  c HB Guide - v26 - i1 - Spring 2015 - p32(1) [51-500]
Hendrix, Scott H. - *Martin Luther: Visionary Reformer*
  BL - v112 - i6 - Nov 15 2015 - p15(2) [51-500]
  LJ - v140 - i19 - Nov 15 2015 - p88(2) [51-500]
Masculinity in the Reformation Era
  CHR - v101 - i2 - Spring 2015 - p366(3) [501+]
Henig, Adam - *Alex Haley's Roots: An Author's Odyssey*
  PW - v262 - i2 - Jan 12 2015 - p54(1) [51-500]
Henkes, Kevin - *Waiting (Illus. by Henkes, Kevin)*
  c HB - v91 - i5 - Sept-Oct 2015 - p81(1) [51-500]
  c KR - June 1 2015 - pNA [51-500]
  c NYTBR - August 23 2015 - p28(L) [51-500]
  c PW - v262 - i23 - June 8 2015 - p59(1) [51-500]
  c PW - v262 - i49 - Dec 2 2015 - p18(2) [51-500]
  c SLJ - v61 - i6 - June 2015 - p82(3) [51-500]
  c BL - v111 - i18 - May 15 2015 - p59(1) [51-500]
When Spring Comes (Illus. by Dronzek, Laura)
  c BL - v112 - i6 - Nov 15 2015 - p59(1) [51-500]
  c KR - Dec 1 2015 - pNA [51-500]
Henn, Sophy - *Pom Pom Panda Gets the Grumps (Illus. by Henn, Sophy)*
  c BL - v112 - i2 - Sept 15 2015 - p69(1) [51-500]
  c KR - August 1 2015 - pNA [501+]
  c PW - v262 - i34 - August 24 2015 - p78(1) [51-500]
  c Sch Lib - v63 - i2 - Summer 2015 - p94(1) [51-500]
  c SLJ - v61 - i9 - Sept 2015 - p122(1) [51-500]
Where Bear? (Illus. by Henn, Sophy)
  c CCB-B - v68 - i8 - April 2015 - p402(1) [51-500]
  c HB Guide - v26 - i2 - Fall 2015 - p37(1) [51-500]
Henneberg, Susan - *Cloning*
  y SLJ - v61 - i9 - Sept 2015 - p151(4) [501+]
Drones
  y SLJ - v61 - i9 - Sept 2015 - p151(4) [501+]
Investigating Ghosts and the Spirit World
  y Teach Lib - v43 - i1 - Oct 2015 - p14(1) [51-500]

Hennen, Tom - *Darkness Sticks to Everything*
  WLT - v89 - i2 - March-April 2015 - p69(2) [501+]
Hennenberg, Fritz - *Victor Fenigstein: Lebensprotokoll, Werkkommentare, Kataloge*
  Notes - v72 - i1 - Sept 2015 - p170(4) [501+]
Hennessey, Jonathan - *The Comic Book Story of Beer: The World's Favorite Beverage from 7000 BC to Today's Craft Brewing Revolution (Illus. by McConnell, Aaron)*
  BL - v112 - i6 - Nov 15 2015 - p33(2) [51-500]
  PW - v262 - i36 - Sept 7 2015 - p54(1) [51-500]
Hennessey, Thomas - *Hunger Strike: Margaret Thatcher's Battle with the IRA, 1980-1981*
  AHR - v120 - i1 - Feb 2015 - p338-339 [501+]
  ILS - v34 - i2 - Spring 2015 - p10(1) [501+]
Hennessy, B.G. - *A Christmas Wish for Corduroy (Illus. by Wheeler, Jody)*
  c HB Guide - v26 - i2 - Fall 2015 - p37(1) [51-500]
Hennessy, Peter - *The Silent Deep: The Royal Navy Submarine Service since 1945*
  Spec - v329 - i9769 - Nov 21 2015 - p48(2) [501+]
Hennig, Nicole - *Apps for Librarians: Using the Best Mobile Technology to Educate, Create, and Engage*
  VOYA - v37 - i6 - Feb 2015 - p91(1) [51-500]
Henrich, Joseph - *The Secret of Our Success: How Culture Is Driving Human Evolution, Domesticating Our Species, and Making Us Smarter*
  KR - Sept 1 2015 - pNA [501+]
  Nature - v527 - i7579 - Nov 26 2015 - p445(1) [51-500]
Henriquez, Cristina - *The Book of Unknown Americans (Read by Avila, Christine). Audiobook Review*
  y BL - v111 - i11 - Feb 1 2015 - p60(1) [51-500]
The Book of Unknown Americans
  y Ent W - i1358 - April 10 2015 - p66(1) [501+]
  y NYTBR - April 19 2015 - p28(L) [501+]
Henry, April - *Blood Will Tell*
  y BL - v111 - i18 - May 15 2015 - p53(1) [51-500]
  y HB Guide - v26 - i2 - Fall 2015 - p122(2) [51-500]
  y SLJ - v61 - i6 - June 2015 - p112(1) [51-500]
  y VOYA - v38 - i2 - June 2015 - p61(1) [51-500]
Henry, Diana - *A Bird in the Hand: Chicken Recipes for Every Day and Every Mood*
  LJ - v140 - i7 - April 15 2015 - p110(1) [51-500]
  NYTBR - May 31 2015 - p24(L) [501+]
Henry, Emily - *The Love That Split the World*
  y KR - Dec 15 2015 - pNA [51-500]
Henry, Jeff - *The Year Yellowstone Burned: A Twenty-Five-Year Perspective*
  BL - v111 - i16 - April 15 2015 - p8(2) [51-500]
Henry, Joe - *Furious Cool: Richard Pryor and the World That Made Him (Read by Graham, Dion). Audiobook Review*
  BL - v111 - i14 - March 15 2015 - p23(2) [51-500]
Henry, Josh - *Monster Goose Nursery Rhymes (Illus. by Larson, Abigail)*
  PW - v262 - i4 - Jan 26 2015 - p171(1) [501+]
Henry, Matt - *Short Stories (Illus. by Henry, Matt)*
  NS - v144 - i5290 - Nov 27 2015 - p52(1) [51-500]
Henry, Murphy Hicks - *Pretty Good for a Girl: Women in Bluegrass*
  JSH - v81 - i1 - Feb 2015 - p237(2) [501+]
Henry, Nancy - *The Life of George Eliot*
  VS - v57 - i3 - Spring 2015 - p544(4) [501+]
Henry of Avranches - *Saints' Lives, 2 vols.*
  Med R - June 2015 - pNA [501+]
Henry, Olivier - *4th Century Karia. Defining a Karian Identity under the Hekatomnids*
  JNES - v74 - i1 - April 2015 - p165(3) [501+]
Henry, Patti Callahan - *The Idea of Love*
  BL - v111 - i19-20 - June 1 2015 - p42(1) [51-500]
Henry, Rosita - *Performing Place, Practising Memories: Aboriginal Australians, Hippies and the State*
  Pac A - v88 - i2 - June 2015 - p373 [501+]
Henry, Steve - *Cat Got a Lot (Illus. by Henry, Steve)*
  c KR - July 15 2015 - pNA [51-500]
  c SLJ - v61 - i11 - Nov 2015 - p89(1) [51-500]
Here Is Big Bunny (Illus. by Henry, Steve)
  c KR - Dec 15 2015 - pNA [51-500]
  c PW - v262 - i48 - Nov 30 2015 - p57(1) [51-500]
Henry, Todd - *Louder Than Words: Harness the Power of Your Authentic Voice*
  BL - v111 - i21 - July 1 2015 - p24(1) [51-500]
Henry, Todd A. - *Assimilating Seoul: Japanese Rule and the Politics of Public Space in Colonial Korea, 1910-1945*
  AHR - v120 - i2 - April 2015 - p600-601 [501+]
  HNet - April 2015 - pNA [501+]
  JAS - v74 - i3 - August 2015 - p763-765 [501+]

Hens, Gregor - *Nicotine*
Spec - v329 - i9772 - Dec 12 2015 - p90(2) [501+]
Henshaw, Mark - *The Fall of Moscow Station*
KR - Dec 15 2015 - pNA [501+]
PW - v262 - i52 - Dec 21 2015 - p131(1) [51-500]
Out of the Line of Fire
KR - Dec 1 2015 - pNA [51-500]
The Snow Kimono
KR - April 1 2015 - pNA [51-500]
Henshaw, Victoria - *Scotland and the British Army, 1700-1750: Defending the Union*
HER - v130 - i545 - August 2015 - p1007(2) [501+]
J Mil H - v79 - i1 - Jan 2015 - p196-197 [501+]
Hensher, Philip - *The Penguin Book of British Short Stories, vol. I: From Daniel Defoe to John Buchan*
Spec - v329 - i9767 - Nov 7 2015 - p38(2) [501+]
The Penguin Book of British Short Stories, vol. II: From P.G. Wodehouse to Zadie Smith
Spec - v329 - i9767 - Nov 7 2015 - p38(2) [501+]
Hensley, Joy N. - *Rites of Passage*
y HB Guide - v26 - i2 - Fall 2015 - p123(1) [51-500]
Hensley, Mary Helen - *Promised by Heaven: A Doctor's Return from the Afterlife to a Destiny of Love and Healing*
LJ - v140 - i15 - Sept 15 2015 - p92(1) [51-500]
Hensley, Michelle - *All the Lights On: Reimagining Theater with Ten Thousand Things*
Am Theat - v32 - i7 - Sept 2015 - p52(2) [501+]
Hensley, Tim - *Ticket Stub*
ABR - v36 - i2 - Jan-Feb 2015 - p6(1) [501+]
Henss, Michael - *The Cultural Monuments of Tibet*
LJ - v140 - i3 - Feb 15 2015 - p128(1) [51-500]
Henstra, Sarah - *Mad Miss Mimic*
y Res Links - v20 - i5 - June 2015 - p26(1) [501+]
Hentea, Marius - *Tata Dada: The Real Life and Celestial Adventures of Tristan Tzara*
TLS - i5851 - May 22 2015 - p21(2) [501+]
Hentges, Gudrun - *Staat und Politische Bildung: Von der "Zentrale fur Heimatdienst" zur "Bundeszentrale fur Politische Bildung"*
HNet - Feb 2015 - pNA [501+]
Hentschke, Reinhard - *Thermodynamics: For Physicists, Chemists and Materials Scientists*
Phys Today - v68 - i9 - Sept 2015 - p54-56 [501+]
Henwood, Karyn - *Too Hot to Moo*
c KR - Dec 15 2015 - pNA [501+]
Heo, Yumi - *Red Light, Green Light (Illus. by Heo, Yumi)*
c PW - v262 - i49 - Dec 2 2015 - p58(1) [51-500]
c KR - July 1 2015 - pNA [51-500]
c PW - v262 - i20 - May 18 2015 - p82(2) [501+]
c SLJ - v61 - i7 - July 2015 - p55(2) [51-500]
Heos, Bridget - *Be Safe around Fire (Illus. by Baroncelli, Silvia)*
c HB Guide - v26 - i1 - Spring 2015 - p176(1) [51-500]
Be Safe around Strangers (Illus. by Baroncelli, Silvia)
c HB Guide - v26 - i1 - Spring 2015 - p176(1) [51-500]
Be Safe around Water
c HB Guide - v26 - i1 - Spring 2015 - p184(1) [51-500]
Be Safe on the Internet (Illus. by Baroncelli, Silvia)
c HB Guide - v26 - i1 - Spring 2015 - p130(1) [51-500]
Be Safe on the Playground (Illus. by Baroncelli, Silvia)
c HB Guide - v26 - i1 - Spring 2015 - p184(1) [51-500]
Be Safe on Your Bike (Illus. by Baroncelli, Silvia)
c HB Guide - v26 - i1 - Spring 2015 - p184(1) [51-500]
Counting Change (Illus. by Longhi, Katya)
c HB Guide - v26 - i1 - Spring 2015 - p148(2) [51-500]
Do You Really Want a Guinea Pig? (Illus. by Longhi, Katya)
c BL - v112 - i2 - Sept 15 2015 - p60(1) [51-500]
Do You Really Want a Lizard? (Illus. by Longhi, Katya)
c BL - v112 - i2 - Sept 15 2015 - p60(1) [51-500]
Do You Really Want a Snake? (Illus. by Longhi, Katya)
c BL - v112 - i2 - Sept 15 2015 - p60(1) [51-500]
Do You Really Want a Turtle? (Illus. by Longhi, Katya)
c BL - v112 - i2 - Sept 15 2015 - p60(1) [51-500]
Do You Really Want to Visit a Coral Reef? (Illus. by Fabbri, Daniele)
c HB Guide - v26 - i1 - Spring 2015 - p154(2) [51-500]
Do You Really Want to Visit a Desert? (Illus. by Fabbri, Daniele)
c HB Guide - v26 - i1 - Spring 2015 - p154(2) [51-500]

Do You Really Want to Visit a Prairie? (Illus. by Fabbri, Daniele)
c HB Guide - v26 - i1 - Spring 2015 - p154(2) [51-500]
Do You Really Want to Visit a Rainforest? (Illus. by Fabbri, Daniele)
c HB Guide - v26 - i1 - Spring 2015 - p154(2) [51-500]
Do You Really Want to Visit a Temperate Forest? (Illus. by Fabbri, Daniele)
c HB Guide - v26 - i1 - Spring 2015 - p154(2) [51-500]
Do You Really Want to Visit a Wetland? (Illus. by Fabbri, Daniele)
c HB Guide - v26 - i1 - Spring 2015 - p154(2) [51-500]
I, Fly: The Buzz about Flies and How Awesome They Are (Illus. by Plecas, Jennifer)
c CCB-B - v68 - i10 - June 2015 - p496(1) [51-500]
c HB - v91 - i2 - March-April 2015 - p120(2) [51-500]
c HB Guide - v26 - i2 - Fall 2015 - p174(1) [51-500]
c NYTBR - April 12 2015 - p19(L) [501+]
It's Getting Hot in Here: The Past, Present, and Future of Climate Change
c KR - Dec 1 2015 - pNA [51-500]
c PW - v262 - i47 - Nov 23 2015 - p70(1) [501+]
Math World Series (Illus. by Longhi, Katya)
c BL - v111 - i12 - Feb 15 2015 - p74(1) [51-500]
Mustache Baby Meets His Match (Illus. by Ang, Joy)
c HB Guide - v26 - i2 - Fall 2015 - p37(1) [51-500]
Telling Time (Illus. by Longhi, Katya)
c HB Guide - v26 - i1 - Spring 2015 - p150(1) [51-500]
Hepburn, Sam - *If You Were Me*
y Sch Lib - v63 - i3 - Autumn 2015 - p183(1) [51-500]
Hepinstall, Becky - *Sisters of Shiloh*
Roundup M - v22 - i4 - April 2015 - p26(1) [501+]
Hepinstall, Kathy - *Sisters of Shiloh*
BL - v111 - i9-10 - Jan 1 2015 - p54(1) [51-500]
KR - Jan 1 2015 - pNA [51-500]
Hepler, Heather - *Frosted Kisses*
y KR - August 15 2015 - pNA [51-500]
y SLJ - v61 - i1 - Oct 2015 - p102(1) [51-500]
y VOYA - v38 - i4 - Oct 2015 - p52(1) [51-500]
Hepola, Sarah - *Blackout: Remembering the Things I Drank to Forget (Read by Hepola, Sarah). Audiobook Review*
LJ - v140 - i17 - Oct 15 2015 - p53(1) [51-500]
PW - v262 - i39 - Sept 28 2015 - p87(2) [51-500]
Blackout: Remembering the Things I Drank to Forget
BooChiTr - July 4 2015 - p14(1) [501+]
KR - April 1 2015 - pNA [51-500]
Mac - v128 - i25 - June 29 2015 - p59(2) [501+]
NS - v144 - i5287 - Nov 6 2015 - p46(2) [501+]
NYT - July 1 2015 - pC1(L) [501+]
PW - v262 - i21 - May 25 2015 - p51(1) [51-500]
Heppell, Timothy - *How Labour Governments Fall: From Ramsay MacDonald to Gordon Brown*
HER - v130 - i542 - Feb 2015 - p253(2) [501+]
Heppermann, Christine - *Backyard Witch: Sadie's Story (Illus. by Marcero, Deborah)*
c CCB-B - v69 - i1 - Sept 2015 - p28(1) [51-500]
c HB - v91 - i4 - July-August 2015 - p135(1) [51-500]
c KR - April 15 2015 - pNA [51-500]
c SLJ - v61 - i3 - March 2015 - p117(1) [51-500]
c BL - v111 - i19-20 - June 1 2015 - p103(1) [51-500]
c PW - v262 - i18 - May 4 2015 - p119(1) [51-500]
Poisoned Apples: Poems for You, My Pretty
y HB Guide - v26 - i1 - Spring 2015 - p188(1) [51-500]
y VOYA - v38 - i2 - June 2015 - p76(1) [51-500]
Hepplewhite, Peter - *Loos, Poos, and Number Twos: A Disgusting Journey through the Bowels of History (Illus. by Morgan-Jones, Tom)*
c BL - v112 - i3 - Oct 1 2015 - p54(2) [51-500]
Hepworth, Adrian - *Costa Rica: A Journey Through Nature*
QRB - v90 - i4 - Dec 2015 - p433(1) [501+]
Hepworth, Sally - *The Things We Keep*
BL - v112 - i7 - Dec 1 2015 - p24(2) [51-500]
KR - Oct 15 2015 - pNA [51-500]
LJ - v140 - i20 - Dec 1 2015 - p90(2) [51-500]
PW - v262 - i44 - Nov 2 2015 - p56(1) [51-500]
Herb, Michael - *The Wages of Oil: Parliaments and Economic Development in Kuwait and the UAE*
For Aff - v94 - i3 - May-June 2015 - pNA [501+]

Herbach, Geoff - *Fat Boy vs. the Cheerleaders (Read by Podehl, Nick). Audiobook Review*
c BL - v111 - i14 - March 15 2015 - p24(2) [501+]
Herbel, D. Oliver - *Turning to Tradition: Converts and the Making of an American Orthodox Church*
Theol St - v76 - i1 - March 2015 - p175(2) [501+]
Herbenick, Debby - *The Coregasm Workout: The Revolutionary Method for Better Sex Through Exercise.*
PW - v262 - i14 - April 6 2015 - p55(1) [51-500]
Herbers, Klaus - *Das begrenzte Papsttum: Spielraumepapstlkhen Handels - Legaten: Delegierte Richter Grenzen*
CHR - v101 - i1 - Wntr 2015 - p153(2) [501+]
Herbert, A.L. - *Murder with Fried Chicken and Waffles*
PW - v262 - i1 - Jan 5 2015 - p54(1) [51-500]
Herbert, Amanda E. - *Female Alliances: Gender, Identity, and Friendship in Early Modern Britain*
AHR - v120 - i1 - Feb 2015 - p326-327 [501+]
Ren Q - v68 - i1 - Spring 2015 - p316-317 [501+]
TLS - i5836 - Feb 6 2015 - p11(2) [501+]
Herbert, Daniel - *Videoland: Movie Culture at the American Video Store*
JAH - v101 - i4 - March 2015 - p1315-1316 [501+]
Herbert, Frank - *Dune*
Esq - v163 - i6-7 - June-July 2015 - p26(2) [501+]
Herbert, Joe - *Testosterone: Sex, Power, and the Will to Win*
BL - v111 - i18 - May 15 2015 - p9(1) [51-500]
LJ - v140 - i9 - May 15 2015 - p98(1) [51-500]
Herbert, Reesa - *Peripheral People*
PW - v262 - i10 - March 9 2015 - p57(1) [51-500]
Herbert, Trevor - *Music and the British Military in the Long Nineteenth Century*
Notes - v71 - i4 - June 2015 - p706(3) [501+]
Herbert, Ulrich - *Geschichte Deutschlands im 20. Jahrhundert*
CEH - v48 - i2 - June 2015 - p249-251 [501+]
GSR - v38 - i3 - Oct 2015 - p680-682 [501+]
Herborn, Daniel - *You're the Kind of Girl I Write Songs About*
y Magpies - v30 - i3 - July 2015 - p40(2) [501+]
Herbst, Ron - *The Deluxe Food Lover's Companion, 2d ed.*
LJ - v140 - i7 - April 15 2015 - p118(1) [51-500]
Hercules, Olia - *Mamushka: A Cookbook: Recipes from Ukraine & Eastern Europe*
LJ - v140 - i20 - Dec 1 2015 - p126(1) [51-500]
NYTBR - Dec 6 2015 - p20(L) [501+]
PW - v262 - i44 - Nov 2 2015 - p80(1) [51-500]
Spec - v329 - i9768 - Nov 14 2015 - p58(1) [501+]
Herder, Johann Gottfried - *Phenomenology of the Spirit*
HT - v65 - i10 - Oct 2015 - p56(2) [501+]
Herdling, Glenn - *Piper Houdini: Apprentice of Coney Island*
y KR - Oct 15 2015 - pNA [501+]
Hering, Scott - *The Hoarders*
CHE - v61 - i28 - March 27 2015 - pNA [501+]
Herissone, Rebecca - *Concepts of Creativity in Seventeenth-Century England*
Sev Cent N - v73 - i3-4 - Fall-Winter 2015 - p116(5) [501+]
Herken, Gregg - *The Georgetown Set: Friends and Rivals in Cold War Washington*
CJR - v53 - i5 - Jan-Feb 2015 - p63(1) [501+]
NYRB - v62 - i4 - March 5 2015 - p38(2) [501+]
Herkert, Barbara - *Mary Cassatt: Extraordinary Impressionist Painter (Illus. by Swiatkowska, Gabi)*
c BL - v112 - i1 - Sept 1 2015 - p94(1) [51-500]
c BL - v112 - i5 - Nov 1 2015 - p48(1) [51-500]
c PW - v262 - i49 - Dec 2 2015 - p48(1) [51-500]
c SLJ - v61 - i10 - Oct 2015 - p125(2) [51-500]
c HB - v91 - i6 - Nov-Dec 2015 - p101(2) [51-500]
c KR - August 15 2015 - pNA [51-500]
c PW - v262 - i29 - July 20 2015 - p190(2) [501+]
Sewing Stories: Harriet Powers' Journey from Slave to Artist (Illus. by Brantley-Newton, Vanessa)
c SLJ - v61 - i8 - August 2015 - p120(2) [51-500]
Sewing Stories: Harriet Powers' Journey from Slave to Artist (Illus. by Newton, Vanessa)
c KR - August 1 2015 - pNA [51-500]
Herkness, Nancy - *The CEO Buys In*
PW - v262 - i19 - May 11 2015 - p41(1) [51-500]
Herman, Arthur - *Freedom's Forge: How American Business Produced Victory in World War II*
RAH - v43 - i1 - March 2015 - p149-155 [501+]
Herman, Daniel - *Zen And The White Whale: A Buddhist Rendering of Moby-Dick*
Am St - v54 - i2 - Summer 2015 - p140-141 [501+]

Herman, David - *Storytelling and the Sciences of Mind*
    MFSF - v61 - i2 - Summer 2015 - p359-369 [501+]
    Poetics T - v36 - i1-2 - June 2015 - p130-133 [501+]
Herman, Eleanor - *Legacy of Kings*
  y BL - v111 - i21 - July 1 2015 - p56(2) [51-500]
  y KR - June 15 2015 - pNA [51-500]
  y PW - v262 - i22 - June 1 2015 - p61(1) [51-500]
  y SLJ - v61 - i6 - June 2015 - p124(1) [51-500]
  y VOYA - v38 - i2 - June 2015 - p61(1) [501+]
Herman, Eric - *The Incredibly Spaced-Out Adventures of Jupiter Jackson*
    CH Bwatch - Jan 2015 - pNA [51-500]
Herman, Gail - *Climbing Everest (Illus. by Amatrula, Michele)*
  c BL - v111 - i19-20 - June 1 2015 - p76(1) [51-500]
  c KR - June 15 2015 - pNA [51-500]
  c SLJ - v61 - i6 - June 2015 - p134(1) [51-500]
Herman, Peter C. - *Approaches to Teaching Milton's 'Paradise Lost'*
    Six Ct J - v46 - i3 - Fall 2015 - p659-664 [501+]
Hermand, Jost - *Vorbilder: Partisanenprofessoren im geteilten Deutschland*
    HNet - April 2015 - pNA [501+]
Hermann Henselmann in seiner Berliner Zeit (1949-1995). Der Architekt, die Macht und die Baukunst. 11. Hermann-Henselmann-Kolloquium
    HNet - March 2015 - pNA [501+]
Hermann, Nellie - *The Season of Migration*
    BL - v111 - i9-10 - Jan 1 2015 - p53(2) [51-500]
    NYTBR - Jan 25 2015 - p13(L) [501+]
    TLS - i5835 - Jan 30 2015 - p21(1) [501+]
Hermann, Pernille - *Minni and Muninn: Memory in Medieval Nordic Culture*
    Med R - Jan 2015 - pNA [501+]
Hernandez, Arturo D. - *Sangama*
    KR - June 15 2015 - pNA [501+]
Hernandez, Carlos - *he Assimilated Cuban's Guide to Quantum Santeria*
    PW - v262 - i45 - Nov 9 2015 - p42(1) [51-500]
Hernandez, Daisy - *A Cup of Water under My Bed: A Memoir*
    BL - v111 - i11 - Feb 1 2015 - p16(1) [501+]
    G&L Rev W - v22 - i2 - March-April 2015 - p44(1) [501+]
Hernandez, Gilbert - *Love and Rockets, vol. 7*
    BL - v111 - i13 - March 1 2015 - p36(1) [51-500]
Hernandez, Marie-Theresa - *The Virgin of Guadalupe and the Conversos: Uncovering Hidden Influences from Spain to Mexico*
    IBMR - v39 - i4 - Oct 2015 - p244(2) [501+]
Hernandez, Sonia - *Working Women into the Borderlands*
    JAH - v101 - i4 - March 2015 - p1265-1266 [501+]
    SHQ - v118 - i3 - Jan 2015 - p334-335 [501+]
Herndon, April Michelle - *Fat Blame: How the War on Obesity Victimizes Women and Children*
    CS - v44 - i5 - Sept 2015 - p744-745 [501+]
Herndon, William H. - *Herndon on Lincoln: Letters*
    LJ - v140 - i19 - Nov 15 2015 - p95(1) [51-500]
Hernon, Peter - *Assessing Service Quality: Satisfying the Expectations of Library Customers, 3d ed.*
    LJ - v140 - i14 - Sept 1 2015 - p126(1) [51-500]
Managing with Data: Using ACRLMetrics and PLAmetrics
    LJ - v140 - i6 - April 1 2015 - p103(1) [51-500]
    R&USQ - v54 - i4 - Summer 2015 - p73(2) [501+]
Herodotus - *Histories Book V*
    TLS - i5843 - March 27 2015 - p10(2) [501+]
Herold, Cameron - *Double Double: How to Double Your Revenue and Profit in 3 Years or Less*
    RVBW - Oct 2015 - pNA [501+]
Herold, Heiko - *Reichsgewalt Bedeutet Seegewalt: Die Kreuzergeschwader der Kaiserlichen Marine als Instrument der Deutschen Kolonial- und Weltpolitik 1885 bis 1914*
    HNet - July 2015 - pNA [501+]
Herrera, Carlos R. - *Juan Boutista de Anza: The King's Governor in New Mexico*
    Roundup M - v23 - i1 - Oct 2015 - p33(1) [501+]
Herrera, Hayden - *Listening to Stone: The Art and Life of Isamu Noguchi*
    BL - v111 - i11 - Feb 1 2015 - p18(1) [51-500]
    BL - v111 - i19-20 - June 1 2015 - p27(1) [51-500]
    KR - Jan 15 2015 - pNA [51-500]
    NY - v91 - i13 - May 18 2015 - p97 [51-500]
    NYTBR - June 28 2015 - p29(L) [501+]
Herrera, Juan Felipe - *Notes on the Assemblage*
    LJ - v140 - i14 - Sept 1 2015 - p102(1) [51-500]
    NYTBR - Dec 27 2015 - p26(L) [501+]

Herrera, Yuri - *Signs Preceding the End of the World*
    NYT - March 26 2015 - pC6(L) [501+]
    TLS - i5850 - May 15 2015 - p21(1) [501+]
Herrero Sanchez, Manuel - *Genova y la Monarquia Hispanica (1528-1713).*
    JMH - v87 - i2 - June 2015 - p403(7) [501+]
Herrick, Dennis - *A Brother's Cold Case*
    Roundup M - v22 - i5 - June 2015 - p38(1) [51-500]
    Roundup M - v22 - i6 - August 2015 - p30(1) [501+]
Herrick, John - *Between These Walls*
    PW - v262 - i9 - March 2 2015 - p73(1) [51-500]
    PW - v262 - i12 - March 23 2015 - p40(2) [501+]
    SPBW - March 2015 - pNA [51-500]
Herrick, Karen E. - *"Grandma, What Is a Soul?" (Illus. by Herrick, Karen E.)*
  c KR - May 15 2015 - pNA [51-500]
Herriman, Nancy - *No Comfort for the Lost*
    PW - v262 - i26 - June 29 2015 - p48(1) [51-500]
Herriman, Nicholas - *The Entangled State: Sorcery, State Control, and Violence in Indonesia*
    JRAI - v21 - i1 - March 2015 - p237(2) [501+]
Herring, Mark Y. - *Are Libraries Obsolete? An Argument for Relevance in the Digital Age*
    LRTS - v59 - i1 - Jan 2015 - p54(2) [501+]
Herring, Peg - *Her Majesty's Mischief*
    KR - May 1 2015 - pNA [51-500]
Herringshaw, Deann - *Rihanna: Grammy-Winning Superstar*
  y HB Guide - v26 - i1 - Spring 2015 - p193(1) [51-500]
Herrington, Lisa M. - *I Broke My Arm*
  c SLJ - v61 - i4 - April 2015 - p72(4) [51-500]
I Lost a Tooth
  c BL - v111 - i15 - April 1 2015 - p63(1) [51-500]
Herrmann, Hans-Christian - *Widerstand, Repression und Verfolgung: Beitrage zur Geschichte des Nationalsozialismus an der Saar*
    HNet - July 2015 - pNA [501+]
Herrnstein, Richard J. - *The Bell Curve: Intelligence and Class Structure in American Life*
    Nation - v300 - i14 - April 6 2015 - p166(1) [501+]
Herron, Matt - *Mississippi Eyes: The Story and Photography of the Southern Documentary Project*
    CSM - March 26 2015 - pNA [51-500]
Herron, Mick - *Nobody Walks*
    RVBW - Nov 2015 - pNA [501+]
Real Tigers
    LJ - v140 - i20 - Dec 1 2015 - p90(1) [51-500]
    PW - v262 - i47 - Nov 23 2015 - p49(1) [51-500]
Herron, Rita - *All the Beautiful Brides*
    PW - v262 - i31 - August 3 2015 - p43(1) [51-500]
Herrschaft durch Esoterik in der intellektuellen Kultur der Weimarer Republik
    HNet - May 2015 - pNA [501+]
Herrschaftserzahlungen. Wilhelm II. in der Kulturgeschichte
    HNet - Jan 2015 - pNA [501+]
Hersant, Beth - *Good Neighbours*
    RVBW - June 2015 - pNA [501+]
Hersh, Kristin - *Don't Suck, Don't Die: Giving Up Vic Chesnutt*
    KR - June 15 2015 - pNA [501+]
    LJ - v140 - i13 - August 1 2015 - p96(2) [51-500]
Hershey, Terry - *Sanctuary: Creating a Space for Grace in Your Life*
    RVBW - May 2015 - pNA [501+]
Hershorn, Tad - *Norman Granz - The Man Who Used Jazz for Justice*
    ERS - v38 - i3 - March 2015 - p487(3) [501+]
Herspring, Dale R. - *The Pentagon and the Presidency: Civil-Military Relations from FDR to George W. Bush*
    APJ - v29 - i4 - July-August 2015 - p93(1) [501+]
Hertel, Ralf - *Staging England in the Elizabethan History Play: Performing National Identity*
    Ren Q - v68 - i2 - Summer 2015 - p773-775 [501+]
    Sev Cent N - v73 - i1-2 - Spring-Summer 2015 - p22(5) [501+]
    Six Ct J - v46 - i3 - Fall 2015 - p695-697 [501+]
    Theat J - v67 - i2 - May 2015 - p369-370 [501+]
Herter, Philip - *The Fabulous Shadow*
    ABR - v36 - i3 - March-April 2015 - p16(1) [501+]
Hertzman, Marc A. - *Making Samba: A New History of Race and Music in Brazil*
    Notes - v71 - i3 - March 2015 - p499(4) [501+]
Hertzog, Nancy B. - *Let's Play!: Discover and Explore the Everyday World with Your Child*
  c CH Bwatch - Oct 2015 - pNA [51-500]

Hervieux, Linda - *Forgotten: The Untold Story of D-Day's Black Heroes, at Home and at War*
    KR - Sept 1 2015 - pNA [501+]
    LJ - v140 - i15 - Sept 15 2015 - p87(3) [51-500]
Herwig, Christopher - *Soviet Bus Stops*
    Spec - v328 - i9759 - Sept 12 2015 - p40(1) [501+]
Herwig, Holger H. - *Long Night of the Tankers: Hitler's War against Caribbean Oil*
    HNet - Sept 2015 - pNA(NA) [501+]
Herz, Henry - *Monster Goose Nursery Rhymes (Illus. by Larson, Abigail)*
  c HB Guide - v26 - i2 - Fall 2015 - p203(2) [51-500]
When You Give an Imp a Penny
  c KR - Oct 15 2015 - pNA [51-500]
Herz, Josh - *Monster Goose Nursery Rhymes (Illus. by Larson, Abigail)*
  c SLJ - v61 - i7 - July 2015 - p62(1) [51-500]
Herzberg, Bob - *Borderline*
    Roundup M - v23 - i1 - Oct 2015 - p30(1) [501+]
Herzig, Rebecca M. - *Plucked: A History of Hair Removal*
    Econ - v414 - i8924 - Feb 7 2015 - p79(US) [501+]
    JAH - v102 - i2 - Sept 2015 - p518-519 [501+]
    Mac - v128 - i11 - March 23 2015 - p60(1) [501+]
    TimHES - i2189 - Feb 5 2015 - p56-56 [501+]
    TLS - i5868 - Sept 18 2015 - p11(2) [501+]
    Wom R Bks - v32 - i6 - Nov-Dec 2015 - p25(3) [501+]
Herzig, Tamar - *Christ Transformed into a Virgin Woman: Lucia Brocadelli, Heinrich Institoris, and the Defense of the Faith*
    AHR - v120 - i2 - April 2015 - p705-706 [501+]
    HER - v130 - i545 - August 2015 - p975(2) [501+]
    Six Ct J - v46 - i2 - Summer 2015 - p474-476 [501+]
Herzog, Amy - *Knit Wear Love: Foolproof Instructions for Knitting Your Best-Fitting Sweaters Ever in the Styles You Love to Wear*
    BL - v111 - i18 - May 15 2015 - p10(1) [51-500]
    LJ - v140 - i6 - April 1 2015 - p93(1) [51-500]
Herzog, Kenny - *Phil Pickle (Illus. by Canby, Kelly)*
  c PW - v262 - i51 - Dec 14 2015 - p84(1) [51-500]
Herzog, Tamar - *Frontiers of Possession: Spain and Portugal in Europe and the Americas*
    HAHR - v95 - i4 - Nov 2015 - p716-717 [501+]
    HNet - Feb 2015 - pNA [501+]
    Six Ct J - v46 - i3 - Fall 2015 - p750-751 [501+]
Herzog, Werner - *Of Walking in Ice*
    KR - March 1 2015 - pNA [51-500]
Hesford, Victoria - *Feeling Women's Liberation*
    Signs - v40 - i2 - Wntr 2015 - p521(4) [501+]
Hesik, Annameekee - *Driving Lessons*
    SLJ - v61 - i2 - Feb 2015 - p102(1) [51-500]
Hesmondhalgh, David - *Why Music Matters*
    Am Q - v67 - i1 - March 2015 - p253-265 [501+]
Hesper, Sam - *Black Widow Spiders*
    SLJ - v61 - i4 - April 2015 - p92(4) [51-500]
Hess, Cordelia - *Social Imagery in Middle Low German: Didactical Literature and Metaphorical Representation, 1470-1517*
    Six Ct J - v46 - i3 - Fall 2015 - p713-714 [501+]
Hess, Earl J. - *The Battle of Ezra Church and the Struggle for Atlanta*
    LJ - v140 - i8 - May 1 2015 - p88(3) [51-500]
Kennesaw Mountain: Sherman, Johnston, and the Atlanta Campaign
    Historian - v77 - i1 - Spring 2015 - p126(2) [501+]
Hess, Frederick M. - *The Cage-Busting Teacher*
    LJ - v140 - i6 - April 1 2015 - p101(2) [51-500]
    TES - i5147 - May 22 2015 - p17(1) [501+]
Hess, Joan - *Pride v. Prejudice: A Claire Malloy Mystery*
    BL - v111 - i13 - March 1 2015 - p25(1) [51-500]
    KR - Feb 15 2015 - pNA [51-500]
    PW - v262 - i6 - Feb 9 2015 - p46(1) [51-500]
Hess, Pamela - *Geschichte als Politikum: Offentliche und Private Kontroversen um die Deutung der DDR-Vergangenheit*
    HNet - March 2015 - pNA [501+]
Hess, Scott Alexander - *The Butcher's Sons*
    KR - Sept 15 2015 - pNA [501+]
Hess, Stephen - *The Professor and the President: Daniel Patrick Moynihan in the Nixon White House*
    Nat R - v67 - i2 - Feb 9 2015 - p46 [501+]
Hesse, Alan J. - *Charles Darwin and the Theory of Natural Selection*
  y Sci & Ch - v53 - i2 - Oct 2015 - p98 [51-500]
  y Sci Teach - v82 - i7 - Oct 2015 - p81 [51-500]
Hesse, Jan-Otmar - *Die Grosse Depression: Die Weltwirtschaftskrise 1929-1939*
    HNet - June 2015 - pNA [501+]

Perspectives on European Economic and Social History - Perspektiven der Europaischen Wirtschafts- und Sozialgeschichte
    HNet - June 2015 - pNA [501+]
Hesse, Monica - *Girl in the Blue Coat*
    y KR - Jan 1 2016 - pNA [51-500]
Hesselberth, Joyce - *Shape Shift (Illus. by Hesselberth, Joyce)*
    c KR - Nov 1 2015 - pNA [51-500]
    c SLJ - v61 - i12 - Dec 2015 - p85(1) [51-500]
Hesser, Amanda - *Food52 Baking: 60 Sensational Treats You Can Pull Off in a Snap*
    NYT - Dec 2 2015 - pD6(L) [501+]
    PW - v262 - i33 - August 17 2015 - p66(1) [51-500]
Hessler, James A. - *Pickett's Charge at Gettysburg*
    RVBW - August 2015 - pNA [501+]
Hessler, John - *Map: Exploring the World*
    LJ - v140 - i16 - Oct 1 2015 - p76(1) [501+]
    NYTBR - Dec 6 2015 - p14(L) [501+]
Hester, Kathy - *The Easy Vegan Cookbook: Make Healthy Home Cooking Practically Effortless*
    LJ - v140 - i20 - Dec 1 2015 - p128(1) [51-500]
    PW - v262 - i38 - Sept 21 2015 - p68(1) [51-500]
Oatrageous Oatmeals
    Veg J - v34 - i3 - July-Sept 2015 - p30(1) [51-500]
Hestermann, Bethanie - *Zoology for Kids: Understanding and Working with Animals*
    c SLJ - v61 - i3 - March 2015 - p177(1) [51-500]
Hestermann, Josh - *Zoology for Kids: Understanding and Working with Animals*
    c BL - v111 - i12 - Feb 15 2015 - p72(1) [51-500]
    c KR - Jan 15 2015 - pNA [51-500]
Heston, Fraser C. - *Desolation Sound*
    SPBW - Sept 2015 - pNA [51-500]
Hetherington, Kregg - *Guerrilla Auditors: The Politics of Transparency in Neoliberal Paraguay*
    Ams - v72 - i2 - April 2015 - p351(3) [501+]
Hetherington, Sands - *Night Buddies Go Sky High (Illus. by Love, Jessica)*
    c CH Bwatch - June 2015 - pNA [501+]
    c CH Bwatch - August 2015 - pNA [51-500]
Hetrick, Hans - *Six Degrees of Peyton Manning: Connecting Football Stars*
    c HB Guide - v26 - i2 - Fall 2015 - p199(1) [51-500]
Heuer, Andreas - *Globales Geschichtsbewusstsein: Die Entstehung der Multipolaren Welt vom 18. Jahrhundert bis in die Gegenwart*
    HNet - July 2015 - pNA [501+]
Heumann, Ina - *Gegenstucke: Populares Wissen im transatlantischen Vergleich*
    HNet - April 2015 - pNA [501+]
Hever, Julieanna - *The Vegiterranean Diet: The New and Improved Mediterranean Eating Plan--with Deliciously Satisfying Vegan Recipes for Optimal Health*
    LJ - v140 - i2 - Feb 1 2015 - p102(2) [51-500]
Hewerdine, Anita - *The Yeomen of the Guard and the Early Tudors: The Formation of a Royal Bodyguard*
    Historian - v77 - i3 - Fall 2015 - p610(2) [501+]
Hewison, Robert - *Cultural Capital: The Rise and Fall of Creative Britain*
    TimHES - i2188 - Jan 29 2015 - p50-51 [501+]
    TLS - i5839 - Feb 27 2015 - p27(1) [501+]
Hewitt, Ben - *The Nourishing Homestead: One Back-to-the-Land Family's Plan for Cultivating Soil, Skills, and Spirit*
    LJ - v140 - i5 - March 15 2015 - p125(1) [51-500]
Hewitt, Jason - *The Dynamite Room*
    BL - v111 - i14 - March 15 2015 - p45(1) [51-500]
    KR - Feb 1 2015 - pNA [51-500]
Hewitt, Kate - *Rainy Day Sisters*
    LJ - v140 - i13 - August 1 2015 - p83(2) [51-500]
Hewitt, Lawrence Lee - *Confederate Generals in the Trans-Mississippi: Essays on America's Civil War*
    SHQ - v118 - i3 - Jan 2015 - p322-323 [501+]
Hewson, David - *The Flood*
    PW - v262 - i34 - August 24 2015 - p60(1) [51-500]
    BL - v112 - i5 - Nov 1 2015 - p30(1) [51-500]
The Killing II
    BL - v111 - i19-20 - June 1 2015 - p54(2) [51-500]
The Killing III: Based on the BAFTA Award-Winning TV Series Written by Soren Sveistrup
    PW - v262 - i31 - August 3 2015 - p38(1) [51-500]
Hexerei und Offentlichkeit
    HNet - May 2015 - pNA [501+]
Hey, Tony - *The Computing Universe: A Journey Through a Revolution*
    TimHES - i2184 - Jan 1 2015 - p66(1) [501+]

Heydemann, Steven - *Middle East Authoritarianisms: Governance, Contestation and Regime Resilience in Syria and Iran*
    IJMES - v47 - i1 - Feb 2015 - p153-168 [501+]
Heyer, Georgette - *An Infamous Army*
    TLS - i5833 - Jan 16 2015 - p16(1) [501+]
Heyer, Kristin E. - *Kinship across Borders: A Christian Ethic of Immigration*
    AM - v212 - i1 - Jan 6 2015 - p38 [501+]
Heylin, Clinton - *It's One for the Money: The Song Snatchers Who Carved Up a Century of Pop and Sparked a Musical Revolution*
    NS - v144 - i5271 - July 17 2015 - p49(1) [501+]
    Spec - v328 - i9749 - July 4 2015 - p34(2) [501+]
Heyman, Alissa - *Twelve Dancing Unicorns (Illus. by Gerard, Justin)*
    c HB Guide - v26 - i1 - Spring 2015 - p144(1) [51-500]
Heyman, Arlene - *Scary Old Sex*
    KR - Jan 1 2016 - pNA [501+]
Heymann, Margret - *"Das Leben ist eine Rutschbahn ... " Albert Steinruck: Eine Biographie des Schauspielers, Malers und Bohemiens*
    Ger Q - v88 - i3 - Summer 2015 - p392(2) [501+]
Heyrman, Christine Leigh - *American Apostles: When Evangelicals Entered the World of Islam*
    BL - v112 - i1 - Sept 1 2015 - p16(1) [51-500]
    CHE - v62 - i6 - Oct 9 2015 - pB17(1) [501+]
    KR - June 1 2015 - pNA [501+]
    LJ - v140 - i11 - June 15 2015 - p97(1) [51-500]
    NY - v91 - i33 - Oct 26 2015 - p79 [51-500]
    PW - v262 - i27 - July 6 2015 - p64(1) [51-500]
Heys, Alistair - *The Anatomy of Bloom: Harold Bloom and the Study of Influence and Anxiety*
    TLS - i5858 - July 10 2015 - p26(1) [501+]
Heywood, Linda - *African Americans in U.S. Foreign Policy: From the Era of Frederick Douglass to the Age of Obama*
    HNet - July 2015 - pNA [501+]
Heyworth, Gregory - *"Eschez d'amours": A Critical Edition of the Poem and its Latin Glosses*
    Specu - v90 - i1 - Jan 2015 - p258-259 [501+]
Heyworth, Stephen J. - *Cynthia: A Companion to the Text of Propertius*
    AJP - v136 - i1 - Spring 2015 - p169-173 [501+]
Hezel, Francis X. - *Making Sense of Micronesia: The Logic of Pacific Island Culture*
    Pac A - v88 - i1 - March 2015 - p238 [501+]
Hiaasen, Carl - *Skink-No Surrender (Read by Heyborne, Kirby). Audiobook Review*
    y BL - v111 - i13 - March 1 2015 - p71(1) [51-500]
Skink-No Surrender. Audiobook Review
    c BL - v111 - i14 - March 15 2015 - p24(2) [51-500]
Skink-No Surrender
    c BL - v111 - i12 - Feb 15 2015 - p76(1) [51-500]
    c BL - v111 - i17 - May 1 2015 - p40(1) [51-500]
    y HB Guide - v26 - i1 - Spring 2015 - p109(1) [51-500]
    y Sch Lib - v63 - i1 - Spring 2015 - p62(1) [51-500]
Hiatt, Joan - *The Watcher*
    c CH Bwatch - Jan 2015 - pNA [51-500]
Hibbs, Gillian - *Tilly's Staycation*
    c HB Guide - v26 - i2 - Fall 2015 - p37(1) [51-500]
Hicken, Sam - *This Time It's Not Personal: Why Science Says Get Over Yourself*
    KR - July 15 2015 - pNA [51-500]
    SPBW - April 2015 - pNA [51-500]
Hickey, Dave - *25 Women: Essays on Their Art*
    BL - v112 - i5 - Nov 1 2015 - p16(1) [501+]
    KR - Dec 1 2015 - pNA [501+]
Hickman, Ben - *John Ashbery and English Poetry*
    MLR - v110 - i3 - July 2015 - p853-855 [501+]
Hickman, Jonathan - *There Is No Us (Illus. by Dragotta, Nick)*
    BL - v111 - i13 - March 1 2015 - p36(1) [51-500]
Hickman, Joseph - *Murder at Camp Delta: A Staff Sergeant's Pursuit of Truth about Guantanamo Bay*
    TLS - i5862 - August 7 2015 - p27(1) [501+]
Hickok, Gregory - *he Myth of Mirror Neurons: The Real Neuroscience of Communication and Cognition*
    AJPsy - v128 - i4 - Winter 2015 - p527(7) [501+]
    AJPsy - v128 - i4 - Winter 2015 - p533(7) [501+]
Hicks, Caitlin - *A Theory of Expanded Love*
    KR - April 1 2015 - pNA [501+]
    PW - v262 - i15 - April 13 2015 - p64(1) [51-500]
Hicks, Michael - *The Mormon Tabernacle Choir: A Biography*
    KR - Jan 15 2015 - pNA [501+]
Hicks, Nola Helen - *Hurry Up, Ilua! (Illus. by Hicks, Nola Helen)*
    c KR - July 15 2015 - pNA [51-500]
    c SLJ - v61 - i10 - Oct 2015 - p78(1) [51-500]

Hicks, Zehra - *All Mine!*
    c Sch Lib - v63 - i2 - Summer 2015 - p94(1) [51-500]
Hidalgo, Carlos - *Driving Demand*
    RVBW - Nov 2015 - pNA [51-500]
Hidalgo, Cesar - *Why Information Grows: The Evolution of Order, from Atoms to Economies*
    Econ - v416 - i8948 - July 25 2015 - p66(US) [501+]
    KR - April 15 2015 - pNA [501+]
Hidayatullah, Aysha A. - *Feminist Edges of the Qur'an*
    JAAR - v83 - i3 - Sept 2015 - p858-861 [501+]
Hidier, Tanuja Desai - *Bombay Blues*
    HB Guide - v26 - i2 - Fall 2015 - p123(1) [51-500]
Hieber, Leanna Renee - *The Eterna Files*
    KR - Jan 15 2015 - pNA [51-500]
Hieber, Lutz - *Politisierung der Kunst: Avantgarde und US-Kunstwelt*
    HNet - Sept 2015 - pNA [501+]
Hiebert, Michael - *A Thorn among the Lilies*
    PW - v262 - i20 - May 18 2015 - p65(1) [51-500]
Hiekkapelto, Kati - *The Hummingbird*
    PW - v262 - i17 - April 27 2015 - p53(1) [51-500]
Hien, Hannah - *Das Beginenwesen in frankischen und bayerischen Bischofsstadten*
    HNet - April 2015 - pNA [501+]
Hiers, Dora - *Rori's Healing*
    PW - v262 - i17 - April 27 2015 - p59(2) [51-500]
Hiestand, Gerald - *The Pastor Theologian: Resurrecting an Ancient Vision*
    Ch Today - v59 - i6 - July-August 2015 - p85(1) [501+]
Higashida, Cheryl - *Black Internationalist Feminism: Woman Writers of the Black Left, 1945-1995*
    AL - v87 - i3 - Sept 2015 - p616-618 [501+]
Higashino, Keigo - *Malice*
    RVBW - Oct 2015 - pNA [51-500]
A Midsummer's Equation
    KR - Dec 15 2015 - pNA [51-500]
    PW - v262 - i50 - Dec 7 2015 - p70(1) [51-500]
Naoko
    CSM - Feb 26 2015 - pNA [51-500]
Higginbotham, Anastasia - *Divorce Is the Worst (Illus. by Higginbotham, Anastasia)*
    c SLJ - v61 - i6 - June 2015 - p134(2) [51-500]
    c PW - v262 - i9 - March 2 2015 - p83(1) [51-500]
Higginbotham, Susan - *Hanging Mary*
    LJ - v140 - i12 - July 1 2015 - p77(1) [51-500]
Higgins, Andrew A. - *Legal Professional Privilege for Corporations: A Guide to Four Major Common Law Jurisdictions*
    Law Q Rev - v131 - Oct 2015 - p676-679 [501+]
Higgins, C.A. - *Lightless*
    KR - July 15 2015 - pNA [51-500]
    PW - v262 - i26 - June 29 2015 - p50(1) [51-500]
    Analog - v135 - i12 - Dec 2015 - p105(1) [501+]
    NYT - Sept 3 2015 - pC1(L) [501+]
Higgins, Charlotte - *This New Noise: The Extraordinary Birth and Troubled Life of the BBC*
    Si & So - v25 - i10 - Oct 2015 - p112(2) [501+]
    Spec - v328 - i9754 - August 8 2015 - p28(2) [501+]
Under Another Sky: Journeys in Roman Britain
    NYTBR - Dec 6 2015 - p46(L) [501+]
    BL - v111 - i21 - July 1 2015 - p20(1) [51-500]
    KR - June 1 2015 - pNA [51-500]
Higgins, Jane - *Havoc*
    y Magpies - v30 - i2 - May 2015 - p41(1) [501+]
    y Magpies - v30 - i3 - July 2015 - p41(1) [501+]
Higgins, Kristan - *Anything for You*
    KR - Oct 1 2015 - pNA [51-500]
If You Only Knew (Read by Rubinate, Amy). Audiobook Review
    LJ - v140 - i20 - Dec 1 2015 - p59(1) [51-500]
If You Only Knew
    BL - v112 - i1 - Sept 1 2015 - p54(1) [51-500]
    KR - June 15 2015 - pNA [51-500]
    LJ - v140 - i13 - August 1 2015 - p86(2) [51-500]
    RVBW - Sept 2015 - pNA [51-500]
Higgins, Kyle - *Batman beyond 2.0, vol. 1: Rewired (Illus. by Wight, Eric)*
    y VOYA - v37 - i6 - Feb 2015 - p50(2) [501+]
C.O.W.L., vol. 2: Principles of Power (Illus. by Reis, Rod)
    y BL - v111 - i9-10 - Jan 1 2015 - p61(1) [51-500]
C.O.W.L., vol. 2: The Greater Good (Illus. by Reis, Rod)
    y BL - v111 - i17 - May 1 2015 - p35(1) [51-500]
Higgins, M.G. - *Rodeo Princess*
    y BL - v112 - i2 - Sept 15 2015 - p64(1) [51-500]
    y PW - v262 - i31 - August 3 2015 - p61(1) [501+]

Higgins, Melissa - *Teen Self-Injury*
   y HB Guide - v26 - i1 - Spring 2015 - p171(1) [51-500]

Higgins, Michelle Perry - *Stocks, Bonds and Soccer Moms*
     RVBW - August 2015 - pNA [51-500]

Higgins, Nadia - *Everything Vikings: All the Incredible Facts and Fierce Fun You Can Plunder*
   c BL - v112 - i7 - Dec 1 2015 - p40(1) [51-500]
Experiment with a Plant's Living Environment
   c HB Guide - v26 - i2 - Fall 2015 - p172(2) [51-500]
Experiment with What a Plant Needs to Grow
   c BL - v111 - i12 - Feb 15 2015 - p75(2) [51-500]
   c CH Bwatch - April 2015 - pNA [51-500]
Last Stand: Causes and Effects of the Battle of the Little Bighorn
   c HB Guide - v26 - i2 - Fall 2015 - p222(1) [51-500]
US Culture Through Infographics (Illus. by Westlund, Laura)
   c HB Guide - v26 - i1 - Spring 2015 - p204(1) [51-500]
US Geography Through Infographics (Illus. by Westlund, Laura)
   c BL - v111 - i9-10 - Jan 1 2015 - p84(1) [501+]
   c HB Guide - v26 - i1 - Spring 2015 - p199(1) [51-500]
US Government through Infographics (Illus. by Westlund, Laura)
   c HB Guide - v26 - i1 - Spring 2015 - p139(1) [51-500]
The World's Oddest Inventions
   c Sch Lib - v63 - i3 - Autumn 2015 - p174(1) [51-500]

Higgins, Nadia Abushanab - *Feminism: Reinventing the F Word*
   y KR - Dec 15 2015 - pNA [51-500]

Higgins, Ryan T. - *Mother Bruce (Illus. by Higgins, Ryan T.)*
   c KR - Sept 15 2015 - pNA [51-500]
   c NYTBR - Dec 20 2015 - p15(L) [501+]
   c PW - v262 - i36 - Sept 7 2015 - p65(1) [51-500]

Higgins, Wendy - *The Great Hunt*
   y KR - Dec 15 2015 - pNA [51-500]
Sweet Temptation
   y SLJ - v61 - i7 - July 2015 - p93(1) [51-500]
   y VOYA - v38 - i4 - Oct 2015 - p72(1) [51-500]

Higginson, Sheila Sweeny - *Doc McStuffins Doctor's Helper*
   c CH Bwatch - Jan 2015 - pNA [51-500]
Minnie in Paris (Illus. by Wall, Mike)
   c HB Guide - v26 - i1 - Spring 2015 - p33(1) [51-500]

Higgns, M.G. - *Rodeo Princess*
   y CH Bwatch - Nov 2015 - pNA [51-500]

Higgs, Catherine - *Chocolate Islands: Cocoa, Slavery, and Colonial Africa*
     AHR - v120 - i4 - Oct 2015 - p1580-1581 [501+]

Higgs, John - *Stranger Than We Can Imagine: Making Sense of the Twentieth Century*
     KR - Sept 1 2015 - pNA [51-500]

High, Casey - *The Anthropology of Ignorance: An Ethnographic Approach*
     JRAI - v21 - i2 - June 2015 - p475(2) [501+]

High, Jeffrey L. - *Heinrich von Kleist: Artistic and Political Legacies*
     MLR - v110 - i2 - April 2015 - p590-592 [501+]

High, Kathy - *The Emergence of Video Processing Tools: Television Becoming Unglued*
     T&C - v56 - i4 - Oct 2015 - p1008-1010 [501+]

High, Linda Oatman - *A Heart Like Ringo Starr*
   y PW - v262 - i14 - April 6 2015 - p60(1) [501+]
   y SLJ - v61 - i3 - March 2015 - p156(1) [51-500]

Higham, N.J. - *Wilfrid: Abbot, Bishop, Saint: Papers from the 1300th Anniversary Conferences*
     HER - v130 - i542 - Feb 2015 - p145(2) [501+]

Higham, Nicholas J. - *The Anglo-Saxon World*
     HER - v130 - i543 - April 2015 - p414(2) [501+]
The Princeton Companion to Applied Mathematics
     LJ - v140 - i17 - Oct 15 2015 - p111(1) [51-500]
     SIAM Rev - v57 - i3 - Sept 2015 - p469-473 [501+]

Highsmith, Patricia - *Strangers on a Train (Read by Pinchot, Bronson). Audiobook Review*
     BL - v112 - i3 - Oct 1 2015 - p86(1) [51-500]

Hightower, Michael J. - *Banking in Oklahoma before Statehood*
     JSH - v81 - i1 - Feb 2015 - p221(2) [501+]
     WHQ - v46 - i1 - Spring 2015 - p83-84 [501+]

Highway, Tomson - *A Tale of Monstrous Extravagance*
     Bwatch - May 2015 - pNA [51-500]

Higonnet, Anne - *A Museum of One's Own: Private Collecting, Public Gift*
     TimHES - i2221 - Sept 17 2015 - p45(1) [501+]

Higson, Charlie - *The Fallen*
   y HB Guide - v26 - i1 - Spring 2015 - p109(1) [51-500]

Hijikata, Tatsumi - *Costume en Face: A Primer of Darkness for Young Boys and Girls*
     NYT - August 30 2015 - p4(L) [51-500]

Hijuelos, Oscar - *Twain and Stanley Enter Paradise*
     BL - v112 - i2 - Sept 15 2015 - p37(1) [51-500]
     KR - Sept 1 2015 - pNA [501+]
     LJ - v140 - i17 - Oct 15 2015 - p73(2) [51-500]
     NYTBR - Dec 13 2015 - p16(L) [501+]
     PW - v262 - i36 - Sept 7 2015 - p44(1) [51-500]

Hilaire-Perez, Liliane - *La piece et le geste: Artisans, marchands et savoir technique a Londres au XVIIIe siecle*
     T&C - v56 - i3 - July 2015 - p752-754 [501+]

Hilary, Sarah - *No Other Darkness: A Detective Inspector Marnie Rome Mystery*
     PW - v262 - i26 - June 29 2015 - p47(1) [51-500]

Hildegard of Bingen - *Solutions to Thirty-Eight Questions*
     Med R - June 2015 - pNA [51-500]

Hilderbrand, Elin - *The Matchmaker (Read by Bennett, Erin). Audiobook Review*
     LJ - v140 - i8 - May 1 2015 - p41(1) [51-500]
The Rumor (Read by McInerney, Kathleen). Audiobook Review
   y BL - v112 - i3 - Oct 1 2015 - p85(1) [51-500]
     Bwatch - Sept 2015 - pNA [501+]
The Rumor
     KR - June 1 2015 - pNA [501+]
     BL - v111 - i19-20 - June 1 2015 - p45(1) [51-500]
Winter Stroll
     BL - v112 - i2 - Sept 15 2015 - p29(1) [51-500]
     KR - August 1 2015 - pNA [501+]

Hile, Lori - *Shang Dynasty China*
   c Sch Lib - v63 - i4 - Winter 2015 - p238(1) [51-500]

Hiley, Matthew S. - *Baseball Dads*
     RVBW - Nov 2015 - pNA [51-500]

Hilger, Stephanie M. - *Gender and Genre: German Women Write the French Revolution*
     Eight-C St - v49 - i1 - Fall 2015 - p91-94 [501+]
     TSWL - v34 - i1 - Spring 2015 - p166-168 [501+]

Hill, Bonnie Hearn - *If Anything Should Happen*
     BL - v112 - i6 - Nov 15 2015 - p28(1) [51-500]
     KR - Oct 1 2015 - pNA [501+]
     PW - v262 - i38 - Sept 21 2015 - p54(2) [51-500]

Hill, Brennan R. - *The Jesus Dialogues: Jesus Speaks with Religious Founders and Leaders*
     RVBW - July 2015 - pNA [51-500]

Hill, Chris - *Lucky*
   c KR - Dec 1 2015 - pNA [51-500]
   c PW - v262 - i48 - Nov 30 2015 - p60(1) [51-500]

Hill, Christopher - *The World Turned Upside Down*
     TimHES - i2211 - July 9 2015 - p49(1) [501+]

Hill, Christopher R. - *Outpost: Life on the Frontlines of American Diplomacy*
     For Aff - v94 - i1 - Jan-Feb 2015 - pNA [501+]

Hill, Christopher William - *The Lily-Livered Prince: Tales from Schwartzgarten, vol. 3*
   c Sch Lib - v63 - i1 - Spring 2015 - p37(2) [51-500]

Hill, David - *First to the Top: Sir Edmund Hillary's Amazing Everest Adventure (Illus. by Morris, Phoebe)*
   c Magpies - v30 - i4 - Sept 2015 - pS7(2) [51-500]
My Brother's War
   c Sch Lib - v63 - i1 - Spring 2015 - p52(2) [51-500]

Hill, Emita Brady - *Bronx Faces and Voices*
     NYT - Jan 11 2015 - p3(L) [51-500]

Hill, Eva - *Faraway Father (Illus. by Hill, Eva)*
   c KR - Dec 15 2015 - pNA [501+]

Hill, Fiona - *Mr. Putin: Operative in the Kremlin*
     For Aff - v94 - i2 - March-April 2015 - pNA [501+]

Hill, Gregory - *The Lonesome Trials of Johnny Riles*
     BL - v111 - i13 - March 1 2015 - p24(1) [51-500]
     RVBW - Oct 2015 - pNA [51-500]

Hill, Henry - *The Lufthansa Heist: Behind the Six-Million Dollar Cash Haul That Shook the World*
     BL - v112 - i1 - Sept 1 2015 - p18(1) [51-500]

Hill, James - *Somewhere between War and Peace*
     NY - v91 - i19 - July 6 2015 - p87 [51-500]

Hill, James Tate - *Academy Gothic*
     BL - v112 - i3 - Oct 1 2015 - p23(1) [51-500]
     PW - v262 - i34 - August 24 2015 - p60(1) [51-500]

Hill, Janet - *Miss Moon: Wise Words from a Dog Governess*
   c KR - Dec 15 2015 - pNA [51-500]

Hill, Joe - *The Best American Science Fiction and Fantasy 2015*
     PW - v262 - i37 - Sept 14 2015 - p46(1) [51-500]
Welcome to Lovecraft
   c LJ - v140 - i7 - April 15 2015 - p126(1) [501+]

Hill, Johnny Bernard - *Prophetic Rage: A Postcolonial Theology of Liberation*
     Theol St - v76 - i3 - Sept 2015 - p647(1) [501+]
     TT - v71 - i4 - Jan 2015 - p471-473 [501+]

Hill, Kat - *Baptism, Brotherhood, and Belief in Reformation Germany: Anabaptism and Lutheranism, 1525-1585*
     TLS - i5862 - August 7 2015 - p25(1) [501+]

Hill, Katie Rain - *Rethinking Normal: A Memoir in Transition*
   y CCB-B - v68 - i6 - Feb 2015 - p297(2) [51-500]
   y HB Guide - v26 - i2 - Fall 2015 - p209(1) [51-500]

Hill, Kirkpatrick - *Bo at Iditarod Creek (Illus. by Pham, LeUyen)*
   y BL - v111 - i16 - April 15 2015 - p57(1) [501+]
   y HB - v91 - i2 - March-April 2015 - p98(1) [51-500]
   y HB Guide - v26 - i2 - Fall 2015 - p86(2) [51-500]

Hill, Lawrence - *The Illegal*
     BL - v112 - i4 - Oct 15 2015 - p16(2) [51-500]
     KR - Oct 15 2015 - pNA [501+]
     LJ - v140 - i20 - Dec 1 2015 - p90(2) [51-500]
     PW - v262 - i41 - Oct 12 2015 - p45(1) [51-500]

Hill, Louella - *Kitchen Creamery: Making Yogurt, Butter and Cheese at Home*
     LJ - v140 - i14 - Sept 1 2015 - p131(2) [51-500]

Hill, Matt - *Graft*
     PW - v262 - i52 - Dec 21 2015 - p138(1) [51-500]

Hill, Melissa - *The Gift of a Charm*
     BL - v112 - i2 - Sept 15 2015 - p41(2) [51-500]

Hill, Michael DeRell - *The Ethics of Swagger: Prizewinning African American Novels, 1977-1993*
     AL - v87 - i3 - Sept 2015 - p622-624 [501+]

Hill, Michael Gibbs - *Lin Shu, Inc.: Translation and the Making of Modern Chinese Culture*
     Clio - v44 - i2 - Spring 2015 - p271-276 [501+]

Hill, Nancy Peterson - *A Very Private Public Citizen: The Life of Grenville Clark*
     RVBW - May 2015 - pNA [501+]

Hill, Pamela Smith - *Pioneer Girl: The Annotated Autobiography*
     Bks & Cult - v21 - i5 - Sept-Oct 2015 - p42(2) [501+]
     Roundup M - v22 - i6 - August 2015 - p37(1) [501+]

Hill, Sandra - *Even Vampires Get the Blues*
     PW - v262 - i32 - August 10 2015 - p44(1) [51-500]

Hill, Steven - *Raw Deal: How the "Uber Economy" and Runaway Capitalism Are Screwing American Workers*
     KR - August 1 2015 - pNA [501+]
     PW - v262 - i31 - August 3 2015 - p50(1) [51-500]

Hill, Susan - *Lassie Come-Home*
   c KR - August 15 2015 - pNA [51-500]
The Soul of Discretion
     NYTBR - Jan 4 2015 - p25(L) [501+]

Hill, Tom - *A Perfect Lie: The Hole Truth*
     KR - April 1 2015 - pNA [51-500]

Hill, Will - *Zero Hour: Department 19, Book 4*
   y VOYA - v37 - i6 - Feb 2015 - p77(1) [51-500]

Hillar, Marian - *From Logos to Trinity: The Evolution of Religious Beliefs from Pythagoras to Tertullian*
     Six Ct J - v46 - i1 - Spring 2015 - p171(2) [501+]

Hillard, Kathleen M. - *Masters, Slaves, and Exchange: Power's Purchase in the Old South*
     AHR - v120 - i2 - April 2015 - p624(1) [501+]

Hillenbrand, Carole - *Introduction to Islam: Beliefs and Practices in Historical Perspective*
     LJ - v140 - i8 - May 1 2015 - p99(1) [51-500]

Hillenbrand, Laura - *Unbroken: An Olympian's Journey from Airman to Castaway to Captive (Read by Herrmann, Edward). Audiobook Review*
   y HB - v91 - i2 - March-April 2015 - p130(2) [51-500]
Unbroken: An Olympian's Journey from Airman to Castaway to Captive
   y HB Guide - v26 - i1 - Spring 2015 - p193(1) [51-500]
   y JAH - v102 - i1 - June 2015 - p317-321 [501+]
Unbroken (Read by Herrmann, Edward). Audiobook Review
   y SLJ - v61 - i2 - Feb 2015 - p50(1) [51-500]

Hillenbrand, Will - *All for a Dime*
   c KR - July 1 2015 - pNA [51-500]
Snowman's Story
   c HB Guide - v26 - i2 - Fall 2015 - p37(1) [51-500]

Hiller, Diana - *Gendered Perceptions of Florentine Last Supper Frescoes, c. 1350-1490*
Ren Q - v68 - i3 - Fall 2015 - p1000-1001 [501+]
Hiller, Jokima - *7 Easy Ways to Show Your Employees You Care! A Booklet for Hotel Managers and Others*
SPBW - August 2015 - pNA [51-500]
Hiller, Mischa - *Disengaged*
KR - March 15 2015 - pNA [51-500]
LJ - v140 - i11 - June 15 2015 - p78(2) [501+]
PW - v262 - i10 - March 9 2015 - p54(1) [51-500]
Hiller von Gaertringen, Hans Georg - *Pop, Politik und Propaganda: Das Amerika Haus Berlin im Wandel der Zeit*
HNet - June 2015 - pNA [501+]
Hillerman, Anne - *Rock with Wings*
BL - v111 - i17 - May 1 2015 - p43(1) [51-500]
PW - v262 - i9 - March 2 2015 - p64(1) [51-500]
Roundup M - v23 - i1 - Oct 2015 - p30(1) [51-500]
Spider Woman's Daughter
RVBW - May 2015 - pNA [51-500]
Hillert, Margaret - *Beginning-to-Read: Dear Dragon (Illus. by Schimmell, David)*
c   HB Guide - v26 - i1 - Spring 2015 - p53(1) [51-500]
Dear Dragon Flies a Kite (Illus. by Pullan, Jack)
c   CH Bwatch - March 2015 - pNA [51-500]
c   HB Guide - v26 - i2 - Fall 2015 - p59(1) [51-500]
Dear Dragon Goes to Grandpa's Farm (Illus. by Pullan, Jack)
c   HB Guide - v26 - i2 - Fall 2015 - p59(1) [51-500]
Dear Dragon Goes to the Aquarium (Illus. by Pullan, Jack)
c   HB Guide - v26 - i2 - Fall 2015 - p59(1) [51-500]
Dear Dragon Goes to the Police Station (Illus. by Pullan, Jack)
c   HB Guide - v26 - i2 - Fall 2015 - p59(1) [51-500]
Hilliard, Kathleen M. - *Masters, Slaves, and Exchange: Power's Purchase in the Old South*
HNet - Jan 2015 - pNA [501+]
JEH - v75 - i1 - March 2015 - p290-291 [501+]
JSH - v81 - i4 - Nov 2015 - p969(2) [501+]
Hillier, Bevis - *Going for a Song: An Anthology of Poems about Antiques*
Sew R - v123 - i1 - Wntr 2015 - pIV-VI [501+]
Hillier, Jennifer - *The Butcher*
RVBW - April 2015 - pNA [51-500]
Hillis, Faith - *Children of Rus': Right-Bank Ukraine and the Invention of a Russian Nation*
JMH - v87 - i3 - Sept 2015 - p762(2) [501+]
Hillman, Bill - *Mozos: A Decade Running with the Bulls of Spain*
PW - v262 - i18 - May 4 2015 - p110(1) [51-500]
Hillman, Brenda - *Seasonal Works with Letters on Fire*
Tikkun - v30 - i2 - Spring 2015 - p45(4) [501+]
Hillman, Bruce J. - *The Man Who Stalked Einstein: How Nazi Scientist Philipp Lenard Changed the Course of History*
BL - v111 - i15 - April 1 2015 - p9(1) [51-500]
KR - March 1 2015 - pNA [501+]
LJ - v140 - i6 - April 1 2015 - p114(1) [51-500]
Hillman, Richard - *French Reflections on the Shakespearean Tragic: Three Case Studies*
MLR - v110 - i1 - Jan 2015 - p239-240 [501+]
Hills, Gregory - *The Lonesome Trials of Johnny Riles*
RVBW - August 2015 - pNA [51-500]
Hills, Rachel - *The Sex Myth: The Gap Between Our Fantasies and Reality*
LJ - v140 - i11 - June 15 2015 - p103(1) [51-500]
NYTBR - Sept 13 2015 - p16(L) [501+]
PW - v262 - i18 - May 4 2015 - p114(1) [51-500]
Hills, Tad - *Drop It, Rocket!*
c   HB Guide - v26 - i1 - Spring 2015 - p53(1) [51-500]
Duck & Goose: Colors! (Illus. by Hills, Tad)
c   KR - July 1 2015 - pNA [51-500]
c   SLJ - v61 - i7 - July 2015 - p55(2) [51-500]
R Is for Rocket: An ABC Book (Illus. by Hills, Tad)
c   KR - May 1 2015 - pNA [51-500]
c   PW - v262 - i23 - June 8 2015 - p60(1) [501+]
c   SLJ - v61 - i6 - June 2015 - p84(1) [51-500]
Rocket et ses mots preferes
c   Res Links - v20 - i3 - Feb 2015 - p45(1) [51-500]
Rocket's 100th Day of School (Illus. by Hills, Tad)
c   CCB-B - v68 - i5 - Jan 2015 - p259(2) [51-500]
c   HB Guide - v26 - i1 - Spring 2015 - p53(1) [51-500]
Hillson, Simon - *Tooth Development in Human Evolution and Bioarchaeology*
QRB - v90 - i2 - June 2015 - p226(2) [501+]
Hillstrom, Laurie Collier - *Plessy v. Ferguson*
y   VOYA - v38 - i3 - August 2015 - p88(2) [51-500]

Hillyer, Lexa - *Proof of Forever (Read by Zeller, Emily Woo). Audiobook Review*
y   SLJ - v61 - i9 - Sept 2015 - p61(1) [51-500]
Proof of Forever
y   BL - v111 - i19-20 - June 1 2015 - p100(1) [51-500]
y   HB Guide - v26 - i2 - Fall 2015 - p123(1) [51-500]
y   PW - v262 - i17 - April 27 2015 - p77(1) [51-500]
y   SLJ - v61 - i3 - March 2015 - p156(1) [51-500]
y   VOYA - v38 - i2 - June 2015 - p76(2) [51-500]
Hillyer, Reiko - *Designing Dixie: Tourism, Memory, and Urban Space in the New South*
HNet - June 2015 - pNA [501+]
HNet - August 2015 - pNA [501+]
Hilmo, Tess - *Skies Like These*
y   HB Guide - v26 - i1 - Spring 2015 - p80(1) [51-500]
Hilsdale, Cecily J. - *Byzantine Art and Diplomacy in an Age of Decline*
Med R - Sept 2015 - pNA [501+]
Hilton, Dan G. - *Biddy Debeau for His Life*
KR - July 1 2015 - pNA [501+]
Hilton, Lisa - *Elizabeth: Renaissance Prince*
HT - v65 - i1 - Jan 2015 - p61(1) [501+]
KR - August 1 2015 - pNA [501+]
LJ - v140 - i17 - Oct 15 2015 - p95(2) [501+]
PW - v262 - i34 - August 24 2015 - p71(1) [51-500]
TLS - i5835 - Jan 30 2015 - p5(1) [501+]
Hilton, Marilyn - *Found Things*
c   HB Guide - v26 - i2 - Fall 2015 - p86(1) [51-500]
Full Cicada Moon
c   BL - v112 - i1 - Sept 1 2015 - p115(1) [51-500]
c   KR - June 15 2015 - pNA [51-500]
c   NYTBR - Nov 8 2015 - p35(L) [501+]
c   PW - v262 - i25 - June 22 2015 - p137(1) [51-500]
c   SLJ - v61 - i8 - August 2015 - p86(2) [51-500]
c   VOYA - v38 - i3 - August 2015 - p62(2) [51-500]
Hilton, Steve - *More Human: Designing a World Where People Come First*
NS - v144 - i5267 - June 19 2015 - p51(1) [501+]
TimHES - i2211 - July 9 2015 - p51(1) [501+]
Hiltzik, Michael - *Big Science: Ernest Lawrence and the Invention That Launched the Military-Industrial Complex (Read by Souer, Bob). Audiobook Review*
BL - v112 - i5 - Nov 1 2015 - p69(1) [51-500]
LJ - v140 - i17 - Oct 15 2015 - p53(1) [51-500]
Big Science: Ernest Lawrence and the Invention that Launched the Military-Industrial Complex
BL - v111 - i18 - May 15 2015 - p8(1) [51-500]
NYTBR - July 19 2015 - p1(L) [501+]
PW - v262 - i18 - May 4 2015 - p107(1) [51-500]
KR - March 1 2015 - pNA [501+]
Himber, Guy - *Steampunk Lego: The Illustrated Researches of Various Fantastical Devices by Sir Herbert Jobson, with Epistles to the Crown, Her Majesty Queen Victoria*
c   HB Guide - v26 - i2 - Fall 2015 - p191(2) [501+]
Himmelman, John - *Noisy Bird Sing-Along (Illus. by Himmelman, John)*
c   CH Bwatch - April 2015 - pNA [51-500]
c   HB Guide - v26 - i2 - Fall 2015 - p177(1) [501+]
c   KR - Jan 1 2015 - pNA [51-500]
c   SLJ - v61 - i5 - May 2015 - p132(2) [51-500]
Tales of Bunjitsu Bunny (Illus. by Himmelman, John)
c   HB - v91 - i1 - Jan-Feb 2015 - p81(2) [51-500]
c   HB Guide - v26 - i1 - Spring 2015 - p60(1) [51-500]
Himmer, Steve - *Fram*
KR - Jan 1 2015 - pNA [501+]
Hindman, Heather - *Mediating the Global: Expatria's Forms and Consequences in Kathmandu*
HNet - March 2015 - pNA [501+]
Hinds, Gareth - *Macbeth: A Play by William Shakespeare (Illus. by Hinds, Gareth)*
y   HB - v91 - i2 - March-April 2015 - p125(2) [51-500]
y   HB Guide - v26 - i2 - Fall 2015 - p202(1) [51-500]
PW - v262 - i2 - Jan 12 2015 - p62(1) [51-500]
Hinduja, Sameer - *Bullying beyond the Schoolyard*
Bwatch - May 2015 - pNA [51-500]
Hine, David - *The Amazing Spider-Man: Edge of Spider-Verse (Illus. by Isanove, Richard)*
c   SLJ - v61 - i10 - Oct 2015 - p118(3) [501+]
Hines, Jerri - *The Belle of Charleston*
PW - v262 - i12 - March 23 2015 - p40(2) [501+]
Hinks, Peter P. - *All Men Free and Brethren: Essays on the History of African American Freemasonry*
ERS - v38 - i3 - March 2015 - p495(2) [501+]
Hinkson, Leslie - *Reproducing Race: An Ethnography of Pregnancy as a Site of Racialization*
SF - v93 - i3 - March 2015 - pe73 [501+]

Hinman, Bonnie - *Life during the Revolutionary War*
c   HB Guide - v26 - i2 - Fall 2015 - p220(1) [51-500]
Hinojosa, Felipe - *Latino Mennonites: Civil Rights, Faith, and Evangelical Culture*
AHR - v120 - i4 - Oct 2015 - p1509-1510 [501+]
CH - v84 - i2 - June 2015 - p480(3) [501+]
JAH - v101 - i4 - March 2015 - p1337-1338 [501+]
Hinsch, Bret - *Masculinities in Chinese History*
JAS - v74 - i1 - Feb 2015 - p196-197 [501+]
Hinter der Front. Der Erste Weltkrieg in Westfalen. 22. Tagung "Fragen der Regionalgeschichte"
HNet - Jan 2015 - pNA [501+]
Hinterberger, Martin - *The Language of Byzantine Learned Literature*
Med R - June 2015 - pNA [501+]
Hinton, James - *The Mass Observers: A History, 1937-1949*
JMH - v87 - i1 - March 2015 - p184(3) [501+]
Hinton, Lynne - *The Case of the Sin City Sister*
BL - v111 - i17 - May 1 2015 - p24(1) [51-500]
LJ - v140 - i6 - April 1 2015 - p66(4) [501+]
Hinton, Marsha - *Zombie Moose of West Bath, Maine*
PW - v262 - i51 - Dec 14 2015 - p66(1) [51-500]
Hinton, Nigel - *Daredevil*
y   Sch Lib - v63 - i2 - Summer 2015 - p118(1) [51-500]
Hinz, Felix - *Mythos Kreuzzuge: Selbst- und Fremdbilder in historischen Romanen*
HNet - April 2015 - pNA [501+]
Hinze, Annika Marlen - *Turkish Berlin: Integration Policy and Urban Space*
ERS - v38 - i3 - March 2015 - p460(3) [501+]
GSR - v38 - i2 - May 2015 - p470-3 [501+]
Hinze, Christine Firer - *Glass Ceilings and Dirt Floors: Women, Work, and the Global Economy*
CC - v132 - i20 - Sept 30 2015 - p42(1) [51-500]
Hirabayashi, Gordon K. - *A Principled Stand: The Story of Hirabayashi v. United States*
PHR - v84 - i1 - Feb 2015 - p115(2) [501+]
Hirabayashi, James A. - *A Principled Stand: The Story of Hirabayashi v. United States*
RAH - v43 - i2 - June 2015 - p320-326 [501+]
Hirahara, Naomi - *Grave on Grand Avenue*
PW - v262 - i8 - Feb 23 2015 - p54(1) [51-500]
Hiranandani, Veera - *Phoebe G. Green: A Passport to Pastries! (Illus. by Dreidemy, Joelle)*
c   HB Guide - v26 - i2 - Fall 2015 - p67(1) [51-500]
Phoebe G. Green: Farm Fresh Fun
c   HB Guide - v26 - i1 - Spring 2015 - p60(1) [51-500]
Phoebe G. Green: Lunch Will Never Be the Same!
c   HB Guide - v26 - i1 - Spring 2015 - p60(1) [51-500]
Hirano, Katsuya - *The Politics of Dialogic Imagination: Power and Popular Culture in Early Modern Japan*
AHR - v120 - i1 - Feb 2015 - p219-220 [501+]
Hirata, Keiko - *Japan: The Paradox of Harmony*
Pac A - v88 - i4 - Dec 2015 - p926 [501+]
TLS - i5875 - Nov 6 2015 - p28(2) [501+]
Hird, Suzanne - *How to Manage Stress*
KR - April 1 2015 - pNA [501+]
Hiro, Dilip - *The Age of Aspiration: Power, Wealth, and Conflict in Globalizing India*
KR - August 15 2015 - pNA [501+]
The Longest August: The Unflinching Rivalry Between India and Pakistan
Econ - v414 - i8926 - Feb 21 2015 - p82(US) [501+]
KR - Jan 15 2015 - pNA [501+]
NYTBR - April 26 2015 - p23(L) [501+]
Hiroshi, Watanabe - *A History of Japanese Political Thought, 1600-1901*
JAS - v74 - i1 - Feb 2015 - p222-223 [501+]
Hirsch, Allan - *The Rainbow Dancer*
c   KR - Sept 1 2015 - pNA [501+]
Hirsch, Andrea Schicke - *Sasquatch*
y   SLJ - v61 - i9 - Sept 2015 - p165(2) [51-500]
Hirsch, Edward - *Gabriel: A Poem*
APR - v44 - i3 - May-June 2015 - p37(2) [501+]
Hirsch, Rebecca - *Our Great States Series*
c   BL - v111 - i18 - May 15 2015 - p51(1) [501+]
Hirsch, Rebecca E. - *American Alligators: Armored Roaring Reptiles*
c   SLJ - v61 - i9 - Sept 2015 - p175(1) [51-500]
Boa Constrictors: Prey-Crushing Reptiles
c   Sci & Ch - v53 - i3 - Nov 2015 - p90 [51-500]
c   SLJ - v61 - i9 - Sept 2015 - p175(1) [51-500]
Comparing Animal Traits
c   HB Guide - v26 - i2 - Fall 2015 - p179(1) [51-500]
Crystals
c   HB Guide - v26 - i1 - Spring 2015 - p151(1) [51-500]

Galapagos Tortoises: Long-Lived Giant Reptiles
   c SLJ - v61 - i9 - Sept 2015 - p175(1) [51-500]
Gray Wolves: Howling Pack Mammals
   c CH Bwatch - April 2015 - pNA [51-500]
King Cobras: Hooded Venomous Reptiles
   c SLJ - v61 - i9 - Sept 2015 - p175(1) [51-500]
Komodo Dragons: Deadly Hunting Reptiles
   c SLJ - v61 - i9 - Sept 2015 - p175(1) [51-500]
Leatherback Sea Turtles: Ancient Swimming Reptiles
   c SLJ - v61 - i9 - Sept 2015 - p175(1) [51-500]
Panther Chameleons: Color-Changing Reptiles
   c SLJ - v61 - i9 - Sept 2015 - p175(1) [51-500]
Platypuses: Web-Footed Billed Mammals
   c BL - v111 - i15 - April 1 2015 - p62(1) [51-500]
Tuataras: Dinosaur-Era Reptiles
   c SLJ - v61 - i9 - Sept 2015 - p175(1) [51-500]
What's Great about Arizona?
   c HB Guide - v26 - i2 - Fall 2015 - p220(1) [51-500]
   c SLJ - v61 - i4 - April 2015 - p116(3) [501+]
What's Great about Washington, DC?
   c HB Guide - v26 - i2 - Fall 2015 - p220(1) [51-500]
Hirsch, Robert - *Exploring Color Photography: From Film to Pixels*
   RVBW - May 2015 - pNA [51-500]
Hirschfeld, Al - *The Hirschfeld Century: Portrait of an Artist and His Age* (Illus. by Hirschfeld, Al)
   BL - v111 - i19-20 - June 1 2015 - p28(2) [51-500]
The Hirschfeld Century: Portrait of an Artist and His Age
   PW - v262 - i21 - May 25 2015 - p49(3) [51-500]
The Hirschfeld Century: Portrait of an Artist and His Age (Illus. by Hirschfeld, Al)
   NYTBR - July 26 2015 - p13(L) [501+]
   KR - May 15 2015 - pNA [51-500]
   LJ - v140 - i12 - July 1 2015 - p82(2) [51-500]
Hirschfeld, Erik - *The World's Rarest Birds*
   QRB - v90 - i1 - March 2015 - p104(2) [501+]
Hirschfeld, Heather - *The End of Satisfaction: Drama and Repentance in the Age of Shakespeare*
   Ren Q - v68 - i3 - Fall 2015 - p1144-1145 [501+]
Hirschfeld, Yair - *Track-Two Diplomacy toward an Israeli-Palestinian Solution, 1978-2014*
   HNet - Sept 2015 - pNA(NA) [501+]
Track-Two Diplomacy: Toward an Israeli-Palestinian Solution 1978-2014
   TLS - i5843 - March 27 2015 - p29(1) [501+]
Hirschfelder, Gunther - *Was der Mensch Essen Darf: Okonomischer Zwang, Okologisches Gewissen und Globale Konflikte*
   HNet - July 2015 - pNA [501+]
Hirschi, Jane S. - *Ripe for Change: Garden-Based Learning in Schools*
   LJ - v140 - i10 - June 1 2015 - p111(1) [51-500]
   Sci & Ch - v53 - i3 - Nov 2015 - p90 [501+]
Hirschiler, Konrad - *The Written Word in the Medieval Arabic Lands: A Social and Cultural History of Reading Practices.*
   Specu - v90 - i3 - July 2015 - p821-822 [501+]
Hirschl, Ran - *Comparative Matters: The Renaissance of Comparative Constitutional Law*
   HLR - v128 - i6 - April 2015 - p1894(1) [1-50]
   Law&PolBR - v25 - i3 - March 2015 - p45(5) [501+]
Hirschland, Deborah - *When Young Children Need Help: Understanding and Addressing Emotional, Behavioral, and Developmental Challenges*
   Bwatch - Oct 2015 - pNA [51-500]
Hirsh, Ananth - *Lucky Penny* (Illus. by Ota, Yuko)
   y PW - v262 - i52 - Dec 21 2015 - p158(1) [51-500]
Hirshberg, Glen - *Good Girls*
   PW - v262 - i52 - Dec 21 2015 - p136(2) [51-500]
Motherless Child
   BL - v111 - i18 - May 15 2015 - p34(1) [501+]
Hirshfield, Jane - *The Beauty*
   BL - v111 - i14 - March 15 2015 - p27(1) [501+]
   WLT - v89 - i3-4 - May-August 2015 - p120(2) [501+]
   CSM - April 27 2015 - pNA [501+]
   HR - v68 - i3 - Autumn 2015 - p481-491 [501+]
   LJ - v140 - i5 - March 15 2015 - p110(1) [501+]
   PW - v262 - i3 - Jan 19 2015 - p70(1) [501+]
Ten Windows: How Great Poems Transform the World
   LJ - v140 - i3 - Feb 15 2015 - p100(3) [51-500]
   PW - v262 - i3 - Jan 19 2015 - p70(1) [501+]
   WLT - v89 - i3-4 - May-August 2015 - p126(2) [501+]
   BL - v111 - i14 - March 15 2015 - p27(1) [501+]
   CSM - April 27 2015 - pNA [501+]
Hirshman, Linda - *Sisters in Law: How Sandra Day O'Connor and Ruth Bader Ginsburg Went to the Supreme Court and Changed the World*
   PW - v262 - i28 - July 13 2015 - p59(2) [51-500]
   BL - v112 - i1 - Sept 1 2015 - p19(2) [51-500]
   KR - August 1 2015 - pNA [51-500]
   LJ - v140 - i13 - August 1 2015 - p112(1) [501+]
   NYTBR - Sept 20 2015 - p1(L) [501+]
Hirsi Ali, Ayaan - *Heretic: Why Islam Needs a Reformation Now*
   Econ - v415 - i8934 - April 18 2015 - p74(US) [501+]
Hirst, Daisy - *The Girl with the Parrot on Her Head*
   c Sch Lib - v63 - i2 - Summer 2015 - p94(1) [51-500]
Hirt, Douglas - *Bone Digger*
   KR - Jan 15 2015 - pNA [51-500]
Hirt, Sonia - *Zoned in the USA: The Origins and Implications of American Land-Use Regulation*
   HNet - March 2015 - pNA [501+]
Hischak, Thomas S. - *The Encyclopedia of Film Composers*
   LJ - v140 - i14 - Sept 1 2015 - p142(2) [51-500]
   BL - v112 - i5 - Nov 1 2015 - p17(1) [501+]
Hislop, Susanna - *Stories in the Stars: An Atlas of Constellations*
   TimHES - i2208 - June 18 2015 - p47(1) [501+]
Hislop, Victoria - *The Sunrise*
   KR - May 1 2015 - pNA [51-500]
   BL - v111 - i18 - May 15 2015 - p25(1) [51-500]
Hissey, Jane - *Jolly Snow*
   c SLJ - v61 - i2 - Feb 2015 - p70(1) [51-500]
Histories of 1914. Debates and Use of Origins of World War One in Southeastern Europe
   HNet - Jan 2015 - pNA [501+]
Histories of American Foodways: Annual Meeting of the Historians in the DGfA
   HNet - April 2015 - pNA [501+]
Historiography and History Education in the South Slavic and Albanian Speaking Regions
   HNet - Jan 2015 - pNA [501+]
History of Heralds in Europe
   HNet - Jan 2015 - pNA [501+]
   HNet - June 2015 - pNA [501+]
Hitchcock, Alfred - *Hitchcock on Hitchcock: Selected Writings and Interviews, vol. 2*
   Lon R Bks - v37 - i11 - June 4 2015 - p19(4) [501+]
   Si & So - v25 - i5 - May 2015 - p104(1) [501+]
Hitchcock, Bonnie-Sue - *The Smell of Other People's Houses*
   y KR - Nov 15 2015 - pNA [51-500]
   y PW - v262 - i45 - Nov 9 2015 - p61(2) [51-500]
Hitchcock, Fleur - *Sunk!*
   Sch Lib - v63 - i4 - Winter 2015 - p228(1) [51-500]
Hitchcock, Shannon - *Ruby Lee and Me*
   c KR - Nov 1 2015 - pNA [51-500]
Ruby Lee & Me
   c BL - v112 - i6 - Nov 15 2015 - p55(1) [51-500]
   c SLJ - v61 - i10 - Oct 2015 - p90(1) [51-500]
Hitchens, Christopher - *And Yet ...*
   KR - Nov 15 2015 - pNA [51-500]
   Mac - v128 - i50 - Dec 21 2015 - p62(2) [501+]
   NYT - Nov 25 2015 - pC1(L) [501+]
Hites, Kati - *Winnie and Waldorf*
   c HB Guide - v26 - i2 - Fall 2015 - p12(1) [51-500]
   c KR - Jan 15 2015 - pNA [51-500]
Hitler und Humor - Geht Das? Der "Fuhrer" als Zielscheibe von Satire und Karikatur
   HNet - Jan 2015 - pNA [501+]
Hixson, Walter L. - *American Settler Colonialism: A History*
   JAH - v101 - i4 - March 2015 - p1227-1228 [501+]
Hjaj, Claire - *Ishmael's Oranges*
   WLT - v89 - i3-4 - May-August 2015 - p110(2) [501+]
Hjalmarson, Leonard - *No Home Like Place: A Christian Theology of Place*
   CC - v132 - i3 - Feb 4 2015 - p35(1) [51-500]
Hjortsberg, William - *Manana*
   PW - v262 - i13 - March 30 2015 - p57(2) [51-500]
Hlasko, Marek - *All Backs Were Turned*
   TLS - i5861 - July 31 2015 - p20(1) [51-500]
Hlawitschka, Eduard - *Die Ahnen der hochmittelalterlichen deutschen Konigen, Kaiser und ihrer Gemahlinnen: Ein kommentiertes Tafelwerk, vol. 3: 1198-1250*
   Med R - June 2015 - pNA [501+]
Ho, Jannie - *Little Bubba Looks For His Elephant*
   c KR - Jan 1 2015 - pNA [51-500]
Ho, Karen - *Liquidated: An Ethnography of Wall Street*
   CS - v44 - i4 - July 2015 - p463-469 [501+]
Hoag, Tami - *The Bitter Season*
   KR - Dec 15 2015 - pNA [501+]
   PW - v262 - i47 - Nov 23 2015 - p50(1) [51-500]
Cold Cold Heart (Read by Whelan, Julia). Audiobook Review
   LJ - v140 - i7 - April 15 2015 - p46(1) [51-500]
   PW - v262 - i12 - March 23 2015 - p70(1) [51-500]
Cold Cold Heart
   SEP - v287 - i1 - Jan-Feb 2015 - p20(1) [501+]
Hoagland, Tony - *Application for Release from the Dream: Poems*
   BL - v112 - i1 - Sept 1 2015 - p29(1) [501+]
   PW - v262 - i29 - July 20 2015 - p165(2) [51-500]
Hoang, Bethany Hanke - *The Justice Calling: Where Passion Meets Perseverance*
   PW - v262 - i51 - Dec 14 2015 - p80(1) [51-500]
Hoang, Jamie Jo - *Blue Sun, Yellow Sky*
   KR - Jan 15 2015 - pNA [501+]
   PW - v262 - i17 - April 27 2015 - p46(2) [51-500]
Hoare, Marko Attila - *The Bosnian Muslims in the Second World War: A History*
   HER - v130 - i544 - June 2015 - p784(3) [501+]
   Slav R - v74 - i1 - Spring 2015 - p168-169 [501+]
Hoban, Russell - *Ace Dragon Ltd.* (Illus. by Blake, Quentin)
   c BL - v112 - i5 - Nov 1 2015 - p64(1) [51-500]
Jim's Lion (Illus. by Deacon, Alexis)
   c CCB-B - v68 - i5 - Jan 2015 - p260(1) [51-500]
   c RVBW - June 2015 - pNA [51-500]
   c HB Guide - v26 - i2 - Fall 2015 - p67(1) [51-500]
Riddley Walker
   NS - v144 - i5282 - Oct 2 2015 - p74(2) [501+]
Hobb, Robin - *Fool's Quest*
   PW - v262 - i28 - July 13 2015 - p50(1) [51-500]
Hobbie, Holly - *Hansel & Gretel* (Illus. by Hobbie, Holly)
   c HB - v91 - i6 - Nov-Dec 2015 - p96(1) [51-500]
   c KR - July 1 2015 - pNA [51-500]
   c PW - v262 - i29 - July 20 2015 - p188(1) [51-500]
   c SLJ - v61 - i8 - August 2015 - p70(1) [51-500]
Hobbs, Allyson - *A Chosen Exile: A History of Racial Passing in America*
   ABR - v36 - i2 - Jan-Feb 2015 - p13(1) [501+]
Hobbs, Jeff - *The Short and Tragic Life of Robert Peace: A Brilliant Young Man Who Left Newark for the Ivy League*
   CrimJR - v40 - i2 - June 2015 - p237-238 [501+]
   Forbes - v196 - i6 - Nov 2 2015 - p42(1) [51-500]
Hobbs, Mitchell - *The Sociology Book: Big Ideas Simply Explained*
   BL - v112 - i2 - Sept 15 2015 - p12(1) [51-500]
Hobbs, Roger - *Vanishing Games* (Read by Weber, Jake). Audiobook Review
   LJ - v140 - i19 - Nov 15 2015 - p52(1) [51-500]
Vanishing Games
   BL - v111 - i19-20 - June 1 2015 - p58(1) [51-500]
   KR - June 1 2015 - pNA [51-500]
   PW - v262 - i21 - May 25 2015 - p34(1) [51-500]
Hobgood, Allison P. - *Passionate Playgoing in Early Modern England*
   Ren Q - v68 - i2 - Summer 2015 - p769-770 [501+]
Hoble, Randooph - *Black Citizenship and Authenticity in the Civil Rights Movement*
   CS - v44 - i2 - March 2015 - p216-218 [501+]
Hobson Faure, Laura - *Un "plan Marshall juif": La presence juive americaine en France apres la Shoah, 1944-1954*
   HNet - August 2015 - pNA [501+]
Hobson, Marian - *Satyre seconde: le neveu de Rameau*
   FS - v69 - i4 - Oct 2015 - p530-531 [501+]
Hoch, Edward D. - *The Judges of Hades: and Other Simon Ark Stories*
   MFSF - v128 - i5-6 - May-June 2015 - p258(1) [501+]
Hoch, Steven L. - *Essays in Russian Social and Economic History*
   Slav R - v74 - i3 - Fall 2015 - p687-687 [501+]
Hochkultur in der Sowjetunion und in ihren Nachfolgestaaten im 20. Jahrhundert in kulturgeschichtlicher Perspektive
   HNet - August 2015 - pNA [501+]
Hochman, Brian - *Savage Preservation: The Ethnographic Origins of Modern Media Technology*
   Afterimage - v42 - i5 - March-April 2015 - p34(1) [501+]
Hochschild, Arlie Russell - *The Managed Heart: Commercialization of Human Feeling*
   TimHES - i2211 - July 9 2015 - p45(1) [501+]

Hochstrasser, Tim - *Natural Law in Theories the Early Enlightenment*
    HT - v65 - i10 - Oct 2015 - p56(2) [501+]

Hockenberry, James - *Over Here*
    SPBW - July 2015 - pNA [51-500]

Hockensmith, Steve - *Fool Me Once*
    PW - v262 - i25 - June 22 2015 - p121(1) [51-500]

Hocker, Katherine - *The Singer in the Stream: A Story of American Dippers*
    c SLJ - v61 - i5 - May 2015 - p133(1) [51-500]

Hockett, Jeffrey D. - *A Storm over This Court: Law, Politics and Supreme Court Decision Making in Brown v. Board of Education*
    JSH - v81 - i1 - Feb 2015 - p242(2) [501+]

Hocking, Amanda - *Crystal Kingdom*
    y SLJ - v61 - i8 - August 2015 - p114(1) [51-500]
    y VOYA - v38 - i4 - Oct 2015 - p72(1) [51-500]
Frostfire
    y HB Guide - v26 - i2 - Fall 2015 - p123(1) [51-500]
    y VOYA - v37 - i6 - Feb 2015 - p77(1) [51-500]
Ice Kissed
    y BL - v111 - i15 - April 1 2015 - p35(1) [501+]
    y BL - v111 - i16 - April 15 2015 - p47(2) [51-500]
    y SLJ - v61 - i3 - March 2015 - p156(1) [51-500]

Hocking, Doug - *Massacre at Point of Rocks*
    Roundup M - v22 - i6 - August 2015 - p30(1) [501+]
Mystery of Chaco Canyon: Dan y Roque
    Roundup M - v22 - i5 - June 2015 - p38(1) [501+]
    Roundup M - v22 - i6 - August 2015 - p30(1) [501+]

Hockney, David - *Derek Roshier: Rethink/Re-entry*
    Art N - v114 - i10 - Nov 2015 - p99(1) [501+]

Hockx, Michel - *Internet Literature in China*
    TLS - i5845 - April 10 2015 - p31(1) [501+]

Hodder, Mark - *The Rise of the Automated Aristocrats*
    BL - v111 - i19-20 - June 1 2015 - p65(1) [51-500]
    KR - June 1 2015 - pNA [501+]
    PW - v262 - i20 - May 18 2015 - p67(1) [51-500]

Hodes, Martha - *Mourning Lincoln*
    AM - v212 - i14 - April 27 2015 - p30(3) [501+]
    HNet - August 2015 - pNA [501+]
    J Mil H - v79 - i3 - July 2015 - p845-846 [501+]
    KR - Jan 1 2015 - pNA [501+]
    NYTBR - Feb 8 2015 - p1(L) [501+]
    NYTBR - Feb 8 2015 - p1(L) [501+]

Hodge, Deborah - *West Coast Wild: A Nature Alphabet (Illus. by Reczuch, Karen)*
    c SLJ - v61 - i11 - Nov 2015 - p131(1) [51-500]
    c KR - July 15 2015 - pNA [51-500]
    c PW - v262 - i49 - Dec 2 2015 - p54(1) [51-500]

Hodge, Rosamund - *Crimson Bound*
    y BL - v111 - i18 - May 15 2015 - p60(1) [51-500]
    y CCB-B - v68 - i10 - June 2015 - p496(2) [51-500]
    HB Guide - v26 - i2 - Fall 2015 - p123(1) [51-500]
    y KR - Feb 15 2015 - pNA [51-500]
    y SLJ - v61 - i3 - March 2015 - p156(1) [51-500]
    y VOYA - v38 - i2 - June 2015 - p77(1) [51-500]

Hodges, Andrew - *Alan Turing: The Enigma*
    G&L Rev W - v22 - i2 - March-April 2015 - p28(4) [501+]
    G&L Rev W - v22 - i2 - March-April 2015 - p28(4) [501+]
    HNet - April 2015 - pNA [501+]
    NYRB - v62 - i2 - Feb 5 2015 - p19(3) [501+]
    NYRB - v62 - i2 - Feb 5 2015 - p19(3) [501+]

Hodges, Cheris - *I Heard a Rumor*
    PW - v262 - i42 - Oct 19 2015 - p61(1) [51-500]
Rumor Has It
    PW - v262 - i9 - March 2 2015 - p69(1) [51-500]

Hodges, Dan - *One Minute to Ten: Cameron, Miliband and Clegg: Three Men, One Ambition and the Price of Power*
    NS - v144 - i5290 - Nov 27 2015 - p52(1) [501+]

Hodges, Laura F. - *Chaucer and Array: Patterns of Costume and Fabric Rhetoric in the Canterbury Tales, Troilus and Criseyde and Other Works*
    Med R - March 2015 - pNA(NA) [501+]
    RES - v66 - i275 - June 2015 - p567-568 [501+]

Hodges, Sam - *London for Lovers: Romantic Days and Nights out in the City*
    LJ - v140 - i8 - May 1 2015 - p92(1) [51-500]

Hodgkins, Fran - *The Secret Galaxy (Illus. by Taylor, Mike)*
    c CH Bwatch - Jan 2015 - pNA [51-500]
    c HB Guide - v26 - i1 - Spring 2015 - p149(1) [51-500]

Hodgkinson, Jo - *A Big Day for Migs!*
    c HB Guide - v26 - i1 - Spring 2015 - p10(1) [51-500]

Hodgkinson, Mark - *Game, Set and Match: Secret Weapons of the World's Top Tennis Players*
    LJ - v140 - i8 - May 1 2015 - p78(2) [51-500]

Hodgkinson, Terrence - *Scupture: The James A. de Rothschild Collection at Waddesdon Manor*
    NYRB - v62 - i11 - June 25 2015 - p29(4) [501+]

Hodgkinson, Will - *The House is Full of Yogis*
    KR - April 15 2015 - pNA [501+]

Hodgman, George - *Bettyville: A Memoir (Read by Woodman, Jeff). Audiobook Review*
    LJ - v140 - i14 - Sept 1 2015 - p69(2) [51-500]
Bettyville: A Memoir
    BL - v111 - i11 - Feb 1 2015 - p5(1) [51-500]
    Econ - v415 - i8933 - April 11 2015 - p77(US) [501+]
    Ent W - i1355-1356 - March 20 2015 - p105(1) [501+]
    LJ - v140 - i10 - June 1 2015 - p120(2) [501+]
    NYTBR - June 21 2015 - p26(L) [501+]

Hodgson, Antonia - *The Last Confession of Thomas Hawkins*
    BL - v112 - i7 - Dec 1 2015 - p29(2) [501+]
    LJ - v140 - i19 - Nov 15 2015 - p77(2) [501+]

Hodgson, Godfrey - *JFK and LBJ: The Last Two Great Presidents*
    KR - April 1 2015 - pNA [501+]

Hodkin, Michelle - *The Retribution of Mara Dyer*
    y HB Guide - v26 - i1 - Spring 2015 - p109(1) [51-500]

Hodkinson, James - *Deploying Orientalism in Culture and History: From Germany to Central and Eastern Europe*
    GSR - v38 - i2 - May 2015 - p409-3 [501+]

Hodorova, Daniela - *A Kingdom of Souls*
    TLS - i5871 - Oct 9 2015 - p30(1) [501+]

Hodson, Jane - *Dialect in Film and Literature*
    TimHES - i2191 - Feb 19 2015 - p49(1) [501+]

Hoeft, Jeanne - *Practicing Care in Rural Congregations and Communities*
    Intpr - v69 - i1 - Jan 2015 - p115(2) [501+]

Hoefte, Rosemarijn - *Suriname in the Long Twentieth Century: Domination, Contestation, Globalization*
    AHR - v120 - i1 - Feb 2015 - p304-305 [501+]

Hoekstra, Misha - *The Snow Queen (Illus. by Arnoux, Lucie)*
    c Spec - v329 - i9772 - Dec 12 2015 - p77(1) [501+]

Hoena, Blake - *The 12 Labors of Hercules: A Graphic Retelling (Illus. by Haus, Estudio)*
    c HB Guide - v26 - i2 - Fall 2015 - p158(1) [51-500]
    c SLJ - v61 - i4 - April 2015 - p70(3) [501+]
Daring (Illus. by Cano, Fernando)
    c HB Guide - v26 - i1 - Spring 2015 - p80(2) [51-500]
Everything Birds of Prey
    c BL - v111 - i19-20 - June 1 2015 - p76(1) [501+]
    c HB Guide - v26 - i2 - Fall 2015 - p177(1) [51-500]
Everything Soccer
    c HB Guide - v26 - i1 - Spring 2015 - p184(1) [51-500]

Hoeres, Peter - *Aussenpolitik und Öffentlichkeit: Massenmedien, Meinungsforschung und Arkanpolitik in den deutsch-amerikanischen Beziehungen von Erhard bis Brandt*
    HNet - April 2015 - pNA [501+]

Hoey, Brian A. - *Opting for Elsewhere: Lifestyle Migration in the American Middle Class*
    Soc - v52 - i2 - April 2015 - p181(1) [501+]

Hof, Dennis - *The Art of the Pimp*
    KR - March 15 2015 - pNA [501+]

Hofberg, Caroline - *Morocco on a Plate: Breads, Entrees and Desserts with Authentic Spice*
    Bwatch - April 2015 - pNA [51-500]

Hofer, Andrew - *Christ in the Life and Teaching of Gregory of Nazianzus*
    CHR - v101 - i3 - Summer 2015 - p598(2) [501+]

Hofer, Theresia - *Bodies in Balance: The Art of Tibetan Medicine*
    MAQ - v29 - i3 - Sept 2015 - pb-11-b-13 [501+]

Hoff, Johannes - *The Analogical Turn: Rethinking Modernity with Nicholas of Cusa*
    TLS - i5843 - March 27 2015 - p30(2) [501+]

Hoffer, Peter Charles - *Clio among the Muses: Essays on History and the Humanities*
    AHR - v120 - i2 - April 2015 - p567-568 [501+]

Hoffer, Wendy Ward - *Minds on Mathematics: Using Math Workshop to Develop Deep Understanding in Grades 4-8*
    TC Math - v21 - i6 - Feb 2015 - p376(2) [501+]

Hoffman, Abraham - *Mono Lake: From Dead Sea to Environmental Treasure*
    Roundup M - v22 - i6 - August 2015 - p37(1) [501+]
    WHQ - v46 - i1 - Spring 2015 - p77-78 [501+]

Hoffman, Alice - *The Marriage of Opposites (Read by Reuben, Gloria). Audiobook Review*
    BL - v112 - i5 - Nov 1 2015 - p71(1) [51-500]
    LJ - v140 - i17 - Oct 15 2015 - p51(1) [51-500]
The Marriage of Opposites
    BL - v111 - i18 - May 15 2015 - p21(1) [51-500]
    KR - June 1 2015 - pNA [501+]
    LJ - v140 - i10 - June 1 2015 - p88(1) [51-500]
    NYTBR - August 16 2015 - p14(L) [501+]
    PW - v262 - i24 - June 15 2015 - p57(1) [51-500]
Nightbird (Read by Lamia, Jenna). Audiobook Review
    PW - v262 - i17 - April 27 2015 - p72(1) [51-500]
    c SLJ - v61 - i6 - June 2015 - p64(1) [51-500]
Nightbird
    c CCB-B - v68 - i9 - May 2015 - p450(1) [51-500]
    c HB Guide - v26 - i2 - Fall 2015 - p86(1) [51-500]
    MFSF - v128 - i5-6 - May-June 2015 - p55(3) [501+]
    BL - v111 - i9-10 - Jan 1 2015 - p103(1) [51-500]
    c HB - v91 - i3 - May-June 2015 - p110(2) [51-500]
    c KR - Jan 1 2015 - pNA [51-500]
    NYTBR - April 12 2015 - p19(L) [501+]
    c PW - v262 - i3 - Jan 19 2015 - p84(1) [51-500]
    y VOYA - v37 - i6 - Feb 2015 - p77(2) [51-500]

Hoffman, Annette - *Jerusalem as Narrative Space / Erzahlraum Jerusalem*
    Specu - v90 - i3 - July 2015 - p823-824 [501+]

Hoffman, Brian - *Naked: A Cultural History of American Nudism*
    KR - March 15 2015 - pNA [501+]
    TLS - i5868 - Sept 18 2015 - p11(2) [501+]

Hoffman, Brian B. - *Adrenaline*
    QRB - v90 - i1 - March 2015 - p108(1) [501+]

Hoffman, Bruce - *Anonymous Soldiers: The Struggle for Israel, 1917-1947*
    BL - v111 - i9-10 - Jan 1 2015 - p33(1) [51-500]
    Econ - v414 - i8930 - March 21 2015 - p74(US) [501+]
    NYRB - v62 - i14 - Sept 24 2015 - p80(4) [501+]
    NYTBR - March 1 2015 - p12(L) [501+]

Hoffman, Cara - *Be Safe I Love You*
    RVBW - May 2015 - pNA [501+]
    TLS - i5861 - July 31 2015 - p20(1) [501+]

Hoffman, David E. - *The Billion Dollar Spy: A True Story of Cold War Espionage and Betrayal (Read by Woren, Dan). Audiobook Review*
    PW - v262 - i35 - August 31 2015 - p84(1) [51-500]
The Billion Dollar Spy: A True Story of Cold War Espionage and Betrayal
    KR - April 15 2015 - pNA [501+]
    PW - v262 - i16 - April 20 2015 - p65(1) [51-500]
    BL - v121 - i21 - July 1 2015 - p10(1) [51-500]
    BooChiTr - July 25 2015 - p12(1) [501+]
    CSM - July 14 2015 - pNA [501+]
    NY - v91 - i28 - Sept 21 2015 - p105 [501+]
    NYT - July 6 2015 - pC4(L) [501+]
    LJ - v140 - i9 - May 15 2015 - p92(1) [51-500]

Hoffman, Eric - *Seth: Conversations*
    Mac - v128 - i8 - March 2 2015 - p61(2) [501+]

Hoffman, Joel M. - *The Bible Doesn't Say That*
    KR - Dec 15 2015 - pNA [501+]

Hoffman, Lars M. - *Eine unbekannte Konzilssynopse aus dem Ende des 9. Jahrhunderts*
    Specu - v90 - i3 - July 2015 - p825-826 [501+]

Hoffman, Lawrence A. - *Naming God: Avinu Malkeinu, Our Father, Our King*
    RVBW - Oct 2015 - pNA [51-500]

Hoffman, Mary - *Angel of Venice*
    c Sch Lib - v63 - i1 - Spring 2015 - p54(1) [501+]
The Great Big Green Book (Illus. by Asquith, Ros)
    c BL - v111 - i17 - May 1 2015 - p74(1) [51-500]
    c BL - v111 - i18 - May 15 2015 - p48(1) [51-500]
    c KR - Feb 1 2015 - pNA [51-500]
    c SLJ - v61 - i5 - May 2015 - p133(1) [51-500]
Welcome to the Family (Illus. by Asquith, Ros)
    c HB - v91 - i1 - Jan-Feb 2015 - p96(2) [51-500]
    c HB Guide - v26 - i1 - Spring 2015 - p136(1) [51-500]

Hoffman, Philip T. - *Why Did Europe Conquer the World?*
    PW - v262 - i17 - April 27 2015 - p61(2) [51-500]

Hoffman, Robert S. - *Goldfrank's Toxicologic Emergencies, 10th ed.*
    Bwatch - July 2015 - pNA [51-500]

Hoffman, Spencer - *The 15 Miracles of Love*
    c PW - v262 - i31 - August 3 2015 - p21(1) [51-500]

Hoffman, Valerie - *The Essentials of Ibadi Islam*
    JR - v95 - i2 - April 2015 - p276(3) [501+]

Hoffman, Warren - *The Great White Way: Race and the Broadway Musical*
    Theat J - v67 - i1 - March 2015 - p152-153 [501+]

Hoffman, William - *The Biologist's Imagination: Innovation in the Biosciences*
    BioSci - v65 - i1 - Jan 2015 - p102(3) [501+]

Hoffmann, Dieter - *Einstein's Berlin: In the Footsteps of a Genius*
    Isis - v106 - i1 - March 2015 - p211(2) [501+]

Hoffmann, Hartmut - *Schreibschulen und Buchmalerei: Handschriften und Texte des 9.-11. Jahrhunderts*
    Med R - August 2015 - pNA [501+]

Hoffmann, Ulrich - *Arbeit an der Literatur: Zur Mythizitat der Artusromane Hartmanns von Aue*
    MLR - v110 - i1 - Jan 2015 - p281-282 [501+]

Hoffmann, Yoel - *Moods*
    KR - April 1 2015 - pNA [501+]
    LJ - v140 - i10 - June 1 2015 - p92(3) [501+]
    PW - v262 - i14 - April 6 2015 - p36(1) [51-500]

Hoffrogge, Ralf - *Werner Scholem: Eine Politische Biographie*
    HNet - Jan 2015 - pNA [501+]

Hofmann, Andreas - *Methods of Molecular Analysis in the Life Sciences*
    QRB - v90 - i4 - Dec 2015 - p444(1) [501+]

Hofmann, Kerstin P. - *Die Wikinger und das Frankische Reich: Identitaten zwischen Konfrontation und Annaherung*
    HNet - July 2015 - pNA [501+]

Hofmann-Maniyar, Ariane - *Ice in the Jungle (Illus. by Hofmann-Maniyar, Ariane)*
    c KR - July 1 2015 - pNA [51-500]
    c SLJ - v61 - i9 - Sept 2015 - p122(1) [51-500]

Hofmann, Michael - *The Dream Songs*
    Atl - v315 - i2 - March 2015 - p51(3) [501+]
    NYRB - v62 - i10 - June 4 2015 - p40(4) [501+]
Where Have You Been? Selected Essays
    NS - v144 - i5275 - August 14 2015 - p38(3) [501+]
    Spec - v327 - i9738 - April 18 2015 - p41(1) [501+]
    TLS - i5850 - May 15 2015 - p25(1) [501+]
    TLS - i5854 - June 12 2015 - p10(2) [501+]
    TLS - i5854 - June 12 2015 - p12(1) [501+]
    WLT - v89 - i6 - Nov-Dec 2015 - p76(2) [501+]

Hofmann, Richie - *Second Empire*
    PW - v262 - i42 - Oct 19 2015 - p53(1) [51-500]

Hofmeyr, David - *Stone Rider (Read by Morgan, Matthew). Audiobook Review*
    y PW - v262 - i39 - Sept 28 2015 - p87(1) [51-500]
    y SLJ - v61 - i12 - Dec 2015 - p78(1) [51-500]
Stone Rider
    y KR - June 1 2015 - pNA [51-500]
    y Sch Lib - v63 - i3 - Autumn 2015 - p183(1) [51-500]
    y SLJ - v61 - i6 - June 2015 - p124(2) [51-500]
    y VOYA - v38 - i3 - August 2015 - p78(1) [51-500]

Hofstadter, Cami - *The Foreign Consuls among Us*
    KR - Sept 15 2015 - pNA [501+]

Hogan, Edward - *The Messengers*
    y KR - Feb 15 2015 - pNA [51-500]
    y SLJ - v61 - i2 - Feb 2015 - p102(1) [51-500]
    y VOYA - v38 - i1 - April 2015 - p79(2) [51-500]
    y CCB-B - v68 - i11 - July-August 2015 - p548(1) [51-500]
    y HB Guide - v26 - i2 - Fall 2015 - p123(1) [51-500]

Hogan, Linda - *Dark, Sweet: New and Selected Poems*
    WLT - v89 - i1 - Jan-Feb 2015 - p75(2) [501+]
Feminist Catholic Theological Ethics: Conversations in the World Church
    Theol St - v76 - i4 - Dec 2015 - p870(2) [501+]

Hogan, Margaret A. - *A Traveled First Lady: Writings of Louisa Catherine Adams*
    Bks & Cult - v21 - i2 - March-April 2015 - p9(2) [501+]
    RAH - v43 - i3 - Sept 2015 - p477-483 [501+]

Hogan, Mitchell - *A Crucible of Souls: Book One of the Sorcery Ascendant Sequence*
    y PW - v262 - i28 - July 13 2015 - p49(1) [51-500]
    y SLJ - v61 - i12 - Dec 2015 - p132(1) [51-500]

Hogan, Phil - *A Pleasure and a Calling (Read by Page, Michael). Audiobook Review*
    BL - v111 - i17 - May 1 2015 - p59(1) [51-500]
    LJ - v140 - i9 - May 15 2015 - p43(1) [51-500]
A Pleasure and a Calling
    NYTBR - Jan 4 2015 - p25(L) [501+]

Hogan, Shanna - *The Stranger She Loved: A Mormon Doctor, His Beautiful Wife, and an Almost Perfect Murder*
    BL - v111 - i13 - March 1 2015 - p8(1) [51-500]
    LJ - v140 - i3 - Feb 15 2015 - p116(1) [51-500]

Hogancamp, Mark - *Welcome to Marwencol*
    BL - v112 - i5 - Nov 1 2015 - p25(2) [51-500]

Hogarth, Ainslie - *The Boy Meets Girl Massacre*
    y KR - July 1 2015 - pNA [51-500]
    y PW - v262 - i28 - July 13 2015 - p68(2) [51-500]
    y SLJ - v61 - i11 - Nov 2015 - p116(1) [51-500]
    y VOYA - v38 - i4 - Oct 2015 - p72(1) [51-500]

Hogarty, Patricia - *Zip It: A Fancy Book of Fastenings (Illus. by Galloway, Fhiona)*
    TES - i5141 - April 10 2015 - p39(1) [51-500]

Hoge, Robert - *Ugly: Young Reader's Edition*
    c Magpies - v30 - i4 - Sept 2015 - p22(1) [51-500]

Hoggart, Richard - *The Uses of Literacy*
    TimHES - i2211 - July 9 2015 - p48-49 [501+]

Hoggarth, Pauline - *Bible in Mission*
    IBMR - v39 - i1 - Jan 2015 - p43(2) [501+]

Hogger, Daniel - *The Oxford Handbook of the History of International Law*
    HNet - August 2015 - pNA [501+]

Hoglund, John - *The American Imperial Gothic: Popular Culture, Empire, Violence*
    SFS - v42 - i1 - March 2015 - p176-178 [501+]

Hogselius, Per - *Red Gas: Russia and the Origins of European Energy Dependence*
    BHR - v89 - i2 - Summer 2015 - p393(4) [501+]

Hohler, Sabine - *Spaceship Earth in the Environmental Age 1960-1990*
    HNet - April 2015 - pNA [501+]

Hohn, Maria - *Over There: Living with the U.S. Military Empire from World War Two to the Present*
    JWH - v27 - i3 - Fall 2015 - p187(7) [501+]

Hohn, Nadia L. - *Malaika's Costume (Illus. by Luxbacher, Irene)*
    c KR - Dec 15 2015 - pNA [51-500]

Hoig, Stan - *Came Men on Horses: The Conquistador Expeditions of Francisco Vazquez de Coronado and Don Juan de Onate*
    HAHR - v95 - i4 - Nov 2015 - p673-675 [501+]

Hoiston, James - *Cities and Citizenship*
    J Urban H - v41 - i1 - Jan 2015 - p143-9 [501+]

Hoke, Chris - *Wanted: A Spiritual Pursuit Through Jail, Among Outlaws, and Across Borders*
    Bks & Cult - v21 - i2 - March-April 2015 - p11(2) [501+]

Hokenson, Terry - *Leif's Journey*
    y CCB-B - v68 - i8 - April 2015 - p402(2) [51-500]
    y SLJ - v61 - i5 - May 2015 - p113(1) [51-500]
    y VOYA - v37 - i6 - Feb 2015 - p57(2) [51-500]

Hoklotubbe, Sara Sue - *Sinking Suspicions*
    Roundup M - v22 - i3 - Feb 2015 - p26(1) [501+]
    Roundup M - v22 - i6 - August 2015 - p30(1) [501+]

Holabird, Katharine - *Angelina's Big City Ballet (Illus. by Craig, Helen)*
    c HB Guide - v26 - i1 - Spring 2015 - p33(1) [51-500]
Angelina's Cinderella (Illus. by Craig, Helen)
    c KR - Sept 1 2015 - pNA [501+]
    c SLJ - v61 - i11 - Nov 2015 - p82(1) [51-500]

Holahan, Cate - *Dark Turns*
    y BL - v112 - i3 - Oct 1 2015 - p25(1) [51-500]
    PW - v262 - i37 - Sept 14 2015 - p43(1) [51-500]

Holbert, John - *Telling the Whole Story: Reading and Preaching Old Testament Stories*
    Intpr - v69 - i1 - Jan 2015 - p111(2) [501+]

Holborn, Mark - *Beaton: Photographs*
    NYTBR - Dec 6 2015 - p38(L) [501+]

Holcombe, Larry - *The Presidents and UFOs: A Secret History from FDR to Obama*
    BL - v111 - i13 - March 1 2015 - p5(1) [51-500]
    PW - v262 - i2 - Jan 12 2015 - p53(1) [51-500]

Holden, Anthony J. - *le Donei des amanz*
    FS - v69 - i2 - April 2015 - p228-2 [501+]

Holden, Wendy - *Born Survivors: Three Young Mothers and Their Extraordinary Story of Courage, Defiance, and Hope*
    y BL - v111 - i19-20 - June 1 2015 - p26(2) [501+]
    LJ - v140 - i8 - May 1 2015 - p84(2) [51-500]
Haatchi & Little B: The Inspiring True Story of One Boy and His Dog
    c Sch Lib - v63 - i2 - Summer 2015 - p105(1) [51-500]

Holder, Alan - *Voices Against Silence*
    y VOYA - v37 - i6 - Feb 2015 - p58(1) [51-500]

Holder, Cindy - *Human Rights: The Hard Questions*
    Ethics - v125 - i2 - Jan 2015 - p581(6) [501+]

Holder, Nancy - *The Rules (Read by Daymond, Robbie). Audiobook Review*
    y SLJ - v61 - i10 - Oct 2015 - p54(1) [51-500]
The Rules
    y CCB-B - v69 - i1 - Sept 2015 - p28(1) [51-500]
    y HB Guide - v26 - i2 - Fall 2015 - p123(1) [51-500]
    y KR - April 15 2015 - pNA [51-500]

Holder, Sara - *Difficult Decisions: Closing and Merging Academic Libraries*
    LJ - v140 - i16 - Oct 1 2015 - p98(1) [51-500]

Holderness, Graham - *Tales from Shakespeare: Creative Collections*
    TLS - i5863 - August 14 2015 - p9(1) [501+]

Holding, Elisabeth Sanxay - *The Obstinate Murderer*
    RVBW - April 2015 - pNA [501+]
Speak of the Devil
    RVBW - April 2015 - pNA [501+]

Holding, Sarah - *SeaBEAN: The SeaBEAN Trilogy, vol. 1*
    c Sch Lib - v63 - i1 - Spring 2015 - p38(1) [51-500]
SeaRISE: The SeaBEAN Trilogy, vol. 3
    c Sch Lib - v63 - i1 - Spring 2015 - p38(1) [51-500]
SeaWAR: The SeaBEAN Trilogy, vol. 2
    c Sch Lib - v63 - i1 - Spring 2015 - p38(1) [51-500]

Holdstock, Nick - *The Casualties*
    BL - v111 - i21 - July 1 2015 - p29(1) [51-500]
China's Forgotten People
    TLS - i5867 - Sept 11 2015 - p25(1) [501+]

Holdsworth, Clare - *Family and Intimate Mobilities*
    CS - v44 - i2 - March 2015 - p289-290 [501+]

Hole, Stian - *Anna's Heaven*
    c HB Guide - v26 - i1 - Spring 2015 - p33(1) [51-500]
    c RVBW - April 2015 - pNA [501+]

Holenstein, Andre - *Mitten in Europa: Verflechtung und Abgrenzung in der Schweizer Geschichte*
    HNet - Sept 2015 - pNA [501+]

Holford, Patrick - *The Stress Cure: How to Resolve Stress, Build Resilience, and Boost Your Energy*
    PW - v262 - i24 - June 15 2015 - p80(1) [51-500]

Holgate, Steve - *Human Expansion*
    KR - April 15 2015 - pNA [501+]

Holingue, Evelyne - *Chronicles from Chateau Moines*
    c PW - v262 - i3 - Jan 19 2015 - p84(1) [51-500]

Holland, Cecelia - *Dragon Heart*
    PW - v262 - i28 - July 13 2015 - p49(1) [51-500]

Holland, Cullen Joe - *Cherokee Newspaper, 1828-1906: Tribal Voice of a People in Transition*
    Roundup M - v23 - i1 - Oct 2015 - p34(1) [501+]

Holland, James - *Battle of Britain*
    y SLJ - v61 - i11 - Nov 2015 - p107(1) [51-500]
The Rise of Germany, 1939-1941: The War in the West, vol. 1
    KR - August 15 2015 - pNA [501+]
    LJ - v140 - i15 - Sept 15 2015 - p88(1) [501+]
    PW - v262 - i34 - August 24 2015 - p70(1) [501+]
    Spec - v329 - i9765 - Oct 24 2015 - p34(2) [501+]

Holland, Janet - *Understanding Families Over Time*
    JGS - v24 - i3 - June 2015 - p370-372 [501+]

Holland, Jesse J. - *The Invisibles*
    KR - Nov 15 2015 - pNA [501+]

Holland, Julie - *Moody Bitches: The Truth about the Drugs You're Taking, the Sleep You're Missing, the Sex You're Not Having, and What's Really Making You Crazy (Read by Campbell, Cassandra). Audiobook Review*
    PW - v262 - i17 - April 27 2015 - p71(1) [51-500]
Moody Bitches: The Truth about the Drugs You're Taking, the Sleep You're Missing, the Sex You're Not Having, and What's Really Making You Crazy
    KR - Jan 1 2015 - pNA [501+]
Moody Bitches: The Truth about the Drugs, You're Taking, the Sleep You're Missing, the Sex You're Not Having, and What's Really Making You Crazy
    Soc - v52 - i5 - Oct 2015 - p499(4) [501+]

Holland, Kate - *The Novel in the Age of Disintegration: Dostoevsky and the Problem of Genre in the 1870s*
    Slav R - v74 - i1 - Spring 2015 - p208-210 [501+]

Holland, Laura - *Dare I Believe*
    Dbt - v82 - i8 - August 2015 - p81(1) [501+]

Holland, Loretta - *Fall Leaves (Illus. by MacKay, Elly)*
    c HB Guide - v26 - i1 - Spring 2015 - p33(1) [51-500]

Holland, Mary - *Animal Eyes*
    c CH Bwatch - April 2015 - pNA [51-500]
    HB Guide - v26 - i1 - Spring 2015 - p155(1) [51-500]

Holland, Max - *Leak: Why Mark Felt Became Deep Throat*
    Historian - v77 - i2 - Summer 2015 - p335(2) [501+]

Holland, Michael - *Desperate Clarity: Chronicles of Intellectual Life, 1942*
    MLR - v110 - i2 - April 2015 - p555-557 [501+]
Into Disaster: Chronicles of Intellectual Life, 1941
    MLR - v110 - i2 - April 2015 - p555-557 [501+]

Holland, Mina - *The World on a Plate: 40 Cuisines, 100 Recipes, and the Stories Behind Them*
    BL - v111 - i15 - April 1 2015 - p10(2) [51-500]
    LJ - v140 - i7 - April 15 2015 - p111(1) [51-500]
    PW - v262 - i14 - April 6 2015 - p52(1) [51-500]

The World on a Plate
    KR - April 1 2015 - pNA [501+]

Holland, Noy - *Bird*
    BL - v112 - i4 - Oct 15 2015 - p31(2) [501+]
    KR - Sept 1 2015 - pNA [501+]
    LJ - v140 - i20 - Dec 1 2015 - p93(1) [51-500]
    NYT - Nov 26 2015 - pC6(L) [501+]
    PW - v262 - i33 - August 17 2015 - p46(1) [51-500]

Holland, Tom - *Dynasty: The Rise and Fall of the House of Caesar*
    KR - Sept 15 2015 - pNA [51-500]
    NS - v144 - i5286 - Oct 30 2015 - p36(3) [501+]
    NYRB - v62 - i20 - Dec 17 2015 - p26(3) [501+]
    NYTBR - Nov 22 2015 - p1(L) [501+]
    Spec - v328 - i9759 - Sept 12 2015 - p43(1) [501+]
    TLS - i5876 - Nov 13 2015 - p21(1) [501+]

Hollandsworth, Skip - *The Midnight Assassin: Panic, Scandal, and the Hunt for America's First Serial Killer*
    PW - v262 - i51 - Dec 14 2015 - p71(1) [51-500]

Hollars, B.J. - *From the Mouths of Dogs: What Our Pets Teach Us about Life, Death, and Being Human*
    KR - July 15 2015 - pNA [51-500]

This Is Only a Test
    KR - Oct 15 2015 - pNA [51-500]

Holleman, Emily - *Cleopatra's Shadows*
    BL - v112 - i4 - Oct 15 2015 - p25(1) [51-500]
    KR - August 1 2015 - pNA [51-500]
    LJ - v140 - i13 - August 1 2015 - p80(1) [501+]
    PW - v262 - i35 - August 31 2015 - p58(1) [51-500]

Holley, Val - *25th Street Confidential: Drama, Decadence, and Dissipation along Ogden's Rowdiest Road*
    Roundup M - v22 - i6 - August 2015 - p38(1) [501+]

Holliday, Graham - *Eating Viet Nam: Dispatches from a Blue Plastic Table*
    KR - Jan 1 2015 - pNA [501+]
    LJ - v140 - i3 - Feb 15 2015 - p122(2) [51-500]
    PW - v262 - i6 - Feb 9 2015 - p60(1) [51-500]

Holliday, Thomas - *Falling Up: The Days and Nights of Carlisle Floyd: The Authorized Biography*
    Notes - v71 - i4 - June 2015 - p703(4) [501+]

Hollihan, Kerrie Logan - *In the Fields and the Trenches: The Famous and the Forgotten on the Battlefields of World War I*
    y BL - v112 - i7 - Dec 1 2015 - p39(1) [51-500]
    y KR - Nov 15 2015 - pNA [51-500]

Hollinger, David A. - *After Cloven Tongues of Fire: Protestant Liberalism in Modern American History*
    JAAR - v83 - i4 - Dec 2015 - p1165-1168 [501+]
    JR - Jan 2015 - p149(3) [501+]

Hollinghurst, Alan - *Offshore*
    Nation - v300 - i19 - May 11 2015 - p27(7) [501+]

Hollingsworth, Amy - *Runaway Radical: A Young Man's Reckless Journey to Save the World*
    Bks & Cult - v21 - i5 - Sept-Oct 2015 - p10(3) [501+]

Hollingworth, Miles - *Saint Augustine of Hippo: An Intellectual Biography*
    Bks & Cult - v21 - i3 - May-June 2015 - p11(2) [501+]

Hollis, James - *Hauntings: Dispelling the Ghosts Who Run Our Lives*
    Parabola - v40 - i2 - Summer 2015 - p112-118 [501+]

Hollis, Rachel - *Smart Girl*
    PW - v262 - i46 - Nov 16 2015 - p63(1) [51-500]

Holloway, Ernest R., III - *Andrew Melville and Humanism in Renaissance Scotland, 1545-1622*
    HER - v130 - i543 - April 2015 - p444(2) [501+]

Holloway, Jonathan Scott - *Jim Crow Wisdom: Memory and Identity in Black America since 1940*
    AHR - v120 - i2 - April 2015 - p657-658 [501+]
    JSH - v81 - i3 - August 2015 - p767(2) [501+]

Holloway, Pippa - *Living in Infamy: Felon Disenfranchisement and the History of American Citizenship*
    AHR - v120 - i2 - April 2015 - p640-641 [501+]

Holm, Chris - *The Killing Kind*
    KR - July 15 2015 - pNA [51-500]
    PW - v262 - i28 - July 13 2015 - p43(2) [51-500]

Holm, Jennifer L. - *Babymouse: Bad Babysitter (Illus. by Holm, Matthew)*
    c HB Guide - v26 - i2 - Fall 2015 - p67(1) [51-500]

Comics Squad: Lunch!
    c KR - Nov 15 2015 - pNA [51-500]
    c PW - v262 - i45 - Nov 9 2015 - p60(1) [51-500]

Comics Squad: Recess!
    c HB Guide - v26 - i1 - Spring 2015 - p187(1) [51-500]

The Fourteenth Goldfish (Read by Perna, Georgette). Audiobook Review
    c HB - v91 - i2 - March-April 2015 - p131(1) [51-500]
    c SLJ - v61 - i2 - Feb 2015 - p38(3) [501+]

The Fourteenth Goldfish
    c BL - v111 - i9-10 - Jan 1 2015 - pS4(8) [501+]
    c HB Guide - v26 - i2 - Fall 2015 - p86(1) [51-500]

Sunny Side Up (Illus. by Holm, Matthew)
    c HB - v91 - i5 - Sept-Oct 2015 - p106(1) [51-500]
    c KR - July 1 2015 - pNA [51-500]
    c SLJ - v61 - i8 - August 2015 - p95(1) [51-500]
    c PW - v262 - i22 - June 1 2015 - p62(1) [51-500]

Holm, Matthew - *Sunny Side Up (Illus. by Holm, Matthew)*
    c CCB-B - v69 - i2 - Oct 2015 - p92(2) [51-500]
    c BL - v111 - i22 - August 1 2015 - p49(1) [51-500]

Holm, Tom - *Anadarko: A Kiowa Country Mystery*
    KR - August 15 2015 - pNA [51-500]
    PW - v262 - i34 - August 24 2015 - p62(1) [51-500]

Holman, Will - *Guerilla Furniture Design: How to Build Lean, Modern Furniture with Salvaged Materials*
    LJ - v140 - i7 - April 15 2015 - p89(1) [51-500]

Holmberg, Charlie N - *The Paper Magician. Audiobook Review*
    y SLJ - v61 - i2 - Feb 2015 - p51(2) [51-500]

Holmberg, Eva Johanna - *Jews in the Early Modern English Imagination: A Scattered Nation*
    HNet - August 2015 - pNA [501+]

Holmene Pelaez, Annelie - *Si Ja, Say Yes to Better Life and Death: An Introduction to Health Literacy and Meditation*
    KR - Nov 1 2015 - pNA [51-500]

Holmes, Amy Austin - *Social Unrest and American Military Bases in Turkey and Germany since 1945*
    HNet - Oct 2015 - pNA [501+]

Holmes, David L. - *The Faiths of the Postwar Presidents: From Truman to Obama*
    Pres St Q - v45 - i1 - March 2015 - p211(2) [501+]
    JAH - v101 - i4 - March 2015 - p1322-1323 [501+]

Holmes, Denzel - *Concho*
    Roundup M - v22 - i6 - August 2015 - p30(1) [501+]

Holmes-Eber, Paula - *Culture in Conflict: Irregular Warfare, Culture Policy, and the Marine Corps*
    Parameters - v45 - i2 - Summer 2015 - p141(3) [501+]

Holmes, Jamie - *Nonsense: The Power of Not Knowing*
    BL - v112 - i1 - Sept 1 2015 - p16(1) [51-500]
    KR - August 1 2015 - pNA [51-500]
    LJ - v140 - i14 - Sept 1 2015 - p124(2) [51-500]

Holmes, Kathryn - *The Distance between Lost and Found*
    y BL - v111 - i9-10 - Jan 1 2015 - p88(1) [51-500]
    y CCB-B - v68 - i7 - March 2015 - p357(1) [51-500]
    y HB Guide - v26 - i2 - Fall 2015 - p123(1) [51-500]

Holmes, Kent - *Wendell Fertig and His Guerrilla Forces in the Philippines: Fighting the Japanese Occupation, 1942-1945*
    HNet - Sept 2015 - pNA [501+]

Holmes, Lauren - *Barbara the Slut and Other People*
    KR - June 1 2015 - pNA [51-500]
    NYTBR - August 2 2015 - p12(L) [501+]
    PW - v262 - i15 - April 13 2015 - p1(1) [51-500]
    Esq - v163 - i6-7 - June-July 2015 - p26(2) [501+]
    BL - v111 - i21 - July 1 2015 - p27(1) [51-500]
    Ent W - i1376 - August 14 2015 - p60(2) [51-500]

Holmes, Leslie - *Corruption: A Very Short Introduction*
    NS - v144 - i5265 - June 5 2015 - p44(2) [501+]

Holmes, Rachel - *Eleanor Marx: A Life*
    NYRB - v62 - i12 - July 9 2015 - p63(3) [501+]
    NYTBR - April 5 2015 - p20(L) [501+]
    Wom R Bks - v32 - i6 - Nov-Dec 2015 - p8(3) [501+]

Holmes, Seth M. - *Fresh Fruit, Broken Bodies: Migrant Farmworkers in the United States*
    CS - v44 - i4 - July 2015 - p517-519 [501+]
    MAQ - v29 - i2 - June 2015 - pb13-b16 [501+]

Holmqvist, Caroline - *Policing Wars: On Military Intervention in the Twenty-First Century*
    J Mil H - v79 - i2 - April 2015 - p552-553 [501+]

Holms, Garret - *Grant of Immunity*
    KR - April 1 2015 - pNA [51-500]
    PW - v262 - i13 - March 30 2015 - p58(1) [51-500]

Holmwood, Anna - *A Perfect Crime*
    LJ - v140 - i9 - May 15 2015 - p68(1) [51-500]

The Holocaust and European Societies. Social Processes and Social Dynamics
    HNet - Jan 2015 - pNA [501+]

The Holocaust in Greece: Genocide and Its Aftermath
    HNet - Jan 2015 - pNA [501+]

Holohan, Amanda - *Unwanted*
    y Magpies - v30 - i2 - May 2015 - p41(1) [501+]

Holsinger, Bruce - *The Invention of Fire*
    BL - v111 - i14 - March 15 2015 - p46(1) [51-500]
    KR - Feb 15 2015 - pNA [51-500]
    PW - v262 - i8 - Feb 23 2015 - p53(1) [51-500]

Holt, Anne - *The Lion's Mouth*
    PW - v262 - i51 - Dec 14 2015 - p59(1) [51-500]

Holt, Christopher - *Journey's End (Illus. by Allen, Douglas)*
    c HB Guide - v26 - i1 - Spring 2015 - p81(1) [51-500]

Holt, Frank L. - *Lost World of the Golden King: In Search of Ancient Afghanistan*
    Historian - v77 - i1 - Spring 2015 - p103(2) [501+]

Holt, Jonathan - *The Absolution*
    BL - v112 - i7 - Dec 1 2015 - p26(1) [51-500]
    PW - v262 - i42 - Oct 19 2015 - p57(1) [51-500]
    KR - Oct 1 2015 - pNA [51-500]
    LJ - v140 - i14 - Sept 1 2015 - p92(2) [51-500]

Holt, K.A. - *House Arrest*
    c BL - v112 - i1 - Sept 1 2015 - p116(2) [51-500]
    c KR - August 1 2015 - pNA [51-500]
    c PW - v262 - i31 - August 3 2015 - p60(2) [51-500]
    c SLJ - v61 - i7 - July 2015 - p86(2) [51-500]

Rhyme Schemer
    c HB Guide - v26 - i1 - Spring 2015 - p81(1) [51-500]

Holt, Kimberly Willis - *Dear Hank Williams*
    c BL - v111 - i16 - April 15 2015 - p59(1) [51-500]
    c CCB-B - v68 - i11 - July-August 2015 - p549(1) [51-500]
    c HB - v91 - i3 - May-June 2015 - p111(2) [501+]
    c HB Guide - v26 - i2 - Fall 2015 - p87(1) [51-500]
    c KR - Feb 15 2015 - pNA [51-500]
    c PW - v262 - i8 - Feb 23 2015 - p75(2) [51-500]
    c VOYA - v38 - i1 - April 2015 - p62(1) [51-500]

Part of Me
    c Teach Lib - v42 - i5 - June 2015 - p47(1) [51-500]

Holt, Maria - *Women in Conflict in the Middle East: Palestinian Refugees and the Response to Violence*
    IJMES - v47 - i2 - May 2015 - p407-409 [501+]

Women, Islam, and Resistance in the Arab World
    IJMES - v47 - i1 - Feb 2015 - p193-194 [501+]

Holt, Marilyn Irvin - *Cold War Kids: Politics and Childhood in Postwar America, 1945-1960*
    AHR - v120 - i3 - June 2015 - p1058-1059 [501+]

Holt, Terrence - *Internal Medicine*
    NY - v91 - i2 - Feb 23 2015 - p179 [51-500]

Holt, Timmothy J. - *Square Affair*
    SPBW - April 2015 - pNA [51-500]

Holt, Tom - *The Good, the Bad and the Smug*
    PW - v262 - i21 - May 25 2015 - p40(1) [51-500]

Holton, John - *ABCDEEG*
    KR - May 15 2015 - pNA [51-500]

Holtz, Thomas R., Jr. - *Digging for Stegosaurus: A Discovery Timeline*
    c HB Guide - v26 - i2 - Fall 2015 - p168(1) [51-500]

Digging for Tyrannosaurus Rex: A Discovery Timeline
    c HB Guide - v26 - i2 - Fall 2015 - p168(1) [51-500]

Digging for Tyrannosaurus Rex: A Discovery Timeline (Illus. by Skrepnick, Michael)
    c BL - v111 - i15 - April 1 2015 - p60(1) [51-500]

Holub, Joan - *Aphrodite the Fair*
    c HB Guide - v26 - i2 - Fall 2015 - p87(1) [51-500]

Ares and the Spear of Fear (Illus. by Phillips, Craig)
    c HB Guide - v26 - i1 - Spring 2015 - p60(2) [51-500]

Athena the Proud
    y HB Guide - v26 - i1 - Spring 2015 - p81(1) [51-500]

Be Careful, Icarus! (Illus. by Patricelli, Leslie)
    c PW - v262 - i31 - August 3 2015 - p58(2) [501+]

Be Patient, Pandora! (Illus. by Patricelli, Leslie)
    c KR - Jan 1 2015 - pNA [51-500]

Brush Your Hair, Medusa! (Illus. by Patricelli, Leslie)
    c KR - July 1 2015 - pNA [51-500]

Cronus and the Threads of Dread (Illus. by Phillips, Craig)
    c HB Guide - v26 - i2 - Fall 2015 - p67(1) [51-500]

Iris the Colorful
    y HB Guide - v26 - i1 - Spring 2015 - p81(1) [51-500]

Itty Bitty Kitty and the Rainy Play Day (Illus. by Burks, James)
   c KR - Dec 15 2015 - pNA [51-500]
Itty Bitty Kitty (Illus. by Burks, James)
   c HB Guide - v26 - i2 - Fall 2015 - p37(1) [51-500]
      KR - Feb 1 2015 - pNA [51-500]
The Knights Before Christmas (Illus. by Magoon, Scott)
   c HB - v91 - i6 - Nov-Dec 2015 - p56(1) [51-500]
   c KR - Sept 1 2015 - pNA [51-500]
   c PW - v262 - i37 - Sept 14 2015 - p76(1) [51-500]
   c SLJ - v61 - i10 - Oct 2015 - p64(1) [51-500]
Make a Wish, Midas! (Illus. by Patricelli, Leslie)
   c KR - July 1 2015 - pNA [51-500]
Please Share, Aphrodite!
   c KR - Jan 1 2016 - pNA [51-500]
Trojans! The Story of the Trojan Horse (Illus. by Jones, Dani)
   c HB Guide - v26 - i2 - Fall 2015 - p159(1) [51-500]
Holzer, Anton - *Rasende Reporter: Eine Kulturgeschichte des Fotojournalismus. Fotografie, Presse und Gesellschaft in Osterreich 1890 bis 1945*
      HNet - May 2015 - pNA [501+]
Holzer, Elizabeth - *The Concerned Women of Buduburam*
      Dis - v62 - i4 - Fall 2015 - p83(1) [501+]
Holzer, Harold - *The Civil War in 50 Objects*
      LJ - v140 - i9 - May 15 2015 - p94(2) [501+]
Exploring Lincoln: Great Historians Reappraise Our Greatest President
      KR - Jan 15 2015 - pNA [501+]
A Just and Generous Nation: Abraham Lincoln and the Fight for American Opportunity
      KR - Sept 1 2015 - pNA [501+]
      LJ - v140 - i14 - Sept 1 2015 - p120(2) [501+]
      CSM - Dec 30 2015 - pNA [501+]
      NYTBR - Dec 20 2015 - p17(L) [501+]
      PW - v262 - i35 - August 31 2015 - p74(1) [51-500]
Lincoln and the Power of the Press: The War for Public Opinion
      NYTBR - Nov 29 2015 - p24(L) [501+]
President Lincoln Assassinated! The Firsthand Story of the Murder, Manhunt, Trial and Mourning
      TLS - i5858 - July 10 2015 - p24(2) [501+]
Homann, Joachim - *Night Vision: Nocturnes In American Art, 1860-1960*
      LJ - v140 - i17 - Oct 15 2015 - p85(1) [51-500]
Homans, Margaret - *The Imprint of Another Life: Adoption Narratives and Human Possibility*
      VS - v57 - i3 - Spring 2015 - p567(3) [501+]
Home Alone: The Classic Illustrated Storybook (Illus. by Smith, Kim)
   c PW - v262 - i37 - Sept 14 2015 - p70(1) [51-500]
Homel, David - *Adrian and the Tree of Secrets (Illus. by Caillou, Marie)*
   y CCB-B - v68 - i6 - Feb 2015 - p315(1) [51-500]
Homer - *The Iliad*
      TLS - i5858 - July 10 2015 - p22(1) [501+]
Homer, Michael W. - *Joseph's Temples: The Dynamic Relationship between Freemasonry and Mormonism*
      AHR - v120 - i3 - June 2015 - p1009-1010 [501+]
Hommels, Anique - *Vulnerability in Technological Cultures: New Directions in Research and Governance*
      T&C - v56 - i2 - April 2015 - p575-576 [501+]
Homza, Kenneth M. - *Your Cash Is Flowing: Why Every Entrepreneur Needs to Think Like a CFO*
      KR - August 1 2015 - pNA [501+]
Hondorp, Paul - *Choral Error Detection: Exercises for Developing Musicianship*
      Teach Mus - v23 - i2 - Oct 2015 - p52(1) [51-500]
Honeck, Mischa - *Germany and the Black Diaspora: Points of Contact, 1250-1914*
      GSR - v38 - i1 - Feb 2015 - p153-155 [501+]
Honey, David B. - *The Southern Garden Poetry Society: Literary Culture and Social Memory in Guangdong*
      AHR - v120 - i2 - April 2015 - p593-594 [501+]
Honey, Elizabeth - *Hop Up! Wriggle Over! (Illus. by Honey, Elizabeth)*
   c Magpies - v30 - i3 - July 2015 - p26(1) [51-500]
Honey, Michael K. - *Sharecropper's Troubadour: John L. Handcox, the Southern Tenant Farmers' Union, and the African American Song Tradition*
      JAH - v101 - i4 - March 2015 - p1311-1312 [501+]
      JSH - v81 - i4 - Nov 2015 - p1024(2) [51-500]
Honeycutt, Kirk - *John Hughes: A Life in Film: The Genius behind Ferris Bueller, The Breakfast Club, Home Alone, and More*
      LJ - v140 - i6 - April 1 2015 - p95(2) [51-500]
Hong, Deuki - *Koreatown*
      PW - v262 - i46 - Nov 16 2015 - p68(1) [501+]
Hong Fincher, Leta - *Leftover Women*
      CSM - Dec 23 2015 - pNA [501+]

Hong, Yinxing - *The China Path to Economic Transition and Development*
      Pac A - v88 - i3 - Sept 2015 - p688 [501+]
Honig, Bonnie - *Antigone, Interrupted*
      AJP - v136 - i1 - Spring 2015 - p158-162 [501+]
Honigstein, Raphael - *Das Reboot: How German Soccer Reinvented Itself and Conquered the World*
      BL - v112 - i3 - Oct 1 2015 - p10(1) [501+]
      LJ - v140 - i17 - Oct 15 2015 - p94(1) [51-500]
Honkasalo, Marja-Liisa - *Culture, Suicide, and the Human Condition*
      MAQ - v29 - i2 - June 2015 - pb4-b6 [501+]
Honnold, Alex - *Alone on the Wall*
      Atl - v316 - i4 - Nov 2015 - p48(3) [501+]
      BL - v112 - i1 - Sept 1 2015 - p32(1) [51-500]
      KR - Sept 15 2015 - pNA [501+]
      LJ - v140 - i14 - Sept 1 2015 - p111(1) [51-500]
Honovich, Nancy - *National Geographic Kids Guide to Photography: Tips and Tricks on How to Be a Great Photographer from the Pros and Your Pals at My Shot*
   y SLJ - v61 - i9 - Sept 2015 - p186(1) [51-500]
Hood, Ann - *Knitting Pearls: Writers Writing about Knitting*
      KR - Sept 1 2015 - pNA [51-500]
      PW - v262 - i33 - August 17 2015 - p60(1) [51-500]
Providence Noir
      PW - v262 - i16 - April 20 2015 - p56(2) [51-500]
Hood-Caddy, Karen - *Saving Crazy*
   c BL - v111 - i17 - May 1 2015 - p100(1) [51-500]
      Nat Post - v17 - i210 - July 11 2015 - pWP5(1) [501+]
   c Res Links - v21 - i1 - Oct 2015 - p14(1) [501+]
   c SLJ - v61 - i6 - June 2015 - p108(1) [51-500]
Hood, Gwyneth - *Book in Honor of Augustus*
      Med R - April 2015 - pNA [501+]
Hood, Joshua - *Clear by Fire*
      KR - June 15 2015 - pNA [501+]
      PW - v262 - i26 - June 29 2015 - p45(1) [51-500]
Hood, Susan - *Leaps and Bounce (Illus. by Cordell, Matthew)*
   c KR - Jan 1 2016 - pNA [51-500]
Mission: New Baby: Top-Secret Info for Big Brothers and Sisters (Illus. by Lundquist, Mary)
   c HB Guide - v26 - i2 - Fall 2015 - p37(1) [51-500]
Pup and Hound's Big Book of Stories (Illus. by Hendry, Linda)
   c HB Guide - v26 - i1 - Spring 2015 - p53(2) [51-500]
Tickly Toes
   c Res Links - v20 - i3 - Feb 2015 - p4(1) [51-500]
Hoof, Florian - *Engel der Effizienz: Eine Mediengeschichte der Unternehmensberatung*
      HNet - Sept 2015 - pNA [501+]
Hoogstad, Alice - *Monster Book*
   c HB Guide - v26 - i1 - Spring 2015 - p10(1) [51-500]
Hooker Jr., Gary - *Gary Sees History: A Child's Journey*
      KR - Feb 1 2015 - pNA [501+]
Hooker, Lynn M. - *Redefining Hungarian Music from Liszt to Bartok*
      Slav R - v74 - i1 - Spring 2015 - p178-179 [501+]
Hooker, Richard - *Of the Laws of Ecclesiastical Polity: A Critical Edition with Modern Spelling*
      Ren Q - v68 - i1 - Spring 2015 - p354-355 [501+]
Hooks, Bell - *Yearning: Race, Gender and Cultural Politics*
      TimHES - i2211 - July 9 2015 - p50(1) [501+]
Hooland, Seth van - *Review of Linked Data for Libraries, Archives and Museums: How to Clean, Link and Publish Your Metadata*
      LR - v64 - i1-2 - Jan-Feb 2015 - p185-186 [501+]
Ho'omanawanui, Ku'ualoha - *Voices of Fire: Reweaving the Literary Lei of Pele and Hi'iaka*
      TLS - i5877 - Nov 20 2015 - p27(1) [501+]
Hooper, Emma - *Etta and Otto and Russell and James*
      Mac - v128 - i3 - Jan 26 2015 - p56(2) [501+]
      Nat Post - v17 - i68 - Jan 17 2015 - pWP10(1) [501+]
      NY - v91 - i3 - March 9 2015 - p95 [501+]
      NYTBR - Feb 8 2015 - p30(L) [501+]
Hooper, John - *The Italians*
      BL - v111 - i9-10 - Jan 1 2015 - p34(1) [51-500]
      HT - v65 - i4 - April 2015 - p64(1) [501+]
      Mac - v128 - i8 - March 2 2015 - p60(1) [501+]
      NYTBR - March 1 2015 - p15(L) [501+]
      Spec - v327 - i9728 - Feb 7 2015 - p45(2) [501+]
      TLS - i5837 - Feb 13 2015 - p30(1) [501+]
Hooper, Judith - *Alice in Bed*
      BL - v112 - i4 - Oct 15 2015 - p30(1) [51-500]
      NYTBR - Nov 22 2015 - p38(L) [501+]
      PW - v262 - i38 - Sept 21 2015 - p49(1) [51-500]

Hooper, Lisa - *Keeping Time: An Introduction to Archival Best Practices for Music Librarians*
      Notes - v71 - i4 - June 2015 - p674(3) [501+]
Hooper, Mary - *Poppy in the Field*
   y Magpies - v30 - i3 - July 2015 - p41(2) [501+]
Hooper, Meredith - *River Story (Illus. by Willey, Bee)*
      Magpies - v30 - i2 - May 2015 - p32(1) [501+]
Hooper, Michael S.D. - *Sexual Politics in the Work of Tennessee Williams: Desire Over Protest*
      Theat J - v67 - i1 - March 2015 - p153-154 [501+]
Hoopmann, Kathy - *Blue Bottle Mystery*
   c KR - Oct 15 2015 - pNA [51-500]
Hoose, Phillip - *The Boys Who Challenged Hitler: Knud Pedersen and the Churchill Club (Read by Hoose, Phillip). Audiobook Review*
   y HB - v91 - i6 - Nov-Dec 2015 - p109(1) [51-500]
The Boys Who Challenged Hitler: Knud Pedersen and the Churchill Club (Read by Braun, Michael). Audiobook Review
   y SLJ - v61 - i9 - Sept 2015 - p61(1) [51-500]
The Boys Who Challenged Hitler: Knud Pedersen and the Churchill Club
   y BL - v111 - i19-20 - June 1 2015 - p86(2) [501+]
   y BL - v111 - i16 - April 15 2015 - p42(1) [51-500]
   y CCB-B - v68 - i11 - July-August 2015 - p549(2) [51-500]
   y HB - v91 - i4 - July-August 2015 - p156(2) [51-500]
   y NYTBR - Sept 13 2015 - p22(L) [501+]
      PW - v262 - i11 - March 16 2015 - p86(2) [51-500]
   y PW - v262 - i49 - Dec 2 2015 - p116(1) [51-500]
   y VOYA - v38 - i2 - June 2015 - p87(2) [51-500]
The Churchill Club: Knud Pedersen and the Boys Who Challenged Hitler
   y SLJ - v61 - i5 - May 2015 - p138(2) [51-500]
Hoover, Colleen - *November 9*
      LJ - v140 - i19 - Nov 15 2015 - p77(1) [51-500]
Hoover, Laurie - *Trash*
      KR - July 1 2015 - pNA [501+]
Hoover, Michelle - *Bottomland*
      KR - Jan 1 2016 - pNA [51-500]
      LJ - v140 - i20 - Dec 1 2015 - p93(1) [51-500]
Hoover, P.J. - *Tut: The Story of My Immortal Life*
   y CH Bwatch - Jan 2015 - pNA [51-500]
   y HB Guide - v26 - i1 - Spring 2015 - p81(1) [51-500]
Hoover, Sunny - *Santa's Secret (Illus. by Hoover, Sunny)*
   c CH Bwatch - Jan 2015 - pNA [51-500]
Hooyman, Kevin - *Conditions on the Ground*
      BL - v112 - i6 - Nov 15 2015 - p34(1) [51-500]
Hope, Christopher - *Jimfish*
      Spec - v328 - i9742 - May 16 2015 - p46(2) [501+]
Hope, Jessamyn - *Safekeeping*
      BL - v111 - i19-20 - June 1 2015 - p45(1) [51-500]
      KR - April 1 2015 - pNA [501+]
      LJ - v140 - i6 - April 1 2015 - p81(1) [51-500]
Hope, John - *Frozen Floppies (Illus. by Adams, Mark Wayne)*
   c CH Bwatch - Jan 2015 - pNA [51-500]
Hope, Lee - *Horsefever*
      KR - Dec 1 2015 - pNA [501+]
      PW - v262 - i48 - Nov 30 2015 - p42(1) [51-500]
Hopgood, Tim - *Hooray for Hoppy!*
   c HB Guide - v26 - i2 - Fall 2015 - p12(1) [51-500]
   c Teach Lib - v42 - i4 - April 2015 - p32(1) [51-500]
Hopkin, David - *Voices of the People in Nineteenth-Century France*
      HER - v130 - i542 - Feb 2015 - p227(2) [501+]
Hopkins, Benjamin D. - *Beyond SWAT: History, Society and Economy along the Afghanistan-Pakistan Frontier*
      JRAI - v21 - i2 - June 2015 - p494(2) [501+]
Hopkins, Cathy - *A Home for Shimmer*
   c Sch Lib - v63 - i2 - Summer 2015 - p105(1) [51-500]
Hopkins, Ellen - *Love Lies Beneath*
   y BL - v111 - i21 - July 1 2015 - p32(1) [51-500]
      KR - May 15 2015 - pNA [51-500]
   y LJ - v140 - i11 - June 15 2015 - p77(1) [51-500]
   y SLJ - v61 - i11 - Nov 2015 - p126(2) [51-500]
Rumble (Read by Heyborne, Kirby). Audiobook Review
      PW - v262 - i5 - Feb 2 2015 - p56(2) [51-500]
      SLJ - v61 - i3 - March 2015 - p80(1) [51-500]
Rumble
   y HB Guide - v26 - i1 - Spring 2015 - p109(1) [51-500]
Traffick
   y BL - v111 - i22 - August 1 2015 - p60(1) [51-500]
   y KR - Sept 1 2015 - pNA [51-500]
   y SLJ - v61 - i9 - Sept 2015 - p166(1) [51-500]

Hopkins, John - *The White Nile Diaries*
    TLS - i5838 - Feb 20 2015 - p27(1) [501+]
Hopkins, Karen Ann - *Embers*
    KR - Feb 15 2015 - pNA [501+]
Hopkins, Lee Bennett - *Amazing Places (Illus. by Hale, Christy)*
    c KR - Sept 1 2015 - pNA [51-500]
Amazing Places (Illus. by Soentpiet, Chris)
    c CH Bwatch - Nov 2015 - pNA [51-500]
    c PW - v262 - i38 - Sept 21 2015 - p75(1) [501+]
    c PW - v262 - i49 - Dec 2 2015 - p54(1) [51-500]
    c SLJ - v61 - i10 - Oct 2015 - p126(1) [51-500]
Jumping Off Library Shelves: A Book of Poems (Illus. by Manning, Jane)
    c BL - v112 - i5 - Nov 1 2015 - p42(1) [51-500]
    c CH Bwatch - Oct 2015 - pNA [51-500]
    c KR - July 15 2015 - pNA [51-500]
    c PW - v262 - i38 - Sept 21 2015 - p75(1) [501+]
Lullaby and Kisses Sweet: Poems to Love With Your Baby (Illus. by Nassner, Alyssa)
    c KR - July 1 2015 - pNA [51-500]
Lullaby and Kisses Sweet: Poems to Love with Your Baby
    c PW - v262 - i6 - Feb 9 2015 - p66(2) [501+]
Manger (Illus. by Cann, Helen)
    c HB Guide - v26 - i1 - Spring 2015 - p188(1) [51-500]
Hopkins, Lisa - *Renaissance Drama on the Edge*
    Six Ct J - v46 - i2 - Summer 2015 - p426-428 [501+]
Hopkinson, Deborah - *Beatrix Potter and the Unfortunate Tale of a Borrowed Guinea Pig (Illus. by Voake, Charlotte)*
    c KR - Nov 15 2015 - pNA [51-500]
    c PW - v262 - i48 - Nov 30 2015 - p57(1) [51-500]
Courage and Defiance: Stories of Spies, Saboteurs, and Survivors in World War II Denmark
    y SLJ - v61 - i7 - July 2015 - p107(2) [51-500]
    y BL - v111 - i21 - July 1 2015 - p49(1) [51-500]
    y CCB-B - v69 - i2 - Oct 2015 - p93(1) [51-500]
    y HB - v91 - i6 - Nov-Dec 2015 - p102(2) [51-500]
    y KR - June 15 2015 - pNA [51-500]
    y VOYA - v38 - i4 - Oct 2015 - p82(2) [51-500]
Hopkinson, Nalo - *Falling in Love with Hominids*
    PW - v262 - i28 - July 13 2015 - p49(2) [501+]
Hopler, Jay - *Before the Door of God: An Anthology of Devotional Poetry*
    Ken R - v37 - i5 - Sept-Oct 2015 - p94(14) [501+]
Hopper, Jessica - *The First Collection of Criticism by a Living Female Rock Critic*
    Nat Post - v17 - i176 - May 30 2015 - pWP5(1) [501+]
    NYT - June 18 2015 - pC1(L) [501+]
    LJ - v140 - i8 - May 1 2015 - p76(1) [51-500]
Hopwood, Jennifer L. - *Best STEM Resources for Nextgen Scientists: The Essential Selection and User's Guide*
    Teach Lib - v43 - i1 - Oct 2015 - p41(3) [501+]
Hopwood, Nick - *Haeckel's Embryos: Images, Evolution, and Fraud*
    Nature - v517 - i7533 - Jan 8 2015 - p143(1) [51-500]
    New Sci - v225 - i3004 - Jan 17 2015 - p41(1) [501+]
Hoque, Aminul - *British-Islamic Identity: Third-Generation Bangladeshis from East London*
    TimHES - i2205 - May 28 2015 - p50-1 [501+]
Horacek, Petr - *The Fly (Illus. by Horacek, Petr)*
    c CCB-B - v68 - i11 - July-August 2015 - p550(1) [51-500]
    c HB Guide - v26 - i2 - Fall 2015 - p37(1) [51-500]
    c KR - March 15 2015 - pNA [51-500]
    c PW - v262 - i10 - March 9 2015 - p70(1) [51-500]
    c SLJ - v61 - i6 - June 2015 - p84(1) [51-500]
The Mouse Who Ate the Moon
    c HB Guide - v26 - i1 - Spring 2015 - p10(1) [51-500]
    c Sch Lib - v63 - i1 - Spring 2015 - p28(1) [51-500]
A Surprise for Tiny Mouse (Illus. by Horacek, Petr)
    c BL - v112 - i6 - Nov 15 2015 - p57(1) [51-500]
    c KR - Jan 1 2016 - pNA [51-500]
    c PW - v262 - i31 - August 3 2015 - p58(2) [501+]
    c SLJ - v61 - i7 - July 2015 - p55(1) [51-500]
Horack, Skip - *The Other Joseph*
    BL - v111 - i13 - March 1 2015 - p21(1) [51-500]
    KR - Feb 15 2015 - pNA [51-500]
Horak, Laura - *Girls Will Be Boys: Cross-Dressed Women, Lesbians, and American Cinema, 1908-1934*
    PW - v262 - i51 - Dec 14 2015 - p74(1) [51-500]
Horan, Daniel P. - *The Franciscan Heart of Thomas Merton: A New Look at the Spiritual Inspiration of His Life, Thought, and Writing*
    AM - v212 - i18 - May 25 2015 - p31(3) [501+]

Horbury, William - *Jewish War under Trajan and Hadrian*
    TLS - i5844 - April 3 2015 - p24(1) [501+]
Hord, Colleen - *From Farm to Restaurant (Illus. by Hord, Colleen)*
    c CH Bwatch - June 2015 - pNA [51-500]
Horden, Peregrine - *A Companion to Mediterranean History*
    HNet - March 2015 - pNA [501+]
Horesh, Niv - *Chinese Money in Global Context: Historic Junctures between 600 BCE and 2012*
    JAS - v74 - i2 - May 2015 - p463-466 [501+]
    Pac A - v88 - i1 - March 2015 - p169 [501+]
Horikoshi, Kohei - *My Hero Academia (Illus. by Horikoshi, Kohei)*
    y SLJ - v61 - i11 - Nov 2015 - p124(2) [51-500]
Horky, Phillip Sydney - *Plato and Pythagoreanism*
    AJP - v136 - i2 - Summer 2015 - p353-356 [501+]
Horler, Sydney - *The Traitor*
    PW - v262 - i39 - Sept 28 2015 - p70(2) [51-500]
Horlyck, Charlotte - *Death, Mourning, and the Afterlife in Korea: From Ancient to Contemporary Times*
    JAS - v74 - i2 - May 2015 - p494-496 [501+]
Horn, Bernd - *Of Courage and Determination: The First Special Service Force, "The Devil's Brigade," 1942-44*
    Beav - v95 - i2 - April-May 2015 - p57(1) [501+]
Horn, John - *The Siege of Petersburg: The Battles for the Weldon Railroad, August 1864*
    J Mil H - v79 - i3 - July 2015 - p844-845 [501+]
Horn, Jonathan - *The Man Who Would Not Be Washington: Robert E. Lee's Civil War and His Decision That Changed American History. Audiobook Review*
    LJ - v140 - i6 - April 1 2015 - p50(1) [51-500]
The Man Who Would Not Be Washington: Robert E. Lee's Civil War and His Decision That Changed American History
    For Aff - v94 - i3 - May-June 2015 - pNA [501+]
    Nat R - v67 - i2 - Feb 9 2015 - p43 [501+]
Horn, Maja - *Masculinity after Trujillo: The Politics of Gender in Dominican Literature*
    Ams - v72 - i1 - Jan 2015 - p166(2) [501+]
    HAHR - v95 - i1 - Feb 2015 - p178-180 [501+]
Horn, Martin - *The Politics of Industrial Collaboration during World War II: Ford France, Vichy and Nazi Germany*
    BHR - v89 - i3 - Autumn 2015 - p612(4) [501+]
Horn, Robert - *It's a Minefield*
    KR - June 15 2015 - pNA [51-500]
Horn, Steven W. - *When Good Men Die*
    KR - Oct 15 2015 - pNA [51-500]
    PW - v262 - i46 - Nov 16 2015 - p58(2) [51-500]
Hornblower, Simon - *The Oxford Companion to Classical Civilization, 2d ed.*
    BL - v111 - i11 - Feb 1 2015 - p13(1) [51-500]
Hornby, Gill - *All Together Now*
    y BL - v111 - i18 - May 15 2015 - p22(1) [51-500]
    y KR - May 15 2015 - pNA [51-500]
    y LJ - v140 - i12 - July 1 2015 - p77(1) [51-500]
Hornby, Hugh - *Bowled Over: The Bowling Greens of Britain*
    Spec - v329 - i9767 - Nov 7 2015 - p49(1) [501+]
Hornby, Jane - *What to Bake & How to Bake It*
    CSM - March 6 2015 - pNA [501+]
Hornby, Nick - *Funny Girl (Read by Fielding, Emma). Audiobook Review*
    BL - v111 - i19-20 - June 1 2015 - p126(1) [51-500]
    LJ - v140 - i6 - April 1 2015 - p48(1) [51-500]
Funny Girl
    CSM - Feb 24 2015 - pNA [501+]
    Ent W - i1348-1349 - Jan 30 2015 - p117(1) [501+]
    Nat Post - v17 - i86 - Feb 7 2015 - pWP11(1) [501+]
    NYT - Jan 29 2015 - pC1(L) [501+]
    NYTBR - Feb 22 2015 - p13(L) [501+]
    SEP - v287 - i1 - Jan-Feb 2015 - p20(1) [501+]
Horne, Alexander - *Parliament and the Law*
    Law&PolBR - v25 - i2 - Feb 2015 - p17(5) [501+]
Horne, Alistair - *Hubris: The Tragedy of War in the Twentieth Century*
    KR - Sept 1 2015 - pNA [51-500]
    LJ - v140 - i15 - Sept 15 2015 - p88(2) [501+]
    NYTBR - Dec 13 2015 - p36(L) [501+]
    PW - v262 - i34 - August 24 2015 - p70(1) [51-500]
    Spec - v329 - i9771 - Dec 5 2015 - p36(2) [501+]
Horne, Gerald - *The Counter-Revolution of 1776: Slave Resistance and the Origins of the United States of America*
    AHR - v120 - i1 - Feb 2015 - p235-236 [501+]
    JAH - v102 - i2 - Sept 2015 - p537-538 [501+]
    JSH - v81 - i3 - August 2015 - p700(2) [501+]
    NEQ - v88 - i1 - March 2015 - p166-169 [501+]

Negro Comrades of the Crown: African-Americans and the British Empire Fight the U.S. Before Emancipation
    S&S - v79 - i4 - Oct 2015 - p614-621 [501+]
Race to Revolution: The United States and Cuba during Slavery and Jim Crow
    AHR - v120 - i4 - Oct 2015 - p1454-1455 [501+]
Horne, John - *War in Peace: Paramilitary Violence in Europe after the Great War*
    J Mil H - v79 - i3 - July 2015 - p865-867 [501+]
Horner, Avril - *Living on Paper: Letters from Iris Murdoch, 1934-1995*
    Spec - v329 - i9766 - Oct 31 2015 - p40(3) [501+]
Horner, David - *Accounting for Non-Accountants, 10th ed.*
    Bwatch - July 2015 - pNA [51-500]
Horner, Ken - *Basic Marquetry and Beyond: Expert Techniques for Crafting Beautiful Images with Veneer and Inlay*
    LJ - v140 - i17 - Oct 15 2015 - p88(2) [51-500]
Hornfischer, James D. - *The Last Stand of the Tin Can Sailors*
    RVBW - July 2015 - pNA [501+]
Horning, Audrey - *Ireland in the Virginian Sea: Colonialism in the British Atlantic*
    AHR - v120 - i1 - Feb 2015 - p197-198 [501+]
    JIH - v45 - i3 - Wntr 2015 - p429-430 [501+]
    JSH - v81 - i2 - May 2015 - p425(2) [501+]
    W&M Q - v72 - i1 - Jan 2015 - p171-174 [501+]
Horning, Sandra - *The Biggest Pumpkin (Illus. by Stone-Barker, Holly)*
    c HB Guide - v26 - i1 - Spring 2015 - p33(1) [51-500]
Horning, Susan Schmidt - *Chasing Sound: Technology, Culture, and the Art of Studio Recording from Edison to the LP*
    AHR - v120 - i1 - Feb 2015 - p261-262 [501+]
    Isis - v106 - i1 - March 2015 - p206(2) [501+]
    T&C - v56 - i3 - July 2015 - p763-765 [501+]
Hornsby, Robert - *Protest, Reform and Repression in Khrushchev's Soviet Union*
    E-A St - v67 - i4 - June 2015 - p688(2) [501+]
Horowitz, Alexandra - *Inside of a Dog*
    c KR - Jan 1 2016 - pNA [51-500]
Horowitz, Anthony - *Moriarty*
    TimHES - i2206 - June 4 2015 - p47(1) [501+]
Trigger Mortis: A James Bond Novel
    NS - v144 - i5284 - Oct 16 2015 - p53(1) [501+]
    NYTBR - Sept 6 2015 - p19(L) [501+]
Horowitz, Brian - *Russian Idea, Jewish Presence: Essays on Russian-Jewish Intellectual Life*
    Slav R - v74 - i1 - Spring 2015 - p190-191 [501+]
Horowitz, Daniel - *On the Cusp: The Yale College Class of 1960 and a World on the Verge of Change*
    Soc - v52 - i4 - August 2015 - p383(1) [501+]
Horowitz, Donald - *Constitutional Change and Democracy in Indonesia: Problems of International Politics*
    Pac A - v88 - i1 - March 2015 - p229 [501+]
Horowitz, Eli - *The Pickle Index*
    y BL - v112 - i1 - Sept 1 2015 - p42(1) [51-500]
    y KR - Sept 1 2015 - pNA [501+]
    y PW - v262 - i38 - Sept 21 2015 - p48(2) [501+]
The Silent History
    WLT - v89 - i2 - March-April 2015 - p53(1) [501+]
Horowitz, Joseph - *"On My Way": The Untold Story of Rouben Mamoulian, George Gershwin, and Porgy and Bess*
    Notes - v71 - i4 - June 2015 - p697(3) [501+]
Horowitz, Lauren Bird - *Shattered Blue*
    y SLJ - v61 - i11 - Nov 2015 - p107(2) [51-500]
Horowitz, Lena - *Dancing with Molly*
    y BL - v111 - i18 - May 15 2015 - p53(1) [51-500]
    y HB Guide - v26 - i2 - Fall 2015 - p123(1) [51-500]
    y KR - April 15 2015 - pNA [51-500]
    y SLJ - v61 - i3 - March 2015 - p156(1) [51-500]
    y VOYA - v38 - i2 - June 2015 - p61(2) [51-500]
Horowitz, Sarah - *Friendship and Politics in Post-Revolutionary France*
    AHR - v120 - i1 - Feb 2015 - p341-342 [501+]
Horrigan, Patrick E. - *Portraits at an Exhibition: A Novel*
    G&L Rev W - v22 - i6 - Nov-Dec 2015 - p48(1) [501+]
    KR - May 15 2015 - pNA [501+]
Horrocks, Dylan - *Incomplete Works*
    PW - v262 - i45 - Nov 9 2015 - p46(1) [51-500]
Sam Zabel and the Magic Pen
    Nat Post - v17 - i74 - Jan 24 2015 - pWP9(1) [501+]
    PW - v262 - i5 - Feb 2 2015 - p44(1) [51-500]
Horschelmann, Kathrin - *Mobilities in Socialist and Post-Socialist States: Societies on the Move*
    E-A St - v67 - i7 - Sept 2015 - p1149(2) [501+]

Horsfall, Nicholas - *Aeneid 6: A Commentary, 2 vols.*
    Class R - v65 - i2 - Oct 2015 - p452-456 [501+]
Horsley, Richard A. - *Jesus and Magic: Freeing the Gospel Stories from Modern Misconceptions*
    CC - v132 - i21 - Oct 14 2015 - p32(2) [501+]
John, Jesus, and the Renewal of Israel
    Intpr - v69 - i4 - Oct 2015 - p493(1) [501+]
Horspool, David - *Alfred the Great*
    Specu - v90 - i3 - July 2015 - p826-2 [501+]
Richard III: A Ruler and His Reputation
    BL - v112 - i5 - Nov 1 2015 - p14(1) [51-500]
    KR - Sept 15 2015 - pNA [51-500]
    LJ - v140 - i17 - Oct 15 2015 - p96(1) [51-500]
    Spec - v329 - i9771 - Dec 5 2015 - p41(1) [501+]
Horst, Baader von - *Florenz!*
    Ren Q - v68 - i1 - Spring 2015 - p241-243 [501+]
Horst, John C. - *Allingham: The Long Journey Home*
    BL - v111 - i18 - May 15 2015 - p29(1) [51-500]
Horst, Jorn Lier - *The Caveman*
    PW - v262 - i27 - July 6 2015 - p49(1) [51-500]
Hort, Jakob - *Architektur der Diplomatie: Reprasentation in europaischen Botschaftsbauten, 1800-1920. Konstantinopel - Rom - Wien - St. Petersburg*
    HNet - April 2015 - pNA [501+]
Hortis, C. Alexander - *The Mob and the City: The Hidden History of How the Mafia Captured New York*
    HNet - Jan 2015 - pNA [501+]
Horton, Aaron D. - *German POWs, Der Ruf, and the Genesis of Group 47: The Political Journey of Alfred Andersch and Hans Werner Richter*
    CEH - v48 - i3 - Sept 2015 - p442-444 [501+]
Horton and the Kwuggerbug and More Lost Stories (Read by Cox, Chris, with Charles Cohen). Audiobook Review
    c SLJ - v61 - i2 - Feb 2015 - p48(1) [51-500]
Horton, Julian - *The Cambridge Companion to the Symphony*
    Notes - v71 - i4 - June 2015 - p679(9) [501+]
Horton, N.L.B. - *The Brothers' Keepers*
    SPBW - Jan 2015 - pNA [51-500]
Horton, NLB - *When Camels Fly*
    SPBW - Jan 2015 - pNA [51-500]
Horton, Scott - *Lords of Secrecy: The National Security Elite and America's Stealth Warfare*
    Reason - v47 - i4 - August-Sept 2015 - p69(3) [501+]
Horton, Valerie - *Library Consortia: Models for Collaboration and Sustainability*
    y VOYA - v38 - i1 - April 2015 - p92(1) [51-500]
Horty, John F. - *Reasons as Defaults*
    Phil R - v124 - i2 - April 2015 - p286(4) [501+]
Horvat, John - *Return to Order: From a Frenzied Economy to an Organic Christian Society - Where We've Been, How We Got Here, and Where We Need to Go*
    RVBW - Nov 2015 - pNA [501+]
Horvath, Gyula - *Spaces and Places in Central and Eastern Europe: Historical Trends and Perspectives*
    E-A St - v67 - i6 - August 2015 - p993(3) [501+]
Horvath, James - *Work, Dogs, Work: A Highway Tail*
    c HB Guide - v26 - i1 - Spring 2015 - p10(1) [51-500]
Hosannah, Vernon - *The Rocky Road of Love*
    c CH Bwatch - Feb 2015 - pNA [51-500]
Hosein-Mohammed, Sherina - *A New World Order*
    y KR - Dec 1 2015 - pNA [501+]
Hosfeld, Rolf - *Karl Marx: An Intellectual Biography*
    Historian - v77 - i3 - Fall 2015 - p611(2) [501+]
Hosford, Kate - *Feeding the Flying Fanellis: And Other Poems from a Circus Chef (Illus. by Kawa, Cosei)*
    c SLJ - v61 - i10 - Oct 2015 - p126(1) [51-500]
    c BL - v112 - i2 - Sept 15 2015 - p57(1) [51-500]
    KR - August 1 2015 - pNA [51-500]
    c PW - v262 - i38 - Sept 21 2015 - p75(1) [51-500]
Hosford, Stephanie - *Bald, Fat & Crazy: How I Beat Cancer While Pregnant with One Daughter and Adopting Another*
    KR - May 15 2015 - pNA [501+]
    LJ - v140 - i9 - May 15 2015 - p100(1) [51-500]
Hosie, Donna - *The Devil's Dreamcatcher*
    y KR - July 1 2015 - pNA [501+]
    y SLJ - v61 - i8 - August 2015 - p104(1) [51-500]
The Devil's Intern
    y HB Guide - v26 - i1 - Spring 2015 - p110(1) [51-500]
Hosier, Jay - *Last of the Sandwalkers (Illus. by Hosier, Jay)*
    BL - v111 - i13 - March 1 2015 - p40(2) [51-500]
    c PW - v262 - i8 - Feb 23 2015 - p78(1) [51-500]
Hosken, Andrew - *Empire of Fear: Inside the Islamic State*
    CSM - Sept 15 2015 - pNA [501+]
    KR - July 15 2015 - pNA [501+]

Hoskin, Michael - *The Construction of the Heavens: William Herschel's Cosmology*
    Isis - v106 - i1 - March 2015 - p189(2) [501+]
Hoskins, Patricia - *How to Make Slipcovers: Designing, Measuring, and Sewing Perfect-Fit Slipcovers for Chairs, Sofas, and Ottomans*
    LJ - v140 - i14 - Sept 1 2015 - p106(1) [51-500]
Hoskyns, Barney - *Small Town Talk: Bob Dylan, The Band, Van Morrison, Janis Joplin, Jimi Hendrix and Friends in the Wild Years of Woodstock*
    KR - Dec 15 2015 - pNA [501+]
Hosle, Vittorio - *The Many Faces of Beauty*
    Dialogue - v54 - i3 - Sept 2015 - p559-560 [501+]
Hosler, Jay - *Last of the Sandwalkers (Illus. by Hosler, Jay)*
    c CCB-B - v68 - i11 - July-August 2015 - p550(2) [51-500]
    c KR - Feb 15 2015 - pNA [51-500]
    c NYTBR - April 12 2015 - p19(L) [501+]
    c SLJ - v61 - i5 - May 2015 - p108(1) [51-500]
Hosmer, Brian - *Tribal Worlds: Critical Studies in American Indian Nation Building*
    HNet - Feb 2015 - pNA [501+]
Hospodar, George - *The Great Loop Experience-From Concept to Completion*
    RVBW - Jan 2015 - pNA [51-500]
Hossain, Saad - *Escape from Baghdad!*
    KR - Jan 15 2015 - pNA [501+]
Hosseini, Khaled - *And the Mountains Echoed (Read by Hosseini, Khaled). Audiobook Review*
    BL - v111 - i15 - April 1 2015 - p86(1) [51-500]
Hotchner, A.E. - *Hemingway in Love: His Own Story*
    BL - v112 - i2 - Sept 15 2015 - p16(1) [51-500]
    KR - June 1 2015 - pNA [51-500]
    LJ - v140 - i12 - July 1 2015 - p83(2) [51-500]
    PW - v262 - i29 - July 20 2015 - p178(1) [51-500]
Hotten, Jon - *My Life and the Beautiful Music*
    Spec - v328 - i9754 - August 8 2015 - p28(1) [501+]
Hottois, Gilbert - *Genealogies Philosophique, Politique, et Imaginaire de la Technoscience*
    SFS - v42 - i1 - March 2015 - p178-181 [501+]
Hotton, Robert - *Would they Lie to You? How to Spin Friends and Manipulate People*
    TimHES - i2226 - Oct 22 2015 - p45(1) [501+]
Houck, Colleen - *Reawakened*
    y BL - v111 - i19-20 - June 1 2015 - p100(1) [51-500]
    y KR - May 15 2015 - pNA [51-500]
    y PW - v262 - i21 - May 25 2015 - p61(1) [51-500]
    y SLJ - v61 - i6 - June 2015 - p112(2) [51-500]
Reawakened (Read by Strole, Phoebe). Audiobook Review
    y SLJ - v61 - i12 - Dec 2015 - p78(2) [51-500]
Reawakened
    y VOYA - v38 - i4 - Oct 2015 - p72(2) [51-500]
Houellebecq, Michel - *Soumission*
    CHE - v61 - i26 - March 13 2015 - pNA [501+]
    Econ - v414 - i8920 - Jan 10 2015 - p75(US) [501+]
    Lon R Bks - v37 - i7 - April 9 2015 - p15(4) [501+]
    NYRB - v62 - i6 - April 2 2015 - p41(3) [501+]
    Spec - v327 - i9725 - Jan 17 2015 - p36(3) [501+]
    TLS - i5840 - March 6 2015 - p19(1) [501+]
Submission
    BL - v112 - i4 - Oct 15 2015 - p17(1) [51-500]
    HM - v331 - i1985 - Oct 2015 - p79(5) [501+]
    KR - August 15 2015 - pNA [501+]
    LJ - v140 - i14 - Sept 1 2015 - p93(1) [51-500]
    New York - Oct 5 2015 - pNA [51-500]
    NYTBR - Nov 8 2015 - p1(L) [501+]
    TimHES - i2230 - Nov 19 2015 - p46(1) [501+]
    CC - v132 - i22 - Oct 28 2015 - p33(4) [501+]
Houen, Alex - *Powers of Possibility: Experimental American Writing since the 1960s*
    MP - v113 - i2 - Nov 2015 - pE133(3) [501+]
Hough, Jason M. - *Zero World*
    Analog - v135 - i12 - Dec 2015 - p105(1) [501+]
    Ent W - i1377 - August 21 2015 - p108(1) [501+]
    PW - v262 - i22 - June 1 2015 - p45(1) [51-500]
Hough, Robert - *Diego's Crossing*
    y BL - v112 - i3 - Oct 1 2015 - p69(1) [51-500]
    y SLJ - v61 - i9 - Sept 2015 - p166(1) [51-500]
The Man Who Saved Henry Morgan
    Nat Post - v17 - i130 - April 4 2015 - pWP5(1) [501+]
Houlden, Leslie - *Jesus in History, Legend, Scripture, and Tradition: A World Encyclopedia*
    BL - v112 - i6 - Nov 15 2015 - p15(1) [51-500]
Houle, Marcy Cottrell - *The Gift of Caring: Saving Our Parents from the Perils of Modern Healthcare*
    BL - v111 - i21 - July 1 2015 - p13(1) [51-500]

Hounam, Donald - *Gifted*
    y Sch Lib - v63 - i2 - Summer 2015 - p118(1) [51-500]
Houran, Lori Haskins - *The $25,000 Flight: How Lindbergh Set a Daring Record... (Illus. by Lowe, Wesley)*
    c HB Guide - v26 - i1 - Spring 2015 - p204(1) [51-500]
A Dozen Cousins (Illus. by Usher, Sam)
    c HB Guide - v26 - i2 - Fall 2015 - p37(2) [51-500]
How to Spy on a Shark (Illus. by Marquez, Francisca)
    c HB Guide - v26 - i2 - Fall 2015 - p176(1) [51-500]
    c KR - Jan 15 2015 - pNA [51-500]
    c SLJ - v61 - i3 - March 2015 - p170(1) [51-500]
Next to You: A Book of Adorableness (Illus. by Hanson, Sydney)
    c KR - Dec 15 2015 - pNA [51-500]
    c PW - v262 - i51 - Dec 14 2015 - p84(1) [51-500]
Hourihane, Colum - *Manuscripta Illuminata: Approaches to Understanding Medieval and Renaissance Manuscripts*
    Six Ct J - v46 - i2 - Summer 2015 - p524-525 [501+]
    Ren Q - v68 - i3 - Fall 2015 - p1095-1096 [501+]
Housden, Martyn - *On Their Own Behalf: Ewald Ammende, Europe's National Minorities and the Campaign for Cultural Autonomy, 1920-1936*
    Slav R - v74 - i3 - Fall 2015 - p614-615 [501+]
Housden, Peter - *So the New Could be Born: The Passing of a Country Grammar School*
    TES - i5159 - August 14 2015 - p14(1) [501+]
    TLS - i5876 - Nov 13 2015 - p11(1) [501+]
House, John C. - *Trail of Deceit*
    KR - July 15 2015 - pNA [501+]
House, Jonathan M. - *Controlling Paris: Armed Forces and Counter-Revolution, 1789-1848*
    HNet - Jan 2015 - pNA [501+]
    JIH - v45 - i3 - Wntr 2015 - p431-432 [501+]
Houser, Heather - *Ecosickness in Contemporary U.S. Fiction: Environment and Affect*
    MFSF - v61 - i3 - Fall 2015 - p539-541 [501+]
Houser, Jason - *Dedicated: Training Your Children to Trust and Follow Jesus*
    RVBW - May 2015 - pNA [51-500]
Housewright, David - *Unidentified Woman #15*
    BL - v111 - i17 - May 1 2015 - p47(1) [51-500]
Unidentified Woman # 15
    KR - April 1 2015 - pNA [51-500]
Unidentified Woman #15
    PW - v262 - i11 - March 16 2015 - p64(1) [51-500]
Housley, Norman - *Crusading and the Ottoman Threat, 1453-1505*
    HER - v130 - i543 - April 2015 - p431(3) [501+]
Houssami, Eyad - *Doomed by Hope: Essays on Arab Theatre*
    IJMES - v47 - i2 - May 2015 - p393-395 [501+]
Houston, Chloe - *The Renaissance Utopia: Dialogue, Travel and the Ideal Society*
    RES - v66 - i276 - Sept 2015 - p770-771 [501+]
    Six Ct J - v46 - i3 - Fall 2015 - p687-688 [501+]
Houston, Philip - *Get the Truth: Former CIA Officers Teach You How to Persuade Anyoneto Tell All. Audiobook Review*
    LJ - v140 - i12 - July 1 2015 - p44(1) [51-500]
Houston, Rob - *When on Earth? History as You've Never Seen it Before!*
    y PW - v262 - i18 - May 4 2015 - p120(1) [51-500]
    y SLJ - v61 - i6 - June 2015 - p142(1) [51-500]
Houston, Stephen - *The Shape of Script: How and Why Writing Systems Change*
    Lang Soc - v44 - i1 - Feb 2015 - p129-130 [501+]
Houston, Victoria - *Dead Repunzel*
    KR - April 1 2015 - pNA [51-500]
    PW - v262 - i16 - April 20 2015 - p57(1) [51-500]
Houts, Amy - *Rachel Maddow: Primetime Political Commentator*
    y BL - v111 - i16 - April 15 2015 - p42(1) [51-500]
Houts, Michelle - *Kammie on First: Baseball's Dottie Kamenshek*
    y HB Guide - v26 - i2 - Fall 2015 - p199(1) [51-500]
    y BL - v111 - i11 - Feb 1 2015 - p34(1) [51-500]
Winterfrost (Read by McFadden, Amy)
    y SLJ - v61 - i2 - Feb 2015 - p50(1) [51-500]
Winterfrost
    y HB Guide - v26 - i1 - Spring 2015 - p81(1) [51-500]
    y RVBW - Jan 2015 - pNA [51-500]
Hovaguimian, Vroni - *Images and Words*
    KR - June 15 2015 - pNA [501+]
Hovland, Ingie - *Mission Station Christianity: Norwegian Missionaries in Colonial Natal and Zululand, Southern Africa, 1850-1890*
    IBMR - v39 - i1 - Jan 2015 - p53(2) [501+]

How We Got to Now: Six innovations That Made the Modern World. Audiobook Review
    Bwatch - Jan 2015 - pNA [51-500]

Howard, A.G. - *Ensnared*
    y HB Guide - v26 - i2 - Fall 2015 - p123(1) [51-500]
    y CCB-B - v68 - i6 - Feb 2015 - p314(1) [51-500]
    y VOYA - v37 - i6 - Feb 2015 - p78(1) [51-500]

Howard, Amy L. - *More Than Shelter: Activism and Community in San Francisco Public Housing*
    AHR - v120 - i2 - April 2015 - p661-663 [501+]
    JAH - v101 - i4 - March 2015 - p1339(1) [501+]

Howard, Billee - *We - Commerce: How to Create, Collaborate, and Succeed in the Sharing Economy*
    BL - v112 - i6 - Nov 15 2015 - p5(1) [51-500]
    PW - v262 - i41 - Oct 12 2015 - p60(1) [51-500]

Howard, Colby - *Brothers Armed: Military Aspects of the Crisis in Ukraine*
    J Mil H - v79 - i2 - April 2015 - p559-560 [501+]

Howard, Deborah - *The Image of Venice: Fialetti's View and Sir Henry Wotton*
    Six Ct J - v46 - i3 - Fall 2015 - p765-767 [501+]

Howard, Elizabeth - *A Day with Bonefish Joe (Illus. by Wege, Diana)*
    c KR - Sept 15 2015 - pNA [51-500]

Howard, Fred - *Transforming Faith: Stories of Change from a Lifelong Spiritual Seeker*
    KR - Feb 15 2015 - pNA [501+]

Howard, Ginnah - *Rope and Bone*
    PW - v262 - i6 - Feb 9 2015 - p44(1) [51-500]

Howard, Gregory - *Hospice*
    KR - Feb 1 2015 - pNA [51-500]

Howard, J.J. - *Tracers*
    y CCB-B - v68 - i6 - Feb 2015 - p314(2) [51-500]
    y HB Guide - v26 - i2 - Fall 2015 - p124(1) [51-500]
    y VOYA - v38 - i1 - April 2015 - p62(1) [51-500]

Howard, John - *The Menzies Era: The Years that Shaped Modern Australia*
    TLS - i5846 - April 17 2015 - p3(3) [501+]

Howard, Jonathan L. - *Carter & Lovecraft*
    BL - v112 - i3 - Oct 1 2015 - p36(1) [51-500]
    KR - August 15 2015 - pNA [51-500]
    PW - v262 - i32 - August 10 2015 - p41(1) [51-500]

Howard, Jules - *Sex on Earth: A Celebration of Animal Reproduction*
    NH - v123 - i1 - Feb 2015 - p46(2) [501+]

Howard, Keith David - *The Reception of Machiavelli in Early Modern Spain*
    Ren Q - v68 - i3 - Fall 2015 - p1068-1069 [501+]

Howard, Linda - *Against the Rules*
    BL - v111 - i21 - July 1 2015 - p43(1) [51-500]

Howard, Patricia - *The Modern Castrato: Gaetano Guadagni and the Coming of a New Operatic Age*
    ON - v80 - i5 - Nov 2015 - p60(2) [501+]
    MT - v156 - i1930 - Spring 2015 - p105-107 [501+]

Howard, Peter - *Creating Magnificence in Renaissance Florence*
    CHR - v101 - i4 - Autumn 2015 - p924(2) [501+]

Howard, Ravi - *Driving the King*
    KR - Jan 1 2015 - pNA [501+]
    People - v83 - i2 - Jan 12 2015 - p29 [501+]
    People - v83 - i2 - Jan 12 2015 - p29 [501+]
    People - v83 - i2 - Jan 12 2015 - p29 [501+]
    People - v83 - i2 - Jan 12 2015 - p29 [501+]
    People - v83 - i2 - Jan 12 2015 - p29 [501+]

Howard, Richard - *A Progressive Education*
    NY - v90 - i45 - Jan 26 2015 - p77 [51-500]

Howard, Ryan - *The Best Bat (Illus. by Madrid, Erwin)*
    c HB Guide - v26 - i2 - Fall 2015 - p67(1) [51-500]
My New Team (Illus. by Madrid, Erwin)
    c HB Guide - v26 - i2 - Fall 2015 - p67(1) [51-500]

Howard, Tim - *The Keeper: A Life of Saving Goals and Achieving Them*
    NYT - Jan 2 2015 - pC23(L) [501+]
The Keeper: The Unguarded Story of Tim Howard
    c HB Guide - v26 - i2 - Fall 2015 - p199(1) [51-500]

Howard, Tyrone C. - *Why Race and Culture Matters in Schools: Closing the Achievement Gap in America's Classrooms*
    JNE - v84 - i1 - Wntr 2015 - p98-101 [501+]

Howard, Vicki - *From Main Street to Mall: The Rise and Fall of the American Department Store*
    LJ - v140 - i10 - June 1 2015 - p109(1) [51-500]

Howard, W. Scott - *An Collins and the Historical Imagination*
    Sev Cent N - v73 - i3-4 - Fall-Winter 2015 - p175(5) [501+]

Howarth, Daniel - *Why I Love Nova Scotia*
    c Res Links - v21 - i1 - Oct 2015 - p22(2) [51-500]

Howarth, Jill - *Jingle Bells (Illus. by Howarth, Jill)*
    c PW - v262 - i37 - Sept 14 2015 - p72(2) [51-500]

Howarth, Kylie - *Fish Jam*
    c HB Guide - v26 - i2 - Fall 2015 - p13(1) [51-500]

Howarth, Naomi - *The Crow's Tale (Illus. by Howarth, Naomi)*
    c SLJ - v61 - i11 - Nov 2015 - p131(2) [51-500]
    c KR - August 15 2015 - pNA [51-500]

Howcroft, Heidi - *First Ladies of Gardening: Designers, Dreamers and Divas*
    LJ - v140 - i6 - April 1 2015 - p109(1) [51-500]

Howe, Cymene - *Intimate Activism: The Struggle for Sexual Rights in Postrevolutionary Nicaragua*
    JRAI - v21 - i3 - Sept 2015 - p589(2) [501+]

Howe, Darcus - *Darcus Howe: a Political Biography*
    ERS - v38 - i3 - March 2015 - p521(3) [501+]

Howe, Fanny - *Second Childhood*
    WLT - v89 - i1 - Jan-Feb 2015 - p61(1) [501+]

Howe, Irving - *A Voice Still Heard: Selected Essays of Irving Howe*
    Soc - v52 - i1 - Feb 2015 - p86(1) [501+]

Howe, Joshua P. - *Behind the Curve: Science and the Politics of Global Warming*
    AHR - v120 - i4 - Oct 2015 - p1526-1527 [501+]
    Isis - v106 - i2 - June 2015 - p503(3) [501+]
    JAH - v102 - i2 - Sept 2015 - p626-627 [501+]

Howe, Katherine - *The Appearance of Annie Van Sinderen (Read by Bernstein, Jesse). Audiobook Review*
    y SLJ - v61 - i12 - Dec 2015 - p79(1) [51-500]
The Appearance of Annie Van Sinderen
    y PW - v262 - i49 - Dec 2 2015 - p100(1) [51-500]
    y SLJ - v61 - i9 - Sept 2015 - p166(2) [51-500]
Conversion
    y HB Guide - v26 - i1 - Spring 2015 - p110(1) [51-500]
The Penguin Book of Witches
    TLS - i5863 - August 14 2015 - p24(1) [501+]

Howe, Lawrence - *Refocusing Chaplin: A Screen Icon through Critical Lenses*
    SAH - v4 - i1 - Annual 2015 - p111-115 [501+]

Howe, Michele - *Empty Nest, What's Next? Parenting Adult Children without Losing Your Mind*
    PW - v262 - i32 - August 10 2015 - p55(2) [51-500]

Howe, Nina - *A Voice Still Heard: Selected Essays of Irving Howe*
    NYRB - v62 - i4 - March 5 2015 - p42(3) [501+]
    NYTBR - Jan 18 2015 - p16(L) [501+]

Howe, Steven - *Heinrich von Kleist and Jean-Jacques Rousseau: Violence, Identity, Nation*
    MLR - v110 - i1 - Jan 2015 - p285-287 [501+]

Howe, Susan - *The Quarry*
    KR - Sept 15 2015 - pNA [501+]
    PW - v262 - i37 - Sept 14 2015 - p57(1) [51-500]

Howe, Zoe - *The Jesus and Mary Chain*
    Bwatch - Jan 2015 - pNA [51-500]

Howell, Angela McMillan - *Raised Up down Yonder: Growing up Black in Rural Alabama*
    Am St - v54 - i2 - Summer 2015 - p85-94 [501+]

Howell, Anthony - *Silent Highway*
    TLS - i5861 - July 31 2015 - p22(1) [501+]

Howell, Brian - *Great Moments in Olympic Snowboarding*
    c HB Guide - v26 - i1 - Spring 2015 - p182(1) [51-500]
Playing Pro Baseball
    c HB Guide - v26 - i1 - Spring 2015 - p182(1) [51-500]
    y VOYA - v38 - i1 - April 2015 - p89(2) [51-500]

Howell, Dorothy - *Swag Bags and Swindlers*
    KR - August 1 2015 - pNA [51-500]

Howell, Hannah - *Highland Guard*
    PW - v262 - i3 - Jan 19 2015 - p68(1) [51-500]
If He's Noble
    PW - v262 - i24 - June 15 2015 - p71(1) [51-500]

Howell, James C. - *Why This Jubilee? Advent Reflections on Songs of the Seasons*
    CC - v132 - i23 - Nov 11 2015 - p42(1) [51-500]

Howell, Jessica - *Exploring Victorian Travel Literature: Disease, Race and Climate*
    Nine-C Lit - v70 - i2 - Sept 2015 - p288(4) [501+]

Howell, Katherine - *Web of Deceit*
    PW - v262 - i41 - Oct 12 2015 - p49(1) [51-500]

Howell, Khristian A. - *Color + Pattern: 50 Playful Exercises for Exploring Pattern Design*
    LJ - v140 - i15 - Sept 15 2015 - p76(1) [51-500]

Howell, Ross, Jr. - *Forsaken*
    KR - Nov 15 2015 - pNA [51-500]

Howell, Sally - *Old Islam in Detroit: Rediscovering the Muslim American Past*
    JAH - v102 - i1 - June 2015 - p205-207 [501+]

Howell, Sara - *Lantern Fish*
    SLJ - v61 - i4 - April 2015 - p92(4) [501+]

Howell, Simmone - *Girl Defective*
    y HB Guide - v26 - i1 - Spring 2015 - p110(1) [51-500]

Howell, Steve N.G. - *The Amazing World of Flyingfish*
    Am Bio T - v77 - i3 - March 2015 - p216(1) [501+]
Rare Birds of North America
    QRB - v90 - i1 - March 2015 - p103(2) [501+]

Howells, Debbie - *The Bones of You*
    LJ - v140 - i10 - June 1 2015 - p88(1) [51-500]
    PW - v262 - i21 - May 25 2015 - p35(1) [51-500]

Howells, Richard - *A Critical Theory of Creativity: Utopia, Aesthetics, Atheism and Design*
    TimHES - i2216 - August 13 2015 - p44(1) [51-500]

Howells, Tania - *Starring Shapes! (Illus. by Howells, Tania)*
    c KR - July 15 2015 - pNA [51-500]
    c SLJ - v61 - i9 - Sept 2015 - p122(1) [51-500]

Howes, David - *Ways of Sensing: Understanding the Senses in Society*
    AHR - v120 - i2 - April 2015 - p568-569 [501+]

Howes, Marjorie - *Yeats and Afterwords: Christ, Culture, and Crisis*
    TLS - i5840 - March 6 2015 - p31(1) [501+]
    ILS - v35 - i1 - Fall 2015 - p21(2) [501+]

Howison, Del - *Midian Unmade: Tales of Clive Barker's Nightbreed*
    PW - v262 - i18 - May 4 2015 - p100(1) [51-500]

Howland, Leila - *The Forget-Me-Not Summer (Illus. by Kim, Ji-Hyuk)*
    c BL - v111 - i16 - April 15 2015 - p49(1) [51-500]
    c KR - March 15 2015 - pNA [51-500]
    c VOYA - v38 - i2 - June 2015 - p61(1) [51-500]

Howlett, David J. - *Kirtland Temple: The Biography of a Shared Mormon Sacred Space*
    CH - v84 - i4 - Dec 2015 - p913(3) [501+]
    JAH - v102 - i2 - Sept 2015 - p515-515 [501+]

Howley, Kerry - *Thrown*
    Spec - v328 - i9749 - July 4 2015 - p41(1) [51-500]

Howling, Eric - *Red Zone Rivals*
    y SLJ - v61 - i9 - Sept 2015 - p151(4) [501+]

Howse, Jan Wooden - *God Does No Wrong*
    SPBW - August 2015 - pNA [51-500]

Howson, Imogen - *Unravel*
    y HB Guide - v26 - i2 - Fall 2015 - p124(1) [51-500]

Hoxie, Frederick E. - *Lewis and Clark among the Nez Perce: Strangers in the Land of the Nimiipuu*
    WHQ - v46 - i1 - Spring 2015 - p103-104 [501+]

Hoy, Marjorie A. - *Insect Molecular Genetics: An Introduction to Principles and Applications*
    QRB - v90 - i1 - March 2015 - p98(1) [501+]

Hoyland, Robert G. - *In God's Path: The Arab Conquests and the Creation of an Islamic Empire*
    HT - v65 - i5 - May 2015 - p57(1) [501+]
    TLS - i5841 - March 13 2015 - p24(1) [501+]

Hoyle, Richard W. - *The Farmer in England, 1650-1980*
    HER - v130 - i544 - June 2015 - p757(3) [501+]

Hoyle, Tom - *Thirteen*
    y HB Guide - v26 - i2 - Fall 2015 - p124(1) [51-500]
    y CCB-B - v68 - i11 - July-August 2015 - p551(1) [51-500]
    y PW - v262 - i14 - April 6 2015 - p61(1) [51-500]
    y KR - March 1 2015 - pNA [51-500]
    y SLJ - v61 - i2 - Feb 2015 - p102(1) [51-500]

Hoyningen-Huene, Paul - *Systematicity: The Nature of Science*
    RM - v69 - i2 - Dec 2015 - p389(3) [501+]

Hoyt, Elizabeth - *Dearest Rogue*
    BL - v111 - i17 - May 1 2015 - p80(1) [51-500]
    PW - v262 - i16 - April 20 2015 - p61(1) [51-500]

Hoyt, Eric - *Hollywood Vault: Film Libraries before Home Video*
    FQ - v68 - i3 - Spring 2015 - p94(3) [501+]

Hoyte, Carol Ann - *Dear Tomato: An International Crop of Food and Agriculture Poems (Illus. by Wasserman, Norie)*
    c Res Links - v21 - i1 - Oct 2015 - p14(1) [51-500]

Hrabal, Bohumil - *Mr. Kafka: And Other Tales from the Time of the Cult*
    PW - v262 - i33 - August 17 2015 - p45(1) [51-500]
    KR - August 15 2015 - pNA [501+]

Hrabowski, Freeman A., III - *Holding Fast to Dreams: Empowering Youth from the Civil Rights Crusade to STEM Achievement*
    KR - March 1 2015 - pNA [501+]
    LJ - v140 - i8 - May 1 2015 - p83(1) [51-500]

Hrbek, Greg - *Not on Fire, but Burning*
    KR - August 1 2015 - pNA [501+]
    NYTBR - Oct 18 2015 - p18(L) [501+]

Hrotic, Steven - *Religion in Science Fiction: The Evolution of an Idea and the Extinction of a Genre*
 SFS - v42 - i2 - July 2015 - p378-380 [501+]
Hruska, Alan - *Pardon the Ravens*
 BL - v111 - i9-10 - Jan 1 2015 - p48(1) [51-500]
 SPBW - August 2015 - pNA [51-500]
Hsia, Chih-tsing - *The Columbia Anthology of Yuan Drama*
 JAS - v74 - i2 - May 2015 - p466-467 [501+]
Hsiu-Lien, Lu - *My Fight for a New Taiwan: One Woman's Journey from Prison to Power*
 Pac A - v88 - i3 - Sept 2015 - p704 [501+]
Hsiung, C. Fong - *Picture Bride*
 WLT - v89 - i5 - Sept-Oct 2015 - p69(1) [501+]
Hsu, Chien-Jung - *The Construction of National Identity in Taiwan's Media, 1896-2012*
 AHR - v120 - i3 - June 2015 - p995-996 [501+]
Hsu, Huan - *The Porcelain Thief*
 TLS - i5857 - July 3 2015 - p5(1) [501+]
 KR - Jan 15 2015 - pNA [501+]
Hsy, Jonathan - *Trading Tongues: Merchants, Multilingualism, and Medieval Literature*
 Med R - Jan 2015 - pNA [501+]
Hsyu, J.C. - *The Dinner That Cooked Itself*
 c CH Bwatch - Nov 2015 - pNA [51-500]
HT 2014: "Gewinner oder Verlierer?" - Das Historische Urteil im Geschichtsunterricht als Qualitatsmerkmal und Desiderat
 HNet - Jan 2015 - pNA [501+]
HT 2014: Gewinner und Verlierer: Das Jahr 1914 im Geschichtsunterricht und Geschichtsbewusstsein aus Internationaler Perspektive
 HNet - Jan 2015 - pNA [501+]
HT 2014: Herrschaft und Ihre Mittlerinstanzen. Lokale Administrationen und Akteure en den im Zweiten Weltkrieg von der Wehrmacht Besetzten Gebieten
 HNet - Jan 2015 - pNA [501+]
HT 2014: Jenseits von Gewinn und Verlust: Entscheidungsfindung in der Fruhen Neuzeit
 HNet - July 2015 - pNA [501+]
HT 2014: Reichtum - Zur Geschichte einer Umstrittenen Sozialfigur
 HNet - June 2015 - pNA [501+]
HT 2014: The Biggest Loser. Gewinnen und Verlieren durch Diaten in Deutschland und den USA zwischen 1860 und 2004
 HNet - April 2015 - pNA [501+]
HT 2014: Veni, Vidi, Vici: (Re)prasentationen von Sieghaftigkeit in der Antike
 HNet - Jan 2015 - pNA [501+]
HT 2014: Verlorenes und Gewonnenes. Geschlechterverhaltnisse und der Wandel des Politischen in der 'Langen Geschichte der Wende' in Ostdeutschland 1980 bis 2000
 HNet - July 2015 - pNA [501+]
HT 2014: Wikipedia und Geschichtswissenschaft. Eine Zwischenbilanz
 HNet - March 2015 - pNA [501+]
Hu, Eileen - *Tofu Power: What Does Tofu Have to Do With Kung Fu? (Illus. by Yumul, Anthony)*
 c CH Bwatch - Nov 2015 - pNA [51-500]
Hu, Ping - *The Thought Remolding Campaign of the Chinese Communist Party-State*
 Pac A - v88 - i4 - Dec 2015 - p898 [501+]
Hu, Tung-Hui - *A Prehistory of the Cloud*
 New Sci - v227 - i3037 - Sept 5 2015 - p45(1) [501+]
Hua, Yu - *The Seventh Day*
 NY - v90 - i44 - Jan 19 2015 - p75 [51-500]
Hua, Zhu - *Exploring Intercultural Communication: Language in Action*
 Lang Soc - v44 - i1 - Feb 2015 - p116-120 [501+]
Huang, Angela Ling - *Textiles and the Medieval Economy: Production, Trade, and Consumption of Textiles, 8th-16th Centuries*
 Specu - v90 - i4 - Oct 2015 - p1193(1) [501+]
Huang, Charlotte - *For the Record*
 y BL - v112 - i5 - Nov 1 2015 - p50(2) [51-500]
 y CSM - Dec 28 2015 - pNA [501+]
 y KR - Sept 15 2015 - pNA [51-500]
 y PW - v262 - i37 - Sept 14 2015 - p79(1) [51-500]
 y SLJ - v61 - i10 - Oct 2015 - p111(1) [51-500]
 y VOYA - v38 - i5 - Dec 2015 - p57(1) [501+]
Hubbard, Ben - *Stories of Women During the Industrial Revolution: Changing Roles, Changing Lives*
 y VOYA - v38 - i1 - April 2015 - p90(1) [51-500]
 Stories of Women's Suffrage: Votes for Women!
 y VOYA - v38 - i1 - April 2015 - p90(1) [51-500]
Hubbard, Charlotte - *Harvest of Blessings*
 PW - v262 - i2 - Jan 12 2015 - p43(1) [501+]
Hubbard, Jenny - *And We Stay*
 y Teach Lib - v42 - i3 - Feb 2015 - p43(1) [51-500]

Hubbard, Kirsten - *Watch the Sky*
 c BL - v111 - i18 - May 15 2015 - p56(1) [51-500]
 c CCB-B - v68 - i11 - July-August 2015 - p551(1) [51-500]
 c HB Guide - v26 - i2 - Fall 2015 - p87(1) [51-500]
 c PW - v262 - i5 - Feb 2 2015 - p61(1) [51-500]
 c SLJ - v61 - i4 - April 2015 - p146(1) [51-500]
 c VOYA - v38 - i1 - April 2015 - p62(1) [51-500]
Hubbard, L. Ron - *Fifty-Fifty O'Brien: A U.S. Marine Sniper in One Hell of a War with One Shot to Survive. Audiobook Review*
 PW - v262 - i5 - Feb 2 2015 - p54(1) [51-500]
Hubbard, Mandy - *Everything But the Truth*
 y BL - v112 - i2 - Sept 15 2015 - p71(2) [51-500]
 y KR - Sept 1 2015 - pNA [51-500]
 y VOYA - v38 - i4 - Oct 2015 - p52(1) [51-500]
Hubbard, Thomas K. - *A Companion to Greek and Roman Sexualities*
 Class R - v65 - i2 - Oct 2015 - p510-512 [501+]
Hubbell, John T. - *Conflict and Command*
 HNet - April 2015 - pNA [501+]
Hubbell, Webb - *Ginger Snaps: A Jack Patterson Thriller*
 LJ - v140 - i9 - May 15 2015 - p71(1) [51-500]
Hubbs, Nadine - *Rednecks, Queers, and Country Music*
 Notes - v71 - i4 - June 2015 - p728(4) [501+]
 PMS - v38 - i2 - May 2015 - p261(3) [501+]
Huber, Anna Lee - *A Study in Death*
 PW - v262 - i22 - June 1 2015 - p43(1) [51-500]
Huber, John J. - *The Purpose-Based Library: Finding Your Path to Survival, Success, and Growth*
 LJ - v140 - i13 - August 1 2015 - p113(1) [501+]
Huber, Laurel Davis - *Margery & Pamela*
 KR - Oct 15 2015 - pNA [501+]
Huber, Linda - *The Cold Cold Sea*
 PW - v262 - i26 - June 29 2015 - p48(2) [51-500]
Huber, Matthew T. - *Lifeblood: Oil, Freedom, and the Forces of Capital*
 CS - v44 - i5 - Sept 2015 - p666-667 [501+]
 RAH - v43 - i2 - June 2015 - p333-339 [501+]
Huber, Mike - *All in One Day (Illus. by Cowman, Joseph)*
 c HB Guide - v26 - i1 - Spring 2015 - p10(1) [51-500]
 The Amazing Erik (Illus. by Cowman, Joseph)
 c HB Guide - v26 - i1 - Spring 2015 - p10(1) [51-500]
 Evette's Invitation (Illus. by Cowman, Joseph)
 c HB Guide - v26 - i1 - Spring 2015 - p10(1) [51-500]
 Rita and the Firefighters (Illus. by Cowman, Joseph)
 c HB Guide - v26 - i1 - Spring 2015 - p10(1) [51-500]
Huber, Raymond - *Peace Warriors*
 Magpies - v30 - i4 - Sept 2015 - pS8(1) [51-500]
Huber, Valeska - *Channelling Mobilities: Migration and Globalisation in the Suez Canal Region and Beyond, 1869-1914*
 IJMES - v47 - i2 - May 2015 - p369-381 [501+]
Huberath, Marek S. - *Nest of Worlds*
 MFSF - v128 - i1-2 - Jan-Feb 2015 - p48(8) [501+]
Hubert - *Adrian and the Tree of Secrets (Illus. by Caillou, Marie)*
 y BL - v111 - i9-10 - Jan 1 2015 - p62(1) [51-500]
 y Can Lit - i224 - Spring 2015 - p126 [501+]
Hubert, Margaret - *Customize Your Crochet: Adjust to Fit; Embellish To Taste*
 LJ - v140 - i19 - Nov 15 2015 - p85(1) [51-500]
Hubery, Julia - *When Grandma Saved Christmas (Illus. by Pedler, Caroline)*
 c HB Guide - v26 - i1 - Spring 2015 - p11(1) [51-500]
Hubler, Angela E. - *Little Red Readings: Historical Materialist Perspectives on Children's Literature*
 Bkbird - v53 - i1 - Wntr 2015 - p94(3) [501+]
Huchtker, Dietlind - *Reden und Schweigen uber religiose Differenz: Tolerieren in epochenubergreifender Perspektive*
 HNet - August 2015 - pNA [501+]
Huchu, Tendai - *The Hairdresser of Harare*
 KR - June 15 2015 - pNA [51-500]
 NYTBR - August 16 2015 - p14(L) [51-500]
 The Maestro, the Magistrate & the Mathematician
 KR - Dec 1 2015 - pNA [51-500]
Huck Magazine - *Paddle against the Flow: Lessons on Life from Doers, Creators, and Cultural Rebels*
 y SLJ - v61 - i7 - July 2015 - p109(1) [51-500]
Huckabay, Calvin - *John Milton: An Annotated Bibliography, 1989-1999*
 MLR - v110 - i2 - April 2015 - p527-528 [501+]

Huckabee, Mike - *God, Guns, Grits, and Gravy*
 LJ - v140 - i2 - Feb 1 2015 - p98(1) [51-500]
 NS - v144 - i5278 - Sept 4 2015 - p40(4) [501+]
 NYRB - v62 - i5 - March 19 2015 - p18(3) [501+]
 Reason - v47 - i4 - August-Sept 2015 - p58(8) [501+]
Huckell, Bruce B. - *Clovis Caches: Recent Discoveries and New Research*
 Am Ant - v80 - i2 - April 2015 - p422(2) [501+]
Huckins, Holly - *The Cat Who Tamed the West*
 c CH Bwatch - March 2015 - pNA [51-500]
Hucks, Tracey E. - *Yoruba Traditions and African American Religious Nationalism*
 Callaloo - v38 - i1 - Wntr 2015 - p234-237 [501+]
Hudgins, Andrew - *The Joker: A Memoir*
 SAH - v4 - i1 - Annual 2015 - p129-131 [501+]
Hudgins, Victoria - *Materially Crafted: A DIY Primer for the Design-Obsessed*
 LJ - v140 - i6 - April 1 2015 - p93(1) [51-500]
Hudis, Peter - *The Complete Works of Rosa Luxemburg: Economic Writings 1, vol. 1*
 E-A St - v67 - i3 - May 2015 - p499(2) [501+]
Hudock, Barry - *Struggle, Condemnation, Vindication: John Courtney Murray's Journey toward Vatican II*
 AM - v213 - i12 - Oct 26 2015 - p32(3) [501+]
 CHR - v101 - i4 - Autumn 2015 - p959(2) [501+]
Hudson, Angela Pulley - *Real Native Genius: How an Ex-Slave and a White Mormon Became Famous Indians*
 LJ - v140 - i11 - June 15 2015 - p97(2) [51-500]
Hudson, Anne - *Two Revisions of Rolle's English Psalter Commentary and the Related Canticles*
 MLR - v110 - i1 - Jan 2015 - p233-234 [501+]
 Two Revisions of Rolle's English Psalter Commentary and the Related Canticles, vol. 2
 Med R - May 2015 - pNA [501+]
Hudson, Charles - *The Cow-Hunter*
 RVBW - Jan 2015 - pNA [501+]
Hudson, David L., Jr. - *The Handy American History Answer Book*
 y LJ - v140 - i15 - Sept 15 2015 - p104(1) [51-500]
 y SLJ - v61 - i10 - Oct 2015 - p57(1) [51-500]
Hudson, James R. - *Special Interest Society: How Membership-Based Organizations Shape America*
 CS - v44 - i3 - May 2015 - p367-368 [501+]
Hudson, Katy - *Bear and Duck (Illus. by Hudson, Katy)*
 c CCB-B - v68 - i11 - July-August 2015 - p552(1) [51-500]
 c HB Guide - v26 - i2 - Fall 2015 - p13(1) [51-500]
 c KR - Feb 15 2015 - pNA [51-500]
 c PW - v262 - i10 - March 9 2015 - p71(1) [51-500]
 c SLJ - v61 - i2 - Feb 2015 - p70(1) [51-500]
 Too Many Carrots (Illus. by Hudson, Katy)
 c KR - Dec 15 2015 - pNA [51-500]
 c PW - v262 - i47 - Nov 23 2015 - p65(1) [51-500]
Hudson, Mark J. - *Beyond Ainu Studies: Changing Academic and Public Perspectives*
 Pac A - v88 - i4 - Dec 2015 - p941 [501+]
Hudson, Nicholas - *A Political Biography of Samuel Johnson*
 Biomag - v38 - i3 - Summer 2015 - p425(12) [501+]
Hudson, Suzanne - *Painting Now*
 LJ - v140 - i7 - April 15 2015 - p92(1) [51-500]
 RVBW - May 2015 - pNA [501+]
Hudson, Valerie M. - *The Hillary Doctrine: Sex and American Foreign Policy*
 KR - March 15 2015 - pNA [501+]
 LJ - v140 - i9 - May 15 2015 - p96(1) [51-500]
Hue - *Dead Letter Office*
 KR - March 15 2015 - pNA [501+]
Hue, Denis - *Lectures de Charles d'Orleans: Les Ballades*
 Specu - v90 - i4 - Oct 2015 - p1192-2 [501+]
Huebener, Rudolf P. - *Conductors, Semiconductors, Superconductors: An Introduction to Solid State Physics*
 Phys Today - v68 - i5 - May 2015 - p52-52 [501+]
Huebner, Daniel - *Becoming Mead: The Social Process of Academic Knowledge*
 CS - v44 - i3 - May 2015 - p305-314 [501+]
Hueller, R.W. - *The Wish*
 y SLJ - v61 - i9 - Sept 2015 - p151(4) [501+]
 Wolf High
 y SLJ - v61 - i9 - Sept 2015 - p151(4) [501+]
Huet, Marie-Helene - *The Culture of Disaster*
 FS - v69 - i1 - Jan 2015 - p119-120 [501+]
Huey, Lois Miner - *Forgotten Bones: Uncovering a Slave Cemetery*
 c BL - v112 - i2 - Sept 15 2015 - p54(1) [51-500]
 c KR - July 15 2015 - pNA [51-500]
 c SLJ - v61 - i8 - August 2015 - p126(2) [51-500]
Huff, Tanya - *The Future Falls*
 MFSF - v128 - i3-4 - March-April 2015 - p67(2) [501+]

Huff, Tobias - *Natur und Industrie im Sozialismus: Eine Umweltgeschichte der DDR*
    HNet - Sept 2015 - pNA [501+]
Huffaker, Nathan - *Stranded*
    y SLJ - v61 - i6 - June 2015 - p125(1) [51-500]
Huffman, Eddie - *John Prine: In Spite of Himself*
    BL - v111 - i13 - March 1 2015 - p13(1) [51-500]
    KR - Jan 15 2015 - pNA [501+]
    PW - v262 - i5 - Feb 2 2015 - p48(2) [51-500]
Huggins, Benjamin L. - *The Papers of George Washington: Revolutionary War Series, vol. 22: 1 August-21 October 1779*
    JSH - v81 - i1 - Feb 2015 - p171(2) [501+]
Hughes, Aaron W. - *The Religious and Spiritual Life of the Jews of Medina*
    JAAR - v83 - i2 - June 2015 - p580-582 [501+]
Hughes, Alison - *Beatrice More Moves In (Illus. by Flook, Helen)*
    c KR - Sept 15 2015 - pNA [51-500]
    Gerbil, Uncurled (Illus. by Del Rizzo, Suzanne)
    c PW - v262 - i36 - Sept 7 2015 - p65(1) [51-500]
    Lost in the Backyard
    c KR - Jan 15 2015 - pNA [51-500]
    c Res Links - v20 - i3 - Feb 2015 - p11(2) [501+]
    c SLJ - v61 - i5 - May 2015 - p102(2) [51-500]
    c VOYA - v38 - i1 - April 2015 - p62(1) [51-500]
    Spare Dog Parts (Illus. by Spires, Ashley)
    c KR - Nov 15 2015 - pNA [51-500]
    c PW - v262 - i44 - Nov 2 2015 - p83(1) [51-500]
Hughes, Amy E. - *Spectacles of Reform: Theater and Activism in Nineteenth-Century America*
    JAH - v102 - i1 - June 2015 - p244-244 [501+]
Hughes, Andrew - *The Convictions of John Delahunt*
    PW - v262 - i14 - April 6 2015 - p38(1) [51-500]
    BL - v111 - i19-20 - June 1 2015 - p50(1) [51-500]
    KR - April 15 2015 - pNA [501+]
    NYTBR - June 21 2015 - p25(L) [501+]
Hughes, Anita - *French Coast*
    BL - v111 - i13 - March 1 2015 - p18(1) [51-500]
    LJ - v140 - i5 - March 15 2015 - p92(2) [51-500]
    Rome in Love
    BL - v111 - i19-20 - June 1 2015 - p45(1) [51-500]
Hughes, Aralyn - *Kid Me Not: An Anthology by Child-Free Women of the '60s, Now in Their 60s*
    PW - v262 - i21 - May 25 2015 - p52(1) [51-500]
Hughes, Caoilinn - *Gathering Evidence*
    TLS - i5853 - June 5 2015 - p25(1) [501+]
Hughes, Catherine D. - *Little Kids First Big Book of Bugs*
    c HB Guide - v26 - i1 - Spring 2015 - p158(1) [51-500]
Hughes, Charles L. - *Country Soul*
    KR - Jan 15 2015 - pNA [501+]
Hughes, David - *The Pillbox*
    NS - v144 - i5282 - Oct 2 2015 - p79(1) [51-500]
Hughes, Dean - *Home and Away: A World War II Christmas Story*
    c PW - v262 - i37 - Sept 14 2015 - p75(1) [51-500]
Hughes, Devon - *Unnaturals: The Battle Begins (Illus. by Richardson, Owen)*
    c KR - July 15 2015 - pNA [51-500]
    c SLJ - v61 - i7 - July 2015 - p78(2) [51-500]
Hughes-Edwards, Mari - *Reading Medieval Anchoritism: Ideology and Spiritual Practices*
    HER - v130 - i544 - June 2015 - p715(6) [501+]
Hughes, Emily - *The Little Gardener (Illus. by Hughes, Emily)*
    c KR - May 1 2015 - pNA [51-500]
    c PW - v262 - i20 - May 18 2015 - p81(1) [51-500]
    c PW - v262 - i49 - Dec 2 2015 - p24(1) [51-500]
    c SLJ - v61 - i6 - June 2015 - p84(1) [51-500]
Hughes, Emma - *Education in Prison: Studying through Distance Learning*
    CS - v44 - i2 - March 2015 - p218-219 [501+]
Hughes, Gerard W. - *Cry of Wonder*
    TLS - i5861 - July 31 2015 - p11(1) [501+]
Hughes, Heather - *The First President: A Life of John L. Dube, Founding President of the ANC*
    Historian - v77 - i2 - Summer 2015 - p317(3) [501+]
Hughes, Holly - *Best Food Writing 2015*
    LJ - v140 - i20 - Dec 1 2015 - p123(1) [51-500]
Hughes, Jenny - *Audrey's Tree House (Illus. by Bentley, Jonathan)*
    c HB Guide - v26 - i2 - Fall 2015 - p38(1) [51-500]
Hughes, Jessica - *Remembering Parthenope: The Reception of Classical Naples from Antiquity to the Present*
    TLS - i5850 - May 15 2015 - p9(1) [51-500]
Hughes, Judith M. - *The Holocaust and the Revival of Psychological History*
    JIH - v46 - i2 - Autumn 2015 - p287-288 [501+]
Hughes, Ken - *Chasing Shadows: The Nixon Tapes, the Chennault Affair, and the Origins of Watergate*
    Lon R Bks - v37 - i21 - Nov 5 2015 - p33(2) [501+]
Hughes, Kyle - *The Scots in Victorian and Edwardian Belfast: A Study in Elite Migration*
    AHR - v120 - i1 - Feb 2015 - p339-340 [501+]
Hughes, Langston - *Sail Away (Illus. by Bryan, Ashley)*
    c KR - July 15 2015 - pNA [51-500]
    c BL - v112 - i1 - Sept 1 2015 - p95(1) [51-500]
    c HB - v91 - i6 - Nov-Dec 2015 - p96(2) [51-500]
    c PW - v262 - i49 - Dec 2 2015 - p56(1) [51-500]
    c SLJ - v61 - i11 - Nov 2015 - p132(1) [51-500]
    Selected Letters of Langston Hughes
    TLS - i5862 - August 7 2015 - p7(2) [501+]
    The Weary Blues
    BL - v111 - i11 - Feb 1 2015 - p18(1) [51-500]
    TLS - i5862 - August 7 2015 - p7(2) [501+]
Hughes, Llewelyn - *Globalizing Oil: Firms and Oil Market Governance in France, Japan, and the United states*
    En Jnl - v36 - i3 - July 2015 - p362(2) [501+]
Hughes, Mary-Beth - *The Loved Ones*
    BL - v111 - i17 - May 1 2015 - p76(1) [51-500]
    KR - April 1 2015 - pNA [501+]
    NY - v91 - i19 - July 6 2015 - p87 [51-500]
    NYT - June 25 2015 - pC4(L) [501+]
    NYTBR - July 26 2015 - p8(L) [501+]
    PW - v262 - i16 - April 20 2015 - p49(2) [51-500]
Hughes, Meredith - *Plants Vs. Meats: The Health, History, and Ethics of What We Eat*
    y KR - Jan 1 2016 - pNA [501+]
Hughes, Neil - *Walking on Custard and the Meaning of Life: A Guide for Anxious Humans*
    PW - v262 - i19 - May 11 2015 - p52(1) [51-500]
Hughes, R. Gerald - *The Postwar Legacy of Appeasement: British Foreign Policy since 1945*
    AHR - v120 - i2 - April 2015 - p719-720 [501+]
Hughes, Robert - *The Fatal Shore*
    TimHES - i2211 - July 9 2015 - p46-47 [501+]
    The Spectacle of Skill: New and Selected Writings of Robert Huges
    KR - July 15 2015 - pNA [501+]
    NYT - Dec 4 2015 - pC25(L) [501+]
    The Spectacle of Skill: New and Selected Writings of Robert Hughes
    BL - v112 - i5 - Nov 1 2015 - p24(2) [51-500]
    CSM - Nov 17 2015 - pNA [501+]
    NYTBR - Dec 6 2015 - p45(L) [501+]
    PW - v262 - i33 - August 17 2015 - p60(1) [51-500]
Hughes, Rose - *Fast-Piece Applique: Easy, Artful Quilts by Machine*
    Bwatch - June 2015 - pNA [501+]
Hughes, Shirley - *Daisy Saves the Day (Illus. by Hughes, Shirley)*
    c BL - v111 - i11 - Feb 1 2015 - p54(1) [51-500]
    c HB Guide - v26 - i2 - Fall 2015 - p38(1) [51-500]
    Digby O'Day and the Great Diamond Robbery (Illus. by Vulliamy, Clara)
    c KR - June 15 2015 - pNA [51-500]
    c SLJ - v61 - i11 - Nov 2015 - p90(2) [51-500]
    Digby O'day in the Fast Lane (Illus. by Vulliamy, Clara)
    c HB Guide - v26 - i1 - Spring 2015 - p61(1) [51-500]
    Out and About: A First Book of Poems
    c HB Guide - v26 - i2 - Fall 2015 - p204(1) [51-500]
    Whistling in the Dark
    c Sch Lib - v63 - i3 - Autumn 2015 - p166(1) [51-500]
Hughes, Simon - *Who Wants to be a Batsman? The Analyst Unveils the Secrets of Batting*
    Econ - v416 - i8946 - July 11 2015 - p77(US) [501+]
Hughes, Susan - *Bijou Needs a Home (Illus. by Franson, Leanne)*
    c Res Links - v20 - i3 - Feb 2015 - p12(1) [51-500]
    Cricket's Close Call (Illus. by Franson, Leanne)
    c Res Links - v21 - i1 - Oct 2015 - p15(1) [51-500]
    Fripon le curieux (Illus. by Franson, Leanne)
    c Res Links - v21 - i1 - Oct 2015 - p51(1) [51-500]
    Piper's First Show (Illus. by Franson, Leanne)
    c Res Links - v20 - i4 - April 2015 - p11(1) [51-500]
Hughes, T. John - *Apparitions: Architecture That Has Disappeared from Our Cities*
    LJ - v140 - i10 - June 1 2015 - p98(2) [501+]
Hughes, Val - *Felt and Fibre Art: A Practical Guide to Making Beautiful Felted Artworks*
    BL - v111 - i11 - Feb 1 2015 - p16(1) [51-500]
Hughes, Wayne P. - *The U.S. Naval Institute on Naval Tactics*
    NWCR - v68 - i3 - Summer 2015 - p166(2) [51-500]
Hughes, William - *That Devil's Trick: Hypnotism in the Victorian Popular Imagination*
    TLS - i5866 - Sept 4 2015 - p27(1) [501+]
Hughey, Matthew W. - *The White Savior Film: Content, Critics, and Consumption*
    Am St - v54 - i2 - Summer 2015 - p137-138 [501+]
Hugo, Victor - *Les Miserables (Illus. by Williams, Marcia)*
    c HB Guide - v26 - i2 - Fall 2015 - p202(1) [51-500]
    Mary Tudor
    FS - v69 - i4 - Oct 2015 - p541-542 [501+]
Huguet, Christine - *George Moore: Across Borders*
    ILS - v34 - i2 - Spring 2015 - p24(2) [501+]
Huhn, Helmut - *Symbol and Intuition: Comparative Studies in Kantian and Romantic-Period Aesthetics*
    MLR - v110 - i3 - July 2015 - p786-788 [501+]
Huiqin, Chen - *Daughter of Good Fortune: A Twentieth-Century Chinese Peasant Memoir*
    TimHES - i2211 - July 9 2015 - p50(1) [501+]
Huitson, Toby - *Stairway to Heaven: The Functions of Medieval Upper Spaces*
    Med R - March 2015 - pNA(NA) [501+]
    Ren Q - v68 - i3 - Fall 2015 - p997-998 [501+]
Hull, Brent - *Building a Timeless House in an Instant Age*
    KR - April 15 2015 - pNA [501+]
Hull, Isabel V. - *A Scrap of Paper: Breaking and Making International Law during the Great War*
    AHR - v120 - i3 - June 2015 - p956-957 [501+]
    CEH - v48 - i2 - June 2015 - p265-266 [501+]
    HNet - May 2015 - pNA [501+]
    Lon R Bks - v37 - i12 - June 18 2015 - p9(2) [501+]
Hull, Linda Joffe - *Sweetheart Deal*
    y BL - v112 - i6 - Nov 15 2015 - p29(1) [51-500]
    KR - Sept 15 2015 - pNA [501+]
Hull, Matthew S. - *Government of Paper: The Materiality of Bureaucracy in Urban Pakistan*
    JRAI - v21 - i3 - Sept 2015 - p707(2) [501+]
Hulme, Alison - *On the Commodity Trail: The Journey of a Bargain Store Product from East to West*
    TimHES - i2204 - May 21 2015 - p50-52 [501+]
Hulme-Cross, Benjamin - *The Marsh Demon (Illus. by Evergreen, Nelson)*
    y SLJ - v61 - i9 - Sept 2015 - p151(4) [501+]
    The Red Thirst (Illus. by Evergreen, Nelson)
    y SLJ - v61 - i9 - Sept 2015 - p151(4) [501+]
    Ship of Death (Illus. by Evergreen, Nelson)
    y PW - v262 - i31 - August 3 2015 - p61(1) [501+]
    y SLJ - v61 - i9 - Sept 2015 - p151(4) [501+]
    Warrior Heroes Series
    c Res Links - v20 - i5 - June 2015 - p26(2) [501+]
Hulse, S.M. - *Black River (Read by Newbern, George). Audiobook Review*
    LJ - v140 - i9 - May 15 2015 - p43(1) [51-500]
Hult, Christine A. - *The Handy English Grammar Answer Book*
    BL - v112 - i6 - Nov 15 2015 - p6(1) [51-500]
Hult, Henrik - *Risk and Portfolio Analysis: Principles and Methods*
    SIAM Rev - v57 - i3 - Sept 2015 - p474-475 [501+]
Hum, Tarry - *Making a Global Immigrant Neighborhood: Brooklyn's Sunset Park*
    AJS - v121 - i2 - Sept 2015 - p607(3) [501+]
Human Rights and Humanitarian Interventions
    HNet - Sept 2015 - pNA [501+]
Humanistic Scholarship and the Anthropocene: Approaching China from a Sustainability Paradigm
    HNet - August 2015 - pNA [501+]
Humaydan, Iman - *Beirut Noir*
    PW - v262 - i41 - Oct 12 2015 - p50(1) [51-500]
    Other Lives
    TSWL - v34 - i1 - Spring 2015 - p189-191 [501+]
Humboldt, Alexander von - *Political Essay on the Island of Cuba*
    HAHR - v95 - i1 - Feb 2015 - p141-142 [501+]
Hume, Clair - *Do You Love Dogs?*
    c Magpies - v30 - i2 - May 2015 - p22(1) [501+]
Hume, Mick - *Trigger Warning: Is the Fear of Being Offensive Killing Free Speech?*
    NS - v144 - i5271 - July 17 2015 - p44(1) [501+]
Humes, James C. - *Churchill: The Prophetic Statesman*
    Historian - v77 - i1 - Spring 2015 - p170(2) [501+]
Humm, Daniel - *The Nomad Cookbook*
    BL - v112 - i4 - Oct 15 2015 - p11(2) [51-500]
    PW - v262 - i42 - Oct 19 2015 - p71(1) [51-500]
Hummel, Karl-Joseph - *Kirche, Krieg und Katholiken: Geschichte und Gedachtnis im 20 Jahrhundert*
    Ger Q - v88 - i2 - Spring 2015 - p257(3) [501+]
Hummer, T.R. - *Skandalon: Poems*
    HR - v68 - i2 - Summer 2015 - p327-335 [501+]

Humphrey, Caroline - *A Monastery in Time: The Making of Mongolian Buddhism*
    JAS - v74 - i1 - Feb 2015 - p216-217 [501+]
Humphrey, Kris - *A Whisper of Wolves*
    c Sch Lib - v63 - i2 - Summer 2015 - p118(1) [51-500]
Humphrey, Ted - *The True History of the Conquest of New Spain*
    HNet - June 2015 - pNA [501+]
Humphreys, C.C. - *The Curse of Anne Boleyn*
    KR - March 15 2015 - pNA [501+]
    RVBW - July 2015 - pNA [51-500]
Humphreys, Helen - *The Evening Chorus*
    Mac - v128 - i9 - March 9 2015 - p55(1) [51-500]
    NYTBR - April 19 2015 - p19(L) [501+]
Humphreys, Jessica Dee - *Child Soldier: When Boys and Girls Are Used in War (Illus. by Chikwanine, Michel)*
    c PW - v262 - i26 - June 29 2015 - p71(1) [51-500]
Child Soldier: When Boys and Girls Are Used in War (Illus. by Davila, Claudia)
    c KR - May 15 2015 - pNA [51-500]
Humphreys, Sara - *Brave the Heat*
    BL - v112 - i1 - Sept 1 2015 - p53(2) [51-500]
    PW - v262 - i27 - July 6 2015 - p52(1) [51-500]
The Good, the Bad, and the Vampire
    BL - v112 - i7 - Dec 1 2015 - p36(1) [51-500]
Humphries, Sam - *Legendary Star-Lord: Face It, I Rule (Illus. by Medina, Paco)*
    BL - v111 - i13 - March 1 2015 - p41(1) [51-500]
Humphries, Stan - *Zillow Talk: The New Rules of Real Estate*
    BL - v111 - i11 - Feb 1 2015 - p7(1) [51-500]
Humphries, Thomas L., Jr. - *Ascetic Pneumatology from John Cassian to Gregory the Great*
    CH - v84 - i4 - Dec 2015 - p866(2) [501+]
Hund, Andrew J. - *Antarctica and the Arctic Circle: A Geographic Encyclopedia of the Earth's Polar Regions*
    BL - v111 - i13 - March 1 2015 - p16(1) [501+]
    R&USQ - v54 - i4 - Summer 2015 - p79(1) [501+]
Hundley, Michael B. - *Gods in Dwellings: Temples and Divine Presence in the Ancient Near East*
    JR - v95 - i2 - April 2015 - p253(3) [501+]
Huneault, Kristina - *Rethinking Professionalism: Women and Art in Canada, 1850-1970*
    CWS - v30 - i2-3 - Fall-Winter 2015 - p142(2) [501+]
Hunermann, Peter - *El Vaticano II como software de la Iglesia actual*
    Theol St - v76 - i4 - Dec 2015 - p850(2) [501+]
Hung, Ho-Fung - *The China Boom: Why China Will Not Rule the World*
    LJ - v140 - i17 - Oct 15 2015 - p98(1) [51-500]
Hunka, George - *The Community and Homo Criticus: Performance in the Age of Neoliberalism*
    PAJ - v37 - i1 - Jan 2015 - p126-129 [501+]
Hunn, Nicole - *Gluten-Free Classic Snacks: 100 Recipes for the Brand-Name Treats You Love*
    LJ - v140 - i8 - May 1 2015 - p94(2) [51-500]
Hunsinger, Deborah van Deusen - *Bearing the Unbearable: Trauma, Gospel, and Pastoral Care*
    PW - v262 - i19 - May 11 2015 - p56(1) [51-500]
Hunt, Alaric - *Godless Country*
    BL - v111 - i19-20 - June 1 2015 - p53(1) [51-500]
    KR - June 15 2015 - pNA [51-500]
    PW - v262 - i25 - June 22 2015 - p121(1) [51-500]
Hunt, Andrew - *A Killing in Zion*
    BL - v111 - i22 - August 1 2015 - p34(1) [51-500]
    PW - v262 - i29 - July 20 2015 - p171(1) [51-500]
Hunt, Angela - *Bathsheba: Reluctant Beauty*
    PW - v262 - i27 - July 6 2015 - p54(2) [51-500]
Hunt, Emily - *Dark Green*
    PW - v262 - i16 - April 20 2015 - p51(1) [51-500]
Hunt, Julie - *Song for a Scarlet Runner*
    c SLJ - v61 - i9 - Sept 2015 - p139(1) [51-500]
Hunt, Kristen - *Blonde Eskimo*
    y SLJ - v61 - i9 - Sept 2015 - p167(1) [51-500]
Hunt, Laird - *Neverhome*
    Econ - v414 - i8922 - Jan 24 2015 - p74(US) [501+]
    NS - v144 - i5249 - Feb 13 2015 - p53(1) [501+]
Hunt, Leo - *Thirteen Days of Midnight*
    y CCB-B - v69 - i2 - Oct 2015 - p93(2) [51-500]
    y HB - v91 - i5 - Sept-Oct 2015 - p107(1) [51-500]
    y KR - June 1 2015 - pNA [51-500]
    y PW - v262 - i19 - May 11 2015 - p62(1) [51-500]
    y PW - v262 - i49 - Dec 2 2015 - p108(1) [51-500]
    y Sch Lib - v63 - i3 - Autumn 2015 - p183(1) [51-500]
    y SLJ - v61 - i6 - June 2015 - p125(1) [51-500]
Hunt, Lynda - *Mullaly Fish in a Tree*
    c HB Guide - v26 - i2 - Fall 2015 - p87(1) [51-500]

Hunt, Lynda Mullaly - *Fish in a Tree (Read by McInerney, Kathleen). Audiobook Review*
    y HB - v91 - i4 - July-August 2015 - p164(2) [51-500]
    y SLJ - v61 - i5 - May 2015 - p68(2) [51-500]
Fish in a Tree
    y CCB-B - v68 - i7 - March 2015 - p357(1) [51-500]
    y HB - v91 - i2 - March-April 2015 - p98(1) [51-500]
    y VOYA - v37 - i6 - Feb 2015 - p58(1) [501+]
One for the Murphys (Read by Hunter, Nora). Audiobook Review
    c SLJ - v61 - i8 - August 2015 - p50(1) [51-500]
Hunt, Lynn - *Writing History in the Global Era*
    For Aff - v94 - i1 - Jan-Feb 2015 - pNA [501+]
    Nation - v300 - i6 - Feb 9 2015 - p27(5) [501+]
Hunt, Peter - *The Food Lover's Anthology*
    TLS - i5845 - April 10 2015 - p30(1) [501+]
Hunt, Rebecca - *Everland*
    KR - July 15 2015 - pNA [51-500]
    NY - v91 - i31 - Oct 12 2015 - p103 [51-500]
    NYTBR - Nov 15 2015 - p20(L) [501+]
Hunt, Roger - *It's Always Sunny and Philosophy*
    RVBW - Nov 2015 - pNA [501+]
Hunt, Samantha - *Mr. Splitfoot*
    KR - Oct 1 2015 - pNA [51-500]
    PW - v262 - i41 - Oct 12 2015 - p45(1) [51-500]
Hunt, Tony - *Writing the Future: Prognostic Texts of Medieval England*
    FS - v69 - i1 - Jan 2015 - p89(2) [501+]
Hunt, Tristram - *Cities of Empire: The British Colonies and the Creation of the Urban World*
    Bks & Cult - v21 - i3 - May-June 2015 - p29(1) [501+]
Hunter, Adriana - *Under the Tripoli Sky*
    TLS - i5833 - Jan 16 2015 - p19(2) [501+]
Hunter, Aislinn - *The World Before Us (Read by Hardingham, Fiona). Audiobook Review*
    LJ - v140 - i17 - Oct 15 2015 - p51(2) [51-500]
The World Before Us
    BL - v111 - i11 - Feb 1 2015 - p25(1) [51-500]
    KR - Jan 15 2015 - pNA [501+]
    NYTBR - April 19 2015 - p12(L) [501+]
    PW - v262 - i4 - Jan 26 2015 - p146(1) [51-500]
    WLT - v89 - i5 - Sept-Oct 2015 - p61(2) [51-500]
Hunter, Anne - *Cricket Song*
    c KR - Jan 1 2016 - pNA [51-500]
Hunter, C.C. - *Almost Midnight*
    y KR - Nov 15 2015 - pNA [51-500]
Eternal
    y HB Guide - v26 - i1 - Spring 2015 - p110(1) [51-500]
    y VOYA - v37 - i6 - Feb 2015 - p78(1) [51-500]
Hunter, C. C. - *Unspoken: Shadow Falls*
    y VOYA - v38 - i5 - Dec 2015 - p70(1) [51-500]
Hunter, David - *Apollinaire in the Great War, 1914-1918*
    TLS - i5845 - April 10 2015 - p30(1) [501+]
Hunter, Denise - *Falling Like Snowflakes*
    BL - v112 - i1 - Sept 1 2015 - p54(1) [51-500]
    PW - v262 - i30 - July 27 2015 - p50(1) [51-500]
Hunter, Erin - *The Blazing Star*
    c HB Guide - v26 - i2 - Fall 2015 - p87(1) [51-500]
The Burning Horizon
    c HB Guide - v26 - i2 - Fall 2015 - p87(1) [51-500]
The Endless Lake
    c HB Guide - v26 - i1 - Spring 2015 - p81(1) [51-500]
A Forest Divided
    c HB Guide - v26 - i2 - Fall 2015 - p87(1) [51-500]
Storm of Dogs
    c HB Guide - v26 - i2 - Fall 2015 - p87(1) [51-500]
Warriors Super Edition: Bramblestar's Storm
    c HB Guide - v26 - i1 - Spring 2015 - p81(1) [51-500]
Hunter, Faith - *Blood in Her Veins: Nineteen Stories from the World of Jane Yellowrock*
    PW - v262 - i51 - Dec 14 2015 - p65(1) [51-500]
Hunter, Ian - *Essays on Church, State and Politics*
    HT - v65 - i10 - Oct 2015 - p56(2) [51-500]
Hunter, Kate - *A Curry for Murray (Illus. by Masciullo, Lucia)*
    c Magpies - v30 - i3 - July 2015 - p28(1) [501+]
Hunter, Maddy - *From Bad to Wurst*
    KR - Oct 1 2015 - pNA [51-500]
Hunter, Madeline - *His Wicked Reputation*
    PW - v262 - i5 - Feb 2 2015 - p43(1) [51-500]
Tall, Dark, and Wicked
    PW - v262 - i37 - Sept 14 2015 - p49(1) [51-500]
Hunter, Marcus Anthony - *Black Citymakers: How The Philadelphia Negro Changed Urban America*
    CS - v44 - i4 - July 2015 - p519-521 [501+]
    ERS - v38 - i3 - March 2015 - p501(3) [501+]

Hunter, Nick - *William Caxton and Tim Berners-Lee*
    c Sch Lib - v63 - i3 - Autumn 2015 - p174(1) [51-500]
Hunter, Phillip - *To Die For*
    BL - v111 - i15 - April 1 2015 - p30(1) [51-500]
Hunter, Rebecca - *Caroline*
    PW - v262 - i42 - Oct 19 2015 - p63(2) [51-500]
Hunter, Richard - *Hesiodic Voices: Studies in the Ancient Reception of Hesiod's Work and Days*
    TLS - i5843 - March 27 2015 - p10(2) [501+]
Hesiodic Voices: Studies in the Ancient Reception of Hesiod's Works and Days
    Class R - v65 - i2 - Oct 2015 - p331-333 [501+]
Hunter, Stephen - *I, Ripper*
    BL - v111 - i17 - May 1 2015 - p37(1) [51-500]
    KR - April 1 2015 - pNA [51-500]
    NYTBR - May 31 2015 - p16(L) [501+]
    PW - v262 - i12 - March 23 2015 - p48(1) [51-500]
Hunter, Troy - *A Philosophy on Life, Family, and Growing Up*
    KR - Dec 1 2015 - pNA [51-500]
Hunting, Robert P. - *What Children Can Teach Adults About Mathematics*
    TC Math - v21 - i6 - Feb 2015 - p378(1) [501+]
Hunton and Williams - *Clean Air Handbook, 4th ed.*
    LJ - v140 - i7 - April 15 2015 - p120(1) [51-500]
Huppen, Hermann - *Station 16*
    BL - v111 - i13 - March 1 2015 - p37(1) [51-500]
Hurd, Brian - *Bitter Waters*
    SPBW - June 2015 - pNA [501+]
Hurd, Holly - *Venture Mom: From Idea to Income in Just 12 Weeks*
    LJ - v140 - i11 - June 15 2015 - p95(1) [51-500]
Hurd, Mary G. - *Kris Kristofferson: Country Highwayman*
    PW - v262 - i21 - May 25 2015 - p51(1) [51-500]
Hurd, Thatcher - *The Pea Patch Jig (Illus. by Hurd, Thatcher)*
    c CH Bwatch - August 2015 - pNA [51-500]
Hurdle, Crystal - *Teacher's Pets*
    y Res Links - v20 - i3 - Feb 2015 - p30(1) [51-500]
Huret, Romain D. - *American Tax Resisters*
    AHR - v120 - i2 - April 2015 - p643(1) [501+]
    JAH - v101 - i4 - March 2015 - p1244(1) [501+]
Hurford, James - *The Origins of Grammar: Language in the Light of Evolution*
    Lon R Bks - v37 - i19 - Oct 8 2015 - p37(2) [501+]
Hurka, Thomas - *British Ethical Theorists from Sidgwick to Ewing*
    TLS - i5855 - June 19 2015 - p11(1) [501+]
Hurley, Andrew Michael - *The Loney*
    NS - v144 - i5281 - Sept 25 2015 - p77(1) [501+]
    TLS - i5877 - Nov 20 2015 - p21(1) [501+]
    Spec - v328 - i9757 - August 29 2015 - p41(1) [501+]
Hurley, Erin - *Theatres of Affect*
    Dance RJ - v47 - i2 - August 2015 - p105-106 [501+]
Hurley, Jorey - *Fetch (Illus. by Hurley, Jorey)*
    c CCB-B - v68 - i8 - April 2015 - p403(1) [51-500]
    c HB Guide - v26 - i2 - Fall 2015 - p13(1) [51-500]
    c PW - v262 - i49 - Dec 2 2015 - p13(1) [51-500]
Hop (Illus. by Hurley, Jorey)
    c KR - Oct 15 2015 - pNA [51-500]
    c PW - v262 - i44 - Nov 2 2015 - p84(1) [501+]
    c SLJ - v61 - i11 - Nov 2015 - p77(1) [51-500]
Nest
    c Teach Lib - v42 - i3 - Feb 2015 - p52(1) [51-500]
Hurley, Katie - *The Happy Kid Handbook: How to Raise Joyful Children in a Stressful World*
    PW - v262 - i38 - Sept 21 2015 - p70(1) [51-500]
Hurley, Michael - *The Vineyard*
    PW - v262 - i7 - Feb 16 2015 - p156(1) [51-500]
Hurley, Susan - *Consciousness in Action*
    TimHES - i2211 - July 9 2015 - p45(1) [501+]
Hurrey, Adam - *Football Cliches: Decoding the Oddball Phrases, Colorful Gestures, and Unwritten Rules of Soccer across the Pond*
    BL - v112 - i1 - Sept 1 2015 - p33(1) [51-500]
Hurst, Kim - *Hidden Natural Histories: Herbs*
    BL - v111 - i19-20 - June 1 2015 - p14(1) [51-500]
Hurst, Melissa E. - *The Edge of Forever*
    y VOYA - v38 - i4 - Oct 2015 - p73(1) [51-500]
Hurst, Rachel Alpha Johnston - *Surface Imaginations: Cosmetic Surgery, Photography, and Skin*
    LJ - v140 - i19 - Nov 15 2015 - p99(1) [51-500]
Hurt, Bryan - *Watchlist*
    PW - v262 - i8 - Feb 23 2015 - p47(1) [51-500]
Hurtgen, Renate - *Ausreise per Antrag: Der Lange Weg nach Druben - Eine Studie uber Herrschaft und Alltag in*

der DDR-Provinz
    HNet - Jan 2015 - pNA [501+]
Hurtut, Caroline - *La mysterieuse boutique de Monsieur Bottom (Illus. by Ben, Magali)*
   c Res Links - v20 - i4 - April 2015 - p40(2) [501+]
Hurwitz, Gregg - *Don't Look Back*
    RVBW - April 2015 - pNA [501+]
Orphan X
    BL - v112 - i5 - Nov 1 2015 - p32(1) [51-500]
    KR - Nov 15 2015 - pNA [501+]
    PW - v262 - i45 - Nov 9 2015 - p34(2) [51-500]
Hurwitz, Laura - *Disappear Home*
   y BL - v111 - i11 - Feb 1 2015 - p47(1) [51-500]
   y HB Guide - v26 - i2 - Fall 2015 - p124(1) [51-500]
   y KR - Jan 15 2015 - pNA [51-500]
   y PW - v262 - i2 - Jan 12 2015 - p60(1) [51-500]
   y SLJ - v61 - i3 - March 2015 - p156(2) [51-500]
   y VOYA - v38 - i1 - April 2015 - p62(1) [51-500]
Husain, Aiyaz - *Mapping the End of Empire: American and British Strategic Visions in the Postwar World*
    AHR - v120 - i2 - April 2015 - p585-586 [501+]
    GR - v105 - i4 - Oct 2015 - p620(3) [501+]
Husain, Tasneem Zehra - *Only the Longest Threads*
    KR - April 1 2015 - pNA [501+]
Husband, Amy - *The Noisy Foxes (Illus. by Husband, Amy)*
   c KR - Nov 1 2015 - pNA [51-500]
   c SLJ - v61 - i12 - Dec 2015 - p90(1) [51-500]
Huser, Glen - *The Elevator Ghost (Illus. by Innerst, Stacy)*
   c HB Guide - v26 - i1 - Spring 2015 - p81(1) [51-500]
The Golden Touch
   c KR - Oct 1 2015 - pNA [51-500]
Hussain, Delwar - *Boundaries Undermined: The Ruins of Progress on the Bangladesh-India Border*
    JAS - v74 - i2 - May 2015 - p511-513 [501+]
Hussain, Musharraf - *Seven Steps to Spiritual Intelligence*
    PW - v262 - i19 - May 11 2015 - p55(2) [501+]
Hussenot, Victor - *The Land of Line (Illus. by Hussenot, Victor)*
   c KR - April 15 2015 - pNA [51-500]
The Land of Lines (Illus. by Hussenot, Victor)
   c HB Guide - v26 - i2 - Fall 2015 - p38(1) [51-500]
The Spectators (Illus. by Hussenot, Victor)
    BL - v111 - i19-20 - June 1 2015 - p67(1) [51-500]
    PW - v262 - i26 - June 29 2015 - p54(1) [51-500]
Hustad, Megan - *More Than Conquerors: A Memoir of Lost Arguments*
    Wom R Bks - v32 - i2 - March-April 2015 - p22(2) [501+]
Huston, Jennifer L. - *U2: Changing the World through Rock 'n' Roll*
   c HB Guide - v26 - i2 - Fall 2015 - p194(1) [51-500]
Hustvedt, Siri - *The Blazing World*
    Wom R Bks - v32 - i1 - Jan-Feb 2015 - p28(2) [501+]
Hustwit, J.R. - *Interreligious Hermeneutics and the Pursuit of Truth*
    RM - v69 - i1 - Sept 2015 - p141(3) [501+]
Hutcheon, Linda - *Four Last Songs: Aging and Creativity in Verdi, Strauss, Messiaen, and Britten*
    LJ - v140 - i11 - June 15 2015 - p91(1) [51-500]
Hutcheon, Phil - *Desperation Passes*
    SPBW - April 2015 - pNA [51-500]
Hutchins, Christina - *Tender the Maker*
    KR - Jan 1 2016 - pNA [501+]
Hutchins, Hazel - *Snap! (Illus. by Petricic, Dusan)*
   c BL - v112 - i5 - Nov 1 2015 - p53(1) [51-500]
   c KR - August 1 2015 - pNA [51-500]
   c SLJ - v61 - i11 - Nov 2015 - p82(1) [51-500]
Hutchins, John M. - *Coronado's Well-Equipped Army: The Spanish Invasion of the American Southwest*
    J Mil H - v79 - i3 - July 2015 - p812-813 [501+]
Hutchins, M.K. - *Drift*
   y HB Guide - v26 - i1 - Spring 2015 - p110(1) [51-500]

Hutchins, Pat - *Rosie's Walk*
   c HB Guide - v26 - i2 - Fall 2015 - p13(1) [51-500]
Titch (Illus. by Hutchins, Pat)
   c HB Guide - v26 - i2 - Fall 2015 - p13(1) [51-500]
   c SLJ - v61 - i7 - July 2015 - p55(2) [51-500]
Where, Oh Where, Is Rosie's Chick?
   c Sch Lib - v63 - i3 - Autumn 2015 - p156(1) [51-500]
Hutchins, Zachary McLeod - *Inventing Eden: Primitivism, Millennialism, and the Making of New England*
    AHR - v120 - i4 - Oct 2015 - p1473-1474 [501+]
    NEQ - v88 - i2 - June 2015 - p338-340 [501+]
Hutchinson, Chris - *Jonas in Frames*
    Can Lit - i224 - Spring 2015 - p116 [501+]
Hutchinson, Francis E. - *Architects of Growth? Sub-national Governments and Industrialization in Asia*
    Pac A - v88 - i2 - June 2015 - p261 [501+]
Hutchinson, Phil - *There Is No Such Thing as a Social Science*
    CS - v44 - i5 - Sept 2015 - p604-614 [501+]
Hutchinson, Robert - *The Audacious Crimes of Colonel Blood*
    TLS - i5855 - June 19 2015 - p34(1) [501+]
    Spec - v328 - i9743 - May 23 2015 - p39(1) [501+]
Hutchinson, Shaun David - *The Five Stages of Andrew Brawley (Illus. by Larsen, Christine)*
   y VOYA - v37 - i6 - Feb 2015 - p58(1) [51-500]
   y HB Guide - v26 - i2 - Fall 2015 - p124(1) [51-500]
Violent Ends
   y VOYA - v38 - i4 - Oct 2015 - p52(2) [51-500]
   y BL - v112 - i1 - Sept 1 2015 - p110(1) [51-500]
   y KR - July 15 2015 - pNA [51-500]
   y SLJ - v61 - i8 - August 2015 - p104(2) [51-500]
We Are the Ants
   y BL - v112 - i3 - Oct 1 2015 - p76(1) [51-500]
   y KR - Oct 1 2015 - pNA [51-500]
   y SLJ - v61 - i11 - Nov 2015 - p116(2) [51-500]
   y VOYA - v38 - i5 - Dec 2015 - p70(2) [51-500]
Hutchison, Hazel - *The War That Used Up Words: American Writers and the First World War*
    CJR - v53 - i6 - March-April 2015 - p63(1) [501+]
    TimHES - i2212 - July 16 2015 - p48-1 [501+]
    TLS - i5871 - Oct 9 2015 - p28(1) [501+]
Hutchison, Katrina - *Women in Philosophy: What Needs to Change?*
    TLS - i5859 - July 17 2015 - p3(2) [501+]
Hutchison, Michele - *Safe as Houses*
    PW - v262 - i2 - Jan 12 2015 - p38(1) [51-500]
Huth, Angela - *Colouring In*
    Spec - v328 - i9746 - June 13 2015 - p34(1) [501+]
Hutson, Matthew - *Beyond Happiness: The Upside of Feeling Down*
    Har Bus R - v93 - i7-8 - July-August 2015 - p130(2) [501+]
Hutson, Shaun - *Monolith*
    PW - v262 - i32 - August 10 2015 - p42(1) [501+]
Hutter, Reinhard - *Dust Bound for Heaven: Explorations in the Theology of Thomas Aquinas*
    JR - v95 - i2 - April 2015 - p263(2) [501+]
Hutton, Andrea - *Bald Is Better with Earrings: A Survivor's Guide to Getting through Breast Cancer*
    BL - v111 - i21 - July 1 2015 - p13(1) [51-500]
    LJ - v140 - i9 - May 15 2015 - p100(1) [501+]
    PW - v262 - i14 - April 6 2015 - p55(1) [501+]
Hutton, John - *Calm Baby Gently*
    KR - Jan 1 2015 - pNA [51-500]
Play (Illus. by Kang, Andrea)
   c KR - Jan 1 2015 - pNA [51-500]
Hutton, Robert - *Would They Lie to You? How to Spin Friends and Manipulate People*
    TimHES - i2208 - June 18 2015 - p47(1) [501+]
Hutton, Will - *How Good We Can Be: Ending the Mercenary Society and Building a Great Country*
    NS - v144 - i5250 - Feb 20 2015 - p49(1) [501+]
    TimHES - i2191 - Feb 19 2015 - p54(1) [501+]
    TLS - i5846 - April 17 2015 - p8(1) [501+]
Huxley, Aldous - *The Devine Within: Selectrd Writings on Enlightenment.*
    Forbes - v196 - i6 - Nov 2 2015 - p42(1) [501+]

Huyssen, David - *Progressive Inequality: Rich and Poor in New York, 1890-1920*
    AHR - v120 - i1 - Feb 2015 - p262(1) [501+]
    Dis - v62 - i2 - Spring 2015 - p145(6) [501+]
    JEH - v75 - i2 - June 2015 - p604-606 [501+]
    JIH - v45 - i4 - Spring 2015 - p592-593 [501+]
    RAH - v43 - i3 - Sept 2015 - p527-531 [501+]
Huzzey, Richard - *Freedom Burning: Anti-slavery and Empire in Victorian Britain*
    VS - v57 - i3 - Spring 2015 - p556(4) [501+]
Hwang, Sog-Yong - *The Shadow of Arms*
    WLT - v89 - i1 - Jan-Feb 2015 - p67(1) [51-500]
Hyde, Catherine Ryan - *Ask Him Why*
    BL - v112 - i6 - Nov 15 2015 - p20(1) [51-500]
Pay It Forward: Young Readers Edition
   c HB Guide - v26 - i1 - Spring 2015 - p81(1) [51-500]
Hyde, Charles K. - *Arsenal of Democracy: The American Automobile Industry in World War II*
    JEH - v75 - i3 - Sept 2015 - p938-939 [501+]
Images from the Arsenal of Democracy
    JEH - v75 - i3 - Sept 2015 - p938-939 [501+]
Hyde, Heidi Smith - *Shanghai Sukkah (Illus. by Tsong, Jing)*
   c KR - May 1 2015 - pNA [51-500]
Shanghai Sukkah (Illus. by Tsong, Jing Jing)
   c BL - v112 - i4 - Oct 15 2015 - p49(1) [51-500]
   c SLJ - v61 - i11 - Nov 2015 - p82(1) [51-500]
Hyde, Michael - *Forty Dreaming*
   y Magpies - v30 - i3 - July 2015 - p42(1) [501+]
Hyde, Natalie - *Classified: Spies at Work*
   c Res Links - v20 - i3 - Feb 2015 - p38(2) [501+]
Cultural Traditions in Sweden
    Res Links - v21 - i1 - Oct 2015 - p22(1) [501+]
Glow-in-the-Dark Creatures
   c Res Links - v20 - i5 - June 2015 - p13(1) [501+]
   c HB Guide - v26 - i2 - Fall 2015 - p171(1) [51-500]
How to Write a Fantasy Story
   c CH Bwatch - April 2015 - pNA [501+]
How to Write an Adventure Story
   c CH Bwatch - March 2015 - pNA [501+]
Ninjas
   c Res Links - v20 - i3 - Feb 2015 - p38(2) [501+]
Stay Strong: A Musician's Journey from Congo
   y CH Bwatch - Oct 2015 - pNA [501+]
The Underground Railroad
   c Res Links - v20 - i5 - June 2015 - p34(1) [501+]
Hyman, John - *Action, Knowledge, and Will*
    TLS - i5876 - Nov 13 2015 - p32(2) [501+]
Hyman, Louis - *Debtor Nation: The History of America In Red America*
    RAH - v43 - i1 - March 2015 - p168-175 [501+]
Hyman, Wendy Beth - *The Automaton in English Renaissance Literature*
    T&C - v56 - i3 - July 2015 - p751-752 [501+]
Hyman, Zachary - *Hockey Hero (Illus. by Pullen, Zachary)*
   c KR - August 15 2015 - pNA [51-500]
Hynde, Chrissie - *Reckless: My Life as a Pretender (Read by Arquette, Rosanna). Audiobook Review*
    LJ - v140 - i19 - Nov 15 2015 - p54(1) [51-500]
    NYTBR - Nov 22 2015 - p21(L) [501+]
Reckless: My Life as a Pretender
    Mac - v128 - i37 - Sept 21 2015 - p56(1) [501+]
    NYT - Sept 2 2015 - pC1(L) [501+]
    Spec - v329 - i9772 - Dec 12 2015 - p83(1) [501+]
Hynes, Samuel - *The Unsubstantial Air: American Fliers in the First World War*
    APH - v62 - i1 - Spring 2015 - p51(1) [501+]
    HNet - August 2015 - pNA [501+]
    J Mil H - v79 - i3 - July 2015 - p858-859 [501+]
    J Mil H - v79 - i4 - Oct 2015 - p1169-1170 [501+]
    TLS - i5853 - June 5 2015 - p22(1) [501+]
Hynickx, Rajsh - *The Maritain Factor: Taking Religion into Postwar Modernism*
    CHR - v101 - i3 - Summer 2015 - p672(3) [501+]
Hysell, Shannon G. - *American Reference Books Annual, vol. 46*
    Teach Lib - v43 - i1 - Oct 2015 - p41(3) [501+]
Recommended Reference Books for Small and Medium-Sized Libraries and Media-Centers, 2015 ed.
    Teach Lib - v43 - i1 - Oct 2015 - p41(3) [501+]
Hyslop, Stephen G. - *Contest for California: From Spanish Colonization to the American Conquest*
    PHR - v84 - i1 - Feb 2015 - p85(2) [501+]
Hyzy, Julie - *Grace Cries Uncle*
    BL - v111 - i22 - August 1 2015 - p34(1) [51-500]

I

I Love You (Illus. by Cottingham, Tracy)
　c　PW - v262 - i41 - Oct 12 2015 - p66(2) [501+]
Iamele, Mike - *Enough Already: Create Success on Your Own Terms*
　　SPBW - May 2015 - pNA [51-500]
Iannini, Christopher P. - *Fatal Revolutions: Natural History, West Indian Slavery and the Routes of American Literature*
　　Isis - v106 - i1 - March 2015 - p190(2) [501+]
Iannone, Gyles - *The Great Maya Droughts in Cultural Context: Case Studies in Resilience and Vulnerability*
　　Lat Ant - v26 - i2 - June 2015 - p281(2) [501+]
Iarskaia-Smirnova, Elena - *Disability in Eastern Europe and the Former Soviet Union: History, Policy and Everyday Life*
　　Slav R - v74 - i1 - Spring 2015 - p160-161 [501+]
Ibanez, Andres - *Brilla, mar del Eden*
　　TLS - i5832 - Jan 9 2015 - p22(1) [501+]
Ibarra, Herminia - *Act Like a Leader, Think Like a Leader*
　　LJ - v140 - i6 - April 1 2015 - p101(1) [51-500]
Ibbotson, Toby - *Mountwood School for Ghosts*
　c　Sch Lib - v63 - i1 - Spring 2015 - p38(1) [51-500]
Ibn Gabirol, Solomon - *The Font of Life*
　　RM - v69 - i1 - Sept 2015 - p143(3) [501+]
Ibrahim, Sonallah - *Beirut, Beirut*
　　CSM - Sept 3 2015 - pNA [501+]
Ibrahim, Vivian - *The Copts of Egypt: The Challenges of Modernisation and Identity*
　　Historian - v77 - i3 - Fall 2015 - p538(2) [501+]
Iceland, John - *A Portrait of America: The Demographic Perspective*
　　CS - v44 - i6 - Nov 2015 - p810-811 [501+]
Icinori - *Issun Boshi: The One-Inch Boy* (Illus. by Icinori)
　c　CCB-B - v68 - i5 - Jan 2015 - p260(2) [51-500]
Ickes, Scott - *African-Brazilian Culture and Regional Identity in Bahia, Brazil*
　　Ams - v72 - i2 - April 2015 - p330(2) [501+]
Icons of Style: Sneakers
　　Bwatch - Sept 2015 - pNA [51-500]
Idel, Moshe - *Mircea Eliade: From Magic to Myth*
　　Slav R - v74 - i3 - Fall 2015 - p643-644 [501+]
Idelson-Shein, Iris - *Difference of a Different Kind: Jewish Constructions of Race during the Long Eighteenth Century*
　　AHR - v120 - i2 - April 2015 - p706-707 [501+]
Idema, Wilt Lukas - *The Resurrected Skeleton: From Zhuangzi to Lu Xun*
　　HNet - Jan 2015 - pNA [501+]
Iding, Marie - *Becoming a Professor: A Guide to a Career in Higher Education*
　　RVBW - May 2015 - pNA [501+]
Idle, Molly - *Flora and the Penguin*
　c　HB Guide - v26 - i1 - Spring 2015 - p11(1) [51-500]
Sea Rex (Illus. by Idle, Molly)
　c　CCB-B - v69 - i1 - Sept 2015 - p29(1) [501+]
　c　HB - v91 - i4 - July-August 2015 - p114(2) [51-500]
　c　KR - March 15 2015 - pNA [51-500]
　c　SLJ - v61 - i4 - April 2015 - p128(1) [51-500]
Idleman, Kyle - *The End of Me: Where Real Life in the Upside-Down Ways of Jesus Begins*
　　PW - v262 - i32 - August 10 2015 - p56(1) [51-500]
Ieronimo, Christine - *A Thirst for Home: A Story of Water across the World* (Illus. by Velasquez, Eric)
　c　HB Guide - v26 - i1 - Spring 2015 - p33(1) [51-500]

Ifkovic, Ed - *Cafe Europa*
　　BL - v111 - i16 - April 15 2015 - p27(2) [51-500]
　　KR - March 1 2015 - pNA [501+]
　　PW - v262 - i9 - March 2 2015 - p66(1) [51-500]
Cold Morning
　　KR - Dec 15 2015 - pNA [501+]
Iggulden, Conn - *Margaret of Anjou*
　　KR - April 15 2015 - pNA [51-500]
Wars of the Roses: Margaret of Anjou
　　LJ - v140 - i8 - May 1 2015 - p62(1) [51-500]
Wars of the Roses: Stormbird (Read by Curless, John). Audiobook Review
　　BL - v111 - i9-10 - Jan 1 2015 - p116(2) [51-500]
Igler, David - *The Great Ocean: Pacific Worlds from Captain Cook to the Gold Rush*
　　PHR - v84 - i2 - May 2015 - p252(2) [501+]
Iglesias, Monica - *You Are a Powerful Creator, My Little One: Creating Happiness* (Illus. by Matheus, Robert Paul)
　c　CH Bwatch - Feb 2015 - pNA [501+]
Igloria, Luisa A. - *Night Willow*
　　NAR - v300 - i2 - Spring 2015 - p44(1) [501+]
Ignatius, Daphne - *My Life as Athena*
　　RVBW - Jan 2015 - pNA [501+]
Ignatow, Amy - *The Popularity Papers: The Less-than-Hidden Secrets and Final Revelations of Lydia Goldblatt and Julie Graham-Chang*
　c　HB Guide - v26 - i1 - Spring 2015 - p82(1) [51-500]
Ihalainen, Pasi - *Scandinavia in the Age of Revolution: Nordic Political Cultures, 1740-1820*
　　HER - v130 - i543 - April 2015 - p464(2) [501+]
Ihrig, Stefan - *Ataturk in the Nazi Imagination*
　　HNet - July 2015 - pNA [501+]
　　IJMES - v47 - i3 - August 2015 - p618-620 [501+]
　　NYRB - v62 - i6 - April 2 2015 - p61(3) [501+]
　　TLS - i5840 - March 6 2015 - p12(1) [501+]
Justifying Genocide
　　KR - Nov 1 2015 - pNA [501+]
Ikeda, Takashi - *Whispered Words*
　　SLJ - v61 - i3 - March 2015 - p165(1) [51-500]
Ikegami, Aiko - *Friends* (Illus. by Ikegami, Aiko)
　c　KR - Dec 15 2015 - pNA [501+]
Ikegami, Lisa Geotus - *A Blanket Quite Rare* (Illus. by Ikegami, Lisa Geotus)
　c　CH Bwatch - August 2015 - pNA [51-500]
Ikenberry, G. John - *Power, Order, and Change in World Politics*
　　HNet - Sept 2015 - pNA [501+]
Ikeyamada, Go - *So Cute It Hurts!!*
　y　SLJ - v61 - i12 - Dec 2015 - p129(2) [51-500]
So Cute It Hurts!!, vol. 1
　y　PW - v262 - i26 - June 29 2015 - p54(1) [51-500]
Ile, Jowhor - *And after Many Days*
　　KR - Dec 1 2015 - pNA [501+]
　　PW - v262 - i52 - Dec 21 2015 - p122(2) [51-500]
Iles, Greg - *The Bone Tree*
　　BL - v111 - i12 - Feb 15 2015 - p34(1) [51-500]
　　KR - Feb 15 2015 - pNA [501+]
　　LJ - v140 - i7 - April 15 2015 - p76(1) [51-500]
　　PW - v262 - i8 - Feb 23 2015 - p51(1) [51-500]
Ilgunas, Ken - *Walden on Wheels: On the Open Road from Debt to Freedom*
　　BL - v111 - i21 - July 1 2015 - p22(2) [51-500]
The Iliad. Audiobook Review
　　LJ - v140 - i2 - Feb 1 2015 - p45(1) [51-500]
Iliffe, John - *The African AIDS Epidemic: A History*
　　CS - v44 - i5 - Sept 2015 - p591-603 [501+]
Illakowicz, Krystyna Lipinska - *Post-Communist Specters: Polish Theatre in the Twenty-First Century*
　　PAJ - v37 - i3 - Sept 2015 - p124-127 [501+]

Illiano, Roberto - *Orchestral Conducting in the Nineteenth Century*
　　Notes - v72 - i2 - Dec 2015 - p360(6) [501+]
Illouz, Eva - *Hard Core Romance: Fifty Shades of Grey, Best-Sellers, and Society*
　　Stud Hum - v41 - i1-2 - March 2015 - p257(3) [501+]
Ilya - *Room for Love* (Illus. by Ilya)
　　BL - v111 - i18 - May 15 2015 - p41(2) [501+]
　　PW - v262 - i15 - April 13 2015 - p65(1) [51-500]
Im Bilde. Visualisierung Vormoderner Geschichte in Modernen Medien
　　HNet - March 2015 - pNA [501+]
Im, Chandler H. - *Global Diasporas and Mission*
　　IBMR - v39 - i2 - April 2015 - p106(2) [501+]
Imaginations and Configurations of Polish Society - From the Middle Ages through the 20th Century
　　HNet - March 2015 - pNA [501+]
Imai, Ayano - *Mr. Brown's Fantastic Hat*
　c　HB Guide - v26 - i1 - Spring 2015 - p33(1) [51-500]
Imarisha, Walidah - *Angels with Dirty Faces*
　　KR - Nov 1 2015 - pNA [501+]
Imig, Ann - *Listen to Your Mother: What She Said Then, What We're Saying Now*
　　KR - Feb 15 2015 - pNA [51-500]
　　PW - v262 - i5 - Feb 2 2015 - p50(1) [51-500]
　　LJ - v140 - i2 - Feb 1 2015 - p99(2) [51-500]
　　Par - v90 - i5 - May 2015 - p18(1) [51-500]
Imlay, Talbot - *The Politics of Industrial Collaboration during World War II: Ford France, Vichy and Nazi Germany*
　　AHR - v120 - i3 - June 2015 - p1129-1130 [501+]
　　HNet - March 2015 - pNA [501+]
Imparato, Lauren - *Retox: Healthy Solutions for Real Life*
　　PW - v262 - i50 - Dec 7 2015 - p82(1) [51-500]
"Imperiale Emotionen" Zur Konzeptualisierung ost-westlicher Affektkulturen angesichts der Ukraine-Krise
　　HNet - April 2015 - pNA [501+]
Impey, Chris - *Beyond: Our Future in Space*
　　BL - v111 - i16 - April 15 2015 - p8(1) [501+]
　　KR - Feb 15 2015 - pNA [501+]
　　LJ - v140 - i8 - May 1 2015 - p97(2) [51-500]
　　Nature - v520 - i7547 - April 16 2015 - p293(1) [501+]
　　NYTBR - May 3 2015 - p19(L) [501+]
　　PW - v262 - i7 - Feb 16 2015 - p169(1) [51-500]
　　TimHES - i2203 - May 14 2015 - p46-2 [501+]
Impey, Oliver - *The Origins of Museums: The Cabinet of Curiosities in Sixteenth- and Seventeenth-Century Europe*
　　HT - v65 - i11 - Nov 2015 - p59(1) [501+]
Imrie, Celia - *Not Quite Nice*
　　BL - v111 - i12 - Feb 15 2015 - p32(1) [51-500]
　　LJ - v140 - i3 - Feb 15 2015 - p87(2) [51-500]
In Poseidons Reich XX, "Land Unter!"
　　HNet - June 2015 - pNA [501+]
Inc. Plaid Enterprises - *The Big Book of Mod Podge: Decoupage Made Easy*
　　LJ - v140 - i12 - July 1 2015 - p84(2) [51-500]
Indiana, Gary - *I Can Give You Anything but Love*
　　BL - v111 - i22 - August 1 2015 - p22(1) [51-500]
　　KR - July 15 2015 - pNA [501+]
　　New York - Sept 7 2015 - pNA [501+]
　　New York - Sept 7 2015 - pNA [501+]
　　New York - Sept 7 2015 - pNA [501+]
　　NYRB - v62 - i19 - Dec 3 2015 - p33(2) [501+]
　　RVBW - Nov 2015 - pNA [51-500]
　　UtneADi - i188 - Fall 2015 - p88(1) [501+]

Indridason, Arnaldur - *Into Oblivion*
    KR - Dec 15 2015 - pNA [51-500]
    PW - v262 - i51 - Dec 14 2015 - p58(2) [51-500]
Reykjavik Nights
    BL - v111 - i14 - March 15 2015 - p48(1) [51-500]
    KR - Feb 15 2015 - pNA [51-500]
    LJ - v140 - i5 - March 15 2015 - p97(1) [51-500]
    NYTBR - April 19 2015 - p29(L) [51-500]
    NYTBR - Dec 6 2015 - p85(L) [501+]
    PW - v262 - i5 - Feb 2 2015 - p36(1) [51-500]
Strange Shores
    RVBW - April 2015 - pNA [51-500]
    RVBW - Sept 2015 - pNA [51-500]
Inequality, Education and Social Power
    HNet - April 2015 - pNA [501+]
Inez, Colette - *The Luba Poems*
    ABR - v36 - i4 - May-June 2015 - p17(2) [501+]
Infante, Guillermo Cabrera - *Mapa dibujado por un espia*
    TLS - i5840 - March 6 2015 - p31(1) [501+]
Infante, Ignacio - *After Translation: The Transfer and Circulation of Modern Poetics across the Atlantic*
    AL - v87 - i1 - March 2015 - p197-199 [501+]
Infelise, Mario - *I padroni dei libri: Il controllo sulla stampa nella prima eta moderna*
    HNet - Oct 2015 - pNA [501+]
Infomaniac: Become an Expert in an Hour (Illus. by Derrick, Stuart)
    SPBW - Nov 2015 - pNA [51-500]
Information Experience: Approaches to Theory and Practice
    LR - v64 - i4-5 - April-May 2015 - p397-398 [501+]
Ing, Dean - *It's Up to Charlie Hardin*
    c CH Bwatch - March 2015 - pNA [51-500]
Inga - *Inga Tells All*
    KR - March 1 2015 - pNA [501+]
Ingalls, Ann - *Biggety Bat: Chow Down, Biggety! (Illus. by Zenz, Aaron)*
    c BL - v111 - i22 - August 1 2015 - p74(1) [51-500]
J Is for Jazz (Illus. by Maidagan, Maria Corte)
    c CH Bwatch - March 2015 - pNA [51-500]
Ingber, Judith Brin - *Seeing Israeli and Jewish Dance*
    Dance RJ - v47 - i1 - April 2015 - p111-115 [501+]
Inge, Denise - *A Tour of Bones: Facing Fear and Looking for Life*
    KR - May 15 2015 - pNA [501+]
    PW - v262 - i26 - June 29 2015 - p60(1) [51-500]
    TLS - i5848 - May 1 2015 - p7(2) [501+]
    TimHES - i2184 - Jan 1 2015 - p64(1) [501+]
Ingerman, Sandra - *Speaking with Nature: Awakening to the Deep Wisdom of the Earth*
    PW - v262 - i19 - May 11 2015 - p55(1) [51-500]
Inglis, Lucy - *City of Halves*
    y BL - v112 - i4 - Oct 15 2015 - p56(1) [51-500]
    y HB - v91 - i6 - Nov-Dec 2015 - p80(2) [51-500]
    y KR - August 1 2015 - pNA [51-500]
    y PW - v262 - i29 - July 20 2015 - p193(1) [51-500]
    y Sch Lib - v63 - i1 - Spring 2015 - p54(1) [51-500]
    y SLJ - v61 - i10 - Oct 2015 - p102(1) [51-500]
    y VOYA - v38 - i4 - Oct 2015 - p73(1) [51-500]
Crow Mountain
    y Sch Lib - v63 - i4 - Winter 2015 - p247(1) [51-500]
Ingman, Heather - *Irish Women's Fiction: From Edgeworth to Enright*
    TSWL - v34 - i1 - Spring 2015 - p169-170 [501+]
Ingold, Tim - *Biosocial Becomings: Integrating Social and Biological Anthropology*
    QRB - v90 - i2 - June 2015 - p219(1) [501+]
Ingram, Catherine - *This Is Dali (Illus. by Rae, Andrew)*
    y HB Guide - v26 - i1 - Spring 2015 - p179(1) [51-500]
This Is Pollock (Illus. by Arkle, Peter)
    y HB Guide - v26 - i1 - Spring 2015 - p179(1) [51-500]
This Is Warhol (Illus. by Rae, Andrew)
    y HB Guide - v26 - i1 - Spring 2015 - p179(1) [51-500]
Ingram, Darcy - *Wildlife, Conservation, and Conflict in Quebec, 1840-1914*
    HNet - March 2015 - pNA [501+]
Ingram, Jay - *The End of Memory: A Natural History of Aging and Alzheimer's*
    BL - v112 - i1 - Sept 1 2015 - p21(1) [51-500]
    KR - June 1 2015 - pNA [501+]
    LJ - v140 - i12 - July 1 2015 - p108(2) [51-500]
    Nat Post - v17 - i56 - Jan 3 2015 - pWP10(1) [501+]
    Nature - v526 - i7573 - Oct 15 2015 - p321(1) [51-500]
    PW - v262 - i35 - August 31 2015 - p77(2) [51-500]
Fatal Flaws: How a Misfolded Protein Baffled Scientists and Changed the Way We Look at the Brain
    QRB - v90 - i1 - March 2015 - p108(1) [501+]
Ingram, Marione - *The Hands of Peace: A Holocaust Survivor's Fight for Civil Rights in the American South*
    KR - May 15 2015 - pNA [501+]
Ingram, Tammy - *Dixie Highway: Road Building and the Making of the Modern South, 1900-1930*
    AHR - v120 - i1 - Feb 2015 - p266-265 [501+]
    JAH - v101 - i4 - March 2015 - p1290(1) [501+]
    JSH - v81 - i2 - May 2015 - p495(2) [501+]
Ingrams, Richard - *The Best of 'Dear Bill': The Collected Letters of Denis Thatcher*
    TimHES - i2193 - March 5 2015 - p49(1) [501+]
Ingrao, Christian - *Believe and Destroy: Intellectuals in the SS War Machine*
    HER - v130 - i542 - Feb 2015 - p244(2) [501+]
Ings, Simon - *City of the Iron Fish*
    BL - v111 - i19-20 - June 1 2015 - p64(1) [51-500]
Hot Head
    BL - v111 - i18 - May 15 2015 - p36(1) [51-500]
    PW - v262 - i19 - May 11 2015 - p41(1) [51-500]
Wolves
    KR - April 15 2015 - pNA [51-500]
    PW - v262 - i12 - March 23 2015 - p50(2) [51-500]
Inhabit Media - *Arctic Animals*
    c KR - Jan 1 2016 - pNA [51-500]
    c PW - v262 - i20 - May 18 2015 - p82(2) [501+]
Inhorn, Marcia C. - *Islam and Assisted Reproductive Technologies: Sunni and Shia Perspectives*
    JRAI - v21 - i1 - March 2015 - p229(2) [501+]
Innenansichten - Deutschland 1945
    HNet - April 2015 - pNA [501+]
Innes, Christopher - *The Cambridge Introduction to Theatre Directing*
    TDR - v59 - i1 - Spring 2015 - p185(2) [501+]
Innes-Parker, Catherine - *Anchoritism in the Middle Ages: Texts and Traditions*
    HER - v130 - i544 - June 2015 - p715(6) [501+]
Innes, Shona - *Friendship Is like a Seesaw (Illus. by Agocs, Irisz)*
    c HB Guide - v26 - i1 - Spring 2015 - p132(1) [51-500]
Life Is like the Wind (Illus. by Agocs, Irisz)
    c HB Guide - v26 - i1 - Spring 2015 - p132(1) [51-500]
Innes, Stephanie - *Bear on the Home Front (Illus. by Deines, Brian)*
    c HB Guide - v26 - i1 - Spring 2015 - p33(1) [51-500]
Innis-Jimenez, Michael - *Steel Barrio: The Great Mexican Migration to South Chicago, 1915-1940*
    Ams - v72 - i3 - July 2015 - p497(3) [501+]
    JAH - v101 - i4 - March 2015 - p1306-1307 [501+]
Innis, Robert Alexander - *Elder Brother and the Law of the People: Contemporary Kinship and Cowessess First Nation*
    Am Ind CRJ - v39 - i2 - Spring 2015 - p135-136 [501+]
Inoue, Yasushi - *The Bullfight*
    ABR - v36 - i2 - Jan-Feb 2015 - p27(2) [501+]
The Hunting Gun
    ABR - v36 - i2 - Jan-Feb 2015 - p27(2) [501+]
    NYTBR - April 5 2015 - p18(L) [501+]
Life of a Counterfeiter
    KR - Jan 1 2015 - pNA [501+]
    ABR - v36 - i2 - Jan-Feb 2015 - p27(2) [501+]
    NYTBR - April 5 2015 - p18(L) [501+]
Insects Close Up Series
    c CH Bwatch - July 2015 - pNA [501+]
Inskeep, Steve - *Jacksonland: President Andrew Jackson, Cherokee Chief John Ross, and a Great American Land Grab (Read by Inskeep, Steve). Audiobook Review*
    LJ - v140 - i17 - Oct 15 2015 - p53(3) [51-500]
Jacksonland: President Andrew Jackson, Cherokee Chief John Ross, and a Great American Land Grab
    CHE - v61 - i38 - June 12 2015 - pB5(1) [501+]
    KR - March 15 2015 - pNA [501+]
    LJ - v140 - i5 - March 15 2015 - p120(2) [51-500]
    PW - v262 - i12 - March 23 2015 - p64(1) [51-500]
Insole, Christopher J. - *Kant and the Creation of Freedom: A Theological Problem*
    Rel St - v51 - i4 - Dec 2015 - p587-593 [501+]

Institut fur Zeitgeschichte Munchen - Berlin im Auftrag des Auswartigen Amts - *Akten zur Auswartigen Politik der Bundesrepublik Deutschland 1983*
    HNet - April 2015 - pNA [501+]
Akten zur Auswartigen Politik der Bundesrepublik Deutschland 1984
    HNet - April 2015 - pNA [501+]
Institute of Chartered Accountants in England and Wales - *Financial Reporting Disclosures: Market and Regulatory Failures*
    AR - v90 - i2 - March 2015 - p819(4) [501+]
Institutionen der Erinnerung
    HNet - August 2015 - pNA [501+]
Intellectual History: Traditions and Perspectives
    HNet - July 2015 - pNA [501+]
Intellectuals Journey: The Translation of Ideas in Enlightenment England, France and Ireland
    FS - v69 - i1 - Jan 2015 - p97-98 [501+]
International Congresses and World History: CISH and NOGWHISTO, August 2015
    HNet - Sept 2015 - pNA [501+]
International Security, Political Crime, and Resistance: The Transnationalisation of Normative Orders and the Formation of Criminal Law Regimes in the 19th and 20th Century
    HNet - May 2015 - pNA [501+]
International Symposium Multidisciplinary Methods in Archaeology: Latest Updates and Outlook
    HNet - Sept 2015 - pNA(NA) [501+]
Internationale Tagung: Der Brief in Seinem Umfeld
    HNet - March 2015 - pNA [501+]
Intner, Sheila S. - *Standard Cataloging for School and Public Libraries, 5th ed.*
    LJ - v140 - i6 - April 1 2015 - p103(1) [51-500]
    Teach Lib - v42 - i3 - Feb 2015 - p43(1) [51-500]
    VOYA - v38 - i1 - April 2015 - p92(1) [51-500]
Into the Open: 1990 - The First Year of Transition
    HNet - Sept 2015 - pNA [501+]
Intondi, Vincent J. - *African Americans against the Bomb: Nuclear Weapons, Colonialism, and the Black Freedom Movement*
    Afr Am R - v48 - i1-2 - Spring-Summer 2015 - p215(4) [501+]
Intrator, Sam M. - *The Quest for Mastery: Positive Youth Development Through Out-of-School Programs*
    HER - v85 - i1 - Spring 2015 - p137-140 [501+]
Ioffe, Carole - *Reproduction and Society: Interdisciplinary Readings*
    Cons - v36 - i1 - Spring 2015 - p42(3) [501+]
Iovine, Julie - *New York in Fifty Design Icons*
    LJ - v140 - i20 - Dec 1 2015 - p106(2) [501+]
Ip, Greg - *Foolproof: Why Safety Can Be Dangerous and How Danger Makes Us Safe*
    KR - August 1 2015 - pNA [501+]
    NYTBR - Oct 25 2015 - p35(L) [501+]
    PW - v262 - i33 - August 17 2015 - p62(1) [51-500]
Ipcar, Dahlov - *Black and White (Illus. by Ipcar, Dahlov)*
    c NYTBR - June 21 2015 - p16(L) [501+]
    c SLJ - v61 - i6 - June 2015 - p84(1) [51-500]
I Like Animals
    c HB Guide - v26 - i1 - Spring 2015 - p11(1) [51-500]
Irelan, Patrick - *The Big Drugstore*
    KR - August 1 2015 - pNA [51-500]
Ireland, D.E. - *Move Your Blooming Corpse*
    BL - v112 - i2 - Sept 15 2015 - p32(1) [51-500]
    PW - v262 - i27 - July 6 2015 - p47(1) [51-500]
Ireland, Justina - *Promise of Shadows*
    y Teach Lib - v42 - i3 - Feb 2015 - p28(4) [501+]
Ireland, Ryan - *Beyond the Horizon*
    KR - Feb 15 2015 - pNA [501+]
    LJ - v140 - i6 - April 1 2015 - p81(1) [51-500]
Irfan, Harris - *Heaven's Bankers: Inside the Hidden World of Islamic Finance*
    LJ - v140 - i3 - Feb 15 2015 - p110(1) [51-500]
    NYTBR - March 22 2015 - p15(L) [501+]
    PW - v262 - i1 - Jan 5 2015 - p64(1) [51-500]
Irigoyen-Garcia, Javier - *The Spanish Arcadia: Sheep Herding, Pastoral Discourse, and Ethnicity in Early Modern Spain*
    MLN - v130 - i2 - March 2015 - p401-402 [501+]
    Six Ct J - v46 - i1 - Spring 2015 - p256-258 [501+]
Irish, Cindy - *The Song That Seduced Paris*
    KR - Oct 1 2015 - pNA [501+]
Irish Countrywomen's Association - *The Irish Countrywomen's Association Book of Crafts: 40 Projects To Make at Home*
    LJ - v140 - i10 - June 1 2015 - p102(2) [51-500]

Iriye, Akira - *Global Interdependence: The World after 1945*
    AHR - v120 - i1 - Feb 2015 - p194-196 [501+]

Iromuanya, Julie - *Mr. and Mrs. Doctor*
    KR - April 15 2015 - pNA [51-500]
    NYTBR - Sept 13 2015 - p34(L) [501+]

Irons, Larry - *Number One Songs: The First Twenty Years*
    PW - v262 - i22 - June 1 2015 - p55(1) [51-500]

Irr, Caren - *Toward the Geopolitical Novel: U.S. Fiction in the Twenty-First Century*
    ABR - v36 - i5 - July-August 2015 - p5(1) [501+]

Irvin, Matthew W. - *The Poetic Voices of John Gower: Politics and Personae in the*
    Ren Q - v68 - i2 - Summer 2015 - p754-755 [501+]

Irvine, Andrew B. - *The Religion of the Future*
    JAAR - v83 - i2 - June 2015 - p554-568 [501+]

Irvine, Leslie - *My Dog Always Eats First: Homeless People and Their Animals*
    CS - v44 - i4 - July 2015 - p521-523 [501+]

Irvine, William B. - *Aha! The Moments of Insight That Shape Our World*
    LJ - v140 - i2 - Feb 1 2015 - p87(1) [51-500]

Irving, Ellie - *Fleeced*
    c Sch Lib - v63 - i4 - Winter 2015 - p229(1) [51-500]

Irving, John - *Avenue of Mysteries*
    BL - v111 - i22 - August 1 2015 - p6(1) [51-500]
    BL - v112 - i3 - Oct 1 2015 - p22(1) [51-500]
    KR - Sept 1 2015 - pNA [501+]
    LJ - v140 - i15 - Sept 15 2015 - p67(1) [51-500]
    NYT - Nov 3 2015 - pC1(L) [501+]
    NYTBR - Nov 29 2015 - p16(L) [501+]
    PW - v262 - i36 - Sept 7 2015 - p42(1) [51-500]

Irving, Terry - *Courier*
    RVBW - Jan 2015 - pNA [51-500]
    PW - v262 - i37 - Sept 14 2015 - p45(2) [51-500]
Day of the Dragonking
    PW - v262 - i38 - Sept 21 2015 - p59(1) [51-500]
Warrior
    KR - August 1 2015 - pNA [501+]

Irving, Washington - *Rip Van Winkle, The Legend of Sleepy Hollow, The Pride of the Village & Spectre Bridegroom (Illus. by Smith, Tod)*
    y HB Guide - v26 - i1 - Spring 2015 - p72(2) [51-500]
Rip Van Winkle, The Legend of Sleepy Hollow, The Pride of the Village & The Spectre Bridegroom (Read by Sims, Adam). Audiobook Review
    y PW - v262 - i17 - April 27 2015 - p69(2) [501+]

Irwin, Ben - *The Story of King Jesus (Illus. by Lee, Nick)*
    c CH Bwatch - July 2015 - pNA [51-500]

Irwin, John T. - *F. Scott Fitzgerald's Fiction: "An Almost Theatrical Innocence"*
    J Am St - v49 - i2 - May 2015 - p431-433 [501+]

Irwin, Kevin W. - *What We Have Done, What We Have Failed to Do: Assessing the Liturgical Reforms of Vatican II*
    Theol St - v76 - i1 - March 2015 - p201(3) [501+]

Irwin, Sue - *Safety Stars: Players Who Fought to Make the Hard-Hitting Game of Professional Hockey Safer*
    y PW - v262 - i31 - August 3 2015 - p61(1) [501+]
    y Res Links - v20 - i5 - June 2015 - p31(1) [501+]
    y SLJ - v61 - i10 - Oct 2015 - p134(1) [51-500]

Irwin, Terence - *The Development of Ethics: A Historical and Critical Study*
    Phil R - v124 - i2 - April 2015 - p279(8) [501+]

Is Shame Necessary? New Uses for an Old Tool
    Econ - v414 - i8929 - March 14 2015 - p84(US) [501+]

Isaac, Joel - *Uncertain Empire: American History and the Idea of the Cold War*
    J Am St - v49 - i1 - Feb 2015 - p211-213 [501+]

Isaacs, Ralph - *Woven Miniatures of Buddhist Art: Sazigyo, Burmese Manuscript Binding Tapes*
    JAS - v74 - i3 - August 2015 - p782-784 [501+]

Isaacson, Walter - *The Innovators: How a Group of Hackers, Geniuses, and Geeks Created the Digital Revolution (Read by Boutsikaris, Dennis). Audiobook Review*
    BL - v111 - i13 - March 1 2015 - p68(2) [51-500]
    BL - v112 - i7 - Dec 1 2015 - p71(1) [501+]
    LJ - v140 - i2 - Feb 1 2015 - p46(3) [51-500]
The Innovators: How a Group of Hackers, Geniuses, and Geeks Created the Digital Revolution
    AJPsy - v128 - i3 - Fall 2015 - p403(5) [501+]
    For Aff - v94 - i1 - Jan-Feb 2015 - pNA [501+]
    NYTBR - Nov 22 2015 - p36(L) [501+]

Isabel, Torres - *Love Poetry in the Spanish Golden Age: Eros, Eris and Empire*
    Hisp R - v83 - i4 - Autumn 2015 - p491-494 [501+]

Isabella, Jude - *The Red Bicycle: The Extraordinary Story of One Ordinary Bicycle (Illus. by Shin, Simone)*
    PW - v262 - i4 - Jan 26 2015 - p174(2) [51-500]
    c BL - v111 - i12 - Feb 15 2015 - p77(1) [51-500]
    c HB - v91 - i3 - May-June 2015 - p88(2) [51-500]
    c HB Guide - v26 - i2 - Fall 2015 - p38(1) [51-500]
    c NYTBR - May 10 2015 - p21(L) [501+]
    c Res Links - v20 - i5 - June 2015 - p5(1) [51-500]
    c SLJ - v61 - i3 - March 2015 - p170(1) [51-500]

Isadora, Rachel - *Bea in The Nutcracker (Illus. by Isadora, Rachel)*
    c BL - v112 - i3 - Oct 1 2015 - p81(1) [51-500]
    c HB - v91 - i6 - Nov-Dec 2015 - p56(1) [51-500]
    c KR - Sept 1 2015 - pNA [51-500]
    c SLJ - v61 - i10 - Oct 2015 - p64(2) [51-500]
I Hear a Pickle: And Smell, See, Touch, and Taste It, Too! (Illus. by Isadora, Rachel)
    c KR - Oct 15 2015 - pNA [51-500]
    c PW - v262 - i42 - Oct 19 2015 - p75(1) [51-500]

Isay, Dave - *StoryCorps OutLoud: Voices of the LGBTQ Community from Across America (Read by Shapiro, Ari). Audiobook Review*
    BL - v111 - i22 - August 1 2015 - p79(1) [51-500]

Isayama, Hajime - *Attack on Titan: The Harsh Mistress of the City, Part 2 (Illus. by Murata, Range)*
    y CH Bwatch - Oct 2015 - pNA [51-500]

Isbell, Jennie - *Finding God in the Verbs: Crafting a Fresh Language of Prayer*
    PW - v262 - i3 - Jan 19 2015 - p76(1) [51-500]

Isbell, Tom - *The Capture*
    y KR - Oct 15 2015 - pNA [51-500]
The Prey
    y CCB-B - v68 - i6 - Feb 2015 - p315(2) [51-500]
    y HB Guide - v26 - i2 - Fall 2015 - p124(1) [51-500]

Isbouts, Jean-Pierre - *Ten Prayers That Changed the World: Extraordinary Stories of Faith That Shaped the Course of History*
    PW - v262 - i51 - Dec 14 2015 - p78(1) [51-500]

Isenbarger, Dennis L. - *Native Americans in Early North Carolina: A Documentary History*
    JSH - v81 - i2 - May 2015 - p537(2) [501+]

Iseppi De Filippis, Laura - *Inventing a Path: Studies in Medieval Rhetoric in Honour of Mary Carruthers*
    Med R - August 2015 - pNA [51-500]

Iserles, Inbali - *Foxcraft: The Taken*
    c Sch Lib - v63 - i4 - Winter 2015 - p229(1) [51-500]
    c KR - July 1 2015 - pNA [51-500]
    c SLJ - v61 - i8 - August 2015 - p86(2) [51-500]

Isern, Susanna - *What are You Scared of, Little Mouse? (Illus. by Hilb, Nora)*
    c SLJ - v61 - i11 - Nov 2015 - p77(1) [51-500]

Ishida, Sanae - *Little Kunoichi, The Ninja Girl (Illus. by Ishida, Sanae)*
    c HB Guide - v26 - i2 - Fall 2015 - p13(1) [51-500]
    c PW - v262 - i14 - April 6 2015 - p57(2) [51-500]
    c KR - March 1 2015 - pNA [51-500]
    c SLJ - v61 - i7 - July 2015 - p62(2) [51-500]

Ishida, Sui - *Tokyo Ghoul, vol. 1*
    PW - v262 - i25 - June 22 2015 - p128(1) [51-500]

Ishiguro, Kazuo - *The Buried Giant (Read by Horovitch, David). Audiobook Review*
    Bwatch - May 2015 - pNA [51-500]
    LJ - v140 - i9 - May 15 2015 - p43(3) [51-500]
The Buried Giant
    Atl - v315 - i2 - March 2015 - p44(3) [51-500]
    BL - v111 - i9-10 - Jan 1 2015 - p35(2) [51-500]
    BooChiTr - March 14 2015 - p14(1) [501+]
    Can Lit - i224 - Spring 2015 - p127 [501+]
    CSM - March 3 2015 - pNA [501+]
    Econ - v414 - i8927 - Feb 28 2015 - p75(US) [501+]
    Ent W - i1354 - March 13 2015 - p62(1) [501+]
    HM - v330 - i1979 - April 2015 - p89(6) [501+]
    KR - Jan 1 2015 - pNA [501+]
    LJ - v140 - i2 - Feb 1 2015 - p72(2) [51-500]
    Lon R Bks - v37 - i5 - March 5 2015 - p17(2) [501+]
    MFSF - v128 - i3-4 - March-April 2015 - p73(8) [501+]
    Nat Post - v17 - i107 - March 7 2015 - pWP5(1) [501+]
    NS - v144 - i5252 - March 6 2015 - p50(2) [501+]
    NY - v91 - i5 - March 23 2015 - p92 [501+]
    NYRB - v62 - i6 - April 2 2015 - p44(2) [501+]
    NYT - Feb 24 2015 - pC1(L) [501+]
    NYTBR - March 1 2015 - p1(L) [501+]
    PW - v262 - i3 - Jan 19 2015 - p54(1) [501+]
    Spec - v327 - i9731 - Feb 28 2015 - p41(1) [501+]
    TLS - i5842 - March 20 2015 - p20(2) [501+]

Ishinomori, Shotaro - *The Legend of Zelda: A Link to the Past (Illus. by Ishinomori, Shotaro)*
    c SLJ - v61 - i7 - July 2015 - p99(2) [51-500]

Islam, Md Saidul - *Development, Power, and the Environment*
    AJS - v120 - i6 - May 2015 - p1876(4) [501+]

Islam, Tanwi Nandini - *Bright Lines*
    BL - v111 - i22 - August 1 2015 - p27(1) [51-500]
    KR - June 1 2015 - pNA [51-500]
    LJ - v140 - i12 - July 1 2015 - p77(2) [51-500]
    Mac - v128 - i31 - August 10 2015 - p57(2) [501+]
    PW - v262 - i24 - June 15 2015 - p59(1) [51-500]

Ismael, Asif - *Over the Tightrope*
    KR - Oct 15 2015 - pNA [51-500]

Ismail, Yasmeen - *Specs for Rex (Illus. by Ismail, Yasmeen)*
    c PW - v262 - i38 - Sept 21 2015 - p71(1) [51-500]
    c Sch Lib - v63 - i2 - Summer 2015 - p94(1) [51-500]
    c SLJ - v61 - i11 - Nov 2015 - p82(1) [51-500]
Specs for Rex
    c KR - Sept 1 2015 - pNA [51-500]

Isol - *The Menino: A Story Based on Real Events (Illus. by Isol)*
    c SLJ - v61 - i11 - Nov 2015 - p82(2) [51-500]
    c CH Bwatch - Oct 2015 - pNA [501+]
    c KR - Sept 15 2015 - pNA [51-500]
    c NYTBR - Nov 8 2015 - p20(L) [501+]

Isom, Chervis - *The Newspaper Boy*
    KR - March 15 2015 - pNA [501+]

Ison, Graham - *Exit Stage Left*
    BL - v111 - i17 - May 1 2015 - p34(1) [51-500]
    PW - v262 - i16 - April 20 2015 - p56(1) [51-500]
Hardcastle's Collector
    PW - v262 - i51 - Dec 14 2015 - p63(1) [51-500]

Ison, Tara - *Ball*
    PW - v262 - i36 - Sept 7 2015 - p43(1) [51-500]
    KR - Sept 1 2015 - pNA [51-500]
Reeling through Life: How I Learned to Live, Love, and Die at the Movies
    BooChiTr - Jan 31 2015 - p14(1) [501+]
    NYTBR - Jan 25 2015 - p11(L) [501+]

Isphording, Bernd - *Biographisches Handbuch des Deutschen Auswartigen Dienstes 1871-1945, vol. 5: T-Z*
    HNet - June 2015 - pNA [501+]

Israel, Jonathan - *Revolutionary Ideas - An Intellectual History of the French Revolution from the 'Rights of Man' to Robespierre*
    FS - v69 - i2 - April 2015 - p252(1) [501+]

Israeli, Raphael - *The Death Camps of Croatia: Visions and Revisions, 1941-1945*
    Historian - v77 - i2 - Summer 2015 - p391(3) [501+]

Issenberg, Sasha - *Outpatients*
    KR - Nov 15 2015 - pNA [501+]

Issitt, Micah L. - *Hidden Religion: The Greatest Mysteries and Symbols of the World's Religious Beliefs*
    R&USQ - v54 - i3 - Spring 2015 - p62(1) [501+]
    BL - v111 - i9-10 - Jan 1 2015 - p20(2) [501+]

Issues in Sports Series
    c BL - v111 - i15 - April 1 2015 - p58(1) [501+]

Istituto per le scienze religiose Bologna - *The General Councils of Latin Christendom: From Constantinople IV (869/870) to Lateran V (1512-1517)*
    CHR - v101 - i3 - Summer 2015 - p573(5) [501+]

Itani, Frances - *Best Friend Trouble (Illus. by Despres, Genevieve)*
    c HB Guide - v26 - i1 - Spring 2015 - p33(1) [51-500]
Tell
    NYTBR - Jan 11 2015 - p18(L) [501+]

Ito, Junji - *Fragments of Horror (Illus. by Ito, Junji)*
    PW - v262 - i20 - May 18 2015 - p72(1) [51-500]
Gyo (Illus. by Ito, Junji)
    y SLJ - v61 - i7 - July 2015 - p99(2) [51-500]

Ito, Kuno - *International Perspectives on Accounting and Corporate Behavior*
    AR - v90 - i3 - May 2015 - p1244(4) [501+]

Ito, Takashi - *London Zoo and the Victorians: 1828-1859*
    JIH - v45 - i4 - Spring 2015 - p576-577 [501+]

Itzkoff, Dave - *Mad as Hell: The Making of Network and the Fateful Vision of the Angriest Man in Movies*
  y NYTBR - April 19 2015 - p28(L) [501+]
Ius, Dawn - *Anne & Henry*
  y BL - v112 - i2 - Sept 15 2015 - p70(1) [51-500]
  y KR - June 15 2015 - pNA [51-500]
  y PW - v262 - i24 - June 15 2015 - p84(2) [51-500]
  y SLJ - v61 - i7 - July 2015 - p93(1) [51-500]
  y VOYA - v38 - i4 - Oct 2015 - p53(1) [51-500]
IV Encuentro Interdisciplinario sobre Estudios de Memoria
  HNet - March 2015 - pNA [501+]
IV ENIUGH Congress "Encounters, Circulations and Conflicts": Conflicts and War
  HNet - Jan 2015 - pNA [501+]
IV ENIUGH Congress "Encounters, Circulations and Conflicts": Gender
  HNet - Jan 2015 - pNA [501+]
IV ENIUGH Congress "Encounters, Circulations and Conflicts": Higher Education
  HNet - Feb 2015 - pNA [501+]
IV ENIUGH Congress "Encounters, Circulations and Conflicts": The Histories of Humanitarianism
  HNet - Feb 2015 - pNA [501+]
IV ENIUGH Congress "Encounters, Circulations and Conflicts": The Ottoman Empire in World and Global History
  HNet - Feb 2015 - pNA [501+]
IV ENIUGH Congress "Encounters, Circulations and Conflicts": Zentrum und Peripherie
  HNet - March 2015 - pNA [501+]
Ivereigh, Austen - *The Great Reformer: Francis and the Making of a Radical Pope*
  CC - v132 - i8 - April 15 2015 - p39(2) [501+]
Ivereigh, Austen - *The Great Reformer: Francis and the Making of a Radical Pope*
  Comw - v142 - i3 - Feb 6 2015 - p26(3) [501+]
  TLS - i5844 - April 3 2015 - p3(2) [501+]
Iversen, Inger - *Incarcerated: Letters from Inmate 92510*
  KR - August 1 2015 - pNA [501+]
Ives, Susanna - *Wicked, My Love*
  PW - v262 - i2 - Jan 12 2015 - p42(1) [51-500]
Ivester, Jo - *The Outskirts of Hope: A Memoir of the 1960s Deep South*
  BL - v111 - i13 - March 1 2015 - p16(1) [51-500]
Ivey, Paul Eli - *Radiance from Halcyon: A Utopian Experiment in Religion and Science*
  Isis - v106 - i2 - June 2015 - p477(2) [501+]
  JR - v95 - i3 - July 2015 - p431(2) [501+]
Ivory, Vincent H. - *Word World*
  KR - Nov 1 2015 - pNA [51-500]
Ivy, Alexandra - *Kill without Mercy*
  PW - v262 - i44 - Nov 2 2015 - p68(1) [51-500]
On the Hunt
  PW - v262 - i28 - July 13 2015 - p52(1) [51-500]
Iwuchukwu, Marinus C. - *Muslim-Christian Dialogue in Postcolonial Northern Nigeria: The Challenges of Inclusive Cultural and Religious Pluralism*
  J Ch St - v57 - i3 - Summer 2015 - p567-569 [501+]
Iyengar, Sujata - *Shakespeare's Medical Language: A Dictionary*
  Ren Q - v68 - i3 - Fall 2015 - p1151-1152 [501+]
Iyer, Deepa - *We Too Sing America: South Asian, Arab, Muslim, and Sikh Immigrants Shape Our Multiracial Future*
  BL - v112 - i4 - Oct 15 2015 - p8(1) [51-500]
  LJ - v140 - i16 - Oct 1 2015 - p99(1) [51-500]
  PW - v262 - i34 - August 24 2015 - p72(2) [51-500]
Iyer, Rani - *Endangered Energy: Investigating the Scarcity of Fossil Fuels*
  c HB Guide - v26 - i2 - Fall 2015 - p155(1) [51-500]
  Endangered Rivers: Investigating Rivers in Crisis
  c HB Guide - v26 - i2 - Fall 2015 - p155(1) [51-500]
Izecksohn, Vitor - *Slavery and War in the Americas: Race, Citizenship, and State Building in the United States and Brazil, 1861-1870*
  AHR - v120 - i4 - Oct 2015 - p1453-1454 [501+]
  JAH - v102 - i2 - Sept 2015 - p565-565 [501+]
Izett, Mary - *Speed Brewing: Techniques and Recipes for Fast-Fermenting Beers, Ciders, Meads, and More*
  LJ - v140 - i17 - Oct 15 2015 - p107(1) [51-500]

J

J. Martineau Paul - *Minor White: Manifestations of the Spirit*
    Parabola - v40 - i1 - Spring 2015 - p96-99 [501+]
J. Paul Getty Museum Science Department - *Art & Science: A Curriculum for K-12 Teachers from the J. Paul Getty Museum*
    Sci Teach - v82 - i9 - Dec 2015 - p74 [51-500]
Jaboulet-Vercherre, Azelina - *The Physician, the Drinker, and the Drunk: Wine's Uses and Abuses in Late Medieval Natural Philosophy*
    Specu - v90 - i4 - Oct 2015 - p1121-1122 [501+]
Jack, Albert - *They Laughed at Galileo: How the Great Inventors Proved Their Critics Wrong*
    LJ - v140 - i12 - July 1 2015 - p108(1) [51-500]
Jack, Jordynn - *Autism and Gender: From Refrigerator Mothers to Computer Geeks*
    Wom R Bks - v32 - i2 - March-April 2015 - p3(2) [501+]
Jacka, Benedict - *Veiled*
    PW - v262 - i28 - July 13 2015 - p50(1) [51-500]
Jackley, Jessica - *Clay Water Brick: Finding Inspiration from Entrepreneurs Who Do the Most with the Least*
    KR - April 15 2015 - pNA [501+]
    BL - v111 - i21 - July 1 2015 - p21(1) [51-500]
    LJ - v140 - i9 - May 15 2015 - p90(1) [51-500]
Jackman, Clifford - *The Winter Family*
    BL - v111 - i12 - Feb 15 2015 - p42(1) [51-500]
    KR - Feb 15 2015 - pNA [51-500]
    NYTBR - August 16 2015 - p30(L) [501+]
    PW - v262 - i8 - Feb 23 2015 - p49(1) [51-500]
Jackson, Aaron P. - *Doctrine, Strategy and Military Culture: Military-Strategic Doctrine Development in Australia, Canada and New Zealand, 1987-2007*
    APH - v62 - i1 - Spring 2015 - p51(2) [501+]
Jackson Albarran, Elena - *Seen and Heard in Mexico: Children and Revolutionary Cultural Nationalism*
    HAHR - v95 - i4 - Nov 2015 - p689-690 [501+]
Jackson, Alvin - *The Oxford Handbook of Modern Irish History*
    TLS - i5838 - Feb 20 2015 - p27(1) [501+]
Jackson, Andrew Grant - *1965: The Most Revolutionary Year in Music*
    BL - v111 - i9-10 - Jan 1 2015 - p30(1) [51-500]
    LJ - v140 - i3 - Feb 15 2015 - p104(1) [51-500]
Jackson, Angela - *It Seems Like a Mighty Long Time*
    BL - v111 - i11 - Feb 1 2015 - p15(1) [51-500]
Jackson, Ashley - *Buildings of Empire*
    AHR - v120 - i2 - April 2015 - p575-576 [501+]
Jackson, Aurelia - *Carmelo Anthony*
    c BL - v111 - i9-10 - Jan 1 2015 - p84(2) [51-500]
Dwayne Wade
    c BL - v111 - i9-10 - Jan 1 2015 - p84(2) [51-500]
LeBron James
    c BL - v111 - i9-10 - Jan 1 2015 - p84(2) [51-500]
Rajon Rondo
    c BL - v111 - i9-10 - Jan 1 2015 - p84(2) [51-500]
Jackson, Blair - *This Is All a Dream We Dreamed: An Oral History of the Grateful Dead*
    BL - v111 - i22 - August 1 2015 - p16(1) [501+]
    KR - Sept 1 2015 - pNA [51-500]
    LJ - v140 - i14 - Sept 1 2015 - p103(1) [51-500]
    PW - v262 - i30 - July 27 2015 - p52(1) [51-500]
Jackson, D.B. - *Dead Man's Reach*
    KR - May 15 2015 - pNA [51-500]
    PW - v262 - i20 - May 18 2015 - p69(1) [51-500]
Jackson, Ellen - *Beastly Babies (Illus. by Wenzel, Brendan)*
    c BL - v111 - i19-20 - June 1 2015 - p108(2) [51-500]
    c KR - May 1 2015 - pNA [51-500]
    c PW - v262 - i18 - May 4 2015 - p118(1) [51-500]
    c SLJ - v61 - i6 - June 2015 - p84(1) [51-500]
Classic Cookies with Modern Twists: 100 Best Recipes for Old and New Favorites
    LJ - v140 - i15 - Sept 15 2015 - p100(1) [51-500]
Tooling Around: Crafty Creatures and the Tools They Use (Illus. by Benoit, Renne)
    c HB Guide - v26 - i1 - Spring 2015 - p155(1) [51-500]
Jackson, Gregg - *Prodigals*
    KR - Jan 1 2016 - pNA [51-500]
Jackson, H.J. - *Those Who Write for Immortality: Romantic Reputations and the Dream of Lasting Fame*
    NYRB - v62 - i19 - Dec 3 2015 - p71(3) [501+]
    AS - v84 - i2 - Spring 2015 - p128(2) [501+]
    CHE - v62 - i1 - Sept 4 2015 - pB17(1) [501+]
    Nat Post - v17 - i125 - March 28 2015 - pWP10(1) [501+]
    New R - v246 - i2-3 - March-April 2015 - p66(4) [501+]
    PW - v262 - i4 - Jan 26 2015 - p165(2) [51-500]
Those Who Write for Immortality. Romantic Reputations and the Dream of Lasting Fame
    TimHES - i2207 - June 11 2015 - p54-55 [501+]
Jackson, Harvey H., III - *The Rise and Decline of the Redneck Riviera: An Insider's History of the Florida-Alabama Coast*
    RAH - v43 - i1 - March 2015 - p116-125 [501+]
Jackson, Holly - *American Blood: The Ends of the Family in American Literature, 1850-1900*
    NEQ - v88 - i2 - June 2015 - p340-343 [501+]
Jackson, Irvin - *The Expeditionary Force Marines Sourcebook*
    RVBW - Sept 2015 - pNA [501+]
Jackson, Jason Baird - *Yuchi Folklore: Cultural Expression in a Southeastern Native American Community*
    WestFolk - v74 - i1 - Wntr 2015 - p96-99 [501+]
Jackson, Jennifer - *The Punkydoos Take the Stage (Illus. by Andreasen, Dan)*
    c HB Guide - v26 - i1 - Spring 2015 - p11(1) [51-500]
Jackson, Joshilyn - *The Opposite of Everyone*
    KR - Dec 15 2015 - pNA [501+]
Jackson, K. David - *Machado de Assis: A Literary Life*
    Spec - v328 - i9755 - August 15 2015 - p34(2) [501+]
    TLS - i5859 - July 17 2015 - p24(1) [501+]
Jackson, Ken - *Shakespeare and Abraham*
    TLS - i5855 - June 19 2015 - p24(1) [501+]
    BL - v111 - i13 - March 1 2015 - p15(1) [51-500]
Jackson, Laura Lynne - *The Light Between Us: Stories from Heaven, Lessons for the Living*
    KR - Sept 15 2015 - pNA [51-500]
    LJ - v140 - i17 - Oct 15 2015 - p103(1) [51-500]
Jackson, Lee - *Dirty Old London: The Victorian Fight against Filth*
    NS - v144 - i5246 - Jan 23 2015 - p41(1) [51-500]
    TLS - i5840 - March 6 2015 - p30(1) [51-500]
Jackson, Lisa - *After She's Gone*
    PW - v262 - i47 - Nov 23 2015 - p50(1) [51-500]
Renegade Son
    BL - v111 - i16 - April 15 2015 - p30(2) [51-500]
Jackson, M. - *While Glaciers Slept: Being Human in a Time of Climate Change*
    LJ - v140 - i10 - June 1 2015 - p128(2) [51-500]
Jackson, MacDonald P. - *Determining the Shakespeare Canon: Arden of Faversham and A Lover's Complaint*
    TLS - i5847 - April 24 2015 - p9(2) [501+]
Jackson, Major - *Roll Deep: Poems*
    BL - v111 - i21 - July 1 2015 - p17(1) [51-500]
    LJ - v140 - i10 - June 1 2015 - p107(1) [51-500]
    NYTBR - Dec 27 2015 - p17(L) [501+]
    PW - v262 - i29 - July 20 2015 - p168(1) [51-500]
Jackson, Maurice - *Jill Bash*
    KR - Nov 1 2015 - pNA [501+]
Jackson, Melanie - *Eye Sore*
    c BL - v111 - i17 - May 1 2015 - p55(1) [51-500]
    c Res Links - v20 - i4 - April 2015 - p30(1) [51-500]
    c VOYA - v38 - i1 - April 2015 - p66(2) [501+]
Jackson, Merima - *Schicksal: Based on a True Story: Two Lives Torn Apart by War, Cradled in the Palm of Fate*
    SPBW - July 2015 - pNA [51-500]
Jackson, Michael - *Harmattan: A Philosophical Fiction*
    KR - Jan 1 2015 - pNA [51-500]
Jackson, Myles W. - *The Genealogy of a Gene: Patents, HIV/AIDS, and Race*
    LJ - v140 - i10 - June 1 2015 - p130(1) [51-500]
Jackson, Naomi - *The Star Side of Bird Hill*
    BL - v111 - i18 - May 15 2015 - p25(1) [51-500]
    Ent W - i1370 - July 3 2015 - p66(1) [51-500]
    KR - May 1 2015 - pNA [51-500]
    LJ - v140 - i10 - June 1 2015 - p88(1) [51-500]
    NY - v91 - i24 - August 24 2015 - p73 [51-500]
    y NYTBR - Sept 20 2015 - p30(L) [501+]
Jackson, Pamela Irving - *Benchmarking Muslim Well-Being in Europe: Reducing Disparities and Polarizations*
    CS - v44 - i1 - Jan 2015 - p138(1) [501+]
Jackson, Peter - *Beyond the Balance of Power: France and the Politics of National Security in the Era of the First World War*
    HER - v130 - i544 - June 2015 - p776(3) [501+]
    J Mil H - v79 - i1 - Jan 2015 - p226-227 [501+]
Jackson, Robert - *Submarines: 1940 to Today*
    c HB Guide - v26 - i1 - Spring 2015 - p137(2) [51-500]
Jackson, Robert H. - *Conflict and Conversion in Sixteenth Century Central Mexico: The Augustinian War on and Beyond the Chichimeca Frontier*
    HER - v130 - i542 - Feb 2015 - p181(2) [501+]
Jackson, Ron J., Jr. - *Joe, the Slave Who Became an Alamo Legend*
    BL - v111 - i11 - Feb 1 2015 - p16(2) [51-500]
    LJ - v140 - i3 - Feb 15 2015 - p112(1) [51-500]
    PW - v262 - i4 - Jan 26 2015 - p161(1) [51-500]
    Roundup M - v23 - i1 - Oct 2015 - p34(1) [501+]
Jackson, Russell - *Shakespeare and the English-Speaking Cinema*
    TLS - i5834 - Jan 23 2015 - p22(1) [501+]
Jackson, Sharley - *Need Big Love - Need it Now*
    KR - Jan 15 2015 - pNA [501+]
Jackson, Shirley - *Let Me Tell You: New Stories, Essays, and Other Writings*
    NYT - July 29 2015 - pC1(L) [501+]
    NYTBR - August 2 2015 - p1(L) [501+]
    PW - v262 - i14 - April 6 2015 - p38(1) [51-500]
    BooChiTr - August 15 2015 - p12(1) [51-500]
Life among the Savages (Read by Lockford, Lesa). Audiobook Review
    PW - v262 - i48 - Nov 30 2015 - p54(1) [51-500]
Jackson, Tom - *The Brain: An Illustrated History of Neuroscience*
    SPBW - Nov 2015 - pNA [501+]
Chilled: How Refrigeration Changed the World and Might Do So Again
    BL - v111 - i21 - July 1 2015 - p12(2) [51-500]
    Bwatch - Nov 2015 - pNA [51-500]
    KR - June 1 2015 - pNA [501+]
    NH - v123 - i9 - Nov 2015 - p46(2) [501+]
    NYTBR - Oct 11 2015 - p20(L) [501+]
    PW - v262 - i23 - June 8 2015 - p49(2) [51-500]
Digital Technology
    c Sch Lib - v63 - i3 - Autumn 2015 - p187(1) [51-500]

L'autobus magic presente series: La Terre
  c Res Links - v21 - i1 - Oct 2015 - p51(1) [51-500]
L'autobus magic presente series: Les creatures marines
  c Res Links - v21 - i1 - Oct 2015 - p51(1) [51-500]
Tracking Animal Movement
  c Sch Lib - v63 - i4 - Winter 2015 - p238(2) [51-500]
Jackson, Tom (b. 1972-) - *Horses around the World*
  c HB Guide - v26 - i1 - Spring 2015 - p168(1) [51-500]
Jackson, Tricia Williams - *Women in Black History: Stories of Courage, Faith, and Resilience*
  c PW - v262 - i48 - Nov 30 2015 - p62(1) [501+]
Jackson, Vanessa Furse - *The Anthropologist's Daughter*
  y CH Bwatch - Oct 2015 - pNA [51-500]
Jackson, Vina - *Spring*
  PW - v262 - i51 - Dec 14 2015 - p68(2) [51-500]
Winter
  LJ - v140 - i16 - Oct 1 2015 - p62(2) [501+]
  PW - v262 - i38 - Sept 21 2015 - p61(1) [51-500]
  KR - Sept 1 2015 - pNA [51-500]
Jacob, Frank - *Die Thule-Gesellschaft und die Kokuryukai: Geheimgesellschaften im Global-Historischen Vergleich*
  HNet - July 2015 - pNA [501+]
Jacob, Margaret C. - *The First Knowledge Economy: Human Capital and the European Economy, 1750-1850*
  AHR - v120 - i2 - April 2015 - p707-708 [501+]
  Historian - v77 - i3 - Fall 2015 - p612(2) [501+]
  Isis - v106 - i2 - June 2015 - p456(2) [501+]
Jacobovici, Simcha - *The Lost Gospel: Decoding the Ancient Texts that Reveals Jesus' Marriage to Mary the Magdalene*
  TLS - i5871 - Oct 9 2015 - p30(1) [501+]
Jacobs, Alan - *The Book of Common Prayer: A Biography*
  MA - v57 - i1 - Wntr 2015 - p81(4) [501+]
The Pleasures of Reading in an Age of Distraction
  T&C - v56 - i4 - Oct 2015 - p957-964 [501+]
Jacobs, Anna - *A Time for Hope*
  BL - v111 - i12 - Feb 15 2015 - p44(1) [51-500]
Jacobs, Carol - *Sebald's Vision*
  PW - v262 - i28 - July 13 2015 - p60(1) [51-500]
  TimHES - i2222 - Sept 24 2015 - p42-43 [501+]
Jacobs, Charlotte DeCroes - *Jonas Salk: A Life*
  AM - v213 - i5 - Nov 16 2015 - p34(3) [501+]
  BL - v111 - i17 - May 1 2015 - p65(2) [501+]
  BL - v111 - i19-20 - June 1 2015 - p27(1) [501+]
  Econ - v415 - i8944 - June 27 2015 - p72(US) [501+]
  KR - March 1 2015 - pNA [501+]
  LJ - v140 - i7 - April 15 2015 - p108(2) [501+]
  NYTBR - June 7 2015 - p24(L) [501+]
  TimHES - i2203 - May 14 2015 - p49(1) [501+]
Jacobs, Evan - *FatherSonFather*
  y BL - v112 - i7 - Dec 1 2015 - p56(1) [51-500]
Skinhead Birdy
  y PW - v262 - i31 - August 3 2015 - p61(1) [501+]
  y SLJ - v61 - i10 - Oct 2015 - p111(1) [51-500]
Varsity 170
  y SLJ - v61 - i5 - May 2015 - p113(2) [51-500]
Jacobs, Frank - *Frank Jacobs (Illus. by Davis, Jack)*
  BL - v111 - i19-20 - June 1 2015 - p66(1) [51-500]
Jacobs, Jaap - *The Worlds of the Seventeenth-Century Hudson Valley*
  JAH - v102 - i1 - June 2015 - p220-231 [501+]
Jacobs, James B. - *The Eternal Criminal Record*
  LJ - v140 - i2 - Feb 1 2015 - p97(1) [51-500]
Jacobs, Jerry A. - *In Defense of Disciplines: Interdisciplinarity and Specialization in the Research University*
  AJS - v121 - i2 - Sept 2015 - p623(3) [501+]
  CS - v44 - i6 - Nov 2015 - p812-813 [501+]
Jacobs, Jessica - *Pelvis with Distance*
  LJ - v140 - i6 - April 1 2015 - p97(2) [51-500]
Jacobs, John Hornor - *The Conformity*
  y HB Guide - v26 - i2 - Fall 2015 - p124(1) [51-500]
  y KR - Feb 1 2015 - pNA [51-500]
    SLJ - v61 - i2 - Feb 2015 - p102(1) [51-500]
Jacobs, Jonnie - *Payback*
  KR - August 1 2015 - pNA [51-500]
Jacobs, Lea - *Film Rhythm after Sound: Technology, Music, and Performance*
  FQ - v68 - i4 - Summer 2015 - p101(2) [501+]
Jacobs, Lily - *The Littlest Bunny in Canada: An Easter Adventure (Illus. by Dunn, Robert)*
  c Res Links - v20 - i4 - April 2015 - p4(1) [51-500]
Jacobs, Margaret D. - *A Generation Removed: The Fostering and Adoption of Indigenous Children in the Postwar World*
  AHR - v120 - i4 - Oct 2015 - p1507-1508 [501+]
  Am Ind CRJ - v39 - i2 - Spring 2015 - p139-141

[501+]
  Am St - v54 - i1 - Spring 2015 - p151-2 [501+]
  PHR - v84 - i4 - Nov 2015 - p537(2) [501+]
  Roundup M - v22 - i5 - June 2015 - p36(1) [501+]
  Roundup M - v22 - i6 - August 2015 - p38(1) [501+]
  WHQ - v46 - i3 - Autumn 2015 - p365-365 [501+]
Jacobs, Martin - *Reorienting the East: Jewish Travelers to the Medieval Muslim World*
  IJMES - v47 - i3 - August 2015 - p627-629 [501+]
  JIH - v46 - i3 - Wntr 2016 - p473-475 [501+]
  TLS - i5857 - July 3 2015 - p8(2) [501+]
Jacobs, Michael - *Everything is Happening: Journey into a Painting*
  HT - v65 - i11 - Nov 2015 - p60(1) [501+]
  NS - v144 - i5279 - Sept 11 2015 - p40(2) [501+]
  TimHES - i2223 - Oct 1 2015 - p49(1) [501+]
Jacobs, Peter - *Stay the Distance: The Life and Times of Marshal of the Royal Air Force Sir Michael Beetham*
  APH - v62 - i2 - Summer 2015 - p57(1) [501+]
Jacobs, Tilia - *Second Helpings at the Serve You Right Cafe*
  KR - May 1 2015 - pNA [501+]
Jacobsen, Annie - *Operation Paperclip*
  APH - v62 - i1 - Spring 2015 - p52(2) [501+]
  NYTBR - Feb 8 2015 - p28(L) [501+]
The Pentagon's Brain: An Uncensored History of DARPA, America's Top-Secret Military Research Agency
  BL - v112 - i1 - Sept 15 2015 - p7(1) [51-500]
  KR - July 1 2015 - pNA [501+]
  LJ - v140 - i12 - July 1 2015 - p94(1) [51-500]
  PW - v262 - i27 - July 6 2015 - p56(2) [51-500]
Jacobsen, Thomas W. - *The New Orleans Jazz Scene, 1970-2000: A Personal Retrospective*
  ABR - v36 - i2 - Jan-Feb 2015 - p14(1) [501+]
Jacobson, Alan - *The Lost Codex: An OPSIG Team Black Novel*
  PW - v262 - i39 - Sept 28 2015 - p68(2) [51-500]
Jacobson, Bernard - *Robert Motherwell: The Making of an American Giant*
  TLS - i5871 - Oct 9 2015 - p31(1) [501+]
Jacobson, Howard - *J: A Novel*
  NYTBR - Sept 6 2015 - p24(L) [501+]
  Quad - v59 - i1-2 - Jan-Feb 2015 - p141(2) [501+]
Shylock Is My Name
  KR - Dec 15 2015 - pNA [501+]
  PW - v262 - i48 - Nov 30 2015 - p35(1) [51-500]
Jacobson, Jennifer Richard - *Paper Things (Read by Rudd, Kate). Audiobook Review*
  c SLJ - v61 - i5 - May 2015 - p69(1) [51-500]
Paper Things
  c CCB-B - v68 - i8 - April 2015 - p403(2) [51-500]
  c HB - v91 - i1 - Jan-Feb 2015 - p82(1) [51-500]
  c HB Guide - v26 - i2 - Fall 2015 - p87(1) [51-500]
Jacobson, Ken - *Carrying Off the Palaces: John Ruskin's Lost Daguerreotypes*
  Apo - v181 - i631 - May 2015 - p106(2) [501+]
  TLS - i5860 - July 24 2015 - p5(1) [501+]
Jacobson, Lynn A. - *Kwajalein: An Island Like No Other*
  KR - August 15 2015 - pNA [51-500]
Jacobson, Rolf A. - *Invitation to the Psalms: A Reader's Guide for Discovery and Engagement*
  Intpr - v69 - i1 - Jan 2015 - p104(1) [501+]
Jacobson, Ryan - *Get a Job at a Business (Illus. by Cannell, Jon)*
  c HB Guide - v26 - i1 - Spring 2015 - p137(1) [51-500]
Get a Job Helping Others (Illus. by Cannell, Jon)
  c HB Guide - v26 - i1 - Spring 2015 - p137(1) [51-500]
  c Teach Lib - v42 - i3 - Feb 2015 - p9(1) [51-500]
Get a Job Making Stuff to Sell (Illus. by Cannell, Jon)
  c HB Guide - v26 - i1 - Spring 2015 - p137(1) [51-500]
Get a Summer Adventure Job (Illus. by Cannell, Jon)
  c HB Guide - v26 - i1 - Spring 2015 - p137(1) [51-500]
Jacobsson, Kerstin - *Beyond NGO-ization: The Development of Social Movements in Central and Eastern Europe*
  CS - v44 - i4 - July 2015 - p523-524 [501+]
Jacobus, Ann - *Romancing the Dark in the City of Light*
  y BL - v112 - i3 - Oct 1 2015 - p73(1) [51-500]
  y KR - August 1 2015 - pNA [51-500]
  y PW - v262 - i31 - August 3 2015 - p63(1) [51-500]
  y SLJ - v61 - i10 - Oct 2015 - p111(2) [51-500]
  y VOYA - v38 - i5 - Dec 2015 - p57(1) [51-500]
Jacoby, Sarah H. - *Love and Liberation: Autobiographical Writings of the Tibetan Buddhist Visionary Sera Khandro*
  JAAR - v83 - i4 - Dec 2015 - p1169-1171 [501+]
  Wom R Bks - v32 - i5 - Sept-Oct 2015 - p27(2) [501+]

Jacoby, Susan - *Strange Gods: A Secular History of Conversion*
  KR - Dec 1 2015 - pNA [501+]
  PW - v262 - i51 - Dec 14 2015 - p79(1) [501+]
Jacques, Juliet - *Trans: A Memoir*
  NS - v144 - i5281 - Sept 25 2015 - p68(2) [501+]
  NYTBR - Nov 15 2015 - p30(L) [501+]
Jacquet, Jennifer - *Is Shame Necessary? New Uses for an Old Tool*
  BooChiTr - April 11 2015 - p14(1) [501+]
  HM - v330 - i1980 - May 2015 - p90(5) [501+]
  Nat Post - v17 - i125 - March 28 2015 - pWP9(1) [501+]
  Nature - v518 - i7539 - Feb 19 2015 - p299(1) [51-500]
  New Sci - v225 - i3013 - March 21 2015 - p46(1) [501+]
  NS - v144 - i5253 - March 13 2015 - p42(3) [501+]
So You've Been Publicly Shamed
  Econ - v414 - i8929 - March 14 2015 - p84(US) [501+]
Jacyna, L. Stephen - *The Neurological Patient in History*
  HNet - Jan 2015 - pNA [501+]
Jaeckel, Jenny - *Siberiak: My Cold War Adventure on the River Ob (Illus. by Jaeckel, Jenny)*
  y CCB-B - v68 - i5 - Jan 2015 - p261(1) [51-500]
Jaeger, Elizabeth - *It's Easter, Little Bunny! (Illus. by Boyer, Robin)*
  c CH Bwatch - March 2015 - pNA [51-500]
Jaeger, Paige - *Think Tank Library: Brain-Based Learning Plans for New Standards, Grades K-5 (Illus. by #)*
  Teach Lib - v42 - i3 - Feb 2015 - p42(1) [51-500]
Think Tank Library: Brain-Based Learning Plans for New Standards, Grades K-5
  VOYA - v38 - i1 - April 2015 - p92(1) [51-500]
Jaeger, Paul T. - *Public Libraries, Public Policies, and Political Processes: Serving and Transforming Communities in Times of Economic and Political Restraint*
  LQ - v85 - i3 - July 2015 - p333(3) [501+]
Jaeggi, Rahel - *Alienation*
  RM - v68 - i3 - March 2015 - p662(3) [501+]
  TimHES - i2195 - March 19 2015 - p49(1) [501+]
Jaeggy, Fleur - *Sono il fratello di XX*
  TLS - i5838 - Feb 20 2015 - p26(1) [501+]
Jaff, Sophie - *Love Is Red (Read by Boehmer, Paul, with Emily Durante). Audiobook Review*
  LJ - v140 - i12 - July 1 2015 - p43(1) [51-500]
Love Is Red
  KR - March 15 2015 - pNA [51-500]
  NYTBR - May 31 2015 - p42(L) [51-500]
Jaffarian, Sue Ann - *A Body to Spare*
  BL - v112 - i3 - Oct 1 2015 - p25(1) [51-500]
  KR - Sept 1 2015 - pNA [51-500]
  PW - v262 - i39 - Sept 28 2015 - p71(1) [51-500]
Jaffe, Harold - *Othello Blues*
  ABR - v36 - i3 - March-April 2015 - p20(1) [501+]
Jaffe, Sara - *Dryland*
  y KR - June 15 2015 - pNA [51-500]
  y LJ - v140 - i12 - July 1 2015 - p80(1) [51-500]
  y NYTBR - Sept 20 2015 - p30(L) [51-500]
  y PW - v262 - i28 - July 13 2015 - p41(1) [51-500]
  y SLJ - v61 - i10 - Oct 2015 - p112(1) [51-500]
Jaffe, Steven - *New York at War: Four Centuries of Combat, Fear and Intrigue in Gotham*
  J Urban H - v41 - i5 - Sept 2015 - p943-950 [501+]
Jaffrey, Madhur - *Vegetarian India: A Journey through the Best of Indian Home Cooking*
  BL - v112 - i7 - Dec 1 2015 - p9(1) [501+]
  LJ - v140 - i13 - August 1 2015 - p120(1) [51-500]
  PW - v262 - i36 - Sept 7 2015 - p60(1) [51-500]
Jager, Rebecca Kay - *Malinche, Pocahontas, and Sacagawea: Indian Women as Cultural Intermediaries and National Symbols*
  LJ - v140 - i16 - Oct 1 2015 - p93(1) [51-500]
Jaggar, Alison M. - *Gender and Global Justice*
  Dialogue - v54 - i2 - June 2015 - p392-393 [501+]
Jagielski, Wojciech - *Burning the Grass: At the Heart of Change in South Africa, 1990-2011*
  PW - v262 - i38 - Sept 21 2015 - p64(1) [51-500]
Jago, Michael - *Rab Butler: The Best Prime Minister We Never Had?*
  Spec - v329 - i9769 - Nov 21 2015 - p51(2) [501+]
Jah, Akim - *Die Deportation der Juden aus Berlin: Die nationalsozialistische Vernichtungspolitik und das Sammellager Grosse Hamburger Strasse*
  HNet - April 2015 - pNA [501+]

Jaher, David - *The Witch of Lime Street: Seance, Seduction, and Houdini in the Spirit World*
    BL - v112 - i4 - Oct 15 2015 - p5(1) [51-500]
    LJ - v140 - i14 - Sept 1 2015 - p117(2) [51-500]
    LJ - v140 - i16 - Oct 1 2015 - p111(1) [501+]
    NYRB - v62 - i20 - Dec 17 2015 - p54(3) [501+]

Jahre, Howard - *The Revenge of the Golf Gods*
    KR - July 15 2015 - pNA [51-500]

Jaillant, Lise - *Modernism, Middlebrow and the Literary Canon*
    TimHES - i2186 - Jan 15 2015 - p51(1) [501+]
    TimHES - i2200 - April 23 2015 - p51(1) [501+]

Jaimet, Kate - *Dunces Rock*
  c BL - v112 - i5 - Nov 1 2015 - p52(1) [501+]
Endangered
  y BL - v111 - i17 - May 1 2015 - p50(1) [51-500]
  y KR - May 1 2015 - pNA [51-500]

Jain, Bapsy - *A Star Called Lucky*
    PW - v262 - i17 - April 27 2015 - p55(1) [51-500]

Jain, Neha - *Perpetrators and Accessories in International Criminal Law: Indivual Modes of Responsibility for Collective Crimes*
    Law&PolBR - v25 - i4 - April 2015 - p62(6) [501+]

Jain, S. Lochlann - *Malignant: How Cancer Becomes Us*
    MAQ - v29 - i1 - March 2015 - p17-19 [501+]

Jakes, H.R. - *The Curious Autobiography of Elaine Jakes*
    SPBW - Sept 2015 - pNA [51-500]

Jakes, T.D. - *Destiny: Step into Your Purpose*
    PW - v262 - i27 - July 6 2015 - p65(2) [51-500]
T.D. Jakes Speaks to Men
    Bwatch - Jan 2015 - pNA [51-500]

Jakle, John A. - *The Garage: Automobility and Building Innovation in America's Early Auto Age*
    BHR - v89 - i1 - Spring 2015 - p173(3) [501+]

Jakub, Lisa - *You Look Like That Girl: A Child Actor Stops Pretending and Finally Grows Up*
    RVBW - Oct 2015 - pNA [501+]

Jakubowska, Longina - *Patrons of History: Nobility, Capital and Political Transitions in Poland*
    HNet - Feb 2015 - pNA [501+]
Patrons of History: Nobility, Capital, and Political Transitions in Poland
    JMH - v87 - i1 - March 2015 - p233(3) [501+]

Jakubowski, Michele - *Big Dog Decisions (Illus. by Montalto, Luisa)*
  c HB Guide - v26 - i1 - Spring 2015 - p61(1) [51-500]

Jalal, Ayesha - *The Oxford Companion to Pakistani History*
    HNet - June 2015 - pNA [501+]
The Struggle for Pakistan: A Muslim Homeland and Global Politics
    NYRB - v62 - i6 - April 2 2015 - p46(3) [501+]
    TLS - i5832 - Jan 9 2015 - p19(1) [501+]

Jalier, David - *The Witch of Lime Street: Seance, Seduction, and Houdini in the Spirit World*
    PW - v262 - i31 - August 3 2015 - p48(1) [51-500]

Jama-Everett, Ayize - *The Entropy of Bones*
    NYTBR - Oct 18 2015 - p18(L) [501+]
    PW - v262 - i18 - May 4 2015 - p99(2) [51-500]
The Liminal War
    KR - May 1 2015 - pNA [51-500]
    PW - v262 - i17 - April 27 2015 - p57(1) [51-500]
    RVBW - Nov 2015 - pNA [51-500]

Jamal, Amina - *Jamaat-e-Islami Women in Pakistan: Vanguard of a New Modernity?*
    CS - v44 - i6 - Nov 2015 - p815-816 [501+]

Jamali, Naveed - *How to Catch a Russian Spy: The True Story of an American Civilian Turned Double Agent*
    KR - April 15 2015 - pNA [501+]
    PW - v262 - i13 - March 30 2015 - p66(1) [51-500]
    LJ - v140 - i7 - April 15 2015 - p102(1) [51-500]
    Mac - v128 - i24 - June 22 2015 - p57(2) [501+]

James, Allison - *Socialising Children*
    CS - v44 - i4 - July 2015 - p579-579 [501+]

James, Ann - *Bird and Bear (Illus. by James, Ann)*
  c BL - v111 - i15 - April 1 2015 - p81(2) [51-500]
  c KR - Feb 15 2015 - pNA [51-500]
    SLJ - v61 - i3 - March 2015 - p117(1) [51-500]

James, Bill - *Blaze Away*
    BL - v111 - i17 - May 1 2015 - p20(1) [51-500]

James, Brant - *Formula One Racing*
  c HB Guide - v26 - i1 - Spring 2015 - p183(1) [51-500]

James, C.L.R. - *Toussaint Louverture: The Story of the Only Successful Slave Revolt in History: A Play in Three Acts*
    TDR - v59 - i1 - Spring 2015 - p194(1) [501+]

James, Carolyn Custis - *Malestrom: Manhood Swept into the Currents of a Changing World*
    PW - v262 - i19 - May 11 2015 - p54(1) [51-500]

James, Cate - *Go Home, Little One!*
  c SLJ - v61 - i11 - Nov 2015 - p84(1) [51-500]

James, Clive - *Latest Readings*
    BL - v111 - i22 - August 1 2015 - p17(1) [51-500]
    HR - v68 - i3 - Autumn 2015 - p501-509 [501+]
    KR - June 1 2015 - pNA [501+]
    NS - v144 - i5275 - August 14 2015 - p38(3) [501+]
    NYRB - v62 - i14 - Sept 24 2015 - p77(3) [501+]
    PW - v262 - i24 - June 15 2015 - p74(2) [51-500]
    Spec - v328 - i9756 - August 22 2015 - p37(2) [501+]
    CC - v132 - i16 - August 5 2015 - p42(1) [51-500]
Poetry Notebook: Reflections on the Intensity of Language
    HR - v68 - i3 - Autumn 2015 - p501-509 [501+]
    New R - v246 - i4 - May 2015 - p84(2) [501+]
    LJ - v140 - i5 - March 15 2015 - p100(2) [51-500]
    NYTBR - Sept 6 2015 - p26(L) [501+]
    BL - v111 - i15 - April 1 2015 - p22(1) [51-500]
    NYRB - v62 - i14 - Sept 24 2015 - p77(3) [501+]
    TLS - i5858 - July 10 2015 - p13(1) [501+]
Sentenced to Life
    HR - v68 - i3 - Autumn 2015 - p501-509 [501+]
    NS - v144 - i5257 - April 10 2015 - p49(1) [501+]
    PW - v262 - i52 - Dec 21 2015 - p128(1) [501+]
    TLS - i5858 - July 10 2015 - p13(1) [501+]
Unreliable Memoirs
    TLS - i5854 - June 12 2015 - p12(1) [501+]

James, Cormac - *The Surfacing*
    PW - v262 - i10 - March 9 2015 - p50(2) [51-500]
    KR - April 1 2015 - pNA [51-500]
    NYTBR - August 16 2015 - p30(L) [501+]

James Corner Field - *The High Line*
    LJ - v140 - i20 - Dec 1 2015 - p106(2) [51-500]

James Corner Field Operations - *The High Line*
    NYTBR - Dec 6 2015 - p66(L) [501+]

James, Dawn - *Playground Math*
  c BL - v111 - i15 - April 1 2015 - p63(1) [51-500]
Store Math
  c Teach Lib - v43 - i1 - Oct 2015 - p17(1) [51-500]

James, E.L. - *Grey*
    Ent W - i1370 - July 3 2015 - p66(1) [51-500]
    KR - July 15 2015 - pNA [501+]
    NYT - June 26 2015 - pC19(L) [501+]
Grey (Read by Webber, Zachary). Audiobook Review
    LJ - v140 - i16 - Oct 1 2015 - p42(1) [51-500]

James, Elliott - *Fearless*
    PW - v262 - i24 - June 15 2015 - p69(1) [51-500]

James, Eloisa - *Four Nights with the Duke*
    BL - v111 - i13 - March 1 2015 - p28(2) [51-500]
    KR - Jan 15 2015 - pNA [501+]
My American Duchess
    BL - v112 - i7 - Dec 1 2015 - p37(1) [51-500]
    KR - Nov 15 2015 - pNA [501+]
    PW - v262 - i46 - Nov 16 2015 - p62(2) [51-500]

James, Erwin - *Redeemable: A Memoir of Darkness and Hope*
    PW - v262 - i45 - Nov 9 2015 - p47(1) [51-500]

James, George Alfred - *Ecology and Religion*
    JAAR - v83 - i2 - June 2015 - p572-574 [501+]
Ecology is Permanent Economy: The Activism and Environmental Philosophy of Sunderlal Bahuguna
    Pac A - v88 - i1 - March 2015 - p215 [501+]

James, Harold - *Krupp: A History of the Legendary German Firm*
    CEH - v48 - i1 - March 2015 - p120-121 [501+]
    T&C - v56 - i4 - Oct 2015 - p990-991 [501+]

James, Helen Foster - *Grandma's Christmas Wish (Illus. by Brown, Petra)*
  c KR - Sept 1 2015 - pNA [501+]
  c SLJ - v61 - i10 - Oct 2015 - p64(1) [51-500]
Grandpa Loves You! (Illus. by Brown, Petra)
  c KR - Dec 1 2015 - pNA [501+]
  c PW - v262 - i47 - Nov 23 2015 - p66(1) [501+]

James, Henry - *The Golden Bowl*
    Nation - v300 - i14 - April 6 2015 - p36(1) [501+]

James, Jessica - *Meant to Be*
    PW - v262 - i21 - May 25 2015 - p33(1) [51-500]
    SPBW - Nov 2015 - pNA [51-500]

James, John Francis - *An Introduction to Practical Laboratory Optics*
    Phys Today v68 - i6 - June 2015 - p56-56 [501+]

James, Julie - *Suddenly One Summer (Read by White, Karen). Audiobook Review*
    LJ - v140 - i17 - Oct 15 2015 - p52(1) [501+]
Suddenly One Summer
    KR - April 15 2015 - pNA [501+]
    PW - v262 - i17 - April 27 2015 - p58(1) [51-500]

James, Kathryn - *Gypsy Girl*
  y Sch Lib - v63 - i2 - Summer 2015 - p118(2) [51-500]

James, Lauren - *The Next Together*
  y Sch Lib - v63 - i3 - Autumn 2015 - p183(1) [51-500]

James, Lawrence - *Churchill and Empire: Portrait of an Imperialist*
    HT - v65 - i1 - Jan 2015 - p56(2) [501+]

James, Leighton S. - *Witnessing the Revolutionary and Napoleonic Wars in German Central Europe*
    HNet - March 2015 - pNA [501+]

James, Liz - *Constantine of Rhodes, On Constantinople and the Church of the Holy Apostles*
    Med R - May 2015 - pNA [501+]

James, Marlon - *The Book of Night Women (Read by Miles, Robin). Audiobook Review*
    BL - v111 - i15 - April 1 2015 - p86(1) [51-500]
A Brief History of Seven Killings
    Lon R Bks - v37 - i21 - Nov 5 2015 - p45(3) [501+]
    Nation - v300 - i22 - June 1 2015 - p26(3) [501+]
    NS - v144 - i5244 - Jan 9 2015 - p39(1) [501+]
    NYRB - v62 - i18 - Nov 19 2015 - p18(2) [501+]
    NYTBR - Oct 25 2015 - p32(L) [501+]
    TLS - i5863 - August 14 2015 - p19(1) [501+]

James, Miranda - *Arsenic and Old Books*
    BL - v111 - i9-10 - Jan 1 2015 - p44(1) [51-500]

James, Peter - *Want You Dead*
    RVBW - July 2015 - pNA [51-500]
    RVBW - Nov 2015 - pNA [51-500]
You Are Dead
    PW - v262 - i34 - August 24 2015 - p57(2) [51-500]
    RVBW - Nov 2015 - pNA [51-500]

James, Ray Anthony - *Veggie Rhapsody: I Want You in My Lunch (Illus. by Jackson, Sommer)*
  c CH Bwatch - August 2015 - pNA [51-500]

James, Russell - *Q Island*
    PW - v262 - i21 - May 25 2015 - p41(1) [51-500]

James, Steven - *Fury*
  y VOYA - v38 - i1 - April 2015 - p80(1) [51-500]
Fury (Read by Podehl, Nick). Audiobook Review
  y SLJ - v61 - i8 - August 2015 - p54(1) [51-500]

James, Tania - *The Tusk That Did the Damage*
    BL - v111 - i11 - Feb 1 2015 - p24(1) [51-500]
    LJ - v140 - i2 - Feb 1 2015 - p73(1) [51-500]
    NYTBR - March 8 2015 - p25(L) [501+]
    PW - v262 - i4 - Jan 26 2015 - p144(1) [51-500]
    TLS - i5852 - May 29 2015 - p21(1) [501+]

Jameson, Stacy M. - *Strip Cultures: Finding America in Las Vegas*
    PW - v262 - i22 - June 1 2015 - p51(1) [51-500]

Jamie, Kathleen - *Findings*
    NS - v144 - i5278 - Sept 4 2015 - p37(1) [51-500]

Jamieson, Alan - *The Hadal Zone: Life in the Deepest Oceans*
    Nature - v523 - i7562 - July 30 2015 - pSB1(1) [51-500]

Jamieson, Alexandra - *Women, Food, and Desire: Embrace Your Cravings, Make Peace with Food, Reclaim Your Body*
    Bwatch - May 2015 - pNA [51-500]

Jamieson, Dale - *Love in the Antropocene*
    PW - v262 - i35 - August 31 2015 - p59(1) [51-500]

Jamieson, Kelly - *Major Misconduct*
    PW - v262 - i34 - August 24 2015 - p68(1) [51-500]

Jamieson, Lynn - *Living Alone: Globalization, Identity, and Belonging*
    AJS - v120 - i4 - Jan 2015 - p1269(3) [501+]
    CS - v44 - i5 - Sept 2015 - p667-669 [501+]

Jamieson, Perry D. - *Spring 1865: The Closing Campaigns of the Civil War*
    KR - Feb 1 2015 - pNA [51-500]
    Roundup M - v22 - i6 - August 2015 - p38(1) [501+]

Jamieson, Scott - *French Visitors to Newfoundland: An Anthology of Nineteenth-Century Travel Writing*
    Can Hist R - v96 - i1 - March 2015 - p116(3) [501+]

Jamieson, Victoria - *Roller Girl (Illus. by Jamieson, Victoria)*
  c BL - v112 - i1 - Sept 1 2015 - p99(1) [501+]
  c CCB-B - v68 - i8 - April 2015 - p404(1) [51-500]
  c HB Guide - v26 - i2 - Fall 2015 - p87(1) [51-500]
  c Nat Post - v17 - i130 - April 4 2015 - pWP5(1) [501+]
  c NYTBR - May 10 2015 - p21(L) [501+]
  c PW - v262 - i49 - Dec 2 2015 - p87(1) [51-500]
  c HB - v91 - i2 - March-April 2015 - p99(1) [51-500]
  c PW - v262 - i4 - Jan 26 2015 - p175(1) [51-500]

Jamiol, Paul - *Bikers Are Animals 3: On the Road : A Children's Book on Motorcycling (Illus. by Jamiol, Paul)*
  c CH Bwatch - Feb 2015 - pNA [501+]

Jamison, Cheryl - *The Barbecue Lover's Big Book of BBQ Sauces: 225 Extraordinary Sauces, Rubs, Marinades, Mops, Bastes, Pastes, and Salsas, for Smoke-Cooking or Grilling*
    LJ - v140 - i11 - June 15 2015 - p108(2) [501+]

Jampoler, Andrew C. A. - *Adak: The Rescue of Alfa Foxtrot 586*
    APJ - v29 - i2 - March-April 2015 - p177(2) [501+]

Jamroziak, Emilia - *The Cistercian Order in Medieval Europe, 1090-1500*
    AHR - v120 - i2 - April 2015 - p695-697 [501+]
Monasteries on the Borders of Medieval Europe: Conflict and Cultural Interaction
    Med R - Jan 2015 - pNA [501+]
    Specu - v90 - i1 - Jan 2015 - p259-260 [501+]
    CHR - v101 - i3 - Summer 2015 - p615(2) [501+]
Survival and Success on Medieval Borders: Cistercian Houses in Medieval Scotland and Pomerania from the Twelth to the Late Fourteenth Century
    Specu - v90 - i3 - July 2015 - p827-829 [501+]

Janacek, Bruce - *Alchemical Belief: Occultism in the Religious Culture of Early Modern England*
    Six Ct J - v46 - i3 - Fall 2015 - p767-768 [501+]

Janc, John J. - *Hernani*
    FS - v69 - i3 - July 2015 - p400-401 [501+]

Jancar, Drago - *I Saw Her That Night*
    KR - Nov 15 2015 - pNA [51-500]

Jance, J.A. - *Cold Betrayal (Read by Ziemba, Karen). Audiobook Review*
    LJ - v140 - i10 - June 1 2015 - p60(1) [51-500]
Cold Betrayal
    BL - v111 - i12 - Feb 15 2015 - p35(1) [51-500]
    KR - Jan 1 2015 - pNA [501+]
    PW - v262 - i2 - Jan 12 2015 - p36(1) [51-500]
    RVBW - April 2015 - pNA [501+]
Dance of the Bones
    BL - v112 - i1 - Sept 1 2015 - p45(1) [51-500]
    PW - v262 - i30 - July 27 2015 - p44(1) [51-500]
    RVBW - Oct 2015 - pNA [51-500]
Remains of Innocence
    RVBW - Feb 2015 - pNA [51-500]
    RVBW - May 2015 - pNA [51-500]

Jane, Pamela - *Little Elfie One (Illus. by Manning, Jane)*
  c BL - v112 - i4 - Oct 15 2015 - p48(1) [51-500]
  c KR - Sept 1 2015 - pNA [51-500]
  c PW - v262 - i37 - Sept 14 2015 - p74(1) [51-500]
  c SLJ - v61 - i10 - Oct 2015 - p64(1) [51-500]

Janea, Irene Cohen - *Mister Doctor: Janusz Korczak and the Orphans of the Warsaw Ghetto (Illus. by Quarello, Maurizio A.C.)*
  c BL - v111 - i21 - July 1 2015 - p74(1) [51-500]

Janeczko, Paul B. - *The Death of the Hat: A Brief History of Poetry in 50 Objects (Illus. by Raschka, Chris)*
  c KR - Jan 1 2015 - pNA [51-500]
  c BL - v111 - i14 - March 15 2015 - p60(1) [51-500]
  c CCB-B - v68 - i9 - May 2015 - p451(1) [51-500]
  c HB - v91 - i2 - March-April 2015 - p116(2) [51-500]
  c HB Guide - v26 - i2 - Fall 2015 - p202(1) [51-500]
  c NYTBR - April 12 2015 - p18(L) [501+]
  c PW - v262 - i6 - Feb 9 2015 - p69(1) [501+]
  c PW - v262 - i49 - Dec 2 2015 - p54(2) [51-500]
Firefly July (Illus. by Sweet, Melissa)
  c BL - v111 - i9-10 - Jan 1 2015 - pS4(8) [51-500]

Janes, Dominic - *Visions of Queer Martyrdom from John Henry Newman to Derek Jarman*
    G&L Rev W - v22 - i5 - Sept-Oct 2015 - p30(3) [501+]

Janes, J. Robert - *Clandestine*
    PW - v262 - i21 - May 25 2015 - p36(2) [51-500]
Sleeper
    KR - Oct 15 2015 - pNA [51-500]

Janes, Rita C. - *Numbers & Stories: Using Children's Literature to Teach Young Children Number Sense*
    TC Math - v21 - i8 - April 2015 - p508(2) [501+]

Janeway, Judith - *The Magician's Daughter*
    Bwatch - April 2015 - pNA [51-500]

Jang, Lucia - *Stars Between the Sun and Moon: One Woman's Life in North Korea and Escape to Freedom (Read by Song, Janet). Audiobook Review*
    LJ - v140 - i19 - Nov 15 2015 - p54(2) [51-500]
Stars between the Sun and Moon: One Woman's Life in North Korea and Escape to Freedom
    KR - August 15 2015 - pNA [501+]
    LJ - v140 - i12 - July 1 2015 - p90(1) [51-500]
    NYTBR - Nov 29 2015 - p26(L) [501+]
    PW - v262 - i26 - June 29 2015 - p55(1) [51-500]

Jangfeldt, Bengt - *Mayakovsky: A Biography*
    Mac - v128 - i1 - Jan 12 2015 - p70(1) [501+]
    NYRB - v62 - i14 - Sept 24 2015 - p86(4) [501+]
    Spec - v327 - i9730 - Feb 21 2015 - p40(1) [501+]
    TLS - i5862 - August 7 2015 - p10(2) [501+]

Janicaud, Dominique - *Heidegger in France*
    J Phil - v112 - i5 - May 2015 - p281(1) [501+]

Janice P. Nimura - *Daughters of the Samurai: A Journey from East to West and Back*
    CSM - May 6 2015 - pNA [501+]

Janikowski, Tom - *The Crawford County Sketchbook*
    KR - June 15 2015 - pNA [501+]

Janisch, Heinz - *The King and the Sea: 21 Extremely Short Stories (Illus. by Erlbruch, Wolf)*
  c KR - June 15 2015 - pNA [51-500]
  c NYTBR - Nov 25 2015 - pNA(L) [501+]
  c PW - v262 - i25 - June 22 2015 - p137(1) [51-500]
  c PW - v262 - i49 - Dec 2 2015 - p23(2) [51-500]
  c Sch Lib - v63 - i3 - Autumn 2015 - p166(1) [51-500]
  c SLJ - v61 - i7 - July 2015 - p63(1) [51-500]

Janken, Kenneth Robert - *The Wilmington Ten: Violence, Injustice, and the Rise of Black Politics in the 1970s*
    KR - Oct 1 2015 - pNA [501+]
    PW - v262 - i39 - Sept 28 2015 - p77(1) [51-500]

Janki, Dadi - *Feeling Great: Creating a Life of Optimism, Enthusiasm and Contentment*
    RVBW - August 2015 - pNA [51-500]

Jankowski, Paul - *Verdun: The Longest Battle of the Great War*
    AHR - v120 - i1 - Feb 2015 - p343-344 [501+]

Janmohamed, Sheniz - *Firesmoke*
    WLT - v89 - i5 - Sept-Oct 2015 - p69(1) [501+]

Janney, Caroline E. - *Remembering the Civil War: Reunion and the Limits of Reconciliation*
    Historian - v77 - i3 - Fall 2015 - p561(1) [501+]
    HNet - June 2015 - pNA [501+]

Janocha, Peter - *Arthur Richard Weber. Ein norddeutscher Kaufmann in Japan zur Zeit der Meiji-Restauration*
    GSR - v38 - i3 - Oct 2015 - p673-675 [501+]

Janosch - *Just One Apple (Illus. by Janosch)*
  c CH Bwatch - May 2015 - pNA [501+]
  c HB Guide - v26 - i1 - Spring 2015 - p33(1) [51-500]

Jans, Donald - *Freaks I've Met*
    KR - April 1 2015 - pNA [501+]

Jansen, Katherine L. - *Center and Periphery: Studies on Power in the Medieval World in Honor of William Chester Jordan*
    CHR - v101 - i3 - Summer 2015 - p621(3) [501+]
    Six Ct J - v46 - i3 - Fall 2015 - p714-716 [501+]
    Specu - v90 - i4 - Oct 2015 - p1123-1124 [501+]

Jansen, Ronald Wilfred - *Anne Frank 80 Years: A Memorial Tour in Current Images*
    SPBW - Feb 2015 - pNA [501+]

Jansen, Yolande - *Secularism, Assimilation, and the Crisis of Multiculturalism*
    RM - v69 - i2 - Dec 2015 - p391(3) [501+]

Jansma, Kristopher - *Why We Came to the City*
    KR - Jan 1 2016 - pNA [501+]

Janssen, Roel - *The Art of Audit: Eight Remarkable Government Auditors on Stage*
    Econ - v416 - i8945 - July 4 2015 - p73(US) [501+]

Janssen, Sarah - *The World Almanac and Book of Facts 2015*
    LJ - v140 - i3 - Feb 15 2015 - p128(1) [51-500]

Jansson, Tove - *The Summer Book*
    TimHES - i2204 - May 21 2015 - p49(1) [501+]

Jantzen, Benjamin C. - *An Introduction to Design Arguments*
    CC - v132 - i14 - July 8 2015 - p33(3) [501+]

Jantzen, Doug - *Henry Hyena, Why Won't You Laugh? (Illus. by Claude, Jean)*
  c BL - v111 - i19-20 - June 1 2015 - p116(1) [51-500]
  c KR - April 15 2015 - pNA [51-500]
  c PW - v262 - i22 - June 1 2015 - p58(1) [501+]
  c SLJ - v61 - i6 - June 2015 - p84(1) [51-500]

January, Brendan - *Information Insecurity: Privacy under Siege*
  y BL - v111 - i22 - August 1 2015 - p50(1) [51-500]
  y KR - June 15 2015 - pNA [51-500]
  y SLJ - v61 - i7 - July 2015 - p107(2) [51-500]
  y VOYA - v38 - i4 - Oct 2015 - p83(3) [51-500]

Januska, Michael - *Maiden Lane*
    BL - v111 - i17 - May 1 2015 - p40(1) [51-500]

Janz, Denis R. - *A People's History of Christianity: One Volume Student Edition*
    Six Ct J - v46 - i1 - Spring 2015 - p189-190 [501+]

Janz, Jonathan - *Wolf Land*
    PW - v262 - i39 - Sept 28 2015 - p72(1) [51-500]

Japp, Andrea - *The Lady Agnes Mystery, vol. 1*
    PW - v262 - i38 - Sept 21 2015 - p55(1) [51-500]
The Lady Agnes Mystery, vol. 2
    PW - v262 - i47 - Nov 23 2015 - p52(1) [51-500]

Jaques, Susan - *The Empress of Art*
    KR - Jan 1 2016 - pNA [501+]

Jarausch, Konrad H. - *Out of Ashes: A New History of Europe in the Twentieth Century*
    HT - v65 - i10 - Oct 2015 - p65(1) [501+]
    KR - April 15 2015 - pNA [501+]
    NYTBR - August 2 2015 - p14(L) [501+]
    PW - v262 - i14 - April 6 2015 - p51(1) [51-500]
    TimHES - i2207 - June 11 2015 - p57(1) [501+]

Jardine, Lisa - *Temptation in the Archives: Essays in Golden Age Dutch Culture*
    TimHES - i2217 - August 20 2015 - p50-50 [501+]

Jarman, Julia - *A Friend in Need (Illus. by Pankhurst, Kate)*
  c SLJ - v61 - i5 - May 2015 - p98(1) [51-500]
Lovely Old Lion (Illus. by Varley, Susan)
  c KR - July 1 2015 - pNA [51-500]
  c Magpies - v30 - i4 - Sept 2015 - p30(1) [51-500]
  c SLJ - v61 - i10 - Oct 2015 - p78(1) [51-500]
The Magic Scooter (Illus. by Hearn, Sam)
  c CH Bwatch - Nov 2015 - pNA [51-500]
Make Friends, Break Friends (Illus. by Pankhurst, Kate)
  c SLJ - v61 - i5 - May 2015 - p98(1) [51-500]
New Friend, Old Friends (Illus. by Pankhurst, Kate)
  c SLJ - v61 - i5 - May 2015 - p98(1) [51-500]

Jarratt, Laura - *Skin Deep*
  y SLJ - v61 - i6 - June 2015 - p112(1) [51-500]

Jarrett, Jonathan - *Problems and Possibilities of Early Medieval Charters*
    Med R - Jan 2015 - pNA [501+]

Jarrow, Gail - *Fatal Fever: Tracking Down Typhoid Mary*
  y CH Bwatch - April 2015 - pNA [51-500]
  y CCB-B - v68 - i8 - April 2015 - p404(2) [51-500]
  y HB Guide - v26 - i2 - Fall 2015 - p184(1) [51-500]
  y KR - Jan 1 2015 - pNA [51-500]
  y PW - v262 - i3 - Jan 19 2015 - p87(1) [51-500]
  y PW - v262 - i49 - Dec 2 2015 - p82(1) [51-500]
  y VOYA - v38 - i4 - Oct 2015 - p83(2) [51-500]
  y BL - v111 - i12 - Feb 15 2015 - p70(1) [51-500]
  y HB - v91 - i2 - March-April 2015 - p121(1) [51-500]

Jarvis - *Alan's Big, Scary Teeth*
  c KR - Dec 15 2015 - pNA [51-500]
  c PW - v262 - i45 - Nov 9 2015 - p58(1) [51-500]
Lazy Dave (Illus. by Jarvis)
  c NYTBR - Dec 20 2015 - p14(L) [501+]
  c SLJ - v61 - i8 - August 2015 - p70(2) [51-500]
Lazy Dave (Illus. by Jarvis, Peter)
  c KR - June 15 2015 - pNA [51-500]
Who Is Happy? (Illus. by Jarvis)
  c KR - Dec 15 2015 - pNA [51-500]

Jarvis, Cynthia A. - *Feasting on the Gospels: Mark*
    Intpr - v69 - i1 - Jan 2015 - p125(1) [51-500]

Jarvis, Dale - *Any Mummers 'lowed in?: Christmas Mummering Traditions*
    Beav - v95 - i5 - Oct-Nov 2015 - p63(2) [501+]

Jarvis, Robin - *Romantic Readers and Transatlantic Travel: Expeditions and Tours in North America, 1760-1840*
    MLR - v110 - i3 - July 2015 - p837-839 [501+]

Jarvis, Stephen - *Death and Mr. Pickwick*
    Atl - v315 - i5 - June 2015 - p38(3) [501+]
    BL - v111 - i16 - April 15 2015 - p32(2) [51-500]
    KR - May 15 2015 - pNA [501+]
    LJ - v140 - i6 - April 1 2015 - p81(1) [51-500]
    NS - v144 - i5261 - May 7 2015 - p46(3) [501+]
    NYTBR - July 19 2015 - p15(L) [501+]
    PW - v262 - i7 - Feb 16 2015 - p152(1) [51-500]
    TLS - i5851 - May 22 2015 - p19(2) [501+]

Jary, David - *Form and Dialectic in Georg Simmel's Sociology: A New Interpretation*
    CS - v44 - i6 - Nov 2015 - p875-876 [501+]

Jarzab, Anna - *Tether*
  y HB Guide - v26 - i2 - Fall 2015 - p124(1) [51-500]
  y KR - Jan 15 2015 - pNA [51-500]
  y SLJ - v61 - i2 - Feb 2015 - p103(1) [51-500]
  y VOYA - v37 - i6 - Feb 2015 - p78(1) [51-500]

Jarzebowski, Claudia - *Childhood and Emotion: Across Cultures, 1450-1800*
    AHR - v120 - i3 - June 2015 - p966-968 [501+]

Jasay, Anthony de - *Indian Rope Trick*
    IndRev - v20 - i1 - Summer 2015 - p147(5) [501+]

Jasinski, Page O'Brien - *Julia's Magic Putter (Illus. by Lindt, Peggy)*
  c CH Bwatch - Feb 2015 - pNA [51-500]

Book Review Index 2016 Cumulation JENNINGS • 231

Jaskulka, Marie - *The Lost Marble Notebook of Forgotten Girl & Random Boy*
y BL - v111 - i16 - April 15 2015 - p48(1) [51-500]
y KR - Feb 15 2015 - pNA [51-500]
y SLJ - v61 - i4 - April 2015 - p165(2) [51-500]
y VOYA - v38 - i2 - June 2015 - p62(1) [51-500]
Jason - *If You Steal*
NYTBR - Oct 18 2015 - p30(L) [501+]
Jason and the Golden Fleece (Illus. by Hartas, Leo)
c Sch Lib - v63 - i1 - Spring 2015 - p41(1) [501+]
Jaspert, Nikolas - *Seeraub im Mittelmeerraum: Piraterie, Korsarentum und maritime Gewalt von der Antike bis zur Neuzeit*
Med R - June 2015 - pNA [501+]
Jaures, Jean - *A Socialist History of the French Revolution*
NS - v144 - i5276 - August 21 2015 - p50(2) [501+]
Javaherbin, Mina - *Elephant in the Dark (Illus. by Yelchin, Eugene)*
c KR - June 15 2015 - pNA [51-500]
c PW - v262 - i24 - June 15 2015 - p82(1) [501+]
c SLJ - v61 - i8 - August 2015 - p71(1) [51-500]
c BL - v111 - i21 - July 1 2015 - p53(1) [51-500]
c HB - v91 - i6 - Nov-Dec 2015 - p67(2) [501+]
Javakhishvili, Mikheil - *Kvachi*
TLS - i5856 - June 26 2015 - p20(2) [501+]
Javier, Nancy - *No-Sew Fleece Throw*
LJ - v140 - i3 - Feb 15 2015 - p98(2) [51-500]
Javier, Paolo - *Court of the Dragon*
PW - v262 - i16 - April 20 2015 - p50(2) [51-500]
Jaworowska, Zofia Kielan - *In Pursuit of Early Mammals*
QRB - v90 - i2 - June 2015 - p207(2) [501+]
Jay, John - *Facing Fearful Odds: My Father's Story of Captivity, Escape and Resistance 1940-45*
TLS - i5839 - Feb 27 2015 - p8(1) [501+]
Jay, Paul - *The Humanities "Crisis" and the Future of Literary Studies*
Col Lit - v42 - i2 - Spring 2015 - p348(4) [501+]
Jay, Stacey - *Of Beast and Beauty (Read by Whelan, Julia). Audiobook Review*
y SLJ - v61 - i10 - Oct 2015 - p54(1) [51-500]
Princess of Thorns (Read by Whelan, Julia). Audiobook Review
y BL - v111 - i18 - May 15 2015 - p72(1) [51-500]
y SLJ - v61 - i4 - April 2015 - p65(1) [51-500]
Princess of Thorns
y CCB-B - v68 - i6 - Feb 2015 - p316(1) [51-500]
y HB Guide - v26 - i1 - Spring 2015 - p110(1) [51-500]
Jayal, Niraja Gopal - *Citizenship and Its Discontents: An Indian History*
HNet - Feb 2015 - pNA [501+]
Pac A - v88 - i1 - March 2015 - p209 [501+]
Jayaraman, Saru - *Forked*
KR - Nov 15 2015 - pNA [501+]
Jayne, Hannah - *The Escape*
y KR - May 1 2015 - pNA [51-500]
y SLJ - v61 - i5 - May 2015 - p120(1) [51-500]
y VOYA - v38 - i2 - June 2015 - p62(1) [51-500]
Jazynka, Kitson - *Mission: Wolf Rescue: All about Wolves and How to Save Them*
c HB Guide - v26 - i1 - Spring 2015 - p164(2) [51-500]
Jealous, Benjamin Todd - *Reach: 40 Black Men Speak on Living, Leading, and Succeeding*
BL - v111 - i11 - Feb 1 2015 - p18(1) [51-500]
Jean, Emiko - *We'll Never Be Apart*
y BL - v112 - i3 - Oct 1 2015 - p76(1) [51-500]
y KR - July 15 2015 - pNA [51-500]
y SLJ - v61 - i10 - Oct 2015 - p112(1) [51-500]
y VOYA - v38 - i5 - Dec 2015 - p57(1) [51-500]
Jeansonne, Glen - *War on the Silver Screen: Shaping Americas Perception of History*
NWCR - v68 - i2 - Spring 2015 - p147(2) [501+]
Jebber, Molly - *Change of Heart*
PW - v262 - i19 - May 11 2015 - p42(1) [51-500]
Jeffers, Dawn - *Beautiful Moon / Bella Luna (Illus. by Leick, Bonnie)*
c CH Bwatch - July 2015 - pNA [51-500]
Jeffers, Honoree Fanonne - *The Glory Gets*
BL - v111 - i17 - May 1 2015 - p72(1) [51-500]
Jeffers, Oliver - *The Hueys: in What's the Opposite? (Illus. by Jeffers, Oliver)*
c BL - v112 - i3 - Oct 1 2015 - p82(1) [51-500]
c KR - Oct 1 2015 - pNA [51-500]
c PW - v262 - i44 - Nov 2 2015 - p84(1) [501+]
c SLJ - v61 - i12 - Dec 2015 - p90(1) [51-500]
Once upon an Alphabet: Short Stories for All the Letters (Illus. by Jeffers, Oliver)
c HB - v91 - i1 - Jan-Feb 2015 - p65(2) [51-500]
c HB Guide - v26 - i1 - Spring 2015 - p34(1) [51-500]
c Sch Lib - v63 - i1 - Spring 2015 - p28(1) [51-500]
Jeffers, Robinson - *The Collected Letters of Robinson Jeffers, with Selected Letters of Una Jeffers, vol. 2 and 3*
AM - v213 - i14 - Nov 9 2015 - p30(3) [501+]
Jefferson, Ann - *Genius in France: An Idea and its Uses*
FS - v69 - i4 - Oct 2015 - p562-563 [501+]
Jefferson, Marci - *Enchantress of Paris*
LJ - v140 - i10 - June 1 2015 - p88(1) [51-500]
Jefferson, Margo - *Negroland: A Memoir*
BL - v111 - i22 - August 1 2015 - p9(1) [51-500]
KR - July 1 2015 - pNA [51-500]
LJ - v140 - i15 - Sept 15 2015 - p85(1) [51-500]
NYT - Sept 11 2015 - pC21(L) [501+]
NYTBR - Sept 20 2015 - p12(L) [501+]
Jefferson, Sam - *Sea Fever: The True Adventures That Inspired Our Greatest Maritime Authors, from Conrad to Masefield, Melville and Hemingway*
LJ - v140 - i7 - April 15 2015 - p84(1) [51-500]
Jeffery, Keith - *1916: A Global History*
KR - Oct 1 2015 - pNA [501+]
PW - v262 - i42 - Oct 19 2015 - p65(1) [51-500]
TimHES - i2222 - Sept 24 2015 - p44-45 [501+]
Jefford, C.G. - *Observers and Navigators: And Other Non-Pilot Aircrew in the RFC, RNAS and RAF*
APH - v62 - i1 - Spring 2015 - p53(1) [501+]
Jefford, Clayton N. - *Didache: The Teaching of the Twelve Apostles*
Class R - v65 - i1 - April 2015 - p83-85 [501+]
Jeffrey, Elizabeth - *Meadowlands*
y BL - v111 - i16 - April 15 2015 - p37(1) [51-500]
Jeffreys, Elaine - *Sex in China*
TimHES - i2188 - Jan 29 2015 - p51(1) [501+]
Jeffreys, Sheila - *Gender Hurts: A Feminist Analysis of the Politics of Transgenderism*
TLS - i5842 - March 20 2015 - p26(1) [501+]
Jeffries, Bayyinah S. - *A Nation Can Rise No Higher Than Its Women: African American Muslim Women in the Movement for Black Self-Determination, 1950-1975*
Wom R Bks - v32 - i4 - July-August 2015 - p7(3) [501+]
Jeffries, Hasan Kwame - *Bloody Lowndes: Civil Rights and Black Power in Alabama's Black Belt*
Am St - v54 - i2 - Summer 2015 - p73-83 [501+]
Jeffries, Sabrina - *The Art of Sinning*
PW - v262 - i24 - June 15 2015 - p71(1) [51-500]
If the Viscount Falls
BL - v111 - i11 - Feb 1 2015 - p30(2) [51-500]
The Study of Seduction
KR - Jan 1 2016 - pNA [51-500]
Jemisin, N.K. - *The Fifth Season: The Broken Earth, Bk. 1*
NYTBR - August 9 2015 - p20(L) [501+]
PW - v262 - i26 - June 29 2015 - p50(1) [51-500]
Jenkins, Beverly - *Destiny's Captive*
PW - v262 - i7 - Feb 16 2015 - pNA [51-500]
For Your Love
BL - v112 - i2 - Sept 15 2015 - p42(2) [501+]
Jenkins, Bowen - *My Name Is Bob (Illus. by Kelley, Gerald)*
c HB Guide - v26 - i1 - Spring 2015 - p23(1) [51-500]
Jenkins, Brian - *Lord Lyons: A Diplomat in an Age of Nationalism and War*
HNet - Jan 2015 - pNA [501+]
Jenkins, Dan - *Unplayable Lies: (The Only Golf Book You'll Ever Need).*
LJ - v140 - i6 - April 1 2015 - p94(1) [501+]
Jenkins, Emily - *A Fine Dessert: Four Centuries, Four Families, One Delicious Treat (Illus. by Blackall, Sophie)*
c CCB-B - v68 - i8 - April 2015 - p405(1) [51-500]
c CH Bwatch - April 2015 - pNA [51-500]
c HB - v91 - i1 - Jan-Feb 2015 - p66(2) [501+]
c HB Guide - v26 - i2 - Fall 2015 - p38(1) [51-500]
c NYT - Nov 7 2015 - pC1(L) [501+]
c NYTBR - March 15 2015 - p16(L) [501+]
The Fun Book of Scary Stuff (Illus. by Yum, Hyewon)
c CCB-B - v69 - i1 - Sept 2015 - p29(1) [51-500]
c HB - v91 - i4 - July-August 2015 - p115(2) [51-500]
c KR - August 1 2015 - pNA [51-500]
c NYTBR - Oct 11 2015 - p16(L) [501+]
c PW - v262 - i21 - May 25 2015 - p57(1) [51-500]
c SLJ - v61 - i9 - Sept 2015 - p106(1) [51-500]
Tiger and Badger (Illus. by Gay, Marie-Louise)
c KR - Nov 15 2015 - pNA [51-500]
c SLJ - v61 - i12 - Dec 2015 - p91(1) [51-500]
Toys Meet Snow (Illus. by Zelinsky, Paul O.)
c PW - v262 - i27 - July 6 2015 - p68(1) [51-500]
c BL - v111 - i21 - July 1 2015 - p65(1) [51-500]
c CH Bwatch - Oct 2015 - pNA [51-500]
c HB - v91 - i5 - Sept-Oct 2015 - p81(2) [51-500]
c KR - July 1 2015 - pNA [51-500]
c NYTBR - Nov 8 2015 - p31(L) [501+]
c PW - v262 - i49 - Dec 2 2015 - p18(1) [51-500]
c SLJ - v61 - i6 - June 2015 - p84(2) [51-500]
Jenkins, Ian - *Defining Beauty: The Body in Ancient Greek Art*
TLS - i5854 - June 12 2015 - p22(1) [501+]
Jenkins, Jerry B. - *Empire's End*
PW - v262 - i20 - May 18 2015 - p38(1) [51-500]
Jenkins, Kathleen E. - *Sacred Divorce: Religion, Therapeutic Culture, and Ending Life Partnerships*
AJS - v121 - i1 - July 2015 - p330(3) [501+]
CS - v44 - i6 - Nov 2015 - p817-818 [501+]
Jenkins, Lyndsey - *Lady Constance Lytton: Aristocrat, Suffragette, Martyr*
Lon R Bks - v37 - i14 - July 16 2015 - p31(2) [501+]
Jenkins, Martin - *Fabulous Frogs (Illus. by Hopgood, Tim)*
c BL - v112 - i7 - Dec 1 2015 - p51(1) [51-500]
c KR - Nov 15 2015 - pNA [51-500]
c Magpies - v30 - i5 - Nov 2015 - p22(1) [501+]
Jenkins, Martin: - *The History of Money: From Bartering to Banking (Illus. by Kitamura, Satoshi)*
c HB Guide - v26 - i1 - Spring 2015 - p139(1) [51-500]
Jenkins, Paul - *Urbanization, Urbanism and Urbanity in an African City: Home Spaces and House Cultures*
HNet - July 2015 - pNA [501+]
Jenkins, Philip - *The Great and Holy War: How World War I Became a Religious Crusade*
NWCR - v68 - i1 - Wntr 2015 - p136(2) [501+]
The Many Faces of Christ: The Thousand-Year Story of the Survival and Influence of the Lost Gospels
Bks & Cult - v21 - i6 - Nov-Dec 2015 - p16(2) [501+]
CC - v132 - i21 - Oct 14 2015 - p50(2) [501+]
LJ - v140 - i11 - June 15 2015 - p92(2) [51-500]
Remembering Armageddon: Religion and the First World War
J Mil H - v79 - i3 - July 2015 - p861-862 [501+]
Jenkins, Richard - *Being Danish: Paradoxes of Identity in Everyday Life*
ERS - v38 - i3 - March 2015 - p534(3) [501+]
Jenkins, Simon - *Mission Accomplished? The Crisis of International Intervention*
NS - v144 - i5280 - Sept 18 2015 - p65(1) [501+]
Jenkins, Steve - *The Animal Book: A Collection of the Fastest, Fiercest, Toughest, Cleverest, Shyest - And Most Surprising-Animals on Earth*
c HB - v91 - i1 - Jan-Feb 2015 - p24(2) [501+]
Creature Features: 25 Animals Explain Why They Look the Way They Do (Illus. by Jenkins, Steve)
c BL - v111 - i9-10 - Jan 1 2015 - pS4(8) [501+]
c HB Guide - v26 - i1 - Spring 2015 - p155(1) [51-500]
c CCB-B - v68 - i5 - Jan 2015 - p261(2) [51-500]
Egg: Nature's Perfect Package (Illus. by Jenkins, Steve)
c CCB-B - v68 - i8 - April 2015 - p405(2) [51-500]
c CH Bwatch - April 2015 - pNA [51-500]
c HB Guide - v26 - i2 - Fall 2015 - p171(1) [51-500]
c KR - Jan 1 2015 - pNA [51-500]
How to Swallow a Pig: Step-by-Step Advice from the Animal Kingdom (Illus. by Jenkins, Steve)
c BL - v112 - i2 - Sept 15 2015 - p54(1) [51-500]
c CCB-B - v69 - i2 - Oct 2015 - p94(1) [51-500]
c PW - v262 - i35 - August 31 2015 - p90(2) [501+]
c KR - June 1 2015 - pNA [51-500]
c PW - v262 - i49 - Dec 2 2015 - p47(1) [51-500]
c SLJ - v61 - i5 - May 2015 - p133(1) [51-500]
Jenkins, William - *Between Raid and Rebellion: The Irish in Buffalo and Toronto, 1867-1916*
AHR - v120 - i1 - Feb 2015 - p225-226 [501+]
JIH - v45 - i3 - Wntr 2015 - p441-442 [501+]
Jenkyns, Richard - *Classical Literature*
KR - Dec 15 2015 - pNA [501+]
TLS - i5852 - May 29 2015 - p11(1) [501+]
Jenne, Mike - *Blue Darker Than Black*
PW - v262 - i47 - Nov 23 2015 - p50(2) [51-500]
Blue Gemini
PW - v262 - i13 - March 30 2015 - p56(2) [51-500]
Jennifer, Donnelly - *Waterfire Saga: 02: Rogue Wave. Audiobook Review*
SLJ - v61 - i4 - April 2015 - p64(1) [51-500]
Jennings, Chris - *Paradise Now: The Story of American Utopianism*
BL - v112 - i5 - Nov 1 2015 - p4(2) [51-500]
KR - Oct 1 2015 - pNA [501+]
PW - v262 - i45 - Nov 9 2015 - p52(1) [51-500]
Jennings, Christian - *At War on the Gothic Line*
KR - Dec 15 2015 - pNA [501+]
Jennings, Garth - *The Deadly 7 (Illus. by Jennings, Garth)*
c KR - Jan 1 2016 - pNA [51-500]
c Sch Lib - v63 - i2 - Summer 2015 - p105(1) [51-500]
c SLJ - v61 - i12 - Dec 2015 - p101(2) [51-500]

Jennings, J. Dalton - *Solomon's Arrow*
KR - May 15 2015 - pNA [51-500]
PW - v262 - i21 - May 25 2015 - p41(2) [51-500]
Jennings, Jack - *Presidents, Congress, and the Public Schools: The Politics of Education Reform*
LJ - v140 - i7 - April 15 2015 - p99(1) [51-500]
RVBW - April 2015 - pNA [501+]
Jennings, Jazz - *I Am Jazz (Illus. by McNicholas, Shelagh)*
c HB Guide - v26 - i1 - Spring 2015 - p32(1) [51-500]
Jennings, Katie - *Things Lost In The Fire*
SPBW - June 2015 - pNA [51-500]
Jennings, Ken - *Ancient Egypt (Illus. by Lowery, Mike)*
c BL - v112 - i6 - Nov 15 2015 - p38(1) [51-500]
c SLJ - v61 - i11 - Nov 2015 - p132(1) [51-500]
The Human Body (Illus. by Lowery, Mike)
c BL - v111 - i17 - May 1 2015 - p84(1) [51-500]
c HB Guide - v26 - i2 - Fall 2015 - p184(1) [51-500]
c SLJ - v61 - i3 - March 2015 - p170(1) [51-500]
Outer Space (Illus. by Lowery, Mike)
c HB Guide - v26 - i1 - Spring 2015 - p149(1) [51-500]
Jennings, Kevin - *One Teacher in Ten in the New Millennium: LGBT Educators Speak Out About What's Gotten Bette ...and What Hasn't*
LJ - v140 - i12 - July 1 2015 - p91(1) [51-500]
One Teacher in Ten in the New Millennium: LGBT Educators Speak Out About What's Gotten Better...and What Hasn't
BL - v111 - i22 - August 1 2015 - p22(2) [51-500]
Jennings, Maureen - *No Known Grave*
y NYTBR - Feb 1 2015 - p25(L) [501+]
Jennings, Patrick - *Guinea Dog 3*
c HB Guide - v26 - i1 - Spring 2015 - p82(1) [51-500]
Hissy Fitz (Illus. by Austin, Michael Allen)
c HB Guide - v26 - i2 - Fall 2015 - p67(1) [51-500]
Jennings, S.L. - *Tryst*
LJ - v140 - i16 - Oct 1 2015 - p62(2) [501+]
Jennings, Sharon - *Connecting Dots*
y Res Links - v20 - i4 - April 2015 - p30(2) [501+]
c SLJ - v61 - i5 - May 2015 - p103(1) [51-500]
Jennings, Terry Catasus - *Sounds of the Savanna*
c KR - July 15 2015 - pNA [51-500]
Jennison, Ruth - *The Zukofsky Era: Modernity, Margins, and the Avant-Garde*
AL - v87 - i3 - Sept 2015 - p618-622 [501+]
Jenny, Tonia - *Zen Doodle: Oodles of Doodles*
Bwatch - March 2015 - pNA [51-500]
Jenoff, Pam - *The Last Summer at Chelsea Beach*
BL - v111 - i22 - August 1 2015 - p40(1) [51-500]
Jensen, Anthony K. - *Nietzsche as a Scholar of Antiquity*
Class R - v65 - i2 - Oct 2015 - p599-601 [501+]
Jensen, Bonnie Rickner - *A Very Merry Christmas Prayer (Illus. by Moore, Natalia)*
c PW - v262 - i37 - Sept 14 2015 - p72(2) [501+]
Jensen, Cordelia - *Skyscraping*
y BL - v111 - i16 - April 15 2015 - p57(1) [51-500]
y HB Guide - v26 - i2 - Fall 2015 - p124(1) [51-500]
y KR - March 15 2015 - pNA [51-500]
y SLJ - v61 - i6 - June 2015 - p125(3) [51-500]
y VOYA - v38 - i2 - June 2015 - p62(1) [501+]
Jensen, Daintry - *The Hidden Forest (Illus. by Baker, Alan)*
c SLJ - v61 - i6 - June 2015 - p100(1) [51-500]
Jensen, Erik N. - *Body by Weimar: Athletes, Gender and German Modernity*
JWH - v27 - i2 - Summer 2015 - p169(6) [501+]
Jensen, Jamie - *Road Trip USA: Cross-Country Adventures on America's Two-Lane Highways*
Bwatch - August 2015 - pNA [51-500]
Jensen, Jane - *Kingdom Come*
KR - Nov 15 2015 - pNA [51-500]
Jensen, Jeff - *Before Tomorrowland (Illus. by Case, Jonathan)*
y BL - v111 - i15 - April 1 2015 - p78(1) [51-500]
y HB Guide - v26 - i2 - Fall 2015 - p124(1) [51-500]
y SLJ - v61 - i4 - April 2015 - p146(1) [51-500]
Before Tomorrowland (Illus. by Case, Jonathon)
y VOYA - v38 - i2 - June 2015 - p77(1) [51-500]
Jensen, Joan M. - *Women on the North American Plains*
WHQ - v46 - i2 - Summer 2015 - p235-236 [501+]
Jensen, Kelly - *It Happens: A Guide to Contemporary Realistic Fiction for the YA Reader*
y SLJ - v61 - i11 - Nov 2015 - p142(1) [51-500]
Skip Trace. E-book Review
PW - v262 - i36 - Sept 7 2015 - p51(1) [51-500]
Jensen-Kimball, Laura - *Momster (Illus. by Mahr, Peter)*
c CH Bwatch - Oct 2015 - pNA [51-500]
Jensen, Marion - *Searching for Super*
y HB Guide - v26 - i2 - Fall 2015 - p87(1) [51-500]
Jensen, Michael - *Woven*
y VOYA - v37 - i6 - Feb 2015 - p78(2) [51-500]
Jensen, Ola Wolfhechel - *Histories of Archaeological Practices: Reflections on Methods, Strategies and Social Organization in Past Fieldwork*
Isis - v106 - i1 - March 2015 - p162(2) [501+]
Jensen, Oscar - *The Yelling Stones*
c Sch Lib - v63 - i3 - Autumn 2015 - p166(1) [51-500]
Jensen, Richard Bach - *The Battle against Anarchist Terrorism: An International History, 1878-1934*
AHR - v120 - i3 - June 2015 - p979-980 [501+]
JAH - v102 - i1 - June 2015 - p264-265 [501+]
Jensen, Robert - *Plain Radical*
KR - July 15 2015 - pNA [501+]
Jensen, Sean - *The Middle School Rules of Brian Urlacher*
c CH Bwatch - May 2015 - pNA [51-500]
Jenson-Elliott, Cindy - *Dig In! (Illus. by Peterson, Mary)*
c KR - Dec 15 2015 - pNA [51-500]
Jenson, Joel - *Tiny Hamster Is a Giant Monster*
c CH Bwatch - August 2015 - pNA [51-500]
Jeremiah, David - *Agents of Babylon: What the Prophecies of Daniel Tell Us about the End of Days*
Bwatch - Nov 2015 - pNA [51-500]
Jeremiah, Emily - *Ethical Approaches in Contemporary German-Language Literature and Culture*
MLR - v110 - i2 - April 2015 - p614-615 [501+]
Nomadic Ethics in Contemporary Women's Writing in German: Strange Subjects
MLR - v110 - i1 - Jan 2015 - p298-299 [501+]
Jerkins, Grant - *Done in One*
BL - v111 - i9-10 - Jan 1 2015 - p45(1) [51-500]
Jernigan, Zachary - *Shower of Stones*
PW - v262 - i19 - May 11 2015 - p40(1) [51-500]
Jeroen de Kloet - *Spectacle and the City: Chinese Urbanities in Art and Popular Culture*
JAS - v74 - i1 - Feb 2015 - p186-188 [501+]
Jerolmack, Colin - *The Global Pigeon*
CS - v44 - i1 - Jan 2015 - p70-71 [501+]
Jersild, Austin - *The Sino-Soviet Alliance: An International History*
AHR - v120 - i1 - Feb 2015 - p205-206 [501+]
Slav R - v74 - i2 - Summer 2015 - p370-371 [501+]
Jerven, Morten - *Africa: Why Economists Get It Wrong*
Econ - v416 - i8948 - July 25 2015 - p67(US) [501+]
Jervis, Simon Swynfen - *Roman Splendour, English Arcadia: The English Taste for Pietre Dure and the Sixtus Cabinet at Stourhead*
Spec - v327 - i9728 - Feb 7 2015 - p41(1) [501+]
Jespersen, Debbie - *Ayala's Dreams*
c CH Bwatch - May 2015 - pNA [51-500]
Jesseman, Deborah J. - *The Common Core in Action: Ready to Use Lesson Plans for K-6 Librarians*
Teach Lib - v43 - i1 - Oct 2015 - p41(3) [501+]
Jessen, John - *Only Trees Need Roots*
SPBW - Sept 2015 - pNA [51-500]
Jessen, Ralph - *Transformations of Retailing in Europe after 1945*
HNet - April 2015 - pNA [501+]
Jessop, Vanessa - *Atlas of the Human Body (Illus. by Mecchubot, Kanitta)*
LJ - v140 - i11 - June 15 2015 - p112(1) [51-500]
Jeter, Derek - *The Contract*
c HB Guide - v26 - i1 - Spring 2015 - p82(1) [51-500]
Hit and Miss
y HB Guide - v26 - i2 - Fall 2015 - p88(1) [51-500]
y SLJ - v61 - i6 - June 2015 - p108(1) [51-500]
Hit & Miss (Read by Williams, Jesse). Audiobook Review
y SLJ - v61 - i7 - July 2015 - p47(1) [51-500]
Jewel - *Never Broken: Songs Are Only Half the Story*
BL - v112 - i1 - Sept 1 2015 - p27(1) [51-500]
KR - August 15 2015 - pNA [51-500]
PW - v262 - i32 - August 10 2015 - p54(1) [51-500]
Jewell, Lisa - *The Third Wife*
BL - v111 - i18 - May 15 2015 - p26(1) [51-500]
KR - April 15 2015 - pNA [501+]
LJ - v140 - i9 - May 15 2015 - p71(1) [51-500]
'Jewish Questions' in International Politics - Diplomacy, Rights and Intervention
HNet - Feb 2015 - pNA [501+]
Jezernik, Bozidar - *Titos Gulag auf der Insel Goli Otok*
HNet - May 2015 - pNA [501+]
Jha, Raj Kamal - *She will Build Him a City*
KR - Jan 15 2015 - pNA [51-500]
Ji, Xianlin - *The Cowshed*
KR - Nov 1 2015 - pNA [501+]
Jian Lee, Deborah - *Rescuing Jesus: How People of Color, Women, and Queer Christians Are Reclaiming Evangelicalism*
LJ - v140 - i17 - Oct 15 2015 - p91(1) [51-500]
Jian, Li - *Ming's Adventure with Confucius in Qufu, A Story in English and Chinese (Illus. by Jian, Li)*
c CH Bwatch - April 2015 - pNA [501+]
Zheng He, the Great Chinese Explorer: A Bilingual Story of Adventure and Discovery
c CH Bwatch - May 2015 - pNA [51-500]
Zheng He, the Great Chinese Explorer: A Bilingual Story of Adventure and Discovery (Illus. by Jian, Li)
c SLJ - v61 - i11 - Nov 2015 - p84(1) [51-500]
Jiang, Jia - *Rejection Proof: How I Beat Fear and Became Invincible through 100 Days of Rejection*
KR - Feb 15 2015 - pNA [51-500]
Jiang, Jiehong - *An Era without Memories: Chinese Contemporary Photography on Urban Transformation*
NS - v144 - i5264 - May 29 2015 - p83(1) [51-500]
Jiang, William - *Guide to Natural Mental Health: Anxiety, Bipolar, Depression, Schizophrenia, and Digital Addiction*
SPBW - Sept 2015 - pNA [501+]
A Schizophrenic Will: A Story of Madness, a Story of Hope
SPBW - Sept 2015 - pNA [51-500]
Jiang, Younglin - *Mandate of Heaven and the Great Ming Code*
HNet - June 2015 - pNA [501+]
Jikell, Gunther - *European Muslim Antisemitism: Why Young Urban Males Say They Don't Like Jews*
TimHES - i2212 - July 16 2015 - p51(1) [501+]
Jiles, Paulette - *News of the World*
LJ - v140 - i20 - Dec 1 2015 - p93(1) [51-500]
Jimenez, Francisco - *Taking Hold: From Migrant Childhood to Columbia University*
y HB - v91 - i3 - May-June 2015 - p126(2) [51-500]
y HB Guide - v26 - i2 - Fall 2015 - p209(1) [51-500]
y SLJ - v61 - i9 - Sept 2015 - p186(2) [51-500]
y VOYA - v38 - i1 - April 2015 - p87(1) [51-500]
y BL - v111 - i17 - May 1 2015 - p93(1) [51-500]
Jimenez, Gidget Roceles - *All about the Philippines: Stories, Songs, Crafts and Games for Kids (Illus. by Dandan-Albano, Corazon)*
c CH Bwatch - August 2015 - pNA [51-500]
c BL - v112 - i2 - Sept 15 2015 - p54(1) [51-500]
c KR - August 15 2015 - pNA [51-500]
c SLJ - v61 - i8 - August 2015 - p121(1) [51-500]
Jimenez, Juan Masullo - *The Power of Staying Put*
Reason - v47 - i7 - Dec 2015 - p56(1) [51-500]
Jimeno, Myriam - *Juan Gregorio Palechor: The Story of My Life*
JRAI - v21 - i2 - June 2015 - p482(2) [501+]
Ams - v72 - i1 - Jan 2015 - p154(3) [501+]
HAHR - v95 - i1 - Feb 2015 - p175-176 [501+]
Jin, Ha - *A Map of Betrayal*
NYRB - v62 - i18 - Nov 19 2015 - p56(5) [501+]
Jin, Susie Lee - *Mine! (Illus. by Jin, Susie Lee)*
c KR - Oct 1 2015 - pNA [51-500]
c PW - v262 - i41 - Oct 12 2015 - p68(1) [51-500]
Jinba, Tenzin - *In the Land of the Eastern Queendom: The Politics of Gender and Ethnicity on the Sino-Tibetan Border*
Signs - v40 - i3 - Spring 2015 - p779(2) [501+]
Jingping, Xi - *Xi Jingping: The Governance of China*
RVBW - Feb 2015 - pNA [501+]
Jinks, Catherine - *The Last Bogler*
c BL - v112 - i6 - Nov 15 2015 - p55(1) [51-500]
c KR - Sept 15 2015 - pNA [51-500]
c SLJ - v61 - i10 - Oct 2015 - p90(2) [51-500]
A Plague of Bogles (Read by Williams, Mandy). Audiobook Review
c BL - v111 - i18 - May 15 2015 - p72(1) [51-500]
A Plague of Bogles (Illus. by Watts, Sarah)
y CCB-B - v68 - i6 - Feb 2015 - p316(1) [51-500]
y HB - v91 - i1 - Jan-Feb 2015 - p82(2) [51-500]
y HB Guide - v26 - i2 - Fall 2015 - p88(1) [51-500]
Theophilus Grey and the Demon Thief
y Magpies - v30 - i4 - Sept 2015 - p34(1) [501+]
JiSeung, Kook - *Ouch! It Stings! (Illus. by JiSeung, Kook)*
c HB Guide - v26 - i1 - Spring 2015 - p26(1) [51-500]
Jiyeoun Song - *Inequality in the Workplace: Labor Market Reform in Japan and Korea*
CS - v44 - i6 - Nov 2015 - p853-855 [501+]
Joan, Torres-Pou - *Asia en la Espana del siglo XIX: literatos, viajeros, intelectuales y diplomaticos ante Oriente*
Hisp R - v83 - i1 - Wntr 2015 - p104-107 [501+]
Joannou, Maroula - *The History of British Women's Writing, 1920-1945: Vol. 8*
Wom HR - v24 - i1 - Feb 2015 - p139-3 [501+]

Joas, Hans - *Faith as an Option: Possible Futures for Christianity*
AJS - v121 - i2 - Sept 2015 - p660(3) [501+]
Theol St - v76 - i3 - Sept 2015 - p607(2) [501+]
TLS - i5869 - Sept 25 2015 - p28(1) [501+]
War in Social Thought: Hobbes to the Present
CS - v44 - i1 - Jan 2015 - p138-140 [501+]

Jobb, Dean - *Empire of Deception: The Incredible Story of a Master Swindler Who Seduced a City and Captivated the Nation (Read by Berkrot, Peter). Audiobook Review*
LJ - v140 - i11 - June 15 2015 - p52(1) [51-500]
Empire of Deception: The Incredible Story of a Master Swindler Who Seduced a City and Captivated the Nation
BL - v111 - i14 - March 15 2015 - p32(1) [51-500]
KR - Feb 15 2015 - pNA [501+]
LJ - v140 - i5 - March 15 2015 - p122(1) [501+]
Mac - v128 - i23 - June 15 2015 - p62(1) [501+]
NYTBR - July 5 2015 - p30(L) [501+]

Jobin-Leeds, Greg - *When We Fight, We Win!*
KR - Oct 1 2015 - pNA [501+]

Jobling, Curtis - *Max Helsing and the Thirteenth Curse*
c BL - v112 - i5 - Nov 1 2015 - p60(1) [51-500]
c KR - Sept 1 2015 - pNA [51-500]
c PW - v262 - i37 - Sept 14 2015 - p78(2) [51-500]
c SLJ - v61 - i10 - Oct 2015 - p91(1) [51-500]

Jobrani, Maz - *I'm Not a Terrorist, But I've Played One on TV: Memoirs of a Middle Eastern Funny Man*
NYT - March 18 2015 - pC1(L) [501+]

Jobs in My School Series
c BL - v111 - i15 - April 1 2015 - p58(1) [501+]

Jocelyn, Marthe - *A Big Dose of Lucky*
y KR - July 15 2015 - pNA [51-500]
y PW - v262 - i28 - July 13 2015 - p66(2) [51-500]
y Res Links - v21 - i1 - Oct 2015 - p35(2) [501+]
y SLJ - v61 - i11 - Nov 2015 - p116(1) [51-500]
y VOYA - v38 - i4 - Oct 2015 - p53(1) [51-500]

Jochnowitz, Eve - *The Yilna Vegetarian Cookbook: Garden-Fresh Recipes Rediscovered and Adapted for Today's Kitchen*
Bwatch - August 2015 - pNA [51-500]

Jockel, Helena - *We Sang in Hushed Voices*
y Res Links - v20 - i3 - Feb 2015 - p39(2) [501+]

Jockers, Matthew L. - *Macroanalysis: Digital Methods and Literary History*
AL - v87 - i2 - June 2015 - p418-420 [501+]

Jockusch, Laura - *Collect and Record! Jewish Holocaust Documentation in Early Postwar Europe*
GSR - v38 - i1 - Feb 2015 - p216-217 [501+]

Jodidio, Philip - *The Japanese House Reinvented*
LJ - v140 - i11 - June 15 2015 - p84(1) [51-500]

Jodorowsky, Alejandro - *Manual of Psychomagic: The Practice of Shamanic Psychotherapy*
Bwatch - August 2015 - pNA [51-500]
PW - v262 - i4 - Jan 26 2015 - p162(1) [51-500]
Showman Killer: Heartless Hero
PW - v262 - i50 - Dec 7 2015 - p75(1) [51-500]
Where the Bird Sings Best
CQ - v65 - i1 - Fall 2015 - p120(4) [501+]

Jodzio, John - *KnockOut*
KR - Jan 1 2016 - pNA [501+]

Joes, Anthony James - *Why South Vietnam Fell*
J Mil H - v79 - i2 - April 2015 - p471-475 [501+]

Johannsen, Birgitte Beggild - *Beyond Scylla and Charybdis*
RVBW - Nov 2015 - pNA [501+]

Johansen, Erika - *Invasion of the Tearling (Read by Porter, Davina). Audiobook Review*
BL - v112 - i2 - Sept 15 2015 - p77(1) [51-500]
The Invasion of the Tearling
BL - v111 - i15 - April 1 2015 - p34(1) [51-500]
Ent W - i1367 - June 12 2015 - p77(1) [501+]
KR - April 15 2015 - pNA [51-500]
PW - v262 - i10 - March 9 2015 - p56(1) [51-500]
SLJ - v61 - i12 - Dec 2015 - p132(2) [51-500]
The Queen of the Tearling (Read by Kellgren, Katherine). Audiobook Review
BL - v111 - i14 - March 15 2015 - p23(2) [501+]
The Queen of the Tearling
BL - v111 - i18 - May 15 2015 - p35(1) [501+]

Johansen, Iris - *Shadow Play: An Eve Duncan Novel*
KR - August 1 2015 - pNA [51-500]
LJ - v140 - i6 - April 1 2015 - p61(1) [501+]
PW - v262 - i30 - July 27 2015 - p43(1) [51-500]
Your Next Breath
BL - v111 - i13 - March 1 2015 - p27(1) [51-500]
KR - March 1 2015 - pNA [501+]
PW - v262 - i8 - Feb 23 2015 - p51(1) [51-500]

Johansen, Roy - *The Naked Eye*
BL - v111 - i19-20 - June 1 2015 - p56(1) [51-500]
PW - v262 - i21 - May 25 2015 - p35(1) [51-500]

Johansson, J.R. - *Cut Me Free*
y CCB-B - v68 - i6 - Feb 2015 - p317(1) [51-500]
y HB Guide - v26 - i2 - Fall 2015 - p124(2) [51-500]
y VOYA - v37 - i6 - Feb 2015 - p58(2) [51-500]
Mania
y KR - May 1 2015 - pNA [51-500]
y VOYA - v38 - i2 - June 2015 - p77(1) [51-500]

Johansson, Karl G. - *Francia et Germania: Studies in Strengleikar and Pidreks saga af Bern*
JEGP - v114 - i1 - Jan 2015 - p115(3) [501+]

Johansson, Kjell-Gunnar - *Googolplex*
SPBW - August 2015 - pNA [51-500]
WLT - v89 - i6 - Nov-Dec 2015 - p69(1) [51-500]

John, Anthony - *Renegade: An Elemental Novel*
y HB Guide - v26 - i1 - Spring 2015 - p110(1) [51-500]

John, Antony - *Imposter*
y KR - June 15 2015 - pNA [51-500]
y SLJ - v61 - i8 - August 2015 - p105(1) [51-500]

John, David - *Nameless*
SPBW - March 2015 - pNA [51-500]

John, Jory - *Goodnight Already! (Illus. by Davies, Benji)*
c CCB-B - v68 - i5 - Jan 2015 - p262(1) [51-500]
c HB Guide - v26 - i1 - Spring 2015 - p34(1) [51-500]
I Love You Already! (Illus. by Davies, Benji)
c KR - Oct 1 2015 - pNA [51-500]
c NYTBR - Nov 8 2015 - p33(L) [501+]
c PW - v262 - i41 - Oct 12 2015 - p66(2) [501+]
c SLJ - v61 - i12 - Dec 2015 - p91(1) [51-500]
I Will Chomp You! (Illus. by Shea, Bob)
c BL - v111 - i22 - August 1 2015 - p72(1) [51-500]
c CCB-B - v69 - i2 - Oct 2015 - p94(2) [51-500]
c HB - v91 - i4 - July-August 2015 - p116(1) [51-500]
c KR - May 1 2015 - pNA [51-500]
c PW - v262 - i20 - May 18 2015 - p81(1) [51-500]
c SLJ - v61 - i7 - July 2015 - p63(1) [51-500]
The Terrible Two (Illus. by Cornell, Kevin)
c HB - v91 - i2 - March-April 2015 - p91(1) [51-500]
c HB Guide - v26 - i2 - Fall 2015 - p74(1) [51-500]
c Sch Lib - v63 - i2 - Summer 2015 - p100(1) [51-500]

John, McQuaid - *Tasty: The Art and Science of What We Eat*
BL - v111 - i9-10 - Jan 1 2015 - p26(2) [51-500]

John, Simon - *Crusading and Warfare in the Middle Ages: Realities and Representations, Essays I nHonour of John France*
Specu - v90 - i3 - July 2015 - p876(1) [501+]

John, Thomas - *Never Argue with a Dead Person: True and Unbelievable Stories from the Other Side*
Bwatch - April 2015 - pNA [51-500]

John-Wenndorf, Carolin - *Der offentliche Autor: Uber die Selbstinszenierung von Schriftstellern*
MLR - v110 - i3 - July 2015 - p918-919 [501+]

John XXIII, St. - *Just for Today (Illus. by Landmann, Bimba)*
c BL - v111 - i19-20 - June 1 2015 - p78(1) [51-500]
c HB Guide - v26 - i2 - Fall 2015 - p150(1) [51-500]
c KR - March 1 2015 - pNA [51-500]
c PW - v262 - i8 - Feb 23 2015 - p79(1) [51-500]

Johncock, Benjamin - *The Last Pilot*
BL - v111 - i21 - July 1 2015 - p31(1) [51-500]
KR - May 1 2015 - pNA [51-500]
LJ - v140 - i10 - June 1 2015 - p90(1) [51-500]
NS - v144 - i5270 - July 10 2015 - p43(1) [501+]
PW - v262 - i16 - April 20 2015 - p49(1) [51-500]
Spec - v328 - i9757 - August 29 2015 - p37(2) [501+]

Johns, Andrew L. - *A Companion to Ronald Reagan*
BL - v111 - i21 - July 1 2015 - p18(1) [51-500]

Johns, Christopher M. S. - *The Visual Culture of Catholic Enlightenment*
Eight-C St - v48 - i4 - Summer 2015 - p549-551 [501+]

Johns, Glyn - *Sound Man: A Life Recording Hits with the Rolling Stones, the Who, Led Zeppelin, the Eagles, Eric Clapton, the Faces (Read by Vance, Simon). Audiobook Review*
LJ - v140 - i15 - Sept 15 2015 - p44(1) [51-500]

Johnsen, Kate - *Grow All You Can Eat in 3 Square Feet*
LJ - v140 - i6 - April 1 2015 - p109(1) [51-500]

Johnsen, Susan K. - *A Teacher's Guide to Using the Common Core State Standards with Mathematically Gifted and Advanced Learners*
TC Math - v22 - i1 - August 2015 - p54(2) [501+]

Johnsgard, Paul A. - *Seasons of the Tallgrass Prairie: A Nebraska Year*
Roundup M - v22 - i4 - April 2015 - p29(2) [501+]
Roundup M - v22 - i6 - August 2015 - p38(1) [501+]
RVBW - Jan 2015 - pNA [51-500]
Yellowstone Wildlife: Ecology and Natural History of the Greater Yellowstone Ecosystem
QRB - v90 - i1 - March 2015 - p83(2) [501+]

Johnson, A.P. - *Religion and Identity in Porphyry of Tyre: The Limits of Hellenism in Late Antiquity*
Class R - v65 - i1 - April 2015 - p93-95 [501+]

Johnson, Aaron P. - *Eusebius*
Class R - v65 - i2 - Oct 2015 - p403-405 [501+]

Johnson, Adam - *The Best American Nonrequired Reading, 2015*
y BL - v112 - i4 - Oct 15 2015 - p14(1) [51-500]
Fortune Smiles: Stories
KR - June 15 2015 - pNA [51-500]
NYTBR - August 16 2015 - p11(L) [501+]
PW - v262 - i25 - June 22 2015 - p118(1) [51-500]
Ent W - i1376 - August 14 2015 - p60(2) [501+]
NYT - Sept 8 2015 - pC1(L) [501+]

Johnson, Alan - *Please, Mr Postman*
TLS - i5833 - Jan 16 2015 - p26(1) [501+]

Johnson, Alaya Dawn - *Love Is the Drug*
y CH Bwatch - March 2015 - pNA [51-500]
y HB Guide - v26 - i1 - Spring 2015 - p110(1) [51-500]

Johnson, Alex - *Improbable Libraries: A Visual Journey to the World's Most Unusual Libraries*
LJ - v140 - i11 - June 15 2015 - p84(2) [51-500]
Mac - v128 - i11 - March 23 2015 - p54(3) [501+]

Johnson, Alissa - *A Talent for Trickery*
BL - v112 - i5 - Nov 1 2015 - p37(1) [51-500]
KR - Sept 1 2015 - pNA [51-500]
PW - v262 - i37 - Sept 14 2015 - p49(1) [51-500]

Johnson, Allan G. - *Not from Here*
KR - March 15 2015 - pNA [51-500]

Johnson, Allen (b. 1946-) - *Pardon My French: How a Grumpy American Fell in Love with France*
BL - v112 - i3 - Oct 1 2015 - p12(1) [51-500]

Johnson-Allen, John - *T.E. Lawrence and the Red Sea Patrol: The Royal Navy's Role in Creating the Legend*
TLS - i5875 - Nov 6 2015 - p30(1) [501+]

Johnson, Allen, Jr. - *The Dead House (Illus. by McMorris, Kelley)*
c CH Bwatch - July 2015 - pNA [51-500]
My Brother's Story (Illus. by McMorris, Kelley)
c CH Bwatch - July 2015 - pNA [51-500]
c SLJ - v61 - i9 - Sept 2015 - p140(1) [51-500]
A Nest of Snakes (Illus. by McMorris, Kelley)
c CH Bwatch - July 2015 - pNA [51-500]

Johnson, Andrew Alan - *Ghosts of the New City: Spirits, Urbanity, and the Ruins of Progress in Chiang Mai*
Pac A - v88 - i4 - Dec 2015 - p962(1) [501+]

Johnson, Anna Marie - *The Reformation as Christianization: Essays on Scott Hendrix's Christianization Thesis*
CHR - v101 - i2 - Spring 2015 - p368(4) [501+]

Johnson, Anne Akers - *Loop Loom Bracelets*
c CH Bwatch - March 2015 - pNA [51-500]

Johnson, Beverly - *The Face That Changed It All: A Memoir*
BL - v111 - i21 - July 1 2015 - p14(1) [51-500]
KR - June 15 2015 - pNA [501+]
PW - v262 - i23 - June 8 2015 - p53(1) [51-500]

Johnson, Bob - *Carbon Nation: Fossil Fuels in the Making of American Culture*
JIH - v46 - i3 - Wntr 2016 - p468-469 [501+]

Johnson, Boris - *The Churchill Factor: How One Man Made History (Read by Shepherd, Simon). Audiobook Review*
LJ - v140 - i8 - May 1 2015 - p43(1) [51-500]
The Churchill Factor: How One Man Made History
TLS - i5836 - Feb 6 2015 - p24(1) [501+]
HT - v65 - i1 - Jan 2015 - p58(1) [501+]
Soc - v52 - i2 - April 2015 - p181(1) [501+]
Think Like Churchill (Illus. by Huxable, Jaime). E-book Review
c SLJ - v61 - i6 - June 2015 - p72(1) [501+]

Johnson, Bryan Stanley - *The Unfortunates*
NS - v144 - i5282 - Oct 2 2015 - p74(2) [501+]

Johnson, Cat - *Midnight Ride*
PW - v262 - i10 - March 9 2015 - p58(1) [51-500]
Midnight Wrangler
PW - v262 - i41 - Oct 12 2015 - p53(1) [51-500]

Johnson, Catherine (b. 1962-) - *The Curious Tale of the Lady Caraboo*
y Sch Lib - v63 - i4 - Winter 2015 - p247(1) [51-500]

Johnson, Charles - *The Adventures of Emery Jones, Boy Science Wonder: The Hard Problems*
    ABR - v36 - i3 - March-April 2015 - p28(2) [501+]
Middle Passage
    NYTBR - July 12 2015 - p4(L) [501+]
Johnson, Christine - *Love's Rescue*
    y BL - v111 - i19-20 - June 1 2015 - p62(1) [51-500]
Johnson, Claudia L. - *Jane Austen's Cults and Cultures*
    Nine-C Lit - v70 - i2 - Sept 2015 - p285(4) [501+]
Johnson, Colin R. - *Just Queer Folks: Gender and Sexuality in Rural America*
    AHR - v120 - i1 - Feb 2015 - p267-268 [501+]
Johnson, Craig - *Any Other Name*
    Roundup M - v22 - i6 - August 2015 - p30(1) [501+]
Dry Bones
    BL - v111 - i17 - May 1 2015 - p34(1) [501+]
    KR - April 15 2015 - pNA [51-500]
    PW - v262 - i13 - March 30 2015 - p52(1) [51-500]
    Roundup M - v23 - i1 - Oct 2015 - p30(1) [501+]
Wait for Signs
    Roundup M - v22 - i3 - Feb 2015 - p26(1) [501+]
    Roundup M - v22 - i6 - August 2015 - p30(1) [501+]
Johnson, Crockett - *Harold and the Purple Crayon (Illus. by Johnson, Crockett)*
    c BL - v112 - i4 - Oct 15 2015 - p53(1) [51-500]
Johnson, Curtis - *Darwin's Dice: The Idea of Chance in the Thought of Charles Darwin*
    QRB - v90 - i4 - Dec 2015 - p418(2) [501+]
Johnson, David - *The Horrell Wars: Feuding in Texas and New Mexico*
    JSH - v81 - i3 - August 2015 - p752(2) [501+]
    Roundup M - v22 - i6 - August 2015 - p38(1) [501+]
    SHQ - v118 - i3 - Jan 2015 - p327-328 [501+]
Johnson, Denis - *The Laughing Monsters*
    NS - v144 - i5252 - March 6 2015 - p53(1) [501+]
    NYRB - v62 - i1 - Jan 8 2015 - p47(2) [501+]
    Spec - v327 - i9735 - March 28 2015 - p43(1) [501+]
Johnson, Dominic - *Glorious Catastrophe: Jack Smith, Performance and Visual Culture*
    TDR - v59 - i1 - Spring 2015 - p189(2) [501+]
Johnson, Don - *Thirteen Months at Manassas/Bull Run: The Two Battles and the Confederate and Union Occupations*
    JSH - v81 - i1 - Feb 2015 - p200(2) [501+]
Johnson, Eleanor - *Practicing Literary Theory in the Middle Ages: Ethics and the Mixed Form in Chaucer, Gower, Usk, and Hoccleve*
    JEGP - v114 - i1 - Jan 2015 - p154(3) [501+]
    MP - v113 - i2 - Nov 2015 - pE73(3) [501+]
Johnson, Elizabeth A. - *Abounding in Kindness: Writing for the People of God*
    AM - v213 - i15 - Nov 16 2015 - p36(2) [501+]
    JAAR - v83 - i2 - June 2015 - pNA [501+]
Ask the Beasts: Darwin and the God of Love
    JR - v95 - i4 - Oct 2015 - p561(2) [501+]
    Theol St - v76 - i1 - March 2015 - p194(2) [501+]
Johnson, Erin - *Grace and the Guiltless*
    y HB Guide - v26 - i1 - Spring 2015 - p110(1) [51-500]
Her Cold Revenge
    y KR - May 1 2015 - pNA [51-500]
    y SLJ - v61 - i8 - August 2015 - p114(1) [51-500]
    y VOYA - v38 - i3 - August 2015 - p63(1) [51-500]
Johnson, Evelyn S. - *Identification and Evaluation of Learning Disabilities*
    Bwatch - April 2015 - pNA [501+]
Johnson-Freese, Joan - *Educating America's Military*
    NWCR - v68 - i2 - Spring 2015 - p147(2) [501+]
Johnson, Giff - *Don't Ever Whisper: Darlene Keju, Pacific Health Pioneer, Champion for Nuclear Survivors*
    Pac A - v88 - i3 - Sept 2015 - p749 [501+]
Johnson, Graham - *Franz Schubert: The Complete Songs*
    TLS - i5848 - May 1 2015 - p3(3) [501+]
    NYRB - v62 - i6 - April 2 2015 - p58(2) [501+]
    Spec - v329 - i9771 - Dec 5 2015 - p45(2) [501+]
Johnson, Hal - *Fearsome Creatures of the Lumberwoods: 20 Chilling Tales from the Wilderness (Illus. by Mead, Tom)*
    c BL - v112 - i2 - Sept 15 2015 - p66(1) [51-500]
    c KR - May 15 2015 - pNA [51-500]
    c PW - v262 - i28 - July 13 2015 - p66(1) [51-500]
    c PW - v262 - i49 - Dec 2 2015 - p77(1) [51-500]
    c SLJ - v61 - i8 - August 2015 - p87(1) [51-500]
Johnson, Holly - *The Grammar of Good Friday: Macaronic Sermons of Late Medieval England*
    Specu - v90 - i1 - Jan 2015 - p265-267 [501+]

Johnson, Ian - *The Middle English Life of Christ: Academic Discourse, Translation, and Vernacular Theology*
    Med R - May 2015 - pNA [501+]
    RES - v66 - i273 - Feb 2015 - p166-168 [501+]
The Pseudo-Bonaventuran Lives of Christ: Exploring the Middle English Tradition
    HER - v130 - i544 - June 2015 - p712(3) [501+]
Johnson, J.J. - *Believarexic*
    y BL - v112 - i2 - Sept 15 2015 - p63(1) [51-500]
    y KR - August 1 2015 - pNA [51-500]
    y SLJ - v61 - i9 - Sept 2015 - p167(2) [51-500]
Johnson, Jaime Gardner - *The Ghost of Donley Farm (Illus. by Klein, Laurie Allen)*
    c CH Bwatch - April 2015 - pNA [51-500]
    c HB Guide - v26 - i1 - Spring 2015 - p34(1) [51-500]
Johnson, Jaleigh - *The Mark of the Dragonfly*
    y Teach Lib - v42 - i3 - Feb 2015 - p32(6) [501+]
The Secrets of Solace
    y KR - Jan 1 2016 - pNA [51-500]
Johnson, Jeff K - *Cash Flow Forever*
    KR - April 15 2015 - pNA [51-500]
Johnson, Jinny - *Clash of the Dinosaurs (Illus. by Croucher, Barry)*
    c Sch Lib - v63 - i1 - Spring 2015 - p47(1) [51-500]
Le hamster et la gerbille
    c Res Links - v20 - i3 - Feb 2015 - p45(2) [51-500]
L'ours brun
    c Res Links - v20 - i3 - Feb 2015 - p46(1) [51-500]
North American Mammals Series
    c HB Guide - v26 - i1 - Spring 2015 - p165(1) [51-500]
Johnson, JoAnn - *An Activity-Based Approach to Early Intervention, 4th ed.*
    RVBW - July 2015 - pNA [501+]
Johnson, Julia Claiborne - *Be Frank with Me*
    LJ - v140 - i20 - Dec 1 2015 - p93(2) [51-500]
Johnson, Julie Christine - *In Another Life*
    LJ - v140 - i20 - Dec 1 2015 - p93(1) [51-500]
Johnson, Junius - *Christ and Analogy: The Christocentric Metaphysics of Hans Urs von Balthasar*
    Theol St - v76 - i2 - June 2015 - p389(2) [501+]
Johnson, Kathryn Lee - *In Peace and Freedom: My Journey in Selma*
    HNet - March 2015 - pNA [501+]
Johnson, Kendall - *Narratives of Free Trade: The Commercial Cultures of Early US-China Relations*
    JAS - v74 - i3 - August 2015 - p737-738 [501+]
Johnson, Kim - *The Funniest One in the Room: The Lives and Legends of Del Close*
    BL - v111 - i19-20 - June 1 2015 - p30(2) [51-500]
Johnson, Kimberly - *Made Flesh: Sacrament and Poetics in Post-Reformation England*
    JR - v95 - i4 - Oct 2015 - p562(3) [501+]
    Ren Q - v68 - i2 - Summer 2015 - p761-763 [501+]
Uncommon Prayer
    HR - v68 - i2 - Summer 2015 - p327-335 [501+]
Johnson, Kristin Lee - *Unattached*
    KR - July 1 2015 - pNA [51-500]
Johnson, L.B. - *The Book of Barkley: Love and Life through the Eyes of a Labrador Retriever*
    KR - March 1 2015 - pNA [501+]
Johnson, Lorraine - *The Ladybird Story: Children's Books for Everyone*
    Sch Lib - v63 - i1 - Spring 2015 - p63(1) [51-500]
Johnson, Maria Morera - *My Badass Book of Saints: Courageous Women Who Showed Me How to Live*
    PW - v262 - i41 - Oct 12 2015 - p63(1) [51-500]
Johnson, Mariana Ruiz - *I Know a Bear*
    c HB Guide - v26 - i1 - Spring 2015 - p11(1) [51-500]
Johnson, Marilyn - *Lives in Ruins: Archaeologists and the Seductive Lure of Human Rubble*
    NYTBR - Jan 11 2015 - p12(L) [501+]
Lives in Ruins: Archaeologists and the Seductive Lure of Human Rubble (Read by Huber, Hillary). Audiobook Review
    PW - v262 - i8 - Feb 23 2015 - p71(1) [51-500]
Johnson, Martin P. - *Writing the Gettysburg Address*
    JSH - v81 - i2 - May 2015 - p471(3) [501+]
Johnson, Mat - *Loving Day*
    NYRB - v62 - i20 - Dec 17 2015 - p68(3) [501+]
    NYT - May 27 2015 - pC1(L) [501+]
    NYTBR - June 7 2015 - p1(L) [501+]

Johnson, Maureen - *The Shadow Cabinet*
    y VOYA - v37 - i6 - Feb 2015 - p79(1) [51-500]
The Shadow Cabinet (Read by Barber, Nicola). Audiobook Review
    y SLJ - v61 - i5 - May 2015 - p70(1) [51-500]
The Shadow Cabinet
    y HB Guide - v26 - i2 - Fall 2015 - p125(1) [51-500]
    y Sch Lib - v63 - i3 - Autumn 2015 - p183(1) [51-500]
Johnson, Michael K - *Hoo-Doo Cowboys and Bronze Buckaroos: Conceptions of the African American West*
    WHQ - v46 - i1 - Spring 2015 - p95-96 [501+]
Johnson, Missy - *Code of Honor*
    PW - v262 - i26 - June 29 2015 - p52(1) [51-500]
Johnson, Nancy - *Shenandoah*
    c KR - Jan 15 2015 - pNA [51-500]
Johnson, Nathan - *Kickboxing and MMA: Winning Ways*
    c BL - v111 - i15 - April 1 2015 - p61(1) [51-500]
Johnson, Nicholas - *Negroes and the Gun: The Black Tradition of Arms*
    JAH - v101 - i4 - March 2015 - p1235-1236 [501+]
Johnson, Nick - *The New York Pizza Project*
    NYT - Dec 27 2015 - p3(L) [501+]
Johnson, Patrick W.T. - *The Mission of Preaching: Equipping the Community for Faithful Witness*
    CC - v132 - i19 - Sept 16 2015 - p30(4) [501+]
Johnson, Paul - *Eisenhower: A Life*
    For Aff - v94 - i1 - Jan-Feb 2015 - pNA [501+]
Mozart: A Life
    Quad - v59 - i1-2 - Jan-Feb 2015 - p140(2) [501+]
Johnson, Peggy - *Fundamentals of Collection Development and Management, 3rd ed.*
    LRTS - v59 - i1 - Jan 2015 - p53(2) [501+]
Johnson, Peter - *The Life and Times of Benny Alvarez*
    c HB Guide - v26 - i1 - Spring 2015 - p82(1) [51-500]
Johnson, Plum - *They Left Us Everything: A Memoir*
    Nat Post - v17 - i107 - March 7 2015 - pWP4(1) [501+]
Johnson, R.W. - *Look Back in Laughter: Oxford's Postwar Golden Age*
    TLS - i5874 - Oct 30 2015 - p32(1) [501+]
Johnson, Rachel - *Fresh Hell*
    Spec - v328 - i9748 - June 27 2015 - p42(2) [501+]
Johnson, Rachel E. - *A Complete Identity: The Youthful Hero in the Work of G.A. Henty and George MacDonald*
    TLS - i5838 - Feb 20 2015 - p26(1) [501+]
Johnson, Rebecca L. - *Chernobyl's Wild Kingdom: Life in the Dead Zone*
    y CCB-B - v68 - i5 - Jan 2015 - p262(2) [51-500]
    y HB Guide - v26 - i1 - Spring 2015 - p155(1) [51-500]
    y Teach Lib - v42 - i3 - Feb 2015 - p28(4) [51-500]
Masters of Disguise
    c KR - Jan 1 2016 - pNA [51-500]
When Lunch Fights Back: Wickedly Clever Animal Defenses (Illus. by Johnson, Rebecca L.)
    c HB Guide - v26 - i1 - Spring 2015 - p155(1) [51-500]
Johnson, Richard William - *How Long Will South Africa Survive? The Looming Crisis*
    Spec - v328 - i9757 - August 29 2015 - p38(2) [501+]
Johnson, Robin - *Light & Sound Waves Close-Up Series*
    c CH Bwatch - Feb 2015 - pNA [51-500]
Pearl Harbor
    c Res Links - v20 - i3 - Feb 2015 - p38(2) [501+]
The Salem Witch Trials
    c Res Links - v20 - i3 - Feb 2015 - p38(2) [501+]
Word Wizard Series, 4 vols.
    c Res Links - v20 - i4 - April 2015 - p19(2) [501+]
The Word Wizard's Book of Adjectives
    c Res Links - v20 - i3 - Feb 2015 - p19(1) [501+]
The Word Wizard's Book of Adverbs
    c Res Links - v20 - i3 - Feb 2015 - p19(1) [501+]
The Word Wizard's Book of Homonyms
    c CH Bwatch - May 2015 - pNA [51-500]
    c SLJ - v61 - i4 - April 2015 - p106(3) [51-500]
The Word Wizard's Book of Nouns
    c Res Links - v20 - i3 - Feb 2015 - p19(1) [501+]
The Word Wizard's Book of Prefixes and Suffixes
    c CH Bwatch - May 2015 - pNA [51-500]
The Word Wizard's Book of Pronouns
    c CH Bwatch - May 2015 - pNA [51-500]
The Word Wizard's Book of Synonyms and Antonyms
    c CH Bwatch - May 2015 - pNA [51-500]
    c CH Bwatch - May 2015 - pNA [51-500]
The Word Wizard's Book of Verbs
    c Res Links - v20 - i3 - Feb 2015 - p19(1) [501+]

Johnson, Ronald Angelo - *Diplomacy in Black and White: John Adams, Toussaint Louverture, and Their Atlantic World Alliance*
    AHR - v120 - i4 - Oct 2015 - p1452-1453 [501+]
    JAH - v102 - i1 - June 2015 - p235-236 [501+]
    JSH - v81 - i2 - May 2015 - p448(3) [501+]

Johnson, Samantha - *How to Build Chicken Coops: Everything You Need To Know*
    LJ - v140 - i15 - Sept 15 2015 - p76(2) [51-500]

Johnson, Sandra - *The Ground Squirrels Take Glacier, Maybe... (Illus. by Johnson, Sandra)*
    c CH Bwatch - July 2015 - pNA [501+]

Johnson, Sarah E. - *The Fear of French Negroes: Transcolonial Collaboration in the Revolutionary Americas*
    Callaloo - v38 - i1 - Wntr 2015 - p231-234 [501+]

Staging Women and the Soul-Body Dynamic in Early Modern England
    Ren Q - v68 - i3 - Fall 2015 - p1138-1140 [501+]
    Sev Cent N - v73 - i1-2 - Spring-Summer 2015 - p26(4) [501+]
    Six Ct J - v46 - i3 - Fall 2015 - p697-699 [501+]

Johnson, Scott Fitzgerald - *The Oxford Handbook of Late Antiquity*
    Class R - v65 - i2 - Oct 2015 - p552-554 [501+]

Johnson-Shelton, Nils - *Endgame: The Calling*
    y HB Guide - v26 - i2 - Fall 2015 - p119(1) [501+]

Sky Key
    y BL - v112 - i3 - Oct 1 2015 - p74(1) [501+]

Johnson, Sherri Franks - *Monastic Women and Religious Orders in Late Medieval Bologna*
    CH - v84 - i4 - Dec 2015 - p873(1) [501+]
    HER - v130 - i545 - August 2015 - p963(3) [501+]
    Med R - August 2015 - pNA [501+]

Johnson, Stephen Burge - *Burnt Cork: Traditions and Legacies of Blackface Minstrelsy*
    Theat J - v67 - i2 - May 2015 - p370-371 [501+]

Johnson, Stephen T. - *Alphabet School (Illus. by Johnson, Stephen T.)*
    c CCB-B - v69 - i2 - Oct 2015 - p95(1) [51-500]
    c HB - v91 - i6 - Nov-Dec 2015 - p68(2) [51-500]
    c KR - June 1 2015 - pNA [51-500]
    c PW - v262 - i22 - June 1 2015 - p59(1) [51-500]
    c SLJ - v61 - i8 - August 2015 - p59(1) [51-500]

Johnson, Steven - *How We Got to Now: Six Innovations That Made the Modern World (Read by Newbern, George). Audiobook Review*
    BL - v111 - i16 - April 15 2015 - p61(1) [51-500]
    BL - v112 - i7 - Dec 1 2015 - p71(1) [501+]

Johnson, Suzanne - *Pirate's Alley*
    KR - Feb 15 2015 - pNA [51-500]
    PW - v262 - i7 - Feb 16 2015 - p164(1) [51-500]

Johnson, T. Geronimo - *Welcome to Braggsville*
    NYTBR - March 1 2015 - p11(L) [501+]

Johnson, Varian - *To Catch a Cheat*
    c KR - Oct 15 2015 - pNA [51-500]
    c SLJ - v61 - i12 - Dec 2015 - p102(2) [51-500]

Johnson, Walter - *River of Dark Dreams: Slavery and Empire in the Cotton Kingdom*
    HNet - Feb 2015 - pNA [501+]
    Historian - v77 - i2 - Summer 2015 - p336(2) [501+]

Johnson, Whitney - *Disrupt Yourself: Disruptive Innovation to Work*
    PW - v262 - i33 - August 17 2015 - p62(1) [51-500]

Johnston, Alexander - *South Africa: Inventing the Nation*
    IJAHS - v48 - i1 - Wntr 2015 - p168-170 [501+]

Johnston, Andrew James - *The Medieval Motion Picture: The Politics of Adaptation*
    Med R - March 2015 - pNA(NA) [501+]

Johnston, Andrew Scott - *Mercury and the Making of California: Mining, Landscape, and Race, 1840-1890*
    T&C - v56 - i3 - July 2015 - p758-759 [501+]

Johnston, Anthony - *Remember Me Like This*
    NYTBR - March 22 2015 - p28(1) [501+]

Johnston, Carolyn Ross - *Voices of Cherokee Women*
    JSH - v81 - i2 - May 2015 - p538(1) [501+]

Johnston, Charles - *The History of Arsaces, Prince of Betlis*
    TLS - i5861 - July 31 2015 - p27(1) [501+]

Johnston, Devin - *Far-Fetched*
    BL - v111 - i15 - April 1 2015 - p13(2) [51-500]
    LJ - v140 - i3 - Feb 15 2015 - p106(1) [51-500]
    NYTBR - July 19 2015 - p14(L) [501+]

Johnston, E.K. - *Exit, Pursued by a Bear*
    y KR - Dec 15 2015 - pNA [51-500]

Prairie Fire
    y BL - v111 - i11 - Feb 1 2015 - p49(1) [51-500]
    y CCB-B - v68 - i10 - June 2015 - p497(1) [51-500]
    y HB - v91 - i2 - March-April 2015 - p99(2) [51-500]
    y HB Guide - v26 - i2 - Fall 2015 - p125(1) [51-500]
    y KR - Jan 1 2015 - pNA [51-500]
    y SLJ - v61 - i3 - March 2015 - p157(1) [51-500]
    y VOYA - v38 - i3 - August 2015 - p78(2) [51-500]

The Story of Owen: Dragon Slayer of Trondheim
    c SLJ - v61 - i6 - June 2015 - p46(6) [501+]

A Thousand Nights
    y BL - v112 - i5 - Nov 1 2015 - p58(2) [51-500]
    y KR - August 15 2015 - pNA [51-500]
    y Sch Lib - v63 - i4 - Winter 2015 - p247(1) [51-500]
    y SLJ - v61 - i10 - Oct 2015 - p112(1) [51-500]
    y VOYA - v38 - i4 - Oct 2015 - p73(1) [51-500]

Johnston, Hugh J.M. - *The Voyage of the Komagata Maru: The Sikh Challenge to Canada's Colour Bar, 3d ed.*
    Can Hist R - v96 - i1 - March 2015 - p128(3) [501+]

Johnston, Joan - *Shameless*
    PW - v262 - i44 - Nov 2 2015 - p67(2) [51-500]

Sinful
    KR - Feb 15 2015 - pNA [51-500]
    PW - v262 - i6 - Feb 9 2015 - p50(1) [51-500]

Johnston, Judith - *Victorian Women and the Economies of Travel, Translation and Culture, 1830-1870*
    MLR - v110 - i3 - July 2015 - p848-849 [501+]

Johnston, Julia - *If Everyone Knew Every Plant and Tree*
    y KR - April 15 2015 - pNA [51-500]

Johnston, Linda M. - *Sports, Peacebuilding and Ethics*
    CS - v44 - i6 - Nov 2015 - p818-820 [501+]

Johnston, Linda O. - *Bite the Biscuit*
    BL - v111 - i17 - May 1 2015 - p20(1) [51-500]
    KR - March 15 2015 - pNA [51-500]

Knock on Wood
    BL - v112 - i2 - Sept 15 2015 - p34(1) [51-500]
    KR - August 1 2015 - pNA [51-500]

Johnston, Lucy - *Digital Handmade: Craftsmanship and the New Industrial Revolution*
    LJ - v140 - i13 - August 1 2015 - p91(2) [51-500]

Johnston, Mary Jo Wisneski - *The Lucky Seven Show (Illus. by Kinra, Richa)*
    c CH Bwatch - Feb 2015 - pNA [501+]

Johnston, Michael - *Romance and the Gentry in Late Medieval England*
    TLS - i5844 - April 3 2015 - p25(1) [501+]

Johnston, Paul - *Heads or Hearts*
    PW - v262 - i26 - June 29 2015 - p48(1) [51-500]

The White Sea
    RVBW - July 2015 - pNA [501+]

Johnston, Robb N. - *Lelani and the Plastic Kingdom*
    c KR - Jan 15 2015 - pNA [51-500]

Johnston, Tim - *Descent (Read by Bray, R.C., with Sands, Xe). Audiobook Review*
    LJ - v140 - i7 - April 15 2015 - p46(1) [51-500]
    PW - v262 - i12 - March 23 2015 - p69(2) [51-500]

Johnston, Timothy S. - *The Void*
    PW - v262 - i4 - Jan 26 2015 - p154(1) [51-500]

Johnston, Tony - *First Grade, Here I Come! (Illus. by Walker, David)*
    c KR - June 1 2015 - pNA [51-500]
    c SLJ - v61 - i8 - August 2015 - p59(1) [51-500]

My Abuelita (Illus. by Morales, Yuyi)
    BL - v111 - i9-10 - Jan 1 2015 - pS18(5) [501+]

Sequoia (Illus. by Minor, Wendell)
    c HB Guide - v26 - i1 - Spring 2015 - p34(1) [51-500]
    c SLJ - v61 - i2 - Feb 2015 - p70(1) [51-500]

Winter Is Coming (Illus. by LaMarche, Jim)
    c HB Guide - v26 - i1 - Spring 2015 - p34(1) [51-500]

Johnston, William M. - *Zur Kulturgeschichte Osterreichs und Ungarns 1890-1938: Auf der Suche nach Verborgenen Gemeinsamkeiten*
    HNet - July 2015 - pNA [501+]

Johnstone, Andrew - *Against Immediate Evil: American Internationalists and the Four Freedoms on the Eve of World War II*
    HNet - Feb 2015 - pNA [501+]

Johnstone, Ian - *The Bell Between Worlds: The Mirror Chronicles*
    y VOYA - v37 - i6 - Feb 2015 - p79(1) [51-500]

The Mirror Chronicles: The Bell Between Worlds
    y CCB-B - v68 - i10 - June 2015 - p497(2) [51-500]

Johnstone, J.A. - *Bloody Sunday*
    Roundup M - v22 - i6 - August 2015 - p31(1) [501+]

Johnstone, Jim - *Dog Ear*
    Can Lit - i224 - Spring 2015 - p115 [501+]

Johnstone, William W. - *Day of Independence*
    Roundup M - v22 - i6 - August 2015 - p31(1) [501+]

Luke Jensen Bounty Hunter: Bloody Sunday
    Roundup M - v22 - i4 - April 2015 - p33(1) [501+]

Winchester 1886
    Roundup M - v22 - i5 - June 2015 - p40(1) [501+]

Joiner, Sara K. - *After the Ashes*
    c BL - v112 - i4 - Oct 15 2015 - p58(1) [51-500]
    c KR - July 15 2015 - pNA [51-500]
    c PW - v262 - i32 - August 10 2015 - p61(1) [51-500]
    c SLJ - v61 - i9 - Sept 2015 - p140(2) [51-500]

Joiner, William H., Jr. - *The Legend of Jake Jackson: The Last of the Great Gunfighters and Comanche Warriors*
    Roundup M - v22 - i5 - June 2015 - p38(1) [501+]

Joinson, Suzanne - *The Photographer's Wife*
    KR - Nov 15 2015 - pNA [51-500]
    LJ - v140 - i20 - Dec 1 2015 - p93(2) [51-500]
    PW - v262 - i51 - Dec 14 2015 - p56(1) [51-500]

Jokulsson, Illugi - *Alex Morgan*
    c HB Guide - v26 - i2 - Fall 2015 - p196(1) [51-500]

World Soccer Legends Series
    c BL - v111 - i18 - May 15 2015 - p51(1) [51-500]

Jolles, Adam - *The Curatorial Avant-Garde: Surrealism and Exhibition Practise in France, 1925-1941*
    FS - v69 - i3 - July 2015 - p418-419 [501+]

Jolley, Dan - *Larp! To Geek or Not to Geek (Illus. by Gunter, Gray)*
    y SLJ - v61 - i12 - Dec 2015 - p130(1) [51-500]

Jollimore, Troy - *Syllabus of Errors: Poems*
    BL - v112 - i3 - Oct 1 2015 - p12(1) [51-500]
    PW - v262 - i42 - Oct 19 2015 - p55(1) [51-500]

Jolly, Alison - *Thank You, Madagascar: The Conservation Diaries of Alison Jolly*
    New Sci - v226 - i3016 - April 11 2015 - p44(1) [501+]

Jolly, Jane - *One Step at a Time (Illus. by Heinrich, Sally)*
    c Magpies - v30 - i1 - March 2015 - p30(1) [501+]

Joly, Herve - *Diriger une grande entreprise au XXe siecle: L'elite industrielle francaise*
    BHR - v89 - i2 - Summer 2015 - p396(3) [501+]

Jonas, Hans - *Essais philosophiques: Du credo ancien a l'homme technologique*
    Dialogue - v54 - i1 - March 2015 - p185-188 [501+]

Jonas, Marieluise - *Tokyo Void: Possibilities in Absence*
    HNet - June 2015 - pNA [501+]

Jonas, Michael - *NS-Diplomatie und Bundnispolitik 1935-1944: Wipert von Blucher, das Dritte Reich und Finnland*
    HER - v130 - i543 - April 2015 - p497(2) [501+]

Jonell, Lynne - *The Sign of the Cat (Illus. by Jonell, Lynne)*
    c BL - v111 - i18 - May 15 2015 - pNA [51-500]
    c HB Guide - v26 - i2 - Fall 2015 - p88(1) [51-500]
    c KR - March 15 2015 - pNA [51-500]
    c PW - v262 - i16 - April 20 2015 - p76(1) [51-500]
    c VOYA - v38 - i2 - June 2015 - p77(2) [51-500]
    c SLJ - v61 - i3 - March 2015 - p136(1) [51-500]

Wild Water Magic (Illus. by Dorman, Brandon)
    c HB Guide - v26 - i1 - Spring 2015 - p61(1) [51-500]

Jones, Adam James - *The Vendetta of Felipe Espinosa*
    Roundup M - v22 - i6 - August 2015 - p31(1) [501+]

Jones, Alan - *Nicolas Winding Refn: The Act of Seeing*
    Si & So - v25 - i12 - Dec 2015 - p107(1) [51-500]

Jones, Amanda - *Dog Years: Faithful Friends, Then and Now*
    PW - v262 - i31 - August 3 2015 - p47(1) [51-500]

Jones, Andrew Meirion - *Prehistoric Materialities: Becoming Material in Prehistoric Britain and Ireland*
    JRAI - v21 - i1 - March 2015 - p226(2) [501+]

Jones, Andy - *The Two of Us*
    PW - v262 - i44 - Nov 2 2015 - p67(1) [51-500]

Jones, Anna - *A Modern Way to Eat: 200+ Satisfying Vegetarian Recipes (That Will Make You Feel Amazing).*
    LJ - v140 - i3 - Feb 15 2015 - p122(4) [501+]
    NYTBR - May 31 2015 - p24(L) [501+]

Jones, Benjamin - *Eisenhower's Guerrillas: The Jedburghs, the Maquis, and the Liberation of France*
    PW - v262 - i52 - Dec 21 2015 - p144(1) [51-500]

Jones, Bill T. - *Story/Time: The Life of an Idea*
    HR - v67 - i4 - Wntr 2015 - p647-652 [501+]

Jones-Branch, Cherisse - *Crossing the Line: Women's Interracial Activism in South Carolina during and after World War II*
    AHR - v120 - i1 - Feb 2015 - p281-282 [501+]
    JAH - v101 - i4 - March 2015 - p1323-1324 [501+]

Jones, Brett - *Pride: The Story of the First Openly Gay Navy Seal*
    KR - Jan 1 2015 - pNA [501+]

Jones, Brian Madison - *Abolishing the Taboo: Dwight D. Eisenhower and American Nuclear Doctrine, 1945-1961*
    Pres St Q - v45 - i1 - March 2015 - p199(7) [501+]

Jones-Brown, Delores D. - *African Americans and Criminal Justice: An Encyclopedia*
    R&USQ - v54 - i3 - Spring 2015 - p57(2) [501+]

Jones, Bryn - *Sixties Radicalism and Social Movement Activism: Retreat or Resurgence?*
    CS - v44 - i1 - Jan 2015 - p71-73 [501+]

Jones, Bryony - *Where's Santa? (Illus. by Whelon, Chuck)*
    c SLJ - v61 - i10 - Oct 2015 - p64(1) [51-500]

Jones, C. Renee - *Science Unshackled: How Obscure, Abstract, Seemingly Useless Scientific Research Turned Out to Be the Basis for Modern Life*
    Bwatch - Feb 2015 - pNA [51-500]

Jones, Candide - *In the Tree Top: A New Lullaby (Illus. by Emery, Steve)*
    c PW - v262 - i39 - Sept 28 2015 - p89(1) [51-500]

Jones, Catherine A. - *Intimate Reconstructions: Children in Postemancipation Virginia*
    HNet - August 2015 - pNA [501+]

Jones, Catherine M. - *An Introduction to the Chansons de Geste: New Perspectives on Medieval Literature--Authors and Traditions*
    Med R - April 2015 - pNA [501+]
An Introduction to the Chansons de Geste
    Specu - v90 - i4 - Oct 2015 - p1124-1125 [501+]

Jones, Cerberus - *The Gateway 1: The Four Fingered Man*
    c Magpies - v30 - i2 - May 2015 - p35(1) [501+]
The Gateway 2: The Warriors of Brin-Hask
    c Magpies - v30 - i2 - May 2015 - p35(1) [501+]

Jones, Charles A. - *More Than Just War: Narratives of the Just War Tradition and Military Life*
    NWCR - v68 - i3 - Summer 2015 - p153(3) [501+]

Jones, Christianne C. - *The Santa Shimmy*
    c KR - Sept 1 2015 - pNA [51-500]
The Santa Shimmy (Illus. by Randall, Emma)
    c PW - v262 - i37 - Sept 14 2015 - p72(2) [501+]
    c SLJ - v61 - i10 - Oct 2015 - p64(1) [51-500]

Jones, Christopher F. - *Routes of Power: Energy and Modern America*
    AHR - v120 - i2 - April 2015 - p636-637 [501+]
    Am Q - v67 - i2 - June 2015 - p529-540 [501+]
    JAH - v101 - i4 - March 2015 - p1283-1284 [501+]
    JIH - v45 - i4 - Spring 2015 - p594-595 [501+]
    T&C - v56 - i2 - April 2015 - p567-568 [501+]

Jones, Christopher P. - *Between Pagan and Christian*
    AHR - v120 - i2 - April 2015 - p693(1) [501+]
    HNet - Feb 2015 - pNA [501+]

Jones, Colin - *The Smile Revolution in Eighteenth-Century Paris*
    Lon R Bks - v37 - i12 - June 18 2015 - p31(2) [501+]
    TLS - i5834 - Jan 23 2015 - p28(2) [501+]

Jones, Cynan - *The Dig*
    KR - Feb 1 2015 - pNA [51-500]
    NYTBR - May 17 2015 - p11(L) [501+]

Jones, Dan - *Magna Carta: The Birth of Liberty*
    LJ - v140 - i16 - Oct 1 2015 - p94(1) [51-500]
    NYTBR - Nov 22 2015 - p24(L) [501+]
Magna Carta: The Making and Legacy of the Great Charter
    KR - Sept 1 2015 - pNA [51-500]
    Lon R Bks - v37 - i8 - April 23 2015 - p15(3) [501+]
The War of the Roses: The Fall of the Plantagenets and the Rise of the Tudors
    NYTBR - Jan 25 2015 - p26(L) [501+]
The Wars of the Roses: The Fall of the Plantagenets and the Rise of the Tudors (Read by Curless, John).
Audiobook Review
    LJ - v140 - i2 - Feb 1 2015 - p47(1) [51-500]

Jones, Darryl - *Horror Stories: Classic Tales from Hoffmann to Hodgson*
    Bks & Cult - v21 - i3 - May-June 2015 - p34(2) [501+]

Jones, Donald W. - *Economic Theory and the Ancient Mediterranean*
    HNet - Feb 2015 - pNA [501+]

Jones, Douglas A., Jr. - *The Captive Stage: Performance and the Proslavery Imagination of the Antebellum North*
    AHR - v120 - i4 - Oct 2015 - p1486-1487 [501+]

Jones, Dylan - *Mr. Mojo: A Biography of Jim Morrison*
    KR - Sept 1 2015 - pNA [51-500]
    LJ - v140 - i13 - August 1 2015 - p99(1) [501+]

Jones, Edward - *Young Milton: The Emerging Author, 1620-1642*
    MLR - v110 - i3 - July 2015 - p827-828 [501+]

Jones, Ena - *Clayton Stone, at Your Service*
    c BL - v111 - i21 - July 1 2015 - p68(1) [51-500]
    c KR - June 15 2015 - pNA [51-500]
    c SLJ - v61 - i7 - July 2015 - p79(1) [51-500]

Jones, Evan C. - *Gateway to the Confederacy: New Perspectives on the Chickamauga and Chattanooga Campaigns, 1862-1863*
    J Mil H - v79 - i3 - July 2015 - p838-840 [501+]
    JSH - v81 - i3 - August 2015 - p738(3) [501+]

Jones, Frankie - *Fall Is Here! (Illus. by Galloway, Fhiona)*
    c KR - Jan 1 2016 - pNA [51-500]
    c PW - v262 - i31 - August 3 2015 - p56(1) [51-500]
Hello Kitty Summertime Fun
    c KR - July 1 2015 - pNA [51-500]
Things That Go
    c KR - Jan 1 2016 - pNA [51-500]

Jones, Gareth P. - *Are You the Pirate Captain? (Illus. by Parsons, Garry)*
    c KR - Dec 1 2015 - pNA [51-500]
The Dinosaurs Are Having a Party! (Illus. by Parsons, Garry)
    c HB Guide - v26 - i2 - Fall 2015 - p38(1) [51-500]
The Leaky Battery Sets Sail
    c Sch Lib - v63 - i2 - Summer 2015 - p106(1) [51-500]
No True Echo
    y BL - v112 - i2 - Sept 15 2015 - p75(1) [51-500]
    y KR - August 1 2015 - pNA [51-500]
    y PW - v262 - i29 - July 20 2015 - p194(1) [51-500]
    y SLJ - v61 - i9 - Sept 2015 - p158(2) [51-500]
    y VOYA - v38 - i3 - August 2015 - p78(2) [51-500]

Jones, Gavin - *Failure and the American Writer: A Literary History*
    RES - v66 - i274 - April 2015 - p394-396 [501+]

Jones, Geoffrey - *Entrepreneurship and Multinationals: Global Business and the Making of the Modern World*
    BHR - v89 - i3 - Autumn 2015 - p578(3) [501+]

Jones, Grace - *I'll Never Write My Memoirs*
    Art N - v114 - i9 - Oct 2015 - p18(2) [501+]
    BL - v112 - i2 - Sept 15 2015 - p15(1) [51-500]
    KR - August 15 2015 - pNA [51-500]
    LJ - v140 - i15 - Sept 15 2015 - p78(1) [51-500]
    Mac - v128 - i41 - Oct 19 2015 - p63(1) [501+]
    NYTBR - Oct 25 2015 - p21(L) [501+]

Jones, Halbert - *The War Has Brought Peace to Mexico: World War II and the Consolidation of the Post-Revolutionary State*
    AHR - v120 - i2 - April 2015 - p680-681 [501+]
    Ams - v72 - i3 - July 2015 - p513(3) [501+]
    HAHR - v95 - i2 - May 2015 - p370-371 [501+]

Jones, Heather - *Quilt Local: Finding Inspiration in the Everyday*
    LJ - v140 - i17 - Oct 15 2015 - p90(1) [51-500]

Jones, Heather Rose - *The Mystic Marriage*
    PW - v262 - i9 - March 2 2015 - p70(1) [51-500]

Jones, Ira - *An Air Fighter's Scrapbook*
    APH - v62 - i2 - Summer 2015 - p50(2) [51-500]

Jones, J.C. - *Run, Pip, Run*
    c Magpies - v30 - i2 - May 2015 - p36(1) [501+]

Jones, J.R. - *The Lives of Robert Ryan*
    LJ - v140 - i10 - June 1 2015 - p105(1) [51-500]
    Si & So - v25 - i7 - July 2015 - p104(2) [501+]

Jones, J. Sydney - *The Third Place: A Viennese Mystery*
    PW - v262 - i32 - August 10 2015 - p40(1) [51-500]

Jones, Jacqueline - *A Dreadful Deceit: The Myth of Race from the Colonial Era to Obama's America*
    JSH - v81 - i2 - May 2015 - p426(2) [501+]

Jones, Jen - *Dog Days for Delaney*
    c HB Guide - v26 - i1 - Spring 2015 - p82(1) [51-500]
Maren Loves Luke Lewis
    c HB Guide - v26 - i1 - Spring 2015 - p82(1) [51-500]

Jones, Jill - *The Beautiful Anxiety*
    Meanjin - v74 - i1 - Autumn 2015 - p68(10) [501+]

Jones, John Bush - *Reinventing Dixie: Tin Pan Alley's Songs and the Creation of the Mythic South*
    TLS - i5870 - Oct 2 2015 - p27(1) [501+]

Jones, Karen - *A Cultural History of Firearms in the Age of Empire*
    T&C - v56 - i3 - July 2015 - p754-755 [501+]

Jones, Kari - *Shimmy*
    y Res Links - v20 - i5 - June 2015 - p27(1) [51-500]
    y VOYA - v38 - i4 - Oct 2015 - p54(2) [51-500]
    y KR - July 1 2015 - pNA [51-500]

Jones, Kaylie - *The Anger Meridian*
    BL - v111 - i17 - May 1 2015 - p18(1) [51-500]
    KR - May 1 2015 - pNA [51-500]
    LJ - v140 - i14 - Sept 1 2015 - p93(2) [51-500]
    PW - v262 - i18 - May 4 2015 - p92(1) [51-500]

Jones, Kelly - *Unusual Chickens for the Exceptional Poultry Farmer (Illus. by Kath, Katie)*
    c CCB-B - v69 - i1 - Sept 2015 - p29(2) [51-500]
    y HB Guide - v26 - i2 - Fall 2015 - p88(1) [51-500]

Jones, Kelly (b. 1948-) - *Evel Knievel Jumps the Snake River Canyon*
    PW - v262 - i7 - Feb 16 2015 - p156(1) [51-500]

Jones, Kelly (b. 1976-) - *Unusual Chickens for the Exceptional Poultry Farmer (Illus. by Kath, Katie)*
    c BL - v111 - i15 - April 1 2015 - p81(1) [51-500]
    c HB - v91 - i3 - May-June 2015 - p112(1) [501+]
    c SLJ - v61 - i2 - Feb 2015 - p87(2) [51-500]

Jones, Kevin B. - *A Smarter, Greener Grid: Forging Environmental Progress through Smart Energy Policies and Technologies*
    RVBW - June 2015 - pNA [501+]

Jones, Larry Eugen - *The German Right in the Weimar Republic: Studies in the History of German Conservatism, Nationalism, and Antisemitism*
    HNet - May 2015 - pNA [501+]

Jones, Lloyd - *The Princess and the Fog: A Story for Children with Depression (Illus. by Jones, Lloyd)*
    c SLJ - v61 - i11 - Nov 2015 - p132(1) [51-500]

Jones, Lynn - *Byzantine Images and Their Afterlives: Essays in Honor of Annemarie Weyl Carr*
    Med R - August 2015 - pNA [501+]
    Specu - v90 - i4 - Oct 2015 - p1126-1127 [501+]

Jones, Marcia Thornton - *Woodford Brave (Illus. by Whipple, Kevin)*
    c KR - July 15 2015 - pNA [51-500]
    c PW - v262 - i32 - August 10 2015 - p61(1) [51-500]

Jones, Marlene - *The Complete Guide to Creating Oils, Soaps, Creams, and Herbal Gels for Your Mind and Body: 101 Natural Body Care Recipes*
    Bwatch - Sept 2015 - pNA [51-500]

Jones, Martha Thorton - *Woodford Brave (Illus. by Whipple, Kevin)*
    c SLJ - v61 - i9 - Sept 2015 - p140(2) [51-500]

Jones, Melissa - *Sheldon: The Antioxidant Super Hero of Jaloonsville*
    c KR - Dec 1 2015 - pNA [501+]

Jones, Merry - *In the Woods*
    BL - v111 - i11 - Feb 1 2015 - p27(1) [51-500]

Jones, Michael - *After Hitler: The Last Days of the Second World War in Europe*
    Spec - v327 - i9729 - Feb 14 2015 - p42(2) [501+]
After Hitler: The Last Days of World War II in Europe
    KR - August 15 2015 - pNA [501+]
Bosworth 1485: The Battle That Transformed England
    KR - June 1 2015 - pNA [51-500]
    LJ - v140 - i11 - June 15 2015 - p98(2) [51-500]
    PW - v262 - i27 - July 6 2015 - p57(1) [51-500]

Jones, Michele H. - *The Beginning Translator's Workbook*
    FS - v69 - i3 - July 2015 - p428(1) [501+]

Jones, Mike - *Birthright*
    BL - v111 - i21 - July 1 2015 - p42(1) [51-500]

Jones, Noah Z. - *Little Red Quacking Hood*
    c HB Guide - v26 - i1 - Spring 2015 - p61(1) [51-500]

Jones, Owen - *The Establishment: And How They Get Away with It*
    KR - April 1 2015 - pNA [501+]
    LJ - v140 - i11 - June 15 2015 - p102(1) [51-500]
    TLS - i5831 - Jan 2 2015 - p3(2) [501+]

Jones, Parneshia - *Vessel*
    PW - v262 - i11 - March 16 2015 - p63(1) [51-500]
    BL - v111 - i14 - March 15 2015 - p39(1) [51-500]

Jones, Patrick - *Always Faithful*
    y SLJ - v61 - i9 - Sept 2015 - p151(4) [501+]
Barrier
    c HB Guide - v26 - i1 - Spring 2015 - p110(1) [51-500]
Collateral Damage
    y KR - Sept 15 2015 - pNA [51-500]
Combat Zone
    y SLJ - v61 - i9 - Sept 2015 - p151(4) [501+]
Doing Right
    y HB Guide - v26 - i2 - Fall 2015 - p125(1) [51-500]
Guarding Secrets
    y CCB-B - v68 - i10 - June 2015 - p498(1) [51-500]
Raising Heaven
    y HB Guide - v26 - i2 - Fall 2015 - p125(1) [51-500]
Taking Sides
    y CCB-B - v68 - i10 - June 2015 - p498(1) [51-500]
Wing Commander: Freedom Flight
    y BL - v112 - i5 - Nov 1 2015 - p54(1) [51-500]
    y KR - Sept 15 2015 - pNA [51-500]

Jones, Peter - *Open Skies: Transparency, Confidence-Building, and the End of the Cold War*
    APJ - v29 - i5 - Sept-Oct 2015 - p103(2) [501+]

Jones, Polly - *Myth, Memory, Trauma: Rethinking the Stalinist Past in the Soviet Union, 1953-70*
    E-A St - v67 - i3 - May 2015 - p494(3) [501+]
    Historian - v77 - i3 - Fall 2015 - p613(2) [501+]
    JMH - v87 - i2 - June 2015 - p506(2) [501+]

Jones, Prof. - *The Basics of Winning Lotto/Lottery*
    RVBW - Oct 2015 - pNA [51-500]

Jones, Rhys - *Changing Behaviors: On the Rise of the Psychological State*
    TimHES - i2212 - July 16 2015 - p47-1 [501+]

Jones, Richard - *House Guests, House Pests: A Natural History of Animals in the Home*
    BL - v111 - i18 - May 15 2015 - p8(1) [51-500]
    Bwatch - August 2015 - pNA [51-500]
    Nature - v518 - i7540 - Feb 26 2015 - p481(1) [51-500]
    NH - v123 - i3 - April 2015 - p46(2) [51-500]

Jones, Rob - *Bernard*
    c Sch Lib - v63 - i2 - Summer 2015 - p94(1) [51-500]

Jones, Rob Lloyd - *Wild Boy and the Black Terror (Read by Clamp, James). Audiobook Review*
    y SLJ - v61 - i8 - August 2015 - p50(2) [51-500]
Wild Boy and the Black Terror
    y BL - v111 - i17 - May 1 2015 - p56(1) [51-500]
    y HB Guide - v26 - i2 - Fall 2015 - p88(1) [51-500]
    y KR - Feb 15 2015 - pNA [51-500]
    y SLJ - v61 - i2 - Feb 2015 - p88(1) [51-500]
    y VOYA - v38 - i1 - April 2015 - p62(2) [51-500]

Jones, Robert E. - *Bread upon the Waters: The St. Petersburg Grain Trade and the Russian Economy, 1703-1811*
    Historian - v77 - i1 - Spring 2015 - p171(2) [501+]
    JEH - v75 - i1 - March 2015 - p281-282 [501+]

Jones, Saeed - *Prelude to Bruise*
    PSQ - v89 - i3 - Fall 2015 - p169(4) [501+]

Jones, Sam - *Yolo*
    c HB Guide - v26 - i1 - Spring 2015 - p111(1) [51-500]

Jones, Sara (b. 1980-) - *Complicity, Censorship and Criticism: Negotiating Space in the GDR Literary Sphere*
    GSR - v38 - i2 - May 2015 - p451-4 [501+]

Jones, Sarah - *Black and White Nighty-Night*
    c KR - July 1 2015 - pNA [51-500]
Lloyd Llama (Illus. by Jones, Sarah)
    c PW - v262 - i16 - April 20 2015 - p75(1) [51-500]
    c SLJ - v61 - i5 - May 2015 - p85(2) [51-500]

Jones, Sarah Rees - *Christians and Jews in Angevin England: The York Massacre of 1190, Narratives and Contexts*
    CHR - v101 - i3 - Summer 2015 - p623(2) [501+]
    J Ch St - v57 - i3 - Summer 2015 - p569-570 [501+]

Jones, Shannon - *KeeKee's Big Adventures in Athens, Greece (Illus. by Uhelski, Casey)*
    c CH Bwatch - Feb 2015 - pNA [51-500]

Jones, Shirley A. - *First Aid, Survival, and CPR: Home and Field Pocket Guide*
    KR - Sept 15 2015 - pNA [501+]

Jones, Simon - *The Test: My Life, and the Inside Story of the Greatest Ashes Series*
    TLS - i5859 - July 17 2015 - p30(1) [501+]

Jones, Stan - *Tundra Kill*
    KR - Nov 15 2015 - pNA [501+]
    PW - v262 - i52 - Dec 21 2015 - p134(1) [51-500]

Jones, Stanleigh H. - *The Bunraku Puppet Theatre of Japan: Honor, Vengeance, and Love in Four Plays of the 18th and 19th Centuries*
    JAS - v74 - i3 - August 2015 - p752-753 [501+]

Jones, Stephanie - *Upstyle Your Furniture: Techniques and Creative Inspiration to Style Your Home*
    LJ - v140 - i8 - May 1 2015 - p73(1) [51-500]
    PW - v262 - i16 - April 20 2015 - p73(1) [51-500]

Jones, Stephen Graham - *The Faster Redder Road: The Best UnAmerican Stories of Stephen Graham Jones*
    Roundup M - v23 - i1 - Oct 2015 - p30(1) [501+]

Jones, Stephen Lloyd - *The String Diaries*
    BL - v111 - i18 - May 15 2015 - p34(1) [501+]
Written in the Blood
    BL - v111 - i15 - April 1 2015 - p34(1) [501+]
    KR - March 1 2015 - pNA [51-500]
    PW - v262 - i11 - March 16 2015 - p65(1) [51-500]

Jones, Susan - *Literature, Modernism, and Dance*
    Dance RJ - v47 - i1 - April 2015 - p103-106 [501+]

Jones, Tod - *Culture, Power, and Authoritarianism in the Indonesian State: Cultural Policy across the Twentieth-Century to the Reform Era*
    Pac A - v88 - i2 - June 2015 - p364 [501+]

Jones, Tom - *Over the Top and Back*
    KR - Nov 1 2015 - pNA [51-500]

Jones, Ursula - *The Princess Who Had No Kingdom (Illus. by Gibb, Sarah)*
    c HB Guide - v26 - i1 - Spring 2015 - p34(1) [51-500]

Jones, Val - *Who Wants Broccoli? (Illus. by Jones, Val)*
    c KR - March 15 2015 - pNA [51-500]
    c SLJ - v61 - i6 - June 2015 - p86(1) [51-500]

Jones, Wendy - *The World is a Wedding*
    BL - v111 - i16 - April 15 2015 - p38(1) [51-500]
    KR - March 1 2015 - pNA [51-500]
    LJ - v140 - i6 - April 1 2015 - p82(1) [51-500]

Jones, William P. - *The March on Washington: Jobs, Freedom, and the Forgotten History of Civil Rights*
    ERS - v38 - i3 - March 2015 - p536(3) [501+]
    JAH - v102 - i2 - Sept 2015 - p614-615 [501+]

Jong, Erica - *Fear of Dying*
    Atl - v316 - i2 - Sept 2015 - p40(2) [501+]
    BL - v111 - i21 - July 1 2015 - p30(1) [51-500]
    KR - July 1 2015 - pNA [501+]
    NYT - Sept 8 2015 - pC1(L) [501+]
    NYTBR - Sept 13 2015 - p12(L) [501+]
    PW - v262 - i19 - May 11 2015 - p28(1) [51-500]
    Spec - v329 - i9770 - Nov 28 2015 - p44(1) [501+]
Fear of Fifty
    Atl - v316 - i2 - Sept 2015 - p40(2) [501+]
Fear of Flying
    Atl - v316 - i2 - Sept 2015 - p40(2) [501+]

Jons, Hal - *Assassin Trail*
    RVBW - May 2015 - pNA [51-500]

Jonsberg, Barry - *The Categorical Universe of Candice Phee*
    c HB Guide - v26 - i1 - Spring 2015 - p82(1) [51-500]

Jonsson, Fredrik Albritton - *Enlightenment's Frontier: The Scottish Highlands and the Origins of Environmentalism*
    Isis - v106 - i2 - June 2015 - p452(2) [501+]
    JMH - v87 - i1 - March 2015 - p175(3) [501+]

Jonsson, Mar - *Arnas Magnaeus Philologus, 1663-1730*
    Med R - June 2015 - pNA [501+]

Jonsson, Maria - *Astrid the Fly (Illus. by Jonsson, Maria)*
    c HB Guide - v26 - i2 - Fall 2015 - p38(1) [51-500]
    c KR - Feb 1 2015 - pNA [51-500]
    c PW - v262 - i9 - March 2 2015 - p82(1) [51-500]
    c SLJ - v61 - i3 - March 2015 - p117(2) [51-500]

Joo, Rachael Miyung - *Transnational Sport: Gender, Media, and Global Korea*
    Signs - v40 - i3 - Spring 2015 - p783(4) [501+]

Joosse, Barbara - *Evermore Dragon (Illus. by Cecil, Randy)*
    c KR - May 15 2015 - pNA [51-500]
    c SLJ - v61 - i8 - August 2015 - p71(1) [51-500]

Joppke, Christian - *Legal Integration of Islam: A Transatlantic Comparison*
    CS - v44 - i4 - July 2015 - p524-525 [501+]

Jordan, Brian Matthew - *Marching Home: Union Veterans and Their Unending Civil War*
    AHR - v120 - i4 - Oct 2015 - p1494(1) [501+]
    For Aff - v94 - i3 - May-June 2015 - pNA [501+]
    J Mil H - v79 - i3 - July 2015 - p848-849 [501+]

Jordan, Bruce F. - *En Recuerdo de: The Dying Art of Mexican Cemeteries in the Southwest*
    y VOYA - v37 - i6 - Feb 2015 - p87(1) [51-500]

Jordan, Carol E. - *Violence Against Women in Kentucky: A History of U.S. and State Legislative Reform*
    JSH - v81 - i3 - August 2015 - p783(2) [501+]

Jordan, Cat - *The Leaving Season*
    y KR - Dec 15 2015 - pNA [51-500]
    y PW - v262 - i52 - Dec 21 2015 - p155(1) [51-500]
    y SLJ - v61 - i12 - Dec 2015 - p112(1) [51-500]

Jordan, David P. - *Paris: Haussmann and After*
    J Urban H - v41 - i3 - May 2015 - p541-549 [501+]

Jordan, Don - *The King's Bed: Sex, Power and the Court of Charles II*
    KR - Dec 1 2015 - pNA [501+]
    Spec - v327 - i9727 - Jan 31 2015 - p37(2) [501+]

Jordan, Jennifer A. - *Edible Memory: The Lure of Heirloom Tomatoes and Other Forgotten Foods*
    NY - v91 - i12 - May 11 2015 - p77 [51-500]
    Spec - v328 - i9744 - May 30 2015 - p36(1) [501+]
    TLS - i5854 - June 12 2015 - p30(1) [501+]

Jordan, Jonathan W. - *American Warlords: How Roosevelt's High Command Led America to Victory in World War II*
    KR - April 1 2015 - pNA [501+]
    LJ - v140 - i8 - May 1 2015 - p88(3) [501+]
Brothers, Rivals, Victors: Eisenhower, Patton, Bradley and the Partnership That Drove the Allied Conquest in Europe
    Pres St Q - v45 - i1 - March 2015 - p199(7) [501+]

Jordan, Larry - *The Dirty Dozen: 12 Nasty Fighting Techniques for Any Self-Defense Situation*
    RVBW - May 2015 - pNA [51-500]

Jordan, Nancy C. - *Number Sense Interventions*
    TC Math - v21 - i7 - March 2015 - p443(1) [501+]

Jordan, Nicole - *The Art of Taming a Rake*
    PW - v262 - i48 - Nov 30 2015 - p45(1) [51-500]

Jordan, Peter - *Technology as Human Social Tradition: Cultural Transmission among Hunter-Gatherers*
    Am Ant - v80 - i4 - Oct 2015 - p788(1) [501+]
The Venetian Origins of the Commedia dell'Arte
    Ren Q - v68 - i1 - Spring 2015 - p374-375 [501+]

Jordan, Sophie - *Reign of Shadows*
    y KR - Dec 15 2015 - pNA [51-500]
    y SLJ - v61 - i12 - Dec 2015 - p113(2) [51-500]
Uninvited
    c HB Guide - v26 - i1 - Spring 2015 - p111(1) [51-500]
Unleashed
    y HB Guide - v26 - i2 - Fall 2015 - p125(1) [51-500]

Jordan, Ulla - *Lost Ground*
    KR - Nov 15 2015 - pNA [501+]

Jordan, William Chester - *From England to France: Felony and Exile in the High Middle Ages*
    HT - v65 - i6 - June 2015 - p58(2) [501+]
    Specu - v90 - i4 - Oct 2015 - p1127-1129 [501+]
Men at the Center: Redemptive Governance under Louis IX
    Specu - v90 - i4 - Oct 2015 - p1129-1131 [501+]

Jorge, Aguirre - *Dragons Beware! (Illus. by Rosado, Rafael)*
    c KR - March 1 2015 - pNA [51-500]

Jorgensen, Jay - *Creating the Illusion: A Fashionable History of Hollywood Costume Designers*
    LJ - v140 - i20 - Dec 1 2015 - p104(1) [501+]

Jorgensen, John - *A Handbook of Korean Zen Practice: A Mirror on the Son School of Buddhism (Son'ga kwigam)*
    HNet - Sept 2015 - pNA(NA) [501+]

Jorgensen, Katrina - *Sports Illustrated Kids: Football Cookbooks*
    c HB Guide - v26 - i2 - Fall 2015 - p188(2) [51-500]

Jorgensen, Timothy J. - *Strange Glow: The Story of Radiation*
    KR - Jan 1 2016 - pNA [501+]

Jorgenson, Kara - *The Earl of Brass*
    PW - v262 - i3 - Jan 19 2015 - p66(1) [51-500]

Joseph, Elizabeth R. - *Twin Reflections*
    SPBW - Nov 2015 - pNA [51-500]

Joseph, Eve - *In the Slender Margin*
    KR - Nov 1 2015 - pNA [501+]

Joseph, Frank - *The Lost Colonies of Ancient America: A Comprehensive Guide to the Pre-Columbian Visitors Who Really Discovered America*
    Am Ant - v80 - i3 - July 2015 - p624(2) [501+]

Joseph, Gilbert M. - *Mexico's Once and Future Revolution: Social Upheaval and the Challenge of Rule since the Late Nineteenth Century*
    Historian - v77 - i2 - Summer 2015 - p337(3) [501+]

Joseph, May - *Fluid New York: Cosmopolitan Urbanism and the Green Imagination*
    CS - v44 - i4 - July 2015 - p526-528 [501+]

Joseph, Miranda - *Debt to Society: Accounting for Life under Capitalism*
    Am St - v54 - i2 - Summer 2015 - p112-114 [501+]

Joseph, Peniel E. - *Stokely: A Life*
    AHR - v120 - i2 - April 2015 - p673-674 [501+]
    JSH - v81 - i2 - May 2015 - p521(2) [501+]
    RAH - v43 - i3 - Sept 2015 - p564-570 [501+]
    Am St - v54 - i2 - Summer 2015 - p133-134 [501+]

Joseph, Robert - *Long Ago and Far Away*
    y KR - May 1 2015 - pNA [501+]

Joseph, Stephen - *What Doesn't Kill Us*
    Amerasia J - v41 - i2 - Spring 2015 - p155-158 [501+]

Joseph, Suzanne E. - *Fertile Bonds: Bedouin Class, Kinship, and Gender in the Bekaa Valley*
    JRAI - v21 - i1 - March 2015 - p221(2) [501+]

Josephson, Jason - *The Invention of Religion in Japan*
    JR - Jan 2015 - p146(2) [501+]

Josephson, Paul - *An Environmental History of Russia*
HNet - July 2015 - pNA [501+]
Slav R - v74 - i1 - Spring 2015 - p199-200 [501+]

Josephson, Paul R. - *The Conquest of the Russian Arctic*
AHR - v120 - i2 - April 2015 - p744-745 [501+]
Isis - v106 - i2 - June 2015 - p497(2) [501+]
JIH - v46 - i2 - Autumn 2015 - p289-291 [501+]
Slav R - v74 - i3 - Fall 2015 - p666-667 [501+]
T&C - v56 - i3 - July 2015 - p761-763 [501+]

Josephson, Sanford - *Jeru's Journey*
Dbt - v82 - i11 - Nov 2015 - p64(1) [501+]

Josephy, Alvin M. - *The Longest Trail: Writings on American Indian History, Culture, and Politics*
LJ - v140 - i15 - Sept 15 2015 - p89(1) [51-500]

Joshi, Khyati Y. - *Asian Americans in Dixie: Race and Migration in the South*
JSH - v81 - i2 - May 2015 - p532(3) [501+]

Joshi, Sunand T. - *H.P. Lovecraft's Collected Fiction: A Variorum Edition, 3 vols.*
TLS - i5835 - Jan 30 2015 - p12(2) [501+]
Lovecraft and a World in Transition: Collected Essays on H.P. Lovecraft
TLS - i5835 - Jan 30 2015 - p12(2) [501+]

Joskowicz, Ari - *The Modernity of Others: Jewish Anti-Catholicism in Germany and France*
CHR - v101 - i4 - Autumn 2015 - p946(2) [501+]
GSR - v38 - i3 - Oct 2015 - p671-673 [501+]
Secularism in Question: Jews and Judaism in Modern Times
JHI - v76 - i4 - Oct 2015 - p667(1) [501+]

Joslin, Mary - *A Treasury of Wisdom*
c BL - v112 - i6 - Nov 15 2015 - p44(2) [51-500]

Jospe, Raphael - *Encounters in Modern Jewish Thought: The Works of Eva Jospe, vol. 1: Martin Buber*
HNet - Feb 2015 - pNA [501+]

Jossa, Stefano - *Un paese senza eroi: L'Italia da Jacopo Ortis a Montalbano*
MLR - v110 - i2 - April 2015 - p565-567 [501+]

Josselsohn, Barbara Solomon - *The Last Dreamer*
BL - v112 - i7 - Dec 1 2015 - p22(1) [51-500]

Jost, Eugen - *Beautiful Geometry*
Math T - v108 - i8 - April 2015 - p638(1) [501+]

Jost, Scott - *Shenandoah Valley Apples*
JSH - v81 - i2 - May 2015 - p544(2) [501+]

Jouanna, Arlette - *Le Pouvoir Absolu: Naissance de l'Imaginaire Politique de la Royauté*
Six Ct J - v46 - i1 - Spring 2015 - p190-192 [501+]

Joubert, Claire - *Le Postcolonial compare: anglophonie, francophonie*
MLR - v110 - i3 - July 2015 - p792-793 [501+]

Joubert, Irma - *The Girl from the Train*
PW - v262 - i27 - July 6 2015 - p54(1) [51-500]

Joubin, Rebecca - *The Politics of Love: Sexuality, Gender, and Marriage in Syrian Television Drama*
IJMES - v47 - i3 - August 2015 - p610-611 [501+]

The Journal of Vincent du Maurier
PW - v262 - i17 - April 27 2015 - p41(2) [501+]

Journeys into the Past: History as a Tourist Attraction in the 19th and 20th Centuries
HNet - March 2015 - pNA [501+]

Jovanovic, Katarina - *The Blue Vase (Illus. by Bisaillon, Josee)*
c KR - Nov 1 2015 - pNA [51-500]

Joy, Breda - *Hidden Kerry: The Keys to the Kingdom*
RVBW - April 2015 - pNA [51-500]

Joy, David - *Where All Light Tends to Go*
BL - v111 - i12 - Feb 15 2015 - p39(1) [51-500]
KR - Jan 1 2015 - pNA [51-500]
LJ - v140 - i3 - Feb 15 2015 - p88(2) [51-500]
NYTBR - March 22 2015 - p29(L) [501+]
PW - v262 - i1 - Jan 5 2015 - p52(1) [51-500]

Joy, LaManda - *Start a Community Food Garden: The Essential Handbook*
LJ - v140 - i2 - Feb 1 2015 - p101(1) [51-500]

Joy, Morny - *Women and the Gift: Beyond the Given and the All-Giving*
JGS - v24 - i3 - June 2015 - p373-376 [501+]

Joy, Susan - *The Joyful Table*
RVBW - Nov 2015 - pNA [51-500]

Joyce, Anna - *Stamp Stencil Paint: Making Extraordinary Patterned Projects by Hand*
BL - v112 - i5 - Nov 1 2015 - p12(1) [51-500]
LJ - v140 - i19 - Nov 15 2015 - p82(1) [51-500]

Joyce, Arthur A. - *Polity and Ecology in Formative Period Coastal Oaxaca*
Six Ct J - v46 - i1 - Spring 2015 - p247-249 [501+]

Joyce, Cynthia - *Please Forward: How Blogging Reconnected New Orleans after Katrina*
KR - May 15 2015 - pNA [501+]
LJ - v140 - i12 - July 1 2015 - p100(2) [501+]

Joyce, Dru, II - *Beyond Championships: A Playbook for Winning at Life*
VOYA - v38 - i2 - June 2015 - p88(1) [51-500]

Joyce, Eddie - *Small Mercies*
BL - v111 - i9-10 - Jan 1 2015 - p42(1) [51-500]
Comw - v142 - i15 - Sept 25 2015 - p34(2) [501+]
Ent W - i1354 - March 13 2015 - p62(1) [51-500]
KR - Jan 1 2015 - pNA [51-500]
NYT - March 26 2015 - pC6(L) [501+]
PW - v262 - i4 - Jan 26 2015 - p145(1) [51-500]

Joyce, Graham - *The Ghost in the Electric Blue Suit (Read by Jackson, Gildart). Audiobook Review*
BL - v111 - i13 - March 1 2015 - p68(1) [51-500]

Joyce, James - *Ulysses*
TLS - i5854 - June 12 2015 - p16(1) [501+]

Joyce, James Dru, II - *Beyond Championships, Teen Edition: A Playbook for Winning at Life*
y SLJ - v61 - i7 - July 2015 - p108(2) [51-500]

Joyce, Patrick - *The State of Freedom: A Social History of the British State since 1800*
JMH - v87 - i2 - June 2015 - p438(2) [501+]

Joyce, Rachel - *The Love Song of Miss Queenie Hennessy*
BL - v111 - i11 - Feb 1 2015 - p23(1) [51-500]
KR - Jan 1 2015 - pNA [51-500]
People - v83 - i11 - March 16 2015 - p41(NA) [501+]

Joyce, Sean Arthur - *Laying the Children's Ghosts to Rest: Canada's Home Children in the West*
Beav - v95 - i4 - August-Sept 2015 - p73(1) [501+]

Joyce, Trevor - *Rome's Wreck*
TLS - i5861 - July 31 2015 - p22(1) [501+]

Joyce, William - *A Bean, a Stalk and a Boy Named Jack (Illus. by Callicutt, Kenny)*
c HB Guide - v26 - i1 - Spring 2015 - p34(1) [51-500]
Billy's Booger (Illus. by Joyce, William)
c HB Guide - v26 - i1 - Fall 2015 - p38(1) [51-500]
c Nat Post - v17 - i188 - June 13 2015 - pWP5(1) [501+]
c BL - v111 - i15 - April 1 2015 - p81(1) [51-500]
c PW - v262 - i16 - April 20 2015 - p74(1) [51-500]
c PW - v262 - i49 - Dec 2 2015 - p33(2) [51-500]
c SLJ - v61 - i4 - April 2015 - p128(1) [51-500]
Jack Frost (Illus. by Joyce, William)
c BL - v112 - i2 - Sept 15 2015 - p67(1) [51-500]
c KR - August 15 2015 - pNA [51-500]
c PW - v262 - i39 - Sept 28 2015 - p90(2) [501+]

Joyner, C. Courtney - *The Rebel: The Complete Series: The Collectors Edition*
Roundup M - v23 - i1 - Oct 2015 - p36(1) [501+]

Joyner, Richard - *Making Marie Curie: Intellectual Property and Celebrity Culture in an Age of Information*
TimHES - i2203 - May 14 2015 - p47(1) [501+]

Juba, Stacy - *Fooling Around with Cinderella*
PW - v262 - i44 - Nov 2 2015 - p71(1) [501+]

Jubak, Jim - *Juggling with Knives: Smart Investing in the Coming Age of Volatility*
KR - Nov 15 2015 - pNA [501+]
LJ - v140 - i20 - Dec 1 2015 - p111(2) [51-500]

Jubermann, David - *Hypercar*
y Magpies - v30 - i4 - May 2015 - pS7(2) [501+]

Juby, Susan - *The Truth Commission. Audiobook Review*
y SLJ - v61 - i7 - July 2015 - p49(1) [51-500]
The Truth Commission
y KR - Jan 15 2015 - pNA [51-500]
y BL - v111 - i15 - April 1 2015 - p71(1) [51-500]
The Truth Commission (Illus. by Cooper, Trevor)
y CCB-B - v68 - i9 - May 2015 - p451(2) [51-500]
The Truth Commission
y HB - v91 - i2 - March-April 2015 - p100(1) [51-500]
y HB Guide - v26 - i2 - Fall 2015 - p125(1) [51-500]
y PW - v262 - i5 - Feb 2 2015 - p63(1) [51-500]
y PW - v262 - i49 - Dec 2 2015 - p99(2) [51-500]
y Res Links - v20 - i3 - Feb 2015 - p30(2) [51-500]
y VOYA - v37 - i6 - Feb 2015 - p59(1) [501+]

Judah, Ben - *Fragile Empire: How Russia Fell in and out of Love with Vladimir Putin*
For Aff - v94 - i2 - March-April 2015 - pNA [501+]
Historian - v77 - i1 - Spring 2015 - p172(2) [501+]

Judd, Jennifer Cole - *Circus Train (Illus. by Matthews, Melanie)*
c HB Guide - v26 - i2 - Fall 2015 - p13(1) [51-500]
c SLJ - v61 - i4 - April 2015 - p128(2) [51-500]

Judd, Richard W. - *Second Nature: An Environmental History of New England*
JAH - v102 - i1 - June 2015 - p211-212 [501+]

Judge, Chris - *The Snow Beast (Illus. by Judge, Chris)*
c KR - July 15 2015 - pNA [51-500]
c SLJ - v61 - i9 - Sept 2015 - p122(2) [51-500]
Tin
c HB Guide - v26 - i1 - Spring 2015 - p34(1) [51-500]
c Sch Lib - v63 - i1 - Spring 2015 - p28(1) [51-500]

Judge, Lita - *Born in the Wild: Baby Mammals and Their Parents (Illus. by Judge, Lita)*
c CCB-B - v68 - i5 - Jan 2015 - p263(1) [51-500]
c HB Guide - v26 - i1 - Spring 2015 - p165(1) [51-500]
Good Morning to Me! (Illus. by Judge, Lita)
c HB - v91 - i4 - July-August 2015 - p116(2) [51-500]
c KR - March 15 2015 - pNA [51-500]
c PW - v262 - i13 - March 30 2015 - p75(1) [51-500]
c PW - v262 - i49 - Dec 2 2015 - p34(1) [51-500]
c SLJ - v61 - i5 - May 2015 - p86(1) [51-500]
Hoot and Peep (Illus. by Judge, Lita)
c KR - Dec 15 2015 - pNA [51-500]
c PW - v262 - i51 - Dec 14 2015 - p81(1) [51-500]

Judge, Malcolm - *Jonny Jakes Investigates the Hamburgers of Doom*
c KR - Jan 1 2016 - pNA [51-500]
c Sch Lib - v63 - i3 - Autumn 2015 - p166(2) [51-500]

Judis, John B. - *Genesis: Truman, American Jews, and the Origins of the Arab/Israeli Conflict*
JTWS - v32 - i1 - Spring 2015 - p349(1) [51-500]
NYTBR - April 5 2015 - p28(L) [501+]

Judith, Anodea - *Anodea Judith's Chakra Yoga*
PW - v262 - i29 - July 20 2015 - p184(1) [51-500]

Judovits, Mordechai - *Find It in the Talmud: An Encyclopedia of Jewish Ethics and Conduct*
LJ - v140 - i2 - Feb 1 2015 - p106(2) [51-500]

Judt, Tony - *When the Facts Change: Essays, 1995-2010*
NS - v144 - i5249 - Feb 13 2015 - p55(1) [51-500]
NYRB - v62 - i9 - May 21 2015 - p31(3) [501+]
NYTBR - Jan 18 2015 - p17(L) [501+]
Spec - v327 - i9728 - Feb 7 2015 - p43(1) [501+]

Jukna, Stasys - *Boolean Functions Complexity: Advances and Frontiers*
SIAM Rev - v57 - i3 - Sept 2015 - p479-480 [501+]

Julavits, Heidi - *The Folded Clock: A Diary (Read by Gilbert, Tavia). Audiobook Review*
LJ - v140 - i16 - Oct 1 2015 - p44(2) [51-500]
The Folded Clock: A Diary
BL - v111 - i16 - April 15 2015 - p11(2) [51-500]
Ent W - i1361 - May 1 2015 - p67(1) [51-500]
HM - v330 - i1979 - April 2015 - p79(81) [501+]
KR - Jan 15 2015 - pNA [501+]
NYTBR - March 29 2015 - p1(L) [501+]
PW - v262 - i5 - Feb 2 2015 - p46(1) [51-500]

Jules, Jacqueline - *Zapato Pozver: Freddie Ramos Stomps the Snow (Illus. by Benitez, Miguel)*
c HB Guide - v26 - i1 - Spring 2015 - p61(1) [51-500]

Julia, Dominique - *Reforme catholique, religion des pretres et "foi des simples": Etudes d'anthropologie religieuse*
CHR - v101 - i3 - Summer 2015 - p639(2) [501+]

Julier, Alice P. - *Eating Together: Food, Friendship, and Inequality*
CS - v44 - i3 - May 2015 - p368-370 [501+]

Juliet S. Erazo - *Governing Indigenous Territories: Enacting Sovereignty in the Ecuadorian Amazon*
Ams - v72 - i2 - April 2015 - p341(1) [501+]

Jullien, Francois - *On the Universal: The Uniform, the Common, and Dialogue Between Cultures*
TLS - i5866 - Sept 4 2015 - p26(1) [501+]

July, Miranda - *The First Bad Man (Read by July, Miranda). Audiobook Review*
BL - v111 - i19-20 - June 1 2015 - p126(1) [51-500]
LJ - v140 - i7 - April 15 2015 - p46(2) [51-500]
PW - v262 - i5 - Feb 2 2015 - p52(1) [51-500]
The First Bad Man
Econ - v414 - i8923 - Jan 31 2015 - p75(US) [501+]
Mac - v128 - i2 - Jan 19 2015 - p57(2) [501+]
Nat Post - v17 - i62 - Jan 10 2015 - pWP10(1) [501+]
NS - v144 - i5252 - March 6 2015 - p52(1) [501+]
NY - v91 - i1 - Feb 16 2015 - p71 [51-500]
NYRB - v62 - i4 - March 5 2015 - p4(2) [501+]
NYT - Jan 12 2015 - pC4(L) [501+]
NYTBR - Jan 18 2015 - p13(L) [501+]
NYTBR - Nov 1 2015 - p28(L) [501+]
Spec - v327 - i9735 - March 28 2015 - p43(2)

[501+]
    TLS - i5840 - March 6 2015 - p20(1) [501+]
No One Belongs Here More Than You
    NYRB - v62 - i4 - March 5 2015 - p4(2) [501+]
Jump, Shirley - *When Somebody Loves You*
    PW - v262 - i36 - Sept 7 2015 - p53(1) [51-500]
Jung, Courtney - *Lactivism: How Feminists and Fundamentalists, Hippies and Yuppies, and Physicians and Politicians Made Breastfeeding Big Business and Bad Policy*
    KR - Sept 1 2015 - pNA [501+]
    NYTBR - Dec 20 2015 - p8(L) [501+]
    PW - v262 - i34 - August 24 2015 - p73(1) [51-500]
Jung, Moon-Ho - *The Rising Tide of Color: Race, State Violence, and Radical Movements across the Pacific*
    AHR - v120 - i3 - June 2015 - p1002-1003 [501+]
    Am St - v54 - i2 - Summer 2015 - p136-137 [501+]
Jung, Sandro - *British Literature and Print Culture*
    BSA-P - v109 - i3 - Sept 2015 - p421-425 [501+]
Jung, Yun - *Shelter*
    PW - v262 - i47 - Nov 23 2015 - p44(1) [51-500]
Jung, Yuson - *Ethical Eating in the Postsocialist and Socialist World*
    JRAI - v21 - i3 - Sept 2015 - p691(2) [501+]

Junger, Ernst - *The Storm Of Steel*
    MLR - v110 - i3 - July 2015 - p902-904 [501+]
Juniper, Tony - *What Nature Does for Britain*
    Nature - v518 - i7538 - Feb 12 2015 - p165(1) [51-500]
Junyk, Ihor - *Foreign Modernism: Cosmopolitanism, Identity, and Style in Paris*
    JMH - v87 - i3 - Sept 2015 - p738(3) [501+]
Jurado, Anabel - *Cleo (Illus. by Pineiro, Azul)*
    c SLJ - v61 - i12 - Dec 2015 - p85(1) [501+]
    Teo (Illus. by Pineiro, Azul)
    c SLJ - v61 - i12 - Dec 2015 - p85(1) [501+]
Jurado, J.G. - *Point of Balance*
    KR - June 1 2015 - pNA [501+]
    PW - v262 - i23 - June 8 2015 - p37(1) [51-500]
Jurafsky, Dan - *The Language of Food: A Linguist Reads the Menu*
    CSM - Feb 5 2015 - pNA [501+]
Jurdjevic, Mark - *A Great and Wretched City: Promise and Failure in Machiavelli's Florentine Political Thought*
    AHR - v120 - i4 - Oct 2015 - p1424-1426 [501+]
Jurevicius, Nathan - *Junction*
    c KR - July 15 2015 - pNA [51-500]
Jurgens, Hanco - *Neue Nachbarschaft: Deutschland und die Niederlande, Bildformung und Beziehungen seit 1990*
    HNet - Sept 2015 - pNA(NA) [501+]

Jurmain, Suzanne Tripp - *Nice Work, Franklin! (Illus. by Day, Larry)*
    c KR - Nov 1 2015 - pNA [51-500]
Jury, Walter - *Burn*
    y BL - v111 - i18 - May 15 2015 - p66(1) [51-500]
    y CCB-B - v68 - i11 - July-August 2015 - p552(1) [51-500]
    y HB Guide - v26 - i2 - Fall 2015 - p125(1) [51-500]
    y KR - March 15 2015 - pNA [51-500]
    y SLJ - v61 - i4 - April 2015 - p155(1) [51-500]
    y VOYA - v38 - i2 - June 2015 - p78(1) [501+]
    Scan (Read by Daniels, Luke). Audiobook Review
    y BL - v111 - i11 - Feb 1 2015 - p61(2) [51-500]
Justice, Steven - *Adam Usk's Secret*
    Med R - Sept 2015 - pNA [501+]
Jute, Annemarie Goldstein - *Putting a Name to It: Diagnosis in Contemporary Society*
    SF - v93 - i3 - March 2015 - pe62 [501+]
Jutel, Annemarie Goldstein - *Social Issues in Diagnosis: An Introduction for Students and Clinicians*
    MAQ - v29 - i1 - March 2015 - p7-9 [501+]
Juul, Pia - *The Murder of Halland*
    KR - July 15 2015 - pNA [51-500]
    Mac - v128 - i38 - Sept 28 2015 - p60(2) [501+]

K

K., Kathleen - *Dark Prince, Heed Thy Queen*
    KR - July 15 2015 - pNA [501+]
Kaaberbol, Lene - *Doctor Death (Read by Barber, Nicola). Audiobook Review*
    LJ - v140 - i8 - May 1 2015 - p41(1) [51-500]
    PW - v262 - i17 - April 27 2015 - p69(1) [51-500]
Doctor Death
    NYTBR - March 1 2015 - p29(L) [501+]
Kaaland, Christie - *Emergency Preparedness and Disaster Recovery in School Libraries: Creating a Safe Haven*
    Teach Lib - v42 - i3 - Feb 2015 - p42(2) [51-500]
    VOYA - v38 - i1 - April 2015 - p92(2) [51-500]
Kabala, James S. - *Church-State Relations in the Early American Republic, 1787-1846*
    RAH - v43 - i2 - June 2015 - p216-222 [501+]
Kabaservice, Geoffrey - *Rule and Ruin: The Downfall of Moderation and the Destruction of the Republican Party, from Eisenhower to the Tea Party*
    AHR - v120 - i2 - April 2015 - p668-669 [501+]
Kabatchnik, Amnon - *Blood on the Stage, 480 B.C. to 1600 A.D.: Milestone Plays of Murder, Mystery, and Mayhem - An Annotated Repertoire*
    R&USQ - v54 - i3 - Spring 2015 - p59(2) [501+]
Kabdebo, Tamas - *Danubius Danubia*
    WLT - v89 - i1 - Jan-Feb 2015 - p69(1) [51-500]
Kacer, Kathy - *The Magician of Auschwitz (Illus. by Newland, Gillian)*
    c HB Guide - v26 - i1 - Spring 2015 - p202(1) [51-500]
Stones on a Grave
    y KR - July 15 2015 - pNA [51-500]
    y Res Links - v21 - i1 - Oct 2015 - p36(1) [501+]
    y SLJ - v61 - i1 - Nov 2015 - p116(1) [51-500]
    y VOYA - v38 - i4 - Oct 2015 - p53(2) [501+]
Kachel, Christian - *Spoils of Olympus: By the Sword*
    KR - March 15 2015 - pNA [501+]
Kachurin, Pamela - *Making Modernism Soviet: The Russian Avant-Garde in the Early Soviet Era, 1918-1928*
    Slav R - v74 - i2 - Summer 2015 - p421-422 [501+]
Kaczmarowski, Jerry - *Sapient*
    KR - June 1 2015 - pNA [501+]
Kaczynski, David - *Every Last Tie*
    KR - Oct 1 2015 - pNA [501+]
Kadane, Matthew - *The Watchful Clothier: The Life of an Eighteenth-Century Protestant Capitalist*
    Bks & Cult - v21 - i1 - Jan-Feb 2015 - p8(1) [501+]
    JMH - v87 - i1 - March 2015 - p174(2) [501+]
Kadare, Ismail - *Twilight of the Eastern Gods*
    HR - v67 - i4 - Wntr 2015 - p685-692 [501+]
Kadish, Matthew - *Earthman Jack vs. the Secret Army*
    KR - Sept 1 2015 - pNA [501+]
Kadman, Noga - *Erased from Space and Consciousness: Israel and the Depopulated Palestinian Villages of 1948*
    PW - v262 - i15 - April 13 2015 - p66(1) [51-500]
Kadohata, Cynthia - *Half a World Away*
    c HB Guide - v26 - i1 - Spring 2015 - p82(1) [51-500]
Kadrey, Richard - *The Everything Box*
    PW - v262 - i51 - Dec 14 2015 - p64(1) [51-500]
Killing Pretty
    BL - v111 - i19-20 - June 1 2015 - p65(1) [51-500]
    PW - v262 - i17 - April 27 2015 - p56(2) [51-500]
Kaell, Hillary - *Walking Where Jesus Walked: American Christians and Holy Land Pilgrimage*
    CH - v84 - i4 - Dec 2015 - p926(3) [501+]
Kaesler, Dirk - *Max Weber: Preusse, Denker, Muttersohn, Eine Biographie*
    TLS - i5860 - July 24 2015 - p8(2) [501+]

Kaeuper, Richard W. - *Holy Warriors: The Religious Ideology of Chivalry*
    CHR - v101 - i1 - Wntr 2015 - p155(3) [501+]
Kafer, Alison - *Feminist, Queer, Crip*
    JGS - v24 - i2 - April 2015 - p247-248 [501+]
Kafka, Rebecca - *Alef Is for Abba / Alef Is for Ima (Illus. by Basaluzzo, Constanza)*
    c HB Guide - v26 - i1 - Spring 2015 - p11(1) [51-500]
Kagan, Donald - *Men of Bronze: Hoplite Warfare in Classical Greece*
    Historian - v77 - i2 - Summer 2015 - p393(2) [501+]
Kagan, Shelly - *The Geometry of Desert*
    Phil R - v124 - i3 - July 2015 - p419(4) [501+]
Kaganovsky, Lilya - *Sound, Speech, Music in Soviet and Post-Soviet Cinema*
    Slav R - v74 - i2 - Summer 2015 - p424-425 [501+]
Kagawa, Julie - *Rogue*
    y SLJ - v61 - i7 - July 2015 - p93(1) [51-500]
Talon
    c HB Guide - v26 - i1 - Spring 2015 - p111(1) [51-500]
    c SLJ - v61 - i6 - June 2015 - p46(6) [51-500]
Kahan, Alex - *Entrepreneurship: Create Your Own Business (Illus. by Crosier, Mike)*
    BL - v111 - i9-10 - Jan 1 2015 - p64(2) [51-500]
Kahaney, Amelia - *The Invisible*
    c HB Guide - v26 - i1 - Spring 2015 - p111(1) [51-500]
Kahanu, Noelle M.K.Y. - *A MAMo State of Mind: Kanaka Maoli Arts and the Review of Three Concurrent Exhibitions*
    Am Q - v67 - i3 - Sept 2015 - p959-967 [501+]
Kahler, A.R. - *Shades of Darkness*
    y KR - Dec 15 2015 - pNA [501+]
    y SLJ - v61 - i12 - Dec 2015 - p121(2) [51-500]
Kahlos, Maijastina - *The Faces of the Other: Religious Rivalry and Ethnic Encounters in the Later Roman World*
    Class R - v65 - i1 - April 2015 - p226-228 [501+]
Kahn, Ava Fran - *Transnational Traditions: New Perspectives on American Jewish History*
    HNet - August 2015 - pNA [501+]
Kahn, Margot - *Horses That Buck: The Story of Champion Bronc Rider Bill Smith*
    Roundup M - v23 - i1 - Oct 2015 - p34(1) [501+]
Kahn, Matt - *Whatever Arises, Love That: A Love Revolution that Begins with You*
    PW - v262 - i45 - Nov 9 2015 - p56(2) [51-500]
Kahn, Michael A. - *The Sirena Quest*
    Bwatch - March 2015 - pNA [51-500]
Kahn, Paul W. - *Finding Ourselves at the Movies: Philosophy for a New Generation*
    TLS - i5837 - Feb 13 2015 - p24(1) [501+]
Kahn, Robert - *Bobby and Mandee's Too Safe for Strangers (Illus. by Cotton, Sue Lynn)*
    c CH Bwatch - August 2015 - pNA [501+]
Kahn, Victoria - *The Future of Illusion: Political Theology and Early Modern Texts*
    MP - v113 - i1 - August 2015 - pE53(3) [501+]
    Ren Q - v68 - i1 - Spring 2015 - p276-277 [501+]
Kaier, Anne - *Home with Henry: A Memoir*
    PW - v262 - i9 - March 2 2015 - p78(1) [51-500]
Kain, Alex - *Beyond the Western Deep (Illus. by Bennett, Rachel)*
    c SLJ - v61 - i5 - May 2015 - p108(2) [51-500]
Kain, Jamie - *The Good Sister*
    c HB Guide - v26 - i1 - Spring 2015 - p111(1) [51-500]

Instructions for the End of the World
    y BL - v112 - i5 - Nov 1 2015 - p55(1) [51-500]
    y HB - v91 - i6 - Nov-Dec 2015 - p81(1) [51-500]
    y KR - Sept 15 2015 - pNA [51-500]
    y PW - v262 - i38 - Sept 21 2015 - p76(1) [51-500]
    y SLJ - v61 - i11 - Nov 2015 - p116(2) [51-500]
    y VOYA - v38 - i5 - Dec 2015 - p57(2) [51-500]
Kainen, Dan - *Polar: A Photicular Book*
    c SLJ - v61 - i10 - Oct 2015 - p126(1) [51-500]
Kainikara, Sanu - *The Bolt from the Blue: Air Power in the Cycle of Strategies*
    APJ - v29 - i3 - May-June 2015 - p94(2) [501+]
Kainulainen, Jaska - *Paolo Sarpi: A Servant of God and State*
    Ren Q - v68 - i2 - Summer 2015 - p714-715 [501+]
    Six Ct J - v46 - i1 - Spring 2015 - p150-151 [501+]
Kaisary, Philip - *The Haitian Revolution in the Literary Imagination: Radical Horizons, Conservative Constraints*
    FS - v69 - i1 - Jan 2015 - p121-122 [501+]
Kaiser, Charles - *The Cost of Courage*
    KR - April 15 2015 - pNA [501+]
    LJ - v140 - i12 - July 1 2015 - p94(1) [51-500]
    PW - v262 - i15 - April 13 2015 - p66(1) [51-500]
Kaiser, David - *No End Save Victory: How FDR Led the Nation into War*
    NWCR - v68 - i4 - Autumn 2015 - p122(3) [501+]
Kaiser, Michael M. - *Curtains? The Future of the Arts in America*
    LJ - v140 - i2 - Feb 1 2015 - p86(2) [51-500]
Kaiser, Robert Blair - *Inside the Jesuits: How Pope Francis is Changing the Church and the World*
    Theol St - v76 - i2 - June 2015 - p356(3) [501+]
Kajander, Ann - *Mathematical Models for Teaching Reasoning without Memorization*
    TC Math - v22 - i1 - August 2015 - p54(1) [501+]
Kajava, Mika - *Studies in Ancient Oracles and Divination*
    Class R - v65 - i2 - Oct 2015 - p492-494 [501+]
Kajuth, Nancy Mramor - *Get Reel: Produce Your Own Life*
    c BL - v112 - i7 - Dec 1 2015 - p34(2) [501+]
Kakoudaki, Despina - *Anatomy of a Robot: Literature, Cinema, and the Cultural Work of Artificial People*
    SFS - v42 - i2 - July 2015 - p380-383 [501+]
Kakoyianni-Doa, Fryni - *Penser le lexique-grammaire: perspectives actuelles*
    FS - v69 - i1 - Jan 2015 - p138-138 [501+]
Kaku, Michio - *The Future of the Mind: The Scientific Quest to Understand, Enhance, and Empower the Mind (Read by Chin, Feodor). Audiobook Review*
    BL - v112 - i7 - Dec 1 2015 - p71(1) [501+]
Kaladeen, Jean - *Larry the Little Orphan Dog*
    c KR - March 15 2015 - pNA [501+]
Kalajian, Douglas - *Stories My Father Never Finished Telling Me: Living with the Armenian Legacy of Loss and Silence*
    KR - Feb 1 2015 - pNA [501+]
Kalanithi, Paul - *When Breath Becomes Air*
    BL - v112 - i6 - Nov 15 2015 - p7(1) [51-500]
    PW - v262 - i44 - Nov 2 2015 - p75(1) [51-500]
    KR - Oct 15 2015 - pNA [501+]
Kalantzis, George - *Christian Political Witness*
    Intpr - v69 - i4 - Oct 2015 - p508(1) [501+]
Kalas, J. Ellsworth - *Preaching in an Age of Distraction*
    CC - v132 - i19 - Sept 16 2015 - p30(4) [501+]
Kalb, Claudia - *Andy Warhol Was a Hoarder: Inside the Minds of History's Great Personalities*
    PW - v262 - i50 - Dec 7 2015 - p79(1) [51-500]
Kalbian, Aline H. - *Sex, Violence, and Justice: Contraception and the Catholic Church*
    Theol St - v76 - i2 - June 2015 - p376(2) [501+]

Kaldellis, Anthony - *Ethnography after Antiquity: Foreign Lands and Peoples in Byzantine Literature*
HER - v130 - i543 - April 2015 - p418(2) [501+]
A New Herodotus: Laonikos Chalkokondyles on the Ottoman Empire, the Fall of Byzantium, and the Emergence of the West
Med R - Sept 2015 - pNA [501+]
Kale, Sunila S. - *Electrifying India: Regional Political Economies of Development*
HNet - Feb 2015 - pNA [501+]
Kalfopoulou, Adrianne - *Ruin: Essays in Exilic Living*
WLT - v89 - i2 - March-April 2015 - p77(2) [501+]
Kalfus, Ken - *Coup de Foudre*
KR - March 15 2015 - pNA [501+]
NYTBR - June 7 2015 - p31(L) [501+]
PW - v262 - i11 - March 16 2015 - p58(2) [51-500]
BL - v111 - i17 - May 1 2015 - p74(1) [51-500]
Spec - v328 - i9750 - July 11 2015 - p34(1) [501+]
Kalimi, Isaac - *Sennacherib at the Gates of Jerusalem: Story, History and Historiography*
JNES - v74 - i1 - April 2015 - p142(3) [501+]
Kaling, Mindy - *Why Not Me? (Read by Kaling, Mindy). Audiobook Review*
NYTBR - Nov 22 2015 - p18(L) [501+]
Kalkipsakis, Thalia - *Lifespan of Starlight*
y Magpies - v30 - i2 - May 2015 - p42(1) [501+]
Kallander, Amy Aisen - *Women, Gender, and the Palace Households in Ottoman Tunisia*
IJMES - v47 - i4 - Nov 2015 - p824-826 [501+]
Kallander, George L. - *Salvation through Dissent: Tonghak Heterodoxy and Early Modern Korea*
Historian - v77 - i1 - Spring 2015 - p151(2) [501+]
Kallanian, Jean-Pierre - *What You Can Learn From Your Teenager*
KR - April 1 2015 - pNA [501+]
Kalleberg, Arne - *Good Jobs, Bad Jobs: The Rise of Polarized and Precarious Employment Systems in the United States, 1970s-2000s*
CS - v44 - i4 - July 2015 - p463-469 [501+]
Kallen, Stuart A. - *Do Aliens Exist?*
y VOYA - v38 - i5 - Dec 2015 - p79(1) [501+]
Running Dry: The Global Water Crisis
y HB Guide - v26 - i2 - Fall 2015 - p155(1) [51-500]
y BL - v111 - i9-10 - Jan 1 2015 - p64(1) [51-500]
Kallendorf, Hilaire - *A Companion to Early Modern Hispanic Theater*
Ren Q - v68 - i3 - Fall 2015 - p1117-1118 [501+]
Kallentoft, Mons - *Autumn Killing*
RVBW - May 2015 - pNA [51-500]
Spring Remains
PW - v262 - i3 - Jan 19 2015 - p61(2) [51-500]
RVBW - Oct 2015 - pNA [51-500]
Kalliney, Peter J. - *Commonwealth of Letters: British Literary Culture and the Emergence of Postcolonial Aesthetics*
Clio - v44 - i2 - Spring 2015 - p261-266 [501+]
Kallio, Jamie - *What's Great about Virginia?*
c HB Guide - v26 - i1 - Spring 2015 - p203(1) [51-500]
Kallos, Stephanie - *Language Arts (Read by Gilbert, Tavia). Audiobook Review*
LJ - v140 - i17 - Oct 15 2015 - p52(1) [51-500]
Language Arts
BL - v111 - i15 - April 1 2015 - p23(2) [51-500]
Language Arts (Read by Gilbert, Tavia). Audiobook Review
BL - v112 - i5 - Nov 1 2015 - p69(1) [51-500]
Language Arts
KR - April 1 2015 - pNA [51-500]
LJ - v140 - i2 - Feb 1 2015 - p73(1) [51-500]
Kalluk, Celina - *Sweetest Kulu (Illus. by Neonakis, Alexandra)*
c Res Links - v20 - i4 - April 2015 - p4(1) [51-500]
Kalman, Bobbie - *All about Animals Close Up*
c CH Bwatch - July 2015 - pNA [501+]
How and What Do Animals Eat?
c Res Links - v20 - i3 - Feb 2015 - p20(1) [501+]
How and What Do Animals Learn?
c Res Links - v21 - i1 - Oct 2015 - p23(2) [501+]
How and Why Do Animals Adapt?
c Res Links - v21 - i1 - Oct 2015 - p23(2) [501+]
How and Why Do Animals Build Homes?
c Res Links - v20 - i3 - Feb 2015 - p20(1) [501+]
How and Why Do Animals Change?
c Res Links - v20 - i3 - Feb 2015 - p20(1) [501+]
How and Why Do Animals Communicate?
c Res Links - v21 - i1 - Oct 2015 - p23(2) [501+]
How and Why Do Animals Move?
c Res Links - v20 - i3 - Feb 2015 - p20(1) [501+]
How and Why Do People Copy Animals?
c CH Bwatch - July 2015 - pNA [501+]
c Res Links - v21 - i1 - Oct 2015 - p23(2) [501+]
What Kinds of Coverings Do Animals Have?
c Res Links - v21 - i1 - Oct 2015 - p23(2) [501+]
Why and Where Are Animals Endangered?
c Res Links - v21 - i1 - Oct 2015 - p23(2) [501+]
Kalman, Maira - *Thomas Jefferson: Life, Liberty and the Pursuit of Everything*
SLJ - v61 - i4 - April 2015 - p59(1) [51-500]
Kalman, Samuel - *French Colonial Fascism: The Extreme Right in Algeria, 1919-1939*
AHR - v120 - i1 - Feb 2015 - p366-367 [501+]
JTWS - v32 - i1 - Spring 2015 - p334(5) [501+]
Kalshoven, Petra T. - *Crafting 'The Indian': Knowledge, Desire, and Play in Indianist Reenactment*
HNet - May 2015 - pNA [501+]
Kalter, Christoph - *Die Entdeckung der Dritten Welt: Dekolonisierung und Neue Radikale Linke in Frankreich*
HNet - Jan 2015 - pNA [501+]
Kalter, Susan - *Old Three Toes and Other Tales of Survival and Extinction*
Roundup M - v22 - i6 - August 2015 - p31(1) [501+]
Kam, Jennifer - *Devin Rhodes Is Dead*
c HB Guide - v26 - i1 - Spring 2015 - p111(1) [51-500]
Kama, Larry - *The Death of Captain America: Civil War Aftermath (Read by Rohan, Richard). Audiobook Review*
BL - v111 - i13 - March 1 2015 - p69(1) [51-500]
Kamata, Suzanne - *Screaming Divas*
y HB Guide - v26 - i1 - Spring 2015 - p111(1) [51-500]
Kambouchner, Denis - *Descartes n'a pas dit [...&rqsb: Un repertoire des fausses idees sur l'auteur da Discours de la mathods, avec les elements utiles et une esquisse d'apologie*
Dialogue - v54 - i3 - Sept 2015 - p545-548 [501+]
Kamenetz, Anya - *The Test: Why Our Schools Are Obsessed With Standardized Testing - But You Don't Have to Be*
NYTBR - Feb 8 2015 - p10(L) [501+]
Kamigaki, Hiro - *Pierre the Maze Detective: The Search for the Stolen Maze Stone*
c CH Bwatch - August 2015 - pNA [51-500]
Kamil, Amos - *Great Is the Truth: Secrecy, Scandal, and the Quest for Justice at the Horace Mann School*
BL - v112 - i1 - Sept 1 2015 - p18(1) [51-500]
Comw - v142 - i17 - Oct 23 2015 - p25(4) [501+]
KR - Sept 1 2015 - pNA [501+]
LJ - v140 - i15 - Sept 15 2015 - p87(1) [51-500]
NYTBR - Nov 1 2015 - p19(L) [501+]
PW - v262 - i34 - August 24 2015 - p71(2) [51-500]
Kaminski, Theresa - *Angels of the Underground*
KR - Sept 1 2015 - pNA [501+]
Kamkwamba, William - *The Boy Who Harnessed the Wind (Read by Jackson, Korey). Audiobook Review*
c SLJ - v61 - i7 - July 2015 - p47(1) [51-500]
The Boy Who Harnessed the Wind (Illus. by Hymas, Anna)
c HB Guide - v26 - i2 - Fall 2015 - p209(1) [51-500]
c VOYA - v37 - i6 - Feb 2015 - p87(2) [51-500]
c HB - v91 - i1 - Jan-Feb 2015 - p97(1) [501+]
Kamm, F.M. - *The Trolley Problem Mysteries*
PW - v262 - i41 - Oct 12 2015 - p60(1) [51-500]
Kamm, Oliver - *Accidence Will Happen: The Non-Pedantic Guide to English Usage*
Spec - v327 - i9732 - March 7 2015 - p43(2) [501+]
TimHES - i2203 - May 14 2015 - p47(1) [501+]
TLS - i5851 - May 22 2015 - p28(1) [501+]
Kammen, Carol - *Zen and the Art of Local History*
JAH - v102 - i1 - June 2015 - p208-208 [501+]
Pub Hist - v37 - i1 - Feb 2015 - p142(3) [501+]
Kammen, Douglas - *The Contours of Mass Violence in Indonesia, 1965-68*
JAS - v74 - i1 - Feb 2015 - p244-246 [501+]
Kammerer, Elsa - *Jean de Vauzelles et le creuset lyonnais: Un humaniste catholique au service de Marguerite de Navarre entre France, Italie et Allemagne*
Ren Q - v68 - i1 - Spring 2015 - p237-238 [501+]
Jean de Vauzelles et le creuset lyonnais: Un humaniste catholique au service de Marguerite de Navarre entre France, Italie et Allemagne, 1520-1550
Six Ct J - v46 - i2 - Summer 2015 - p471-472 [501+]
Kampf um die Ressourcen - Relevanz der Energiepreise fur deutsche Unternehmen
HNet - May 2015 - pNA [501+]
Kampff, Joseph - *Ray Bradbury and the Cold War*
y BL - v111 - i9-10 - Jan 1 2015 - p85(1) [501+]
Kamph, Jamie - *Tricks of the Trade: Confessions of a Bookbinder*
TLS - i5875 - Nov 6 2015 - p31(1) [501+]
Kampmann, Eric - *Getting to Know Jesus: An Invitation to Walk with the Lord Day by Day*
PW - v262 - i37 - Sept 14 2015 - p60(1) [51-500]
Kampourakis, Kostas - *Understanding Evolution*
Am Bio T - v77 - i2 - Feb 2015 - p150(2) [501+]
QRB - v90 - i2 - June 2015 - p215(2) [501+]
Kamrava, Mehran - *Beyond the Arab Spring: The Evolving Ruling Bargain in the Middle East*
HNet - August 2015 - pNA [501+]
Kamteka, Rachana - *Virtue and Happiness: Essays in Honour of Julia Annas*
Phil R - v124 - i2 - April 2015 - p292(4) [501+]
Kamusella, Tomasz - *The Politics of Language and Nationalism in Modern Central Europe*
AHR - v120 - i2 - April 2015 - p737-738 [501+]
Kanaris, Leo - *Codename Xenophon*
PW - v262 - i17 - April 27 2015 - p54(1) [51-500]
Kanata, Konami - *The Complete Chi's Sweet Home, vol. 1 (Illus. by Kanata, Konami)*
c CH Bwatch - August 2015 - pNA [51-500]
c SLJ - v61 - i11 - Nov 2015 - p104(2) [51-500]
Kander, Astrid - *Power to the People: Energy in Europe over the Last Five Centuries*
JEH - v75 - i3 - Sept 2015 - p936-937 [501+]
Kandil, Hazem - *Inside the Brotherhood*
For Aff - v94 - i3 - May-June 2015 - pNA [501+]
Kane, Andrea - *The Silence That Speaks*
BL - v111 - i17 - May 1 2015 - p44(1) [51-500]
The Silence That Speaks (Read by Huber, Hillary). Audiobook Review
LJ - v140 - i15 - Sept 15 2015 - p41(2) [51-500]
The Silence That Speaks
PW - v262 - i12 - March 23 2015 - p49(2) [51-500]
Kane, Arnold - *Marriage Can Be Hazardous to Your Health*
KR - April 1 2015 - pNA [501+]
Kane, D.S. - *Baksheesh (Bribes).*
KR - Oct 1 2015 - pNA [501+]
GrayNet
KR - Sept 15 2015 - pNA [501+]
Kane, Joseph Nathan - *Famous First Facts: A Record of First Happenings, Discoveries, and Inventions in American History, 7th ed.*
BL - v111 - i21 - July 1 2015 - p15(1) [51-500]
Kane, Kim - *Esther's Rainbow (Illus. by Acton, Sara)*
c Sch Lib - v63 - i2 - Summer 2015 - p96(1) [51-500]
Kane, Paula M. - *Sister Thorn and Catholic Mysticism in Modern America*
AM - v212 - i1 - Jan 6 2015 - p40 [501+]
CH - v84 - i3 - Sept 2015 - p686(3) [501+]
JR - v95 - i4 - Oct 2015 - p566(2) [501+]
Kane, Sharon Smith - *Kitty and Me*
c HB Guide - v26 - i2 - Fall 2015 - p38(1) [51-500]
Kane, Tim - *Bleeding Talent: How the U.S. Military Mismanages Great Leaders and Why It's Time for a Revolution*
NWCR - v68 - i1 - Wntr 2015 - p140(2) [501+]
Kanefield, Maureen Stolar - *The Magic of Maxwell and His Tail*
c CH Bwatch - Feb 2015 - pNA [51-500]
Kanefield, Teri - *The Girl from the Tar Paper School: Barbara Rose Johns and the Advent of the Civil Rights Movement*
y SE - v79 - i3 - May-June 2015 - p144(1) [501+]
Guilty? Crime, Punishment, and the Changing Face of Justice
c HB Guide - v26 - i1 - Spring 2015 - p140(1) [51-500]
Kaneko, Yuki - *Into the Snow (Illus. by Saito, Masamitsu)*
c KR - Jan 1 2016 - pNA [51-500]
c PW - v262 - i42 - Oct 19 2015 - p75(1) [51-500]
Kaner, Etta - *Friend or Foe: The Whole Truth about Animals People Love to Hate (Illus. by Anderson, David)*
c KR - July 15 2015 - pNA [51-500]
c SLJ - v61 - i12 - Dec 2015 - p136(1) [51-500]
Kanevsky, Polly - *Here Is the Baby (Illus. by Yoo, Taeeun)*
c HB - v91 - i1 - Jan-Feb 2015 - p67(2) [51-500]
c HB Guide - v26 - i1 - Spring 2015 - p11(1) [51-500]
Kanfer, Stefan - *Ball of Fire: The Tumultuous Life and Comic Art of Lucille Ball*
BL - v111 - i19-20 - June 1 2015 - p30(2) [501+]
Groucho: The Life and Times of Julius Henry Marx
BL - v111 - i19-20 - June 1 2015 - p30(2) [501+]
Kang, Anna - *That's (Not) Mine (Illus. by Weyant, Christopher)*
c KR - July 15 2015 - pNA [51-500]
c SLJ - v61 - i9 - Sept 2015 - p123(1) [51-500]
Kang, Han - *The Vegetarian*
LJ - v140 - i20 - Dec 1 2015 - p94(1) [51-500]
Kang, Joshua Choonmin - *Spirituality of Gratitude: The Unexpected Blessings of Thankfulness*
PW - v262 - i19 - May 11 2015 - p53(1) [51-500]

Kang, Lydia - *Catalyst*
  y HB Guide - v26 - i2 - Fall 2015 - p125(1) [51-500]
  y KR - Jan 15 2015 - pNA [51-500]
  y VOYA - v37 - i6 - Feb 2015 - p79(1) [51-500]
Kang, Mandip S. - *The Doctor's Kidney Diets: A Nutritional Guide to Managing and Slowing the Progression of Chronic Kidney Disease*
    BL - v112 - i4 - Oct 15 2015 - p10(1) [51-500]
    LJ - v140 - i15 - Sept 15 2015 - p96(1) [51-500]
Kang, Manjit S. - *Combating Climate Change: An Agricultural Perspective*
    QRB - v90 - i1 - March 2015 - p85(1) [501+]
Kang, Maria - *The No More Excuses Diet: 3 Days to Bust Any Excuse, 3 Weeks to Easy New Eating Habits, 3 Months to Total Transformation*
    PW - v262 - i3 - Jan 19 2015 - p74(1) [51-500]
Kang, Sun Woo - *Epigenetics, Environment, and Genes*
    QRB - v90 - i1 - March 2015 - p97(2) [501+]
Kang, Yong-sook - *Rina*
    KR - Oct 15 2015 - pNA [501+]
Kanipe, Jeff - *Annals of the Deep Sky: A Survey of Galactic and Extragalactic Objects*
    S&T - v130 - i6 - Dec 2015 - p65(2) [501+]
    S&T - v130 - i2 - August 2015 - p38(1) [51-500]
Kann, Victoria - *Aqualicious*
  c HB Guide - v26 - i2 - Fall 2015 - p38(1) [51-500]
Pinkalicious and the Pink Parakeet (Illus. by Kann, Victoria)
  c BL - v111 - i22 - August 1 2015 - p75(1) [51-500]
  c HB Guide - v26 - i2 - Fall 2015 - p60(1) [51-500]
Kanner, Rebecca - *Esther*
    BL - v112 - i6 - Nov 15 2015 - p16(1) [51-500]
    KR - Sept 1 2015 - pNA [51-500]
Kanon, Joseph - *Leaving Berlin (Read by Brill, Corey). Audiobook Review*
    BL - v111 - i19-20 - June 1 2015 - p126(1) [51-500]
    LJ - v140 - i11 - June 15 2015 - p50(2) [51-500]
Leaving Berlin
    BL - v111 - i9-10 - Jan 1 2015 - p47(1) [51-500]
    KR - Jan 1 2015 - pNA [51-500]
    NYTBR - March 29 2015 - p15(L) [501+]
Kanon, Tom - *Tennesseans at War, 1812-1815: Andrew Jackson, the Creek War, and the Battle of New Orleans*
    JSH - v81 - i4 - Nov 2015 - p963(2) [501+]
    Pres St Q - v45 - i3 - Sept 2015 - p625(2) [501+]
Kanter, Rosabeth Moss - *Move: Putting America's Infrastructure Back in the Lead*
    BL - v111 - i16 - April 15 2015 - p7(1) [51-500]
    KR - March 15 2015 - pNA [501+]
    Nature - v522 - i7544 - June 4 2015 - p33(1) [51-500]
    NYTBR - June 14 2015 - p14(L) [501+]
Kantor, Joan - *Fading into Focus*
    KR - April 15 2015 - pNA [501+]
Kantor, Keith - *The Green Box League of Nutritious Justice*
  c CH Bwatch - April 2015 - pNA [51-500]
Kantor, MacKinlay - *Andersonville (Read by Gardner, Grover). Audiobook Review*
    BL - v111 - i19-20 - June 1 2015 - p132(1) [51-500]
Kantor, Melissa - *Better Than Perfect*
  y HB Guide - v26 - i2 - Fall 2015 - p125(1) [51-500]
  y Sch Lib - v63 - i3 - Autumn 2015 - p183(2) [51-500]
  y VOYA - v38 - i1 - April 2015 - p63(1) [51-500]
Maybe One Day
  y Teach Lib - v42 - i3 - Feb 2015 - p28(4) [501+]
Kantor, Paul - *Struggling Giants: City-Region Governance in London, New York, Paris and Tokyo*
    CS - v44 - i1 - Jan 2015 - p73-75 [501+]
Kantorovitz, Sylvie - *Zig and the Magic Umbrella (Illus. by Kantorovitz, Sylvie)*
  c BL - v111 - i12 - Feb 15 2015 - p89(1) [51-500]
  c HB - v91 - i3 - May-June 2015 - p89(1) [51-500]
  c HB Guide - v26 - i2 - Fall 2015 - p13(1) [51-500]
Kao, Grace - *Education and Immigration*
    CS - v44 - i2 - March 2015 - p219-222 [51-500]
Kapell, Matthew Wilhelm - *Playing with the Past: Digital Games and the Simulation of History*
    JIH - v45 - i3 - Wntr 2015 - p423-424 [501+]
Kapferer, Bruce - *2001 and Counting: Kubrick, Nietzsche, and Anthropology*
    JRAI - v21 - i2 - June 2015 - p489(2) [501+]
Kapil, Bhanu - *Ban en Banlieue*
    PW - v262 - i3 - Jan 19 2015 - p58(2) [51-500]

Kaplan, Arie - *Saturday Night Live: Shaping TV Comedy and American Culture*
  y HB Guide - v26 - i1 - Spring 2015 - p181(1) [51-500]
Swashbuckling Scoundrels
  y KR - July 1 2015 - pNA [51-500]
Kaplan, Basha - *SoulMating: The Secret to Finding Everlasting Love and Passion*
    SPBW - Feb 2015 - pNA [51-500]
Kaplan, Benjamin J. - *Cunegonde's Kidnapping: A Story of Religious Conflict in the Age of Enlightenment*
    Comw - v142 - i16 - Oct 9 2015 - p40(5) [501+]
    HT - v65 - i10 - Oct 2015 - p58(1) [501+]
    TimHES - i2185 - Jan 8 2015 - p46-47 [501+]
    TLS - i5851 - May 22 2015 - p25(1) [501+]
Kaplan, Bruce Eric - *I Was a Child*
    BL - v111 - i13 - March 1 2015 - p13(1) [51-500]
    KR - Feb 1 2015 - pNA [501+]
    PW - v262 - i9 - March 2 2015 - p76(1) [51-500]
Kaplan, Carter - *Emanations: Foray into Forever*
    WLT - v89 - i2 - March-April 2015 - p74(1) [501+]
Kaplan, Fred - *A New Birth of Freedom: Selected Writings of Abraham Lincoln*
    TLS - i5858 - July 10 2015 - p24(2) [501+]
Kaplan, J.D. - *The Scary Girls*
    SPBW - June 2015 - pNA [51-500]
Kaplan, James - *Sinatra: The Chairman*
    BL - v112 - i5 - Nov 1 2015 - p15(2) [51-500]
    KR - Oct 1 2015 - pNA [501+]
    LJ - v140 - i17 - Oct 15 2015 - p86(2) [51-500]
    NYT - Nov 17 2015 - pC1(L) [501+]
    NYTBR - Dec 6 2015 - p74(L) [501+]
    PW - v262 - i38 - Sept 21 2015 - p67(1) [501+]
    Spec - v329 - i9767 - Nov 7 2015 - p46(2) [501+]
Kaplan, Janice - *The Gratitude Diaries: How a Year Looking on the Bright Side Transformed My Life*
    PW - v262 - i18 - May 4 2015 - p107(1) [51-500]
    KR - May 15 2015 - pNA [51-500]
Kaplan, Jerry - *Humans Need Not Apply: A Guide to Wealth and Work in the Age of Artificial Intelligence*
    LJ - v140 - i13 - August 1 2015 - p120(2) [51-500]
    TimHES - i2217 - August 20 2015 - p48-48 [501+]
Kaplan, Matt - *Science of the Magical: From the Holy Grail to Love Potions to Superpowers*
    KR - August 15 2015 - pNA [501+]
    LJ - v140 - i14 - Sept 1 2015 - p127(1) [51-500]
    PW - v262 - i32 - August 10 2015 - p46(1) [51-500]
Kaplan, Michael B. - *Betty Bunny Didn't Do It (Read by Kellgren, Katherine). Audiobook Review*
  c BL - v111 - i13 - March 1 2015 - p70(1) [51-500]
  c SLJ - v61 - i3 - March 2015 - p76(1) [51-500]
  c SLJ - v61 - i4 - April 2015 - p52(2) [51-500]
Betty Bunny Loves Easter (Illus. by Jorisch, Stephane)
  c CCB-B - v68 - i7 - March 2015 - p358(1) [51-500]
  c KR - Feb 1 2015 - pNA [501+]
    PW - v262 - i2 - Jan 12 2015 - p62(2) [51-500]
Kaplan, Robert D. - *Asia's Cauldron: The South China Sea and the End of a Stable Pacific*
    JTWS - v32 - i1 - Spring 2015 - p317(2) [501+]
    NS - v144 - i5267 - June 19 2015 - p42(3) [501+]
    NYTBR - Feb 1 2015 - p24(L) [501+]
    Parameters - v45 - i1 - Spring 2015 - p146(2) [501+]
    Soc - v52 - i3 - June 2015 - p284(3) [501+]
In Europe's Shadow: Two Cold Wars and a Thirty-Year Journey Through Romania and Beyond
    KR - Dec 1 2015 - pNA [51-500]
    PW - v262 - i51 - Dec 14 2015 - p71(1) [501+]
Kaplan, Roberta - *Then Comes Marriage: United States v. Windsor and the Defeat of Doma*
    KR - August 1 2015 - pNA [501+]
    LJ - v140 - i15 - Sept 15 2015 - p90(1) [51-500]
    Ms - v25 - i3 - Summer 2015 - p41(1) [501+]
    PW - v262 - i32 - August 10 2015 - p48(1) [51-500]
Kaplan, Ron - *The Jewish Olympics*
    KR - May 1 2015 - pNA [501+]
Kapoor, Deepti - *A Bad Character*
    LJ - v140 - i3 - Feb 15 2015 - p88(1) [51-500]
    NYTBR - Feb 15 2015 - p20(L) [501+]
    NYTBR - Dec 20 2015 - p24(L) [501+]
Kappeler, Manfred - *Lessings Kiste: Nicolais Plan und das Grimm'sche Worterbuch*
    HNet - July 2015 - pNA [501+]
Kappelhoff, Hermann - *Mobilisierung der Sinne: Der Hollywood-Kriegsfilm zwischen Genrekino und Historie*
    HNet - Sept 2015 - pNA [501+]
Kappler, Kathryn J. - *My Own Pioneers, 3 vols.*
    SPBW - April 2015 - pNA [501+]

Kapsch, Robert J. - *Over the Alleghenies: Early Canals and Railroads of Pennsylvania*
    T&C - v56 - i2 - April 2015 - p540-542 [501+]
Kapur, Jyotsna - *The Politics of Time and Youth in Brand India: Bargaining with Capital*
    JAS - v74 - i1 - Feb 2015 - p231-233 [501+]
Karadzic, Radovan - *The Opening Statement of Dr. Radovan Karadzic Before the International Criminal Tribunal for the Former Yugoslavia in The Hague March 1-2, 2010*
    KR - Sept 15 2015 - pNA [501+]
Karalis, Sylvia - *Jimmy Handstand (Illus. by Cowen, Linda)*
  c CH Bwatch - Oct 2015 - pNA [51-500]
Karalius, Kimberly - *Love Fortunes and Other Disasters*
  y SLJ - v61 - i5 - May 2015 - p120(1) [51-500]
Karam, Stephen - *The Humans*
    Am Theat - v32 - i10 - Dec 2015 - p8(1) [51-500]
Karamichas, John - *The Olympic Games and the Environment*
    CS - v44 - i1 - Jan 2015 - p75-77 [501+]
Karan, Donna - *My Journey*
    BL - v112 - i3 - Oct 1 2015 - p9(1) [51-500]
    KR - Oct 1 2015 - pNA [51-500]
Karas, G. Brian - *As an Oak Tree Grows*
  c HB Guide - v26 - i1 - Spring 2015 - p34(1) [51-500]
On the Farm, At the Market (Illus. by Karas, G. Brian)
  c KR - Jan 1 2016 - pNA [51-500]
Karatani, Kojin - *The Structure of World History: From Modes of Production to Modes of Exchange*
    HNet - April 2015 - pNA [501+]
    HNet - April 2015 - pNA [501+]
Karban, Richard - *How to Do Ecology: A Concise Handbook*
    QRB - v90 - i3 - Sept 2015 - p324(2) [501+]
Plant Sensing and Communication
    New Sci - v226 - i3023 - May 30 2015 - p46(2) [501+]
Kardashian West, Kim - *Selfish*
    Nat Post - v17 - i159 - May 9 2015 - pWP4(1) [501+]
    Spec - v328 - i9744 - May 30 2015 - p38(1) [501+]
Kardos, Michael - *Before He Finds Her (Illus. by Whelan, Julia). Audiobook Review*
  y PW - v262 - i12 - March 23 2015 - p69(1) [51-500]
Before He Finds Her
  y NYTBR - Feb 1 2015 - p25(L) [501+]
  y SLJ - v61 - i6 - June 2015 - p132(1) [51-500]
Kareem, Sarah Tindal - *Eighteenth-Century Fiction and the Reinvention of Wonder*
    RES - v66 - i276 - Sept 2015 - p788-790 [501+]
    TLS - i5861 - July 31 2015 - p10(2) [501+]
Karet, Evelyn - *The Antonio II Badile Album of Drawings: The Origins of Collecting Drawings in Early Modern Northern Italy*
    Ren Q - v68 - i2 - Summer 2015 - p643-644 [501+]
Karim-Cooper, Farah - *Shakespeare's Theatres and the Effects of Performance*
    Shakes Q - v66 - i1 - Spring 2015 - p95-97 [501+]
Karimi, Pamela - *Domesticity and Consumer Culture in Iran: Interior Revolutions of the Modern Era*
    HNet - May 2015 - pNA [501+]
    IJMES - v47 - i4 - Nov 2015 - p830-831 [501+]
Karjel, Robert - *The Swede (Read by Harding, Jeff). Audiobook Review*
    LJ - v140 - i17 - Oct 15 2015 - p52(1) [51-500]
The Swede
    Ent W - i1370 - July 3 2015 - p62(1) [501+]
    BL - v111 - i21 - July 1 2015 - p40(1) [51-500]
    PW - v262 - i21 - May 25 2015 - p35(2) [51-500]
Karkkainen, Veli-Matti - *Trinity and Revelation, vol. 2*
    IBMR - v39 - i1 - Jan 2015 - p44(1) [501+]
Karlgaard, Rich - *Team Genius: The New Science of High-Performing Organizations*
    BL - v111 - i19-20 - June 1 2015 - p14(1) [51-500]
    KR - May 1 2015 - pNA [501+]
    LJ - v140 - i10 - June 1 2015 - p109(2) [51-500]
Karlin, Marlise - *The Simplicity of Stillness Method: 3 Steps to Rewire Your Brain and Access Your Highest Potential*
    PW - v262 - i30 - July 27 2015 - p56(1) [51-500]
Karlip, Joshua M. - *The Tragedy of a Generation: The Rise and Fall of Jewish Nationalism in Eastern Europe*
    JMH - v87 - i3 - Sept 2015 - p765(3) [501+]
Karlsdottir, Alice - *Norse Goddess Magic: Trancework, Mythology, and Ritual*
    Bwatch - July 2015 - pNA [51-500]

Karlson, Kevin T. - *Birding by Impression: A Different Approach to Knowing and Identifying Birds*
    LJ - v140 - i3 - Feb 15 2015 - p125(1) [51-500]
Peterson Reference Guide: Birding by Impression - A Different Approach to Knowing and Identifying Birds
    BL - v111 - i12 - Feb 15 2015 - p16(1) [51-500]

Karlsson, Jonas - *The Room*
    TLS - i5839 - Feb 27 2015 - p20(1) [501+]

Karman, James - *Robinson Jeffers: Poet and Prophet*
    BL - v111 - i22 - August 1 2015 - p18(1) [501+]
    PW - v262 - i26 - June 29 2015 - p60(1) [51-500]

Karmi, Ghada - *Return: A Palestinian Memoir*
    NS - v144 - i5269 - July 3 2015 - p46(3) [501+]

Karn, Nicholas - *English Episcopal Acta 42: Ely 1198-1256*
    Specu - v90 - i1 - Jan 2015 - p267-268 [501+]

Karnad, Raghu - *Farthest Field: An Indian Story of the Second World War*
    KR - June 1 2015 - pNA [51-500]
    LJ - v140 - i11 - June 15 2015 - p98(1) [51-500]
    NS - v144 - i5270 - July 10 2015 - p36(3) [501+]
    PW - v262 - i25 - June 22 2015 - p133(2) [51-500]
    Spec - v328 - i9746 - June 13 2015 - p36(1) [501+]

Karnes, Michelle - *Imagination, Meditation, and Cognition in the Middle Ages*
    CHR - v101 - i2 - Spring 2015 - p360(3) [501+]

Karo, Aaron - *Galgorithm*
    y BL - v111 - i19-20 - June 1 2015 - p98(1) [51-500]
    y HB Guide - v26 - i2 - Fall 2015 - p125(1) [51-500]
    y SLJ - v61 - i6 - June 2015 - p126(1) [51-500]

Karon, Jan - *Come Rain or Come Shine*
    BL - v111 - i22 - August 1 2015 - p27(1) [51-500]
    KR - July 15 2015 - pNA [51-500]
    LJ - v140 - i14 - Sept 1 2015 - p95(2) [51-500]

Karon, Karen - *Advanced Chain Maille Jewelry Workshop: Weaving with Rings and Scale Maille*
    LJ - v140 - i11 - June 15 2015 - p86(1) [51-500]

Karp, Josh - *Orson Welles's Last Movie: The Making of The Other Side of the Wind*
    BL - v111 - i14 - March 15 2015 - p37(1) [51-500]
    Ent W - i1362 - May 8 2015 - p57(1) [501+]
    KR - Feb 1 2015 - pNA [51-500]
Orson Welles's Last Movie: The Making of "The Other Side of the Wind"
    NYT - April 23 2015 - pC1(L) [501+]
Orson Welles's Last Movie: The Making of The Other Side of the Wind
    NYTBR - May 31 2015 - p34(L) [501+]
    PW - v262 - i7 - Feb 16 2015 - p172(2) [51-500]
    Si & So - v25 - i9 - Sept 2015 - p107(1) [501+]

Karp, Karen S. - *Using Research to Improve Instruction*
    TC Math - v21 - i6 - Feb 2015 - p376(1) [501+]

Karplus, Ilan - *Symbiosis in Fishes: The Biology of Interspecific Partnerships*
    QRB - v90 - i2 - June 2015 - p208(2) [501+]

Karpowitz, Christopher F. - *The Silent Sex: Gender, Deliberation and Institutions*
    Wom R Bks - v32 - i3 - May-June 2015 - p12(2) [501+]

Karpp, Gerhard - *Mittelalterliche Bibelhandschriften am Niederrhein*
    Specu - v90 - i2 - April 2015 - p554-555 [501+]

Karpyshyn, Drew - *Chaos Unleashed*
    PW - v262 - i34 - August 24 2015 - p65(1) [51-500]

Karr, Mary - *The Art of Memoir*
    KR - July 1 2015 - pNA [501+]
    LJ - v140 - i12 - July 1 2015 - p98(1) [51-500]
    NYT - Sept 17 2015 - pC1(L) [501+]
    NYTBR - Oct 25 2015 - p20(L) [501+]
    PW - v262 - i27 - July 6 2015 - p60(1) [51-500]

Karre, Elizabeth - *All You Are*
    y HB Guide - v26 - i1 - Spring 2015 - p111(1) [51-500]
Calling the Shots
    y HB Guide - v26 - i1 - Spring 2015 - p111(1) [51-500]
Certain Signals
    y HB Guide - v26 - i1 - Spring 2015 - p111(1) [51-500]
No Regrets
    y HB Guide - v26 - i1 - Spring 2015 - p111(1) [51-500]

Karsh, Efraim - *The Tail Wags the Dog: International Politics and the Middle East*
    Bwatch - Oct 2015 - pNA [51-500]
    KR - June 1 2015 - pNA [501+]
    PW - v262 - i19 - May 11 2015 - p47(2) [51-500]

Karst, Ken - *Area 51*
    c HB Guide - v26 - i1 - Spring 2015 - p133(1) [51-500]
Atlantis
    c HB Guide - v26 - i1 - Spring 2015 - p144(1) [51-500]

Karst, Patrice - *The Smile That Went Around the World (Illus. by Christy, Jana)*
    c CH Bwatch - March 2015 - pNA [51-500]

Kartaloff, Kiril Plamen - *La Sollecitudine Ecclesiale di Monsignor Roncalli in Bulgaria (1925-1934)*
    CHR - v101 - i1 - Wntr 2015 - p176(2) [501+]

Karten, Toby J. - *Inclusion Strategies That Work! Research-Based Methods for the Classroom*
    Bwatch - July 2015 - pNA [51-500]

Karthas, Ilyana - *When Ballet Became French: Modern Ballet and the Cultural Politics of France, 1909-1939*
    LJ - v140 - i13 - August 1 2015 - p97(1) [51-500]

Kasapovic, Mirjana - *Kombinirani izborni sustavi u Europi 1945-2014: Parne komparacije Njemacke i Italije, Bugarske i Hrvatske*
    Slav R - v74 - i1 - Spring 2015 - p184-185 [501+]

Kasdan, Mallory - *Ella (Illus. by Chin, Marcos)*
    c CH Bwatch - June 2015 - pNA [51-500]
    c HB Guide - v26 - i2 - Fall 2015 - p39(1) [51-500]
    c Nat Post - v17 - i62 - Jan 10 2015 - pWP9(1) [501+]

Kasdepke, Grzegorz - *The Beast in My Belly (Illus. by Kozlowski, Tomasz)*
    c KR - June 1 2015 - pNA [51-500]

Kasfir, Sidney Littlefield - *African Art and Agency in the Workshop*
    IJAHS - v48 - i1 - Wntr 2015 - p131-132 [501+]

Kashani-Sabet, Firoozeh - *Conceiving Citizens: Women and the Politics of Motherhood in Iran*
    AHR - v120 - i1 - Feb 2015 - p371-372 [501+]

Kashua, Sayed - *Native: Dispatches from an Israeli-Palestinian Life*
    KR - Dec 1 2015 - pNA [501+]
    PW - v262 - i41 - Oct 12 2015 - p55(1) [51-500]

Kashyap, Anurag - *Bombay Velvet*
    Si & So - v25 - i7 - July 2015 - p70(2) [501+]

Kasischke, Lou - *After the Wind: 1996 Everest Tragedy: One Survivor's Story*
    c BL - v112 - i3 - Oct 1 2015 - p32(2) [51-500]
    PW - v262 - i16 - April 20 2015 - p70(1) [51-500]

Kasparov, Garry - *Winter Is Coming: Why Vladimir Putin and the Enemies of the Free World Must Be Stopped*
    KR - August 1 2015 - pNA [501+]
    LJ - v140 - i19 - Nov 15 2015 - p96(1) [51-500]
    NYTBR - Nov 8 2015 - p13(L) [501+]
    PW - v262 - i34 - August 24 2015 - p73(1) [51-500]

Kasper, Agent - *Supernotes*
    BL - v112 - i7 - Dec 1 2015 - p32(1) [51-500]
    KR - Oct 15 2015 - pNA [51-500]
    PW - v262 - i46 - Nov 16 2015 - p56(2) [51-500]

Kasper, Leagan E. - *The Deceptive Fibionary*
    SPBW - Sept 2015 - pNA [51-500]
Love
    RVBW - Oct 2015 - pNA [51-500]
    SPBW - August 2015 - pNA [51-500]

Kasper, Walter - *The Gospel of the Family*
    Theol St - v76 - i2 - June 2015 - p379(3) [501+]
Mercy: The Essence of the Gospel and the Key to Christian Life
    CC - v132 - i2 - Jan 21 2015 - p35(2) [501+]
Pope Francis' Revolution of Tenderness and Love: Theological and Pastoral Perspectives
    Theol St - v76 - i3 - Sept 2015 - p619(2) [501+]

Kassel, Douglas - *The Organ: An Encyclopaedia*
    TLS - i5855 - June 19 2015 - p29(1) [501+]

Kasson, John F. - *The Little Girl Who Fought the Great Depression: Shirley Temple and 1930s America*
    AHR - v120 - i4 - Oct 2015 - p1504-1505 [501+]
    JAH - v101 - i4 - March 2015 - p1313(1) [501+]

Kastan, David Scott - *A Will to Believe: Shakespeare and Religion*
    MP - v113 - i1 - August 2015 - pE30(3) [501+]
    Ren Q - v68 - i1 - Spring 2015 - p397-398 [501+]
    Six Ct J - v46 - i2 - Summer 2015 - p504-507 [501+]
    TLS - i5860 - July 24 2015 - p10(2) [501+]

Kastner, Alexander - *Gottlicher Zorn und Menschliches Mass: Religiose Abweichung in Fruhneuzeitlichen Stadtgemeinschaften*
    HNet - Feb 2015 - pNA [501+]

Kastner, Fatima - *Transitional Justice in der Weltgesellschaft*
    HNet - July 2015 - pNA [501+]

Kasurak, Peter - *A National Force: The Evolution of Canada's Army, 1950-2000*
    Parameters - v45 - i1 - Spring 2015 - p161(2) [501+]

Kasza, Keiko - *Finders Keepers (Illus. by Kasza, Keiko)*
    c HB - v91 - i5 - Sept-Oct 2015 - p82(2) [51-500]
    c KR - May 15 2015 - pNA [51-500]
    c SLJ - v61 - i6 - June 2015 - p86(1) [51-500]

Katagiri, Yasuhiro - *Black Freedom, White Resistance, and Red Menace: Civil Rights and Anticommunism in the Jim Crow South*
    AHR - v120 - i4 - Oct 2015 - p1516-1517 [501+]

Katajala-Peltomaa, Sari - *Mental (Dis)Order in Later Medieval Europe*
    Med R - Sept 2015 - pNA [501+]
    Ren Q - v68 - i3 - Fall 2015 - p1025-1027 [501+]

Katauskas, Fiona - *The Amazing True Story of How Babies Are Made*
    Magpies - v30 - i4 - Sept 2015 - p24(1) [501+]

Katchadjian, Pablo - *What To Do*
    KR - Dec 1 2015 - pNA [51-500]

Katcher, Brian - *The Improbable Theory of Ana & Zak*
    y BL - v111 - i15 - April 1 2015 - p66(1) [51-500]
    y CCB-B - v69 - i1 - Sept 2015 - p30(1) [51-500]
    y HB Guide - v26 - i2 - Fall 2015 - p125(1) [51-500]
    y KR - March 15 2015 - pNA [51-500]
    y Nat Post - v17 - i176 - May 30 2015 - pWP4(1) [501+]
    y PW - v262 - i11 - March 16 2015 - p86(1) [51-500]
    y SLJ - v61 - i2 - Feb 2015 - p103(2) [51-500]
    y VOYA - v38 - i1 - April 2015 - p63(1) [51-500]

Katchoura, Jean-Luc - *Tal Farlow: A Life In Jazz Guitar*
    Dbt - v82 - i6 - June 2015 - p78(1) [501+]

Katchur, Karen - *The Secrets of Lake Road*
    LJ - v140 - i10 - June 1 2015 - p90(1) [51-500]

Kate, Lauren - *Unforgiven*
    y BL - v112 - i6 - Nov 15 2015 - p52(1) [51-500]
    y KR - Oct 15 2015 - pNA [51-500]

Kateb, George - *Lincoln's Political Thought*
    Dis - v62 - i2 - Spring 2015 - p150(5) [501+]

Kates, Steven - *Defending the History of Economic Thought*
    BHR - v89 - i3 - Autumn 2015 - p573(3) [501+]

Kats, Jewel - *Hansel and Gretel: A Fairy Tale with a Down Syndrome Twist (Illus. by Lenart, Claudia Maria)*
    c CH Bwatch - Feb 2015 - pNA [51-500]

Katsaropoulos, Chris - *Entrevoir*
    BL - v111 - i16 - April 15 2015 - p23(1) [51-500]
    SPBW - June 2015 - pNA [501+]

Katsiaficas, George - *Asia's Unknown Uprisings, Vol. 2: People Power in the Philippines, Burma, Tibet, China, Taiwan, Bangladesh, Nepal, Thailand, and Indonesia*
    JAS - v74 - i1 - Feb 2015 - p176-178 [501+]

Katz, Alan - *The Day the Mustache Took Over (Illus. by Easler, Kris)*
    c PW - v262 - i26 - June 29 2015 - p68(1) [51-500]
    c KR - July 1 2015 - pNA [51-500]
    c SLJ - v61 - i8 - August 2015 - p87(1) [51-500]

Katz, Alyssa - *The Influence Machine: The U.S. Chamber of Commerce and the Corporate Capture of American Life*
    BL - v111 - i19-20 - June 1 2015 - p12(2) [51-500]
    KR - May 15 2015 - pNA [51-500]
    PW - v262 - i20 - May 18 2015 - p78(1) [51-500]

Katz, Amy - *Seed Bead Chic: 25 Elegant Projects Inspired by Fine Jewelry*
    LJ - v140 - i3 - Feb 15 2015 - p99(2) [51-500]

Katz, Brian P. - *Distilling Ideas: An Introduction to Mathematical Thinking*
    Math T - v108 - i7 - March 2015 - p558(1) [501+]

Katz, Charles - *Peter and Lisa: A Mental Illness Children's Story (Illus. by Suico, Mitchi)*
    c CH Bwatch - Oct 2015 - pNA [51-500]

Katz, Harry L. - *Mark Twain's America: A Celebration in Words and Images*
    NYTBR - Feb 22 2015 - p16(L) [501+]

Katz, James E. - *The Social Media President: Barack Obama and the Politics of Digital Engagement*
    Pres St Q - v45 - i1 - March 2015 - p212(3) [501+]

Katz, Jeff - *Split Season, 1981: Fernandomania, the Bronx Zoo, and the Strike That Saved Baseball*
    KR - Feb 1 2015 - pNA [51-500]
    LJ - v140 - i3 - Feb 15 2015 - p103(2) [51-500]

Katz, Karen - *Rosie Goes to Preschool (Illus. by Katz, Karen)*
    c KR - June 1 2015 - pNA [51-500]
    c SLJ - v61 - i8 - August 2015 - p57(1) [51-500]
What Does Baby Love? (Illus. by Katz, Karen)
    c KR - Jan 1 2015 - pNA [51-500]

Katz, Michael R. - *The Kreutzer Sonata Variations: Lev Tolstoy's Novella and Counterstories by Sofiya Tolstaya and Lev Lvovich Tolstoy*
    TLS - i5842 - March 20 2015 - p11(2) [501+]
Katz, Pamela - *The Partnership: Brecht, Weill, Three Women, and Germany on the Brink*
    NY - v91 - i2 - Feb 23 2015 - p179 [51-500]
    NYT - Jan 6 2015 - pC4(L) [501+]
Katz, Paul R. - *Religion in China and Its Modern Fate*
    AHR - v120 - i4 - Oct 2015 - p1464-1465 [501+]
Katz, Samuel M - *The Ghost Warriors*
    KR - Dec 1 2015 - pNA [501+]
Katz, Susan B. - *ABC School's for Me! (Illus. by Munsinger, Lynn)*
    c KR - June 1 2015 - pNA [51-500]
    c SLJ - v61 - i8 - August 2015 - p57(1) [51-500]
All Year Round (Illus. by Ojala, Eiko)
    c KR - Oct 15 2015 - pNA [51-500]
    c SLJ - v61 - i11 - Nov 2015 - p77(1) [51-500]
Katzenbach, John - *The Dead Student*
    BL - v111 - i22 - August 1 2015 - p33(1) [51-500]
    KR - August 1 2015 - pNA [51-500]
    LJ - v140 - i16 - Oct 1 2015 - p69(1) [51-500]
    PW - v262 - i31 - August 3 2015 - p34(1) [51-500]
Katzir, Shaul - *Traditions and Transformations in the History of Quantum Physics*
    Isis - v106 - i1 - March 2015 - p214(2) [501+]
Katznelson, Ira - *Fear Itself: The New Deal and the Origins of Our Time*
    RAH - v43 - i1 - March 2015 - p1-13 [501+]
Kaube, Jurgen - *Max Weber: Ein Leben zwischen den Epochen*
    CS - v44 - i1 - Jan 2015 - p77-78 [501+]
    HNet - Feb 2015 - pNA [501+]
Kauffman, Connie - *Little Gem: 15 Paper-Pieced Miniature Quilts*
    Bwatch - May 2015 - pNA [501+]
Kauffman, Kenton - *Pulling The Dragon's Tail*
    KR - April 1 2015 - pNA [501+]
Kaufman, Alex - *Time Flies*
    KR - Oct 1 2015 - pNA [501+]
Kaufman, Amie - *Illuminae*
    y BL - v112 - i2 - Sept 15 2015 - p64(1) [51-500]
    y KR - July 15 2015 - pNA [51-500]
    y Magpies - v30 - i5 - Nov 2015 - p40(2) [501+]
    y PW - v262 - i29 - July 20 2015 - p195(1) [51-500]
    y PW - v262 - i49 - Dec 2 2015 - p109(2) [51-500]
    y SLJ - v61 - i6 - June 2015 - p112(2) [51-500]
    y VOYA - v38 - i3 - August 2015 - p79(1) [501+]
These Broken Stars
    y Magpies - v30 - i1 - March 2015 - p40(2) [501+]
This Shattered World (Read by Various readers). Audiobook Review
    y SLJ - v61 - i4 - April 2015 - p65(1) [51-500]
This Shattered World
    y HB Guide - v26 - i1 - Spring 2015 - p112(1) [51-500]
    y Magpies - v30 - i1 - March 2015 - p40(2) [501+]
Kaufman, Asher - *Contested Frontiers in the Syria-Lebanon-Israel Region: Cartography, Sovereignty, and Conflict*
    AHR - v120 - i3 - June 2015 - p1146-1147 [501+]
Kaufman, Gayle - *Superdads: How Fathers Balance Work and Family in the 21st Century*
    CS - v44 - i2 - March 2015 - p222-223 [501+]
Kaufman, Peter - *Skull in the Ashes: Murder, a Gold Rush Manhunt, and the Birth of Circumstantial Evidence in America*
    Historian - v77 - i3 - Fall 2015 - p562(2) [501+]
Kaufman, Peter Iver - *Religion Around Shakespeare*
    JR - v95 - i2 - April 2015 - p292(3) [501+]
    CH - v84 - i3 - Sept 2015 - p669(1) [501+]
Kaufman, Ruth - *At His Command: Historical Romance Version*
    PW - v262 - i13 - March 30 2015 - p62(2) [51-500]
Follow Your Heart
    PW - v262 - i29 - July 20 2015 - p177(1) [51-500]
Kaufman, Sarah L. - *The Art of Grace: On Moving Well through Life*
    BL - v112 - i4 - Oct 15 2015 - p6(1) [51-500]
    KR - Sept 1 2015 - pNA [501+]
    NYTBR - Dec 20 2015 - p10(L) [501+]
Kaufman, Scott Barry - *Wired to Create: Unraveling the Mysteries of the Creative Mind*
    KR - Sept 15 2015 - pNA [501+]
    PW - v262 - i45 - Nov 9 2015 - p53(1) [501+]
Kaufman, Sharon R. - *Ordinary Medicine: Extraordinary Treatments, Longer Lives, and Where to Draw the Line*
    LJ - v140 - i8 - May 1 2015 - p93(2) [51-500]
    PW - v262 - i17 - April 27 2015 - p63(1) [51-500]

Kaufman, Stuart J. - *Nationalists Passions*
    Dis - v62 - i4 - Fall 2015 - p83(1) [501+]
Kaufmann, Carol - *Polar: A Photicular Book*
    c BL - v112 - i4 - Oct 15 2015 - p40(1) [51-500]
Kaufmann, Dorte - *Anton Friedrich Justus Thibaut (1772-1840): Ein Heidelberger Professor zwischen Wissenschaft und Politik*
    HNet - August 2015 - pNA [501+]
Kaufmann, Eric - *Whither the Child?: Causes and Consequences of Low Fertility*
    CS - v44 - i2 - March 2015 - p223-225 [501+]
Kaufmann, Matthias - *A Companion to Luis de Molina*
    Ren Q - v68 - i1 - Spring 2015 - p328-329 [501+]
Kaufmann, Walter - *Nietzsche: Philosopher, Psychologist, Antichrist*
    HT - v65 - i10 - Oct 2015 - p56(2) [501+]
Kaul, Aashish - *The Queen's Play*
    RVBW - June 2015 - pNA [501+]
Kaul, Chandrika - *Communications, Media and the Imperial Experience: Britain and India in the Twentieth Century*
    HNet - June 2015 - pNA [501+]
Kauntze, Mark - *Authority and Imitation: A Study of the Cosmographia of Bernard Silvestris*
    Med R - August 2015 - pNA [501+]
Kaur, Inderjit - *The Oxford Handbook of the Economics of the Pacific Rim*
    Pac A - v88 - i1 - March 2015 - p145 [501+]
Kaushik, Bhavya - *The Bullied Anthology: Stories of Success*
    KR - Sept 1 2015 - pNA [501+]
Kavacs, Ed - *The Russian Bride*
    PW - v262 - i5 - Feb 2 2015 - p36(1) [51-500]
Kavanagh, Emma - *After We Fall*
    PW - v262 - i15 - April 13 2015 - p60(1) [51-500]
Kavanagh, Marianne - *Don't Get Me Wrong*
    BL - v111 - i21 - July 1 2015 - p30(1) [51-500]
Kavanaugh, Dorothy - *Feeling Unloved? Girls Dealing with Feelings*
    y VOYA - v37 - i6 - Feb 2015 - p89(2) [51-500]
Hassled Girl? Girls Dealing with Feelings
    y VOYA - v37 - i6 - Feb 2015 - p89(2) [51-500]
Shamans, Witch Doctors, Wizards, Sorcerers, and Alchemists
    y CH Bwatch - April 2015 - pNA [501+]
Kaveney, Roz - *Tiny Pieces of Skull: A Lesson in Manners*
    TLS - i5860 - July 24 2015 - p19(1) [501+]
Kaveny, M. Cathleen - *Law's Virtues: Fostering Autonomy and Solidarity in American Society*
    Theol St - v76 - i3 - Sept 2015 - p622(2) [501+]
Kawakami, Akane - *Photobiography: Photographic Self-Writing in Proust, Guibert, Ernaux, Mace*
    MLR - v110 - i2 - April 2015 - p550-551 [501+]
Kawakami, Ryo - *Attack on Titan: The Harsh Mistress of the City, Part 1 (Illus. by Murata, Range)*
    y CH Bwatch - Sept 2015 - pNA [501+]
Kawamori, Shoji - *Aquarion Evol (Illus. by Aogiri)*
    y SLJ - v61 - i7 - July 2015 - p100(1) [51-500]
Kawano, Satsuki - *Capturing Contemporary Japan: Differentiation and Uncertainty*
    TLS - i5875 - Nov 6 2015 - p28(2) [501+]
Kawasaki, Guy - *APE: Author, Publisher, Entrepreneur - How To Publish a Book*
    LJ - v140 - i11 - June 15 2015 - p46(1) [51-500]
The Art of the Start 2.0: The Time-Tested, Battle-Hardened Guide for Anyone Starting Anything
    LJ - v140 - i5 - March 15 2015 - p114(3) [501+]
Kawashima, Yasuhide - *The Tokyo Rose Case: Treason on Trial, by Aiko Takeuchi-Demirci*
    PHR - v84 - i3 - August 2015 - p388(2) [501+]
Kay, Alex J. - *Nazi Policy on the Eastern Front, 1941: Total War, Genocide, and Radicalization*
    Slav R - v74 - i2 - Summer 2015 - p408-409 [501+]
Kay, Emma - *Dining with the Georgians: A Delicious History*
    TLS - i5860 - July 24 2015 - p3(2) [501+]
Kay, Jackie - *Red Dust Road*
    TimHES - i2211 - July 9 2015 - p45(1) [501+]
Kay, Jim - *The Great War*
    c KR - Jan 1 2015 - pNA [501+]
Kay, John - *Other People's Money: The Real Business of Fame*
    Econ - v416 - i8952 - August 22 2015 - p69(US) [501+]
    KR - August 1 2015 - pNA [501+]
    LJ - v140 - i14 - Sept 1 2015 - p114(1) [51-500]
Other People's Money: The Real Business of Finance
    BL - v112 - i1 - Sept 1 2015 - p21(1) [51-500]
    Fortune - v172 - i5 - Oct 1 2015 - p24(1) [501+]
    NS - v144 - i5290 - Nov 27 2015 - p48(2) [501+]
    NYTBR - Oct 11 2015 - p14(L) [501+]

Kay, Michael F. - *The Feel Rich Project: Reinventing Your Understanding of True Wealth to Find True Happiness*
    PW - v262 - i51 - Dec 14 2015 - p30(3) [501+]
Kay, Philip - *Rome's Economic Revolution*
    TLS - i5832 - Jan 9 2015 - p24(1) [501+]
Kay, Richard - *The Glorious Revolution and the Continuity Law*
    Lon R Bks - v37 - i18 - Sept 24 2015 - p19(2) [501+]
Kaye, Harvey J. - *The Fight for the Four Freedoms: What Made FDR and the Greatest Generation Truly Great*
    Pres St Q - v45 - i4 - Dec 2015 - p817(2) [501+]
Kaye, Jenni - *Mommy Is a Worrywart (Illus. by Kaye, Jenni)*
    c CH Bwatch - August 2015 - pNA [51-500]
Kaye, Joel - *A History of Balance, 1250-1375: The Emergence of a New Model of Equilibrium and Its Impact on Medieval Thought*
    Ren Q - v68 - i3 - Fall 2015 - p1022-1024 [501+]
Kaye, Laura - *Hard to Let Go*
    KR - May 15 2015 - pNA [51-500]
Kaylor, Noel Harold, Jr. - *A Companion to Boethius in the Middle Ages*
    JEGP - v114 - i1 - Jan 2015 - p134(4) [501+]
Kaymer, Lin - *Who Is Mackie Spence?*
    y HB Guide - v26 - i2 - Fall 2015 - p126(1) [51-500]
Kaysen, Susanna - *Cambridge*
    NYTBR - March 8 2015 - p32(L) [501+]
Kayser, Eric - *The Larousse Book of Bread: 80 Recipes to Make at Home*
    LJ - v140 - i8 - May 1 2015 - p95(1) [51-500]
    TLS - i5850 - May 15 2015 - p26(1) [501+]
Kazanjian, Howard - *The Death Row All Stars: A Story of Baseball, Corruption, and Murder*
    Roundup M - v22 - i4 - April 2015 - p30(1) [501+]
    Roundup M - v22 - i6 - August 2015 - p38(1) [501+]
Kazden, J. Joseph - *Totls*
    KR - Nov 1 2015 - pNA [501+]
Kazemi, Elham - *Intentional Talk: How to Structure and Lead Productive Mathematical Discussions*
    TC Math - v21 - i8 - April 2015 - p509(1) [501+]
Kazemzadeh, Firuz - *Russia and Britain in Persia: Imperial Ambitions in Qajar Iran*
    Historian - v77 - i3 - Fall 2015 - p539(2) [501+]
Kazerooni, Abbas - *On Two Feet and Wings (Read by Kazerooni, Abbas). Audiobook Review*
    SLJ - v61 - i2 - Feb 2015 - p52(1) [51-500]
Kazin, Michael - *American Dreamers: How the Left Changed a Nation*
    RAH - v43 - i2 - June 2015 - p281-287 [501+]
Kdrkkdinen, Veli-Matti - *Christ and Reconciliation*
    IBMR - v39 - i2 - April 2015 - p100(1) [501+]
Keane, Ann - *Let's Catch That Rainbow (Illus. by Keane, Ann)*
    c Magpies - v30 - i5 - Nov 2015 - pS6(1) [501+]
Keane, Claire - *Once upon a Cloud (Illus. by Keane, Claire)*
    c HB Guide - v26 - i2 - Fall 2015 - p13(1) [51-500]
    PW - v262 - i2 - Jan 12 2015 - p56(1) [51-500]
    c SLJ - v61 - i2 - Feb 2015 - p70(1) [51-500]
Keane, Dave - *Monster School: The Spooky Sleepover*
    c HB Guide - v26 - i1 - Spring 2015 - p54(1) [51-500]
Keane, Marc Peter - *Moss: Stories from the Edge of Nature*
    SPBW - Oct 2015 - pNA [51-500]
Kearby, Mike - *Texas Tales Illustrated: The Trail Drives (Illus. by White, Mack)*
    c Roundup M - v22 - i6 - August 2015 - p25(1) [501+]
Kearney, Chris - *The Monkey's Mask: Identity, Memory, Narrative and Voice*
    TimHES - i2211 - July 9 2015 - p47(1) [501+]
Kearney, Eileen - *Irish Women Dramatists, 1908-2001*
    TLS - i5853 - June 5 2015 - p11(1) [501+]
Kearney, Jill - *The Dog Thief*
    KR - Jan 1 2015 - pNA [501+]
Kearney, Richard - *Reimagining the Sacred: Richard Kearney Debates God*
    PW - v262 - i41 - Oct 12 2015 - p64(1) [51-500]
Kearns, Gerry - *Spatial Justice and the Irish Crisis*
    TimHES - i2196 - March 26 2015 - p51(1) [501+]
Kearns, J.M. - *The Deep End*
    PW - v262 - i12 - March 23 2015 - p45(2) [51-500]
Kearns, Rosalie Morales - *The Female Complaint: Tales of Unruly Women*
    RVBW - Oct 2015 - pNA [51-500]
    KR - Sept 1 2015 - pNA [51-500]

Kearsley, Susanna - *A Desperate Fortune*
    BL - v111 - i13 - March 1 2015 - p28(1) [51-500]
    LJ - v140 - i2 - Feb 1 2015 - p73(1) [51-500]

Keates, Jonathan - *William III and Mary II: Partners in Revolution*
    TLS - i5859 - July 17 2015 - p23(1) [501+]

Keating, Ana Louise - *Transformation Now! Toward a Post-Oppositional Politics of Change*
    Wom R Bks - v32 - i2 - March-April 2015 - p29(2) [501+]

Keating, Celine - *Play for Me*
    BL - v111 - i15 - April 1 2015 - p26(2) [51-500]

Keating, Jess - *How to Outfox Your Friends When You Don't Have a Clue*
    c KR - August 15 2015 - pNA [51-500]
Pink Is for Blobfish: Discovering the World's Perfectly Pink Animals (Illus. by DeGrand, David)
    c BL - v112 - i7 - Dec 1 2015 - p51(1) [51-500]
    c SLJ - v61 - i12 - Dec 2015 - p136(1) [51-500]
    c KR - Nov 15 2015 - pNA [51-500]
    c PW - v262 - i46 - Nov 16 2015 - p75(1) [501+]

Keating, Kevin P. - *The Captive Condition*
    KR - May 1 2015 - pNA [501+]
    LJ - v140 - i8 - May 1 2015 - p62(1) [51-500]
    PW - v262 - i21 - May 25 2015 - p32(1) [51-500]

Keatinge, Joe - *Shutter, vol 1: Wanderlost (Illus. by Duca, Leila Del)*
    BL - v111 - i13 - March 1 2015 - p36(2) [51-500]

Keaton, David James - *The Last Projector*
    KR - August 15 2015 - pNA [501+]
Stealing Propeller Hats from the Dead
    PW - v262 - i35 - August 31 2015 - p65(2) [51-500]

Keaton, Trica Danielle - *Black France/France Noire: The History and Politics of Blackness*
    JMH - v87 - i1 - March 2015 - p194(3) [501+]

Keats, Ezra Jack - *The Snowy Day (Illus. by Keats, Ezra Jack)*
    c BL - v112 - i4 - Oct 15 2015 - p53(1) [51-500]

Kebbi, Yann - *Americanine: A Haute Dog in New York (Illus. by Kebbi, Yann)*
    c KR - May 1 2015 - pNA [51-500]
    c SLJ - v61 - i10 - Oct 2015 - p78(1) [51-500]

Keck, Edward - *Island Park*
    SPBW - Jan 2015 - pNA [51-500]

Keck, Leander - *Christ's First Theologian: The Shape of Paul's Thought*
    CC - v132 - i21 - Oct 14 2015 - p32(2) [501+]

Kee, Joan - *Contemporary Korean Art: Tansaekhwa and the Urgency of Method*
    JAS - v74 - i1 - Feb 2015 - p225-226 [501+]

Keeble, Neil Howard - *The Complete Works of John Milton, vol. 6: Vernacular Regicide and Republican Writings*
    TLS - i5831 - Jan 2 2015 - p20(1) [501+]

Keedus, Liisi - *The Crisis of German Historicism*
    HT - v65 - i10 - Oct 2015 - p56(2) [501+]

Keefe, Susan - *Explanationes symboli aevi carolini*
    Med R - May 2015 - pNA [501+]

Keegan, William - *Mr. Osborne's Economic Experiment: Austerity 1945-51 and 2010*
    NS - v144 - i5260 - May 1 2015 - p50(1) [501+]

Keelan, Claudia - *Truth of My Songs: Poems of the Trobairitz*
    LJ - v140 - i2 - Feb 1 2015 - p87(1) [51-500]

Keeley, D.A. - *Fallen Sparrow*
    KR - April 1 2015 - pNA [501+]

Keeley, Page - *Science Formative Assessment, vol. 2*
    Sci & Ch - v52 - i7 - March 2015 - p98 [501+]
    Sci Teach - v82 - i3 - March 2015 - p71 [51-500]
Uncovering Student Ideas in Physical Science: 39 New Electricity and Magnetism Formative Assessment Probes
    Sci & Ch - v52 - i9 - Summer 2015 - p28 [51-500]

Keen, Andrew - *The Internet Is Not the Answer*
    BL - v111 - i13 - March 1 2015 - p7(1) [51-500]
    CSM - Jan 14 2015 - pNA [501+]
    Econ - v414 - i8921 - Jan 17 2015 - p81(US) [501+]
    LJ - v140 - i2 - Feb 1 2015 - p105(1) [51-500]
    Nature - v518 - i7539 - Feb 19 2015 - p299(1) [51-500]
    New Sci - v225 - i3008 - Feb 14 2015 - p46(2) [501+]
    NS - v144 - i5253 - March 13 2015 - p42(3) [501+]

Keen, Caroline - *Princely India and the British: Political Development and the Operation of Empire*
    VS - v57 - i2 - Wntr 2015 - p294(3) [501+]

Keen, Mary - *Paradise and Plenty: A Rothschild Family Garden*
    PW - v262 - i52 - Dec 21 2015 - p149(1) [51-500]

Keen, Paul - *Literature, Commerce, and the Spectacle of Modernity, 1750a-1800*
    MP - v112 - i4 - May 2015 - pE322(5) [501+]

Keen, Sam - *Prodigal Father Wayward Son: A Roadmap to Reconciliation*
    RVBW - June 2015 - pNA [51-500]

Keenan-Bolger, Andrew - *Jack & Louisa: Act 1 (Illus. by Wetherhead, Kate)*
    y BL - v111 - i9-10 - Jan 1 2015 - p101(1) [51-500]
    y CCB-B - v68 - i7 - March 2015 - p358(1) [51-500]
    y HB Guide - v26 - i2 - Fall 2015 - p88(1) [51-500]
Jack & Louisa: Act 2
    y KR - Nov 15 2015 - pNA [51-500]
    y SLJ - v61 - i12 - Dec 2015 - p102(1) [51-500]

Keenan, Edward - *The Art of the Possible: An Everyday Guide to Politics (Illus. by McLaughlin, Julie)*
    c BL - v112 - i3 - Oct 1 2015 - p37(1) [51-500]
    c KR - July 15 2015 - pNA [51-500]
    c PW - v262 - i34 - August 24 2015 - p82(1) [501+]
    c SLJ - v61 - i9 - Sept 2015 - p187(2) [51-500]

Keenan, Sheila - *Castle*
    c HB Guide - v26 - i2 - Fall 2015 - p216(1) [51-500]
Eye: How It Works
    c HB Guide - v26 - i2 - Fall 2015 - p184(1) [51-500]

Keene, Brian - *The Castaways*
    c LJ - v140 - i7 - April 15 2015 - p126(1) [501+]

Keene, Carolyn - *The Magician's Secret*
    y HB Guide - v26 - i2 - Fall 2015 - p88(1) [51-500]
Nancy Drew Diaries (Read by Marie, Jorjeana). Audiobook Review
    y CH Bwatch - June 2015 - pNA [51-500]
Nancy Drew: Identity Revealed
    c Teach Lib - v42 - i3 - Feb 2015 - p55(1) [51-500]
Nancy Drew: Identity Theft
    c Teach Lib - v42 - i3 - Feb 2015 - p55(1) [51-500]
Nancy Drew: Secret Identity
    c Teach Lib - v42 - i3 - Feb 2015 - p55(1) [51-500]
Nancy Drew: The Clue at Black Creek Farm (Read by Marie, Jorjeana). Audiobook Review
    c CH Bwatch - July 2015 - pNA [51-500]
The Phantom of Nantucket
    c HB Guide - v26 - i1 - Spring 2015 - p82(1) [51-500]
Secret at Mystic Lake
    c HB Guide - v26 - i1 - Spring 2015 - p82(1) [51-500]

Keene, John - *Counternarratives: Stories and Novellas*
    HM - v330 - i1980 - May 2015 - p79(3) [501+]
    KR - April 1 2015 - pNA [51-500]
    PW - v262 - i13 - March 30 2015 - p46(1) [51-500]
    RVBW - Nov 2015 - pNA [51-500]
    Nation - v301 - i16 - Oct 19 2015 - p27(3) [501+]

Keene, Melanie - *Science in Wonderland: The Scientific Fairy Tales of Victorian Britain*
    New Sci - v226 - i3016 - April 11 2015 - p43(1) [501+]
    TLS - i5866 - Sept 4 2015 - p24(1) [501+]

Keene, Nancy - *Your Child in the Hospital: A Practical Guide for Parents. 3d ed.*
    LJ - v140 - i9 - May 15 2015 - p66(2) [501+]

Keener, Peggy - *Potato in a Rice Bowl*
    KR - July 15 2015 - pNA [501+]

Keeney, Bradford - *Way of the Bushman as Told by the Tribal Elders: Spiritual Teachings and Practices of the Kalahari Jul'hoansi*
    Bwatch - August 2015 - pNA [51-500]

Keeney, L. Douglas - *The Eleventh Hour: How Great Britain, the Soviet Union, and the U.S. Brokered an Unlikely Deal That Won the War*
    BL - v111 - i13 - March 1 2015 - p16(1) [51-500]

Keffer, David J. - *A Bestiary of East Tennessee: Illustrated in Felt*
    SPBW - Nov 2015 - pNA [51-500]

Kegan, Stephanie - *Golden State*
    BL - v111 - i11 - Feb 1 2015 - p22(1) [51-500]

Kehlmann, Daniel - *F*
    Lon R Bks - v37 - i2 - Jan 22 2015 - p31(4) [501+]
    NS - v144 - i5246 - Jan 23 2015 - p42(1) [51-500]
    NYTBR - Sept 13 2015 - p32(L) [501+]

Kehoe, Alice beck - *A Passion for the True and Just: Felix and Lucy Kramer Cohen and the Indian New Deal*
    WHQ - v46 - i1 - Spring 2015 - p106-107 [501+]

Kehoe, Genevieve M. - *Presidents and Terminal Logic Behavior: Term Limits and Executive Action in the United States, Brazil and Argentina*
    Pres St Q - v45 - i2 - June 2015 - p412(3) [501+]

Kehret, Peg - *Dangerous Deception*
    c HB Guide - v26 - i1 - Spring 2015 - p82(1) [51-500]

Keighery, Chrissie - *Whisper*
    y SLJ - v61 - i9 - Sept 2015 - p158(2) [51-500]

Keil, Soeren - *The Foreign Policies of Post-Yugoslav States: From Yugoslavia to Europe*
    E-A St - v67 - i8 - Oct 2015 - p1341(2) [501+]

Keilson, Hans - *Tagebuch 1944: Und 46 Sonette*
    TLS - i5851 - May 22 2015 - p27(1) [51-500]

Keire, Anita E. - *Resurrection Dialogues with Skeptics and Believers*
    PW - v262 - i15 - April 13 2015 - p76(1) [51-500]

Keiter, Robert B. - *To Conserve Unimpaired: The Evolution of the National Park Idea*
    QRB - v90 - i1 - March 2015 - p87(2) [501+]

Keith, Barbara Benson - *I Love You to Pieces!*
    c CH Bwatch - Jan 2015 - pNA [51-500]

Keith, Charles - *Catholic Vietnam: A Church from Empire to Nation*
    CH - v84 - i1 - March 2015 - p263(3) [501+]

Keith, Chris - *Jesus against the Scribal Elite: The Origins of the Conflict*
    Theol St - v76 - i2 - June 2015 - p384(1) [501+]

Keith, Joseph - *Unbecoming Americans: Writing Race and Nation from the Shadows of Citizenship, 1945-1960*
    AL - v87 - i2 - June 2015 - p396-398 [501+]

Keith, Michael - *China Constructing Capitalism: Economic Life and Urban Change*
    Pac A - v88 - i2 - June 2015 - p274 [501+]

Keith, Pat - *Chester the Cedar Christmas Tree (Illus. by Houston, Bobbie)*
    c CH Bwatch - Jan 2015 - pNA [51-500]

Kekes, John - *How Should We Live? A Practical Approach to Everyday Morality*
    RM - v68 - i4 - June 2015 - p856(2) [501+]

Kelen, Sarah A. - *Renaissance Retrospections: Tudor Views of the Middle Ages*
    JEGP - v114 - i2 - April 2015 - p303(3) [501+]
    Six Ct J - v46 - i1 - Spring 2015 - p212-213 [501+]

Kelin-Higger, Joni - *Rainbow of Friendship (Illus. by Goldenberg, Eileen)*
    c CH Bwatch - August 2015 - pNA [51-500]

Kell, Brynn - *Deception Island*
    PW - v262 - i48 - Nov 30 2015 - p44(1) [51-500]

Kell, Carl L. - *The Exiled Generations: Legacies of the Southern Baptist Convention Holy Wars*
    RVBW - June 2015 - pNA [51-500]
    Bwatch - July 2015 - pNA [51-500]

Kellenbach, Katharina von - *The Mark of Cain: Guilt and Denial in the Post-War Lives of Nazi Perpetrator*
    TT - v72 - i1 - April 2015 - p125-126 [501+]

Keller, Catherine - *Cloud of the Impossible: Negative Theology and Planetary Entanglement*
    CC - v132 - i15 - July 22 2015 - p35(3) [501+]

Keller, Daniel - *Neighbours and Successors of Rome: Traditions of Glass Production and Use in Europe and the Middle East in the Later First Millennium AD*
    Med R - May 2015 - pNA [501+]

Keller, David H. - *The Devil and the Doctor*
    MFSF - v128 - i1-2 - Jan-Feb 2015 - p258(1) [501+]

Keller, Elinoar - *Just Like I Wanted (Illus. by Gordon-Noy, Aya)*
    c KR - June 1 2015 - pNA [51-500]
    c SLJ - v61 - i9 - Sept 2015 - p123(2) [51-500]

Keller, Julia - *Last Ragged Breath*
    BL - v111 - i19-20 - June 1 2015 - p55(1) [51-500]
    KR - June 15 2015 - pNA [51-500]
    PW - v262 - i22 - June 1 2015 - p41(1) [51-500]

Keller, Peter - *"Die Wehrmacht der Deutschen Republik ist die Reichswehr": Die Deutsche Armee 1918-1921*
    HNet - March 2015 - pNA [501+]

Keller, Philip - *Advanced Math for Young Students: A First Course in Algebra*
    SPBW - Oct 2015 - pNA [501+]

Keller, Reuben P. - *Invasive Species in a Globalized World: Ecological, Social and Legal Perspectives on Policy*
    BioSci - v65 - i6 - June 2015 - p623(2) [501+]

Keller, Sarah - *Maya Deren: Incomplete Control*
    FQ - v69 - i1 - Fall 2015 - p104(2) [501+]

Keller, Timothy - *Prayer: Experiencing Awe and Intimacy with God*
    Ch Today - v59 - i1 - Jan-Feb 2015 - p61(3) [501+]
Preaching: Communicating Faith in an Age of Skepticism
    CC - v132 - i19 - Sept 16 2015 - p30(4) [501+]

Kellerman, Faye - *Murder 101*
    RVBW - April 2015 - pNA [51-500]

The Theory of Death
    BL - v112 - i4 - Oct 15 2015 - p24(1) [51-500]
    KR - Sept 1 2015 - pNA [501+]
    NYTBR - Nov 15 2015 - p29(L) [501+]
    PW - v262 - i33 - August 17 2015 - p52(1) [51-500]

Kellerman, Henry - *Anatomy of Delusion*
    SPBW - May 2015 - pNA [51-500]

Kellerman, Jonathan - *The Golem of Paris*
    KR - Sept 1 2015 - pNA [51-500]
    NYTBR - Nov 15 2015 - p29(L) [501+]
    PW - v262 - i38 - Sept 21 2015 - p53(2) [51-500]

Killer
    RVBW - Feb 2015 - pNA [51-500]

Motive
    BL - v111 - i12 - Feb 15 2015 - p38(1) [51-500]
    RVBW - Sept 2015 - pNA [51-500]

The Murderer's Daughter
    BL - v111 - i22 - August 1 2015 - p35(1) [51-500]
    PW - v262 - i26 - June 29 2015 - p45(1) [51-500]

Kelley, Donald R. - *Taking the Measure: The Presidency of George W. Bush*
    JSH - v81 - i1 - Feb 2015 - p250(2) [501+]

Kelley, Frank J. - *The People's Lawyer: The Life and Times of Frank J. Kelley, the Nation's Longest-Serving Attorney General*
    RVBW - Nov 2015 - pNA [501+]

Kelley, Gretchen - *Superheroes Don't Eat Veggie Burgers*
    c KR - Oct 1 2015 - pNA [51-500]
    c SLJ - v61 - i11 - Nov 2015 - p96(1) [51-500]
    c PW - v262 - i42 - Oct 19 2015 - p77(1) [51-500]

Kelley, Jane - *The Book of Dares for Lost Friends*
    c PW - v262 - i18 - May 4 2015 - p119(1) [51-500]
    c KR - April 15 2015 - pNA [51-500]
    c VOYA - v38 - i3 - August 2015 - p63(1) [51-500]

Kelley, Joseph T. - *What Are They Saying About Augustine?*
    Theol St - v76 - i3 - Sept 2015 - p641(2) [501+]

Kelley, K.C. - *Astronauts!*
    c BL - v112 - i1 - Sept 1 2015 - p97(1) [501+]

Kelley, True - *Where Is Mount Rushmore? (Illus. by Hinderliter, John)*
    SLJ - v61 - i3 - March 2015 - p170(1) [51-500]

Kellogg, Danielle L. - *Marathon Fighters and Men of Maple: Ancient Acharnai*
    Class R - v65 - i1 - April 2015 - p172-174 [501+]

Kellough, Janet - *The Burying Ground*
    BL - v111 - i19-20 - June 1 2015 - p48(1) [51-500]
    PW - v262 - i23 - June 8 2015 - p40(2) [51-500]

Kellow, Brian - *Can I Go Now? The Life of Sue Mengers, Hollywood's First Superagent*
    BL - v112 - i1 - Sept 1 2015 - p24(1) [51-500]
    KR - July 1 2015 - pNA [501+]
    LJ - v140 - i13 - August 1 2015 - p97(2) [51-500]
    NYT - August 21 2015 - pC1(L) [501+]
    NYTBR - Sept 13 2015 - p8(L) [501+]

Kells, Claire - *Girl Underwater (Read by Whelan, Julia). Audiobook Review*
    LJ - v140 - i11 - June 15 2015 - p50(2) [51-500]

Girl Underwater
    y KR - Feb 1 2015 - pNA [51-500]
    y PW - v262 - i3 - Jan 19 2015 - p53(1) [51-500]
    y SLJ - v61 - i10 - Oct 2015 - p122(1) [51-500]

Kelly, Anthony J. - *Upward: Faith, Church, and the Ascension of Christ*
    Theol St - v76 - i1 - March 2015 - p184(2) [501+]

Kelly, April - *Valentine's Day*
    KR - Nov 15 2015 - pNA [501+]

Kelly, Barbara L. - *Music and Ultra-Modernism in France: A Fragile Consensus, 1913-1939*
    Notes - v71 - i3 - March 2015 - p509(4) [501+]

Kelly, Carla - *Marco and Devil's Bargain*
    Roundup M - v22 - i6 - August 2015 - p31(1) [501+]

Vegan al Fresco
    Veg J - v34 - i2 - April-June 2015 - p30(1) [51-500]

Kelly, Cathy - *It Started with Paris*
    KR - June 1 2015 - pNA [51-500]

Kelly, Catriona - *St Petersburg: Shadows of the Past*
    AHR - v120 - i1 - Feb 2015 - p183-185 [501+]
    HNet - Feb 2015 - pNA [501+]
    Slav R - v74 - i1 - Spring 2015 - p196-197 [501+]

Kelly, Christopher - *America Invades*
    KR - March 15 2015 - pNA [51-500]
    SPBW - June 2015 - pNA [51-500]

Theodosius II: Rethinking the Roman Empire in Late Antiquity
    Class R - v65 - i1 - April 2015 - p236-238 [501+]
    HER - v130 - i543 - April 2015 - p413(2) [501+]

Kelly, Dasha - *Almost Crimson*
    KR - March 1 2015 - pNA [51-500]

Kelly, David A. - *The Rookie Blue Jay (Illus. by Meyers, Mark)*
    c HB Guide - v26 - i2 - Fall 2015 - p67(1) [51-500]

Kelly, Deborah - *Dinosaur Disco (Illus. by Parton, Daron)*
    c Magpies - v30 - i4 - Sept 2015 - p28(1) [51-500]

Jam for Nana (Illus. by Stewart, Lisa)
    c SLJ - v61 - i2 - Feb 2015 - p71(1) [51-500]

Kelly, Debra - *A History of the French in London: Liberty, Equality, Opportunity*
    HT - v65 - i6 - June 2015 - p60(1) [51-500]
    FS - v69 - i1 - Jan 2015 - p122-122 [501+]
    TLS - i5863 - August 14 2015 - p10(1) [501+]

Kelly, Douglas - *Machaut and the Medieval Apprenticeship Tradition: Truth, Fiction and Poetic Craft*
    Ren Q - v68 - i2 - Summer 2015 - p730-731 [501+]

Kelly, Elaine - *Art outside the Lines: New Perspectives on GDR Art Culture*
    MLR - v110 - i2 - April 2015 - p607-609 [501+]

Kelly, Erika - *I Want You to Want Me*
    BL - v111 - i19-20 - June 1 2015 - p62(1) [51-500]

Kelly, Erin Entrada - *Blackbird Fly*
    c KR - Jan 1 2015 - pNA [51-500]
    c BL - v111 - i11 - Feb 1 2015 - p45(1) [51-500]
    c CCB-B - v68 - i8 - April 2015 - p406(2) [51-500]
    c HB Guide - v26 - i2 - Fall 2015 - p88(1) [51-500]
    c PW - v262 - i49 - Dec 2 2015 - p69(1) [51-500]

The Land of Forgotten Girls
    y KR - Dec 15 2015 - pNA [51-500]
    c SLJ - v61 - i12 - Dec 2015 - p102(1) [51-500]

Kelly, Fanny - *My Captivity: A Pioneer Woman's Story of Her Life among the Sioux*
    Roundup M - v22 - i6 - August 2015 - p38(1) [501+]

Kelly, J.A. - *Willamina Mermaid & the Quest for the Crystal of Light*
    c KR - Oct 15 2015 - pNA [51-500]

Kelly, Jacqueline - *The Curious World of Calpurnia Tate (Read by Ross, Natalie). Audiobook Review*
    c BL - v112 - i3 - Oct 1 2015 - p86(1) [51-500]
    c HB - v91 - i6 - Nov-Dec 2015 - p109(2) [51-500]
    c SLJ - v61 - i10 - Oct 2015 - p52(1) [51-500]

The Curious World of Calpurnia Tate
    c PW - v262 - i18 - May 4 2015 - p121(1) [51-500]
    c BL - v111 - i16 - April 15 2015 - p59(1) [51-500]
    c CCB-B - v69 - i1 - Sept 2015 - p30(2) [51-500]
    c HB - v91 - i4 - July-August 2015 - p135(2) [51-500]
    c KR - April 15 2015 - pNA [51-500]
    c PW - v262 - i49 - Dec 2 2015 - p79(2) [51-500]
    c SLJ - v61 - i3 - March 2015 - p137(2) [51-500]

Kelly, James - *Sport in Ireland, 1600-1840*
    Six Ct J - v46 - i3 - Fall 2015 - p745-747 [501+]

Kelly, Jim - *At Death's Window*
    BL - v111 - i9-10 - Jan 1 2015 - p44(1) [51-500]
    RVBW - Nov 2015 - pNA [501+]

Death on Demand
    BL - v112 - i4 - Oct 15 2015 - p20(1) [51-500]
    KR - Sept 15 2015 - pNA [51-500]
    PW - v262 - i36 - Sept 7 2015 - p46(1) [51-500]

Kelly, Joe - *Bang! Tango (Illus. by Sibar, Michael)*
    y LJ - v140 - i9 - May 15 2015 - p61(3) [501+]

Kelly, John B. - *Fighting the Retreat from Arabia and the Gulf: The Collected Essays and Reviews of J.B. Kelly*
    Nat R - v67 - i1 - Jan 26 2015 - p47 [501+]

The Oil Cringe of the West: The Collected Essays and Reviews of J.B. Kelly
    Nat R - v67 - i1 - Jan 26 2015 - p47 [501+]

Kelly, Katy - *Melonhead and the Later Gator Plan (Illus. by Johnson, Gillian)*
    c HB Guide - v26 - i2 - Fall 2015 - p88(1) [51-500]

Kelly, Lee - *City of Savages*
    y BL - v111 - i11 - Feb 1 2015 - p32(1) [51-500]
    y Teach Lib - v42 - i3 - Feb 2015 - p28(4) [501+]

A Criminal Magic
    PW - v262 - i52 - Dec 21 2015 - p137(1) [51-500]

Kelly, Linda Armstrong - *Deceptions*
    KR - June 15 2015 - pNA [51-500]

Kelly, Margo - *Who R U Really?*
    y HB Guide - v26 - i1 - Spring 2015 - p112(1) [51-500]

Kelly, Mark - *Astrotwins: Project Blastoff*
    c BL - v111 - i11 - Feb 1 2015 - p33(1) [51-500]
    c BL - v111 - i12 - Feb 15 2015 - p84(2) [51-500]
    c HB Guide - v26 - i2 - Fall 2015 - p88(1) [51-500]
    c KR - Jan 1 2015 - pNA [51-500]
    c SLJ - v61 - i3 - March 2015 - p136(2) [51-500]
    c CH Bwatch - July 2015 - pNA [51-500]

Kelly, Mary Anne - *Twillyweed: A Claire Breslinsky Mystery*
    PW - v262 - i30 - July 27 2015 - p44(2) [51-500]

Kelly, Mary Louise - *The Bullet*
    KR - Jan 1 2015 - pNA [51-500]
    PW - v262 - i2 - Jan 12 2015 - p35(1) [51-500]

Kelly, Mary Pat - *Of Irish Blood*
    BL - v111 - i9-10 - Jan 1 2015 - p53(1) [51-500]

Kelly, Matthew - *Quartz and Feldspar: Dartmoor - A British Landscape in Modern Times*
    Spec - v328 - i9746 - June 13 2015 - p41(1) [501+]
    TimHES - i2211 - July 9 2015 - p47(1) [501+]
    TLS - i5876 - Nov 13 2015 - p27(1) [501+]

Kelly, Michael - *Encyclopedia of Aesthetics, 2d ed.*
    TLS - i5844 - April 3 2015 - p10(1) [501+]

The Governor's Wife
    NYTBR - June 7 2015 - p37(L) [501+]

Interpreting the Peace: Peace Operations, Conflict and Language in Bosnia-Herzegovina
    Lang Soc - v44 - i1 - Feb 2015 - p125-126 [501+]

Kelly, Michelle - *Downward Facing Death*
    BL - v112 - i7 - Dec 1 2015 - p27(1) [51-500]
    PW - v262 - i46 - Nov 16 2015 - p57(1) [51-500]

Kelly, Nikki - *Lailah*
    y HB Guide - v26 - i2 - Fall 2015 - p126(1) [51-500]

Kelly, Peter A. - *The Postal History of the Type Sage Issue of France 1876-1900*
    Phil Lit R - v64 - i2 - Spring 2015 - p132(3) [501+]

Kelly, Stephen - *The Language of the Dead: A World War II Mystery*
    BL - v111 - i13 - March 1 2015 - p24(1) [51-500]
    KR - Feb 15 2015 - pNA [51-500]
    LJ - v140 - i8 - May 1 2015 - p103(1) [51-500]
    PW - v262 - i5 - Feb 2 2015 - p35(2) [51-500]

Kelly, Susan Croce - *Father of Route 66: The Story of Cy Avery*
    Roundup M - v22 - i4 - April 2015 - p30(1) [501+]
    Roundup M - v22 - i6 - August 2015 - p38(1) [501+]

Kelly, Suzanne - *Greening Death: Reclaiming Burial Practices and Restoring Our Tie to the Earth*
    BL - v112 - i3 - Oct 1 2015 - p5(1) [51-500]

Kelly, Thomas Forrest - *Capturing Music: The Story of Notation*
    ON - v80 - i2 - August 2015 - p60(1) [501+]

Kelly, Tracey - *Ancient Sumer*
    c Sch Lib - v63 - i3 - Autumn 2015 - p187(2) [51-500]

Kelly, Victoria - *Mrs. Houdini*
    KR - Jan 1 2016 - pNA [51-500]

Kelman, Ari - *Battle Lines: A Graphic History of the Civil War (Illus. by Fetter-Vorm, Jonathan)*
    y LJ - v140 - i9 - May 15 2015 - p61(3) [501+]
    SLJ - v61 - i8 - August 2015 - p115(1) [51-500]

A Misplaced Massacre: Struggling over the Memory of Sand Creek
    Pub Hist - v37 - i1 - Feb 2015 - p123(2) [501+]

Kelman, James - *A Lean Third*
    NS - v144 - i5260 - May 1 2015 - p47(1) [51-500]

Kelman, Jennifer - *The Disappearing Dolphins (Read by Swaim, Michael)*
    c CH Bwatch - August 2015 - pNA [51-500]

Kelman, Nic - *How to Pass as Human*
    PW - v262 - i44 - Nov 2 2015 - p72(1) [51-500]

Kelman, Stephen - *Man on Fire*
    BL - v112 - i7 - Dec 1 2015 - p22(1) [51-500]
    KR - Nov 15 2015 - pNA [51-500]
    LJ - v140 - i20 - Dec 1 2015 - p94(1) [51-500]
    PW - v262 - i42 - Oct 19 2015 - p48(1) [51-500]

Kelsey, Annie - *Pippa Morgan's Diary (Illus. by Larsen, Kate)*
    c BL - v112 - i6 - Nov 15 2015 - p55(1) [51-500]
    c KR - Oct 1 2015 - pNA [51-500]
    c SLJ - v61 - i9 - Sept 2015 - p134(1) [51-500]

Kelsey, Elin - *Wild Ideas: Let Nature Inspire Your Thinking (Illus. by Kim, Soyeon)*
    c BL - v111 - i18 - May 15 2015 - p48(1) [51-500]
    c CH Bwatch - May 2015 - pNA [51-500]
    c HB Guide - v26 - i2 - Fall 2015 - p39(1) [51-500]
    c Res Links - v20 - i5 - June 2015 - p13(2) [51-500]
    c SLJ - v61 - i5 - May 2015 - p86(1) [51-500]

Kelsey, Marie - *Cataloging for School Librarians*
    Sch Lib - v63 - i2 - Summer 2015 - p127(1) [51-500]

Kelsey, Penelope Myrtle - *Reading the Wampum: Essay on Hodinohsoni' Visual Code Epistemological Recovery*
    Am Ind CRJ - v39 - i2 - Spring 2015 - p153-155 [501+]

Kelsey, Robin - *Photography and the Art of Chance*
    Apo - v181 - i631 - May 2015 - p103(1) [51-500]
    PW - v262 - i14 - April 6 2015 - p51(3) [50-500]
Kelsky, Karen - *The Professor Is In: The Essential Guide to Turning Your Ph.D. into a Job*
    BL - v111 - i21 - July 1 2015 - p24(2) [51-500]
    KR - May 1 2015 - pNA [51-500]
    LJ - v140 - i10 - June 1 2015 - p111(1) [51-500]
Kelton, Elmer - *The Wolf and the Buffalo*
    Roundup M - v22 - i3 - Feb 2015 - p13(1) [501+]
Kemmerer, Brigid - *Storm*
    c Sch Lib - v63 - i1 - Spring 2015 - p54(1) [51-500]
Thicker Than Water
    y KR - Nov 15 2015 - pNA [51-500]
    y VOYA - v38 - i5 - Dec 2015 - p71(1) [51-500]
Kemmerer, Lisa - *Eating Earth: Environmental Ethics and Dietary Choice*
    TLS - i5843 - March 27 2015 - p31(1) [501+]
Kemp, Anna - *Rhinos Don't Eat Pancakes (Illus. by Ogilvie, Sara)*
    c BL - v111 - i16 - April 15 2015 - p55(1) [51-500]
    c HB - v91 - i3 - May-June 2015 - p89(2) [51-500]
    c HB Guide - v26 - i2 - Fall 2015 - p39(1) [51-500]
    c KR - March 1 2015 - pNA [51-500]
Kemp, Gene - *The Turbulent Term of Tyke Tiler*
    c Sch Lib - v63 - i2 - Summer 2015 - p73(3) [501+]
Kemp, Martin - *Art in History: 600 BC to 2000 AD*
    Spec - v327 - i9728 - Feb 7 2015 - p44(2) [501+]
Kempe, Margery - *The Book of Margery Kempe*
    TLS - i5855 - June 19 2015 - p22(2) [501+]
Kemper, Bitsy - *Budgeting, Spending, and Saving*
    c HB Guide - v26 - i2 - Fall 2015 - p153(1) [51-500]
    SLJ - v61 - i4 - April 2015 - p76(4) [501+]
Kemper, Steve - *A Splendid Savage: The Restless Life of Frederick Russell Burnham*
    KR - Nov 1 2015 - pNA [501+]
    LJ - v140 - i19 - Nov 15 2015 - p93(1) [51-500]
Kemper, Theodore D. - *Status, Power and Ritual Interaction: A Relational Reading of Durkheim, Goffman, and Collins*
    SF - v94 - i2 - Dec 2015 - pNA [501+]
Kempinski, Bernard - *Model Railroads Go to War*
    Bwatch - Feb 2015 - pNA [51-500]
Kempner, Joanna - *Not Tonight: Migraine and the Politics of Gender and Health*
    MAQ - v29 - i3 - Sept 2015 - pb-8-b-10 [501+]
    Wom R Bks - v32 - i3 - May-June 2015 - p23(3) [501+]
Kempowski, Walter - *Swansong 1945: A Collective Diary of the Last Days of the Third Reich*
    KR - Jan 1 2015 - pNA [501+]
    PW - v262 - i8 - Feb 23 2015 - p68(1) [501+]
Swansong 1945
    CSM - April 23 2015 - pNA [501+]
Kempshall, Chris - *The First World War in Computer Games*
    TLS - i5877 - Nov 20 2015 - p31(1) [501+]
Ken, Ivy - *Closure: The Rush to End Grief and What It Costs Us*
    SF - v93 - i3 - March 2015 - pe80 [501+]
Kenah, Katharine - *The Very Stuffed Turkey (Illus. by Talib, Binny)*
    c KR - May 1 2015 - pNA [51-500]
    c PW - v262 - i34 - August 24 2015 - p80(1) [51-500]
    c SLJ - v61 - i10 - Oct 2015 - p78(1) [51-500]
Kendall, Grace - *I See Reality: Twelve Short Stories about Real Life*
    y KR - Oct 1 2015 - pNA [51-500]
    y SLJ - v61 - i12 - Dec 2015 - p122(1) [51-500]
Kendall, Seth - *The Struggle for Roman Citizenship: Romans, Allies, and the Wars of 91-77 BCE*
    J Mil H - v79 - i3 - July 2015 - p806-807 [501+]
Kendig, Rome - *Falcon*
    LJ - v140 - i6 - April 1 2015 - p66(4) [501+]
Kendrick, Beth - *New Uses for Old Boyfriends*
    BL - v111 - i11 - Feb 1 2015 - p31(1) [51-500]
    LJ - v140 - i2 - Feb 1 2015 - p73(1) [51-500]
Put a Ring on It
    BL - v112 - i2 - Sept 15 2015 - p46(1) [51-500]
    KR - Oct 1 2015 - pNA [51-500]
Kendrick, Patrick - *The Savants*
    KR - Oct 15 2015 - pNA [51-500]
Kendrick, Robert L. - *Singing Jeremiah: Music and Meaning in Holy Week*
    Ren Q - v68 - i3 - Fall 2015 - p1091-1093 [501+]
Keneally, Thomas - *Shame and the Captives*
    BL - v111 - i9-10 - Jan 1 2015 - p54(1) [51-500]
    LJ - v140 - i3 - Feb 15 2015 - p88(2) [51-500]
    NYTBR - April 19 2015 - p19(L) [501+]
Keniston, Ann - *Ghostly Figures: Memory and Belatedness in Postwar American Poetry*
    RVBW - Oct 2015 - pNA [501+]

Kennan, George F. - *The Kennan Diaries*
    JMH - v87 - i3 - Sept 2015 - p715(2) [501+]
    Soc - v52 - i1 - Feb 2015 - p97(5) [501+]
Kennard, Matt - *The Racket: A Rogue Reporter vs. the Masters of the Universe*
    NS - v144 - i5265 - June 5 2015 - p44(2) [501+]
Kenneally, Christine - *The Invisible History of the Human Race: How DNA and History Shape Our Identities and Our Futures*
    NYTBR - Nov 22 2015 - p36(L) [501+]
Kenneally, Miranda - *Breathe, Annie, Breathe*
    y HB Guide - v26 - i1 - Spring 2015 - p112(1) [51-500]
Jesse's Girl
    y KR - May 1 2015 - pNA [51-500]
    SLJ - v61 - i4 - April 2015 - p166(1) [51-500]
    y VOYA - v38 - i2 - June 2015 - p62(1) [51-500]
Kennedy, A.L. - *The Drosten's Curse*
    NS - v144 - i5272 - July 24 2015 - p48(1) [501+]
Kennedy, Anne Vittur - *Ragweed's Farm Dog Handbook (Illus. by Kennedy, Anne Vittur)*
    c CCB-B - v69 - i1 - Sept 2015 - p31(1) [51-500]
    c KR - June 15 2015 - pNA [51-500]
    c PW - v262 - i20 - May 18 2015 - p81(1) [51-500]
    c SLJ - v61 - i12 - Dec 2015 - p91(1) [51-500]
Kennedy, Catriona - *Narratives of War: Military and Civilian Experience in Britain and Ireland, 1793-1815*
    HER - v130 - i542 - Feb 2015 - p123(14) [501+]
Soldiering in Britain and Ireland, 1750-1850: Men of Arms
    HER - v130 - i542 - Feb 2015 - p123(14) [501+]
Kennedy, Cecilia - *Whatever You Wear*
    y SLJ - v61 - i7 - July 2015 - p86(1) [51-500]
Kennedy, Claire - *After Hours*
    y HB Guide - v26 - i2 - Fall 2015 - p126(1) [51-500]
    SLJ - v61 - i4 - April 2015 - p166(1) [51-500]
    y VOYA - v38 - i2 - June 2015 - p62(2) [51-500]
Kennedy, Dane - *The Last Blank Spaces: Exploring Africa and Australia*
    IJAHS - v48 - i1 - Wntr 2015 - p156-157 [501+]
Kennedy, David - *Eat Your Greens: The Surprising Power of Homegrown Leaf Crops*
    Bwatch - Jan 2015 - pNA [501+]
Kennedy, David M. - *The Modern American Military*
    RAH - v43 - i2 - June 2015 - p300-306 [501+]
Kennedy, David O. - *Plants and the Human Brain*
    BioSci - v65 - i1 - Jan 2015 - p104(2) [51-500]
Kennedy, Douglas - *The Blue Hour*
    KR - Dec 1 2015 - pNA [501+]
The Heat of Betrayal
    NS - v144 - i5260 - May 1 2015 - p47(1) [501+]
Kennedy, Eliza - *I Take You (Read by Whelan, Julia). Audiobook Review*
    y BL - v112 - i2 - Sept 15 2015 - p76(2) [51-500]
I Take You
    y BL - v111 - i16 - April 15 2015 - p24(1) [51-500]
    KR - March 15 2015 - pNA [51-500]
    y NYTBR - May 31 2015 - p23(L) [501+]
    PW - v262 - i9 - March 2 2015 - p63(1) [51-500]
Kennedy, Elle - *Claimed*
    PW - v262 - i36 - Sept 7 2015 - p53(1) [51-500]
Kennedy, Gregory M.W. - *Something of a Peasant Paradise?: Comparing Rural Societies in Acadie and the Loudunais, 1604-1755*
    Can Hist R - v96 - i1 - March 2015 - p112(3) [501+]
Kennedy, John Patrick - *Weresisters*
    KR - May 15 2015 - pNA [501+]
Kennedy, Kathleen E. - *The Courtly and Commercial Art of the Wycliffite Bible*
    Med R - May 2015 - pNA [51-500]
    Specu - v90 - i4 - Oct 2015 - p1131-1133 [501+]
Medieval Hackers
    Med R - August 2015 - pNA [501+]
Kennedy, Kelly - *The Emperor's New Uniform*
    c CH Bwatch - July 2015 - pNA [501+]
Kennedy, Pagan - *Inventology: How We Dream Up Things That Change the World*
    KR - Nov 1 2015 - pNA [501+]
    PW - v262 - i46 - Nov 16 2015 - p70(1) [501+]
Kennedy, Rick - *The First American Evangelical: A Short Life of Cotton Mather*
    Ch Today - v59 - i4 - May 2015 - p59(1) [51-500]
    MA - v57 - i3 - Summer 2015 - p57(4) [501+]
Kennedy, Rory - *Last Days in Vietnam*
    Pub Hist - v37 - i3 - August 2015 - p156(3) [501+]
Kennedy, Sarah - *City of Ladies*
    Six Ct J - v46 - i1 - Spring 2015 - p205-207 [501+]
Kennedy, Thomas E. - *Kerrigan in Copenhagen: A Love Story, by Thomas E. Kennedy*
    NYTBR - Feb 1 2015 - p24(L) [501+]

Kennedy, X.J. - *A Hoarse Half-Human Cheer*
    KR - June 1 2015 - pNA [501+]
Kennel, Sarah - *Charles Marville: Photographer of Paris*
    FS - v69 - i1 - Jan 2015 - p132-133 [501+]
Kenner, Julie - *Under My Skin*
    PW - v262 - i32 - August 10 2015 - p44(1) [51-500]
Kenney, Karen Latchana - *Ancient Aztecs*
    c BL - v111 - i15 - April 1 2015 - p59(1) [51-500]
Economics through Infographics (Illus. by Stankiewicz, Steven)
    c BL - v!11 - i9-10 - Jan 1 2015 - p84(1) [501+]
    c HB Guide - v26 - i1 - Spring 2015 - p139(1) [51-500]
Stephen Hawking: Extraordinary Theoretical Physicist
    c HB Guide - v26 - i1 - Spring 2015 - p190(2) [51-500]
Teen Pregnancy
    y HB Guide - v26 - i1 - Spring 2015 - p137(1) [51-500]
US History Through Infographics (Illus. by Westlund, Laura)
    c HB Guide - v26 - i1 - Spring 2015 - p204(1) [51-500]
World Geography through Infographics (Illus. by Stankiewicz, Steven)
    c BL - v111 - i9-10 - Jan 1 2015 - p84(1) [501+]
    c HB Guide - v26 - i1 - Spring 2015 - p199(1) [51-500]
You Have a Pet What?! Sugar Glider
    c BL - v112 - i1 - Sept 1 2015 - p97(1) [51-500]
Kenney, Sean - *Cool Creations in 101 Pieces*
    c HB Guide - v26 - i2 - Fall 2015 - p192(1) [51-500]
Kenny, Nicholas - *The Feel of the City: Experiences of Urban Transformation*
    Can Hist R - v96 - i1 - March 2015 - p124(2) [501+]
Kent, Alan M. - *The Theatre of Cornwall: Space, Place and Performance*
    TimHES - i2194 - March 12 2015 - p49(1) [501+]
Kent, Alison - *The Sweetness of Honey (Read by Ross, Natalie). Audiobook Review*
    LJ - v140 - i3 - Feb 15 2015 - p57(1) [51-500]
Kent, Allegra - *Ballerina Gets Ready (Illus. by Stock, Catherine)*
    c KR - Dec 15 2015 - pNA [51-500]
Kent, Christobel - *The Crooked House*
    LJ - v140 - i16 - Oct 1 2015 - p69(2) [51-500]
    PW - v262 - i44 - Nov 2 2015 - p60(1) [51-500]
    KR - Oct 1 2015 - pNA [51-500]
The Killing Room: A Mystery in Florence
    BL - v111 - i21 - July 1 2015 - p38(1) [51-500]
    NYTBR - August 16 2015 - p29(L) [501+]
    PW - v262 - i23 - June 8 2015 - p37(1) [51-500]
Kent, Claire - *Darker the Release*
    PW - v262 - i36 - Sept 7 2015 - p53(1) [51-500]
Kent, Derek Taylor - *El Perro con Sombrero: A Bilingual Doggy Tale (Illus. by Henry, Jed)*
    c BL - v111 - i18 - May 15 2015 - p57(2) [51-500]
    c HB Guide - v26 - i2 - Fall 2015 - p39(1) [51-500]
    c KR - March 1 2015 - pNA [51-500]
    c SLJ - v61 - i4 - April 2015 - p130(1) [51-500]
Kent, Gabrielle - *Alfie Bloom and the Secrets of Hexbridge Castle*
    Sch Lib - v63 - i4 - Winter 2015 - p229(1) [51-500]
Kent, James - *Testament of Youth*
    Queens Q - v122 - i3 - Fall 2015 - p326(12) [501+]
Kent, Mike - *A Life at the Chalkface: The Memoir of a London Headteacher*
    TES - i5149 - June 5 2015 - p17(1) [501+]
Kent, Neil - *The Sami Peoples of the North: A Social and Cultural History*
    HNet - April 2015 - pNA [501+]
Kent, Susan Kingsley - *Queen Victoria: Gender and Empire*
    TimHES - i2228 - Nov 5 2015 - p47(1) [501+]
Kenworthy, Lane - *Progress for the Poor*
    CS - v44 - i3 - May 2015 - p370-371 [501+]
Social Democratic America
    RAH - v43 - i2 - June 2015 - p281-287 [501+]
Kenyeres, Nick - *Mind-set Adjustments*
    KR - May 15 2015 - pNA [501+]
Kenyon, J. Douglas - *Paradigm Busters: Beyond Science, Lost History, Ancient Wisdom*
    Bwatch - May 2015 - pNA [51-500]
Kenyon, Sherrilyn - *Born of Defiance (Read by Berman, Fred). Audiobook Review*
    BL - v112 - i2 - Sept 15 2015 - p78(1) [51-500]
Instinct
    y HB Guide - v26 - i2 - Fall 2015 - p126(1) [51-500]

Kephart, Beth - *One Thing Stolen*
    BL - v111 - i14 - March 15 2015 - p65(1) [51-500]
    y CCB-B - v68 - i9 - May 2015 - p452(1) [51-500]
    y HB - v91 - i4 - July-August 2015 - p136(1) [51-500]
    y KR - Feb 15 2015 - pNA [51-500]
    y PW - v262 - i8 - Feb 23 2015 - p78(1) [51-500]
    y SLJ - v61 - i3 - March 2015 - p157(1) [51-500]
    y VOYA - v38 - i2 - June 2015 - p63(1) [501+]

Keplinger, Kody - *Lying Out Loud*
    y HB Guide - v26 - i2 - Fall 2015 - p126(1) [51-500]
    y KR - March 1 2015 - pNA [51-500]
    y SLJ - v61 - i4 - April 2015 - p166(2) [51-500]
    y VOYA - v38 - i2 - June 2015 - p63(1) [51-500]

Kepner, Susan Fulop - *A Civilized Woman: M.L. Boonlua Debyasuvarn and the Thai Twentieth Century*
    JAS - v74 - i2 - May 2015 - p519-521 [501+]

Kepnes, Caroline - *Hidden Bodies*
    BL - v112 - i1 - Sept 1 2015 - p47(1) [51-500]
    LJ - v140 - i16 - Oct 1 2015 - p70(2) [51-500]
    PW - v262 - i44 - Nov 2 2015 - p60(1) [501+]

Ker, Ian - *Newman on Vatican II*
    TLS - i5840 - March 6 2015 - p26(1) [501+]

Ker, James - *Elizabethan Seneca: Three Tragedies*
    MLR - v110 - i1 - Jan 2015 - p238-239 [501+]

Kerbs, John J. - *Senior Citizens Behind Bars: Challenges for the Criminal Justice System*
    CS - v44 - i6 - Nov 2015 - p874(1) [501+]

Keret, Etgar - *The Seven Good Years: A Memoir (Read by Karpovsky, Alex). Audiobook Review*
    PW - v262 - i35 - August 31 2015 - p84(1) [51-500]

The Seven Good Years: A Memoir
    CSM - July 13 2015 - pNA [501+]
    KR - April 15 2015 - pNA [501+]
    LJ - v140 - i11 - June 15 2015 - p95(1) [51-500]
    NY - v91 - i27 - Sept 14 2015 - p91 [51-500]
    NYTBR - July 5 2015 - p21(L) [501+]
    PW - v262 - i16 - April 20 2015 - p69(1) [51-500]
    TLS - i5866 - Sept 4 2015 - p27(1) [501+]

Kerick, Mia - *Love Spell*
    KR - July 15 2015 - pNA [501+]
    y VOYA - v38 - i3 - August 2015 - p63(2) [51-500]

The Red Sheet
    y KR - Oct 1 2015 - pNA [51-500]

Kerley, Barbara - *A Home for Mr. Emerson (Illus. by Fotheringham, Edwin)*
    c HB Guide - v26 - i1 - Spring 2015 - p193(1) [51-500]

With a Friend by Your Side
    c HB Guide - v26 - i2 - Fall 2015 - p147(1) [51-500]
    c KR - March 1 2015 - pNA [51-500]
    c SLJ - v61 - i4 - April 2015 - p130(1) [51-500]

Kerman, Judith B. - *The Fantastic in Holocaust Literature and Film: Critical Perspectives*
    SFS - v42 - i2 - July 2015 - p383-385 [501+]

Kermani, Houshang Moradi - *The Water Urn*
    y Bkbird - v53 - i4 - Fall 2015 - p78(1) [501+]

Kermode, Mark - *Silent Running*
    Si & So - v25 - i3 - March 2015 - p106(1) [501+]

Kern, Karen M. - *Imperial Citizen: Marriage and Citizenship in the Ottoman Frontier Provinces of Iraq*
    JWH - v27 - i2 - Summer 2015 - p182(12) [501+]

Kern, Peggy - *Little Peach*
    y BL - v111 - i12 - Feb 15 2015 - p82(1) [51-500]
    y CCB-B - v68 - i8 - April 2015 - p407(1) [51-500]
    y HB Guide - v26 - i2 - Fall 2015 - p126(1) [51-500]
    y KR - Feb 15 2015 - pNA [51-500]
    y VOYA - v37 - i6 - Feb 2015 - p59(1) [51-500]

Kern, Ronni - *Wondering Boy*
    KR - Dec 1 2015 - pNA [501+]

Kerner, Susan - *Mama's Right Here (Illus. by Corke, Estelle)*
    c HB Guide - v26 - i2 - Fall 2015 - p39(1) [51-500]

Kerns, Brian - *Gregory the Great, Moral Reflections on the Book of Job, vol. 1: Preface and Books 1-5*
    Med R - August 2015 - pNA [51-500]

Kerr, Esme - *The Girl with the Glass Bird*
    c BL - v111 - i11 - Feb 1 2015 - p51(1) [51-500]
    c CCB-B - v68 - i8 - April 2015 - p407(2) [51-500]
    c CH Bwatch - May 2015 - pNA [501+]
    c HB Guide - v26 - i2 - Fall 2015 - p89(1) [51-500]
    c NYTBR - May 10 2015 - p25(L) [501+]
    c PW - v262 - i4 - Jan 26 2015 - p169(1) [51-500]

Kerr, Greg - *Dream Cities: Utopia and Prose by Poets in Nineteenth-Century France*
    MLR - v110 - i3 - July 2015 - p870-871 [501+]

Kerr, Jeannette - *Before Sliced Bread*
    KR - Jan 1 2016 - pNA [501+]

Kerr, Judith - *The Crocodile Under the Bed (Illus. by Kerr, Judith)*
    c HB - v91 - i6 - Nov-Dec 2015 - p69(2) [51-500]

Judith Kerr's Creatures (Illus. by Kerr, Judith)
    y BL - v112 - i5 - Nov 1 2015 - p48(1) [51-500]

Kerr, M.E. - *Edge: Collected Stories*
    y BL - v112 - i4 - Oct 15 2015 - p45(1) [51-500]
    y KR - August 1 2015 - pNA [51-500]
    y SLJ - v61 - i8 - August 2015 - p105(1) [51-500]

Kerr, Margee - *Scream: Chilling Advebture in the Science of Fear*
    KR - July 15 2015 - pNA [501+]

Scream: Chilling Adventures in the Science of Fear
    LJ - v140 - i13 - August 1 2015 - p114(1) [51-500]
    PW - v262 - i33 - August 17 2015 - p63(1) [51-500]

Kerr, Meera Patricia - *Big Yoga for Less Stress*
    RVBW - August 2015 - pNA [51-500]

Kerr, Philip - *The Lady from Zagreb (Read by Lee, John). Audiobook Review*
    PW - v262 - i21 - May 25 2015 - p53(1) [51-500]

The Lady from Zagreb
    BL - v111 - i13 - March 1 2015 - p24(1) [51-500]
    KR - Feb 1 2015 - pNA [51-500]
    NYTBR - April 5 2015 - p29(L) [51-500]
    PW - v262 - i8 - Feb 23 2015 - p51(2) [51-500]

The Winter Horses
    c Sch Lib - v63 - i1 - Spring 2015 - p54(1) [51-500]

Kerr-Ritchie, Jeffrey R. - *Freedom's Seekers: Essays on Comparative Emancipation*
    AHR - v120 - i3 - June 2015 - p970-971 [501+]
    JAH - v101 - i4 - March 2015 - p1229-1230 [501+]

Kerrin, Jessica Scott - *The Missing Dog Is Spotted*
    c BL - v111 - i18 - May 15 2015 - p56(1) [51-500]
    c HB Guide - v26 - i2 - Fall 2015 - p89(1) [51-500]
    c Nat Post - v17 - i107 - March 7 2015 - pWP5(1) [501+]
    c Res Links - v21 - i1 - Oct 2015 - p15(1) [51-500]
    c SLJ - v61 - i6 - June 2015 - p108(2) [51-500]

Kersey, Geoff - *Painting Successful Watercolours from Photographs*
    LJ - v140 - i5 - March 15 2015 - p106(1) [51-500]

Kershaw, Alex - *Avenue of Spies: A True Story of Terror, Espionage, and One American Family's Heroic Resistance in Nazi-Occupied Paris*
    BL - v111 - i21 - July 1 2015 - p18(1) [51-500]
    BooChiTr - August 22 2015 - p14(1) [501+]
    KR - June 1 2015 - pNA [51-500]
    LJ - v140 - i10 - June 1 2015 - p112(2) [51-500]
    NYTBR - August 30 2015 - p30(L) [501+]

Kershaw, Anne Louise - *Essential Articles 2015: Understanding Our World: Articles, Opinions, Arguments, Personal Accounts, Opposing Viewpoints*
    y Sch Lib - v63 - i1 - Spring 2015 - p61(1) [51-500]

Kershaw, Ian - *To Hell and Back: Europe 1914-1949*
    KR - Sept 1 2015 - pNA [51-500]
    LJ - v140 - i17 - Oct 15 2015 - p100(2) [51-500]
    NS - v144 - i5282 - Oct 2 2015 - p58(4) [501+]
    NYTBR - Nov 29 2015 - p10(L) [501+]
    PW - v262 - i33 - August 17 2015 - p59(2) [51-500]
    Spec - v329 - i9760 - Sept 19 2015 - p49(1) [501+]
    TimHES - i2221 - Sept 17 2015 - p49(1) [501+]

Kershaw, Robert - *24 Hours at Waterloo: 18 June 1815*
    TLS - i5833 - Jan 16 2015 - p12(2) [501+]

Kerten, Alex - *Goodbye Parkinson's, Hello Life! The Gyro-Kinetic Method for Eliminating Symptoms and Reclaiming Your Good Health*
    LJ - v140 - i20 - Dec 1 2015 - p123(1) [51-500]

Kertesz, Imre - *A vegso kocsma*
    WLT - v89 - i3-4 - May-August 2015 - p111(2) [501+]

Kertzer, David I. - *The Pope and Mussolini: The Secret History of Pius XI and the Rise of Fascism in Europe*
    AHR - v120 - i4 - Oct 2015 - p1560-1561 [501+]
    NYRB - v62 - i7 - April 23 2015 - p48(3) [501+]

Kerven, Rosalind - *Viking Myths and Sagas: Retold from Ancient Norse Texts*
    TLS - i5862 - August 7 2015 - p26(1) [501+]

Kerzoncuf, Alain - *Hitchcock Lost and Found: The Forgotten Films*
    LJ - v140 - i8 - May 1 2015 - p76(2) [51-500]
    Si & So - v25 - i5 - May 2015 - p104(1) [51-500]

Kespert, Deborah - *Genius! The Most Astonishing Inventions of All Time*
    c Magpies - v30 - i3 - July 2015 - p24(1) [51-500]
    y PW - v262 - i18 - May 4 2015 - p120(1) [51-500]
    c SLJ - v61 - i6 - June 2015 - p142(2) [51-500]
    c VOYA - v38 - i3 - August 2015 - p87(1) [51-500]

Kessemeier, Gesa - *Ein Feentempel der Mode oder Eine vergessene Familie, ein ausgeloschter Ort: Die Familie Freudenberg und das Modehaus "Herrmann Gerson"*
    GSR - v38 - i1 - Feb 2015 - p177-179 [501+]

Kessler, Deirdre - *Born! A Foal, Five Kittens and Confederation (Illus. by Jones, Brenda)*
    c Res Links - v20 - i3 - Feb 2015 - p12(1) [51-500]

Kessler, Lauren - *Raising the Barre: Big Dreams, False Starts, and My Midlife Quest to Dance the Nutcracker*
    KR - Oct 15 2015 - pNA [51-500]

Kessler, Liz - *Has Anyone Seen Jessica Jenkins?*
    c HB Guide - v26 - i2 - Fall 2015 - p89(1) [51-500]

Poppy the Pirate Dog and the Missing Treasure (Illus. by Phillips, Mike)
    c HB Guide - v26 - i2 - Fall 2015 - p67(1) [51-500]
    c SLJ - v61 - i5 - May 2015 - p95(1) [51-500]

Read Me Like A Book
    y Sch Lib - v63 - i4 - Winter 2015 - p247(1) [51-500]

Kessler, Todd - *The Good Dog (Illus. by Olson, Jennifer Gray)*
    c CH Bwatch - Jan 2015 - pNA [501+]

Kett, Joseph F. - *Merit: The History of a Founding Ideal from the American Revolution to the Twenty-First Century*
    JAH - v102 - i1 - June 2015 - p213-214 [501+]

Kettelhut, Martin - *Listen ... till You Disappear*
    SPBW - July 2015 - pNA [51-500]

Ketteman, Helen - *The Ghosts Go Haunting (Illus. by Record, Adam)*
    c HB Guide - v26 - i1 - Spring 2015 - p34(1) [51-500]

Go to School, Little Monster (Illus. by Leick, Bonnie)
    c SLJ - v61 - i8 - August 2015 - p59(1) [51-500]

Kettle, Martin - *Churchill and the Archangel Fiasco*
    HT - v65 - i1 - Jan 2015 - p56(2) [501+]

Kettler, Todd - *Modern Curriculum for Gifted and Advanced Academic Students*
    RVBW - Nov 2015 - pNA [501+]

Kettmann, Steve - *Baseball Maverick: How Sandy Alderson Revolutionized Baseball and Revived the Mets*
    BL - v111 - i12 - Feb 15 2015 - p20(1) [51-500]
    KR - March 1 2015 - pNA [51-500]
    LJ - v140 - i5 - March 15 2015 - p111(1) [51-500]
    PW - v262 - i12 - March 23 2015 - p60(2) [51-500]

Keupp, Jan - *Konstanz 1414-1418: Eine Stadt und ihr Konzil*
    HNet - Feb 2015 - pNA [501+]

Kevin Ashton - *How to Fly a Horse: The Secret History of Creation, Invention, and Discovery*
    Nature - v518 - i7538 - Feb 12 2015 - p165(1) [51-500]

Kevorkian, Raymond - *The Armenian Genocide: A Complete History*
    HT - v65 - i7 - July 2015 - p56(2) [501+]

Kewes, Paulina - *The Oxford Handbook of Holinshed's Chronicles*
    Six Ct J - v46 - i1 - Spring 2015 - p221-223 [501+]

Key, Harrison Scott - *The World's Largest Man*
    KR - April 1 2015 - pNA [51-500]

Key, Watt - *Terror at Bottle Creek*
    c KR - Oct 15 2015 - pNA [51-500]
    c PW - v262 - i41 - Oct 12 2015 - p70(1) [51-500]
    c SLJ - v61 - i11 - Nov 2015 - p96(1) [51-500]

Keyes, Charles - *Finding Their Voice: Northeastern Villagers and the Thai State*
    JAS - v74 - i3 - August 2015 - p784-785 [501+]

Keyes, Diane E. - *Peas Let Her Be a Princess (Illus. by Mericle, Hannah)*
    c PW - v262 - i51 - Dec 14 2015 - p81(1) [51-500]

Keyes, Marian - *The Woman Who Stole My Life (Read by McMahon, Aoife). Audiobook Review*
    LJ - v140 - i20 - Dec 1 2015 - p59(1) [51-500]

The Woman Who Stole My Life
    BL - v111 - i14 - March 15 2015 - p56(1) [51-500]
    KR - May 1 2015 - pNA [51-500]
    LJ - v140 - i8 - May 1 2015 - p62(2) [51-500]

Keyes, Marian Therese - *Politics and Ideology in Children's Literature*
    Bkbird - v53 - i4 - Fall 2015 - p66(2) [501+]

Keyes, Mary - *Codifying Contract Law: International and Consumer Law Perspectives*
    Law Q Rev - v131 - July 2015 - p499-502 [501+]

Keyes, Raven - *The Healing Light of Angels: Transforming Your Past, Present, and Future with Divine Energy*
    PW - v262 - i6 - Feb 9 2015 - p62(1) [51-500]

Keyi, Sheng - *Death Fugue*
    NYRB - v62 - i18 - Nov 19 2015 - p56(5) [501+]

Keys, Barbara J. - *Reclaiming American Virtue: The Human Rights Revolution of the 1970s*
    AHR - v120 - i1 - Feb 2015 - p296-297 [501+]
    HNet - Jan 2015 - pNA [501+]

Keys, Sheila McCauley - *Our Auntie Rosa: The Family of Rosa Parks Remembers Her Life and Lessons*
    BL - v111 - i9-10 - Jan 1 2015 - p24(1) [51-500]

Keyser, Amber J. - *Sneaker Century: A History of Athletic Shoes*
    y HB Guide - v26 - i2 - Fall 2015 - p199(1) [51-500]
The V-Word: True Stories About First-Time Sex
    y KR - Nov 1 2015 - pNA [51-500]
    y PW - v262 - i47 - Nov 23 2015 - p71(1) [51-500]
The Way Back from Broken
    y BL - v112 - i2 - Sept 15 2015 - p65(1) [51-500]
    y KR - July 15 2015 - pNA [51-500]
    y SLJ - v61 - i9 - Sept 2015 - p168(1) [51-500]
    y VOYA - v38 - i5 - Dec 2015 - p58(1) [51-500]

Keyt, Andrew - *Myths and Mortals: Family Business Leadership and Succession Planning*
    BL - v111 - i21 - July 1 2015 - p24(1) [51-500]

Keyzer, Patrick - *Preventive Detention: Asking the Fundamental Questions*
    Crim J & B - v42 - i2 - Feb 2015 - p237-239 [501+]

Khaal, Abu Bakr - *African Titanics*
    TLS - i5868 - Sept 18 2015 - p28(1) [501+]

Khadra, Yasmina - *The African Equation*
    LJ - v140 - i2 - Feb 1 2015 - p73(1) [51-500]
    TLS - i5844 - April 3 2015 - p21(1) [501+]

Khakpour, Porochista - *The Last Illusion*
    TLS - i5831 - Jan 2 2015 - p18(1) [501+]

Khalaf, Samir - *Lebanon Adrift: From Battleground to Playground*
    IJMES - v47 - i2 - May 2015 - p399-402 [501+]

Khalil, Mohammad Hassan - *Islam and the Fate of Others: The Salvation Question*
    JNES - v74 - i2 - Oct 2015 - p392(3) [501+]

Khan, Ausma Zehanat - *The Language of Secrets*
    KR - Dec 1 2015 - pNA [501+]
    PW - v262 - i48 - Nov 30 2015 - p38(2) [51-500]
The Unquiet Dead. Audiobook Review
    LJ - v140 - i6 - April 1 2015 - p48(1) [51-500]

Khan, Babar Shah - *How and Why God Evolved*
    KR - Dec 1 2015 - pNA [501+]

Khan, Ramla - *Fairy Tale Baking: More Than 50 Enchanting Cakes, Bakes, and Decorations*
    y KR - Nov 15 2015 - pNA [51-500]

Khan, Rehan - *Last of the Tasburai*
    SPBW - Nov 2015 - pNA [51-500]

Khan, Vaseem - *The Unexpected Inheritance of Inspector Chopra: A Baby Ganesh Agency Investigation*
    PW - v262 - i31 - August 3 2015 - p37(1) [51-500]
The Unexpected Inheritance of Inspector Chopra
    BL - v112 - i1 - Sept 1 2015 - p50(1) [51-500]

Khan, Yasmin - *India at War: The Subcontinent and the Second World War*
    NYTBR - Nov 29 2015 - p17(L) [501+]
The Raj at War: A People's History of India's Second World War
    NS - v144 - i5270 - July 10 2015 - p36(3) [51-500]
    Spec - v328 - i9752 - July 25 2015 - p28(2) [501+]

Khanmohamadi, Shirin A. - *In Light of Another's Word: European Ethnography in the Middle Ages*
    AHR - v120 - i2 - April 2015 - p694-695 [501+]

Khanna, Nikki - *Biracial in America: Forming and Performing Racial Identity*
    CS - v44 - i1 - Jan 2015 - p79-80 [501+]

Khanna, Rachel - *Live, Eat, Cook Healthy: Simple, Fresh and Delicious Recipes for Balanced Living*
    SPBW - June 2015 - pNA [501+]

Khanna, Rajan - *Rising Tide*
    BL - v112 - i4 - Oct 15 2015 - p28(1) [51-500]
    PW - v262 - i34 - August 24 2015 - p65(1) [51-500]

Khanna, Vikas - *Rivers: Recipes and Memories of the Himalayan River Valleys*
    Bwatch - May 2015 - pNA [51-500]

Kharbichi, Amal - *Paris*
    KR - Dec 1 2015 - pNA [51-500]

Kharms, Daniil - *The Old Woman*
    NYRB - v62 - i8 - May 7 2015 - p36(3) [501+]

Khater, Akram Fouad - *Embracing the Divine: Passion and Politics in the Christian Middle East*
    CHR - v101 - i2 - Spring 2015 - p374(3) [501+]

Khatib, Lina - *Taking to the Streets: The Transformation of Arab Activism*
    For Aff - v94 - i1 - Jan-Feb 2015 - pNA [501+]

Khatri, Chhote La - *Two-Minute Silence*
    WLT - v89 - i2 - March-April 2015 - p70(1) [501+]

Khayat, David - *The Anticancer Diet: Reduce Cancer Risk through the Foods You Eat*
    PW - v262 - i1 - Jan 5 2015 - p67(1) [51-500]

Khazeni, Arash - *Sky Blue Stone: The Turquoise Trade in World History*
    AHR - v120 - i3 - June 2015 - p965-966 [501+]

Khegay, Nuriya - *More Monster Knits for Little Monsters: 20 Super-Cute Animal-Themed Hat and Mitten Sets to Knit*
    BL - v111 - i13 - March 1 2015 - p14(1) [51-500]

Kheraj, Sean - *Inventing Stanley Park: An Environmental History*
    PHR - v84 - i1 - Feb 2015 - p96(2) [501+]

Kherdian, David - *A Stopinder Anthology*
    Parabola - v40 - i3 - Fall 2015 - p118-121 [501+]

Khilnani, Sunil - *An Indian Social Democracy: Integrating Markets, Democracy and Social Justice, 2 vols.*
    Pac A - v88 - i2 - June 2015 - p337 [501+]

Khlevniuk, Oleg V. - *Stalin: New Biography of a Dictator*
    KR - April 1 2015 - pNA [51-500]
    LJ - v140 - i7 - April 15 2015 - p94(1) [51-500]
    NYRB - v62 - i18 - Nov 19 2015 - p60(3) [501+]
    TLS - i5863 - August 14 2015 - p23(1) [501+]
    Spec - v328 - i9743 - May 23 2015 - p41(2) [501+]
    TimHES - i2205 - May 28 2015 - p51(1) [501+]

Kho, Kian Lam - *Phoenix Claws and Jade Trees: Essential Techniques of Authentic Chinese Cooking*
    PW - v262 - i36 - Sept 7 2015 - p61(1) [51-500]

Khomskii, Daniel I. - *Transition Metal Compounds*
    Phys Today - v68 - i8 - August 2015 - p55-56 [501+]

Khoury, Dina Rizk - *Iraq in Wartime: Soldiering, Martyrdom, and Remembrance*
    AHR - v120 - i2 - April 2015 - p750-751 [501+]

Khoury, Elias - *Broken Mirrors*
    KR - Nov 1 2015 - pNA [501+]

Khoury-Ghata, Venus - *Where Are the Trees Going?*
    WLT - v89 - i5 - Sept-Oct 2015 - p77(2) [501+]

Khoury, Jessica - *The Forbidden Wish*
    y KR - Dec 15 2015 - pNA [51-500]
    y PW - v262 - i47 - Nov 23 2015 - p68(2) [51-500]
Kalahari
    y CCB-B - v68 - i7 - March 2015 - p359(1) [51-500]
    y CH Bwatch - July 2015 - pNA [51-500]
    y HB Guide - v26 - i2 - Fall 2015 - p126(1) [51-500]

Khoury, Joseph - *The Adventures of Brusanus, Prince of Hungaria*
    Six Ct J - v46 - i2 - Summer 2015 - p457-458 [501+]

Khromeychuk, Olesya - *"Undetermined" Ukrainians: Post-War Narratives of the Waffen SS "Galicia" Division*
    Slav R - v74 - i1 - Nov 2015 - p153-156 [501+]

Khumalo, Sihle - *Almost Sleeping My Way to Timbuktu: West Africa on a Shoestring by Public Transport with No French*
    Bwatch - June 2015 - pNA [51-500]

Kibuishi, Kazu - *Explorer: The Hidden Doors: Seven Graphic Stories*
    y HB - v91 - i1 - Jan-Feb 2015 - p83(1) [51-500]
    c HB Guide - v26 - i1 - Spring 2015 - p187(1) [51-500]

Kick, Russ - *The Graphic Canon of Children's Literature: The World's Greatest Kids' Lit as Comics and Visuals*
    y Sch Lib - v63 - i2 - Summer 2015 - p123(1) [51-500]
The Graphic Canon of Children's Literature: The World's Greatest Kid's Lit as Comics and Visuals
    y BL - v111 - i9-10 - Jan 1 2015 - p61(1) [51-500]

Kidd, Ronald - *Night on Fire*
    c BL - v112 - i1 - Sept 1 2015 - p117(1) [51-500]
    c KR - July 15 2015 - pNA [51-500]
    c SLJ - v61 - i8 - August 2015 - p87(2) [501+]

Kidd, Sue Monk - *The Invention of Wings (Read by Lamia, Jenna). Audiobook Review*
    BL - v111 - i14 - March 15 2015 - p23(2) [501+]
The Mermaid Chair
    LJ - v140 - i17 - Oct 15 2015 - p118(1) [501+]

Kidd, Thomas S. - *Baptists in America: A History*
    Bks & Cult - v21 - i5 - Sept-Oct 2015 - p27(1) [501+]
    BL - v111 - i18 - May 15 2015 - p15(1) [51-500]
    Econ - v415 - i8942 - June 13 2015 - p80(US) [501+]
    KR - March 1 2015 - pNA [501+]
    LJ - v140 - i8 - May 1 2015 - p78(1) [51-500]
George Whitefield: America's Spiritual Founding Father
    Bks & Cult - v21 - i1 - Jan-Feb 2015 - p16(2) [501+]
    JAH - v102 - i2 - Sept 2015 - p534-535 [501+]

Kidner, Derek - *Psalms 1-72*
    BTB - v45 - i2 - May 2015 - p116(2) [501+]

Kidula, Jean Ngoya - *Music in Kenya Christianity: Logooli Religious Song*
    IJAHS - v48 - i1 - Wntr 2015 - p159-161 [501+]

Kiefer, Christian - *The Animals*
    BL - v111 - i11 - Feb 1 2015 - p25(1) [51-500]
    KR - Jan 15 2015 - pNA [51-500]
    PW - v262 - i4 - Jan 26 2015 - p144(2) [51-500]

Kiehl, Jeffrey T. - *Facing Climate Change*
    KR - Jan 1 2016 - pNA [501+]

Kiel und die Marine 1865-2015: 150 Jahre Gemeinsame Geschichte
    HNet - June 2015 - pNA [501+]

Kielinger, Thomas - *Winston Churchill: Der Spate Held*
    HT - v65 - i1 - Jan 2015 - p57(1) [501+]
    TLS - i5836 - Feb 6 2015 - p24(1) [501+]
    TimHES - i2185 - Jan 8 2015 - p47-47 [501+]

Kiely, Jan - *The Compelling Ideal: Thought Reform and the Prison in China, 1901-1956*
    AHR - v120 - i3 - June 2015 - p991-992 [501+]
    HNet - Feb 2015 - pNA [501+]
    JAS - v74 - i2 - May 2015 - p467-469 [501+]
    Pac A - v88 - i3 - Sept 2015 - p698 [501+]

Kiely, Tracy - *Murder with a Twist*
    KR - March 1 2015 - pNA [51-500]

Kiem, Elizabeth - *Hider Seeker Secret Keeper*
    y HB Guide - v26 - i2 - Fall 2015 - p126(1) [51-500]

Kieran, David - *Forever Vietnam: How a Divisive War Changed American Public Memory*
    AHR - v120 - i3 - June 2015 - p1073-1074 [501+]
    Am St - v54 - i2 - Summer 2015 - p117-118 [501+]
    Pub Hist - v37 - i3 - August 2015 - p144(3) [501+]
The War of My Generation: Youth Culture and the War on Terror
    CHE - v62 - i5 - Oct 2 2015 - pB17(1) [501+]

Kierkegaard, Soren - *Kierkegaard's Journals and Notebooks*
    CC - v132 - i15 - July 22 2015 - p39(2) [501+]

Kiernan, Celine - *Into the Grey*
    y HB Guide - v26 - i1 - Spring 2015 - p112(1) [51-500]

Kiernan, Celine - *Resonance*
    y Magpies - v30 - i2 - May 2015 - p42(1) [501+]

Kiernan, Peter D. - *American Mojo: Lost and Found: Restoring Our Middle Class before the Wind Blows By*
    PW - v262 - i17 - April 27 2015 - p65(1) [51-500]

Kiernan, Stephen P. - *The Hummingbird*
    BL - v112 - i1 - Sept 1 2015 - p40(1) [51-500]
    KR - July 1 2015 - pNA [501+]
    LJ - v140 - i14 - Sept 1 2015 - p95(1) [51-500]

Kierstead, Matt - *From Copperas to Cleanup: The History of Vermont's Elizabeth Copper Mine*
    Pub Hist - v37 - i3 - Feb 2015 - p132(3) [501+]

Kieschinick, John - *India in the Chinese Imagination: Myth, Religion, and Thought*
    JAS - v74 - i2 - May 2015 - p469-471 [501+]

Kiffmeyer, Thomas - *Reformers to Radicals: The Appalachian Volunteers and the War on Poverty*
    Am St - v54 - i2 - Summer 2015 - p73-83 [501+]

Kihn, Greg - *Painted Black*
    BL - v111 - i16 - April 15 2015 - p29(1) [51-500]

Kiib, Hans - *Catalyst Architecture: Rio de Janeiro, New York, Tokyo, Copenhagen*
    SPBW - August 2015 - pNA [51-500]

Kikuchi, Yoshiyuki - *Anglo-American Connections in Japanese Chemistry: The Lab as Contact Zone*
    AHR - v120 - i1 - Feb 2015 - p207-208 [501+]

Kilbride, Daniel - *Being American in Europe, 1750-1860*
    RAH - v43 - i1 - March 2015 - p47-53 [501+]

Kilcup, Karen L. - *Fallen Forests: Emotion, Embodiment and Ethics in American Women's Environmental Writing, 1781-1924*
    Wom R Bks - v32 - i1 - Jan-Feb 2015 - p5(4) [501+]

Kiley, Charles - *Writing the War: Chronicles of a World War II Correspondent*
    BL - v112 - i2 - Sept 15 2015 - p18(1) [51-500]

Kilgore, James - *Understanding Mass Incarceration: A People's Guide to the Key Civil Rights Struggle of Our Time*
    KR - July 1 2015 - pNA [501+]
    PW - v262 - i28 - July 13 2015 - p60(1) [51-500]
    RVBW - Nov 2015 - pNA [501+]

Kilham, Chris - *The Ayahuasca Test Pilots Handbook*
    UtneAdi - i186 - Spring 2015 - p90(2) [501+]

Kilian, Jan - *Michel Stuelers Gedenkbuch (1629-1649): Alltagsleben in Bohmen zur Zeit des Dreissigjahrigen Krieges*
    HNet - July 2015 - pNA [501+]

Killeen, Dan - *Tillie and Clementine Noises in the Night (Illus. by Killeen, Dan)*
    c CH Bwatch - March 2015 - pNA [51-500]

Killeen, Kevin - *Thomas Browne*
NYRB - v62 - i16 - Oct 22 2015 - p67(3) [501+]
Sev Cent N - v73 - i1-2 - Spring-Summer 2015 - p4(6) [501+]
Ren Q - v68 - i2 - Summer 2015 - p799-800 [501+]

Killelea, Grace - *The Confidence Effect: Every Woman's Guide to the Attitude that Attracts Success*
PW - v262 - i47 - Nov 23 2015 - p63(1) [51-500]

Killigrew, Anne - *"My Rare Wit Killing Sin": Poems of a Restoration Courtier*
Ren Q - v68 - i1 - Spring 2015 - p415-416 [501+]

Killion, Bette - *Princess Rosie's Rainbows (Illus. by Jacobs, Kim)*
c KR - August 1 2015 - pNA [51-500]

Kilmeade, Brian - *Thomas Jefferson and the Tripoli Pirates: The Forgotten War That Changed American History*
LJ - v140 - i17 - Oct 15 2015 - p101(2) [51-500]

Kilner, John F. - *Dignity and Destiny: Humanity in the Image of God*
Bwatch - August 2015 - pNA [51-500]
Ch Today - v59 - i1 - Jan-Feb 2015 - p68(1) [501+]

Kilpack, Josi S. - *A Heart Revealed*
KR - Feb 15 2015 - pNA [51-500]
PW - v262 - i7 - Feb 16 2015 - p165(1) [51-500]
Lord Fenton's Folly
y BL - v112 - i2 - Sept 15 2015 - p74(1) [51-500]
KR - August 1 2015 - pNA [501+]
y PW - v262 - i24 - June 15 2015 - p69(1) [51-500]

Kilpatrick, Nancy - *Expiration Date*
PW - v262 - i13 - March 30 2015 - p60(2) [51-500]
Nevermore! Tales of Murder, Mystery and the Macabre: Neo-Gothic Fiction Inspired by the Imagination of Edgar Allan Poe
y PW - v262 - i36 - Sept 7 2015 - p48(1) [51-500]
y VOYA - v38 - i4 - Oct 2015 - p54(1) [51-500]

Kilpatrick, Sally - *Bittersweet Creek*
LJ - v140 - i17 - Oct 15 2015 - p82(2) [501+]

Kilroy, Gerard - *Edmund Campion: A Scholarly Life*
Spec - v329 - i9765 - Oct 24 2015 - p45(2) [501+]

Kilson, Martin - *Transformation of the African American Intelligentsia, 1880-2012*
JAH - v102 - i1 - June 2015 - p260-261 [501+]

Kilworth, Garry - *The Songbirds of Pain*
TLS - i5832 - Jan 9 2015 - p14(1) [501+]

Kilzer, Lou - *Fatal Redemption*
PW - v262 - i42 - Oct 19 2015 - p59(1) [51-500]

Kim, Annabelle J. - *Tiger Pelt*
KR - June 1 2015 - pNA [51-500]

Kim, Cecil - *Friendship Quilt (Illus. by Jeong, Hajin)*
c HB Guide - v26 - i1 - Spring 2015 - p26(1) [51-500]
Mommy and Daddy Love You (Illus. by Ladecka, Anna)
c HB Guide - v26 - i2 - Fall 2015 - p39(1) [51-500]
The Three Pig Sisters (Illus. by Park, Keun)
c CH Bwatch - May 2015 - pNA [51-500]
c HB Guide - v26 - i2 - Fall 2015 - p39(1) [51-500]
c SLJ - v61 - i5 - May 2015 - p86(1) [51-500]

Kim, Chi-Young - *The Investigation*
BL - v111 - i17 - May 1 2015 - p38(2) [51-500]
PW - v262 - i25 - June 22 2015 - p118(1) [51-500]

Kim, Dae Soon - *The Transition to Democracy in Hungary: Arpad Goncz and the Post-Communist Hungarian Presidency*
E-A St - v67 - i5 - July 2015 - p839(2) [501+]

Kim, Eleana J. - *Adopted Territory: Transnational Korean Adoptees and the Politics of Belonging*
JWH - v27 - i1 - Spring 2015 - p168(10) [501+]

Kim, Eunsun - *A Thousand Miles to Freedom: My Escape from North Korea (Read by Zeller, Emily Woo)*. Audiobook Review
LJ - v140 - i17 - Oct 15 2015 - p54(1) [51-500]
A Thousand Miles to Freedom: My Escape from North Korea
LJ - v140 - i10 - June 1 2015 - p126(1) [501+]

Kim, Gyeong-Uk - *God Has No Grandchildren*
KR - Oct 15 2015 - pNA [51-500]

Kim, Hanmin - *Tiptoe Tapirs (Illus. by Kim, Hanmin)*
c KR - August 15 2015 - pNA [51-500]
c SLJ - v61 - i10 - Oct 2015 - p78(2) [51-500]

Kim, JeongHo - *Oh That Snow! (Illus. by Ok, SeoJeong)*
c HB Guide - v26 - i2 - Fall 2015 - p39(1) [51-500]

Kim, JiYu - *Zippy the Runner (Illus. by Seon, Jeong-Hyeon)*
c HB Guide - v26 - i1 - Spring 2015 - p26(1) [51-500]

Kim, Joseph - *Under the Same Sky: From Starvation in North Korea to Salvation in America*
CSM - June 10 2015 - pNA [501+]
KR - March 15 2015 - pNA [501+]
NYTBR - Nov 29 2015 - p26(L) [501+]
PW - v262 - i10 - March 9 2015 - p61(1) [51-500]
BL - v111 - i13 - March 1 2015 - p8(1) [51-500]

Kim, Kyung Hyun - *The Korean Popular Culture Reader*
JAS - v74 - i1 - Feb 2015 - p226-228 [501+]
Pac A - v88 - i2 - June 2015 - p330 [501+]

Kim, Marie Seong-Hak - *Law and Custom in Korea: Comparative Legal History*
AHR - v120 - i3 - June 2015 - p998-999 [501+]

Kim, Patti - *Here I Am (Illus. by Sanchez, Sonia)*
c Sch Lib - v63 - i2 - Summer 2015 - p96(1) [51-500]

Kim, Rebecca Y. - *The Spirit Moves West: Korean Missionaries in America*
CC - v132 - i21 - Oct 14 2015 - p33(2) [501+]

Kim, Sue - *Boutique Bags: Classic Style for Modern Living*
LJ - v140 - i11 - June 15 2015 - p89(1) [51-500]

Kim, Suk-Young - *DMZ Crossing: Performing Emotional Citizenship along the Korean Border*
AHR - v120 - i3 - June 2015 - p999-1000 [501+]
JAS - v74 - i2 - May 2015 - p496-497 [501+]

Kim, Suki - *Without You, There Is No Us: My Time with the Sons of North Korea's Elite*
NYRB - v62 - i10 - June 4 2015 - p46(3) [501+]

Kim, Sun Joo - *Wrongful Deaths: Selected Inquest Records from Nineteenth-Century Korea*
JAS - v74 - i1 - Feb 2015 - p228-230 [501+]

Kim, Susan - *Guardians*
y HB Guide - v26 - i2 - Fall 2015 - p126(1) [501+]

Kim, W. Chan - *Blue Ocean Strategy: How to Create Uncontested Market Space and Make the Competition Irrelevant*
RVBW - May 2015 - pNA [51-500]

Kim, YeShil - *My Best Buddy (Illus. by Tanco, Miguel)*
c CCB-B - v68 - i10 - June 2015 - p498(2) [51-500]
c SLJ - v61 - i6 - June 2015 - p86(1) [51-500]
We Are Proud of You (Illus. by The Pope Twins)
c HB Guide - v26 - i1 - Spring 2015 - p26(1) [51-500]

Kim, YoeongAh - *Shooting Stars Soccer Team (Illus. by Lee, Hyeongjin)*
c HB Guide - v26 - i1 - Spring 2015 - p26(1) [51-500]

Kim, Yosep - *The Identity and the Life of the Church: John Calvin's Ecclesiology in the Perspective of His Anthropology*
Six Ct J - v46 - i3 - Fall 2015 - p838-839 [501+]

Kim, Youn-Mi - *New Perspectives on Early Korean Art: From Silla to Koryo*
JAS - v74 - i2 - May 2015 - p497-498 [501+]

Kim, Yung Sik - *Questioning Science in East Asian Contexts: Essays on Science, Confucianism, and the Comparative History of Science*
Isis - v106 - i2 - June 2015 - p415(2) [501+]
JAS - v74 - i3 - August 2015 - p726-727 [501+]

Kimber, Edd - *Patisserie Made Simple*
NYT - Dec 2 2015 - pD6(L) [501+]

Kimber, Stephen - *What Lies Across the Water: The Real Story of the Cuban Five*
S&S - v79 - i1 - Jan 2015 - p138-140 [501+]

Kimble, James J. - *Prairie Forge: The Extraordinary Story of the Nebraska Scrap Metal Drive of World War II*
JAH - v102 - i1 - June 2015 - p286-287 [501+]

Kimbriel, Samuel - *Friendship as Sacred Knowing: Overcoming Isolation*
Theol St - v76 - i4 - Dec 2015 - p859(2) [501+]

Kimbrough, R. Keller - *Publishing the Stage: Print and Performance in Early Modern Japan*
JAS - v74 - i2 - May 2015 - p437-441 [501+]
Wondrous Brutal Fictions: Eight Buddhist Tales from the Early Japanese Puppet Theater
JAS - v74 - i2 - May 2015 - p437-441 [501+]

Kimmel, Allison Crotzer - *The Montgomery Bus Boycott: A Primary Source Exploration of the Protest for Equal Treatment*
c SLJ - v61 - i2 - Feb 2015 - p116(1) [51-500]
A Primary Source History of Slavery in the United States
c HB Guide - v26 - i2 - Fall 2015 - p220(1) [51-500]

Kimmel, Elizabeth - *Cody Secret of the Mountain Dog*
c HB Guide - v26 - i1 - Spring 2015 - p83(1) [51-500]

Kimmel, Elizabeth Cody - *Secret of the Mountain Dog*
y CH Bwatch - Feb 2015 - pNA [501+]
c Teach Lib - v42 - i4 - April 2015 - p43(1) [51-500]

Kimmel, Eric A. - *Hershel and the Hanukkah Goblins: 25th Anniversary Edition (Illus. by Hyman, Trina Schart)*
c HB Guide - v26 - i1 - Spring 2015 - p35(1) [51-500]
The Runaway Tortilla
c KR - July 1 2015 - pNA [51-500]
Scarlett and Sam: Escape from Egypt (Illus. by Stevanovic, Ivica)
c HB Guide - v26 - i2 - Fall 2015 - p67(2) [51-500]
PW - v262 - i2 - Jan 12 2015 - p63(1) [51-500]
Simon and the Bear (Illus. by Trueman, Matthew)
c HB Guide - v26 - i1 - Spring 2015 - p35(1) [51-500]

Kimmel, Meike - *Motive und Rollen des Autors in Vergils Eklogen, den Oden des Horaz und den Elegien des Properz*
Class R - v65 - i2 - Oct 2015 - pNA [501+]

Kimmel, Michael - *Cultural Encyclopedia of the Penis*
BL - v111 - i12 - Feb 15 2015 - p12(1) [51-500]

Kimmel, Michael S. - *Cultural Encyclopedia of the Penis*
G&L Rev W - v22 - i6 - Nov-Dec 2015 - p44(1) [51-500]

Kimmel, Mike - *Scenes for Teens: 50 Original Comedy and Drama Scenes for Teenage Actors*
SPBW - Sept 2015 - pNA [51-500]

Kimmelman, Leslie - *Everybody Says Shalom (Illus. by Shipman, Talitha)*
c HB Guide - v26 - i2 - Fall 2015 - p39(1) [51-500]
Trick ARRR Treat: A Pirate Halloween (Illus. by Monlongo, Jorge)
c BL - v112 - i4 - Oct 15 2015 - p49(1) [51-500]
c HB - v91 - i5 - Sept-Oct 2015 - p67(2) [51-500]
c KR - August 1 2015 - pNA [51-500]
c PW - v262 - i30 - July 27 2015 - p64(1) [51-500]
c PW - v262 - i49 - Dec 2 2015 - p63(1) [51-500]
c SLJ - v61 - i9 - Sept 2015 - p106(2) [51-500]

Kimmich, F. Scott - *The Apostles of Satan*
KR - March 15 2015 - pNA [501+]

Kimport, Katrina - *Queering Marriage Challenging Family Formation in the United States*
AJS - v120 - i4 - Jan 2015 - p1276(3) [501+]
Queering Marriage: Challenging Family Formation in the United States
CS - v44 - i1 - Jan 2015 - p140(1) [501+]

Kimura, Aya Hirata - *Hidden Hunger: Gender and the Politics of Smarter Foods*
CS - v44 - i2 - March 2015 - p225-226 [501+]

Kimura, Ken - *999 Frogs and a Little Brother (Illus. by Murakami, Yasunari)*
c HB Guide - v26 - i2 - Fall 2015 - p13(1) [51-500]

Kimura, Yasuko - *Pakkun the Wolf and His Dinosaur Friends (Illus. by Kimura, Yasuko)*
c KR - March 1 2015 - pNA [51-500]
c SLJ - v61 - i5 - May 2015 - p86(1) [51-500]

Kimyongur, Angela - *Rewriting Wrongs: French Crime Fiction and the Palmpsest*
FS - v69 - i3 - July 2015 - p421-422 [501+]

Kinard, Rhonda - *A Life Ignited*
KR - Nov 15 2015 - pNA [51-500]

Kincaid, Kimberly - *Reckless*
PW - v262 - i47 - Nov 23 2015 - p54(2) [51-500]

Kincaid, Paul - *Call and Response*
SFS - v42 - i2 - July 2015 - p386-388 [501+]

Kincaid, S.J. - *Catalyst*
y HB Guide - v26 - i1 - Spring 2015 - p112(1) [51-500]

Kincheloe, Jennifer - *The Secret Life of Anna Blanc*
BL - v112 - i3 - Oct 1 2015 - p28(1) [51-500]
PW - v262 - i37 - Sept 14 2015 - p44(2) [51-500]

Kincy, Karen - *Storms of Lazarus*
PW - v262 - i42 - Oct 19 2015 - p60(1) [51-500]

Kindall, Brian - *Blue Sky*
KR - July 15 2015 - pNA [51-500]

Kinder, John M. - *Paying With Their Bodies: American War and the Problem of the Disabled Veteran*
LJ - v140 - i5 - March 15 2015 - p124(1) [51-500]
PW - v262 - i8 - Feb 23 2015 - p67(2) [51-500]
TLS - i5859 - July 17 2015 - p7(2) [501+]

Kinder und Krieg. Epochenubergreifende Analysen zu Kriegskindheiten im Wandel
HNet - June 2015 - pNA [501+]

Kindi, Patrice - *A School for Brides*
y BL - v111 - i19-20 - June 1 2015 - p100(1) [51-500]

Kindl, Patrice - *A School for Brides: A Story of Maidens, Mystery, and Matrimony*
y HB - v91 - i4 - July-August 2015 - p136(2) [51-500]
y SLJ - v61 - i5 - May 2015 - p114(1) [51-500]
A School for Brides
y KR - April 15 2015 - pNA [51-500]
y VOYA - v38 - i2 - June 2015 - p63(2) [501+]

Kindler, Robert - *Stalins Nomaden: Herrschaft und Hunger in Kasachstan*
    HNet - Jan 2015 - pNA [501+]

Kindt, Matt - *Armor Hunters*
    PW - v262 - i8 - Feb 23 2015 - p60(1) [51-500]

King, A.S. - *Glory O'Brien's History of the Future (Read by Lakin, Christine). Audiobook Review*
    c BL - v111 - i14 - March 15 2015 - p24(2) [501+]
Glory O'Brien's History of the Future
    y HB - v91 - i1 - Jan-Feb 2015 - p83(2) [51-500]
    y HB Guide - v26 - i1 - Spring 2015 - p112(2) [51-500]
    y Teach Lib - v42 - i3 - Feb 2015 - p39(1) [51-500]
I Crawl through It (Read by King, A.S.). Audiobook Review
    y SLJ - v61 - i12 - Dec 2015 - p79(1) [51-500]
I Crawl through It
    y BL - v111 - i22 - August 1 2015 - p64(1) [51-500]
    y CCB-B - v69 - i2 - Oct 2015 - p95(2) [51-500]
    y HB - v91 - i5 - Sept-Oct 2015 - p107(2) [51-500]
    y KR - July 15 2015 - pNA [51-500]
    y NYTBR - Oct 25 2015 - p34(L) [501+]
    y PW - v262 - i24 - June 15 2015 - p86(2) [51-500]
    y PW - v262 - i49 - Dec 2 2015 - p102(1) [51-500]
    y SLJ - v61 - i7 - July 2015 - p93(2) [51-500]
    y VOYA - v38 - i3 - August 2015 - p79(2) [51-500]

King, Andrew - *Engibear's Bridge (Illus. by Johnston, Benjamin)*
    c Magpies - v30 - i1 - March 2015 - p30(1) [501+]

King, Anthony - *The Blunders of Our Governments*
    TimHES - i2202 - May 7 2015 - p49(1) [501+]
The Combat Soldier: Infantry Tactics and Cohesion in the Twentieth and Twenty-First Centuries
    Parameters - v45 - i1 - Spring 2015 - p153(3) [501+]
Who Governs Britain?
    NS - v144 - i5260 - May 1 2015 - p48(1) [501+]

King, Bart - *The Big Book of Superheroes (Illus. by Paprocki, Greg)*
    c HB Guide - v26 - i1 - Spring 2015 - p177(1) [51-500]

King, C. Richard - *Redskins: Insult and Brand*
    KR - Jan 1 2016 - pNA [501+]

King, Charles - *Midnight at the Pera Palace: The Birth of Modern Istanbul*
    NYTBR - Nov 29 2015 - p24(L) [501+]

King, Daren - *Frightfully Friendly Ghosties: Ghostly Holler-Day (Illus. by Roberts, David)*
    c HB Guide - v26 - i1 - Spring 2015 - p61(1) [51-500]

King, David Powers - *Woven*
    y CCB-B - v68 - i8 - April 2015 - p406(1) [51-500]
    c CH Bwatch - June 2015 - pNA [51-500]

King, Don W. - *Yet One More Spring: A Critical Study of Joy Davidman*
    LJ - v140 - i16 - Oct 1 2015 - p79(1) [51-500]

King, Edward - *Science Fiction and Digital Technologies in Argentine and Brazilian Culture*
    MLN - v130 - i2 - March 2015 - p403-405 [501+]

King, Francis - *A Domestic Animal*
    TLS - i5849 - May 8 2015 - p19(2) [501+]
Yesterday Came Suddenly
    TLS - i5849 - May 8 2015 - p16(1) [501+]

King, George - *Contacts with the Gods from Space*
    SPBW - Feb 2015 - pNA [51-500]

King, Greg - *Lusitania: Triumph, Tragedy, and the End of the Edwardian Age*
    BL - v111 - i11 - Feb 1 2015 - p11(1) [51-500]
    LJ - v140 - i2 - Feb 1 2015 - p92(1) [501+]

King, Helen - *The One-Sex Body on Trial: The Classical and Early Modern Evidence*
    Six Ct J - v46 - i2 - Summer 2015 - p419-421 [501+]

King, Hiram - *Broken Ranks*
    Roundup M - v22 - i3 - Feb 2015 - p13(1) [501+]

King, Jason - *God Has Begun a Great Work in Us: Embodied Love in Consecrated Life and Ecclesial Movements*
    JAAR - v83 - i2 - June 2015 - pNA [501+]

King, John - *Notes on the Death of Culture*
    KR - April 15 2015 - pNA [51-500]
Physics Project Lab
    Phys Today - v68 - i8 - August 2015 - p56-57 [501+]

King, Jonathon - *Don't Lose Her*
    PW - v262 - i16 - April 20 2015 - p57(2) [51-500]

King, K.L. - *Little Golden Bear (Illus. by Terrano, Doina Cociuba)*
    c CH Bwatch - Sept 2015 - pNA [51-500]

King, Laurie R. - *In the Company of Sherlock Holmes: Stories Inspired by the Holmes Canon*
    NYTBR - Jan 11 2015 - p26(L) [501+]

King, Lily - *Euphoria*
    TLS - i5836 - Feb 6 2015 - p19(1) [501+]
    HR - v67 - i4 - Wntr 2015 - p685-692 [501+]
    NYTBR - May 3 2015 - p28(L) [501+]
    Wom R Bks - v32 - i4 - July-August 2015 - p15(2) [501+]

King, Linda A.W. - *Invitations from Afar*
    KR - Jan 1 2015 - pNA [501+]

King, Lindsey - *Spiritual Currency in Northeast Brazil*
    HAHR - v95 - i4 - Nov 2015 - p711-712 [501+]

King, Margaret L. - *Renaissance Humanism: An Anthology of Sources*
    Six Ct J - v46 - i2 - Summer 2015 - p482-484 [501+]
    Ren Q - v68 - i1 - Spring 2015 - p232-234 [501+]

King, Mary Anna - *Bastards: A Memoir (Read by Delaine, Christina). Audiobook Review*
    LJ - v140 - i19 - Nov 15 2015 - p54(1) [51-500]
Bastards: A Memoir
    BL - v111 - i17 - May 1 2015 - p62(1) [51-500]
    KR - March 15 2015 - pNA [51-500]
    NYTBR - August 2 2015 - p26(L) [501+]

King, Mary Elizabeth - *Gandhian Nonviolent Struggle and Untouchability in South India: The 1924-25 Vykom Satyagraha and Mechanisms of Change*
    TimHES - i2204 - May 21 2015 - p49(1) [501+]

King-Meadows, Tyson D. - *African American Leadership: A Concise Reference Guide*
    LJ - v140 - i20 - Dec 1 2015 - p130(1) [51-500]

King, Melanie - *Secrets in a Dead Fish: The Spying Game in the First World War*
    J Mil H - v79 - i3 - July 2015 - p857-858 [501+]

King, Melissa - *DIY Nut Milks, Nut Butters, And More*
    Veg J - v34 - i4 - Oct-Dec 2015 - p31(1) [51-500]

King, Michelle T. - *Between Birth and Death: Female Infanticide in Nineteenth-Century China*
    AHR - v120 - i2 - April 2015 - p595-596 [501+]
    HNet - April 2015 - pNA [501+]
    JAS - v74 - i1 - Feb 2015 - p197-199 [501+]

King, Nancy - *Changing Spaces*
    KR - May 1 2015 - pNA [501+]

King, Owen - *Intro to Alien Invasion (Illus. by Ahn, Nancy)*
    BL - v112 - i2 - Sept 15 2015 - p50(1) [51-500]
    KR - July 15 2015 - pNA [51-500]
Intro to Alien Invasion
    PW - v262 - i37 - Sept 14 2015 - p51(1) [51-500]

King, Peter - *The Antimodern Condition: An Argument against Progress*
    MA - v57 - i3 - Summer 2015 - p40(9) [501+]

King, Richard - *Original Rockers*
    Econ - v415 - i8941 - June 6 2015 - p76(US) [501+]

King, Richard H. - *Arendt and America*
    LJ - v140 - i16 - Oct 1 2015 - p84(1) [51-500]
In Time We Shall Know Ourselves
    Am St - v54 - i1 - Spring 2015 - p160-2 [501+]

King, Ross - *Florence: The Paintings and Frescoes, 1250-1743*
    LJ - v140 - i17 - Oct 15 2015 - p85(1) [51-500]

King, Stephen - *The Bazaar of Bad Dreams*
    BL - v111 - i22 - August 1 2015 - p6(1) [51-500]
    BL - v112 - i2 - Sept 15 2015 - p38(1) [51-500]
    PW - v262 - i37 - Sept 14 2015 - p47(1) [51-500]
    CSM - Dec 4 2015 - pNA [501+]
    Esq - v164 - i4 - Nov 2015 - p36(1) [501+]
    KR - Sept 1 2015 - pNA [501+]
    LJ - v140 - i16 - Oct 1 2015 - p74(1) [51-500]
    NYTBR - Nov 1 2015 - p22(L) [501+]
Drunken Fireworks (Read by Sample, Tim). Audiobook Review
    BL - v112 - i2 - Sept 15 2015 - p76(1) [51-500]
    LJ - v140 - i16 - Oct 1 2015 - p42(2) [51-500]
Finders Keepers (Read by Patton, Will). Audiobook Review
    BL - v111 - i21 - July 1 2015 - p78(1) [51-500]
Finders Keepers
    BL - v111 - i16 - April 15 2015 - p28(1) [51-500]
    CSM - June 9 2015 - pNA [51-500]
    KR - April 15 2015 - pNA [51-500]
    LJ - v140 - i7 - April 15 2015 - p76(1) [51-500]
    NYT - June 1 2015 - pC1(L) [501+]
    NYTBR - May 31 2015 - p14(L) [501+]
    PW - v262 - i16 - April 20 2015 - p54(1) [51-500]
    PW - v262 - i24 - June 15 2015 - p16(1) [51-500]
    Spec - v328 - i9745 - June 6 2015 - p41(1) [501+]
Mr. Mercedes
    LJ - v140 - i9 - May 15 2015 - p74(3) [501+]
Revival (Read by Morse, David). Audiobook Review
    LJ - v140 - i6 - April 1 2015 - p48(1) [51-500]
    PW - v262 - i5 - Feb 2 2015 - p54(1) [51-500]
Revival
    BL - v111 - i18 - May 15 2015 - p34(1) [501+]

King, Stephen Michael - *My Dad Is a Giraffe (Illus. by King, Stephen Michael)*
    c Magpies - v30 - i5 - Nov 2015 - p28(1) [501+]

King, T. Jackson - *The Memory Singer*
    c Analog - v135 - i1-2 - Jan-Feb 2015 - p183(1) [501+]

King, Thomas - *The Inconvenient Indian*
    HNet - August 2015 - pNA [501+]

King, Tiffany - *A Shattered Moment*
    PW - v262 - i10 - March 9 2015 - p58(1) [51-500]

King, Wesley - *Dragons vs. Drones*
    y KR - Jan 1 2016 - pNA [51-500]
The Incredible Space Raiders from Space!
    c CCB-B - v68 - i6 - Feb 2015 - p317(1) [51-500]
    c HB Guide - v26 - i2 - Fall 2015 - p89(1) [51-500]

King-White, Ryan - *Dominican Baseball: New Pride, Old Prejudice*
    SSJ - v32 - i2 - June 2015 - p220-4 [501+]

King, William S. - *Till the Dark Angel Comes: Abolitionism and the Road to the Second American Revolution*
    PW - v262 - i47 - Nov 23 2015 - p62(1) [51-500]
To Raise Up a Nation: John Brown, Frederick Douglass, and the Making of a Free Country
    JSH - v81 - i2 - May 2015 - p460(3) [501+]

Kingloff, Amanda - *Project Kid: 100 Ingenious*
    c HB Guide - v26 - i1 - Spring 2015 - p177(1) [51-500]

King'oo, Clare Costley - *Miserere Mei: The Penitential Psalms in Late Medieval and Early Modern England*
    MLR - v110 - i2 - April 2015 - p520-522 [501+]

Kingsberg, Miriam - *Moral Nation: Modern Japan and Narcotics in Global History*
    AHR - v120 - i1 - Feb 2015 - p221-222 [501+]
    Pac A - v88 - i2 - June 2015 - p306 [501+]

Kingsbury, Karen - *Chasing Sunsets*
    BL - v111 - i15 - April 1 2015 - p23(1) [51-500]

Kingsbury, Noel - *Hidden Natural Histories: Trees*
    BL - v111 - i19-20 - June 1 2015 - p14(1) [51-500]

Kingshill, Sophia - *Mermaids*
    TLS - i5859 - July 17 2015 - p26(2) [501+]
    Spec - v328 - i9750 - July 11 2015 - p37(1) [501+]

Kingsley, Charles - *The Water-Babies: A Fairy Tale for a Land Baby*
    VS - v57 - i3 - Spring 2015 - p387(8) [501+]

Kingsley, Jennifer P. - *The Bernward Gospels: Art, Memory and the Episcopate in Medieval Germany*
    Med R - Feb 2015 - pNA [501+]

Kingsnorth, Paul - *The Wake*
    BL - v112 - i1 - Sept 1 2015 - p53(1) [51-500]
    LJ - v140 - i15 - Sept 15 2015 - p68(1) [51-500]
    NYTBR - Sept 6 2015 - p15(L) [501+]
    KR - July 1 2015 - pNA [51-500]
    PW - v262 - i27 - July 6 2015 - p43(1) [51-500]

Kingwell, Jen - *Quilt Lovely: 15 Vibrant Projects Using Piecing and Applique*
    LJ - v140 - i10 - June 1 2015 - p104(1) [51-500]

Kingwell, Mark - *Measure Yourself against the Earth: Essays*
    KR - July 1 2015 - pNA [51-500]
    LJ - v140 - i20 - Dec 1 2015 - p105(1) [51-500]

Kinkley, Jeffrey C. - *Visions of Dystopia in China's New Historical Novels*
    HNet - August 2015 - pNA [501+]

Kinnamon, Michael - *Can a Renewal Movement Be Renewed?: Questions for the Future of Ecumenism*
    CC - v132 - i10 - May 13 2015 - p39(2) [501+]
    IBMR - v39 - i1 - Jan 2015 - p42(2) [501+]

Kinnard, Jacob N. - *The Norton Anthology of World Religions*
    JAAR - v83 - i2 - June 2015 - p591-596 [501+]

Kinney, David - *The Dylanologists: Adventures in the Land of Bob*
    NYTBR - June 14 2015 - p24(L) [501+]

Kinney, Jeff - *Commentarii de Inepto Puero*
    c KR - August 1 2015 - pNA [51-500]
Diary of a Wimpy Kid: The Long Haul
    c HB Guide - v26 - i2 - Fall 2015 - p89(1) [51-500]

Kinsella, Kajsa - *Nordicana: 100 Icons of Scandi Culture and Nordic Cool*
    Bwatch - July 2015 - pNA [51-500]

Kinsella, Sophie - *Finding Audrey (Read by Whelan, Gemma). Audiobook Review*
   y BL - v112 - i2 - Sept 15 2015 - p80(1) [51-500]
   y HB - v91 - i6 - Nov-Dec 2015 - p110(1) [51-500]
   y PW - v262 - i35 - August 31 2015 - p86(1) [51-500]
   y SLJ - v61 - i10 - Oct 2015 - p54(2) [51-500]
Finding Audrey
   y BL - v111 - i13 - March 1 2015 - p47(1) [501+]
   y BL - v111 - i17 - May 1 2015 - p91(1) [501+]
   y CCB-B - v69 - i1 - Sept 2015 - p31(2) [51-500]
   y CH Bwatch - July 2015 - pNA [51-500]
   y HB - v91 - i4 - July-August 2015 - p137(1) [51-500]
   y KR - April 15 2015 - pNA [51-500]
   y Magpies - v30 - i4 - Sept 2015 - p41(1) [501+]
   y PW - v262 - i15 - April 13 2015 - p82(1) [51-500]
   y Sch Lib - v63 - i3 - Autumn 2015 - p184(1) [51-500]
   y SLJ - v61 - i6 - June 2015 - p114(1) [51-500]
   y VOYA - v38 - i2 - June 2015 - p64(1) [51-500]
Shopaholic to the Stars (Read by Corbett, Clare). Audiobook Review
   y BL - v111 - i14 - March 15 2015 - p85(1) [51-500]
Shopaholic to the Stars
   y Bwatch - Jan 2015 - pNA [51-500]
Kinsella, W.P. - *The Essential W.P. Kinsella*
     PW - v262 - i7 - Feb 16 2015 - p164(1) [51-500]
     BL - v111 - i14 - March 15 2015 - p43(1) [51-500]
Kinser, Brent E. - *The American Civil War and the Shaping of British Democracy*
     VS - v57 - i2 - Wntr 2015 - p354(4) [501+]
Kinsky, Esther - *Am Fluss*
     TimHES - i2205 - May 28 2015 - p47(1) [501+]
Kinsman, Sharla - *My Mother Always Tells Me (Illus. by Nadeau, Sonia)*
   c Res Links - v20 - i4 - April 2015 - p4(1) [51-500]
Kinvig, Douglas - *Churchill's Crusade: The British Invasion of Russia, 1918-20*
     HT - v65 - i1 - Jan 2015 - p56(2) [501+]
Kiper, Richard L. - *Spare Not the Brave: The Special Activities Group in Korea*
     J Mil H - v79 - i1 - Jan 2015 - p256-257 [501+]
Kipling, Rudyard - *How the Elephant Got Her Trunk (Illus. by Tjornehoj, T.G.)*
   c CH Bwatch - Nov 2015 - pNA [51-500]
The Jungle Book
   c KR - Jan 1 2016 - pNA [51-500]
Just So Stories for Little Children, vol. 2 (Illus. by Wallace, Ian)
   c Bkbird - v53 - i3 - Summer 2015 - p101(1) [501+]
Puck of Pook's Hill (Read by Kenny, Peter). Audiobook Review
   c CH Bwatch - August 2015 - pNA [51-500]
Kipnis, Igor - *The Harpsichord and Clavichord: An Encyclopaedia, 2d ed*
     TLS - i5855 - June 19 2015 - p29(1) [501+]
Kipnis, Laura - *Men: Notes from an Ongoing Investigation*
     Dis - v62 - i1 - Wntr 2015 - p141(5) [501+]
Kiraly, Stephen J. - *Your Healthy Brain*
     KR - Dec 1 2015 - pNA [51-500]
Kirby, Denise - *88 Lime Street: The Way In*
   c Magpies - v30 - i2 - May 2015 - p36(1) [501+]
Kirby, Jessi - *Things We Know by Heart*
   y CCB-B - v68 - i10 - June 2015 - p499(1) [501+]
   y HB Guide - v26 - i2 - Fall 2015 - p126(1) [51-500]
   y KR - Feb 15 2015 - pNA [51-500]
   y VOYA - v38 - i1 - April 2015 - p63(2) [51-500]
Kirby, Leslie Dana - *The Perfect Game*
     PW - v262 - i2 - Jan 12 2015 - p37(1) [51-500]
     Bwatch - May 2015 - pNA [51-500]
     KR - Jan 1 2015 - pNA [51-500]
Kirby, Matthew J. - *The Arctic Code*
     BL - v111 - i14 - March 15 2015 - p72(2) [51-500]
   c CCB-B - v68 - i10 - June 2015 - p499(2) [51-500]
   c HB Guide - v26 - i2 - Fall 2015 - p89(1) [51-500]
     KR - Feb 15 2015 - pNA [51-500]
   c SLJ - v61 - i2 - Feb 2015 - p88(1) [51-500]
Kirby, Peter - *Child Workers and Industrial Health in Britain, 1780-1850*
     HT - v65 - i2 - Feb 2015 - p57(2) [501+]
Kirby, Stan - *Captain Awesome and the Easter Egg Bandit (Illus. by O'Connor, George)*
   c HB Guide - v26 - i2 - Fall 2015 - p68(1) [51-500]
Captain Awesome Gets a Hole-in-One (Illus. by O'Connor, George)
   c HB Guide - v26 - i1 - Spring 2015 - p61(1) [51-500]
Captain Awesome vs. the Evil Babysitter (Illus. by O'Connor, George)
   c HB Guide - v26 - i1 - Spring 2015 - p61(1) [51-500]

Kirby, Torrance - *Paul's Cross and the Culture of Persuasion in England, 1520-1640*
     Six Ct J - v46 - i1 - Spring 2015 - p145-147 [501+]
Kirby, William S. - *Vienna*
     KR - July 1 2015 - pNA [51-500]
     PW - v262 - i31 - August 3 2015 - p37(1) [51-500]
Kirche vor Ort: Pfarreikulturen im vormodernen Europa
     HNet - Sept 2015 - pNA [501+]
Kircher, Timothy - *Living Well in Renaissance Italy: The Virtues of Humanism and the Irony of Leon Battista Alberti*
     Ren Q - v68 - i2 - Summer 2015 - p622-623 [501+]
Neo-Latin and the Humanities: Essays in Honour of Charles E. Fantazzi
     Ren Q - v68 - i1 - Spring 2015 - p234-235 [501+]
Kirchhoffer, David G. - *Human Dignity in Contemporary Ethics*
     Theol St - v76 - i4 - Dec 2015 - p895(2) [501+]
Kirchner, Andreas - *Boethius as a Paradigm of Late Ancient Thought*
     Med R - August 2015 - pNA [501+]
Kirchner, Bharti - *Goddess of Fire*
     KR - Dec 1 2015 - pNA [51-500]
Kirin, Asen - *Exuberance of Meaning: The Art Patronage of Catherine the Great*
     Slav R - v74 - i2 - Summer 2015 - p411-412 [501+]
Kirk, Brian - *We Are Monsters*
     BL - v111 - i22 - August 1 2015 - p44(1) [51-500]
     LJ - v140 - i16 - Oct 1 2015 - p111(1) [501+]
Kirk, Daniel - *Ten Thank-You Letters*
   c HB Guide - v26 - i1 - Spring 2015 - p35(1) [51-500]
The Thing about Spring (Illus. by Kirk, Daniel)
   c CH Bwatch - July 2015 - pNA [51-500]
   c HB Guide - v26 - i2 - Fall 2015 - p39(1) [51-500]
   c KR - Jan 1 2015 - pNA [51-500]
You Are Not My Friend, But I Miss You (Illus. by Kirk, Daniel)
   c CCB-B - v68 - i5 - Jan 2015 - p263(1) [51-500]
   c HB Guide - v26 - i1 - Spring 2015 - p35(1) [51-500]
Kirk, David - *Oh So Brave Dragon (Illus. by Kirk, David)*
   c SLJ - v61 - i6 - June 2015 - p46(6) [501+]
Sword of Honor
     BL - v112 - i4 - Oct 15 2015 - p26(1) [51-500]
     KR - Sept 1 2015 - pNA [51-500]
     LJ - v140 - i13 - August 1 2015 - p86(2) [51-500]
Kirk, Joe - *Bun Bun and Milby Go Walkabout*
   c Magpies - v30 - i1 - March 2015 - p27(1) [51-500]
Kirk, Randy - *Retired Broke*
     KR - June 15 2015 - pNA [51-500]
Kirk, Robert - *The Conceptual Link from Physical to Mental*
     Dialogue - v54 - i3 - Sept 2015 - p590-594 [501+]
Kirk, Shannon - *Method 15/33*
     BL - v111 - i17 - May 1 2015 - p25(1) [51-500]
     PW - v262 - i10 - March 9 2015 - p54(1) [51-500]
Kirkegaard, Peter - *Blues for folkhemmet: Noranalyse af Arne Dahls Europa Blues*
     Scan St - v87 - i2 - Summer 2015 - p312(4) [501+]
Kirkham, Anne - *Wounds in the Middle Ages*
     Med R - June 2015 - pNA [501+]
Kirkham, David M. - *State Responses to Minority Religions*
     J Ch St - v57 - i2 - Spring 2015 - p364-366 [501+]
Kirkham, Victoria - *Boccaccio: A Critical Guide to the Complete Works*
     Ren Q - v68 - i3 - Fall 2015 - p1108-1110 [501+]
     Specu - v90 - i4 - Oct 2015 - p1133-1134 [501+]
Kirkman, Robert - *Outcast: A Darkness Surrounds Him (Illus. by Azaceta, Paul)*
     BL - v111 - i16 - April 15 2015 - p39(1) [51-500]
Kirkpatrick, Frank G. - *The Mystery and Agency of God: Divine Being and Action in the World*
     Theol St - v76 - i1 - March 2015 - p214(1) [501+]
Kirkpatrick, Jane - *A Light in the Wilderness*
     Roundup M - v22 - i6 - August 2015 - p31(1) [501+]
The Memory Weaver
     PW - v262 - i30 - July 27 2015 - p50(1) [51-500]
Kirkpatrick, Katherine - *Between Two Worlds*
   y BL - v111 - i19-20 - June 1 2015 - p86(2) [51-500]
The Snow Baby: The Arctic Childhood of Robert E. Peary's Daring Daughter
   y BL - v111 - i19-20 - June 1 2015 - p86(2) [501+]

Kirman, Robin - *Bradstreet Gate*
     BL - v111 - i18 - May 15 2015 - p26(2) [51-500]
     KR - May 1 2015 - pNA [501+]
     PW - v262 - i21 - May 25 2015 - p32(1) [51-500]
Kirsch, Adam - *Emblems of the Passing World: Poems after Photographs by August Sander*
     NYTBR - Dec 27 2015 - p17(L) [501+]
Rocket and Lightship: Essays on Literature and Ideas
     HM - v330 - i1977 - Feb 2015 - p84(6) [501+]
     TLS - i5840 - March 6 2015 - p22(1) [501+]
Kirsch, Vincent X. - *Freddie and Gingersnap Find a Cloud to Keep*
   c CH Bwatch - March 2015 - pNA [51-500]
   c HB Guide - v26 - i2 - Fall 2015 - p39(2) [51-500]
Kirschke, Amy Helene - *Protest and Propaganda: W.E.B. Du Bois, "The Crisis," and American History*
     AHR - v120 - i3 - June 2015 - p1047-1048 [501+]
Kirschman, Ellen - *Burying Ben*
     RVBW - Nov 2015 - pNA [501+]
The Right Wrong Thing
     PW - v262 - i33 - August 17 2015 - p54(1) [51-500]
Kirscht, Judith - *Home Fires*
     KR - Jan 15 2015 - pNA [51-500]
Kirshenbaum, Richard - *Isn't That Rich*
     KR - May 1 2015 - pNA [501+]
Kirshner, Ben - *Youth Activism in an Era of Education Inequality*
   y VOYA - v38 - i3 - August 2015 - p92(2) [501+]
Kirshner, Jonathan - *American Power after the Financial Crisis*
     HNet - August 2015 - pNA [501+]
Kirsten, Sven - *Tiki Pop: America Imagines Its Own Polynesian Paradise*
     Cont Pac - v27 - i2 - Fall 2015 - p560(6) [501+]
Kirwan, Wednesday - *Baby Loves to Party! (Illus. by Kirwan, Wednesday)*
   c KR - July 1 2015 - pNA [51-500]
Kirylo, James D. - *Education Essential for Global Competitiveness: A Critical Pedagogy of Resistance: 34 Pedagogues We Need to Know*
     IJCM - v25 - i1 - Spring 2015 - p133(3) [501+]
Kis, Danilo - *The Encyclopaedia of the Dead*
     NS - v144 - i5270 - July 10 2015 - p42(1) [501+]
Kishik, David - *The Manhattan Project*
     KR - Feb 1 2015 - pNA [51-500]
Kishimoto, Elyse - *The Dining and Social Club for Time Travellers (Illus. by Feaver, Doug)*
   c SLJ - v61 - i11 - Nov 2015 - p97(1) [51-500]
Kishira, Mayuko - *Who's Next Door? (Illus. by Takabakate, Jun)*
   c HB Guide - v26 - i1 - Spring 2015 - p35(1) [51-500]
Kishlansky, Mark - *Charles I: An Abbreviated Life*
     TLS - i5841 - March 13 2015 - p10(2) [501+]
Kisor, Henry - *Tracking the Beast*
     BL - v112 - i7 - Dec 1 2015 - p32(1) [51-500]
     KR - Oct 15 2015 - pNA [51-500]
Kissane, Andy - *Radiance*
     Meanjin - v74 - i1 - Autumn 2015 - p68(10) [501+]
Kissas, Konstantinos - *The Corinthia and the Northeast Peloponnese: Topography and History from Prehistoric Times until the End of Antiquityq*
     HNet - August 2015 - pNA [501+]
Kissinger, Henry - *World Order*
     APH - v62 - i2 - Summer 2015 - p51(1) [501+]
     For Aff - v94 - i2 - March-April 2015 - pNA [501+]
     NWCR - v68 - i3 - Summer 2015 - p138(10) [501+]
     NYRB - v62 - i5 - March 19 2015 - p10(24) [501+]
     NYTBR - Sept 20 2015 - p28(L) [501+]
     Soc - v52 - i3 - June 2015 - p284(3) [501+]
     TimHES - i2190 - Feb 12 2015 - p49(1) [501+]
Kitanov, Severin Valentinov - *Beatific Enjoyment in Medieval Scholastic Debates: The Complex Legacy of Saint Augustine and Peter Lombard*
     RM - v68 - i3 - March 2015 - p664(2) [501+]
     Six Ct J - v46 - i2 - Summer 2015 - p527-529 [501+]
Kitchen, James E. - *The British Imperial Army in the Middle East: Morale and Military Identity in the Sinai and Palestine Campaigns, 1916-1918*
     J Mil H - v79 - i1 - Jan 2015 - p237-238 [501+]
     J Mil H - v79 - i4 - Oct 2015 - p1161-1162 [501+]

Book Review Index 2016 Cumulation **KLEYPAS • 253**

Kitchen, Judith - *Brief Encounters: A Collection of Contemporary Nonfiction*
BL - v112 - i1 - Sept 1 2015 - p28(1) [51-500]
KR - August 1 2015 - pNA [501+]
LJ - v140 - i14 - Sept 1 2015 - p100(2) [51-500]
PW - v262 - i20 - May 18 2015 - p73(1) [51-500]
Kitchen, Martin - *Speer: Hitler's Architect*
NYRB - v62 - i20 - Dec 17 2015 - p36(3) [501+]
KR - Sept 15 2015 - pNA [501+]
Kitcher, Philip - *Deaths in Venice: The Cases of Gustav von Aschenbach*
GSR - v38 - i1 - Feb 2015 - p192-193 [501+]
Life after Faith: The Case for Secular Humanism
NYRB - v62 - i7 - April 23 2015 - p42(2) [501+]
Comw - v142 - i9 - May 15 2015 - p29(2) [501+]
TLS - i5846 - April 17 2015 - p28(1) [501+]
Kitchings, Taylor - *Yard War*
c BL - v111 - i21 - July 1 2015 - p77(1) [51-500]
c KR - July 1 2015 - pNA [51-500]
c SLJ - v61 - i6 - June 2015 - p100(2) [51-500]
Kite, Melissa - *The Girl Who Couldn't Stop Arguing*
Spec - v327 - i9736 - April 4 2015 - p36(1) [501+]
Kitromilides, Paschalis M. - *Enlightenment and Revolution: The Making of Modern Greece*
AHR - v120 - i2 - April 2015 - p734-735 [501+]
HER - v130 - i544 - June 2015 - p760(3) [501+]
Kittelstrom, Amy - *The Religion and the American Moral Tradition: Seven Liberals and the American Moral Tradition*
CHE - v61 - i38 - June 12 2015 - pB5(1) [501+]
The Religion of Democracy: Seven Liberals and the American Moral Tradition
BL - v111 - i18 - May 15 2015 - p5(1) [51-500]
CC - v132 - i25 - Dec 9 2015 - p41(3) [501+]
KR - Feb 15 2015 - pNA [501+]
PW - v262 - i6 - Feb 9 2015 - p2(1) [51-500]
Kittrie, Orde F. - *Lawfare: Law as a Weapon of War*
PW - v262 - i45 - Nov 9 2015 - p51(2) [51-500]
Kittscher, Kristen - *The Tiara on the Terrace*
c KR - Oct 1 2015 - pNA [51-500]
c SLJ - v61 - i12 - Dec 2015 - p102(2) [51-500]
Kitz, Anne Marie - *Cursed Are You! The Phenomenology of Cursing in Cuneiform and Hebrew Texts*
JNES - v74 - i2 - Oct 2015 - p355(4) [501+]
Kitzerow, Phyllis - *Women Attorneys and the Changing Workplace: High Hopes, Mixed Outcomes*
CrimJR - v40 - i1 - March 2015 - p107-109 [501+]
Kitzing, Michael - *Fur den christlichen und sozialen Volksstaat: Die Badische Zentrumspartei in der Weimarer Republik*
AHR - v120 - i2 - April 2015 - p735-736 [501+]
Kivelson, Valerie - *Desperate Magic: The Moral Economy of Witchcraft in Seventeenth-Century Russia*
AHR - v120 - i4 - Oct 2015 - p1426-1429 [501+]
Kivirahk, Andrus - *The Man Who Spoke Snakish*
BL - v112 - i4 - Oct 15 2015 - p28(1) [51-500]
KR - Sept 1 2015 - pNA [51-500]
PW - v262 - i27 - July 6 2015 - p49(1) [51-500]
Kivisto, Peter - *Debating Multiculturalism in the Nordic Welfare States*
ERS - v38 - i3 - March 2015 - p491(3) [501+]
Kivisto, Sari - *The Vices of Learning: Morality and Knowledge at Early Modern Universities*
Ren Q - v68 - i3 - Fall 2015 - p1021-1022 [501+]
Kjaernes, Unni - *Trust in Food: A Comparative and Institutional Analysis*
CS - v44 - i2 - March 2015 - p226-228 [501+]
Kjelle, Marylou - *The Quest to End World Hunger*
c BL - v111 - i16 - April 15 2015 - p45(1) [51-500]
Kjelle, Marylou Morano - *Bill Gates: Microsoft Founder and Philanthropist*
c HB Guide - v26 - i2 - Fall 2015 - p209(2) [51-500]
Line Dances around the World
BL - v111 - i9-10 - Jan 1 2015 - p84(1) [51-500]
Klaassen, Frank - *The Transformations of Magic: Illicit Learned Magic in the Later Middle Ages and the Renaissance*
Historian - v77 - i1 - Spring 2015 - p173(2) [501+]
Klaber, William - *The Rebellion of Miss Lucy Ann Lobdell*
BL - v111 - i11 - Feb 1 2015 - p30(1) [51-500]
LJ - v140 - i3 - Feb 15 2015 - p89(1) [51-500]
NYTBR - March 15 2015 - p14(L) [501+]
Klapczynski, Gregor - *Katholischer Historismus? Zum historischen Denken in der Deutschsprachigen Kirchengeschichte um 1900 Heinrich Schrors - Albert Ehrhard - Joseph Schnitzer*
CHR - v101 - i1 - Wntr 2015 - p169(2) [501+]
Klass, David - *Losers Take All*
y BL - v112 - i1 - Sept 1 2015 - p100(1) [51-500]
y KR - August 1 2015 - pNA [51-500]
y PW - v262 - i32 - August 10 2015 - p62(1) [51-500]
y SLJ - v61 - i9 - Sept 2015 - p160(1) [51-500]
Klassen, Jon - *Ce n'est pas mon chapeau (Illus. by Klassen, Jon)*
c Res Links - v21 - i1 - Oct 2015 - p51(1) [51-500]
Klassen, Julie - *The Painter's Daughter*
y BL - v112 - i6 - Nov 15 2015 - p19(1) [51-500]
Klaus, Ian - *Forging Capitalism: Rogues, Swindlers, Frauds and the Rise of Modern Finance*
BHR - v89 - i3 - Autumn 2015 - p580(4) [501+]
HNet - Sept 2015 - pNA(NA) [501+]
Spec - v327 - i9728 - Feb 7 2015 - p40(2) [501+]
Klause, Inna - *Der Klang des Gulag: Musik und Musiker in den Sowjetischen Zwangsarbeitslagern der 1920er- bis 1950er-Jahre*
HNet - July 2015 - pNA [501+]
Klaussmann, Liza - *Villa America*
BL - v111 - i21 - July 1 2015 - p43(1) [51-500]
Ent W - i1376 - August 14 2015 - p61(1) [501+]
KR - June 1 2015 - pNA [501+]
PW - v262 - i26 - June 29 2015 - p42(2) [51-500]
Klautke, Egbert - *The Mind of the Nation: Volkerpsychologie in Germany, 1851-1955*
GSR - v38 - i1 - Feb 2015 - p181-183 [501+]
HNet - Feb 2015 - pNA [501+]
Klavan, Andrew - *Hostage Run*
y BL - v111 - i15 - April 1 2015 - p68(1) [51-500]
y SLJ - v61 - i3 - March 2015 - p137(1) [51-500]
Werewolf Cop
BL - v111 - i11 - Feb 1 2015 - p29(1) [51-500]
Ch Today - v59 - i2 - March 2015 - p62(1) [51-500]
KR - Jan 15 2015 - pNA [51-500]
PW - v262 - i4 - Jan 26 2015 - p149(1) [51-500]
Klay, Phil - *Redeployment (Read by Klein, Craig). Audiobook Review*
BL - v111 - i16 - April 15 2015 - p61(1) [51-500]
Redeployment
HM - v331 - i1983 - August 2015 - p84(6) [501+]
NYRB - v62 - i9 - May 21 2015 - p48(3) [501+]
NYTBR - March 8 2015 - p32(L) [501+]
Prog - v79 - i2 - Feb 2015 - p44(4) [501+]
TLS - i5854 - June 12 2015 - p19(2) [501+]
Klee, Miles - *True False*
TLS - i5869 - Sept 25 2015 - p20(1) [501+]
Kleeman, Alexandra - *You Too Can Have a Body Like Mine*
KR - June 15 2015 - pNA [51-500]
NYT - Sept 24 2015 - pC6(L) [501+]
NYTBR - Sept 6 2015 - p19(L) [501+]
PW - v262 - i19 - May 11 2015 - p33(1) [51-500]
Kleeman, Faye Yuan - *In Transit: The Formation of the Colonial East Asian Cultural Sphere*
Pac A - v88 - i4 - Dec 2015 - p936 [501+]
Klehr, Dawn - *If You Wrong Us*
y BL - v112 - i3 - Oct 1 2015 - p69(2) [51-500]
y KR - August 1 2015 - pNA [51-500]
y SLJ - v61 - i9 - Sept 2015 - p168(1) [51-500]
y VOYA - v38 - i4 - Oct 2015 - p54(1) [51-500]
Kleiman, Irit Ruth - *Philippe de Commynes: Memory, Betrayal, Text*
HER - v130 - i545 - August 2015 - p973(3) [501+]
Klein, Alan - *Dominican Baseball: New Pride, Old Prejudice*
CS - v44 - i6 - Nov 2015 - p820-821 [501+]
Klein, Carol Swartout - *Painting for Peace in Ferguson*
c CH Bwatch - April 2015 - pNA [51-500]
c SLJ - v61 - i7 - July 2015 - p103(2) [51-500]
Klein, Caroline - *Ai Weiwei Architecture*
Bwatch - May 2015 - pNA [51-500]
Klein, Christine A. - *Mississippi River Tragedies: A Century of Unnatural Disaster*
JSH - v81 - i3 - August 2015 - p758(2) [501+]
Klein, Christopher - *Strong Boy: The Life and Times of John L. Sullivan, America's First Sports Hero*
AM - v212 - i5 - Feb 16 2015 - p36(2) [501+]
Klein, Daniel - *Every Time I Find the Meaning of Life, They Change It: Wisdom of the Great Philosophers on How to Live*
BL - v112 - i1 - Sept 1 2015 - p16(1) [51-500]
KR - July 1 2015 - pNA [501+]
LJ - v140 - i14 - Sept 1 2015 - p109(2) [51-500]
Klein, Grady - *The Cartoon Introduction to Statistics*
Math T - v108 - i6 - Feb 2015 - p476-477 [501+]
Klein, Hilary - *Companeras: Zapatista Women's Stories*
Wom R Bks - v32 - i4 - July-August 2015 - p12(2) [501+]
Klein, Jen - *Jillian Cade: (Fake) Paranormal Investigator*
y BL - v112 - i3 - Oct 1 2015 - p70(1) [51-500]
y KR - July 15 2015 - pNA [51-500]
y PW - v262 - i27 - July 6 2015 - p75(1) [51-500]
y SLJ - v61 - i9 - Sept 2015 - p168(1) [51-500]
y VOYA - v38 - i4 - Oct 2015 - p73(1) [51-500]
Klein, Joe - *Charlie Mike: A True Story of Heroes Who Brought Their Mission Home*
BL - v112 - i3 - Oct 1 2015 - p5(1) [51-500]
KR - July 15 2015 - pNA [501+]
LJ - v140 - i13 - August 1 2015 - p108(2) [51-500]
NYTBR - Nov 22 2015 - p24(L) [501+]
PW - v262 - i30 - July 27 2015 - p51(1) [51-500]
Klein, Joel - *Lessons of Hope: How to Fix Our Schools*
NYRB - v62 - i4 - March 5 2015 - p8(2) [501+]
Klein, Laurie - *Photographing the Female Form with Digital Infrared*
Bwatch - Feb 2015 - pNA [51-500]
Klein, Mason - *Helena Rubinstein: Beauty is Power*
TLS - i5846 - April 17 2015 - p26(1) [501+]
Klein, Maury - *A Call to Arms: Mobilizing America for World War II*
RAH - v43 - i1 - March 2015 - p149-155 [501+]
Klein, Menachem - *Lives in Common: Arabs and Jews in Jerusalem, Jaffa and Hebron*
HT - v65 - i5 - May 2015 - p65(1) [501+]
Klein, Naomi - *This Changes Everything: Capitalism vs. the Climate (Read by Archer, Ellen). Audiobook Review*
BL - v111 - i15 - April 1 2015 - p85(2) [51-500]
This Changes Everything: Capitalism vs. The Climate
Barron's - v95 - i22 - June 1 2015 - p37(2) [501+]
CS - v44 - i3 - May 2015 - p314-321 [501+]
HNet - Jan 2015 - pNA [501+]
TLS - i5876 - Nov 13 2015 - p22(2) [501+]
Klein, Philip - *Overcoming Obamacare: Three Approaches to Reversing the Government Takeover of Health Care*
Reason - v47 - i1 - May 2015 - p54(7) [501+]
Klein, Richard - *Musikphilosophie zur Einfuhrung*
HNet - March 2015 - pNA [501+]
Klein, Shawn E. - *Steve Jobs and Philosophy: For Those Who Think Different*
Bwatch - June 2015 - pNA [51-500]
Klein, Stefan - *We Are All Stardust*
BL - v112 - i6 - Nov 15 2015 - p6(2) [51-500]
Nature - v528 - i7581 - Dec 10 2015 - p191(1) [51-500]
Klein, Todd - *The Sandman: Overture*
CSM - Nov 11 2015 - pNA [501+]
Kleinbard, Edward D. - *We Are Better Than This: How Government Should Spend Our Money*
IndRev - v20 - i2 - Fall 2015 - p313(4) [501+]
Kleinberg, Aviad M. - *The Sensual God: How the Senses Make the Almighty Senseless*
LJ - v140 - i16 - Oct 1 2015 - p64(2) [501+]
Kleine, Andrea - *Calf: A Novel*
KR - August 1 2015 - pNA [501+]
LJ - v140 - i17 - Oct 15 2015 - p75(1) [51-500]
PW - v262 - i20 - May 18 2015 - p1(1) [51-500]
Kleine Erinnerungen: Raume, Praktiken und Akteure landlicher Erinnerungen
HNet - May 2015 - pNA [501+]
Kleiner, Morris M. - *Stages of Occupational Regulation: Analysis of Case Studies*
CS - v44 - i3 - May 2015 - p371-373 [501+]
Kleinhendler, Howard - *Running for the House*
KR - Jan 1 2015 - pNA [501+]
Klemann, Hein - *Occupied Economies: An Economic History of Nazi-Occupied Europe, 1939-1945*
HNet - Jan 2015 - pNA [501+]
Klepeis, Alicia Z. - *Francisco's Kites / Las cometas de Francisco (Illus. by Undercuffler, Gary)*
c CH Bwatch - June 2015 - pNA [51-500]
c HB Guide - v26 - i2 - Fall 2015 - p40(1) [51-500]
c KR - March 15 2015 - pNA [51-500]
Francisco's Kites/Las cometas de Francisco (Illus. by Undercuffler, Gary)
c SLJ - v61 - i4 - April 2015 - p130(1) [51-500]
Kletter, Kerry - *The First Time She Drowned*
KR - Dec 15 2015 - pNA [51-500]
PW - v262 - i52 - Dec 21 2015 - p155(2) [51-500]
Kleveman, Lutz - *Wanderjahre: A Reporter's Journey in a Mad World*
TLS - i5832 - Jan 9 2015 - p26(1) [501+]
Kleymeyer, Charles David - *Yeshu*
SPBW - Jan 2015 - pNA [501+]
Kleypas, Lisa - *Brown-Eyed Girl*
BL - v111 - i21 - July 1 2015 - p43(1) [51-500]
KR - May 15 2015 - pNA [501+]
PW - v262 - i15 - April 13 2015 - p62(1) [51-500]

Cold-Hearted Rake
BL - v112 - i4 - Oct 15 2015 - p26(1) [51-500]
KR - August 15 2015 - pNA [51-500]
PW - v262 - i38 - Sept 21 2015 - p60(1) [51-500]
Kliegel, Ewald - *Reflexology Made Easy: Self-Help Techniques for Everyday Ailments*
RVBW - Nov 2015 - pNA [51-500]
Kliger, Ilya - *The Narrative Shape of Truth: Veridiction in Modern European Literature*
MLR - v110 - i1 - Jan 2015 - p225-227 [501+]
Klima, John - *The Game Must Go On: Hank Greenberg, Pete Gray, and the Great Days of Baseball on the Home Front in WWII*
LJ - v140 - i5 - March 15 2015 - p111(1) [51-500]
KR - Feb 15 2015 - pNA [501+]
Kliman, Daniel - *Fateful Transitions: How Democracies Manage Rising Powers, from the Eve of World War I to China's Ascendance*
For Aff - v94 - i3 - May-June 2015 - pNA [501+]
Klimo, Kate - *Dash (Illus. by Jessell, Tim)*
c HB Guide - v26 - i1 - Spring 2015 - p61(1) [51-500]
Dr. Seuss (Illus. by Krull, Kathleen)
c KR - Jan 1 2016 - pNA [51-500]
Sweetie (Illus. by Jessell, Tim)
c HB Guide - v26 - i2 - Fall 2015 - p68(1) [51-500]
Kline, Nancy - *Living with Time to Think: The Goddaughter Letters*
Bwatch - Sept 2015 - pNA [51-500]
Time to Think: Listening to Ignite the Human Mind
Bwatch - Sept 2015 - pNA [51-500]
Kline, Ronald R. - *The Cybernetics Moment: Or Why We Call Our Age the Information Age*
LJ - v140 - i11 - June 15 2015 - p107(1) [51-500]
Kline, Suzy - *Horrible Harry and the Hallway Bully (Read by Heller, Johnny). Audiobook Review*
c SLJ - v61 - i5 - May 2015 - p68(2) [51-500]
Klinenberg, Eric - *Modern Romance*
Spec - v328 - i9747 - June 20 2015 - p36(2) [501+]
Nat Post - v17 - i194 - June 20 2015 - pWP5(1) [501+]
PW - v262 - i18 - May 4 2015 - p111(2) [51-500]
Spec - v328 - i9747 - June 20 2015 - p36(2) [501+]
Klingemann, August - *The Nightwatches of Bonaventura*
TLS - i5855 - June 19 2015 - p13(1) [501+]
Klingen, Henning - *Extra Ecclesiam ... : Zur Institution und Kritik von Kirche*
Theol St - v76 - i1 - March 2015 - p187(2) [501+]
Klinger, Leslie S. - *In the Shadow of Edgar Allan Poe: Classic Tales of Terror 1816-1914*
PW - v262 - i33 - August 17 2015 - p54(1) [51-500]
The New Annotated H.P. Lovecraft
TLS - i5835 - Jan 30 2015 - p12(2) [501+]
Klink, Joanna - *Excerpts from a Secret Prophecy*
HR - v68 - i2 - Summer 2015 - p327-335 [501+]
Klinkowitz, Jerome - *Frank Lloyd Wright and his Manner of Thought*
Am St - v54 - i2 - Summer 2015 - p120(1) [501+]
Klise, Kari Allente - *The Circus Goes to Sea (Illus. by Klise, M. Sarah)*
c HB Guide - v26 - i1 - Spring 2015 - p83(1) [51-500]
Klise, Kate - *43 Old Cemetery Road: The Loch Ness Punster (Illus. by Klise, M. Sarah)*
c CH Bwatch - July 2015 - pNA [51-500]
c HB Guide - v26 - i2 - Fall 2015 - p89(1) [51-500]
c SLJ - v61 - i5 - May 2015 - p98(2) [51-500]
Pop Goes the Circus! (Illus. by Klise, M. Sarah)
c SLJ - v61 - i5 - May 2015 - p99(1) [51-500]
Three-Ring Rascals, Books 1-2: The Show Must Go On! - The Greatest Star on Earth. Audiobook Review
c SLJ - v61 - i9 - Sept 2015 - p62(1) [51-500]
Three-Ring Rascals, Books 3-4: The Circus Goes to Sea - Pop Goes the Circus!. Audiobook Review
c SLJ - v61 - i9 - Sept 2015 - p62(1) [51-500]
Klitzman, Robert L. - *Am I My Genes? Confronting Fate and Family Secrets in the Age of Genetic Testing*
CS - v44 - i4 - July 2015 - p528-530 [501+]
The Ethics Police: The Struggle to Make Human Research Safe
Soc - v52 - i5 - Oct 2015 - p503(4) [501+]
Klobuchar, Amy - *The Senator Next Door: A Memoir from the Heartland*
KR - July 15 2015 - pNA [501+]
LJ - v140 - i13 - August 1 2015 - p111(1) [51-500]
Klockler, Jurgen - *Ulrich Richental: Chronik des Konzils zu Konstanz, 1414-1418*
HNet - Feb 2015 - pNA [501+]
Kloeble, Christopher - *Almost Everything Very Fast*
KR - Dec 1 2015 - pNA [51-500]
PW - v262 - i48 - Nov 30 2015 - p35(1) [51-500]
Kloepfer, John - *Galaxy's Most Wanted (Illus. by Edwards, Nick)*
c HB Guide - v26 - i2 - Fall 2015 - p89(1) [51-500]
Into the Dorkness (Illus. by Edwards, Nick)
c KR - March 1 2015 - pNA [51-500]
c HB Guide - v26 - i2 - Fall 2015 - p89(1) [51-500]
Zombies of the Carribbean (Illus. by DeGrand, David)
c HB Guide - v26 - i1 - Spring 2015 - p83(1) [51-500]
Klose, Alexander - *The Container Principle: How a Box Changes the Way We Think*
Nature - v519 - i7544 - March 26 2015 - p413(1) [51-500]
Klose, Carol - *The Best of Carol Klose: Fifteen Original Piano Solos*
Am MT - v65 - i3 - Dec 2015 - p48(2) [501+]
Klose, Robert - *Long Live Grover Cleveland*
BL - v111 - i21 - July 1 2015 - p32(1) [51-500]
Kloss, Robert - *The Revelator*
KR - July 15 2015 - pNA [501+]
Klosterman, Robert J. - *The Four Horsemen of the Investor's Apocalypse*
KR - Sept 1 2015 - pNA [501+]
Klostermann, Penny Parker - *There Was an Old Dragon Who Swallowed a Knight (Illus. by Mantle, Ben)*
c KR - May 1 2015 - pNA [51-500]
c SLJ - v61 - i7 - July 2015 - p63(1) [51-500]
Klosty, James - *John Cage Was*
HR - v67 - i4 - Wntr 2015 - p647-652 [501+]
Klotz, David - *Caesar in the City of Amun: Egyptian Temple Construction and Theology in Roman Thebes*
Class R - v65 - i1 - April 2015 - p218-220 [501+]
Klubock, Thomas Miller - *La Frontera: Forests and Ecological Conflict in Chile's Frontier Territory*
AHR - v120 - i3 - June 2015 - p1082-1083 [501+]
HAHR - v95 - i2 - May 2015 - p371-373 [501+]
Kluge, Alexander - *30 April 1945*
BL - v112 - i2 - Sept 15 2015 - p36(1) [51-500]
K'Meyer, Tracy E. - *From Brown to Meredith: The Long Struggle for School Desegration in Louisville, Kentucky, 1954-2007*
RAH - v43 - i1 - March 2015 - p177-183 [501+]
Kmiec, Douglas - *Secularism, Catholicism, and the Future of Public Life*
JAAR - v83 - i2 - June 2015 - pNA [501+]
Knaak, Richard A. - *Black City Saint*
KR - Dec 15 2015 - pNA [51-500]
Knaap, Anna C. - *Art, Music, and Spectacle in the Age of Rubens: The Pompa Introitus Ferdinandi*
Ren Q - v68 - i1 - Spring 2015 - p247-249 [501+]
Six Ct J - v46 - i3 - Fall 2015 - p704-705 [501+]
Knapman, Timothy - *Hamlet (Illus. by Shimony, Yaniv)*
c HB Guide - v26 - i2 - Fall 2015 - p202(1) [51-500]
c Sch Lib - v63 - i3 - Autumn 2015 - p174(1) [51-500]
Mom's the Word (Illus. by Littler, Jamie)
c HB Guide - v26 - i1 - Spring 2015 - p11(1) [51-500]
A Monster Moved In! (Illus. by Schauer, Loretta)
c HB Guide - v26 - i2 - Fall 2015 - p40(1) [51-500]
c KR - Jan 1 2015 - pNA [51-500]
c SLJ - v61 - i2 - Feb 2015 - p71(1) [51-500]
Soon (Illus. by Benson, Patrick)
c Magpies - v30 - i1 - March 2015 - p26(1) [501+]
c BL - v111 - i18 - May 15 2015 - p59(1) [51-500]
c CH Bwatch - March 2015 - pNA [51-500]
c HB Guide - v26 - i2 - Fall 2015 - p13(1) [51-500]
SLJ - v61 - i3 - March 2015 - p118(1) [51-500]
A Very Pirate Christmas (Illus. by Ayto, Russell)
c PW - v262 - i37 - Sept 14 2015 - p66(1) [51-500]
c SLJ - v61 - i10 - Oct 2015 - p65(1) [51-500]
Knapp, A. Bernard - *The Archaeology of Cyprus: From Earliest Prehistory through the Bronze Age*
JNES - v74 - i1 - April 2015 - p162(165) [501+]
Knapp, Gwendolyn - *After a While You Just Get Used to It: A Tale of Family Clutter*
New Or - v49 - i9 - June 2015 - p38(1) [501+]
Knarr, Stephanie Weiland - *Dr. Stephanie's Relationship Repair for Couples: A Customer Service Approach for Minimizing Conflict and Creating Lasting Love in Your Relationships*
SPBW - Oct 2015 - pNA [51-500]
Knauer, Christine - *Let Us Fight as Free Men: Black Soldiers and Civil Rights*
AHR - v120 - i4 - Oct 2015 - p1515-1516 [501+]
HLR - v128 - i5 - March 2015 - p1560(1) [1-50]
JAH - v101 - i4 - March 2015 - p1310-1311 [501+]
Knaus, John Kenneth - *Beyond Shangri-La: America and Tibet's Move into the Twenty-First Century*
AHR - v120 - i1 - Feb 2015 - p207(1) [501+]
Knausgaard, Karl Ove - *Dancing in the Dark*
KR - Feb 15 2015 - pNA [51-500]
NYT - April 21 2015 - pC1(L) [501+]
NYTBR - April 26 2015 - p1(L) [501+]
PW - v262 - i8 - Feb 23 2015 - p2(1) [51-500]
TLS - i5842 - March 20 2015 - p22(1) [501+]
My Struggle, bk. 3
NYTBR - May 17 2015 - p32(L) [501+]
My Struggle Book Four
AM - v212 - i19 - June 8 2015 - p36(2) [501+]
BL - v111 - i16 - April 15 2015 - p26(1) [51-500]
NYRB - v62 - i11 - June 25 2015 - p24(3) [501+]
My Struggle: Book Four
LJ - v140 - i10 - June 1 2015 - p92(3) [501+]
My Struggle: Book One (Read by Ballerini, Edoardo). Audiobook Review
LJ - v140 - i12 - July 1 2015 - p43(1) [51-500]
My Struggle: Boyhood
AM - v212 - i8 - March 9 2015 - p35(3) [501+]
Knausgaard, Linda Bostrom - *The Helios Disaster*
TLS - i5854 - June 12 2015 - p13(1) [501+]
TLS - i5859 - July 17 2015 - p27(1) [501+]
Knausgard, Karl Ove - *Dancing in the Dark*
Nat Post - v17 - i153 - May 2 2015 - pWP6(1) [501+]
Knazev, Sergey - *The Fame Game: A Superstar's Guide to Getting Rich and Famous*
LJ - v140 - i14 - Sept 1 2015 - p125(1) [51-500]
Knecht, Robert J. - *Hero or Tyrant? Henry III, King of France, 1574-89*
FS - v69 - i2 - April 2015 - p240(1) [501+]
HER - v130 - i544 - June 2015 - p732(2) [501+]
Hero or Tyrant?: Henry III, King of France, 1574-89
Six Ct J - v46 - i3 - Fall 2015 - p676-677 [501+]
Knecht, Rosalie - *Relief Map*
KR - Jan 1 2016 - pNA [51-500]
Kneece, Mark - *The Art of Comic Book Writing: The Definitive Guide to Outlining, Scripting, and Pitching Your Sequential Art Stories*
BL - v112 - i2 - Sept 15 2015 - p50(1) [51-500]
LJ - v140 - i16 - Oct 1 2015 - p89(1) [51-500]
Kneen, Krissy - *The Adventures of Holly White and the Incredible Sex Machine*
KR - Nov 15 2015 - pNA [501+]
PW - v262 - i48 - Nov 30 2015 - p44(1) [51-500]
Kneidel, Sally - *Creepy Crawlies and the Scientific Method: More Than 100 Hands-On Science Experiments for Children*
c RVBW - June 2015 - pNA [51-500]
Knepper, Paul - *International Crime in the 20th Century: The League of Nations Era, 1919-1939*
CS - v44 - i2 - March 2015 - p291-292 [501+]
Knier, Maria - *The Bezert (Illus. by Knier, Maria)*
c CH Bwatch - Jan 2015 - pNA [51-500]
Knight, Alisha - *Pauline Hopkins and the American Dream: An African American Writer's Re-Visionary Gospel of Success*
Callaloo - v38 - i1 - Wntr 2015 - p210-214 [501+]
Knight, Angela - *Without Restraint*
PW - v262 - i23 - June 8 2015 - p45(2) [51-500]
Knight, Eric - *KLassie Come-Home: An Adaptation of Eric Knight's Classic Story (Illus. by Ivanov, Olga)*
c SLJ - v61 - i9 - Sept 2015 - p124(1) [51-500]
Knight, Erika - *500 Crochet Stitches: The Ultimate Crochet Stitch Bible*
LJ - v140 - i15 - Sept 15 2015 - p77(1) [51-500]
Knight, Florence - *One: A Cook and Her Cupboard*
TLS - i5831 - Jan 2 2015 - p11(1) [501+]
Knight, G. Roger - *Commodities and Colonialism: The Story of Big Sugar in Indonesia, 1880-1942*
BHR - v89 - i1 - Spring 2015 - p197(4) [501+]
Knight, Gladys L. - *Pop Culture Places: An Encyclopedia of Places in American Popular Culture*
R&USQ - v54 - i3 - Spring 2015 - p65(1) [501+]
Knight, Henry - *Tropic of Hopes: California, Florida, and the Selling of American Paradise, 1869-1929*
RAH - v43 - i1 - March 2015 - p116-125 [501+]
Knight, Julia - *Swords and Scoundrels*
y BL - v112 - i3 - Oct 1 2015 - p36(1) [51-500]
PW - v262 - i37 - Sept 14 2015 - p46(1) [51-500]
Knight, Kelly Ray - *Addicted.pregnant.poor*
TimHES - i2223 - Oct 1 2015 - p53(1) [501+]
Knight, L.A. - *Dog Training the American Male*
KR - March 15 2015 - pNA [501+]
Knight, Leah - *Reading Green in Early Modern England*
Ren Q - v68 - i2 - Summer 2015 - p766-767

[501+]
    RES - v66 - i274 - April 2015 - p371-372 [501+]
    Sev Cent N - v73 - i3-4 - Fall-Winter 2015 - p107(5) [501+]
Knight, Mary - *Saving Wonder*
    c KR - Dec 15 2015 - pNA [51-500]
    c PW - v262 - i45 - Nov 9 2015 - p59(2) [51-500]
Knight, Michael Muhammad - *Why I Am a Salafi*
    KR - June 1 2015 - pNA [501+]
    PW - v262 - i23 - June 8 2015 - p54(1) [51-500]
Knight, Molly - *The Best Team Money Can Buy: The Los Angeles Dodgers' Wild Struggle to Build a Baseball Powerhouse*
    KR - June 1 2015 - pNA [51-500]
    LJ - v140 - i12 - July 1 2015 - p89(2) [51-500]
Knight, Renee - *Disclaimer*
    BL - v111 - i16 - April 15 2015 - p28(1) [51-500]
    KR - March 15 2015 - pNA [501+]
    LJ - v140 - i6 - April 1 2015 - p86(1) [501+]
    NYT - May 28 2015 - pC1(L) [501+]
    PW - v262 - i11 - March 16 2015 - p64(1) [51-500]
Knight, Rob - *Follow Your Gut: The Enormous Impact of Tiny Microbes*
    Spec - v328 - i9742 - May 16 2015 - p37(1) [501+]
Knight, Roger - *Britain against Napoleon: The Organization of Victory 1793-1815*
    HER - v130 - i542 - Feb 2015 - p123(14) [501+]
Knight, Sarah - *The Life-Changing Magic of Not Giving a F*ck: How to Stop Spending Time You Don't Have with People You Don't Like Doing Things You Don't Want to Do*
    NYTBR - Dec 6 2015 - p87(L) [501+]
Knightley, Erin - *The Duke Can Go to the Devil*
    PW - v262 - i20 - May 18 2015 - p70(1) [51-500]
Knighton, Charles S. - *Elizabethan Naval Administration*
    Six Ct J - v46 - i1 - Spring 2015 - p136-3 [501+]
Knights, Sarah - *Bloomsbury's Outsider: A Life of David Garnett*
    Spec - v328 - i9748 - June 27 2015 - p36(2) [501+]
    TLS - i5877 - Nov 20 2015 - p11(1) [501+]
Knirck, Jason - *Afterimage of the Revolution: Cumann na Ngaedheal and Irish Politics, 1922-1932*
    ILS - v34 - i2 - Spring 2015 - p9(1) [501+]
Knisley, Lucy - *Displacement (Illus. by Knisley, Lucy)*
    BL - v111 - i13 - March 1 2015 - p32(2) [51-500]
    LJ - v140 - i5 - March 15 2015 - p88(3) [501+]
Knittel, Susanne C. - *The Historical Uncanny: Disability, Ethnicity, and the Politics of Holocaust Memory*
    HNet - August 2015 - pNA [501+]
Knock, Thomas J. - *The Rise of a Prairie Statesman*
    KR - Dec 1 2015 - pNA [501+]
Knoll, Jessica - *Luckiest Girl Alive*
    BL - v111 - i16 - April 15 2015 - p26(1) [51-500]
    Ent W - i1362 - May 8 2015 - p56(1) [501+]
    KR - March 1 2015 - pNA [501+]
    Mac - v128 - i19-20 - May 18 2015 - p77(1) [501+]
    PW - v262 - i13 - March 30 2015 - p46(1) [51-500]
Knopf, Chris - *A Billion Ways to Die*
    RVBW - July 2015 - pNA [501+]
Cop Job
    BL - v111 - i22 - August 1 2015 - p32(1) [51-500]
    KR - July 15 2015 - pNA [501+]
    PW - v262 - i27 - July 6 2015 - p47(1) [51-500]
Knopf, Kelly Jones - *Unusual Chickens for the Exceptional Poultry Farmer (Illus. by Kath, Katie)*
    c CH Bwatch - July 2015 - pNA [51-500]
Knopper, Steve - *MJ: The Genius of Michael Jackson*
    BL - v112 - i2 - Sept 15 2015 - p15(1) [51-500]
    KR - August 15 2015 - pNA [501+]
    PW - v262 - i34 - August 24 2015 - p77(1) [51-500]
Knoppers, Gary N. - *Jews and Samaritans. The Origins and History of Their Early Relations*
    JNES - v74 - i1 - April 2015 - p160(2) [501+]
Knoppers, Laura Lunger - *The Oxford Handbook of Literature and the English Revolution*
    MP - v112 - i4 - May 2015 - pE316(3) [501+]
Knott, Betty I. - *Collected Works of Erasmus, vols. 37-38: Apophthegmata*
    Six Ct J - v46 - i3 - Fall 2015 - p814-816 [501+]
Knott, Robert - *Robert B. Parker's Blackjack*
    KR - Dec 1 2015 - pNA [501+]
Knott, Stephen F. - *Washington and Hamilton: The Alliance That Forged America*
    LJ - v140 - i14 - Sept 1 2015 - p120(2) [51-500]
    KR - July 1 2015 - pNA [501+]

Knowing Things: Circulations and Transitions of Objects in Natural History
    HNet - May 2015 - pNA [501+]
Knowles, Anne Kelly - *Geographies of the Holocaust*
    HNet - March 2015 - pNA [501+]
Mastering Iron: The Struggle to Modernize an American Iron Industry, 1800-1868
    RAH - v43 - i3 - Sept 2015 - p471-476 [501+]
Knowles, Elizabeth - *Oxford Dictionary of Quotations, 8th ed.*
    BL - v111 - i16 - April 15 2015 - p12(1) [51-500]
    TLS - i5835 - Jan 30 2015 - p25(1) [501+]
Knowles, Jo - *Read Between the Lines*
    y BL - v111 - i12 - Feb 15 2015 - p83(2) [51-500]
    y CCB-B - v68 - i9 - May 2015 - p452(2) [51-500]
    y HB - v91 - i3 - May-June 2015 - p113(1) [51-500]
    y HB Guide - v26 - i2 - Fall 2015 - p127(1) [51-500]
    y KR - Jan 1 2015 - pNA [51-500]
    y PW - v262 - i2 - Jan 12 2015 - p61(2) [51-500]
    y VOYA - v37 - i6 - Feb 2015 - p59(1) [51-500]
Knowles, Katie - *Shakespeare's Boys: A Cultural History*
    Ren Q - v68 - i2 - Summer 2015 - p783-784 [501+]
Knowlton, Timothy W. - *Maya Creation Myths: Words and Worlds of the Chilam Balam*
    Six Ct J - v46 - i1 - Spring 2015 - p249(1) [501+]
Knox, Cynthia - *CP Horses: A Complete Guide to Drawing Horses in Colored Pencil*
    LJ - v140 - i7 - April 15 2015 - p88(1) [51-500]
Knox, Jennifer L. - *Days of Shame & Failure*
    NYTBR - Dec 27 2015 - p18(L) [501+]
    PW - v262 - i42 - Oct 19 2015 - p54(1) [51-500]
Knudsen, Michelle - *Evil Librarian (Read by Foster, Emily). Audiobook Review*
    y BL - v111 - i18 - May 15 2015 - p70(1) [51-500]
Evil Librarian. Audiobook Review
    y SLJ - v61 - i3 - March 2015 - p80(2) [51-500]
Evil Librarian
    y HB Guide - v26 - i1 - Spring 2015 - p112(1) [51-500]
The Mage of Trelian
    y KR - Nov 1 2015 - pNA [51-500]
Marilyn's Monster (Illus. by Phelan, Matt)
    c BL - v111 - i12 - Feb 15 2015 - p88(1) [51-500]
    c CCB-B - v68 - i9 - May 2015 - p453(1) [51-500]
    c CH Bwatch - May 2015 - pNA [51-500]
    c HB Guide - v26 - i2 - Fall 2015 - p40(1) [51-500]
    c KR - Jan 1 2015 - pNA [51-500]
    c PW - v262 - i4 - Jan 26 2015 - p168(1) [51-500]
    c PW - v262 - i49 - Dec 2 2015 - p16(1) [51-500]
    c SLJ - v61 - i2 - Feb 2015 - p71(2) [51-500]
Knudsen, Rachel Ahern - *Homeric Speech and the Origins of Rhetoric*
    Class R - v65 - i2 - Oct 2015 - p325-327 [501+]
Knudsen, Shannon - *I'll Haunt You! Meet a Ghost (Illus. by Buccheri, Chiara)*
    c HB Guide - v26 - i1 - Spring 2015 - p143(1) [51-500]
I'm Undead and Hungry! Meet a Zombie (Illus. by Buccheri, Chiara)
    c HB Guide - v26 - i1 - Spring 2015 - p143(1) [51-500]
Testing the Truth
    y VOYA - v38 - i5 - Dec 2015 - p65(1) [501+]
Knupfer, Anne Meis - *Food Co-ops in America: Communities, Consumption, and Economic Democracy*
    BHR - v89 - i1 - Spring 2015 - p160(3) [501+]
    RAH - v43 - i1 - March 2015 - p126-133 [501+]
Knuteman, Jerzhy - *The Vatican Files*
    SPBW - May 2015 - pNA [501+]
Knuth, Wendy - *Moore Zombies: The Search for Gargoy (Illus. by Allen, Brian)*
    c CH Bwatch - Feb 2015 - pNA [51-500]
Knutsen, Kimberly - *The Lost Journals of Sylvia Plath*
    BL - v112 - i4 - Oct 15 2015 - p33(1) [51-500]
    KR - August 1 2015 - pNA [501+]
Ko, Sangmi - *A Dog Wearing Shoes (Illus. by Ko, Sangmi)*
    c BL - v112 - i1 - Sept 1 2015 - p119(1) [51-500]
    c CH Bwatch - Nov 2015 - pNA [51-500]
    c KR - July 15 2015 - pNA [51-500]
    c NYTBR - Dec 20 2015 - p14(L) [51-500]
    c SLJ - v61 - i6 - June 2015 - p86(2) [51-500]
Ko, Un - *Maninbo: Peace & War*
    WLT - v89 - i5 - Sept-Oct 2015 - p73(2) [51-500]
Koba, Susan - *Hard-to-Teach Biology Concepts, 2d ed.*
    Sci Teach - v82 - i1 - Jan 2015 - p65 [51-500]
Kobald, Irena - *My Two Blankets (Illus. by Blackwood, Freya)*
    c BL - v112 - i1 - Sept 1 2015 - p122(1) [51-500]
    c KR - July 1 2015 - pNA [51-500]
    c NYTBR - August 23 2015 - p24(L) [51-500]

Kobayashi, Yoshiaki - *Malfunctioning Democracy in Japan: Quantitative Analysis in a Civil Society*
    JAS - v74 - i2 - May 2015 - p443-447 [501+]
Kobrin, Kirill - *Eleven Prague Corpses: Stories*
    KR - Dec 15 2015 - pNA [51-500]
    PW - v262 - i46 - Nov 16 2015 - p48(1) [51-500]
Kobrin, Rebecca - *Chosen Capital: The Jewish Encounter with American Capitalism*
    BHR - v89 - i1 - Spring 2015 - p165(4) [501+]
Koch, Aidan - *Impressions*
    ABR - v36 - i2 - Jan-Feb 2015 - p7(1) [501+]
Koch, Erin - *Free Market Tuberculosis: Managing Epidemics in Post-Soviet Georgia*
    Isis - v106 - i2 - June 2015 - p506(2) [501+]
    MAQ - v29 - i1 - March 2015 - p22-25 [501+]
Koch, Jim - *Quench Your Own Thirst: Business Lessons Learned over a Beer or Two*
    PW - v262 - i52 - Dec 21 2015 - p142(1) [51-500]
Koch, Nadia J. - *Paradeigma: Die antike Kunstschriftstellerei als Grundlage der fruhneuzeitlichen Kunsttheorie*
    Six Ct J - v46 - i2 - Summer 2015 - p486-487 [501+]
Koch, Pat - *Letters to Santa Claus: The Elves*
    NYT - Nov 27 2015 - pC28(L) [501+]
Kochalka, James - *The Glorkian Warrior Eats Adventure Pie (Illus. by Kochalka, James)*
    c CCB-B - v68 - i8 - April 2015 - p408(1) [51-500]
    c SLJ - v61 - i3 - March 2015 - p146(1) [51-500]
    c KR - Jan 15 2015 - pNA [51-500]
    c HB Guide - v26 - i2 - Fall 2015 - p68(1) [51-500]
Kociejowski, Marius - *Zoroaster's Children*
    Mac - v128 - i46 - Nov 23 2015 - p56(2) [501+]
Kocol, Cleo Fellers - *The Last Aloha*
    Hum - v75 - i6 - Nov-Dec 2015 - p42(2) [501+]
Kocurek, Carly A. - *Coin-Operated Americans: Rebooting Boyhood at the Video Game Arcade*
    LJ - v140 - i15 - Sept 15 2015 - p95(1) [51-500]
Koechlin, Carol - *Q Tasks: How to Empower Students to Ask Questions and Care About the Answers, 2d ed.*
    Res Links - v20 - i3 - Feb 2015 - p41(1) [501+]
Koehler, Elisa - *A Dictionary for the Modern Trumpet Player*
    BL - v111 - i22 - August 1 2015 - p8(1) [51-500]
    LJ - v140 - i12 - July 1 2015 - p111(1) [51-500]
Fanfares and Finesse: A Performer's Guide to Trumpet History and Literature
    Notes - v72 - i2 - Dec 2015 - p382(3) [501+]
Koehler, Fred - *Super Jumbo (Illus. by Koehler, Fred)*
    c KR - Dec 1 2015 - pNA [51-500]
    c SLJ - v61 - i12 - Dec 2015 - p91(1) [51-500]
Koehler, Jeff - *Darjeeling: The Colorful History and Precarious Fate of the World's Greatest Tea*
    Bwatch - July 2015 - pNA [51-500]
    KR - Feb 1 2015 - pNA [501+]
    LJ - v140 - i5 - March 15 2015 - p121(1) [51-500]
Koehler, Lora - *The Little Snowplow (Illus. by Parker, Jake)*
    c KR - July 1 2015 - pNA [51-500]
    c SLJ - v61 - i9 - Sept 2015 - p124(1) [51-500]
Koehler, Marc - *Leading with Purpose: How to Engage, Empower and Encourage Your People to Reach Their Full Potential*
    RVBW - Nov 2015 - pNA [51-500]
Koehler-Pentacoff, Elizabeth - *The Missing Kennedy: Rosemary Kennedy and the Secret Bonds of Four Women*
    KR - June 15 2015 - pNA [501+]
    LJ - v140 - i16 - Oct 1 2015 - p90(1) [51-500]
Koelsch, William A. - *Geography and the Classical World: Unearthing Historical Geography's Forgotten Past*
    GR - v105 - i2 - April 2015 - p255(4) [501+]
Koeneman, Keith - *First Son: The Biography of Richard M. Daley*
    Historian - v77 - i2 - Summer 2015 - p339(3) [501+]
Koenig, Leah - *Modern Jewish Cooking: Recipes and Customs for Today's Kitchen*
    LJ - v140 - i10 - June 1 2015 - p131(1) [501+]
    PW - v262 - i7 - Feb 16 2015 - p173(1) [51-500]
Koenig, Minerva - *South of Nowhere*
    KR - Dec 15 2015 - pNA [501+]
    PW - v262 - i50 - Dec 7 2015 - p71(1) [51-500]
Koenker, Diane P. - *Club Red: Vacation Travel and the Soviet Dream*
    BHR - v89 - i3 - Autumn 2015 - p617(4) [501+]
    JMH - v87 - i3 - Sept 2015 - p767(3) [501+]
Koeppel, Gerard - *City on a Grid: How New York Became New York*
    KR - August 15 2015 - pNA [501+]
    NY - v91 - i30 - Oct 5 2015 - p80 [501+]
    NYT - Dec 13 2015 - p8(L) [501+]
    PW - v262 - i37 - Sept 14 2015 - p52(1) [51-500]

Koeppen, Wolfgang - *Youth: Autobiographical Writings*
TLS - i5850 - May 15 2015 - p24(1) [501+]

Koerber, Jennifer - *Emerging Technologies: A Primer for Librarians*
LJ - v140 - i19 - Nov 15 2015 - p97(1) [51-500]

Koesel, Karrie J. - *Religion and Authoritarianism: Cooperation, Conflict, and the Consequences*
Slav R - v74 - i2 - Summer 2015 - p372-373 [501+]

Koestenbaum, Wayne - *The Pink Trance Notebooks*
PW - v262 - i38 - Sept 21 2015 - p52(1) [51-500]

Koester, Nancy - *Harriet Beecher Stowe: A Spiritual Life*
CHR - v101 - i4 - Autumn 2015 - p954(2) [501+]
JSH - v81 - i2 - May 2015 - p458(2) [501+]
RAH - v43 - June 2015 - p249-253 [501+]

Koestler, Arthur - *Darkness at Noon*
Nat R - v67 - i21 - Nov 19 2015 - p78(2) [501+]

Koethe, John - *The Swimmer*
LJ - v140 - i20 - Dec 1 2015 - p107(1) [51-500]

Koetting, Alexis - *Encore*
KR - July 1 2015 - pNA [51-500]

Koffsky, Ann D. - *Kayla and Kugel (Illus. by Koffsky, Ann D.)*
c CH Bwatch - August 2015 - pNA [51-500]
Kayla and Kugel (Illus. by Koffsky, Ann D)
c KR - June 15 2015 - pNA [51-500]
Shabbat Shalom, Hey! (Illus. by Koffsky, Ann D.)
c BL - v111 - i15 - April 1 2015 - p84(1) [51-500]
Shabbat Shalom, Hey! (Illus. by Koffsky, Ann D)
c HB Guide - v26 - i2 - Fall 2015 - p13(1) [51-500]
Shabbat Shalom, Hey! (Illus. by Koffsky, Ann D.)
c KR - Feb 15 2015 - pNA [51-500]

Kofler, Werner - *At the Writing Desk*
KR - Nov 15 2015 - pNA [501+]

Kogawa, Joy - *Obasan*
y Res Links - v20 - i3 - Feb 2015 - p31(1) [501+]

Kogel, Lynne Alcott - *Christianity in Stained Glass*
KR - March 1 2015 - pNA [501+]

Kohara, Kazuno - *El pequeno mago (Illus. by Kohara, Kazuno)*
c SLJ - v61 - i12 - Dec 2015 - p91(1) [51-500]

Kohen, Yael - *We Killed: The Rise of Women in American Comedy*
BL - v111 - i19-20 - June 1 2015 - p30(2) [501+]

Kohl, Margaret - *Jurgen Moltmann: Collected Readings*
Theol St - v76 - i4 - Dec 2015 - p894(2) [501+]

Kohler, Joyce Webb - *Like Water, Like Bread*
KR - Nov 15 2015 - pNA [51-500]

Kohlhagen, Steven W. - *Chief of Thieves*
Roundup M - v23 - i1 - Oct 2015 - p30(1) [51-500]

Kohlmann, Benjamin - *Committed Styles: Modernism, Politics, and Left-Wing Literature in the 1930s*
RES - v66 - i276 - Sept 2015 - p797-799 [501+]
TLS - i5843 - March 27 2015 - p24(1) [501+]
Edward Upward and Left-Wing Literary Culture in Britain
RES - v66 - i274 - April 2015 - p398-400 [501+]

Kohlrausch, Martin - *Building Europe on Expertise: Innovators, Organizers, Networkers*
HNet - April 2015 - pNA [501+]

Kohn, Alan J. - *Conus of the Southeastern United States and Caribbean*
QRB - v90 - i2 - June 2015 - p218(1) [501+]

Kohn, Edward P. - *Heir to the Empire City: New York and the Making of Theodore Roosevelt*
RAH - v43 - June 2015 - p307-313 [501+]

Kohn, Karen C. - *Collection Evaluation in Academic Libraries: A Practical Guide for Librarians*
LJ - v140 - i16 - Oct 1 2015 - p98(1) [51-500]

Koinova, Maria - *Ethnonationalist Conflict in Postcommunist States: Varieties of Governance in Bulgaria, Macedonia, and Kosovo: National and Ethnic Conflict in the Twenty-First Century*
E-A St - v67 - i5 - July 2015 - p833(3) [501+]

Koistinen, David - *Confronting Decline: The Political Economy of Deindustrialization in Twentieth-Century New England*
AHR - v120 - i1 - Feb 2015 - p271-272 [501+]
BHR - v89 - i1 - Spring 2015 - p189(4) [501+]
CS - v44 - i5 - Sept 2015 - p669-670 [501+]

Kojeve, Alexandre - *The Notion of Authority*
GSR - v38 - i2 - May 2015 - p438-2 [501+]

Kokoris, Jim - *It's. Nice. Outside*
BL - v112 - i6 - Nov 15 2015 - p21(2) [51-500]
KR - Oct 1 2015 - pNA [501+]

Kolanovic, Dubravka - *This Little Light of Mine*
c KR - Jan 1 2015 - pNA [51-500]

Kolata, Gina - *The New York Times Book of Medicine: More Than 150 Years of Reporting on the Evolution of Medicine*
BL - v111 - i18 - May 15 2015 - p15(2) [51-500]

Kolaya, Chrissy - *Charmed Particles*
BL - v112 - i4 - Oct 15 2015 - p32(1) [51-500]
KR - Sept 1 2015 - pNA [501+]

Kolb, Andrew - *Edmund Unravels (Read by Poe, Richard). Audiobook Review*
c SLJ - v61 - i12 - Dec 2015 - p74(2) [51-500]
Edmund Unravels (Illus. by Kolb, Andrew)
c PW - v262 - i4 - Jan 26 2015 - p169(1) [51-500]
c HB Guide - v26 - i2 - Fall 2015 - p14(1) [51-500]
c KR - Jan 1 2015 - pNA [51-500]
c Res Links - v21 - i1 - Oct 2015 - p6(1) [51-500]
c SLJ - v61 - i2 - Feb 2015 - p72(1) [51-500]

Kolb, Robert - *The Oxford Handbook of Martin Luther's Theology*
Theol St - v76 - i2 - June 2015 - p362(3) [501+]
CH - v84 - i2 - June 2015 - p438(3) [501+]

Kolbell, Erik - *When Your Life is on Fire, What Would You Save?*
Intpr - v69 - i1 - Jan 2015 - p125(2) [51-500]

Kolberg, Sharael - *A Year Unplugged: A Family's Life without Technology*
PW - v262 - i28 - July 13 2015 - p62(1) [51-500]

Kolbert, Elizabeth - *The Sixth Extinction: An Unnatural History*
Bks & Cult - v21 - i1 - Jan-Feb 2015 - p29(2) [501+]
CC - v132 - i2 - Jan 21 2015 - p38(2) [501+]
QRB - v90 - i2 - June 2015 - p214(1) [501+]

Koll, Hilary - *Design a Skyscraper (Illus. by Aleksic, Vladimir)*
y HB Guide - v26 - i2 - Fall 2015 - p164(1) [51-500]
Design a Skyscraper (You Do the Math). (Illus. by Aleksic, Vladimir)
c Sch Lib - v63 - i1 - Spring 2015 - p47(1) [51-500]
Fly a Jet Fighter (Illus. by Mills, Steve)
y SLJ - v61 - i6 - June 2015 - p146(1) [51-500]
y HB Guide - v26 - i2 - Fall 2015 - p164(1) [51-500]
Launch a Rocket into Space
y SLJ - v61 - i6 - June 2015 - p146(1) [51-500]
Launch a Rocket into Space (Illus. by Aleksic, Vladimir)
y HB Guide - v26 - i2 - Fall 2015 - p164(1) [51-500]
y KR - April 1 2015 - pNA [51-500]
Solve a Crime (Illus. by Aleksic, Vladimir)
y HB Guide - v26 - i2 - Fall 2015 - p164(1) [51-500]
You Do the Math Series
c BL - v111 - i19-20 - June 1 2015 - p82(1) [51-500]

"Kollektive Akteure" und Gewalt. Macht und Ohnmacht im 20. Jahrhundert
HNet - May 2015 - pNA [501+]

Koller, Alexander - *Imperator und Pontifex: Forschungen zum Verhaltnis von Kaiserhof und romischer Kurie im Zeitalter der Konfessionalisierung, 1555-1648*
Six Ct J - v46 - i1 - Spring 2015 - p127(1) [501+]

Koller, Sabine - *Marc Chagall: Grenzgange zwischen Literatur und Malerei*
Slav R - v74 - i1 - Spring 2015 - p210-211 [501+]

Kolodko, Grzegorz - *Whither the World: The Political Economy of the Future, Volume I*
E-A St - v67 - i7 - Sept 2015 - p1145(4) [501+]
Whither the World: The Political Economy of the Future, Volume II
E-A St - v67 - i7 - Sept 2015 - p1145(4) [501+]

Kolodny, Annette - *In Search of First Contact: The Vikings of Vinland, the Peoples of the Dawnland, and the Anglo-American Anxiety of Discovery*
AL - v87 - i3 - Sept 2015 - p603-605 [501+]

Koloski-Ostrow, Ann Olga - *The Archaeology of Sanitation in Roman Italy: Toilets, Sewers, and Water Systems*
LJ - v140 - i11 - June 15 2015 - p99(1) [51-500]
Nature - v520 - i7547 - April 16 2015 - p293(1) [51-500]
Spec - v327 - i9738 - April 18 2015 - p40(1) [501+]
TLS - i5848 - May 1 2015 - p12(1) [501+]

Kolosov, Jacqueline - *Along the Way*
y HB Guide - v26 - i2 - Fall 2015 - p127(1) [51-500]

Kolpin, Molly - *Why Do I Burp?*
c HB Guide - v26 - i2 - Fall 2015 - p184(1) [51-500]
Why Do I Hiccup?
c HB Guide - v26 - i2 - Fall 2015 - p184(1) [51-500]

Kolrud, Kristine - *Iconoclasm from Antiquity to Modernity*
CHR - v101 - i3 - Summer 2015 - p590(3) [501+]
Six Ct J - v46 - i2 - Summer 2015 - p407-409 [501+]

Kolsto, Pal - *Strategies of Symbolic Nation Building in South Eastern Europe*
E-A St - v67 - i7 - Sept 2015 - p1154(2) [501+]

Komara, Edward - *100 Books Every Blues Fan Should Own*
Notes - v71 - i4 - June 2015 - p726(3) [501+]

Komlosy, Andrea - *Arbeit: Eine Globalhistorische Perspektive. 13. bis 21. Jahrhundert*
HNet - March 2015 - pNA [501+]

Komori, Shigetaka - *Innovating Out of Crisis: How Fujifilm Survived (and Thrived) as Its Core Business Was Vanishing*
RVBW - Oct 2015 - pNA [501+]

Komunyakaa, Yusef - *The Emperor of Water Clocks*
LJ - v140 - i16 - Oct 1 2015 - p85(1) [51-500]
PW - v262 - i33 - August 17 2015 - p47(2) [51-500]

Kon, Satoshi - *Satoshi Kon's Opus*
LJ - v140 - i5 - March 15 2015 - p88(3) [51-500]

Kondo, Marie - *The Life-Changing Magic of Tidying Up: The Japanese Art of Decluttering and Organizing. Audiobook Review*
LJ - v140 - i6 - April 1 2015 - p50(1) [51-500]

Kondracke, Morton - *Jack Kemp: The Bleeding-Heart Conservative Who Changed America*
NYTBR - Nov 8 2015 - p14(L) [501+]

Kong, Debra Purdy - *The Deep End*
RVBW - June 2015 - pNA [501+]

Koni, Ibrahim al- - *A Sleepless Eye: Aphorisms from the Sahara*
WLT - v89 - i1 - Jan-Feb 2015 - p69(1) [51-500]

Konicek-Moran, Richard - *Teaching for Conceptual Understanding in Science*
Sci & Ch - v52 - i9 - Summer 2015 - p29 [51-500]
Sci & Ch - v53 - i1 - Sept 2015 - p93 [501+]
Sci Teach - v82 - i6 - Sept 2015 - p72 [51-500]

Konieczny, Mary Ellen - *The Spirit's Tether: Family, Work, and Religion among American Catholics*
CS - v44 - i3 - May 2015 - p373-375 [501+]
JR - v95 - i4 - Oct 2015 - p567(3) [501+]

Konig, Christian - *Fluchtlinge und Vertriebene in der DDR-Aufbaugeneration: Sozial- und Biographiegeschichtliche Studien*
HNet - July 2015 - pNA [501+]

Konig, Eva - *The Orphan in Eighteenth-Century Fiction: The Vicissitudes of the Eighteenth-Century Subject*
RES - v66 - i276 - Sept 2015 - p787-788 [501+]

Konig, Jason - *Encyclopaedism from Antiquity to the Renaissance*
Class R - v65 - i2 - Oct 2015 - p487-488 [501+]
Ren Q - v68 - i2 - Summer 2015 - p627-629 [501+]

Konigsberg, Bill - *The Porcupine of Truth*
y PW - v262 - i14 - April 6 2015 - p63(1) [51-500]
y BL - v111 - i13 - March 1 2015 - p59(1) [51-500]
y CCB-B - v69 - i2 - Oct 2015 - p96(1) [51-500]
y HB Guide - v26 - i2 - Fall 2015 - p127(1) [51-500]
y KR - March 1 2015 - pNA [51-500]
y SLJ - v61 - i3 - March 2015 - p158(1) [51-500]
y Teach Lib - v43 - i1 - Oct 2015 - p22(1) [51-500]

Konnecke, Ole - *The Big Book of Animals of the World (Illus. by Konnecke, Ole)*
c BL - v112 - i6 - Nov 15 2015 - p57(1) [51-500]
c KR - Jan 1 2016 - pNA [51-500]
c Magpies - v30 - i4 - Sept 2015 - p26(1) [51-500]
c NYTBR - Dec 6 2015 - p32(L) [501+]
c PW - v262 - i32 - August 10 2015 - p60(1) [51-500]
c SLJ - v61 - i10 - Oct 2015 - p79(1) [51-500]
You Can Do It, Bert! (Illus. by Konnecke, Ole)
c HB - v91 - i2 - March-April 2015 - p77(2) [51-500]
c HB Guide - v26 - i2 - Fall 2015 - p14(1) [51-500]
c Magpies - v30 - i2 - May 2015 - p26(1) [51-500]
PW - v262 - i2 - Jan 12 2015 - p57(1) [51-500]
c PW - v262 - i49 - Dec 2 2015 - p19(1) [51-500]

Konner, Melvin - *Women After All: Sex, Evolution, and the End of Male Supremacy*
BL - v111 - i11 - Feb 1 2015 - p6(1) [51-500]
Nature - v518 - i7540 - Feb 26 2015 - p481(1) [51-500]
Soc - v52 - i5 - Oct 2015 - p499(4) [501+]
TimHES - i2196 - March 26 2015 - p52-53 [501+]
TLS - i5850 - May 15 2015 - p3(2) [501+]

Konnikova, Maria - *The Confidence Game: Why We Fall for It...Every Time*
LJ - v140 - i20 - Dec 1 2015 - p120(2) [51-500]
The Confidence Game: Why We Fall for ItaEvery Time
KR - Oct 15 2015 - pNA [501+]

Kono, Erin Eitter - *Caterina and the Best Beach Day*
c KR - March 15 2015 - pNA [51-500]

Konopinski, Natalie - *Doing Anthropological Research: A Practical Guide*
JRAI - v21 - i2 - June 2015 - p476(2) [501+]

Konrad, Deborah - *The Blessing of Movement*
KR - Oct 15 2015 - pNA [501+]

Konstan, David - *Beauty: The Fortunes of an Ancient Greek Idea*
    TLS - i5854 - June 12 2015 - p22(1) [501+]

Kontis, Aletheia - *Dearest*
  y HB Guide - v26 - i2 - Fall 2015 - p127(1) [51-500]
  y VOYA - v37 - i6 - Feb 2015 - p79(1) [51-500]

Konzepte des Authentischen - Prozesse der Authentisierung
    HNet - June 2015 - pNA [501+]

Konzeptionelle Uberlegungen zur Edition von Rechnungen und Amtsbuchern des Spaten Mittelalters
    HNet - March 2015 - pNA [501+]

Koob, Jeff - *Ad Nauseam*
    KR - August 1 2015 - pNA [501+]

Koontz, Christie - *Marketing and Social Media: A Guide for Libraries, Archives, and Museums*
    LR - v64 - i4-5 - April-May 2015 - p400-401 [501+]

Koontz, Dean - *Ashley Bell*
  y BL - v112 - i6 - Nov 15 2015 - p31(2) [51-500]
    KR - Oct 15 2015 - pNA [51-500]
The City (Read by Jackson, Korey). Audiobook Review
    BL - v111 - i11 - Feb 1 2015 - p58(1) [51-500]
Saint Odd (Read by Baker, David Aaron). Audiobook Review
    BL - v111 - i21 - July 1 2015 - p78(2) [51-500]

Koontz, Robin - *Binoculars*
  c CH Bwatch - April 2015 - pNA [51-500]
The Science of a Sinkhole
  c BL - v112 - i4 - Oct 15 2015 - p42(1) [51-500]
The Science of a Tsunami
  c BL - v112 - i4 - Oct 15 2015 - p42(1) [51-500]
Volcanologists
  c BL - v112 - i3 - Oct 1 2015 - p64(1) [51-500]

Koopmans, Loek - *The Three Wise Men*
  c HB Guide - v26 - i1 - Spring 2015 - p11(1) [51-500]

Koops, Egbert - *Law & Equity: Approaches in Roman Law and Common Law*
    Law Q Rev - v131 - July 2015 - p495-496 [501+]

Koortbojian, Michael - *The Divinization of Caesar and Augustus: Precedents, Consequences, Implications*
    Class R - v65 - i1 - April 2015 - p266-268 [501+]

Koosed, Jennifer L. - *The Bible and Posthumanism*
    Intpr - v69 - i1 - Jan 2015 - p123(1) [51-500]

Kooser, Ted - *Splitting an Order*
    Bks & Cult - v21 - i2 - March-April 2015 - p38(1) [501+]
    CC - v132 - i16 - August 5 2015 - p41(1) [501+]

Kootstra, Kara - *The Boy in Number Four (Illus. by Thomson, Regan)*
  c HB Guide - v26 - i2 - Fall 2015 - p199(1) [51-500]
  c Res Links - v20 - i3 - Feb 2015 - p4(2) [51-500]

Kopaczyk, Joanna - *The Legal Language of Scottish Burghs: Standardization and Lexical Bundles*
    Specu - v90 - i1 - Jan 2015 - p268-269 [501+]

Kopee, Danny - *Test, Evaluate and Improve Your Chess: A Knowledge-Based Approach*
    RVBW - August 2015 - pNA [501+]

Kopelman, Judy Tal - *Grandpa's Third Drawer*
  c CH Bwatch - March 2015 - pNA [51-500]

Kopelson, Heather Miyano - *Childhood and Emotion: Across Cultures, 1450-1800*
    AHR - v120 - i3 - June 2015 - p968-969 [501+]
Faithful Bodies: Performing Religion and Race in the Puritan Atlantic
    CH - v84 - i4 - Dec 2015 - p899(2) [501+]
    Col Lit - v42 - i4 - Fall 2015 - p725(3) [51-500]
    JAH - v102 - i1 - June 2015 - p227-228 [501+]
    W&M Q - v72 - i2 - April 2015 - p367-369 [501+]

Kopitzke, Becky - *The Supermom Myth*
    PW - v262 - i41 - Oct 12 2015 - p64(1) [51-500]

Kopp, Hermann - *From the Molecular World: A Nineteenth-Century Science Fantasy*
    Isis - v106 - i1 - March 2015 - p202(2) [501+]

Kopp, Megan - *Be the Change Series*
  c Res Links - v20 - i4 - April 2015 - p14(1) [501+]
How to Write a Drama
  c CH Bwatch - Feb 2015 - pNA [51-500]
  c CH Bwatch - April 2015 - pNA [51-500]
Text Styles: How to Write Science Fiction
  c CH Bwatch - August 2015 - pNA [51-500]

Kopp, Shannon - *Pound for Pound: A Story of One Woman's Recovery and the Shelter Dogs Who Loved Her Back to Life*
    BL - v112 - i4 - Oct 15 2015 - p10(1) [51-500]
    KR - August 15 2015 - pNA [51-500]

Kopp, Vanina - *Spiele und Machtspiele in der Vormoderne. Politische und soziale Aspekte von Gesellschaft in hiofischen Gesellschaften*
    HNet - August 2015 - pNA [501+]

Koppel, Ted - *Lights Out: A Cyberattack, a Nation Unprepared, Surviving the Aftermath*
    BL - v112 - i3 - Oct 1 2015 - p6(1) [51-500]
    KR - August 1 2015 - pNA [51-500]
    NYTBR - Nov 22 2015 - p23(L) [501+]

Koppelman, Amy - *Hesitation Wounds*
    BL - v112 - i5 - Nov 1 2015 - p27(1) [51-500]

Kopperman, Paul - *"Regimental Practice". E-book Review*
    Isis - v106 - i2 - June 2015 - p450(2) [501+]

Kopperude, Amy - *Complete Photo Guide to Bead Crafts*
  c CH Bwatch - Oct 2015 - pNA [51-500]

Kopshidze, Nicholas - *Urgent Interventional Therapies*
    Bwatch - August 2015 - pNA [51-500]

Kopytek, Bruce Allen - *Eaton's: The Trans-Canada Store*
    Beav - v95 - i4 - August-Sept 2015 - p68(2) [501+]

Korb, Alexander - *Im Schatten des Weltkriegs: Massengewalt der Ustasa gegen Serben, Juden und Roma in Kroatien 1941-1945*
    Slav R - v74 - i1 - Spring 2015 - p169-170 [501+]

Korczynski, Marek - *Songs of the Factory: Pop Music, Culture, and Resistance*
    TimHES - i2188 - Jan 29 2015 - p50(1) [501+]

Korda, Lerryn - *So Cozy (Illus. by Korda, Lerryn)*
  c CCB-B - v68 - i10 - June 2015 - p500(1) [51-500]
  c HB - v91 - i4 - July-August 2015 - p117(2) [51-500]
  c SLJ - v61 - i3 - March 2015 - p118(1) [51-500]

Kordzaia-Samadashvili, Ana - *Me, Margarita*
    TLS - i5856 - June 26 2015 - p20(2) [501+]

Koresky, Michael - *Terrence Davies*
    Si & So - v25 - i4 - April 2015 - p104(2) [501+]

Koretsky, J. Lea - *Mandated Reporter*
    KR - Nov 1 2015 - pNA [51-500]

Korey, Marie Elena - *A Long way from the Armstrong Beer Parlour: A Life in Rare Books - Essays by Richard Landon*
    TLS - i5835 - Jan 30 2015 - p27(1) [501+]

Koritz, Amy - *Culture Makers: Urban Performance and Literature in the 1920s*
    J Urban H - v41 - i1 - Jan 2015 - p157-8 [501+]

Korman, Gordon - *The 39 Clues: Unstoppable Book 4: Flashpoint*
  y HB Guide - v26 - i1 - Spring 2015 - p83(1) [51-500]
The 39th Clues
  y CH Bwatch - Jan 2015 - pNA [501+]
Criminal Destiny
  c KR - Nov 1 2015 - pNA [51-500]
The Dragonfly Effect
  c Res Links - v21 - i1 - Oct 2015 - p15(1) [51-500]
  c SLJ - v61 - i6 - June 2015 - p109(1) [51-500]
Masterminds
  c CCB-B - v68 - i7 - March 2015 - p359(1) [51-500]
  c NYTBR - May 10 2015 - p22(L) [501+]
  c Teach Lib - v42 - i5 - June 2015 - p15(1) [51-500]
  c HB Guide - v26 - i2 - Fall 2015 - p89(1) [51-500]
  c Res Links - v20 - i3 - Feb 2015 - p12(1) [51-500]
Memory Maze
  c HB Guide - v26 - i1 - Spring 2015 - p83(1) [51-500]
  c Res Links - v21 - i1 - Oct 2015 - p15(2) [501+]
Outlaws 2.0
  c SLJ - v61 - i12 - Dec 2015 - p104(1) [51-500]
Schooled
  c Teach Lib - v43 - i1 - Oct 2015 - p48(1) [51-500]
Ungifted
  c Teach Lib - v43 - i1 - Oct 2015 - p48(1) [51-500]
Unleashed (Read by Ross, Jonathan Todd). Audiobook Review
  c SLJ - v61 - i8 - August 2015 - p50(1) [51-500]
Unleashed
    Res Links - v20 - i4 - April 2015 - p11(2) [501+]
  c HB Guide - v26 - i2 - Fall 2015 - p89(1) [51-500]

Korman, Keith - *End Time*
    KR - June 15 2015 - pNA [51-500]
    PW - v262 - i25 - June 22 2015 - p125(1) [51-500]

Korn, Peter - *Why We Make Things and Why It Matters: The Education of a Craftsman*
    TLS - i5852 - May 29 2015 - p28(1) [501+]

Kornbluth, Jesse - *Married Sex*
    KR - June 15 2015 - pNA [51-500]
    NYTBR - Sept 27 2015 - p30(L) [501+]
    PW - v262 - i26 - June 29 2015 - p43(1) [501+]

Kornegay, Jamie - *Soil*
    BL - v111 - i12 - Feb 15 2015 - p39(1) [51-500]
    KR - Jan 15 2015 - pNA [51-500]
    PW - v262 - i4 - Jan 26 2015 - p142(1) [51-500]
Soil (Read by Hutchinson, Brian). Audiobook Review
    LJ - v140 - i12 - July 1 2015 - p43(1) [51-500]

Kornetis, Kostis - *Children of the Dictatorship: Student Resistance, Cultural Politics, and the "Long 1960s" in Greece*
    AHR - v120 - i4 - Oct 2015 - p1563-1565 [501+]

Korngold, Jamie - *Mazel Tov! It's a Boy/Mazel Tov! It's a Girl*
  c SLJ - v61 - i5 - May 2015 - p79(1) [51-500]
Mazel Tov! It's a Boy/Mazel Tov! It's a Girl (Illus. by Finkelstein, Jeff)
  c HB Guide - v26 - i2 - Fall 2015 - p14(1) [51-500]
Mazel Tov! It's a Boy/Mazel Tov! It's a Girl
  c KR - March 1 2015 - pNA [51-500]
Sadie and Ori and the Blue Blanket (Illus. by Fortenberry, Julie)
  c KR - August 1 2015 - pNA [51-500]
  c PW - v262 - i39 - Sept 28 2015 - p90(2) [501+]
Sadie, Ori, and Nuggles Go to Camp (Illus. by Fortenberry, Julie)
  c HB Guide - v26 - i1 - Spring 2015 - p35(1) [51-500]

Kornher-Stace, Nicole - *Archivist Wasp*
  y KR - March 1 2015 - pNA [51-500]
  y PW - v262 - i9 - March 2 2015 - p85(2) [51-500]
  y SLJ - v61 - i3 - March 2015 - p158(1) [51-500]

Korobeinikov, Dimitri - *Byzantium and the Turks in the Thirteenth Century*
    HER - v130 - i544 - June 2015 - p699(2) [501+]

Korom, Frank J. - *The Anthropology of Performance: A Reader*
    JRAI - v21 - i2 - June 2015 - p490(2) [501+]

Korra, Monika - *Kill the Silence: A Survivor's Life Reclaimed*
  y BL - v111 - i21 - July 1 2015 - p11(1) [51-500]
    KR - May 15 2015 - pNA [51-500]

Korschun, Daniel - *We Are Market Basket: The Story of the Unlikely Grassroots Movement that Saved a Beloved Business*
    PW - v262 - i26 - June 29 2015 - p59(2) [51-500]

Korson, Kim - *I Don't Have a Happy Place: Cheerful Stories of Despondency and Gloom*
    KR - Jan 1 2015 - pNA [501+]
    PW - v262 - i1 - Jan 5 2015 - p60(2) [51-500]

Korteweg, Anna - *The Headscarf Debates: Conflicts of National Belonging*
    AJS - v121 - i2 - Sept 2015 - p629(3) [501+]
    ERS - v38 - i8 - August 2015 - p1441(3) [501+]

Koryta, Michael - *Last Words*
    BL - v111 - i19-20 - June 1 2015 - p55(1) [51-500]
    KR - June 15 2015 - pNA [51-500]
    LJ - v140 - i10 - June 1 2015 - p91(1) [51-500]
    NYTBR - August 16 2015 - p29(L) [501+]
    PW - v262 - i22 - June 1 2015 - p40(1) [51-500]
Last Words (Read by Petkoff, Robert). Audiobook Review
    BL - v112 - i5 - Nov 1 2015 - p69(1) [51-500]
Those Who Wish Me Dead
    RVBW - Jan 2015 - pNA [501+]
    RVBW - August 2015 - pNA [501+]

Koshiro, Yukiko - *Imperial Eclipse: Japan's Strategic Thinking about Continental Asia before August 1945*
    HER - v130 - i542 - Feb 2015 - p246(2) [501+]

Kositsky, Lynne - *With Fearful Bravery*
  y Res Links - v20 - i3 - Feb 2015 - p31(1) [51-500]

Koskela, Doug - *Calling and Clarity: Discovering What God Wants for Your Life*
    CC - v132 - i15 - July 22 2015 - p37(2) [501+]

Kosman, Aryeh - *Virtues of Thought: Essays on Plato and Aristotle*
    RM - v68 - i3 - March 2015 - p666(2) [501+]

Kosmatka, Ted - *The Flicker Men*
  y BL - v111 - i19-20 - June 1 2015 - p53(1) [51-500]
    KR - May 15 2015 - pNA [51-500]
  y LJ - v140 - i9 - May 15 2015 - p71(1) [51-500]
    NYT - July 30 2015 - pC6(L) [501+]
    PW - v262 - i18 - May 4 2015 - p96(2) [51-500]
  y SLJ - v61 - i11 - Nov 2015 - p126(2) [51-500]

Kosmin, Paul J. - *The Land of the Elephant Kings: Space, Territory, and Ideology in the Seleucid Empire*
    HNet - Feb 2015 - pNA [501+]

Kostecki-Shaw, Jenny Sue - *Luna & Me: The True Story of a Girl Who Lived in a Tree to Save a Forest*
  c HB Guide - v26 - i2 - Fall 2015 - p210(1) [51-500]
Luna & Me: The True Story of a Girl Who Lived in a Tree to Save a Forest (Illus. by Kostecki-Shaw, Jenny Sue)
  c KR - Feb 1 2015 - pNA [51-500]
  c PW - v262 - i17 - April 27 2015 - p74(1) [501+]
Luna & Me: The True Story of Girl Who Lived in a Tree to Save a Forest (Illus. by Kostecki-Shaw, Jenny Sue)
  c SLJ - v61 - i5 - May 2015 - p133(2) [51-500]

Koster, Fredy - *Das Ende des Konigreichs Hannover und Preussen: Die Jahre 1865 und 1866*
    HNet - April 2015 - pNA [501+]

Kostick, Conor - *The Crusades and the Near East: Cultural Histories*
    HER - v130 - i544 - June 2015 - p701(2) [501+]

Kostigen, Thomas M. - *Extreme Weather: Surviving Tornadoes, Sandstorms, Hailstorms, Blizzards, Hurricanes, and More!*
    c HB Guide - v26 - i1 - Spring 2015 - p151(1) [51-500]

Kostoff, Lynn - *Words to Die For*
    BL - v111 - i12 - Feb 15 2015 - p40(1) [51-500]
    PW - v262 - i7 - Feb 16 2015 - p163(1) [51-500]

Kot, Mark - *A First Course in the Calculus of Variations*
    SIAM Rev - v57 - i2 - June 2015 - p314-314 [501+]

Kotb, Hoda - *Where We Belong*
    KR - Dec 15 2015 - pNA [51-500]

Kotin, Lisa - *My Confection*
    KR - Oct 1 2015 - pNA [51-500]

Kotkin, Joel - *The New Class Conflict*
    Nat R - v67 - i6 - April 6 2015 - p47 [501+]
    Soc - v52 - i3 - June 2015 - p295(3) [501+]

Kotkin, Stephen - *Historical Legacies of Communism in Russia and Eastern Europe*
    E-A St - v67 - i5 - July 2015 - p831(2) [501+]
  Stalin, vol. 1: Paradoxes of Power, 1878-1928
    For Aff - v94 - i1 - Jan-Feb 2015 - pNA [51-500]
    J Mil H - v79 - i2 - April 2015 - p499-500 [501+]
    NYT - Jan 9 2015 - pC31(L) [501+]
    AS - v84 - i1 - Wntr 2015 - p101(3) [501+]
    E-A St - v67 - i7 - Sept 2015 - p1130(15) [501+]
    Reason - v46 - i9 - Feb 2015 - p56(5) [501+]
  Stalin, vol. I: Paradoxes of Power, 1878-1928
    Slav R - v74 - i3 - Fall 2015 - p604-606 [501+]

Kotler, Philip - *Confronting Capitalism: Real Solutions for a Troubled Economic System*
    LJ - v140 - i7 - April 15 2015 - p95(2) [51-500]

Kotler, Steven - *Tomorrowland: Our Journey from Science Fiction to Science Fact (Read by Parks, Tom). Audiobook Review*
    LJ - v140 - i13 - August 1 2015 - p49(1) [51-500]
  Tomorrowland: Our Journey from Science Fiction to Science Fact
    LJ - v140 - i7 - April 15 2015 - p113(2) [51-500]
    KR - March 15 2015 - pNA [51-500]

Kotlikoff, Laurence J. - *Get What's Yours: The Secrets to Maxing Out Your Social Security (Read by Cumming, Jeff). Audiobook Review*
    LJ - v140 - i10 - June 1 2015 - p61(2) [51-500]
  Get What's Yours: The Secrets to Maxing Out Your Social Security
    LJ - v140 - i3 - Feb 15 2015 - p110(1) [51-500]

Kotowski, Mariusz - *Pola Negri: Hollywood's First Femme Fatale*
    Lon R Bks - v37 - i4 - Feb 19 2015 - p33(2) [501+]

Kott, Sandrine - *Sozialstaat und Gesellschaft: Das Deutsche Kaiserreich in Europa*
    HNet - July 2015 - pNA [501+]

Kottaras, E. Katherine - *How to Be Brave*
    y BL - v112 - i4 - Oct 15 2015 - p45(1) [51-500]
    y KR - Sept 1 2015 - pNA [51-500]
    y PW - v262 - i35 - August 31 2015 - p94(1) [51-500]
    y SLJ - v61 - i12 - Dec 2015 - p122(2) [51-500]
    y VOYA - v38 - i5 - Dec 2015 - p58(1) [51-500]

Kotte, Andreas - *Theatergeschichte: Eine Einfuhrung*
    HNet - Feb 2015 - pNA [501+]

Kotter, Jan-Markus - *Zwischen Kaisern und Aposteln: Das Akakianische Schisma (484-519) als Kirchlicher Ordnungskonflikt der Spatantike*
    HNet - Jan 2015 - pNA [501+]

Koudounaris, Paul - *Memento Mori: The Dead among Us*
    LJ - v140 - i14 - Sept 1 2015 - p98(2) [51-500]

Koulias, Adriana - *The Seal*
    RVBW - July 2015 - pNA [51-500]

Kounalakis, Eleni - *Madam Ambassador: Three Years of Diplomacy, Dinner Parties, and Democracy in Budapest*
    BL - v111 - i13 - March 1 2015 - p7(2) [51-500]
    KR - Feb 15 2015 - pNA [501+]

Kounios, John - *The Eureka Factor: Aha Moments, Creative Insight, and the Brain*
    BL - v111 - i14 - March 15 2015 - p34(1) [51-500]
    KR - Feb 1 2015 - pNA [51-500]
    LJ - v140 - i8 - May 1 2015 - p125(2) [51-500]

Kourik, Robert - *Understanding Roots: Discover How to Make Your Garden Flourish*
    SPBW - Oct 2015 - pNA [51-500]

Kousky, Vern - *Otto the Owl Who Loved Poetry*
    c CH Bwatch - June 2015 - pNA [501+]
    c HB Guide - v26 - i2 - Fall 2015 - p40(1) [51-500]

Koutstaal, Wilma - *Innovating Minds: Rethinking Creativity to Inspire Change*
    LJ - v140 - i7 - Oct 15 2015 - p105(1) [51-500]

Kovacs, Alex - *The Currency of Paper*
    TLS - i5855 - June 19 2015 - p19(2) [501+]

Kovacs, Arpad - *Animals in Photographs*
    LJ - v140 - i5 - Sept 15 2015 - p81(3) [51-500]

Kovacs, Ed - *The Russian Bride*
    KR - Feb 1 2015 - pNA [51-500]

Kovaly, Heda Margolius - *Innocence, or, Murder on Steep Street*
    BL - v111 - i18 - May 15 2015 - p27(2) [51-500]
    LJ - v140 - i8 - May 1 2015 - p63(1) [51-500]
    PW - v262 - i14 - April 6 2015 - p41(1) [51-500]
    TLS - i5861 - July 31 2015 - p21(1) [501+]

Kovalyova, Irina - *Specimen: Stories*
    Mac - v128 - i25 - June 29 2015 - p56(1) [501+]
    Nat Post - v17 - i182 - June 6 2015 - pWP5(1) [501+]

Kove, T.T. - *More Than Words*
    PW - v262 - i22 - June 1 2015 - p48(1) [51-500]

Kovecses, Anna - *One Thousand Things (Illus. by Kovecses, Anna)*
    c KR - July 15 2015 - pNA [51-500]
    c Sch Lib - v63 - i3 - Autumn 2015 - p156(1) [51-500]
    c SLJ - v61 - i10 - Oct 2015 - p70(1) [51-500]

Koven, Seth - *The Match Girl and the Heiress*
    CSM - Jan 20 2015 - pNA [501+]
    Spec - v327 - i9727 - Jan 31 2015 - p40(1) [501+]
    TLS - i5843 - March 27 2015 - p5(1) [501+]
    Wom R Bks - v32 - i6 - Nov-Dec 2015 - p16(3) [501+]
    NYTBR - Jan 25 2015 - p16(L) [501+]
    NYRB - v62 - i20 - Dec 17 2015 - p94(4) [501+]

Kovite, Gavin - *War of the Encyclopaedists*
    Esq - v163 - i5 - May 2015 - p22(1) [501+]

Kovner, Sarah - *Occupying Power: Sex Workers and Servicemen in Postwar Japan*
    AHR - v120 - i1 - Feb 2015 - p224-225 [501+]
    JWH - v27 - i3 - Fall 2015 - p187(7) [501+]

Kowalik, Tadeusz - *From Solidarity to Sellout: The Restoration of Capitalism in Poland*
    S&S - v79 - i1 - Jan 2015 - p135-138 [501+]

Kowallis, J. - *Afterimage*
    PW - v262 - i47 - Nov 23 2015 - p54(1) [501+]

Kowalski, Kathiann M. - *Be Smart about Credit: Credit and Debit Management*
    y HB Guide - v26 - i1 - Spring 2015 - p138(1) [51-500]
  Be Smart about Investing: Planning, Saving, and the Stock Market
    y HB Guide - v26 - i1 - Spring 2015 - p138(1) [51-500]
  Be Smart about Shopping: The Critical Consumer and Civic Financial Responsibility
    y HB Guide - v26 - i1 - Spring 2015 - p138(1) [51-500]

Kowalski, William - *Epic Game*
    KR - Jan 1 2016 - pNA [51-500]

Kowalzig, Barbara - *Dithyramb in Context*
    Class R - v65 - i1 - April 2015 - p16-18 [501+]

Koyczan, Shane - *To This Day: For the Bullied and Beautiful*
    y HB Guide - v26 - i2 - Fall 2015 - p204(1) [501+]
    c SLJ - v61 - i12 - Dec 2015 - p64(4) [501+]

Kozloff, Max - *Saul Leiter: Early Black and White, 2 vols.*
    NYRB - v62 - i12 - July 9 2015 - p10(3) [501+]
    NYRB - v62 - i12 - July 9 2015 - p10(3) [501+]

Kozlov, Denis - *The Readers of "Novyi Mir": Coming to Terms with the Stalinist Past*
    JMH - v87 - i2 - June 2015 - p502(3) [501+]
  The Thaw: Soviet Society and Culture during the 1950s and 1960s
    JMH - v87 - i2 - June 2015 - p504(2) [501+]

Kozol, Jonathan - *The Theft of Memory: Losing My Father, One Day at a Time*
    NYTBR - June 21 2015 - p26(L) [501+]
    PW - v262 - i15 - April 13 2015 - p70(2) [501+]
    BL - v111 - i17 - May 1 2015 - p68(1) [51-500]
    KR - April 1 2015 - pNA [51-500]

Kozol, Wendy - *Distant Wars Visible: The Ambivalence of Witnessing*
    HNet - April 2015 - pNA [501+]

Kozuchowski, Adam - *The Afterlife of Austria-Hungary: The Image of the Habsburg Monarchy in Interwar Europe*
    AHR - v120 - i1 - Feb 2015 - p353-354 [501+]
    CEH - v48 - i2 - June 2015 - p267-268 [501+]
    HNet - Feb 2015 - pNA [501+]

Kraatz, Jeramey - *Fall of Heroes*
    c HB Guide - v26 - i1 - Spring 2015 - p83(1) [51-500]

Krache, Diane L. - *Walking in Credence: An Administrative History of George Washington Carver National Monument*
    Pub Hist - v37 - i2 - May 2015 - p150(3) [501+]

Kracht, Christian - *Imperium: A Fiction of the South Seas*
    KR - May 1 2015 - pNA [501+]
    LJ - v140 - i12 - July 1 2015 - p78(1) [51-500]
    NYT - July 30 2015 - pC6(L) [501+]
    NYTBR - July 26 2015 - p19(L) [501+]
    PW - v262 - i17 - April 27 2015 - p1(1) [51-500]
    TLS - i5874 - Oct 30 2015 - p21(1) [501+]
    WLT - v89 - i6 - Nov-Dec 2015 - p60(2) [501+]

Krackow, Eric T. - *The Lollipop Monster's Christmas*
    c HB Guide - v26 - i1 - Spring 2015 - p35(1) [51-500]

Kraegel, Kenneth - *The Song of Delphine (Illus. by Kraegel, Kenneth)*
    c BL - v111 - i15 - April 1 2015 - p84(1) [51-500]
    c HB Guide - v26 - i2 - Fall 2015 - p40(1) [51-500]
    c KR - Feb 1 2015 - pNA [51-500]

Kraft, Betsy Harvey - *The Fantastic Ferris Wheel: The Story of Inventor George Ferris (Illus. by Salerno, Steven)*
    c KR - August 15 2015 - pNA [51-500]
    c SLJ - v61 - i8 - August 2015 - p121(1) [51-500]
    c BL - v112 - i2 - Sept 15 2015 - p57(1) [51-500]

Kragl, Florian - *Nibelungenlied und Nibelungensage: Kommentierte Bibliographie 1945-2010*
    MLR - v110 - i2 - April 2015 - p583(1) [501+]

Kraig, Michael R. - *Shaping US Military Forces for the Asia-Pacific: Lessons from Conflict Management in Past Great Power Eras*
    Parameters - v45 - i2 - Summer 2015 - p135(3) [501+]

Krakauer, Jon - *Missoula: Rape and the Justice System in a College Town (Read by Marno, Mozhan). Audiobook Review*
    LJ - v140 - i12 - July 1 2015 - p44(2) [51-500]
  Missoula: Rape and the Justice System in a College Town
    CHE - v62 - i2 - Sept 11 2015 - pA14(1) [501+]
    CJR - v54 - i2 - July-August 2015 - p42(3) [501+]
    Ent W - i1361 - May 1 2015 - p62(1) [501+]
    LJ - v140 - i10 - June 1 2015 - p118(1) [51-500]
    NYT - April 20 2015 - pC1(L) [501+]
    NYTBR - May 3 2015 - p11(L) [501+]
    y SLJ - v61 - i8 - August 2015 - p115(1) [51-500]

Krall, Dan - *Sick Simon (Illus. by Krall, Dan)*
    c HB Guide - v26 - i2 - Fall 2015 - p40(1) [51-500]

Krall, Elizabeth - *Too Close*
    PW - v262 - i1 - Jan 5 2015 - p58(2) [51-500]

Krallis, Dimitris - *Michael Attaleiates and the Politics of Imperial Decline in Eleventh-Century*
    Specu - v90 - i2 - April 2015 - p555-556 [501+]

Kralovansky, Susan - *Crocodile or Alligator?*
    c HB Guide - v26 - i2 - Fall 2015 - p175(1) [51-500]
  Frog or Toad?
    c HB Guide - v26 - i2 - Fall 2015 - p175(1) [51-500]
  Monkey or Ape?
    c HB Guide - v26 - i2 - Fall 2015 - p179(1) [51-500]
  Moth or Butterfly?
    c HB Guide - v26 - i2 - Fall 2015 - p174(1) [51-500]

Kram, Mark, Jr. - *Great Men Die Twice: The Selected Works of Mark Kram*
    BL - v111 - i13 - March 1 2015 - p14(1) [51-500]
    KR - April 15 2015 - pNA [51-500]
    NYT - June 22 2015 - pC4(L) [501+]

Kramer, Adam - *The Law of Contract Damages*
    Law Q Rev - v131 - April 2015 - p325-328 [501+]

Kramer, Barbara - *National Geographic Readers: Nelson Mandela*
    c HB Guide - v26 - i1 - Spring 2015 - p192(1) [51-500]

Kramer, Bruce H. - *We Know How This Ends: Living While Dying*
    CC - v132 - i13 - June 24 2015 - p43(1) [51-500]

Kramer, Felix - *Monet and the Birth of Impressionism*
    LJ - v140 - i16 - Oct 1 2015 - p75(2) [51-500]

Kramer, Joan - *In the Company of Legends*
    RVBW - May 2015 - pNA [51-500]

Kramer, Johanna - *Between Earth and Heaven: Liminality and the Ascencion of Christ in Anglo-Saxon Literature*
    RES - v66 - i275 - June 2015 - p565-566 [501+]

Kramer, Larry - *The American People, vol. 1: Search for My Heart*
    G&L Rev W - v22 - i3 - May-June 2015 - p18(3) [501+]
    KR - Feb 1 2015 - pNA [501+]
    LJ - v140 - i6 - April 1 2015 - p82(2) [51-500]
    Nat Post - v17 - i147 - April 25 2015 - pWP5(1)

[501+]
  NYT - March 27 2015 - pC21(L) [501+]
  NYTBR - May 17 2015 - p20(L) [501+]
  PW - v262 - i4 - Jan 26 2015 - p143(1) [501+]
Kramer, Lynne Adair - *The Brockhurst File*
  KR - Jan 15 2015 - pNA [501+]
Kramer, Michael J. - *The Republic of Rock: Music and Citizenship in the Sixties Counterculture*
  HNet - April 2015 - pNA [501+]
Kramer, Peter - *Dr. Strangelove, or, How I Learned to Stop Worrying and Love the Bomb*
  TLS - i5837 - Feb 13 2015 - p26(2) [501+]
Kramer, Stephan - *On What, There Is for Things to Be*
  RM - v69 - i2 - Dec 2015 - p393(3) [501+]
Kramer, Wendy - *Saqueo en el archivo: El paradero de los tesoros documentales guatemaltecos*
  HAHR - v95 - i1 - Feb 2015 - p148-149 [501+]
Kranjc, Gregor Joseph - *To Walk with the Devil: Slovene Collaboration and Axis Occupation, 1941-1945*
  JMH - v87 - i2 - June 2015 - p499(2) [501+]
Krans, Kim - *ABC Dream*
  c KR - Oct 1 2015 - pNA [51-500]
Krantz, Steven G. - *Differential Equations: Theory, Technique, and Practice. Second Edition*
  SIAM Rev - v57 - i2 - June 2015 - p314-315 [501+]
  A Guide to Functional Analysis
  Math T - v108 - i6 - Feb 2015 - p477(1) [501+]
Kranz, Jonathan David - *Our Brothers at the Bottom of the Bottom of the Sea*
  y HB Guide - v26 - i2 - Fall 2015 - p127(1) [51-500]
  y PW - v262 - i17 - April 27 2015 - p78(1) [51-500]
  y SLJ - v61 - i4 - April 2015 - p166(3) [51-500]
  y VOYA - v38 - i2 - June 2015 - p64(1) [51-500]
Krasner, Barbara - *Goldie Takes a Stand! Golda Meir's First Crusade (Illus. by Garrity-Riley, Kelsey)*
  c HB Guide - v26 - i1 - Spring 2015 - p193(2) [51-500]
  Native Nations of the Great Basin and Plateau
  c CH Bwatch - Oct 2015 - pNA [51-500]
  Native Nations of the Northeast
  c CH Bwatch - Oct 2015 - pNA [51-500]
  Native Nations of the Southwest
  c CH Bwatch - Oct 2015 - pNA [51-500]
Krasno, Jeff - *Wanderlust: A Modern Yogi's Guide to Discovering Your Best Self*
  PW - v262 - i16 - April 20 2015 - p72(1) [51-500]
Krass, Peter - *Clarion Call of the Last Kallus*
  KR - August 1 2015 - pNA [51-500]
Krasznahorkai, Laszlo - *Destruction and Sorrow beneath the Heavens*
  PW - v262 - i41 - Oct 12 2015 - p56(1) [51-500]
Kratzner, Anita - *Die Universitaten der DDR und der Mauerbau 1961*
  HNet - April 2015 - pNA [501+]
Kraulis, Julie - *An Armadillo in Paris*
  c HB Guide - v26 - i1 - Spring 2015 - p35(1) [51-500]
  c Res Links - v20 - i3 - Feb 2015 - p5(1) [51-500]
Kraus, Alexander - *Weltmeere: Wissen und Wahrnehmung im Langen 19. Jahrhundert*
  HNet - March 2015 - pNA [501+]
Kraus, Daniel - *At the Edge of Empire*
  y KR - August 1 2015 - pNA [51-500]
  The Death and Life of Zebulon Finch: At the Edge of Empire
  y SLJ - v61 - i9 - Sept 2015 - p168(2) [51-500]
  The Death and Life of Zebulon Finch, vol. 1: At the Edge of Empire
  y BL - v112 - i3 - Oct 1 2015 - p72(1) [501+]
  y PW - v262 - i31 - August 3 2015 - p62(2) [51-500]
  y VOYA - v38 - i5 - Dec 2015 - p71(1) [51-500]
  Talking with: Lorenzo Pace
  BL - v111 - i11 - Feb 1 2015 - p42(1) [501+]
  Trollhunters (Illus. by Murray, Sean)
  c Spec - v328 - i9759 - Sept 12 2015 - p46(2) [501+]
Kraus, Hans-Christof - *Bismarck: Grosse - Grenzen - Leistungen*
  HNet - July 2015 - pNA [501+]
Kraus, Nicola - *How to Be a Grown-Up*
  NYTBR - July 26 2015 - p26(L) [501+]
Krause, Jens - *Animal Social Networks*
  QRB - v90 - i4 - Dec 2015 - p437(1) [501+]
Krause, Jonathan - *The Greater War: Other Combatants and Other Fronts, 1914-1918*
  J Mil H - v79 - i4 - Oct 2015 - p1140-1141 [501+]
Krause, Ute - *Oscar and the Very Hungry Dragon (Illus. by Krause, Ute)*
  c SLJ - v61 - i12 - Dec 2015 - p91(1) [51-500]
Krausman, Paul R. - *Wildlife Management and Conservation: Contemporary Principles and Practices*
  QRB - v90 - i1 - March 2015 - p86(2) [501+]

Krauss, Kenneth - *Male Beauty: Postwar Masculinity in Theater, Film, and Physique Magazines*
  G&L Rev W - v22 - i1 - Jan-Feb 2015 - p39(1) [501+]
Kraut, Alan M. - *Ethnic Historians and the Mainstream: Shaping American's Immigration Story*
  JIH - v45 - i3 - Wntr 2015 - p447-448 [501+]
Kravchenko, Elena - *The Prose of Sasha Sokolov: Reflections on/of the Real*
  MLR - v110 - i2 - April 2015 - p623-625 [501+]
  Slav R - v74 - i1 - Spring 2015 - p214-215 [501+]
Kravitz, Asher - *The Jewish Dog*
  y KR - May 1 2015 - pNA [51-500]
  SPBW - June 2015 - pNA [51-500]
Krawchuk, Andrii - *Eastern Orthodox Encounters of Identity and Otherness: Values, Self-Reflection, Dialogue*
  HNet - May 2015 - pNA [501+]
Kraybill, Donald B. - *Renegade Amish: Beard Cutting, Hate Crimes, and the Trial of the Bergholz Barbers*
  J Ch St - v57 - i3 - Summer 2015 - p592-594 [501+]
Kreamer, Anne - *Risk/Reward: Why Intelligent Leaps and Daring Choices Are the Best Career Moves You Can Make*
  LJ - v140 - i10 - June 1 2015 - p111(2) [51-500]
Krebber, Jochen - *Wurttemberger in Nordamerika: Migration von der Schwabischen Alb im 19. Jahrhundert*
  JAH - v102 - i2 - Sept 2015 - p561-562 [501+]
Krebs, Daniel - *A Generous and Merciful Enemy: Life for German Prisoners of War during the American Revolution*
  RAH - v43 - i3 - Sept 2015 - p441-446 [501+]
Krebs, Justin - *Blue in a Red State*
  KR - Dec 1 2015 - pNA [51-500]
Kredensor, Diane - *Buck's Tooth (Illus. by Kredensor, Diane)*
  c HB Guide - v26 - i2 - Fall 2015 - p68(1) [51-500]
  c KR - March 1 2015 - pNA [51-500]
  Buck's Tooth
  SLJ - v61 - i4 - April 2015 - p141(2) [51-500]
Krefting, Rebecca - *All Joking Aside: American Humor and Its Discontents*
  SAH - v4 - i1 - Annual 2015 - p109-111 [501+]
Kreiner, Jamie - *The Social Life of Hagiography in the Merovingian Kingdom*
  Med R - March 2015 - pNA(NA) [501+]
Kreis, Georg - *Die Geschichte der Schweiz*
  HNet - Feb 2015 - pNA [501+]
Kreis, Reinhild - *Diplomatie mit Gefuhl: Vertrauen, Misstrauen und die Aussenpolitik der Bundesrepublik Deutschland*
  HNet - May 2015 - pNA [501+]
Kreiser, Lawrence A. - *The Civil War in Popular Culture: Memory and Meaning*
  JSH - v81 - i2 - May 2015 - p477(3) [501+]
  Defeating Lee: A History of the Second Corps, Army of the Potomac
  J Mil H - v79 - i2 - April 2015 - p498-499 [501+]
Kreisman, Rachelle - *Being a Good Citizen: A Kids' Guide to Community Involvement (Illus. by Haggerty, Tim)*
  c BL - v112 - i1 - Sept 1 2015 - p97(1) [51-500]
  People Who Help: A Kids' Guide to Community Heroes (Illus. by Haggerty, Tim)
  c BL - v112 - i1 - Sept 1 2015 - p97(1) [51-500]
  Places We Go: A Kids' Guide to Community Buildings (Illus. by Haggerty, Tim)
  c BL - v112 - i1 - Sept 1 2015 - p97(1) [51-500]
  Things We Do: A Kids' Guide to Community Activity (Illus. by Haggerty, Tim)
  c BL - v112 - i1 - Sept 1 2015 - p97(1) [51-500]
  What's That Smell? A Kids' Guide to Keeping Clean (Illus. by Haggerty, Tim)
  c HB Guide - v26 - i1 - Spring 2015 - p176(1) [51-500]
Krell, David - *Our Bums: The Brooklyn Dodgers in History, Memory and Popular Culture*
  NYT - Nov 1 2015 - p3(L) [501+]
Krell, David Farrell - *Derrida and Our Animal Others: Derrida's Final Seminar, 'The Beast and the Sovereign'*
  FS - v69 - i3 - July 2015 - p416-417 [501+]
Kreller, Susan - *You Can't See the Elephants*
  c BL - v112 - i5 - Nov 1 2015 - p63(1) [51-500]
  y KR - Sept 1 2015 - pNA [51-500]
  c PW - v262 - i30 - July 27 2015 - p68(1) [51-500]
  c PW - v262 - i49 - Dec 2 2015 - p74(1) [51-500]
  c SLJ - v61 - i11 - Nov 2015 - p97(1) [51-500]
Krementsov, Nikolai - *Revolutionary Experiments: The Quest for Immortality in Bolshevik Science and Fiction*
  Slav R - v74 - i2 - Summer 2015 - p404-406 [501+]

Kremer, Richard L. - *Johannes Hevelius and His World: Astronomer, Cartographer, Philosopher, and Correspondent*
  Isis - v106 - i2 - June 2015 - p445(2) [501+]
Kremi, William P. - *The Bias of Temperament in American Politics, 2d ed.*
  RVBW - June 2015 - pNA [501+]
Krensky, Stephen - *The Deep Dish on Pizza! (Illus. by Guidera, Daniel)*
  c HB Guide - v26 - i1 - Spring 2015 - p175(1) [51-500]
  I Am So Brave! (Illus. by Gillingham, Sara)
  c KR - Jan 1 2015 - pNA [51-500]
  The Last Christmas Tree (Illus. by Campion, Pascal)
  c HB Guide - v26 - i1 - Spring 2015 - p35(1) [51-500]
  Open Wide! (Illus. by Burks, James)
  c KR - Jan 1 2015 - pNA [51-500]
  The Sweet Story of Hot Chocolate! (Illus. by McClurkan, Rob)
  c HB Guide - v26 - i2 - Fall 2015 - p189(1) [51-500]
Krentz, Jayne Ann - *Secret Sisters*
  BL - v112 - i4 - Oct 15 2015 - p27(1) [51-500]
  PW - v262 - i41 - Oct 12 2015 - p53(1) [51-500]
  KR - Oct 1 2015 - pNA [51-500]
Krepinevich, Andrew F. - *The Last Warrior: Andrew Marshall and the Shaping of Modern American Defense Strategy*
  For Aff - v94 - i3 - May-June 2015 - pNA [501+]
  HNet - May 2015 - pNA [501+]
  NWCR - v68 - i2 - Spring 2015 - p141(2) [501+]
Kreps, Sonja N. - *Tale of Miss Susie and Her Steamboat: And Other Songs from your Childhood Explained*
  SPBW - August 2015 - pNA [501+]
Kreslehner, Gabi - *I Don't Live Here Anymore*
  y KR - Sept 15 2015 - pNA [51-500]
  y SLJ - v61 - i10 - Oct 2015 - p112(1) [51-500]
Kress, Nancy - *The Best of Nancy Kress*
  PW - v262 - i35 - August 31 2015 - p66(2) [51-500]
Kress, Stephen W. - *Project Puffin: The Improbable Quest to Bring a Beloved Seabird Back to Egg Rock*
  New Sci - v226 - i3027 - June 27 2015 - p44(1) [501+]
Kretsedemas, Philip - *The Immigration Crucible: Transforming Race, Nation and the Limits of the Law*
  CS - v44 - i1 - Jan 2015 - p80-81 [501+]
Kreutzer, Susanne - *Arbeits- und Lebensalltag Evangelischer Krankenpflege: Organisation, Soziale Praxis und Biographische Erfahrungen, 1945-1980*
  HNet - March 2015 - pNA [501+]
Kreutzmann, Bill - *Deal: My Three Decades of Drumming, Dreams, and Drugs with the Grateful Dead*
  Dbt - v82 - i9 - Sept 2015 - p75(1) [501+]
  KR - March 15 2015 - pNA [501+]
  LJ - v140 - i5 - March 15 2015 - p101(1) [501+]
  NS - v144 - i5266 - June 12 2015 - p48(2) [501+]
  PW - v262 - i15 - April 13 2015 - p72(1) [51-500]
Kreyling, Michael - *A Late Encounter with the Civil War*
  JSH - v81 - i3 - August 2015 - p755(2) [501+]
Kriebel, Sabine T. - *Revolutionary Beauty: The Radical Photomontages of John Heartfield*
  AHR - v120 - i2 - April 2015 - p736-737 [501+]
Kriechbaumer, Robert - *Zwischen Osterreich und Grossdeutschland: Eine politische Geschichte der Salzburger Festspiele, 1933-1944*
  HER - v130 - i543 - April 2015 - p495(3) [501+]
Krieg der Welten: Wissenschaftliche Tagung zur Geschichte des Kalten Krieges
  HNet - May 2015 - pNA [501+]
  HNet - May 2015 - pNA [501+]
Krieg, Katherine - *What We Get from Norse Mythology*
  c BL - v112 - i15 - April 1 2015 - p62(1) [51-500]
Kriegel, Jay L. - *John V. Lindsay: 50th Anniversary Commemoration*
  NYT - Nov 1 2015 - p3(L) [501+]
Krieger, Butch - *Figure Drawing Studio: Drawing and Painting the Nude Figure from Pose Photos*
  LJ - v140 - i13 - August 1 2015 - p94(1) [51-500]
Krieger, Ellie - *You Have It Made: Delicious, Healthy, Do-Ahead Meals*
  LJ - v140 - i20 - Dec 1 2015 - p128(1) [51-500]
  PW - v262 - i44 - Nov 2 2015 - p79(1) [51-500]
Krieger, Henry - *Side Show*
  Theat J - v67 - i2 - May 2015 - p295-309 [501+]
  Theat J - v67 - i2 - May 2015 - p295-309 [501+]
Kriegman, Mitchell - *Being Audrey Hepburn*
  y HB Guide - v26 - i1 - Spring 2015 - p112(1) [51-500]
  Things I Can't Explain
  y BL - v112 - i5 - Nov 1 2015 - p29(1) [51-500]

260 • KRIEGSERFAHRUNGEN

Kriegserfahrungen erzahlen
    HNet - May 2015 - pNA [501+]
Kriegslandschaften. Gewalt, Zerstorung und Erinnerung
    HNet - July 2015 - pNA [501+]
Krien, Anna - *Night Games: Sex, Power and a Journey Into the Dark Heart of Sport*
    NS - v144 - i5245 - Jan 16 2015 - p46(2) [501+]
Krigseisen, Wojciech - *Odrodzenie i Reformacja w Polsce*
    Six Ct J - v46 - i3 - Fall 2015 - p783-784 [501+]
Krimmer, Elisabeth - *Religion, Reason, and Culture in the Age of Goethe*
    Ger Q - v88 - i1 - Wntr 2015 - p105(3) [501+]
Krimsky, Sheldon - *Genetic Explanations: Sense and Nonsense*
    QRB - v90 - i1 - March 2015 - p96(2) [501+]
Stem Cell Dialogues: A Philosophical and Scientific Inquiry into Medical Frontiers
    LJ - v140 - i9 - May 15 2015 - p102(2) [51-500]
Krimtataren in Geschichte und Gegenwart
    HNet - June 2015 - pNA [501+]
Kripal, Jeffrey J. - *The Super Natural*
    KR - Nov 15 2015 - pNA [501+]
Krippe, Kuche, Kombinat - Frauen im Kommunismus. 7. Hohenschonhausen-Forum
    HNet - March 2015 - pNA [501+]
Krippner, Greta R. - *Capitalizing on Crisis: The Political Origins of the Rise of Finance*
    CS - v44 - i4 - July 2015 - p449-462 [501+]
Krisak, Len - *Ovid's Erotic Poems: Amores and Ars Amatoria*
    Sew R - v123 - i2 - Spring 2015 - p350-357 [501+]
Krisher, Trudy - *An Affectionate Farewell: The Story of Old Bob and Old Abe (Illus. by Dodson, Bert)*
    c CH Bwatch - May 2015 - pNA [51-500]
    c HB Guide - v26 - i2 - Fall 2015 - p210(1) [51-500]
Krishnaswami, Uma - *Bright Sky, Starry City (Illus. by Sicuro, Aimee)*
    c CCB-B - v69 - i1 - Sept 2015 - p32(1) [51-500]
    c CH Bwatch - June 2015 - pNA [51-500]
    c HB - v91 - i4 - July-August 2015 - p118(1) [51-500]
    c KR - March 15 2015 - pNA [51-500]
    c PW - v262 - i14 - April 6 2015 - p59(1) [51-500]
    c Res Links - v20 - i5 - June 2015 - p5(1) [501+]
    c SLJ - v61 - i5 - May 2015 - p86(1) [51-500]
Krisp, Caleb - *Anyone but Ivy Pocket (Illus. by Cantini, Barbara)*
    c CCB-B - v68 - i11 - July-August 2015 - p553(1) [51-500]
    c HB Guide - v26 - i2 - Fall 2015 - p90(1) [51-500]
    c KR - Feb 15 2015 - pNA [51-500]
    c Magpies - v30 - i2 - May 2015 - p36(1) [501+]
    c SLJ - v61 - i3 - March 2015 - p137(1) [51-500]
    c BL - v111 - i14 - March 15 2015 - p68(2) [51-500]
Krist, Gary - *Empire of Sin: A Story of Sex, Jazz, Murder, and the Battle for New Orleans (Read by Dean, Robertson). Audiobook Review*
    PW - v262 - i8 - Feb 23 2015 - p71(1) [51-500]
Empire of Sin: A Story of Sex, Jazz, Murder, and the Battle for New Orleans
    LJ - v140 - i7 - April 15 2015 - p48(1) [51-500]
Kristensen, Troels Myrup - *Making and Breaking the Gods: Christian Reponses to Pagan Sculpture in Late Antiquity*
    Class R - v65 - i1 - April 2015 - p262-263 [501+]
Kristeva, Julia - *Teresa, My Love: An Imagined Life of the Saint of Avila*
    RVBW - Feb 2015 - pNA [51-500]
Kristof, Agota - *The Illiterate*
    TLS - i5854 - June 12 2015 - p10(2) [501+]
The Notebook
    TLS - i5854 - June 12 2015 - p13(1) [501+]
The Proof
    TLS - i5844 - April 3 2015 - p20(1) [501+]
    TLS - i5854 - June 12 2015 - p12(1) [501+]
The Third Lie
    TLS - i5844 - April 3 2015 - p20(1) [501+]
    TLS - i5854 - June 12 2015 - p12(1) [501+]
Kristofferson, Sara - *Design by IKEA: A Cultural History*
    BHR - v89 - i2 - Summer 2015 - p364(4) [501+]
Kristofic, Jim - *The Hero Twins: A Navajo-English Story of the Monster Slayers (Illus. by James, Nolan Karras)*
    c Roundup M - v22 - i4 - April 2015 - p27(1) [501+]
    c Roundup M - v22 - i6 - August 2015 - p25(1) [501+]
Kristufek, Peter - *The House of the Deaf Man*
    TLS - i5844 - April 3 2015 - p21(1) [501+]
Krobb, Florian - *Weimar Colonialism: Discourses and Legacies of Post-Imperialism in Germany after 1918*
    HNet - July 2015 - pNA [501+]
    MLR - v110 - i3 - July 2015 - p901-902 [501+]

Kroener, Inga - *CCTV: A Technology under the Radar?*
    CS - v44 - i3 - May 2015 - p436(1) [501+]
Kroesen, Justin - *Die mittelalterliche Sakramentsnische auf Gotland (Schweden): Kunst und Liturgie*
    Specu - v90 - i4 - Oct 2015 - p1136-1137 [501+]
Kroetsch, Robert - *Badlands*
    RVBW - Nov 2015 - pNA [51-500]
Kroger, Joseph - *Aztec Goddesses and Christian Madonnas: Images of the Divine Feminine in Mexico*
    JAAR - v83 - i3 - Sept 2015 - p866-3 [501+]
Krogh, Tyge - *A Lutheran Plague: Murdering to Die in the Eighteenth Century*
    CHR - v101 - i1 - Wntr 2015 - p168(2) [501+]
Krohn, Leena - *Leena Krohn: Collected Fiction*
    KR - Oct 15 2015 - pNA [501+]
Krokos, Dan - *The Black Stars*
    y CH Bwatch - Jan 2015 - pNA [51-500]
    c HB Guide - v26 - i1 - Spring 2015 - p83(1) [51-500]
False Future
    y HB Guide - v26 - i2 - Fall 2015 - p127(1) [51-500]
The Planet Thieves
    c BL - v112 - i1 - Sept 1 2015 - p114(1) [501+]
Krol, Marcin - *Europa w obliczu konca*
    Nation - v300 - i1 - Jan 5 2015 - p27(10) [501+]
Kroll-Smith, Steve - *Left to Chance: Hurricane Katrina and the Story of Two New Orleans Neighborhoods*
    NYTBR - August 9 2015 - p34(L) [501+]
Krolow, Karl - *Puppets in the Wind*
    PSQ - v89 - i2 - Summer 2015 - p171(3) [501+]
Kronenfeld, Jennie Jacobs - *Healthcare Reform in America, 2d ed.*
    BL - v111 - i21 - July 1 2015 - p10(2) [51-500]
Krosoczka, Jarrett J. - *It's Tough to Lose Your Balloon (Illus. by Krosoczka, Jarrett J.)*
    c CCB-B - v69 - i2 - Oct 2015 - p96(1) [51-500]
    c KR - July 1 2015 - pNA [51-500]
    c PW - v262 - i23 - June 8 2015 - p57(1) [51-500]
    c SLJ - v61 - i7 - July 2015 - p63(1) [51-500]
Last Panda Standing
    c KR - March 1 2015 - pNA [51-500]
Lunch Lady and the Schoolwide Scuffle
    c HB Guide - v26 - i1 - Spring 2015 - p83(1) [51-500]
Peanut Butter and Jellyfish (Read by Krosoczka, Jarrett J.). Audiobook Review
    c SLJ - v61 - i8 - August 2015 - p47(2) [51-500]
Peanut Butter and Jellyfish (Illus. by Krosoczka, Jarrett J.)
    c CH Bwatch - May 2015 - pNA [51-500]
Platypus Police Squad: Last Panda Standing
    c HB Guide - v26 - i2 - Fall 2015 - p90(1) [51-500]
Krossing, Karen - *Punch Like a Girl*
    y PW - v262 - i8 - Feb 23 2015 - p77(1) [51-500]
    y VOYA - v38 - i1 - April 2015 - p64(1) [51-500]
Krotz, Ulrich - *Shaping Europe: France, Germany, and Embedded Bilateralism from the Elysee Treaty to Twenty-First Century Politics*
    For Aff - v94 - i1 - Jan-Feb 2015 - pNA [501+]
Krotzl, Christian - *On Old Age: Approaching Death in Antiquity and the Middle Ages*
    Class R - v65 - i1 - April 2015 - p242-244 [501+]
Krovatin, Christopher - *Entombed*
    c HB Guide - v26 - i1 - Spring 2015 - p83(1) [51-500]
Krueger, Derek - *Liturgical Subjects: Christian Ritual, Biblical Narrative, and the Formation of the Self in Byzantium*
    CHR - v101 - i3 - Summer 2015 - p602(2) [501+]
Krueger, Kate - *British Women Writers and the Short Story, 1850-1930: Reclaiming Social Space*
    TSWL - v34 - i1 - Spring 2015 - p170-172 [501+]
Krueger, William Kent - *Windigo Island*
    RVBW - March 2015 - pNA [51-500]
    RVBW - Nov 2015 - pNA [51-500]
Kruft, Anton - *Jan Sluijters Oorlogsprenten, 1915-1919: Politieke Oorlogsprenten uit de Nieuwe Amsterdammer*
    HNet - July 2015 - pNA [501+]
Krug, Ken - *No, Silly! (Illus. by Krug, Ken)*
    c CCB-B - v68 - i8 - April 2015 - p408(2) [51-500]
    c HB Guide - v26 - i2 - Fall 2015 - p14(1) [51-500]
Kruger, Mark H. - *Overtaken*
    y VOYA - v38 - i2 - June 2015 - p78(1) [51-500]
    y HB Guide - v26 - i2 - Fall 2015 - p127(1) [51-500]
    y KR - March 15 2015 - pNA [51-500]
Kruger, Michael - *Last Day of the Year: Selected Poems*
    WLT - v89 - i2 - March-April 2015 - p70(2) [501+]

Krull, Kathleen - *Coretta Scott King (Illus. by Freeman, Laura)*
    c KR - Sept 1 2015 - pNA [51-500]
    c SLJ - v61 - i8 - August 2015 - p121(2) [51-500]
    c BL - v112 - i7 - Dec 1 2015 - p39(2) [51-500]
Dolley Madison (Illus. by Johnson, Steve)
    c HB Guide - v26 - i2 - Fall 2015 - p210(1) [51-500]
    c SLJ - v61 - i3 - March 2015 - p170(2) [51-500]
Hillary Rodham Clinton: Dreams Taking Flight (Illus. by Bates, Amy June)
    c SLJ - v61 - i7 - July 2015 - p104(1) [51-500]
Lives of the Explorers: Discoveries, Disasters (and What the Neighbors Thought). (Illus. by Hewitt, Kathryn)
    c HB Guide - v26 - i1 - Spring 2015 - p199(2) [51-500]
Mary Todd Lincoln (Illus. by Baddley, Elizabeth)
    c SLJ - v61 - i8 - August 2015 - p121(2) [51-500]
Sacajawea (Illus. by Collins, Matt)
    c CCB-B - v69 - i1 - Sept 2015 - p33(1) [51-500]
    c HB Guide - v26 - i2 - Fall 2015 - p223(1) [51-500]
Sonia Sotomayor (Illus. by Dominguez, Angela)
    c CCB-B - v69 - i1 - Sept 2015 - p33(1) [51-500]
Krull, Lena - *Prozessionen in Preussen: Katholisches Leben in Berlin, Breslau, Essen und Munster im 19. Jahrhundert*
    HNet - May 2015 - pNA [501+]
Krulos, Tea - *Monster Hunters: On the Trail with Ghost Hunters, Bigfooters, Ufologists, and Other Paranormal Investigators*
    BL - v111 - i18 - May 15 2015 - p5(1) [51-500]
    LJ - v140 - i8 - May 1 2015 - p87(2) [51-500]
Krummel, John W.M. - *Nashida Kitaro's Chiasmatic Chorology: Palce of Dialectic, Dialectic of Palce*
    J Phil - v112 - i5 - May 2015 - p281(1) [501+]
Krummen, Eveline - *Cult, Myth, and Occasion in Pindar's Victory Odes: A Study of Isthmian 4, Pythian 5, Olympian 1, and Olympian 3*
    Class R - v65 - i1 - April 2015 - p13-15 [501+]
Krumwiede, Lana - *Just Itzy (Illus. by Pizzoli, Greg)*
    c CCB-B - v68 - i9 - May 2015 - p453(2) [51-500]
    c HB - v91 - i1 - Jan-Feb 2015 - p68(2) [51-500]
    c HB Guide - v26 - i2 - Fall 2015 - p40(1) [51-500]
    c NYTBR - April 12 2015 - p19(L) [501+]
True Son
    c BL - v111 - i15 - April 1 2015 - p68(1) [51-500]
    y HB Guide - v26 - i2 - Fall 2015 - p90(1) [51-500]
    c KR - Feb 15 2015 - pNA [51-500]
    c SLJ - v61 - i4 - April 2015 - p155(1) [51-500]
    y VOYA - v38 - i1 - April 2015 - p80(1) [51-500]
Krupat, Arnold - *"That the People Might Live": Loss and Renewal in Native American Elegy*
    AL - v87 - i1 - March 2015 - p194-197 [501+]
Kruse, Donald W. - *Hey, Charlie! (Illus. by Crank, Donny)*
    c CH Bwatch - Jan 2015 - pNA [51-500]
Waldo, Blue, and Glad Max Too! (Illus. by Crank, Donny)
    c CH Bwatch - August 2015 - pNA [51-500]
Kruse, Kevin M. - *One Nation under God: How Corporate America Invented Christian America*
    AM - v212 - i20 - June 22 2015 - p33(2) [501+]
    Bks & Cult - v21 - i4 - July-August 2015 - p5(1) [501+]
    Comw - v142 - i8 - May 1 2015 - p38(3) [501+]
    For Aff - v94 - i4 - July-August 2015 - pNA [501+]
    HNet - June 2015 - pNA [501+]
    Hum - v75 - i4 - July-August 2015 - p42(2) [501+]
    KR - Jan 1 2015 - pNA [501+]
    LJ - v140 - i3 - Feb 15 2015 - p112(3) [501+]
    Nation - v300 - i23 - June 8 2015 - p40(4) [501+]
    New R - v246 - i4 - May 2015 - p86(4) [501+]
    NYTBR - May 17 2015 - p27(L) [501+]
    PW - v262 - i6 - Feb 9 2015 - p58(1) [501+]
    Reason - v47 - i7 - Dec 2015 - p56(4) [501+]
Kruse, Megan - *Call Me Home*
    BL - v111 - i12 - Feb 15 2015 - p30(1) [51-500]
    PW - v262 - i3 - Jan 19 2015 - p53(1) [51-500]
Krusie, Curtis - *The World as We Know It*
    PW - v262 - i37 - Sept 14 2015 - p51(1) [51-500]
Krusoe, Jim - *The Sleep Garden*
    KR - Dec 1 2015 - pNA [51-500]
Kruszelnicki, Karl - *Dr Karl's Biggest Book of Science Stuff and Nonsense (Illus. by Jeffery, Russell)*
    c Magpies - v30 - i5 - Nov 2015 - p26(1) [501+]
Kruuk, Hans - *The Spotted Hyena: A Study of Predation and Social Behavior*
    Bwatch - May 2015 - pNA [51-500]
Kruvant, Jonah - *The Last Book Ever Written*
    KR - June 1 2015 - pNA [501+]

Krys, Michelle - *Charmed (Read by Ricci, Tai Alexandra). Audiobook Review*
  y SLJ - v61 - i10 - Oct 2015 - p55(1) [51-500]
Charmed
  y BL - v111 - i18 - May 15 2015 - p60(1) [51-500]
  y KR - March 1 2015 - pNA [51-500]
  y Res Links - v21 - i1 - Oct 2015 - p36(2) [501+]
  y SLJ - v61 - i3 - March 2015 - p158(1) [51-500]
  y VOYA - v38 - i2 - June 2015 - p78(1) [51-500]
Hexed
  y HB Guide - v26 - i1 - Spring 2015 - p112(1) [51-500]
  y Sch Lib - v63 - i1 - Spring 2015 - p62(1) [51-500]

Krzoska, Markus - *Ein Land unterwegs: Kulturgeschichte Polens seit 1945*
    HNet - Sept 2015 - pNA(NA) [501+]

Ktna, Jonathon - *Don't Lose Her*
    BL - v111 - i17 - May 1 2015 - p32(1) [51-500]

Ku, Robert Ji-Song - *Eating Asian America: A Food Studies Reader*
    RAH - v43 - i2 - June 2015 - p390-395 [501+]

Kubica, Mary - *Pretty Baby (Read by Campbell, Cassandra). Audiobook Review*
    BL - v112 - i4 - Oct 15 2015 - p64(1) [51-500]
    PW - v262 - i39 - Sept 28 2015 - p86(1) [51-500]
Pretty Baby
    BL - v111 - i17 - May 1 2015 - p42(1) [51-500]
    BooChiTr - August 22 2015 - p12(1) [501+]
    KR - June 1 2015 - pNA [51-500]
    LJ - v140 - i11 - June 15 2015 - p77(1) [51-500]
    PW - v262 - i24 - June 15 2015 - p64(1) [51-500]

Kuc, Kamila - *The Struggle for Form: Perspectives on Polish Avant-Garde Film 1916-1989*
    Slav R - v74 - i3 - Fall 2015 - p639-640 [501+]

Kucharski, Adam - *The Perfect Bet*
    KR - Dec 15 2015 - pNA [501+]

Kuchler, Christian - *NS-Propaganda im 21. Jahrhundert: Zwischen Verbot und öffentlicher Auseinandersetzung*
    HNet - April 2015 - pNA [501+]

Kucia, John F. - *Leadership in Balance: New Habits of the Mind*
    CHE - v61 - i26 - March 13 2015 - pNA [51-500]

Kudela, Katy R. - *My First Book of Mandarin Chinese Words*
  c Sch Lib - v63 - i3 - Autumn 2015 - p174(1) [51-500]

Kuderick, Madeleine - *Kiss of Broken Glass*
  y HB Guide - v26 - i1 - Spring 2015 - p112(2) [51-500]

Kudlinski, Kathleen V. - *Boy, Were We Wrong about the Human Body! (Illus. by Tilley, Debbie)*
  c BL - v112 - i3 - Oct 1 2015 - p39(1) [51-500]
  c KR - August 1 2015 - pNA [51-500]
  c SLJ - v61 - i8 - August 2015 - p122(1) [51-500]
Boy, Were We Wrong about the Weather! (Illus. by Serra, Sebastia)
  c BL - v111 - i21 - July 1 2015 - p53(1) [51-500]
  c CCB-B - v69 - i2 - Oct 2015 - p97(1) [51-500]
  c HB - v91 - i4 - July-August 2015 - p157(2) [51-500]
  c KR - April 15 2015 - pNA [51-500]
  c SLJ - v61 - i5 - May 2015 - p134(1) [51-500]
History's All-Stars (Illus. by Henderson, Meryl)
  c HB Guide - v26 - i2 - Fall 2015 - p210(1) [51-500]
Rebel with a Cause: The Daring Adventure of Dicey Langston, Girl Spy of the American Revolution (Illus. by Faber, Rudy)
  c BL - v112 - i6 - Nov 15 2015 - p42(1) [51-500]

Kuefler, Joseph - *Beyond the Pond (Illus. by Kuefler, Joseph)*
  c BL - v112 - i3 - Oct 1 2015 - p81(1) [51-500]
  c KR - August 1 2015 - pNA [51-500]
  c PW - v262 - i31 - August 3 2015 - p55(2) [51-500]
  c PW - v262 - i49 - Dec 2 2015 - p12(1) [51-500]
  c SLJ - v61 - i7 - July 2015 - p63(2) [51-500]

Kuefler, Mathew - *The Making and Unmaking of a Saint: Hagiography and Memory in the Cult of Gerald of Aurillac*
    AHR - v120 - i2 - April 2015 - p698-699 [501+]
The Making and Unmaking of a Saint: Hagiography and Memory in the Cult of Gerald of Aurillac
    CHR - v101 - i3 - Summer 2015 - p610(2) [501+]

Kuehn Julia - *Diasporic Chineseness after the Rise of China: Communities and Cultural Production*
    Pac A - v88 - i2 - June 2015 - p292 [501+]

Kuehn, Stephanie - *Delicate Monsters*
  c BL - v111 - i17 - May 1 2015 - p49(1) [51-500]
  y CCB-B - v69 - i1 - Sept 2015 - p33(2) [51-500]
  y HB - v91 - i4 - July-August 2015 - p138(1) [51-500]
    KR - April 1 2015 - pNA [51-500]
  y PW - v262 - i15 - April 13 2015 - p83(1) [51-500]
  y PW - v262 - i49 - Dec 2 2015 - p112(1) [51-500]
    SLJ - v61 - i4 - April 2015 - p167(1) [51-500]

Kuethe, Allan J. - *La defensa del imperio.: JuliauN De Arriaga En La Armada*
    HAHR - v95 - i3 - August 2015 - p526-528 [501+]
The Spanish Atlantic World in the Eighteenth Century: War and the Bourbon Reforms, 1713-1796
    HAHR - v95 - i3 - August 2015 - p528-529 [501+]

Kugelmeier, Christoph - *Marsilio Ficino: Index Rerum*
    Sev Cent N - v73 - i1-2 - Spring-Summer 2015 - p66(2) [501+]

Kugler, Tina - *In Mary's Garden (Illus. by Kugler, Tina)*
  c CCB-B - v68 - i10 - June 2015 - p500(2) [51-500]
  c HB - v91 - i2 - March-April 2015 - p121(2) [51-500]
  c HB Guide - v26 - i2 - Fall 2015 - p193(1) [51-500]
  c KR - Jan 15 2015 - pNA [51-500]
  c NYTBR - May 10 2015 - p23(L) [51+]
  c PW - v262 - i3 - Jan 19 2015 - p80(1) [51-500]
  c Teach Lib - v42 - i5 - June 2015 - p44(1) [51-500]

Kuhlman, Evan - *Great Ball of Light (Illus. by Holmes, Jeremy)*
  c BL - v111 - i12 - Feb 15 2015 - p86(1) [51-500]
  c CCB-B - v68 - i11 - July-August 2015 - p553(1) [51-500]
  c HB Guide - v26 - i2 - Fall 2015 - p90(1) [51-500]
Great Ball of Light
  c KR - Jan 1 2015 - pNA [51-500]

Kuhlmann, Torben - *Moletown (Illus. by Kuhlmann, Torben)*
  c BL - v112 - i1 - Sept 1 2015 - p121(2) [51-500]
  c KR - August 1 2015 - pNA [51-500]
  c PW - v262 - i29 - July 20 2015 - p189(1) [51-500]
  c SLJ - v61 - i11 - Nov 2015 - p84(1) [51-500]

Kuhn, Cornelia - *Die Kunst Gehort dem Volke? Volkskunst in der Fruhen DDR zwischen Politischer Lenkung und Asthetischer Praxis*
    HNet - July 2015 - pNA [501+]

Kuhn, Shane - *Hostile Takeover*
    BL - v111 - i18 - May 15 2015 - p27(1) [51-500]
    KR - May 1 2015 - pNA [51-500]
    PW - v262 - i21 - May 25 2015 - p34(2) [51-500]

Kuhn, Thomas S. - *The Copernican Revolution: Planetary Astronomy in the Development of Western Thought*
    TimHES - i2211 - July 9 2015 - p51(1) [501+]

Kuhn, William - *Mrs. Queen Takes the Train*
    VOYA - v38 - i3 - August 2015 - p10(2) [501+]

Kuhner, Timothy K. - *Capitalism v. Democracy: Money in Politics and the Free Market Constitution*
    HLR - v128 - i6 - April 2015 - p1894(2) [1-50]

Kuhns, Eleanor - *Cradle to Grave (Read by Berneis, Susie). Audiobook Review*
    LJ - v140 - i13 - August 1 2015 - p47(1) [51-500]
    PW - v262 - i30 - July 27 2015 - p60(1) [51-500]
Death in Salem (Read by Berneis, Susie). Audiobook Review
    LJ - v140 - i16 - Oct 1 2015 - p43(1) [51-500]
Death in Salem
    BL - v111 - i17 - May 1 2015 - p30(1) [51-500]
    KR - April 15 2015 - pNA [501+]
    PW - v262 - i20 - May 18 2015 - p55(2) [51-500]

Kuipers, Alice - *Violet and Victor Write the Best-Ever Bookworm Book (Illus. by Murguia, Bethanie Deeney)*
  c HB Guide - v26 - i1 - Spring 2015 - p35(1) [51-500]
Violet and Victor Write the Most Fabulous Fairy Tale (Illus. by Murguia, Bethanie Deeney)
  c KR - Oct 15 2015 - pNA [51-500]
  c SLJ - v61 - i8 - August 2015 - p71(2) [51-500]

Kuittinen, Riikka - *Street Craft: Guerilla Gardening, Yarnbombing, Light Graffiti, Street Sculpture, and More*
    Am Craft - v75 - i3 - June-July 2015 - p20(1) [501+]
    LJ - v140 - i6 - April 1 2015 - p96(1) [51-500]
    PW - v262 - i8 - Feb 23 2015 - p68(2) [51-500]

Kukielski, Peter - *Roses without Chemicals: 150 Disease-Free Varieties That Will Change the Way You Grow Roses*
    LJ - v140 - i2 - Feb 1 2015 - p101(1) [51-500]

Kuklin, Susan - *Beyond Magenta: Transgender Teens Speak Out (Read by Eby, Tanya). Audiobook Review*
  y BL - v111 - i9-10 - Jan 1 2015 - p117(1) [51-500]

Kuklis, David - *Escape from Netherworld*
    SPBW - Nov 2015 - pNA [51-500]

Kukowski, Martin - *Kriegswirtschaft und Arbeitseinsatz bei der Auto Union AG Chemnitz im Zweiten Weltkrieg*
    HNet - May 2015 - pNA [501+]

Kulaga, Jaime - *The SuperWoman's Guide to Super Fulfillment*
    RVBW - April 2015 - pNA [51-500]

Kulakov, Konstantin - *Excavating the Sky*
    CC - v132 - i24 - Nov 25 2015 - p42(1) [51-500]
    KR - Nov 15 2015 - pNA [501+]

Kuligin, Victor - *The Language of Salvation: Discovering the Riches of What It Means to Be Saved*
    RVBW - Nov 2015 - pNA [51-500]

Kulka, Joe - *The Christmas Coal Man (Illus. by Kulka, Joe)*
  c KR - Sept 1 2015 - pNA [51-500]
  c PW - v262 - i37 - Sept 14 2015 - p77(1) [51-500]
  c SLJ - v61 - i10 - Oct 2015 - p65(1) [51-500]

Kullck, Don - *Loneliness and Its Opposite: Sex, Disability, and the Ethics of Engagement*
    TimHES - i2214 - July 30 2015 - p49-49 [501+]

Kulling, Monica - *Grant and Tillie Go Walking (Illus. by Smith, Sydney)*
  c CH Bwatch - August 2015 - pNA [501+]
  c KR - July 1 2015 - pNA [51-500]
  c Res Links - v21 - i1 - Oct 2015 - p6(2) [51-500]
  c SLJ - v61 - i10 - Oct 2015 - p79(1) [51-500]
Spic-and-Span! Lillian Gilbreth's Wonder Kitchen (Illus. by Parkins, David)
  c HB Guide - v26 - i1 - Spring 2015 - p194(1) [51-500]
To the Rescue! Garrett Morgan Underground (Illus. by Parkins, David)
  c PW - v262 - i51 - Dec 14 2015 - p82(2) [501+]
The Tweedles Go Electric (Illus. by Lafrance, Marie)
  c Bkbird - v53 - i1 - Wntr 2015 - p99(1) [501+]
The Tweedles Go Online (Illus. by Lafrance, Marie)
  c CH Bwatch - April 2015 - pNA [501+]
  c HB Guide - v26 - i2 - Fall 2015 - p40(1) [51-500]
  c KR - March 15 2015 - pNA [51-500]
  c Res Links - v20 - i5 - June 2015 - p5(1) [51-500]

Kulper, Kendall - *Drift & Dagger*
  y KR - July 15 2015 - pNA [51-500]
  y SLJ - v61 - i7 - July 2015 - p86(2) [51-500]
Salt & Storm
  y HB Guide - v26 - i1 - Spring 2015 - p113(1) [51-500]

Kulturelle Phanomene des Altertums zwischen Regularitat, Distinktion und Devianz
    HNet - April 2015 - pNA [501+]

Kumamoto, Robert - *The Historical Origins of Terrorism in America, 1644-1880*
    AHR - v120 - i2 - April 2015 - p611-612 [501+]

Kumar, A. Vinod - *India and the Nuclear Non-Proliferation Regime: The Perennial Outlier*
    HNet - May 2015 - pNA [501+]

Kumar, Alok - *Sciences of the Ancient Hindus: Unlocking Nature in the Pursuit of Salvation*
    LJ - v140 - i11 - June 15 2015 - p107(1) [51-500]

Kumar, Amit - *Short Selling: Finding Uncommon Short Ideas*
    PW - v262 - i36 - Sept 7 2015 - p58(2) [51-500]

Kumar, Amitava - *Lunch with a Bigot*
    KR - March 15 2015 - pNA [501+]

Kumar, Shiv K. - *Where Have the Dead Gone? And Other Poems*
    WLT - v89 - i3-4 - May-August 2015 - p121(1) [501+]

Kumin, Maxine - *Lizzie! (Illus. by Gilbert, Elliott)*
  c HB Guide - v26 - i1 - Spring 2015 - p83(1) [51-500]
The Pawnbroker's Daughter: A Memoir
    KR - April 15 2015 - pNA [51-500]
    NY - v91 - i21 - July 27 2015 - p71 [51-500]
    Wom R Bks - v32 - i5 - Sept-Oct 2015 - p18(2) [501+]

Kummerling-Meibauer, Bettina - *Picturebooks: Representation and Narration*
    Bkbird - v53 - i1 - Wntr 2015 - p93(2) [501+]

Kumpfmuller, Michael - *The Glory of Life*
    TLS - i5836 - Feb 6 2015 - p20(1) [501+]

Kun, Josh - *Black and Brown in Los Angeles: Beyond Conflict and Coalition*
    ERS - v38 - i8 - August 2015 - p1473(3) [501+]
    PHR - v84 - i3 - August 2015 - p382(2) [501+]

Kunce, Jeanna - *Darien and the Lost Paints of Telinoria (Illus. by Kunce, Craig)*
  c PW - v262 - i35 - August 31 2015 - p92(1) [51-500]
Darien and the Seed of Obreget (Illus. by Kunce, Craig)
  c SLJ - v61 - i11 - Nov 2015 - p97(2) [51-500]

Kundera, Milan - *The Festival of Insignificance*
    Atl - v316 - i1 - July-August 2015 - p40(3) [501+]
    BL - v111 - i17 - May 1 2015 - p75(1) [51-500]
    Econ - v415 - i8942 - June 13 2015 - p81(US) [501+]
    Ent W - i1370 - July 3 2015 - p66(1) [501+]
    KR - April 15 2015 - pNA [501+]
    Lon R Bks - v37 - i13 - July 2 2015 - p19(2) [501+]
    Nat Post - v17 - i194 - June 20 2015 - pWP4(1) [501+]
    Nat R - v67 - i12 - July 6 2015 - p45 [501+]
    NS - v144 - i5266 - June 12 2015 - p50(2) [501+]
    NYRB - v62 - i17 - Nov 5 2015 - p45(3) [501+]
    NYT - June 15 2015 - pC1(L) [501+]
    PW - v262 - i12 - March 23 2015 - p42(1) [51-500]
    Spec - v328 - i9747 - June 20 2015 - p36(1) [501+]
    TLS - i5855 - June 19 2015 - p21(1) [501+]
  La Fete de l'insignificance
    TLS - i5834 - Jan 23 2015 - p27(1) [501+]
Kundnani, Hans - *The Paradox of German Power*
    TLS - i5857 - July 3 2015 - p12(2) [501+]
Kunetka, James W. - *The General and the Genius: Groves and Oppenheimer: The Unlikely Partnership That Built the Atom Bomb*
    KR - April 15 2015 - pNA [51-500]
    LJ - v140 - i8 - May 1 2015 - p88(3) [501+]
    PW - v262 - i19 - May 11 2015 - p50(1) [501+]
Kunicki, Mikolaj Stanislaw - *Between the Brown and the Red*
    HNet - March 2015 - pNA [501+]
Kunkel, Mike - *Brother vs. Brother (Illus. by Kunkel, Mike)*
  c HB Guide - v26 - i2 - Fall 2015 - p68(1) [51-500]
  Magic Words! (Illus. by Kunkel, Mike)
  c HB Guide - v26 - i2 - Fall 2015 - p68(1) [51-500]
Kunkel, Thomas - *Man in Profile: Joseph Mitchell of The New Yorker*
    Atl - v315 - i5 - June 2015 - p44(3) [501+]
    BL - v111 - i11 - Feb 1 2015 - p10(2) [51-500]
    CJR - v54 - i2 - July-August 2015 - p38(4) [501+]
    Econ - v415 - i8938 - May 16 2015 - p76(US) [501+]
    KR - Feb 1 2015 - pNA [501+]
    LJ - v140 - i5 - March 15 2015 - p114(1) [501+]
    Lon R Bks - v37 - i12 - June 18 2015 - p15(4) [501+]
    Nation - v301 - i31 - August 3 2015 - p32(4) [501+]
    NYRB - v62 - i7 - April 23 2015 - p60(3) [501+]
    NYT - June 25 2015 - pC4(L) [501+]
    NYTBR - May 24 2015 - p18(L) [501+]
    PW - v262 - i6 - Feb 9 2015 - p57(3) [51-500]
Kunow, Jurgen - *Archaologie und Bodendenkmalpflege in der Rheinprovinz 1920-1945*
    HNet - Jan 2015 - pNA [501+]
Kunst im Deutschen Orden
    HNet - March 2015 - pNA [501+]
Kunst- und Ausstellungshalle der Bundesrepublik Deutschland - *1914: The Avant-Gardes at War*
    Ger Q - v88 - i3 - Summer 2015 - p384(9) [501+]
Kunter, Katharina - *Globalisierung der Kirchen: Der Okumenische Rat der Kirchen und die Entdeckung der Dritten Welt in den 1960er und 1970er Jahren*
    HNet - Jan 2015 - pNA [501+]
Kuo, Mei-Fen - *Making Chinese Australia: Urban Elites, Newspapers and the Formation of Chinese-Australian Identity, 1892-1912*
    JAS - v74 - i3 - August 2015 - p728-729 [501+]
Kuper, Adam - *Anthropology and Anthropologists: The British School in the Twentieth Century*
    TLS - i5873 - Oct 23 2015 - p27(1) [501+]
Kuper, Peter - *Ruins (Illus. by Kuper, Peter)*
    BL - v112 - i4 - Oct 15 2015 - p35(2) [51-500]
    PW - v262 - i36 - Sept 7 2015 - p54(1) [51-500]
Kuper, Tonya - *Anomaly*
  y KR - Jan 1 2015 - pNA [501+]
Kupersmith, Violet - *The Frangipani Hotel*
  y NYTBR - April 19 2015 - p28(L) [501+]
Kureishi, Hanif - *The Last Word*
    BL - v111 - i12 - Feb 15 2015 - p31(2) [51-500]
    KR - Jan 1 2015 - pNA [51-500]
    Nat Post - v119 - i17 - March 21 2015 - pWP5(1) [501+]
    NY - v91 - i14 - May 25 2015 - p73 [501+]
    NYT - March 26 2015 - pC6(L) [501+]
    PW - v262 - i3 - Jan 19 2015 - p54(1) [501+]
Kuri, Frederick - *Beyond the Great Water*
    KR - Dec 1 2015 - pNA [501+]

Kurian, George Thomas - *Encyclopedia of Christian Education, 3 vols.*
    BL - v112 - i6 - Nov 15 2015 - p12(2) [501+]
    LJ - v140 - i14 - Sept 1 2015 - p138(1) [51-500]
Kurihara, Ken - *Celestial Wonders in Reformation Germany*
    Isis - v106 - i2 - June 2015 - p441(1) [501+]
    Ren Q - v68 - i1 - Spring 2015 - p343-344 [501+]
Kurin, Richard - *The Smithsonian's History of America in 101 Objects*
    LJ - v140 - i9 - May 15 2015 - p94(2) [501+]
Kurjan, Kristy - *Nap-A-Roo (Illus. by Parker, Tyler)*
  c CH Bwatch - August 2015 - pNA [51-500]
  c PW - v262 - i20 - May 18 2015 - p82(2) [501+]
Kurkjian, Stephen - *Master Thieves: The Boston Gangsters Who Pulled Off the World's Greatest Art Heist*
    KR - Jan 15 2015 - pNA [501+]
    LJ - v140 - i3 - Feb 15 2015 - p116(1) [51-500]
  Master Thieves: The Boston Gangsters Who Pulled Off the World's Greatest Art Heist (Read by Chamberlain, Mike). Audiobook Review
    LJ - v140 - i11 - June 15 2015 - p52(2) [51-500]
  Master Thieves: The Boston Gangsters Who Pulled Off the World's Greatest Art Heist
    BL - v111 - i14 - March 15 2015 - p32(2) [51-500]
    NYTBR - June 28 2015 - p22(L) [501+]
Kurlansky, Mark - *City Beasts: Fourteen Stories of Uninvited Wildlife*
    BL - v111 - i9-10 - Jan 1 2015 - p36(1) [51-500]
    NYTBR - Feb 1 2015 - p26(L) [501+]
  Cod: A Biography of the Fish That Changed the World
    Under Nat - v36 - i1 - Fall 2015 - p38(1) [51-500]
  Frozen in Time: Clarence Birdseye's Outrageous Idea about Frozen Food
  y HB Guide - v26 - i1 - Spring 2015 - p194(1) [51-500]
Kurniawan, Eka - *Beauty Is a Wound*
    BL - v112 - i2 - Sept 15 2015 - p26(1) [51-500]
    KR - July 1 2015 - pNA [501+]
    New R - v246 - i11 - Fall 2015 - p72(4) [501+]
    NYRB - v62 - i16 - Oct 22 2015 - p60(3) [501+]
    NYT - Sept 18 2015 - pC27(L) [501+]
    NYTBR - Sept 13 2015 - p9(L) [501+]
    PW - v262 - i23 - June 8 2015 - p1(1) [51-500]
    WLT - v89 - i6 - Nov-Dec 2015 - p71(1) [51-500]
  Man Tiger
    KR - August 15 2015 - pNA [501+]
    NYTBR - Sept 13 2015 - p9(L) [501+]
    PW - v262 - i30 - July 27 2015 - p39(1) [51-500]
Kurr, Ryan - *Sugar Burn*
    PW - v262 - i25 - June 22 2015 - p135(1) [51-500]
Kurson, Robert - *Pirate Hunters: Treasure, Obsession, and the Search for a Legendary Pirate Ship (Read by Porter, Ray). Audiobook Review*
    LJ - v140 - i16 - Oct 1 2015 - p45(1) [501+]
  Pirate Hunters: Treasure, Obsession, and the Search for a Legendary Pirate Ship
    BL - v111 - i12 - Feb 15 2015 - p22(1) [51-500]
    BooChiTr - July 18 2015 - p12(1) [501+]
    CSM - June 25 2015 - pNA [501+]
    Esq - v163 - i6-7 - June-July 2015 - p26(2) [501+]
    KR - April 1 2015 - pNA [501+]
    LJ - v140 - i6 - April 1 2015 - p100(1) [501+]
    NYT - June 12 2015 - pC24(L) [501+]
    PW - v262 - i6 - Feb 9 2015 - p53(1) [51-500]
    Under Nat - v36 - i1 - Fall 2015 - p38(1) [51-500]
Kurtagich, Dawn - *The Dead House*
  y BL - v112 - i1 - Sept 1 2015 - p103(1) [51-500]
  y KR - July 15 2015 - pNA [51-500]
  y SLJ - v61 - i7 - July 2015 - p94(2) [51-500]
  y VOYA - v38 - i4 - Oct 2015 - p73(1) [51-500]
  y PW - v262 - i27 - July 6 2015 - p75(1) [51-500]
Kurti, Richard - *Monkey Wars*
  y CCB-B - v68 - i8 - April 2015 - p409(1) [51-500]
  y HB Guide - v26 - i2 - Fall 2015 - p127(1) [51-500]
  y PW - v262 - i49 - Dec 2 2015 - p104(1) [51-500]
  y VOYA - v37 - i6 - Feb 2015 - p79(2) [51-500]
Kurtis, Arlene - *Lila's Hamsa*
    PW - v262 - i34 - August 24 2015 - p68(1) [51-500]
Kurtz, Glenn - *Three Minutes in Poland: Discovering a Lost World in a 1938 Family Film*
    NY - v91 - i1 - Feb 16 2015 - p71 [51-500]
Kurtz, Jane - *Celebrating Pennsylvania: 50 States to Celebrate (Illus. by Canga, C.B.)*
  c BL - v111 - i22 - August 1 2015 - p74(1) [51-500]
Kurtz, Kevin - *What Makes Sports Gear Safer?*
  c BL - v112 - i1 - Sept 1 2015 - p98(2) [51-500]
Kurzweil, Allen - *Whipping Boy: The Forty-Year Search for My Twelve-Year-Old Bully*
    BL - v111 - i9-10 - Jan 1 2015 - p32(1) [51-500]
    NYTBR - August 2 2015 - p26(L) [501+]

Kushner, Aleksandr - *Apollo in the Grass: Selected Poems*
    BL - v111 - i21 - July 1 2015 - p17(1) [51-500]
    PW - v262 - i29 - July 20 2015 - p166(2) [51-500]
Kushner, Aviya - *The Grammar of God: A Journey into the Words and Worlds of the Bible (Read by Kushner, Aviya). Audiobook Review*
    LJ - v140 - i20 - Dec 1 2015 - p61(1) [51-500]
  The Grammar of God: A Journey into the Words and Worlds of the Bible
    KR - June 1 2015 - pNA [501+]
    LJ - v140 - i11 - June 15 2015 - p93(1) [51-500]
    Nat Post - v17 - i240 - August 22 2015 - pWP4(1) [501+]
    PW - v262 - i19 - May 11 2015 - p53(1) [51-500]
Kushner, Barak - *Men to Devils, Devils to Men: Japanese War Crimes and Chinese Justice*
    For Aff - v94 - i3 - May-June 2015 - pNA [501+]
    J Mil H - v79 - i2 - April 2015 - p534-536 [501+]
Kushner, David - *Alligator Candy: A Memoir*
    KR - Jan 1 2016 - pNA [501+]
Kushner, Harold S. - *Nine Essential Things I've Learned about Life*
    CC - v132 - i20 - Sept 30 2015 - p42(1) [51-500]
Kushner, Kim - *The New Kosher: Simple Recipes to Savor & Share*
    BL - v112 - i3 - Oct 1 2015 - p18(2) [51-500]
Kushner, Nina - *Erotic Exchanges: The World of Elite Prostitution in Eighteenth-Century Paris*
    AHR - v120 - i2 - April 2015 - p724-725 [501+]
    Eight-C St - v48 - i3 - Spring 2015 - p356-359 [501+]
    JIH - v45 - i4 - Spring 2015 - p578-580 [501+]
  Women and Work in Eighteenth-Century France
    JIH - v46 - i3 - Wntr 2016 - p443-444 [501+]
Kushner, Rachel - *The Strange Case of Rachel K.*
    NYTBR - July 12 2015 - p30(L) [501+]
Kushner, Seth - *Schmuck*
    PW - v262 - i38 - Sept 21 2015 - p62(1) [51-500]
Kuskin, William - *Recursive Origins: Writing at the Transition to Modernity*
    Six Ct J - v46 - i1 - Spring 2015 - p251-253 [501+]
Kuskowski, Alex - *Biggest, Baddest Book of Caves*
  c HB Guide - v26 - i2 - Fall 2015 - p167(1) [51-500]
  c BL - v111 - i16 - April 15 2015 - p45(1) [501+]
  Cool Breads & Biscuits: Easy & Fun Comfort Food
  c HB Guide - v26 - i2 - Fall 2015 - p189(1) [51-500]
  Cool Cake Mix Cupcakes: Fun & Easy Baking Recipes for Kids!
  c HB Guide - v26 - i1 - Spring 2015 - p175(1) [51-500]
  Cool Crocheting for Kids: A Fun and Creative Introduction to Fiber Art
  c HB Guide - v26 - i1 - Spring 2015 - p177(1) [51-500]
  Cool Embroidery for Kids: A Fun and Creative Introduction to Fiber Art
  c HB Guide - v26 - i1 - Spring 2015 - p177(1) [51-500]
  Cool Punch Needle for Kids: A Fun and Creative Introduction to Fiber Art
  c HB Guide - v26 - i1 - Spring 2015 - p177(1) [51-500]
  Cool Sewing for Kids: A Fun and Creative Introduction to Fiber Art
  c HB Guide - v26 - i1 - Spring 2015 - p177(1) [51-500]
  Penguins
  c HB Guide - v26 - i2 - Fall 2015 - p177(1) [51-500]
  SandCastle: Zoo Animals
  c HB Guide - v26 - i2 - Fall 2015 - p180(1) [51-500]
  Super SandCastle: Super Simple Gardening
  c HB Guide - v26 - i2 - Fall 2015 - p187(1) [51-500]
  Super Simple Australian Art: Fun and Easy Art from around the World
  c HB Guide - v26 - i1 - Spring 2015 - p177(2) [51-500]
  Super Simple European Art: Fun and Easy Art from around the World
  c HB Guide - v26 - i1 - Spring 2015 - p177(2) [51-500]
  Super Simple Hanging Gardens: A Kid's Guide to Gardening
  c BL - v111 - i12 - Feb 15 2015 - p75(1) [51-500]
  Super Simple Indian Art: Fun and Easy Art from around the World
  c HB Guide - v26 - i1 - Spring 2015 - p177(2) [51-500]
  Super Simple Japanese Art: Fun and Easy Art from around the World
  c HB Guide - v26 - i1 - Spring 2015 - p177(2) [51-500]

Kusno, Abidin - *After the New Order: Space, Politics and Jakarta*
    Pac A - v88 - i2 - June 2015 - p362 [501+]

Kusoglu, Mehmet Zeki - *The Ottoman Touch: Traditional Decorative Arts and Crafts*
    LJ - v140 - i17 - Oct 15 2015 - p85(1) [51-500]

Kuster, Volker - *Muslim-Christian Relations Observed: Comparative Studies from Indonesia and the Netherlands*
    IBMR - v39 - i2 - April 2015 - p107(2) [501+]

Kutch, Lynn M. - *Tatort Germany: The Curious Case of German-Language Crime Fiction*
    TLS - i5864-5865 - August 21 2015 - p33(1) [501+]

Kuter, Alexa - *Zwischen Republik und Kaiserzeit: Die Munzmeisterpragung unter Augustus*
    HNet - June 2015 - pNA [501+]

Kutner, Laura - *The Soda Bottle School: A True Story of Recycling, Teamwork, and One Crazy Idea (Illus. by Darragh, Aileen)*
    c HB Guide - v26 - i1 - Spring 2015 - p141(1) [51-500]

Kutner, Richard - *Theseus and the Minotaur (Illus. by Pommaux, Yvan)*
    c HB Guide - v26 - i1 - Spring 2015 - p145(1) [51-500]

Kutz, Michael - *If, by Miracle*
    y Res Links - v20 - i3 - Feb 2015 - p40(1) [501+]

Kutzinski, Vera M. - *The Words of Langston Hughes: Modernism and Translation in the Americas*
    AL - v87 - i1 - March 2015 - p197-199 [501+]
    The Worlds of Langston Hughes: Modernism and Translation in the Americas
    J Am St - v49 - i1 - Feb 2015 - p173-179 [501+]

Kuukkanen, Jouni-Matti - *Postnarrativist Philosophy of Historiography*
    HNet - July 2015 - pNA [501+]

Kuwata, Jiro - *Batman: The Jiro Kuwata Batmanga, vol. 2 (Illus. by Kuwata, Jiro)*
    c BL - v111 - i22 - August 1 2015 - p49(1) [51-500]
    LJ - v140 - i5 - March 15 2015 - p88(3) [501+]

Kuzmany, Borries - *Brody: Eine Galizische Grenzstadt im Langen 19. Jahrhundert*
    HNet - July 2015 - pNA [501+]

Kvach, John F. - *De Bow's Review: The Antebellum Vision of a New South*
    AHR - v120 - i2 - April 2015 - p624-625 [501+]
    Historian - v77 - i2 - Summer 2015 - p341(2) [501+]
    JSH - v81 - i2 - May 2015 - p462(2) [501+]

Kwak, Nancy H. - *A World of Homeowners: American Power and the Politics of Housing Aid*
    TimHES - i2227 - Oct 29 2015 - p48-49 [501+]

Kwakkel, Erik - *Turning Over a New Leaf: Change and Development in the Medieval Book*
    Med R - Jan 2015 - pNA [501+]
    Specu - v90 - i4 - Oct 2015 - p1137-1139 [501+]

Kwan, Coleen - *Courting the Cop. E-book Review*
    PW - v262 - i37 - Sept 14 2015 - p50(1) [51-500]

Kwan, James - *Dear Yeti (Illus. by Kwan, James)*
    c BL - v112 - i6 - Nov 15 2015 - p58(1) [51-500]
    c KR - Sept 1 2015 - pNA [51-500]
    c PW - v262 - i35 - August 31 2015 - p89(1) [51-500]
    c PW - v262 - i49 - Dec 2 2015 - p13(1) [51-500]
    c SLJ - v61 - i10 - Oct 2015 - p79(2) [51-500]

Kwan, Kevin - *China Rich Girlfriend (Read by Look, Lydia). Audiobook Review*
    LJ - v140 - i16 - Oct 1 2015 - p43(2) [51-500]
    China Rich Girlfriend
    BL - v111 - i18 - May 15 2015 - p22(1) [51-500]
    Ent W - i1368 - June 19 2015 - p64(1) [501+]
    KR - June 15 2015 - pNA [501+]
    LJ - v140 - i8 - May 1 2015 - p63(1) [51-500]
    Mac - v128 - i26-27 - July 6 2015 - p66(2) [51-500]
    NYT - June 29 2015 - pC4(L) [501+]
    NYTBR - July 12 2015 - p14(L) [501+]

Kwarteng, Kwasi - *Thatcher's Trial: 180 Days That Created a Conservative Icon*
    KR - Sept 15 2015 - pNA [501+]
    LJ - v140 - i17 - Oct 15 2015 - p102(1) [51-500]

Kwasny, Melissa - *Pictograph*
    PW - v262 - i7 - Feb 16 2015 - p159(1) [51-500]

Kwass, Michael - *Contraband: Louis Mandrin and the Making of a Global Underground*
    JEH - v75 - i2 - June 2015 - p595-597 [501+]
    JIH - v45 - i4 - Spring 2015 - p577-578 [501+]
    Lon R Bks - v37 - i1 - Jan 8 2015 - p35(2) [501+]

Kwaymullina, Ezekiel - *We All Sleep (Illus. by Morgan, Sally)*
    c Magpies - v30 - i5 - Nov 2015 - p27(1) [501+]

Kwiatkowski-Celofiga, Tina - *Verfolgte Schuler: Ursachen und Folgen von Diskriminierung im Schulwesen der DDR*
    HNet - Feb 2015 - pNA [501+]

Kwilecki, Paul - *One Place: Paul Kwilecki and Four Decades of Photographs from Decatur County, Georgia (Illus. by Kwilecki, Paul)*
    JSH - v81 - i2 - May 2015 - p543(1) [501+]

Kwitney, Alisa - *New Avengers: Breakout. Audiobook Review*
    LJ - v140 - i7 - April 15 2015 - p47(1) [51-500]

Kwong-chiu, Chiu - *What Was It Like, Mr. Emperor? Life in China's Forbidden City*
    c KR - Nov 15 2015 - pNA [51-500]

Kyger, Joanner - *On Time: Poems 2005-2014*
    PW - v262 - i20 - May 18 2015 - p61(1) [51-500]

Kylie, Aaron - *Kylie, Aaron: Canadian Geographic Biggest and Best of Canada: 1000 Facts and Figures*
    c Res Links - v20 - i3 - Feb 2015 - p20(1) [51-500]

Kynaston, David - *Modernity Britain, 1957-1962*
    NYT - Jan 21 2015 - pC1(L) [501+]
    NYTBR - Jan 25 2015 - p17(L) [501+]

Kypta, Ulla - *Die Autonomie der Routine: Wie im 12. Jahrhundert das Englische Schatzamt Entstand*
    HNet - Jan 2015 - pNA [501+]

Kyrychenko, Alexander - *The Roman Army and the Expansion of the Gospel: The Role of the Centurion in Luke-Acts*
    Theol St - v76 - i4 - Dec 2015 - p837(2) [501+]

Kytle, Ethan J. - *Romantic Reformers and the Antislavery Struggle in the Civil War Era*
    JAH - v102 - i2 - Sept 2015 - p564-564 [501+]

L

La Bella, Laura - *Careers for Tech Girls in Video Game Development*
　y　BL - v112 - i7 - Dec 1 2015 - p44(1) [51-500]
La Berge, Leigh Claire - *Scandals and Abstraction: Financial Fiction of the Long 1980s*
　　TLS - i5855 - June 19 2015 - p19(2) [501+]
La Coccinella - *Farm Animals*
　c　KR - July 1 2015 - pNA [51-500]
Happy Birthday, Elephant!
　c　KR - July 1 2015 - pNA [51-500]
La Farge, Tom - *The Broken House*
　　ABR - v36 - i4 - May-June 2015 - p21(1) [501+]
　　PW - v262 - i16 - April 20 2015 - p59(1) [51-500]
La Suer, Carrie - *The Home Place (Read by Nichols, Andrus). Audiobook Review*
　　BL - v111 - i14 - March 15 2015 - p23(2) [51-500]
La Vere, David - *The Tuscarora War: Indians, Settlers, and the Fight for the Carolina Colonies*
　　Historian - v77 - i3 - Fall 2015 - p563(2) [501+]
　　HNet - March 2015 - pNA [501+]
　　J Mil H - v79 - i1 - Jan 2015 - p197-198 [501+]
　　JSH - v81 - i1 - Feb 2015 - p162(2) [501+]
Laats, Adam - *The Other School Reformers: Conservative Activism in American Education*
　　HNet - Sept 2015 - pNA [501+]
LaBan, Elizabeth - *The Restaurant Critic's Wife*
　　BL - v112 - i6 - Nov 15 2015 - p24(1) [51-500]
　　LJ - v140 - i16 - Oct 1 2015 - p72(1) [501+]
Laband, John - *Zulu Warriors: The Battle for the South African Frontier*
　　AHR - v120 - i3 - June 2015 - p1156-1157 [501+]
Labbe, Carlos - *Loquela*
　　KR - Oct 15 2015 - pNA [51-500]
Labbe, Joni - *Why Is Mid-Life Mooching Your Mojo? Solutions to Banish Fuzziness and Fatigue Forever!*
　　SPBW - August 2015 - pNA [51-500]
Labe, Louise - *Love Sonnets and Elegies*
　　TLS - i5856 - June 26 2015 - p22(1) [501+]
Labelle, Kathryn Magee - *Dispersed but Not Destroyed: A History of the Seventeenth-Century Wendat People*
　　Can Hist R - v96 - i3 - Sept 2015 - p424(3) [501+]
Labinger, Jay A. - *Up from Generality: How Inorganic Chemistry Finally Became a Respectable Field*
　　J Chem Ed - v92 - i6 - June 2015 - p971-972 [501+]
Labor, Earle - *Jack London: An American Life*
　　HNet - April 2015 - pNA [501+]
Laborie, Christian - *The Rocheforts*
　　KR - March 1 2015 - pNA [501+]
Labov, William - *The language of life and death: The transformation of experience in oral narrative*
　　Lang Soc - v44 - i5 - Nov 2015 - p733-736 [501+]
Labrecque, Ellen - *Living beside a River*
　c　SLJ - v61 - i4 - April 2015 - p116(3) [501+]
Living in a City
　c　HB Guide - v26 - i2 - Fall 2015 - p156(1) [51-500]
Living in a Desert
　c　HB Guide - v26 - i2 - Fall 2015 - p156(1) [51-500]
Living on a Mountain
　c　HB Guide - v26 - i2 - Fall 2015 - p156(1) [51-500]
The Science of a Triple Axel
　c　BL - v112 - i3 - Oct 1 2015 - p64(1) [51-500]
Labrie, Pierre - *Un gouffre sous mon lit*
　y　Res Links - v20 - i3 - Feb 2015 - p46(1) [51-500]
Labriola, Jerry - *Diamonds and Pirates*
　　SPBW - April 2015 - pNA [51-500]
Lacamara, Laura - *Floating on Mama's Song / Flotando en la cancion de mama (Illus. by Morales, Yuyi)*
　c　BL - v111 - i9-10 - Jan 1 2015 - pS18(5) [51-500]
LaCapra, Dominick - *History, Literature, Critical Theory*
　　Clio - v44 - i2 - Spring 2015 - p298-306 [501+]

Lacerda, Daniel - *2,100 Asanas: The Complete Yoga Poses*
　　LJ - v140 - i19 - Nov 15 2015 - p100(1) [51-500]
Lacey, Brian - *Medieval and Monastic Derry: Sixth Century to 1600*
　　CHR - v101 - i3 - Summer 2015 - p606(2) [501+]
Lacey, Catherine - *Nobody Is Ever Missing*
　　Spec - v327 - i9730 - Feb 21 2015 - p42(1) [501+]
Lacey, Jim - *The First Clash: The Miraculous Greek Victory at Marathon - and Its Impact on the Western Civilization*
　　RVBW - June 2015 - pNA [501+]
Lacey, Josh - *The Dragonsitter (Illus. by Parsons, Garry)*
　c　KR - June 15 2015 - pNA [51-500]
　c　PW - v262 - i30 - July 27 2015 - p69(1) [51-500]
　c　SLJ - v61 - i7 - July 2015 - p72(1) [51-500]
Lacey, Minna - *Big Book of the Boy*
　c　KR - Nov 15 2015 - pNA [51-500]
Lacey, Rachel - *Ever After*
　　PW - v262 - i27 - July 6 2015 - p52(1) [51-500]
Lacey, Robert - *Model Woman: Eileen Ford and the Business of Beauty*
　　LJ - v140 - i8 - May 1 2015 - p80(1) [51-500]
　　BL - v111 - i17 - May 1 2015 - p65(1) [51-500]
　　KR - April 1 2015 - pNA [51-500]
Lacey, Saskia - *How to Build a Car*
　c　KR - Sept 15 2015 - pNA [51-500]
Lacey, Sharon Tosi - *Pacific Blitzkrieg: World War II in the Central Pacific*
　　Mar Crp G - v99 - i4 - April 2015 - p84(2) [501+]
Lachenicht Susanne - *Europeans Engaging the Atlantic: Knowledge and Trade, 1500-1800*
　　HNet - Sept 2015 - pNA(NA) [501+]
Lachman, Gary - *The Cartaker of the Cosmos: Living Responsibly in an Unfinished World*
　　Parabola - v40 - i1 - Spring 2015 - p110-114 [501+]
The Secret Teachers of the Western World
　　KR - Oct 15 2015 - pNA [51-500]
　　LJ - v140 - i19 - Nov 15 2015 - p89(1) [51-500]
　　PW - v262 - i41 - Oct 12 2015 - p58(1) [51-500]
Lachman, Kathryn - *Borrowed Forms: The Music and Ethics of Transnational Fiction*
　　FS - v69 - i3 - July 2015 - p423(1) [501+]
Lachter, Hartley - *Kabbalistic Revolution: Reimagining Judaism in Medieval Spain*
　　HNet - April 2015 - pNA [501+]
Lackberg, Camilla - *The Drowning*
　　BL - v111 - i21 - July 1 2015 - p37(1) [51-500]
　　KR - July 15 2015 - pNA [51-500]
　　PW - v262 - i27 - July 6 2015 - p46(2) [51-500]
The Hidden Child
　　RVBW - Jan 2015 - pNA [51-500]
　　RVBW - June 2015 - pNA [51-500]
Lackey, Mercedes - *Hunter*
　y　BL - v112 - i3 - Oct 1 2015 - p69(1) [51-500]
　y　KR - July 15 2015 - pNA [51-500]
　y　NYTBR - Oct 25 2015 - p34(L) [51-500]
　y　PW - v262 - i28 - July 13 2015 - p68(1) [51-500]
　y　SLJ - v61 - i10 - Oct 2015 - p104(1) [51-500]
　y　VOYA - v38 - i4 - Oct 2015 - p74(1) [51-500]
Lacombe, Jean - *Marcello*
　c　Res Links - v20 - i5 - June 2015 - p39(1) [51-500]
LaCombe, Michael A. - *Political Gastronomy: Food and Authority in the English Atlantic World*
　　W&M Q - v72 - i3 - July 2015 - p553-556 [501+]
Lacroix, Melissa Morelli - *A Most Beautiful Deception*
　　Can Lit - i224 - Spring 2015 - p128 [501+]
Lacy, James V. - *Taxifornia 2016: 14 Essays on the Future of California*
　　KR - Nov 1 2015 - pNA [501+]

Lacy, Peter - *Waste to Wealth: The Circular Economy Advantage*
　　Nature - v525 - i7567 - Sept 3 2015 - p31(1) [51-500]
　　RVBW - Nov 2015 - pNA [501+]
Lacy, Tim - *The Dream of a Democratic Culture: Mortimer J. Adler and the Great Books Idea*
　　AHR - v120 - i1 - Feb 2015 - p271(1) [501+]
Ladd, Helen F. - *Handbook of Research in Education Finance and Policy*
　　RVBW - April 2015 - pNA [501+]
Laden, Nina - *Peek-A-Boo*
　c　KR - Jan 1 2016 - pNA [51-500]
Laderman, Scott - *Empire in Waves: A Political History of Surfing*
　　AHR - v120 - i3 - June 2015 - p985-986 [501+]
　　HNet - Jan 2015 - pNA [501+]
　　JAH - v101 - i4 - March 2015 - p1239-1240 [501+]
　　PHR - v84 - i4 - Nov 2015 - p568(2) [501+]
Four Decades On: Vietnam, the United States, and the Legacies of the Second Indochina War
　　Parameters - v45 - i1 - Spring 2015 - p171(3) [501+]
　　PHR - v84 - i2 - May 2015 - p246(2) [501+]
Ladich, Friedrich - *Sound Communication in Fishes*
　　QRB - v90 - i3 - Sept 2015 - p337(1) [501+]
Ladouceur, Ben - *Otter*
　　Nat Post - v17 - i188 - June 13 2015 - pWP4(1) [501+]
Ladouceur, Bob - *Chasing Perfection: The Principles Behind Winning Football the De La Salle Way*
　y　BL - v112 - i1 - Sept 1 2015 - p32(1) [51-500]
Lafaye, Vanessa - *Under a Dark Summer Sky*
　　KR - April 15 2015 - pNA [51-500]
　　LJ - v140 - i5 - March 15 2015 - p93(1) [51-500]
　　PW - v262 - i16 - April 20 2015 - p46(2) [51-500]
Lafayette, Madame de - *Complete Works*
　　TLS - i5850 - May 15 2015 - p8(1) [501+]
LaFevers, Robin - *Mortal Heart (Read by Grace, Jennifer). Audiobook Review*
　y　BL - v111 - i18 - May 15 2015 - p72(1) [51-500]
Mortal Heart
　y　HB Guide - v26 - i1 - Spring 2015 - p113(1) [51-500]
　y　Sch Lib - v63 - i1 - Spring 2015 - p54(2) [51-500]
Lafferty, Renee N. - *The Guardianship of Best Interests: Institutional Care for the Children of the Poor in Halifax, 1850-1960*
　　Can Hist R - v96 - i1 - March 2015 - p122(3) [501+]
LaFlaur, Mark - *What Fresh Hell: The Best of Levees Not War: Blogging on Post-Katrina New Orleans and America, 2005-2015*
　　PW - v262 - i45 - Nov 9 2015 - p54(1) [51-500]
Lafon, Lola - *We Are the Birds of the Coming Storm*
　　WLT - v89 - i2 - March-April 2015 - p65(1) [51-500]
LaFosse, Michael G. - *LaFosse and Alexander's Origami Jewelry: Easy-to-Make Paper Pendants, Bracelets, Necklaces and Earrings*
　　LJ - v140 - i20 - Dec 1 2015 - p101(1) [51-500]
Laframboise, Michele - *La Reine Margot*
　y　Res Links - v20 - i4 - April 2015 - p41(1) [501+]
LaGamma, Alisa - *Kongo: Power and Majesty*
　　PW - v262 - i38 - Sept 21 2015 - p66(2) [51-500]
Lagasse, Emeril - *Essential Emeril: Favorite Recipes and Hard-Won Wisdom from My Life in the Kitchen*
　　BL - v112 - i7 - Dec 1 2015 - p8(1) [51-500]
　　LJ - v140 - i17 - Oct 15 2015 - p108(1) [51-500]
　　New Or - v50 - i1 - Oct 2015 - p44(1) [501+]
　　PW - v262 - i38 - Sept 21 2015 - p68(2) [51-500]

Lagasse, Paul - *Channel 37: Season One!*
Analog - v135 - i3 - March 2015 - p107(1) [501+]

Lagercrantz, David - *The Girl in the Spider's Web (Read by Vance, Simon). Audiobook Review*
BL - v112 - i5 - Nov 1 2015 - p69(1) [51-500]
The Girl in the Spider's Web
Esq - v164 - i5 - Dec 2015 - p52(1) [51-500]
KR - Sept 1 2015 - pNA [501+]
NS - v144 - i5284 - Oct 16 2015 - p53(1) [501+]
NYT - August 27 2015 - pC1(L) [501+]
NYTBR - Sept 6 2015 - p1(L) [501+]

Lagercrantz, Rose - *My Heart Is Laughing (Illus. by Eriksson, Eva)*
c CH Bwatch - Jan 2015 - pNA [51-500]
c HB Guide - v26 - i1 - Spring 2015 - p61(1) [51-500]
When I Am Happiest (Illus. by Eriksson, Eva)
c HB - v91 - i5 - Sept-Oct 2015 - p108(1) [51-500]
c KR - June 15 2015 - pNA [51-500]
c Sch Lib - v63 - i4 - Winter 2015 - p229(1) [51-500]
c Magpies - v30 - i3 - July 2015 - p32(1) [501+]
c SLJ - v61 - i8 - August 2015 - p80(2) [51-500]

Lagerlof, Margaretha Rossholm - *Fate, Glory, and Love in Early Modern Gallery Decoration: Visualizing Supreme Power*
Sev Cent N - v73 - i1-2 - Spring-Summer 2015 - p55(5) [501+]
Ren Q - v68 - i1 - Spring 2015 - p259-261 [501+]

Lagerlof, Selma - *What the Shepherd Saw (Illus. by Dusikova, Maja)*
c HB Guide - v26 - i2 - Fall 2015 - p40(1) [51-500]

Lago, Don - *Canyon of Dreams: Stories from Grand Canyon History*
Roundup M - v22 - i6 - August 2015 - p38(1) [501+]

LaGrandeur, Kevin - *Androids and Intelligent Networks in Early Modern Literature and Culture: Artificial Slaves*
AHR - v120 - i1 - Feb 2015 - p320-321 [501+]

LaGreca, Jody R. - *Forever in Vein*
SPBW - Sept 2015 - pNA [51-500]

Lahens, Yanick - *Bain de lune*
WLT - v89 - i5 - Sept-Oct 2015 - p62(2) [501+]

Lahey, Jessica - *The Gift of Failure: How the Best Parents Learn to Let Go So Their Children Can Succeed*
KR - May 15 2015 - pNA [501+]
NYTBR - August 23 2015 - p22(L) [501+]
PW - v262 - i20 - May 18 2015 - p79(1) [51-500]

Lahiri, Jhumpa - *In Other Words*
KR - Nov 15 2015 - pNA [501+]
PW - v262 - i45 - Nov 9 2015 - p2(1) [51-500]
BL - v112 - i6 - Nov 15 2015 - p8(1) [51-500]
The Lowland
ABR - v36 - i5 - July-August 2015 - p8(2) [501+]
Redeployment
LJ - v140 - i10 - June 1 2015 - p139(1) [501+]

Lahiri, Nayanjot - *Ashoka in Ancient India*
Mac - v128 - i37 - Sept 21 2015 - p56(2) [501+]

Lahr, John - *Joy Ride: Show People and their Shows*
AM - v213 - i8 - Dec 7 2015 - p40(2) [501+]
BL - v111 - i22 - August 1 2015 - p15(2) [51-500]
KR - June 15 2015 - pNA [501+]
LJ - v140 - i13 - August 1 2015 - p98(2) [51-500]
NYTBR - Dec 6 2015 - p75(L) [501+]
PW - v262 - i25 - June 22 2015 - p130(1) [51-500]
Tennessee Williams: Mad Pilgrimage of the Flesh
HR - v67 - i4 - Wntr 2015 - p692-699 [501+]

Lahusen, Christiane - *Zukunft am Ende: Autobiographische Sinnstiftungen von DDR-Geisteswissenschaftlern nach 1989*
HNet - July 2015 - pNA [501+]

Lai, Larissa - *Slanting I, Imagining We: Asian Canadian Literary Production in the 1980s and 1990s*
Pac A - v88 - i3 - Sept 2015 - p685 [501+]

Lai, Thanhha - *Listen, Slowly (Read by Lam, Lulu). Audiobook Review*
y SLJ - v61 - i5 - May 2015 - p69(1) [51-500]
Listen, Slowly
y CCB-B - v68 - i7 - March 2015 - p360(1) [51-500]
y HB - v91 - i2 - March-April 2015 - p100(2) [51-500]
c HB Guide - v26 - i2 - Fall 2015 - p90(1) [51-500]
c NYTBR - May 10 2015 - p24(L) [501+]
c PW - v262 - i49 - Dec 2 2015 - p72(1) [51-500]
y Teach Lib - v42 - i4 - April 2015 - p28(1) [51-500]

Lain, Douglas - *In the Shadow of the Towers: Speculative Fiction in a Post-9/11 World*
PW - v262 - i31 - August 3 2015 - p40(1) [501+]

Lainer-Vos, Dan - *Sinews of the Nation: Constructing Irish and Zionist Bonds in the United States*
CS - v44 - i1 - Jan 2015 - p82-83 [501+]

Laing, Alastair - *Drawings for Architecture Design and Ornament: The James A. de Rothschild Bequest at Waddesdon Manor, 2 vols.*
NYRB - v62 - i11 - June 25 2015 - p29(4) [501+]

Laing, Annette - *Don't Know Where, Don't Know When*
KR - July 1 2015 - pNA [501+]

Laing, Olivia - *The Trip to Echo Spring: On Writers and Drinking*
Sew R - v123 - i2 - Spring 2015 - pXXIII-XXV [501+]

Laird, Elizabeth - *Dindy and the Elephant*
c Sch Lib - v63 - i3 - Autumn 2015 - p168(1) [51-500]

Laird, Mark - *A Natural History of English Gardening, 1650-1800*
Nature - v522 - i7555 - June 11 2015 - p155(1) [51-500]
NS - v144 - i5273 - July 31 2015 - p66(2) [501+]
Spec - v328 - i9743 - May 23 2015 - p38(2) [501+]
TLS - i5861 - July 31 2015 - p12(1) [501+]

Lakatos, Menyhert - *The Color of Smoke*
KR - July 1 2015 - pNA [501+]

Lake, Deryn - *The Moonlit Door*
BL - v111 - i13 - March 1 2015 - p25(1) [51-500]
PW - v262 - i3 - Jan 19 2015 - p64(1) [51-500]

Lake, Joanna - *Lionel and Molly: Colors (Illus. by Racklyeft, Jess)*
c KR - July 1 2015 - pNA [501+]

Lake, Nick - *There Will Be Lies*
y CCB-B - v68 - i6 - Feb 2015 - p318(1) [51-500]
y Ent W - i1348-1349 - Jan 30 2015 - p117(1) [501+]
y HB - v91 - i2 - March-April 2015 - p101(1) [51-500]
y HB Guide - v26 - i2 - Fall 2015 - p127(1) [51-500]
y Sch Lib - v63 - i2 - Summer 2015 - p119(1) [51-500]
y VOYA - v37 - i6 - Feb 2015 - p59(1) [51-500]

Lakeland, Paul - *A Council That Will Never End: "Lumen Gentium" and the Church Today*
AM - v213 - i12 - Oct 26 2015 - p32(3) [501+]

Lakomaki, Sami - *Gathering Together: The Shawnee People through Diaspora and Nationhood, 1600-1870*
AHR - v120 - i4 - Oct 2015 - p1477-1478 [501+]
JAH - v102 - i2 - Sept 2015 - p530-531 [501+]
W&M Q - v72 - i2 - April 2015 - p351-366 [501+]
Seasons of Change: Labour, Treaty Rights, and Ojibwe Nationhood
WHQ - v46 - i3 - Autumn 2015 - p370-371 [501+]

Lakritz, Deborah - *Joey and the Giant Box (Illus. by Byrne, Mike)*
c HB Guide - v26 - i2 - Fall 2015 - p40(1) [51-500]
c KR - March 1 2015 - pNA [501+]
c PW - v262 - i11 - March 16 2015 - p87(1) [51-500]

Lakshman, Vijay - *Mythborn II: Bane of the Warforged*
PW - v262 - i27 - July 6 2015 - p52(1) [51-500]

Lal, Ruby - *Coming of Age in Nineteenth-Century India: The Girl-Child and the Art of Playfulness*
JAS - v74 - i1 - Feb 2015 - p233-235 [501+]

Lalami, Laila - *The Moor's Account*
NYTBR - Sept 20 2015 - p28(L) [501+]
TLS - i5874 - Oct 30 2015 - p20(1) [501+]

Lalire, Gregory J. - *Captured: From the Frontier Diary of Infant Danny Duly*
Roundup M - v22 - i6 - August 2015 - p31(1) [501+]

Lall, Vikram - *The Golden Lands: Cambodia, Indonesia, Laos, Myanmar, Thailand and Vietnam*
LJ - v140 - i3 - Feb 15 2015 - p97(1) [51-500]

Lallemand, Orianne - *The Wolf Who Travels Back in Time (Illus. by Thuillier, Eleonore)*
c CH Bwatch - Jan 2015 - pNA [51-500]
The Wolf Who Wanted to Change His Color (Illus. by Thuillier, Eleonore)
c CH Bwatch - June 2015 - pNA [51-500]

Lalo, Eduardo - *Simone*
KR - August 1 2015 - pNA [501+]
LJ - v140 - i15 - Sept 15 2015 - p68(2) [51-500]

Lam, Angela - *Red Eggs and Good Luck*
y BL - v112 - i2 - Sept 15 2015 - p18(1) [51-500]

Lam, Desmond - *Chopsticks and Gambling*
CS - v44 - i1 - Jan 2015 - p140-141 [501+]

Lam, Francis - *Cornbread Nation 7: The Best of Southern Food Writing*
JSH - v81 - i4 - Nov 2015 - p1049(2) [501+]
SHQ - v118 - i3 - Jan 2015 - p319-320 [501+]

Lam, Q.S. - *Schizophrenics Can Be Good Mothers Too*
LJ - v140 - i8 - May 1 2015 - p92(1) [51-500]

Lam, Thao - *Skunk on a String (Illus. by Lam, Thao)*
c KR - Dec 15 2015 - pNA [501+]
c PW - v262 - i52 - Dec 21 2015 - p152(1) [51-500]

Lam, Willy Wo-Lap - *Chinese Politics in the Era of Xi Jinping: Renaissance, Reform, or Retrogression?*
NYRB - v62 - i13 - August 13 2015 - p32(3) [501+]
TimHES - i2198 - April 9 2015 - p51(1) [501+]

Lamanda, Al - *This Side of Midnight*
BL - v111 - i17 - May 1 2015 - p46(1) [51-500]
KR - May 1 2015 - pNA [51-500]

LaMarche, Una - *Don't Fail Me Now (Read by Ojo, Adenrele). Audiobook Review*
y SLJ - v61 - i12 - Dec 2015 - p79(2) [51-500]
Don't Fail Me Now
y VOYA - v38 - i4 - Oct 2015 - p54(1) [51-500]
y KR - July 15 2015 - pNA [51-500]
y PW - v262 - i26 - June 29 2015 - p69(2) [51-500]
y SLJ - v61 - i8 - August 2015 - p97(1) [51-500]
Five Summers (Read by Revasch, Abigail). Audiobook Review
y SLJ - v61 - i10 - Oct 2015 - p55(1) [51-500]
Like No Other (Read by Odom, Leslie, with Phoebe Strole). Audiobook Review
y BL - v112 - i5 - Nov 1 2015 - p72(1) [51-500]
y SLJ - v61 - i11 - Nov 2015 - p73(1) [51-500]
Like No Other
y HB Guide - v26 - i1 - Spring 2015 - p113(1) [51-500]
Unabrow: Misadventures of a Late Bloomer
PW - v262 - i2 - Jan 12 2015 - p51(2) [51-500]

Lamb, Christina - *Farewell Kabul: From Afghanistan to a More Dangerous World*
NS - v144 - i5265 - June 5 2015 - p42(3) [501+]
TLS - i5870 - Oct 2 2015 - p11(2) [501+]

Lamb, S.D. - *Pathologist of the Mind: Adolf Meyer and the Origins of American Psychiatry*
TLS - i5863 - August 14 2015 - p11(2) [501+]

Lamb, Scott - *Huckabee: The Authorized Biography*
LJ - v140 - i17 - Oct 15 2015 - p104(1) [51-500]

Lamb-Shapiro, Jessica - *Promise Land: My Journey through America's Self-Help Culture*
NYTBR - Feb 22 2015 - p32(L) [501+]

Lamb, Sybil - *I've Got a Time Bomb*
Wom R Bks - v32 - i6 - Nov-Dec 2015 - p15(1) [51-500]

Lamb, Victoria - *Witchrise*
y VOYA - v37 - i6 - Feb 2015 - p80(1) [51-500]

Lamb, Warren - *Nicaea Trilogy*
PW - v262 - i52 - Dec 21 2015 - p141(1) [51-500]

Lamb, William - *Scripture: A Guide for the Perplexed*
Intpr - v69 - i1 - Jan 2015 - p125(1) [51-500]
Theol St - v76 - i2 - June 2015 - p383(1) [51-500]

Lambdin, Dewey - *Kings and Emperors*
Bwatch - May 2015 - pNA [51-500]

Lamberson, Gregory - *Black Creek*
PW - v262 - i45 - Nov 9 2015 - p40(1) [51-500]
Human Monsters
BL - v111 - i13 - March 1 2015 - p30(1) [51-500]
PW - v262 - i5 - Feb 2 2015 - p40(2) [51-500]

Lambert, Charles - *The Children's Home*
BL - v112 - i4 - Oct 15 2015 - p16(1) [51-500]
KR - Oct 1 2015 - pNA [51-500]
NYT - Dec 31 2015 - pC7(L) [501+]
PW - v262 - i44 - Nov 2 2015 - p60(2) [51-500]

Lambert, Craig - *Shadow Work: The Unpaid, Unseen Jobs That Fill Your Day*
Atl - v315 - i4 - May 2015 - p57(1) [51-500]
KR - March 15 2015 - pNA [51-500]
LJ - v140 - i7 - April 15 2015 - p105(2) [51-500]
Mac - v128 - i21 - June 1 2015 - p58(1) [51-500]
NYTBR - May 17 2015 - p1(L) [501+]
PW - v262 - i8 - Feb 23 2015 - p63(1) [51-500]

Lambert, David - *Mastering the Niger: James MacQueen's African Geography and the Struggle over Atlantic Slavery*
HNet - Feb 2015 - pNA [501+]
Isis - v106 - i2 - June 2015 - p458(2) [501+]

Lambert, J.L.F. - *The Quiet Tides of Bordeaux*
KR - Sept 1 2015 - pNA [501+]

Lambert, Josh - *Unclean Lips: Obscenity, Jews, and American Culture*
J Am St - v49 - i3 - August 2015 - p626-628 [501+]
JAH - v101 - i4 - March 2015 - p1338(1) [501+]

Lambert, Ken - *Conkers: British Twins in Nazi Germany*
KR - August 15 2015 - pNA [501+]

Lambert, Megan Dowd - *A Crow of His Own (Illus. by Costello, David Hyde)*
c BL - v111 - i15 - April 1 2015 - p82(1) [51-500]
c HB - v91 - i2 - March-April 2015 - p78(1) [51-500]
c HB Guide - v26 - i2 - Fall 2015 - p41(1) [51-500]
c KR - Feb 15 2015 - pNA [51-500]
Reading Picture Books with Children
KR - Sept 15 2015 - pNA [51-500]

Lambert, Megan Dowd. A Crow of His Own.(Brief article)(Book review)(Children's review) - *A Crow of His Own (Illus. by Costello, David Hyde)*
c SLJ - v61 - i4 - April 2015 - p131(1) [51-500]
Lamberton, Ken - *Chasing Arizona: One Man's Yearlong Obsession with the Grand Canyon State*
Bwatch - May 2015 - pNA [51-500]
Roundup M - v23 - i1 - Oct 2015 - p34(1) [501+]
RVBW - April 2015 - pNA [501+]
Lambin, Gerard - *Timothee de Milet : le poete et le musicien*
AJP - v136 - i2 - Summer 2015 - p361-364 [501+]
Lambirth, Andrew - *Patrick George*
Spec - v327 - i9725 - Jan 17 2015 - p39(1) [501+]
Lambright, W. Henry - *Why Mars: NASA and the Politics of Space Exploration*
AHR - v120 - i2 - April 2015 - p664(1) [501+]
Lamele, Mike - *Enough Already: Create Success on Your Own Terms*
Bwatch - July 2015 - pNA [51-500]
Lamm, Gina - *Kiss the Earl*
BL - v111 - i14 - March 15 2015 - p49(2) [51-500]
Lammle, Rebecca - *Poetik des Satyrspiels*
Class R - v65 - i2 - Oct 2015 - p356-358 [501+]
Lamond, Margrete - *Once upon a Timeless Tale Collection (Read by Margolyes, Miriam). Audiobook Review*
c SLJ - v61 - i7 - July 2015 - p45(1) [51-500]
Lamont, Brian - *Norfolk Broadsides*
TimHES - i2217 - August 20 2015 - p47-47 [501+]
Lamott, Anne - *Small Victories: Spotting Improbable Moments of Grace (Read by Lamott, Anne). Audiobook Review*
BL - v111 - i14 - March 15 2015 - p85(1) [51-500]
LaMotte, David - *Worldchanging 101: Challenging the Myth of Powerlessness*
PW - v262 - i10 - March 9 2015 - p66(1) [51-500]
L'Amour, Louis - *Diamond of Jeru. Audiobook Review*
LJ - v140 - i15 - Sept 15 2015 - p42(2) [51-500]
Lampe, Evan - *Work, Class, and Power in the Borderlands of the Early American Pacific: The Labors of Empire*
AHR - v120 - i1 - Feb 2015 - p236-238 [501+]
Lampedusa, Giuseppe Tomasi di - *The Leopard*
Nat R - v67 - i21 - Nov 19 2015 - p82(1) [501+]
Lampert, Catherine - *Frank Auerbach: Speaking and Painting*
Art N - v114 - i6 - June 2015 - p77(1) [501+]
Spec - v328 - i9745 - June 6 2015 - p40(2) [501+]
Lampman, Peggy - *Simmer and Smoke*
KR - August 15 2015 - pNA [501+]
Lamptey, Jerusha Tanner - *Never Wholly Other: A Muslima Theology of Religious Pluralism*
Theol St - v76 - i3 - Sept 2015 - p614(3) [501+]
Lampton, David M. - *Following the Leader: Ruling China, from Deng Xiaoping to Xi Jinping*
Pac A - v88 - i3 - Sept 2015 - p690 [501+]
Lan Lan - *Canyon in the Body*
WLT - v89 - i3-4 - May-August 2015 - p121(2) [501+]
Lancaster, Ashley Craig - *The Angelic Mother and the Predatory Seductress: Poor White Women in Southern Literature of the Great Depression*
MFSF - v61 - i1 - Spring 2015 - p198-200 [501+]
Lancaster, Guy - *Racial Cleansing in Arkansas, 1883-1924: Politics, Land, Labor, and Criminality*
JSH - v81 - i4 - Nov 2015 - p1007(2) [501+]
Lancaster, Jen - *The Best of Enemies*
BL - v111 - i22 - August 1 2015 - p26(1) [51-500]
I Regret Nothing: A Memoir
BL - v111 - i18 - May 15 2015 - p11(1) [51-500]
Bwatch - July 2015 - pNA [51-500]
KR - April 1 2015 - pNA [51-500]
Lancaster, Jill - *Aquatic Entomology*
QRB - v90 - i1 - March 2015 - p100(1) [501+]
Lancaster, Mike A. - *Dotwav*
y VOYA - v38 - i4 - Oct 2015 - p74(1) [51-500]
Lancaster, Osbert - *Osbert Lancaster's Cartoons, Columns and Curlicues: Includes "Pillar to Post," "Homes Sweet Homes" and "Drayneflete Revealed"*
Spec - v329 - i9772 - Dec 12 2015 - p84(2) [501+]
Lance, Kathryn - *Pandora's Promise*
Analog - v135 - i12 - Dec 2015 - p106(1) [501+]
Lancet, Barry - *Pacific Burn*
KR - Dec 1 2015 - pNA [51-500]
PW - v262 - i52 - Dec 21 2015 - p130(2) [51-500]
Lanchester, John - *Capital*
TimHES - i2190 - Feb 12 2015 - p49(1) [501+]
Land, Jon - *Black Scorpion: The Tyrant Reborn*
BL - v111 - i13 - March 1 2015 - p21(1) [51-500]
PW - v262 - i8 - Feb 23 2015 - p52(2) [51-500]
Strong Darkness
Roundup M - v22 - i3 - Feb 2015 - p26(1) [501+]
Roundup M - v22 - i6 - August 2015 - p31(1) [501+]
Strong Light of Day
BL - v112 - i1 - Sept 1 2015 - p50(1) [51-500]
PW - v262 - i32 - August 10 2015 - p37(2) [51-500]
Landau, Alexis - *The Empire of the Senses (Read by Lane, Christopher). Audiobook Review*
BL - v112 - i2 - Sept 15 2015 - p76(1) [51-500]
The Empire of the Senses
BL - v111 - i9-10 - Jan 1 2015 - p52(1) [51-500]
BL - v111 - i16 - April 15 2015 - p34(1) [501+]
KR - Jan 15 2015 - pNA [51-500]
LJ - v140 - i3 - Feb 15 2015 - p89(1) [51-500]
PW - v262 - i2 - Jan 12 2015 - p33(1) [51-500]
Landau, Deborah - *The Uses of the Body*
NY - v91 - i12 - May 11 2015 - p78 [501+]
PW - v262 - i16 - April 20 2015 - p53(1) [51-500]
Landau, Elaine - *The Alamo: Would You Join the Fight?*
c HB Guide - v26 - i1 - Spring 2015 - p204(1) [51-500]
The Boston Tea Party: Would You Join the Revolution?
c HB Guide - v26 - i1 - Spring 2015 - p204(1) [51-500]
Discovering a New World: Would You Sail with Columbus?
c HB Guide - v26 - i1 - Spring 2015 - p200(1) [51-500]
The Salem Witchcraft Trials: Would You Join the Madness?
c HB Guide - v26 - i1 - Spring 2015 - p204(1) [51-500]
The Underground Railroad: Would You Help Them Escape?
c HB Guide - v26 - i1 - Spring 2015 - p204(1) [51-500]
Landau, Emily Epstein - *Spectacular Wickedness: Sex, Race, and Memory in Storyville, New Orleans*
RAH - v43 - i2 - June 2015 - p223-230 [501+]
Landau, Laura - *The Life Balance Playbook*
KR - August 15 2015 - pNA [501+]
Landau, Mark J. - *The Power of Metaphor: Examining Its Influence on Social Life*
Lang Soc - v44 - i3 - June 2015 - p435-438 [501+]
Landau, Orna - *Leopardpox! (Illus. by Hoffman, Omer)*
c BL - v111 - i11 - Feb 1 2015 - p56(1) [51-500]
c HB Guide - v26 - i2 - Fall 2015 - p41(1) [51-500]
Leopardpox! (Illus. by Hoffmann, Omer)
c CH Bwatch - March 2015 - pNA [51-500]
c CH Bwatch - April 2015 - pNA [51-500]
Landemare, Georgina - *Churchill's Cookbook*
TLS - i5858 - July 10 2015 - p26(1) [501+]
Landers, Clifford E. - *The Body Snatcher*
PW - v262 - i29 - July 20 2015 - p170(1) [51-500]
Landers, Melissa - *Invaded*
y BL - v111 - i9-10 - Jan 1 2015 - p94(2) [51-500]
y CCB-B - v68 - i8 - April 2015 - p409(1) [51-500]
y CH Bwatch - April 2015 - pNA [51-500]
y HB Guide - v26 - i2 - Fall 2015 - p127(1) [51-500]
y VOYA - v37 - i6 - Feb 2015 - p80(1) [51-500]
Starflight
y KR - Nov 1 2015 - pNA [51-500]
y SLJ - v61 - i12 - Dec 2015 - p114(1) [51-500]
Landesmuseum, Badisches - *Das Konstanzer Konzil 1414-1418: Weltereignis des Mittelalters. Katalog zur Grossen Landesausstellung Baden-Wurttemberg in Konstanz vom 27. April bis zum 21. September 2014*
HNet - Feb 2015 - pNA [501+]
Landman, Seth - *Confidence*
PW - v262 - i29 - July 20 2015 - p167(1) [51-500]
Landman, Todd - *Human Rights and Democracy: The Precarious Rights of Ideals*
E-A St - v67 - i1 - Jan 2015 - p158(3) [501+]
Landmann, Bimba - *In Search of the Little Prince: The Story of Antoine de Saint-Exupery (Illus. by Landmann, Bimba)*
c HB - v91 - i1 - Jan-Feb 2015 - p97(2) [51-500]
c HB Guide - v26 - i1 - Spring 2015 - p194(1) [51-500]
Landon, Carolyn - *Banksia Lady: Celia Rosser, Botanical Artist*
RVBW - August 2015 - pNA [501+]
Landon, Sydney - *Watch over Me*
PW - v262 - i28 - July 13 2015 - p52(1) [51-500]
Landon, William J. - *Lorenzo di Filippo Strozzi and Niccolo Machiavelli: Patron, Client, and the Pistola fatta per la peste / An Epistle Written Concerning the Plague*
JMH - v87 - i3 - Sept 2015 - p745(3) [501+]
Landra, Maie - *Wrapped in Color: 30 Shawls to Knit*
LJ - v140 - i7 - April 15 2015 - p90(1) [51-500]
Landreth, David - *The Face of Mammon: The Matter of Money in English Renaissance Literature*
MP - v112 - i3 - Feb 2015 - pE238(E240) [501+]
Landry, Stan M. - *Ecumenism, Memory and German Nationalism, 1817-1917*
CH - v84 - i2 - June 2015 - p457(3) [501+]
Landsberry, Belinda - *Anzac Ted (Illus. by Landsberry, Belinda)*
c Magpies - v30 - i1 - March 2015 - pS5(1) [501+]
c Sch Lib - v63 - i2 - Summer 2015 - p106(1) [51-500]
Landsem, Stephanie - *The Tomb*
LJ - v140 - i2 - Feb 1 2015 - p67(3) [501+]
Landstrom, Lena - *Where Is Pim? (Illus. by Landstrom, Olof)*
c CCB-B - v68 - i10 - June 2015 - p501(1) [51-500]
c HB - v91 - i3 - May-June 2015 - p90(2) [51-500]
c HB Guide - v26 - i2 - Fall 2015 - p14(1) [51-500]
"Landwirtschaft und Dorfgesellschaft im Ausgehenden Mittelalter." Herbsttagung des Konstanzer Arbeitskreises fur Mittelalterliche Geschichte e.V
HNet - March 2015 - pNA [501+]
Landy, Linda - *Textured Bead Embroidery: Learn to Make Inspired Pins, Pendants, Earrings, and More*
Bwatch - Feb 2015 - pNA [51-500]
Lane, Amy - *Winter Ball*
PW - v262 - i44 - Nov 2 2015 - p70(2) [51-500]
Lane, Andrew - *Shadow Creatures*
y Sch Lib - v63 - i1 - Spring 2015 - p55(1) [51-500]
Snake Bite
y HB Guide - v26 - i2 - Fall 2015 - p128(1) [51-500]
Lane, Barbara Miller - *Houses for a New World: Builders and Buyers in American Suburbs, 1945-1965*
LJ - v140 - i15 - Sept 15 2015 - p75(1) [501+]
Lane, Belden C. - *Backpacking with the Saints: Wilderness Hiking as Spiritual Practice*
TT - v72 - i3 - Oct 2015 - p339-340 [501+]
Lane, Calvin - *The Laudians and the Elizabethan Church: Conformity and Religious Identity in Post-Reformation England*
HER - v130 - i542 - Feb 2015 - p194(2) [501+]
Lane, Carrie - *A Company of One: Insecurity, Independence and the New World of White Collar Unemployment*
CS - v44 - i4 - July 2015 - p463-469 [501+]
Lane, Christel - *The Cultivation of Taste: Chefs and the Organization of Fine Dining*
AJS - v120 - i5 - March 2015 - p1590(3) [501+]
Lane, Christina - *Comfort and Joy: Cooking for Two: Small Batch Meals for Every Occasion*
LJ - v140 - i17 - Oct 15 2015 - p108(1) [51-500]
Lane, David - *The Capitalist Transformation of State Socialism: The Making and Breaking of State Social Society, and What Followed*
E-A St - v67 - i6 - August 2015 - p989(2) [501+]
Lane, Harriet - *Her*
Ent W - i1348-1349 - Jan 30 2015 - p117 [501+]
NY - v91 - i6 - March 30 2015 - p74 [51-500]
People - v83 - i2 - Jan 12 2015 - p29 [501+]
SEP - v287 - i1 - Jan-Feb 2015 - p20(1) [501+]
Lane, Jeremy F. - *Jazz and Machine-Age Imperialism: Music, "Race," and Intellectuals in France, 1918-1945*
JMH - v87 - i2 - June 2015 - p458(2) [501+]
Lane, Jodi - *Fear of Crime in the United States: Causes, Consequences, and Contradictions*
CrimJR - v40 - i2 - June 2015 - p230-231 [501+]
Lane, Laura - *Two Mothers One Prayer*
KR - June 1 2015 - pNA [501+]
Lane, Lindsey - *Evidence of Things Not Seen*
y HB Guide - v26 - i1 - Spring 2015 - p113(1) [51-500]
Lane, M.S. - *A Poet's Reich: Politics and Culture in the George Circle*
HNet - August 2015 - pNA [501+]
Lane, Nathan - *Naughty Mabel (Illus. by Krall, Dan)*
c BL - v112 - i3 - Oct 1 2015 - p83(1) [51-500]
c KR - July 15 2015 - pNA [51-500]
c PW - v262 - i27 - July 6 2015 - p68(1) [51-500]
c SLJ - v61 - i8 - August 2015 - p72(1) [51-500]
Lane, Nick - *The Vital Question: Energy, Evolution, and the Origins of Complex Life*
BL - v111 - i21 - July 1 2015 - p12(1) [51-500]
BL - v112 - i7 - Dec 1 2015 - p13(1) [501+]
KR - April 15 2015 - pNA [501+]
LJ - v140 - i10 - June 1 2015 - p130(2) [51-500]
NYT - July 21 2015 - pD3(L) [501+]
PW - v262 - i19 - May 11 2015 - p47(1) [51-500]
The Vital Question: Why Is Life the Way It Is?
Econ - v415 - i8936 - May 2 2015 - p75(US) [501+]
Nature - v523 - i7562 - July 30 2015 - pSB1(1)

[51-500]
New Sci - v226 - i3018 - April 25 2015 - p46(2) [501+]
TimHES - i2203 - May 14 2015 - p50(1) [501+]
Lane, Patrick - *Washita*
Can Lit - i224 - Spring 2015 - p113 [501+]
Lane, Prescott - *Perfectly Broken*
PW - v262 - i12 - March 23 2015 - p56(1) [51-500]
Lane, Robert - *The Cardinal's Sin*
PW - v262 - i51 - Dec 14 2015 - p63(2) [51-500]
Lane, Sandra M. - *The Moment You Were Born: A Story for You and Your Premature Baby (Illus. by Hehenberger, Shelly)*
c CH Bwatch - Nov 2015 - pNA [51-500]
Lane, Soraya - *Cowboy Take Me Away*
PW - v262 - i44 - Nov 2 2015 - p68(1) [51-500]
The Devil Wears Spurs
PW - v262 - i13 - March 30 2015 - p61(1) [51-500]
Lane, Stewart F. - *Black Broadway: African Americans on the Great White Way*
Am Theat - v32 - i2 - Feb 2015 - p58(2) [501+]
PW - v262 - i2 - Jan 12 2015 - p54(1) [51-500]
Lang, Anthony F., Jr. - *Just War: Authority, Tradition, and Practice*
J Ch St - v57 - i2 - Spring 2015 - p370-371 [501+]
Lang, Diana - *Opening to Meditation: A Gentle, Guided Approach*
RVBW - June 2015 - pNA [51-500]
Lang, Heather - *Fearless Flyer: Ruth Law and Her Flying Machine (Illus. by Colon, Raul)*
c KR - Jan 1 2016 - pNA [51-500]
c PW - v262 - i51 - Dec 14 2015 - p82(1) [51-500]
The Original Cowgirl: The Wild Adventures of Lucille Mulhall (Illus. by Beaky, Suzanne)
c CCB-B - v68 - i9 - May 2015 - p454(1) [51-500]
c KR - Jan 1 2015 - pNA [51-500]
c HB Guide - v26 - i2 - Fall 2015 - p210(1) [51-500]
Lang, John - *Understanding Ron Rash*
Sew R - v123 - i2 - Spring 2015 - p345-350 [501+]
Lang, John Patrick - *The Big Bitch*
PW - v262 - i24 - June 15 2015 - p66(1) [51-500]
Lang, Kimberly - *Everything at Last*
PW - v262 - i47 - Nov 23 2015 - p55(2) [51-500]
Lang, Maya - *The Sixteenth of June (Read by Whelan, Julia). Audiobook Review*
BL - v111 - i14 - March 15 2015 - p84(1) [51-500]
Lang, Peter - *The Poetics of Sight*
TimHES - i2212 - July 16 2015 - p47-1 [501+]
Lang, Robert - *New Tunisian Cinema*
IJMES - v47 - i2 - May 2015 - p397-399 [501+]
Lang, Sean - *First World War for Dummies*
y VOYA - v38 - i1 - April 2015 - p87(1) [51-500]
Lang, Suzanne - *Families, Families, Families! (Illus. by Lang, Max)*
c HB Guide - v26 - i2 - Fall 2015 - p41(1) [51-500]
c NYTBR - July 12 2015 - p19(L) [501+]
Hooray for Kids
c KR - Dec 15 2015 - pNA [51-500]
Lang, Zoe Alexis - *The Legacy of Johann Strauss*
GSR - v38 - i3 - Oct 2015 - p668-671 [501+]
Lange, Erin Jade - *Rebel, Bully, Geek, Pariah*
y BL - v111 - Nov 15 2015 - pNA [51-500]
y PW - v262 - i47 - Nov 23 2015 - p69(2) [51-500]
y SLJ - v61 - i12 - Dec 2015 - p123(2) [51-500]
Lange, Matthew - *Educations in Ethnic Violence: Identity, Educational Bubbles, and Resource Mobilization*
SF - v93 - i3 - March 2015 - pe70 [501+]
Lange, Patricia A. - *Kids on YouTube: Technical Identities and Digital Literacies*
Biomag - v38 - i3 - Summer 2015 - p457(4) [501+]
Lange, Tyler - *The First French Reformation: Church Reform and the Origins of the Old Regime*
AHR - v120 - i3 - June 2015 - p1120-1121 [501+]
Six Ct J - v46 - i2 - Summer 2015 - p452-453 [501+]
Langedijk, Jack A. - *Because*
KR - August 15 2015 - pNA [501+]
SPBW - Nov 2015 - pNA [51-500]
Langelett, George - *How Do I Keep My Employees Motivated?:The Practice of Empathy-Based Management*
Per Psy - v68 - i4 - Wntr 2015 - p929(2) [501+]
Langer, Cassandra - *Romaine Brooks: A Life*
BL - v111 - i22 - August 1 2015 - p24(1) [51-500]
Bwatch - Nov 2015 - pNA [51-500]
Langerak, Edward - *Civil Disagreement: Personal Integrity in a Pluralistic Society*
Theol St - v76 - i2 - June 2015 - p396(2) [501+]

Langford, Julie - *Maternal Megalomania. Julia Domna and the Imperial Politics of Motherhood*
Class R - v65 - i1 - April 2015 - p200-202 [501+]
Langfur, Hal - *Native Brazil: Beyond the Convert and the Cannibal, 1500-1900*
AHR - v120 - i2 - April 2015 - p683-684 [501+]
HAHR - v95 - i3 - August 2015 - p504-507 [501+]
Langhamer, Claire - *The English in Love: The Intimate Story of an Emotional Revolution*
JWH - v27 - i3 - Fall 2015 - p194(10) [501+]
Langland, Victoria - *Speaking of Flowers: Student Movements and the Making and Remembering of 1968 in Military Brazil*
Historian - v77 - i2 - Summer 2015 - p342(3) [501+]
Langland, William - *Piers Plowman: A Modern Verse Translation*
TLS - i5855 - June 19 2015 - p22(2) [501+]
Langley, Andrew - *Every Place Has a History*
y HB Guide - v26 - i1 - Spring 2015 - p200(1) [51-500]
Hurricane: Perspectives on Storm Disasters
y VOYA - v38 - i1 - April 2015 - p89(1) [51-500]
Stories of Women in World War II: We Can Do It!
y VOYA - v38 - i1 - April 2015 - p90(1) [51-500]
Langlois, Dominic - *Le tresor de Memramcook (Illus. by Cormiere, Maurice)*
c Res Links - v20 - i5 - June 2015 - p39(2) [51-500]
Langston-George, Rebecca - *For the Right to Learn: Malala Yousafzai's Story (Illus. by Bock, Janna)*
c BL - v112 - i6 - Nov 15 2015 - p42(1) [51-500]
Langston, Laura - *Stepping Out*
y KR - Nov 15 2015 - pNA [51-500]
Langum, David J., Sr. - *Quite Contrary: The Litigious Life of Mary Bennett Love*
Roundup M - v22 - i6 - August 2015 - p38(1) [501+]
Lanh, Andrew - *Return to Dust*
KR - August 15 2015 - pNA [51-500]
PW - v262 - i35 - August 31 2015 - p63(1) [51-500]
Lanicek, Jan - *Czechs, Slovaks, and the Jews, 1938-48: Beyond Idealisation and Condemnation*
Slav R - v74 - i3 - Fall 2015 - p617-618 [501+]
Lanier, Wendy H. - *Life during the Great Depression*
c HB Guide - v26 - i2 - Fall 2015 - p220(1) [51-500]
Lankov, Andrei - *The Real North Korea: Life and Politics in the Failed Stalinist Utopia*
NYTBR - Feb 15 2015 - p28(L) [501+]
Lanna, Sara - *Mesomedes: Inno a phi nu sigma iota sigma*
Class R - v65 - i2 - Oct 2015 - pNA [501+]
Lansbury, Jennifer H. - *A Spectacular Leap: Black Women Athletes in Twentieth-Century America*
JAH - v102 - i1 - June 2015 - p279-280 [501+]
Lansdale, Joe R. - *Hell's Bounty*
PW - v262 - i46 - Nov 16 2015 - p59(1) [51-500]
Honky Tonk Samurai
KR - Jan 1 2016 - pNA [51-500]
PW - v262 - i52 - Dec 21 2015 - p133(1) [51-500]
Paradise Sky
BL - v111 - i13 - March 1 2015 - p28(1) [51-500]
KR - April 15 2015 - pNA [51-500]
PW - v262 - i14 - April 6 2015 - p40(1) [51-500]
Lansens, Lori - *The Mountain Story*
y BL - v111 - i16 - April 15 2015 - p26(1) [51-500]
Can Lit - i224 - Spring 2015 - p101 [501+]
KR - March 1 2015 - pNA [51-500]
LJ - v140 - i2 - Feb 1 2015 - p76(1) [501+]
Mac - v128 - i16 - April 27 2015 - p56(1) [501+]
Nat Post - v17 - i135 - April 11 2015 - pWP5(1) [501+]
PW - v262 - i9 - March 2 2015 - p61(2) [51-500]
Lanser, Amanda - *The American Revolution by the Numbers*
y SLJ - v61 - i9 - Sept 2015 - p151(4) [501+]
The Civil War by the Numbers
y SLJ - v61 - i9 - Sept 2015 - p151(4) [501+]
Food Science: You Are What You Eat
y HB Guide - v26 - i2 - Fall 2015 - p189(1) [51-500]
Otzi the Iceman
y HB Guide - v26 - i1 - Spring 2015 - p200(2) [51-500]
School Lunches: Healthy Choices vs. Crowd Pleasers
VOYA - v38 - i2 - June 2015 - p89(1) [51-500]
World War I by the Numbers
y SLJ - v61 - i9 - Sept 2015 - p151(4) [501+]
World War II by the Numbers
y SLJ - v61 - i9 - Sept 2015 - p151(4) [501+]
Lanser, Susan S. - *The Sexuality of History: Modernity and the Sapphic, 1565-1830*
G&L Rev W - v22 - i4 - July-August 2015 - p34(2) [501+]
Wom R Bks - v32 - i5 - Sept-Oct 2015 - p29(2) [501+]
Lansky, Sam - *The Gilded Razor: A Memoir*
KR - Oct 1 2015 - pNA [501+]
Lansley, Stewart - *Breadline Britain: The Rise of Mass Poverty*
Lon R Bks - v37 - i8 - April 23 2015 - p19(2) [501+]
TLS - i5842 - March 20 2015 - p26(1) [501+]
Lanzetta, Beverly - *Nine Jewels of Night: One Soul's Journey into God*
SPBW - May 2015 - pNA [51-500]
Laoutaris, Chris - *Shakespeare and the Countess: The Battle That Gave Birth to the Globe*
KR - March 15 2015 - pNA [501+]
LJ - v140 - i7 - April 15 2015 - p102(2) [51-500]
Lon R Bks - v37 - i1 - Jan 8 2015 - p29(3) [501+]
NYTBR - May 24 2015 - p16(L) [501+]
PW - v262 - i14 - April 6 2015 - p50(1) [51-500]
Lapadula, Erminia - *The Chora of Metaponto 4: The Late Roman Farmhouse at San Biagio*
Class R - v65 - i1 - April 2015 - p270-272 [501+]
Lapatin, Kenneth - *The Berthouville Silver Treasure and Roman Luxury*
TLS - i5866 - Sept 4 2015 - p26(2) [501+]
LaPlante, Alice - *Coming of Age at the End of Days*
y BL - v111 - i21 - July 1 2015 - p29(1) [51-500]
y KR - June 1 2015 - pNA [501+]
y LJ - v140 - i12 - July 1 2015 - p78(1) [51-500]
y PW - v262 - i23 - June 8 2015 - p35(1) [51-500]
LaPlante, Walter - *The Presidential Seal*
c BL - v111 - i15 - April 1 2015 - p63(1) [51-500]
LaPoma, Jonathan - *Developing Minds*
KR - August 15 2015 - pNA [501+]
LaPorte, David J. - *Paranoid: Exploring Suspicion from the Dubious to the Delusional*
PW - v262 - i25 - June 22 2015 - p131(1) [51-500]
Lappano, Jon-Erik - *Tokyo Digs a Garden (Illus. by Hatanaka, Kellen)*
c KR - Jan 1 2016 - pNA [51-500]
Laqua-O'Donnell, Simone - *Women and the Counter-Reformation in Early Modern Munster*
CEH - v48 - i3 - Sept 2015 - p424-425 [501+]
Laquer, Walter - *Putinism: Russia and Its Future with the West*
PW - v262 - i16 - April 20 2015 - p68(2) [51-500]
Laqueur, Thomas W. - *The Work of the Dead: A Cultural History of Mortal Remains*
TimHES - i2230 - Nov 19 2015 - p44-45 [501+]
Laqueur, Walter - *Putinism: Russia and Its Future with the West*
BL - v111 - i18 - May 15 2015 - p13(1) [51-500]
KR - May 1 2015 - pNA [501+]
NYT - July 21 2015 - pC1(L) [501+]
Lara, Maria Pia - *The Disclosure of Politics: Struggles over the Semantics of Secularization*
J Ch St - v57 - i2 - Spring 2015 - p371-373 [501+]
Larabee, Ann - *The Wrong Hands: Popular Weapons Mannuals and Their Historic Challenges to a Democratic Society*
TimHES - i2228 - Nov 5 2015 - p49(1) [501+]
Larbalestier, Justine - *Razorhurst*
y CCB-B - v68 - i10 - June 2015 - p501(2) [51-500]
y HB - v91 - i2 - March-April 2015 - p102(1) [51-500]
y HB Guide - v26 - i2 - Fall 2015 - p128(1) [51-500]
y NYTBR - May 31 2015 - p54(L) [501+]
y PW - v262 - i3 - Jan 19 2015 - p86(1) [51-500]
y PW - v262 - i49 - Dec 2 2015 - p104(2) [51-500]
Lardas, Mark - *Shenandoah, 1864: Sheridan's Valley Campaign*
Bwatch - Feb 2015 - pNA [51-500]
Lardy, Nicholas R. - *Markets over Mao: The Rise of Private Business in China*
For Aff - v94 - i1 - Jan-Feb 2015 - pNA [501+]
Lareau, Annette - *Choosing Homes, Choosing Schools: Residential Segregation and the Search for a Good School*
AJS - v121 - i2 - Sept 2015 - p616(3) [501+]
HER - v85 - i2 - Summer 2015 - p279-293 [501+]
Largent, Mark A. - *Keep Out of Reach of Children: Reye's Syndrome, Aspirin, and the Politics of Public Health*
LJ - v140 - i2 - Feb 1 2015 - p102(1) [51-500]
Lark Crafts - *Fat Quarters: Small Fabrics, More Than 50 Big Bags*
LJ - v140 - i6 - April 1 2015 - p92(2) [51-500]
Lark, Lolita - *The Vivisection Mambo*
KR - Sept 1 2015 - pNA [501+]

Larkin, Joan - *Blue Hanuman*
    Wom R Bks - v32 - i5 - Sept-Oct 2015 - p21(3) [501+]
Larkin, John - *The Pause*
    y Magpies - v30 - i2 - May 2015 - p43(1) [501+]
LaRoche, Amelia - *Amusing Animal Jokes to Tickle Your Funny Bone*
    c HB Guide - v26 - i1 - Spring 2015 - p181(1) [51-500]
    Funniest Bone Animal Jokes Series (Illus. by Mitchell, Susan K.)
    c BL - v111 - i12 - Feb 15 2015 - p74(1) [501+]
    Toad Chicken Jokes to Tickle Your Funny Bone
    c HB Guide - v26 - i1 - Spring 2015 - p181(1) [51-500]
LaRoche, Cheryl Janifer - *Free Black Communities and the Underground Railroad: The Geography of Resistance*
    AHR - v120 - i1 - Feb 2015 - p253-254 [501+]
    JAH - v101 - i4 - March 2015 - p1264-1265 [501+]
    JSH - v81 - i3 - August 2015 - p721(2) [501+]
LaRoque, George, III - *Getting More for Less: The Gravity of America's Choices*
    SPBW - Jan 2015 - pNA [51-500]
LaRosa, Michael J. - *Neighborly Adversaries: Readings in U.S.-Latin American Relations, 3d ed.*
    Bwatch - Sept 2015 - pNA [51-500]
Larouche, Nadya - *Comme un tour de magie*
    y Res Links - v20 - i4 - April 2015 - p41(1) [51-500]
Larranaga, Ana - *If You See a Cow*
    c KR - July 1 2015 - pNA [51-500]
Larrimore, Mark - *The Book of Job: A Biography*
    TT - v72 - i3 - Oct 2015 - p345-346 [501+]
Larrington, Carolyne - *The Land of the Green Man: A Journey through the Supernatural Landscapes of the British Isles*
    NS - v144 - i5280 - Sept 18 2015 - p66(2) [501+]
    Spec - v329 - i9760 - Sept 19 2015 - p50(1) [501+]
Larry, H.I. - *Horror House (Illus. by Monnier, Ron)*
    c Res Links - v21 - i1 - Oct 2015 - p19(1) [51-500]
    Zac Power: Mission Swamp Race (Illus. by Hook, Andy)
    c Res Links - v20 - i4 - April 2015 - p12(1) [51-500]
Larsen, Andrew - *Charlie's Dirt Day (Illus. by Hudon-Verrelli, Jacqueline)*
    c CH Bwatch - June 2015 - pNA [51-500]
    c HB Guide - v26 - i2 - Fall 2015 - p41(1) [51-500]
    c Res Links - v20 - i4 - April 2015 - p5(1) [51-500]
    See You Next Year (Illus. by Stewart, Todd)
    c BL - v111 - i17 - May 1 2015 - p102(2) [51-500]
    c CCB-B - v68 - i10 - June 2015 - p502(1) [51-500]
    c CH Bwatch - June 2015 - pNA [51-500]
    c HB - v91 - i4 - July-August 2015 - p119(1) [51-500]
    Res Links - v21 - i1 - Oct 2015 - p7(1) [51-500]
    SLJ - v61 - i3 - March 2015 - p119(1) [51-500]
Larsen, Jeffrey A. - *On Limited Nuclear War in the 21st Century*
    APJ - v29 - i5 - Sept-Oct 2015 - p106(2) [501+]
Larsen, Jen - *Future Perfect*
    y BL - v112 - i4 - Oct 15 2015 - p56(1) [51-500]
    y KR - July 15 2015 - pNA [51-500]
    y PW - v262 - i31 - August 3 2015 - p62(1) [51-500]
    y SLJ - v61 - i8 - August 2015 - p105(1) [51-500]
    y VOYA - v38 - i5 - Dec 2015 - p58(1) [51-500]
Larsen, K.J. - *Bye, Bye Love*
    BL - v111 - i13 - March 1 2015 - p22(1) [51-500]
    KR - Feb 1 2015 - pNA [51-500]
    PW - v262 - i8 - Feb 23 2015 - p53(1) [51-500]
Larsen, Mylisa - *How to Put Your Parents to Bed (Illus. by Cole, Babette)*
    c KR - Nov 1 2015 - pNA [51-500]
    c PW - v262 - i48 - Nov 30 2015 - p57(2) [51-500]
Larsen, Reif - *I Am Radar*
    LJ - v140 - i3 - Feb 15 2015 - p89(2) [51-500]
    Mac - v128 - i11 - March 23 2015 - p60(2) [51-500]
    NYT - Feb 20 2015 - pC24(L) [51+]
    TLS - i5853 - June 5 2015 - p19(1) [501+]
Larsen, Timothy - *The Slain God: Anthropologists and the Christian Faith*
    Bks & Cult - v21 - i4 - July-August 2015 - p11(2) [501+]
    IBMR - v39 - i4 - Oct 2015 - p238(1) [501+]
    Theol St - v76 - i4 - Dec 2015 - p854(3) [501+]
    TLS - i5862 - August 7 2015 - p25(1) [501+]
Larsen, Ward - *Passenger 19*
    BL - v112 - i7 - Dec 1 2015 - p30(1) [51-500]
    LJ - v140 - i19 - Nov 15 2015 - p77(1) [51-500]
    PW - v262 - i44 - Nov 2 2015 - p64(1) [51-500]
Larson, Barbara - *Darwin and Theories of Aesthetics and Cultural History*
    VS - v57 - i3 - Spring 2015 - p535(3) [501+]

Larson, Edward J. - *The Return of George Washington, 1783-1789*
    JSH - v81 - i4 - Nov 2015 - p954(2) [501+]
Larson, Ellen - *In Retrospect*
    LJ - v140 - i19 - Nov 15 2015 - p110(1) [51-500]
Larson, Erik - *Dead Wake: The Last Crossing of the Lusitania (Read by Brick, Scott). Audiobook Review*
    LJ - v140 - i9 - May 15 2015 - p45(2) [51-500]
    PW - v262 - i17 - April 27 2015 - p71(2) [51-500]
    Dead Wake: The Last Crossing of the Lusitania
    BL - v111 - i9-10 - Jan 1 2015 - p33(2) [51-500]
    CSM - March 10 2015 - pNA [51-500]
    Ent W - i1354 - March 13 2015 - p58(1) [501+]
    LJ - v140 - i2 - Feb 1 2015 - p92(1) [51-500]
    Mac - v128 - i10 - March 16 2015 - p56(2) [51-500]
    NY - v91 - i6 - March 30 2015 - p74 [51-500]
    NYT - March 5 2015 - pC1(L) [501+]
    NYTBR - March 8 2015 - p1(L) [501+]
    PW - v262 - i1 - Jan 5 2015 - p64(1) [51-500]
    TLS - i5848 - May 1 2015 - p27(1) [501+]
Larson, Frances - *Severed: A History of Heads Lost and Heads Found*
    NY - v90 - i43 - Jan 12 2015 - p71 [51-500]
Larson, Jean Russell - *Norwegian Folk Tales*
    c CH Bwatch - Nov 2015 - pNA [51-500]
Larson, Jeanette - *Children's Services Today: A Practical Guide for Librarians*
    CCB-B - v69 - i1 - Sept 2015 - p67(1) [51-500]
    Sch Lib - v63 - i3 - Autumn 2015 - p191(1) [51-500]
Larson, John W. - *The German Friend*
    KR - August 1 2015 - pNA [501+]
Larson, Karin - *Bedtime Kisses (Illus. by Nielson, Ginger)*
    c CH Bwatch - Feb 2015 - pNA [51-500]
Larson, Kate Clifford - *Rosemary: The Hidden Kennedy Daughter*
    BL - v112 - i4 - Oct 15 2015 - p7(1) [51-500]
    LJ - v140 - i16 - Oct 1 2015 - p90(1) [501+]
    Nat R - v67 - i20 - Nov 2 2015 - p41(3) [501+]
    NYTBR - Oct 11 2015 - p12(L) [501+]
    KR - August 1 2015 - pNA [501+]
Larson, Kirby - *Audacity Jones to the Rescue*
    c BL - v112 - i6 - Nov 15 2015 - p53(1) [51-500]
    c KR - Oct 15 2015 - pNA [51-500]
    Dash
    c HB Guide - v26 - i1 - Spring 2015 - p84(1) [51-500]
Larson, Kirsten W. - *Zombies in Nature*
    c BL - v112 - i3 - Oct 1 2015 - p64(1) [51-500]
Larson, M.A. - *Pennyroyal Academy (Read by Duerden, Susan). Audiobook Review*
    c BL - v111 - i18 - May 15 2015 - p72(1) [51-500]
    Pennyroyal Academy
    c HB Guide - v26 - i1 - Spring 2015 - p84(1) [51-500]
Larson, Nathan - *The Immune System*
    BL - v111 - i15 - April 1 2015 - p29(2) [51-500]
    KR - March 1 2015 - pNA [501+]
    PW - v262 - i5 - Feb 2 2015 - p35(1) [51-500]
    Stockholm Noir
    KR - Dec 15 2015 - pNA [51-500]
Larson, Sara B. - *Endure*
    y KR - Oct 1 2015 - pNA [51-500]
    y SLJ - v61 - i11 - Nov 2015 - p108(1) [51-500]
    y VOYA - v38 - i5 - Dec 2015 - p71(1) [51-500]
    Ignite
    y HB Guide - v26 - i2 - Fall 2015 - p128(1) [51-500]
Larson, Theresa - *Warrior: A Memoir*
    KR - Jan 1 2016 - pNA [51-500]
Larsson, Asa - *Until Thy Wrath Be Past*
    RVBW - Jan 2015 - pNA [501+]
LaRue, Angelina - *The Whole Enchilada: Fresh and Nutritious Southwestern Cuisine*
    LJ - v140 - i17 - Oct 15 2015 - p108(2) [51-500]
LaRue, Teresa - *A Talent for Murder*
    KR - Sept 1 2015 - pNA [51-500]
Laruelle, Francois - *Dictionary of Non-Philosophy*
    Dialogue - v54 - i1 - March 2015 - p200-202 [501+]
    Philosphy and Non-Philosophy
    Dialogue - v54 - i1 - March 2015 - p200-202 [501+]
LaSalle, Gerard - *Isthmus*
    SPBW - July 2015 - pNA [51-500]
LaSalle, Peter - *The City at Three P.M.: Writing, Reading, and Traveling*
    NYTBR - Dec 6 2015 - p46(L) [501+]
    KR - Sept 15 2015 - pNA [501+]
    LJ - v140 - i19 - Nov 15 2015 - p99(1) [51-500]
    PW - v262 - i41 - Oct 12 2015 - p59(1) [51-500]

LaSalvia, Jimmy - *No Hope: Why I Left the GOP (and You Should, Too).*
    BL - v112 - i2 - Sept 15 2015 - p6(2) [51-500]
Lasater, Ike - *Choosing Peace: New Ways to Communicate to Reduce Stress, Create Connection, and Resolve Conflict*
    Hum - v75 - i1 - Jan-Feb 2015 - p45(2) [501+]
Lascalles, Alice - *Ten Cocktails: The Art of Convivial Drinking*
    TLS - i5859 - July 17 2015 - p26(1) [501+]
Lasdun, James - *Bluestone: New and Selected Poems*
    BL - v111 - i17 - May 1 2015 - p72(1) [501+]
Laser, Michael - *My Impending Death*
    KR - July 1 2015 - pNA [51-500]
Lashner, William - *Bagmen*
    RVBW - April 2015 - pNA [501+]
    Guaranteed Heroes
    PW - v262 - i27 - July 6 2015 - p44(1) [51-500]
Laskas, Jeanne Marie - *Concussion*
    PW - v262 - i42 - Oct 19 2015 - p68(1) [51-500]
    KR - Oct 1 2015 - pNA [51-500]
    BL - v112 - i4 - Oct 15 2015 - p9(2) [51-500]
    LJ - v140 - i17 - Oct 15 2015 - p92(2) [501+]
Lasko-Gross, Miss - *Henni (Illus. by Lasko-Gross, Miss)*
    y SLJ - v61 - i5 - May 2015 - p127(1) [51-500]
Lasky, Kathryn - *Star Rise*
    c HB Guide - v26 - i2 - Fall 2015 - p90(1) [51-500]
Laslett, John - *Sunshine Was Never Enough: Los Angeles Workers, 1880-2010*
    JEH - v75 - i1 - March 2015 - p287-288 [501+]
Lasnoski, Kent J. - *Vocation to Virtue: Christian Marriage as a Consecrated Life*
    Theol St - v76 - i4 - Dec 2015 - p896(2) [501+]
Lassalle-Klein, Robert - *Blood and Ink: Ignacio Ellacuria, Jon Sobrino, and the Jesuit Martyrs of the University of Central America*
    Ams - v72 - i3 - July 2015 - p519(3) [501+]
    IBMR - v39 - i2 - April 2015 - p108(2) [501+]
    Theol St - v76 - i1 - March 2015 - p177(2) [501+]
Lassen, Annette - *The Legendary Sagas: Origins and Development*
    JEGP - v114 - i1 - Jan 2015 - p132(3) [501+]
    Specu - v90 - i3 - July 2015 - p829-830 [501+]
Lassen, Jason - *Hollywood Clown: An Inside Look into the Competitive and Political World of Children's Birthday Parties of Hollywood's Rich and Famous*
    SPBW - Oct 2015 - pNA [51-500]
Lassieur, Allison - *Are Crop Circles Real?*
    c BL - v112 - i4 - Oct 15 2015 - p43(1) [51-500]
    At Battle in the Civil War: An Interactive Battlefield Adventure
    c HB Guide - v26 - i2 - Fall 2015 - p220(1) [51-500]
    Fruits
    c BL - v111 - i12 - Feb 15 2015 - p76(1) [51-500]
    c CH Bwatch - July 2015 - pNA [51-500]
    Is Atlantis Real?
    c BL - v112 - i4 - Oct 15 2015 - p43(1) [51-500]
    Is the Bermuda Triangle Real?
    c BL - v112 - i4 - Oct 15 2015 - p43(1) [51-500]
    Is the Loch Ness Monster Real?
    c BL - v112 - i4 - Oct 15 2015 - p43(1) [51-500]
    Where Does Our Food Come From? Series
    c HB Guide - v26 - i1 - Spring 2015 - p174(1) [51-500]
Lassner, Jacob - *Jews, Christians, and the Abode of Islam: Modern Scholarship, Medieval Realities*
    Specu - v90 - i4 - Oct 2015 - p1141-1143 [501+]
Latham, Irene - *Dear Wandering Wildebeest and Other Poems from the Water Hole (Illus. by Wadham, Anna)*
    c CCB-B - v68 - i5 - Jan 2015 - p264(1) [51-500]
    c HB Guide - v26 - i2 - Fall 2015 - p204(1) [51-500]
    Fresh Delicious: Poems from the Farmers' Market (Illus. by Moriuchi, Mique)
    c KR - Dec 15 2015 - pNA [51-500]
    c PW - v262 - i52 - Dec 21 2015 - p156(2) [501+]
    When the Sun Shines on Antarctica: And Other Poems About the Frozen Continent (Illus. by Wadham, Anna)
    c KR - Nov 15 2015 - pNA [51-500]
    c PW - v262 - i52 - Dec 21 2015 - p156(2) [501+]
Latham, Jennifer - *Scarlett Undercover*
    c BL - v111 - i17 - May 1 2015 - p52(2) [51-500]
    y CCB-B - v68 - i11 - July-August 2015 - p554(1) [51-500]
    y HB - v91 - i4 - July-August 2015 - p138(2) [51-500]
    y KR - March 1 2015 - pNA [51-500]
    y PW - v262 - i14 - April 6 2015 - p61(1) [51-500]
    y Teach Lib - v43 - i1 - Oct 2015 - p22(1) [51-500]
    y VOYA - v38 - i1 - April 2015 - p64(1) [51-500]
Latham, Kat - *Taming the Legend*
    PW - v262 - i13 - March 30 2015 - p61(2) [51-500]

Leadbetter, David - *The A Swing: The Alternative Approach to Great Golf*
    LJ - v140 - i6 - April 1 2015 - p94(1) [501+]
Leader, Zachary - *The Life of Saul Bellow: To Fame and Fortune, 1915-1964*
    BL - v111 - i13 - March 1 2015 - p15(1) [51-500]
    Econ - v415 - i8940 - May 30 2015 - p83(US) [501+]
    HM - v330 - i1980 - May 2015 - p85(6) [501+]
    HR - v68 - i1 - Spring 2015 - p158-166 [501+]
    KR - March 1 2015 - pNA [501+]
    LJ - v140 - i8 - May 1 2015 - p70(1) [51-500]
    Lon R Bks - v37 - i10 - May 21 2015 - p9(3) [501+]
    Mac - v128 - i18 - May 11 2015 - p59(2) [501+]
    NYRB - v62 - i10 - June 4 2015 - p10(4) [501+]
    NYT - April 29 2015 - pC6(L) [501+]
    NYTBR - May 3 2015 - p1(L) [501+]
    PW - v262 - i10 - March 9 2015 - p65(1) [51-500]
    Spec - v327 - i9740 - May 2 2015 - p36(2) [501+]
    TLS - i5851 - May 22 2015 - p3(2) [501+]
Leaf, Christina - *Great Horned Owls*
    c BL - v111 - i15 - April 1 2015 - p63(1) [51-500]
Leaf, Munroe - *How to Be: Six Simple Rules for Being the Best Kid You Can Be*
    RVBW - Oct 2015 - pNA [51-500]
Leaf, Sue - *Portage: A Family, a Canoe, and the Search for the Good Life*
    KR - August 15 2015 - pNA [51-500]
Leahy, Stephen - *Your Water Footprint*
    y VOYA - v38 - i5 - Dec 2015 - p77(1) [51-500]
Lealos, Ron - *Don't Mean Nuthin'*
    BL - v111 - i11 - Feb 1 2015 - p26(1) [51-500]
Leaming, Barbara - *Jacqueline Bouvier Kennedy Onassis: The Untold Story*
    NYTBR - Dec 13 2015 - p44(L) [501+]
Lean, Nathan - *The Islamophobia Industry: How the Right Manufactures Fear of Muslims*
    ERS - v38 - i8 - August 2015 - p1423(3) [501+]
Lean, Sarah - *Harry and Hope*
    c Sch Lib - v63 - i3 - Autumn 2015 - p168(1) [51-500]
Hero
    c HB Guide - v26 - i2 - Fall 2015 - p90(1) [51-500]
Leander, Hans - *Discourses of Empire: The Gospel of Mark from a Postcolonial Perspective*
    Intpr - v69 - i4 - Oct 2015 - p496(1) [501+]
Leane, Elizabeth - *Antarctica in Fiction: Imaginative Narratives of the Far South*
    AL - v87 - i2 - June 2015 - p408-410 [501+]
Leaney, Glynn - *Parodies Lost*
    SPBW - Jan 2015 - pNA [51-500]
Leap, Jorja - *Project Fatherhood: A Story of Courage and Healing in One of America's Toughest Communities*
    KR - March 15 2015 - pNA [51-500]
    PW - v262 - i14 - April 6 2015 - p54(1) [501+]
Lear, Edward - *Nonsense Limericks (Illus. by Robins, Arthur)*
    c Sch Lib - v63 - i1 - Spring 2015 - p49(1) [51-500]
The Owl and the Pussy-Cat (Illus. by Galdone, Paul)
    c HB Guide - v26 - i2 - Fall 2015 - p204(1) [51-500]
The Owl and the Pussy Cat (Illus. by Voake, Charlotte)
    c Sch Lib - v63 - i1 - Spring 2015 - p28(2) [51-500]
Lear, Norman - *Even This I Get to Experience (Read by Lear, Norman). Audiobook Review*
    BL - v111 - i16 - April 15 2015 - p61(1) [501+]
Learmont, David - *The Foster Factory*
    TimHES - i2205 - May 28 2015 - p47(1) [501+]
Leary, James P. - *Folksongs of Another America: Field Recordings from the Upper Midwest, 1937-1946*
    LJ - v140 - i15 - Sept 15 2015 - p106(1) [51-500]
Leary, Jan English - *Thicker Than Blood*
    KR - August 15 2015 - pNA [51-500]
Leary, Timothy John - *Symphosius: The Aenigmata: An Introduction, Text and Commentary*
    Class R - v65 - i2 - Oct 2015 - p485-486 [501+]
Leask, Nigel - *The Oxford Edition of the Works of Robert Burns, vol. 1: Commonplace Books, Tour Journals and Miscellaneous Prose*
    RES - v66 - i275 - June 2015 - p585-586 [501+]
    TLS - i5834 - Jan 23 2015 - p3(2) [501+]
Leathers, Philippa - *How to Catch a Mouse (Illus. by Leathers, Philippa)*
    c BL - v111 - i15 - April 1 2015 - p82(2) [51-500]
    c CCB-B - v68 - i11 - July-August 2015 - p554(2) [51-500]
    c HB Guide - v26 - i2 - Fall 2015 - p41(1) [51-500]
    c KR - Jan 15 2015 - pNA [51-500]
    c Sch Lib - v63 - i3 - Autumn 2015 - p156(1) [51-500]
    c SLJ - v61 - i6 - June 2015 - p74(1) [51-500]

Leaton, Stephen K. - *Vivienne's Blog*
    KR - Jan 1 2015 - pNA [501+]
Leavell, Linda - *Holding On Upside Down: The Life and Work of Marianne Moore*
    Ant R - v73 - i2 - Spring 2015 - p381(2) [501+]
    CSM - Feb 19 2015 - pNA [51-500]
    NYTBR - Jan 4 2015 - p24(L) [501+]
Leavell, Peter - *West for the Black Hills*
    PW - v262 - i9 - March 2 2015 - p72(2) [501+]
Leaver, Trisha - *Hardwired*
    c KR - Sept 15 2015 - pNA [51-500]
The Secrets We Keep (Read by Rudd, Kate). Audiobook Review
    y SLJ - v61 - i7 - July 2015 - p49(1) [51-500]
The Secrets We Keep
    y BL - v111 - i13 - March 1 2015 - p59(1) [51-500]
    y CCB-B - v68 - i10 - June 2015 - p502(2) [51-500]
    y HB Guide - v26 - i2 - Fall 2015 - p128(1) [51-500]
    y KR - Feb 15 2015 - pNA [51-500]
    y PW - v262 - i7 - Feb 16 2015 - p181(1) [51-500]
    y SLJ - v61 - i10 - Oct 2015 - p104(1) [51-500]
    y VOYA - v37 - i6 - Feb 2015 - p59(2) [51-500]
Sweet Madness
    y KR - July 15 2015 - pNA [51-500]
    y VOYA - v38 - i3 - August 2015 - p64(1) [501+]
Leavey, JoAnn Elizabeth - *Living Recovery: Youth Speak Out on "Owning" Mental Illness*
    RVBW - June 2015 - pNA [501+]
Leavey, Peggy Dymond - *Mary Pickford: Canada's Silent Siren, America's Sweetheart*
    CWS - v30 - i2-3 - Fall-Winter 2015 - p128(1) [501+]
Leavitt, Amie - *Emergency Aid*
    c BL - v111 - i16 - April 15 2015 - p45(1) [501+]
Leavitt, Lindsey - *The Pages between Us (Illus. by Dening, Abby)*
    c KR - Dec 1 2015 - pNA [51-500]
    c SLJ - v61 - i12 - Dec 2015 - p104(1) [51-500]
Leavitt, Martine - *Blue Mountain*
    c HB Guide - v26 - i1 - Spring 2015 - p84(1) [51-500]
    c Res Links - v20 - i3 - Feb 2015 - p12(1) [51-500]
Calvin
    y BL - v111 - i22 - August 1 2015 - p63(1) [51-500]
    y HB - v91 - i6 - Nov-Dec 2015 - p81(2) [51-500]
    y KR - Sept 1 2015 - pNA [51-500]
    y PW - v262 - i35 - August 31 2015 - p94(1) [51-500]
    y SLJ - v61 - i9 - Sept 2015 - p169(1) [51-500]
    y VOYA - v38 - i5 - Dec 2015 - p58(2) [51-500]
Lebar, Mark - *The Value of Living Well*
    RM - v68 - i3 - March 2015 - p667(3) [501+]
Lebedev, Anna Colin - *Le cour politique des meres: Analyse du mouvement des meres de soldats en Russie*
    Slav R - v74 - i1 - Spring 2015 - p201-202 [501+]
Lebedev, Sergei - *Oblivion*
    KR - Oct 15 2015 - pNA [51-500]
Leberecht, Tim - *The Business Romantic: Give Everything, Quantify Nothing, and Create Something Greater Than Yourself*
    BL - v111 - i12 - Feb 15 2015 - p14(1) [51-500]
    New R - v246 - i2-3 - March-April 2015 - p57(3) [501+]
Leblanc, Catherine - *Here She Is! (Illus. by Tharlet, Eve)*
    c HB Guide - v26 - i2 - Fall 2015 - p41(1) [51-500]
    c SLJ - v61 - i5 - May 2015 - p79(1) [51-500]
How to Zap Zombies (Illus. by Garrigue, Roland)
    c HB Guide - v26 - i1 - Spring 2015 - p36(1) [51-500]
LeBlanc, Donna - *Explorations of Commander Josh, Book 1: In Space (Illus. by Servetnik, Anton)*
    c CH Bwatch - Jan 2015 - pNA [51-500]
    c CH Bwatch - Feb 2015 - pNA [51-500]
LeBor, Adam - *The Washington Stratagem*
    RVBW - August 2015 - pNA [51-500]
LeBoutillier, Linda - *Unusual and Awesome Jobs Using Technology: Roller Coaster Designer, Space Robotics Engineer, and More*
    c HB Guide - v26 - i2 - Fall 2015 - p152(1) [51-500]
LeBoutillier, Nate - *The Story of the Oklahoma City Thunder*
    c HB Guide - v26 - i2 - Fall 2015 - p198(1) [51-500]
Lebovic, Nitzan - *The Philosophy of Life and Death: Ludwig Klages and the Rise of a Nazi Biopolitics*
    AHR - v120 - i3 - June 2015 - p1135-1136 [501+]
    CEH - v48 - i1 - March 2015 - p129-130 [501+]
Lebow, Katherine - *Unfinished Utopia: Nowa Huta, Stalinism, and Polish Society, 1949-56*
    JMH - v87 - i2 - June 2015 - p494(2) [501+]

Lebow, Laura - *The Figaro Murders*
    BL - v111 - i13 - March 1 2015 - p23(1) [51-500]
    KR - Jan 15 2015 - pNA [51-500]
    ON - v80 - i2 - August 2015 - p59(1) [501+]
    PW - v262 - i2 - Jan 12 2015 - p38(1) [51-500]
LeBox, Annette - *Peace Is an Offering (Illus. by Graegin, Stephanie)*
    c HB Guide - v26 - i2 - Fall 2015 - p41(1) [51-500]
    c KR - Jan 15 2015 - pNA [51-500]
    c PW - v262 - i3 - Jan 19 2015 - p79(1) [51-500]
Peace Is an Offering
    c Res Links - v20 - i5 - June 2015 - p5(2) [51-500]
Lebreton, Christophe - *Born from the Gaze of God: The Tibhirine Journal of a Martyr Monk*
    Comw - v142 - i2 - Jan 23 2015 - p28(1) [501+]
L'echange - Der Austausch. 7. Interdisziplinarer deutsch-franzosischer Workshop fur Nachwuchswissenschaftler/innen
    HNet - April 2015 - pNA [501+]
Lechevalier, Sebastien - *The Great Transformation of Japanese Capitalism*
    Pac A - v88 - i4 - Dec 2015 - p924 [501+]
Leck, James - *After Dark*
    c KR - May 15 2015 - pNA [51-500]
Leckie, Ann - *Ancillary Mercy*
    KR - August 1 2015 - pNA [51-500]
    PW - v262 - i36 - Sept 7 2015 - p50(1) [51-500]
LeClair, Jenifer - *Apparition Island*
    PW - v262 - i3 - Jan 19 2015 - p64(1) [51-500]
LeClair, Tom - *Lincoln's Billy*
    KR - Feb 15 2015 - pNA [51-500]
    NYTBR - August 16 2015 - p30(L) [501+]
LeCoeur, Ursula - *The Willing Widow*
    PW - v262 - i47 - Nov 23 2015 - p56(1) [51-500]
Lecomber, Phil - *Mask of the Verdoy*
    KR - June 1 2015 - pNA [51-500]
Lecouteux, Claude - *Demons and Spirits of the Land: Ancestral Lore and Practices*
    Bwatch - Sept 2015 - pNA [501+]
LeCraw, Holly - *The Half Brother*
    BL - v111 - i9-10 - Jan 1 2015 - p36(2) [51-500]
Ledder, Glenn - *Undergraduate Mathematics for the Life Sciences: Models, Processes, and Directions*
    Math T - v108 - i8 - April 2015 - p639(1) [501+]
Ledeneva, Alena - *Can Russia Modernise?: 'Sistema,' Power Networks and Informal Governance*
    Lon R Bks - v37 - i3 - Feb 5 2015 - p13(3) [501+]
Leder, Andrzej - *Przesniona rewolucja: Cwiczenie z logiki historycznej*
    Nation - v300 - i1 - Jan 5 2015 - p27(10) [501+]
Lederer, Paul Joseph - *On Cimarron*
    BL - v111 - i18 - May 15 2015 - p30(1) [51-500]
    Roundup M - v23 - i1 - Oct 2015 - p31(2) [501+]
Ledo, Jorge - *Moira de Erasmo Roterodamo: A Critical Edition of the Early Modern Spanish Translation of Erasmus's 'Encomium Moriae'*
    Six Ct J - v46 - i3 - Fall 2015 - p707-710 [501+]
LeDoux, Joseph - *Anxious: The Modern Mind in the Age of Anxiety*
    TimHES - i2222 - Sept 24 2015 - p44(1) [501+]
Anxious: Using the Brain to Understand and Treat Fear and Anxiety
    BL - v111 - i21 - July 1 2015 - p13(1) [51-500]
    KR - May 15 2015 - pNA [501+]
    Nature - v524 - i7563 - August 6 2015 - p34(1) [501+]
    PW - v262 - i19 - May 11 2015 - p48(1) [51-500]
Leduc, Emilie - *All Year Round (Illus. by Leduc, Emilie)*
    c KR - July 1 2015 - pNA [51-500]
    c PW - v262 - i29 - July 20 2015 - p192(1) [501+]
    c SLJ - v61 - i10 - Oct 2015 - p70(1) [51-500]
Lee, A. Robert - *The Native American Renaissance: Literary Imagination and Achievement*
    Am Ind CRJ - v39 - i1 - Wntr 2015 - p142-145 [501+]
Lee, Alexander - *The Ugly Renaissance: Sex, Greed, Violence and Depravity in an Age of Beauty (Read by Morey, Arthur). Audiobook Review*
    LJ - v140 - i6 - April 1 2015 - p50(3) [51-500]
The Ugly Renaissance: Sex, Greed, Violence and Depravity in an Age of Beauty
    NYRB - v62 - i16 - Oct 22 2015 - p63(2) [501+]
Lee-Brownie, Martin - *Delius and His Music*
    MT - v156 - i1932 - Autumn 2015 - p99-102 [501+]
Lee, C.B. - *Seven Tears at High Tide*
    y SLJ - v61 - i10 - Oct 2015 - p113(1) [51-500]
Lee, Carl - *Everything Is Connected to Everything Else: 101 Stories about 21st Century Geography*
    TimHES - i2204 - May 21 2015 - p9(1) [501+]
Lee, Catherine - *Fictive Kinship: Family Reunification and the Meaning of Race and Nation in American*

272 • LEE

Immigration
   ERS - v38 - i3 - March 2015 - p456(3) [501+]
Lee, Chang-Rae - *On Such a Full Sea*
   ABR - v36 - i5 - July-August 2015 - p14(2) [501+]
Lee, Charlotte - *The Very Late Goethe: Self-Consciousness and the Art of Ageing*
   MLR - v110 - i2 - April 2015 - p587-588 [501+]
Lee, Christina - *Two of Hearts*
   BL - v111 - i17 - May 1 2015 - p81(1) [51-500]
Lee, Dan - *The Civil War in the Jackson Purchase, 1861-1862: The Pro-Confederate Struggle and Defeat in Southwest Kentucky*
   JSH - v81 - i2 - May 2015 - p466(2) [501+]
Lee, Daniel - *Petain's Jewish Children: French Jewish Youth and the Vichy Regime, 1940-42*
   HT - v65 - i5 - May 2015 - p61(2) [501+]
   TLS - i5872 - Oct 16 2015 - p24(1) [501+]
Lee, Day's - *Guitar Hero*
   KR - August 1 2015 - pNA [501+]
Lee, Deborah - *Aboriginal and Visible Minority Librarians: Oral Histories from Canada*
   LR - v64 - i4-5 - April-May 2015 - p393-394 [501+]
Lee, Deborah Jian - *Rescuing Jesus: How People of Color, Women, and Queer Christians Are Reclaiming Evangelicalism*
   PW - v262 - i37 - Sept 14 2015 - p63(1) [501+]
Lee, Dennis - *Melvis and Elvis (Illus. by Tankard, Jeremy)*
   c Res Links - v20 - i5 - June 2015 - p6(1) [51-500]
Lee, Erika - *The Making of Asian America: A History*
   KR - June 1 2015 - pNA [501+]
   LJ - v140 - i10 - June 1 2015 - p113(1) [51-500]
   NYTBR - Sept 6 2015 - p17(L) [501+]
   Prog - v79 - i10 - Oct 2015 - p43(3) [501+]
   PW - v262 - i23 - June 8 2015 - p50(1) [501+]
Lee, Fiona - *Playtime*
   c KR - Jan 1 2016 - pNA [51-500]
Lee, Fonda - *Zeroboxer*
   KR - Feb 1 2015 - pNA [51-500]
   y PW - v262 - i9 - March 2 2015 - p86(1) [51-500]
   y SLJ - v61 - i3 - March 2015 - p158(2) [51-500]
   y VOYA - v37 - i6 - Feb 2015 - p80(1) [51-500]
Lee, Francis L.F. - *Communication, Public Opinion, and Globalization in Urban China*
   Pac A - v88 - i1 - March 2015 - p174 [501+]
Lee, Grace - *American Revolutionary: The Evolution of Grace Lee Boggs*
   NWSA Jnl - v27 - i1 - Spring 2015 - p201-203 [501+]
Lee, HaeDa - *Ida's Present (Illus. by Kim, IhHyeon)*
   c SLJ - v61 - i7 - July 2015 - p64(1) [51-500]
Lee, Harper - *Go Set a Watchman (Read by Witherspoon, Reese). Audiobook Review*
   BL - v112 - i1 - Sept 1 2015 - p139(1) [51-500]
   LJ - v140 - i15 - Sept 15 2015 - p42(1) [51-500]
   Go Set a Watchman
   BooChiTr - July 11 2015 - p12(1) [501+]
   CC - v132 - i21 - Oct 14 2015 - p24(4) [501+]
   CSM - July 12 2015 - pNA [501+]
   CSM - July 30 2015 - pNA [501+]
   Econ - v416 - i8947 - July 18 2015 - p71(US) [501+]
   Ent W - i1373 - July 24 2015 - p61(1) [501+]
   Hum - v75 - i5 - Sept-Oct 2015 - p44(2) [501+]
   KR - August 1 2015 - pNA [501+]
   LJ - v140 - i13 - August 1 2015 - p86(1) [501+]
   Nat Post - v17 - i210 - July 11 2015 - pA8(1) [501+]
   Nat Post - v17 - i215 - July 18 2015 - pWP3(1) [501+]
   New R - v246 - i9-10 - Sept-Oct 2015 - p61(7) [501+]
   NS - v144 - i5271 - July 17 2015 - p42(2) [501+]
   NY - v91 - i21 - July 27 2015 - p66 [501+]
   NYRB - v62 - i14 - Sept 24 2015 - p22(3) [501+]
   NYT - July 11 2015 - pA1(L) [501+]
   NYT - July 11 2015 - pNA(L) [501+]
   NYTBR - August 2 2015 - p8(L) [501+]
   PW - v262 - i29 - July 20 2015 - p3(1) [501+]
   SEP - v287 - i3 - May-June 2015 - p24(1) [501+]
   Spec - v328 - i9751 - July 18 2015 - p32(2) [501+]
   TLS - i5866 - Sept 4 2015 - p20(2) [501+]
   To Kill a Mockingbird
   NYT - Sept 1 2015 - pB4(L) [501+]
Lee, Heath Hardage - *Winnie Davis: Daughter of the Lost Cause*
   JSH - v81 - i4 - Nov 2015 - p1001(2) [501+]

Lee, Hermione - *Penelope Fitzgerald: A Life*
   CC - v132 - i11 - May 27 2015 - p39(3) [501+]
   HM - v330 - i1976 - Jan 2015 - p89(6) [501+]
   Nation - v300 - i19 - May 11 2015 - p27(7) [501+]
   NYTBR - Nov 29 2015 - p24(L) [501+]
   Wom R Bks - v32 - i6 - Nov-Dec 2015 - p30(2) [501+]
Lee, Hong Yung - *Colonial Rule and Social Change in Korea, 1910-1945*
   Historian - v77 - i1 - Spring 2015 - p153(2) [501+]
Lee, Hyeon-Ju - *Mina's White Canvas (Illus. by Lee, Hyeon-Ju)*
   c SLJ - v61 - i10 - Oct 2015 - p80(1) [51-500]
Lee, Hyeonseo - *The Girl with Seven Names: A North Korean Defector's Story*
   KR - June 1 2015 - pNA [501+]
   Mac - v128 - i28 - July 20 2015 - p56(1) [501+]
   NS - v144 - i5282 - Oct 2 2015 - p71(1) [501+]
   NYTBR - Nov 29 2015 - p26(L) [501+]
Lee, Ingrid - *Chicken House*
   c Teach Lib - v42 - i5 - June 2015 - p61(1) [51-500]
Lee, J.M. - *The Investigation*
   LJ - v140 - i13 - August 1 2015 - p87(2) [51-500]
Lee, Jackie - *See It Grow Series*
   c SLJ - v61 - i5 - Nov 1 2015 - p47(1) [51-500]
Lee, Jade - *50 Ways to Ruin a Rake*
   PW - v262 - i12 - March 23 2015 - p55(1) [51-500]
Lee, James - *From House of Lords to Supreme Court, Judges, Jurists and the Process of Judging*
   Law&PolBR - v25 - i2 - Feb 2015 - p22(5) [501+]
Lee, Janice Y.K. - *The Expatriates*
   BL - v112 - i6 - Nov 15 2015 - p21(1) [51-500]
   KR - Nov 15 2015 - pNA [51-500]
   PW - v262 - i41 - Oct 12 2015 - p44(1) [51-500]
Lee, Jen - *Vacancy (Illus. by Lee, Jen)*
   c SLJ - v61 - i9 - Sept 2015 - p148(3) [51-500]
Lee, JiHyeon - *Pool (Illus. by Lee, JiHyeon)*
   c HB - v91 - i4 - July-August 2015 - p119(2) [51-500]
   c KR - March 15 2015 - pNA [51-500]
   c Nat Post - v17 - i230 - August 8 2015 - pWP5(1) [501+]
   c NYTBR - May 31 2015 - p45(L) [501+]
   c PW - v262 - i10 - March 9 2015 - p70(1) [51-500]
   c PW - v262 - i49 - Dec 2 2015 - p17(1) [51-500]
   c SLJ - v61 - i5 - May 2015 - p86(2) [51-500]
Lee, Jonathan - *High Dive*
   KR - Jan 1 2016 - pNA [51-500]
   PW - v262 - i45 - Nov 9 2015 - p33(1) [51-500]
   Spec - v329 - i9765 - Oct 24 2015 - p47(1) [501+]
Lee, Jonathan H.X. - *History of Asian Americans: Exploring Diverse Roots*
   y BL - v111 - i19-20 - June 1 2015 - p25(1) [51-500]
Lee, Julia - *Our Gang: A Racial History of 'The Little Rascals'*
   Atl - v316 - i5 - Dec 2015 - p36(1) [51-500]
Lee, Kanani K.M. - *The Incredible Plate Tectonics Comic (Illus. by Wallenta, Adam)*
   y CH Bwatch - Jan 2015 - pNA [51-500]
Lee, Kathleen - *All Things Tending towards the Eternal*
   BL - v111 - i11 - Feb 1 2015 - p20(1) [51-500]
Lee, Laurie - *Village Christmas: And Other Notes on the English Year*
   c Spec - v329 - i9772 - Dec 12 2015 - p77(1) [501+]
Lee, Linda Francis - *The Glass Kitchen (Read by Whelan, Julia). Audiobook Review*
   BL - v111 - i14 - March 15 2015 - p85(1) [51-500]
Lee, Lloyd L. - *Dine Perspectives: Revitalizing and Reclaiming Navajo Thought*
   Am Ind CRJ - v39 - i1 - Wntr 2015 - p119-120 [501+]
   Roundup M - v22 - i6 - August 2015 - p38(1) [501+]
   WHQ - v46 - i3 - Autumn 2015 - p373-374 [501+]
Lee, Mackenzi - *This Monstrous Thing*
   y BL - v112 - i1 - Sept 1 2015 - p109(2) [51-500]
   y CCB-B - v69 - i2 - Oct 2015 - p98(1) [51-500]
   y HB - v91 - i5 - Sept-Oct 2015 - p109(1) [51-500]
   y KR - July 1 2015 - pNA [51-500]
   y PW - v262 - i23 - June 8 2015 - p62(1) [51-500]
   y SLJ - v61 - i8 - August 2015 - p106(1) [51-500]
   y VOYA - v38 - i5 - Dec 2015 - p71(2) [51-500]
Lee, Mary Elizabeth - *Beveled Edges and Mitered Corners: Poems*
   KR - Nov 1 2015 - pNA [51-500]
Lee, Mi-ae - *A Day at Grandma's (Illus. by Choi, Yangsook)*
   c KR - March 1 2015 - pNA [51-500]
   c SLJ - v61 - i8 - August 2015 - p120(1) [51-500]

Lee, Michael J. - *Creating Conservatism: Postwar Words That Made an American Movement*
   AHR - v120 - i3 - June 2015 - p1056-1057 [501+]
   Am St - v54 - i2 - Summer 2015 - p110-111 [501+]
Lee, Michelle - *Living Luxe Gluten Free*
   PW - v262 - i18 - May 4 2015 - p114(1) [51-500]
Lee, Mike - *Our Lost Constitution: The Willful Subversion of America's Founding Document*
   Nat R - v67 - i10 - June 1 2015 - p43 [501+]
Lee, Mireille M. - *Body, Dress, and Identity in Ancient Greece*
   TLS - i5854 - June 12 2015 - p22(1) [501+]
Lee, Monica K.K. - *Makena's Shadow*
   y SLJ - v61 - i7 - July 2015 - p94(1) [51-500]
Lee, Nancy - *The Island*
   RVBW - Nov 2015 - pNA [51-500]
Lee, Niclaus - *The Adventures Of Jon Paul Chavalier*
   SPBW - Jan 2015 - pNA [51-500]
Lee, Okhee - *NGSS for All Students*
   Sci & Ch - v52 - i9 - Summer 2015 - p28 [51-500]
   Sci & Ch - v53 - i2 - Oct 2015 - p97 [501+]
   Sci Teach - v82 - i7 - Oct 2015 - p81 [51-500]
Lee, Patrick - *Signal*
   BL - v111 - i17 - May 1 2015 - p44(1) [51-500]
   PW - v262 - i18 - May 4 2015 - p98(1) [51-500]
Lee, Paul R., II - *Parks, Postmarks & Postmasters: Post Offices within the National Park System*
   Phil Lit R - v64 - i2 - Spring 2015 - p141(3) [501+]
Lee, R. Alton - *Sunflower Justice: A New History of the Kansas Supreme Court*
   WHQ - v46 - i1 - Spring 2015 - p84-85 [501+]
Lee, Rena - *Ports of Recall*
   KR - Oct 1 2015 - pNA [501+]
Lee, Richard E. - *The Longue Duree and World-Systems Analysis*
   HNet - April 2015 - pNA [501+]
Lee, Sera - *Tiptoe Tapirs (Illus. by Kim, Hanmin)*
   c PW - v262 - i35 - August 31 2015 - p92(1) [51-500]
Lee Si-young - *Patterns*
   WLT - v89 - i3-4 - May-August 2015 - p122(2) [501+]
Lee, Sonia Song-Ha - *Building a Latino Civil Rights Movement: Puerto Ricans, African Americans, and the Pursuit of Racial Justice in New York City*
   AHR - v120 - i3 - June 2015 - p1069-1070 [501+]
   Soc Ser R - v89 - i1 - March 2015 - p203(5) [501+]
Lee, Stacey - *Under a Painted Sky*
   y BL - v111 - i11 - Feb 1 2015 - p44(1) [51-500]
   y HB Guide - v26 - i2 - Fall 2015 - p128(1) [51-500]
   y PW - v262 - i4 - Jan 26 2015 - p173(1) [51-500]
   y PW - v262 - i49 - Dec 2 2015 - p115(2) [51-500]
   y VOYA - v37 - i6 - Feb 2015 - p60(1) [51-500]
Lee, Stan - *Amazing Fantastic Incredible: A Marvelous Memoir (Illus. by Doran, Colleen)*
   y BL - v112 - i6 - Nov 15 2015 - p33(1) [51-500]
   KR - Sept 1 2015 - pNA [51-500]
   PW - v262 - i46 - Nov 16 2015 - p64(1) [51-500]
   Convergence (Illus. by Tong, Andie)
   y BL - v111 - i9-10 - Jan 1 2015 - p87(2) [51-500]
   y CCB-B - v68 - i7 - March 2015 - p361(1) [51-500]
   c HB Guide - v26 - i2 - Fall 2015 - p90(1) [51-500]
Lee, Sukhee - *Negotiated Power: The State, Elites, and Local Governance in Twelfth- to Fourteenth-Century China*
   JIH - v46 - i3 - Wntr 2016 - p476-477 [501+]
Lee, Susanna Michele - *Claiming the Union: Citizenship in the Post-Civil War South*
   AHR - v120 - i2 - April 2015 - p634-635 [501+]
   JAH - v101 - i4 - March 2015 - p1279-1280 [501+]
   JSH - v81 - i3 - August 2015 - p749(2) [501+]
Lee, Thomas H. - *Eugene Braumwald and the Rise of Modern Medicine*
   RAH - v43 - i3 - Sept 2015 - p531-536 [501+]
Lee, Tony - *Messenger: The Legend of Joan of Arc (Illus. by Hart, Sam)*
   y KR - Sept 15 2015 - pNA [51-500]
   y SLJ - v61 - i11 - Nov 2015 - p140(2) [51-500]
Lee, Tosca - *The Legend of Sheba*
   RVBW - July 2015 - pNA [51-500]
Lee, Trisha - *Princesses, Dragons and Helicopter Stories*
   RVBW - Oct 2015 - pNA [51-500]
Lee, Wayne E. - *Barbarians and Brothers: Anglo-American Warfare, 1500-1865*
   Six Ct J - v46 - i2 - Summer 2015 - p503-504 [501+]
   W&M Q - v72 - i1 - Jan 2015 - p175-178 [501+]

Book Review Index 2016 Cumulation **LEITER • 273**

Lee, WonKyeong - *The Chirping Band (Illus. by Jang, EunJoo)*
c HB Guide - v26 - i2 - Fall 2015 - p39(1) [51-500]
Lee, Y.S. - *Rivals in the City*
y HB Guide - v26 - i2 - Fall 2015 - p128(1) [51-500]
y KR - Jan 1 2015 - pNA [51-500]
Leech, Christine - *Fresh Prints: 25 Easy and Enticing Printing Projects to Make at Home*
LJ - v140 - i8 - May 1 2015 - p72(1) [51-500]
Leech, Emma V. - *The Dark Prince*
KR - August 1 2015 - pNA [501+]
Leedy, Loreen - *Amazing Plant Powers: How Plants Fly, Fight, Hide, Hunt, and Change the World*
c HB Guide - v26 - i2 - Fall 2015 - p173(1) [51-500]
c KR - March 1 2015 - pNA [51-500]
c SLJ - v61 - i3 - March 2015 - p171(1) [51-500]
Leeming, David A. - *The Handy Mythology Answer Book*
VOYA - v37 - i6 - Feb 2015 - p90(1) [51-500]
Leenders, Reinoud - *Spoils of Truce: Corruption and State-Building in Postwar Lebanon*
IJMES - v47 - i1 - Feb 2015 - p204-205 [501+]
Leerhsen, Charles - *Ty Cobb: A Terrible Beauty*
KR - March 15 2015 - pNA [501+]
NYTBR - May 31 2015 - p18(L) [501+]
y SLJ - v61 - i8 - August 2015 - p115(2) [51-500]
LJ - v140 - i7 - April 15 2015 - p92(1) [51-500]
PW - v262 - i12 - March 23 2015 - p67(1) [51-500]
Lees, Clare A. - *The Cambridge History of Early Medieval English Literature*
Specu - v90 - i1 - Jan 2015 - p270-271 [501+]
Lees, William B. - *Recalling Deeds Immortal: Florida Monuments to the Civil War*
JSH - v81 - i4 - Nov 2015 - p1003(2) [501+]
Lees William B. - *Recalling Deeds Immortal: Florida Monuments to the Civil War*
Pub Hist - v37 - i2 - May 2015 - p146(3) [501+]
Lefebure, Leo D. - *True and Holy: Christian Scripture and Other Religions*
IBMR - v39 - i1 - Jan 2015 - p50(2) [501+]
Theol St - v76 - i1 - March 2015 - p208(2) [501+]
Lefebvre, Benjamin - *The L.M. Montgomery Reader, vol. 3: A Legacy in Review*
TLS - i5846 - April 17 2015 - p26(1) [501+]
Lefer, David - *The Founding Conservatives: How a Group of Unsung Heroes Saved the American Revolution*
Historian - v77 - i3 - Fall 2015 - p564(2) [501+]
LeFevre, John - *Straight to Hell: True Tales of Deviance, Debauchery, and Billion-Dollar Deals*
Barron's - v95 - i36 - Sept 7 2015 - p44(1) [501+]
KR - May 15 2015 - pNA [51-500]
NW - v165 - i8 - August 28 2015 - pNA [501+]
PW - v262 - i19 - May 11 2015 - p51(2) [51-500]
PW - v262 - i30 - July 27 2015 - p10(1) [51-500]
Leffingwell, Randy - *Corvette: Seven Generations of American High Performance*
Bwatch - May 2015 - pNA [51-500]
Leffler, Rebecca - *Tres Green, Tres Clean, Tres Chic: Eat (and Live!) the New French Way with Plant-Based, Gluten-Free Recipes for Every Season*
LJ - v140 - i11 - June 15 2015 - p106(1) [51-500]
Lefranc, Karin - *I Want to Eat Your Books (Illus. by Parker, Tyler)*
c KR - August 1 2015 - pNA [51-500]
c PW - v262 - i30 - July 27 2015 - p63(1) [51-500]
LeFrancois, Brenda A. - *Mad Matters: A Critical Reader in Canadian Mad Studies*
HNet - Feb 2015 - pNA [501+]
Left, Lisa Moses - *The Archive Thief: The Man Who Salvaged French Jewish History in the Wake of the Holocaust*
BL - v111 - i19-20 - June 1 2015 - p26(1) [51-500]
The Legacies of Jean-Luc Godard
FS - v69 - i3 - July 2015 - p424-425 [501+]
Legat, Alexandra - *The Incomparables*
Can Lit - i224 - Spring 2015 - p116 [501+]
Legault, Stephen - *Black Sun Descending*
RVBW - Jan 2015 - pNA [51-500]
Leger, Dimitry Elias - *God Loves Haiti*
KR - Jan 15 2015 - pNA [501+]
NY - v91 - i9 - April 20 2015 - p89 [51-500]
NYTBR - Feb 8 2015 - p30(L) [501+]
WLT - v89 - i6 - Nov-Dec 2015 - p61(2) [501+]
Leger, Nathalie - *Suite for Barbara Loden*
TLS - i5851 - May 22 2015 - p27(1) [501+]
Legg, Stephen - *Prostitution and the Ends of Empire: Scale, Governmentalities, and Interwar India*
AHR - v120 - i4 - Oct 2015 - p1460(1) [501+]
Legge, David - *Bamboozled, 21st Anniversary ed.*
c Magpies - v30 - i3 - July 2015 - p29(1) [501+]
Leggiere, Michael V. - *Napoleon and the Struggle for Germany: The Franco-Prussian War of 1813, 2 vols.*
TLS - i5876 - Nov 13 2015 - p29(1) [501+]
Legler, John M. - *The Turtles of Mexico: Land and Freshwater Forms*
QRB - v90 - i2 - June 2015 - p237(1) [501+]
Legrand, Claire - *Winterspell*
y HB Guide - v26 - i2 - Fall 2015 - p128(1) [51-500]
Legro, Ron - *The Man Who Painted the Universe: The Story of a Planetarium in the Heart of the North Woods*
RVBW - August 2015 - pNA [51-500]
LJ - v140 - i11 - June 15 2015 - p107(3) [51-500]
Lehane, Dennis - *World Gone By (Read by Frangione, Jim). Audiobook Review*
LJ - v140 - i10 - June 1 2015 - p61(1) [51-500]
World Gone By
BL - v111 - i12 - Feb 15 2015 - p40(1) [51-500]
KR - Jan 1 2015 - pNA [51-500]
LJ - v140 - i5 - March 15 2015 - p93(1) [51-500]
Mac - v128 - i13-14 - April 6 2015 - p75(1) [501+]
NYT - April 2 2015 - pC1(L) [501+]
NYTBR - April 5 2015 - p29(L) [501+]
NYTBR - Dec 6 2015 - p85(L) [501+]
RVBW - May 2015 - pNA [51-500]
Lehberger, Reiner - *Loki Schmidt: Die Biographie*
HNet - April 2015 - pNA [501+]
Lehman, Barbara A. - *Creating Books for the Young in the New South Africa: Essays on Authors and Illustrators of Children's and Young Adult Literature*
Bkbird - v53 - i2 - Spring 2015 - p81(2) [501+]
Bkbird - v53 - i3 - Summer 2015 - p88(1) [501+]
Lehman, Dale E. - *The Fibonacci Murders*
SPBW - Jan 2015 - pNA [51-500]
Lehman, Dana - *Remember When ... (Illus. by Lehman, Judy)*
c CH Bwatch - July 2015 - pNA [51-500]
Lehman, David - *Sinatra's Century: One Hundred Notes on the Man and His World*
NYTBR - Dec 6 2015 - p74(L) [501+]
The State of the Art: A Chronicle of American Poetry, 1988-2014
HR - v68 - i3 - Autumn 2015 - p474-480 [501+]
LJ - v140 - i6 - April 1 2015 - p88(1) [51-500]
NYTBR - Sept 6 2015 - p26(L) [501+]
Lehman, Eric D. - *Homegrown Terror: Benedict Arnold and the Burning of New London*
NEQ - v88 - i3 - Sept 2015 - p545-547 [501+]
Lehman, Katherine - *Interacting with History: Teaching with Primary Sources*
R&USQ - v54 - i3 - Spring 2015 - p53(2) [501+]
Those Girls: Single Women in Sixties and Seventies Popular Culture
JWH - v27 - i3 - Fall 2015 - p176(11) [501+]
Lehman-Wilzig, Tami - *Stork's Landing (Illus. by Shuttlewood, Anna)*
c HB Guide - v26 - i2 - Fall 2015 - p41(1) [51-500]
Lehmann, Alan W. - *Hamlet*
KR - Sept 15 2015 - pNA [501+]
Lehmann, Angela - *Transnational Lives in China: Expatriates in a Globalizing City*
AJS - v120 - i5 - March 2015 - p1574(3) [501+]
TimHES - i2216 - August 13 2015 - p43(1) [501+]
Lehmann, Devra - *Spinoza: The Outcast Thinker*
y HB Guide - v26 - i1 - Spring 2015 - p194(1) [51-500]
y CCB-B - v68 - i5 - Jan 2015 - p264(1) [51-500]
Lehmann, Roland - *Die Transformation des Kirchenbegriffs in der Fruhaufklarung*
HNet - July 2015 - pNA [501+]
Lehnert, Detlef - *Gemeinschaftsdenken in Europa: Das Gesellschaftskonzept 'Volksheim' im Vergleich 1900-1938*
HER - v130 - i544 - June 2015 - p778(3) [501+]
Konstitutionalismus in Europa: Entwicklung und Interpretation
HNet - June 2015 - pNA [501+]
Lehning, James R. - *European Colonialism since 1700*
HNet - March 2015 - pNA [501+]
LeHoullier, Craig - *Epic Tomatoes: How to Select and Grow the Best Varieties of All Time*
Bwatch - June 2015 - pNA [51-500]
Lehr, Dick - *The Birth of a Nation: How a Legendary Filmmaker and a Crusading Editor Reignited America's Civil War*
JAH - v102 - i2 - Sept 2015 - p579-579 [501+]
Lehrer, Erica T. - *Jewish Poland Revisited: Heritage Tourism in Unquiet Places*
HNet - April 2015 - pNA [501+]
Slav R - v74 - i3 - Fall 2015 - p622-623 [501+]
Lehrhaupt, Adam - *Please, Open This Book! (Illus. by Forsythe, Matthew)*
c KR - August 1 2015 - pNA [51-500]
c PW - v262 - i39 - Sept 28 2015 - p90(2) [501+]
Lehrman, Maggie - *The Cost of All Things*
y HB Guide - v26 - i2 - Fall 2015 - p128(1) [51-500]
y KR - Feb 15 2015 - pNA [51-500]
y PW - v262 - i13 - March 30 2015 - p77(1) [51-500]
y VOYA - v38 - i1 - April 2015 - p80(1) [51-500]
Leicht, Johannes - *Heinrich Cla beta 1868-1953: Die politische Biographie eines Alldeutschen*
GSR - v38 - i1 - Feb 2015 - p187-189 [501+]
Leicht, Martin - *The World Forgot*
y KR - Feb 1 2015 - pNA [51-500]
y VOYA - v38 - i1 - April 2015 - p80(1) [51-500]
Leicht, Stina - *Cold Iron*
BL - v111 - i21 - July 1 2015 - p46(1) [51-500]
PW - v262 - i21 - May 25 2015 - p40(1) [51-500]
Leichtentritt, Hugo - *A Musical Life in Two Worlds: The Autobiography of Hugo Leichtentritt*
Notes - v72 - i2 - Dec 2015 - p343(3) [501+]
"Leidenschaften". 20. Fachtagung des Arbeitskreises Geschlechtergeschichte der Fruhen Neuzeit
HNet - Feb 2015 - pNA [501+]
Leidich, Shari Koolik - *Two Moms in the Raw: Simple, Clean, Irresistible Recipes for Your Family's Health*
PW - v262 - i18 - May 4 2015 - p113(1) [51-500]
Leifer, John - *After You Hear It's Cancer: A Guide to Navigating the Difficult Journey Ahead*
LJ - v140 - i11 - June 15 2015 - p110(1) [501+]
Leigh, Eva - *Forever Your Earl*
PW - v262 - i36 - Sept 7 2015 - p52(1) [51-500]
Scandal Takes the Stage
BL - v112 - i4 - Oct 15 2015 - p27(1) [51-500]
Leigh, Fiona - *The Eudemian Ethics on the Voluntary, Friendship, and Luck: The Sixth S.V. Keeling Colloquium in Ancient Philosophy*
Class R - v65 - i1 - April 2015 - p66-68 [501+]
Leigh, Garrett - *Misfits*
BL - v111 - i13 - March 1 2015 - p29(1) [51-500]
PW - v262 - i1 - Jan 5 2015 - p57(1) [51-500]
Leigh, Geoffrey - *SIV & the Blood Moon*
KR - June 15 2015 - pNA [501+]
Leigh, John - *Touche: The Duel in Literature*
NS - v144 - i5267 - June 19 2015 - p46(2) [501+]
PW - v262 - i15 - April 13 2015 - p71(1) [51-500]
Leigh, Lora - *Wicked Lies*
PW - v262 - i25 - June 22 2015 - p126(1) [51-500]
Leigh, Philip - *Trading with the Enemy: The Covert Economy During the American Civil War*
JSH - v81 - i4 - Nov 2015 - p989(2) [501+]
Leigh, Spencer - *Frank Sinatra: An Extraordinary Life*
Spec - v329 - i9767 - Nov 7 2015 - p46(2) [501+]
Leighton, M. - *Strong Enough*
PW - v262 - i26 - June 29 2015 - p52(1) [51-500]
Leine, Kim - *The Prophets of Eternal Fjord*
BL - v111 - i19-20 - June 1 2015 - p60(1) [51-500]
BooChiTr - July 25 2015 - p13(1) [501+]
KR - May 1 2015 - pNA [501+]
Leiner, Jorge - *On the Edge of Destiny*
c PW - v262 - i31 - August 3 2015 - p21(1) [51-500]
Leininger, Rob - *Gumshoe*
BL - v112 - i5 - Nov 1 2015 - p30(1) [51-500]
LJ - v140 - i15 - Sept 15 2015 - p72(1) [51-500]
PW - v262 - i36 - Sept 7 2015 - p45(1) [51-500]
Leins, Amanda - *Wanderlust Quilts: 10 Modern Projects Inspired by Classic Art and Architecture*
LJ - v140 - i15 - Sept 15 2015 - p77(1) [51-500]
PW - v262 - i31 - August 3 2015 - p53(1) [51-500]
Leipciger, Sarah - *The Mountain Can Wait*
BL - v111 - i16 - April 15 2015 - p26(1) [51-500]
KR - March 15 2015 - pNA [51-500]
NYTBR - Sept 13 2015 - p34(L) [501+]
Leipert, Beverly - *Rural Women's Health*
CWS - v30 - i2-3 - Fall-Winter 2015 - p149(2) [501+]
Leitao, D.D. - *The Pregnant Male as Myth and Metaphor in Classical Greek Literature*
Class R - v65 - i1 - April 2015 - p18-20 [501+]
Leitch, Thomas - *Wikipedia U: Knowledge, Authority and Liberal Education in the Digital Age*
TimHES - i2188 - Jan 29 2015 - p48(1) [501+]
Leiter, Richard - *The Flying Hand of Marco B. (Illus. by Kober, Shahar)*
c BL - v111 - i17 - May 1 2015 - p101(1) [51-500]
c KR - Feb 15 2015 - pNA [51-500]
c SLJ - v61 - i5 - May 2015 - p87(1) [51-500]

Leitman, Margot - *Long Story Short: The Only Storytelling Guide You'll Ever Need*
    LJ - v140 - i16 - Oct 1 2015 - p89(1) [51-500]

Leitz, Beatrice - *La dea di Erice e la sua diffusione nel Mediterraneo. Un culto tra Fenici, Greci e Romani*
    Class R - v65 - i1 - April 2015 - p202-204 [501+]

Lejeune, Maud - *Pourtraits divers de Jean de Tournes: Edition critique et fac-simile du tirage de 1556*
    Ren Q - v68 - i1 - Spring 2015 - p252-253 [501+]

Leland, John - *Readings in Wood: What the Forest Taught Me*
    RVBW - April 2015 - pNA [501+]

Lelchuk, Alan - *Searching for Wallenberg*
    SPBW - June 2015 - pNA [51-500]
    SPBW - July 2015 - pNA [51-500]

LeMahieu, Michael - *Fictions of Fact and Value: The Erasure of Logical Positivism in American Literature, 1945-1975*
    AL - v87 - i3 - Sept 2015 - p611-613 [501+]
    Col Lit - v42 - i1 - Wntr 2015 - p171(3) [501+]

Lemaitre, Pierre - *Camille*
    BL - v111 - i17 - May 1 2015 - p22(2) [51-500]
    The Great Swindle
    KR - July 15 2015 - pNA [501+]
    NYT - Oct 5 2015 - pC1(L) [501+]
    PW - v262 - i28 - July 13 2015 - p43(1) [51-500]
    TLS - i5876 - Nov 13 2015 - p20(1) [501+]

LeMaster, Michelle - *Creating and Contesting Carolina: Proprietary Era Histories*
    JSH - v81 - i2 - May 2015 - p427(3) [501+]
    JAH - v102 - i2 - Sept 2015 - p529-529 [501+]
    W&M Q - v72 - i1 - Jan 2015 - p179-181 [501+]

Lembeck, Harry - *Taking on Theodore Roosevelt: How One Senator Defied the President on Brownsville and Shook American Politics*
    J Mil H - v79 - i2 - April 2015 - p502-503 [501+]

Lemberger, Michal - *After Abel and Other Stories*
    BL - v111 - i13 - March 1 2015 - p27(1) [51-500]
    KR - Feb 15 2015 - pNA [501+]
    PW - v262 - i6 - Feb 9 2015 - p51(1) [51-500]

Lemelin, Harvey Raynald - *The Management of Insects in Recreation and Tourism*
    QRB - v90 - i2 - June 2015 - p212(2) [501+]

LeMenager, Stephanie - *Living Oil: Petroleum Culture in the American Century*
    Am Q - v67 - i2 - June 2015 - p529-540 [501+]
    JAH - v102 - i1 - June 2015 - p313-314 [501+]

Lemerle, Frederique - *Architectures de papier: La France et l'Europe*
    Ren Q - v68 - i1 - Spring 2015 - p256-258 [501+]

Lemieux, Genevieve - *La lecon de trombone (Illus. by Eid, Jean-Paul)*
    c Res Links - v20 - i5 - June 2015 - p40(1) [51-500]

Lemire, Jeff - *Bloodshot Reborn: Colorado*
    PW - v262 - i25 - June 22 2015 - p128(1) [51-500]
    The Valiant
    PW - v262 - i19 - May 11 2015 - p44(1) [51-500]

Lemke, Donald - *Book-o-Beards: A Wearable Book (Illus. by Nassner, Alyssa)*
    c PW - v262 - i6 - Feb 9 2015 - p66(2) [51-500]
    Superman: A Giant Attack (Illus. by Ferguson, Lee)
    c BL - v111 - i22 - August 1 2015 - p75(1) [51-500]

Lemke, Lisa - *The Summer Table: Recipes and Menus for Casual Outdoor Entertaining*
    LJ - v140 - i7 - April 15 2015 - p110(2) [51-500]

Lemke, Michael - *Vor der Mauer. Berlin in der Ost-West-Konkurrenz 1948 bis 1961*
    GSR - v38 - i2 - May 2015 - p445-3 [501+]

Lemmer, T.J. - *The Wizard and the Quient*
    c CH Bwatch - July 2015 - pNA [51-500]

Lemmon, Alfred E. - *French Baroque Music of New Orleans: Spiritual Songs from the Ursuline Convent*
    Notes - v72 - i2 - Dec 2015 - p410(5) [501+]

Lemmon, Gayle Tzemach - *Ashley's War: The Untold Story of a Team of Women Soldiers on the Special Ops Battlefield*
    CSM - May 18 2015 - pNA [51-500]
    LJ - v140 - i12 - July 1 2015 - p90(1) [51-500]
    Parameters - v45 - i2 - Summer 2015 - p152(2) [501+]

Lemnitzer, Jan Martin - *Power, Law and the End of Privateering*
    AHR - v120 - i2 - April 2015 - p580-581 [501+]
    NWCR - v68 - i2 - Spring 2015 - p139(2) [501+]

Lemonier, Aurelien - *Frank Gehry*
    LJ - v140 - i10 - June 1 2015 - p98(1) [51-500]

Lemov, Michael R. - *Car Safety Wars: One Hundred Years of Technology, Politics, and Death*
    RVBW - July 2015 - pNA [501+]

Lemov, Rebecca - *Database of Dreams*
    KR - Oct 1 2015 - pNA [501+]

Lempke, Donald - *Book-o-Beards: A Wearable Book (Illus. by Lentz, Bob)*
    c KR - July 1 2015 - pNA [51-500]

Lenain, Philippe - *Histoire litteraire des benedictins de Saint-Maur, Tome Quatrieme (1724-1787)*
    CHR - v101 - i4 - Autumn 2015 - p942(2) [501+]

Lende, Heather - *Find the Good: Unexpected Life Lessons from a Small-Town Obituary Writer (Read by Lende, Heather). Audiobook Review*
    LJ - v140 - i14 - Sept 1 2015 - p69(1) [51-500]
    PW - v262 - i30 - July 27 2015 - p65(1) [51-500]
    Find the Good: Unexpected Life Lessons from a Small-Town Obituary Writer
    BL - v111 - i12 - Feb 15 2015 - p4(1) [501+]
    Bwatch - July 2015 - pNA [51-500]
    KR - Feb 1 2015 - pNA [51-500]
    NYTBR - May 10 2015 - p38(L) [501+]
    PW - v262 - i8 - Feb 23 2015 - p66(1) [51-500]

Lendler, Ian - *The Stratford Zoo Midnight Revue Presents Romeo and Juliet (Illus. by Giallongo, Zack)*
    c BL - v112 - i2 - Sept 15 2015 - p53(1) [51-500]
    c KR - July 15 2015 - pNA [51-500]

Lendroth, Susan - *Old Manhattan Has Some Farms (Illus. by Endle, Kate)*
    c HB Guide - v26 - i1 - Spring 2015 - p175(1) [51-500]

Lengel, Edward G. - *First Entrepreneur*
    KR - Dec 15 2015 - pNA [501+]
    The Papers of George Washington, Vol. 17: 1 October 1794-31 March 1795
    JSH - v81 - i1 - Feb 2015 - p175(2) [501+]
    Thunder and Flames: Americans in the Crucible of Combat, 1917-1918
    J Mil H - v79 - i4 - Oct 2015 - p1174-1175 [501+]

Lenger, Friedrich - *Metropolen der Moderne: Eine europaische Stadtgeschichte seit 1850*
    AHR - v120 - i1 - Feb 2015 - p179-181 [501+]

Lenhard-Schramm, Niklas - *Konstrukteure der Nation: Geschichtsprofessoren als Politische Akteure in Vormarz und Revolution 1848/49*
    HNet - July 2015 - pNA [501+]

Lennie, Charles - *Apatosaurus*
    c HB Guide - v26 - i1 - Spring 2015 - p152(1) [51-500]
    Bulldozers
    c HB Guide - v26 - i1 - Spring 2015 - p173(1) [51-500]
    Pteranodon
    c HB Guide - v26 - i1 - Spring 2015 - p152(1) [51-500]
    Stegosaurus
    c HB Guide - v26 - i1 - Spring 2015 - p152(1) [51-500]
    Triceratops
    c HB Guide - v26 - i1 - Spring 2015 - p152(1) [51-500]

Lennon, J.L. - *Pollution and Religion in Ancient Rome*
    Class R - v65 - i1 - April 2015 - p208-210 [501+]

Lennon, J. Robert - *See You in Paradise: Stories*
    NYTBR - Jan 18 2015 - p12(L) [501+]

Lennon, Maria T. - *Watch Out, Hollywood!: More Confessions of a So-Called Middle Child*
    c HB Guide - v26 - i2 - Fall 2015 - p91(1) [51-500]

Lennox, John C. - *Against the Flow: The Inspiration of Daniel in an Age of Relativism*
    Ch Today - v59 - i4 - May 2015 - p65(1) [51-500]
    RVBW - June 2015 - pNA [501+]

Lennox, Michael - *Llewellyn's Complete Dictionary of Dreams: Over 1,000 Dream Symbols and Their Universal Meanings*
    LJ - v140 - i6 - April 1 2015 - p115(2) [51-500]
    RVBW - July 2015 - pNA [51-500]

Lennox, Patricia - *Shakespeare and Costume*
    TLS - i5857 - July 3 2015 - p26(1) [501+]

Leno, Katrina - *The Half Life of Molly Pierce*
    y HB Guide - v26 - i1 - Spring 2015 - p113(1) [51-500]

Lenoir, Frederic - *Happiness: A Philosopher's Guide*
    Har Bus R - v93 - i7-8 - July-August 2015 - p130(2) [501+]
    KR - Jan 15 2015 - pNA [501+]
    LJ - v140 - i5 - March 15 2015 - p108(1) [51-500]

Lent, Jeffrey - *A Slant of Light*
    BL - v111 - i12 - Feb 15 2015 - p41(1) [51-500]
    KR - Feb 1 2015 - pNA [501+]
    LJ - v140 - i2 - Feb 1 2015 - p74(2) [51-500]
    NYTBR - August 16 2015 - p30(L) [501+]
    PW - v262 - i8 - Feb 23 2015 - p47(1) [51-500]

Lent, John A. - *Asian Comics*
    TLS - i5849 - May 8 2015 - p27(1) [51-500]

Lenz, Karmen - *Raed and Frofer: Christian Poetics in the Old English "Froferboc" Meters*
    Med R - April 2015 - pNA [501+]

Lenzer, Suzanne - *Truly Madly Pizza: One Incredibly Easy Crust, Countless Inspired Combinations and Other Irresistible Tidbits to Make Handmade Pizza a Nightly Affair*
    BL - v111 - i19-20 - June 1 2015 - p21(1) [51-500]

Lenzi, Christy - *Stone Field*
    y KR - Dec 15 2015 - pNA [501+]
    y SLJ - v61 - i12 - Dec 2015 - p123(1) [51-500]

Leo, Per - *Der Wille zum Wesen: Weltanschauungskultur, Charakterologisches Denken und Judenfeindschaft in Deutschland 1890-1940*
    HNet - Feb 2015 - pNA [501+]
    Flut und Boden: Roman einer Familie
    HNet - Jan 2015 - pNA [501+]

LeoGrande, William M. - *Back Channel to Cuba: The Hidden History of Negotiations Between Washington and Havana*
    JAH - v102 - i2 - Sept 2015 - p604-605 [501+]
    NYRB - v62 - i6 - April 2 2015 - p51(3) [501+]

Leon, Donna - *By Its Cover*
    RVBW - April 2015 - pNA [501+]
    Falling in Love
    BL - v111 - i13 - March 1 2015 - p23(1) [51-500]
    KR - Feb 15 2015 - pNA [501+]
    NYTBR - April 5 2015 - p29(L) [501+]
    PW - v262 - i4 - Jan 26 2015 - p147(1) [51-500]
    The Waters of Eternal Youth
    KR - Jan 1 2016 - pNA [501+]

Leon, Luis - *Religion and American Cultures: Tradition, Diversity, and Popular Expression, 2d ed.*
    BL - v111 - i15 - April 1 2015 - p5(1) [51-500]

Leon, Miguel Lopez de - *Galadria: Peter Huddleston & The Mists of the Three Lakes*
    SPBW - Jan 2015 - pNA [51-500]

Leon, Sharon M. - *An Image of God: The Catholic Struggle with Eugenics*
    AHR - v120 - i1 - Feb 2015 - p272-273 [501+]

Leonard, Candy - *Beatleness*
    RVBW - Feb 2015 - pNA [51-500]

Leonard, Christopher - *The Meat Racket: The Secret Takeover of America's Food Business*
    NYTBR - April 5 2015 - p28(L) [501+]
    VQR - v91 - i2 - Spring 2015 - p218-222 [501+]

Leonard, Elmore - *Charlie Martz and Other Stories: The Unpublished Stories*
    BL - v111 - i17 - May 1 2015 - p26(1) [51-500]
    BooChiTr - July 4 2015 - p12(1) [501+]
    KR - April 15 2015 - pNA [501+]
    LJ - v140 - i10 - June 1 2015 - p96(2) [51-500]
    PW - v262 - i14 - April 6 2015 - p35(1) [51-500]
    NYRB - v62 - i14 - Sept 24 2015 - p50(3) [501+]
    Four Novels of the 1970s: Fifty-Two Pickup, Swag, Unknown Man No. 89, The Switch
    NYRB - v62 - i14 - Sept 24 2015 - p50(3) [501+]
    NYTBR - Jan 11 2015 - p26(L) [501+]
    Four Novels of the 1980s: City Primeval, LaBrava, Glitz, Freaky Deaky
    NYRB - v62 - i14 - Sept 24 2015 - p50(3) [501+]

Leonard, John - *Faithful Labourers: A Reception History of Paradise Lost, 1667-1970*
    MP - v112 - i3 - Feb 2015 - p569(589) [501+]

Leonard, Kendra Preston - *Louise Talma: A Life in Composition*
    Notes - v72 - i2 - Dec 2015 - p339(3) [501+]

Leonard, Louise Wareham - *52 Men*
    KR - June 1 2015 - pNA [51-500]

Leonard, M.G. - *Beetle Boy*
    c KR - Nov 15 2015 - pNA [51-500]

Leonard, Mary Helen - *The Natural Beauty Solution: Break Free from Commercial Beauty Products Using Simple Recipes and Natural Ingredients*
    LJ - v140 - i19 - Nov 15 2015 - p83(2) [51-500]

Leonard, Max - *Lanterne Rouge: The Last Man in the Tour de France*
    KR - April 15 2015 - pNA [51-500]
    LJ - v140 - i10 - June 1 2015 - p108(2) [51-500]
    NYTBR - May 31 2015 - p30(L) [501+]

Leonard, Miriam - *Tragic Modernities*
    TimHES - i2217 - August 20 2015 - p50-51 [501+]

Leonard, Richard - *What Are We Doing on Earth for Christ's Sake?*
    AM - v213 - i17 - Nov 30 2015 - p33(3) [501+]
    RVBW - April 2015 - pNA [51-500]

Leonard, Sarah - *The Future We Want: Radical Ideas for the New Century*
    KR - Dec 15 2015 - pNA [501+]

Leonard, Scott A. - *Myths and Legends of Africa*
   c BL - v112 - i6 - Nov 15 2015 - p42(2) [501+]
Myths and Legends of Scandinavia
   c BL - v112 - i6 - Nov 15 2015 - p42(2) [501+]
Myths and Legends of South Asia and Southeast Asia
   c BL - v112 - i6 - Nov 15 2015 - p42(2) [501+]
Leonard, Scott Carol - *Privatization and Transition in Russia in the Early 1990s*
   Slav R - v74 - i2 - Summer 2015 - p428-430 [501+]
Leonard, Stephen Pax - *The Polar North: Ways of Speaking, Ways of Belonging*
   TLS - i5847 - April 24 2015 - p24(1) [501+]
Leone, George - *Kierkegaard's Existentialism*
   KR - August 1 2015 - pNA [501+]
Leone, Josh - *Calling Tower*
   KR - Dec 1 2015 - pNA [501+]
Leonetti, Mike - *Iginla Sparks the Flames (Illus. by McLaughlin, Gary)*
   c Res Links - v20 - i3 - Feb 2015 - p6(1) [501+]
Leonhard, Jorn - *Die Buchse der Pandora: Geschichte des Ersten Weltkrieges*
   HER - v130 - i543 - April 2015 - p490(4) [501+]
Leonhardt, Jurgen - *Latin: Story of a World Language*
   Lon R Bks - v37 - i1 - Jan 8 2015 - p32(3) [501+]
Leoni, Francesca - *Eros and Sexuality in Islamic Art*
   Six Ct J - v46 - i3 - Fall 2015 - p679-681 [501+]
Leontiades, Louisa - *The Husband Swap: A True Story of Unconventional Love*
   RVBW - June 2015 - pNA [51-500]
Leotta, Allison - *A Good Killing*
   KR - March 1 2015 - pNA [501+]
   PW - v262 - i9 - March 2 2015 - p65(1) [51-500]
Leovy, Jill - *Ghettoside: A True Story of Murder in America (Read by Lowman, Rebecca). Audiobook Review*
   LJ - v140 - i8 - May 1 2015 - p43(2) [51-500]
Ghettoside: A True Story of Murder in America
   Econ - v414 - i8928 - March 7 2015 - p86(US) [501+]
   NYT - Jan 23 2015 - pC32(L) [501+]
   NYTBR - Jan 25 2015 - p1(L) [501+]
Ghettoside: Investigating a Homicide Epidemic
   NS - v144 - i5263 - May 22 2015 - p50(2) [501+]
   TimHES - i2211 - July 9 2015 - p51(1) [501+]
Lepenies, Wolf - *Auguste Comte: Die Macht der Zeichen*
   CS - v44 - i3 - May 2015 - p305-314 [501+]
Leporatti, Roberto - *Il Poeta e il suo pubblico: Lettura e commento dei testi lirici nel Cinquecento Convegno internazionale di Studi*
   Ren Q - v68 - i2 - Summer 2015 - p743-745 [501+]
Lepore, Jill - *The Secret History of Wonder Woman (Read by Lepore, Jill). Audiobook Review*
   LJ - v140 - i2 - Feb 1 2015 - p47(1) [51-500]
The Secret History of Wonder Woman
   Nation - v300 - i23 - June 8 2015 - p35(5) [501+]
   Reason - v46 - i10 - March 2015 - p62(1) [51-500]
   TLS - i5839 - Feb 27 2015 - p30(1) [501+]
   Wom R Bks - v32 - i3 - May-June 2015 - p5(3) [501+]
Lepp, Bil - *The King of Little Things (Illus. by Wenzel, David T.)*
   RVBW - Jan 2015 - pNA [51-500]
Lepucki, Edan - *California*
   y HR - v68 - i1 - Spring 2015 - p151-157 [501+]
Lerangis, Peter - *The Curse of the King (Illus. by Norstrand, Torstein)*
   c HB Guide - v26 - i2 - Fall 2015 - p91(1) [501+]
Lerman, Amy E. - *Arresting Citizenship: The Democratic Consequences of American Crime Control*
   AJS - v121 - i1 - July 2015 - p308(3) [501+]
   CrimJR - v40 - i2 - June 2015 - p238-240 [501+]
Lerman, Dawn - *My Fat Dad*
   KR - July 15 2015 - pNA [501+]
Lerman, Eleanor - *Radiomen*
   G&L Rev W - v22 - i3 - May-June 2015 - p41(2) [501+]
Lerner, Ben - *10:04 (Read by Summerer, Eric Michael). Audiobook Review*
   PW - v262 - i5 - Feb 2 2015 - p55(1) [51-500]
10:04
   Lon R Bks - v37 - i4 - Feb 19 2015 - p25(2) [501+]
   Nation - v300 - i9 - March 2 2015 - p27(5) [501+]
   NS - v144 - i5245 - Jan 16 2015 - p51(1) [501+]
   Spec - v327 - i9723 - Jan 3 2015 - p26(1) [501+]
Leaving the Atocha Station
   Obs - Jan 4 2015 - p31 [501+]
Lerner, Helene - *The Confidence Myth: Why Women Undervalue Their Skills and How To Get Over It*
   LJ - v140 - i2 - Feb 1 2015 - p92(1) [51-500]

Lerner, Scott - *The Fraternity Of The Soul Eater*
   RVBW - June 2015 - pNA [51-500]
Leroi, Armand Marie - *The Lagoon: How Aristotle Invented Science*
   Lon R Bks - v37 - i13 - July 2 2015 - p25(2) [501+]
   NYTBR - Dec 27 2015 - p24(L) [501+]
   TLS - i5841 - March 13 2015 - p22(1) [501+]
Lertzman, Richard A. - *The Life and Times of Mickey Rooney*
   KR - Sept 1 2015 - pNA [501+]
   NYTBR - Dec 6 2015 - p70(L) [501+]
Les Becquets, Diane - *Breaking Wild*
   BL - v112 - i5 - Nov 1 2015 - p29(1) [51-500]
   KR - Nov 1 2015 - pNA [51-500]
   LJ - v140 - i19 - Nov 15 2015 - p77(2) [51-500]
   PW - v262 - i44 - Nov 2 2015 - p57(1) [51-500]
Lescroart, John - *The Fall (Read by Colacci, David). Audiobook Review*
   PW - v262 - i26 - June 29 2015 - p62(1) [51-500]
The Fall
   BL - v111 - i17 - May 1 2015 - p34(1) [51-500]
   KR - March 1 2015 - pNA [51-500]
   PW - v262 - i9 - March 2 2015 - p64(1) [51-500]
Leshay, Tracy - *She Yelled, I Screamed ... She Pulled My Hair!*
   c CH Bwatch - May 2015 - pNA [51-500]
She Yelled, I Screamed ... She Pulled My Hair! (Illus. by Renald, James)
   c KR - Feb 1 2015 - pNA [51-500]
Lesiv, Mariya - *The Return of Ancestral Gods: Modern Ukrainian Paganism as an Alternative Vision for a Nation*
   WestFolk - v74 - i1 - Wntr 2015 - p91-93 [501+]
Leslie, Alex - *The Things I Heard about You*
   Can Lit - i224 - Spring 2015 - p128 [501+]
Leslie, Barbra - *Cracked*
   BL - v112 - i4 - Oct 15 2015 - p18(1) [51-500]
   KR - Sept 15 2015 - pNA [51-500]
   PW - v262 - i37 - Sept 14 2015 - p44(1) [51-500]
Leslie, David - *Tourism Enterprise: Developments, Management and Sustainability*
   RVBW - August 2015 - pNA [51-500]
Leslie, Ian - *Curious: The Desire to Know and Why Your Future Depends on It*
   CC - v132 - i1 - Jan 7 2015 - p35(3) [501+]
Leslie, Mark Alan - *True North: Tice's Story*
   PW - v262 - i17 - April 27 2015 - p60(1) [51-500]
Lesowitz, Nina - *The Grateful Life: The Secret to Happiness, and the Science of Contentment*
   RVBW - Feb 2015 - pNA [501+]
Lessac, Frane - *A Is for Australia: A Factastic Tour*
   c Magpies - v30 - i1 - March 2015 - p22(1) [501+]
Lesser, Jeffrey - *Immigration, Ethnicity, and National Identity in Brazil, 1808 to the Present*
   HAHR - v95 - i4 - Nov 2015 - p680-681 [501+]
   JIH - v45 - i3 - Wntr 2015 - p449-451 [501+]
Lesser, Rachel Levy - *Who's Going to Watch My Kids? Working Mothers' Humorous and Heartfelt Struggles to Find and Hold on to the Elusive Perfect Nanny*
   SPBW - June 2015 - pNA [501+]
Lesser, Wendy - *Why I Read: The Serious Pleasure of Books*
   NYTBR - March 22 2015 - p28(L) [501+]
Lesser, Zachary - *Hamlet after Q1: An Uncanny History of the Shakespearean Text*
   PQ - v94 - i1-2 - Wntr-Spring 2015 - p195(5) [501+]
   TLS - i5866 - Sept 4 2015 - p8(1) [501+]
Lessing, Doris - *The Sun between Their Fleet*
   TimHES - i2229 - Nov 12 2015 - p46(1) [51-500]
The Sweetest Dream
   Lon R Bks - v37 - i17 - Sept 10 2015 - p27(2) [501+]
Lessing, Gotthold Ephraim - *Lessing's Hamburg Dramaturgy: A New and Complete Translation*
   Theat J - v67 - i2 - May 2015 - p347-359 [501+]
Lester, Alan - *Colonization and the Origins of Humanitarian Governance: Protecting Aborigines across the Nineteenth-Century British Empire*
   JIH - v46 - i1 - Summer 2015 - p115-116 [501+]
Lester, Alison - *Noni the Pony Goes to the Beach (Illus. by Lester, Alison)*
   c SLJ - v61 - i10 - Oct 2015 - p70(2) [501+]
Lester, Anne E. - *Creating Cistercian Nuns: The Women's Religious Movement and Its Reform in Thirteenth-Century Champagne*
   Specu - v90 - i4 - Oct 2015 - p1143-1145 [501+]

Lester, Helen - *Laugh-Along Lessons: 5 Minute Stories (Illus. by Munsinger, Lynn)*
   c CH Bwatch - May 2015 - pNA [51-500]
   c HB Guide - v26 - i2 - Fall 2015 - p41(1) [51-500]
Pookins Gets Her Way (Illus. by Munsinger, Lynn)
   c CH Bwatch - March 2015 - pNA [51-500]
Score One for the Sloths (Illus. by Munsinger, Lynn)
   c CH Bwatch - March 2015 - pNA [51-500]
The Sheep in Wolf's Clothing (Illus. by Munsinger, Lynn)
   c HB Guide - v26 - i1 - Spring 2015 - p36(1) [51-500]
Tacky and the Haunted Igloo (Illus. by Munsinger, Lynn)
   c BL - v111 - i19-20 - June 1 2015 - p125(1) [51-500]
   c CH Bwatch - August 2015 - pNA [501+]
   c HB - v91 - i5 - Sept-Oct 2015 - p68(1) [51-500]
   c KR - August 1 2015 - pNA [501+]
   c PW - v262 - i30 - July 27 2015 - p67(1) [51-500]
   c SLJ - v61 - i9 - Sept 2015 - p107(1) [51-500]
The Wizard, the Fairy, and the Magic Chicken (Illus. by Munsinger, Lynn)
   c HB Guide - v26 - i1 - Spring 2015 - p36(1) [51-500]
Lester, Julius - *Pharaoh's Daughter*
   y BL - v111 - i16 - April 15 2015 - p58(1) [501+]
Lester, Meera - *A Beeline to Murder*
   PW - v262 - i34 - August 24 2015 - p61(1) [51-500]
Lester, Paul - *In Search of Pharrell Williams*
   y BL - v112 - i5 - Nov 1 2015 - p21(2) [501+]
   LJ - v140 - i16 - Oct 1 2015 - p81(1) [51-500]
Lester, Valerie - *Giambattista Bodoni: His Life and His World*
   BL - v112 - i5 - Nov 1 2015 - p17(2) [51-500]
   RVBW - Oct 2015 - pNA [501+]
Lesynski, Loris - *Crazy about Hockey! (Illus. by Rasmussen, Gerry)*
   c Res Links - v21 - i1 - Oct 2015 - p8(1) [51-500]
Leszczak, Bob - *Encyclopedia of Pop Music Aliases, 1950-2000*
   BL - v112 - i5 - Nov 1 2015 - p26(1) [51-500]
From Small Screen to Vinyl: A Guide to Television Stars Who Made Records, 1950-2000
   BL - v112 - i2 - Sept 15 2015 - p12(1) [51-500]
Who Did It First? Great Pop Cover Songs and Their Original Artists
   PMS - v38 - i2 - July 2015 - p400(4) [501+]
Lethbridge, Lucy - *Servants: A Downstairs History of Britain from the Nineteenth Century to Modern Times*
   Historian - v77 - i3 - Fall 2015 - p614(2) [501+]
Lethem, Jonathan - *The Best American Comics 2015*
   BL - v112 - i4 - Oct 15 2015 - p35(1) [51-500]
   PW - v262 - i42 - Oct 19 2015 - p64(1) [51-500]
Lucky Alan and Other Stories
   NYT - March 3 2015 - pC6(L) [501+]
   NYTBR - Feb 22 2015 - p23(L) [501+]
   Spec - v328 - i9756 - August 22 2015 - p36(1) [501+]
   TLS - i5864-5865 - August 21 2015 - p22(1) [501+]
Letherland, Lucy - *Atlas of Adventures*
   c Sch Lib - v63 - i1 - Spring 2015 - p48(1) [51-500]
Letourneau, Jocelyn - *Je me souviens? Le passe du Quebec dans la conscience de sa jeunesse*
   Can Hist R - v96 - i2 - June 2015 - p323(3) [501+]
Letourneau, Roger - *Operation KE: The Cactus Air Force and the Japanese Withdrawal from Guadalcanal*
   APJ - v29 - i2 - March-April 2015 - p171(2) [501+]
Lett, Travis - *Gjelina: Cooking from Venice, California*
   NYTBR - Dec 6 2015 - p20(L) [501+]
   NYTBR - Dec 6 2015 - p20(L) [501+]
Lettrick, Robert - *The Murk*
   c BL - v111 - i15 - April 1 2015 - p80(1) [51-500]
   c HB Guide - v26 - i2 - Fall 2015 - p91(1) [51-500]
   c KR - Feb 15 2015 - pNA [51-500]
   SLJ - v61 - i4 - April 2015 - p147(2) [51-500]
Letts, Tracy - *August: Osage County (Read by Various readers). Audiobook Review*
   LJ - v140 - i3 - Feb 15 2015 - p57(2) [51-500]
August: Osage County (Read by a full cast of performers). Audiobook Review
   PW - v262 - i5 - Feb 2 2015 - p54(1) [51-500]
Leuchtenburg, William E. - *The American President: From Teddy Roosevelt to Bill Clinton*
   KR - Oct 1 2015 - pNA [51-500]
Leun Yang, Gene - *Boxers & Saints (Illus. by Pien, Lark)*
   c HB - v91 - i1 - Jan-Feb 2015 - p41(2) [501+]
Leung, Bryce - *Little Miss Evil*
   c SLJ - v61 - i5 - May 2015 - p103(1) [501+]

Leung, For-Hing - *Da shi dai li de xiao za zhi : "Xin er tong" ban yue kan, 1941-1949*
   Bkbird - v53 - i1 - Wntr 2015 - p97(2) [501+]
Leung, Ping-Chung - *Health, Wellbeing, Competence and Aging*
   QRB - v90 - i1 - March 2015 - p108(1) [501+]
Leustean, Lucian N. - *Orthodox Christianity and Nationalism in Nineteenth Century Southeastern Europe*
   CH - v84 - i3 - Sept 2015 - p678(1) [501+]
   Orthodox Christianity and Nationalism in Nineteenth-Century Southeastern Europe
   E-A St - v67 - i6 - August 2015 - p992(2) [501+]
   J Ch St - v57 - i3 - Summer 2015 - p572-574 [501+]
Leutner, Mechthild - *Preussen, Deutschland und China: Entwicklungslinien und Akteure (1842-1911)*.
   HNet - July 2015 - pNA [501+]
Leutzsch, Andreas - *European National Identities. Elements, Transitions, Conflicts*
   E-A St - v67 - i9 - Nov 2015 - p1504(3) [501+]
Levack, Brian P. - *The Devil Within: Possession and Exorcism in the Christian West*
   HER - v130 - i542 - Feb 2015 - p140(2) [501+]
   Historian - v77 - i1 - Spring 2015 - p175(2) [501+]
   JMH - v87 - i1 - March 2015 - p142(3) [501+]
LeVan, A. Carl - *Dictatorships and Democracy in African Development: The Political Economy of Public Goods Provision in Nigeria*
   Africa T - v62 - i1 - Fall 2015 - p138(4) [501+]
Levander, Caroline Field - *Hotel Life: The Story of a Place Where Anything Can Happen*
   PW - v262 - i6 - Feb 9 2015 - p55(2) [51-500]
Levant, Nina - *The Multisensory Museum: Cross-Disciplinary Perspectives on Touch, Sounds, Smell, Memory, and Space*
   Pub Hist - v37 - i2 - May 2015 - p154(3) [501+]
Levasseur, Brent - *Aoleon the Martian Girl*
   c   SLJ - v61 - i9 - Sept 2015 - p141(1) [51-500]
Levatino, Audrey - *Woman-Powered Farm: Manual for a Self-Sufficient Lifestyle from Homestead to Field*
   LJ - v140 - i11 - June 15 2015 - p105(1) [51-500]
Leveen, Tom - *Random*
   y   HB Guide - v26 - i1 - Spring 2015 - p113(1) [51-500]
   Shackled
   y   KR - May 1 2015 - pNA [51-500]
   y   SLJ - v61 - i7 - July 2015 - p94(1) [51-500]
LeVen, Pauline A. - *The Many-Headed Muse: Tradition and Innovation in Late Classical Greek Lyric Poetry*
   AJP - v136 - i2 - Summer 2015 - p357-361 [501+]
   The Many-Headed Muse. Tradition and Innovation in Late Classical Greek Lyric Poetry
   Class R - v65 - i1 - April 2015 - p20-22 [501+]
Levene, Mark - *The Crisis of Genocide, vol. 1, Devastation: The European Rimlands, 1912-1938*
   HT - v65 - i1 - Jan 2015 - p62(3) [501+]
   The Crisis of Genocide, vol. 2, Annihilation: The European Rimlands, 1939-1953
   HT - v65 - i1 - Jan 2015 - p62(3) [501+]
   Political Fiction
   BL - v111 - i18 - May 15 2015 - p15(1) [51-500]
Levenson, Christopher - *Night Vision*
   Can Lit - i224 - Spring 2015 - p108 [501+]
Levenson, Deborah T. - *Adios Nino: The Gangs of Guatemala City and the Politics of Death*
   CS - v44 - i3 - May 2015 - p375-377 [501+]
   Historian - v77 - i1 - Spring 2015 - p127(2) [501+]
Levenson, Eleanor - *The Election (Illus. by Jagucki, Marek)*
   c   Sch Lib - v63 - i2 - Summer 2015 - p96(1) [51-500]
Levenson, Jon D. - *The Love of God: Divine Gift, Human Gratitude, and Mutual Faithfulness in Judaism*
   CC - v132 - i21 - Oct 14 2015 - p45(3) [501+]
   Comw - v142 - i16 - Oct 9 2015 - p35(2) [501+]
   LJ - v140 - i16 - Oct 1 2015 - p64(2) [501+]
Levenson, Thomas - *The Hunt for Vulcan: And How Albert Einstein Destroyed a Planet, Discovered Relativity, and Deciphered the Universe*
   KR - Sept 15 2015 - pNA [501+]
   Nature - v528 - i7581 - Dec 10 2015 - p191(1) [51-500]
   PW - v262 - i33 - August 17 2015 - p59(1) [501+]
Leventhal, Josh - *A History of Baseball in 100 Objects: A Tour through the Bats, Balls, Uniforms, Awards, Documents, and Other Artifacts That Tell the Story of the National Pastime*
   LJ - v140 - i9 - May 15 2015 - p94(2) [501+]
   LJ - v140 - i11 - June 15 2015 - p112(2) [51-500]

Lever, Jill - *The Worm Who Knew Karate! (Illus. by Denton, Terry)*
   c   Magpies - v30 - i3 - July 2015 - p27(1) [501+]
Leverentz, Andrea M. - *The Ex-Prisoner's Dilemma: How Women Negotiate Competing Narratives of Reentry and Desistance*
   AJS - v120 - i6 - May 2015 - p1864(1) [501+]
Levete, Sarah - *Undercover Story: The Hidden Story of Eating Disorders*
   c   CH Bwatch - Feb 2015 - pNA [51-500]
Levett, John - *The Nick of Time*
   TLS - i5872 - Oct 16 2015 - p23(1) [501+]
Levey, Joel - *Living in Balance*
   SPBW - March 2015 - pNA [51-500]
Levi, Primo - *The Complete Works of Primo Levi*
   Atl - v316 - i5 - Dec 2015 - p84(13) [501+]
   HM - v331 - i1987 - Dec 2015 - p82(6) [501+]
   Nat R - v67 - i18 - Oct 5 2015 - p40(2) [501+]
   NY - v91 - i29 - Sept 28 2015 - p68 [501+]
   NYRB - v62 - i17 - Nov 5 2015 - p28(3) [501+]
   KR - July 1 2015 - pNA [51-500]
Leviant, Curt - *King of Yiddish*
   KR - Oct 15 2015 - pNA [51-500]
Levick, Barbara M. - *Faustina I and II: Imperial Women of the Golden Age*
   Class R - v65 - i2 - Oct 2015 - p539-541 [501+]
Levie, Sophie - *La rivista 'Commerce' e Marguerite Caetani, vol. 2: Giuseppe Ungaretti - lettere a Marguerite Caetani*
   MLR - v110 - i3 - July 2015 - p884-885 [501+]
Levien, David - *Signature Kill*
   BL - v111 - i11 - Feb 1 2015 - p28(1) [51-500]
   KR - Jan 15 2015 - pNA [51-500]
   PW - v262 - i3 - Jan 19 2015 - p62(1) [51-500]
Levin, Adam - *Swiped: How to Protect Yourself in a World Full of Scammers, Phishers, and Identity Thieves*
   Har Bus R - v93 - i11 - Nov 2015 - p150(2) [501+]
   KR - Sept 15 2015 - pNA [51-500]
Levin, Meyer - *Compulsion*
   PW - v262 - i8 - Feb 23 2015 - p53(1) [51-500]
   SPBW - May 2015 - pNA [51-500]
Levin Rojo, Danna A. - *Return to Aztlan: Indians, Spaniards, and the Invention of Nuevo Mexico*
   AHR - v120 - i3 - June 2015 - p1078-1079 [501+]
   SHQ - v118 - i4 - April 2015 - p427-428 [501+]
Levin, Rona - *Comic, Curious and Quirky: News Stories from Centuries Past*
   TLS - i5836 - Feb 6 2015 - p27(1) [501+]
Levin, Sheila - *Musical Chairs*
   SPBW - August 2015 - pNA [51-500]
Levin, Yuval - *The Great Debate: Edmund Burke, Thomas Paine, and the Birth of Right and Left*
   Historian - v77 - i3 - Fall 2015 - p616(2) [501+]
   MA - v57 - i1 - Wntr 2015 - p57(8) [501+]
   NYTBR - Feb 22 2015 - p32(L) [501+]
   RAH - v43 - i2 - June 2015 - p193-202 [501+]
Levine, Adam Seth - *American Insecurity: Why Our Economic Fears Lead to Political Inaction*
   LJ - v140 - i3 - Feb 15 2015 - p116(1) [51-500]
Levine, Alex - *Darwinistas: The Construction of Evolutionary Thought in Nineteenth Century Argentina*
   Isis - v106 - i1 - March 2015 - p197(2) [501+]
Levine, Allan - *Toronto: Biography of a City*
   Beav - v95 - i3 - June-July 2015 - p54(1) [501+]
Levine, Amy-Jill - *Short Stories by Jesus: The Enigmatic Parables of a Controversial Rabbi*
   CC - v132 - i6 - March 18 2015 - p41(2) [501+]
Levine, Anna - *Jodie's Shabbat Surprise (Illus. by Topaz, Ksenia)*
   c   HB Guide - v26 - i2 - Fall 2015 - p42(1) [51-500]
   c   KR - March 15 2015 - pNA [51-500]
   c   PW - v262 - i11 - March 16 2015 - p87(1) [51-500]
Levine, Carol - *Living in the Land of Limbo: Fiction and Poetry about Family Caregiving*
   TLS - i5841 - March 13 2015 - p5(1) [501+]
Levine, Caroline - *Forms: Whole, Rhythm, Hierarchy, Network*
   Lon R Bks - v37 - i16 - August 27 2015 - p11(2) [501+]
   TLS - i5861 - July 31 2015 - p27(1) [501+]
Levine, Deborah A. - *The Icing on the Cake*
   c   KR - July 15 2015 - pNA [51-500]
   Kitchen Chaos
   c   HB Guide - v26 - i2 - Fall 2015 - p91(1) [51-500]
Levine, Emily J. - *Dreamland of Humanists: Warburg, Cassirer, Panofsky, and the Hamburg School*
   AHR - v120 - i3 - June 2015 - p1133-1134 [501+]
   CEH - v48 - i1 - March 2015 - p124-126 [501+]
   GSR - v38 - i1 - Feb 2015 - p198-201 [501+]

Levine, Frances - *Battles and Massacres on the Southwestern Frontier: Historical and Archaeological Perspectives*
   Roundup M - v22 - i6 - August 2015 - p41(1) [501+]
Levine, Gail Carson - *Stolen Magic*
   c   HB Guide - v26 - i2 - Fall 2015 - p91(1) [51-500]
   y   HB - v91 - i2 - March-April 2015 - p102(2) [51-500]
   KR - Feb 1 2015 - pNA [51-500]
   SLJ - v61 - i3 - March 2015 - p138(1) [51-500]
   y   VOYA - v38 - i1 - April 2015 - p80(1) [51-500]
   Writer to Writer: From Think to Ink
   y   CCB-B - v68 - i6 - Feb 2015 - p319(1) [51-500]
   c   HB Guide - v26 - i1 - Spring 2015 - p187(1) [51-500]
Levine, Judith A. - *Ain't No Trust: How Bosses, Boyfriends, and Bureaucrats Fail Low-Income Mothers and Why It Matters*
   CS - v44 - i3 - May 2015 - p377-378 [501+]
   Soc Ser R - v89 - i1 - March 2015 - p214(5) [501+]
Levine, Kristin - *The Paper Cowboy (Read by Hoppe, Lincoln). Audiobook Review*
   c   BL - v111 - i16 - April 15 2015 - p64(1) [51-500]
   SLJ - v61 - i2 - Feb 2015 - p50(1) [51-500]
   The Paper Cowboy
   y   BL - v111 - i16 - April 15 2015 - p57(1) [501+]
   y   HB - v91 - i1 - Jan-Feb 2015 - p84(1) [51-500]
   c   HB Guide - v26 - i1 - Spring 2015 - p84(1) [51-500]
Levine, Lee I. - *Visual Judaism in Late Antiquity: Historical Contexts of Jewish Art*
   HNet - August 2015 - pNA [501+]
Levine, Marc N. - *Obsidian Reflections: Symbolic Dimensions of Obsidian in Mesoamerica*
   Lat Ant - v26 - i2 - June 2015 - p279(2) [501+]
Levine, Martha Peaslee - *The Twelve Days of Christmas in Pennsylvania (Illus. by Dougherty, Rachel)*
   c   HB Guide - v26 - i1 - Spring 2015 - p22(1) [51-500]
Levine, Michelle - *Allergies*
   c   HB Guide - v26 - i1 - Spring 2015 - p171(1) [51-500]
   Animal Kingdom Series
   c   HB Guide - v26 - i1 - Spring 2015 - p160(1) [51-500]
   Fish
   c   HB Guide - v26 - i1 - Spring 2015 - p161(1) [51-500]
   Mammals
   c   CH Bwatch - March 2015 - pNA [51-500]
   c   HB Guide - v26 - i1 - Spring 2015 - p165(1) [51-500]
Levine, Ondrea - *The Healing I Took Birth For: Practicing the Art of Compassion*
   PW - v262 - i15 - April 13 2015 - p75(1) [51-500]
Levine, Paul - *Bum Rap*
   BL - v111 - i17 - May 1 2015 - p22(1) [51-500]
   KR - May 1 2015 - pNA [51-500]
   PW - v262 - i17 - April 27 2015 - p55(1) [51-500]
Levine, Robert S. - *The Lives of Frederick Douglas*
   KR - Nov 15 2015 - pNA [501+]
Levine, Sarah - *Tooth by Tooth (Illus. by Spookytooth, T. S.)*
   c   KR - Dec 15 2015 - pNA [51-500]
LeVine, Steve - *The Powerhouse: Inside the Invention of a Battery to Save the World*
   Econ - v414 - i8927 - Feb 28 2015 - p76(US) [501+]
   Nature - v518 - i7540 - Feb 26 2015 - p481(1) [51-500]
Leving, Yuri - *Marketing Literature and Posthumous Legacies: The Symbolic Capital of Leonid Andreev and Vladimir Nabokov*
   Slav R - v74 - i3 - Fall 2015 - p672-673 [501+]
Levinson, Cynthia - *Hillary Rodham Clinton: Do All the Good You Can*
   c   BL - v112 - i5 - Nov 1 2015 - p38(1) [501+]
   c   PW - v262 - i42 - Oct 19 2015 - p78(1) [501+]
   y   SLJ - v61 - i11 - Nov 2015 - p134(1) [51-500]
   y   VOYA - v38 - i5 - Dec 2015 - p77(1) [51-500]
   Watch Out for Flying Kids! How Two Circuses, Two Countries, and Nine Kids Confront Conflict and Build Community
   c   BL - v111 - i19-20 - June 1 2015 - p79(1) [51-500]
   c   KR - May 15 2015 - pNA [51-500]
   c   SLJ - v61 - i8 - August 2015 - p128(1) [51-500]
Levinson, Gary - *The Books of Jonathan: Four Men, One God*
   Tikkun - v30 - i1 - Wntr 2015 - pNA [51-500]

Book Review Index 2016 Cumulation LEWIS • 277

Levinson, Sanford - *An Argument Open to All: Reading The Federalist in the Twenty-First Century*
PW - v262 - i37 - Sept 14 2015 - p55(1) [51-500]
Levinson, Steve - *The Power to Get Things Done (Whether You Feel Like It or Not).*
PW - v262 - i48 - Nov 30 2015 - p52(1) [51-500]
Levis, Caron - *Ida, Always (Illus. by Santoso, Charles)*
c KR - Dec 1 2015 - pNA [51-500]
c PW - v262 - i48 - Nov 30 2015 - p60(1) [51-500]
Levis, Larry - *The Darkening Trapeze: Last Poems*
PW - v262 - i52 - Dec 21 2015 - p127(1) [51-500]
Levison, Jack - *40 Days with the Holy Spirit*
CC - v132 - i6 - March 18 2015 - p43(1) [51-500]
Inspired: The Holy Spirit and the Mind of Faith
Intpr - v69 - i4 - Oct 2015 - p493(3) [501+]
Leviston, Frances - *Disinformation*
NS - v144 - i5262 - May 15 2015 - p46(2) [501+]
Levithan, David - *Another Day (Read by McInerney, Kathleen). Audiobook Review*
y SLJ - v61 - i11 - Nov 2015 - p73(1) [51-500]
Another Day
y BL - v111 - i19-20 - June 1 2015 - p94(1) [51-500]
y HB - v91 - i4 - July-August 2015 - p139(1) [51-500]
y KR - June 1 2015 - pNA [51-500]
y Magpies - v30 - i4 - Sept 2015 - p41(2) [501+]
y SLJ - v61 - i7 - July 2015 - p94(2) [51-500]
Hold Me Closer: The Tiny Cooper Story
y BL - v111 - i12 - Feb 15 2015 - p80(1) [51-500]
y CCB-B - v68 - i8 - April 2015 - p410(1) [51-500]
y HB - v91 - i2 - March-April 2015 - p103(1) [51-500]
y HB Guide - v26 - i2 - Fall 2015 - p129(1) [51-500]
y KR - Jan 15 2015 - pNA [51-500]
y Magpies - v30 - i1 - March 2015 - p41(1) [501+]
y PW - v262 - i2 - Jan 12 2015 - p61(1) [51-500]
y PW - v262 - i49 - Dec 2 2015 - p92(1) [51-500]
y SLJ - v61 - i3 - March 2015 - p159(1) [51-500]
y Teach Lib - v42 - i5 - June 2015 - p18(1) [51-500]
Levitin, Daniel - *The Organised Mind: Thinking Straight in the Age of Information Overload*
NS - v144 - i5266 - June 12 2015 - p46(2) [501+]
Levitsky, Sandra R. - *Caring for Our Own: Why There Is No Political Demand for New American Social Welfare Rights*
AJS - v120 - i6 - May 2015 - p1857(3) [501+]
Soc Ser R - v89 - i2 - June 2015 - p417(4) [501+]
Levitt, Peggy - *Artifacts and Allegiances: How Museums Put the Nation and the World on Display*
LJ - v140 - i14 - Sept 1 2015 - p99(1) [51-500]
UtneADi - i188 - Fall 2015 - p89(1) [501+]
Levitt, Steven D. - *When to Rob a Bank ... and 131 More Warped Suggestions and Well-Intended Rants*
KR - April 15 2015 - pNA [501+]
LJ - v140 - i8 - May 1 2015 - p82(2) [51-500]
Levmore, Saul - *American Guy: Masculinity in American Law and Literature*
G&L Rev W - v22 - i2 - March-April 2015 - p42(2) [501+]
TLS - i5834 - Jan 23 2015 - p27(1) [501+]
Levocz, Reynold J. - *The Spear of Longinus*
SPBW - Nov 2015 - pNA [51-500]
Levoy, Jill - *Ghettoside: A True Story of Murder in America (Read by Lowman, Rebecca). Audiobook Review*
PW - v262 - i17 - April 27 2015 - p71(2) [51-500]
Levs, Josh - *All In: How Our Work-First Culture Fails Dads, Families, and Businesses--and How We Can Fix It Together*
KR - March 1 2015 - pNA [501+]
PW - v262 - i11 - March 16 2015 - p80(1) [51-500]
Levy, Aidan - *Dirty Blvd.: The Life and Music of Lou Reed*
BL - v112 - i3 - Oct 1 2015 - p8(1) [51-500]
KR - August 15 2015 - pNA [501+]
Dirty Blvd: The Life and Music of Lou Reed
LJ - v140 - i15 - Sept 15 2015 - p78(2) [51-500]
Levy, Andrea - *The Long Song*
TimHES - i2221 - Sept 17 2015 - p45(1) [501+]
Levy, Andrew - *Huck Finn's America: Mark Twain and the Era That Shaped His Masterpiece*
BL - v111 - i9-10 - Jan 1 2015 - p30(2) [51-500]
Mac - v128 - i3 - Jan 26 2015 - p56(1) [501+]
NY - v91 - i5 - March 23 2015 - p91 [51-500]
NYT - Feb 5 2015 - pC6(L) [501+]
NYTBR - Feb 22 2015 - p16(L) [501+]
Levy, Anne Boles - *The Temple of Doubt*
y KR - June 15 2015 - pNA [51-500]
y VOYA - v38 - i3 - August 2015 - p80(1) [51-500]
Levy, Ariel - *The Best American Essays 2015*
LJ - v140 - i15 - Sept 15 2015 - p74(2) [51-500]
PW - v262 - i35 - August 31 2015 - p76(2) [51-500]
Levy-Bertherat, Deborah - *The Travels of Daniel Ascher*
BL - v111 - i13 - March 1 2015 - p21(1) [51-500]
KR - March 15 2015 - pNA [51-500]
LJ - v140 - i10 - June 1 2015 - p92(3) [501+]
PW - v262 - i9 - March 2 2015 - p63(2) [51-500]
Levy, Ceri - *Nextinction (Illus. by Steadman, Ralph)*
NS - v144 - i5280 - Sept 18 2015 - p62(1) [51-500]
Levy, Dana Alison - *The Misadventures of the Family Fletcher*
c HB Guide - v26 - i1 - Spring 2015 - p84(1) [51-500]
Levy, Debbie - *Dozer's Run: A True Story of a Dog and His Race (Illus. by Panza, Rosana)*
c HB Guide - v26 - i1 - Spring 2015 - p36(1) [51-500]
Levy, Deborah - *Beautiful Mutants and Swallowing Geography: Two Early Novels*
LJ - v140 - i8 - May 1 2015 - p63(2) [51-500]
PW - v262 - i14 - April 6 2015 - p35(2) [51-500]
Black Vodka: Ten Stories
Wom R Bks - v32 - i1 - Jan-Feb 2015 - p30(2) [501+]
Things I Don't Want to Know: On Writing
Wom R Bks - v32 - i1 - Jan-Feb 2015 - p30(2) [501+]
The Unloved
KR - Jan 1 2015 - pNA [51-500]
Levy, Emanuel - *Gay Directors, Gay Films? Pedro Almodovar, Terence Davies, Todd Haynes, Gus Van Sant, John Waters*
BL - v111 - i21 - July 1 2015 - p15(1) [51-500]
KR - May 15 2015 - pNA [501+]
LJ - v140 - i13 - August 1 2015 - p98(1) [51-500]
PW - v262 - i24 - June 15 2015 - p77(1) [51-500]
Levy, Evonne - *Lexikon of the Hispanic Baroque: Transatlantic Exchange and Transformation*
Ren Q - v68 - i2 - Summer 2015 - p686-687 [501+]
Levy, Ian Christopher - *The Bible in Medieval Tradition: The Letter to the Romans*
Specu - v90 - i1 - Jan 2015 - p271-272 [501+]
Nicholas of Cusa and Islam: Polemic and Dialogue in the Late Middle Ages
Ren Q - v68 - i3 - Fall 2015 - p1059-1060 [501+]
Levy, Jack S. - *The Outbreak of the First World War: Structure, Politics and Decision-Making*
J Mil H - v79 - i4 - Oct 2015 - p1146-1147 [501+]
J Mil H - v79 - i1 - Jan 2015 - p230-231 [501+]
Levy, Janey - *History's Mysteries Series*
c BL - v111 - i19-20 - June 1 2015 - p82(1) [501+]
c BL - v111 - i19-20 - June 1 2015 - p82(1) [51-500]
Levy, Janice - *Papa Gave Me a Stick (Illus. by Shin, Simone)*
c CH Bwatch - August 2015 - pNA [51-500]
c HB Guide - v26 - i2 - Fall 2015 - p42(1) [51-500]
c SLJ - v61 - i8 - August 2015 - p72(2) [51-500]
Levy, Lawrence H. - *Brooklyn on Fire*
KR - Nov 1 2015 - pNA [51-500]
PW - v262 - i44 - Nov 2 2015 - p63(1) [51-500]
Second Street Station
BL - v111 - i17 - May 1 2015 - p44(1) [51-500]
KR - April 1 2015 - pNA [51-500]
PW - v262 - i14 - April 6 2015 - p42(1) [51-500]
Levy, Lital - *Poetic Trespass: Writing between Hebrew and Arabic in Israel/Palestine*
IJMES - v47 - i3 - August 2015 - p605-607 [501+]
Levy, Michelle - *Not after Everything*
y BL - v112 - i2 - Sept 15 2015 - p64(1) [51-500]
y KR - May 15 2015 - pNA [51-500]
y PW - v262 - i20 - May 18 2015 - p87(1) [51-500]
y SLJ - v61 - i5 - May 2015 - p120(2) [51-500]
y VOYA - v38 - i2 - June 2015 - p64(1) [501+]
Levy, Neil - *Addiction and Self-Control: Perspectives from Philosophy, Psychology and Neuroscience*
Ethics - v125 - i2 - Jan 2015 - p586(5) [501+]
Levy, Peter B. - *The Civil Rights Movement in America: From Black Nationalism to the Women's Political Council*
BL - v112 - i2 - Sept 15 2015 - p5(1) [51-500]
Levy, Philip - *George Washington Written upon the Land*
KR - Oct 1 2015 - pNA [501+]
Where the Cherry Tree Grew: The Story of Ferry Farm, George Washington's Boyhood Home
JSH - v81 - i1 - Feb 2015 - p167(2) [501+]
Levy, Reynold - *They Told Me Not to Take That Job: Tumult, Betrayal, Heroics, and the Transformation of Lincoln Center*
Mac - v128 - i22 - June 8 2015 - p57(1) [501+]
NYTBR - May 31 2015 - p46(L) [501+]
SEP - v287 - i3 - May-June 2015 - p24(1) [501+]
Levy, Robert - *The Glittering World*
LJ - v140 - i2 - Feb 1 2015 - p74(1) [51-500]
y SLJ - v61 - i10 - Oct 2015 - p122(2) [51-500]
Levy, Tatiana Salem - *The House in Smyrna*
TLS - i5862 - August 7 2015 - p19(1) [501+]
Lew, Young Ick - *The Making of the First Korean President: Syngman Rhee's Quest for Independence, 1875-1948*
Pac A - v88 - i3 - Sept 2015 - p717 [501+]
Lewando, Fania - *The Vilna Vegetarian Cookbook: Garden-Fresh Recipes Rediscovered and Adapted for Today's Kitchen*
BL - v111 - i16 - April 15 2015 - p10(1) [51-500]
Lewandowska, Eliza - *From Solidarity to Sellout: The Restoration of Capitalism in Poland*
Nation - v300 - i1 - Jan 5 2015 - p27(10) [501+]
Lewens, Tim - *The Meaning of Science: An Introduction to the Philosophy of Science*
KR - Nov 15 2015 - pNA [501+]
PW - v262 - i52 - Dec 21 2015 - p144(2) [51-500]
Lewin, Betsy - *Good Night, Knight (Illus. by Lewin, Betsy)*
c BL - v111 - i19-20 - June 1 2015 - p116(1) [51-500]
c HB Guide - v26 - i2 - Fall 2015 - p60(1) [51-500]
c KR - March 1 2015 - pNA [51-500]
SLJ - v61 - i3 - March 2015 - p119(2) [51-500]
Lewin, Jill - *Shark Island (Illus. by Marnat, Annette)*
c HB Guide - v26 - i2 - Fall 2015 - p71(1) [51-500]
Lewin, Ted - *Animals Work*
c HB Guide - v26 - i1 - Spring 2015 - p168(1) [51-500]
How to Babysit a Leopard: And Other True Stories from Our Travels across Six Continents (Illus. by Lewin, Betsy)
c CCB-B - v69 - i1 - Sept 2015 - p34(2) [51-500]
c HB Guide - v26 - i2 - Fall 2015 - p210(1) [51-500]
c KR - March 15 2015 - pNA [51-500]
How to Babysit a Leopard and Other True Stories from Our Travels across Six Continents (Illus. by Lewin, Betsy)
c PW - v262 - i17 - April 27 2015 - p79(1) [51-500]
How to Babysit a Leopard: And Other True Stories from Our Travels across Six Continents (Illus. by Lewin, Betsy)
SLJ - v61 - i3 - March 2015 - p177(2) [51-500]
How to Babysit a Leopard and Other True Stories from Our Travels across Six Continents (Illus. by Lewin, Ted)
c BL - v111 - i16 - April 15 2015 - p42(2) [51-500]
I See and See (Illus. by Lewin, Ted)
c KR - Dec 1 2015 - pNA [51-500]
Lewinnek, Elaine - *The Working Man's Reward: Chicago's Early Suburbs and the Roots of American Sprawl*
AHR - v120 - i2 - April 2015 - p635-636 [501+]
Lewis, Ali - *Timber Creek Station*
y KR - Dec 15 2015 - pNA [51-500]
Lewis, Amey Parsons - *Nipper of Drayton Hall (Illus. by McElroy, Gerry)*
c KR - August 1 2015 - pNA [51-500]
Lewis, Anne Margaret - *Puddle Jumpers*
c KR - Nov 15 2015 - pNA [51-500]
The Runaway Pumpkin (Illus. by Schindler, S.D.)
c KR - August 1 2015 - pNA [51-500]
The Runaway Santa: A Christmas Adventure Story (Illus. by Zenz, Aaron)
c KR - Sept 1 2015 - pNA [51-500]
Lewis, Bower - *Patience, My Dear*
PW - v262 - i2 - Jan 12 2015 - p41(1) [51-500]
Lewis, C.S. - *The Abolition of Man*
Nat R - v67 - i21 - Nov 19 2015 - p74(2) [501+]
Spenser's Images of Life
Six Ct J - v46 - i1 - Spring 2015 - p172(2) [501+]
Lewis, Charlene M. Boyer - *Elizabeth Patterson Bonaparte: An American Aristocrat in the Early Republic*
HNet - March 2015 - pNA [501+]
Lewis, Clare - *Education through the Years: How Going to School Has Changed in Living Memory*
c HB Guide - v26 - i2 - Fall 2015 - p153(1) [51-500]
Through the Years: How Having Fun Has Changed in Living Memory
c HB Guide - v26 - i2 - Fall 2015 - p157(1) [51-500]
Lewis, Daniel - *The History of Argentina. 2d ed.*
BL - v111 - i13 - March 1 2015 - p14(1) [51-500]
Lewis, David H. - *Hopelessly Hollywood*
KR - May 1 2015 - pNA [51-500]
Lewis, George - *A Power Stronger Than Itself*
TLS - i5854 - June 12 2015 - p10(1) [501+]
Lewis, Gill - *Gorilla Dawn*
c Sch Lib - v63 - i4 - Winter 2015 - p229(1) [51-500]
Moon Bear (Illus. by Gottardo, Alessandro)
c BL - v111 - i12 - Feb 15 2015 - p77(1) [51-500]
c PW - v262 - i4 - Jan 26 2015 - p169(2) [51-500]
c CCB-B - v68 - i10 - June 2015 - p503(1) [51-500]
c HB Guide - v26 - i2 - Fall 2015 - p91(1) [51-500]

Lewis, Gwyneth - *Quantum Poetics: Newcastle/Bloodaxe Poetry Lectures*
    Sch Lib - v63 - i2 - Summer 2015 - p113(1) [51-500]

Lewis, J. Patrick - *Bigfoot Is Missing! (Illus. by MinaLima)*
    c BL - v111 - i16 - April 15 2015 - p44(1) [51-500]
    c HB Guide - v26 - i2 - Fall 2015 - p204(1) [51-500]
    c PW - v262 - i49 - Dec 2 2015 - p54(1) [51-500]
    c SLJ - v61 - i6 - June 2015 - p136(1) [51-500]
Book of Nature Poetry
    c SLJ - v61 - i12 - Dec 2015 - p136(1) [51-500]
Everything Is a Poem: The Best of J. Patrick Lewis (Illus. by Pritelli, Maria Cristina)
    c HB Guide - v26 - i1 - Spring 2015 - p188(1) [51-500]
Harlem Hellfighters (Illus. by Kelley, Gary)
    c HB Guide - v26 - i1 - Spring 2015 - p188(1) [51-500]
Just Joking: Animal Riddles
    c HB Guide - v26 - i2 - Fall 2015 - p195(1) [51-500]
M Is for Monster: A Fantastic Creatures Alphabet (Illus. by Kelley, Gerald)
    c HB Guide - v26 - i1 - Spring 2015 - p144(1) [51-500]
National Geographic Book of Nature Poetry: More Than 200 Poems with Photographs That Float, Zoom, and Bloom!
    c PW - v262 - i49 - Dec 2 2015 - p55(1) [51-500]
The Wren and the Sparrow (Illus. by Nayberg, Yevgenia)
    c CCB-B - v68 - i10 - June 2015 - p503(2) [51-500]
    c HB Guide - v26 - i2 - Fall 2015 - p42(1) [51-500]
    c SLJ - v61 - i4 - April 2015 - p148(1) [51-500]

Lewis, James R. - *Controversial New Religions*
    TLS - i5867 - Sept 11 2015 - p28(1) [501+]

Lewis, Jeremy - *Shades of Greene: One Generation of an English Family*
    TimHES - i2208 - June 18 2015 - p47(1) [501+]

Lewis, John - *Across That Bridge*
    CSM - June 1 2015 - pNA [51-500]
March, Book 2 (Illus. by Powell, Nate)
    y HB - v91 - i3 - May-June 2015 - p127(1) [501+]
    y HB Guide - v26 - i2 - Fall 2015 - p153(1) [51-500]
    y KR - Jan 15 2015 - pNA [51-500]
    LJ - v140 - i3 - Feb 15 2015 - p5(1) [51-500]
    Nat Post - v17 - i74 - Jan 24 2015 - pWP9(1) [501+]
    PW - v262 - i4 - Jan 26 2015 - p157(1) [51-500]

Lewis, Katherine J. - *Kingship and Masculinity in Late Medieval England*
    AHR - v120 - i1 - Feb 2015 - p315-316 [501+]
    HER - v130 - i544 - June 2015 - p725(3) [501+]

Lewis, Linda M. - *Dickens, His Parables, and His Reader*
    VS - v57 - i2 - Wntr 2015 - p325(4) [501+]

Lewis, Marc - *The Biology of Desire: Why Addiction Is Not a Disease*
    KR - June 1 2015 - pNA [501+]
    LJ - v140 - i11 - June 15 2015 - p103(2) [51-500]
    Mac - v128 - i34-35 - August 31 2015 - p78(2) [501+]
    PW - v262 - i21 - May 25 2015 - p49(1) [51-500]

Lewis, Mark - *The Birth of the New Justice: The Internationalization of Crime and Punishment, 1919-1950*
    HNet - May 2015 - pNA [501+]

Lewis, Mary Dewhurst - *Divided Rule: Sovereignty and Empire in French Tunisia, 1881-1938*
    Historian - v77 - i3 - Fall 2015 - p540(2) [501+]

Lewis, Matt - *Last Man Off*
    KR - April 1 2015 - pNA [501+]

Lewis-McCoy, R. L'Heureux - *Inequality in the Promised Land: Race, Resources and Suburban Schooling*
    AJS - v121 - i1 - July 2015 - p292(3) [501+]

Lewis, Michael G. - *The Great Pirate Christmas Battle (Illus. by Jaskiel, Stan)*
    c HB Guide - v26 - i1 - Spring 2015 - p36(1) [51-500]

Lewis, Michael M. - *Flash Boys: A Wall Street Revolt*
    y NYTBR - April 19 2015 - p28(L) [501+]
The New New Thing: A Silicon Valley Story
    CJR - v53 - i5 - Jan-Feb 2015 - p50(5) [501+]

Lewis, Norman - *An Empire of the East: Travels in Indonesia*
    TLS - i5872 - Oct 16 2015 - p8(1) [501+]

Lewis, R.C. - *Spinning Starlight*
    y KR - August 15 2015 - pNA [51-500]
    y VOYA - v38 - i4 - Oct 2015 - p74(1) [51-500]
Stitching Snow
    c SLJ - v61 - i3 - March 2015 - p81(1) [51-500]
    y HB Guide - v26 - i1 - Spring 2015 - p114(1) [51-500]

Lewis, Rachel - *Cook's Coloring Book: Simple Recipes for Beginners (Illus. by Lewis, Rachel)*
    c CH Bwatch - April 2015 - pNA [51-500]

Lewis, Robert E. - *Break Free*
    KR - Jan 15 2015 - pNA [51-500]

Lewis, Robert K. - *Innocent Damage*
    KR - Feb 1 2015 - pNA [51-500]

Lewis, Robin Coste - *Voyage of the Sable Venus and Other Poems*
    LJ - v140 - i17 - Oct 15 2015 - p89(2) [51-500]
    NYT - Dec 2 2015 - pC1(L) [501+]
    PW - v262 - i42 - Oct 19 2015 - p52(1) [51-500]

Lewis, Ronald L. - *Aspiring to Greatness: West Virginia University Since World War II*
    JSH - v81 - i1 - Feb 2015 - p247(2) [501+]

Lewis, Susan - *No Place to Hide*
    LJ - v140 - i14 - Sept 1 2015 - p95(1) [51-500]
Too Close to Home
    KR - Sept 15 2015 - pNA [51-500]
    LJ - v140 - i16 - Oct 1 2015 - p71(1) [51-500]
    BL - v112 - i5 - Nov 1 2015 - p29(1) [51-500]

Lewis, Suzanne - *A Penguin Named Patience: A Hurricane Katrina Rescue Story (Illus. by Anchin, Lisa)*
    c CH Bwatch - March 2015 - pNA [51-500]
    c HB Guide - v26 - i2 - Fall 2015 - p42(1) [51-500]

Lewis, Ted - *GBH*
    BL - v111 - i12 - Feb 15 2015 - p36(2) [51-500]
    KR - April 1 2015 - pNA [51-500]
    LJ - v140 - i2 - Feb 1 2015 - p74(2) [51-500]
    PW - v262 - i8 - Feb 23 2015 - p52(1) [51-500]

Lewis, Thabiti - *Conversations with Toni Cade Bambara*
    Callaloo - v38 - i1 - Wntr 2015 - p202-203 [501+]

Lewis, Todd - *Buddhists: Understanding Buddhism through the Lives of Practitioners*
    HNet - June 2015 - pNA [501+]

Lewis, Tom - *Washington: A History of Our National City*
    LJ - v140 - i14 - Sept 1 2015 - p118(1) [51-500]
    KR - August 15 2015 - pNA [501+]
    PW - v262 - i32 - August 10 2015 - p51(1) [51-500]

Lewman, David - *First Contact (Illus. by Spaziante, Patrick)*
    c HB Guide - v26 - i1 - Spring 2015 - p62(1) [51-500]
New Developments (Illus. by Spaziante, Patrick)
    c HB Guide - v26 - i1 - Spring 2015 - p62(1) [51-500]

Leyerle, Blake - *Ascetic Culture: Essays in Honor of Philip Rousseau*
    CH - v84 - i2 - June 2015 - p423(3) [501+]

Leyner, Mark - *Gone with the Mind*
    KR - Jan 1 2016 - pNA [51-500]

Leypoldt, Gunter - *Intellectual Authority and Literary Culture in the U.S., 1790-1900*
    JAH - v101 - i4 - March 2015 - p1259-1260 [501+]

Leys, Simon - *La Mort de Napoleon*
    TLS - i5854 - June 12 2015 - p12(2) [51-500]

Leyser, Henrietta - *Beda: A Journey through the Seven Kingdoms in the Age of Bede*
    Spec - v328 - i9755 - August 15 2015 - p33(2) [501+]
    TLS - i5875 - Nov 6 2015 - p34(1) [501+]

Leznoff, Glenda - *Heartache and Other Natural Shocks*
    y KR - August 15 2015 - pNA [51-500]
    y Res Links - v21 - i1 - Oct 2015 - p37(1) [501+]
    y SLJ - v61 - i10 - Oct 2015 - p113(1) [51-500]

Li, Jie - *Shanghai Homes: Palimpsests of Private Life*
    TimHES - i2187 - Jan 22 2015 - p50-51 [501+]

Li, Larry - *MeditationSwerve: Your Very Own Jackass Sweetheart Meditation Companion*
    KR - June 15 2015 - pNA [501+]

Li, Maggie - *Bug Detective: Amazing Facts, Myths, and Quirks of Nature (Illus. by Rossi, Francesca)*
    c BL - v111 - i16 - April 15 2015 - p42(1) [51-500]
    c SLJ - v61 - i8 - August 2015 - p122(1) [51-500]
    c HB Guide - v26 - i2 - Fall 2015 - p174(1) [51-500]
    c KR - Jan 15 2015 - pNA [51-500]

Li, Stephanie - *Playing in the White: Black Writers, White Subjects*
    TLS - i5877 - Nov 20 2015 - p5(1) [501+]
Signifying without Specifying: Racial Discourse in the Age of Obama
    Callaloo - v38 - i1 - Wntr 2015 - p204-205 [501+]

Li, Xiaobing - *China's Battle for Korea: The 1951 Spring Offensive*
    AHR - v120 - i3 - June 2015 - p992-993 [501+]
    J Mil H - v79 - i3 - July 2015 - p879-880 [501+]
    Pac A - v88 - i3 - Sept 2015 - p702 [501+]

Oil: A Cultural and Geographic Encyclopedia of Black Gold
    BL - v111 - i12 - Feb 15 2015 - p14(1) [51-500]
    R&USQ - v54 - i4 - Summer 2015 - p83(1) [501+]

Li, Yishan - *How to Draw Manga Boys: In Simple Steps*
    LJ - v140 - i12 - July 1 2015 - p84(1) [51-500]
How to Draw Manga Girls: In Simple Steps
    LJ - v140 - i12 - July 1 2015 - p84(1) [51-500]

Li, Yiyun - *Kinder Than Solitude*
    NYRB - v62 - i18 - Nov 19 2015 - p56(5) [501+]
    NYTBR - Feb 8 2015 - p28(L) [501+]

Lianas, Sheila Griffin - *Caleb Davis Bradham: Pepsi-Cola Inventor*
    c HB Guide - v26 - i1 - Spring 2015 - p194(1) [51-500]
Ettore Boiardi: Chef Boyar dee Manufacturer
    c HB Guide - v26 - i1 - Spring 2015 - p194(1) [51-500]
John Pemberton: Coca-Cola Developer
    c HB Guide - v26 - i1 - Spring 2015 - p194(1) [51-500]
Tom Monaghan: Domino's Pizza Innovator
    c HB Guide - v26 - i1 - Spring 2015 - p194(1) [51-500]

Liang, David - *Blue Ink*
    KR - Dec 1 2015 - pNA [501+]

Lianke, Yan - *The Four Books*
    BL - v111 - i12 - Feb 15 2015 - p30(1) [51-500]
    KR - Jan 1 2015 - pNA [51-500]
    LJ - v140 - i2 - Feb 1 2015 - p78(1) [51-500]

Lianos, Michalis - *Dangerous Others, Insecure Societies: Fear and Social Division*
    CS - v44 - i1 - Jan 2015 - p141(1) [51-500]
    ERS - v38 - i3 - March 2015 - p483(3) [501+]

Liasson, Miranda - *This Thing Called Love*
    PW - v262 - i13 - March 30 2015 - p62(1) [51-500]

Liautaud, Martine - *Culture Monitoring*
    Forbes - v196 - i6 - Nov 2 2015 - p42(1) [501+]

Libbrecht, Kenneth - *The Snowflake: Winter's Frozen Artistry*
    Nature - v582 - i7582 - Dec 17 2015 - p331(1) [501+]

Liberalismus und Bismarck. Liberale Wahrnehmungen des "Eisernen Kanzlers" in zwei Jahrhunderten
    HNet - April 2015 - pNA [501+]

Liberati, Tami - *First Creatures: A Journey through Grief*
    KR - Feb 1 2015 - pNA [501+]

Liberman, Kenneth - *More Studies in Ethnomethodology*
    CS - v44 - i5 - Sept 2015 - p604-614 [501+]

Licence, Amy - *Living in Squares, Loving in Triangles: The Lives and Loves of Virginia Woolf and the Bloomsbury Group*
    TLS - i5863 - August 14 2015 - p17(1) [501+]

Licence, Tom - *Bury St Edmunds and the Norman Conquest*
    CHR - v101 - i4 - Autumn 2015 - p911(2) [501+]

Lichtenberg, Judith - *Distant Strangers: Ethics, Psychology, and Global Poverty*
    AM - v213 - i14 - Nov 9 2015 - p42(2) [501+]

Lichtenstein, Nelson - *The Right and Labor in America: Politics, Ideology, and Imagination*
    J Am St - v49 - i1 - Feb 2015 - p216-219 [501+]

Lidchi, Henrietta - *Surviving Desires: Making and Selling Native Jewellery in the American Southwest*
    Roundup M - v22 - i6 - August 2015 - p38(1) [501+]

Liddington, Jill - *Vanishing for the Vote: Suffrage, Citizenship and the Battle for the Census*
    HT - v65 - i2 - Feb 2015 - p61(1) [501+]

Liddle, J.D. - *Shattered Hand: Sarah's Secret War*
    SPBW - August 2015 - pNA [501+]

Liddle, Roger - *The Risk of Brexit*
    Econ - v415 - i8932 - April 4 2015 - p78(US) [501+]

Lidh, Jessica - *The Number 7*
    y HB Guide - v26 - i1 - Spring 2015 - p114(1) [51-500]

Lieb, Josh - *Ratscalibur (Read by Ballerini, Edoardo). Audiobook Review*
    c BL - v112 - i4 - Oct 15 2015 - p64(1) [51-500]
    c SLJ - v61 - i8 - August 2015 - p50(1) [51-500]
Ratscalibur (Illus. by Lintern, Tom)
    c BL - v111 - i15 - April 1 2015 - p80(1) [51-500]
    c CCB-B - v68 - i11 - July-August 2015 - p555(1) [51-500]
    c HB Guide - v26 - i2 - Fall 2015 - p91(1) [51-500]
    c KR - March 1 2015 - pNA [51-500]
    c NYTBR - June 21 2015 - p18(L) [501+]
    c SLJ - v61 - i5 - May 2015 - p103(1) [51-500]

Liebal, Katja - *Primate Communication: A Multimodal Approach*
    QRB - v90 - i2 - June 2015 - p220(1) [501+]
Lieber, James B. - *Killer Care*
    KR - Oct 1 2015 - pNA [501+]
Lieber, Laura Suzanne - *A Vocabulary of Desire: The Song of Songs in the Early Synagogue*
    HNet - May 2015 - pNA [501+]
Lieber, Ron - *The Opposite of Spoiled: Raising Kids Who Are Grounded, Generous, and Smart about Money*
    BL - v111 - i9-10 - Jan 1 2015 - p27(2) [51-500]
    NYTBR - March 22 2015 - p16(L) [501+]
    The Opposite of Spoiled: Raising Kids Who Are Grounded, Generous and Smart About Money
    Par - v90 - i3 - March 2015 - p18(1) [501+]
Lieberman, Jeffrey A. - *Shrinks: The Untold Story of Psychiatry*
    BL - v111 - i13 - March 1 2015 - p11(1) [51-500]
    KR - Jan 1 2015 - pNA [501+]
    Mac - v128 - i10 - March 16 2015 - p56(1) [501+]
    Nat Post - v17 - i101 - Feb 28 2015 - pWP5(1) [501+]
    NYTBR - March 29 2015 - p17(L) [501+]
Lieberman, Lisa - *All the Wrong Places*
    KR - Feb 1 2015 - pNA [51-500]
Liebermann, Lowell - *Three Lullabies for Two Pianos*
    Am MT - v65 - i3 - Dec 2015 - p51(1) [51-500]
Liebert, Emily - *Those Secrets We Keep*
    LJ - v140 - i10 - June 1 2015 - p90(1) [51-500]
Liebert, Hugh - *Thinking beyond Boundaries: Transnational Challenges to US Foreign Policy*
    Parameters - v45 - i2 - Summer 2015 - p117(2) [501+]
Liebmann, Marion - *Art Therapy with Neurological Conditions*
    Bwatch - Nov 2015 - pNA [51-500]
    Art Therapy with Physical Conditions
    Bwatch - Nov 2015 - pNA [51-500]
Liebscher, Martin - *Analytical Psychology in Exile: The Correspondence of C.G. Jung and Erich Neumann*
    PW - v262 - i1 - Jan 5 2015 - p60(1) [51-500]
Lief, Jacob - *I Am Because You Are*
    KR - March 1 2015 - pNA [501+]
Liehr, Dorothee - *Skandal und Nation: Politische Deutungskampfe in der Schweiz 1988-1991*
    HNet - Feb 2015 - pNA [501+]
Lies, Brian - *Bats in the Band*
    c HB Guide - v26 - i1 - Spring 2015 - p36(1) [51-500]
Lietz, Cecilia - *A Dragon's Mage*
    SPBW - Jan 2015 - pNA [51-500]
Lieven, Dominic - *The End of Tsarist Russia: The March to World War I and Revolution*
    PW - v262 - i21 - May 25 2015 - p46(1) [51-500]
    KR - June 1 2015 - pNA [501+]
    LJ - v140 - i12 - July 1 2015 - p94(2) [51-500]
    NYT - August 31 2015 - pC4(L) [501+]
    NYTBR - August 30 2015 - p19(L) [501+]
    Towards the Flame: Empire, War and the End of Tsarist Russia
    Econ - v415 - i8938 - May 16 2015 - p76(US) [501+]
    Spec - v328 - i9744 - May 30 2015 - p34(1) [501+]
Liew, Sonny - *The Art of Charlie Chan Hock Chye*
    KR - Jan 1 2016 - pNA [501+]
Life in Squares
    TLS - i5863 - August 14 2015 - p17(1) [501+]
Lifschitz, Avi - *Language and Enlightenment: The Berlin Debates of the Eighteenth Century*
    JMH - v87 - i2 - June 2015 - p481(2) [501+]
Lifset, Robert - *American Energy Policy in the 1970s*
    JAH - v102 - i1 - June 2015 - p312-313 [501+]
    BHR - v89 - i2 - Summer 2015 - p389(3) [501+]
Lifset, Robert D. - *Power on the Hudson: Storm King Mountain and the Emergence of Modern American Environmentalism*
    AHR - v120 - i4 - Oct 2015 - p1524-1525 [501+]
    JAH - v102 - i2 - Sept 2015 - p626-626 [501+]
Liftin, Hilary - *Movie Star by Lizzie Pepper*
    Ent W - i1374 - July 31 2015 - p62(1) [501+]
    KR - May 15 2015 - pNA [501+]
    LJ - v140 - i8 - May 1 2015 - p64(1) [501+]
    PW - v262 - i18 - May 4 2015 - p92(2) [501+]
Liggett, Kim - *Blood and Salt*
    y BL - v112 - i2 - Sept 15 2015 - p70(1) [51-500]
    y KR - July 1 2015 - pNA [51-500]
    y SLJ - v61 - i7 - July 2015 - p95(2) [51-500]
    y VOYA - v38 - i3 - August 2015 - p64(1) [501+]
Light, Aimee Upjohn - *God at the Margins: Making Theological Sense of Religious Plurality*
    Theol St - v76 - i2 - June 2015 - p365(3) [501+]

Light, Alison - *Common People: In Pursuit of My Ancestors*
    BL - v112 - i1 - Sept 1 2015 - p17(1) [501+]
    KR - August 15 2015 - pNA [501+]
    NYTBR - Sept 20 2015 - p15(L) [501+]
    PW - v262 - i27 - July 6 2015 - p56(1) [51-500]
    Common People: The History of an English Family
    Lon R Bks - v37 - i4 - Feb 19 2015 - p31(2) [501+]
    TLS - i5831 - Jan 2 2015 - p5(1) [501+]
Light, Caroline E. - *That Pride of Race and Character: The Roots of Jewish Benevolence in the Jim Crow South*
    Am St - v54 - i1 - Spring 2015 - p169-2 [501+]
    HNet - Sept 2015 - pNA [501+]
Light, Donald W. - *Good Pharma: The Public-Health Model of the Mario Negri Institute*
    TimHES - i2221 - Sept 17 2015 - p46(1) [501+]
Light, Ivan - *Deadly Secret of the Lusitania*
    RVBW - Oct 2015 - pNA [51-500]
Light, Kelly - *Louise Loves Art (Illus. by Light, Kelly)*
    c HB Guide - v26 - i1 - Spring 2015 - p36(1) [51-500]
Light, Steve - *Boats Go (Illus. by Light, Steve)*
    c CCB-B - v68 - i10 - June 2015 - p504(1) [51-500]
    c KR - July 1 2015 - pNA [51-500]
    c SLJ - v61 - i7 - July 2015 - p56(1) [51-500]
    Have You Seen My Dragon? (Illus. by Light, Steve)
    c SLJ - v61 - i6 - June 2015 - p46(6) [501+]
    Have You Seen My Monster? (Illus. by Light, Steve)
    BL - v111 - i14 - March 15 2015 - p77(1) [51-500]
    c HB Guide - v26 - i2 - Fall 2015 - p14(1) [51-500]
    c KR - Jan 15 2015 - pNA [51-500]
    c SLJ - v61 - i2 - Feb 2015 - p72(1) [51-500]
    Planes Go (Illus. by Light, Steve)
    c KR - Jan 1 2015 - pNA [51-500]
    Swap! (Illus. by Light, Steve)
    c KR - Nov 15 2015 - pNA [51-500]
    c PW - v262 - i44 - Nov 2 2015 - p82(1) [51-500]
Light, Zuzka - *15 Minutes to Fit: The Simple 30-Day Guide to Total Fitness, 15 Minutes at a Time*
    PW - v262 - i44 - Nov 2 2015 - p81(1) [51-500]
Lightburn, Ron - *Frankenstink! Garbage Gone Bad (Illus. by Lightburn, Ron)*
    c HB Guide - v26 - i2 - Fall 2015 - p42(1) [51-500]
    c Res Links - v20 - i5 - June 2015 - p6(1) [51-500]
Lighte, Peter Rupert - *Host of Memories*
    KR - June 1 2015 - pNA [501+]
    PW - v262 - i23 - June 8 2015 - p53(2) [51-500]
    SPBW - May 2015 - pNA [51-500]
Lightman, Alan - *Screening Room: Family Pictures*
    NYTBR - August 2 2015 - p26(L) [501+]
Lightman, Bernard - *The Age of Scientific Naturalism: Tyndall and His Contemporaries*
    Isis - v106 - i2 - June 2015 - p463(2) [501+]
Lignel, Benjamin - *Shows and Tales: On Jewelry Exhibition-Making*
    Am Craft - v75 - i5 - Oct-Nov 2015 - p24(1) [501+]
Ligotti, Thomas - *Songs of a Dead Dreamer and Grimscribe*
    NYT - Oct 30 2015 - pC35(L) [501+]
    NYTBR - Nov 1 2015 - p22(L) [501+]
Likhachev, D.S. - *The Poetics of Early Russian Literature*
    MLR - v110 - i3 - July 2015 - p920-921 [501+]
Lilja, Mona - *Resisting Gendered Norms: Civil Society, the Juridical and Political Space in Cambodia*
    Pac A - v88 - i2 - June 2015 - p358 [501+]
Lilley, James D. - *Common Things: Romance and the Aesthetics of Belonging in Atlantic Modernity*
    AL - v87 - i2 - June 2015 - p387-389 [501+]
Lillington, Joe - *Toby and the Ice Giants (Illus. by Lillington, Joe)*
    c KR - April 15 2015 - pNA [501+]
    c PW - v262 - i20 - May 18 2015 - p85(1) [501+]
    c SLJ - v61 - i9 - Sept 2015 - p124(2) [51-500]
Lilly, Paul R. - *The Lake of Far: Stories*
    KR - Jan 1 2015 - pNA [501+]
Lillywhite, Harvey B. - *How Snakes Work: Structure, Function, and Behavior of the World's Snakes*
    Am Bio T - v77 - i3 - March 2015 - p216(1) [501+]
    QRB - v90 - i3 - Sept 2015 - p350(1) [501+]
Lilti, Antoine - *Figures publiques: L'Invention de la celebrite, 1750-1850*
    NYRB - v62 - i9 - May 21 2015 - p8(2) [501+]
Lim, Dennis - *David Lynch: The Man from Another Place*
    BL - v112 - i5 - Nov 1 2015 - p17(1) [501+]
    KR - Sept 15 2015 - pNA [501+]
    NYTBR - Dec 6 2015 - p70(L) [501+]
    PW - v262 - i36 - Sept 7 2015 - p58(1) [51-500]

Lim, Jeanette - *Big Little Felt Fun: 60+ Projects That Jump, Swim, Roll, Sprout and Roar*
    LJ - v140 - i2 - Feb 1 2015 - p82(2) [51-500]
Lim, Louisa - *The People's Republic of Amnesia: Tiananmen Revisited*
    Comw - v142 - i2 - Jan 23 2015 - p26(2) [501+]
    NYTBR - Nov 1 2015 - p28(L) [501+]
    TLS - i5876 - Nov 13 2015 - p31(1) [501+]
Lim, Rebecca - *Afterlight*
    y Magpies - v30 - i4 - Sept 2015 - p42(1) [501+]
    The Astrologer's Daughter
    y CCB-B - v69 - i1 - Sept 2015 - p35(1) [501+]
    y KR - April 15 2015 - pNA [51-500]
    y SLJ - v61 - i6 - June 2015 - p126(1) [51-500]
Lim, Sandra - *The Wilderness*
    Ant R - v73 - i2 - Spring 2015 - p382(2) [51-500]
Lim, Song Hwee - *Tsai Ming-liang and a Cinema of Slowness*
    FQ - v68 - i3 - Spring 2015 - p96(3) [501+]
Lim, Suchen Christine - *River's Song*
    KR - July 15 2015 - pNA [501+]
Lima, Frank - *Incidents of Travel in Poetry: New and Selected Poems*
    PW - v262 - i52 - Dec 21 2015 - p126(1) [51-500]
Lima, Manuel - *The Book of Trees: Visualizing Branches of Knowledge*
    Bks & Cult - v21 - i2 - March-April 2015 - p33(2) [501+]
Lime, Liz - *That Day in September and Other Rhymes for the Times*
    c KR - Jan 1 2015 - pNA [501+]
Limon, Ada - *Bright Dead Things*
    LJ - v140 - i10 - June 1 2015 - p107(1) [51-500]
    NYTBR - Dec 27 2015 - p26(L) [501+]
    PW - v262 - i33 - August 17 2015 - p48(1) [51-500]
Limon, Jose E. - *Americo Paredes: Culture and Critique*
    AL - v87 - i3 - Sept 2015 - p624-627 [501+]
Limon, Martin - *The Iron Sickle*
    RVBW - March 2015 - pNA [51-500]
    RVBW - July 2015 - pNA [51-500]
    The Ville Rat
    BL - v111 - i22 - August 1 2015 - p38(1) [51-500]
    KR - August 1 2015 - pNA [51-500]
    PW - v262 - i32 - August 10 2015 - p39(2) [51-500]
Lin, Derek - *The Tao of Happiness: Stories from Chuang Tzu for Your Spiritual Journey*
    PW - v262 - i37 - Sept 14 2015 - p63(1) [51-500]
    BL - v112 - i6 - Nov 15 2015 - p16(1) [51-500]
Lin, Ed - *Ghost Month*
    RVBW - April 2015 - pNA [51-500]
    RVBW - July 2015 - pNA [51-500]
Lin, Grace - *Ling & Ting: Twice as Silly (Illus. by Lin, Grace)*
    c HB - v91 - i1 - Jan-Feb 2015 - p85(1) [51-500]
    c HB Guide - v26 - i1 - Spring 2015 - p54(1) [51-500]
    The Year of the Dog (Read by Wu, Nancy). Audiobook Review
    c SLJ - v61 - i2 - Feb 2015 - p38(3) [501+]
Lin, Hsiang-ju - *Slippery Noodles: A Culinary History of China*
    TLS - i5860 - July 24 2015 - p27(1) [501+]
Lin, Wei-Cheng - *Building a Sacred Mountain: The Buddhist Architecture of China's Mount Wutai*
    AHR - v120 - i2 - April 2015 - p591-592 [501+]
    JAS - v74 - i1 - Feb 2015 - p199-200 [501+]
Linch, Kevin - *Britain and Wellington's Army: Recruitment, Society and Tradition, 1807-13*
    HER - v130 - i542 - Feb 2015 - p123(14) [501+]
Lincoln, Evelyn - *Brilliant Discourse: Pictures and Readers in Early Modern Rome*
    Six Ct J - v46 - i2 - Summer 2015 - p534-536 [501+]
Lincoln, Margarette - *British Pirates and Society, 1680-1730*
    HT - v65 - i3 - March 2015 - p58(1) [501+]
Lind, Stephen J. - *A Charlie Brown Religion*
    Mac - v128 - i46 - Nov 23 2015 - p57(1) [501+]
Linda, David - *Tales from Concrete Jungles: Urban Birding around the World*
    New Sci - v227 - i3033 - August 8 2015 - p43(1) [501+]
Lindberg, Marian E. - *The End of the Rainy Season: Discovering My Family's Hidden Past in Brazil*
    BL - v111 - i16 - April 15 2015 - p13(2) [51-500]
    KR - Jan 15 2015 - pNA [501+]
Lindberg, Richard - *Gangland Chicago: Criminality and Lawlessness in the Windy City*
    PW - v262 - i42 - Oct 19 2015 - p68(1) [51-500]

Lindeen, Mary - *Read and Discover Series*
c   BL - v112 - i5 - Nov 1 2015 - p47(1) [51-500]

Lindeland, Turid - *Yarn Happy: Traditional Norwegian Designs for Modern Knit and Crochet*
LJ - v140 - i16 - Oct 1 2015 - p83(1) [51-500]
RVBW - Sept 2015 - pNA [51-500]

Lindelauf, Benny - *Nine Open Arms*
c   HB Guide - v26 - i1 - Spring 2015 - p84(2) [51-500]

Lindeman, Michael - *From Prehistoric Villages to Cities: Settlement Aggregation and Community Transformation*
Am Ant - v80 - i1 - Jan 2015 - p210(2) [501+]

Lindeman, Peter V. - *The Map Turtle and Sawback Atlas: Ecology, Evolution, Distribution, and Conservation*
QRB - v90 - i1 - March 2015 - p102(2) [501+]

Lindemann, Danielle J. - *Dominatrix: Gender, Eroticism and Control in the Dungeon*
CS - v44 - i1 - Jan 2015 - p83-85 [501+]

Linden, Caroline - *Love in the Time of Scandal*
BL - v111 - i18 - May 15 2015 - p31(1) [51-500]
KR - April 15 2015 - pNA [51-500]
PW - v262 - i7 - Feb 16 2015 - p165(1) [51-500]

Linden, David J. - *Touch: The Science of Hand, Heart, and Mind*
Am Sci - v103 - i5 - Sept-Oct 2015 - p362(2) [501+]
Bwatch - April 2015 - pNA [51-500]
LJ - v140 - i3 - Feb 15 2015 - p126(1) [51-500]
Nature - v517 - i7536 - Jan 29 2015 - p551(1) [51-500]
Spec - v327 - i9737 - April 11 2015 - p41(1) [501+]

Linden, Emily - *UnSlut: A Diary and a Memoir*
y   PW - v262 - i38 - Sept 21 2015 - p78(1) [51-500]

Linden, Joanne - *Ben & Zip: Two Short Friends (Illus. by Goldsmith, Tom)*
c   HB Guide - v26 - i1 - Spring 2015 - p36(1) [51-500]

Linden, Joshua - *The Sound of Water*
SPBW - March 2015 - pNA [501+]

Lindeperg, Sylvie - *"Night and Fog": A Film in History*
TLS - i5863 - August 14 2015 - p26(1) [501+]

Linder, Shirley Ayn - *Doc Holiday in Film and Literature*
Roundup M - v22 - i6 - August 2015 - p38(1) [501+]
Doc Holliday in Film and Literature
SHQ - v118 - i3 - Jan 2015 - p328(1) [501+]
WHQ - v46 - i1 - Spring 2015 - p97-97 [501+]

Lindgren, James M. - *Preserving South Street Seaport: The Dream and Reality of a New York Urban Renewal District*
JAH - v102 - i1 - June 2015 - p315-315 [501+]

Lindin, Emily - *UnSlut: A Diary and a Memoir*
y   BL - v112 - i4 - Oct 15 2015 - p38(1) [51-500]
y   KR - Oct 1 2015 - pNA [51-500]
y   SLJ - v61 - i9 - Sept 2015 - p187(2) [51-500]
y   VOYA - v38 - i5 - Dec 2015 - p77(1) [51-500]

Lindner, April - *Love, Lucy*
y   HB Guide - v26 - i2 - Fall 2015 - p129(1) [51-500]

Lindner, Dee - *Sew Cute and Collectible Sock Monkeys: For Red-Heel Sock Monkey Crafters and Collectors*
LJ - v140 - i15 - Sept 15 2015 - p77(1) [51-500]

Lindoff, Hannah - *Mary's Wild Winter Feast (Illus. by Koch, Nobu)*
c   HB Guide - v26 - i1 - Spring 2015 - p37(1) [51-500]

Lindop, Grevel - *Charles Williams: The Third Inkling*
Spec - v329 - i9768 - Nov 14 2015 - p48(1) [501+]

Lindquist, Lynn - *Secret of the Sevens*
c   BL - v111 - i17 - May 1 2015 - p53(1) [51-500]
y   SLJ - v61 - i8 - August 2015 - p106(1) [51-500]
y   VOYA - v38 - i2 - June 2015 - p64(2) [51-500]

Lindsay, Brendan C. - *Murder State: California's Native American Genocide, 1846-1873*
HNet - April 2015 - pNA [501+]

Lindsay, Jeff - *Dexter Is Dead*
BL - v111 - i19-20 - June 1 2015 - p52(1) [51-500]
KR - June 1 2015 - pNA [51-500]
PW - v262 - i20 - May 18 2015 - p64(1) [51-500]
Red Tide
BL - v112 - i3 - Oct 1 2015 - p28(1) [51-500]
PW - v262 - i34 - August 24 2015 - p61(1) [51-500]

Lindsay, Lisa A. - *Biography and the Black Atlantic*
JIH - v45 - i4 - Spring 2015 - p606-607 [501+]

Lindsay, Virginia - *Pretty Birds: 18 Simple Projects to Sew and Love*
PW - v262 - i3 - Jan 19 2015 - p75(1) [51-500]

Lindsey, Johanna - *Wildfire in His Arms (Read by Branson, Ted). Audiobook Review*
LJ - v140 - i16 - Oct 1 2015 - p43(1) [51-500]

Lindsey, Marta - *Little Gray's Great Migration (Illus. by Gabriel, Andrea)*
c   CH Bwatch - April 2015 - pNA [51-500]
c   HB Guide - v26 - i1 - Spring 2015 - p37(1) [51-500]

Lindstrom, Eric - *Not If I See You First*
y   BL - v112 - i4 - Oct 15 2015 - p57(1) [51-500]
y   HB - v91 - i6 - Nov-Dec 2015 - p82(1) [51-500]
y   KR - Oct 1 2015 - pNA [51-500]
y   PW - v262 - i38 - Sept 21 2015 - p76(1) [51-500]
y   VOYA - v38 - i5 - Dec 2015 - p59(1) [51-500]

Lindstrom, Martin - *Small Data: The Tiny Clues That Uncover Huge Trends*
KR - Jan 1 2016 - pNA [501+]

Lindvall, Terry - *God Mocks: A History of Religious Satire from the Hebrew Prophets to Stephen Colbert*
Ch Today - v59 - i9 - Nov 2015 - p69(3) [501+]
LJ - v140 - i16 - Oct 1 2015 - p86(1) [51-500]

Linehan, Moira - *Incarnate Grace: Poems*
LJ - v140 - i5 - March 15 2015 - p110(1) [51-500]

Lines, David A. - *Rethinking Virtue, Reforming Society: New Directions in Renaissance Ethics, c.1350 - c.1650*
Med R - June 2015 - pNA [501+]

Lines, Kate - *Crime Seen*
Nat Post - v17 - i147 - April 25 2015 - pWP5(1) [501+]

Ling, David - *What Do Cats Have Tails? (Illus. by Thatcher, Stephanie)*
Magpies - v30 - i3 - July 2015 - pS4(1) [501+]

Ling, Nancy Tupper - *Double Happiness (Illus. by Chau, Alina)*
c   KR - July 1 2015 - pNA [501+]
c   SLJ - v61 - i8 - August 2015 - p73(1) [51-500]
The Story I'll Tell (Illus. by Lanan, Jessica)
c   PW - v262 - i35 - August 31 2015 - p92(1) [51-500]
c   KR - Sept 1 2015 - pNA [51-500]
c   PW - v262 - i49 - Dec 2 2015 - p32(1) [51-500]

Ling, Peter J. - *John F. Kennedy*
HNet - June 2015 - pNA [501+]
J Am St - v49 - i1 - May 2015 - p441-444 [501+]

Lingane, Mark - *Sucker*
PW - v262 - i23 - June 8 2015 - p44(1) [51-500]

Lingard, Joan - *The Sign of the Black Dagger*
c   CCB-B - v68 - i5 - Jan 2015 - p265(1) [51-500]
Trouble on Cable Street
y   Sch Lib - v63 - i1 - Spring 2015 - p55(1) [51-500]

Lingen, Kerstin von - *Allen Dulles, the OSS, and Nazi War Criminals: The Dynamics of Selective Prosecution*
JMH - v87 - i2 - June 2015 - p490(2) [501+]

Lingenfelter, Richard E. - *Bonanzas & Borrascas: Copper Kings and Stock Frenzies, 1885-1918*
PHR - v84 - i2 - May 2015 - p231(3) [501+]
Bonanzas & Borrascas: Gold Lust and Silver Sharks, 1848-1884
PHR - v84 - i2 - May 2015 - p231(3) [501+]

Linhard, Tabea Alexa - *Jewish Spain: A Mediterranean Memory*
HNet - May 2015 - pNA [501+]

Liniers - *Escrito y Dibujado por Enriqueta (Illus. by Liniers)*
c   SLJ - v61 - i9 - Sept 2015 - p133(1) [51-500]
Macanudo No. 2 (Illus. by Liniers)
c   HB Guide - v26 - i2 - Fall 2015 - p91(1) [51-500]
What There Is Before There Is Anything There: A Scary Story (Illus. by Liniers)
c   HB Guide - v26 - i1 - Spring 2015 - p37(1) [51-500]
Written and Drawn by Henrietta (Illus. by Liniers)
c   BL - v112 - i2 - Sept 15 2015 - p53(1) [51-500]
c   HB - v91 - i6 - Nov-Dec 2015 - p83(1) [51-500]
c   KR - June 1 2015 - pNA [51-500]
c   PW - v262 - i25 - June 22 2015 - p143(1) [51-500]
c   PW - v262 - i49 - Dec 2 2015 - p40(1) [51-500]
c   SLJ - v61 - i9 - Sept 2015 - p133(1) [51-500]

Link, Eric Carl - *The Cambridge Companion to American Science Fiction*
SFS - v42 - i3 - Nov 2015 - p590-593 [501+]

Link, Kelly - *Get in Trouble: Stories (Read by several narrators). Audiobook Review*
LJ - v140 - i14 - Sept 1 2015 - p66(1) [51-500]
PW - v262 - i12 - March 23 2015 - p69(1) [51-500]
Get in Trouble: Stories
BL - v111 - i9-10 - Jan 1 2015 - p36(1) [51-500]
Ent W - i1353 - March 6 2015 - p73(1) [501+]
MFSF - v128 - i5-6 - May-June 2015 - p65(6) [501+]
NYT - Feb 26 2015 - pC6(L) [501+]
NYTBR - Feb 15 2015 - p17(L) [501+]
Monstrous Affections: An Anthology of Beastly Tales
y   HB Guide - v26 - i1 - Spring 2015 - p187(1) [51-500]

Link, Mardi Jo - *The Drummond Girls*
KR - May 15 2015 - pNA [51-500]

Link, Perry - *An Anatomy of Chinese: Rhythm, Metaphor, Politics*
JAS - v74 - i1 - Feb 2015 - p200-202 [501+]

Link, Roland - *Love in Vain: The Story of the Ruts and Ruts DC*
NS - v144 - i5276 - August 21 2015 - p49(1) [501+]

Link, Tim - *Talking with Dogs and Cats: Joining the Conversation to Improve Behavior and Bond with Your Animals*
LJ - v140 - i11 - June 15 2015 - p105(1) [51-500]

Link, William A. - *Atlanta, Cradle of the New South: Race and Remembering in the Civil War's Aftermath*
Historian - v77 - i1 - Spring 2015 - p128(2) [501+]
HNet - April 2015 - pNA [501+]
JAH - v102 - i1 - June 2015 - p259-259 [501+]
Creating Citizenship in the Nineteenth-Century South
J Am St - v49 - i1 - Feb 2015 - p181-185 [501+]

Linka, Catherine - *A Girl Undone*
y   BL - v111 - i19-20 - June 1 2015 - p98(1) [51-500]
y   KR - April 15 2015 - pNA [51-500]
y   VOYA - v38 - i2 - June 2015 - p78(1) [51-500]

Linke, Alexander - *Typologie in der fruhen Neuzeit: Genese und Semantik heilsgeschichtlicher Bildprogramme von der Cappella Sistina (1480) bis San Giovanni in Laterano, 1650*
Six Ct J - v46 - i2 - Summer 2015 - p529-531 [501+]

Linklater, Andro - *Owning the Earth: The Transforming History of Land Ownership*
IBMR - v39 - i1 - Jan 2015 - p46(1) [501+]

Linn, Brian McAllister - *The U.S. Army and Counterinsurgency in the Philippine War*
NWCR - v68 - i2 - Spring 2015 - p142(3) [501+]

Linn, Jennifer - *Animals Have Feelings Too: Eight Original Piano Solos*
Am MT - v65 - i3 - Dec 2015 - p46(2) [501+]

Linna, Vaino - *Unknown Soldiers*
TLS - i5853 - June 5 2015 - p20(1) [501+]

Linnett, Richard - *In the Godfather Garden: The Long Life and Times of Richie "the Boot" Boiardo*
Historian - v77 - i2 - Summer 2015 - p344(3) [501+]

Linse, Tamara - *Earth's Imagined Corners*
PW - v262 - i12 - March 23 2015 - p35(5) [501+]
PW - v262 - i24 - June 15 2015 - p60(1) [51-500]

Lint Sagarena, Roberto Ramon - *Aztlan and Arcadia: Religion, Ethnicity, and the Creation of Place*
JAH - v102 - i2 - Sept 2015 - p511-512 [501+]

Lintner, Bertil - *Great Game East: India, China, and the Struggle for Asia's Most Volatile Frontier*
For Aff - v94 - i3 - May-June 2015 - pNA [501+]

Linton, Eliza Lynn - *Sowing the Wind*
TLS - i5867 - Sept 11 2015 - p26(1) [501+]

Linton, Marisa - *Choosing Terror: Virtue, Friendship, and Authenticity in the French Revolution*
HER - v130 - i543 - April 2015 - p468(2) [501+]
JIH - v45 - i3 - Wntr 2015 - p432-434 [501+]

Linton, Suzannah - *Hong Kong's War Crimes Trials*
J Mil H - v79 - i3 - July 2015 - p876-877(1) [501+]

Lion, Susan Andra - *How the Trees Got Their Voices (Illus. by Lion, Susan Andra)*
c   CH Bwatch - Sept 2015 - pNA [51-500]
c   CH Bwatch - Oct 2015 - pNA [51-500]

Lionni, Leo - *Alexander and the Wind-Up Mouse (Illus. by Lionni, Leo)*
c   HB Guide - v26 - i1 - Spring 2015 - p54(1) [51-500]
Frederick (Illus. by Lionni, Leo)
c   HB Guide - v26 - i1 - Spring 2015 - p54(1) [51-500]
Swimmy
c   Sch Lib - v63 - i3 - Autumn 2015 - p156(2) [51-500]

Liontas, Annie - *Let Me Explain You*
BL - v111 - i21 - July 1 2015 - p31(2) [51-500]
KR - May 1 2015 - pNA [501+]
LJ - v140 - i11 - June 15 2015 - p77(2) [51-500]
NYTBR - July 19 2015 - p10(L) [501+]
A Manner of Being: Writers on Their Mentors
y   BL - v112 - i7 - Dec 1 2015 - p10(1) [51-500]
KR - Oct 15 2015 - pNA [501+]
LJ - v140 - i19 - Nov 15 2015 - p85(1) [51-500]

Lipan, Sabine - *Mom, There's a Bear at the Door (Illus. by Olten, Manuela)*
   c KR - Dec 15 2015 - pNA [51-500]
Lipman, Andrew - *The Saltwater Frontier: Indians and the Contest for the American Coast*
   PW - v262 - i38 - Sept 21 2015 - p63(2) [51-500]
Lipman, Victor - *The Type B Manager: Leading Successfully in a Type A World*
   BL - v111 - i21 - July 1 2015 - p25(1) [51-500]
   LJ - v140 - i10 - June 1 2015 - p110(1) [51-500]
   PW - v262 - i18 - May 4 2015 - p107(1) [51-500]
Lipp, Karlheinz - *Berliner Friedenspfarrer und der Erste Weltkrieg: Ein Lesebuch*
   HNet - Feb 2015 - pNA [501+]
Lippard, George - *The Killers: A Narrative of Real Life in Philadelphia*
   Nine-C Lit - v70 - i1 - June 2015 - p150(8) [501+]
Lippert-Martin, Kristen - *Tabula Rasa (Read by Rudd, Kate). Audiobook Review*
   y BL - v111 - i15 - April 1 2015 - p87(1) [51-500]
Tabula Rasa
   y HB Guide - v26 - i1 - Spring 2015 - p114(1) [51-500]
Lippert-Rasmussen, Kasper - *Born Free and Equal? A Philosophical Inquiry into the Nature of Discrimination*
   Ethics - v125 - i4 - July 2015 - p1204(7) [501+]
Lippman, Laura - *Hush, Hush (Read by Maxwell, Jan). Audiobook Review*
   LJ - v140 - i9 - May 15 2015 - p44(1) [51-500]
Hush Hush
   RVBW - Oct 2015 - pNA [501+]
Lipscomb, John - *The Painting and the Piano*
   KR - Dec 15 2015 - pNA [501+]
Lipscombe, Nick - *Waterloo: The Decisive Victory*
   TLS - i5833 - Jan 16 2015 - p12(2) [501+]
Wellington's Guns: The Untold Story of Wellington and His Artillery in the Peninsula and at Waterloo
   HER - v130 - i542 - Feb 2015 - p123(14) [501+]
Lipsey, Jennifer - *I Love to Paint!*
   c BL - v112 - i5 - Nov 1 2015 - p50(1) [501+]
Lipsey, Roger - *Make Peace before the Sun Goes Down: The Long Encounter of Thomas Merton and His Abbot, James Fox*
   PW - v262 - i15 - April 13 2015 - p74(1) [51-500]
Lipsyte, Robert - *The Twin Powers*
   c HB Guide - v26 - i2 - Fall 2015 - p91(1) [51-500]
Lipszyc, Rywka - *Rywka's Diary: The Writings of a Jewish Girl from the Lodz Ghetto*
   KR - August 1 2015 - pNA [51-500]
   LJ - v140 - i13 - August 1 2015 - p109(1) [51-500]
Lipton, Sara - *Dark Mirror: The Medieval Origins of Anti-Jewish Iconography*
   Comw - v142 - i16 - Oct 9 2015 - p40(5) [501+]
   NY - v90 - i47 - Feb 9 2015 - p69 [51-500]
   NYRB - v62 - i12 - July 9 2015 - p49(3) [501+]
   Specu - v90 - i2 - April 2015 - p556-558 [501+]
Lischer, Richard - *Reading the Parables: Interpretation: Resources for the Use of Scripture in the Church*
   TT - v72 - i3 - Oct 2015 - p344-345 [501+]
Lish, Atticus - *Preparation for the Next Life*
   ABR - v36 - i2 - Jan-Feb 2015 - p16(1) [501+]
   CSM - May 11 2015 - pNA [51-500]
   NS - v144 - i5255 - March 27 2015 - p72(1) [501+]
   NYRB - v62 - i2 - Feb 5 2015 - p16(3) [501+]
   TLS - i5852 - May 29 2015 - p20(1) [501+]
Lish, Gordon - *Cess*
   KR - August 1 2015 - pNA [501+]
Lisi, Clemente A. - *A History of the World Cup: 1930-2014*
   LJ - v140 - i5 - March 15 2015 - p130(1) [51-500]
Lisi, Leonardo F. - *Marginal Modernity: The Aesthetics of Dependency from Kierkegaard to Joyce*
   Scan St - v87 - i2 - Summer 2015 - p281(11) [501+]
Lisicky, Paul - *The Narrow Door: A Memoir of Friendship*
   KR - Oct 15 2015 - pNA [501+]
   PW - v262 - i45 - Nov 9 2015 - p49(2) [51-500]
Liska, Vivian - *Fremde Gemeinschaft: Deutsch-judische Literatur der Moderne*
   MLR - v110 - i1 - Jan 2015 - p303-305 [501+]
Lispector, Clarice - *Collected Stories*
   TLS - i5866 - Sept 4 2015 - p21(1) [501+]
The Complete Stories
   NYTBR - August 2 2015 - p1(L) [501+]
   BL - v111 - i22 - August 1 2015 - p27(1) [51-500]
   NYRB - v62 - i20 - Dec 17 2015 - p61(3) [501+]
   NYT - August 12 2015 - pC1(L) [501+]
   KR - June 1 2015 - pNA [501+]
   LJ - v140 - i9 - May 15 2015 - p79(1) [51-500]
   Nation - v301 - i21-22 - Nov 23 2015 - p31(4) [501+]
   PW - v262 - i25 - June 22 2015 - p117(1) [501+]
   TLS - i5854 - June 12 2015 - p11(2) [501+]
The Hour of the Star
   Nation - v301 - i21-22 - Nov 23 2015 - p31(4) [501+]
The Passion According to G.H.
   Nation - v301 - i21-22 - Nov 23 2015 - p31(4) [501+]
Liss, David - *The Day of Atonement (Read by Roukin, Samuel). Audiobook Review*
   LJ - v140 - i5 - March 15 2015 - p72(1) [51-500]
Randoms
   c BL - v111 - i21 - July 1 2015 - p76(1) [51-500]
   c BL - v112 - i1 - Sept 1 2015 - p114(1) [501+]
   y CCB-B - v69 - i2 - Oct 2015 - p98(1) [51-500]
   c KR - May 15 2015 - pNA [51-500]
   c PW - v262 - i19 - May 11 2015 - p62(1) [51-500]
   c SLJ - v61 - i8 - August 2015 - p88(1) [51-500]
Lista, Michael - *The Scarborough*
   Can Lit - i224 - Spring 2015 - p123 [501+]
Lister, Charles R. - *The Syrian Jihad: Al-Qaeda, the Islamic State and the Evolution of an Insurgency*
   KR - Jan 1 2016 - pNA [51-500]
Lister-Kaye, John - *Gods of the Morning: A Bird's-Eye View of a Changing World*
   KR - June 15 2015 - pNA [501+]
   PW - v262 - i22 - June 1 2015 - p52(2) [51-500]
Gods of the Morning: A Bird's-Eye View of a Changing Year
   Spec - v327 - i9732 - March 7 2015 - p41(2) [501+]
Lister, Michael - *The Big Bout*
   BL - v112 - i2 - Sept 15 2015 - p29(1) [51-500]
   PW - v262 - i31 - August 3 2015 - p37(1) [51-500]
Blood Money
   PW - v262 - i38 - Sept 21 2015 - p56(1) [51-500]
Blood Moon
   KR - Oct 1 2015 - pNA [501+]
Innocent Blood
   PW - v262 - i10 - March 9 2015 - p55(1) [51-500]
Lisy-Wagner, Laura - *Islam, Christianity, and the Making of Czech Identity, 1453-1683*
   JMH - v87 - i3 - Sept 2015 - p752(3) [501+]
Litan, Robert E. - *Trillion Dollar Economists: How Economists and Their Ideas Have Transformed Business*
   For Aff - v94 - i1 - Jan-Feb 2015 - pNA [51-500]
Litt, Jerome Z. - *Litt's Drug Eruption and Reaction Manual, 21st ed.*
   Bwatch - April 2015 - pNA [51-500]
Litt, Toby - *Life-Like*
   WLT - v89 - i3-4 - May-August 2015 - p115(1) [51-500]
Littauer, Amanda H. - *Bad Girls: Young Women, Sex, and Rebellion before the Sixties*
   LJ - v140 - i13 - August 1 2015 - p114(2) [51-500]
Littell, Jonathan - *Syrian Notebooks: Inside the Homs Uprising*
   NS - v144 - i5263 - May 22 2015 - p42(2) [501+]
   Lon R Bks - v37 - i14 - July 16 2015 - p5(6) [501+]
Little, Bentley - *The Consultant*
   BL - v112 - i1 - Sept 1 2015 - p54(2) [51-500]
Little, Catherine C. - *Transforming Work: Early Modern Pastoral and Late Medieval Poetry*
   MLR - v110 - i3 - July 2015 - p813-815 [501+]
Little, Charlene Pillow - *The Song of Sarah*
   KR - April 1 2015 - pNA [501+]
Little, Don - *Effective Discipling in Muslim Communities: Scripture, History, and Seasoned Practices*
   Ch Today - v59 - i6 - July-August 2015 - p91(1) [51-500]
Little, Jason - *Borb*
   PW - v262 - i8 - Feb 23 2015 - p60(1) [51-500]
Little, Jean - *Do Not Open until Christmas*
   c Res Links - v20 - i4 - April 2015 - p12(1) [501+]
Little, John R. - *Soul Mates*
   PW - v262 - i27 - July 6 2015 - p51(1) [501+]
Little, Kimberley Griffiths - *Forbidden*
   y BL - v111 - i16 - April 15 2015 - p57(1) [501+]
   y CCB-B - v68 - i5 - Jan 2015 - p265(1) [51-500]
   y HB Guide - v26 - i1 - Spring 2015 - p114(1) [51-500]
The Time of the Fireflies
   c HB Guide - v26 - i1 - Spring 2015 - p84(1) [51-500]
Little, Linda - *Work and More Work (Illus. by Perez, Oscar T.)*
   c CH Bwatch - Feb 2015 - pNA [51-500]
   c CH Bwatch - April 2015 - pNA [51-500]
   c HB Guide - v26 - i2 - Fall 2015 - p42(1) [51-500]
   c KR - Jan 15 2015 - pNA [51-500]
   c PW - v262 - i4 - Jan 26 2015 - p169(1) [51-500]
   c Res Links - v20 - i4 - April 2015 - p5(1) [501+]
Little, Peter C. - *Toxic Town: IBM, Pollution, and Industrial Risks*
   MAQ - v29 - i2 - June 2015 - pb21-b23 [501+]
Little, Shauna Sare - *The Gamers*
   y KR - May 1 2015 - pNA [501+]
Little, Thomas J. - *The Origins of Southern Evangelicalism: Religious Revivalism in the South Carolina Lowcountry, 1670-1760*
   JR - v95 - i2 - April 2015 - p287(3) [501+]
   JSH - v81 - i2 - May 2015 - p429(2) [501+]
Little, Tom - *Loving Learning: How Progressive Education Can Save America's Schools*
   BL - v111 - i13 - March 1 2015 - p7(1) [51-500]
   Bwatch - May 2015 - pNA [51-500]
   LJ - v140 - i2 - Feb 1 2015 - p92(2) [51-500]
   PW - v262 - i2 - Jan 12 2015 - p51(1) [51-500]
Loving Learning
   KR - Jan 1 2015 - pNA [501+]
Little, Tony - *An Intelligent Person's Guide to Education*
   Spec - v328 - i9756 - August 22 2015 - p40(2) [501+]
   NS - v144 - i5273 - July 31 2015 - p69(1) [51-500]
   TES - i5155 - July 17 2015 - p16(1) [501+]
Little, Troy - *Hunter S. Thompson's Fear and Loathing in Las Vegas*
   PW - v262 - i45 - Nov 9 2015 - p46(1) [51-500]
Littlefield, Bill - *The Top of His Game: The Best Sportswriting of W.C. Heinz*
   CSM - March 11 2015 - pNA [501+]
The Top of His Game: The Best Sportswriting of W. C. Heinz
   NYT - March 17 2015 - pC7(L) [501+]
Littlefield, Nick - *Lion of the Senate: When Ted Kennedy Rallied the Democrats in a GOP Congress*
   BL - v112 - i4 - Oct 15 2015 - p15(1) [51-500]
   KR - August 15 2015 - pNA [501+]
   LJ - v140 - i15 - Sept 15 2015 - p92(1) [51-500]
   PW - v262 - i32 - August 10 2015 - p46(2) [51-500]
Littlefield, Sophie - *The Guilty One (Read by Eby, Tanya). Audiobook Review*
   LJ - v140 - i19 - Nov 15 2015 - p52(1) [51-500]
The Guilty One
   LJ - v140 - i11 - June 15 2015 - p76(1) [51-500]
   RVBW - Sept 2015 - pNA [501+]
Infected
   y CCB-B - v68 - i6 - Feb 2015 - p319(1) [51-500]
   y HB Guide - v26 - i2 - Fall 2015 - p129(1) [51-500]
   y SLJ - v61 - i3 - March 2015 - p159(1) [51-500]
   y VOYA - v37 - i6 - Feb 2015 - p80(1) [51-500]
Littlejohn, Marion - *Life in Colonial Australia*
   c Magpies - v30 - i4 - Sept 2015 - p24(1) [501+]
Littlewood, Kathryn - *Rose Bliss Cooks Up Magic*
   y Sch Lib - v63 - i4 - Winter 2015 - p229(1) [51-500]
Littman, Sarah Darer - *Backlash*
   y BL - v111 - i12 - Feb 15 2015 - p79(1) [51-500]
   c CH Bwatch - June 2015 - pNA [501+]
   y HB Guide - v26 - i2 - Fall 2015 - p129(1) [51-500]
   PW - v262 - i2 - Jan 12 2015 - p60(1) [51-500]
Litton, Jonathan - *Boo! A Book of Spooky Surprises (Illus. by Galloway, Fhiona)*
   c KR - Jan 1 2016 - pNA [51-500]
   c PW - v262 - i30 - July 27 2015 - p66(1) [501+]
Farm: Barnyard Fun
   c KR - July 1 2015 - pNA [51-500]
Hoot
   c KR - Jan 1 2015 - pNA [51-500]
I Like to Squeak! How Do You Speak? (Illus. by Galloway, Fhiona)
   c KR - Jan 1 2016 - pNA [51-500]
   c PW - v262 - i27 - July 6 2015 - p70(2) [501+]
Mechanical Marvels (Illus. by Connell, Tom)
   c BL - v111 - i16 - April 15 2015 - p52(1) [51-500]
Noisy Dinosaurs
   c KR - Jan 1 2016 - pNA [51-500]
One Two, Baa Moo: A Pop-Up Book of Counting (Illus. by Verrall, Lisa)
   c PW - v262 - i27 - July 6 2015 - p70(2) [501+]
Peek-Through Forest
   c KR - Jan 1 2016 - pNA [51-500]
Red Car, Blue Car (Illus. by Verrall, Lisa)
   c KR - Dec 1 2015 - pNA [51-500]
Snap (Illus. by Galloway, Fhiona)
   c KR - Jan 1 2015 - pNA [51-500]
Snip Snap Pop-Up Fun (Illus. by Nowowiejska, Kasia)
   c BL - v111 - i16 - April 15 2015 - p52(1) [51-500]
   c KR - Dec 1 2015 - pNA [51-500]
   c PW - v262 - i5 - Feb 2 2015 - p60(1) [501+]
What's the Time Clockodile?
   c KR - Dec 1 2015 - pNA [51-500]

Litwack, David - *The Children of Darkness*
  KR - August 1 2015 - pNA [501+]
Litwin, Eric - *The Nuts: Bedtime at the Nut House (Illus. by Magoon, Scott)*
  c HB Guide - v26 - i1 - Spring 2015 - p37(1) [51-500]
  The Nuts: Sing and Dance in Your Polka-Dot Pants (Illus. by Magoon, Scott)
  c SLJ - v61 - i11 - Nov 2015 - p84(1) [51-500]
Litwin, Mike - *Crown of the Cowibbean (Illus. by Litwin, Mike)*
  c HB Guide - v26 - i1 - Spring 2015 - p62(1) [51-500]
Liu, Cixin - *The Dark Forest*
  KR - June 15 2015 - pNA [501+]
  The Three-Body Problem
  MFSF - v128 - i3-4 - March-April 2015 - p73(8) [501+]
  New Sci - v227 - i3032 - August 1 2015 - p44(2) [501+]
  TLS - i5872 - Oct 16 2015 - p20(1) [501+]
  WLT - v89 - i5 - Sept-Oct 2015 - p63(2) [501+]
Liu, Cynthea - *Bike On, Bear! (Illus. by Litten, Kristyna)*
  c HB Guide - v26 - i2 - Fall 2015 - p42(1) [51-500]
  c KR - March 15 2015 - pNA [51-500]
  c SLJ - v61 - i6 - June 2015 - p87(1) [51-500]
Liu, Ken - *The Grace of Kings*
  PW - v262 - i8 - Feb 23 2015 - p57(1) [51-500]
Liu, Liana - *The Memory Key*
  BL - v111 - i12 - Feb 15 2015 - p82(2) [51-500]
  c HB Guide - v26 - i2 - Fall 2015 - p129(1) [51-500]
  y KR - Jan 1 2015 - pNA [51-500]
  PW - v262 - i2 - Jan 12 2015 - p61(1) [51-500]
  y VOYA - v37 - i6 - Feb 2015 - p80(2) [51-500]
Liu, Lydia H. - *The Birth of Chinese Feminism: Essential Texts in Transnational Theory*
  Bks & Cult - v21 - i2 - March-April 2015 - p37(1) [501+]
Liu, Robert K. - *Photography of Personal Adornment*
  Am Craft - v75 - i5 - Oct-Nov 2015 - p24(1) [501+]
Liu, Siyuan - *Performing Hybridity in Colonial-Modern China*
  JAS - v74 - i1 - Feb 2015 - p202-203 [501+]
Liu, Sylvia - *A Morning with Grandpa (Illus. by Forshay, Christina)*
  c PW - v262 - i47 - Nov 23 2015 - p66(1) [501+]
Liu, Xia - *Empty Chairs*
  BL - v112 - i5 - Nov 1 2015 - p12(1) [51-500]
  PW - v262 - i46 - Nov 16 2015 - p53(2) [51-500]
Liukas, Linda - *Hello Ruby*
  c KR - Sept 15 2015 - pNA [51-500]
LiuPerkins, Christine - *At Home In Her Tomb (Illus. by Brannen, Sarah S.)*
  c BL - v111 - i9-10 - Jan 1 2015 - pS4(8) [501+]
Livanios, Eleni - *Best Grandma in the World*
  c KR - July 15 2015 - pNA [51-500]
  The Best Grandpa in the World! (Illus. by Lutje, Susanne)
  c PW - v262 - i26 - June 29 2015 - p67(1) [501+]
  c SLJ - v61 - i9 - Sept 2015 - p111(1) [51-500]
Lively, Padgett - *Odette Speex*
  y PW - v262 - i46 - Nov 16 2015 - p77(1) [51-500]
Liverani, Mario - *The Ancient Near East: History, Society and Economy*
  Class R - v65 - i1 - April 2015 - p165-167 [501+]
Living in European Borderlands
  HNet - Jan 2015 - pNA [501+]
Livings, Jack - *The Dog: Stories*
  NYRB - v62 - i18 - Nov 19 2015 - p56(5) [501+]
  Spec - v328 - i9756 - August 22 2015 - p36(1) [501+]
Livingston, A.A. - *B. Bear & Lolly: Off to School*
  c HB Guide - v26 - i2 - Fall 2015 - p42(1) [51-500]
  Catch That Cookie! (Illus. by Chou, Joey)
  c SLJ - v61 - i5 - May 2015 - p87(1) [51-500]
Livingston, Billie - *The Crooked Heart of Mercy*
  KR - Jan 1 2016 - pNA [51-500]
Livingston, Eric - *Ethnographies of Reason*
  CS - v44 - i5 - Sept 2015 - p604-614 [501+]
Livingston, Jane - *The New York School: Photographs, 1936-1963*
  NYRB - v62 - i12 - July 9 2015 - p10(3) [501+]
  NYRB - v62 - i12 - July 9 2015 - p10(3) [501+]
Livingston, Lenora - *Where's Stephanie? A Story of Love, Faith, and Courage*
  SPBW - May 2015 - pNA [51-500]
Livingston, Lesley - *Transcendent: A Starling Novel*
  y HB Guide - v26 - i1 - Spring 2015 - p114(1) [51-500]
Livingston, Michael - *The Shards of Heaven*
  KR - Sept 15 2015 - pNA [51-500]
  PW - v262 - i38 - Sept 21 2015 - p58(1) [51-500]

Livingston, Sonja - *Queen of the Fall: A Memoir of Girls and Goddesses*
  KR - March 1 2015 - pNA [501+]
Livingstone, David N. - *Dealing with Darwin: Place, Politics, and Rhetoric in Religious Engagements with Evolution*
  AHR - v120 - i2 - April 2015 - p582-583 [501+]
  CH - v84 - i3 - Sept 2015 - p680(1) [501+]
Livingstone, Natalie - *The Mistresses of Cliveden: Three Centuries of Scandal, Power and Intrigue*
  Spec - v328 - i9751 - July 18 2015 - p34(1) [501+]
Livington, Lesley - *Transcendent: A Starling Novel*
  y Res Links - v20 - i4 - April 2015 - p31(1) [51-500]
Lixey, Kevin - *Sport and Christianity: A Sign of the Times in the Light of Faith*
  CHR - v101 - i3 - Summer 2015 - p597(2) [501+]
Lizhi, Fang - *The Most Wanted Man in China: My Journey from Scientist to Enemy of the State*
  PW - v262 - i48 - Nov 30 2015 - p49(1) [51-500]
Lizzi, Ken - *Under Strange Suns*
  PW - v262 - i44 - Nov 2 2015 - p66(1) [51-500]
Ljungkvist, Laura - *A Line Can Be (Illus. by Ljungkvist, Laura)*
  c SLJ - v61 - i7 - July 2015 - p56(1) [51-500]
  Search and Spot: Animals! (Illus. by Ljungkvist, Laura)
  c HB - v91 - i6 - Nov-Dec 2015 - p71(2) [51-500]
  c KR - August 1 2015 - pNA [51-500]
  c SLJ - v61 - i6 - June 2015 - p87(1) [51-500]
Llenas, Anna - *The Color Monster: A Pop-Up Book of Feelings (Illus. by Llenas, Anna)*
  c KR - Dec 1 2015 - pNA [51-500]
  c SLJ - v61 - i12 - Dec 2015 - p85(1) [51-500]
Llewellyn, Claire - *African Savanna*
  c HB Guide - v26 - i2 - Fall 2015 - p218(1) [51-500]
  Amazing Animal Senses (Illus. by Llewellyn, Claire)
  c HB Guide - v26 - i2 - Fall 2015 - p171(1) [51-500]
  Spiders: Deadly Predators
  c HB Guide - v26 - i1 - Spring 2015 - p158(2) [51-500]
Llewellyn, Kathleen M. - *Representing Judith in Early Modern French Litterature*
  FS - v69 - i4 - Oct 2015 - p522-523 [501+]
Llewellyn, Tom - *The Shadow of Seth*
  c BL - v111 - i17 - May 1 2015 - p53(1) [51-500]
  y KR - May 15 2015 - pNA [51-500]
Llewelyn, Christopher - *Tyranno-sort-of-Rex (Illus. by Tulloch, Scott)*
  Magpies - v30 - i3 - July 2015 - pS4(2) [501+]
Lliteras, D.S. - *Viet Man*
  BL - v111 - i15 - April 1 2015 - p28(1) [51-500]
  PW - v262 - i6 - Feb 9 2015 - p43(1) [51-500]
Lloret, Albert - *Printing Ausias March: Material Culture and Renaissance Poetics*
  MLN - v130 - i2 - March 2015 - p405-407 [501+]
  Ren Q - v68 - i1 - Spring 2015 - p375-377 [501+]
Llosa, Mario Vargas - *The Discreet Hero*
  BL - v111 - i9-10 - Jan 1 2015 - p36(1) [51-500]
  KR - Jan 1 2015 - pNA [51-500]
  NS - v144 - i5255 - March 27 2015 - p73(1) [501+]
  NYTBR - March 15 2015 - p15(L) [501+]
  Spec - v327 - i9739 - April 25 2015 - p42(2) [501+]
  Notes on the Death of Culture: Essays on Spectacle and Society
  NYTBR - August 23 2015 - p12(L) [501+]
Lloyd, Ann - *Gizmo the Lonely Robucket (Illus. by Forbus, Tiffanie)*
  c CH Bwatch - Jan 2015 - pNA [51-500]
Lloyd, Anthony - *Labour Markets and Identity on the Post-Industrial Assembly Line*
  CS - v44 - i5 - Sept 2015 - p672-674 [501+]
Lloyd, Brett - *Scugnizzi*
  NS - v144 - i5250 - Feb 20 2015 - p50(1) [51-500]
Lloyd, Catherine - *Death Comes to Kurland Hall*
  KR - Sept 15 2015 - pNA [51-500]
Lloyd, Christopher D. - *Social-Spatial Segregation: Concepts, Processes and Outcomes*
  AJS - v121 - i2 - Sept 2015 - p614(2) [501+]
Lloyd, Donal Blaise - *Geo Power: Stay Warm, Keep Cool and Save Money with Geothermal Heating and Cooling*
  LJ - v140 - i12 - July 1 2015 - p108(1) [51-500]
Lloyd, Jennifer - *Murilla Gorilla and the Hammock Problem (Illus. by Lee, Jacqui)*
  c HB Guide - v26 - i1 - Spring 2015 - p54(2) [51-500]
  Taffy Time (Illus. by Lee, Jacqui)
  c CH Bwatch - June 2015 - pNA [51-500]
  c SLJ - v61 - i7 - July 2015 - p64(1) [51-500]
Lloyd, John - *1,411 Quite Interesting Facts to Knock You Sideways*
  LJ - v140 - i16 - Oct 1 2015 - p109(1) [51-500]

Lloyd-Jones, Emily - *Deceptive*
  y SLJ - v61 - i10 - Oct 2015 - p104(1) [51-500]
  Illusive
  y HB Guide - v26 - i1 - Spring 2015 - p114(1) [51-500]
Lloyd-Jones, Sally - *Bunny's First Spring (Illus. by McPhail, David)*
  c SLJ - v61 - i2 - Feb 2015 - p72(1) [51-500]
  The House That's Your Home (Illus. by Dyer, Jane)
  c HB - v91 - i1 - Jan-Feb 2015 - p69(1) [51-500]
  HB Guide - v26 - i2 - Fall 2015 - p14(1) [51-500]
  Sally Poor Doreen: A Fishy Tale (Illus. by Boiger, Alexandra)
  c HB Guide - v26 - i1 - Spring 2015 - p37(1) [51-500]
  Skip to the Loo, My Darling! A Potty Book (Illus. by Jeram, Anita)
  c PW - v262 - i50 - Dec 7 2015 - p86(1) [501+]
Lloyd, Kalan Chapman - *Home Is Where Your Boots Are*
  KR - May 1 2015 - pNA [501+]
  These Boots Are Made for Butt Kickin'
  KR - June 15 2015 - pNA [501+]
Lloyd, Natalie - *A Snicker of Magic (Read by Morris, Cassandra). Audiobook Review*
  c SLJ - v61 - i2 - Feb 2015 - p38(3) [501+]
Lloyd, Nick - *Hundred Days: The Campaign That Ended World War I*
  AHR - v120 - i1 - Feb 2015 - p343-344 [501+]
  J Mil H - v79 - i4 - Oct 2015 - p1178-1179 [501+]
Lloyd, Stephen - *Constant Lambert: Beyond the Rio Grande*
  Lon R Bks - v37 - i2 - Jan 22 2015 - p28(2) [501+]
Llwyd, Humphrey - *"The Breviary of Britain" (1573), with Selections from "The History of Cambria" (1584).*
  MLR - v110 - i2 - April 2015 - p522-523 [501+]
Llywelyn, Dorian - *America's Church: The National Shrine and Catholic Presence in the Nation's Capital*
  JAAR - v83 - i2 - June 2015 - p587-591 [501+]
Lo Bello, Anthony - *Origins of Mathematical Words: A Comprehensive Dictionary of Latin, Greek, and Arabic Roots*
  Math T - v108 - i8 - April 2015 - p638-639 [501+]
Lo, Bobo - *Russia and the New World Disorder*
  Econ - v416 - i8949 - August 1 2015 - p73(US) [501+]
Lo, Malinda - *Adaptation*
  y Sch Lib - v63 - i1 - Spring 2015 - p55(1) [51-500]
  Inheritance
  y Sch Lib - v63 - i1 - Spring 2015 - p55(1) [51-500]
Lo Monaco, Gerard - *Madame Sonia Delaunay*
  c KR - Dec 1 2015 - pNA [51-500]
  The Small World of Paper Toys
  c KR - Dec 1 2015 - pNA [51-500]
Loan-Wilsey, Anna - *A Deceptive Homecoming*
  PW - v262 - i23 - June 8 2015 - p39(2) [51-500]
Lobbes, Louis - *Des Apophtegmes a la Polyanthee: Erasme et le Genre des Dits Memorables*
  Sev Cent N - v73 - i1-2 - Spring-Summer 2015 - p69(5) [501+]
Lobe, Mira - *Hoppelpopp and the Best Bunny (Illus. by Kaufmann, Angelika)*
  c KR - Jan 1 2015 - pNA [51-500]
  SLJ - v61 - i3 - March 2015 - p121(1) [51-500]
Lobel, Anita - *Playful Pigs from A to Z (Illus. by Lobel, Anita)*
  c BL - v111 - i18 - May 15 2015 - p58(2) [51-500]
  c HB - v91 - i4 - July-August 2015 - p120(1) [51-500]
  c KR - April 15 2015 - pNA [51-500]
  c PW - v262 - i23 - June 8 2015 - p60(1) [51-500]
  c SLJ - v61 - i5 - May 2015 - p87(2) [51-500]
Lobel, Cindy R. - *Urban Appetites: Food and Culture in Nineteenth-Century New York*
  JAH - v102 - i1 - June 2015 - p265-266 [501+]
Lobell, Nathan D. - *Of Things That Used to Be: A Childhood on Fox Street in the Bronx in the Early Twentieth Century*
  NYT - Jan 11 2015 - p3(L) [501+]
LoBiondo, Gina - *Button Nose the Sad Little Bear (Illus. by Wilder, Brittany)*
  c CH Bwatch - Sept 2015 - pNA [51-500]
Locher, Mira - *Japanese Architecture*
  Bwatch - July 2015 - pNA [51-500]
LoCicero, Alice - *Why "Good Kids" Turn into Deadly Terrorists: Deconstructing the Accused Boston Marathon Bombers and Others Like Them*
  KR - Feb 15 2015 - pNA [501+]
Lock, Andrew - *Master of Thin Air: Life and Death on the World's Highest Peaks*
  LJ - v140 - i15 - Sept 15 2015 - p84(1) [501+]

Lock, Norman - *American Meteor (Read by Bramhall, Mark). Audiobook Review*
y BL - v112 - i4 - Oct 15 2015 - p60(1) [51-500]
American Meteor
BL - v111 - i17 - May 1 2015 - p78(1) [51-500]
KR - April 15 2015 - pNA [501+]
LJ - v140 - i10 - June 1 2015 - p91(1) [51-500]

Locke, Attica - *Pleasantville*
BL - v111 - i13 - March 1 2015 - p25(1) [51-500]
KR - Feb 15 2015 - pNA [51-500]
LJ - v140 - i6 - April 1 2015 - p83(1) [51-500]
PW - v262 - i5 - Feb 2 2015 - p37(1) [51-500]
Spec - v327 - i9738 - April 18 2015 - p44(1) [501+]
TLS - i5854 - June 12 2015 - p10(1) [501+]

Locke, Brian S. - *Otakar Zich: Vina - Opera in Three Acts Based on the Play by Jaroslav Hilbert: Part 1: Introductory Materials and Act 1*
Notes - v71 - i4 - June 2015 - p752(4) [501+]
Otakar Zich: Vina - Opera in Three Acts Based on the Play by Jaroslav Hilbert: Part 2, Act 2
Notes - v71 - i4 - June 2015 - p752(4) [501+]
Otakar Zich: Vina - Opera in Three Acts Based on the Play by Jaroslav Hilbert: Part 3, Act 3 and Critical Report
Notes - v71 - i4 - June 2015 - p752(4) [501+]

Locke, Edwin A. - *New Developments in Goal Setting and Task Performance*
Per Psy - v68 - i3 - Autumn 2015 - p709(3) [501+]

Locke, Hillary Bell - *Collar Robber*
KR - March 1 2015 - pNA [51-500]
PW - v262 - i9 - March 2 2015 - p65(2) [51-500]

Locker, Jesse M. - *Artemisia Gentileschi: The Language of Painting*
LJ - v140 - i10 - June 1 2015 - p100(1) [51-500]

Locker, Ray - *Nixon's Gamble: How a President's Own Secret Government Destroyed His Administration*
LJ - v140 - i14 - Sept 1 2015 - p120(2) [501+]
PW - v262 - i35 - August 31 2015 - p79(1) [51-500]

Lockhart, E. - *The Disreputable History of Frankie Landau-Banks*
y Magpies - v30 - i1 - March 2015 - p41(1) [501+]
How to Be Bad
y Magpies - v30 - i3 - July 2015 - p42(1) [501+]
y Sch Lib - v63 - i4 - Winter 2015 - p253(1) [501+]
We Were Liars (Read by Meyers, Ariadne). Audiobook Review
c BL - v111 - i14 - March 15 2015 - p24(2) [51-500]
We Were Liars
y Teach Lib - v42 - i3 - Feb 2015 - p43(1) [501+]

Lockhart, Paul - *A Mathematician's Lament: How School Cheats Us Out of Our Most Fascinating and Imaginative Art Form*
CHE - v62 - i6 - Oct 9 2015 - pA16(1) [51-500]

Lockhart, Ross E. - *Giallo Fantastique: Tales of Crime and Terror*
PW - v262 - i12 - March 23 2015 - p51(2) [51-500]

Lockley, Nigeria - *Seasoned with Grace*
PW - v262 - i20 - May 18 2015 - p38(1) [51-500]

Locklin, Reid B. - *Liturgy of Liberation: A Christian Commentary on Shankara's "Upadesasahasri"*
JR - v95 - i3 - July 2015 - p413(3) [501+]

Lockwood, Lewis - *Beethoven's Symphonies: An Artistic Vision*
BL - v112 - i1 - Sept 1 2015 - p24(1) [51-500]
KR - August 1 2015 - pNA [501+]
LJ - v140 - i13 - August 1 2015 - p98(1) [51-500]
NYRB - v62 - i19 - Dec 3 2015 - p40(3) [501+]

Lockwood, Vicki - *The Magnificent Lizzie Brown and the Devil's Hound*
c HB Guide - v26 - i1 - Spring 2015 - p84(1) [51-500]
The Magnificent Lizzie Brown and the Mysterious Phantom
y Teach Lib - v42 - i3 - Feb 2015 - p32(6) [501+]
c HB Guide - v26 - i1 - Spring 2015 - p84(1) [51-500]

Loconte, Joseph - *A Hobbit, a Wardrobe, and a Great War: How J.R.R. Tolkien and C.S. Lewis Rediscovered Faith, Friendship, and Heroism in the Cataclysm of 1914-1918*
BL - v111 - i21 - July 1 2015 - p17(1) [51-500]

Lodge, David - *Lives in Writing: Essays*
Lon R Bks - v37 - i4 - Feb 19 2015 - p13(3) [501+]
Quite a Good Time to Be Born: A Memoir, 1935-1975
Lon R Bks - v37 - i4 - Feb 19 2015 - p13(3) [501+]
NS - v144 - i5247 - Jan 30 2015 - p46(2) [501+]
Spec - v327 - i9726 - Jan 24 2015 - p40(2) [501+]
TimHES - i2224 - Oct 8 2015 - p43(1) [501+]
TLS - i5848 - May 1 2015 - p8(1) [501+]

Lodge, Jo - *Happy Birthday, Mr. Croc! (Illus. by Lodge, Jo)*
c BL - v111 - i16 - April 15 2015 - p52(1) [51-500]
Happy Birthday, Mr Croc! (Illus. by Lodge, Jo)
c KR - Dec 1 2015 - pNA [51-500]
Happy Birthday, Mr. Croc! (Illus. by Lodge, Jo)
c PW - v262 - i5 - Feb 2 2015 - p60(1) [501+]

Lodge, Nancy Kunhardt - *The Crystal Navigator: A Perilous Journey through Time*
y CH Bwatch - Jan 2015 - pNA [51-500]
KR - May 1 2015 - pNA [501+]

Loe, Steve - *The Glimpsing Book*
c CH Bwatch - May 2015 - pNA [51-500]

Loehfelm, Bill - *Doing the Devil's Work*
BL - v111 - i9-10 - Jan 1 2015 - p45(1) [51-500]
NYTBR - Jan 18 2015 - p25(L) [501+]

Loesch, Kevin - *Small Government My A***
RVBW - March 2015 - pNA [51-500]

Loewen, Nancy - *Besties, Sleepovers, and Drama Queens: Questions and Answers about Friends (Illus. by Mora, Julissa)*
c HB Guide - v26 - i2 - Fall 2015 - p147(1) [51-500]
People of the World
c Sch Lib - v63 - i4 - Winter 2015 - p219(1) [51-500]
Siblings, Curfews, and How to Deal: Questions and Answers about Family Life (Illus. by Mora, Julissa)
c HB Guide - v26 - i2 - Fall 2015 - p151(1) [51-500]
Walt Whitman (Illus. by Day, Rob)
c HB Guide - v26 - i1 - Spring 2015 - p191(1) [51-500]

Loewenstein, David - *Treacherous Faith: The Specter of Heresy in Early Modern English Literature and Culture*
Ren Q - v68 - i2 - Summer 2015 - p760-761 [501+]

Loewy, Ronny - *"Der Letzte der Ungerechten": Der "Judenalteste" Benjamin Murmelstein in Filmen 1942-1975*
HNet - Feb 2015 - pNA [501+]

Lofchie, Michael F. - *The Political Economy of Tanzania: Decline and Recovery*
IJAHS - v48 - i1 - Wntr 2015 - p130-131 [501+]

Loffelbein, Nils - *Ehrenburger der Nation: Die Kriegsbeschadigten des Ersten Weltkriegs in Politik und Propaganda des Nationalsozialismus*
HNet - June 2015 - pNA [501+]

Lofgren, Mike - *The Deep State: The Fall of the Constitution and the Rise of a Shadow Government*
KR - Oct 15 2015 - pNA [501+]

Loftin, Nikki - *Wish Girl*
c CCB-B - v68 - i9 - May 2015 - p454(1) [51-500]
c HB Guide - v26 - i2 - Fall 2015 - p91(1) [51-500]
c NYTBR - March 15 2015 - p17(L) [501+]
c SLJ - v61 - i2 - Feb 2015 - p88(2) [51-500]
y VOYA - v37 - i6 - Feb 2015 - p60(1) [51-500]

Lofting, Hugh - *Doctor Dolittle (Illus. by Chwast, Seymour)*
c SLJ - v61 - i10 - Oct 2015 - p98(1) [51-500]

Loftis, Sonya Freeman - *Shakespeare's Surrogates: Rewriting Renaissance Drama*
Six Ct J - v46 - i2 - Summer 2015 - p504-507 [501+]

Logan, Kirsty - *The Gracekeepers*
BL - v111 - i14 - March 15 2015 - p50(1) [51-500]
BL - v111 - i18 - May 15 2015 - p35(1) [51-500]
KR - March 15 2015 - pNA [501+]
LJ - v140 - i6 - April 1 2015 - p119(1) [51-500]
LJ - v140 - i9 - May 15 2015 - p74(3) [51-500]
y SLJ - v61 - i10 - Oct 2015 - p122(2) [51-500]

Logan, Laura - *Little Butterfly*
c KR - Dec 1 2015 - pNA [51-500]

Logan, Michael - *World War Moo*
y BL - v111 - i19-20 - June 1 2015 - p65(1) [51-500]
KR - April 1 2015 - pNA [501+]
LJ - v140 - i9 - May 15 2015 - p57(4) [501+]
PW - v262 - i15 - April 13 2015 - p62(1) [51-500]

Logan, Sadye L.M. - *The Spirit of an Activist: The Life and Work of I. DeQuincey Newman*
JSH - v81 - i3 - August 2015 - p772(2) [501+]

Logan, Samuel T., Jr. - *Reformed Means Missional: Following Jesus into the World*
IBMR - v39 - i1 - Jan 2015 - p44(1) [501+]

Logemann, Jan L. - *Trams or Tailfins? Public and Private Prosperity in Postwar West Germany and the United States*
T&C - v56 - i1 - Jan 2015 - p283-284 [501+]

Logothetis, Paul - *Cristiano Ronaldo: International Soccer Star*
c BL - v112 - i4 - Oct 15 2015 - p43(1) [51-500]
Lionel Messi: Soccer Sensation
c BL - v112 - i4 - Oct 15 2015 - p43(1) [51-500]
Rory McIlroy: Golf Champion
c BL - v112 - i4 - Oct 15 2015 - p43(1) [51-500]

Logoz, Dinu - *John Mayall: The Blues Crusader*
Dbt - v83 - i1 - Jan 2016 - p76(1) [501+]

Logue, Christopher - *War Music*
TLS - i5854 - June 12 2015 - p10(1) [501+]

Loh, Kah Seng - *Squatters into Citizens: The 1961 Bukit Ho Swee Fire and the Making of Modern Singapore*
Pac A - v88 - i3 - Sept 2015 - p739 [501+]
The University Socialist Club and the Contest for Malaya: Tangled Strands of Modernity
Pac A - v88 - i1 - March 2015 - p226 [501+]

Loh, Maria H. - *Still Lives: Death, Desire, and the Portrait of the Old Master*
TimHES - i2209 - June 25 2015 - p50(1) [51-500]

Lohfink, Gerhard - *No Irrelevant Jesus: On Jesus and the Church Today*
Theol St - v76 - i2 - June 2015 - p371(2) [501+]

Lohlein, Susanne - *Hamster Monster (Illus. by Lohlein, Henning)*
c HB Guide - v26 - i1 - Spring 2015 - p37(1) [51-500]

Lohr, Steve - *Data-ism: Inside the Big Data Revolution*
Nature - v518 - i7540 - Feb 26 2015 - p480(2) [501+]
Data-ism: The Revolution Transforming Decision Making, Consumer Behavior, and Almost Everything Else
PW - v262 - i3 - Jan 19 2015 - p72(1) [501+]

Lohre, Mike - *Six Degrees of LeBron James: Connecting Basketball Stars*
c HB Guide - v26 - i2 - Fall 2015 - p199(1) [51-500]

Loigman, Lynda Cohen - *The Two-Family House*
KR - Jan 1 2016 - pNA [51-500]

Lois, Jennifer - *Home Is Where the School Is: The Logic of Homeschooling and the Emotional Labor of Mothering*
SF - v94 - i2 - Dec 2015 - pNA [501+]

Loiselle, Kenneth - *Brotherly Love: Freemasonry and Male Friendship in Enlightenment France*
AHR - v120 - i3 - June 2015 - p1124-1125 [501+]

Lok, Joan - *Chinese Brush Painting: Flowers*
LJ - v140 - i8 - May 1 2015 - p72(1) [51-500]

Lokale Geschichte(n), (Macht-)Politik und die Suche nach Historischer Authentizitat
HNet - July 2015 - pNA [501+]

Loker, Chris - *One Hundred Books Famous in Children's Literature*
TLS - i5864-5865 - August 21 2015 - p27(1) [501+]

Lokere, Jillian - *Epidemiology: The Fight Against Ebola & Other Diseases*
y HB Guide - v26 - i2 - Fall 2015 - p184(1) [51-500]

LoLordo, Antonia - *Locke's Moral Man*
Phil R - v124 - i2 - April 2015 - p261(3) [501+]

Lomax, Raeder - *Stand Your Ground*
KR - Dec 1 2015 - pNA [501+]

Lombardi, Elena - *Dantean Dialogues: Engaging with the Legacy of Amilcare Iannucci*
Med R - Sept 2015 - pNA [501+]

Lombardi, John V. - *How Universities Work*
J Hi E - v86 - i4 - July-August 2015 - p663(4) [501+]

Lombardi, Kristine A. - *Lovey Bunny*
c HB Guide - v26 - i2 - Fall 2015 - p14(1) [51-500]
PW - v262 - i2 - Jan 12 2015 - p57(1) [51-500]
c PW - v262 - i7 - Feb 16 2015 - p33(34) [501+]

Lombardo, Constance - *Mr. Puffball: Stunt Cat to the Stars (Illus. by Lombardo, Constance)*
c PW - v262 - i27 - July 6 2015 - p73(1) [501+]
c SLJ - v61 - i7 - July 2015 - p80(1) [51-500]
Stunt Cat to the Stars (Illus. by Lombardo, Constance)
c KR - June 1 2015 - pNA [51-500]

Lomberg, Michelle - *The Iroquois*
c BL - v112 - i1 - Sept 1 2015 - p96(1) [51-500]
The Ojibwa
c BL - v112 - i1 - Sept 1 2015 - p96(1) [51-500]

Lomborg, Bjorn - *Prioritizing the World: Cost-Benefit to Identify the Smartest Targets for the Next 15 Years*
For Aff - v94 - i3 - May-June 2015 - pNA [501+]

Lomer, Kathryn - *Talk under Water*
y Magpies - v30 - i4 - Sept 2015 - p42(1) [501+]

Lomnitz, Claudio - *The Return of Comrade Ricardo Flores Magon*
AHR - v120 - i2 - April 2015 - p558-561 [501+]

Londero, Rudolfo Rurato - *Futuro Esquecido: A Recepcao da Ficcao Cyberpunk na America Latina. E-book Review*
SFS - v42 - i1 - March 2015 - p181-182 [501+]

London, C. Alexander - *The Wild Ones*
    c KR - April 15 2015 - pNA [51-500]
    c SLJ - v61 - i8 - August 2015 - p88(1) [51-500]
London, Jack - *The People of the Abyss*
    TLS - i5843 - March 27 2015 - p22(1) [501+]
London, Jonathan - *Desolation Canyon*
    c CH Bwatch - Feb 2015 - pNA [51-500]
    KR - May 1 2015 - pNA [501+]
Froggy Goes to the Library (Illus. by Remkiewicz, Frank)
    c KR - Jan 1 2016 - pNA [51-500]
Froggy's Birthday Wish (Read by McDonough, John). Audiobook Review
    c SLJ - v61 - i10 - Oct 2015 - p50(2) [51-500]
Froggy's Birthday Wish (Illus. by Remkiewicz, Frank)
    c CH Bwatch - June 2015 - pNA [501+]
    c HB Guide - v26 - i2 - Fall 2015 - p42(1) [51-500]
    c KR - Jan 15 2015 - pNA [51-500]
Hippos Are Huge! (Illus. by Trueman, Matthew)
    c HB - v91 - i2 - March-April 2015 - p122(2) [51-500]
    c CCB-B - v68 - i9 - May 2015 - p455(1) [51-500]
    c CH Bwatch - June 2015 - pNA [501+]
    c HB Guide - v26 - i2 - Fall 2015 - p180(1) [51-500]
    c KR - Jan 1 2015 - pNA [51-500]
Little Puffin's First Flight (Illus. by Van Zyle, Jon)
    c HB Guide - v26 - i2 - Fall 2015 - p177(1) [51-500]
    c KR - Jan 15 2015 - pNA [51-500]
Ollie's First Year (Illus. by Van Zyle, Jon)
    c HB Guide - v26 - i1 - Spring 2015 - p37(1) [51-500]
Otters Love to Play (Illus. by So, Meilo)
    c KR - Dec 15 2015 - pNA [51-500]
London, Julia - *The Devil Takes a Bride*
    BL - v111 - i9-10 - Jan 1 2015 - p56(1) [51-500]
The Perfect Homecoming
    BL - v111 - i11 - Feb 1 2015 - p31(1) [51-500]
    KR - Jan 1 2015 - pNA [501+]
    PW - v262 - i2 - Jan 12 2015 - p43(1) [51-500]
The Scoundrel and the Debutante
    PW - v262 - i9 - March 2 2015 - p71(1) [51-500]
The Trouble with Honor (Read by Landor, Rosalyn). Audiobook Review
    BL - v111 - i12 - Feb 15 2015 - p104(1) [51-500]
London, Matt - *Welcome to the Jungle*
    c HB Guide - v26 - i2 - Fall 2015 - p92(1) [51-500]
Lonely Planet - *Adventures in Famous Places*
    c PW - v262 - i18 - May 4 2015 - p117(1) [501+]
From the Source: Italy: Authentic Recipes from the People That Know Them Best
    LJ - v140 - i19 - Nov 15 2015 - p102(1) [51-500]
You Only Live Once: A Lifetime of Experiences for the Explorer in All of Us
    Bwatch - Jan 2015 - pNA [51-500]
Lonely Planet Kids - *The Lonely Planet Kids Travel Book: Mind-Blowing Stuff on Every Country in the World*
    c CH Bwatch - Oct 2015 - pNA [51-500]
Long, A.A. - *Greek Models of Mind and Self*
    Nation - v301 - i19 - Nov 9 2015 - p37(1) [501+]
    RM - v69 - i1 - Sept 2015 - p145(2) [501+]
Long, Christopher - *Kem Weber: Designer and Architect*
    Mag Antiq - v182 - i1 - Jan-Feb 2015 - p102(2) [501+]
Long, D. Stephen - *Saving Karl Barth: Hans Urs von Balthasar's Preoccupation*
    TT - v72 - i2 - July 2015 - p242-243 [501+]
Long, David - *Diary of a Time Traveler* (Illus. by Stevenson, Nicholas)
    c PW - v262 - i41 - Oct 12 2015 - p69(1) [51-500]
    c SLJ - v61 - i10 - Oct 2015 - p126(1) [51-500]
Diary of a Time Traveller (Illus. by Stevenson, Nicholas)
    c KR - Sept 1 2015 - pNA [51-500]
Long, Dustin - *NASCAR Racing*
    c HB Guide - v26 - i1 - Spring 2015 - p183(1) [51-500]
Long, Ethan - *Big Cat* (Illus. by Long, Ethan)
    c KR - Dec 15 2015 - pNA [51-500]
Fright Club (Illus. by Long, Ethan)
    c HB - v91 - i5 - Sept-Oct 2015 - p68(1) [51-500]
    c KR - August 1 2015 - pNA [51-500]
    c PW - v262 - i30 - July 27 2015 - p66(2) [51-500]
    c PW - v262 - i49 - Dec 2 2015 - p60(1) [51-500]
    c SLJ - v61 - i9 - Sept 2015 - p107(1) [51-500]
Good Night!
    c KR - Jan 1 2016 - pNA [51-500]
    c SLJ - v61 - i7 - July 2015 - p56(1) [51-500]
Hi! (Illus. by Long, Ethan)
    c KR - July 1 2015 - pNA [51-500]
    c PW - v262 - i15 - April 13 2015 - p78(2) [51-500]
    c SLJ - v61 - i6 - June 2015 - p56(1) [51-500]
In, Over and On! (the Farm). (Illus. by Long, Ethan)
    c NYTBR - August 23 2015 - p26(L) [51-500]
    c SLJ - v61 - i11 - Nov 2015 - p84(1) [51-500]
Lion and Tiger and Bear: Tag! You're It! (Illus. by Long, Ethan)
    c PW - v262 - i52 - Dec 21 2015 - p153(2) [51-500]
Ms. Spell (Illus. by Long, Ethan)
    c KR - July 15 2015 - pNA [51-500]
    c SLJ - v61 - i8 - August 2015 - p59(2) [51-500]
The Wing Wing Brothers Geometry Palooza!
    c HB - v91 - i1 - Jan-Feb 2015 - p106(2) [51-500]
Long, Hayley - *Being a Girl*
    y Sch Lib - v63 - i4 - Winter 2015 - p251(1) [51-500]
Sophie Someone
    y Sch Lib - v63 - i4 - Winter 2015 - p247(2) [51-500]
Long, Julie Anne - *The Legend of Lyon Redmond*
    BL - v112 - i2 - Sept 15 2015 - p44(2) [51-500]
    PW - v262 - i33 - August 17 2015 - p57(2) [51-500]
Long, Kelly - *The Amish Heart of Ice Mountain*
    PW - v262 - i36 - Sept 7 2015 - p51(1) [51-500]
An Amish Man of Ice Mountain
    PW - v262 - i10 - March 9 2015 - p58(1) [51-500]
Long, Loren - *Little Tree* (Illus. by Long, Loren)
    c BL - v112 - i1 - Sept 1 2015 - p120(1) [51-500]
    c KR - July 15 2015 - pNA [51-500]
    c NYTBR - Sept 13 2015 - p21(L) [501+]
    c PW - v262 - i26 - June 29 2015 - p68(1) [51-500]
    c PW - v262 - i49 - Dec 2 2015 - p30(1) [51-500]
    c SLJ - v61 - i7 - July 2015 - p64(1) [51-500]
Otis and the Scarecrow (Illus. by Long, Loren)
    c HB Guide - v26 - i1 - Spring 2015 - p37(1) [51-500]
Long, Lucy M. - *Ethnic American Food Today*
    BL - v112 - i3 - Oct 1 2015 - p15(1) [51-500]
Long, Maebh - *Assembling Flann O'Brien*
    TLS - i5853 - June 5 2015 - p9(2) [501+]
Long, Matty - *Super Happy Magic Forest*
    c KR - Dec 1 2015 - pNA [51-500]
Long, Michael G. - *Gay Is Good: The Life and Letters of Gay Rights Pioneer Franklin Kameny*
    G&L Rev W - v22 - i4 - July-August 2015 - p40(2) [501+]
Long, Nicholas J. - *Being Malay in Indonesia: Histories, Hopes and Citizenship in the Riau Archipelago*
    Pac A - v88 - i3 - Sept 2015 - p742 [501+]
Sociality: New Directions
    JRAI - v21 - i2 - June 2015 - p477(2) [501+]
Long, Pamela - *Artisan/Practitioners and the Rise of the New Sciences, 1400-1600*
    Specu - v90 - i3 - July 2015 - p830-832 [501+]
Long, Ruth Frances - *A Crack in Everything*
    y Sch Lib - v63 - i1 - Spring 2015 - p55(1) [51-500]
Long, Stephen D. - *Saving Karl Barth: Hans Urs von Balthasars Preoccupation*
    Ger Q - v88 - i1 - Wntr 2015 - p138(2) [501+]
Longacre, Edward G. - *The Early Morning of War: Bull Run, 1861*
    J Mil H - v79 - i2 - April 2015 - p495-496 [501+]
    JSH - v81 - i4 - Nov 2015 - p994(3) [501+]
Longenecker, Steve - *Gettysburg Religion: Refinement, Diversity, and Race in the Antebellum and Civil War Border North*
    AHR - v120 - i2 - April 2015 - p625-626 [501+]
    CHR - v101 - i4 - Autumn 2015 - p955(2) [501+]
    JAH - v101 - i4 - March 2015 - p1276-1277 [501+]
Longerich, Peter - *Goebbels: A Biography*
    BL - v111 - i19-20 - June 1 2015 - p28(1) [51-500]
    LJ - v140 - i5 - March 15 2015 - p113(1) [51-500]
    Nat R - v67 - i14 - August 10 2015 - p43 [501+]
    NS - v144 - i5268 - June 26 2015 - p42(3) [501+]
    NYTBR - May 17 2015 - p24(L) [501+]
    PW - v262 - i9 - March 2 2015 - p74(2) [51-500]
    SEP - v287 - i3 - May-June 2015 - p24(1) [501+]
    TimHES - i2211 - July 9 2015 - p46(1) [501+]
    KR - March 1 2015 - pNA [51-500]
    TimHES - i2208 - June 18 2015 - p50(1) [501+]
Heinrich Himmler: A Life
    HNet - August 2015 - pNA [501+]
Longino, Helen E. - *Studying Human Behavior: How Scientists Investigate Aggression and Sexuality*
    CS - v44 - i1 - Jan 2015 - p85-87 [501+]
Longley, Michael - *Robert Graves: Selected Poems*
    Lon R Bks - v37 - i9 - May 7 2015 - p33(3) [501+]
The Stairwell
    RVBW - Jan 2015 - pNA [51-500]
Longmeyer, Carole Marsh - *The Kudzu Cookbook: Cooking Up a Storm with That Wild and Crazy Vine That Grows in Miles-Per-Hour!* (Illus. by French, Kristen)
    c CH Bwatch - Sept 2015 - pNA [51-500]
Longo, Jennifer - *Six Feet over It*
    y HB Guide - v26 - i1 - Spring 2015 - p114(1) [51-500]
    y Teach Lib - v42 - i3 - Feb 2015 - p28(4) [501+]
Up to This Pointe
    y BL - v112 - i7 - Dec 1 2015 - p58(2) [51-500]
    y KR - Nov 1 2015 - pNA [51-500]
    y PW - v262 - i44 - Nov 2 2015 - p86(1) [51-500]
Longworth, Karina - *Hollywood Frame by Frame: The Unseen Silver Screen in Contact Sheets, 1951-1997*
    FQ - v68 - i3 - Spring 2015 - p93(2) [501+]
Longworth, M.L. - *The Mystery of the Lost Cezanne*
    BL - v111 - i22 - August 1 2015 - p36(1) [51-500]
    KR - August 1 2015 - pNA [51-500]
    PW - v262 - i31 - August 3 2015 - p36(1) [51-500]
Lonie, Nicola - *Online Safety for Children and Teens on the Autism Spectrum*
    Bwatch - April 2015 - pNA [501+]
Loo, Tze May - *Heritage Politics: Shuri Castle and Okinawa's Incorporation into Modern Japan, 1879-2000*
    AHR - v120 - i3 - June 2015 - p1000-1001 [501+]
    Pub Hist - v37 - i3 - August 2015 - p146(3) [501+]
Loofton, Kathryn - *Oprah: The Gospel of an Icon*
    Am Q - v67 - i1 - March 2015 - p241-252 [501+]
Look, Lenore - *Alvin Ho: Allergic to the Great Wall, the Forbidden Palace, and Other Tourist Attractions* (Illus. by Pham, LeUyen)
    c HB Guide - v26 - i1 - Spring 2015 - p62(1) [51-500]
Looman, Mary D. - *A Country Called Prison: Mass Incarceration and the Making of a New Nation*
    LJ - v140 - i9 - May 15 2015 - p98(1) [51-500]
    PW - v262 - i19 - May 11 2015 - p50(1) [51-500]
Loomis, Susan Herrmann - *In a French Kitchen: Tales and Traditions of Everyday Home Cooking in France*
    KR - March 15 2015 - pNA [51-500]
    LJ - v140 - i10 - June 1 2015 - p128(1) [51-500]
    PW - v262 - i18 - May 4 2015 - p108(1) [51-500]
Loory, Ben - *The Baseball Player and the Walrus* (Illus. by Latimer, Alex)
    c BL - v111 - i16 - April 15 2015 - p51(1) [51-500]
    c HB Guide - v26 - i2 - Fall 2015 - p43(1) [51-500]
    c KR - March 1 2015 - pNA [51-500]
Loose, Gerry - *An Oakwoods Almanac*
    TLS - i5864-5865 - August 21 2015 - p34(1) [501+]
Loose, Margaret A. - *The Chartist Imaginary: Literary Form in Working-Class Political Theory and Practice*
    Nine-C Lit - v70 - i2 - Sept 2015 - p274(4) [501+]
Loosen, Livia - *Deutsche Frauen in den Sudsee-Kolonien des Kaiserreichs: Alltag und Beziehungen zur indigenen Bevolkerung, 1884-1919*
    HNet - April 2015 - pNA [501+]
Lopate, Phillip - *Portrait inside My Head*
    TLS - i5855 - June 19 2015 - p30(1) [501+]
Lopes, Cristina Videira - *Exercises in Programming Style*
    Bwatch - March 2015 - pNA [501+]
    Bwatch - June 2015 - pNA [501+]
Lopes, Henri - *Le Meridional*
    WLT - v89 - i6 - Nov-Dec 2015 - p62(1) [501+]
Lopes, Milton E. - *Lenten Reflections: From the Desert to the Resurrection*
    KR - July 1 2015 - pNA [501+]
Lopez-Alt, J. Kenji - *The Food Lab: Better Home Cooking through Science*
    Am Sci - v103 - i6 - Nov-Dec 2015 - p424(3) [501+]
    LJ - v140 - i11 - June 15 2015 - p108(2) [501+]
Lopez-Alt, J. Kenji - *The Food Lab: Better Home Cooking through Science*
    NYT - Sept 30 2015 - pD4(L) [501+]
Lopez-Alt, J. Kenji - *The Food Lab: Better Home Cooking through Science*
    NYTBR - Dec 6 2015 - p20(L) [501+]
    NYTBR - Dec 6 2015 - p20(L) [501+]
    PW - v262 - i29 - July 20 2015 - p183(1) [51-500]
Lopez, Donald S., Jr. - *In Search of the Christian Buddha: How an Asian Sage Became a Medieval Saint*
    Bks & Cult - v21 - i2 - March-April 2015 - p28(1) [501+]
The Scientific Buddha: His Short and Happy Life
    JR - Jan 2015 - p141(3) [501+]
Lopez-Farjeat, Luis Xavier - *Philosophical Psychology in Arabic Thought and the Latin Aristotelianism of the 13th Century*
    RM - v68 - i4 - June 2015 - p863(3) [501+]
Lopez, Jennifer - *The Boy Next Door*
    Spec - v327 - i9731 - Feb 28 2015 - p53(1) [501+]

Lopez, Kathleen - *Chinese Cubans: A Transnational History*
    Ams - v72 - i2 - April 2015 - p344(2) [501+]
Lopez, Raul Necochea - *A History of Family Planning in Twentieth-Century Peru*
    JIH - v46 - i2 - Autumn 2015 - p302-303 [501+]
Lopez, Robert - *Good People*
    KR - Oct 1 2015 - pNA [51-500]
    PW - v262 - i45 - Nov 9 2015 - p33(1) [51-500]
Lopez, Sarah Lynn - *The Remittance Landscape: Spaces of Migration in Rural Mexico and Urban USA*
    HNet - July 2015 - pNA [501+]
Lopresti, Kirsten - *Bright Coin Moon*
  y SLJ - v61 - i3 - March 2015 - p159(1) [51-500]
Lora, Francesco - *Giovanni Paolo Colonna: Oratorii*
    Notes - v71 - i3 - March 2015 - p563(4) [501+]
Lora, Loris - *Eventually Everything Connects (Illus. by Lora, Loris)*
  c SLJ - v61 - i5 - May 2015 - p138(1) [51-500]
Loranger, Danielle - *Une etoile sur la dune*
  c Res Links - v21 - i1 - Oct 2015 - p52(1) [501+]
Lorayne, Elizabeth - *The Adventures of Piratess Tilly (Illus. by Watson, Karen)*
  c KR - July 1 2015 - pNA [51-500]
  c PW - v262 - i32 - August 10 2015 - p58(2) [51-500]
Lorbeer, Lukas - *Die Sterbe- und Ewigkeitslieder in Deutschen Lutherischen Gesangbuchern des 17. Jahrhunderts*
    HNet - Feb 2015 - pNA [501+]
Lorber, Martin Barnes - *A Token of Elegance: Cigarette Holders in Vogue*
    NYT - Nov 27 2015 - pC28(L) [501+]
Lorbiecki, Marybeth - *The Prairie That Nature Built (Illus. by Morrison, Cathy)*
  c HB Guide - v26 - i1 - Spring 2015 - p156(1) [51-500]
Lord, Carnes - *Rebalancing U.S. Forces: Basing and Forward Presence in the Asia-Pacific*
    APJ - v29 - i4 - July-August 2015 - p96(3) [501+]
Lord, Cynthia - *A Handful of Stars (Read by Cabezas, Maria). Audiobook Review*
  c SLJ - v61 - i12 - Dec 2015 - p76(1) [51-500]
A Handful of Stars
  c KR - March 15 2015 - pNA [51-500]
  c BL - v111 - i16 - April 15 2015 - p50(1) [51-500]
  c CCB-B - v69 - i1 - Sept 2015 - p35(2) [51-500]
  c HB Guide - v26 - i2 - Fall 2015 - p92(1) [51-500]
  c SLJ - v61 - i6 - June 2015 - p101(1) [51-500]
  c Teach Lib - v42 - i5 - June 2015 - p47(1) [51-500]
Hot Rod Hamster and the Awesome ATV Adventure! (Illus. by Anderson, Derek)
  c HB Guide - v26 - i2 - Fall 2015 - p60(1) [51-500]
  c SLJ - v61 - i2 - Feb 2015 - p72(1) [51-500]
Hot Rod Hamster and the Haunted Halloween Party! (Illus. by Anderson, Derek)
  c KR - August 1 2015 - pNA [51-500]
  c SLJ - v61 - i9 - Sept 2015 - p108(1) [51-500]
Hot Rod Hamster and the Wacky Whatever Race! (Illus. by Paprocki, Greg)
  c HB Guide - v26 - i1 - Spring 2015 - p54(1) [51-500]
Jelly Bean (Illus. by McGuire, Erin)
  c HB Guide - v26 - i1 - Spring 2015 - p62(1) [51-500]
The Rules
  c Teach Lib - v42 - i5 - June 2015 - p47(1) [51-500]
Lord, Emery - *The Start of Me and You*
  y BL - v111 - i12 - Feb 15 2015 - p84(1) [51-500]
  y CCB-B - v68 - i10 - June 2015 - p504(2) [51-500]
  y HB Guide - v26 - i2 - Fall 2015 - p129(1) [51-500]
  y VOYA - v37 - i6 - Feb 2015 - p60(1) [51-500]
Lord, Karen - *The Galaxy Game*
    Analog - v135 - i6 - June 2015 - p105(2) [51-500]
Lord, Michelle - *Animal School: What Class Are You? (Illus. by Garland, Michael)*
  c HB Guide - v26 - i1 - Spring 2015 - p156(1) [51-500]
Lord, Scott Richard - *The Logic Bomb*
    SPBW - March 2015 - pNA [51-500]
Lord, Susanne - *In Search of Scandal*
    BL - v112 - i5 - Nov 1 2015 - p36(1) [51-500]
    PW - v262 - i45 - Nov 9 2015 - p44(1) [51-500]
Lordan, Dave - *Young Irelanders*
    TLS - i5862 - August 7 2015 - p27(1) [51-500]
Lore, Pittacus - *The Revenge of Seven*
  y HB Guide - v26 - i1 - Spring 2015 - p114(1) [51-500]
Loren, Roni - *Call on Me*
    PW - v262 - i19 - May 11 2015 - p41(2) [51-500]
Off the Clock
    PW - v262 - i47 - Nov 23 2015 - p55(1) [51-500]

Lorentz, Dayna - *No Dawn without Darkness*
  y HB Guide - v26 - i1 - Spring 2015 - p114(1) [51-500]
Lorenz, Johnny - *A Breath of Life*
    Nation - v301 - i21-22 - Nov 23 2015 - p31(4) [501+]
Lorenzo, David J. - *Conceptions of Chinese Democracy: Reading Sun Yat-sen, Chiang Kai-shek, and Chiang Ching-kuo*
    JAS - v74 - i2 - May 2015 - p471-472 [501+]
Lorge, Peter A. - *Debating War in Chinese History*
    Six Ct J - v46 - i1 - Spring 2015 - p163(2) [501+]
Lorimer, Jamie - *Wildlife in the Anthropocene*
    TLS - i5854 - June 12 2015 - p11(1) [501+]
Lorinc, John - *The Ward: The Life and Loss of Toronto's First Immigrant Neighbourhood*
    Mac - v128 - i22 - June 8 2015 - p56(2) [501+]
Lorini, Andrea - *Trick or Treat? (Illus. by Rigo, Laura)*
  c PW - v262 - i30 - July 27 2015 - p66(1) [501+]
Lorke, Christoph - *Armut im geteilten Deutschland: Die Wahrnehmung sozialer Randlagen in der Bundesrepublik und der DDR*
    HNet - May 2015 - pNA [501+]
Lorrain, Jean - *Nightmares of an Ether-Drinker*
    PW - v262 - i52 - Dec 21 2015 - p138(1) [501+]
Lorrimer, Claire - *Trust Me*
    BL - v111 - i21 - July 1 2015 - p45(1) [51-500]
    PW - v262 - i18 - May 4 2015 - p102(2) [51-500]
Lorway, Robert - *Namibia's Rainbow Project: Gay Rights in an African Nation*
    G&L Rev W - v22 - i1 - Jan-Feb 2015 - p40(2) [501+]
Lorz, Julienne - *Louise Bourgeois: Structures of Existence - The Cells*
    LJ - v140 - i13 - August 1 2015 - p92(1) [51-500]
Lose, David J. - *Preaching at the Crossroads: How the World--and our Preaching--Is Changing*
    Intpr - v69 - i4 - Oct 2015 - p500(2) [501+]
Loshe, Toko - *Shades of Africa*
    KR - August 1 2015 - pNA [501+]
Loske, Judith - *Sadako's Cranes (Illus. by Loske, Judith)*
  c KR - August 1 2015 - pNA [51-500]
Loskoutoff, Yvan - *Heraldique et numismatique I: Moyen Age - Temps modernes*
    Ren Q - v68 - i1 - Spring 2015 - p262-264 [501+]
Losos, Jonathan B. - *The Princeton Guide to Evolution*
    Am Bio T - v77 - i2 - Feb 2015 - p151(1) [501+]
    QRB - v90 - i2 - June 2015 - p214(2) [501+]
Losure, Mary - *Backwards Moon*
  c HB Guide - v26 - i1 - Spring 2015 - p84(1) [51-500]
Loth, Wilfried - *Europas Einigung: Eine Unvollendete Geschichte*
    HNet - June 2015 - pNA [501+]
Lothar, Ernst - *The Vienna Melody*
    WLT - v89 - i5 - Sept-Oct 2015 - p13(1) [501+]
Lotman, Yuri - *High Society Dinners: Dining in Tsarist Russia*
    Slav R - v74 - i2 - Summer 2015 - p412-413 [501+]
    TLS - i5831 - Jan 2 2015 - p10(1) [501+]
Lott, David B. - *Sally McFague: Collected Readings*
    Theol St - v76 - i1 - March 2015 - p225(2) [501+]
Lott, Johnny W. - *Mathematics Lessons Learned from across the World, Prekindergarten-Grade 8*
  c TC Math - v22 - i1 - August 2015 - p52(1) [501+]
Lott, Tim - *The Last Summer of the Water Strider*
    TimHES - i2217 - August 20 2015 - p47-47 [501+]
Lott, Trent - *Crisis Point: Why We Must--and How We Can--Overcome Our Broken Politics in Washington and across America*
    KR - Oct 1 2015 - pNA [501+]
    PW - v262 - i41 - Oct 12 2015 - p57(1) [501+]
Lotz, Amanda - *Cable Guys: Television and Masculinities in the Twenty-First Century*
    JGS - v24 - i3 - June 2015 - p366-368 [501+]
Lotz, Sarah - *Day Four (Read by Rawlins, Penelope). Audiobook Review*
    LJ - v140 - i14 - Sept 1 2015 - p66(1) [51-500]
Day Four
    BL - v111 - i18 - May 15 2015 - p34(1) [51-500]
    Ent W - i1369 - June 26 2015 - p66(1) [51-500]
    KR - April 15 2015 - pNA [51-500]
    LJ - v140 - i11 - June 15 2015 - p79(2) [51-500]
    NYTBR - June 21 2015 - p25(L) [51-500]
    PW - v262 - i14 - April 6 2015 - p41(1) [51-500]
Loudon, George - *Object Lessons: The Visualisation of Nineteenth-Century Life Sciences*
    TLS - i5868 - Sept 18 2015 - p34(1) [501+]
Lough, Amber - *The Fire Wish*
  y HB Guide - v26 - i2 - Fall 2015 - p129(1) [51-500]

Lough, David - *No More Champagne: Churchill and His Money*
    PW - v262 - i39 - Sept 28 2015 - p81(1) [501+]
    KR - Sept 1 2015 - pNA [501+]
    LJ - v140 - i15 - Sept 15 2015 - p94(1) [501+]
Lough, James - *Short Flights: Thirty-Two Modern Writers Share Aphorisms of Insight, Inspiration, and Wit*
    PW - v262 - i39 - Sept 28 2015 - p81(2) [501+]
Loughead, Deb - *Beyond Crazy*
  y SLJ - v61 - i9 - Sept 2015 - p151(4) [501+]
Rise of the Zombie Scarecrows
  c BL - v111 - i17 - May 1 2015 - p52(1) [51-500]
  y KR - Feb 15 2015 - pNA [51-500]
  y PW - v262 - i14 - April 6 2015 - p60(1) [501+]
  c Res Links - v20 - i3 - Feb 2015 - p31(2) [51-500]
Loughlin, Marie H. - *Same-Sex Desire in Early Modern England, 1550-1735: An Anthology of Literary Texts and Contexts*
    HNet - Sept 2015 - pNA [501+]
Loughnane, Rory - *Staged Transgression in Shakespeare's England*
    RES - v66 - i275 - June 2015 - p577-579 [501+]
Louie, Vivian - *Keeping the Immigrant Bargain: The Costs and Rewards of Success in America*
    CS - v44 - i2 - March 2015 - p228-229 [501+]
Louis, Jenn - *Pasta by Hand: A Collection of Italy's Regional Hand-Shaped Pasta (Illus. by Anderson, Ed)*
    PW - v262 - i16 - April 20 2015 - p71(1) [51-500]
Louise, Kate - *Tough Cookie (Illus. by Sandford, Grace)*
  c KR - Sept 15 2015 - pNA [51-500]
Louise, Zanni - *Too Busy Sleeping (Illus. by Pignataro, Anna)*
  c Magpies - v30 - i4 - Sept 2015 - p26(2) [51-500]
Loukaki, Argyro - *The Geographical Unconscious*
    GR - v105 - i2 - April 2015 - p251(5) [501+]
Lourd, Blaine - *Born on the Bayou: A Memoir*
    KR - June 1 2015 - pNA [51-500]
    PW - v262 - i26 - June 29 2015 - p60(2) [51-500]
Lourey, Jess - *February Fever*
    BL - v111 - i9-10 - Jan 1 2015 - p46(1) [51-500]
Lourey, Jessica - *The Catalain Book of Secrets*
    PW - v262 - i36 - Sept 7 2015 - p44(2) [51-500]
Louth, Charlie - *A C.H. Sisson Reader*
    TLS - i5849 - May 8 2015 - p23(1) [51-500]
Louv, Richard - *Last Child in the Woods: Saving Our Children from Nature-Deficit Disorder*
    Bwatch - July 2015 - pNA [51-500]
Lovano, Michael - *All Things Julius Caesar: An Encyclopedia of Caesar's World and Legacy*
    BL - v111 - i14 - March 15 2015 - p41(1) [501+]
    R&USQ - v54 - i4 - Summer 2015 - p78(2) [501+]
Lovatt, Helen - *Epic Visions: Visuality in Greek and Latin Epic and its Reception*
    Class R - v65 - i2 - Oct 2015 - p468-470 [501+]
Love, David K. - *Kepler and the Universe: How One Man Revolutionized Astronomy*
    PW - v262 - i38 - Sept 21 2015 - p65(1) [501+]
Love, Jessica - *In Real Life*
  y KR - Jan 1 2016 - pNA [51-500]
Love, Preston, Jr. - *Economic Cataracts, vol. 1*
    RVBW - August 2015 - pNA [51-500]
Love, Reggie - *Power Forward: My Presidential Education*
    BL - v111 - i9-10 - Jan 1 2015 - p24(1) [51-500]
Love, Robert - *Number 13 (Illus. by Walker, David (b. 1965-))*
  y VOYA - v37 - i6 - Feb 2015 - p50(2) [501+]
Love, Shannon - *Twisting My Kaleidoscope*
    SPBW - August 2015 - pNA [51-500]
Love, Susan M. - *Dr. Susan Love's Breast Book, 6th ed*
    LJ - v140 - i14 - Sept 1 2015 - p130(2) [501+]
Lovejoy, Alice - *Army Film and the Avent Garde: Cinema and Experiment in the Czechoslovak Millitary*
    FQ - v68 - i4 - Summer 2015 - p96(3) [501+]
Lovejoy, Sharon - *Running Out of Night*
  c HB Guide - v26 - i1 - Spring 2015 - p84(2) [51-500]
Lovelace, Sharia - *Loving the Chase*
    PW - v262 - i22 - June 1 2015 - p48(1) [51-500]
Loveland, Anne C. - *Change and Conflict in the U.S. Army Chaplain Corps since 1945*
    CH - v84 - i4 - Dec 2015 - p919(4) [501+]
    J Ch St - v57 - i3 - Summer 2015 - p583-585 [501+]
    JR - v95 - i4 - Oct 2015 - p569(2) [501+]
Loveland, Helena - *Ylsnavan, Realms of Elsvanische*
  y CH Bwatch - July 2015 - pNA [501+]
Lovell, Julia - *The Opium War: Drugs, Dreams and the Making of China*
    JAS - v74 - i2 - May 2015 - p472-474 [501+]
Lovell, Stephen - *Russia in the Microphone Age: A History of Soviet Radio*
    TimHES - i2203 - May 14 2015 - p49(1) [501+]

Lovell, W. George - *"Strange Lands and Different Peoples": Spaniards and Indians in Colonial Guatemala*
  Am Ind CRJ - v39 - i2 - Spring 2015 - p160-162 [501+]
  Ams - v72 - i1 - Jan 2015 - p156(2) [501+]
  HAHR - v95 - i2 - May 2015 - p348-350 [501+]
Lovelock, James - *A Rough Ride to the Future*
  BL - v111 - i12 - Feb 15 2015 - p27(2) [51-500]
  Lon R Bks - v37 - i4 - Feb 19 2015 - p18(3) [501+]
Loveman, Kate - *Samuel Pepys and His Books: Reading, Newsgathering, and Sociability, 1660-1703*
  TimHES - i2221 - Sept 17 2015 - p46-47 [501+]
Lovesey, Peter - *Down among the Dead Men*
  BL - v111 - i17 - May 1 2015 - p32(1) [51-500]
  KR - May 1 2015 - pNA [501+]
  NYTBR - July 19 2015 - p25(L) [501+]
  NYTBR - Dec 6 2015 - p85(L) [501+]
  PW - v262 - i19 - May 11 2015 - p37(1) [51-500]
Lovett, Bobby L. - *"A Touch of Greatness": A History of Tennessee State University*
  JSH - v81 - i4 - Nov 2015 - p1021(2) [501+]
Lovick, Elizabeth - *Magical Shetland Lace Shawls to Knit: Feather Soft and Incredibly Light: 15 Great Patterns and Full Instructions*
  LJ - v140 - i20 - Dec 1 2015 - p103(1) [51-500]
Lovin, Dale - *Strangers, Lovers and the Winds of Time*
  Roundup M - v22 - i4 - April 2015 - p33(1) [501+]
  Roundup M - v22 - i6 - August 2015 - p31(1) [501+]
Loving, Jerome - *Confederate Bushwhacker: Mark Twain in the Shadow of the Civil War*
  JSH - v81 - i1 - Feb 2015 - p216(2) [501+]
Low, Jacqueline - *The Chicago School Diaspora: Epistemology and Substance*
  CS - v44 - i5 - Sept 2015 - p674-675 [501+]
Low, Rachel - *Girl's Guide to DIY Fashion: Design & Sew 5 Complete Outfits*
  PW - v262 - i1 - Jan 5 2015 - p69(1) [51-500]
Low, William - *Daytime Nighttime (Illus. by Low, William)*
  c SLJ - v61 - i7 - July 2015 - p56(1) [51-500]
Lowdon, Claire - *Left of the Bang*
  NS - v144 - i5267 - June 19 2015 - p50(1) [501+]
  TLS - i5855 - June 19 2015 - p20(1) [501+]
Lowe, E.J. - *Forms of Thought: A Study in Philosophical Logic*
  RM - v68 - i3 - March 2015 - p669(2) [501+]
Lowe, George - *The Crossing of Antarctica: Original Photographs from the Epic Journey That Fulfilled Shackleton's Dream*
  TLS - i5840 - March 6 2015 - p28(2) [501+]
Lowe, Hannah - *Ormonde*
  TLS - i5853 - June 5 2015 - p25(1) [501+]
Lowe, Helen - *Daughter of Blood*
  PW - v262 - i48 - Nov 30 2015 - p44(1) [51-500]
Lowe, Natasha - *The Courage of Cat Campbell*
  c CCB-B - v68 - i8 - April 2015 - p410(1) [51-500]
  y HB Guide - v26 - i2 - Fall 2015 - p92(1) [51-500]
Lowe, Stuart - *Cosmos: The Infographic Book of Space*
  Nature - v526 - i7575 - Oct 29 2015 - p639(1) [51-500]
Lowe, Tower - *In Gallup, Greed*
  PW - v262 - i7 - Feb 16 2015 - p163(1) [51-500]
Loweecey, Alice - *Second to Nun*
  BL - v112 - i2 - Sept 15 2015 - p34(2) [51-500]
  PW - v262 - i31 - August 3 2015 - p38(1) [51-500]
Lowell, Catherine - *The Madwoman Upstairs*
  KR - Jan 1 2016 - pNA [501+]
Lowell, D.L. - *Soulmate*
  SPBW - Jan 2015 - pNA [51-500]
Lowell, David W. - *Unbelievable Me*
  KR - Jan 15 2015 - pNA [51-500]
Lowell, Elizabeth - *Perfect Touch*
  BL - v111 - i19-20 - June 1 2015 - p64(1) [51-500]
Lowenstein-Malz, Ronit - *Escape in Time (Illus. by McGaw, Laurie)*
  c BL - v111 - i16 - April 15 2015 - p59(1) [51-500]
  KR - May 1 2015 - pNA [51-500]
Lowenstein, Roger - *America's Bank: The Epic Struggle to Create the Federal Reserve*
  Fortune - v172 - i5 - Oct 1 2015 - p24(1) [501+]
  KR - August 1 2015 - pNA [501+]
  LJ - v140 - i15 - Sept 15 2015 - p86(1) [51-500]
  NYTBR - Oct 25 2015 - p1(L) [501+]
  PW - v262 - i33 - August 17 2015 - p60(2) [51-500]
  SEP - v287 - i5 - Sept-Oct 2015 - p24(1) [501+]
Lowery, Lawrence F. - *Our Very Own Tree*
  Sci & Ch - v53 - i4 - Dec 2015 - p97 [501+]

Lowery, Lynda Blackmon - *Turning 15 on the Road to Freedom: My Story of the 1965 Selma Voting Rights March (Illus. by Loughran, P.J.)*
  c CCB-B - v68 - i6 - Feb 2015 - p295(2) [501+]
  y HB Guide - v26 - i2 - Fall 2015 - p210(1) [51-500]
  y VOYA - v37 - i6 - Feb 2015 - p88(1) [51-500]
  y HB - v91 - i1 - Jan-Feb 2015 - p98(2) [51-500]
Lowery, Mark - *The Jam Doughnut That Ruined My Life (Illus. by Shaw, Hannah)*
  c Sch Lib - v63 - i4 - Winter 2015 - p229(2) [51-500]
Lowinger, Kathy - *Give Me Wings: How a Choir of Former Slaves Took on the World*
  y KR - June 1 2015 - pNA [51-500]
  y SLJ - v61 - i8 - August 2015 - p128(1) [51-500]
Lowitz, Leza - *Up from the Sea*
  y SLJ - v61 - i12 - Dec 2015 - p123(3) [51-500]
  y VOYA - v38 - i5 - Dec 2015 - p59(1) [51-500]
Lownie, Andrew - *Stalin's Englishman: The Lives of Guy Burgess*
  NS - v144 - i5281 - Sept 25 2015 - p66(3) [501+]
  Spec - v329 - i9771 - Dec 5 2015 - p42(3) [501+]
Lowrey, Janette Sebring - *The Poky Little Puppy*
  c HB Guide - v26 - i2 - Fall 2015 - p60(1) [51-500]
Lowrey, Lois - *Number the Stars*
  c HB Guide - v26 - i1 - Spring 2015 - p85(1) [51-500]
Lowry, Malcolm - *In the Ballast to the White Sea: A Scholarly Edition*
  TLS - i5846 - April 17 2015 - p19(1) [501+]
  Under the Volcano
  Obs - Jan 4 2015 - p33 [501+]
Lowry, Richard - *The Photographer and the President: Abraham Lincoln, Alexander Gardner, and the Images That Made a Presidency*
  LJ - v140 - i5 - March 15 2015 - p121(1) [51-500]
Loxton, Daniel - *Abominable Science! Origins of the Yeti, Nessie, and Other Famous Cryptids*
  Bks & Cult - v21 - i5 - Sept-Oct 2015 - p19(2) [501+]
Loy, Jessica - *Weird and Wild Animal Facts (Illus. by Loy, Jessica)*
  c HB Guide - v26 - i2 - Fall 2015 - p171(1) [51-500]
Loyd, Alexander - *Beyond Willpower: The Secret Principle to Achieving Success in Life, Love, and Happiness (Read by Singer, Erik). Audiobook Review*
  BL - v111 - i21 - July 1 2015 - p79(1) [51-500]
  Beyond Willpower: The Secret Principle to Achieving Success in Life, Love, and Happiness
  Bwatch - June 2015 - pNA [51-500]
Lozano, Jeff - *Paws on Ice (Illus. by Reiland, Lizette)*
  c CH Bwatch - Feb 2015 - pNA [51-500]
Lozano, Jose - *Little Chanclas (Illus. by Crosthwaite, Luis Humberto)*
  c SLJ - v61 - i5 - May 2015 - p88(1) [51-500]
  Little Chanclas (Illus. by Lozano, Jose)
  c CCB-B - v68 - i11 - July-August 2015 - p555(2) [51-500]
  c HB Guide - v26 - i2 - Fall 2015 - p43(1) [51-500]
  c KR - March 15 2015 - pNA [51-500]
Lozo, Ignaz - *Der Putsch gegen Gorbatschow und das Ende der Sowjetunion*
  Slav R - v74 - i1 - Spring 2015 - p203-204 [501+]
Lu, Marie - *The Evertree*
  c CH Bwatch - July 2015 - pNA [51-500]
  The Rose Society
  y BL - v112 - i3 - Oct 1 2015 - p73(1) [51-500]
  y KR - Sept 1 2015 - pNA [51-500]
  y PW - v262 - i49 - Dec 2 2015 - p105(1) [51-500]
  y SLJ - v61 - i10 - Oct 2015 - p113(2) [51-500]
  y VOYA - v38 - i5 - Dec 2015 - p72(1) [51-500]
  The Young Elites
  y HB - v91 - i1 - Jan-Feb 2015 - p85(1) [51-500]
  y HB Guide - v26 - i1 - Spring 2015 - p114(1) [51-500]
  y Teach Lib - v42 - i3 - Feb 2015 - p28(4) [501+]
Lubar, David - *The Bully Bug (Illus. by Calo, Marcos)*
  c HB Guide - v26 - i1 - Spring 2015 - p85(1) [51-500]
  Character, Driven
  y KR - Jan 1 2016 - pNA [51-500]
  y PW - v262 - i52 - Dec 21 2015 - p155(1) [51-500]
  The Gloomy Ghost (Illus. by Calo, Marcos)
  c HB Guide - v26 - i1 - Spring 2015 - p85(1) [51-500]
  Numbed!
  c CH Bwatch - Jan 2015 - pNA [51-500]
  Sophomores and Other Oxymorons (Read by Goldstrom, Michael). Audiobook Review
  y SLJ - v61 - i12 - Dec 2015 - p80(1) [51-500]
  Sophomores and Other Oxymorons
  y SLJ - v61 - i8 - August 2015 - p97(1) [51-500]
  y VOYA - v38 - i4 - Oct 2015 - p56(1) [51-500]
Lubektin, M. John - *Custer's Gold*
  Roundup M - v23 - i1 - Oct 2015 - p31(1) [501+]
Lubert, Allison - *Baking You Happy: Gluten-Free Recipes from Sweet Freedom Bakery (100 Percent Vegan).*
  Veg J - v34 - i3 - July-Sept 2015 - p30(1) [51-500]
Lubetzky, Daniel - *Do the Kind Thing: Think Boundlessly, Work Purposefully, Live Passionately*
  BL - v111 - i13 - March 1 2015 - p9(1) [51-500]
Lubienski, Christopher A. - *The Public School Advantage: Why Public Schools Outperform Private Schools*
  CS - v44 - i4 - July 2015 - p530-532 [501+]
Lubin, Alex - *Geographies of Liberation: The Making of an Afro-Arab Political Imaginary*
  AHR - v120 - i4 - Oct 2015 - p1448-1449 [501+]
  JAH - v101 - i4 - March 2015 - p1324-1325 [501+]
Lubin, David M. - *Flags and Faces: The Visual Culture of America's First World War*
  HNet - Sept 2015 - pNA [501+]
Lubitz, Rob - *Breaking Free*
  PW - v262 - i10 - March 9 2015 - p55(2) [51-500]
Lublin, Elizabeth Dorn - *Reforming Japan: The Women's Christian Temperance Union in the Meiji Period*
  JWH - v27 - i1 - Spring 2015 - p187(10) [501+]
Lubonja, Fatos - *The False Apocalypse: From Stalinism to Capitalism*
  TLS - i5845 - April 10 2015 - p28(1) [501+]
Lubow, Mike - *Paper and Ink: Stories*
  KR - June 1 2015 - pNA [501+]
Lucado, Denalyn - *Lucado Treasury of Bedtime Prayers (Read by Garver, Kathy). Audiobook Review*
  c CH Bwatch - May 2015 - pNA [51-500]
Lucado, Max - *Miracle at the Higher Ground Cafe*
  BL - v111 - i11 - Feb 1 2015 - p23(1) [51-500]
Lucas, Caroline - *Honourable Friends? Parliament and the Fight for Change*
  Lon R Bks - v37 - i9 - May 7 2015 - p27(2) [501+]
Lucas, Ed - *Seeing Home: The Ed Lucas Story: A Blind Broadcaster's Story of Overcoming Life's Greatest Obstacles*
  BL - v111 - i16 - April 15 2015 - p11(1) [51-500]
  KR - March 15 2015 - pNA [51-500]
Lucas, Edward - *Cyberphobia: Identity, Trust, Security and the Internet*
  BL - v112 - i4 - Oct 15 2015 - p6(1) [51-500]
  KR - Sept 1 2015 - pNA [501+]
  LJ - v140 - i16 - Oct 1 2015 - p105(1) [51-500]
  PW - v262 - i39 - Sept 28 2015 - p78(2) [51-500]
  TLS - i5877 - Nov 20 2015 - p24(2) [501+]
Lucas-Hall, Renae - *Tokyo Tales*
  RVBW - May 2015 - pNA [51-500]
Lucas, Jen - *Sock-Yarn Shawls II: 16 Patterns for Lace Knitting*
  Bwatch - March 2015 - pNA [51-500]
Lucas, Peter J. - *The Medieval Manuscripts at Maynooth: Explorations in the Unknown*
  TLS - i5856 - June 26 2015 - p27(1) [501+]
Lucas, Samuel Roundfield - *Just Who Loses?: Discrimination in the United States, vol. 2*
  CS - v44 - i2 - March 2015 - p229-232 [501+]
Luce, Ed - *Wuvable Oaf*
  PW - v262 - i23 - June 8 2015 - p47(1) [51-500]
Luce, Stephanie - *What Works for Workers? Public Policies and Innovative Strategies for Low-Wage Workers*
  AJS - v121 - i2 - Sept 2015 - p648(3) [501+]
Luchinger, Peter - *Eine Stadt im Krieg: Bremen 1914-1918: Szenische Lesung: Auswahl und Zusammenstellung der Originaldokumente*
  HNet - April 2015 - pNA [501+]
Luciani, Brigitte - *The Carnival (Illus. by Tharlet, Eve)*
  c HB Guide - v26 - i1 - Spring 2015 - p37(1) [51-500]
Luciani, Joseph J. - *Thin from Within: The Powerful Self-Coaching Program for Permanent Weight Loss*
  PW - v262 - i52 - Dec 21 2015 - p149(1) [51-500]
Luck, Joyce - *The Master Yeshua: The Undiscovered Gospel of Joseph*
  KR - July 1 2015 - pNA [501+]
Luckadoo, Robert - *Grit in Your Craw*
  SPBW - March 2015 - pNA [51-500]

Lucke, Deb - *The Lunch Witch (Illus. by Lucke, Deb)*
   y CH Bwatch - June 2015 - pNA [51-500]
   c PW - v262 - i49 - Dec 2 2015 - p86(1) [51-500]
   c SLJ - v61 - i3 - March 2015 - p146(1) [51-500]
   c PW - v262 - i4 - Jan 26 2015 - p175(1) [51-500]
   y VOYA - v38 - i1 - April 2015 - p80(2) [51-500]
Luckett, Dave - *Sian, a New Australian*
   c Magpies - v30 - i4 - Sept 2015 - p34(1) [501+]
Luckhurst, Roger - *Zombies: A Cultural History*
   TLS - i5874 - Oct 30 2015 - p7(1) [501+]
Lucks, Daniel S. - *Selma to Saigon: The Civil Rights Movement and the Vietnam War*
   AHR - v120 - i3 - June 2015 - p1071-1072 [501+]
   HNet - Sept 2015 - pNA [501+]
   JSH - v81 - i4 - Nov 2015 - p1041(2) [501+]
Ludicke, Lars - *Constantin von Neurath: Eine Politische Biographie*
   Ger Q - v88 - i1 - Wntr 2015 - p137(2) [501+]
Ludington, Charles - *The Politics of Wine in Britain: A New Cultural History*
   JMH - v87 - i3 - Sept 2015 - p725(3) [501+]
Ludlow, Elizabeth - *Christina Rossetti and the Bible*
   TLS - i5870 - Oct 2 2015 - p23(1) [501+]
Ludmerer, Kenneth M. - *Let Me Heal: The Opportunity to Preserve Excellence in American Medicine*
   NYRB - v62 - i10 - June 4 2015 - p60(3) [501+]
Ludolf und Wansleben - Orientalistik, Politik und Geschichte zwischen Gotha und Afrika 1650-1700
   HNet - July 2015 - pNA [501+]
Ludovici, Anne Marie - *Change Your Mind, Change Your Health*
   RVBW - Jan 2015 - pNA [501+]
Ludvigsen, Karl - *Professor Porsche's Wars*
   Spec - v329 - i9767 - Nov 7 2015 - p43(1) [501+]
Ludwig, Elisa - *Pretty Wanted*
   y HB Guide - v26 - i2 - Fall 2015 - p129(1) [51-500]
   y KR - Jan 1 2015 - pNA [51-500]
Ludwigstein: Annaherungen an die Geschichte der Burg im 20. Jahrhundert. Archivtagung im Archiv der Deutschen Jugendbewegung
   HNet - March 2015 - pNA [501+]
Ludy, Mark - *Noah (AA) Picture story)*
   c HB Guide - v26 - i1 - Spring 2015 - p134(1) [51-500]
Luebke, David M. - *Mixed Matches: Transgressive Unions in Germany from the Reformation to the Enlightenment*
   RVBW - Oct 2015 - pNA [501+]
Lugo-Ortiz, Agnes - *Slave Portraiture in the Atlantic World*
   J Am St - v49 - i2 - May 2015 - p417-419 [501+]
Luibheid, Eithne - *Pregnant on Arrival: Making the Illegal Immigrant*
   NWSA Jnl - v27 - i2 - Summer 2015 - p203-205 [501+]
Luidens, Lyz - *Screening Silk*
   c BL - v112 - i7 - Dec 1 2015 - p42(1) [51-500]
Luiselli, Valeria - *The Story of My Teeth*
   KR - July 15 2015 - pNA [51-500]
   LJ - v140 - i13 - August 1 2015 - p87(1) [51-500]
   NY - v91 - i32 - Oct 19 2015 - p88 [51-500]
   NYT - Sept 24 2015 - pC6(L) [501+]
   NYTBR - Sept 13 2015 - p11(L) [501+]
   PW - v262 - i10 - March 9 2015 - p51(1) [51-500]
   TLS - i5850 - May 15 2015 - p21(1) [501+]
Lujan, Jorge - *Movila mano / I Moved My Hand (Illus. by Sadat, Mandana)*
   c HB Guide - v26 - i1 - Spring 2015 - p37(1) [51-500]
Numeralia (Illus. by Isol)
   c Bkbird - v53 - i1 - Wntr 2015 - p99(1) [501+]
Lukacs, John - *A Short History of the Twentieth Century*
   RAH - v43 - i3 - Sept 2015 - p557-563 [501+]
Lukavics, Amy - *Daughters unto Devils*
   y BL - v112 - i2 - Sept 15 2015 - p63(1) [51-500]
   y KR - July 15 2015 - pNA [51-500]
   LJ - v140 - i16 - Oct 1 2015 - p111(1) [501+]
   y SLJ - v61 - i10 - Oct 2015 - p113(1) [501+]
Luke, Bob - *Soldiering for Freedom: How the Union Army Recruited, Trained, and Deployed the U.S. Colored Troops*
   J Mil H - v79 - i3 - July 2015 - p837-838 [501+]
Luke, Timothy W. - *Gun Violence and Public Life*
   CS - v44 - i6 - Nov 2015 - p871(1) [51-500]
Lulushi, Albert - *Donovan's Devils: OSS Commandos behind Enemy Lines: Europe, World War II*
   KR - Nov 15 2015 - pNA [51-500]
   PW - v262 - i50 - Dec 7 2015 - p76(2) [51-500]
Lum, Kathryn Gin - *Damned Nation: Hell in America from the Revolution to Reconstruction*
   Bks & Cult - v21 - i2 - March-April 2015 - p19(2) [501+]
   CC - v132 - i21 - Oct 14 2015 - p33(2) [501+]
   JAH - v102 - i2 - Sept 2015 - p514-515 [501+]
Lumbard, Alexis York - *Pine and the Winter Sparrow (Illus. by Vidal, Beatriz)*
   c CH Bwatch - March 2015 - pNA [51-500]
   c CH Bwatch - April 2015 - pNA [51-500]
   c HB Guide - v26 - i2 - Fall 2015 - p159(1) [51-500]
When the Animals Saved Earth (Illus. by Demi)
   c CH Bwatch - June 2015 - pNA [51-500]
   c CH Bwatch - July 2015 - pNA [51-500]
   c KR - Feb 15 2015 - pNA [51-500]
   c PW - v262 - i8 - Feb 23 2015 - p79(1) [51-500]
   c SLJ - v61 - i8 - August 2015 - p122(1) [51-500]
Lumley, Brian - *Tales of the Primal Land*
   PW - v262 - i9 - March 2 2015 - p67(1) [51-500]
Lumsden, Linda J. - *Black, White, and Red All Over: A Cultural History of the Radical Press in Its Heyday, 1900-1917*
   HNet - August 2015 - pNA [501+]
Lumsden, Roddy - *Not All Honey*
   TLS - i5844 - April 3 2015 - p23(1) [501+]
Lumsden, Simon - *Self-Consciousness and the Critique of the Subject: Hegel, Heidegger, and the Poststructuralists*
   RM - v69 - i2 - Dec 2015 - p395(3) [501+]
Luna, Concetta - *Proclus. Commentaire sur le Parmenide de Platon. Tome V: Livre V*
   Class R - v65 - i2 - Oct 2015 - p410-412 [501+]
Luna, Francisco Vidal - *The Economic and Social History of Brazil since 1889*
   JEH - v75 - i3 - Sept 2015 - p944-946 [501+]
Luna, James - *The Place Where You Live / El lugar donde vives (Illus. by Muraida, Thelma)*
   c KR - Sept 15 2015 - pNA [51-500]
Luna, Juan Pablo - *The Resilience of the Latin American Right*
   For Aff - v94 - i1 - Jan-Feb 2015 - pNA [51-500]
Luna, Tania - *Surprise: Embrace the Unpredictable and Engineer the Unexpected*
   PW - v262 - i2 - Jan 12 2015 - p48(1) [51-500]
The Lunatic
   BL - v111 - i14 - March 15 2015 - p27(1) [51-500]
Lunbeck, Elizabeth - *The Americanization of Narcissism*
   AHR - v120 - i2 - April 2015 - p561-563 [501+]
   AM - v212 - i17 - May 18 2015 - p45(2) [501+]
   JAH - v101 - i4 - March 2015 - p1353-1354 [501+]
   Soc - v52 - i3 - June 2015 - p287(5) [501+]
Lundahl, Bev - *Entangled Roots: The Mystery of Peterborough's Headless Corpse*
   Beav - v95 - i4 - August-Sept 2015 - p72(2) [501+]
Lunde, Darrin P. - *Dirty Rats? (Illus. by Gustavson, Adam)*
   c Sci & Ch - v53 - i1 - Sept 2015 - p96 [501+]
   c HB Guide - v26 - i2 - Fall 2015 - p180(1) [51-500]
Lunden, Joan - *Had I Known: A Memoir of Survival (Read by Lunden, Joan). Audiobook Review*
   BL - v112 - i7 - Dec 1 2015 - p69(1) [51-500]
Had I Known: A Memoir of Survival
   BL - v112 - i1 - Sept 1 2015 - p21(2) [51-500]
   KR - August 1 2015 - pNA [51-500]
   LJ - v140 - i14 - Sept 1 2015 - p130(1) [51-500]
   PW - v262 - i30 - July 27 2015 - p59(1) [51-500]
Lundestad, Geir - *International Relations since the End of the Cold War: New and Old Dimensions*
   E-A St - v67 - i3 - May 2015 - p506(2) [501+]
Lundquist, Jenny - *The Opal Crown*
   y CH Bwatch - Jan 2015 - pNA [51-500]
Lundquist, Mary - *Cat & Bunny (Illus. by Lundquist, Mary)*
   c BL - v111 - i9-10 - Jan 1 2015 - p104(1) [51-500]
   c CCB-B - v68 - i7 - March 2015 - p361(2) [51-500]
   c HB Guide - v26 - i2 - Fall 2015 - p43(1) [51-500]
   c PW - v262 - i49 - Dec 2 2015 - p13(1) [51-500]
   c Teach Lib - v42 - i4 - April 2015 - p32(1) [51-500]
Lundskaer-Nielsen, Tom - *Prepositions in English Grammars until 1801, with a Survey of the Western European Background*
   MLR - v110 - i2 - April 2015 - p517-519 [501+]
Lundwall, John Knight - *Mythos and Cosmos: Mind and Meaning in the Oral Age*
   KR - July 1 2015 - pNA [501+]
Lundy, J.T. - *Saving Grapes*
   KR - March 15 2015 - pNA [51-500]
Lunetta, Demitria - *In the End*
   y HB Guide - v26 - i1 - Spring 2015 - p114(2) [51-500]
Lung, Sam - *Francis Poulenc: His Life & Work with Authoritative Text and Selected Music*
   Am MT - v64 - i4 - Feb-March 2015 - p62(1) [501+]

Lunis, Natalie - *Eerie Inns*
   c HB Guide - v26 - i1 - Spring 2015 - p133(1) [51-500]
Gravity-Defying Animals
   c HB Guide - v26 - i1 - Spring 2015 - p156(1) [51-500]
Lifeguard Dogs
   c HB Guide - v26 - i1 - Spring 2015 - p168(1) [51-500]
Shape-Shifting Animals
   c HB Guide - v26 - i1 - Spring 2015 - p156(1) [51-500]
Luo, Liang - *The Avant-Garde and the Popular in Modern China: Tian Han and the Intersection of Performance and Politics*
   Theat J - v67 - i3 - Oct 2015 - p584-586 [501+]
Lupack, Barbara Tepa - *Richard E. Norman and Race Filmmaking*
   JAH - v102 - i1 - June 2015 - p278-279 [501+]
Lupica, Mike - *Fantasy League*
   c HB Guide - v26 - i1 - Spring 2015 - p85(1) [51-500]
Fast Break
   c BL - v112 - i1 - Sept 1 2015 - p100(1) [51-500]
   c KR - Sept 1 2015 - pNA [51-500]
The Only Game (Read by Nobbs, Keith). Audiobook Review
   c BL - v112 - i1 - Sept 1 2015 - p142(1) [51-500]
   c PW - v262 - i21 - May 25 2015 - p56(1) [51-500]
   c SLJ - v61 - i5 - May 2015 - p69(1) [51-500]
The Only Game
   c CCB-B - v68 - i8 - April 2015 - p411(1) [51-500]
   c HB Guide - v26 - i2 - Fall 2015 - p92(1) [51-500]
Lupton, Robert D. - *Charity Detox: What Charity Would Look Like If We Cared about Results*
   KR - April 15 2015 - pNA [51-500]
   LJ - v140 - i8 - May 1 2015 - p78(1) [51-500]
Toxic Charity: How Churches and Charities Hurt Those They Help (and How to Reverse It). (Read by Lawlor, Patrick). Audiobook Review
   LJ - v140 - i10 - June 1 2015 - p62(1) [51-500]
Lupton, Rosamund - *The Quality of Silence*
   KR - Dec 15 2015 - pNA [501+]
   PW - v262 - i52 - Dec 21 2015 - p131(2) [51-500]
Luraghi, Nino - *The Splendors and Miseries of Ruling Alone. Encounters with Monarchy from Archaic Greece to the Hellenistic Mediterranean*
   Class R - v65 - i1 - April 2015 - p185-187 [501+]
Lurie, Alison - *The Language of Houses: How Buildings Speak to Us*
   TimHES - i2199 - April 16 2015 - p57-1 [501+]
Lurie, Jonathan - *William Howard Taft: The Travails of a Progressive Conservative*
   Pres St Q - v45 - i1 - March 2015 - p214(2) [501+]
Luscher, Jonas - *Barbarian Spring*
   WLT - v89 - i3-4 - May-August 2015 - p117(1) [51-500]
Lussu, Emilio - *A Soldier on the Southern Front: The Classic Italian Memoir of World War I*
   HT - v65 - i2 - Feb 2015 - p62(2) [501+]
Lusted, Marcia Amidon - *Civic Unrest: Investigate the Struggle for Social Change (Illus. by Chandhok, Lena)*
   c BL - v111 - i21 - July 1 2015 - p52(1) [51-500]
The US National Guard
   y HB Guide - v26 - i1 - Spring 2015 - p138(2) [51-500]
Luthens, John - *Taconite Creek*
   SPBW - May 2015 - pNA [51-500]
Luther, Daisy - *The Prepper's Water Survival Guide*
   RVBW - July 2015 - pNA [51-500]
Lutterbach, Hubertus - *Das Tauferreich von Munster: Ursprunge und Merkmale eines religiosen Aufbruchs*
   CHR - v101 - i2 - Spring 2015 - p372(2) [501+]
Lutz, Deborah - *The Bronte Cabinet: Three Lives in Nine Objects*
   PW - v262 - i2 - Jan 12 2015 - p46(1) [51-500]
   BL - v111 - i15 - April 1 2015 - p12(2) [51-500]
   LJ - v140 - i8 - May 1 2015 - p70(2) [51-500]
   TimHES - i2209 - June 25 2015 - p46-47 [501+]
Lutz, Lisa - *How to Start a Fire*
   BL - v111 - i12 - Feb 15 2015 - p31(1) [51-500]
   KR - March 1 2015 - pNA [51-500]
   LJ - v140 - i6 - April 1 2015 - p83(2) [51-500]
   PW - v262 - i12 - March 23 2015 - p46(1) [51-500]
The Passenger
   BL - v112 - i7 - Dec 1 2015 - p31(1) [51-500]
   KR - Jan 1 2016 - pNA [51-500]
   LJ - v140 - i19 - Nov 15 2015 - p78(2) [51-500]

Lutz, Martin - *Carl von Siemens, 1829-1906: Ein Leben zwischen Familie und Weitfirma*
    JMH - v87 - i1 - March 2015 - p155(3) [501+]

Lutzeler, Paul Michael - *Hermann Broch und die Romantik*
    Ger Q - v88 - i3 - Summer 2015 - p398(3) [501+]
Transatlantische Germanistik. Kontakt, Transfer, Dialogik
    GSR - v38 - i2 - May 2015 - p466-2 [501+]

Lux, Courtney - *Small Wonders*
    PW - v262 - i29 - July 20 2015 - p176(1) [51-500]

Lux, Thomas - *Selected Poems*
    c Sch Lib - v63 - i1 - Spring 2015 - p49(1) [501+]

Luxbacher, Irene - *Mr. Frank (Illus. by Luxbacher, Irene)*
    c HB Guide - v26 - i1 - Spring 2015 - p38(1) [51-500]

Luzzatto, Sergio - *Primo Levi's Resistance: Rebels and Collaborators in Occupied Italy*
    KR - Oct 1 2015 - pNA [501+]
    PW - v262 - i48 - Nov 30 2015 - p51(1) [51-500]

Luzzi, Joseph - *In a Dark Wood: What Dante Taught Me about Grief, Healing, and the Mysteries of Love*
    BL - v111 - i16 - April 15 2015 - p12(2) [51-500]
    NYTBR - July 5 2015 - p20(L) [501+]
    TLS - i5868 - Sept 18 2015 - p28(2) [501+]
    KR - March 1 2015 - pNA [501+]
    PW - v262 - i15 - April 13 2015 - p71(2) [51-500]
My Two Italies
    Comw - v142 - i1 - Jan 9 2015 - p24(2) [501+]
    NYTBR - Sept 13 2015 - p32(L) [501+]
    WLT - v89 - i2 - March-April 2015 - p67(1) [51-500]

Lyandres, Semion - *The Fall of Tsarism: Untold Stories of the February 1917 Revolution*
    Historian - v77 - i1 - Spring 2015 - p176(2) [501+]
    HNet - April 2015 - pNA [501+]

Lybeck-Robinson, Lynda - *Composer Showcase: An Awesome Adventure, Eight Original Piano Solos*
    Am MT - v65 - i1 - August-Sept 2015 - p59(2) [501+]

Lydon, John - *Anger Is an Energy: My Life Uncensored (Read by Perkins, Derek). Audiobook Review*
    LJ - v140 - i20 - Dec 1 2015 - p59(1) [51-500]
Anger Is an Energy: My Life Uncensored
    BL - v111 - i14 - March 15 2015 - p36(2) [51-500]
    LJ - v140 - i6 - April 1 2015 - p95(1) [51-500]
    TLS - i5833 - Jan 16 2015 - p21(1) [501+]
    KR - Feb 1 2015 - pNA [51-500]

Lyga, Barry - *After the Red Rain*
    c BL - v111 - i11 - Feb 1 2015 - p33(1) [51-500]
    y BL - v111 - i18 - May 15 2015 - p60(1) [51-500]
    y CCB-B - v69 - i2 - Oct 2015 - p99(1) [51-500]
    y KR - June 1 2015 - pNA [51-500]
    y PW - v262 - i21 - May 25 2015 - p61(1) [51-500]
    y SLJ - v61 - i5 - May 2015 - p121(2) [51-500]
    y VOYA - v38 - i2 - June 2015 - p78(2) [501+]
Blood of My Blood
    c BL - v111 - i17 - May 1 2015 - p40(1) [51-500]
    y HB - v91 - i1 - Jan-Feb 2015 - p86(1) [51-500]
    y HB Guide - v26 - i1 - Spring 2015 - p115(1) [51-500]

Lyle, Dixie - *A Deadly Tail*
    KR - Dec 15 2015 - pNA [51-500]

Lyly, John - *Pap with an Hatchet: An Annotated Modern-Spelling Edition*
    TLS - i5866 - Sept 4 2015 - p26(1) [501+]

Lynch, Anabelle - *Let's Visit England*
    c Sch Lib - v63 - i3 - Autumn 2015 - p175(1) [51-500]

Lynch, Annabelle - *France*
    c HB Guide - v26 - i1 - Spring 2015 - p202(1) [51-500]

Lynch, Chris - *Alive and Kicking*
    y HB Guide - v26 - i2 - Fall 2015 - p129(1) [51-500]
Dead in the Water
    y HB Guide - v26 - i1 - Spring 2015 - p115(1) [51-500]
Hit Count
    y BL - v111 - i15 - April 1 2015 - p65(2) [51-500]
    c BL - v112 - i1 - Sept 1 2015 - p99(1) [501+]
    y CCB-B - v68 - i10 - June 2015 - p505(1) [51-500]
    y HB - v91 - i3 - May-June 2015 - p113(2) [51-500]
    y HB Guide - v26 - i2 - Fall 2015 - p129(2) [51-500]
    y KR - March 15 2015 - pNA [51-500]
    y NYTBR - August 23 2015 - p25(L) [501+]
    y PW - v262 - i11 - March 16 2015 - p86(1) [51-500]
    y SLJ - v61 - i3 - March 2015 - p159(1) [51-500]
    y VOYA - v38 - i1 - April 2015 - p65(1) [51-500]
Killing Time in Crystal City
    y CCB-B - v68 - i7 - March 2015 - p362(1) [51-500]
    y HB Guide - v26 - i2 - Fall 2015 - p130(1) [51-500]
    y VOYA - v37 - i6 - Feb 2015 - p60(1) [51-500]
Walking Wounded
    y HB Guide - v26 - i1 - Spring 2015 - p115(1) [51-500]

Lynch, Deidre Shauna - *Loving Literature: A Cultural History*
    TLS - i5842 - March 20 2015 - p7(2) [501+]
    VQR - v91 - i1 - Wntr 2015 - p188-192 [501+]

Lynch, Helen - *Milton and the Politics of Public Speech*
    Sev Cent N - v73 - i3-4 - Fall-Winter 2015 - p94(4) [501+]

Lynch, Jack - *You Could Look It Up: The Reference Shelf from Ancient Babylon to Wikipedia*
    KR - Nov 1 2015 - pNA [501+]
    PW - v262 - i44 - Nov 2 2015 - p74(2) [51-500]

Lynch, Jane - *Marlene, Marlene, Queen of Mean (Illus. by Tusa, Tricia)*
    c HB Guide - v26 - i1 - Spring 2015 - p38(1) [51-500]

Lynch, John - *New Worlds: A Religious History of Latin America*
    HNet - Sept 2015 - pNA [501+]

Lynch, Katie - *Confucius Jane*
    LJ - v140 - i20 - Dec 1 2015 - p94(1) [51-500]
    PW - v262 - i46 - Nov 16 2015 - p61(1) [51-500]

Lynch, Marc - *The Arab Uprisings Explained: New Contentious Politics in the Middle East*
    For Aff - v94 - i1 - Jan-Feb 2015 - pNA [501+]

Lynch, Margaret M. - *Tapping Into Wealth: How Emotional Freedom Techniques (EFT) Can Help You Clear the Path to Making More Money*
    RVBW - Feb 2015 - pNA [51-500]

Lynch, Michael Patrick - *The Internet of Us*
    KR - Dec 15 2015 - pNA [51-500]

Lynch, Patrick James - *The Boy Who Fell off the Mayflower, or, John Howland's Good Fortune (Illus. by Lynch, Patrick James)*
    c BL - v112 - i1 - Sept 1 2015 - p93(1) [51-500]
    c KR - July 1 2015 - pNA [51-500]
    c PW - v262 - i24 - June 15 2015 - p87(1) [51-500]
    c PW - v262 - i49 - Dec 2 2015 - p44(1) [51-500]
    c SLJ - v61 - i11 - Nov 2015 - p132(3) [51-500]

Lynch, Paul - *The Black Snow*
    BL - v111 - i16 - April 15 2015 - p32(1) [51-500]
    KR - March 1 2015 - pNA [501+]
    PW - v262 - i10 - March 9 2015 - p49(1) [51-500]

Lynds, Gayle - *The Assassins*
    LJ - v140 - i11 - June 15 2015 - p78(2) [51-500]
    PW - v262 - i17 - April 27 2015 - p49(1) [51-500]
    RVBW - Sept 2015 - pNA [51-500]

Lyndsey, Anna - *Girl in the Dark: A Memoir (Read by Curtis, Hannah). Audiobook Review*
    LJ - v140 - i10 - June 1 2015 - p62(2) [51-500]
Girl in the Dark: A Memoir
    LJ - v140 - i12 - July 1 2015 - p118(1) [501+]
    NYTBR - March 8 2015 - p15(L) [501+]
    PW - v262 - i3 - Jan 19 2015 - p71(1) [51-500]

Lynerd, Benjamin T. - *Republican Theology: The Civil Religion of American Evangelicals*
    CH - v84 - i3 - Sept 2015 - p701(4) [501+]
    TLS - i5857 - July 3 2015 - p23(1) [501+]

Lynn, Alvin R. - *Kit Carson and the First Battle of Adobe Walls: A Tale of Two Journeys*
    Roundup M - v22 - i4 - April 2015 - p30(1) [501+]
    Roundup M - v22 - i6 - August 2015 - p38(1) [501+]

Lynn, Barry W. - *God and Government: Twenty-Five Years of Fighting for Equality, Secularism, and Freedom of Conscience*
    Cons - v36 - i2 - Summer 2015 - p45(3) [501+]

Lynn, Cynthia - *Are You Empowered??? The Basics*
    SPBW - June 2015 - pNA [51-500]

Lynn, Kirk - *Rules for Werewolves*
    KR - August 1 2015 - pNA [501+]
    LJ - v140 - i16 - Oct 1 2015 - p71(1) [51-500]
    PW - v262 - i32 - August 10 2015 - p34(1) [51-500]

Lynn, Richard - *The Sarcastic Lens*
    KR - May 15 2015 - pNA [51-500]

Lynn, Sarah - *The Boulder Brothers: Meet Mo and Jo (Illus. by Collet-Derby, Pierre)*
    BL - v111 - i13 - March 1 2015 - p43(1) [51-500]
    c CCB-B - v68 - i7 - March 2015 - p362(2) [51-500]
    c HB Guide - v26 - i2 - Fall 2015 - p68(1) [51-500]
    c SLJ - v61 - i3 - March 2015 - p129(2) [51-500]

Lyon, George Ella - *Boats Float! (Illus. by Wiggins, Mick)*
    c HB - v91 - i5 - Sept-Oct 2015 - p83(1) [51-500]
    c KR - July 15 2015 - pNA [51-500]
    c PW - v262 - i49 - Dec 2 2015 - p19(1) [51-500]
    c SLJ - v61 - i9 - Sept 2015 - p124(1) [51-500]
Voices from the March on Washington
    c HB Guide - v26 - i1 - Spring 2015 - p189(1) [51-500]
What Forest Knows (Illus. by Hall, August)
    c HB Guide - v26 - i1 - Spring 2015 - p38(1) [51-500]

Lyons, Adam - *The 1711 Expedition to Quebec: Politics and the Limitations of British Global Strategy*
    Historian - v77 - i3 - Fall 2015 - p617(2) [501+]

Lyons, Amelia H. - *The Civilizing Mission in the Metropole: Algerian Families and the French Welfare State during Decolonization*
    FS - v69 - i1 - Jan 2015 - p118-119 [501+]

Lyons, C.J. - *Watched*
    y HB Guide - v26 - i2 - Fall 2015 - p130(1) [51-500]

Lyons, Malcolm C. - *Tales of the Marvellous and News of the Strange*
    LJ - v140 - i5 - March 15 2015 - p106(2) [51-500]
    Lon R Bks - v37 - i1 - Jan 8 2015 - p27(2) [501+]
    TLS - i5833 - Jan 16 2015 - p8(2) [501+]
    TLS - i5833 - Jan 16 2015 - p9(2) [501+]

Lyons, Stefanie - *Dating Down*
    y BL - v111 - i15 - April 1 2015 - p64(1) [51-500]
    KR - Feb 1 2015 - pNA [51-500]
    y SLJ - v61 - i7 - July 2015 - p95(2) [51-500]
    y VOYA - v38 - i2 - June 2015 - p65(1) [51-500]

Lyris, Sonia Orin - *The Seer*
    PW - v262 - i50 - Dec 7 2015 - p72(1) [51-500]

Lythcott-Haims, Julie - *How to Raise an Adult: Break Free of the Overparenting Trap and Prepare Your Kid for Success*
    CC - v132 - i23 - Nov 11 2015 - p36(2) [501+]
    KR - April 1 2015 - pNA [51-500]
    NYTBR - June 21 2015 - p1(L) [501+]
    PW - v262 - i14 - April 6 2015 - p54(1) [51-500]

Lythell, Jane - *The Lie of You*
    BL - v111 - i19-20 - June 1 2015 - p55(1) [51-500]
    PW - v262 - i17 - April 27 2015 - p54(1) [51-500]

Lyttleton, Ben - *Twelve Yards: The Art and Psychology of the Perfect Penalty Kick*
    BL - v111 - i21 - July 1 2015 - p16(1) [51-500]
    LJ - v140 - i12 - July 1 2015 - p89(1) [51-500]

Lytton, Deborah - *Silence*
    y SLJ - v61 - i6 - June 2015 - p114(2) [51-500]

Lytton, Timothy D. - *Kosher: Private Regulation in the Age of Industrial Food*
    Historian - v77 - i1 - Spring 2015 - p203(2) [501+]

Lyubomirsky, Sonja - *The Myths of Happiness: What Should Make You Happy, but Doesn't, What Shouldn't Make You Happy, but Does*
    AJPsy - v128 - i1 - Spring 2015 - p125(4) [501+]

M

Ma, Daishu - *Leaf (Illus. by Ma, Daishu)*
  y BL - v112 - i4 - Oct 15 2015 - p36(1) [51-500]
Ma, Jean - *Sounding the Modern Woman: The Songstress in Chinese Cinema*
  HNet - Sept 2015 - pNA [501+]
Ma, Kathryn - *The Year She Left Us*
  NYTBR - May 24 2015 - p28(L) [501+]
Ma, Roger - *The Zombie Combat Field Guide*
  c CH Bwatch - Feb 2015 - pNA [51-500]
Ma, Suzanne - *Meet Me in Venice: A Chinese Immigrant's Journey from the Far East to the Faraway West*
  y BL - v111 - i12 - Feb 15 2015 - p12(2) [51-500]
Ma, Wonsuk - *Pentecostal Mission and Global Christianity*
  IBMR - v39 - i1 - Jan 2015 - p52(2) [501+]
Maangchi - *Maangchi's Real Korean Cooking: Authentic Dishes for the Home Cook*
  LJ - v140 - i5 - March 15 2015 - p126(2) [501+]
  PW - v262 - i9 - March 2 2015 - p78(2) [51-500]
Maas, John R. - *Defending a New Nation, 1783-1811*
  J Mil H - v79 - i1 - Jan 2015 - p181-185 [501+]
Maas, Michael - *The Cambridge Companion to the Age of Attila*
  J Mil H - v79 - i1 - Jan 2015 - p192-193 [501+]
Maas, Sarah J. - *A Court of Thorns and Roses*
  y BL - v111 - i17 - May 1 2015 - p90(1) [51-500]
  y CCB-B - v68 - i11 - July-August 2015 - p556(1) [51-500]
  y HB Guide - v26 - i2 - Fall 2015 - p130(1) [51-500]
  PW - v262 - i12 - March 23 2015 - p78(1) [51-500]
  y SLJ - v61 - i5 - May 2015 - p121(1) [51-500]
Heir of Fire (Read by Evans, Elizabeth). Audiobook Review
  y SLJ - v61 - i2 - Feb 2015 - p52(2) [51-500]
Heir of Fire
  y HB Guide - v26 - i1 - Spring 2015 - p115(1) [51-500]
Queen of Shadows
  y BL - v111 - i22 - August 1 2015 - p64(1) [51-500]
  y KR - August 1 2015 - pNA [51-500]
  y Magpies - v30 - i5 - Nov 2015 - p45(1) [501+]
  y SLJ - v61 - i10 - Oct 2015 - p114(1) [51-500]
Maass, John R. - *The French and Indian War in North Carolina: The Spreading Flames of War*
  JSH - v81 - i2 - May 2015 - p439(2) [501+]
Mabalon, Dawn Bohulano - *Little Manila Is in the Heart: The Making of the Filipina/o American Community in Stockton, California*
  PHR - v84 - i1 - Feb 2015 - p116(3) [501+]
Mabanckou, Alain - *Letter to Jimmy: On the Twentieth Anniversary of Your Death*
  WLT - v89 - i2 - March-April 2015 - p77(3) [501+]
The Lights of Pointe-Noire
  Econ - v415 - i8941 - June 6 2015 - p76(US) [501+]
  TLS - i5873 - Oct 23 2015 - p27(1) [501+]
  KR - Dec 1 2015 - pNA [51-500]
  NS - v144 - i5263 - May 22 2015 - p54(1) [501+]
Mabbitt, Will - *Mabel Jones and the Forbidden City*
  c KR - Nov 15 2015 - pNA [51-500]
The Unlikely Adventures of Mabel Jones (Illus. by Collins, Ross)
  c BL - v111 - i19-20 - June 1 2015 - p108(1) [51-500]
  c HB Guide - v26 - i2 - Fall 2015 - p92(1) [51-500]
  KR - April 1 2015 - pNA [51-500]
  c PW - v262 - i17 - April 27 2015 - p76(1) [51-500]
  c PW - v262 - i49 - Dec 2 2015 - p69(1) [51-500]
  c Sch Lib - v63 - i3 - Autumn 2015 - p168(1) [51-500]
  SLJ - v61 - i3 - March 2015 - p138(1) [51-500]

Mabbott, Lizzie - *Chinatown Kitchen: From Noodles to Nuoc Cham: Delicious Dishes from Southeast Asian Ingredients*
  LJ - v140 - i12 - July 1 2015 - p106(1) [51-500]
Maberry, Jonathan - *Bits and Pieces*
  y BL - v111 - i21 - July 1 2015 - p55(1) [51-500]
  y KR - July 15 2015 - pNA [51-500]
Deadlands: Ghostwalkers
  BL - v112 - i2 - Sept 15 2015 - p38(1) [51-500]
The Orphan Army
  c BL - v111 - i18 - May 15 2015 - p67(1) [51-500]
  c CCB-B - v69 - i1 - Sept 2015 - p36(1) [51-500]
  c HB Guide - v26 - i2 - Fall 2015 - p92(1) [51-500]
  c KR - Feb 15 2015 - pNA [51-500]
  c PW - v262 - i13 - March 30 2015 - p76(1) [51-500]
  c SLJ - v61 - i3 - March 2015 - p138(2) [51-500]
Rot & Ruin: Warrior Smart (Illus. by Vargas, Tony)
  c LJ - v140 - i7 - April 15 2015 - p126(1) [51-500]
  y SLJ - v61 - i8 - August 2015 - p111(2) [51-500]
Mabey, Richard - *The Cabaret of Plants: Botany and the Imagination*
  Nature - v526 - i7574 - Oct 22 2015 - p503(1) [51-500]
  NS - v144 - i5286 - Oct 30 2015 - p42(1) [501+]
  Spec - v329 - i9764 - Oct 17 2015 - p45(1) [501+]
The Cabaret of Plants: Forty Thousand Years of Plant Life and the Human Imagination
  BL - v112 - i7 - Dec 1 2015 - p12(1) [51-500]
  KR - Oct 1 2015 - pNA [51-500]
  PW - v262 - i45 - Nov 9 2015 - p51(1) [51-500]
Dreams of the Good Life: The Life of Flora Thompson and the Creation of 'Lake Rise to Candleford'
  Lon R Bks - v37 - i4 - Feb 19 2015 - p27(3) [501+]
Mabry, Tristan James - *Divided Nations and European Integration*
  ERS - v38 - i3 - March 2015 - p523(3) [501+]
Mac Donald, Glenn P. - *The Caloris Rim Project*
  KR - Jan 1 2015 - pNA [51-500]
MacAfee, M.A. - *Song of the Wild*
  KR - Jan 15 2015 - pNA [501+]
Macala, Robert M. - *The Immigrant Expert*
  KR - June 1 2015 - pNA [501+]
MacAller, Natasha - *Vanilla Table: The Essence of Exquisite Cooking from the World's Best Chefs*
  BL - v111 - i16 - April 15 2015 - p10(1) [51-500]
  LJ - v140 - i5 - March 15 2015 - p126(2) [501+]
Macallister, Greer - *The Magician's Lie (Read by Podehl, Nick). Audiobook Review*
  BL - v111 - i19-20 - June 1 2015 - p130(1) [51-500]
  LJ - v140 - i7 - April 15 2015 - p47(1) [51-500]
The Magician's Lie
  People - v83 - i3 - Jan 19 2015 - p29 [501+]
  People - v83 - i3 - Jan 19 2015 - p29 [501+]
  People - v83 - i3 - Jan 19 2015 - p29 [501+]
  People - v83 - i3 - Jan 19 2015 - p29 [501+]
  People - v83 - i3 - Jan 19 2015 - p29 [501+]
  People - v83 - i3 - Jan 19 2015 - p29 [501+]
Macan, Turner - *The Persian Interpreter: The Life and Career of Turner Macan*
  TimHES - i2210 - July 2 2015 - p47-1 [501+]
Macari, Anne Marie - *Red Deer*
  BL - v111 - i14 - March 15 2015 - p39(1) [51-500]
MacArthur, Brian - *The Penguin Book of Modern Speeches*
  LJ - v140 - i11 - June 15 2015 - p114(1) [51-500]
MacArthur, John - *Why Believe the Bible?*
  RVBW - March 2015 - pNA [51-500]
MacAskill, William - *Doing Good Better: Effective Altruism and A Radical New Way to Make A Difference*
  Lon R Bks - v37 - i18 - Sept 24 2015 - p3(3) [501+]
  TLS - i5877 - Nov 20 2015 - p3(2) [501+]
Doing Good Better: Effective Altruism and How You Can Make a Difference
  KR - June 1 2015 - pNA [51-500]
  LJ - v140 - i12 - July 1 2015 - p102(1) [51-500]
  NYT - August 16 2015 - p6(L) [501+]
Macaulay, David - *Black and White*
  c JE - v195 - i2 - Spring 2015 - p57-58 [501+]
How Machines Work: Zoo Break! (Illus. by Macaulay, David)
  c PW - v262 - i49 - Dec 2 2015 - p59(1) [51-500]
  c BL - v112 - i6 - Nov 15 2015 - p38(1) [51-500]
  c KR - Dec 1 2015 - pNA [51-500]
  c NYTBR - Dec 6 2015 - p32(L) [501+]
Jet Plane
  c HB Guide - v26 - i2 - Fall 2015 - p186(1) [51-500]
Toilet
  c HB Guide - v26 - i2 - Fall 2015 - p186(1) [51-500]
Macauley, Jo - *Inferno*
  y HB Guide - v26 - i1 - Spring 2015 - p115(1) [51-500]
Macbain, Bruce - *Odin's Child*
  SPBW - August 2015 - pNA [51-500]
MacBird, Bonnie - *Art in the Blood*
  KR - Sept 15 2015 - pNA [501+]
  PW - v262 - i27 - July 6 2015 - p47(1) [51-500]
MacBride, Samantha - *Recycling Reconsidered: The Present Failure and Future Promise of Environmental Action in the United States*
  SF - v93 - i3 - March 2015 - pe83 [501+]
  SF - v93 - i3 - March 2015 - pe83 [501+]
MacBride, Stuart - *The Missing and the Dead*
  KR - April 15 2015 - pNA [51-500]
  PW - v262 - i14 - April 6 2015 - p41(1) [51-500]
A Song for the Dying
  RVBW - Jan 2015 - pNA [51-500]
  RVBW - April 2015 - pNA [51-500]The Maccabees - *Unfaithful Music & Disappearing Ink*
  CSM - Oct 9 2015 - pNA [501+]
Maccarone, Grace - *The Three Little Pigs Count to 100 (Illus. by Pistacchio)*
  c KR - July 15 2015 - pNA [51-500]
  c SLJ - v61 - i8 - August 2015 - p73(1) [51-500]
MacColl, Michaela - *Always Emily*
  y Teach Lib - v42 - i3 - Feb 2015 - p28(4) [501+]
Freedom's Price
  c KR - August 1 2015 - pNA [51-500]
  c SLJ - v61 - i8 - August 2015 - p88(1) [51-500]
The Revelation of Louisa May
  y BL - v111 - i16 - April 15 2015 - p56(2) [51-500]
  y CCB-B - v68 - i11 - July-August 2015 - p556(2) [51-500]
  y HB Guide - v26 - i2 - Fall 2015 - p130(1) [51-500]
  y PW - v262 - i7 - Feb 16 2015 - p181(1) [51-500]
Rory's Promise
  c HB Guide - v26 - i1 - Spring 2015 - p85(1) [51-500]
MacCuish, Al - *The Bee Who Spoke: The Wonderful World of Belle and the Bee (Illus. by Gibbon, Rebecca)*
  c CH Bwatch - Jan 2015 - pNA [51-500]
  c HB Guide - v26 - i1 - Spring 2015 - p38(1) [51-500]
MacCulloch, Diarmaid - *Silence: A Christian History*
  Quad - v59 - i1-2 - Jan-Feb 2015 - p52(6) [501+]
MacDonald, Ann-Marie - *Adult Onset*
  G&L Rev W - v22 - i5 - Sept-Oct 2015 - p44(1)

[501+]
    KR - Feb 1 2015 - pNA [501+]
    LJ - v140 - i6 - April 1 2015 - p83(1) [51-500]
    NYT - April 30 2015 - pC6(L) [501+]
    NYTBR - May 10 2015 - p10(L) [501+]
    PW - v262 - i6 - Feb 9 2015 - p43(2) [51-500]
    TLS - i5855 - June 19 2015 - p20(1) [501+]
MacDonald, Betty - *The Egg and I (Read by Henderson, Heather). Audiobook Review*
    PW - v262 - i35 - August 31 2015 - p85(1) [51-500]
Macdonald, David S. - *2015 Brookman*
    Phil Lit R - v64 - i2 - Spring 2015 - p127(2) [501+]
Macdonald, David W. - *Key Topics in Conservation Biology 2*
    QRB - v90 - i1 - March 2015 - p87(2) [501+]
Wildlife Conservation on Framland
    TimHES - i2220 - Sept 10 2015 - p47(1) [501+]
MacDonald, Dennis R. - *Mythologizing Jesus: From Jewish Teacher to Epic Hero*
    PW - v262 - i15 - April 13 2015 - p75(1) [51-500]
    RVBW - August 2015 - pNA [51-500]
MacDonald, Eve - *Hannibal: A Hellenistic Life*
    HT - v65 - i8 - August 2015 - p59(1) [501+]
    NY - v91 - i10 - April 27 2015 - p77 [51-500]
MacDonald, Fiona - *Do You Want to Be a Medieval Knight? (Illus. by Bergin, Mark)*
    c HB Guide - v26 - i2 - Fall 2015 - p216(1) [501+]
    c SLJ - v61 - i4 - April 2015 - p113(4) [501+]
You Wouldn't Want to Live without Dentists! (Illus. by Antram, David)
    c BL - v111 - i18 - May 15 2015 - p51(1) [501+]
MacDonald, George - *The Princess and the Goblin (Read by Heldman, Brooke). Audiobook Review*
    c BL - v111 - i18 - May 15 2015 - p72(1) [501+]
    c CH Bwatch - Feb 2015 - pNA [51-500]
Macdonald, Helen - *H Is for Hawk (Read by Macdonald, Helen). Audiobook Review*
    BL - v112 - i1 - Sept 1 2015 - p140(1) [51-500]
    BL - v112 - i7 - Dec 1 2015 - p71(1) [501+]
H Is for Hawk
    BL - v112 - i7 - Dec 1 2015 - p13(1) [501+]
    BooChiTr - March 14 2015 - p14(1) [501+]
    Ent W - i1353 - March 6 2015 - p71(1) [501+]
    HR - v68 - i3 - Autumn 2015 - p517-527 [501+]
    LJ - v140 - i12 - July 1 2015 - p118(1) [51-500]
    Mac - v128 - i9 - March 9 2015 - p54(1) [501+]
    NS - v144 - i5278 - Sept 4 2015 - p37(1) [51-500]
    NYRB - v62 - i7 - April 23 2015 - p32(2) [501+]
    NYT - Feb 18 2015 - pC1(L) [501+]
    NYTBR - Feb 22 2015 - p1(L) [501+]
    NYTBR - Dec 13 2015 - p12(L) [501+]
    TLS - i5854 - June 12 2015 - p12(1) [501+]
    Wom R Bks - v32 - i5 - Sept-Oct 2015 - p3(2) [501+]
    BL - v111 - i12 - Feb 15 2015 - p27(1) [501+]
Macdonald, Hugh - *Bizet*
    MT - v156 - i1932 - Autumn 2015 - p102-105 [501+]
    ON - v80 - i2 - August 2015 - p59(1) [501+]
MacDonald, Hugh - *Morgan's Boat Ride (Illus. by Bald, Anna)*
    c Res Links - v20 - i3 - Feb 2015 - p6(1) [51-500]
Macdonald, James - *When Globalization Fails: The Rise and Fall of Pax Americana*
    BL - v111 - i9-10 - Jan 1 2015 - p25(1) [51-500]
MacDonald, Margaret R. - *Storyteller's Sampler: Tales from Tellers around the World*
    Teach Lib - v43 - i1 - Oct 2015 - p41(3) [501+]
MacDonald, Margaret Read - *Party Croc! A Folktale from Zimbabwe (Illus. by Sullivan, Derek)*
    c KR - Jan 15 2015 - pNA [51-500]
    c PW - v262 - i4 - Jan 26 2015 - p168(1) [51-500]
Macdonald, Mark - *Why Kids Make You Fat ... And How to Get Your Body Back*
    PW - v262 - i16 - April 20 2015 - p72(2) [51-500]
MacDonald, Marylee - *Bonds of Love & Blood*
    KR - Oct 15 2015 - pNA [501+]
Montpelier Tomorrow
    KR - Jan 15 2015 - pNA [501+]
MacDonald, Michael - *Overreach: Delusions of Regime Change in Iraq*
    J Mil H - v79 - i1 - Jan 2015 - p266-267 [501+]
Macdonald, Mike - *Choose Your Own Misery: The Office Adventure*
    PW - v262 - i46 - Nov 16 2015 - p69(1) [51-500]
MacDonald, Nicholas - *In Search of 'La Grande Illusion': A Critical Appreciation of Jean Renoir's Elusive Masterpiece*
    FS - v69 - i2 - April 2015 - p285-286 [501+]

MacDonald, Patrick - *We're Going on a Moa Hunt*
    c Magpies - v30 - i4 - Sept 2015 - pS5(1) [501+]
Macdonald, Peggy - *Marjorie Harris Carr: Defender of Florida's Environment*
    JSH - v81 - i2 - May 2015 - p514(2) [501+]
MacDonald, Scott B. - *Separating Fools from their Money*
    Bwatch - July 2015 - pNA [501+]
MacDonald, Siobhan - *Twisted River*
    KR - Dec 15 2015 - pNA [51-500]
MacDougall, Pauleena M.' - *Fannie Hardy Eckstorm and Her Quest for Local Knowledge, 1865-1946*
    WestFolk - v74 - i1 - Wntr 2015 - p104-107 [501+]
MacDougall, Philip - *Naval Resistance to Britain's Growing Power in India, 1660-1800: The Saffron Banner and the Tiger of Mysore*
    HNet - July 2015 - pNA [501+]
MacDougall, Phillip - *Naval Resistance to Britain's Growing Power in India, 1600-1800: The Saffron Banner and the Tiger of Mysore*
    J Mil H - v79 - i3 - July 2015 - p814-815 [501+]
MacDougall, Robert - *The People's Network: The Political Economy of the Telephone in the Gilded Age*
    AHR - v120 - i1 - Feb 2015 - p259-260 [501+]
    JAH - v101 - i4 - March 2015 - p1284-1285 [501+]
Mace, Darryl - *In Remembrance of Emmett Till: Regional Stories and Media Responses to the Black Freedom Struggle*
    AHR - v120 - i3 - June 2015 - p1066-1067 [501+]
    JAH - v102 - i1 - June 2015 - p303-304 [501+]
Macedo, Regina H. - *Sexual Selection: Perspectives and Models from the Neotropics*
    QRB - v90 - i2 - June 2015 - p221(2) [501+]
Macedo, Stephen - *Just Married: Same-Sex Couples, Monogamy & the Future of Marriage*
    LJ - v140 - i10 - June 1 2015 - p118(2) [51-500]
MacFarlane-Barrow, Magnus - *The Shed that Fed a Million Children: The Extraordinary Story of Mary's Meals*
    KR - March 15 2015 - pNA [501+]
    PW - v262 - i11 - March 16 2015 - p76(2) [51-500]
Macfarlane, Daniel - *Negotiating a River: Canada, the US, and the Creation of the St. Lawrence Seaway*
    Can Hist R - v96 - i3 - Sept 2015 - p451(3) [501+]
MacFarlane, John - *Stormstruck!*
    c SLJ - v61 - i9 - Sept 2015 - p141(2) [501+]
Macfarlane, Robert - *Landmarks*
    Lon R Bks - v37 - i18 - Sept 24 2015 - p23(1) [501+]
    New Sci - v225 - i3014 - March 28 2015 - p47(1) [501+]
    Spec - v327 - i9731 - Feb 28 2015 - p36(2) [501+]
    TimHES - i2192 - Feb 26 2015 - p52(1) [501+]
    TLS - i5841 - March 13 2015 - p24(1) [501+]
    New Sci - v228 - i3045 - Oct 31 2015 - p45(1) [501+]
MacFarquhar, Larissa - *Strangers Drowning: Grappling with Impossible Idealism, Drastic Choices, and the Overpowering Urge to Help (Read by MacFarquhar, Larissa). Audiobook Review*
    PW - v262 - i48 - Nov 30 2015 - p55(2) [51-500]
Strangers Drowning: Grappling with Impossible Idealism, Drastic Choices, and the Overpowering Urge to Help
    Atl - v316 - i3 - Oct 2015 - p52(1) [501+]
    KR - July 1 2015 - pNA [501+]
    Mac - v128 - i39 - Oct 5 2015 - p58(1) [501+]
    Nat Post - v17 - i266 - Sept 26 2015 - pWP5(1) [501+]
    Nation - v301 - i21-22 - Nov 23 2015 - p27(4) [501+]
    NS - v144 - i5282 - Oct 2 2015 - p20(1) [501+]
    NYRB - v62 - i20 - Dec 17 2015 - p58(3) [501+]
    NYT - Sept 25 2015 - pC21(L) [501+]
    NYTBR - Oct 11 2015 - p13(L) [501+]
    PW - v262 - i27 - July 6 2015 - p60(1) [51-500]
    Spec - v329 - i9764 - Oct 17 2015 - p44(2) [501+]
MacFfarlane, John - *Stormstruck!*
    c KR - July 15 2015 - pNA [501+]
MacGinnis, John - *The Arrows of the Sun: Armed Forces in Sippar in the First Millennium BC*
    JNES - v74 - i1 - April 2015 - p155(5) [501+]
MacGregor, Christopher - *Mummy's Home! (Illus. by Yarlett, Emma)*
    c Sch Lib - v63 - i3 - Autumn 2015 - p158(1) [51-500]
MacGregor, Neil - *Germany: Memories of a Nation*
    KR - August 1 2015 - pNA [501+]
    PW - v262 - i31 - August 3 2015 - p48(1) [51-500]
    LJ - v140 - i15 - Sept 15 2015 - p88(1) [501+]

A History of the World in 100 Objects
    LJ - v140 - i9 - May 15 2015 - p94(2) [501+]
Shakespeare's Restless World: A Portrait of an Era in Twenty Objects
    LJ - v140 - i9 - May 15 2015 - p94(2) [501+]
MacGregor, Roy - *Reality Check in Detroit*
    c Res Links - v20 - i4 - April 2015 - p12(2) [51-500]
Machado, Ana Maria - *Until the Day Arrives*
    c CCB-B - v68 - i5 - Jan 2015 - p266(1) [51-500]
    c HB - v91 - i2 - March-April 2015 - p103(2) [51-500]
    y HB Guide - v26 - i2 - Fall 2015 - p92(1) [51-500]
Machado de Assis, Joaquim Maria - *Lord Taciturn*
    TLS - i5848 - May 1 2015 - p27(1) [501+]
Machajewski, Sarah - *A Kid's Life during the American Civil War*
    c SLJ - v61 - i4 - April 2015 - p113(4) [501+]
MacHale, D.J. - *Project Alpha*
    c KR - June 15 2015 - pNA [51-500]
    c PW - v262 - i23 - June 8 2015 - p61(1) [51-500]
Machale, D.J. - *Project Alpha*
    c SLJ - v61 - i10 - Oct 2015 - p91(2) [501+]
MacHale, D.J. - *Sylo (Read by Bates, Andrew S.). Audiobook Review*
    y SLJ - v61 - i6 - June 2015 - p53(3) [501+]
Voyagers: Project Alpha
    c BL - v111 - i21 - July 1 2015 - p77(1) [51-500]
Machcewicz, Pawel - *Poland's War on Radio Free Europe, 1950-1989*
    HNet - June 2015 - pNA [501+]
Machiavelli - *The Prince*
    TimHES - i2211 - July 9 2015 - p44(1) [501+]
Machielsen, Jan - *Martin Delrio: Demonology and Scholarship in the Counter-Reformation*
    TLS - i5855 - June 19 2015 - p9(1) [501+]
    CHR - v101 - i4 - Autumn 2015 - p941(2) [501+]
Machon, Josephine - *Immersive Theatres: Intimacy and Immediacy in Contemporary Performance*
    PAJ - v37 - i3 - Sept 2015 - p131-132 [501+]
Machtan, Lothar - *Prinz Max von Baden: Der Letzte Kanzler des Kaisers*
    HNet - March 2015 - pNA [501+]
Maciag, Drew - *Edmund Burke in America: The Contested Career of the Father of Modern Conservatism*
    Historian - v77 - i3 - Fall 2015 - p633(2) [501+]
    MA - v57 - i1 - Wntr 2015 - p73(3) [501+]
    RAH - v43 - i2 - June 2015 - p193-202 [501+]
Macias-Gonzalez, Victor M. - *Masculinity and Sexuality in Modern Mexico*
    HNet - June 2015 - pNA [501+]
Macinnis, Peter - *The Big Book of Australian History, 2d ed.*
    c Magpies - v30 - i2 - May 2015 - p24(1) [501+]
MacIntosh, Harold J. - *Mastering Negative Impulsive Thoughts*
    SPBW - Feb 2015 - pNA [501+]
Macintyre, Ben - *A Spy among Friends: Kim Philby and the Great Betrayal*
    NYTBR - June 7 2015 - p36(L) [501+]
Macintyre, Magnus - *Whirlgig*
    KR - June 1 2015 - pNA [51-500]
Whirligig
    BL - v111 - i21 - July 1 2015 - p34(1) [501+]
MacIver, Juliette - *Grasshoppers Dance (Illus. by Rycroft, Nina)*
    c Magpies - v30 - i2 - May 2015 - pS4(1) [501+]
Toucan Can! (Illus. by Davis, Sarah)
    c HB Guide - v26 - i1 - Spring 2015 - p38(1) [501+]
Yak and Gnu (Illus. by Chapman, Cat)
    c CCB-B - v69 - i1 - Sept 2015 - p36(1) [501+]
    c CH Bwatch - August 2015 - pNA [51-500]
    c HB Guide - v26 - i2 - Fall 2015 - p43(1) [51-500]
    c KR - April 1 2015 - pNA [51-500]
    c Magpies - v30 - i1 - March 2015 - p27(1) [501+]
    c SLJ - v61 - i8 - August 2015 - p74(1) [501+]
Mack - *Countries: Mack's World of Wonder (Illus. by Mack)*
    c SLJ - v61 - i10 - Oct 2015 - p128(1) [51-500]
Mack, Burton L. - *A Myth of Innocence: Mark and Christian Origins*
    JAAR - v83 - i3 - Sept 2015 - p826-857 [501+]
Mack, Daniel C. - *Assessing Liaison Librarians: Documenting Impact for Positive Change*
    LJ - v140 - i8 - May 1 2015 - p84(1) [501+]
Mack, Dwayne A. - *Black Spokane: The Civil Rights Struggle in the Inland Northwest*
    PHR - v84 - i4 - Nov 2015 - p553(554) [501+]
Mack, Janey - *Choked Up*
    PW - v262 - i44 - Nov 2 2015 - p62(1) [51-500]
Time's Up
    PW - v262 - i21 - May 25 2015 - p38(1) [51-500]

Book Review Index 2016 Cumulation MACMICHAEL • 291

Mack, Jeff - *Duck in the Fridge (Illus. by Mack, Jeff)*
c CCB-B - v68 - i5 - Jan 2015 - p267(1) [51-500]
Look! (Illus. by Mack, Jeff)
c BL - v111 - i14 - March 15 2015 - p78(1) [51-500]
c HB - v91 - i2 - March-April 2015 - p78(2) [51-500]
c HB Guide - v26 - i2 - Fall 2015 - p14(1) [51-500]
c KR - Jan 15 2015 - pNA [51-500]
c PW - v262 - i5 - Feb 2 2015 - p57(1) [51-500]
c PW - v262 - i49 - Dec 2 2015 - p35(1) [51-500]
Who Needs a Bath? (Illus. by Mack, Jeff)
y BL - v112 - i3 - Oct 1 2015 - p84(1) [51-500]
c KR - July 1 2015 - pNA [51-500]
c SLJ - v61 - i6 - June 2015 - p88(1) [51-500]
Who Wants a Hug? (Illus. by Mack, Jeff)
c CCB-B - v68 - i7 - March 2015 - p363(1) [51-500]
c HB Guide - v26 - i2 - Fall 2015 - p43(1) [51-500]
Mack, Lia - *Waiting for Paint to Dry*
KR - Nov 1 2015 - pNA [501+]
Mack, W.C. - *Changement de ligne*
c Res Links - v20 - i4 - April 2015 - p41(2) [501+]
Mackall, Dandi Daley - *The Super Gifts of Spring (Illus. by Blackmore, Katherine)*
c CH Bwatch - March 2015 - pNA [51-500]
Mackavey, Maria G. - *Yiayia Visits Amalia*
KR - Jan 1 2016 - pNA [51-500]
MacKay, Elly - *Butterfly Park (Illus. by MacKay, Elly)*
c HB Guide - v26 - i2 - Fall 2015 - p43(1) [51-500]
c KR - March 15 2015 - pNA [51-500]
c PW - v262 - i10 - March 9 2015 - p71(1) [51-500]
c SLJ - v61 - i7 - July 2015 - p64(2) [51-500]
Shadow Chasers
c HB Guide - v26 - i1 - Spring 2015 - p11(1) [51-500]
Mackay, Finn - *Radical Feminism: Feminist Activism in Movement*
TimHES - i2191 - Feb 19 2015 - p50-51 [501+]
Mackay, Gregory - *Anders and the Comet*
y Magpies - v30 - i1 - March 2015 - p35(1) [501+]
Mackay, Janis - *The Selkie Girl (Illus. by Mhasane, Ruchi)*
c SLJ - v61 - i2 - Feb 2015 - p72(2) [51-500]
MacKay, Jennifer - *Sports Nutrition*
y VOYA - v38 - i3 - August 2015 - p89(2) [51-500]
MacKay, Jenny - *Do Haunted Houses Exist?*
y VOYA - v38 - i5 - Dec 2015 - p79(1) [501+]
Mackay, Jordan - *Franklin Barbecue: A Meat-Smoking Manifesto*
NYTBR - May 31 2015 - p24(L) [501+]
Mackay, Malcolm - *The Necessary Death of Lewis Winter*
PW - v262 - i7 - Feb 16 2015 - p162(1) [501+]
MacKay, Robert B. - *Gardens of Eden: Long Island's Early Twentieth-Century Planned Communities*
HM - v330 - i1978 - March 2015 - p79(3) [501+]
LJ - v140 - i15 - Sept 15 2015 - p75(1) [501+]
MacKeen, Dawn Anahid - *The Hundred-Year Walk: An Armenian Odyssey*
KR - Oct 15 2015 - pNA [51-500]
LJ - v140 - i20 - Dec 1 2015 - p115(2) [51-500]
Macken, JoAnn Early - *Poet's Workshop*
c CH Bwatch - August 2015 - pNA [51-500]
Poet's Workshop Series: Read, Recite, and Write Nursery Rhymes
c Res Links - v20 - i3 - Feb 2015 - p22(1) [501+]
Read, Recite, and Write Cinquains
c Res Links - v21 - i1 - Oct 2015 - p24(1) [501+]
Read, Recite, and Write Concrete Poems
c Res Links - v21 - i1 - Oct 2015 - p24(1) [501+]
Read, Recite, and Write Free Verse Poems
c Res Links - v20 - i3 - Feb 2015 - p22(1) [501+]
Read, Recite, and Write Haiku
c Res Links - v21 - i1 - Oct 2015 - p24(1) [501+]
Read, Recite, and Write Limericks
c Res Links - v20 - i3 - Feb 2015 - p22(1) [501+]
Read, Recite, and Write List Poems
c Res Links - v21 - i1 - Oct 2015 - p24(1) [501+]
c CH Bwatch - July 2015 - pNA [501+]
Read, Recite, and Write Narrative Poems
c Res Links - v20 - i3 - Feb 2015 - p22(1) [501+]
MacKendrick, Karmen - *Divine Enticement: Theological Seductions*
JR - v95 - i2 - April 2015 - p267(3) [501+]
Mackenzie, Anna - *Evie's War*
Magpies - v30 - i3 - July 2015 - pS6(1) [501+]
Mackenzie, Catriona - *Vulnerability: New Essays in Ethics and Feminist Philosophy*
Ethics - v125 - i4 - July 2015 - p1210(6) [501+]
Mackenzie, Emily - *Wanted! Ralfy Rabbit, Book Burglar*
c Sch Lib - v63 - i2 - Summer 2015 - p96(1) [51-500]
Mackenzie, Jackson - *Psychopath Free (Expanded Edition): Recovering from Emotionally Abusive Relationships with Narcissists, Sociopaths, and Other Toxic People*
LJ - v140 - i16 - Oct 1 2015 - p98(1) [51-500]
Mackenzie, Kenneth - *The Refuge*
KR - Sept 1 2015 - pNA [51-500]
MacKenzie, S.P. - *The Imjin and Kapyong Battles, Korea, 1951*
HNet - Jan 2015 - pNA [501+]
Mackenzie, Sally - *What to Do with a Duke*
PW - v262 - i31 - August 3 2015 - p42(1) [51-500]
Mackert, Nina - *Jugenddelinquenz: Die Produktivitat eines Problems in den USA der Spaten 1940er bis 1960er Jahre*
HNet - June 2015 - pNA [501+]
Mackey, Alison - *Annual Review of Applied Linguistics*
Lang Soc - v44 - i4 - Sept 2015 - p608-1 [501+]
Mackey, Heather - *Dreamwood*
c HB Guide - v26 - i1 - Spring 2015 - p85(1) [51-500]
Mackey, Nathaniel - *Blue Fasa*
LJ - v140 - i11 - June 15 2015 - p92(1) [51-500]
PW - v262 - i16 - April 20 2015 - p52(1) [51-500]
Mackey, Thomas P. - *Metaliteracy: Reinventing Information Literacy to Empower Learners*
LR - v64 - i1-2 - Jan-Feb 2015 - p180-182 [501+]
Mackil, Emily - *Creating a Common Polity: Religion, Economy, and Politics in the Making of the Greek Koinon*
Historian - v77 - i3 - Fall 2015 - p618(2) [501+]
Mackin, Jeanne - *A Lady of Good Family*
NYTBR - July 5 2015 - p18(L) [501+]
MacKinnon, Dolly - *Earls Colne's Early Modern Landscapes*
AHR - v120 - i3 - June 2015 - p1109-1110 [501+]
MacKinnon, J.B. - *The Once and Future World: Nature As It Was, As It Is, As It Could Be*
Can Lit - i224 - Spring 2015 - p129 [501+]
Mackintosh, David - *Lucky (Illus. by Mackintosh, David)*
c HB Guide - v26 - i1 - Spring 2015 - p38(1) [51-500]
c NYTBR - Jan 18 2015 - p18(L) [501+]
Mackler, Carolyn - *Best Friend Next Door (Read by Sands, Tara, with Cassandra Morris). Audiobook Review*
c BL - v112 - i1 - Sept 1 2015 - p143(1) [51-500]
c SLJ - v61 - i10 - Oct 2015 - p52(1) [51-500]
Best Friend Next Door
c BL - v111 - i17 - May 1 2015 - p94(1) [51-500]
c CCB-B - v69 - i1 - Sept 2015 - p37(1) [51-500]
y HB - v91 - i3 - May-June 2015 - p114(1) [501+]
y HB Guide - v26 - i2 - Fall 2015 - p92(1) [51-500]
c KR - March 15 2015 - pNA [51-500]
SLJ - v61 - i4 - April 2015 - p148(1) [51-500]
Infinite in Between (Read by Yuen, Erin). Audiobook Review
y SLJ - v61 - i11 - Nov 2015 - p73(1) [51-500]
Infinite in Between
c BL - v112 - i1 - Sept 1 2015 - p104(1) [51-500]
y KR - July 15 2015 - pNA [51-500]
y PW - v262 - i28 - July 13 2015 - p69(1) [51-500]
y PW - v262 - i49 - Dec 2 2015 - p93(1) [51-500]
y SLJ - v61 - i9 - Sept 2015 - p160(1) [51-500]
y VOYA - v38 - i4 - Oct 2015 - p56(1) [51-500]
MacKnight, Elizabeth C. - *Aristocratic Families in Republican France, 1870-1940*
HER - v130 - i543 - April 2015 - p476(2) [501+]
Mackrell, Judith - *Flappers: Six Women of a Dangerous Generation*
NYTBR - March 8 2015 - p32(L) [501+]
Mackrory, KaraLynne - *Haunting Mr. Darcy: A Spirited Courtship*
PW - v262 - i29 - July 20 2015 - p177(1) [51-500]
PW - v262 - i30 - July 27 2015 - p32(1) [51-500]
Macks, Jon - *Monologue: What Makes America Laugh before Bed (Read by Heller, Johnny). Audiobook Review*
LJ - v140 - i12 - July 1 2015 - p45(1) [51-500]
PW - v262 - i30 - July 27 2015 - p62(1) [51-500]
Monologue: What Makes America Laugh before Bed
BL - v111 - i15 - April 1 2015 - p11(1) [51-500]
KR - March 1 2015 - pNA [51-500]
MacLachlan, Bonnie - *Women in Ancient Rome: A Sourcebook*
Class R - v65 - i1 - April 2015 - p193-195 [501+]
MacLachlan, Colin M. - *Imperialism and the Origins of Mexican Culture*
LJ - v140 - i9 - May 15 2015 - p92(1) [51-500]
NYRB - v62 - i12 - July 9 2015 - p58(3) [501+]
Maclachlan, Ian - *Marking Time: Derrida, Blanchot, Beckett, des Forets, Klossowski, Laporte*
MLR - v110 - i3 - July 2015 - p871-873 [501+]
MacLachlan, Patricia - *The Iridescence of Birds: A Book about Henri Matisse (Illus. by Hooper, Hadley)*
c HB Guide - v26 - i1 - Spring 2015 - p179(1) [51-500]
c Teach Lib - v42 - i5 - June 2015 - p44(1) [51-500]
MacLaine, Shirley - *Above the Line*
KR - Dec 15 2015 - pNA [51-500]
MacLauchlin, Cory - *Butterfly in the Typewriter: The Tragic Life of John Kennedy Toole and the Remarkable Story of a Confederacy of Dunces*
JSH - v81 - i3 - August 2015 - p782(2) [501+]
MacLaughlin, Nina - *Hammer Head: The Making of a Carpenter*
BL - v111 - i12 - Feb 15 2015 - p16(1) [51-500]
Ent W - i1357 - April 3 2015 - p66(1) [501+]
LJ - v140 - i10 - June 1 2015 - p120(2) [501+]
NYTBR - May 10 2015 - p38(L) [501+]
MacLean, Andrew - *ApocalyptiGirl: An Aria for the End Times*
BL - v111 - i22 - August 1 2015 - p46(1) [51-500]
PW - v262 - i23 - June 8 2015 - p47(1) [51-500]
MacLean, Harry N. - *The Joy of Killing*
KR - May 1 2015 - pNA [51-500]
PW - v262 - i20 - May 18 2015 - p67(1) [51-500]
MacLean, Ken - *The Government of Mistrust: Illegibility and Bureaucratic Power in Socialist Vietnam*
Pac A - v88 - i3 - Sept 2015 - p733 [501+]
Maclean, Norman - *A Less Green and Pleasant Land: Our Threatened Wildlife*
TimHES - i2206 - June 4 2015 - p50(1) [501+]
MacLean, Rory - *Back in the USSR: Heroic Adventures in Transnistria (Illus. by Danziger, Nick)*
NS - v144 - i5248 - Feb 6 2015 - p40(2) [501+]
TLS - i5849 - May 8 2015 - p12(2) [501+]
Berlin: Imagine a City
TLS - i5852 - May 29 2015 - p26(1) [501+]
MacLean, Sarah - *The Rogue Not Taken*
KR - Nov 1 2015 - pNA [501+]
PW - v262 - i42 - Oct 19 2015 - p62(1) [51-500]
Maclear, Kyo - *The Good Little Book (Illus. by Arbona, Marion)*
c CH Bwatch - Sept 2015 - pNA [51-500]
c CH Bwatch - Nov 2015 - pNA [51-500]
c KR - May 1 2015 - pNA [51-500]
c Res Links - v21 - i1 - Oct 2015 - p8(1) [501+]
c SLJ - v61 - i10 - Oct 2015 - p80(1) [51-500]
Julia, Child (Illus. by Morstad, Julie)
c HB Guide - v26 - i2 - Fall 2015 - p43(1) [51-500]
The Specific Ocean (Illus. by Maurey, Katty)
c CH Bwatch - Oct 2015 - pNA [501+]
c KR - June 1 2015 - pNA [51-500]
c PW - v262 - i21 - May 25 2015 - p57(1) [51-500]
c SLJ - v61 - i8 - August 2015 - p74(1) [51-500]
MacLellan, David E. - *The National Home Maintenance Manual: The Complete Guide to Caring for Your Home*
LJ - v140 - i12 - July 1 2015 - p86(1) [51-500]
MacLellan, Vanessa - *Three Great Lies*
PW - v262 - i26 - June 29 2015 - p49(1) [51-500]
MacLennan, Alan - *Information Governance and Assurance: Reducing Risk, Promoting Policy*
LR - v64 - i1-2 - Jan-Feb 2015 - p186-188 [501+]
MacLennan, Carol A. - *Sovereign Sugar: Industry and Environment in Hawai'i*
AHR - v120 - i2 - April 2015 - p603-604 [501+]
WHQ - v46 - i2 - Summer 2015 - p230-231 [501+]
MacLeod, D. Peter - *Northern Armageddon: The Battle of the Plains of Abraham and the Making of the American Revolution*
KR - Dec 15 2015 - pNA [501+]
MacLeod, Elizabeth - *Bunny the Brave War Horse: Based on a True Story (Illus. by Lafance, Marie)*
c HB Guide - v26 - i2 - Fall 2015 - p217(1) [51-500]
Galloping through History: Amazing True Horse Stories
c BL - v111 - i17 - May 1 2015 - p84(1) [51-500]
c Res Links - v20 - i5 - June 2015 - p14(1) [51-500]
MacLeod, Janice - *Paris Letters (Read by Gilbert, Tavia). Audiobook Review*
BL - v111 - i11 - Feb 1 2015 - p58(1) [51-500]
MacLeod, John - *Scottish Theology*
RVBW - Nov 2015 - pNA [501+]
MacManus, James - *Sleep in Peace Tonight*
Spec - v327 - i9728 - Feb 7 2015 - p47(1) [501+]
TLS - i5840 - March 6 2015 - p21(1) [501+]
MacManus, Richard - *Health Trackers: How Technology Is Helping Us Monitor and Improve Our Health*
BL - v112 - i7 - Dec 1 2015 - p13(2) [51-500]
PW - v262 - i38 - Sept 21 2015 - p69(1) [51-500]
MacMichael, Simon - *Niccolo Machiavelli: An Intellectual Biography*
Historian - v77 - i2 - Summer 2015 - p406(2) [501+]
JMH - v87 - i1 - March 2015 - p202(3) [501+]

Macmillan, Gilly - *What She Knew*
BL - v112 - i7 - Dec 1 2015 - p32(2) [51-500]
PW - v262 - i47 - Nov 23 2015 - p49(1) [51-500]

MacMillan, Kathy - *Sword and Verse*
y   BL - v112 - i7 - Dec 1 2015 - p58(1) [51-500]
y   KR - Nov 1 2015 - pNA [51-500]
y   SLJ - v61 - i11 - Nov 2015 - p118(1) [51-500]

MacMillan, Margaret - *History's People: Personalities and the Past*
KR - Sept 1 2015 - pNA [501+]
PW - v262 - i35 - August 31 2015 - p82(1) [51-500]

The War That Ended Peace
J Mil H - v79 - i4 - Oct 2015 - p1147-1149 [501+]

Macmillan, Palgrave - *How Politics Makes Us Sick: Neoliberal Epidemics*
TimHES - i2225 - Oct 15 2015 - p43-1 [501+]

MacNeal, Susan Elia - *Mrs. Roosevelt's Confidante*
BL - v112 - i2 - Sept 15 2015 - p32(1) [51-500]
KR - August 15 2015 - pNA [501+]
PW - v262 - i36 - Sept 7 2015 - p46(1) [51-500]

MacNeil, Karen - *The Wine Bible, 2d ed.*
LJ - v140 - i13 - August 1 2015 - p123(1) [51-500]

MacNiven, Ian S. - *"Literchoor Is My Beat": A Life of James Laughlin, Publisher of New Directions*
AS - v84 - i1 - Wntr 2015 - p111(4) [501+]
Nation - v300 - i12 - March 23 2015 - p35(3) [501+]
NY - v91 - i2 - Feb 23 2015 - p179 [51-500]
NYRB - v62 - i6 - April 2 2015 - p36(3) [501+]
NYT - Jan 16 2015 - pC34(L) [501+]
TLS - i5840 - March 6 2015 - p24(1) [501+]

Macomber, Debbie - *Marriage of Inconvenience*
BL - v111 - i18 - May 15 2015 - p31(1) [51-500]

Silver Linings
BL - v112 - i2 - Sept 15 2015 - p42(2) [501+]

Maconie, Robin - *Experiencing Stravinsky: A Listener's Companion*
Notes - v71 - i4 - June 2015 - p687(4) [501+]

Maconie, Stuart - *The Pie at Night: in Search of the North at Play*
NS - v144 - i5287 - Nov 6 2015 - p47(1) [51-500]

MacPhail, Catherine - *Stars Shall Be Bright*
c   Sch Lib - v63 - i2 - Summer 2015 - p106(1) [51-500]

MacPhail, Cathy - *Devil You Know*
y   Sch Lib - v63 - i2 - Summer 2015 - p119(1) [51-500]

Macpherson, David - *All Lies: A Story of the Portland Spies*
TimHES - i2213 - July 23 2015 - p45(1) [501+]

MacQuarrie, Kim - *Life and Death in the Andes: On the Trail of Bandits, Heroes, and Revolutionaries*
KR - Sept 15 2015 - pNA [501+]
LJ - v140 - i17 - Oct 15 2015 - p102(1) [51-500]
NYTBR - Dec 6 2015 - p46(L) [501+]
PW - v262 - i37 - Sept 14 2015 - p52(1) [51-500]

MacRae, Sigrid von Hoyningen-Huene - *A World Elsewhere: An American Woman in Wartime Germany*
WLT - v89 - i2 - March-April 2015 - p74(3) [501+]

Macri, Thomas - *The Story of Ironman (Illus. by Rousseau, Craig)*
c   HB Guide - v26 - i2 - Fall 2015 - p61(1) [51-500]

The Story of Spider-Man
c   HB Guide - v26 - i2 - Fall 2015 - p61(1) [51-500]

The Story of the Avengers (Illus. by Olliffe, Pat)
c   HB Guide - v26 - i2 - Fall 2015 - p61(1) [51-500]

Macrides, Ruth - *Pseudo-Kodinos and the Constantinopolitan Court: Offices and Ceremonies*
HER - v130 - i545 - August 2015 - p949(4) [501+]
Specu - v90 - i3 - July 2015 - p832-833 [501+]

MacShane, Denis - *Brexit: How Britain Will Leave Europe*
TLS - i5846 - April 17 2015 - p7(1) [501+]

Macsovits, Rebecca Wilson - *Guion the Lion: A Colorful World (Illus. by Morales, Joseba)*
c   CH Bwatch - Jan 2015 - pNA [51-500]
c   CH Bwatch - Feb 2015 - pNA [51-500]

Macy, Joanna - *Coming Back to Life: The Updated Guide to The Work That Reconnects*
Bwatch - Feb 2015 - pNA [51-500]

Macy, Sue - *Miss Mary Reporting: The True Story of Sportswriter Mary Garber (Illus. by Payne, C.F.)*
c   BL - v112 - i5 - Nov 1 2015 - p42(1) [51-500]
c   KR - Dec 1 2015 - pNA [51-500]
c   PW - v262 - i51 - Dec 14 2015 - p82(2) [501+]

Roller Derby Rivals (Illus. by Collins, Matt)
c   CH Bwatch - Feb 2015 - pNA [51-500]
c   HB Guide - v26 - i1 - Spring 2015 - p184(1) [51-500]

Sally Ride: Life on a Mission
c   HB Guide - v26 - i1 - Spring 2015 - p194(1) [51-500]
Sci & Ch - v53 - i2 - Oct 2015 - p99 [51-500]

Madden, Patrick - *Sublime Physick: Essays*
KR - Dec 15 2015 - pNA [51-500]
PW - v262 - i48 - Nov 30 2015 - p49(1) [51-500]

Madden, Thomas - *The Concise History of the Crusades*
Specu - v90 - i3 - July 2015 - p834(1) [501+]

Maddison, Ben - *Class and Colonialism in Antarctic Exploration, 1750-1920*
AHR - v120 - i4 - Oct 2015 - p1447-1448 [501+]

Maddox, Cynthia - *Walking with Spirit: Consciously Continuing Your Spiritual Journey*
SPBW - July 2015 - pNA [51-500]

Maddox, Jake - *Gridiron Showdown*
c   HB Guide - v26 - i1 - Spring 2015 - p85(1) [51-500]

Second-Chance Soccer
c   HB Guide - v26 - i1 - Spring 2015 - p85(1) [51-500]

Maddox, Lucy - *The Parker Sisters: A Border Kidnapping*
LJ - v140 - i20 - Dec 1 2015 - p115(1) [51-500]
PW - v262 - i47 - Nov 23 2015 - p58(2) [51-500]

Madeira, Victor - *Britannia and the Bear: The Anglo-Russian Intelligence Wars, 1917-1929*
HNet - July 2015 - pNA [501+]

Madelung, Wilferd - *Studies in Medieval Muslim Thought and History*
Specu - v90 - i1 - Jan 2015 - p273-275 [501+]

Maden, Mike - *Drone Command*
PW - v262 - i33 - August 17 2015 - p52(1) [51-500]

Mader, C. Roger - *Tiptop Cat (Read by Mitchell, Lizan). Audiobook Review*
c   SLJ - v61 - i5 - May 2015 - p68(1) [51-500]

Tiptop Cat (Illus. by Mader, C. Roger)
c   CH Bwatch - Jan 2015 - pNA [51-500]
c   HB Guide - v26 - i1 - Spring 2015 - p38(1) [51-500]

Madhavan, Guru - *Applied Minds: How Engineers Think*
KR - May 1 2015 - pNA [501+]
LJ - v140 - i10 - June 1 2015 - p130(1) [51-500]
Nature - v524 - i7564 - August 13 2015 - p159(1) [501+]
New Sci - v227 - i3036 - August 29 2015 - p43(1) [501+]
PW - v262 - i20 - May 18 2015 - p75(1) [51-500]

Madhok, Sumi - *Rethinking Agency: Developmentalism, Gender and Rights*
TimHES - i2186 - Jan 15 2015 - p49(1) [501+]

Madigan, Jamie - *Getting Gamers: The Psychology of Video Games and Their Impact on the People Who Play Them*
PW - v262 - i35 - August 31 2015 - p78(1) [51-500]

Madigan, Kevin - *Medieval Christianity: A New History (Read by Larkin, Pete). Audiobook Review*
LJ - v140 - i15 - Sept 15 2015 - p44(1) [51-500]

Medieval Christianity: A New History
CC - v132 - i13 - June 24 2015 - p38(2) [51-500]
Comw - v142 - i8 - May 1 2015 - p33(2) [51-500]

Madigan, Robert - *How Memory Works--and How to Make It Work for You*
PW - v262 - i21 - May 25 2015 - p50(1) [51-500]

Madison, Catherine - *The War Came Home with Him: A Daughter's Memoir*
KR - July 1 2015 - pNA [51-500]
LJ - v140 - i13 - August 1 2015 - p106(1) [51-500]

Madison, James H. - *Hoosiers: A New History of Indiana*
JAH - v102 - i1 - June 2015 - p208-209 [501+]

Madison, Juliet - *Sight: The Delta Girls*
y   SLJ - v61 - i7 - July 2015 - p96(1) [51-500]

Madison, Paula Williams - *Finding Samuel Lowe: China, Jamaica, Harlem*
BL - v111 - i11 - Feb 1 2015 - p15(1) [51-500]
KR - Feb 1 2015 - pNA [501+]

Madison, William V. - *Madeline Kahn: Being the Music: A Life*
LJ - v140 - i8 - May 1 2015 - p77(1) [51-500]

Madland, David - *Hollowed Out: Why the Economy Doesn't Work without a Middle Class*
KR - May 15 2015 - pNA [501+]
TimHES - i2217 - August 20 2015 - p47-47 [501+]

Madsen, Ole Jacob - *The Therapeutic Turn: How Psychology Altered Western Culture*
Soc - v52 - i2 - April 2015 - p181(1) [501+]

Mae, Cassie - *No Interest in Love. E-book Review*
PW - v262 - i42 - Oct 19 2015 - p61(1) [51-500]

Maeda, Martha - *How to Solar Power Your Home: Everything You Need to Know Explained Simply*
Bwatch - Sept 2015 - pNA [51-500]

Maes, Sientje - *Souveranitat-Feindschaft-Masse: Theatralikund Rhetorikdes Politischen in den Dramen Christian Dietrich Grabbes*
Ger Q - v88 - i1 - Wntr 2015 - p107(3) [501+]

Maetani, Valynne E. - *Ink and Ashes*
y   BL - v111 - i21 - July 1 2015 - p55(1) [51-500]
y   CCB-B - v69 - i1 - Sept 2015 - p37(1) [51-500]
y   CH Bwatch - July 2015 - pNA [51-500]
y   HB Guide - v26 - i2 - Fall 2015 - p130(1) [51-500]
y   KR - April 15 2015 - pNA [501+]
y   SLJ - v61 - i5 - May 2015 - p114(1) [51-500]

Maffie, James - *Aztec Philosophy: Understanding a World in Motion*
Ams - v72 - i2 - April 2015 - p336(2) [501+]

Magaziner, Lauren - *The Only Thing Worse Than Witches*
c   HB Guide - v26 - i1 - Spring 2015 - p85(1) [51-500]

Pilfer Academy: A School So Bad It's Criminal
c   KR - Nov 15 2015 - pNA [51-500]
c   SLJ - v61 - i12 - Dec 2015 - p104(1) [51-500]

Magerl, Caroline - *Rose and the Wish Thing*
c   KR - Jan 1 2016 - pNA [51-500]

Magesa, Laurenti - *What Is Not Sacred? African Spirituality*
Theol St - v76 - i2 - June 2015 - p378(2) [501+]

Maggay, Melba Padilla - *The Gospel in Culture: Contextualization Issues through Asian Eyes*
IBMR - v39 - i3 - July 2015 - p165(2) [501+]

Maggi, Nicole - *The Blue Woods*
y   KR - Oct 15 2015 - pNA [51-500]

In the Mouth of the Wolf
y   VOYA - v38 - i3 - August 2015 - p80(1) [51-500]

Maggiore, Lisa - *Ava the Monster Slayer (Illus. by Felten, Ross)*
c   KR - June 1 2015 - pNA [51-500]
c   SLJ - v61 - i10 - Oct 2015 - p80(1) [51-500]

Maggs, Sam - *The Fangirl's Guide to the Galaxy: A Handbook for Girl Geeks*
y   CH Bwatch - July 2015 - pNA [51-500]
RVBW - June 2015 - pNA [51-500]

Magi, Trina - *Intellectual Freedom Manual, 9th ed.*
LJ - v140 - i15 - Sept 15 2015 - p93(1) [51-500]

Magic Science Series
c   BL - v111 - i15 - April 1 2015 - p58(1) [501+]

Magid, Shaul - *Hasidism Incarnate: Hasidism, Christianity, and the Construction of Modern Judaism*
HNet - Sept 2015 - pNA(NA) [501+]

Magidor, Ofra - *Category Mistakes*
Phil R - v124 - i2 - April 2015 - p289(4) [501+]

Magliocca, Gerard N. - *American Founding Son: John Bingham and the Invention of the Fourteenth Amendment*
Historian - v77 - i3 - Fall 2015 - p566(2) [501+]

Magner, Scott James - *Homefront*
SPBW - March 2015 - pNA [51-500]

Magnet, Shoshana Amielle - *When Biometrics Fail: Gender, Race and the Technology of Identity*
CWS - v30 - i2-3 - Fall-Winter 2015 - p134(2) [501+]

Magny, Ariane - *Porphyry in Fragments: Reception of an Anti-Christian Text in Late Antiquity*
Class R - v65 - i2 - Oct 2015 - p405-407 [501+]

Magoon, Kekla - *How It Went Down (Read by several narrators). Audiobook Review*
y   HB - v91 - i4 - July-August 2015 - p165(1) [51-500]
y   SLJ - v61 - i6 - June 2015 - p67(1) [51-500]

How It Went Down
y   HB Guide - v26 - i1 - Spring 2015 - p115(1) [51-500]
c   SLJ - v61 - i12 - Dec 2015 - p64(4) [501+]
y   Teach Lib - v42 - i4 - April 2015 - p23(1) [51-500]

Shadows of Sherwood
c   BL - v111 - i18 - May 15 2015 - p67(2) [51-500]
c   HB - v91 - i4 - July-August 2015 - p139(2) [51-500]
c   KR - June 15 2015 - pNA [51-500]
c   NYTBR - August 23 2015 - p29(L) [501+]
c   PW - v262 - i20 - May 18 2015 - p84(2) [51-500]
c   SLJ - v61 - i7 - July 2015 - p80(1) [51-500]

X
y   HB - v91 - i3 - May-June 2015 - p117(2) [501+]
y   HB Guide - v26 - i2 - Fall 2015 - p138(1) [51-500]
y   Magpies - v30 - i3 - July 2015 - p44(1) [501+]
y   PW - v262 - i49 - Dec 2 2015 - p116(1) [51-500]

Magorian, Michelle - *Impossible!*
c   Sch Lib - v63 - i1 - Spring 2015 - p40(1) [51-500]

Magro, Mark - *Surfacing*
y   VOYA - v38 - i5 - Dec 2015 - p72(1) [51-500]

Magruder, James - *Let Me See It*
  Ga R - v69 - i1 - Spring 2015 - p130-132 [501+]
Magson, Adrian - *Close Quarters*
  BL - v111 - i19-20 - June 1 2015 - p48(2) [51-500]
  PW - v262 - i24 - June 15 2015 - p64(2) [51-500]
  The Locker
  BL - v112 - i5 - Nov 1 2015 - p31(1) [501+]
  KR - Oct 15 2015 - pNA [51-500]
Magueijo, Joao - *Bifes Mal Passados: Passeios e outras catastrofes por terra de Sua Majestade*
  TLS - i5847 - April 24 2015 - p26(1) [501+]
Maguire, Gregory - *After Alice*
  y BL - v112 - i3 - Oct 1 2015 - p34(1) [51-500]
  KR - Sept 1 2015 - pNA [51-500]
  LJ - v140 - i16 - Oct 1 2015 - p71(1) [51-500]
  NYTBR - Nov 1 2015 - p21(L) [501+]
  PW - v262 - i37 - Sept 14 2015 - p46(2) [51-500]
  Egg & Spoon
  y HB Guide - v26 - i1 - Spring 2015 - p115(1) [51-500]
Maguire, Kay - *Nature's Day: Discover the World of Wonder on Your Doorstep (Illus. by Kroll, Danielle)*
  c Sch Lib - v63 - i2 - Summer 2015 - p96(1) [51-500]
  Red Hot Chili Grower: The Complete Guide to Planting, Picking, and Preserving Chilis
  Bwatch - Nov 2015 - pNA [51-500]
  LJ - v140 - i19 - Nov 15 2015 - p105(1) [501+]
Maguire, Nora - *Childness and the Writing of the German Past: Tropes of Childhood in Contemporary German Literature*
  MLR - v110 - i3 - July 2015 - p912-913 [501+]
Magura, Sandra - *HippoDuck: Trouble at the Airport (Illus. by Haufiller, Gaston)*
  c CH Bwatch - April 2015 - pNA [51-500]
Magziner, Lauren - *Pilfer Academy: A School So Bad It's Criminal*
  c PW - v262 - i47 - Nov 23 2015 - p68(1) [51-500]
Mah, Alice - *Port Cities and Global Legacies: Hardcover Urban Identity, Waterfront Work, and Radicalism*
  HNet - June 2015 - pNA [501+]
Mahadevan, Kumar - *From India: Over 100 Recipes to Celebrate Food, Family & Tradition*
  NYTBR - Dec 6 2015 - p20(L) [501+]
  NYTBR - Dec 6 2015 - p20(L) [501+]
Mahaffey, Jerome D. - *The Accidental Revolutionary: George Whitefield and the Creation of America*
  Bks & Cult - v21 - i1 - Jan-Feb 2015 - p17(2) [501+]
Mahajan, Karan - *The Association of Small Bombs*
  KR - Jan 1 2016 - pNA [51-500]
Mahajan, Sanjoy - *The Art of Insight in Science and Engineering: Mastering Complexity*
  Phys Today - v68 - i9 - Sept 2015 - p53-53 [501+]
  RM - v69 - i2 - Dec 2015 - p397(2) [501+]
Mahaney, Ian F. - *Author*
  c CH Bwatch - April 2015 - pNA [51-500]
Mahard, Martha - *The Preservation Management Handbook: A 21st Century Guide for Libraries, Archives, and Museums*
  LR - v64 - i6-7 - June-July 2015 - p505-506 [501+]
Mahbubani, Kishore - *Can Singapore Survive?*
  TLS - i5868 - Sept 18 2015 - p30(1) [501+]
Mahdi, Musin - *The Thousand and One Nights (Alf Layla Wa-Layla), 2 vols.*
  TLS - i5846 - April 17 2015 - p12(2) [501+]
Mahe, Vincent - *750 Years in Paris*
  BL - v112 - i6 - Nov 15 2015 - p33(1) [51-500]
Maher, Damian - *This One Thing*
  KR - May 15 2015 - pNA [501+]
Maher, Naramore Susan - *Deep Map Country: Literary Cartography of the Great Plains*
  J Am St - v49 - i3 - August 2015 - p644-645 [501+]
Mahin, Shanna - *Oh! You Pretty Things*
  BL - v111 - i13 - March 1 2015 - p20(1) [51-500]
  KR - Feb 15 2015 - pNA [51-500]
  LJ - v140 - i5 - March 15 2015 - p93(1) [51-500]
  NYT - May 7 2015 - pC6(L) [501+]
  NYTBR - May 31 2015 - p27(L) [501+]
  PW - v262 - i5 - Feb 2 2015 - p31(1) [51-500]
Mahiri, Jabari - *The First Year of Teaching: Classroom Research to Increase Student Learning*
  JE - v195 - i2 - Spring 2015 - p49-53 [501+]
Mahmoody, Mahtob - *My Name Is Mahtob: The Story That Began in the Global Phenomenon 'Not without My Daughter' Continues*
  PW - v262 - i37 - Sept 14 2015 - p60(1) [51-500]

Mahn, Churnjeet - *British Women's Travel to Greece, 1840-1914: Travels in the Palimpsest*
  MLR - v110 - i2 - April 2015 - p535-536 [501+]
Mahnken, Thomas G. - *Strategy in Asia: The Past, Present, and Future of Regional Security*
  HNet - Feb 2015 - pNA [501+]
  J Mil H - v79 - i1 - Jan 2015 - p263-264 [501+]
Mahon, Annette - *Slay Bells*
  BL - v112 - i4 - Oct 15 2015 - p23(1) [51-500]
  KR - Sept 1 2015 - pNA [51-500]
Mahoney, Bill - *Vagabonding through Retirement: Unusual Wanders Far From Our Paris Houseboat*
  SPBW - Oct 2015 - pNA [51-500]
Mahoney, Daniel J. - *The Other Solzhenitsyn: Telling the Truth about a Misunderstood Writer and Thinker*
  MA - v57 - i4 - Fall 2015 - p73(3) [501+]
  Soc - v52 - i2 - April 2015 - p185(4) [501+]
Mahoney, Dennis - *Bell Weather*
  BL - v111 - i21 - July 1 2015 - p46(1) [51-500]
  KR - May 1 2015 - pNA [51-500]
  PW - v262 - i18 - May 4 2015 - p94(1) [51-500]
Mahoney, Ellen - *Nellie Bly and Investigative Journalism for Kids: Mighty Muckrakers from the Golden Age to Today, with 21 Activities*
  c BL - v111 - i19-20 - June 1 2015 - p79(1) [51-500]
  c SLJ - v61 - i5 - May 2015 - p138(2) [51-500]
Mahoney, Michel R. - *The Other Zulus: The Spread of Zulu Ethnicity in Colonial South Africa*
  AHR - v120 - i3 - June 2015 - p1155-1156 [501+]
Mahs, Jurgen von - *Down and Out in Los Angeles and Berlin: The Sociospatial Exclusion of Homeless People*
  CS - v44 - i5 - Sept 2015 - p726-728 [501+]
Mahy, Margaret - *The Great White Man-Eating Shark (Illus. by Allen, Jonathan)*
  c Magpies - v30 - i4 - Sept 2015 - pS6(1) [501+]
Mai Jia - *Decoded*
  NYTBR - May 10 2015 - p36(L) [501+]
Maibom, Heidi L. - *Empathy and Morality*
  TLS - i5872 - Oct 16 2015 - p11(2) [501+]
Maiden, Ramon - *Inking the Borders of Heaven and Hell: The Art of Ramon Maiden*
  LJ - v140 - i20 - Dec 1 2015 - p99(1) [51-500]
Maidment, Brian - *Comedy, Caricature and The Social Order, 1820-50*
  Historian - v77 - i3 - Fall 2015 - p620(2) [501+]
Maienschein, Jane - *Embryos under the Microscope: The Diverging Meanings of Life*
  Comw - v142 - i12 - July 10 2015 - p29(2) [501+]
  QRB - v90 - i3 - Sept 2015 - p340(1) [501+]
Maifreda, Germano - *From Oikonomia to Political Economy: Constructing Economic Knowledge from the Renaissance to the Scientific Revolution*
  Historian - v77 - i2 - Summer 2015 - p413(2) [501+]
Maihack, Mike - *The Thief and the Sword (Illus. by Maihack, Mike)*
  c BL - v111 - i16 - April 15 2015 - p40(1) [51-500]
  c SLJ - v61 - i5 - May 2015 - p110(2) [51-500]
  y HB Guide - v26 - i2 - Fall 2015 - p92(1) [51-500]
Mailander, Elissa - *Female SS Guards and Workaday Violence: The Majdanek Concentration Camp, 1942-1944*
  NYRB - v62 - i12 - July 9 2015 - p52(3) [501+]
Maillard, Mary - *The Belles of Williamsburg*
  KR - April 1 2015 - pNA [51-500]
Main, Suzanne - *How I Alienated My Grandma (Illus. by Williamson, Fraser)*
  c Magpies - v30 - i2 - May 2015 - pS6(1) [501+]
Mainardi, Diogo - *The Fall: A Father's Memoir in 424 Steps*
  WLT - v89 - i2 - March-April 2015 - p67(1) [51-500]
Mair, Victor H. - *Chinese Lives: The People Who Made a Civilization*
  Historian - v77 - i1 - Spring 2015 - p154(2) [501+]
Mairs, Rachel - *The Hellenistic Far East: Archaeology, Language, and Identity in Greek Central Asia*
  TLS - i5867 - Sept 11 2015 - p25(1) [501+]
Maisky, Ivan - *The Maisky Diaries: Red Ambassador to the Court of St. James's, 1932-1943*
  NS - v144 - i5284 - Oct 16 2015 - p49(1) [501+]
Maitland, Barry - *Crucifixion Creek*
  BL - v112 - i1 - Sept 1 2015 - p45(1) [51-500]
  KR - Sept 1 2015 - pNA [51-500]
  PW - v262 - i37 - Sept 14 2015 - p43(1) [51-500]
Maizel, Rebecca - *Between Us and the Moon*
  y BL - v111 - i16 - April 15 2015 - p47(1) [51-500]
  SLJ - v61 - i4 - April 2015 - p167(1) [51-500]
Maizels, Jennie - *Pop-up New York (Illus. by Maizels, Jennie)*
  c HB Guide - v26 - i1 - Spring 2015 - p204(1) [51-500]

Maizes, Sarah - *On My Way to School (Illus. by Paraskevas, Michael)*
  c HB Guide - v26 - i1 - Spring 2015 - p38(1) [51-500]
Majd, Hooman - *The Ministry of Guidance Invites You to Not Stay*
  TLS - i5869 - Sept 25 2015 - p23(1) [501+]
Majic, Samantha - *Sex Work Politics: From Protest to Service Provision*
  Wom R Bks - v32 - i1 - Jan-Feb 2015 - p12(2) [501+]
Majka, Sara - *Cities I've Never Lived In: Stories*
  KR - Dec 15 2015 - pNA [51-500]
  PW - v262 - i45 - Nov 9 2015 - p32(1) [51-500]
Major, Aaron - *Architects of Austerity: International Finance and the Politics of Growth*
  AJS - v120 - i6 - May 2015 - p1874(3) [501+]
Major, Amy - *Toward the Light: Rescuing Spirits, Trapped Souls, and Earthbound Ghosts*
  Bwatch - July 2015 - pNA [51-500]
Major, Debra A. - *Handbook of Work-Life Integration among Professionals: Challenges and Opportunities*
  Per Psy - v68 - i3 - Autumn 2015 - p697(3) [501+]
Major, Philip - *Thomas Killigrew and the Seventeenth-Century English Stage: New Perspectives*
  Ren Q - v68 - i2 - Summer 2015 - p800-802 [501+]
  RES - v66 - i274 - April 2015 - p378-380 [501+]
Majumdar, Simon - *Fed, White, and Blue: Finding America with My Fork*
  Bwatch - June 2015 - pNA [51-500]
Mak, Elaine - *Judicial Decision-Making in a Globalized World: A Comparative Analysis of the Changing Practices of Western Highest Courts*
  Law&PolBR - v25 - i2 - Feb 2015 - p27(4) [501+]
Mak, Geert - *In America: Travels with John Steinbeck*
  Spec - v327 - i9723 - Jan 3 2015 - p28(2) [501+]
Makalani, Minkah - *In the Cause of Freedom: Radical Black Internationalism from Harlem to London, 1917-1939*
  HNet - June 2015 - pNA [501+]
Makari, George - *Soul Machine: The Invention of the Modern Mind*
  BL - v111 - i22 - August 1 2015 - p6(1) [51-500]
  KR - June 15 2015 - pNA [51-500]
  LJ - v140 - i13 - August 1 2015 - p112(1) [51-500]
  PW - v262 - i33 - August 17 2015 - p60(1) [51-500]
  TimHES - i2227 - Oct 29 2015 - p48(1) [501+]
Makdisi, Saree - *Making England Western: Occidentalism, Race, and Imperial Culture*
  AHR - v120 - i2 - April 2015 - p715-716 [501+]
  Reading William Blake
  TLS - i5856 - June 26 2015 - p27(1) [501+]
Maker, Azmaira H. - *Family Changes: Explaining Divorce to Children (Illus. by Lovsin, Polona)*
  c CH Bwatch - Oct 2015 - pNA [51-500]
  c SPBW - July 2015 - pNA [51-500]
Makhlouf, Jack - *Millie the Octopus Learns to Hula Dance (Illus. by Thompson, Leslie)*
  c CH Bwatch - Feb 2015 - pNA [51-500]
Makhoul, Bashir - *The Origins of Palestinian Art*
  HNet - May 2015 - pNA [501+]
Maki, Craig - *Detroit Country Music: Mountaineers, Cowboys, and Rockabillies*
  Am St - v54 - i1 - Spring 2015 - p137-2 [501+]
Makin, Amir - *Aisha the Navigator Trains a Leader! (Illus. by Hilley, Thomas)*
  c CH Bwatch - August 2015 - pNA [501+]
Makine, Andrei - *Brief Loves That Live Forever*
  KR - June 1 2015 - pNA [51-500]
  NY - v91 - i27 - Sept 14 2015 - p91 [51-500]
  NYTBR - August 16 2015 - p18(L) [501+]
  PW - v262 - i26 - June 29 2015 - p41(1) [51-500]
  A Woman Loved
  KR - June 1 2015 - pNA [51-500]
  NYTBR - August 16 2015 - p18(L) [501+]
  PW - v262 - i22 - June 1 2015 - p38(2) [51-500]
  WLT - v89 - i6 - Nov-Dec 2015 - p71(1) [51-500]
The Making of Middle Classes: Social Mobility and Boundary Work in Global Perspective
  HNet - Jan 2015 - pNA [501+]
Makkai, Rebecca - *The Hundred-Year House*
  NYTBR - Oct 4 2015 - p28(L) [501+]
  Music for Wartime: Stories
  BL - v111 - i21 - July 1 2015 - p33(1) [51-500]
  BooChiTr - August 1 2015 - p12(1) [501+]
  NY - v91 - i23 - August 10 2015 - p77 [51-500]
  NYT - July 8 2015 - pC1(L) [501+]
  RVBW - July 2015 - pNA [51-500]

Makley, Michael J. - *Saving Lake Tahoe: An Environmental History of a National Treasure*
    PHR - v84 - i4 - Nov 2015 - p527(2) [501+]
    WHQ - v46 - i1 - Spring 2015 - p78-79 [501+]

Makonin, Anna - *Puddles or Lunch? (Illus. by Makonin, Anna)*
    c Res Links - v20 - i3 - Feb 2015 - p6(2) [51-500]

Makos, Adam - *Devotion: An Epic Story of Heroism, Friendship, and Sacrifice*
    KR - July 1 2015 - pNA [501+]
    LJ - v140 - i11 - June 15 2015 - p99(1) [51-500]
    PW - v262 - i31 - August 3 2015 - p45(2) [51-500]

Makowski, Elizabeth - *English Nuns and the Law in the Middle Ages: Cloistered Nuns and their Lawyers, 1293-1540*
    HER - v130 - i543 - April 2015 - p421(2) [501+]

Maksudyan, Nazan - *Women and the City, Women in the City: A Gendered Perspective of Ottoman Urban History*
    RVBW - July 2015 - pNA [51-500]

Malacrida, Claudia - *A Special Hell: Institutional Life in Alberta's Eugenic Years*
    Beav - v95 - i3 - June-July 2015 - p59(1) [501+]

Malaev, Alibek Kazhgalievich - *Vizual'nyi arkhetip*
    E-A St - v67 - i8 - Oct 2015 - p1338(3) [501+]

Malafarina, Gianfranco - *The Basilica of St. Francis in Assisi*
    CC - v132 - i11 - May 27 2015 - p41(2) [501+]

Malam, Rosalind - *Rustle Up a Rhythm (Illus. by Anderson, Sarah Nelisiwe)*
    c Magpies - v30 - i2 - May 2015 - pS4(2) [501+]

Malamud, Bernard - *The Assistant*
    NYT - Feb 8 2015 - p5(L) [51-500]
The Complete Stories
    New R - v246 - i9-10 - Sept-Oct 2015 - p82(4) [501+]
Novels and Stories of the 1940s and 50s
    NYRB - v62 - i6 - April 2 2015 - p80(3) [501+]
    TLS - i5838 - Feb 20 2015 - p7(2) [501+]
Novels and Stories of the 1960s
    NYRB - v62 - i6 - April 2 2015 - p80(3) [501+]
    TLS - i5838 - Feb 20 2015 - p7(2) [501+]
Pictures of Fidelman
    TLS - i5838 - Feb 20 2015 - p16(1) [501+]

Malanga, Gerard - *Malanga Chasing Vallejo: Selected Poems of Cesar Vallejo: New Translations and Notes*
    PSQ - v89 - i2 - Summer 2015 - p167(3) [501+]

Malaspina, Ann - *Vivian and Victor Learn About Verbs (Illus. by Prater, Linda)*
    CH Bwatch - Feb 2015 - pNA [51-500]

Malatesta, Errico - *Life and Ideas: The Anarchist Writings of Errico Malatesta*
    PW - v262 - i19 - May 11 2015 - p46(1) [51-500]

Malave, Idelisse - *Latino Stats: American Hispanics by the Numbers*
    BL - v111 - i11 - Feb 1 2015 - p17(1) [51-500]

Malcolm, Ellen R. - *When Women Win*
    KR - Dec 15 2015 - pNA [501+]

Malcolm, Noel - *Agents of Empire: Knights, Corsairs, Jesuits and Spies in the Sixteenth-Century Mediterranean World*
    Econ - v415 - i8939 - May 23 2015 - p73(US) [501+]
    Spec - v328 - i9744 - May 30 2015 - p32(2) [501+]
    TLS - i5852 - May 29 2015 - p7(2) [501+]

Malcolmson, Patricia - *A Free-Spirited Woman: The London Diaries of Gladys Langford, 1938-1940*
    HT - v65 - i3 - March 2015 - p61(2) [501+]

Maldonado, Frank E. - *The Chimera Murders*
    SPBW - Nov 2015 - pNA [51-500]

Malegam, Jehangir Yezdi - *The Sleep of Behemoth: Disputing Peace and Violence in Medieval Europe, 1000-1200*
    J Ch St - v57 - i1 - Wntr 2015 - p179-181 [501+]

Malek, Rami - *Mr. Robot*
    New R - v246 - i11 - Fall 2015 - p62(2) [51-500]

Malet, David - *Foreign Fighters: Transnational Identity in Civil Conflicts*
    HNet - May 2015 - pNA [501+]

Malfi, Ronald - *Little Girls*
    PW - v262 - i21 - May 25 2015 - p41(1) [51-500]

Malhotra, Anshu - *Punjab Reconsidered: History, Culture, and Practice*
    JAS - v74 - i2 - May 2015 - p514-516 [501+]

Malhotra, Ravi - *Exploring Disability Identity and Disability Rights through Narratives: Finding a Voice of Their Own*
    HNet - Feb 2015 - pNA [501+]

Malicote, Sandra - *Aiol: A Chanson de Geste: Modern Edition and First English Translation*
    Specu - v90 - i3 - July 2015 - p834-836 [501+]

Malik, Liesa - *Sliced Vegetarian*
    BL - v111 - i17 - May 1 2015 - p45(1) [51-500]
    KR - June 1 2015 - pNA [51-500]
    PW - v262 - i24 - June 15 2015 - p66(1) [51-500]

Malin, Brenton J. - *Feeling Mediated: A History of Media Technology and Emotion in America*
    AHR - v120 - i3 - June 2015 - p1042-1043 [501+]
    JAH - v102 - i2 - Sept 2015 - p579-580 [501+]

Malina, Judith - *Full Moon Stages: Personal Notes from 50 Years of The Living Theatre*
    LJ - v140 - i19 - Nov 15 2015 - p86(1) [51-500]

Malkes, Simon - *The Righteous of the Wehrmacht*
    HNet - July 2015 - pNA [501+]

Malkin, Craig - *Rethinking Narcissism: The Bad--and Surprising Good--about Feeling Special*
    KR - April 1 2015 - pNA [501+]
    LJ - v140 - i8 - May 1 2015 - p92(1) [51-500]
    NYTBR - Sept 27 2015 - p13(L) [501+]
    PW - v262 - i16 - April 20 2015 - p65(1) [51-500]

Mallery, Mary - *Technology Disaster Response and Recovery Planning: A LITA Guide*
    LJ - v140 - i12 - July 1 2015 - p99(1) [51-500]

Mallery, Susan - *The Girls of Mischief Bay (Read by Eby, Tanya). Audiobook Review*
    BL - v111 - i19-20 - June 1 2015 - p126(1) [51-500]
The Girls of Mischief Bay
    BL - v111 - i12 - Feb 15 2015 - p44(1) [51-500]
    KR - Jan 15 2015 - pNA [51-500]
Susan Mallery
    PW - v262 - i8 - Feb 23 2015 - p58(1) [51-500]
Thrill Me
    BL - v112 - i2 - Sept 15 2015 - p42(2) [51-500]

Malleson, Tom - *After Occupy: Economic Democracy for the 21st Century*
    TLS - i5845 - April 10 2015 - p28(1) [51-500]

Mallet, Alex - *Popular Muslim Reactions to the Franks in the Levant, 1097-1291*
    Specu - v90 - i1 - Jan 2015 - p275-277 [501+]

Mallett, Alex - *Popular Muslim Reactions to the Franks in the Levant, 1097-1291*
    AHR - v120 - i3 - June 2015 - p1345-1346 [501+]

Mallia-Milanes, Victor - *Al Seruizio della Repubblica di Venezia: Le lettere di Massimiliano Buzzaccarini Gonzaga, Commendatore di Malta, inviate alia Magistratura dei Cinque Savii alia Mercanzia 1754-1776*
    CHR - v101 - i3 - Summer 2015 - p665(2) [501+]

Malliet, G.M. - *A Demon Summer (Read by Page, Michael). Audiobook Review*
    BL - v111 - i17 - May 1 2015 - p57(1) [51-500]
The Haunted Season
    BL - v112 - i4 - Oct 15 2015 - p21(1) [51-500]
    KR - August 1 2015 - pNA [51-500]
    PW - v262 - i34 - August 24 2015 - p59(2) [51-500]

Mallinson, Allan - *Words of Command*
    Spec - v327 - i9740 - May 2 2015 - p45(1) [501+]

Mallis, Fern - *Fashion Lives: Fashion Icons with Fern Mallis*
    PW - v262 - i12 - March 23 2015 - p67(2) [51-500]

Mallon, Thomas - *Finale*
    BL - v111 - i21 - July 1 2015 - p42(1) [51-500]
    KR - July 15 2015 - pNA [501+]
    LJ - v140 - i13 - August 1 2015 - p87(1) [51-500]
    Nat R - v67 - i22 - Dec 7 2015 - p46(2) [51-500]
    NYT - Sept 24 2015 - pC1(L) [501+]
    NYTBR - Sept 20 2015 - p14(L) [501+]
    PW - v262 - i28 - July 13 2015 - p42(1) [51-500]

Mallory, Alex - *Wild*
    y HB Guide - v26 - i1 - Spring 2015 - p115(1) [51-500]

Mallory, Carolyn - *Painted Skies (Illus. by Zhao, Amei)*
    c KR - Sept 1 2015 - pNA [51-500]
    c Res Links - v21 - i1 - Oct 2015 - p8(1) [51-500]

Malnor, Carol L. - *Wild Ones: Critters in the City (Illus. by Morrison, Cathy)*
    c KR - Dec 15 2015 - pNA [51-500]

Malo, Robyn - *Relics and Writing in Late Medieval England*
    MP - v112 - i4 - May 2015 - pE288(4) [501+]
    Specu - v90 - i2 - April 2015 - p558-560 [501+]

Malone, Aubrey - *Maureen O'Hara: The Biography*
    ILS - v34 - i2 - Spring 2015 - p27(2) [501+]

Malone, Cheryl Lawton - *Dario and the Whale (Illus. by Masseva, Bistra)*
    c PW - v262 - i52 - Dec 21 2015 - p152(1) [51-500]

Malone, Jen - *You're Invited*
    c BL - v111 - i16 - April 15 2015 - p51(1) [51-500]
    y HB Guide - v26 - i2 - Fall 2015 - p92(1) [51-500]
You're Invited Too
    y KR - Nov 15 2015 - pNA [51-500]

Malone, Lee Gjertsen - *The Last Boy at St. Edith's*
    c BL - v112 - i5 - Nov 1 2015 - p60(1) [51-500]
    c KR - Oct 15 2015 - pNA [51-500]

Malone, Marianne - *The Secret of the Key (Read by Campbell, Cassandra). Audiobook Review*
    c BL - v111 - i14 - March 15 2015 - p88(1) [51-500]
The Secret of the Key (Illus. by Call, Greg)
    c HB Guide - v26 - i1 - Spring 2015 - p85(1) [51-500]

Maloney, Brenna - *Ready Rabbit Gets Ready! (Illus. by Kennedy, Chuck)*
    c CCB-B - v68 - i10 - June 2015 - p505(2) [51-500]
    c HB Guide - v26 - i2 - Fall 2015 - p14(1) [51-500]
    c PW - v262 - i49 - Dec 2 2015 - p38(1) [51-500]
    c Teach Lib - v42 - i4 - April 2015 - p32(1) [51-500]

Malouf, David - *Earth Hour*
    Meanjin - v74 - i1 - Autumn 2015 - p68(10) [501+]

Malouf, Juman - *The Trilogy of Two (Illus. by Malouf, Juman)*
    c PW - v262 - i39 - Sept 28 2015 - p93(1) [51-500]
    c BL - v112 - i5 - Nov 1 2015 - p52(2) [51-500]
    y KR - Oct 1 2015 - pNA [51-500]
    c SLJ - v61 - i11 - Nov 2015 - p100(1) [51-500]

Maloy, Heather - *I Hate Pinatas: Surviving Life's Unexpected Surprises*
    KR - Sept 1 2015 - pNA [51-500]

Malsberger, John W. - *The General and the Politician: Dwight Eisenhower, Richard Nixon, and American Politics*
    AHR - v120 - i2 - April 2015 - p666-667 [501+]
    Pres St Q - v45 - i2 - June 2015 - p414(2) [501+]

Malvinni, David - *Grateful Dead and the Art of Rock Improvisation*
    Notes - v71 - i3 - March 2015 - p486(4) [501+]

Malycha, Andreas - *Die SED in der Ara Honecker: Machtstrukturen, Entscheidungsmechanismen und Konfliktfelder in der Staatspartei 1971 bis 1989*
    HNet - Jan 2015 - pNA [501+]

Mamatha, B. - *The House They Couldn't Build*
    PW - v262 - i11 - March 16 2015 - p59(2) [51-500]

Man, John - *Marco Polo: The Journey That Changed the World (Read by Vance, Simon). Audiobook Review*
    LJ - v140 - i16 - Oct 1 2015 - p45(1) [51-500]
The Mongol Empire: Genghis Khan, His Heirs and the Founding of Modern China
    TLS - i5845 - April 10 2015 - p26(1) [501+]
Saladin: The Life, the Legend and the Islamic Empire
    NS - v144 - i5269 - July 3 2015 - p50(2) [501+]

Managing Mass Culture: Serialization, Standardization and Modernity, 1880-1940
    HNet - June 2015 - pNA [501+]

Manale, Shizumi Shigeto - *Running with Cosmos Flowers: The Children of Hiroshima*
    y HB Guide - v26 - i2 - Fall 2015 - p130(1) [51-500]

Manalo, Ricky - *The Liturgy of Life: The Interrelationship of Sunday Eucharist and Everyday Worship Practices*
    Theol St - v76 - i4 - Dec 2015 - p898(1) [51-500]

Manasek, F.J. - *Collecting Old Maps*
    SPBW - Oct 2015 - pNA [51-500]

Manaugh, Geoff - *A Burglar's Guide to the City*
    PW - v262 - i45 - Nov 9 2015 - p47(2) [51-500]

Manceau, Edouard - *Hatch, Little Egg (Illus. by Manceau, Edouard)*
    c HB Guide - v26 - i2 - Fall 2015 - p15(1) [51-500]
    c Res Links - v20 - i3 - Feb 2015 - p7(1) [51-500]
Look! (Illus. by Manceau, Edouard)
    c PW - v262 - i5 - Feb 2 2015 - p60(1) [51-500]
    c SLJ - v61 - i7 - July 2015 - p56(1) [51-500]
Once upon a Rainy Day (Illus. by Manceau, Edouard)
    c CH Bwatch - Oct 2015 - pNA [51-500]
    c KR - July 1 2015 - pNA [51-500]
    c SLJ - v61 - i8 - August 2015 - p74(1) [51-500]
Tickle Monster (Illus. by Manceau, Edouard)
    c KR - May 15 2015 - pNA [51-500]
    c SLJ - v61 - i10 - Oct 2015 - p71(1) [51-500]

Manchette, Jean-Patrick - *Fatale*
    NS - v144 - i5253 - March 13 2015 - p50(2) [501+]
The Gunman
    NS - v144 - i5253 - March 13 2015 - p50(2) [501+]
The Mad and the Bad
    NS - v144 - i5253 - March 13 2015 - p50(2) [501+]

Mancini, Lee Ann - *Fast Freddy (Illus. by Sharp, Dan)*
    c CH Bwatch - July 2015 - pNA [51-500]

Mancusi, Mari - *Golden Girl*
 y KR - Oct 1 2015 - pNA [51-500]
Scorched
 c SLJ - v61 - i6 - June 2015 - p46(6) [501+]
Smoked
 y KR - July 15 2015 - pNA [51-500]
 y VOYA - v38 - i4 - Oct 2015 - p74(1) [51-500]

Mancuso, Jackie Clark - *Hudson in Provence: A Paris-Chien Adventure*
 c CH Bwatch - July 2015 - pNA [51-500]

Mancuso, Stefano - *Brilliant Green: The Surprising History and Science of Plant Intelligence*
 LJ - v140 - i3 - Feb 15 2015 - p126(1) [501+]
 Mac - v128 - i11 - March 23 2015 - p62(1) [501+]
 New Sci - v226 - i3023 - May 30 2015 - p46(2) [501+]

Mandel, Emily St. John - *Station Eleven (Read by Potter, Kirsten). Audiobook Review*
 BL - v111 - i9-10 - Jan 1 2015 - p116(1) [51-500]
 BL - v111 - i14 - March 15 2015 - p23(2) [501+]
Station Eleven
 y HR - v68 - i1 - Spring 2015 - p151-157 [501+]
 NYTBR - June 7 2015 - p36(L) [501+]
 TLS - i5854 - June 12 2015 - p11(1) [501+]

Mandel, Harvey - *Snake Box*
 Dbt - v82 - i8 - August 2015 - p81(1) [501+]

Mandel, Joey - *Anxiety: Deal with it before it Ties You Up in Knots (Illus. by Heeley, Ted)*
 c Res Links - v20 - i3 - Feb 2015 - p22(2) [51-500]
Stop the Stress in Schools: Mental Health Strategies Teachers Can Use to Build a Kinder Gentler Classroom
 Res Links - v20 - i4 - April 2015 - p35(2) [501+]

Mandel, Maud S. - *Muslims and Jews in France: History of a Conflict*
 AHR - v120 - i4 - Oct 2015 - p1556-1557 [501+]
 FS - v69 - i1 - Jan 2015 - p128-129 [501+]
 HER - v130 - i545 - August 2015 - p1052(3) [501+]

Mandel, Oscar - *Otherwise Fables*
 WLT - v89 - i1 - Jan-Feb 2015 - p71(1) [501+]

Mandelbrote, Giles - *The Arcadian Library: Bindings and Provenance*
 TLS - i5837 - Feb 13 2015 - p23(1) [501+]

Mandelbrote, Scott - *Dissent and the Bible in Britain, c. 1650-1950*
 CH - v84 - i3 - Sept 2015 - p673(3) [501+]

Mandell, Bob - *Stroke Victor: How to Go From Stroke Victim to Stroke Victor*
 SPBW - August 2015 - pNA [51-500]

Mandell, Charlotte - *Syrian Notebooks: Inside the Homs Uprising*
 TLS - i5869 - Sept 25 2015 - p7(2) [501+]

Mander, Jerry - *The Capitalism Papers: Fatal Flaws of an Obsolete System*
 CS - v44 - i3 - May 2015 - p314-321 [501+]

Mandeville, Chris - *52 Ways to Get Unstuck: Exercises to Break through Writer's Block*
 PW - v262 - i25 - June 22 2015 - p135(1) [501+]

Mandle, Jon - *A Companion to Rawls*
 Ethics - v125 - i2 - Jan 2015 - p591(6) [501+]

Mandler, Peter - *Return from the Natives: How Margaret Mead Won the Second World War and Lost the Cold War*
 PHR - v84 - i1 - Feb 2015 - p103(2) [501+]

Mandvi, Aasif - *No Land's Man: A Perilous Journey through Romance, Islam, and Brunch (Read by Mandvi, Aasif). Audiobook Review*
 PW - v262 - i8 - Feb 23 2015 - p71(2) [501+]

Manea, Norman - *Captives*
 NYTBR - Feb 22 2015 - p34(L) [501+]

Manecke, Kirt - *Smile and Succeed for Teens: A Crash Course in Face-to-Face Communication*
 y CH Bwatch - Feb 2015 - pNA [51-500]

Manent, Pierre - *Metamorphoses of the City: On the Western Dynamic*
 MA - v57 - i1 - Wntr 2015 - p85(4) [501+]
Seeing Things Politically
 RM - v69 - i2 - Dec 2015 - p398(3) [501+]

Manes, Yael - *Motherhood and Patriarchal Masculinities in Sixteenth-Century Italian Comedy*
 MLR - v110 - i3 - July 2015 - p878-879 [501+]

Manetti, Giannozzo - *De Terremotu*
 Ren Q - v68 - i1 - Spring 2015 - p228-229 [501+]

Manfredi, Valerio Massimo - *Spartan*
 HT - v65 - i8 - August 2015 - p56(2) [501+]

Manfredonia, Rosa - *La Passione di Felice Martire, vescovo di Nola (BHL): Edizione critica e traduzione*
 Specu - v90 - i3 - July 2015 - p836-2 [501+]

Mangabeira, Roberto - *The Religion of the Future*
 JR - v95 - i4 - Oct 2015 - p534(5) [501+]

Manganelli, Kimberly Snyder - *Transatlantic Spectacles of Race: The Tragic Mulatta and the Tragic Muse*
 AL - v87 - i3 - Sept 2015 - p609-611 [501+]
 Callaloo - v38 - i2 - Spring 2015 - p405-408 [501+]

Mangham, Andrew - *The Cambridge Companion to Sensation Fiction*
 Poetics T - v36 - i1-2 - June 2015 - p133-136 [501+]

Mangini, Cara - *The Vegetable Butcher: How to Select, Prep, Slice, Dice, and Masterfully Cook Vegetables from Artichokes to Zucchini*
 LJ - v140 - i20 - Dec 1 2015 - p129(1) [51-500]
 PW - v262 - i46 - Nov 16 2015 - p71(1) [51-500]

Manguel, Alberto - *Curiosity*
 Econ - v415 - i8933 - April 11 2015 - p77(US) [501+]
 KR - Jan 15 2015 - pNA [501+]
 NS - v144 - i5275 - August 14 2015 - p38(3) [501+]
 NYRB - v62 - i16 - Oct 22 2015 - p72(2) [501+]
 PW - v262 - i2 - Jan 12 2015 - p49(2) [51-500]
 TLS - i5867 - Sept 11 2015 - p23(1) [501+]

Manguso, Sarah - *Ongoingness: The End of a Diary*
 Atl - v315 - i3 - April 2015 - p44(3) [501+]
 NYTBR - May 24 2015 - p30(L) [501+]
 NYT - March 4 2015 - pC4(L) [501+]
 PW - v262 - i2 - Jan 12 2015 - p51(1) [501+]

Mani, Danielle R. - *The Divine One*
 y KR - May 1 2015 - pNA [501+]

Manicom, James - *Bridging Troubled Waters: China, Japan, and Maritime Order in the East China Sea*
 NWCR - v68 - i1 - Wntr 2015 - p137(2) [501+]
 Pac A - v88 - i3 - Sept 2015 - p681 [501+]

Manigault-Bryant, LeRhonda S. - *Talking to the Dead: Religion, Music, and Lived Memory among Gullah/Geechee Women*
 JAH - v102 - i2 - Sept 2015 - p508-509 [501+]

Mankekar, Purnima - *Media, Erotics, and Transnational Asia*
 Signs - v40 - i3 - Spring 2015 - p773(7) [501+]

Mankiewicz, Frank - *So As I Was Saying ... My Somewhat Eventful Life*
 LJ - v140 - i20 - Dec 1 2015 - p110(1) [51-500]

Mankoff, Bob - *How about Never--Is Never Good for You?: My Life in Cartoons*
 NYTBR - Dec 20 2015 - p24(L) [501+]

Manktelow, Emily J. - *Missionary Families: Race, Gender, and Generation on the Spiritual Frontier*
 JMH - v87 - i2 - June 2015 - p435(3) [501+]

Manlevelt, Thomas - *Questiones Libri Porphirii*
 RM - v69 - i2 - Dec 2015 - p400(2) [501+]

Manley, Lawrence - *Lord Strange's Men and Their Plays*
 Ren Q - v68 - i3 - Fall 2015 - p1140-1142 [501+]

Mann, Charles C. - *1493 for Young People: From Columbus's Voyage to Globalization*
 y KR - Nov 15 2015 - pNA [51-500]

Mann, Don - *Seal Team Six: Hunt the Fox*
 KR - April 15 2015 - pNA [501+]

Mann, James - *George W. Bush*
 BL - v111 - i9-10 - Jan 1 2015 - p34(1) [51-500]
 CSM - Feb 3 2015 - pNA [51-500]

Mann, Jennifer Ann - *Sunny Sweet Can So Get Lost*
 y HB Guide - v26 - i2 - Fall 2015 - p93(1) [51-500]

Mann, Jennifer K. - *I Will Never Get a Star on Mrs. Benson's Blackboard (Illus. by Mann, Jennifer K.)*
 c CCB-B - v69 - i2 - Oct 2015 - p99(2) [51-500]
 c CH Bwatch - August 2015 - pNA [51-500]
 c HB Guide - v26 - i2 - Fall 2015 - p43(1) [51-500]
 c KR - June 1 2015 - pNA [51-500]
 c PW - v262 - i49 - Dec 2 2015 - p13(2) [51-500]
 c SLJ - v61 - i8 - August 2015 - p60(1) [51-500]
 PW - v262 - i15 - April 13 2015 - p80(1) [51-500]

Mann, Jill - *Life in Words: Essays on Chaucer, the Gawain-Poet, and Malory*
 Med R - June 2015 - pNA [501+]
 Ren Q - v68 - i3 - Fall 2015 - p1126-1128 [501+]
 Six Ct J - v46 - i3 - Fall 2015 - p816-818 [501+]
Ysengrimus
 Med R - May 2015 - pNA [501+]

Mann, John Paul - *Pleomorph*
 KR - Oct 15 2015 - pNA [501+]

Mann, Lucas - *Lord Fear*
 BL - v111 - i14 - March 15 2015 - p32(1) [51-500]
 KR - March 1 2015 - pNA [51-500]

Mann, Michael - *The Sources of Social Power, vol. 1: A History of Power from the Beginning to AD 1760*
 RAH - v43 - i3 - Sept 2015 - p401-410 [501+]
The Sources of Social Power, vol. 2: The Rise of Classes and Nation-States, 1760-1914
 RAH - v43 - i3 - Sept 2015 - p401-410 [501+]
The Sources of Social Power, vol. 3: Global Empires and Revolution, 1890-1945
 RAH - v43 - i3 - Sept 2015 - p401-410 [501+]
The Sources of Social Power, vol. 4: Globalizations, 1945-2011
 RAH - v43 - i3 - Sept 2015 - p401-410 [501+]

Mann, Natalie - *Doing Harder Time? The Experiences of an Ageing Male Prison Population in England and Wales*
 CS - v44 - i6 - Nov 2015 - p874-875 [501+]

Mann, Sally - *Hold Still: A Memoir with Photographs*
 Atl - v316 - i1 - July-August 2015 - p44(3) [501+]
 BL - v111 - i16 - April 15 2015 - p10(2) [51-500]
 Ent W - i1364 - May 22 2015 - p66(1) [51-500]
 NYT - May 6 2015 - pC1(L) [501+]
 NYTBR - May 10 2015 - p13(L) [501+]
 SEP - v287 - i3 - May-June 2015 - p24(1) [501+]
 y SLJ - v61 - i8 - August 2015 - p116(1) [51-500]
 TLS - i5854 - June 12 2015 - p11(1) [501+]
 TLS - i5871 - Oct 9 2015 - p14(1) [501+]
 Wom R Bks - v32 - i6 - Nov-Dec 2015 - p3(3) [501+]
 KR - March 1 2015 - pNA [501+]
 LJ - v140 - i7 - April 15 2015 - p94(1) [501+]
 PW - v262 - i8 - Feb 23 2015 - p62(2) [501+]

Mann, Sandra - *The Generous Dead*
 KR - July 15 2015 - pNA [501+]

Mann, Traci - *Secrets from the Eating Lab: The Science of Weight Loss, the Myth of Willpower, and Why You Should Never Diet Again*
 BL - v111 - i14 - March 15 2015 - p34(2) [51-500]

Mann, William E. - *Augustine's Confessions: Philosophy in Autobiography*
 RM - v69 - i1 - Sept 2015 - p117(2) [501+]

Mannering, Derek - *Mario Lanza: Singing to the Gods*
 ON - v80 - i5 - Nov 2015 - p60(1) [501+]

Mannering, Rose - *Boo's Beard (Illus. by Straker, Bethany)*
 c KR - August 1 2015 - pNA [51-500]

Manney, P.J. - *(R)Evolution*
 PW - v262 - i6 - Feb 9 2015 - p49(1) [501+]
Revolution
 BL - v111 - i18 - May 15 2015 - p40(1) [51-500]

Mannherz, Julia - *Modern Occultism in Late Imperial Russia*
 HER - v130 - i543 - April 2015 - p479(3) [501+]
 JMH - v87 - i1 - March 2015 - p243(3) [501+]

Manning, Christel - *Losing Our Religion: How Unaffiliated Parents Are Raising Their Children*
 KR - Sept 1 2015 - pNA [501+]

Manning, Dorothy Thurgood - *The True Spirit of Christmas (Illus. by Manning, Dorothy Thurgood)*
 c CH Bwatch - Nov 2015 - pNA [51-500]

Manning, Mick - *Dino-Dinners (Illus. by Granstrom, Brita)*
 c Magpies - v30 - i5 - Nov 2015 - p26(1) [501+]
The Story of Britain
 c Sch Lib - v63 - i2 - Summer 2015 - p112(1) [51-500]
Wild Adventures: Look, Make, Explore--in Nature's Playground (Illus. by Manning, Mick)
 c Sch Lib - v63 - i2 - Summer 2015 - p112(1) [51-500]
 c SLJ - v61 - i5 - May 2015 - p134(1) [51-500]
William Shakespeare: Scenes from the Life of the World's Greatest Writer (Illus. by Manning, Mick)
 y Magpies - v30 - i2 - May 2015 - p24(1) [501+]
 c Sch Lib - v63 - i4 - Winter 2015 - p239(1) [51-500]
 c SLJ - v61 - i10 - Oct 2015 - p128(1) [51-500]

Manning, Molly Guptill - *When Books Went to War: The Stories That Helped Us Win World War II (Read by Dunne, Bernadette). Audiobook Review*
 LJ - v140 - i5 - March 15 2015 - p73(1) [51-500]
When Books Went to War: The Stories that Helped Us Win World War II
 TLS - i5841 - March 13 2015 - p21(1) [501+]
 NYTBR - Jan 25 2015 - p18(L) [501+]

Manning, Olivia - *The Balkan Trilogy*
 Nation - v301 - i11-12 - Sept 14 2015 - p31(4) [501+]
The Levant Trilogy
 Nation - v301 - i11-12 - Sept 14 2015 - p31(4) [501+]
Mongrels or Marvels: The Levantine Writings of Jacqueline Shohet Kabarnoff
 Nation - v301 - i11-12 - Sept 14 2015 - p31(4) [501+]

Manning, Paul - *Nile River*
 c BL - v112 - i3 - Oct 1 2015 - p62(1) [51-500]

Manning, Susan - *Poetics of Character: Transatlantic Encounters, 1700-1900*
 AL - v87 - i2 - June 2015 - p387-389 [501+]
 J Am St - v49 - i1 - Feb 2015 - p159-171 [501+]

Mannion, Jenny - *A Short Path to Change: 30 Ways to Transform Your Life*
    PW - v262 - i45 - Nov 9 2015 - p55(1) [51-500]

Manoukian, Setrag - *City of Knowledge in Twentieth-Century Iran: Shiraz, History and Poetry*
    HNet - April 2015 - pNA [501+]

Manrique, Michelangelo - *Blender for Animation and Film-Based Production*
    Bwatch - June 2015 - pNA [501+]

Mansbach, Adam - *Benjamin Franklin: Huge Pain in My ... (Illus. by Zweibel, Alan)*
    c KR - July 15 2015 - pNA [51-500]
    c SLJ - v61 - i11 - Nov 2015 - p100(1) [51-500]
The Devil's Bag Man
    BL - v111 - i19-20 - June 1 2015 - p64(1) [51-500]
    KR - May 15 2015 - pNA [51-500]
    PW - v262 - i21 - May 25 2015 - p40(1) [51-500]
Seriously, You Have to Eat (Illus. by Brozman, Owen)
    c CH Bwatch - Nov 2015 - pNA [51-500]
    c KR - August 15 2015 - pNA [51-500]
    c PW - v262 - i31 - August 3 2015 - p55(1) [51-500]
    c SLJ - v61 - i10 - Oct 2015 - p80(1) [51-500]

Manseau, Peter - *One Nation, Under Gods: A New American History*
    NYTBR - March 15 2015 - p30(L) [501+]
    Reason - v47 - i7 - Dec 2015 - p56(4) [501+]

Mansel, Philip - *The Eagle in Splendour: Inside the Court of Napoleon*
    TLS - i5877 - Nov 20 2015 - p30(1) [501+]

Mansell, Jill - *Falling for You*
    BL - v111 - i21 - July 1 2015 - p44(1) [51-500]
    PW - v262 - i20 - May 18 2015 - p70(1) [51-500]
The Unexpected Consequences of Love
    BL - v111 - i9-10 - Jan 1 2015 - p58(1) [51-500]
    LJ - v140 - i2 - Feb 1 2015 - p74(1) [51-500]

Mansell, Nigel - *Staying on Track: The Autobiography*
    NYT - Dec 5 2015 - pNA(L) [501+]
    Spec - v329 - i9768 - Nov 14 2015 - p63(1) [501+]

Mansell, Robina - *The International Encyclopedia of Digital Communication and Society, 3 vols.*
    BL - v111 - i19-20 - June 1 2015 - p10(1) [51-500]

Mansfield, Andy - *Fish Food (Illus. by Lohlein, Henning)*
    c KR - Dec 1 2015 - pNA [51-500]
    c PW - v262 - i13 - March 30 2015 - p74(1) [51-500]
Journey to the Moon: A Pop-Up Lunar Adventure
    c KR - Dec 1 2015 - pNA [51-500]
    c PW - v262 - i27 - July 6 2015 - p70(2) [501+]
    c PW - v262 - i49 - Dec 2 2015 - p59(1) [51-500]

Mansfield, Elaine - *Leaning into Love: A Spiritual Journey through Grief*
    SPBW - Feb 2015 - pNA [51-500]

Mansfield, Gwen - *Roll Call*
    y KR - Sept 15 2015 - pNA [501+]

Mansky, Matthias - *Cornelius von Ayrenhoff: Ein Wiener Theaterdichter*
    Ger Q - v88 - i1 - Wntr 2015 - p109(2) [501+]

Manson, Chris - *Lionheart: The Diaries of Richard I*
    KR - Jan 15 2015 - pNA [51-500]

Mansouri, Fethi - *Migration, Citizenship and Intercultural Relations: Looking through the Lens of Social Inclusion*
    CS - v44 - i4 - July 2015 - p532-533 [501+]

Mantchev, Lisa - *Strictly No Elephants (Illus. by Yoo, Taeeun)*
    c BL - v112 - i3 - Oct 1 2015 - p84(1) [51-500]
    c KR - August 15 2015 - pNA [51-500]
    c PW - v262 - i29 - July 20 2015 - p189(1) [51-500]
    c SLJ - v61 - i10 - Oct 2015 - p80(1) [51-500]

Mantel, Hilary - *The Assassination of Margaret Thatcher: Stories (Read by Carr, Jane). Audiobook Review*
    PW - v262 - i5 - Feb 2 2015 - p55(1) [51-500]
The Assassination of Margaret Thatcher: Stories
    Nation - v300 - i19 - May 11 2015 - p27(7) [501+]
    NYTBR - Oct 25 2015 - p32(L) [501+]
    TimHES - i2200 - April 23 2015 - p51(1) [501+]

Mantena, Karuna - *Alibis of Empire: Henry Maine and the Ends of Liberal Imperialism*
    JAS - v74 - i3 - August 2015 - p711-722 [501+]

Mantena, Rama Sundari - *The Origins of Modern Historiography in India: Antiquarianism and Philology, 1780-1880*
    VS - v57 - i2 - Wntr 2015 - p296(3) [501+]

Manthorpe, William H.J., Jr. - *A Century of Service: The U.S. Navy on Cape Henlopen, Lewes, Delaware, 1898-1996*
    NWCR - v68 - i2 - Spring 2015 - p147(2) [501+]

Mantle, Ben - *The Best Birthday Present Ever!*
    c Sch Lib - v63 - i2 - Summer 2015 - p96(2) [51-500]

Mantler, Gordon K. - *Power to the Poor: Black-Brown Coalition and the Fight for Economic Justice, 1960-1974*
    Aztlan - v40 - i2 - Fall 2015 - p275-279 [501+]
    PHR - v84 - i1 - Feb 2015 - p118(2) [501+]
    RAH - v43 - i2 - June 2015 - p369-377 [501+]

Mantovani, Ennio - *The Dema and the Christ: My Engagement and Inner Dialogue with the Cultures and Religions of Melanesia*
    IBMR - v39 - i2 - April 2015 - p106(1) [501+]

Manuel, Zenju Earthlyn - *The Way of Tenderness: Awakening Through Race, Sexuality, and Gender*
    PW - v262 - i3 - Jan 19 2015 - p77(1) [51-500]

Manushkin, Fran - *Happy in Our Skin (Illus. by Tobia, Lauren)*
    c KR - June 1 2015 - pNA [51-500]
    c PW - v262 - i22 - June 1 2015 - p57(1) [51-500]
    c PW - v262 - i49 - Dec 2 2015 - p26(1) [51-500]
    c SLJ - v61 - i6 - June 2015 - p74(1) [51-500]
Katie and the Fancy Substitute (Illus. by Lyon, Tammie)
    c HB Guide - v26 - i1 - Spring 2015 - p62(1) [51-500]
Keep Dancing, Katie (Illus. by Lyon, Tammie)
    c HB Guide - v26 - i1 - Spring 2015 - p62(1) [51-500]

Manz, Stefan - *Constructing a German Diaspora: The "Greater German Empire," 1871-1914*
    HNet - July 2015 - pNA [501+]

Manzano, Sonia - *Becoming Maria: Love and Chaos in the South Bronx*
    y BL - v111 - i19-20 - June 1 2015 - p83(1) [51-500]
    y HB - v91 - i5 - Sept-Oct 2015 - p129(1) [51-500]
    y KR - June 15 2015 - pNA [51-500]
    y SLJ - v61 - i9 - Sept 2015 - p187(1) [501+]
Miracle on 133rd Street (Illus. by Priceman, Marjorie)
    c BL - v111 - i11 - Sept 1 2015 - p121(1) [51-500]
    c CH Bwatch - Nov 2015 - pNA [51-500]
    c HB - v91 - i6 - Nov-Dec 2015 - p56(2) [51-500]
    c KR - Sept 1 2015 - pNA [51-500]
    c PW - v262 - i37 - Sept 14 2015 - p74(1) [51-500]
    c PW - v262 - i49 - Dec 2 2015 - p62(1) [51-500]
    c SLJ - v61 - i10 - Oct 2015 - p65(2) [51-500]
No Dogs Allowed! (Illus. by Muth, Jon J.)
    c BL - v111 - i9-10 - Jan 1 2015 - pS18(5) [51-500]

Manzer, Jenny - *Save Me, Kurt Cobain*
    y KR - Dec 15 2015 - pNA [51-500]

Manzini, Antonio - *Black Run*
    KR - Feb 15 2015 - pNA [51-500]
    PW - v262 - i6 - Feb 9 2015 - p45(2) [51-500]

Manzione, Lisa - *Christmas in New York City! (Illus. by Lucco, Kristine)*
    c PW - v262 - i37 - Sept 14 2015 - p77(1) [51-500]
    c SLJ - v61 - i10 - Oct 2015 - p65(1) [51-500]

Manzo, Lynne C. - *Place Attachment: Advances in Theory, Methods and Applications*
    GR - v105 - i1 - Jan 2015 - p129(4) [501+]

Manzoni, Alessandro - *The Betrothed*
    HT - v65 - i11 - Nov 2015 - p56(2) [501+]

Mao, Sally Wen - *Mad Honey Symposium*
    Poet - v205 - i5 - Feb 2015 - p501(3) [501+]

Mar, Alex - *Witches of America*
    BL - v112 - i2 - Sept 15 2015 - p4(1) [51-500]
    KR - August 15 2015 - pNA [501+]
    LJ - v140 - i15 - Sept 15 2015 - p80(2) [51-500]
    NYTBR - Nov 1 2015 - p12(L) [501+]
    PW - v262 - i34 - August 24 2015 - p72(1) [51-500]

Mara, Wil - *Deep-Sea Exploration*
    y BL - v111 - i14 - March 15 2015 - p63(1) [51-500]
Paul Revere
    c BL - v112 - i4 - Oct 15 2015 - p43(1) [51-500]
Robotics: From Concept to Consumer
    y VOYA - v38 - i5 - Dec 2015 - p78(2) [51-500]
Space Exploration: Science, Technology, and Engineering
    c Teach Lib - v42 - i3 - Feb 2015 - p9(1) [51-500]

Marable, Manning - *Malcolm X: A Life of Reinvention*
    Am St - v54 - i2 - Summer 2015 - p9-20 [501+]

Marafioti, Nicole - *The King's Body: Burial and Succession in Late Anglo-Saxon England*
    HER - v130 - i544 - June 2015 - p686(3) [501+]
    Specu - v90 - i4 - Oct 2015 - p1146-1147 [501+]

Maran, Meredith - *Why We Write About Ourselves: Twenty Memoirists on Why They Expose Themselves (and Others) in the Name of Literature*
    PW - v262 - i44 - Nov 2 2015 - p76(1) [51-500]
    KR - Oct 15 2015 - pNA [501+]
    LJ - v140 - i19 - Nov 15 2015 - p93(1) [51-500]

Maranda, Marta - *What It Looks Like*
    SPBW - Feb 2015 - pNA [51-500]

Marani, Diego - *God's Dog*
    PW - v262 - i1 - Jan 5 2015 - p52(2) [51-500]

Maraniss, David - *Once in a Great City: A Detroit Story (Read by Maraniss, David). Audiobook Review*
    BL - v112 - i7 - Dec 1 2015 - p68(2) [51-500]
Once in a Great City: A Detroit Story
    BL - v111 - i21 - July 1 2015 - p19(1) [51-500]
    CSM - Sept 18 2015 - pNA [501+]
    KR - July 1 2015 - pNA [501+]
    LJ - v140 - i12 - July 1 2015 - p96(1) [51-500]
    NY - v91 - i30 - Oct 5 2015 - p80 [501+]
    NYT - Sept 15 2015 - pC1(L) [501+]
    NYTBR - Sept 27 2015 - p23(L) [501+]
    PW - v262 - i27 - July 6 2015 - p59(1) [51-500]

Marasco, Gabriele - *Political Autobiographies and Memories in Antiquity: A Brill Companion*
    Class R - v65 - i2 - Oct 2015 - p368-370 [501+]

Marble, Sanders - *Skilled and Resolute: A History of the 12th Evacuation Hospital and the 212th MASH, 1917-2006*
    J Mil H - v79 - i1 - Jan 2015 - p242-243 [501+]

Marburger, John H., III - *Science Policy Up Close*
    Nature - v517 - i7534 - Jan 15 2015 - p268(2) [501+]

Marcal, Katrine - *Who Cooked Adam Smith's Dinner?*
    NS - v144 - i5252 - March 6 2015 - p47(1) [501+]

Marceau, Fani - *In This Book (Illus. by Jolivet, Joelle)*
    c HB Guide - v26 - i1 - Spring 2015 - p12(1) [51-500]

Marcellus, Rabb - *Prince of Tyrants*
    KR - Sept 1 2015 - pNA [501+]

March, Emily - *Heartsong Cottage*
    BL - v112 - i3 - Oct 1 2015 - p31(2) [51-500]
    PW - v262 - i38 - Sept 21 2015 - p60(1) [51-500]

March, J.D. - *Dance with the Devil, Book 1: The Devil's Own*
    Roundup M - v22 - i6 - August 2015 - p31(1) [501+]

March, JD - *An Uneasy Alliance*
    BL - v111 - i19-20 - June 1 2015 - p60(2) [51-500]
    KR - July 1 2015 - pNA [51-500]

March, Kerstin - *Branching Out*
    BL - v112 - i7 - Dec 1 2015 - p22(1) [51-500]

March, Lucy - *For Love or Magic*
    PW - v262 - i42 - Oct 19 2015 - p62(1) [51-500]

March, Richard - *The Tamburitza Tradition: From the Balkans to the American Midwest*
    WestFolk - v74 - i2 - Spring 2015 - p229-232 [501+]

Marchand, Peter J. - *Life and Times of a Big River: An Uncommon Natural History of Alaska's Upper Yukon*
    RVBW - June 2015 - pNA [501+]

Marchant, Alicia - *The Revolt of Owain Glynd?r in Medieval English Chronicles*
    Specu - v90 - i4 - Oct 2015 - p1147-1149 [501+]

Marchant, Jo - *Cure: A Journey into the Science of Mind over Body*
    KR - Dec 1 2015 - pNA [501+]
    PW - v262 - i48 - Nov 30 2015 - p50(2) [51-500]

Marchant, Nancy - *Knitting Fresh Brioche: Creating Two-Color Twists and Turns*
    Bwatch - Feb 2015 - pNA [51-500]

Marche, Stephen - *The Hunger of the Wolf*
    Mac - v128 - i8 - March 2 2015 - p60(2) [501+]
    Nat Post - v17 - i80 - Jan 31 2015 - pWP7(1) [501+]

Marchetta, Melina - *Froi of the Exiles (Read by Cartwright, Grant). Audiobook Review*
    BL - v111 - i13 - March 1 2015 - p71(1) [51-500]

Marchetti, Domenica - *Ciao Biscotti: Sweet and Savory Recipes Celebrating Italy's Favorite Cookie*
    LJ - v140 - i7 - April 15 2015 - p112(1) [51-500]

Marchetto, Marisa Acocella - *Ann Tenna*
    KR - July 1 2015 - pNA [51-500]
    PW - v262 - i19 - May 11 2015 - p44(1) [51-500]

Marchiaro, Michaelangiola - *La bibilioteca di Pietro Crinito: Manoscritti e libri a stampa della raccolta libraria di un umanista fiorentino (Textes et Etudes du Moyen Age 60.) Porto: federation international des instituts d'etudes medievales*
    Specu - v90 - i3 - July 2015 - p837-839 [501+]

Marchildon, Daniel - *Zazette, la chatte des ouendats (Illus. by Lamarre, Adeline)*
    c Res Links - v20 - i5 - June 2015 - p40(1) [501+]

Marchive, Laurane - *The Green Teen Cookbook: Recipes for All Seasons*
    y Teach Lib - v42 - i3 - Feb 2015 - p28(4) [501+]

Marciano, Francesca - *The Othe Language: Stories*
    NYTBR - June 14 2015 - p24(L) [501+]

Marciano, John Bemelmans - *Mischief Season*
  c   KR - Jan 1 2016 - pNA [51-500]
  Whatever Happened to the Metric System?: How America Kept Its Feet
    NYTBR - Oct 18 2015 - p28(L) [501+]
Marciniak, Kristin - *The US Coast Guard*
  y   HB Guide - v26 - i1 - Spring 2015 - p138(2) [51-500]
Marcionette, Jake - *Just Jake: Dog Eat Dog (Illus. by Villa, Victor Rivas)*
    SLJ - v61 - i3 - March 2015 - p140(1) [51-500]
Marciotte, Jake - *Dog Eat Dog*
  c   KR - Jan 15 2015 - pNA [51-500]
Marcott, Lindsay - *The Producer's Daughter*
    BL - v112 - i5 - Nov 1 2015 - p32(1) [51-500]
    PW - v262 - i39 - Sept 28 2015 - p68(1) [51-500]
    RVBW - Nov 2015 - pNA [51-500]
Marcovit, Hal - *Life during the Renaissance*
  y   SLJ - v61 - i9 - Sept 2015 - p176(1) [51-500]
Marcovitz, Hal - *Exposing Torture: Centuries of Cruelty*
  y   HB Guide - v26 - i2 - Fall 2015 - p155(1) [51-500]
  Life in Nazi Germany
  y   BL - v111 - i16 - April 15 2015 - p46(1) [51-500]
  Life in the Time of Shakespeare
  y   BL - v111 - i16 - April 15 2015 - p46(1) [51-500]
  y   VOYA - v38 - i3 - August 2015 - p89(1) [501+]
  The Rise of the Nazis
  y   VOYA - v38 - i2 - June 2015 - p89(1) [501+]
Marcus Aurelius - *Meditations*
    CSM - Jan 19 2015 - pNA [51-500]
Marcus, Ben - *New American Stories*
    KR - June 1 2015 - pNA [51-500]
    NS - v144 - i5276 - August 21 2015 - p47(1) [501+]
    TLS - i5870 - Oct 2 2015 - p27(1) [501+]
Marcus, Elena N. - *Devon: The Wild Adventures of Devon and Friends*
  c   CH Bwatch - June 2015 - pNA [51-500]
Marcus, Gary - *The Future of the Brain: Essays by the World's Leading Neuroscientists*
    Nature - v517 - i7533 - Jan 8 2015 - p143(1) [51-500]
    New Sci - v225 - i3011 - March 7 2015 - p46(2) [501+]
Marcus, Greil - *History of Rock 'n' Roll in Ten Songs*
    New R - v246 - i11 - Fall 2015 - p64(2) [501+]
  Real Life Rock: The Complete Top Ten Columns
    NYT - Nov 27 2015 - pC31(L) [501+]
  Three Songs, Three Singers, Three Nations: The William E. Massey Sr. Lectures in the History of American Civilization, 2013
    BL - v112 - i1 - Sept 1 2015 - p28(1) [51-500]
Marcus, Mary - *Lavina*
    BL - v111 - i16 - April 15 2015 - p24(1) [51-500]
Mardis, Marcia - *The Collection's at the Core: Revitalizing Your Library with Innovative Resources for the Common Cores and STEM*
    Teach Lib - v42 - i3 - Feb 2015 - p41(1) [501+]
Mardou - *Sky in Stereo (Illus. by Mardou)*
  y   BL - v112 - i4 - Oct 15 2015 - p36(1) [51-500]
Marechal, Paul - *Andy Warhol: The Complete Commissioned Record Covers, 1949-1987, 2d ed.*
    LJ - v140 - i7 - Oct 15 2015 - p85(2) [51-500]
Marek, Lillian - *Lady Emily's Exotic Journey*
    BL - v111 - i22 - August 1 2015 - p41(1) [51-500]
    PW - v262 - i23 - June 8 2015 - p45(1) [51-500]
Marenbon, John - *Abelard in Four Dimensions: A Twelfth-Century Philosopher in His Context and Ours*
    Med R - Jan 2015 - pNA [501+]
    Specu - v90 - i1 - Jan 2015 - p277-278 [501+]
  Pagans and Philosophers: The Problem of Paganism from Augustine to Leibniz
    HNet - Oct 2015 - pNA [501+]
Marent, Thomas - *Butterflies*
    LJ - v140 - i20 - Dec 1 2015 - p128(2) [51-500]
Maresca, Beth Anne - *Megan Owlet (Illus. by Maresca, Beth Anne)*
  c   SLJ - v61 - i6 - June 2015 - p88(1) [51-500]
Maresca, Marshall Ryan - *The Alchemy of Chaos*
    PW - v262 - i52 - Dec 21 2015 - p137(1) [51-500]
Margaret, Anne - *The Runaway Pumpkin (Illus. by Zenz, Aaron)*
  c   PW - v262 - i30 - July 27 2015 - p63(1) [51-500]
Margaret, Eby - *South Toward Home: Travels in Southern Literature*
    New Or - v50 - i1 - Oct 2015 - p44(1) [51-500]
Margetson, Evan K. - *Night Falling on the Tree of Cups*
    KR - March 1 2015 - pNA [501+]
Margocsy, Daniel - *Commercial Visions: Science, Trade, and Visual Culture in the Dutch Golden Age*
    Sev Cent N - v73 - i1-2 - Spring-Summer 2015 - p59(5) [501+]

Margolin, Phillip - *Violent Crimes*
    KR - Nov 1 2015 - pNA [51-500]
    PW - v262 - i51 - Dec 14 2015 - p59(1) [51-500]
  Woman with a Gun (Read by Huber, Hillary). Audiobook Review
    BL - v111 - i14 - March 15 2015 - p85(1) [51-500]
    PW - v262 - i5 - Feb 2 2015 - p52(1) [51-500]
Margolin, Victor - *World History of Design, 2 vols.*
    LJ - v140 - i16 - Oct 1 2015 - p108(1) [51-500]
Margolis, Leslie - *If I Were You*
  c   CCB-B - v69 - i1 - Sept 2015 - p38(1) [51-500]
  y   HB Guide - v26 - i2 - Fall 2015 - p93(1) [51-500]
  c   PW - v262 - i13 - March 30 2015 - p76(1) [51-500]
  c   SLJ - v61 - i6 - June 2015 - p102(1) [51-500]
  y   VOYA - v38 - i3 - August 2015 - p80(1) [51-500]
  Monkey Business
  y   HB Guide - v26 - i2 - Fall 2015 - p93(1) [51-500]
Margolis, Sue - *Losing Me*
    LJ - v140 - i12 - July 1 2015 - p78(1) [51-500]
Margotin, Philippe - *Bob Dylan: All the Songs: The Story behind Every Track*
    BL - v112 - i5 - Nov 1 2015 - p16(1) [501+]
    LJ - v140 - i19 - Nov 15 2015 - p86(2) [51-500]
Mariani, Lucio - *Traces of Time*
    WLT - v89 - i6 - Nov-Dec 2015 - p73(1) [51-500]
Mariani, Paul - *The Whole Harmonium: The Life of Wallace Stevens*
    PW - v262 - i47 - Nov 23 2015 - p58(1) [51-500]
Mariani, Philomena - *The Weegee Guide to New York: Roaming the City with Its Greatest Tabloid Photographer*
    LJ - v140 - i7 - April 15 2015 - p83(1) [51-500]
    NYT - Feb 8 2015 - p7(L) [501+]
Mariano, Marco - *L'America nell' "Occidente": Storia della dottrina Monroe*
    JAH - v102 - i2 - Sept 2015 - p562-563 [501+]
Marianski, Stanley - *The Art of Making Vegetarian Sausages*
    SPBW - Sept 2015 - pNA [51-500]
Marias, Javier - *Asi empieza lo malo*
    TLS - i5844 - April 3 2015 - p19(1) [501+]
Mariconda, Barbara - *The Voyage of Lucy P. Simmons: The Emerald Shore*
  c   HB Guide - v26 - i1 - Spring 2015 - p85(1) [51-500]
Marie, Farzana - *Load Poems Like Guns: Women's Poetry from Herat, Afghanistan*
    RVBW - May 2015 - pNA [51-500]
Marie, Naja - *Rock, Paper, Scissors*
    PW - v262 - i19 - May 11 2015 - p30(1) [51-500]
Marillier, Juliet - *The Caller*
  y   HB Guide - v26 - i1 - Spring 2015 - p115(1) [51-500]
  Tower of Thorns
    BL - v112 - i4 - Oct 15 2015 - p28(1) [51-500]
    PW - v262 - i38 - Sept 21 2015 - p58(1) [51-500]
Marin, Humberto - *Clinical Psychopharmacology: A Practical Approach*
    QRB - v90 - i2 - June 2015 - p225(1) [51-500]
Marina, Peter - *Getting the Holy Ghost: Urban Ethnography in a Brooklyn Pentecostal Tongue-Speaking Church*
    CS - v44 - i1 - Jan 2015 - p87-89 [501+]
Marinaccio, Dave - *Admen, Mad Men, and the Real World of Advertising: Essential Lessons for Business and Life*
    LJ - v140 - i17 - Oct 15 2015 - p98(1) [51-500]
Marinaccio, Isabella Clough - *Global Rome: Changing Faces of the Eternal City*
    HNet - Feb 2015 - pNA [51-500]
Marinelli-Konig, Gertraud - *Die bohmischen Lander in den Wiener Zeitschriften und Almanachen des Vormarz, 1805-1848*
    HNet - April 2015 - pNA [501+]
Marino, Gianna - *Night Animals (Illus. by Marino, Gianna)*
  c   BL - v111 - i19-20 - June 1 2015 - p122(1) [51-500]
  c   KR - May 1 2015 - pNA [51-500]
  c   PW - v262 - i16 - April 20 2015 - p74(1) [51-500]
  c   SLJ - v61 - i5 - May 2015 - p88(1) [51-500]
Marino, Rick - *I Love You Very Muchly ... : The Story of the Brave Little Girl*
  c   CH Bwatch - April 2015 - pNA [51-500]
  I Miss You Very Muchly: City of the Cats: Nika's Trek to Find Big Brother (Illus. by Contento, Dindo)
  c   CH Bwatch - Feb 2015 - pNA [51-500]
Marino, Salvatore - *Ospedali e citta nel Regno di Napoli: le Annunziate: istituzioni, archivi, e fonti*
    CHR - v101 - i4 - Autumn 2015 - p897(2) [501+]
Marino, Soraya M. Castro - *Fifty Years of Revolution: Perspectives on Cuba, the United States, and the World*
    RAH - v43 - i1 - March 2015 - p184-191 [501+]

Marinovich, Matt - *The Winter Girl*
    BL - v112 - i4 - Oct 15 2015 - p24(1) [51-500]
    KR - Sept 15 2015 - pNA [51-500]
    LJ - v140 - i15 - Sept 15 2015 - p69(1) [51-500]
    PW - v262 - i44 - Nov 2 2015 - p61(1) [51-500]
Mario, Helaine - *The Lost Concerto*
    LJ - v140 - i11 - June 15 2015 - p80(1) [51-500]
    PW - v262 - i21 - May 25 2015 - p38(2) [51-500]
Marion, Nancy E. - *Drugs in American Society: An Encyclopedia of History, Politics, Culture, and the Law*
  y   BL - v111 - i15 - April 1 2015 - p6(1) [51-500]
    R&USQ - v54 - i4 - Summer 2015 - p80(2) [501+]
Marion, Paul - *Mill Power: The Origin and Impact of Lowell National Historical Park*
    Pub Hist - v37 - i3 - August 2015 - p150(3) [501+]
Mariotte, Jeffrey J. - *Empty Rooms*
    BL - v111 - i11 - Feb 1 2015 - p26(1) [51-500]
Mariotti, Celine Rose - *Minister's Shoes*
    SPBW - Feb 2015 - pNA [51-500]
Marisco, Katie - *I Can't Eat Peanuts*
    BL - v111 - i14 - March 15 2015 - p63(1) [51-500]
  I Get Sunburned
    BL - v111 - i14 - March 15 2015 - p63(1) [51-500]
Marissen, Michael - *Tainted Glory in Handel's Messiah: The Unsettling History of the World's Most Beloved Choral Work*
    TLS - i5874 - Oct 30 2015 - p17(1) [501+]
Maristain, Monica - *Bolano: A Biography in Conversations*
    TLS - i5842 - March 20 2015 - p3(2) [501+]
Mark, David - *Sorrow Bound*
    RVBW - Feb 2015 - pNA [501+]
    RVBW - July 2015 - pNA [501+]
  Taking Pity
    BL - v111 - i18 - May 15 2015 - p29(1) [51-500]
    KR - May 1 2015 - pNA [51-500]
    NYTBR - July 5 2015 - p29(L) [501+]
    PW - v262 - i21 - May 25 2015 - p37(1) [51-500]
Mark, Mary Ellen - *Mary Ellen Mark: Tiny, Streetwise Revisited*
    CSM - Dec 22 2015 - pNA [51-500]
    LJ - v140 - i19 - Nov 15 2015 - p81(2) [51-500]
Markarian, Marianne - *Mariam's Easter Parade (Illus. by Wasielewski, Margaret Markarian)*
  c   CH Bwatch - March 2015 - pNA [51-500]
Markegard, Blake - *Alberto Del Rio*
  c   BL - v111 - i9-10 - Jan 1 2015 - p85(1) [51-500]
  John Cena
  c   BL - v111 - i9-10 - Jan 1 2015 - p85(1) [51-500]
  Rey Mysterio
  c   BL - v111 - i9-10 - Jan 1 2015 - p85(1) [51-500]
  Sheamus
  c   BL - v111 - i9-10 - Jan 1 2015 - p85(1) [51-500]
Markel, Adam - *Pivot: The Art and Science of Reinventing Your Life*
    PW - v262 - i52 - Dec 21 2015 - p146(1) [51-500]
Markel, Michelle - *Brave Girl: Clara and the Shirtwaist Makers' Strike of 1909 (Read by Lockford, Lesa). Audiobook Review*
  c   BL - v111 - i9-10 - Jan 1 2015 - p117(1) [51-500]
  Hillary Rodham Clinton: Some Girls Are Born to Lead (Illus. by Pham, LeUyen)
  c   BL - v112 - i5 - Nov 1 2015 - p38(1) [501+]
  c   KR - Nov 15 2015 - pNA [51-500]
  c   PW - v262 - i42 - Oct 19 2015 - p78(1) [501+]
  c   SLJ - v61 - i12 - Dec 2015 - p136(2) [51-500]
Markert, Jenny - *Tigers*
  c   BL - v111 - i22 - August 1 2015 - p54(1) [51-500]
Markey, Karen - *Designing Online Information Literacy Games Students Want to Play*
    LR - v64 - i6-7 - June-July 2015 - p503-504 [501+]
Markham, Laura - *Peaceful Parent, Happy Siblings: How to Stop the Fighting and Raise Friends for Life*
    PW - v262 - i9 - March 2 2015 - p80(1) [51-500]
Markle, Sandra - *Build, Beaver, Build!: Life at the Longest Beaver Dam*
  c   KR - Jan 1 2016 - pNA [51-500]
  The Case of the Vanishing Little Brown Bats: A Scientific Mystery
  c   HB Guide - v26 - i1 - Spring 2015 - p165(1) [51-500]
  The Great Monkey Rescue: Saving the Golden Lion Tamarins
  c   BL - v112 - i3 - Oct 1 2015 - p38(2) [51-500]
  c   KR - August 15 2015 - pNA [51-500]
  c   SLJ - v61 - i9 - Sept 2015 - p179(1) [51-500]
  Toad Weather (Illus. by Gonzalez, Thomas)
  c   BL - v111 - i12 - Feb 15 2015 - p77(1) [51-500]
  c   HB Guide - v26 - i2 - Fall 2015 - p43(1) [51-500]
  c   KR - Jan 15 2015 - pNA [51-500]
  c   SLJ - v61 - i5 - May 2015 - p88(1) [51-500]
  What If You Had Animal Feet!? (Illus. by McWilliam, Howard)
  c   HB Guide - v26 - i2 - Fall 2015 - p171(1) [51-500]

Marklund, Liza - *Borderline*
    KR - Feb 15 2015 - pNA [51-500]
    BL - v111 - i13 - March 1 2015 - p22(1) [51-500]
    PW - v262 - i6 - Feb 9 2015 - p47(1) [51-500]

Marko, Cyndi - *The Birdy Snatchers (Illus. by Marko, Cyndi)*
    c HB Guide - v26 - i1 - Spring 2015 - p62(1) [51-500]

Heroes on the Side
    c HB Guide - v26 - i2 - Fall 2015 - p68(1) [51-500]

Markoff, John - *Machines of Loving Grace: The Quest for Common Ground between Humans and Robots*
    BL - v111 - i22 - August 1 2015 - p8(1) [51-500]
    KR - June 15 2015 - pNA [501+]
    Nature - v526 - i7573 - Oct 15 2015 - p320(2) [501+]
    New Sci - v227 - i3034 - August 15 2015 - p42(2) [501+]
    NYTBR - August 23 2015 - p13(L) [501+]
    PW - v262 - i23 - June 8 2015 - p51(1) [51-500]

Markopoulos, Gregory J. - *Film as Film: The Collected Writings of Gregory J. Markopoulos*
    TLS - i5834 - Jan 23 2015 - p23(1) [501+]

Markova, Dawna - *Collaborative Intelligence*
    Har Bus R - v93 - i9 - Sept 2015 - p122(2) [51-500]
    KR - June 1 2015 - pNA [501+]

Markovics, Joyce - *Blizzard*
    c HB Guide - v26 - i1 - Spring 2015 - p151(1) [51-500]

Bow-Wow! Dog Helpers
    c HB Guide - v26 - i1 - Spring 2015 - p168(2) [51-500]

Earth: No Place Like Home
    c SLJ - v61 - i4 - April 2015 - p82(4) [501+]

Earthquake
    c HB Guide - v26 - i1 - Spring 2015 - p151(1) [51-500]

Mars: Red Rocks and Dust
    c BL - v111 - i17 - May 1 2015 - p87(2) [51-500]

Terremoto
    c SLJ - v61 - i5 - May 2015 - p132(1) [51-500]

Tormenta De Nieve
    c SLJ - v61 - i5 - May 2015 - p132(1) [51-500]

Tsunami
    c HB Guide - v26 - i1 - Spring 2015 - p151(1) [51-500]
    c SLJ - v61 - i5 - May 2015 - p132(1) [51-500]

Markovits, Benjamin - *You Don't Have to Live Like This*
    BL - v111 - i22 - August 1 2015 - p31(1) [51-500]
    KR - May 1 2015 - pNA [501+]
    PW - v262 - i20 - May 18 2015 - p58(2) [51-500]
    Spec - v328 - i9749 - July 4 2015 - p37(2) [501+]
    TLS - i5858 - July 10 2015 - p19(1) [501+]

Markovits, Julia - *Moral Reason*
    Ethics - v125 - i4 - July 2015 - p1215(5) [501+]

Markowitz, Fran - *Ethnographic Encounters in Israel: Poetics and Ethics of Fieldwork*
    HNet - March 2015 - pNA [501+]

Marks, Andreas - *Japan Journeys: Famous Woodblock Prints of Cultural Sights in Japan*
    LJ - v140 - i9 - May 15 2015 - p80(1) [51-500]
    PW - v262 - i12 - March 23 2015 - p67(2) [51-500]

Marks, Elizabeth - *Growing Together across the Autism Spectrum*
    c CH Bwatch - August 2015 - pNA [51-500]

Marks, Erika - *The Mermaid Collector*
    LJ - v140 - i17 - Oct 15 2015 - p118(1) [501+]

Marks, Howard - *Mr Smiley: My Last Pill and Testament*
    Spec - v329 - i9768 - Nov 14 2015 - p63(1) [501+]

Marks, Lara - *The Lock and Key of Medicine: Monoclonal Antibodies and the Transformation of Healthcare*
    Nature - v523 - i7558 - July 2 2015 - p34(1) [501+]

Marks, Walter - *The Battle of Jericho: A Detective Jericho Novel*
    PW - v262 - i41 - Oct 12 2015 - p51(1) [51-500]

Markus, Julia - *Lady Byron and Her Daughters*
    KR - August 1 2015 - pNA [501+]
    LJ - v140 - i14 - Sept 1 2015 - p112(1) [51-500]
    Nature - v528 - i7581 - Dec 10 2015 - p191(1) [51-500]
    NYTBR - Dec 6 2015 - p79(L) [501+]
    PW - v262 - i32 - August 10 2015 - p52(1) [51-500]

Markus, Parvati - *Love Everyone: The Transcendent Wisdom of Neem Karoii Baba Told through the Stories of the Westerners Whose Lives He Transformed*
    PW - v262 - i37 - Sept 14 2015 - p61(1) [51-500]

Markwyn, Abigail M. - *Empress San Francisco: The Pacific Rim, the Great West, & California at the Panama-Pacific International Exposition*
    Am St - v54 - i2 - Summer 2015 - p115-116 [501+]
    JAH - v102 - i2 - Sept 2015 - p588-589 [501+]
    Roundup M - v22 - i3 - Feb 2015 - p24(1) [501+]
    Roundup M - v22 - i6 - August 2015 - p38(2) [501+]
    WHQ - v46 - i2 - Summer 2015 - p254-255 [501+]

Marland, Hilary - *Health and Girlhood in Britain, 1874-1920*
    VS - v57 - i3 - Spring 2015 - p539(4) [501+]

Marler, Penny Long - *American Religion: Contemporary Trends*
    SF - v93 - i3 - March 2015 - pe75 [501+]

Marler, Scott P. - *The Merchants' Capital: New Orleans and the Political Economy of the Nineteenth-Century South*
    BHR - v89 - i3 - Autumn 2015 - p607(3) [501+]
    RAH - v43 - i1 - March 2015 - p83-91 [501+]

Marley, Anna O. - *The Artist's Garden: American Impressionism and the Garden Movement*
    LJ - v140 - i5 - March 15 2015 - p99(1) [501+]

Marley, Cedella - *Every Little Thing (Illus. by Brantley-Newton, Vanessa)*
    c SLJ - v61 - i7 - July 2015 - p56(1) [51-500]

Marley, Christopher - *Biophilia*
    NYT - April 14 2015 - pD2(L) [501+]

Marley, David F. - *Mexico at War: From the Struggle for Independence to 21st Century Drug Wars*
    R&USQ - v54 - i3 - Spring 2015 - p64(1) [501+]

Marlow, Susan K. - *Thick as Thieves*
    y CH Bwatch - June 2015 - pNA [51-500]

Marlowe, Elizabeth - *Shaky Ground: Context, Connoisseurship and the History of Roman Art*
    Class R - v65 - i1 - April 2015 - p272-273 [501+]

Marlowe, Mia - *Never Resist a Rake*
    PW - v262 - i11 - March 16 2015 - p69(1) [51-500]
    BL - v111 - i18 - May 15 2015 - p31(2) [51-500]
    KR - April 1 2015 - pNA [501+]

Marmell, Ari - *Covenant's End*
    y CH Bwatch - April 2015 - pNA [51-500]
    y VOYA - v37 - i6 - Feb 2015 - p81(1) [51-500]

Marmodoro, Anna - *Aristotle on Perceiving Objects*
    TLS - i5841 - March 13 2015 - p22(1) [501+]

The Author's Voice in Classical and Late Antiquity
    Class R - v65 - i2 - Oct 2015 - p323-324 [501+]

Marmor, Andrei - *The Language of Law*
    Law Q Rev - v131 - July 2015 - p502-504 [501+]

Marmot, Michael - *The Health Gap: The Challenge of an Unequal World*
    BL - v112 - i5 - Nov 1 2015 - p4(1) [51-500]
    KR - July 15 2015 - pNA [501+]
    LJ - v140 - i17 - Oct 15 2015 - p104(1) [51-500]
    NS - v144 - i5282 - Oct 2 2015 - p67(1) [501+]
    TimHES - i2226 - Oct 22 2015 - p46-1 [501+]

Marmureanu, Peter - *Beyond My Dreams*
    c BL - v112 - i3 - Oct 1 2015 - p32(2) [501+]

Marney, Ellie - *Every Breath*
    y HB Guide - v26 - i1 - Spring 2015 - p116(1) [51-500]

Every Word
    y Res Links - v21 - i1 - Oct 2015 - p38(2) [501+]
    y VOYA - v38 - i5 - Dec 2015 - p59(2) [51-500]

Marno, Mozhan - *Missoula: Rape and the Justice System in a College Town (Read by Brick, Scott). Audiobook Review*
    BL - v111 - i22 - August 1 2015 - p77(2) [51-500]

Maroh, Julie - *Blue Is the Warmest Color*
    Stud Hum - v41 - i1-2 - March 2015 - p261(3) [501+]

Marolda, Maria - *Working with the Math Balance*
    TC Math - v22 - i2 - Sept 2015 - p119(1) [501+]

Marom, Malka - *Joni Mitchell: In Her Own Words*
    Wom R Bks - v32 - i4 - July-August 2015 - p23(2) [501+]

Maron, Margaret - *Long upon the Land*
    BL - v111 - i22 - August 1 2015 - p35(1) [51-500]
    NYTBR - Sept 6 2015 - p25(L) [501+]
    PW - v262 - i25 - June 22 2015 - p120(1) [51-500]

Marotti, William - *Money, Trains, and Guillotines: Art and Revolution in 1960s Japan*
    JAS - v74 - i1 - Feb 2015 - p219-220 [501+]
    Pac A - v88 - i1 - March 2015 - p198 [501+]

Marouan, Maha - *Race and Displacement: Nation, Migration, and Identity in the Twenty-First Century*
    J Am St - v49 - i2 - May 2015 - p433-434 [501+]

Maroun, Taren - *A Hot Glue Gun Mess: Funny Stories, Pretty DIY Projects*
    LJ - v140 - i13 - August 1 2015 - p94(2) [51-500]

Marovich, Robert M. - *A City Called Heaven: Chicago and the Birth of Gospel Music*
    LJ - v140 - i6 - April 1 2015 - p95(2) [51-500]

Marquardt, Marie - *Dream Things True*
    y BL - v112 - i2 - Sept 15 2015 - p70(2) [51-500]
    y KR - June 15 2015 - pNA [51-500]
    y PW - v262 - i23 - June 8 2015 - p62(1) [51-500]
    y SLJ - v61 - i9 - Sept 2015 - p169(2) [51-500]
    y VOYA - v38 - i4 - Oct 2015 - p56(1) [51-500]

Marquardt, Meg - *The Science of a Flood*
    c BL - v112 - i4 - Oct 15 2015 - p42(1) [51-500]

The Science of a Nuclear Plant Explosion
    c BL - v112 - i4 - Oct 15 2015 - p42(1) [51-500]

Marques, Sandra Moreira - *Now and at the Hour of Our Death*
    TLS - i5868 - Sept 18 2015 - p29(1) [501+]

Marquet, L. David - *Turn the Ship Around! A True Story of Turning Followers into Leaders*
    NWCR - v68 - i1 - Wntr 2015 - p145(2) [501+]

Marquez, Benjamin - *Democratizing Texas Politics: Race, Identity, and Mexican American Empowerment, 1945-2002*
    ERS - v38 - i8 - August 2015 - p1455(3) [501+]
    JSH - v81 - i2 - May 2015 - p504(2) [501+]
    WHQ - v46 - i2 - Summer 2015 - p239-240 [501+]

Marquez, John D. - *Black-Brown Solidarity: Racial Politics in the New Gulf South*
    ERS - v38 - i8 - August 2015 - p1429(3) [501+]

Marquez, Vicki - *The Rootlets: Super Rootabilities (Illus. by Russnak, Jeremy)*
    c CH Bwatch - April 2015 - pNA [51-500]
    c KR - June 15 2015 - pNA [501+]

Marquis, Kathy - *Local History Reference Collections for Public Libraries*
    RVBW - Oct 2015 - pNA [501+]
    LJ - v140 - i20 - Dec 1 2015 - p116(1) [51-500]

Marquis, Samuel - *The Slush Pile Brigade*
    KR - Nov 15 2015 - pNA [501+]

Marquis, Sarah - *Wild by Nature: From Siberia to Australia, Three Years Alone in the Wilderness on Foot*
    KR - Nov 15 2015 - pNA [501+]
    PW - v262 - i47 - Nov 23 2015 - p59(2) [51-500]

Marquis, Timothy Luckritz - *Transient Apostle: Paul, Travel, and the Rhetoric of Empire*
    Intpr - v69 - i1 - Jan 2015 - p107(2) [501+]

Marr, Andrew - *Head of the State: A Political Entertainment*
    BL - v111 - i11 - Feb 1 2015 - p22(1) [51-500]
    NYTBR - Feb 22 2015 - p14(L) [501+]

We British: The Poetry of a People
    NS - v144 - i5287 - Nov 6 2015 - p47(1) [501+]

Marr, Melissa - *Bunny Roo, I Love You (Illus. by White, Teagan)*
    c HB Guide - v26 - i2 - Fall 2015 - p15(1) [51-500]
    c PW - v262 - i6 - Feb 9 2015 - p64(1) [51-500]
    c SLJ - v61 - i5 - May 2015 - p79(2) [51-500]

Made for You
    y HB Guide - v26 - i1 - Spring 2015 - p116(1) [51-500]

Seven Black Diamonds
    y BL - v112 - i5 - Nov 1 2015 - p56(1) [51-500]
    y SLJ - v61 - i12 - Dec 2015 - p124(1) [51-500]

Untamed City: Carnival of Secrets
    y VOYA - v38 - i5 - Dec 2015 - p72(1) [51-500]

Marra, Anthony - *The Tsar of Love and Techno: Stories*
    KR - Sept 1 2015 - pNA [501+]
    BL - v112 - i3 - Oct 1 2015 - p23(1) [51-500]
    LJ - v140 - i15 - Sept 15 2015 - p72(1) [51-500]
    NYT - Oct 8 2015 - pC1(L) [501+]
    NYT - Nov 27 2015 - pC31(L) [501+]
    NYTBR - Oct 25 2015 - p17(L) [501+]
    PW - v262 - i31 - August 3 2015 - p33(1) [51-500]

Marren, Peter - *Rainbow Dust: Three Centuries of Delight in British Butterflies*
    New Sci - v227 - i3033 - August 8 2015 - p43(1) [501+]
    TLS - i5869 - Sept 25 2015 - p22(1) [501+]

Marren, Susannah - *Between the Tides*
    BL - v111 - i16 - April 15 2015 - p23(1) [51-500]
    KR - May 15 2015 - pNA [51-500]

Marrin, Albert - *FDR and the American Crisis*
    y CCB-B - v68 - i6 - Feb 2015 - p320(1) [51-500]
    y HB - v91 - i1 - Jan-Feb 2015 - p99(1) [51-500]
    y HB Guide - v26 - i2 - Fall 2015 - p211(1) [51-500]

Thomas Paine: Crusader for Liberty: How One Man's Ideas Helped Form a New Nation
    y CCB-B - v68 - i6 - Feb 2015 - p320(1) [51-500]
    y HB Guide - v26 - i1 - Spring 2015 - p194(1) [51-500]

Marriott, Zoe - *Darkness Hidden*
  y KR - Sept 15 2015 - pNA [51-500]
  c SLJ - v61 - i10 - Oct 2015 - p104(2) [51-500]
The Name of the Blade
  y HB Guide - v26 - i2 - Fall 2015 - p130(1) [51-500]
Marrison, James - *The Drowning Ground*
    BL - v111 - i19-20 - June 1 2015 - p50(1) [51-500]
    KR - June 15 2015 - pNA [51-500]
    PW - v262 - i18 - May 4 2015 - p96(1) [51-500]
Marro, Elizabeth - *Casualties*
    KR - Dec 1 2015 - pNA [51-500]
Marrow, Stanley B. - *Paul for Today's Church: A Commentary on First Corinthians*
    Theol St - v76 - i1 - March 2015 - p169(2) [501+]
Marrs, Jim - *Population Control*
    KR - April 15 2015 - pNA [51-500]
Marrs, Suzanne - *Meanwhile There Are Letters: The Correspondence of Eudora Welty and Ross Macdonald*
    KR - April 15 2015 - pNA [501+]
    LJ - v140 - i10 - June 1 2015 - p103(1) [51-500]
    NYT - July 14 2015 - pC1(L) [501+]
    PW - v262 - i19 - May 11 2015 - p50(2) [51-500]
Mars, Brigitte - *The Home Reference to Holistic Health & Healing: Easy-To-Use Natural Remedies, Herbs, Flower Essences, Essential Oils, Supplements, and Therapeutic Practices for Health, Happiness, and Well-Being.*
    LJ - v140 - i2 - Feb 1 2015 - p107(2) [501+]
Mars, Emma - *Elle*
    KR - Feb 15 2015 - pNA [51-500]
    PW - v262 - i5 - Feb 2 2015 - p42(1) [51-500]
Mars-Jones, Adam - *Kid Gloves: a Voyage Round My Father*
    NS - v144 - i5277 - August 28 2015 - p41(1) [501+]
    Spec - v328 - i9757 - August 29 2015 - p40(2) [501+]
Marschner, Joanna - *Queen Caroline: Cultural Politics at the Early Eighteenth-Century Court*
    HT - v65 - i8 - August 2015 - p63(1) [501+]
    TLS - i5846 - April 17 2015 - p10(2) [501+]
Marsden, Ben - *Uncommon Contexts: Encounters Between Science and Literature, 1800-1914*
    VS - v57 - i3 - Spring 2015 - p529(5) [501+]
Marsden, George M. - *The Twilight of the American Enlightenment: The 1950s and the Crisis of Liberal Belief*
    AHR - v120 - i1 - Feb 2015 - p283-284 [501+]
    CHR - v101 - i4 - Autumn 2015 - p960(2) [501+]
    Historian - v77 - i3 - Fall 2015 - p567(2) [501+]
    JAH - v102 - i1 - June 2015 - p290-291 [501+]
    RAH - v43 - i3 - Sept 2015 - p557-563 [501+]
Marsden, Lee - *The Ashgate Research Companion to Religion and Conflict Resolution*
    J Ch St - v57 - i1 - Wntr 2015 - p160-162 [501+]
Marsden, Peter - *Social Trends in American Life: Findings from the General Social Survey since 1972*
    CS - v44 - i6 - Nov 2015 - p823-825 [501+]
Marsden, Philip - *Rising Ground: A Search for the Spirit of Place*
    KR - Jan 1 2016 - pNA [51-500]
    Lon R Bks - v37 - i5 - March 5 2015 - p31(1) [501+]
    TLS - i5831 - Jan 2 2015 - p26(1) [501+]
Marsh, Ava - *Untouchable*
    PW - v262 - i34 - August 24 2015 - p60(1) [51-500]
Marsh, Charles - *Strange Glory: A Life of Dietrich Bonhoeffer*
    NYRB - v62 - i19 - Dec 3 2015 - p53(3) [501+]
Marsh, Dawn G. - *A Lenape among the Quakers: The Life of Hannah Freeman*
    AHR - v120 - i1 - Feb 2015 - p232-233 [501+]
    HNet - Feb 2015 - pNA [501+]
    WHQ - v46 - i1 - Spring 2015 - p102-103 [501+]
Marsh, Henry - *Do No Harm: Stories of Life, Death, and Brain Surgery (Read by Barclay, Jim). Audiobook Review*
    LJ - v140 - i17 - Oct 15 2015 - p54(1) [51-500]
Do No Harm: Stories of Life, Death, and Brain Surgery
    PW - v262 - i10 - March 9 2015 - p62(1) [51-500]
    BL - v111 - i15 - April 1 2015 - p9(1) [51-500]
    BL - v112 - i7 - Dec 1 2015 - p13(1) [501+]
    CC - v132 - i22 - Oct 28 2015 - p39(3) [501+]
    KR - March 15 2015 - pNA [51-500]
    LJ - v140 - i12 - July 1 2015 - p118(1) [501+]
    NY - v91 - i13 - May 18 2015 - p98 [501+]
    NYT - May 19 2015 - pC1(L) [501+]
    NYT - July 28 2015 - pC1(L) [501+]
    NYTBR - May 24 2015 - p13(L) [501+]
    TimHES - i2195 - March 19 2015 - p49(1) [501+]
    TimHES - i2197 - April 2 2015 - p53(1) [501+]

Marsh, John - *In Walt We Trust: How a Queer Socialist Poet Can Save America From Itself*
    G&L Rev W - v22 - i4 - July-August 2015 - p43(1) [501+]
    LJ - v140 - i2 - Feb 1 2015 - p82(2) [501+]
    RVBW - June 2015 - pNA [501+]
Marsh, Katherine - *The Door by the Staircase (Illus. by Murphy, Kelly)*
  c KR - Oct 1 2015 - pNA [51-500]
  c SLJ - v61 - i12 - Dec 2015 - p104(2) [51-500]
Marsh, Laura - *Alligators and Crocodiles*
  c HB Guide - v26 - i2 - Fall 2015 - p175(1) [51-500]
Les poneys
  c Res Links - v20 - i3 - Feb 2015 - p47(2) [51-500]
Owls
  c HB Guide - v26 - i1 - Spring 2015 - p162(1) [51-500]
Sea Otters
  c HB Guide - v26 - i1 - Spring 2015 - p165(2) [51-500]
Marsh, Selina Tusitala - *Dark Sparring: Poems*
    Cont Pac - v27 - i1 - Spring 2015 - p298(3) [501+]
Marshall, Alex - *A Crown for Cold Silver*
    BL - v111 - i13 - March 1 2015 - p29(2) [51-500]
    BL - v111 - i18 - May 15 2015 - p35(1) [501+]
    KR - March 1 2015 - pNA [51-500]
    PW - v262 - i5 - Feb 2 2015 - p39(1) [51-500]
Marshall, Alison R. - *Cultivating Connections: The Making of Chinese Prairie Canada*
    WHQ - v46 - i3 - Autumn 2015 - p392-393 [501+]
Marshall-Ball, Sara - *Hush*
    KR - Sept 1 2015 - pNA [501+]
Marshall, Colby - *Double Vision*
    PW - v262 - i8 - Feb 23 2015 - p53(1) [51-500]
Marshall, Dan - *Home Is Burning: A Memoir*
    BL - v112 - i2 - Sept 15 2015 - p6(1) [51-500]
    KR - August 15 2015 - pNA [501+]
    SEP - v287 - i5 - Sept-Oct 2015 - p24(1) [51-500]
    Spec - v329 - i9767 - Nov 7 2015 - p44(2) [501+]
Marshall, David - *Prayer: Christian and Muslim Perspectives*
    Theol St - v76 - i1 - March 2015 - p226(2) [501+]
Marshall, Gail - *Shakespeare in the Nineteenth Century*
    VS - v57 - i2 - Wntr 2015 - p319(3) [501+]
Marshall III, Joseph M. - *In the Footsteps of Crazy Horse (Illus. by Yellowhawk, Jim)*
  y KR - Sept 1 2015 - pNA [51-500]
Marshall, Jeffrey - *Little Miss Sure Shot*
    SPBW - Feb 2015 - pNA [51-500]
Marshall, Joseph, III - *In the Footsteps of Crazy Horse (Illus. by Yellowhawk, Jim)*
  c BL - v112 - i4 - Oct 15 2015 - p51(1) [51-500]
  c PW - v262 - i37 - Sept 14 2015 - p78(1) [51-500]
  c SLJ - v61 - i10 - Oct 2015 - p92(2) [51-500]
  y VOYA - v38 - i4 - Oct 2015 - p56(2) [51-500]
Marshall, Julia - *Where Is Pim? (Illus. by Landstrom, Olof)*
  c KR - Feb 15 2015 - pNA [51-500]
    SLJ - v61 - i3 - March 2015 - p118(2) [51-500]
Marshall, Linda Elovitz - *Talia and the Very Yum Kippur (Illus. by Assirelli, Francesca)*
  c KR - June 15 2015 - pNA [51-500]
  c SLJ - v61 - i7 - July 2015 - p65(1) [51-500]
Marshall, Mac - *Drinking Smoke: The Tobacco Syndemic in Oceania*
    JRAI - v21 - i1 - March 2015 - p230(2) [501+]
    MAQ - v29 - i2 - June 2015 - pb37-b39 [501+]
    Pac A - v88 - i3 - Sept 2015 - p751 [501+]
Marshall, Melanie L. - *Sexualities, Textualities, Art and Music in Early Modern Italy: Playing with Boundaries*
    Ren Q - v68 - i3 - Fall 2015 - pNA [501+]
Marshall, Natalie - *The Big Book of Happy (Illus. by Marshall, Natalie)*
  c KR - July 1 2015 - pNA [51-500]
  c PW - v262 - i20 - May 18 2015 - p82(2) [51-500]
  c SLJ - v61 - i9 - Sept 2015 - p111(1) [51-500]
The Big Book of Silly (Illus. by Marshall, Natalie)
  c SLJ - v61 - i9 - Sept 2015 - p111(1) [51-500]
Five Little Monkeys
  c KR - Jan 1 2016 - pNA [51-500]
This Little Piggy
  c KR - July 1 2015 - pNA [51-500]
Marshall, Nate - *Wild Hundreds*
    PW - v262 - i33 - August 17 2015 - p50(1) [51-500]
Marshall, Paul - *The Tail: How England's Schools Fail One Child in Five And What Can Be Done*
    TimHES - i2196 - March 26 2015 - p51(1) [501+]
Marshall, Perry - *Evolution 2.0: Breaking the Deadlock between Darwin and Design*
    LJ - v140 - i15 - Sept 15 2015 - p103(1) [501+]

Marshall, Peter - *The Oxford Illustrated History of the Reformation*
    TLS - i5877 - Nov 20 2015 - p12(2) [501+]
Marshall, Susan - *Mind's Eye: Stories from Whapmagoostui*
    Can Lit - i224 - Spring 2015 - p131 [501+]
Marshall, Tim - *Prioners of Geography: Ten Maps That Explain Everything About the World*
    NYTBR - Dec 6 2015 - p14(L) [501+]
Marshall, Woodville K. - *From Plantations to University Campus: The Social History of Cave Hill, Barbados*
    HNet - Feb 2015 - pNA [501+]
Marsico, Katie - *Ball Game Math*
  c HB Guide - v26 - i1 - Spring 2015 - p149(1) [51-500]
Get a Good Night's Sleep! (Illus. by Marsico, Katie)
  c BL - v111 - i15 - April 1 2015 - p60(1) [51-500]
Key Discoveries in Physical Science
  y HB Guide - v26 - i2 - Fall 2015 - p166(1) [51-500]
Leeches
  c BL - v112 - i7 - Dec 1 2015 - p42(2) [51-500]
Math on the Move
  c Teach Lib - v43 - i1 - Oct 2015 - p17(1) [51-500]
Marsoobian, Armen T. - *Fragments of a Lost Homeland: Remembering Armenia*
    NS - v144 - i5259 - April 24 2015 - p46(3) [501+]
Marston, Daniel - *The Indian Army and the End of the Raj*
    J Mil H - v79 - i2 - April 2015 - p539-540 [501+]
Marston, Ewart, Claire - *Marston, Elsa (Illus. by Ewart, Claire)*
  c CH Bwatch - Feb 2015 - pNA [51-500]
Marston, Gwen - *Free Range Triangle Quilts*
    Bwatch - Oct 2015 - pNA [51-500]
Marston, John A. - *Ethnicity, Borders, and the Grassroots Interface with the State: Studies on Southeast Asia in Honor of Charles F. Keyes*
    JAS - v74 - i3 - August 2015 - p785-787 [501+]
Marszalek, John F. - *Lincoln and the Military*
    JSH - v81 - i4 - Nov 2015 - p983(3) [501+]
Martaud, Alain - *Les Mineraux de Sainte-Marie-Aux-Mines*
    RocksMiner - v90 - i2 - March-April 2015 - p187(2) [501+]
Martel, Gordon - *The Month That Changed The World: July 2014*
    HT - v65 - i8 - August 2015 - p65(1) [501+]
Twentieth-Century War and Conflict: A Concise Encyclopedia
    HT - v65 - i11 - Nov 2015 - p64(2) [501+]
Martel, Marcel - *Canada the Good: A Short History of Vice since 1500*
    Can Hist R - v96 - i1 - March 2015 - p137(3) [501+]
Martel, Tina - *Not in the Pink*
    PW - v262 - i10 - March 9 2015 - p66(1) [51-500]
Martel, William C. - *Grand Strategy in Theory and Practice: The Need for an Effective American Foreign Policy*
    HNet - August 2015 - pNA [501+]
Martel, Yann - *The High Mountains of Portugal*
    BL - v112 - i3 - Oct 1 2015 - p4(1) [51-500]
    KR - Dec 1 2015 - pNA [501+]
    PW - v262 - i51 - Dec 14 2015 - p54(1) [51-500]
Martell, Jon - *Katya*
    SPBW - Nov 2015 - pNA [51-500]
Martelle, Scott - *The Madman and the Assassin*
    KR - Jan 15 2015 - pNA [501+]
Marten, James - *America's Corporal: James Tanner in War and Peace*
    JAH - v102 - i1 - June 2015 - p262-263 [501+]
    JSH - v81 - i3 - August 2015 - p746(2) [501+]
Children and Youth during the Gilded Age and Progressive Era
    JAH - v102 - i2 - Sept 2015 - p569-570 [501+]
Marti, Gerardo - *The Deconstructed Church: Understanding Emerging Christianity*
    AJS - v121 - i1 - July 2015 - p327(3) [501+]
    CS - v44 - i6 - Nov 2015 - p825-827 [501+]
Martikainen, Tuomas - *Religion, Migration, Settlement: Reflections on Post-1990 Immigration to Finland*
    BTB - v45 - i2 - May 2015 - p125(2) [501+]
Martin, Adrian - *Mise en Scene and Film Style: From Classical Hollywood to New Media Art*
    Si & So - v25 - i4 - April 2015 - p106(2) [501+]
Martin, Adrienne M. - *How We Hope: A Moral Psychology*
    Ethics - v125 - i2 - Jan 2015 - p596(5) [501+]
Martin, Alexander M. - *Enlightened Metropolis: Constructing Imperial Moscow, 1762-1855*
    HNet - March 2015 - pNA [501+]
    JMH - v87 - i1 - March 2015 - p240(2) [501+]

Martin, Amy E. - *Alter-Nations: Nationalisms, Terror and the State in Nineteenth-Century Britain and Ireland*
    VS - v57 - i2 - Wntr 2015 - p348(3) [501+]

Martin, Andrew - *Belles and Whistles: Five Journeys through Time on Britain's Train*
    TLS - i5845 - April 10 2015 - p32(1) [501+]

Martin, Andy - *Reacher Said Nothing: Lee Child and the Making of "Make Me"*
    NS - v144 - i5290 - Nov 27 2015 - p50(2) [501+]

Martin, Ann M. - *The Doll People Set Sail (Illus. by Helquist, Brett)*
    c HB - v91 - i1 - Jan-Feb 2015 - p86(1) [51-500]
    c HB Guide - v26 - i1 - Spring 2015 - p86(1) [51-500]
Home Is the Place (Read by Siegfried, Mandy, with Lorna Raver). Audiobook Review
    SLJ - v61 - i4 - April 2015 - p63(1) [51-500]
Home Is the Place
    c CH Bwatch - June 2015 - pNA [501+]
    y HB Guide - v26 - i2 - Fall 2015 - p93(1) [51-500]
Rain Reign (Read by Hamilton, Laura). Audiobook Review
    c BL - v111 - i15 - April 1 2015 - p87(1) [51-500]
    SLJ - v61 - i3 - March 2015 - p78(1) [51-500]
Rain Reign
    c BL - v111 - i9-10 - Jan 1 2015 - pS4(8) [501+]
    c HB Guide - v26 - i1 - Spring 2015 - p86(1) [51-500]

Martin, Annie - *The Magical World of Moss Gardening*
    LJ - v140 - i13 - August 1 2015 - p116(1) [51-500]
    PW - v262 - i31 - August 3 2015 - p54(1) [51-500]
    RVBW - Nov 2015 - pNA [51-500]

Martin, Benjamin Franklin - *Years of Plenty, Years of Want: France and the Legacy of the Great War*
    Historian - v77 - i2 - Summer 2015 - p396(2) [501+]

Martin, Bill, Jr. - *Brown Bear, Brown Bear, What Do You See? (Illus. by Carle, Eric)*
    c BL - v112 - i4 - Oct 15 2015 - p53(1) [51-500]
Listen to Our World (Illus. by Sweet, Melissa)
    c KR - Dec 15 2015 - pNA [51-500]
Panda Bear, Panda Bear, What Do You See? (Illus. by Carle, Eric)
    c HB Guide - v26 - i1 - Spring 2015 - p12(1) [51-500]

Martin, C.E. - *Mythical*
    RVBW - Jan 2015 - pNA [51-500]

Martin, C.K. Kelly - *The Sweetest Thing You Can Sing*
    y Res Links - v20 - i3 - Feb 2015 - p32(1) [51-500]

Martin, Carol Ann - *Underneath a Cow (Illus. by Wood, Ben)*
    c Magpies - v30 - i4 - Sept 2015 - p28(1) [501+]

Martin, Chris - *The Falling Down Dance*
    PW - v262 - i42 - Oct 19 2015 - p52(2) [51-500]

Martin, Christopher - *Constituting Old Age in Early Modern English Literature, from Queen Elizabeth to 'King Lear'*
    MLR - v110 - i1 - Jan 2015 - p237-238 [501+]

Martin, Chuck - *Gunsmoke Bonanza*
    RVBW - June 2015 - pNA [51-500]

Martin, Clancy - *Bad Sex*
    NYTBR - Sept 27 2015 - p30(L) [501+]
    PW - v262 - i30 - July 27 2015 - p38(1) [51-500]
Love and Lies: An Essay on Truthfulness, Deceit, and the Growth and Care of Erotic Love
    PW - v262 - i1 - Jan 5 2015 - p68(1) [51-500]
    LJ - v140 - i2 - Feb 1 2015 - p87(1) [51-500]
    NYTBR - Feb 8 2015 - p20(L) [501+]
    TLS - i5871 - Oct 9 2015 - p30(2) [501+]

Martin, Claude - *On the Edge: The State and Fate of the World's Tropical Rainforests*
    Nature - v521 - i7553 - May 28 2015 - p421(1) [51-500]

Martin, Claudia - *My Little Book of Volcanoes and Earthquakes*
    c Sch Lib - v63 - i2 - Summer 2015 - p112(1) [51-500]
Spiders and Bugs around the World
    c HB Guide - v26 - i1 - Spring 2015 - p159(1) [51-500]

Martin, Craig - *Subverting Aristotle: Religion, History, and Philosophy in Early Modern Science*
    Ren Q - v68 - i1 - Spring 2015 - p267-268 [501+]
    Six Ct J - v46 - i1 - Spring 2015 - p200-204 [501+]

Martin, Daniel D. - *The Politics of Sorrow: Families, Victims, and the Micro-Organization of Youth Homicide*
    CS - v44 - i4 - July 2015 - p533-535 [501+]

Martin, Darragh - *The Keeper*
    y SLJ - v61 - i7 - July 2015 - p87(1) [51-500]

Martin, David (b. 1929-) - *The Education of David Martin: The Making of an Unlikely Sociologist*
    Soc - v52 - i5 - Oct 2015 - p513(3) [501+]

Martin, David (b. 1944-) - *Peep and Ducky Rainy Day (Illus. by Walker, David)*
    c HB Guide - v26 - i2 - Fall 2015 - p15(1) [51-500]
Peep and Ducky: Rainy Day (Illus. by Walker, David)
    SLJ - v61 - i3 - March 2015 - p120(2) [51-500]
Shh! Bears Sleeping (Illus. by Johnson, Steve)
    c KR - Nov 1 2015 - pNA [51-500]
    c SLJ - v61 - i12 - Dec 2015 - p92(1) [51-500]

Martin, Desiree A. - *Borderlands Saints: Secular Sanctity in Chicano/a and Mexican Culture*
    AL - v87 - i2 - June 2015 - p405-408 [501+]

Martin, Elisabeth - *"Ich habe mich nur an das geltende Recht gehalten": Herkunft, Arbeitsweise und Mentalitat der Warter und Vernehmer der Stasi-Untersuchungshaftanstalt Berlin-Hohenschonhausen*
    HNet - April 2015 - pNA [501+]

Martin, Emily - *Winfield Day Dreamers: A Journey of Imagination*
    c HB Guide - v26 - i1 - Spring 2015 - p12(1) [51-500]

Martin, Emily (b. 1987-) - *The Year We Fell Apart*
    y BL - v112 - i6 - Nov 15 2015 - p52(2) [51-500]
    y KR - Oct 1 2015 - pNA [51-500]
    y SLJ - v61 - i11 - Nov 2015 - p118(2) [51-500]

Martin, Emily Winfield - *The Wonderful Things You Will Be (Illus. by Martin, Emily Winfield)*
    c BL - v111 - i22 - August 1 2015 - p76(1) [51-500]
    c KR - June 15 2015 - pNA [51-500]
    c PW - v262 - i19 - May 11 2015 - p57(1) [51-500]
    c PW - v262 - i49 - Dec 2 2015 - p42(2) [51-500]
    c SLJ - v61 - i6 - June 2015 - p74(1) [51-500]

Martin, Felix - *Money: The Unauthorized Biography--from Coinage to Cryptocurrencies*
    NYTBR - March 22 2015 - p28(L) [501+]

Martin, Francis - *The Ecological Genomics of Fungi*
    QRB - v90 - i3 - Sept 2015 - p348(1) [501+]

Martin, Geoffrey - *American Geographers and Geography: Toward Geographic Science*
    TimHES - i207 - June 11 2015 - p53(1) [501+]

Martin, George R.R. - *A Game of Thrones, 5 vols. (Read by Dotrice, Roy). Audiobook Review*
    BooChiTr - July 18 2015 - p13(1) [501+]
The Ice Dragon (Illus. by Royo, Luis)
    Bwatch - Jan 2015 - pNA [51-500]
    c CCB-B - v68 - i6 - Feb 2015 - p321(1) [51-500]
    c HB Guide - v26 - i1 - Spring 2015 - p86(1) [51-500]
A Knight of the Seven Kingdoms
    BL - v112 - i5 - Nov 1 2015 - p37(1) [51-500]
    KR - Oct 15 2015 - pNA [501+]
Old Venus
    KR - Jan 1 2015 - pNA [501+]
    Analog - v135 - i5 - May 2015 - p105(1) [501+]

Martin, George W. - *Opera at the Bandstand: Then and Now*
    Notes - v72 - i1 - Sept 2015 - p143(4) [501+]

Martin, Isabel - *A Library Field Trip*
    c HB Guide - v26 - i2 - Fall 2015 - p146(1) [51-500]
A Zoo Field Trip (Illus. by Martin, Isabel)
    c HB Guide - v26 - i2 - Fall 2015 - p171(1) [51-500]

Martin, Jacqueline Briggs - *Alice Waters and the Trip to Delicious (Read by Hamilton, Laura). Audiobook Review*
    BL - v111 - i12 - Feb 15 2015 - p104(1) [51-500]
Farmer Will Allen and the Growing Table (Illus. by Larkin, Eric-Shabazz)
    c SLJ - v61 - i12 - Dec 2015 - p64(4) [51-500]

Martin, James (b. 1960-) - *The Abbey*
    AM - v213 - i11 - Oct 19 2015 - p38(3) [501+]
    PW - v262 - i32 - August 10 2015 - p45(1) [51-500]
Seven Last Words: An Invitation to a Deeper Friendship with Jesus
    PW - v262 - i51 - Dec 14 2015 - p79(1) [51-500]

Martin, James P. - *Cloud Computing and Electronic Discovery*
    Bwatch - Feb 2015 - pNA [51-500]

Martin, Jean - *Un siecle d'oubli: Les Canadiens et la Premiere Guerre mondiale, 1914-2014*
    J Mil H - v79 - i2 - April 2015 - p512-513 [501+]

Martin, Jenny - *Tracked*
    y BL - v111 - i18 - May 15 2015 - p64(2) [51-500]
    y HB Guide - v26 - i2 - Fall 2015 - p130(1) [51-500]
    y KR - March 15 2015 - pNA [51-500]
    y SLJ - v61 - i4 - April 2015 - p167(2) [51-500]
    y VOYA - v38 - i2 - June 2015 - p79(1) [51-500]

Martin, Joel W. - *Atlas of Crustacean Larvae*
    QRB - v90 - i2 - June 2015 - p217(2) [501+]

Martin, John F. - *In Character: Opera Portraiture*
    ON - v79 - i11 - May 2015 - p71(1) [501+]

Martin, Jon Edward - *Shades of Artemis*
    HT - v65 - i8 - August 2015 - p56(2) [501+]

Martin, Justin - *Rebel Souls: Walt Whitman and America's First Bohemians*
    G&L Rev W - v22 - i3 - May-June 2015 - p38(2) [501+]

Martin, Jynne Dilling - *We Mammals in Hospitable Times*
    KR - Feb 1 2015 - pNA [51-500]
    LJ - v140 - i7 - April 15 2015 - p90(2) [51-500]
    NYTBR - March 1 2015 - p30(L) [51-500]

Martin, Karen Wooley - *Isabel Allende's House of the Spirits Trilogy: Narrative Geographies*
    MLR - v110 - i2 - April 2015 - p575-577 [501+]

Martin, Kat - *Into the Fury*
    PW - v262 - i51 - Dec 14 2015 - p68(1) [51-500]

Martin, Keir - *The Death of the Big Men and the Rise of the Big Shots: Custom and Conflict in East New Britain*
    Pac A - v88 - i1 - March 2015 - p239 [501+]

Martin, Lee - *Shadow on the Mesa*
    Roundup M - v22 - i6 - August 2015 - p31(1) [501+]

Martin, Lerone A. - *Preaching on Wax: The Phonograph and the Shaping of Modern African American Religion*
    CH - v84 - i4 - Dec 2015 - p917(3) [501+]

Martin, Lisa - *Anton and Cecil: Cats on Track (Illus. by Murphy, Kelly)*
    c SLJ - v61 - i8 - August 2015 - p88(1) [51-500]

Martin, Lori Latrice - *Black Asset Poverty and the Enduring Racial Divide*
    CS - v44 - i2 - March 2015 - p232-233 [501+]
    ERS - v38 - i3 - March 2015 - p473(3) [501+]

Martin, Luisge - *The Same City*
    KR - July 1 2015 - pNA [51-500]
    PW - v262 - i28 - July 13 2015 - p42(2) [51-500]

Martin, Lynn B. - *Integrative Organismal Biology*
    QRB - v90 - i4 - Dec 2015 - p431(2) [501+]

Martin, Madeline - *Deception of a Highlander*
    PW - v262 - i9 - March 2 2015 - p69(2) [51-500]
    y VOYA - v38 - i2 - June 2015 - p65(1) [51-500]
Enchantment of a Highlander
    PW - v262 - i46 - Nov 16 2015 - p62(1) [51-500]
Possession of a Highlander
    PW - v262 - i23 - June 8 2015 - p45(1) [51-500]
    RVBW - August 2015 - pNA [501+]

Martin, Marc - *A River (Illus. by Martin, Marc)*
    c Magpies - v30 - i1 - March 2015 - p30(1) [501+]

Martin, Margaret - *Judging Positivism*
    Law Q Rev - v131 - April 2015 - p335-338 [501+]

Martin, Michael - *Literature and the Encounter with God in Post-Reformation England*
    Ren Q - v68 - i3 - Fall 2015 - p1054-1056 [501+]
    Sev Cent N - v73 - i1-2 - Spring-Summer 2015 - p29(7) [501+]

Martin, Nancy - *Miss Ruffles Inherits Everything*
    BL - v112 - i3 - Oct 1 2015 - p27(1) [51-500]
    KR - Sept 1 2015 - pNA [51-500]
    PW - v262 - i37 - Sept 14 2015 - p43(2) [51-500]

Martin, Philippe - *Hyper Nature*
    LJ - v140 - i20 - Dec 1 2015 - p126(1) [51-500]

Martin, Randall - *Shakespeare and Ecology*
    TimHES - i2226 - Oct 22 2015 - p47(1) [501+]

Martin, Randolph M. - *Realistic Retirement for Realistic People: Look Before You Leap*
    SPBW - July 2015 - pNA [51-500]

Martin, Richard - *Coal Wars*
    KR - Feb 15 2015 - pNA [501+]

Martin, Roberto - *Roberto's New Vegan Cooking: 125 Easy, Delicious, Real Food Recipes*
    PW - v262 - i20 - May 18 2015 - p79(1) [51-500]

Martin, Roderick - *Constructing Capitalisms: Transforming Business Systems in Central and Eastern Europe*
    E-A St - v67 - i9 - Nov 2015 - p1501(2) [501+]

Martin, Roger L. - *Getting beyond Better: How Social Entrepreneurship Works*
    LJ - v140 - i19 - Nov 15 2015 - p94(1) [51-500]

Martin, Ruth - *My Amazing Body (Illus. by Sanders, Allan)*
    c SLJ - v61 - i6 - June 2015 - p136(1) [51-500]
On the Move (Illus. by Sanders, Allan)
    c SLJ - v61 - i6 - June 2015 - p136(1) [51-500]

Martin, Sasha - *Life from Scratch: A Memoir of Food, Family, and Forgiveness*
    BL - v111 - i11 - Feb 1 2015 - p8(1) [51-500]
    LJ - v140 - i5 - March 15 2015 - p128(2) [51-500]
    People - v83 - i11 - March 16 2015 - p41(NA) [501+]
    PW - v262 - i1 - Jan 5 2015 - p66(1) [51-500]

Martin, Stephen W. - *Robot Smash! (Illus. by Solon, Juan Carlos)*
    c HB Guide - v26 - i2 - Fall 2015 - p15(1) [51-500]
    KR - Feb 1 2015 - pNA [51-500]

Martin, Steve - *The Wacky and Wonderful World through Numbers: Over 2,000 Figures and Facts*
  c SLJ - v61 - i5 - May 2015 - p140(3) [51-500]
Martin, Steve (b. 1962-) - *Numerolandia: El Mundo en Mas de 2,000 Cifras y Datos (Illus. by Pinder, Andrew)*
  c SLJ - v61 - i7 - July 2015 - p108(1) [51-500]
Martin, Steve J. - *The Small Big: Small Changes That Spark Big Influence (Read by Chamberlain, Mike). Audiobook Review*
  BL - v111 - i16 - April 15 2015 - p62(1) [51-500]
Martin, Thomas R. - *Alexander the Great. The Story of an Ancient Life*
  Class R - v65 - i1 - April 2015 - p177-179 [501+]
  Ancient Rome: From Romulus to Justinian
  Class R - v65 - i2 - Oct 2015 - p519-520 [501+]
Martin, Timothy - *Grief, Folly, Love: Searching for Truth in War*
  KR - August 1 2015 - pNA [501+]
Martin, Tovah - *The Indestructible Houseplant: 200 Beautiful Plants That Everyone Can Grow*
  BL - v111 - i19-20 - June 1 2015 - p18(2) [51-500]
  NYTBR - May 31 2015 - p36(L) [501+]
Martin, Valerie - *The Ghost of the Mary Celeste*
  NYTBR - April 26 2015 - p28(L) [501+]
  Sea Lovers: Selected Stories
  KR - June 15 2015 - pNA [501+]
  NYTBR - August 9 2015 - p21(L) [501+]
Martin, Vanessa - *Iran between Islamic Nationalism and Secularism: The Constitutional Revolution of 1906*
  AHR - v120 - i2 - April 2015 - p751-752 [501+]
Martin, Waldo E. - *Black against Empire: The History and Politics of the Black Panther Party*
  AJS - v121 - i1 - July 2015 - p303(4) [501+]
  Historian - v77 - i2 - Summer 2015 - p323(2) [501+]
Martin, Wednesday - *Primates of Park Avenue*
  Econ - v415 - i8943 - June 20 2015 - p82(US) [501+]
  Ent W - i1367 - June 12 2015 - p81(1) [501+]
  LJ - v140 - i10 - June 1 2015 - p120(2) [501+]
  NYT - June 4 2015 - pC1(L) [501+]
  NYTBR - May 31 2015 - p21(L) [501+]
  Spec - v328 - i9751 - July 18 2015 - p35(1) [501+]
  NYT - June 8 2015 - pB6(L) [501+]
  Bus W - i4430 - June 8 2015 - p83(1) [501+]
  KR - April 1 2015 - pNA [501+]
Martin, William Patrick - *The Mother of All Booklists: The 500 Most Recommended Nonfiction Reads for Ages 3 to 103*
  LJ - v140 - i2 - Feb 1 2015 - p107(2) [51-500]
Martineau, Chantal - *How the Gringos Stole Tequila*
  KR - March 1 2015 - pNA [501+]
Martineau, Paul - *Minor White: Manifestations of the Spirit*
  G&L Rev W - v22 - i5 - Sept-Oct 2015 - p26(3) [501+]
Martineau, Susan - *Slimy Science and Awesome Experiments (Illus. by Ursell, Martin)*
  SLJ - v61 - i3 - March 2015 - p171(1) [51-500]
Martinello, Marian - *Chili Queen: Mi Historia*
  y KR - Jan 15 2015 - pNA [51-500]
  y SLJ - v61 - i3 - March 2015 - p160(2) [51-500]
Martinez, Angie - *Healthy Latin Eating: Our Favorite Family Recipes Remixed*
  LJ - v140 - i3 - Feb 15 2015 - p122(4) [501+]
Martinez, Anne M. - *Catholic Borderlands: Mapping Catholicism onto American Empire, 1905-1935*
  HAHR - v95 - i4 - Nov 2015 - p721-723 [501+]
  HNet - June 2015 - pNA [501+]
Martinez, Claudia Guadalupe - *Pig Park*
  y CCB-B - v68 - i5 - Jan 2015 - p267(1) [51-500]
  y HB Guide - v26 - i1 - Spring 2015 - p116(1) [51-500]
  RVBW - Jan 2015 - pNA [51-500]
Martinez, Domingo - *My Heart Is a Drunken Compass: A Memoir*
  NYTBR - Jan 11 2015 - p12(L) [501+]
Martinez, Ernesto Javier - *On Making Sense: Queer Race Narratives of Intelligibility*
  AL - v87 - i2 - June 2015 - p415-417 [501+]
Martinez, J. Michael - *Coming for to Carry Me Home: Race in America from Abolitionism to Jim Crow*
  Historian - v77 - i1 - Spring 2015 - p130(2) [501+]
Martinez, Jaime Amanda - *Confederate Slave Impressment in the Upper South*
  JSH - v81 - i1 - Feb 2015 - p202(2) [501+]
Martinez, Jessica - *Kiss Kill Vanish*
  y HB Guide - v26 - i1 - Spring 2015 - p116(1) [51-500]
  y Res Links - v20 - i3 - Feb 2015 - p32(1) [51-500]

Martinez, Maria Del Carmen - *Veracruz 1519: Los bombres de Cortes*
  HAHR - v95 - i1 - Feb 2015 - p149-150 [501+]
Martinez, Michael J. - *The Venusian Gambit*
  PW - v262 - i13 - March 30 2015 - p59(2) [51-500]
Martinez, Oscar - *A History of Violence*
  KR - Jan 1 2016 - pNA [501+]
Martinez, Pedro - *Pedro*
  CSM - July 23 2015 - pNA [501+]
Martinez, Peggy - *Time Warper: Fated*
  y SLJ - v61 - i12 - Dec 2015 - p124(1) [51-500]
Martini, Steve - *The Enemy Inside: A Paul Madriani Novel*
  PW - v262 - i13 - March 30 2015 - p52(1) [51-500]
Martiniello, Marco - *An Introduction to International Migration Studies: European Perspectives*
  ERS - v38 - i3 - March 2015 - p499(3) [501+]
Martins, Isabel Minhos - *The World in a Second (Illus. by Carvalho, Bernardo)*
  c HB Guide - v26 - i2 - Fall 2015 - p43(1) [51-500]
  c KR - March 1 2015 - pNA [51-500]
  c PW - v262 - i8 - Feb 23 2015 - p73(2) [51-500]
  c SLJ - v61 - i5 - May 2015 - p88(2) [51-500]
Martinsen, Joel - *The Dark Forest*
  BL - v111 - i22 - August 1 2015 - p42(1) [51-500]
  TLS - i5872 - Oct 16 2015 - p20(1) [501+]
  PW - v262 - i28 - July 13 2015 - p50(1) [51-500]
Marts, Doreen Mulryan - *Even Monsters Say Good Night (Illus. by Marts, Doreen Mulryan)*
  c KR - August 1 2015 - pNA [51-500]
  c PW - v262 - i20 - May 18 2015 - p64(1) [51-500]
Martschini, Elisabeth - *Nibelungenlied und Nibelungensage: Kommentierte Bibliographie 1945-2010*
  JEGP - v114 - i1 - Jan 2015 - p127(3) [501+]
Martschukat, Jurgen - *Violence and Visibility in Modern History*
  HNet - Feb 2015 - pNA [501+]
Marugg, Tip - *The Roar of Morning*
  PW - v262 - i35 - August 31 2015 - p59(1) [51-500]
Maruno, Jennifer - *Cherry Blossom Baseball*
  c KR - Sept 15 2015 - pNA [51-500]
Marvel, William - *Lincoln's Autocrat: The Life of Edwin Stanton*
  J Mil H - v79 - i3 - July 2015 - p833-835 [501+]
  LJ - v140 - i3 - Feb 15 2015 - p108(1) [51-500]
Marven, Lyn - *Emerging German-Language Novelists of the Twenty-First Century*
  MLR - v110 - i3 - July 2015 - p914-915 [501+]
Marvin, Cate - *Oracle*
  BL - v111 - i14 - March 15 2015 - p39(2) [51-500]
  LJ - v140 - i5 - March 15 2015 - p110(1) [51-500]
  PW - v262 - i7 - Feb 16 2015 - p158(2) [51-500]
Marwood, Alex - *The Killer Next Door (Read by Church, Imogen). Audiobook Review*
  LJ - v140 - i3 - Feb 15 2015 - p58(1) [51-500]
  The Killer Next Door
  PW - v262 - i8 - Feb 23 2015 - p70(1) [51-500]
Marwood, Lorraine - *Celebrating Australia*
  y Magpies - v30 - i1 - March 2015 - p38(1) [51-500]
Marx, Ive - *Minimum Income Protection in FLux*
  CS - v44 - i2 - March 2015 - p233-234 [501+]
Marx, Patricia - *Let's Be Less Stupid: An Attempt to Maintain My Mental Faculties*
  KR - May 15 2015 - pNA [51-500]
  Nature - v523 - i7559 - July 9 2015 - p157(1) [51-500]
  NYT - August 6 2015 - pC1(L) [501+]
  PW - v262 - i21 - May 25 2015 - p50(2) [51-500]
Marx, Ursula - *Walter Benjamin's Archive: Images, Texts, Signs*
  NS - v144 - i5284 - Oct 16 2015 - p44(3) [501+]
Marx, W. David - *Ametora: How Japan Saved American Style*
  LJ - v140 - i20 - Dec 1 2015 - p99(2) [501+]
  PW - v262 - i39 - Sept 28 2015 - p71(2) [51-500]
Marxistische Geschichtskulturen und soziale Bewegungen wahrend des Kalten Krieges in Westeuropa
  HNet - May 2015 - pNA [501+]
Marxsen, Patti M. - *Helene Schweitzer: A Life of Her Own*
  RVBW - Oct 2015 - pNA [501+]
Marzluff, John - *Welcome to Subirdia: Sharing Our Neighborhoods with Wrens, Robins, Woodpeckers, and Other Wildlife*
  Am Bio T - v77 - i6 - August 2015 - p469(2) [501+]
Marzo, Bridget - *Tiz and Ott's Big Draw (Illus. by Marzo, Bridget)*
  c KR - Sept 15 2015 - pNA [51-500]
  c SLJ - v61 - i11 - Nov 2015 - p84(1) [51-500]

Mascareno, Aldo - *Legitimization in World Society*
  CS - v44 - i1 - Jan 2015 - p89-90 [501+]
Maschari, Jennifer - *The Remarkable Journey of Charlie Price*
  c KR - Nov 15 2015 - pNA [51-500]
Masciola, Carol - *The Yearbook*
  y KR - Sept 15 2015 - pNA [51-500]
  y SLJ - v61 - i10 - Oct 2015 - p114(1) [51-500]
  y VOYA - v38 - i4 - Oct 2015 - p75(1) [51-500]
Mascolo, Michael F. - *8 Keys to Old School Parenting for Modern-Day Families*
  Bwatch - August 2015 - pNA [51-500]
  PW - v262 - i14 - April 6 2015 - p54(1) [51-500]
Masear, Terry - *Fastest Things on Wings: Rescuing Hummingbirds in Hollywood*
  BL - v111 - i18 - May 15 2015 - p8(1) [51-500]
  KR - April 15 2015 - pNA [501+]
Masello, Robert - *The Einstein Prophecy*
  PW - v262 - i11 - March 16 2015 - p67(1) [51-500]
Masessa, Ed - *Scarecrow Magic (Illus. by Myers, Matt)*
  c HB - v91 - i5 - Sept-Oct 2015 - p68(2) [51-500]
  c KR - August 1 2015 - pNA [51-500]
  c PW - v262 - i30 - July 27 2015 - p63(1) [51-500]
  c PW - v262 - i49 - Dec 2 2015 - p63(1) [51-500]
  c SLJ - v61 - i9 - Sept 2015 - p108(1) [51-500]
Mash, Holly - *The Holistic Cat: A Complete Guide to Natural Health Care*
  LJ - v140 - i9 - May 15 2015 - p99(1) [51-500]
Maskame, Estelle - *Did I Mention I Love You?*
  y SLJ - v61 - i12 - Dec 2015 - p124(2) [51-500]
  y VOYA - v38 - i5 - Dec 2015 - p60(1) [51-500]
Maskill, Alexander - *The Hive Construct*
  PW - v262 - i45 - Nov 9 2015 - p41(1) [51-500]
Mason, Conrad - *The Watchmen of Port Fayt*
  c CCB-B - v69 - i2 - Oct 2015 - p100(1) [51-500]
  c KR - June 1 2015 - pNA [51-500]
  c SLJ - v61 - i9 - Sept 2015 - p142(1) [51-500]
Mason, Courtney W. - *Spirits of the Rockies: Reasserting an Indigenous Presence in Banff National Park*
  Beav - v95 - i4 - August-Sept 2015 - p71(2) [501+]
  Can Hist R - v96 - i2 - June 2015 - p303(2) [501+]
Mason, Eric E. - *Reading 1-2 Peter and Jude: A Resource for Students*
  Intpr - v69 - i1 - Jan 2015 - p124(1) [51-500]
Mason, J.D. - *Finding Amos*
  BL - v112 - i4 - Oct 15 2015 - p16(1) [51-500]
Mason, Mary Ann - *Do Babies Matter? Gender and Family in the Ivory Tower*
  J Hi E - v86 - i2 - March-April 2015 - p326(4) [501+]
Mason, Michael - *Oldenglen*
  c PW - v262 - i50 - Dec 7 2015 - p85(2) [51-500]
Mason, Paul (b. 1960-) - *PostCapitalism: A Guide to Our Future*
  KR - Nov 15 2015 - pNA [501+]
  NS - v144 - i5276 - August 21 2015 - p48(1) [501+]
  PW - v262 - i51 - Dec 14 2015 - p73(2) [51-500]
  TLS - i5869 - Sept 25 2015 - p3(2) [501+]
Mason, Paul
  TLS - i5854 - June 12 2015 - p13(1) [501+]
Mason, Paul (b. 1967-) - *Understanding Computer Safety*
  c Sch Lib - v63 - i3 - Autumn 2015 - p175(1) [51-500]
  Understanding Computing Series
  c HB Guide - v26 - i2 - Fall 2015 - p146(1) [51-500]
Mason, Prue - *Zafir: Through My Eyes*
  y Magpies - v30 - i2 - May 2015 - p36(1) [51-500]
Mason, Rhonda - *The Empress Game*
  BL - v111 - i21 - July 1 2015 - p46(1) [51-500]
  PW - v262 - i23 - June 8 2015 - p43(1) [51-500]
Mason, Robert - *Seeking a New Majority: The Republican Party and American Politics, 1960-1980*
  Historian - v77 - i1 - Spring 2015 - p131(2) [501+]
Mason, Robin - *Oldenglen*
  KR - Nov 15 2015 - pNA [51-500]
Mason, Roger A. - *Andrew Melville (1545-1622): Writings, Reception, and Reputation*
  Sev Cent N - v73 - i1-2 - Spring-Summer 2015 - p15(5) [501+]
  Six Ct J - v46 - i3 - Fall 2015 - p678-679 [501+]
Mason, Sandy - *Silver Voyage*
  KR - August 15 2015 - pNA [51-500]
Mason, Sophie - *Hunter's Moon*
  y Magpies - v30 - i3 - July 2015 - p42(2) [501+]
Mason, Susan Anne - *A Worthy Heart*
  PW - v262 - i45 - Nov 9 2015 - p45(1) [51-500]
Mason, Thomas A. - *Writing Local History Today: A Guide to Researching, Publishing, and Marketing Your*

Book
Pub Hist - v37 - i1 - Feb 2015 - p144(3) [501+]

Mass, Wendy - *Graceful (Read by McInerney, Kathleen). Audiobook Review*
c SLJ - v61 - i8 - August 2015 - p50(1) [51-500]
Graceful
y HB Guide - v26 - i2 - Fall 2015 - p93(1) [51-500]
c Teach Lib - v42 - i5 - June 2015 - p61(1) [51-500]
Space Taxi: Archie Takes Flight
c BL - v111 - i9-10 - Jan 1 2015 - p39(2) [501+]
Water Planet Rescue (Illus. by Gravel, Elise)
c HB Guide - v26 - i1 - Spring 2015 - p62(1) [51-500]

Massa, Michael A. - *The Boy Who Stopped Time (Illus. by Joharapurkar, Pritali)*
c CH Bwatch - Oct 2015 - pNA [51-500]

Massaad, Barbara Abdeni - *Soup for Syria: Recipes to Celebrate Our Shared Humanity*
LJ - v140 - i20 - Dec 1 2015 - p124(3) [51-500]

Massey, Cynthia L. - *Death of a Texas Ranger: A True Story of Murder and Vengeance on the Texas Frontier*
SHQ - v118 - i4 - April 2015 - p436-437 [501+]

Massey, David - *Taken*
y HB Guide - v26 - i1 - Spring 2015 - p116(1) [51-500]

Massey, Douglas S. - *Climbing Mount Laurel: The Struggle for Affordable Housing and Social Mobility in an American Suburb*
AJS - v121 - i1 - July 2015 - p290(3) [501+]
CS - v44 - i1 - Jan 2015 - p91-92 [501+]

Massey, Edward - *Every Soul Is Free*
Roundup M - v22 - i6 - August 2015 - p31(1) [501+]

Massey, Jeremy - *The Last Four Days of Paddy Buckley*
BL - v111 - i18 - May 15 2015 - p28(1) [51-500]
KR - April 1 2015 - pNA [51-500]

Massey, Joseph - *Illocality*
NYTBR - Dec 27 2015 - p19(L) [501+]
PW - v262 - i29 - July 20 2015 - p166(1) [51-500]

Massey, Peter - *Beginner's Guide to Mosaic*
LJ - v140 - i20 - Dec 1 2015 - p101(1) [51-500]

Massey, Sujata - *The Kizuna Coast*
PW - v262 - i4 - Jan 26 2015 - p152(1) [51-500]

Massey, Tyler James - *Chasing the Moon (Illus. by Chatterjee, Somnath)*
c CH Bwatch - April 2015 - pNA [51-500]

Massie, Allan - *End Games in Bordeaux*
Spec - v329 - i9763 - Oct 10 2015 - p41(1) [501+]

Massie, Felix - *Terry Perkins and his Upside Down Frown*
c Sch Lib - v63 - i4 - Winter 2015 - p219(2) [51-500]

Massing, J.M. - *King's College Chapel 1515-2015: Art, Music and Religion in Cambridge*
TLS - i5864-5865 - August 21 2015 - p26(2) [501+]

Massini, Sarah - *Love Always Everywhere (Illus. by Massini, Sarah)*
c HB Guide - v26 - i2 - Fall 2015 - p15(1) [51-500]
c NYTBR - Feb 8 2015 - p24(L) [501+]

Massle, Allan - *Klaus*
WLT - v89 - i2 - March-April 2015 - p69(1) [51-500]

Masson, Andre - *Glossaire j'y serre mes gloses*
FS - v69 - i3 - July 2015 - p410-411 [501+]

Massoudi, Cyrus - *Land of the Turquoise Mountains: Journeys Across Iran*
TLS - i5869 - Sept 25 2015 - p23(1) [501+]

Massumi, Brian - *Ontopower: War, Powers, and the State of Perception*
LJ - v140 - i10 - June 1 2015 - p106(2) [51-500]

Mast, Jason L. - *The Performative Presidency: Crisis and Resurrection during the Clinton Years*
CS - v44 - i4 - July 2015 - p535-537 [501+]

Masterman, Becky - *Fear the Darkness (Read by Toren, Suzanne). Audiobook Review*
BL - v111 - i21 - July 1 2015 - p78(1) [51-500]
LJ - v140 - i8 - May 1 2015 - p41(1) [51-500]
Fear the Darkness (Illus. by Masterman, Becky)
BL - v111 - i9-10 - Jan 1 2015 - p46(1) [51-500]
NYT - Jan 15 2015 - pC6(L) [501+]

Masters, Ben - *Branded*
RVBW - June 2015 - pNA [51-500]

Masters, Blake - *Zero to One: Notes on Startups, or How to Build the Future*
Barron's - v95 - i1 - Jan 5 2015 - p17(1) [501+]
Har Bus R - v93 - i3 - March 2015 - p126(2) [501+]

Masters, Bruce - *The Arabs of the Ottoman Empire, 1516-1918: A Social and Cultural History*
AHR - v120 - i1 - Feb 2015 - p362(1) [501+]

Masters, Priscilla - *Guilty Waters*
BL - v111 - i13 - March 1 2015 - p24(1) [51-500]
PW - v262 - i4 - Jan 26 2015 - p152(1) [51-500]
Recalled to Death
BL - v112 - i2 - Sept 15 2015 - p32(2) [51-500]
PW - v262 - i33 - August 17 2015 - p54(2) [51-500]

Masters, Riley - *Fortune Hunters*
KR - Jan 1 2015 - pNA [501+]

Masterson, Mark - *Man to Man: Desire, Homosociality, and Authority in Late-Roman Manhood*
HNet - April 2015 - pNA [501+]

Masterton, Graham - *Blood Sisters*
PW - v262 - i50 - Dec 7 2015 - p72(1) [501+]
Figures of Fear
BL - v111 - i11 - Feb 1 2015 - p32(1) [51-500]

Mastriano, Douglas V. - *Alvin York: A New Biography of the Hero of the Argonne*
J Mil H - v79 - i4 - Oct 2015 - p1170-1171 [501+]
Parameters - v45 - i2 - Summer 2015 - p149(2) [501+]

Mastrocinque, A. - *Demeter, Isis, Vestra, and Cybele. Studies in Greek and Roman Religion in Honour of Giulia Sfameni Gasparro*
Class R - v65 - i1 - April 2015 - p170-172 [501+]

Masur, Louis P. - *Lincoln's Last Speech: Wartime Reconstruction and the Crisis of Reunion*
KR - Feb 1 2015 - pNA [501+]
Roundup M - v22 - i4 - April 2015 - p26(1) [501+]
TimHES - i2203 - May 14 2015 - p49(1) [501+]

Mata, Julie - *Bride of Slug Man*
c KR - March 15 2015 - pNA [51-500]
Kate Walden Directs: Bride of Slug Man
c CCB-B - v69 - i1 - Sept 2015 - p38(1) [51-500]
y HB Guide - v26 - i2 - Fall 2015 - p93(1) [51-500]

Matalon, Ronit - *The Sound of Our Steps*
BL - v111 - i21 - July 1 2015 - p33(1) [51-500]
KR - June 1 2015 - pNA [51-500]

Mateland, Vanessa - *Cortes Connection*
KR - August 1 2015 - pNA [51-500]

Mateo, Jose Manuel - *Migrant (Illus. by Pedro, Javier Martinez)*
c BL - v111 - i9-10 - Jan 1 2015 - pS4(8) [501+]

Mateos, Pablo - *Names, Ethnicity and Populations: Tracing Identity in Space*
ERS - v38 - i8 - August 2015 - p1427(3) [501+]

Matera, Frank J. - *God's Saving Grace: A Pauline Theology*
BTB - v45 - i3 - August 2015 - p187(3) [501+]

Matera, Marc - *The Women's War of 1929: Gender and Violence in Colonial Nigeria*
AHR - v120 - i1 - Feb 2015 - p374-375 [501+]

Matharu, Taran - *The Novice*
y KR - March 1 2015 - pNA [51-500]
c Sch Lib - v63 - i2 - Summer 2015 - p119(1) [51-500]
y SLJ - v61 - i3 - March 2015 - p160(1) [51-500]
y VOYA - v38 - i1 - April 2015 - p81(1) [51-500]

Matheny, Bill - *Catwoman Gets Busted by the Batman (Illus. by Jones, Christopher)*
c HB Guide - v26 - i1 - Spring 2015 - p86(1) [51-500]
Frozen Solid by Mr. Freeze! (Illus. by Jones, Christopher)
c HB Guide - v26 - i1 - Spring 2015 - p86(1) [51-500]

Matheny, Mike - *The Matheny Manifesto: A Young Manager's Old-School Views on Success in Sports and Life*
LJ - v140 - i3 - Feb 15 2015 - p103(2) [51-500]

Mathers, Petra - *When Aunt Mattie Got Her Wings (Illus. by Mathers, Petra)*
c BL - v112 - i6 - Nov 15 2015 - p48(1) [51-500]
c HB Guide - v26 - i1 - Spring 2015 - p38(1) [51-500]

Mathes, Valerie Sherer - *The Woman's National Indian Association: A History*
Roundup M - v23 - i1 - Oct 2015 - p34(1) [501+]

Matheson, Christie - *Touch the Brightest Star (Illus. by Matheson, Christie)*
c BL - v111 - i18 - May 15 2015 - p59(1) [51-500]
c HB - v91 - i3 - May-June 2015 - p92(2) [51-500]
c HB Guide - v26 - i2 - Fall 2015 - p15(1) [51-500]
c KR - Feb 1 2015 - pNA [51-500]
SLJ - v61 - i3 - March 2015 - p121(1) [51-500]

Matheson, M.J. - *Hokey Dowa Gerda and the Snowflake Girl*
c Res Links - v20 - i5 - June 2015 - p6(1) [51-500]

Matheson, Neil - *The Machine and the Ghost: Technology and Spiritualism in Nineteenth-to Twenty-First-Century Art and Culture*
T&C - v56 - i1 - Jan 2015 - p286-287 [501+]

Mathew, Nicholas - *Political Beethoven*
Notes - v72 - i2 - Dec 2015 - p341(3) [501+]

Mathews, Ellen - *A Match to Die For*
KR - May 15 2015 - pNA [501+]

Mathews, Francine - *Too Bad to Die (Read by Brenher, Matthew). Audiobook Review*
LJ - v140 - i10 - June 1 2015 - p61(1) [51-500]
Too Bad to Die (Read by Brenner, Matthew). Audiobook Review
PW - v262 - i21 - May 25 2015 - p54(1) [51-500]
Too Bad to Die
BL - v111 - i11 - Feb 1 2015 - p28(2) [51-500]
KR - Jan 1 2015 - pNA [501+]
NYTBR - May 31 2015 - p16(L) [501+]
PW - v262 - i4 - Jan 26 2015 - p149(1) [51-500]

Mathews, John Joseph - *Old Three Toes and Other Tales of Survival and Extinction*
Roundup M - v22 - i5 - June 2015 - p39(1) [501+]

Mathieu, Jennifer - *Devoted (Read by Grace, Jennifer). Audiobook Review*
y SLJ - v61 - i12 - Dec 2015 - p80(1) [51-500]
Devoted
y BL - v111 - i19-20 - June 1 2015 - p95(1) [51-500]
y CCB-B - v69 - i2 - Oct 2015 - p100(2) [51-500]
y HB Guide - v26 - i2 - Fall 2015 - p130(1) [51-500]
y KR - April 15 2015 - pNA [51-500]
y PW - v262 - i16 - April 20 2015 - p76(2) [51-500]
y SLJ - v61 - i5 - May 2015 - p114(1) [51-500]
y VOYA - v38 - i3 - August 2015 - p64(2) [51-500]
The Truth about Alice (Read by several narrators). Audiobook Review
y SLJ - v61 - i6 - June 2015 - p67(1) [51-500]

Mathys, Ted - *Null Set*
PW - v262 - i20 - May 18 2015 - p62(1) [51-500]

Matilsky, Barbara C. - *Vanishing Ice: Alpine and Polar Landscapes in Art, 1775-2012*
HNet - July 2015 - pNA [501+]

Matis, Aspen - *Girl in the Woods: A Memoir*
y BL - v112 - i1 - Sept 1 2015 - p29(1) [51-500]
KR - July 15 2015 - pNA [51-500]
NYTBR - Nov 15 2015 - p30(L) [501+]

Matison, Jimbo - *I'm Going to Catch My Tail!*
c HB Guide - v26 - i2 - Fall 2015 - p15(1) [51-500]

Matossian, Bedross Der - *Shattered Dreams of Revolution: From Liberty to Violence in the Late Ottoman Empire*
IJMES - v47 - i4 - Nov 2015 - p821-824 [501+]

Matovina, Timothy - *Recollections of a Tejano Life: Antonio Menchaca in Texas History*
JSH - v81 - i2 - May 2015 - p450(2) [501+]

Matras, Varon - *The Romani Gypsies*
For Aff - v94 - i3 - May-June 2015 - pNA [501+]

Matras, Yaron - *I Met Lucky People: The Story of the Romani Gypsies*
TLS - i5844 - April 3 2015 - p26(1) [501+]

Matray, James I. - *The Ashgate Research Companion to the Korean War*
J Mil H - v79 - i1 - Jan 2015 - p257-258 [501+]
Northeast Asia and the Legacy of Harry S. Truman: Japan, China, and the Two Koreas
HNet - Jan 2015 - pNA [501+]

Matson, Lynne - *Nil*
y Teach Lib - v42 - i3 - Feb 2015 - p28(4) [501+]
Nil Unlocked
y BL - v111 - i18 - May 15 2015 - p66(1) [51-500]
y HB Guide - v26 - i2 - Fall 2015 - p130(1) [51-500]
y KR - Feb 15 2015 - pNA [51-500]
y SLJ - v61 - i3 - March 2015 - p160(1) [51-500]
y VOYA - v38 - i2 - June 2015 - p79(2) [51-500]

Matson, Stacey - *A Year in the Life of a Complete and Total Genius*
c BL - v112 - i5 - Nov 1 2015 - p63(1) [51-500]
c PW - v262 - i34 - August 24 2015 - p81(1) [51-500]
c Res Links - v20 - i3 - Feb 2015 - p14(1) [501+]
y Sch Lib - v63 - i4 - Winter 2015 - p248(1) [51-500]
c SLJ - v61 - i10 - Oct 2015 - p104(1) [51-500]

Matt, Susan J. - *Doing Emotions History*
AHR - v120 - i1 - Feb 2015 - p187-188 [501+]

Matta, William - *The Solution: A Blueprint for Change and Happiness*
SPBW - Nov 2015 - pNA [51-500]

Mattehews, Gary R. - *More American Than Southern: Kentucky, Slavery, and the War for an American Ideology, 1828-1861*
JSH - v81 - i4 - Nov 2015 - p968(2) [501+]

Matteoni, Norman E. - *Prairie Man: The Struggle Between Sitting Bull and the Indian Agent James McLaughlin*
LJ - v140 - i9 - May 15 2015 - p92(1) [51-500]

Matter, E. Ann - *From Knowledge to Beatitude: St. Victor, Twelfth-Century Schools, and Beyond: Essays in Honor*

of Grover A. Zinn, Jr.
    CHR - v101 - i3 - Summer 2015 - p618(2) [501+]
Mattern, Joanne - *Careers in Finance*
  y SLJ - v61 - i9 - Sept 2015 - p176(1) [51-500]
Helping Children with Life-Threatening Medical Issues
  c BL - v111 - i16 - April 15 2015 - p45(1) [501+]
Wyatt Earp
  c BL - v112 - i1 - Sept 1 2015 - p96(2) [501+]
Mattern, Susan P. - *The Prince of Medicine: Galen in the Roman Empire*
    Class R - v65 - i1 - April 2015 - p85-87 [501+]
Matterson, Stephen - *Melville: Fashioning in Modernity*
    TLS - i5836 - Feb 6 2015 - p21(1) [501+]
Mattes, Kyle - *The Positive Case for Negative Campaigning*
    Pub Op Q - v79 - i3 - Fall 2015 - p825(3) [501+]
Matthaus, Jurgen - *War, Pacification, and Mass Murder, 1939: The Einsatzgruppen in Poland*
    J Mil H - v79 - i3 - July 2015 - p874-875 [501+]
Matthee, Rudi - *Persia in Crisis: Safavaid Decline and the Fall of Isfahan*
    IJMES - v47 - i4 - Nov 2015 - p815-818 [501+]
Matthes, Dave - *Bar Nights*
    RVBW - Oct 2015 - pNA [51-500]
Matthew, Adam - *American History, 1493-1945*
    BL - v112 - i2 - Sept 15 2015 - p9(1) [51-500]
History of America in 50 Documents
    LJ - v140 - i9 - May 15 2015 - p94(2) [501+]
Matthew, Dayna Bowen - *Just Medicine*
    KR - Oct 15 2015 - pNA [501+]
Matthews, Ben - *The Pursuit of Justice*
    KR - March 15 2015 - pNA [501+]
Matthews, David - *Medievalism: A Critical History*
    Med R - Sept 2015 - pNA [501+]
    TLS - i5874 - Oct 30 2015 - p12(1) [501+]
Matthews-Grieco, Sara F. - *Erotic Cultures of Renaissance Italy*
    HER - v130 - i543 - April 2015 - p434(2) [501+]
Matthews, Jason - *Palace of Treason (Read by Bobb, Jeremy). Audiobook Review*
    PW - v262 - i30 - July 27 2015 - p60(1) [51-500]
Palace of Treason
    BL - v111 - i17 - May 1 2015 - p42(1) [51-500]
    KR - May 1 2015 - pNA [501+]
    LJ - v140 - i11 - June 15 2015 - p78(2) [51-500]
    NYTBR - May 31 2015 - p35(L) [501+]
    PW - v262 - i17 - April 27 2015 - p51(1) [51-500]
Matthews, Jenny - *Children Growing Up with War*
  c HB Guide - v26 - i1 - Spring 2015 - p137(1) [51-500]
Matthews, John T. - *William Faulkner in Context*
    TLS - i5846 - April 17 2015 - p26(1) [501+]
Matthews, Michael - *The Civilizing Machine: A Cultural History of Mexican Railroads, 1876-1910*
    AHR - v120 - i1 - Feb 2015 - p299-300 [501+]
    WHQ - v46 - i2 - Summer 2015 - p231-232 [501+]
Matthews, Owen - *Glorious Misadventures: Nikolai Rezanov and the Dream of a Russian America*
    RAH - v43 - i3 - Sept 2015 - p522-527 [501+]
How to Win at High School
  y CCB-B - v68 - i9 - May 2015 - p455(1) [51-500]
  c Nat Post - v17 - i101 - Feb 28 2015 - pWP5(1) [501+]
  y Res Links - v20 - i3 - Feb 2015 - p32(2) [51-500]
Matthews, Penny - *1854: Do You Dare? Eureka Boys*
  y Magpies - v30 - i2 - May 2015 - p38(1) [501+]
Matthews, Peter J. - *On the Trail of Taro: An Exploration of Natural and Cultural History*
    JRAI - v21 - i4 - Dec 2015 - p944(2) [501+]
Matthews, Rupert - *Ninjas*
  c BL - v112 - i3 - Oct 1 2015 - p62(1) [51-500]
Matthews, Samantha - *That Thing You Do with Your Mouth*
    KR - April 1 2015 - pNA [501+]
Matthews, Wade - *The New Left, National Identity, and the Break-up of Britain*
    HER - v130 - i545 - August 2015 - p1058(2) [501+]
    TimHES - i2199 - April 16 2015 - p57-1 [501+]
Matthies, Janna - *Two Is Enough (Illus. by Mourning, Tuesday)*
  c CH Bwatch - Nov 2015 - pNA [51-500]
  c KR - Sept 1 2015 - pNA [51-500]
  c NYTBR - Dec 20 2015 - p15(L) [501+]
  c PW - v262 - i34 - August 24 2015 - p79(1) [51-500]
  c SLJ - v61 - i11 - Nov 2015 - p84(2) [51-500]
Matthiessen, Peter - *In Paradise*
    NYTBR - March 8 2015 - p32(L) [501+]
    Comw - v142 - i5 - March 6 2015 - p28(3) [501+]
Mattich, Alen - *Killing Pilgrim*
    KR - Oct 15 2015 - pNA [51-500]

Zagreb Cowboy
    BL - v111 - i21 - July 1 2015 - p41(1) [51-500]
Mattick, Lindsay - *Finding Winnie: The True Story of the World's Most Famous Bear (Illus. by Blackall, Sophie)*
  c BL - v112 - i1 - Sept 1 2015 - p116(1) [51-500]
  c HB - v91 - i5 - Sept-Oct 2015 - p129(2) [51-500]
  c KR - July 15 2015 - pNA [51-500]
  c NYTBR - Nov 8 2015 - p33(L) [501+]
  c PW - v262 - i29 - July 20 2015 - p195(1) [51-500]
  c PW - v262 - i49 - Dec 2 2015 - p46(1) [51-500]
  c SLJ - v61 - i8 - August 2015 - p122(2) [51-500]
Mattioli, Marco - *Savoia-Marchetti S.79 Sparviero Torpedo-Bomber Units*
    Bwatch - Feb 2015 - pNA [51-500]
Maturana, Andrea - *Life without Nico (Illus. by Olea, Francisco Javier)*
  c KR - Jan 1 2016 - pNA [51-500]
Matustik, Martin Beck - *Out of Silence*
    KR - May 15 2015 - pNA [501+]
Matynia, Elzbieta - *An Uncanny Era: Conversations between Vaclav Havel and Adam Michnik*
    NYRB - v62 - i6 - April 2 2015 - p73(3) [501+]
Matzelle, Helo - *Halo Found Hope: A Memoir*
    RVBW - May 2015 - pNA [501+]
    KR - Feb 1 2015 - pNA [501+]
Matzke, Ann - *You Have a Pet What?! Hedgehog*
  c BL - v112 - i1 - Sept 1 2015 - p97(1) [51-500]
You Have a Pet What?! Mini Horse
  c BL - v112 - i1 - Sept 1 2015 - p97(1) [51-500]
Mauger, Matthew - *Empire of Tea: The Asian Leaf That Conquered the World*
    TLS - i5871 - Oct 9 2015 - p34(1) [501+]
Maul, Stefan M. - *Die Wahrsagekunst im Alten Orient: Zeichen des Himmels und der Erde*
    JNES - v74 - i1 - April 2015 - p133(3) [501+]
Maulucci, Thomas W. Jr. - *GIs in Germany: The Social, Economic, Cultural, and Political History of the American Military Presence*
    GSR - v38 - i1 - Feb 2015 - p218-220 [501+]
Maunsell, Jerome Boyd - *Susan Sontag*
    TLS - i5834 - Jan 23 2015 - p8(2) [501+]
Maupassant, Guy de - *The Necklace and Other Stories: Maupassant for Modern Times*
    LJ - v140 - i9 - May 15 2015 - p84(1) [51-500]
Maupin, Armistead - *Three Days of Anna Madrigal*
    NYTBR - Feb 8 2015 - p28(L) [501+]
Maurer, Gretchen - *Call Me Isis: Egyptian Goddess of Magic (Illus. by Bridges, Shirin Yim)*
  y HB Guide - v26 - i1 - Spring 2015 - p71(1) [51-500]
Maurer, John H. - *At the Crossroads between War and Peace: The London Naval Conference of 1930*
    J Mil H - v79 - i3 - July 2015 - p867-868 [501+]
Maurer, Kathrin - *Visualizing the Past: The Power of the Image in German Historicism*
    GSR - v38 - i3 - Oct 2015 - p661-664 [501+]
Maurer, Michael - *Wales: Die Entdeckung einer Landschaft und eines Volkes durch Deutsche Reisende (1780-1860).*
    Ger Q - v88 - i1 - Wntr 2015 - p111(2) [501+]
Maurer, Tracy Nelson - *Outrageous Car Racing Rivalries*
  c HB Guide - v26 - i2 - Fall 2015 - p198(1) [51-500]
Maurice, Alice - *The Cinema and Its Shadow: Race and Technology in Early Cinema*
    ERS - v38 - i3 - March 2015 - p510(2) [501+]
Mauries, Patrick - *Maison Goossens: Haute Couture Jewelry*
    RVBW - March 2015 - pNA [51-500]
Mauritzson, Erik - *Grendel's Game*
    KR - May 15 2015 - pNA [501+]
    PW - v262 - i20 - May 18 2015 - p65(1) [51-500]
Maus, Derek C. - *Post-Soul Satire: Black Identity after Civil Rights*
    Afr Am R - v48 - i1-2 - Spring-Summer 2015 - p220(3) [501+]
Mavhunga, Clapperton Chakanetsa - *Transient Workspaces: Technologies of Everyday Innovation in Zimbabwe*
    T&C - v56 - i4 - Oct 2015 - p1002-1003 [501+]
Mawby, Spencer - *Ordering Independence: The End of Empire in the Anglophone Caribbean, 1947-69*
    HNet - June 2015 - pNA [501+]
Mawer, Simon - *Tightrope*
    BL - v112 - i6 - Nov 15 2015 - p29(1) [51-500]
    KR - Sept 1 2015 - pNA [501+]
    LJ - v140 - i15 - Sept 15 2015 - p69(1) [51-500]
    NYT - Oct 15 2015 - pC1(L) [501+]
    PW - v262 - i36 - Sept 7 2015 - p43(2) [51-500]
Max - *True Tails from the Dog Park (Illus. by Stricklin, Julie Ann)*
  c CH Bwatch - Jan 2015 - pNA [51-500]

Maxey, Trent E. - *The "Greatest Problem": Religion and State Formation in Meiji Japan*
    HNet - May 2015 - pNA [501+]
    Pac A - v88 - i3 - Sept 2015 - p711 [501+]
Maxim, Hiram S. - *My Life*
    Nature - v520 - i7548 - April 23 2015 - p443(1) [51-500]
Maximos the Confessor - *On Difficulties in the Church Fathers: The Ambigua, vols. 1-2*
    Med R - August 2015 - pNA [501+]
Maxon, H.A. - *Comfort: A Novel of the Reverse Underground Railroad*
    PW - v262 - i20 - May 18 2015 - p60(2) [51-500]
Maxwell, Alyssa - *Murder at Beechwood*
    PW - v262 - i17 - April 27 2015 - p53(1) [51-500]
Murder Most Malicious
    BL - v112 - i7 - Dec 1 2015 - p30(1) [51-500]
    KR - Oct 15 2015 - pNA [51-500]
    PW - v262 - i44 - Nov 2 2015 - p64(1) [51-500]
Maxwell, Angie - *The Indicted South: Public Criticism, Southern Inferiority, and the Politics of Whiteness*
    JSH - v81 - i3 - August 2015 - p762(2) [501+]
The Ongoing Burden of Southern History: Politics and Identity in the Twenty-First-Century South
    JSH - v81 - i1 - Feb 2015 - p251(4) [501+]
Maxwell, Cassandre - *Fur, Fins, and Feathers: Abraham Dee Bartlett and the Invention of the Modern Zoo (Illus. by Maxwell, Cassandre)*
  c KR - May 1 2015 - pNA [51-500]
  c PW - v262 - i29 - July 20 2015 - p190(2) [501+]
  c SLJ - v61 - i9 - Sept 2015 - p179(1) [51-500]
Furs, Fins, and Feathers: Abraham Dee Bartlett and the Invention of the Modern Zoo (Illus. by Maxwell, Cassandre)
  c BL - v112 - i2 - Sept 15 2015 - p57(1) [51-500]
Maxwell, Cathy - *The Match of the Century: Marrying the Duke*
    KR - Sept 15 2015 - pNA [51-500]
    PW - v262 - i42 - Oct 19 2015 - p60(2) [51-500]
Maxwell, Edith - *Farmed and Dangerous*
    BL - v111 - i19-20 - June 1 2015 - p52(2) [51-500]
    KR - March 15 2015 - pNA [51-500]
    PW - v262 - i15 - April 13 2015 - p59(1) [51-500]
Maxwell, John C. - *Sometimes You Win--Sometimes You Learn (Illus. by Bjorkman, Steve)*
  c KR - Nov 15 2015 - pNA [51-500]
Maxwell, Kathleen - *Between Constantinople and Rome: An Illuminated Byzantine Gospel Book (Paris gr. 54) and the Union of Churches*
    Med R - August 2015 - pNA [501+]
Maxwell, Lisa - *Gathering Deep*
  y KR - August 1 2015 - pNA [51-500]
  y SLJ - v61 - i9 - Sept 2015 - p161(1) [51-500]
  y VOYA - v38 - i4 - Oct 2015 - p75(1) [501+]
Unhooked
    KR - Jan 1 2016 - pNA [51-500]
Maxwell, Marcia - *The Rogue Queen*
    PW - v262 - i34 - August 24 2015 - p57(1) [51-500]
Maxwell, Marie - *Maggie: A Girl of the Streets*
  y BL - v111 - i18 - May 15 2015 - p24(1) [51-500]
Maxwell, Nicholas - *Global Philosophy: What Philosophy Ought to Be*
    TimHES - i2185 - Jan 8 2015 - p50-51 [501+]
Maxwell, Virginia - *Istanbul*
    Bwatch - May 2015 - pNA [51-500]
Maxwell, William J. - *F.B. Eyes: How J. Edgar Hoover's Ghostreaders Framed African American Literature*
    Afr Am R - v48 - i1-2 - Spring-Summer 2015 - p215(4) [501+]
    CHE - v61 - i21 - Feb 6 2015 - pNA [501+]
    Nation - v300 - i21 - May 25 2015 - p34(3) [501+]
    TLS - i5852 - May 29 2015 - p13(1) [501+]
May, Allyson N. - *The Fox-Hunting Controversy, 1781-2004*
    HER - v130 - i545 - August 2015 - p1067(2) [501+]
    Historian - v77 - i1 - Spring 2015 - p178(2) [501+]
May, Brian - *Brian May's Red Special*
    RVBW - Jan 2015 - pNA [501+]
May, Edwin C. - *Anomalous Cognition: Remote Viewing Research and Theory*
    JP - v79 - i1 - Spring 2015 - p108(8) [501+]
ESP Wars
    JP - v79 - i1 - Spring 2015 - p115(4) [501+]

May, Eleanor - *Albert Adds Up! (Illus. by Melmon, Deborah)*
  c HB Guide - v26 - i1 - Spring 2015 - p28(1) [51-500]
  c TC Math - v22 - i1 - August 2015 - p52(2) [501+]
  Albert Is Not Scared (Illus. by Melmon, Deborah)
    TC Math - v21 - i6 - Feb 2015 - p382(1) [501+]
  Albert Starts School (Illus. by Melmon, Deborah)
  c CH Bwatch - March 2015 - pNA [51-500]
  c HB Guide - v26 - i2 - Fall 2015 - p44(1) [51-500]
  c KR - June 1 2015 - pNA [51-500]
  Albert the Muffin-Maker (Illus. by Melmon, Deborah)
  c HB - v91 - i1 - Jan-Feb 2015 - p106(2) [501+]
    TC Math - v21 - i6 - Feb 2015 - p382(1) [501+]
  A Beach for Albert (Illus. by Melmon, Deborah)
    TC Math - v21 - i6 - Feb 2015 - p382(1) [501+]
  Lost in the Mouseum (Illus. by Melmon, Deborah)
  c HB Guide - v26 - i2 - Fall 2015 - p44(1) [51-500]
May, Gary - *Bending toward Justice: The Voting Rights Act and the Transformation of American Democracy*
    Am St - v54 - i2 - Summer 2015 - p73-83 [501+]
May, Kayla - *Lulu la tres chic*
  c Res Links - v21 - i1 - Oct 2015 - p52(1) [51-500]
May, Megan - *Raw Organic Goodness: 100 Recipes, 100 Percent Raw and Plant Based, for Everyone Who Loves Food*
    BL - v112 - i5 - Nov 1 2015 - p7(1) [51-500]
May, Nancy - *Dogs Don't Talk*
  c BL - v112 - i3 - Oct 1 2015 - p32(2) [501+]
  y VOYA - v38 - i4 - Oct 2015 - p57(1) [51-500]
May, Peter - *The Black House*
    RVBW - May 2015 - pNA [51-500]
  Entry Island
    KR - July 15 2015 - pNA [51-500]
    Mac - v128 - i39 - Oct 5 2015 - p58(2) [501+]
    PW - v262 - i24 - June 15 2015 - p63(2) [51-500]
  The Lewis Man
    RVBW - June 2015 - pNA [51-500]
  Runaway
    PW - v262 - i51 - Dec 14 2015 - p61(1) [51-500]
May, Reuben A. Buford - *Urban Nightlife: Entertaining Race, Class, and Culture in Public Space*
    AJS - v121 - i2 - Sept 2015 - p609(3) [501+]
May, Robert E. - *Slavery, Race, and Conquest in the Tropics: Lincoln, Douglas, and the Future of Latin America*
    AHR - v120 - i3 - June 2015 - p983-984 [501+]
    JSH - v81 - i3 - August 2015 - p727(2) [501+]
May, Robert L. - *Rudolph Shines Again (Illus. by Caparo, Antonio Javier)*
  c KR - Sept 1 2015 - pNA [51-500]
  c PW - v262 - i37 - Sept 14 2015 - p68(1) [51-500]
  c SLJ - v61 - i10 - Oct 2015 - p65(2) [51-500]
  Rudolph the Red-Nosed Reindeer (Illus. by Caparo, Antonio Javier)
  c HB Guide - v26 - i1 - Spring 2015 - p39(1) [51-500]
May, Stephen - *Wake Up Happy Every Day*
    NYTBR - March 22 2015 - p22(L) [501+]
May, Theresa - *Salmon Is Everything: Community-Based Theatre in the Klamath Watershed*
    Theat J - v67 - i3 - Oct 2015 - p569-571 [501+]
May, Tracy - *Keeping Mother's Secrets*
    PW - v262 - i39 - Sept 28 2015 - p84(1) [51-500]
Mayer, Catherine - *Born to Be King*
    KR - March 1 2015 - pNA [501+]
    People - v83 - i11 - March 16 2015 - p41(NA) [501+]
  Charles: The Heart of a King
    Quad - v59 - i7-8 - July-August 2015 - p140(3) [501+]
    NS - v144 - i5257 - April 10 2015 - p46(2) [501+]
Mayer, Dale - *The Complete Guide to Companion Planting: Everything You Need to Know to Make Your Garden Successful*
    Bwatch - July 2015 - pNA [51-500]
Mayer, Ellen - *A Fish to Feed (Illus. by Hu, Ying-Hwa)*
  c CH Bwatch - Sept 2015 - pNA [51-500]
  c KR - July 1 2015 - pNA [51-500]
  Red Socks (Illus. by Hu, Ying-Hwa)
  c KR - July 1 2015 - pNA [51-500]
Mayer, Hans Eberhard - *Die Siegel der lateinischen Konige von Jerusalem*
    Med R - Sept 2015 - pNA [501+]
Mayer, Hansjorg - *Typo*
    TLS - i5848 - May 1 2015 - p26(1) [501+]
Mayer, Mercer - *Just a Little Love (Illus. by Mayer, Mercer)*
  c HB Guide - v26 - i1 - Spring 2015 - p54(1) [51-500]
  Just a Special Thanksgiving
  c PW - v262 - i34 - August 24 2015 - p80(1) [51-500]

Mayer, Roland - *Horace: Odes Book I*
    Class R - v65 - i1 - April 2015 - p139-141 [501+]
Mayer, Ruth - *Serial Fu Manchu: The Chinese Supervillain and the Spread of Yellow Peril Ideology*
    PHR - v84 - i2 - May 2015 - p271(2) [501+]
Mayer, Thomas F. - *Reforming Reformation*
    CHR - v101 - i4 - Autumn 2015 - p933(3) [501+]
  The Roman Inquisition: A Papal Bureaucracy and Its Laws in the Age of Galileo
    HER - v130 - i542 - Feb 2015 - p189(2) [501+]
    Historian - v77 - i2 - Summer 2015 - p397(2) [501+]
  The Roman Inquisition on the Stage of Italy, c. 1590-1640
    AHR - v120 - i2 - April 2015 - p733-734 [501+]
    CH - v84 - i2 - June 2015 - p443(2) [501+]
    CHR - v101 - i3 - Summer 2015 - p659(3) [501+]
    Isis - v106 - i2 - June 2015 - p436(2) [501+]
  The Roman Inquisition: Trying Galileo
    CH - v84 - i4 - Dec 2015 - p891(3) [501+]
Mayes, April J. - *The Mulatto Republic: Class, Race, and Dominican National Identity*
    AHR - v120 - i1 - Feb 2015 - p308-309 [501+]
    HAHR - v95 - i4 - Nov 2015 - p686-687 [501+]
    HNet - March 2015 - pNA [51-500]
Mayes, Benjamin T.G. - *Luther's Works, vol. 75: Church Postil I*
    Six Ct J - v46 - i2 - Summer 2015 - p460-461 [501+]
  Luther's Works, vol. 76: Church Postil II
    Six Ct J - v46 - i1 - Spring 2015 - p178(3) [501+]
Mayes, Carrie - *Good Posture Made Easy: Look and Feel Your Best for Life*
    SPBW - August 2015 - pNA [51-500]
Mayes, Vernon O. - *Nanise', A Navajo Herbal*
    RVBW - Oct 2015 - pNA [51-500]
Mayew, William J. - *Speech Analysis in Financial Markets*
    AR - v90 - i1 - Jan 2015 - p395(4) [501+]
Mayfield, Dan - *Jasper and the Magpie: Enjoying Special Interests Together (Illus. by Merry, Alex)*
  c CH Bwatch - Feb 2015 - pNA [51-500]
  c CH Bwatch - March 2015 - pNA [51-500]
Mayfield, John E. - *The Engine of Complexity: Evolution as Computation*
    QRB - v90 - i1 - March 2015 - p90(2) [501+]
Mayfield, Kate - *The Undertaker's Daughter*
    Econ - v414 - i8919 - Jan 3 2015 - p69(US) [501+]
Mayhew, Emily - *Wounded: A New History of the Western Front in World War I*
    HNet - Sept 2015 - pNA(NA) [501+]
    J Mil H - v79 - i4 - Oct 2015 - p1133-1134 [501+]
    JMH - v87 - i2 - June 2015 - p440(2) [501+]
Mayhew, Graham - *The Monks of Saint Pancras: Lewes Priory, England's Premier Cluniac Monastery and its Dependencies, 1076-1537*
    HER - v130 - i545 - August 2015 - p965(3) [501+]
Mayhew, James - *Ella Bella Ballerina and A Midsummer Night's Dream (Illus. by Mayhew, James)*
  c BL - v112 - i5 - Nov 1 2015 - p53(1) [51-500]
  c PW - v262 - i39 - Sept 28 2015 - p90(2) [51-500]
Mayhew, Julie - *The Big Lie*
  y Sch Lib - v63 - i4 - Winter 2015 - p248(1) [51-500]
  Red Ink
  y KR - Dec 1 2015 - pNA [51-500]
  y PW - v262 - i46 - Nov 16 2015 - p77(2) [51-500]
Mayhew, Robert J. - *Malthus: The Life and Legacies of an Untimely Prophet*
    AHR - v120 - i1 - Feb 2015 - p331-332 [501+]
    Bks & Cult - v21 - i1 - Jan-Feb 2015 - p31(1) [501+]
    HNet - April 2015 - pNA [501+]
Mayle, Peter - *The Diamond Caper*
    BL - v112 - i2 - Sept 15 2015 - p31(1) [51-500]
    PW - v262 - i35 - August 31 2015 - p61(1) [51-500]
Maynard, Joyce - *Under the Influence*
    KR - Dec 15 2015 - pNA [501+]
    PW - v262 - i51 - Dec 14 2015 - p54(1) [501+]
Maynard, Lee - *Cinco Becknell*
    KR - Feb 15 2015 - pNA [501+]
  Magnetic North
    KR - Feb 15 2015 - pNA [501+]
Mayne, Andrew - *Name of the Devil*
    BL - v111 - i21 - July 1 2015 - p39(1) [501+]
    PW - v262 - i20 - May 18 2015 - p66(1) [501+]
Mayne, Kienzle - *Solutions to Thirty-Eight Questions, Cistercian Studies, 253*
    Med R - April 2015 - pNA [501+]
Mayne, Seymour - *Cusp: Word Sonnets (Illus. by Frye, Sebastian)*
    Can Lit - i224 - Spring 2015 - p133 [51-500]

Maynor, Megan - *Ella and Penguin Stick Together (Illus. by Bonnet, Rosalinde)*
  c KR - Oct 1 2015 - pNA [501+]
  c PW - v262 - i42 - Oct 19 2015 - p75(1) [51-500]
Mayo, C.M. - *Metaphysical Odyssey into the Mexican Revolution*
    KR - Feb 1 2015 - pNA [501+]
Mayo, Michael - *Everybody Goes to Jimmy's*
    BL - v111 - i9-10 - Jan 1 2015 - p46(1) [51-500]
Mayor, Adrienne - *The Amazons: Lives and Legends of Warrior Women Across the Ancient World*
    For Aff - v94 - i3 - May-June 2015 - pNA [501+]
    Lon R Bks - v37 - i20 - Oct 22 2015 - p15(2) [501+]
    NS - v144 - i5245 - Jan 16 2015 - p48(2) [501+]
    TLS - i5840 - March 6 2015 - p10(1) [501+]
  The Griffin and the Dinosaur: How Adrienne Mayor Discovered a Fascinating Link between Myth and Science (Read by Rowar, Graham). Audiobook Review
  c SLJ - v61 - i8 - August 2015 - p48(1) [51-500]
Mayor, Archer - *The Company She Kept*
    BL - v111 - i22 - August 1 2015 - p32(1) [51-500]
    PW - v262 - i27 - July 6 2015 - p45(1) [51-500]
  Proof Positive
    RVBW - May 2015 - pNA [51-500]
Mayr-Harting, Henry - *Religion, Politics and Society in Britain, 1066-1272*
    CHR - v101 - i2 - Spring 2015 - p355(2) [501+]
Mayrhofer, Bernadette - *Orchestrierte Vertreibung: Unerwunschte Wiener Philharmoniker. Verfolgung, Ermordung und Exil*
    HNet - April 2015 - pNA [501+]
Mayrock, Aija - *The Survival Guide to Bullying: Written by a Teen*
  c PW - v262 - i25 - June 22 2015 - p141(1) [501+]
  c SLJ - v61 - i10 - Oct 2015 - p134(2) [51-500]
  y VOYA - v38 - i4 - Oct 2015 - p84(1) [51-500]
Mays, Andrea - *The Millionaire and the Bard: Henry Folger's Obsessive Hunt for Shakespeare's First Folio*
    BL - v111 - i16 - April 15 2015 - p47(1) [51-500]
    Ent W - i1364 - May 22 2015 - p66(1) [501+]
    KR - March 15 2015 - pNA [501+]
    LJ - v140 - i7 - April 15 2015 - p84(1) [51-500]
    PW - v262 - i12 - March 23 2015 - p64(1) [51-500]
Maysonet, Melody - *A Work of Art*
  y BL - v111 - i12 - Feb 15 2015 - p84(1) [51-500]
  y HB Guide - v26 - i2 - Fall 2015 - p131(1) [51-500]
  y KR - Jan 15 2015 - pNA [501+]
  y VOYA - v38 - i1 - April 2015 - p65(1) [51-500]
Maze, Stephanie - *Keeping Fit from A to Z / Mantente en forma de la A a la Z*
  c CH Bwatch - June 2015 - pNA [51-500]
Mazer, Ben - *The Collected Poems of John Crowe Ransom*
    TLS - i5875 - Nov 6 2015 - p10(1) [501+]
Mazierska, Ewa - *Polish Cinema in a Transnational Context*
    Slav R - v74 - i3 - Fall 2015 - p637-638 [501+]
Mazo, Margarita del - *Lucy's Light*
  c KR - August 15 2015 - pNA [51-500]
Mazur, Allan - *Energy and Electricity in Industrial Nations: The Sociology and Technology of Energy*
    T&C - v56 - i2 - April 2015 - p565-566 [501+]
Mazur, Amy G. - *The Politics of State Feminism: Innovation in Comparative Research*
    SF - v93 - i3 - March 2015 - pe61 [501+]
Mazur, Joseph - *Enlightening Symbols: A Short History of Mathematical Notation and Its Hidden Powers*
    AJPsy - v128 - i3 - Fall 2015 - p411(4) [501+]
    Isis - v106 - i2 - June 2015 - p425(2) [501+]
Mazur, Robert - *The Infiltrator*
    TLS - i5867 - Sept 11 2015 - p27(1) [501+]
Mazzantini, Margaret - *Morning Sea*
    BL - v111 - i13 - March 1 2015 - p20(1) [501+]
    KR - Feb 15 2015 - pNA [501+]
    WLT - v89 - i3-4 - May-August 2015 - p117(1) [51-500]
Mazzucato, Mariana - *The Entrepreneurial State: Debunking Public vs. Private Sector Myths*
    LJ - v140 - i16 - Oct 1 2015 - p89(2) [51-500]
Mazzuco, Melania G. - *Limbo*
    TLS - i5854 - June 12 2015 - p19(2) [501+]
McAdam, Claudia Cangilla - *The Mermaid's Gift (Illus. by Wagoner, Traci Van)*
  c SLJ - v61 - i12 - Dec 2015 - p91(2) [51-500]
McAdam, Nan - *Saving Mim (Illus. by Bickel, Chuck)*
  c CH Bwatch - April 2015 - pNA [51-500]
McAdams, Frank - *Vietnam Rough Riders: A Convoy Commander's Memoir*
    HNet - March 2015 - pNA [501+]

McAdams, Molly - *Trusting Liam*
 BL - v111 - i18 - May 15 2015 - p32(1) [51-500]
 PW - v262 - i13 - March 30 2015 - p61(1) [51-500]

McAdoo, Monty L. - *The Student's Survival Guide to Research*
 LJ - v140 - i20 - Dec 1 2015 - p116(1) [51-500]

McAfee, Andrew - *The Second Machine Age: Work, Progress, and Prosperity in a Time of Brilliant Technologies*
 Lon R Bks - v37 - i5 - March 5 2015 - p3(5) [501+]
 NS - v144 - i5245 - Jan 16 2015 - p44(3) [501+]

McAllister, Angela - *Mommy's Little Sunflowers (Illus. by Edgson, Alison)*
 c HB Guide - v26 - i1 - Spring 2015 - p12(1) [51-500]
A Mouse So Small (Illus. by Pedler, Caroline)
 c KR - July 15 2015 - pNA [51-500]
Winter's Child (Illus. by Baker-Smith, Grahame)
 c RVBW - Nov 2015 - pNA [501+]

McAllister, Bruce - *Berlin Airlift: Air Bridge to Freedom: A Photographic History of the Great Airlift*
 APH - v62 - i2 - Summer 2015 - p58(1) [501+]

McAllister, Cameron - *The Tin Snail (Illus. by Usher, Sam)*
 c KR - Oct 1 2015 - pNA [51-500]
 c SLJ - v61 - i11 - Nov 2015 - p99(1) [51-500]

McAllister, Ian - *Great Bear Wild: Dispatches from a Northern Rainforest*
 RVBW - May 2015 - pNA [51-500]

McAllister, Jenn - *Really Professional Internet Person*
 y SLJ - v61 - i12 - Dec 2015 - p145(1) [51-500]
 y VOYA - v38 - i4 - Oct 2015 - p84(1) [51-500]

McAllister, John - *Barlow by the Book*
 PW - v262 - i39 - Sept 28 2015 - p69(1) [51-500]

McAllister, Margaret - *15 Things Not to Do with a Baby (Illus. by Sterling, Holly)*
 c KR - Feb 1 2015 - pNA [51-500]

McAllister, Marvin - *Whiting Up: Whiteface Minstrels and Stage Europeans in African American Performance*
 Callaloo - v38 - i2 - Spring 2015 - p411-416 [501+]

McAllister, William V.M., III - *Malee: A Tear in the Ocean*
 SPBW - July 2015 - pNA [51-500]

McAlpine, Fraser - *Stuff Brits Like: A Guide to What's Great About Great Britain*
 LJ - v140 - i12 - July 1 2015 - p83(1) [51-500]

McAlpine, Gordon - *The Pet and the Pendulum (Illus. by Zippardi, Sam)*
 c CH Bwatch - August 2015 - pNA [51-500]
The Pet and the Pendulum (Illus. by Zuppardi, Sam)
 y HB Guide - v26 - i2 - Fall 2015 - p93(1) [51-500]
Woman with a Blue Pencil
 BL - v112 - i3 - Oct 1 2015 - p30(1) [51-500]
 PW - v262 - i39 - Sept 28 2015 - p68(1) [51-500]

Mcandrew, Marie - *Fragile Majorities and Education: Belgium, Catalonia, Northern Ireland and Quebec*
 ERS - v38 - i3 - March 2015 - p468(2) [501+]

McAndrews, Lawrence J. - *What They Wished For: American Catholics and American Presidents, 1960-2004*
 AHR - v120 - i3 - June 2015 - p1075-1076 [501+]
 J Ch St - v57 - i2 - Spring 2015 - p384-386 [501+]
 JAH - v101 - i4 - March 2015 - p1349-1350 [501+]
 Pres St Q - v45 - i4 - Dec 2015 - p817(2) [501+]

McAnulty, Stacy - *A Mysterious Egg (Illus. by Boldt, Mike)*
 c KR - Sept 15 2015 - pNA [51-500]
 c SLJ - v61 - i11 - Nov 2015 - p91(2) [51-500]

McArdle, Megan M. - *The Readers' Advisory Guide to Genre Blends*
 R&USQ - v54 - i4 - Summer 2015 - p76(1) [51-500]

McArdle, Sean - *Extra Math Practice: Grade 4 Workbook*
 TC Math - v21 - i6 - Feb 2015 - p380(1) [501+]
Extra Math Practice: K Workbook
 TC Math - v21 - i6 - Feb 2015 - p380(1) [501+]

McAulay, Karen - *Our Ancient National Airs: Scottish Song Collecting from the Enlightenment to the Romantic Era*
 Notes - v71 - i4 - June 2015 - p714(3) [501+]

McAuley, Paul - *Evening's Empires*
 BL - v111 - i18 - May 15 2015 - p35(1) [51-500]
 PW - v262 - i16 - April 20 2015 - p59(2) [51-500]
In the Mouth of the Whale
 BL - v111 - i19-20 - June 1 2015 - p65(1) [51-500]
 LJ - v140 - i9 - May 15 2015 - p57(4) [501+]
 PW - v262 - i13 - March 30 2015 - p58(1) [51-500]

McAuliffe, Mary - *Twilight of the Belle Epoque: The Paris of Picasso, Stravinsky, Proust, Renault, Marie Curie, Gertrude Stein, and Their Friends through the Great War*
 G&L Rev W - v22 - i3 - May-June 2015 - p40(1) [501+]

McBain, Ed - *Cut Me In*
 BL - v112 - i6 - Nov 15 2015 - p25(1) [51-500]
 KR - Oct 15 2015 - pNA [51-500]
 PW - v262 - i46 - Nov 16 2015 - p58(1) [51-500]
So Nude, So Dead
 BL - v111 - i17 - May 1 2015 - p45(1) [51-500]
 PW - v262 - i19 - May 11 2015 - p39(1) [51-500]

McBee, Randy D. - *Born to be Wild*
 KR - May 1 2015 - pNA [51-500]

McBride, Anne E. - *Payard Cookies*
 LJ - v140 - i17 - Oct 15 2015 - p109(1) [51-500]

McBride, Kristina - *A Million Times Goodnight*
 y VOYA - v38 - i2 - June 2015 - p665(1) [501+]

McBride, Lish - *Firebug (Read by Ahn, Ali). Audiobook Review*
 SLJ - v61 - i3 - March 2015 - p81(1) [51-500]
Firebug
 y HB Guide - v26 - i1 - Spring 2015 - p116(1) [51-500]

McBride, Susan - *Very Bad Things*
 y HB Guide - v26 - i1 - Spring 2015 - p116(1) [51-500]

McBride, Tim - *Saltwater Cowboy: The Rise and Fall of a Marijuana Empire*
 KR - Jan 15 2015 - pNA [51-500]

McCabe, M.P. - *For God and Ireland: The Fight for Moral Superiority in Ireland 1922-1932*
 CHR - v101 - i1 - Wntr 2015 - p174(3) [501+]

McCade, Cole - *The Lost*
 PW - v262 - i47 - Nov 23 2015 - p56(1) [51-500]

McCafferty, Kathleen - *Baby Brights: 30 Colorful Crochet Accessories*
 LJ - v140 - i13 - August 1 2015 - p96(1) [51-500]
 PW - v262 - i14 - April 6 2015 - p56(1) [51-500]

McCafferty, Keith - *Crazy Mountain Kiss*
 BL - v111 - i17 - May 1 2015 - p26(2) [51-500]
 KR - April 15 2015 - pNA [501+]
 PW - v262 - i15 - April 13 2015 - p58(1) [51-500]
Dead Man's Fancy
 Roundup M - v22 - i6 - August 2015 - p31(1) [501+]

McCafferty, Megan - *The (Totally Not) Guaranteed Guide to Friends, Foes, & Faux Friends*
 y HB Guide - v26 - i1 - Spring 2015 - p116(1) [51-500]
 y VOYA - v37 - i6 - Feb 2015 - p61(1) [51-500]

McCaffery, Steve - *The Darkness of the Present: Poetics, Anachronism, and the Anomaly*
 AL - v87 - i3 - Sept 2015 - p618-622 [501+]

McCaffrey, James M. - *Going for Broke: Japanese American Soldiers in the War against Nazi Germany*
 PHR - v84 - i1 - Feb 2015 - p113(2) [501+]

McCaffrey, Laura Williams - *Marked (Illus. by Cantirino, Sally)*
 c KR - Dec 1 2015 - pNA [51-500]
 y SLJ - v61 - i12 - Dec 2015 - p114(2) [51-500]

McCaffrey, Mark S. - *Climate Smart & Energy Wise: Advancing Science Literacy, Knowledge, and Know-How*
 Bwatch - Jan 2015 - pNA [51-500]
 c Sci & Ch - v52 - i6 - Feb 2015 - p81 [501+]
 c Sci Teach - v82 - i2 - Feb 2015 - p65 [501+]

McCahill, Elizabeth - *Reviving the Eternal City: Rome and the Papal Court, 1420-1447*
 AHR - v120 - i2 - April 2015 - p701-702 [501+]

McCaig, Donald - *Rhett Butler's People*
 NYTBR - Feb 8 2015 - p28(L) [501+]

McCall, Deanna Dickinson - *Mustang Spring*
 Roundup M - v22 - i6 - August 2015 - p24(1) [501+]

McCall, Fiona - *Baal's Priests: The Loyalist Clergy and the English Revolution*
 CH - v84 - i1 - March 2015 - p247(3) [501+]
 HER - v130 - i544 - June 2015 - p748(3) [501+]

McCall, Leslie - *The Underserving Rich: American Beliefs about Inequality, Opportunity, and Redistribution*
 CS - v44 - i4 - July 2015 - p449-462 [501+]
 CS - v44 - i4 - July 2015 - p537-539 [501+]

McCall Smith, Alexander - *Bertie's Guide to Life and Mothers*
 BL - v111 - i11 - Feb 1 2015 - p20(1) [51-500]
 CSM - April 6 2015 - pNA [51-500]
Emma: A Modern Retelling
 KR - Feb 1 2015 - pNA [501+]
 LJ - v140 - i3 - Feb 15 2015 - p90(1) [51-500]
 NYTBR - May 31 2015 - p20(L) [501+]
Good Dog Lion (Illus. by Dean, David)
 c Sch Lib - v63 - i1 - Spring 2015 - p38(1) [51-500]
The Mystery of the Missing Lion (Read by Andoh, Adjoa). Audiobook Review
 SLJ - v61 - i2 - Feb 2015 - p47(1) [51-500]
The Novel Habits of Happiness
 BL - v111 - i19-20 - June 1 2015 - p44(1) [51-500]
 KR - May 15 2015 - pNA [501+]
 PW - v262 - i22 - June 1 2015 - p42(1) [51-500]

McCallum, Ann - *Eat Your Science Homework: Recipes for Inquiring Minds (Illus. by Hernandez, Leeza)*
 c HB Guide - v26 - i1 - Spring 2015 - p148(1) [51-500]
Eat Your U.S. History Homework: Recipies for Revolutionary Minds (Illus. by Hernandez, Leeza)
 c KR - August 15 2015 - pNA [51-500]
 c SLJ - v61 - i10 - Oct 2015 - p126(2) [51-500]

McCallum, David - *Once a Crooked Man*
 KR - Nov 1 2015 - pNA [51-500]
 LJ - v140 - i20 - Dec 1 2015 - p94(1) [51-500]
 PW - v262 - i45 - Nov 9 2015 - p36(1) [51-500]

McCallum, E.L. - *The Cambridge History of Gay and Lesbian Literature*
 G&L Rev W - v22 - i4 - July-August 2015 - p41(1) [51-500]

McCallum, Jamie K. - *Global Unions, Local Power: The New Spirit of Transnational Labor Organizing*
 AJS - v121 - i1 - July 2015 - p341(3) [501+]
 CS - v44 - i5 - Sept 2015 - p675-677 [501+]

McCallum, Mary - *Dappled Annie and the Tigrish (Illus. by Hayward, Annie)*
 c HB Guide - v26 - i1 - Spring 2015 - p86(1) [51-500]

McCallum, Mary Fane Logan - *Indigenous Women, Work, and History, 1940-1980*
 Can Hist R - v96 - i1 - March 2015 - p143(3) [501+]

McCalman, Iain - *The Reef: A Passionate History*
 HNet - Sept 2015 - pNA [501+]
 NYTBR - June 7 2015 - p36(L) [501+]
 TLS - i5837 - Feb 13 2015 - p22(1) [501+]

McCalmon, Barbara - *Your Weight or Your Life?: Balancing the Scale for A Healthy Life*
 RVBW - March 2015 - pNA [51-500]

McCambridge, Peter - *The Adventures of Radisson 2: Back to the New World*
 y VOYA - v38 - i3 - August 2015 - p60(1) [501+]

McCammon, Holly J. - *The US Women's Jury Movements and Strategic Adaptation: A More Just Verdict*
 SF - v94 - i2 - Dec 2015 - pNA [501+]

McCammon, Robert - *The Border*
 BL - v111 - i18 - May 15 2015 - p33(1) [51-500]
 LJ - v140 - i9 - May 15 2015 - p57(4) [501+]
 PW - v262 - i13 - March 30 2015 - p59(1) [51-500]

McCammon, Ross - *Works Well with Others: An Outsider's Guide to Shaking Hands, Shutting Up, Handling Jerks, and Other Crucial Skills in Business That No One Ever Teaches You*
 BL - v111 - i21 - July 1 2015 - p25(1) [51-500]
 KR - July 1 2015 - pNA [501+]
 NYTBR - Dec 6 2015 - p87(L) [501+]
 PW - v262 - i31 - August 3 2015 - p50(1) [51-500]

McCandless, Bruce, III - *Beatrice and the Basilisk*
 KR - Nov 1 2015 - pNA [51-500]

McCann, Bryan - *Hard Times in the Marvelous City: From Dictatorship to Democracy in the Favelas of Rio de Janeiro*
 AHR - v120 - i2 - April 2015 - p684-685 [501+]
 AJS - v120 - i4 - Jan 2015 - p1267(3) [501+]
 JIH - v45 - i4 - Spring 2015 - p603-606 [501+]

McCann, Colum - *Thirteen Ways of Looking (Read by McCann, Colum). Audiobook Review*
 PW - v262 - i48 - Nov 30 2015 - p54(1) [51-500]
Thirteen Ways of Looking
 NYT - Oct 12 2015 - pC1(L) [501+]
 KR - August 1 2015 - pNA [501+]
 PW - v262 - i29 - July 20 2015 - p164(1) [51-500]
 NYTBR - Nov 22 2015 - p13(L) [501+]

McCann, Graham - *A Very Courageous Decision: The Inside Story of Yes Minister*
 TimHES - i2186 - Jan 15 2015 - p50(1) [501+]

McCardie, Amanda - *A Book of Feelings (Illus. by Rubbino, Salvatore)*
 c Sch Lib - v63 - i4 - Winter 2015 - p220(1) [51-500]

McCargo, Duncan - *Mapping National Anxieties: Thailand's Southern Conflict*
 JAS - v74 - i3 - August 2015 - p787-789 [501+]

McCarney, Rosemary - *Because I Am a Girl I Can Change the World*
  c CCB-B - v68 - i5 - Jan 2015 - p268(1) [51-500]
  c Res Links - v20 - i3 - Feb 2015 - p20(1) [51-500]
Dear Malala, We Stand with You
  c HB Guide - v26 - i2 - Fall 2015 - p153(2) [51-500]
Tilt Your Head, Rosie the Red (Illus. by Cathcart, Yvonne)
  c CH Bwatch - July 2015 - pNA [51-500]
  c HB Guide - v26 - i2 - Fall 2015 - p44(1) [51-500]
  c KR - Feb 15 2015 - pNA [51-500]
  c Res Links - v20 - i4 - April 2015 - p5(1) [51-500]
The Way to School
  c SLJ - v61 - i9 - Sept 2015 - p179(1) [51-500]
  c KR - July 15 2015 - pNA [51-500]
Mccarney, Rosemary - *The Way to School*
  c Res Links - v21 - i1 - Oct 2015 - p24(1) [501+]
McCarroll, Pamela R. - *The End of Hope - the Beginning: Narratives of Hope in the Face of Death and Trauma*
  Intpr - v69 - i1 - Jan 2015 - p121(1) [51-500]
McCarron, Leon - *The Road Headed West: A 6,000-Mile Cycling Odyssey Through North America*
  LJ - v140 - i12 - July 1 2015 - p102(1) [51-500]
  BL - v111 - i19-20 - June 1 2015 - p34(1) [51-500]
McCarry, Charles - *The Mulberry Bush*
  BL - v112 - i1 - Sept 1 2015 - p48(1) [51-500]
  KR - Sept 1 2015 - pNA [501+]
  LJ - v140 - i11 - June 15 2015 - p78(2) [501+]
  PW - v262 - i35 - August 31 2015 - p61(1) [51-500]
McCarry, Sarah - *About a Girl*
  y BL - v111 - i22 - August 1 2015 - p55(1) [51-500]
  y KR - May 1 2015 - pNA [51-500]
  y SLJ - v61 - i6 - June 2015 - p126(1) [51-500]
  y VOYA - v38 - i3 - August 2015 - p65(1) [51-500]
Dirty Wings
  y HB Guide - v26 - i2 - Fall 2015 - p131(1) [51-500]
McCarter, Robert - *Steven Holl*
  PW - v262 - i44 - Nov 2 2015 - p78(1) [51-500]
McCarthy, Andrew - *The Best American Travel Writing, 2015*
  BL - v112 - i3 - Oct 1 2015 - p12(1) [51-500]
Journeys Home: Inspiring Stories, Plus Tips and Strategies to Find Your Family History
  LJ - v140 - i3 - Feb 15 2015 - p119(1) [51-500]
McCarthy, Cori - *Breaking Sky*
  y CCB-B - v68 - i9 - May 2015 - p456(1) [51-500]
  y KR - Jan 1 2015 - pNA [51-500]
  PW - v262 - i1 - Jan 5 2015 - p74(2) [51-500]
You Were Here
  y KR - Dec 15 2015 - pNA [51-500]
McCarthy, Cormac - *All the Pretty Horses*
  CSM - April 20 2015 - pNA [1-50]
McCarthy, Ellen - *The Real Thing: Lessons on Love and Life from a Wedding Reporter's Notebook*
  BL - v111 - i13 - March 1 2015 - p8(1) [51-500]
  KR - Jan 1 2015 - pNA [51-500]
  LJ - v140 - i3 - Feb 15 2015 - p118(1) [51-500]
  PW - v262 - i5 - Feb 2 2015 - p51(1) [51-500]
McCarthy, Gary - *Sisters of the Wyoming Mountains: Book I*
  Roundup M - v22 - i4 - April 2015 - p33(2) [501+]
  Roundup M - v22 - i6 - August 2015 - p31(1) [501+]
Sisters of the Wyoming Plains: Book II
  Roundup M - v22 - i4 - April 2015 - p33(2) [501+]
  Roundup M - v22 - i6 - August 2015 - p31(1) [501+]
McCarthy, Kerry - *Byrd*
  MT - v156 - i1931 - Summer 2015 - p118-120 [501+]
  Notes - v72 - i1 - Sept 2015 - p175(2) [501+]
McCarthy, Lauren A. - *Trafficking Justice*
  Dis - v62 - i4 - Fall 2015 - p83(1) [501+]
McCarthy, Matt - *The Real Doctor Will See You Shortly: A Physician's First Year*
  BL - v111 - i13 - March 1 2015 - p10(2) [51-500]
  Ent W - i1359-1360 - April 17 2015 - p116(1) [501+]
  PW - v262 - i8 - Feb 23 2015 - p68(1) [51-500]
McCarthy, Meghan - *Daredevil: The Daring Life of Betty Skelton. Audiobook Review*
  SLJ - v61 - i2 - Feb 2015 - p47(2) [51-500]
Earmuffs for Everyone! How Chester Greenwood Became Known as the Inventor of Earmuffs (Illus. by McCarthy, Meghan)
  c CCB-B - v68 - i6 - Feb 2015 - p321(2) [51-500]
  c HB Guide - v26 - i2 - Fall 2015 - p211(1) [51-500]
  PW - v262 - i49 - Dec 2 2015 - p45(1) [51-500]

The Wildest Race Ever: The Story of the 1904 Olympic Marathon (Illus. by McCarthy, Meghan)
  c KR - Jan 1 2016 - pNA [51-500]
  c PW - v262 - i50 - Dec 7 2015 - p87(2) [51-500]
McCarthy, Michael - *The Moth Snowstorm: Nature and Joy*
  Spec - v328 - i9745 - June 6 2015 - p41(2) [501+]
  TLS - i5849 - May 8 2015 - p30(1) [501+]
McCarthy, Molly - *The Accidental Diarist: A History of the Daily Planner in America*
  RAH - v43 - i1 - March 2015 - p54-59 [501+]
McCarthy, Pat - *Chicago Street Cop*
  KR - Jan 1 2016 - pNA [51-500]
McCarthy, Susan Carol - *A Place We Knew Well*
  BL - v112 - i1 - Sept 1 2015 - p52(1) [51-500]
  KR - July 15 2015 - pNA [501+]
McCarthy, T.J.H. - *Chronicles of the Investiture Contest: Frutolf of Michelsberg and His Continuators*
  Med R - May 2015 - pNA [501+]
McCarthy, Thomas J.H. - *Chronicles of the Investiture Contest: Frutolf of Michelsberg and His Continuato*
  Ger Q - v88 - i3 - Summer 2015 - p412(3) [501+]
McCarthy, Tom - *Satin Island*
  BL - v111 - i1 - Feb 1 2015 - p24(1) [51-500]
  HM - v330 - i1977 - Feb 2015 - p77(3) [501+]
  Lon R Bks - v37 - i10 - May 21 2015 - p21(3) [501+]
  Nat Post - v17 - i113 - March 14 2015 - pWP5(1) [501+]
  Nation - v300 - i22 - June 1 2015 - p35(8) [501+]
  New R - v246 - i2-3 - March-April 2015 - p72(4) [501+]
  NS - v144 - i5252 - March 6 2015 - p50(2) [501+]
  NY - v91 - i4 - March 16 2015 - p83 [501+]
  NYRB - v62 - i17 - Nov 5 2015 - p60(2) [501+]
  NYTBR - Feb 22 2015 - p22(L) [501+]
  TLS - i5839 - Feb 27 2015 - p19(1) [501+]
McCartney, James - *America's War Machine: Vested Interests, Endless Conflicts*
  LJ - v140 - i16 - Oct 1 2015 - p94(1) [51-500]
McCartney, Tania - *An Aussie Year: Twelve Months in the Life of Australian Kids*
  c Sch Lib - v63 - i2 - Summer 2015 - p97(1) [51-500]
Australian Kids through the Years (Illus. by Joyner, Andrew)
  c Magpies - v30 - i5 - Nov 2015 - p23(1) [501+]
An English Year: Twelve Months in the Life of England's Kids
  KR - Oct 15 2015 - pNA [51-500]
  c Sch Lib - v63 - i4 - Winter 2015 - p220(1) [51-500]
Peas in a Pod (Illus. by Snerling, Tina)
  c KR - July 1 2015 - pNA [51-500]
  c Sch Lib - v63 - i4 - Winter 2015 - p220(1) [51-500]
  c SLJ - v61 - i10 - Oct 2015 - p80(1) [51-500]
This is Captain Cook (Illus. by Booth, Christina)
  c Magpies - v30 - i2 - May 2015 - p32(1) [501+]
McCarty, Nolan - *Polarized America: The Dance of Ideology and Unequal Riches*
  CS - v44 - i4 - July 2015 - p449-462 [501+]
McCarty, Peter - *Bunny Dreams (Illus. by McCarty, Peter)*
  c BL - v112 - i6 - Nov 15 2015 - p56(2) [51-500]
  c KR - Oct 15 2015 - pNA [51-500]
  c SLJ - v61 - i11 - Nov 2015 - p77(1) [501+]
First Snow (Illus. by McCarty, Peter)
  c CCB-B - v68 - i6 - Feb 2015 - p322(1) [51-500]
  c HB - v91 - i1 - Jan-Feb 2015 - p69(2) [51-500]
  c HB Guide - v26 - i2 - Fall 2015 - p15(1) [51-500]
  c NYTBR - Jan 18 2015 - p20(L) [51-500]
McCarty, Susan - *Anatomies: Stories*
  KR - April 15 2015 - pNA [51-500]
McCaskill, Claire - *Plenty Ladylike*
  BL - v111 - i19-20 - June 1 2015 - p12(1) [51-500]
  KR - May 15 2015 - pNA [501+]
  PW - v262 - i21 - May 25 2015 - p48(1) [51-500]
McCaslin, Susan - *The Disarmed Heart*
  CWS - v30 - i2-3 - Fall-Winter 2015 - p125(1) [501+]
McCaughan, Edward J. - *Art and Social Movements: Cultural Politics in Mexico*
  CS - v44 - i3 - May 2015 - p380-382 [501+]
McCauley, Debbie - *Motiti Blue and the Oil Spill*
  c Magpies - v30 - i1 - March 2015 - pS7(1) [501+]
McCauley, Robert N. - *Why Religion Is Natural and Science Is Not*
  JR - Jan 2015 - p160(3) [501+]

McCauley, Terrence - *Sympathy for the Devil*
  BL - v111 - i21 - July 1 2015 - p40(1) [51-500]
  KR - May 15 2015 - pNA [51-500]
  LJ - v140 - i13 - June 15 2015 - p78(2) [501+]
  PW - v262 - i19 - May 11 2015 - p38(1) [51-500]
McCauley, Tiffany - *Clean Eating Freezer Meals*
  LJ - v140 - i3 - Feb 15 2015 - p122(4) [501+]
McChesney, Robert W. - *Blowing the Roof off the Twenty-First Century*
  RVBW - Feb 2015 - pNA [501+]
Digital Disconnect: How Capitalism Is Turning the Internet against Democracy
  NYRB - v62 - i10 - June 4 2015 - p43(3) [501+]
McChrystal, Stanley - *Team of Teams: New Rules of Engagement for a Complex World*
  KR - April 1 2015 - pNA [501+]
  Mar Crp G - v99 - i6 - June 2015 - p86(2) [501+]
  Parameters - v45 - i2 - Summer 2015 - p157(2) [501+]
  PW - v262 - i12 - March 23 2015 - p65(1) [51-500]
McClaren, Meredith - *Clockwork City (Illus. by McClaren, Meredith)*
  c SLJ - v61 - i5 - May 2015 - p110(2) [51-500]
McClay, Wilfred M. - *Why Place Matters: Geography, Identity, and Civic Life in Modern America*
  CC - v132 - i3 - Feb 4 2015 - p35(1) [51-500]
McCleave, Sarah - *Dance in Handel's London Operas*
  Notes - v71 - i3 - March 2015 - p517(3) [501+]
McClellan, Brian - *The Autumn Republic*
  KR - Jan 1 2015 - pNA [51-500]
McClelland, Mac - *Irritable Hearts: A PTSD Love Story*
  NYTBR - Feb 22 2015 - p19(L) [501+]
McClelland, Peter - *The American Search for Economic Justice*
  Nat R - v67 - i21 - Nov 19 2015 - p74(1) [501+]
McClements, Richard - *Death Poem*
  c BL - v112 - i7 - Dec 1 2015 - p34(2) [501+]
McClenahan, William, Jr. - *Eisenhower and the Cold War Economy*
  Pres St Q - v45 - i1 - March 2015 - p199(7) [501+]
McCleskey, Turk - *The Road to Black Ned's Forge: A Story of Race, Sex, and Trade on the Colonial American Frontier*
  AHR - v120 - i3 - June 2015 - p1007-1008 [501+]
  HNet - May 2015 - pNA [501+]
  JAH - v102 - i2 - Sept 2015 - p536-537 [501+]
  JSH - v81 - i4 - Nov 2015 - p943(2) [501+]
McClintock, Barbara - *Emma and Julia Love Ballet (Illus. by McClintock, Barbara)*
  c BL - v112 - i7 - Dec 1 2015 - p66(1) [51-500]
  c KR - Dec 1 2015 - pNA [51-500]
McClintock, James - *A Naturalist Goes Fishing: Casting in Fragile Waters from the Gulf of Mexico to New Zealand's South Island*
  KR - August 15 2015 - pNA [51-500]
  PW - v262 - i37 - Sept 14 2015 - p53(1) [51-500]
McClintock, Norah - *My Life before Me*
  y KR - July 15 2015 - pNA [51-500]
  y Res Links - v21 - i1 - Oct 2015 - p37(1) [501+]
  y SLJ - v61 - i11 - Nov 2015 - p118(1) [51-500]
  y VOYA - v38 - i4 - Oct 2015 - p57(1) [51-500]
Tru Detective (Illus. by Hughes, Steven P.)
  y Res Links - v21 - i1 - Oct 2015 - p37(2) [501+]
  y VOYA - v38 - i2 - June 2015 - p65(1) [51-500]
McCloskey, Kevin - *We Dig Worms!*
  c HB Guide - v26 - i2 - Fall 2015 - p174(1) [51-500]
We Dig Worms! (Illus. by McCloskey, Kevin)
  c BL - v111 - i16 - April 15 2015 - p41(1) [51-500]
  c KR - Feb 15 2015 - pNA [51-500]
  c NYTBR - April 12 2015 - p19(L) [501+]
  c SLJ - v61 - i3 - March 2015 - p130(1) [51-500]
We Dig Worms!
  c PW - v262 - i49 - Dec 2 2015 - p51(1) [51-500]
McCloud, Carol - *Bucket Filling from A to Z: The Key to Being Happy (Illus. by Zimmer, Glenn)*
  c CH Bwatch - April 2015 - pNA [51-500]
McCloud, Scott - *The Sculptor (Illus. by McCloud, Scott)*
  Mac - v128 - i5-6 - Feb 9 2015 - p76(1) [501+]
  MFSF - v128 - i3-4 - March-April 2015 - p68(3) [501+]
  Nat Post - v17 - i113 - March 14 2015 - pWP4(1) [501+]
  NS - v144 - i5249 - Feb 13 2015 - p51(2) [501+]
  TLS - i5840 - March 6 2015 - p31(1) [501+]
  NYTBR - May 31 2015 - p31(L) [501+]
McClung, Nellie L. - *Painted Fires*
  Can Lit - i224 - Spring 2015 - p134 [501+]
McClure, Monica - *Tender Data*
  PW - v262 - i24 - June 15 2015 - p61(1) [51-500]

McClure, Nikki - *In (Illus. by McClure, Nikki)*
c BL - v111 - i14 - March 15 2015 - p78(1) [51-500]
c HB Guide - v26 - i2 - Fall 2015 - p15(1) [51-500]
c PW - v262 - i3 - Jan 19 2015 - p79(1) [51-500]
c PW - v262 - i49 - Dec 2 2015 - p20(1) [51-500]
c SLJ - v61 - i4 - April 2015 - p122(1) [51-500]
McClure, Wendy - *On Track for Treasure*
y HB Guide - v26 - i2 - Fall 2015 - p93(1) [51-500]
McClurkan, Rob - *Aw, Nuts! (Illus. by McClurkan, Rob)*
c HB Guide - v26 - i1 - Spring 2015 - p39(1) [51-500]
McCluskey, Fergal - *Tyrone: The Irish Revolution, 1912-23*
ILS - v35 - i1 - Fall 2015 - p10(2) [501+]
McCollim, Gary B. - *Louis XIV's Assault on Privilege: Nicolas Desmaretz and the Tax on Wealth*
JMH - v87 - i2 - June 2015 - p447(2) [501+]
McComb Sinclair, James C., II - *Box of Cigar Bands*
NYT - Nov 27 2015 - pC28(L) [501+]
McCombie, Karen - *The Girl with the Sunshine Smile (Illus. by Brett, Cathy)*
c Sch Lib - v63 - i1 - Spring 2015 - p38(1) [51-500]
McConchie, Lyn - *Vestiges of Flames*
PW - v262 - i22 - June 1 2015 - p45(1) [51-500]
McConnel, James - *The Irish Parliamentary Party and the Third Home Rule Crisis*
HER - v130 - i543 - April 2015 - p487(2) [501+]
McConnel, Jen - *Daughter of Chaos*
y VOYA - v37 - i6 - Feb 2015 - p81(1) [51-500]
McConnell, Judy - *A Penny a Kiss*
RVBW - Feb 2015 - pNA [51-500]
RVBW - May 2015 - pNA [51-500]
McConville, Sean - *Irish Political Prisoners, 1920-1962: Pilgrimage of Desolation*
AHR - v120 - i1 - Feb 2015 - p340-341 [501+]
McCoog, Thomas M. - *"And Touching Our Society": Fashioning Jesuit Identity in Elizabethan England*
CHR - v101 - i3 - Summer 2015 - p655(3) [501+]
Six Ct J - v46 - i2 - Summer 2015 - p520-522 [501+]
McCoola, Marika - *Baba Yaga's Assistant (Illus. by Carroll, Emily)*
c BL - v111 - i19-20 - June 1 2015 - p67(1) [51-500]
c CCB-B - v69 - i2 - Oct 2015 - p73(2) [501+]
y HB - v91 - i5 - Sept-Oct 2015 - p109(2) [51-500]
c KR - June 15 2015 - pNA [51-500]
c PW - v262 - i21 - May 25 2015 - p61(2) [51-500]
c SLJ - v61 - i8 - August 2015 - p95(1) [51-500]
y VOYA - v38 - i3 - August 2015 - p80(1) [51-500]
McCord, Gretchen - *What You Need to Know about Privacy Law: A Guide for Librarians and Educators*
LQ - v85 - i3 - July 2015 - p336(3) [501+]
McCorkel, Jill A. - *Breaking Women: Gender, Race, and the New Politics of Imprisonment*
Soc Ser R - v89 - i3 - Sept 2015 - p579(4) [501+]
McCormac, P. - *Wild Justice*
RVBW - May 2015 - pNA [51-500]
McCormack, Derek P. - *Refrains for Moving Bodies: Experience and Experiment in Affective Spaces*
Dance RJ - v47 - i1 - April 2015 - p118-121 [501+]
McCormack, John - *Jamaal's Journey*
KR - April 1 2015 - pNA [501+]
McCormack, Kathleen - *George Eliot and Intoxication*
TLS - i5857 - July 3 2015 - p16(1) [501+]
George Eliot in Society: Travels Abroad and Sundays at the Priory
VS - v57 - i3 - Spring 2015 - p544(4) [501+]
McCormick, Anita Louise - *The Industrial Revolution in United States History*
y HB Guide - v26 - i1 - Spring 2015 - p203(1) [51-500]
McCormick, Joseph B. - *Level 4: Virus Hunters of the CDC: Tracking Ebola and the World's Deadliest Viruses*
LJ - v140 - i5 - March 15 2015 - p129(1) [51-500]
McCormick, Michael - *Across the Pond*
KR - June 1 2015 - pNA [51-500]
Charlemagne's Survey of the Holy Land: Wealth, Personnel, and Buildings of a Mediterranean Church between Antiquity and the Middle Ages, with a Critical Edition and Translation of the Original Text
HER - v130 - i542 - Feb 2015 - p150(3) [501+]
McCormick, Scott - *Mr. Pants: It's Go Time!*
c HB Guide - v26 - i1 - Spring 2015 - p62(1) [51-500]
Mr. Pants: Slacks, Camera, Action! (Illus. by Lazzell, R.H.)
c HB Guide - v26 - i2 - Fall 2015 - p68(1) [51-500]
Mr. Pants: Trick or Feet! (Illus. by Lazzell, R.H.)
c SLJ - v61 - i10 - Oct 2015 - p98(1) [51-500]
McCormick, Stephen D. - *Euryhaline Fishes*
QRB - v90 - i2 - June 2015 - p235(2) [501+]
McCoskey, Denise Eileen - *Latin Love Poetry*
Class R - v65 - i2 - Oct 2015 - p446-448 [501+]
Race: Antiquity and Its Legacy
AJP - v136 - i3 - Fall 2015 - p525-528 [501+]
McCoy, Alfred W. - *Policing America's Empire: The United States, the Philippines, and the Rise of the Surveillance State*
JAS - v74 - i3 - August 2015 - p789-791 [501+]
McCoy, Ann - *High-Yield Routines for Grades K-8*
TC Math - v21 - i9 - May 2015 - p566(1) [501+]
McCoy, Chris - *The Prom Goer's Interstellar Excursion*
BL - v111 - i14 - March 15 2015 - p65(1) [51-500]
y CCB-B - v68 - i9 - May 2015 - p456(1) [51-500]
y HB Guide - v26 - i2 - Fall 2015 - p131(1) [51-500]
y KR - Feb 1 2015 - pNA [51-500]
PW - v262 - i7 - Feb 16 2015 - p181(1) [51-500]
McCoy, John A. - *A Still and Quiet Conscience: The Archbishop Who Challenged a Pope, a President, and a Church*
AM - v213 - i9 - Oct 5 2015 - p34(3) [501+]
Bwatch - Sept 2015 - pNA [51-500]
Bwatch - July 2015 - pNA [51-500]
McCoy, Mary - *Dead to Me*
y BL - v111 - i12 - Feb 15 2015 - p80(1) [51-500]
y CCB-B - v68 - i7 - March 2015 - p363(2) [51-500]
y HB Guide - v26 - i2 - Fall 2015 - p131(1) [51-500]
y KR - Jan 1 2015 - pNA [51-500]
y PW - v262 - i4 - Jan 26 2015 - p172(1) [51-500]
y VOYA - v38 - i1 - April 2015 - p65(1) [51-500]
McCoy, Sarah - *The Mapmaker's Children*
y BL - v111 - i16 - April 15 2015 - p37(1) [51-500]
KR - March 1 2015 - pNA [51-500]
LJ - v140 - i7 - April 15 2015 - p76(1) [51-500]
PW - v262 - i10 - March 9 2015 - p52(1) [51-500]
McCoy, Shirlee - *The Orchard at the Edge of Town*
PW - v262 - i22 - June 1 2015 - p48(1) [51-500]
McCracken, Allison - *Real Men Don't Sing: Crooning in American Culture*
LJ - v140 - i13 - August 1 2015 - p98(1) [51-500]
McCracken, Elizabeth - *Thunderstruck and Other Stories*
TLS - i5854 - June 12 2015 - p10(2) [501+]
McCrae, Shane - *The Animal Too Big to Kill*
PW - v262 - i52 - Dec 21 2015 - p128(2) [51-500]
McCraith, Sheila - *Yell Less, Love More: How the Orange Rhino Mom Stopped Yelling at Her Kids--and How You Can Too!*
RVBW - April 2015 - pNA [501+]
McCrate, Colin - *High-Yield Vegetable Gardening: Grow More of What You Want in the Space You Have*
LJ - v140 - i20 - Dec 1 2015 - p124(1) [501+]
McCraw, Thomas K. - *The Founders and Finance: How Hamilton, Gallatin, and Other Immigrants Forged a New Economy*
BHR - v89 - i1 - Spring 2015 - p129(25) [501+]
McCray, Linzee Kull - *Art Quilts of the Midwest*
Bwatch - May 2015 - pNA [51-500]
McCray, W. Patrick - *The Visioneers: How a Group of Elite Scientists Pursued Space Colonies, Nanotechnologies, and a Limitless Future*
T&C - v56 - i1 - Jan 2015 - p289-291 [501+]
McCrea, Brian - *Frances Burney and Narrative Prior to Ideology*
Eight-C St - v49 - i1 - Fall 2015 - p106-107 [501+]
McCrea, Gavin - *Mrs. Engels*
BL - v112 - i1 - Sept 1 2015 - p52(1) [51-500]
KR - August 1 2015 - pNA [51-500]
LJ - v140 - i13 - August 1 2015 - p87(1) [51-500]
NYTBR - Nov 22 2015 - p38(L) [501+]
PW - v262 - i25 - June 22 2015 - p119(1) [51-500]
Spec - v328 - i9742 - May 16 2015 - p49(1) [501+]
McCready, Amy - *The Me, Me, Me Epidemic: A Step-by-Step Guide to Raising Capable, Grateful Kids in an Over-Entitled World*
KR - May 15 2015 - pNA [501+]
PW - v262 - i20 - May 18 2015 - p80(1) [51-500]
McCready, William D. - *Odiosa Sanctitas: St Peter Damian, Simony, and Reform*
Specu - v90 - i4 - Oct 2015 - p1149-1150 [501+]
McCreedy, J.L. - *The Orphan of Torundi*
PW - v262 - i2 - Jan 12 2015 - p60(2) [51-500]
McCreely, Havelock - *Attack of the Zombie Clones*
c SLJ - v61 - i6 - June 2015 - p109(1) [51-500]
My Zombie Hamster
c HB Guide - v26 - i1 - Spring 2015 - p86(1) [51-500]
McCreight, Kimberly - *Where They Found Her*
BL v111 - i14 - March 15 2015 - p48(1) [51-500]
KR - Feb 15 2015 - pNA [51-500]
PW - v262 - i6 - Feb 9 2015 - p45(1) [51-500]
y SLJ - v61 - i6 - June 2015 - p132(1) [501+]
McCrossen, Alexis - *Marking Modern Times: A History of Clocks, Watches, and Other Timekeepers in American Life*
RAH - v43 - i1 - March 2015 - p54-59 [501+]
T&C - v56 - i4 - Oct 2015 - p965-969 [501+]
McCruden, Kevin - *A Body You Have Prepared for Me: The Spirituality of the Letter to the Hebrews*
Intpr - v69 - i1 - Jan 2015 - p110(1) [501+]
McCullin, Don - *Unreasonable Behavior: The Updated Autobiography*
TLS - i5876 - Nov 13 2015 - p30(1) [501+]
McCulloch, Amy - *The Oathbreaker's Shadow*
y BL - v111 - i9-10 - Jan 1 2015 - p96(1) [51-500]
y VOYA - v37 - i6 - Feb 2015 - p81(1) [51-500]
The Shadow's Curse
y KR - Dec 1 2015 - pNA [51-500]
c Res Links - v21 - i1 - Oct 2015 - p38(1) [51-500]
McCullough, Amy - *The Box Wine Sailors: Misadventures of a Broke Young Couple at Sea*
BL - v112 - i3 - Oct 1 2015 - p12(1) [51-500]
McCullough, David - *1776: The Illustrated Edition*
y JE - v195 - i1 - Wntr 2015 - p54-55 [501+]
Brave Companions (Read by McCullough, David). Audiobook Review
BL - v112 - i7 - Dec 1 2015 - p68(1) [51-500]
The Wright Brothers. Audiobook Review
LJ - v140 - i12 - July 1 2015 - p45(1) [51-500]
The Wright Brothers
BL - v111 - i16 - April 15 2015 - p8(1) [51-500]
BL - v111 - i19-20 - June 1 2015 - p27(1) [501+]
CSM - May 5 2015 - pNA [501+]
Econ - v415 - i8935 - April 25 2015 - p78(US) [501+]
Ent W - i1365-1366 - May 29 2015 - p109(1) [501+]
Forbes - v196 - i6 - Nov 2 2015 - p42(1) [501+]
KR - March 15 2015 - pNA [501+]
LJ - v140 - i6 - April 1 2015 - p99(1) [51-500]
Lon R Bks - v37 - i17 - Sept 10 2015 - p3(4) [501+]
Nat R - v67 - i11 - June 22 2015 - p36 [501+]
NYRB - v62 - i13 - August 13 2015 - p4(2) [501+]
NYTBR - May 10 2015 - p11(L) [501+]
y BL - v111 - i22 - August 1 2015 - p79(1) [501+]
NYT - May 4 2015 - pC1(L) [501+]
PW - v262 - i11 - March 16 2015 - p74(1) [51-500]
McCullough, Kelly - *School for Sidekicks*
c BL - v111 - i21 - July 1 2015 - p76(2) [51-500]
c CCB-B - v69 - i2 - Oct 2015 - p101(1) [51-500]
y KR - April 15 2015 - pNA [51-500]
c PW - v262 - i49 - Dec 2 2015 - p68(1) [51-500]
SLJ - v61 - i3 - March 2015 - p138(2) [51-500]
y VOYA - v38 - i3 - August 2015 - p80(2) [51-500]
McCullough, Lissa - *The Religious Philosophy of Simone Weil: An Introduction*
TLS - i5840 - March 6 2015 - p26(1) [501+]
McCullough, Matthew - *The Cross of War: Christian Nationalism and U.S. Expansion in the Spanish-American War*
AHR - v120 - i4 - Oct 2015 - p1496-1497 [501+]
CC - v132 - i5 - March 4 2015 - p32(2) [501+]
CH - v84 - i4 - Dec 2015 - p915(3) [501+]
JAH - v102 - i2 - Sept 2015 - p575-576 [501+]
JR - v95 - i4 - Oct 2015 - p571(2) [501+]
McCullough, Megan B. - *Reconstructing Obesity: The Meaning of Measures and the Measure of Meanings*
MAQ - v29 - i1 - March 2015 - p1-3 [501+]
McCully, Emily Arnold - *3, 2, 1, Go! (Illus. by McCully, Emily Arnold)*
c BL - v111 - i18 - May 15 2015 - p57(1) [51-500]
c HB Guide - v26 - i2 - Fall 2015 - p60(1) [51-500]
c KR - March 1 2015 - pNA [51-500]
SLJ - v61 - i3 - March 2015 - p120(1) [51-500]
Ida M. Tarbell: The Woman Who Challenged Big Business--and Won!
y HB Guide - v26 - i1 - Spring 2015 - p194(2) [51-500]
Pete Makes a Mistake (Illus. by McCully, Emily Arnold)
c KR - June 15 2015 - pNA [51-500]
c SLJ - v61 - i11 - Nov 2015 - p89(1) [51-500]
Queen of the Diamond: The Lizzie Murphy Story (Illus. by McCully, Emily Arnold)
c CCB-B - v68 - i8 - April 2015 - p411(1) [51-500]
c HB Guide - v26 - i2 - Fall 2015 - p199(1) [51-500]
c BL - v112 - i1 - Sept 1 2015 - p99(1) [501+]
c HB - v91 - i1 - Jan-Feb 2015 - p99(2) [51-500]
c KR - March 1 2015 - pNA [51-500]
Strongheart: The World's First Movie Star Dog
c HB Guide - v26 - i2 - Fall 2015 - p44(1) [51-500]

McCulough, Kelly - *School for Sidekicks*
   c PW - v262 - i20 - May 18 2015 - p86(1) [51-500]
McCune, Joshua - *Invisible Monsters*
   y KR - May 1 2015 - pNA [51-500]
   y SLJ - v61 - i8 - August 2015 - p114(1) [51-500]
McCurley, T. Mark - *Hunter Killer: Inside America's Unmanned Air War*
     KR - July 15 2015 - pNA [51-500]
     LJ - v140 - i15 - Sept 15 2015 - p89(1) [51-500]
McCurry, Kristen - *The Wizard of Oz Counting*
     TC Math - v21 - i9 - May 2015 - p567(2) [501+]
McCurry, Steve - *From These Hands: A Journey along the Coffee Trail*
     RVBW - Oct 2015 - pNA [51-500]
McDaniel, Iain - *Adam Ferguson in the Scottish Enlightenment: The Roman Past and Europe's Future*
     Historian - v77 - i1 - Spring 2015 - p179(2) [501+]
McDaniel, L. Bailey - *(Re)Constructing Maternal Performance In Twentieth-Century American Drama*
     Theat J - v67 - i2 - May 2015 - p366-367 [501+]
McDaniel, Lurlene - *The Year of Chasing Dreams*
   y HB Guide - v26 - i1 - Spring 2015 - p116(1) [51-500]
McDaniel, W. Caleb - *The Problem of Democracy in the Age of Slavery: Garrisonian Abolitionists and Transatlantic Reform*
     RAH - v43 - i1 - March 2015 - p60-69 [501+]
McDaniels, Edison - *The Matriarch of Ruins*
     KR - Dec 15 2015 - pNA [501+]
McDermid, Jane - *The Schooling of Girls in Britain and Ireland, 1800-1900*
     VS - v57 - i3 - Spring 2015 - p539(4) [501+]
McDermid, Val - *Forensics: The Anatomy of Crime*
     KR - June 1 2015 - pNA [501+]
Forensics: What Bugs, Burns, Prints, DNA, and More Tell Us about Crime
     LJ - v140 - i11 - June 15 2015 - p102(1) [51-500]
     PW - v262 - i19 - May 11 2015 - p50(1) [51-500]
Northanger Abbey (Read by McDermid, Val). Audiobook Review
     LJ - v140 - i7 - April 15 2015 - p47(1) [51-500]
The Skeleton Road
     RVBW - June 2015 - pNA [501+]
Splinter the Silence
     BL - v112 - i3 - Oct 1 2015 - p28(1) [51-500]
     KR - Oct 1 2015 - pNA [51-500]
     NYTBR - Dec 20 2015 - p25(L) [51-500]
McDermott, Gerald R. - *A Trinitarian Theology of Religions: An Evangelical Proposal*
     IBMR - v39 - i2 - April 2015 - p98(1) [501+]
     Theol St - v76 - i3 - Sept 2015 - p620(3) [501+]
McDermott, John D. - *Red Cloud: Oglala Legend*
     RVBW - Oct 2015 - pNA [501+]
McDermott, Joseph P. - *The Making of a New Rural Order in South China, vol. 1: Village, Land, and Lineage in Huizhou, 900-1600*
     AHR - v120 - i3 - June 2015 - p989-990 [501+]
McDermott, Kevin - *The 1989 Revolutions in Central and Eastern Europe: From Communism to Pluralism*
     Slav R - v74 - i3 - Fall 2015 - p646-647 [501+]
McDermott, Nancie - *Southern Soups and Stews: More Than 75 Recipes from Burgoo and Gumbo to Etouffee and Fricassee*
     LJ - v140 - i20 - Dec 1 2015 - p128(2) [51-500]
McDermott, Thomas - *Filled with All the Fullness of God: An Introduction to Catholic Spirituality*
     Theol St - v76 - i2 - June 2015 - p397(1) [501+]
McDiarmid, Lucy - *Poets and the Peacock Dinner: The Literary History of a Meal*
     RES - v66 - i276 - Sept 2015 - p793-795 [501+]
     Spec - v327 - i9723 - Jan 3 2015 - p27(1) [501+]
     TimHES - i2189 - Feb 5 2015 - p59-59 [501+]
     TLS - i5861 - July 31 2015 - p5(1) [501+]
McDonagh, Sorcha - *Death in Brittany*
     BL - v111 - i17 - May 1 2015 - p30(1) [51-500]
McDonald, Ann A. - *The Oxford Inheritance*
     KR - Nov 15 2015 - pNA [51-500]
McDonald, Courtney Greene - *Putting the User First: 30 Strategies for Transforming Library Services*
     R&USQ - v54 - i4 - Summer 2015 - p75(2) [501+]
McDonald, David A. - *My Voice Is My Weapon: Music, Nationalism, and the Poetics of Palestinian Resistance*
     Notes - v72 - i1 - Sept 2015 - p146(3) [501+]
McDonald, Deborah - *A Very Dangerous Woman: The Lives, Loves and Lies of Russia's Most Seductive Spy*
     KR - March 15 2015 - pNA [51-500]
     LJ - v140 - i7 - April 15 2015 - p102(1) [51-500]
     PW - v262 - i16 - April 20 2015 - p68(1) [51-500]
McDonald, Donna - *The Shaman's Mate*
     RVBW - Sept 2015 - pNA [51-500]

McDonald, Ian - *Luna: New Moon*
     BL - v112 - i2 - Sept 15 2015 - p38(1) [51-500]
     PW - v262 - i32 - August 10 2015 - p42(1) [51-500]
McDonald, Jason - *Social Media Marketing Workbook*
     SPBW - Nov 2015 - pNA [51-500]
McDonald, Kim Chanlder - *Flat World Navigation: Collaboration and Networking in the Global Digital Economy*
     RVBW - Oct 2015 - pNA [51-500]
McDonald, Lee Martin - *The Story of Jesus in History and Faith: An Introduction*
     Intpr - v69 - i4 - Oct 2015 - p492(1) [501+]
McDonald, Mary Ann - *Boas*
   c BL - v111 - i22 - August 1 2015 - p54(1) [51-500]
McDonald, Megan - *Amy Namey in Ace Reporter (Illus. by Madrid, Erwin)*
   c HB Guide - v26 - i1 - Spring 2015 - p62(2) [51-500]
Frank Pearl in the Awful Waffle Kerfuffle (Illus. by Madrid, Erwin)
   c HB Guide - v26 - i1 - Spring 2015 - p62(2) [51-500]
Judy Moody, Mood Martian (Read by Rosenblat, Barbara). Audiobook Review
   c SLJ - v61 - i2 - Feb 2015 - p38(3) [501+]
Judy Moody, Mood Martian (Illus. by Reynolds, Peter H.)
   c HB Guide - v26 - i1 - Spring 2015 - p63(1) [51-500]
Shoe Dog (Illus. by Tillotson, Katherine)
   c HB Guide - v26 - i1 - Spring 2015 - p39(1) [51-500]
Stink Moody in Master of Disaster (Illus. by Madrid, Erwin)
   c HB Guide - v26 - i2 - Fall 2015 - p68(2) [51-500]
The Wishbone Wish (Illus. by Reynolds, Peter H.)
   c BL - v111 - i21 - July 1 2015 - p73(1) [51-500]
   c PW - v262 - i34 - August 24 2015 - p80(1) [51-500]
McDonald, Peter - *Sound Intentions: The Workings of Rhyme in Nineteenth-Century Poetry*
     VS - v57 - i2 - Wntr 2015 - p338(2) [501+]
McDonald, Robert I. - *Conservation for Cities: How to Plan and Build Natural Infrastructure*
     LJ - v140 - i13 - August 1 2015 - p121(1) [51-500]
McDonald, Robert M.S. - *Sons of the Father: George Washington and His Proteges*
     JSH - v81 - i1 - Feb 2015 - p173(2) [501+]
     MA - v57 - i2 - Spring 2015 - p61(4) [501+]
McDonald, Wren - *Cyber Realm*
     PW - v262 - i27 - July 6 2015 - p55(1) [51-500]
McDonnell, Duggan - *Drinking the Devil's Acre: A Love Letter from San Francisco and Her Cocktails*
     LJ - v140 - i15 - Sept 15 2015 - p97(1) [51-500]
McDonnell, Michael A. - *Masters of Empire: Great Lakes Indians and the Making of America*
     KR - Oct 1 2015 - pNA [501+]
     LJ - v140 - i17 - Oct 15 2015 - p102(1) [51-500]
Mcdonnell, Michael A. - *Remembering the Revolution: Memory, History, and Nation Making from Independence to the Civil War*
     Pub Hist - v37 - i3 - August 2015 - p137(3) [501+]
McDonnell, Patrick - *Me ... Jane (Read by Kellgren, Katherine). Audiobook Review*
     BL - v111 - i13 - March 1 2015 - p70(1) [51-500]
A Perfectly Messed-Up Story (Illus. by McDonnell, Patrick)
   c HB Guide - v26 - i1 - Spring 2015 - p12(1) [51-500]
Thank You and Good Night (Illus. by McDonnell, Patrick)
   c BL - v112 - i3 - Oct 1 2015 - p84(1) [51-500]
   c HB - v91 - i5 - Sept-Oct 2015 - p83(2) [51-500]
   c KR - August 1 2015 - pNA [51-500]
   c NYTBR - Nov 8 2015 - p29(L) [51-500]
   c PW - v262 - i31 - August 3 2015 - p55(1) [51-500]
   c PW - v262 - i49 - Dec 2 2015 - p39(1) [51-500]
   c SLJ - v61 - i8 - August 2015 - p73(2) [51-500]
McDonough, Frank - *The Gestapo: The Myth and Reality of Hitler's Secret Polic*
     TimHES - i2227 - Oct 29 2015 - p50-51 [501+]
McDonough, Kelly S. - *The Learned Ones: Nahua Intellectuals in Postconquest Mexico*
     CH - v84 - i4 - Dec 2015 - p886 [501+]
The Learned Ones: Nahua Intellectuals in Postconquest Mexico (Illus. by McDonough, Kelly S.)
     Ams - v72 - i2 - April 2015 - p343(2) [501+]
McDonough, Peter - *The Catholic Labyrinth: Power, Apathy, and a Passion for Reform in the American Church*
     Am St - v54 - i2 - Summer 2015 - p33-42 [501+]
     Theol St - v76 - i1 - March 2015 - p204(3) [501+]
     JR - v95 - i2 - April 2015 - p285(3) [501+]
McDonough, Susan Alice - *Witnesses, Neighbors, and Community in Late Medieval Marseille: The New Middle Ages*
     AHR - v120 - i3 - June 2015 - p1098-1099 [501+]
     Med R - Feb 2015 - pNA [501+]
McDonough, Yona Zeldis - *Little Author in the Big Woods: A Biography of Laura Ingalls Wilder (Illus. by Thermes, Jennifer)*
   c CCB-B - v68 - i5 - Jan 2015 - p268(2) [51-500]
   c HB Guide - v26 - i1 - Spring 2015 - p195(1) [51-500]
McDougal, Dennis - *Dylan: The Biography*
     Bwatch - Feb 2015 - pNA [51-500]
McDougall, Christopher - *Natural Born Heroes: How a Daring Band of Misfits Mastered the Lost Secrets of Strength and Endurance (Read by Smith, Nicholas Guy). Audiobook Review*
     PW - v262 - i26 - June 29 2015 - p65(1) [51-500]
Natural Born Heroes: How a Daring Band of Misfits Mastered the Lost Secrets of Strength and Endurance
     BL - v111 - i14 - March 15 2015 - p42(1) [51-500]
     KR - Feb 1 2015 - pNA [501+]
     PW - v262 - i5 - Feb 2 2015 - p51(1) [51-500]
     TimHES - i2227 - Oct 29 2015 - p47(1) [501+]
McDougall, Chros - *The Best Soccer Players of All Time*
   c HB Guide - v26 - i2 - Fall 2015 - p197(2) [51-500]
McDougall, Sara - *Bigamy and Christian Identity in Late Medieval Champagne*
     CH - v84 - i1 - March 2015 - p238(3) [501+]
McDougall, Sophia - *Mars Evacuees*
   y HB Guide - v26 - i2 - Fall 2015 - p93(1) [51-500]
   c Res Links - v20 - i3 - Feb 2015 - p13(1) [501+]
Space Hostages
   c KR - Nov 15 2015 - pNA [51-500]
   c SLJ - v61 - i10 - Oct 2015 - p91(1) [51-500]
McDowell, Catherine W. - *Now You Hear My Horn: The Journal of James Wilson Nichols, 1820-1887*
     Roundup M - v22 - i5 - June 2015 - p22(1) [501+]
McDowell, Deborah E. - *The Punitive Turn: New Approaches to Race and Incarceration*
     CS - v44 - i5 - Sept 2015 - p677-680 [501+]
McDowell, Megan - *My Documents*
     NY - v91 - i17 - June 22 2015 - p77 [501+]
     TLS - i5849 - May 8 2015 - p20(1) [501+]
Private Lives of Trees
     NY - v91 - i17 - June 22 2015 - p77 [501+]
McDowell, Pamela - *Arts and Crafts*
   c Res Links - v20 - i3 - Feb 2015 - p20(3) [501+]
Ceremonies and Celebrations
   c Res Links - v20 - i3 - Feb 2015 - p20(3) [501+]
Clothing
   c Res Links - v20 - i3 - Feb 2015 - p20(3) [501+]
Gorillas
   c BL - v112 - i6 - Nov 15 2015 - p42(1) [51-500]
Music and Dance
   c Res Links - v20 - i3 - Feb 2015 - p20(3) [501+]
Tools and Weapons
   c Res Links - v20 - i3 - Feb 2015 - p20(3) [501+]
McDuffie, Erik S. - *Sojourning for Freedom: Black Women, American Communism, and the Making of Black Left Feminism*
     JWH - v27 - i3 - Fall 2015 - p204(7) [501+]
McElhinney, James L. - *Art Students League of New York on Painting: Lessons and Meditations on Mediums, Styles, and Methods*
     LJ - v140 - i20 - Dec 1 2015 - p100(1) [51-500]
McElligott, Anthony - *Rethinking the Weimar Republic: Authority and Authoritarianism, 1916-1936*
     HER - v130 - i545 - August 2015 - p1038(3) [501+]
McElligott, Matthew - *Mad Scientist Academy: The Dinosaur Disaster (Illus. by McElligott, Matthew)*
   c BL - v111 - i19-20 - June 1 2015 - p68(1) [51-500]
     KR - April 1 2015 - pNA [51-500]
   c SLJ - v61 - i6 - June 2015 - p87(2) [51-500]
McEnroe, Kevin - *Our Town*
     BL - v111 - i17 - May 1 2015 - p79(1) [51-500]
     KR - April 15 2015 - pNA [501+]
     PW - v262 - i13 - March 30 2015 - p48(2) [51-500]
McEnteer, James - *Acting Like It Matters: John Malpede and the Los Angeles Poverty Department*
     Am Theat - v32 - i7 - Sept 2015 - p52(2) [501+]
McEntire, Mark - *Portraits of a Mature God: Choices in Old Testament Theology*
     Intpr - v69 - i4 - Oct 2015 - p491(2) [501+]

McEntyre, Marilyn Chandler - *A Faithful Farewell: Living Your Last Chapter with Love*
    Bwatch - July 2015 - pNA [51-500]

McEvoy, John - *High Stakes*
    RVBW - April 2015 - pNA [51-500]

McEwan, Ian - *Amsterdam*
    TimHES - i2199 - April 16 2015 - p57-1 [501+]
  The Children Act
    Comw - v142 - i2 - Jan 23 2015 - p22(3) [501+]
    HR - v67 - i4 - Wntr 2015 - p685-692 [501+]
    Hum - v75 - i1 - Jan-Feb 2015 - p41(2) [501+]
    NYTBR - May 24 2015 - p28(L) [501+]
    Quad - v59 - i5 - May 2015 - p102(3) [501+]
  The Comfort of Strangers
    TimHES - i2201 - April 30 2015 - p51(1) [501+]

McEwan, Paul - *The Birth of a Nation*
    Si & So - v25 - i10 - Oct 2015 - p114(1) [501+]

McEwen, Katharine - *Bear Hug (Illus. by McEwen, Katharine)*
    c HB Guide - v26 - i1 - Spring 2015 - p39(1) [51-500]

McEwen, Rory - *The Colours of Reality*
    Spec - v328 - i9752 - July 25 2015 - p32(2) [501+]

McEwen, Scott - *American Sniper*
    NYRB - v62 - i6 - April 2 2015 - p6(2) [501+]
  The Sniper and the Wolf: A Sniper Elite Novel
    PW - v262 - i10 - March 9 2015 - p52(1) [51-500]
  Target America
    RVBW - Feb 2015 - pNA [51-500]

McFadden, C. A. - *Love, or, the Witches of Windward Circle*
    KR - March 1 2015 - pNA [501+]

McFadden, David W. - *Shouting Your Name Down the Well: Tankas and Haiku*
    Can Lit - i224 - Spring 2015 - p108 [501+]

McFadden, Jane - *James Welling: The Mind on Fire*
    LJ - v140 - i3 - Feb 15 2015 - p106(1) [501+]

McFadden, Jesse - *A Construction Worker's Tools*
    c BL - v112 - i3 - Oct 1 2015 - p48(1) [51-500]

McFadden, Johnjoe - *Life on the Edge: The Coming of Age of Quantum Biology*
    BL - v111 - i19-20 - June 1 2015 - p14(2) [51-500]
    KR - May 15 2015 - pNA [501+]
    LJ - v140 - i13 - August 1 2015 - p121(1) [51-500]

McFadden, Laura - *Knitless: 50 No-Knit, Stash-Busting Yarn Projects*
    LJ - v140 - i17 - Oct 15 2015 - p88(1) [51-500]

McFall, Claire - *Black Cairn Point*
    y Magpies - v30 - i5 - Nov 2015 - p41(1) [501+]

McFarland, Ben - *The Thinking Drinker's Guide to Alcohol: A Cocktail of Amusing Anecdotes and Opinion on the Art of Imbibing*
    LJ - v140 - i3 - Feb 15 2015 - p122(2) [51-500]

McFarland, Clive - *A Bed for Bear (Illus. by McFarland, Clive)*
    c HB Guide - v26 - i2 - Fall 2015 - p44(1) [51-500]

McFarland, Gerald W. - *The Last of Our Kind*
    KR - Dec 1 2015 - pNA [501+]

McFarland, Ian A. - *From Nothing: A Theology of Creation*
    Theol St - v76 - i2 - June 2015 - p388(2) [501+]
    TT - v72 - i3 - Oct 2015 - p336-337 [501+]

McFarlane, Bonnie - *You're Better Than Me: A Memoir*
    KR - Dec 15 2015 - pNA [501+]
    PW - v262 - i46 - Nov 16 2015 - p66(2) [501+]

McFarlane, Brian - *Peter Puck and the Runaway Zamboni Machine (Illus. by Storey, Geri)*
    c HB Guide - v26 - i2 - Fall 2015 - p69(1) [51-500]
    c Res Links - v20 - i3 - Feb 2015 - p13(1) [51-500]
  Peter Puck and the Stolen Stanley Cup (Illus. by Storey, Geri)
    c HB Guide - v26 - i2 - Fall 2015 - p69(1) [51-500]
    c Res Links - v20 - i4 - April 2015 - p12(1) [51-500]

McFarlane, Fiona - *The Night Guest*
    NYTBR - Jan 4 2015 - p24(L) [501+]

McFarlane, Mhairi - *It's Not Me It's You*
    BL - v111 - i18 - May 15 2015 - p23(1) [51-500]
    LJ - v140 - i7 - April 15 2015 - p77(1) [51-500]

McFarlane, Sheryl - *Jessie's Island (Illus. by Lott, Sheena)*
    c SLJ - v61 - i7 - July 2015 - p64(1) [51-500]

McFate, Sean - *The Modern Mercenary: Private Armies and What They Mean for World Order*
    Econ - v414 - i8920 - Jan 10 2015 - p75(US) [501+]
    For Aff - v94 - i4 - July-August 2015 - pNA [501+]
    HNet - July 2015 - pNA [501+]

McFawn, Monica - *Bright Shards of Someplace Else*
    PSQ - v89 - i1 - Spring 2015 - p159(3) [501+]

McFetridge, John - *A Little More Free*
    PW - v262 - i30 - July 27 2015 - p45(2) [51-500]

McGann, Jerome - *A New Republic of Letters: Memory and Scholarship in the Age of Digital Reproduction*
    Isis - v106 - i2 - June 2015 - p426(2) [501+]
  The Poet Edgar Allan Poe: Alien Angel
    Bks & Cult - v21 - i2 - March-April 2015 - p29(1) [501+]
    TLS - i5836 - Feb 6 2015 - p7(1) [501+]

McGann, Oisin - *Ancient Appetites*
    y BL - v112 - i2 - Sept 15 2015 - p62(1) [51-500]
    y KR - May 1 2015 - pNA [51-500]
    y SLJ - v61 - i8 - August 2015 - p106(1) [51-500]
  Rat Runners
    y BL - v111 - i9-10 - Jan 1 2015 - p100(1) [51-500]
  Strangled Silence
    BL - v111 - i14 - March 15 2015 - p68(1) [51-500]
    SLJ - v61 - i2 - Feb 2015 - p105(2) [51-500]
    y VOYA - v38 - i1 - April 2015 - p65(1) [51-500]

McGarrigle, Anna - *Mountain City Girls*
    Mac - v128 - i45 - Nov 16 2015 - p58(1) [501+]

McGarrity, Michael - *Backlands*
    Roundup M - v22 - i6 - August 2015 - p31(1) [501+]

McGarry, Katie - *Nowhere but Here*
    y BL - v111 - i21 - July 1 2015 - p57(2) [51-500]
    y HB Guide - v26 - i2 - Fall 2015 - p131(1) [51-500]
    y SLJ - v61 - i5 - May 2015 - p121(1) [51-500]

McGaughy, Chris - *Supporting the Dream: High School-College Partnerships for College and Career Readiness*
    Bwatch - August 2015 - pNA [501+]

McGee, J. Sears - *An Industrious Mind: The Worlds of Sir Simonds D'Ewes*
    TLS - i5872 - Oct 16 2015 - p25(1) [501+]

McGee, James - *The Blooding*
    BL - v111 - i19-20 - June 1 2015 - p47(1) [51-500]
    KR - May 15 2015 - pNA [501+]
    LJ - v140 - i11 - June 15 2015 - p78(2) [51-500]
    PW - v262 - i19 - May 11 2015 - p36(1) [51-500]

McGee, Joe - *Peanut Butter & Brains: A Zombie Culinary Tale (Illus. by Santoso, Charles)*
    c HB - v91 - i5 - Sept-Oct 2015 - p69(1) [51-500]
    c KR - August 1 2015 - pNA [51-500]
    c PW - v262 - i20 - May 18 2015 - p84(1) [51-500]
    c SLJ - v61 - i9 - Sept 2015 - p108(2) [51-500]

McGee, Laurelin - *Love Struck*
    PW - v262 - i51 - Dec 14 2015 - p68(1) [51-500]
  Miss Match
    PW - v262 - i11 - March 16 2015 - p69(1) [51-500]

McGee, Marni - *Bear Can't Sleep! (Illus. by Julian, Sean)*
    c KR - July 15 2015 - pNA [51-500]

McGee, Randel - *Fun and Festive Fall Crafts: Leaf Rubbings, Dancing Scarecrows, and Pinecone Turkeys*
    c HB Guide - v26 - i1 - Spring 2015 - p178(1) [51-500]
  Fun and Festive Spring Crafts: Flower Puppets, Bunny Masks, and Mother's Day Pop-Up Cards
    c HB Guide - v26 - i1 - Spring 2015 - p178(1) [51-500]
  Fun and Festive Summer Crafts: Tie-Dyed Shirts, Bug Cages, and Sand Castles
    c HB Guide - v26 - i1 - Spring 2015 - p178(1) [51-500]
  Fun and Festive Winter Crafts: Snow Globes, Groundhog Puppets, and Fairy Masks
    c HB Guide - v26 - i1 - Spring 2015 - p178(1) [51-500]

McGehee, Claudia - *My Wilderness: An Alaskan Adventure (Illus. by McGehee, Claudia)*
    c HB Guide - v26 - i2 - Fall 2015 - p44(1) [51-500]
    c SLJ - v61 - i5 - May 2015 - p88(1) [51-500]
  My Wilderness (Illus. by McGehee, Claudia)
    c KR - Jan 15 2015 - pNA [51-500]

McGevna, Matthew - *Little Beasts*
    KR - May 15 2015 - pNA [51-500]
    PW - v262 - i20 - May 18 2015 - p60(1) [51-500]

McGhee, Alison - *Firefly Hollow (Illus. by Denise, Christopher)*
    c CCB-B - v69 - i2 - Oct 2015 - p101(2) [51-500]
    c CH Bwatch - Oct 2015 - pNA [51-500]
    c HB - v91 - i4 - July-August 2015 - p140(1) [51-500]
    c KR - April 15 2015 - pNA [51-500]
    c PW - v262 - i21 - May 25 2015 - p59(2) [51-500]
    c PW - v262 - i49 - Dec 2 2015 - p65(2) [51-500]
    c SLJ - v61 - i6 - June 2015 - p101(2) [51-500]
    c NYTBR - Sept 13 2015 - p22(L) [501+]
  Making a Friend (Read by Berneis, Susie). Audiobook Review
    c SLJ - v61 - i3 - March 2015 - p76(1) [51-500]
  Star Bright: A Christmas Story (Illus. by Reynolds, Peter H.)
    c HB Guide - v26 - i1 - Spring 2015 - p12(1) [51-500]

The Sweetest Witch Around (Illus. by Bliss, Harry)
    c HB Guide - v26 - i1 - Spring 2015 - p39(1) [51-500]

McGhee, George R., Jr. - *When the Invasion of Land Failed: The Legacy of the Devonian Extinctions*
    QRB - v90 - i1 - March 2015 - p81(1) [501+]

McGill, Leslie - *The Game*
    y SLJ - v61 - i9 - Sept 2015 - p151(4) [501+]
  Gearhead
    y SLJ - v61 - i9 - Sept 2015 - p151(4) [501+]

McGill, Ralph - *A Church, a School: Pulitzer Prize-Winning Civil Rights Editorials from the Atlanta Constitution*
    JSH - v81 - i4 - Nov 2015 - p1059(2) [501+]

McGillick, Paul - *Sustainable Luxury: The New Singapore House, Solutions for a Livable Future*
    PW - v262 - i3 - Jan 19 2015 - p72(2) [51-500]

McGilligan, Patrick - *Young Orson: The Years of Luck and Genius on the Path to Citizen Kane*
    BL - v112 - i3 - Oct 1 2015 - p10(1) [51-500]
    KR - Oct 1 2015 - pNA [501+]
    LJ - v140 - i15 - Sept 15 2015 - p79(1) [51-500]
    Spec - v329 - i9772 - Dec 12 2015 - p82(1) [501+]

McGinley, Paige A. - *Staging the Blues: From Tent Shows to Tourism*
    JAH - v102 - i2 - Sept 2015 - p591-592 [501+]

McGinley, Patrick - *Cold Spring*
    ILS - v34 - i2 - Spring 2015 - p14(1) [501+]

McGinn, Bernard - *Thomas Aquinas's Summa Theologiae: A Biography*
    Bks & Cult - v21 - i2 - March-April 2015 - p35(2) [501+]
    CH - v84 - i2 - June 2015 - p430(2) [501+]
    TT - v71 - i4 - Jan 2015 - p468-470 [501+]
    Theol St - v76 - i3 - Sept 2015 - p637(1) [501+]

McGinn, Colin - *Prehension: The Hand and the Emergence of Humanity*
    New Sci - v227 - i3038 - Sept 12 2015 - p41(1) [501+]

McGinnis, Maggie - *Forever This Time*
    BL - v112 - i5 - Nov 1 2015 - p36(1) [51-500]

McGinnis, Mindy - *In a Handful of Dust*
    y HB Guide - v26 - i1 - Spring 2015 - p116(1) [51-500]
  A Madness So Discreet
    y KR - August 15 2015 - pNA [51-500]
    y SLJ - v61 - i8 - August 2015 - p106(2) [51-500]
    y VOYA - v38 - i5 - Dec 2015 - p60(1) [51-500]

McGinty, Alice B. - *Rabbi Benjamin's Buttons (Illus. by Reinhardt, Jennifer Black)*
    c HB Guide - v26 - i1 - Spring 2015 - p39(1) [51-500]

McGinty, Brian - *Lincoln's Greatest Case: The River, the Bridge, and the Making of America*
    BL - v111 - i9-10 - Jan 1 2015 - p34(1) [51-500]
    BooChiTr - Feb 21 2015 - p12(1) [501+]
    CSM - Feb 16 2015 - pNA [501+]

McGinty, Ian - *Hello Kitty: It's about Time*
    BL - v111 - i9-10 - Jan 1 2015 - p63(1) [51-500]

McGirr, Lisa - *The War on Alcohol: Prohibition and the Rise of the American State*
    KR - August 15 2015 - pNA [501+]
    LJ - v140 - i16 - Oct 1 2015 - p94(2) [51-500]
    PW - v262 - i33 - August 17 2015 - p60(1) [51-500]

McGlynn, Sean - *Blood Cries Afar: The Forgotten Invasion of England, 1216*
    HT - v65 - i6 - June 2015 - p56(2) [501+]

McGoey, Linsey - *No Such Thing as a Free Gift: The Gates Foundation and the Price of Philanthropy*
    KR - August 15 2015 - pNA [501+]
    Mac - v128 - i42 - Oct 26 2015 - p56(2) [501+]
    PW - v262 - i35 - August 31 2015 - p79(1) [51-500]

McGonigal, Jane - *SuperBetter: A Revolutionary Approach to Getting Stronger, Happier, Braver and More Resilient: Powered by the Science of Games*
    y BL - v112 - i1 - Sept 1 2015 - p22(1) [51-500]
    KR - June 1 2015 - pNA [501+]
    NS - v144 - i5290 - Nov 27 2015 - p46(3) [501+]
    NY - v91 - i27 - Sept 14 2015 - p86 [501+]
    NYTBR - Oct 18 2015 - p10(L) [501+]
    PW - v262 - i29 - July 20 2015 - p180(1) [51-500]

McGonigal, Kelly - *The Upside of Stress: Why Stress Is Good for You and How to Get Good at It*
    Har Bus R - v93 - i7-8 - July-August 2015 - p130(2) [501+]
    PW - v262 - i13 - March 30 2015 - p70(1) [51-500]

McGoran, Jon - *Deadout*
    RVBW - April 2015 - pNA [51-500]
    RVBW - July 2015 - pNA [51-500]

McGough, Julie V. - *The Power of Questioning*
 Sci & Ch - v52 - i9 - Summer 2015 - p29 [51-500]
 Sci & Ch - v53 - i1 - Sept 2015 - p92 [51-500]
McGough, Roger - *I Never Liked Wednesdays (Illus. by Broad, Michael)*
 c Sch Lib - v63 - i3 - Autumn 2015 - p168(1) [51-500]
 You Tell Me (Illus. by Paul, Korky)
 c Sch Lib - v63 - i2 - Summer 2015 - p113(1) [51-500]
McGovern, Cammie - *Just My Luck*
 c KR - Nov 1 2015 - pNA [51-500]
 PW - v262 - i45 - Nov 9 2015 - p59(1) [51-500]
 c SLJ - v61 - i12 - Dec 2015 - p104(1) [51-500]
 y VOYA - v38 - i5 - Dec 2015 - p60(1) [51-500]
 A Step toward Falling
 y BL - v112 - i3 - Oct 1 2015 - p75(1) [51-500]
 y HB - v91 - i5 - Sept-Oct 2015 - p110(2) [51-500]
 y KR - July 1 2015 - pNA [51-500]
 y NYTBR - Nov 8 2015 - p30(L) [501+]
 y PW - v262 - i30 - July 27 2015 - p71(1) [51-500]
 y PW - v262 - i49 - Dec 2 2015 - p98(1) [51-500]
 y SLJ - v61 - i9 - Sept 2015 - p169(1) [51-500]
 y VOYA - v38 - i4 - Oct 2015 - p57(1) [51-500]
McGovern, Kate - *Rules for 50/50 Chances*
 y BL - v112 - i2 - Sept 15 2015 - p75(1) [51-500]
 y HB - v91 - i6 - Nov-Dec 2015 - p83(2) [501+]
 y KR - Sept 1 2015 - pNA [51-500]
 y PW - v262 - i37 - Sept 14 2015 - p79(1) [51-500]
 y SLJ - v61 - i10 - Oct 2015 - p114(1) [51-500]
 y VOYA - v38 - i5 - Dec 2015 - p60(1) [51-500]
McGowan, Andrew B. - *Ancient Christian Worship: Early Church Practices in Social, Historical, and Theological Perspective*
 Theol St - v76 - i3 - Sept 2015 - p628(2) [501+]
McGowan, Anthony - *Pike*
 y Sch Lib - v63 - i3 - Autumn 2015 - p184(1) [51-500]
McGowan, Claire - *The Dead Ground*
 BL - v111 - i21 - July 1 2015 - p36(1) [51-500]
 PW - v262 - i20 - May 18 2015 - p66(1) [51-500]
McGowan, Jayme - *One Bear Extraordinaire (Illus. by McGowan, Jayme)*
 c BL - v112 - i2 - Sept 15 2015 - p69(1) [51-500]
 c KR - July 15 2015 - pNA [51-500]
 c PW - v262 - i24 - June 15 2015 - p83(1) [51-500]
 c SLJ - v61 - i9 - Sept 2015 - p125(1) [51-500]
McGowan, Jennifer - *Maid of Deception*
 y HB Guide - v26 - i1 - Spring 2015 - p117(1) [51-500]
 Maid of Wonder
 y KR - June 15 2015 - pNA [51-500]
 y SLJ - v61 - i8 - August 2015 - p114(2) [51-500]
McGowan, Margaret M. - *Dynastic Marriages 1612/1615: A Celebration of the Habsburg and Bourbon Unions*
 Historian - v77 - i3 - Fall 2015 - p621(2) [501+]
 Ren Q - v68 - i1 - Spring 2015 - p290-291 [501+]
McGowan, Michael - *When the Devil Flies*
 KR - Oct 1 2015 - pNA [501+]
McGowen, Georgia Lee - *Dear Mom and Dad*
 KR - Oct 15 2015 - pNA [501+]
McGrade, Arthur Stephen - *Richard Hooker: Of the "Laws of Ecclesiastical Polity" - A Critical Edition with Modern Spelling*
 RES - v66 - i275 - June 2015 - p575-577 [501+]
McGranaghan, Mary K. - *Thinking Good Thoughts about Me*
 KR - June 15 2015 - pNA [501+]
McGrath, Alister - *The Big Question: Why We Can't Stop Talking about Science, Faith, and God*
 BL - v112 - i6 - Nov 15 2015 - p11(2) [51-500]
 KR - Sept 1 2015 - pNA [501+]
McGrath, Alister E. - *The Big Question: Why We Can't Stop Talking about Science, Faith, and God*
 Ch Today - v59 - i10 - Dec 2015 - p74(1) [51-500]
 LJ - v140 - i17 - Oct 15 2015 - p91(2) [51-500]
 Emil Brunner: A Reappraisal
 TT - v72 - i1 - April 2015 - p109-110 [501+]
 The Spirit of Grace: A Guide for Study and Devotion
 CC - v132 - i19 - Sept 16 2015 - p42(1) [51-500]
McGrath, Barbara Barbieri - *Teddy Bear Addition (Illus. by Nihoff, Tim)*
 c HB - v91 - i1 - Jan-Feb 2015 - p106(2) [51-500]
McGrath, Brendan - *Landscape and Society in Contemporary Ireland*
 GR - v105 - i1 - Jan 2015 - p123(4) [501+]
McGrath, Paula - *Generation*
 NS - v144 - i5277 - August 28 2015 - p43(1) [51-500]
McGrath, Rick - *Deep Ends: The J.G. Ballard Anthology 2014*
 SFS - v42 - i2 - July 2015 - p388-390 [501+]

McGrath, Wendy - *North East*
 RVBW - May 2015 - pNA [51-500]
McGraw, Jason - *The Work of Recognition: Caribbean Colombia and the Postemancipation Struggle for Citizenship*
 HAHR - v95 - i2 - May 2015 - p361-363 [501+]
 JIH - v46 - i1 - Summer 2015 - p143-144 [501+]
McGraw, Peter - *The Humor Code: A Global Search for What Makes Things Funny*
 SAH - v4 - i2 - Dec 15 2015 - p281-284 [501+]
McGraw, Seamus - *Betting the Farm on a Drought: Stories from the Front Lines of Climate Change*
 BL - v111 - i12 - Feb 15 2015 - p25(1) [51-500]
 KR - Jan 15 2015 - pNA [501+]
McGregor, James H. S. - *Back to the Garden: Nature and the Mediterranean World from Prehistory to the Present*
 TimHES - i2194 - March 12 2015 - p52(1) [501+]
McGregor, Michael N. - *Pure Act: The Uncommon Life of Robert Lax*
 AM - v213 - i13 - Nov 2 2015 - p36(2) [501+]
 NYTBR - Dec 27 2015 - p18(L) [501+]
McGregor, Robert Kuhn - *A Calculus of Color: The Integration of Baseball's American League*
 LJ - v140 - i3 - Feb 15 2015 - p103(2) [501+]
McGuane, Thomas - *Crow Fair: Stories*
 KR - Jan 1 2015 - pNA [501+]
 NYT - March 26 2015 - pC6(L) [501+]
 NYTBR - March 29 2015 - p11(L) [501+]
McGuigan, Mary Ann - *Crossing into Brooklyn*
 y KR - May 1 2015 - pNA [51-500]
 y SLJ - v61 - i5 - May 2015 - p121(1) [51-500]
 y VOYA - v38 - i2 - June 2015 - p65(2) [51-500]
McGuinness, Lisa - *Catarina's Ring*
 SPBW - Nov 2015 - pNA [51-500]
McGuire, Beverley Foulks - *Living Karma: The Religious Practices of Ouyi Zhixu*
 HNet - July 2015 - pNA [51-500]
 JAS - v74 - i2 - May 2015 - p474-475 [501+]
McGuire, Ian - *The North Water*
 BL - v112 - i6 - Nov 15 2015 - p28(1) [51-500]
McGuire, Kara - *All about the Green: The Teens' Guide to Finding Work and Making Money*
 y Teach Lib - v42 - i3 - Feb 2015 - p10(1) [51-500]
McGuire, Richard - *Here (Illus. by McGuire, Richard)*
 ABR - v36 - i2 - Jan-Feb 2015 - p25(1) [501+]
 NS - v144 - i5249 - Feb 13 2015 - p51(2) [501+]
 NYT - Nov 27 2015 - pC31(L) [501+]
 NYTBR - Oct 18 2015 - p12(L) [501+]
McGuire, Sarah - *Valiant*
 y BL - v111 - i19-20 - June 1 2015 - p102(2) [51-500]
 y HB Guide - v26 - i2 - Fall 2015 - p93(1) [51-500]
 c KR - March 15 2015 - pNA [51-500]
 c SLJ - v61 - i5 - May 2015 - p103(2) [51-500]
McGuire, Seanan - *Every Heart a Doorway*
 PW - v262 - i44 - Nov 2 2015 - p65(1) [51-500]
 Indexing
 MFSF - v128 - i1-2 - Jan-Feb 2015 - p37(4) [501+]
 Sparrow Hill Road
 MFSF - v128 - i1-2 - Jan-Feb 2015 - p37(4) [501+]
McGuirk, Leslie - *Gobble, Gobble, Tucker!*
 c KR - Jan 1 2015 - pNA [51-500]
McHugh, Adam - *The Listening Life: Embracing Attentiveness in a World of Distraction*
 Ch Today - v59 - i9 - Nov 2015 - p72(1) [501+]
 PW - v262 - i41 - Oct 12 2015 - p63(1) [51-500]
McHugh, Arianne - *Seven Ancient Wonders of the World*
 y SLJ - v61 - i9 - Sept 2015 - p151(4) [501+]
McHugh, Dominic - *Alan Jay Lerner: A Father's Letters*
 TLS - i5837 - Feb 13 2015 - p21(1) [501+]
McHugh, Matt - *Radioland*
 PW - v262 - i23 - June 8 2015 - p43(2) [501+]
McHugo, John - *Syria: A History of the Last Hundred Years*
 KR - Jan 15 2015 - pNA [501+]
 PW - v262 - i4 - Jan 26 2015 - p164(2) [51-500]
McInelly, Brett C. - *Textual Warfare and the Making of Methodism*
 CH - v84 - i4 - Dec 2015 - p895(4) [501+]
McInerney, Lisa - *The Glorious Heresies*
 Spec - v328 - i9742 - May 16 2015 - p49(1) [501+]
McInerney, Paul-Brian - *From Social Movement to Moral Market: How the Circuit Riders Sparked an IT Revolution and Created a Technology Market*
 CS - v44 - i5 - Sept 2015 - p680-682 [501+]
McInnes, Mitchell - *The Canadian Law of Unjust Enrichment and Restitution*
 Law Q Rev - v131 - April 2015 - p323-325 [501+]

McInnis, David - *Lost Plays in Shakespeare's England*
 RES - v66 - i275 - June 2015 - p579-581 [501+]
 TLS - i5855 - June 19 2015 - p24(1) [501+]
McInnis, Maurie D. - *Slaves Waiting for Sale: Abolitionist Art and the American Slave Trade*
 VS - v57 - i3 - Spring 2015 - p556(4) [501+]
McInroy, Mark - *Balthasar on the Spiritual Senses: Perceiving Splendor*
 JAAR - v83 - i4 - Dec 2015 - p1163-1165 [501+]
 Balthasar on the Spiritual Senses: Perceiving Splendour
 JR - v95 - i4 - Oct 2015 - p572(3) [501+]
McInton, Marjorie Keniston - *Poor Relief in England, 1350-1600*
 HER - v130 - i543 - April 2015 - p437(2) [501+]
McIntosh, D.J. - *Angel of Eden*
 Nat Post - v17 - i205 - July 4 2015 - pWP4(1) [501+]
McIntosh, Fiona - *The Whisperer*
 c CH Bwatch - July 2015 - pNA [51-500]
 c CCB-B - v68 - i9 - May 2015 - p457(1) [51-500]
 c BL - v111 - i14 - March 15 2015 - p76(1) [51-500]
 y HB Guide - v26 - i2 - Fall 2015 - p94(1) [51-500]
 c KR - Feb 1 2015 - pNA [51-500]
 c SLJ - v61 - i2 - Feb 2015 - p88(1) [51-500]
McIntosh, Janet - *The Edge of Islam: Personhood, and Ethnoreligious Boundaries on the Kenya Coast*
 JTWS - v32 - i1 - Spring 2015 - p338(3) [501+]
McIntosh, Will - *Burning Midnight*
 y KR - Nov 1 2015 - pNA [51-500]
McIntyre, Sarah - *Dinosaur Police*
 c Sch Lib - v63 - i3 - Autumn 2015 - p158(1) [51-500]
 Jampires (Illus. by O'Connell, David)
 c NYTBR - June 21 2015 - p17(L) [501+]
 c NYTBR - June 21 2015 - p17(L) [501+]
 c SLJ - v61 - i5 - May 2015 - p88(1) [51-500]
McIntyre, W. David - *Winding Up the British Empire in the Pacific Islands*
 HNet - June 2015 - pNA [51-500]
McIsaac, Meaghan - *The Boys of Fire and Ash*
 c BL - v111 - i15 - April 1 2015 - p78(1) [51-500]
 y CCB-B - v69 - i1 - Sept 2015 - p38(2) [51-500]
 y HB Guide - v26 - i2 - Fall 2015 - p94(1) [51-500]
 y KR - March 1 2015 - pNA [51-500]
 c SLJ - v61 - i4 - April 2015 - p155(3) [51-500]
 y VOYA - v38 - i1 - April 2015 - p81(1) [51-500]
McIver, Katherine A. - *Cooking and Eating in Renaissance Italy: From Kitchen to Table*
 TLS - i5847 - April 24 2015 - p30(1) [501+]
McKay, Don - *Angular Unconformity: Collected Poems, 1970-2014*
 Can Lit - i224 - Spring 2015 - p135 [501+]
McKay, George - *Shakin' All Over: Popular Music and Disability*
 PMS - v38 - i1 - Feb 2015 - p102(3) [501+]
McKay, Hilary - *Binny in Secret (Illus. by Player, Micah)*
 c CCB-B - v69 - i1 - Sept 2015 - p39(1) [51-500]
 c HB - v91 - i4 - July-August 2015 - p140(2) [51-500]
 c KR - April 15 2015 - pNA [51-500]
 c Sch Lib - v63 - i3 - Autumn 2015 - p168(1) [51-500]
 c SLJ - v61 - i6 - June 2015 - p102(1) [51-500]
 Lulu and the Hamster in the Night (Illus. by Lamont, Priscilla)
 c HB Guide - v26 - i2 - Fall 2015 - p69(1) [51-500]
 c BL - v111 - i17 - May 1 2015 - p98(1) [51-500]
 c HB - v91 - i3 - May-June 2015 - p114(2) [51-500]
 c SLJ - v61 - i2 - Feb 2015 - p58(1) [51-500]
McKay, Kirsty - *Killer Game*
 c Sch Lib - v63 - i4 - Winter 2015 - p253(2) [51-500]
 Unfed (Read by Shindler, Amy). Audiobook Review
 y SLJ - v61 - i3 - March 2015 - p81(2) [51-500]
McKay, Laurie - *Quest Maker*
 c KR - Oct 15 2015 - pNA [51-500]
 Villain Keeper
 y HB Guide - v26 - i2 - Fall 2015 - p94(1) [51-500]
 c SLJ - v61 - i6 - June 2015 - p46(6) [501+]
McKay, Matthew - *Seeking Jordan: How I Learned the Truth about Death and the Invisible Universe*
 PW - v262 - i51 - Dec 14 2015 - p78(1) [51-500]
McKay, Sharon E. - *The End of the Line*
 c Res Links - v20 - i3 - Feb 2015 - p13(1) [51-500]
 Prison Boy
 y KR - Feb 1 2015 - pNA [51-500]
 y Res Links - v21 - i1 - Oct 2015 - p38(1) [51-500]
 SLJ - v61 - i4 - April 2015 - p156(1) [51-500]
 War Brothers: The Graphic Novel (Illus. by Lafrance, Daniel)
 y Magpies - v30 - i1 - March 2015 - p41(2) [501+]

McKay, Sindy - *Big Cats, Little Cats*
   c CH Bwatch - April 2015 - pNA [51-500]
McKean, Alan T. - *The Scent of Eternity*
     SPBW - Feb 2015 - pNA [51-500]
McKee, David - *Elmer*
   c HB Guide - v26 - i1 - Spring 2015 - p12(1) [51-500]
Elmer and Butterfly (Illus. by McKee, David)
   c HB Guide - v26 - i2 - Fall 2015 - p44(1) [51-500]
Elmer and the Flood (Illus. by McKee, David)
   c SLJ - v61 - i9 - Sept 2015 - p125(1) [51-500]
Elmer and the Monster (Illus. by McKee, David)
   c HB Guide - v26 - i2 - Fall 2015 - p44(1) [51-500]
McKegney, Sam - *Masculindians: Conversations about Indigenous Manhood*
     Am Ind CRJ - v39 - i2 - Spring 2015 - p144-146 [501+]
McKelvey, Katrina - *Dandelions (Illus. by Lonergan, Kirrili)*
   c KR - Oct 1 2015 - pNA [51-500]
McKendrick, Scot - *Codex Sinaiticus: New Perspectives on the Ancient Biblical Manuscript*
     TLS - i5875 - Nov 6 2015 - p32(1) [501+]
McKenna, Cara - *Burn It Up*
     PW - v262 - i38 - Sept 21 2015 - p59(1) [51-500]
Crosstown Crush
     PW - v262 - i30 - July 27 2015 - p49(2) [51-500]
Give It All
     PW - v262 - i1 - Jan 5 2015 - p58(1) [51-500]
McKenna, Lindsay - *Running Fire*
     PW - v262 - i12 - March 23 2015 - p54(1) [51-500]
Taking Fire
     BL - v111 - i11 - Feb 1 2015 - p31(1) [51-500]
McKenna, Marla - *Mom's Big Catch*
   c CH Bwatch - March 2015 - pNA [51-500]
Sadie's Big Steal
   c CH Bwatch - March 2015 - pNA [51-500]
McKenna, Martin - *The Crocodolly*
   c Magpies - v30 - i4 - Sept 2015 - p27(1) [501+]
The Octopuppy (Illus. by McKenna, Martin)
   c BL - v111 - i19-20 - June 1 2015 - p122(2) [51-500]
   c HB Guide - v26 - i2 - Fall 2015 - p44(1) [51-500]
   c KR - Feb 15 2015 - pNA [51-500]
   c PW - v262 - i8 - Feb 23 2015 - p74(1) [51-500]
McKenna, Michael - *Real People and the Rise of Reality Television*
     BL - v112 - i3 - Oct 1 2015 - p11(1) [51-500]
McKenzie, C.B. - *Bad Country*
     Roundup M - v22 - i4 - April 2015 - p34(1) [501+]
     Roundup M - v22 - i6 - August 2015 - p31(1) [501+]
McKenzie, Catherine - *Smoke*
     BL - v112 - i1 - Sept 1 2015 - p42(2) [51-500]
McKenzie, Elizabeth - *The Portable Veblen*
   y BL - v112 - i7 - Dec 1 2015 - p24(1) [51-500]
     KR - Nov 15 2015 - pNA [501+]
     PW - v262 - i38 - Sept 21 2015 - p48(1) [51-500]
McKenzie, Grant - *Speak the Dead*
     KR - July 15 2015 - pNA [51-500]
     PW - v262 - i29 - July 20 2015 - p171(1) [51-500]
McKenzie, Heath - *My Rules for Being a Pretty Princess (Illus. by McKenzie, Heath)*
   c CH Bwatch - August 2015 - pNA [51-500]
   c HB Guide - v26 - i2 - Fall 2015 - p44(1) [51-500]
   c KR - Feb 15 2015 - pNA [51-500]
Mckenzie, Lisa - *Getting By: Estates, Class and Culture in Austerity Britain*
     TimHES - i2188 - Jan 29 2015 - p49(1) [501+]
McKenzie, Mia - *Black Girl Dangerous: On Race, Queerness, Class, and Gender*
     Stud Hum - v41 - i1-2 - March 2015 - p253(2) [501+]
McKenzie, Paige - *The Haunting of Sunshine Girl (Read by McKenzie, Paige). Audiobook Review*
   y BL - v112 - i6 - Nov 15 2015 - p63(1) [51-500]
   y SLJ - v61 - i12 - Dec 2015 - p80(1) [51-500]
The Haunting of Sunshine Girl
   y CH Bwatch - April 2015 - pNA [51-500]
   y PW - v262 - i4 - Jan 26 2015 - p172(1) [51-500]
   y Sch Lib - v63 - i4 - Winter 2015 - p248(1) [51-500]
   y SLJ - v61 - i3 - March 2015 - p159(2) [51-500]
   y VOYA - v38 - i1 - April 2015 - p81(1) [51-500]
The Hunting of Sunshine Girl
   y KR - Jan 15 2015 - pNA [51-500]
McKenzie, Robert Tracy - *The First Thanksgiving: What the Real Story Tells Us about Loving God and Learning from History*
     Intpr - v69 - i4 - Oct 2015 - p504(1) [501+]

McKenzie, Shelly - *Getting Physical: The Rise of Fitness Culture in America*
     AHR - v120 - i1 - Feb 2015 - p284-285 [501+]
     Am St - v54 - i2 - Summer 2015 - p23-30 [501+]
McKenzie, Sophie - *Every Second Counts*
   y KR - Dec 15 2015 - pNA [51-500]
In a Split Second
   y BL - v111 - i12 - Feb 15 2015 - p82(1) [51-500]
   y KR - Jan 1 2015 - pNA [51-500]
   y VOYA - v37 - i6 - Feb 2015 - p61(1) [51-500]
You Can Trust Me
     KR - Feb 15 2015 - pNA [51-500]
     PW - v262 - i7 - Feb 16 2015 - p160(1) [51-500]
McKenzie, William - *Shakespeare and I*
     Six Ct J - v46 - i1 - Spring 2015 - p182(2) [501+]
McKeon, Belinda - *Tender*
     KR - Dec 1 2015 - pNA [501+]
     PW - v262 - i51 - Dec 14 2015 - p54(2) [501+]
     TLS - i5867 - Sept 11 2015 - p22(1) [501+]
McKeown, Patrick - *The Oxygen Advantage: The Simple, Scientifically Proven Breathing Techniques for a Healthier, Slimmer, Faster, and Fitter You*
     PW - v262 - i31 - August 3 2015 - p53(1) [51-500]
McKersie, Robert B. - *A Decisive Decade: An Insider's View of the Civil Rights Movement during the 1960s*
     ABR - v36 - i4 - May-June 2015 - p23(2) [501+]
McKevett, G.A. - *Killer Gourmet*
     BL - v111 - i14 - March 15 2015 - p46(1) [51-500]
     KR - Feb 1 2015 - pNA [51-500]
     PW - v262 - i1 - Jan 5 2015 - p51(1) [51-500]
Mckiernan-Gonzalez, John - *Fevered Measures: Public Health and Race at the Texas-Mexico Border, 1848-1942*
     Ams - v72 - i1 - Jan 2015 - p171(3) [501+]
McKillen, Elizabeth - *Making the World Safe for Workers: Labor, the Left, and Wilsonian Internationalism*
     AHR - v120 - i2 - April 2015 - p648-649 [501+]
McKillip, Patricia A. - *Kingfisher*
     KR - Dec 15 2015 - pNA [501+]
McKimmie, Chris - *Lara of Newtown*
   c Magpies - v30 - i4 - Sept 2015 - p30(1) [501+]
McKinlay, Jenn - *At the Drop of a Hat*
     BL - v111 - i9-10 - Jan 1 2015 - p44(1) [51-500]
McKinlay, Meg - *A Single Stone*
   y Magpies - v30 - i2 - May 2015 - p42(1) [501+]
McKinley, Mary - *Rusty Summer*
   y SLJ - v61 - i8 - August 2015 - p107(1) [51-500]
   y VOYA - v38 - i4 - Oct 2015 - p57(1) [51-500]
McKinley, Robin - *Beauty (Read by Parry, Charlotte). Audiobook Review*
   y SLJ - v61 - i6 - June 2015 - p53(3) [51-500]
McKinley, Shepherd W. - *Stinking Stones and Rocks of Gold: Phosphate, Fertilizer, and Industrialization in Postbellum South Carolina*
     AHR - v120 - i1 - Feb 2015 - p255-256 [501+]
     JAH - v101 - i4 - March 2015 - p1282-1283 [501+]
     JSH - v81 - i3 - August 2015 - p750(3) [501+]
McKinney, April - *The Outdoor Table: The Ultimate Cookbook for Your Next Backyard BBQ, Front-Porch Meal, Tailgate, or Picnic*
     Bwatch - August 2015 - pNA [51-500]
McKinney, Joe - *The Dead Won't Die*
     PW - v262 - i35 - August 31 2015 - p67(1) [51-500]
McKinney-Whitaker, Courtney - *The Last Sister*
   y HB Guide - v26 - i2 - Fall 2015 - p131(1) [51-500]
   y Roundup M - v22 - i4 - April 2015 - p27(1) [501+]
   y Roundup M - v22 - i6 - August 2015 - p25(1) [501+]
McKinty, Adrian - *Gun Street Girl*
     BL - v111 - i11 - Feb 1 2015 - p27(1) [51-500]
     KR - Jan 1 2015 - pNA [51-500]
     PW - v262 - i2 - Jan 12 2015 - p39(1) [51-500]
McKissack, Jennifer - *Sanctuary*
   y BL - v112 - i1 - Sept 1 2015 - p108(2) [51-500]
   y KR - June 15 2015 - pNA [51-500]
   y SLJ - v61 - i7 - July 2015 - p96(1) [51-500]
McKissack, Patricia C. - *A Friendship for Today*
   c Teach Lib - v42 - i5 - June 2015 - p61(1) [51-500]
McKitterick, Rosamond - *Old Saint Peter's, Rome*
     Med R - August 2015 - pNA [51-500]
     Specu - v90 - i1 - Jan 2015 - p279-281 [501+]
McKnight, Brian D. - *We Fight for Peace: Twenty-Three American Soldiers, Prisoners of War and 'Turncoats' in the Korean War*
     J Mil H - v79 - i2 - April 2015 - p543-544 [501+]
McKnight, Kirk - *The Voices of Baseball: The Game's Greatest Broadcasters Reflect on America's Pastime*
     BL - v111 - i22 - August 1 2015 - p17(1) [51-500]
     PW - v262 - i28 - July 13 2015 - p62(1) [51-500]

McKnight, Scott - *Sharing God's Love: The Jesus Creed for Children (Illus. by Hill, Dave)*
   c CH Bwatch - Jan 2015 - pNA [51-500]
McLachlan, Campbell - *Foreign Relations Law*
     Law Q Rev - v131 - Oct 2015 - p673-676 [501+]
McLachlan, J.A. - *The Occasional Diamond Thief*
   y VOYA - v38 - i3 - August 2015 - p82(1) [51-500]
McLachlan, Jane Ann - *The Occasional Diamond Thief*
     PW - v262 - i14 - April 6 2015 - p61(1) [51-500]
McLachlan, Jenny - *Flirty Dancing*
     BL - v111 - i14 - March 15 2015 - p65(1) [51-500]
   y HB Guide - v26 - i2 - Fall 2015 - p131(1) [51-500]
   y KR - Feb 1 2015 - pNA [51-500]
   y SLJ - v61 - i2 - Feb 2015 - p88(2) [51-500]
   y VOYA - v37 - i6 - Feb 2015 - p61(1) [51-500]
Love Bomb
   y Sch Lib - v63 - i2 - Summer 2015 - p119(1) [51-500]
   y SLJ - v61 - i12 - Dec 2015 - p114(1) [51-500]
Sunkissed
   y Sch Lib - v63 - i4 - Winter 2015 - p248(1) [51-500]
McLain, Paula - *Circling the Sun (Read by McEwan, Katharine). Audiobook Review*
     BL - v112 - i6 - Nov 15 2015 - p60(1) [51-500]
     LJ - v140 - i16 - Oct 1 2015 - p43(1) [51-500]
Circling the Sun
     BL - v111 - i19-20 - June 1 2015 - p59(1) [51-500]
     CSM - July 26 2015 - pNA [501+]
     Ent W - i1375 - August 7 2015 - p64(1) [501+]
     KR - June 1 2015 - pNA [501+]
     LJ - v140 - i9 - May 15 2015 - p71(3) [501+]
     NYTBR - August 2 2015 - p13(L) [501+]
     SEP - v287 - i3 - May-June 2015 - p24(1) [501+]
McLane, LuAnn - *Written in the Stars*
     PW - v262 - i34 - August 24 2015 - p66(1) [51-500]
McLane, Maureen N. - *This Blue*
     NYTBR - May 3 2015 - p28(L) [501+]
McLarney, Ellen Anne - *Soft Force: Women in Egypt's Islamic Awakening*
     JAAR - v83 - i2 - June 2015 - pNA [501+]
     TimHES - i2220 - Sept 10 2015 - p48-49 [501+]
McLaughlin, Brian A. - *A Flight without Wings: My Experience with Heaven*
     SPBW - April 2015 - pNA [51-500]
McLaughlin, Dionne V. - *Insights: How Expert Principals Make Difficult Decisions*
     Bwatch - August 2015 - pNA [51-500]
McLaughlin, Emma - *How to Be a Grown-Up*
     BL - v111 - i19-20 - June 1 2015 - p40(2) [51-500]
     KR - May 15 2015 - pNA [51-500]
     LJ - v140 - i11 - June 15 2015 - p79(2) [51-500]
     PW - v262 - i19 - May 11 2015 - p28(2) [51-500]
McLaughlin, Jen - *Dare to Run*
     PW - v262 - i52 - Dec 21 2015 - p139(2) [51-500]
McLaughlin, Malcolm - *The Long, Hot Summer of 1967: Urban Rebellion in America*
     JAH - v102 - i1 - June 2015 - p304-305 [501+]
McLaughlin, Tom - *The Accidental Prime Minister*
   c Sch Lib - v63 - i2 - Summer 2015 - p106(1) [51-500]
The Cloudspotter (Illus. by McLaughlin, Tom)
   c Sch Lib - v63 - i4 - Winter 2015 - p220(1) [51-500]
McLaurin, Thad H. - *Full-Body Fitness for Runners*
     KR - Feb 15 2015 - pNA [51-500]
McLean, Allan Campbell - *The Hill of the Red Fox*
   y Sch Lib - v63 - i4 - Winter 2015 - p230(1) [51-500]
McLean, B.H. - *Biblical Interpretation and Philosophical Hermeneutics*
     JR - v95 - i3 - July 2015 - p427(3) [501+]
Hellenistic and Biblical Greek: A Graduated Reader
     Theol St - v76 - i3 - Sept 2015 - p635(2) [501+]
McLean, Bethany - *Shaky Ground: The Strange Saga of the U.S. Mortgage Giants*
     KR - August 1 2015 - pNA [501+]
     PW - v262 - i28 - July 13 2015 - p61(1) [51-500]
McLean, Gill - *When I Grow Up*
     KR - April 1 2015 - pNA [51-500]
   c Sch Lib - v63 - i1 - Spring 2015 - p30(1) [51-500]
McLean, Ian W. - *Why Australia Prospered: The Shifting Sources of Economic Growth*
     HER - v130 - i543 - April 2015 - p485(3) [501+]
McLean, Robin - *Reptile House*
     PW - v262 - i11 - March 16 2015 - p58(1) [51-500]

McLean, Russel D. - *Cry Uncle*
    BL - v111 - i9-10 - Jan 1 2015 - p45(1) [51-500]
    PW - v262 - i3 - Jan 19 2015 - p63(1) [51-500]

McLean, Thomas - *The Other East and Nineteenth-Century British Literature: Imagining Poland and the Russian Empire*
    MLR - v110 - i3 - July 2015 - p842-843 [501+]

McLeish, Tom - *Faith and Wisdom in Science*
    CC - v132 - i7 - April 1 2015 - p42(2) [501+]

McLellan, Josie - *Love in the Time of Communism: Intimacy and Sexuality in the GDR*
    JWH - v27 - i3 - Fall 2015 - p194(10) [501+]

McLellan, Stephanie - *Tweezle into Everything (Illus. by Griffiths, Dean)*
    c CH Bwatch - July 2015 - pNA [51-500]

McLelland, Nicola - *German through English Eyes: A History of Language Teaching and Learning in Britain 1500-2000*
    TimHES - i2220 - Sept 10 2015 - p47(1) [501+]

McLemore, Anna-Marie - *The Weight of Feathers*
    y KR - June 1 2015 - pNA [51-500]
    y CCB-B - v69 - i2 - Oct 2015 - p102(1) [51-500]
    y PW - v262 - i26 - June 29 2015 - p70(2) [51-500]
    y SLJ - v61 - i9 - Sept 2015 - p160(2) [51-500]

McLeod, Alan - *Ontario Beer: A Heady History of Brewing from the Great Lakes to Hudson Bay*
    Beav - v95 - i3 - June-July 2015 - p59(1) [501+]

McLeod, Kembrew - *Pranksters: Making Mischief in the Modern World*
    NS - v144 - i5252 - March 6 2015 - p49(1) [501+]
    SAH - v4 - i2 - Dec 15 2015 - p299-303 [501+]

McLeod, Shane - *The Beginning of Scandinavian Settlement in England: The Viking 'Great Army' and Early Settlers, c. 865-900*
    Med R - August 2015 - pNA [501+]

McLeRoy, Sherrie S. - *Texas Adoption Activist Edna Gladney: A Life and Legacy Of Love*
    SHQ - v118 - i3 - Jan 2015 - p335-336 [501+]

McLoughlin, Jane - *The Crowham Martyrs*
    c Sch Lib - v63 - i3 - Autumn 2015 - p168(2) [51-500]

McLynn, Frank - *Genghis Khan: His Conquests, His Empire, His Legacy*
    BL - v111 - i21 - July 1 2015 - p19(1) [51-500]
    KR - May 15 2015 - pNA [501+]
    LJ - v140 - i11 - June 15 2015 - p95(1) [51-500]
    PW - v262 - i20 - May 18 2015 - p77(1) [51-500]
Genghis Khan: The Man Who Conquered the World
    Mac - v128 - i29-30 - July 27 2015 - p69(1) [501+]
    NS - v144 - i5269 - July 3 2015 - p50(2) [501+]
    Spec - v328 - i9748 - June 27 2015 - p38(1) [501+]

McMahon, Christopher - *Public Capitalism: The Political Authority of Corporate Executives*
    Phil R - v124 - i3 - July 2015 - p422(4) [501+]

McMahon, Darrin M. - *Divine Fury: A History of Genius*
    Historian - v77 - i2 - Summer 2015 - p414(2) [501+]
    JMH - v87 - i3 - Sept 2015 - p701(2) [501+]
Rethinking Modern European Intellectual History
    HNet - Jan 2015 - pNA [501+]
    AHR - v120 - i4 - Oct 2015 - p1445-1446 [501+]

McMahon, Elisabeth - *Slavery and Emancipation in Islamic East Africa: From Honor to Respectability*
    AHR - v120 - i1 - Feb 2015 - p373-374 [501+]
    IJAHS - v48 - i1 - Wntr 2015 - p154-156 [501+]

McMahon, Jennifer - *The Night Sister (Read by Campbell, Cassandra). Audiobook Review*
    LJ - v140 - i19 - Nov 15 2015 - p52(1) [51-500]
The Night Sister
    PW - v262 - i26 - June 29 2015 - p46(1) [51-500]

McMahon, Kara - *It's the Great Pumpkin, Charlie Brown (Illus. by Jeralds, Scott)*
    c SLJ - v61 - i9 - Sept 2015 - p109(1) [51-500]

McMahon, Marci R. - *Domestic Negotiations: Gender, Nation, and Self-Fashioning in US Mexicana and Chicana Literature and Art*
    AL - v87 - i2 - June 2015 - p405-408 [501+]
    Aztlan - v40 - i2 - Fall 2015 - p269-273 [501+]

McMahon, Matt - *The Blue Folio*
    PW - v262 - i25 - June 22 2015 - p64(1) [51-500]

McMahon, Orlene Denice - *Listening to the French New Wave: The Film Music and Composers of Postwar French Art Cinema*
    FS - v69 - i3 - July 2015 - p425-426 [501+]

McMahon, Richard - *Homicide in Pre-Famine and Famine Ireland*
    AHR - v120 - i2 - April 2015 - p709-710 [501+]
    JIH - v45 - i3 - Wntr 2015 - p430-431 [501+]
A Web of Evil
    PW - v262 - i47 - Nov 23 2015 - p52(2) [51-500]

McMan, Ann - *Backcast*
    LJ - v140 - i20 - Dec 1 2015 - p94(1) [51-500]

McManaman, Doug - *Why Be Afraid?*
    CI - v23 - i2 - Feb 2015 - p34(1) [51-500]

McMann, Kelly M. - *Corruption as a Last Resort: Adapting to the Market in Central Asia*
    For Aff - v94 - i3 - May-June 2015 - pNA [501+]

McMann, Lisa - *Gasp*
    y HB Guide - v26 - i1 - Spring 2015 - p117(1) [51-500]
Island of Legends
    c HB Guide - v26 - i1 - Spring 2015 - p86(1) [51-500]
Island of Shipwrecks
    y HB Guide - v26 - i2 - Fall 2015 - p94(1) [51-500]

McManus, James - *The Education of a Poker Player*
    y BL - v112 - i4 - Oct 15 2015 - p25(1) [51-500]
    KR - August 1 2015 - pNA [501+]

McManus, John - *Fox Tooth Heart*
    KR - Sept 1 2015 - pNA [51-500]
Fox Tooth Heart: Stories
    NYTBR - Dec 13 2015 - p34(L) [501+]
    PW - v262 - i38 - Sept 21 2015 - p46(1) [51-500]

McManus, Sean - *How to Code in 10 Easy Lessons: Learn How to Design and Code Your Very Own Computer Game (Illus. by Foster, Walter, Jr.)*
    c BL - v112 - i5 - Nov 1 2015 - p40(1) [51-500]
Raspberry Pi for Dummies
    Bwatch - Feb 2015 - pNA [51-500]

McManus, Sophie - *The Unfortunates*
    BL - v111 - i18 - May 15 2015 - p26(1) [51-500]
    KR - March 15 2015 - pNA [51-500]
    LJ - v140 - i9 - May 15 2015 - p73(1) [51-500]
    NYTBR - Sept 13 2015 - p34(L) [501+]

McMaster, Bec - *Of Silk and Steam*
    BL - v111 - i12 - Feb 15 2015 - p44(1) [51-500]
    KR - Jan 15 2015 - pNA [51-500]

McMeekin, Sean - *The Ottoman Endgame: War, Revolution, and the Making of the Modern Middle East, 1908-1923*
    KR - August 15 2015 - pNA [501+]
    LJ - v140 - i15 - Sept 15 2015 - p89(1) [51-500]
    PW - v262 - i37 - Sept 14 2015 - p53(1) [51-500]

McMenamin, Michael - *Becoming Winston Churchill*
    HT - v65 - i1 - Jan 2015 - p56(2) [501+]

McMichael, James - *If You Can Tell*
    LJ - v140 - i20 - Dec 1 2015 - p107(2) [51-500]

McMichael, Pate - *Klandestine: How a Klan Lawyer and a Checkbook Journalist Helped James Earl Ray Cover Up His Crime*
    BL - v111 - i15 - April 1 2015 - p7(1) [51-500]
    KR - Feb 1 2015 - pNA [51-500]

McMillan, Dan - *How Could This Happen: Explaining the Holocaust*
    Lon R Bks - v37 - i2 - Jan 22 2015 - p17(3) [501+]

McMillan, Dawn - *Doctor Grundy's Undies (Illus. by Kinnaird, Ross)*
    c Magpies - v30 - i1 - March 2015 - pS4(1) [501+]
Mister Spears and His Hairy Ears (Illus. by Kinnaird, Ross)
    c Magpies - v30 - i5 - Nov 2015 - pS6(2) [501+]

McMillan, Gloria - *Orbiting Ray Bradbury's Mars: Biographical, Anthropological, Literary, Scientific and Other Perspectives*
    SFS - v42 - i2 - July 2015 - p390-391 [501+]

McMillan, Jonathan - *The End of Banking: Money, Credit, and the Digital Revolution*
    PW - v262 - i16 - April 20 2015 - p70(1) [501+]

McMillan, Tracy - *Multiple Listings*
    KR - Jan 1 2016 - pNA [51-500]
    LJ - v140 - i17 - Oct 15 2015 - p82(2) [51-500]

McMillen, Christian W. - *Discovering Tuberculosis: A Global History, 1900 to the Present*
    BL - v111 - i19-20 - June 1 2015 - p18(1) [51-500]
    LJ - v140 - i9 - May 15 2015 - p99(1) [51-500]
    Nature - v523 - i7559 - July 9 2015 - p157(1) [51-500]
    TimHES - i2217 - August 20 2015 - p48-49 [501+]

McMillen, R.J. - *Black Tide Rising*
    BL - v111 - i17 - May 1 2015 - p20(1) [51-500]

McMillen, Sally G. - *Lucy Stone: An Unapologetic Life*
    CC - v132 - i10 - May 13 2015 - p42(1) [51-500]
Seneca Falls and the Origins of the Women's Rights Movement
    JWH - v27 - i2 - Summer 2015 - p159(10) [501+]

McMillin, Mark M. - *The Butcher's Daughter*
    KR - Sept 1 2015 - pNA [501+]

McMorris, Kristina - *Edge of Lost*
    y VOYA - v38 - i5 - Dec 2015 - p60(2) [51-500]

McMullan, Kate - *Get Lost, Odysseus!*
    c HB Guide - v26 - i1 - Spring 2015 - p86(1) [51-500]
I Stink (Illus. by McMullan, Jim)
    c BL - v112 - i4 - Oct 15 2015 - p53(1) [51-500]
I'm Brave (Read by Banks, Jonathan). Audiobook Review
    c SLJ - v61 - i11 - Nov 2015 - p69(1) [51-500]
I'm Cool! (Illus. by McMullan, Jim)
    c HB - v91 - i5 - Sept-Oct 2015 - p84(2) [51-500]
    c KR - July 15 2015 - pNA [51-500]
    c PW - v262 - i39 - Sept 28 2015 - p90(2) [51-500]
    c SLJ - v61 - i8 - August 2015 - p74(1) [51-500]
Pinocchio (Illus. by Lemaitre, Pascal)
    c CCB-B - v68 - i5 - Jan 2015 - p269(1) [51-500]

McMullan, Margaret - *Aftermath Lounge*
    Wom R Bks - v32 - i6 - Nov-Dec 2015 - p19(2) [501+]
Every Father's Daughter: Twenty-Four Women Writers Remember Their Fathers
    BL - v111 - i16 - April 15 2015 - p5(1) [51-500]
    KR - Feb 1 2015 - pNA [501+]

McMullin, Julie Ann - *Aging and Working in the New Economy: Changing Career Structures in Small IT Firms*
    CS - v44 - i1 - Jan 2015 - p141-142 [501+]

McMullin, Neridah - *Knockabout Cricket: A Story of Sporting Legend Johnny Mullagh (Illus. by Walters, Ainsley)*
    c Magpies - v30 - i2 - May 2015 - p32(1) [51-500]

McMurchy-Barber, Gina - *A Bone to Pick*
    c KR - Oct 1 2015 - pNA [51-500]

McMurtry, Larry - *Duane's Depressed*
    Roundup M - v22 - i5 - June 2015 - p40(1) [501+]
The Last Kind Words Saloon: A Novel
    Roundup M - v22 - i6 - August 2015 - p31(1) [501+]
Lonesome Dove
    Esq - v163 - i6-7 - June-July 2015 - p26(2) [501+]

McMyne, Mary - *Wolf Skin*
    ABR - v36 - i3 - March-April 2015 - p20(2) [501+]

McNab, Chris - *Uniforms: 1944 to Today*
    c HB Guide - v26 - i1 - Spring 2015 - p137(2) [51-500]

Mcnally, Dennis - *On Highway 61*
    Dbt - v82 - i2 - Feb 2015 - p78(1) [501+]

McNally, John - *The Forbidden City*
    c Sch Lib - v63 - i4 - Winter 2015 - p230(1) [51-500]

McNally, Robert - *I Had Jelly on My Nose and a Hole in My Breeches*
    SPBW - April 2015 - pNA [501+]

McNally, Robert Aquinas - *Simply to Know Its Name*
    Roundup M - v23 - i1 - Oct 2015 - p28(1) [501+]

McNamara, Laurie - *Simply Scratch: 120 Wholesome Recipes Made Easy*
    LJ - v140 - i19 - Nov 15 2015 - p102(2) [51-500]

McNamara, Margaret - *Christmas Fairy Magic (Illus. by Collingridge, Catharine)*
    c HB Guide - v26 - i1 - Spring 2015 - p63(1) [51-500]
A Poem in Your Pocket (Illus. by Karas, G. Brian)
    c BL - v111 - i9-10 - Jan 1 2015 - p108(1) [51-500]
    c HB - v91 - i1 - Jan-Feb 2015 - p70(1) [51-500]
    c HB Guide - v26 - i2 - Fall 2015 - p44(1) [51-500]

McNaughton, Janet - *Flame and Ashes: The Great Fire Diary of Triffie Winsor*
    c Res Links - v20 - i3 - Feb 2015 - p13(2) [501+]

McNear, Mary - *Moonlight on Butternut Lake*
    BL - v111 - i18 - May 15 2015 - p24(1) [51-500]
    LJ - v140 - i7 - April 15 2015 - p77(1) [51-500]

McNee, Alan - *The Cockney Who Sold the Alps: Albert Smith and the Ascent of Mont Blanc*
    TLS - i5869 - Sept 25 2015 - p26(1) [501+]

McNeil, Brenda Salter - *Roadmap to Reconciliation: Moving into Unity, Wholeness and Justice*
    PW - v262 - i45 - Nov 9 2015 - p56(1) [51-500]

McNeil, Bryan T. - *Combating Mountaintop Removal: New Directions in the Fight against Big Coal*
    SF - v93 - i3 - March 2015 - pe86 [501+]
Removing Mountains: Extracting Nature and Identity in the Appalachian Coalfields
    SF - v93 - i3 - March 2015 - pNA [501+]

McNeil, Genna Rae - *Witness: Two Hundred Years of African-American Faith and Practice at the Abyssinian Baptist Church of Harlem, New York*
    JAH - v101 - i4 - March 2015 - p1236-1237 [501+]

McNeil, Gretchen - *Get Dirty*
y BL - v111 - i19-20 - June 1 2015 - p96(1) [51-500]
KR - April 1 2015 - pNA [51-500]
y VOYA - v38 - i3 - August 2015 - p65(1) [51-500]
Get Even
y CCB-B - v68 - i5 - Jan 2015 - p269(1) [51-500]
McNeill, John - *Romanesque and the Past: Retrospection in the Art and Architecture of Romanesque Europe*
Specu - v90 - i2 - April 2015 - p562-564 [501+]
McNeill, Laura - *Center of Gravity*
BL - v111 - i19-20 - June 1 2015 - p48(1) [51-500]
McNeill, Lynne S. - *Folklore Rules: A Fun, Quick, and Useful Introduction to the Field of Academic Folklore Studies*
WestFolk - v74 - i1 - Wntr 2015 - p80-83 [501+]
McNeill, Suzanne - *FloraBunda Style: Super Simple Art Doodles to Color, Craft and Draw*
LJ - v140 - i16 - Oct 1 2015 - p82(1) [51-500]
McNeur, Catherine - *Taming Manhattan: Environmental Battles in the Antebellum City*
JIH - v46 - i2 - Autumn 2015 - p297-298 [501+]
TLS - i5839 - Feb 27 2015 - p9(2) [501+]
McNicoll, Sylvia - *Best Friends through Eternity*
y CH Bwatch - March 2015 - pNA [51-500]
y HB Guide - v26 - i2 - Fall 2015 - p131(1) [51-500]
y Res Links - v20 - i3 - Feb 2015 - p32(1) [501+]
SLJ - v61 - i3 - March 2015 - p139(1) [51-500]
McNiff, Dawn - *Little Celeste*
c Sch Lib - v63 - i1 - Spring 2015 - p38(2) [51-500]
McNulty, Amy - *Nobody's Goddess*
y SLJ - v61 - i5 - May 2015 - p121(2) [51-500]
McNutt, Jennifer Powell - *Calvin Meets Voltaire: The Clergy of Geneva in the Age of Enlightenment, 1685-1798*
AHR - v120 - i1 - Feb 2015 - p349-350 [501+]
CH - v84 - i2 - June 2015 - p447(4) [501+]
McParland, Robert - *Beyond Gatsby: How Fitzgerald, Hemingway, and Writers of the 1920s Shaped American Culture*
LJ - v140 - i6 - April 1 2015 - p88(2) [51-500]
McPartlin, Anna - *The Last Days of Rabbit Hayes*
BL - v111 - i21 - July 1 2015 - p31(1) [51-500]
KR - May 15 2015 - pNA [51-500]
McPeck, Eleanor M. - *Elizabeth Bishop: The North Haven Journal, 1974-1979*
G&L Rev W - v22 - i6 - Nov-Dec 2015 - p47(2) [501+]
McPhail, David - *Andrew Draws*
c HB Guide - v26 - i2 - Fall 2015 - p45(1) [51-500]
Baby Pig Pig Walks (Illus. by McPhail, David)
c KR - Jan 1 2015 - pNA [51-500]
Beatrix Potter and Her Paint Box (Illus. by McPhail, David)
c KR - July 15 2015 - pNA [51-500]
c SLJ - v61 - i10 - Oct 2015 - p128(1) [51-500]
Brothers
c HB Guide - v26 - i1 - Spring 2015 - p12(1) [51-500]
I Get Dressed (Illus. by McPhail, David)
c SLJ - v61 - i7 - July 2015 - p56(1) [51-500]
I Play (Illus. by McPhail, David)
c KR - Jan 1 2016 - pNA [51-500]
c SLJ - v61 - i7 - July 2015 - p56(1) [51-500]
Peter Loves Penguin
c KR - Jan 1 2015 - pNA [51-500]
McPhee, John - *Coming into the Country*
TLS - i5871 - Oct 9 2015 - p33(1) [501+]
The Control of Nature
Nature - v523 - i7562 - July 30 2015 - p528(1) [51-500]
McPherson, Alan L. - *The Invaded: How Latin Americans and their Allies Fought and Ended U.S. Occupations*
HNet - May 2015 - pNA [501+]
McPherson, Ben - *A Line of Blood*
Esq - v164 - i1 - August 2015 - p32(1) [501+]
KR - July 15 2015 - pNA [51-500]
LJ - v140 - i11 - June 15 2015 - p76(1) [501+]
PW - v262 - i27 - July 6 2015 - p47(1) [51-500]
McPherson, Catriona - *The Child Garden*
KR - July 1 2015 - pNA [501+]
NYTBR - Oct 4 2015 - p29(L) [501+]
PW - v262 - i27 - July 6 2015 - p49(1) [51-500]
Come to Harm
BL - v111 - i17 - May 1 2015 - p26(1) [51-500]
KR - March 1 2015 - pNA [51-500]
NYTBR - June 7 2015 - p37(L) [501+]
PW - v262 - i11 - March 16 2015 - p66(2) [51-500]
McPherson, James M. - *Embattled Rebel: Jefferson Davis as Commander in Chief*
Parameters - v45 - i1 - Spring 2015 - p164(2) [501+]
NYRB - v62 - i18 - Nov 19 2015 - p41(3) [501+]
War on the Waters: The Union and Confederate Navies, 1861-1865
HNet - June 2015 - pNA [501+]
The War That Forged a Nation: Why the Civil War Still Matters
Ch Today - April 2015 - p77(1) [501+]
For Aff - v94 - i3 - May-June 2015 - pNA [501+]
KR - Jan 1 2015 - pNA [501+]
NYRB - v62 - i18 - Nov 19 2015 - p41(3) [501+]
McPherson, Robert S. - *Life in a Corner: Cultural Episodes in Southeastern Utah, 1880-1950*
Roundup M - v23 - i1 - Oct 2015 - p34(1) [501+]
McPherson, Stephanie Sammartino - *Arctic Thaw: Climate Change and the Global Race for Energy*
y HB Guide - v26 - i1 - Spring 2015 - p141(1) [51-500]
McPhillips, Shirley - *Poem Central: Word Journeys with Readers and Writers*
RVBW - April 2015 - pNA [51-500]
McPike, Elizabeth - *Little Bitty Friends (Illus. by Barton, Patrice)*
c KR - Dec 1 2015 - pNA [51-500]
Little Sleepyhead (Illus. by Barton, Patrice)
c BL - v111 - i14 - March 15 2015 - p78(1) [51-500]
c HB Guide - v26 - i2 - Fall 2015 - p15(1) [51-500]
c KR - Jan 15 2015 - pNA [51-500]
McPike, K.J. - *Xodus*
y KR - Dec 1 2015 - pNA [501+]
McQuaid, John - *Tasty: The Art and Science of What We Eat (Read by Perkins, Tom). Audiobook Review*
LJ - v140 - i8 - May 1 2015 - p43(1) [51-500]
PW - v262 - i21 - May 25 2015 - p56(1) [51-500]
Tasty: The Art and Science of What we Eat
Bus W - i4412 - Jan 26 2015 - p68(1) [501+]
Bwatch - April 2015 - pNA [51-500]
McQueen, Janie - *The Motherless Child Project*
y SLJ - v61 - i5 - May 2015 - p114(1) [51-500]
McQuein, Joisin L. - *Arclight*
y Sch Lib - v63 - i1 - Spring 2015 - p55(1) [51-500]
Meridian
y Sch Lib - v63 - i1 - Spring 2015 - p55(1) [51-500]
McQuerry, Maureen Doyle - *The Telling Stone*
c BL - v111 - i18 - May 15 2015 - p68(1) [51-500]
y HB Guide - v26 - i2 - Fall 2015 - p94(1) [51-500]
c KR - March 1 2015 - pNA [51-500]
SLJ - v61 - i3 - March 2015 - p139(1) [51-500]
y VOYA - v37 - i6 - Feb 2015 - p81(1) [51-500]
McQuestion, Karen - *From a Distant Star (Read by Rudd, Kate). Audiobook Review*
y SLJ - v61 - i8 - August 2015 - p54(2) [51-500]
From a Distant Star
y SLJ - v61 - i8 - August 2015 - p98(1) [51-500]
McQuiddy, Steve - *Here on the Edge: How a Small Group of World War II Conscientious Objectors Took Art and Peace from the Margins to the Mainstream*
PHR - v84 - i3 - August 2015 - p394(2) [501+]
McQuillan, Martin - *The Paul de Man Notebooks*
Lon R Bks - v37 - i1 - Jan 8 2015 - p11(4) [501+]
McQuillen, Colleen - *The Modernist Masquerade: Stylizing Life, Literature, and Costumes in Russia*
Slav R - v74 - i3 - Fall 2015 - p670-672 [501+]
McQuinn, Anna - *Lola Plants a Garden (Illus. by Beardshaw, Rosalind)*
c HB Guide - v26 - i1 - Spring 2015 - p12(1) [51-500]
Lulu Loves Flowers (Illus. by Beardshaw, Rosalind)
c Sch Lib - v63 - i3 - Autumn 2015 - p158(1) [51-500]
McQuiston, Jennifer - *Diary of an Accidental Wallflower*
BL - v111 - i13 - March 1 2015 - p28(1) [51-500]
KR - Jan 15 2015 - pNA [51-500]
The Spinster's Guide to Scandalous Behavior
BL - v112 - i7 - Dec 1 2015 - p37(1) [51-500]
KR - Oct 15 2015 - pNA [51-500]
Mcrae, Donald - *A Man's World: The Double Life of Emile Griffith*
Spec - v329 - i9762 - Oct 3 2015 - p44(2) [501+]
McShane, Melissa - *Servant of the Crown*
PW - v262 - i42 - Oct 19 2015 - p63(1) [51-500]
McSkimming, Geoffrey - *Phyllis Wong and the Return of the Conjuror*
c SLJ - v61 - i7 - July 2015 - p80(1) [51-500]
Phyllis Wong and the Waking of the Wizard
c Magpies - v30 - i3 - July 2015 - p36(1) [501+]
McSmith, Andy - *Fear and the Muse Kept Watch: The Russian Masters--from Akhmatova and Pasternak to Shostakovich and Eisenstein--under Stalin*
BL - v111 - i21 - July 1 2015 - p14(2) [51-500]
KR - May 1 2015 - pNA [501+]
PW - v262 - i20 - May 18 2015 - p77(1) [51-500]
McStay, Moriah - *Everything That Makes You*
y CCB-B - v68 - i10 - June 2015 - p506(1) [51-500]
y HB Guide - v26 - i2 - Fall 2015 - p131(1) [51-500]
y KR - Jan 1 2015 - pNA [51-500]
c PW - v262 - i1 - Jan 5 2015 - p74(1) [51-500]
y VOYA - v38 - i2 - June 2015 - p66(1) [51-500]
McTeer, James E., II - *Minnow*
KR - March 15 2015 - pNA [51-500]
LJ - v140 - i8 - May 1 2015 - p64(2) [51-500]
PW - v262 - i10 - March 9 2015 - p51(1) [51-500]
SPBW - Nov 2015 - pNA [51-500]
McVety, Allison - *Lighthouses*
TLS - i5853 - June 5 2015 - p25(1) [501+]
McVicar, Michael J. - *Christian Reconstruction: R.J. Rushdoony and American Religious Conservatism*
Bks & Cult - v21 - i4 - July-August 2015 - p17(1) [501+]
HNet - August 2015 - pNA [501+]
LJ - v140 - i5 - March 15 2015 - p111(1) [501+]
PW - v262 - i3 - Jan 19 2015 - p75(2) [51-500]
McVoy, Terra - *Elan in Deep*
c HB Guide - v26 - i1 - Spring 2015 - p117(1) [51-500]
McVoy, Terra Elan - *Drive Me Crazy*
BL - v111 - i14 - March 15 2015 - p73(1) [51-500]
y CCB-B - v68 - i10 - June 2015 - p506(2) [51-500]
y HB Guide - v26 - i2 - Fall 2015 - p94(1) [51-500]
c KR - Jan 15 2015 - pNA [51-500]
y SLJ - v61 - i3 - March 2015 - p139(2) [51-500]
y VOYA - v38 - i1 - April 2015 - p65(2) [51-500]
McWarren, Mila - *The Luckiest*
PW - v262 - i21 - May 25 2015 - p43(1) [51-500]
McWatt, Tessa - *Higher Ed*
Mac - v128 - i12 - March 30 2015 - p55(2) [501+]
TLS - i5868 - Sept 18 2015 - p21(1) [501+]
McWhorter, John H. - *The Language Hoax: Why the World Looks the Same in Any Language*
Soc - v52 - i3 - June 2015 - p292(3) [501+]
TLS - i5843 - March 27 2015 - p25(1) [501+]
McWilliam, Candia - *The Blue Flower*
Nation - v300 - i19 - May 11 2015 - p27(7) [501+]
McWilliams, Douglas - *The Flat White Economy*
NS - v144 - i5262 - May 15 2015 - p51(1) [501+]
McWilliams, James - *The Modern Savage: Our Unthinking Decision to Eat Animals*
BL - v111 - i9-10 - Jan 1 2015 - p20(1) [51-500]
Veg J - v34 - i4 - Oct-Dec 2015 - p30(1) [501+]
McWilliams, John P. - *New Mexico: A Glimpse Into an Enchanted Land*
Roundup M - v22 - i6 - August 2015 - p39(1) [501+]
Mda, Zakes - *Black Diamond*
NY - v90 - i45 - Jan 26 2015 - p77 [51-500]
Me, Tara Sue - *The Master*
PW - v262 - i51 - Dec 14 2015 - p66(2) [51-500]
Meacham, Jon - *Destiny and Power: The American Odyssey of George Herbert Walker Bush*
BL - v111 - i22 - August 1 2015 - p6(1) [51-500]
CSM - Dec 2 2015 - pNA [501+]
NYT - Nov 16 2015 - pC1(L) [501+]
NYTBR - Nov 15 2015 - p12(L) [501+]
Thomas Jefferson: President and Philosopher (Read by Hermann, Edward). Audiobook Review
c BL - v111 - i14 - March 15 2015 - p24(2) [501+]
Thomas Jefferson: President and Philosopher
y HB Guide - v26 - i1 - Spring 2015 - p195(1) [51-500]
Mead, Gary - *Victoria's Cross*
Spec - v328 - i9745 - June 6 2015 - p42(1) [501+]
Mead, Jane - *Money Money Money Water Water Water*
Ant R - v73 - i1 - Wntr 2015 - p190(2) [501+]
Mead, Maggie - *Suffrage Sisters: The Fight for Liberty (Illus. by Feeney, Siri Weber)*
SLJ - v61 - i3 - March 2015 - p171(2) [51-500]
Mead, Rebecca - *My Life in Middlemarch*
NYTBR - Feb 1 2015 - p24(L) [501+]
Mead, Richelle - *Soundless*
y BL - v112 - i4 - Oct 15 2015 - p46(1) [51-500]
y KR - Sept 1 2015 - pNA [51-500]
y SLJ - v61 - i9 - Sept 2015 - p161(2) [51-500]
y VOYA - v38 - i4 - Oct 2015 - p75(1) [51-500]
Meader, Kate - *Playing with Fire*
PW - v262 - i36 - Sept 7 2015 - p52(1) [51-500]
Meadows, Daisy - *Lucy Longwhiskers Gets Lost*
SLJ - v61 - i2 - Feb 2015 - p58(1) [51-500]
Tiffany la fee du tennis: Les fees des sports
c Res Links - v20 - i5 - June 2015 - p40(2) [51-500]
Meadows, Jodi - *The Orphan Queen*
y BL - v111 - i12 - Feb 15 2015 - p83(1) [51-500]
y CCB-B - v68 - i9 - May 2015 - p457(1) [51-500]
y HB Guide - v26 - i2 - Fall 2015 - p131(1) [51-500]
y KR - Jan 1 2015 - pNA [51-500]

Meadows, Sally - *The Two Trees (Illus. by Olfert, Trudi)*
c Res Links - v21 - i1 - Oct 2015 - p9(1) [501+]

Meagher, Robert Emmett - *Killing from the Inside Out: Moral Injury and Just War*
AM - v213 - i13 - Nov 2 2015 - p35(2) [501+]

Meale, Carol M. - *Makers and Users of Medieval Books: Essays in Honour of A.S.G. Edwards*
Med R - Jan 2015 - pNA [501+]
TLS - i5850 - May 15 2015 - p26(2) [501+]

Meany, Paul - *Vitals*
New Or - v50 - i1 - Oct 2015 - p44(1) [501+]

Mears, Gillian - *The Cat with the Coloured Tail (Illus. by Dabarera, Dinalie)*
c Magpies - v30 - i4 - Sept 2015 - p34(1) [501+]

Mears, Natalie - *National Prayers: Special Worship since the Reformation, vol. 1: Special Prayers, Fasts and Thanksgivings in the British Isles, 1533-1688*
CHR - v101 - i3 - Summer 2015 - p650(2) [501+]
Worship and the Parish Church in Early Modern Britain
CHR - v101 - i3 - Summer 2015 - p647(2) [501+]

Mebane, Jeanie - *At the Marsh in the Meadow (Illus. by Guerlais, Gerald)*
c KR - Nov 1 2015 - pNA [51-500]

Mecham, June L. - *Sacred Communities, Shared Devotions: Gender, Material Culture, and Monasticism in Late Medieval Germany*
CHR - v101 - i4 - Autumn 2015 - p919(3) [501+]

Mechefske, Lindy - *Sir John's Table: The Culinary Life and Times of Canada's First Prime Minister*
Nat Post - v17 - i277 - Oct 10 2015 - pWP6(1) [501+]

Meckel, Richard A. - *Classrooms and Clinics: Urban Schools and the Protection and Promotion of Child Health, 1870-1930*
JAH - v101 - i4 - March 2015 - p1297-1298 [501+]

Mecklenburg-Schwerin, Friedrich Franz von, II - *Vormarz und Revolution: Die Tagebucher des Grossherzogs Friedrich Franz II. von Mecklenburg-Schwerin 1841-1854, kommentiert, eingeleitet und hrsg. v. Rene Wiese*
HNet - May 2015 - pNA [501+]

Meconi, Vince - *A Practical Guide to Government Management*
BL - v111 - i18 - May 15 2015 - p16(1) [51-500]

Meddaugh, Susan - *Teacher's Pets*
c HB Guide - v26 - i1 - Spring 2015 - p63(1) [51-500]

Meddens, Frank - *Inca Sacred Space: Landscape, Site and Symbol in the Andes*
Lat Ant - v26 - i3 - Sept 2015 - p426(3) [501+]

Meddour, Wendy - *How the Library (Not the Prince) Saved Rapunzel (Illus. by Ashdown, Rebecca)*
c Sch Lib - v63 - i1 - Spring 2015 - p30(1) [51-500]

Medearis, Carl - *Adventures in Saying Yes: A Journey from Fear to Faith*
Ch Today - v59 - i5 - June 2015 - p76(1) [51-500]

Media and the Cold War, 1975-1991
HNet - Feb 2015 - pNA [501+]

Mediano, Fernando Rodriguez - *The Orient in Spain. Converted Muslims, the Forged Lead Books of Granada, and the Rise of Orientalism*
JNES - v74 - i1 - April 2015 - p174(3) [501+]

Medina, K.T. - *White Crocodile*
BL - v111 - i17 - May 1 2015 - p48(1) [51-500]
KR - April 15 2015 - pNA [501+]
LJ - v140 - i11 - June 15 2015 - p80(1) [51-500]
PW - v262 - i9 - March 2 2015 - p64(1) [51-500]

Medina, Meg - *Mango, Abuela, and Me (Illus. by Dominguez, Angela)*
c BL - v111 - i21 - July 1 2015 - p64(1) [51-500]
c HB - v91 - i5 - Sept-Oct 2015 - p85(1) [51-500]
c KR - May 1 2015 - pNA [51-500]
c PW - v262 - i21 - May 25 2015 - p59(1) [51-500]
c PW - v262 - i49 - Dec 2 2015 - p31(1) [51-500]
c SLJ - v61 - i7 - July 2015 - p65(2) [51-500]
Tia Isa Wants a Car (Illus. by Munoz, Claudio)
c BL - v111 - i9-10 - Jan 1 2015 - pS18(5) [501+]

Medina, Susana - *Philosophical Toys*
KR - April 15 2015 - pNA [51-500]

Medizin und Religion, Heilkunde und Seelsorge. Jahrestagung 2015 des Vereins fur Sozialgeschichte der Medizin - Geschichte(n) von Gesundheit und Krankheit
HNet - July 2015 - pNA [501+]

Medley, Keith Weldon - *Black Life in Old New Orleans*
Roundup M - v22 - i4 - April 2015 - p30(1) [501+]
Roundup M - v22 - i6 - August 2015 - p39(1) [501+]

Medoff, Rafael - *FDR and the Holocaust: A Breach of Faith*
RAH - v43 - i2 - June 2015 - p314-319 [501+]

Medrano, Adan - *Truly Texas Mexican: A Native Culinary Heritage in Recipes*
Roundup M - v22 - i6 - August 2015 - p39(1) [501+]

Medvedev, Kirill - *It's No Good*
TLS - i5877 - Nov 20 2015 - p31(1) [501+]

Meehan, Ciara - *A Just Society for Ireland? 1964-1987*
ILS - v35 - i1 - Fall 2015 - p15(1) [501+]

Meehan, Peter - *Lucky Peach Presents: 101 Easy Asian Recipes*
NYTBR - Dec 6 2015 - p20(L) [501+]
NYTBR - Dec 6 2015 - p20(L) [501+]
PW - v262 - i33 - August 17 2015 - p65(1) [51-500]

Meek, Edwin E. - *Riot: Witness to Anger and Change*
LJ - v140 - i15 - Sept 15 2015 - p81(3) [501+]

Meek, James - *Private Island: Why Britain Now Belongs to Someone Else*
TLS - i5831 - Jan 2 2015 - p3(2) [501+]

Meek, Tim - *Learning Outdoors with the Meek Family*
c Sch Lib - v63 - i4 - Winter 2015 - p254(1) [51-500]

Meeker, Lauren - *Sounding Out Heritage: Cultural Politics and the Social Practice of Quan Ho Folk Song in Northern Vietnam*
Pac A - v88 - i2 - June 2015 - p356 [501+]

Meens, Rob - *Penance in Medieval Europe, 600-1200*
Med R - June 2015 - pNA [501+]

Meeuf, Russell - *John Wayne's World: Transnational Masculinity in the Fifties*
Roundup M - v22 - i6 - August 2015 - p39(1) [501+]

Megan, Gross - *The Inclusive Toolbox: Strategies and Techniques for All Teachers*
Bwatch - April 2015 - pNA [501+]

Megdal, Howard - *The Cardinals Way: How One Team Embraced Tradition and Moneyball at the Same Time*
KR - Dec 15 2015 - pNA [51-500]
LJ - v140 - i20 - Dec 1 2015 - p108(1) [51-500]
PW - v262 - i45 - Nov 9 2015 - p49(1) [51-500]

Megier, Elisabeth - *Christliche Weltgeschichte im 12: Jahrhundert - Themen, Variationen und Kontraste - Untersuchungen zu Hugo von Fleury, Ordericus Vitalis, und Otto von Freising*
CHR - v101 - i2 - Spring 2015 - p359(2) [501+]

Mehigan, Joshua - *Accepting the Disaster*
Ant R - v73 - i1 - Wntr 2015 - p189(1) [501+]
HR - v67 - i4 - Wntr 2015 - p667-676 [501+]
TLS - i5849 - May 8 2015 - p27(1) [501+]

Mehlman, Peter - *It Won't Always Be This Great*
RVBW - June 2015 - pNA [501+]

Mehltretter, Jeffrey P. - *Speaking with the People's Voice: How Presidents Invoke Public Opinion*
Pres St Q - v45 - i2 - June 2015 - p408(3) [501+]

Mehrotra, Ajay K. - *Making the Modern American Fiscal State: Law, Politics, and the Rise of Progressive Taxation, 1877-1929*
AHR - v120 - i3 - June 2015 - p1034-1035 [501+]
JEH - v75 - i3 - Sept 2015 - p939-941 [501+]

Mehrotra, Arvind Krishna - *Collected Poems: 1969-2014*
WLT - v89 - i2 - March-April 2015 - p71(3) [501+]

Mehrotra, Ajay K. - *Making the Modern American Fiscal State: Law, Politics, and the Rise of Progressive Taxation, 1877-1929*
JAH - v101 - i4 - March 2015 - p1225-1226 [501+]

Mehta, Jal - *The Allure of Order: High Hopes, Dashed Expectations, and the Troubled Quest to Remake American Schooling*
CS - v44 - i2 - March 2015 - p234-235 [501+]

Mehta, Rupa - *The Nalini Method: 7 Workouts for 7 Moods*
PW - v262 - i46 - Nov 16 2015 - p72(2) [51-500]

Mehta, Uday Singh - *Liberalism and Empire: A Study in Nineteenth-Century British Liberal Thought*
JAS - v74 - i3 - August 2015 - p711-722 [501+]

Mei-en, Lo Kwa - *The Yearling*
PW - v262 - i11 - March 16 2015 - p63(1) [51-500]

Meier, Anna - *Curious George Discovers the Sun*
c HB Guide - v26 - i2 - Fall 2015 - p31(1) [51-500]

Meier, Kathryn Shively - *Nature's Civil War: Common Soldiers and the Environment in 1862 Virginia*
HNet - Jan 2015 - pNA [501+]
JSH - v81 - i1 - Feb 2015 - p201(2) [501+]

Meier, Leslie - *Candy Corn Murder*
BL - v112 - i1 - Sept 1 2015 - p44(2) [51-500]
KR - July 1 2015 - pNA [51-500]
PW - v262 - i28 - July 13 2015 - p46(1) [51-500]

Meier, Robert - *Wertheim 1628: Eine Stadt in Krieg und Hexenverfolgung*
HNet - Sept 2015 - pNA [501+]

Meierz, Christie - *Farryn's War*
KR - Nov 1 2015 - pNA [501+]

Meijer, Maarten - *Louis van Gaal: The Biography*
NS - v144 - i5251 - Feb 27 2015 - p44(2) [501+]

Meijer, Roel - *The Muslim Brotherhood in Europe*
J Ch St - v57 - i1 - Wntr 2015 - p155-157 [501+]

Meikle, William - *Sherlock Holmes: The London Terrors*
SPBW - July 2015 - pNA [51-500]

Meiling Cheng - *Beijing Xingwei: Contemporary Chinese Time-Based Art*
Theat J - v67 - i1 - March 2015 - p158-159 [501+]

Meiners, Antonia - *Die Stunde der Frauen: Zwischen Monarchie, Weltkrieg und Wahlrecht 1913-1919*
HNet - July 2015 - pNA [501+]

Meiners, Cheri J. - *Cool Down and Work Through Anger/Calmate y supera la ira*
SLJ - v61 - i3 - March 2015 - p121(1) [51-500]
Stand Tall! A Book about Integrity (Illus. by Allen, Elizabeth)
c HB Guide - v26 - i2 - Fall 2015 - p147(1) [51-500]

Meinhardt, Matthias - *Religion, Macht, Politik: Hofgeistlichkeit im Europa der Fruhen Neuzeit*
Six Ct J - v46 - i2 - Summer 2015 - p480-482 [501+]

Meinking, Mary - *Machu Picchu*
y HB Guide - v26 - i1 - Spring 2015 - p200(2) [51-500]
What's Great about Colorado?
c HB Guide - v26 - i1 - Spring 2015 - p203(1) [51-500]
What's Great about South Dakota?
c HB Guide - v26 - i2 - Fall 2015 - p220(1) [51-500]
c SLJ - v61 - i4 - April 2015 - p116(3) [51-500]

Meinstein, Menucha - *My Eyes Looking Back at Me: Insight into a Survivor's Soul*
KR - July 1 2015 - pNA [501+]

Meisel, Peter - *Stinky Spike the Pirate Dog (Illus. by Meisel, Peter)*
c SLJ - v61 - i9 - Sept 2015 - p134(1) [51-500]

Meisler, Stanley - *Shocking Paris: Soutine, Chagall, and the Outsiders of Montparnasse*
BL - v111 - i15 - April 1 2015 - p4(1) [501+]
BL - v112 - i5 - Nov 1 2015 - p18(2) [501+]
NYTBR - June 28 2015 - p24(L) [501+]

Meiss-Even, Marjorie - *Les Guise et leur paraitre*
Six Ct J - v46 - i1 - Spring 2015 - p241-242 [501+]
Les Guise et paraitre
AHR - v120 - i3 - June 2015 - p1121-1122 [501+]

Meissner, Susan - *Secrets of a Charmed Life*
BL - v111 - i9-10 - Jan 1 2015 - p54(1) [51-500]
Stars over Sunset Boulevard
KR - Dec 1 2015 - pNA [51-500]

Meister, Car - *Sea Dragons*
c SLJ - v61 - i6 - June 2015 - p46(6) [501+]

Meister, Cari - *Do You Really Want to Meet a Crocodile? (Illus. by Fabbri, Daniele)*
c HB Guide - v26 - i1 - Spring 2015 - p160(1) [51-500]
Do You Really Want to Meet a Swan? (Illus. by Fabbri, Daniele)
c HB Guide - v26 - i1 - Spring 2015 - p162(1) [51-500]

Meister, Ernst - *Of Entirety Say the Sentence*
PW - v262 - i38 - Sept 21 2015 - p51(2) [51-500]

Mejsnar, Jiri A. - *The Evolution Myth: or, The Genes Cry Out Their Urgent Song, Mister Darwin Got It Wrong*
QRB - v90 - i4 - Dec 2015 - p436(2) [501+]

McKenzie, Sophie - *You Can Trust Me*
BL - v111 - i12 - Feb 15 2015 - p40(1) [51-500]

Mekhennet, Souad - *The Eternal Nazi: From Mauthausen to Cairo, the Relentless Pursuit of SS Doctor Aribert Heim*
NYTBR - Jan 11 2015 - p24(L) [501+]

Mela, Charles - *Variations sur l'Amour et le Graal*
Specu - v90 - i3 - July 2015 - p839-340 [501+]

Melancon, Robert - *Pour une poesie impure*
Can Lit - i224 - Spring 2015 - p136 [501+]

Melancon, Trimiko - *Unbought and Unbossed: Transgressive Black Women, Sexuality, and Representation*
Wom R Bks - v32 - i4 - July-August 2015 - p27(2) [501+]

Melanson, Carl - *Amlethus*
SPBW - Feb 2015 - pNA [51-500]

Book Review Index 2016 Cumulation MERGEN • 315

Melber, Henning - *Understanding Namibia: The Trials of Independence*
HNet - Feb 2015 - pNA [501+]
TLS - i5850 - May 15 2015 - p27(1) [501+]
Melchior, Riegels - *Fashion and Museums: Theory and Practice*
LJ - v140 - i5 - March 15 2015 - p102(3) [501+]
Mele, Alfred R. - *Free: Why Science Hasn't Disproved Free Will*
NS - v144 - i5260 - May 1 2015 - p42(3) [501+]
Meleagrou, Ivi - *Eastern Mediterranean*
TLS - i5875 - Nov 6 2015 - p30(1) [501+]
Melendez Salinas, Claudia - *A Fighting Chance*
y KR - Sept 15 2015 - pNA [51-500]
y SLJ - v61 - i11 - Nov 2015 - p119(1) [51-500]
Melillo, Edward Dallam - *Strangers on Familiar Soil: Rediscovering the Chile-California Connection*
PW - v262 - i39 - Sept 28 2015 - p79(1) [51-500]
Melinek, Judy - *Working Stiff: Two Years, 262 Bodies, and the Making of a Medical Examiner (Read by Eby, Tanya). Audiobook Review*
BL - v111 - i9-10 - Jan 1 2015 - p117(1) [51-500]
Melion, Walter S. - *Imago Exegetica: Visual Images as Exegetical Instruments, 1400-1700*
Ren Q - v68 - i3 - Fall 2015 - p994-995 [501+]
Melki-Wegner, Skye - *Chasing the Valley*
c BL - v112 - i7 - Dec 1 2015 - p59(2) [51-500]
y VOYA - v38 - i5 - Dec 2015 - p72(1) [51-500]
The Hush
y Magpies - v30 - i1 - March 2015 - p42(1) [501+]
Mellick, Carlton, III - *Clownfellas: Tales of the Bozo Family*
PW - v262 - i14 - April 6 2015 - p43(1) [51-500]
Melling, David - *We Love You, Hugless Douglas!*
c HB Guide - v26 - i1 - Spring 2015 - p12(1) [51-500]
Mello, Deborah Fletcher - *Playing for Keeps*
BL - v112 - i2 - Sept 15 2015 - p46(1) [51-500]
PW - v262 - i35 - August 31 2015 - p72(1) [51-500]
Playing with Fire
PW - v262 - i2 - Jan 12 2015 - p43(1) [51-500]
Mellody, Maureen - *Training Students to Extract Value from Big Data: Summary of a Workshop*
RVBW - March 2015 - pNA [501+]
Mellom, Robin - *Trick Out My School! (Illus. by Gilpin, Stephen)*
c HB Guide - v26 - i1 - Spring 2015 - p86(1) [51-500]
Mellor, Leo - *Reading the Ruins: Modernism, Bombsites and British Culture*
MP - v113 - i2 - Nov 2015 - pE129(4) [501+]
Mellyn, Elizabeth W. - *Mad Tuscans and Their Families: A History of Mental Disorder in Early Modern Italy*
AHR - v120 - i4 - Oct 2015 - p1557-1558 [501+]
CHR - v101 - i3 - Summer 2015 - p654(2) [501+]
Ren Q - v68 - i2 - Summer 2015 - p678-680 [501+]
Six Ct J - v46 - i1 - Spring 2015 - p253-255 [501+]
Mellynchuk, Steve - *The Prayer Warrior: A Tale of the Last Battle of General Stonewall Jackson*
SPBW - Oct 2015 - pNA [51-500]
Melmon, Deborah - *Hey Diddle Diddle (Illus. by Melmon, Deborah)*
c CH Bwatch - Feb 2015 - pNA [51-500]
Meloy, Maile - *The After-Room*
c KR - Sept 15 2015 - pNA [51-500]
c Magpies - v30 - i5 - Nov 2015 - p36(1) [501+]
c SLJ - v61 - i10 - Oct 2015 - p93(1) [51-500]
y VOYA - v38 - i5 - Dec 2015 - p72(2) [51-500]
Meloy, Paul - *The Night Clock*
KR - Sept 1 2015 - pNA [51-500]
PW - v262 - i29 - July 20 2015 - p172(2) [51-500]
Melton, H. Keith - *Ultimate Spy: Inside the Secret World of Espionage, 4th ed.*
y SLJ - v61 - i7 - July 2015 - p108(1) [51-500]
Meltzer, Brad - *I Am Albert Einstein (Illus. by Eliopoulos, Christopher)*
c HB Guide - v26 - i1 - Spring 2015 - p195(1) [51-500]
I Am Jackie Robinson (Illus. by Eliopoulos, Christopher)
c BL - v111 - i11 - Feb 1 2015 - p43(1) [51-500]
c HB Guide - v26 - i2 - Fall 2015 - p199(1) [51-500]
I am Rosa Parks (Illus. by Eliopoulos, Christopher)
c HB Guide - v26 - i1 - Spring 2015 - p195(1) [51-500]
The President's Shadow
BL - v111 - i17 - May 1 2015 - p43(1) [51-500]
KR - April 15 2015 - pNA [501+]
LJ - v140 - i8 - May 1 2015 - p65(3) [51-500]
PW - v262 - i16 - April 20 2015 - p55(1) [51-500]
Meltzoff, Sarah Keene - *Listening to Sea Lions: Currents of Change from Galapagos to Patagonia*
JRAI - v21 - i2 - June 2015 - p474(2) [501+]
Melville, Diane - *The Community College Advantage: Your Guide to a Low-Cost, High-Reward College Experience*
BL - v111 - i21 - July 1 2015 - p22(2) [501+]
Melville, Herman - *Redburn: His First Voyage*
TimHES - i2227 - Oct 29 2015 - p47-1 [501+]
Melvin, Alice - *Grandma's House (Illus. by Melvin, Alice)*
c PW - v262 - i41 - Oct 12 2015 - p69(1) [51-500]
c SLJ - v61 - i12 - Dec 2015 - p92(1) [51-500]
Melzer, Arthur M. - *Philosophy Between the Lines: The Lost History of Esoteric Writing*
RM - v69 - i1 - Sept 2015 - p147(3) [501+]
Melzer, Patricia - *Death in the Shape of a Young Girl: Women's Political Violence in the Red Army Faction*
TimHES - i2206 - June 4 2015 - p50-51 [501+]
Membrino, Anna - *I Want to Be a Ballerina (Illus. by Coh, Smiljana)*
c HB Guide - v26 - i1 - Spring 2015 - p13(1) [51-500]
Memoirs of a Neurotic Zombie: Escape from Camp
c Sch Lib - v63 - i4 - Winter 2015 - p230(1) [51-500]
Menaker, Daniel - *My Mistake: A Memoir*
NYTBR - Jan 11 2015 - p24(L) [501+]
Menand, Louis - *The Marketplace of Ideas: Reform and Resistance in the American University*
J Hi E - v86 - i1 - Jan-Feb 2015 - p156(15) [501+]
Menard, Lawrence - *The Collective Legacy*
KR - June 15 2015 - pNA [501+]
Menchi, Silvana Seidel - *I-8 Ordinis primi tomus octavus: Iusus Exclusus, De civilitate morum puerilium, Conflictus Thaliae et Barbariei*
Six Ct J - v46 - i3 - Fall 2015 - p706-707 [501+]
Menchin, Scott - *Goodnight Selfie (Illus. by Collet-Derby, Pierre)*
c PW - v262 - i31 - August 3 2015 - p57(1) [51-500]
Grandma in Blue with Red Hat (Illus. by Bliss, Harry)
c HB - v91 - i2 - March-April 2015 - p79(1) [51-500]
c HB Guide - v26 - i2 - Fall 2015 - p45(1) [51-500]
c KR - Feb 15 2015 - pNA [51-500]
c PW - v262 - i5 - Feb 2 2015 - p59(1) [51-500]
c PW - v262 - i7 - Feb 16 2015 - p33(34) [501+]
c SLJ - v61 - i2 - Feb 2015 - p73(1) [51-500]
Mendel, Lori - *The Place I Live, the People I Know: Profiles from the Eastern Mediterranean*
PW - v262 - i41 - Oct 12 2015 - p64(1) [51-500]
Mendelsohn, Adam D. - *The Rag Race: How Jews Sewed Their Way to Success in America and the British Empire*
BHR - v89 - i3 - Autumn 2015 - p588(3) [501+]
Mendelsohn, Barak - *Combating Jihadism: American Hegemony and Interstate Cooperation in the War on Terrorism*
CS - v44 - i1 - Jan 2015 - p142-143 [501+]
Mendelson, Edward - *The Complete Works of W.H. Auden: Prose, vol. 6, 1969-1973*
PW - v262 - i17 - April 27 2015 - p65(1) [51-500]
Moral Agents: Eight Twentieth-Century American Writers
LJ - v140 - i2 - Feb 1 2015 - p83(2) [51-500]
Nat R - v67 - i3 - Feb 23 2015 - p42 [501+]
NYTBR - May 24 2015 - p30(L) [501+]
TLS - i5857 - July 3 2015 - p24(1) [501+]
AM - v212 - i20 - June 22 2015 - p31(3) [501+]
Comw - v142 - i8 - May 1 2015 - p35(2) [501+]
Lon R Bks - v37 - i16 - August 27 2015 - p13(2) [501+]
Mendelsund, Peter - *Cover*
TLS - i5856 - June 26 2015 - p28(1) [501+]
Mendenhall, Allen P. - *Literature and Liberty: Essays in Libertarian Literary Criticism*
IndRev - v19 - i3 - Wntr 2015 - p452(4) [501+]
Mendes, Ana Cristina - *Salman Rushdie in the Cultural Marketplace*
RES - v66 - i274 - April 2015 - p400-401 [501+]
Mendes, Kaitlynn - *Slutwalk: Feminism, Activism and Media*
TimHES - i2217 - August 20 2015 - p46-2 [501+]
Mendez, Chip - *The Millionaire in the Next Cubicle: A Corporate Everyman's Blueprint to Financial Independence*
KR - March 15 2015 - pNA [501+]
Mendicino, Valentina - *Le veritable abominable homme des neiges*
c Res Links - v20 - i5 - June 2015 - p41(1) [501+]
Mendoza, Elmer - *Silver Bullets*
TLS - i5850 - May 15 2015 - p21(1) [501+]
Menefy, Diana - *1915: Wounds of War*
Magpies - v30 - i2 - May 2015 - p56(2) [501+]
Menell, Esther - *Loose Connections: From Narva Maantee to Great Russell Street*
TLS - i5841 - March 13 2015 - p26(1) [501+]
Meng, Cece - *Always Remember (Illus. by Jago)*
c KR - Nov 1 2015 - pNA [51-500]
c SLJ - v61 - i12 - Dec 2015 - p92(1) [51-500]
Meng, Kaari - *French General: A Year of Jewelry: 36 Projects with Vintage Beads*
PW - v262 - i1 - Jan 5 2015 - p69(1) [51-500]
Menger, Pierre-Michel - *The Economics of Creativity: Art and Achievement Under Uncertainty*
TLS - i5857 - July 3 2015 - p28(1) [501+]
Mengestu, Dinaw - *All Our Names*
NYTBR - March 1 2015 - p28(L) [501+]
Mengisteab, Kidane - *The Horn of Africa*
For Aff - v94 - i1 - Jan-Feb 2015 - pNA [51-500]
Mengue, Philippe - *Faire l'idiot: La politique de Deleuze*
FS - v69 - i2 - April 2015 - p264-2 [501+]
Menikoff, Aaron - *Politics and Piety: Baptist Social Reform in America, 1770-1860*
JSH - v81 - i3 - August 2015 - p699(2) [501+]
Menjivar, Mark - *The Luck Archive: Exploring Belief, Superstition, and Tradition*
PW - v262 - i19 - May 11 2015 - p52(1) [51-500]
Menning, Daniel - *Standesgemasse Ordnung in der Moderne: Adlige Familienstrategien und Gesellschaftsentwurfe in Deutschland 1840-1945*
HNet - May 2015 - pNA [501+]
Meno, Joe - *Chicago Noir: The Classics*
BL - v111 - i22 - August 1 2015 - p32(1) [51-500]
PW - v262 - i28 - July 13 2015 - p45(1) [51-500]
Marvel and a Wonder
y BL - v112 - i2 - Sept 15 2015 - p27(2) [51-500]
KR - July 1 2015 - pNA [51-500]
LJ - v140 - i15 - Sept 15 2015 - p69(1) [51-500]
NYTBR - Sept 13 2015 - p13(L) [501+]
PW - v262 - i28 - July 13 2015 - p42(1) [51-500]
Menon, Jisha - *The Performance of Nationalism: India, Pakistan, and the Memory of Partition*
Theat J - v67 - i3 - Oct 2015 - p583-584 [501+]
Menoret, Pascal - *Joyriding in Riyadh: Oil, Urbanism, and Road Revolt*
AHR - v120 - i3 - June 2015 - p1149-1150 [501+]
Mensch, Jennifer - *Kant's Organicism: Epigenesis and the Development of Critical Philosophy*
GSR - v38 - i1 - Feb 2015 - p162-163 [501+]
Mentyka, Sharon - *B in the World (Illus. by Schlott, Stephen)*
c SLJ - v61 - i5 - May 2015 - p95(2) [51-500]
Mentzer, Raymond A. - *Les registres des consistoires des Eglises Reformees de France, XVIe-XVIIe siecles: Un inventaire*
CHR - v101 - i3 - Summer 2015 - p643(2) [501+]
Menuez, Doug - *Fearless Genius: The Digital Revolution in Silicon Valley, 1985-2000*
Am Sci - v103 - i2 - March-April 2015 - p153(2) [501+]
Mercer, Bobby - *Junk Drawer Chemistry: 50 Awesome Experiments That Don't Cost a Thing*
c BL - v112 - i3 - Oct 1 2015 - p39(1) [51-500]
c CH Bwatch - Oct 2015 - pNA [51-500]
c CH Bwatch - Nov 2015 - pNA [51-500]
Merchant, Eli - *The Collectivistic Premise*
KR - March 15 2015 - pNA [501+]
Merchant, Holt - *South Carolina Fire-Eater: The Life of Laurence Massillon Keitt, 1824-1864*
JSH - v81 - i3 - August 2015 - p707(3) [501+]
Mercier, Deb - *Real Stories about Werewolves*
y CH Bwatch - April 2015 - pNA [51-500]
Mercier, Johanne - *La machine a mesurer l'amour*
y Res Links - v20 - i3 - Feb 2015 - p46(1) [51-500]
Merdjanova, Ina - *Rediscovering the Umma: Muslims in the Balkans between Nationalism and Transnationalism*
E-A St - v67 - i9 - Nov 2015 - p1509(3) [501+]
Meredith, Anthony - *W.G. Grace: In the Steps of a Legend*
TLS - i5876 - Nov 13 2015 - p10(1) [501+]
Meredith, Jane - *Circle of Eight: Creating Magic for Your Place on Earth*
Bwatch - July 2015 - pNA [51-500]
Meredith, Martin - *The Fortunes of Africa: A 5,000-Year History of Wealth, Greed and Endeavour*
TLS - i5844 - April 3 2015 - p8(1) [501+]
Meredith, Samantha - *Itsy Bitsy Spider and Other Rhymes (Illus. by Meredith, Samantha)*
c KR - July 1 2015 - pNA [51-500]
Merey, Ryszard I. - *A Father for Lilja*
LJ - v140 - i12 - July 1 2015 - p80(1) [51-500]
Merezhkovsky, Dmitry - *Leonardo Da Vinci: The Resurrection of the Gods*
TLS - i5873 - Oct 23 2015 - p21(1) [501+]
Mergen, Bernard - *At Pyramid Lake*
WHQ - v46 - i1 - Spring 2015 - p79-79 [501+]

Merijian, Ara H. - *Giorgio de Chirico and the Metaphysical City: Nietzsche, Modernism*
    FS - v69 - i3 - July 2015 - p411-412 [501+]
Merino, Gemma - *The Cow Who Climbed a Tree (Illus. by Merino, Gemma)*
    c KR - Jan 1 2016 - pNA [51-500]
    c Sch Lib - v63 - i4 - Winter 2015 - p220(2) [51-500]
Merino, Noel - *Teen Rights and Freedoms: Drugs*
    y VOYA - v38 - i3 - August 2015 - p90(1) [51-500]
Teen Rights and Freedoms: Emancipation
    y VOYA - v38 - i3 - August 2015 - p90(1) [51-500]
Teen Rights and Freedoms: Health Care
    y VOYA - v38 - i3 - August 2015 - p90(1) [51-500]
Merisotis, Jamie - *America Needs Talent: Attracting, Educating and Deploying the 21st-Century Workforce*
    BL - v112 - i1 - Sept 1 2015 - p20(1) [51-500]
Merjian, Ara H. - *Giorgio de Chirico and the Metaphysical City: Nietzche, Modernism, Paris*
    TLS - i5866 - Sept 4 2015 - p5(1) [501+]
Merkatz, David - *Wrongly Charged: A Look at the Legal System*
    SPBW - August 2015 - pNA [501+]
Merle, Robert - *The Brethren*
    KR - Jan 15 2015 - pNA [51-500]
    LJ - v140 - i2 - Feb 1 2015 - p74(2) [51-500]
    NYTBR - May 31 2015 - p39(L) [501+]
    TLS - i5868 - Sept 18 2015 - p19(2) [501+]
City of Wisdom and Blood
    TLS - i5868 - Sept 18 2015 - p19(2) [501+]
Merlino, Doug - *Beast: Blood, Struggle, and Dreams at the Heart of Mixed Martial Arts*
    y BL - v112 - i2 - Sept 15 2015 - p16(1) [51-500]
    KR - July 15 2015 - pNA [501+]
    LJ - v140 - i12 - July 1 2015 - p89(1) [51-500]
    PW - v262 - i28 - July 13 2015 - p55(2) [51-500]
Merlino, Stephen C. - *The Jack of Souls*
    SPBW - April 2015 - pNA [51-500]
Merlis, Mark - *JD: A Novel*
    G&L Rev W - v22 - i3 - May-June 2015 - p41(1) [501+]
    KR - Feb 1 2015 - pNA [51-500]
    RVBW - April 2015 - pNA [51-500]
Merlo, Carol - *Create a Happy Business: How to Be a Successful SoloPreneur*
    SPBW - June 2015 - pNA [51-500]
Merola, Caroline - *The Story Starts Here! (Illus. by Merola, Caroline)*
    c HB Guide - v26 - i1 - Spring 2015 - p39(1) [51-500]
Meron, Ehud - *Nonlinear Physics of Ecosystems*
    Phys Today - v68 - i10 - Oct 2015 - p46-50 [501+]
Merriam, Joanne - *How to Live on Other Planets: A Handbook for Aspiring Aliens*
    PW - v262 - i4 - Jan 26 2015 - p153(1) [51-500]
Merrick, Patrick - *Avalanches*
    c BL - v111 - i15 - April 1 2015 - p60(1) [51-500]
Easter Bunnies
    c CH Bwatch - Feb 2015 - pNA [51-500]
Merridale, Catherine - *Red Fortress: The Secret Heart of Russia's History*
    HNet - March 2015 - pNA [501+]
Merrill, Gary F. - *Our Aging Bodies*
    BL - v111 - i11 - Feb 1 2015 - p8(1) [51-500]
Merrill, Jean - *The Elephant Who Liked to Smash Small Cars (Illus. by Solbert, Ronni)*
    c HB Guide - v26 - i2 - Fall 2015 - p45(1) [51-500]
The Pushcart War (Illus. by Solbert, Ronni)
    c HB Guide - v26 - i1 - Spring 2015 - p86(1) [51-500]
    c Sch Lib - v63 - i2 - Summer 2015 - p106(1) [51-500]
Merriman, John - *The Life and Death of the Paris Commune*
    HT - v65 - i3 - March 2015 - p63(2) [501+]
Massacre: The Life and Death of the Paris Commune
    AM - v212 - i15 - May 4 2015 - p37(2) [501+]
    AS - v84 - i1 - Wntr 2015 - p107(3) [501+]
    JIH - v46 - i2 - Autumn 2015 - p282-284 [501+]
    Lon R Bks - v37 - i13 - July 2 2015 - p21(2) [501+]
    Mac - v128 - i1 - Jan 12 2015 - p68(1) [501+]
    NYRB - v62 - i3 - Feb 19 2015 - p26(3) [501+]
    TLS - i5855 - June 19 2015 - p8(1) [501+]
Merritt, Carolyn - *Tango Nuevo*
    Dance RJ - v47 - i1 - April 2015 - p121-123 [501+]
Merritt, J.F. - *Westminster 1640-60: A Royal City in a Time of Revolution*
    AHR - v120 - i1 - Feb 2015 - p325-326 [501+]
    HER - v130 - i544 - June 2015 - p746(3) [501+]

Merritt, Kory - *The Dreadful Fate of Jonathan York: A Yarn for the Strange at Heart*
    y KR - August 1 2015 - pNA [51-500]
    c PW - v262 - i33 - August 17 2015 - p75(1) [51-500]
    c SLJ - v61 - i11 - Nov 2015 - p105(2) [51-500]
Mertha, Andrew - *Brothers in Arms: Chinese Aid to the Khmer Rouge, 1975-1979*
    HNet - March 2015 - pNA [501+]
    Pac A - v88 - i2 - June 2015 - p263 [501+]
Merton, Charlotte - *Välkommen hem Mr. Swanson: Svenska emigranter och svenskhet pa film*
    Scan St - v87 - i2 - Summer 2015 - p309(4) [501+]
Meruane, Lina - *Seeing Red*
    KR - Jan 1 2016 - pNA [51-500]
Merullo, Roland - *Dinner with Buddha*
    BL - v111 - i19-20 - June 1 2015 - p39(1) [51-500]
    KR - March 15 2015 - pNA [501+]
    LJ - v140 - i6 - April 1 2015 - p83(1) [51-500]
    PW - v262 - i16 - April 20 2015 - p1(1) [51-500]
Merwin, Ted - *Pastrami on Rye: An Overstuffed History of the Jewish Deli*
    BL - v112 - i3 - Oct 1 2015 - p20(1) [51-500]
    KR - August 15 2015 - pNA [501+]
    NYTBR - Oct 11 2015 - p20(L) [501+]
Merz, Bruno - *Fluff and Other Stuff (Illus. by Blow, Dreda)*
    c KR - August 1 2015 - pNA [51-500]
Merzer, Glen - *Off the Reservation*
    KR - April 15 2015 - pNA [501+]
Mesara-Dogan, Gulden - *Mommy Goes to the Office*
    c KR - June 15 2015 - pNA [501+]
Mesce, Bill, Jr. - *Inside the Rise of HBO: A Personal History of the Company That Transformed Television*
    Bwatch - Nov 2015 - pNA [51-500]
    RVBW - Oct 2015 - pNA [501+]
Meschenmoser, Sebastian - *Mr. Squirrel and the Moon (Illus. by Meschenmoser, Sebastian)*
    c BL - v111 - i9-10 - Jan 1 2015 - p106(1) [51-500]
    c CH Bwatch - July 2015 - pNA [51-500]
    c HB Guide - v26 - i2 - Fall 2015 - p45(1) [51-500]
Meserve, Adria - *Don't Kick Up a Fuss, Gus! (Illus. by Meserve, Adria)*
    c SLJ - v61 - i9 - Sept 2015 - p125(2) [51-500]
Meshorer, Sean - *Thriving with Chronic Pain : A Holistic Guide to Reclaiming Your Life*
    KR - April 15 2015 - pNA [501+]
Mesler, Bill - *A Brief History of Creation: Science and the Search for the Origin of Life*
    BL - v112 - i4 - Oct 15 2015 - p9(1) [51-500]
    KR - Sept 15 2015 - pNA [501+]
    LJ - v140 - i19 - Nov 15 2015 - p104(1) [501+]
    PW - v262 - i41 - Oct 12 2015 - p58(1) [51-500]
Mesmer, Sharon - *Greetings from My Girlie Leisure Place*
    PW - v262 - i52 - Dec 21 2015 - p129(1) [51-500]
Mesnil, Emmanuelle Tixier du - *Desordres createurs : L'invention politique a la faveur des troubles*
    Specu - v90 - i3 - July 2015 - p877-878 [501+]
Mesqui, Jean - *Cesaree Maritime: Ville fortifiee du Proche-Orient*
    Med R - Sept 2015 - pNA [501+]
Mesrobian, Carrie - *Cut Both Ways*
    y BL - v111 - i22 - August 1 2015 - p55(1) [51-500]
    y KR - July 15 2015 - pNA [51-500]
    y PW - v262 - i25 - June 22 2015 - p143(1) [51-500]
    y SLJ - v61 - i7 - July 2015 - p96(1) [51-500]
    y VOYA - v38 - i3 - August 2015 - p65(1) [51-500]
Perfectly Good White Boy
    y HB Guide - v26 - i1 - Spring 2015 - p117(1) [51-500]
Messenger, David A. - *Hunting Nazis in Franco's Spain*
    GSR - v38 - i2 - May 2015 - p442-2 [501+]
Messenger, Jon - *Wolves of the Northern Rift*
    PW - v262 - i1 - Jan 5 2015 - p55(1) [51-500]
Messenger, Shannon - *Everblaze*
    c HB Guide - v26 - i2 - Fall 2015 - p94(1) [51-500]
Messengill, Rebekah Peeples - *Wal-Mart Wars: Moral Populism in the Twenty-First Century*
    CS - v44 - i3 - May 2015 - p379-380 [501+]
Messer, Neil - *Flourishing: Health, Disease, and Bioethics in Theological Perspective*
    JR - v95 - i4 - Oct 2015 - p574(2) [501+]
Messier, Mireille - *Le voilier d'Olivier: Une aventure en anagrammes*
    c Res Links - v20 - i3 - Feb 2015 - p47(1) [51-500]
Messier, Ron - *Jesus: One Man, Two Faiths: A Dialough between Christians & Muslims*
    KR - Nov 1 2015 - pNA [51-500]
Messier, William S. - *Townships*
    Can Lit - i224 - Spring 2015 - p137 [501+]

Messina, Lynn - *Prejudice and Pride*
    KR - Oct 15 2015 - pNA [501+]
Messina, Virginia - *Never Too Late to Go Vegan*
    Veg J - v34 - i2 - April-June 2015 - p31(1) [51-500]
Messing, Scott - *Marching to the Canon: The Life of Schubert's Marche Militaire*
    HNet - Oct 2015 - pNA [501+]
Messinger, Holly - *The Curse of Jacob Tracy*
    BL - v112 - i7 - Dec 1 2015 - p38(1) [51-500]
    PW - v262 - i41 - Oct 12 2015 - p52(1) [51-500]
Messner, Kate - *59 Reasons to Write: Mini-Lessons, Prompts, and Inspiration for Teachers*
    Bwatch - August 2015 - pNA [51-500]
    RVBW - Feb 2015 - pNA [501+]
    VOYA - v38 - i2 - June 2015 - p89(2) [51-500]
All the Answers
    c CCB-B - v68 - i9 - May 2015 - p458(1) [51-500]
    c HB Guide - v26 - i2 - Fall 2015 - p94(1) [51-500]
    c SLJ - v61 - i3 - March 2015 - p140(1) [51-500]
Danger in Ancient Rome
    c KR - March 15 2015 - pNA [501+]
How to Read a Story (Illus. by Siegel, Mark)
    c CCB-B - v69 - i1 - Sept 2015 - p39(2) [51-500]
    c SLJ - v61 - i7 - July 2015 - p66(1) [51-500]
Manhunt
    c HB Guide - v26 - i1 - Spring 2015 - p87(1) [51-500]
Ranger in Time: Rescue on the Oregon Trail
    c HB Guide - v26 - i2 - Fall 2015 - p69(1) [51-500]
Tree of Wonder: The Many Marvelous Lives of a Rainforest Tree (Illus. by Mulazzani, Simona)
    c BL - v112 - i4 - Oct 15 2015 - p41(1) [51-500]
    c SLJ - v61 - i8 - August 2015 - p123(1) [51-500]
Up in the Garden and Down in the Dirt (Illus. by Neal, Christopher Silas)
    c SLJ - v61 - i3 - March 2015 - p172(1) [51-500]
    c HB - v91 - i3 - May-June 2015 - p93(1) [51-500]
    c HB Guide - v26 - i2 - Fall 2015 - p45(1) [51-500]
Up in the Garden and Down in ther Dirt (Illus. by Neal, Christopher Silas)
    c NYTBR - May 10 2015 - p23(L) [501+]
Mester, Benjamin - *The Banished Lands*
    SPBW - Oct 2015 - pNA [51-500]
Metaphrog - *The Red Shoes and Other Tales (Illus. by Metaphrog)*
    c BL - v112 - i2 - Sept 15 2015 - p53(1) [51-500]
    c PW - v262 - i28 - July 13 2015 - p64(1) [501+]
    c KR - August 1 2015 - pNA [51-500]
    c SLJ - v61 - i5 - May 2015 - p110(1) [51-500]
Metatawabin, Edmund - *Up Ghost River: A Chief's Journey through the Turbulent Waters of Native History*
    Beav - v95 - i5 - Oct-Nov 2015 - p62(2) [501+]
Metaxas, Eric - *7 Women: And the Secret of Their Greatness*
    Ch Today - v59 - i8 - Oct 2015 - p76(1) [501+]
Bonhoeffer: Pastor, Martyr, Prophet, Spy (Read by Hillgartner, Malcolm). Audiobook Review
    y SLJ - v61 - i8 - August 2015 - p54(1) [51-500]
Bonhoeffer: Pastor, Martyr, Prophet, Spy, student ed.
    y BL - v111 - i19-20 - June 1 2015 - p83(1) [51-500]
    y SLJ - v61 - i7 - July 2015 - p108(1) [51-500]
Miracles: What They Are, Why They Happen, and How They Can Change Your Life (Read by Sanders, Fred). Audiobook Review
    LJ - v140 - i5 - March 15 2015 - p73(1) [51-500]
Metcalf, Ben - *Against the Country*
    NY - v90 - i47 - Feb 9 2015 - p69 [51-500]
    NYTBR - Jan 25 2015 - p9(L) [501+]
    y SLJ - v61 - i10 - Oct 2015 - p123(1) [51-500]
    TLS - i5870 - Oct 2 2015 - p20(1) [501+]
Metcalf, Gabriel - *Democratic by Design: How Carsharing, Co-Ops and Community Land Trusts Are Reinventing America*
    KR - Sept 1 2015 - pNA [501+]
Metcalf, Paul - *Genoa*
    KR - May 15 2015 - pNA [501+]
Metcalf, Paula - *A Guide to Sisters (Illus. by Barton, Suzanne)*
    c CCB-B - v69 - i2 - Oct 2015 - p102(2) [51-500]
    c KR - May 1 2015 - pNA [51-500]
    c Sch Lib - v63 - i1 - Spring 2015 - p30(1) [51-500]
    c SLJ - v61 - i6 - June 2015 - p88(1) [51-500]
Metcalf, Peter - *The Life of the Longhouse: An Archaeology of Ethnicity*
    JAS - v74 - i2 - May 2015 - p523-524 [501+]
Metcalfe, Stephen - *The Tragic Age*
    y BL - v111 - i12 - Feb 15 2015 - p84(1) [51-500]
    y CCB-B - v68 - i9 - May 2015 - p458(1) [51-500]
    y KR - Jan 1 2015 - pNA [51-500]
    PW - v262 - i1 - Jan 5 2015 - p75(1) [51-500]

Metheny, Richard - *The Person Leaders Really Need to Know*
   KR - Jan 1 2016 - pNA [501+]

Metoyer, Herbert R., Jr. - *Small Fires in the Sun*
   KR - March 15 2015 - pNA [501+]

Metropolitan Temporalities
   HNet - April 2015 - pNA [501+]

Mettler, Suzanne - *Degrees of Inequality: How the Politics of Higher Education Sabotaged the American Dream*
   BL - v111 - i21 - July 1 2015 - p22(2) [501+]

Metz, Christian - *Impersonal Enunciation, or the Place of Film*
   PW - v262 - i39 - Sept 28 2015 - p77(1) [51-500]

Metz, Thaddeus - *Meaning in Life: An Analytic Study*
   Ethics - v125 - i2 - Jan 2015 - p600(6) [501+]

Metzger, Birgit - *"Erst stirbt der Wald, dann du!": Das Waldsterben als westdeutsches Politikum*
   HNet - Sept 2015 - pNA [501+]

Metzger, Folker - *Gustav Adolph Comaro Riecke: Schulpolitik und Schulpadagogik zur Zeit des Vormarz, und der Revolution von 1848/49*
   Ger Q - v88 - i2 - Spring 2015 - p259(3) [501+]

Metzger, Steve - *Twinkle, Twinkle, I Love You (Illus. by Corke, Estelle)*
   c SLJ - v61 - i2 - Feb 2015 - p73(1) [51-500]
Waiting for Santa (Illus. by Edgson, Alison)
   c KR - Sept 1 2015 - pNA [51-500]
   c PW - v262 - i37 - Sept 14 2015 - p67(2) [51-500]
   c SLJ - v61 - i10 - Oct 2015 - p65(2) [51-500]

Metzler, Mark - *Capital as Will and Imagination: Schumpeter's Guide to the Postwar Japanese Miracle*
   JAS - v74 - i3 - August 2015 - p753-754 [501+]

Metzler, Sally - *Bartholomeus Spranger: Splendor and Eroticism in Imperial Prague*
   Mag Antiq - v182 - i1 - Jan-Feb 2015 - p104(1) [501+]

Metzler, Tobias - *Tales of Three Cities: Urban Jewish Cultures in London, Berlin, and Paris*
   HNet - April 2015 - pNA [501+]

Meuwese, Mark - *Brothers in Arms, Partners in Trade: Dutch-Indigenous Alliances in the Atlantic World, 1595-1674*
   Ren Q - v68 - i2 - Summer 2015 - p705-706 [501+]

Mewburn, Kyle - *Fire! (Illus. by Bixley, Donovan)*
   c Magpies - v30 - i1 - March 2015 - pS6(1) [501+]
Rats! (Illus. by Bixley, Donovan)
   c Magpies - v30 - i2 - May 2015 - pS6(1) [501+]
Rosie's Radical Rescue Ride
   c Magpies - v30 - i1 - March 2015 - pS5(1) [501+]

Mewshaw, Michael - *Sympathy for the Devil: Four Decades of Friendship with Gore Vidal*
   Nat Post - v17 - i56 - Jan 3 2015 - pWP11(1) [501+]
   TLS - i5842 - March 20 2015 - p4(2) [501+]
   G&L Rev W - v22 - i3 - May-June 2015 - p10(3) [51-500]
   NY - v91 - i33 - Oct 26 2015 - p83 [501+]

Mexal, Stephen J. - *Reading for Liberalism: The Overland Monthly and the Writing of the Modern American West*
   PHR - v84 - i1 - Feb 2015 - p89(2) [501+]

Meyer, Carolyn - *Anastasia and Her Sisters*
   y BL - v111 - i19-20 - June 1 2015 - p86(2) [501+]
   y BL - v111 - i16 - April 15 2015 - p56(1) [51-500]
   y HB Guide - v26 - i2 - Fall 2015 - p132(1) [51-500]
   y PW - v262 - i9 - March 2 2015 - p86(1) [51-500]
   y VOYA - v38 - i1 - April 2015 - p66(1) [51-500]
Diary of a Waitress: The Not-So-Glamorous Life of a Harvey Girl
   c CCB-B - v68 - i9 - May 2015 - p459(1) [51-500]
   y HB Guide - v26 - i2 - Fall 2015 - p132(1) [51-500]
   c KR - Jan 15 2015 - pNA [51-500]
   y SLJ - v61 - i2 - Feb 2015 - p89(1) [51-500]

Meyer, Christopher Paul - *Icarus Falling: The True Story of a Nightclub Bouncer Who Wanted to Be a Fucking Movie Star But Settled for Being a Fucking Man*
   KR - March 1 2015 - pNA [501+]

Meyer, Deon - *Cobra*
   RVBW - June 2015 - pNA [51-500]
Icarus
   BL - v112 - i1 - Sept 1 2015 - p47(1) [51-500]
   KR - August 15 2015 - pNA [51-500]
   PW - v262 - i33 - August 17 2015 - p50(1) [51-500]

Meyer, Eileen R. - *Sweet Dreams, Wild Animals! A Story of Sleep (Illus. by Caple, Laurie)*
   c CH Bwatch - June 2015 - pNA [51-500]
   c CH Bwatch - Nov 2015 - pNA [51-500]
   c HB Guide - v26 - i2 - Fall 2015 - p171(1) [51-500]
   c SLJ - v61 - i5 - May 2015 - p135(1) [51-500]

Meyer, Elizabeth - *Good Mourning: A Memoir*
   BL - v111 - i19-20 - June 1 2015 - p28(1) [51-500]
   PW - v262 - i21 - May 25 2015 - p48(2) [51-500]

Meyer, Hans-Caspar - *Greco-Scythian Art and the Birth of Eurasia: From Classical Antiquity to Russian Modernity*
   Class R - v65 - i1 - April 2015 - p258-260 [501+]

Meyer, Heinz-Dieter - *PISA, Power, and Policy: The Emergence of Global Educational Governance*
   TimHES - i2191 - Feb 19 2015 - p49(1) [501+]

Meyer, Jerrold S. - *Psychopharmacology: Drugs, the Brain, and Behavior*
   QRB - v90 - i2 - June 2015 - p225(1) [501+]

Meyer, Joyce - *The Battle Belongs to the Lord: Overcoming Life's Struggles through Worship (Read by Carlisle, Jodi). Audiobook Review*
   Bwatch - July 2015 - pNA [51-500]
Get Your Hopes Up! Expect Something Good to Happen to You Every Day
   LJ - v140 - i9 - May 15 2015 - p64(2) [501+]

Meyer, Karl - *The China Collectors: America's Century-Long Hunt for Asian Art Treasures*
   Econ - v415 - i8935 - April 25 2015 - p79(US) [501+]

Meyer, Karl E. - *The China Collector: America's Century-Long Hunt for Asian Art Treasures*
   BL - v111 - i13 - March 1 2015 - p12(1) [51-500]
The China Collectors: America's Century-Long Hunt for Asian Art Treasures
   LJ - v140 - i2 - Feb 1 2015 - p79(1) [51-500]
   PW - v262 - i2 - Jan 12 2015 - p49(1) [51-500]

Meyer, Kerstin - *The Pirate Pig (Illus. by Latsch, Oliver)*
   c SLJ - v61 - i2 - Feb 2015 - p69(1) [51-500]

Meyer, Kimberly - *The Book of Wanderings: A Mother-Daughter Pilgrimage*
   BL - v111 - i14 - March 15 2015 - p29(1) [51-500]
   Bwatch - July 2015 - pNA [51-500]

Meyer, L.A. - *Wild Rover No More: Being the Last Recorded Account of the Life and Times of Jacky Faber*
   c HB Guide - v26 - i1 - Spring 2015 - p117(1) [51-500]
   y VOYA - v37 - i6 - Feb 2015 - p61(1) [51-500]
Wild Rover No More: Being the Last Recorded Account of the Life & Times of Jacky Faber (Read by Kellgren, Katherine). Audiobook Review
   SLJ - v61 - i4 - April 2015 - p65(1) [51-500]

Meyer, Madonna Harrington - *Grandmothers at Work: Juggling Families and Jobs*
   AJS - v120 - i6 - May 2015 - p1903(3) [501+]

Meyer, Marissa - *Fairest (Read by Soler, Rebecca). Audiobook Review*
   y SLJ - v61 - i5 - May 2015 - p72(1) [51-500]
Fairest
   y CCB-B - v68 - i11 - July-August 2015 - p557(1) [51-500]
   y HB Guide - v26 - i2 - Fall 2015 - p132(1) [51-500]
   SLJ - v61 - i4 - April 2015 - p168(2) [51-500]
Winter
   y BL - v111 - i21 - July 1 2015 - p49(1) [501+]
   y BL - v112 - i4 - Oct 15 2015 - p46(2) [51-500]
   y PW - v262 - i34 - August 24 2015 - p81(1) [51-500]
   y SLJ - v61 - i11 - Nov 2015 - p119(1) [51-500]

Meyer, Michael - *In Manchuria: a Village Called Wasteland and the Transformation of Rural China*
   NS - v144 - i5260 - May 1 2015 - p44(2) [501+]
   NYRB - v62 - i10 - June 4 2015 - p46(3) [501+]
   NYT - March 9 2015 - pC4(L) [501+]
   TLS - i5856 - June 26 2015 - p24(1) [501+]

Meyer, Michael A. - *Between Jewish Tradition and Modernity: Rethinking an Old Opposition: Essays in Honor of David Ellenson*
   HNet - June 2015 - pNA [501+]

Meyer, Nicole L. - *Cups, Sticks & Nibbles: Unlock Your Inner Hosting Confidence with Stress-Free Tips & Recipes*
   SPBW - Sept 2015 - pNA [501+]

Meyer, Pamela - *The Agility Shift: Creating Agile and Effective Leaders, Teams, and Organizations*
   PW - v262 - i30 - July 27 2015 - p57(1) [51-500]

Meyer, Ralph - *XIII Mystery: The Mongoose (Illus. by Dorison, Xavier)*
   y Sch Lib - v63 - i2 - Summer 2015 - p124(2) [51-500]

Meyer, Richard J. - *Wang Renmei: The Wildcat of Shanghai*
   Pac A - v88 - i2 - June 2015 - p294 [501+]
   Pac A - v88 - i2 - June 2015 - p294 [501+]

Meyer, Susan Lynn - *New Shoes (Illus. by Velasquez, Eric)*
   c BL - v111 - i11 - Feb 1 2015 - p46(1) [51-500]
   c CCB-B - v68 - i8 - April 2015 - p412(1) [51-500]
   c HB Guide - v26 - i2 - Fall 2015 - p45(1) [51-500]
   c PW - v262 - i49 - Dec 2 2015 - p16(2) [51-500]
   c SLJ - v61 - i2 - Feb 2015 - p73(1) [51-500]

Meyer, Taro - *Emma G. Loves Boyz*
   y KR - Oct 1 2015 - pNA [501+]

Meyer, Terry Teague - *Female Genital Cutting*
   y BL - v112 - i7 - Dec 1 2015 - p44(1) [51-500]
The Vo-Tech Track to Success in Information Technology
   y Teach Lib - v42 - i3 - Feb 2015 - p10(1) [51-500]

Meyerhofer, Michael - *Wytchfire*
   PW - v262 - i22 - June 1 2015 - p46(1) [51-500]

Meyerhoff, Jenny - *Green Thumbs-Up! (Illus. by Chatelain, Eva)*
   c BL - v111 - i21 - July 1 2015 - p72(2) [51-500]
   c KR - June 15 2015 - pNA [51-500]
   c PW - v262 - i24 - June 15 2015 - p85(1) [501+]
   c SLJ - v61 - i5 - May 2015 - p96(2) [51-500]

Meyers, Cynthia B. - *A Word from Our Sponsor: Admen, Advertising, and the Golden Age of Radio*
   AHR - v120 - i1 - Feb 2015 - p278-279 [501+]

Meyers, Jeffrey - *Robert Lowell in Love*
   LJ - v140 - i20 - Dec 1 2015 - p101(2) [51-500]

Meyers, Robert A. - *Epigenetic Regulation and Epigenomics*
   QRB - v90 - i2 - June 2015 - p228(2) [501+]

Meyers, Robin - *Spiritual Defiance: Building a Beloved Community of Resistance*
   LJ - v140 - i9 - May 15 2015 - p64(2) [501+]

Meyers, Ruth A. - *Missional Worship, Worshipful Mission: Gathering as God's People, Going Out in God's Name*
   IBMR - v39 - i3 - July 2015 - p158(1) [501+]

Meyers, Steven Key - *My Mad Russian*
   KR - May 1 2015 - pNA [501+]

Meylan, Nicolas - *Magic and Kingship in Medieval Iceland: The Construction of a Discourse of Political Resistance*
   Med R - Feb 2015 - pNA [501+]

Meyn, Laura Samuel - *Meatless in Cowtown: A Vegetarian Guide to Food and Wine, Texas Style*
   BL - v111 - i19-20 - June 1 2015 - p20(2) [51-500]
   LJ - v140 - i11 - June 15 2015 - p108(2) [51-500]

Meynell, Mark - *A Wilderness of Mirrors: Trusting Again in a Cynical World*
   PW - v262 - i15 - April 13 2015 - p76(1) [51-500]

Meyrick, Denzil - *The Last Witness*
   BL - v112 - i4 - Oct 15 2015 - p22(1) [51-500]
   KR - Oct 15 2015 - pNA [51-500]
   LJ - v140 - i19 - Nov 15 2015 - p78(1) [51-500]
   PW - v262 - i41 - Oct 12 2015 - p48(1) [51-500]

Mez, Kristin Kobes Du - *A New Gospel for Women: Katherine Bushnell and the Challenge of Christian Feminism*
   TimHES - i2218 - August 27 2015 - p46-47 [501+]

Mezaros, Julia - *Sacrifice and Modern Thought*
   Theol St - v76 - i1 - March 2015 - p218(2) [51-500]

Mezrich, Ben - *Bringing Down the Mouse*
   c HB Guide - v26 - i1 - Spring 2015 - p87(1) [51-500]
Once upon a Time in Russia: The Rise of the Oligarchs: A True Story of Ambition, Wealth, Betrayal, and Murder (Read by Bobb, Jeremy). Audiobook Review
   PW - v262 - i35 - August 31 2015 - p84(1) [51-500]
Once upon a Time in Russia: The Rise of the Oligarchs: A True Story of Ambition, Wealth, Betrayal, and Murder
   BL - v111 - i18 - May 15 2015 - p13(1) [51-500]
   KR - March 15 2015 - pNA [501+]
   LJ - v140 - i8 - May 1 2015 - p80(1) [51-500]
   Mac - v128 - i26-27 - July 6 2015 - p68(1) [501+]
   PW - v262 - i9 - March 2 2015 - p75(1) [501+]

Miachi, Tom A. - *The Incarnate Being Phenomenon in African Culture: Anthropological Perspectives on the Igala of North-Central Nigeria*
   HNet - August 2015 - pNA [501+]

Mian, Zanib - *It Must Have Been You! (Illus. by Mian, Fatima)*
   c Sch Lib - v63 - i3 - Autumn 2015 - p158(1) [51-500]
Oddsockosaurus (Illus. by Bolton, Bill)
   c PW - v262 - i33 - August 17 2015 - p71(1) [51-500]

Michael, Eilenberg - *At the Edges of States: Dynamics of State Formation in the Indonesian Borderlands*
   JAS - v74 - i1 - Feb 2015 - p239-241 [501+]

Michael, Ethan - *The Defender: How the Legendary Black Newspaper Changed America*
   PW - v262 - i45 - Nov 9 2015 - p51(1) [51-500]

Michael, Livi - *Succession*
   NYTBR - Sept 20 2015 - p18(L) [501+]

Michael, Pamela - *Edible Wild Plants and Herbs: A Compendium of Recipes and Remedies*
   TLS - i5872 - Oct 16 2015 - p30(1) [501+]

Michael, T.T. - *Fire War*
   KR - Dec 1 2015 - pNA [501+]

Michaeli, Ethan - *The Defender: How the Legendary Black Newspaper Changed America*
    BL - v111 - i21 - July 1 2015 - p4(1) [51-500]
    KR - Oct 1 2015 - pNA [501+]
    LJ - v140 - i19 - Nov 15 2015 - p93(1) [51-500]

Michaels, Anne - *The Adventures of Miss Petitfour (Illus. by Block, Emma)*
    c KR - August 15 2015 - pNA [51-500]
    c PW - v262 - i38 - Sept 21 2015 - p77(1) [501+]
    c Res Links - v21 - i1 - Oct 2015 - p19(1) [51-500]
    c SLJ - v61 - i12 - Dec 2015 - p99(1) [51-500]

Michaels, Kasey - *An Improper Arrangement*
    PW - v262 - i46 - Nov 16 2015 - p63(1) [51-500]

Michaels, Nicole - *Start Me Up*
    PW - v262 - i2 - Jan 12 2015 - p42(1) [51-500]

Michaels, Nikka - *In the Distance*
    PW - v262 - i16 - April 20 2015 - p61(1) [51-500]

Michaels, Paula A. - *Lamaze: An International History*
    AHR - v120 - i2 - April 2015 - p587-588 [501+]
    JIH - v45 - i4 - Spring 2015 - p570-571 [501+]
    Lon R Bks - v37 - i11 - June 4 2015 - p17(2) [501+]

Michaels, Sean - *Us Conductors*
    WLT - v89 - i1 - Jan-Feb 2015 - p67(3) [501+]

Michaels, Shawn - *Wrestling for My Life: The Legend, the Reality, and the Faith of a WWE Superstar*
    BL - v111 - i11 - Feb 1 2015 - p10(1) [51-500]

Michalson, Gordon E. - *Kant's Religion within the Boundaries of Mere Reason: A Critical Guide*
    Rel St - v51 - i1 - March 2015 - p125-130 [501+]

Michaud, Nicolas - *Dracula and Philosophy*
    RVBW - Oct 2015 - pNA [501+]

Michaux, Henri - *Thousand Times Broken, 3 vols.*
    TLS - i5864-5865 - August 21 2015 - p24(1) [501+]

Michel, Lincoln - *Upright Beast*
    KR - August 1 2015 - pNA [51-500]
Upright Beasts: Stories
    NYTBR - Oct 4 2015 - p30(L) [501+]
    PW - v262 - i33 - August 17 2015 - p46(1) [51-500]

Michel, Misja Fitzgerald - *Dreams Are Made for Children (Illus. by Green Ilya)*
    RVBW - Oct 2015 - pNA [51-500]

Michelakis, Pantelis - *Greek Tragedy on Screen*
    Class R - v65 - i1 - April 2015 - p289-291 [501+]

Michele, Hope Schenk-de - *Devil's Daughter*
    PW - v262 - i14 - April 6 2015 - p43(1) [51-500]

Micheletta, Luca - *L'Italia e la guerra di Libia cent'anni dopo*
    J Mil H - v79 - i4 - Oct 2015 - p1121-1126 [501+]

Michell, David - *Slade House*
    NS - v144 - i5286 - Oct 30 2015 - p43(1) [501+]

Michelle, Caswell - *Archiving the Unspeakable: Silence, Memory, and the Photographic Record in Cambodia*
    JAS - v74 - i1 - Feb 2015 - p236-239 [501+]

Michelle, P.T. - *Mister Black*
    PW - v262 - i47 - Nov 23 2015 - p56(1) [51-500]

Michelson, Emily - *The Pulpit and the Press in Reformation Italy*
    Historian - v77 - i2 - Summer 2015 - p398(2) [501+]

Michelson, Leslie D. - *The Patient's Playbook: How to Save Your Life and the Lives of Those You Love*
    BL - v111 - i22 - August 1 2015 - p12(2) [51-500]
    BL - v112 - i7 - Dec 1 2015 - p13(1) [501+]
    KR - August 15 2015 - pNA [51-500]
    LJ - v140 - i13 - August 1 2015 - p116(2) [51-500]

Michelson, Patrick Lally - *Thinking Orthodox in Modern Russia: Culture, History, Context*
    Slav R - v74 - i2 - Summer 2015 - p401-403 [501+]

Michelson, Richard - *More Money Than God*
    WLT - v89 - i6 - Nov-Dec 2015 - p73(1) [51-500]

Michie, Jonathan - *Why the Social Sciences Matter*
    TimHES - i2196 - March 26 2015 - p55(1) [501+]

Michlin, Monica - *Black Intersectionalities: A Critique for the 21st Century*
    JGS - v24 - i2 - April 2015 - p242-244 [501+]

Michnik, Adam - *The Church and the Left*
    Nation - v300 - i1 - Jan 5 2015 - p27(10) [501+]
The Trouble With History: Morality, Revolution, and Counterrevolution
    Nation - v300 - i1 - Jan 5 2015 - p27(10) [501+]
    NYRB - v62 - i6 - April 2 2015 - p73(3) [501+]
    TLS - i5841 - March 13 2015 - p26(2) [501+]

Michon, Cedric - *Le Cardinal Jean du Bellay: Diplomatie et culture dans l'Europe de la Renaissance*
    FS - v69 - i2 - April 2015 - p237-238 [501+]
    Six Ct J - v46 - i1 - Spring 2015 - p239-240 [501+]

Micka, Rene - *Charlie's Birthday Wish (Illus. by Sauer, Scott)*
    c CH Bwatch - April 2015 - pNA [51-500]

Mickey, Robert - *Paths Out of Dixie: The Democratization of Authoritarian Enclaves in America's Deep South, 1944-1972*
    HNet - August 2015 - pNA [501+]

Mickiewicz, Ellen - *No Illusions: The Voices of Russia's Future Leaders*
    For Aff - v94 - i1 - Jan-Feb 2015 - pNA [501+]

Micklos, John., Jr. - *The 1918 Flu Pandemic: Core Events of a Worldwide Outbreak*
    SLJ - v61 - i2 - Feb 2015 - p114(1) [51-500]

Micros, Matt - *Five Days*
    SPBW - Jan 2015 - pNA [51-500]

Middlebrook, Diana - *Young Ovid: A Life Recreated*
    Sew R - v123 - i2 - Spring 2015 - p350-357 [501+]

Middlecamp, Catherine H. - *Chemistry in Context: Applying Chemistry to Society, 8th ed.*
    J Chem Ed - v92 - i8 - August 2015 - p1284-1285 [501+]

Middlekauff, Robert - *Washington's Revolution: The Making of America's First Leader*
    NYTBR - March 29 2015 - p23(L) [501+]
    y BL - v111 - i9-10 - Jan 1 2015 - p34(1) [51-500]
    LJ - v140 - i2 - Feb 1 2015 - p94(1) [501+]
    Nat R - v67 - i8 - May 4 2015 - p45 [501+]

Middleton, J. Richard - *A New Heaven and a New Earth: Reclaiming Biblical Eschatology*
    CC - v132 - i9 - April 29 2015 - p51(1) [501+]

Middleton, Patrick - *Eureka Man*
    KR - Jan 15 2015 - pNA [501+]
    PW - v262 - i39 - Sept 28 2015 - p64(1) [51-500]

Middleton, Richard - *Studying Popular Music*
    TimHES - i2211 - July 9 2015 - p49(1) [501+]

Midthun, Joseph - *Animal Behavior*
    SLJ - v61 - i2 - Feb 2015 - p116(1) [51-500]

Mieczkowski, Yanek - *Eisenhower's Sputnik Moment: The Race for Space and World Prestige*
    Pres St Q - v45 - i1 - March 2015 - p199(7) [501+]

Miernowski, Jan - *Le Sublime et le grotesque*
    FS - v69 - i3 - July 2015 - p407-408 [501+]

Miert, Dirk van - *Communicating Observations in Early Modern Letters (1500-1675): Epistolography and Epistemology in the Age of the Scientific Revolution*
    Isis - v106 - i2 - June 2015 - p437(2) [501+]

Miesnik, Liz - *Second Chance*
    RVBW - Jan 2015 - pNA [51-500]

Mieville, China - *This Census-Taker*
    KR - Dec 1 2015 - pNA [501+]
    PW - v262 - i50 - Dec 7 2015 - p73(1) [51-500]
Three Moments of an Explosion
    KR - June 1 2015 - pNA [501+]
    BL - v111 - i19-20 - June 1 2015 - p46(1) [51-500]
    Ent W - i1375 - August 7 2015 - p66(1) [501+]
    NS - v144 - i5276 - August 21 2015 - p52(1) [501+]
    PW - v262 - i17 - April 27 2015 - p46(1) [501+]
    TLS - i5860 - July 24 2015 - p19(1) [501+]

Miglore, Kristen - *Food52 Genius Recipes: 100 Recipes That Will Change the Way You Cook*
    NYTBR - May 31 2015 - p24(L) [501+]
    PW - v262 - i11 - March 16 2015 - p79(1) [51-500]

Mignolo, Walter D. - *The Darker Side of Western Modernity*
    Tikkun - v30 - i1 - Wntr 2015 - pNA [501+]

Migraine-George, Therese - *From Francophonie to World Literature in French: Ethics, Poetics, and Politics*
    FS - v69 - i1 - Jan 2015 - p120-121 [501+]

Migration in and out of East and Southeast Europe: Values, Networks, Well-Being
    HNet - Sept 2015 - pNA [501+]

Migration und Familie
    HNet - April 2015 - pNA [501+]

Miguelez-Cavero, Laura - *Triphiodorus, the Sack of Troy: A General Study and a Commentary*
    Class R - v65 - i2 - Oct 2015 - p399-401 [501+]

Migy - *And Away We Go! (Illus. by Migy)*
    c HB Guide - v26 - i2 - Fall 2015 - p45(1) [51-500]

Mikalatos, Matt - *Sky Lantern: The Story of a Father's Love for His Children and the Healing Power of the Smallest Act of Kindness*
    Ch Today - v59 - i10 - Dec 2015 - p74(1) [51-500]

Mikhaelevitch, Alexandre - *Balzac et Bianchon*
    FS - v69 - i1 - Jan 2015 - p99-100 [501+]

Miklian, Jason - *India's Human Security: Lost Debates, Forgotten People, Intractable Challenges*
    Pac A - v88 - i3 - Sept 2015 - p725 [501+]

Mikrokosmos und Makrokosmos. Meistersinger als mentalitats- und ideengeschichtlicher Ausdruck der Stadt im spaten Mittelalter und Fruher Neuzeit
    HNet - May 2015 - pNA [501+]

Mikulencak, Mandy - *Burn Girl*
    c BL - v112 - i2 - Sept 15 2015 - p63(1) [51-500]
    y KR - July 1 2015 - pNA [51-500]
    y SLJ - v61 - i8 - August 2015 - p107(1) [51-500]
    y VOYA - v38 - i5 - Dec 2015 - p61(1) [51-500]

Milan, Victor - *The Dinosaur Lords*
    PW - v262 - i21 - May 25 2015 - p40(1) [51-500]

Milanes, Cecilia Rodriguez - *Oye What I'm Gonna Tell You*
    KR - Feb 15 2015 - pNA [501+]
    BL - v111 - i16 - April 15 2015 - p27(1) [51-500]
    NYTBR - May 3 2015 - p30(L) [501+]

Milanesio, Natalia - *Workers Go Shopping in Argentina: The Rise of Popular Consumer Culture*
    CS - v44 - i2 - March 2015 - p236-237 [501+]

Milani, Milad - *Sufism in the Secret History of Persia*
    JR - v95 - i3 - July 2015 - p415(2) [501+]

Milanovic, Therese - *Learning and Teaching Healthy Piano Technique: Training as an Instructor in the Taubman Approach*
    Am MT - v64 - i4 - Feb-March 2015 - p58(2) [501+]

Milazzo, Richard - *Like Branches to Wind: Poems 2008*
    WLT - v89 - i1 - Jan-Feb 2015 - p75(2) [501+]
A Prayer in a Wolf's Mouth: Poems 2013-2014
    WLT - v89 - i1 - Jan-Feb 2015 - p75(2) [501+]

Milburn, Colin - *Mondo Nano: Fun and Games in the World of Digital Matter*
    SFS - v42 - i3 - Nov 2015 - p593-597 [501+]
    New Sci - v226 - i3024 - June 6 2015 - p46(1) [501+]
    Phys Today - v68 - i7 - July 2015 - p46-1 [501+]

Milburn, Olivia - *Cherishing Antiquity: The Cultural Construction of an Ancient Chinese Kingdom*
    JAS - v74 - i1 - Feb 2015 - p204-205 [501+]

Milchman, Jenny - *As Night Falls (Read by Berneis, Susie). Audiobook Review*
    BL - v112 - i7 - Dec 1 2015 - p68(1) [51-500]
    LJ - v140 - i19 - Nov 15 2015 - p52(1) [51-500]
As Night Falls
    BL - v111 - i21 - July 1 2015 - p34(1) [51-500]
    PW - v262 - i20 - May 18 2015 - p64(1) [51-500]
Ruin Falls
    RVBW - May 2015 - pNA [51-500]

Mildenberger, Florian - *Medizinische Belehrung fur das Burgertum: Medikale Kulturen in der Zeitschrift "Die Gartenlaube"*
    Isis - v106 - i1 - March 2015 - p200(2) [501+]

Mildon, Emma - *The Soul Searcher's Handbook: The Modern Girl's Guide to the New Age World*
    PW - v262 - i37 - Sept 14 2015 - p63(1) [51-500]

Mildred's - *Mildreds: The Cookbook*
    BL - v112 - i3 - Oct 1 2015 - p18(1) [51-500]

Miles, Barry - *Call Me Burroughs: A Life*
    NYTBR - March 1 2015 - p28(L) [501+]

Miles, Brenda S. - *Stickley Sticks To It! A Frog's Guide to Getting Things Done (Illus. by Mack, Steve)*
    c CH Bwatch - June 2015 - pNA [51-500]

Miles, David - *Book (Illus. by Hoopes, Natalie)*
    c CH Bwatch - March 2015 - pNA [51-500]
    c KR - April 1 2015 - pNA [51-500]
    c PW - v262 - i18 - May 4 2015 - p116(1) [51-500]

Miles, Ellen - *Bandit*
    c Res Links - v21 - i1 - Oct 2015 - p52(1) [501+]
Mona
    c Res Links - v20 - i4 - April 2015 - p42(1) [51-500]
Oscar
    c Res Links - v21 - i1 - Oct 2015 - p54(1) [51-500]

Miles, Jack - *The Norton Anthology of World Religions, 2 vols.*
    Comw - v142 - i10 - June 1 2015 - p23(4) [501+]

Miles, Jon Lindsay - *Southeaster*
    TLS - i5869 - Sept 25 2015 - p21(1) [501+]

Miles, Justin - *Ultimate Explorer Guide for Kids*
    c Sch Lib - v63 - i3 - Autumn 2015 - p175(1) [51-500]

Miles, Lisa - *Ballet Spectacular: A Young Ballet Lover's Guide and an Insight into a Magical World*
    c HB Guide - v26 - i1 - Spring 2015 - p181(1) [51-500]

Miles, Liz - *Celebrating Islamic Festivals*
    c Sch Lib - v63 - i4 - Winter 2015 - p239(1) [51-500]

Miles, Rachael - *Jilting the Duke*
    PW - v262 - i47 - Nov 23 2015 - p54(1) [51-500]

Miles, Tiya - *The Cherokee Rose*
  KR - Feb 1 2015 - pNA [51-500]
  LJ - v140 - i6 - April 1 2015 - p83(1) [51-500]
  PW - v262 - i6 - Feb 9 2015 - p42(2) [51-500]
  RVBW - March 2015 - pNA [51-500]

Miles, Valerie - *A Thousand Forests in One Acorn: An Anthology of Spanish-Language Fiction*
  WLT - v89 - i2 - March-April 2015 - p77(1) [501+]

Milford, Kate - *Greenglass House (Read by Coffey, Chris Henry). Audiobook Review*
  c SLJ - v61 - i6 - June 2015 - p64(1) [51-500]
  Greenglass House (Illus. by Zollars, Jaime)
  c BL - v111 - i17 - May 1 2015 - p40(1) [51-500]
  c HB Guide - v26 - i1 - Spring 2015 - p87(1) [51-500]

Milgrim, David - *Wild Feelings (Illus. by Milgrim, David)*
  c KR - June 15 2015 - pNA [51-500]
  c PW - v262 - i22 - June 1 2015 - p58(1) [501+]
  c SLJ - v61 - i5 - May 2015 - p89(1) [51-500]

Milham, Alea - *Prep-Ahead Meals from Scratch: Make Healthy Home Cooking Practically Effortless (Illus. by Holloman, Chris)*
  PW - v262 - i50 - Dec 7 2015 - p82(1) [51-500]

Milhander, Laura Aron - *Not for All the Hamantaschen in Town (Illus. by Chernyak, Inna)*
  c KR - Dec 1 2015 - pNA [51-500]
  c PW - v262 - i48 - Nov 30 2015 - p63(1) [51-500]

Milisic, Roman - *Apes a-Go-Go! (Illus. by Allen, A. Richard)*
  c KR - May 1 2015 - pNA [51-500]
  c SLJ - v61 - i9 - Sept 2015 - p126(1) [51-500]

Militarhistorische Sammlungen in Bibliotheken - Bewahren, Erschliessen, Prasentieren
  HNet - Jan 2015 - pNA [501+]

Milk Carton Kids - *Monterey*
  CSM - May 29 2015 - pNA [501+]

Milkman, Ruth - *New Labor in New York: Precarious Workers and the Future of the Labor Movement*
  CS - v44 - i6 - Nov 2015 - p827-828 [501+]
  Unfinished Business: Paid Family Leave in California and the Future of U.S. Work-Family Policy
  CS - v44 - i5 - Sept 2015 - p682-683 [501+]
  Soc Ser R - v89 - i1 - March 2015 - p207(5) [501+]

Millar, David - *The Racer*
  Spec - v329 - i9768 - Nov 14 2015 - p61(2) [501+]

Millar, Goldie - *F Is for Feelings (Illus. by Mitchell, Flazel)*
  c HB Guide - v26 - i1 - Spring 2015 - p132(1) [51-500]

Millar, Mark - *Civil War*
  LJ - v140 - i9 - May 15 2015 - p110(1) [501+]
  Jupiter's Legacy
  PW - v262 - i18 - May 4 2015 - p104(1) [51-500]

Millar, Martin - *The Goddess of Buttercups and Daisies*
  LJ - v140 - i5 - March 15 2015 - p93(2) [501+]
  PW - v262 - i13 - March 30 2015 - p47(1) [51-500]

Millar, Peter - *Marrakech Express*
  WLT - v89 - i1 - Jan-Feb 2015 - p73(1) [51-500]
  LJ - v140 - i2 - Feb 1 2015 - p100(1) [51-500]

Millar, Robert McColl - *Lexical Variation and Attrition in the Scottish Fishing Communities*
  Lang Soc - v44 - i5 - Nov 2015 - p746-747 [501+]

Millard, Glenda - *Once a Shepherd (Illus. by Lesnie, Phil)*
  c HB Guide - v26 - i1 - Spring 2015 - p39(1) [51-500]
  Plum Pudding and Paper Moons
  c Sch Lib - v63 - i1 - Spring 2015 - p40(1) [51-500]

Miller, A.D. - *The Faithful Couple*
  TimHES - i2226 - Oct 22 2015 - p45(1) [501+]
  Spec - v327 - i9732 - March 7 2015 - p46(1) [501+]

Miller, Aaron L. - *Discourses of Discipline: An Anthropology of Corporal Punishment in Japan's Schools and Sports*
  Pac A - v88 - i4 - Dec 2015 - p932 [501+]

Miller, Adrian - *Soul Food*
  JSH - v81 - i1 - Feb 2015 - p257(2) [501+]

Miller, Amy - *The Carbon Rush: The Truth Behind the Carbon Market Smokescreen*
  Sci Teach - v82 - i6 - Sept 2015 - p74 [51-500]

Miller, Andrew - *The Crossing*
  NS - v144 - i5277 - August 28 2015 - p43(1) [501+]
  Spec - v328 - i9758 - Sept 5 2015 - p38(2) [501+]

Miller, Barnabas - *The Girl with the Wrong Name*
  y BL - v112 - i5 - Nov 1 2015 - p54(1) [51-500]
  y KR - Sept 15 2015 - pNA [51-500]
  y PW - v262 - i38 - Sept 21 2015 - p76(1) [51-500]
  y SLJ - v61 - i10 - Oct 2015 - p114(1) [51-500]

Miller, Bobbi - *The Girls of Gettysburg*
  c HB Guide - v26 - i1 - Spring 2015 - p87(1) [51-500]

Miller, Brandon Marie - *Women of Colonial America: 13 Stories of Courage and Survival in the New World*
  KR - Dec 1 2015 - pNA [51-500]
  PW - v262 - i48 - Nov 30 2015 - p62(1) [501+]

Miller, Burton Richard - *Rural Unrest during the First Russian Revolution: Kursk Province, 1905-1906*
  AHR - v120 - i1 - Feb 2015 - p356-357 [501+]
  Slav R - v74 - i3 - Fall 2015 - p650-652 [501+]

Miller, Caroline - *Heart Land: A Place Called Ockley Green*
  SPBW - Nov 2015 - pNA [51-500]

Miller, Char - *Death Valley National Park: A History*
  PHR - v84 - i2 - May 2015 - p233(4) [501+]

Miller, Christopher R. - *Surprise: The Poetics of the Unexpected from Milton to Austen*
  TLS - i5876 - Nov 13 2015 - p31(1) [501+]

Miller, Daniel Jude - *Earclaw and Eddie*
  c PW - v262 - i32 - August 10 2015 - p58(1) [51-500]

Miller, Davis - *Approaching Ali: A Reclamation in Three Acts*
  KR - Sept 15 2015 - pNA [51-500]
  PW - v262 - i44 - Nov 2 2015 - p78(1) [51-500]

Miller, Debbie S. - *Arctic Lights, Arctic Nights*
  Sci & Ch - v53 - i4 - Dec 2015 - p16 [501+]
  Grizzly Bears of Alaska: Explore the Wild World of Bears (Illus. by Endres, Patrick J.)
  c HB Guide - v26 - i1 - Spring 2015 - p166(1) [51-500]
  A King Salmon Journey (Illus. by Van Zyle, Jon)
  c HB Guide - v26 - i1 - Spring 2015 - p161(1) [51-500]

Miller, Donald - *Scary Close: Dropping the Act and Finding True Intimacy*
  PW - v262 - i3 - Jan 19 2015 - p77(1) [51-500]

Miller, Donald (b. 1934-) - *Lafayette: His Extraordinary Life and Legacy*
  KR - Nov 15 2015 - pNA [501+]
  SPBW - Nov 2015 - pNA [51-500]

Miller, Donald L. - *Supreme City: How Jazz Age Manhattan Gave Birth to Modern America*
  NYTBR - May 31 2015 - p52(L) [501+]

Miller, Donna - *Mad Random*
  KR - March 1 2015 - pNA [51-500]

Miller, Edward - *Recycling Day (Illus. by Miller, Edward)*
  c HB Guide - v26 - i1 - Spring 2015 - p39(1) [51-500]

Miller, Edward Garvey - *Misalliance: Ngo Dinh Diem, the United States, and the Fate of South Vietnam*
  HNet - June 2015 - pNA [501+]
  J Mil H - v79 - i1 - Jan 2015 - p259-260 [501+]

Miller, Edward H. - *Nut Country: Right-Wing Dallas and the Birth of the Southern Strategy*
  NYTBR - Dec 20 2015 - p12(L) [501+]
  PW - v262 - i33 - August 17 2015 - p64(1) [51-500]

Miller, Elaine P. - *Head Cases: Julia Kristeva on Philosophy and Art in Depressed Times*
  FS - v69 - i2 - April 2015 - p265-266 [501+]

Miller, Emma - *Plain Dead*
  BL - v112 - i7 - Dec 1 2015 - p31(1) [51-500]
  KR - Nov 15 2015 - pNA [51-500]
  PW - v262 - i45 - Nov 9 2015 - p37(1) [51-500]

Miller, Eric - *18 Wheels of Horror*
  RVBW - Nov 2015 - pNA [51-500]

Miller, Evie Yoder - *Everyday Mercies*
  SPBW - Feb 2015 - pNA [51-500]

Miller, Flagg - *The Audacious Ascetic: What Bin Laden Sound Archive Reveals about al-Qa'ida*
  KR - July 1 2015 - pNA [51-500]
  The Audacious Ascetic: What Obama Bin Laden's Sound Archive Reveals about al-Qa'ida
  PW - v262 - i28 - July 13 2015 - p60(2) [51-500]

Miller, Frank - *Dark Knight III: The Master Race*
  NYT - Nov 23 2015 - pC1(L) [501+]
  Ronin: The Deluxe Edition
  LJ - v140 - i5 - March 15 2015 - p88(3) [501+]

Miller, G. Wayne - *Car Crazy: The Battle for Supremacy between Ford and Olds and the Dawn of the Automobile Age*
  KR - Sept 15 2015 - pNA [51-500]
  LJ - v140 - i16 - Oct 1 2015 - p95(1) [51-500]

Miller, Ian - *Water: A Global History*
  TLS - i5870 - Oct 2 2015 - p9(2) [501+]

Miller, Ian Jared - *Japan at Nature's Edge: The Environmental Context of a Global Power*
  HNet - March 2015 - pNA [501+]
  JAS - v74 - i1 - Feb 2015 - p220-221 [501+]
  The Nature of the Beasts: Empire and Exhibition at the Tokyo Imperial Zoo
  JAS - v74 - i3 - August 2015 - p754-756 [501+]
  Pac A - v88 - i1 - March 2015 - p200 [501+]

Miller, Jason - *Down Don't Bother Me*
  BL - v111 - i12 - Feb 15 2015 - p36(1) [51-500]
  PW - v262 - i3 - Jan 19 2015 - p62(1) [51-500]

Miller, Jax - *Freedom's Child*
  BL - v111 - i13 - March 1 2015 - p23(1) [51-500]
  KR - April 1 2015 - pNA [51-500]
  NYTBR - June 7 2015 - p37(L) [501+]
  PW - v262 - i14 - April 6 2015 - p2(1) [51-500]

Miller, Jeff - *Close Encounters of the Nerd Kind*
  c HB Guide - v26 - i2 - Fall 2015 - p94(1) [51-500]

Miller, Jeffrey - *No Solid Ground*
  KR - April 1 2015 - pNA [501+]

Miller, Jeffrey B. - *Behind the Lines: WWI's Little-Known Story of German Occupation, Belgian Resistance, and the Band of Yanks Who Helped Save Millions from Starvation*
  c BL - v112 - i7 - Dec 1 2015 - p34(2) [501+]

Miller, Jennifer - *The Heart You Carry Home*
  BL - v112 - i4 - Oct 15 2015 - p16(1) [51-500]
  KR - Sept 1 2015 - pNA [501+]
  LJ - v140 - i17 - Oct 15 2015 - p82(2) [51-500]

Miller, John - *Empire and the Animal Body: Violence, Identity and Ecology in Victorian Adventure Fiction*
  VS - v57 - i2 - Wntr 2015 - p285(3) [501+]

Miller, John (b. 1934-) - *Red Spider Hero (Illus. by Cucco, Giuliano)*
  c KR - Oct 15 2015 - pNA [51-500]

Miller, John H. - *A Crude Look at the Whole: The Science of Complex Systems in Business, Life, and Society*
  BL - v112 - i7 - Dec 1 2015 - p12(1) [51-500]
  KR - Oct 1 2015 - pNA [501+]
  PW - v262 - i46 - Nov 16 2015 - p70(1) [51-500]

Miller, Johnny - *The Mood Guide to Fabric and Fashion: The Essential Guide from the World's Most Famous Fabric Store*
  LJ - v140 - i16 - Oct 1 2015 - p83(1) [51-500]

Miller, Jon James - *Garbo's Last Stand*
  KR - Feb 1 2015 - pNA [51-500]

Miller, Jonathan - *On Further Reflection: 60 Years of Writing*
  NYRB - v62 - i6 - April 2 2015 - p78(2) [501+]

Miller, Jonathan R. - *Frend*
  KR - Feb 1 2015 - pNA [501+]

Miller, Joseph C. - *The Princeton Companion to Atlantic History*
  BL - v111 - i15 - April 1 2015 - p22(1) [51-500]
  TLS - i5863 - August 14 2015 - p24(2) [501+]

Miller, Judith - *The Story: A Reporter's Journey*
  KR - May 1 2015 - pNA [501+]
  LJ - v140 - i10 - June 1 2015 - p109(1) [51-500]
  NYT - April 8 2015 - pC6(L) [501+]

Miller, K.D. - *All Saints*
  Can Lit - i224 - Spring 2015 - p139 [501+]

Miller, Kathy M. - *Chippy Chipmunk: Friends in the Garden*
  c CH Bwatch - March 2015 - pNA [51-500]

Miller, Keith - *Suburban Christianity: God's Work in Unhip Places*
  Ch Today - v59 - i7 - Sept 2015 - p73(1) [51-500]

Miller, Keith A. - *Love under Repair: How to Save Your Marriage and Survive Couples Therapy*
  KR - July 15 2015 - pNA [51-500]

Miller, Kelsey - *Big Girl: How I Gave Up Dieting and Got a Life*
  KR - Oct 1 2015 - pNA [51-500]
  PW - v262 - i42 - Oct 19 2015 - p71(1) [51-500]

Miller, Ken - *Dangerous Guests: Enemy Captives and Revolutionary Communities during the War for Independence*
  AHR - v120 - i3 - June 2015 - p1013-1014 [501+]
  HNet - Sept 2015 - pNA [501+]
  J Mil H - v79 - i2 - April 2015 - p488-490 [501+]
  JAH - v102 - i2 - Sept 2015 - p539-540 [501+]
  W&M Q - v72 - i1 - Jan 2015 - p182-187 [501+]

Miller, Kirsten - *Nightmares! (Illus. by Kwasny, Karl)*
  c HB Guide - v26 - i1 - Spring 2015 - p91(2) [51-500]

Miller, L.S. - *Nectar of the Gods*
  KR - July 15 2015 - pNA [501+]

Miller-Lachmann - *Surviving Santiago*
  y KR - March 15 2015 - pNA [51-500]

Miller-Lachmann, Lyn - *Surviving Santiago*
  y BL - v111 - i16 - April 15 2015 - p57(2) [51-500]
  y HB Guide - v26 - i2 - Fall 2015 - p132(1) [51-500]
  y SLJ - v61 - i3 - March 2015 - p160(2) [51-500]
  y VOYA - v38 - i2 - June 2015 - p66(1) [51-500]

Miller, Lisa - *The Spiritual Child: The New Science on Parenting for Health and Lifelong Thriving*
  KR - March 1 2015 - pNA [501+]
  PW - v262 - i11 - March 16 2015 - p80(1) [51-500]

Miller, Marilyn G. - *Tango Lessons: Movement, Sound, Image, and Text in Contemporary Practice*
  HAHR - v95 - i4 - Nov 2015 - p709-710 [501+]

Miller, Marla - *Rebecca Dickinson: Independence for a New England Woman*
  Historian - v77 - i3 - Fall 2015 - p568(2) [501+]

Miller, Mary - *The Last Days of California*
  Wom R Bks - v32 - i2 - March-April 2015 - p22(2) [501+]

Miller, Mary E. - *Painting a Map of Sixteenth-Century Mexico City: Land, Writing, and Native Rule*
  HER - v130 - i543 - April 2015 - p436(2) [501+]

Miller, Mary Ellen - *Maya Art and Architecture, 2d ed.*
  Lat Ant - v26 - i3 - Sept 2015 - p425(2) [501+]

Miller, Matthew - *Performance Artist Database*
  Theat J - v67 - i2 - May 2015 - p347-359 [501+]

Miller, Maureen C. - *Clothing the Clergy: Virtue and Power in Medieval Europe, c. 800-1200*
  AHR - v120 - i4 - Oct 2015 - p1538-1539 [501+]
  CHR - v101 - i4 - Autumn 2015 - p908(3) [501+]
  Med R - August 2015 - pNA [501+]

Miller-McLemore, E. Rhodes - *Christian Theology in Practice: Discovering a Discipline*
  Intpr - v69 - i1 - Jan 2015 - p94(3) [501+]

Miller, Michael B. - *Europe and the Maritime World: A Twentieth-Century History*
  HNet - May 2015 - pNA [501+]

Miller, Michelle - *The Underwriting*
  KR - March 15 2015 - pNA [501+]
  PW - v262 - i12 - March 23 2015 - p43(1) [51-500]

Miller, Pat Zietlow - *Sharing the Bread: An Old-Fashioned Thanksgiving Story (Illus. by McElmurry, Jill)*
  c BL - v111 - i19-20 - June 1 2015 - p124(1) [51-500]
  c CH Bwatch - Nov 2015 - pNA [51-500]
  c HB - v91 - i6 - Nov-Dec 2015 - p57(1) [51-500]
  c KR - June 15 2015 - pNA [51-500]
  c PW - v262 - i34 - August 24 2015 - p80(1) [51-500]
  c PW - v262 - i49 - Dec 2 2015 - p63(1) [51-500]
  c SLJ - v61 - i7 - July 2015 - p66(1) [51-500]
Wherever You Go
  c KR - Feb 15 2015 - pNA [51-500]
Wherever You Go (Illus. by Wheeler, Eliza)
  c BL - v111 - i18 - May 15 2015 - p59(1) [51-500]
  c HB Guide - v26 - i2 - Fall 2015 - p45(1) [51-500]
  c PW - v262 - i49 - Dec 2 2015 - p42(1) [51-500]

Miller, Patricia - *Good Catholics: The Battle over Abortion in the Catholic Church*
  Wom R Bks - v32 - i2 - March-April 2015 - p5(3) [501+]

Miller, Patrick D. - *The Lord of the Psalms*
  TT - v71 - i4 - Jan 2015 - p466-467 [501+]
Stewards of the Mysteries of God: Preaching the Old Testament and the New
  Intpr - v69 - i1 - Jan 2015 - p110(2) [501+]

Miller, Peter Benson - *Go Figure! New Perspectives on Guston*
  PW - v262 - i8 - Feb 23 2015 - p66(3) [501+]

Miller, Peter N. - *Peiresc's Mediterranean World*
  NYRB - v62 - i18 - Nov 19 2015 - p63(3) [501+]
  Spec - v328 - i9744 - May 30 2015 - p32(2) [501+]
Philology: The Forgotten Origins of the Modern Humanities
  TLS - i5843 - March 27 2015 - p26(2) [501+]
The Sea: Thalassography and Historiography
  JMH - v87 - i1 - March 2015 - p136(2) [501+]

Miller, Robert Worth - *Populist Cartoons: An Illustrated History of the Third-Party Movement in the 1890s*
  SAH - v4 - i1 - Annual 2015 - p124-126 [501+]

Miller, Rod - *Goodnight Goes Riding and Other Poems*
  Roundup M - v22 - i4 - April 2015 - p27(1) [501+]
  Roundup M - v22 - i6 - August 2015 - p24(1) [501+]

Miller, Ron - *The Art of Space*
  MFSF - v128 - i3-4 - March-April 2015 - p70(2) [501+]

Chasing the Storm: Tornadoes, Meteorology, and Weather Watching
  y HB Guide - v26 - i1 - Spring 2015 - p151(1) [51-500]

Miller, Ruth A. - *Snarl: In Defense of Stalled Traffic and Faulty Networks*
  AHR - v120 - i1 - Feb 2015 - p190-191 [501+]

Miller, Sarah Elizabeth - *The Borden Murders: Lizzie Borden & the Trial of the Century*
  BL - v112 - i6 - Nov 15 2015 - p37(1) [51-500]
  y KR - Oct 1 2015 - pNA [51-500]
  y SLJ - v61 - i11 - Nov 2015 - p134(2) [51-500]

Miller, Sasha L. - *Slaying Dragons*
  PW - v262 - i31 - August 3 2015 - p42(1) [51-500]

Miller, Serena B. - *More Than Happy: The Wisdom of Amish Parenting*
  BL - v111 - i11 - Feb 1 2015 - p8(1) [51-500]
  LJ - v140 - i3 - Feb 15 2015 - p81(3) [51-500]

Miller, Shannon - *It's Not about Perfect: Competing for My Country and Fighting for My Life*
  BL - v111 - i18 - May 15 2015 - p10(1) [51-500]
  PW - v262 - i18 - May 4 2015 - p112(1) [51-500]

Miller, Shauna - *Penny Chic: How to Be Stylish on a Real Girl's Budget*
  y HB Guide - v26 - i1 - Spring 2015 - p142(1) [51-500]

Miller, Stephen - *Walking New York: Reflections of American Writers from Walt Whitman to Teju Cole*
  TLS - i5855 - June 19 2015 - p25(1) [501+]

Miller, Steve (b. 1950-) - *Dragon in Exile*
  Bwatch - Oct 2015 - pNA [501+]
  LJ - v140 - i9 - May 15 2015 - p57(4) [501+]
  PW - v262 - i15 - April 13 2015 - p62(1) [51-500]

Miller, Steven E. - *The Next Great War? The Roots of World War I and the Risk of U.S.-China Conflict*
  For Aff - v94 - i3 - May-June 2015 - pNA [501+]

Miller, Steven P. - *The Age of Evangelicalism: America's Born-Again Years*
  AHR - v120 - i2 - April 2015 - p674-675 [501+]
  J Ch St - v57 - i3 - Summer 2015 - p587-589 [501+]

Miller, Sue - *The Arsonist*
  y Ent W - i1358 - April 10 2015 - p66(1) [501+]
  NYTBR - Oct 18 2015 - p28(L) [501+]

Miller, Susan Cummins - *Chasm*
  PW - v262 - i2 - Jan 12 2015 - p39(1) [501+]
  Roundup M - v22 - i5 - June 2015 - p39(1) [501+]
  Roundup M - v22 - i6 - August 2015 - p31(2) [501+]

Miller, Tanya Stabler - *The Beguines of Medieval Paris: Gender, Patronage, and Spiritual Authority*
  JGS - v24 - i2 - April 2015 - p244-245 [501+]
  JIH - v46 - i1 - Summer 2015 - p117-118 [501+]

Miller, Tim - *To the House of the Sun*
  SPBW - Feb 2015 - pNA [501+]

Miller, Todd - *Border Patrol Nation: Dispatches from the Front Lines of Homeland Security*
  CC - v132 - i3 - Feb 4 2015 - p33(3) [501+]

Miller, Vivien - *Cross-Cultural Connections in Crime Fictions*
  MLR - v110 - i1 - Jan 2015 - p230-231 [501+]

Miller, Whitney A. - *The Crimson Gate*
  y KR - Jan 1 2015 - pNA [51-500]
  y SLJ - v61 - i7 - July 2015 - p96(1) [51-500]
  y VOYA - v38 - i2 - June 2015 - p80(1) [51-500]

Miller, William Ian - *'Why Is Your Axe Bloody?': A Reading of Njal's Saga*
  Lon R Bks - v37 - i13 - July 2 2015 - p23(2) [501+]
  TLS - i5833 - Jan 16 2015 - p25(1) [501+]

Miller-Young, Mireille - *A Taste for Brown Sugar: Black Women in Pornography*
  Wom R Bks - v32 - i5 - Sept-Oct 2015 - p30(2) [501+]

Millet, Lydia - *Mermaids in Paradise (Read by Campbell, Cassandra). Audiobook Review*
  LJ - v140 - i2 - Feb 1 2015 - p45(2) [501+]
  PW - v262 - i5 - Feb 2 2015 - p53(1) [501+]
Mermaids in Paradise
  LJ - v140 - i17 - Oct 15 2015 - p118(1) [501+]
  NY - v90 - i44 - Jan 19 2015 - p75 [501+]
  NYTBR - Jan 4 2015 - p13(L) [501+]
Pills and Starships
  c HB Guide - v26 - i1 - Spring 2015 - p117(1) [51-500]
  y Sch Lib - v63 - i1 - Spring 2015 - p56(1) [51-500]
Sweet Lamb of Heaven
  PW - v262 - i51 - Dec 14 2015 - p53(1) [51-500]

Millett, Alan R. - *For the Common Defense: A Military History of the United States from 1607 to 2012*
  J Mil H - v79 - i3 - July 2015 - p783-802 [501+]

Millett, Allan R. - *The War for Korea, 1950-1951: They Came from the North*
  APJ - v29 - i5 - Sept-Oct 2015 - p104(3) [501+]

Millett, Peter - *Johnny Danger DIY Spy: Failure Is Not an Option*
  c Magpies - v30 - i2 - May 2015 - p38(1) [501+]

Millhauser, Steven - *Voices in the Night*
  KR - Feb 1 2015 - pNA [501+]
  LJ - v140 - i3 - Feb 15 2015 - p95(1) [51-500]
Voices in the Night: Stories
  BL - v111 - i9-10 - Jan 1 2015 - p43(1) [51-500]
  NYT - April 30 2015 - pC6(L) [501+]
  NYTBR - May 17 2015 - p22(L) [501+]
  PW - v262 - i5 - Feb 2 2015 - p32(1) [51-500]

Millhiser, Ian - *Injustices: The Supreme Court's History of Comforting the Comfortable and Afflicting the Afflicted*
  KR - Jan 1 2015 - pNA [501+]
  PW - v262 - i5 - Feb 2 2015 - p47(2) [501+]

Milligan, Gerry - *The Poetics of Masculinity in Early Modern Italy and Spain*
  Six Ct J - v46 - i1 - Spring 2015 - p177(2) [501+]

Milligan, Ian - *Rebel Youth: 1960s Labour Unrest, Young Workers, and New Leftists in English Canada*
  Can Hist R - v96 - i2 - June 2015 - p320(4) [501+]

Milligan, Peter N. - *Bulls before Breakfast: Running with the Bulls and Celebrating Fiesta de San Fermin in Pamplona, Spain*
  BL - v111 - i18 - May 15 2015 - p12(1) [51-500]

Milliken, Doug - *Testimony of the Protected*
  SPBW - July 2015 - pNA [51-500]

Mills, Claudia - *Ethics and Children's Literature*
  Bkbird - v53 - i2 - Spring 2015 - p85(2) [501+]
Izzy Barr, Running Star (Illus. by Shepperson, Rob)
  c HB - v91 - i6 - Nov-Dec 2015 - p84(1) [51-500]
The Trouble with Ants (Illus. by Kath, Katie)
  c PW - v262 - i49 - Dec 2 2015 - p65(1) [51-500]
  c BL - v111 - i21 - July 1 2015 - p75(1) [51-500]
  c CCB-B - v69 - i2 - Oct 2015 - p103(1) [51-500]
  c HB - v91 - i5 - Sept-Oct 2015 - p111(1) [51-500]
  c KR - July 1 2015 - pNA [51-500]
  c PW - v262 - i22 - June 1 2015 - p59(1) [51-500]
  c SLJ - v61 - i7 - July 2015 - p80(1) [51-500]

Mills, David E. - *Dividing the Nile: Egypt's Economic Nationalists in the Sudan 1918-56*
  RVBW - May 2015 - pNA [501+]

Mills, Emma - *First & Then*
  y BL - v112 - i2 - Sept 15 2015 - p74(1) [51-500]
  y KR - August 1 2015 - pNA [51-500]
  y PW - v262 - i30 - July 27 2015 - p71(1) [51-500]
  y SLJ - v61 - i8 - August 2015 - p107(2) [51-500]
  y VOYA - v38 - i5 - Dec 2015 - p61(1) [51-500]

Mills, Greg - *Why States Recover: Changing Walking Societies into Winning Nations, from Afghanistan to Zimbabwe*
  For Aff - v94 - i3 - May-June 2015 - pNA [501+]

Mills, Jean - *Virginia Woolf, Jane Ellen Harrison and the Spirit of Modernist Classicism*
  ABR - v36 - i3 - March-April 2015 - p14(1) [501+]

Mills, Jon L. - *Privacy in the New Media Age*
  BL - v111 - i14 - March 15 2015 - p33(1) [51-500]

Mills, Lauren A. - *Minna's Patchwork Coat (Illus. by Mills, Lauren A.)*
  c SLJ - v61 - i9 - Sept 2015 - p142(1) [501+]

Mills, Magnus - *The Field of the Cloth of Gold*
  Spec - v327 - i9738 - April 18 2015 - p43(1) [501+]
The Maintenance of Headway
  KR - March 1 2015 - pNA [51-500]
  LJ - v140 - i6 - April 1 2015 - p83(2) [51-500]
  NYT - May 28 2015 - pC6(L) [501+]
  PW - v262 - i10 - March 9 2015 - p50(1) [51-500]

Mills, Marja - *The Mockingbird Next Door: Life with Harper Lee*
  AM - v212 - i16 - May 11 2015 - p44(2) [501+]
  TLS - i5831 - Jan 2 2015 - p19(1) [501+]

Mills, Quincy T. - *Cutting along the Color Line: Black Barbers and Barber Shops in America*
  JSH - v81 - i1 - Feb 2015 - p184(2) [501+]

Mills, Robert - *Seeing Sodomy in the Middle Ages*
  Med R - Sept 2015 - pNA [501+]
  TimHES - i2195 - March 19 2015 - p50(1) [501+]

Mills, Sally Hill - *Jimmy: Toughest. Dog. Ever.*
  KR - July 15 2015 - pNA [51-500]

Mills, Steve - *Launch a Rocket into Space (Illus. by Aleksic, Vladimir)*
  c Sch Lib - v63 - i1 - Spring 2015 - p47(1) [51-500]

Mills, Wendy - *Positively Beautiful*
   y   BL - v111 - i13 - March 1 2015 - p59(1) [51-500]
   y   CCB-B - v68 - i9 - May 2015 - p459(1) [51-500]
   y   HB Guide - v26 - i2 - Fall 2015 - p132(1) [51-500]
   y   PW - v262 - i2 - Jan 12 2015 - p61(1) [51-500]
   y   VOYA - v38 - i1 - April 2015 - p66(1) [51-500]

Millward, Myfanwy - *Rosie's Special Present (Illus. by Millward, Gwen)*
   c   Sch Lib - v63 - i4 - Winter 2015 - p222(1) [51-500]

Milne, A.A. - *The Collected Stories of Winnie the Pooh (Read by Dench, Judi). Audiobook Review*
   y   SLJ - v61 - i6 - June 2015 - p53(3) [501+]

Milne, Anna-Louise - *The Cambridge Companion to the Literature of Paris*
      Poetics T - v36 - i1-2 - June 2015 - p136-138 [501+]

Milne, David - *Worldmaking: The Art and Science of American Diplomacy*
      BL - v111 - i22 - August 1 2015 - p10(1) [51-500]
      KR - August 1 2015 - pNA [501+]
      LJ - v140 - i14 - Sept 1 2015 - p124(1) [51-500]
      NYRB - v62 - i18 - Nov 19 2015 - p29(2) [501+]
      PW - v262 - i22 - June 1 2015 - p51(1) [51-500]

Milne, Kirsty - *At Vanity Fair: From Bunyan to Thackeray*
      TLS - i5872 - Oct 16 2015 - p28(1) [501+]

Milner, H. Richard - *Rac(e)ing to Class: Confronting Poverty and Race in Schools and Classrooms*
      LJ - v140 - i9 - May 15 2015 - p90(1) [51-500]

Milner, Marc - *Stopping the Panzers: The Untold Story of D-Day*
      Parameters - v45 - i1 - Spring 2015 - p162(2) [501+]

Milner, Murray, Jr. - *Elites: A General Model*
      JRAI - v21 - i3 - Sept 2015 - p708(2) [501+]
      Soc - v52 - i3 - June 2015 - p283(1) [501+]

Milosevic, Irena - *Phobias: The Psychology of Irrational Fear*
      BL - v112 - i2 - Sept 15 2015 - p8(1) [51-500]

Milovanovic, Dragan - *Quantum Holographic Criminology: Paradigm Shift in Criminology, Law, and Transformative Justice*
      CrimJR - v40 - i2 - June 2015 - p231-233 [501+]

Milqueen, Michael - *Small Navies: Strategy and Policy for Small Navies in War and Peace*
      NWCR - v68 - i1 - Wntr 2015 - p145(2) [501+]

Milroy, Sarah - *From the Forest to the Sea: Emily Carr in British Columbia*
      RVBW - Oct 2015 - pNA [51-500]

Milstein, Joanna - *The Gondi: Family Strategy and Survival in Early Modern France*
      Six Ct J - v46 - i3 - Fall 2015 - p688-690 [501+]

Milteer, Lee - *Reclaim the Magic: The Real Secrets to Manifesting Anything You Want*
      RVBW - August 2015 - pNA [501+]

Milton, Cynthia E. - *Art from a Fractured Past: Memory and Truth-Telling in Post-Shining Path Peru*
      Ams - v72 - i3 - July 2015 - p500(3) [501+]

Milton, Giles - *When Hitler Took Cocaine and Lenin Lost His Brain*
      KR - Oct 15 2015 - pNA [501+]
      LJ - v140 - i19 - Nov 15 2015 - p95(1) [51-500]
      PW - v262 - i45 - Nov 9 2015 - p52(1) [51-500]

Milton, Jon - *Punk Science: The Intergalactic, Supermassive Space Book (Illus. by Hope, Dan)*
   c   PW - v262 - i28 - July 13 2015 - p67(1) [501+]

Milton, Nina - *Beneath the Tor*
      KR - Oct 1 2015 - pNA [501+]
      PW - v262 - i42 - Oct 19 2015 - p58(2) [51-500]

Milton, Stephanie - *Minecraft Combat Handbook*
   y   CH Bwatch - Jan 2015 - pNA [501+]

Milward, Andrew Malan - *I Was a Revolutionary: Stories*
      KR - June 15 2015 - pNA [501+]
      NYTBR - Oct 4 2015 - p30(L) [501+]
      PW - v262 - i22 - June 1 2015 - p40(1) [51-500]

Milway, Alex - *Pigsticks and Harold and the Incredible Journey (Illus. by Milway, Alex)*
   c   HB Guide - v26 - i1 - Spring 2015 - p63(1) [51-500]
      Pigsticks and Harold and the Tuptown Thief
   c   SLJ - v61 - i11 - Nov 2015 - p91(2) [51-500]

Mims, Lee - *Saving Cecil*
      KR - Feb 1 2015 - pNA [501+]
      PW - v262 - i8 - Feb 23 2015 - p54(1) [51-500]

Min, Pyong Gap - *Koreans in North America: Their Twenty-First Century Experiences*
      CS - v44 - i3 - May 2015 - p382-384 [501+]

Min, SooHyeon - *The Drummer Boy (Illus. by Nille, Peggy)*
   c   HB Guide - v26 - i2 - Fall 2015 - p39(1) [51-500]
   c   SLJ - v61 - i6 - June 2015 - p88(1) [51-500]

Mina, Denise - *Blood, Salt, Water*
      BL - v112 - i4 - Oct 15 2015 - p18(1) [51-500]
      KR - Sept 15 2015 - pNA [501+]
      PW - v262 - i42 - Oct 19 2015 - p57(1) [51-500]
      The Red Road
      Ent W - i1364 - May 22 2015 - p66(1) [51-500]
      RVBW - April 2015 - pNA [501+]

Minchilli, Elizabeth - *Eating Rome: Living the Good Life in the Eternal City*
      LJ - v140 - i6 - April 1 2015 - p108(1) [51-500]
      PW - v262 - i7 - Feb 16 2015 - p173(1) [51-500]

Minchow-Proffitt, Terry - *Seven Last Words*
      SPBW - May 2015 - pNA [51-500]

Mindell, David A. - *Our Robots, Ourselves: Robotics and the Myths of Autonomy*
      BL - v112 - i1 - Sept 1 2015 - p21(1) [51-500]
      KR - August 15 2015 - pNA [501+]
      LJ - v140 - i14 - Sept 1 2015 - p137(2) [51-500]
      Nature - v526 - i7573 - Oct 15 2015 - p320(2) [501+]
      PW - v262 - i31 - August 3 2015 - p47(1) [51-500]

Mineo, Bernard - *A Companion to Livy*
      HNet - March 2015 - pNA [501+]

Miner, Dylan A.T. - *Creating Aztlan: Chicano Art, Indigenous Sovereignty, and Lowriding Across Turtle*
      WHQ - v46 - i3 - Autumn 2015 - p375-376 [501+]

Miner, Matt - *Rage Ignition*
      PW - v262 - i16 - April 20 2015 - p63(1) [51-500]

Minghuan, Li - *Seeing Transnationally: How Chinese Migrants Make Their Dreams Come True*
      Pac A - v88 - i4 - Dec 2015 - p907 [501+]

Mingkwan, Chat - *Buddha's Table*
      Veg J - v34 - i2 - April-June 2015 - p34(1) [51-500]

Mingle, Jonathan - *Fire and Ice: Soot, Solidarity, and Survival on the Roof of the World*
      BL - v111 - i12 - Feb 15 2015 - p26(1) [51-500]
      KR - Jan 15 2015 - pNA [501+]
      LJ - v140 - i3 - Feb 15 2015 - p126(1) [51-500]
      PW - v262 - i4 - Jan 26 2015 - p160(1) [51-500]

Minich, Julie Avril - *Accessible Citizenships: Disability, Nation, and the Cultural Politics of Greater Mexico*
      Aztlan - v40 - i1 - Spring 2015 - p243-246 [501+]

Minichiello, Victor - *Male Sex Work and Society*
      G&L Rev W - v22 - i1 - Jan-Feb 2015 - p37(2) [501+]
      TimHES - i2185 - Jan 8 2015 - p47-47 [501+]

Minier, Bernard - *The Circle*
      PW - v262 - i34 - August 24 2015 - p60(1) [51-500]

Minier, David - *Rafiki*
      KR - June 15 2015 - pNA [501+]

Ministerialität, Ritterschaft und landständischer Adel im Rheinland, 11.-19. Jahrhundert
      HNet - May 2015 - pNA [501+]

Mink, George - *History, Memory and Politics in Central and Eastern Europe: Memory Games*
      E-A St - v67 - i1 - Jan 2015 - p148(2) [501+]

Minnema, Cheryl - *Hungry Johnny (Illus. by Ballinger, Wesley)*
   c   HB Guide - v26 - i1 - Spring 2015 - p39(1) [51-500]

Minnis, Alastair - *From Eden to Eternity: Creations of Paradise in the Later Middle Ages*
      JHI - v76 - i4 - Oct 2015 - p666(1) [501+]

Minnis, Paul E. - *New Lives for Ancient and Extinct Crops*
      Am Ant - v80 - i2 - April 2015 - p418(2) [501+]

Minor, Florence - *If You Were a Panda Bear (Read by Stechschulte, Tom). Audiobook Review*
   c   BL - v111 - i19-20 - June 1 2015 - p140(2) [51-500]

Minor, Wendell - *Daylight Starlight Wildlife (Illus. by Minor, Wendell)*
   c   HB - v91 - i4 - July-August 2015 - p158(2) [51-500]
   c   SLJ - v61 - i5 - May 2015 - p135(1) [51-500]
      PW - v262 - i11 - March 16 2015 - p82(1) [51-500]
   c   KR - March 1 2015 - pNA [501+]

Minot, Susan - *Thirty Girls*
      Bks & Cult - v21 - i4 - July-August 2015 - p30(1) [501+]
      NYTBR - March 22 2015 - p28(L) [501+]

Minteer, Ben A. - *After Preservation: Saving American Nature in the Age of Humans*
      BioSci - v65 - i10 - Oct 2015 - p1025(3) [501+]
      BL - v111 - i12 - Feb 15 2015 - p25(1) [51-500]
      LJ - v140 - i5 - March 15 2015 - p128(1) [51-500]

Minter, Kendall - *Understanding and Negotiating 360 Ancillary Rights Deals*
      SPBW - July 2015 - pNA [501+]

Mintie, L.L. - *Moonfin: Through the Watery Door*
   c   PW - v262 - i33 - August 17 2015 - p72(1) [51-500]

Mintz, Steven - *The Prime of Life: A History of Modern Adulthood*
      BL - v111 - i14 - March 15 2015 - p33(1) [51-500]
      KR - Feb 1 2015 - pNA [501+]
      LJ - v140 - i6 - April 1 2015 - p107(2) [51-500]
      Nature - v520 - i7547 - April 16 2015 - p293(1) [51-500]
      NYTBR - June 21 2015 - p1(L) [501+]
      NYTBR - June 21 2015 - p1(L) [501+]
      Spec - v327 - i9740 - May 2 2015 - p41(1) [501+]
      TimHES - i2201 - April 30 2015 - p54-55 [501+]

Miraldi, Robert - *Seymour Hersh, Scoop Artist*
      AM - v213 - i4 - Nov 9 2015 - p34(2) [51-500]

Miralles, Francesc - *Love in Lowercase*
      KR - Nov 1 2015 - pNA [501+]
      PW - v262 - i51 - Dec 14 2015 - p76(2) [501+]

Miranda, Megan - *Soulprint*
   y   CCB-B - v68 - i8 - April 2015 - p412(1) [51-500]
   y   HB Guide - v26 - i2 - Fall 2015 - p132(1) [51-500]
   y   PW - v262 - i49 - Dec 2 2015 - p111(1) [51-500]
   y   SLJ - v61 - i4 - April 2015 - p156(2) [51-500]

Mirande, Alfredo - *Jalos, USA: Transnational Community and Identity*
      CS - v44 - i6 - Nov 2015 - p830-832 [501+]

Miraucourt, Christophe - *Pirate Treasure (Illus. by Vaufrey, Delphine)*
   c   CH Bwatch - Nov 2015 - pNA [501+]

Mirbeau, Octave - *21 Days of a Neurasthenic*
      KR - May 1 2015 - pNA [501+]

Mires, Charlene - *Capital of the World: The Race to Host the United Nations*
      Historian - v77 - i2 - Summer 2015 - p415(3) [501+]

Mirolla, Michael - *Lessons in Relationship Dyads*
      KR - August 15 2015 - pNA [501+]

Mirriam-Goldberg, Caryn - *Chasing Weather: Tornadoes, Tempests, and Thunderous Skies in Word and Image*
      SPBW - June 2015 - pNA [51-500]

Misa, Thomas J. - *Digital State: The Story of Minnesota's Computing Industry*
      JAH - v101 - i4 - March 2015 - p1316-1317 [501+]
      T&C - v56 - i1 - Jan 2015 - p296-298 [501+]

Mischel, Walter - *The Marshmallow Test: Mastering Self-Control*
      AJPsy - v128 - i3 - Fall 2015 - p414(4) [501+]
      The Marshmallow Test: Understanding Self-Control and How to Master It
      TLS - i5873 - Oct 23 2015 - p27(1) [501+]

Mischke, Werner - *The Global Gospel: Achieving Missional Impact in Our Multicultural World*
      IBMR - v39 - i4 - Oct 2015 - p236(2) [501+]

Misconi, N.Y. - *An Immigrant's Journey into the Cosmos*
      KR - Oct 1 2015 - pNA [501+]

Misencik, Paul R. - *George Washington and the Half-King Chief Tanacharison: An Alliance That Began the French and Indian War*
      HNet - Feb 2015 - pNA [501+]

Mishal, Shaul - *Understanding Shiite Leadership: The Art of the Middle Ground in Iran and Lebanon*
      IJMES - v47 - i3 - August 2015 - p651-653 [501+]

Mishani, D.A. - *A Possibility of Violence*
      WLT - v89 - i2 - March-April 2015 - p69(1) [51-500]

Misri, Deepti - *Beyond Partition: Gender, Violence, and Representation in Postcolonial India*
      HNet - Sept 2015 - pNA(NA) [501+]

Mistry, Kaeten - *The United States, Italy, and the Origins of the Cold War: Waging Political Warfare, 1945-1950*
      JAH - v102 - i2 - Sept 2015 - p605-606 [501+]

Mit der Antike Schule Machen? Das Integrative Potenzial der Alten Geschichte fur das Historische Lernen
      HNet - March 2015 - pNA [501+]

Mitchael, Anna - *Copygirl*
      LJ - v140 - i19 - Nov 15 2015 - p78(1) [51-500]
      PW - v262 - i35 - August 31 2015 - p58(1) [51-500]

Mitchard, Jacquelyn - *Two If by Sea*
      KR - Dec 15 2015 - pNA [501+]

Mitchell, Alanna - *Malignant Metaphor: Finding the Hidden Meaning of Cancer*
      PW - v262 - i33 - August 17 2015 - p65(1) [51-500]

Mitchell, Andie - *It Was Me All Along: A Memoir (Read by Mitchell, Andie). Audiobook Review*
      LJ - v140 - i7 - April 15 2015 - p48(1) [51-500]
      It Was Me All Along: A Memoir
      People - v83 - i3 - Jan 19 2015 - p29 [501+]

Mitchell, Colin P. - *New Perspectives on Safavid Iran: Empire and Society*
    IJMES - v47 - i4 - Nov 2015 - p813-815 [501+]

Mitchell-Cook, Amy - *A Sea of Misadventures: Shipwreck and Survival in Early America*
    RAH - v43 - i3 - Sept 2015 - p434-440 [501+]
    W&M Q - v72 - i3 - July 2015 - p509-512 [501+]

Mitchell, David - *The Bone Clocks (Read by Various readers). Audiobook Review*
    LJ - v140 - i2 - Feb 1 2015 - p45(1) [51-500]
The Bone Clocks
    BL - v111 - i18 - May 15 2015 - p35(1) [501+]
    HR - v67 - i4 - Wntr 2015 - p685-692 [501+]
    y HR - v68 - i1 - Spring 2015 - p151-157 [501+]
    WLT - v89 - i3-4 - May-August 2015 - p113(3) [501+]
Slade House
    KR - Sept 1 2015 - pNA [51-500]
    LJ - v140 - i14 - Sept 1 2015 - p95(2) [51-500]
    PW - v262 - i28 - July 13 2015 - p40(1) [51-500]

Mitchell, David Stephen - *The Bone Clocks*
    NYRB - v62 - i19 - Dec 3 2015 - p55(3) [501+]
Slade House
    BL - v112 - i2 - Sept 15 2015 - p38(1) [51-500]
    BooChiTr - Nov 7 2015 - p14(1) [501+]
    Nat Post - v18 - i21 - Nov 21 2015 - pWP8(1) [501+]
    NYRB - v62 - i19 - Dec 3 2015 - p55(3) [501+]
    NYT - Oct 23 2015 - pC21(L) [501+]
    NYTBR - Nov 15 2015 - p18(L) [501+]
    Spec - v329 - i9765 - Oct 24 2015 - p37(2) [501+]

Mitchell, Dennis J. - *A New History of Mississippi*
    JAH - v102 - i1 - June 2015 - p209-210 [501+]
    JSH - v81 - i4 - Nov 2015 - p932(3) [501+]

Mitchell, Edgar - *Earthrise: My Adventures as an Apollo 14 Astronaut*
    y HB Guide - v26 - i1 - Spring 2015 - p195(1) [51-500]

Mitchell, Emily - *Viral: Stories*
    KR - May 15 2015 - pNA [501+]
    NYTBR - July 12 2015 - p30(L) [501+]
    PW - v262 - i17 - April 27 2015 - p43(1) [51-500]

Mitchell, George - *The Negotiator: A Memoir*
    BL - v111 - i17 - May 1 2015 - p63(1) [501+]

Mitchell, Graham - *Never Safe, Always Fun!*
    KR - July 15 2015 - pNA [501+]

Mitchell, J. Allan - *Becoming Human: The Matter of the Medieval Child*
    Ren Q - v68 - i3 - Fall 2015 - p1027-1028 [501+]

Mitchell, J. Barton - *Valley of Fires*
    c HB Guide - v26 - i1 - Spring 2015 - p117(1) [51-500]

Mitchell, Jolyon - *Promoting Peace, Inciting Violence: The Role of Religion and the Media*
    J Ch St - v57 - i1 - Wntr 2015 - p164-166 [501+]

Mitchell, Jon - *In Real Life: Searching for Connection in High-Tech Times*
    RVBW - March 2015 - pNA [51-500]

Mitchell, Joseph - *Up in the Old Hotel*
    Nat R - v67 - i21 - Nov 19 2015 - p80(2) [501+]

Mitchell, Judith Claire - *A Reunion of Ghosts*
    BL - v111 - i11 - Feb 1 2015 - p24(1) [501+]
    KR - Jan 15 2015 - pNA [501+]
    LJ - v140 - i2 - Feb 1 2015 - p75(1) [51-500]
    PW - v262 - i3 - Jan 19 2015 - p53(2) [51-500]

Mitchell, Kaye - *Sarah Waters: Contemporary Critical Perspectives*
    JGS - v24 - i3 - June 2015 - p376-377 [501+]

Mitchell, Laine - *Maman, je t'aime tant! (Illus. by Fleming, Kim)*
    c Res Links - v20 - i5 - June 2015 - p41(1) [51-500]
Mommy, You're Special to Me (Illus. by Fleming, Kim)
    c Res Links - v20 - i5 - June 2015 - p6(2) [51-500]

Mitchell, Maggie - *Pretty Is*
    LJ - v140 - i10 - June 1 2015 - p91(2) [51-500]
    NYT - July 17 2015 - pC19(L) [501+]
    y NYTBR - Oct 11 2015 - p30(L) [501+]
    PW - v262 - i19 - May 11 2015 - p30(2) [51-500]
    y SLJ - v61 - i10 - Oct 2015 - p123(1) [51-500]

Mitchell, Marea - *Continuation to Sidney's Arcadia, 1607-1867, 4 vols.*
    TLS - i5868 - Sept 18 2015 - p24(2) [501+]

Mitchell, Maria D. - *The Origins of Christian Democracy: Politics and Confession in Modern Germany*
    GSR - v38 - i1 - Feb 2015 - p220-222 [501+]
    HER - v130 - i542 - Feb 2015 - p252(2) [501+]
    JMH - v87 - i1 - March 2015 - p237(2) [501+]

Mitchell, Peter (b. 1962-) - *Horse Nations: The Worldwide Impact of the Horse on Indigenous Societies*
    TLS - i5858 - July 10 2015 - p3(3) [501+]

Mitchell, Peter M. - *The Coup at Catholic University: The 1968 Revolution in American Catholic Education*
    Comw - v142 - i16 - Oct 9 2015 - p28(3) [501+]

Mitchell, Piers D. - *Sanitation, Latrines and Intestinal Parasites in Past Populations*
    Specu - v90 - i4 - Oct 2015 - p1193(1) [501+]

Mitchell, Rebecca - *Modern Love, and Other Poems*
    Lon R Bks - v37 - i12 - June 18 2015 - p19(3) [501+]

Mitchell, Robert - *Experimental Life: Vitalism in Romantic Science and Literature*
    Isis - v106 - i1 - March 2015 - p196(2) [501+]

Mitchell, Sara - *The Acadians*
    c Res Links - v20 - i3 - Feb 2015 - p23(2) [501+]
The French
    c Res Links - v20 - i3 - Feb 2015 - p23(2) [501+]
The United Empire Loyalists
    c Res Links - v20 - i3 - Feb 2015 - p23(2) [501+]

Mitchell, Saundra - *50 Impressive Kids and Their Amazing (and True!) Stories*
    y KR - Dec 1 2015 - pNA [51-500]
50 Unbelievable Women and Their Fascinating (and True!) Stories (Illus. by Petrus, Cara)
    c BL - v112 - i6 - Nov 15 2015 - p37(2) [501+]
    c KR - Nov 15 2015 - pNA [51-500]
    c PW - v262 - i48 - Nov 30 2015 - p62(1) [501+]

Mitchell, Shay - *Bliss*
    y BL - v111 - i21 - July 1 2015 - p29(1) [51-500]
    KR - August 1 2015 - pNA [51-500]

Mitchell, Stephen A. - *Witchcraft and Magic in the Nordic Middle Ages*
    CHR - v101 - i2 - Spring 2015 - p358(2) [501+]
    HER - v130 - i542 - Feb 2015 - p166(2) [501+]

Mitchell, Susan K. - *Humorous Small Critter Jokes to Tickle Your Funny Bone*
    c HB Guide - v26 - i1 - Spring 2015 - p181(1) [51-500]

Mitchell, Syne - *Inventive Weaving on a Little Loom: Discover the Full Potential of the Rigid-Heddle Loom, for Beginners and Beyond*
    LJ - v140 - i17 - Oct 15 2015 - p90(1) [51-500]

Mitchell, Timothy - *Carbon Democracy: Political Power in the Age of Oil*
    RAH - v43 - i2 - June 2015 - p333-339 [501+]

Mitchell, William D. - *Paper Contracting*
    RVBW - March 2015 - pNA [501+]

Mitchison, Naomi - *Black Sparta*
    HT - v65 - i8 - August 2015 - p56(2) [501+]
The Corn King and the Spring Queen
    HT - v65 - i8 - August 2015 - p56(2) [501+]
The Delicate Fire
    TLS - i5841 - March 13 2015 - p16(1) [501+]
The Fourth Pig
    TLS - i5841 - March 13 2015 - p3(3) [501+]

Mitenbuler, Reid - *Bourbon Empire: The Past and Future of America's Whiskey*
    KR - April 1 2015 - pNA [501+]
    LJ - v140 - i9 - May 15 2015 - p100(3) [501+]
    PW - v262 - i13 - March 30 2015 - p71(1) [51-500]

Mitra, Diditi - *Punjabi Immigrant Mobility in the United States: Adaptation through Race and Class*
    CS - v44 - i6 - Nov 2015 - p875(1) [501+]

Mitsiou, Ekaterini - *Emperor Sigismund and the Orthodox World*
    CHR - v101 - i2 - Spring 2015 - p362(3) [501+]

Mittag, Jurgen - *Theoretische Ansatze und Konzepte der Forschung uber soziale Bewegungen in der Geschichtswissenschaft*
    HNet - April 2015 - pNA [501+]

Mitten, Mark - *Sipping Whiskey in a Shallow Grave*
    Roundup M - v22 - i6 - August 2015 - p32(1) [501+]

Mittlefehldt, Sarah - *Tangled Roots: The Appalachian Trail and American Environmental Politics*
    JSH - v81 - i1 - Feb 2015 - p233(2) [501+]

Mittleman, Alan L. - *Human Nature and Jewish Thought: Judaism's Case for Why Persons Matter*
    BL - v111 - i19-20 - June 1 2015 - p6(2) [501+]
    KR - Feb 15 2015 - pNA [501+]
    PW - v262 - i15 - April 13 2015 - p75(1) [51-500]

Mittler, Barbara - *A Continuous Revolution: Making Sense of Cultural Revolution Culture*
    Pac A - v88 - i4 - Dec 2015 - p902 [501+]

Mittman, Asa Simon - *Inconceivable Beasts: The Wonders of the East in the Beowulf Manuscript*
    Med R - August 2015 - pNA [501+]
    RES - v66 - i274 - April 2015 - p364-365 [501+]

Mitton, Tony - *Snowy Bear (Illus. by Brown, Alison)*
    c KR - July 15 2015 - pNA [51 500]
    c PW - v262 - i31 - August 3 2015 - p58(2) [51-500]
    c SLJ - v61 - i7 - July 2015 - p58(1) [51-500]
Sounds (Illus. by Parker, Ant)
    c KR - Jan 1 2016 - pNA [51-500]

Mitzen, Jennifer - *Power in Concert: The Nineteenth-Century Origins of Global Governance*
    JIH - v45 - i4 - Spring 2015 - p568-570 [501+]

Mitzner, Adam - *Losing Faith*
    BL - v111 - i12 - Feb 15 2015 - p38(1) [51-500]
    KR - Feb 1 2015 - pNA [51-500]
    PW - v262 - i5 - Feb 2 2015 - p37(1) [51-500]

Miura, Taro - *The Big Princess (Illus. by Miura, Taro)*
    c CCB-B - v69 - i1 - Sept 2015 - p40(1) [51-500]
    c HB - v91 - i3 - May-June 2015 - p93(2) [501+]
    c HB Guide - v26 - i2 - Fall 2015 - p45(1) [51-500]
    c KR - March 15 2015 - pNA [51-500]
    c Sch Lib - v63 - i1 - Spring 2015 - p30(1) [51-500]
    c SLJ - v61 - i5 - May 2015 - p89(1) [51-500]

Miville, China - *Three Moments of an Explosion*
    NYT - August 4 2015 - pC1(L) [501+]

Miyakoshi, Akiko - *The Tea Party in the Woods (Illus. by Miyakoshi, Akiko)*
    c BL - v111 - i22 - August 1 2015 - p73(1) [51-500]
    c CH Bwatch - August 2015 - pNA [501+]
    c KR - May 1 2015 - pNA [51-500]
    c PW - v262 - i20 - May 18 2015 - p81(1) [51-500]
    c PW - v262 - i49 - Dec 2 2015 - p18(1) [51-500]
    c SLJ - v61 - i7 - July 2015 - p66(1) [51-500]

Miyanishi, Tatsuya - *Mr. Reaper (Illus. by Miyanishi, Tatsuya)*
    c BL - v112 - i6 - Nov 15 2015 - p48(1) [51-500]
You Look Yummy! (Illus. by Miyanishi, Tatsuya)
    c KR - Oct 1 2015 - pNA [51-500]
    c PW - v262 - i38 - Sept 21 2015 - p71(2) [51-500]
    c SLJ - v61 - i12 - Dec 2015 - p92(2) [51-500]

Miyaoka, Hiroe - *Perfect Gift Wrapping Ideas: 101 Ways to Personalize Your Gift Using Simple, Everyday Materials*
    PW - v262 - i33 - August 17 2015 - p68(1) [51-500]

Miyares, Daniel - *Float (Illus. by Miyares, Daniel)*
    c BL - v111 - i19-20 - June 1 2015 - p116(1) [51-500]
    c CH Bwatch - Sept 2015 - pNA [501+]
    c HB - v91 - i3 - May-June 2015 - p94(1) [501+]
    c HB Guide - v26 - i2 - Fall 2015 - p45(1) [51-500]
    c KR - March 15 2015 - pNA [51-500]
    c PW - v262 - i16 - April 20 2015 - p74(2) [51-500]
    c SLJ - v61 - i3 - March 2015 - p121(3) [51-500]

Mize, Britt - *Traditional Subjectivities: The Old English Poetics of Mentality*
    MP - v113 - i2 - Nov 2015 - pE66(3) [501+]

Mizejewski, Linda - *Pretty/Funny: Women Comedians and Body Politics*
    SAH - v4 - i1 - Annual 2015 - p106-108 [501+]

Mizelle, Richard M., Jr. - *Backwater Blues: The Mississippi Flood of 1927 in the African American Imagination*
    AHR - v120 - i3 - June 2015 - p1049-1050 [501+]
    JAH - v102 - i1 - June 2015 - p281-281 [501+]

Mizielinska, Aleksandra - *The World of Mamoko in the Time of Dragons*
    c HB Guide - v26 - i1 - Spring 2015 - p181(1) [51-500]
The World of Mamoko in the Time of Dragons (Illus. by Mizielinski, Daniel)
    c SLJ - v61 - i3 - March 2015 - p130(1) [51-500]

Mizruchi, Mark - *The Fracturing of the American Corporate Elite*
    CS - v44 - i4 - July 2015 - p449-462 [501+]

Mizruchi, Susan L. - *Brando's Smile: His Life, Thought, and Work*
    Bwatch - Sept 2015 - pNA [51-500]
    NYRB - v62 - i1 - Jan 8 2015 - p18(2) [501+]

Mizuki, Shigeru - *Shigeru Mizuki's Hitler*
    PW - v262 - i45 - Nov 9 2015 - p46(1) [51-500]
Showa 1944-1953: A History of Japan (Illus. by Mizuki, Shigeru)
    BL - v111 - i13 - March 1 2015 - p33(1) [51-500]
Showa 1953-1989: A History of Japan (Illus. by Mizuki, Shigeru)
    BL - v112 - i6 - Nov 15 2015 - p35(1) [51-500]

Mizumura, Minae - *The Fall of Language in the Age of English*
    CHE - v61 - i22 - Feb 13 2015 - pNA [501+]
    TLS - i5855 - June 19 2015 - p3(2) [501+]
    WLT - v89 - i6 - Nov-Dec 2015 - p77(2) [501+]
A True Novel
    NYTBR - Jan 11 2015 - p24(L) [501+]

Mizushima, Margaret - *Killing Trail*
    BL - v112 - i6 - Nov 15 2015 - p28(1) [51-500]
    KR - Oct 1 2015 - pNA [501+]
Mlambo, Alois S. - *A History of Zimbabwe*
    JIH - v46 - i1 - Summer 2015 - p149-150 [501+]
Mlawer, Teresa - *A Color of His Own: Spanish-English Bilingual Edition (Illus. by Lionni, Leo)*
    c SLJ - v61 - i12 - Dec 2015 - p85(1) [51-500]
Little Red Riding Hood/Caperucita Roja (Illus. by Cuellar, Olga)
    c SLJ - v61 - i2 - Feb 2015 - p72(1) [51-500]
The Three Little Pigs/Los tres cerditos (Illus. by Cuellar, Olga)
    c SLJ - v61 - i2 - Feb 2015 - p72(1) [51-500]
Mlinko, Ange - *Marvelous Things Overheard*
    Poet - v205 - i4 - Jan 2015 - p392(5) [501+]
Mlodinow, Leonard - *The Upright Thinkers: The Human Journey from Living in Trees to Understanding the Cosmos (Read by Mlodinow, Leonard). Audiobook Review*
    LJ - v140 - i17 - Oct 15 2015 - p54(1) [51-500]
The Upright Thinkers: The Human Journey from Living in Trees to Understanding the Cosmos
    BL - v111 - i16 - April 15 2015 - p8(1) [51-500]
    KR - March 1 2015 - pNA [501+]
    Nature - v521 - i7550 - May 7 2015 - p31(1) [51-500]
    PW - v262 - i10 - March 9 2015 - p63(2) [51-500]
Mlynowski, Sarah - *Bad Hair Day*
    c Res Links - v20 - i5 - June 2015 - p11(1) [51-500]
    c HB Guide - v26 - i1 - Spring 2015 - p87(1) [51-500]
Cold as Ice
    c HB Guide - v26 - i2 - Fall 2015 - p94(1) [51-500]
    c Res Links - v20 - i4 - April 2015 - p13(1) [501+]
Dream On
    c Res Links - v20 - i3 - Feb 2015 - p14(1) [51-500]
Upside-Down Magic
    c KR - July 15 2015 - pNA [51-500]
    c BL - v111 - i21 - July 1 2015 - p77(1) [51-500]
    c HB - v91 - i5 - Sept-Oct 2015 - p111(2) [51-500]
    c PW - v262 - i24 - June 15 2015 - p83(2) [51-500]
    c SLJ - v61 - i9 - Sept 2015 - p142(1) [51-500]
Mo, Yan - *Frog*
    AM - v213 - i7 - Sept 21 2015 - p37(2) [501+]
    NY - v90 - i46 - Feb 2 2015 - p65 [51-500]
    NYTBR - Feb 8 2015 - p14(L) [501+]
    TLS - i5835 - Jan 30 2015 - p19(1) [501+]
Moalem, Sharon - *Inheritance: How Our Genes Change Our Lives and Our Lives Change Our Genes*
    Am Bio T - v77 - i5 - May 2015 - p393(2) [501+]
Moazami, Behrooz - *State, Religion, and Revolution in Iran, 1796 to the Present*
    AHR - v120 - i3 - June 2015 - p1151-1152 [501+]
Moberg, Julia - *Historical Animals: The Dogs, Cats, Horses, Snakes, Goats, Rats, Dragons, Bears, Elephants, Rabbits, and Other Creatures That Changed the World (Illus. by Jeff Albrecht Studios)*
    c HB Guide - v26 - i2 - Fall 2015 - p215(1) [51-500]
    c BL - v111 - i9-10 - Jan 1 2015 - p72(1) [51-500]
    y SLJ - v61 - i3 - March 2015 - p172(1) [51-500]
Moberry, Jonathan - *Fall of Night*
    BL - v111 - i18 - May 15 2015 - p34(1) [501+]
Mobilitat und Umwelt
    HNet - July 2015 - pNA [501+]
Mobley, Jeannie - *Searching for Silverheels*
    c HB Guide - v26 - i2 - Fall 2015 - p95(1) [51-500]
Mobley, Joe A. - *The Papers of Zebulon Baird Vance, vol. 3: 1864-1865*
    JSH - v81 - i2 - May 2015 - p474(2) [501+]
Moch, Leslie Page - *The Pariahs of Yesterday: Breton Migrants in Paris*
    HNet - Jan 2015 - pNA [501+]
Mock, Janice - *Not All Bad Comes to Harm You*
    KR - Jan 1 2016 - pNA [501+]
Mock, Melanie Springer - *The Spirit of Adoption: Writers on Religion, Adoption, Faith, and More*
    Ch Today - v59 - i1 - Jan-Feb 2015 - p68(1) [501+]
Mockel, Benjamin - *Erfahrungsbruch und Generationsbehauptung: Die gt;Kriegsjugendgeneration< in den beiden deutschen Nachkriegsgesellschaften*
    HNet - April 2015 - pNA [501+]
Mockett, Marie Mutsuki - *Where the Dead Pause, and the Japanese Say Goodbye*
    BL - v111 - i9-10 - Jan 1 2015 - p21(1) [51-500]
    Bwatch - April 2015 - pNA [501+]
    NYTBR - Jan 25 2015 - p10(L) [501+]
Modern Family - *The Modern Family Cookbook*
    BL - v112 - i3 - Oct 1 2015 - p18(1) [51-500]

Modern India in German Archives, 1706-1989: Inaugural Project Workshop
    HNet - Sept 2015 - pNA [501+]
Moderow, Debbie Clarke - *Fast into the Night: A Woman, Her Dogs, and Their Journey North on the Iditarod Trail*
    BL - v112 - i7 - Dec 1 2015 - p10(1) [51-500]
    KR - Nov 1 2015 - pNA [501+]
    LJ - v140 - i20 - Dec 1 2015 - p108(2) [51-500]
Modesitt, L.E., Jr. - *Madness in Solidar*
    KR - Jan 1 2015 - pNA [501+]
The One-Eyed Man
    Analog - v135 - i10 - Oct 2015 - p108(1) [51-500]
Solar Express
    KR - Sept 1 2015 - pNA [501+]
    PW - v262 - i38 - Sept 21 2015 - p56(1) [51-500]
Modesto, Michelle - *Revenge and the Wild*
    y KR - Nov 15 2015 - pNA [51-500]
    y PW - v262 - i46 - Nov 16 2015 - p78(1) [51-500]
    y SLJ - v61 - i12 - Dec 2015 - p125(1) [51-500]
Modiano, Patrick - *After the Circus*
    LJ - v140 - i14 - Sept 1 2015 - p94(1) [501+]
Honeymoon
    NY - v91 - i30 - Oct 5 2015 - p75 [501+]
In the Cafe of Lost Youth
    KR - Jan 1 2016 - pNA [501+]
The Occupation Trilogy
    KR - July 15 2015 - pNA [501+]
    HM - v331 - i1985 - Oct 2015 - p73(3) [501+]
    LJ - v140 - i14 - Sept 1 2015 - p94(1) [501+]
Paris Nocturne
    BL - v112 - i4 - Oct 15 2015 - p23(1) [51-500]
    LJ - v140 - i14 - Sept 1 2015 - p94(1) [501+]
    PW - v262 - i34 - August 24 2015 - p55(1) [51-500]
Pedigree
    PW - v262 - i26 - June 29 2015 - p60(1) [51-500]
So You Don't Get Lost in the Neighborhood
    BL - v112 - i1 - Sept 1 2015 - p44(1) [51-500]
    KR - July 15 2015 - pNA [501+]
    LJ - v140 - i14 - Sept 1 2015 - p94(1) [501+]
    NY - v91 - i30 - Oct 5 2015 - p75 [501+]
    PW - v262 - i27 - July 6 2015 - p42(1) [51-500]
Suspended Sentences: Three Novellas
    NYT - Jan 14 2015 - pC1(L) [501+]
Young Once
    KR - Jan 1 2016 - pNA [501+]
Moe-Lobeda, Cynthia D. - *Resisting Structural Evil: Love as Ecological-Economic Vocation*
    Intpr - v69 - i4 - Oct 2015 - p506(1) [501+]
Moehring, Eugene P. - *Reno, Las Vegas, and the Strip: A Tale of Three Cities*
    WHQ - v46 - i4 - Winter 2015 - p529-530 [501+]
Moerbe, Mary J. - *Whisper, Whisper: Learning about Church (Illus. by Aviles, Martha)*
    c CH Bwatch - August 2015 - pNA [51-500]
Moerder, Lynne - *Things That Go Burp! in the Night*
    c HB Guide - v26 - i2 - Fall 2015 - p15(1) [51-500]
Moffatt, Ann - *Constantine Porphyrogennetos: The Book of Ceremonies, with the Greek Edition of the Corpus Scriptorum Historiae Byzantinae: Bonn, 1829*
    HER - v130 - i545 - August 2015 - p949(4) [501+]
Moffit, Mitchell - *AsapScience: Answers to the World's Weirdest Questions, Most Persistent Rumors, and Unexplained Phenomena*
    PW - v262 - i1 - Jan 5 2015 - p62(2) [51-500]
Moffitt, Donald - *Children of the Comet*
    PW - v262 - i29 - July 20 2015 - p173(1) [51-500]
Moger, Jourden Travis - *Priestly Resistance to the Early Reformation in Germany*
    CHR - v101 - i3 - Summer 2015 - p641(3) [501+]
    Ger Q - v88 - i2 - Spring 2015 - p261(2) [501+]
Moger, Susan - *Of Better Blood*
    y KR - Dec 15 2015 - pNA [501+]
Mogford, Thomas - *Sleeping Dogs*
    BL - v111 - i17 - May 1 2015 - p45(1) [51-500]
    KR - May 1 2015 - pNA [501+]
    PW - v262 - i18 - May 4 2015 - p97(2) [51-500]
Moggach, Deborah - *Heartbreak Hotel*
    KR - Dec 15 2015 - pNA [501+]
    BL - v111 - i13 - March 1 2015 - p18(1) [51-500]
In the Dark
    BL - v112 - i3 - Oct 1 2015 - p30(1) [51-500]
    NYTBR - Oct 25 2015 - p23(L) [501+]
Mogilner, Marina - *Homo Imperii: A History of Physical Anthropology in Russia*
    HNet - August 2015 - pNA [501+]
Moglia, Paul - *Salem Health: Psychology and Behavioral Health, 4th ed.*
    BL - v112 - i7 - Dec 1 2015 - p21(1) [51-500]

Mohamed, Feisal G. - *Milton and Questions of History: Essays by Canadians Past and Present*
    Ren Q - v68 - i1 - Spring 2015 - p412-414 [501+]
Mohamed, Nadifa - *The Orchard of Lost Souls*
    TLS - i5854 - June 12 2015 - p13(1) [501+]
Mohammad, Akikur - *The Anatomy of Addiction*
    KR - Dec 15 2015 - pNA [501+]
Mohan, Rohini - *The Seasons of Trouble: Life amid the Ruins of Sri Lanka's Civil War*
    NYRB - v62 - i4 - March 5 2015 - p31(3) [501+]
Mohr, James C. - *Licensed to Practice: The Supreme Court Defines the American Medical Profession*
    JAH - v101 - i4 - March 2015 - p1294-1295 [501+]
Mohr, Joshua - *All This Life*
    y BL - v111 - i19-20 - June 1 2015 - p38(1) [51-500]
    KR - May 1 2015 - pNA [51-500]
    PW - v262 - i18 - May 4 2015 - p96(1) [51-500]
Mohr, Michel - *Buddhism, Unitarianism, and the Meiji Competition for Universality*
    IBMR - v39 - i4 - Oct 2015 - p240(1) [501+]
Mohr, Tim - *Just Call Me Superhero*
    WLT - v89 - i2 - March-April 2015 - p54(2) [501+]
Mohrbacher, Paul - *Brothers*
    KR - Dec 15 2015 - pNA [501+]
Mohrig, Jerry R. - *Laboratory Techniques in Organic Chemistry: Supporting Inquiry-Driven Experiments, 4th ed.*
    J Chem Ed - v92 - i9 - Sept 2015 - p1433-1434 [501+]
Moin, Baqer - *Khomeini: Life of a Ayatollah*
    TimHES - i2211 - July 9 2015 - p48(1) [501+]
Mojola, Sanyu A. - *Love, Money, and HIV: Becoming a Modern African Woman in the Age of AIDS*
    CS - v44 - i5 - Sept 2015 - p591-603 [501+]
Mok, Carmen - *Ride the Big Machines Across Canada (Illus. by Mok, Carmen)*
    c Res Links - v21 - i1 - Oct 2015 - p26(1) [51-500]
Mokhtari, Tara - *The Bloomsbury Introduction to Creative Writing*
    RVBW - May 2015 - pNA [51-500]
Mola, Francesc Zamora - *150 Best Mini Interior Ideas*
    LJ - v140 - i7 - April 15 2015 - p91(1) [51-500]
Molander, Beverly - *Heartfelt Memorial Services: Your Guide for Planning Meaningful Funerals, Celebrations of Life and Times of Remembrance*
    SPBW - July 2015 - pNA [501+]
Molaro, Anthony - *The Library Innovation Toolkit: Ideas, Strategies, and Programs*
    LJ - v140 - i9 - May 15 2015 - p97(1) [501+]
Moldavsky, Goldy - *Kill the Boy Band*
    y KR - Dec 15 2015 - pNA [51-500]
Moldoveanu, Mihnea C. - *Epinets: The Epistemic Structure and Dynamics of Social Networks*
    AJS - v121 - i1 - July 2015 - p322(3) [501+]
Mole, Noelle J. - *Labor Disorders in Neoliberal Italy: Mobbing, Well-being, and the Workplace*
    MAQ - v29 - i1 - March 2015 - p10-13 [501+]
Molekamp, Femke - *Women and the Bible in Early Modern England: Religious Reading and Writing*
    MP - v112 - i4 - May 2015 - pNA [501+]
Molesini, Andrea - *Not All Bastards Are from Vienna*
    KR - Nov 15 2015 - pNA [501+]
    PW - v262 - i47 - Nov 23 2015 - p46(1) [51-500]
Molesky, Mark - *This Gulf of Fire: The Destruction of Lisbon, or Apocalypse in the Age of Science and Reason*
    BL - v112 - i4 - Oct 15 2015 - p15(1) [51-500]
    CSM - Nov 9 2015 - pNA [501+]
    KR - August 15 2015 - pNA [501+]
    LJ - v140 - i16 - Oct 1 2015 - p95(1) [51-500]
Molina, Antonio Munoz - *Como la sombra que se va*
    WLT - v89 - i5 - Sept-Oct 2015 - p64(2) [501+]
Molina, Bengie - *Molina: The Story of the Father Who Raised an Unlikely Baseball Dynasty*
    KR - April 15 2015 - pNA [501+]
    y BL - v111 - i18 - May 15 2015 - p10(1) [51-500]
    LJ - v140 - i9 - May 15 2015 - p87(1) [51-500]
Molina, Concepcion - *The Problem with Math Is English: A Language-Focused Approach to Helping All Students Develop a Deeper Understanding of Mathematics*
    TC Math - v21 - i7 - March 2015 - p444(1) [501+]
Molina, Michelle - *To Overcome Oneself: The Jesuit Ethic and Spirit of Global Expansion, 1520-1767*
    Historian - v77 - i3 - Fall 2015 - p622(3) [501+]
Molina, Natalia - *How Race Is Made in America: Immigration, Citizenship, and the Historical Power of Racial Scripts*
    AHR - v120 - i1 - Feb 2015 - p274-275 [501+]
    PHR - v84 - i3 - August 2015 - p384(2) [501+]
    RAH - v43 - i3 - Sept 2015 - p550-556 [501+]
    WHQ - v46 - i2 - Summer 2015 - p241-242 [501+]

White Elephants on Campus: The Decline of the University Chapel in America, 1920-1960
    AHR - v120 - i1 - Feb 2015 - p274-275 [501+]
Moliner, Sara - *The Whispering City*
    BL - v112 - i1 - Sept 1 2015 - p51(1) [51-500]
    KR - Sept 15 2015 - pNA [51-500]
    PW - v262 - i37 - Sept 14 2015 - p42(2) [51-500]
Molino, Anthony - *Traces of Time*
    PW - v262 - i29 - July 20 2015 - p168(1) [51-500]
Molk, Laurel - *Eeny, Meeny, Miney, Mo and Flo! (Illus. by Molk, Laurel)*
  c CCB-B - v69 - i2 - Oct 2015 - p103(2) [51-500]
Molkentin, Michael - *Australia and the War in the Air*
    APH - v62 - i2 - Summer 2015 - p51(2) [501+]
Moll, Cathy de - *Think South: How We Got Six Men and Forty Dogs Across Antarctica*
    LJ - v140 - i15 - Sept 15 2015 - p84(1) [501+]
Moller, Esther - *Orte der Zivilisierungsmission: Französische Schulen im Libanon 1909-1943*
    HNet - June 2015 - pNA [501+]
Moller, Frank - *Das Buch Witsch: Das schwindelerregende Leben des Verlegers Joseph Caspar Witsch*
    Ger Q - v88 - i2 - Spring 2015 - p249(4) [501+]
    HNet - April 2015 - pNA [501+]
Molles, D.J. - *Extinction*
    PW - v262 - i20 - May 18 2015 - p69(1) [51-500]
Molloy, Aimee - *However Long the Night: Molly Melching's journey to Help Millions of African Women and Girls Triumph*
    Forbes - v196 - i6 - Nov 2 2015 - p42(1) [501+]
Molnar, Virag - *Building the State: Architecture, Politics and State Formation in Post-War Central Europe*
    E-A St - v67 - i8 - Oct 2015 - p1334(3) [501+]
Moloney, Brian - *Francis of Assisi and His Canticle of Brother Sun Reassessed*
    MLR - v110 - i2 - April 2015 - p562-564 [501+]
Moloney, James - *The Beauty Is in the Walking*
  y Magpies - v30 - i4 - Sept 2015 - p42(2) [501+]
Bridget: A New Australian
  y Magpies - v30 - i1 - March 2015 - p35(2) [501+]
Molotch, Harvey - *Against Security: How We Go Wrong at Airports, Subways, and Other Sites of Ambiguous Danger*
    CS - v44 - i5 - Sept 2015 - p684-685 [501+]
Moltz, James Clay - *Crowded Orbits: Conflict and Cooperation in Space*
    APJ - v29 - i4 - July-August 2015 - p94(3) [501+]
Molvarec, Stephen J. - *A Fish out of Water? From Contemplative Solitude to Carthusian Involvement in Pastoral Care and Reform Activity*
    CHR - v101 - i4 - Autumn 2015 - p915(2) [501+]
Mombauer, Annika - *The Origins of the First World War: Diplomatic and Military Documents*
    HNet - Feb 2015 - pNA [501+]
Mommsen, Peter - *Homage to a Broken Man*
    RVBW - Oct 2015 - pNA [51-500]
Monaco, Gerard Lo - *Madame Sonia Delaunay*
  c PW - v262 - i13 - March 30 2015 - p74(1) [51-500]
Monaghan, Tess - *Hush, Hush*
    NYTBR - Feb 15 2015 - p29(L) [51-500]
Monagle, Clare - *Orthodoxy and Controversy in Twelfth-century Religious Discourse: Peter Lombard's Sentences and the Development of Theology*
    Med R - Jan 2015 - pNA [501+]
Monahan, Brent - *The St. Simons Island Club: A John Le Brun Novel*
    PW - v262 - i42 - Oct 19 2015 - p58(1) [51-500]
Monahan, Hillary - *Mary: The Summoning*
  c HB Guide - v26 - i1 - Spring 2015 - p117(1) [51-500]
Monahan, Seth - *Mahler's Symphonic Sonatas*
    MT - v156 - i1932 - Autumn 2015 - p111-114 [501+]
    NYRB - v62 - i20 - Dec 17 2015 - p75(3) [501+]
Monahan, Sherry - *The Cowboy's Cookbook: Recipes and Tales from Campfires, Cookouts, and Chuck Wagons*
    PW - v262 - i33 - August 17 2015 - p66(1) [51-500]
Monahan, W. Gregory - *Let God Arise: The War and Rebellion of the Camisards*
    AHR - v120 - i2 - April 2015 - p723(1) [501+]
Monckton, Linda - *Coventry: Medieval Art, Architecture and Archaeology in the City and Its Vicinity*
    Specu - v90 - i4 - Oct 2015 - p1151-1152 [501+]
Monday, T.T. - *Double Switch*
    KR - Jan 1 2016 - pNA [51-500]
    PW - v262 - i48 - Nov 30 2015 - p38(1) [51-500]
Mong, Ambrose - *Are Non-Christians Saved? Joseph Ratzinger's Thoughts on Religious Pluralism*
    AM - v213 - i4 - August 17 2015 - p43(2) [501+]

Monir, Alexandra - *Suspicion*
  y CCB-B - v68 - i6 - Feb 2015 - p322(2) [51 500]
  y HB Guide - v26 - i2 - Fall 2015 - p132(1) [51-500]
Moniz, Richard - *The Personal Librarian: Enhancing the Student Experience*
    LJ - v140 - i2 - Feb 1 2015 - p97(1) [51-500]
    R&USQ - v54 - i4 - Summer 2015 - p75(1) [501+]
    VOYA - v37 - i6 - Feb 2015 - p91(2) [51-500]
Monk, Connie - *The Fleeting Years*
    BL - v111 - i17 - May 1 2015 - p78(1) [51-500]
Monk, Devon - *Crucible Zero*
    PW - v262 - i29 - July 20 2015 - p173(1) [51-500]
Infinity Bell
    PW - v262 - i5 - Feb 2 2015 - p40(1) [51-500]
Monk, Ray - *Robert Oppenheimer: A Life inside the Center*
    T&C - v56 - i3 - July 2015 - p774-775 [501+]
Monmonier, Mark - *The History of Cartography: Cartography in the Twentieth Century, 2 vols.*
    LJ - v140 - i13 - August 1 2015 - p123(1) [51-500]
Lake Effect: Tales of Large Lakes, Arctic Winds, and Recurrent Snows
    GR - v105 - i1 - Jan 2015 - p128(2) [501+]
Monnig, Alex - *Drag Racing*
  c HB Guide - v26 - i1 - Spring 2015 - p183(1) [51-500]
Monninger, Joseph - *Whippoorwill*
  y CCB-B - v69 - i2 - Oct 2015 - p104(1) [51-500]
  y HB - v91 - i6 - Nov-Dec 2015 - p84(2) [51-500]
  y KR - June 1 2015 - pNA [51-500]
  y SLJ - v61 - i6 - June 2015 - p115(1) [51-500]
  y VOYA - v38 - i4 - Oct 2015 - p57(1) [51-500]
Monod, Paul Kleber - *Solomon's Secret Arts: The Occult in the Age of Enlightenment*
    AHR - v120 - i1 - Feb 2015 - p324-325 [501+]
    Historian - v77 - i2 - Summer 2015 - p400(2) [501+]
    JMH - v87 - i2 - June 2015 - p421(3) [501+]
Monro, Alexander - *The Paper Trail: An Unexpected History of the World's Greatest Invention*
    TLS - i5846 - April 17 2015 - p22(2) [501+]
Monroe, Alexei - *Laibach und NSK: Die Inquisitionsmaschine im Kreuzverhor*
    HNet - July 2015 - pNA [501+]
Monroe, Barbara - *Plateau Indian Ways with Words: The Rhetorical Tradition of the Tribes of the Inland Pacific Northwest*
    Am Ind CRJ - v39 - i1 - Wntr 2015 - p148-150 [501+]
Monroe, Chris - *Bug on a Bike (Illus. by Monroe, Chris)*
  c HB Guide - v26 - i1 - Spring 2015 - p39(2) [51-500]
Monroe, Debra - *My Unsentimental Education*
    KR - Sept 1 2015 - pNA [51-500]
    RVBW - Oct 2015 - pNA [51-500]
Monroe, Gary - *Mary Ann Carroll: First Lady of the Highwaymen*
    HNet - Jan 2015 - pNA [501+]
Monroe, J. Cameron - *The Precolonial State in West Africa: Building Power in Dahomey*
    IJAHS - v48 - i1 - Wntr 2015 - p133-135 [501+]
Monroe, Katrina - *Sacrificial Lamb Cake*
    PW - v262 - i4 - Jan 26 2015 - p154(1) [51-500]
Monroe, Lucy - *Wild Heat*
    PW - v262 - i12 - March 23 2015 - p54(2) [51-500]
Monroe, Randall - *Thing Explainer: Complicated Stuff in Simple Words*
    PW - v262 - i50 - Dec 7 2015 - p13(1) [51-500]
Monshipouri, Mahmood - *Democratic Uprisings in the New Middle East: Youth, Technology, Human Rights, and US Foreign Policy*
    HNet - April 2015 - pNA [501+]
Monso, Imma - *A Man of His Word*
    TLS - i5839 - Feb 27 2015 - p26(1) [51-500]
Monson, Ander - *Letter to a Future Lover: Marginalia, Errata, Secrets, Inscriptions, and Other Ephemera Found in Libraries*
    LJ - v140 - i3 - Feb 15 2015 - p101(1) [51-500]
    NYTBR - May 24 2015 - p30(L) [501+]
Montague, Conor - *George Moore: Dublin, Paris, Hollywood*
    VS - v57 - i2 - Wntr 2015 - p345(4) [501+]
Montana, Bob - *Archie Archives: Prom Pranks and Other Stories*
  y SLJ - v61 - i12 - Dec 2015 - p110(1) [51-500]
Montana, Ismael M. - *The Abolition of Slavery in Ottoman Tunisia*
    Historian - v77 - i1 - Spring 2015 - p104(3) [501+]
Montanari, Massimo - *Medieval Tastes: Food, Cooking, and the Table*
    TLS - i5863 - August 14 2015 - p30(1) [501+]

Montanari, Richard - *The Doll Maker*
    BL - v111 - i15 - April 1 2015 - p29(1) [51-500]
    PW - v262 - i8 - Feb 23 2015 - p51(1) [51-500]
Shutter Man
    KR - Dec 1 2015 - pNA [51-500]
    PW - v262 - i52 - Dec 21 2015 - p130(1) [51-500]
Montanari, Susan McElroy - *My Dog's a Chicken (Illus. by Wilsdorf, Anne)*
  c KR - Nov 1 2015 - pNA [51-500]
  c PW - v262 - i45 - Nov 9 2015 - p58(1) [51-500]
  c SLJ - v61 - i12 - Dec 2015 - p93(1) [51-500]
Montandon, Pat - *Peeing on Hot Coals*
    KR - Feb 15 2015 - pNA [501+]
    PW - v262 - i12 - March 23 2015 - p68(1) [51-500]
Montarese, Francesco - *Lucretius and His Sources: A Study of Lucretius, De Rerum Natura I 635-920*
    Class R - v65 - i1 - April 2015 - p114-116 [501+]
Montebello, Philippe de - *Rendez-vous with Art*
    NYRB - v62 - i11 - June 25 2015 - p46(2) [501+]
Montefiore, Santa - *The Beekeeper's Daughter*
    BL - v111 - i12 - Feb 15 2015 - p30(1) [51-500]
Monteith, Sharon - *The Cambridge Companion to the Literature of the American South*
    JSH - v81 - i2 - May 2015 - p534(3) [501+]
Montes, Christian - *American Capitals: A Historical Geography*
    AHR - v120 - i1 - Feb 2015 - p241-242 [501+]
    JAH - v101 - i4 - March 2015 - p1245-1246 [501+]
Montes, Raphael - *Perfect Days*
    KR - Dec 1 2015 - pNA [501+]
    LJ - v140 - i19 - Nov 15 2015 - p78(1) [51-500]
    PW - v262 - i47 - Nov 23 2015 - p47(1) [51-500]
Montez de Oca, Jeffrey - *Discipline and Indulgence: College Football, Media, and the American Way of Life during the Cold War*
    CS - v44 - i3 - May 2015 - p384-385 [501+]
Montfort, Anne - *Sonia Delaunay*
    TLS - i5851 - May 22 2015 - p18(1) [501+]
Montgomerie, Bob - *Ten Thousand Birds: Ornithology since Darwin*
    QRB - v90 - i1 - March 2015 - p103(2) [501+]
Montgomery, Ben - *Grandma Gatewood's Walk: The Inspiring Story of the Woman Who Saved the Appalachian Trail (Read by Lawlor, Patrick). Audiobook Review*
    LJ - v140 - i8 - May 1 2015 - p43(1) [51-500]
    PW - v262 - i8 - Feb 23 2015 - p71(1) [51-500]
Montgomery, David R. - *The Hidden Half of Nature: The Microbial Roots of Life and Health*
    BL - v112 - i5 - Nov 1 2015 - p6(1) [51-500]
    KR - Sept 1 2015 - pNA [51-500]
    LJ - v140 - i17 - Oct 15 2015 - p110(2) [51-500]
    Nature - v582 - i7582 - Dec 17 2015 - p331(1) [501+]
Montgomery, James E. - *Al-Jahiz: In Praise of Books*
    TLS - i5842 - March 20 2015 - p10(1) [501+]
Montgomery, L.M. - *The Complete Journals of L.M. Montgomery: The PEI Years, 1889-1900*
    MLR - v110 - i1 - Jan 2015 - p249-250 [501+]
Montgomery, Lewis B. - *The Case of the Buried Bones (Illus. by Wummer, Amy)*
  c HB Guide - v26 - i1 - Spring 2015 - p63(1) [51-500]
Montgomery, Lucy Maud - *Anne of Green Gables (Read by Frasier, Shelly). Audiobook Review*
  c SLJ - v61 - i2 - Feb 2015 - p38(3) [501+]
Montgomery, Michela - *The Cave*
    SPBW - June 2015 - pNA [51-500]
Montgomery, Scott L. - *Does Science Need a Global Language? English and the Future of Research*
    T&C - v56 - i1 - Jan 2015 - p261-263 [501+]
The Shape of the New: Four Big Ideas and How They Made the Modern World
    NYTBR - August 23 2015 - p14(L) [501+]
    PW - v262 - i17 - April 27 2015 - p63(2) [51-500]
    Soc - v52 - i4 - August 2015 - p383(1) [501+]
The Shape of the New
    KR - April 15 2015 - pNA [501+]
Montgomery, Sy - *The Octopus Scientists: Exploring the Mind of a Mollusk (Illus. by Ellenbogen, Keith)*
  c BL - v111 - i18 - May 15 2015 - p46(1) [51-500]
  c CCB-B - v68 - i11 - July-August 2015 - p557(2) [51-500]
  c CH Bwatch - Oct 2015 - pNA [51-500]
  y HB - v91 - i4 - July-August 2015 - p159(3) [51-500]
  y SLJ - v61 - i7 - July 2015 - p108(2) [51-500]
The Soul of an Octopus: A Surprising Exploration into the Wonder of Consciousness (Read by Montgomery, Sy). Audiobook Review
  y BL - v112 - i2 - Sept 15 2015 - p78(2) [51-500]
    BL - v112 - i7 - Dec 1 2015 - p71(1) [501+]
    LJ - v140 - i11 - June 15 2015 - p52(1) [51-500]

The Soul of an Octopus: A Surprising Exploration into the Wonder of Consciousness
  y BL - v111 - i17 - May 1 2015 - p66(1) [51-500]
     KR - April 1 2015 - pNA [51-500]
     LJ - v140 - i10 - June 1 2015 - p130(2) [51-500]
     NS - v144 - i5275 - August 14 2015 - p41(1) [501+]
     TLS - i5855 - June 19 2015 - p12(1) [501+]
Temple Grandin: How the Girl Who Loved Cows Embraced Autism and Changed the World
  c SLJ - v61 - i12 - Dec 2015 - p64(4) [501+]

Montgomery, Thaddaeus U. - *Beyond Expectations: Out of the Surf*
     SPBW - Jan 2015 - pNA [51-500]

Montgomery Ward - *Montgomery Ward & Co. Catalogue & Buyers' Guide 1895*
     Bwatch - June 2015 - pNA [51-500]

Monti, Daniel J., Jr. - *Engaging Strangers: Civil Rites, Civic Capitalism, and Public Order in Boston*
     CS - v44 - i1 - Jan 2015 - p93-94 [501+]
Engaging Strangers: Civil Rites, Civil Capitalism, and Public Order in Boston
     J Urban H - v41 - i1 - Jan 2015 - p143-9 [501+]

Montiglio, Silvia - *Love and Providence: Recognition in Ancient Novel*
     AJP - v136 - i1 - Spring 2015 - p166-169 [501+]

Montileaux, Donald F. - *Tasunka: A Lakota Horse Legend (Illus. by Montileaux, Donald F.)*
  y Roundup M - v22 - i5 - June 2015 - p37(1) [501+]
  c Roundup M - v22 - i6 - August 2015 - p25(1) [501+]

Montillo, Roseanne - *The Wilderness of Ruin: A Tale of Madness, Fire and the Hunt for America's Youngest Serial Killer (Read by Zeller, Emily Woo). Audiobook Review*
     LJ - v140 - i17 - Oct 15 2015 - p54(1) [51-500]
The Wilderness of Ruin: A Tale of Madness, Fire, and the Hunt for America's Youngest Serial Killer
     LJ - v140 - i2 - Feb 1 2015 - p94(1) [51-500]
     NYTBR - July 5 2015 - p30(L) [501+]
The Wilderness of Ruin
     KR - Jan 15 2015 - pNA [501+]

Montillo, Rosearme - *The Wilderness of Ruin: A Tale of Madness, Boston's Great Fire, and the Hunt for America's Youngest Serial Killer*
     PW - v262 - i3 - Jan 19 2015 - p73(1) [51-500]

Montolieu, Isabelle de - *Caroline of Lichtfield*
     TLS - i5831 - Jan 2 2015 - p23(1) [501+]

Montoya, Maceo - *Letters to the Poet from His Brother*
     Aztlan - v40 - i2 - Fall 2015 - p287-290 [501+]

Montparker, Carol - *The Composer's Landscape: The Pianist as Explorer, Interpreting the Scores of Eight Masters*
     Am MT - v64 - i6 - June-July 2015 - p64(1) [501+]

Montross, Sarah J. - *Past Futures: Science Fiction, Space Travel, and Postwar Art of the Americas*
     SFS - v42 - i3 - Nov 2015 - p597-599 [501+]
     Nature - v520 - i7546 - April 9 2015 - p155(1) [51-500]

Monture, Rick - *We Share Our Matters: Two Centuries of Writing and Resistance at Six Nations of the Grand River*
     RVBW - Jan 2015 - pNA [501+]
     RVBW - March 2015 - pNA [501+]

Monush, Barry - *The Sound of Music FAQ: All That's Left to Know About Maria, the Von Trapps, and Our Favorite Things*
     Bwatch - July 2015 - pNA [501+]

Moo, Douglas J. - *Galatians*
     Intpr - v69 - i4 - Oct 2015 - p482(3) [501+]

Moodie, Susanna - *Flora Lyndsay: Or, Passages in an Eventful Life*
     Can Lit - i224 - Spring 2015 - p134 [501+]

Moody, A. David - *Ezra Pound: Poet: A Portrait of the Man and His Work, 2 vols.*
     MP - v113 - i1 - August 2015 - pE50(3) [501+]
Ezra Pound: Poet: A Portrait of the Man and His Work, vol. 2, The Epic Years, 1921-1939
     ABR - v36 - i3 - March-April 2015 - p15(1) [501+]
Ezra Pound: Poet, A Portrait of the Man and His Work, vol. 2, The Epic Years, 1921-1939
     HR - v67 - i4 - Wntr 2015 - p660-666 [501+]
Ezra Pound: Poet: A Portrait of the Man and His Work, vol. 2: The Epic Years, 1921-1939
     NYRB - v62 - i8 - May 7 2015 - p24(3) [501+]
     RES - v66 - i275 - June 2015 - p595-597 [501+]
Ezra Pound: Poet: A Portrait of the Man and His Work, vol. 2, The Epic Years, 1921-1939
     TLS - i5861 - July 31 2015 - p3(3) [501+]

Ezra Pound: Poet: A Portrait of the Man and His Work, vol. 3: The Tragic Years
     PW - v262 - i41 - Oct 12 2015 - p59(1) [51-500]
     TLS - i5875 - Nov 6 2015 - p5(2) [501+]

Moody, Rick - *Hotels of North America*
     BL - v112 - i4 - Oct 15 2015 - p16(1) [501+]
     KR - Sept 1 2015 - pNA [501+]
     LJ - v140 - i19 - Nov 15 2015 - p78(1) [51-500]
     NYT - Nov 10 2015 - pC1(L) [501+]
     NYTBR - Dec 20 2015 - p9(L) [501+]
     PW - v262 - i37 - Sept 14 2015 - p37(1) [51-500]

Moody-Turner, Shirley - *Black Folklore and the Politics of Racial Representation*
     WestFolk - v74 - i1 - Wntr 2015 - p84-87 [501+]
     JSH - v81 - i2 - May 2015 - p490(2) [501+]

Moodysson, Coco - *Never Goodnight*
     PW - v262 - i36 - Sept 7 2015 - p54(1) [51-500]

Mooers, John - *A Farewell to Windemere*
     KR - April 1 2015 - pNA [501+]

Moon, Alison - *Bad Dyke: Salacious Stories from a Queer Life*
     PW - v262 - i9 - March 2 2015 - p77(2) [51-500]

Moon, David - *The Plough that Broke the Steppes: Agriculture and Environment on Russia's Grasslands, 1700-1914*
     HNet - Feb 2015 - pNA [501+]

Moon, JooHee - *The Tiger Who Would Be King (Illus. by Moon, JooHee)*
  c CH Bwatch - Nov 2015 - pNA [51-500]

Moon, Munir - *The Beltway Beast*
     KR - Jan 15 2015 - pNA [501+]

Moon, Yumi - *Populist Collaborators: The Ilchinhoe and the Japanese Colonization of Korea, 1896-1910*
     Historian - v77 - i2 - Summer 2015 - p370(2) [501+]

Mooney, Carla - *Asking Questions about How the News Is Created*
  c BL - v112 - i3 - Oct 1 2015 - p42(1) [51-500]
The Brain: Journey through the Universe Inside Your Head (Illus. by Casteel, Tom)
  c PW - v262 - i28 - July 13 2015 - p67(1) [501+]
  y Sci Teach - v82 - i7 - Oct 2015 - p80 [501+]
Comparative Religion: Investigate the World through Religious Tradition (Illus. by Chandhok, Lena)
  c BL - v112 - i6 - Nov 15 2015 - p44(1) [51-500]
Isaac Newton: Genius Mathematician and Physicist
  c HB Guide - v26 - i1 - Spring 2015 - p190(2) [51-500]
Privacy in the Online World: Online Privacy and Social Media
  y VOYA - v37 - i6 - Feb 2015 - p90(1) [501+]
Recycling
  c HB Guide - v26 - i1 - Spring 2015 - p141(1) [51-500]
  c Sci & Ch - v52 - i5 - Jan 2015 - p86 [501+]
What Is Anxiety Disorder?
  y BL - v112 - i7 - Dec 1 2015 - p48(1) [51-500]
What Is Panic Disorder?
  y VOYA - v38 - i5 - Dec 2015 - p80(1) [51-500]

Mooney, Carol Garhart - *Theories of Practice: Raising the Standards of Early Childhood Education*
     Bwatch - April 2015 - pNA [501+]

Mooney, J.E. - *Shadows of the New Sun*
     Analog - v135 - i10 - Oct 2015 - p107(1) [501+]

Mooney, Katherine C. - *Race Horse Men: How Slavery and Freedom Were Made at the Racetrack*
     AHR - v120 - i2 - April 2015 - p616-617 [501+]
     JAH - v102 - i1 - June 2015 - p248-249 [501+]
     JSH - v81 - i3 - August 2015 - p719(2) [501+]

Mooney, Linne R. - *Scribes and the City: London Guildhall Clerks and the Dissemination of Middle English Literature 1375-1425*
     JEGP - v114 - i1 - Jan 2015 - p97(18) [501+]
     Specu - v90 - i3 - July 2015 - p840-842 [501+]

Moor, Becka - *Foxtrot (Illus. by Moor, Becka)*
  c SLJ - v61 - i11 - Nov 2015 - p85(1) [51-500]

Moorcock, Michael - *The Knight of the Swords*
     NYTBR - Oct 18 2015 - p18(L) [501+]
The Whispering Swarm
     KR - Jan 1 2015 - pNA [51-500]
     Spec - v328 - i9754 - August 8 2015 - p30(2) [501+]
     TLS - i5872 - Oct 16 2015 - p20(1) [501+]

Moore, Aaron William - *Writing War: Soldiers Record the Japanese Empire*
     JAS - v74 - i3 - August 2015 - p738-740 [501+]

Moore, Andrew - *Pawpaw: In Search of America's Forgotten Fruit*
     BL - v111 - i22 - August 1 2015 - p11(1) [51-500]

Moore, Brenda L. - *Life-Course Perspectives on Military Services*
     CS - v44 - i2 - March 2015 - p278-280 [501+]

Moore, Carole - *Au coeur de la jungle (Illus. by Lavoie, Camille)*
  c Res Links - v20 - i5 - June 2015 - p41(1) [51-500]

Moore, Charles - *Margaret Thatcher: The Authorised Biography, vol. 2: Everything She Wants*
     BL - v112 - i3 - Oct 1 2015 - p4(1) [51-500]
     KR - Dec 1 2015 - pNA [501+]
     NS - v144 - i5286 - Oct 30 2015 - p40(3) [501+]
     Spec - v329 - i9764 - Oct 17 2015 - p36(3) [501+]
     TLS - i5876 - Nov 13 2015 - p3(3) [501+]

Moore, Christopher - *The Court of Appeal for Ontario: Defining the Right of Appeal, 1792- 2013*
     Can Hist R - v96 - i3 - Sept 2015 - p441(5) [501+]
Secondhand Souls (Read by Stevens, Fisher). Audiobook Review
     BL - v112 - i5 - Nov 1 2015 - p70(1) [501+]

Moore, Clement C. - *The Night before Christmas: A Brick Story (Illus. by Brack, Amanda)*
  c PW - v262 - i37 - Sept 14 2015 - p68(1) [51-500]
The Night before Christmas (Illus. by Duvoisin, Roger)
  c HB Guide - v26 - i1 - Spring 2015 - p189(1) [51-500]
The Night before Christmas (Illus. by Engelbreit, Mary)
  c KR - Sept 1 2015 - pNA [51-500]
The Night before Christmas (Illus. by Ercolini, David)
  c BL - v112 - i4 - Oct 15 2015 - p48(2) [51-500]
  c HB - v91 - i6 - Nov-Dec 2015 - p57(2) [51-500]
  c PW - v262 - i37 - Sept 14 2015 - p66(1) [51-500]
  c PW - v262 - i49 - Dec 2 2015 - p62(1) [51-500]
  c SLJ - v61 - i10 - Oct 2015 - p66(1) [51-500]
The Night before Christmas (Illus. by Reid, Barbara)
  c HB Guide - v26 - i1 - Spring 2015 - p189(1) [51-500]
'Twas the Night before Christmas (Illus. by Kirk, Daniel)
  c PW - v262 - i37 - Sept 14 2015 - p74(1) [51-500]
  c SLJ - v61 - i10 - Oct 2015 - p66(1) [51-500]
'Twas the Night before Christmas (Illus. by Marshall, Mark)
  c KR - Sept 1 2015 - pNA [51-500]
A Visit from St. Nicholas
  c KR - Sept 1 2015 - pNA [51-500]
  c KR - Sept 1 2015 - pNA [51-500]

Moore, Colten - *Catching the Sky: Two Brothers, One Family, and Our Dream to Fly*
     PW - v262 - i46 - Nov 16 2015 - p67(1) [51-500]

Moore, David L. - *That Dream Shall Have a Name: Native Americans Rewriting America*
     AL - v87 - i3 - Sept 2015 - p603-605 [501+]
     Am Ind CRJ - v39 - i2 - Spring 2015 - p165-167 [501+]

Moore, Deborah Dash - *Urban Origins of American Judaism*
     JAH - v102 - i2 - Sept 2015 - p513-514 [501+]

Moore, Dinty W. - *Dear Mister Essay Writer Guy: Advice and Confessions on Writing, Love, and Cannibals*
     LJ - v140 - i9 - May 15 2015 - p89(2) [51-500]

Moore, E.B. - *Stones in the Road*
     KR - Sept 15 2015 - pNA [51-500]
An Unseemly Wife
     KR - July 1 2015 - pNA [501+]

Moore, Erin - *That's Not English: Britishisms, Americanisms, and What Our English Says About Us*
     KR - Feb 1 2015 - pNA [501+]

Moore, Gareth - *Seeing Is Believing (Illus. by Moore, Gareth)*
  c KR - April 15 2015 - pNA [51-500]

Moore, Jeff M. - *The Thai Way of Counterinsurgency*
     J Mil H - v79 - i2 - April 2015 - p547-548 [501+]

Moore, Jennifer - *Simply Anna*
     PW - v262 - i34 - August 24 2015 - p68(1) [51-500]

Moore, Jodi - *When a Dragon Moves in Again (Illus. by McWilliam, Howard)*
  c CH Bwatch - Nov 2015 - pNA [51-500]
  c KR - July 15 2015 - pNA [51-500]

Moore, John S. - *Counting People: A DIY Manual for Local and Family Historians*
     Six Ct J - v46 - i2 - Summer 2015 - p497-498 [501+]

Moore, Jonathan - *The Poison Artist*
     KR - Dec 1 2015 - pNA [501+]
     PW - v262 - i45 - Nov 9 2015 - p36(1) [51-500]

Moore, Joyce Elson - *The Stockholm Castle Mystery*
     KR - June 1 2015 - pNA [51-500]
     PW - v262 - i25 - June 22 2015 - p121(1) [51-500]

Moore, Julianne - *Freckleface Strawberry: Backpacks!* (Illus. by Pham, LeUyen)
  c KR - June 1 2015 - pNA [51-500]
  c SLJ - v61 - i8 - August 2015 - p79(1) [51-500]
Freckleface Strawberry: Loose Tooth! (Illus. by Pham, LeUyen)
  c PW - v262 - i45 - Nov 9 2015 - p60(1) [501+]
Freckleface Strawbery: Lunch, or What's That? (Illus. by Pham, LeUyen)
  c KR - June 1 2015 - pNA [51-500]
  c SLJ - v61 - i8 - August 2015 - p79(1) [51-500]

Moore, Kathleen Dean - *Great Tide Rising*
  KR - Nov 15 2015 - pNA [501+]

Moore, Laurie - *Dawn of the Deb*
  KR - July 1 2015 - pNA [51-500]
  PW - v262 - i30 - July 27 2015 - p45(1) [51-500]

Moore. Lilian - *My First Counting Book* (Illus. by Williams, Garth)
  c SLJ - v61 - i7 - July 2015 - p56(1) [51-500]

Moore, Lorrie - *100 Years of the Best American Short Stories*
  KR - August 1 2015 - pNA [501+]
  NYT - Nov 27 2015 - pC31(L) [501+]
Bark: Stories
  TimHES - i2212 - July 16 2015 - p47-1 [501+]

Moore, M.D. - *Waiting for the Cool Kind of Crazy*
  SPBW - Oct 2015 - pNA [51-500]

Moore, Meg Mitchell - *The Admissions*
  y BL - v112 - i1 - Sept 1 2015 - p40(1) [51-500]
  KR - July 15 2015 - pNA [501+]

Moore, Megan - *Exchanges in Exoticism: Cross-Cultural Marriage and the Making of the Mediterranean in Old French Romance*
  MLR - v110 - i2 - April 2015 - p540-541 [501+]
  Specu - v90 - i4 - Oct 2015 - p1152-1153 [501+]

Moore, Meredith - *Fiona*
  y KR - Jan 1 2016 - pNA [51-500]
I Am Her Revenge
  y CCB-B - v68 - i9 - May 2015 - p460(1) [51-500]
  y HB Guide - v26 - i2 - Fall 2015 - p132(1) [51-500]
  y KR - Feb 1 2015 - pNA [51-500]
  y PW - v262 - i6 - Feb 9 2015 - p70(1) [51-500]
  SLJ - v61 - i2 - Feb 2015 - p106(1) [51-500]
  y VOYA - v37 - i6 - Feb 2015 - p61(2) [51-500]

Moore, Michael F. - *Agostino*
  TLS - i5869 - Sept 25 2015 - p13(1) [501+]

Moore, Michele - *The Cigar Factory*
  KR - Nov 15 2015 - pNA [51-500]

Moore, Mike - *Dragons and Hot Sauce and Other Imaginations* (Illus. by Young, Andy)
  c CH Bwatch - April 2015 - pNA [51-500]

Moore, Nancy Jane - *The Weave*
  PW - v262 - i22 - June 1 2015 - p45(2) [51-500]

Moore, Naoko Takei - *Donabe: Classic and Modern Japanese Clay Pot Cooking*
  LJ - v140 - i16 - Oct 1 2015 - p102(1) [51-500]

Moore, Nicole - *Censorship and the Limits of the Literary: A Global View*
  TLS - i5873 - Oct 23 2015 - p26(2) [501+]

Moore, Peter - *The Weather Experiment: The Pioneers Who Sought to See the Future*
  NYTBR - July 19 2015 - p1(L) [501+]
  BL - v111 - i17 - May 1 2015 - p67(1) [501+]
  Ch Today - v59 - i8 - Oct 2015 - p74(1) [51-500]
  KR - April 15 2015 - pNA [501+]
  Nature - v521 - i7550 - May 7 2015 - p31(1) [51-500]
  PW - v262 - i17 - April 27 2015 - p64(1) [51-500]
  Spec - v328 - i9749 - July 4 2015 - p40(1) [51-500]
  TLS - i5851 - May 22 2015 - p13(1) [501+]

Moore, Peter (b. 1983-) - *The Story of the British and Their Weather*
  TLS - i5851 - May 22 2015 - p13(1) [501+]

Moore, Phyllis - *Pegasus Colony*
  PW - v262 - i5 - Feb 2 2015 - p41(1) [51-500]

Moore, Rebecca - *Women in Christian Traditions*
  CHR - v101 - i4 - Autumn 2015 - p890(2) [501+]

Moore, Richard O. - *Particulars of Place*
  PW - v262 - i11 - March 16 2015 - p62(1) [51-500]

Moore, Ronnie - *Folk Healing and Health Care Practices in Britain and Ireland: Stethoscopes, Wands and Crystals*
  JRAI - v21 - i2 - June 2015 - p479(2) [501+]

Moore, Russell - *This Is Camino*
  LJ - v140 - i17 - Oct 15 2015 - p109(2) [51-500]
  PW - v262 - i29 - July 20 2015 - p183(1) [51-500]

Moore, Saiphin - *Rosa's Thai Cafe*
  BL - v111 - i17 - May 1 2015 - p68(1) [51-500]
  LJ - v140 - i9 - May 15 2015 - p102(2) [51-500]

Moore, Sandra - *The Peace Tree from Hiroshima* (Illus. by Wilds, Kazumi)
  c CH Bwatch - August 2015 - pNA [51-500]
The Peace Tree from Hiroshima: The Little Bonsai with a Big Story (Illus. by Wilds, Kazumi)
  c PW - v262 - i18 - May 4 2015 - p119(1) [51-500]
  c SLJ - v61 - i8 - August 2015 - p123(1) [51-500]

Moore, Sarah J. - *Empire on Display: San Francisco's Panama-Pacific International Exposition of 1915*
  HNet - April 2015 - pNA [501+]

Moore, Shannon Baker - *King Tut's Tomb*
  y HB Guide - v26 - i1 - Spring 2015 - p200(2) [51-500]

Moore, Stephanie - *Sharp Sisters Series*
  c HB Guide - v26 - i1 - Spring 2015 - p117(1) [51-500]

Moore, Stephanie Perry - *Back That Thing*
  y SLJ - v61 - i5 - May 2015 - p122(1) [51-500]
Feel Real Good
  y HB Guide - v26 - i2 - Fall 2015 - p132(1) [51-500]
Give It Up
  BL - v111 - i14 - March 15 2015 - p65(2) [51-500]
  y PW - v262 - i14 - April 6 2015 - p60(1) [51-500]
  y SLJ - v61 - i5 - May 2015 - p122(1) [51-500]
On Your Knees
  y HB Guide - v26 - i2 - Fall 2015 - p132(1) [51-500]
  y SLJ - v61 - i5 - May 2015 - p122(1) [51-500]

Moore, Stephen L. - *Texas Rising*
  LJ - v140 - i6 - April 1 2015 - p102(2) [51-500]

Moore, Stephen T. - *Bootleggers and Borders: The Paradox of Prohibition on a Canada-U.S. Borderland*
  JAH - v102 - i2 - Sept 2015 - p591-591 [501+]

Moore, Susanna - *Paradise of the Pacific: Approaching Hawaii*
  BL - v111 - i21 - July 1 2015 - p20(1) [51-500]
  LJ - v140 - i10 - June 1 2015 - p113(1) [51-500]
  NY - v91 - i32 - Oct 19 2015 - p88 [51-500]
  NYRB - v62 - i19 - Dec 3 2015 - p47(3) [501+]
  NYT - Sept 22 2015 - pC1(L) [501+]
  NYTBR - August 30 2015 - p17(L) [501+]
  PW - v262 - i22 - June 1 2015 - p45(1) [51-500]

Moore, Suzi - *Whoops!* (Illus. by Ayto, Russell)
  c KR - Dec 1 2015 - pNA [51-500]
  c PW - v262 - i46 - Nov 16 2015 - p74(1) [51-500]

Moore, Tim - *Gironimo! Riding the Very Terrible 1914 Tour of Italy*
  NYTBR - May 31 2015 - p30(L) [501+]
  BL - v111 - i14 - March 15 2015 - p40(1) [51-500]
  Bwatch - July 2015 - pNA [51-500]

Moore, Wendy - *How to Create the Perfect Wife: Britain's Most Ineligible Bachelor and His Enlightened Quest to Train the Ideal Mate*
  Historian - v77 - i1 - Spring 2015 - p180(2) [501+]

Moore, Wes - *This Way Home*
  y BL - v112 - i5 - Nov 1 2015 - p58(1) [51-500]
  y KR - Sept 15 2015 - pNA [51-500]
  y PW - v262 - i35 - August 31 2015 - p95(1) [51-500]
  y SLJ - v61 - i10 - Oct 2015 - p114(2) [51-500]
The Work: My Search for a Life That Matters (Read by Moore, Wes). Audiobook Review
  LJ - v140 - i9 - May 15 2015 - p45(1) [51-500]

Moorehead, Alan - *Gallipoli*
  Spec - v327 - i9736 - April 4 2015 - p32(2) [501+]
  Lon R Bks - v37 - i10 - May 21 2015 - p39(3) [501+]

Moorehead, Caroline - *Dancing to the Precipice: Lucie De La Tour Du Pin and the French Revolution*
  CWS - v30 - i2-3 - Fall-Winter 2015 - p129(3) [501+]

Moorhouse, Roger - *The Devils' Alliance: Hitler's Pact with Stalin, 1939-1941*
  HNet - Jan 2015 - pNA [501+]
  J Mil H - v79 - i2 - April 2015 - p521-522 [501+]
  NYRB - v62 - i7 - April 23 2015 - p30(2) [501+]
  Parameters - v45 - i1 - Spring 2015 - p170(2) [501+]

Moorhouse, Tom - *The Adventures of Mr. Toad* (Illus. by Roberts, David)
  c Sch Lib - v63 - i1 - Spring 2015 - p30(1) [51-500]

Moosa, Ebrahim - *Modern Islamic Thought in a Radical Age: Religious Authority and Internal Criticism*
  JAAR - v83 - i2 - June 2015 - p569-572 [501+]

Moosbrugger, Mathias - *Die Rehabilitierung des Opfers: Zum Dialog zwischen Rene Girard und Raymund Schwager um die Zentralinhalte des Opfers im christlichen Kontext*
  Theol St - v76 - i1 - March 2015 - p192(2) [501+]

Mora, G. Cristina - *Making Hispanics: How Activists, Bureaucrats, and Media Constructed a New American*
  AJS - v120 - i5 - March 2015 - p1548(3) [501+]
  Aztlan - v40 - i1 - Spring 2015 - p265-269 [501+]
  RAH - v43 - i3 - Sept 2015 - p550-556 [501+]

Mora, Pat - *A Birthday Basket for Tia* (Illus. by Lang, Cecily)
  c BL - v111 - i9-10 - Jan 1 2015 - pS18(5) [501+]
Bravo, Chico Canta! Bravo! (Illus. by Carling, Amelia Lau)
  c Bkbird - v53 - i1 - Wntr 2015 - p9(1) [501+]
I Pledge Allegiance (Illus. by Barton, Patrice)
  c SLJ - v61 - i12 - Dec 2015 - p64(4) [501+]
The Remembering Day / El Dia de Los Muertos (Illus. by Casilla, Robert)
  c CH Bwatch - Nov 2015 - pNA [51-500]
The Remembering Day / El Dia de Los Muertos
  c KR - Sept 1 2015 - pNA [51-500]
Water Rolls, Water Rises / El agua rueda, el agua sube (Illus. by So, Meilo)
  c BL - v111 - i9-10 - Jan 1 2015 - pS4(8) [501+]
  c HB Guide - v26 - i1 - Spring 2015 - p189(1) [51-500]

Morabia, Alfredo - *Enigmas of Health and Disease: How Epidemiology Helps Unravel Scientific Mysteries*
  QRB - v90 - i3 - Sept 2015 - p352(2) [501+]

Moracho, Cristina - *Althea & Oliver*
  y CCB-B - v68 - i5 - Jan 2015 - p270(1) [51-500]
  y HB Guide - v26 - i1 - Spring 2015 - p118(1) [51-500]

Morais, Fernando - *The Last Soldiers of the Cold War: The Story of the Cuban Five*
  LJ - v140 - i9 - May 15 2015 - p96(1) [51-500]

Moral als Kapital in Antiken Gesellschaften
  HNet - Feb 2015 - pNA [501+]

Morales Dominguez, Esteban - *Race in Cuba: Essays on the Revolution and Racial Inequality*
  S&S - v79 - i3 - July 2015 - p477-480 [501+]

Morales, Jennifer - *Meet Me Halfway: Milwaukee Stories*
  RVBW - May 2015 - pNA [501+]

Morales, Oscar Recio - *Redes de nacion y espacios de poder. La Comunidad irlandesa en Espana y la America Espanola, 1600-1825*
  HER - v130 - i544 - June 2015 - p753(3) [501+]

Morales, Yuyi - *Nino Wrestles the World* (Read by Sananes, Adriana). Audiobook Review
  c SLJ - v61 - i8 - August 2015 - p48(1) [51-500]
Viva Frida (Illus. by O'Meara, Tim)
  c HB Guide - v26 - i1 - Spring 2015 - p179(1) [51-500]

Moran, Jan - *Scent of Triumph*
  BL - v111 - i13 - March 1 2015 - p28(1) [51-500]

Moran, Kelly - *All of Me*
  PW - v262 - i29 - July 20 2015 - p176(1) [51-500]
Return to Me
  BL - v111 - i12 - Feb 15 2015 - p44(1) [51-500]
  KR - Jan 15 2015 - pNA [501+]
  PW - v262 - i1 - Jan 5 2015 - p57(1) [51-500]

Moran, Martin - *Atlanta's Living Legacy: A History of Grady Memorial Hospital and Its People*
  JSH - v81 - i1 - Feb 2015 - p224(2) [501+]

Moran, Michelle - *Rebel Queen*
  BL - v111 - i12 - Feb 15 2015 - p41(1) [51-500]

Moran, Rachel - *Paid For: My Journey through Prostitution*
  BL - v112 - i1 - Sept 1 2015 - p19(1) [51-500]
  KR - June 1 2015 - pNA [501+]
  LJ - v140 - i13 - August 1 2015 - p115(1) [51-500]
  New R - v246 - i9-10 - Sept-Oct 2015 - p73(5) [501+]
  NY - v91 - i32 - Oct 19 2015 - p88 [51-500]
  NYTBR - Sept 13 2015 - p12(L) [501+]

Moran, Victoria - *The Good Karma Diet: Eat Gently, Feel Amazing, Age in Slow Motion*
  LJ - v140 - i8 - May 1 2015 - p94(1) [51-500]
  PW - v262 - i16 - April 20 2015 - p72(1) [51-500]

Morana, Mabel - *Arguedas/Vargas Llosa: Dilemas y ensamblajes*
  Hisp R - v83 - i3 - Summer 2015 - p367-370 [501+]

Morand, Paul - *The Man in a Hurry*
  KR - July 1 2015 - pNA [501+]
  PW - v262 - i30 - July 27 2015 - p36(1) [51-500]
  TLS - i5857 - July 3 2015 - p20(1) [501+]

Moranda, Scott - *The People's Own Landscape: Nature, Tourism, and Dictatorship in East Germany*
  CEH - v48 - i1 - March 2015 - p142-142 [501+]

More, Anna - *Baroque Sovereignty: Carlos De Siguenza Y Gongora and the Creole Archive of Colonial Mexico*
  Comp L - v67 - i2 - June 2015 - p228-232 [501+]

More, Nicholas D. - *Nietzsche's Last Laugh: Ecce Homo as Satire*
    MLN - v130 - i3 - April 2015 - p679-682 [501+]

Moreau, A. Scott - *Effective Intercultural Communication: A Christian Perspective*
    IBMR - v39 - i3 - July 2015 - p160(1) [501+]

Moreau, Gary - *Understanding China: There Is Reason for the Difference*
    KR - Jan 1 2016 - pNA [501+]

Moreau, J.M. - *Eschatological Subjects: Divine and Literary Judgment in Fourteenth-Century French Poetry*
    Med R - Sept 2015 - pNA [501+]

Moreau, Laurent - *My Wild Family (Illus. by Moreau, Laurent)*
    c KR - August 15 2015 - pNA [51-500]
    c PW - v262 - i39 - Sept 28 2015 - p88(1) [51-500]
    c SLJ - v61 - i10 - Oct 2015 - p80(2) [51-500]

Morel, Olivier - *Walking Wounded: Uncut Stories from Iraq (Illus. by Mael)*
    BL - v112 - i4 - Oct 15 2015 - p36(1) [51-500]

Morell, Michael - *The Great War of Our Time: The CIA's Fight against Terrorism from al Qa'ida to ISIS*
    CSM - May 12 2015 - pNA [501+]
    Nat R - v67 - i12 - July 6 2015 - p44 [501+]
    Parameters - v45 - i2 - Summer 2015 - p122(3) [501+]

Morell, Sally Fallon - *Nourishing Broth: An Old-Fashioned Remedy for the Modern World*
    LJ - v140 - i3 - Feb 15 2015 - p123(1) [51-500]

Morellet, Andre - *Memoires sur le XVIIIe siecle et sur la Revolution*
    MLR - v110 - i1 - Jan 2015 - p261-262 [501+]

Morelli, Laura - *Venice: A Travel Guide to Murano Glass, Carnival Masks, Gondolas, Lace, Paper, and More*
    PW - v262 - i17 - April 27 2015 - p67(1) [51-500]

Morelli, Licia - *The Lemonade Hurricane: A Story about Mindfulness and Meditation (Illus. by Morris, Jennifer E.)*
    c KR - June 15 2015 - pNA [51-500]
    c PW - v262 - i22 - June 1 2015 - p58(1) [51-500]

Morello, Gustavo - *The Catholic Church and Argentina's Dirty War*
    Comw - v142 - i16 - Oct 9 2015 - p38(2) [501+]

Moreno, Alvaro - *Biological Autonomy: A Philosophical and Theoretical Inquiry*
    RM - v69 - i2 - Dec 2015 - p402(2) [501+]

Moreno-Garcia, Silvia - *Signal to Noise*
    PW - v262 - i1 - Jan 5 2015 - p55(1) [51-500]

Moreno, Jonathan D. - *Progress in Bioethics: Science, Policy and Politics*
    CS - v44 - i1 - Jan 2015 - p94-96 [501+]

Moreno-Luzon, Javier - *Modernizing the Nation: Spain during the Reign of Alfonso XIII, 1902-1931*
    JMH - v87 - i2 - June 2015 - p474(2) [501+]

Moreno, Marisel C. - *Family Matters: Puerto Rican Women Authors on the Island and the Mainland*
    MFSF - v61 - i3 - Fall 2015 - p559-562 [501+]

Morent, Stefan - *Das Mittelalter im 19. Jahrhundert: Ein Beitrag zur Kompositionsgeschichte in Frankreich*
    Notes - v71 - i4 - June 2015 - p692(3) [501+]

Morenzoni, Franco - *Preaching and Political Society: From Late Antiquity to the End of the Middle Ages / Depuis l'Antiquite tardive jusqu'a la fin du Moyen*
    Med R - Feb 2015 - pNA [501+]

Moresco, Antonio - *Distant Light*
    KR - Dec 15 2015 - pNA [51-500]

Moretta, Alison - *Harriet Beecher Stowe and the Abolitionist Movement*
    y BL - v111 - i9-10 - Jan 1 2015 - p85(1) [501+]

Moretti, Franco - *Distant Reading*
    Nation - v300 - i22 - June 1 2015 - p28(6) [501+]

Morey, Allan - *Birds*
    c HB Guide - v26 - i1 - Spring 2015 - p162(1) [51-500]
Camels Are Awesome!
    c BL - v112 - i3 - Oct 1 2015 - p64(2) [51-500]
Insects
    c HB Guide - v26 - i1 - Spring 2015 - p159(1) [51-500]
A Timeline History of the Declaration of Independence
    c HB Guide - v26 - i2 - Fall 2015 - p220(1) [51-500]
A Timeline History of the Early American Republic
    c BL - v111 - i15 - April 1 2015 - p62(1) [51-500]
    c HB Guide - v26 - i2 - Fall 2015 - p220(1) [51-500]

Morgan, Alex - *Breakaway: Beyond the Goal*
    y BL - v112 - i1 - Sept 1 2015 - p98(1) [51-500]
    y SLJ - v61 - i8 - August 2015 - p128(2) [51-500]
    y VOYA - v38 - i3 - August 2015 - p87(1) [51-500]

Morgan, Angie - *Shouty Arthur*
    c Sch Lib - v63 - i1 - Spring 2015 - p30(2) [51-500]

Morgan, Ann - *Beside Myself*
    BL - v112 - i4 - Oct 15 2015 - p31(1) [51-500]
    KR - Oct 1 2015 - pNA [51-500]
    LJ - v140 - i16 - Oct 1 2015 - p71(1) [51-500]
    PW - v262 - i41 - Oct 12 2015 - p47(1) [51-500]
Reading the World: Confessions of Literary Explorer
    NS - v144 - i5249 - Feb 13 2015 - p55(1) [51-500]
    Spec - v327 - i9731 - Feb 28 2015 - p41(2) [501+]
The World between Two Covers: Reading the Globe
    BL - v111 - i15 - April 1 2015 - p13(1) [51-500]
    LJ - v140 - i6 - April 1 2015 - p90(1) [51-500]
    NYTBR - August 23 2015 - p38(L) [501+]
    KR - Feb 1 2015 - pNA [501+]
    PW - v262 - i7 - Feb 16 2015 - p168(1) [51-500]

Morgan, Ben - *On Becoming God: Late Medieval Mysticism and the Modern Western Self*
    MLR - v110 - i1 - Jan 2015 - p224-225 [501+]
    MLR - v110 - i2 - April 2015 - p617-619 [501+]

Morgan, Bill - *I Greet You at the Beginning of a Great Career: The Selected Correspondence of Lawrence Ferlinghetti and Allen Ginsberg, 1955-1997*
    PW - v262 - i17 - April 27 2015 - p66(2) [51-500]

Morgan-Cole, Trudy J. - *A Sudden Sun*
    RVBW - April 2015 - pNA [51-500]

Morgan, Edwin - *The Midnight Letterbox: Selected Letters 1950-2010*
    TLS - i5863 - August 14 2015 - p21(1) [501+]

Morgan, Emily - *Next Time You See a Maple Seed*
    c Sci & Ch - v52 - i6 - Feb 2015 - p76 [51-500]

Morgan, Emily Kathryn - *Street Life in London: Context and Commentary*
    HT - v65 - i4 - April 2015 - p59(1) [501+]

Morgan, G.A. - *Chantarelle*
    c KR - May 15 2015 - pNA [51-500]
    y VOYA - v38 - i3 - August 2015 - p82(1) [51-500]

Morgan, George - *Global Islamophobia: Muslims and Moral Panic in the West*
    CS - v44 - i1 - Jan 2015 - p96-98 [501+]

Morgan, George G. - *How to Do Everything: Genealogy, 4th ed.*
    Bwatch - May 2015 - pNA [51-500]

Morgan, James G. - *Into New Territory: American Historians and the Concept of US Imperialism*
    AHR - v120 - i3 - June 2015 - p1063-1064 [501+]
    J Am St - v49 - i3 - August 2015 - p649-651 [501+]
    JAH - v102 - i2 - Sept 2015 - p510-510 [501+]

Morgan, Jeff - *The Covenant Kitchen: Food and Wine for the New Jewish Table*
    LJ - v140 - i5 - March 15 2015 - p128(1) [51-500]

Morgan, Jessica - *The Royal We*
    LJ - v140 - i5 - March 15 2015 - p91(1) [51-500]
    VOYA - v38 - i3 - August 2015 - p10(2) [51-500]

Morgan, Kass - *Day 21*
    y HB Guide - v26 - i1 - Spring 2015 - p118(1) [51-500]

Morgan, Keith N. - *Community by Design: The Olmsted Form and the Development of Brookline, Massachusetts*
    T&C - v56 - i2 - April 2015 - p544-545 [501+]

Morgan, Marcyliena H. - *Speech communities*
    Lang Soc - v44 - i2 - April 2015 - p273-276 [501+]

Morgan, Max - *Black Ice*
    KR - May 15 2015 - pNA [501+]

Morgan, Michaela - *Respect: The Walter Tull Story*
    y Sch Lib - v63 - i1 - Spring 2015 - p60(1) [51-500]

Morgan, Michelle - *The Ice Cream Blonde: The Whirlwind Life and Mysterious Death of Screwball Comedienne Thelma Todd*
    BL - v112 - i5 - Nov 1 2015 - p21(1) [51-500]
The Mammoth Book of Madonna
    LJ - v140 - i10 - June 1 2015 - p105(1) [51-500]

Morgan, Page - *The Wondrous and the Wicked*
    y HB Guide - v26 - i2 - Fall 2015 - p132(1) [51-500]
    y KR - Feb 1 2015 - pNA [51-500]
    SLJ - v61 - i2 - Feb 2015 - p106(1) [51-500]
    y VOYA - v37 - i6 - Feb 2015 - p81(2) [51-500]

Morgan, Rhys - *The Welsh and the Shaping of Early Modern Ireland*
    Sev Cent N - v73 - i3-4 - Fall-Winter 2015 - p143(5) [501+]

Morgan, Richard - *Thirteen*
    LJ - v140 - i19 - Nov 15 2015 - p110(1) [51-500]

Morgan, Robert - *Dark Energy*
    LJ - v140 - i8 - May 1 2015 - p77(2) [51-500]

Morgan, Robert P. - *Becoming Heinrich Schenker: Music Theory and Ideology*
    Notes - v72 - i2 - Dec 2015 - p391(2) [501+]

Morgan, Ruthie - *Skylark*
    KR - July 15 2015 - pNA [501+]

Morgan, Sally - *Flying High (Illus. by Smith, Craig)*
    c Magpies - v30 - i3 - July 2015 - p32(1) [501+]
Magpie Learns a Lesson (Illus. by Erzinger, Tania)
    c Magpies - v30 - i1 - March 2015 - p27(2) [501+]
The Memory Shed (Illus. by Smith, Craig)
    c Magpies - v30 - i1 - March 2015 - p31(1) [501+]
Sister Heart
    y Magpies - v30 - i4 - Sept 2015 - p43(1) [501+]
Where Is Galah?
    c Magpies - v30 - i2 - May 2015 - p30(1) [501+]

Morgan, Sarah - *First Time in Forever*
    BL - v111 - i11 - Feb 1 2015 - p30(1) [51-500]
    KR - Jan 15 2015 - pNA [51-500]

Morgan, Victoria - *The Daughter of an Earl*
    PW - v262 - i20 - May 18 2015 - p71(2) [51-500]

Morgan, Winifred - *The Trickster Figure in American Literature*
    SAH - v4 - i2 - Dec 15 2015 - p303-308 [501+]

Morgenstern, Erin - *The Night Circus*
    LJ - v140 - i6 - April 1 2015 - p119(1) [501+]

Morgenstern, Matthias - *Gerholm Scholem in Deutschland: Zwischen Seelenverwandtschaft und Sprachlosigkeit*
    TLS - i5845 - April 10 2015 - p27(1) [501+]

Morgridge, Carrie - *Every Gift Matters: How Your Passion Can Change the World*
    PW - v262 - i13 - March 30 2015 - p67(1) [51-500]
    RVBW - June 2015 - pNA [501+]

Mori, Toshio - *Yokohama, California*
    KR - Jan 15 2015 - pNA [51-500]

Morial, Sybil Haydel - *Witness to Change*
    KR - June 15 2015 - pNA [501+]

Moriarty, Donald Peter, II - *A Fine Body of Men: The Orleans Light Horse Louisiana Cavalry, 1861-1865*
    JSH - v81 - i4 - Nov 2015 - p1055(1) [51-500]

Moriarty, Jaclyn - *A Tangle of Gold*
    y KR - Dec 15 2015 - pNA [51-500]

Moriarty, Liane - *Big Little Lies (Read by Lee, Caroline). Audiobook Review*
    BL - v111 - i11 - Feb 1 2015 - p58(1) [51-500]
    LJ - v140 - i5 - March 15 2015 - p134(1) [501+]

Moricz, Klara - *Funeral Games in Honor of Arthur Vincent Lourie*
    MT - v156 - i1930 - Spring 2015 - p107-111 [501+]

Moriggi, Marco - *A Corpus of Syriac Incantation Bowls: Syriac Magical Texts from Late-Antique Mesopotamia*
    JNES - v74 - i2 - Oct 2015 - p361(3) [501+]

Morimoto, Junko - *My Hiroshima*
    y Magpies - v30 - i1 - March 2015 - p33(1) [501+]

Morin, Christopher - *A Tale of Life & War*
    KR - Sept 15 2015 - pNA [51-500]

Morin, Frank - *Set in Stone: The Petralist*
    SPBW - July 2015 - pNA [51-500]

Morin, Tomas Q. - *Canto General, Canto II, The Heights of Macchu Picchu*
    APR - v44 - i6 - Nov-Dec 2015 - p33(3) [501+]

Moritz, Isenmann - *Merkantilismus: Wiederaufnahme einer Debatte*
    HNet - March 2015 - pNA [501+]
    HNet - Feb 2015 - pNA [501+]

Moriyama, Takeshi - *Crossing Boundaries in Tokugawa Society: Suzuki Bokushi, a Rural Elite Commoner*
    AHR - v120 - i4 - Oct 2015 - p1467(1) [501+]

Morlan, Robert - *The Atheism That Saved Me*
    RVBW - Nov 2015 - pNA [51-500]

Morley, Morris H. - *Reagan and Pinochet: The Struggle over U.S. Policy toward Chile*
    HNet - August 2015 - pNA [501+]

Morley, Neville - *Thucydides and the Idea of History*
    Class R - v65 - i2 - Oct 2015 - p347-349 [501+]

Morofsky, Scott A. - *The Daily Breath: Transform Your Life One Breath at a Time*
    SPBW - Nov 2015 - pNA [51-500]

Moroney, Shannon - *Through the Glass*
    Ant R - v73 - i1 - Wntr 2015 - p188(2) [501+]

Moroni, Lisa - *Watch Out for the Crocodile (Illus. by Eriksson, Eva)*
    c HB Guide - v26 - i1 - Spring 2015 - p40(1) [51-500]

Morpurgo, Michael - *Half a Man (Illus. by O'Callaghan, Gemma)*
    c BL - v111 - i12 - Feb 15 2015 - p86(1) [51-500]
    c HB Guide - v26 - i2 - Fall 2015 - p95(1) [51-500]
    c Sch Lib - v63 - i1 - Spring 2015 - p40(1) [51-500]
Listen to the Moon
    c BL - v112 - i1 - Sept 1 2015 - p105(1) [51-500]
    c KR - July 15 2015 - pNA [51-500]
    c Sch Lib - v63 - i1 - Spring 2015 - p40(1) [51-500]
    c SLJ - v61 - i9 - Sept 2015 - p143(1) [51-500]

328 • MORREALE Book Review Index 2016 Cumulation

Morreale, Marie - *Pharrell Williams*
c BL - v111 - i19-20 - June 1 2015 - p90(2) [51-500]
Morreale, P. - *Bullpen*
Roundup M - v23 - i1 - Oct 2015 - p31(1) [501+]
Morrell, David - *Inspector of the Dead*
BL - v111 - i11 - Feb 1 2015 - p27(1) [51-500]
KR - Jan 15 2015 - pNA [51-500]
PW - v262 - i2 - Jan 12 2015 - p39(1) [51-500]
y SLJ - v61 - i12 - Dec 2015 - p132(1) [51-500]
Morretta, Alison - *F. Scott Fitzgerald and the Jazz Age*
y BL - v111 - i9-10 - Jan 1 2015 - p85(1) [501+]
Morrill, Lauren - *The Trouble with Destiny*
y BL - v112 - i5 - Nov 1 2015 - p51(1) [51-500]
y KR - Sept 15 2015 - pNA [51-500]
y PW - v262 - i39 - Sept 28 2015 - p93(1) [51-500]
y SLJ - v61 - i11 - Nov 2015 - p119(2) [51-500]
Morris, Aldon D. - *The Scholar Denied: W.E.B. Du Bois and the Birth of Modern Sociology*
KR - June 1 2015 - pNA [501+]
LJ - v140 - i10 - June 1 2015 - p124(2) [51-500]
PW - v262 - i19 - May 11 2015 - p47(1) [51-500]
Morris, Bob - *Bobby Wonderful: An Imperfect Son Buries His Parents*
BL - v111 - i14 - March 15 2015 - p28(1) [51-500]
KR - March 15 2015 - pNA [51-500]
NYTBR - June 21 2015 - p26(L) [501+]
PW - v262 - i14 - April 6 2015 - p51(1) [51-500]
Morris, Catherine - *Judith Scott: Bound and Unbound*
LJ - v140 - i2 - Feb 1 2015 - p85(1) [501+]
Morris, Chris - *Los Lobos: Dream in Blue*
BL - v111 - i22 - August 1 2015 - p16(1) [51-500]
KR - July 1 2015 - pNA [501+]
Morris, Christopher - *Modernism and the Cult of Mountains: Music, Opera, Cinema*
GSR - v38 - i1 - Feb 2015 - p194-196 [501+]
Morris, D.C. - *And Then the Hawk Said ...*
KR - July 1 2015 - pNA [51-500]
Morris, Daniel - *Understanding and Overcoming Temptation*
SPBW - July 2015 - pNA [501+]
Morris, David J. - *The Evil Hours: A Biography of Post-Traumatic Stress Disorder (Read by Chamberlain, Mike). Audiobook Review*
LJ - v140 - i9 - May 15 2015 - p45(1) [51-500]
The Evil Hours: A Biography of Post-Traumatic Stress Disorder
BL - v111 - i9-10 - Jan 1 2015 - p28(1) [51-500]
NWCR - v68 - i3 - Summer 2015 - p151(3) [501+]
NYTBR - Feb 22 2015 - p18(L) [501+]
TLS - i5859 - July 17 2015 - p7(2) [501+]
Morris, Desmond - *Bison*
TLS - i5871 - Oct 9 2015 - p31(1) [501+]
Morris, Edd - *Exploring English Castles*
BL - v111 - i18 - May 15 2015 - p15(1) [51-500]
Morris, Edward L. - *Wall Streeters: The Creators and Corruptors of American Finance*
PW - v262 - i35 - August 31 2015 - p80(1) [51-500]
Morris, Edward W. - *Learning the Hard Way: Masculinity, Place, and the Gender Gap in Education*
CS - v44 - i1 - Jan 2015 - p98-100 [501+]
SF - v94 - i2 - Dec 2015 - pNA [501+]
Morris, Eric - *Jacob Jump*
KR - June 15 2015 - pNA [51-500]
Morris, Frances - *Agnes Martin*
TLS - i5867 - Sept 11 2015 - p17(3) [501+]
Morris, Harold C. - *Seven Tales for the Seven Dark Seas*
KR - May 15 2015 - pNA [501+]
Morris, Ian - *Foragers, Farmers, and Fossil Fuels: How Human Values Evolve*
Hum - v75 - i6 - Nov-Dec 2015 - p44(2) [501+]
TLS - i5874 - Oct 30 2015 - p12(1) [501+]
KR - Feb 15 2015 - pNA [501+]
War! What Is It Good For? Conflict and the Progress of Civilization from Primates to Robots
Reason - v47 - i3 - July 2015 - p62(6) [501+]
Morris, J. Brent - *Oberlin, Hotbed of Abolitionism: College, Community, and the Fight for Freedom and Equality in Antebellum America*
AHR - v120 - i4 - Oct 2015 - p1491-1492 [501+]
JAH - v102 - i1 - June 2015 - p243-244 [501+]
Morris, Jackie - *Something about a Bear*
c Sch Lib - v63 - i1 - Spring 2015 - p32(1) [51-500]
Morris, James McGrath - *Eye on the Struggle: Ethel Payne, the First Lady of the Black Press*
BL - v111 - i11 - Feb 1 2015 - p14(1) [501+]
BL - v111 - i19-20 - June 1 2015 - p27(1) [501+]
LJ - v140 - i2 - Feb 1 2015 - p90(1) [501+]
NYT - Feb 13 2015 - pC27(L) [501+]
NYTBR - April 5 2015 - p14(L) [501+]
Wom R Bks - v32 - i4 - July-August 2015 - p29(3) [501+]
Morris, Jan - *Ciao, Carpaccio! An Infatuation*
TLS - i5840 - March 6 2015 - p31(1) [501+]
Morris, Jayne - *Burnout to Brilliance: Strategies for Sustainable Success*
RVBW - May 2015 - pNA [51-500]
Morris, Jeannie - *Behind the Smile: A Story of Carol Moseley Braun's Historic Senate Campaign*
KR - August 1 2015 - pNA [501+]
PW - v262 - i31 - August 3 2015 - p49(2) [51-500]
Morris, Jeremy - *The Informal Post-Socialist Economy: Embedded Practices and Livelihoods*
E-A St - v67 - i3 - May 2015 - p503(2) [501+]
Mastering Chaos: The Metafictional Worlds of Evgeny Popov
MLR - v110 - i1 - Jan 2015 - p310-312 [501+]
Morris, Jessica L. - *Dewdrops*
SPBW - June 2015 - pNA [51-500]
Morris, Keith Lee - *Travelers Rest*
KR - Nov 1 2015 - pNA [51-500]
LJ - v140 - i19 - Nov 15 2015 - p78(2) [51-500]
PW - v262 - i42 - Oct 19 2015 - p60(1) [51-500]
Morris, Kerry - *Are We There Yeti? (Illus. by Freshley, Taylor)*
c CH Bwatch - August 2015 - pNA [51-500]
Morris, Leon - *Homage to New Orleans*
New Or - v49 - i11 - August 2015 - p42(1) [501+]
Morris, M. Michelle Jarrett - *Under Household Government: Sex and Family in Puritan Massachusetts*
W&M Q - v72 - i3 - July 2015 - p517-522 [501+]
Morris, Marc - *A Great and Terrible King: Edward I and the Forging of Britain*
LJ - v140 - i2 - Feb 1 2015 - p94(2) [51-500]
PW - v262 - i2 - Jan 12 2015 - p50(1) [51-500]
King John: Treachery and Tyranny in Medieval England: The Road to Magna Carta
KR - July 1 2015 - pNA [51-500]
LJ - v140 - i14 - Sept 1 2015 - p118(1) [51-500]
PW - v262 - i29 - July 20 2015 - p178(1) [51-500]
King John: Treachery, Tyranny and the Road to Magna Carta
Spec - v327 - i9737 - April 11 2015 - p47(1) [501+]
HT - v65 - i6 - June 2015 - p56(2) [501+]
TLS - i5854 - June 12 2015 - p9(1) [501+]
Morris, Mary - *Between You and Me: Confessions of a Comma Queen*
BL - v111 - i14 - March 15 2015 - p34(1) [51-500]
The Jazz Palace
BL - v111 - i16 - April 15 2015 - p36(1) [51-500]
KR - Feb 15 2015 - pNA [51-500]
NYTBR - June 7 2015 - p38(L) [501+]
Morris, Michelle Jarrett - *Under Household Government: Sex and Family in Puritan Massachusetts*
Historian - v77 - i1 - Spring 2015 - p132(3) [501+]
Morris, Nicholas - *Capital Failure: Rebuilding Trust in Financial Services*
TLS - i5845 - April 10 2015 - p28(1) [501+]
Morris, Paula - *The Eternal City*
y BL - v111 - i18 - May 15 2015 - p61(1) [51-500]
y HB Guide - v26 - i2 - Fall 2015 - p133(1) [51-500]
y SLJ - v61 - i3 - March 2015 - p140(2) [51-500]
c VOYA - v38 - i1 - April 2015 - p81(1) [51-500]
Morris, Peter J.T. - *The Matter Factory: A History of the Chemistry Laboratory*
Nature - v521 - i7553 - May 28 2015 - p422(1) [501+]
TimHES - i2213 - July 23 2015 - p44-45 [501+]
Morris, Richard T. - *Ceci est un orignal (Illus. by Lichtenheld, Tom)*
c Res Links - v20 - i5 - June 2015 - p41(2) [51-500]
Morris, Roy, Jr. - *American Vandal: Mark Twain Abroad*
KR - Jan 15 2015 - pNA [501+]
LJ - v140 - i5 - March 15 2015 - p101(1) [501+]
TLS - i5854 - June 12 2015 - p24(1) [501+]
Morris, Sandra - *Discovering New Zealand Trees*
Magpies - v30 - i4 - Sept 2015 - pS8(1) [501+]
Welcome to New Zealand: A Nature Journal (Illus. by Morris, Sandra)
c BL - v112 - i7 - Dec 1 2015 - p51(1) [51-500]
c SLJ - v61 - i12 - Dec 2015 - p138(1) [51-500]
Morris, Susana M. - *Close Kin and Distant Relatives: The Paradox of Respectability in Black Women's Literature*
Callaloo - v38 - i1 - Wntr 2015 - p222-225 [501+]
Morris, Sylvia Jukes - *Price of Fame: The Honorable Clare Boothe Luce*
NYTBR - May 3 2015 - p28(L) [501+]
Morris, Theresa - *Cut It Out: The C-Section Epidemic in America*
AJS - v120 - i5 - March 2015 - p1583(3) [501+]
CS - v44 - i3 - May 2015 - p385-387 [501+]
Morris, Thomas - *We Don't Know What We're Doing*
TLS - i5854 - June 12 2015 - p12(1) [501+]
TLS - i5864-5865 - August 21 2015 - p22(1) [501+]
Morris, Tisha - *Decorating with the Five Elements of Feng Shui*
PW - v262 - i29 - July 20 2015 - p185(1) [51-500]
PW - v262 - i29 - July 20 2015 - p185(1) [51-500]
Morris, Tom - *The Oasis Within*
RVBW - Nov 2015 - pNA [51-500]
Morris, William - *The Well at the World's End*
MFSF - v128 - i1-2 - Jan-Feb 2015 - p42(3) [501+]
Morrison, Blake - *Shingle Street*
TLS - i5853 - June 5 2015 - p24(1) [501+]
Morrison, Kenneth - *The Sandzak: A History*
HER - v130 - i545 - August 2015 - p1031(2) [501+]
Morrison, Megan - *Grounded: The Adventures of Rapunzel*
c BL - v111 - i16 - April 15 2015 - p50(1) [51-500]
c CCB-B - v68 - i10 - June 2015 - p507(1) [51-500]
c HB Guide - v26 - i2 - Fall 2015 - p95(1) [51-500]
KR - Feb 1 2015 - pNA [51-500]
c PW - v262 - i9 - March 2 2015 - p85(1) [51-500]
y SLJ - v61 - i3 - March 2015 - p141(1) [51-500]
c Teach Lib - v43 - i1 - Oct 2015 - p48(1) [51-500]
y VOYA - v38 - i2 - June 2015 - p80(1) [51-500]
Morrison, Minion K.C. - *Aaron Henry of Mississippi: Inside Agitator*
KR - March 15 2015 - pNA [501+]
LJ - v140 - i9 - May 15 2015 - p88(1) [51-500]
Morrison, Richard T. - *Sovereignty Betrayed: Imperium Proditum*
SPBW - Nov 2015 - pNA [51-500]
Morrison, Scott Allan - *Terms of Use*
PW - v262 - i47 - Nov 23 2015 - p51(1) [51-500]
Morrison, Stephen - *A Late Fifteenth-Century Dominical Sermon Cycle*
JEGP - v114 - i2 - April 2015 - p300(4) [501+]
Morrison, Susan Signe - *Grendel's Mother*
KR - Sept 1 2015 - pNA [51-500]
Morrison, Toni - *God Help the Child (Read by Morrison, Toni). Audiobook Review*
LJ - v140 - i11 - June 15 2015 - p51(1) [51-500]
PW - v262 - i26 - June 29 2015 - p63(1) [51-500]
God Help the Child
Bks & Cult - v21 - i4 - July-August 2015 - p35(1) [501+]
BL - v111 - i11 - Feb 1 2015 - p4(1) [51-500]
BL - v111 - i12 - Feb 15 2015 - p30(2) [51-500]
CC - v132 - i9 - April 29 2015 - p39(2) [501+]
HM - v330 - i1979 - April 2015 - p79(81) [501+]
KR - Jan 15 2015 - pNA [51-500]
LJ - v140 - i5 - March 15 2015 - p94(1) [51-500]
Mac - v128 - i17 - May 4 2015 - p55(1) [501+]
Ms - v25 - i2 - Spring 2015 - p41(1) [501+]
Nat Post - v17 - i188 - June 13 2015 - pWP5(1) [501+]
NS - v144 - i5258 - April 17 2015 - p63(1) [501+]
NYRB - v62 - i8 - May 7 2015 - p11(3) [501+]
NYT - April 17 2015 - pC1(L) [501+]
NYTBR - April 19 2015 - p1(L) [501+]
Spec - v327 - i9740 - May 2 2015 - p40(2) [501+]
Wom R Bks - v32 - i6 - Nov-Dec 2015 - p13(2) [501+]
Morrison-Topping, Alan - *Naomi and Her Friends*
KR - April 1 2015 - pNA [501+]
Morrison, Yvonne - *Little Red Riding Hood: Not Quite (Illus. by Bixley, Donovan)*
c Magpies - v30 - i1 - March 2015 - pS6(1) [501+]
Morrisroe, Patricia - *9 1/2 Narrow: My Life in Shoes*
KR - Feb 15 2015 - pNA [501+]
PW - v262 - i10 - March 9 2015 - p65(2) [51-500]
Morrissey - *Autobiography*
Notes - v71 - i3 - March 2015 - p489(4) [501+]
List of the Lost
NS - v144 - i5282 - Oct 2 2015 - p77(1) [501+]
Morrissey, Patricia Aguilar - *Magdalena's Picnic/El Picnic de Magdalena (Illus. by Deahl, Gretchen)*
c SLJ - v61 - i6 - June 2015 - p88(2) [51-500]
Morrissey, Robert - *The Economy of Glory: From Ancien Regime France to the Fall of Napoleon*
MLR - v110 - i2 - April 2015 - p548-549 [501+]
Morrissey, Sinead - *Parallax and Selected Poems*
BL - v111 - i18 - May 15 2015 - p11(1) [51-500]
Morrissey, Thomas E. - *Conciliarism and Church Law in the Fifteenth Century: Studies on Franciscus Zabarella and the Council of Constance*
HNet - June 2015 - pNA [501+]
CHR - v101 - i3 - Summer 2015 - p633(2) [501+]
Morrow, Bradford - *The Forgers*
RVBW - August 2015 - pNA [501+]

Morrow, James D. - *Order within Anarchy: The Laws of War as an International Institution*
    HNet - August 2015 - pNA [501+]

Morrow, Susan Brind - *The Dawning Moon of the Mind: Unlocking the Pyramid Texts*
    KR - Sept 15 2015 - pNA [501+]
    LJ - v140 - i17 - Oct 15 2015 - p91(2) [51-500]

Morse, Deborah Denenholz - *Reforming Trollope: Race, Gender, and Englishness in the Novels of Anthony Trollope*
    MLR - v110 - i3 - July 2015 - p851-852 [501+]

Morse, Eric - *What Is Punk? (Illus. by Yi, Anny)*
    c KR - August 1 2015 - pNA [51-500]
    c PW - v262 - i32 - August 10 2015 - p63(1) [51-500]

Morstad, Julie - *This Is Sadie*
    c CH Bwatch - Oct 2015 - pNA [51-500]

Mort, Terry - *The Monet Murders*
    BL - v111 - i22 - August 1 2015 - p35(1) [51-500]
    KR - July 15 2015 - pNA [51-500]
    PW - v262 - i26 - June 29 2015 - p45(1) [51-500]
Thieves' Road: The Black Hills Betrayal and Custer's Path to Little Bighorn
    Bwatch - April 2015 - pNA [51-500]

Mortensen, Lori - *Chicken Lily (Illus. by Crittenden, Nina Victor)*
    c KR - Dec 1 2015 - pNA [51-500]
    c PW - v262 - i50 - Dec 7 2015 - p84(2) [51-500]
Voices of the Civil Rights Movement: A Primary Source Exploration of the Struggle for Racial Equality
    c SLJ - v61 - i2 - Feb 2015 - p116(1) [51-500]

Mortier, Erwin - *While the Gods Were Sleeping*
    NY - v91 - i10 - April 27 2015 - p77 [51-500]

Mortimer, Adam Egypt - *Ballistic*
    PW - v262 - i12 - March 23 2015 - p57(1) [51-500]

Mortimer, Ian - *Centuries of Change: Which Century Saw the Most Change and Why It Matters to Us*
    HT - v65 - i5 - May 2015 - p58(1) [501+]
    TLS - i5840 - March 6 2015 - p8(1) [501+]
Human Race
    NS - v144 - i5289 - Nov 20 2015 - p52(2) [501+]

Mortimer, J.R. - *This or That? 2: More Wacky Choices to Reveal the Hidden You*
    c HB Guide - v26 - i2 - Fall 2015 - p147(1) [51-500]

Mortimer, Rachel - *Jack and the Jelly Bean Stalk (Illus. by Pichon, Liz)*
    c HB Guide - v26 - i1 - Spring 2015 - p40(1) [51-500]

Mortley, Raoul - *Plotinus, Self and the World*
    Class R - v65 - i1 - April 2015 - p87-89 [501+]

Morton, Andrew - *17 Carnations: The Royals, the Nazis, and the Biggest Cover-up in History*
    BL - v111 - i12 - Feb 15 2015 - p22(2) [51-500]
    KR - Jan 1 2015 - pNA [501+]
    LJ - v140 - i2 - Feb 1 2015 - p95(1) [51-500]

Morton, Brian - *Florence Gordon*
    BooChiTr - Jan 24 2015 - p14(1) [501+]

Morton, Carole J. - *Entering Your Own Heart: A Guide to Developing Self Love, Inner Peace and Happiness*
    SPBW - June 2015 - pNA [51-500]

Morton, Clay - *Why Johnny Doesn't Flap: NT is OK!*
    c SLJ - v61 - i12 - Dec 2015 - p138(1) [51-500]

Morton, Kate - *The Lake House*
    BL - v112 - i4 - Oct 15 2015 - p22(1) [51-500]
    CSM - Nov 6 2015 - pNA [51-500]
    KR - August 15 2015 - pNA [501+]
    LJ - v140 - i13 - August 1 2015 - p88(1) [501+]
    PW - v262 - i30 - July 27 2015 - p36(1) [51-500]

Morton, Lisa - *Ghosts: A Haunted History*
    TLS - i5874 - Oct 30 2015 - p7(1) [501+]

Morton, Oliver - *The Planet Remade: How Geoengineering Could Change the World*
    KR - Sept 15 2015 - pNA [501+]
    Nature - v526 - i7571 - Oct 1 2015 - p38(2) [501+]
    New Sci - v228 - i3045 - Oct 31 2015 - p45(1) [501+]

Morton, Orde - *Rio*
    KR - June 15 2015 - pNA [501+]

Morton, Peter - *Lusting for London: Australian Expatriate Writers at the Hub of Empire, 1870-1950*
    VS - v57 - i2 - Wntr 2015 - p352(3) [501+]

Morton, Suzanne - *Wisdom, Justice, and Charity: Canadian Social Welfare through the Life of Jane B. Wisdom, 1884-1975*
    AHR - v120 - i4 - Oct 2015 - p1498-1499 [501+]
    Can Hist R - v96 - i3 - Sept 2015 - p451(3) [501+]

Morvan, Jean-David - *Omaha Beach on D-Day*
    BL - v112 - i4 - Oct 15 2015 - p35(1) [51-500]

Morwood, James - *A Little Greek Reader*
    Class R - v65 - i2 - Oct 2015 - p620-620 [501+]

Mosby, Steve - *The Nightmare Place*
    BL - v111 - i17 - May 1 2015 - p41(2) [51-500]
    KR - April 15 2015 - pNA [51-500]
    PW - v262 - i12 - March 23 2015 - p46(1) [51-500]

Mosca, Sal - *The Talk of the Town*
    Dbt - v82 - i8 - August 2015 - p80(1) [51-500]

Moscaliuc, Mihaela - *Immigrant Model*
    ABR - v36 - i4 - May-June 2015 - p12(2) [501+]

Mosco, Vincent - *To the Cloud: Big Data in a Turbulent World*
    CS - v44 - i3 - May 2015 - p436-437 [501+]

Moscowitz, Leigh - *The Battle over Marriage: Gay Rights Activism through the Media*
    CS - v44 - i1 - Jan 2015 - p143(1) [501+]

Mosegaard Hansen, Maj-Britt - *The Diachrony of Negation*
    FS - v69 - i4 - Oct 2015 - p574-575 [501+]

Moseley, Carys - *Nationhood, Providence, and Witness: Israel in Modern Theology and Social Theory*
    Intpr - v69 - i4 - Oct 2015 - p498(2) [501+]

Moseley, Keith - *Where's the Fairy? (Illus. by Harris, Nick)*
    c HB Guide - v26 - i2 - Fall 2015 - p45(2) [51-500]

Moser, Barry - *We Were Brothers*
    y BL - v112 - i3 - Oct 1 2015 - p9(2) [51-500]
    KR - June 15 2015 - pNA [501+]

Moser, Lisa - *Stories from Bug Garden (Illus. by Millward, Gwen)*
    c KR - Dec 15 2015 - pNA [51-500]
    c PW - v262 - i52 - Dec 21 2015 - p153(1) [51-500]

Moser, Michael - *Language Policy and the Discourse on Languages in Ukraine under President Viktor Yanukovych*
    E-A St - v67 - i9 - Nov 2015 - p1512(3) [501+]

Moses, Hary Morgan - *Obvious Power: Getting to Know-How*
    RVBW - Jan 2015 - pNA [51-500]

Moses, Itamar - *The Fortress of Solitude*
    Theat J - v67 - i2 - May 2015 - p295-309 [501+]
    Theat J - v67 - i2 - May 2015 - p295-309 [501+]

Moses, Nancy - *Stolen, Smuggled, Sold: On the Hunt for Cultural Treasures*
    LJ - v140 - i11 - June 15 2015 - p92(1) [501+]

Moses, Paul - *An Unlikely Union: The Love-Hate Story of New York's Irish and Italians*
    Comw - v142 - i12 - July 10 2015 - p32(4) [501+]
    KR - April 15 2015 - pNA [501+]
    PW - v262 - i16 - April 20 2015 - p66(1) [51-500]

Moses, Robert Ewusie - *Practices of Power: Revisiting the Principality and Powers in the Pauline Letters*
    Theol St - v76 - i3 - Sept 2015 - p603(3) [501+]

Moses, Will - *Fairy Tales for Little Folks (Illus. by Moses, Will)*
    c KR - July 1 2015 - pNA [51-500]
    c PW - v262 - i28 - July 13 2015 - p64(1) [51-500]
    c SLJ - v61 - i10 - Oct 2015 - p81(1) [51-500]

Moshenska, Joe - *Feeling Pleasures: The Sense of Touch in Renaissance England*
    TLS - i5874 - Oct 30 2015 - p11(1) [501+]

Mosher, Howard Frank - *God's Kingdom*
    BL - v112 - i3 - Oct 1 2015 - p22(2) [51-500]
    KR - August 1 2015 - pNA [51-500]
    LJ - v140 - i20 - Dec 1 2015 - p5(1) [51-500]

Moshfegh, Ottessa - *Eileen*
    Ent W - i1377 - August 21 2015 - p104(1) [501+]
    KR - June 15 2015 - pNA [501+]
    Mac - v128 - i34-35 - August 31 2015 - p79(1) [501+]
    Nation - v301 - i18 - Nov 2 2015 - p36(2) [501+]
    NY - v91 - i25 - August 31 2015 - p89 [51-500]
    NYTBR - August 16 2015 - p1(L) [501+]
    PW - v262 - i19 - May 11 2015 - p28(1) [51-500]
    BL - v111 - i19-20 - June 1 2015 - p52(1) [51-500]
    LJ - v140 - i10 - June 1 2015 - p94(1) [501+]

Moshier, Joe - *Go, Pea. Go! (Illus. by Sonnenburg, Chris)*
    c HB Guide - v26 - i2 - Fall 2015 - p16(1) [51-500]
    c KR - Feb 15 2015 - pNA [51-500]

Moshiri, Farnoosh - *The Drum Tower*
    RVBW - Jan 2015 - pNA [51-500]

Mosier, John - *Verdun: The Lost History of the Most Important Battle of the World War I, 1914-1918*
    J Mil H - v79 - i4 - Oct 2015 - p1180-1181 [501+]

Moskovitz, Rick - *The Methuselarity Transformation*
    SPBW - Jan 2015 - pNA [51-500]

Moskowitz, Anita Fiderer - *Forging Authenticity: Bastianini and the Neo-Renaissance in Nineteenth-Century Florence*
    Six Ct J - v46 - i3 - Fall 2015 - p760-761 [501+]

Moskowitz, Hannah - *A History of Glitter and Blood (Illus. by Johnson, Cathy G.)*
    c BL - v112 - i1 - Sept 1 2015 - p103(1) [51-500]
    y CCB-B - v69 - i1 - Sept 2015 - p40(2) [51-500]
    y HB - v91 - i6 - Nov-Dec 2015 - p85(1) [51-500]
    y KR - June 1 2015 - pNA [51-500]
A History of Glitter and Blood (Illus. by Johnson, Cathy G.)
    y SLJ - v61 - i8 - August 2015 - p108(1) [51-500]
A History of Glitter and Blood (Illus. by Johnson, Cathy G.)
    y VOYA - v38 - i3 - August 2015 - p82(1) [51-500]
Not Otherwise Specified
    y BL - v111 - i12 - Feb 15 2015 - p83(1) [51-500]
    y CCB-B - v68 - i11 - July-August 2015 - p558(1) [51-500]
    y HB Guide - v26 - i2 - Fall 2015 - p133(1) [51-500]
    y KR - Jan 1 2015 - pNA [51-500]
    y PW - v262 - i4 - Jan 26 2015 - p173(1) [51-500]

Moskowitz, Marc L. - *Go Nation: Chinese Masculinities and the Game of Weiqi in China*
    JAS - v74 - i2 - May 2015 - p476-477 [501+]
    Signs - v40 - i3 - Spring 2015 - p783(4) [501+]

Moslener, Sara - *Virgin Nation: Sexual Purity and American Adolescence*
    LJ - v140 - i10 - June 1 2015 - p108(1) [501+]
    PW - v262 - i23 - June 8 2015 - p55(1) [51-500]

Mosler, Layne - *Driving Hungry*
    BL - v111 - i21 - July 1 2015 - p14(1) [51-500]
Driving Hungry: A Memoir
    LJ - v140 - i13 - August 1 2015 - p114(1) [501+]
    NYTBR - Dec 6 2015 - p46(L) [501+]
    PW - v262 - i21 - May 25 2015 - p49(1) [51-500]
Driving Hungry
    KR - May 1 2015 - pNA [501+]

Mosley, Eric - *The Power of Thanks: How Social Recognition Empowers Employees and Creates a Best Place to Work*
    Econ - v415 - i8934 - April 18 2015 - p77(US) [501+]

Mosley, Max - *Formula One and Beyond: The Autobiography*
    Spec - v328 - i9749 - July 4 2015 - p39(1) [501+]

Mosley, Nicholas - *Metamorphoses*
    WLT - v89 - i1 - Jan-Feb 2015 - p73(1) [501+]

Mosley, Walter - *And Sometimes I Wonder about You (Read by Onayemi, Prentice). Audiobook Review*
    PW - v262 - i26 - June 29 2015 - p62(1) [51-500]
And Sometimes I Wonder about You
    BL - v111 - i17 - May 1 2015 - p18(1) [51-500]
    LJ - v140 - i9 - May 15 2015 - p79(1) [51-500]
    NYTBR - May 17 2015 - p33(L) [501+]
    PW - v262 - i12 - March 23 2015 - p1(1) [51-500]
Inside a Silver Box
    Analog - v135 - i6 - June 2015 - p107(2) [501+]
Rose Gold (Read by Jackson, J.D.). Audiobook Review
    BL - v111 - i11 - Feb 1 2015 - p60(1) [51-500]
Rose Gold
    RVBW - May 2015 - pNA [51-500]

Moss, Barbara Klein - *The Language of Paradise*
    LJ - v140 - i3 - Feb 15 2015 - p94(1) [51-500]
    PW - v262 - i7 - Feb 16 2015 - p152(1) [51-500]

Moss, Candida R. - *Ancient Christian Martyrdom: Diverse Practices, Theologies, and Traditions*
    BTB - v45 - i2 - May 2015 - p123(2) [501+]
Reconceiving Infertility: Biblical Perspective on Procreation and Childlessness
    TimHES - i2229 - Nov 12 2015 - p49(1) [501+]

Moss, Charlotte - *Garden Inspirations*
    NYT - April 15 2015 - p3(L) [51-500]

Moss, Daniel D. - *The Ovidian Vogue: Literary Fashion and Imitative Practice in Late Elizabethan England*
    Six Ct J - v46 - i3 - Fall 2015 - p820-821 [501+]

Moss, Dixie - *First Bites: Tidbits of American History for the Young and Young at Heart*
    c CH Bwatch - Jan 2015 - pNA [51-500]

Moss, Elizabeth - *Wolf Bride*
    PW - v262 - i12 - March 23 2015 - p55(1) [51-500]

Moss, Marissa - *Amelia's Middle-School Graduation Yearbook*
    c SLJ - v61 - i5 - May 2015 - p104(1) [51-500]
    c KR - Feb 15 2015 - pNA [51-500]

Moss, Rachel E. - *Fatherhood and Its Representations in Middle English Texts*
    Specu - v90 - i2 - April 2015 - p564-565 [501+]
    HER - v130 - i544 - June 2015 - p724(2) [501+]

Moss, Sarah - *Bodies of Light*
    TLS - i5862 - August 7 2015 - p19(1) [501+]
Signs for Lost Children
    TLS - i5862 - August 7 2015 - p19(1) [501+]

330 • MOSS Book Review Index 2016 Cumulation

Moss, Tina - *Code Black*
PW - v262 - i29 - July 20 2015 - p175(1) [51-500]
Moss, Todd - *Minute Zero*
BL - v112 - i2 - Sept 15 2015 - p34(1) [51-500]
KR - July 15 2015 - pNA [51-500]
PW - v262 - i25 - June 22 2015 - p119(2) [51-500]
Moss, Wendy L. - *Bounce Back: How to Be a Resilient Kid*
c PW - v262 - i25 - June 22 2015 - p141(1) [501+]
c SLJ - v61 - i11 - Nov 2015 - p136(1) [51-500]
The Survival Guide for Kids with Physical Disabilities and Challenges
CH Bwatch - Nov 2015 - pNA [51-500]
The Tween Book: A Growing-Up Guide for the Changing You
c SLJ - v61 - i9 - Sept 2015 - p187(2) [51-500]
Mossakowski, Stanislaw - *King Sigismund Chapel at Cracow Cathedral, 1515-1533*
Six Ct J - v46 - i1 - Spring 2015 - p199-200 [501+]
Mossman, Kenneth L. - *The Complexity Paradox: The More Answers We Find, the More Questions We Have*
QRB - v90 - i4 - Dec 2015 - pNA [501+]
Most, Andrea - *Making Americans: Jews and the Broadway Musical*
J Urban H - v41 - i1 - Jan 2015 - p157-8 [501+]
Mostaccio, Silvia - *Early Modern Jesuits between Obedience and Conscience during the Generalate of Claudio Acquaviva (1581-1615).*
CHR - v101 - i3 - Summer 2015 - p658(2) [501+]
Ren Q - v68 - i3 - Fall 2015 - p1042-1043 [501+]
Mostert, Marco - *Uses of the Written Word in Medieval Towns: Medieval Urban Literacy, 2 vols.*
Med R - Jan 2015 - pNA [501+]
Mostert, Natasha - *Dark Prayer*
KR - Jan 1 2015 - pNA [501+]
Motadel, David - *Islam and Nazi Germany's War*
J Mil H - v79 - i2 - April 2015 - p520-521 [501+]
NYRB - v62 - i6 - April 2 2015 - p61(3) [501+]
TimHES - i2187 - Jan 22 2015 - p53(1) [501+]
TLS - i5840 - March 6 2015 - p12(1) [501+]
Mote, Ian - *From Chicken Feet to Crystal Baths: An Englishman's Travels throughout China*
RVBW - Oct 2015 - pNA [51-500]
Moten, Fred - *The Little Edges*
LJ - v140 - i2 - Feb 1 2015 - p87(2) [51-500]
Moten, Matthew - *Presidents & Their Generals: An American History of Command in War*
J Mil H - v79 - i1 - Jan 2015 - p199-200 [501+]
NWCR - v68 - i2 - Spring 2015 - p137(3) [501+]
Motion, Andrew - *The New World*
BL - v111 - i18 - May 15 2015 - p30(1) [51-500]
KR - May 1 2015 - pNA [501+]
LJ - v140 - i9 - May 15 2015 - p73(1) [51-500]
PW - v262 - i21 - May 25 2015 - p31(2) [51-500]
Motley, Bryan - *Embracing Cuba*
BL - v112 - i2 - Sept 15 2015 - p25(1) [51-500]
Motomura, Hiroshi - *Immigration Outside the Law*
HLR - v128 - i5 - March 2015 - p1405(44) [501+]
Motoya, Yukiko - *Granta 127: Japan*
TLS - i5848 - May 1 2015 - p25(1) [501+]
Motschenbacher, Heiko - *New Perspectives on English as a European Linguafranca*
Lang Soc - v44 - i4 - Sept 2015 - p600-601 [501+]
Mott, Jason - *The Wonder of All Things (Read by Whelan, Julia). Audiobook Review*
LJ - v140 - i3 - Feb 15 2015 - p58(1) [51-500]
Mott, Toby - *Skinhead: An Archive*
TLS - i5848 - May 1 2015 - p30(1) [501+]
Mottalini, Chris - *After You Left/They Took It Apart*
NYRB - v62 - i2 - Feb 5 2015 - p34(3) [501+]
Moubayed, Sami - *Syria and the USA: Washington's Relations with Damascus from Wilson to Eisenhower*
AHR - v120 - i2 - April 2015 - p643-644 [501+]
Moudud, Jamee K. - *Alternative Theories of Competition: Challenges to the Orthodoxy*
S&S - v79 - i4 - Oct 2015 - p635-638 [501+]
Mouillot, Miranda Richmond - *A Fifty-Year Silence: Love, War, and a Ruined House in France*
BL - v111 - i9-10 - Jan 1 2015 - p34(1) [51-500]
Mac - v128 - i5-6 - Feb 9 2015 - p75(2) [501+]
Mould, David H. - *Postcards from Stanland*
KR - Dec 15 2015 - pNA [501+]
Moulin, Jules - *Ally Hughes Has Sex Sometimes*
y BL - v111 - i21 - July 1 2015 - p27(1) [51-500]
Ent W - i1377 - August 21 2015 - p108(1) [501+]
LJ - v140 - i12 - July 1 2015 - p78(1) [51-500]
NYTBR - July 26 2015 - p26(L) [501+]
PW - v262 - i25 - June 22 2015 - p118(1) [51-500]
Mouline, Nabil - *The Clerics of Islam: Religious Authority and Political Power in Saudi Arabia*
For Aff - v94 - i3 - May-June 2015 - pNA [501+]
Moulson, Roger - *What Flows across the Glass*
TLS - i5872 - Oct 16 2015 - p23(1) [501+]
Moulson, Tom - *The Millionaires' Squadron: The Remarkable Story of 601 Squadron and the Flying Sword*
APH - v62 - i2 - Summer 2015 - p59(2) [501+]
Moulton, Erin E. - *Keepers of the Labyrinth*
y KR - May 1 2015 - pNA [51-500]
c SLJ - v61 - i6 - June 2015 - p102(1) [51-500]
y VOYA - v38 - i2 - June 2015 - p66(1) [51-500]
Moulton, Ian Frederick - *Love in Print in the Sixteenth Century: The Popularization of Romance*
Ren Q - v68 - i2 - Summer 2015 - p740-742 [501+]
Six Ct J - v46 - i2 - Summer 2015 - p517-518 [501+]
Moulton, Mo - *Ireland and the Irish in Interwar England*
HT - v65 - i3 - March 2015 - p61(1) [501+]
Moulton, Sara - *Home Cooking 101: How to Make Everything Taste Better*
PW - v262 - i52 - Dec 21 2015 - p147(2) [51-500]
Mount, Ferdinand - *The Tears of the Rajas: Mutiny, Money and Marriage in India 1805-1905*
HT - v65 - i10 - Oct 2015 - p62(2) [501+]
Quad - v59 - i7-8 - July-August 2015 - p134(3) [501+]
Spec - v327 - i9733 - March 14 2015 - p38(2) [501+]
TLS - i5847 - April 24 2015 - p22(2) [501+]
Mount, Harry - *Harry Mount's Odyssey: Ancient Greece in the Footsteps of Odysseus*
Spec - v328 - i9752 - July 25 2015 - p33(1) [501+]
TLS - i5871 - Oct 9 2015 - p31(1) [501+]
Mountjoy, Joseph - *El Pantano y Otros Sitios del Formativo Medio en el Valle de Mascota, Jalisco*
Lat Ant - v26 - i2 - June 2015 - p280(2) [501+]
Mourad, Kenize - *In the City of Gold and Silver: The Story of Begum Hazrat Mahal*
WLT - v89 - i3-4 - May-August 2015 - p114(2) [501+]
Mouritsen, Ole G. - *Umami: Unlocking the Secrets of the Fifth Taste*
Am Sci - v103 - i1 - Jan-Feb 2015 - p68(2) [501+]
Moussavi, Sam - *Detroit*
y BL - v112 - i7 - Dec 1 2015 - p53(2) [51-500]
Moustafa, Ahmed - *The Cosmic Script: Sacred Geometry and the Science of Arabic Penmanship, 2 vols.*
TLS - i5864-5865 - August 21 2015 - p32(1) [501+]
Mouton, Alice - *Luwian Identities. Culture, Language and Religion between Anatolia and the Aegean*
JNES - v74 - i1 - April 2015 - p151(3) [501+]
Mowry, Barbara - *Crystal and Breanna: The Secret of Blackridge Farm (Illus. by Fletcher, Christina)*
c SLJ - v61 - i6 - June 2015 - p102(2) [51-500]
Mowry, Tia - *Twintuition: Double Vision*
c SLJ - v61 - i6 - June 2015 - p109(1) [51-500]
Moya, Horacio Castellanos - *The Dream of My Return*
KR - Jan 15 2015 - pNA [51-500]
NYT - March 16 2015 - pC6(L) [501+]
PW - v262 - i4 - Jan 26 2015 - p144(1) [51-500]
Moyad, Mark - *The Supplement Handbook: A Trusted Expert's Guide to What Works and What's Worthless for More Than 100 Conditions*
BL - v111 - i9-10 - Jan 1 2015 - p29(1) [51-500]
Moyaert, Marianne - *In Response to the Religious Other: Ricoeur and the Fragility of Interreligious Encounters*
Theol St - v76 - i4 - Dec 2015 - p867(2) [501+]
Moyar, Mark - *Strategic Failure: How President Obama's Drone Warfare, Defense Cuts, and Military Amateurism Have Imperiled America*
Nat R - v67 - i16 - Sept 7 2015 - p43 [501+]
Moyd, Michelle R. - *Violent Intermediaries: African Soldiers, Conquest, and Everyday Colonialism in German East Africa*
AHR - v120 - i2 - April 2015 - p756-757 [501+]
HNet - Feb 2015 - pNA [501+]
Moyer, Ian S. - *Egypt and the Limits of Hellenism*
JNES - v74 - i2 - Oct 2015 - p370(4) [501+]
Moyer, Jamie Lee - *Against a Brightening Sky*
BL - v112 - i2 - Sept 15 2015 - p37(2) [51-500]
PW - v262 - i31 - August 3 2015 - p39(1) [51-500]
Moyes, Jojo - *After You*
KR - August 15 2015 - pNA [501+]
LJ - v140 - i15 - Sept 15 2015 - p69(1) [51-500]
Moylan, Tom - *Demand the Impossible: Science Fiction and the Utopian Imagination*
SFS - v42 - i3 - Nov 2015 - p566-573 [501+]
Moyn, Samuel - *Christian Human Rights*
Comw - v142 - i17 - Oct 23 2015 - p28(3) [501+]
Global Intellectual History
JMH - v87 - i2 - June 2015 - p395(2) [501+]
Human Rights and the Uses of History
HNet - Jan 2015 - pNA [501+]
Moynahan, Brian - *Leningrad: Siege and Symphony*
AM - v213 - i3 - August 3 2015 - p33(3) [501+]
Moynahan, Jean - *The Black Fountain Goddess*
SPBW - March 2015 - pNA [51-500]
Moynihan, Dan - *Hiding Dinosaurs (Illus. by Moynihan, Dan)*
c KR - July 15 2015 - pNA [51-500]
c SLJ - v61 - i12 - Dec 2015 - p98(1) [51-500]
Moynihan, Michael P., Jr. - *Fighting Shadows in Vietnam: A Combat Memoir*
HNet - June 2015 - pNA [501+]
Moynihan, Ray - *Sex, Lies and Pharmaceuticals: How Drug Companies Plan to Profit from Female Sexual Dysfunction*
CWS - v30 - i2-3 - Fall-Winter 2015 - p137(2) [501+]
Moyson, Graham - *Storyline*
c Sch Lib - v63 - i4 - Winter 2015 - p230(1) [51-500]
Mozina, Andy - *Contrary Motion*
KR - Dec 15 2015 - pNA [501+]
Mozingo, Louise A. - *Pastoral Capitalism: A History of Suburban Corporate Landscapes*
J Urban H - v41 - i1 - Jan 2015 - p171-10 [501+]
Mu, Yang - *Memories of Mount Qilai*
WLT - v89 - i6 - Nov-Dec 2015 - p75(1) [51-500]
Muchembled, Robert - *Mysterieuse Madame de Pompadour*
TLS - i5852 - May 29 2015 - p5(1) [501+]
Muchler, Gunter - *1813: Napoleon, Metternich und das Weltgeschichtliche Duell von Dresden*
HNet - Feb 2015 - pNA [501+]
Muck, Terry C. - *Handbook of Religion: A Christian Engagement with Traditions, Teachings, and Practices*
LJ - v140 - i2 - Feb 1 2015 - p106(1) [51-500]
Mucke, Lukas - *Die allgemeine Altersrentenversorgung in der*
HNet - August 2015 - pNA [501+]
Muckle, John - *Little White Bull: British Fiction in the 50s and 60s*
TLS - i5831 - Jan 2 2015 - p7(1) [501+]
Mudd, Joseph C. - *Eucharist as Meaning: Critical Metaphysics and Contemporary Sacramental Theology*
AM - v212 - i10 - March 23 2015 - p34(3) [501+]
Theol St - v76 - i4 - Dec 2015 - p876(2) [501+]
Mudge, Lewis S. - *We Can Make the World Economy a Sustainable Global Home*
Intpr - v69 - i4 - Oct 2015 - p505(1) [501+]
Mudgett, Kathryn - *Writing the Seaman's Tale in Law and Literature: Dana, Melville, and Justice Story*
AL - v87 - i3 - Sept 2015 - p607-609 [501+]
Mudhai, Okoth F. - *Civic Engagement, Digital Networks, and Political Reform in Africa*
JTWS - v32 - i1 - Spring 2015 - p365(12) [501+]
Mueggenberg, Brent - *The Czecho-Slovak Struggle for Independence, 1914-1920*
HNet - Jan 2015 - pNA [501+]
Muehlbauer, Matthew S. - *Ways of War: American Military History from the Colonial Era to the Twenty-First Century*
J Mil H - v79 - i3 - July 2015 - p783-802 [501+]
Muehlenbeck, Philip E. - *Betting on the Africans: John F. Kennedy's Courting of African Nationalist Leaders*
HNet - Jan 2015 - pNA [501+]
Muehlmann, Shaylih - *When I Wear My Alligator Boots: Narco-Culture in the U.S.-Mexico Borderlands*
CS - v44 - i5 - Sept 2015 - p686-687 [501+]
Where the River Ends: Contested Indigeneity in the Mexican Colorado Delta
JRAI - v21 - i1 - March 2015 - p217(2) [501+]
Mueller, Alex - *Translating Troy: Provincial Politics in Alliterative Romance*
JEGP - v114 - i1 - Jan 2015 - p149(4) [501+]
Mueller, James E. - *Shooting Arrows and Slinging Mud: Custer, the Press, and the Little Bighorn*
WHQ - v46 - i2 - Summer 2015 - p250-251 [501+]
Mueller, Ken S. - *Senator Benton and the People: Master Race Democracy on the Early American Frontiers*
JSH - v81 - i4 - Nov 2015 - p964(2) [501+]
Mueller, Kirk Jay - *Harriet Can Carry It (Illus. by Vonthron-Laver, Sarah)*
c HB Guide - v26 - i2 - Fall 2015 - p46(1) [51-500]
Mueller-Stahl, Annin - *Dreimal Deutschland und Zuruck*
Ger Q - v88 - i1 - Wntr 2015 - p121(2) [501+]
Mugglestone, Lynda - *The Oxford History of English: Updated Edition*
MLR - v110 - i1 - Jan 2015 - p231-233 [501+]
Samuel Johnson and the Journey into Words
TimHES - i2222 - Sept 24 2015 - p42(1) [501+]

Mugur, Paul Doru - *The Vanishing Point That Whistles: An Anthology of Contemporary Romanian Poetry*
    HNet - July 2015 - pNA [501+]
Muhl-Benninghaus, Wolfgang - *Geschichte der Medienokonomie: Eine Einfuhrung in die Traditionelle Medienwirtschaft von 1750 bis 2000*
    HNet - Jan 2015 - pNA [501+]
Muhlberger, Steven - *Charny's Men-at-Arms: Questions Concerning the Joust, Tournaments, and War*
    Med R - May 2015 - pNA [501+]
Muhle, Susanne - *Auftrag: Menschenraub - Entfuhrungen von Westberlinern und Bundesburgern durch das Ministerium fur Staatssicherheit der DDR*
    HNet - May 2015 - pNA [501+]
Muhlfried, Florian - *Being a State and States of Being in Highland Georgia*
    Slav R - v74 - i2 - Summer 2015 - p395-395 [501+]
Muhling, Jens - *A Journey into Russia*
    TLS - i5832 - Jan 9 2015 - p22(1) [501+]
Muhs, Gabriella Gutierrez - *Rebozos De Palabras: An Helena Maria Viramontes Critical Reader*
    Aztlan - v40 - i1 - Spring 2015 - p277-280 [501+]
Muhsam, Erich - *Tagebucher: Band 6, 1919*
    Ger Q - v88 - i1 - Wntr 2015 - p119(3) [501+]
Muihauser, Travis - *Sweetgirl*
    y BL - v112 - i5 - Nov 1 2015 - p27(2) [51-500]
Muir, Rory - *Wellington: Waterloo and the Fortunes of Peace, 1814-1852*
    HT - v65 - i7 - July 2015 - p58(2) [501+]
    TLS - i5864-5865 - August 21 2015 - p3(3) [501+]
Muir, Sally - *Knit Your Own Pet: Easy-to-Follow Patterns for a Cat, Mouse, Guinea Pig, Pony, and More Adorable Companions*
    LJ - v140 - i11 - June 15 2015 - p89(1) [51-500]
Muir, Sharona - *Invisible Beasts: Tales of the Animals That Go Unseen among Us*
    Wom R Bks - v32 - i1 - Jan-Feb 2015 - p22(2) [501+]
Muir, T. Frank - *A Life for a Life*
    BL - v111 - i22 - August 1 2015   p35(1) [51-500]
Life for a Life
    PW - v262 - i29 - July 20 2015 - p171(2) [501+]
Mujila, Fiston Mwanza - *Tram 83*
    KR - July 15 2015 - pNA [51-500]
    PW - v262 - i30 - July 27 2015 - p40(1) [51-500]
    TLS - i5877 - Nov 20 2015 - p21(1) [501+]
Mukasonga, Scholastique - *Our Lady of the Nile*
    WLT - v89 - i2 - March-April 2015 - p60(1) [501+]
Mukerjee, Madhusree - *Churchill's Secret War: The British Empire and the Ravaging of India during World War II*
    HT - v65 - i1 - Jan 2015 - p56(2) [501+]
Mukhamediev, Konyr - *Kazakh Oneri: 5 Tomdyk*
    E-A St - v67 - i1 - Jan 2015 - p151(3) [501+]
Mukherjee, Janam - *Hungry Bengal: War, Famine and the End of Empire*
    HT - v65 - i11 - Nov 2015 - p65(1) [501+]
Mukherjee, Neel - *The Lives of Others*
    NY - v90 - i42 - Jan 5 2015 - p73 [51-500]
    NYRB - v62 - i16 - Oct 22 2015 - p65(3) [501+]
Mukherjee, Siddhartha - *The Laws of Medicine: Field Notes from an Uncertain Science (Read by Fontana, Santino). Audiobook Review*
    LJ - v140 - i20 - Dec 1 2015 - p61(1) [51-500]
The Laws of Medicine: Field Notes from an Uncertain Science
    BL - v112 - i4 - Oct 15 2015 - p10(1) [51-500]
    KR - August 15 2015 - pNA [501+]
Mukhina, Irina - *Women and the Birth of Russian Capitalism. A History of the Shuttle Trade*
    E-A St - v67 - i7 - Sept 2015 - p1158(2) [501+]
Mulcahy, Greg - *O'Hearn*
    KR - Feb 1 2015 - pNA [51-500]
Mulcahy, Matthew - *Hubs of Empire: The Southeastern Lowcountry and British Caribbean*
    JSH - v81 - i4 - Nov 2015 - p939(2) [501+]
Mulcair, Thomas - *Strength of Conviction*
    Nat Post - v17 - i230 - August 8 2015 - pWP5(1) [501+]
Mulder, Michelle - *Trash Talk: Moving toward a Zero-Waste World*
    c BL - v111 - i12 - Feb 15 2015 - p75(1) [51-500]
    c HB Guide - v26 - i2 - Fall 2015 - p155(1) [51-500]
    c KR - Feb 15 2015 - pNA [51-500]
    c Res Links - v20 - i4 - April 2015 - p20(1) [51-500]
Muldoon, Paul - *Mules*
    TLS - i5850 - May 15 2015 - p16(1) [501+]
One Thousand Things Worth Knowing
    TLS - i5850 - May 15 2015 - p10(1) [501+]
Muldoon, Sean - *The Dead Rabbit Drinks Manual: Secret Recipes and Barroom Tales from Two Belfast Boys Who Conquered the Cocktail World*
    BL - v112 - i1 - Sept 1 2015 - p23(1) [51-500]
    LJ - v140 - i13 - August 1 2015 - p118(3) [51-500]
    PW - v262 - i36 - Sept 7 2015 - p61(2) [51-500]
Mulford, Carolyn - *Show Me The Ashes*
    KR - Oct 15 2015 - pNA [51-500]
Mulgrew, Kate - *Born with Teeth: A Memoir (Read by Mulgrew, Kate). Audiobook Review*
    BL - v112 - i3 - Oct 1 2015 - p85(1) [51-500]
    LJ - v140 - i12 - July 1 2015 - p45(1) [51-500]
Born with Teeth: A Memoir
    BL - v111 - i16 - April 15 2015 - p10(1) [51-500]
    KR - March 1 2015 - pNA [51-500]
    LJ - v140 - i7 - April 15 2015 - p88(3) [51-500]
    PW - v262 - i6 - Feb 9 2015 - p59(1) [51-500]
    PW - v262 - i7 - Feb 16 2015 - pNA [1-50]
    PW - v262 - i12 - March 23 2015 - p26(2) [51-500]
Mulhauser, Travis - *Sweetgirl*
    KR - Nov 15 2015 - pNA [51-500]
    PW - v262 - i42 - Oct 19 2015 - p48(1) [51-500]
Mulhern, Julie - *Guaranteed to Bleed*
    BL - v112 - i2 - Sept 15 2015 - p31(1) [51-500]
    PW - v262 - i35 - August 31 2015 - p65(1) [51-500]
Mull, Brandon - *Crystal Keepers (Read by Nobbs, Keith). Audiobook Review*
    c SLJ - v61 - i8 - August 2015 - p50(1) [51-500]
Crystal Keepers
    c HB Guide - v26 - i2 - Fall 2015 - p95(1) [51-500]
Rogue Knight (Read by Nobbs, Keith). Audiobook Review
    SLJ - v61 - i2 - Feb 2015 - p50(1) [51-500]
Rogue Knight
    c HB Guide - v26 - i1 - Spring 2015 - p87(1) [51-500]
Tales of the Great Beasts: Special Edition
    c HB Guide - v26 - i1 - Spring 2015 - p187(1) [51-500]
Wild Born (Read by Barber, Nicola). Audiobook Review
    y SLJ - v61 - i6 - June 2015 - p53(3) [501+]
Mullaly, Katie - *Land of Or (Illus. by Allen, Toby)*
    c PW - v262 - i44 - Nov 2 2015 - p83(1) [51-500]
Mullaney, Dean - *King of the Comics: One Hundred Years of King Features Syndicate*
    CSM - Nov 13 2015 - pNA [501+]
Mullarkey, Lisa - *Get Ella to the Apollo (Illus. by Bernard, Courtney)*
    c HB Guide - v26 - i2 - Fall 2015 - p95(1) [51-500]
Mary Molds a Monster (Illus. by Bernard, Courtney)
    c HB Guide - v26 - i2 - Fall 2015 - p95(1) [51-500]
Monet Changes Mediums (Illus. by Bernard, Courtney)
    c HB Guide - v26 - i2 - Fall 2015 - p95(1) [51-500]
Shakespeare Saves the Globe (Illus. by Bernard, Courtney)
    c HB Guide - v26 - i2 - Fall 2015 - p95(1) [51-500]
Mullen, Bill V. - *Un-American: W.E.B. Du Bois and the Century of World Revolution*
    LJ - v140 - i16 - Oct 1 2015 - p88(1) [51-500]
Mullen, Diane C. - *Tagged*
    y HB Guide - v26 - i2 - Fall 2015 - p133(1) [51-500]
    y KR - Jan 15 2015 - pNA [51-500]
    y SLJ - v61 - i5 - May 2015 - p114(2) [51-500]
Mullen, Laura - *Complicated Grief*
    KR - Sept 1 2015 - pNA [501+]
    PW - v262 - i46 - Nov 16 2015 - p53(1) [51-500]
Mullenbach, Cheryl - *The Great Depression for Kids: Hardship and Hope in 1930s America, with 21 Activities*
    c BL - v111 - i22 - August 1 2015 - p52(1) [51-500]
    y PW - v262 - i18 - May 4 2015 - p120(1) [51-500]
    c SLJ - v61 - i7 - July 2015 - p108(2) [51-500]
Muller, Birte - *Farley Farts*
    c HB Guide - v26 - i1 - Spring 2015 - p40(1) [51-500]
Muller, Charles - *Korea's Great Buddhist-Confucian Debate: The Treatises of Chong Tojon (Sambong) and Hamho Tukt'ong*
    JAAR - v83 - i4 - Dec 2015 - p1175-1177 [501+]
Muller, Gerda - *The Town Musicians of Bremen*
    c Sch Lib - v63 - i2 - Summer 2015 - p97(1) [51-500]
Muller, Heribert - *Die Kirchliche Krise des Spatmittelalters: Schisma, Konziliarismus und Konzilien*
    HNet - Feb 2015 - pNA [501+]
Muller, Hildegard - *The Cowboy*
    c HB Guide - v26 - i2 - Fall 2015 - p60(1) [51-500]
    c KR - March 1 2015 - pNA [51-500]
    c PW - v262 - i10 - March 9 2015 - p71(1) [51-500]
    c SLJ - v61 - i3 - March 2015 - p122(1) [51-500]
Muller, Isabel - *The Green Sea Turtle*
    c HB Guide - v26 - i2 - Fall 2015 - p175(1) [51-500]
Muller, Lothar - *White Magic: The Age of Paper*
    NYRB - v62 - i13 - August 13 2015 - p67(2) [501+]
    TLS - i5846 - April 17 2015 - p22(2) [501+]
Muller, Marcia - *The Night Searchers*
    RVBW - March 2015 - pNA [51-500]
    RVBW - May 2015 - pNA [51-500]
Muller, Martin Anton - *Hermann Bahr: Osterreichischer Kritiker europaischer Avantgarden*
    MLR - v110 - i2 - April 2015 - p593-594 [501+]
Muller, Matthias - *Kulturtransfer am Furstenhof: Hofische Austauschprozesse und Ihre Medien im Zeitalter Kaiser Maximilians I*
    HNet - Jan 2015 - pNA [501+]
Muller, Rachel Dunstan - *When the Curtain Rises*
    c Teach Lib - v42 - i4 - April 2015 - p43(1) [51-500]
Muller, Reinhard - *Evidence of Editing: Growth and Change of Texts in the Hebrew Bible*
    Intpr - v69 - i1 - Jan 2015 - p124(1) [51-500]
Muller, Rolf-Dieter - *Enemy in the East: Hitler's Secret Plans to Invade the Soviet Union*
    HT - v65 - i7 - July 2015 - p62(2) [501+]
    TimHES - i2190 - Feb 12 2015 - p52-53 [501+]
Muller-Simmerling, Chantal - *The Rainbow Piano: A Method for Children 4-7 Years Old*
    Am MT - v64 - i5 - April-May 2015 - p49(2) [51-500]
Muller, Sven Oliver - *Das Publikum macht die Musik: Musikleben in Berlin, London und Wien im 19. Jahrhundert*
    HNet - May 2015 - pNA [501+]
Mullett-Bowlsby, Shannon - *Designer Crochet: 32 Patterns to Elevate Your Style, Sizes Small to 5X*
    BL - v111 - i17 - May 1 2015 - p69(1) [51-500]
    LJ - v140 - i8 - May 1 2015 - p73(1) [51-500]
    PW - v262 - i14 - April 6 2015 - p56(1) [51-500]
Mullett, Michael A. - *Martin Luther, 2d ed.*
    Six Ct J - v46 - i3 - Fall 2015 - p777-778 [51-500]
Mulligan, Andy - *The Boy with Two Heads*
    y BL - v112 - i6 - Nov 15 2015 - p50(1) [51-500]
    y SLJ - v61 - i10 - Oct 2015 - p104(2) [51-500]
Ribblestrop
    c HB Guide - v26 - i1 - Spring 2015 - p87(1) [51-500]
Mulligan, William - *The Great War for Peace*
    J Mil H - v79 - i4 - Oct 2015 - p1134-1135 [501+]
Mullin, Chris - *A Very British Coup*
    TimHES - i2227 - Oct 29 2015 - p47(1) [501+]
Mullin, Gerard E. - *The Gut Balance Revolution: Boost Your Metabolism, Restore Your Inner Ecology, and Lose the Weight for Good!*
    PW - v262 - i18 - May 4 2015 - p114(1) [51-500]
Mullin, Michael - *Simon*
    y PW - v262 - i26 - June 29 2015 - p70(1) [51-500]
Mullins, Charlotte - *Picturing People: The New State of the Art*
    LJ - v140 - i16 - Oct 1 2015 - p76(1) [51-500]
    PW - v262 - i34 - August 24 2015 - p75(1) [51-500]
Mullins, Juliet - *Envisioning Christ on the Cross: Ireland and the Early Medieval West*
    Specu - v90 - i1 - Jan 2015 - p281-283 [501+]
Mulloy, D.J. - *The World of the John Birch Society: Conspiracy, Conservatism, and the Cold War*
    AHR - v120 - i4 - Oct 2015 - p1517-1518 [501+]
    JAH - v102 - i2 - Sept 2015 - p607-608 [501+]
Mulqueen, Michael - *Small Navies: Strategy and Policy for Small Navies in War and Peace*
    NWCR - v68 - i2 - Spring 2015 - p136(2) [501+]
Mulrooney, Kristin J. - *Teaching and Learning in Bilingual Classrooms: New Scholarship*
    Bwatch - Oct 2015 - pNA [51-500]
Mulryne, J.R. - *Ceremonial Entries in Early Modern Europe: The Iconography of Power*
    HT - v65 - i8 - August 2015 - p61(2) [501+]
The Guild and Guild Buildings of Shakespeare's Stratford: Society: Religion, Education and Stage
    Sev Cent N - v73 - i1-2 - Spring-Summer 2015 - p9(3) [501+]
Mulzet, Ottilie - *Seiobo There Below*
    Econ - v415 - i8939 - May 23 2015 - p72(US) [501+]
    NS - v144 - i5266 - June 12 2015 - p53(1) [501+]

Mumme, Sarah - *Guess Who's My Pet*
   c KR - Jan 1 2016 - pNA [51-500]
Mun-yol, Yi - *Son of Man*
     KR - Oct 1 2015 - pNA [51-500]
Munaweera, Nayomi - *What Lies between Us*
     KR - Dec 15 2015 - pNA [501+]
Muncaster, Harriet - *Happy Halloween, Witch's Cat!*
(Illus. by Muncaster, Harriet)
   c HB - v91 - i5 - Sept-Oct 2015 - p69(1) [51-500]
   c KR - August 1 2015 - pNA [51-500]
   c PW - v262 - i30 - July 27 2015 - p67(1) [51-500]
   c SLJ - v61 - i9 - Sept 2015 - p108(1) [51-500]
I Am a Witch's Cat
   c HB Guide - v26 - i1 - Spring 2015 - p40(1) [51-500]
Muncy, Robyn - *Relentless Reformer: Josephine Roche and Progressivism in Twentieth Century America*
     Wom R Bks - v32 - i3 - May-June 2015 - p16(2) [501+]
Munday, Alicia - *Squishy Squashy Birds (Illus. by Van Wijk, Carl)*
   c Magpies - v30 - i2 - May 2015 - pS5(1) [501+]
Munday, Evan - *Loyalist to a Fault*
   y KR - July 15 2015 - pNA [51-500]
Muniz, Maria de las Nieves Muniz - *Lo 'Zibaldone' di Leopardi come ipertesto: Atti del Convegno internazionale Barcellona, Universitat de Barcelona, 26-27 ottobre 2012*
     MLR - v110 - i3 - July 2015 - p879-881 [501+]
Munleyand, Kathleen P. - *The Freach and Keen Murders: The True Story of the Crime That Shocked and Changed a Community Forever*
     PW - v262 - i15 - April 13 2015 - p68(2) [51-500]
Munnell, Alicia H. - *The Funding of State and Local Pensions: 2014-2018*
     Econ - v415 - i8944 - June 27 2015 - p60(US) [501+]
Munnich, Nicole - *Belgrad zwischen Sozialistischem Herrschaftsanspruch und Gesellschaftlichem Eigensinn: Die Jugoslawische Hauptstadt als Entwurf und Urbane Erfahrung*
     HNet - Feb 2015 - pNA [501+]
     Slav R - v74 - i1 - Spring 2015 - p173-174 [501+]
Munoz, C.J. - *Could Be a Crowd*
     PW - v262 - i39 - Sept 28 2015 - p76(1) [51-500]
Munoz, Daniel - *Alpha Docs: The Making of a Cardiologist*
     PW - v262 - i22 - June 1 2015 - p52(1) [51-500]
     BL - v111 - i22 - August 1 2015 - p11(2) [51-500]
     KR - May 15 2015 - pNA [51-500]
     LJ - v140 - i12 - July 1 2015 - p104(1) [51-500]
Munoz, Maria Jose - *The Compilation of Knowledge in the Middle Ages*
     Specu - v90 - i4 - Oct 2015 - p1194(1) [501+]
Munro, Alice - *Family Furnishings: Selected Stories, 1995-2014*
     Bks & Cult - v21 - i1 - Jan-Feb 2015 - p35(1) [501+]
     HR - v68 - i2 - Summer 2015 - p343-351 [501+]
     NYRB - v62 - i2 - Feb 5 2015 - p28(2) [501+]
Lives of Girls and Women
     TLS - i5848 - May 1 2015 - p19(1) [501+]
Munro, Eileen - *ABC's Down on the Farm (Illus. by Munro, Eileen)*
   c Res Links - v20 - i4 - April 2015 - p5(1) [51-500]
Munro, Lucy - *Archaic Style in English Literature, 1590-1674*
     Ren Q - v68 - i1 - Spring 2015 - p384-386 [501+]
     RES - v66 - i273 - Feb 2015 - p172-174 [501+]
     TLS - i5857 - July 3 2015 - p11(1) [501+]
Munro, Rona - *The James Plays*
     Theat J - v67 - i2 - May 2015 - p328-332 [501+]
Munro, Roxie - *Christmastime in New York City*
   c HB Guide - v26 - i2 - Fall 2015 - p221(1) [51-500]
The Inside-Outside Book of London
     HB Guide - v26 - i2 - Fall 2015 - p218(1) [51-500]
Market Maze (Illus. by Munro, Roxie)
   c HB Guide - v26 - i2 - Fall 2015 - p195(1) [51-500]
   c BL - v111 - i15 - April 1 2015 - p37(1) [51-500]
   c CH Bwatch - June 2015 - pNA [51-500]
   c KR - March 1 2015 - pNA [51-500]
Munroe, Randall - *Thing Explainer: Complicated Stuff in Simple Words*
     Am Sci - v103 - i6 - Nov-Dec 2015 - p422(2) [501+]
What If?: Serious Scientific Answers to Absurd Hypothetical Questions
     J Chem Ed - v92 - i7 - July 2015 - p1143-1145

[501+]
     Nature - v523 - i7562 - July 30 2015 - p530(1) [51-500]
Munsch, Robert - *Deep Snow (Illus. by Martchenko, Michael)*
   c Res Links - v20 - i4 - April 2015 - p5(2) [51-500]
Journee pyjama (Illus. by Martchenko, Michael)
     Res Links - v20 - i4 - April 2015 - p42(1) [51-500]
L'avion de Julie (Illus. by Martchenko, Michael)
     Res Links - v20 - i3 - Feb 2015 - p47(1) [51-500]
Le Papa de David (Illus. by Martchenko, Michael)
     Res Links - v20 - i4 - April 2015 - p47(1) [51-500]
Ou es-tu, Catherine? (Illus. by Martchenko, Michael)
     Res Links - v21 - i1 - Oct 2015 - p54(1) [51-500]
Papasorsnous de la! (Illus. by Martchenko, Michael)
     Res Links - v20 - i4 - April 2015 - p42(1) [51-500]
Pyjama Day (Illus. by Martchenko, Michael)
     Res Links - v20 - i4 - April 2015 - p6(1) [501+]
Munson, Victoria - *British Trees*
     Sch Lib - v63 - i3 - Autumn 2015 - p175(1) [51-500]
Munstedt, Peter - *Money for the Asking: Fundraising in Music Libraries*
     Notes - v71 - i4 - June 2015 - p676(3) [51-500]
Munsterhjelm, Mark - *Living Dead in the Pacific: Contested Sovereignty and Racism in Genetic Research on Taiwan Aborigines*
     Pac A - v88 - i2 - June 2015 - p302 [501+]
Mura, David - *The Last Incantations*
     WLT - v89 - i1 - Jan-Feb 2015 - p75(1) [51-500]
Muradov, Roman - *(In a Sense) Lost and Found*
     BL - v111 - i9-10 - Jan 1 2015 - p62(1) [51-500]
Murakami, Haruki - *Colorless Tsukuru Tazaki and His Years of Pilgrimage (Read by Locke, Bruce). Audiobook Review*
     BL - v111 - i12 - Feb 15 2015 - p103(1) [51-500]
Colorless Tsukuru Tazaki and His Years of Pilgrimage (Illus. by Locke, Bruce) (Read by Locke, Bruce). Audiobook Review
     LJ - v140 - i2 - Feb 1 2015 - p45(1) [51-500]
Colorless Tsukuru Tazaki and His Years of Pilgrimage (Read by Locke, Bruce). Audiobook Review
     NYTBR - May 17 2015 - p12(L) [501+]
Colorless Tsukuru Tazaki and His Years of Pilgrimage
     HR - v67 - i4 - Wntr 2015 - p685-692 [501+]
     NYTBR - May 31 2015 - p52(L) [501+]
The Strange Library (Read by Heyborne, Kirby). Audiobook Review
     NYTBR - May 17 2015 - p12(L) [501+]
     PW - v262 - i5 - Feb 2 2015 - p52(1) [51-500]
The Strange Library
     TLS - i5833 - Jan 16 2015 - p27(1) [501+]
Wind/Pinball (Read by Heyborne, Kirby). Audiobook Review
     LJ - v140 - i19 - Nov 15 2015 - p52(1) [51-500]
     PW - v262 - i39 - Sept 28 2015 - p85(1) [51-500]
Wind/Pinball
     BL - v111 - i22 - August 1 2015 - p30(2) [51-500]
     KR - June 15 2015 - pNA [51-500]
     LJ - v140 - i13 - August 1 2015 - p87(2) [51-500]
     NYTBR - August 16 2015 - p16(L) [51-500]
The Wind-Up Bird Chronicle
     Esq - v163 - i6-7 - June-July 2015 - p26(2) [501+]
Murakami, Masahiko - *Nichiren (Illus. by Tanaka, Ken)*
   y KR - August 15 2015 - pNA [51-500]
   y SLJ - v61 - i11 - Nov 2015 - p125(1) [51-500]
Murakawa, Naomi - *The First Civil Right: How Liberals Built Prison America*
     Dis - v62 - i2 - Spring 2015 - p137(4) [501+]
     Reason - v46 - i8 - Jan 2015 - p68(4) [501+]
Murat, Laure - *The Man Who Thought He Was Napoleon: Towards a Political History of Madness*
     Lon R Bks - v37 - i10 - May 21 2015 - p17(3) [501+]
Muratori, Cecilia - *Ethical Perspectives on Animals in the Renaissance and Early Modern Period*
     Ren Q - v68 - i3 - Fall 2015 - p1030-1032 [501+]
Murav, Harriet - *Soviet Jews in World War II: Fighting, Witnessing, Remembering*
     Slav R - v74 - i3 - Fall 2015 - p657-659 [501+]
Muravchik, Joshua - *Making David into Goliath: How the World Turned against Israel*
     Soc - v52 - i4 - August 2015 - p394(4) [501+]
Murdoch, Brian - *Gregorius: An Incestuous Saint in Medieval Europe and Beyond*
     MLR - v110 - i3 - July 2015 - p782-783 [501+]
Murdoch, H. Adlai - *Francophone Cultures and Geographies of Identity*
     FS - v69 - i2 - April 2015 - p274-275 [501+]

Murdoch, Iris - *Living on Paper: Letters from Iris Murdoch 1934-1995*
     KR - Nov 15 2015 - pNA [501+]
     PW - v262 - i52 - Dec 21 2015 - p145(1) [51-500]
Murdock, Rebecca Merry - *Wild Cats: Around the Globe with Suki & Finch*
     CH Bwatch - June 2015 - pNA [51-500]
Murguia, Bethanie - *Deeney I Feel Five!*
   c HB Guide - v26 - i1 - Spring 2015 - p40(1) [51-500]
Murguia, Bethanie Deeney - *The Best Parts of Christmas (Illus. by Murguia, Bethanie Deeney)*
   c KR - Sept 1 2015 - pNA [51-500]
   c PW - v262 - i37 - Sept 14 2015 - p67(1) [51-500]
   c SLJ - v61 - i10 - Oct 2015 - p66(1) [51-500]
Cockatoo, Too (Illus. by Murguia, Bethanie Deeney)
   c KR - Oct 15 2015 - pNA [51-500]
   c PW - v262 - i41 - Oct 12 2015 - p65(1) [51-500]
   c SLJ - v61 - i11 - Nov 2015 - p85(1) [51-500]
Muriel, Michelle - *Essie's Roses*
     SPBW - August 2015 - pNA [501+]
Murnane, Gerald - *A Million Windows*
     WLT - v89 - i1 - Jan-Feb 2015 - p68(2) [51-500]
Murphet, Julian - *Flann O'Brien and Modernism*
     TLS - i5853 - June 5 2015 - p9(2) [501+]
Murphy, Angela - *The Tricks and Treats of Halloween! (Illus. by Wake, Rich)*
   c HB Guide - v26 - i1 - Spring 2015 - p142(1) [51-500]
Murphy, Anne - *The Materiality of the Past: History and Representation in Sikh Tradition*
     AHR - v120 - i1 - Feb 2015 - p208-209 [501+]
Murphy, Audrey - *Bird's Flight*
     KR - July 15 2015 - pNA [501+]
Murphy, Brenda - *Brewing Identities: Globalisation, Guinness and the Production of Irishness*
     TimHES - i2211 - July 9 2015 - p44(1) [501+]
Murphy, Brendan - *Ready for School, Murphy? (Illus. by Murphy, Brendan)*
   c HB Guide - v26 - i2 - Fall 2015 - p46(1) [51-500]
   c KR - June 1 2015 - pNA [51-500]
Murphy, Brian - *81 Days below Zero: The Incredible Survival Story of a World War II Pilot in Alaska's Frozen Wilderness*
     BL - v111 - i18 - May 15 2015 - p12(1) [51-500]
     KR - April 15 2015 - pNA [51-500]
Murphy, Catherine - *Maestra. Film.*
     Ams - v72 - i1 - Jan 2015 - p178(2) [501+]
Murphy, Daniel - *William Washington, American Light Dragoon: A Continental Cavalry Leader in the War of Independence*
     J Mil H - v79 - i2 - April 2015 - p487-488 [501+]
Murphy, Dervla - *Between River and Sea: Encounters in Israel and Palestine*
     NS - v144 - i5269 - July 3 2015 - p46(3) [501+]
Murphy, Douglas A. - *Two Armies on the Rio Grande: The First Campaign of the US-Mexican War*
     J Mil H - v79 - i2 - April 2015 - p493-494 [501+]
Murphy, Erin E. - *Inside the Cell: The Dark Side of Forensic DNA*
     LJ - v140 - i15 - Sept 15 2015 - p90(1) [51-500]
Inside the Cell: The Dark Side of Forensic DNA (Illus. by Murphy, Erin E.)
     KR - August 1 2015 - pNA [51-500]
Murphy, Fiona - *Integration in Ireland: The Everyday Lives of African Migrants*
     JRAI - v21 - i1 - March 2015 - p234(2) [501+]
Murphy, G. Ronald - *Tree of Salvation: Yggdrasil and the Cross in the North*
     CH - v84 - i1 - March 2015 - p231(1) [501+]
Murphy, Gareth - *Cowboys and Indies: The Epic History of the Record Industry*
     NS - v144 - i5265 - June 5 2015 - p46(2) [501+]
     Spec - v327 - i9730 - Feb 21 2015 - p44(1) [501+]
Murphy, James B. - *Becoming the Beach Boys, 1961-1963*
     LJ - v140 - i14 - Sept 1 2015 - p103(1) [51-500]
Murphy, James G. - *War's Ends: Human Rights, International Order, and the Ethics of Peace*
     AM - v212 - i4 - Feb 9 2015 - p34(3) [501+]
Murphy, Jill - *The Worst Witch to the Rescue*
   c HB Guide - v26 - i1 - Spring 2015 - p87(1) [51-500]
Murphy, Jim (b. 1947-) - *Breakthrough! How Three People Saved "Blue Babies" and Changed Medicine Forever*
   c BL - v112 - i7 - Dec 1 2015 - p44(1) [51-500]
   c HB - v91 - i6 - Nov-Dec 2015 - p103(1) [51-500]
   c KR - Sept 15 2015 - pNA [51-500]
   c PW - v262 - i49 - Dec 2 2015 - p82(1) [51-500]
   c SLJ - v61 - i11 - Nov 2015 - p136(2) [51-500]

Murphy, Jonell Patricia - *Pull (Illus. by Kumar, Rohit)*
   c CH Bwatch - August 2015 - pNA [51-500]
Murphy, Julie - *Dumplin' (Read by Stevens, Eileen).*
Audiobook Review
   y SLJ - v61 - i11 - Nov 2015 - p73(1) [51-500]
Dumplin'
   y BL - v111 - i22 - August 1 2015 - p63(2) [51-500]
   y HB - v91 - i6 - Nov-Dec 2015 - p86(1) [51-500]
   y KR - June 1 2015 - pNA [51-500]
   y PW - v262 - i22 - June 1 2015 - p61(1) [51-500]
   y PW - v262 - i49 - Dec 2 2015 - p90(1) [51-500]
   y SLJ - v61 - i8 - August 2015 - p108(2) [51-500]
   y VOYA - v38 - i3 - August 2015 - p65(1) [51-500]
Murphy, Kathryn - *The Emergence of Impartiality*
   Ren Q - v68 - i3 - Fall 2015 - p1024-1025 [501+]
Murphy, Kevin D. - *Studies in Ephemera: Text and Image in Eighteenth-Century Print*
   TLS - i5874 - Oct 30 2015 - p31(1) [501+]
Murphy, Liam - *What Makes Law: An Introduction to the Philosophy of Law*
   HLR - v128 - i4 - Feb 2015 - p1330(1) [1-50]
Murphy, Lucy Eldersveld - *Great Lakes Creoles: A French-Indian Community on the Northern Borderlands, Prairie Du Chien, 1750-1860*
   AHR - v120 - i4 - Oct 2015 - p1484-1485 [501+]
Murphy, Mary - *Are You My Mommy? (Illus. by Murphy, Mary)*
   c KR - July 1 2015 - pNA [51-500]
   c PW - v262 - i15 - April 13 2015 - p78(2) [501+]
Good Night Like This
   c KR - Dec 1 2015 - pNA [51-500]
Murphy, Maureen O'Rourke - *Compassionate Stranger: Asenath Nicholson and the Great Irish Famine*
   ILS - v35 - i1 - Fall 2015 - p6(2) [501+]
Murphy, Michelle - *Seizing the Means of Reproduction*
   T&C - v56 - i3 - July 2015 - p782-784 [501+]
Murphy, Monica - *Never Tear Us Apart*
   BL - v112 - i7 - Dec 1 2015 - p37(1) [51-500]
   PW - v262 - i50 - Dec 7 2015 - p75(1) [51-500]
Stealing Rose
   BL - v111 - i13 - March 1 2015 - p29(1) [51-500]
   PW - v262 - i2 - Jan 12 2015 - p42(1) [51-500]
Murphy-O'Connor, Cormac - *An English Spring: Memoirs*
   TLS - i5859 - July 17 2015 - p8(2) [501+]
Murphy, Pat - *Lego Chain Reactions*
   c CH Bwatch - March 2015 - pNA [51-500]
Murphy, Peter - *And Is There Honey Still for Tea?*
   KR - Dec 1 2015 - pNA [501+]
   PW - v262 - i52 - Dec 21 2015 - p134(1) [51-500]
Murphy, Philip - *Monarchy and the End of Empire: The House of Windsor, the British Government, and the Postwar Commonwealth*
   AHR - v120 - i1 - Feb 2015 - p337-338 [501+]
Murphy, Richard - *The Joy of Tax*
   TimHES - i2230 - Nov 19 2015 - p50(1) [501+]
Murphy, Robert Lee - *Eagle Talons*
   y Roundup M - v22 - i3 - Feb 2015 - p26(2) [501+]
   Roundup M - v22 - i6 - August 2015 - p32(1) [501+]
Murphy, Sally - *Australia's Great War: 1915*
   y Magpies - v30 - i1 - March 2015 - p36(1) [501+]
Fly-in Fly-out Dad (Illus. by Dawson, Janine)
   c Magpies - v30 - i3 - July 2015 - p29(1) [501+]
Murphy, Seamus - *I am the Beggar of the World: Landays from contemporary Afghanistan*
   TimHES - i2184 - Jan 1 2015 - p63(1) [501+]
Murphy, Shawn - *The Optimistic Workplace: Creating an Environment that Energizes Everyone*
   LJ - v140 - i16 - Oct 1 2015 - p90(1) [51-500]
Murphy, Stacy Anne - *ASL Tales: Annie's Tails (Illus. by Pierleoni, Gina)*
   c CH Bwatch - July 2015 - pNA [51-500]
Murphy, Stephen - *The Puma Blues: The Complete Saga*
   PW - v262 - i48 - Nov 30 2015 - p47(1) [51-500]
Murphy, Taggart - *Japan and the Shackles of the Past*
   Econ - v414 - i8920 - Jan 10 2015 - p74(US) [501+]
Murphy, Todd - *Go Fast, Goo*
   c CH Bwatch - March 2015 - pNA [51-500]
Murphy, William - *Political Imprisonment and the Irish, 1912-1921*
   AHR - v120 - i2 - April 2015 - p710-711 [501+]
Murr, Karl Borromaus - *Lassalles "Sudliche Avantgarde": Protokollbuch des Allgemeinen Deutschen Arbeitervereins der Gemeinde Augsburg (1864-1867).*
   HNet - Feb 2015 - pNA [501+]

Murray, Alison - *Hickory Dickory Dog*
   c HB Guide - v26 - i1 - Spring 2015 - p13(1) [51-500]
The House That Zack Built (Illus. by Murray, Alison)
   c KR - Nov 15 2015 - pNA [51-500]
   c SLJ - v61 - i12 - Dec 2015 - p93(1) [51-500]
Murray, Charles - *By the People: Rebuilding Liberty without Permission*
   Nat R - v67 - i13 - July 20 2015 - p37 [501+]
   NYTBR - July 5 2015 - p1(L) [501+]
Murray, David - *The Happy Christian: Ten Ways To Be a Joyful Believer in a Gloomy World*
   LJ - v140 - i9 - May 15 2015 - p64(2) [501+]
Murray, Diane M. - *Cabinet of Mathematical Curiosities at Teachers College: David Eugene Smith's Collection*
   Math T - v108 - i7 - March 2015 - p559(1) [501+]
Murray, Donald S. - *Herring Tales: How the Silver Darlings Shaped Human Taste and History*
   Spec - v329 - i9760 - Sept 19 2015 - p44(1) [501+]
Murray, E.C. - *A Long Way from Paris*
   PW - v262 - i27 - July 6 2015 - p61(1) [51-500]
Murray, Elizabeth A. - *Overturning Wrongful Convictions: Science Serving Justice*
   y HB Guide - v26 - i2 - Fall 2015 - p155(1) [51-500]
Murray, Eva - *Island Birthday (Illus. by Hogan, Jamie)*
   c CH Bwatch - August 2015 - pNA [51-500]
   c KR - March 15 2015 - pNA [51-500]
Murray, George - *Wow Wow and Haw Haw (Illus. by Pittman, Michael)*
   c CH Bwatch - May 2015 - pNA [51-500]
Murray, J.J. - *Let's Stay Together*
   PW - v262 - i11 - March 16 2015 - p70(1) [51-500]
Murray, James - *The Long Rifle Season*
   Roundup M - v22 - i4 - April 2015 - p34(1) [501+]
   Roundup M - v22 - i6 - August 2015 - p32(1) [501+]
Murray, James T. - *Store Front II: A History Preserved: The Disappearing Face of New York*
   LJ - v140 - i20 - Dec 1 2015 - p106(2) [501+]
Murray, Jeanette - *Against the Ropes*
   PW - v262 - i35 - August 31 2015 - p67(2) [51-500]
Below the Belt
   PW - v262 - i8 - Feb 23 2015 - p59(1) [51-500]
Murray, Jennifer M. - *On a Great Battlefield: The Making, Management, and Memory of Gettysburg National Military Park, 1933-2013*
   JAH - v102 - i2 - Sept 2015 - p592-593 [501+]
   JSH - v81 - i4 - Nov 2015 - p1027(2) [501+]
Murray, Jonathan - *The New Scottish Cinema*
   Si & So - v25 - i9 - Sept 2015 - p105(1) [51-500]
Murray, Joseph - *Gallipoli 1915*
   Lon R Bks - v37 - i10 - May 21 2015 - p39(3) [501+]
Murray, Julie - *Birds*
   c SLJ - v61 - i9 - Sept 2015 - p175(2) [51-500]
Boats
   c HB Guide - v26 - i1 - Spring 2015 - p173(1) [51-500]
Cars
   c HB Guide - v26 - i1 - Spring 2015 - p173(1) [51-500]
Cats
   c SLJ - v61 - i9 - Sept 2015 - p175(2) [51-500]
Chickens
   c SLJ - v61 - i9 - Sept 2015 - p176(1) [51-500]
Cows
   c SLJ - v61 - i9 - Sept 2015 - p176(1) [51-500]
Day of the Dead
   c HB Guide - v26 - i1 - Spring 2015 - p142(1) [51-500]
Dizvali
   c HB Guide - v26 - i1 - Spring 2015 - p135(1) [51-500]
Earth Day
   c HB Guide - v26 - i1 - Spring 2015 - p142(1) [51-500]
Fish
   c SLJ - v61 - i9 - Sept 2015 - p175(2) [51-500]
Goats
   c SLJ - v61 - i9 - Sept 2015 - p176(1) [51-500]
Greece
   HB Guide - v26 - i2 - Fall 2015 - p218(1) [51-500]

Groundhog Day
   c HB Guide - v26 - i1 - Spring 2015 - p142(1) [51-500]
Hamsters
   c SLJ - v61 - i9 - Sept 2015 - p175(2) [51-500]
Hermit Crabs
   c SLJ - v61 - i9 - Sept 2015 - p175(2) [51-500]
Horses
   c SLJ - v61 - i9 - Sept 2015 - p176(1) [51-500]
Norway
   HB Guide - v26 - i2 - Fall 2015 - p218(1) [51-500]
Pigs
   c SLJ - v61 - i9 - Sept 2015 - p176(1) [51-500]
Piranhas
   c HB Guide - v26 - i1 - Spring 2015 - p161(1) [51-500]
Planes
   c HB Guide - v26 - i1 - Spring 2015 - p173(1) [51-500]
Poison Dart Frogs
   c HB Guide - v26 - i1 - Spring 2015 - p160(1) [51-500]
Sheep
   c SLJ - v61 - i9 - Sept 2015 - p176(1) [51-500]
Sloths
   c HB Guide - v26 - i1 - Spring 2015 - p166(1) [51-500]
South American Animals: Toucans
   c HB Guide - v26 - i1 - Spring 2015 - p162(1) [51-500]
Spaceships
   c HB Guide - v26 - i1 - Spring 2015 - p174(1) [51-500]
United States Air Force
   c HB Guide - v26 - i1 - Spring 2015 - p139(1) [51-500]
United States Army
   c HB Guide - v26 - i1 - Spring 2015 - p139(1) [51-500]
United States Marine Corps
   c HB Guide - v26 - i1 - Spring 2015 - p139(1) [51-500]
United States Navy
   c HB Guide - v26 - i1 - Spring 2015 - p139(1) [51-500]
Murray, Julie (b. 1969-) - *New Zealand*
   c HB Guide - v26 - i2 - Fall 2015 - p223(1) [51-500]
Pakistan
   c HB Guide - v26 - i2 - Fall 2015 - p218(1) [51-500]
Murray, Kara - *Abbreviations*
   c SLJ - v61 - i4 - April 2015 - p106(3) [501+]
Murray, Kirsty - *Eat the Sky, Drink the Ocean*
   y Magpies - v30 - i1 - March 2015 - p42(1) [501+]
Murray, Laura (b. 1970-) - *The Gingerbread Man Loose at Christmas (Illus. by Lowery, Mike)*
   c BL - v112 - i4 - Oct 15 2015 - p48(1) [51-500]
   c HB - v91 - i6 - Nov-Dec 2015 - p58(1) [51-500]
   c KR - Sept 1 2015 - pNA [51-500]
   c PW - v262 - i37 - Sept 14 2015 - p76(1) [51-500]
   c SLJ - v61 - i10 - Oct 2015 - p66(1) [51-500]
Murray, Laura K. - *Bean*
   c BL - v112 - i2 - Sept 15 2015 - p60(2) [51-500]
Corn
   c BL - v112 - i2 - Sept 15 2015 - p60(2) [51-500]
Penguin
   c BL - v112 - i2 - Sept 15 2015 - p60(2) [51-500]
Spiders
   c BL - v112 - i7 - Dec 1 2015 - p43(1) [51-500]
The Story of AT&T
   y SLJ - v61 - i9 - Sept 2015 - p176(1) [51-500]
Worms
   c BL - v112 - i7 - Dec 1 2015 - p43(1) [51-500]
Murray, Les - *New Selected Poems*
   Bks & Cult - v21 - i5 - Sept-Oct 2015 - p29(2) [501+]
   HR - v67 - i4 - Wntr 2015 - p667-676 [501+]
Murray, Lucy Miller - *Chamber Music: An Extensive Guide for Listeners*
   BL - v111 - i22 - August 1 2015 - p14(2) [51-500]
Murray, Martine - *Molly and Pim and the Millions of Stars*
   c Magpies - v30 - i4 - Sept 2015 - p36(1) [501+]
Murray, Nicholas - *The Rocky Road to the Great War: The Evolution of the Trench Warfare to 1914*
   J Mil H - v79 - i4 - Oct 2015 - p1149-1150 [501+]

Murray, Paul - *The Mark and the Void*
 BL - v112 - i2 - Sept 15 2015 - p27(1) [51-500]
 KR - Sept 1 2015 - pNA [51-500]
 LJ - v140 - i17 - Oct 15 2015 - p75(2) [51-500]
 NS - v144 - i5276 - August 21 2015 - p47(1) [51-500]
 NYTBR - Dec 13 2015 - p22(L) [501+]
 PW - v262 - i34 - August 24 2015 - p55(1) [51-500]

Murray, Peter (1920-1992) - *The Oxford Dictionary of Christian Art & Architecture, 2d ed*
 LJ - v140 - i2 - Feb 1 2015 - p108(1) [51-500]

Murray, Peter (b. 1952-) - *Chameleons*
 c BL - v111 - i22 - August 1 2015 - p54(1) [51-500]

Murray, Stuart A.P. - *World War II: Step into the Action and Behind Enemy Lines from Hitler's Rise to Japan's Surrender*
 y SLJ - v61 - i9 - Sept 2015 - p188(1) [51-500]

Murray, Tamsyn - *Accidental Genius (Illus. by Miller, Antonia)*
 c Sch Lib - v63 - i3 - Autumn 2015 - p169(1) [51-500]

Murray, Tessa - *Thomas Morley: Elizabethan Music Publisher*
 MT - v156 - i1931 - Summer 2015 - p118-120 [501+]

Murray, Victoria Christopher - *Stand Your Ground*
 y BL - v111 - i19-20 - June 1 2015 - p45(1) [51-500]

Murray, Williamson - *The Iran-Iraq War: A Military and Strategic History*
 J Mil H - v79 - i2 - April 2015 - p550-551 [501+]

Murrin, Michael - *Trade and Romance*
 MLR - v110 - i3 - July 2015 - p781-782 [501+]
 Ren Q - v68 - i1 - Spring 2015 - p408-409 [501+]

Murry, Gregory - *The Medicean Succession: Monarchy and Sacral Politics in Duke Cosimo dei Medici's Florence*
 AHR - v120 - i2 - April 2015 - p732-733 [501+]
 CHR - v101 - i3 - Summer 2015 - p652(3) [501+]
 Six Ct J - v46 - i1 - Spring 2015 - p196-197 [501+]

Murtagh, Ciaran - *Stuntboy: The Fincredible Diary of Fin Spencer (Illus. by Wesson, Tim)*
 c Sch Lib - v63 - i3 - Autumn 2015 - p169(1) [51-500]

Murthy, Vasudev - *Sherlock Holmes, the Missing Years: Japan*
 BL - v111 - i13 - March 1 2015 - p25(1) [51-500]
 KR - Jan 15 2015 - pNA [51-500]
 PW - v262 - i2 - Jan 12 2015 - p38(2) [51-500]
 Sherlock Holmes, the Missing Years: Timbuktu
 BL - v112 - i6 - Nov 15 2015 - p29(1) [51-500]
 KR - Oct 15 2015 - pNA [51-500]
 PW - v262 - i45 - Nov 9 2015 - p37(2) [51-500]

Murthy, Viren - *The Challenge of Linear Time: Nationhood and the Politics of History in East Asia*
 AHR - v120 - i2 - April 2015 - p589-591 [501+]

Mury, Megan - *Bound with Love*
 PW - v262 - i15 - April 13 2015 - p63(1) [51-500]

Musa, Omar - *Here Come the Dogs*
 KR - Oct 15 2015 - pNA [51-500]
 PW - v262 - i41 - Oct 12 2015 - p45(2) [51-500]

Musacchio, Aldo - *Reinventing State Capitalism: Leviathan in Business, Brazil and Beyond*
 BHR - v89 - i1 - Spring 2015 - p158(3) [501+]

Muschert, Glenn W. - *Responding to School Violence: Confronting the Columbine Effect*
 CS - v44 - i4 - July 2015 - p539-541 [501+]

Musegades, Benjamin - *Furstliche Erziehung und Ausbildung im Spatmittelalterlichen Reich*
 HNet - July 2015 - pNA [501+]

Museumsverband des Landes Brandenburg - *Entnazifizierte Zone? Zum Umgang mit der Zeit des Nationalsozialismus in ostdeutschen Stadt- und Regionalmuseen*
 HNet - Oct 2015 - pNA [501+]

Musgrave, Susan - *More Blueberries! (Illus. by Melo, Esperanca)*
 c KR - July 1 2015 - pNA [51-500]
 c PW - v262 - i15 - April 13 2015 - p78(2) [501+]
 c Res Links - v20 - i4 - April 2015 - p6(1) [51-500]
 c SLJ - v61 - i7 - July 2015 - p56(2) [51-500]

Musgrave, Toby - *Paradise Gardens: Spiritual Inspiration and Earthly Expression*
 LJ - v140 - i20 - Dec 1 2015 - p123(1) [51-500]

Musialkowski, Lechoslaw - *Bomber Aircraft of 305 Squadron*
 APH - v62 - i2 - Summer 2015 - p52(1) [501+]

Music, Debra - *Theo Chocolate: Recipes and Sweet Secrets from Seattle's Favorite Chocolate Maker*
 LJ - v140 - i12 - July 1 2015 - p106(1) [51-500]

Musick, Michael P. - *"I Am Busy Drawing Pictures": The Civil War Art and Letters of Private John Jacob Omenhausser, CSA*
 JSH - v81 - i4 - Nov 2015 - p997(2) [501+]

Musik und Vergnugen am Hohen Ufer. Fest- und Kulturtransfer von Venedig nach Hannover in der Fruhen Neuzeit
 HNet - Jan 2015 - pNA [501+]

Musikwissenschaft: Generationen, Netzwerke, Denkstrukturen
 HNet - June 2015 - pNA [501+]

Musil, Brian - *Rachel Carson and Her Sisters: Extraordinary Women Who Have Shaped America's Environment*
 Wom R Bks - v32 - i1 - Jan-Feb 2015 - p5(4) [501+]

Musil, Robert - *Wien in der Weltwirtschaft: Die Positionsbestimmung der Stadtregion Wien in der Internationalen Stadtehierarchie*
 HNet - July 2015 - pNA [501+]

Musomandera, Elise Rida - *Le Livre d'Elise*
 WLT - v89 - i3-4 - May-August 2015 - p127(1) [501+]

Musser, George - *Spooky Action at a Distance: The Phenomenon That Reimagines Space and Time--and What It Means for Black Holes, the Big Bang, and Theories of Everything*
 KR - August 15 2015 - pNA [501+]
 Nature - v527 - i7577 - Nov 12 2015 - p163(1) [51-500]
 NH - v123 - i9 - Nov 2015 - p46(2) [51-500]
 PW - v262 - i32 - August 10 2015 - p46(1) [51-500]

Musser, Susan - *Parenting*
 y Teach Lib - v42 - i3 - Feb 2015 - p28(4) [51-500]

Musson, Jeremy - *The Country House Ideal: Recent Work by ADAM Architecture*
 TimHES - i2223 - Oct 1 2015 - p49(1) [501+]

Mustacich, Suzanne - *Thirsty Dragon: China's Lust for Bordeaux and the Threat to the World's Best Wines*
 KR - Sept 1 2015 - pNA [501+]
 PW - v262 - i44 - Nov 2 2015 - p78(1) [51-500]

Mustin, Bob - *We Are Strong, But We Are Fragile*
 KR - May 15 2015 - pNA [501+]

Mutala, Marion - *Grateful*
 c Res Links - v20 - i3 - Feb 2015 - p7(1) [51-500]

Mutch, Maria - *Know the Night: A Memoir of Survival in the Small Hours*
 Can Lit - i224 - Spring 2015 - p129 [501+]

Mutch, Robert E. - *Buying the Vote: A History of Campaign Finance Reform*
 AHR - v120 - i3 - June 2015 - p1038-1039 [501+]
 JIH - v46 - i2 - Autumn 2015 - p298-299 [501+]

Mutchler, Terry - *Under This Beautiful Dome: A Senator, A Journalist, and the Politics of Gay Love in America*
 G&L Rev W - v22 - i1 - Jan-Feb 2015 - p40(1) [501+]

Muten, Burleigh - *Miss Emily (Illus. by Matt Phelan,)*
 c RVBW - March 2015 - pNA [501+]

Muth, Jon J. - *Zen Socks (Illus. by Muth, Jon J.)*
 c BL - v111 - i19-20 - June 1 2015 - p125(1) [51-500]
 c KR - June 15 2015 - pNA [51-500]
 c PW - v262 - i29 - July 20 2015 - p189(2) [51-500]
 c PW - v262 - i49 - Dec 2 2015 - p23(1) [51-500]
 c SLJ - v61 - i7 - July 2015 - p66(1) [51-500]

Mutter, John C. - *The Disaster Profiteers: How Natural Disasters Make the Rich Richer and the Poor Even Poorer*
 LJ - v140 - i12 - July 1 2015 - p102(1) [51-500]
 The Disaster Profiteers
 KR - June 15 2015 - pNA [501+]

Mutz, Diana C. - *In-Your-Face Politics: The Consequences of Uncivil Media*
 KR - Feb 1 2015 - pNA [501+]

Muus, Kate - *Secret of the Seeds*
 y SLJ - v61 - i10 - Oct 2015 - p115(1) [51-500]

Muzanenhamo, Togara - *Gumiguru*
 TLS - i5872 - Oct 16 2015 - p23(1) [501+]

Muzekari, Nick - *A Gift for Matthew (Illus. by Lobastov, Masha)*
 c CH Bwatch - Oct 2015 - pNA [51-500]

Muzzarelli, Maria Giuseppina - *From Words to Deeds: The Effectiveness of Preaching in the Late Middle Ages*
 Med R - May 2015 - pNA [501+]
 Specu - v90 - i3 - July 2015 - p877(1) [501+]

Myer, Andy - *Henry Hubble's Book of Troubles (Illus. by Myer, Andy)*
 c CCB-B - v68 - i10 - June 2015 - p507(2) [51-500]
 c HB Guide - v26 - i2 - Fall 2015 - p95(1) [51-500]

Myer, Ilana C. - *Last Song before Night*
 PW - v262 - i27 - July 6 2015 - p50(1) [51-500]

Myers, Amy - *Classic Cashes In*
 BL - v111 - i9-10 - Jan 1 2015 - p50(1) [51-500]
 Classic in the Dock
 BL - v112 - i1 - Sept 1 2015 - p45(1) [51-500]
 PW - v262 - i29 - July 20 2015 - p172(1) [51-500]

Myers, Ann - *The Stem Shift: A Guide for School Leaders*
 Bwatch - Nov 2015 - pNA [501+]

Myers, Anna - *Tumbleiveeo Baby (Illus. by Vess, Charles)*
 c HB Guide - v26 - i1 - Spring 2015 - p40(1) [51-500]
 Tumbleweed Baby (Illus. by Vess, Charles)
 y Roundup M - v22 - i5 - June 2015 - p37(1) [501+]
 c Roundup M - v22 - i6 - August 2015 - p25(1) [501+]

Myers, B.R. - *Asp of Ascension: A Nefertari Hughes Mystery*
 y SLJ - v61 - i8 - August 2015 - p108(1) [51-500]

Myers, Benjamin J. - *The Grindle Witch*
 c Sch Lib - v63 - i2 - Summer 2015 - p119(1) [51-500]

Myers, Christopher - *H.O.R.S.E.: A Game of Basketball and Imagination (Read by Graham, Dion). Audiobook Review*
 c SLJ - v61 - i3 - March 2015 - p76(1) [51-500]
 My Pen (Illus. by Myers, Christopher)
 c BL - v111 - i11 - Feb 1 2015 - p56(2) [51-500]
 c CH Bwatch - April 2015 - pNA [51-500]
 c HB - v91 - i4 - July-August 2015 - p121(1) [51-500]
 c KR - Jan 15 2015 - pNA [51-500]
 c PW - v262 - i2 - Jan 12 2015 - p56(1) [51-500]
 c PW - v262 - i49 - Dec 2 2015 - p21(1) [51-500]
 c SLJ - v61 - i2 - Feb 2015 - p73(2) [51-500]

Myers, E.C. - *The Silence of Six*
 y CCB-B - v68 - i6 - Feb 2015 - p323(1) [51-500]

Myers, Gary - *Brady vs Manning: The Untold Story of the Rivalry That Transformed the NFL*
 LJ - v140 - i17 - Oct 15 2015 - p92(2) [501+]

Myers, Kate Kae - *Inherit Midnight*
 y BL - v111 - i9-10 - Jan 1 2015 - p94(1) [51-500]
 y CCB-B - v68 - i8 - April 2015 - p413(1) [51-500]
 Ent W - i1352 - Feb 27 2015 - p61(1) [501+]
 y HB Guide - v26 - i2 - Fall 2015 - p133(1) [51-500]
 SLJ - v61 - i4 - April 2015 - p168(1) [51-500]
 y VOYA - v37 - i6 - Feb 2015 - p62(1) [51-500]

Myers, Marc - *Why Jazz Happened*
 Notes - v71 - i4 - June 2015 - p723(4) [501+]

Myers, Perry - *German Visions of India, 1871-1918: Commandeering the Holy Ganges during the Kaiserreich*
 GSR - v38 - i1 - Feb 2015 - p183-185 [501+]

Myers, Steven Lee - *The New Tsar: The Rise and Reign of Vladimir Putin*
 LJ - v140 - i14 - Sept 1 2015 - p112(1) [51-500]
 PW - v262 - i28 - July 13 2015 - p55(1) [51-500]
 BL - v112 - i1 - Sept 1 2015 - p31(1) [51-500]
 CSM - Sept 30 2015 - pNA [501+]
 KR - July 15 2015 - pNA [51-500]
 NYTBR - Nov 8 2015 - p12(L) [501+]

Myers, Suzanne - *I'm from Nowhere*
 y KR - Nov 1 2015 - pNA [51-500]
 y VOYA - v38 - i5 - Dec 2015 - p61(1) [51-500]
 Stone Cove Island
 y CCB-B - v68 - i5 - Jan 2015 - p270(1) [51-500]
 c HB Guide - v26 - i1 - Spring 2015 - p118(1) [51-500]

Myers, Tim J. - *The Christmas Stick (Illus. by Yilmaz, Necdet)*
 c CH Bwatch - Jan 2015 - pNA [51-500]
 The Thunder Egg (Illus. by Coleman, Winfield)
 c CH Bwatch - August 2015 - pNA [51-500]
 c KR - May 1 2015 - pNA [51-500]
 c SLJ - v61 - i12 - Dec 2015 - p93(1) [51-500]

Myers, Walter Dean - *An African Princess: From African Orphan to Queen Victoria's Favourite*
 c Sch Lib - v63 - i2 - Summer 2015 - p112(1) [51-500]
 Crystal (Read by Johnson, Sisi Aisha). Audiobook Review
 y SLJ - v61 - i6 - June 2015 - p67(1) [51-500]
 Juba!
 y BL - v111 - i21 - July 1 2015 - p56(1) [51-500]
 y CCB-B - v69 - i2 - Oct 2015 - p104(2) [51-500]
 y HB - v91 - i6 - Nov-Dec 2015 - p86(2) [51-500]
 y KR - July 15 2015 - pNA [51-500]
 y PW - v262 - i29 - July 20 2015 - p194(1) [51-500]

y   SLJ - v61 - i8 - August 2015 - p98(1) [51-500]
y   VOYA - v38 - i5 - Dec 2015 - p61(1) [51-500]
Monster (Illus. by Anyabwile, Dawud)
y   BL - v111 - i22 - August 1 2015 - p48(1) [51-500]
y   KR - August 15 2015 - pNA [51-500]
y   SLJ - v61 - i8 - August 2015 - p112(1) [51-500]
On a Clear Day
y   HB Guide - v26 - i1 - Spring 2015 - p118(1) [51-500]

Myers, William David - *Death and a Maiden: Infanticide and the Tragical History of Grethe Schmidt*
    GSR - v38 - i1 - Feb 2015 - p155-157 [501+]

Myka, Lenore - *King of the Gypsies*
    KR - July 15 2015 - pNA [501+]

Myklusch, Matt - *The Lost Prince*
c   KR - March 15 2015 - pNA [51-500]

c   SLJ - v61 - i2 - Feb 2015 - p89(1) [51-500]
c   BL - v111 - i15 - April 1 2015 - p80(1) [51-500]
c   HB Guide - v26 - i2 - Fall 2015 - p95(1) [51-500]

Myles, Eileen - *Chelsea Girls*
    NYT - Sept 29 2015 - pC1(L) [501+]
I Must Be Living Twice: New and Selected Poems 1975-2014
    NYT - Sept 29 2015 - pC1(L) [501+]
    NYTBR - Dec 27 2015 - p8(L) [501+]
    PW - v262 - i38 - Sept 21 2015 - p51(1) [51-500]

Mylnowski, Sarah - *Beauty Queen*
c   Res Links - v21 - i1 - Oct 2015 - p19(1) [51-500]

Mylonas, Harris - *The Politics of Nation-Building: Making Co-Nationals, Refugees and Minorities*
    ERS - v38 - i3 - March 2015 - p475(3) [501+]

Myracle, Lauren - *The Life of Ty: Friends of a Feather (Illus. by Henry, Jed)*
c   BL - v111 - i15 - April 1 2015 - p68(1) [51-500]
c   HB Guide - v26 - i2 - Fall 2015 - p69(1) [51-500]
    KR - Feb 1 2015 - pNA [51-500]
c   SLJ - v61 - i5 - May 2015 - p99(2) [51-500]
Yolo
y   HB Guide - v26 - i1 - Spring 2015 - p118(1) [51-500]

Myscofski, Carole A. - *Amazons, Wives, Nuns & Witches: Women and the Catholic Church in Colonial Brazil, 1500-1822*
    Ams - v72 - i2 - April 2015 - p356(3) [501+]
    CHR - v101 - i3 - Summer 2015 - p688(2) [501+]

Mytting, Lars - *Norwegian Wood: Chopping, Stacking, and Drying Wood the Scandinavian Way*
    TLS - i5876 - Nov 13 2015 - p31(1) [501+]

N

N., Jose Angel - *Illegal: Reflections of an Undocumented Immigrant*
    AJE - v121 - i3 - May 2015 - p470(5) [501+]
    CS - v44 - i1 - Jan 2015 - p143-144 [501+]

Na, Il Sung - *Welcome Home, Bear: A Book of Animal Habitats*
    c KR - May 1 2015 - pNA [51-500]

Welcome Home, Bear: A Book of Animal Habitats (Illus. by Na, Il Sung)
    c SLJ - v61 - i5 - May 2015 - p89(2) [51-500]

Naam, Ramez - *Apex*
    Reason - v47 - i4 - August-Sept 2015 - p66(1) [51-500]

Naas, Michael - *The End of the World and Other Teachable Moments : Jacques Derrida's Final Seminar*
    FS - v69 - i3 - July 2015 - p416-417 [501+]

Naber, Therese - *Native Nations of California*
    c CH Bwatch - Oct 2015 - pNA [51-500]

Native Nations of the Southeast
    c CH Bwatch - Oct 2015 - pNA [51-500]

Naberhaus, Sarvinder - *Boom Boom (Illus. by Chodos-Irvine, Margaret)*
    c CCB-B - v68 - i6 - Feb 2015 - p323(2) [51-500]
    c HB Guide - v26 - i1 - Spring 2015 - p13(1) [51-500]

Nabhan, David - *The Pilots of Borealis*
    PW - v262 - i26 - June 29 2015 - p50(1) [51-500]

Nabokov, Peter - *How the World Moves: The Odyssey of an American Indian Family*
    BL - v112 - i2 - Sept 15 2015 - p18(1) [51-500]
    KR - August 1 2015 - pNA [501+]
    LJ - v140 - i14 - Sept 1 2015 - p118(2) [51-500]
    PW - v262 - i32 - August 10 2015 - p49(1) [51-500]

Nabokov, Vladimir - *Letters to Vera*
    KR - July 15 2015 - pNA [501+]
    LJ - v140 - i12 - July 1 2015 - p83(2) [51-500]
    NYRB - v62 - i18 - Nov 19 2015 - p22(3) [51-500]
    NYTBR - Nov 15 2015 - p1(L) [51-500]
    PW - v262 - i26 - June 29 2015 - p57(1) [51-500]

Lolita
    New R - v246 - i7-8 - July-August 2015 - p70(4) [501+]
    Obs - Feb 22 2015 - p45 [501+]

Pnin
    TimHES - i2201 - April 30 2015 - p51(1) [501+]

Nabonnand, Philippe - *Justifier en mathematiques*
    Isis - v106 - i2 - June 2015 - p417(3) [501+]

Nach dem Konstruktivismus? Aktuelle Strategien der Kontextualisierung in der Neuen Ideengeschichte
    HNet - Jan 2015 - pNA [501+]

Nachenberg, Carey - *The Florentine Deception*
    KR - Jan 1 2015 - pNA [501+]

Nachtomy, Ohad - *The Life Sciences in Early Modern Philosophy*
    Isis - v106 - i2 - June 2015 - p438(2) [501+]
    QRB - v90 - i4 - Dec 2015 - p424(2) [501+]

Nachwuchssymposium "An die Arbeit! Minderheiten und Erwerbserfahrungen im 19. und 20. Jahrhundert"
    HNet - Sept 2015 - pNA [501+]

Nackenoff, Carol - *Statebuilding from the Margins: Between Reconstruction and the New Deal*
    AHR - v120 - i3 - June 2015 - p1032-1034 [501+]
    JAH - v102 - i1 - June 2015 - p268-268 [501+]

Nackerdien, Zeena - *The Heroine Next Door*
    SPBW - Nov 2015 - pNA [51-500]

Nacoste, Rupert W. - *Taking on Diversity: How We Can Move from Anxiety to Respect: A Diversity Doctor's Best Lessons from the Campus*
    PW - v262 - i2 - Jan 12 2015 - p48(1) [51-500]

Nadasen, Premilla - *Household Workers Unite: The Untold Story of African American Women Who Built a Movement*
    KR - June 15 2015 - pNA [501+]
    LJ - v140 - i12 - July 1 2015 - p96(1) [51-500]
    Ms - v25 - i3 - Summer 2015 - p43(1) [501+]

Nadeau, Yvan - *Dog Bites Caesar! A Reading of Juvenal's Satire 5*
    Class R - v65 - i1 - April 2015 - p151-153 [501+]

Nadel, Jessica - *Greens 24/7: More Than 100 Quick, Easy, and Delicious Recipes for Eating Leafy Greens and Other Green Vegetables, at Every Meal*
    CSM - Jan 16 2015 - pNA [501+]
    Veg J - v34 - i3 - July-Sept 2015 - p31(1) [51-500]

Nadel, Matt - *Amazing Aaron to Zero Zippers: An Introduction to Baseball History*
    c SLJ - v61 - i5 - May 2015 - p140(2) [51-500]
    SPBW - March 2015 - pNA [51-500]

Nadelson, Scott - *Between You and Me*
    KR - Sept 1 2015 - pNA [501+]

Nader, Helen - *The First Letter from New Spain: The Lost Petition of Cortes and His Company, June 20, 1519*
    Six Ct J - v46 - i1 - Spring 2015 - p255-256 [501+]

Nader, Ralph - *Unstoppable: The Emerging Left-Right Alliance to Dismantle the Corporate State*
    IndRev - v19 - i3 - Wntr 2015 - p447(3) [501+]

Nadin, Joanna - *Eden*
    y Sch Lib - v63 - i1 - Spring 2015 - p62(2) [51-500]

Joe All Alone
    y Sch Lib - v63 - i3 - Autumn 2015 - p169(1) [51-500]

Nading, Alex - *Mosquito Trails: Ecology, Health, and the Politics of Entanglement*
    MAQ - v29 - i2 - June 2015 - pb40-b42 [501+]

Nadis, Steve - *From the Great Wall to the Great Collider: China and the Quest to Uncover the Inner Workings of the Universe*
    Nature - v528 - i7581 - Dec 10 2015 - p191(1) [51-500]
    RVBW - Nov 2015 - pNA [501+]

A History in Sum: 150 Years of Mathematics at Harvard (1825-1975).
    Isis - v106 - i2 - June 2015 - p466(2) [501+]

Nadkarni, Saroj - *STEP into Storytime: Using StoryTime Effective Practice to Strengthen the Development of Newborns to Five-Year-Olds*
    R&USQ - v54 - i3 - Spring 2015 - p55(1) [501+]

Nadler, Ben - *The Sea Beach Line*
    KR - August 15 2015 - pNA [501+]
    LJ - v140 - i13 - August 1 2015 - p89(1) [51-500]

Nadler, Steven - *The Philosopher, the Priest, and the Painter: A Portrait of Descartes*
    Historian - v77 - i1 - Spring 2015 - p182(2) [501+]
    JMH - v87 - i1 - March 2015 - p212(2) [501+]

Nadol, Jen - *This Is How It Ends*
    y CCB-B - v68 - i5 - Jan 2015 - p271(1) [51-500]
    c HB Guide - v26 - i1 - Spring 2015 - p118(1) [51-500]

Nadrigny, Xavier - *Information et opinion publique a toulouse a la fin du moyen age*
    Specu - v90 - i3 - July 2015 - p842-844 [501+]

Naepels, Michel - *Conjurer la Guerre: Violence et Pouvoir a Houailou*
    Cont Pac - v27 - i2 - Fall 2015 - p565(4) [501+]

Nafisi, Azar - *The Republic of Imagination: A Case for Fiction*
    TLS - i5832 - Jan 9 2015 - p5(1) [501+]

The Republic of Imagination: A Life in Books
    ABR - v36 - i5 - July-August 2015 - p13(2) [501+]
    NYTBR - Oct 18 2015 - p28(L) [501+]

The Republic of Imagination: America in Three Books
    NY - v90 - i42 - Jan 5 2015 - p73 [51-500]
    Comw - v142 - i10 - June 1 2015 - p27(3) [501+]

Nagara, Innosanto - *Counting on Community (Illus. by Nagara, Innosanto)*
    c KR - Jan 1 2016 - pNA [51-500]
    c PW - v262 - i31 - August 3 2015 - p58(2) [51-500]
    c SLJ - v61 - i7 - July 2015 - p56(1) [51-500]

Nagase-Reimer, Keiko - *Mining, Monies, and Culture in Early Modern Societies: East Asian and Global Perspectives*
    T&C - v56 - i1 - Jan 2015 - p267-268 [501+]

Nagata, Linda - *The Red: First Light*
    PW - v262 - i8 - Feb 23 2015 - p55(1) [51-500]

Nagel, Anne C. - *Johannes Popitz (1884-1945): Gorings Finanzminister und Verschworer Gegen Hitler: Eine Biographie*
    HNet - March 2015 - pNA [501+]

Nagel, Gunter - *Wissenschaft fur den Krieg: Die geheimen Arbeiten des Heereswaffenamtes*
    HNet - May 2015 - pNA [501+]

Nagl, John A. - *Knife Fights: A Memoir of Modern War in Theory and Practice*
    Parameters - v45 - i1 - Spring 2015 - p142(3) [501+]
    J Mil H - v79 - i1 - Jan 2015 - p265-266 [501+]

Naglehout, Ryan - *Clownfish/ Peces Payaso*
    c CH Bwatch - Jan 2015 - pNA [51-500]

Nagoski, Emily - *Come As You Are: The Surprising New Science That Will Transform Your Sex Life*
    LJ - v140 - i5 - March 15 2015 - p125(1) [51-500]

Nagy, J.F. - *Writing Down the Myths*
    Class R - v65 - i1 - April 2015 - p103-105 [501+]

Nahm, David Connerley - *Ancient Oceans of Central Kentucky*
    ABR - v36 - i2 - Jan-Feb 2015 - p18(2) [501+]

Naidoo, Beverley - *Who Is King? Ten Magical Stories from Africa (Illus. by Grobler, Piet)*
    c BL - v111 - i18 - May 15 2015 - p46(1) [51-500]
    c KR - Feb 15 2015 - pNA [51-500]

Naifeh, Ted - *Princess Ugg (Illus. by Naifeh, Ted)*
    y SLJ - v61 - i5 - May 2015 - p127(2) [51-500]

Naik, Anita - *How to Be a Girl: The Common Sense Guide to Girlhood*
    y Sch Lib - v63 - i1 - Spring 2015 - p60(1) [51-500]

Naim, Moises - *The End of Power: From Boardrooms to Battlefields and Churches to States, Why Being in Charge Isn't What It Used to Be*
    Historian - v77 - i1 - Spring 2015 - p204(2) [501+]

Nair, Neeti - *Changing Homelands: Hindu Politics and the Partition of India*
    JAS - v74 - i2 - May 2015 - p516-517 [501+]

Nair, Prakash - *Blueprint for Tomorrow: Redesigning Schools for Student-Centered Learning*
    RVBW - July 2015 - pNA [501+]

Nairn, Ian - *Nairn's London*
    TLS - i5832 - Jan 9 2015 - p22(2) [501+]

Nakamura, Fuminori - *The Gun*
    BL - v112 - i4 - Oct 15 2015 - p21(1) [51-500]
    KR - Oct 1 2015 - pNA [51-500]
    LJ - v140 - i16 - Oct 1 2015 - p71(2) [51-500]
    PW - v262 - i45 - Nov 9 2015 - p36(1) [51-500]

Last Winter, We Parted
    RVBW - Sept 2015 - pNA [501+]

Nakamura, Lisa - *Race after the Internet*
    Am St - v54 - i2 - Summer 2015 - p97-98 [501+]

Nakamura, Mariko - *Stitch, Wear, Play: 20 Charming Patterns for Boys & Girls*
    LJ - v140 - i7 - April 15 2015 - p90(1) [51-500]

Nakassis, Dimitri - *Individuals and Society in Mycenaean Pylos*
    Class R - v65 - i1 - April 2015 - p249-252 [501+]

Nakaya, Andrea C. - *Climate Change*
  y VOYA - v38 - i3 - August 2015 - p90(1) [501+]
Euthanasia
  y VOYA - v38 - i3 - August 2015 - p90(1) [501+]
How Do Cell Phones Affect Health?
  y VOYA - v38 - i1 - April 2015 - p88(2) [501+]
How Do Cell Phones Affect Society?
  y VOYA - v38 - i1 - April 2015 - p88(2) [501+]
Teens and Sex
  y VOYA - v38 - i5 - Dec 2015 - p79(2) [501+]
Thinking Critically: Mass Shootings
  y BL - v112 - i2 - Sept 15 2015 - p60(1) [51-500]
Threats to Privacy and Security
  y VOYA - v38 - i1 - April 2015 - p88(2) [501+]
Video Games and Youth
  y VOYA - v38 - i4 - Oct 2015 - p86(1) [51-500]
Nakhimovsky, Alice - *Dear Mendl, Dear Reyzl: Yiddish Letter Manuals from Russia and America*
    Slav R - v74 - i2 - Summer 2015 - p403-404 [501+]
Nakhjavani, Bahiyyih - *The Woman Who Read Too Much*
    BL - v111 - i16 - April 15 2015 - p38(1) [51-500]
    KR - March 15 2015 - pNA [51-500]
Nakhjavani, Bahlyylh - *The Woman Who Read too Much: A Novel*
    WLT - v89 - i6 - Nov-Dec 2015 - p62(2) [501+]
Nalkowska, Zofia - *Choucas*
    TLS - i5841 - March 13 2015 - p28(1) [501+]
The Romance of Teresa Hennert
    TLS - i5852 - May 29 2015 - p27(1) [501+]
Nall, Gail - *Breaking the Ice*
  c SLJ - v61 - i2 - Feb 2015 - p89(1) [51-500]
Nama, Adilifu - *Race on the QT: Blackness and the Films of Quentin Tarantino*
    TimHES - i2213 - July 23 2015 - p46-47 [501+]
Name, Billy - *Billy Name--the Silver Age: Black & White Photographs from Andy Warhol's Factory*
    Afterimage - v42 - i6 - May-June 2015 - p39(3) [501+]
Nance, Susan - *Entertaining Elephants: Animal Agency and the Business of the American Circus*
    BHR - v89 - i2 - Summer 2015   p371(4) [501+]
Nance, Terry - *Awaken: Letters of a Spiritual Father to This Generation*
    PW - v262 - i45 - Nov 9 2015 - p56(1) [51-500]
Nancy, Jean-Luc - *Identity: Fragments, Frankness*
    ABR - v36 - i3 - March-April 2015 - p23(2) [501+]
Nannestad, Katrina - *When Mischief Came to Town*
  c BL - v112 - i6 - Nov 15 2015 - p56(1) [51-500]
  c KR - Oct 1 2015 - pNA [51-500]
  c SLJ - v61 - i9 - Sept 2015 - p143(1) [51-500]
  c PW - v262 - i42 - Oct 19 2015 - p77(1) [51-500]
Naoshi - *Ice Cream Work (Illus. by Naoshi)*
  c PW - v262 - i35 - August 31 2015 - p88(2) [51-500]
Napoleon, Landon J. - *Angels Three: The Karen Perry Story*
    KR - July 15 2015 - pNA [501+]
Napoleoni, Loretta - *The Islamist Phoenix: The Islamic State and the Redrawing of the Middle East*
    LJ - v140 - i2 - Feb 1 2015 - p98(1) [51-500]
    Parameters - v45 - i1 - Spring 2015 - p158(2) [501+]
Napoli, Donna Jo - *Dark Shimmer*
  y BL - v111 - i22 - August 1 2015 - p63(1) [51-500]
  y CCB-B - v69 - i2 - Oct 2015 - p105(1) [51-500]
  y HB - v91 - i6 - Nov-Dec 2015 - p87(1) [51-500]
  y KR - July 1 2015 - pNA [51-500]
  y PW - v262 - i27 - July 6 2015 - p74(1) [51-500]
  y PW - v262 - i49 - Dec 2 2015 - p101(1) [51-500]
  y SLJ - v61 - i7 - July 2015 - p96(1) [51-500]
Hidden
  y CCB-B - v68 - i7 - March 2015 - p364(1) [51-500]
  y HB - v91 - i1 - Jan-Feb 2015 - p87(1) [51-500]
Hidden: An Irish Princess' Tale
  c HB Guide - v26 - i1 - Spring 2015 - p118(1) [51-500]
Storm
  y BL - v111 - i16 - April 15 2015 - p58(1) [501+]
Treasury of Norse Mythology: Stories of Intrigue, Trickery, Love, and Revenge (Illus. by Balit, Christina)
  c SLJ - v61 - i10 - Oct 2015 - p136(1) [51-500]
  c BL - v112 - i5 - Nov 1 2015 - p44(1) [51-500]
Napoli, Linda - *Sailing Away on a Windy Day (Illus. by Kudemus, Raynald)*
  c CH Bwatch - Feb 2015 - pNA [51-500]
Napolitano, Andrew P. - *Suicide Pact: The Radical Expansion of Presidential Powers and the Lethal Threat to American Liberty*
    IndRev - v20 - i2 - Fall 2015 - p297(5) [501+]

Nappaaluk, Mitiarjuk Attasie - *Sanaaq: An Inuit Novel*
    Can Lit - i224 - Spring 2015 - p131 [501+]
Napthali, Sarah - *Buddhism for Couples: A Calm Approach to Relationships*
    LJ - v140 - i11 - June 15 2015 - p85(2) [501+]
Naranch, Bradley - *German Colonialism in a Global Age*
    HNet - July 2015 - pNA [501+]
Narangoa, Li - *Historical Atlas of Northeast Asia, 1590-2010: Korea, Manchuria, Mongolia, Eastern Siberia*
    LJ - v140 - i3 - Feb 15 2015 - p128(1) [51-500]
Narasimhan, M. Amu - *The Little Parrot and the Angel's Tears*
  c CH Bwatch - Feb 2015 - pNA [51-500]
Nardizzi, Vin - *Wooden Os: Shakespeare's Theatres and England's Trees*
    Ren Q - v68 - i1 - Spring 2015 - p401-403 [501+]
    Shakes Q - v66 - i1 - Spring 2015 - p104-107 [501+]
Nardo, Anna K. - *Oculto a los Ojos Mortales: Introduction a "El Paraiso Perdido" de John Milton*
    Sev Cent N - v73 - i3-4 - Fall-Winter 2015 - p89(6) [501+]
Nardo, Don - *Daily Life in Ancient Egypt*
  c HB Guide - v26 - i2 - Fall 2015 - p216(1) [501+]
Daily Life in the Islamic Golden Age
  c HB Guide - v26 - i2 - Fall 2015 - p216(1) [501+]
The Golden Spike: How a Photograph Celebrated the Transcontinental Railroad
  c HB Guide - v26 - i2 - Fall 2015 - p221(1) [501+]
Life in Ancient Egypt
  y VOYA - v38 - i3 - August 2015 - p89(1) [501+]
Life in Ancient Greece
  y SLJ - v61 - i9 - Sept 2015 - p176(1) [51-500]
Mythology of the Egyptians
  y HB Guide - v26 - i1 - Spring 2015 - p144(1) [51-500]
Nazi War Criminals
  y VOYA - v38 - i5 - Dec 2015 - p80(1) [51-500]
Sir Henry Morgan
  c BL - v112 - i7 - Dec 1 2015 - p43(1) [51-500]
Slavery through the Ages
  y VOYA - v38 - i3 - August 2015 - p90(1) [501+]
Sleep Problems
  y VOYA - v38 - i3 - August 2015 - p89(2) [51-500]
Narita, Ryohgo - *Durarara!! (Illus. by Yasuda, Suzuhito)*
  y SLJ - v61 - i9 - Sept 2015 - p162(1) [51-500]
Narratives of Europe and European Integration. 11th Annual Conference of the History of European Integration Research Society
    HNet - June 2015 - pNA [501+]
Narsimhan, Mahtab - *Mission Mumbai*
  c KR - Jan 1 2016 - pNA [51-500]
Nary, Henry - *The Northwest Passage*
    KR - Nov 15 2015 - pNA [501+]
Nas, Peter J. M. - *Cities Full of Symbols: A Theory of Urban Space and Culture*
    CS - v44 - i1 - Jan 2015 - p100-101 [501+]
Naseem, Linda - *Nothing*
    KR - Oct 15 2015 - pNA [501+]
Nash, Geoffrey P. - *Reading Arabia: British Orientalism in the Age of Mass Publication, 1880-1930*
    IJMES - v47 - i1 - Feb 2015 - p182-184 [501+]
Nash, George H. - *The Conservative Intellectual Movement in America since 1945*
    Nat R - v67 - i21 - Nov 19 2015 - p78(1) [51-500]
Nash, Jennifer C. - *The Black Body in Ecstasy: Reading Race, Reading Pornography*
    JGS - v24 - i3 - June 2015 - p362-364 [501+]
    Wom R Bks - v32 - i5 - Sept-Oct 2015 - p30(2) [501+]
Nasir, Na'ilah Suad - *Mathematics for Equity: A Framework for Successful Practice*
    Math T - v108 - i6 - Feb 2015 - p475(1) [501+]
Nasmyth, Peter - *Literature and Landscape in East Devon*
    TLS - i5852 - May 29 2015 - p26(2) [501+]
Nason, Bill - *The Autism Discussion Page on Anxiety, Behavior, School, and Parenting Strategies: A Toolbox for Helping Children with Autism Feel Safe, Accepted and Competent*
    Bwatch - April 2015 - pNA [501+]
    Bwatch - July 2015 - pNA [501+]
The Autism Discussion Page on the Core Challenges of Autism: A Toolbox for Helping Children with Autism Feel Safe, Accepted, and Competent
    Bwatch - April 2015 - pNA [501+]
    Bwatch - July 2015 - pNA [501+]
Nassar, Issam - *The Storyteller of Jerusalem: The Life and Times of Wasif Jawhariyyeh, 1904-1948*
    TLS - i5855 - June 19 2015 - p28(1) [501+]
Nasser, Amjad - *Petra: The Concealed Rose*
    WLT - v89 - i6 - Nov-Dec 2015 - p74(1) [501+]

Nastenlieva, Vanya - *Mo and Beau (Illus. by Nastenlieva, Vanya)*
  c SLJ - v61 - i9 - Sept 2015 - p111(1) [51-500]
Nasti, Paola - *Interpreting Dante: Essays on the Traditions of Dante Commentary*
    Ren Q - v68 - i2 - Summer 2015 - p742-743 [501+]
    Six Ct J - v46 - i3 - Fall 2015 - p798-799 [501+]
    Specu - v90 - i2 - April 2015 - p566-567 [501+]
Nat, Gowri - *Little Jessie's Beach Fun*
  c KR - August 1 2015 - pNA [51-500]
Nath, Michael - *British Story: A Romance*
    TimHES - i2209 - June 25 2015 - p47(1) [501+]
    TLS - i5840 - March 6 2015 - p21(1) [501+]
Nathan, Amy - *The Music Parent's Survival Guide*
    KR - Jan 15 2015 - pNA [501+]
Nathan, Amy Sue - *The Good Neighbor*
    BL - v112 - i3 - Oct 1 2015 - p23(1) [51-500]
Nathan, Sarah - *Disney Frozen, Special Edition: Junior Novelization*
  c HB Guide - v26 - i1 - Spring 2015 - p59(1) [51-500]
Nation, Mark Thiessen - *Bonhoeffer the Assassin? Challenging the Myth, Recovering His Call to Peacemaking*
    BTB - v45 - i3 - August 2015 - p190(2) [501+]
    Intpr - v69 - i1 - Jan 2015 - p91(3) [501+]
National Association of the Deaf - *Legal Rights: The Guide for Deaf and Hard of Hearing People, 6th ed.*
    LJ - v140 - i11 - June 15 2015 - p101(1) [51-500]
National Council of Teachers of Mathematics - *Principles to Actions: Ensuring Mathematical Success for All*
    TC Math - v22 - i1 - August 2015 - p51(1) [501+]
National Geographic - *National Geographic Kids Almanac 2016*
  c Res Links - v21 - i1 - Oct 2015 - p24(2) [51-500]
National Geographic Kids - *125 Cool Inventions: Supersmart Machines and Wacky Gadgets You Never Knew You Wanted!*
  c BL - v111 - i21 - July 1 2015 - p50(2) [51-500]
Bizarre mais vrai! 300fets renversants
  c Res Links - v20 - i4 - April 2015 - p36(1) [51-500]
National Geographic Kids Weird but True! Ripped from the Headlines: Real-Life Stories You Have to Read to Believe
  c HB Guide - v26 - i1 - Spring 2015 - p130(1) [51-500]
National Geographic Society (U.S.) - *Abroad at Home: The 600 Best International Travel Experiences in North America*
    LJ - v140 - i7 - April 15 2015 - p106(1) [51-500]
Atlas of the World, 21st ed.
  c BL - v111 - i9-10 - Jan 1 2015 - p28(1) [51-500]
National Minorities in the Soviet Bloc after 1945
    HNet - March 2015 - pNA [501+]
National Research Council - *Guide to Implementing the Next Generation Science Standards*
    Sci & Ch - v53 - i2 - Oct 2015 - p96 [501+]
    Sci Teach - v82 - i7 - Oct 2015 - p82 [501+]
National Research Council (U.S.). Committee to Review the State of Postdoctoral Experience in Scientists and Engineers - *The Postdoctoral Experience Revisited*
    RVBW - Feb 2015 - pNA [51-500]
National Science Teachers Association - *Chemical Reactions*
    Sci Teach - v82 - i3 - March 2015 - p71 [501+]
Nature Protection, Environmental Policy, and Social Movements in Communist and Capitalist Countries during the Cold War
    HNet - June 2015 - pNA [501+]
Naturel, Mireille - *Proust Pluriel*
    FS - v69 - i4 - Oct 2015 - p551-552 [501+]
Naude, S.J. - *The Alphabet of Birds*
    WLT - v89 - i5 - Sept-Oct 2015 - p65(2) [501+]
Naughton, Michael - *The Innocent and the Criminal Justice System: A Sociological Analysis of Miscarriages of Justice*
    CS - v44 - i3 - May 2015 - p387-389 [501+]
Naugle, Ronald C. - *History of Nebraska, 4th ed.*
    Roundup M - v22 - i4 - April 2015 - p30(2) [501+]
    Roundup M - v22 - i6 - August 2015 - p39(1) [501+]
Nava, Alex - *Wonder and Exile in the New World*
    CH - v84 - i2 - June 2015 - p445(2) [501+]
Navai, Ramita - *City of Lies: Love, Sex, Death and the Search for Truth in Tehran (Read by Lisle, Sylvia). Audiobook Review*
    LJ - v140 - i5 - March 15 2015 - p73(2) [51-500]

Navarro, Jaume - *A History of the Electron: J.J. and G.P. Thomson*
    Isis - v106 - i1 - March 2015 - p204(2) [501+]
Navarro, Mireya - *Stepdog: A Memoir*
    PW - v262 - i5 - Feb 2 2015 - p48(1) [51-500]
Navarro, Peter - *Crouching Tiger: What China's Militarism Means for the World*
    PW - v262 - i37 - Sept 14 2015 - p52(2) [51-500]
Navasky, Victor S. - *The Art of Controversy: Political Cartoons and Their Enduring Power*
    SAH - v4 - i2 - Dec 15 2015 - p308-311 [501+]
Nayak, Hari - *The Cafe Spice Cookbook: 84 Quick and Easy Indian Recipes for Everyday Meals*
    BL - v111 - i14 - March 15 2015 - p36(1) [51-500]
Naylor, Elaine - *Frontier Boosters: Port Townsend and the Culture of Development in the American West, 1850-1895*
    WHQ - v46 - i4 - Winter 2015 - p528-529 [501+]
Naylor, Ernest - *Moonstruck: How Lunar Cycles Affect Life*
    Nature - v526 - i7574 - Oct 22 2015 - p503(1) [51-500]
Naylor, Phyllis Reynolds - *Going Where It's Dark*
  y BL - v112 - i7 - Dec 1 2015 - p56(1) [51-500]
  c KR - Oct 1 2015 - pNA [51-500]
  c PW - v262 - i42 - Oct 19 2015 - p77(1) [51-500]
  c SLJ - v61 - i12 - Dec 2015 - p105(1) [51-500]
A Shiloh Christmas
  c HB - v91 - i6 - Nov-Dec 2015 - p58(1) [51-500]
  c KR - July 15 2015 - pNA [51-500]
  c PW - v262 - i37 - Sept 14 2015 - p75(1) [51-500]
  c PW - v262 - i49 - Dec 2 2015 - p73(1) [51-500]
  c SLJ - v61 - i10 - Oct 2015 - p66(1) [51-500]
Naylor, Roger - *Boots and Burgers: An Arizona Handbook for Hungry Hikers*
    Roundup M - v22 - i3 - Feb 2015 - p24(1) [501+]
    Roundup M - v22 - i6 - August 2015 - p39(1) [501+]
Naylor, Sean - *Relentless Strike: The Secret History of Joint Special Operations Command*
    KR - July 1 2015 - pNA [501+]
    LJ - v140 - i12 - July 1 2015 - p96(1) [51-500]
    PW - v262 - i28 - July 13 2015 - p59(1) [51-500]
Nayyar, Deepak - *Catch Up: Developing Countries in the World Economy*
    Pac A - v88 - i4 - Dec 2015 - p889 [501+]
Nayyar, Kunal - *Yes, My Accent Is Real: And Some Other Things I Haven't Told You*
    LJ - v140 - i15 - Sept 15 2015 - p79(1) [51-500]
    KR - August 15 2015 - pNA [51-500]
Nazar, Hina - *Enlightened Sentiments: Judgement and Antonymy in the Age of Sensibility*
    Eight-C St - v48 - i2 - Wntr 2015 - p239-245 [501+]
Nazemoff, Valeh - *The Four Intelligences of the Business Mind: How to Rewire Your Brain and Your Business for Success*
    RVBW - April 2015 - pNA [501+]
Ncube, Mthuli - *The Emerging Middle Class in Africa*
    IJAHS - v48 - i1 - Wntr 2015 - p171-173 [501+]
NDiaye, Marie - *Self-Portrait in Green*
    TLS - i5839 - Feb 27 2015 - p20(1) [501+]
Ndiaye, Papa Samba - *Les Organisations Internationales Africaines et le Maintien de la Paix : L'exemple de la CEDEAO, Liberia, Sierra Leone, Guinee-Bissau, Cote d'Ivoire*
    HNet - March 2015 - pNA [501+]
Ndibe, Okey - *Arrows of Rain*
    LJ - v140 - i3 - Feb 15 2015 - p90(2) [51-500]
Foreign Gods, Inc.
    NYTBR - June 14 2015 - p24(L) [501+]
Neagoy, Monica - *Planting the Seeds of Algebra, 3-5: Explorations for the Upper Elementary Grades*
    Bwatch - March 2015 - pNA [501+]
Neal, Bill - *Skullduggery, Secrets, and Murders: The 1894 Wells Fargo Scam That Backfired*
    Roundup M - v23 - i1 - Oct 2015 - p34(1) [501+]
Neal, Lana - *The Earliest Instrument: Ritual Power and Fertility Magic of the Flute in Upper Paleolithic Culture*
    RVBW - August 2015 - pNA [501+]
Neal, Mark Anthony - *Looking for Leroy: Illegible Black Masculinities*
    Am St - v54 - i1 - Spring 2015 - p145-3 [501+]
    ERS - v38 - i3 - March 2015 - p471(3) [501+]
Neal, Toby - *Island Fire*
  y PW - v262 - i15 - April 13 2015 - p82(1) [51-500]
Neale, Margaret A. - *Getting (More of) What You Want: How the Secrets of Economics and Psychology Can Help You Negotiate Anything, in Business and in Life*
    Forbes - v196 - i6 - Nov 2 2015 - p42(1) [501+]
    KR - May 1 2015 - pNA [501+]
Nease, Bob - *The Power of Fifty Bits*
    KR - Nov 1 2015 - pNA [501+]

Neddo, Nick - *The Organic Artist: Make Your Own Paint, Paper, Pigments, Prints, and More from Nature*
    LJ - v140 - i6 - April 1 2015 - p92(1) [51-500]
Nedelcu, Ovi - *Just Like Daddy (Illus. by Nedelcu, Ovi)*
  c PW - v262 - i15 - April 13 2015 - p81(1) [51-500]
  c SLJ - v61 - i5 - May 2015 - p80(1) [51-500]
Nedo, Michael - *Ludwig Wittgenstein: Ein biographisches Album*
    Quad - v59 - i5 - May 2015 - p106(3) [501+]
Nee, Victor - *Capitalism from Below: Markets and Institutional Change in China*
    Pac A - v88 - i1 - March 2015 - p165 [501+]
Needell, Claire - *The Word for Yes*
  y KR - Dec 1 2015 - pNA [51-500]
Needham, Andrew - *Power Lines: Phoenix and the Making of the Modern Southwest*
    JAH - v102 - i1 - June 2015 - p288-288 [501+]
Neeleman, John - *Logos*
    KR - March 1 2015 - pNA [501+]
Neely, Mark E., Jr. - *Lincoln and the Triumph of the Nation: Constitutional Conflict in the American Civil War*
    JSH - v81 - i1 - Feb 2015 - p207(3) [501+]
Neer, Robert M. - *Napalm: An American Biography*
    Historian - v77 - i1 - Spring 2015 - p134(2) [501+]
Nef, Annliese - *A Companion to Medieval Palermo: The History of a Mediterranean City from 600 to 1500*
    HER - v130 - i545 - August 2015 - p956(3) [501+]
Neff, Charles - *Hidden Impact*
    RVBW - Jan 2015 - pNA [501+]
Neff, James - *Vendetta: Bobby Kennedy Versus Jimmy Hoffa*
    CSM - July 7 2015 - pNA [501+]
    LJ - v140 - i10 - June 1 2015 - p113(2) [51-500]
    PW - v262 - i18 - May 4 2015 - p110(1) [51-500]
Vendetta
    KR - April 15 2015 - pNA [501+]
Neff, Stephen C. - *Justice among Nations: A History of International Law*
    AHR - v120 - i2 - April 2015 - p571-572 [501+]
    RM - v68 - i3 - March 2015 - p671(3) [501+]
Neftzger, Amy - *The War of Words*
    KR - Nov 15 2015 - pNA [501+]
Neggers, Carla - *Echo Lake*
    BL - v111 - i9-10 - Jan 1 2015 - p56(1) [51-500]
    BL - v112 - i2 - Sept 15 2015 - p42(2) [501+]
Keeper's Reach
    PW - v262 - i29 - July 20 2015 - p168(2) [51-500]
Negley, Keith - *Tough Guys Have Feelings Too (Illus. by Negley, Keith)*
  c KR - Sept 15 2015 - pNA [51-500]
  c SLJ - v61 - i12 - Dec 2015 - p93(1) [51-500]
Negri, Antonio - *Spinoza for our Time: Politics and Postmodernity*
    Dialogue - v54 - i3 - Sept 2015 - p548-550 [501+]
Nehring, Holger - *Politics of Security: British and West German Protest Movements and the Early Cold War, 1945-1970*
    HER - v130 - i543 - April 2015 - p500(3) [501+]
Neibaur, James L. - *The Clint Eastwood Westerns*
    BL - v111 - i11 - Feb 1 2015 - p8(2) [51-500]
Neiberg, Michael - *Potsdam: The End of World War II and the Remaking of Europe*
    KR - March 1 2015 - pNA [501+]
    LJ - v140 - i5 - March 15 2015 - p121(1) [51-500]
    NYRB - v62 - i16 - Oct 22 2015 - p28(4) [501+]
    PW - v262 - i9 - March 2 2015 - p75(2) [51-500]
Neiderman, Andrew - *Lost in His Eyes*
    BL - v112 - i5 - Nov 1 2015 - p36(1) [51-500]
    KR - Oct 15 2015 - pNA [51-500]
Neidorf, Leonard - *The Dating of Beowulf: A Reassessment*
    MP - v113 - i1 - August 2015 - pE1(3) [501+]
Neil, Bronwen - *Questions of Gender in Byzantine Society*
    CHR - v101 - i1 - Wntr 2015 - p148(2) [501+]
Neill, Anna - *Primitive Minds: Evolution and Spiritual Experience in the Victorian Novel*
    Nine-C Lit - v69 - i4 - March 2015 - p551(4) [501+]
Neill, Calum - *Without Ground: Lacanian Ethics and the Assumption of Subjectivity*
    FS - v69 - i3 - July 2015 - p413-414 [501+]
Neill, Chloe - *Dark Debt*
    PW - v262 - i5 - Feb 2 2015 - p41(1) [51-500]
The Veil
    PW - v262 - i27 - July 6 2015 - p51(1) [51-500]
Neill, Michael - *The Spanish Tragedy*
    Six Ct J - v46 - i2 - Summer 2015 - p495-496 [501+]
Neill, Ted - *City on a Hill*
    KR - April 1 2015 - pNA [501+]

Neiman, Susan - *Evil in Modern thought: An Alternative histoty of Philosophy*
    J Phil - v112 - i5 - May 2015 - p281(1) [501+]
Why Grow Up? Subversive Thoughts for an Infantile Age
    KR - Feb 15 2015 - pNA [501+]
    LJ - v140 - i7 - April 15 2015 - p90(1) [51-500]
    NYTBR - June 21 2015 - p1(L) [501+]
Neis, Rachel - *The Sense of Sight in Rabbinic Culture: Jewish Ways of Seeing in Late Antiquity*
    AHR - v120 - i2 - April 2015 - p690-691 [501+]
Neiwert, David - *Of Orcas and Men: What Killer Whales Can Teach Us*
    BL - v111 - i18 - May 15 2015 - p8(1) [51-500]
    KR - April 15 2015 - pNA [501+]
    LJ - v140 - i7 - April 15 2015 - p114(1) [51-500]
Nelsn, Theresa - *The Year We Sailed the Sun*
  c HB - v91 - i2 - March-April 2015 - p104(1) [51-500]
Nelson, Alice - *After This: Survivors of the Holocaust Speak*
    Magpies - v30 - i3 - July 2015 - p22(1) [501+]
Nelson, Alondra - *The Social Life of DNA*
    KR - Nov 15 2015 - pNA [501+]
Nelson, Amanda S. - *The Buttermilk Biscuit Boy (Illus. by Klein, Laurie)*
  c HB Guide - v26 - i2 - Fall 2015 - p159(1) [51-500]
Nelson, B.C. - *Maddoc*
    KR - Nov 15 2015 - pNA [501+]
Nelson, Brent - *Digitizing Medieval and Early Modern Material Culture*
    Ren Q - v68 - i1 - Spring 2015 - p264-265 [501+]
Nelson, Bryce - *The Academic Library Administrator's Field Guide*
    R&USQ - v54 - i4 - Summer 2015 - p70(2) [51-500]
Nelson, Cary - *The Oxford Handbook of Modern and Contemporary American Poetry*
    MP - v112 - i3 - Feb 2015 - pE272(E275) [501+]
Nelson, Claudia - *British Family Life, 1780-1914, vol. 1: Growing Up*
    HER - v130 - i545 - August 2015 - p1015(3) [501+]
Nelson, Colleen - *250 Hours*
  y KR - August 15 2015 - pNA [51-500]
  y SLJ - v61 - i10 - Oct 2015 - p105(1) [51-500]
  y VOYA - v38 - i4 - Oct 2015 - p57(2) [51-500]
Nelson, D-L - *Murder in Ely*
    KR - Feb 15 2015 - pNA [51-500]
    PW - v262 - i11 - March 16 2015 - p67(1) [51-500]
Nelson, Daniel - *Wild Gourmet: Naturally Healthy Game, Fish and Fowl Recipes for Everyday Chefs*
    Bwatch - August 2015 - pNA [51-500]
Nelson, David L. - *David & Lee Roy: A Vietnam Story*
    APJ - v29 - i2 - March-April 2015 - p179(2) [501+]
Nelson, Dick - *The Prince and the Scorpion*
    SPBW - Jan 2015 - pNA [501+]
Nelson, Dorothy - *In Night's City*
    NS - v144 - i5282 - Oct 2 2015 - p74(2) [501+]
Nelson, Emmanuel S. - *Ethnic American Literature: An Encyclopedia for Students*
  y BL - v111 - i19-20 - June 1 2015 - p24(1) [51-500]
    LJ - v140 - i10 - June 1 2015 - p133(1) [51-500]
Nelson, Eric - *The Royalist Revolution: Monarchy and the American Founding*
    J Mil H - v79 - i3 - July 2015 - p817-819 [501+]
    Nation - v300 - i12 - March 23 2015 - p27(5) [501+]
    TLS - i5841 - March 13 2015 - p23(1) [501+]
Nelson, Eric A. - *Calculations in Chemistry: An Introduction*
    J Chem Ed - v92 - i8 - August 2015 - p1286-1287 [501+]
Nelson, Eric (b. 1977-) - *The Royalist Revolution: Monarchy and the American Founding*
    AHR - v120 - i4 - Oct 2015 - p1479(1) [501+]
    JAH - v102 - i2 - Sept 2015 - p541-541 [501+]
    NYRB - v62 - i16 - Oct 22 2015 - p53(3) [501+]
Nelson, Greg - *Fostering Children's Number Sense in Grades K-2: Turning Math Inside Out*
    TC Math - v21 - i7 - March 2015 - p442(2) [501+]
Nelson, Harold B. - *Little Dreams in Glass and Metal: Enameling in America*
    Am Craft - v75 - i6 - Dec 2015 - p26(1) [501+]
Nelson, James L. - *The French Prize*
    LJ - v140 - i11 - June 15 2015 - p80(2) [51-500]

Nelson, Jandy - *I'll Give You the Sun (Read by Whelan, Julia, with Jesse Bernstein). Audiobook Review*
   y BL - v111 - i16 - April 15 2015 - p63(1) [51-500]
   y PW - v262 - i8 - Feb 23 2015 - p72(1) [51-500]
I'll Give You the Sun
   c HB Guide - v26 - i1 - Spring 2015 - p118(1) [51-500]
   y Sch Lib - v63 - i2 - Summer 2015 - p126(1) [51-500]
   y Teach Lib - v42 - i4 - April 2015 - p23(1) [51-500]
   y VOYA - v37 - i6 - Feb 2015 - p62(1) [51-500]
Nelson, Jennifer - *Aim at the Centaur Stealing Your Wife*
     PW - v262 - i52 - Dec 21 2015 - p128(1) [51-500]
Nelson, Jo - *Historium (Illus. by Wilkinson, Richard)*
   c BL - v112 - i5 - Nov 1 2015 - p48(1) [51-500]
   c KR - August 15 2015 - pNA [51-500]
   c Magpies - v30 - i5 - Nov 2015 - p22(1) [501+]
   c PW - v262 - i32 - August 10 2015 - p60(1) [51-500]
   c Sch Lib - v63 - i4 - Winter 2015 - p239(1) [51-500]
   c SLJ - v61 - i10 - Oct 2015 - p136(2) [51-500]
Nelson, John K. - *Experimental Buddhism: Innovation and Activism in Contemporary Japan*
     HNet - March 2015 - pNA [501+]
     Pac A - v88 - i2 - June 2015 - p326 [501+]
Nelson, Kadir - *Baby Bear*
   c BL - v112 - i4 - Oct 15 2015 - p53(1) [51-500]
If You Plant a Seed (Illus. by Nelson, Kadir)
   c HB Guide - v26 - i2 - Fall 2015 - p16(1) [51-500]
   c KR - Jan 15 2015 - pNA [51-500]
   c NYTBR - May 10 2015 - p23(L) [501+]
   c PW - v262 - i7 - Feb 16 2015 - p72(32) [501+]
   c PW - v262 - i49 - Dec 2 2015 - p14(1) [51-500]
Nelson, Kevin - *The Golden Game: The Story of California Baseball*
     Roundup M - v22 - i6 - August 2015 - p39(1) [501+]
Nelson, Lydia Loretta - *Dreamy Quilts: 14 Timeless Projects to Welcome You Home*
     PW - v262 - i9 - March 2 2015 - p81(1) [51-500]
Nelson, Maggie - *The Argonauts*
     Lon R Bks - v37 - i20 - Oct 22 2015 - p11(3) [501+]
     NY - v91 - i14 - May 25 2015 - p73 [51-500]
     PW - v262 - i15 - April 13 2015 - p8(1) [51-500]
     KR - Feb 1 2015 - pNA [501+]
     NYTBR - May 10 2015 - p26(L) [501+]
     PW - v262 - i11 - March 16 2015 - p78(1) [51-500]
Nelson, Marilyn - *American Ace*
   y BL - v112 - i7 - Dec 1 2015 - p53(1) [51-500]
   y KR - Oct 1 2015 - pNA [51-500]
   y SLJ - v61 - i12 - Dec 2015 - p125(1) [51-500]
My Seneca Village
   y BL - v112 - i1 - Sept 1 2015 - p92(1) [51-500]
   y HB - v91 - i6 - Nov-Dec 2015 - p97(2) [51-500]
   c SLJ - v61 - i12 - Dec 2015 - p105(1) [51-500]
   y VOYA - v38 - i5 - Dec 2015 - p61(2) [51-500]
   c KR - Sept 1 2015 - pNA [51-500]
Nelson, Mark Daniel - *Learn to Paint in Acrylics with 50 Small Paintings: Pick Up the Skills, Put on the Paint, Hang Up Your Art*
     LJ - v140 - i10 - June 1 2015 - p102(1) [51-500]
Nelson, Michael - *Resilient America: Electing Nixon in 1968, Channeling Dissent, and Dividing Government*
     JAH - v101 - i4 - March 2015 - p1348-1349 [501+]
Nelson, Michael Alan - *Hexed*
   y VOYA - v38 - i2 - June 2015 - p80(1) [501+]
   c KR - March 15 2015 - pNA [51-500]
Nelson, Michael (b. 1949-) - *Resilient America: Electing Nixon in 1968, Channeling Dissent, and Dividing Government*
     JSH - v81 - i3 - August 2015 - p780(2) [501+]
Nelson, Michelle - *The Urban Homesteading Cookbook: Forage, Farm, Ferment and Feast for a Better World*
     LJ - v140 - i14 - Sept 1 2015 - p131(2) [51-500]
Nelson, Paul T. - *Wrecks of Human Ambition: A History of Utah's Canyon Country to 1936*
     Roundup M - v22 - i6 - August 2015 - p39(1) [501+]
     WHQ - v46 - i3 - Autumn 2015 - p384-385 [501+]
Nelson, Peter - *Creature Keepers and the Hijacked Hydro-Hide (Illus. by Rohitash Rao)*
   c HB Guide - v26 - i1 - Spring 2015 - p87(1) [51-500]
Creature Keepers and the Swindled Soil-Soles
   c KR - July 1 2015 - pNA [51-500]
Nelson, Randy H. - *The Second Decison*
     RVBW - June 2015 - pNA [501+]

Nelson, Robin - *Start to Finish: Sports Gear Series*
   c HB Guide - v26 - i1 - Spring 2015 - p173(2) [51-500]
Nelson, Ruth D. - *Searching for Marquette: A Pilgrimage in Art*
     AM - v212 - i4 - Feb 9 2015 - p25(2) [501+]
Nelson, S. D. - *Digging a Hole to Heaven: Coal Miner Boys*
   c HB Guide - v26 - i1 - Spring 2015 - p40(1) [51-500]
Nelson, S.D. - *Digging a Hole to Heaven*
   c BL - v111 - i12 - Feb 15 2015 - p76(1) [51-500]
Sitting Bull: Lakota Warrior and Defender of His People (Illus. by Nelson, S.D.)
   c BL - v112 - i3 - Oct 1 2015 - p39(1) [51-500]
   c HB - v91 - i6 - Nov-Dec 2015 - p103(2) [51-500]
   c KR - August 15 2015 - pNA [51-500]
   c PW - v262 - i38 - Sept 21 2015 - p78(1) [51-500]
   c PW - v262 - i49 - Dec 2 2015 - p84(1) [51-500]
   c SLJ - v61 - i9 - Sept 2015 - p188(2) [501+]
Nelson-Schmidt, Michelle - *Bob Is a Unicorn (Illus. by Nelson-Schmidt, Michelle)*
   c CH Bwatch - March 2015 - pNA [51-500]
Dog and Mouse (Illus. by Nelson-Schmidt, Michelle)
   c CH Bwatch - July 2015 - pNA [51-500]
   c PW - v262 - i27 - July 6 2015 - p69(1) [51-500]
Nelson, Suzanne - *Le lac aux mysteres*
   c Res Links - v20 - i3 - Feb 2015 - p48(1) [51-500]
Serendipity's Footsteps
   y BL - v112 - i5 - Nov 1 2015 - p56(1) [51-500]
   y KR - Sept 15 2015 - pNA [51-500]
   y SLJ - v61 - i10 - Oct 2015 - p115(2) [51-500]
   y VOYA - v38 - i5 - Dec 2015 - p62(1) [51-500]
Nelson, Theresa - *The Year We Sailed the Sun*
   c BL - v111 - i16 - April 15 2015 - p60(1) [51-500]
   c CCB-B - v68 - i8 - April 2015 - p413(1) [51-500]
   c HB Guide - v26 - i2 - Fall 2015 - p95(1) [51-500]
   c KR - Jan 1 2015 - pNA [51-500]
   c RVBW - May 2015 - pNA [501+]
Nelson, Vaunda Micheaux - *The Book Itch: Freedom, Truth & Harlem's Greatest Bookstore (Illus. by Christie, R. Gregory)*
   c BL - v112 - i3 - Oct 1 2015 - p78(1) [51-500]
   c HB - v91 - i6 - Nov-Dec 2015 - p104(2) [51-500]
   c KR - Sept 15 2015 - pNA [51-500]
   c PW - v262 - i38 - Sept 21 2015 - p74(1) [51-500]
   c SLJ - v61 - i9 - Sept 2015 - p179(2) [51-500]
Don't Call Me Grandma (Illus. by Zunon, Elizabeth)
   c KR - Dec 1 2015 - pNA [51-500]
   c PW - v262 - i47 - Nov 23 2015 - p66(1) [501+]
Nelson, Victoria - *The Secret Life of Puppets*
     TimHES - i2211 - July 9 2015 - p47(1) [501+]
Nelson, William E. - *The Common Law in Colonial America, vol. 2: The Middle Colonies and the Carolinas, 1660-1730*
     JSH - v81 - i1 - Feb 2015 - p160(2) [51-500]
Nelson, Willie - *It's a Long Story: My Life (Illus. by Ritz, David)*
     KR - March 1 2015 - pNA [51-500]
     LJ - v140 - i7 - April 15 2015 - p89(1) [51-500]
     Mac - v128 - i19-20 - May 18 2015 - p77(2) [501+]
     PW - v262 - i14 - April 6 2015 - p52(1) [51-500]
Nembhard, Jessica Gordon - *Collective Courage: A History of African American Cooperative Economic Thought and Practice*
     JAH - v102 - i2 - Sept 2015 - p568-569 [501+]
Neme, Laurel - *Orangutan Houdini (Illus. by Kelleher, Kathie)*
   c HB Guide - v26 - i1 - Spring 2015 - p166(1) [51-500]
Nemer, Lawrence - *The Great Age of Mission: Some Historical Studies in Mission History*
     CHR - v101 - i3 - Summer 2015 - p595(3) [501+]
Nemeth, Eduard - *Romische Militargeschichte*
     HNet - July 2015 - pNA [501+]
Nemirovsky, Irene - *The Fires of Autumn*
     KR - Jan 1 2015 - pNA [501+]
Neorassismus im Spannungsfeld der Kulturen - (k)ein Bildungsproblem!?
     HNet - May 2015 - pNA [501+]
Nepo, Mark - *Inside the Miracle: Enduring Suffering, Approaching Wholeness*
     PW - v262 - i42 - Oct 19 2015 - p39(1) [501+]
Neri, G. - *Hello, I'm Johnny Cash (Illus. by Ford, A.G.)*
   c HB - v91 - i1 - Jan-Feb 2015 - p100(2) [501+]
   c HB Guide - v26 - i1 - Spring 2015 - p195(1) [51-500]
Knockout Games
   y HB Guide - v26 - i1 - Spring 2015 - p118(1) [51-500]

Tru and Nelle
   c KR - Dec 15 2015 - pNA [51-500]
   c PW - v262 - i51 - Dec 14 2015 - p85(1) [51-500]
   c SLJ - v61 - i10 - Oct 2015 - p93(1) [51-500]
Nerjordet, Arne - *30 Slippers to Knit and Felt: Fabulous Projects You Can Make, Wear, and Share*
     BL - v112 - i5 - Nov 1 2015 - p7(1) [51-500]
Neroni, Hilary - *Feminist Film Theory and 'Cleo from 5 to 7'*
     PW - v262 - i45 - Nov 9 2015 - p53(1) [51-500]
Nersessian, Anahid - *Utopia, Limited: Romanticism and Adjustment*
     TimHES - i2207 - June 11 2015 - p56-57 [501+]
Nesbet, Anne - *The Wrinkled Crown*
   c PW - v262 - i36 - Sept 7 2015 - p68(1) [51-500]
   c HB - v91 - i6 - Nov-Dec 2015 - p87(2) [51-500]
   c KR - Sept 1 2015 - pNA [51-500]
   c SLJ - v61 - i8 - August 2015 - p88(2) [51-500]
Nesbit, E. - *Five Children and It*
   c Magpies - v30 - i1 - March 2015 - p14(2) [501+]
Nesbit, TaraShea - *The Wives of Los Alamos*
     Wom R Bks - v32 - i2 - March-April 2015 - p17(2) [501+]
Nesbitt, Claire - *Experiencing Byzantium*
     Specu - v90 - i2 - April 2015 - p567-568 [501+]
Nesbitt, John D. - *Across the Cheyenne River*
     Roundup M - v22 - i6 - August 2015 - p32(1) [501+]
Don't Be a Stranger
     BL - v111 - i9-10 - Jan 1 2015 - p52(1) [51-500]
     Roundup M - v22 - i5 - June 2015 - p39(1) [501+]
     Roundup M - v22 - i6 - August 2015 - p32(1) [501+]
Justice at Redwillow
     BL - v112 - i1 - Sept 1 2015 - p52(1) [51-500]
     KR - July 1 2015 - pNA [51-500]
     Roundup M - v23 - i1 - Oct 2015 - p31(1) [501+]
Nesbitt, Kenn - *Believe It or Not, My Brother Has a Monster! (Illus. by Slonim, David)*
   c KR - August 1 2015 - pNA [51-500]
   c PW - v262 - i30 - July 27 2015 - p64(1) [51-500]
   c SLJ - v61 - i5 - May 2015 - p90(1) [51-500]
Nesbo, Jo - *Blood on Snow (Read by Smith, Patti). Audiobook Review*
     LJ - v140 - i15 - Sept 15 2015 - p42(1) [51-500]
     NYTBR - May 17 2015 - p15(L) [501+]
     PW - v262 - i17 - April 27 2015 - p68(1) [51-500]
Blood on Snow
     BL - v111 - i13 - March 1 2015 - p22(1) [51-500]
     KR - Feb 1 2015 - pNA [51-500]
     LJ - v140 - i5 - March 15 2015 - p94(2) [51-500]
     NYT - April 9 2015 - pC1(L) [501+]
     PW - v262 - i7 - Feb 16 2015 - p162(1) [501+]
Doctor Proctor's Fart Powder (Read by Dufris, William). Audiobook Review
   c SLJ - v61 - i5 - May 2015 - p69(1) [51-500]
Midnight Sun
     KR - Dec 15 2015 - pNA [51-500]
     PW - v262 - i52 - Dec 21 2015 - p130(1) [51-500]
Nesi, Annalisa - *Storia della lingua italiana e storia dell'Italia unita: l'italiano e lo stato nazionale*
     MLR - v110 - i1 - Jan 2015 - p266-268 [501+]
Nesin, Kate - *Cy Twombly's Things*
     TLS - i5845 - April 10 2015 - p12(1) [501+]
Nesquens, Daniel - *Mister H (Illus. by Lozano, Luciano)*
   c BL - v111 - i12 - Feb 15 2015 - p86(2) [51-500]
   c HB Guide - v26 - i2 - Fall 2015 - p69(1) [51-500]
   c SLJ - v61 - i2 - Feb 2015 - p74(1) [51-500]
Ness, Gregory - *The Sword of Agrippa: Antioch. E-book Review*
     PW - v262 - i3 - Jan 19 2015 - p65(2) [501+]
     PW - v262 - i3 - Jan 19 2015 - p65(2) [501+]
Ness, Immanuel - *Guest Workers and Resistance to U.S. Corporate Despotism*
     SF - v94 - i2 - Dec 2015 - pNA [501+]
Ness, Patrick - *The Rest of Us Just Live Here*
   y BL - v111 - i21 - July 1 2015 - p59(1) [51-500]
   y CCB-B - v69 - i2 - Oct 2015 - p105(2) [51-500]
   y HB - v91 - i5 - Sept-Oct 2015 - p112(1) [51-500]
   y KR - August 1 2015 - pNA [51-500]
   c Magpies - v30 - i3 - July 2015 - p18(1) [501+]
   y NYTBR - Nov 8 2015 - p35(L) [501+]
   y PW - v262 - i31 - August 3 2015 - p63(1) [51-500]
   y Sch Lib - v63 - i3 - Autumn 2015 - p184(1) [51-500]
   y SLJ - v61 - i9 - Sept 2015 - p170(1) [51-500]
   y VOYA - v38 - i5 - Dec 2015 - p73(1) [51-500]
Nesselrath, Heinz-Günther - *Libanios: Zeuge einer schwindenden Welt*
     CHR - v101 - i2 - Spring 2015 - p351(2) [501+]

Nesser, Hakan - *Hour of the Wolf*
BL - v112 - i6 - Nov 15 2015 - p25(1) [51-500]
KR - Oct 15 2015 - pNA [51-500]

Nester, William - *The Age of Jackson and the Art of American Power, 1815-1848*
JSH - v81 - i1 - Feb 2015 - p182(2) [501+]

Nester, William R. - *The French and Indian War and the Conquest of New France*
Can Hist R - v96 - i2 - June 2015 - p292(3) [501+]
Roundup M - v22 - i3 - Feb 2015 - p24(1) [501+]
Roundup M - v22 - i6 - August 2015 - p39(1) [501+]

Nesteroff, Kliph - *The Comedians: Drunks, Thieves, Scoundrels, and the History of American Comedy*
BL - v112 - i5 - Nov 1 2015 - p16(1) [51-500]
KR - July 15 2015 - pNA [501+]
LJ - v140 - i12 - July 1 2015 - p88(1) [51-500]
Mac - v128 - i46 - Nov 23 2015 - p58(1) [501+]
NYTBR - Dec 6 2015 - p58(L) [501+]

Nestle, Marion - *Soda Politics: Taking on Big Soda (and Winning)*
KR - July 15 2015 - pNA [501+]
LJ - v140 - i13 - August 1 2015 - p117(2) [51-500]
Nature - v526 - i7571 - Oct 1 2015 - p34(2) [501+]
NYTBR - Nov 22 2015 - p15(L) [501+]

Nestvogel, Renate - *Afrikanerinnen in Deutschland: Lebenslagen, Eifahrungen und Erwartungen*
Ger Q - v88 - i2 - Spring 2015 - p263(2) [501+]

Nettel, Guadalupe - *The Body Where I Was Born*
NYTBR - July 5 2015 - p18(L) [501+]
PW - v262 - i17 - April 27 2015 - p43(2) [51-500]
Natural Stories
HR - v68 - i3 - Autumn 2015 - p510-516 [501+]

Nettelfield, Lara J. - *Courting Democracy in Bosnia and Herzegovina: The Hague Tribunal's Impact in a Postwar State*
E-A St - v67 - i1 - Jan 2015 - p153(2) [501+]

Netting, Lara Jaishree - *A Perpetual Fire: John C. Ferguson and His Quest for Chinese Art and Culture*
JAS - v74 - i3 - August 2015 - p729-731 [501+]

Nettleton, Melinda - *Special Needs and Legal Entitlement: The Essential Guide to Getting Out of the Maze*
Bwatch - May 2015 - pNA [51-500]

Netzley, Patricia D. - *Do Witches Exist?*
y BL - v112 - i3 - Oct 1 2015 - p40(1) [51-500]
y VOYA - v38 - i5 - Dec 2015 - p79(1) [501+]
Is Legalized Marijuana Good for Society?
BL - v111 - i21 - July 1 2015 - p54(1) [51-500]
Teens and Sexting
y VOYA - v38 - i5 - Dec 2015 - p79(2) [501+]
Video Games, Violence, and Crime
y VOYA - v38 - i4 - Oct 2015 - p86(1) [51-500]

Neu, Charles E. - *Colonel House: A Biography of Woodrow Wilson's Silent Partner*
HNet - June 2015 - pNA [501+]

Neubecker, Robert - *Days of the Knights (Illus. by Neubecker, Robert)*
c SLJ - v61 - i6 - June 2015 - p46(6) [501+]
Racing the Waves (Illus. by Neubecker, Robert)
y CH Bwatch - Jan 2015 - pNA [501+]
c HB Guide - v26 - i1 - Spring 2015 - p54(1) [51-500]

Neuborne, Burt - *Madison's Music: On Reading the First Amendment*
NYRB - v62 - i17 - Nov 5 2015 - p24(3) [501+]

Neuburger, Mary C. - *Balkan Smoke: Tobacco and the Making of Modern Bulgaria*
JMH - v87 - i3 - Sept 2015 - p760(2) [501+]

Neue Forschungen zu Spatmittelalterlichen Landtransfers und Bodenmarkten zwischen Rhein und Alpen
HNet - July 2015 - pNA [501+]

Neue Soziale Bewegungen in der 'Provinz' 1970-1990
HNet - Jan 2015 - pNA [501+]

Neue Tendenzen der Italienforschung zu Mittelalter und Renaissance
HNet - March 2015 - pNA [501+]

Neue Vielfalt. Medienpluralitat und -konkurrenz in historischer Perspektive
HNet - April 2015 - pNA [501+]

Neuere Forschungen zur Frauen - und Geschlechtergeschichte
HNet - May 2015 - pNA [501+]

Neuere Tendenzen in der Historiographiegeschichte
HNet - Sept 2015 - pNA(NA) [501+]

Neufeld, Michael J. - *Spacefarers: Images of Astronauts and Cosmonauts in the Heroic Era of Spaceflight*
T&C - v56 - i1 - Jan 2015 - p288-289 [501+]

Neuffer, Julie Debra - *Helen Andelin and the Fascinating Womanhood Movement*
KR - August 15 2015 - pNA [501+]

Neuhaus, Nele - *I Am Your Judge*
PW - v262 - i46 - Nov 16 2015 - p56(1) [51-500]

Neuheuser, Hanns Peter - *Bischofsbild und Bischofssitz: Geistige und geistliche Impulse aus regionalen Zentren des Hochmittelalters*
Specu - v90 - i4 - Oct 2015 - p1195(1) [501+]

Neuman, Andres - *The Things We Don't Do*
KR - July 1 2015 - pNA [501+]
LJ - v140 - i13 - August 1 2015 - p90(1) [51-500]
NYT - Sept 24 2015 - pC6(L) [501+]
PW - v262 - i30 - July 27 2015 - p40(3) [51-500]

Neuman, Lisa K. - *Indian Play: Indigenous Identities at Bacone College*
JSH - v81 - i2 - May 2015 - p486(2) [501+]

Neuman, Meredith Marie - *Jeremiah's Scribes: Creating Sermon Literature in Puritan New England*
Historian - v77 - i3 - Fall 2015 - p570(2) [501+]
JR - v95 - i3 - July 2015 - p418(3) [501+]

Neuman, Susan B. - *Go, Cub!*
c HB Guide - v26 - i1 - Spring 2015 - p166(1) [51-500]
Hang On, Monkey!
c HB Guide - v26 - i1 - Spring 2015 - p166(1) [51-500]
Hop, Bunny!: Explore the Forest
c HB Guide - v26 - i1 - Spring 2015 - p156(1) [51-500]
Jump, Pup!
c HB Guide - v26 - i1 - Spring 2015 - p169(1) [51-500]
Swim, Fish!: Explore the Coral Reef
c HB Guide - v26 - i1 - Spring 2015 - p156(1) [51-500]
Swing, Sloth!: Explore the Rain Forest
SLJ - v61 - i4 - April 2015 - p61(1) [51-500]

Neumann, Ann - *The Good Death: An Exploration of Dying in America*
KR - Nov 1 2015 - pNA [51-500]
LJ - v140 - i20 - Dec 1 2015 - p121(2) [51-500]

Neumann, Annja - *Durchkreuzte Zeit: Zur asthetischen Temporalitat der spaten Gedichte von Nelly Sachs und Paul Celan*
MLR - v110 - i3 - July 2015 - p909-910 [501+]

Neumann, Stella - *Contrastive Register Variation: A Quantitative Approach to the Comparison of English and German*
MLR - v110 - i2 - April 2015 - p578-579 [501+]

Neumann-Thein, Philipp - *Parteidisziplin und Eigenwilligkeit: Das Internationale Komitee Buchenwald-Dora und Kommandos*
HNet - March 2015 - pNA [501+]

Neumark, Heidi B. - *Hidden Inheritance: Family Secrets, Memory, and Faith*
CC - v132 - i21 - Oct 14 2015 - p28(4) [501+]

Neumeier, Rachel - *The Keeper of the Mist*
y KR - Dec 15 2015 - pNA [51-500]

Neurath, A. Robert - *Newcomers' Accomplishments: Jewish Immigrants from Upper Hungary/Slovakia, 1806-1953*
SPBW - Nov 2015 - pNA [501+]

Neuschwander, Cindy - *Sir Cumference and the Off-the-Charts Dessert (Illus. by Geehan, Wayne)*
TC Math - v22 - i2 - Sept 2015 - p118(1) [501+]
Sir Cumference and the Roundabout Battle: A Math Adventure (Illus. by Geehan, Wayne)
c SLJ - v61 - i8 - August 2015 - p123(1) [51-500]

Neve, Tim - *Sand Castles: Interiors Inspired by the Coast*
LJ - v140 - i12 - July 1 2015 - p87(1) [51-500]

Nevill, Adam - *No One Gets Out Alive*
y BL - v111 - i14 - March 15 2015 - p50(1) [51-500]
Bwatch - July 2015 - pNA [51-500]
KR - Feb 15 2015 - pNA [501+]
PW - v262 - i9 - March 2 2015 - p67(1) [51-500]

Neville, Cynthia J. - *Regesta Regum Scottorum IV, Pt 1: The Acts of Alexander III*
Med R - March 2015 - pNA(NA) [501+]

Neville, Mark - *London/ Pittsburgh*
NS - v144 - i5252 - March 6 2015 - p49(1) [51-500]

Neville, Stuart - *The Final Silence*
RVBW - July 2015 - pNA [501+]
RVBW - August 2015 - pNA [501+]
Those We Left Behind
BL - v111 - i21 - July 1 2015 - p40(2) [51-500]
KR - July 15 2015 - pNA [501+]
NYTBR - Oct 4 2015 - p29(L) [501+]
NYTBR - Dec 6 2015 - p85(L) [501+]
PW - v262 - i28 - July 13 2015 - p46(1) [51-500]

Nevin, Thomas R. - *The Last Years op' Saint Therese: Doubt and Darkness: 1895-1897*
CHR - v101 - i2 - Spring 2015 - p386(2) [501+]

Nevison, Susanna - *Teratology: Poems*
PW - v262 - i20 - May 18 2015 - p63(1) [51-500]

New Classics to Moderns Series
Am MT - v64 - i6 - June-July 2015 - p69(1) [501+]

A New Organon: Science Studies in Poland between the Wars
HNet - July 2015 - pNA [501+]

New York Genealogical and Biographical Society - *New York Family History Research Guide and Gazetteer*
NYT - April 19 2015 - p2(L) [501+]

Newbery, Georgie - *The Flower Farmer's Year: How to Grow Cut Flowers for Pleasure and Profit*
PW - v262 - i1 - Jan 5 2015 - p68(2) [51-500]
Grow Your Own Wedding Flowers: How to Grow and Arrange Your Own Rowers for All Special Occasions
PW - v262 - i52 - Dec 21 2015 - p149(1) [51-500]

Newbery, Linda - *The Brockenspectre (Illus. by Smy, Pam)*
c Sch Lib - v63 - i1 - Spring 2015 - p40(1) [51-500]
Some Other War
c Sch Lib - v63 - i2 - Summer 2015 - p108(1) [51-500]

Newcomb, Tim - *Engineering*
y BL - v111 - i17 - May 1 2015 - p88(1) [51-500]

Newcomer, Ron - *The Adventures of Marlin the Monkey*
c KR - Oct 15 2015 - pNA [501+]

Newdick, Thomas - *Modern Military Aircraft: The World's Great Weapons*
APH - v62 - i1 - Spring 2015 - p54(2) [501+]

Newell, John Philip - *The Rebirthing of God: Christianity's Struggle for New Beginnings*
CC - v132 - i13 - June 24 2015 - p41(1) [501+]

Newell, Lizzie - *Sappho's Agency*
KR - July 15 2015 - pNA [51-500]

Newhall Barbara Falconer - *Wrestling With God: Stories of Doubt and Faith*
PW - v262 - i3 - Jan 19 2015 - p77(1) [51-500]

Newkirk, Pamela - *Spectacle: The Astonishing Life of Ota Benga (Read by Turpin, Bahni). Audiobook Review*
BL - v112 - i6 - Nov 15 2015 - p62(1) [51-500]
LJ - v140 - i13 - August 1 2015 - p49(1) [51-500]
Spectacle: The Astonishing Life of Ota Benga
BL - v111 - i19-20 - June 1 2015 - p34(1) [51-500]
KR - April 1 2015 - pNA [501+]
LJ - v140 - i7 - April 15 2015 - p103(1) [51-500]
NY - v91 - i23 - August 10 2015 - p77 [501+]
NYTBR - June 7 2015 - p26(L) [501+]
PW - v262 - i14 - April 6 2015 - p50(1) [51-500]

Newland, Courttia - *Writing Short Stories*
TLS - i5849 - May 8 2015 - p23(1) [501+]

Newman, Aline Alexander - *Animal Superstars and More True Stories of Amazing Animal Talents (Read by Heller, Johnny). Audiobook Review*
c SLJ - v61 - i8 - August 2015 - p50(2) [51-500]
How to Speak Cat: A Guide to Decoding Cat Language
c CCB-B - v68 - i8 - April 2015 - p414(1) [51-500]
BL - v111 - i13 - March 1 2015 - p48(1) [51-500]

Newman, Barbara - *Medieval Crossover: Reading the Secular against the Sacred*
MP - v113 - i2 - Nov 2015 - pE69(4) [501+]

Newman, Barbara Johansen - *Glamorous Garbage (Illus. by Newman, Barbara Johansen)*
c BL - v111 - i12 - Feb 15 2015 - p77(1) [51-500]
c KR - Jan 1 2015 - pNA [51-500]
Glamorous Garbage (Illus. by Newman, Barbara Johnson)
c SLJ - v61 - i2 - Feb 2015 - p74(1) [51-500]

Newman, Elizabeth Terese - *Biography of a Hacienda: Work and Revolution in Rural Mexico*
HAHR - v95 - i1 - Feb 2015 - p164-165 [501+]

Newman, Janis Cooke - *A Master Plan for Rescue*
y BL - v111 - i19-20 - June 1 2015 - p44(1) [51-500]
KR - May 1 2015 - pNA [51-500]

Newman, Joni Marie - *The Complete Guide to Even More Vegan Food Substitutions: The Latest and Greatest Methods for Veganizing Anything Using More Natural, Plant-Based Ingredients*
LJ - v140 - i16 - Oct 1 2015 - p102(1) [51-500]

Newman, Joshua I. - *Sport, Spectacle, and NASCAR Nation: Consumption and the Cultural Politics of Neoliberalism*
SSJ - v32 - i1 - March 2015 - p106-109 [501+]

Newman, Karen - *Early Modern Cultures of Translation*
JHI - v76 - i4 - Oct 2015 - p666(1) [501+]
RVBW - Oct 2015 - pNA [501+]

Newman, Katherine S. - *Taxing the Poor: Doing Damage to the Truly Disadvantaged*
SF - v93 - i3 - March 2015 - pe68 [501+]

Newman, Kathryn - *Who Cares? Public Ambivalence and Government Activism from the New Deal to the Second Gilded Age*
    CS - v44 - i4 - July 2015 - p449-462 [501+]
Newman, Kim - *Quatermass and the Pit: Five Million Years to Earth*
    Si & So - v25 - i2 - Feb 2015 - p105(1) [501+]
    TLS - i5842 - March 20 2015 - p27(1) [501+]
Newman, Leslea - *Heather Has Two Mommies (Illus. by Cornell, Laura)*
  c HB - v91 - i3 - May-June 2015 - p140(2) [51-500]
  c HB Guide - v26 - i2 - Fall 2015 - p16(1) [51-500]
  c KR - Jan 15 2015 - pNA [51-500]
  c NYTBR - July 12 2015 - p19(L) [501+]
  c Sch Lib - v63 - i3 - Autumn 2015 - p158(1) [51-500]
  c SLJ - v61 - i2 - Feb 2015 - p74(1) [51-500]
Here Is the World: A Year of Jewish Holidays (Illus. by Gal, Susan)
  c HB Guide - v26 - i1 - Spring 2015 - p135(1) [51-500]
Ketzel, the Cat Who Composed (Illus. by Bates, Amy June)
  c BL - v111 - i21 - July 1 2015 - p63(1) [51-500]
  c KR - August 1 2015 - pNA [51-500]
  c PW - v262 - i32 - August 10 2015 - p63(1) [51-500]
  c PW - v262 - i49 - Dec 2 2015 - p48(1) [51-500]
  c SLJ - v61 - i8 - August 2015 - p74(2) [51-500]
My Name Is Aviva (Illus. by Jatkowska, Ag)
  c KR - July 15 2015 - pNA [51-500]
  c PW - v262 - i31 - August 3 2015 - p55(1) [51-500]
  c SLJ - v61 - i8 - August 2015 - p75(1) [51-500]
Newman, Mark - *Moon Bears (Illus. by Newman, Mark)*
  c PW - v262 - i35 - August 31 2015 - p90(2) [501+]
  c BL - v112 - i4 - Oct 15 2015 - p41(1) [51-500]
  c KR - August 15 2015 - pNA [51-500]
Newman, Michael Z. - *Video Revolutions. On the History of a Medium*
    T&C - v56 - i4 - Oct 2015 - p1010-1011 [501+]
Newman, Patricia - *Ebola: Fears and Facts*
  y BL - v112 - i3 - Oct 1 2015 - p37(1) [51-500]
  c KR - July 15 2015 - pNA [51-500]
  c SLJ - v61 - i8 - August 2015 - p128(2) [51-500]
Newman, Renee - *Exotic Gems, vols. 2 and 3*
    RocksMiner - v90 - i2 - March-April 2015 - p188(2) [501+]
Newman, Roberta J. - *Black Baseball, Black Business: Race Enterprise and the Fate of the Segregated Dollar*
    Am St - v54 - i2 - Summer 2015 - p106-108 [501+]
Newman, Robin - *The Case of the Missing Carrot Cake (Illus. by Zemke, Deborah)*
  c BL - v111 - i17 - May 1 2015 - p56(1) [51-500]
  c KR - Feb 15 2015 - pNA [51-500]
  c SLJ - v61 - i5 - May 2015 - p96(1) [51-500]
Newman, Sandra - *The Country of Ice Cream Star*
  y NYTBR - March 29 2015 - p18(L) [501+]
    NYTBR - Dec 20 2015 - p24(L) [501+]
Newman, Simon P. - *A New World of Labor: The Development of Plantation Slavery in the British Atlantic*
    RAH - v43 - i1 - March 2015 - p20-25 [501+]
Paine and Jefferson in the Age of Revolutions
    JAH - v101 - i4 - March 2015 - p1253-1254 [501+]
    JSH - v81 - i4 - Nov 2015 - p952(3) [501+]
Newman, Tracy - *Hanukkah Is Coming! (Illus. by Garofoli, Viviana)*
  c HB - v91 - i6 - Nov-Dec 2015 - p59(1) [51-500]
  c KR - Sept 1 2015 - pNA [51-500]
  c PW - v262 - i37 - Sept 14 2015 - p72(2) [501+]
  c SLJ - v61 - i10 - Oct 2015 - p66(1) [51-500]
Uncle Eli's Wedding (Illus. by Isik, Sernur)
  c HB Guide - v26 - i2 - Fall 2015 - p46(1) [51-500]
  c KR - Jan 15 2015 - pNA [51-500]
Newman, Wendy - *121 First Dates: How to Succeed at Online Dating, Fall in Love, and Live Happily Ever After*
    PW - v262 - i51 - Dec 14 2015 - p76(2) [501+]
Newport, Cal - *Deep Work: Rules for Focused Success in a Distracted World*
    PW - v262 - i45 - Nov 9 2015 - p53(1) [51-500]
Newquist, H.P. - *Abracadabra: The Story of Magic through the Ages (Illus. by Ivanov, Aleksey)*
  c BL - v112 - i6 - Nov 15 2015 - p38(1) [51-500]
  c SLJ - v61 - i10 - Oct 2015 - p136(1) [51-500]
The Human Body: The Story of How We Protect, Repair, and Make Ourselves Stronger
  c BL - v112 - i6 - Nov 15 2015 - p38(2) [51-500]
  c KR - Oct 15 2015 - pNA [51-500]
Newsome, Hampton - *Richmond Must Fall: The Richmond-Petersburg Campaign, October 1864*
    Historian - v77 - i1 - Spring 2015 - p135(2) [501+]

Newth, Michael A.H. - *Heroines of the French Epic: A Second Selection of Chansons de geste*
    Specu - v90 - i3 - July 2015 - p834-836 [501+]
Newton, Charlie - *Traitor's Gate*
    KR - April 1 2015 - pNA [501+]
    LJ - v140 - i11 - June 15 2015 - p78(2) [501+]
    PW - v262 - i12 - March 23 2015 - p50(1) [51-500]
Newton, David E. - *Fracking: A Reference Handbook*
  y BL - v111 - i19-20 - June 1 2015 - p22(1) [51-500]
GMO Food
  y BL - v111 - i9-10 - Jan 1 2015 - p27(1) [51-500]
Wind Energy
  y BL - v111 - i19-20 - June 1 2015 - p12(1) [51-500]
Newton, Douglas - *The Darkest Days: The Truth behind Britain's Rush to War, 1914*
    J Mil H - v79 - i1 - Jan 2015 - p229-230 [501+]
    J Mil H - v79 - i4 - Oct 2015 - p1150-1152 [501+]
    Lon R Bks - v37 - i1 - Jan 8 2015 - p17(4) [501+]
Newton, Jim - *Eisenhower: The White House Years*
    Pres St Q - v45 - i1 - March 2015 - p199(7) [501+]
Newton, Michael - *Famous Assassinations in World History: An Encyclopedia*
    R&USQ - v54 - i4 - Summer 2015 - p81(1) [501+]
White Robes and Burning Crosses: A History of the Ku Klux Klan from 1866
    HNet - Feb 2015 - pNA [501+]
Newton-Small, Jay - *Broad Influence*
    KR - Nov 1 2015 - pNA [501+]
Neyer, Andrew - *Letters Are for Learning*
  c KR - Jan 1 2016 - pNA [51-500]
Neyfakh, Leon - *The Next Next Level*
    PW - v262 - i22 - June 1 2015 - p54(2) [51-500]
    Mac - v128 - i26-27 - July 6 2015 - p67(1) [51-500]
Neysmith, Sheila M. - *Beyond Caring Labour to Provisioning Work*
    CWS - v30 - i2-3 - Fall-Winter 2015 - p148(2) [501+]
Ng, Celeste - *Everything I Never Told You*
    Ent W - i1364 - May 22 2015 - p66(1) [501+]
Ngalamulume, Kalala - *Colonial Pathologies, Environment, and Western Medicine in Saint-Louis-du-Senegal, 1867-1920*
    AHR - v120 - i3 - June 2015 - p1153-1154 [501+]
Ngo, Fiona I.B. - *Imperial Blues: Geographies of Race and Sex in Jazz Age New York*
    AHR - v120 - i2 - April 2015 - p650-651 [501+]
    JAH - v101 - i4 - March 2015 - p1303(1) [501+]
Ngo Tu Lap - *Black Stars*
    WLT - v89 - i1 - Jan-Feb 2015 - p71(1) [51-500]
Nguyen, Dustin - *Christmas and New Year's Eve (Illus. by Nguyen, Dustin)*
  c HB Guide - v26 - i1 - Spring 2015 - p88(1) [51-500]
Halloween and Thanksgiving (Illus. by Nguyen, Dustin)
  c HB Guide - v26 - i1 - Spring 2015 - p88(1) [51-500]
Valentine's Day and the Lunar New Year (Illus. by Nguyen, Dustin)
  c HB Guide - v26 - i1 - Spring 2015 - p88(1) [51-500]
Nguyen, Hoa - *Red Juice*
    APR - v44 - i1 - Jan-Feb 2015 - p9(3) [501+]
Nguyen, Lien-Hang T. - *Hanoi's War: An International History of the War for Peace in Vietnam*
    APH - v62 - i1 - Spring 2015 - p55(1) [501+]
    Pac A - v88 - i2 - June 2015 - p353 [501+]
Nguyen Tan Hoang - *A View from the Bottom: Asian American Masculinity and Sexual Representation*
    G&L Rev W - v22 - i2 - March-April 2015 - p43(2) [501+]
Nguyen, Viet Thanh - *The Sympathizer*
    BL - v111 - i16 - April 15 2015 - p38(1) [51-500]
    KR - Feb 1 2015 - pNA [51-500]
    LJ - v140 - i3 - Feb 15 2015 - p91(1) [51-500]
    NY - v91 - i18 - June 29 2015 - p71 [501+]
    NYT - August 28 2015 - pC9(L) [501+]
    NYTBR - April 5 2015 - p1(L) [501+]
    PW - v262 - i2 - Jan 12 2015 - p34(1) [51-500]
Ni, Zhange - *The Pagan Writes Back: When World Religion Meets World Literature*
    JAAR - v83 - i2 - June 2015 - pNA [501+]
Nibert, David A. - *Animal Oppression and Human Violence: Domesecration, Capitalism, and Global Conflict*
    QRB - v90 - i1 - March 2015 - p76(1) [501+]
Nicassio, Theresa - *Yum*
    KR - Dec 1 2015 - pNA [501+]
Nicastro, Nick - *The Isle of Stone*
    HT - v65 - i8 - August 2015 - p56(2) [501+]

Novel of Ancient Sparta
    HT - v65 - i8 - August 2015 - p56(2) [501+]
Nichol, Christina - *Waiting for Electricity*
    Wom R Bks - v32 - i4 - July-August 2015 - p25(2) [501+]
Nichol, Shellie - *Destination Hope: A Guidethrough Life's Unexpected Journeys*
    SPBW - Nov 2015 - pNA [51-500]
Nicholas, Douglas - *Throne of Darkness*
    PW - v262 - i8 - Feb 23 2015 - p57(1) [51-500]
    BL - v111 - i13 - March 1 2015 - p31(1) [51-500]
Nicholas, J.W. - *The Freedom to Kill*
    KR - August 15 2015 - pNA [501+]
Nicholas, Kristin - *Crafting a Colorful Home: A Room-by-Room Guide to Personalizing Your Space with Color*
    LJ - v140 - i2 - Feb 1 2015 - p83(1) [51-500]
Nicholas, Ralph W. - *Night of the Gods: Durga Puja and the Legitimation of Power in Rural Bengal*
    JRAI - v21 - i3 - Sept 2015 - p709(2) [501+]
Nicholl, Colin - *The Great Christ Comet: Revealing the True Star of Bethlehem*
    Spec - v329 - i9772 - Dec 12 2015 - p85(1) [501+]
Nicholls, David - *Us (Read by Haig, David). Audiobook Review*
    LJ - v140 - i2 - Feb 1 2015 - p45(1) [51-500]
    PW - v262 - i5 - Feb 2 2015 - p53(1) [51-500]
Us
    NYTBR - Jan 4 2015 - p17(L) [501+]
Nicholls, John G. - *Pioneers of Neurobiology: My Brilliant Eccentric Heroes*
    Nature - v518 - i7537 - Feb 5 2015 - p33(1) [51-500]
Nicholls, Sally - *An Island of Our Own*
  c Sch Lib - v63 - i2 - Summer 2015 - p120(1) [51-500]
Nicholls, Walter J. - *The DREAMers: How the Undocumented Youth Movement Transformed the Immigrant Rights Debate*
    AJS - v120 - i5 - March 2015 - p1552(4) [501+]
    CS - v44 - i3 - May 2015 - p389-391 [501+]
    ERS - v38 - i3 - March 2015 - p452(3) [501+]
    J Hi E - v86 - i6 - Nov-Dec 2015 - p955(5) [501+]
Nichols, Amy K. - *Now That You're Here*
  y CCB-B - v68 - i6 - Feb 2015 - p324(1) [51-500]
  y HB Guide - v26 - i2 - Fall 2015 - p133(1) [51-500]
While You Were Gone
  y KR - June 1 2015 - pNA [51-500]
  y BL - v111 - i21 - July 1 2015 - p60(1) [51-500]
  y SLJ - v61 - i8 - August 2015 - p108(1) [51-500]
  y VOYA - v38 - i3 - August 2015 - p82(1) [51-500]
Nichols, Joel A. - *Teaching Internet Basics: The Can-Do Guide*
    Teach Lib - v42 - i3 - Feb 2015 - p43(1) [51-500]
Nichols, Kate - *Greece and Rome at the Crystal Palace: Classical Sculpture and Modern Britain, 1854-1936*
    TimHES - i2208 - June 18 2015 - p51(1) [501+]
Nichols, Lori - *Maple (Read by Nielsen, Stina). Audiobook Review*
  c SLJ - v61 - i9 - Sept 2015 - p56(2) [51-500]
Maple & Willow Apart (Illus. by Nichols, Lori)
  c BL - v112 - i2 - Sept 15 2015 - p67(2) [51-500]
  c KR - June 1 2015 - pNA [51-500]
  c SLJ - v61 - i8 - August 2015 - p60(1) [51-500]
Maple & Willow Together
  c HB Guide - v26 - i1 - Spring 2015 - p13(1) [51-500]
Nichols, Naomi - *Youth Work: An Institutional Ethnography of Youth Homelessness*
    CS - v44 - i5 - Sept 2015 - p745(1) [501+]
Nichols, Peter - *The Rocks*
    BL - v111 - i18 - May 15 2015 - p30(2) [51-500]
    CSM - June 23 2015 - pNA [501+]
    CSM - July 24 2015 - pNA [501+]
    Ent W - i1365-1366 - May 29 2015 - p108(1) [501+]
    KR - March 15 2015 - pNA [501+]
    LJ - v140 - i7 - April 15 2015 - p77(1) [51-500]
    NYTBR - May 24 2015 - p15(L) [501+]
    Par - v90 - i8 - August 2015 - p22(1) [501+]
    PW - v262 - i13 - March 30 2015 - p50(1) [51-500]
Nichols, Roger L. - *American Indians in U.S. History, 2d ed.*
    Roundup M - v22 - i6 - August 2015 - p39(1) [501+]
Warrior Nations: The United States and Indian Peoples
    JAH - v102 - i1 - June 2015 - p234-235 [501+]
Nichols, Travis - *Fowl Play (Illus. by Nichols, Travis)*
  c KR - June 15 2015 - pNA [51-500]
  c SLJ - v61 - i9 - Sept 2015 - p126(1) [51-500]

Nicholson, Catherine - *Uncommon Tongues: Eloquence and Eccentricity in the English Renaissance*
    Ren Q - v68 - i2 - Summer 2015 - p757-758 [501+]
    TLS - i5857 - July 3 2015 - p11(1) [501+]

Nicholson, Cecily - *From the Poplars*
    Can Lit - i224 - Spring 2015 - p140 [501+]

Nicholson, Christopher - *Winter*
    BL - v112 - i6 - Nov 15 2015 - p30(2) [51-500]
    KR - Oct 1 2015 - pNA [501+]
    NYT - Dec 31 2015 - pC7(L) [501+]
    PW - v262 - i42 - Oct 19 2015 - p51(1) [51-500]

Nicholson, David - *Flying Home: Seven Stories of the Secret City*
    NYTBR - Oct 4 2015 - p30(L) [501+]

Nicholson, Hope - *Moonshot: The Indigenous Comics Collection*
    c SLJ - v61 - i11 - Nov 2015 - p125(2) [51-500]

Nicholson, Julia - *In Their Shoes: Fairy Tales and Folktales*
    c Sch Lib - v63 - i4 - Winter 2015 - p234(1) [501+]

Nicholson, Lorna Schultz - *Fragile Bones: Harrison & Anna*
    y Res Links - v20 - i4 - April 2015 - p32(1) [501+]
    y VOYA - v38 - i3 - August 2015 - p65(2) [51-500]

Nicholson, Simon - *The Demon Curse*
    c BL - v111 - i19-20 - June 1 2015 - p108(1) [51-500]
    The Magician's Fire
    y HB Guide - v26 - i1 - Spring 2015 - p88(1) [51-500]
    c Sch Lib - v63 - i2 - Summer 2015 - p108(1) [51-500]

Nicholson, Virginia - *Perfect Wives in Ideal Homes: The Story of Women in the 1950s*
    Spec - v327 - i9733 - March 14 2015 - p40(1) [501+]

Nicholson, William - *Amherst*
    BL - v111 - i9-10 - Jan 1 2015 - p51(2) [51-500]
    NYTBR - June 14 2015 - p26(L) [501+]
    The Lovers of Amherst
    NS - v144 - i5261 - May 7 2015 - p46(3) [501+]

Nichter, Luke A. - *The Nixon Tapes: 1973*
    NYTBR - Oct 25 2015 - p12(L) [501+]

Nichter, Mimi - *Lighting Up: The Rise of Social Smoking on College Campuses*
    VOYA - v38 - i2 - June 2015 - p90(1) [501+]

Nichtern, Ethan - *The Road Home: A Contemporary Exploration of the Buddhist Path*
    KR - Feb 15 2015 - pNA [501+]
    LJ - v140 - i3 - Feb 15 2015 - p107(1) [51-500]
    PW - v262 - i10 - March 9 2015 - p68(1) [51-500]

Nici, John B. - *Famous Works of Art--and How They Got That Way*
    BL - v112 - i5 - Nov 1 2015 - p17(1) [51-500]
    PW - v262 - i29 - July 20 2015 - p182(1) [51-500]

Nickel, Barbara - *A Boy Asked the Wind*
    KR - Jan 1 2016 - pNA [51-500]

Nickel, Rainer - *Der verbannte Stratege: Xenophon und der Tod des Thukydides*
    HNet - Sept 2015 - pNA [501+]

Nickerson, Sara - *The Secrets of Blueberries, Brothers, Moose & Me*
    c BL - v111 - i19-20 - June 1 2015 - p106(1) [51-500]
    c CCB-B - v69 - i1 - Sept 2015 - p41(1) [51-500]
    c HB Guide - v26 - i2 - Fall 2015 - p95(1) [51-500]
    KR - April 1 2015 - pNA [51-500]
    c NYTBR - July 12 2015 - p19(L) [501+]
    c SLJ - v61 - i5 - May 2015 - p104(1) [51-500]
    y VOYA - v38 - i2 - June 2015 - p66(1) [501+]

Nickson, Chris - *Skin Like Silver*
    KR - Jan 1 2016 - pNA [51-500]
    Two Bronze Pennies
    BL - v111 - i19-20 - June 1 2015 - p58(1) [51-500]
    KR - June 1 2015 - pNA [51-500]
    PW - v262 - i26 - June 29 2015 - p48(1) [51-500]

Nicolaides, Becky M. - *The Suburb Reader*
    J Urban H - v41 - i1 - Jan 2015 - p171-10 [501+]

Nicolaides, Demetris - *In the Light of Science: Our Ancient Quest for Knowledge and the Measure of Modern Physics*
    Phys Today - v68 - i4 - April 2015 - p53-54 [501+]

Nicolaisen, Peter - *Cosmopolitanism and Nationhood in the Age of Jefferson*
    JAH - v102 - i1 - June 2015 - p237-238 [501+]

Nicolas, Louis - *The Codex Canadensis and the Writings of Louis Nicolas*
    AM - v213 - i4 - August 17 2015 - p29(3) [501+]

Nicoletti, Cara - *Voracious: A Hungry Reader Cooks Her Way through Great Books*
    KR - June 15 2015 - pNA [51-500]
    PW - v262 - i23 - June 8 2015 - p52(1) [51-500]
    BL - v111 - i19-20 - June 1 2015 - p21(1) [51-500]
    LJ - v140 - i7 - April 15 2015 - p111(3) [51-500]

Nicosia, Francis R. - *Jewish Life in Nazi Germany: Dilemmas and Responses*
    HNet - March 2015 - pNA [501+]

Niebruegge, Kersti - *Mistake Wisconsin*
    y CH Bwatch - March 2015 - pNA [51-500]
    y PW - v262 - i16 - April 20 2015 - p79(1) [51-500]

Niebuhr, Reinhold - *Major Works on Religion and Politics*
    NYRB - v62 - i13 - August 13 2015 - p74(2) [501+]

Nielsen, Chris P. - *Clearer Skies over China: Reconciling Air Quality, Climate, and Economic Goals*
    Pac A - v88 - i2 - June 2015 - p285 [501+]

Nielsen, Gert Holmgaard - *Walking a Tightrope: Defending Human Rights in China*
    Pac A - v88 - i4 - Dec 2015 - p900 [501+]

Nielsen, Jennifer A. - *Le souverain dans l'ombre*
    y Res Links - v20 - i5 - June 2015 - p42(1) [51-500]
    Mark of the Thief (Read by Andrews, Macleod). Audiobook Review
    c SLJ - v61 - i7 - July 2015 - p47(1) [51-500]
    Mark of the Thief
    c BL - v111 - i9-10 - Jan 1 2015 - p101(1) [51-500]
    y CCB-B - v68 - i8 - April 2015 - p414(1) [51-500]
    c HB Guide - v26 - i2 - Fall 2015 - p96(1) [51-500]
    c Teach Lib - v42 - i5 - June 2015 - p15(1) [51-500]
    y VOYA - v37 - i6 - Feb 2015 - p82(1) [51-500]
    A Night Divided (Read by Sinrses, Kate). Audiobook Review
    c SLJ - v61 - i12 - Dec 2015 - p76(1) [51-500]
    A Night Divided
    c BL - v111 - i22 - August 1 2015 - p68(1) [51-500]
    c KR - June 15 2015 - pNA [51-500]
    c PW - v262 - i22 - June 1 2015 - p60(1) [51-500]
    c SLJ - v61 - i7 - July 2015 - p80(3) [51-500]
    y VOYA - v38 - i4 - Oct 2015 - p58(1) [51-500]
    Rise of the Wolf
    c KR - Oct 15 2015 - pNA [51-500]

Nielsen, Kim E. - *A Disability History of the United States*
    JWH - v27 - i1 - Spring 2015 - p178(9) [501+]

Nielsen, Susin - *We Are All Made of Molecules (Read by Bernstein, Jesse). Audiobook Review*
    y BL - v112 - i2 - Sept 15 2015 - p80(1) [51-500]
    y HB - v91 - i6 - Nov-Dec 2015 - p110(1) [51-500]
    y SLJ - v61 - i8 - August 2015 - p54(1) [51-500]
    We Are All Made of Molecules
    y BL - v111 - i15 - April 1 2015 - p71(1) [51-500]
    y CCB-B - v68 - i11 - July-August 2015 - p558(2) [51-500]
    y HB Guide - v26 - i2 - Fall 2015 - p133(1) [51-500]
    y KR - March 1 2015 - pNA [51-500]
    y Magpies - v30 - i3 - July 2015 - p43(1) [501+]
    y Res Links - v20 - i5 - June 2015 - p27(1) [501+]
    y Sch Lib - v63 - i2 - Summer 2015 - p120(1) [51-500]
    y SLJ - v61 - i2 - Feb 2015 - p90(2) [51-500]
    y Teach Lib - v42 - i5 - June 2015 - p18(1) [51-500]
    y VOYA - v38 - i1 - April 2015 - p66(1) [51-500]

Nielsen, Wendy C. - *Women Warriors in Romantic Drama*
    Eight-C St - v49 - i1 - Fall 2015 - p91-94 [501+]

Nielson, Carmen J. - *Private Women and the Public Good: Charity and State Formation in Hamilton, Ontario, 1846-93*
    Can Hist R - v96 - i3 - Sept 2015 - p447(3) [501+]

Niemann, Christoph - *The Potato King (Illus. by Niemann, Christoph)*
    c CH Bwatch - April 2015 - pNA [51-500]
    c HB Guide - v26 - i2 - Fall 2015 - p46(1) [51-500]
    c KR - Feb 15 2015 - pNA [51-500]
    c Nat Post - v17 - i147 - April 25 2015 - pWP4(1) [501+]
    c NYTBR - May 10 2015 - p23(L) [501+]
    c PW - v262 - i49 - Dec 2 2015 - p24(1) [51-500]
    c Res Links - v20 - i5 - June 2015 - p7(1) [51-500]
    SLJ - v61 - i3 - March 2015 - p122(1) [51-500]

Niemeyer, Charles P. - *The Chesapeake Campaign 1813-1814*
    J Mil H - v79 - i1 - Jan 2015 - p181-185 [501+]

Niemeyer, Christin - *Der Deutsche Film im Kalten Krieg/Cinema Allemand et Guerre Froid*
    HNet - July 2015 - pNA [501+]

Nieres-Chevrel, Isabelle - *Dictionnaire du livre de jeunesse: la litterature d'enfance et de jeunesse en France*
    Bkbird - v53 - i3 - Summer 2015 - p88(2) [501+]

Niesser, Jacqueline - *Angewandte Geschichte: Neue Perspektiven auf Geschichte in der Offentlichkeit*
    HNet - Feb 2015 - pNA [501+]

Nieto, Sandra Rodriguez - *The Story of Vicente, Who Murdered His Mother, His Father, and His Sister: Life and Death in Juarez*
    LJ - v140 - i20 - Dec 1 2015 - p118(2) [51-500]

Nievo, Ippolito - *Confessions of an Italian*
    NYRB - v62 - i6 - April 2 2015 - p64(3) [501+]

Niffenegger, Audrey - *Ghostly: A Collection of Ghost Stories*
    LJ - v140 - i17 - Oct 15 2015 - p84(1) [51-500]
    PW - v262 - i36 - Sept 7 2015 - p48(2) [51-500]

Nigg, Joseph - *Sea Monsters: A Voyage around the World's Most Beguiling Map*
    Ren Q - v68 - i1 - Spring 2015 - p273-274 [501+]

Night and Day Studios - *Peekaboo Presents (Illus. by Lunn, Corey)*
    c KR - Sept 1 2015 - pNA [51-500]

Nightingale, Steven - *Granada: A Pomegranate in the Hand of God*
    BL - v111 - i9-10 - Jan 1 2015 - p33(1) [51-500]
    PW - v262 - i2 - Jan 12 2015 - p53(2) [51-500]

Niimi, Nankichi - *Gon, the Little Fox (Illus. by Mita, Genjirou)*
    c KR - March 15 2015 - pNA [51-500]
    c SLJ - v61 - i5 - May 2015 - p90(1) [51-500]

Niimura, Ken - *Henshin (Illus. by Niimura, Ken)*
    BL - v111 - i16 - April 15 2015 - p39(1) [51-500]

Nijkamp, Marieke - *This Is Where It Ends*
    y KR - Oct 15 2015 - pNA [51-500]
    y PW - v262 - i44 - Nov 2 2015 - p87(1) [51-500]

Nika, D.J. - *The Oracle*
    BL - v112 - i2 - Sept 15 2015 - p32(1) [51-500]

Nikitas, Derek - *Extra Life*
    y BL - v112 - i3 - Oct 1 2015 - p69(1) [51-500]
    y SLJ - v61 - i11 - Nov 2015 - p108(2) [51-500]

Niklas, Karl - *Plant Physics*
    BioSci - v65 - i2 - Feb 2015 - p215(2) [501+]

Nikola-Lisa, W. - *The Men Who Made the Yankees: The Odyssey of the World's Greatest Team from Baltimore to the Bronx*
    PW - v262 - i19 - May 11 2015 - p52(2) [51-500]

Nikolaidou, Sophia - *The Scapegoat*
    TLS - i5837 - Feb 13 2015 - p19(1) [501+]

Nikoloutsos, K.P. - *Ancient Greek Women in Film*
    Class R - v65 - i1 - April 2015 - p291-293 [501+]

Nil, Santianez - *Topographies of Fascism: Habitus, Space, and Writing in Twentieth-Century Spain*
    Hisp R - v83 - i1 - Wntr 2015 - p107-110 [501+]

Nilsen, Anders - *Poetry Is Useless (Illus. by Nilsen, Anders)*
    BL - v112 - i2 - Sept 15 2015 - p51(1) [51-500]
    PW - v262 - i28 - July 13 2015 - p53(1) [51-500]

Nilsson, Magnus - *The Nordic Cookbook*
    NYTBR - Dec 6 2015 - p20(L) [501+]
    NYTBR - Dec 6 2015 - p20(L) [501+]
    PW - v262 - i42 - Oct 19 2015 - p70(2) [51-500]
    Spec - v329 - i9768 - Nov 14 2015 - p58(1) [501+]

Nilsson, Ulf - *Detective Gordon: The First Case (Illus. by Spee, Gitte)*
    c HB Guide - v26 - i2 - Fall 2015 - p69(1) [51-500]
    c BL - v111 - i17 - May 1 2015 - p54(2) [51-500]
    c KR - Feb 15 2015 - pNA [51-500]
    c HB - v91 - i3 - May-June 2015 - p115(1) [51-500]
    c Magpies - v30 - i2 - May 2015 - p34(1) [501+]
    SLJ - v61 - i3 - March 2015 - p122(1) [51-500]

Niman, Nicolette Hahn - *Defending Beef: The Case for Sustainable Meat Production*
    Bwatch - Jan 2015 - pNA [51-500]
    VQR - v91 - i2 - Spring 2015 - p218-222 [501+]

Nimura, Janice P. - *Daughters of the Samurai: A Journey from East to West and Back*
    KR - Jan 15 2015 - pNA [51-500]
    LJ - v140 - i5 - March 15 2015 - p121(1) [51-500]
    PW - v262 - i10 - March 9 2015 - p62(1) [51-500]
    y BL - v111 - i16 - April 15 2015 - p14(1) [51-500]
    Bwatch - June 2015 - pNA [51-500]
    NYTBR - May 31 2015 - p26(L) [501+]

Nin, Anais - *The Novel of the Future*
    RVBW - Jan 2015 - pNA [501+]

Ninham, Sally - *Ten African Cardinals*
    AM - v212 - i3 - Feb 2 2015 - p43(3) [501+]

Ninkovich, Frank - *The Global Republic: America's Inadvertent Rise to World Power*
    JAH - v102 - i1 - June 2015 - p212-212 [501+]

Nippert-Eng, Christena - *Islands of Privacy*
    SF - v93 - i3 - March 2015 - pe79 [501+]

Nirenberg, David - *Anti-Judaism: The History of a Way of Thinking*
    Lon R Bks - v37 - i10 - May 21 2015 - p31(4) [501+]
    Anti-Judaism: The Western Tradition
    JR - Jan 2015 - p94(13) [501+]

Neighboring Faiths: Christianity, Islam, and Judaism in the Middle Ages and Today
    CC - v132 - i23 - Nov 11 2015 - p38(3) [501+]
    Lon R Bks - v37 - i10 - May 21 2015 - p31(4) [501+]
    RM - v69 - i1 - Sept 2015 - p149(3) [501+]
Nisbet, Gideon - *Greek Epigram in Reception. J.A. Symonds, Oscar Wilde, and the Invention of Desire, 1805-1929*
    Class R - v65 - i1 - April 2015 - p284-285 [501+]
Nisbet, H.B. - *Gotthold Ephraim Lessing: His Life, Works, and Thought*
    GSR - v38 - i2 - May 2015 - p411-4 [501+]
Nisbett, Richard E. - *Mindware: Tools for Smart Thinking*
    LJ - v140 - i10 - June 1 2015 - p124(1) [51-500]
    Nature - v524 - i7564 - August 13 2015 - p159(1) [501+]
    NYTBR - Oct 18 2015 - p23(L) [501+]
    PW - v262 - i23 - June 8 2015 - p51(1) [51-500]
Nishiyama, Takashi - *Engineering War and Peace in Modern Japan, 1868-1964*
    AHR - v120 - i2 - April 2015 - p598-599 [501+]
    J Mil H - v79 - i1 - Jan 2015 - p218-219 [501+]
    T&C - v56 - i2 - April 2015 - p545-547 [501+]
Nissenbaum, Dion - *A Street Divided*
    KR - June 15 2015 - pNA [501+]
Nissley, Claudia - *Consultation and Cultural Heritage: Let Us Reason Together*
    Pub Hist - v37 - i1 - Feb 2015 - p148(2) [501+]
Niven, Felicia Lowenstein - *Hilarious Huge Animal Jokes to Tickle Your Funny Bone*
    c HB Guide - v26 - i1 - Spring 2015 - p181(1) [51-500]
Hysterical Dog Jokes to Tickle Your Funny Bone
    c HB Guide - v26 - i1 - Spring 2015 - p181(1) [51-500]
Niven, Jennifer - *All the Bright Places (Read by Heyborne, Kirby, with Ari Meyers). Audiobook Review*
    y BL - v111 - i19-20 - June 1 2015 - p140(1) [51-500]
All the Bright Places (Read by Heyborne, Kirby). Audiobook Review
    y PW - v262 - i8 - Feb 23 2015 - p72(2) [51-500]
All the Bright Places
    y CCB-B - v68 - i7 - March 2015 - p364(2) [51-500]
    y Ent W - i1346 - Jan 16 2015 - p66(1) [501+]
    y Magpies - v30 - i2 - May 2015 - p42(1) [501+]
    c Nat Post - v17 - i56 - Jan 3 2015 - pWP11(1) [501+]
    y NYTBR - Jan 18 2015 - p20(L) [501+]
    y PW - v262 - i49 - Dec 2 2015 - p88(1) [51-500]
    y Sch Lib - v63 - i1 - Spring 2015 - p56(1) [51-500]
    y VOYA - v37 - i6 - Feb 2015 - p62(1) [501+]
Niven, Larry - *Red Tide*
    Analog - v135 - i3 - March 2015 - p107(2) [501+]
Nivola, Claire A. - *Star Child*
    c HB Guide - v26 - i1 - Spring 2015 - p40(1) [51-500]
Nivola, Pietro S. - *What So Proudly We Hailed: Essays on the Contemporary Meanings of the War of 1812*
    J Am St - v49 - i1 - Feb 2015 - p188-190 [501+]
Nix, Echol, Jr. - *In the Beginning: The Martin Luther King Jr. International Chapel at Morehouse College*
    RVBW - Oct 2015 - pNA [51-500]
Nix, Garth - *Clariel (Read by Malcolm, Graeme). Audiobook Review*
    y BL - v111 - i15 - April 1 2015 - p87(1) [51-500]
Clariel
    y CCB-B - v68 - i5 - Jan 2015 - p271(1) [51-500]
    y HB Guide - v26 - i1 - Spring 2015 - p118(1) [51-500]
    y Sch Lib - v63 - i1 - Spring 2015 - p56(1) [51-500]
    y Teach Lib - v42 - i3 - Feb 2015 - p28(4) [501+]
Newt's Emerald
    y BL - v112 - i2 - Sept 15 2015 - p74(1) [51-500]
    y KR - July 15 2015 - pNA [51-500]
    y Magpies - v30 - i4 - Sept 2015 - p43(1) [501+]
    y PW - v262 - i29 - July 20 2015 - p193(2) [51-500]
    y SLJ - v61 - i8 - August 2015 - p98(1) [51-500]
    y VOYA - v38 - i4 - Oct 2015 - p75(1) [51-500]
To Hold the Bridge
    y BL - v111 - i13 - March 1 2015 - p60(1) [51-500]
    y Magpies - v30 - i3 - July 2015 - p43(1) [501+]
    y SLJ - v61 - i5 - May 2015 - p122(1) [51-500]
    y VOYA - v38 - i4 - April 2015 - p81(2) [51-500]
    y HB Guide - v26 - i2 - Fall 2015 - p133(2) [51-500]
    y PW - v262 - i15 - April 13 2015 - p82(2) [51-500]
    y Sch Lib - v63 - i4 - Winter 2015 - p248(2) [51-500]
Nixon, James - *BMX Champion*
    c Sch Lib - v63 - i3 - Autumn 2015 - p188(1) [51-500]
Football (Illus. by Humphrey, Booby)
    c Sch Lib - v63 - i1 - Spring 2015 - p48(1) [51-500]

Nixon, Mark - *Echo's Bones*
    NYRB - v62 - i5 - March 19 2015 - p34(3) [501+]
Samuel Beckett's Library
    MLR - v110 - i3 - July 2015 - p789-790 [501+]
Nixon, Sam - *The Adventures of Long Arm (Illus. by Bitskoff, Aleksei)*
    c Sch Lib - v63 - i4 - Winter 2015 - p230(1) [51-500]
Nixon, Sterling - *Seven Days*
    PW - v262 - i2 - Jan 12 2015 - p34(2) [51-500]
Nizri, Michael - *Ottoman High Politics and the Ulema Household*
    IJMES - v47 - i4 - Nov 2015 - p826-828 [501+]
Nizynska, Joanna - *The Kingdom of Insignificance: Miron Bialoszewski and the Quotidian, the Queer, and the Traumatic*
    Slav R - v74 - i2 - Summer 2015 - p389-391 [501+]
Noanoa, Julie - *Maori Art for Kids*
    c Magpies - v30 - i1 - March 2015 - pS7(1) [501+]
Nobit, John - *Collapsed World*
    KR - April 1 2015 - pNA [501+]
Noble, Carrie Anne - *The Mermaid's Sister*
    y CCB-B - v68 - i11 - July-August 2015 - p559(1) [51-500]
    y SLJ - v61 - i3 - March 2015 - p160(2) [51-500]
    y CH Bwatch - May 2015 - pNA [51-500]
Noble, Justin - *Artie's Party (Featuring the Vita-Men!). (Illus. by Bonin, Anna)*
    CH Bwatch - Sept 2015 - pNA [51-500]
Noble, Karyn - *Lonely Planet's Ultimate Travel: Our List of the 500 Best Places on the Planet - Ranked*
    LJ - v140 - i20 - Dec 1 2015 - p122(1) [51-500]
Noble, Kate - *The Lie and the Lady*
    PW - v262 - i46 - Nov 16 2015 - p61(1) [51-500]
Noble, Shelley - *Whisper Beach*
    BL - v111 - i19-20 - June 1 2015 - p47(1) [51-500]
Noble, Trinka Hakes - *Lizzie and the Last Day of School (Illus. by McLeod, Kris Aro)*
    c BL - v111 - i12 - Feb 15 2015 - p88(1) [51-500]
    c CH Bwatch - April 2015 - pNA [51-500]
    c KR - Jan 15 2015 - pNA [51-500]
    SLJ - v61 - i3 - March 2015 - p123(1) [51-500]
Noblin, Annie England - *Sit! Stay! Speak!*
    BL - v112 - i2 - Sept 15 2015 - p28(1) [51-500]
    KR - July 1 2015 - pNA [51-500]
    LJ - v140 - i14 - Sept 1 2015 - p96(1) [51-500]
Nocentelli, Carmen - *Empires of Love: Europe, Asia and the Making of Early Modern Identity*
    MP - v112 - i3 - Feb 2015 - pE220(E223) [501+]
Noe, Alva - *Strange Tools: Art and Human Nature*
    KR - May 15 2015 - pNA [501+]
    LJ - v140 - i10 - June 1 2015 - p107(1) [51-500]
    New Sci - v228 - i3042 - Oct 10 2015 - p47(1) [501+]
    PW - v262 - i26 - June 29 2015 - p55(1) [501+]
Noe, Kenneth W. - *The Yellowhammer War: The Civil War and Reconstruction in Alabama*
    JAH - v102 - i1 - June 2015 - p256-257 [501+]
Noel, Erick - *Dictionnaire des Gens de Couleur dans la France Moderne (Debut XVIe s.-1792), vol. 2: La Bretagne*
    HNet - Jan 2015 - pNA [501+]
Noel, Linda C. - *Debating American Identity: Southwestern Statehood and Mexican Immigration*
    AHR - v120 - i3 - June 2015 - p1044(1) [501+]
    JAH - v101 - i4 - March 2015 - p1305-1306 [501+]
    PHR - v84 - i4 - Nov 2015 - p535(3) [501+]
    SHQ - v118 - i3 - Jan 2015 - p331-332 [501+]
Noel-Maw, Marline - *Louis Riel: Combattant metis*
    c Res Links - v20 - i3 - Feb 2015 - p48(1) [51-500]
Noel, Michel - *Pineshish: La pie bleue (Illus. by Lavoie, Camille)*
    c Res Links - v21 - i1 - Oct 2015 - p54(1) [51-500]
Noel, Thomas J. - *Colorado: A Historical Atlas*
    Roundup M - v22 - i6 - August 2015 - p39(1) [501+]
Noel, Urayoan - *Buzzing Hemisphere/Rumor Hemisferico*
    BL - v112 - i2 - Sept 15 2015 - p17(1) [51-500]
Nogelmeier, Puakea - *I Ulu I Ke Kumu*
    Cont Pac - v27 - i2 - Fall 2015 - p587(4) [501+]
Nogerbek, Bauyrzhan - *Kazakhskoie igrovoie kino: Ekranno-follornie traditsii i obraz geroia*
    E-A St - v67 - i7 - Sept 2015 - p1164(2) [501+]
Noiville, Florence - *Attachment*
    TLS - i5861 - July 31 2015 - p19(1) [501+]
    WLT - v89 - i3-4 - May-August 2015 - p119(1) [501+]
Nolan, Dennis - *Hunters of the Great Forest*
    c HB Guide - v26 - i1 - Spring 2015 - p40(1) [51-500]

Nolan, Frederick - *Gunslingers and Cowboys*
    c BL - v111 - i15 - April 1 2015 - p54(1) [51-500]
    c HB Guide - v26 - i2 - Fall 2015 - p221(1) [51-500]
Outlaws and Rebels
    c HB Guide - v26 - i2 - Fall 2015 - p221(1) [51-500]
Trailblazing the Way West
    c HB Guide - v26 - i2 - Fall 2015 - p221(1) [51-500]
The Wild West: Native Peoples
    c HB Guide - v26 - i2 - Fall 2015 - p223(1) [51-500]
Nolan, Janet - *PB and J Hooray! (Illus. by Patton, Julia)*
    c HB Guide - v26 - i1 - Spring 2015 - p175(1) [51-500]
Nolan, Karen J. - *Be Positive, No Matter What*
    SPBW - March 2015 - pNA [51-500]
Nolan, Nina - *Mahalia Jackson: Walking with Kings and Queens (Illus. by Holyfield, John)*
    c HB - v91 - i2 - March-April 2015 - p123(1) [51-500]
    c HB Guide - v26 - i2 - Fall 2015 - p211(1) [51-500]
Nolane, Richard D. - *Millennium*
    PW - v262 - i5 - Feb 2 2015 - p44(1) [51-500]
Nolen, Jerdine - *Backyard Camp-Out (Illus. by Henninger, Michelle)*
    c KR - July 1 2015 - pNA [51-500]
    c SLJ - v61 - i5 - May 2015 - p94(1) [51-500]
Block Party Surprise (Illus. by Henninger, Michelle)
    c BL - v111 - i22 - August 1 2015 - p74(1) [51-500]
    c KR - July 1 2015 - pNA [51-500]
    c SLJ - v61 - i11 - Nov 2015 - p91(2) [51-500]
Irene's Wish (Illus. by Ford, A.G.)
    c CH Bwatch - Feb 2015 - pNA [51-500]
    c HB Guide - v26 - i1 - Spring 2015 - p40(1) [51-500]
Nolen, Jeremy - *New German Cooking: Recipes for Classics Revisited*
    Ent W - i1346 - Jan 16 2015 - p67(1) [501+]
    LJ - v140 - i5 - March 15 2015 - p126(2) [51-500]
    PW - v262 - i3 - Jan 19 2015 - p74(2) [51-500]
Nolen-Weathington, Eric - *Paolo Rivera*
    Bwatch - May 2015 - pNA [51-500]
Noll, Mark A. - *From Every Tribe and Nation: A Historian's Discovery of the Global Christian Story*
    IBMR - v39 - i3 - July 2015 - p164(1) [501+]
In the Beginning Was the Word: The Bible in American Public Life, 1492-1783
    Bks & Cult - v21 - i6 - Nov-Dec 2015 - p20(2) [501+]
Noni, Lynette - *Akarnae: The Medoran Chronicles Begin*
    y CH Bwatch - May 2015 - pNA [51-500]
Nonnenmacher, Frank - *"Du Hattest es Besser als Ich": 2 Bruder im 20. Jahrhundert*
    HNet - June 2015 - pNA [501+]
Noon, Dane - *Stoner Mug Cakes*
    Bwatch - Sept 2015 - pNA [51-500]
Noonan, Diana - *Quaky Cat Helps Out (Illus. by Bishop, Gavin)*
    c Magpies - v30 - i4 - Sept 2015 - pS5(1) [501+]
Noonan, Mary - *Echo's Voice: The Theatres of Sarrante, Duras, Cixous and Renaude*
    FS - v69 - i2 - April 2015 - p262-263 [501+]
Noonan, Peggy - *The Time of Our Lives: Collected Writings*
    BL - v112 - i6 - Nov 15 2015 - p4(1) [51-500]
    KR - Oct 1 2015 - pNA [501+]
    PW - v262 - i39 - Sept 28 2015 - p80(1) [51-500]
Noone, Roni - *Little Bean's Funderwear Day! (Illus. by Zobel, David)*
    c CH Bwatch - Jan 2015 - pNA [51-500]
Noord, Alex - *Religious Minorities and Cultural Diversity in the Dutch Republic: Studies Presented to Piet Visser on the Occasion of His 65th Birthday*
    Six Ct J - v46 - i2 - Summer 2015 - p446-448 [501+]
Noordhof, Gina - *A Puffin Playing by the Sea: The Twelve Days of Christmas in Newfoundland and Labrador (Illus. by Peddle, Derek)*
    c Res Links - v20 - i4 - April 2015 - p6(2) [501+]
Noorwood, Stephan H. - *Antisemitism and the American Far Left*
    J Am St - v49 - i3 - August 2015 - p624-626 [501+]
Nooteboom, Cees - *Letters to Poseidon*
    TLS - i5846 - April 17 2015 - p29(1) [501+]
Nor, Grandma - *The Magic Stones (Illus. by Vincent-Sy, Jan Michael)*
    c CH Bwatch - April 2015 - pNA [51-500]
Norbury, Katharine - *The Fish Ladder: A Journey Upstream*
    KR - May 15 2015 - pNA [501+]
    New Sci - v225 - i3014 - March 28 2015 - p47(1) [501+]
    PW - v262 - i23 - June 8 2015 - p53(1) [51-500]
Norcliffe, James - *The Pirates and the Nightmaker*
    Magpies - v30 - i2 - May 2015 - pS6(1) [501+]

Nordberg, Jenny - *The Underground Girls of Kabul: In Search of a Hidden Resistance in Afghanistan*
    SLJ - v61 - i2 - Feb 2015 - p113(1) [501+]
Nordhaus, Hannah - *American Ghost: A Family's Haunted Past in the Desert Southwest (Read by Sands, Xe). Audiobook Review*
    LJ - v140 - i10 - June 1 2015 - p62(1) [51-500]
American Ghost: A Family's Haunted Past in the Desert Southwest
    Bwatch - May 2015 - pNA [51-500]
Nordland, Rod - *The Lovers: Afghanistan's Romeo and Juliet: The True Story of How They Defied Their Families and Escaped an Honor Killing*
    PW - v262 - i42 - Oct 19 2015 - p65(1) [51-500]
Nordland, Rod: The Lovers.(Book review) - *The Lovers: Afghanistan's Romeo and Juliet: The True Story of How They Defied Their Families and Escaped an Honor Killing*
    KR - Nov 15 2015 - pNA [501+]
Nordling, Lee - *BirdCatDog: A Graphic Novel (Illus. by Bosch, Meritxell)*
    c HB - v91 - i1 - Jan-Feb 2015 - p70(2) [51-500]
    c HB Guide - v26 - i1 - Spring 2015 - p41(1) [51-500]
Fish-FishFish (Illus. by Bosch, Meritxell)
    c SLJ - v61 - i2 - Feb 2015 - p82(1) [51-500]
SheHeWe (Illus. by Bosch, Meritxell)
    c KR - August 1 2015 - pNA [51-500]
Nordlinger, Jay - *Children of Monsters: An Inquiry into the Sons and Daughters of Dictators*
    HM - v331 - i1984 - Sept 2015 - p79(3) [501+]
    Nat R - v67 - i18 - Oct 5 2015 - p38(2) [501+]
    Spec - v329 - i9765 - Oct 24 2015 - p38(2) [501+]
Nordqvist, Sven - *The Birthday Cake: The Adventures of Pettson and Findus (Illus. by Nordqvist, Sven)*
    c HB Guide - v26 - i2 - Fall 2015 - p46(1) [51-500]
Findus Disappears! (Illus. by Nordqvist, Sven)
    c CH Bwatch - June 2015 - pNA [51-500]
    c HB Guide - v26 - i1 - Spring 2015 - p41(1) [51-500]
The Fox Chase (Illus. by Nordqvist, Sven)
    c KR - July 15 2015 - pNA [51-500]
    c SLJ - v61 - i12 - Dec 2015 - p93(1) [51-500]
Nordstrom, Eugene - *Cape Deception*
    KR - Nov 15 2015 - pNA [501+]
Nordstrom, Lori - *Maximizing Profits: A Practical Guide for Portrait Photographers*
    Bwatch - June 2015 - pNA [51-500]
Norgren, Jill - *Rebels at the Bar: The Fascinating, Forgotten Stories of America's First Women Lawyers*
    Wom HR - v24 - i1 - Feb 2015 - p148(3) [501+]
Norlen, Paul - *The Intruder*
    BL - v111 - i19-20 - June 1 2015 - p54(1) [51-500]
Norm und Realitat in der Uberlieferung des Fruhen Mittelalters
    HNet - July 2015 - pNA [501+]
Norman, Brian - *Dead Women Talking: Figures of Injustice in American Literature*
    MFSF - v61 - i3 - Fall 2015 - p568-570 [501+]
    AL - v87 - i1 - March 2015 - p200-202 [501+]
Norman, Dean - *City Birds (Illus. by Norman, Dean)*
    c KR - May 1 2015 - pNA [51-500]
Spook the Halloween Cat (Illus. by Norman, Dean)
    c KR - August 1 2015 - pNA [51-500]
Norman, Donald - *The Design of Everyday Things*
    T&C - v56 - i3 - July 2015 - p785-787 [501+]
Norman, Jesse - *Edmund Burke: The First Conservative*
    RAH - v43 - i2 - June 2015 - p193-202 [501+]
Norman, Jill - *Herbs & Spices: The Cook's Reference*
    BL - v111 - i18 - May 15 2015 - p15(1) [51-500]
    LJ - v140 - i9 - May 15 2015 - p105(1) [51-500]
Norman, Kim - *This Old Van (Illus. by Conahan, Carolyn)*
    c KR - June 15 2015 - pNA [51-500]
    c SLJ - v61 - i7 - July 2015 - p66(2) [51-500]
Norman, Mark - *Funny Families*
    c Magpies - v30 - i1 - March 2015 - p23(2) [51-500]
Norman, Russell - *Spuntino: Comfort Food*
    Spec - v329 - i9768 - Nov 14 2015 - p58(1) [501+]
Norminton, Gregory - *The Little Prince (Illus. by Saint-Exupery, Antoine de)*
    c Sch Lib - v63 - i4 - Winter 2015 - p232(1) [51-500]
Normore, Christina - *A Feast for the Eyes: Art, Performance, and the Late Medieval Banquet*
    TimHES - i2209 - June 25 2015 - p51(1) [501+]
Norrell, Robert J. - *Alex Haley: And the Books That Changed a Nation*
    BL - v112 - i4 - Oct 15 2015 - p15(1) [51-500]
    KR - August 15 2015 - pNA [501+]
    LJ - v140 - i16 - Oct 1 2015 - p79(1) [51-500]
    NYT - Dec 9 2015 - pC1(L) [501+]
    PW - v262 - i32 - August 10 2015 - p47(2) [51-500]

Norrgard, Chantal - *Seasons of Change: Labor, Treaty Rights, and Ojibwe Nationhood*
    AHR - v120 - i4 - Oct 2015 - p1506-1507 [501+]
    WHQ - v46 - i3 - Autumn 2015 - p369-370 [501+]
Norris, Ashley P. Watson - *How to Canoe and Kayak like a Pro*
    c HB Guide - v26 - i1 - Spring 2015 - p183(1) [51-500]
How to Hike like a Pro
    c HB Guide - v26 - i1 - Spring 2015 - p183(1) [51-500]
Norris, Eryl - *What's That in the Water?*
    c KR - Dec 1 2015 - pNA [51-500]
Norris, Gloria - *KooKooLand*
    BL - v112 - i6 - Nov 15 2015 - p10(1) [51-500]
    KR - Oct 15 2015 - pNA [501+]
    PW - v262 - i46 - Nov 16 2015 - p67(3) [51-500]
Norris, John - *Mary McGrory: The First Queen of Journalism*
    BL - v112 - i1 - Sept 1 2015 - p16(1) [51-500]
    CJR - v54 - i3 - Sept-Oct 2015 - p30(3) [501+]
    Comw - v142 - i17 - Oct 23 2015 - p33(2) [501+]
    KR - July 1 2015 - pNA [501+]
    LJ - v140 - i12 - July 1 2015 - p90(2) [51-500]
    NYTBR - Oct 4 2015 - p14(L) [501+]
    PW - v262 - i30 - July 27 2015 - p57(1) [51-500]
Norris, Mary - *Between You and Me: Confessions of a Comma Queen (Read by Norris, Mary). Audiobook Review*
    LJ - v140 - i12 - July 1 2015 - p45(2) [51-500]
Between You and Me: Confessions of a Comma Queen
    Ent W - i1359-1360 - April 17 2015 - p114(1) [501+]
Between You & Me: Confessions of a Comma Queen (Read by Norris, Mary). Audiobook Review
    PW - v262 - i26 - June 29 2015 - p64(1) [51-500]
Between You & Me: Confessions of a Comma Queen
    Spec - v328 - i9742 - May 16 2015 - p47(2) [501+]
    TLS - i5855 - June 19 2015 - p26(1) [501+]
    KR - Jan 1 2015 - pNA [501+]
    LJ - v140 - i3 - Feb 15 2015 - p108(2) [51-500]
    New R - v246 - i2-3 - March-April 2015 - p70(2) [501+]
    NYTBR - April 19 2015 - p18(L) [501+]
    PW - v262 - i6 - Feb 9 2015 - p56(1) [501+]
Norris, Pippa - *Making Democratic Governance Work: How Regimes Shape Prosperity, Welfare and Peace*
    CS - v44 - i1 - Jan 2015 - p101-103 [501+]
Norriss, Andrew - *Friends for Life*
    c BL - v111 - i21 - July 1 2015 - p72(1) [51-500]
    c CCB-B - v69 - i2 - Oct 2015 - p106(1) [51-500]
    y HB - v91 - i5 - Sept-Oct 2015 - p113(1) [51-500]
    c KR - May 15 2015 - pNA [51-500]
    c PW - v262 - i20 - May 18 2015 - p84(1) [51-500]
    c PW - v262 - i49 - Dec 2 2015 - p77(2) [51-500]
    c SLJ - v61 - i7 - July 2015 - p87(2) [51-500]
Jessica's Ghost
    y Sch Lib - v63 - i2 - Summer 2015 - p120(1) [501+]
Nors, Dorthe - *Karate Chop/Minna Needs Rehearsal Space*
    NS - v144 - i5258 - April 17 2015 - p61(1) [51-500]
    TLS - i5847 - April 24 2015 - p20(1) [51-500]
North, Anna - *The Life and Death of Sophie Stark (Read by Dolan, Amanda). Audiobook Review*
    LJ - v140 - i17 - Oct 15 2015 - p52(2) [51-500]
The Life and Death of Sophie Stark
    BL - v111 - i15 - April 1 2015 - p26(1) [51-500]
    KR - March 15 2015 - pNA [501+]
    LJ - v140 - i9 - May 15 2015 - p73(2) [51-500]
    NYTBR - June 28 2015 - p38(L) [501+]
    Par - v90 - i8 - August 2015 - p22(1) [501+]
    PW - v262 - i13 - March 30 2015 - p47(2) [51-500]
North, Claire - *Touch*
    BL - v111 - i12 - Feb 15 2015 - p45(1) [51-500]
North, Laura - *The Big Bad Wolf and the Robot Pig (Illus. by Cross, Kevin)*
    c CH Bwatch - Feb 2015 - pNA [501+]
    c Res Links - v20 - i3 - Feb 2015 - p14(2) [501+]
The Boy with the Sweet-Treat Touch (Illus. by Chapman, Neil)
    c CH Bwatch - April 2015 - pNA [51-500]
    c Res Links - v20 - i3 - Feb 2015 - p14(2) [501+]
Cinderella: The Terrible Truth (Illus. by Dreidemy, Joelle)
    c CH Bwatch - April 2015 - pNA [51-500]
    c Res Links - v20 - i3 - Feb 2015 - p14(2) [501+]
Hansel and Gretel and the Green Witch
    c CH Bwatch - July 2015 - pNA [51-500]
The Pied Piper and the Wrong Song
    c CH Bwatch - July 2015 - pNA [501+]

North, Phoebe - *Starbreak*
    c HB Guide - v26 - i1 - Spring 2015 - p119(1) [51-500]
North, Ryan - *The Unbeatable Squirrel Girl, vol. 1: Squirrel Power (Illus. by Henderson, Erica)*
    NYTBR - Oct 18 2015 - p30(L) [501+]
    c SLJ - v61 - i12 - Dec 2015 - p110(1) [51-500]
North, Vanessa - *Blueberry Boys*
    PW - v262 - i39 - Sept 28 2015 - p76(1) [51-500]
Rough Road
    PW - v262 - i27 - July 6 2015 - p52(2) [51-500]
Northcott, Michael S. - *A Political Theology of Climate Change*
    CC - v132 - i5 - March 4 2015 - p38(3) [501+]
Northfield, Gary - *Rumble with the Romans!*
    y KR - Jan 1 2016 - pNA [501+]
    c Sch Lib - v63 - i2 - Summer 2015 - p108(1) [51-500]
Northrop, Michael - *Amulet Keepers*
    c HB Guide - v26 - i2 - Fall 2015 - p96(1) [51-500]
    c SLJ - v61 - i6 - June 2015 - p109(1) [51-500]
Book of the Dead (Read by De Ocampo, Ramon). Audiobook Review
    c SLJ - v61 - i5 - May 2015 - p69(2) [51-500]
Book of the Dead
    BL - v111 - i9-10 - Jan 1 2015 - p101(1) [51-500]
    y VOYA - v37 - i6 - Feb 2015 - p82(1) [51-500]
Surrounded by Sharks
    c HB Guide - v26 - i1 - Spring 2015 - p119(1) [51-500]
Northrup, Christiane - *Goddesses Never Age: The Secret Prescription for Radiance, Vitality, and Well-Being*
    PW - v262 - i11 - March 16 2015 - p15(1) [51-500]
Northrup, David - *How English Became the Global Language*
    NWCR - v68 - i1 - Wntr 2015 - p141(3) [501+]
Northrup, Michael - *Tombquest: Book of the Dead*
    c CH Bwatch - July 2015 - pNA [51-500]
Norton, Andre - *Tales of High Hallack: The Collected Short Stories*
    MFSF - v128 - i1-2 - Jan-Feb 2015 - p44(3) [501+]
Norton, Anne - *On the Muslim Question*
    ERS - v38 - i3 - March 2015 - p532(3) [501+]
Norton, Bill - *American Bomber Aircraft Development in World War II*
    APH - v62 - i2 - Summer 2015 - p58(1) [501+]
Norton, Carla - *What Doesn't Kill Her (Read by Delaine, Christina). Audiobook Review*
    BL - v112 - i6 - Nov 15 2015 - p63(1) [51-500]
    LJ - v140 - i19 - Nov 15 2015 - p52(2) [51-500]
What Doesn't Kill Her
    BL - v111 - i17 - May 1 2015 - p48(1) [51-500]
    KR - April 15 2015 - pNA [501+]
    PW - v262 - i15 - April 13 2015 - p56(1) [51-500]
Norton, Elizabeth - *The Temptation of Elizabeth Tudor: Elizabeth I, Thomas Seymour, and the Making of a Virgin Queen*
    KR - Oct 15 2015 - pNA [501+]
    PW - v262 - i50 - Dec 7 2015 - p81(1) [51-500]
Norton, Jeff - *Memoirs of a Neurotic Zombie, 2: Escape from Camp*
    c Sch Lib - v63 - i1 - Spring 2015 - p41(1) [51-500]
    c Sch Lib - v63 - i4 - Winter 2015 - p230(1) [51-500]
Norwich, John Julius - *Darling Monster: The Letters of Lady Diana Cooper to Her Son John Julius Norwich, 1939-1952*
    NYRB - v62 - i10 - June 4 2015 - p33(3) [501+]
The Duff Cooper Diaries
    NYRB - v62 - i10 - June 4 2015 - p33(3) [501+]
Sicily: A Short History from the Ancient Greeks to Cosa Nostra
    Spec - v328 - i9745 - June 6 2015 - p44(2) [501+]
    TLS - i5862 - August 7 2015 - p30(1) [501+]
Sicily: An Island at the Crossroads of History
    KR - June 1 2015 - pNA [51-500]
    LJ - v140 - i13 - August 1 2015 - p109(1) [51-500]
Trying to Please: A Memoir
    NYRB - v62 - i10 - June 4 2015 - p33(3) [501+]
Nostlinger, Christine - *Good Dragon, Bad Dragon (Illus. by Rassmus, Jens)*
    c CH Bwatch - July 2015 - pNA [51-500]
    c HB Guide - v26 - i2 - Fall 2015 - p46(1) [51-500]
Nosy Crow - *Arf! Arf! (Illus. by Braun, Sebastien)*
    c KR - July 1 2015 - pNA [51-500]
Dinosaur Safari
    c KR - Jan 1 2016 - pNA [51-500]
Growl! Growl! (Illus. by Braun, Sebastien)
    c KR - Jan 1 2015 - pNA [51-500]
Hoot! Hoot!
    c KR - Jan 1 2016 - pNA [51-500]
Jack and the Beanstalk. E-book Review
    SLJ - v61 - i3 - March 2015 - p71(1) [51-500]

Nothomb, Amelie - *Petronille*
   KR - August 1 2015 - pNA [501+]
   PW - v262 - i34 - August 24 2015 - p56(1) [51-500]

Nottage, Luke - *Who Rules Japan? Popular Participation in the Japanese Legal Process*
   RVBW - August 2015 - pNA [51-500]

Nouraie-Simone, Fereshteh - *The Shipwrecked: Contemporary Stories by Women from Iran*
   Bwatch - March 2015 - pNA [51-500]
   WLT - v89 - i2 - March-April 2015 - p63(2) [501+]

Nouzille, Jean - *Le Prince Eugene de Savoie et le Sud-Est Europeen (1683-1736).*
   HER - v130 - i543 - April 2015 - p457(2) [501+]

Novak, Ali - *The Heartbreakers*
   y KR - June 1 2015 - pNA [51-500]
   y PW - v262 - i21 - May 25 2015 - p60(1) [51-500]
   y SLJ - v61 - i6 - June 2015 - p126(1) [51-500]

Novak, Andrew - *The Global Decline of the Mandatory Death Penalty: Constitutional Jurisprudence and Legislative Reform in Africa, Asia, and the Caribbean*
   Law&PolBR - v25 - i2 - Feb 2015 - p31(5) [501+]

Novak, B.J. - *The Book with No Pictures*
   c HB Guide - v26 - i1 - Spring 2015 - p13(1) [51-500]

Novak, B. J. - *One More Thing: Stories and Other Stories*
   NYTBR - March 15 2015 - p28(L) [501+]

Novak, Brenda - *A Matter of Grave Concern (Read by Page, Michael). Audiobook Review*
   LJ - v140 - i3 - Feb 15 2015 - p58(1) [51-500]
The Secret Sister
   BL - v111 - i22 - August 1 2015 - p41(1) [51-500]
This Heart of Mine
   y BL - v111 - i15 - April 1 2015 - p33(1) [501+]
   BL - v112 - i2 - Sept 15 2015 - p42(2) [501+]

Novak, Chase - *Brood (Read by Rodgers, Elisabeth S.). Audiobook Review*
   y BL - v111 - i18 - May 15 2015 - p69(1) [51-500]

Novak, David - *Japanoise: Music at the Edge of Circulation*
   Notes - v71 - i3 - March 2015 - p512(3) [501+]

Novak, Kathleen - *Do Not Find Me*
   KR - Nov 1 2015 - pNA [501+]
   PW - v262 - i51 - Dec 14 2015 - p59(1) [51-500]

Novak, Rick - *The Doctor and Mr. Dylan.*
   KR - Sept 1 2015 - pNA [501+]

Novak, Robby - *Kid President's Guide to Being Awesome*
   c BL - v111 - i17 - May 1 2015 - p84(1) [51-500]
   c HB Guide - v26 - i2 - Fall 2015 - p190(1) [51-500]

Novdl, Adam - *The House of Small Shadows*
   BL - v111 - i18 - May 15 2015 - p34(1) [501+]

November, Nancy - *Beethoven's Theatrical Quartets: Opp. 59, 74 and 95*
   Notes - v71 - i4 - June 2015 - p690(3) [501+]

Novesky, Amy - *Cloth Lullaby: The Woven Life of Louise Bourgeois (Illus. by Arsenault, Isabelle)*
   c PW - v262 - i51 - Dec 14 2015 - p82(2) [51-500]

Novey, Idra - *Ways to Disappear*
   BL - v112 - i4 - Oct 15 2015 - p34(1) [51-500]
   KR - Nov 1 2015 - pNA [51-500]

Novic, Sara - *Girl at War*
   BL - v111 - i15 - April 1 2015 - p23(1) [51-500]
   KR - March 15 2015 - pNA [51-500]
   LJ - v140 - i5 - March 15 2015 - p94(1) [501+]
   NS - v144 - i5275 - August 14 2015 - p45(1) [51-500]
   NYT - May 28 2015 - pC6(L) [501+]
   NYTBR - June 7 2015 - p28(L) [501+]
   PW - v262 - i9 - March 2 2015 - p60(2) [51-500]
   PW - v262 - i11 - March 16 2015 - p44(2) [501+]

Novik, Naomi - *Uprooted (Read by Emelin, Julia). Audiobook Review*
   LJ - v140 - i13 - August 1 2015 - p47(1) [51-500]
Uprooted
   NYTBR - May 31 2015 - p38(L) [501+]
   PW - v262 - i11 - March 16 2015 - p2(1) [51-500]
   CSM - July 6 2015 - pNA [501+]
   Par - v90 - i8 - August 2015 - p22(1) [501+]

Novikoff, Alex J. - *The Medieval Culture of Disputation: Pedagogy, Practice, and Performance*
   AHR - v120 - i4 - Oct 2015 - p1541-1542 [501+]

Nowadnick, Deanna - *Signs in Life: Finding Direction in Our Travels with God*
   SPBW - Sept 2015 - pNA [51-500]

Nowak, Lisa - *Running Wide Open*
   y KR - Nov 15 2015 - pNA [501+]

Nowak, Martin A. - *Evolution, Games, and God: The Principle of Cooperation*
   Comw - v142 - i1 - Jan 9 2015 - p26(2) [501+]

Nowak, Pamela - *Escaping Yesterday*
   BL - v112 - i2 - Sept 15 2015 - p40(1) [51-500]
   KR - August 1 2015 - pNA [51-500]
   Roundup M - v23 - i1 - Oct 2015 - p31(1) [51-500]

Nowell, Irene - *Jonah, Tobit, Judith*
   RVBW - July 2015 - pNA [51-500]

Nowell, Iris - *Harold Town*
   Beav - v95 - i4 - August-Sept 2015 - p69(2) [501+]

Nowotny, Helga - *The Cunning of Uncertainty*
   TimHES - i2225 - Oct 15 2015 - p42-2 [501+]

Nowra, Louis - *Prince of Afghanistan*
   y Magpies - v30 - i1 - March 2015 - p42(1) [501+]

Noyce, Pendred E. - *Magnificent Minds: 16 Pioneering Women in Science & Medicine*
   y VOYA - v38 - i1 - April 2015 - p87(1) [51-500]
Remarkable Minds: 17 More Pioneering Women in Science & Medicine
   y CH Bwatch - Oct 2015 - pNA [51-500]
   y SLJ - v61 - i10 - Oct 2015 - p136(2) [51-500]
   y VOYA - v38 - i4 - Oct 2015 - p84(1) [51-500]

Noyed, Robert B. - *Smiles: The Sound of Long I*
   c BL - v112 - i3 - Oct 1 2015 - p66(1) [51-500]

Noyes, Deborah - *Ten Days a Madwoman: The Daring Life and Turbulent Times of the Original "Girl" Reporter Nellie Bly*
   y KR - Nov 15 2015 - pNA [51-500]
   y PW - v262 - i47 - Nov 23 2015 - p71(1) [51-500]
   y SLJ - v61 - i12 - Dec 2015 - p145(2) [51-500]

nplusone - *Happiness: Ten Years of n+1*
   HM - v330 - i1977 - Feb 2015 - p84(6) [501+]

Ntarangwi, Mwenda - *East African Hip Hop: Youth Culture and Globalization*
   Callaloo - v38 - i2 - Spring 2015 - p418-421 [501+]

Ntleko, Abegail - *Empty Hands: A Memoir*
   KR - May 15 2015 - pNA [51-500]

Nuckolls, Janis - *Evidentiality in interaction*
   Lang Soc - v44 - i4 - Sept 2015 - p591-594 [501+]

Nudo, Sal - *The Millionaire's Cross*
   KR - Oct 1 2015 - pNA [51-500]

Nugent, Alida - *You Don't Have to Like Me: Essays on Growing Up, Speaking Out, and Finding Feminism*
   PW - v262 - i34 - August 24 2015 - p73(2) [51-500]

Nukamp, Marieke - *This Is Where It Ends*
   y SLJ - v61 - i11 - Nov 2015 - p120(1) [51-500]

Null, Matthew Neill - *Honey from the Lion*
   BL - v111 - i22 - August 1 2015 - p40(1) [51-500]
   LJ - v140 - i12 - July 1 2015 - p78(2) [51-500]

Nulo, Naktsang - *My Tibetan Childhood: When Ice Shattered Stone*
   Lon R Bks - v37 - i5 - March 5 2015 - p22(2) [501+]

Numata, Mahokaru - *Nan-Core*
   WLT - v89 - i6 - Nov-Dec 2015 - p75(1) [51-500]

Numbers, Ronald L. - *Newton's Apple and Other Myths about Science*
   PW - v262 - i35 - August 31 2015 - p76(1) [51-500]

Numeroff, Laura - *Cora, tu veux une crepe? (Illus. by Bond, Felicia)*
   c Res Links - v21 - i1 - Oct 2015 - p54(2) [51-500]
Souris, tu viens au cinema? (Illus. by Bond, Felicia)
   c Res Links - v20 - i3 - Feb 2015 - p48(1) [51-500]

Numismatik Lehren in Europa
   HNet - July 2015 - pNA [501+]

Nunez, Quirino Olivera - *Arqueologia Alto Amazonica: Los Origenes de la Civilizacion en el Peru*
   Lat Ant - v26 - i3 - Sept 2015 - p429(2) [501+]

Nunki, Hope Russell - *Release*
   PW - v262 - i15 - April 13 2015 - p56(1) [51-500]

Nunn, Kem - *Chance*
   NYTBR - Feb 22 2015 - p32(L) [51-500]

Nunn, Lisa M. - *Defining Student Success: The Role of School and Culture*
   AJS - v120 - i6 - May 2015 - p1886(3) [501+]
   CS - v44 - i1 - Jan 2015 - p144(1) [51-500]

Nunn, Malla - *Present Darkness*
   RVBW - Jan 2015 - pNA [51-500]

Nunnally, Tiina - *Dark Angel*
   RVBW - Feb 2015 - pNA [51-500]

Nunnally, Tiina - *Pippi Won't Grow Up (Illus. by Nyman, Ingrid Vang)*
   c SLJ - v61 - i3 - March 2015 - p129(1) [51-500]

Nunokawa, Jeff - *Note Book*
   KR - April 15 2015 - pNA [501+]
   PW - v262 - i7 - Feb 16 2015 - p167(2) [51-500]
   TLS - i5870 - Oct 2 2015 - p24(1) [501+]

Nuovo, Angela - *The Book Trade in the Italian Renaissance*
   BSA-P - v109 - i2 - June 2015 - p270-272 [501+]

Nuowen, Mollie Lewis - *Oy, My Buenos Aires: Jewish Immigrants and the Creation of Argentine National Identity*
   Ams - v72 - i1 - Jan 2015 - p179(2) [501+]

Nur, Ofer Nordheimer - *Eros and Tragedy: Jewish Male Fantasies and the Masculine Revolution of Zionism*
   HNet - Feb 2015 - pNA [501+]

Nutini, Hugo G. - *Native Evangelism in Central America*
   Ams - v72 - i2 - April 2015 - p358(2) [501+]

Nutt, Amy Ellis - *Becoming Nicole: The Transformation of an American Family*
   NYT - Oct 22 2015 - pC1(L) [501+]
   NYTBR - Nov 8 2015 - p16(L) [501+]
The Teenage Brain: A Neuroscientist's Survival Guide to Raising Adolescents and Young Adults
   NYTBR - April 5 2015 - p30(L) [501+]

Nuwer, Hank - *Sons of the Dawn: A Basque Odyssey*
   Roundup M - v22 - i6 - August 2015 - p32(1) [501+]

Nyad, Diana - *Find a Way: One Wild and Precious Life*
   BL - v112 - i1 - Sept 1 2015 - p33(1) [51-500]
   KR - August 15 2015 - pNA [51-500]
   LJ - v140 - i15 - Sept 15 2015 - p85(1) [51-500]
   PW - v262 - i32 - August 10 2015 - p54(1) [51-500]

Nyberg, Jason - *Popular Piano Solos for All Piano Methods*
   Am MT - v64 - i5 - April-May 2015 - p48(2) [501+]

Nyburg, Anna - *Emigres: The Transformation of Art Publishing in Britain*
   TLS - i5832 - Jan 9 2015 - p10(2) [501+]

Nye, David E. - *America's Assembly Line*
   Historian - v77 - i1 - Spring 2015 - p136(3) [501+]
   T&C - v56 - i4 - Oct 2015 - p991-993 [501+]

Nye, Eric - *John Kemble's Gibraltar Journal: The Spanish Expedition of the Cambridge Apostles, 1830-1831*
   Lon R Bks - v37 - i17 - Sept 10 2015 - p29(3) [501+]

Nye, Jody Lynn - *Rhythm of the Imperium*
   PW - v262 - i44 - Nov 2 2015 - p66(1) [51-500]

Nye, Joseph S. - *Is the American Century Over?*
   Econ - v414 - i8928 - March 7 2015 - p86(US) [501+]
   NS - v144 - i5267 - June 19 2015 - p42(3) [501+]
   RVBW - June 2015 - pNA [51-500]

Nye, Mary Jo - *Michael Polanyi and His Generation: Origins of the Social Construction of Science*
   AHR - v120 - i1 - Feb 2015 - p352-353 [501+]

Nye, Naomi - *The Turtle of Oman (Illus. by Peterschmidt, Betsy)*
   c HB Guide - v26 - i1 - Spring 2015 - p88(1) [51-500]

Nyeck, S.N. - *Sexual Diversity in Africa: Politics, Theory, and Citizenship*
   AHR - v120 - i4 - Oct 2015 - p1581-1582 [501+]
   IJAHS - v48 - i1 - Wntr 2015 - p122-124 [501+]

Nygreen, Kysa - *These Kids: Identity, Agency, and Social Justice at a Last Chance High School*
   CS - v44 - i6 - Nov 2015 - p832-834 [501+]

Nykanen, Harri - *Behind God's Back*
   RVBW - March 2015 - pNA [51-500]

Nyman, Ingrid - *Do You Know Pippi Longstocking?*
   c Sch Lib - v63 - i4 - Winter 2015 - p219(1) [51-500]

Nyquist, Mary - *Arbitrary Rule: Slavery, Tyranny, and the Power of Life and Death*
   MP - v113 - i2 - Nov 2015 - pE90(6) [501+]

Nystrom, Eric C. - *Seeing Underground: Maps, Models, and Mining Engineering in America*
   AHR - v120 - i3 - June 2015 - p1037-1038 [501+]
   JAH - v101 - i4 - March 2015 - p1286-1287 [501+]
   PHR - v84 - i4 - Nov 2015 - p530(2) [501+]
   T&C - v56 - i4 - Oct 2015 - p986-988 [501+]
   WHQ - v46 - i2 - Summer 2015 - p226-226 [501+]

Nystul, Jill - *One Good Life: My Tips, My Wisdom, My Story*
   PW - v262 - i15 - April 13 2015 - p71(1) [51-500]
   BL - v111 - i17 - May 1 2015 - p68(1) [51-500]

Nytra, David - *Windmill Dragons (Illus. by Nytra, David)*
   c KR - July 1 2015 - pNA [51-500]
   c BL - v112 - i2 - Sept 15 2015 - p53(1) [51-500]
   c SLJ - v61 - i9 - Sept 2015 - p136(1) [51-500]

O

O Baoill, Donall - *Saltair Saiochta, Sanasaiochta agus Senchais: A Festschrift for Gearoid Mac Eoin*
    Med R - June 2015 - pNA [501+]
O Cadhain, Mairtin - *The Dirty Dust: Cre na Cille*
    ILS - v35 - i1 - Fall 2015 - p2(1) [501+]
    LJ - v140 - i5 - March 15 2015 - p101(1) [501+]
    Mac - v128 - i19-20 - May 18 2015 - p76(2) [501+]
    NS - v144 - i5259 - April 24 2015 - p52(2) [501+]
    TLS - i5853 - June 5 2015 - p7(2) [501+]
O Cathain, Gearoid Cheaist - *The Loneliest Boy in the World: The Last Child of the Great Blasket Island*
    ILS - v35 - i1 - Fall 2015 - p25(2) [501+]
O Ciosain, Niall - *Ireland in Official Print Culture, 1800-1850: A New Reading of the Poor Inquiry*
    HER - v130 - i545 - August 2015 - p1019(2) [501+]
O Clabaigh, Colman - *The Friars in Ireland, 1224-1540*
    HER - v130 - i544 - June 2015 - p714(2) [501+]
O hEigeartaigh, Cian - *Sairseal agus Dill, 1947-1981: Sceal foilsitheora*
    TLS - i5853 - June 5 2015 - p7(2) [501+]
Oak, B.B. - *Thoreau in Phantom Bog*
    BL - v112 - i2 - Sept 15 2015 - p35(1) [51-500]
    KR - July 1 2015 - pNA [51-500]
    PW - v262 - i29 - July 20 2015 - p171(1) [51-500]
Oak, Raven - *Amaskan's Blood*
    PW - v262 - i7 - Feb 16 2015 - p164(2) [51-500]
    PW - v262 - i12 - March 23 2015 - p40(2) [501+]
Oakdale, Suzanne - *Fluent Selves: Autobiography, Person, and History in Lowland South America*
    HAHR - v95 - i3 - August 2015 - p544-546 [501+]
Oakes, Cary Putman - *Dinosaur Boy*
    c SLJ - v61 - i2 - Feb 2015 - p90(1) [51-500]
Oakes, Colleen - *The Crown*
    SLJ - v61 - i2 - Feb 2015 - p106(2) [51-500]
Stars
    y KR - Sept 1 2015 - pNA [51-500]
    y SLJ - v61 - i9 - Sept 2015 - p170(1) [51-500]
Oakes, Cory Putman - *Dinosaur Boy Saves Mars*
    c KR - Nov 15 2015 - pNA [51-500]
Oakes, James - *The Scorpion's Sting: Antislavery and the Coming of the Civil War*
    JSH - v81 - i3 - August 2015 - p725(3) [501+]
    NYRB - v62 - i5 - March 19 2015 - p30(4) [501+]
Oakes, Peter - *Galatians*
    RVBW - July 2015 - pNA [51-500]
Oakes, Rita - *Comrades-in-Arms*
    PW - v262 - i32 - August 10 2015 - p42(1) [51-500]
Oakes, Stephanie - *Minnow*
    BL - v111 - i17 - May 1 2015 - p89(1) [501+]
The Sacred Lies of Minnow Bly
    y HB Guide - v26 - i2 - Fall 2015 - p133(1) [51-500]
    y Magpies - v30 - i3 - July 2015 - p43(1) [501+]
    c Nat Post - v17 - i225 - August 1 2015 - pWP5(1) [501+]
    y PW - v262 - i17 - April 27 2015 - p78(1) [501+]
    y PW - v262 - i49 - Dec 2 2015 - p113(1) [501+]
    y SLJ - v61 - i4 - April 2015 - p168(2) [51-500]
    y VOYA - v38 - i3 - August 2015 - p61(1) [51-500]
Oakley, Ann - *Father and Daughter: Patriarchy, Gender and Social Science*
    Lon R Bks - v37 - i19 - Oct 8 2015 - p29(4) [501+]
Oakley, Tyler - *Binge (Read by Oakley, Tyler). Audiobook Review*
    PW - v262 - i48 - Nov 30 2015 - p55(1) [51-500]
Oakman, Douglas E. - *Jesus, Debt, and the Lord's Prayer: First-Century Debt and Jesus' Intentions*
    Intpr - v69 - i4 - Oct 2015 - p487(1) [501+]

Oard, Brian - *Flying Hung-Over*
    SPBW - June 2015 - pNA [51-500]
Oates-Bockenstedt, Catherine - *Earth Science Success, 2d ed.: 55 Table-Ready, Notebook-Based Lessons*
    Sci Teach - v82 - i5 - Summer 2015 - p71 [51-500]
Oates, Joyce Carol - *Jack of Spades (Read by Barrett, Joe). Audiobook Review*
    BL - v112 - i2 - Sept 15 2015 - p77(2) [51-500]
    LJ - v140 - i14 - Sept 1 2015 - p66(1) [51-500]
    PW - v262 - i26 - June 29 2015 - p62(1) [51-500]
Jack of Spades
    BL - v111 - i17 - May 1 2015 - p39(1) [51-500]
    KR - March 15 2015 - pNA [51-500]
    LJ - v140 - i6 - April 1 2015 - p86(1) [51-500]
    NYRB - v62 - i19 - Dec 3 2015 - p44(2) [501+]
    PW - v262 - i12 - March 23 2015 - p48(1) [51-500]
The Lost Landscape: A Writer's Coming of Age
    BL - v111 - i22 - August 1 2015 - p17(1) [51-500]
    KR - June 15 2015 - pNA [51-500]
    NYRB - v62 - i19 - Dec 3 2015 - p44(2) [501+]
    NYTBR - Sept 20 2015 - p16(L) [501+]
    PW - v262 - i27 - July 6 2015 - p59(1) [51-500]
    LJ - v140 - i12 - July 1 2015 - p84(2) [51-500]
    LJ - v140 - i6 - April 1 2015 - p61(1) [51-500]
The Man without a Shadow
    KR - Dec 1 2015 - pNA [51-500]
The Sacrifice
    CSM - Feb 20 2015 - pNA [51-500]
    NYRB - v62 - i19 - Dec 3 2015 - p44(2) [501+]
    NYTBR - Feb 1 2015 - p13(L) [501+]
Oates, Matthew - *In Pursuit of Butterflies: A Fifty-Year Affair*
    TLS - i5869 - Sept 25 2015 - p22(1) [501+]
Oatman, Linda High - *Otherwise*
    y Teach Lib - v42 - i3 - Feb 2015 - p28(4) [501+]
Obadare, Ebenezer - *Civic Agency in Africa: Arts of Resistance in the 21st Century*
    JIH - v45 - i4 - Spring 2015 - p609-611 [501+]
O'Banion, Patrick J. - *The Sacrament of Penance and Religious Life in Golden Age Spain*
    JMH - v87 - i1 - March 2015 - p211(2) [501+]
Obasogie, Osagie K. - *Blinded by Sight: Seeing Race through the Eyes of the Blind*
    CS - v44 - i5 - Sept 2015 - p688-689 [501+]
Obata, Fumio - *Just So Happens*
    PW - v262 - i7 - Feb 16 2015 - p166(1) [51-500]
Ober, Damien - *Doctor Benjamin Franklin's Dream America*
    ABR - v36 - i3 - March-April 2015 - p18(1) [501+]
Ober, Josiah - *The Rise and Fall of Classical Greece*
    HT - v65 - i8 - August 2015 - p58(1) [501+]
    Mac - v128 - i23 - June 15 2015 - p60(2) [501+]
    Spec - v328 - i9750 - July 11 2015 - p36(1) [501+]
    TimHES - i2213 - July 23 2015 - p50-51 [501+]
    TLS - i5854 - June 12 2015 - p13(1) [501+]
    TLS - i5864-5865 - August 21 2015 - p25(1) [501+]
Oberfield, Zachary W. - *Becoming Bureaucrats: Socialization at the Front Lines of Government Service*
    Soc Ser R - v89 - i1 - March 2015 - p211(4) [501+]
Oberg, Barbara B. - *The Papers of Thomas Jefferson, vol. 40: 4 March to 10 July 1803*
    JSH - v81 - i3 - August 2015 - p703(2) [501+]
Obermayer, Hans Peter - *Deutsche Altertumswissenschaftler im Amerikanischen Exil: Eine Rekonstruktion*
    HNet - July 2015 - pNA [501+]

Obermeier, Pat - *The President Factor*
    KR - Sept 15 2015 - pNA [501+]
Obermeier, Wanda - *Mama Bird Papa Bird (Illus. by Thomas, Faith)*
    c CH Bwatch - June 2015 - pNA [51-500]
Oberski, Jona - *A Childhood*
    TLS - i5832 - Jan 9 2015 - p23(1) [501+]
Obertone, Laurent - *Utoya: Norvege, 22 juillet 2011, 77 morts*
    Quad - v59 - i5 - May 2015 - p98(5) [501+]
Obioma, Chigozie - *The Fishermen*
    NS - v144 - i5280 - Sept 18 2015 - p69(1) [501+]
    WLT - v89 - i6 - Nov-Dec 2015 - p63(2) [501+]
    Econ - v414 - i8931 - March 28 2015 - p86(US) [501+]
    KR - March 1 2015 - pNA [501+]
    LJ - v140 - i5 - March 15 2015 - p94(1) [501+]
    Mac - v128 - i18 - May 11 2015 - p60(1) [501+]
    NY - v91 - i20 - July 20 2015 - p71 [51-500]
    NYTBR - April 19 2015 - p10(L) [501+]
    PW - v262 - i8 - Feb 23 2015 - p50(1) [51-500]
    TLS - i5841 - March 13 2015 - p19(1) [501+]
Oborne, Peter - *Wounded Tiger: A History of Cricket in Pakistan*
    NS - v144 - i5285 - Oct 23 2015 - p51(1) [501+]
Obradovic-Wochnik, Jelena - *Ethnic Conflict and War Crimes in the Balkans: The Narratives of Denial in Post-Conflict Serbia*
    E-A St - v67 - i9 - Nov 2015 - p1506(2) [501+]
O'Brady, Tara - *Seven Spoons: My Favorite Recipes for Any and Every Day*
    LJ - v140 - i5 - March 15 2015 - p126(2) [501+]
O'Brien, Anne Sibley - *Abracadabra! It's Spring! (Illus. by Gal, Susan)*
    c KR - Jan 1 2016 - pNA [51-500]
I'm New Here (Illus. by O'Brien, Anne Sibley)
    c BL - v111 - i22 - August 1 2015 - p72(1) [51-500]
    c CH Bwatch - Nov 2015 - pNA [51-500]
    c KR - June 1 2015 - pNA [51-500]
    c NYTBR - August 23 2015 - p24(L) [501+]
    c SLJ - v61 - i8 - August 2015 - p60(1) [51-500]
O'Brien, Caragh M. - *The Rule of Mirrors*
    y KR - Dec 15 2015 - pNA [51-500]
Vault of Dreamers (Read by Zeller, Emily Woo). Audiobook Review
    y SLJ - v61 - i5 - May 2015 - p72(1) [51-500]
The Vault of Dreamers
    y HB Guide - v26 - i2 - Fall 2015 - p133(1) [51-500]
O'Brien, Charles - *Death at Tammany Hall*
    PW - v262 - i19 - May 11 2015 - p38(1) [51-500]
O'Brien, Colleen C. - *Race, Romance, and Rebellion: Literatures of the Americas in the Nineteenth Century*
    J Am St - v49 - i2 - May 2015 - p424-425 [501+]
O'Brien, Cynthia - *Amazing Brain Mysteries*
    c Res Links - v20 - i5 - June 2015 - p14(2) [51-500]
Lost Treasures
    c Res Links - v20 - i5 - June 2015 - p14(2) [51-500]
Mystery Files Series
    c BL - v111 - i21 - July 1 2015 - p54(1) [51-500]
O'Brien, Dan - *Scarsdale*
    TLS - i5844 - April 3 2015 - p23(1) [501+]
Wild Idea: Buffalo and Family in a Difficult Land
    Roundup M - v22 - i5 - June 2015 - p36(1) [501+]
    Roundup M - v22 - i6 - August 2015 - p39(1) [501+]
O'Brien, Daniel (b. 1967-) - *Classical Masculinity and the Spectacular Body on Film: the Mighty Sons of Hercules*
    TimHES - i2185 - Jan 8 2015 - p51-51 [501+]
O'Brien, Edna - *The Little Red Chairs*
    Lon R Bks - v37 - i20 - Oct 22 2015 - p37(1)

[501+]
    NS - v144 - i5288 - Nov 13 2015 - p42(1) [501+]
    PW - v262 - i45 - Nov 9 2015 - p32(1) [51-500]
    Spec - v329 - i9768 - Nov 14 2015 - p62(2) [501+]
    TLS - i5877 - Nov 20 2015 - p20(1) [501+]
The Love Object: Selected Stories
    BL - v111 - i14 - March 15 2015 - p51(1) [501+]
    KR - March 1 2015 - pNA [501+]
    LJ - v140 - i6 - April 1 2015 - p87(1) [51-500]
    NYT - May 8 2015 - pC19(L) [501+]
    NYTBR - June 14 2015 - p10(L) [501+]
    PW - v262 - i9 - March 2 2015 - p60(1) [51-500]
O'Brien, Flann - *At Swim-Two-Birds*
    NS - v144 - i5282 - Oct 2 2015 - p74(2) [501+]
O'Brien, Gillian - *Blood Runs Green: The Murder That Transfixed Gilded Age Chicago*
    LJ - v140 - i5 - March 15 2015 - p122(1) [51-500]
    NY - v91 - i9 - April 20 2015 - p89 [51-500]
    NYTBR - July 5 2015 - p30(L) [501+]
    TimHES - i2193 - March 5 2015 - p51(1) [501+]
O'Brien, Julia M. - *The Oxford Encyclopedia of the Bible and Gender Studies, 2 vols.*
    BL - v111 - i14 - March 15 2015 - p29(1) [501+]
    LJ - v140 - i3 - Feb 15 2015 - p129(1) [501+]
O'Brien, Payson - *How The War Was Won: Air-Sea Power and Allied Victory in World War II*
    TimHES - i2199 - April 16 2015 - p61(1) [501+]
O'Brien, Sean - *The Beautiful Librarians*
    TLS - i5860 - July 24 2015 - p21(1) [501+]
O'Brien, Susan - *The Gluten-Free Vegetarian Family Cookbook: 150 Healthy Recipes for Meals, Snacks, Sides, Desserts, and More*
    Bwatch - May 2015 - pNA [51-500]
O'Brien, Tim - *The Things They Carried (Read by Cranston, Bryan). Audiobook Review*
    BL - v111 - i14 - March 15 2015 - p23(2) [501+]
O'Brien, William Patrick - *Merchants of Independence: International Trade on the Santa Fe Trail, 1827-1860*
    WHQ - v46 - i1 - Spring 2015 - p82-83 [501+]
Obrist, Hans Ulrich - *Lives of the Artists, Lives of the Architects*
    Spec - v328 - i9742 - May 16 2015 - p40(2) [501+]
    TLS - i5856 - June 26 2015 - p26(1) [501+]
Ways of Curating
    Lon R Bks - v37 - i11 - June 4 2015 - p13(2) [501+]
Oby, Maduka Sunny - *The Whispering Voice*
    SPBW - Sept 2015 - pNA [51-500]
O'Byrne, Nicola - *Use Your Imagination (Illus. by O'Byrne, Nicola)*
    c KR - May 15 2015 - pNA [51-500]
    c Sch Lib - v63 - i1 - Spring 2015 - p32(1) [51-500]
Oca, Jeffrey Montez - *Religion and sports in American Culture*
    SSJ - v32 - i2 - June 2015 - p224-3 [501+]
O'Callaghan, Conor - *The Sun King*
    ILS - v35 - i1 - Fall 2015 - p23(1) [501+]
O'Callaghan, Joseph F. - *The Last Crusade in the West: Castile and the Conquest of Granada*
    Med R - March 2015 - pNA(NA) [501+]
    Specu - v90 - i2 - April 2015 - p572-574 [501+]
Ocampo, Silvina - *Silvina Ocampo*
    TLS - i5858 - July 10 2015 - p20(1) [501+]
Thus Were Their Faces: Selected Stories
    HM - v330 - i1979 - April 2015 - p79(81) [501+]
    TLS - i5858 - July 10 2015 - p20(1) [501+]
Ocasio, Rafael - *Afro-Cuban Costumbrismo: From Plantations to the Slums*
    Callaloo - v38 - i1 - Wntr 2015 - p225-228 [501+]
Ocean, Davy - *The Boy Who Cried Shark (Illus. by Blecha, Aaron)*
    c HB Guide - v26 - i2 - Fall 2015 - p69(1) [51-500]
Shark School Series (Illus. by Blecha, Aaron)
    c HB Guide - v26 - i1 - Spring 2015 - p63(1) [51-500]
Ochiagha, Terri - *Achebe and Friends at Umuahia: The Making of a Literary Elite*
    TimHES - i2210 - July 2 2015 - p50-1 [501+]
    TLS - i5872 - Oct 16 2015 - p28(1) [501+]
Ochiltree, Dianne - *It's a Seashell Day (Illus. by Kreloff, Elliot)*
    c CH Bwatch - July 2015 - pNA [51-500]
    c KR - Feb 15 2015 - pNA [51-500]
    c SLJ - v61 - i9 - Sept 2015 - p126(1) [51-500]
Ochoa, Gilda L. - *Profiling: Latinos, Asian Americans and the Achievement Gap*
    AJS - v120 - i4 - Jan 2015 - p1239(2) [501+]
Ochoa, Marcia - *Queen for a Day: Transformistas, Beauty Queens, and the Performance of Femininity in Venezuela*
    HAHR - v95 - i2 - May 2015 - p382-384 [501+]

Ochonu, Moses E. - *Colonialism by Proxy: Hausa Imperial Agents and Middle Belt Consciousness in Nigeria*
    AHR - v120 - i3 - June 2015 - p1154-1155 [501+]
Ochs, Steve - *Midmen*
    KR - June 15 2015 - pNA [501+]
Ochshorn, Susan - *Squandering America's Future: Why ECE Policy Matters for Equality, Our Economy, and Our Children*
    LJ - v140 - i10 - June 1 2015 - p112(2) [51-500]
Ockler, Sarah - *Scandal*
    c HB Guide - v26 - i1 - Spring 2015 - p119(1) [51-500]
The Summer of Chasing Mermaids
    y CCB-B - v68 - i11 - July-August 2015 - p559(2) [51-500]
    y HB Guide - v26 - i2 - Fall 2015 - p133(1) [51-500]
    y KR - March 15 2015 - pNA [51-500]
    y SLJ - v61 - i4 - April 2015 - p168(1) [51-500]
    y VOYA - v38 - i2 - June 2015 - p66(2) [51-500]
O'Collins, Gerald - *The Second Vatican Council: Message and Meaning*
    Theol St - v76 - i2 - June 2015 - p370(2) [501+]
The Second Vatican Council on Other Religions
    JR - Jan 2015 - p127(3) [501+]
The Spirituality of the Second Vatican Council
    Theol St - v76 - i1 - March 2015 - p222(2) [501+]
O'Connell, Aaron B. - *Underdogs: The Making of the Modern Marine Corps*
    NWCR - v68 - i4 - Autumn 2015 - p137(2) [51-500]
O'Connell, Caitlin - *Elephant Don: The Politics of a Pachyderm Posse*
    Nature - v522 - i7555 - June 11 2015 - p155(1) [51-500]
    TLS - i5866 - Sept 4 2015 - p23(1) [501+]
O'Connell, Kevin - *Pearl Harbor: The Missing Motive*
    KR - Nov 1 2015 - pNA [501+]
O'Connell, Rebecca - *Baby Party (Illus. by Poole, Susie)*
    c HB Guide - v26 - i2 - Fall 2015 - p16(1) [51-500]
    c KR - Jan 15 2015 - pNA [51-500]
    c SLJ - v61 - i2 - Feb 2015 - p74(1) [51-500]
O'Connell, Robert L. - *Fierce Patriot: The Tangled Lives of William Tecumseh Sherman*
    JSH - v81 - i4 - Nov 2015 - p981(2) [501+]
O'Connell, Ryan - *I'm Special: And Other Lies We Tell Ourselves to Get through Our Twenties*
    PW - v262 - i14 - April 6 2015 - p49(1) [51-500]
O'Connell, Susan - *Putting the Practices Into Action: Implementing the Common Core Standards for Mathematical Practice K-8*
    TC Math - v21 - i7 - March 2015 - p444(2) [501+]
O'Connor, Eimear - *Sean Keating: Art, Politics and Building the Irish Nation*
    ILS - v35 - i1 - Fall 2015 - p26(2) [501+]
O'Connor, George - *Apollo*
    c KR - Dec 1 2015 - pNA [51-500]
Ares: Bringer of War (Illus. by O'Connor, George)
    c HB Guide - v26 - i2 - Fall 2015 - p159(1) [51-500]
    SLJ - v61 - i3 - March 2015 - p179(1) [51-500]
If I Had a Triceratops (Illus. by O'Connor, George)
    c BL - v111 - i9-10 - Jan 1 2015 - p106(1) [51-500]
    c CCB-B - v68 - i8 - April 2015 - p415(1) [51-500]
    c CH Bwatch - May 2015 - pNA [51-500]
    c HB Guide - v26 - i2 - Fall 2015 - p46(1) [51-500]
O'Connor, Heather M. - *Betting Game*
    y BL - v112 - i1 - Sept 1 2015 - p99(1) [51-500]
    y KR - August 15 2015 - pNA [51-500]
    y Res Links - v21 - i1 - Oct 2015 - p39(1) [501+]
    y SLJ - v61 - i9 - Sept 2015 - p151(4) [501+]
O'Connor, J. Patrick - *Truth Seeker*
    SPBW - Jan 2015 - pNA [51-500]
O'Connor, Jacqueline - *Documentary Trial Plays in Contemporary American Theater*
    Theat J - v67 - i1 - March 2015 - p135-146 [501+]
O'Connor, Jane - *Cueillette au verger (Je lis avec Mademoiselle Nancy). (Illus. by Glasser, Robin Preiss)*
    c Res Links - v20 - i3 - Feb 2015 - p48(2) [51-500]
Fancy Nancy and the Wedding of the Century (Illus. by Glasser, Robin Preiss)
    c HB Guide - v26 - i1 - Spring 2015 - p41(1) [51-500]
Fancy Nancy's Fabulous Fall Storybook Collection (Illus. by Glasser, Robin Preiss)
    c HB Guide - v26 - i1 - Spring 2015 - p41(1) [51-500]
Le trefle a quatre feuilles (Illus. by Glasser, Robin Preiss)
    c Res Links - v20 - i5 - June 2015 - p42(1) [51-500]
Lulu and the Witch Baby (Illus. by Sinclair, Bella)
    c HB Guide - v26 - i1 - Spring 2015 - p54(1) [51-500]

Nancy Clancy, Secret of the Silver Key (Illus. by Glasser, Robin Preiss)
    c HB Guide - v26 - i1 - Spring 2015 - p63(1) [51-500]
Nancy Clancy, Star of Stage and Screen (Illus. by Glasser, Robin Preiss)
    c HB Guide - v26 - i2 - Fall 2015 - p69(1) [51-500]
Peanut Butter and Jellyfish (Illus. by Enik, Ted)
    c HB Guide - v26 - i2 - Fall 2015 - p60(1) [51-500]
Super Secret Surprise Party (Illus. by Enik, Ted)
    c HB Guide - v26 - i2 - Fall 2015 - p60(1) [51-500]
O'Connor, Jim - *Where Is the Grand Canyon? (Illus. by Colon, Daniel)*
    c SLJ - v61 - i8 - August 2015 - p118(1) [51-500]
O'Connor, Kathleen M. - *Jeremiah: Pain and Promise*
    Intpr - v69 - i1 - Jan 2015 - p122(1) [51-500]
O'Connor, Liz Gelb - *The Wanderer's Children*
    PW - v262 - i3 - Jan 19 2015 - p65(1) [51-500]
O'Connor, M.R. - *Resurrection Science: Conservation, De-Extinction and the Precarious Future of Wild Things*
    KR - June 15 2015 - pNA [501+]
    LJ - v140 - i14 - Sept 1 2015 - p133(1) [51-500]
O'Connor, Mike - *A Commercial Republic: America's Enduring Debate over Democratic Capitalism*
    AHR - v120 - i3 - June 2015 - p1016-1017 [501+]
    JAH - v101 - i4 - March 2015 - p1243-1244 [501+]
    JIH - v45 - i4 - Spring 2015 - p589-590 [501+]
O'Connor, Nuala - *Miss Emily*
    BL - v111 - i21 - July 1 2015 - p42(1) [51-500]
    LJ - v140 - i12 - July 1 2015 - p80(1) [51-500]
O'Connor, Ralph - *The Destruction of Da Derga's Hostel: Kingship and Narrative Artistry in a Mediaeval Irish Saga*
    JEGP - v114 - i3 - July 2015 - p451(3) [501+]
O'Connor, Steven - *Irish Officers in the British Forces, 1922-1945*
    HER - v130 - i545 - August 2015 - p1044(2) [501+]
O'Connor, T.J. - *Dying to Tell*
    KR - Nov 1 2015 - pNA [51-500]
O'Dair, Marcus - *Different Every Time: The Authorised Biography of Robert Wyatt*
    KR - July 1 2015 - pNA [51-500]
    TimHES - i2187 - Jan 22 2015 - p49(1) [501+]
Ode, Eric - *Bigfoot Does Not Like Birthday Parties (Illus. by Temairik, Jamie)*
    c KR - August 1 2015 - pNA [51-500]
Busy Trucks on the Go (Illus. by Culotta, Kent)
    c HB Guide - v26 - i1 - Spring 2015 - p13(1) [51-500]
Elliott the Otter: The Totally Untrue Story of Elliott, Boss of the Bay (Illus. by Skewes, John)
    c HB Guide - v26 - i2 - Fall 2015 - p46(1) [51-500]
    c SLJ - v61 - i2 - Feb 2015 - p80(1) [51-500]
Larry Gets Lost under the Sea (Illus. by Skewes, John)
    c HB Guide - v26 - i2 - Fall 2015 - p46(1) [51-500]
Odede, Kennedy - *Find Me Unafraid: Love, Loss, and Hope in an African Slum*
    y BL - v112 - i1 - Sept 15 2015 - p5(1) [51-500]
    KR - July 1 2015 - pNA [501+]
    PW - v262 - i25 - June 22 2015 - p129(2) [51-500]
Odell, Amy - *Tales from the Back Row: An Outsider's View from Inside the Fashion Industry*
    BL - v112 - i2 - Sept 15 2015 - p15(1) [501+]
    KR - June 15 2015 - pNA [501+]
    NYTBR - Nov 8 2015 - p50(L) [501+]
O'Dell, Dino - *Zar and the Broken Spaceship (Illus. by Germano, Santiago)*
    c CH Bwatch - Oct 2015 - pNA [51-500]
O'Dell, Tawni - *Angels Burning*
    BL - v112 - i7 - Dec 1 2015 - p26(2) [501+]
    KR - Oct 15 2015 - pNA [501+]
    LJ - v140 - i16 - Oct 1 2015 - p72(1) [51-500]
    PW - v262 - i44 - Nov 2 2015 - p64(1) [51-500]
One of Us
    RVBW - April 2015 - pNA [51-500]
Odendaal, Andre - *The Founders: The Origins of the ANC and the Struggle for Democracy in South Africa*
    AHR - v120 - i2 - April 2015 - p760-761 [501+]
Oderman, Kevin - *Cannot Stay: Essays on Travel*
    LJ - v140 - i9 - May 15 2015 - p98(1) [51-500]
Odgers, Darrel - *Pup Patrol: Farm Rescue (Illus. by Dawson, Janine)*
    c Magpies - v30 - i1 - March 2015 - p31(1) [501+]
Odgers, Sally - *Good Night, Truck (Illus. by McKenzie, Heath)*
    c KR - Nov 1 2015 - pNA [51-500]
    c SLJ - v61 - i12 - Dec 2015 - p93(2) [51-500]

Odo, Franklin - *Voices from the Canefields: Folksongs from Japanese Immigrant Workers in Hawai'i*
Amerasia J - v41 - i1 - Wntr 2015 - p126-128 [501+]
O'Doherty, David - *Danger Is Everywhere: A Handbook for Avoiding Danger (Illus. by Judge, Chris)*
c CCB-B - v68 - i7 - March 2015 - p365(1) [51-500]
c HB Guide - v26 - i1 - Spring 2015 - p88(1) [51-500]
O'Doherty, Marianne - *The Indies and the Medieval West: Thought, Report, Imagination*
AHR - v120 - i1 - Feb 2015 - p201-202 [501+]
O'Donell, James J. - *The End of Traditional Religion and the Rise of Christianity*
NYTBR - March 15 2015 - p30(L) [501+]
O'Donnell, Angela Alaimo - *Flannery O'Connor: Fiction Fired by Faith*
AM - v213 - i16 - Nov 23 2015 - p35(4) [501+]
Mortal Blessings: A Sacramental Farewell
AM - v212 - i8 - March 9 2015 - p34(2) [501+]
O'Donnell, Edward T. - *Henry George and the Crisis of Inequality: Progress and Poverty in the Gilded Age*
KR - April 1 2015 - pNA [501+]
PW - v262 - i16 - April 20 2015 - p66(2) [51-500]
O'Donnell, Helen - *The Irish Brotherhood: John F. Kennedy, His Inner Circle and the Improbable Rise to the Presidency*
KR - Jan 1 2015 - pNA [51-500]
LJ - v140 - i3 - Feb 15 2015 - p113(1) [51-500]
PW - v262 - i4 - Jan 26 2015 - p161(1) [51-500]
O'Donnell, James J. - *Pagans: The End of Traditional Religion and the Rise of Christianity*
KR - Jan 1 2015 - pNA [51-500]
LJ - v140 - i2 - Feb 1 2015 - p88(1) [501+]
NY - v91 - i14 - May 25 2015 - p73 [51-500]
PW - v262 - i3 - Jan 19 2015 - p76(1) [51-500]
O'Donnell, Liam - *The Case of the Battling Bots*
c KR - Dec 1 2015 - pNA [51-500]
The Case of the Slime Stampede (Illus. by Deas, Mike)
c CCB-B - v68 - i9 - May 2015 - p460(1) [51-500]
c BL - v111 - i11 - Feb 1 2015 - p53(1) [51-500]
The Case of the Snack Snatcher (Illus. by Grand, Aurelie)
c KR - Sept 1 2015 - pNA [51-500]
c PW - v262 - i30 - July 27 2015 - p69(1) [501+]
c SLJ - v61 - i9 - Sept 2015 - p135(1) [51-500]
O'Donnell, Patrick - *A Temporary Future: The Fiction of David Mitchell*
LJ - v140 - i2 - Feb 1 2015 - p84(1) [51-500]
O'Donnell, Patrick Ian - *Final Words*
SPBW - Oct 2015 - pNA [51-500]
O'Donnell, Patrick K. - *Dog Company: The Boys of Pointe du Hoc: The Rangers Who Accomplished D-Day's Toughest Mission and Led the Way Across Europe*
J Mil H - v79 - i1 - Jan 2015 - p252-254 [501+]
Washington's Immortals: The Untold Story of an Elite Regiment Who Changed the Course of the Revolution
KR - Nov 1 2015 - pNA [501+]
O'Donnell, Peter J. - *Essential Dynamics and Relativity*
Bwatch - April 2015 - pNA [51-500]
O'Donoghue, Heather - *English Poetry and Old Norse Myth: A History*
RES - v66 - i275 - June 2015 - p563-565 [501+]
O'Donohoe, Benedict - *Severally Seeking Sartre*
FS - v69 - i1 - Jan 2015 - p109-109 [501+]
O'Donovan, Oliver - *Finding and Seeking*
Theol St - v76 - i4 - Dec 2015 - p871(2) [501+]
Self, World, and Time: Ethics as Theology
TLS - i5837 - Feb 13 2015 - p28(1) [501+]
O'Dowd, Chris - *Moone Boy: The Blunder Years (Read by O'Dowd, Chris, and Nick V. Murphy). Audiobook Review*
BL - v112 - i4 - Oct 15 2015 - p62(1) [51-500]
c SLJ - v61 - i10 - Oct 2015 - p52(1) [51-500]
Moone Boy: The Blunder Years (Illus. by Giampaglia, Walter)
c BL - v111 - i17 - May 1 2015 - p100(1) [51-500]
c Sch Lib - v63 - i1 - Spring 2015 - p41(1) [51-500]
y VOYA - v38 - i2 - June 2015 - p67(1) [51-500]
Odozor, Paulinus Ikechukwu - *Morality: Truly Christian, Truly African: Foundational, Methodological, and Theological Considerations*
Theol St - v76 - i4 - Dec 2015 - p873(2) [501+]
Odyssey, Shawn Thomas - *The Magician's Dream: An Oona Crate Mystery*
c SLJ - v61 - i2 - Feb 2015 - p90(1) [51-500]
y VOYA - v38 - i1 - April 2015 - p82(1) [51-500]
Oe, Kenzaburo - *Death by Water*
BL - v112 - i2 - Sept 15 2015 - p26(1) [51-500]
HM - v331 - i1985 - Oct 2015 - p73(3) [501+]
KR - August 1 2015 - pNA [501+]
LJ - v140 - i17 - Oct 15 2015 - p75(2) [51-500]
NYTBR - Oct 4 2015 - p9(L) [501+]
PW - v262 - i31 - August 3 2015 - p32(1) [51-500]
OEGarra, Anne - *Immunity and Tolerance*
QRB - v90 - i1 - March 2015 - p108(1) [501+]
Oelschlager, Vanita - *The Pullman Porter: An American Journey (Illus. by Blanc, Mike)*
CH Bwatch - April 2015 - pNA [51-500]
Oettinger, Marion - *Raymundo Gonzalez: Magical Realism in Mexico*
SPBW - April 2015 - pNA [51-500]
Ofanansky, Allison - *New Moon, New Moon (Illus. by Alpern, Eliyahu)*
c HB Guide - v26 - i1 - Spring 2015 - p135(1) [51-500]
Offe, Claus - *Europe Entrapped*
For Aff - v94 - i3 - May-June 2015 - pNA [501+]
TimHES - i2189 - Feb 5 2015 - p58-59 [501+]
Offen, Hilda - *Blue Balloons and Rabbit Ears*
c Sch Lib - v63 - i1 - Spring 2015 - p49(1) [51-500]
Offene Lizenzen in den Digitalen Geisteswissenschaften
HNet - June 2015 - pNA [501+]
Offerman, Nick - *Gumption: Relighting the Torch of Freedom with America's Gutsiest Troublemakers (Read by Offerman, Nick). Audiobook Review*
LJ - v140 - i13 - August 1 2015 - p49(2) [51-500]
PW - v262 - i30 - July 27 2015 - p61(2) [51-500]
Gumption: Relighting the Torch of Freedom with America's Gutsiest Troublemakers
KR - April 15 2015 - pNA [501+]
Offill, Jenny - *While You Were Napping (Illus. by Blitt, Barry)*
c HB Guide - v26 - i1 - Spring 2015 - p13(1) [51-500]
Offit, Paul A. - *Bad Faith: When Religious Belief Undermines Modern Medicine*
KR - Jan 1 2015 - pNA [501+]
NYRB - v62 - i4 - March 5 2015 - p29(3) [501+]
NYT - March 11 2015 - pC4(L) [501+]
NYTBR - April 12 2015 - p14(L) [501+]
PW - v262 - i3 - Jan 19 2015 - p76(2) [51-500]
TimHES - i2208 - June 18 2015 - p49(1) [501+]
Offley, Ed - *The Burning Shore: How Hitler's U-Boats Brought World War II to America*
HNet - Feb 2015 - pNA [501+]
Offutt, Chris - *My Father, the Pornographer: A Memoir*
KR - Dec 1 2015 - pNA [501+]
PW - v262 - i48 - Nov 30 2015 - p48(1) [51-500]
O'Flaherty, Dennis - *King of the Cracksmen*
BL - v111 - i9-10 - Jan 1 2015 - p60(1) [51-500]
O'Flaherty, Patrick - *Scotland's Pariah: The Life and Work of John Pinkerton, 1759-1826*
TLS - i5867 - Sept 11 2015 - p27(1) [501+]
Ogain, Rionach Ui - *The Otherworld: Music and Song from Irish Tradition*
ILS - v34 - i2 - Spring 2015 - p17(1) [501+]
O'Gara, Margaret - *No Turning Back: The Future of Ecumenism*
Comw - v142 - i7 - April 10 2015 - p26(3) [501+]
Theol St - v76 - i4 - Dec 2015 - p892(2) [501+]
Ogden, Daniel - *Dragons, Serpents, and Slayers in the Classical and Early Christian Worlds: A Sourcebook*
Class R - v65 - i2 - Oct 2015 - p333-334 [501+]
Oge, Margo - *Driving the Future: Combating Climate Change with Cleaner, Smarter Cars*
BL - v111 - i16 - April 15 2015 - p8(1) [51-500]
KR - Feb 15 2015 - pNA [501+]
LJ - v140 - i7 - April 15 2015 - p116(1) [51-500]
Ogien, Ruwen - *Human Kindness and the Smell of Warm Croissants: An Introduction to Ethics*
BL - v111 - i18 - May 15 2015 - p4(1) [51-500]
LJ - v140 - i5 - March 15 2015 - p108(2) [51-500]
Ogilvie, Isabel - *The Luchair Stones*
c SLJ - v61 - i6 - June 2015 - p103(1) [51-500]
O'Gorman, Francis - *Worrying: A Literary and Cultural History*
Ch Today - v59 - i5 - June 2015 - p70(1) [501+]
Econ - v416 - i8949 - August 1 2015 - p72(US) [501+]
Spec - v328 - i9752 - July 25 2015 - p30(1) [501+]
O'Gorman, Patricia - *The Resilient Woman: Mastering the 7 Steps to Personal Power*
NACEJou - v75 - i4 - April 2015 - p12-13 [501+]
O'Grady, Paul - *Open the Cage, Murphy*
Spec - v329 - i9768 - Nov 14 2015 - p63(1) [501+]
Oh, Arissa H. - *To Save the Children of Korea: The Cold War Origins of International Adoption*
TimHES - i2220 - Sept 10 2015 - p45-1 [501+]
Oh, Ellen - *King*
y HB Guide - v26 - i2 - Fall 2015 - p133(2) [51-500]
y KR - Jan 1 2015 - pNA [51-500]
Oh, Young Kyun - *Engraving Virtue: The Printing History of a Premodern Korean Moral Primer*
JAS - v74 - i3 - August 2015 - p765-767 [501+]
O'Hagan, Andrew - *The Illuminations*
NYRB - v62 - i12 - July 9 2015 - p36(3) [501+]
TLS - i5843 - March 27 2015 - p19(1) [501+]
HR - v68 - i2 - Summer 2015 - p343-351 [501+]
KR - Jan 1 2015 - pNA [51-500]
NYTBR - March 15 2015 - p20(L) [501+]
Spec - v327 - i9730 - Feb 21 2015 - p46(2) [501+]
The Missing
TLS - i5843 - March 27 2015 - p16(1) [501+]
Ohanesian, Aline - *Orhan's Inheritance (Read by Cohen, Assaf). Audiobook Review*
LJ - v140 - i12 - July 1 2015 - p43(1) [51-500]
Orhan's Inheritance
BL - v111 - i14 - March 15 2015 - p44(1) [51-500]
Bwatch - June 2015 - pNA [51-500]
CSM - April 8 2015 - pNA [501+]
KR - Feb 1 2015 - pNA [51-500]
LJ - v140 - i7 - April 15 2015 - p77(2) [51-500]
NYTBR - June 7 2015 - p31(L) [501+]
PW - v262 - i11 - March 16 2015 - p6(1) [51-500]
O'Hanlon, Michael - *The Pitt Rivers Museum: A World Within*
HT - v65 - i5 - May 2015 - p63(1) [501+]
O'Hara, Frank - *Lunch Poems*
Poet - v205 - i4 - Jan 2015 - p383(9) [501+]
O'Hara, Mo - *The Fintastic Fishsitter (Illus. by Jagucki, Marek)*
c KR - Dec 15 2015 - pNA [51-500]
My Big Fat Zombie Goldfish (Read by Gebauer, Christopher). Audiobook Review
c SLJ - v61 - i8 - August 2015 - p48(1) [51-500]
My Big Fat Zombie Goldfish: Fins of Fury (Illus. by Jagucki, Marek)
c HB Guide - v26 - i2 - Fall 2015 - p96(1) [51-500]
O'Hara, Vincent P. - *To Crown the Waves: The Great Navies of the First World War*
Historian - v77 - i3 - Fall 2015 - p635(2) [501+]
GSR - v38 - i2 - May 2015 - p430-3 [501+]
O'Hear, Natasha - *Picturing the Apocalypse: The Book of Revelation in the Arts over Two Millennia*
Spec - v328 - i9749 - July 4 2015 - p35(2) [501+]
O'Hearn, Kate - *Origins of Olympus*
c HB Guide - v26 - i2 - Fall 2015 - p96(1) [51-500]
Valkyrie
c KR - Nov 1 2015 - pNA [51-500]
c PW - v262 - i46 - Nov 16 2015 - p76(1) [51-500]
c SLJ - v61 - i12 - Dec 2015 - p105(2) [51-500]
Ohi, Debbie Ridpath - *Where Are My Books? (Illus. by Ohi, Debbie Ridpath)*
KR - Feb 1 2015 - pNA [51-500]
c PW - v262 - i13 - March 30 2015 - p75(1) [51-500]
SLJ - v61 - i3 - March 2015 - p123(2) [51-500]
Ohi, Ruth - *Fox and Squirrel Make a Friend*
c Res Links - v20 - i3 - Feb 2015 - p7(1) [51-500]
Ohle, Kathrin - *The Decision-Maker's Guide to Long-Term Financing*
KR - Sept 15 2015 - pNA [501+]
Ohlgren, Thomas H. - *Early Rymes of Robyn Hood: An Edition of the Texts, ca. 1425 to ca. 1600*
Med R - June 2015 - pNA [501+]
Ohlig, Karl-Heinz - *Early Islam: A Critical Reconstruction Based on Contemporary Sources*
JAAR - v83 - i3 - Sept 2015 - p868-872 [501+]
Ohlin, Nancy - *Consent*
y BL - v112 - i5 - Nov 1 2015 - p49(1) [51-500]
y KR - Sept 1 2015 - pNA [51-500]
y SLJ - v61 - i9 - Sept 2015 - p170(1) [501+]
y VOYA - v38 - i5 - Dec 2015 - p62(1) [51-500]
Ohlsson, Kristina - *The Disappeared*
RVBW - April 2015 - pNA [51-500]
The Glass Children
c Sch Lib - v63 - i1 - Spring 2015 - p56(1) [51-500]
Hostage
BL - v112 - i3 - Oct 1 2015 - p26(2) [51-500]
Ohmura, Tomoko - *Line Up, Please!*
c Magpies - v30 - i2 - May 2015 - p26(1) [501+]
Ohora, Zachariah - *My Cousin Momo (Illus. by OHora, Zachariah)*
c BL - v111 - i19-20 - June 1 2015 - p120(2) [51-500]
OHora, Zachariah - *My Cousin Momo (Illus. by OHora, Zachariah)*
c CCB-B - v69 - i1 - Sept 2015 - p41(2) [51-500]
c HB - v91 - i4 - July-August 2015 - p121(2) [51-500]
c PW - v262 - i15 - April 13 2015 - p77(1) [51-500]
Ohrenstein, Dora - *The Crocheter's Skill-Building Workshop: Essential Techniques for Becoming a More Versatile*
LJ - v140 - i2 - Feb 1 2015 - p83(1) [51-500]

Oil, Gas and Pipelines: New Perspectives on the Role of Soviet Energy during the Cold War
HNet - March 2015 - pNA [501+]
Oja, Carol J. - *Bernstein Meets Broadway: Collaborative Art in a Time of War*
Am Theat - v32 - i5 - May-June 2015 - p64(2) [501+]
Bks & Cult - v21 - i1 - Jan-Feb 2015 - p25(3) [501+]
TLS - i5862 - August 7 2015 - p24(1) [501+]
Ojeda, Oscar Riera - *Sagrada Familia: Gaudi's Unfinished Masterpiece, Geometry, Construction and Site*
NYRB - v62 - i11 - June 25 2015 - p56(3) [501+]
Ojendal, Joakim - *Beyond Democracy in Cambodia: Political Reconstruction in a Post-Conflict Society*
JAS - v74 - i1 - Feb 2015 - p246-248 [501+]
Okamba, Emmanuel - *La comptabilite fondamentale*
AR - v90 - i3 - May 2015 - p1248(2) [501+]
Okamoto, Naomi - *The Art of Sumi-E: Beautiful Ink Painting Using Japanese Brushwork*
LJ - v140 - i19 - Nov 15 2015 - p82(1) [51-500]
O'Keefe, M. - *Everything I Left Unsaid*
KR - July 15 2015 - pNA [501+]
PW - v262 - i28 - July 13 2015 - p51(1) [51-500]
O'Keefe, Molly - *The Truth about Him*
KR - Sept 15 2015 - pNA [51-500]
PW - v262 - i45 - Nov 9 2015 - p44(1) [51-500]
O'Keefe, Paul - *Waterloo: The Aftermath*
Econ - v415 - i8939 - May 23 2015 - p71(US) [501+]
HT - v65 - i7 - July 2015 - p58(2) [501+]
O'Keeffe, Katherine O'Brien - *Stealing Obedience: Narratives of Agency and Identity in Later Anglo-Saxon England*
JEGP - v114 - i1 - Jan 2015 - p143(3) [501+]
Specu - v90 - i1 - Jan 2015 - p283-284 [501+]
O'Keeffe, Paul - *Waterloo: The Aftermath*
KR - March 1 2015 - pNA [51-500]
PW - v262 - i12 - March 23 2015 - p62(2) [501+]
RVBW - August 2015 - pNA [51-500]
TLS - i5833 - Jan 16 2015 - p12(2) [501+]
Okerstrom, Dennis R. - *The Final Mission of Bottoms Up: A World War II Pilot's Story*
APJ - v29 - i2 - March-April 2015 - p181(2) [501+]
Okihiro, Gary Y. - *The Great American Mosaic: An Exploration of Diversity in Primary Documents*
R&USQ - v54 - i4 - Summer 2015 - p81(2) [501+]
Oklap, Ekin - *A Strangeness in My Mind*
TLS - i5871 - Oct 9 2015 - p22(1) [501+]
Okoli, Kate - *In Silence and Dignity: The Single Mother Story*
SPBW - May 2015 - pNA [501+]
Okorafor, Nnedi - *The Book of Phoenix*
LJ - v140 - i9 - May 15 2015 - p57(4) [501+]
NYTBR - May 31 2015 - p38(L) [501+]
PW - v262 - i16 - April 20 2015 - p60(1) [51-500]
Okparanta, Chinelo - *Under the Udala Trees*
y BL - v112 - i1 - Sept 1 2015 - p44(1) [51-500]
CSM - Dec 1 2015 - pNA [501+]
KR - July 15 2015 - pNA [501+]
LJ - v140 - i11 - June 15 2015 - p81(1) [51-500]
Ms - v25 - i3 - Summer 2015 - p42(1) [501+]
NYTBR - Oct 25 2015 - p11(L) [501+]
Okpewho, Isidore - *Blood on the Tides: The Ozidi Saga and Oral Epic Narratology*
MP - v113 - i1 - August 2015 - pE59(3) [501+]
Oksanen, Sofi - *When the Doves Disappeared*
BL - v111 - i9-10 - Jan 1 2015 - p55(1) [51-500]
Econ - v415 - i8936 - May 2 2015 - p74(US) [501+]
NY - v91 - i6 - March 30 2015 - p74 [51-500]
Oktober, Tricia - *Blue Moon (Illus. by Oktober, Tricia)*
c Magpies - v30 - i1 - March 2015 - p28(1) [501+]
Olbrys, Brooks - *The Adventures of Blue Ocean Bob: A Challenging Job (Illus. by Keele, Kevin)*
c CH Bwatch - Feb 2015 - pNA [51-500]
SLJ - v61 - i4 - April 2015 - p141(1) [51-500]
Oldenziel, Ruth - *Consumers, Tinkerers, Rebels: The People Who Shaped Europe*
T&C - v56 - i4 - Oct 2015 - p993-995 [501+]
Older, Daniel Jose - *Midnight Taxi Tango*
PW - v262 - i48 - Nov 30 2015 - p43(1) [51-500]
Shadowshaper
y BL - v111 - i18 - May 15 2015 - p64(1) [51-500]
y KR - March 15 2015 - pNA [51-500]
c NYTBR - July 12 2015 - p20(L) [501+]
y PW - v262 - i15 - April 13 2015 - p83(1) [51-500]
y PW - v262 - i49 - Dec 2 2015 - p105(1) [51-500]
y SLJ - v61 - i4 - April 2015 - p157(2) [51-500]
y Teach Lib - v43 - i1 - Oct 2015 - p23(1) [51-500]
Oldfield, Dawn Bluemel - *Venus: Super Hot*
c HB Guide - v26 - i2 - Fall 2015 - p164(2) [51-500]
Oldfield, J.R. - *Transatlantic Abolitionism in the Age of Revolution: An International History of Anti-Slavery, c.1787-1820*
HER - v130 - i545 - August 2015 - p1005(3) [501+]
Oldfield, Paul - *Sanctity and Pilgrimage in Medieval Southern Italy, 1000-1200*
Med R - August 2015 - pNA [501+]
Oldham, Nick - *Edge*
BL - v111 - i13 - March 1 2015 - p22(2) [51-500]
KR - Feb 1 2015 - pNA [51-500]
PW - v262 - i7 - Feb 16 2015 - p163(1) [51-500]
Unforgiving
BL - v112 - i1 - Sept 1 2015 - p50(1) [51-500]
PW - v262 - i39 - Sept 28 2015 - p70(1) [51-500]
Oldland, Nicholas - *Les amis qui ne pensaient qu'a gagner*
c Res Links - v21 - i1 - Oct 2015 - p55(1) [51-500]
Walk on the Wild Side (Illus. by Oldland, Nicholas)
c HB Guide - v26 - i2 - Fall 2015 - p46(1) [51-500]
c Res Links - v21 - i1 - Oct 2015 - p9(1) [51-500]
c SLJ - v61 - i2 - Feb 2015 - p74(2) [51-500]
Oldstone-Moore, Christopher - *Of Beards and Men: The Revealing History of Facial Hair*
NYTBR - Dec 6 2015 - p48(L) [501+]
O'Leary, Don - *Irish Catholicism and Science: From Godless Colleges to the Celtic Tiger*
CHR - v101 - i2 - Spring 2015 - p380(3) [501+]
Isis - v106 - i1 - March 2015 - p203(2) [501+]
O'Leary, John - *Goldilocks: A Pop-Up Book*
c KR - Dec 1 2015 - pNA [51-500]
c PW - v262 - i27 - July 6 2015 - p70(2) [501+]
O'Leary, Sara - *This Is Sadie (Illus. by Morstad, Julie)*
y Nat Post - v17 - i176 - May 30 2015 - pWP4(1) [501+]
c PW - v262 - i10 - March 9 2015 - p70(2) [51-500]
c Res Links - v20 - i5 - June 2015 - p7(1) [51-500]
c SLJ - v61 - i4 - April 2015 - p188(1) [501+]
Olejniczak, Julian M. - *To Be a Soldier*
KR - Dec 15 2015 - pNA [501+]
Olen, Helaine - *The Index Card: Why Personal Finance Doesn't Have to be Complicated*
PW - v262 - i47 - Nov 23 2015 - p63(1) [51-500]
PW - v262 - i51 - Dec 14 2015 - p30(3) [501+]
Oles, James - *Art and Architecture in Mexico*
HAHR - v95 - i3 - August 2015 - p503-504 [501+]
Olien, Jessica - *Shark Detective! (Illus. by Olien, Jessica)*
c BL - v112 - i2 - Sept 15 2015 - p69(1) [51-500]
c KR - July 1 2015 - pNA [51-500]
c PW - v262 - i25 - June 22 2015 - p136(2) [51-500]
c SLJ - v61 - i6 - June 2015 - p89(1) [51-500]
Olin, Sean - *Reckless Hearts*
y KR - Sept 15 2015 - pNA [51-500]
y VOYA - v38 - i5 - Dec 2015 - p62(1) [51-500]
Wicked Games
c HB Guide - v26 - i1 - Spring 2015 - p119(1) [51-500]
Olivas, Aimee - *Survival Time: A Handbook for Surviving a Violent Incident*
KR - Jan 1 2016 - pNA [501+]
Olive, John - *Tell Me a Story In the Dark: A Guide to Creating Magical Bedtime Stories for Young Children*
SPBW - March 2015 - pNA [51-500]
Oliveira, Patrick Luiz Sullivan De - *Parisian Palimpsest: Monuments, Ruins, and Preservation in the Long Nineteenth Century*
J Urban H - v41 - i4 - July 2015 - p739-745 [501+]
Olivelle, Patrick - *Governance, and Law in Ancient India: Kautuilya's Arthasastra*
HNet - April 2015 - pNA [501+]
Oliver, Andrew - *American Travelers on the Nile: Early US Visitors to Egypt, 1774-1839*
RVBW - May 2015 - pNA [501+]
Oliver, Carmen - *Bears Make the Best Reading Buddies*
c KR - Jan 1 2016 - pNA [51-500]
Oliver, Dave - *Against the Tide: Rickover's Leadership Principles and the Rise of the Nuclear Navy*
J Mil H - v79 - i2 - April 2015 - p541-543 [501+]
NWCR - v68 - i4 - Autumn 2015 - p133(3) [51-500]
RVBW - March 2015 - pNA [51-500]
Oliver, Ilanit - *Are You My Daddy? (Illus. by Parker-Rees, Guy)*
c KR - July 1 2015 - pNA [51-500]
Eight Jolly Reindeer (Illus. by Rogers, Jacqueline)
c KR - Jan 1 2015 - pNA [51-500]
Oliver, Isaac - *Intimacy Idiot*
KR - April 15 2015 - pNA [51-500]
BL - v111 - i17 - May 1 2015 - p71(1) [51-500]
Ent W - i1367 - June 12 2015 - p80(1) [501+]
Oliver, Jana - *Briar Rose*
y SLJ - v61 - i5 - May 2015 - p115(1) [51-500]
Oliver, Kendrick - *To Touch the Face of God: The Sacred, the Profane, and the American Space Program, 1957-1975*
RAH - v43 - i2 - June 2015 - p378-383 [501+]
Oliver, L. J. - *The Humbug Murders: An Ebenezer Scrooge Mystery*
RVBW - Nov 2015 - pNA [51-500]
Oliver, Lauren - *The Shrunken Head (Read by Steinbruner, Greg). Audiobook Review*
BL - v112 - i7 - Dec 1 2015 - p70(1) [51-500]
The Shrunken Head (Illus. by Lacombe, Benjamin)
c BL - v111 - i21 - July 1 2015 - p68(2) [51-500]
c KR - June 15 2015 - pNA [51-500]
c PW - v262 - i27 - July 6 2015 - p73(1) [51-500]
The Shrunken Head
c SLJ - v61 - i6 - June 2015 - p103(1) [51-500]
Vanishing Girls (Read by Maarleveld, Saskia). Audiobook Review
y BL - v111 - i19-20 - June 1 2015 - p141(1) [51-500]
Vanishing Girls
y CCB-B - v68 - i7 - March 2015 - p365(2) [51-500]
y HB Guide - v26 - i2 - Fall 2015 - p134(1) [51-500]
y KR - Jan 1 2015 - pNA [51-500]
y PW - v262 - i2 - Jan 12 2015 - p62(1) [51-500]
y PW - v262 - i49 - Dec 2 2015 - p113(1) [51-500]
y VOYA - v37 - i6 - Feb 2015 - p62(1) [51-500]
Oliver, Mary - *Blue Horses: Poems*
AM - v212 - i5 - Feb 16 2015 - p25(3) [501+]
Felicity: Poems
LJ - v140 - i19 - Nov 15 2015 - p88(2) [51-500]
PW - v262 - i38 - Sept 21 2015 - p50(1) [51-500]
Oliver, Narelle - *Sand Swimmers: The Secret Life of Australia's Desert Wilderness (Illus. by Oliver, Narelle)*
c BL - v111 - i9-10 - Jan 1 2015 - p76(1) [51-500]
Oliver, Neil - *Master of Shadows*
TimHES - i2229 - Nov 12 2015 - p47(1) [501+]
Olivera, Ramon - *ABCs on Wings (Illus. by Olivera, Ramon)*
c KR - April 15 2015 - pNA [51-500]
c PW - v262 - i23 - June 8 2015 - p60(1) [501+]
c SLJ - v61 - i6 - June 2015 - p89(1) [51-500]
Olko, Justyna - *Insignia of Rank in the Nahua World: From the Fifteenth to the Seventeenth Century*
HAHR - v95 - i3 - August 2015 - p509-511 [501+]
Oller, John - *American Queen: The Rise and Fall of Kate Chase Sprague, Civil War "Belle of the North" and Gilded Age Woman of Scandal*
NYTBR - Jan 11 2015 - p15(L) [501+]
Ollikainen, Aki - *White Hunger*
TimHES - i2207 - June 11 2015 - p53(1) [501+]
TLS - i5853 - June 5 2015 - p20(1) [501+]
Ollison, Rashod - *Soul Serenade: Rhythm, Blues and Coming of Age through Vinyl*
KR - Oct 1 2015 - pNA [51-500]
PW - v262 - i50 - Dec 7 2015 - p80(2) [51-500]
Ollmann, Joe - *Happy Stories about Well Adjusted People*
BL - v111 - i9-10 - Jan 1 2015 - p61(1) [51-500]
Olmstead, Kathleen - *Silver Penny Stories (Illus. by Olafsdottir, Linda)*
c HB Guide - v26 - i1 - Spring 2015 - p145(1) [51-500]
Olmsted, Frederick Law - *Plans and Views of Public Parks*
LJ - v140 - i10 - June 1 2015 - p100(1) [501+]
Olmsted, Kathryn S. - *Right Out of California: The 1930s and the Big Business Roots of Modern Conservatism*
KR - July 15 2015 - pNA [501+]
NYTBR - Dec 20 2015 - p12(L) [501+]
PW - v262 - i28 - July 13 2015 - p55(1) [51-500]
O'Loghlin, James - *Daisy Malone and the Blue Glowing Stone*
c Magpies - v30 - i2 - May 2015 - p38(1) [501+]
Olopade, Dayo - *The Bright Continent: Breaking Rules and Making Change in Modern Africa*
AM - v212 - i9 - March 16 2015 - p34(3) [501+]
NYTBR - April 12 2015 - p28(L) [501+]
Olsen, Bjornar - *Ruin Memories: Materialities, Aesthetics and the Archaeology of the Recent Past*
Am Ant - v80 - i2 - April 2015 - p416(2) [501+]
Olsen, Darcy - *The Right to Try: How the Federal Government Prevents Americans from Getting the Life-Saving Treatments They Need*
BL - v112 - i4 - Oct 15 2015 - p7(1) [51-500]
KR - Sept 15 2015 - pNA [501+]
Olsen, David C. - *Saying No to Say Yes: Everyday Boundaries and Pastoral Excellence*
CC - v132 - i10 - May 13 2015 - p42(1) [51-500]
Olsen, Flemming - *The Literary Criticism of Matthew Arnold: Letters to Clough, the 1853 Preface, and Some*

Essays
  TLS - i5858 - July 10 2015 - p12(2) [501+]
Olsen, Stephanie - *Juvenile Nation: Youth, Emotions and the Making of the Modern British Citizen, 1880-1914*
  AHR - v120 - i2 - April 2015 - p717-718 [501+]
Olsen, Sue - *The Plant Lover's Guide to Ferns*
  NYTBR - May 31 2015 - p36(L) [501+]
Olsen, Sylvia - *Life Cycle of a Lie*
  y Res Links - v20 - i4 - April 2015 - p31(2) [51-500]
Olshan, Matthew - *Marshlands*
  NYTBR - Sept 20 2015 - p28(L) [501+]
Olshanskii, Maxim A. - *Iterative Methods for Linear Systems and Applications*
  SIAM Rev - v57 - i2 - June 2015 - p305-307 [501+]
Olshin, Benjamin B. - *The Mysteries of the Marco Polo Maps*
  Spec - v327 - i9726 - Jan 24 2015 - p46(1) [501+]
  TLS - i5852 - May 29 2015 - p25(1) [501+]
Olson, Christa J. - *Constitutive Visions: Indigeneity and Commonplaces of National Identity in Republican Ecuador*
  Ams - v72 - i1 - Jan 2015 - p180(3) [501+]
Olson, Gordon L. - *The Notorious Isaac Earl and His Scouts: Union Soldiers, Prisoners, Spies*
  JSH - v81 - i4 - Nov 2015 - p996(2) [501+]
Olson, James S. - *American Economic History: A Dictionary and Chronology*
  BL - v112 - i3 - Oct 1 2015 - p11(1) [51-500]
  LJ - v140 - i14 - Sept 1 2015 - p143(1) [51-500]
  The Industrial Revolution: Key Themes and Documents
  BL - v111 - i13 - March 1 2015 - p14(1) [51-500]
Olson, Jennifer Gray - *Ninja Bunny (Illus. by Olson, Jennifer Gray)*
  c HB - v91 - i4 - July-August 2015 - p122(2) [51-500]
  c KR - March 15 2015 - pNA [51-500]
  c SLJ - v61 - i5 - May 2015 - p90(1) [51-500]
Olson, Jonas - *Moral Error Theory: History, Critique, Defence*
  Dialogue - v54 - i3 - Sept 2015 - p594-596 [501+]
  Ethics - v125 - i4 - July 2015 - p1219(7) [501+]
Olson, Karen E. - *Hidden*
  KR - Sept 15 2015 - pNA [51-500]
Olson, Laura J. - *The Worlds of Russian Village Women: Tradition, Transgression, Compromise*
  Historian - v77 - i1 - Spring 2015 - p183(2) [501+]
Olson, Maria - *Music Room Posters Set 1: Sousa, Vaughan Williams, Holst, Grainger*
  Teach Mus - v23 - i1 - August 2015 - p60(1) [51-500]
Olson, Melissa F. - *Hunter's Trail*
  MFSF - v128 - i5-6 - May-June 2015 - p58(2) [501+]
Olson, Norah - *Twisted Fate*
  y CCB-B - v68 - i6 - Feb 2015 - p324(2) [51-500]
  y HB Guide - v26 - i2 - Fall 2015 - p134(1) [51-500]
Olson, Randy - *Houston, We Have a Narrative: Why Science Needs Story*
  Nature - v526 - i7573 - Oct 15 2015 - p321(1) [51-500]
  TimHES - i2226 - Oct 22 2015 - p48(1) [501+]
Olson, Rebecca - *Arras Hanging: The Textile that Determined Early Modern Literature and Drama*
  Six Ct J - v46 - i1 - Spring 2015 - p250-251 [501+]
Olson, Roger E. - *Reclaiming Pietism: Retrieving an Evangelical Tradition*
  Bks & Cult - v21 - i5 - Sept-Oct 2015 - p24(2) [501+]
  HNet - May 2015 - pNA [501+]
Olson, Rosanne - *ABCs of Beautiful Light: A Complete Course in Lighting for Photographers*
  Bwatch - Feb 2015 - pNA [51-500]
Olson, Steve - *Eruption: The Untold Story of Mount St. Helens*
  KR - Jan 1 2016 - pNA [501+]
Olson, Theodore B. - *Redeeming the Dream: The Case for Marriage Equality*
  G&L Rev W - v22 - i2 - March-April 2015 - p34(2) [501+]
  HLR - v128 - i4 - Feb 2015 - p1328(1) [1-50]
Olsson, Jan - *Hitchcock a la Carte*
  LJ - v140 - i3 - Feb 15 2015 - p97(1) [501+]
  Lon R Bks - v37 - i11 - June 4 2015 - p19(4) [501+]
  TLS - i5862 - August 7 2015 - p21(1) [501+]
Olsson, Karen - *All the Houses*
  BL - v112 - i1 - Sept 15 2015 - p26(1) [51-500]
  KR - Sept 1 2015 - pNA [51-500]
  LJ - v140 - i17 - Oct 15 2015 - p82(2) [501+]

Olstad, Tyra A. - *Zen of the Plains: Experiencing Wild Western Places*
  GR - v105 - i3 - July 2015 - p386(3) [501+]
Olvera, Enrique - *Mexico from the Inside Out*
  NYTBR - Dec 6 2015 - pNA(L) [501+]
Olwell, Victoria - *The Genius of Democracy: Fictions of Gender and Citizenship in the United States, 1860-1945*
  AL - v87 - i1 - March 2015 - p187-189 [501+]
Olzewski, Edward J. - *Parmigianino's 'Madonna of the Long Neck': A Grace Beyond the Reach of Art*
  Six Ct J - v46 - i3 - Fall 2015 - p673-674 [501+]
O'Mahony, Niamh - *Essays on the Poetry of Trevor Joyce*
  TLS - i5861 - July 31 2015 - p22(1) [501+]
O'Malley, Gregory E. - *Final Passages: The Intercolonial Slave Trade of British America, 1619-1807*
  AHR - v120 - i4 - Oct 2015 - p1449-1450 [501+]
  BHR - v89 - i2 - Summer 2015 - p362(3) [501+]
  JAH - v102 - i2 - Sept 2015 - p526-527 [501+]
  JSH - v81 - i4 - Nov 2015 - p938(2) [501+]
  NEQ - v88 - i3 - Sept 2015 - p542-545 [501+]
  W&M Q - v72 - i2 - April 2015 - p370-372 [501+]
O'Malley, John W. - *Catholic History for Today's Church: How Our Past Illuminates Our Present*
  LJ - v140 - i16 - Oct 1 2015 - p64(2) [501+]
  Saints or Devils Incarnate? Studies in Jesuit History
  Six Ct J - v46 - i1 - Spring 2015 - p147-148 [501+]
  Trent: What Happened at the Council
  Theol St - v76 - i1 - March 2015 - p173(3) [501+]
  JMH - v87 - i1 - March 2015 - p144(3) [501+]
O'Malley, Michelle - *Painting under Pressure: Fame, Reputation and Demand in Renaissance Florence*
  Ren Q - v68 - i3 - Fall 2015 - p1003-1004 [501+]
O'Malley, Padraig - *The Two-State Delusion: Israel and Palestine--a Tale of Two Narratives*
  BL - v111 - i14 - March 15 2015 - p42(1) [51-500]
  CC - v132 - i23 - Nov 11 2015 - p40(2) [51-500]
  KR - Feb 1 2015 - pNA [501+]
  LJ - v140 - i5 - March 15 2015 - p123(1) [51-500]
  The Two-State Delusion: Israel and Palestine -- a Tale of Two Narratives
  PW - v262 - i9 - March 2 2015 - p76(2) [51-500]
O'Malley, Seamus - *Making History New: Modernism and Historical Narrative*
  TLS - i5858 - July 10 2015 - p26(1) [501+]
O'Malley, Thomas - *Serpents in the Cold*
  NYTBR - Jan 18 2015 - p25(L) [501+]
O'Mara, Shane - *Why Torture Doesn't Work: The Neuroscience of Interrogation*
  KR - Sept 1 2015 - pNA [501+]
  LJ - v140 - i19 - Nov 15 2015 - p96(3) [51-500]
O'Mara, Tim - *Dead Red*
  RVBW - Sept 2015 - pNA [51-500]
Omdahl, Kristin - *Crochet So Lovely: 21 Carefree Lace Designs*
  LJ - v140 - i11 - June 15 2015 - p89(1) [51-500]
O'Meara, Kristi - *The Pattern Base: Over 550 Contemporary Textile and Surface Designs*
  PW - v262 - i18 - May 4 2015 - p112(3) [51-500]
O'Meara, Richard Michael - *Going Home for Apples and Other Stories*
  KR - Nov 1 2015 - pNA [501+]
Omenyo, Cephas N. - *Trajectories of Religion in Africa: Essays in Honour of John S. Pobee*
  IBMR - v39 - i2 - April 2015 - p102(1) [501+]
Omer, Atalia - *When Peace Is Not Enough: How the Israeli Peace Camp Thinks about Religion, Nationalism, and Justice*
  AJS - v120 - i5 - March 2015 - p1592(3) [501+]
Omo-Osagie, Solomon Iyobosa, II - *Commercial Poultry Production on Maryland's Lower Eastern Shore: The Role of African Americans, 1930s to 1990s*
  JSH - v81 - i1 - Feb 2015 - p234(2) [501+]
Omololu, C.J. - *The Third Twin*
  y CCB-B - v68 - i7 - March 2015 - p366(1) [51-500]
  y HB Guide - v26 - i2 - Fall 2015 - p134(1) [51-500]
O'Nan, Stewart - *West of Sunset (Read by Lane, Christopher). Audiobook Review*
  BL - v111 - i21 - July 1 2015 - p79(1) [501+]
  West of Sunset
  BooChiTr - Feb 7 2015 - p10(1) [501+]
  Ent W - i1346 - Jan 16 2015 - p66(1) [501+]
  NY - v91 - i7 - April 6 2015 - p81 [51-500]
  NYTBR - Feb 22 2015 - p15(L) [501+]
  SEP - v287 - i1 - Jan-Feb 2015 - p20(1) [501+]
Ondaatje, Griffin - *The Mosquito Brothers (Illus. by Salcedo, Erica)*
  c HB Guide - v26 - i2 - Fall 2015 - p69(1) [51-500]
  c PW - v262 - i16 - April 20 2015 - p77(1) [51-500]
  c SLJ - v61 - i5 - May 2015 - p96(3) [51-500]
  c Res Links - v21 - i1 - Oct 2015 - p19(2) [51-500]

Ondjaki - *Granma Nineteen and the Soviet's Secret*
  HNet - Sept 2015 - pNA [501+]
Ondra, Nancy J. - *Container Theme Gardens: 42 Combinations, Each Using 5 Perfectly Matched Plants (Illus. by Cardillo, Rob)*
  LJ - v140 - i16 - Oct 1 2015 - p100(1) [51-500]
  PW - v262 - i33 - August 17 2015 - p68(1) [51-500]
One - *One-Punch Man (Illus. by Murata, Yusuke)*
  y SLJ - v61 - i12 - Dec 2015 - p130(1) [51-500]
O'Neal, John c - *The Progressive Poetics of Confusion in the French Enlightenment*
  Eight-C St - v48 - i2 - Wntr 2015 - p239-245 [501+]
O'Neal, Shaquille - *Little Shaq (Illus. by Taylor, Theodore, III)*
  c KR - August 1 2015 - pNA [51-500]
  c PW - v262 - i30 - July 27 2015 - p69(1) [501+]
  c SLJ - v61 - i9 - Sept 2015 - p135(1) [51-500]
O'Neil, Patrick - *Gun, Needle, Spoon: A Memoir*
  ABR - v36 - i5 - July-August 2015 - p25(2) [51-500]
O'Neill, Ellie - *Reluctantly Charmed*
  y BL - v111 - i12 - Feb 15 2015 - p32(1) [51-500]
  KR - Jan 1 2015 - pNA [501+]
O'Neill, Gemma - *Monty's Magnificent Mane (Illus. by O'Neill, Gemma)*
  c CH Bwatch - April 2015 - pNA [51-500]
  c CH Bwatch - May 2015 - pNA [51-500]
O'Neill, Heather - *Daydreams of Angels*
  Mac - v128 - i16 - April 27 2015 - p54(2) [501+]
  Daydreams of Angels: Stories
  KR - August 1 2015 - pNA [51-500]
  PW - v262 - i33 - August 17 2015 - p46(2) [51-500]
  The Girl Who Was Saturday Night
  NYTBR - Dec 27 2015 - p24(L) [501+]
O'Neill, Joe - *Wrath of the Caid*
  y KR - March 15 2015 - pNA [501+]
O'Neill, Joseph - *The Dog*
  ABR - v36 - i5 - July-August 2015 - p10(2) [501+]
  NYRB - v62 - i5 - March 19 2015 - p6(2) [501+]
O'Neill, Josh - *Little Nemo's Big New Dreams*
  y BL - v111 - i22 - August 1 2015 - p48(1) [51-500]
  y KR - July 1 2015 - pNA [51-500]
  y SLJ - v61 - i9 - Sept 2015 - p174(1) [51-500]
O'Neill, Joshua - *Little Nemo: Dream another Dream*
  PW - v262 - i17 - April 27 2015 - p41(2) [501+]
  PW - v262 - i12 - March 23 2015 - p57(1) [51-500]
O'Neill, Kevin Lewis - *Secure the Soul: Christian Piety and Gang Prevention in Guatemala*
  Bks & Cult - v21 - i4 - July-August 2015 - p25(3) [501+]
  CC - v132 - i21 - Oct 14 2015 - p33(2) [501+]
O'Neill, Laura - *Van Leeuwen Artisan Ice Cream: Classic Flavors and New Favorites: 100 Recipes Made in Brooklyn (Illus. by Bensimon, Sidney)*
  LJ - v140 - i13 - August 1 2015 - p119(1) [51-500]
  Van Leeuwen Artisan Ice Cream: Classic Flavors and New Favorites: 100 Recipes Made in Brooklyn
  BL - v111 - i19-20 - June 1 2015 - p21(1) [51-500]
  PW - v262 - i20 - May 18 2015 - p79(1) [51-500]
O'Neill, Lindsay - *The Opened Letter: Networking in the Early Modern British World*
  JIH - v46 - i2 - Autumn 2015 - p274-275 [501+]
O'Neill, Louise - *Only Ever Yours*
  PW - v262 - i14 - April 6 2015 - p62(1) [51-500]
  y PW - v262 - i49 - Dec 2 2015 - p110(2) [51-500]
  y SLJ - v61 - i6 - June 2015 - p126(2) [51-500]
O'Neill, Michael - *Gangs of Shadow*
  TLS - i5853 - June 5 2015 - p25(1) [501+]
  The Oxford Handbook of Percy Bysshe Shelley
  MLR - v110 - i1 - Jan 2015 - p245-246 [501+]
O'Neill, Sarah - *Play in the Garden: Fun Projects for Kids to Enjoy Outdoors (Illus. by Unka, Vasanti)*
  c Magpies - v30 - i2 - May 2015 - pS8(1) [51-500]
O'Neill, Timothy - *The Irish Hand: Scribes and their Manuscripts from the Earliest Times*
  RVBW - April 2015 - pNA [51-500]
  TLS - i5862 - August 7 2015 - p27(1) [501+]
O'Neill, Tracy - *The Hopeful*
  KR - April 15 2015 - pNA [51-500]
  PW - v262 - i16 - April 20 2015 - p46(1) [51-500]
Onfray, Michel - *Appetites for Thought: Philosophers and Food*
  New Sci - v225 - i3014 - March 28 2015 - p48(1) [501+]
  TLS - i5842 - March 20 2015 - p27(1) [501+]
  A Hedonist Manifesto
  PW - v262 - i37 - Sept 14 2015 - p61(1) [51-500]

Oniga, Renato - *Latin: A Linguistic Introduction*
   Class R - v65 - i2 - Oct 2015 - p421-423 [501+]
Onishi, Yuichiro - *Transpacific Antiracism: Afro-Asian Solidarity in 20th-Century Black America, Japan, and Okinawa*
   PHR - v84 - i2 - May 2015 - p256(2) [501+]
Onsgard, Bethany - *Daily Life in U.S. History Series*
   c BL - v111 - i19-20 - June 1 2015 - p80(2) [501+]
   Life on the Frontier
   c HB Guide - v26 - i2 - Fall 2015 - p220(1) [501+]
Onstad, David W. - *Insect Resistance Management: Biology, Economics, and Prediction*
   QRB - v90 - i3 - Sept 2015 - p328(1) [501+]
Ontiveros, Randy J. - *In the Spirit of a New People: The Cultural Politics of the Chicano Movement*
   Aztlan - v40 - i1 - Spring 2015 - p247-251 [501+]
Onuora, Emy - *Pitch Black*
   NS - v144 - i5261 - May 7 2015 - p54(2) [501+]
Oortman, Annie - *'Til Death Do Us Part*
   PW - v262 - i23 - June 8 2015 - p46(1) [51-500]
Ophuijsen, J.M. van - *Protagoras of Abdera: the Man, His Measure*
   Class R - v65 - i2 - Oct 2015 - p372-374 [501+]
O'Porter, Dawn - *Goose*
   y KR - July 15 2015 - pNA [51-500]
   y SLJ - v61 - i8 - August 2015 - p108(2) [51-500]
   y VOYA - v38 - i4 - Oct 2015 - p58(1) [51-500]
   Paper Airplanes
   y HB Guide - v26 - i1 - Spring 2015 - p119(1) [51-500]
Opotowsky, Anne - *Nocturne (Illus. by Hoffmeister, Angie)*
   BL - v111 - i16 - April 15 2015 - p40(1) [51-500]
Oppegaard, David - *The Firebug of Balrog County*
   KR - June 1 2015 - pNA [51-500]
   y PW - v262 - i25 - June 22 2015 - p142(1) [51-500]
   y SLJ - v61 - i7 - July 2015 - p96(2) [51-500]
   y VOYA - v38 - i3 - August 2015 - p66(1) [51-500]
Oppel, Kenneth - *The Boundless (Read by Podehl, Nick). Audiobook Review*
   c BL - v111 - i16 - April 15 2015 - p64(1) [51-500]
   The Boundless
   c BL - v111 - i9-10 - Jan 1 2015 - pS4(8) [501+]
   y Sch Lib - v63 - i1 - Spring 2015 - p56(1) [51-500]
   The Nest (Illus. by Klassen, Jon)
   c BL - v111 - i21 - July 1 2015 - p75(1) [51-500]
   c HB - v91 - i5 - Sept-Oct 2015 - p113(2) [51-500]
   c KR - August 1 2015 - pNA [51-500]
   c NYTBR - Oct 11 2015 - p17(L) [501+]
   c PW - v262 - i29 - July 20 2015 - p194(1) [51-500]
   c PW - v262 - i49 - Dec 2 2015 - p68(1) [51-500]
   c Res Links - v21 - i1 - Oct 2015 - p39(1) [51-500]
   c SLJ - v61 - i8 - August 2015 - p89(1) [51-500]
Oppenheim, Shulamith - *Where Do I End and You Begin? (Illus. by Felix, Monique)*
   c KR - July 15 2015 - pNA [51-500]
   c PW - v262 - i49 - Dec 2 2015 - p42(1) [51-500]
   c SLJ - v61 - i9 - Sept 2015 - p126(2) [51-500]
Oppenheimer, Daniel - *Exit Right: The People Who Left the Left and Reshaped the American Century*
   KR - Nov 15 2015 - pNA [501+]
   LJ - v140 - i19 - Nov 15 2015 - p96(1) [51-500]
Oppenheimer, Jerry - *RFK, Jr.: Robert F. Kennedy, Jr. and the Dark Side of the Dream*
   LJ - v140 - i14 - Sept 1 2015 - p112(2) [51-500]
   PW - v262 - i30 - July 27 2015 - p56(1) [51-500]
Oppenheimer, Margaret A. - *The Remarkable Rise of Eliza Jumel: A Story of Marriage and Money in the Early Republic*
   BL - v112 - i4 - Oct 15 2015 - p15(1) [51-500]
   LJ - v140 - i17 - Oct 15 2015 - p96(1) [51-500]
   PW - v262 - i38 - Sept 21 2015 - p63(1) [51-500]
Oppenlander, Annette - *Escape from the Past: The Duke's Wrath*
   y CH Bwatch - Oct 2015 - pNA [51-500]
Oppo, Andrea - *Shapes of Apocalypse: Arts and Philosophy in Slavic Thought*
   Slav R - v74 - i2 - Summer 2015 - p419-420 [501+]
O'Quinn, Lynne Robertson - *I Am with You Always (Illus. by Duckworth, Jeffrey)*
   c CH Bwatch - Jan 2015 - pNA [51-500]
Oral, Feridun - *The Red Apple*
   c KR - August 1 2015 - pNA [51-500]
Oravecz, Johannes Miroslav - *God as Love: The Concept and Spiritual Aspect of Agape in Modern Russian Religious Thought*
   Theol St - v76 - i2 - June 2015 - p393(2) [501+]
Orbach, Hilary - *Choice*
   KR - Jan 1 2016 - pNA [501+]
   Transgressions and Other Stories
   KR - March 1 2015 - pNA [501+]

Orbeck-Nilssen, Constance - *I'm Right Here (Illus. by Duzakin, Akin)*
   c BL - v112 - i6 - Nov 15 2015 - p48(1) [501+]
   c KR - Sept 1 2015 - pNA [51-500]
Orchard, Eric - *Maddy Kettle: The Adventure of the Thimblewitch (Illus. by Orchard, Eric)*
   c CCB-B - v68 - i5 - Jan 2015 - p271(2) [51-500]
Orcutt, Chris - *One Hundred Miles from Manhattan*
   PW - v262 - i6 - Feb 9 2015 - p44(1) [51-500]
   A Truth Stranger Than Fiction
   PW - v262 - i28 - July 13 2015 - p48(1) [51-500]
"Ordo inversus": Formen und Funktionen einer Denkfigur um 1800. Jahrestagung des Zentrums fur Klassikforschung
   HNet - May 2015 - pNA [501+]
Ordonez, Juan Thomas - *Jornalero: Being a Day Laborer in the USA*
   TimHES - i2217 - August 20 2015 - p49-49 [501+]
Orecchio, Christa - *How to Conceive Naturally: And Have a Healthy Pregnancy after 30*
   LJ - v140 - i16 - Oct 1 2015 - p101(1) [51-500]
O'Reiley, Mary - *Kick Her Again: She's Irish*
   SPBW - March 2015 - pNA [51-500]
O'Reilly, Bill - *Bill O'Reilly's Legends and Lies: The Real West*
   Roundup M - v22 - i6 - August 2015 - p35(1) [501+]
   Hitler's Last Days: The Death of the Nazi Regime and the World's Most Notorious Dictator
   y VOYA - v38 - i4 - Oct 2015 - p84(1) [51-500]
   Killing Lincoln: The Shocking Assassination That Changed America
   Nat R - v67 - i22 - Dec 7 2015 - p8(1) [51-500]
   Killing Reagan: The Violent Assault That Changed a Presidency
   Nat R - v67 - i22 - Dec 7 2015 - p8(1) [51-500]
   The Last Days of Jesus: His Life and Times
   c HB Guide - v26 - i1 - Spring 2015 - p134(1) [51-500]
O'Reilly, Caitriona - *Geis*
   Sch Lib - v63 - i3 - Autumn 2015 - p177(2) [501+]
O'Reilly, James T. - *The Clergy Sex Abuse Crisis and the Legal Responses*
   AM - v212 - i15 - May 4 2015 - p35(3) [501+]
O'Reilly, Sean - *Watermark*
   TLS - i5845 - April 10 2015 - p31(1) [501+]
Oren, Michael B. - *Ally: My Journey across the American-Israeli Divide (Read by Oren, Michael B.). Audiobook Review*
   LJ - v140 - i16 - Oct 1 2015 - p45(1) [51-500]
   Ally: My Journey across the American-Israeli Divide
   Econ - v416 - i8946 - July 11 2015 - p74(US) [501+]
   NYTBR - July 12 2015 - p1(L) [501+]
Orenduff, J. Michael - *The Pot Thief Who Studied Georgia O'Keeffe: A Pot Thief Mystery*
   PW - v262 - i44 - Nov 2 2015 - p63(1) [51-500]
Orenstein, John M. - *Hummingbirds*
   Am Bio T - v77 - i6 - August 2015 - p469(2) [501+]
Orenstein, Peggy - *Girls and Sex: Navigating the Complicated New Landscape*
   KR - Jan 1 2016 - pNA [501+]
   LJ - v140 - i20 - Dec 1 2015 - p122(1) [51-500]
   PW - v262 - i47 - Nov 23 2015 - p58(1) [51-500]
Oreskes, Naomi - *The Collapse of Western Civilization: A View from the Future*
   CS - v44 - i3 - May 2015 - p314-321 [501+]
Orfalea, Gregory - *Journey to the Sun: Junipero Serra's Dream and the Founding of California*
   RAH - v43 - i3 - Sept 2015 - p447-455 [501+]
Orgain, Diana - *Yappy Hour*
   y BL - v112 - i6 - Nov 15 2015 - p30(1) [51-500]
   KR - Sept 1 2015 - pNA [51-500]
   PW - v262 - i39 - Sept 28 2015 - p68(1) [51-500]
The Organization of Korean Historians - *Everyday Life in Joseon-Era Korea: Economy and Society*
   JAS - v74 - i3 - August 2015 - p768-770 [501+]
Orgel, Stephen - *The Reader in the Book*
   TimHES - i2226 - Oct 22 2015 - p47(1) [501+]
   Spectacular Performances: Essays on Theatre, Imagery, Books, and Selves in Early Modern England
   Ren Q - v68 - i2 - Summer 2015 - p772-773 [501+]
Oria, Shelly - *New York 1, Tel Aviv 0*
   NYTBR - Feb 1 2015 - p26(L) [501+]
Orians, Gordon H. - *Snakes, Sunrises, and Shakespeare: How Evolution Shapes Our Loves and Fears*
   QRB - v90 - i3 - Sept 2015 - p335(1) [501+]

Originator - *Endless Spanish/Infinity Espanol. E-book Review*
   SLJ - v61 - i10 - Oct 2015 - p58(1) [501+]
Oriola, Temitope B. - *Criminal Resistance?: The Politics of Kidnapping Oil Workers*
   CS - v44 - i3 - May 2015 - p391-392 [501+]
Orion, Tao - *Beyond the War on Invasive Species: A Permaculture Approach to Ecosystem Restoration*
   LJ - v140 - i13 - August 1 2015 - p121(2) [51-500]
Orlandi, Nico - *The Innocent Eye: Why Vision Is Not a Cognitive Process*
   TLS - i5837 - Feb 13 2015 - p24(1) [501+]
Orlando, Richard J. - *Legacy: The Hidden Keys to Optimizing Your Family Wealth Decisions*
   KR - May 15 2015 - pNA [501+]
Orlin, Lena Cowen - *Othello: The State of Play*
   Ren Q - v68 - i3 - Fall 2015 - p1148-1149 [501+]
Orloff, Karen Kaufman - *I Wanna Go Home (Illus. by Catrow, David)*
   c HB Guide - v26 - i1 - Spring 2015 - p41(1) [51-500]
Ormand, Kate - *The Wanderers*
   y KR - July 15 2015 - pNA [51-500]
   y SLJ - v61 - i10 - Oct 2015 - p105(2) [51-500]
   y VOYA - v38 - i4 - Oct 2015 - p75(2) [51-500]
Orme, Nicholas - *The Church in Devon, 400-1560*
   HER - v130 - i543 - April 2015 - p428(2) [501+]
   Fleas, Flies, and Friars: Children's Poetry from the Middle Ages
   Specu - v90 - i3 - July 2015 - p844-845 [501+]
   The Minor Clergy of Exeter Cathedral: Biographies, 1250-1548
   Specu - v90 - i3 - July 2015 - p845-846 [501+]
   Specu - v90 - i3 - July 2015 - p845-846 [501+]
Ormerod, Jan - *The Baby Swap (Illus. by Joyner, Andrew)*
   c CCB-B - v68 - i9 - May 2015 - p461(1) [51-500]
   c HB Guide - v26 - i2 - Fall 2015 - p47(1) [51-500]
   c NYTBR - March 15 2015 - p18(L) [501+]
   c NYTBR - March 15 2015 - p18(L) [501+]
   c PW - v262 - i49 - Dec 2 2015 - p26(1) [51-500]
   c SLJ - v61 - i2 - Feb 2015 - p75(1) [51-500]
Ormond, Richard - *Sargent: Portraits of Artists and Friends*
   LJ - v140 - i14 - Sept 1 2015 - p99(3) [51-500]
Ormsbee, K.E. - *The Water and the Wild*
   c HB Guide - v26 - i2 - Fall 2015 - p96(1) [51-500]
   c KR - Feb 15 2015 - pNA [51-500]
   c PW - v262 - i6 - Feb 9 2015 - p68(1) [51-500]
   c SLJ - v61 - i7 - July 2015 - p81(1) [51-500]
   y VOYA - v38 - i4 - April 2015 - p82(1) [51-500]
Orna, Mary Virginia - *The Chemical History of Color*
   J Chem Ed - v92 - i10 - Oct 2015 - p1600-1601 [501+]
Ornbratt, Susan - *The Particular Appeal of Gillian Pugsley*
   KR - Feb 15 2015 - pNA [501+]
Ornellas, Kevin De - *The Horse in Early Modern English Culture: Bridled, Curbed, and Tamed*
   Ren Q - v68 - i3 - Fall 2015 - p1032-1033 [501+]
O'Rorke, Torena - *The Killer of Cancer Rising*
   KR - Feb 15 2015 - pNA [501+]
Orosz, Attila - *The Beginner's Book of Meditation*
   SPBW - May 2015 - pNA [501+]
O'Rourke, Erica - *Dissonance*
   y HB Guide - v26 - i1 - Spring 2015 - p119(1) [51-500]
   Resonance
   y KR - May 15 2015 - pNA [51-500]
   y SLJ - v61 - i6 - June 2015 - p128(1) [51-500]
   y VOYA - v38 - i3 - August 2015 - p82(1) [51-500]
O'Rourke, P.J. - *Thrown under the Omnibus: A Reader*
   NYTBR - Dec 6 2015 - p58(L) [501+]
O'Rourke, Tim - *Flashes*
   y BL - v112 - i5 - Nov 1 2015 - p54(1) [51-500]
   y KR - August 1 2015 - pNA [51-500]
   y SLJ - v61 - i10 - Oct 2015 - p116(1) [51-500]
   y VOYA - v38 - i4 - Oct 2015 - p76(1) [51-500]
Orozco, Lourdes - *Theater & Animals*
   Theat J - v67 - i1 - March 2015 - p162-163 [501+]
   Theat J - v67 - i1 - March 2015 - p162-163 [501+]
Orr, Cynthia - *Crash Course in Readers' Advisory*
   SLJ - v61 - i6 - June 2015 - p147(1) [51-500]
   Teach Lib - v42 - i3 - Feb 2015 - p41(2) [51-500]
   VOYA - v38 - i3 - August 2015 - p93(1) [51-500]
Orr, David - *The Road Not Taken: Finding America in the Poem Everyone Loves and Almost Everyone Gets Wrong*
   CSM - August 17 2015 - pNA [501+]
   KR - May 1 2015 - pNA [501+]
   LJ - v140 - i9 - May 15 2015 - p84(1) [51-500]
   NYTBR - August 23 2015 - p15(L) [501+]
   PW - v262 - i16 - April 20 2015 - p64(1) [51-500]

Orr, Peter - *Christ Absent and Present: A Study in Pauline Christology*
    Theol St - v76 - i2 - June 2015 - p349(2) [501+]

Orr, Sally - *When a Rake Falls*
    PW - v262 - i9 - March 2 2015 - p71(1) [51-500]

Orr, Stephen - *One Boy Missing*
    KR - May 15 2015 - pNA [51-500]

Orr, Tamar B. - *I See Falling Stars*
    BL - v111 - i14 - March 15 2015 - p63(1) [51-500]

Orr, Tamra - *Markus "Notch" Persson*
    c SLJ - v61 - i10 - Oct 2015 - p125(1) [51-500]
    My Friend Is Buddhist
    c SLJ - v61 - i8 - August 2015 - p126(1) [51-500]

Orszag-Land, Thomas - *Survivors: Hungarian Jewish Poets of the Holocaust*
    WLT - v89 - i5 - Sept-Oct 2015 - p77(1) [51-500]

Ortabasi, Melek - *The Undiscovered Country: Text, Translation, and Modernity in the Work of Yanagita Kunio*
    HNet - Sept 2015 - pNA [501+]

Ortberg, John - *All the Places to Go: How Will You Know?*
    Bwatch - June 2015 - pNA [51-500]

Ortberg, Mallory - *Texts from Jane Eyre: And Other Conversations with Your Favorite Literary Characters (Read by Landon, Amy). Audiobook Review*
    LJ - v140 - i7 - April 15 2015 - p49(1) [51-500]

Ortega, Brenda - *Fault Lines*
    y CH Bwatch - June 2015 - pNA [51-500]

Orthodoxa Confessio? Konfessionsbildung, Konfessionalisierung und ihre Folgen in der östlichen Christenheit Europas
    HNet - April 2015 - pNA [501+]

Ortiz, Ana Patuieia - *Authentic Portuguese Cooking*
    PW - v262 - i42 - Oct 19 2015 - p70(1) [51-500]

Ortiz Cuadra, Cruz Miguel - *Eating Puerto Rico: A History of Food, Culture, and Identity*
    HAHR - v95 - i2 - May 2015 - p343-344 [501+]
    RAH - v43 - i2 - June 2015 - p390-395 [501+]

Ortiz, Joseph M. - *Broken Harmony: Shakespeare and the Politics of Music*
    Shakes Q - v66 - i1 - Spring 2015 - p99-101 [501+]
    Shakespeare and the Culture of Romanticism
    Theat J - v67 - i3 - Oct 2015 - p573-575 [501+]

Ortiz, Raquel M. - *Sofi and the Magic, Musical Mural/Sofi y el magico musical (Illus. by Dominguez, Maria)*
    c CH Bwatch - May 2015 - pNA [51-500]
    c HB Guide - v26 - i2 - Fall 2015 - p47(1) [51-500]
    c KR - March 15 2015 - pNA [51-500]

Ortlieb, Gilles - *Guide Bleu*
    TLS - i5868 - Sept 18 2015 - p28(1) [501+]

Ortman, Scott G. - *Winds from the North: Tewa Origins and Historical Anthropology*
    Am Ant - v80 - i1 - Jan 2015 - p206(2) [501+]

Ortner, Kathleen - *Stealing Shiva*
    KR - July 1 2015 - pNA [501+]

Ortner, Sherry B. - *Not Hollywood: Independent Film at the Twilight of the American Dream*
    J Am St - v49 - i1 - Feb 2015 - p222-223 [501+]

Orton, D.L. - *Crossing in Time: The First Disaster*
    PW - v262 - i46 - Nov 16 2015 - p60(1) [51-500]

Orullian, Peter - *Trial of Intentions*
    BL - v111 - i18 - May 15 2015 - p40(1) [51-500]
    KR - March 15 2015 - pNA [51-500]
    The Unremembered
    KR - Feb 1 2015 - pNA [51-500]

Orvell, Miles - *Rethinking the American City: An International Dialogue*
    JAH - v102 - i1 - June 2015 - p210-211 [501+]
    T&C - v56 - i4 - Oct 2015 - p1005-1006 [501+]

Orvis, Linda - *Rough Cut*
    KR - Nov 1 2015 - pNA [501+]

Orwell, George - *Homage to Catalonia*
    Nat R - v67 - i21 - Nov 19 2015 - p79(2) [51-500]
    Nineteen Eighty-Four
    Obs - Jan 18 2015 - p39 [501+]
    Obs - Jan 18 2015 - p39 [501+]
    Seeing Things as They Are: Selected Journalism and Other Writings
    TimHES - i2198 - April 9 2015 - p49(1) [501+]

O'Ryan, Ray - *The Annoying Crush (Illus. by Kraft, Jason)*
    c HB Guide - v26 - i2 - Fall 2015 - p70(1) [51-500]
    Drake Makes a Splash (Illus. by Jack, Colin)
    c HB Guide - v26 - i1 - Spring 2015 - p63(1) [51-500]
    Return to Earth! (Illus. by Kraft, Jason)
    c HB Guide - v26 - i2 - Fall 2015 - p70(1) [51-500]

Orzel, Chad - *Eureka! Discovering Your Inner Scientist*
    New Sci - v225 - i3003 - Jan 10 2015 - p42(2) [501+]

Osborn, Matthew Warner - *Rum Maniacs: Alcoholic Insanity in the Early American Republic*
    AHR - v120 - i1 - Feb 2015 - p238(1) [501+]
    JAH - v101 - i4 - March 2015 - p1292-1293 [501+]

Osborne, Lawrence - *The Ballad of a Small Player*
    NYTBR - March 1 2015 - p28(L) [501+]
    Hunters in the Dark
    BL - v112 - i5 - Nov 1 2015 - p31(1) [51-500]
    KR - Sept 15 2015 - pNA [51-500]
    LJ - v140 - i20 - Dec 1 2015 - p94(3) [51-500]
    NS - v144 - i5263 - May 22 2015 - p55(1) [501+]
    PW - v262 - i47 - Nov 23 2015 - p46(2) [51-500]

Osborne, Mary A. - *Alchemy's Daughter*
    y KR - March 1 2015 - pNA [51-500]
    SLJ - v61 - i4 - April 2015 - p168(2) [51-500]
    y VOYA - v38 - i2 - June 2015 - p67(1) [51-500]

Osborne, Mary Pope - *Danger in the Darkest Hour (Read by Osborne, Mary Pope). Audiobook Review*
    SLJ - v61 - i4 - April 2015 - p61(1) [51-500]
    Danger in the Darkest Hour: Super Edition (Illus. by Murdocca, Sal)
    c HB Guide - v26 - i2 - Fall 2015 - p96(1) [51-500]
    Magic Tree House Survival Guide (Illus. by Murdocca, Sal)
    c HB Guide - v26 - i1 - Spring 2015 - p130(1) [51-500]
    Soccer: A Nonfiction Companion to Soccer on Sunday (Illus. by Murdocca, Sal)
    c HB Guide - v26 - i1 - Spring 2015 - p184(1) [51-500]

Osborne, Michael A. - *The Emergence of Tropical Medicine in France*
    AHR - v120 - i3 - June 2015 - p1126-1127 [501+]

Osborne, Myles - *The Life and Times of General China: Mau Mau and the End of Empire in Kenya*
    IJAHS - v48 - i1 - Wntr 2015 - p152-154 [501+]

Osborne, Peter - *No Grain, No Pain: A 30-Day Diet for Eliminating the Root Cause of Chronic Pain*
    PW - v262 - i46 - Nov 16 2015 - p73(1) [51-500]

Osborne, Steve - *The Job: True Tales from the Life of a New York City Cop (Read by Osborne, Steve). Audiobook Review*
    LJ - v140 - i13 - August 1 2015 - p49(1) [51-500]
    PW - v262 - i26 - June 29 2015 - p65(1) [51-500]
    The Job: True Tales from the Life of a New York City Cop
    KR - Feb 1 2015 - pNA [51-500]
    NYTBR - May 10 2015 - p38(L) [501+]
    NY - v91 - i15 - June 1 2015 - p75 [51-500]
    BL - v111 - i13 - March 1 2015 - p7(1) [51-500]
    PW - v262 - i12 - March 23 2015 - p68(1) [51-500]

Osborne, William - *Winter's Bullet*
    y BL - v112 - i6 - Nov 15 2015 - p52(1) [51-500]
    y KR - Oct 1 2015 - pNA [51-500]
    y Sch Lib - v63 - i1 - Spring 2015 - p41(1) [51-500]
    y SLJ - v61 - i12 - Dec 2015 - p106(1) [51-500]

Osborough, W.N. - *The Law School of University College Dublin: A History*
    Law Q Rev - v131 - July 2015 - p505-507 [501+]

Osburn, Katherine M.B. - *Choctaw Resurgence in Mississippi: Race, Class, and Nation Building in the Jim Crow South, 1830-1977*
    JAH - v102 - i1 - June 2015 - p259-260 [501+]
    JSH - v81 - i4 - Nov 2015 - p1025(2) [501+]

Osburn, Terri - *His First and Last*
    PW - v262 - i11 - March 16 2015 - p71(1) [51-500]

Oschema, Klaus - *Bilder von Europa im Mittelalter*
    HNet - August 2015 - pNA [501+]

Oselin, Sharon S. - *Leaving Prostitution: Getting Out and Staying Out of Sex Work*
    AJS - v120 - i6 - May 2015 - p1866(3) [501+]
    CrimJR - v40 - i1 - March 2015 - p104-105 [501+]
    CS - v44 - i6 - Nov 2015 - p834-835 [501+]

Oseman, Alice - *Solitaire*
    BL - v111 - i13 - March 1 2015 - p59(2) [51-500]
    y PW - v262 - i3 - Jan 19 2015 - p85(1) [51-500]
    y VOYA - v38 - i1 - April 2015 - p67(1) [51-500]
    y CCB-B - v68 - i9 - May 2015 - p461(2) [51-500]
    y HB Guide - v26 - i2 - Fall 2015 - p134(1) [51-500]
    y KR - Jan 15 2015 - pNA [51-500]

Osentowski, Jerome - *The Forest Garden Greenhouse: How to Design and Manage an Indoor Permaculture Oasis*
    BL - v112 - i4 - Oct 15 2015 - p11(1) [51-500]
    PW - v262 - i36 - Sept 7 2015 - p63(1) [51-500]

Oser, Stefan - *Easy Studies for Acoustic and Electric Guitar*
    Am MT - v65 - i1 - August-Sept 2015 - p62(2) [501+]

Osgood, Kenneth - *Winning While Losing: Civil Rights, the Conservative Movement, and the Presidency from Nixon to Obama*
    AHR - v120 - i1 - Feb 2015 - p292-293 [501+]
    JSH - v81 - i2 - May 2015 - p527(3) [501+]

O'Shaughnessy, Tam - *Sally Ride: A Photobiography of America's Pioneering Woman in Space*
    c BL - v112 - i7 - Dec 1 2015 - p50(1) [51-500]

O'Shea, Joseph - *Gap Year: How Delaying College Changes People in Ways the World Needs*
    J Hi E - v86 - i3 - May-June 2015 - p484(4) [501+]

Oskarsson, Bardur - *The Flat Rabbit (Illus. by Oskarsson, Bardur)*
    c BL - v112 - i6 - Nov 15 2015 - p48(1) [51-500]
    c HB Guide - v26 - i1 - Spring 2015 - p41(1) [51-500]

Osle, Janessa - *Learn to Draw Cats and Kittens: Step-by-Step Instructions for More Than 25 Favorite Feline Friends (Illus. by Cuddy, Robin)*
    c SLJ - v61 - i8 - August 2015 - p120(1) [51-500]

Osmani, Rashid - *Pause and Ponder*
    KR - April 15 2015 - pNA [501+]

Osnos, Evan - *Age of Ambition: Chasing Fortune, Truth, and Faith in the New China*
    NYTBR - June 14 2015 - p24(L) [501+]

Osoegawa, Taku - *Syria and Lebanon: International Relations and Diplomacy in the Middle East*
    MEQ - v22 - i1 - Wntr 2015 - pNA [501+]

Osseo-Asare, Abena Dove - *Bitter Roots: The Search for Healing Plants in Africa*
    IJAHS - v48 - i1 - Wntr 2015 - p162-163 [501+]
    MAQ - v29 - i1 - March 2015 - pB43-B45 [501+]
    QRB - v90 - i2 - June 2015 - p231(2) [501+]

Ossip, Kathleen - *The Do-Over*
    NYTBR - April 26 2015 - p18(L) [501+]

Ossman, Susan - *Moving Matters: Paths of Serial Migration*
    ERS - v38 - i3 - March 2015 - p479(3) [501+]

Ost, David - *The Defeat of Solidarity: Anger and Politics in Postcommunist Europe*
    Nation - v300 - i1 - Jan 5 2015 - p27(10) [501+]

Ostashevsky, Eugene - *Oberiu: An Anthology of Russian Absurdism*
    NYRB - v62 - i8 - May 7 2015 - p36(3) [501+]

Osteen, Joel - *The Power of I Am: Two Words That Will Change Your Life Today*
    PW - v262 - i32 - August 10 2015 - p55(1) [51-500]

Oster, Carolin - *Die Farben hofischer Korper: Farbattribuierung und hofische Identitat in mittelhochdeutschen Artus- und Tristanromane*
    MLR - v110 - i3 - July 2015 - p889-892 [501+]
    Sakramentale Reprasentation: Substanz, Zeichen und Prasenz in der fruhen Neuzeit
    MLR - v110 - i3 - July 2015 - p892-893 [501+]

Osterhage, Jeff - *Parker Strip*
    KR - Dec 15 2015 - pNA [501+]

Osterhammel, Jurgen - *The Transformation of the World: A Global History of the Nineteenth Century*
    AHR - v120 - i4 - Oct 2015 - p1440-1441 [501+]
    JAH - v101 - i4 - March 2015 - p1262-1263 [501+]
    NYRB - v62 - i8 - May 7 2015 - p54(4) [501+]
    PHR - v84 - i4 - Nov 2015 - p571(572) [501+]

Osteuropaexperten und Politik im 20. Jahrhundert
    HNet - July 2015 - pNA [501+]

Ostler, Nicholas - *Passwords to Paradise*
    KR - Dec 15 2015 - pNA [501+]

Ostler, Rosemarie - *Founding Grammars: How Early America's War over Words Shaped Today's Language*
    BL - v111 - i15 - April 1 2015 - p8(1) [51-500]
    KR - Feb 1 2015 - pNA [501+]
    LJ - v140 - i9 - May 15 2015 - p84(1) [51-500]
    PW - v262 - i6 - Feb 9 2015 - p53(1) [51-500]

Ostlund, Lori - *After the Parade*
    BL - v111 - i21 - July 1 2015 - p27(1) [51-500]
    KR - July 15 2015 - pNA [51-500]
    LJ - v140 - i12 - July 1 2015 - p80(1) [51-500]
    NYTBR - Nov 1 2015 - p20(L) [501+]
    PW - v262 - i27 - July 6 2015 - p43(1) [51-500]
    The Bigness of the World
    KR - Nov 15 2015 - pNA [51-500]

Ostlundh, Hakan - *The Intruder*
    KR - June 15 2015 - pNA [51-500]
    PW - v262 - i23 - June 8 2015 - p37(1) [51-500]

Ostow, Micol - *Amity*
   y HB Guide - v26 - i1 - Spring 2015 - p119(1) [51-500]
The Devil and Winnie Flynn (Illus. by Ostow, David)
   y BL - v112 - i4 - Oct 15 2015 - p45(1) [51-500]
   y KR - Sept 15 2015 - pNA [51-500]
   y PW - v262 - i33 - August 17 2015 - p73(1) [51-500]
   y SLJ - v61 - i10 - Oct 2015 - p116(1) [51-500]
Louise Trapeze Did Not Lose the Juggling Chickens
   c KR - Nov 15 2015 - pNA [51-500]
Louise Trapeze Is Totally 100 Percent Fearless (Illus. by Barrager, Brigette)
   c BL - v111 - i21 - July 1 2015 - p74(1) [51-500]
   c CCB-B - v69 - i2 - Oct 2015 - p106(2) [51-500]
   c KR - April 15 2015 - pNA [51-500]
   c PW - v262 - i24 - June 15 2015 - p85(1) [501+]
   c SLJ - v61 - i5 - May 2015 - p97(1) [51-500]
Ostrander, Susan A. - *Citizenship and Governance in a Changing City: Somerville, MA*
   CS - v44 - i3 - May 2015 - p392-394 [501+]
Ostrom, Lizzie - *Perfume: Century of Scents*
   Spec - v329 - i9772 - Dec 12 2015 - p86(1) [501+]
Ostrovski, Emil - *Away We Go*
   y KR - Nov 15 2015 - pNA [51-500]
   y SLJ - v61 - i12 - Dec 2015 - p126(1) [51-500]
O'Sullivan, Brian - *Butcher a Hog*
   KR - Jan 1 2015 - pNA [51-500]
O'Sullivan, Helen - *Language Learner Narrative: An Exploration of 'Mundigkeit' in Intercultural Literature*
   MLR - v110 - i3 - July 2015 - p908-909 [501+]
O'Sullivan, Joanne - *Migration Nation: Animals on the Go from Coast to Coast*
   c BL - v111 - i19-20 - June 1 2015 - p79(1) [51-500]
   c HB Guide - v26 - i2 - Fall 2015 - p171(1) [51-500]
   c PW - v262 - i18 - May 4 2015 - p120(1) [51-500]
   c SLJ - v61 - i5 - May 2015 - p141(1) [51-500]
O'Sullivan, Joanne: Migration Nation.(Children's review)(Brief article)(Book review) - *Migration Nation: Animals on the Go from Coast to Coast*
   c KR - March 15 2015 - pNA [51-500]
O'Sullivan, Kathryn - *Neighing with Fire*
   BL - v111 - i6 - April 15 2015 - p29(1) [51-500]
   KR - March 1 2015 - pNA [51-500]
   PW - v262 - i10 - March 9 2015 - p54(2) [51-500]
O'Sullivan, Kevin - *Ireland, Africa, and the End of Empire: Small State Identity in the Cold War, 1955-75*
   AHR - v120 - i3 - June 2015 - p1107-1108 [501+]
Oswald, Nancy - *Edward Wynkoop: Soldier and Indian Agent*
   y Roundup M - v22 - i5 - June 2015 - p37(1) [501+]
   y Roundup M - v22 - i6 - August 2015 - p25(1) [501+]
Oswalt, Patton - *Silver Screen Fiend: Learning about Life from an Addiction to Film (Read by Oswalt, Patton). Audiobook Review*
   LJ - v140 - i8 - May 1 2015 - p43(1) [51-500]
   PW - v262 - i12 - March 23 2015 - p72(1) [51-500]
Silver Screen Fiend: Learning about Life from an Addiction to Film
   Ent W - i1347 - Jan 23 2015 - p64(1) [501+]
   NYTBR - Jan 25 2015 - p11(L) [501+]
   NYTBR - Dec 13 2015 - p44(L) [501+]
Oswell, David - *The Agency of Children: From Family to Global Human Rights*
   CS - v44 - i3 - May 2015 - p394-396 [501+]
Otfinoski, Steven - *Air Travel: Science, Technology, Engineering*
   y BL - v111 - i14 - March 15 2015 - p63(1) [51-500]
   y VOYA - v38 - i5 - Dec 2015 - p78(2) [51-500]
Day of Infamy: The Story of the Attack on Pearl Harbor
   y SLJ - v61 - i9 - Sept 2015 - p151(4) [51-500]
Patriots and Redcoats: Stories of American Revolutionary War Leaders
   c HB Guide - v26 - i2 - Fall 2015 - p221(1) [51-500]
The Story of Juneteenth: An Interactive History Adventure
   c HB Guide - v26 - i2 - Fall 2015 - p221(1) [51-500]
Yankees and Rebels: Stories of the U.S. Civil War Leaders
   c HB Guide - v26 - i2 - Fall 2015 - p219(1) [51-500]
Otis, Bernard S. - *How to Prepare for Old Age: Without Taking the Fun Out of Life*
   SPBW - Oct 2015 - pNA [51-500]
Otis, Ginger Adams - *Firefight: The Century-Long Battle to Integrate New York's Bravest*
   LJ - v140 - i8 - May 1 2015 - p82(1) [501+]
Otmazgin, Nissim Kadosh - *Regionalizing Culture: The Political Economy of Japanese Popular Culture in Asia*
   Pac A - v88 - i2 - June 2015 - p324 [501+]

Otomo, Yuko - *Study & Other Poems of Art*
   ABR - v36 - i4 - May-June 2015 - p14(2) [501+]
O'Toole, Christopher - *Bees: A Natural History*
   QRB - v90 - i3 - Sept 2015 - p349(2) [501+]
O'Toole, Emer - *Girls Will Be Girls: Dressing Up, Playing Parts and Daring to Act Differently*
   Spec - v327 - i9730 - Feb 21 2015 - p45(2) [501+]
O'Toole, Fintan - *A History of Ireland in 100 Objects*
   LJ - v140 - i9 - May 15 2015 - p94(2) [501+]
O'Toole, Tina - *The Irish New Woman*
   ILS - v35 - i1 - Fall 2015 - p5(2) [501+]
Otoshi, Kathryn - *Beautiful Hands (Illus. by Otoshi, Kathryn)*
   c BL - v111 - i21 - July 1 2015 - p61(1) [51-500]
   c PW - v262 - i26 - June 29 2015 - p66(1) [51-500]
   c SLJ - v61 - i7 - July 2015 - p67(1) [51-500]
Two (Illus. by Otoshi, Kathryn)
   c BL - v111 - i9-10 - Jan 1 2015 - pS4(8) [51-500]
Otroshenko, Vladislav - *Addendum to a Photo Album*
   KR - Jan 1 2015 - pNA [501+]
   TLS - i5870 - Oct 2 2015 - p26(1) [501+]
   WLT - v89 - i6 - Nov-Dec 2015 - p77(1) [51-500]
Ott, Frank-Thomas - *Die Zweite Philippica als Flugschrift in der Spaten Republik*
   HNet - Jan 2015 - pNA [501+]
Ott, John - *Manufacturing the Modern Patron in Victorian California: Cultural Philanthropy, Industrial Capital, and Social Authority*
   WHQ - v46 - i1 - Spring 2015 - p88-89 [501+]
Ottati, Douglas F. - *Theology for Liberal Protestants: God the Creator*
   Intpr - v69 - i1 - Jan 2015 - p88(3) [501+]
Ottaviano, Patricia - *Girl World: How to Ditch the Drama and Find Your Inner Amazing*
   y BL - v112 - i3 - Oct 1 2015 - p37(1) [51-500]
   c PW - v262 - i25 - June 22 2015 - p141(1) [501+]
   y SLJ - v61 - i9 - Sept 2015 - p189(1) [51-500]
Otte, T.G. - *The Foreign Office Mind: The Making of British Foreign Policy, 1865-1914*
   VS - v57 - i2 - Wntr 2015 - p291(2) [501+]
An Historian in Peace and War: The Diaries of Harold Temperley
   J Mil H - v79 - i1 - Jan 2015 - p244-245 [501+]
Ottenheym, Koen - *Public Buildings in Early Modern Europe*
   Six Ct J - v46 - i1 - Spring 2015 - p143-145 [501+]
Otto, Eric C. - *Green Speculations: Science Fiction and Transformative Environmentalism*
   AL - v87 - i2 - June 2015 - p413-415 [501+]
Otto, Kate - *Everyday Ambassador*
   y KR - March 15 2015 - pNA [51-500]
Otto, Shawn Lawrence - *Sins of Our Fathers*
   RVBW - May 2015 - pNA [51-500]
Ottolenghi, Yotam - *NOPI: The Cookbook (Illus. by Lovekin, Jonathan)*
   BL - v112 - i4 - Oct 15 2015 - p12(1) [51-500]
   LJ - v140 - i15 - Sept 15 2015 - p100(1) [51-500]
   NYTBR - Dec 6 2015 - p20(L) [501+]
   NYTBR - Dec 6 2015 - p20(L) [501+]
   PW - v262 - i38 - Sept 21 2015 - p68(1) [51-500]
Plenty More: Vibrant Vegetable Cooking from London's Ottolenghi
   Ent W - i1346 - Jan 16 2015 - p67(1) [501+]
Otwell, Margaret - *Schirmer Performance Editions: Burgmuller: 25 Progressive Studies, Opus 100*
   Am MT - v65 - i1 - August-Sept 2015 - p60(2) [501+]
Schirmer Performance Editions: Kabalevsky: 24 Pieces for Children, Opus 39
   Am MT - v65 - i1 - August-Sept 2015 - p61(2) [501+]
Oudolf, Piet - *Hummelo: A Journey through a Plantsman's Life*
   NYTBR - May 31 2015 - p36(L) [501+]
Ould, Chris - *The Blood Strand*
   KR - Dec 15 2015 - pNA [51-500]
   PW - v262 - i52 - Dec 21 2015 - p132(2) [51-500]
Oulton, Harry - *A Pig Called Heather*
   c CH Bwatch - July 2015 - pNA [51-500]
   c HB Guide - v26 - i2 - Fall 2015 - p96(1) [51-500]
   c SLJ - v61 - i3 - March 2015 - p141(2) [51-500]
Oumraou, Leny - *Pourquoi les mathematiques sont-elles difficiles?*
   Dialogue - v54 - i2 - June 2015 - p389-392 [501+]
Oust, Gail - *Cinnamon Toasted*
   BL - v112 - i6 - Nov 15 2015 - p24(1) [51-500]
   KR - Oct 15 2015 - pNA [51-500]
   PW - v262 - i42 - Oct 19 2015 - p58(1) [51-500]
Ouyang, Wen-chin - *The Arabian Nights: An Anthology*
   TLS - i5846 - April 17 2015 - p12(2) [501+]

Overdeck, Laura - *Bedtime Math 2: This Time It's Personal (Illus. by Paillot, Jim)*
   c HB Guide - v26 - i1 - Spring 2015 - p149(1) [51-500]
Bedtime Math: The Truth Comes Out (Illus. by Paillot, Jim)
   c HB Guide - v26 - i2 - Fall 2015 - p164(1) [51-500]
Overman, Steven J. - *The Protestant Ethic and Spirit of Sport: How Calvinism and Capitalism Shaped America's Games*
   JR - Jan 2015 - p155(3) [501+]
Overton, Iain - *Gun Baby Gun: A Bloody Journey into the World of the Gun*
   Spec - v327 - i9739 - April 25 2015 - p39(2) [501+]
Overton, Margaret - *Hope for a Cool Pillow*
   KR - Nov 15 2015 - pNA [501+]
Overturf, Brenda J. - *Vocabularians: Integrated Word Study in the Middle Grades*
   Bwatch - Sept 2015 - pNA [51-500]
Overy, Richard - *The Bombers and the Bombed: Allied Air War over Europe, 1940-1945*
   JAH - v102 - i1 - June 2015 - p285-286 [501+]
   NYTBR - Oct 25 2015 - p32(L) [501+]
Der Bombenkrieg: Europa 1939-1945
   HNet - August 2015 - pNA [501+]
A History of War in 100 Battles
   J Mil H - v79 - i2 - April 2015 - p475(1) [501+]
The Oxford Illustrated History of World War Two
   BL - v111 - i22 - August 1 2015 - p8(1) [51-500]
   KR - March 15 2015 - pNA [501+]
Ovid - *The Offense of Love: Ars Amatoria, Remedia Amoris and Tristia*
   Sew R - v123 - i2 - Spring 2015 - p350-357 [501+]
   TLS - i5848 - May 1 2015 - p12(1) [501+]
Ovid's Erotic Poems: Amores and Ars Amatoria
   TLS - i5848 - May 1 2015 - p12(1) [501+]
Owen-Crocker, Gale R. - *Kingship, Legislation and Power in Anglo-Saxon England*
   Med R - Jan 2015 - pNA [501+]
Owen, David - *Panther*
   y Sch Lib - v63 - i2 - Summer 2015 - p126(1) [51-500]
Owen, David (b. 1938-) - *The Hidden Perspective: The Military Conversations 1906-1914*
   J Mil H - v79 - i1 - Jan 2015 - p224-225 [501+]
   J Mil H - v79 - i4 - Oct 2015 - p1152-1153 [501+]
Owen, Howard - *The Bottom*
   BL - v111 - i19-20 - June 1 2015 - p47(2) [51-500]
   KR - June 15 2015 - pNA [51-500]
   PW - v262 - i23 - June 8 2015 - p39(1) [51-500]
Owen, James - *Labour and the Caucus: Working-Class Radicalism and Organised Liberalism in England, 1868-88*
   AHR - v120 - i3 - June 2015 - p1116-1117 [501+]
Owen, John Bailey - *Prehistoric: Follow the Dinosaurs*
   c HB Guide - v26 - i2 - Fall 2015 - p96(1) [51-500]
Presidents: Follow the Leaders
   c SLJ - v61 - i10 - Oct 2015 - p128(1) [51-500]
Owen, Lauren - *The Quick*
   NYTBR - April 12 2015 - p28(L) [501+]
Owen, Mark - *No Hero: The Evolution of a Navy SEAL (Read by Michael, Paul). Audiobook Review*
   PW - v262 - i12 - March 23 2015 - p72(1) [51-500]
Owen, Robin - *Boudoir Lighting: Simple Techniques for Dramatic Photography*
   Bwatch - Feb 2015 - pNA [51-500]
Owen, Roger - *The Rise and Fall of Arab Presidents for Life*
   IJMES - v47 - i1 - Feb 2015 - p153-168 [501+]
Owen, Ruth - *Asteroid Hunters*
   c BL - v112 - i3 - Oct 1 2015 - p44(1) [51-500]
Owen, Taylor - *Disruptive Power: The Crisis of the State in the Digital Age*
   LJ - v140 - i9 - May 15 2015 - p96(1) [51-500]
Owens, Ann-Maureen - *Our Flag: The Story of Canada's Maple Leaf (Illus. by Slavin, Bill)*
   c HB Guide - v26 - i2 - Fall 2015 - p221(1) [51-500]
Owens, Robert M. - *Red Dreams, White Nightmares: Pan-Indian Alliances in the Anglo-Indian Mind, 1963-1815*
   Roundup M - v23 - i1 - Oct 2015 - p34(1) [501+]
Owings, Lisa - *From Bulb to Tulip*
   c HB Guide - v26 - i2 - Fall 2015 - p187(1) [51-500]
Ghost Ships
   c Teach Lib - v42 - i5 - June 2015 - p9(1) [51-500]
Igneous Rocks
   c HB Guide - v26 - i1 - Spring 2015 - p151(1) [51-500]

Katy Perry: Chart-Topping Superstar
  c BL - v111 - i19-20 - June 1 2015 - p88(2) [51-500]
Punishing Bullies: Zero Tolerance vs. Working Together
  c HB Guide - v26 - i2 - Fall 2015 - p155(1) [51-500]
      VOYA - v38 - i2 - June 2015 - p89(1) [501+]
Rev Up Your Writing Series (Illus. by Gallagher-Cole, Mernie)
      BL - v112 - i5 - Nov 1 2015 - p47(1) [501+]
  c CH Bwatch - Sept 2015 - pNA [51-500]
Start to Finish, Second Series: Nature's Treasures
  c HB Guide - v26 - i2 - Fall 2015 - p189(1) [51-500]
What Are Legends, Folktales, and Other Classic Stories?
  c HB Guide - v26 - i1 - Spring 2015 - p145(1) [51-500]
What Are Plays?
  c HB Guide - v26 - i1 - Spring 2015 - p181(1) [51-500]

Ownby, Ted - *The Civil Rights Movement in Mississippi*
      JSH - v81 - i2 - May 2015 - p517(2) [501+]

Owsley, Douglas M. - *Kennewick Man: The Scientific Investigation of an Ancient American Skeleton*
      Am Ant - v80 - i4 - Oct 2015 - p781(3) [501+]

Owuor, Yvonne Adhiambo - *Dust*
      TLS - i5864-5865 - August 21 2015 - p23(1) [501+]

Oxenstierna, Susanne - *Russian Energy and Security up to 2030*
      E-A St - v67 - i6 - August 2015 - p995(2) [501+]

Oxlade, Chris - *Animal Infographics*
      TC Math - v21 - i6 - Feb 2015 - p380(1) [501+]
Be a Survivor (Illus. by Sassin, Eva)
  c PW - v262 - i30 - July 27 2015 - p70(1) [501+]
  c KR - Sept 15 2015 - pNA [51-500]
Making Machines with Pulleys
  c HB Guide - v26 - i2 - Fall 2015 - p166(1) [51-500]
Making Machines with Ramps and Wedges
  c HB Guide - v26 - i2 - Fall 2015 - p166(1) [51-500]
Making Machines with Springs
  c HB Guide - v26 - i2 - Fall 2015 - p166(1) [51-500]
Population Infographics
      TC Math - v21 - i6 - Feb 2015 - p380(1) [501+]

Oxley, Jennifer - *Peg + Cat: The Race Car Problem*
  c KR - July 1 2015 - pNA [51-500]
Peg + Cat: The Race Car Problem (Illus. by Oxley, Jennifer)
  c SLJ - v61 - i8 - August 2015 - p75(1) [51-500]

Oyer, Gordon - *Pursuing the Spiritual Roots of Protest: Merton, Berrigan, Yoder, and Muste at the Gethsemani Abbey Peacemakers Retreat*
      CC - v132 - i19 - Sept 16 2015 - p42(1) [51-500]

Oyeyemi, Helen - *Boy, Snow, Bird*
      NYTBR - April 12 2015 - p28(L) [501+]
What Is Not Yours Is Not Yours
      KR - Jan 1 2016 - pNA [501+]

Oz, Lisa - *The Oz Family Kitchen: More than 100 Simple and Delicious Real-Food Recipes from Our Home to Yours*
      PW - v262 - i31 - August 3 2015 - p52(1) [51-500]

Ozbudun, Ergun - *Party Politics and Social Changes in Turkey*
      IJMES - v47 - i1 - Feb 2015 - p207-210 [501+]

Ozeki, Ruth - *The Face: A Time Code*
      KR - Dec 15 2015 - pNA [501+]
A Tale for the Time Being
      ABR - v36 - i5 - July-August 2015 - p7(2) [501+]

Ozouf, Mona - *Jules Ferry: La liberte et la tradition*
      TLS - i5842 - March 20 2015 - p26(2) [501+]

Ozyurek, Esra - *Being German, Becoming Muslim: Race, Religion, and Conversion in the New Europe*
      JAAR - v83 - i2 - June 2015 - pNA [501+]
      TimHES - i2195 - March 19 2015 - p53(1) [501+]

P

P., Rosa - *Great New Ways with Granny Squares*
 LJ - v140 - i9 - May 15 2015 - p83(1) [51-500]
Paajanen, Terri - *The Complete Guide to Drying Foods at Home*
 Bwatch - Sept 2015 - pNA [51-500]
Pacat, C.S. - *Captive Prince*
 PW - v262 - i8 - Feb 23 2015 - p59(1) [51-500]
 Prince's Gambit
 PW - v262 - i21 - May 25 2015 - p43(1) [51-500]
Pace, Lilah - *Asking for It*
 PW - v262 - i17 - April 27 2015 - p58(1) [51-500]
 Begging for It
 PW - v262 - i30 - July 27 2015 - p48(2) [51-500]
Pacheco, Rebecca - *Do Your Om Thing: Bending Yoga Tradition to Fit Your Modern Life*
 PW - v262 - i1 - Jan 5 2015 - p68(1) [51-500]
Pacholok, Shelley - *Into the Fire: Disaster and the Remaking of Gender*
 CS - v44 - i1 - Jan 2015 - p144-145 [501+]
Pacini, Greg - *Journey beyond Hardship: A Practical, Hopeful Guide for Getting through Tough Times*
 SPBW - Nov 2015 - pNA [51-500]
Pack, C.A. - *Second Chronicles of Illumination*
 KR - August 1 2015 - pNA [501+]
Pack, Robert - *Clayfeld Holds On*
 LJ - v140 - i17 - Oct 15 2015 - p90(2) [51-500]
Packard, Mary - *Origami Aircraft*
 Bwatch - April 2015 - pNA [51-500]
Packer, Ann - *The Children's Crusade (Read by Smith, Cotter). Audiobook Review*
 BL - v111 - i22 - August 1 2015 - p77(1) [51-500]
 PW - v262 - i26 - June 29 2015 - p63(2) [51-500]
 The Children's Crusade
 CSM - May 18 2015 - pNA [501+]
 NY - v91 - i15 - June 1 2015 - p75 [51-500]
 NYT - April 16 2015 - pC1(L) [501+]
 NYTBR - April 12 2015 - p11(L) [501+]
 People - v83 - i15 - April 13 2015 - p41(NA) [501+]
 PW - v262 - i5 - Feb 2 2015 - p31(1) [51-500]
 Slaughterhouse-Five
 BL - v111 - i11 - Feb 1 2015 - p22(1) [51-500]
 KR - Feb 15 2015 - pNA [51-500]
Packer, Craig - *Lions in the Balance: Man-Eaters, Manes, and Men with Guns*
 LJ - v140 - i4 - Sept 1 2015 - p133(2) [51-500]
 New Sci - v227 - i3032 - August 1 2015 - p43(1) [501+]
Packer, Nigel - *The Restoration of Otto Laird*
 BL - v112 - i4 - Oct 15 2015 - p34(1) [51-500]
 KR - Sept 15 2015 - pNA [51-500]
Packer, Sarit - *Honey & Co.: Food from the Middle East*
 LJ - v140 - i9 - May 15 2015 - p102(2) [501+]
Packer, Tina - *Women of Will: Following the Feminine in Shakespeare's Plays*
 LJ - v140 - i5 - March 15 2015 - p101(2) [501+]
 Am Theat - v32 - i3 - March 2015 - p54(2) [501+]
 BL - v111 - i11 - Feb 1 2015 - p11(1) [51-500]
 CSM - April 9 2015 - pNA [501+]
 NYT - May 5 2015 - pC6(L) [501+]
 NYTBR - May 24 2015 - p16(L) [501+]
Paddison, Joshua - *American Heathens: Religion, Race, and Reconstruction in California*
 PHR - v84 - i1 - Feb 2015 - p91(3) [501+]
Paddock, Bonner - *One More Step: My Story of Living with Cerebral Palsy, Climbing Kilimanjaro, and Surviving the Hardest Race on Earth*
 PW - v262 - i6 - Feb 9 2015 - p60(1) [51-500]
Paddock, Troy R.E. - *World War I and Propaganda*
 J Mil H - v79 - i1 - Jan 2015 - p241-242 [501+]
 J Mil H - v79 - i4 - Oct 2015 - p1136-1137 [501+]

Pade, Marianne - *Plutarchi Chaeronensis Vita Dionis et Comparatio et de Bruto ac Dione Iucidium Guarino Veronensi Interprete*
 Six Ct J - v46 - i3 - Fall 2015 - p747-748 [501+]
Padfield, Tim - *Copyright for Archivists and Records Managers, 5th ed.*
 RVBW - Nov 2015 - pNA [51-500]
Padgett, Ron - *Alone and Not Alone*
 NYT - July 9 2015 - pC6(L) [501+]
 PW - v262 - i20 - May 18 2015 - p62(1) [51-500]
 Oklahoma Tough
 NYTBR - June 28 2015 - p16(L) [501+]
Padmanahan, Thanu - *Sleeping Beauties in Theoretical Physics: 26 Surprising Insights*
 Phys Today - v68 - i11 - Nov 2015 - p54-55 [501+]
Padowicz, Julian - *When the Diamonds Were Gone*
 KR - May 1 2015 - pNA [501+]
Padua, Sydney - *The Thrilling Adventures of Lovelace and Babbage: The (Mostly) True Story of the First Computer*
 BL - v111 - i13 - March 1 2015 - p40(1) [51-500]
 KR - Feb 15 2015 - pNA [501+]
 LJ - v140 - i5 - March 15 2015 - p88(3) [501+]
 NYTBR - June 7 2015 - p27(L) [501+]
 PW - v262 - i4 - Jan 26 2015 - p156(2) [51-500]
 TLS - i5858 - July 10 2015 - p27(1) [501+]
Paeth, Scott R. - *Shaping Public Theology: Selections from the Writings of Max L. Stackhouse*
 CC - v132 - i12 - June 10 2015 - p41(2) [501+]
Pagan, Camille - *Life and Other Near-Death Experiences*
 BL - v112 - i4 - Oct 15 2015 - p17(1) [51-500]
Pagden, Anthony - *The Burdens of Empire: 1539 to the Present*
 TimHES - i2208 - June 18 2015 - p48-49 [501+]
Page, Alan - *Constitutional Law of Scotland*
 Lon R Bks - v37 - i18 - Sept 24 2015 - p21(2) [501+]
Page, Anita - *Murder New York Style: Family Matters*
 RVBW - June 2015 - pNA [501+]
Page, Christian - *The Iron Golem*
 y CH Bwatch - April 2015 - pNA [51-500]
 KR - Feb 1 2015 - pNA [501+]
Page, Geoff - *New Selected Poems*
 Meanjin - v74 - i1 - Autumn 2015 - p68(10) [501+]
Page, Joseph T., II - *Holloman Air Force Base, Images of America*
 APJ - v29 - i3 - May-June 2015 - p92(2) [501+]
Page, Katharine Hall - *The Body in the Birches: A Faith Fairchild Mystery*
 PW - v262 - i12 - March 23 2015 - p48(1) [51-500]
Page, Katherine Hall - *The Body in the Belfry (Read by Eby, Tanya). Audiobook Review*
 BL - v111 - i17 - May 1 2015 - p58(1) [51-500]
 The Body in the Birches
 BL - v111 - i18 - May 15 2015 - p26(1) [51-500]
Page, Kathy - *Frankie Styne and the Silver Man*
 KR - Sept 15 2015 - pNA [51-500]
 PW - v262 - i48 - Nov 30 2015 - p37(2) [51-500]
Page, Robin - *A Chicken Followed Me Home! Questions and Answers about a Familiar Fowl (Illus. by Page, Robin)*
 c BL - v111 - i18 - May 15 2015 - p48(1) [51-500]
 c CCB-B - v69 - i1 - Sept 2015 - p42(1) [51-500]
 c HB - v91 - i3 - May-June 2015 - p128(1) [51-500]
 c HB Guide - v26 - i2 - Fall 2015 - p188(1) [51-500]
 c KR - Feb 1 2015 - pNA [51-500]
 c PW - v262 - i20 - May 18 2015 - p85(1) [501+]
 c PW - v262 - i49 - Dec 2 2015 - p44(1) [51-500]
Page, Sophie - *Magic in the Cloister: Pious Motives, Illicit Interests, and Occult Approaches to the Medieval Universe*
 AHR - v120 - i1 - Feb 2015 - p314(1) [501+]
 CH - v84 - i2 - June 2015 - p432(3) [501+]
 Med R - June 2015 - pNA [501+]
Page, Warren - *Applications of Mathematics in Economics*
 Math T - v108 - i6 - Feb 2015 - p476(1) [501+]
Paget, Karen M. - *Patriotic Betrayal: The Inside Story of the CIA's Secret Campaign to Enroll American Students in the Crusade against Communism*
 HM - v330 - i1978 - March 2015 - p84(5) [501+]
 KR - Jan 1 2015 - pNA [501+]
 NY - v91 - i5 - March 23 2015 - p84 [501+]
Pahomov, Larissa - *Authentic Learning in the Digital Age: Engaging Students through Inquiry*
 Teach Lib - v42 - i3 - Feb 2015 - p40(1) [501+]
Pai, Hyung Il - *Heritage Management in Korea and Japan: The Politics of Antiquity and Identity*
 JAS - v74 - i3 - August 2015 - p767-768 [501+]
Pai, Raja - *No Room for Dabha*
 KR - July 1 2015 - pNA [501+]
Pai, Sudha - *Dalit Assertion*
 Pac A - v88 - i1 - March 2015 - p211 [501+]
Paige, Danielle - *Dorothy Must Die Stories: No Place Like Oz*
 SLJ - v61 - i4 - April 2015 - p169(1) [51-500]
 The Wicked Will Rise
 y CCB-B - v68 - i10 - June 2015 - p508(1) [51-500]
 SLJ - v61 - i4 - April 2015 - p169(1) [51-500]
Paige, Laurelin - *First Touch*
 KR - Oct 15 2015 - pNA [51-500]
 PW - v262 - i42 - Oct 19 2015 - p63(1) [51-500]
Painchaud, Michelle - *Pretending to Be Erica*
 y BL - v111 - i21 - July 1 2015 - p58(1) [51-500]
 y CCB-B - v69 - i2 - Oct 2015 - p107(1) [51-500]
 y KR - May 1 2015 - pNA [51-500]
 y SLJ - v61 - i5 - May 2015 - p122(1) [51-500]
 y VOYA - v38 - i3 - August 2015 - p66(1) [51-500]
Paine, Jed - *Ferrari*
 y BL - v112 - i3 - Oct 1 2015 - p40(1) [51-500]
Paine, Lauran - *Renegades of Perdition Range*
 BL - v111 - i11 - Feb 1 2015 - p30(1) [51-500]
 Roundup M - v22 - i5 - June 2015 - p39(1) [501+]
 Rough Justice
 Roundup M - v22 - i4 - April 2015 - p34(1) [501+]
Paine, S.C.M. - *The Wars for Asia, 1911-1949*
 J Mil H - v79 - i3 - July 2015 - p852-853 [501+]
Paine, Tom - *A Boy's Book of Nervous Breakdowns*
 PW - v262 - i31 - August 3 2015 - p33(1) [51-500]
Painter, Kristen - *Garden of Dreams and Desires*
 PW - v262 - i8 - Feb 23 2015 - p55(1) [51-500]
Pairault, Thierry - *Chine-Algerie: Une Relation Singuliere en Afrique*
 HNet - March 2015 - pNA [501+]
Paisner, Daniel - *I Feel Like Going On: Life, Game, and Glory*
 LJ - v140 - i20 - Dec 1 2015 - p108(1) [51-500]
Paiva, Johannah Gilman - *See How They Work and Look inside Big Rigs (Illus. by Tegg, Simon)*
 c BL - v112 - i6 - Nov 15 2015 - p43(1) [501+]
 See How They Work and Look inside Diggers (Illus. by Tegg, Simon)
 c BL - v112 - i6 - Nov 15 2015 - p43(1) [501+]
 See How They Work and Look inside Farm Equipment (Illus. by Tegg, Simon)
 c BL - v112 - i6 - Nov 15 2015 - p43(1) [501+]
 See How They Work and Look inside Fire Trucks
 c BL - v112 - i6 - Nov 15 2015 - p43(1) [501+]

Pajalunga, Lorena V. - *Yoga for Kids: Simple Animal Poses for Any Age (Illus. by Forlati, Anna)*
   c BL - v112 - i6 - Nov 15 2015 - p48(1) [51-500]
   c SLJ - v61 - i9 - Sept 2015 - p111(1) [51-500]
   c KR - Oct 1 2015 - pNA [51-500]

Pajcic, Kathrin - *Frauenstimmen in der Spatmittelalterlichen Stadt? Testamente von Frauen aus Luneburg, Hamburg und Wien als Soziale Kommunikation*
   HNet - June 2015 - pNA [501+]

Pakenham, Thomas - *The Company of Trees: A Year in a Lifetime's Quest*
   Spec - v329 - i9761 - Sept 26 2015 - p42(1) [501+]

Pakkala, Christina - *Jasmine and Maddie*
   y Teach Lib - v42 - i3 - Feb 2015 - p32(6) [501+]

Pakkala, Christine - *Last-but-Not-Least: Lola and the Cupcake Queens (Illus. by Hoppe, Paul)*
   c SLJ - v61 - i5 - May 2015 - p99(1) [51-500]
Last-but-Not-Least Lola and the Wild Chicken (Illus. by Hoppe, Paul)
   c HB Guide - v26 - i2 - Fall 2015 - p70(1) [51-500]

Pal, Carol - *Republic of Women: Rethinking the Republic of Letters in the Seventeenth Century*
   HER - v130 - i545 - August 2015 - p996(2) [501+]

Pal, Ruma - *An Introduction to Phytoplanktons: Diversity and Ecology*
   QRB - v90 - i1 - March 2015 - p83(2) [501+]

Palacio, R.J. - *365 Days of Wonder: Mr. Browne's Book of Precepts*
   c HB Guide - v26 - i1 - Spring 2015 - p187(1) [51-500]
Auggie and Me: Three Wonder Stories
   c Magpies - v30 - i5 - Nov 2015 - p36(2) [501+]
Pluto (Read by Merriman, Scott). Audiobook Review
   c SLJ - v61 - i6 - June 2015 - p64(1) [51-500]
Shingaling (Read by Krahn, Taylor Ann). Audiobook Review
   c SLJ - v61 - i10 - Oct 2015 - p52(3) [51-500]

Palahniuk, Chuck - *Make Something Up: Stories You Can't Unread*
   y BL - v111 - i15 - April 1 2015 - p34(1) [51-500]
     LJ - v140 - i9 - May 15 2015 - p79(1) [51-500]
     PW - v262 - i10 - March 9 2015 - p49(1) [51-500]

Palaia, Marian - *The Given World*
   BL - v111 - i13 - March 1 2015 - p18(1) [51-500]
   KR - March 1 2015 - pNA [51-500]
   LJ - v140 - i3 - Feb 15 2015 - p91(1) [51-500]
   NYTBR - June 7 2015 - p28(L) [501+]
   PW - v262 - i5 - Feb 2 2015 - p34(1) [51-500]

Palanisamy, Akil - *The Paleovedic Diet: A Complete Program to Burn Fat, Increase Energy, and Reverse Disease*
   PW - v262 - i44 - Nov 2 2015 - p80(1) [51-500]

Palatini, Margie - *No Nap! Yes Nap! (Illus. by Yaccarino, Dan)*
   c HB Guide - v26 - i1 - Spring 2015 - p13(1) [51-500]
Under a Pig Tree: A History of the Noble Fruit (Illus. by Groenink, Chuck)
   c BL - v111 - i14 - March 15 2015 - p82(1) [51-500]
   c HB Guide - v26 - i2 - Fall 2015 - p47(1) [51-500]
   c KR - Feb 15 2015 - pNA [51-500]
   c PW - v262 - i8 - Feb 23 2015 - p73(1) [51-500]

Palau, Kevin - *Unlikely: Setting Aside Our Differences to Live Out the Gospel*
   LJ - v140 - i10 - June 1 2015 - p107(2) [51-500]
   PW - v262 - i19 - May 11 2015 - p55(1) [51-500]

Paleja, Shaker - *Power Up! A Visual Exploration of Energy (Illus. by Tse, Glenda)*
   c KR - June 15 2015 - pNA [51-500]
   c SLJ - v61 - i6 - June 2015 - p136(1) [51-500]
   c Res Links - v21 - i1 - Oct 2015 - p25(1) [51-500]

Palermo, Tonya M. - *Managing Your Child's Chronic Pain*
   LJ - v140 - i5 - March 15 2015 - p123(1) [51-500]

Paley-Bain, Renee - *Murder She Wrote: The Ghost and Mrs. Fletcher*
   Bwatch - Nov 2015 - pNA [51-500]

Paley, Dan - *Luigi and the Barefoot Races (Illus. by Boyd, Aaron)*
   c KR - August 15 2015 - pNA [51-500]

Paley-Phillips, Giles - *Little Bell and the Moon (Illus. by Deppe, Iris)*
   c Sch Lib - v63 - i4 - Winter 2015 - p222(1) [51-500]

Palfreman, Jon - *Brain Storms: The Race to Unlock the Mysteries of Parkinson's Disease*
   BL - v111 - i22 - August 1 2015 - p12(1) [51-500]
   KR - June 1 2015 - pNA [51-500]
   LJ - v140 - i11 - June 15 2015 - p105(1) [51-500]
   PW - v262 - i27 - July 6 2015 - p57(2) [51-500]
   TLS - i5877 - Nov 20 2015 - p26(1) [501+]

Palfrey, John - *BiblioTech: Why Libraries Matter More Than Ever in the Age of Google (Read by Zingarelli, Tom). Audiobook Review*
   LJ - v140 - i16 - Oct 1 2015 - p45(1) [51-500]
BiblioTech: Why Libraries Matter More Than Ever in the Age of Google
   KR - Feb 15 2015 - pNA [501+]
   LJ - v140 - i7 - April 15 2015 - p107(1) [51-500]
   NYTBR - August 23 2015 - p38(L) [501+]
   PW - v262 - i15 - April 13 2015 - p69(1) [501+]
   VOYA - v38 - i2 - June 2015 - p92(2) [51-500]

Palfrey, Simon - *Poor Tom: Living "King Lear"*
   Six Ct J - v46 - i3 - Fall 2015 - p788-789 [501+]
   TLS - i5834 - Jan 23 2015 - p22(1) [501+]
Shakespeare's Possible Worlds
   TLS - i5834 - Jan 23 2015 - p22(1) [501+]

Palin, Michael - *Travelling to Work: Diaries 1988-1998*
   KR - Sept 1 2015 - pNA [51-500]
   LJ - v140 - i15 - Sept 15 2015 - p79(1) [51-500]
   NYTBR - Dec 6 2015 - p58(L) [501+]

Palka, Joel W. - *Maya Pilgrimage to Natural Landscapes: Insights from Archaeology, History, and Ethnography*
   HAHR - v95 - i4 - Nov 2015 - p669-670 [501+]

Pallace, Chris - *Get Mooned (Illus. by Pallace, Chris)*
   c CCB-B - v68 - i9 - May 2015 - p462(1) [51-500]
   c KR - Jan 1 2015 - pNA [51-500]

Palley, Elizabeth - *In Our Hands: The Struggle for U.S. Child Care Policy*
   HLR - v128 - i6 - April 2015 - p1895(1) [1-50]

Pallotta, Jerry - *Butterfly Counting (Illus. by Bersani, Shennen)*
   c BL - v111 - i15 - April 1 2015 - p37(1) [51-500]
   c HB Guide - v26 - i2 - Fall 2015 - p174(1) [51-500]
   c KR - Jan 15 2015 - pNA [51-500]
   c PW - v262 - i8 - Feb 23 2015 - p76(1) [501+]
Qui aidera le pere Noel? (Illus. by Biedrzycki, David)
   c Res Links - v20 - i3 - Feb 2015 - p49(1) [51-500]

Palma, Felix J. - *The Map of Chaos*
   BL - v111 - i18 - May 15 2015 - p38(1) [51-500]
   KR - April 15 2015 - pNA [501+]
   PW - v262 - i16 - April 20 2015 - p54(2) [51-500]

Palma, Pina - *Savoring Power, Consuming the Times: The Metaphors of Food in Medieval and Renaissance Italian Literature*
   MLR - v110 - i1 - Jan 2015 - p268-269 [501+]
   MP - v113 - i1 - August 2015 - pE11(13) [501+]

Palmer, Aaron J. - *A Rule of Law: Elite Political Authority and the Coming of the Revolution in the South Carolina Lowcountry, 1763-1776*
   JSH - v81 - i4 - Nov 2015 - p944(2) [501+]

Palmer, Ada - *Reading Lucretius in the Renaissance*
   Ren Q - v68 - i3 - Fall 2015 - p986-987 [501+]
   Sev Cent N - v73 - i3-4 - Fall-Winter 2015 - p205(4) [501+]
   Six Ct J - v46 - i3 - Fall 2015 - p753-755 [501+]

Palmer, Alex - *The Santa Claus Man: The Rise and Fall of a Jazz Age Con Man and the Invention of Christmas in New York*
   PW - v262 - i32 - August 10 2015 - p49(1) [51-500]
   NYT - Nov 27 2015 - pC28(L) [501+]

Palmer, Amanda - *The Art of Asking, or, How I Learned to Stop Worrying and Let People Help (Read by Palmer, Amanda). Audiobook Review*
   LJ - v140 - i6 - April 1 2015 - p51(1) [51-500]
   PW - v262 - i5 - Feb 2 2015 - p55(2) [51-500]

Palmer, Andrew - *Smart Money: How High-Stakes Financial Innovation Is Reshaping Our World--for the Better*
   BL - v111 - i11 - Feb 1 2015 - p7(1) [51-500]
   KR - Feb 15 2015 - pNA [501+]
   NYTBR - May 10 2015 - p28(L) [51-500]
   PW - v262 - i2 - Jan 12 2015 - p48(1) [51-500]

Palmer, Charlie - *Charlie Palmer's American Fare: Everyday Recipes from My Kitchen to Yours*
   PW - v262 - i14 - April 6 2015 - p53(1) [51-500]

Palmer, Daniel - *Constant Fear (Read by Berkrot, Peter). Audiobook Review*
   LJ - v140 - i14 - Sept 1 2015 - p67(1) [51-500]
Constant Fear
   y BL - v111 - i17 - May 1 2015 - p26(1) [51-500]
     LJ - v140 - i9 - May 15 2015 - p73(1) [51-500]
     PW - v262 - i15 - April 13 2015 - p57(1) [51-500]
Trauma
   BL - v111 - i16 - April 15 2015 - p30(1) [51-500]
   PW - v262 - i11 - March 16 2015 - p65(2) [51-500]

Palmer, Dexter - *Version Control*
   KR - Dec 15 2015 - pNA [501+]
   PW - v262 - i51 - Dec 14 2015 - p60(1) [51-500]

Palmer, Diana - *Untamed*
   PW - v262 - i20 - May 18 2015 - p71(1) [51-500]

Palmer, Douglas - *Firefly Encyclopedia of Dinosaurs and Prehistoric Animals*
   SLJ - v61 - i2 - Feb 2015 - p56(1) [51-500]

Palmer, Erin - *Recycling, Yes or No*
   c BL - v112 - i6 - Nov 15 2015 - p43(1) [51-500]

Palmer, James T. - *The Apocalypse in the Early Middle Ages*
   Specu - v90 - i2 - April 2015 - p574-576 [501+]

Palmer, Jenny - *A Little ABC Book*
   c Magpies - v30 - i1 - March 2015 - pS4(1) [501+]

Palmer, Jessica - *The Art of Papercutting*
   LJ - v140 - i17 - Oct 15 2015 - p88(1) [51-500]

Palmer, Lacretia - *Billy the Bully (Illus. by Vasquez, Romney)*
   c CH Bwatch - April 2015 - pNA [51-500]

Palmer, Linda F. - *Baby Poop: What Your Pediatrician May Not Tell You*
   LJ - v140 - i9 - May 15 2015 - p66(2) [501+]

Palmer, Matthew - *Secrets of State*
   BL - v111 - i16 - April 15 2015 - p29(1) [51-500]
   KR - March 15 2015 - pNA [501+]
   LJ - v140 - i9 - May 15 2015 - p73(1) [51-500]
   PW - v262 - i9 - March 2 2015 - p65(1) [51-500]

Palmer, Ocean - *Portable Dad: Stuff to Know Without the Lecture*
   RVBW - June 2015 - pNA [51-500]

Palmer, Patricia - *The Severed Head and the Grafted Tongue: Literature, Translation and Violence in Early Modern Ireland*
   Ren Q - v68 - i1 - Spring 2015 - p298-299 [501+]

Palmer, Rob - *Mr. P.C.: The Life and Music of Paul Chambers*
   Notes - v71 - i3 - March 2015 - p492(6) [501+]

Palmer, Robert L. - *The Survivors*
   BL - v112 - i2 - Sept 15 2015 - p35(1) [51-500]
   PW - v262 - i32 - August 10 2015 - p39(1) [51-500]

Palmer, Robin - *Once upon a Kiss*
   y KR - Oct 1 2015 - pNA [51-500]

Palmer, Roderick Byron - *The Ballad of David and Israel*
   KR - May 15 2015 - pNA [501+]

Palmer, Sharon - *Plant-Powered for Life*
   Veg J - v34 - i1 - Jan-March 2015 - p30(1) [51-500]

Palmieri, Robert - *The Piano: An Encyclopaedia, 2d ed.*
   TLS - i5855 - June 19 2015 - p29(1) [501+]

Palmieri, Suzanne - *The Witch of Bourbon Street*
   BL - v111 - i19-20 - June 1 2015 - p47(1) [51-500]

Palombo, Alyssa - *The Violinist of Venice*
   KR - Sept 15 2015 - pNA [51-500]

Palser, Barb - *Choosing News: What Gets Reported and Why*
   c CH Bwatch - Jan 2015 - pNA [51-500]
Selling Ourselves: Marketing Body Images
   c CH Bwatch - Jan 2015 - pNA [51-500]

Palumbi, Stephen R. - *The Extreme Life of the Sea*
   Am Bio T - v77 - i1 - Jan 2015 - p80(1) [51-500]
   QRB - v90 - i3 - Sept 2015 - p326(2) [51-500]

Palumbo, Dennis - *Phantom Limb*
   RVBW - May 2015 - pNA [51-500]

Palumbo-Liu, David - *The Deliverance of Others: Reading Literature in a Global Age*
   Comp L - v67 - i2 - June 2015 - p238-240 [501+]

Pamuk, Orhan - *Kafamda Bir Tuhaflik*
   WLT - v89 - i3-4 - May-August 2015 - p116(1) [501+]
A Strangeness in My Mind
   BL - v112 - i2 - Sept 15 2015 - p28(1) [51-500]
   BooChiTr - Oct 31 2015 - p14(1) [501+]
   KR - Sept 1 2015 - pNA [501+]
   LJ - v140 - i15 - Sept 15 2015 - p69(1) [51-500]
   NS - v144 - i5279 - Sept 11 2015 - p46(3) [501+]
   NYRB - v62 - i17 - Nov 5 2015 - p52(3) [501+]
   NYT - Oct 21 2015 - pC1(L) [501+]
   NYTBR - Oct 25 2015 - p13(L) [501+]
   PW - v262 - i34 - August 24 2015 - p8(1) [51-500]

Panagore, Peter Baldwin - *Heaven Is Beautiful*
   PW - v262 - i32 - August 10 2015 - p57(1) [51-500]

Panayi, Panikos - *Fish and Chips: A History*
   HT - v65 - i2 - Feb 2015 - p58(3) [501+]

Pancake, Ann - *Me and My Daddy Listen to Bob Marley: Novellas & Stories*
   BL - v111 - i11 - Feb 1 2015 - p23(1) [51-500]

Panchyk, Richard - *Basketball History for Kids*
   c KR - Dec 15 2015 - pNA [51-500]

Pande, Amrita - *Wombs in Labor: Transnational Commercial Surrogacy in India*
    AJS - v121 - i2 - Sept 2015 - p653(3) [501+]
    Wom R Bks - v32 - i3 - May-June 2015 - p21(3) [501+]

Pandian, Anand - *Ayya's Accounts: A Ledger of Hope in Modern India*
    JRAI - v21 - i3 - Sept 2015 - p697(2) [501+]

Pandian, Gigi - *The Accidental Alchemist*
    Veg J - v34 - i4 - Oct-Dec 2015 - p31(1) [51-500]
Artifact (Read by Ryan, Allyson). Audiobook Review
    LJ - v140 - i15 - Sept 15 2015 - p42(1) [51-500]
The Masquerading Magician
    KR - Nov 1 2015 - pNA [51-500]

Panetta, Leon - *Worthy Fights: A Memoir of Leadership in War and Peace*
    For Aff - v94 - i1 - Jan-Feb 2015 - pNA [51-500]

Pangle, Lorraine Smith - *Virtue Is Knowledge. The Moral Foundations of Socratic Political Philosophy*
    Class R - v65 - i1 - April 2015 - p47-49 [501+]

Panhorst, Michael W. - *The Memorial Art and Architecture of Vicksburg National Military Park*
    J Mil H - v79 - i3 - July 2015 - p849-850 [501+]

Panich, Lee - *Indigenous Landscapes and Spanish Missions: New Perspectives from Archaeology and Ethnohistory*
    WHQ - v46 - i2 - Summer 2015 - p249(1) [501+]

Panich, Lee M. - *Indigenous Landscapes and Spanish Missions: New Perspectives from Archaeology and Ethnohistory*
    HAHR - v95 - i3 - August 2015 - p519-521 [501+]

Panikkar, Raimon - *Mysticism and Spirituality, Part I: Mysticism, Fullness of Life*
    Theol St - v76 - i2 - June 2015 - p390(2) [501+]

Panitch, Amanda - *Damage Done*
    y BL - v111 - i21 - July 1 2015 - p55(1) [51-500]
    y CCB-B - v69 - i2 - Oct 2015 - p107(2) [51-500]
    y SLJ - v61 - i8 - August 2015 - p109(1) [51-500]

Pankhurst, Emmeline - *Suffragette: My Own Story*
    PW - v262 - i16 - April 20 2015 - p66(1) [51-500]

Pankhurst, Kate - *The Huge Hair Scare*
    c SLJ - v61 - i6 - June 2015 - p109(1) [51-500]
The Mystery Of the Cursed Poodle
    c SLJ - v61 - i6 - June 2015 - p109(1) [51-500]
The Spaghetti Yeti (Illus. by Pankhurst, Kate)
    c SLJ - v61 - i6 - June 2015 - p109(1) [51-500]

Pankhurst, Sheila - *Zoo Animals: Behaviour, Management and Welfare*
    QRB - v90 - i1 - March 2015 - p107(1) [501+]

Panowich, Brian - *Bull Mountain (Read by Troxell, Brian). Audiobook Review*
    BL - v112 - i7 - Dec 1 2015 - p68(1) [51-500]
Bull Mountain
    BL - v111 - i17 - May 1 2015 - p22(1) [51-500]
    KR - May 1 2015 - pNA [51-500]
    LJ - v140 - i10 - June 1 2015 - p94(2) [51-500]
    NYTBR - July 19 2015 - p25(L) [501+]

Pantell, Robert H. - *Taking Care of Your Child: A Parent's Illustrated Guide to Complete Medical Care*
    RVBW - August 2015 - pNA [51-500]

Panter-Downes, Mollie - *London War Notes*
    TLS - i5854 - June 12 2015 - p26(2) [51-500]

Panton, Kenneth J. - *Historical Dictionary of the British Empire*
    BL - v112 - i2 - Sept 15 2015 - p18(1) [51-500]
    LJ - v140 - i13 - August 1 2015 - p123(1) [51-500]

Pantsov, Alexander V. - *Deng Xiaoping: A Revolutionary Life*
    BL - v111 - i17 - May 1 2015 - p73(1) [51-500]
    Econ - v415 - i8944 - June 27 2015 - p73(US) [501+]
    For Aff - v94 - i3 - May-June 2015 - pNA [501+]
    NYRB - v62 - i16 - Oct 22 2015 - p35(2) [501+]
    TimHES - i2216 - August 13 2015 - p45(1) [501+]
    KR - Feb 1 2015 - pNA [501+]
Mao: The Real Story
    Pac A - v88 - i1 - March 2015 - p187 [501+]

Pantucci, Raffaello - *'We Love Death as You Love Life': Britain's Suburban Terrorists*
    Lon R Bks - v37 - i16 - August 27 2015 - p9(2) [501+]

Paoletti, Jo B. - *Sex and Unisex: Fashion, Feminism, and the Sexual Revolution*
    G&L Rev W - v22 - i6 - Nov-Dec 2015 - p40(2) [501+]
    PW - v262 - i1 - Jan 5 2015 - p65(2) [51-500]

Paoli, Maria Pia - *Nel laboratorio della storia: Una guida alle fonti dell'eta' moderna*
    Six Ct J - v46 - i1 - Spring 2015 - p175-176 [501+]

Paolini, Gregory - *Arts and Crafts Furniture Projects: A Skill-Building Guide Featuring 9 Beautiful Projects*
    LJ - v140 - i11 - June 15 2015 - p88(1) [51-500]

Papadakis, Maxine A. - *Current Medical Diagnosis and Treament 2015*
    Bwatch - March 2015 - pNA [51-500]

Papadatos, Alecos - *Democracy (Illus. by Di Donna, Annie)*
    y BL - v111 - i22 - August 1 2015 - p46(1) [51-500]
Democracy (Illus. by Papadatos, Alecos)
    KR - July 1 2015 - pNA [501+]
    PW - v262 - i33 - August 17 2015 - p58(1) [51-500]

Papademetriou, Lisa - *A Tale of Highly Unusual Magic*
    c KR - August 1 2015 - pNA [51-500]
    c BL - v112 - i1 - Sept 1 2015 - p118(1) [51-500]
    c SLJ - v61 - i9 - Sept 2015 - p143(2) [51-500]
    c SLJ - v61 - i12 - Dec 2015 - p106(1) [51-500]

Papanikolaou, Aristotle - *The Mystical as Political: Democracy and Non-Radical Orthodoxy*
    J Ch St - v57 - i2 - Spring 2015 - p376-378 [501+]
    JR - v95 - i4 - Oct 2015 - p575(3) [501+]

Papantoniou, G. - *Religion and Social Transformations in Cyprus: From the Cypriots Basileis to the Hellenistic Strategos*
    Class R - v65 - i1 - April 2015 - p254-256 [501+]

Paparone, Chris - *The Sociology of Military Science: Prospects for Postinstitutional Military Design*
    CS - v44 - i3 - May 2015 - p396-398 [501+]

Papas, Phillip - *Renegade Revolutionary: The Life of General Charles Lee*
    J Am St - v49 - i3 - August 2015 - p628-629 [501+]
    AHR - v120 - i1 - Feb 2015 - p236(1) [501+]

Papernick, Jonathan - *The Book of Stone*
    BL - v111 - i17 - May 1 2015 - p22(1) [51-500]
    LJ - v140 - i7 - April 15 2015 - p79(1) [51-500]

Papke, Edgar - *True Alignment: Linking Company Culture with Customer Needs for Extraordinary Results*
    Per Psy - v68 - i4 - Wntr 2015 - p939(3) [501+]

Papp, Hannah - *The Mystical Backpacker: How to Discover Your Destiny in the Modern World*
    BL - v111 - i16 - April 15 2015 - p14(1) [51-500]
    LJ - v140 - i7 - April 15 2015 - p107(1) [51-500]
    PW - v262 - i15 - April 13 2015 - p75(1) [51-500]

Pappano, Marilyn - *Chance of a Lifetime*
    PW - v262 - i45 - Nov 9 2015 - p43(1) [51-500]
A Promise of Forever
    PW - v262 - i21 - May 25 2015 - p44(1) [51-500]

Pappos, Ioannis - *Hotel Living*
    BL - v111 - i17 - May 1 2015 - p75(1) [51-500]
    KR - May 1 2015 - pNA [51-500]

Papson, Don - *Secret Lives of the Underground Railroad in New York City: Sydney Howard Gay, Louis Napoleon and the Record of Fugitives*
    NYT - July 19 2015 - p2(L) [501+]

Papstgeschichte des Hohen Mittelalters: Digitale und Hilfswissenschaftliche Zugangsweisen zu einer Kulturgeschichte Europas
    HNet - June 2015 - pNA [501+]

Paquet, Pierre - *A Glance Backward (Illus. by Sandoval, Tony)*
    y BL - v111 - i22 - August 1 2015 - p47(2) [51-500]

Paquette, Ammi-Joan - *Princess Juniper of the Hourglass*
    c BL - v111 - i21 - July 1 2015 - p76(1) [51-500]
    c KR - April 15 2015 - pNA [51-500]
    c SLJ - v61 - i6 - June 2015 - p103(2) [51-500]

Paquette, Gabriel B. - *Imperial Portugal in the Age of Atlantic Revolutions: The Luso-Brazilian World, c. 1770-1850*
    HNet - Jan 2015 - pNA [501+]

Parachini, Jodie - *The Snake Who Said Shh ...*
    KR - April 1 2015 - pNA [51-500]

Paraclete Press - *Life Is a Gift: A Book for Thankful Hearts*
    RVBW - Jan 2015 - pNA [51-500]

Paradis, Odile - *Mystere a la montagne du Diable*
    c Res Links - v20 - i5 - June 2015 - p42(2) [51-500]

Parajuly, Prajwal - *The Gurkha's Daughter*
    PSQ - v89 - i2 - Summer 2015 - p169(3) [501+]

Parani, Maria - *Court Ceremonies and the Rituals of Power in Byzantium and the Medieval Mediterranean: Comparative Perspectives*
    HER - v130 - i545 - August 2015 - p947(2) [501+]

Parascandola, Louis J. - *A Coney Island Reader*
    WLT - v89 - i3-4 - May-August 2015 - p111(1) [51-500]

Paraschas, Sotirios - *The Realist Author and Sympathetic Imagination*
    MLR - v110 - i2 - April 2015 - p516-517 [501+]

Paravicini-Bagliani, Agostino - *Morte e elezione del papa: Norme, riti e conflitti: Il medioevo*
    HER - v130 - i543 - April 2015 - p422(3) [501+]

Pardee, Jessica Warner - *Surviving Katrina: The Experiences of Low-Income African American Women*
    CS - v44 - i3 - May 2015 - p437-438 [501+]

Pardo, Alona - *Constructing Worlds: Photography and Architecture in the Modern Age*
    LJ - v140 - i9 - May 15 2015 - p80(1) [51-500]

Pare, Arleen - *Lake of Two Mountains*
    Can Lit - i224 - Spring 2015 - p123 [501+]

Pare, Simon - *The Little Paris Bookshop*
    BL - v111 - i17 - May 1 2015 - p76(1) [51-500]

Paredes, Mario J. - *The History of the National Encuentros: Hispanic Americans in the One Catholic Church*
    AM - v213 - i9 - Oct 5 2015 - p36(2) [501+]

Parent, Jason - *Seeing Evil*
    PW - v262 - i45 - Nov 9 2015 - p40(1) [51-500]

Parenteau, Shirley - *Bears and a Birthday (Illus. by Walker, David)*
    c HB Guide - v26 - i2 - Fall 2015 - p16(1) [51-500]
Dolls of Hope
    c HB - v91 - i5 - Sept-Oct 2015 - p114(1) [51-500]
    c KR - July 1 2015 - pNA [51-500]
    c SLJ - v61 - i9 - Sept 2015 - p144(1) [51-500]
Ship of Dolls (Read by Reinders, Kate). Audiobook Review
    c BL - v111 - i9-10 - Jan 1 2015 - p118(1) [51-500]
Ship of Dolls
    y HB Guide - v26 - i1 - Spring 2015 - p88(1) [51-500]
    y Magpies - v30 - i1 - March 2015 - p36(1) [51-500]
    RVBW - Jan 2015 - pNA [51-500]

Pares, Luis Nicolau - *The Formation of Candomble: Vodun History and Ritual in Brazil*
    AHR - v120 - i4 - Oct 2015 - p1533-1534 [501+]
    WestFolk - v74 - i2 - Spring 2015 - p233-234 [501+]

Paretsky, Sara - *Brush Back (Read by Peakes, Karen). Audiobook Review*
    PW - v262 - i39 - Sept 28 2015 - p86(1) [51-500]
Brush Back
    BL - v111 - i19-20 - June 1 2015 - p48(1) [51-500]
    KR - June 1 2015 - pNA [51-500]
    NYTBR - August 2 2015 - p25(L) [51-500]
    PW - v262 - i21 - May 25 2015 - p37(1) [51-500]

Parfitt, Tudor - *Black Jews in Africa and the Americas*
    JR - Jan 2015 - p107(14) [501+]

Pariat, Janice - *Seahorse*
    KR - Nov 15 2015 - pNA [51-500]

Parini, Jay - *Empire of Self: A Life of Gore Vidal*
    BL - v111 - i22 - August 1 2015 - p21(1) [501+]
    Econ - v416 - i8952 - August 22 2015 - p70(US) [501+]
    KR - August 1 2015 - pNA [501+]
    LJ - v140 - i14 - Sept 1 2015 - p101(1) [501+]
    Nat R - v67 - i22 - Dec 7 2015 - p43(3) [501+]
    NY - v91 - i33 - Oct 26 2015 - p83 [501+]
    NYT - Oct 19 2015 - pC1(L) [501+]
    NYTBR - Nov 29 2015 - p12(L) [501+]
    PW - v262 - i32 - August 10 2015 - p52(1) [51-500]
Every Time a Friend Succeeds Something inside Me Dies: The Life of Gore Vidal
    Spec - v328 - i9758 - Sept 5 2015 - p36(1) [501+]
    TLS - i5872 - Oct 16 2015 - p12(2) [501+]

Parins, James W. - *Literacy and Intellectual Life in the Cherokee Nation: 1820-1906*
    Am Ind CRJ - v39 - i1 - Wntr 2015 - p131-134 [501+]

Paris, Alain - *Throne of Ice*
    PW - v262 - i18 - May 4 2015 - p104(1) [51-500]

Paris, Harper - *The Mystery across the Secret Bridge (Illus. by Calo, Marcos)*
    c HB Guide - v26 - i2 - Fall 2015 - p70(1) [51-500]
The Mystery in the Forbidden City (Illus. by Calo, Marcos)
    c HB Guide - v26 - i1 - Spring 2015 - p64(1) [51-500]
The Mystery of the Suspicious Spices (Illus. by Calo, Marcos)
    c HB Guide - v26 - i2 - Fall 2015 - p70(1) [51-500]

Paris Match. Audiobook Review
    Bwatch - Jan 2015 - pNA [51-500]

Parish, Helen - *Clerical Celibacy in the West: c. 1100-1700*
    CHR - v101 - i2 - Spring 2015 - p349(3) [501+]
The Search for Authority in Reformation Europe
    Ren Q - v68 - i1 - Spring 2015 - p341-343 [501+]

Parish, Herman - *Amelia Bedelia Chalks One Up (Illus. by Avril, Lynne)*
  c   HB Guide - v26 - i2 - Fall 2015 - p60(1) [51-500]
Amelia Bedelia Is for the Birds (Illus. by Avril, Lynne)
  c   HB Guide - v26 - i2 - Fall 2015 - p60(1) [51-500]
Amelia Bedelia Shapes Up (Illus. by Avril, Lynne)
  c   HB Guide - v26 - i1 - Spring 2015 - p64(1) [51-500]
Amelia Bedelia's First Day of School (Illus. by Avril, Lynne)
  c   SLJ - v61 - i8 - August 2015 - p60(1) [51-500]
Parisot, Eric - *Graveyard Poetry: Religion, Aesthetics and the Mid-Eighteenth-Century Poetic Condition*
  RES - v66 - i273 - Feb 2015 - p176-178 [501+]
Park, Adele - *Gadzooks! A Comically Quirky Audio Book (Read by several narrators). Audiobook Review*
  c   PW - v262 - i8 - Feb 23 2015 - p71(1) [51-500]
Park, Albert L. - *Encountering Modernity: Christianity in East Asia and Asian America*
  Pac A - v88 - i2 - June 2015 - p268 [501+]
Park, Bae-gyoon - *Locating Neoliberalism in East Asia: Neoliberalizing Spaces in Developmental States*
  CS - v44 - i3 - May 2015 - p398-399 [501+]
Park, David - *The Truth Commissioner*
  TimHES - i2218 - August 27 2015 - p43(1) [501+]
Park, Ed - *Buffalo Noir*
  KR - Sept 15 2015 - pNA [51-500]
  PW - v262 - i36 - Sept 7 2015 - p46(2) [51-500]
Park, Eugene Y. - *A Family of No Prominence: The Descendants of Pak Tokhwa and the Birth of Modern Korea*
  AHR - v120 - i3 - June 2015 - p997-998 [501+]
  Pac A - v88 - i4 - Dec 2015 - p943 [501+]
Park, Graham - *The Making of Europe: A Geological History*
  SPBW - Jan 2015 - pNA [51-500]
Park, Linda Sue - *Forest of Wonders (Illus. by Madsen, Jim)*
  c   KR - Dec 15 2015 - pNA [51-500]
  c   PW - v262 - i52 - Dec 21 2015 - p154(1) [51-500]
Yaks Yak: Animal Word Pairs (Illus. by Reinhardt, Jennifer Black)
  c   KR - Dec 15 2015 - pNA [51-500]
  c   PW - v262 - i51 - Dec 14 2015 - p84(1) [51-500]
  c   SLJ - v61 - i12 - Dec 2015 - p94(1) [51-500]
Park, Nani - *Hanok: The Korean House (Illus. by Lee, Jongkeun)*
  LJ - v140 - i3 - Feb 15 2015 - p101(1) [51-500]
Park, Patricia - *Re Jane*
  y   BL - v111 - i17 - May 1 2015 - p77(1) [51-500]
  CSM - May 13 2015 - pNA [501+]
  Ent W - i1362 - May 8 2015 - p57(1) [501+]
  KR - March 15 2015 - pNA [501+]
  LJ - v140 - i10 - June 1 2015 - p95(1) [51-500]
  NYTBR - May 31 2015 - p20(L) [501+]
  PW - v262 - i11 - March 16 2015 - p57(1) [51-500]
Park, Paul - *All Those Vanished Engines*
  MFSF - v128 - i1-2 - Jan-Feb 2015 - p48(8) [501+]
Park, Peter K.J. - *Africa, Asia, and the History of Philosophy: Racism in the Formation of the Philosophical Canon, 1780-1830*
  GSR - v38 - i1 - Feb 2015 - p164-165 [501+]
Park, Sooyong - *Great Soul of Siberia: Passion, Obsession, and One Man's Quest for the World's Most Elusive Tiger*
  KR - August 15 2015 - pNA [501+]
Park, Tony - *Ivory*
  BL - v112 - i4 - Oct 15 2015 - p22(1) [51-500]
  KR - Sept 15 2015 - pNA [51-500]
  PW - v262 - i36 - Sept 7 2015 - p47(1) [51-500]
Park, Yeonmi - *In Order to Live: A North Korean Girl's Journey to Freedom*
  KR - August 15 2015 - pNA [501+]
  NS - v144 - i5282 - Oct 2 2015 - p71(1) [501+]
  NYTBR - Nov 29 2015 - p26(L) [501+]
Park, Yung Chul - *How Finance Is Shaping the Economies of China, Japan, and Korea*
  Pac A - v88 - i3 - Sept 2015 - p677 [501+]
Parker, Amy - *Beasts & Children: Stories*
  y   BL - v112 - i6 - Nov 15 2015 - p20(1) [51-500]
  KR - Oct 15 2015 - pNA [51-500]
The Plans I Have for You (Illus. by Brantley-Newton, Vanessa)
  c   BL - v112 - i6 - Nov 15 2015 - p49(1) [51-500]
  c   KR - June 15 2015 - pNA [51-500]
Parker, Amy Christine - *Astray*
  y   HB Guide - v26 - i1 - Spring 2015 - p119(1) [51-500]
Parker, Barry - *The Physics of War: From Arrows to Atoms*
  RAH - v43 - i2 - June 2015 - p300-306 [501+]

Parker, C.L. - *Playing Dirty*
  LJ - v140 - i6 - April 1 2015 - p70(2) [501+]
  PW - v262 - i12 - March 23 2015 - p54(1) [51-500]
Parker, Danny - *Lola's Toybox: The Patchwork Picnic (Illus. by Shield, Guy)*
  c   Magpies - v30 - i4 - Sept 2015 - p32(1) [501+]
Perfect (Illus. by Blackwood, Freya)
  c   Magpies - v30 - i4 - Sept 2015 - p26(1) [501+]
Parker, Derek - *This Tattooed Land*
  Quad - v59 - i5 - May 2015 - p108(3) [501+]
Parker, Emily - *Now I Know What My Comrades Are: Voices from the Internet Underground*
  NYTBR - March 15 2015 - p28(L) [501+]
Parker, Geoffrey - *Global Crisis: War, Climate Change and Catastrophe in the Seventeenth Century*
  AHR - v120 - i4 - Oct 2015 - p1429-1431 [501+]
  GSR - v38 - i1 - Feb 2015 - p157-159 [501+]
  Historian - v77 - i3 - Fall 2015 - p636(2) [501+]
  Lon R Bks - v37 - i5 - March 5 2015 - p29(2) [501+]
Imprudent King: A New Life of Philip II
  Bks & Cult - v21 - i6 - Nov-Dec 2015 - p22(2) [501+]
  Six Ct J - v46 - i3 - Fall 2015 - p829-831 [501+]
  TLS - i5835 - Jan 30 2015 - p3(2) [501+]
War, Climate Change and Catastrophe in the Seventeenth Century
  W&M Q - v72 - i1 - Jan 2015 - p159-167 [501+]
Parker, Gewanda J. - *It Only Hurts When I Can't Run: One Girl's Story*
  SPBW - August 2015 - pNA [51-500]
Parker, Greig - *Probate Inventories of French Immigrants in Early Modern London*
  FS - v69 - i3 - July 2015 - p390-391 [501+]
  Six Ct J - v46 - i1 - Spring 2015 - p133-134 [501+]
Parker, Jake - *Missile Mouse: The Star Crusher (Illus. by Parker, Jake)*
  c   BL - v112 - i1 - Sept 1 2015 - p114(1) [501+]
Parker, Jeff - *Batman '66, vol. 1 (Illus. by Case, Jonathan)*
  y   VOYA - v37 - i6 - Feb 2015 - p50(2) [501+]
Parker, Jeri - *Unmoored*
  c   BL - v112 - i7 - Dec 1 2015 - p34(2) [501+]
Parker, Joanne - *Britannia Obscura: Mapping Hidden Britain*
  TimHES - i2184 - Jan 1 2015 - p67(1) [501+]
  TLS - i5849 - May 8 2015 - p26(1) [501+]
Parker, John - *The Oxford Handbook of Modern African History*
  HER - v130 - i544 - June 2015 - p795(4) [501+]
Parker, John L. - *Racing the Rain*
  y   BL - v111 - i19-20 - June 1 2015 - p44(1) [51-500]
Parker, K.J. - *The Last Witness*
  PW - v262 - i35 - August 31 2015 - p67(1) [51-500]
Savages
  PW - v262 - i20 - May 18 2015 - p68(1) [51-500]
Parker, Kate - *The Royal Assassin*
  PW - v262 - i21 - May 25 2015 - p36(1) [51-500]
Sade's Sensibilities
  FS - v69 - i4 - Oct 2015 - p531-532 [501+]
Parker, M.E. - *Jonesbridge: Echoes of Hinterland*
  y   VOYA - v38 - i2 - June 2015 - p80(1) [501+]
Parker, Marjorie Blain - *I Love You Near and Far (Illus. by Henry, Jed)*
  c   HB Guide - v26 - i2 - Fall 2015 - p16(1) [51-500]
Parker, Mary-Louise - *Dear Mr. You*
  BL - v112 - i4 - Oct 15 2015 - p14(1) [51-500]
  LJ - v140 - i17 - Oct 15 2015 - p87(1) [51-500]
  KR - Sept 1 2015 - pNA [51-500]
  PW - v262 - i32 - August 10 2015 - p48(1) [51-500]
Parker, Matt - *Things to Make and Do in the Fourth Dimension: A Mathematician's Journey through Narcissistic Numbers, Optimal Dating Algorithms, at Least Two Kinds of Infinity, and More*
  Math T - v109 - i2 - Sept 2015 - p159-159 [501+]
Parker, Matthew - *Goldeneye: Where Bond Was Born: Ian Fleming's Jamaica*
  BL - v111 - i12 - Feb 15 2015 - p20(1) [51-500]
  PW - v262 - i2 - Jan 12 2015 - p50(1) [501+]
Willoughbyland: England's Lost Colony
  Spec - v328 - i9754 - August 8 2015 - p26(2) [501+]
Parker, Morgan - *Other People's Comfort Keeps Me Up at Night*
  PW - v262 - i20 - May 18 2015 - p63(1) [51-500]

Parker, Natalie C. - *Behold the Bones*
  y   KR - Dec 1 2015 - pNA [51-500]
Beware the Wild
  y   HB Guide - v26 - i1 - Spring 2015 - p119(1) [51-500]
Parker, Robert (b. 1950-) - *Personal Names in Ancient Anatolia: Proceedings of the British Academy*
  Class R - v65 - i1 - April 2015 - p3-5 [501+]
Parker, Robert Nash - *Alcohol and Violence: The Nature of the Relationship and the Promise of Prevention*
  CS - v44 - i1 - Jan 2015 - p145(1) [501+]
Parker, S.M. - *The Girl Who Fell*
  y   PW - v262 - i52 - Dec 21 2015 - p158(1) [51-500]
Parker, Stephen - *Bertolt Brecht: A Literary Life*
  MLR - v110 - i2 - April 2015 - p596-597 [501+]
Parker, Steve - *Evolution: The Whole Story*
  y   BL - v112 - i7 - Dec 1 2015 - p13(1) [51-500]
  New Sci - v227 - i3038 - Sept 12 2015 - p42(1) [501+]
A Journey through the Human Body
  c   KR - Oct 1 2015 - pNA [51-500]
Race to the Moon
  c   Sci & Ch - v53 - i4 - Dec 2015 - p99 [501+]
  c   Sch Lib - v63 - i3 - Autumn 2015 - p175(1) [51-500]
Parkhurst, Melissa - *To Win the Indian Heart: Music at Chemawa Indian School*
  Am Ind CRJ - v39 - i2 - Spring 2015 - p169-171 [501+]
  WHQ - v46 - i2 - Summer 2015 - p247-248 [501+]
Parkin, Simon - *Death by Video Game: Tales of Obsession from the Virtual Frontline*
  NS - v144 - i5290 - Nov 27 2015 - p46(3) [501+]
  TLS - i5875 - Nov 6 2015 - p29(1) [501+]
Parkinson, Gavin - *Futures of Surrealism: Myth, Science Fiction and Fantastic Art in France, 1936-1969*
  Apo - v181 - i631 - May 2015 - p108(2) [501+]
Parkinson, Kate - *Grace (Illus. by Parkinson, Kate)*
  c   HB Guide - v26 - i2 - Fall 2015 - p60(1) [51-500]
  c   KR - Feb 15 2015 - pNA [501+]
  SLJ - v61 - i4 - April 2015 - p139(1) [51-500]
Parks, Brad - *The Fraud*
  BL - v111 - i19-20 - June 1 2015 - p53(1) [51-500]
  KR - May 1 2015 - pNA [51-500]
  PW - v262 - i18 - May 4 2015 - p99(1) [51-500]
Parks, Carrie Stuart - *The Bones Will Speak*
  KR - June 1 2015 - pNA [51-500]
Parks, Cecily - *O'Nights*
  PW - v262 - i7 - Feb 16 2015 - p157(1) [51-500]
Parks, Conon - *Empty Bottle of Gin*
  KR - Nov 15 2015 - pNA [51-500]
Some Kind of Ending
  KR - Dec 15 2015 - pNA [51-500]
Parks, Kathy - *The Lifeboat Clique*
  y   PW - v262 - i51 - Dec 14 2015 - p86(1) [51-500]
  y   SLJ - v61 - i12 - Dec 2015 - p126(1) [51-500]
Parks, Peggy - *How Serious a Problem Is Synthetic Drug Use?*
  y   SLJ - v61 - i9 - Sept 2015 - p176(1) [51-500]
Parks, Peggy J. - *HPV*
  y   VOYA - v38 - i3 - August 2015 - p88(1) [51-500]
Smoking
  c   HB Guide - v26 - i1 - Spring 2015 - p142(1) [51-500]
Parks, Robin - *Egg Heaven*
  ABR - v36 - i5 - July-August 2015 - p28(1) [51-500]
Parks, Ronald D. - *The Darkest Period: The Kanza Indians and Their Last Homeland, 1846-1873*
  Roundup M - v22 - i6 - August 2015 - p39(1) [501+]
  WHQ - v46 - i2 - Summer 2015 - p250(1) [501+]
Parks, Suzan-Lori - *Father Comes Home from the Wars*
  Am Theat - v32 - i6 - July-August 2015 - p8(1) [51-500]
Parks, Tim - *Indian Nocturne*
  NYRB - v62 - i10 - June 4 2015 - p63(3) [501+]
A Literary Tour of Italy
  Spec - v328 - i9750 - July 11 2015 - p32(2) [501+]
Painting Death
  BL - v112 - i4 - Oct 15 2015 - p23(1) [51-500]
  NYTBR - Oct 11 2015 - p23(L) [501+]
  PW - v262 - i34 - August 24 2015 - p59(1) [51-500]
Where I'm Reading From: The Changing World of Books
  BL - v111 - i18 - May 15 2015 - p4(1) [51-500]
  LJ - v140 - i5 - March 15 2015 - p104(1) [51-500]
  NYTBR - August 23 2015 - p38(L) [501+]
  PW - v262 - i8 - Feb 23 2015 - p63(2) [501+]
  TLS - i5831 - Jan 2 2015 - p23(1) [501+]
  KR - March 1 2015 - pNA [501+]

The Woman of Porto Pim
    NYRB - v62 - i10 - June 4 2015 - p63(3) [501+]

Parlamentarismuskritik und Antiparlamentarismus in Europa
    HNet - Sept 2015 - pNA [501+]

Parlett, Graham - *Ralph Vaughan Williams: Fantasia for Piano and Orchestra - Study Score*
    Notes - v71 - i3 - March 2015 - p573(5) [501+]

Parmar, Priya - *Vanessa and Her Sister (Read by Fox, Emilia). Audiobook Review*
    Bwatch - March 2015 - pNA [51-500]
Vanessa and Her Sister (Read by Fox Emilia). Audiobook Review
    PW - v262 - i12 - March 23 2015 - p71(2) [51-500]
Vanessa and Her Sister
    CSM - Jan 21 2015 - pNA [501+]
    Ent W - i1347 - Jan 23 2015 - p65(1) [501+]
    G&L Rev W - v22 - i3 - May-June 2015 - p32(2) [501+]
Vanessa and Her Sister. Audiobook Review
    LJ - v140 - i7 - April 15 2015 - p47(1) [51-500]
Vanessa and Her Sister
    Nat Post - v17 - i68 - Jan 17 2015 - pWP9(1) [501+]
    NS - v144 - i5261 - May 7 2015 - p46(3) [501+]
    NYTBR - Jan 11 2015 - p11(L) [501+]
    NYTBR - Nov 22 2015 - p36(L) [501+]

Parodi, Laura E. - *The Visual World of Muslim India: The Art, Culture and Society of the Deccan in the Early Modern Era*
    NYRB - v62 - i11 - June 25 2015 - p36(3) [501+]

Parr, Adrian - *The Wrath of Capital: Neoliberalism and Climate Change Politics*
    CS - v44 - i3 - May 2015 - p314-321 [501+]

Parr, Delia - *The Midwife's Choice*
    BL - v112 - i6 - Nov 15 2015 - p18(1) [51-500]
The Midwife's Tale
    BL - v111 - i18 - May 15 2015 - p31(1) [51-500]

Parr, Maria - *Adventures with Waffles (Read by Daniels, Luke). Audiobook Review*
    c SLJ - v61 - i9 - Sept 2015 - p59(1) [51-500]
Adventures with Waffles (Illus. by Forrester, Kate)
    c BL - v111 - i15 - April 1 2015 - p76(1) [51-500]
    c CCB-B - v69 - i1 - Sept 2015 - p42(2) [51-500]
    c HB - v91 - i3 - May-June 2015 - p115(2) [501+]
    c HB Guide - v26 - i2 - Fall 2015 - p70(1) [51-500]
    c KR - March 1 2015 - pNA [51-500]
    c SLJ - v61 - i3 - March 2015 - p142(1) [51-500]

Parr, Rolf - *Die Fremde als Heimat: Heimatkunst, Kolonialismus, Expeditionen*
    MLR - v110 - i3 - July 2015 - p900-901 [501+]

Parr, Todd - *The Goodbye Book (Illus. by Parr, Todd)*
    c KR - Sept 15 2015 - pNA [51-500]
    c PW - v262 - i39 - Sept 28 2015 - p88(1) [51-500]
    c SLJ - v61 - i8 - August 2015 - p75(2) [51-500]
It's Okay to Make Mistakes
    c HB Guide - v26 - i1 - Spring 2015 - p13(1) [51-500]

Parramon Editorial Team - *Paint Like the Masters*
    RVBW - April 2015 - pNA [501+]

Parrett, Favel - *When the Night Comes*
    BL - v111 - i12 - Feb 15 2015 - p33(1) [51-500]
    KR - Feb 15 2015 - pNA [501+]
    LJ - v140 - i6 - April 1 2015 - p84(1) [51-500]

Parrillo, Nicholas R. - *Against the Profit Motive: The Salary Revolution in American Government, 1780-1940*
    AHR - v120 - i2 - April 2015 - p613-614 [501+]
    RAH - v43 - i2 - June 2015 - p274-280 [501+]

Parrington, John - *The Deeper Genome: Why There Is More to the Human Genome Than Meets the Eye*
    LJ - v140 - i10 - June 1 2015 - p130(1) [51-500]
    TimHES - i2215 - August 6 2015 - p48-48 [501+]

Parrish, Emma - *Flutterby Butterfly (Illus. by Parrish, Emma)*
    c KR - July 1 2015 - pNA [51-500]
    c PW - v262 - i15 - April 13 2015 - p78(2) [501+]

Parrish, Susan Scott - *The History and Present State of Virginia*
    Historian - v77 - i2 - Summer 2015 - p322(2) [501+]
    RAH - v43 - i2 - June 2015 - p210-215 [501+]

Parry, Leslie - *Church of Marvels*
    BL - v111 - i16 - April 15 2015 - p32(1) [51-500]
    KR - March 1 2015 - pNA [51-500]
    NYTBR - May 31 2015 - p43(L) [501+]
    PW - v262 - i13 - March 30 2015 - p46(2) [51-500]

Parry, Rosanne - *The Turn of the Tide*
    c BL - v112 - i6 - Nov 15 2015 - p56(1) [51-500]
    c KR - Oct 15 2015 - pNA [51-500]
    c PW - v262 - i41 - Oct 12 2015 - p68(2) [51-500]
    c SLJ - v61 - i11 - Nov 2015 - p100(3) [51-500]

Parshall, Karen Hunger - *Bridging Traditions: Alchemy, Chemistry, and Paracelsian Practices in the Early Modern Era*
    RVBW - Nov 2015 - pNA [51-500]

Parsley, Elise - *If You Ever Want to Bring an Alligator to School, Don't! (Illus. by Parsley, Elise)*
    c SLJ - v61 - i7 - July 2015 - p67(1) [51-500]

Parsons, Ash - *Still Waters*
    y BL - v111 - i13 - March 1 2015 - p60(1) [51-500]
    y KR - Feb 1 2015 - pNA [51-500]
    y PW - v262 - i6 - Feb 9 2015 - p71(1) [51-500]
    y VOYA - v37 - i6 - Feb 2015 - p62(2) [51-500]

Parsons, Chuck - *Texas Ranger N.O. Reynolds, The Intrepid*
    Roundup M - v22 - i3 - Feb 2015 - p24(1) [501+]
    Roundup M - v22 - i6 - August 2015 - p39(1) [501+]

Parsons, Keith - *It Started with Copernicus: Vital Questions about Science*
    QRB - v90 - i2 - June 2015 - p201(1) [501+]

Parsons, Michael - *Reformation Faith: Exegesis and Theology in the Protestant Reformations*
    CH - v84 - i3 - Sept 2015 - p662(3) [501+]
    Six Ct J - v46 - i1 - Spring 2015 - p236-237 [501+]

Parsons, Michelle A. - *Dying Unneeded: The Cultural Context of the Russian Mortality Crisis*
    HNet - May 2015 - pNA [501+]
    MAQ - v29 - i3 - Sept 2015 - pb-5-b-7 [501+]

Parsons, Timothy H. - *The Second British Empire: In the Crucible of the Twentieth Century*
    AHR - v120 - i4 - Oct 2015 - p1550-1551 [501+]
    IJAHS - v48 - i1 - Wntr 2015 - p166-168 [501+]

Parsons, Tony - *The Murder Bag (Read by Mace, Colin). Audiobook Review*
    BL - v111 - i17 - May 1 2015 - p58(2) [51-500]
    LJ - v140 - i6 - April 1 2015 - p48(1) [51-500]
The Slaughter Man
    BL - v112 - i1 - Sept 1 2015 - p50(1) [51-500]
    KR - July 15 2015 - pNA [51-500]
    PW - v262 - i23 - June 8 2015 - p36(1) [51-500]

Parssinen, Keija - *The Unraveling of Mercy Louis*
    BL - v111 - i11 - Feb 1 2015 - p29(1) [51-500]
    KR - Jan 15 2015 - pNA [51-500]
    LJ - v140 - i3 - Feb 15 2015 - p91(1) [51-500]
    NYTBR - March 15 2015 - p14(L) [501+]
    PW - v262 - i2 - Jan 12 2015 - p34(1) [51-500]
    y SLJ - v61 - i12 - Dec 2015 - p132(1) [51-500]

Partington, Gill - *Book Destruction from the Medieval to the Contemporary*
    TLS - i5843 - March 27 2015 - p27(1) [51-500]

Partridge, Christopher - *The Lyre of Orpheus: Popular Music, the Sacred, & the Profane*
    JAAR - v83 - i4 - Dec 2015 - p1160-1163 [501+]

Partridge, Damani J. - *Hypersexuality and Headscarves: Race, Sex, and Citizenship in the New Germany*
    GSR - v38 - i3 - Oct 2015 - p709-710 [501+]

Partridge, Derek Velez - *The Book of Kringle: Legend of the North Pole (Illus. by Wenzel, David)*
    c PW - v262 - i37 - Sept 14 2015 - p70(1) [51-500]

Partridge, Frances - *Memories*
    TimHES - i2186 - Jan 15 2015 - p49(1) [501+]

Pascale, Lorraine - *Everyday Easy*
    PW - v262 - i1 - Jan 5 2015 - p67(1) [51-500]

Pascente, Fred - *Mob Cop: My Life of Crime in the Chicago Police Department*
    KR - April 15 2015 - pNA [501+]
    LJ - v140 - i10 - June 1 2015 - p119(1) [51-500]

Paschkis, Julie - *Flutter & Hum: Animal Poems / Aleteo y Zumbido: Poemas de Animales (Illus. by Paschkis, Julie)*
    c CCB-B - v68 - i11 - July-August 2015 - p533(2) [501+]
    c HB - v91 - i5 - Sept-Oct 2015 - p123(1) [51-500]
    c PW - v262 - i49 - Dec 2 2015 - p55(1) [51-500]
    c SLJ - v61 - i5 - May 2015 - p135(1) [51-500]
P. Zonka Lays an Egg (Read by Morton, Elizabeth). Audiobook Review
    c SLJ - v61 - i12 - Dec 2015 - p74(1) [51-500]
P. Zonka Lays an Egg (Illus. by Paschkis, Julie)
    c CH Bwatch - March 2015 - pNA [51-500]
    c CH Bwatch - May 2015 - pNA [51-500]
    c HB - v91 - i2 - March-April 2015 - p79(2) [51-500]
    c HB Guide - v26 - i2 - Fall 2015 - p47(1) [51-500]
    c KR - Jan 15 2015 - pNA [51-500]
    c PW - v262 - i2 - Jan 12 2015 - p63(1) [51-500]
    c PW - v262 - i49 - Dec 2 2015 - p17(1) [51-500]
    c SLJ - v61 - i2 - Feb 2015 - p75(1) [51-500]

Pasciak, Adam - *Jones' After the Smoke Clears: Surviving the Police Shooting--an Analysis of the Post Officer-Involved Shooting Trauma*
    RVBW - June 2015 - pNA [501+]

Pascuzzi, Robert - *The Ravine*
    KR - Oct 1 2015 - pNA [501+]

Pasdzierny, Matthias - *Wiederaufnahme? Ruckkehr aus dem Exil und das Westdeutsche Musikleben nach 1945*
    HNet - Jan 2015 - pNA [501+]

Pash, Melinda L. - *In the Shadow of the Greatest Generation: The Americans Who Fought the Korean War*
    J Mil H - v79 - i1 - Jan 2015 - p262-263 [501+]

Pash, Sidney - *The Currents of War: A New History of American-Japanese Relations, 1899-1941*
    J Mil H - v79 - i1 - Jan 2015 - p222-223 [501+]

Pashley, Hilton - *Gabriel's Clock*
    y HB Guide - v26 - i1 - Spring 2015 - p88(1) [51-500]

Pashley, Jennifer - *The Scamp*
    PW - v262 - i23 - June 8 2015 - p34(1) [51-500]
    KR - June 1 2015 - pNA [51-500]

Pask, Colin - *Magnificent Principia: Exploring Isaac Newton's Masterpiece*
    Phys Today - v68 - i1 - Jan 2015 - p45-46 [501+]

Pasley, Jeffrey L. - *The First Presidential Contest: 1796 and the Founding of American Democracy*
    Historian - v77 - i3 - Fall 2015 - p571(2) [501+]

Pasmore, Victoria Micklish - *Stars of the Rock 'N' Roll Highway*
    c KR - Nov 15 2015 - pNA [51-500]

Pasquale, Frank - *The Black Box Society: The Secret Algorithms That Control Money and Information*
    New Sci - v225 - i3004 - Jan 17 2015 - p40(2) [501+]
    TimHES - i2194 - March 12 2015 - p50(1) [501+]

Pasquier, Roger F. - *Painting Central Park*
    LJ - v140 - i15 - Sept 15 2015 - p73(1) [51-500]

Pass, Emma - *Acid. Audiobook Review*
    c BL - v111 - i14 - March 15 2015 - p24(2) [51-500]
The Fearless
    y CCB-B - v68 - i10 - June 2015 - p508(2) [51-500]
    y HB Guide - v26 - i2 - Fall 2015 - p134(1) [51-500]
    y KR - Feb 1 2015 - pNA [51-500]
    y PW - v262 - i5 - Feb 2 2015 - p63(1) [51-500]
    y VOYA - v38 - i2 - June 2015 - p81(1) [51-500]

Passarlay, Gulwali - *The Lightless Sky*
    KR - Dec 15 2015 - pNA [51-500]

Passmore, Jonathan - *The Wiley-Blackwell Handbook of the Psychology of Coaching and Mentoring*
    Per Psy - v68 - i4 - Wntr 2015 - p934(3) [501+]

Passmore, Kevin - *The Right in France from the Third Republic to Vichy*
    JMH - v87 - i2 - June 2015 - p455(4) [501+]

Passo, Elizabeth - *Birthday Party SBD (Illus. by Badon, Joe)*
    c CH Bwatch - Nov 2015 - pNA [51-500]

Passos, John Dos - *Manhattan Transfer*
    TimHES - i2194 - March 12 2015 - p49(1) [501+]

Past, Elena - *Methods of Murder: Beccarian Introspection and Lombrosian Vivisection in Italian Crime Fiction*
    MLR - v110 - i2 - April 2015 - p569-572 [501+]

Pastan, Linda - *Insomnia: Poems*
    BL - v112 - i5 - Nov 1 2015 - p14(1) [51-500]
    LJ - v140 - i13 - August 1 2015 - p101(2) [51-500]

Paster, Thomas - *The Role of Business in the Development of the Welfare State and Labor Markets in Germany: Containing Social Reforms*
    GSR - v38 - i1 - Feb 2015 - p222-224 [501+]

Pastis, Stephan - *Sanitized for Your Protection (Illus. by Pastis, Stephan)*
    c KR - August 1 2015 - pNA [51-500]
Timmy Failure: Sanitized for Your Protection (Illus. by Pastis, Stephan)
    c BL - v112 - i2 - Sept 15 2015 - p66(2) [51-500]
Timmy Failure: We Meet Again
    c HB Guide - v26 - i1 - Spring 2015 - p88(1) [51-500]
We Meet Again (Read by Goldsmith, Jared). Audiobook Review
    SLJ - v61 - i3 - March 2015 - p78(1) [51-500]

Pastis, Stephan T. - *Skip School, Fly to Space (Illus. by Pastis, Stephan T.)*
    c SLJ - v61 - i9 - Sept 2015 - p149(1) [51-500]

Pastor, Ben - *Tin Sky*
    PW - v262 - i13 - March 30 2015 - p58(1) [51-500]

Pastor, David - *Sleep Softly (Illus. by Nouren, Elodie)*
    c CH Bwatch - April 2015 - pNA [51-500]

Pastore, Christopher L. - *Between Land and Sea: The Atlantic Coast and the Transformation of New England*
    AHR - v120 - i4 - Oct 2015 - p1472-1473 [501+]
    JAH - v102 - i2 - Sept 2015 - p527-528 [501+]
    JIH - v46 - i2 - Autumn 2015 - p291-292 [501+]

Pasulka, Diana Walsh - *Heaven Can Wait: Purgatory in Catholic Devotional and Popular Culture*
    AM - v213 - i14 - Nov 9 2015 - p37(4) [501+]

Pataki, Allison - *Accidental Empress*
    LJ - v140 - i3 - Feb 15 2015 - p91(2) [51-500]

Patal, Shona - *Flame Tree Road*
    KR - May 1 2015 - pNA [501+]

Patalano, Alessio - *Post-war Japan as a Sea Power: Imperial Legacy, Wartime Experience and the Making of a Navy*
    NWCR - v68 - i4 - Autumn 2015 - p132(2) [51-500]

Patalsky, Kathy - *Happy Healthy Vegan Kitchen*
    PW - v262 - i16 - April 20 2015 - p71(1) [51-500]

Patch, Robert W. - *Indians and the Political Economy of Colonial Central America, 1670-1810*
    Am Ind CRJ - v39 - i1 - Wntr 2015 - p125-127 [501+]
    Ams - v72 - i1 - Jan 2015 - p157(3) [501+]

Patchett, Ann - *This Is the Story of A Happy Marriage (Read by Patchett, Ann). Audiobook Review*
    LJ - v140 - i5 - March 15 2015 - p134(1) [501+]

Pate, SooJin - *From Orphan to Adoptee: U.S. Empire and Genealogies of Korean Adoption*
    AHR - v120 - i2 - April 2015 - p665(1) [501+]
    Amerasia J - v41 - i2 - Spring 2015 - p153-158 [501+]
    JAS - v74 - i2 - May 2015 - p499-500 [501+]

Patel, Kiran Klaus - *European Integration and the Atlantic Community in the 1980s*
    HNet - Jan 2015 - pNA [501+]
The New Deal: A Global History
    KR - Oct 15 2015 - pNA [501+]
    LJ - v140 - i19 - Nov 15 2015 - p95(1) [51-500]

Patel, Meera Lee - *Daily Zen Doodles: 365 Tangle Creations for Inspiration, Relaxation and Mindfulness*
    Bwatch - Jan 2015 - pNA [51-500]

Patel, Sahera - *I'm Not a Celebrity, I am a Muslim: One Woman's Journey to a World of Faith*
    TimHES - i2206 - June 4 2015 - p47(1) [501+]

Patel, Shona - *Flame Tree Road*
    BL - v111 - i18 - May 15 2015 - p29(1) [51-500]
    LJ - v140 - i9 - May 15 2015 - p73(2) [51-500]

Patella, Michael - *Word and Image: The Hermeneutics of the Saint John's Bible*
    Intpr - v69 - i4 - Oct 2015 - p507(1) [501+]

Patent, Dorothy Hinshaw - *The Call of the Osprey (Illus. by Munoz, William)*
    y BL - v111 - i19-20 - June 1 2015 - p70(1) [51-500]
    c CCB-B - v69 - i1 - Sept 2015 - p43(1) [51-500]
    c CH Bwatch - Oct 2015 - pNA [51-500]
    y HB - v91 - i4 - July-August 2015 - p160(1) [51-500]
    y KR - April 15 2015 - pNA [51-500]
    c SLJ - v61 - i7 - July 2015 - p109(3) [51-500]
Decorated Horses (Illus. by Brett, Jeannie)
    c CH Bwatch - June 2015 - pNA [51-500]
    c HB Guide - v26 - i2 - Fall 2015 - p182(1) [51-500]
Super Sniffers: Dog Detectives on the Job
    c HB Guide - v26 - i2 - Fall 2015 - p182(1) [51-500]

Paterculus, Velleius - *The Roman History: From Romulus and the Foundation of Rome to the Reign of the Emperor Tiberius*
    HNet - Jan 2015 - pNA [501+]

Paterniti, Michael - *Love and Other Ways of Dying: Essays*
    CJR - v53 - i6 - March-April 2015 - p60(2) [501+]
    Esq - v163 - i4 - April 2015 - p40(1) [501+]
    LJ - v140 - i5 - March 15 2015 - p104(1) [51-500]
    PW - v262 - i2 - Jan 12 2015 - p50(2) [51-500]

Paterson, Alan - *Final Judgment: The Last Law Lords and the Supreme Court*
    Law Q Rev - v131 - April 2015 - p321-322 [501+]

Paterson, Allison Marlow - *Anzac Sons: Young Peoples Edition*
    c Magpies - v30 - i2 - May 2015 - p24(1) [501+]

Paterson, Katherine - *Stories of My Life (Read by Birmingham, Laurie). Audiobook Review*
    LJ - v140 - i9 - May 15 2015 - p45(2) [51-500]
Stories of My Life
    Bks & Cult - v21 - i2 - March-April 2015 - p9(2) [501+]
    y HB Guide - v26 - i1 - Spring 2015 - p195(1) [51-500]

Paterson, Lindsay - *Social Radicalism and Liberal Education*
    TimHES - i2213 - July 23 2015 - p45(1) [501+]

Patricelli, Leslie - *Boo! (Illus. by Patricelli, Leslie)*
    c HB - v91 - i5 - Sept-Oct 2015 - p69(2) [51-500]
    c KR - Jan 1 2016 - pNA [51-500]
    c PW - v262 - i30 - July 27 2015 - p66(1) [51-500]
    c SLJ - v61 - i9 - Sept 2015 - p108(1) [51-500]
Hop! Hop! (Illus. by Patricelli, Leslie)
    c KR - July 1 2015 - pNA [51-500]
    c SLJ - v61 - i2 - Feb 2015 - p75(1) [51-500]

Patricios, Nicholas N. - *The Sacred Architecture of Byzantium: Art, Liturgy and Symbolism in Early Christian Churches*
    CHR - v101 - i3 - Summer 2015 - p599(2) [501+]

Patrick, Bethanne - *The Books That Changed my Life*
    KR - Dec 15 2015 - pNA [501+]

Patrick, David - *18th-Century English Organ Music: A Graded Anthology, 4 vols.*
    TimHES - i2196 - March 26 2015 - p51(1) [501+]

Patrick, Den - *The Boy with the Porcelain Blade*
    LJ - v140 - i9 - May 15 2015 - p57(4) [501+]
    PW - v262 - i13 - March 30 2015 - p58(1) [51-500]

Patrick, Denise Lewis - *Finding Someplace*
    c BL - v111 - i21 - July 1 2015 - p72(1) [51-500]
    c CCB-B - v69 - i2 - Oct 2015 - p108(1) [51-500]
    c KR - May 1 2015 - pNA [51-500]
    c NYTBR - August 9 2015 - p16(L) [501+]
    c PW - v262 - i21 - May 25 2015 - p59(1) [51-500]
    c SLJ - v61 - i6 - June 2015 - p104(1) [51-500]
    y VOYA - v38 - i3 - August 2015 - p66(1) [51-500]

Patrick-Goudreau, Colleen - *The 30-Day Vegan Challenge*
    PW - v262 - i9 - March 2 2015 - p79(1) [51-500]

Patrick, Kat - *I am Doodle Cat (Illus. by Marriott, Lauren)*
    c Magpies - v30 - i1 - March 2015 - pS5(1) [51-500]

Patrick, Seth - *Lost Souls*
    BL - v112 - i5 - Nov 1 2015 - p37(1) [51-500]
    PW - v262 - i37 - Sept 14 2015 - p44(1) [51-500]

Patrick, Wendy L. - *Red Flags: How to Spot Frenemies, Underminers, and Toxic People in Your Life*
    LJ - v140 - i7 - April 15 2015 - p106(1) [51-500]
    PW - v262 - i2 - Jan 12 2015 - p46(1) [51-500]

Patriquin, Larry - *Economic Equality and Direct Democracy in Ancient Athens*
    Class R - v65 - i2 - Oct 2015 - p500-502 [501+]

Patry, Sylvie - *Discovering the Impressionists: Paul Durand-Ruel and the New Painting*
    LJ - v140 - i14 - Sept 1 2015 - p98(1) [51-500]

Pattee, Phillip G. - *At War in Distant Waters: British Colonial Defense in the Great War*
    NWCR - v68 - i3 - Summer 2015 - p157(2) [501+]

Patten, Brian - *Can I Come Too? (Illus. by Bayley, Nicola)*
    c HB Guide - v26 - i1 - Spring 2015 - p41(1) [51-500]

Patten, Marguerite - *A Century of British Cooking*
    TLS - i5860 - July 24 2015 - p3(2) [501+]

Patten, Timothy - *Money, Family, Murder*
    SPBW - August 2015 - pNA [51-500]

Pattenden, Miles - *Pius IV and the Fall of the Carafa: Nepotism and Papal Authority in Counter-Reformation Rome*
    Ren Q - v68 - i3 - Fall 2015 - p1035-1036 [501+]

Patterson, Annabel - *The International Novel*
    ABR - v36 - i5 - July-August 2015 - p6(1) [501+]

Patterson, A. - *1-2-3 A Calmer Me: Helping Children Cope When Emotions Get Out of Control (Illus. by Keay, Claire)*
    c CH Bwatch - Oct 2015 - pNA [51-500]

Patterson, Eric - *Military Chaplains in Afghanistan, Iraq, and Beyond*
    NWCR - v68 - i2 - Spring 2015 - p147(2) [501+]

Patterson, James - *Alert (Read by Leyva, Henry, with Danny Mastrogiorigio). Audiobook Review*
    Bwatch - Nov 2015 - pNA [51-500]
The Best American Mystery Stories 2015
    PW - v262 - i35 - August 31 2015 - p60(2) [51-500]
    BL - v112 - i3 - Oct 1 2015 - p23(2) [51-500]
    KR - August 15 2015 - pNA [51-500]
Daniel X: Lights Out (Read by Landon, Aaron). Audiobook Review
    c CH Bwatch - Nov 2015 - pNA [51-500]
Hope to Die (Read by Boatman, Michael, with Scott Sowers). Audiobook Review
    Bwatch - Feb 2015 - pNA [51-500]
House of Robots (Read by Patterson, Jack). Audiobook Review
    PW - v262 - i5 - Feb 2 2015 - p56(1) [51-500]
    SLJ - v61 - i2 - Feb 2015 - p50(1) [51-500]
I Totally Funniest (Read by Seratch, Frankie). Audiobook Review
    SLJ - v61 - i4 - April 2015 - p63(1) [51-500]
Just My Rotten Luck (Read by Kennedy, Bryan). Audiobook Review
    c SLJ - v61 - i12 - Dec 2015 - p76(1) [51-500]
Private India: City on Fire
    Bwatch - Jan 2015 - pNA [501+]
Public School Superhero (Read by Boone, Joshua). Audiobook Review
    c SLJ - v61 - i8 - August 2015 - p51(2) [51-500]
Public School Superhero (Illus. by Thomas, Cory)
    c BL - v111 - i14 - March 15 2015 - p74(1) [51-500]
    c KR - Feb 1 2015 - pNA [51-500]
    c SLJ - v61 - i4 - April 2015 - p148(1) [51-500]
Treasure Hunters: Danger Down the Nile (Illus. by Neufeld, Juliana)
    c HB Guide - v26 - i1 - Spring 2015 - p88(1) [51-500]
Treasure Hunters: Secret of the Forbidden City (Read by Kennedy, Bryan). Audiobook Review
    c CH Bwatch - Oct 2015 - pNA [51-500]
Truth or Die (Read by Ballerini, Edoardo). Audiobook Review
    Bwatch - Sept 2015 - pNA [501+]

Patterson, James T. - *The Eve of Destruction: How 1965 Transformed America*
    Am St - v54 - i2 - Summer 2015 - p73-83 [501+]

Patterson, Jonathan - *Representing Avarice in Late Renaissance France*
    TLS - i5849 - May 8 2015 - p27(1) [501+]

Patterson, Orlando - *The Cultural Matrix: Understanding Black Youth*
    NY - v90 - i47 - Feb 9 2015 - p62 [501+]

Patterson, Rebecca - *The Christmas Show*
    c HB Guide - v26 - i1 - Spring 2015 - p14(1) [51-500]
    c RVBW - Jan 2015 - pNA [51-500]

Patterson, Robert P. - *Arming the Nation for War: Mobilization, Supply, and the American War Effort in World War II*
    J Mil H - v79 - i1 - Jan 2015 - p247-248 [501+]

Patterson, Thomas C. - *From Acorns to Warehouses: Historical Political Economy of Southern California's Inland Empire*
    WHQ - v46 - i4 - Winter 2015 - p527-528 [501+]

Patterson, Victoria - *The Little Brother*
    KR - June 1 2015 - pNA [51-500]
    BL - v111 - i21 - July 1 2015 - p32(1) [51-500]

Patterson, W.B. - *William Perkins and the Making of a Protestant England*
    CH - v84 - i4 - Dec 2015 - p884(3) [501+]
    TimHES - i2187 - Jan 22 2015 - p51(1) [501+]

Patterson, Wayne - *In the Service of His Korean Majesty: William Nelson Lovatt, the Pusan Customs, and Sino-Korea Relations, 1876-1888*
    AHR - v120 - i3 - June 2015 - p996-997 [501+]
    Pac A - v88 - i2 - June 2015 - p335 [501+]

Patterson, William H., Jr. - *Robert A. Heinlein in Dialogue with His Century, vol. 2, 1948-88: The Man Who Learned Better*
    SFS - v42 - i1 - March 2015 - p151-157 [501+]

Patti, Caroline T. - *Into the Dark*
    y SLJ - v61 - i10 - Oct 2015 - p116(1) [51-500]

Pattillo, Edward - *Carolina Planters on the Alabama Frontier: The Spencer-Robeson-McKenzie Family Papers*
    JSH - v81 - i1 - Feb 2015 - p179(2) [501+]

Pattison, Darcy - *I Want a Cat: My Opinion Essay (Illus. by O'Neill, Ewa)*
    c SLJ - v61 - i5 - May 2015 - p90(1) [51-500]
I Want a Dog: My Opinion Essay (Illus. by O'Neill, Ewa)
    c SLJ - v61 - i5 - May 2015 - p90(1) [51-500]
Kell and the Detectives (Illus. by Davis, Rich)
    c SLJ - v61 - i2 - Feb 2015 - p75(1) [51-500]
My Crazy Dog: My Narrative Essay (Illus. by O'Neill, Ewa)
    c SLJ - v61 - i11 - Nov 2015 - p85(1) [51-500]

Pattison, Eliot - *Soul of the Fire*
    RVBW - August 2015 - pNA [51-500]

Pattison, James - *The Morality of Private War*
    TLS - i5870 - Oct 2 2015 - p12(1) [501+]

Pattison, Rosie Gowsell - *Just Joking 6: 300 Hilarious Jokes about Everything, Including Tongue Twisters, Riddles, and More!*
    c HB Guide - v26 - i1 - Spring 2015 - p181(1) [51-500]

Patton, Cindy - *L.A. Plays itself / Boys in the Sand*
    FQ - v68 - i4 - Summer 2015 - p98(2) [501+]

Patton, Jack - *The Lizard War*
    c KR - March 15 2015 - pNA [51-500]
    SLJ - v61 - i2 - Feb 2015 - p58(1) [51-500]

Patton, Michael F. - *The Cartoon Introduction to Philosophy*
    KR - Jan 1 2015 - pNA [501+]
    PW - v262 - i4 - Jan 26 2015 - p157(1) [51-500]

Patz, Harry, Jr. - *The Naive Guys: A Memoir of Friendship, Love and Tech in the Early 1990s*
SPBW - June 2015 - pNA [51-500]
The Naive Guys
SPBW - August 2015 - pNA [51-500]

Patzold, Steffen - *Ich und Karl der Grosse: Das Leben des Höflings Einhard*
HNet - Jan 2015 - pNA [501+]

Pauer-Studer, Herlinde - *Konrad Morgen: The Conscience of a Nazi Judge*
TimHES - i2211 - July 9 2015 - p44(1) [501+]

Paui, Miranda - *One Plastic Bag: Isatou Ceesay and the Recycling Women of the Gambia (Illus. by Zunon, Elizabeth)*
c BL - v111 - i12 - Feb 15 2015 - p77(1) [51-500]

Paul, Alison - *The Plan (Illus. by Lehman, Barbara)*
c BL - v112 - i5 - Nov 1 2015 - p66(1) [51-500]
c HB - v91 - i6 - Nov-Dec 2015 - p72(1) [51-500]
c KR - August 15 2015 - pNA [51-500]
c PW - v262 - i33 - August 17 2015 - p69(2) [51-500]
c PW - v262 - i49 - Dec 2 2015 - p31(2) [51-500]
c SLJ - v61 - i6 - June 2015 - p89(1) [51-500]

Paul, Andy - *Amp Up Your Sales*
RVBW - Jan 2015 - pNA [501+]

Paul, David C. - *Charles Ives in the Mirror: American Histories of an Iconic Composer*
Notes - v71 - i3 - March 2015 - p507(3) [501+]

Paul, Donita K. - *Two Renegade Realms*
c SLJ - v61 - i3 - March 2015 - p142(1) [51-500]

Paul, Ellis - *The Hero in You (Illus. by Padron, Angela)*
c HB Guide - v26 - i1 - Spring 2015 - p198(1) [51-500]
The Night the Lights Went Out on Christmas (Illus. by Brundage, Scott)
c KR - Sept 1 2015 - pNA [51-500]
c PW - v262 - i37 - Sept 14 2015 - p70(1) [51-500]
c SLJ - v61 - i10 - Oct 2015 - p66(2) [51-500]

Paul, L.A. - *Transformative Experience*
Comw - v142 - i5 - March 6 2015 - p31(4) [501+]
TLS - i5854 - June 12 2015 - p8(1) [501+]

Paul, Marcy Beller - *Underneath Everything*
y BL - v112 - i4 - Oct 15 2015 - p57(2) [51-500]
y KR - August 1 2015 - pNA [51-500]
y PW - v262 - i32 - August 10 2015 - p62(2) [51-500]
y SLJ - v61 - i10 - Oct 2015 - p116(1) [51-500]

Paul, Miranda - *One Plastic Bag: Isatou Ceesay and the Recycling Women of the Gambia (Illus. by Zunon, Elizabeth)*
c HB Guide - v26 - i2 - Fall 2015 - p155(2) [51-500]
c HB - v91 - i1 - Jan-Feb 2015 - p101(2) [51-500]
Water Is Water: A Book About the Water Cycle (Illus. by Chin, Jason)
c HB Guide - v26 - i2 - Fall 2015 - p167(1) [51-500]
c BL - v111 - i14 - March 15 2015 - p62(1) [51-500]
c CCB-B - v68 - i11 - July-August 2015 - p560(1) [51-500]
c HB - v91 - i3 - May-June 2015 - p128(2) [51-500]
c KR - Feb 15 2015 - pNA [51-500]
c PW - v262 - i49 - Dec 2 2015 - p51(1) [51-500]
c SLJ - v61 - i3 - March 2015 - p172(1) [51-500]
Whose Hands Are These?
c KR - Dec 1 2015 - pNA [51-500]

Paul, Nicholas L. - *To Follow in Their Footsteps: The Crusades and Family Memory in the High Middle Ages*
Specu - v90 - i1 - Jan 2015 - p285-286 [501+]

Paul, Rand - *Taking a Stand: Moving Beyond Partisan Politics to Unite America*
NS - v144 - i5278 - Sept 4 2015 - p40(4) [501+]

Paul, Richard - *We Could Not Fail: The First African Americans in the Space Program*
BL - v111 - i12 - Feb 15 2015 - p18(1) [51-500]
LJ - v140 - i6 - April 1 2015 - p103(2) [51-500]
NYTBR - April 26 2015 - p30(L) [501+]

Paul, Robert A. - *Mixed Messages: Cultural and Genetic Inheritance in the Constitution of Human Society*
New Sci - v226 - i3021 - May 16 2015 - p44(2) [501+]

Paul, Ruth - *Bad Dog Flash*
c HB Guide - v26 - i1 - Spring 2015 - p14(1) [51-500]
Bye-Bye Grumpy Fly (Illus. by Paul, Ruth)
c Magpies - v30 - i3 - July 2015 - pS4(1) [501+]
Go Home Flash (Illus. by Paul, Ruth)
c PW - v262 - i39 - Sept 28 2015 - p90(2) [51-500]
c SLJ - v61 - i10 - Oct 2015 - p81(1) [51-500]
What's the Time, Dinosaur? (Illus. by Paul, Ruth)
c Magpies - v30 - i5 - Nov 2015 - pS5(1) [501+]

Paul, T.V. - *The Warrior State: Pakistan in the Contemporary World*
Pac A - v88 - i2 - June 2015 - p347 [501+]
TLS - i5832 - Jan 9 2015 - p19(1) [501+]

Pauli, Laline - *The Bees (Read by Cassidy, Orlagh). Audiobook Review*
BL - v111 - i14 - March 15 2015 - p23(2) [51-500]

Pauli, Lorenz - *You Call That Brave? (Illus. by Scharer, Kathrin)*
c HB Guide - v26 - i2 - Fall 2015 - p47(1) [51-500]

Paulicelli, Eugenia - *Writing Fashion in Early Modern Italy: From Sprezzatura to Satire*
Ren Q - v68 - i3 - Fall 2015 - p1111-1113 [501+]

Paulle, Bowen - *Toxic Schools: High-Poverty Education in New York and Amsterdam*
CS - v44 - i6 - Nov 2015 - p835-837 [501+]

Paulos, John Allen - *A Numerate Life: A Mathematician Explores the Vagaries of Life, His Own and Probably Yours*
LJ - v140 - i19 - Nov 15 2015 - p101(1) [51-500]

Pauls, Alan - *A History of Money*
BL - v111 - i18 - May 15 2015 - p22(2) [51-500]
KR - April 1 2015 - pNA [501+]
LJ - v140 - i10 - June 1 2015 - p92(3) [501+]
Mac - v128 - i25 - June 29 2015 - p55(1) [501+]
PW - v262 - i12 - March 23 2015 - p44(1) [51-500]
TLS - i5855 - June 19 2015 - p19(2) [501+]

Paulsen, Gary - *Family Ties (Read by Bernstein, Jesse). Audiobook Review*
c BL - v111 - i9-10 - Jan 1 2015 - p117(2) [51-500]
Family Ties
y HB Guide - v26 - i1 - Spring 2015 - p88(1) [51-500]
Field Trip
c BL - v111 - i19-20 - June 1 2015 - p104(1) [51-500]
c KR - June 1 2015 - pNA [51-500]
This Side of Wild: Mutts, Mares, and Laughing Dinosaurs (Read by Sanders, Fred). Audiobook Review
c SLJ - v61 - i12 - Dec 2015 - p77(1) [51-500]
This Side of Wild: Mutts, Mares, and Laughing Dinosaurs (Illus. by Jessell, Tim)
c BL - v112 - i2 - Sept 15 2015 - p57 [51-500]
c SLJ - v61 - i10 - Oct 2015 - p137(2) [51-500]
Vote
c Teach Lib - v42 - i5 - June 2015 - p61(1) [51-500]

Paulsen, Michael Stokes - *The Constitution: An Introduction*
BL - v111 - i15 - April 1 2015 - p6(1) [51-500]
KR - March 15 2015 - pNA [51-500]
Nat R - v67 - i10 - June 1 2015 - p45 [501+]

Paulsen, Roland - *Empty Labor: Idleness and Workplace Resistance*
AJS - v121 - i2 - Sept 2015 - p651(3) [501+]

Paulson, Elizabeth - *Dead upon a Time*
y CCB-B - v69 - i2 - Oct 2015 - p108(2) [51-500]
y KR - June 1 2015 - pNA [51-500]
y VOYA - v38 - i3 - August 2015 - p82(2) [51-500]

Paulson, Henry M., Jr. - *Dealing with China: An Insider Unmasks the New Economic Superpower (Read by Stillwell, Kevin). Audiobook Review*
Bwatch - July 2015 - pNA [51-500]

Pauw, Amy Plantinga - *Proverbs and Ecclesiastes: A Theological Commentary on the Bible*
CC - v132 - i8 - April 15 2015 - p41(1) [51-500]
RVBW - May 2015 - pNA [501+]

Pauw, Marion - *Girl in the Dark*
PW - v262 - i52 - Dec 21 2015 - p131(1) [51-500]

Paver, Michelle - *The Crocodile Tomb*
c Sch Lib - v63 - i4 - Winter 2015 - p230(2) [51-500]
The Eye of the Falcon
c HB Guide - v26 - i2 - Fall 2015 - p96(1) [51-500]
y VOYA - v38 - i1 - April 2015 - p82(1) [51-500]

Pavilion Books - *750 Knitting Stitches: The Ultimate Knit Stitch Bible*
LJ - v140 - i14 - Sept 1 2015 - p105(1) [51-500]

Pavlic, Ed - *Let's Let That Are Not Yet: Inferno*
NYTBR - Dec 27 2015 - p12(L) [501+]
Who Can Afford to Improvise? James Baldwin and Black Music, the Lyric and the Listeners
RVBW - Nov 2015 - pNA [51-500]
LJ - v140 - i10 - June 1 2015 - p103(2) [51-500]

Pavlidis, Adele - *Sport, Gender and Power: The Rise of Roller Derby*
CS - v44 - i5 - Sept 2015 - p745-746 [501+]

Pavlouskova, Nela - *Cy Twombly: Late Paintings, 2003-2011*
NYTBR - June 28 2015 - p12(L) [501+]

Pavlov, Oleg - *The Matiushin Case*
TLS - i5861 - July 31 2015 - p19(1) [501+]
WLT - v89 - i2 - March-April 2015 - p60(2) [501+]
Requiem for a Soldier
TLS - i5861 - July 31 2015 - p19(1) [501+]

Pavone, Chris - *The Accident*
RVBW - Feb 2015 - pNA [501+]

Pawar, Urmila - *Motherwit*
WLT - v89 - i3-4 - May-August 2015 - p119(1) [51-500]

Pawel, Miriam - *The Crusades of Cesar Chavez: A Biography*
BL - v111 - i11 - Feb 1 2015 - p16(1) [51-500]
JAH - v102 - i2 - Sept 2015 - p624-625 [501+]
NYTBR - May 10 2015 - p36(L) [501+]

Pawlikowski, John T. - *Restating the Catholic Church's Relationship with the Jewish People: The Challenge of Super-Sessionary Theology*
Theol St - v76 - i1 - March 2015 - p186(2) [501+]

Paxton, Frederick S. - *The Death Ritual at Cluny in the Central Middle Ages / Le rituel de la mort a Cluny au Moyen Age central*
Specu - v90 - i1 - Jan 2015 - p286-288 [501+]

Payard, Francois - *Payard Cookies*
NYT - Dec 2 2015 - pD6(L) [501+]
PW - v262 - i33 - August 17 2015 - p65(1) [51-500]

Payne, Bryson - *Teach Your Kids to Code: A Parent-Friendly Guide to Python Programming*
Bwatch - August 2015 - pNA [51-500]
c KR - July 15 2015 - pNA [51-500]

Payne, David - *Barefoot to Avalon: A Brother's Story*
KR - May 15 2015 - pNA [501+]
NYT - August 27 2015 - pC4(L) [501+]
PW - v262 - i20 - May 18 2015 - p75(1) [51-500]

Payne, Ed - *Molly and the Bully (Illus. by Sekulic, Britt)*
c CH Bwatch - March 2015 - pNA [51-500]

Payne, J.T. - *The Academy*
SPBW - Oct 2015 - pNA [51-500]

Payne, Jackie - *I Saw the Blues*
Dbt - v82 - i8 - August 2015 - p81(1) [501+]

Payne, Lauren Murphy - *Just Because I Am: A Child's Book of Affirmation (Illus. by Iwai, Melissa)*
c SLJ - v61 - i12 - Dec 2015 - p138(1) [51-500]
We Can Get Along: A Child's Book of Choices (Illus. by Iwai, Melissa)
c SLJ - v61 - i12 - Dec 2015 - p138(1) [51-500]

Payne, Lyla - *Mistletoe and Mr. Right*
y KR - August 1 2015 - pNA [51-500]

Payne, Stanley G. - *Franco: A Personal and Political Biography*
Lon R Bks - v37 - i5 - March 5 2015 - p32(2) [501+]
Nat R - v67 - i1 - Jan 26 2015 - p42 [501+]
TLS - i5840 - March 6 2015 - p3(2) [51-500]

Payne, Tom - *The Ancient Art of Growing Old*
Spec - v327 - i9733 - March 14 2015 - p43(1) [501+]

Payton, Belle - *Double or Nothing*
y HB Guide - v26 - i1 - Spring 2015 - p89(1) [51-500]
Even the Score
c HB Guide - v26 - i2 - Fall 2015 - p97(1) [51-500]
Go! Fight! Twin!
c HB Guide - v26 - i2 - Fall 2015 - p97(1) [51-500]
Two Cool for School
y HB Guide - v26 - i1 - Spring 2015 - p89(1) [51-500]

Payton, Theresa M. - *Privacy in the Age of Big Data: Recognizing Threats, Defending Your Rights, and Protecting Your Family*
Har Bus R - v93 - i11 - Nov 2015 - p150(2) [501+]

Peabody, Rebecca - *The Unruly PhD: Doubts, Detours, Departures, and Other Success Stories*
TimHES - i2185 - Jan 8 2015 - p52-53 [501+]

Peacey, Jason - *Print and Public Politics in the English Revolution*
HER - v130 - i545 - August 2015 - p992(3) [501+]
HT - v65 - i1 - Jan 2015 - p60(1) [501+]

Peacham, Henry - *Compleat Gentleman, 1634*
TLS - i5837 - Feb 13 2015 - p16(1) [501+]

Peacock, Caro - *Friends in High Places*
BL - v111 - i22 - August 1 2015 - p33(2) [51-500]
PW - v262 - i24 - June 15 2015 - p66(1) [51-500]

Peacock, Kathleen - *Willowgrove*
y HB Guide - v26 - i2 - Fall 2015 - p134(1) [51-500]
y VOYA - v37 - i6 - Feb 2015 - p82(1) [51-500]

Peacock, Margaret - *Innocent Weapons: The Soviet and American Politics of Childhood in the Cold War*
JAH - v102 - i1 - June 2015 - p293-294 [501+]

Peak, Tony - *Inherit the Stars*
  PW - v262 - i38 - Sept 21 2015 - p58(1) [51-500]
Peak, William - *The Oblate's Confession*
  KR - Feb 1 2015 - pNA [501+]
Peake, Ernest Cromwell - *This Divided Island: Stories from the Sri Lankan War*
  TLS - i5844 - April 3 2015 - p29(1) [501+]
Peake, Robert - *The Knowledge*
  WLT - v89 - i6 - Nov-Dec 2015 - p74(2) [501+]
Peakman, Julie - *Peg Plunkett: Memoirs of a Whore*
  NS - v144 - i5268 - June 26 2015 - p46(1) [501+]
Peale, Titian Ramsay, II - *The Butterflies of North America, Diurnal Lepidoptera: Whence They Come, Where They Go, and What They Do*
  NYT - August 25 2015 - pD6(L) [501+]
Pearce, Andy - *Holocaust Consciousness in Contemporary Britain*
  AHR - v120 - i2 - April 2015 - p720-721 [501+]
Pearce, Bryony - *Phoenix Rising*
  c Sch Lib - v63 - i3 - Autumn 2015 - p169(1) [51-500]
Pearce, Clemency - *Three Little Words (Illus. by Beardshaw, Rosalind)*
  c HB Guide - v26 - i1 - Spring 2015 - p14(1) [51-500]
Pearce, Fred - *The New Wild: Why Invasive Species Will Be Nature's Salvation*
  BL - v111 - i12 - Feb 15 2015 - p27(1) [51-500]
  KR - Jan 1 2015 - pNA [51-500]
  Mac - v128 - i16 - April 27 2015 - p54(1) [501+]
  Nature - v519 - i7544 - March 26 2015 - p413(1) [51-500]
Pearce-Higgins, James W. - *Birds and Climate Change: Impacts and Conservation Responses*
  QRB - v90 - i3 - Sept 2015 - p333(1) [501+]
Pearce, Jackson - *Cold Spell*
  y Sch Lib - v63 - i1 - Spring 2015 - p56(2) [51-500]
  The Doublecross (and Other Skills I Learned as a Superspy).
  c BL - v111 - i21 - July 1 2015 - p69(1) [51-500]
  c KR - April 15 2015 - pNA [51-500]
  y Magpies - v30 - i5 - Nov 2015 - p37(1) [501+]
  c PW - v262 - i18 - May 4 2015 - p119(2) [51-500]
  c SLJ - v61 - i3 - March 2015 - p142(1) [51-500]
  Pip Bartlett's Guide to Magical Creatures (Read by Morris, Cassandra). Audiobook Review
  c PW - v262 - i35 - August 31 2015 - p85(1) [51-500]
  c SLJ - v61 - i9 - Sept 2015 - p59(2) [51-500]
  Pip Bartlett's Guide to Magical Creatures (Illus. by Stiefvater, Maggie)
  y BL - v111 - i15 - April 1 2015 - p35(1) [501+]
  c BL - v111 - i16 - April 15 2015 - p50(1) [51-500]
  c CCB-B - v68 - i9 - May 2015 - p462(1) [51-500]
  c HB - v91 - i4 - July-August 2015 - p141(1) [51-500]
  c KR - Feb 15 2015 - pNA [51-500]
  y PW - v262 - i8 - Feb 23 2015 - p75(1) [51-500]
  c SLJ - v61 - i7 - July 2015 - p81(1) [51-500]
Pearce, Kate - *Tribute: The Complete Collection*
  PW - v262 - i39 - Sept 28 2015 - p75(1) [51-500]
Pearce, Michael - *The Mouth of the Crocodile*
  BL - v111 - i1 - Feb 1 2015 - p27(2) [51-500]
  KR - Jan 1 2015 - pNA [51-500]
  PW - v262 - i4 - Jan 26 2015 - p150(1) [51-500]
Pearce, Sarah - *The Image and its Prohibition in Jewish Antiquity*
  Class R - v65 - i2 - Oct 2015 - p535-536 [501+]
Pearl, Matthew - *The Last Bookaneer (Read by Vance, Simon). Audiobook Review*
  BL - v112 - i1 - Sept 1 2015 - p140(2) [51-500]
  LJ - v140 - i14 - Sept 1 2015 - p67(1) [51-500]
  The Last Bookaneer
  BL - v111 - i16 - April 15 2015 - p36(1) [51-500]
  CSM - May 20 2015 - pNA [501+]
  KR - March 15 2015 - pNA [501+]
  LJ - v140 - i6 - April 1 2015 - p84(1) [51-500]
  NYTBR - May 31 2015 - p47(L) [501+]
  PW - v262 - i12 - March 23 2015 - p43(2) [51-500]
Pearle, Ida - *The Moon Is Going to Addy's House (Illus. by Pearle, Ida)*
  c KR - May 1 2015 - pNA [51-500]
  c PW - v262 - i18 - May 4 2015 - p116(1) [51-500]
  c PW - v262 - i49 - Dec 2 2015 - p42(1) [51-500]
  c SLJ - v61 - i6 - June 2015 - p89(2) [51-500]
Pearline, Jaikumar - *Holidays, Festivals, and Celebrations of the World Dictionary, 5th ed.*
  y VOYA - v38 - i5 - Dec 2015 - p81(1) [51-500]

Pearlman, Edith - *Honeydew: Stories*
  Bwatch - April 2015 - pNA [501+]
  CSM - Jan 13 2015 - pNA [501+]
  Econ - v414 - i8924 - Feb 7 2015 - p80(US) [501+]
  NS - v144 - i5248 - Feb 6 2015 - p43(1) [51-500]
  NYTBR - Jan 4 2015 - p1(L) [501+]
  Spec - v327 - i9724 - Jan 10 2015 - p26(2) [501+]
  TLS - i5845 - April 10 2015 - p20(1) [501+]
  NYTBR - Oct 4 2015 - p28(L) [501+]
Pearlman, Robb - *Groundhog's Day Off (Illus. by Helquist, Brett)*
  c KR - Oct 1 2015 - pNA [51-500]
  c PW - v262 - i36 - Sept 7 2015 - p65(1) [51-500]
  c PW - v262 - i49 - Dec 2 2015 - p60(1) [51-500]
  c SLJ - v61 - i11 - Nov 2015 - p85(2) [501+]
Pears, Iain - *Arcadia*
  BL - v112 - i3 - Oct 1 2015 - p4(1) [51-500]
  KR - Dec 1 2015 - pNA [501+]
  PW - v262 - i51 - Dec 14 2015 - p56(2) [51-500]
  y SLJ - v61 - i10 - Oct 2015 - p58(1) [501+]
  Spec - v328 - i9758 - Sept 5 2015 - p36(1) [501+]
Pearsall, Jennifer L.S. - *The Big Book of Bacon: Savory Flirtations, Dalliances, and Indulgences with the Underbelly of the Pig*
  Bwatch - April 2015 - pNA [501+]
Pearsall, Shelley - *The Seventh Most Important Thing*
  c BL - v111 - i22 - August 1 2015 - p68(2) [51-500]
  c KR - July 1 2015 - pNA [51-500]
  c SLJ - v61 - i7 - July 2015 - p81(2) [51-500]
Pearse-Otene, Helen - *The Matawehi Fables: Arohanui: Revenge of the Fey*
  c Magpies - v30 - i4 - Sept 2015 - pS6(1) [501+]
  The Matawehi Fables: Meariki: The Quest for Truth
  c Magpies - v30 - i4 - Sept 2015 - pS6(1) [501+]
Pearson, Drew - *Washington Merry-Go-Round*
  NY - v91 - i29 - Sept 28 2015 - p76 [501+]
Pearson, Ivan L. G. - *In the Name of Oil: Anglo-American Relations in the Middle East, 1950-1958*
  IJMES - v47 - i1 - Feb 2015 - p169-174 [501+]
Pearson, Kit - *The Lights Go On Again*
  c Res Links - v20 - i3 - Feb 2015 - p16(1) [501+]
  Looking at the Moon
  c Res Links - v20 - i3 - Feb 2015 - p15(2) [501+]
  The Sky is Falling
  c Res Links - v20 - i3 - Feb 2015 - p16(2) [501+]
Pearson, Luke - *Hilda and the Black Hound (Illus. by Pearson, Luke)*
  c BL - v111 - i17 - May 1 2015 - p40(1) [51-500]
Pearson, Maggie - *Dragons vs Dinos (Illus. by Redlich, Ben)*
  c Res Links - v20 - i3 - Feb 2015 - p14(2) [51-500]
  The Pop Star Pirates (Illus. by Chernett, Dan)
  c CH Bwatch - Nov 2015 - pNA [501+]
  Rumpelstiltskin Returns (Illus. by Stone, Steve)
  c CH Bwatch - April 2015 - pNA [51-500]
Pearson, Mary E. - *The Heart of Betrayal (Read by Lee, Ann Marie). Audiobook Review*
  y SLJ - v61 - i10 - Oct 2015 - p55(1) [51-500]
  The Heart of Betrayal
  y BL - v111 - i16 - April 15 2015 - p47(1) [51-500]
  y HB - v91 - i4 - July-August 2015 - p142(1) [51-500]
  y KR - May 1 2015 - pNA [51-500]
  SLJ - v61 - i4 - April 2015 - p169(1) [51-500]
  y VOYA - v38 - i2 - June 2015 - p81(1) [51-500]
  The Kiss of Deception
  y HB Guide - v26 - i1 - Spring 2015 - p119(1) [51-500]
Pearson, Ridley - *Disney Lands*
  c BL - v111 - i16 - April 15 2015 - p49(1) [51-500]
  c CH Bwatch - July 2015 - pNA [51-500]
Pearson, Timothy G. - *Becoming Holy in Early Canada*
  Can Hist R - v96 - i2 - June 2015 - p291(2) [501+]
Peart-Binns, Byjohn S. - *Herbert Hensley Henson: A Biography*
  CHR - v101 - i3 - Summer 2015 - p669(2) [501+]
Peart, Daniel - *Era of Experimentation: American Political Practices in the Early Republic*
  AHR - v120 - i1 - Feb 2015 - p238-239 [501+]
  J Am St - v49 - i2 - May 2015 - p416-417 [501+]
  JAH - v102 - i1 - June 2015 - p239-240 [501+]
Pease, Allison - *The Cambridge Companion to "To the Lighthouse"*
  TLS - i5852 - May 29 2015 - p27(1) [501+]
  Modernism, Feminism and the Culture of Boredom
  MFSF - v61 - i1 - Spring 2015 - p189-192 [501+]
Pease, D. Robert - *Dream Warriors. E-book Review*
  y PW - v262 - i18 - May 4 2015 - p122(1) [51-500]
Pease Garcia-Yrigoyen, Franklin - *Los Incas en la colonia: Estudios sobre los siglos XVI, XVII y XVIII en los Andes*
  HAHR - v95 - i4 - Nov 2015 - p670-671 [501+]
Peatman, Jared - *The Long Shadow of Lincoln's Gettysburg Address*
  JSH - v81 - i2 - May 2015 - p471(3) [501+]
  Pres St Q - v45 - i4 - Dec 2015 - p820(2) [501+]
Peattie, Thomas - *Gustav Mahler's Symphonic Landscapes*
  NYRB - v62 - i20 - Dec 17 2015 - p75(3) [501+]
Peavy, Linda - *Full-Court Quest: The Girls from Fort Shaw Indian School, Basketball Champions of the World*
  Roundup M - v22 - i6 - August 2015 - p39(1) [501+]
Pebay, Alice - *Regenerative Biology of the Eye*
  QRB - v90 - i4 - Dec 2015 - p444(1) [501+]
Pech, Julie - *Dare to Pair: The Ultimate Guide to Chocolate and Wine Pairing*
  KR - July 1 2015 - pNA [51-500]
Pechenik, Jan A. - *The Readable Darwin: The Origin of Species: Edited for Modern Readers*
  QRB - v90 - i2 - June 2015 - p217(1) [501+]
Peck, Dale - *Visions and Revisions: Coming of Age in the Age of AIDS (Read by Woodman, Jeff). Audiobook Review*
  LJ - v140 - i15 - Sept 15 2015 - p44(1) [51-500]
  Visions and Revisions: Coming of Age in the Age of AIDS
  BL - v111 - i14 - March 15 2015 - p40(1) [51-500]
  KR - Jan 15 2015 - pNA [51-500]
  NYTBR - July 19 2015 - p26(L) [501+]
  LJ - v140 - i5 - March 15 2015 - p124(1) [51-500]
Peckham, Robert - *Imperial Contagions: Medicine, Hygiene, and Cultures of Planning in Asia*
  J Urban H - v41 - i1 - Jan 2015 - p165-6 [501+]
Pecknold, Diane - *Hidden in the Mix: The African American Presence in Country Music*
  JSH - v81 - i1 - Feb 2015 - p235(3) [501+]
  JAH - v102 - i2 - Sept 2015 - p521-522 [501+]
  WestFolk - v74 - i1 - Wntr 2015 - p107-108 [501+]
Peddana, Allasani - *The Story of Manu*
  NYRB - v62 - i14 - Sept 24 2015 - p64(3) [501+]
Peddle, Francis - *Young, Well-Educated, and Adaptable: Chilean Exiles in Ontario and Quebec, 1973-2010*
  Can Hist R - v96 - i3 - Sept 2015 - p457(3) [501+]
Peden, Knox - *Spinoza Contra Phenomenology: French Rationalism from Cavailles to Deleuze*
  AHR - v120 - i4 - Oct 2015 - p1555-1556 [501+]
Pedersen, David - *American Value: Migrants, Money, and Meaning in El Salvador and the United States*
  CS - v44 - i1 - Jan 2015 - p103-105 [501+]
Pedersen, Laura - *Ava's Adventure (Illus. by Weber, Penny)*
  c HB Guide - v26 - i1 - Spring 2015 - p41(1) [51-500]
  Life in New York: How I Learned to Love Squeegee Men, Token Suckers, Trash Twisters, and Subway Sharks
  RVBW - August 2015 - pNA [51-500]
Pedersen, Susan - *The Guardians: The League of Nations and the Crisis of Empire*
  Lon R Bks - v37 - i20 - Oct 22 2015 - p7(2) [501+]
  Nation - v301 - i20 - Nov 16 2015 - p32(5) [501+]
  PW - v262 - i15 - April 13 2015 - p67(2) [51-500]
  TimHES - i2210 - July 2 2015 - p46-2 [501+]
Pederson, Rena - *The Burma Spring: Aung San Suu Kyi and the New Struggle for the Soul of a Nation*
  BL - v111 - i1 - Feb 1 2015 - p12(1) [51-500]
  Bwatch - June 2015 - pNA [51-500]
  LJ - v140 - i2 - Feb 1 2015 - p98(1) [51-500]
Pedley, Paul - *Practical Copyright for Library and Information Professionals*
  RVBW - Oct 2015 - pNA [501+]
Peebles, Alice - *Demons and Dragons (Illus. by Chilvers, Nigel)*
  c KR - August 1 2015 - pNA [51-500]
  Giants and Trolls (Illus. by Chilvers, Nigel)
  c PW - v262 - i33 - August 17 2015 - p74(1) [501+]
Peek, Caspar - *Of Giants and Other Men*
  KR - April 15 2015 - pNA [51-500]
Peeler, Nicole - *Jinn and Juice*
  PW - v262 - i8 - Feb 23 2015 - p58(1) [51-500]
Peeples, Edward H. - *Scalawag: A White Southerner's Journey through Segregation to Human Rights Activism*
  JSH - v81 - i4 - Nov 2015 - p1059(1) [501+]
Peet, Amanda - *Dear Santa, Love, Rachel Rosenstein (Illus. by Davenier, Christine)*
  c HB - v91 - i6 - Nov-Dec 2015 - p59(1) [51-500]
  c KR - Sept 1 2015 - pNA [51-500]
  c PW - v262 - i37 - Sept 14 2015 - p66(1) [51-500]
  c SLJ - v61 - i10 - Oct 2015 - p67(1) [51-500]

Book Review Index 2016 Cumulation **PEPPIS • 363**

Peet, Mal - *The Murdstone Trilogy*
y BL - v111 - i22 - August 1 2015 - p44(1) [51-500]
y KR - August 1 2015 - pNA [51-500]
y PW - v262 - i25 - June 22 2015 - p142(1) [51-500]
y Sch Lib - v63 - i2 - Summer 2015 - p126(1) [51-500]
y VOYA - v38 - i5 - Dec 2015 - p73(1) [51-500]
Night Sky Dragons (Illus. by Benson, Patrick)
c HB Guide - v26 - i2 - Fall 2015 - p70(1) [51-500]
c CCB-B - v68 - i5 - Jan 2015 - p272(1) [51-500]
c RVBW - Jan 2015 - pNA [501+]
c SLJ - v61 - i6 - June 2015 - p46(6) [501+]
Peete, Holly Robinson - *Same But Different: Teen Life on the Autism Express*
y KR - Dec 15 2015 - pNA [51-500]
y PW - v262 - i48 - Nov 30 2015 - p61(1) [51-500]
Peevyhouse, Parker - *Where Futures End*
y KR - Dec 1 2015 - pNA [51-500]
y PW - v262 - i46 - Nov 16 2015 - p76(1) [51-500]
Pegau, Cathy - *Murder on the Last Frontier*
PW - v262 - i41 - Oct 12 2015 - p49(1) [51-500]
Peglau, Andreas - *Unpolitische Wissenschaft? Wilhelm Reich und die Psychoanalyse im Nationalsozialismus*
HNet - March 2015 - pNA [501+]
Pehe, Jiri - *Three Faces of an Angel*
KR - Dec 1 2015 - pNA [501+]
TLS - i5854 - June 12 2015 - p21(1) [501+]
Peikoff, Kira - *Die Again Tomorrow*
BL - v112 - i4 - Oct 15 2015 - p20(1) [51-500]
Peill-Meninghaus, Jessica - *The Gnome Project: One Woman's Wild and Woolly Adventure*
PW - v262 - i14 - April 6 2015 - p55(2) [51-500]
Peirce, Lincoln - *Big Nate Lives It Up*
c HB Guide - v26 - i2 - Fall 2015 - p97(1) [51-500]
Say Good-bye to Dork City
SLJ - v61 - i4 - April 2015 - p151(1) [51-500]
Peirse, Alison - *Korean Horror Cinema*
HNet - April 2015 - pNA [501+]
Pekelder, Jacco - *Neue Nachbarschaft: Deutschland und die Niederlande, Bildformung und Beziehungen seit 1990*
HNet - Sept 2015 - pNA(NA) [501+]
Pekkanen, Sarah - *Things You Won't Say*
BL - v111 - i14 - March 15 2015 - p56(1) [51-500]
KR - March 15 2015 - pNA [501+]
LJ - v140 - i7 - April 15 2015 - p79(2) [51-500]
Pelc, Milan - *Theatrum Humanum: Illustrierte Flugblatter und Druckgrafik des 17. Jahrhunderts als Spiegel der Zeit: Beispiele aus dem Bestand der Sammlung Valvasor des Zagreber Erzbistum*
Ren Q - v68 - i1 - Spring 2015 - p250-252 [501+]
Pelecanos, George - *The Martini Shot: A Novella and Stories (Read by Graham, Dion). Audiobook Review*
PW - v262 - i12 - March 23 2015 - p71(1) [51-500]
The Martini Shot: A Novella and Stories
NYT - Jan 8 2015 - pC1(L) [501+]
The Martini Shot and Other Stories
NS - v144 - i5251 - Feb 27 2015 - p48(2) [501+]
Pelevin, Victor - *S.N.U.F.F.: A Utopia*
New Sci - v227 - i3032 - August 1 2015 - p44(2) [501+]
Spec - v328 - i9751 - July 18 2015 - p34(2) [501+]
TLS - i5859 - July 17 2015 - p21(1) [501+]
Pelfrey, Matt - *John Ball's In the Heat of the Night. Audiobook Review*
PW - v262 - i12 - March 23 2015 - p69(1) [51-500]
Pelham, Jacqueline - *A Promise to Die For*
KR - April 1 2015 - pNA [51-500]
Pelizzon, V. Penelope - *Whose Flesh Is Flame, Whose Bone Is Time*
HR - v68 - i3 - Autumn 2015 - p481-491 [501+]
Pell, Eve - *Love, Again: The Wisdom of Unexpected Romance*
NYTBR - Feb 15 2015 - p30(L) [501+]
Pellant, Chris - *Rocks and Minerals*
LJ - v140 - i3 - Feb 15 2015 - p130(1) [51-500]
Pellegrino, Charles - *To Hell and Back: The Last Train from Hiroshima*
KR - July 1 2015 - pNA [501+]
Pelletier, Cathie - *The Summer Experiment*
c BL - v111 - i9-10 - Jan 1 2015 - p39(2) [501+]
Pelletier, Dominique - *C'est la fete des Peres!*
c Res Links - v21 - i1 - Oct 2015 - p55(1) [51-500]
C'est Noel!
c Res Links - v21 - i1 - Oct 2015 - p55(1) [51-500]
C'est Paques!
c Res Links - v20 - i5 - June 2015 - p42(1) [51-500]
Je suis capable! Series
c Res Links - v20 - i3 - Feb 2015 - p49(1) [51-500]
Le verbe Aimer au present de l'indicatif
c Res Links - v20 - i5 - June 2015 - p43(1) [51-500]
Le verbe Avoir au present de Vindicatif
c Res Links - v20 - i3 - Feb 2015 - p49(1) [51-500]
Le verbe Etre au present de l'indicatif
c Res Links - v20 - i3 - Feb 2015 - p49(1) [51-500]
Le verbe Finir au present de l'indicatif
c Res Links - v20 - i5 - June 2015 - p43(1) [51-500]
Pelletier, Mia - *A Children's Guide to Arctic Birds (Illus. by Christopher, Danny)*
c CH Bwatch - July 2015 - pNA [501+]
c CH Bwatch - June 2015 - pNA [51-500]
c KR - Feb 1 2015 - pNA [51-500]
c Res Links - v20 - i4 - April 2015 - p20(1) [51-500]
c SLJ - v61 - i3 - March 2015 - p172(1) [51-500]
Pelletier, Sue - *Collage Paint Draw: Explore Mixed Media Techniques & Materials*
Bwatch - July 2015 - pNA [51-500]
Pellicioli, Anna - *Where You End*
KR - April 1 2015 - pNA [51-500]
y BL - v111 - i19-20 - June 1 2015 - p103(1) [51-500]
SLJ - v61 - i4 - April 2015 - p169(1) [51-500]
Pelling, Christopher - *Twelve Voices from Greece and Rome: Ancient Ideas for Modern Times*
HT - v65 - i2 - Feb 2015 - p60(2) [501+]
TLS - i5840 - March 6 2015 - p9(1) [501+]
Pells, Richard - *War Babies: The Generation That Changed America*
Bwatch - April 2015 - pNA [51-500]
Pelster, Angela - *Limber*
PSQ - v89 - i3 - Fall 2015 - p172(3) [501+]
Pelttari, Aaron - *The Space That Remains: Reading Latin Poetry in Late Antiquity*
Class R - v65 - i2 - Oct 2015 - p483-484 [501+]
Peltzer, Ulrich - *Part of the Solution*
TimHES - i2185 - Jan 8 2015 - p47-47 [501+]
Pemnot, Jean Paul - *Calculus without Derivatives*
SIAM Rev - v57 - i2 - June 2015 - p310-313 [501+]
Pendleton, Steve - *Collecting Easter Island Stamps and Postal History*
Phil Lit R - v64 - i1 - Wntr 2015 - p54(2) [501+]
Penick, Pam - *The Water-Saving Garden: How to Grow a Gorgeous Garden with a Lot Less Water*
PW - v262 - i46 - Nov 16 2015 - p72(1) [51-500]
Penkov, Miroslav - *Stork Mountain*
PW - v262 - i52 - Dec 21 2015 - p122(1) [51-500]
Penman, Michael - *Monuments and Monumentality across Medieval and Early Modern Europe: Proceedings of the 2011 Stirling Conference*
Specu - v90 - i1 - Jan 2015 - p288-289 [501+]
Penn, Amy Phillips - *Elaine's: The Rise of One of New York's Most Legendary Restaurants from Those Who Were There*
BL - v111 - i19-20 - June 1 2015 - p20(1) [51-500]
Penn, Elaine - *The Magic Screen: A History of Regent Street Cinema*
Si & So - v25 - i10 - Oct 2015 - p114(1) [501+]
Penn, Michael Philip - *Envisioning Islam: Syriac Christians and the Early Muslim World*
Bks & Cult - v21 - i5 - Sept-Oct 2015 - p8(2) [501+]
When Christians First Met Muslims: A Sourcebook of the Earliest Syriac Writings on Islam
Bks & Cult - v21 - i5 - Sept-Oct 2015 - p8(2) [501+]
Penner, Barbara - *Bathroom*
T&C - v56 - i3 - July 2015 - p787-788 [501+]
Penniman, W. David - *Mergers and Alliances: The Wider View, the Operational View and Cases*
LR - v64 - i3 - March 2015 - p264-265 [501+]
Pennington, Bill - *Billy Martin: Baseball's Flawed Genius*
BL - v111 - i15 - April 1 2015 - p12(1) [51-500]
CSM - July 23 2015 - pNA [501+]
KR - March 1 2015 - pNA [501+]
LJ - v140 - i5 - March 15 2015 - p111(2) [51-500]
NYTBR - June 7 2015 - p23(L) [501+]
PW - v262 - i12 - March 23 2015 - p60(2) [501+]
Pennington, Lee - *Casualties of History: Wounded Japanese Servicemen and the Second World War*
HNet - July 2015 - pNA [501+]
Penny, H. Glenn - *Kindred by Choice: Germans and American Indians since 1800*
CEH - v48 - i1 - March 2015 - p118-120 [501+]
GSR - v38 - i2 - May 2015 - p418-3 [501+]
JMH - v87 - i2 - June 2015 - p484(3) [501+]
WHQ - v46 - i2 - Summer 2015 - p252-253 [501+]
Penny, Louise - *The Long Way Home (Read by Cosham, Ralph). Audiobook Review*
BL - v111 - i11 - Feb 1 2015 - p58(1) [51-500]
The Long Way Home
RVBW - April 2015 - pNA [501+]
RVBW - August 2015 - pNA [501+]
The Nature of the Beast (Read by Bathurst, Robert). Audiobook Review
BL - v112 - i6 - Nov 15 2015 - p60(2) [51-500]
LJ - v140 - i20 - Dec 1 2015 - p60(1) [51-500]
PW - v262 - i39 - Sept 28 2015 - p85(1) [51-500]
The Nature of the Beast
BL - v111 - i21 - July 1 2015 - p39(1) [51-500]
KR - July 15 2015 - pNA [501+]
PW - v262 - i24 - June 15 2015 - p65(1) [51-500]
Pennypacker, Sara - *Completely Clementine (Read by Almasy, Jessica). Audiobook Review*
c HB - v91 - i6 - Nov-Dec 2015 - p111(1) [51-500]
c SLJ - v61 - i10 - Oct 2015 - p50(1) [51-500]
Completely Clementine (Illus. by Frazee, Marla)
c HB Guide - v26 - i2 - Fall 2015 - p70(1) [51-500]
c BL - v111 - i11 - Feb 1 2015 - p54(1) [51-500]
c HB - v91 - i2 - March-April 2015 - p105(1) [51-500]
c KR - Jan 15 2015 - pNA [51-500]
c SLJ - v61 - i2 - Feb 2015 - p75(1) [51-500]
Meet the Dullards (Illus. by Salmieri, Daniel)
c CCB-B - v68 - i9 - May 2015 - p463(1) [51-500]
c HB - v91 - i2 - March-April 2015 - p81(2) [51-500]
c HB Guide - v26 - i2 - Fall 2015 - p47(1) [51-500]
c NYTBR - May 10 2015 - p18(L) [501+]
c PW - v262 - i7 - Feb 16 2015 - p72(32) [501+]
c SLJ - v61 - i2 - Feb 2015 - p75(1) [51-500]
Pax (Illus. by Klassen, Jon)
c BL - v112 - i5 - Nov 1 2015 - p61(2) [51-500]
c KR - Nov 1 2015 - pNA [51-500]
c PW - v262 - i46 - Nov 16 2015 - p77(1) [51-500]
c SLJ - v61 - i12 - Dec 2015 - p106(2) [501+]
Pensalfini, Rob - *Prison Shakespeare: For These Deep Shames and Great Indignities*
TimHES - i2223 - Oct 1 2015 - p51(1) [501+]
Penslar, Derek J. - *Jews and the Military: A History*
JMH - v87 - i2 - June 2015 - p412(3) [501+]
Pentcheva, Bissera V. - *The Sensual Icon: Space, Ritual, and the Senses in Byzantium*
CHR - v101 - i3 - Summer 2015 - p601(2) [501+]
Penzler, Otto - *The Big Book of Sherlock Holmes Stories*
BL - v112 - i4 - Oct 15 2015 - p18(1) [51-500]
PW - v262 - i33 - August 17 2015 - p52(1) [51-500]
LJ - v140 - i13 - August 1 2015 - p90(1) [51-500]
NYTBR - Nov 1 2015 - p10(L) [501+]
Peot, Margaret - *Crow Made a Friend (Illus. by Peot, Margaret)*
c CH Bwatch - Nov 2015 - pNA [51-500]
c KR - July 15 2015 - pNA [51-500]
c SLJ - v61 - i12 - Dec 2015 - p98(1) [51-500]
Inkblot: Drip, Splat, and Squish Your Way to Creativity (Illus. by Peot, Margaret)
c BL - v112 - i5 - Nov 1 2015 - p50(1) [501+]
Pepin, Claudine - *Kids Cook French*
c CH Bwatch - March 2015 - pNA [51-500]
Pepin, Jacques - *Heart and Soul in the Kitchen*
BL - v112 - i7 - Dec 1 2015 - p9(1) [51-500]
LJ - v140 - i12 - July 1 2015 - p106(2) [51-500]
PW - v262 - i31 - August 3 2015 - p52(1) [51-500]
The Origin of AIDS
CS - v44 - i5 - Sept 2015 - p591-603 [501+]
Peppard, Christiana Z. - *Just Sustainablility: Technology, Ecology, and Resource Extraction*
JAAR - v83 - i2 - June 2015 - pNA [501+]
Just Water: Theology, Ethics, and the Global Water Crisis
Theol St - v76 - i2 - June 2015 - p395(1) [501+]
Peppas, Lynn - *Cultural Traditions in Germany*
Res Links - v21 - i1 - Oct 2015 - p22(1) [501+]
Cultural Traditions in Iran
Res Links - v21 - i1 - Oct 2015 - p22(1) [501+]
Cultural Traditions in Jamaica
Res Links - v21 - i1 - Oct 2015 - p22(1) [501+]
Forensics: The Scene of the Crime
c Res Links - v20 - i3 - Feb 2015 - p38(2) [501+]
Robotics
c Res Links - v20 - i3 - Feb 2015 - p38(2) [501+]
Peppas, Lynn Leslie - *The Holocaust*
c Res Links - v20 - i5 - June 2015 - p34(1) [501+]
Peppiatt, Michael - *Francis Bacon in Your Blood: A Memoir*
BL - v112 - i1 - Sept 1 2015 - p25(1) [51-500]
KR - Sept 1 2015 - pNA [501+]
NS - v144 - i5276 - August 21 2015 - p47(1) [51-500]
NYT - Dec 31 2015 - pC7(L) [501+]
PW - v262 - i30 - July 27 2015 - p51(1) [51-500]
Spec - v328 - i9758 - Sept 5 2015 - p39(1) [501+]
Peppis, Paul - *Sciences of Modernism: Ethnography, Sexology, and Psychology*
MP - v113 - i2 - Nov 2015 - pE126(3) [501+]

Peppler, Kylie - *Soft Circuits: Crafting e-Fashion with DIY Electronics*
    Sci & Ch - v53 - i1 - Sept 2015 - p97 [51-500]
    Sci Teach - v82 - i6 - Sept 2015 - p73 [51-500]

Pepys, Samuel - *The Diary of Samuel Pepys, 1660-1669, 3 vols. (Read by Pugh, Leighton). Audiobook Review*
    Spec - v328 - i9756 - August 22 2015 - p41(1) [501+]

Per Aspera ad Astra - Soziale Hierarchien und Ihre Praxis in der Antike. 3. Gottinger Nachwuchsforum
    HNet - July 2015 - pNA [501+]

Perabo, Susan - *Why They Run the Way They Do*
    KR - Dec 15 2015 - pNA [501+]

Peralta, Dan-el Padilla - *Undocumented: A Dominican Boy's Odyssey from a Homeless Shelter to the Ivy League*
    y BL - v111 - i18 - May 15 2015 - p6(1) [51-500]
    KR - May 1 2015 - pNA [501+]
    LJ - v140 - i9 - May 15 2015 - p88(1) [51-500]
    PW - v262 - i23 - June 8 2015 - p53(1) [51-500]

The Perception of Apartheid in Western Europe, 1960-1990
    HNet - Sept 2015 - pNA [501+]

Perchard, Tom - *After Django: Making Jazz in Postwar France*
    NYRB - v62 - i12 - July 9 2015 - p55(3) [501+]
    TimHES - i2202 - May 7 2015 - p54-55 [501+]
    TimHES - i2211 - July 9 2015 - p46-47 [501+]

Percival, Chap - *Go See the Eclipse and Take a Kid with You*
    Sci & Ch - v53 - i2 - Oct 2015 - p97 [51-500]

Percival, Tom - *Bubble Trouble*
    c HB Guide - v26 - i2 - Fall 2015 - p47(1) [51-500]
    c KR - April 1 2015 - pNA [51-500]
    c Sch Lib - v63 - i1 - Spring 2015 - p32(1) [51-500]
    c SLJ - v61 - i10 - Oct 2015 - p81(2) [51-500]
Herman's Letter (Illus. by Percival, Tom)
    c HB Guide - v26 - i2 - Fall 2015 - p47(1) [51-500]
Herman's Vacation (Illus. by Percival, Tom)
    c SLJ - v61 - i12 - Dec 2015 - p94(1) [51-500]

Percy, Benjamin - *The Dead Lands (Read by Graham, Holter). Audiobook Review*
    BL - v112 - i3 - Oct 1 2015 - p85(1) [51-500]
    Bwatch - Sept 2015 - pNA [501+]
    LJ - v140 - i10 - June 1 2015 - p61(1) [51-500]
    PW - v262 - i26 - June 29 2015 - p63(1) [51-500]
The Dead Lands
    BL - v111 - i13 - March 1 2015 - p30(1) [51-500]
    y HR - v68 - i1 - Spring 2015 - p151-157 [501+]
    KR - April 1 2015 - pNA [51-500]
    NYTBR - May 31 2015 - p16(L) [501+]
    PW - v262 - i6 - Feb 9 2015 - p48(1) [51-500]

Perdew, Laura - *Bullying*
    y HB Guide - v26 - i1 - Spring 2015 - p132(1) [51-500]
A Kid's Guide to the Middle East Series
    c BL - v111 - i12 - Feb 15 2015 - p74(1) [501+]

Perec, Georges - *Le Condottiere*
    TLS - i5854 - June 12 2015 - p10(1) [501+]
Portrait of a Man Known as Il Condottiere
    KR - Feb 15 2015 - pNA [501+]
    NY - v91 - i21 - July 27 2015 - p71 [51-500]

Pereira, Elaine C. - *I Will Never Forget: A Daughter's Story of Her Mother's Arduous and Humorous Journey through Dementia*
    SPBW - May 2015 - pNA [501+]

Perelman, Helen - *Frozen Treats (Illus. by Water, Erica-Jane)*
    c HB Guide - v26 - i1 - Spring 2015 - p64(1) [51-500]
Sweet Secrets (Illus. by Waters, Erica-Jane)
    c HB Guide - v26 - i2 - Fall 2015 - p70(1) [51-500]

Perepeczko, Jenny - *Moses: The True Story of an Elephant Baby*
    c HB Guide - v26 - i1 - Spring 2015 - p166(1) [51-500]

Peres, Tanya M. - *Trends and Traditions in Southeastern Zooarchaeology*
    Am Ant - v80 - i1 - Jan 2015 - p213(2) [501+]

Perez, Ashley Hope - *Out of Darkness*
    y BL - v112 - i1 - Sept 1 2015 - p108(1) [51-500]
    y KR - June 1 2015 - pNA [51-500]
    y SLJ - v61 - i6 - June 2015 - p128(1) [51-500]

Perez-Brown, Maria - *Zuri Pi Wonders Why: Do I Have to Go to School? (Illus. by Gonzales, Chuck)*
    c CH Bwatch - Sept 2015 - pNA [51-500]

Perez-Giese, Tony - *Send More Idiots*
    KR - April 1 2015 - pNA [501+]

Perez, Kristina - *The Myth of Morgan la Fey*
    FS - v69 - i2 - April 2015 - p230-231 [501+]

Perez, Louis A., Jr. - *The Structure of Cuban History: Meanings and Purpose of the Past*
    Ams - v72 - i1 - Jan 2015 - p174(3) [501+]

Perez, Monica - *Curious George Discovers Space*
    c CH Bwatch - Nov 2015 - pNA [51-500]

Perez, Rene S., II - *Seeing off the Johns*
    y BL - v112 - i3 - Oct 1 2015 - p74(1) [51-500]
    y KR - June 1 2015 - pNA [51-500]
    y PW - v262 - i39 - Sept 28 2015 - p95(1) [51-500]
    y SLJ - v61 - i11 - Nov 2015 - p120(2) [51-500]
    y VOYA - v38 - i5 - Dec 2015 - p62(1) [51-500]

Perez-Soba, J.J. - *Gospel of the Family: Going beyond Cardinal Kasper's Proposal in the Debate on Marriage, Civil Re-Marriage, and Communion in the Church*
    Theol St - v76 - i2 - June 2015 - p379(3) [501+]

Perez-Villanueva, Sonia - *The Life of Catalina de Erauso, the Lieutenant Nun: An Early Modern Autobiography*
    Biomag - v38 - i3 - Summer 2015 - p441(4) [501+]

Performing Local and Regional Level Administration and Politics: Ceremonies, Rituals and Routines, 16th-18th c.
    HNet - April 2015 - pNA [501+]

Pericolo, Lorenzo - *Caravaggio: Reflections and Refractions*
    Ren Q - v68 - i3 - Fall 2015 - p1009-1011 [501+]
    Sev Cent N - v73 - i1-2 - Spring-Summer 2015 - p47(9) [501+]
    Six Ct J - v46 - i3 - Fall 2015 - p690-692 [501+]

Perin, Raffaella - *Chiesa Cattolica e Minoranze in Italia nella Prima Meta del Novecento: Il Caso Veneto a Confronto*
    CHR - v101 - i1 - Wntr 2015 - p171(2) [501+]

Perino, Dana - *And the Good News Is ... : Lessons and Advice from the Bright Side*
    KR - Feb 15 2015 - pNA [501+]
    Nat R - v67 - i8 - May 4 2015 - p51 [501+]

Perinot, Sophie - *Medicis Daughter*
    KR - Oct 1 2015 - pNA [51-500]
    LJ - v140 - i17 - Oct 15 2015 - p76(1) [501+]

Perkins, Dwight H. - *East Asian Development: Foundations and Strategies*
    Pac A - v88 - i4 - Dec 2015 - p891 [501+]

Perkins, John - *The New Confessions of an Economic Hit Man*
    PW - v262 - i52 - Dec 21 2015 - p146(2) [51-500]

Perkins, Lynne Rae - *Nuts to You (Read by Almasy, Jessica). Audiobook Review*
    y HB - v91 - i4 - July-August 2015 - p165(2) [51-500]
    c SLJ - v61 - i6 - June 2015 - p64(2) [51-500]
Nuts to You (Illus. by Perkins, Lynne Rae)
    c BL - v111 - i12 - Feb 15 2015 - p76(1) [51-500]
    c CCB-B - v68 - i5 - Jan 2015 - p272(2) [51-500]
    c HB Guide - v26 - i1 - Spring 2015 - p89(2) [51-500]

Perkins, Maripat - *Rodeo Red (Illus. by Idle, Molly)*
    c BL - v111 - i12 - Feb 15 2015 - p88(1) [51-500]
    c CH Bwatch - April 2015 - pNA [51-500]
    c HB - v91 - i2 - March-April 2015 - p82(1) [51-500]
    c HB Guide - v26 - i2 - Fall 2015 - p47(1) [51-500]
    c KR - Jan 15 2015 - pNA [51-500]
    c NYTBR - March 15 2015 - p18(L) [501+]
    c NYTBR - March 15 2015 - p18(L) [501+]
    c SLJ - v61 - i2 - Feb 2015 - p75(2) [51-500]

Perkins, Mitali - *Tiger Boy (Illus. by Hogan, Jamie)*
    BL - v111 - i14 - March 15 2015 - p76(1) [51-500]
    c HB - v91 - i2 - March-April 2015 - p105(2) [51-500]
    c HB Guide - v26 - i2 - Fall 2015 - p97(1) [51-500]
    c KR - Jan 15 2015 - pNA [51-500]
    c PW - v262 - i5 - Feb 2 2015 - p61(1) [51-500]
    c SLJ - v61 - i2 - Feb 2015 - p90(2) [51-500]

Perkins, Nicholas - *Medieval Romance and Material Culture*
    TLS - i5853 - June 5 2015 - p26(1) [501+]

Perkins, Richard - *The Verses in Eric the Red's Saga, and Again: Norse Visits to America*
    Med R - May 2015 - pNA [501+]

Perkins, Stephanie - *Isla and the Happily Ever After*
    y HB Guide - v26 - i1 - Spring 2015 - p120(1) [51-500]
My True Love Gave to Me: Twelve Holiday Stories
    y HB Guide - v26 - i1 - Spring 2015 - p187(1) [51-500]
    y Teach Lib - v42 - i3 - Feb 2015 - p28(4) [501+]

Perkins-Valdez, Dolen - *Balm*
    BL - v111 - i16 - April 15 2015 - p32(1) [51-500]
    LJ - v140 - i7 - April 15 2015 - p80(1) [51-500]

Perkiss, Abigail - *Making Good Neighbors: Civil Rights, Liberalism, and Integration in Postwar Philadelphia*
    AHR - v120 - i4 - Oct 2015 - p1512-1514 [501+]
    JAH - v101 - i4 - March 2015 - p1333-1334 [501+]

Perkovich, Beth - *Which Way Did She Go?*
    KR - Nov 1 2015 - pNA [501+]

Perkowski, Piotr - *Gdansk: Miasto od Nowa*
    HNet - July 2015 - pNA [501+]

Perl, Erica S. - *Goatilocks and the Three Bears (Illus. by Howard, Arthur)*
    c HB Guide - v26 - i1 - Spring 2015 - p41(1) [51-500]
Totally Tardy Marty (Illus. by Krosoczka, Jarrett J.)
    c CH Bwatch - Oct 2015 - pNA [51-500]
    c KR - July 15 2015 - pNA [51-500]
    c SLJ - v61 - i10 - Oct 2015 - p82(1) [51-500]

Perl, Jed - *New Art City: Manhattan at Mid-Century*
    BL - v112 - i5 - Nov 1 2015 - p18(2) [501+]

Perl, Lila - *Lilli's Quest*
    y BL - v112 - i3 - Oct 1 2015 - p70(2) [51-500]
    y KR - Sept 15 2015 - pNA [51-500]
    y PW - v262 - i35 - August 31 2015 - p94(1) [51-500]

Perlman, Janice - *Favela: Four Decades of Living on the Edge in Rio de Janeiro*
    SF - v93 - i3 - March 2015 - pe72 [501+]

Perloff, Carey - *Beautiful Chaos: A Life in the Theater*
    BL - v111 - i14 - March 15 2015 - p37(1) [51-500]
    KR - Feb 1 2015 - pNA [501+]
    TLS - i5852 - May 29 2015 - p27(1) [501+]

Perloff, Marjorie - *Poetics in a New Key: Interviews and Essays*
    TLS - i5836 - Feb 6 2015 - p26(1) [501+]

Perlstein, Rick - *The Invisible Bridge (Read by de Vries, David). Audiobook Review*
    BL - v111 - i11 - Feb 1 2015 - p58(1) [51-500]
The Invisible Bridge
    HNet - April 2015 - pNA [501+]
    Lon R Bks - v37 - i21 - Nov 5 2015 - p33(2) [501+]
    NYTBR - Oct 4 2015 - p28(L) [501+]
    TimHES - i2202 - May 7 2015 - p49(1) [501+]

Perona, Blandine - *Prosopopee et persona a la Renaissance*
    Ren Q - v68 - i3 - Fall 2015 - p1121-1123 [501+]

Perona, Elizabeth - *Murder on the Bucket List*
    KR - May 1 2015 - pNA [51-500]

Perrat, Charles - *Bullarium Cyprium, vol. 3: Lettres papales relatives a Chypre, 1316-1378*
    HER - v130 - i543 - April 2015 - p384(16) [501+]

Perreiah, Alan R. - *Renaissance Truths: Humanism, Scholasticism and the Search for the Perfect Language*
    Ren Q - v68 - i2 - Summer 2015 - p619-620 [501+]
    Six Ct J - v46 - i3 - Fall 2015 - p685-686 [501+]

Perret, Delphine - *Pedro and George (Illus. by Perret, Delphine)*
    c HB Guide - v26 - i2 - Fall 2015 - p47(1) [51-500]
    c KR - April 15 2015 - pNA [51-500]
    c PW - v262 - i17 - April 27 2015 - p75(1) [51-500]
    c SLJ - v61 - i6 - June 2015 - p90(1) [51-500]
    c Teach Lib - v43 - i1 - Oct 2015 - p28(1) [51-500]

Perret, Gene - *Comedy Writing Self-Taught: The Professional Skill-Building Course in Writing Stand-Up, Sketch, and Situation Comedy*
    Bwatch - April 2015 - pNA [51-500]

Perrett, Lisa - *Sparkling Princess Opposites (Illus. by Perrett, Lisa)*
    c KR - Jan 1 2015 - pNA [51-500]

Perrin, Andrew J. - *American Democracy: From Tocqueville to Town Halls to Twitter*
    AJS - v120 - i5 - March 2015 - p1562(4) [501+]
    CS - v44 - i2 - March 2015 - p292(1s) [501+]

Perritano, John - *Bomb Squad Technician*
    c BL - v112 - i3 - Oct 1 2015 - p44(2) [51-500]
The Comet of Doom (Illus. by Laughead, Mike)
    c HB Guide - v26 - i1 - Spring 2015 - p89(1) [51-500]
The Egyptian Prophecy (Illus. by Laughead, Mike)
    c HB Guide - v26 - i1 - Spring 2015 - p89(1) [51-500]
Fault Lines
    y SLJ - v61 - i9 - Sept 2015 - p151(4) [501+]
The Madness of Captain Cyclops (Illus. by Laughead, Mike)
    c HB Guide - v26 - i1 - Spring 2015 - p89(1) [51-500]
Monsters of the Deep
    y SLJ - v61 - i9 - Sept 2015 - p151(4) [501+]
Monsters on Land
    y SLJ - v61 - i9 - Sept 2015 - p151(4) [501+]
The Snickerblooms and the Age Bug (Illus. by Laughead, Mike)
    c HB Guide - v26 - i1 - Spring 2015 - p89(1) [51-500]

Book Review Index 2016 Cumulation **PETERSON • 365**

Virtual Reality
y SLJ - v61 - i9 - Sept 2015 - p151(4) [501+]
Wormholes
y SLJ - v61 - i9 - Sept 2015 - p151(4) [501+]
Perros, Georges - *Paper Collage*
TLS - i5869 - Sept 25 2015 - p27(1) [501+]
Perrot, Jean - *Henry James's Enigmas: Turning the Screw of Eternity?*
TLS - i5840 - March 6 2015 - p22(1) [501+]
Perrun, Jody - *The Patriotic Consensus: Unity, Morale, and the Second World War in Winnipeg*
Beav - v95 - i2 - April-May 2015 - p54(2) [501+]
Perry, Adele - *Place and Replace: Essays on Western Canada*
WHQ - v46 - i1 - Spring 2015 - p98-98 [501+]
Perry, Alex - *The Rift: A New Africa Breaks Free*
KR - Oct 1 2015 - pNA [51-500]
LJ - v140 - i19 - Nov 15 2015 - p99(2) [51-500]
PW - v262 - i37 - Sept 14 2015 - p54(1) [51-500]
Perry, Anne - *Corridors of the Night*
BL - v112 - i2 - Sept 15 2015 - p30(1) [51-500]
PW - v262 - i31 - August 3 2015 - p36(1) [51-500]
Perry, Carol J. - *Look Both Ways*
KR - Sept 1 2015 - pNA [51-500]
Perry, Chrissie - *Penelope Perfect: Project Best Friend*
y Magpies - v30 - i1 - March 2015 - p36(1) [501+]
Perry, Gill - *Placing Faces: The Portrait and the English Country House in the Long Eighteenth Century*
HT - v65 - i1 - Jan 2015 - p62(1) [501+]
Perry, Grayson - *Playing to the Gallery: Helping Contemporary Art in Its Struggle to Be Understood*
CHE - v61 - i38 - June 12 2015 - pB5(1) [501+]
LJ - v140 - i5 - March 15 2015 - p99(1) [501+]
NYTBR - June 28 2015 - p15(L) [501+]
PW - v262 - i10 - March 9 2015 - p64(2) [51-500]
Perry, Jolene - *Has to Be Love*
c BL - v112 - i1 - Sept 1 2015 - p103(1) [51-500]
y KR - July 15 2015 - pNA [51-500]
y SLJ - v61 - i8 - August 2015 - p109(1) [51-500]
Stonger Than You Know
y HB Guide - v26 - i1 - Spring 2015 - p120(1) [51-500]
Perry, Keisha-Khan Y. - *Black Women against the Land Grab: The Fight for Racial Justice in Brazil*
Ams - v72 - i3 - July 2015 - p522(3) [501+]
CS - v44 - i5 - Sept 2015 - p689-691 [501+]
ERS - v38 - i8 - August 2015 - p1425(3) [501+]
Perry, M.J. - *Gender, Manumission, and the Roman Freedwoman*
Class R - v65 - i1 - April 2015 - p197-199 [501+]
Perry, Marta - *When Secrets Strike*
PW - v262 - i39 - Sept 28 2015 - p75(1) [51-500]
Where Secrets Sleep
PW - v262 - i4 - Jan 26 2015 - p155(2) [51-500]
Perry, Michael - *The Jesus Cow*
BL - v111 - i16 - April 15 2015 - p24(1) [51-500]
KR - March 15 2015 - pNA [51-500]
LJ - v140 - i6 - April 1 2015 - p84(1) [51-500]
PW - v262 - i13 - March 30 2015 - p51(1) [51-500]
The Scavengers (Read by Rustin, Sandy). Audiobook Review
c SLJ - v61 - i6 - June 2015 - p64(1) [51-500]
The Scavengers
c HB Guide - v26 - i1 - Spring 2015 - p89(1) [51-500]
c BL - v111 - i9-10 - Jan 1 2015 - p39(2) [501+]
Perry, Nandra - *Imitatio Christi: The Poetics of Piety in Early Modern England*
Ren Q - v68 - i3 - Fall 2015 - p1134-1135 [501+]
Perry, Richard J. - *Killer Apes, Naked Apes, and Just Plain Nasty People: The Misuse and Abuse of Science in Political Discourse*
PW - v262 - i29 - July 20 2015 - p181(1) [51-500]
TimHES - i2229 - Nov 12 2015 - p49(1) [501+]
Perry, Sue - *Nica of Los Angeles*
KR - Sept 1 2015 - pNA [501+]
Perry, Thomas - *Forty Thieves*
BL - v112 - i7 - Dec 1 2015 - p28(1) [51-500]
KR - Oct 15 2015 - pNA [51-500]
LJ - v140 - i19 - Nov 15 2015 - p79(1) [51-500]
A String of Beads (Read by Bean, Joyce). Audiobook Review
BL - v111 - i17 - May 1 2015 - p60(1) [51-500]
A String of Beads
NYTBR - Jan 4 2015 - p25(L) [501+]
RVBW - Sept 2015 - pNA [51-500]
Perry, William J. - *My Journey at the Nuclear Brink*
KR - Sept 15 2015 - pNA [501+]
Pershing, Douglas - *Ordinaries*
KR - March 1 2015 - pNA [501+]
Pershing, John J. - *My Life before the World War, 1860-1917: A Memoir*
Historian - v77 - i3 - Fall 2015 - p572(2) [501+]
Person, Katarzyna - *Assimilated Jews in the Warsaw Ghetto, 1940-1943*
Slav R - v74 - i3 - Fall 2015 - p620-621 [501+]
Person, M.G. - *A Presentist Path to World Peace*
SPBW - Feb 2015 - pNA [51-500]
Personlicher Einfluss auf den Herrscher in der Romischen Kaiserzeit und dem Fruhen Mittelalter
HNet - Jan 2015 - pNA [501+]
Pesce, Dolores - *Liszt's Final Decade*
TLS - i5844 - April 3 2015 - p9(1) [501+]
Peschel, Lisa - *Performing Captivity, Performing Escape: Cabarets and Plays from the Terezin/Theresienstadt Ghetto*
TDR - v59 - i1 - Spring 2015 - p193(1) [501+]
Peschio, Joe - *The Poetics of Impudence and Intimacy in the Age of Pushkin*
Slav R - v74 - i3 - Fall 2015 - p668-669 [501+]
Peschke, Marci - *Green Queen (Illus. by Mourning, Tuesday)*
c HB Guide - v26 - i1 - Spring 2015 - p64(1) [51-500]
Pesco, Daniela del - *La citta del Seicento*
Ren Q - v68 - i2 - Summer 2015 - p652-654 [501+]
Pesic, Peter - *Music and the Making of Modern Science*
Isis - v106 - i2 - June 2015 - p412(2) [501+]
Phys Today - v68 - i3 - March 2015 - p50-50 [501+]
TLS - i5871 - Oct 9 2015 - p24(1) [501+]
Peskanov, Alexander - *Ozark Waltz*
c Am MT - v64 - i6 - June-July 2015 - p67(2) [501+]
Song of Remembrance
c Am MT - v64 - i6 - June-July 2015 - p67(2) [501+]
Pessah, Jon - *The Game: Inside the Secret World of Major League Baseball's Power Brokers*
LJ - v140 - i9 - May 15 2015 - p87(2) [51-500]
NYTBR - June 7 2015 - p22(L) [501+]
Pestilli, Livio - *Paolo de Matteis: Neapolitan Painting and Cultural History in Baroque Europe*
Sev Cent N - v73 - i3-4 - Fall-Winter 2015 - p167(9) [501+]
Petel, Gilies - *Under the Channel*
PW - v262 - i3 - Jan 19 2015 - p63(1) [51-500]
Peterfreund, Diana - *Omega City*
BL - v111 - i13 - March 1 2015 - p61(1) [51-500]
c CCB-B - v68 - i10 - June 2015 - p509(1) [51-500]
c HB Guide - v26 - i2 - Fall 2015 - p97(1) [51-500]
c KR - Jan 1 2015 - pNA [51-500]
c PW - v262 - i7 - Feb 16 2015 - p179(1) [51-500]
c SLJ - v61 - i2 - Feb 2015 - p91(1) [51-500]
y VOYA - v38 - i2 - June 2015 - p81(1) [51-500]
Peterman, Steven - *The Sketchbook Project World Tour*
LJ - v140 - i9 - May 15 2015 - p80(2) [51-500]
Peternell, Cal - *Twelve Recipes*
Bwatch - Feb 2015 - pNA [51-500]
Ent W - i1346 - Jan 16 2015 - p67(1) [501+]
Peters, Andrew Fusek - *The Color Thief: A Family's Story of Depression (Illus. by Littlewood, Karin)*
c KR - August 15 2015 - pNA [51-500]
The Colour Thief: A Family's Story of Depression (Illus. by Littlewood, Karin)
c Sch Lib - v63 - i1 - Spring 2015 - p32(1) [51-500]
Peters, Bernadette - *Stella and Charlie, Friends Forever (Illus. by Murphy, Liz)*
c SLJ - v61 - i11 - Nov 2015 - p86(1) [51-500]
Peters, Chris - *Rethinking Journalism: Trust and Participation in a Transformed News Landscape*
NYRB - v62 - i10 - June 4 2015 - p43(3) [501+]
Peters, Christabelle - *Cuban Identity and the Angolan Experience*
HAHR - v95 - i3 - August 2015 - p543-544 [501+]
Peters, Greg - *The Story of Monasticism: Retrieving an Ancient Tradition for Contemporary Spirituality*
PW - v262 - i27 - July 6 2015 - p66(2) [51-500]
Peters, Jenny - *21 Songs in 6 Days: Learn Ukulele the Easy Way*
Am MT - v64 - i6 - June-July 2015 - p70(1) [501+]
Peters, John (b. 1963-) - *Boom, Bust and Crisis: Labour, Corporate Power and Politics in Canada*
CS - v44 - i3 - May 2015 - p399-401 [501+]
Peters, John Durham - *The Marvelous Clouds: Toward a Philosophy of Elemental Media*
LJ - v140 - i9 - May 15 2015 - p86(1) [51-500]
Peters, Julie Anne - *Define Normal (Read by Lakin, Christine). Audiobook Review*
c BL - v111 - i14 - March 15 2015 - p24(2) [501+]
Peters, Justin - *The Idealist: Aaron Swartz and the Rise of Free Culture on the Internet*
BL - v112 - i7 - Dec 1 2015 - p5(1) [501+]
KR - Nov 15 2015 - pNA [501+]
LJ - v140 - i19 - Nov 15 2015 - p105(1) [51-500]
PW - v262 - i45 - Nov 9 2015 - p53(2) [51-500]
Peters, Marilee - *10 Rivers That Shaped The World (Illus. by Rosen, Kim)*
c BL - v111 - i21 - July 1 2015 - p50(1) [51-500]
c KR - May 15 2015 - pNA [51-500]
c Res Links - v21 - i1 - Oct 2015 - p25(2) [51-500]
Patient Zero: Solving the Mysteries of Deadly Epidemics
y VOYA - v38 - i1 - April 2015 - p87(2) [51-500]
Peters, Nancy J. - *Dreams of Dreams and the Last Three Days of Fernando Pessoa*
NYRB - v62 - i10 - June 4 2015 - p63(3) [501+]
Peters, Ralph - *Valley of the Shadow*
BL - v111 - i16 - April 15 2015 - p38(1) [51-500]
KR - March 15 2015 - pNA [501+]
Peters, Rebecca Todd - *Solidarity Ethics: Transformation in a Globalized World*
Intpr - v69 - i4 - Oct 2015 - p506(1) [501+]
Peters, Robbie - *Surabaya, 1945-2010: Neighbourhood, State and Economy in Indonesia's City of Struggle*
Pac A - v88 - i2 - June 2015 - p369 [501+]
Petersen, Keith C. - *John Mullan: The Tumultuous Life of a Western Road Builder*
Bwatch - August 2015 - pNA [51-500]
PHR - v84 - i4 - Nov 2015 - p531(2) [501+]
WHQ - v46 - i3 - Autumn 2015 - p381-382 [501+]
Petersen, Leif Inge Ree - *Siege Warfare and Military Organization in the Successor States (400-800 AD): Byzantium, the West and Islam*
HNet - March 2015 - pNA [501+]
Petersik, John - *Lovable, Livable Home: How to Add Beauty, Get Organized, and Make Your House Work for You*
PW - v262 - i29 - July 20 2015 - p185(1) [51-500]
Petersik, Sherry - *Lovable Livable Home: How to Add Beauty, Get Organized, and Make Your House Work for You*
LJ - v140 - i15 - Sept 15 2015 - p78(1) [51-500]
Peterson, Allan - *Precarious*
Ant R - v73 - i1 - Wntr 2015 - p190(1) [501+]
Peterson, Alyson - *Ian Quicksilver: The Warrior's Return*
y SLJ - v61 - i6 - June 2015 - p115(1) [51-500]
Peterson, Amanda - *The U.S. Civil War: A Chronology of a Divided Nation*
c HB Guide - v26 - i2 - Fall 2015 - p219(1) [51-500]
Peterson, Bryan - *Learning to See Creatively: Design, Color, and Composition in Photography, 3d ed.*
LJ - v140 - i17 - Oct 15 2015 - p88(1) [51-500]
Peterson, Charlotte - *The Mindful Parent: Strategies from Peaceful Cultures to Raise Compassionate, Well-Balanced Kids*
PW - v262 - i42 - Oct 19 2015 - p72(2) [51-500]
Peterson, Cheryl - *Who Is the Church? An Ecclesiology for the Twenty-First Century*
Intpr - v69 - i1 - Jan 2015 - p112(2) [501+]
Peterson, David - *Happiness Is a Warm Carcass: Assorted Sordid Stories from the Photographer in the Midst*
RVBW - August 2015 - pNA [51-500]
Peterson, David J. - *The Art of Language Invention: From Horse-Lords to Dark Elves, the Words Behind World-Building*
KR - July 15 2015 - pNA [501+]
LJ - v140 - i14 - Sept 1 2015 - p114(1) [51-500]
PW - v262 - i31 - August 3 2015 - p48(1) [51-500]
Peterson, Derek R. - *Ethnic Patriotism and the East Africa Revival: A History of Dissent 1935-1972*
IJAHS - v48 - i1 - Wntr 2015 - p120-122 [501+]
Peterson, Jeanette Favrot - *Visualizing Guadalupe: From Black Madonna to Queen of the Americas*
Ams - v72 - i2 - April 2015 - p335(336) [501+]
HAHR - v95 - i3 - August 2015 - p515-517 [501+]
Peterson, Joel L. - *Dreams of My Mothers: A Story of Love Transcendent*
SPBW - April 2015 - pNA [51-500]
Peterson, Jonathan - *Social Security for Dummies, 2d ed.*
Bwatch - June 2015 - pNA [51-500]
Peterson, Kristin - *Speculative Markets: Drug Circuits and Derivative Life in Nigeria*
MAQ - v29 - i2 - June 2015 - pb49-b51 [501+]
Peterson, Lawrence K. - *Confederate Combat Commander: The Remarkable Life of Brigadier General Alfred Jefferson Vaughan Jr.*
JSH - v81 - i3 - August 2015 - p740(2) [501+]
Peterson, Linda Lee - *The Spy on the Tennessee Walker*
BL - v112 - i3 - Oct 1 2015 - p26(1) [51-500]
PW - v262 - i39 - Sept 28 2015 - p69(2) [51-500]

366 • PETERSON Book Review Index 2016 Cumulation

Peterson, Lois - *Three Good Things*
y KR - Sept 15 2015 - pNA [51-500]
y Res Links - v21 - i1 - Oct 2015 - p39(1) [501+]
Peterson, Mark Allen - *Connected in Cairo: Growing Up Cosmopolitan in the Modern Middle East*
IJMES - v47 - i4 - Nov 2015 - p831-833 [501+]
Peterson, Martin - *The Dimensions of Consequentialism*
Dialogue - v54 - i3 - Sept 2015 - p588-589 [501+]
Peterson, Mary Pflum - *White Dresses*
KR - July 15 2015 - pNA [501+]
Peterson, Megan Cooley - *Chimpanzees Are Awesome!*
c Sch Lib - v63 - i3 - Autumn 2015 - p158(1) [51-500]
Peterson, Oscar - *Oscar Lives Next Door: A Story Inspired by Oscar Peterson's Childhood (Illus. by Lafrance, Marie)*
c Nat Post - v17 - i277 - Oct 10 2015 - pWP5(1) [501+]
Peterson, Peter G. - *Steering Clear: How to Avoid a Debt Crisis and Secure Our Economic Future*
NYRB - v62 - i4 - March 5 2015 - p48(3) [501+]
Peterson, Sarah Jo - *Planning the Home Front: Building Bombers and Communities at Willow Run*
RAH - v43 - i1 - March 2015 - p161-167 [501+]
Peterson, Teri - *Who's Got Time? Spirituality for a Busy Generation*
Intpr - v69 - i4 - Oct 2015 - p502(2) [501+]
Peterson, Tina L. - *Oscar and the Amazing Gravity Repellent*
c KR - July 15 2015 - pNA [51-500]
Peterson, Trade - *Refining Fire*
PW - v262 - i23 - June 8 2015 - p46(2) [51-500]
Peterson, Troy Everett - *The Last Comanche Moon*
Roundup M - v22 - i3 - Feb 2015 - p27(1) [501+]
Roundup M - v22 - i6 - August 2015 - p32(1) [501+]
Peterson, Valerie - *Cookie Craft: Baking and Decorating Techniques for Fun and Festive Occasions*
Bwatch - June 2015 - pNA [51-500]
Peterson, Vicki - *Notes to Screenwriters: Advancing Your Story, Screenplay, and Career with Whatever Hollywood Throws at You*
Bwatch - Feb 2015 - pNA [51-500]
Petosa, Jess - *Exceptional (Read by Durante, Emily). Audiobook Review*
SLJ - v61 - i3 - March 2015 - p81(1) [51-500]
Petra, Daniel - *Missing Links: Practical and Surprisingly Effective Tools for Self-Transformation ... and Behavior Modification*
SPBW - June 2015 - pNA [51-500]
Petram, Lodewijk - *The World's First Stock Exchange*
BHR - v89 - i1 - Spring 2015 - p181(4) [501+]
Petras, James - *Imperialism and Capitalism in the Twenty-First Century: A System in Crisis*
CS - v44 - i5 - Sept 2015 - p691-692 [501+]
Petravic, Robin - *Tile Makes the Room: Good Design from Heath Ceramics*
Am Craft - v75 - i6 - Dec 2015 - p26(1) [501+]
BL - v112 - i1 - Sept 1 2015 - p28(1) [51-500]
LJ - v140 - i14 - Sept 1 2015 - p107(1) [51-500]
Petre, James - *Crusader Castles of Cyprus: The Fortifications of Cyprus under the Lusignans, 1191-1489*
HER - v130 - i543 - April 2015 - p384(16) [501+]
Petrella, R.J. - *Days of the Giants*
SPBW - Jan 2015 - pNA [51-500]
Petri, Alexandra - *A Field Guide to Awkward Silences*
y BL - v111 - i19-20 - June 1 2015 - p5(1) [51-500]
Petricic, Dusan - *Ma grande famille*
c Res Links - v20 - i5 - June 2015 - p43(1) [501+]
My Family Tree and Me (Illus. by Petricic, Dusan)
c BL - v111 - i11 - Feb 1 2015 - p46(1) [51-500]
c HB - v91 - i3 - May-June 2015 - p129(2) [51-500]
c HB Guide - v26 - i2 - Fall 2015 - p152(1) [51-500]
c KR - Feb 1 2015 - pNA [51-500]
c NYTBR - July 12 2015 - p19(L) [501+]
c Res Links - v20 - i5 - June 2015 - p8(1) [51-500]
c SLJ - v61 - i3 - March 2015 - p124(1) [51-500]
Petrie, Kristin - *Affenpinschers*
c HB Guide - v26 - i1 - Spring 2015 - p169(1) [51-500]
American Crows
c HB Guide - v26 - i2 - Fall 2015 - p177(1) [51-500]
Cottontail Rabbits
c HB Guide - v26 - i2 - Fall 2015 - p180(1) [51-500]
Garter Snakes
c HB Guide - v26 - i2 - Fall 2015 - p175(1) [51-500]
Hummingbirds
c HB Guide - v26 - i2 - Fall 2015 - p177(1) [51-500]
Petrie, Nicholas - *The Drifter*
KR - Nov 15 2015 - pNA [501+]
PW - v262 - i46 - Nov 16 2015 - p55(1) [51-500]
Petrie, Thomas - *Following Oil: Four Decades of Cycle-Testing Experiences and What They Foretell about U.S. Energy Independence*
For Aff - v94 - i3 - May-June 2015 - pNA [501+]
Petro, Anthony M. - *After the Wrath of God: AIDS, Sexuality, and American Religion*
LJ - v140 - i10 - June 1 2015 - p108(1) [51-500]
Petroff, Bryan - *Big Gay Ice Cream: Saucy Stories and Frozen Treats: Going All the Way With Ice Cream*
NYTBR - May 31 2015 - p24(L) [501+]
Petroff, Shani - *Ash: A Destined Novel*
y SLJ - v61 - i5 - May 2015 - p122(1) [51-500]
Petroski, Henry - *The Road Taken: The History and Future of America's Infrastructure*
BL - v112 - i6 - Nov 15 2015 - p7(1) [51-500]
KR - Sept 15 2015 - pNA [501+]
PW - v262 - i44 - Nov 2 2015 - p74(1) [51-500]
Petrovic, Mina - *Manga Crash Course: Drawing Manga Characters and Scenes from Start to Finish*
LJ - v140 - i12 - July 1 2015 - p84(1) [51-500]
RVBW - May 2015 - pNA [51-500]
Petrovsky-Shtern, Yohanan - *The Golden Age of Shtetl: A New History of Jewish Life in Eastern Europe*
TLS - i5838 - Feb 20 2015 - p11(2) [501+]
Shtetl: The Golden Age: A New History of Jewish Life in East Europe
HT - v65 - i1 - Jan 2015 - p64(2) [501+]
Petrovszky, Konrad - *Geschichte schreiben im osmanischen Sudosteuropa: Eine Kulturgeschichte orthodoxer Historiographie des 16. und 17. Jahrhunderts*
Slav R - v74 - i3 - Fall 2015 - p613-614 [501+]
Petrucci, Federico - *Epistolarum Iuvenilium Libri Octo Petri Candidi Decembrii*
Ren Q - v68 - i3 - Fall 2015 - p970-971 [501+]
Petrucci, Kellyann - *Dr. Kellyann's Bone Broth Diet: Lose up to 15 Pounds, 4 Inches, and Your Wrinkles in Just 21 Days*
PW - v262 - i44 - Nov 2 2015 - p81(1) [51-500]
Petrucci, Mario - *Crib*
TLS - i5844 - April 3 2015 - p23(1) [501+]
Petrus, Kevin A. - *Philippians*
KR - Dec 15 2015 - pNA [501+]
Petrusich, Amanda - *Do Not Sell at Any Price: The Wild, Obsessive Hunt for the World's Rarest 78 rpm Records*
NYTBR - Sept 13 2015 - p32(L) [501+]
Petry, Carl F. - *The Criminal Underworld in a Medieval Islamic Society: Narratives from Cairo and Damascus under the Mamluks*
AHR - v120 - i3 - June 2015 - p1147-1148 [501+]
JNES - v74 - i2 - Oct 2015 - p394(3) [501+]
Pett, Mark - *Lizard from the Park (Illus. by Pett, Mark)*
c BL - v111 - i22 - August 1 2015 - p72(2) [51-500]
c KR - June 15 2015 - pNA [51-500]
c PW - v262 - i24 - June 15 2015 - p83(1) [51-500]
c SLJ - v61 - i6 - June 2015 - p90(1) [51-500]
Pettegree, Andrew - *Brand Luther: How an Unheralded Monk Turned His Small Town into a Center of Publishing, Made Himself the Most Famous Man in Europe--and Started the Protestant Reformation*
Ch Today - v59 - i9 - Nov 2015 - p76(1) [501+]
KR - August 15 2015 - pNA [501+]
How an Unheralded Monk Turned His Small Town into a Center of Publishing, Made Himself the Most Famous Man in Europe--and Started the Protestant Reformation
LJ - v140 - i15 - Sept 15 2015 - p89(1) [51-500]
PW - v262 - i35 - August 31 2015 - p73(1) [51-500]
The Invention of News: How the World Came to Know about Itself
AHR - v120 - i4 - Oct 2015 - p1546-1547 [501+]
CJR - v53 - i6 - March-April 2015 - p63(1) [501+]
Ren Q - v68 - i2 - Summer 2015 - p739-740 [501+]
Pettersen, Bev - *A Pony for Christmas*
c KR - Feb 15 2015 - pNA [51-500]
Pettersen, Per - *I Refuse*
NY - v91 - i18 - June 29 2015 - p71 [51-500]
Petterson, Per - *Ashes in My Mouth, Sand in My Shoes: Stories*
KR - Feb 1 2015 - pNA [501+]
NYRB - v62 - i13 - August 13 2015 - p57(2) [501+]
NYT - April 30 2015 - pC6(L) [501+]
PW - v262 - i5 - Feb 2 2015 - p34(1) [501+]
I Refuse
BL - v111 - i12 - Feb 15 2015 - p31(1) [51-500]
CSM - April 7 2015 - pNA [501+]
KR - Feb 1 2015 - pNA [501+]
NYTBR - April 26 2015 - p1(L) [501+]
PW - v262 - i5 - Feb 2 2015 - p34(1) [501+]
Pettersson, Vicki - *Swerve*
PW - v262 - i19 - May 11 2015 - p38(1) [51-500]
Pettiford, Rebecca - *Roller Coasters*
c BL - v112 - i3 - Oct 1 2015 - p62(2) [51-500]
Pettigrew, William A. - *Freedom's Debt: The Royal African Company and the Politics of the Atlantic Slave Trade, 1672-1752*
HER - v130 - i544 - June 2015 - p755(3) [501+]
HNet - Feb 2015 - pNA [501+]
JIH - v45 - i3 - Wntr 2015 - p424-426 [501+]
JSH - v81 - i2 - May 2015 - p430(3) [501+]
Pettit, Becky - *Invisible Men: Mass Incarceration and the Myth of Black Progress*
CS - v44 - i1 - Jan 2015 - p105-106 [501+]
SF - v93 - i3 - March 2015 - pe89 [501+]
SF - v93 - i3 - March 2015 - pNA [501+]
Pettit, Michael - *The Science of Deception: Psychology and Commerce in America*
Isis - v106 - i2 - June 2015 - p475(3) [501+]
Pettrey, Dani - *Cold Shot*
PW - v262 - i47 - Nov 23 2015 - p57(1) [51-500]
Sabotaged
BL - v111 - i11 - Feb 1 2015 - p31(1) [51-500]
Petty, Adrienne Monteith - *Standing Their Ground: Small Farmers in North Carolina since the Civil War*
AHR - v120 - i4 - Oct 2015 - p1494-1495 [501+]
JSH - v81 - i2 - May 2015 - p484(2) [501+]
Petty, Dev - *I Don't Want to Be a Frog (Illus. by Boldt, Mike)*
c CCB-B - v68 - i10 - June 2015 - p509(2) [51-500]
c CH Bwatch - May 2015 - pNA [51-500]
c HB Guide - v26 - i2 - Fall 2015 - p48(1) [51-500]
c PW - v262 - i49 - Dec 2 2015 - p35(1) [51-500]
Petty, Heather W. - *Lock & Mori*
y BL - v112 - i1 - Sept 1 2015 - p105(1) [51-500]
y KR - July 1 2015 - pNA [51-500]
y SLJ - v61 - i9 - Sept 2015 - p170(1) [51-500]
y VOYA - v38 - i4 - Oct 2015 - p58(1) [51-500]
Petz, Moritz - *The Day Everything Went Wrong (Illus. by Jackowski, Amelie)*
c BL - v111 - i19-20 - June 1 2015 - p112(1) [51-500]
c HB Guide - v26 - i2 - Fall 2015 - p48(1) [51-500]
Pevsner, Nikolaus - *The Englishness of English Art*
TimHES - i2197 - April 2 2015 - p53(1) [501+]
Pewsey, Arthur - *Circular Statistics in R*
QRB - v90 - i2 - June 2015 - p203(2) [501+]
Peyo - *Forever Smurfette*
c CH Bwatch - March 2015 - pNA [51-500]
Peyser, Marc - *Hissing Cousins: The Untold Story of Eleanor Roosevelt and Alice Roosevelt Longworth*
BL - v111 - i19-20 - June 1 2015 - p27(1) [501+]
BL - v111 - i14 - March 15 2015 - p41(1) [51-500]
CSM - March 31 2015 - pNA [501+]
KR - Jan 15 2015 - pNA [501+]
LJ - v140 - i2 - Feb 1 2015 - p95(1) [51-500]
Nat R - v67 - i7 - April 20 2015 - p40 [501+]
PW - v262 - i7 - Feb 16 2015 - p170(1) [51-500]
Pezzotti, Barbara - *The Importance of Place in Contemporary Italian Crime Fiction: A Bloody Journey*
MLR - v110 - i2 - April 2015 - p569-572 [501+]
Pfaff, Eugene E. - *Keep on Walkin', Keep on Talkin': An Oral History of the Greensboro Civil Rights Movement*
LJ - v140 - i17 - Oct 15 2015 - p102(1) [51-500]
Pfau, Thomas - *Minding the Modern: Human Agency, Intellectual Traditions, and Responsible Knowledge*
Comw - v142 - i3 - Feb 6 2015 - p32(4) [501+]
RM - v68 - i4 - June 2015 - p865(3) [501+]
Pfeffer, Jeffrey - *Leadership BS: Fixing Workplaces and Careers One Truth at a Time*
NYTBR - Dec 6 2015 - p87(L) [501+]
PW - v262 - i28 - July 13 2015 - p61(1) [51-500]
Pfeffer, Yehoshua - *Prophecies and Providence: A Biblical Approach to Modern Jewish History*
RVBW - March 2015 - pNA [51-500]
Pfeifer, Mark Edward - *Diversity in Diaspora: Hmong Americans in the Twenty-First Century*
ERS - v38 - i3 - March 2015 - p527(3) [501+]
Pfeifer, Michael J. - *Lynching beyond Dixie: American Mob Violence outside the South*
JSH - v81 - i1 - Feb 2015 - p218(3) [501+]
WHQ - v46 - i1 - Spring 2015 - p99-100 [501+]
Pfeifer, Will - *Blinded by the Light (Illus. by Rocafort, Kenneth)*
y SLJ - v61 - i10 - Oct 2015 - p119(1) [51-500]
Pfister, Marcus - *The Adventures of Rainbow Fish (Illus. by Pfister, Marcus)*
c HB Guide - v26 - i2 - Fall 2015 - p48(1) [51-500]
c CH Bwatch - May 2015 - pNA [51-500]
Happiness Is ... (Illus. by Pfister, Marcus)
c CH Bwatch - August 2015 - pNA [51-500]
c HB Guide - v26 - i1 - Spring 2015 - p41(1) [51-500]

The Little Moon Raven
   c HB Guide - v26 - i1 - Spring 2015 - p41(2) [51-500]
Milo and the Mysterious Island
   c HB Guide - v26 - i1 - Spring 2015 - p42(1) [51-500]

Pfitzinger, Pete - *Faster Road Racing: 5K to Half Marathon*
   Bwatch - Feb 2015 - pNA [51-500]

Pflugfelder, Bob - *Nick and Tesla's Special Effects Spectacular: A Mystery with Animatronics, Alien Makeup, Camera Gear, and Other Movie Magic You Can Make Yourself! (Illus. by Garrett, Scott)*
   SLJ - v61 - i4 - April 2015 - p148(2) [51-500]
   c CH Bwatch - May 2015 - pNA [51-500]
Nick and Tesla's Special Effects Spectacular: A Mystery with Animatronics, Alien Makeup, Camera Gear, and Other Movie Magic You Can Make Yourself (Illus. by Garrett, Scott)
   c HB Guide - v26 - i2 - Fall 2015 - p97(1) [51-500]
Nick and Tesla's Super-Cyborg Gadget Glove: A Mystery with a Blinking, Beeping, Voice-Recording Gadget Glove You Can Build Yourself (Illus. by Garrett, Scott)
   c HB Guide - v26 - i1 - Spring 2015 - p89(1) [51-500]

Pfundt, Andreas Peter - *The Diary of a Suicidal Artist*
   KR - March 15 2015 - pNA [501+]

Pham, LeUyen - *There's No Such Thing as Little (Illus. by Pham, LeUyen)*
   c BL - v111 - i14 - March 15 2015 - p80(2) [51-500]
   c CH Bwatch - June 2015 - pNA [51-500]
   c HB Guide - v26 - i2 - Fall 2015 - p48(1) [51-500]
   c PW - v262 - i5 - Feb 2 2015 - p59(1) [51-500]
The Twelve Days of Christmas (Illus. by Pham, LeUyen)
   c HB Guide - v26 - i1 - Spring 2015 - p180(1) [51-500]

Phan-Le, Marie-Rose - *Talking Story: One Woman's Quest to Preserve Ancient Spiritual and Healing Traditions*
   Bwatch - June 2015 - pNA [51-500]

Pharand, Michel W. - *Benjamin Disraeli Letters, vol. IX: 1865-1867*
   Historian - v77 - i1 - Spring 2015 - p184(3) [501+]
   Historian - v77 - i2 - Summer 2015 - p380(2) [501+]

Phelan, Donna M. - *Women, Money and Prosperity: A Sister's Perspective on How to Retire Well*
   SPBW - Jan 2015 - pNA [51-500]

Phelan, James - *The Last Thirteen: Book Thirteen: 1*
   y Res Links - v20 - i5 - June 2015 - p27(2) [51-500]
The Last Thirteen
   y VOYA - v38 - i4 - Oct 2015 - p76(1) [51-500]

Phelan, Matt - *Druthers (Illus. by Phelan, Matt)*
   c HB Guide - v26 - i1 - Spring 2015 - p14(1) [51-500]

Phelan, Peggy - *Live Art in LA: Performance in Southern California, 1970-1983*
   PAJ - v37 - i2 - May 2015 - p103-110 [501+]

Phelps, Adelaide Poniatowski - *Coretta Scott King Award Books Discussion Guide: Pathways to Democracy*
   SLJ - v61 - i2 - Feb 2015 - p131(1) [51-500]

Phelps, Earl R. - *How to Draw Reptiles and Mammals: An Educational Guide*
   SPBW - Sept 2015 - pNA [51-500]

Phelps, Edmund S. - *Mass Flourishing: How Grassroots Innovation Created Jobs, Challenge, and Change*
   IndRev - v19 - i3 - Wntr 2015 - p449(4) [501+]
   NYRB - v62 - i18 - Nov 19 2015 - p53(3) [501+]
Seven Schools of Macroeconomic Thought
   TimHES - i2229 - Nov 12 2015 - p47(1) [501+]

Phelps, Nicole M. - *U.S.-Habsburg Relations from 1815 to the Paris Peace Conference: Sovereignty Transformed*
   RAH - v43 - i2 - June 2015 - p237-244 [501+]

Phelps, Rebekah Lea - *Psalm of My Heart: Who We Are in Christ*
   KR - Nov 1 2015 - pNA [501+]

Phelps, Robert - *The Letters of James Agee to Father Flye*
   Comw - v142 - i15 - Sept 25 2015 - p32(2) [51-500]

Phelps, Wesley G. - *A People's War on Poverty: Urban Politics and Grassroots Activists in Houston*
   JSH - v81 - i3 - August 2015 - p778(2) [501+]
   RAH - v43 - i2 - June 2015 - p369-377 [501+]
   SHQ - v118 - i4 - April 2015 - p439-440 [501+]

Philbrick, Nathaniel - *Bunker Hill: A City, a Siege, a Revolution*
   Historian - v77 - i1 - Spring 2015 - p138(2) [501+]

Philbrick, Rodman - *The Big Dark*
   c BL - v112 - i6 - Nov 15 2015 - p53(1) [51-500]
   c KR - Oct 1 2015 - pNA [51-500]
   c PW - v262 - i44 - Nov 2 2015 - p83(2) [51-500]
Poetics of Character: Transatlantic Encounters, 1700-1900
   c SLJ - v61 - i11 - Nov 2015 - p101(1) [51-500]

Philbrook, Burnham - *Conclave Conspiracy*
   SPBW - Nov 2015 - pNA [51-500]

Philip, Aaron - *This Kid Can Fly: It's about Ability (Not Disability).*
   c BL - v112 - i6 - Nov 15 2015 - p39(2) [51-500]
   c KR - Nov 15 2015 - pNA [51-500]
   c PW - v262 - i47 - Nov 23 2015 - p71(1) [51-500]
   c SLJ - v61 - i12 - Dec 2015 - p145(2) [51-500]

Philip, Gillian - *Icefall*
   KR - Jan 1 2015 - pNA [51-500]
   PW - v262 - i1 - Jan 5 2015 - p55(2) [51-500]

Philip, M. NourbeSe - *Zong!*
   ABR - v36 - i4 - May-June 2015 - p6(2) [501+]

Philips, Fleur - *Beautiful Girl*
   y SLJ - v61 - i6 - June 2015 - p128(1) [51-500]

Phillip, Michael - *The Flip*
   PW - v262 - i27 - July 6 2015 - p49(1) [51-500]

Phillips, Adam - *Becoming Freud: The Making of a Psychoanalyst*
   Tikkun - v30 - i2 - Spring 2015 - p49(11) [501+]

Phillips, Andrea - *Revision*
   PW - v262 - i14 - April 6 2015 - p43(1) [501+]

Phillips, Barnaby - *Another Man's War: The Story of Burma Boy in Britain's Forgotten African Army*
   TLS - i5832 - Jan 9 2015 - p21(1) [501+]

Phillips, Billy - *Once Upon a Zombie, bk. 1: The Color of Fear*
   y CH Bwatch - Nov 2015 - pNA [51-500]
   KR - April 15 2015 - pNA [51-500]

Phillips, Brent - *Charles Walters: The Director Who Made Hollywood Dance*
   LJ - v140 - i2 - Feb 1 2015 - p87(1) [51-500]

Phillips, Carl - *Reconnaissance*
   BL - v111 - i22 - August 1 2015 - p18(1) [51-500]
   LJ - v140 - i13 - August 1 2015 - p102(1) [51-500]

Phillips, Caryl - *The Lost Child*
   HM - v330 - i1978 - March 2015 - p79(3) [501+]
   HR - v68 - i1 - Summer 2015 - p343-351 [501+]
   KR - Jan 1 2015 - pNA [501+]
   NYTBR - May 10 2015 - p27(L) [501+]
   Spec - v327 - i9738 - April 18 2015 - p41(2) [501+]
   TLS - i5847 - April 24 2015 - p19(1) [501+]

Phillips, Christopher - *The Civil War in the Border South*
   JSH - v81 - i4 - Nov 2015 - p992(2) [501+]

Phillips, Dee - *Meerkat's Burrow*
   c HB Guide - v26 - i1 - Spring 2015 - p166(1) [51-500]
Snowshoe Hare
   c BL - v111 - i15 - April 1 2015 - p62(1) [51-500]
Yesterday's Voices Series
   c CH Bwatch - Feb 2015 - pNA [51-500]

Phillips, Diane - *The Everyday Rice Cooker: Soups, Sides, Grains, Mains, and More (Illus. by Causey, Jennifer)*
   LJ - v140 - i11 - June 15 2015 - p108(2) [51-500]

Phillips, George Harwood - *Chiefs and Challengers: Indian Resistance and Cooperation in Southern California, 1769-1906*
   Roundup M - v22 - i3 - Feb 2015 - p24(1) [501+]
   Roundup M - v22 - i6 - August 2015 - p39(2) [501+]

Phillips, Gin - *A Little Bit of Spectacular*
   c BL - v111 - i15 - April 1 2015 - p80(1) [51-500]
   c CCB-B - v68 - i9 - May 2015 - p463(1) [51-500]
   c HB Guide - v26 - i2 - Fall 2015 - p97(1) [51-500]
   c KR - Feb 15 2015 - pNA [51-500]
   c PW - v262 - i9 - March 2 2015 - p85(1) [51-500]

Phillips, Helen - *The Beautiful Bureaucrat*
   BL - v111 - i21 - July 1 2015 - p27(1) [51-500]
   KR - June 1 2015 - pNA [501+]
   LJ - v140 - i10 - June 1 2015 - p95(2) [51-500]
   NYT - August 24 2015 - pC1(L) [501+]
   NYTBR - August 9 2015 - p12(L) [501+]
   PW - v262 - i22 - June 1 2015 - p37(1) [51-500]

Phillips, Jason - *Storytelling, History, and the Postmodern South*
   JSH - v81 - i2 - May 2015 - p515(2) [501+]
   South CR - v47 - i2 - Spring 2015 - p168-169 [501+]

Phillips, Kim M. - *Before Orientalism: Asian Peoples and Cultures in European Travel Writing, 1245-1510*
   AHR - v120 - i1 - Feb 2015 - p202-203 [501+]
   HER - v130 - i543 - April 2015 - p429(3) [501+]
   HNet - August 2015 - pNA [501+]
   Med R - August 2015 - pNA [501+]

Phillips, Kyra - *The Whole Life Fertility Plan: Understanding What Affects Your Fertility to Help You Get Pregnant When You Want To*
   LJ - v140 - i3 - Feb 15 2015 - p121(2) [51-500]

Phillips, Linda Vigen - *Crazy*
   y CCB-B - v68 - i5 - Jan 2015 - p273(1) [51-500]
   y RVBW - June 2015 - pNA [501+]

Phillips, Lisa A. - *Unrequited: Women and Romantic Obsession*
   BL - v111 - i9-10 - Jan 1 2015 - p20(1) [51-500]
   LJ - v140 - i2 - Feb 1 2015 - p99(1) [51-500]
   Mac - v128 - i10 - March 16 2015 - p59(1) [501+]

Phillips, Logan - *Sonoran Strange*
   Roundup M - v22 - i4 - April 2015 - p27(2) [501+]
   Roundup M - v22 - i6 - August 2015 - p24(1) [501+]

Phillips, Louise - *The Doll's House*
   BL - v111 - i12 - Feb 15 2015 - p36(1) [51-500]

Phillips, Mark Salber - *On Historical Distance*
   Clio - v44 - i2 - Spring 2015 - p256-261 [501+]
   Eight-C St - v48 - i3 - Spring 2015 - p363-365 [501+]

Phillips, Nickie D. - *Comic Book Crime: Truth, Justice, and the American Way*
   CS - v44 - i3 - May 2015 - p401-403 [501+]

Phillips, Nicola - *The Profligate Son: Or, A True Story of Family Conflict, Fashionable Vice, and Financial Ruin in Regency Britain*
   HER - v130 - i545 - August 2015 - p1018(2) [501+]

Phillips, Patrick - *Elegy for a Broken Machine*
   PW - v262 - i7 - Feb 16 2015 - p158(1) [51-500]
   HR - v68 - i3 - Autumn 2015 - p481-491 [501+]

Phillips, Paul T. - *Contesting the Moral High Ground: Popular Moralists in Mid-Twentieth-Century Britain*
   CH - v84 - i1 - March 2015 - p270(1) [501+]

Phillips, Rebecca - *Faking Perfect*
   y VOYA - v38 - i3 - August 2015 - p66(2) [51-500]

Phillips, Rod - *Alcohol: A History*
   JIH - v46 - i1 - Summer 2015 - p105-107 [501+]
   TLS - i5845 - April 10 2015 - p29(1) [51-500]

Phillips, Rowan Ricardo - *Heaven: Poems*
   BL - v111 - i19-20 - June 1 2015 - p24(1) [51-500]
   PW - v262 - i20 - May 18 2015 - p61(1) [51-500]

Phillips, Ruby Ann - *The Great and Powerful (Illus. by Isik, Krystal)*
   c HB Guide - v26 - i1 - Spring 2015 - p64(1) [51-500]

Phillips, Samuel R. - *Torn by War: The Civil War Journal of Mary Adelia Byers*
   JSH - v81 - i2 - May 2015 - p539(1) [51-500]

Phillips, Steve - *Brown Is the New White*
   KR - Dec 15 2015 - pNA [51-500]

Phillips, Stevie - *Judy & Liza & Robert & Freddie & David & Sue & Me ... : A Memoir*
   BL - v111 - i19-20 - June 1 2015 - p32(1) [51-500]
   KR - April 15 2015 - pNA [51-500]
   LJ - v140 - i10 - June 1 2015 - p105(2) [51-500]
   Mac - v128 - i23 - June 15 2015 - p61(2) [51-500]
   NYTBR - May 31 2015 - p34(L) [501+]

Phillips, Tom - *A Beginner's Life: The Adventures of Tom Phillips*
   KR - August 15 2015 - pNA [501+]

Phillips, Whitney - *This Is Why We Can't Have Nice Things: Mapping the Relationship between Online Trolling and Mainstream Culture*
   Spec - i9745 - June 6 2015 - p45(1) [501+]
   TimHES - i2202 - May 7 2015 - p50-51 [501+]

Phillips, William D. - *Slavery in Medieval and Early Modern Iberia*
   AHR - v120 - i1 - Feb 2015 - p317-318 [501+]
   Ams - v72 - i2 - April 2015 - p332(2) [501+]
   Ren Q - v68 - i1 - Spring 2015 - p287-289 [501+]
   Specu - v90 - i1 - Jan 2015 - p289-291 [501+]

Phillips, William D., Jr. - *Slavery in Medieval and Early Modern Iberia*
   JIH - v45 - i3 - Wntr 2015 - p434-435 [501+]

Phillips, Winifred - *A Composer's Guide to Game Music*
   Teach Mus - v22 - i3 - Jan 2015 - p61(1) [51-500]

Philosophy, Theory and History in Germany since 1945
   HNet - Feb 2015 - pNA [501+]

Philp, Mark - *Reforming Ideas in Britain: Politics and Language in the Shadow of the French Revolution, 1789-1815*
   HER - v130 - i545 - August 2015 - p1014(2) [501+]

Philpot, Chelsey - *Even in Paradise*
   y CCB-B - v68 - i5 - Jan 2015 - p273(1) [51-500]
   y HB Guide - v26 - i1 - Spring 2015 - p120(1) [51-500]
   y Teach Lib - v42 - i3 - Feb 2015 - p28(4) [501+]

Philpott, Ian M. - *The Birth of the Royal Air Force: An Encyclopedia of British Air Power Before and During the*

Great War 1914 to 1918
    APH - v62 - i2 - Summer 2015 - p52(1) [501+]
Philpott, Maryam - *Air and Sea Power in World War I: Combat Experience in the Royal Flying Corps and the Royal Navy*
    J Mil H - v79 - i4 - Oct 2015 - p1181-1182 [501+]
Philpott, William - *Attrition: Fighting the First World War*
    TLS - i5832 - Jan 9 2015 - p8(1) [501+]
Vacationland: Tourism and Environment in the Colorado High Country
    PHR - v84 - i1 - Feb 2015 - p97(3) [501+]
    RAH - v43 - i2 - June 2015 - p346-354 [501+]
Phoenix, Adrian - *Thinning the Herd*
    PW - v262 - i48 - Nov 30 2015 - p43(1) [51-500]
Pholsena, Vatthana - *Interactions with a Violent Past: Reading Post-Conflict Landscapes in Cambodia, Lao, and Vietnam*
    Pac A - v88 - i2 - June 2015 - p352 [501+]
Phuntsho, Karma - *The History of Bhutan*
    HT - v65 - i7 - July 2015 - p61(1) [501+]
Pi, M. Naresh - *The Goddess' Daughter*
    KR - May 15 2015 - pNA [501+]
Piana, Mathias - *Archaeology and Architecture of the Military Orders: New Studies*
    Med R - August 2015 - pNA [501+]
    Specu - v90 - i3 - July 2015 - p877(1) [501+]
Piasecki, Bruce - *New World Companies: The Future of Capitalism*
    KR - Dec 15 2015 - pNA [501+]
    PW - v262 - i48 - Nov 30 2015 - p49(1) [51-500]
Piazza, Carmelo - *Crazy for Science with Carmelo the Science Fellow (Illus. by Geran, Chad)*
    c HB Guide - v26 - i2 - Fall 2015 - p163(1) [51-500]
Piazza, Daniela - *The Temple of Light*
    KR - April 15 2015 - pNA [501+]
Piazza, Tom - *A Free State*
    KR - July 15 2015 - pNA [501+]
    LJ - v140 - i13 - August 1 2015 - p89(1) [51-500]
    NY - v91 - i32 - Oct 19 2015 - p88 [51-500]
Pic, Anne-Sophie - *Le Livre blanc*
    TLS - i5831 - Jan 2 2015 - p11(1) [501+]
Pica, Rae - *What If Everybody Understood Child Development? Straight Talk about Bettering Education and Children's Lives*
    Bwatch - Oct 2015 - pNA [51-500]
Picard, Jean-Michel - *Le Prince, son peuple et le bien commun de l'Antiquite tardive a la fin du Moyen Age*
    HER - v130 - i543 - April 2015 - p408(2) [501+]
Picchi, Debra - *A Woman's Guide to the Sailing Lifestyle*
    KR - Dec 1 2015 - pNA [501+]
Picciolin, Christian - *Romantic Violence: Memoirs of an American Skinhead*
    SPBW - May 2015 - pNA [501+]
Pichon, L. - *Tom Gates: Excellent Excuses and Other Good Stuff (Illus. by Pichon, L.)*
    c CCB-B - v68 - i11 - July-August 2015 - p561(1) [51-500]
Pichon, Liz - *The Brilliant World of Tom Gates*
    c HB Guide - v26 - i1 - Spring 2015 - p89(1) [51-500]
Tom Gates Absolutely Brilliant Book
    c Res Links - v21 - i1 - Oct 2015 - p20(1) [51-500]
Tom Gates: Excellent Excuses (and Other Good Stuff).
    c KR - March 15 2015 - pNA [51-500]
Tom Gates: Excellent Excuses (and Other Good Stuff). (Illus. by Pichon, Liz)
    c BL - v111 - i19-20 - June 1 2015 - p107(1) [51-500]
    c BL - v112 - i5 - Nov 1 2015 - p52(1) [501+]
    c HB Guide - v26 - i2 - Fall 2015 - p97(1) [51-500]
    c SLJ - v61 - i5 - May 2015 - p104(3) [51-500]
Pick, Alison - *Between Gods: A Memoir*
    BL - v112 - i1 - Sept 1 2015 - p16(2) [51-500]
    KR - June 15 2015 - pNA [501+]
    LJ - v140 - i12 - July 1 2015 - p90(1) [51-500]
    NYTBR - Nov 15 2015 - p30(L) [501+]
Pick, Daniel - *The Pursuit of the Nazi Mind: Hitler, Hess, and the Analysts*
    HER - v130 - i544 - June 2015 - p788(2) [501+]
    Historian - v77 - i1 - Spring 2015 - p186(2) [501+]
Pickavance, Norman - *The Reconnected Leader: An Executive's Guide to Creating Responsible, Purposeful and Valuable Organizations*
    Bwatch - June 2015 - pNA [501+]
    RVBW - Feb 2015 - pNA [501+]
Pickenpaugh, Roger - *Captives in Blue: The Civil War Prisons of the Confederacy*
    Historian - v77 - i1 - Spring 2015 - p139(2) [501+]
Pickering, Travis Rayne - *Rough and Tumble: Aggression, Hunting, and Human Evolution*
    QRB - v90 - i1 - March 2015 - p92(1) [51-500]

Pickett, Michelle K. - *Milayna*
    y KR - Jan 15 2015 - pNA [51-500]
    SLJ - v61 - i3 - March 2015 - p161(1) [51-500]
Unspeakable
    SLJ - v61 - i3 - March 2015 - p161(1) [51-500]
Pickrell, John - *Flying Dinosaurs: How Fearsome Reptiles Became Birds*
    QRB - v90 - i3 - Sept 2015 - p334(2) [501+]
Picon, Deanna - *The Autism Parents' Guide to Reclaiming Your Life: How to Build the Best Life While Successfully Raising A Child with Autism*
    SPBW - May 2015 - pNA [51-500]
Picou, Lin - *Pink Toys, Yes or No*
    c BL - v112 - i6 - Nov 15 2015 - p43(1) [51-500]
Picoult, Jodi - *Off the Page (Read by Various readers). Audiobook Review*
    y BL - v112 - i2 - Sept 15 2015 - p80(1) [51-500]
    y SLJ - v61 - i9 - Sept 2015 - p61(1) [51-500]
Off the Page (Illus. by Gilbert, Yvonne)
    y BL - v111 - i17 - May 1 2015 - p92(1) [51-500]
    y HB Guide - v26 - i2 - Fall 2015 - p134(1) [51-500]
    y SLJ - v61 - i5 - May 2015 - p115(1) [51-500]
    y VOYA - v38 - i2 - June 2015 - p81(1) [51-500]
Piechota, Toni - *Real Solutions Weight Loss Workbook, 2d ed.*
    RVBW - April 2015 - pNA [51-500]
Pien, Lark - *Long Tail Kitty: Come Out and Play (Illus. by Pien, Lark)*
    c KR - Feb 15 2015 - pNA [51-500]
    c SLJ - v61 - i7 - July 2015 - p72(2) [51-500]
Pienkowski, Jan - *Easter: The King James Version (Illus. by Pienkowski, Jan)*
    c HB Guide - v26 - i2 - Fall 2015 - p150(1) [51-500]
The First Christmas: The King James Version (Illus. by Pienkowski, Jan)
    c HB Guide - v26 - i1 - Spring 2015 - p135(1) [51-500]
Piepenbring, Meike - *Introduction to Mycology in the Tropics*
    RVBW - August 2015 - pNA [51-500]
Pierce, Cahterine J. - *Knight Writings: Three Tragedies and a Romance*
    SPBW - Oct 2015 - pNA [51-500]
Pierce, Christa - *Did You Know That I Love You? (Illus. by Pierce, Christa)*
    c NYTBR - Feb 8 2015 - p24(L) [501+]
Pierce, Gretchen - *Alcohol in Latin America: A Social and Cultural History*
    HAHR - v95 - i1 - Feb 2015 - p146-147 [501+]
Pierce, James - *General Paul von Lettow-Vorbeck: My Life*
    J Mil H - v79 - i3 - July 2015 - p853-854 [501+]
Pierce, Lawrence - *A New Little Ice Age Has Started: How to Survive and Prosper during the Next 50 Difficult Years*
    RVBW - August 2015 - pNA [501+]
Pierce, Nicola - *Behind the Walls: A City Beseiged*
    Sch Lib - v63 - i3 - Autumn 2015 - p169(1) [51-500]
Pierce, Thomas - *Hall of Small Mammals*
    BL - v111 - i9-10 - Jan 1 2015 - p38(1) [51-500]
    LJ - v140 - i10 - June 1 2015 - p139(1) [501+]
    NYT - Jan 13 2015 - pC1(L) [501+]
    NYTBR - Feb 1 2015 - pNA [501+]
Pierce, Wendell - *The Wind in the Reeds: A Storm, a Play, and the City That Would Not Be Broken*
    BL - v112 - i1 - Sept 1 2015 - p28(1) [51-500]
    KR - July 1 2015 - pNA [51-500]
Piercy, Marge - *Made in Detroit: Poems*
    BL - v111 - i14 - March 15 2015 - p38(1) [51-500]
Piere, Jaime - *Ideologias, practicas y discursos. La construccion cultural del mundo social, siglos XVII-XIX*
    HAHR - v95 - i1 - Feb 2015 - p155-157 [501+]
Pieri, Bruna - *Intacti saltus: Studi sull III libro delle Georgiche*
    Class R - v65 - i1 - April 2015 - p131-132 [501+]
Pieri, Giuliana - *Italian Crime Fiction*
    MLR - v110 - i2 - April 2015 - p569-572 [501+]
Pierpoint, Eric - *The Secret Mission of William Tuck*
    c KR - June 1 2015 - pNA [51-500]
    c SLJ - v61 - i9 - Sept 2015 - p144(1) [51-500]
Pierpont, James Lord - *Jingle Bells: A Magical Cut-Paper Edition (Illus. by Puttapipat, Niroot)*
    c KR - Sept 1 2015 - pNA [51-500]
    c KR - Sept 1 2015 - pNA [51-500]
    c PW - v262 - i37 - Sept 14 2015 - p72(2) [51-500]
    c PW - v262 - i49 - Dec 2 2015 - p60(2) [51-500]
    RVBW - Nov 2015 - pNA [51-500]
    c SLJ - v61 - i10 - Oct 2015 - p67(1) [51-500]
Pierpont, Julia - *Among the Ten Thousand Things*
    BL - v111 - i19-20 - June 1 2015 - p38(1) [51-500]

    KR - May 1 2015 - pNA [501+]
    LJ - v140 - i7 - April 15 2015 - p80(2) [51-500]
    NY - v91 - i22 - August 3 2015 - p73 [501+]
    NYT - July 23 2015 - pC1(L) [501+]
    NYTBR - July 12 2015 - p11(L) [501+]
    PW - v262 - i5 - Feb 2 2015 - p32(1) [51-500]
    Spec - v328 - i9757 - August 29 2015 - p37(2) [501+]
Pierre, D.B.C. - *Mexico20: New Voices, Old Traitors*
    TLS - i5856 - June 26 2015 - p27(1) [501+]
Piers, Helen - *How to Look After Your Kitten*
    c Sch Lib - v63 - i4 - Winter 2015 - p239(1) [51-500]
Piersall, Wendy - *Coloring Animal Mandalas*
    c CH Bwatch - Jan 2015 - pNA [51-500]
Pierson, Katie - *'89 Walls*
    y SLJ - v61 - i8 - August 2015 - p109(1) [51-500]
Pierson, Melissa Holbrook - *The Secret History of Kindness: Learning from How Dogs Learn.*
    LJ - v140 - i6 - April 1 2015 - p109(2) [51-500]
    PW - v262 - i7 - Feb 16 2015 - p171(2) [51-500]
Pierson, Paul - *Winner-Take-All Politics: How Washington Made the Rich Richer--and Turned Its Back on the Middle Class*
    CS - v44 - i4 - July 2015 - p449-462 [501+]
Pierson, Sharon Gay - *Laboratory of Learning: HBCU Laboratory Schools and Alabama State College Lab High in the Era of Jim Crow*
    HER - v85 - i1 - Spring 2015 - p134-137 [501+]
    JSH - v81 - i2 - May 2015 - p496(2) [501+]
Pieterse, Jan Nederveen - *Globalization and Culture: Global Melange*
    Bwatch - May 2015 - pNA [51-500]
Globalization and Development in East Asia
    CS - v44 - i1 - Jan 2015 - p107-109 [501+]
Pietra, Cheryl Della - *Gonzo Girl*
    BL - v111 - i21 - July 1 2015 - p31(1) [51-500]
    KR - May 15 2015 - pNA [501+]
    LJ - v140 - i10 - June 1 2015 - p96(1) [51-500]
Pietrek, Daniel - *Ich Erschreibe mich Selbst: (Autor)Biografisches Schreiben bei Horst Bienek*
    Ger Q - v88 - i1 - Wntr 2015 - p122(3) [501+]
Pietri, Pedro - *Pedro Pietri: Selected Poetry*
    PW - v262 - i29 - July 20 2015 - p167(2) [51-500]
Pietron, Barbara - *Soulshifter*
    y KR - Sept 1 2015 - pNA [51-500]
    y VOYA - v38 - i5 - Dec 2015 - p73(1) [51-500]
Pietrow-Ennker, Bianca - *Russlands Imperiale Macht: Integrationsstrategien und Ihre Reichweite in Transnationaler Perspektive*
    HNet - March 2015 - pNA [501+]
Pietrusza, David - *1932: The Rise of Hitler & FDR: Two Tales of Politics, Betrayal, and Unlikely Destiny*
    KR - June 15 2015 - pNA [501+]
Pietrzyk, Leslie - *This Angel on My Chest*
    KR - August 1 2015 - pNA [501+]
Pietsch, Tamson - *Empire of Scholars: Universities, Networks, and the British Academic World, 1850-1939*
    JMH - v87 - i3 - Sept 2015 - p731(3) [501+]
Pietschmann, Klaus - *Schubert: Interpretationen*
    Ger Q - v88 - i3 - Summer 2015 - p379(5) [501+]
Pietz, David A. - *The Yellow River: The Problem of Water in Modern China*
    Nature - v517 - i7533 - Jan 8 2015 - p144(1) [501+]
Piggott, Michael - *Archives and Societal Provenance: Australian Essays*
    Archiv - i79 - Spring 2015 - p192(4) [501+]
Pignat, Caroline - *The Gospel Truth*
    y Res Links - v20 - i3 - Feb 2015 - p33(1) [501+]
Pignataro, Anna - *Agatha (Illus. by Pignataro, Anna)*
    c KR - Sept 15 2015 - pNA [51-500]
    c PW - v262 - i36 - Sept 7 2015 - p65(2) [51-500]
    c SLJ - v61 - i10 - Oct 2015 - p82(1) [51-500]
Pigneguy, Dee - *Exploring Nature's Pattern Magic*
    y Magpies - v30 - i4 - Sept 2015 - pS8(1) [501+]
Pignone, Charles - *Sinatra 100*
    LJ - v140 - i20 - Dec 1 2015 - p104(2) [51-500]
    Spec - v329 - i9767 - Nov 7 2015 - p46(2) [501+]
Pigza, Jessica - *BiblioCraft: The Modern Crafter's Guide to Using Library Resources to Jumpstart Creative Projects*
    TimHES - i2194 - March 12 2015 - p49(1) [501+]
Pike, Aprilynne - *Earthquake*
    y HB Guide - v26 - i2 - Fall 2015 - p134(1) [51-500]
Pike, Charlotte - *Fermented: A Beginner's Guide to Making Your Own Sourdough, Yogurt, Sauerkraut, Kefir, Kimchi, and More*
    BL - v112 - i3 - Oct 1 2015 - p15(1) [51-500]

Pike, Christopher - *Black Knight*
  y HB Guide - v26 - i1 - Spring 2015 - p120(1) [51-500]
The Howling Ghost
  c HB Guide - v26 - i1 - Spring 2015 - p89(1) [51-500]
The Secret Path
  c HB Guide - v26 - i1 - Spring 2015 - p89(1) [51-500]
Strange Girl
  y BL - v112 - i4 - Oct 15 2015 - p46(1) [51-500]
  c KR - Sept 15 2015 - pNA [51-500]
  y SLJ - v61 - i11 - Nov 2015 - p120(1) [51-500]
  y VOYA - v38 - i4 - Oct 2015 - p58(2) [51-500]
Pike, Francis - *Hirohito's War: The Pacific War, 1941-1945*
  NS - v144 - i5272 - July 24 2015 - p44(2) [501+]
  Spec - v328 - i9749 - July 4 2015 - p36(2) [501+]
Piker, Joshua - *The Four Deaths of Acorn Whistler: Telling Stories in Colonial America*
  Historian - v77 - i2 - Summer 2015 - p346(2) [501+]
  JSH - v81 - i3 - August 2015 - p698(2) [501+]
Piketty, Thomas - *Capital in the Twenty-First Century*
  AHR - v120 - i2 - April 2015 - p564-566 [501+]
  IndRev - v20 - i1 - Summer 2015 - p133(7) [501+]
  IndRev - v20 - i2 - Fall 2015 - p285(5) [501+]
  Wom R Bks - v32 - i1 - Jan-Feb 2015 - p8(2) [501+]
Das Kapital im 21. Jahrhundert
  HNet - March 2015 - pNA [501+]
The Economics of Inequality
  KR - June 1 2015 - pNA [51-500]
  LJ - v140 - i12 - July 1 2015 - p91(1) [51-500]
  NYT - August 3 2015 - pC1(L) [501+]
  PW - v262 - i26 - June 29 2015 - p59(1) [51-500]
  TLS - i5869 - Sept 25 2015 - p3(2) [501+]
Pilcher, Steve - *Over There (Illus. by Pilcher, Steve)*
  c HB Guide - v26 - i1 - Spring 2015 - p42(1) [51-500]
Pilger, Seamus - *Fart Squad (Illus. by Gilpin, Stephen)*
  c CCB-B - v68 - i10 - June 2015 - p510(1) [51-500]
  c HB Guide - v26 - i2 - Fall 2015 - p70(1) [51-500]
  c BL - v111 - i15 - April 1 2015 - p78(1) [51-500]
  c SLJ - v61 - i2 - Feb 2015 - p76(1) [51-500]
Pilger, Zoe - *Eat My Heart Out*
  BL - v111 - i17 - May 1 2015 - p74(1) [51-500]
  KR - March 15 2015 - pNA [51-500]
  PW - v262 - i10 - March 9 2015 - p49(1) [51-500]
Pilkey, Dav - *Big Dog and Little Dog (Illus. by Pilkey, Dav)*
  c HB Guide - v26 - i2 - Fall 2015 - p61(1) [51-500]
  c SLJ - v61 - i6 - June 2015 - p96(1) [51-500]
Captain Underpants and the Sensational Saga of Sir Stinks-a-Lot (Illus. by Pilkey, Dav)
  c KR - June 15 2015 - pNA [51-500]
  c SLJ - v61 - i8 - August 2015 - p81(1) [51-500]
  c BL - v111 - i21 - July 1 2015 - p68(1) [51-500]
Captain Underpants and the Tyrannical Retaliation of the Turbo Toilet 2000 (Illus. by Pilkey, Dav)
  c CH Bwatch - March 2015 - pNA [501+]
  c HB Guide - v26 - i2 - Fall 2015 - p70(1) [51-500]
Ricky Ricotta's Mighty Robot vs. the Jurassic Jackrabbits from Jupiter (Illus. by Santat, Dan)
  c HB Guide - v26 - i2 - Fall 2015 - p71(1) [51-500]
Ricky Ricotta's Mighty Robot vs. the Mecha-Monkeys from Mars (Illus. by Santat, Dan)
  c HB Guide - v26 - i1 - Spring 2015 - p64(1) [51-500]
Ricky Ricotta's Mighty Robot vs. the Mutant Mosquitoes from Mercury (Illus. by Santat, Dan)
  c HB Guide - v26 - i1 - Spring 2015 - p64(1) [51-500]
Ricky Ricotta's Mighty Robot vs. the Stupid Stinkbugs from Saturn (Illus. by Santat, Dan)
  c HB Guide - v26 - i2 - Fall 2015 - p71(1) [51-500]
Ricky Ricotta's Mighty Robot vs. the Voodoo Vultures from Venus (Illus. by Santat, Dan)
  c HB Guide - v26 - i1 - Spring 2015 - p64(1) [51-500]
Pilkington, John - *Marbeck and the Gunpowder Plot*
  BL - v112 - i1 - Sept 1 2015 - p48(1) [51-500]
  PW - v262 - i30 - July 27 2015 - p45(1) [51-500]
Pillar, Paul R. - *Why America Misunderstands the World*
  KR - Jan 1 2016 - pNA [501+]
Pilling, David - *Bending Adversity: Japan and the Art of Survival*
  NYTBR - April 12 2015 - p28(L) [501+]
Pillsbury, Michael - *The Hundred-Year Marathon: China's Secret Strategy to Replace America as the Global Superpower*
  Bwatch - April 2015 - pNA [51-500]
  CSM - Feb 2 2015 - pNA [501+]
  For Aff - v94 - i1 - Jan-Feb 2015 - pNA [501+]
  Mac - v128 - i5-6 - Feb 9 2015 - p74(2) [501+]
  NW - v164 - i12 - March 27 2015 - pNA [501+]
  NWCR - v68 - i3 - Summer 2015 - p148(4) [501+]
  Parameters - v45 - i1 - Spring 2015 - p149(2) [501+]
Pillsworth, Anne M. - *Fathomless*
  y KR - Sept 15 2015 - pNA [501+]
  y SLJ - v61 - i10 - Oct 2015 - p106(1) [51-500]
Summoned
  y HB Guide - v26 - i1 - Spring 2015 - p120(1) [51-500]
Pilon, Mary - *The Monopolists: Obsession, Fury, and the Scandal behind the World's Favorite Board Game*
  Bus W - i4416 - Feb 23 2015 - p66(1) [51-500]
  CSM - Feb 17 2015 - pNA [501+]
  Har Bus R - v93 - i1-2 - Jan-Feb 2015 - p118(2) [501+]
  LJ - v140 - i2 - Feb 1 2015 - p90(1) [51-500]
  New R - v246 - i1 - Feb 2015 - p56(2) [501+]
  NS - v144 - i5267 - June 19 2015 - p47(1) [501+]
  NYTBR - March 22 2015 - p10(L) [501+]
  Spec - v327 - i9739 - April 25 2015 - p40(2) [501+]
Pilutti, Deb - *Bear and Squirrel Are Friends ... Yes, Really! (Illus. by Pilutti, Deb)*
  c KR - July 15 2015 - pNA [51-500]
  c PW - v262 - i27 - July 6 2015 - p68(2) [51-500]
  c SLJ - v61 - i9 - Sept 2015 - p127(1) [51-500]
Ten Rules of Being a Superhero
  c HB Guide - v26 - i1 - Spring 2015 - p42(1) [51-500]
Pilzer, Joshua D. - *Hearts of Pine: Songs in the Lives of Three Korean Survivors of the Japanese "Comfort Women"*
  PMS - v38 - i2 - May 2015 - p265(3) [501+]
Pimsleur, Julia - *Million Dollar Women: Raise Capital and Take Your Business Further, Faster*
  BL - v112 - i1 - Sept 1 2015 - p20(2) [51-500]
  LJ - v140 - i13 - August 1 2015 - p108(1) [51-500]
  PW - v262 - i32 - August 10 2015 - p51(1) [51-500]
Pina, Marco - *The Evolution of Social Communication in Primates: A Multidisciplinary Approach*
  QRB - v90 - i3 - Sept 2015 - p336(2) [501+]
Pinborough, Sarah - *Mayhem*
  c LJ - v140 - i7 - April 15 2015 - p126(1) [501+]
Pinckney, Darryl - *Black Deutschland*
  KR - Nov 1 2015 - pNA [501+]
Blackballed: The Black Vote and U.S. Democracy
  Comw - v142 - i9 - May 15 2015 - p25(1) [501+]
  Nation - v300 - i19 - May 11 2015 - p37(1) [501+]
"O, Write My Name": American Portraits, Harlem Heroes
  NYTBR - Dec 6 2015 - p38(L) [501+]
Pinckney, David - *Fight Like a Girl: Learning Curve (Illus. by Lee, Soo)*
  y SLJ - v61 - i8 - August 2015 - p112(1) [51-500]
Pindar - *Pindar*
  Class R - v65 - i2 - Oct 2015 - p339-341 [501+]
Pinder, Eric - *How to Share with a Bear (Illus. by Graegin, Stephanie)*
  c KR - July 15 2015 - pNA [51-500]
  c SLJ - v61 - i8 - August 2015 - p76(1) [51-500]
Pine, Shaaren - *Torn Together: One Family's Journey through Addiction, Treatment, and the Restaurant Industry*
  SPBW - May 2015 - pNA [51-500]
Pineda, Jorge - *Vegan Holiday Cooking from Candle Cafe: Celebratory Menus and Recipes from New York's Premier Plant-Based Restaurants*
  Veg J - v34 - i4 - Oct-Dec 2015 - p30(1) [51-500]
Pineiro, Claudia - *Betty Boo*
  PW - v262 - i51 - Dec 14 2015 - p63(1) [51-500]
Pineiro, R.J. - *The Fall*
  PW - v262 - i19 - May 11 2015 - p36(1) [51-500]
Pines, Paul - *Message from the Memoirist*
  ABR - v36 - i5 - July-August 2015 - p26(2) [501+]
Pinfold, Levi - *Greenling (Illus. by Pinfold, Levi)*
  c KR - Dec 1 2015 - pNA [51-500]
  c PW - v262 - i47 - Nov 23 2015 - p65(2) [51-500]
Pingk, Rubin - *Samurai Santa: A Very Ninja Christmas (Illus. by Pingk, Rubin)*
  c HB - v91 - i6 - Nov-Dec 2015 - p59(2) [51-500]
  c KR - Sept 1 2015 - pNA [51-500]
  c PW - v262 - i37 - Sept 14 2015 - p76(1) [51-500]
  c PW - v262 - i49 - Dec 2 2015 - p63(1) [51-500]
  c SLJ - v61 - i10 - Oct 2015 - p67(2) [51-500]
Pinheiro, Futre - *Intende, Lector: Echoes of Myth, Religion and Ritual in the Ancient Novel*
  Class R - v65 - i2 - Oct 2015 - p474-476 [501+]
Pinheiro, John C. - *Missionaries of Republicanism: A Religious History of the Mexican-American War*
  JAH - v101 - i4 - March 2015 - p1266(1) [501+]
Pini, Richard - *Elfquest*
  PW - v262 - i17 - April 27 2015 - p60(1) [51-500]
Pinkard, John E. - *African American Felon Disenfranchisement: Case Studies in Modern Racism and Political Exclusion*
  CrimJR - v40 - i1 - March 2015 - p100-101 [501+]
Pinkard, Terry - *German Philosophy, 1760-1860*
  HT - v65 - i10 - Oct 2015 - p63(1) [501+]
Pinker, Steven - *The Sense of Style: The Thinking Person's Guide to Writing in the 21st Century*
  J Chem Ed - v92 - i7 - July 2015 - p1140-1142 [501+]
  Sew R - v123 - i2 - Spring 2015 - pXIII-XVIII [501+]
  TLS - i5833 - Jan 16 2015 - p30(1) [501+]
Pinkham, Allen V. - *Lewis and Clark among the Nez Perce: Strangers in the Land of the Nimíipuu*
  Am Ind CRJ - v39 - i2 - Spring 2015 - p141-144 [501+]
  PHR - v84 - i2 - May 2015 - p262(2) [501+]
Pinkney, Andrea Davis - *The Red Pencil (Illus. by Evans, Shane W.)*
  c BL - v111 - i9-10 - Jan 1 2015 - pS4(8) [501+]
  y HB Guide - v26 - i1 - Spring 2015 - p120(1) [51-500]
  y Magpies - v30 - i1 - March 2015 - p42(3) [501+]
Rhythm Ride: A Road Trip through the Motown Sound
  c BL - v112 - i2 - Sept 15 2015 - p56(2) [51-500]
  y HB - v91 - i5 - Sept-Oct 2015 - p130(1) [51-500]
  c KR - July 15 2015 - pNA [51-500]
  c SLJ - v61 - i8 - August 2015 - p129(1) [51-500]
Pinkney, Brian - *On the Ball (Illus. by Pinkney, Brian)*
  c BL - v112 - i1 - Sept 1 2015 - p101(1) [51-500]
  c KR - July 15 2015 - pNA [51-500]
  c PW - v262 - i23 - June 8 2015 - p57(1) [51-500]
  c SLJ - v61 - i10 - Oct 2015 - p82(1) [51-500]
  c HB - v91 - i6 - Nov-Dec 2015 - p72(2) [51-500]
Pinkney, Jerry - *The Grasshopper and the Ants (Illus. by Pinkney, Jerry)*
  c HB - v91 - i2 - March-April 2015 - p115(1) [501+]
  c NYTBR - April 12 2015 - p19(L) [501+]
The Grasshopper & the Ants (Illus. by Pinkney, Jerry)
  c BL - v111 - i12 - Feb 15 2015 - p87(1) [51-500]
  c HB Guide - v26 - i2 - Fall 2015 - p159(2) [51-500]
  c KR - Feb 15 2015 - pNA [51-500]
  c PW - v262 - i5 - Feb 2 2015 - p57(1) [51-500]
  c PW - v262 - i49 - Dec 2 2015 - p23(1) [51-500]
  c SLJ - v61 - i2 - Feb 2015 - p76(1) [51-500]
The Lion & the Mouse (Illus. by Pinkney, Jerry)
  c BL - v112 - i4 - Oct 15 2015 - p53(1) [51-500]
Pinkwater, Daniel - *Bear and Bunny (Illus. by Hillenbrand, Will)*
  c BL - v112 - i5 - Nov 1 2015 - p64(1) [51-500]
  c KR - Sept 15 2015 - pNA [51-500]
  c SLJ - v61 - i10 - Oct 2015 - p82(1) [51-500]
Beautiful Yetta's Hanukkah Kitten (Illus. by Pinkwater, Jill)
  c HB Guide - v26 - i1 - Spring 2015 - p42(1) [51-500]
Mrs. Noodlekugel and Drooly the Bear (Illus. by Stower, Adam)
  c HB Guide - v26 - i2 - Fall 2015 - p71(1) [51-500]
  c BL - v111 - i17 - May 1 2015 - p98(1) [51-500]
  c KR - March 1 2015 - pNA [51-500]
  c SLJ - v61 - i4 - April 2015 - p141(2) [51-500]
Pinney, Melissa Ann - *Two*
  BL - v111 - i16 - April 15 2015 - p11(1) [51-500]
  KR - Feb 1 2015 - pNA [501+]
Pins, Arthur de - *March of the Crabs, vol. 1: The Crabby Condition*
  PW - v262 - i5 - Feb 2 2015 - p44(1) [51-500]
Pinsky, Mark I. - *Met Her on the Mountain: A Forty-Year Quest to Solve the Appalachian Cold-Case Murder of Nancy Morgan*
  JSH - v81 - i2 - May 2015 - p530(3) [501+]
Pinson, Anita - *Voices across the Lakes (Illus. by Hall, Emmeline)*
  c CH Bwatch - Oct 2015 - pNA [51-500]
Pinson, Isabel - *Bubbe's Belated Bat Mitzvah (Illus. by Cis, Valeria)*
  c HB Guide - v26 - i1 - Spring 2015 - p42(1) [51-500]
Pinto, Giuliano - *I Centri Minori Della Toscana Nel Medioevo*
  Six Ct J - v46 - i3 - Fall 2015 - p762-763 [501+]

Pinto, Sarah - *Daughters of Parvati: Women and Madness in Contemporary India*
    JRAI - v21 - i3 - Sept 2015 - p701(2) [501+]
Pintoff, Stefanie - *Hostage Taker (Read by Eby, Tanya). Audiobook Review*
    LJ - v140 - i19 - Nov 15 2015 - p53(1) [51-500]
Hostage Taker
    BL - v111 - i21 - July 1 2015 - p37(1) [51-500]
    KR - June 15 2015 - pNA [501+]
    LJ - v140 - i12 - July 1 2015 - p76(1) [51-500]
    PW - v262 - i22 - June 1 2015 - p40(1) [51-500]
Piot, Peter - *AIDS: Between Science and Politics*
    LJ - v140 - i3 - Feb 15 2015 - p126(1) [51-500]
Piotrovsky, Mikhail - *My Hermitage: How the Hermitage Survived Tsars, Wars, and Revolution to Become the Greatest Museum in the World*
    Spec - v329 - i9763 - Oct 10 2015 - p38(1) [501+]
Piper, Andrew - *Book Was There*
    T&C - v56 - i4 - Oct 2015 - p957-964 [501+]
Piper, Ernst - *Nacht uber Europa: Kulturgeschichte des Ersten Weltkrieges*
    HNet - July 2015 - pNA [501+]
Piper, Karen - *The Price of Thirst: Global Water Inequality and the Coming Chaos*
    Am St - v54 - i2 - Summer 2015 - p135-136 [501+]
Pippidi, Andrei - *Visions of the Ottoman World in Renaissance Europe*
    HER - v130 - i543 - April 2015 - p431(3) [501+]
Pippin, Robert B. - *After the Beautiful: Hegel and the Philosophy of Pictorial Modernism*
    Dialogue - v54 - i2 - June 2015 - p396-398 [501+]
Pirani, Simon - *The Russian Gas Matrix: How Markets are Driving Change*
    E-A St - v67 - i4 - June 2015 - p675(2) [501+]
Pirotta, Saviour - *The Ghosts Who Danced*
    c Sch Lib - v63 - i4 - Winter 2015 - p232(1) [51-500]
The Twelve Tasks of Hercules (Illus. by Kelly, Gerald)
    c Sch Lib - v63 - i1 - Spring 2015 - p41(1) [501+]
Pirrone, D.M. - *For You Were Strangers*
    PW - v262 - i42 - Oct 19 2015 - p58(1) [51-500]
Pisani, Elizabeth - *Indonesia Etc.: Exploring the Improbable Nation*
    TLS - i5872 - Oct 16 2015 - p8(1) [501+]
Pisani, Michael V. - *Music for the Melodramatic Theater in Nineteenth-Century London and New York*
    Theat J - v67 - i1 - March 2015 - p149-151 [501+]
Pisano, Claudia Moreno - *Amiri Baraka & Edward Dorn: The Collected Letters*
    Am St - v54 - i1 - Spring 2015 - p134-135 [501+]
    Bks & Cult - v21 - i4 - July-August 2015 - p38(1) [501+]
Piskor, Ed - *Hip Hop Family Tree, vol. 3: 1983-1984 (Illus. by Piskor, Ed)*
    BL - v112 - i2 - Sept 15 2015 - p51(1) [51-500]
Pissock, Jonathan - *World Fishing*
    c Res Links - v20 - i4 - April 2015 - p18(1) [51-500]
Pitamic, Maja - *Modern Art Adventures: 36 Creative, Hands-on Projects Inspired by Artists from Monet to Banksy*
    c PW - v262 - i49 - Dec 2 2015 - p82(1) [51-500]
    c PW - v262 - i18 - May 4 2015 - p117(1) [51-500]
    c SLJ - v61 - i5 - May 2015 - p141(1) [51-500]
Pitch, Anthony S. - *The Last Lynching*
    KR - Jan 1 2016 - pNA [501+]
Pitcher, Annabel - *Silence Is Goldfish*
    y Sch Lib - v63 - i4 - Winter 2015 - p249(1) [51-500]
Pitcher, Chelsea - *The Last Faerie Queen*
    y KR - Sept 15 2015 - pNA [51-500]
Pitici, Mircea - *The Best Writing on Mathematics 2013*
    Math T - v108 - i6 - Feb 2015 - p476(1) [501+]
The Best Writing on Mathematics 2014
    Math T - v109 - i1 - August 2015 - p79-79 [501+]
The Best Writing on Mathematics 2015
    LJ - v140 - i20 - Dec 1 2015 - p125(1) [51-500]
    PW - v262 - i46 - Nov 16 2015 - p67(1) [51-500]
Pitlor, Heidi - *The Daylight Marriage*
    BL - v111 - i13 - March 1 2015 - p17(1) [51-500]
    Ent W - i1363 - May 15 2015 - p61(1) [51-500]
    KR - March 1 2015 - pNA [51-500]
    LJ - v140 - i7 - April 15 2015 - p80(1) [51-500]
    NYTBR - May 31 2015 - p16(L) [501+]
Pitre, Michael - *Fives and Twenty-Fives (Read by five participants). Audiobook Review*
    LJ - v140 - i16 - Oct 1 2015 - p43(2) [51-500]
Fives and Twenty-Fives
    HM - v331 - i1983 - August 2015 - p84(6) [501+]
    TLS - i5854 - June 12 2015 - p19(2) [501+]

Pitt, Darrell - *The Broken Sun: Book III in the Jack Mason Adventures*
    y Magpies - v30 - i1 - March 2015 - p36(2) [501+]
The Lost Sword
    c Magpies - v30 - i5 - Nov 2015 - p37(1) [501+]
The Monster Within
    y KR - Sept 15 2015 - pNA [51-500]
    y Magpies - v30 - i2 - May 2015 - p38(1) [501+]
Pitt, Leonard - *My Brain on Fire*
    KR - Dec 15 2015 - pNA [51-500]
Pitt, Richard - *Divine Callings: Understanding the Call to Ministry in Black Pentecostalism*
    SF - v94 - i2 - Dec 2015 - pNA [501+]
Pittman, Allison - *On Shifting Sand*
    BL - v111 - i16 - April 15 2015 - p37(1) [51-500]
    PW - v262 - i9 - March 2 2015 - p72(1) [51-500]
Pittman, Janet - *Applique: The Basics & Beyond*
    Bwatch - August 2015 - pNA [501+]
Pittrof, Thomas - *Freie Anerkennung ubergeschichtlicher Bindungen: Katholische Geschichtswahrnehmung im deutschsprachigen Raum des 20 Jahrhutiderts*
    CHR - v101 - i3 - Summer 2015 - p671(2) [501+]
Pitts, Leonard, Jr. - *Grant Park*
    BL - v111 - i22 - August 1 2015 - p27(2) [51-500]
    KR - August 1 2015 - pNA [501+]
    NYTBR - Oct 25 2015 - p16(L) [501+]
    PW - v262 - i31 - August 3 2015 - p31(1) [51-500]
Pivato, Joseph - *Sheila Watson: Essays on Her Works*
    Can Lit - i224 - Spring 2015 - p141 [501+]
Piven, Hanoch - *Let's Make Faces (Illus. by Piven, Hanoch)*
    c BL - v112 - i5 - Nov 1 2015 - p50(1) [501+]
Pizarnik, Alejandra - *Extracting the Stone of Madness: Poems 1962-1972*
    HM - v331 - i1987 - Dec 2015 - p77(3) [501+]
    PW - v262 - i42 - Oct 19 2015 - p54(1) [51-500]
Pizer, Carol - *Witchcraft*
    y SLJ - v61 - i9 - Sept 2015 - p151(4) [51-500]
Pizio, Barbara - *Penthouse Variations on Oral*
    RVBW - Jan 2015 - pNA [51-500]
Pizzi, Katia - *Pinocchio, Puppets and Modernity: The Mechanical Body*
    MLR - v110 - i2 - April 2015 - p564-565 [501+]
Pizzitola, Renita - *Just a Little Kiss*
    PW - v262 - i26 - June 29 2015 - p53(1) [51-500]
Pizzolatto, Nic - *Between Here and the Yellow Sea (Read by Heyborne, Kirby). Audiobook Review*
    PW - v262 - i30 - July 27 2015 - p60(1) [51-500]
Pizzoli, Greg - *Templeton Gets His Wish (Illus. by Pizzoli, Greg)*
    c BL - v111 - i16 - April 15 2015 - p55(1) [51-500]
    c CCB-B - v69 - i1 - Sept 2015 - p43(2) [501+]
    c HB - v91 - i3 - May-June 2015 - p94(2) [51-500]
    c HB Guide - v26 - i2 - Fall 2015 - p48(1) [51-500]
    c KR - March 15 2015 - pNA [51-500]
    c PW - v262 - i9 - March 2 2015 - p82(1) [51-500]
    c SLJ - v61 - i5 - May 2015 - p90(1) [51-500]
Tricky Vic: The Impossibly True Story of the Man Who Sold the Eiffel Tower (Illus. by Pizzoli, Greg)
    c CCB-B - v68 - i8 - April 2015 - p415(1) [51-500]
    c HB - v91 - i3 - May-June 2015 - p130(2) [51-500]
    c HB Guide - v26 - i2 - Fall 2015 - p211(1) [51-500]
    c PW - v262 - i3 - Jan 19 2015 - p86(2) [51-500]
Pizzolo, Matt - *Godkiller, vol. 1 (Illus. by Wieszczyk, Anna)*
    KR - March 1 2015 - pNA [51-500]
Occupy Comics: Art + Stories Inspired by Occupy Wall Street
    y LJ - v140 - i9 - May 15 2015 - p61(3) [51-500]
    PW - v262 - i9 - March 2 2015 - p73(1) [51-500]
Pla, Josep - *The Gray Notebook*
    TLS - i5838 - Feb 20 2015 - p10(1) [501+]
Life Embitters
    TLS - i5861 - July 31 2015 - p26(1) [501+]
    KR - April 1 2015 - pNA [501+]
Place, Vanessa - *Boycott*
    Stud Hum - v41 - i1-2 - March 2015 - p263(3) [501+]
Plaff, Donald W. - *The Altruistic Brain: How We Are Naturally Good*
    New Sci - v225 - i3006 - Jan 31 2015 - p44(1) [501+]
Plain, Nancy - *This Strange Wilderness: The Life and Art of John James Audubon*
    y BL - v111 - i15 - April 1 2015 - p35(1) [51-500]
    c KR - Jan 15 2015 - pNA [51-500]
    c Roundup M - v22 - i5 - June 2015 - p37(1) [501+]
    c Roundup M - v22 - i6 - August 2015 - p25(1) [501+]
    y SLJ - v61 - i5 - May 2015 - p141(3) [51-500]
Plakcy, Neil - *Take This Man*
    PW - v262 - i21 - May 25 2015 - p44(1) [51-500]

Plamper, Jan - *The History of Emotions: An Introduction*
    TimHES - i2205 - May 28 2015 - p47(1) [501+]
    TLS - i5860 - July 24 2015 - p24(2) [501+]
Planck, M.C. - *Gold Throne in Shadow*
    PW - v262 - i34 - August 24 2015 - p63(1) [51-500]
Plane, Ann Marie - *Dreams and the Invisible World in Colonial New England: Indians, Colonists, and the Seventeenth Century*
    JAH - v102 - i2 - Sept 2015 - p532-533 [501+]
    RAH - v43 - i3 - Sept 2015 - p427-433 [501+]
    Ren Q - v68 - i3 - Fall 2015 - p1078-1079 [501+]
    Sev Cent N - v73 - i1-2 - Spring-Summer 2015 - p35(2) [501+]
Dreams, Dreamers and Visions: The Early Modern Atlantic World
    RAH - v43 - i3 - Sept 2015 - p427-433 [501+]
Plank, Geoffrey - *John Woolman's Path to the Peaceable Kingdom: A Quaker in the British Empire*
    HER - v130 - i542 - Feb 2015 - pNA [501+]
Plant, David J. - *Hungry Roscoe (Illus. by Plant, David J.)*
    c BL - v111 - i21 - July 1 2015 - p63(1) [51-500]
    c KR - April 15 2015 - pNA [51-500]
    c NYTBR - June 21 2015 - p17(L) [501+]
    c NYTBR - June 21 2015 - p17(L) [501+]
    c PW - v262 - i15 - April 13 2015 - p77(1) [51-500]
    c Sch Lib - v63 - i3 - Autumn 2015 - p158(2) [51-500]
    c SLJ - v61 - i6 - June 2015 - p90(2) [51-500]
Plante, David - *Worlds Apart: A Memoir*
    BL - v111 - i22 - August 1 2015 - p24(2) [51-500]
    LJ - v140 - i13 - August 1 2015 - p94(2) [51-500]
    TLS - i5874 - Oct 30 2015 - p32(1) [501+]
Plantinga, Cornelius, Jr. - *Reading for Preaching: The Preacher in Conversation with Storytellers, Biographers, Poets, and Journalists*
    Intpr - v69 - i4 - Oct 2015 - p500(2) [501+]
Plato - *The Republic*
    Nat R - v67 - i21 - Nov 19 2015 - p73(1) [51-500]
Platoni, Kara - *We Have the Technology: How Biohackers, Foodies, Physicians, and Scientists Are Transforming Human Perception, One Sense at a Time*
    KR - Oct 15 2015 - pNA [501+]
    PW - v262 - i42 - Oct 19 2015 - p66(2) [51-500]
Platt, Larry - *Every Day I Fight*
    BL - v111 - i14 - March 15 2015 - p37(2) [51-500]
    LJ - v140 - i8 - May 1 2015 - p79(1) [51-500]
Platt, Randall - *Incommunicado*
    c SLJ - v61 - i2 - Feb 2015 - p91(2) [51-500]
Plecas, Jennifer - *Bah! Said the Baby (Illus. by Plecas, Jennifer)*
    CCB-B - v68 - i11 - July-August 2015 - p561(1) [501+]
    c HB Guide - v26 - i2 - Fall 2015 - p16(1) [51-500]
    c KR - Jan 15 2015 - pNA [51-500]
Pleins, J. David - *The Evolving God: Charles Darwin on the Naturalness of Religion*
    TT - v72 - i2 - July 2015 - p237-239 [501+]
Plender, John - *Capitalism: Money, Morals and Markets*
    Econ - v416 - i8951 - August 15 2015 - p75(US) [501+]
    TLS - i5869 - Sept 25 2015 - p3(2) [501+]
Plenderleith, Ian - *Rock 'n' Roll Soccer: The Short Life and Fast Times of the North American Soccer League*
    BL - v112 - i1 - Sept 1 2015 - p38(1) [51-500]
    LJ - v140 - i13 - August 1 2015 - p104(2) [51-500]
    PW - v262 - i28 - July 13 2015 - p56(2) [51-500]
Plenel, Edwy - *Pour les Musulmans*
    TLS - i5852 - May 29 2015 - p10(2) [501+]
Pleska, Cat - *Riding on Comets*
    BL - v111 - i18 - May 15 2015 - p5(1) [51-500]
    KR - Feb 15 2015 - pNA [51-500]
Plesko, Les - *No Stopping Train*
    WLT - v89 - i2 - March-April 2015 - p71(1) [51-500]
Plessini, Karel - *The Perils of Normalcy: George L. Mosse and the Remaking of Cultural History*
    AHR - v120 - i1 - Feb 2015 - p189-190 [501+]
Pleysier, Elizabeth - *Henry VIII and the Anabaptists*
    CH - v84 - i3 - Sept 2015 - p665(2) [501+]
Plichota, Anne - *Oksa Pollock Series*
    c Sch Lib - v63 - i2 - Summer 2015 - p108(1) [51-500]
Pliley, Jessica R. - *Policing Sexuality: The Mann Act and the Making of the FBI*
    Am St - v54 - i2 - Summer 2015 - p127-128 [501+]
    JAH - v102 - i2 - Sept 2015 - p583-584 [501+]
    Wom R Bks - v32 - i5 - Sept-Oct 2015 - p10(2) [501+]

Pliscou, Lisa - *Young Jane Austen: Becoming a Writer (Illus. by Mongiardo, Massimo)*
   y VOYA - v38 - i2 - June 2015 - p67(1) [51-500]

Plokhy, Serhii - *The Gates of Europe: A History of Ukraine*
     KR - Sept 15 2015 - pNA [501+]
     LJ - v140 - i17 - Oct 15 2015 - p102(1) [51-500]
The Last Empire: The Final Days of the Soviet Union
     E-A St - v67 - i3 - May 2015 - p497(3) [501+]
     Slav R - v74 - i1 - Spring 2015 - p202-203 [501+]

Plonsker, Madeleine - *The Light in Cuban Eyes: Lake Forest College's Madeleine P. Plonsker Collection of Contemporary Cuban Photography*
     LJ - v140 - i9 - May 15 2015 - p80(1) [51-500]

Plouffe, Manon - *Jeanne Mance: Cofondatrice de Montreal*
   c Res Links - v20 - i3 - Feb 2015 - p49(2) [51-500]

Plowman, Peter - *Voyage to Gallipoli*
     HNet - May 2015 - pNA [501+]

Plum, Amy - *Until the Beginning*
   y BL - v111 - i17 - May 1 2015 - p98(1) [51-500]
   y KR - March 1 2015 - pNA [51-500]

Plumly, Stanley - *The Immortal Evening: A Legendary Dinner with Keats, Wordsworth and Lamb*
     Spec - v327 - i9723 - Jan 3 2015 - p27(1) [501+]

Plummer, Ken - *Cosmopolitan Sexualities: Hope and the Humanist Imagination*
     TimHES - i2207 - June 11 2015 - p52-53 [501+]

Plumpe, Werner - *Unternehmer - Fakten und Fiktionen: Historisch-biographische Studien*
     HNet - April 2015 - pNA [501+]

Pluss, Caroline - *Living Intersections: Transnational Migrant Identifications in Asia*
     ERS - v38 - i8 - August 2015 - p1452(2) [501+]

Poague, Michele - *The Candy Store*
     KR - Sept 1 2015 - pNA [501+]

Poblete, Joanna - *Islanders in the Empire: Filipino and Puerto Rican Laborers in Hawai'i*
     AHR - v120 - i4 - Oct 2015 - p1470-1471 [501+]

Poblocki, Dan - *The Book of Bad Things*
   y HB Guide - v26 - i1 - Spring 2015 - p89(1) [51-500]
The House on Stone's Throw Island
   c KR - June 1 2015 - pNA [51-500]
   y SLJ - v61 - i9 - Sept 2015 - p144(2) [51-500]
   y VOYA - v38 - i4 - Oct 2015 - p76(1) [51-500]

Pochmara, Ana - *The Making of the New Negro: Black Authorship, Masculinity, and Sexuality in the Harlem Renaissance*
     Callaloo - v38 - i1 - Wntr 2015 - p209-210 [501+]

Podell, Albert - *Around the World in 50 Years: My Adventure to Every Country on Earth*
     BL - v111 - i11 - Feb 1 2015 - p11(1) [51-500]
     KR - Jan 1 2015 - pNA [501+]
     PW - v262 - i2 - Jan 12 2015 - p49(1) [51-500]

Podos, Rebecca - *The Mystery of Hollow Places*
   y BL - v112 - i4 - Oct 15 2015 - p56(1) [51-500]
   y KR - Oct 1 2015 - pNA [51-500]
   y PW - v262 - i41 - Oct 12 2015 - p70(2) [51-500]
   y SLJ - v61 - i11 - Nov 2015 - p120(1) [51-500]

Poe, Deborah - *Between Worlds: An Anthology of Contemporart Fiction and Criticism*
     Aztlan - v40 - i2 - Fall 2015 - p291-295 [501+]

Poehler, Amy - *Yes Please (Read by Poehler, Amy). Audiobook Review*
     BL - v111 - i9-10 - Jan 1 2015 - p116(1) [51-500]

Poetiken des Pazifiks
     HNet - Sept 2015 - pNA [501+]

Pogrebin, Letty Cottin - *Single Jewish Male Seeking Soul Mate*
     BL - v111 - i17 - May 1 2015 - p77(1) [51-500]
     KR - April 1 2015 - pNA [501+]

Pohl, Nicole - *The Letters of Sarah Scott*
     Eight-C St - v48 - i4 - Summer 2015 - p543-545 [501+]

Pohl, Walter - *Post-Roman Transitions: Christian and Barbarian Identities in the Early Medieval West*
     Med R - May 2015 - pNA [501+]

Pohlen, Jerome - *Gay & Lesbian History for Kids: The Century-Long Struggle for LGBT Rights, with 21 Activities*
   c BL - v111 - i22 - August 1 2015 - p55(1) [51-500]
   y KR - August 15 2015 - pNA [51-500]
   c SLJ - v61 - i10 - Oct 2015 - p138(1) [51-500]

Poisson, Eric - *Gravity: Newtonian, Post-Newtonian, Relativistic*
     Phys Today - v68 - i10 - Oct 2015 - p50-52 [501+]

Poitier, Anton - *Flippy Floppy Ocean Animals (Illus. by Touliatou, Sophia)*
   c CH Bwatch - June 2015 - pNA [51-500]
Numbers
   c KR - Jan 1 2016 - pNA [51-500]

Pojmann, Wendy - *Italian Women and International Cold War Politics, 1944-1968*
     HNet - June 2015 - pNA [501+]
     JWH - v27 - i3 - Fall 2015 - p204(7) [51-500]

Polacco, Patricia - *An A from Miss Keller (Illus. by Polacco, Patricia)*
   c BL - v111 - i21 - July 1 2015 - p60(1) [51-500]
   c CH Bwatch - Nov 2015 - pNA [51-500]
   c KR - June 1 2015 - pNA [51-500]
   c SLJ - v61 - i10 - Oct 2015 - p82(1) [51-500]
Fiona's Lace
   c HB Guide - v26 - i1 - Spring 2015 - p42(1) [51-500]
Mr. Wayne's Masterpiece (Illus. by Polacco, Patricia)
   c CH Bwatch - Jan 2015 - pNA [51-500]
   c HB Guide - v26 - i2 - Fall 2015 - p48(1) [51-500]
Tucky Jo and Little Heart (Illus. by Polacco, Patricia)
   c KR - June 15 2015 - pNA [51-500]
   c SLJ - v61 - i9 - Sept 2015 - p127(1) [51-500]

Polak, Monique - *Learning the Ropes*
   y BL - v111 - i17 - May 1 2015 - p91(1) [51-500]
   y KR - March 1 2015 - pNA [51-500]
   y VOYA - v38 - i1 - April 2015 - p64(2) [51-500]
Passover: Festival of Freedom
   c BL - v112 - i6 - Nov 15 2015 - p44(1) [51-500]
   c KR - Nov 15 2015 - pNA [51-500]

Poland, Tom - *Georgialina: A Southland as We Knew It*
     KR - Sept 15 2015 - pNA [51-500]

Polansky, Daniel - *The Builders*
     BL - v112 - i6 - Nov 15 2015 - p32(1) [51-500]
     PW - v262 - i39 - Sept 28 2015 - p72(2) [51-500]

Polanyi, Karl - *For a New West: Essays, 1919-1958*
     TimHES - i2198 - April 9 2015 - p49(1) [501+]

Polar, Antonio Cornejo - *Writing in the Air: Heterogeneity and the Persistence of Oral Tradition in Andean Literature*
     Hisp R - v83 - i1 - Wntr 2015 - p110-113 [501+]

Polasky, Janet - *Revolutions without Borders: The Call to Liberty in the Atlantic World*
     Econ - v415 - i8936 - May 2 2015 - p74(US) [501+]
     HNet - July 2015 - pNA [501+]
     NYRB - v62 - i13 - August 13 2015 - p50(2) [501+]

Polatin, Betsy - *The Actor's Secret: Techniques for Transforming Habitual Patterns and Improving Performance*
     Am Theat - v32 - i1 - Jan 2015 - p92(2) [501+]

Polenberg, Richard - *Hear My Sad Story: The True Tales That Inspired "Stagolee," "John Henry," and Other Traditional American Folk Songs*
     LJ - v140 - i19 - Nov 15 2015 - p88(1) [501+]
     NYTBR - Dec 6 2015 - p72(L) [501+]

Poletti, Frances - *Miss Todd and Her Wonderful Flying Machine (Illus. by Yee, Kristina)*
   c BL - v111 - i19-20 - June 1 2015 - p105(1) [51-500]

Policastro, Margaret M. - *Formative Assessment in the New Balanced Literacy Classroom*
     Teach Lib - v43 - i1 - Oct 2015 - p41(3) [501+]

Polillo, Simone - *Conservatives versus Wildcats: A Sociology of Financial Conflict*
     CS - v44 - i6 - Nov 2015 - p837-839 [501+]

Poliner, Elizabeth - *As Close to Us as Breathing*
     KR - Dec 15 2015 - pNA [501+]

Poling-Kempes, Lesley - *Ladies of the Canyons: A League of Extraordinary Women and Their Adventures in the American Southwest*
     LJ - v140 - i13 - August 1 2015 - p110(1) [51-500]

Politi, Marco - *Pope Francis among the Wolves: The Inside Story of a Revolution*
     LJ - v140 - i14 - Sept 1 2015 - p108(1) [501+]
     BL - v112 - i2 - Sept 15 2015 - p4(1) [51-500]

The Political Cult of the Dead in Ukraine: Traditions and Dimensions from Soviet Time to Today
     HNet - Sept 2015 - pNA [501+]

Politik und Versammlung im Fruhmittelalter
     HNet - March 2015 - pNA [501+]

Pollack, Amy - *The Course of Nature: A Book of Drawings on Natural Selection and Its Consequences*
     Am Bio T - v77 - i6 - August 2015 - p470(1) [501+]

Pollack, Eileen - *The Only Woman in the Room: Why Science Is Still a Boys' Club*
   y BL - v112 - i1 - Sept 1 2015 - p19(1) [51-500]
     KR - July 1 2015 - pNA [51-500]
     LJ - v140 - i16 - Oct 1 2015 - p104(1) [51-500]

Pollan, Michael - *The Omnivore's Dilemma: The Secrets behind What You Eat (Read by Andrews, MacLeod). Audiobook Review*
   y BL - v112 - i3 - Oct 1 2015 - p87(1) [51-500]
   y SLJ - v61 - i11 - Nov 2015 - p74(1) [51-500]

Pollard, Natalie - *Don Paterson: Contemporary Critical Essays*
     TLS - i5837 - Feb 13 2015 - p26(1) [501+]

Polli, Miriam - *In a Vertigo of Silence*
     KR - May 15 2015 - pNA [51-500]

Pollitt, J.J. - *The Cambridge History of Painting in the Classical World*
     HT - v65 - i8 - August 2015 - p58(2) [501+]

Pollitt, Katha - *Pro: Reclaiming Abortion Rights*
     Cons - v36 - i2 - Summer 2015 - p39(2) [501+]
     NYTBR - Oct 18 2015 - p28(L) [501+]
     Wom R Bks - v32 - i4 - July-August 2015 - p3(3) [501+]

Pollitt, Phoebe - *The History of Professional Nursing in North Carolina, 1902-2002*
     JSH - v81 - i4 - Nov 2015 - p1017(2) [501+]

Pollock, Benjamin - *Franz Rosenzweig's Conversions: World Denial and World Redemption*
     JR - v95 - i4 - Oct 2015 - p577(3) [501+]

Pollock, Mary Sanders - *Storytelling Apes: Primatology Narratives Past and Future*
     LJ - v140 - i9 - May 15 2015 - p103(2) [51-500]

Pollock, Sheldon - *Murty Classical Library of India*
     HT - v65 - i10 - Oct 2015 - p63(1) [501+]
     NS - v144 - i5251 - Feb 27 2015 - p40(3) [501+]

Polonsky, Ami - *Gracefully Grayson*
   c CCB-B - v68 - i6 - Feb 2015 - p325(1) [51-500]
   c CH Bwatch - Feb 2015 - pNA [51-500]
   c HB Guide - v26 - i1 - Spring 2015 - p120(1) [51-500]

Polt, Richard - *The Typewriter Revolution: A Typist's Companion for the 21st Century*
   y BL - v112 - i6 - Nov 15 2015 - p5(1) [51-500]
     LJ - v140 - i16 - Oct 1 2015 - p95(1) [51-500]
     PW - v262 - i34 - August 24 2015 - p72(1) [51-500]

Poluchowicz, Krzysztof - *Brooklyn ABC: A Scrapbook of Everyone's Favorite Borough*
   c PW - v262 - i14 - April 6 2015 - p58(1) [51-500]

Pomare, Carla - *Byron and the Discourses of History*
     Clio - v44 - i2 - Spring 2015 - p217-237 [501+]

Pomerantsev, Peter - *Nothing Is True and Everything Is Possible: Adventures in Modern Russia*
     NS - v144 - i5248 - Feb 6 2015 - p40(2) [501+]
     Spec - v327 - i9729 - Feb 14 2015 - p43(2) [501+]
Nothing Is True and Everything Is Possible: The Surreal Heart of the New Russia
     Dis - v62 - i3 - Summer 2015 - p135(140) [501+]
     Nat R - v67 - i5 - March 23 2015 - p45 [501+]
     TLS - i5831 - Jan 2 2015 - p10(1) [501+]

Pomerleau, Clark A. - *Califia Women: Feminist Education against Sexism, Classism, and Racism*
     AHR - v120 - i1 - Feb 2015 - p295-296 [501+]
     PHR - v84 - i3 - August 2015 - p391(2) [501+]

Pomeroy, S.B. - *Pythagorean Women: Their History and Writings*
     Class R - v65 - i1 - April 2015 - p96-97 [501+]

Pommaux, Yvan - *Orpheus in the Underworld (Illus. by Pommaux, Yvan)*
   c BL - v111 - i19-20 - June 1 2015 - p68(1) [51-500]
   c CCB-B - v69 - i1 - Sept 2015 - p44(1) [51-500]
   c HB Guide - v26 - i2 - Fall 2015 - p160(1) [51-500]
   c SLJ - v61 - i5 - May 2015 - p110(1) [51-500]
Orpheus in the Underworld
   c KR - March 1 2015 - pNA [51-500]

Pon, Cindy - *Serpentine*
   y KR - July 15 2015 - pNA [51-500]
   y SLJ - v61 - i7 - July 2015 - p97(2) [51-500]
   y VOYA - v38 - i4 - Oct 2015 - p76(1) [51-500]

Ponce de Leon, Charles L. - *That's the Way It Is: A History of Television News in America*
     LJ - v140 - i8 - May 1 2015 - p81(1) [51-500]

Ponce, Pearl T. - *To Govern the Devil in Hell: The Political Crisis in Territorial Kansas*
     JSH - v81 - i4 - Nov 2015 - p979(2) [501+]

Poncet, Charles - *Camus et l'imposible treve civile: suivi d'une correspondance avec Amar Ouzegane*
     TLS - i5875 - Nov 6 2015 - p26(1) [501+]

Ponepinto, Joseph - *Curtain Calls*
     KR - May 1 2015 - pNA [51-500]

Poniatowska, Elena - *Leonora*
     Spec - v327 - i9735 - March 28 2015 - p41(2)

Pons, Bruno - *Architecture and Panelling: The James A. de Rothschild Bequest at Waddesdon Manor*
     NYRB - v62 - i11 - June 25 2015 - p29(4) [501+]

Pons, Silvio - *The Global Revolution: A History of International Communism 1917-1991*
HNet - July 2015 - pNA [501+]
TLS - i5869 - Sept 25 2015 - p25(1) [501+]

Ponsaers, Paul - *Social Analysis of Security: Financial, Economic and Ecological Crime - Crime, (In)security and (Dis)trust - Public and Private Policing*
CS - v44 - i3 - May 2015 - p403-404 [501+]

Pont, Jean-Claude - *Le destin douloureux de Walther Ritz (1878-1909): Physicien theoricien de genie*
Isis - v106 - i1 - March 2015 - p201(2) [501+]

Pontano, Giovanni Gioviano - *On Married Love: Eridanus*
Ren Q - v68 - i3 - Fall 2015 - p972-974 [501+]

Ponti, Crystal - *Clash of the Couples: A Humorous Collection of Completely Absurd Lovers' Squabbles and Relationship Spats*
PW - v262 - i5 - Feb 2 2015 - p51(1) [51-500]

Pontynen, Arthur - *Cultural Renewal: Restoring the Liberal and Fine Arts*
RM - v68 - i3 - March 2015 - p673(3) [501+]

Poo, Ai-jen - *The Age of Dignity: Preparing for the Elder Boom in a Changing America*
Ms - v25 - i1 - Wntr 2015 - p55(1) [501+]
NYTBR - March 1 2015 - p18(L) [501+]

Pooker, J.D. - *The Ifs Return (Illus. by Walls, Frank)*
c SPBW - July 2015 - pNA [51-500]

Pookie Pop Plays Hide-and-Seek (Illus. by Ho, Jannie)
c CH Bwatch - March 2015 - pNA [51-500]

Pool, Gail - *Lost among the Baining: Adventure, Marriage, and Other Fieldwork*
RVBW - Oct 2015 - pNA [501+]

Poole, Andrea Geddes - *Philanthropy and the Construction of Victorian Women's Citizenship: Lady Frederick Cavendish and Miss Emma Cons*
AHR - v120 - i1 - Feb 2015 - p330-331 [501+]

Poole, De Witt Clinton - *An American Diplomat in Bolshevik Russia*
E-A St - v67 - i9 - Nov 2015 - p1507(3) [501+]

The Poorer Nationa: A Possible History of the Global South
Am Q - v67 - i1 - March 2015 - p219-229 [501+]

Poothullil, John M. - *Eat, Chew, Live: 4 Revolutionary Ideas to Prevent Diabetes, Lose Weight and Enjoy Food*
LJ - v140 - i10 - June 1 2015 - p128(1) [51-500]

Pope, Dan - *Housebreaking*
BL - v111 - i13 - March 1 2015 - p18(1) [51-500]
HR - v68 - i2 - Summer 2015 - p343-351 [501+]
KR - March 1 2015 - pNA [51-500]
LJ - v140 - i9 - May 15 2015 - p76(2) [51-500]
NYTBR - May 17 2015 - p25(L) [501+]

Pope Francis: Untying the Knots
NYRB - v62 - i3 - Feb 19 2015 - p11(3) [501+]

Pope, Greg - *I'm a Big Girl: A Story for Dads and Daughters (Illus. by Wells, Lea)*
c CH Bwatch - April 2015 - pNA [51-500]

Pope-Levison, Priscilla - *Building the Old Time Religion: Women Evangelists in the Progressive Era*
JAH - v101 - i4 - March 2015 - p1298-1299 [501+]

Pope, Paul - *The Fall of the House of West (Illus. by Rubin, David)*
c BL - v112 - i4 - Oct 15 2015 - p36(1) [51-500]
y SLJ - v61 - i12 - Dec 2015 - p130(1) [51-500]
c KR - Sept 15 2015 - pNA [51-500]

Pope, Thomas - *A Call to Arms*
PW - v262 - i34 - August 24 2015 - p64(1) [51-500]

Popescu, Delia - *Political Action in Vaclav Havel's Thought: The Responsibility of Resistance*
Soc - v52 - i1 - Feb 2015 - p87(6) [501+]

Popescu, Toader - *Proiectul Feroviar Romanesc*
HNet - March 2015 - pNA [51-500]

Popkin, Ruth Shamir - *Jewish Identity: The Challenge of Peoplehood Today*
RVBW - Oct 2015 - pNA [501+]

Popky, Linda J. - *Marketing above the Noise: Achieve Strategic Advantage with Marketing That Matters*
SPBW - May 2015 - pNA [51-500]
SPBW - May 2015 - pNA [51-500]
SPBW - June 2015 - pNA [51-500]

Poploff, Michelle - *Where Triplets Go, Trouble Follows (Illus. by Jamieson, Victoria)*
c HB Guide - v26 - i2 - Fall 2015 - p71(1) [51-500]
c BL - v111 - i21 - July 1 2015 - p77(1) [51-500]
c KR - March 1 2015 - pNA [51-500]
c PW - v262 - i16 - April 20 2015 - p77(1) [51-500]
c SLJ - v61 - i4 - April 2015 - p142(2) [51-500]

Popoff, Alexandra - *Tolstoy's False Disciple: The Untold Story of Leo Tolstoy and Vladimir Chertkov*
NY - v90 - i46 - Feb 2 2015 - p65 [51-500]
Spec - v327 - i9726 - Jan 24 2015 - p48(1) [501+]

Popovich, C.A. - *The Courage to Try*
PW - v262 - i36 - Sept 7 2015 - p52(2) [51-500]

Popowski, Mark D. - *The Rise and Fall of Triumph: The History of a Radical Roman Catholic Magazine, 1966-1976*
CHR - v101 - i2 - Spring 2015 - p396(2) [501+]

Popper, Nathaniel - *Digital Gold: Bitcoin and the Inside Story of the Misfits and Millionaires Trying to Reinvent Money*
BL - v111 - i18 - May 15 2015 - p6(1) [51-500]
Har Bus R - v93 - i6 - June 2015 - p118(2) [51-500]
LJ - v140 - i9 - May 15 2015 - p90(1) [51-500]
NYTBR - July 5 2015 - p17(L) [501+]
Digital Gold
KR - April 1 2015 - pNA [501+]

Popper, Nicholas - *Walter Ralegh's "History of the World" and the Historical Culture of the Late Renaissance*
AHR - v120 - i2 - April 2015 - p713-714 [501+]

Porch, Dorris D. - *Murder in Memphis*
PW - v262 - i11 - March 16 2015 - p3(1) [51-500]

Porcher, Richard Dwight, Jr. - *The Market Preparation of Carolina Rice: An Illustrated History of Innovations in the Lowcountry Rice Kingdom*
JSH - v81 - i4 - Nov 2015 - p940(2) [51-500]

Poreba, Christine - *Rough Knowledge*
PW - v262 - i52 - Dec 21 2015 - p126(2) [51-500]

Porpora, Douglas V. - *Post-Ethical Society: The Iraq War, Abu Ghraib, and the Moral Failure of the Secular*
CS - v44 - i4 - July 2015 - p541-543 [501+]

Port, Elisa - *The New Generation Breast Cancer Book: How to Navigate Your Diagnosis and Treatment Options--and Remain Optimistic--in an Age of Information Overload*
LJ - v140 - i14 - Sept 1 2015 - p130(2) [501+]
PW - v262 - i33 - August 17 2015 - p67(1) [51-500]

Portas, Mary - *Shop Girl*
Spec - v327 - i9733 - March 14 2015 - p46(2) [501+]

Porter, Amy M. - *Their Lives, Their Wills: Women in the Borderlands, 1750-1846*
Bwatch - Nov 2015 - pNA [51-500]

Porter, Anna - *Buying a Better World: George Soros and Billionaire Philanthropy*
Mac - v128 - i10 - March 16 2015 - p57(2) [501+]

Porter, Anne - *Mobile Pastoralism and the Formation of Near Eastern Civilizations: Weaving Together Society*
JNES - v74 - i1 - April 2015 - p153(3) [501+]

Porter, Bill - *The Silk Road: Taking the Bus to Pakistan*
KR - Dec 1 2015 - pNA [51-500]
South of the Clouds: Travels in Southwest China
BL - v112 - i2 - Sept 15 2015 - p25(1) [51-500]
KR - Sept 15 2015 - pNA [51-500]

Porter, James - *Time, History and Literature: Selected Essays of Erich Auerbach*
Lon R Bks - v37 - i5 - March 5 2015 - p19(3) [501+]

Porter, Jane - *It's You*
BL - v111 - i19-20 - June 1 2015 - p42(1) [51-500]

Porter, Janelle - *Arlene Shechet: All at Once*
BL - v112 - i1 - Sept 1 2015 - p26(1) [51-500]

Porter, Jenelle - *Fiber: Sculpture 1960-Present*
LJ - v140 - i2 - Feb 1 2015 - p85(1) [501+]
Am Craft - v75 - i1 - Feb-March 2015 - p26(2) [501+]

Porter, Margaret - *A Pledge of Better Times*
PW - v262 - i27 - July 6 2015 - p44(1) [51-500]

Porter, Matthew - *Fox on the Loose! (Illus. by Porter, Matthew)*
c KR - Jan 1 2015 - pNA [51-500]
The Rise and Fall of Oscar the Magician (Illus. by Porter, Matthew)
c KR - April 15 2015 - pNA [51-500]

Porter, Max - *Grief Is the Thing with Feathers*
NS - v144 - i5280 - Sept 18 2015 - p63(1) [501+]
Spec - v329 - i9761 - Sept 26 2015 - p42(2) [501+]
TLS - i5873 - Oct 23 2015 - p19(1) [501+]

Porter, Patrick - *The Global Village Myth: Distance, War, and the Limits of Power*
Parameters - v45 - i2 - Summer 2015 - p115(2) [501+]

Porter-Reynolds, Daisy - *Streamlined Library Programming: How to Improve Services and Cut Costs*
LQ - v85 - i3 - July 2015 - p338(2) [501+]

Porter, Susan Eva - *Bully Nation: Why America's Approach to Childhood Aggression Is Bad for Everyone*
CS - v44 - i3 - May 2015 - p438(1) [501+]

Porter-Szucs, Brian - *Poland in the Modern World: Beyond Martyrdom*
HNet - Feb 2015 - pNA [501+]
Nation - v300 - i1 - Jan 5 2015 - p27(10) [501+]

Porterfield, Amanda - *Conceived in Doubt: Religion and Politics in the New American Nation*
RAH - v43 - i2 - June 2015 - p216-222 [501+]

Porterfield, Jason - *Working as a Tattoo Artist in Your Community*
y BL - v112 - i3 - Oct 1 2015 - p40(2) [51-500]

Portes, Andrea - *Anatomy of a Misfit*
y HB Guide - v26 - i1 - Spring 2015 - p120(1) [51-500]

Portes, Pedro R. - *U.S. Latinos and Educational Policy: Research-Based Directions for Change*
HER - v85 - i3 - Fall 2015 - p502-513 [501+]

Portier, William L. - *Divided Friends: Portraits of the Roman Catholic Modernist Crisis in the United States*
CH - v84 - i3 - Sept 2015 - p698(3) [501+]
CHR - v101 - i3 - Summer 2015 - p684(1) [501+]

Portis, Antoinette - *Wait (Illus. by Portis, Antoinette)*
c CCB-B - v69 - i2 - Oct 2015 - p109(1) [51-500]
c HB - v91 - i4 - July-August 2015 - p123(1) [51-500]
c KR - May 1 2015 - pNA [51-500]
c PW - v262 - i18 - May 4 2015 - p116(2) [51-500]
c PW - v262 - i49 - Dec 2 2015 - p33(1) [51-500]
c SLJ - v61 - i5 - May 2015 - p80(1) [51-500]

Portman, Frank - *King Dork Approximately*
y CCB-B - v68 - i5 - Jan 2015 - p274(1) [51-500]
y HB Guide - v26 - i1 - Spring 2015 - p120(1) [51-500]

Portnoy, Bruce - *First, the 'Saturday People', and Then the....*
SPBW - Nov 2015 - pNA [51-500]

Portraying the Prince in the Renaissance: The Humanist Depiction of Rulers in Historiographical and Biographical Texts
HNet - Feb 2015 - pNA [501+]

Portuese, Orazio - *Il carme 67 di Catullo*
Class R - v65 - i1 - April 2015 - p122-124 [501+]

Portugal, Franklin H. - *The Least Likely Man: Marshall Nirenberg and the Discovery of the Genetic Code*
New Sci - v226 - i3019 - May 2 2015 - p46(1) [501+]
Nature - v519 - i7544 - March 26 2015 - p413(1) [51-500]
TimHES - i2193 - March 5 2015 - p52-53 [501+]

Posada, Jorge - *The Journey Home: My Life in Pinstripes*
LJ - v140 - i9 - May 15 2015 - p87(1) [51-500]

Posada, Mia - *Who Was Here? Discovering Wild Animal Tracks (Illus. by Posada, Mia)*
c HB Guide - v26 - i2 - Fall 2015 - p171(2) [51-500]

Posamentier, Alfred S. - *Magnificent Mistakes in Mathematics*
Math T - v108 - i8 - April 2015 - p638(1) [501+]
Mathematical Couriosities: A Treasure Trove of Unexpected Entertainments
Math T - v109 - i2 - Sept 2015 - p159-159 [501+]
Numbers: Their Tales, Types, and Treasures
Bwatch - Oct 2015 - pNA [51-500]
PW - v262 - i24 - June 15 2015 - p75(2) [51-500]

Posen, Barry R. - *Restraint: A New Foundation for U.S. Grand Strategy*
For Aff - v94 - i3 - May-June 2015 - pNA [501+]
NWCR - v68 - i4 - Autumn 2015 - p115(3) [501+]
Parameters - v45 - i1 - Spring 2015 - p139(3) [501+]
TLS - i5875 - Nov 6 2015 - p13(1) [501+]

Poser, Norman - *Lord Mansfield: Justice in the Age of Reason*
Lon R Bks - v37 - i2 - Jan 22 2015 - p20(3) [501+]

Poshoglian, Yvette - *Frankie Fox Girl Spy: Ready Set Spy*
y Magpies - v30 - i1 - March 2015 - p36(1) [501+]

Posnanski, Joe - *The Secret of Golf: The Story of Tom Watson and Jack Nicklaus*
BL - v111 - i19-20 - June 1 2015 - p22(1) [51-500]
KR - May 1 2015 - pNA [51-500]
LJ - v140 - i10 - June 1 2015 - p108(1) [51-500]
PW - v262 - i19 - May 11 2015 - p52(1) [51-500]

Posner, Dassia N. - *The Routledge Companion to Puppetry and Material Performance*
Theat J - v67 - i2 - May 2015 - p375-376 [501+]

Posner, Eric - *The Twilight of Human Rights Law*
For Aff - v94 - i1 - Jan-Feb 2015 - pNA [51-500]

Posner, Gerald - *God's Bankers: A History of Money & Power at the Vatican*
    AM - v213 - i2 - July 20 2015 - p31(2) [501+]
    BL - v111 - i9-10 - Jan 1 2015 - p25(1) [51-500]
    Comw - v142 - i8 - May 1 2015 - p40(3) [501+]
    LJ - v140 - i2 - Feb 1 2015 - p95(1) [51-500]
    NYTBR - March 22 2015 - p14(L) [501+]
Posner, Richard A. - *Divergent Paths: The Academy and the Judiciary*
    PW - v262 - i46 - Nov 16 2015 - p67(1) [51-500]
Pospieszna, Paulina - *Democracy Assistance from the Third Wave: Polish Engagement in Belarus and Ukraine*
    E-A St - v67 - i3 - May 2015 - p504(3) [501+]
    E-A St - v67 - i6 - August 2015 - p996(2) [501+]
Possenti, Vittorio - *Nihilism and Metaphysics: The Third Voyage*
    RM - v69 - i2 - Dec 2015 - p403(3) [501+]
Possieri, Andrea - *Garibaldi*
    HNet - Feb 2015 - pNA [501+]
Post, Andrew - *Sired by Stone*
    y VOYA - v38 - i2 - June 2015 - p81(2) [51-500]
Post-Colonial Germany
    HT - v65 - i10 - Oct 2015 - p56(2) [501+]
Post, Eric - *Ecology of Climate Change: The Importance of Biotic Interactions*
    QRB - v90 - i2 - June 2015 - p213(2) [501+]
Post, Robert C. - *Citizens Divided: Campaign Finance Reform and the Constitution*
    HLR - v128 - i4 - Feb 2015 - p1330(2) [1-50]
Who Owns America's Past? The Smithsonian and the Problem of History
    Isis - v106 - i1 - March 2015 - p216(2) [501+]
    T&C - v56 - i1 - Jan 2015 - p248-251 [501+]
Postgate, Daniel - *Rumpled Stilton Skin*
    c CH Bwatch - July 2015 - pNA [501+]
Posthuma, Sieb - *Where Is Rusty? (Illus. by Posthuma, Sieb)*
    c CH Bwatch - Oct 2015 - pNA [51-500]
    c HB Guide - v26 - i2 - Fall 2015 - p48(1) [51-500]
    c KR - Jan 15 2015 - pNA [501+]
Postle, Martin - *Richard Wilson and the Transformation of European Landscape Painting*
    TLS - i5853 - June 5 2015 - p12(1) [501+]
Postman, Neil - *Amusing Ourselves to Death*
    CSM - April 9 2015 - pNA [51-500]
Poston, Lawrence - *The Antagonist Principle: John Henry Newman and the Paradox of Personality*
    CHR - v101 - i4 - Autumn 2015 - p947(3) [501+]
Potter, Alicia - *Miss Hazeltine's Home for Shy and Fearful Cats (Illus. by Sif, Birgitta)*
    c CCB-B - v68 - i11 - July-August 2015 - p561(2) [51-500]
    c HB - v91 - i3 - May-June 2015 - p95(2) [51-500]
    c HB Guide - v26 - i2 - Fall 2015 - p48(1) [51-500]
    c KR - Feb 1 2015 - pNA [501+]
    c Sch Lib - v63 - i3 - Autumn 2015 - p160(1) [51-500]
Potter, David - *The Left Behinds: The iPhone That Saved George Washington (Read by Heyborne, Kirby). Audiobook Review*
    c BL - v111 - i18 - May 15 2015 - p70(2) [51-500]
The Left Behinds: The iPhone That Saved George Washington
    c HB Guide - v26 - i2 - Fall 2015 - p97(1) [51-500]
Potter, David (b. 1955-) - *Abe Lincoln and the Selfie That Saved the Union*
    c KR - Oct 1 2015 - pNA [51-500]
Potter, David (B. 1955-) - *The Left Behinds: The iPhone That Saved George Washington (Read by Heyborne, Kirby). Audiobook Review*
    SLJ - v61 - i4 - April 2015 - p63(2) [501+]
The Left Behinds: The iPhone that Saved George Washington
    c CCB-B - v68 - i6 - Feb 2015 - p325(1) [51-500]
Potter, David (b. 1955-) - *The Left Behinds: The iPhone that Saved George Washington*
    y VOYA - v37 - i6 - Feb 2015 - p82(2) [51-500]
Potter, David S. (b. 1957-) - *Constantine the Emperor*
    Lon R Bks - v37 - i8 - April 23 2015 - p25(2) [501+]
    Class R - v65 - i2 - Oct 2015 - p545-547 [501+]
Theodora: Actress, Emperor, Saint
    PW - v262 - i32 - August 10 2015 - p46(1) [51-500]
Theodora: Actress, Empress, Saint
    NYRB - v62 - i18 - Nov 19 2015 - p34(2) [501+]
Potter, Dennis - *The Art of Invective: Selected Non-Fiction, 1953-94*
    Spec - v328 - i9750 - July 11 2015 - p38(2) [501+]

Potter, Ellen - *Piper Green and the Fairy Tree (Illus. by Leng, Qin)*
    c HB - v91 - i4 - July-August 2015 - p142(2) [51-500]
    c KR - June 15 2015 - pNA [501+]
    c PW - v262 - i24 - June 15 2015 - p85(1) [501+]
    c PW - v262 - i49 - Dec 2 2015 - p64(2) [501+]
    y SLJ - v61 - i7 - July 2015 - p72(1) [51-500]
Potter, Giselle - *Tell Me What to Dream About (Illus. by Potter, Giselle)*
    c BL - v111 - i14 - March 15 2015 - p80(1) [51-500]
    c CH Bwatch - May 2015 - pNA [501+]
    c HB Guide - v26 - i2 - Fall 2015 - p48(1) [51-500]
    c KR - Jan 15 2015 - pNA [501+]
    c NYTBR - June 21 2015 - p16(L) [501+]
    c PW - v262 - i6 - Feb 9 2015 - p64(1) [501+]
    c SLJ - v61 - i2 - Feb 2015 - p76(1) [501+]
Potter, Jesse - *Crisis at Work: Identity and the End of Career*
    TimHES - i2216 - August 13 2015 - p42-43 [501+]
Potter, Joan Monk - *Sweet Dreams*
    KR - Sept 1 2015 - pNA [501+]
Potter, Sarah - *Everybody Else: Adoption and the Politics of Domestic Diversity in Postwar America*
    CS - v44 - i2 - March 2015 - p292-293 [501+]
    JAH - v102 - i2 - Sept 2015 - p599-600 [501+]
Potter, Simon J. - *Broadcasting Empire: The BBC and the British World, 1922-1970*
    JMH - v87 - i1 - March 2015 - p183(2) [501+]
    T&C - v56 - i3 - July 2015 - p770-772 [501+]
Potter, Wendell - *Nation on the Take: How Big Money Corrupts Our Democracy and What We Can Do about It*
    BL - v112 - i7 - Dec 1 2015 - p6(1) [51-500]
    KR - Nov 15 2015 - pNA [501+]
    PW - v262 - i52 - Dec 21 2015 - p142(2) [51-500]
Potts, D.T. - *Nomadism in Iran: From Antiquity to the Modern Era*
    JNES - v74 - i1 - April 2015 - p144(2) [51-500]
Potts, Sue Davis - *Get Fit with Video Workouts*
    BL - v111 - i9-10 - Jan 1 2015 - p84(1) [51-500]
Potzsch, Oliver - *The Werewolf of Bamberg*
    BL - v112 - i6 - Nov 15 2015 - p29(2) [51-500]
    KR - Oct 15 2015 - pNA [501+]
    LJ - v140 - i19 - Nov 15 2015 - p80(1) [51-500]
Poucher, Judith G. - *State of Defiance: Challenging the Johns Committee's Assault on Civil Liberties*
    JAH - v101 - i4 - March 2015 - p1318-1319 [501+]
Pouillon, Nora - *My Organic Life: How a Pioneering Chef Helped Shape the Way We Eat Today*
    BL - v111 - i14 - March 15 2015 - p36(1) [51-500]
    KR - Feb 1 2015 - pNA [501+]
Poulenc, Francis - *Articles and Interviews: Notes from the Heart*
    TLS - i5842 - March 20 2015 - p24(1) [501+]
Poulsen, David A. - *Numbers*
    y BL - v112 - i5 - Nov 1 2015 - p56(1) [501+]
Poulton, Dionne Wright - *It's Not Always Racist ... But Sometimes It Is*
    KR - June 15 2015 - pNA [501+]
Pounder, Sibeal - *Witch Wars (Illus. by Anderson, Laura Ellen)*
    c KR - Oct 1 2015 - pNA [501+]
    c Sch Lib - v63 - i2 - Summer 2015 - p108(1) [51-500]
    c SLJ - v61 - i9 - Sept 2015 - p145(1) [501+]
    c BL - v112 - i4 - Oct 15 2015 - p59(1) [501+]
Pounds, Robbi - *Rubble Fever*
    KR - Nov 15 2015 - pNA [501+]
Pournelle, Jerry - *Lord of Janissaries*
    Bwatch - Nov 2015 - pNA [51-500]
Pouroulis, Anita - *Nina Goes Barking Mad! (Illus. by Krawczyk, Agata)*
    c Sch Lib - v63 - i3 - Autumn 2015 - p160(1) [51-500]
Poursat, J.C. - *Fouilles executees a Malia. Le Quartier Mu V. Vie quotidienne at techniques au Minoen Moyen II*
    Class R - v65 - i2 - Oct 2015 - p556-558 [501+]
Powell, Allen Kent - *Nels Anderson's World War I Diary*
    J Mil H - v79 - i4 - Oct 2015 - p1171-1173 [501+]
Powell, Allison Markin - *Last Winter, We Parted*
    RVBW - July 2015 - pNA [501+]
Powell, Anthony - *A Dance to the Music of Time*
    BL - v111 - i9-10 - Jan 1 2015 - p120(1) [501+]
Powell, Anton - *Hindsight in Greek and Roman History*
    Class R - v65 - i2 - Oct 2015 - p512-514 [501+]
Powell, Caleb - *I Think You're Totally Wrong: A Quarrel*
    CSM - Jan 9 2015 - pNA [501+]
Powell, Corey S. - *Unstoppable: Harnessing Science to Change the World*
    LJ - v140 - i20 - Dec 1 2015 - p126(2) [501+]

Powell, Eve Troutt - *Tell This in My Memory: Stories of Enslavement from Egypt, Sudan, and the Ottoman Empire*
    Historian - v77 - i2 - Summer 2015 - p319(2) [501+]
Powell, Holly - *The Audition Bible*
    SPBW - March 2015 - pNA [501+]
Powell, Huw - *The Last Sword*
    c KR - Nov 15 2015 - pNA [51-500]
Spacejackers
    c BL - v111 - i18 - May 15 2015 - p68(1) [51-500]
    c BL - v112 - i1 - Sept 1 2015 - p114(1) [501+]
    c HB Guide - v26 - i2 - Fall 2015 - p97(1) [51-500]
    c KR - March 15 2015 - pNA [501+]
    c Sch Lib - v63 - i1 - Spring 2015 - p41(1) [51-500]
    c SLJ - v61 - i3 - March 2015 - p142(1) [51-500]
Powell, James Lawrence - *Four Revolutions in the Earth Sciences: From Heresy to Truth*
    Nature - v518 - i7537 - Feb 5 2015 - p33(1) [51-500]
Powell, Jason - *Authority and Diplomacy from Dante to Shakespeare*
    Six Ct J - v46 - i2 - Summer 2015 - p404-405 [501+]
Powell, Jessie Bishop - *The Case of the Red-Handed Thesus*
    KR - Sept 15 2015 - pNA [501+]
Powell, Jillian - *China*
    c HB Guide - v26 - i1 - Spring 2015 - p202(1) [51-500]
Egypt
    c HB Guide - v26 - i1 - Spring 2015 - p202(1) [51-500]
India
    c HB Guide - v26 - i1 - Spring 2015 - p202(1) [51-500]
Powell, Jonathan - *Talking to Terrorists: How to End Armed Conflicts*
    TLS - i5834 - Jan 23 2015 - p24(1) [501+]
Terrorists at the Table: Why Negotiating is the Only Way to Peace
    KR - April 1 2015 - pNA [501+]
    LJ - v140 - i10 - June 1 2015 - p122(1) [51-500]
    PW - v262 - i15 - April 13 2015 - p70(1) [51-500]
Powell, Kelley - *The Merit Birds*
    y BL - v111 - i17 - May 1 2015 - p92(1) [51-500]
    y Res Links - v20 - i3 - Feb 2015 - p33(2) [501+]
    SLJ - v61 - i4 - April 2015 - p169(2) [51-500]
Powell, Kevin (b. 1966-) - *The Education of Kevin Powell: A Boy's Journey into Manhood*
    KR - August 15 2015 - pNA [501+]
    PW - v262 - i37 - Sept 14 2015 - p57(2) [51-500]
Powell, Kevin M. - *A Strengths-Based Approach for Intervention with At-Risk Youth*
    RVBW - Sept 2015 - pNA [51-500]
Powell, Larry - *Dark Money, Stiper PACs, and the 2012 Election*
    Pres St Q - v45 - i4 - Dec 2015 - p823(3) [501+]
Powell, Lynn - *Planting My Values (Illus. by Thinkstock)*
    c CH Bwatch - August 2015 - pNA [51-500]
Powell, Marie - *Don't Trip, Pip! (Illus. by Cartwright, Amy)*
    c HB Guide - v26 - i2 - Fall 2015 - p161(2) [51-500]
Get Wet! (Illus. by Cartwright, Amy)
    c HB Guide - v26 - i2 - Fall 2015 - p161(2) [51-500]
Native Nations of the Arctic and Subarctic
    c CH Bwatch - Oct 2015 - pNA [51-500]
Not a Lot, Robot! (Illus. by Cartwright, Amy)
    c HB Guide - v26 - i2 - Fall 2015 - p161(2) [51-500]
Please Take Jake! (Illus. by Cartwright, Amy)
    c HB Guide - v26 - i2 - Fall 2015 - p161(2) [51-500]
Quit It! (Illus. by Cartwright, Amy)
    c HB Guide - v26 - i2 - Fall 2015 - p161(2) [51-500]
Stay, Kay!
    c HB Guide - v26 - i2 - Fall 2015 - p161(2) [51-500]
Unsolved
    c Res Links - v20 - i5 - June 2015 - p14(2) [51-500]
Powell, Mark Allan - *Jesus as a Figure in History: How Modern Historians View the Man from Galilee*
    BTB - v45 - i2 - May 2015 - p118(2) [501+]
Powell, Mike - *Information Management for Development Organisations*
    JTWS - v32 - i1 - Spring 2015 - p365(12) [501+]
Powell, Nate - *You Don't Say: Stories 2004-2013 (Illus. by Powell, Nate)*
    y BL - v111 - i18 - May 15 2015 - p43(1) [51-500]
    PW - v262 - i14 - April 6 2015 - p47(1) [51-500]
Powell, Padgett - *Cries for Help, Various: Stories*
    KR - July 1 2015 - pNA [51-500]
    NYTBR - Oct 4 2015 - p19(L) [501+]
    PW - v262 - i26 - June 29 2015 - p41(1) [51-500]

Powell, Patricia Hruby - *Josephine: The Dazzling Life of Josephine Baker (Illus. by Robinson, Christian)*
   c HB - v91 - i1 - Jan-Feb 2015 - p26(1) [51-500]
Powell, Simon G. - *Magic Mushroom Explorer: Psilocybin and the Awakening Earth*
     RVBW - May 2015 - pNA [51-500]
Powell-Tuck, Maudie - *Pirates Aren't Afraid of the Dark! (Illus. by Edgson, Alison)*
   c HB Guide - v26 - i1 - Spring 2015 - p14(1) [51-500]
Pumpkin Party! (Illus. by Guile, Gill)
   c KR - Jan 1 2016 - pNA [51-500]
   c PW - v262 - i30 - July 27 2015 - p66(1) [501+]
Powell, V.K. - *Side Effects*
     PW - v262 - i27 - July 6 2015 - p53(1) [51-500]
Powell, William Campbell - *Expiration Day*
   y HB Guide - v26 - i1 - Spring 2015 - p120(1) [51-500]
Power, Amanda - *Roger Bacon and the Defence of Christendom*
     CHR - v101 - i3 - Summer 2015 - p625(3) [501+]
     JR - Jan 2015 - p129(3) [501+]
Power, Andrew J. - *Late Shakespeare, 1608-1613*
     MLR - v110 - i3 - July 2015 - p822-823 [501+]
     Ren Q - v68 - i1 - Spring 2015 - p403-404 [501+]
Power, Carla - *If the Oceans Were Ink: An Unlikely Friendship and a Journey to the Heart of the Qur'an*
     BL - v111 - i13 - March 1 2015 - p6(1) [51-500]
     KR - Jan 1 2015 - pNA [501+]
     PW - v262 - i4 - Jan 26 2015 - p158(1) [51-500]
Power-Greene, Ousmane K. - *Against Wind and Tide: The African American Struggle against the Colonization Movement*
     AHR - v120 - i3 - June 2015 - p1025-1026 [501+]
     JAH - v102 - i2 - Sept 2015 - p550-550 [501+]
     JIH - v46 - i3 - Wntr 2016 - p460-461 [501+]
Power-Relationships in Court Societies: Marriage, Concubinage, Friendship, Kinship, and Patronage in Historical Perspective: International Research Workshop
     HNet - May 2015 - pNA [501+]
Power, Tristan - *Suetonius the Biographer: Studies in Roman Lives*
     HNet - Feb 2015 - pNA [501+]
     TLS - i5837 - Feb 13 2015 - p11(1) [501+]
Powers, Devon - *Writing the Record: The Village Voice and the Birth of Rock Criticism*
     CS - v44 - i1 - Jan 2015 - p145-146 [501+]
Powers, J.L. - *Amina*
   y BL - v111 - i18 - May 15 2015 - p53(1) [51-500]
   y KR - April 15 2015 - pNA [51-500]
   y Sch Lib - v63 - i1 - Spring 2015 - p57(1) [51-500]
Colors of the Wind: The Story of Blind Artist and Champion Runner George Mendoza (Illus. by Mendoza, George)
   c CH Bwatch - Jan 2015 - pNA [51-500]
   c HB Guide - v26 - i1 - Spring 2015 - p179(1) [51-500]
Powers, Jane - *The Irish Garden*
     RVBW - June 2015 - pNA [51-500]
Powers, Kevin - *The Yellow Birds*
     HM - v331 - i1983 - August 2015 - p84(6) [501+]
Powers, Kim - *Dig Two Graves*
     BL - v112 - i4 - Oct 15 2015 - p20(1) [51-500]
     KR - Sept 15 2015 - pNA [51-500]
     PW - v262 - i41 - Oct 12 2015 - p49(1) [51-500]
Powers, Kirsten - *The Silencing: How the Left Is Killing Free Speech*
     Bwatch - August 2015 - pNA [51-500]
     Nat R - v67 - i13 - July 20 2015 - p38 [501+]
     Prog - v79 - i7-8 - July-August 2015 - p59(3) [501+]
Powers, Thomas - *American Carnage: Wounded Knee, 1890*
     WHQ - v46 - i2 - Summer 2015 - p251-252 [501+]
Powers, Tim - *Medusa's Web*
     BL - v112 - i7 - Dec 1 2015 - p38(1) [51-500]
Powers, William - *New Slow City: Living Simply in the World's Fastest City*
     RVBW - Feb 2015 - pNA [51-500]
Powery, Luke A. - *Dem Dry Bones: Preaching, Death, and Hope*
     CC - v132 - i19 - Sept 16 2015 - p30(4) [501+]
Powning, Beth - *Home: Chronicles of a North Country Life*
     Can Lit - i224 - Spring 2015 - p129 [501+]
Powys, Llewelyn - *Earth Memories*
     TLS - i5863 - August 14 2015 - p8(1) [501+]
Poyer, David - *Tipping Point*
     BL - v112 - i3 - Oct 1 2015 - p26(1) [51-500]
     Ch Today - v59 - i10 - Dec 2015 - p70(1) [51-500]
     KR - Sept 15 2015 - pNA [51-500]
     PW - v262 - i37 - Sept 14 2015 - p40(1) [51-500]

Poyiadgi, Andy - *Lost Property (Illus. by Poyiadgi, Andy)*
   c KR - May 1 2015 - pNA [51-500]
Poyo, Gerald E. - *Exile and Revolution: Jose' D. Poyo, Key West, and Cuban Independence*
     JSH - v81 - i4 - Nov 2015 - p1008(2) [501+]
Pozorski, Aimee - *Falling after 9/11: Crisis in American Art and Literature*
     TLS - i5849 - May 8 2015 - p26(2) [501+]
Pozrikidis, Constantine - *Introduction to Finite and Spectral Element Methods Using MATLAB*
     SIAM Rev - v57 - i1 - March 2015 - p161-161 [501+]
Prachett, Terry - *Raising Steam*
     TimHES - i2187 - Jan 22 2015 - p49(1) [501+]
The Practices of Structural Policy in Western Market Economies since the 1960s
     HNet - July 2015 - pNA [501+]
Prado, Ignacio M. Sanchez - *Screening Neoliberalism: Transforming Mexican Cinema 1988-2012*
     Ams - v72 - i2 - April 2015 - p338(2) [501+]
Prager, Ellen - *Sea Slime: It's Eeuwy, Gooey, and Under the Sea (Illus. by Bersani, Shennen)*
   c HB Guide - v26 - i1 - Spring 2015 - p156(1) [51-500]
Prager, Jeffrey Kenneth - *Managing Your Business with 7 Key Numbers*
     SPBW - Sept 2015 - pNA [51-500]
Prain, Leanne - *Strange Material: Storytelling through Textiles*
     LJ - v140 - i2 - Feb 1 2015 - p85(1) [501+]
Prak, Maarten - *Technology, Skills and the Pre-Modern Economy in the East and the West*
     HNet - April 2015 - pNA [501+]
     JEH - v75 - i1 - March 2015 - p268-270 [501+]
Prakash, A.K. - *Impressionism in Canada: A Journey of Rediscovery*
     Apo - v181 - i631 - May 2015 - p103(1) [51-500]
Prakash, Saikrishna Bangalore - *Imperial from the Beginning: The Constitution of the Original Executive*
     Pres St Q - v45 - i4 - Dec 2015 - p821(3) [501+]
Prakash, Uday - *The Walls of Delhi*
     WLT - v89 - i1 - Jan-Feb 2015 - p75(1) [51-500]
Pramuk, Christopher - *Hope Sings, So Beautiful: Graced Encounters across the Color Line*
     JR - v95 - i4 - Oct 2015 - p579(2) [501+]
Prange, Martine - *Nietzsche, Wagner, Europe*
     GSR - v38 - i2 - May 2015 - p421-3 [501+]
Prap, Lila - *Cat Whys*
   c HB Guide - v26 - i2 - Fall 2015 - p182(1) [51-500]
Dinosaurs?! (Illus. by Prap, Lila)
   c CCB-B - v69 - i1 - Sept 2015 - p44(2) [51-500]
Prasad, Amit - *Imperial Technoscience: Transnational Histories of MRI in the United States, Britain, and India*
     T&C - v56 - i2 - April 2015 - p562-563 [501+]
Prasad, Monica - *The Land of Too Much: American Abundance and the Paradox of Poverty*
     CS - v44 - i3 - May 2015 - p404-406 [501+]
     CS - v44 - i4 - July 2015 - p449-462 [501+]
     SF - v94 - i2 - Dec 2015 - pNA [501+]
Prasad, Vinayak K. - *Ending Medical Reversal*
     NYT - Nov 3 2015 - pD3(L) [501+]
Prasadam-Halls, Smitri - *Pumpkins, Pumpkins Everywhere (Illus. by Alvarez, Lorena)*
   c PW - v262 - i30 - July 27 2015 - p67(2) [51-500]
Prasadam-Halls, Smriti - *My Alien and Me (Illus. by McLaughlin, Tom)*
   c Sch Lib - v63 - i4 - Winter 2015 - p222(1) [51-500]
Prashad, Vijay - *The Poorer Nations: A Possible History of the Global South*
     Am Q - v67 - i1 - March 2015 - p219-229 [501+]
Pratchett, Terry - *A Blink of the Screen: Collected Shorter Fiction*
   y BL - v111 - i12 - Feb 15 2015 - p45(1) [51-500]
     KR - Jan 15 2015 - pNA [51-500]
     NYTBR - May 31 2015 - p38(L) [501+]
     PW - v262 - i5 - Feb 2 2015 - p40(1) [51-500]
Darwin's Watch: The Science of Discworld III
   y BL - v111 - i19-20 - June 1 2015 - p24(1) [51-500]
Dodger (Read by Briggs, Stephen). Audiobook Review
   y SLJ - v61 - i6 - June 2015 - p53(3) [501+]
Dragons at Crumbling Castle and Other Tales (Read by Rhind-Tutt, Julian). Audiobook Review
     PW - v262 - i17 - April 27 2015 - p72(1) [51-500]

Dragons at Crumbling Castle and Other Tales (Illus. by Beech, Mark)
   c CCB-B - v68 - i9 - May 2015 - p464(1) [51-500]
   c HB Guide - v26 - i2 - Fall 2015 - p97(2) [51-500]
   c Sch Lib - v63 - i1 - Spring 2015 - p42(1) [51-500]
   c SLJ - v61 - i2 - Feb 2015 - p92(1) [51-500]
The Shepherd's Crown (Read by Briggs, Stephen). Audiobook Review
   y BL - v112 - i7 - Dec 1 2015 - p71(2) [51-500]
The Shepherd's Crown
   y BL - v112 - i3 - Oct 1 2015 - p74(1) [51-500]
   y CSM - Sept 4 2015 - pNA [501+]
   y KR - Sept 15 2015 - pNA [51-500]
   y Magpies - v30 - i5 - Nov 2015 - p41(2) [501+]
   y PW - v262 - i49 - Dec 2 2015 - p108(1) [51-500]
   y Sch Lib - v63 - i4 - Winter 2015 - p249(1) [51-500]
   y SLJ - v61 - i10 - Oct 2015 - p106(1) [51-500]
A Slip of the Keyboard: Collected Nonfiction
     Analog - v135 - i4 - April 2015 - p107(1) [501+]
Pratt, Hugo - *Corto Maltese: Under the Sign of Capricorn*
     LJ - v140 - i5 - March 15 2015 - p88(3) [501+]
Pratt, J. Kristian - *The Father of Modern Landmarkism: The Life of Ben M. Bogard*
     JSH - v81 - i1 - Feb 2015 - p232(2) [501+]
Pratt, Joseph A. - *Energy Capitals: Local Impact, Global Influence*
     JAH - v101 - i4 - March 2015 - p1245(1) [501+]
     T&C - v56 - i4 - Oct 2015 - p1000-1001 [501+]
Pratt, Mary K. - *A Timeline History of the Thirteen Colonies*
   c HB Guide - v26 - i2 - Fall 2015 - p220(1) [51-500]
The US Army
   y HB Guide - v26 - i1 - Spring 2015 - p138(2) [51-500]
Pratt, Non - *Remix*
   y Sch Lib - v63 - i3 - Autumn 2015 - p190(1) [51-500]
Pratt, Zane - *Introduction to Global Missions*
     IBMR - v39 - i1 - Jan 2015 - p51(2) [501+]
Pravilova, Ekaterina - *A Public Empire: Property and the Quest for the Common Good in Imperial Russia*
     AHR - v120 - i3 - June 2015 - p1140-1141 [501+]
     Slav R - v74 - i2 - Summer 2015 - p357-360 [501+]
Prebble, John - *The Buffalo Soldiers*
     Roundup M - v22 - i3 - Feb 2015 - p13(1) [501+]
Prebble, Stuart - *The Insect Farm*
     BL - v111 - i19-20 - June 1 2015 - p54(1) [51-500]
     KR - May 15 2015 - pNA [51-500]
     LJ - v140 - i11 - June 15 2015 - p81(1) [51-500]
     PW - v262 - i18 - May 4 2015 - p98(1) [51-500]
Preble, Joy - *Finding Paris*
   y BL - v111 - i14 - March 15 2015 - p65(1) [51-500]
   y CCB-B - v68 - i10 - June 2015 - p510(1) [51-500]
   y HB Guide - v26 - i2 - Fall 2015 - p134(1) [51-500]
   y KR - Jan 15 2015 - pNA [51-500]
   y VOYA - v38 - i1 - April 2015 - p67(1) [51-500]
Prehn, Ulrich - *Max Hildebert Boehm: Radikales Ordnungsdenken vom Ersten Weltkrieg bis in die Bundesrepublik*
     HER - v130 - i543 - April 2015 - p499(2) [501+]
Preiss, Richard - *Clowning and Authorship in Early Modern Theatre*
     RES - v66 - i274 - April 2015 - p372-374 [501+]
Prelinger, Megan - *Inside the Machine: Art and Invention in the Electronic Age*
     KR - May 15 2015 - pNA [501+]
     Nature - v524 - i7564 - August 13 2015 - p159(1) [501+]
     PW - v262 - i13 - March 30 2015 - p64(1) [51-500]
     Reason - v47 - i8 - Jan 2016 - p54(1) [501+]
Preller, James - *The Fall*
   c BL - v111 - i21 - July 1 2015 - p72(1) [51-500]
   c KR - July 1 2015 - pNA [51-500]
   y SLJ - v61 - i7 - July 2015 - p88(1) [51-500]
   y VOYA - v38 - i3 - August 2015 - p67(1) [51-500]
Nightmareland (Illus. by Bruno, Iacopo)
   y HB Guide - v26 - i1 - Spring 2015 - p90(1) [51-500]
Premchand, A. - *Contemporary India: Society and Its Governance*
     CS - v44 - i5 - Sept 2015 - p692-693 [501+]
Prendergast, Gabrielle - *The Frail Days*
   y KR - Feb 15 2015 - pNA [51-500]
   y Res Links - v20 - i3 - Feb 2015 - p34(1) [501+]
   y VOYA - v38 - i1 - April 2015 - p64(2) [51-500]
Prendergast, Maria Theresa Micaela - *Railing, Reviling and Invective in English Literary Culture, 1588-1617:*

The Anti-Poetics of Theater and Print
    MLR - v110 - i2 - April 2015 - p526-527 [501+]
Prendergast, Stephanie A. - *Pelvic Pain Explained: What Everyone Needs to Know*
    BL - v112 - i7 - Dec 1 2015 - p20(1) [51-500]
Prentiss, Anna Marie - *People of the Middle Fraser Canyon: An Archaeological History*
    Am Ant - v80 - i1 - Jan 2015 - p212(2) [501+]
Prentiss, Craig R. - *Staging Faith: Religion and African American Theater from the Harlem Renaissance to World War II*
    CH - v84 - i2 - June 2015 - p466(3) [501+]
    JAH - v101 - i4 - March 2015 - p1309-1310 [501+]
Prentiss, Mara - *Energy Revolution: The Physics and the Promise of Efficient Technology*
    LJ - v140 - i7 - April 15 2015 - p116(2) [51-500]
    Nature - v518 - i7540 - Feb 26 2015 - p481(1) [51-500]
Prentiss, Sean - *Finding Abbey: The Search for Edward Abbey and His Hidden Desert Grave*
    KR - March 1 2015 - pNA [51-500]
    LJ - v140 - i11 - June 15 2015 - p109(2) [51-500]
    Roundup M - v23 - i1 - Oct 2015 - p35(1) [501+]
Prescott, Tara - *Neil Gaiman in the 21st Century: Essays on the Novels, Children's Stories, Online Writings, Comics and Other Works*
    LJ - v140 - i6 - April 1 2015 - p90(2) [51-500]
Press, Lowell H. - *The Kingdom of the Sun and Moon*
    c CH Bwatch - Feb 2015 - pNA [51-500]
Pressfield, Steven - *Gates of Fire*
    HT - v65 - i8 - August 2015 - p56(2) [501+]
The Lion's Gate: on the Front Lines of the Six Day War
    APH - v62 - i1 - Spring 2015 - p56(1) [501+]
Pressly, Paul M. - *On the Rim of the Caribbean: Colonial Georgia and the British Atlantic World*
    RAH - v43 - i1 - March 2015 - p26-31 [501+]
Pressman, Jessica - *Digital Modernism: Making it New in New Media*
    RES - v66 - i273 - Feb 2015 - p200-201 [501+]
Preston B.G. - *Obsidian Portal*
    SPBW - Nov 2015 - pNA [51-500]
Preston, Deborah Bray - *The Challenges of Being a Rural Gay Man: Coping with Stigma*
    CS - v44 - i4 - July 2015 - p543-545 [501+]
Preston, Diana - *A Higher Form of Killing: Six Weeks in World War I That Forever Changed the Nature of Warfare*
    BL - v111 - i11 - Feb 1 2015 - p12(2) [51-500]
    NYTBR - April 5 2015 - p12(L) [501+]
Lusitania: An Epic Tragedy
    Bwatch - July 2015 - pNA [51-500]
Preston, Douglas - *Blue Labyrinth (Read by Auberjonois, Rene). Audiobook Review*
    Bwatch - Feb 2015 - pNA [51-500]
    PW - v262 - i5 - Feb 2 2015 - p52(2) [51-500]
Crimson Shore
    KR - Sept 1 2015 - pNA [51-500]
Preston-Gannon, Frann - *Deep Deep Sea (Illus. by Preston-Gannon, Frann)*
    c BL - v111 - i19-20 - June 1 2015 - p110(1) [51-500]
    c KR - Jan 1 2016 - pNA [51-500]
    c PW - v262 - i20 - May 18 2015 - p82(2) [501+]
Pepper & Poe (Illus. by Preston-Gannon, Frann)
    c HB - v91 - i4 - July-August 2015 - p123(2) [51-500]
    c KR - May 1 2015 - pNA [51-500]
    c NYTBR - Oct 11 2015 - p17(L) [501+]
    c SLJ - v61 - i5 - May 2015 - p90(2) [51-500]
Sloth Slept On
    c KR - July 15 2015 - pNA [51-500]
What a Hoot!
    c PW - v262 - i20 - May 18 2015 - p82(2) [51-500]
Preston, Natasha - *Awake*
    y PW - v262 - i22 - June 1 2015 - p61(2) [51-500]
    y SLJ - v61 - i8 - August 2015 - p109(1) [51-500]
    y VOYA - v38 - i4 - Oct 2015 - p59(1) [51-500]
Preston, Paul - *The Last Stalinist: The Life of Santiago Carrillo*
    LJ - v140 - i2 - Feb 1 2015 - p95(2) [51-500]
    TLS - i5833 - Jan 16 2015 - p7(1) [501+]
Preston, Todd - *King Alfred's Book of Laws: A Study of the Domboc and Its Influence on English Identity*
    JEGP - v114 - i1 - Jan 2015 - p140(3) [501+]
    Specu - v90 - i1 - Jan 2015 - p291-292 [501+]
Prestowitz, Clyde - *Japan Restored: How Japan Can Reinvent Itself and Why This Is Important for America and the World*
    BL - v111 - i22 - August 1 2015 - p8(1) [51-500]
    LJ - v140 - i15 - Sept 15 2015 - p92(1) [51-500]
    PW - v262 - i33 - August 17 2015 - p59(1) [51-500]
Preus, Margi - *The Bamboo Sword*
    y BL - v111 - i19-20 - June 1 2015 - p94(2) [51-500]
    c HB - v91 - i6 - Nov-Dec 2015 - p88(1) [51-500]
    c KR - June 1 2015 - pNA [51-500]
    c PW - v262 - i26 - June 29 2015 - p69(1) [51-500]
    c SLJ - v61 - i8 - August 2015 - p89(3) [51-500]
    y VOYA - v38 - i4 - Oct 2015 - p59(1) [51-500]
Enchantment Lake
    y BL - v111 - i12 - Feb 15 2015 - p80(1) [51-500]
    c CCB-B - v69 - i1 - Sept 2015 - p45(1) [51-500]
    y HB Guide - v26 - i2 - Fall 2015 - p134(1) [51-500]
    y KR - Jan 15 2015 - pNA [51-500]
    c PW - v262 - i4 - Jan 26 2015 - p170(1) [51-500]
    y SLJ - v61 - i3 - March 2015 - p142(2) [51-500]
    y VOYA - v38 - i1 - April 2015 - p67(1) [51-500]
Heart of a Samurai
    y BL - v111 - i19-20 - June 1 2015 - p86(2) [501+]
West of the Moon
    c BL - v111 - i9-10 - Jan 1 2015 - pS4(8) [501+]
    y Teach Lib - v42 - i3 - Feb 2015 - p32(6) [501+]
    y Magpies - v30 - i2 - May 2015 - p39(1) [501+]
Prevette, Bill - *Child, Church, and Compassion: Towards Child Theology in Romania*
    IBMR - v39 - i4 - Oct 2015 - p238(2) [501+]
Prevot, Franck - *Wangari Maathai: The Woman Who Planted Millions of Trees (Illus. by Fronty, Aurelia)*
    c BL - v111 - i12 - Feb 15 2015 - p76(1) [501+]
    c CCB-B - v68 - i6 - Feb 2015 - p326(1) [51-500]
Wangari Maathai: The Woman Who Planted Millions of Trees (Illus. by Clement, Dominique)
    c PW - v262 - i49 - Dec 2 2015 - p51(1) [51-500]
Wangari Maathai: The Woman Who Planted Millions of Trees (Illus. by Fronty, Aurelia)
    c HB Guide - v26 - i2 - Fall 2015 - p211(1) [51-500]
    c PW - v262 - i3 - Jan 19 2015 - p80(1) [51-500]
Prewitt, J. Everett - *The Long Way Back*
    KR - Sept 1 2015 - pNA [51-500]
Prez, Ashley Hope - *Out of Darkness*
    y NYTBR - Nov 8 2015 - p32(L) [501+]
Price, Asher - *Year of the Dunk: A Modest Defiance of Gravity*
    BL - v111 - i13 - March 1 2015 - p15(1) [51-500]
    KR - March 15 2015 - pNA [51-500]
    PW - v262 - i8 - Feb 23 2015 - p64(1) [51-500]
Price, Ben Joel - *Earth Space Moon Base*
    c HB Guide - v26 - i1 - Spring 2015 - p42(1) [51-500]
In the Deep Dark Deep (Illus. by Price, Ben Joel)
    c KR - May 15 2015 - pNA [51-500]
    c SLJ - v61 - i10 - Oct 2015 - p82(1) [51-500]
Price, Catherine - *Vitamania: Our Obsessive Quest for Nutritional Perfection*
    NYT - March 3 2015 - pD5(L) [51-500]
Price, Charlie - *Dead Investigation*
    y KR - August 15 2015 - pNA [51-500]
    y SLJ - v61 - i10 - Oct 2015 - p116(1) [51-500]
Price, Gin - *On Edge*
    c KR - Dec 1 2015 - pNA [51-500]
    y PW - v262 - i46 - Nov 16 2015 - p77(1) [51-500]
Price, Huw - *Expressivism, Pragmatism and Representationalism*
    Dialogue - v54 - i3 - Sept 2015 - p573-576 [501+]
Price, Jay M. - *Temples for a Modern God: Religious Architecture in Postwar America*
    JR - Jan 2015 - p148(2) [501+]
Price, Joan - *The Ultimate Guide to Sex after Fifty: How to Maintain--or Regain--a Spicy, Satisfying Sex Life*
    RVBW - March 2015 - pNA [51-500]
Price, Jordan Castillo - *Charmed and Dangerous: Ten Tales of Gay Paranormal Romance and Urban Fantasy*
    PW - v262 - i47 - Nov 23 2015 - p57(1) [51-500]
Price, Lance - *The Modi Effect: Inside Narendra Modi's Campaign to Transform India*
    Lon R Bks - v37 - i17 - Sept 10 2015 - p33(2) [501+]
    NS - v144 - i5257 - April 10 2015 - p50(1) [51-500]
Price, Richard - *The Whites*
    NYTBR - Feb 15 2015 - p1(L) [501+]
Price-Spratlen, Townsand - *Reconstructing Rage: Transformative Reentry in the Era of Mass Incarceration*
    CS - v44 - i1 - Jan 2015 - p109-110 [501+]
Price, Wayne - *The Mercy Seat*
    NS - v144 - i5258 - April 17 2015 - p61(1) [51-500]
Prickett, Stephen - *The Edinburgh Companion to the Bible and the Arts*
    IBMR - v39 - i3 - July 2015 - p165(1) [501+]
Priebe, Craig - *The United States of Pizza: America's Favorite Pizzas, from Thin Crust to Deep Dish, to Sourdough and Gluten-Free*
    NYTBR - Dec 6 2015 - pNA(L) [501+]
Priess, David - *The President's Book of Secrets*
    KR - Dec 1 2015 - pNA [501+]
Priest, Alicia - *A Rock Fell on the Moon: Dad and the Great Yukon Silver Ore Heist*
    Beav - v95 - i2 - April-May 2015 - p55(2) [501+]
    RVBW - Jan 2015 - pNA [501+]
Priest, Cherie - *Chapelwood*
    PW - v262 - i31 - August 3 2015 - p40(1) [51-500]
I Am Princess X (Illus. by Ciesemier, Kali)
    y PW - v262 - i13 - March 30 2015 - p77(1) [51-500]
    y BL - v111 - i14 - March 15 2015 - p68(1) [51-500]
    c BL - v111 - i17 - May 1 2015 - p40(1) [51-500]
    c CCB-B - v69 - i1 - Sept 2015 - p45(1) [51-500]
    y HB Guide - v26 - i2 - Fall 2015 - p135(1) [51-500]
    y KR - March 15 2015 - pNA [51-500]
    y PW - v262 - i49 - Dec 2 2015 - p112(2) [51-500]
    y SLJ - v61 - i4 - April 2015 - p157(1) [51-500]
    c Teach Lib - v42 - i5 - June 2015 - p15(1) [51-500]
Maplecroft (Read by Parker, Johanna)
    LJ - v140 - i5 - March 15 2015 - p72(1) [51-500]
Priest, Robert - *Second Kiss*
    c Res Links - v20 - i3 - Feb 2015 - p34(1) [51-500]
Priestley, Chris - *Anything That Isn't This*
    y Magpies - v30 - i5 - Nov 2015 - p42(1) [501+]
The Last of the Spirits
    c Sch Lib - v63 - i1 - Spring 2015 - p57(1) [51-500]
    c Spec - v329 - i9772 - Dec 12 2015 - p77(1) [501+]
Priestley, Jessica - *Herodotus and Hellenistic Culture: Literary Studies in the Reception of "Histories"*
    TLS - i5843 - March 27 2015 - p10(2) [501+]
Priestman, Martin - *The Poetry of Erasmus Darwin: Enlightened Spaces, Romantic Times*
    RES - v66 - i275 - June 2015 - p583-585 [501+]
    TLS - i5833 - Jan 16 2015 - p5(1) [501+]
Prieto, Eric - *Litterature, Geography, and the Postmodern Poetics of Place*
    FS - v69 - i2 - April 2015 - p275-276 [501+]
Priewe, Marc - *Textualizing Illness: Medicine and Culture in New England, 1620-1730*
    AHR - v120 - i4 - Oct 2015 - p1474-1475 [501+]
Prigge, Matthew J. - *Milwaukee Mayhem: Murder and Mystery in the Cream City's First Century*
    PW - v262 - i25 - June 22 2015 - p132(1) [51-500]
Prill, Scott Douglas - *Into the Realm of Time*
    KR - Sept 15 2015 - pNA [501+]
Primack, Richard B. - *Essentials of Conservation Biology*
    QRB - v90 - i4 - Dec 2015 - p434(1) [501+]
Walden Warming: Climate Change Comes to Walden Woods
    NEQ - v88 - i1 - March 2015 - p149-158 [501+]
Primavera, Elise - *Ms. Rapscott's Girls (Read by Kellgren, Katherine). Audiobook Review*
    c SLJ - v61 - i7 - July 2015 - p47(1) [51-500]
Ms. Rapscott's Girls (Illus. by Primavera, Elise)
    c BL - v111 - i9-10 - Jan 1 2015 - p101(2) [51-500]
    c HB Guide - v26 - i2 - Fall 2015 - p98(1) [51-500]
    c NYTBR - May 10 2015 - p25(L) [501+]
Prime, Rebecca - *Hollywood Exiles in Europe: The Blacklist and Cold War Film Culture*
    AHR - v120 - i1 - Feb 2015 - p199(1) [501+]
Primm, Beny J. - *The Healer*
    KR - March 15 2015 - pNA [501+]
Prince, K. Stephen - *Stories of the South: Race and the Reconstruction of Southern Identity, 1865-1915*
    AHR - v120 - i3 - June 2015 - p1030-1031 [501+]
    AHR - v120 - i3 - June 2015 - p1030-1031 [501+]
    HNet - March 2015 - pNA [501+]
    JAH - v101 - i4 - March 2015 - p1280-1281 [501+]
Prince, Liz - *Tomboy: A Graphic Memoir (Illus. by Prince, Liz)*
    y HB - v91 - i1 - Jan-Feb 2015 - p102(2) [51-500]
    y HB Guide - v26 - i1 - Spring 2015 - p195(1) [51-500]
Prince, Ruth J. - *Making and Unmaking Public Health in Africa: Ethnographic and Historical Perspectives*
    IJAHS - v48 - i1 - Wntr 2015 - p137-138 [501+]
    MAQ - v29 - i2 - June 2015 - pb28-b30 [501+]
Prince, Sue Ann - *Of Elephants and Roses: French Natural History, 1790-1830*
    Isis - v106 - i2 - June 2015 - p457(2) [501+]
Prince, T.M. - *Leeching the Sirens*
    c BL - v112 - i7 - Dec 1 2015 - p34(2) [501+]
Princenthal, Nancy - *Agnes Martin: Her Life and Art*
    Art N - v114 - i6 - June 2015 - p77(1) [501+]
    BL - v111 - i19-20 - June 1 2015 - p26(1) [51-

500]
    KR - March 15 2015 - pNA [51-500]
    TLS - i5867 - Sept 11 2015 - p17(3) [501+]
Principe, Lawrence - *The Secrets of Alchemy*
    Historian - v77 - i1 - Spring 2015 - p187(2) [501+]
Prineas, Sarah - *Ash & Bramble*
  y BL - v112 - i2 - Sept 15 2015 - p70(1) [51-500]
  y KR - June 15 2015 - pNA [51-500]
  y SLJ - v61 - i7 - July 2015 - p97(1) [51-500]
  y VOYA - v38 - i4 - Oct 2015 - p76(2) [51-500]
The Magic Thief: Home (Illus. by Caparo, Antonio Javier)
  c HB Guide - v26 - i1 - Spring 2015 - p90(1) [51-500]
Pringle, Laurence - *Octopuses! Strange and Wonderful (Illus. by Henderson, Meryl)*
  c BL - v111 - i12 - Feb 15 2015 - p70(2) [51-500]
  c HB - v91 - i2 - March-April 2015 - p123(2) [51-500]
  c HB Guide - v26 - i2 - Fall 2015 - p174(1) [51-500]
  c KR - Jan 15 2015 - pNA [51-500]
The Secret Life of the Woolly Bear Caterpillar (Illus. by Paley, Joan)
  c HB Guide - v26 - i1 - Spring 2015 - p159(1) [51-500]
Prinja, Raman - *Mon guide du del et des etoiles*
  c Res Links - v20 - i5 - June 2015 - p43(2) [501+]
Prins, Marcel - *Hidden: True Stories of Children Who Survived World War II*
  Sch Lib - v63 - i2 - Summer 2015 - p112(2) [501+]
Prinster, Tari - *Yoga for Cancer: A Guide to Managing Side Effects, Boosting Immunity, and Improving Recovery for Cancer Survivors*
  Bwatch - Feb 2015 - pNA [51-500]
Printy, Jen - *My Soul Immortal*
  PW - v262 - i5 - Feb 2 2015 - p44(1) [51-500]
Prinz, Jesse - *The Conscious Brain: How Attention Engenders Experience*
  Phil R - v124 - i1 - Jan 2015 - p163(5) [501+]
Prinz, Yvonne - *If You're Lucky*
  c BL - v112 - i1 - Sept 1 2015 - p103(2) [51-500]
  y KR - August 15 2015 - pNA [51-500]
  y PW - v262 - i29 - July 20 2015 - p194(2) [51-500]
  y SLJ - v61 - i9 - Sept 2015 - p170(2) [51-500]
  y VOYA - v38 - i4 - Oct 2015 - p59(1) [51-500]
Prior, Karen Swallow - *Fierce Convictions: The Extraordinary Life of Hannah More*
  Bks & Cult - v21 - i1 - Jan-Feb 2015 - p32(1) [501+]
Prior, Loani - *Pretty Funny Tea Cosies and Other Beautiful Knitted Things*
  BL - v111 - i21 - July 1 2015 - p15(2) [51-500]
Prior, Mark E. - *Shadowlands*
  SPBW - Feb 2015 - pNA [51-500]
Prior, Robin - *Churchill's 'World Crisis' as History*
  HT - v65 - i1 - Jan 2015 - p56(2) [501+]
Pritchard, Forrest - *Growing Tomorrow: A Farm-to-Table Journey in Photos and Recipes: Behind the Scenes with 18 Extraordinary Sustainable Farmers Who Are Changing the Way We Eat*
  LJ - v140 - i15 - Sept 15 2015 - p96(1) [51-500]
Pritchard, John - *Methodists and Their Missionary Societies, 1760-1900*
  CH - v84 - i1 - March 2015 - p251(3) [501+]
Pritchard, Melissa - *A Solemn Pleasure: To Imagine, Witness, and Write*
  KR - March 1 2015 - pNA [501+]
  LJ - v140 - i7 - April 15 2015 - p84(2) [51-500]
Solemn Pleasure: To Imagine, Witness, and Write
  PW - v262 - i11 - March 16 2015 - p75(1) [501+]
Pritchett, Georgia - *Wilf the Mighty Worrier: Saves the World (Illus. by Littler, Jamie)*
  c KR - August 15 2015 - pNA [51-500]
  c PW - v262 - i38 - Sept 21 2015 - p77(1) [501+]
  c SLJ - v61 - i7 - July 2015 - p72(1) [51-500]
Pritchett, Laura - *Red Lighting*
  BL - v111 - i17 - May 1 2015 - p77(1) [51-500]
Red Lightning
  LJ - v140 - i9 - May 15 2015 - p76(2) [51-500]
Pritz, Alan L. - *Meditation as a Way of Life: Philosophy and Practice*
  RVBW - March 2015 - pNA [51-500]
Pritzker, Olivia Batker - *House of Harwood*
  KR - April 1 2015 - pNA [501+]
Pritzker, Sonya E. - *Living Translation: Language and the Search for Resonance in U.S. Chinese Medicine*
  MAQ - v29 - i3 - Sept 2015 - pb-1-b-4 [501+]
Prizant, Barry M. - *Uniquely Human: A Different Way of Seeing Autism (Read by Ochlan, P.J.). Audiobook Review*
  BL - v112 - i3 - Oct 1 2015 - p86(1) [51-500]
  BL - v112 - i7 - Dec 1 2015 - p71(1) [501+]

Uniquely Human: A Different Way of Seeing Autism
  BL - v111 - i22 - August 1 2015 - p13(1) [501+]
  KR - June 1 2015 - pNA [501+]
  LJ - v140 - i13 - August 1 2015 - p113(1) [51-500]
  Nature - v523 - i7562 - July 30 2015 - pSB2(1) [501+]
Probst, Christopher J. - *Demonizing the Jews: Luther and the Protestant Church in Nazi Germany*
  HNet - Jan 2015 - pNA [501+]
Processes of Social Decline among the European Nobility
  HNet - Jan 2015 - pNA [501+]
Prochaska, Frank - *Eminent Victorians on American Democracy: The View from Albion*
  VS - v57 - i2 - Wntr 2015 - p354(4) [501+]
Prochnik, George - *The Impossible Exile: Stefan Zweig at the End of the World*
  NYTBR - Oct 18 2015 - p28(L) [501+]
  TLS - i5841 - March 13 2015 - p12(1) [501+]
Proctor, Alan Robert - *The Sweden File: Memoir of an American Expatriate*
  KR - Nov 15 2015 - pNA [501+]
Proctor, Bob - *The ABCs of Success: The Essential Principles from America's Greatest Prosperity Teacher*
  LJ - v140 - i11 - June 15 2015 - p104(1) [51-500]
Proctor, Robert (b. 1973-) - *Building the Modern Church: Roman Catholic Church Architecture in Britain, 1955 to 1975*
  CH - v84 - i4 - Dec 2015 - p922(2) [51-500]
Prodan, Sarah Rolfe - *Michelangelo's Christian Mysticism: Spirituality, Poetry and Art in Sixteenth-Century Italy*
  CHR - v101 - i3 - Summer 2015 - p644(3) [501+]
Produkte und Produktinnovationen. 37. Technikgeschichtliche Tagung der Eisenbibliothek
  HNet - April 2015 - pNA [501+]
Proescholdt, Kevin - *Glimpses of Wilderness*
  RVBW - August 2015 - pNA [51-500]
Proffet, Paul - *Crossover*
  KR - March 1 2015 - pNA [501+]
Progler, Daniela - *English Students at Leiden University, 1575-1650: Advancing Your Abilities in Learning and Bettering Your Understanding of the World and State Affairs*
  Isis - v106 - i1 - March 2015 - p185(2) [501+]
Proimos, James - *The Complete Adventures of Johnny Mutton*
  c HB Guide - v26 - i1 - Spring 2015 - p65(1) [51-500]
Waddle! Waddle! (Illus. by Proimos, James)
  c BL - v112 - i5 - Nov 1 2015 - p68(1) [51-500]
  c HB - v91 - i6 - Nov-Dec 2015 - p73(1) [501+]
  c KR - Sept 1 2015 - pNA [51-500]
  c PW - v262 - i34 - August 24 2015 - p79(1) [51-500]
  c PW - v262 - i49 - Dec 2 2015 - p39(1) [51-500]
  c SLJ - v61 - i11 - Nov 2015 - p86(1) [51-500]
Proimos, James, III - *Apocalypse Bow Wow (Illus. by Proimos, James, Jr.)*
  c CCB-B - v68 - i8 - April 2015 - p416(1) [51-500]
  c HB Guide - v26 - i2 - Fall 2015 - p98(1) [51-500]
  c SLJ - v61 - i3 - March 2015 - p130(1) [51-500]
Projansky, Sarah - *Spectacular Girls: Media Fascination and Celebrity Culture*
  Wom R Bks - v32 - i2 - March-April 2015 - p25(3) [501+]
Prokopowicz, Jen - *Look Out for Bugs*
  KR - Feb 1 2015 - pNA [501+]
Promey, Sally - *Sensational Religion: Sensory Cultures in Material Practice*
  CH - v84 - i2 - June 2015 - p482(3) [501+]
Pronzini, Bill - *The Vixen*
  BL - v111 - i17 - May 1 2015 - p47(2) [51-500]
  KR - April 15 2015 - pNA [501+]
  PW - v262 - i16 - April 20 2015 - p56(1) [51-500]
Proops, Greg - *The Smartest Book in the World: A Lexicon of Literacy, a Rancorous Reportage, a Concise Curriculum of Cool (Read by Proops, Greg). Audiobook Review*
  PW - v262 - i30 - July 27 2015 - p61(1) [51-500]
The Smartest Book in the World: A Lexicon of Literacy, a Rancorous Reportage, a Concise Curriculum of Cool
  KR - Feb 15 2015 - pNA [51-500]
  PW - v262 - i9 - March 2 2015 - p76(1) [51-500]
Propst, Andy - *You Fascinate Me So: The Life and Times of Cy Coleman*
  LJ - v140 - i7 - April 15 2015 - p89(2) [51-500]
ProQuest Statistical Abstract of the United States, 2015
  BL - v111 - i12 - Feb 15 2015 - p21(1) [51-500]

Prose, Francine - *Lovers at the Chameleon Club, Paris 1932*
  NYTBR - May 31 2015 - p52(L) [501+]
  Wom R Bks - v32 - i1 - Jan-Feb 2015 - p27(1) [501+]
Peggy Guggenheim: The Shock of the Modern
  BL - v112 - i2 - Sept 15 2015 - p15(2) [501+]
  KR - July 15 2015 - pNA [501+]
  LJ - v140 - i13 - August 1 2015 - p92(1) [501+]
  NYRB - v62 - i20 - Dec 17 2015 - p32(2) [501+]
  TLS - i5876 - Nov 13 2015 - p25(2) [501+]
  New R - v246 - i12 - Nov 2015 - p66(3) [501+]
  PW - v262 - i29 - July 20 2015 - p181(2) [501+]
Prosser, Daniel F. - *Thirteeners: Why Only 13 Percent of Companies Successfully Execute Their Strategy--and How Yours Can Be One of Them*
  PW - v262 - i2 - Jan 12 2015 - p52(2) [501+]
Protestantismus im geteilten Deutschland. Forschungsperspektiven
  HNet - Sept 2015 - pNA(NA) [501+]
Protevi, John - *Life, War, Earth: Deleuze and the Sciences*
  Isis - v106 - i2 - June 2015 - p499(2) [501+]
Prothero, Donald R. - *Bringing Fossils to Life: An Introduction to Paleobiology*
  QRB - v90 - i1 - March 2015 - p81(2) [501+]
The Story of Life in 25 Fossils
  KR - June 1 2015 - pNA [501+]
The Story of Life in 25 Fossils: Tales of Intrepid Fossil Hunters and the Wonders of Evolution
  LJ - v140 - i11 - June 15 2015 - p110(2) [51-500]
  PW - v262 - i25 - June 22 2015 - p132(1) [51-500]
Prothero, Stephen - *Why Liberals Win the Culture Wars (Even When They Lose Elections): The Battles That Define America from Jefferson's Heresies to Gay Marriage*
  KR - Oct 15 2015 - pNA [501+]
  LJ - v140 - i20 - Dec 1 2015 - p120(1) [51-500]
  PW - v262 - i45 - Nov 9 2015 - p52(1) [501+]
Proud, Louis - *Strange Electromagnetic Dimensions: The Science of the Unexplainable*
  Bwatch - Feb 2015 - pNA [51-500]
Proudfit, Benjamin - *Building the White House*
  c BL - v111 - i16 - April 15 2015 - p46(1) [51-500]
Proudfoot, Lindsay J. - *Imperial Spaces: Placing the Irish and Scots in Colonial Australia*
  VS - v57 - i3 - Spring 2015 - p554(3) [501+]
Provencal, Vernon L. - *Sophist Kings: Persians as Other in Herodotus*
  TimHES - i2215 - August 6 2015 - p48-49 [501+]
Provensen, Alice - *Murphy in the City (Illus. by Provensen, Alice)*
  c BL - v112 - i5 - Nov 1 2015 - p65(1) [51-500]
  c KR - Oct 1 2015 - pNA [51-500]
  c PW - v262 - i39 - Sept 28 2015 - p90(2) [501+]
Provincializing the Social Sciences: International Workshop
  HNet - Sept 2015 - pNA [501+]
Provoost, Anne - *In the Shadow of the Ark*
  y BL - v111 - i16 - April 15 2015 - p58(1) [501+]
Provost, Stephen H. - *Fresno Growing Up: A City Comes of Age: 1945-1985*
  RVBW - Sept 2015 - pNA [51-500]
Pruessen, Linda - *Saving Eyesight: Adventures of Seva around the World*
  c BL - v112 - i7 - Dec 1 2015 - p50(2) [51-500]
  c SLJ - v61 - i12 - Dec 2015 - p138(2) [51-500]
Pruitt, Bernadette - *The Other Great Migration: The Movement of Rural African Americans to Houston, 1900-1941*
  JSH - v81 - i1 - Feb 2015 - p227(2) [501+]
Pruitt, Jenny - *Beneath His Wings*
  PW - v262 - i51 - Dec 14 2015 - p80(1) [51-500]
Prutsch, Markus J. - *Making Sense of Constitutional Monarchism in Post-Napoleonic France and Germany*
  HER - v130 - i544 - June 2015 - p762(3) [501+]
Pryce-Jones, David - *Fault Lines*
  Nat R - v67 - i20 - Nov 2 2015 - p43(3) [501+]
Pryce, Thomas - *Cosmosis*
  KR - Jan 1 2016 - pNA [501+]
Pryce, Trevor - *The Rainbow Serpent (Illus. by Greene, Sanford)*
  c HB Guide - v26 - i2 - Fall 2015 - p98(1) [51-500]
Pryce, Vicky - *It's the Economy, Stupid*
  NS - v144 - i5251 - Feb 27 2015 - p48(1) [51-500]
  TLS - i5848 - May 1 2015 - p23(1) [501+]
Pryor, Alton - *Frontier Doctors and Snake Oil Peddlers: A Journal of Early Medical Procedures*
  SPBW - June 2015 - pNA [51-500]
Pryor, Katherine - *Zora's Zucchini (Illus. by Raff, Anna)*
  c KR - July 15 2015 - pNA [51-500]
  c SLJ - v61 - i12 - Dec 2015 - p94(1) [51-500]

Pryor, Mark - *Hollow Man*
 BL - v111 - i22 - August 1 2015 - p34(1) [51-500]
 KR - July 1 2015 - pNA [51-500]
 PW - v262 - i28 - July 13 2015 - p45(1) [51-500]
The Reluctant Matador
 BL - v111 - i18 - May 15 2015 - p28(1) [51-500]
 KR - April 1 2015 - pNA [51-500]
 PW - v262 - i16 - April 20 2015 - p56(1) [51-500]
Pryor, Michael - *Leo Da Vinci vs the Ice-Cream Domination League (Illus. by Faber, Jules)*
 c Magpies - v30 - i3 - July 2015 - p36(2) [501+]
Przybyszewski, Linda - *The Lost Art of Dress: The Women Who Once Made America Stylish*
 AHR - v120 - i3 - June 2015 - p1052-1053 [501+]
Ptacin, Mira - *Poor Your Soul: A Memoir*
 KR - Dec 15 2015 - pNA [501+]
 PW - v262 - i46 - Nov 16 2015 - p69(1) [51-500]
Ptak, Claire - *The Violet Bakery Cookbook: Baking All Day on Wilton Way*
 PW - v262 - i29 - July 20 2015 - p184(1) [51-500]
The Violet Bakery Cookbook
 NYT - Dec 2 2015 - pD6(L) [501+]
 NYTBR - Dec 6 2015 - pNA(L) [501+]
Puaca, Laura Micheletti - *Searching for Scientific Womanpower: Technocratic Feminism and the Politics of National Security, 1940-1980*
 AHR - v120 - i3 - June 2015 - p1059-1061 [501+]
 JAH - v102 - i2 - Sept 2015 - p622-622 [501+]
 Wom R Bks - v32 - i2 - March-April 2015 - p8(3) [501+]
Pucci, Joseph Michael - *Augustine's Virgilian Retreat: Reading the Auctores at Cassiciacum*
 Class R - v65 - i2 - Oct 2015 - p481-483 [501+]
Puccini, Giacomo - *Manon Lescaut*
 Notes - v72 - i1 - Sept 2015 - p226(5) [501+]
Puchner, Willy - *The ABC of Fantastic Princes (Illus. by Puchner, Willy)*
 c HB Guide - v26 - i2 - Fall 2015 - p48(1) [51-500]
Puckett, Dan J. - *In the Shadow of Hitler: Alabama's Jews, the Second World War, and the Holocaust*
 J Am St - v49 - i2 - May 2015 - p437-440 [501+]
 JSH - v81 - i3 - August 2015 - p769(3) [501+]
Puckett, Kelley - *Batman's Dark Secret (Illus. by Muth, Jon J.)*
 c KR - Sept 15 2015 - pNA [51-500]
 c SLJ - v61 - i11 - Nov 2015 - p86(1) [51-500]
Pue, A. Sean - *I Too Have Some Dreams: N. M. Rashed and Modernism in Urdu Poetry*
 TLS - i5855 - June 19 2015 - p23(1) [501+]
Pugh, David - *Sea-Level Science: Understanding Tides, Surges, Tsunamis and Mean Sea-Level Changes*
 Phys Today - v68 - i4 - April 2015 - p56-57 [501+]
Pugh, Emily - *Architecture, Politics and Identity in Divided Berlin*
 CEH - v48 - i2 - June 2015 - p277-278 [501+]
Pugh, Megan - *America Dancing: From the Cakewalk to the Moonwalk*
 KR - Sept 15 2015 - pNA [51-500]
 LJ - v140 - i17 - Oct 15 2015 - p87(1) [51-500]
 NYT - Dec 31 2015 - pC1(L) [501+]
 NYTBR - Dec 6 2015 - p52(L) [501+]
Pugh, Tison - *Chaucer's (Anti-)Eroticisms and the Queer Middle Ages*
 Med R - August 2015 - pNA [501+]
Truman Capote: A Literary Life at the Movies
 G&L Rev W - v22 - i3 - May-June 2015 - p43(2) [501+]
Pugliese, Peter T. - *The Cookie Doctor*
 PW - v262 - i1 - Jan 5 2015 - p66(1) [51-500]
Puglisi, Catherine R. - *New Perspectives on the Man of Sorrows*
 Med R - Jan 2015 - pNA [501+]
 Six Ct J - v46 - i1 - Spring 2015 - p210-211 [501+]
 Specu - v90 - i2 - April 2015 - p579-581 [501+]
Pugmire, John - *The House That Kills*
 PW - v262 - i11 - March 16 2015 - p66(1) [51-500]
Puk, Alexander - *Das romische Spielewesen in der Spatantike*
 HNet - April 2015 - pNA [501+]
Pukhov, Ruslan - *Brothers Armed: Military Aspects of the Crisis in Ukraine*
 E-A St - v67 - i7 - Sept 2015 - p1157(2) [501+]
Pule, John Puhiatau - *The Bond of Time: An Epic Love Poem*
 Cont Pac - v27 - i1 - Spring 2015 - p296(3) [501+]

Pulford, Elizabeth - *Finding Monkey Moon (Illus. by Wilkinson, Kate)*
 c BL - v112 - i5 - Nov 1 2015 - p64(2) [51-500]
 c KR - August 15 2015 - pNA [51-500]
 c Magpies - v30 - i2 - May 2015 - p27(1) [51-500]
 c NYTBR - Nov 8 2015 - p29(L) [501+]
 c SLJ - v61 - i11 - Nov 2015 - p86(1) [51-500]
Sanspell
 Magpies - v30 - i3 - July 2015 - pS6(1) [501+]
Pulju, Rebecca J. - *Women and Mass Consumer Society in Postwar France*
 HER - v130 - i545 - August 2015 - p934(11) [501+]
Pullen, M.J. - *The Marriage Pact*
 BL - v112 - i3 - Oct 1 2015 - p23(1) [51-500]
Regrets Only
 KR - Jan 1 2016 - pNA [51-500]
Pulley, D.M. - *The Dead Key*
 KR - Jan 1 2015 - pNA [51-500]
Pulley, Natasha - *The Watchmaker of Filigree Street*
 y BL - v111 - i18 - May 15 2015 - p40(1) [51-500]
 KR - May 15 2015 - pNA [51-500]
 LJ - v140 - i6 - April 1 2015 - p119(1) [501+]
 LJ - v140 - i9 - May 15 2015 - p57(4) [501+]
 NYTBR - August 2 2015 - p16(L) [501+]
 PW - v262 - i8 - Feb 23 2015 - p57(1) [51-500]
 Spec - v328 - i9757 - August 29 2015 - p37(2) [501+]
 TimHES - i2218 - August 27 2015 - p43(1) [501+]
Pulliam, June Michele - *Encyclopedia of the Zombie: The Walking Dead in Popular Culture and Myth*
 SLJ - v61 - i2 - Feb 2015 - p56(1) [51-500]
 R&USQ - v54 - i3 - Spring 2015 - p61(2) [51-500]
Pullman, Peter - *Wail: The Life of Bud Powell*
 Notes - v71 - i3 - March 2015 - p492(6) [501+]
Pullman, Philip - *The Golden Compass: The Graphic Novel, vol. 1 (Illus. by Oubrerie, Clement)*
 y KR - July 15 2015 - pNA [51-500]
 y BL - v111 - i22 - August 1 2015 - p48(1) [51-500]
 c PW - v262 - i26 - June 29 2015 - p71(1) [51-500]
 c PW - v262 - i49 - Dec 2 2015 - p85(1) [51-500]
 y SLJ - v61 - i7 - July 2015 - p84(1) [51-500]
Pulter, Lady Hester - *Poems, Emblems, and the Unfortunate Florinda*
 Ren Q - v68 - i3 - Fall 2015 - p1087-1088 [501+]
Pulvers, Roger - *Once upon a Time in Japan*
 c PW - v262 - i35 - August 31 2015 - p93(1) [501+]
Pupa, D.A. - *The Magician*
 PW - v262 - i25 - June 22 2015 - p123(1) [51-500]
Purcell, Hugh - *A Very Private Celebrity: The Nine Lives of John Freeman*
 NS - v144 - i5270 - July 10 2015 - p39(1) [51-500]
 Spec - v328 - i9755 - August 15 2015 - p35(1) [501+]
Purdie, Kathryn - *Burning Glass*
 y KR - Jan 1 2016 - pNA [51-500]
 y SLJ - v61 - i12 - Dec 2015 - p126(1) [51-500]
Purdom, Tom - *Romance on Four Worlds: A Casanova Quartet*
 Analog - v135 - i9 - Sept 2015 - p107(1) [501+]
 PW - v262 - i11 - March 16 2015 - p68(1) [51-500]
Purdue, A.W. - *The First World War*
 TimHES - i2202 - May 7 2015 - p55(1) [501+]
Purdy, Jedediah - *After Nature: A Politics for the Anthropocene*
 CHE - v62 - i9 - Oct 30 2015 - pB17(1) [501+]
 HM - v331 - i1984 - Sept 2015 - p79(3) [501+]
 KR - July 1 2015 - pNA [51-500]
 NYRB - v62 - i16 - Oct 22 2015 - p37(3) [501+]
Purdy, Ray - *Evidence from Earth Observation Satellites: Emerging Legal Issues*
 APJ - v29 - i2 - March-April 2015 - p183(3) [501+]
Purnell, Brian - *Fighting Jim Crow in the County of Kings: The Congress of Racial Equality in Brooklyn*
 J Urban H - v41 - i5 - Sept 2015 - p943-950 [501+]
Purnell, Sonia - *Clementine: The Life of Mrs. Winston Churchill*
 KR - August 1 2015 - pNA [51-500]
 LJ - v140 - i15 - Sept 15 2015 - p94(1) [51-500]
 NY - v91 - i35 - Nov 9 2015 - p81 [51-500]
 NYTBR - Dec 6 2015 - p12(L) [501+]
 PW - v262 - i39 - Sept 28 2015 - p81(1) [501+]
Purpura, Lia - *It Shouldn't Have Been Beautiful*
 PW - v262 - i38 - Sept 21 2015 - p51(1) [51-500]

Pursell, J.J. - *The Herbal Apothecary: 100 Medicinal Herbs and How to Use Them*
 PW - v262 - i42 - Oct 19 2015 - p72(1) [51-500]
Purser, Ann - *Suspicion at Seven*
 Bwatch - March 2015 - pNA [51-500]
Purtolas, Romain - *The Extraordinary Journey of the Fakir Who Got Trapped in Ikea Wardrobe*
 NYTBR - March 8 2015 - p34(L) [501+]
Puryear, Tony - *Concrete Park, vol 1: You Send Me (Illus. by Puryear, Tony)*
 BL - v111 - i13 - March 1 2015 - p32(1) [51-500]
Putnam, David - *The Replacements*
 BL - v111 - i9-10 - Jan 1 2015 - p50(1) [51-500]
The Squandered
 PW - v262 - i52 - Dec 21 2015 - p134(1) [51-500]
Putnam, Robert D. - *Our Kids: The American Dream in Crisis*
 BL - v111 - i14 - March 15 2015 - p33(1) [51-500]
 CC - v132 - i25 - Dec 9 2015 - p39(3) [501+]
 Comw - v142 - i11 - June 12 2015 - p25(2) [501+]
 CSM - March 12 2015 - pNA [501+]
 Econ - v414 - i8930 - March 21 2015 - p73(US) [501+]
 Esq - v163 - i4 - April 2015 - p41(1) [501+]
 KR - Feb 15 2015 - pNA [501+]
 LJ - v140 - i5 - March 15 2015 - p124(1) [51-500]
 Nat R - v67 - i9 - May 18 2015 - p43 [501+]
 Nature - v520 - i7546 - April 9 2015 - p155(1) [51-500]
 NYRB - v62 - i9 - May 21 2015 - p25(3) [501+]
 NYTBR - March 8 2015 - p14(L) [501+]
 TimHES - i2206 - June 4 2015 - p53(1) [501+]
 TimHES - i2224 - Oct 8 2015 - p43(1) [501+]
Puttock, Simon - *Mouse's First Night at Moonlight School (Illus. by Pye, Ali)*
 c KR - June 1 2015 - pNA [51-500]
 c BL - v111 - i21 - July 1 2015 - p64(1) [51-500]
 c CH Bwatch - August 2015 - pNA [51-500]
 c HB Guide - v26 - i2 - Fall 2015 - p16(1) [51-500]
 c SLJ - v61 - i8 - August 2015 - p60(2) [51-500]
Pycior, Julie Leininger - *Democratic Renewal and the Mutual Aid Legacy of US Mexicans*
 WHQ - v46 - i2 - Summer 2015 - p240-241 [501+]
Pye, Michael - *The Edge of the World: A Cultural History of the North Sea and the Transformation of Europe*
 KR - Jan 15 2015 - pNA [51-500]
 NYTBR - June 7 2015 - p25(L) [501+]
 PW - v262 - i6 - Feb 9 2015 - p54(2) [51-500]
Japanese Buddhist Pilgrimage
 HNet - May 2015 - pNA [501+]
Pye, Omari - *Curse of the King*
 SPBW - Feb 2015 - pNA [501+]
Pye, Virginia - *Dreams of the Red Phoenix*
 KR - August 1 2015 - pNA [51-500]
Pykett, Lyn - *The Nineteenth-Century Sensation Novel, 2d ed.*
 MLR - v110 - i3 - July 2015 - p846-848 [501+]
Pyle, Barbara - *Bruce Springsteen and the E Street Band 1975: Photographs*
 CSM - Dec 8 2015 - pNA [501+]
Pyle, Nate - *Man Enough: How Jesus Redefines Manhood*
 PW - v262 - i32 - August 10 2015 - p57(1) [51-500]
Pyle, Ryan - *Chinese Turkestan: A Photographic Journey through an Ancient Civilization (Illus. by Pyle, Ryan)*
 KR - Nov 1 2015 - pNA [51-500]
Sacred Mountains of China
 KR - Jan 1 2016 - pNA [501+]
Pyper, Andrew - *The Damned*
 NYTBR - May 31 2015 - p42(L) [501+]
Pyron, Bobbie - *Lucky Strike*
 c BL - v111 - i11 - Feb 1 2015 - p52(1) [51-500]
 c CCB-B - v68 - i8 - April 2015 - p416(1) [51-500]
 c HB - v91 - i2 - March-April 2015 - p106(1) [51-500]
 c HB Guide - v26 - i2 - Fall 2015 - p98(1) [51-500]
 y Teach Lib - v42 - i4 - April 2015 - p28(1) [51-500]
 y VOYA - v37 - i6 - Feb 2015 - p63(1) [51-500]
Pyros, Andrea - *My Year of Epic Rock*
 c BL - v112 - i5 - Nov 1 2015 - p52(1) [501+]
Pytell, Timothy E. - *Viktor Frankl's Search for Meaning: An Emblematic 20th-Century Life*
 LJ - v140 - i14 - Sept 1 2015 - p125(1) [51-500]
Pyzhikov, A.V. - *Grani russkogo raskola: Zametki o nashei istorii ot XVII veka do 1917 goda*
 Slav R - v74 - i1 - Spring 2015 - p185-187 [501+]

Q R

Qadiri, Sura - *Postcolonial Fiction and Sacred Scripture: Rewriting the Divine?*
    FS - v69 - i4 - Oct 2015 - p566-567 [501+]
Qian, Kefei - *Die Donau von 1740 bis 1875: Eine kulturwissenschaftliche Untersuchung*
    Ger Q - v88 - i1 - Wntr 2015 - p139(3) [501+]
Qitsualik-Tinsley, Rachel - *How Things Came to Be: Inuit Stories of Creation (Illus. by Fiegenschuh, Emily)*
    Res Links - v21 - i1 - Oct 2015 - p20(1) [501+]
Lesson for the Wolf (Illus. by Cook, Alan)
    c KR - July 15 2015 - pNA [51-500]
    c Res Links - v21 - i1 - Oct 2015 - p9(2) [51-500]
Tuniit
    c KR - April 15 2015 - pNA [51-500]
The Walrus who Escaped (Illus. by Brennan, Anthony)
    c Res Links - v20 - i4 - April 2015 - p7(2) [501+]
Qitsualik-Tinsley, Sean - *Tuniit: Mysterious People of the Arctic (Illus. by Brigham, Sean)*
    c Res Links - v21 - i1 - Oct 2015 - p20(1) [51-500]
The Walrus Who Escaped (Illus. by Brennan, Anthony)
    c CH Bwatch - July 2015 - pNA [501+]
Qiu, Peipei - *Chinese Comfort Women: Testimonies from Imperial Japan's Sex Slaves*
    Pac A - v88 - i1 - March 2015 - p188 [501+]
    Wom R Bks - v32 - i5 - Sept-Oct 2015 - p5(3) [501+]
Qiu, Xiaolong - *Shanghai Redemption*
    KR - July 15 2015 - pNA [51-500]
    PW - v262 - i30 - July 27 2015 - p43(1) [51-500]
Quaas, Ruben - *Fair Trade: Eine global-lokale Geschichte am Beispiel des Kaffees*
    HNet - Sept 2015 - pNA [501+]
Quade, Kirstin Valdez - *Night at the Fiestas: Stories*
    LJ - v140 - i10 - June 1 2015 - p139(1) [501+]
    Atl - v315 - i2 - March 2015 - p46(1) [51-500]
    BL - v111 - i11 - Feb 1 2015 - p23(1) [51-500]
    KR - Feb 1 2015 - pNA [51-500]
    LJ - v140 - i5 - March 15 2015 - p97(1) [501+]
    NYT - March 26 2015 - pC6(L) [501+]
    NYTBR - March 29 2015 - p19(L) [501+]
    PW - v262 - i1 - Jan 5 2015 - p49(1) [51-500]
Quaglia, Russell J. - *Student Voice: Turn Up the Volume K-8 Activity Book*
    Bwatch - August 2015 - pNA [501+]
Quammen, David - *The Chimp and the River: How AIDS Emerged from an African Forest*
    Nature - v519 - i7542 - March 12 2015 - p155(1) [51-500]
    NYT - March 31 2015 - pD4(L) [501+]
Quark, Amy A. - *Global Rivalries: Standards Wars and the Transnational Cotton Trade*
    CS - v44 - i3 - May 2015 - p406-408 [501+]
Quarles, Angela - *Steam Me Up, Rawley*
    PW - v262 - i12 - March 23 2015 - p55(2) [51-500]
Quartey, Kwei - *Murder at Cape Three Points*
    RVBW - March 2015 - pNA [501+]
Quartz, Steven - *Cool: How the Brain's Hidden Quest for Cool Drives Our Economy and Shapes Our World*
    Har Bus R - v93 - i4 - April 2015 - p110(2) [501+]
    KR - Feb 1 2015 - pNA [51-500]
Quash, Ben - *Found Theology: History, Imagination and the Holy Spirit*
    CC - v132 - i1 - Jan 7 2015 - p37(4) [501+]
Quattlebaum, Mary - *Mighty Mole and Super Soil (Illus. by Wallace, Chad)*
    c CH Bwatch - Oct 2015 - pNA [501+]
    c CH Bwatch - Nov 2015 - pNA [501+]
    c KR - July 15 2015 - pNA [501+]

Quayson, Ato - *Oxford Street, Accra: City Life and the Itineraries of Transnationalism*
    IJAHS - v48 - i1 - Wntr 2015 - p138-140 [501+]
Quddus, Marguerite Elias - *In Hiding*
    y Res Links - v20 - i3 - Feb 2015 - p40(2) [501+]
Queirolo, Rosario - *The Success of the Left in Latin America: Untainted Parties, Market Reforms, and Voting Behavior*
    CS - v44 - i5 - Sept 2015 - p694-695 [501+]
Quezada, Sergio - *Maya Lords and Lordship: The Formation of Colonial Society in Yucatan, 1350-1600*
    JIH - v45 - i4 - Spring 2015 - p595-597 [501+]
Quiccheberg, Samuel - *The First Treatise on Museums: Samuel Quiccheberg's "Inscriptiones," 1565*
    Six Ct J - v46 - i2 - Summer 2015 - p477-479 [501+]
Quick, Amanda - *Garden of Lies (Read by Underwood, Louise Jane). Audiobook Review*
    LJ - v140 - i12 - July 1 2015 - p44(1) [51-500]
Garden of Lies
    BL - v111 - i16 - April 15 2015 - p30(1) [51-500]
    KR - April 1 2015 - pNA [51-500]
Quick, Matthew - *Love May Fail*
    BL - v111 - i16 - April 15 2015 - p24(2) [51-500]
    KR - April 1 2015 - pNA [51-500]
    LJ - v140 - i7 - April 15 2015 - p80(1) [51-500]
    PW - v262 - i7 - Feb 16 2015 - p151(1) [51-500]
Quickenden, Kenneth - *Matthew Boulton: Enterprising Industrialist of the Enlightenment*
    Historian - v77 - i2 - Summer 2015 - p401(2) [501+]
Quigley, Joan - *Just Another Southern Town: Mary Church Terrell and the Struggle for Racial Justice in the Nation's Capita*
    KR - Jan 1 2016 - pNA [501+]
    LJ - v140 - i20 - Dec 1 2015 - p115(2) [51-500]
Quigley, John - *The Six-Day War and Israeli Self-Defense: Questioning the Legal Basis for Preventive War*
    J Mil H - v79 - i3 - July 2015 - p881-883 [501+]
    IJMES - v47 - i4 - Nov 2015 - p843-845 [501+]
Quigley, Megan - *Modernist Fiction and Vagueness: Philosophy, Form, and Language*
    TLS - i5871 - Oct 9 2015 - p27(2) [501+]
Quill, Sarah - *Ruskin's Venice: The Stones Revisited*
    Apo - v181 - i631 - May 2015 - p106(2) [501+]
Quillen, C.L. - *Read On ... Romance: Reading Lists for Every Taste*
    BL - v111 - i14 - March 15 2015 - p48(1) [51-500]
Quin, Ann - *Berg*
    NS - v144 - i5282 - Oct 2 2015 - p74(2) [501+]
Quin, Edel - *Safe Dance Practice*
    RVBW - August 2015 - pNA [501+]
Quin, Sally - *Bauhaus on the Swan: Elise Blumann, an Emigre Artist in Western Australia, 1938-1948*
    RVBW - Nov 2015 - pNA [501+]
Quinault, Roland - *William Gladstone: New Studies and Perspectives*
    VS - v57 - i3 - Spring 2015 - p561(3) [501+]
Quinby, Roger P. - *Postal Censorship in Finland 1914-1918*
    Phil Lit R - v64 - i3 - Summer 2015 - p211(2) [501+]
Quindlen, Anna - *Miller's Valley*
    PW - v262 - i51 - Dec 14 2015 - p53(1) [51-500]
Quinlan, Jessica - *Vater, Tochter, Schwiegersohn: Die erzahlerische Ausgestaltung einer familiaren Dreierkonstellation im Artusroman franzosischer und deutscher Sprache um 1200*
    JEGP - v114 - i2 - April 2015 - p308(4) [501+]
Quinlan, Nigel - *The Maloneys' Magical Weatherbox*
    c KR - May 15 2015 - pNA [501+]
    c SLJ - v61 - i7 - July 2015 - p82(1) [51-500]

Quinlivan, Ada - *Blake the Baker: Develop Understanding of Fractions and Numbers*
    c Teach Lib - v43 - i1 - Oct 2015 - p17(1) [51-500]
Quinlivan, Davina - *Filming the Body in Crisis: Trauma, Healing and Hopefulness*
    TimHES - i2223 - Oct 1 2015 - p50-51 [501+]
Quinn, Anthony - *Curtain Call*
    NS - v144 - i5247 - Jan 30 2015 - p47(1) [51-500]
    Spec - v327 - i9733 - March 14 2015 - p43(2) [501+]
Quinn, Caisey - *Loving Dallas*
    BL - v111 - i19-20 - June 1 2015 - p62(1) [51-500]
Quinn, Colin - *Coloring Book*
    KR - May 15 2015 - pNA [501+]
Quinn, Darlene - *Conflicting Webs*
    RVBW - June 2015 - pNA [51-500]
Quinn, Gene R. - *Current Medical Diagnosis and Treatment Study Guide*
    Bwatch - March 2015 - pNA [51-500]
Quinn, James - *Adventures in the Lives of Others: Ethical Dilemmas in Factual Filmmaking*
    Si & So - v25 - i12 - Dec 2015 - p105(1) [501+]
Quinn, Jane Bryant - *How to Make Your Money Last: The Indispensable Retirement Guide*
    BL - v112 - i6 - Nov 15 2015 - p4(1) [501+]
    LJ - v140 - i20 - Dec 1 2015 - p118(1) [51-500]
    PW - v262 - i44 - Nov 2 2015 - p77(1) [51-500]
    PW - v262 - i51 - Dec 14 2015 - p30(3) [501+]
Quinn, Jason - *The Kaurava Empire: The Vengeance of Ashwatthama (Illus. by Nagar, Sachin)*
    y SLJ - v61 - i5 - May 2015 - p127(2) [51-500]
Quinn, Jordan - *Adventures in Flatfrost (Illus. by McPhillips, Robert)*
    c HB Guide - v26 - i1 - Spring 2015 - p65(1) [51-500]
Beneath the Stone Forest (Illus. by McPhillips, Robert)
    c HB Guide - v26 - i2 - Fall 2015 - p71(1) [51-500]
Let the Games Begin! (Illus. by McPhillips, Robert)
    c HB Guide - v26 - i2 - Fall 2015 - p71(1) [51-500]
Sea Monster! (Illus. by McPhillips, Robert)
    c HB Guide - v26 - i1 - Spring 2015 - p65(1) [51-500]
The Witch's Curse (Illus. by McPhillips, Robert)
    c HB Guide - v26 - i1 - Spring 2015 - p65(1) [51-500]
Quinn, Julia - *The Secrets of Sir Richard Kenworthy*
    BL - v111 - i9-10 - Jan 1 2015 - p58(1) [51-500]
Quinn, Kate - *Black Power in the Caribbean*
    AHR - v120 - i1 - Feb 2015 - p306-307 [501+]
Quinn, Kennedy - *The Last Best Lie*
    KR - Sept 15 2015 - pNA [51-500]
Quinn, Malcolm - *Utilitarianism and the Art School in Nineteenth-Century Britain*
    VS - v57 - i3 - Spring 2015 - p537(3) [501+]
Quinn, Paula - *The Taming of Malcolm Grant*
    PW - v262 - i35 - August 31 2015 - p67(1) [51-500]
Quinn, Spencer - *Paw and Order: A Chet and Bernie Mystery*
    RVBW - April 2015 - pNA [501+]
    RVBW - May 2015 - pNA [501+]
Scents and Sensibility
    PW - v262 - i22 - June 1 2015 - p42(2) [51-500]
Woof (Read by Frangione, Jim). Audiobook Review
    c BL - v112 - i2 - Sept 15 2015 - p80(1) [51-500]
Woof
    c HB Guide - v26 - i2 - Fall 2015 - p98(1) [51-500]
    c KR - Feb 15 2015 - pNA [51-500]
    c SLJ - v61 - i2 - Feb 2015 - p92(1) [51-500]

Quinn, Susan Kaye - *Faery Swap*
   c PW - v262 - i6 - Feb 9 2015 - p68(1) [51-500]
Third Daughter
     PW - v262 - i2 - Jan 12 2015 - p44(1) [51-500]

Quinn, William A. - *Olde Clerkis Speche: Chaucer's Troilus and Criseyde and the Implications of Authorial Recital*
     Med R - Feb 2015 - pNA [501+]

Quinones, John - *What Would You Do? Words of Wisdom about Doing the Right Thing*
     Bwatch - June 2015 - pNA [51-500]

Quinones, Sam - *Dreamland: The True Tale of America's Opiate Epidemic*
     BL - v111 - i11 - Feb 1 2015 - p5(1) [51-500]
     CSM - April 28 2015 - pNA [501+]
     Econ - v416 - i8949 - August 1 2015 - p72(US) [501+]
     Ent W - i1361 - May 1 2015 - p67(1) [501+]
     KR - Feb 1 2015 - pNA [501+]
     PW - v262 - i5 - Feb 2 2015 - p45(2) [51-500]
     Spec - v328 - i9751 - July 18 2015 - p39(1) [501+]

Quint, David - *Inside Paradise Lost: Reading the Designs of Milton's Epic*
     Bks & Cult - v21 - i1 - Jan-Feb 2015 - p38(1) [501+]

Quint, M. - *The Defiant*
   c KR - July 15 2015 - pNA [51-500]

Quintero, Andres - *Hairy Harold and His Extraordinary Trip to New York*
   c PW - v262 - i38 - Sept 21 2015 - p71(1) [51-500]

Quintero, Isabel - *Gabi: A Girl in Pieces*
   y CCB-B - v68 - i5 - Jan 2015 - p274(2) [51-500]
   y CH Bwatch - April 2015 - pNA [51-500]
   y HB Guide - v26 - i1 - Spring 2015 - p121(1) [51-500]
   y SLJ - v61 - i12 - Dec 2015 - p64(4) [501+]

Quintero, Sofia - *Show and Prove*
   y BL - v111 - i21 - July 1 2015 - p59(1) [51-500]
   y HB - v91 - i5 - Sept-Oct 2015 - p114(2) [51-500]
   y KR - May 15 2015 - pNA [51-500]
   y PW - v262 - i18 - May 4 2015 - p121(2) [51-500]
   y SLJ - v61 - i12 - Dec 2015 - p126(2) [51-500]
   y VOYA - v38 - i3 - August 2015 - p67(2) [51-500]

Quinton, Sasha - *Florabelle (Illus. by Barrager, Brigette)*
   c HB Guide - v26 - i2 - Fall 2015 - p48(2) [51-500]
     KR - Feb 1 2015 - pNA [51-500]
   c SLJ - v61 - i2 - Feb 2015 - p76(1) [51-500]

Quiring, Bjorn - *Shakespeare's Curse: The Aporias of Ritual Exclusion in Early Modern Royal Drama*
     Ren Q - v68 - i1 - Spring 2015 - p392-393 [501+]
     Theat J - v67 - i1 - March 2015 - p148-149 [501+]

Quiroga, Alejandro - *Right-Wing Spain in the Civil War Era: Soldiers of God and Apostles of the Fatherland, 1914-45*
     HER - v130 - i545 - August 2015 - p1037(2) [501+]

Quiroga Puertas, A.J. - *The Purpose of Rhetoric in Late Antiquity: From Performance to Exegesis*
     Class R - v65 - i1 - April 2015 - p101-103 [501+]

Quist, John W. - *James Buchanan and the Coming of the Civil War*
     JSH - v81 - i1 - Feb 2015 - p192(3) [501+]
     Pres St Q - v45 - i2 - June 2015 - p415(3) [501+]

Quo vadis Zeitgeschichte?/L'histoire du Temps Present et ses Defis au XXIe Siecle
     HNet - Feb 2015 - pNA [501+]

Quodbach, Esmee - *Holland's Golden Age in America: Collecting the Arts of Rembrandt, Vermeer, and Hals*
     Six Ct J - v46 - i2 - Summer 2015 - p518-520 [501+]

Qureshi, Saqib - *Reconstructing Strategy*
     KR - May 15 2015 - pNA [501+]

Qutob, Fida Fayez - *Sarah in the City of Moon (Illus. by Qutob, Dalia)*
   c KR - Jan 15 2015 - pNA [501+]

Raasch, Sara - *Ice Like Fire*
   y KR - July 15 2015 - pNA [51-500]
   y SLJ - v61 - i9 - Sept 2015 - p171(2) [51-500]
   y VOYA - v38 - i5 - Dec 2015 - p73(1) [51-500]
Snow Like Ashes
   y CCB-B - v68 - i5 - Jan 2015 - p275(1) [51-500]
   y HB Guide - v26 - i1 - Spring 2015 - p121(1) [51-500]

Raban, Sandra - *The Accounts of Godfrey of Crowland, Abbot of Peterborough 1299-1321*
     HER - v130 - i543 - April 2015 - p420(2) [501+]

Rabault-Feuerhahn, Pascale - *Archives of Origins: Sanskrit, Philology, Anthropology in Nineteenth Century Germany*
     Isis - v106 - i2 - June 2015 - p461(2) [501+]

Rabb, Margo - *Kissing in America*
   y BL - v111 - i15 - April 1 2015 - p67(1) [51-500]
   y CCB-B - v69 - i1 - Sept 2015 - p46(1) [51-500]
   y HB - v91 - i3 - May-June 2015 - p163(1) [51-500]
   y HB Guide - v26 - i2 - Fall 2015 - p135(1) [51-500]
   y KR - March 1 2015 - pNA [51-500]
   y NYTBR - May 31 2015 - p54(L) [501+]
   y PW - v262 - i14 - April 6 2015 - p62(2) [51-500]
   y PW - v262 - i49 - Dec 2 2015 - p93(2) [51-500]
   y SLJ - v61 - i3 - March 2015 - p161(1) [51-500]

Rabe, Tish - *Huff and Puff Have Too Much Stuff (Illus. by Guile, Gill)*
   c HB Guide - v26 - i1 - Spring 2015 - p54(1) [51-500]
Out of Sight till Tonight! All about Nocturnal Animals (Illus. by Mathieu, Joe)
   c SLJ - v61 - i5 - May 2015 - p136(1) [51-500]
Out of Sight till Tonight! All About Nocturnal Animals (Illus. by Ruiz, Aristides)
   c HB Guide - v26 - i2 - Fall 2015 - p172(1) [51-500]
!Te amo, te abrazo, leo contigo! Love You, Hug You, Read to You! (Illus. by Endersby, Frank)
   c SLJ - v61 - i12 - Dec 2015 - p85(1) [51-500]

Rabei, Carolina - *Crunch! (Illus. by Rabei, Carolina)*
   c KR - Jan 1 2016 - pNA [51-500]
   c Sch Lib - v63 - i4 - Winter 2015 - p222(1) [51-500]

Rabikowska, Marta - *The Everyday of Memory: Between Communism and Post-Communism*
     Slav R - v74 - i1 - Spring 2015 - p182-184 [501+]

Rabinovici, Doron - *Elsewhere*
     WLT - v89 - i3-4 - May-August 2015 - p116(2) [501+]

Rabinowitz, Paula - *American Pulp: How Paperbacks Brought Modernism to Main Street*
     NS - v144 - i5244 - Jan 9 2015 - p41(1) [501+]
     TLS - i5836 - Feb 6 2015 - p23(1) [501+]

Race, Gender, and Military Heroism in U.S. History: From World War I to 9/11
     HNet - May 2015 - pNA [501+]

Race, Jody Sullivan - *Poo and Puke Eaters of the Animal World*
   c Sch Lib - v63 - i3 - Autumn 2015 - p175(1) [51-500]

Rachel, Lea - *The Other Shakespeare*
     SPBW - Feb 2015 - pNA [51-500]

Racine, Philip N. - *Living a Big War in a Small Place: Spartanburg, South Carolina, during the Confederacy*
     JSH - v81 - i2 - May 2015 - p467(2) [501+]

Rackham, Oliver - *The Ash Tree*
     Ch Today - v59 - i4 - May 2015 - p60(1) [51-500]
     TLS - i5840 - March 6 2015 - p27(1) [501+]

Raczka, Bob - *Presidential Misadventures: Poems That Poke Fun at the Man in Charge (Illus. by Burr, Dan E.)*
   c HB Guide - v26 - i2 - Fall 2015 - p204(1) [51-500]
     SLJ - v61 - i3 - March 2015 - p172(2) [51-500]
Santa Clauses: Short Poems from the North Pole (Illus. by Groenink, Chuck)
   c HB Guide - v26 - i1 - Spring 2015 - p189(1) [51-500]
Wet Cement: A Mix of Concrete Poems
   c KR - Jan 1 2016 - pNA [51-500]
   c PW - v262 - i52 - Dec 21 2015 - p156(2) [51-500]

Radakovich, Tropical Tom - *The Overthrow of Hawaii*
     KR - Sept 1 2015 - pNA [51-500]

Radchenko, Sergey - *Unwanted Visionaries: The Soviet Failure in Asia at the End of the Cold War*
     Slav R - v74 - i2 - Summer 2015 - p376-378 [501+]

Radcliff, Benjamin - *The Political Economy of Human Happiness: How Voters' Choices Determine the Quality of Life*
     CS - v44 - i1 - Jan 2015 - p110-112 [501+]

Raddatz, Fritz J. - *Tagebucher 2002-2012*
     Ger Q - v88 - i3 - Summer 2015 - p394(2) [501+]

Radelet, Steven - *The Great Surge: The Ascent of the Developing World*
     KR - Sept 15 2015 - pNA [501+]
     LJ - v140 - i17 - Oct 15 2015 - p98(1) [51-500]
     PW - v262 - i34 - August 24 2015 - p73(1) [51-500]

Raden, Aja - *Stoned: Jewelry, Obsession, and How Desire Shapes the World*
     BL - v112 - i6 - Nov 15 2015 - p8(1) [51-500]
     KR - Sept 15 2015 - pNA [501+]
     LJ - v140 - i17 - Oct 15 2015 - p103(1) [51-500]
     PW - v262 - i41 - Oct 12 2015 - p59(2) [51-500]

Rader-Day, Lori - *Little Pretty Things*
     BL - v111 - i17 - May 1 2015 - p40(1) [51-500]
     Bwatch - Sept 2015 - pNA [51-500]
     KR - May 1 2015 - pNA [51-500]
     PW - v262 - i16 - April 20 2015 - p53(1) [51-500]

Rader, Karen A. - *Life on Display: Revolutionizing U.S. Museums of Science and Natural History in the Twentieth Century*
     NEQ - v88 - i3 - Sept 2015 - p534-537 [501+]

Radford, Alexandra Walton - *Top Student, Top School?: How Social Class Shapes Where Valedictorians Go to College*
     CS - v44 - i2 - March 2015 - p238-239 [501+]

Radford, Andrew - *Mary Butts and British Neo-Romanticism: The Enchantment of Place*
     RES - v66 - i276 - Sept 2015 - p799-801 [501+]

Radford, Gail - *The Rise of the Public Authority: Statebuilding and Economic Development in Twentieth-Century America*
     AHR - v120 - i1 - Feb 2015 - p269-270 [501+]
     Historian - v77 - i2 - Summer 2015 - p347(2) [501+]
     JAH - v102 - i2 - Sept 2015 - p580-581 [501+]
     RAH - v43 - i2 - June 2015 - p327-332 [501+]

Radice, Giles - *Odd Couples: The Great Political Pairings of Modern Britain*
     NS - v144 - i5258 - April 17 2015 - p61(1) [51-500]
     TLS - i5851 - May 22 2015 - p23(1) [501+]

Radikalisierung des Antisemitismus wahrend des Ersten Weltkrieges? Antisemitische Akteure und judische Kriegserfahrungen im europaischen Vergleich
     HNet - May 2015 - pNA [501+]

Radin, Stacey - *Brave Girls: Raising Young Women with Passion and Purpose to Become Powerful Leaders*
     LJ - v140 - i3 - Feb 15 2015 - p81(3) [501+]

Radisson, Pierre-Esprit - *The Collected Writings, vol. 2: The Port Nelson Relations*
     Sev Cent N - v73 - i3-4 - Fall-Winter 2015 - p127(4) [501+]

Radkau, Joachim - *The Age of Ecology: A Global History*
     HNet - May 2015 - pNA [501+]

Radko, Timour - *Double-Diffusive Convection*
     SIAM Rev - v57 - i2 - June 2015 - p295-305 [501+]

Radner, John B. - *Johnson and Boswell: A Biography of a Friendship*
     Historian - v77 - i2 - Summer 2015 - p402(2) [501+]

Radner, Karen - *State Correspondence in the Ancient World: From New Kingdom Egypt to the Roman Empire*
     HNet - May 2015 - pNA [501+]

Radojicic, Snezana - *Zakotrljaj me oko sveta*
     WLT - v89 - i1 - Jan-Feb 2015 - p79(1) [501+]

Radomski, Kassandra - *Battle for a New Nation: Causes and Effects of the Revolutionary War*
   c HB Guide - v26 - i2 - Fall 2015 - p221(1) [51-500]

Rae, Issa - *The Misadventures of Awkward Black Girl*
     KR - Jan 1 2015 - pNA [51-500]

Rae, Kristin - *What You Always Wanted*
   y KR - Jan 1 2016 - pNA [51-500]

Raeburn, Daniel - *Vessels: A Love Story*
     KR - Dec 15 2015 - pNA [51-500]

Raeder, Leah - *Black Iris*
     BL - v111 - i16 - April 15 2015 - p30(1) [51-500]

Rael, Patrick - *Eighty-Eight Years: The Long Death of Slavery in the United States, 1777-1865*
     KR - May 1 2015 - pNA [51-500]
     LJ - v140 - i10 - June 1 2015 - p116(1) [51-500]
     PW - v262 - i23 - June 8 2015 - p51(1) [51-500]

Raeymaekers, Dries - *One Foot in the Palace: The Habsburg Court of Brussels and the Politics of Access in the Reign of Albert and Isabella, 1598-1621*
     HER - v130 - i544 - June 2015 - p743(2) [501+]

Raeymaekers, Timothy - *Violent Capitalism and Hybrid Identity in the Eastern Congo: Power to the Margins*
     For Aff - v94 - i3 - May-June 2015 - pNA [51-500]

Raff, Sarah - *Jane Austen's Erotic Advice*
     Nine-C Lit - v69 - i4 - March 2015 - p543(4) [501+]

Rafferty, Colin - *Hallow This Ground*
     KR - Dec 15 2015 - pNA [501+]

Raffman, Diana - *Unruly Words*
     Phil R - v124 - i3 - July 2015 - p415(5) [501+]

Raford, Noah - *Warlords, Inc.: Black Markets, Broken States, and the Rise of the Warlord Entrepreneur*
     PW - v262 - i12 - March 23 2015 - p66(1) [51-500]

Rafter, Nicole - *The Crime of All Crimes: Toward a Criminology of Genocide*
     KR - Jan 1 2016 - pNA [501+]

Raftery, Deirder - *Educating Ireland: Schooling and Social Change, 1700-2000*
ILS - v34 - i2 - Spring 2015 - p5(2) [501+]
Ragai, Jehane - *The Scientist and the Forger: Insights into the Scientific Detection of Forgery in Paintings*
TimHES - i2229 - Nov 12 2015 - p46(1) [501+]
Ragazzi, Grazia Mangano - *Obeying the Truth: Discretion in the Spiritual Writings of Saint Catherine of Siena*
Theol St - v76 - i1 - March 2015 - p197(2) [501+]
Obeying the Truth: Discretion in the Spiritual Writings of Saint Catherine of Sienna
CH - v84 - i3 - Sept 2015 - p658(3) [501+]
Ragen, Naomi - *The Devil in Jerusalem*
BL - v112 - i4 - Oct 15 2015 - p20(1) [51-500]
Ragep, F. Jamil - *The "Herbal" of al-Ghafiq?: A Facsimile Edition with Critical Essays*
Specu - v90 - i4 - Oct 2015 - p1158-1160 [501+]
Raghavan, Srinath - *1971: A Global History of the Creation of Bangladesh*
Pac A - v88 - i4 - Dec 2015 - p952 [501+]
Ragosta, John - *Religious Freedom: Jefferson's Legacy, America's Creed*
J Ch St - v57 - i3 - Summer 2015 - p576-578 [501+]
JSH - v81 - i1 - Feb 2015 - p176(2) [501+]
Ragsdale, Alison - *The Father-Daughter Club*
KR - March 15 2015 - pNA [501+]
Ragsdale, Amy - *Crossing the River: A Life in Brazil*
BL - v112 - i4 - Oct 15 2015 - p14(2) [51-500]
KR - Sept 15 2015 - pNA [501+]
Raham, R. Gary - *Confessions of a Time Traveler*
KR - May 1 2015 - pNA [501+]
Rahane, Huw Barker - *Who's Who in Thomas Hardy*
TLS - i5842 - March 20 2015 - p27(1) [501+]
Rahbar, Mitra - *Miraculous Silence: A Journey to Illumination and Healing through Prayer*
PW - v262 - i45 - Nov 9 2015 - p55(1) [51-500]
Raheb, Mitri - *Faith in the Face of Empire: The Bible through Palestinian Eyes*
IBMR - v39 - i2 - April 2015 - p81(3) [501+]
Theol St - v76 - i2 - June 2015 - p351(2) [501+]
Rahman, Raad - *Framed Butterflies*
G&L Rev W - v22 - i3 - May-June 2015 - p33(1) [51-500]
Rahman, Zia Haider - *In the Light of What We Know*
NYTBR - May 17 2015 - p32(L) [501+]
Raidt, Gerda - *In the New World: A Family in Two Centuries (Illus. by Holtei, Christa)*
c CCB-B - v68 - i10 - June 2015 - p511(1) [51-500]
c CH Bwatch - June 2015 - pNA [501+]
c HB Guide - v26 - i2 - Fall 2015 - p221(1) [51-500]
c KR - Jan 15 2015 - pNA [51-500]
c PW - v262 - i2 - Jan 12 2015 - p59(1) [51-500]
Raikhel, Eugene - *Addiction Trajectories*
CS - v44 - i2 - March 2015 - p239-241 [501+]
JRAI - v21 - i1 - March 2015 - p231(2) [501+]
Rail, Ted - *Snowden*
PW - v262 - i32 - August 10 2015 - p45(1) [51-500]
LJ - v140 - i15 - Sept 15 2015 - p60(3) [501+]
Railey, John - *Rage to Redemption in the Sterilization Age: A Confrontation with American Genocide*
Ch Today - v59 - i5 - June 2015 - p76(1) [51-500]
Raimbault, Alain - *Alexander Graham Bell: Inventeur de genie*
c Res Links - v20 - i3 - Feb 2015 - p50(1) [51-500]
Raimey, Jusin - *Fiji Random Garage Maid Special 01--Preparation*
RVBW - May 2015 - pNA [51-500]
Raimey, Terry L. - *Knights of 2nd Earth: Tears of an Honorable King (Illus. by Raimey, Justin)*
c CH Bwatch - Sept 2015 - pNA [51-500]
Raimondo, Lynne - *Dante's Dilemma*
KR - June 1 2015 - pNA [51-500]
PW - v262 - i24 - June 15 2015 - p65(1) [51-500]
Rainer, Helga - *State of the Apes 2013*
QRB - v90 - i2 - June 2015 - p240(1) [501+]
Rainey, Anne - *Body Shots*
PW - v262 - i31 - August 3 2015 - p41(1) [51-500]
Rainey, Cortez R. - *Free Your Mind: An African American Guide to Meditation and Freedom*
KR - Nov 1 2015 - pNA [501+]
Rainey, Paul B. - *There's No Time Like the Present*
TLS - i5872 - Oct 16 2015 - p27(1) [501+]
Rainini, Marco - *Corrado de Hirsau e il "Dialogus de cruce": Per la recostruzione del profilo di un autore monastico del XII secolo*
CHR - v101 - i3 - Summer 2015 - p614(2) [501+]
Rains, Valerie - *Country Living Smart Storage Solutions: Creative Closets, Stylish Shelves and More*
LJ - v140 - i2 - Feb 1 2015 - p83(1) [51-500]
Rainsford, Marcus - *An Historical Account of the Black Empire of Hayti*
Historian - v77 - i2 - Summer 2015 - p366(4) [501+]
Raiser, Jennifer - *Burning Man: Art on Fire*
LJ - v140 - i2 - Feb 1 2015 - p79(2) [51-500]
Raisor, Philip - *Headhunting and Other Sports Poems*
Sew R - v123 - i1 - Wntr 2015 - pI-II [501+]
Raith, Charles, II - *Aquinas and Calvin on Romans: God's Justification and Our Participation*
CH - v84 - i3 - Sept 2015 - p666(3) [501+]
Six Ct J - v46 - i3 - Fall 2015 - p847-848 [501+]
Raj, Shilpa Anthony - *The Elephant Chaser's Daughter*
KR - July 15 2015 - pNA [501+]
Raj, Zain - *Marketing for Tomorrow, Not Yesterday*
SPBW - Nov 2015 - pNA [51-500]
Rajah, Jaishen - *A Year of Learning, Laughter, and Life: 365 Motivational Parables*
KR - August 1 2015 - pNA [501+]
Rajan, Kaushik Sunder - *Lively Capital: Biotechnologies, Ethics, and Governance in Global Markets*
MAQ - v29 - i1 - March 2015 - pB39-B42 [501+]
Rajaniemi, Hannu - *The Causal Angel*
Analog - v135 - i1-2 - Jan-Feb 2015 - p182(1) [501+]
Rajczak, Kristen - *Famous Graveyards*
c Teach Lib - v42 - i5 - June 2015 - p9(1) [51-500]
Rajczak, Michael - *Christopher Columbus*
c BL - v111 - i16 - April 15 2015 - p46(1) [501+]
Rake, Jody Sullivan - *Carcass Chewers of the Animal World*
c HB Guide - v26 - i2 - Fall 2015 - p172(1) [51-500]
Poop and Puke Eaters of the Animal World
c HB Guide - v26 - i2 - Fall 2015 - p172(1) [51-500]
Rake, Matthew - *Creatures of the Deep (Illus. by Mendez, Simon)*
c PW - v262 - i35 - August 31 2015 - p90(2) [501+]
Creepy, Crawly Creatures (Illus. by Mendez, Simon)
c KR - August 15 2015 - pNA [51-500]
The Dawn of Planet Earth
c KR - June 15 2015 - pNA [51-500]
Dinosaurs Rule (Illus. by Minister, Peter)
c BL - v112 - i3 - Oct 1 2015 - p48(2) [51-500]
Rakoff, David - *The Uncollected David Rakoff: Including the Entire Text of Love, Dishonor, Marry, Die, Cherish, Perish*
KR - July 15 2015 - pNA [51-500]
LJ - v140 - i14 - Sept 1 2015 - p102(1) [51-500]
NYTBR - Dec 6 2015 - p78(L) [501+]
Rakoff, Joanna - *My Salinger Year*
Ent W - i1364 - May 22 2015 - p66(1) [501+]
NYTBR - June 21 2015 - p24(L) [501+]
Rakovan, Monica Tsang - *A Quest for Shiny Purple Crystals: Johnny and Max's Rock Hunting Adventure*
c RocksMiner - v90 - i3 - May-June 2015 - p285(1) [501+]
Rakow, Mary - *This Is Why I Came*
KR - Oct 1 2015 - pNA [51-500]
PW - v262 - i39 - Sept 28 2015 - p62(1) [51-500]
Rall, Ted - *Bernie*
KR - Jan 1 2016 - pNA [501+]
Ralph, Ann - *Grow a Little Fruit Tree*
NYTBR - May 31 2015 - p36(L) [501+]
Ralphs, Matt - *Fire Girl*
y Sch Lib - v63 - i4 - Winter 2015 - p249(1) [51-500]
Ram, Kalpana - *Fertile Disorder: Spirit Possession and Its Provocation of the Modern*
JRAI - v21 - i3 - Sept 2015 - p712(2) [501+]
Phenomenology in Anthropology: A Sense of Perspective
J Phil - v112 - i5 - May 2015 - p281(1) [501+]
Ramadier, Cedric - *Help! The Wolf Is Coming! (Illus. by Bourgeau, Vincent)*
c BL - v112 - i6 - Nov 15 2015 - p57(1) [51-500]
c KR - Jan 1 2016 - pNA [51-500]
c Magpies - v30 - i3 - July 2015 - p27(1) [501+]
Ramazani, Jahan - *A Transnational Poetics*
TimHES - i2211 - July 9 2015 - p49(1) [501+]
Rambaran-Olm, M.R. - *John the Baptist's Prayer or The Descent into Hell from the Exeter Book: Text, Translation and Critical Study*
Med R - May 2015 - pNA [501+]
Rambelli, Fabio - *Zen Anarchism: The Egalitarian Dharma of Uchiyama Gudo*
HNet - June 2015 - pNA [501+]
Rambo, Shelly - *Spirit and Trauma: A Theology of Remaining*
Intpr - v69 - i1 - Jan 2015 - p121(2) [51-500]
Ramet, Sabrina P. - *Bosnia-Herzegovina since Dayton: Civic and Uncivic Values*
E-A St - v67 - i5 - July 2015 - p837(2) [501+]
Religion and Politics in Post-Socialist Central and Southeastern Europe: Challenges since 1989
E-A St - v67 - i7 - Sept 2015 - p1159(3) [501+]
Ramey, Lynn T. - *Black Legacies: Race and the European Middle Ages*
Col Lit - v42 - i2 - Spring 2015 - p355(4) [501+]
Med R - May 2015 - pNA [501+]
Ramey, Stacie - *The Sister Pact*
y KR - Sept 15 2015 - pNA [51-500]
y VOYA - v38 - i5 - Dec 2015 - p62(2) [51-500]
Ramirez, Joy - *Toot: The World's Tiniest Whale (Illus. by Chapman, Mike)*
c Magpies - v30 - i5 - Nov 2015 - pS5(1) [501+]
Ramirez, Michael - *Give Me Liberty or Give Me Obama-care*
Nat R - v67 - i22 - Dec 7 2015 - p47(3) [501+]
Ramirez, Sergio - *Divine Punishment*
BL - v111 - i17 - May 1 2015 - p78(1) [51-500]
KR - March 1 2015 - pNA [501+]
LJ - v140 - i6 - April 1 2015 - p85(1) [51-500]
PW - v262 - i12 - March 23 2015 - p42(1) [51-500]
WLT - v89 - i5 - Sept-Oct 2015 - p73(1) [51-500]
Ramnanan, Sabrina - *Nothing Like Love*
Mac - v128 - i16 - April 27 2015 - p55(2) [501+]
Ramone, Marky - *Punk Rock Blitzkrieg: My Life as a Ramone*
NYT - Feb 8 2015 - p7(L) [501+]
Ramos, Dania - *Who's Ju?*
y SLJ - v61 - i6 - June 2015 - p115(2) [51-500]
y VOYA - v38 - i4 - Oct 2015 - p60(1) [51-500]
Ramos, Gabriela - *Indigenous Intellectuals: Knowledge, Power, and Colonial Culture in Mexico and the Andes*
AHR - v120 - i4 - Oct 2015 - p1528-1530 [501+]
Ramos, Jason - *Smokejumper: A Memoir by One of America's Most Select Airborne Firefighters*
LJ - v140 - i12 - July 1 2015 - p118(1) [501+]
Ramos, Manuel - *The Skull of Pancho Villa and Other Stories*
BL - v111 - i14 - March 15 2015 - p44(1) [51-500]
Rampersad, Arnold - *The Selected Letters of Langston Hughes*
HM - v330 - i1978 - March 2015 - p89(6) [501+]
Ramsay, Caro - *The Tears of Angels*
BL - v111 - i22 - August 1 2015 - p37(2) [51-500]
PW - v262 - i29 - July 20 2015 - p169(2) [51-500]
Ramsay, Frederick - *The Vulture*
KR - Sept 15 2015 - pNA [51-500]
PW - v262 - i41 - Oct 12 2015 - p50(1) [51-500]
Ramsay, Nigel - *Heralds and Heraldry in Shakespeare's England*
Six Ct J - v46 - i3 - Fall 2015 - p841-842 [501+]
TLS - i5834 - Jan 23 2015 - p21(1) [501+]
Ramsden, Evelyn - *Seacrow Island*
c HB - v91 - i6 - Nov-Dec 2015 - p115(2) [501+]
Ramsden, John - *Man of the Century: Winston Churchill and His Legend since 1945*
HT - v65 - i1 - Jan 2015 - p56(2) [501+]
Ramsey, Hope - *Last Chance Hero*
PW - v262 - i19 - May 11 2015 - p43(1) [51-500]
Ramsey, Jo - *Work Boots and Tees*
y KR - Sept 1 2015 - pNA [51-500]
Ramsey, Luke - *Intelligent Sentient?*
PW - v262 - i13 - March 30 2015 - p63(1) [51-500]
Ramsey, Paul J. - *Bilingual Public Schooling in the United States: A History of America's "Polyglot Boardinghouse".*
AJE - v121 - i3 - May 2015 - p465(5) [501+]
Ramsey, Sherry D. - *The Seventh Crow*
y VOYA - v38 - i4 - Oct 2015 - p78(1) [51-500]
Ramsom, Jeanie Franz - *The Crown Affair (Illus. by Axelsen, Stephen)*
c PW - v262 - i49 - Dec 2 2015 - p34(1) [51-500]
Ramstein, Anne-Margot - *Before After (Illus. by Ramstein, Anne-Margot)*
c HB - v91 - i1 - Jan-Feb 2015 - p71(2) [51-500]
Ramuz, Charles-Ferdinand - *Riversong of the Rhone*
TLS - i5864-5865 - August 21 2015 - p24(1) [501+]
Rana, Yadvinder S. - *The 4PS Framework*
KR - Feb 15 2015 - pNA [501+]
Ranamurthy, Anandi - *Black Star: Britain's Asian Youth Movements*
JMH - v87 - i3 - Sept 2015 - p733(2) [501+]
Ranciere, Jacques - *The Intervals of Cinema*
Afterimage - v42 - i5 - March-April 2015 - p32(2) [501+]
Rancourt, Sylvie - *Melody: Story of a Nude Dancer (Illus. by Rancourt, Sylvie)*
BL - v112 - i2 - Sept 15 2015 - p50(1) [51-500]
Nat Post - v17 - i200 - June 27 2015 - pWP4(1)

[501+]
   PW - v262 - i25 - June 22 2015 - p128(1) [51-500]
Rand, Archie - *The 613*
   KR - Sept 1 2015 - pNA [501+]
Rand, Ayn - *Ideal: The Novel and the Play*
   KR - June 1 2015 - pNA [51-500]
   New R - v246 - i7-8 - July-August 2015 - p74(5) [501+]
   NYT - August 11 2015 - pC1(L) [501+]
Rand, Emily - *A Dog Day (Illus. by Rand, Emily)*
   c NYTBR - July 12 2015 - p18(L) [501+]
   c SLJ - v61 - i6 - June 2015 - p91(1) [51-500]
Rand, Violetta - *Sin*
   PW - v262 - i14 - April 6 2015 - p47(1) [51-500]
Randall, Alice - *Soul Food Love: Healthy Recipes Inspired by One Hundred Years of Cooking in a Black Family*
   NYTBR - May 31 2015 - p24(L) [501+]
Randall, Catharine - *The Wisdom of Animals: Creatureliness in Early Modern French Spirituality*
   MLR - v110 - i3 - July 2015 - p860-862 [501+]
   Ren Q - v68 - i2 - Summer 2015 - p726-728 [501+]
   Six Ct J - v46 - i3 - Fall 2015 - p796-798 [501+]
Randall, David K. - *The King and Queen of Malibu*
   KR - Dec 15 2015 - pNA [501+]
Randall, Gregory C. - *Diamonds for Death*
   SPBW - Feb 2015 - pNA [51-500]
Randall, Lisa - *Dark Matter and the Dinosaurs: The Astounding Interconnectedness of the Universe*
   BL - v112 - i2 - Sept 15 2015 - p7(1) [51-500]
   BL - v112 - i7 - Dec 1 2015 - p13(1) [501+]
   KR - Sept 15 2015 - pNA [501+]
   Nature - v526 - i7571 - Oct 1 2015 - p40(2) [501+]
   NYTBR - Nov 29 2015 - p14(L) [501+]
   PW - v262 - i36 - Sept 7 2015 - p59(1) [51-500]
Randall, Margaret - *Haydee Santamaria, Cuban Revolutionary: She Led by Transgression*
   KR - May 1 2015 - pNA [501+]
   PW - v262 - i21 - May 25 2015 - p47(1) [51-500]
Randazzo, Joe - *Funny on Purpose: The Definitive Guide to an Unpredictable Career in Comedy*
   NYTBR - May 31 2015 - p22(L) [501+]
   PW - v262 - i12 - March 23 2015 - p60(1) [51-500]
Randazzo, Kirk A. - *Checking the Courts: Law, Ideology, and Contingent Discretion*
   HLR - v128 - i7 - May 2015 - p2107(2) [1-50]
Randel, Weina Dai - *The Moon in the Palace*
   LJ - v140 - i15 - Sept 15 2015 - p69(2) [51-500]
Randi, Don - *You've Heard These Hands: From the Wall of Sound to the Wrecking Crew and Other Incredible Stories*
   RVBW - Nov 2015 - pNA [51-500]
Randisi, Robert J. - *When Somebody Kills You*
   BL - v111 - i21 - July 1 2015 - p41(1) [51-500]
   PW - v262 - i27 - July 6 2015 - p49(1) [51-500]
Randle, Kevin D. - *The UFO Dossier: 100 Years of Government Secrets, Conspiracies, and Cover-Ups*
   y VOYA - v38 - i5 - Dec 2015 - p77(2) [51-500]
Randol, Anna - *Sins of a Wicked Princess*
   LJ - v140 - i3 - Feb 15 2015 - p133(1) [501+]
Randolph, Sherie M. - *Florynce "Flo" Kennedy: The Life of a Black Feminist Radical*
   LJ - v140 - i16 - Oct 1 2015 - p88(1) [51-500]
Randolph, Tina M. - *Breath of Dragons: Vanished*
   RVBW - Jan 2015 - pNA [501+]
Raney, James Matlack - *Jim Morgan and the Door at the Edge of the World*
   c KR - Feb 15 2015 - pNA [501+]
Rangarajan, Mahesh - *Shifting Ground: People, Mobility, and Animals in India's Environmental Histories*
   HNet - March 2015 - pNA [501+]
Range, Peter Ross - *1924*
   KR - Dec 1 2015 - pNA [51-500]
Ranisch, Robert - *Post- and Transhumanism: An Introduction*
   Col Lit - v42 - i3 - Summer 2015 - p532(4) [501+]
   SFS - v42 - i2 - July 2015 - p391-395 [501+]
Rankin, Deana - *Landgartha: A Tragicomedy by Henry Burnell*
   RES - v66 - i274 - April 2015 - p376-378 [501+]
Rankin, Ian - *The Beat Goes On: The Complete Rebus Stories*
   BL - v111 - i22 - August 1 2015 - p31(1) [51-500]
   KR - July 1 2015 - pNA [51-500]
   NS - v144 - i5251 - Feb 27 2015 - p48(2) [501+]
   PW - v262 - i26 - June 29 2015 - p47(1) [51-500]
   Even Dogs in the Wild
   KR - Nov 15 2015 - pNA [51-500]
   Mac - v128 - i46 - Nov 23 2015 - p57(2) [501+]
   PW - v262 - i47 - Nov 23 2015 - p49(1) [51-500]
   Saints of the Shadow Bible
   RVBW - March 2015 - pNA [51-500]
Rankin, Lissa - *The Anatomy of a Calling: A Doctor's Journey from the Head to the Heart and a Prescription for Finding Your Life's Purpose*
   PW - v262 - i41 - Oct 12 2015 - p63(1) [51-500]
Rankin, Peter - *Joan Littlewood: Dreams and Realities: The Official Biography*
   Am Theat - v32 - i7 - Sept 2015 - p54(2) [501+]
   TLS - i5870 - Oct 2 2015 - p30(1) [501+]
Rankin, Tom - *One Place: Paul Kwilecki and Four Decades of Photographs*
   Am St - v54 - i2 - Summer 2015 - p85-94 [501+]
Rankine, Camille - *Incorrect Merciful Impulses*
   BL - v112 - i6 - Nov 15 2015 - p19(1) [51-500]
   PW - v262 - i42 - Oct 19 2015 - p53(1) [51-500]
Rankine, Claudia - *Citizen: An American Lyric (Read by Johnson, Allyson). Audiobook Review*
   LJ - v140 - i16 - Oct 1 2015 - p45(1) [51-500]
   Citizen: An American Lyric
   Comw - v142 - i13 - August 14 2015 - p34(4) [501+]
   TLS - i5868 - Sept 18 2015 - p23(1) [501+]
   APR - v44 - i1 - Jan-Feb 2015 - p9(3) [501+]
   NYRB - v62 - i7 - April 23 2015 - p39(3) [501+]
Ranney, Karen - *An American in Scotland*
   KR - Dec 15 2015 - pNA [51-500]
   PW - v262 - i52 - Dec 21 2015 - p139(1) [51-500]
Ransom, Candice - *Cross-Pollination*
   c SLJ - v61 - i4 - April 2015 - p86(4) [51-500]
   Endangered and Extinct Amphibians
   c HB Guide - v26 - i1 - Spring 2015 - p159(1) [51-500]
   Parts of a Flower
   c CH Bwatch - March 2015 - pNA [51-500]
   Pumpkin Day! (Illus. by Meza, Erika)
   c BL - v111 - i22 - August 1 2015 - p75(1) [51-500]
   c KR - May 15 2015 - pNA [51-500]
   c SLJ - v61 - i9 - Sept 2015 - p108(2) [51-500]
Ransom, Jeanie Franz - *The Crown Affair: From the Files of a Hard-Boiled Detective (Illus. by Axelsen, Stephen)*
   c CCB-B - v68 - i9 - May 2015 - p464(2) [51-500]
   c SLJ - v61 - i2 - Feb 2015 - p76(2) [51-500]
   The Crown Affair: From the Files of a Hard-Boiled Detective (Illus. by Axelson, Stephen)
   c HB Guide - v26 - i2 - Fall 2015 - p49(1) [51-500]
Ransom, Michael - *The Ripper Gene*
   PW - v262 - i23 - June 8 2015 - p38(2) [51-500]
Ransome, Arthur - *Swallowdale*
   y HB Guide - v26 - i1 - Spring 2015 - p90(1) [51-500]
Ranzan, David A. - *Hero of Fort Schuyler: Selected Revolutionary War Correspondence of Brigadier General Peter Gansevoort, Jr.*
   HNet - May 2015 - pNA [501+]
Rao, Vani - *The Traumatized Brain: A Family Guide to Understanding Mood, Memory, and Behavior After Brain Injury*
   BL - v112 - i5 - Nov 1 2015 - p7(1) [51-500]
   LJ - v140 - i16 - Oct 1 2015 - p101(1) [51-500]
Rapacz, Mark - *City Kaiju*
   PW - v262 - i12 - March 23 2015 - p53(1) [51-500]
Rapaille, Clotaire - *The Global Code: How a New Culture of Universal Values Is Reshaping Business and Marketing*
   LJ - v140 - i13 - August 1 2015 - p108(1) [51-500]
   PW - v262 - i28 - July 13 2015 - p61(1) [51-500]
   Move Up: Why Some Cultures Advance While Others Don't
   Spec - v327 - i9739 - April 25 2015 - p46(1) [501+]
Raphael, Kate Jessica - *Murder under the Bridge*
   BL - v112 - i5 - Nov 1 2015 - p31(1) [51-500]
Raphael, Lev - *Assault with a Deadly Lie*
   RVBW - July 2015 - pNA [51-500]
Raphael, Ray - *The Spirit of '74: How the American Revolution Began*
   KR - July 15 2015 - pNA [501+]
   PW - v262 - i25 - June 22 2015 - p132(1) [51-500]
Raphael, Steven - *The New Scarlet Letter? Negotiating the U.S. Labor Market with a Criminal Record*
   IndRev - v19 - i3 - Wntr 2015 - p462(4) [501+]
Rapp, Adam - *Know Your Beholder*
   y BL - v111 - i9-10 - Jan 1 2015 - p38(1) [501+]
   Ent W - i1355-1356 - March 20 2015 - p104(1) [501+]
   KR - Jan 1 2015 - pNA [501+]
   PW - v262 - i3 - Jan 19 2015 - p54(2) [501+]
Rapp, Bill - *Tears of Innocence*
   RVBW - April 2015 - pNA [501+]
   Tears of Innocense
   RVBW - May 2015 - pNA [501+]
Rapp, J.R. - *Ordinary Oblivion and the Self Unmoored: Reading Plato's Phaedrus and Writing the Soul*
   Class R - v65 - i2 - Oct 2015 - p378-380 [501+]
Rapp, Jennifer R. - *Ordinary Oblivion and the Self Unmoored: Reading Plato's "Phaedrus" and Writing the Soul*
   Rel St - v51 - i1 - March 2015 - p130-135 [501+]
Rapp, Stephen H., Jr. - *The Sasanian World through Georgian Eyes: Caucasia and the Iranian Commonwealth in Late Antique Georgian Literature*
   HNet - Sept 2015 - pNA [501+]
Rappaport, Doreen - *Elizabeth Started All the Trouble*
   c KR - Nov 15 2015 - pNA [501+]
   Frederick's Journey: The Life of Frederick Douglass (Illus. by Ladd, London)
   c BL - v112 - i4 - Oct 15 2015 - p40(2) [501+]
   c KR - Sept 1 2015 - pNA [51-500]
   c SLJ - v61 - i10 - Oct 2015 - p130(1) [51-500]
   Lady Liberty: A Biography (Illus. by Tavares, Matt)
   c HB Guide - v26 - i1 - Spring 2015 - p204(1) [51-500]
Rappaport, Joanne - *The Disappearing Mestizo: Configuring Difference in the Colonial New Kingdom of Granada*
   AHR - v120 - i3 - June 2015 - p1087-1088 [501+]
   Ams - v72 - i1 - Jan 2015 - p159(2) [501+]
   HAHR - v95 - i3 - August 2015 - p521-523 [501+]
Rappaport, Nina - *Cultural Cues: Joe Day, Adib Cure and Carie Penabad, Tom Wiscombe*
   RVBW - Nov 2015 - pNA [501+]
Rappaport, Steve - *If Jack Had*
   SPBW - Sept 2015 - pNA [501+]
Rasch, Wolfgang - *Karl Gutzkow: Erinnerungen, Berichte und Urteile seiner Zeitgenossen. Eine Dokumentation*
   MLR - v110 - i1 - Jan 2015 - p287-289 [501+]
Raschka, Chris - *Alphabetabum: An Alphabet Album*
   c HB Guide - v26 - i2 - Fall 2015 - p204(1) [51-500]
   Give and Take
   c HB Guide - v26 - i1 - Spring 2015 - p42(1) [51-500]
   Thingy Things Series (Illus. by Raschka, Chris)
   c HB Guide - v26 - i1 - Spring 2015 - p14(1) [51-500]
Rasco, Hanna - *Jon-Lorond Saves the Day (Illus. by Flowers, Luke)*
   c PW - v262 - i52 - Dec 21 2015 - p153(1) [51-500]
Rash, Andy - *Archie the Daredevil Penguin (Illus. by Rash, Andy)*
   c BL - v111 - i22 - August 1 2015 - p70(1) [51-500]
   c KR - June 15 2015 - pNA [51-500]
   c PW - v262 - i25 - June 22 2015 - p136(1) [51-500]
Rash, Ron - *Above the Waterfall*
   BL - v111 - i22 - August 1 2015 - p26(1) [51-500]
   Esq - v164 - i2 - Sept 2015 - p58(1) [51-500]
   KR - July 1 2015 - pNA [51-500]
   PW - v262 - i28 - July 13 2015 - p40(2) [51-500]
   y SLJ - v61 - i11 - Nov 2015 - p126(2) [51-500]
   Something Rich and Strange: Selected Stories
   CC - v132 - i14 - July 8 2015 - p35(1) [51-500]
Rashid, Maemar Ibn - *The Expeditions: An Early Biography of Muhammad*
   Specu - v90 - i2 - April 2015 - p560-562 [501+]
Rashidi, Feridon - *Tales of Iran*
   KR - March 15 2015 - pNA [501+]
   Tales of Iran 2
   KR - July 1 2015 - pNA [51-500]
Rashin - *There Was an Old Lady Who Swallowed a Fly (Illus. by Rashin)*
   c HB Guide - v26 - i1 - Spring 2015 - p42(1) [51-500]
Rashke, Richard - *The Whistleblower's Dilemma: Snowden, Silkwood and Their Quest for the Truth*
   KR - Nov 15 2015 - pNA [501+]
Raskin, Jonah - *A Terrible Beauty: The Wilderness of American Literature*
   BL - v111 - i12 - Feb 15 2015 - p28(1) [51-500]
Raskin, Joyce - *My Misadventures as a Teenage Rock Star*
   c BL - v112 - i5 - Nov 1 2015 - p52(1) [501+]
Raskino, Mark - *Digital to the Core: Remastering Leadership for Your Industry, Your Enterprise, and Yourself*
   LJ - v140 - i17 - Oct 15 2015 - p98(1) [51-500]
Rasmussen, Birgit Brander - *Queequeg's Coffin: Indigenous Literacies and Early American Literature*
   MLR - v110 - i3 - July 2015 - p783-784 [501+]
Rasmussen, Nicolas - *Gene Jockeys: Life Science and the Rise of Biotech Enterprise*
   AHR - v120 - i2 - April 2015 - p675-676 [501+]
   JAH - v101 - i4 - March 2015 - p1352-1353 [501+]

Rasmussen, Seth C. - *How Glass Changed the World: The History and Chemistry of Glass from Antiquity to the 13th Century*
    J Chem Ed - v92 - i3 - March 2015 - p406-407 [501+]

Rassas, Lori B. - *The Perpetual Paycheck: 5 Secrets to Getting a Job, Keeping a Job, and Earning Income for Life in the Loyalty-Free Workplace*
    PW - v262 - i26 - June 29 2015 - p61(1) [51-500]

Rasula, Jed - *Destruction Was My Beatrice: Dada and the Unmaking of the Twentieth Century*
    Econ - v415 - i8943 - June 20 2015 - p83(US) [501+]
    KR - May 1 2015 - pNA [501+]
    LJ - v140 - i8 - May 1 2015 - p69(1) [51-500]
    NY - v91 - i25 - August 31 2015 - p89 [51-500]
    NYTBR - June 28 2015 - p31(L) [501+]
    PW - v262 - i14 - April 6 2015 - p48(1) [51-500]

Ratcliffe, Marjorie - *Mujeres epicas espanolas: silencios, olvidos e ideologias*
    MLR - v110 - i1 - Jan 2015 - p271-273 [501+]

Rath, Aaron - *The Eight-Bit Bard*
    RVBW - July 2015 - pNA [501+]

Rath, Tom - *The Rechargeables: Eat Move Sleep*
    c KR - August 1 2015 - pNA [51-500]

Rathbone, Olivia - *The Occidental Arts & Ecology Center Cookbook: Fresh-from-the-Garden Recipes for Gatherings Large and Small*
    BL - v111 - i15 - April 1 2015 - p10(1) [51-500]
    Bwatch - June 2015 - pNA [51-500]
    PW - v262 - i18 - May 4 2015 - p113(1) [51-500]

Rathbun, Brian C. - *Diplomacy's Value: Creating Security in 1920s Europe and the Contemporary Middle East*
    HNet - March 2015 - pNA [501+]

Rathmayr, Bernhard - *Armut und Fursorge: Einfuhrung in die Geschichte der Sozialen Arbeit von der Antike bis zur Gegenwart*
    HNet - May 2015 - pNA [501+]

Ratliff, Ben - *Every Song Ever: Twenty Ways to Listen in an Age of Musical Plenty*
    KR - Nov 15 2015 - pNA [501+]
    LJ - v140 - i20 - Dec 1 2015 - p105(1) [51-500]

Ratner-Rosenhagen, Jennifer - *American Nietzsche: A History of an Icon and His Ideas*
    Clio - v44 - i2 - Spring 2015 - p277-282 [501+]

Rattenburg, Richard C. - *A Legacy in Arms: American Firearm Manufacture, Design, and Artistry, 1800-1900*
    Roundup M - v22 - i4 - April 2015 - p31(1) [501+]
    Roundup M - v22 - i6 - August 2015 - p40(1) [501+]

Ratti, Carlo - *Open Source Architecture*
    TimHES - i2207 - June 11 2015 - p55(1) [501+]

Rattle, Alison - *The Beloved*
    Sch Lib - v63 - i3 - Autumn 2015 - p190(1) [51-500]

Rau, Brad - *The Ghost, Josephine*
    KR - Nov 15 2015 - pNA [51-500]

Rau, Dana Meachen - *Kids Top 10 Pet Cats*
    c CH Bwatch - July 2015 - pNA [51-500]
Recipes from Italy
    Sch Lib - v63 - i1 - Spring 2015 - p61(1) [51-500]

Raub, Raubkunst und Verwertung Judischen Eigentums. 26. Tagung zur Geschichte und Kultur der Juden in Schwaben
    HNet - March 2015 - pNA [501+]

Rauch, Alan - *Dolphin*
    Am Bio T - v77 - i4 - April 2015 - p301(2) [501+]

Rauch, Georg - *Unlikely Warrior: A Jewish Soldier in Hitler's Army*
    y CCB-B - v68 - i10 - June 2015 - p511(2) [51-500]
    y HB Guide - v26 - i2 - Fall 2015 - p211(1) [51-500]
    y PW - v262 - i49 - Dec 2 2015 - p117(2) [51-500]
    y VOYA - v38 - i1 - April 2015 - p88(1) [51-500]

Rauch, Steven J. - *The Campaign of 1812*
    J Mil H - v79 - i1 - Jan 2015 - p181-185 [501+]

Rauchway, Eric - *The Money Makers: How Roosevelt and Keynes Ended the Depression, Defeated Fascism, and Secured a Prosperous Peace*
    KR - August 1 2015 - pNA [501+]
    LJ - v140 - i15 - Sept 15 2015 - p89(2) [51-500]
    NYTBR - Nov 22 2015 - p31(L) [501+]
    PW - v262 - i37 - Sept 14 2015 - p53(1) [51-500]

Rauer, Christine - *The Old English Martyrology: Edition, Translation and Commentary*
    JEGP - v114 - i3 - July 2015 - p447(3) [501+]
    Med R - Jan 2015 - pNA [501+]
    Specu - v90 - i4 - Oct 2015 - p1161-1163 [501+]

Rauh, Cornelia - *Ausnahmezustande: Entgrenzungen und Regulierungen in Europa Wahrend des Kalten Krieges*
    HNet - June 2015 - pNA [501+]

Raulerson, Joshua - *Singularities: Technoculture, Transhumanism, and Science Fiction in the 21st Century*
    SFS - v42 - i1 - March 2015 - p182-185 [501+]

Raum, Elizabeth - *Bearded Dragons*
    c HB Guide - v26 - i1 - Spring 2015 - p160(1) [51-500]
Egyptian Pyramids
    c CH Bwatch - Feb 2015 - pNA [51-500]
    c HB Guide - v26 - i1 - Spring 2015 - p201(1) [51-500]
Great Wall of China
    c HB Guide - v26 - i1 - Spring 2015 - p201(1) [51-500]
Machu Picchu
    c HB Guide - v26 - i1 - Spring 2015 - p201(1) [51-500]
Statues of Easter Island
    c HB Guide - v26 - i1 - Spring 2015 - p201(1) [51-500]
Stonehenge
    c HB Guide - v26 - i1 - Spring 2015 - p201(1) [51-500]
Taj Mahal
    c HB Guide - v26 - i1 - Spring 2015 - p201(1) [51-500]

Raum - Ort - Ding: Kultur- und Sozialwissenschaftliche Perspektiven
    HNet - Feb 2015 - pNA [501+]

Raume, Orte, Konstruktionen. (Trans)Lokale Wirklichkeiten im Mittelalter und der Fruhen Neuzeit
    HNet - July 2015 - pNA [501+]

Raumzeitlichkeit des Imperialen
    HNet - Jan 2015 - pNA [501+]

Rausch, Jane M. - *Colombia and World War I: The Experience of a Neutral Latin American Nation during the Great War and Its Aftermath, 1914-1921*
    Ams - v72 - i3 - July 2015 - p515(2) [501+]
    HAHR - v95 - i2 - May 2015 - p368-369 [501+]

Rautenberg, Karen Rita - *Castle in Danger*
    y CH Bwatch - Sept 2015 - pNA [51-500]

Raven, James - *Bookscape: Geographies of Printing and Publishing in London before 1800*
    Eight-C St - v49 - i1 - Fall 2015 - p94-97 [501+]
Publishing Business in Eighteenth-Century England
    BHR - v89 - i2 - Summer 2015 - p374(3) [501+]
    Eight-C St - v49 - i1 - Fall 2015 - p94-97 [501+]

Raven, Margot - *Theis Rags, Hero Dog of WWI: A True Story (Illus. by Brown, Petra)*
    c HB Guide - v26 - i2 - Fall 2015 - p217(1) [51-500]

Ravenne, Jacques - *Shadow Ritual*
    PW - v262 - i1 - Jan 5 2015 - p55(1) [51-500]

Raver, Sharon A. - *Family-Centered Early Intervention: Supporting Infants and Toddlers in Natural Environments*
    RVBW - March 2015 - pNA [501+]

Raverat, Gwen - *Period Piece*
    Nature - v523 - i7562 - July 30 2015 - p529(1) [51-500]

Ravinthiran, Vidyan - *Grun-Tu-Molani*
    TLS - i5832 - Jan 9 2015 - p25(1) [501+]

Ravishankar, Anushka - *Captain Coconut & the Case of the Missing Bananas (Illus. by Sundram, Priya)*
    c CCB-B - v69 - i1 - Sept 2015 - p46(1) [51-500]
    KR - April 1 2015 - pNA [501+]
    c PW - v262 - i16 - April 20 2015 - p77(1) [51-500]
    c PW - v262 - i49 - Dec 2 2015 - p64(1) [51-500]
    y Sch Lib - v63 - i1 - Spring 2015 - p57(1) [51-500]
    c SLJ - v61 - i4 - April 2015 - p142(1) [51-500]

Raviv, Yael - *Falafel: A National Icon*
    KR - Sept 1 2015 - pNA [501+]

Ravizza, Bridget Burke - *Project Holiness: Marriage as a Workshop for Everyday Saints*
    RVBW - Nov 2015 - pNA [501+]

Rawcliffe, Carole - *Urban Bodies: Communal Health in Late Medieval English Towns and Cities*
    AHR - v120 - i1 - Feb 2015 - p313-314 [501+]
    HER - v130 - i543 - April 2015 - p426(3) [501+]
    Isis - v106 - i1 - March 2015 - p171(2) [501+]

Rawl, Paige - *Positive: Surviving My Bullies, Finding Hope, and Living to Change the World*
    y HB Guide - v26 - i1 - Spring 2015 - p195(1) [51-500]

Rawlence, Ben - *City of Thorns: Nine Lives in the World's Largest Refugee Camp*
    y BL - v112 - i6 - Nov 15 2015 - p10(1) [51-500]
    KR - Oct 1 2015 - pNA [501+]
    PW - v262 - i34 - August 24 2015 - p69(1) [51-500]

Rawley, James A. - *A Lincoln Dialogue*
    JSH - v81 - i4 - Nov 2015 - p986(2) [501+]

Rawlings, Annette - *Upsidedown and Backwards*
    RVBW - June 2015 - pNA [51-500]

Rawlings, William - *A Killing on Ring Jaw Bluff: The Great Recession and the Death of Small Town Georgia*
    Historian - v77 - i3 - Fall 2015 - p574(2) [501+]

Rawls, Wilson - *Where the Red Fern Grows*
    Ent W - i1355-1356 - March 20 2015 - p106(1) [501+]

Rawn, Melanie - *Window Wall*
    KR - Feb 1 2015 - pNA [51-500]
    PW - v262 - i7 - Feb 16 2015 - p164(1) [51-500]

Rawson, Claude - *Swift and Others*
    TimHES - i2210 - July 2 2015 - p48-2 [501+]
Swift's Angers
    Eight-C St - v49 - i1 - Fall 2015 - p104-106 [501+]

Rawson, K. - *Hitlist*
    y KR - July 15 2015 - pNA [501+]

Ray, Alice - *Born for Greatness: Me, You, and the Dalai Lama (Illus. by Roberts, Monica)*
    c CH Bwatch - July 2015 - pNA [51-500]

Ray, Benjamin C. - *Satan and Salem: The Witch-Hunt Crisis of 1692*
    JAAR - v83 - i2 - June 2015 - pNA [501+]
    NYRB - v62 - i19 - Dec 3 2015 - p21(3) [501+]

Ray, David Eugene - *The Little Mouse Santi (Illus. by Germano, Santiago)*
    c CH Bwatch - May 2015 - pNA [51-500]
    c KR - Jan 15 2015 - pNA [51-500]
    c SLJ - v61 - i5 - May 2015 - p91(1) [51-500]

Ray, Deborah Kogan - *The Impossible Voyage of Kon-Tiki (Illus. by Ray, Deborah Kogan)*
    c SLJ - v61 - i12 - Dec 2015 - p139(2) [51-500]
    c HB - v91 - i6 - Nov-Dec 2015 - p105(2) [51-500]
    c KR - July 15 2015 - pNA [51-500]

Ray, Delia - *Finding Fortune (Illus. by Ray, Delia)*
    c BL - v112 - i6 - Nov 15 2015 - p54(1) [51-500]
    c HB - v91 - i6 - Nov-Dec 2015 - p88(2) [51-500]
    c PW - v262 - i34 - August 24 2015 - p81(1) [51-500]
    c SLJ - v61 - i7 - July 2015 - p82(1) [51-500]
    c KR - Sept 1 2015 - pNA [51-500]

Ray, G. Carleton - *Marine Conservation: Science, Policy, and Management*
    QRB - v90 - i3 - Sept 2015 - p332(1) [501+]

Ray, Jonathan - *After Expulsion: 1492 and the Making of Sephardic Jewry*
    AHR - v120 - i3 - June 2015 - p1139-1140 [501+]
    JMH - v87 - i3 - Sept 2015 - p702(3) [501+]

Ray, Mary Lyn - *Go to Sleep, Little Farm (Read by Cabezas, Maria). Audiobook Review*
    SLJ - v61 - i4 - April 2015 - p61(2) [51-500]
Go to Sleep, Little Farm (Illus. by Neal, Christopher Silas)
    c HB Guide - v26 - i1 - Spring 2015 - p14(1) [51-500]
Goodnight, Good Dog (Illus. by Malone, Rebecca)
    c BL - v112 - i6 - Nov 15 2015 - p58(1) [51-500]
    c HB - v91 - i6 - Nov-Dec 2015 - p73(2) [51-500]
    c KR - August 1 2015 - pNA [51-500]
    c PW - v262 - i35 - August 31 2015 - p89(1) [51-500]
    c PW - v262 - i49 - Dec 2 2015 - p41(2) [51-500]
    c SLJ - v61 - i11 - Nov 2015 - p86(1) [51-500]
A Lucky Author Has a Dog (Illus. by Henry, Steven)
    c BL - v111 - i21 - July 1 2015 - p63(2) [51-500]
    c CH Bwatch - Oct 2015 - pNA [51-500]
    c KR - May 1 2015 - pNA [51-500]
    c SLJ - v61 - i10 - Oct 2015 - p82(2) [51-500]
A Violin for Elva (Illus. by Tusa, Tricia)
    c CCB-B - v68 - i7 - March 2015 - p366(2) [51-500]
    c CH Bwatch - March 2015 - pNA [51-500]
    c HB Guide - v26 - i2 - Fall 2015 - p49(1) [51-500]

Ray, Max - *Powerful Problem Solving*
    TC Math - v21 - i7 - March 2015 - p443(2) [501+]

Ray, Rachael - *Everyone Is Italian on Sunday!*
    BL - v112 - i7 - Dec 1 2015 - p8(1) [51-500]
    LJ - v140 - i19 - Nov 15 2015 - p103(1) [51-500]
    PW - v262 - i44 - Nov 2 2015 - p79(2) [51-500]

Ray, Shann - *American Copper*
    BL - v112 - i2 - Sept 15 2015 - p36(1) [51-500]
    Esq - v164 - i4 - Nov 2015 - p38(1) [51-500]
    KR - Sept 1 2015 - pNA [51-500]
    LJ - v140 - i16 - Oct 1 2015 - p72(1) [51-500]
    PW - v262 - i39 - Sept 28 2015 - p63(2) [51-500]

Raybon, Patricia - *Undivided: A Muslim Daughter, Her Christian Mother, Their Path to Peace (Read by Althens, Suzie). Audiobook Review*
    PW - v262 - i30 - July 27 2015 - p62(1) [51-500]
Undivided: A Muslim Daughter, Her Christian Mother, Their Path to Peace
    BL - v111 - i15 - April 1 2015 - p6(1) [51-500]
    LJ - v140 - i6 - April 1 2015 - p98(1) [51-500]
    PW - v262 - i10 - March 9 2015 - p68(1) [51-500]

Raybourn, Deanna - *A Curious Beginning*
KR - August 1 2015 - pNA [51-500]
PW - v262 - i28 - July 13 2015 - p46(1) [51-500]
Raye, Kimberly - *Texas Thunder*
PW - v262 - i31 - August 3 2015 - p42(1) [51-500]
Raymond Arsenault - *Dixie Redux: Essays in Honor of Sheldon Hackney*
JSH - v81 - i1 - Feb 2015 - p253(3) [501+]
Raymond, Cathy - *Sing What You Cannot Say*
KR - Oct 1 2015 - pNA [501+]
Raymond, Jay - *Mangle Boards of Northern Europe: A Definitive Guide to the Geographic Origins of Mangle Boards*
Mag Antiq - v182 - i4 - July-August 2015 - p40(2) [501+]
Raymond, Jon - *The World Split Open: Great Authors on How and Why We Write*
Ga R - v69 - i1 - Spring 2015 - p138-141 [501+]
Raymundo, Peter - *The Monkey and the Bee (Illus. by Bloom, C.P.)*
c KR - Feb 1 2015 - pNA [51-500]
c PW - v262 - i7 - Feb 16 2015 - p33(34) [501+]
Raynaud, Dominique - *Optics and the Rise of Perspective: A Study in Network Knowledge Diffusion*
Specu - v90 - i4 - Oct 2015 - p1163-1165 [501+]
Rayne, Sarah - *Deadlight Hall*
BL - v111 - i13 - March 1 2015 - p30(1) [51-500]
KR - Feb 1 2015 - pNA [51-500]
Raynor, John S. - *A Chronicle of Intimacies*
SPBW - Jan 2015 - pNA [51-500]
Rayor, Diane J. - *Sappho: A New Translation of the Complete Works*
Lon R Bks - v37 - i22 - Nov 19 2015 - p21(2) [501+]
NYRB - v62 - i8 - May 7 2015 - p48(3) [501+]
Rayven, Leisa - *Broken Juliet*
BL - v111 - i15 - April 1 2015 - p30(2) [51-500]
Raz, Mical - *What's Wrong with the Poor? Psychiatry, Race, and the War on Poverty*
JSH - v81 - i2 - May 2015 - p523(2) [501+]
RAH - v43 - i2 - June 2015 - p369-377 [501+]
Raz, Rachel - *The Colors of Israel*
c KR - August 1 2015 - pNA [51-500]
Razsa, Maple - *Bastards of Utopia: Living Radical Politics After Socialism*
PW - v262 - i2 - Jan 12 2015 - p46(2) [51-500]
Rea, Melissa - *Conjuring Casanova*
KR - Dec 15 2015 - pNA [501+]
Read, Benjamin - *Night Post (Illus. by Trinder, Laura)*
MFSF - v128 - i5-6 - May-June 2015 - p60(2) [501+]
Read, Calia - *Unhinge*
PW - v262 - i50 - Dec 7 2015 - p75(1) [51-500]
Read, Christopher - *War and Revolution in Russia, 1914-22: The Collapse of Tsarism and the Establishment of Soviet Power*
E-A St - v67 - i4 - June 2015 - p672(2) [501+]
Read, Piers Paul - *Monk Dawson*
TLS - i5849 - May 8 2015 - p19(2) [501+]
Scarpia
BL - v112 - i6 - Nov 15 2015 - p30(1) [51-500]
KR - Jan 1 2016 - pNA [51-500]
LJ - v140 - i20 - Dec 1 2015 - p96(1) [51-500]
Spec - v329 - i9766 - Oct 31 2015 - p38(1) [501+]
Read, Sara - *Menstruation and the Female Body in Early Modern England*
Six Ct J - v46 - i2 - Summer 2015 - p512-513 [501+]
Read, Simon - *Winston Churchill Reporting: Adventures of a Young War Correspondent*
KR - July 15 2015 - pNA [501+]
LJ - v140 - i15 - Sept 15 2015 - p94(1) [501+]
Readman, Angela - *Don't Try This At Home*
KR - March 1 2015 - pNA [51-500]
TLS - i5856 - June 26 2015 - p21(1) [501+]
Ready, Emmy Smith - *Migrant (Illus. by Pedro, Javier Martinez)*
c HB Guide - v26 - i1 - Spring 2015 - p38(1) [51-500]
Ready, Oliver - *Before and During*
NYRB - v62 - i12 - July 9 2015 - p71(3) [501+]
Reagan, Jean - *How to Catch Santa (Illus. by Wildish, Lee)*
c HB - v91 - i6 - Nov-Dec 2015 - p60(1) [51-500]
c KR - Sept 1 2015 - pNA [51-500]
c PW - v262 - i37 - Sept 14 2015 - p71(1) [51-500]
c SLJ - v61 - i10 - Oct 2015 - p68(1) [51-500]
How to Surprise a Dad (Illus. by Wildish, Lee)
c HB Guide - v26 - i2 - Fall 2015 - p49(1) [51-500]
c PW - v262 - i15 - April 13 2015 - p81(1) [51-500]

Reagan, Leslie J. - *Dangerous Pregnancies: Mothers, Disabilities, and Abortion in Modern America*
JWH - v27 - i1 - Spring 2015 - p178(9) [501+]
Reagan, Susan - *Slipper and Flipper in the Quest for the Golden Sun (Illus. by Reagan, Susan)*
c KR - July 15 2015 - pNA [51-500]
c SLJ - v61 - i10 - Oct 2015 - p83(1) [51-500]
Reagle, Joseph M., Jr. - *The Net Is Dark and Full of Terrors*
TimHES - i2218 - August 27 2015 - p46-1 [501+]
Reading the Comments: Likers, Haters, and Manipulators at the Bottom of the Web
LJ - v140 - i12 - July 1 2015 - p109(1) [51-500]
Spec - v328 - i9745 - June 6 2015 - p45(1) [501+]
Reale, Michelle - *Becoming an Embedded Librarian: Making Connections in the Classroom*
LJ - v140 - i20 - Dec 1 2015 - p116(1) [51-500]
Realini, Carol - *Financial Inclusion at the Bottom of the Pyramid*
KR - Nov 15 2015 - pNA [501+]
Reardon, Bryan - *Finding Jake*
BL - v111 - i9-10 - Jan 1 2015 - p46(1) [51-500]
NYTBR - March 1 2015 - p29(L) [501+]
y SLJ - v61 - i6 - June 2015 - p132(1) [501+]
Reardon, Carol - *A Field Guide to Gettysburg: Experiencing the Battlefield through Its History, Places, and People*
JSH - v81 - i2 - May 2015 - p539(2) [501+]
Reasoner, James - *Wind River*
RVBW - March 2015 - pNA [51-500]
Reay, Barry - *Sex Addiction: A Critical History*
TLS - i5875 - Nov 6 2015 - p31(1) [51-500]
Reay, Katherine - *The Bronte Plot*
y BL - v112 - i6 - Nov 15 2015 - p16(1) [51-500]
KR - Sept 1 2015 - pNA [51-500]
PW - v262 - i37 - Sept 14 2015 - p50(2) [51-500]
Rebanks, James - *The Shepherd's Life: A Tale of the Lake District*
NS - v144 - i5278 - Sept 4 2015 - p37(1) [51-500]
TimHES - i2208 - June 18 2015 - p47(1) [501+]
TLS - i5850 - May 15 2015 - p5(1) [501+]
The Shepherd's Life: Modern Dispatches from an Ancient Landscape
NY - v91 - i28 - Sept 21 2015 - p105 [51-500]
NYT - June 2 2015 - pC1(L) [501+]
Rebeck, Theresa - *I'm Glad about You*
KR - Dec 1 2015 - pNA [51-500]
Rebhorn, Matthew - *Pioneer Performances: Staging the Frontier*
MLR - v110 - i2 - April 2015 - p532-533 [501+]
Rebman, Renee - *Are You Doing Risky Things? Cutting, Bingeing, Snorting, and Other Dangers*
y HB Guide - v26 - i1 - Spring 2015 - p132(1) [51-500]
Rebman, Renee C. - *Are You Doing Risky Things? Cutting, Bingeing, Snorting, and Other Dangers*
VOYA - v38 - i2 - June 2015 - p88(2) [51-500]
Rebok, Sandra - *Humboldt and Jefferson: A Transatlantic Friendship of the Enlightenment*
AHR - v120 - i2 - April 2015 - p617-618 [501+]
JAH - v102 - i1 - June 2015 - p237-238 [501+]
Rector, John - *Ruthless*
BL - v111 - i18 - May 15 2015 - p29(1) [51-500]
PW - v262 - i16 - April 20 2015 - p58(1) [51-500]
Red Pine - *Finding Them Gone: Visiting China's Poets of the Past*
BL - v112 - i6 - Nov 15 2015 - p8(1) [51-500]
PW - v262 - i39 - Sept 28 2015 - p80(2) [51-500]
Redding, Arthur - *Haints: American Ghosts, Millennial Passions, and Contemporary Gothic Fictions*
AL - v87 - i1 - March 2015 - p200-202 [501+]
Reddy, Gerry - *Land Access and Resettlement: A Guide to Best Practice*
Bwatch - July 2015 - pNA [51-500]
Reddy, Nancy - *Double Jinx*
LJ - v140 - i17 - Oct 15 2015 - p91(1) [51-500]
PW - v262 - i29 - July 20 2015 - p166(1) [51-500]
Reddy, Srikanth - *Changing Subjects: Digressions in Modern American Poetry*
MLR - v110 - i1 - Jan 2015 - p251-253 [501+]
AL - v87 - i3 - Sept 2015 - p618-622 [501+]
Reddy, William M. - *The Making of Romantic Love: Longing and Sexuality in Europe, South Asia, and Japan, 900-1200 CE*
HER - v130 - i545 - August 2015 - p958(3) [501+]
Reden, Sitta von - *Antike Wirtschaft*
HNet - July 2015 - pNA [501+]
Redfern, Jon - *Children of the Tide: A Victorian Detective Story*
PW - v262 - i1 - Jan 5 2015 - p55(1) [51-500]
Redfern, Keith - *Apportionment of Blame*
RVBW - Jan 2015 - pNA [51-500]

Redfern, Nick - *The Bigfoot Book: The Encyclopedia of Sasquatch, Yeti, and Cryptid Primates*
LJ - v140 - i14 - Sept 1 2015 - p144(1) [51-500]
y SLJ - v61 - i10 - Oct 2015 - p57(1) [51-500]
Secret History: Conspiracies from Ancient Aliens to the New World Order
LJ - v140 - i12 - July 1 2015 - p110(1) [51-500]
VOYA - v38 - i2 - June 2015 - p88(1) [501+]
The Zombie Book: The Encyclopedia of the Living Dead
R&USQ - v54 - i3 - Spring 2015 - p61(2) [501+]
Redfield, Mark - *Theory at Yale: The Strange Case of Deconstruction in America*
PW - v262 - i32 - August 10 2015 - p48(1) [51-500]
Redfield, Peter - *Life in Crisis: The Ethical Journey of Doctors without Borders*
MAQ - v29 - i2 - June 2015 - pb55-b57 [501+]
Redfield, Wesley - *Sangre de Cristo: The Blood of Christ*
KR - August 15 2015 - pNA [501+]
Redgate, Riley - *Seven Ways We Lie*
y KR - Dec 15 2015 - pNA [51-500]
Redgold, Eliza - *Naked*
BL - v111 - i19-20 - June 1 2015 - p60(1) [51-500]
Rediker, Marcus - *The Amistad Rebellion: An Atlantic Odyssey of Slavery and Freedom*
AHR - v120 - i1 - Feb 2015 - p243-244 [501+]
JAH - v101 - i4 - March 2015 - p1263-1264 [501+]
S&S - v79 - i3 - July 2015 - p483-485 [501+]
Outlaws of the Atlantic: Sailors, Pirates, and Motley Crews in the Age of Sail
AHR - v120 - i1 - Feb 2015 - p198-199 [501+]
Redling, S.G. - *Baggage*
PW - v262 - i50 - Dec 7 2015 - p71(2) [51-500]
Redman, Winston K. - *Quest of a Bipolar Soldier*
y VOYA - v38 - i4 - Oct 2015 - p84(2) [51-500]
Redmond, Lea - *Knit the Sky: Cultivate Your Creativity with a Playful Way of Knitting*
LJ - v140 - i14 - Sept 1 2015 - p106(1) [51-500]
Redmond, Shana L. - *Anthem: Social Movements and the Sound of Solidarity in the African Diaspora*
AHR - v120 - i1 - Feb 2015 - p185-186 [501+]
JAH - v101 - i4 - March 2015 - p1325-1326 [501+]
Redner, Rebecca - *The Gateways Haggadah: A Seder for the Whole FamilyThe Gateways Haggadah: A Seder for the Whole Family*
PW - v262 - i2 - Jan 12 2015 - p62(1) [51-500]
Redniss, Lauren - *Thunder and Lightning: Weather Past, Present, Future*
KR - August 15 2015 - pNA [501+]
NYTBR - Oct 18 2015 - p11(L) [501+]
Redwine, C.J. - *Deliverance*
y HB Guide - v26 - i1 - Spring 2015 - p121(1) [51-500]
The Shadow Queen
y BL - v112 - i7 - Dec 1 2015 - p57(2) [51-500]
y KR - Oct 15 2015 - pNA [51-500]
y PW - v262 - i48 - Nov 30 2015 - p63(1) [51-500]
y SLJ - v61 - i12 - Dec 2015 - p126(1) [51-500]
Reece, Debbie - *The Worst Day Ever! (Illus. by Head, Ron)*
c CH Bwatch - Nov 2015 - pNA [51-500]
Reece, Henry - *The Army in Cromwellian England, 1649-1660*
Historian - v77 - i3 - Fall 2015 - p624(2) [501+]
Reece, Julie - *The Artisans*
y SLJ - v61 - i5 - May 2015 - p122(2) [51-500]
Reece, Spencer - *The Road to Emmaus*
Ga R - v69 - i1 - Spring 2015 - p122-129 [501+]
Tikkun - v30 - i1 - Wntr 2015 - p47(2) [501+]
Reed, Amy - *Damaged*
y HB Guide - v26 - i1 - Spring 2015 - p121(1) [51-500]
Invincible
y BL - v111 - i14 - March 15 2015 - p68(1) [51-500]
y CCB-B - v68 - i10 - June 2015 - p512(1) [51-500]
y HB Guide - v26 - i2 - Fall 2015 - p135(1) [51-500]
y KR - Feb 15 2015 - pNA [51-500]
y SLJ - v61 - i5 - May 2015 - p123(1) [51-500]
Reed, Austin - *The Life and the Adventures of a Haunted Convict*
KR - Nov 15 2015 - pNA [501+]
PW - v262 - i47 - Nov 23 2015 - p63(2) [51-500]
Reed, Christopher Robert - *Knock at the Door of Opportunity: Black Migration to Chicago, 1900-1919*
AHR - v120 - i4 - Oct 2015 - p1500-1501 [501+]
JAH - v102 - i2 - Sept 2015 - p589-590 [501+]
Reed, Cristie - *You Have a Pet What?! Mini Pig*
c BL - v112 - i1 - Sept 1 2015 - p97(1) [51-500]
Reed, Eli - *Eli Reed: A Long Walk Home*
CSM - Dec 29 2015 - pNA [501+]

Reed, Eric - *The Guardian Stones*
    KR - Oct 1 2015 - pNA [51-500]
    PW - v262 - i44 - Nov 2 2015 - p61(1) [51-500]

Reed, Ishmael - *Flight to Canada*
    Nation - v300 - i14 - April 6 2015 - p154(2) [501+]

Reed, Kit - *Where*
    KR - March 1 2015 - pNA [51-500]
    PW - v262 - i12 - March 23 2015 - p52(1) [51-500]

Reed, Lissa - *Definitely, Maybe, Yours*
    PW - v262 - i24 - June 15 2015 - p69(2) [51-500]

Reed, M.K. - *Palefire*
    y BL - v112 - i6 - Nov 15 2015 - p36(1) [51-500]

Reed, Marguerite - *Archangel*
    PW - v262 - i9 - March 2 2015 - p68(1) [51-500]

Reed, Mary - *Murder in Megara*
    KR - August 1 2015 - pNA [51-500]
    PW - v262 - i32 - August 10 2015 - p39(1) [51-500]

Reed, Peter - *Acid Rain and the Rise of the Environmental Chemist in Nineteenth-Century Britain: The Life and Work of Robert Angus Smith*
    Isis - v106 - i2 - June 2015 - p468(2) [501+]

Reed, Philip - *Off and Running*
    PW - v262 - i24 - June 15 2015 - p66(1) [51-500]

Reed, S. Alexander - *Assimilate: A Critical History of Industrial Music*
    PMS - v38 - i1 - Feb 2015 - p104(3) [501+]

Reed, T.J. - *Light in Germany: Scenes from an Unknown Enlightenment*
    HT - v65 - i10 - Oct 2015 - p57(2) [501+]
    TLS - i5873 - Oct 23 2015 - p23(1) [501+]

Reed, T.V. - *Robert Cantwell and the Literary Left: A Northwest Writer Reworks American Fiction*
    JAH - v102 - i1 - June 2015 - p282-283 [501+]

Reeder, Marilou T. - *The Daring Prince Dashing (Illus. by West, Karl)*
    c KR - Sept 15 2015 - pNA [51-500]
    c SLJ - v61 - i12 - Dec 2015 - p94(1) [51-500]

Reeder, Stephanie Owen - *Lennie the Legend: Solo to Sydney by Pony*
    y Magpies - v30 - i1 - March 2015 - p38(1) [51-500]

Reeds, Manuela Mischke - *8 Keys to Practicing Mindfulness: Practical Strategies for Emotional Health and Well-Being*
    BL - v111 - i19-20 - June 1 2015 - p6(1) [51-500]

Reedy, Trent - *Burning Nation*
    c CH Bwatch - May 2015 - pNA [501+]
    y HB Guide - v26 - i2 - Fall 2015 - p135(1) [51-500]
    y PW - v262 - i49 - Dec 2 2015 - p112(1) [51-500]
    y VOYA - v37 - i6 - Feb 2015 - p83(1) [51-500]

Divided We Fall (Read by Eiden, Andrew). Audiobook Review
    c BL - v111 - i14 - March 15 2015 - p24(2) [501+]

If You're Reading This
    y CH Bwatch - Feb 2015 - pNA [501+]
    y HB Guide - v26 - i1 - Spring 2015 - p121(1) [51-500]

Reef, Catherine - *The Bronte Sisters*
    y BL - v111 - i19-20 - June 1 2015 - p86(2) [501+]

Frida and Diego: Art, Love, Life
    y HB Guide - v26 - i1 - Spring 2015 - p179(1) [51-500]

The Life of Paul Laurence Dunbar: Portrait of a Poet
    y HB Guide - v26 - i1 - Spring 2015 - p192(1) [51-500]

Noah Webster: Man of Many Words
    y BL - v111 - i19-20 - June 1 2015 - p83(1) [51-500]
    c CH Bwatch - Nov 2015 - pNA [51-500]
    y HB - v91 - i4 - July-August 2015 - p160(2) [51-500]
    c KR - June 15 2015 - pNA [51-500]

Reekles, Beth - *Out of Tune*
    c Sch Lib - v63 - i1 - Spring 2015 - p57(1) [51-500]

Reel, Jerome V. - *The High Seminaiy, vol. 2: A History of Clemson University, 1964-2000*
    JSH - v81 - i1 - Feb 2015 - p248(2) [501+]

Reep, D.C. - *The Dangerous Summer of Jesse Turner*
    y PW - v262 - i30 - July 27 2015 - p71(1) [51-500]

Rees, Brian - *Detained: Emails and Musings from a Spiritual Journey through Abu Ghraib, Kandahar, and Other Garden Spots*
    KR - Oct 15 2015 - pNA [51-500]

Rees, E.A. - *Iron Lazar: A Political Biography of Lazar Kaganovich*
    E-A St - v67 - i3 - May 2015 - p500(3) [501+]
    Slav R - v74 - i1 - Spring 2015 - p192-193 [501+]

Rees, Hedley - *Find It, File It, Flog It: Pharma's Crippling Addiction and How to Cure it*
    KR - Jan 1 2016 - pNA [501+]

Reese, Abbie - *Dedicated to God: An Oral History of Cloistered Nuns*
    CH - v84 - i2 - June 2015 - p485(3) [501+]

Reese, Linda W. - *Main Street Oklahoma: Stories of Twentieth-Century America*
    JSH - v81 - i1 - Feb 2015 - p222(3) [501+]

Reese, Linda Williams - *Trail Sisters: Freedwomen in Indian Territory, 1850-1890*
    JSH - v81 - i1 - Feb 2015 - p194(2) [501+]

Reese, Terence - *Imaginative Card Play*
    RVBW - Jan 2015 - pNA [51-500]

Reese, William J. - *Testing Wars in the Public Schools: A Forgotten History*
    AJE - v121 - i4 - August 2015 - p629(4) [501+]

Reeve, Philip - *Cakes in Space (Illus. by McIntyre, Sarah)*
    c BL - v111 - i15 - April 1 2015 - p78(1) [51-500]
    c CCB-B - v69 - i1 - Sept 2015 - p46(2) [51-500]
    c HB Guide - v26 - i2 - Fall 2015 - p98(1) [51-500]
    c KR - March 1 2015 - pNA [51-500]
    c PW - v262 - i13 - March 30 2015 - p75(1) [51-500]
    c SLJ - v61 - i2 - Feb 2015 - p77(1) [51-500]

Oliver and the Seawigs Novel) (Illus. by McIntyre, Sarah)
    c HB Guide - v26 - i1 - Spring 2015 - p90(1) [51-500]

Pugs of the Frozen North (Illus. by McIntyre, Sarah)
    c BL - v112 - i6 - Nov 15 2015 - p55(1) [51-500]
    c KR - Oct 1 2015 - pNA [51-500]
    c SLJ - v61 - i11 - Nov 2015 - p91(1) [51-500]

Railhead
    y Sch Lib - v63 - i4 - Winter 2015 - p249(1) [51-500]

Reeve-Tucker, Alice - *Utopianism, Modernism, and Literature in the Twentieth Century*
    Clio - v44 - i2 - Spring 2015 - p307-311 [501+]

Reeves, Diane Lindsey - *I Declare, Charlie Brown! (Illus. by Brannon, Tom)*
    c KR - July 1 2015 - pNA [51-500]

Reeves, Eileen - *Evening News: Optics, Astronomy, and Journalism in Early Modern Europe*
    AHR - v120 - i3 - June 2015 - p1102-1103 [501+]
    JIH - v46 - i1 - Summer 2015 - p111-112 [501+]
    Ren Q - v68 - i3 - Fall 2015 - p1017-1018 [501+]
    Six Ct J - v46 - i3 - Fall 2015 - p802-803 [501+]

Reeves-Ellington, Barbara - *Domestic Frontiers: Gender, Reform, and American Interventions in the Ottoman Balkans and the Near East, 1831-1908*
    HNet - June 2015 - pNA [501+]
    JWH - v27 - i1 - Spring 2015 - p187(10) [501+]

Reeves, Madeleine - *Border Work: Spatial Lives of the State in Rural Central Asia*
    E-A St - v67 - i3 - May 2015 - p493(2) [501+]

Reeves, Martin - *Your Strategy Needs a Strategy*
    Econ - v415 - i8940 - May 30 2015 - p66(US) [501+]

Reeves, Richard - *Infamy: The Shocking Story of the Japanese American Internment in World War II*
    BL - v111 - i12 - Feb 15 2015 - p23(1) [501+]
    KR - Jan 1 2015 - pNA [501+]
    LJ - v140 - i3 - Feb 15 2015 - p113(1) [51-500]
    NYTBR - April 26 2015 - p14(L) [501+]
    PW - v262 - i7 - Feb 16 2015 - p170(1) [51-500]
    TLS - i5867 - Sept 11 2015 - p5(1) [501+]

Reeves, Virginia - *Work Like Any Other*
    KR - Jan 1 2016 - pNA [51-500]

Reformation vor Ort. Zum Quellenwert von Visitationsprotokollen
    HNet - Jan 2015 - pNA [501+]

Reformationsgeschichte und Kulturgeschichte der Reformation. Symposium zum Gedenken an Ernst Walter Zeeden
    HNet - Jan 2015 - pNA [501+]

Regal, Bryan - *Searching for Sasquatch: Crackpots, Eggheads, and Cryptozoology*
    AHR - v120 - i2 - April 2015 - p586-587 [501+]

Regan, Dian Curtis - *Space Boy and His Dog (Illus. by Neubecker, Robert)*
    c BL - v111 - i15 - April 1 2015 - p84(1) [51-500]
    c CH Bwatch - July 2015 - pNA [51-500]
    c HB Guide - v26 - i2 - Fall 2015 - p49(1) [51-500]
    c KR - Feb 1 2015 - pNA [51-500]
    c PW - v262 - i8 - Feb 23 2015 - p73(1) [51-500]

Space Boy and His Sister Dog (Illus. by Neubecker, Robert)
    c HB - v91 - i3 - May-June 2015 - p96(1) [51-500]

Space Boy and the Space Pirate
    c KR - Dec 15 2015 - pNA [51-500]

Regan, Margaret - *Detained and Deported: Stories of Immigrant Families Under Fire*
    BL - v111 - i12 - Feb 15 2015 - p8(1) [51-500]

Regan, Richard J. - *The American Constitution and Religion*
    J Ch St - v57 - i3 - Summer 2015 - p574-576 [501+]

Regionale Produzenten oder Global Player? Zur Internationalisierung der Wirtschaft im 19. und 20. Jahrhundert
    HNet - Jan 2015 - pNA [501+]

Regis, Ed - *Monsters: The Hindenburg Disaster and the Birth of Pathological Technology*
    KR - June 15 2015 - pNA [501+]
    LJ - v140 - i15 - Sept 15 2015 - p103(1) [51-500]
    Mac - v128 - i36 - Sept 14 2015 - p76(1) [501+]
    PW - v262 - i26 - June 29 2015 - p56(1) [51-500]

Regulska, Joanna - *Women and Gender in Postwar Europe: From Cold War to European Union*
    HER - v130 - i545 - August 2015 - p934(11) [501+]

Rehm, Diane - *On My Own*
    KR - Dec 15 2015 - pNA [51-500]
    PW - v262 - i51 - Dec 14 2015 - p74(2) [51-500]

Rehman, Yasmin - *Moving in the Shadows: Violence in the Lives of Minority Women and Children*
    CS - v44 - i2 - March 2015 - p241-242 [501+]

Rehr, Henrik - *Terrorist: Gavrilo Princip, the Assassin Who Ignited World War I (Illus. by Rehr, Henrik)*
    y PW - v262 - i7 - Feb 16 2015 - p182(1) [51-500]
    y PW - v262 - i49 - Dec 2 2015 - p118(1) [51-500]
    y CCB-B - v68 - i10 - June 2015 - p512(2) [51-500]
    y KR - Feb 1 2015 - pNA [51-500]
    y LJ - v140 - i5 - March 15 2015 - p88(3) [51-500]
    y VOYA - v38 - i1 - April 2015 - p68(1) [51-500]
    y BL - v111 - i13 - March 1 2015 - p42(2) [51-500]
    y HB Guide - v26 - i2 - Fall 2015 - p218(1) [51-500]

Reich, Christopher - *Invasion of Privacy (Read by Michael, Paul). Audiobook Review*
    LJ - v140 - i19 - Nov 15 2015 - p53(1) [51-500]

Invasion of Privacy
    PW - v262 - i14 - April 6 2015 - p40(1) [51-500]
    BL - v111 - i17 - May 1 2015 - p38(1) [51-500]

Reich, Kass - *Up Hamster, Down Hamster (Illus. by Reich, Kass)*
    c KR - Jan 1 2016 - pNA [51-500]
    c PW - v262 - i31 - August 3 2015 - p58(2) [501+]
    c PW - v262 - i49 - Dec 2 2015 - p58(1) [51-500]
    c Res Links - v21 - i1 - Oct 2015 - p10(1) [51-500]

Reich, Robert B. - *Saving Capitalism: For the Many, Not the Few*
    BL - v111 - i21 - July 1 2015 - p25(1) [51-500]
    KR - August 15 2015 - pNA [51-500]
    LJ - v140 - i14 - Sept 1 2015 - p114(2) [51-500]
    NYRB - v62 - i20 - Dec 17 2015 - p16(2) [501+]
    NYTBR - Nov 15 2015 - p13(L) [501+]
    PW - v262 - i35 - August 31 2015 - p79(1) [51-500]

Reich, Simon - *Good-Bye Hegemony!: Power and Influence in the Global System*
    J Am St - v49 - i3 - August 2015 - p651-652 [501+]

Reich, Susanna - *Fab Four Friends: The Boys Who Became the Beatles (Illus. by Gustavson, Adam)*
    c BL - v111 - i21 - July 1 2015 - p52(1) [51-500]
    c HB - v91 - i4 - July-August 2015 - p161(2) [51-500]
    c KR - June 15 2015 - pNA [51-500]

Reichardt, Marisa - *Underwater*
    y BL - v112 - i4 - Oct 15 2015 - p58(1) [51-500]
    y KR - Oct 15 2015 - pNA [51-500]
    y PW - v262 - i44 - Nov 2 2015 - p86(1) [51-500]
    y SLJ - v61 - i11 - Nov 2015 - p120(1) [51-500]

Reichart, David - *Every Able Body*
    PW - v262 - i8 - Feb 23 2015 - p55(1) [51-500]

Reichert, Amy E. - *The Coincidence of Coconut Cake*
    BL - v111 - i21 - July 1 2015 - p43(2) [51-500]

Reichert, Mickey Zucker - *Fields of Wrath*
    Bwatch - June 2015 - pNA [51-500]

Issac Asimov's I, Robot: To Obey
    Analog - v135 - i1-2 - Jan-Feb 2015 - p182(1) [501+]

Reichert, Ramon - *Big Data: Analysen zum Digitalen Wandel von Wissen, Macht und Okonomie*
    HNet - Feb 2015 - pNA [501+]

Reicherter, Daryn - *The Cambodian Dancer: Sophany's Gift of Hope (Illus. by Hale, Christy)*
    c BL - v112 - i6 - Nov 15 2015 - p58(1) [51-500]

Cambodian Dancer: Sophany's Gift of Hope (Illus. by Hale, Christy)
    c SLJ - v61 - i7 - July 2015 - p104(1) [51-500]

Reichl, Karl - *Medieval Oral Literature*
    Specu - v90 - i1 - Jan 2015 - p294-296 [501+]

Book Review Index 2016 Cumulation **RENTZENBRINK • 385**

Reichl, Ruth - *My Kitchen Year: 136 Recipes That Saved My Life (Illus. by Vang, Mikel)*
BL - v112 - i1 - Sept 1 2015 - p23(2) [51-500]
NYTBR - Dec 6 2015 - pNA(L) [501+]
PW - v262 - i27 - July 6 2015 - p61(1) [51-500]
Reichs, Kathy - *Speaking in Bones*
BL - v111 - i21 - July 1 2015 - p40(1) [51-500]
PW - v262 - i22 - June 1 2015 - p42(1) [51-500]
Terminal
c KR - Jan 1 2015 - pNA [51-500]
y VOYA - v38 - i1 - April 2015 - p82(1) [51-500]
Reid, Carlton - *Roads Were Not Built for Cars*
RVBW - June 2015 - pNA [51-500]
Reid, Christopher - *The Curiosities*
TLS - i5872 - Oct 16 2015 - p23(1) [501+]
Imprison'd Wranglers: The Rhetorical Culture of the House of Commons, 1760-1800
HER - v130 - i543 - April 2015 - p462(3) [501+]
Reid, Jamie - *Doped: The Real Life Story of the 1960s Racehorse Doping Gang*
BL - v111 - i21 - July 1 2015 - p16(1) [51-500]
Reid, Jan - *Let the People In*
Historian - v77 - i1 - Spring 2015 - p140(2) [501+]
Reid, Joy-Ann - *Fracture: Barack Obama, the Clintons, and the Racial Divide*
KR - August 1 2015 - pNA [501+]
PW - v262 - i30 - July 27 2015 - p56(2) [51-500]
Reid, Lindsay Ann - *Ovidian Bibliofictions and the Tudor Book: Metamorphosing Classical Heroines in Late Medieval and Renaissance England*
Six Ct J - v46 - i3 - Fall 2015 - p845-847 [501+]
Reid-Maroney, Nina - *The Reverend Jennie Johnson and African Canadian History, 1868-1967*
Can Hist R - v96 - i2 - June 2015 - p313(3) [501+]
Reid, Megan H. - *Law and Piety in Medieval Islam*
JNES - v74 - i2 - Oct 2015 - p396(2) [501+]
Reid, Michael - *Brazil: The Troubled Rise of a Global Power*
TLS - i5848 - May 1 2015 - p28(1) [501+]
Reid, Raziel - *When Everything Feels Like the Movies*
y Can Lit - i224 - Spring 2015 - p126 [501+]
SLJ - v61 - i3 - March 2015 - p161(1) [51-500]
Reid, Richard M. - *African Canadians in Union Blue: Enlisting for the Cause in the Civil War*
AHR - v120 - i4 - Oct 2015 - p1493(1) [501+]
African Canadians in Union Blue: Volunteering for the Cause in the Civil War
Can Hist R - v96 - i3 - Sept 2015 - p439(3) [501+]
Reid, Rob - *Animal Shenanigans: 24 Creative, Interactive Story Programs for Preschoolers*
Bwatch - April 2015 - pNA [51-500]
SLJ - v61 - i4 - April 2015 - p186(2) [51-500]
Reid, Robert - *Aspects of Dostoevskii: Art, Ethics and Faith*
MLR - v110 - i2 - April 2015 - p621-623 [501+]
Reid, Taylor - *Maybe in Another Life*
KR - May 1 2015 - pNA [51-500]
Reid, Taylor Jenkins - *Maybe in Another Life*
LJ - v140 - i10 - June 1 2015 - p96(1) [51-500]
Reidy, Alejandro Garcia - *Las musas rameras: Oficio dramatico y conciencia profesional en Lope de Vega*
MP - v112 - i3 - Feb 2015 - pE244(E246) [501+]
Reidy, Dave - *The Voiceover Artist*
KR - Sept 1 2015 - pNA [51-500]
PW - v262 - i39 - Sept 28 2015 - p64(1) [51-500]
Reidy, David A. - *A Companion to Rawls*
Dialogue - v54 - i1 - March 2015 - p192-193 [501+]
Reilly, Christine - *Sunday's on the Phone to Monday*
PW - v262 - i50 - Dec 7 2015 - p62(1) [51-500]
Reilly, Kathleen M. - *Explore Soil! With 25 Great Projects*
c BL - v112 - i5 - Nov 1 2015 - p39(1) [51-500]
Explore Solids and Liquids! With 25 Great Projects
c Sci & Ch - v52 - i6 - Feb 2015 - p77 [51-500]
Reilly, Matthew - *The Tournament (Read by Firth, Katie). Audiobook Review*
LJ - v140 - i19 - Nov 15 2015 - p53(1) [51-500]
The Tournament
BL - v111 - i17 - May 1 2015 - p47(1) [51-500]
KR - May 15 2015 - pNA [51-500]
LJ - v140 - i9 - May 15 2015 - p77(1) [51-500]
PW - v262 - i21 - May 25 2015 - p38(1) [51-500]
Reilly, Maura - *Women Artists: The Linda Nochlin Reader*
PW - v262 - i16 - April 20 2015 - p68(2) [51-500]
Art N - v114 - i6 - June 2015 - p77(1) [501+]
TLS - i5869 - Sept 25 2015 - p26(1) [501+]
Reilly, Nichola - *Drowned*
y HB Guide - v26 - i2 - Fall 2015 - p135(1) [51-500]
Reily, Suzel Ana - *Brass Bands of the World: Militarism, Colonial Legacies, and Local Music Making*
Notes - v71 - i3 - March 2015 - p504(4) [501+]
Reina, Mary - *Make Money Choices*
c HB Guide - v26 - i2 - Fall 2015 - p154(1) [51-500]
Save Money
c HB Guide - v26 - i2 - Fall 2015 - p154(1) [51-500]
Reinarz, Jonathan - *Past Scents: Historical Perspectives on Smell*
AHR - v120 - i4 - Oct 2015 - p1446-1447 [501+]
JIH - v45 - i4 - Spring 2015 - p567-568 [501+]
Reinburg, Virginia - *French Books of Hours: Making an Archive of Prayer, c.1400-1600*
Specu - v90 - i2 - April 2015 - p581-583 [501+]
Reiner, Desiree Ramos - *Democracy and Justice: Collected Writings*
NYRB - v62 - i9 - May 21 2015 - p20(3) [501+]
Reinhardt, Bob H. - *The End of a Global Pox: America and the Eradication of Smallpox in the Cold War Era*
LJ - v140 - i12 - July 1 2015 - p104(1) [51-500]
Reinhardt, Eric - *L'amour et les forets*
TLS - i5840 - March 6 2015 - p20(1) [501+]
Reinisch, Jessica - *The Perils of Peace: The Public Health Crisis in Occupied Germany*
HNet - March 2015 - pNA [501+]
Reinke-Williams, Tim - *Women, Work and Sociability in Early Modern London*
AHR - v120 - i3 - June 2015 - p1108-1109 [501+]
Reis, Ronald A. - *Henry Ford for Kids: His Life and Ideas, with 21 Activities*
y KR - Oct 15 2015 - pNA [51-500]
The US Congress for Kids: Over 200 Years of Lawmaking, Deal Breaking, and Compromising, with 21 Activities
BL - v111 - i9-10 - Jan 1 2015 - p64(1) [51-500]
Reiser, Lynn - *Tortillas and Lullabies / Tortillas y cancioncitas (Illus. by Valientes, Corazones)*
c BL - v111 - i9-10 - Jan 1 2015 - pS18(5) [501+]
Reisman, Nancy - *Trompe l'Oeil*
BL - v111 - i12 - Feb 15 2015 - p33(1) [51-500]
KR - March 1 2015 - pNA [51-500]
NYTBR - June 28 2015 - p26(L) [501+]
PW - v262 - i13 - March 30 2015 - p49(2) [51-500]
Reiss, Karla - *Leadership Coaching for Educators*
Bwatch - July 2015 - pNA [501+]
Reiss, Suzanna - *We Sell Drugs: The Alchemy of US Empire*
AHR - v120 - i3 - June 2015 - p1062-1063 [501+]
Am Q - v67 - i2 - June 2015 - p505-515 [501+]
Am St - v54 - i1 - Spring 2015 - p178-179 [501+]
JAH - v102 - i2 - Sept 2015 - p598-599 [501+]
Reason - v47 - i8 - Jan 2016 - p55(5) [501+]
Reist, Melinda Tankard - *Big Porn Inc: Exposing the Harms of the Global Pornography Industry*
CWS - v30 - i2-3 - Fall-Winter 2015 - p136(2) [501+]
Reitano, Joanne - *The Restless City: A Short History of New York from Colonial Times to the Present*
J Urban H - v41 - i5 - Sept 2015 - p943-950 [501+]
Reiter, Yitzhak - *Contesting Symbolic Landscape in Jerusalem: Jewish/Islamic Conflict over the Museum of Tolerance at Mamilla Cemetery*
IJMES - v47 - i3 - August 2015 - p629-632 [501+]
Rejino, Mona - *Miniatures in Style: Six Original Piano Solos in Baroque, Classical, Romantic, Impressionist, and Contemporary Styles*
Am MT - v65 - i3 - Dec 2015 - p47(2) [501+]
Rekonstruktive Wissensbildung. Historische und gegenwartige Perspektiven einer gegenstandsbezogenen Theorie der Sozialen Arbeit
HNet - April 2015 - pNA [501+]
Religious Press and Print Culture
HNet - Feb 2015 - pNA [501+]
Remarque, Erich Maria - *The Promised Land*
Lon R Bks - v37 - i9 - May 7 2015 - p3(1) [501+]
NS - v144 - i5248 - Feb 6 2015 - p38(2) [501+]
Remenar, Kristen - *Groundhog's Dilemma (Illus. by Faulkner, Matt)*
c KR - Oct 1 2015 - pNA [51-500]
c SLJ - v61 - i11 - Nov 2015 - p86(1) [51-500]
Remender, Rick - *The Delirium of Hope*
LJ - v140 - i15 - Sept 15 2015 - p60(3) [501+]
Remensnyder, Amy G. - *La Conquistadora: The Virgin Mary at War and Peace in the Old and New Worlds*
AHR - v120 - i1 - Feb 2015 - p298-299 [501+]
Remick, Elizabeth J. - *Regulating Prostitution in China: Gender and Local Statebuilding, 1900-1937*
AHR - v120 - i2 - April 2015 - p596-597 [501+]
Pac A - v88 - i4 - Dec 2015 - p911 [501+]
Remington, Thomas F. - *Presidential Decrees in Russia: A Comparative Perspective*
For Aff - v94 - i1 - Jan-Feb 2015 - pNA [51-500]
Remphry, Martin - *Pirates Are Stealing Our Cows*
c CH Bwatch - Feb 2015 - pNA [501+]
Wanted Prince Charming (Illus. by Fiorin, Fabiano)
c Res Links - v20 - i3 - Feb 2015 - p14(2) [501+]
Renard, Amelie Le - *A Society of Young Women: Oppurtunities of Place, Power and Reform in Saudi Arabia*
IJMES - v47 - i2 - May 2015 - p404-406 [501+]
Renard, John - *The Handy Islam Answer Book*
LJ - v140 - i3 - Feb 15 2015 - p129(2) [51-500]
y SLJ - v61 - i6 - June 2015 - p71(1) [51-500]
Renaud, Anne - *Pier 21: Stories From Near and Far, 2d ed.*
c Res Links - v20 - i5 - June 2015 - p15(1) [51-500]
Renault, Mary - *The Last of the Wine*
HT - v65 - i8 - August 2015 - p56(2) [501+]
Renaut, Olivier - *Platon: La mediation des emotions. L'education du thymos dans les dialogues*
Class R - v65 - i2 - Oct 2015 - p374-376 [501+]
Renberg, Tore - *See You Tomorrow*
KR - Jan 15 2015 - pNA [51-500]
RVBW - Oct 2015 - pNA [51-500]
Rende, Richard - *Raising Can-Do Kids: Giving Children the Tools to Thrive in a Fast-Changing World*
KR - June 1 2015 - pNA [501+]
PW - v262 - i27 - July 6 2015 - p63(1) [51-500]
Rendell, Ruth - *Dark Corners*
BL - v112 - i3 - Oct 1 2015 - p4(1) [51-500]
BL - v112 - i4 - Oct 15 2015 - p18(2) [51-500]
NS - v144 - i5284 - Oct 16 2015 - p50(2) [501+]
NYTBR - Nov 1 2015 - p29(L) [501+]
Spec - v329 - i9764 - Oct 17 2015 - p38(1) [501+]
Rendle, Gil - *Doing the Math of Mission: Fruits, Faithfulness, and Metrics*
CC - v132 - i8 - April 15 2015 - p41(1) [51-500]
Rendon, Jim - *Upside: The New Science of Post-Traumatic Growth*
KR - June 1 2015 - pNA [501+]
LJ - v140 - i12 - July 1 2015 - p100(1) [51-500]
Renee, Rachel - *Dork Diaries 9: Tales from a Not-So-Dorky Drama Queen*
PW - v262 - i24 - June 15 2015 - p16(1) [51-500]
Renehan, John - *The Valley*
BL - v111 - i11 - Feb 1 2015 - p24(1) [51-500]
KR - Feb 1 2015 - pNA [51-500]
LJ - v140 - i2 - Feb 1 2015 - p75(2) [51-500]
PW - v262 - i2 - Jan 12 2015 - p35(1) [51-500]
PW - v262 - i7 - Feb 16 2015 - p8(1) [51-500]
Renn, Diana - *Blue Voyage*
y KR - August 15 2015 - pNA [51-500]
y PW - v262 - i32 - August 10 2015 - p61(1) [51-500]
y SLJ - v61 - i9 - Sept 2015 - p162(1) [51-500]
y VOYA - v38 - i4 - Oct 2015 - p60(1) [51-500]
Latitude Zero
y HB Guide - v26 - i2 - Fall 2015 - p135(1) [51-500]
Renner, James - *The Great Forgetting*
BL - v112 - i2 - Sept 15 2015 - p31(1) [51-500]
KR - Sept 1 2015 - pNA [51-500]
PW - v262 - i37 - Sept 14 2015 - p38(1) [51-500]
Renner, Michael - *Vital Signs, Volume 20*
QRB - v90 - i1 - March 2015 - p86(1) [501+]
Rennie, Kriston R. - *The Foundations of Medieval Papal Legation*
Med R - Jan 2015 - pNA [501+]
Specu - v90 - i3 - July 2015 - p847-848 [501+]
Rennie, Neil - *Treasure Neverland: Real and Imaginary Pirates*
Nine-C Lit - v69 - i4 - March 2015 - p558(3) [501+]
Rennie, Susan - *The 12 Days o' Yule: A Scots Christmas Rhyme (Illus. by Land, Matthew)*
c KR - Oct 15 2015 - pNA [51-500]
c PW - v262 - i37 - Sept 14 2015 - p69(1) [51-500]
Rennison, Nick - *The Rivals of Dracula*
Spec - v329 - i9771 - Dec 5 2015 - p52(1) [501+]
Renoff, Greg - *Van Halen Rising: How a Southern California Backyard Party Band Saved Heavy Metal*
BL - v112 - i3 - Oct 1 2015 - p9(1) [51-500]
PW - v262 - i34 - August 24 2015 - p75(1) [51-500]
Renshaw, Layla - *Exhuming Loss: Memory, Materiality and Mass Graves of the Spanish Civil War*
HER - v130 - i542 - Feb 2015 - p239(2) [501+]
Rentfrow, James C. - *Home Squadron: The U.S. Navy on the North Atlantic Station*
AHR - v120 - i2 - April 2015 - p632-633 [501+]
Rentzenbrink, Cathy - *The Last Act of Love: The Story of My Brother and His Sister*
NS - v144 - i5268 - June 26 2015 - p44(2) [501+]

Renwick, Robin - *The End of Apartheid: Diary of a Revolution*
    Econ - v414 - i8929 - March 14 2015 - p85(US) [501+]

Repila, Ivan - *The Boy Who Stole Attila's Horse*
    NS - v144 - i5263 - May 22 2015 - p53(1) [501+]
    TLS - i5844 - April 3 2015 - p27(1) [501+]

Repino, Robert - *Mort(e): A Novel (Read by Pinchot, Bronson).* Audiobook Review
    PW - v262 - i12 - March 23 2015 - p70(1) [51-500]
    Mort(e).
    CQ - v65 - i1 - Fall 2015 - p124(3) [501+]

Repousis, Angelo - *Greek-American Relations from Monroe to Truman*
    RAH - v43 - i2 - June 2015 - p237-244 [501+]

Resau, Laura - *The Lightning Queen*
    c BL - v112 - i3 - Oct 1 2015 - p79(1) [51-500]
    c KR - August 15 2015 - pNA [51-500]
    c PW - v262 - i33 - August 17 2015 - p72(1) [51-500]
    c SLJ - v61 - i9 - Sept 2015 - p145(3) [51-500]
    y VOYA - v38 - i4 - Oct 2015 - p60(1) [51-500]

Rescher, Nicholas - *A Journey Through Philosophy in 101 Anecdotes*
    BL - v111 - i19-20 - June 1 2015 - p6(1) [51-500]
    LJ - v140 - i11 - June 15 2015 - p92(1) [51-500]

Reside, Mark - *Stunno's Surf Adventure (Illus. by Jacobson, Tina)*
    c CH Bwatch - Oct 2015 - pNA [501+]

Ressler, Kim - *When I Grow Up I Want To Be ... a Veterinarian!*
    c CH Bwatch - Feb 2015 - pNA [501+]

Reston, James, Jr. - *Luther's Fortress: Martin Luther and His Reformation under Siege*
    KR - Feb 15 2015 - pNA [501+]
    PW - v262 - i10 - March 9 2015 - p63(1) [51-500]

Reszke, Katka - *Return of the Jew: Identity Narratives of the Third Post-Holocaust Generation of Jews in Poland*
    ERS - v38 - i3 - March 2015 - p469(3) [501+]
    HNet - July 2015 - pNA [501+]

Rettstatt, Linda - *The Real Thing.* E-book Review
    PW - v262 - i46 - Nov 16 2015 - p61(1) [51-500]
    Rescued
    PW - v262 - i6 - Feb 9 2015 - p51(1) [51-500]

Reus, Katie - *Shattered Duty*
    PW - v262 - i16 - April 20 2015 - p63(1) [51-500]

Revell, Donald - *Drought-Adapted Vine*
    PW - v262 - i29 - July 20 2015 - p166(1) [51-500]
    LJ - v140 - i15 - Sept 15 2015 - p80(1) [51-500]
    Essay: A Critical Memoir
    PW - v262 - i7 - Feb 16 2015 - p156(1) [51-500]

Revell, Mike - *Stonebird*
    c BL - v111 - i19-20 - June 1 2015 - p107(1) [51-500]
    c Sch Lib - v63 - i2 - Summer 2015 - p108(2) [51-500]
    c SLJ - v61 - i11 - Nov 2015 - p101(2) [51-500]

Revelle, Rick - *Algonquin Spring*
    y Res Links - v21 - i1 - Oct 2015 - p39(2) [51-500]

Revelli, Nuto - *Mussolini's Death March: Eyewitness Accounts of Italian Soldiers on the Eastern Front*
    Historian - v77 - i1 - Spring 2015 - p188(2) [501+]

Reverte, Jorge M. - *Guerreros y traidores: De la Guerra de Espana a la Guerra fria*
    J Mil H - v79 - i3 - July 2015 - p871-872 [501+]

Revis, Beth - *Body Electric*
    PW - v262 - i14 - April 6 2015 - p63(1) [51-500]

Revisiting Humboldtian Science
    HNet - June 2015 - pNA [501+]

Revoyr, Nina - *Lost Canyon*
    BL - v111 - i21 - July 1 2015 - p32(1) [51-500]
    KR - June 15 2015 - pNA [51-500]
    PW - v262 - i26 - June 29 2015 - p41(1) [51-500]

Rework America - *America's Moment: Creating Opportunity in the Connected Age*
    Econ - v416 - i8945 - July 4 2015 - p73(US) [501+]

Rex, Adam - *Smek for President! (Read by Turpin, Bahni).* Audiobook Review
    c BL - v111 - i19-20 - June 1 2015 - p141(1) [51-500]
    y HB - v91 - i4 - July-August 2015 - p166(1) [51-500]
    c SLJ - v61 - i5 - May 2015 - p70(2) [51-500]
    Smek for President!
    c HB Guide - v26 - i2 - Fall 2015 - p98(1) [51-500]
    Smek for President (Illus. by Rex, Adam)
    y CCB-B - v68 - i6 - Feb 2015 - p326(2) [51-500]

Rex, Michael - *The Hole to China*
    c HB Guide - v26 - i1 - Spring 2015 - p65(1) [51-500]

Rey, H.A. - *It's Ramadan, Curious George (Illus. by Young, Mary O'Keefe)*
    c BL - v112 - i6 - Nov 15 2015 - p49(1) [51-500]

Rey, Hans Augusto - *Curious George Makes Maple Syrup (Illus. by Rey, Hans Augusto)*
    c HB Guide - v26 - i1 - Spring 2015 - p27(1) [51-500]

Rey, Margret - *Sweet Dreams: 5-Minute Bedtime Stories*
    c HB Guide - v26 - i2 - Fall 2015 - p53(1) [51-500]

Rey, Rainer - *Cosmosis*
    Bwatch - March 2015 - pNA [51-500]

Rey Rosa, Rodrigo - *Severina*
    WLT - v89 - i2 - March-April 2015 - p61(2) [501+]

Rey, Terry - *Crossing the Water and Keeping the Faith: Haitian Religion in Miami*
    CS - v44 - i6 - Nov 2015 - p839-841 [501+]

Reyes, Barbara Jane - *Diwata*
    NAR - v300 - i2 - Spring 2015 - p44(1) [501+]

Reyes, M.G. - *The Emancipated*
    c BL - v111 - i17 - May 1 2015 - p49(2) [51-500]
    y HB Guide - v26 - i2 - Fall 2015 - p135(1) [51-500]
    y PW - v262 - i10 - March 9 2015 - p74(2) [51-500]
    SLJ - v61 - i3 - March 2015 - p161(2) [51-500]
    y VOYA - v37 - i6 - Feb 2015 - p63(1) [51-500]

Reynaud, Emmanuel G. - *Imaging Marine Life: Macrophotography and Microscopy Approaches for Marine Biology*
    QRB - v90 - i2 - June 2015 - p242(2) [501+]

Reynaud, Stephane - *Book of Tripe*
    PW - v262 - i27 - July 6 2015 - p62(1) [51-500]

Reynhout, Kenneth A. - *Interdisciplinary Interpretation: Paul Ricoeur and the Hermeneutics of Theology and Science*
    TT - v72 - i2 - July 2015 - p234-236 [501+]

Reynolds, Aaron - *Creepy Carrots.* Audiobook Review
    c SLJ - v61 - i4 - April 2015 - p52(2) [501+]
    Las zanahorias maleficas (Illus. by Brown, Peter)
    c SLJ - v61 - i12 - Dec 2015 - p94(1) [51-500]
    Nerdy Birdy (Illus. by Davies, Matt)
    c BL - v111 - i21 - July 1 2015 - p64(1) [51-500]
    c KR - June 15 2015 - pNA [51-500]
    c PW - v262 - i23 - June 8 2015 - p59(1) [51-500]
    President Squid (Illus. by Varon, Sara)
    c KR - Jan 1 2016 - pNA [51-500]
    c PW - v262 - i51 - Dec 14 2015 - p85(1) [51-500]

Reynolds, Alastair - *Slow Bullets*
    PW - v262 - i17 - April 27 2015 - p57(1) [51-500]

Reynolds, Alison - *A New Friend for Marmalade (Illus. by McKenzie, Heath)*
    c HB Guide - v26 - i1 - Spring 2015 - p43(1) [51-500]
    Why I Love My Dad (Illus. by Geddes, Serena)
    c HB Guide - v26 - i2 - Fall 2015 - p16(2) [51-500]
    KR - April 1 2015 - pNA [51-500]

Reynolds, Benjamin E. - *Reconsidering the Relationship between Biblical and Systematic Theology in the New Testament*
    Theol St - v76 - i4 - Dec 2015 - p839(2) [501+]

Reynolds, Bill - *Hope: A School, a Team, a Dream*
    BL - v112 - i7 - Dec 1 2015 - p10(1) [51-500]
    LJ - v140 - i19 - Nov 15 2015 - p89(1) [51-500]

Reynolds, Burt - *But Enough about Me: A Memoir*
    BL - v112 - i6 - Nov 15 2015 - p7(1) [51-500]
    KR - Oct 15 2015 - pNA [501+]

Reynolds, David - *In Command of History: Churchill Fighting and Writing the Second*
    HT - v65 - i1 - Jan 2015 - p56(2) [501+]

Reynolds, Debbie - *Make 'Em Laugh: Short-Term Memories of Longtime Friends*
    BL - v112 - i6 - Nov 15 2015 - p8(1) [51-500]
    NYTBR - Dec 6 2015 - p70(L) [501+]

Reynolds, Jason - *All American Boys*
    y BL - v112 - i2 - Sept 15 2015 - p62(1) [51-500]
    y HB - v91 - i6 - Nov-Dec 2015 - p89(1) [51-500]
    y KR - August 15 2015 - pNA [51-500]
    y NYTBR - Dec 20 2015 - p15(L) [501+]
    y PW - v262 - i49 - Dec 2 2015 - p88(1) [51-500]
    y SLJ - v61 - i9 - Sept 2015 - p172(2) [51-500]
    The Boy in the Black Suit (Read by Allen, Corey). Audiobook Review
    y HB - v91 - i4 - July-August 2015 - p166(1) [51-500]
    y SLJ - v61 - i6 - June 2015 - p67(1) [51-500]
    The Boy in the Black Suit
    y BL - v111 - i11 - Feb 1 2015 - p44(1) [51-500]
    y CCB-B - v68 - i6 - Feb 2015 - p327(1) [51-500]
    y HB - v91 - i2 - March-April 2015 - p107(1) [51-500]
    y HB Guide - v26 - i2 - Fall 2015 - p135(1) [51-500]
    y VOYA - v37 - i6 - Feb 2015 - p63(1) [51-500]
    When I was the Greatest (Read by Adkins, J.B.). Audiobook Review
    c BL - v111 - i14 - March 15 2015 - p24(2) [51-500]

Reynolds, Kate E. - *Ellie Needs to Go*
    c CH Bwatch - March 2015 - pNA [51-500]
    Things Ellie Likes
    c CH Bwatch - March 2015 - pNA [51-500]
    What's Happening to Ellie?
    c CH Bwatch - March 2015 - pNA [51-500]

Reynolds, L.D. - *Scribes and Scholars: a Guide to the Transmission of Greek and Latin Literature*
    Class R - v65 - i2 - Oct 2015 - p618-619 [501+]

Reynolds, L.M. - *Spies In Our Midst*
    KR - April 1 2015 - pNA [501+]

Reynolds, Luke - *Bedtime Blastoff!*
    c KR - Oct 15 2015 - pNA [501+]
    The Looney Experiment
    c SLJ - v61 - i8 - August 2015 - p90(1) [51-500]

Reynolds, Marcia - *The Discomfort Zone: How Leaders Turn Difficult Conversations Into Breakthroughs*
    Bwatch - Jan 2015 - pNA [51-500]

Reynolds, Matthew - *Likenesses: Translation, Illustration, Interpretation*
    MLR - v110 - i3 - July 2015 - p793-794 [501+]

Reynolds, Paul A. - *Sydney & Simon: Full Steam Ahead! (Illus. by Reynolds, Peter H.)*
    c HB Guide - v26 - i1 - Spring 2015 - p65(1) [51-500]
    Sydney & Simon: Go Green! (Illus. by Reynolds, Peter H.)
    c KR - August 15 2015 - pNA [51-500]
    c SLJ - v61 - i12 - Dec 2015 - p99(1) [51-500]

Reynolds, R.R. - *Masters' Mysterium*
    KR - June 15 2015 - pNA [51-500]

Reynolds, Susan - *The Middle Ages without Feudalism: Essays in Criticism and Comparison on the Medieval West*
    HER - v130 - i545 - August 2015 - p962(2) [501+]

Reynolds, Toby - *Extreme Earth*
    c SLJ - v61 - i5 - May 2015 - p142(1) [51-500]

Reys, Barbara J. - *We Need Another Revolution: Five Decades of Mathematics Curriculum Papers by Zalman Usiskin*
    TC Math - v22 - i2 - Sept 2015 - p116(2) [501+]

Reysmann, Theodor - *De Obitu Lohannis Stoefler Lustingani Mathematici Tubingensis elegia (Augsburg 1531): Ein Gedicht auf den Tod des Tubinger Astronomen Johannes Stoffler*
    Sev Cent N - v73 - i1-2 - Spring-Summer 2015 - p67(3) [501+]

Reza, Seema - *When the World Breaks Open*
    KR - Dec 15 2015 - pNA [501+]

Reza, Yasmina - *Happy Are the Happy*
    CSM - Jan 28 2015 - pNA [501+]
    NY - v91 - i2 - Feb 23 2015 - p179 [501+]
    NYTBR - Feb 1 2015 - p12(L) [501+]
    TLS - i5839 - Feb 27 2015 - p20(1) [501+]

Rgev, Motti - *Pop-Rock Music: Aesthetic Cosmopolitanism in Late Modernity*
    Am Q - v67 - i1 - March 2015 - p253-265 [501+]

Rhatigan, Joe - *Alice in Wonderland: Down the Rabbit Hole (Illus. by Puybaret, Eric)*
    c CH Bwatch - April 2015 - pNA [51-500]
    c HB Guide - v26 - i2 - Fall 2015 - p42(1) [51-500]
    c Sch Lib - v63 - i2 - Summer 2015 - p97(1) [51-500]
    Inventions That Could Have Changed the World ... But Didn't! (Illus. by Owsley, Anthony)
    c BL - v111 - i9-10 - Jan 1 2015 - p72(2) [51-500]
    c CCB-B - v68 - i8 - April 2015 - p417(1) [51-500]
    c HB Guide - v26 - i2 - Fall 2015 - p186(1) [51-500]
    c Sci & Ch - v52 - i9 - Summer 2015 - p91 [51-500]
    My First Book of Funny Animals
    c KR - July 1 2015 - pNA [51-500]
    c PW - v262 - i6 - Feb 9 2015 - p66(2) [51-500]

Rhee, Helen - *Loving the Poor, Saving the Rich: Wealth, Poverty, and Early Christian Formation*
    CH - v84 - i3 - Sept 2015 - p644(3) [51-500]

Rhoades, J.D. - *Devils and Dust*
    BL - v111 - i9-10 - Jan 1 2015 - p45(1) [51-500]
    Ice Chest
    PW - v262 - i52 - Dec 21 2015 - p133(1) [51-500]

Rhoads, Loren - *The Dangerous Type*
    KR - May 15 2015 - pNA [51-500]
    PW - v262 - i18 - May 4 2015 - p101(1) [51-500]
    In the Wake of the Templars: Kill by Numbers
    PW - v262 - i30 - July 27 2015 - p47(1) [51-500]

Rhodes, Bill - *An Introduction to Military Ethics: A Reference Handbook*
    APJ - v29 - i5 - Sept-Oct 2015 - p109(2) [501+]

Rhodes-Courter, Ashley - *Three More Words*
    y BL - v111 - i22 - August 1 2015 - p50(1) [51-500]

Rhodes, Dan - *When the Professor Got Stuck in the Snow*
    Spec - v329 - i9769 - Nov 21 2015 - p56(2) [501+]

Rhodes, Gary D. - *Ted Browning's Dracula*
    Si & So - v25 - i2 - Feb 2015 - p106(1) [501+]
Rhodes, Harold - *The Blameless Victim*
    KR - May 1 2015 - pNA [501+]
Rhodes, James - *Instrumental: A Memoir of Madness, Medication and Music*
    NS - v144 - i5266 - June 12 2015 - p49(1) [501+]
    Spec - v328 - i9747 - June 20 2015 - p37(2) [501+]
Rhodes, Jewell Parker - *Bayou Magic (Read by Turpin, Bahni). Audiobook Review*
    c SLJ - v61 - i11 - Nov 2015 - p70(1) [51-500]
    Bayou Magic
    BL - v111 - i14 - March 15 2015 - p73(1) [51-500]
    c CCB-B - v69 - i1 - Sept 2015 - p47(1) [51-500]
    c HB Guide - v26 - i2 - Fall 2015 - p98(1) [51-500]
    c KR - Feb 15 2015 - pNA [51-500]
    c SLJ - v61 - i2 - Feb 2015 - p92(1) [51-500]
Rhodes, Kate - *The Winter Foundlings*
    LJ - v140 - i2 - Feb 1 2015 - p76(1) [51-500]
Rhodes, Lisa - *Animals of Alaska: A Coloring and Activity Book (Illus. by Rhodes, Lisa)*
    c CH Bwatch - March 2015 - pNA [51-500]
Rhodes, Morgan - *A Book of Spirits and Thieves*
    y BL - v111 - i18 - May 15 2015 - p60(1) [51-500]
    y HB Guide - v26 - i2 - Fall 2015 - p135(1) [51-500]
    y SLJ - v61 - i5 - May 2015 - p123(2) [51-500]
    y VOYA - v38 - i2 - June 2015 - p82(1) [501+]
    Gathering Darkness
    y HB Guide - v26 - i1 - Spring 2015 - p121(1) [51-500]
    c Res Links - v20 - i3 - Feb 2015 - p34(2) [51-500]
Rhodes, Neil - *English Renaissance Translation Theory*
    Ren Q - v68 - i1 - Spring 2015 - p382-384 [501+]
Rhodes, P.J. - *A Short History of Ancient Greece*
    Class R - v65 - i2 - Oct 2015 - p614-615 [501+]
Rhodes, Peter J. - *Atthis: The Ancient Histories of Athens*
    HNet - March 2015 - pNA [501+]
Rhodes-Pitts, Sharifa - *Jake Makes a World: Jacob Lawrence, a Young Artist in Harlem (Illus. by Myers, Christopher)*
    c CH Bwatch - August 2015 - pNA [51-500]
    c SLJ - v61 - i11 - Nov 2015 - p133(1) [51-500]
Rhodes, Richard - *Hell and Good Company: The Spanish Civil War and the World It Made*
    Econ - v414 - i8923 - Jan 31 2015 - p74(US) [501+]
    Nature - v518 - i7538 - Feb 12 2015 - p165(1) [501+]
    NYTBR - March 1 2015 - p19(L) [501+]
Rhodes, Rita - *Empire and Co-operation: How the British Empire Used Co-Operatives in Its Development Strategies 1900-1970*
    ILR - v154 - i1 - March 2015 - p115(6) [501+]
Rhodes, Ryan - *Free Electricity*
    KR - Feb 15 2015 - pNA [501+]
Rhodes, Sammy - *This Is Awkward: How Life's Uncomfortable Moments Open the Door to Intimacy and Connection*
    PW - v262 - i51 - Dec 14 2015 - p76(2) [51-500]
Riall, Lucy - *Under the Volcano: Revolution in a Sicilian Town*
    JMH - v87 - i1 - March 2015 - p206(2) [501+]
Ribar, Lindsay - *The Fourth Wish*
    y HB Guide - v26 - i1 - Spring 2015 - p121(1) [51-500]
Ribay, Randy - *An Infinite Number of Parallel Universes*
    y HB - v91 - i6 - Nov-Dec 2015 - p90(1) [51-500]
    y KR - Sept 1 2015 - pNA [51-500]
    y PW - v262 - i35 - August 31 2015 - p95(1) [51-500]
    y SLJ - v61 - i9 - Sept 2015 - p172(1) [51-500]
Ribchester, Lucy - *The Hourglass Factory*
    y BL - v112 - i6 - Nov 15 2015 - p25(1) [51-500]
Ribeiro, Edgard Telles - *His Own Man*
    For Aff - v94 - i1 - Jan-Feb 2015 - pNA [501+]
Ribowsky, Mark - *Dreams to Remember: Otis Redding, Stax Records, and the Transformation of Southern Soul*
    Mac - v128 - i23 - June 15 2015 - p60(1) [501+]
    BL - v111 - i17 - May 1 2015 - p69(1) [51-500]
    Dbt - v82 - i10 - Oct 2015 - p68(1) [501+]
    KR - April 1 2015 - pNA [501+]
    NYTBR - May 31 2015 - p28(L) [501+]
    PW - v262 - i19 - May 11 2015 - p52(2) [501+]
    Whiskey Bottles and Brand-New Cars: The Fast Life and Sudden Death of Lynyrd Skynyrd
    BL - v111 - i13 - March 1 2015 - p13(2) [501+]
    KR - Feb 1 2015 - pNA [501+]
Ricard, Anouk - *Anna & Froga: Thrills, Spills and Gooseberries*
    BL - v111 - i13 - March 1 2015 - p43(1) [501+]
    c SLJ - v61 - i3 - March 2015 - p130(1) [51-500]

Ricard, Matthieu - *Altruism*
    KR - May 15 2015 - pNA [501+]
    Caring Economics: Conversations on Altruism and Compassion, between Scientists, Economists, and the Dalai Lama
    LJ - v140 - i5 - March 15 2015 - p114(1) [501+]
Riccards, Michael P. - *Faith and Leadership: The Papacy and the Roman Catholic Church*
    CHR - v101 - i4 - Autumn 2015 - p899(3) [501+]
Ricciardelli, Rose - *Surviving Incarceration: Inside Canadian Prisons*
    CS - v44 - i6 - Nov 2015 - p841-843 [501+]
Ricciardi, Holly - *Magpie: Sweets and Savories from Philadelphia's Favorite Pie Boutique*
    LJ - v140 - i15 - Sept 15 2015 - p100(2) [51-500]
Riccio, Anthony V. - *Farms, Factories, and Families: Italian American Women of Connecticut*
    HNet - Jan 2015 - pNA [501+]
Rice, Anne - *Beauty's Kingdom*
    KR - March 1 2015 - pNA [51-500]
    LJ - v140 - i6 - April 1 2015 - p70(2) [501+]
    PW - v262 - i9 - March 2 2015 - p70(1) [501+]
    Prince Lestat: The Vampire Chronicles (Read by Vance, Simon). Audiobook Review
    PW - v262 - i12 - March 23 2015 - p71(1) [51-500]
Rice, Earle - *The Vietnam War*
    y BL - v112 - i6 - Nov 15 2015 - p43(1) [51-500]
Rice, James - *Alice and the Fly*
    TLS - i5848 - May 1 2015 - p19(2) [501+]
Rice, Luanne - *The Secret Language of Sisters*
    y KR - Nov 15 2015 - pNA [51-500]
    y PW - v262 - i45 - Nov 9 2015 - p61(1) [51-500]
    y SLJ - v61 - i12 - Dec 2015 - p114(2) [51-500]
Rice, Patricia - *Formidable Lord Quentin*
    PW - v262 - i5 - Feb 2 2015 - p43(1) [501+]
Rice, Tom - *Hearing and the Hospital: Sound, Listening, Knowledge, and Experience*
    MAQ - v29 - i2 - June 2015 - pb52-b54 [501+]
Rice, William B. - *The Story of Fossil Fuels*
    c BL - v112 - i2 - Sept 15 2015 - p60(2) [51-500]
Rich, A.J. - *The Hand That Feeds You*
    BL - v111 - i21 - July 1 2015 - p37(1) [51-500]
    KR - April 15 2015 - pNA [501+]
    LJ - v140 - i8 - May 1 2015 - p68(1) [501+]
    NYTBR - July 26 2015 - p15(L) [501+]
    PW - v262 - i20 - May 18 2015 - p59(1) [501+]
Rich, Harold - *Fort Worth: Outpost, Cowtown, Boomtown*
    Roundup M - v22 - i4 - April 2015 - p31(1) [501+]
    Roundup M - v22 - i6 - August 2015 - p40(1) [501+]
    WHQ - v46 - i3 - Autumn 2015 - p389-390 [501+]
Rich, Jamie - *Madame Frankenstein*
    PW - v262 - i11 - March 16 2015 - p72(1) [51-500]
Rich, Mari - *Big-Animal Vets!*
    c BL - v112 - i1 - Sept 1 2015 - p97(1) [51-500]
    Cyber Spy Hunters!
    c BL - v112 - i1 - Sept 1 2015 - p97(1) [51-500]
Rich, Matthew A. - *A Week from Next Tuesday: Joy Keeps Showing Up (Because Christ Keeps Showing Up).*
    Intpr - v69 - i1 - Jan 2015 - p114(2) [501+]
Rich, Nathaniel - *Odds Against Tomorrow*
    Math T - v108 - i6 - Feb 2015 - p478(1) [501+]
Rich, Simon - *Spoiled Brats: Stories*
    NYTBR - June 21 2015 - p24(L) [501+]
Rich, Steve - *Mrs. Carter's Butterfly Garden*
    c Sci & Ch - v52 - i8 - April-May 2015 - p74 [51-500]
    My School Yard Garden
    c Sci & Ch - v52 - i9 - Summer 2015 - p88 [51-500]
Richard, Carl J. - *When the United States Invaded Russia: Woodrow Wilson's Siberian Disaster*
    Historian - v77 - i3 - Fall 2015 - p575(3) [501+]
Richard, Julian - *Water for the City, Fountains for the People: Monumental Fountains in the Roman East. An Archaeological Study of Water Management*
    Class R - v65 - i1 - April 2015 - p268-270 [501+]
Richard, Laurent - *The Championship! (Illus. by Ryser, Nicolas)*
    c HB Guide - v26 - i1 - Spring 2015 - p65(1) [51-500]
    Wild Animals! (Illus. by Ryser, Nicolas)
    c HB Guide - v26 - i1 - Spring 2015 - p65(1) [51-500]
Richards, Bernard - *The Greatest Books You'll Never Read: Unpublished Masterpieces by the World's Greatest Writers*
    LJ - v140 - i16 - Oct 1 2015 - p78(2) [51-500]

Richards, C.J. - *Battle of the Bots*
    c KR - Sept 15 2015 - pNA [51-500]
    The Junkyard Bot (Illus. by Fujita, Goro)
    c HB Guide - v26 - i1 - Spring 2015 - p90(1) [51-500]
    Lots of Bots (Illus. by Fujita, Goro)
    c BL - v111 - i18 - May 15 2015 - p66(1) [51-500]
    c HB Guide - v26 - i2 - Fall 2015 - p98(1) [51-500]
Richards, Carl - *The One-Page Financial Plan: A Simple Way to Be Smart about Your Money*
    BL - v111 - i16 - April 15 2015 - p7(1) [51-500]
    LJ - v140 - i7 - April 15 2015 - p98(1) [51-500]
Richards, D. Manning - *Gift of Sydney*
    SPBW - April 2015 - pNA [501+]
Richards, Dan - *The Problem with Not Being Scared of Kids (Illus. by Neubecker, Robert)*
    c KR - June 15 2015 - pNA [51-500]
    c SLJ - v61 - i8 - August 2015 - p76(1) [51-500]
    The Problem with Not Being Scared of Monsters (Illus. by Neubecker, Robert)
    c HB Guide - v26 - i2 - Fall 2015 - p49(1) [51-500]
Richards, Jasmine - *Secrets of Valhalla*
    c KR - Oct 1 2015 - pNA [51-500]
    c SLJ - v61 - i11 - Nov 2015 - p102(1) [51-500]
Richards, Jeffrey - *The Golden Age of Pantomime: Slapstick, Spectacle and Subversion in Victorian England*
    HT - v65 - i4 - April 2015 - p61(2) [501+]
Richards, Jon - *Record-Breaking Animals (Illus. by Simkins, Ed)*
    c Sch Lib - v63 - i3 - Autumn 2015 - p175(2) [51-500]
    Record-Breaking Earth and Space Facts
    c BL - v111 - i22 - August 1 2015 - p54(1) [51-500]
    Record-Breaking People
    c BL - v111 - i22 - August 1 2015 - p54(1) [51-500]
Richards, Justin - *The Suicide Exhibition*
    KR - Jan 1 2015 - pNA [51-500]
Richards, Keith - *Gus & Me: The Story of My Granddad and My First Guitar (Illus. by Richards, Theodora)*
    c HB Guide - v26 - i1 - Spring 2015 - p195(1) [51-500]
    c Sch Lib - v63 - i1 - Spring 2015 - p32(1) [51-500]
Richards, Laurie - *Barren Branches*
    KR - May 1 2015 - pNA [501+]
Richards, Leonard - *Who Freed the Slaves?*
    PW - v262 - i2 - Jan 12 2015 - p53(1) [501+]
Richards, Michael - *After the Civil War: Making Memory and Re-making Spain since 1936*
    AHR - v120 - i1 - Feb 2015 - p345-346 [501+]
    JMH - v87 - i3 - Sept 2015 - p750(3) [501+]
Richards, Natalie D. - *My Secret to Tell*
    y KR - July 15 2015 - pNA [51-500]
    y PW - v262 - i33 - August 17 2015 - p73(1) [51-500]
    y SLJ - v61 - i10 - Oct 2015 - p116(2) [51-500]
    y VOYA - v38 - i4 - Oct 2015 - p60(1) [51-500]
Richards, Pamela Spence - *A History of Modern Librarianship: Constructing the Heritage of Western Cultures*
    LJ - v140 - i15 - Sept 15 2015 - p93(1) [51-500]
Richards, Patricia - *Race and the Chilean Miracle: Neoliberalism, Democracy, and Indigenous Rights*
    HAHR - v95 - i4 - Nov 2015 - p706-707 [501+]
Richards, Peter - *India: Future Tense*
    KR - Sept 15 2015 - pNA [501+]
Richards, Robert J. - *Was Hitler a Darwinian? Disputed Questions in the History of Evolutionary Theory*
    Isis - v106 - i2 - June 2015 - p488(3) [501+]
    QRB - v90 - i1 - March 2015 - p73(2) [501+]
Richardson, Bobby - *Impact Player*
    CSM - April 13 2015 - pNA [51-500]
Richardson, Chad - *The Informal and Underground Economy of the South Texas Border*
    SF - v94 - i2 - Dec 2015 - pNA [501+]
Richardson, Christopher - *Empire of the Waves: Voyage of the Moon Child*
    c Magpies - v30 - i3 - July 2015 - p38(1) [501+]
Richardson, Edmund - *Classical Victorians. Scholars, Scoundrels and Generals in Pursuit of Antiquity*
    Class R - v65 - i2 - Oct 2015 - p597-599 [501+]
Richardson, Glenn - *The Field of Cloth of Gold*
    AHR - v120 - i2 - April 2015 - p722-723 [501+]
    HER - v130 - i544 - June 2015 - p727(2) [501+]
    Ren Q - v68 - i1 - Spring 2015 - p295-296 [501+]
    Six Ct J - v46 - i1 - Spring 2015 - p261-263 [501+]
Richardson, Heather Cox - *To Make Men Free: A History of the Republican Party*
    JAH - v102 - i2 - Sept 2015 - p567-567 [501+]
    NYTBR - Jan 4 2015 - p10(L) [501+]

Richardson, John - *The Oxford Handbook of New Audiovisual Aesthetics*
  PMS - v38 - i3 - July 2015 - p391(5) [501+]
  Notes - v71 - i3 - March 2015 - p514(4) [501+]
Richardson, Justin - *And Tango Makes Three (Illus. by Cole, Henry)*
  c SLJ - v61 - i7 - July 2015 - p56(2) [51-500]
Richardson, Kim Michele - *Liar's Bench*
  BL - v111 - i14 - March 15 2015 - p53(1) [51-500]
  PW - v262 - i8 - Feb 23 2015 - p48(2) [51-500]
Richardson, Lloyd - *The Golden Arrow*
  KR - Sept 1 2015 - pNA [501+]
Richardson, Matt - *The Queer Limit of Black Memory: Black Lesbian Literature and Irresolution*
  Signs - v40 - i2 - Wntr 2015 - p515(7) [501+]
Richardson, Paddy - *Swimming in the Dark*
  PW - v262 - i3 - Jan 19 2015 - p64(1) [51-500]
Richardson, Peter - *No Simple Highway: A Cultural History of the Grateful Dead*
  Bwatch - April 2015 - pNA [51-500]
  HM - v330 - i1976 - Jan 2015 - p82(4) [501+]
  KR - Jan 1 2015 - pNA [501+]
  LJ - v140 - i5 - March 15 2015 - p101(1) [501+]
Richardson, Sara - *No Better Man*
  PW - v262 - i16 - April 20 2015 - p61(1) [51-500]
Richardson, Sarah S. - *Sex Itself: The Search for Male and Female in the Human Genome*
  Isis - v106 - i2 - June 2015 - p496(2) [501+]
Richardson, Selden - *The Tri-State Gang in Richmond: Murder and Robery in the Great Depression*
  KR - Dec 15 2015 - pNA [501+]
Richardson, Tarn - *The Damned: The Darkest Hand Trilogy*
  PW - v262 - i47 - Nov 23 2015 - p53(1) [51-500]
Richardson, Theodor - *Microsoft Powerpoint 2013 Pocket Primer*
  Bwatch - March 2015 - pNA [51-500]
Richardson, Tim - *Oxford College Gardens*
  TLS - i5876 - Nov 13 2015 - p12(2) [501+]
  NYTBR - Dec 6 2015 - p66(L) [501+]
The Responsible Leader: Developing a Culture of Responsibility in an Uncertain World
  RVBW - March 2015 - pNA [51-500]
Richardson, Todd - *The Undead President*
  KR - Sept 1 2015 - pNA [501+]
Riche, Barnabe - *The Adventures of Brusanus, Prince of Hungaria*
  Ren Q - v68 - i2 - Summer 2015 - p793-794 [501+]
Richemont, Enid - *The Night of the Were-boy (Illus. by Mazali, Gustavo)*
  c CH Bwatch - Nov 2015 - pNA [501+]
Riches, Daniel - *Protestant Cosmopolitanism and Diplomatic Culture: Brandenburg-Swedish Relations in the Seventeenth Century*
  CEH - v48 - i2 - June 2015 - p253-255 [501+]
Riches, Samantha - *St George: A Saint for All*
  Spec - v327 - i9739 - April 25 2015 - p38(1) [501+]
Richey, Russell E. - *Methodism in the American Forest*
  CC - v132 - i21 - Oct 14 2015 - p33(2) [501+]
Richie, Beth E. - *Arrested Justice: Black Women, Violence, and America's Prison Nation*
  CS - v44 - i1 - Jan 2015 - p112-113 [501+]
Richlin, Amy - *Arguments with Silence: Writing the History of Roman Women*
  TLS - i5837 - Feb 13 2015 - p27(1) [501+]
Richman, Adam - *Straight Up Tasty*
  PW - v262 - i16 - April 20 2015 - p70(2) [51-500]
Richman, Joe - *Teenage Diaries Then and Now. Audiobook Review*
  y SLJ - v61 - i7 - July 2015 - p49(1) [51-500]
Richman, Kimberly D. - *License to Wed: What Legal Marriage Means to Same-Sex Couples*
  CS - v44 - i5 - Sept 2015 - p695-697 [501+]
Richmond, Benjamin - *What Are the Three Branches of Government? And Other Questions about the U.S. Constitution*
  c HB Guide - v26 - i2 - Fall 2015 - p153(1) [51-500]
Why Is the Sea Salty?: And Other Questions About Oceans
  c HB Guide - v26 - i1 - Spring 2015 - p156(1) [51-500]
Richmond, Caroline Tung - *The Only Thing to Fear*
  y CH Bwatch - Feb 2015 - pNA [501+]
  y HB Guide - v26 - i1 - Spring 2015 - p121(1) [51-500]
Richmond, Douglas W. - *The Mexican Revolution: Conflict and Consolidation, 1910-1940*
  HAHR - v95 - i1 - Feb 2015 - p189-190 [501+]
Richmond, Peter - *Always a Catch*
  y HB Guide - v26 - i2 - Fall 2015 - p135(1) [51-500]

Richmond, T.R. - *What She Left*
  y BL - v112 - i4 - Oct 15 2015 - p34(1) [51-500]
  KR - Oct 1 2015 - pNA [51-500]
  LJ - v140 - i17 - Oct 15 2015 - p76(1) [51-500]
  PW - v262 - i46 - Nov 16 2015 - p54(1) [51-500]
Richmond, Vivienne - *Clothing the Poor in Nineteenth-Century England*
  HT - v65 - i2 - Feb 2015 - p58(1) [501+]
Richtel, Matt - *A Deadly Wandering: A Mystery, a Landmark Investigation, and the Astonishing Science of Attention in the Digital Age*
  NYTBR - Sept 20 2015 - p28(L) [501+]
The Doomsday Equation
  BL - v111 - i9-10 - Jan 1 2015 - p45(2) [51-500]
  NYTBR - May 31 2015 - p16(L) [501+]
Richter, Andrea - *Hans Schmithals (1878-1964): Malerei zwischen Jugendstil und Abstraktion*
  Ger Q - v88 - i1 - Wntr 2015 - p124(2) [501+]
Richter, Antje - *Letters and Epistolary Culture in Early Medieval China*
  JAS - v74 - i2 - May 2015 - p477-478 [501+]
Richter, Daniel K. - *Trade, Land, Power: The Struggle for Eastern North America*
  Historian - v77 - i2 - Summer 2015 - p348(2) [501+]
  RAH - v43 - i1 - March 2015 - p14-19 [501+]
Richter, Murray - *Lucky Rocks*
  c PW - v262 - i36 - Sept 7 2015 - p68(1) [51-500]
Richter, Simon - *Goethe's Ghosts: Reading and the Persistence of Literature*
  MLR - v110 - i3 - July 2015 - p893-894 [501+]
  Eight-C St - v49 - i1 - Fall 2015 - p108-109 [501+]
Women, Pleasure, Film: What Lolas Want
  GSR - v38 - i1 - Feb 2015 - p201-204 [501+]
Richter, Thomas - *Der Bildhauer Hans Juncker: Wunderkind zwischen Spatrenaissance und Barock*
  Ren Q - v68 - i2 - Summer 2015 - p646-647 [501+]
Richter, Uwe - *Mineralogische Sammlung Deutschland: Das Krugerhaus in Freiberg*
  RocksMiner - v90 - i1 - Jan-Feb 2015 - p93(1) [501+]
Rickard, David - *Pyrite: A Natural History of Fool's Gold*
  LJ - v140 - i7 - April 15 2015 - p114(1) [51-500]
  New Sci - v227 - i3031 - July 25 2015 - p43(1) [501+]
Rickards, James - *The Death of Money: The Coming Collapse of the International Monetary System*
  NWCR - v68 - i2 - Spring 2015 - p140(2) [501+]
Rickert, Mary - *You Have Never Been Here*
  y BL - v112 - i6 - Nov 15 2015 - p32(1) [51-500]
  KR - Oct 1 2015 - pNA [51-500]
Rickett, Joel - *Q Is for Quinoa: A Modern Parent's ABC (Illus. by Wilson, Spencer)*
  c HB Guide - v26 - i1 - Spring 2015 - p43(1) [51-500]
Ricketts, Philadelphia - *High-Ranking Widows in Medieval Iceland and Yorkshire: Property, Power, Marriage and Identity in the Twelfth and Thirteenth Centuries*
  HER - v130 - i542 - Feb 2015 - p164(2) [501+]
Ricketts, Rita - *Scholars, Poets and Radicals: Discovering Forgotten Lives in Blackwell Collections*
  TLS - i5854 - June 12 2015 - p25(1) [501+]
Ricketts, Wendell - *Blue, Too: More Writing by (for or about) Working-Class Queers*
  G&L Rev W - v22 - i1 - Jan-Feb 2015 - p42(1) [501+]
Rickman, Sarah Byrn - *Nancy Love and the WASP Ferry Pilots of World War II*
  HNet - August 2015 - pNA [501+]
Rico, Monica - *Nature's Noblemen: Transatlantic Masculinities and the Nineteenth-Century American West*
  PHR - v84 - i2 - May 2015 - p269(3) [501+]
Ricotta, Ricky - *Mighty Robot vs. The Stupid Stinkbugs from Saturn*
  c CH Bwatch - July 2015 - pNA [51-500]
Ridarsky, Christine L. - *Susan B. Anthony and the Struggle for Equal Rights*
  JWH - v27 - i2 - Summer 2015 - p159(10) [501+]
Riddell, Chris - *Goth Girl and the Fete Worse than Death*
  c Sch Lib - v63 - i1 - Spring 2015 - p42(1) [501+]
Riddle, A.G. - *Departure*
  KR - August 15 2015 - pNA [501+]
  PW - v262 - i34 - August 24 2015 - p64(1) [51-500]
Riddle, Christopher A. - *Disability and Justice: The Capabilities Approach in Practice*
  Dialogue - v54 - i3 - Sept 2015 - p567-569 [501+]

Riddle, Tohby - *The Greatest Gatsby: A Visual Book of Grammar*
  Magpies - v30 - i2 - May 2015 - p22(1) [501+]
Unforgotten (Illus. by Riddle, Tohby)
  y Sch Lib - v63 - i2 - Summer 2015 - p120(1) [51-500]
Rideout, Helen - *Employee Risk Management: How to Protect Your Business Reputation and Reduce Your Legal Liability*
  Bwatch - Feb 2015 - pNA [501+]
Rider, Jordan C. - *Leaving Waden*
  y KR - March 1 2015 - pNA [501+]
Rider, Z. - *Man Made Murder: The Blood Road Trilogy*
  PW - v262 - i32 - August 10 2015 - p41(1) [51-500]
Suckers
  BL - v111 - i9-10 - Jan 1 2015 - p60(1) [51-500]
Ridge, Mia - *Crowdsourcing Our Cultural Heritage*
  LR - v64 - i6-7 - June-July 2015 - p506-507 [501+]
Ridge, Rachel Anne - *Flash: The Homeless Donkey Who Taught Me about Life, Faith and Second Chances*
  PW - v262 - i15 - April 13 2015 - p74(1) [51-500]
Ridgway, Christie - *Keep On Loving You*
  PW - v262 - i48 - Nov 30 2015 - p45(2) [51-500]
Make Me Lose Control
  BL - v111 - i9-10 - Jan 1 2015 - p56(1) [51-500]
Ridha, Jennifer - *Criminal That I Am: A Memoir*
  BL - v111 - i18 - May 15 2015 - p4(2) [51-500]
  KR - April 1 2015 - pNA [51-500]
  PW - v262 - i11 - March 16 2015 - p77(2) [51-500]
Ridley, Erica - *The Captain's Bluestocking Mistress*
  PW - v262 - i18 - May 4 2015 - p103(1) [51-500]
The Earl's Defiant Wallflower
  PW - v262 - i12 - March 23 2015 - p56(1) [51-500]
Ridley, Frances - *Nelson Mandela*
  c BL - v111 - i19-20 - June 1 2015 - p90(1) [51-500]
Ridley, Hugh - *Darwin Becomes Art: Aesthetic Vision in the Wake of Darwin, 1870-1920*
  MLR - v110 - i3 - July 2015 - p898-900 [501+]
Ridley, Jane - *Victoria: Queen, Matriarch, Empress*
  TLS - i5859 - July 17 2015 - p23(1) [501+]
  TimHES - i2214 - July 30 2015 - p48-48 [501+]
Ridley, Kimberly - *The Secret Bay (Illus. by Raye, Rebekah)*
  c PW - v262 - i35 - August 31 2015 - p90(2) [501+]
  c CH Bwatch - Nov 2015 - pNA [501+]
  c KR - August 1 2015 - pNA [501+]
Ridley, Matt - *The Evolution of Everything: How New Ideas Emerge*
  BL - v112 - i5 - Nov 1 2015 - p4(1) [51-500]
  KR - July 1 2015 - pNA [501+]
  LJ - v140 - i16 - Oct 1 2015 - p104(1) [51-500]
  Nat R - v67 - i24 - Dec 31 2015 - p35(2) [501+]
  Nature - v526 - i7571 - Oct 1 2015 - p36(2) [501+]
  New Sci - v228 - i3044 - Oct 24 2015 - p42(1) [501+]
  NS - v144 - i5289 - Nov 20 2015 - p52(2) [501+]
  NYTBR - Nov 29 2015 - p15(L) [501+]
  PW - v262 - i27 - July 6 2015 - p56(1) [51-500]
  Reason - v47 - i8 - Jan 2016 - p52(3) [501+]
  Spec - v329 - i9760 - Sept 19 2015 - p53(1) [501+]
Ridyard, Jennifer - *Empire*
  PW - v262 - i1 - Jan 5 2015 - p56(1) [51-500]
Rieber, Alfred J. - *Salami Tactics Revisited: Hungarian Communists on the Road to Power*
  E-A St - v67 - i7 - Sept 2015 - p1161(3) [501+]
The Struggle for the Eurasian Borderlands: From the Rise of Early Modern Empires to the End of the First World War
  AHR - v120 - i3 - June 2015 - p973-974 [501+]
Riebling, Mark - *Church of Spies: The Pope's Secret War against Hitler*
  KR - July 15 2015 - pNA [501+]
  LJ - v140 - i13 - August 1 2015 - p110(1) [51-500]
  Nat R - v67 - i19 - Oct 19 2015 - p54(2) [501+]
Riedel, Michael - *Razzle Dazzle: The Battle for Broadway*
  BL - v112 - i1 - Sept 1 2015 - p27(2) [51-500]
  KR - August 1 2015 - pNA [501+]
  LJ - v140 - i15 - Sept 15 2015 - p79(1) [51-500]
  NYTBR - Dec 6 2015 - p22(L) [501+]

Rieff, David - *The Reproach of Hunger: Food, Justice, and Money in the Twenty-First Century*
    KR - June 15 2015 - pNA [501+]
    LJ - v140 - i14 - Sept 1 2015 - p124(1) [51-500]
    NS - v144 - i5288 - Nov 13 2015 - p38(3) [501+]
    NY - v91 - i31 - Oct 12 2015 - p103 [51-500]
    NYTBR - Nov 8 2015 - p15(L) [501+]
    PW - v262 - i32 - August 10 2015 - p51(1) [51-500]

Rieger, Bernhard - *The People's Car: A Global History of the Volkswagen Beetle*
    Historian - v77 - i1 - Spring 2015 - p190(2) [501+]

Rieger, Byjoerg - *Across Borders: Latin Perspectives in the Americas Reshaping Religion, Theology, and Life*
    Theol St - v76 - i1 - March 2015 - p224(2) [501+]

Riehecky, Janet Ellen - *Velociraptor*
    y Sci & Ch - v52 - i8 - April-May 2015 - p75 [51-500]

Riehle, Mary Ann McCabe - *The Little Kids' Table (Illus. by Uhles, Mary)*
    c KR - July 1 2015 - pNA [51-500]
The Little Kids' Table (Illus. by Uhles, Mary Reaves)
    c CH Bwatch - Oct 2015 - pNA [51-500]
    c SLJ - v61 - i10 - Oct 2015 - p83(1) [51-500]

Riehle, Wolfgang - *The Secret Within: Hermits, Recluses, and Spiritual Outsiders in Medieval England*
    AHR - v120 - i2 - April 2015 - p699-700 [501+]

Ries, Frank W.D. - *The Dance Theatre of Jean Cocteau*
    RVBW - Nov 2015 - pNA [51-500]

Riesz, Janos - *Sudlich der Sahara: Afrikanische Literatur in franzosischer Sprache*
    MLR - v110 - i2 - April 2015 - p553-554 [501+]

Riether, Achim - *Bettler, Diebe, Unterwelt: Leonaert Bramer illustriert spanische Romane*
    Ren Q - v68 - i1 - Spring 2015 - p249-250 [501+]

Rifbjerg, Klaus - *Terminal Innocence*
    NS - v144 - i5272 - July 24 2015 - p47(1) [501+]
    TLS - i5870 - Oct 2 2015 - p27(1) [501+]

Rifkin, Mark - *Settler Common Sense: Queerness and Everyday Colonialism in the American Renaissance*
    Am Ind CRJ - v39 - i2 - Spring 2015 - p158-159 [501+]

Rigal, Emily-Anne - *Flawd: How to Stop Hating on Yourself, Others, and the Things That Make You Who You Are (Read by Rigal, Emily-Anne). Audiobook Review*
    y SLJ - v61 - i11 - Nov 2015 - p74(1) [51-500]

Rigby, Alexander - *The Second Chances of Priam Wood*
    PW - v262 - i33 - August 17 2015 - p47(1) [51-500]

Riggs, Carol - *The Body Institute*
    y SLJ - v61 - i12 - Dec 2015 - p127(1) [51-500]
    y VOYA - v38 - i5 - Dec 2015 - p74(1) [51-500]

Riggs, Cynthia - *Poison Ivy*
    PW - v262 - i4 - Jan 26 2015 - p150(2) [51-500]

Riggs, Kate - *Amazing Animals Series*
    c BL - v111 - i18 - May 15 2015 - p50(1) [51-500]
    c HB Guide - v26 - i2 - Fall 2015 - p177(1) [51-500]
Asteroids
    c HB Guide - v26 - i2 - Fall 2015 - p165(1) [51-500]
Beavers
    c HB Guide - v26 - i2 - Fall 2015 - p180(1) [51-500]
Camels
    c HB Guide - v26 - i1 - Spring 2015 - p166(1) [51-500]
    c HB Guide - v26 - i2 - Fall 2015 - p180(1) [51-500]
Comets
    c BL - v111 - i15 - April 1 2015 - p62(1) [51-500]
    c HB Guide - v26 - i2 - Fall 2015 - p165(1) [51-500]
Eagles
    c HB Guide - v26 - i1 - Spring 2015 - p162(2) [51-500]
Fire Trucks
    c BL - v112 - i7 - Dec 1 2015 - p43(1) [51-500]
Galaxies
    c HB Guide - v26 - i2 - Fall 2015 - p165(1) [51-500]
Geckos
    c HB Guide - v26 - i2 - Fall 2015 - p176(1) [51-500]
Helicopters
    c BL - v112 - i7 - Dec 1 2015 - p43(1) [51-500]
Hummingbirds
    c HB Guide - v26 - i1 - Spring 2015 - p163(1) [51-500]
Moons
    c HB Guide - v26 - i2 - Fall 2015 - p165(1) [51-500]
On the Farm (Illus. by Dogi, Fiammetta)
    c KR - July 1 2015 - pNA [51-500]
    c PW - v262 - i6 - Feb 9 2015 - p66(2) [501+]
On the Farm (Illus. by Kubinyi, Laszlo)
    c SLJ - v61 - i7 - July 2015 - p57(1) [51-500]
Planets
    c HB Guide - v26 - i2 - Fall 2015 - p165(1) [51-500]
Sea Lions
    c HB Guide - v26 - i1 - Spring 2015 - p167(1) [51-500]
Sea Turtles
    c HB Guide - v26 - i2 - Fall 2015 - p176(1) [51-500]
Seedlings
    c HB Guide - v26 - i2 - Fall 2015 - p186(1) [51-500]
The Sun
    c HB Guide - v26 - i2 - Fall 2015 - p165(1) [51-500]
Time to Build (Illus. by Dogi, Fiammetta)
    c KR - July 1 2015 - pNA [51-500]
    c SLJ - v61 - i7 - July 2015 - p57(1) [51-500]
Tortoises
    c HB Guide - v26 - i1 - Spring 2015 - p160(1) [51-500]

Riggs, Ransom - *Hollow City (Read by Heyborne, Kirby). Audiobook Review*
    c BL - v111 - i14 - March 15 2015 - p24(2) [51-500]
Library of Souls
    y BL - v112 - i3 - Oct 1 2015 - p70(1) [51-500]
    y SLJ - v61 - i10 - Oct 2015 - p106(2) [51-500]

Righter, Robert W. - *Peaks, Politics and Passion: Grand Teton National Park Comes of Age*
    WHQ - v46 - i3 - Autumn 2015 - p386-387 [501+]

Rigney, Heather - *Waking the Merrow*
    PW - v262 - i50 - Dec 7 2015 - p73(2) [501+]

Rigoni, Isabelle - *Mediating Cultural Diversity in a Globalised Public Space*
    ERS - v38 - i8 - August 2015 - p1464(3) [501+]

Riley, Alexander T. - *Angel Patriots: The Crash of United Flight 93 and the Myth of America*
    Soc - v52 - i3 - June 2015 - p283(1) [501+]

Riley, Brendan - *The Great Latin American Novel*
    PW - v262 - i50 - Dec 7 2015 - p79(1) [51-500]

Riley, Charlotte S. - *A Mysterious Life and Calling: From Slavery to Ministry in South Carolina*
    PW - v262 - i45 - Nov 9 2015 - p55(1) [51-500]

Riley, Gretchen - *Famous Trees of Texas*
    Bwatch - August 2015 - pNA [51-500]

Riley, James - *The Stolen Chapters*
    c KR - Sept 15 2015 - pNA [51-500]
Story Thieves
    c HB Guide - v26 - i2 - Fall 2015 - p98(1) [51-500]

Riley, Jason L. - *Please Stop Helping Us: How Liberals Make It Harder for Blacks to Succeed*
    NYTBR - March 8 2015 - p12(L) [501+]

Riley, Lia - *Inside Out*
    PW - v262 - i30 - July 27 2015 - p50(1) [51-500]
Sideswiped
    PW - v262 - i20 - May 18 2015 - p70(1) [51-500]
Upside Down
    PW - v262 - i19 - May 11 2015 - p43(1) [51-500]
With Every Breath
    PW - v262 - i47 - Nov 23 2015 - p55(1) [51-500]

Riley, Lucinda - *The Seven Sisters (Read by Lucienne, Emily). Audiobook Review*
    LJ - v140 - i15 - Sept 15 2015 - p42(1) [51-500]
The Seven Sisters
    BL - v111 - i17 - May 1 2015 - p79(1) [51-500]
    KR - March 1 2015 - pNA [501+]

Riley, Michael - *Reading the Streets*
    KR - Dec 1 2015 - pNA [501+]

Riley, Naomi Schaefer - *'Til Faith Do Us Part: How Interfaith Marriage Is Transforming America*
    Comw - v142 - i1 - Jan 9 2015 - p29(2) [501+]
    CS - v44 - i4 - July 2015 - p545-546 [501+]

Riley, Peter - *Life Cycles*
    c Sch Lib - v63 - i3 - Autumn 2015 - p176(1) [51-500]
Rocks and Soil
    c Sch Lib - v63 - i4 - Winter 2015 - p239(1) [51-500]

Riley, Reba - *Post-Traumatic Church Syndrome: A Memoir of Humor and Healing in 30 Religions*
    BL - v111 - i22 - August 1 2015 - p6(1) [51-500]
    PW - v262 - i10 - March 9 2015 - p68(2) [51-500]

Riley, Zane - *Go Your Own Way*
    PW - v262 - i11 - March 16 2015 - p71(1) [51-500]

Rim, Sujean - *Birdie's Big-Girl School Day (Illus. by Rim, Sujean)*
    c SLJ - v61 - i2 - Feb 2015 - p77(1) [51-500]
Birdie's First Day of School (Illus. by Rim, Sujean)
    c KR - June 1 2015 - pNA [51-500]

Rimer, J. Thomas - *The Columbia Anthology of Modern Japanese Drama*
    TLS - i5848 - May 1 2015 - p25(1) [501+]

Rimler, Walter - *The Man That Got Away: The Life and Songs of Harold Arlen*
    LJ - v140 - i13 - August 1 2015 - p98(2) [51-500]

Rinaldi, Robin - *The Wild Oats Project: One Woman's Midlife Quest for Passion at Any Cost*
    PW - v262 - i4 - Jan 26 2015 - p167(2) [51-500]
    BL - v111 - i13 - March 1 2015 - p8(2) [51-500]
    LJ - v140 - i5 - March 15 2015 - p113(1) [51-500]

Rinaldo, Rachel - *Mobilizing Piety: Islam and Feminism in Indonesia*
    AJS - v120 - i6 - May 2015 - p1881(3) [501+]
    Pac A - v88 - i3 - Sept 2015 - p744 [501+]

Rinck, Maranke - *The Other Rabbit (Illus. by van der Linden, Martijn)*
    c KR - Sept 15 2015 - pNA [51-500]
    c PW - v262 - i35 - August 31 2015 - p88(1) [51-500]
    c SLJ - v61 - i12 - Dec 2015 - p95(1) [51-500]

Rindlisbacher, Stephan - *Leben fur die Sache: Vera Figner, Vera Zasulic und das radikale Milieu im spaten Zarenreich*
    HNet - May 2015 - pNA [501+]
    Slav R - v74 - i2 - Summer 2015 - p397-398 [501+]

Rinehart, J.D. - *Crown of Three*
    y HB - v91 - i4 - July-August 2015 - p143(1) [51-500]
    c HB Guide - v26 - i2 - Fall 2015 - p99(1) [51-500]
    c PW - v262 - i16 - April 20 2015 - p76(1) [51-500]

Rinehart, Richard - *Re-Collection: Art, New Media, and Social Memory*
    Afterimage - v42 - i5 - March-April 2015 - p33(2) [501+]

Rinella, Steven - *The Complete Guide to Hunting, Butchering, and Cooking Wild Game, vol. 1: Big Game*
    PW - v262 - i27 - July 6 2015 - p62(1) [51-500]
The Complete Guide to Hunting, Butchering, and Cooking Wild Game, vol. 2: Small Game and Fowl
    PW - v262 - i42 - Oct 19 2015 - p70(1) [51-500]

Riney-Kehrberg, Pamela - *The Nature of Childhood: An Environmental History of Growing Up in America since 1865*
    AHR - v120 - i4 - Oct 2015 - p1499-1500 [501+]

Ring, Jennifer - *A Game of Their Own: Voices of Contemporary Women in Baseball*
    BL - v111 - i15 - April 1 2015 - p12(1) [51-500]

Ringe, Wolf-Georg - *Legal Challenges in the Global Financial Crisis: Bail-outs, the Euro and Regulation*
    Law Q Rev - v131 - April 2015 - p333-335 [501+]

Ringel, Jed - *Stuck in the Passing Lane: A Memoir*
    SPBW - August 2015 - pNA [51-500]
    SPBW - Sept 2015 - pNA [51-500]

Ringel, Lance - *Flower of Iowa*
    KR - March 1 2015 - pNA [501+]

Ringer, Monica M. - *Pious Citizens: Reforming Zoroastrianism in India and Iran*
    IJMES - v47 - i4 - Nov 2015 - p833-835 [501+]

Ringgold, Faith - *Harlem Renaissance Party (Illus. by Ringgold, Faith)*
    c HB - v91 - i3 - May-June 2015 - p96(2) [51-500]
    c HB Guide - v26 - i2 - Fall 2015 - p49(1) [51-500]

Ringness, Mari - *The Dragonfly Club: A Friend In Need*
    c CH Bwatch - Oct 2015 - pNA [51-500]

Ringo, John - *A Hymn before Battle*
    RVBW - Feb 2015 - pNA [51-500]

Ringquist, Rebecca - *Rebecca Ringquist's Embroidery Workshops: A Bend-the-Rules Primer*
    LJ - v140 - i10 - June 1 2015 - p104(1) [51-500]

Ringstad, Arnold - *Wild Cats Series*
    c HB Guide - v26 - i1 - Spring 2015 - p167(1) [51-500]

Ringwald, Whitaker - *The Secret Cipher*
    c HB Guide - v26 - i2 - Fall 2015 - p99(1) [51-500]

Rink, Martina - *Fashion Germany*
    LJ - v140 - i5 - March 15 2015 - p102(3) [501+]

Rinke, Stefan - *Im Sog der Katastrophe: Lateinamerika und der Erste Weltkrieg*
    HNet - Oct 2015 - pNA [501+]

Rinker, Sherri Duskey - *Silly Wonderful You (Illus. by McDonnell, Patrick)*
    c KR - Nov 1 2015 - pNA [51-500]
    c PW - v262 - i45 - Nov 9 2015 - p59(1) [51-500]
    c SLJ - v61 - i12 - Dec 2015 - p95(1) [51-500]

Rinne, Katherine Wentworth - *The Waters of Rome: Aqueducts, Fountains, and the Birth of the Baroque City*
    J Urban H - v41 - i1 - Jan 2015 - p152-5 [501+]

Rinpoche, Chokyi Nyima - *Medicine and Compassion: A Tibetan Lama and an American Doctor on How to Provide Care with Compassion and Wisdom*
    RVBW - May 2015 - pNA [501+]

Rintoul, Fiona - *The Leipzig Affair*
    KR - Nov 1 2015 - pNA [501+]

Riolo, Amy - *The Ultimate Mediterranean Diet Cookbook: Harness the Power of the World's Healthiest Diet to Live Better, Longer*
    BL - v111 - i17 - May 1 2015 - p68(2) [51-500]

Riordan Hall, Deirdre - *Sugar*
    y SLJ - v61 - i5 - May 2015 - p124(1) [51-500]

Riordan, J.F. - *North of the Tension Line*
    Nat R - v67 - i7 - April 20 2015 - p45 [501+]
    RVBW - April 2015 - pNA [51-500]
Riordan, John P. - *They Are All My Family: A Daring Rescue in the Chaos of Saigon's Fall*
    KR - Feb 1 2015 - pNA [501+]
    PW - v262 - i6 - Feb 9 2015 - p59(1) [51-500]
Riordan, Kate - *Fiercombe Manor*
    BL - v111 - i9-10 - Jan 1 2015 - p52(1) [51-500]
    KR - Jan 15 2015 - pNA [51-500]
Riordan, Michael - *Tunnel Visions: The Rise and Fall of the Superconducting Super Collider*
    Nature - v528 - i7581 - Dec 10 2015 - p191(1) [51-500]
Riordan, Rick - *The Blood of Olympus*
    c CH Bwatch - Feb 2015 - pNA [51-500]
    y HB Guide - v26 - i1 - Spring 2015 - p90(1) [51-500]
The Lost Hero: The Graphic Novel (Illus. by Powell, Nate)
    y HB Guide - v26 - i1 - Spring 2015 - p90(1) [51-500]
Magnus Chase and the Gods of Asgard: The Sword of Summer
    c NYTBR - Nov 8 2015 - p23(L) [501+]
Percy Jackson and the Lightning Thief
    TES - i5157 - July 31 2015 - p37(1) [501+]
Percy Jackson's Greek Gods (Read by Bernstein, Jesse). Audiobook Review
    c BL - v111 - i15 - April 1 2015 - p87(1) [51-500]
Percy Jackson's Greek Gods (Illus. by Rocco, John)
    c HB Guide - v26 - i1 - Spring 2015 - p145(1) [51-500]
Percy Jackson's Greek Heroes (Read by Bernstein, Jesse). Audiobook Review
    y SLJ - v61 - i12 - Dec 2015 - p80(1) [51-500]
Percy Jackson's Greek Heroes (Illus. by Rocco, John)
    c PW - v262 - i35 - August 31 2015 - p93(1) [501+]
    c BL - v112 - i3 - Oct 1 2015 - p79(1) [51-500]
    c SLJ - v61 - i11 - Nov 2015 - p136(1) [51-500]
    c VOYA - v38 - i4 - Oct 2015 - p78(1) [51-500]
The Sword of Summer
    y KR - Sept 15 2015 - pNA [51-500]
    y BL - v111 - i21 - July 1 2015 - p49(1) [501+]
    y BL - v112 - i3 - Oct 1 2015 - p75(1) [51-500]
    c PW - v262 - i32 - August 10 2015 - p61(1) [51-500]
    c SLJ - v61 - i12 - Dec 2015 - p107(1) [51-500]
    y VOYA - v38 - i5 - Dec 2015 - p74(1) [51-500]
Rios, Alberto - *A Small Story about the Sky*
    PW - v262 - i16 - April 20 2015 - p52(1) [51-500]
Rios, Christopher M. - *After the Monkey Trial: Evangelical Scientists and a New Creationism*
    JIH - v46 - i3 - Wntr 2016 - p465-466 [501+]
    QRB - v90 - i2 - June 2015 - p202(1) [501+]
Rios, Julia - *Year's Best Young Adult Speculative Fiction 2014*
    y SLJ - v61 - i12 - Dec 2015 - p127(1) [51-500]
Riots in Regions of Heavy Industry: Violence, Conflict and Protest in the 20th Century
    HNet - Feb 2015 - pNA [501+]
Rioux, Anne Boyd - *Constance Fenimore Woolson: Portrait of a Lady Novelist*
    KR - Nov 15 2015 - pNA [501+]
    LJ - v140 - i20 - Dec 1 2015 - p102(2) [51-500]
    PW - v262 - i45 - Nov 9 2015 - p48(1) [51-500]
Ripley, J.R. - *Buried in Beignets*
    PW - v262 - i41 - Oct 12 2015 - p50(2) [51-500]
Ripley, Mike - *Mr. Campion's Fox*
    BL - v111 - i17 - May 1 2015 - p41(1) [51-500]
    PW - v262 - i15 - April 13 2015 - p59(1) [51-500]
Ripley, W.L. - *Storme Warning*
    BL - v111 - i12 - Feb 15 2015 - p39(1) [51-500]
Ripley's Entertainment, Inc. - *Ripley's Believe It or Not! Special Edition 2015*
    c HB Guide - v26 - i1 - Spring 2015 - p130(1) [51-500]
Ripley's Entertainment Inc. - *Special Edition 2015 of Ripley's Believe It Or Not!*
    c CH Bwatch - March 2015 - pNA [51-500]
Rippin, Sally - *Billie's Great Desert Adventure (Illus. by Coburn, Alisa)*
    c Magpies - v30 - i2 - May 2015 - p28(1) [501+]
Hey Jack! The Star of the Week
    c Magpies - v30 - i2 - May 2015 - p33(1) [51-500]
Spooky House (Illus. by Fukuoka, Aki)
    c BL - v111 - i17 - May 1 2015 - p56(1) [51-500]
Ripplemeyer, Kay - *The Civilian Conservation Corps in Southern Illinois, 1933-1942*
    RVBW - May 2015 - pNA [501+]
Rippon, Blythe - *Stowe Away*
    PW - v262 - i48 - Nov 30 2015 - p45(1) [51-500]

Rische, Stephanie - *I Was Blind (Dating), but Now I See: My Misadventures in Dating, Waiting, and Stumbling into Love*
    PW - v262 - i51 - Dec 14 2015 - p80(1) [51-500]
Risco, Elle D. - *Disney Mickey and Friends: Mickey's Birthday*
    c HB Guide - v26 - i2 - Fall 2015 - p61(1) [51-500]
Risen, Clay - *The Bill of the Century*
    NYTBR - May 24 2015 - p28(L) [501+]
Risen, James - *Pay Any Price: Greed, Power, and Endless War*
    NYRB - v62 - i3 - Feb 19 2015 - p18(3) [501+]
    NYTBR - Oct 11 2015 - p28(L) [501+]
Rislov, Casey - *Love Is Forever (Illus. by Balsaitis, Rachael)*
    c CH Bwatch - April 2015 - pNA [51-500]
Risser, Nicole Dombrowski - *France under Fire: German Invasion, Civilian Flight, and Family Survival during World War II*
    JMH - v87 - i1 - March 2015 - p196(3) [501+]
Rissi, Anica Mrose - *Anna, Banana, and the Friendship Split (Illus. by Park, Meg)*
    c CCB-B - v69 - i1 - Sept 2015 - p48(1) [51-500]
    c HB Guide - v26 - i2 - Fall 2015 - p71(1) [51-500]
    c KR - March 1 2015 - pNA [51-500]
    SLJ - v61 - i3 - March 2015 - p124(1) [51-500]
Anna, Banana, and the Monkey in the Middle (Illus. by Park, Meg)
    c CCB-B - v69 - i1 - Sept 2015 - p48(1) [51-500]
Rissman, Rebecca - *The Black Power Movement*
    c HB Guide - v26 - i1 - Spring 2015 - p139(1) [51-500]
Calm Girl: Yoga for Stress Relief
    c HB Guide - v26 - i2 - Fall 2015 - p199(2) [51-500]
Smart Girl: Yoga for Brain Power
    c HB Guide - v26 - i2 - Fall 2015 - p199(2) [51-500]
Yoga for You
    y VOYA - v38 - i4 - Oct 2015 - p86(1) [51-500]
Yoga for Your Mind and Body: A Teenage Practice for a Healthy, Balanced Life
    y BL - v111 - i16 - April 15 2015 - p42(1) [51-500]
Risso, Linda - *Propaganda and Intelligence in the Cold War: The NATO Information Service*
    HNet - Jan 2015 - pNA [51-500]
Ristvet, Lauren - *Ritual, Performance, and Politics in the Ancient Near East*
    TimHES - i2192 - Feb 26 2015 - p49(1) [501+]
Ritchell, Ross - *The Knife*
    BooChiTr - Feb 14 2015 - p16(1) [501+]
    LJ - v140 - i3 - Feb 15 2015 - p93(1) [51-500]
    Nat Post - v17 - i101 - Feb 28 2015 - pWP4(1) [501+]
Ritchey, Sara - *Holy Matter: Changing Perceptions of the Material World in Late Medieval Christianity*
    AHR - v120 - i3 - June 2015 - p1094-1095 [501+]
    CHR - v101 - i3 - Summer 2015 - p620(2) [501+]
    Med R - May 2015 - pNA [51-500]
Ritchie, Alison - *Me and My Dad! (Illus. by Edgson, Alison)*
    c HB Guide - v26 - i1 - Spring 2015 - p14(1) [51-500]
The Tortoise and the Hare (Illus. by Noj, Nahta)
    c HB Guide - v26 - i2 - Fall 2015 - p160(1) [51-500]
    c KR - March 15 2015 - pNA [51-500]
Ritchie, Brendan - *Carousel*
    y Magpies - v30 - i2 - May 2015 - p43(1) [501+]
Ritchie, Fiona - *Wayfaring Strangers: The Musical Voyage from Scotland and Ulster to Appalachia*
    Notes - v72 - i2 - Dec 2015 - p378(3) [501+]
    TLS - i5848 - May 1 2015 - p13(1) [501+]
Ritchie, Jason - *The New Arab Man: Emergent Masculinities, Technologies, and Islam in the Middle East*
    IJMES - v47 - i1 - Feb 2015 - p189-191 [501+]
Ritchie, Scot - *Look Where We Live! A First Book of Community Building (Illus. by Ritchie, Scot)*
    c HB Guide - v26 - i2 - Fall 2015 - p157(1) [51-500]
    c Res Links - v21 - i1 - Oct 2015 - p26(1) [51-500]
    c BL - v111 - i14 - March 15 2015 - p78(1) [51-500]
    c KR - Feb 1 2015 - pNA [51-500]
My House Is Alive!
    c KR - Dec 15 2015 - pNA [51-500]
P'esk'a and the First Salmon Ceremony (Illus. by Ritchie, Scot)
    c BL - v112 - i4 - Oct 15 2015 - p41(1) [51-500]
    c KR - July 15 2015 - pNA [51-500]
Riter, Bob - *When Your Life Is Touched by Cancer: Practical Advice and Insights for Patients, Professionals and Those Who Care*
    Bwatch - March 2015 - pNA [51-500]
Riti, Marsha - *Marion Strikes a Pose*
    c HB Guide - v26 - i1 - Spring 2015 - p56(1) [51-500]

Ritland, Mike - *Navy SEAL Dogs: My Tale of Training Canines for Combat (Read by Kramer, Michael). Audiobook Review*
    LJ - v140 - i7 - April 15 2015 - p49(1) [51-500]
Team Dog: How to Train Your Dog - the Navy SEAL Way
    LJ - v140 - i3 - Feb 15 2015 - p120(1) [51-500]
Ritter, Bill - *Powering Forward*
    KR - Dec 15 2015 - pNA [501+]
Ritter, Gerhard A. - *Hans-Dietrich Genscher, das Auswartige Amt, und die deutsche Vereinigung*
    JMH - v87 - i2 - June 2015 - p497(2) [501+]
Ritter Runkel in seiner Zeit. Mittelalter und Zeitgeschichte im Spiegel eines Geschichtscomics
    HNet - Sept 2015 - pNA [501+]
Ritter, William - *Beastly Bones*
    y HB - v91 - i6 - Nov-Dec 2015 - p90(1) [51-500]
    y KR - June 1 2015 - pNA [51-500]
    y SLJ - v61 - i7 - July 2015 - p88(2) [51-500]
    y VOYA - v38 - i2 - June 2015 - p82(1) [51-500]
Jackaby (Read by Barber, Nicola). Audiobook Review
    BL - v111 - i13 - March 1 2015 - p71(1) [51-500]
    c BL - v111 - i14 - March 15 2015 - p24(2) [501+]
Jackaby
    HB Guide - v26 - i1 - Spring 2015 - p121(1) [51-500]
Rittersporn, Gabor T. - *Anguish, Anger, and Folkways in Soviet Russia*
    HNet - July 2015 - pNA [501+]
Rittner, Carol - *Rape: Weapon of War and Genocide*
    HNet - Feb 2015 - pNA [501+]
Ritz, David - *It's a Long Story: My Life (Read by Grant, Ryan Christopher). Audiobook Review*
    BooChiTr - July 18 2015 - p13(1) [501+]
It's a Long Story: My Life
    BL - v111 - i19-20 - June 1 2015 - p32(1) [51-500]
Respect: The Life of Aretha Franklin
    BL - v111 - i19-20 - June 1 2015 - p27(1) [501+]
Ritzenberg, Aaron - *The Sentimental Touch: The Language of Feeling in the Age of Managerialism*
    J Am St - v49 - i1 - Feb 2015 - p203-205 [501+]
Ritzenhoff, Karen A. - *Heroism and Gender in War Films*
    JGS - v24 - i2 - April 2015 - p245-247 [501+]
Ritzi, Christian - *Gymnasium im Strukturellen Wandel: Befunde und Perspektiven von den Preussischen Reformen bis zur Reform der Gymnasialen Oberstufe*
    HNet - Jan 2015 - pNA [51-500]
Rivera-Ashford, Roni Capin - *My Tata's Remedies / Los remedios de mi Tata (Illus. by Castro, Antonio)*
    c BL - v111 - i21 - July 1 2015 - p64(1) [51-500]
    c CH Bwatch - July 2015 - pNA [51-500]
    c HB Guide - v26 - i2 - Fall 2015 - p49(1) [51-500]
    c KR - April 15 2015 - pNA [51-500]
    c SLJ - v61 - i6 - June 2015 - p91(1) [51-500]
Rivera, Lauren A. - *Pedigree: How Elite Students Get Elite Jobs*
    TimHES - i2211 - July 9 2015 - p50(1) [501+]
    TimHES - i2212 - July 16 2015 - p46-2 [501+]
Rivera, Mariano - *The Closer*
    c HB Guide - v26 - i1 - Spring 2015 - p184(1) [51-500]
Rivera-Sylva, Hector E. - *Dinosaurs and Other Reptiles from the Mesozoic of Mexico*
    QRB - v90 - i4 - Dec 2015 - p427(2) [501+]
Rivera, Tomas - *Y no se lo Trago la Tierra / And the Earth Did Not Devour Him*
    KR - July 15 2015 - pNA [51-500]
Rivers, Karen - *Finding Ruby Starling*
    y HB Guide - v26 - i1 - Spring 2015 - p90(1) [51-500]
The Girl in the Well Is Me
    c KR - Dec 15 2015 - pNA [51-500]
    c PW - v262 - i51 - Dec 14 2015 - p85(1) [51-500]
Rivers, Melissa - *The Book of Joan: Tales of Mirth, Mischief, and Manipulation (Read by Rivers, Melissa). Audiobook Review*
    PW - v262 - i26 - June 29 2015 - p64(1) [51-500]
Rivett, Sarah - *The Science of the Soul in Colonial New England*
    AL - v87 - i1 - March 2015 - p190-192 [501+]
Riviere, Sam - *Kim Kardashian's Marriage*
    NS - v144 - i5262 - May 15 2015 - p46(2) [501+]
Rivlin, Gary - *Katrina: After the Flood*
    AM - v213 - i8 - Sept 28 2015 - p42(3) [501+]
    BL - v111 - i22 - August 1 2015 - p8(1) [51-500]
    KR - July 1 2015 - pNA [501+]
    LJ - v140 - i12 - July 1 2015 - p100(2) [501+]
    Nature - v524 - i7563 - August 6 2015 - p33(1) [51-500]
    NYTBR - August 9 2015 - p11(L) [501+]
    PW - v262 - i24 - June 15 2015 - p74(1) [51-500]

Rivlin-Gutman, Annette - *Just Breathe (Illus. by Bailey, Melissa)*
  c CH Bwatch - June 2015 - pNA [51-500]
  c CH Bwatch - July 2015 - pNA [51-500]
Rivoal, Marine - *Three Little Peas*
  c HB Guide - v26 - i1 - Spring 2015 - p15(1) [51-500]
Rix, Jamie - *The Last Chocolate Chip Cookie (Illus. by Elsom, Clare)*
  c KR - June 15 2015 - pNA [51-500]
  c SLJ - v61 - i11 - Nov 2015 - p86(2) [51-500]
Rix, Len - *The Door*
  NYTBR - Feb 8 2015 - p12(L) [501+]
Journey by Moonlight
  Nation - v300 - i6 - Feb 9 2015 - p37(1) [501+]
Rizal, Jose - *The Reign of Greed*
  AJS - v121 - i1 - July 2015 - p346(7) [501+]
The Social Cancer
  AJS - v121 - i1 - July 2015 - p346(7) [501+]
Rizga, Kristina - *Mission High: One School, How Experts Tried to Fail It, and the Students and Teachers Who Made It Triumph*
  KR - June 1 2015 - pNA [51-500]
  LJ - v140 - i11 - June 15 2015 - p97(1) [51-500]
Rizzo, Raffaela Marie - *Thank You For the Shoes*
  KR - Nov 1 2015 - pNA [501+]
Rizzolo, S.K. - *Die I Will Not*
  Bwatch - Jan 2015 - pNA [51-500]
On a Desert Shore
  KR - Jan 1 2016 - pNA [51-500]
Roach, Edward J. - *The Wright Company: From Invention to Industry*
  AHR - v120 - i1 - Feb 2015 - p264-265 [501+]
  BHR - v89 - i2 - Summer 2015 - p339(5) [501+]
  T&C - v56 - i3 - July 2015 - p765-766 [501+]
Roach, Joyce Gibson - *The Land of Rain Shadow: Horned Toad, Texas*
  RVBW - Oct 2015 - pNA [51-500]
Roach, Levi - *Kingship and Consent in Anglo-Saxon England, 871-978: Assemblies and the State in the Early Middle Ages*
  HER - v130 - i544 - June 2015 - p685(2) [501+]
Roach, Mary - *Gulp: Adventures on the Alimentary Canal*
  J Chem Ed - v92 - i7 - July 2015 - p1143-1145 [501+]
Roadmap Nation - *Roadmap: The Get-It-Together Guide for Figuring Out What to Do with Your Life*
  SLJ - v61 - i4 - April 2015 - p184(1) [51-500]
Roane, Caris - *Savage Chains*
  PW - v262 - i3 - Jan 19 2015 - p66(1) [51-500]
Roat, Sharon Huss - *Between the Notes*
  y BL - v111 - i17 - May 1 2015 - p90(1) [51-500]
  y HB Guide - v26 - i2 - Fall 2015 - p135(1) [51-500]
  y KR - April 1 2015 - pNA [51-500]
  y SLJ - v61 - i4 - April 2015 - p170(1) [51-500]
  y VOYA - v38 - i1 - April 2015 - p68(1) [51-500]
Robaard, Jedda - *If My Dad Were an Animal (Illus. by Robaard, Jedda)*
  c HB Guide - v26 - i2 - Fall 2015 - p17(1) [51-500]
  c PW - v262 - i15 - April 13 2015 - p81(1) [501+]
If My Mom Were a Bird (Illus. by Robaard, Jedda)
  c HB Guide - v26 - i2 - Fall 2015 - p17(1) [51-500]
  c KR - April 1 2015 - pNA [51-500]
The Little Bird Who Lost His Song
  c KR - July 1 2015 - pNA [51-500]
Milo and Millie
  c HB Guide - v26 - i1 - Spring 2015 - p15(1) [51-500]
Robach, Amy - *Better: How I Let Go of Control, Held on to Hope, and Found Joy in My Darkest Hour*
  LJ - v140 - i14 - Sept 1 2015 - p130(2) [501+]
Robb, J.D. - *Devoted in Death*
  BL - v112 - i2 - Sept 15 2015 - p30(2) [51-500]
  PW - v262 - i31 - August 3 2015 - p36(1) [51-500]
Down the Rabbit Hole
  PW - v262 - i36 - Sept 7 2015 - p51(2) [51-500]
Festive in Death
  Bwatch - Jan 2015 - pNA [51-500]
Obsession in Death
  BL - v111 - i11 - Feb 1 2015 - p28(1) [51-500]
Robbins, Alexandra - *The Nurses: A Year with the Heroes behind the Hospital Curtain*
  Ent W - i1359-1360 - April 17 2015 - p116(1) [501+]
  PW - v262 - i13 - March 30 2015 - p70(1) [51-500]
Robbins, Dean - *Two Friends: Susan B. Anthony and Frederick Douglass (Illus. by Qualls, Sean)*
  c BL - v112 - i4 - Oct 15 2015 - p41(1) [51-500]
  c KR - Nov 1 2015 - pNA [51-500]
  c PW - v262 - i42 - Oct 19 2015 - p75(2) [51-500]

Robbins, Karen E. - *James McHenry, Forgotten Federalist*
  JSH - v81 - i2 - May 2015 - p445(2) [501+]
Robbins, Michael - *Yes! Poems and Paintings by Michael Robbins*
  KR - Jan 1 2016 - pNA [501+]
Robbins Rose, Judith - *Look Both Ways in the Barrio Blanco*
  y VOYA - v38 - i4 - Oct 2015 - p60(1) [51-500]
Robbins, Vernon K. - *Who Do People Say I Am? Rewriting Gospel in Emerging Christianity*
  Bks & Cult - v21 - i6 - Nov-Dec 2015 - p16(2) [501+]
Robcis, Camille - *The Law of Kinship: Anthropology, Pyschoanalysis, and the Family in France*
  JMH - v87 - i2 - June 2015 - p452(3) [501+]
Robeck, Cecil M., Jr. - *The Cambridge Companion to Pentecostalism*
  IBMR - v39 - i3 - July 2015 - p164(2) [51-500]
Robenalt, James - *January 1973*
  KR - March 1 2015 - pNA [51-500]
Roberds, William - *The Origins, History, and Future of the Federal Reserve: A Return to Jekyll Island*
  BHR - v89 - i1 - Spring 2015 - p175(3) [501+]
Roberge, Rob - *Liar: A Memoir*
  KR - Nov 15 2015 - pNA [501+]
  PW - v262 - i51 - Dec 14 2015 - p75(1) [51-500]
Roberton, Fiona - *A Tale of Two Beasts (Illus. by Roberton, Fiona)*
  c BL - v111 - i12 - Feb 15 2015 - p89(1) [51-500]
  c HB Guide - v26 - i2 - Fall 2015 - p49(1) [51-500]
  c KR - Jan 15 2015 - pNA [51-500]
  c SLJ - v61 - i8 - August 2015 - p76(1) [51-500]
Roberts, Adam - *Landor's Cleanness: A Study of Walter Savage Landor*
  TLS - i5858 - July 10 2015 - p12(2) [51-500]
Twenty Trillion Leagues under the Sea
  BL - v111 - i9-10 - Jan 1 2015 - p60(1) [51-500]
Roberts, Allen F. - *A Dance of Assassins: Performing Early Colonial Hegemony in the Congo*
  HNet - Jan 2015 - pNA [501+]
  JRAI - v21 - i1 - March 2015 - p241(2) [501+]
Roberts, Amanda - *Crazy Dumplings*
  PW - v262 - i22 - June 1 2015 - p56(1) [51-500]
Roberts, Andrew - *Elegy: The First Day on the Somme*
  Spec - v328 - i9758 - Sept 5 2015 - p34(2) [501+]
Napoleon: A Life (Read by Lee, John Rafter). Audiobook Review
  LJ - v140 - i6 - April 1 2015 - p51(3) [501+]
Napoleon: A Life
  CSM - March 13 2015 - pNA [501+]
  MA - v57 - i3 - Summer 2015 - p71(3) [501+]
  Nat R - v67 - i2 - Feb 9 2015 - p41 [501+]
  Nation - v300 - i24 - June 15 2015 - p35(5) [501+]
Napoleon the Great
  HT - v65 - i7 - July 2015 - p58(2) [501+]
Roberts, Bethany - *Birthday Mice! (Illus. by Cushman, Doug)*
  c HB Guide - v26 - i2 - Fall 2015 - p61(1) [51-500]
Christmas Mice! (Illus. by Cushman, Doug)
  c HB Guide - v26 - i1 - Spring 2015 - p55(1) [51-500]
Roberts, Blain - *Pageants, Parlors, & Pretty Women: Race and Beauty in the Twentieth-Century South*
  AHR - v120 - i1 - Feb 2015 - p268-269 [501+]
  HNet - Jan 2015 - pNA [501+]
  J Am St - v49 - i2 - May 2015 - p436-437 [501+]
  JAH - v101 - i4 - March 2015 - p1304-1305 [501+]
Roberts, Cas - *As Country as It Gets: Short Stories from Appalachia*
  RVBW - April 2015 - pNA [51-500]
Roberts, Cokie - *Capital Dames: The Civil War and the Women of Washington, 1848-1868*
  BL - v111 - i18 - May 15 2015 - p12(2) [51-500]
  LJ - v140 - i8 - May 1 2015 - p86(1) [51-500]
Roberts, David - *Letters to His Children from an Uncommon Attorney*
  KR - Jan 15 2015 - pNA [501+]
The Lost World of the Old Ones: Discoveries in the Ancient Southwest
  BL - v111 - i15 - April 1 2015 - p22(1) [51-500]
  KR - Feb 15 2015 - pNA [501+]
  LJ - v140 - i6 - April 1 2015 - p100(1) [501+]
  Nature - v521 - i7550 - May 7 2015 - p31(1) [51-500]
The Total Work of Art in European Modernism
  MLR - v110 - i1 - Jan 2015 - p227-228 [501+]
Roberts, Diane - *Tribal: College Football and the Secret Heart of America*
  BL - v112 - i2 - Sept 15 2015 - p16(1) [51-500]
  LJ - v140 - i17 - Oct 15 2015 - p92(1) [501+]
  PW - v262 - i37 - Sept 14 2015 - p58(2) [51-500]

Roberts, Elizabeth - *The Sandzak: A History*
  E-A St - v67 - i6 - August 2015 - p998(2) [501+]
Roberts, Elizabeth F.S. - *God's Laboratory: Assisted Conception in the Andes*
  MAQ - v29 - i1 - March 2015 - p30-32 [501+]
Roberts, Gareth - *Robert Recorde: The Life and Times of a Tudor Mathematician*
  Isis - v106 - i1 - March 2015 - p180(2) [501+]
Roberts, Gregory David - *The Mountain Shadow*
  NYTBR - Dec 13 2015 - p23(L) [501+]
Roberts, Hilary - *Lee Miller: A Woman's War*
  BL - v112 - i7 - Dec 1 2015 - p9(1) [51-500]
Roberts, Jeyn - *The Bodies We Wear*
  c CH Bwatch - Jan 2015 - pNA [501+]
  y HB Guide - v26 - i1 - Spring 2015 - p121(1) [51-500]
Roberts, Jillian - *Where Do Babies Come From? Our First Talk about Birth (Illus. by Revell, Cindy)*
  c BL - v112 - i6 - Nov 15 2015 - p40(1) [51-500]
  c KR - August 15 2015 - pNA [51-500]
  c Res Links - v21 - i1 - Oct 2015 - p26(2) [51-500]
  c SLJ - v61 - i10 - Oct 2015 - p130(1) [51-500]
Roberts, Josephine - *Total Tractor!*
  c BL - v111 - i18 - May 15 2015 - p46(1) [51-500]
  c SLJ - v61 - i7 - July 2015 - p110(2) [51-500]
Roberts, Justin - *Slavery and the Enlightenment in the British Atlantic, 1750-1807*
  JMH - v87 - i2 - June 2015 - p428(3) [501+]
  W&M Q - v72 - i2 - April 2015 - p373-376 [501+]
Roberts, Keller - *Miseryland*
  PW - v262 - i22 - June 1 2015 - p49(1) [51-500]
Roberts, Les - *The Ashtabula Hat Trick*
  RVBW - Nov 2015 - pNA [501+]
Roberts, Linda - *The Whale Savers: Returning Wera to the Ocean (Illus. by Potter, Bruce)*
  c Magpies - v30 - i2 - May 2015 - pS5(1) [501+]
Roberts, Lisa Brown - *How (Not) to Fall in Love*
  y KR - March 15 2015 - pNA [501+]
Roberts, M.J. - *Montana Winter*
  PW - v262 - i13 - March 30 2015 - p62(1) [51-500]
Roberts, Mary Louise - *D-Day through French Eyes: Normandy 1944*
  HNet - August 2015 - pNA [501+]
What Soldiers Do: Sex and the American GI in World War II France
  JMH - v87 - i2 - June 2015 - p460(2) [501+]
  RAH - v43 - i1 - March 2015 - p156-160 [501+]
Roberts, Michael James - *Tell Tchaikovsky the News: Rock 'n' Roll, the Labor Question, and the Musicians' Union, 1942-1968*
  AJS - v120 - i5 - March 2015 - p1569(3) [501+]
  JAH - v101 - i4 - March 2015 - p1312(1) [501+]
Roberts, Ngaere - *Hoiho Paku (Illus. by Roberts, Ngaere)*
  c Magpies - v30 - i1 - March 2015 - pS4(2) [501+]
Roberts, Nora - *The Liar (Read by LaVoy, January). Audiobook Review*
  BL - v111 - i22 - August 1 2015 - p77(1) [51-500]
The Liar
  BL - v111 - i14 - March 15 2015 - p50(1) [51-500]
Stars of Fortune
  BL - v112 - i4 - Oct 15 2015 - p27(1) [51-500]
Roberts, Patrick S. - *Disasters and the American State*
  KR - March 1 2015 - pNA [501+]
Roberts, Paul G. - *Style Icons: Golden Boys*
  RVBW - Feb 2015 - pNA [51-500]
Roberts, Penny - *Peace and Authority during the French Religious Wars, c. 1560-1600*
  CHR - v101 - i3 - Summer 2015 - p657(2) [501+]
  JMH - v87 - i2 - June 2015 - p445(2) [501+]
Roberts, Priscilla - *Arab-Israeli Conflict: The Essential Reference Guide*
  R&USQ - v54 - i3 - Spring 2015 - p58(1) [501+]
Roberts, Randy - *Blood Brothers: The Fatal Friendship between Muhammad Ali and Malcolm X*
  KR - Dec 15 2015 - pNA [501+]
  PW - v262 - i52 - Dec 21 2015 - p147(1) [501+]
Roberts, Richard - *Becoming Fluent: How Cognitive Science Can Help Adults Learn a Foreign Language*
  LJ - v140 - i16 - Oct 1 2015 - p98(2) [51-500]
Roberts, Russ - *How Adam Smith Can Change Your Life: An Unexpected Guide to Human Nature and Happiness*
  IndRev - v20 - i2 - Fall 2015 - p301(4) [501+]
  TLS - i5876 - Nov 13 2015 - p30(2) [501+]
Roberts, Sam - *America's Mayor: John V. Lindsay and the Reinvention of New York*
  Am St - v54 - i2 - Summer 2015 - p45-55 [501+]
A History of New York in 101 Objects
  LJ - v140 - i9 - May 15 2015 - p94(2) [501+]
Roberts, Sean E. - *Printing a Mediterranean World: Florence, Constantinople, and the Renaissance of*

Geography
 JMH - v87 - i1 - March 2015 - p141(2) [501+]
Visual Cultures of Secrecy in Early Modern Europe
 Isis - v106 - i1 - March 2015 - p176(2) [501+]
Roberts, Sheila - *A Wedding on Primrose Street*
 BL - v111 - i22 - August 1 2015 - p42(1) [51-500]
 BL - v112 - i2 - Sept 15 2015 - p42(2) [501+]
Roberts, Sian Silyn - *Gothic Subjects: The Transformation of Individualism in American Fiction, 1790-1861*
 Nine-C Lit - v70 - i1 - June 2015 - p153(5) [501+]
Roberts, Siobhan - *Genius at Play: The Curious Mind of John Horton Conway*
 BL - v111 - i19-20 - June 1 2015 - p27(2) [51-500]
 KR - May 15 2015 - pNA [501+]
 Mac - v128 - i31 - August 10 2015 - p58(1) [501+]
 Nature - v523 - i7561 - July 23 2015 - p406(2) [501+]
 PW - v262 - i18 - May 4 2015 - p109(1) [51-500]
Wind Wizard: Alan G. Davenport and the Art of Wind Engineering
 T&C - v56 - i1 - Jan 2015 - p281-283 [501+]
Roberts-Smith, Jennifer - *Simulated Environment for Theatre*
 Theat J - v67 - i2 - May 2015 - p347-359 [501+]
Roberts, Steven C. - *Winning the Money Game in College, Book 1: Finance*
 RVBW - April 2015 - pNA [51-500]
Roberts, Tyler - *Encountering Religion: Responsibility and Criticism after Secularism*
 JR - v95 - i2 - April 2015 - p274(3) [501+]
Roberts, Victoria - *Kilts and Daggers*
 BL - v111 - i16 - April 15 2015 - p30(1) [51-500]
 PW - v262 - i11 - March 16 2015 - p71(1) [51-500]
My Highland Spy
 LJ - v140 - i3 - Feb 15 2015 - p133(1) [501+]
Robertson, Barry - *Royalists at War in Scotland and Ireland, 1638-1650*
 Six Ct J - v46 - i1 - Spring 2015 - p131-133 [501+]
Robertson, Ben - *The Last Generation*
 y PW - v262 - i4 - Jan 26 2015 - p173(1) [51-500]
Robertson, Brian J. - *Holacracy: The New Management System for a Rapidly Changing World*
 BL - v111 - i18 - May 15 2015 - p6(1) [51-500]
 KR - April 15 2015 - pNA [501+]
 LJ - v140 - i9 - May 15 2015 - p90(1) [51-500]
 PW - v262 - i12 - March 23 2015 - p58(1) [51-500]
Robertson-Buchanan, Angela - *Bonny Grows Her Feathers and Learns to Fly*
 c Magpies - v30 - i4 - Sept 2015 - p23(2) [501+]
Robertson, Donald - *Mitford at the Fashion Zoo*
 c KR - June 1 2015 - pNA [51-500]
Robertson, Geoffrey - *An Inconvenient Genocide: Who Now Remembers the Armenians?*
 HT - v65 - i7 - July 2015 - p56(2) [501+]
 NS - v144 - i5259 - April 24 2015 - p46(3) [501+]
Robertson, James - *The Testament of Gideon Mack*
 TimHES - i2187 - Jan 22 2015 - p49(1) [501+]
Robertson, James I., Jr. - *Diary of a Southern Refugee during the War*
 JSH - v81 - i4 - Nov 2015 - p1056(2) [501+]
Robertson, John - *Iraq: A History*
 LJ - v140 - i10 - June 1 2015 - p116(1) [51-500]
 PW - v262 - i15 - April 13 2015 - p68(1) [51-500]
Robertson, Kay - *D Is for Duck Calls (Illus. by Hanson, Sydney)*
 c HB Guide - v26 - i1 - Spring 2015 - p43(1) [51-500]
Robertson, Leigh - *Southern Rocky Mountain Wildflowers*
 Bwatch - Sept 2015 - pNA [51-500]
Robertson, Rachel - *When You Just Have to Roar! (Illus. by Prentice, Priscilla)*
 c KR - Feb 15 2015 - pNA [51-500]
 c SLJ - v61 - i9 - Sept 2015 - p111(1) [51-500]
Robertson, Renee - *The Coaching Solution*
 KR - Jan 1 2016 - pNA [501+]
Robertson, Ritchie - *Lessing and the German Enlightenment*
 Eight-C St - v48 - i2 - Wntr 2015 - p253-255 [501+]
Robertson, Robbie - *Hiawatha and the Peacemaker (Illus. by Shannon, David)*
 c BL - v112 - i1 - Sept 1 2015 - p116(1) [51-500]
 c CH Bwatch - Oct 2015 - pNA [501+]
 c KR - June 1 2015 - pNA [51-500]
 c NYTBR - Nov 8 2015 - p28(L) [501+]
 c PW - v262 - i27 - July 6 2015 - p72(1) [51-500]
 c SLJ - v61 - i8 - August 2015 - p129(1) [51-500]

Robertson, Robin - *Robin Robertson's Vegan without Borders: Easy Everyday Meals from around the World*
 Bwatch - Feb 2015 - pNA [51-500]
 Veg J - v34 - i3 - July-Sept 2015 - p31(1) [51-500]
Sailing the Forest: Selected Poems
 Ant R - v73 - i2 - Spring 2015 - p383(2) [51-500]
 NYTBR - Jan 11 2015 - p16(L) [501+]
Robertson, Sebastian - *Rock & Roll Highway: The Robbie Robertson Story (Illus. by Gustavson, Adam)*
 c HB Guide - v26 - i1 - Spring 2015 - p196(1) [51-500]
Robetti, Italo - *La Comunicazione Epistolare da e per Torino, Volume II - Vittorio Amedeo II e le prime Tariffe per la Posta delle Lettere*
 Phil Lit R - v64 - i2 - Spring 2015 - p134(4) [501+]
Robins, Lane - *Renovation*
 PW - v262 - i12 - March 23 2015 - p52(1) [51-500]
Robinson, Alex - *Our Expanding Universe*
 PW - v262 - i46 - Nov 16 2015 - p64(1) [51-500]
Robinson, Andrew - *Traces of the Trinity: Signs, Sacraments, and Sharing God's Life*
 Theol St - v76 - i3 - Sept 2015 - p613(2) [501+]
Robinson, Brett T. - *Appletopia: Media Technology and the Religious Imagination of Steve Jobs*
 T&C - v56 - i1 - Jan 2015 - p291-293 [501+]
Robinson, Bruce - *They All Love Jack: Busting the Ripper*
 Spec - v329 - i9770 - Nov 28 2015 - p53(1) [501+]
Robinson, Charles M., III - *The Diaries of John Gregory Bourke, vol. 5: May 23, 1881-August 26, 1881*
 JAH - v102 - i1 - June 2015 - p261-262 [501+]
 Roundup M - v22 - i6 - August 2015 - p40(1) [501+]
Robinson, Charles R., II - *Remembrances in Black: Personal Perspective of the African American Experience at the University of Arkansas 1940-2000s*
 JNE - v84 - i1 - Wntr 2015 - p94-3 [501+]
Robinson, Christian - *Last Stop on Market Street*
 c Nat Post - v119 - i17 - March 21 2015 - pWP5(1) [501+]
Robinson, Christopher - *War of the Encyclopaedists (Read by Robinson, Christopher). Audiobook Review*
 BooChiTr - July 18 2015 - p13(1) [501+]
War of the Encyclopaedists
 BL - v111 - i13 - March 1 2015 - p21(1) [51-500]
 HR - v68 - i3 - Autumn 2015 - p510-516 [501+]
 KR - Feb 15 2015 - pNA [51-500]
 LJ - v140 - i3 - Feb 15 2015 - p93(1) [51-500]
 NYT - May 12 2015 - pC1(L) [501+]
 PW - v262 - i10 - March 9 2015 - p50(1) [51-500]
 TLS - i5854 - June 12 2015 - p20(1) [501+]
Robinson, Daniel - *Death of a Century: A Novel of the Lost Generation*
 PW - v262 - i16 - April 20 2015 - p56(1) [501+]
Robinson, David Myles - *Tropical Judgments*
 SPBW - Nov 2015 - pNA [51-500]
Robinson, D'Wayne - *The Luvya Tree (Illus. by Thinkstock)*
 c CH Bwatch - Jan 2015 - pNA [51-500]
Robinson, Edna - *The Trouble with the Truth*
 BL - v111 - i9-10 - Jan 1 2015 - p55(1) [51-500]
Robinson, Gary - *Paranormal*
 y KR - March 1 2015 - pNA [51-500]
Robinson, Gina - *Agent Ex*
 LJ - v140 - i3 - Feb 15 2015 - p133(1) [501+]
Robinson, Hilary - *Croc by the Rock (Illus. by Gordon, Mike)*
 SLJ - v61 - i4 - April 2015 - p139(1) [51-500]
Tom's Sunflower (Illus. by Stanley, Mandy)
 c Sch Lib - v63 - i3 - Autumn 2015 - p160(1) [51-500]
Robinson, Holly - *Chance Harbor*
 BL - v112 - i2 - Sept 15 2015 - p26(1) [51-500]
Robinson, J.J. - *The Maldives: Islamic Republic, Tropical Autocracy*
 Spec - v329 - i9771 - Dec 5 2015 - p46(1) [501+]
Robinson, Jessica - *Undead Obsessed: Finding Meaning in Zombies*
 RVBW - June 2015 - pNA [51-500]
Robinson, Joan G. - *When Marnie Was There (Read by Duerden, Susan). Audiobook Review*
 c PW - v262 - i8 - Feb 23 2015 - p72(1) [51-500]
Robinson, Joanna L. - *Contested Water: The Struggle against Water Privatization in the United States and Canada*
 CS - v44 - i2 - March 2015 - p243-244 [501+]
Robinson, Julian - *The Fine Art of Fashion Illustration*
 LJ - v140 - i19 - Nov 15 2015 - p82(1) [51-500]
 Spec - v329 - i9772 - Dec 12 2015 - p78(2) [501+]

Robinson, Keith - *The Broken Compass: Parental Involvement with Children's Education*
 CS - v44 - i5 - Sept 2015 - p697-699 [501+]
Robinson, Ken - *Creative Schools: The Grassroots Revolution That's Transforming Education*
 LJ - v140 - i8 - May 1 2015 - p83(2) [51-500]
Robinson, Kim Stanley - *Aurora*
 KR - June 1 2015 - pNA [501+]
 PW - v262 - i13 - March 30 2015 - p59(1) [51-500]
 BL - v111 - i18 - May 15 2015 - p33(1) [51-500]
 New Sci - v227 - i3032 - August 1 2015 - p44(2) [501+]
Red Mars
 LJ - v140 - i11 - June 15 2015 - p118(1) [501+]
Robinson, Kirk Ward - *The Appalachian*
 KR - Oct 1 2015 - pNA [501+]
Robinson, Lee - *Lawyer for the Dog*
 BL - v111 - i19-20 - June 1 2015 - p44(1) [51-500]
Robinson, Linda Orst - *Sunday Morning, Shamwana*
 CSM - April 1 2015 - pNA [51-500]
Robinson, Lorin R. - *The Warming: Speculative Fiction about the Human Impact of the Climate Crisis*
 SPBW - August 2015 - pNA [51-500]
Robinson, Luke - *Independent Chinese Documentary: From the Studio to the Street*
 JAS - v74 - i2 - May 2015 - p478-480 [501+]
Robinson, Marilynne - *The Death of Adam*
 New R - v246 - i12 - Nov 2015 - p78(2) [501+]
The Givenness of Things: Essays
 BL - v112 - i3 - Oct 1 2015 - p10(1) [51-500]
 CSM - Oct 26 2015 - pNA [501+]
 KR - August 1 2015 - pNA [501+]
 LJ - v140 - i15 - Sept 15 2015 - p82(2) [51-500]
 Mac - v128 - i44 - Nov 9 2015 - p124(1) [51-500]
 NYRB - v62 - i20 - Dec 17 2015 - p13(2) [501+]
 NYTBR - Dec 13 2015 - p20(L) [501+]
Lila
 AM - v212 - i17 - May 18 2015 - p42(1) [501+]
 BL - v111 - i16 - April 15 2015 - p34(1) [501+]
 CC - v132 - i9 - April 29 2015 - p3(1) [501+]
 HR - v67 - i4 - Wntr 2015 - p685-692 [501+]
 Nation - v300 - i4 - Jan 26 2015 - p27(3) [501+]
 TLS - i5864-5865 - August 21 2015 - p21(2) [501+]
Robinson, Michael F. - *The Lost White Tribe*
 KR - Nov 15 2015 - pNA [501+]
Robinson, Michelle - *A Beginner's Guide to Bear Spotting (Illus. by Roberts, David)*
 c KR - Nov 15 2015 - pNA [51-500]
 c PW - v262 - i44 - Nov 2 2015 - p82(1) [51-500]
 c SLJ - v61 - i12 - Dec 2015 - p95(2) [51-500]
Goodnight Santa: The Perfect Bedtime Book (Illus. by East, Nick)
 c PW - v262 - i37 - Sept 14 2015 - p64(1) [51-500]
There's a Lion in My Cornflakes (Illus. by Field, Jim)
 c HB Guide - v26 - i2 - Fall 2015 - p49(1) [51-500]
 c KR - March 15 2015 - pNA [51-500]
 c SLJ - v61 - i7 - July 2015 - p67(2) [51-500]
Robinson, Nick - *Election Notebook: The Inside Story of the Battle over Britain's Future and My Personal Battle to Report It*
 TLS - i5869 - Sept 25 2015 - p9(2) [501+]
Traditional Japanese Origami Kit
 Bwatch - Sept 2015 - pNA [51-500]
Robinson, Nikki Slade - *Muddle & Mo*
 c Magpies - v30 - i2 - May 2015 - pS4(1) [501+]
The Roadman Boogie (Illus. by Robinson, Nikki Slade)
 c Magpies - v30 - i5 - Nov 2015 - pS6(1) [501+]
Robinson, Patrick - *The Lion of Sabray: The Afghani Warrior Who Defied the Taliban and Saved the Life of Navy SEAL Marcus Luttrell*
 KR - Sept 1 2015 - pNA [501+]
 LJ - v140 - i16 - Oct 1 2015 - p94(1) [501+]
 PW - v262 - i38 - Sept 21 2015 - p63(1) [51-500]
Robinson, Peter - *Children of the Revolution*
 RVBW - March 2015 - pNA [51-500]
In the Dark Places
 BL - v111 - i17 - May 1 2015 - p37(2) [51-500]
 KR - May 15 2015 - pNA [501+]
 PW - v262 - i25 - June 22 2015 - p120(1) [51-500]
No Cure for Love
 PW - v262 - i52 - Dec 21 2015 - p132(1) [51-500]
Robinson, Sharon - *The Hero Two Doors Down: Based on the True Story of Friendship Between a Boy and a Baseball Legend*
 c KR - Nov 1 2015 - pNA [501+]
 c PW - v262 - i42 - Oct 19 2015 - p77(1) [51-500]
Robinson, Shira - *Citizen Strangers: Palestinians and the Birth of Israel's Liberal Settler State*
 AHR - v120 - i1 - Feb 2015 - p370-371 [501+]

Robinson, Stacy - *Surface*
  PW - v262 - i4 - Jan 26 2015 - p145(2) [51-500]
Robinson, Tom - *Fibonacci Zoo (Illus. by Wald, Christina)*
  c CH Bwatch - July 2015 - pNA [51-500]
Robinson-Tomsett, Emma - *Women, Travel and Identity: Journeys by Rail and Sea, 1870-1940*
  Wom HR - v24 - i1 - Feb 2015 - p132-134 [501+]
Robinson, Tony - *Sir Tony Robinson's Weird World of Wonders: Pets (Illus. by Thorpe, Del)*
  c Sch Lib - v63 - i1 - Spring 2015 - p48(1) [51-500]
  c Sch Lib - v63 - i2 - Summer 2015 - p113(1) [51-500]
Robinson, Zandria F. - *This Ain't Chicago: Race, Class, and Regional Identity in the Post-Soul South*
  AJS - v121 - i1 - July 2015 - p301(3) [501+]
Robison, John - *Switched On*
  KR - Dec 15 2015 - pNA [501+]
Robles, Antonio J. - *The Refugee Centaur*
  MFSF - v128 - i3-4 - March-April 2015 - p258(1) [501+]
Robotham, Michael - *Life or Death*
  KR - Jan 1 2015 - pNA [501+]
  NYTBR - March 22 2015 - p29(L) [501+]
  PW - v262 - i2 - Jan 12 2015 - p36(2) [51-500]
Robson, Art - *A Medieval Latin Miscellany: An Intermediate Reader*
  Med R - April 2015 - pNA [501+]
Robson, Cecy - *Once Pure*
  PW - v262 - i11 - March 16 2015 - p69(2) [51-500]
Robson, Jennifer - *Moonlight over Paris*
  KR - Dec 1 2015 - pNA [51-500]
Robson, Jenny - *Balaclava Boy (Illus. by Mitchell, Sandy)*
  c Sch Lib - v63 - i2 - Summer 2015 - p109(1) [51-500]
  Granite
  y Bkbird - v53 - i4 - Fall 2015 - p19(1) [501+]
Robson, Lane - *Shasta and Her Cubs*
  KR - Dec 15 2015 - pNA [501+]
Robson, Peter A. - *Raincoast Chronicles 23*
  RVBW - August 2015 - pNA [501+]
Robuck, Erika - *The House of Hawthorne*
  BL - v111 - i16 - April 15 2015 - p35(1) [51-500]
  NYTBR - June 28 2015 - p38(L) [501+]
  PW - v262 - i9 - March 2 2015 - p61(1) [51-500]
Roby, Kimberla Lawson - *Best Friends Forever*
  KR - Nov 1 2015 - pNA [51-500]
  The Ultimate Betrayal
  BL - v111 - i18 - May 15 2015 - p26(1) [51-500]
  KR - April 15 2015 - pNA [51-500]
Roby, Kinley - *An Anecdotal Death*
  BL - v111 - i13 - March 1 2015 - p21(1) [51-500]
  KR - Feb 1 2015 - pNA [51-500]
Roca, Jordi - *The Desserts of Jordi Roca: More Than 80 Sweet Recipes*
  BL - v112 - i1 - Sept 1 2015 - p23(1) [51-500]
Roca, Nuria - *The Earth (Illus. by Bonilla, Rocio)*
  c CH Bwatch - March 2015 - pNA [51-500]
Roca, Paco - *Wrinkles*
  y LJ - v140 - i9 - May 15 2015 - p61(3) [501+]
Rocco, John - *Blizzard (Illus. by Rocco, John)*
  c CH Bwatch - Feb 2015 - pNA [51-500]
  c HB Guide - v26 - i1 - Spring 2015 - p43(1) [51-500]
  c NYTBR - Jan 18 2015 - p20(L) [501+]
Rocha, K.E. - *Secrets of Bearhaven (Illus. by Dearsley, Ross)*
  c KR - Nov 1 2015 - pNA [51-500]
  c SLJ - v61 - i10 - Oct 2015 - p93(2) [51-500]
Roche, Helen - *Sparta's German Children: The Ideal of Ancient Sparta in the Royal Prussian Cadet Corps, 1818-1920, and in National Socialist Elite Schools (the Napolas), 1933-1945*
  Class R - v65 - i1 - April 2015 - p285-287 [501+]
Roche, Suzanne - *Kidding around NYC*
  c KR - Oct 1 2015 - pNA [501+]
  Making It Home
  c KR - Oct 15 2015 - pNA [501+]
Rochet, Quentin - *Les filles de saint Bruno au Moyen Age: Les moniales cartusiennes et l'exemple de Premol*
  Specu - v90 - i1 - Jan 2015 - p296-298 [501+]
Rock, J.A. - *Minotaur*
  y BL - v112 - i3 - Oct 1 2015 - p34(1) [51-500]
  PW - v262 - i34 - August 24 2015 - p64(1) [51-500]
  Pain Slut
  PW - v262 - i51 - Dec 14 2015 - p68(1) [51-500]
  The Subs Club
  PW - v262 - i44 - Nov 2 2015 - p68(2) [51-500]
  Tempest
  PW - v262 - i1 - Jan 5 2015 - p58(1) [51-500]

Rock, Maya - *Scripted (Read by Almasy, Jessica). Audiobook Review*
  y SLJ - v61 - i6 - June 2015 - p67(2) [51-500]
  Scripted
  y BL - v111 - i9-10 - Jan 1 2015 - p100(1) [51-500]
  y CCB-B - v68 - i8 - April 2015 - p417(2) [51-500]
  y HB Guide - v26 - i2 - Fall 2015 - p136(1) [51-500]
  y NYTBR - Jan 18 2015 - p19(L) [501+]
Rock, Peter - *Klickitat*
  c KR - Jan 1 2016 - pNA [51-500]
Rock, Suzanne - *At His Service*
  KR - April 15 2015 - pNA [501+]
  PW - v262 - i14 - April 6 2015 - p45(1) [51-500]
Rock, Zack - *Homer Henry Hudson's Curio Museum (Illus. by Rock, Zack)*
  c HB Guide - v26 - i2 - Fall 2015 - p49(2) [51-500]
Rockett, Paul - *100 Trillion Good Bacteria Living in the Human Body (Illus. by Ruffle, Mark)*
  c BL - v112 - i3 - Oct 1 2015 - p42(1) [51-500]
Rockhill, Gabriel - *Radical History and the Politics of Art*
  HNet - April 2015 - pNA [501+]
Rockliff, Mara - *Chik Chak Shabbat (Illus. by Brooker, Kyrsten)*
  c HB Guide - v26 - i1 - Spring 2015 - p43(1) [51-500]
  Gingerbread for Liberty! How a German Baker Helped Win the American Revolution (Illus. by Kirsch, Vincent X.)
  c CCB-B - v68 - i6 - Feb 2015 - p327(1) [51-500]
  c HB Guide - v26 - i2 - Fall 2015 - p221(1) [51-500]
  c PW - v262 - i49 - Dec 2 2015 - p47(1) [51-500]
  The Grudge Keeper (Read by McDonough, John). Audiobook Review
  c SLJ - v61 - i5 - May 2015 - p68(1) [51-500]
  Mesmerized: How Ben Franklin Solved a Mystery That Baffled All of France (Illus. by Bruno, Iacopo)
  c HB Guide - v26 - i2 - Fall 2015 - p163(1) [51-500]
  c PW - v262 - i49 - Dec 2 2015 - p20(2) [51-500]
  c CCB-B - v68 - i7 - March 2015 - p367(1) [51-500]
  c CH Bwatch - June 2015 - pNA [51-500]
  c HB - v91 - i1 - Jan-Feb 2015 - p103(1) [51-500]
Rocklin, Joanne - *Fleabrain Loves Franny*
  c HB Guide - v26 - i1 - Spring 2015 - p90(2) [51-500]
  I Say Shehechiyanu (Illus. by Filipina, Monika)
  c HB Guide - v26 - i2 - Fall 2015 - p150(1) [51-500]
Rockmore, Tom - *Art and Truth after Plato*
  RM - v69 - i2 - Dec 2015 - p407(3) [501+]
Rockoff, Adam - *The Horror of It All: One Moviegoer's Love Affair with Masked Maniacs, Frightened Virgins, and the Living Dead*
  KR - Feb 15 2015 - pNA [501+]
  NYTBR - May 31 2015 - p34(L) [501+]
  PW - v262 - i8 - Feb 23 2015 - p64(1) [51-500]
Rockwell, Anne - *Apples and Pumpkins (Illus. by Rockwell, Lizzy)*
  c HB Guide - v26 - i1 - Spring 2015 - p15(1) [51-500]
  At the Beach (Illus. by Rockwell, Harlow)
  c HB Guide - v26 - i1 - Spring 2015 - p15(1) [51-500]
  The First Snowfall
  c HB Guide - v26 - i1 - Spring 2015 - p15(1) [51-500]
  Hey Charleston! The True Story of the Jenkins Orphanage Band (Illus. by Bootman, Colin)
  c SE - v79 - i3 - May-June 2015 - p143(1) [501+]
  Let's Go to the Hardware Store (Illus. by Iwai, Melissa)
  c KR - Dec 15 2015 - pNA [51-500]
  Library Day (Illus. by Rockwell, Lizzy)
  c KR - Oct 1 2015 - pNA [51-500]
  c PW - v262 - i42 - Oct 19 2015 - p76(1) [51-500]
  My Spring Robin (Illus. by Rockwell, Harlow)
  c HB Guide - v26 - i2 - Fall 2015 - p17(1) [51-500]
Rockwell, Lizzy - *A Bird Is a Bird (Illus. by Rockwell, Lizzy)*
  c HB Guide - v26 - i2 - Fall 2015 - p178(1) [51-500]
  c KR - Feb 15 2015 - pNA [51-500]
  SLJ - v61 - i3 - March 2015 - p173(1) [51-500]
  c BL - v111 - i17 - May 1 2015 - p84(1) [51-500]
  c CCB-B - v69 - i1 - Sept 2015 - p48(1) [51-500]
  Plants Feed Me
  c CH Bwatch - April 2015 - pNA [51-500]
Rodabaugh, Katrina - *The Paper Playhouse: Awesome Art Projects for Kids Using Paper, Boxes, and Books*
  c CH Bwatch - April 2015 - pNA [51-500]
Rodale, Maya - *Lady Bridget's Diary*
  PW - v262 - i52 - Dec 21 2015 - p140(1) [51-500]
Rodan, Garry - *The Politics of Accountability in Southeast Asia: The Dominance of Moral Ideologies*
  Pac A - v88 - i4 - Dec 2015 - p955 [501+]

Rodarmor, William - *Oh My, Oh No! (Illus. by Domergue, Agnes)*
  c HB Guide - v26 - i1 - Spring 2015 - p7(1) [51-500]
Rodda, Emily - *Star of Deltora: Shadows of the Master Magpies*
  v30 - i3 - July 2015 - p12(1) [51-500]
Rodden, John - *The Cambridge Introduction to George Orwell*
  MLR - v110 - i3 - July 2015 - p852-853 [501+]
Roden, Nadia - *Ice Pops! 50 Delicious, Fresh, and Fabulous Icy Treats*
  LJ - v140 - i11 - June 15 2015 - p108(2) [501+]
Rodenas, Adriana Mendez - *Transatlantic Travels in Nineteenth-Century Latin America: European Women Pilgrims*
  MLN - v130 - i2 - March 2015 - p408-410 [501+]
Rodenbeck, Judith F. - *Radical Prototypes: Allan Kaprow and the Invention of Happenings*
  Critm - v57 - i1 - Wntr 2015 - pNA [501+]
Rodenborn, Steven M. - *Hope in Action: Subversive Eschatology in the Theology of Edward Schillebeeckx and Johann Baptist Metz*
  Theol St - v76 - i3 - Sept 2015 - p646(2) [501+]
Roderick, Stacey - *Dinosaurs from Head to Tail (Illus. by Moriya, Kwanchai)*
  c BL - v111 - i17 - May 1 2015 - p73(2) [51-500]
  c HB Guide - v26 - i2 - Fall 2015 - p168(1) [51-500]
  c Res Links - v20 - i5 - June 2015 - p15(2) [51-500]
  c SLJ - v61 - i7 - July 2015 - p68(1) [51-500]
Rodgers, Greg - *Chukfi Rabbit's Big, Bad Bellyache: A Trickster Tale (Illus. by Widender, Leslie Stall)*
  c HB Guide - v26 - i1 - Spring 2015 - p145(1) [51-500]
Rodgers, Kathleen - *Welcome to Resistervilk: American Dissidents in British Columbia*
  Can Hist R - v96 - i3 - Sept 2015 - p455(3) [501+]
Rodgers, Marion Elizabeth - *The Days Trilogy, Expanded Edition*
  Am St - v54 - i1 - Spring 2015 - p159-2 [501+]
Rodgers, Richard - *South Pacific: The Complete Book and Lyrics of the Broadway Musical*
  RVBW - Jan 2015 - pNA [501+]
Rodgers, Rick - *Flavors of Aloha: Cooking with Tommy Bahama*
  LJ - v140 - i9 - May 15 2015 - p102(2) [501+]
Rodgers, Sally-Christine - *Convergence: A Voyage through French Polynesia*
  Bwatch - March 2015 - pNA [51-500]
Rodkey, Geoff - *The Tapper Twins Go to War (with Each Other)*
  BL - v111 - i14 - March 15 2015 - p74(2) [51-500]
  c HB Guide - v26 - i2 - Fall 2015 - p99(1) [51-500]
  The Tapper Twins Go to War
  c KR - Jan 1 2015 - pNA [51-500]
  The Tapper Twins Go to War with Each Other
  c PW - v262 - i5 - Feb 2 2015 - p63(1) [51-500]
  The Tapper Twins Go to War (With Each Other).
  c PW - v262 - i49 - Dec 2 2015 - p73(1) [51-500]
  The Tapper Twins Tear Up New York
  c KR - June 15 2015 - pNA [51-500]
  c SLJ - v61 - i7 - July 2015 - p82(1) [51-500]
Rodman, Sean - *Tap Out*
  y Res Links - v20 - i3 - Feb 2015 - p35(1) [51-500]
Rodoreda, Merce - *War, So Much War*
  KR - Sept 1 2015 - pNA [51-500]
  LJ - v140 - i20 - Dec 1 2015 - p96(1) [51-500]
  PW - v262 - i38 - Sept 21 2015 - p47(1) [51-500]
Rodrigue, John C. - *Lincoln and Reconstruction*
  RAH - v43 - i3 - Sept 2015 - p512-521 [501+]
Rodrigue, Michel - *Sybil the Backpack Fairy 5: The Dragon's Dance (Illus. by Dalena, Antonello)*
  c CH Bwatch - May 2015 - pNA [51-500]
Rodrigue, Wendy W. - *The Other Side of the Painting*
  Roundup M - v22 - i6 - August 2015 - p40(1) [501+]
Rodriguez, Andrew J. - *Santa Rita Stories*
  PW - v262 - i3 - Jan 19 2015 - p55(2) [51-500]
Rodriguez, Ashley - *Date Night In: More than 120 Recipes to Nourish Your Relationship*
  PW - v262 - i2 - Jan 5 2015 - p67(1) [51-500]
Rodriguez, Cindy L. - *When Reason Breaks*
  y BL - v111 - i9-10 - Jan 1 2015 - p100(1) [51-500]
  y CCB-B - v68 - i8 - April 2015 - p418(1) [51-500]
  y HB Guide - v26 - i2 - Fall 2015 - p136(1) [51-500]
  y VOYA - v38 - i1 - April 2015 - p68(1) [51-500]
Rodriguez, Ed - *Kiki Kokt: La leyenda encantada del coqui (Illus. by Rodriguez, Ed)*
  c HB Guide - v26 - i1 - Spring 2015 - p146(1) [51-500]
  c KR - Feb 1 2015 - pNA [51-500]

Rodriguez Garcia, Jose Manuel - *La cruzada en tiempos de Alfonso X*
  Med R - Jan 2015 - pNA [501+]
Rodriguez, Guadalupe - *Handmade Crafts: By Children for Children (Illus. by Montero, Manuela)*
  c SLJ - v61 - i2 - Feb 2015 - p21(2) [51-500]
Rodriguez, Jarbel - *Muslim and Christian Contact in the Middle Ages*
  Bwatch - Sept 2015 - pNA [51-500]
Rodriguez, Jason - *Colonial Comics: New England, 1620-1750*
  BL - v111 - i9-10 - Jan 1 2015 - p62(1) [51-500]
Rodriguez, Jessamyn Waldman - *The Hot Bread Kitchen Cookbook: Artisanal Baking from Around the World*
  LJ - v140 - i4 - Sept 1 2015 - p132(1) [51-500]
Rodriguez O., Jaime E. - *"We Are Now the True Spaniards": Sovereignty, Revolution, Independence, and the Emergence of the Federal Republic of Mexico, 1808-1824*
  AHR - v120 - i2 - April 2015 - p678-679 [501+]
  Ams - v72 - i1 - Jan 2015 - p182(3) [501+]
  HAHR - v95 - i1 - Feb 2015 - p157-159 [501+]
  JIH - v46 - i1 - Summer 2015 - p142-143 [501+]
Rodriguez-Pereyra, Gonzalo - *Leibniz's Principle of Identity of Indiscernibles*
  TLS - i5840 - March 6 2015 - p32(1) [501+]
Rodriguez, Roberto Cintli - *Our Sacred Maiz Is Our Mother: Indigeneity and Belonging in the Americas*
  WHQ - v46 - i3 - Autumn 2015 - p374-375 [501+]
Rodriguez, Sarah B. - *Female Circumcision and Clitoridectomy in the United States: A History of a Medical Treatment*
  JAH - v102 - i2 - Sept 2015 - p517-518 [501+]
Rodriguez, Sergio Gonzales - *Campo de guerra: Premio Anagrama de Ensayo*
  ABR - v36 - i4 - May-June 2015 - p7(1) [501+]
Rodriguez, Vanessa - *The Teaching Brain*
  RVBW - Jan 2015 - pNA [501+]
Rodrik, Dani - *Economics Rules: The Rights and Wrongs of the Dismal Science*
  KR - June 15 2015 - pNA [501+]
  LJ - v140 - i13 - August 1 2015 - p108(1) [51-500]
  NYTBR - Nov 22 2015 - p25(L) [501+]
  PW - v262 - i23 - June 8 2015 - p48(1) [51-500]
Rodriquez, Jason - *Labors of Love: Nursing Homes and the Structures of Care Work*
  AJS - v121 - i3 - Nov 2015 - p987(3) [501+]
  Soc - v52 - i1 - Feb 2015 - p86(1) [501+]
Rodwell, Warwick - *The Coronation Chair and Stone of Scone: History, Archaeology and Conservation*
  Med R - Jan 2015 - pNA [501+]
Roe, Andrew - *The Miracle Girl*
  BL - v111 - i13 - March 1 2015 - p20(1) [51-500]
  KR - Feb 15 2015 - pNA [501+]
  NYTBR - May 3 2015 - p30(L) [501+]
Roe, Joann - *The Columbia River: A Historical Travel Guide*
  Roundup M - v22 - i6 - August 2015 - p40(1) [501+]
Roe, Sue - *In Montmartre: Picasso, Matisse and Modernism in Paris, 1900-1910*
  NYTBR - June 28 2015 - p24(L) [501+]
  In Montmartre: Picasso, Matisse and the Birth of Modernist Art (Read by Bering, Emma). Audiobook Review
  LJ - v140 - i13 - August 1 2015 - p49(1) [51-500]
  In Montmartre: Picasso, Matisse and the Birth of Modernist Art
  BL - v111 - i16 - April 15 2015 - p11(1) [51-500]
  BL - v112 - i5 - Nov 1 2015 - p18(2) [501+]
  CSM - April 22 2015 - pNA [501+]
  KR - Feb 15 2015 - pNA [501+]
  LJ - v140 - i8 - May 1 2015 - p69(1) [51-500]
  NY - v91 - i11 - May 4 2015 - p70 [501+]
  PW - v262 - i11 - March 16 2015 - p75(2) [51-500]
Roeber, A.G. - *Hopes for Better Spouses: Protestant Marriage and Church Renewal in Early Modern Europe, India, and North America*
  CHR - v101 - i1 - Wntr 2015 - p166(2) [501+]
Roeder, Katherine - *Wide Awake in Slumberland: Fantasy, Mass Culture, and Modernism in the Art of Winsor McCay*
  Col Lit - v42 - i1 - Wntr 2015 - p178(4) [501+]
Roediger, David - *Seizing Freedom: Slave Emancipation and Liberty for All*
  AHR - v120 - i4 - Oct 2015 - p1436-1439 [501+]
Roemer, Robin Chin - *Meaningful Metrics: A 21st Century Librarian's Guide to Bibliometrics, Altmetrics, and Research Impact*
  LJ - v140 - i13 - August 1 2015 - p113(1) [501+]

Roesen, Tine - *Vladimir Sorokin's Languages*
  MLR - v110 - i2 - April 2015 - p625-627 [501+]
Roffe, Stephen - *Beyond Hercules*
  SPBW - March 2015 - pNA [51-500]
Roffer, Michael H. - *The Law Book: From Hammurabi to the International Criminal Court, 250 Milestones in the History of Law*
  LJ - v140 - i20 - Dec 1 2015 - p130(1) [51-500]
Rogak, Lisa - *Angry Optimist: The Life and Times of Jon Stewart*
  BL - v111 - i19-20 - June 1 2015 - p30(2) [51-500]
  Cats on the Job: 50 Fabulous Felines Who Purr, Mouse, and Even Sing for Their Supper
  LJ - v140 - i16 - Oct 1 2015 - p100(1) [51-500]
Rogan, Eugene - *The Fall of the Ottomans: The Great War in the Middle East*
  CC - v132 - i16 - August 5 2015 - p42(1) [51-500]
  Econ - v414 - i8928 - March 7 2015 - p85(US) [501+]
  J Mil H - v79 - i4 - Oct 2015 - p1164-1165 [501+]
  KR - Jan 1 2015 - pNA [501+]
  LJ - v140 - i3 - Feb 15 2015 - p114(1) [51-500]
  NY - v91 - i9 - April 20 2015 - p89 [51-500]
  NYRB - v62 - i8 - May 7 2015 - p46(2) [501+]
  NYTBR - April 19 2015 - p16(L) [501+]
  PW - v262 - i3 - Jan 19 2015 - p70(2) [51-500]
  Spec - v327 - i9740 - May 2 2015 - p38(2) [501+]
  TLS - i5850 - May 15 2015 - p7(1) [501+]
Roganm, Johnny - *Ray Davies: A Complicated Life*
  NS - v144 - i5252 - March 6 2015 - p44(2) [501+]
Rogel-Salazar, Jesus - *Essential MATLAB and Octave*
  Bwatch - March 2015 - pNA [51-500]
Roger, Bernard - *The Initiatory Path in Fairy Tales: The Alchemical Secrets of Mother Goose*
  Bwatch - Sept 2015 - pNA [51-500]
Roger, Motti - *Pop-Rock Music: Aesthetic Cosmopolitanism in Late Modernity*
  CS - v44 - i3 - May 2015 - p408-410 [501+]
Rogers, Alan - *The Child Cases: How America's Religious Exemption Laws Harm Children*
  AHR - v120 - i4 - Oct 2015 - p1522-1523 [501+]
  J Ch St - v57 - i2 - Spring 2015 - p392-394 [501+]
Rogers, Ariel - *Cinematic Appeals: The Experience of New Movie Technologies*
  T&C - v56 - i2 - April 2015 - p558-560 [501+]
Rogers, Brett M. - *Classical Traditions in Science Fiction*
  TLS - i5857 - July 3 2015 - p27(1) [501+]
Rogers, David - *By Royal Appointment: Tales from the Privy Council--the Unknown Arm of Government*
  Lon R Bks - v37 - i20 - Oct 22 2015 - p29(2) [501+]
Rogers, Frank, Jr. - *Practicing Compassion*
  RVBW - July 2015 - pNA [51-500]
Rogers, Garry - *Corr Syl the Terrible*
  y KR - July 15 2015 - pNA [501+]
Rogers, Gayle - *Modernism and the New Spain: Britain, Cosmopolitan Europe, and Literary History*
  Comp L - v67 - i2 - June 2015 - p232-234 [501+]
Rogers, Guy MacLean - *The Mysteries of Artemis of Ephesos: Cult, Polis, and Change in the Graeco-Roman World*
  AHR - v120 - i2 - April 2015 - p692(1) [501+]
Rogers, James Silas - *Northhern Orchards: Places near the Dead*
  ILS - v35 - i1 - Fall 2015 - p27(1) [501+]
Rogers, Jaqueline McLeod - *Finding McLuhan: The Mind/The Man/The Message*
  RVBW - Oct 2015 - pNA [51-500]
Rogers, Jedediah S. - *Roads in the Wilderness: Conflict in Canyon Country*
  Roundup M - v22 - i6 - August 2015 - p40(1) [501+]
Rogers, Jim E. - *Lighting the World: Transforming Our Energy Future by Bringing Electricity to Everyone*
  KR - June 1 2015 - pNA [501+]
  LJ - v140 - i12 - July 1 2015 - p91(1) [51-500]
  New Sci - v227 - i3038 - Sept 12 2015 - p41(1) [501+]
Rogers, Lola - *When the Doves Disappeared*
  NYRB - v62 - i10 - June 4 2015 - p79(2) [501+]
Rogers, Mary Beth - *Turning Texas Blue: What It Will Take to Break the GOP Grip on America's Reddest State*
  KR - Nov 1 2015 - pNA [501+]
  PW - v262 - i44 - Nov 2 2015 - p77(1) [51-500]
Rogers, Rebecca - *A Frenchwoman's Imperial Story: Madame Luce in Nineteenth-Century Algeria*
  JMH - v87 - i1 - March 2015 - p191(2) [501+]
Rogers, Sarah A. - *Arab Art Histories: The Khalid Shoman Collection*
  HNet - August 2015 - pNA [51-500]

Rogers, Simon - *Information Graphics: Space (Illus. by Daniel, Jennifer)*
  SLJ - v61 - i4 - April 2015 - p184(2) [51-500]
Rogin, Ellen - *Picture Your Prosperity: Smart Money Moves to Turn Your Vision into Reality (Read by Rogin, Ellen). Audiobook Review*
  BL - v111 - i21 - July 1 2015 - p79(1) [51-500]
Rohan, Timothy M. - *The Architecture of Paul Rudolph*
  NYRB - v62 - i2 - Feb 5 2015 - p34(3) [501+]
Rohde, George - *A Prairie Year*
  Sci & Ch - v52 - i7 - March 2015 - p96 [501+]
Rohde, Klaus - *The Balance of Nature and Human Impact*
  QRB - v90 - i2 - June 2015 - p211(2) [501+]
Rohl, John - *Wilhelm II: Into the Abyss of War and Exile, 1900-41*
  Lon R Bks - v37 - i8 - April 23 2015 - p23(2) [501+]
Rohl, John C. - *Kaiser Wilhelm II*
  BL - v111 - i11 - Feb 1 2015 - p13(1) [51-500]
Rohl, Vera Regine - *Es gibt kein Himmelreich auf Erden: Heinrich Margulies - ein sakularer Zionist*
  HNet - May 2015 - pNA [51-500]
Rohmann, Eric - *Kitten Tale (Illus. by Rohmann, Eric)*
  c BL - v112 - i4 - Oct 15 2015 - p53(1) [51-500]
Rohnert, Jan - *Die Metaphorik der Autobahn: Literatur, Kunst, Film und Architektur nach 1945*
  HNet - March 2015 - pNA [501+]
Rohr, Richard - *Eager to Love: The Alternative Way of Francis of Assisi*
  CC - v132 - i12 - June 10 2015 - p37(3) [501+]
  What the Mystics Know: Seven Pathways to Your Deeper Self
  RVBW - June 2015 - pNA [51-500]
Rohrbach, Augusta - *Thinking Outside the Book*
  AL - v87 - i3 - Sept 2015 - p630-632 [501+]
Rohrbough, Malcolm J. - *Rush to Gold: The French and the California Gold Rush, 1848-1854*
  RAH - v43 - i1 - March 2015 - p92-97 [501+]
Rohrer, Matthew - *Surrounded by Friends*
  PW - v262 - i7 - Feb 16 2015 - p157(1) [51-500]
Roig-DeBellis, Kaitlin - *Choosing Hope: Moving Forward from Life's Darkest Hours*
  KR - July 15 2015 - pNA [51-500]
  PW - v262 - i28 - July 13 2015 - p55(1) [51-500]
Roiphe, Anne - *Ballad of the Black and Blue Mind*
  BL - v111 - i18 - May 15 2015 - p22(1) [51-500]
  HR - v68 - i3 - Autumn 2015 - p510-516 [501+]
  NYT - May 28 2015 - pC6(L) [501+]
Roiphe, Katie - *The Violet Hour: Great Writers at the End*
  KR - Dec 15 2015 - pNA [501+]
  PW - v262 - i47 - Nov 23 2015 - p58(1) [51-500]
Roisman, Hanna - *The Encyclopedia of Greek Tragedy, 3 vols.*
  Class R - v65 - i1 - April 2015 - p22-24 [501+]
Rojas, Agustin de - *A Legend of the Future*
  ABR - v36 - i4 - May-June 2015 - p26(2) [501+]
Rojas, Carlos - *The Four Books*
  PW - v262 - i4 - Jan 26 2015 - p142(1) [51-500]
Rojek, Chris - *Fame Attack: The Inflation of Celebrity and Its Consequences*
  CS - v44 - i2 - March 2015 - p245-246 [501+]
Rojo, Danna A. Levin - *Return to Aztlan: Indians, Spaniards, and the Invention of Nuevo Mexico*
  HAHR - v95 - i2 - May 2015 - p350-352 [501+]
Rojstczer, Stuart - *The Mathematician's Shiva*
  Math T - v109 - i3 - Oct 2015 - p239-239 [501+]
Roker, Al - *Been There, Done That: Family Wisdom for Modern Times*
  PW - v262 - i50 - Dec 7 2015 - p83(1) [51-500]
  The Storm of the Century: Tragedy, Heroism, Survival, and the Epic True Story of America's Deadliest Natural Disaster: The Great Gulf Hurricane of 1900
  BL - v111 - i21 - July 1 2015 - p20(1) [51-500]
  BooChiTr - August 29 2015 - p12(1) [501+]
  KR - May 15 2015 - pNA [501+]
  LJ - v140 - i10 - June 1 2015 - p116(1) [51-500]
  PW - v262 - i24 - June 15 2015 - p76(1) [51-500]
Roksa, Josipa - *Aspiring Adults Adrift: Tentative Transitions of College Graduates*
  CS - v44 - i6 - Nov 2015 - p773-774 [501+]
Roland, L. Kaifa - *Cuban Color in Tourism and La Lucha: An Ethnography of Racial Meanings*
  Signs - v40 - i2 - Wntr 2015 - p525(7) [501+]
Roland, Paul - *The Curious Case of H.P. Lovecraft*
  TLS - i5849 - May 8 2015 - p24(1) [501+]
Roland, Rebecca - *Fractured Days*
  SPBW - Oct 2015 - pNA [51-500]
  Shards of History
  SPBW - Oct 2015 - pNA [51-500]

Book Review Index 2016 Cumulation ROOTS • 395

Roland, Timothy - *Monkey Me and the New Neighbor*
c HB Guide - v26 - i1 - Spring 2015 - p65(1) [51-500]
Monkey Me and the School Ghost
y CH Bwatch - Jan 2015 - pNA [501+]
c HB Guide - v26 - i1 - Spring 2015 - p65(1) [51-500]
Rolf, Veronica Mary - *Julian's Gospel: Illuminating the Life and Revelations of Julian of Norwich*
TLS - i5832 - Jan 9 2015 - p20(1) [501+]
Rolfe, Glenn - *Blood and Rain. E-book Review*
PW - v262 - i36 - Sept 7 2015 - p50(2) [51-500]
Roling, Bernd - *Physica Sacra: Wunder, Naturwissenschaft und historischer Schriftsinn zwischen Mittelalter und Fruher Neuzeit*
Isis - v106 - i1 - March 2015 - p174(2) [501+]
Six Ct J - v46 - i1 - Spring 2015 - p161(3) [501+]
Rollason, David - *Early Medieval Europe, 300-1050: The Birth of Western Society*
Med R - August 2015 - pNA [501+]
Roller, Alexander - *Imperator et Pontifex: Forschungen zum Verhaltnis von Kaiserhof und Romischer Kurie im Zeitalter der Konfessionalisierung*
CHR - v101 - i1 - Wntr 2015 - p162(2) [501+]
Roller, Duane W. - *The Geography of Strabo: An English Translation, with Introduction and Notes*
Class R - v65 - i2 - Oct 2015 - p608-608 [501+]
GR - v105 - i3 - July 2015 - p383(4) [501+]
Roller, Heather F - *Amazonian Routes: Indigenous Mobility and Colonial Communities in Northern Brazil*
Eight-C St - v48 - i3 - Spring 2015 - p353-356 [501+]
Roller, Leonard H. - *The Ash and the Thorn: God on Trial?*
SPBW - August 2015 - pNA [51-500]
Rollin, Catherine - *Museum Masterpieces: Piano Solos Inspired by Great Works of Art, 4 vols.*
Am MT - v64 - i6 - June-July 2015 - p68(2) [501+]
Rollins, Danielle - *Burning*
y SLJ - v61 - i12 - Dec 2015 - p127(1) [51-500]
Rollins, Jack - *Bonhomme de neige (Illus. by Williams, Sam)*
c Res Links - v20 - i3 - Feb 2015 - p50(1) [51-500]
Rollins, James - *The Bone Labyrinth*
BL - v112 - i7 - Dec 1 2015 - p27(1) [51-500]
KR - Oct 15 2015 - pNA [501+]
Rollins, Kent - *A Taste of Cowboy: Ranch Recipes and Tales from the Trail*
LJ - v140 - i7 - April 15 2015 - p112(1) [51-500]
PW - v262 - i14 - April 6 2015 - p53(1) [51-500]
Rollins, Suzy Pepper - *Learning in the Fast Lane: 8 Ways to Put ALL Students on the Road to Academic Success*
Teach Lib - v42 - i3 - Feb 2015 - p40(1) [501+]
Rolls, Alistair - *Paris and the Fetish: Primal Crime Scenes*
FS - v69 - i3 - July 2015 - p420-421 [501+]
Rollyson, Carol - *Marilyn Monroe Day by Day: A Timeline of People, Places, and Events*
BL - v111 - i12 - Feb 15 2015 - p21(1) [51-500]
Roma, Catherine - *A City That Sings: Cincinnati's Choral Tradition 1800-2012*
RVBW - April 2015 - pNA [51-500]
Romain, Theresa - *A Gentleman's Game*
PW - v262 - i48 - Nov 30 2015 - p44(2) [51-500]
Roman, Carole P. - *Captain No Beard and the Aurora Borealis (Illus. by Roman, Carole P.)*
c CH Bwatch - Jan 2015 - pNA [501+]
c KR - Jan 15 2015 - pNA [501+]
Fribbet the Frog and the Tadpoles (Illus. by Roman, Carole P.)
c KR - May 15 2015 - pNA [501+]
If You Were Me and Lived in ... Greece
KR - March 1 2015 - pNA [501+]
If You Were Me and Lived in ... Scotland (Illus. by Roman, Carole P.)
c CH Bwatch - March 2015 - pNA [51-500]
KR - May 15 2015 - pNA [51-500]
Roman, Dave - *The Race for Boatlantis*
y KR - July 15 2015 - pNA [51-500]
Teen Boat! The Race for Boatlantis (Illus. by Green, John)
c SLJ - v61 - i9 - Sept 2015 - p174(1) [51-500]
Roman, Richard - *Continental Crucible: Big Business, Workers and Unions in the Transformation of North America*
CS - v44 - i5 - Sept 2015 - p699-700 [501+]
Romanek, Trudee - *Raising the Stakes*
c Res Links - v21 - i1 - Oct 2015 - p40(1) [51-500]
Romani, Gabriella - *Postal Culture: Writing and Reading Letters in Post-Unification Italy*
MP - v113 - i2 - Nov 2015 - pE118(4) [501+]
Romani, Ludovico - *Attilio Grisafi*
Specu - v90 - i4 - Oct 2015 - p1145-1146 [501+]
Romaniuk, Jenni - *How Brands Grow: Part 2*
TimHES - i2229 - Nov 12 2015 - p47(1) [501+]
Romankiewicz, Tanja - *The Medieval Kirk, Cemetery and Hospice at Kirk Ness, North Berwick: The Scottish Seabird Center Excavations 1999-2006*
Med R - Sept 2015 - pNA [501+]
Romano, Florence Ann - *Nanny and Me (Illus. by Kruger, Sydni)*
c CH Bwatch - April 2015 - pNA [51-500]
Romano, John F. - *Liturgy and Society in Early Medieval Rome*
CH - v84 - i3 - Sept 2015 - p651(3) [501+]
CHR - v101 - i4 - Autumn 2015 - p907(2) [501+]
Med R - May 2015 - pNA [501+]
Romano, Juliana - *First There Was Forever*
y BL - v111 - i9-10 - Jan 1 2015 - p92(1) [51-500]
y HB Guide - v26 - i2 - Fall 2015 - p136(1) [51-500]
y KR - Jan 15 2015 - pNA [51-500]
y PW - v262 - i8 - Feb 23 2015 - p78(1) [51-500]
y PW - v262 - i49 - Dec 2 2015 - p91(1) [51-500]
y VOYA - v37 - i6 - Feb 2015 - p63(1) [51-500]
Romano-Lax, Andromeda - *Behave*
KR - Dec 15 2015 - pNA [501+]
Romano, Nina - *Lemon Blossoms*
PW - v262 - i47 - Nov 23 2015 - p44(1) [51-500]
Romano, Renee C. - *Racial Reckoning: Prosecuting America's Civil Rights Murders*
JAH - v102 - i2 - Sept 2015 - p631-632 [501+]
Romanska, Magda - *The Routledge Companion to Dramaturgy*
Am Theat - v32 - i8 - Oct 2015 - p126(2) [501+]
Rombes, Nicholas - *The Absolution of Roberto Acestes Laing*
ABR - v36 - i2 - Jan-Feb 2015 - p17(1) [501+]
Rome, Adam - *The Genius of Earth Day: How a 1970 Teach-In Unexpectedly Made the First Green Generation*
PHR - v84 - i3 - August 2015 - p368(1) [501+]
Romer, Franz - *Fasti Austriae 1736: Ein naulateinisches Gedicht in funfzehn europaischen Sprachen*
Sev Cent N - v73 - i3-4 - Fall-Winter 2015 - p197(3) [501+]
Romer, Thomas - *The Invention of God*
Mac - v128 - i47 - Nov 30 2015 - p58(2) [501+]
Romero, Patricia W. - *African Women: A Historical Panorama*
IJAHS - v48 - i1 - Wntr 2015 - p170-171 [501+]
Romero, Terry Hope - *Salad Samurai*
Veg J - v34 - i1 - Jan-March 2015 - p30(2) [51-500]
Romhild, Juliane - *Femininity and Authorship in the Novels of Elizabeth Von Arnim: At Her Most Radiant Moment*
TSWL - v34 - i1 - Spring 2015 - p181-184 [501+]
Romirowsky, Asaf - *Religion, Politics, and the Origins of Palestine Refugee Relief*
MEQ - v22 - i1 - Wntr 2015 - pNA [501+]
Romm, James - *Dying Every Day: Seneca at the Court of Nero*
Lon R Bks - v37 - i12 - June 18 2015 - p33(3) [501+]
NYTBR - Jan 4 2015 - p24(L) [501+]
Romney, Susanah Shaw - *New Netherland Connections: Intimate Networks and Atlantic Ties in Seventeenth-Century America*
AHR - v120 - i2 - April 2015 - p609-610 [501+]
JAH - v102 - i2 - Sept 2015 - p525-526 [501+]
W&M Q - v72 - i1 - Jan 2015 - p188-192 [501+]
Romo, Anadelia A. - *Brazil's Living Museum: Race, Reform, and Tradition in Bahia*
HAHR - v95 - i4 - Nov 2015 - p691-692 [501+]
Romo, Kelly A. - *Whistling Women*
BL - v112 - i6 - Nov 15 2015 - p30(1) [51-500]
Rona-Tas, Akos - *Plastic Money: Constructing Markets for Credit Cards in Eight Postcommunist Countries*
AJS - v121 - i1 - July 2015 - p315(3) [501+]
CS - v44 - i4 - July 2015 - p546-548 [501+]
Ronald, Susan - *Hitler's Art Thief: Hildebrand Gurlitt, the Nazis and the Looting of Europe's Treasures*
BL - v112 - i2 - Sept 15 2015 - p14(1) [51-500]
LJ - v140 - i14 - Sept 1 2015 - p122(2) [51-500]
NY - v91 - i35 - Nov 9 2015 - p81 [51-500]
Ronau, Robert N. - *Putting Essential Understanding of Fractions into Practice in Grades 9-12*
Math T - v108 - i6 - Feb 2015 - p475-476 [501+]
Roncagliolo, Santiago - *La Pena Maxima*
TLS - i5839 - Feb 27 2015 - p26(1) [501+]
Rondo, Marie - *Spark Joy*
PW - v262 - i42 - Oct 19 2015 - p36(1) [51-500]
Roney, Jessica Choppin - *Governed by a Spirit of Opposition: The Origins of American Political Practice in Colonial Philadelphia*
JEH - v75 - i1 - March 2015 - p297-299 [501+]
Ronnen, Tal - *Crossroads: Extraordinary Recipes from the Restaurant That Is Reinventing Vegan Cuisine*
LJ - v140 - i15 - Sept 15 2015 - p102(1) [51-500]
PW - v262 - i31 - August 3 2015 - p52(1) [51-500]
Ronning, Kari A. - *The Song of the Lark*
MLR - v110 - i2 - April 2015 - p536-537 [501+]
Ronson, Jon - *So You've Been Publicly Shamed (Read by Ronson, Jon). Audiobook Review*
LJ - v140 - i10 - June 1 2015 - p62(1) [51-500]
So You've Been Publicly Shamed
BL - v111 - i13 - March 1 2015 - p5(1) [51-500]
BooChiTr - April 11 2015 - p14(1) [501+]
Bwatch - July 2015 - pNA [51-500]
CHE - v61 - i38 - June 12 2015 - pB5(1) [501+]
HM - v330 - i1980 - May 2015 - p90(5) [501+]
KR - Feb 1 2015 - pNA [501+]
Lon R Bks - v37 - i7 - April 9 2015 - p12(2) [501+]
Nat Post - v17 - i125 - March 28 2015 - pWP9(1) [501+]
New Sci - v225 - i3013 - March 21 2015 - p46(1) [501+]
NS - v144 - i5253 - March 13 2015 - p42(3) [501+]
NYT - March 30 2015 - pC1(L) [501+]
NYTBR - April 19 2015 - p13(L) [501+]
PW - v262 - i4 - Jan 26 2015 - p164(1) [51-500]
PW - v262 - i15 - April 13 2015 - p13(1) [51-500]
Soc - v52 - i4 - August 2015 - p383(1) [501+]
UtneADi - i186 - Spring 2015 - p91(2) [501+]
Ronson, Mark - *Uptown Special*
People - v83 - i2 - Jan 12 2015 - p29 [501+]
People - v83 - i2 - Jan 12 2015 - p29 [501+]
People - v83 - i2 - Jan 12 2015 - p29 [501+]
People - v83 - i2 - Jan 12 2015 - p29 [501+]
People - v83 - i2 - Jan 12 2015 - p29 [501+]
Roodhouse, Mark - *Black Market Britain, 1939-1955*
HNet - Jan 2015 - pNA [501+]
Rooke, Margaret - *Creative, Successful, Dyslexic: 23 High Achievers Share Their Stories*
y SLJ - v61 - i12 - Dec 2015 - p146(1) [51-500]
Rooks, Erin Kerr - *In Between Dreams*
KR - Jan 15 2015 - pNA [501+]
Rooney, Anne - *Agricultural Engineering and Feeding the Future*
c BL - v112 - i4 - Oct 15 2015 - p42(1) [51-500]
Earthquake: Perspectives on Earthquake Disasters
y VOYA - v38 - i1 - April 2015 - p89(1) [51-500]
A Math Journey through Planet Earth
c BL - v111 - i9-10 - Jan 1 2015 - p84(1) [51-500]
A Math Journey through Space
c BL - v111 - i9-10 - Jan 1 2015 - p84(1) [51-500]
c Res Links - v20 - i3 - Feb 2015 - p24(1) [501+]
A Math Journey through the Animal Kingdom
c Res Links - v20 - i3 - Feb 2015 - p24(1) [501+]
A Math Journey through the Human Body
c BL - v111 - i9-10 - Jan 1 2015 - p84(1) [51-500]
c Res Links - v20 - i3 - Feb 2015 - p24(1) [501+]
A Math Journey through the Planet Earth
c Res Links - v20 - i3 - Feb 2015 - p24(1) [501+]
Rooney, E. Ashley - *Contemporary American Print Makers*
Bwatch - April 2015 - pNA [51-500]
Bwatch - July 2015 - pNA [51-500]
Rooney, Morgan - *The French Revolution Debate and the British Novel, 1790-1814: The Struggle for History's Authority*
Clio - v44 - i2 - Spring 2015 - p253-256 [501+]
Roorda, Rhonda M. - *In Their Voices: Black Americans on Transracial Adoption*
PW - v262 - i37 - Sept 14 2015 - p55(2) [51-500]
Roosevelt, Eleanor - *The Autobiography of Eleanor Roosevelt (Read by Gilbert, Tavia). Audiobook Review*
LJ - v140 - i3 - Feb 15 2015 - p60(1) [51-500]
Roosevelt, Grace G. - *Creating a College That Works: Audrey Cohen and Metropolitan College of New York*
HNet - April 2015 - pNA [501+]
Root, Damon - *Overruled: The Long War for Control of the U.S. Supreme Court*
Nat R - v67 - i4 - March 9 2015 - p44 [501+]
Root, Dan - *Tsunami: Images of Resilience*
SPBW - June 2015 - pNA [51-500]
Root, Phyllis - *Snowy Sunday (Illus. by Craig, Helen)*
c KR - July 15 2015 - pNA [51-500]
c SLJ - v61 - i10 - Oct 2015 - p71(1) [51-500]
Roots, James - *The 100 Greatest Silent Film Comedians*
BL - v112 - i5 - Nov 1 2015 - p16(1) [51-500]

Ropal, Monica - *When You Leave*
  y BL - v111 - i17 - May 1 2015 - p53(2) [51-500]
     KR - Feb 1 2015 - pNA [51-500]
     SLJ - v61 - i3 - March 2015 - p162(1) [51-500]
Roper, J.R. - *The Hunter Awakens*
  y CH Bwatch - Feb 2015 - pNA [501+]
Roper, Robert - *Nabokov in America: On the Road to Lolita*
     BL - v111 - i17 - May 1 2015 - p71(2) [51-500]
     KR - April 15 2015 - pNA [501+]
     LJ - v140 - i8 - May 1 2015 - p72(2) [51-500]
     NYRB - v62 - i18 - Nov 19 2015 - p22(3) [501+]
     NYTBR - Nov 15 2015 - p1(L) [501+]
     PW - v262 - i16 - April 20 2015 - p68(1) [51-500]
     Spec - v328 - i9756 - August 22 2015 - p39(2) [501+]
     TLS - i5877 - Nov 20 2015 - p8(2) [501+]
     Econ - v416 - i8951 - August 15 2015 - p76(US) [501+]
     NYT - June 11 2015 - pC1(L) [501+]
Ropper, Allan H. - *Reaching Down the Rabbit Hole: A Renowned Neurologist Explains the Mystery and Drama of Brain Disease (Read by Boehmer, Paul). Audiobook Review*
     LJ - v140 - i11 - June 15 2015 - p52(1) [51-500]
  Reaching Down the Rabbit Hole: A Renowned Neurologist Explains the Mystery and Drama of Brain Disease
     NYT - July 7 2015 - pD3(L) [501+]
Roques, Dominique - *Anna Banana and the Chocolate Explosion! (Illus. by Dormal, Alexis)*
  c HB Guide - v26 - i2 - Fall 2015 - p17(1) [51-500]
     KR - April 1 2015 - pNA [51-500]
  c NYTBR - June 21 2015 - p17(L) [501+]
  c NYTBR - June 21 2015 - p17(L) [501+]
  Sleep Tight, Anna Banana! (Illus. by Dormal, Alexis)
  c HB Guide - v26 - i1 - Spring 2015 - p15(1) [51-500]
Rorby, Ginny - *How to Speak Dolphin*
  c BL - v111 - i17 - May 1 2015 - p100(1) [51-500]
  c HB Guide - v26 - i2 - Fall 2015 - p99(1) [51-500]
  c KR - March 1 2015 - pNA [51-500]
  c SLJ - v61 - i3 - March 2015 - p143(1) [51-500]
  c Teach Lib - v42 - i5 - June 2015 - p47(1) [51-500]
Rorick, Kate - *The Secret Diary of Lizzie Bennet*
  y Sch Lib - v63 - i1 - Spring 2015 - p63(1) [51-500]
Ros, Ana - *The Post-Dictatorship Generation in Argentina, Chile, and Uruguay: Collective Memory and Cultural Production*
     Ams - v72 - i1 - Jan 2015 - p176(3) [501+]
Rosa, Eugene A. - *The Risk Society Revisited: Social Theory and Governance*
     AJS - v120 - i5 - March 2015 - p1565(3) [501+]
Rosa, John P. - *Local Story: The Massie-Kahahawai Case and the Culture of History*
     PHR - v84 - i4 - Nov 2015 - p563(2) [501+]
Rosa, Sonia - *When the Slave Esperanca Garcia Wrote a Letter (Illus. by Hees, Luciana Justiniani)*
  c BL - v112 - i6 - Nov 15 2015 - p40(1) [51-500]
  c KR - Sept 15 2015 - pNA [51-500]
  c SLJ - v61 - i10 - Oct 2015 - p130(1) [51-500]
Rosales, Allen C. - *Mathematizing: An Emergent Math Curriculum Approach for Young Children*
     Bwatch - Oct 2015 - pNA [51-500]
Rosario, Vanessa Perez - *Hispanic Caribbean Literature of Migration: Narratives of Displacement*
     Callaloo - v38 - i1 - Wntr 2015 - p215-216 [501+]
Rosati, Massimo - *Multiple Modernities and Postsecular Societies*
     J Ch St - v57 - i1 - Wntr 2015 - p175-177 [501+]
Roscoe, Lily - *The Night Parade (Illus. by Walker, David)*
  c CH Bwatch - Jan 2015 - pNA [51-500]
  c HB Guide - v26 - i1 - Spring 2015 - p15(1) [51-500]
Rose, Alexander - *Men of War: The American Soldier in Combat at Bunker Hill, Gettysburg, and Iwo Jima*
     KR - March 15 2015 - pNA [501+]
     LJ - v140 - i8 - May 1 2015 - p88(3) [501+]
     Mar Crp G - v99 - i10 - Oct 2015 - p78(2) [501+]
     Nat R - v67 - i13 - July 20 2015 - p42 [501+]
     NYTBR - July 26 2015 - p16(L) [501+]
Rose, Amber - *How to Be a Bad Bitch*
     NYTBR - Dec 6 2015 - p87(L) [501+]
Rose, Andreas - *The Wars before the Great War: Conflict and International Politics before the Outbreak of the First World War*
     J Mil H - v79 - i4 - Oct 2015 - p1121-1126 [501+]
Rose, Caroline - *Starr Blue Birds*
  c HB Guide - v26 - i2 - Fall 2015 - p99(1) [51-500]

Rose, Caroline Starr - *Blue Birds*
  c BL - v111 - i13 - March 1 2015 - p60(2) [51-500]
  c KR - Jan 1 2015 - pNA [51-500]
  c PW - v262 - i3 - Jan 19 2015 - p84(1) [51-500]
  c SLJ - v61 - i2 - Feb 2015 - p92(1) [51-500]
  y VOYA - v37 - i6 - Feb 2015 - p63(2) [501+]
  Over in the Wetlands (Illus. by Dunlavey, Rob)
  c KR - May 1 2015 - pNA [51-500]
  c SLJ - v61 - i6 - June 2015 - p92(1) [51-500]
Rose, Chanelle N. - *The Struggle for Black Freedom in Miami: Civil Rights and America's Tourist Paradise, 1896-1968*
     HNet - Sept 2015 - pNA [501+]
Rose, Charles Brian - *The Archaeology of Greek and Roman Troy*
     TLS - i5843 - March 27 2015 - p7(2) [501+]
Rose, Cirilia - *Magpies, Homebodies, and Nomads: A Modern Knitter's Guide to Discovering and Exploring Style (Illus. by Flood, Jared)*
     LJ - v140 - i3 - Feb 15 2015 - p100(2) [51-500]
Rose, Clare - *Art Nouveau Fashion*
     LJ - v140 - i5 - March 15 2015 - p102(3) [501+]
Rose, Daniel - *Making a Living, Making a Life*
     KR - April 15 2015 - pNA [51-500]
Rose, E.M. - *The Murder of William of Norwich: The Origins of the Blood Libel in Medieval Europe*
     TLS - i5873 - Oct 23 2015 - p27(1) [501+]
Rose, Elizabeth - *Yo Miz!*
     KR - July 1 2015 - pNA [501+]
     SPBW - July 2015 - pNA [51-500]
Rose, Jacqueline - *Women in Dark Times*
     TLS - i5870 - Oct 2 2015 - p7(2) [501+]
     NY - v91 - i33 - Oct 26 2015 - p79 [501+]
Rose, Jessica - *Bead and Wire Fashion Jewelry: A Collection of Stunning Statement Pieces to Make*
     LJ - v140 - i13 - August 1 2015 - p97(2) [51-500]
Rose, Jonathan - *The Literary Churchill: Author, Reader, Actor*
     HT - v65 - i1 - Jan 2015 - p56(2) [501+]
Rose, Joseph A. - *Grant under Fire: An Expose of Generalship and Character in the American Civil War*
     J Mil H - v79 - i4 - Oct 2015 - p1109-11 [501+]
     SPBW - August 2015 - pNA [501+]
Rose, Judith Robbins - *Look Both Ways in the Barrio Blanco*
  c BL - v112 - i1 - Sept 1 2015 - p117(1) [51-500]
  c PW - v262 - i25 - June 22 2015 - p140(1) [51-500]
  Look Both Ways in the Barrio Blanco (Illus. by Rose, Judith Robbins)
  c KR - June 1 2015 - pNA [51-500]
  Look Both Ways in the Barrio Blanco
  c SLJ - v61 - i7 - July 2015 - p82(2) [51-500]
Rose, Karen - *Alone in the Dark*
     PW - v262 - i51 - Dec 14 2015 - p67(2) [51-500]
Rose, Kathryn - *Avalon Rising*
  y KR - March 1 2015 - pNA [51-500]
  y SLJ - v61 - i8 - August 2015 - p114(1) [51-500]
  y VOYA - v38 - i2 - June 2015 - p82(1) [51-500]
Rose, Katie - *The Heat Is On*
     PW - v262 - i48 - Nov 30 2015 - p46(1) [51-500]
Rose, Kenneth - *Pluralism: The Future of Religion*
     JR - v95 - i3 - July 2015 - p410(3) [501+]
Rose, Lisa - *Shmulik Paints the Town (Illus. by Echeverri, Catalina)*
  c KR - Dec 15 2015 - pNA [51-500]
Rose, Lisa M. - *Midwest Foraging: 115 Wild and Flavorful Edibles from Burdock to Wild Peach*
     LJ - v140 - i12 - July 1 2015 - p111(1) [51-500]
Rose, Lisle A. - *Farewell to Prosperity: Wealth, Identity, and Conflict in Postwar America*
     JSH - v81 - i4 - Nov 2015 - p1031(3) [501+]
Rose, M.J. - *The Witch of Painted Sorrows (Read by Ross, Natalie). Audiobook Review*
     LJ - v140 - i9 - May 15 2015 - p44(1) [51-500]
  The Witch of Painted Sorrows
  y BL - v111 - i13 - March 1 2015 - p28(1) [51-500]
     BL - v111 - i22 - August 1 2015 - p79(1) [51-500]
     KR - Feb 1 2015 - pNA [501+]
     LJ - v140 - i3 - Feb 15 2015 - p93(2) [51-500]
     PW - v262 - i4 - Jan 26 2015 - p150(1) [51-500]
Rose, Martin - *My Loaded Gun, My Lonely Heart*
     PW - v262 - i38 - Sept 21 2015 - p58(1) [51-500]
Rose, Nancy - *Merry Christmas, Squirrels! (Illus. by Rose, Nancy)*
  c PW - v262 - i37 - Sept 14 2015 - p66(1) [51-500]
  c SLJ - v61 - i10 - Oct 2015 - p68(2) [51-500]
  The Secret Life of Squirrels (Illus. by Rose, Nancy)
  c HB Guide - v26 - i1 - Spring 2015 - p43(1) [51-500]
  c Res Links - v20 - i3 - Feb 2015 - p7(2) [51-500]

Rose, Richard - *Paying Bribes for Public Services: A Global Guide to Grass Roots Corruption*
     TimHES - i2205 - May 28 2015 - p48-49 [501+]
Rose, Simon - *The House of Commons*
  c Res Links - v20 - i4 - April 2015 - p20(2) [51-500]
  The Senate
  c Res Links - v20 - i4 - April 2015 - p20(2) [51-500]
  The Sphere of Septimus
  c Res Links - v21 - i1 - Oct 2015 - p20(2) [51-500]
Rose-Solomon, Diane - *JJ Goes to Puppy Class*
  c CH Bwatch - Feb 2015 - pNA [51-500]
Rose, Todd - *The End of Average: How We Succeed in a World That Values Sameness*
     KR - Nov 1 2015 - pNA [501+]
     LJ - v140 - i19 - Nov 15 2015 - p98(1) [51-500]
Rose, Tony - *America: The Black Point of View: An Investigation and Study of the White People of America and Western Europe and the Autobiography of an American Ghetto Boy, the 1950s and 1960s*
     SPBW - Oct 2015 - pNA [501+]
Rose-Vallee, Jayne M. - *Dinosaurs Living in My Hair (Illus. by Matsick, Anni)*
  c KR - Oct 15 2015 - pNA [51-500]
Rose, William Todd - *Bleedovers*
     PW - v262 - i29 - July 20 2015 - p174(2) [51-500]
Roseman, Bruce - *The Addictocarb Diet: Avoid the 9 Highly Addictive Carbs While Eating Anything Else You Want*
     PW - v262 - i20 - May 18 2015 - p80(1) [51-500]
Rosemont, Henry - *Against Individualism: A Confucian Rethinking of the Foundations of Morality, Politics, Family, and Religion*
     RM - v69 - i2 - Dec 2015 - p409(2) [501+]
Rosen, David - *The Watchman in Pieces: Surveillance, Literature, and Liberal Personhood*
     JMH - v87 - i2 - June 2015 - p409(2) [501+]
Rosen, Deborah - *Border Law: The First Seminole War and American Nationhood*
     J Mil H - v79 - i3 - July 2015 - p827-828 [501+]
Rosen Digital's Spotlight on Science and Social Studies Series. Audiobook Review
     SLJ - v61 - i12 - Dec 2015 - p82(2) [501+]
Rosen, Elliot A. - *The Republican Party in the Age of Roosevelt: Sources of Anti-Government Conservatism in the United States*
     AHR - v120 - i3 - June 2015 - p1055-1056 [501+]
     JSH - v81 - i2 - May 2015 - p502(2) [501+]
     Pres St Q - v45 - i3 - Sept 2015 - p627(2) [501+]
Rosen, Kara M.L. - *Plenish: Juices to Boost, Cleanse and Heal*
     RVBW - March 2015 - pNA [51-500]
Rosen, Klaus - *Konstantin der Grosse: Kaiser zwischen Machtpolitik und Religion*
     HNet - April 2015 - pNA [501+]
Rosen, Lev - *Woundabout (Illus. by Rosen, Ellis)*
  c BL - v111 - i18 - May 15 2015 - p68(1) [51-500]
  c CCB-B - v69 - i1 - Sept 2015 - p49(1) [51-500]
  c HB Guide - v26 - i2 - Fall 2015 - p99(1) [51-500]
  c KR - March 15 2015 - pNA [51-500]
  c PW - v262 - i16 - April 20 2015 - p76(1) [51-500]
  c SLJ - v61 - i2 - Feb 2015 - p92(2) [51-500]
Rosen, Lev AC - *Depth*
     LJ - v140 - i9 - May 15 2015 - p57(4) [501+]
Rosen, Martin A. - *Return to Roswell*
     KR - Dec 1 2015 - pNA [501+]
     KR - Dec 15 2015 - pNA [501+]
Rosen, Michael - *Alphabetical: How Every Letter Tells a Story*
     BL - v111 - i9-10 - Jan 1 2015 - p25(1) [51-500]
     LJ - v140 - i3 - Feb 15 2015 - p101(1) [51-500]
  The Bus Is for Us! (Illus. by Tyler, Gillian)
     BL - v111 - i14 - March 15 2015 - p77(1) [51-500]
  c CH Bwatch - June 2015 - pNA [501+]
  c KR - Jan 15 2015 - pNA [51-500]
  c NYTBR - May 10 2015 - p21(L) [501+]
  c Sch Lib - v63 - i2 - Summer 2015 - p97(1) [51-500]
  Don't Forget Tiggs! (Illus. by Ross, Tony)
  c Sch Lib - v63 - i3 - Autumn 2015 - p160(1) [51-500]
  A Great Big Cuddle: Poems for the Very Young (Illus. by Riddell, Chris)
  c BL - v112 - i2 - Sept 15 2015 - p58(1) [51-500]
  c KR - August 15 2015 - pNA [51-500]
  c SLJ - v61 - i10 - Oct 2015 - p71(2) [51-500]
  The Wicked Tricks of Till Owlyglass (Illus. by Wenger, Fritz)
  c Sch Lib - v63 - i1 - Spring 2015 - p42(1) [51-500]

Rosen, Michael J. - *Girls vs. Guys: Surprising Differences between the Sexes*
   y HB Guide - v26 - i1 - Spring 2015 - p171(1) [51-500]
   c KR - Dec 1 2015 - pNA [51-500]
   y SLJ - v61 - i12 - Dec 2015 - p146(1) [51-500]
The Maine Coon's Haiku: And Other Poems for Cat Lovers (Illus. by White, Lee)
   c BL - v111 - i14 - March 15 2015 - p60(2) [51-500]
   c CCB-B - v68 - i9 - May 2015 - p465(1) [51-500]
   c HB Guide - v26 - i2 - Fall 2015 - p204(1) [51-500]
   c PW - v262 - i6 - Feb 9 2015 - p69(1) [501+]
   c PW - v262 - i49 - Dec 2 2015 - p55(1) [51-500]
Place Hacking: Venturing Off Limits
   y HB Guide - v26 - i2 - Fall 2015 - p214(1) [51-500]
   y SLJ - v61 - i3 - March 2015 - p178(1) [51-500]
   y CCB-B - v68 - i8 - April 2015 - p418(2) [51-500]
The Tale of Rescue (Illus. by Fellows, Stan)
   c KR - August 15 2015 - pNA [51-500]
   c PW - v262 - i49 - Dec 2 2015 - p68(1) [51-500]
   c SLJ - v61 - i11 - Nov 2015 - p102(1) [51-500]
Rosen, Renee - *White Collar Girl*
   BL - v112 - i3 - Oct 1 2015 - p31(1) [51-500]
Rosen, Stanley - *The Idea of Hegel's Science of Logic*
   Dialogue - v54 - i2 - June 2015 - p382-384 [501+]
Rosen, Steven A. - *An Investigation into Early Desert Pastoralism: Excavations at the Camel Site, Negev*
   JNES - v74 - i2 - Oct 2015 - p363(2) [501+]
Rosen, Suri - *Playing with Matches*
   y CCB-B - v68 - i5 - Jan 2015 - p275(1) [51-500]
Rosenbaum, Andrea - *Meg Goldberg on Parade (Illus. by Lyles, Christopher)*
   c SLJ - v61 - i11 - Nov 2015 - p87(1) [51-500]
Rosenbaum, Andria - *Meg Goldberg on Parade (Illus. by Lyles, Christopher)*
   c KR - August 15 2015 - pNA [51-500]
Rosenbaum, S.P. - *The Bloomsbury Group Memoir Club*
   ABR - v36 - i2 - Jan-Feb 2015 - p23(1) [501+]
Rosenberg, Alex - *The Girl from Krakow*
   BL - v111 - i22 - August 1 2015 - p40(1) [51-500]
   PW - v262 - i29 - July 20 2015 - p164(2) [51-500]
Rosenberg, David - *Rebel Footprints: A Guide to Uncovering London's Radical History*
   TimHES - i2193 - March 5 2015 - p52(1) [501+]
Rosenberg, Emily S. - *Body and Nation: The Global Realm of U.S. Body Politics in the Twentieth Century*
   HNet - May 2015 - pNA [501+]
   J Am St - v49 - i2 - May 2015 - p447-449 [501+]
Rosenberg, Eugene - *The Hologenome Concept: Human, Animal and Plant Microbiota*
   QRB - v90 - i2 - June 2015 - p230(1) [501+]
Rosenberg, Goran - *Brief Stop on the Road from Auschwitz*
   BL - v111 - i11 - Feb 1 2015 - p11(2) [51-500]
Rosenberg, Jonathan - *How Google Works*
   Forbes - v196 - i6 - Nov 2 2015 - p42(1) [501+]
Rosenberg, Liz - *What James Said (Illus. by Myers, Matt)*
   c BL - v111 - i18 - May 15 2015 - p59(1) [51-500]
   c CCB-B - v69 - i1 - Sept 2015 - p49(1) [51-500]
   c HB - v91 - i4 - July-August 2015 - p124(2) [51-500]
   c PW - v262 - i16 - April 20 2015 - p75(1) [51-500]
   c SLJ - v61 - i10 - Oct 2015 - p83(1) [51-500]
Rosenberg, Madelyn - *How to Behave at a Dog Show (Illus. by Ross, Heather)*
   c KR - June 15 2015 - pNA [51-500]
   c SLJ - v61 - i6 - June 2015 - p91(2) [51-500]
How to Behave at a Tea Party (Illus. by Ross, Heather)
   c HB Guide - v26 - i1 - Spring 2015 - p43(1) [51-500]
Nanny X (Illus. by Donnelly, Karen)
   c HB Guide - v26 - i1 - Spring 2015 - p91(1) [51-500]
Nanny X Returns
   c KR - August 1 2015 - pNA [51-500]
Rosenberger, Nancy - *Dilemmas of Adulthood: Japanese Women and the Nuances of Long-Term Resistance*
   Pac A - v88 - i2 - June 2015 - p312 [501+]
Rosenberger, Peter - *Hope for the Caregiver*
   Ch Today - v59 - i4 - May 2015 - p60(1) [51-500]
Rosenblatt, Roger - *The Book of Love: Improvisations on a Crazy Little Thing*
   CSM - Feb 9 2015 - pNA [501+]
   NYTBR - Feb 15 2015 - p30(L) [501+]
Thomas Murphy
   KR - Nov 1 2015 - pNA [501+]
   PW - v262 - i44 - Nov 2 2015 - p58(2) [501+]
Rosenbloom, David Scott - *Greek Drama IV: Texts, Contexts, Performance*
   Class R - v65 - i1 - April 2015 - p36-38 [501+]

Rosenblum, David - *Welwyn Ardsley and the Cosmic Ninjas: Preparing Your Child, and Yourself for Anesthesia and Surgery*
   c KR - Sept 1 2015 - pNA [501+]
Rosenblum, Gregg - *City 1*
   y HB Guide - v26 - i2 - Fall 2015 - p136(1) [51-500]
Rosendorf, Neal M. - *Franco Sells Spain to America: Hollywood, Tourism, and Public Relations as Postwar Spanish Soft Power*
   JAH - v101 - i4 - March 2015 - p1313-1314 [501+]
Rosenfeld, Alvin H. - *Das Ende des Holocaust*
   HNet - Sept 2015 - pNA [501+]
Deciphering the New Antisemitism
   KR - Oct 1 2015 - pNA [501+]
Rosenfeld, Ben - *Russian Optimism: Dark Nursery Rhymes to Cheer You Right Up*
   PW - v262 - i13 - March 30 2015 - p63(1) [51-500]
Rosenfeld, Dina - *It's Called Kibud Av Va'Eim! A Story about Honoring Parents (Illus. by Ebert, Len)*
   c HB Guide - v26 - i1 - Spring 2015 - p15(1) [51-500]
Rosenfeld, Gavriel D. - *Hi Hitler! How the Nazi Past Is Being Normalized in Contemporary Culture*
   HT - v65 - i3 - March 2015 - p64(2) [501+]
   TLS - i5867 - Sept 11 2015 - p7(1) [501+]
Rosenfeld, Jake - *What Unions No Longer Do*
   AJS - v120 - i5 - March 2015 - p1567(3) [501+]
Rosenfeld, Jessica - *Ethics and Enjoyment in Late Medieval Poetry: Love after Aristotle*
   MP - v112 - i3 - Feb 2015 - pE217(E219) [501+]
Rosenfeld, Shterni - *Tuky*
   c KR - Sept 1 2015 - pNA [51-500]
Rosenfelt, David - *Blackout*
   PW - v262 - i47 - Nov 23 2015 - p49(2) [51-500]
Hounded
   RVBW - August 2015 - pNA [501-500]
   RVBW - Feb 2015 - pNA [501-500]
Lessons from Tara: Life Advice from the World's Most Brilliant Dog
   BL - v111 - i19-20 - June 1 2015 - p14(1) [51-500]
Who Let the Dog Out?
   BL - v111 - i19-20 - June 1 2015 - p58(1) [51-500]
   KR - May 15 2015 - pNA [51-500]
   PW - v262 - i19 - May 11 2015 - p37(1) [51-500]
Rosenfield, Kat - *Inland*
   y HB Guide - v26 - i1 - Spring 2015 - p121(1) [51-500]
Rosengren, Gayle - *Cold War on Maplewood Street (Read by Rubinate, Amy). Audiobook Review*
   c BL - v112 - i7 - Dec 1 2015 - p70(1) [51-500]
   c SLJ - v61 - i11 - Nov 2015 - p70(1) [51-500]
Cold War on Maplewood Street
   c BL - v111 - i21 - July 1 2015 - p68(1) [51-500]
   c KR - May 1 2015 - pNA [51-500]
   c PW - v262 - i21 - May 25 2015 - p59(1) [51-500]
   c SLJ - v61 - i6 - June 2015 - p104(1) [51-500]
   y VOYA - v38 - i3 - August 2015 - p68(1) [51-500]
What the Moon Said (Read by Merlington, Laural). Audiobook Review
   c SLJ - v61 - i12 - Dec 2015 - p77(1) [51-500]
Rosenkrantz, Linda - *Talk*
   HM - v331 - i1982 - July 2015 - p85(3) [501+]
   Nation - v301 - i24 - Dec 14 2015 - p33(3) [501+]
   New R - v246 - i7-8 - July-August 2015 - p78(2) [501+]
   NS - v144 - i5277 - August 28 2015 - p42(2) [501+]
   NYT - July 30 2015 - pC6(L) [501+]
Rosensaft, Menachem - *God, Faith and Identity from the Ashes: Reflections of Children and Grandchildren of Holocaust Survivors*
   BL - v111 - i14 - March 15 2015 - p41(1) [51-500]
Rosenshield, Gary - *Challenging the Bard: Dostoevsky and Pushkin. A Study of a Literary Relationship*
   MLR - v110 - i1 - Jan 2015 - p306-307 [501+]
Rosenstock, Barb - *Ben Franklin's Big Splash: The Mostly True Story of His First Invention (Read by Berneis, Susie). Audiobook Review*
   c SLJ - v61 - i5 - May 2015 - p70(1) [51-500]
Ben Franklin's Big Splash: The Mostly True Story of His First Invention (Illus. by Schindler, S.D.)
   c HB Guide - v26 - i1 - Spring 2015 - p196(1) [51-500]

Dorothea's Eyes: Dorothea Lange Photographs the Truth (Illus. by DuBois, Gerard)
   c KR - Dec 1 2015 - pNA [51-500]
   c PW - v262 - i51 - Dec 14 2015 - p82(2) [501+]
The Noisy Paint Box: The Colors and Sounds of Kandinsky's Abstract Art (Illus. by GrandPre, Mary)
   c Teach Lib - v42 - i5 - June 2015 - p44(1) [51-500]
Rosenstock, Gabriel - *The Flea Market in Valparaiso*
   WLT - v89 - i1 - Jan-Feb 2015 - p77(1) [51-500]
Rosenthal, Amy Krouse - *Awake Beautiful Child (Illus. by Lam, Gracia)*
   c KR - Sept 1 2015 - pNA [51-500]
   c PW - v262 - i49 - Dec 2 2015 - p40(1) [51-500]
Friendshape: An Uplifting Celebration of Friendship (Illus. by Lichtenheld, Tom)
   c BL - v112 - i2 - Sept 15 2015 - p67(1) [51-500]
   c PW - v262 - i22 - June 1 2015 - p57(1) [51-500]
   c SLJ - v61 - i6 - June 2015 - p92(1) [51-500]
I Wish You More (Illus. by Lichtenheld, Tom)
   c BL - v111 - i17 - May 1 2015 - p101(1) [51-500]
   c HB Guide - v26 - i2 - Fall 2015 - p50(1) [51-500]
   c KR - March 1 2015 - pNA [51-500]
   c SLJ - v61 - i6 - June 2015 - p74(1) [51-500]
Little Miss, Big Sis (Illus. by Reynolds, Peter H.)
   Nat Post - v17 - i210 - July 11 2015 - pWP5(1) [501+]
   SLJ - v61 - i10 - Oct 2015 - p83(2) [51-500]
Little Pea (Illus. by Corace, Jen)
   c SLJ - v61 - i7 - July 2015 - p57(1) [51-500]
Uni the Unicorn (Illus. by Barrager, Brigette)
   c HB Guide - v26 - i1 - Spring 2015 - p15(1) [51-500]
Rosenthal, Betsy R. - *An Ambush of Tigers: A Wild Gathering of Collective Nouns (Illus. by Jago)*
   c PW - v262 - i49 - Dec 2 2015 - p43(1) [51-500]
   c BL - v111 - i15 - April 1 2015 - p37(1) [51-500]
   c CCB-B - v68 - i11 - July-August 2015 - p562(1) [51-500]
   c HB Guide - v26 - i2 - Fall 2015 - p162(1) [51-500]
   c KR - Feb 15 2015 - pNA [51-500]
Rosenthal, Caroline - *New York and Toronto Novels after Postmodernism: Explorations of the Urban*
   Callaloo - v38 - i2 - Spring 2015 - p401-405 [501+]
Rosenthal, Lecia - *Radio Benjamin*
   Nation - v301 - i23 - Dec 7 2015 - p30(7) [501+]
   TLS - i5839 - Feb 27 2015 - p5(1) [501+]
Rosenthal, Leslie - *The River Pollution Dilemma in Victorian England: Nuisance Law versus Economic Efficiency*
   HNet - June 2015 - pNA [501+]
Rosenthal, Marc - *Big Bot, Small Bot: A Book of Robot Opposites (Illus. by Rosenthal, Marc)*
   c PW - v262 - i21 - May 25 2015 - p58(1) [501+]
   c SLJ - v61 - i9 - Sept 2015 - p127(2) [51-500]
Rosenthal, Naomi M. - *Missing Insects*
   KR - May 1 2015 - pNA [501+]
Rosenzweig, Paul - *Thinking about Cybersecurity: From Cyber Crime to Cyber Warfare (Read by Rosenzweig, Paul). Audiobook Review*
   LJ - v140 - i5 - March 15 2015 - p74(1) [51-500]
Rosero, Evelio - *Feast of the Innocents*
   TLS - i5846 - April 17 2015 - p20(1) [501+]
Rosetree, Rose - *The Empowered Empath: Owning, Embracing, and Managing Your Special Gifts*
   SPBW - May 2015 - pNA [51-500]
Roskifte, Kristin - *Animal Beauty (Illus. by Roskifte, Kristin)*
   c KR - July 15 2015 - pNA [51-500]
   c PW - v262 - i27 - July 6 2015 - p72(1) [51-500]
   c SLJ - v61 - i12 - Dec 2015 - p96(1) [51-500]
Roskrow, Dominic - *Whiskey: What to Drink Next: Craft Whiskeys, Classic Flavors, New Distilleries, Future Trends*
   BL - v111 - i22 - August 1 2015 - p14(1) [51-500]
Rosner, Jennifer - *The Mitten String (Illus. by Swarner, Kristina)*
   c CCB-B - v68 - i6 - Feb 2015 - p328(1) [51-500]
   c HB Guide - v26 - i1 - Spring 2015 - p43(1) [51-500]
Rosner, Victoria - *The Cambridge Companion to the Bloomsbury Group*
   TLS - i5863 - August 14 2015 - p26(1) [501+]
Ross, Alec - *The Industries of the Future*
   KR - Dec 1 2015 - pNA [501+]
   PW - v262 - i50 - Dec 7 2015 - p79(1) [51-500]
Ross, Ann B. - *Miss Julia Lays down the Law*
   BL - v111 - i13 - March 1 2015 - p24(2) [51-500]
   KR - Feb 1 2015 - pNA [51-500]
   PW - v262 - i7 - Feb 16 2015 - p161(1) [51-500]
Ross, Charlene - *Frosted Cowboy*
   PW - v262 - i51 - Dec 14 2015 - p67(1) [51-500]

Ross, Cheri Barton - *Cloning Noah*
  KR - Jan 1 2016 - pNA [501+]
Ross, Dennis - *Doomed to Succeed: The U.S.-Israel Relationship from Truman to Obama*
  KR - July 15 2015 - pNA [501+]
  LJ - v140 - i16 - Oct 1 2015 - p96(2) [51-500]
  NY - v91 - i33 - Oct 26 2015 - p75 [501+]
  NYTBR - Oct 25 2015 - p14(L) [501+]
  PW - v262 - i30 - July 27 2015 - p55(1) [51-500]
Ross, Don - *Trails*
  KR - July 15 2015 - pNA [501+]
Ross, Douglas E. - *An Archaeology of Asian Transnationalism*
  PHR - v84 - i2 - May 2015 - p248(2) [501+]
Ross, Edward - *Filmish: A Graphic Journey through Film (Illus. by Ross, Edward)*
  y BL - v112 - i6 - Nov 15 2015 - p34(1) [51-500]
Ross, Emily - *Half in Love with Death*
  c KR - Oct 15 2015 - pNA [501+]
  y SLJ - v61 - i11 - Nov 2015 - p108(2) [51-500]
Ross, Fran - *Oreo*
  KR - May 15 2015 - pNA [501+]
  NYT - July 15 2015 - pC1(L) [501+]
  NYT - Nov 27 2015 - pC31(L) [501+]
Ross, Helen Klein - *What Was Mine*
  KR - Oct 1 2015 - pNA [501+]
  LJ - v140 - i20 - Dec 1 2015 - p96(1) [51-500]
  PW - v262 - i44 - Nov 2 2015 - p58(1) [51-500]
Ross, Iain - *Oscar Wilde and Ancient Greece*
  Class R - v65 - i2 - Oct 2015 - p621-621 [501+]
  VS - v57 - i2 - Wntr 2015 - p343(3) [501+]
Ross, Ian James - *War at the Edge of the World*
  RVBW - August 2015 - pNA [501+]
Ross, James - *Thought and World: The Hidden Necessities*
  RM - v68 - i4 - June 2015 - p867(4) [501+]
Ross, Janice - *Like a Bomb Going Off: Leonid Yakobson and Ballet as Resistance in Soviet Russia*
  Atl - v315 - i5 - June 2015 - p40(3) [501+]
  CHE - v61 - i31 - April 17 2015 - pNA [501+]
  NY - v91 - i12 - May 11 2015 - p77 [501+]
  NYT - Feb 23 2015 - pC4(L) [501+]
  Spec - v327 - i9735 - March 28 2015 - p47(1) [501+]
Ross, Jeff - *At Ease*
  y Res Links - v21 - i1 - Oct 2015 - p40(1) [51-500]
  Set You Free
  y KR - August 1 2015 - pNA [501+]
  y Res Links - v21 - i1 - Oct 2015 - p40(1) [51-500]
  y SLJ - v61 - i9 - Sept 2015 - p172(1) [51-500]
  y VOYA - v38 - i4 - Oct 2015 - p61(1) [51-500]
Ross, Jeffrey Ian - *The Globalization of Supermax Prisons*
  CS - v44 - i4 - July 2015 - p548-550 [501+]
Ross, Joel - *The Fog Diver*
  c BL - v111 - i17 - May 1 2015 - p98(2) [51-500]
  c CCB-B - v68 - i11 - July-August 2015 - p562(2) [51-500]
  c HB Guide - v26 - i2 - Fall 2015 - p99(1) [51-500]
  c KR - March 15 2015 - pNA [51-500]
  c SLJ - v61 - i3 - March 2015 - p142(2) [51-500]
  y VOYA - v38 - i1 - April 2015 - p83(1) [51-500]
Ross, John F. - *Enduring Courage: Ace Pilot Eddie Rickenbacker and the Dawn of the Age of Speed (Read by Herrmann, Edward). Audiobook Review*
  LJ - v140 - i5 - March 15 2015 - p134(1) [501+]
Ross, Kat - *Some Fine Day (Read by Kowal, Mary Robinette). Audiobook Review*
  y SLJ - v61 - i6 - June 2015 - p68(1) [51-500]
Ross, Kristin - *Communal Luxury: The Political Imaginary of the Paris Commune*
  Lon R Bks - v37 - i13 - July 2 2015 - p21(2) [501+]
Ross, Lawrence - *Blackballed: The Black & White Politics of Race on America's Campuses*
  KR - Nov 15 2015 - pNA [501+]
  PW - v262 - i51 - Dec 14 2015 - p73(1) [51-500]
Ross, Lillian - *Reporting Always: Writings from The New Yorker*
  BL - v112 - i4 - Oct 15 2015 - p5(1) [51-500]
  CSM - Dec 10 2015 - pNA [501+]
  KR - Sept 15 2015 - pNA [501+]
  NYTBR - Dec 6 2015 - p50(L) [501+]
Ross, Loretta - *Death and the Brewmaster's Widow*
  KR - Nov 15 2015 - pNA [501+]
  PW - v262 - i52 - Dec 21 2015 - p135(1) [51-500]
Ross, Margaret - *A Timeshare*
  PW - v262 - i42 - Oct 19 2015 - p53(2) [51-500]
Ross, Melanie C. - *Evangelical versus Liturgical? Defying a Dichotomy*
  Theol St - v76 - i3 - Sept 2015 - p629(2) [501+]
  TT - v72 - i1 - April 2015 - p116-118 [501+]

Ross, Michael - *Designing Fictions: Literature Confronts Advertising*
  Nat Post - v17 - i230 - August 8 2015 - pWP5(1) [501+]
Ross, Michael Elsohn - *She Takes a Stand: 16 Fearless Activists Who Have Changed the World*
  c PW - v262 - i34 - August 24 2015 - p82(1) [501+]
  y SLJ - v61 - i7 - July 2015 - p110(1) [51-500]
  y VOYA - v38 - i3 - August 2015 - p87(2) [501+]
Ross, Richard - *Girls in Justice*
  SLJ - v61 - i8 - August 2015 - p116(2) [51-500]
Ross, Robert - *The Borders of Race in Colonial South Africa: The Kat River Settlement, 1829-1856*
  AHR - v120 - i1 - Feb 2015 - p376-377 [501+]
  IJAHS - v48 - i1 - Wntr 2015 - p173-174 [501+]
Ross, Susan - *Kiki and Jacques*
  c BL - v112 - i1 - Sept 1 2015 - p101(1) [51-500]
  c KR - August 15 2015 - pNA [501+]
  c PW - v262 - i30 - July 27 2015 - p68(1) [51-500]
  c SLJ - v61 - i9 - Sept 2015 - p146(1) [51-500]
Ross, Theodora - *A Cancer in the Family*
  KR - Dec 1 2015 - pNA [501+]
Ross, Tony - *I Feel Sick! (Illus. by Ross, Tony)*
  c HB Guide - v26 - i2 - Fall 2015 - p50(1) [51-500]
  I Want to Go Home! (Illus. by Ross, Tony)
  c HB Guide - v26 - i1 - Spring 2015 - p44(1) [51-500]
  Rita's Rhino (Illus. by Ross, Tony)
  c BL - v111 - i15 - April 1 2015 - p83(2) [51-500]
  c HB Guide - v26 - i2 - Fall 2015 - p50(1) [51-500]
  c KR - Jan 15 2015 - pNA [501+]
Rossberg, Axel G. - *Food Webs and Biodiversity: Foundations, Models, Data*
  QRB - v90 - i1 - March 2015 - p87(2) [501+]
Rossell, Judith - *Withering-by-Sea*
  c KR - Dec 15 2015 - pNA [501+]
Rossen, Rebecca - *Dancing Jewish: Jewish Identity in American Modern and Postmodern Dance*
  Dance RJ - v47 - i2 - August 2015 - p86-88 [501+]
Rosser, J. Allyn - *Mimi's Trapese*
  HR - v67 - i4 - Wntr 2015 - p667-676 [501+]
Rossetto, Luca - *Il commissario distrettuale nel Veneto asburgico: Un funzionario dell' Impero tra mediazione politica e controllo sociale*
  AHR - v120 - i1 - Feb 2015 - p346-347 [501+]
Rossi, Chef - *The Raging Skillet: The True Life Story of Chef Rossi: A Memoir with Recipes*
  KR - August 15 2015 - pNA [501+]
  PW - v262 - i37 - Sept 14 2015 - p58(1) [51-500]
Rossi, Lauren Faulkner - *Wehrmacht Priests: Catholicism and the Nazi War of Annihilation*
  CHR - v101 - i4 - Autumn 2015 - p950(3) [501+]
Rossi, Nickolas - *Heaven Adores You*
  Si & So - v25 - i7 - July 2015 - p77(2) [501+]
Rossi, Sophia - *A Tale of Two Besties (Read by Brisbin, Anna, with Nora Hunter). Audiobook Review*
  c SLJ - v61 - i9 - Sept 2015 - p60(1) [51-500]
  A Tale of Two Besties
  y HB Guide - v26 - i2 - Fall 2015 - p136(1) [51-500]
  y KR - March 15 2015 - pNA [501+]
  y SLJ - v61 - i4 - April 2015 - p157(2) [51-500]
  y VOYA - v38 - i1 - April 2015 - p68(2) [51-500]
Rossi, Veronica - *Riders*
  y BL - v112 - i7 - Dec 1 2015 - p57(1) [51-500]
  y KR - Nov 15 2015 - pNA [51-500]
  y PW - v262 - i46 - Nov 16 2015 - p77(1) [51-500]
  y SLJ - v61 - i12 - Dec 2015 - p127(3) [51-500]
Rossi, Wynn-Anne - *Triumphant Journey*
  c Am MT - v64 - i6 - June-July 2015 - p67(2) [501+]
Rossini, Seton - *Sweet Envy: Deceptively Easy Desserts, Designed to Steal the Show*
  LJ - v140 - i20 - Dec 1 2015 - p129(1) [51-500]
Rossiter, William T. - *Wyatt Abroad: Tudor Diplomacy and the Translation of Power*
  TLS - i5872 - Oct 16 2015 - p25(1) [501+]
Rossland, Ingelin - *Minus Me*
  y SLJ - v61 - i6 - June 2015 - p116(1) [51-500]
Rosslenbroich, Bernd - *On the Origin of Autonomy*
  QRB - v90 - i1 - March 2015 - p77(2) [501+]
Rossman, Gabriel - *Climbing the Charts: What Radio Airplay Tells Us about the Diffusion of Innovation*
  CS - v44 - i1 - July 2015 - p550-552 [501+]
Rosso, Nico - *Countdown to Zero Hour*
  PW - v262 - i51 - Dec 14 2015 - p66(1) [51-500]
Rossoliski-Liebe, Grzegorz - *Stepan Bandera: The Life and Afterlife of a Ukrainian Nationalist: Fascism, Genocide, and Cult*
  HNet - April 2015 - pNA [501+]

Rossum, Ralph A. - *Understanding Clarence Thomas: The Jurisprudence of Constitutional Restoration*
  Pers PS - v44 - i4 - Oct-Dec 2015 - p260-261 [501+]
Rosta, Joseph - *Swimming the Elements*
  KR - April 15 2015 - pNA [501+]
Rostila, Mikael - *Social Capital and Health Inequality in European Welfare States*
  CS - v44 - i5 - Sept 2015 - p700-702 [501+]
Rostoker-Gruber, Karen - *Farmer Kobi's Hanukkah Match (Illus. by Decker, C.B.)*
  c CH Bwatch - Nov 2015 - pNA [51-500]
  c KR - Sept 1 2015 - pNA [51-500]
  c PW - v262 - i37 - Sept 14 2015 - p76(1) [51-500]
  c SLJ - v61 - i10 - Oct 2015 - p68(1) [51-500]
  Ferret Fun in the Sun (Illus. by de Tagyos, Paul Ratz)
  c HB Guide - v26 - i2 - Fall 2015 - p50(1) [51-500]
  c SLJ - v61 - i6 - June 2015 - p92(1) [51-500]
Rota, Emanuel - *A Pact with Vichy: Angelo Tasca from Italian Socialism to French Collaboration*
  HNet - June 2015 - pNA [501+]
Rotbard, Sharon - *White City, Black City: Architecture and War in Tel Aviv and Jaffa*
  Econ - v414 - i8924 - Feb 7 2015 - p78(US) [501+]
  TLS - i5849 - May 8 2015 - p22(1) [501+]
Rotella, Bob - *How Champions Think: In Sports and in Life*
  KR - March 15 2015 - pNA [501+]
  PW - v262 - i11 - March 16 2015 - p76(1) [51-500]
Rotenberg, Marc - *Privacy in the Modern Age: The Search for Solutions*
  LJ - v140 - i8 - May 1 2015 - p98(1) [51-500]
Roth, Alvin E. - *Who Gets What--and Why: The New Economics of Matchmaking and Market Design (Read by Berkrot, Peter). Audiobook Review*
  PW - v262 - i39 - Sept 28 2015 - p87(1) [501+]
  Who Gets What--and Why: The New Economics of Matchmaking and Market Design
  KR - May 1 2015 - pNA [501+]
  LJ - v140 - i11 - June 15 2015 - p95(2) [51-500]
  Mac - v128 - i26-27 - July 6 2015 - p67(2) [501+]
  PW - v262 - i16 - April 20 2015 - p68(1) [51-500]
Roth, Andrew J. - *Managing Prostate Cancer: A Guide for Living Better*
  BL - v112 - i7 - Dec 1 2015 - p20(1) [51-500]
  LJ - v140 - i19 - Nov 15 2015 - p100(1) [51-500]
Roth, Bernard - *The Achievement Habit: Stop Wishing, Start Doing, and Take Command of Your Life*
  KR - May 1 2015 - pNA [501+]
  LJ - v140 - i11 - June 15 2015 - p96(1) [51-500]
  PW - v262 - i17 - April 27 2015 - p61(1) [51-500]
Roth, Carol - *Five Little Ducklings Go to School (Illus. by Julian, Sean)*
  c SLJ - v61 - i9 - Sept 2015 - p112(1) [51-500]
Roth, Christopher F. - *Let's Split! A Complete Guide to Separatist Movements and Aspirant Nations, from Abkhazia to Zanzibar*
  LJ - v140 - i6 - April 1 2015 - p115(1) [51-500]
Roth, Gerhard - *The Calm Ocean*
  TimHES - i2197 - April 2 2015 - p53(1) [501+]
Roth, Henry - *Mercy of a Rude Stream: The Complete Novels*
  NYRB - v62 - i7 - April 23 2015 - p34(3) [501+]
Roth, Joseph - *The Hotel Years*
  PW - v262 - i30 - July 27 2015 - p56(1) [51-500]
  NYTBR - Sept 6 2015 - p16(L) [501+]
Roth, Kathleen Bittner - *Josette*
  PW - v262 - i32 - August 10 2015 - p43(1) [51-500]
Roth, Mitchel P. - *An Eye for an Eye: A Global History of Crime and Punishment*
  HT - v65 - i7 - July 2015 - p57(1) [501+]
Roth, Philip - *Nemesis*
  Nat R - v67 - i21 - Nov 19 2015 - p82(1) [501+]
Roth, Rachel - *Here There Is No Why*
  KR - June 15 2015 - pNA [501+]
Roth, Ralf - *Eastern European Railways in Transition: Nineteenth to Twenty-First Centuries*
  Historian - v77 - i3 - Fall 2015 - p625(2) [501+]
  T&C - v56 - i2 - April 2015 - p549-551 [501+]
Roth, Sarah N. - *Gender and Race in Antebellum Popular Culture*
  AHR - v120 - i3 - June 2015 - p1023-1024 [501+]
  JSH - v81 - i4 - Nov 2015 - p972(3) [501+]
Roth, Susan L. - *Prairie Dog Song (Illus. by Trumbore, Cindy)*
  c KR - Jan 1 2016 - pNA [51-500]
Roth, Timothy P. - *Economists and the State: What Went Wrong*
  IndRev - v20 - i1 - Summer 2015 - p139(3) [501+]

Roth, Ulrike - *By the Sweat of your Brow: Roman Slavery in its Socio-Economic Setting*
    Class R - v65 - i1 - April 2015 - p228-230 [501+]
Roth, Wendy - *Race Migrations: Latinos and the Cultural Transformation of Race*
    SF - v94 - i2 - Dec 2015 - pNA [501+]
Rothenberg, David - *Bug Music: How Insects Gave us Rhythm and Noise*
    Am Bio T - v77 - i5 - May 2015 - p392(2) [501+]
Rotherham, Lee - *The Discerning Gentleman's Guidebook to Britain's American Colonies: The 1770's Edition*
    Sch Lib - v63 - i2 - Summer 2015 - p123(1) [51-500]
Rothfels, Nigel - *Elephant House (Illus. by Blau, Dick)*
    PW - v262 - i41 - Oct 12 2015 - p62(1) [51-500]
Rothfuss, Joan - *Topless Cellist: The Improbable Life of Charlotte Moorman*
    Wom R Bks - v32 - i3 - May-June 2015 - p3(2) [501+]
Rothfuss, Patrick - *The Slow Regard of Silent Things (Read by Rothfuss, Patrick). Audiobook Review*
    BL - v111 - i18 - May 15 2015 - p69(1) [51-500]
The Slow Regard of Silent Things
    MFSF - v128 - i3-4 - March-April 2015 - p73(8) [501+]
Rothko, Christopher - *Mark Rothko*
    KR - Sept 15 2015 - pNA [501+]
Rothman, Claire Holden - *My October*
    Can Lit - i224 - Spring 2015 - p112 [501+]
Rothman, Hal K. - *Death Valley National Park: A History*
    JAH - v101 - i4 - March 2015 - p1342-1343 [501+]
Rothman, Julia - *Nature Anatomy: The Curious Parts and Pieces of the Natural World*
    y BL - v111 - i12 - Feb 15 2015 - p27(1) [51-500]
    Bwatch - July 2015 - pNA [51-500]
Rothman, Stephen - *The Paradox of Evolution: The Strange Relationship Between Natural Selection and Reproduction*
    LJ - v140 - i19 - Nov 15 2015 - p104(1) [501+]
Rothmund, Christophe - *History of Rocketry and Astronautics: AAS History Series, Vol. 40*
    APH - v62 - i1 - Spring 2015 - p56(2) [501+]
Rothschild, Ferdinand - *Personal Characteristics from French History*
    NYRB - v62 - i11 - June 25 2015 - p29(4) [501+]
Rothschild, Hannah - *The Improbability of Love*
    BL - v112 - i1 - Sept 15 2015 - p27(1) [51-500]
    Econ - v416 - i8945 - July 4 2015 - p70(US) [501+]
    KR - July 1 2015 - pNA [501+]
    LJ - v140 - i12 - July 1 2015 - p80(2) [51-500]
    NYT - Dec 3 2015 - pC1(L) [501+]
    PW - v262 - i38 - Sept 21 2015 - p48(1) [51-500]
Rothschild, James de, Mrs. - *The Rothschilds at Waddesdon Manor*
    NYRB - v62 - i11 - June 25 2015 - p29(4) [501+]
Rothschild, Nan A. - *The Archaeology of American Cities*
    JIH - v46 - i2 - Autumn 2015 - p301-302 [501+]
Rothstein, Adam - *Drone*
    TLS - i5854 - June 12 2015 - p28(1) [501+]
Rothstein, Irving - *It Couldn't Have Been the Pay: A Life of Teaching and Learning in Public Schools*
    SPBW - July 2015 - pNA [501+]
Rotner, Shelley - *Body Bones (Illus. by Rotner, Shelley)*
    c HB Guide - v26 - i1 - Spring 2015 - p156(1) [51-500]
Families (Illus. by Rotner, Shelley)
    c BL - v111 - i21 - July 1 2015 - p53(1) [51-500]
    c HB Guide - v26 - i2 - Fall 2015 - p152(1) [51-500]
    c KR - Feb 15 2015 - pNA [51-500]
    c SLJ - v61 - i3 - March 2015 - p173(1) [51-500]
Whose Eye Am I? (Illus. by Rotner, Shelley)
    c KR - Jan 1 2016 - pNA [51-500]
    c PW - v262 - i46 - Nov 16 2015 - p75(1) [501+]
Rotsler, William - *Patron of the Arts*
    PW - v262 - i21 - May 25 2015 - p42(1) [51-500]
Rotstein, Robert - *The Bomb Maker's Son*
    BL - v111 - i17 - May 1 2015 - p22(1) [51-500]
    KR - April 1 2015 - pNA [501+]
    PW - v262 - i15 - April 13 2015 - p58(2) [51-500]
Rotter, Jeffrey - *The Only Words That Are Worth Remembering*
    BL - v111 - i13 - March 1 2015 - p20(2) [51-500]
    KR - Feb 1 2015 - pNA [501+]
    PW - v262 - i8 - Feb 23 2015 - p57(2) [51-500]
Rouaud, Antoine - *The Path of Anger*
    PW - v262 - i29 - July 20 2015 - p174(1) [51-500]
Rouda, Bill - *Nashville's Lower Broad*
    BL - v112 - i5 - Nov 1 2015 - p18(2) [501+]

Roufa, M.E. - *The Norma Gene*
    KR - June 15 2015 - pNA [51-500]
    PW - v262 - i24 - June 15 2015 - p67(1) [51-500]
Roufs, Kathleen S. - *Sweet Treats around the World: An Encyclopedia of Food and Culture*
    R&USQ - v54 - i4 - Summer 2015 - p84(1) [501+]
Roughgarden, Joan - *RAM-2050*
    PW - v262 - i9 - March 2 2015 - p68(2) [51-500]
Rouleau, Brian - *With Sails Whitening Every Sea: Mariners and the Making of an American Maritime Empire*
    HNet - June 2015 - pNA [501+]
Roumanis, Alexis - *Baboons*
    c BL - v112 - i6 - Nov 15 2015 - p42(1) [51-500]
Saturn
    c BL - v112 - i3 - Oct 1 2015 - p66(1) [51-500]
Rouse, Martyn - *Learning to See Invisible Children: Inclusion of Children with Disabilities in Central Asia*
    E-A St - v67 - i9 - Nov 2015 - p1511(2) [501+]
Rousmaniere, Kate - *The Principal's Office: A Social History of the American School Principal*
    Am St - v54 - i1 - Spring 2015 - p149-2 [501+]
Rouss, Sylvia A. - *Sammy Spider's First Mitzvah (Illus. by Kahn, Katherine Janus)*
    c HB Guide - v26 - i1 - Spring 2015 - p44(1) [51-500]
Sammy Spider's First Taste of Hanukkah: A Cookbook (Illus. by Kahn, Katherine Janus)
    c PW - v262 - i37 - Sept 14 2015 - p72(2) [501+]
    c SLJ - v61 - i10 - Oct 2015 - p68(1) [51-500]
Sammy Spider's First Taste of Hanukkah (Illus. by Kahn, Katherine Janus)
    c KR - Sept 1 2015 - pNA [51-500]
Rousseau, George - *Rachmaninoff's Cape: A Nostalgia Memoir*
    TLS - i5858 - July 10 2015 - p10(2) [501+]
Roussen, Jean - *Beautiful Birds (Illus. by Walker, Emmanuelle)*
    c KR - Jan 15 2015 - pNA [51-500]
    c PW - v262 - i8 - Feb 23 2015 - p73(1) [51-500]
Routhier, Gilles - *Cinquante ans apres Vatican II: Que reste-t-il a mettre en oeuvre?*
    Theol St - v76 - i2 - June 2015 - p367(2) [501+]
Routledge, Joonmo Son - *Social Capital and Institutional Constraints: A Comparative Analysis of China, Taiwan and the US*
    SF - v94 - i2 - Dec 2015 - pNA [501+]
Roux, Madeleine - *Catacomb*
    y VOYA - v38 - i3 - August 2015 - p83(1) [51-500]
Sanctum
    y HB Guide - v26 - i1 - Spring 2015 - p122(1) [51-500]
    y VOYA - v38 - i5 - Dec 2015 - p74(1) [51-500]
Rouy, Maryse - *L'Epopee de Petit-Jules*
    y Res Links - v21 - i1 - Oct 2015 - p55(1) [51-500]
Rove, Karl - *The Triumph of William McKinley: Why the Election of 1896 Still Matters*
    KR - Nov 1 2015 - pNA [501+]
    LJ - v140 - i20 - Dec 1 2015 - p117(1) [51-500]
    Nat R - v67 - i23 - Dec 21 2015 - p42(3) [501+]
Rovelli, Carlo - *Seven Brief Lessons on Physics*
    Nature - v526 - i7571 - Oct 1 2015 - p37(2) [501+]
    NS - v144 - i5283 - Oct 9 2015 - p49(1) [501+]
    KR - Dec 15 2015 - pNA [51-500]
Rovner, Adam - *In the Shadow of Zion: Promised Lands Before Israel*
    TLS - i5853 - June 5 2015 - p22(1) [501+]
Rowbotham, Judith - *Crime News in Modern Britain: Press Reporting and Responsibility, 1820-2010*
    AHR - v120 - i1 - Feb 2015 - p332-333 [501+]
Rowbotham, Sheila - *Friends of Alice Wheeldon: The Anti-War Activist Accused of Plotting to Kill Lloyd George*
    TimHES - i2206 - June 4 2015 - p47(1) [501+]
Rowden, Clair - *Performing Salome, Revealing Stories*
    Notes - v71 - i3 - March 2015 - p519(4) [501+]
Rowe, Karen Paysse - *Letters from Galveston*
    KR - Sept 1 2015 - pNA [51-500]
Rowe, Laura - *Taste: The Infographic Book of Food*
    NYTBR - Dec 6 2015 - pNA(L) [501+]
Rowe, Rosemary - *The Fateful Day*
    BL - v111 - i9-10 - Jan 1 2015 - p46(1) [51-500]
Rowell, Diana - *Paris: The 'New Rome' of Napoleon*
    Class R - v65 - i1 - April 2015 - p282-283 [501+]
Rowell, Rainbow - *Attachments*
    LJ - v140 - i13 - August 1 2015 - p126(1) [501+]

Carry On: The Rise and Fall of Simon Snow
    y NYTBR - Oct 25 2015 - p34(L) [501+]
    y PW - v262 - i49 - Dec 2 2015 - p102(1) [501+]
    y SLJ - v61 - i11 - Nov 2015 - p121(2) [51-500]
Eleanor & Park
    BL - v111 - i9-10 - Jan 1 2015 - p120(1) [501+]
Rowell, Rebecca - *Amazing America Series*
    c BL - v111 - i19-20 - June 1 2015 - p80(1) [51-500]
Pink: Pop Singer and Songwriter
    y HB Guide - v26 - i1 - Spring 2015 - p193(1) [51-500]
Social Media: Like It or Leave It
    c HB Guide - v26 - i2 - Fall 2015 - p155(1) [51-500]
    VOYA - v38 - i2 - June 2015 - p89(1) [501+]
    c BL - v111 - i16 - April 15 2015 - p44(1) [51-500]
Rowell, Rosie - *Almost Grace*
    y Sch Lib - v63 - i4 - Winter 2015 - p250(1) [51-500]
Rowland, Amy - *The Transcriptionist*
    NYTBR - Jan 25 2015 - p24(L) [501+]
Rowland, Joanna - *Always Mom, Forever Dad (Illus. by Weber, Penny)*
    c HB Guide - v26 - i1 - Spring 2015 - p44(1) [51-500]
Rowland, Laura Jon - *The Iris Fan (Read by Dunnem, Bernadette). Audiobook Review*
    BL - v111 - i17 - May 1 2015 - p58(1) [51-500]
Rowlands, Guy - *The Financial Decline of a Great Power: War, Influence, and Money in Louis XIV's France*
    Historian - v77 - i1 - Spring 2015 - p191(2) [501+]
Rowlands, Jennifer L. - *The Locket*
    PW - v262 - i15 - April 13 2015 - p64(1) [51-500]
Rowley, Aidan Donnelley - *The Ramblers*
    KR - Nov 15 2015 - pNA [501+]
    PW - v262 - i46 - Nov 16 2015 - p50(1) [51-500]
Rowley, Alison - *Open Letters: Russian Popular Culture and the Picture Postcard, 1880-1922*
    JMH - v87 - i3 - Sept 2015 - p763(3) [501+]
    Slav R - v74 - i2 - Summer 2015 - p398-400 [501+]
Rowling, J.K. - *Harry Potter and the Sorcerer's Stone (Illus. by Kay, Jim)*
    y BL - v111 - i21 - July 1 2015 - p49(1) [51-500]
    Forbes - v195 - i8 - June 15 2015 - p22(1) [51-500]
    c NYTBR - Dec 6 2015 - p32(L) [501+]
Very Good Lives
    KR - May 1 2015 - pNA [501+]
Rowson, Martin - *Carol Carnage: Malicious Mishearings of Your Yuletide Favourites*
    c Spec - v329 - i9772 - Dec 12 2015 - p77(1) [501+]
Rowson, Pauline - *Fatal Catch*
    KR - Nov 1 2015 - pNA [501+]
    PW - v262 - i45 - Nov 9 2015 - p39(1) [51-500]
Silent Running
    BL - v111 - i17 - May 1 2015 - p44(2) [51-500]
    PW - v262 - i22 - June 1 2015 - p43(1) [51-500]
Roy, Anuradha - *Sleeping on Jupiter*
    TLS - i5874 - Oct 30 2015 - p20(1) [501+]
Roy, Arundhati - *The God of Small Things*
    NYTBR - June 28 2015 - p16(L) [501+]
Roy-Bhattacharya, Joydeep - *The Watch*
    HM - v331 - i1983 - August 2015 - p84(6) [501+]
Roy, David Tod - *The Plum in the Golden Vase*
    NYRB - v62 - i7 - April 23 2015 - p56(3) [501+]
Roy, Denny - *Return of the Dragon: Rising China and Regional Security*
    Pac A - v88 - i1 - March 2015 - p171 [501+]
Roy, Haimanti - *Partitioned Lives: Migrants, Refugees, Citizens in India and Pakistan, 1947-1965*
    Historian - v77 - i3 - Fall 2015 - p590(2) [501+]
    HNet - July 2015 - pNA [501+]
Roy, Jennifer - *Jars of Hope: How One Woman Helped Save 2,500 Children during the Holocaust (Illus. by Owenson, Meg)*
    c BL - v112 - i6 - Nov 15 2015 - p42(1) [51-500]
    c KR - June 15 2015 - pNA [51-500]
    c PW - v262 - i29 - July 20 2015 - p190(2) [501+]
    c SLJ - v61 - i9 - Sept 2015 - p180(1) [51-500]
Roy, Katherine - *Neighborhood Sharks: Hunting with the Great Whites of California's Farallon Islands (Illus. by Roy, Katherine)*
    c HB Guide - v26 - i1 - Spring 2015 - p161(1) [51-500]
Roy, Kaushik - *Military Transition in Early Modern Asia, 1400-1750: Cavalry, Guns, Government and Ships*
    J Mil H - v79 - i3 - July 2015 - p810-812 [501+]
Roy, Lauren - *The Fire Children*
    y KR - April 15 2015 - pNA [51-500]
    y VOYA - v38 - i3 - August 2015 - p83(1) [51-500]

Roy, Lori - *Let Me Die in His Footsteps*
   y BL - v111 - i17 - May 1 2015 - p40(1) [51-500]
      KR - April 1 2015 - pNA [51-500]
      LJ - v140 - i6 - April 1 2015 - p85(1) [51-500]
      NYTBR - June 21 2015 - p25(L) [501+]
      NYTBR - Dec 6 2015 - p85(L) [501+]
      PW - v262 - i15 - April 13 2015 - p58(1) [51-500]

Roy, Philip - *Eco Warrior*
   y Res Links - v21 - i1 - Oct 2015 - p41(2) [501+]
   Jellybean Mouse (Illus. by Balsara, Andrea Torrey)
   c Res Links - v20 - i3 - Feb 2015 - p8(1) [51-500]

Roy, Ron - *December Dog (Illus. by Gurney, John Steven)*
   c HB Guide - v26 - i1 - Spring 2015 - p65(1) [51-500]
   New Year's Eve Thieves
   c HB Guide - v26 - i1 - Spring 2015 - p65(1) [51-500]
   November Night (Illus. by Gurney, John Steven)
   c HB Guide - v26 - i1 - Spring 2015 - p65(1) [51-500]

Roy, Tui De - *Penguins: The Ultimate Guide*
      QRB - v90 - i3 - Sept 2015 - p350(2) [501+]

Royal, Priscilla - *Land of Shadows*
      KR - Nov 1 2015 - pNA [51-500]
      PW - v262 - i50 - Dec 7 2015 - p70(1) [51-500]

Royalty, Robert M., Jr. - *The Origin of Heresy: A History of Discourse in Second Temple Judaism and Early Christianity*
      CH - v84 - i1 - March 2015 - p222(4) [501+]

Royes, Gillian - *The Rhythm of the August Rain*
      BL - v111 - i21 - July 1 2015 - p39(2) [51-500]
      KR - June 1 2015 - pNA [51-500]
      PW - v262 - i21 - May 25 2015 - p37(2) [51-500]

Royston, Angela - *Birds*
   c HB Guide - v26 - i2 - Fall 2015 - p178(1) [51-500]
   Mammals
   c HB Guide - v26 - i2 - Fall 2015 - p181(1) [51-500]
   Reptiles
   c HB Guide - v26 - i2 - Fall 2015 - p176(1) [51-500]

Roza, Greg - *Greatest Movie Monsters Series*
   c BL - v112 - i5 - Nov 1 2015 - p46(2) [501+]

Rozbicki, Michal Jan - *Culture and Liberty in the Age of the American Revolution*
      AL - v87 - i1 - March 2015 - p187-189 [501+]

Rozema, Mark - *Road Trip*
      KR - July 1 2015 - pNA [501+]

Rozier, Lucy Margaret - *Jackrabbit McCabe and the Electric Telegraph (Illus. by Espinosa, Leo)*
   c BL - v111 - i22 - August 1 2015 - p72(1) [51-500]
   c KR - July 1 2015 - pNA [51-500]
   c PW - v262 - i24 - June 15 2015 - p81(1) [51-500]
   c PW - v262 - i49 - Dec 2 2015 - p16(1) [51-500]
   c SLJ - v61 - i9 - Sept 2015 - p180(1) [51-500]

Rozman, Gilbert - *The Sino-Russian Challenge to the World Order: National Identities, Bilateral Relations, and East Versus West in the 2010s*
      For Aff - v94 - i3 - May-June 2015 - pNA [501+]
      JAS - v74 - i3 - August 2015 - p731-732 [501+]

Rozycki, Tomasz - *Colonies*
      TLS - i5856 - June 26 2015 - p12(1) [501+]
   Twelve Stations
      TLS - i5856 - June 26 2015 - p12(1) [501+]

Rubart, James L. - *The Five Times I Met Myself*
      KR - Sept 1 2015 - pNA [51-500]
      PW - v262 - i34 - August 24 2015 - p68(1) [51-500]

Ruben, Kelly Easton - *A Place for Elijah (Illus. by Friar, Joanne)*
   c PW - v262 - i50 - Dec 7 2015 - p88(1) [51-500]

Rubenstein, Eli - *Witness: Passing the Torch of the Holocaust Memory to New Generations*
   y SLJ - v61 - i10 - Oct 2015 - p138(1) [51-500]

Rubenstein, Mary-jane - *Worlds without End: The Many Lives of Multiverse*
      Phys Today - v68 - i2 - Feb 2015 - p48-49 [501+]

Rubenstein, Roberta - *Literary Half-Lives: Doris Lessing, Clancy Sigal, and Roman a Clef*
      TLS - i5840 - March 6 2015 - p11(1) [501+]

Rubin, Adam - *Big Dad Bubble (Illus. by Salmieri, Daniel)*
   c HB Guide - v26 - i1 - Spring 2015 - p44(1) [51-500]
   Robo-Sauce (Illus. by Salmieri, Daniel)
   c BL - v112 - i3 - Oct 1 2015 - p83(1) [51-500]
   c KR - August 1 2015 - pNA [51-500]
   c PW - v262 - i28 - July 13 2015 - p65(1) [51-500]
   c PW - v262 - i49 - Dec 2 2015 - p38(1) [51-500]
   c SLJ - v61 - i11 - Nov 2015 - p87(1) [51-500]

Rubin, Anne Sarah - *Through the Heart of Dixie: Sherman's March and American Memory*
      HNet - Jan 2015 - pNA [501+]

Rubin, David - *The Hero*
      PW - v262 - i27 - July 6 2015 - p55(1) [51-500]

Rubin, Elihu - *Insuring the City: The Prudential Center and the Postwar Urban Landscap*
      J Urban H - v41 - i5 - Sept 2015 - p936-942 [501+]

Rubin, Gretchen - *Better Than Before: Mastering the Habits of Our Everyday Lives (Read by Rubin, Gretchen). Audiobook Review*
      LJ - v140 - i9 - May 15 2015 - p46(1) [51-500]
   Better than Before: Mastering the Habits of Our Everyday Lives
      Bwatch - June 2015 - pNA [51-500]
      Mac - v128 - i9 - March 9 2015 - p48(4) [501+]
      NYTBR - April 12 2015 - p15(L) [501+]
      NYTBR - Dec 27 2015 - p24(L) [501+]

Rubin, Jacob - *The Poser*
      BL - v111 - i11 - Feb 1 2015 - p23(1) [51-500]
      KR - March 1 2015 - pNA [501+]
      NYTBR - April 12 2015 - p13(L) [501+]
      PW - v262 - i4 - Jan 26 2015 - p146(1) [51-500]

Rubin, Jasper - *A Negotiated Landscape: The Transformation of San Francisco's Waterfront Since 1950*
      J Urban H - v41 - i5 - Sept 2015 - p936-942 [501+]

Rubin, Jay - *The Suns Gods*
      KR - April 15 2015 - pNA [501+]

Rubin, Jeffrey W. - *Sustaining Activism: A Brazilian Women's Movement and a Father-Daughter Collaboration*
      CS - v44 - i5 - Sept 2015 - p746-747 [501+]

Rubin, Julius H. - *Tears of Repentance: Christian Indian Identity and Community in Colonial Southern New England*
      CH - v84 - i1 - March 2015 - p254(2) [501+]
      Eight-C St - v49 - i1 - Fall 2015 - p102-103 [501+]

Rubin, Lance - *Denton Little's Deathdate (Read by Rubin, Lance). Audiobook Review*
   y BL - v112 - i2 - Sept 15 2015 - p79(1) [51-500]
   y HB - v91 - i4 - July-August 2015 - p166(1) [51-500]
   y SLJ - v61 - i7 - July 2015 - p49(3) [51-500]
   Denton Little's Deathdate
   y CCB-B - v68 - i10 - June 2015 - p513(1) [51-500]
   y HB - v91 - i2 - March-April 2015 - p107(2) [51-500]
   y HB Guide - v26 - i2 - Fall 2015 - p136(1) [51-500]
   y KR - Jan 15 2015 - pNA [51-500]
   y PW - v262 - i6 - Feb 9 2015 - p71(1) [51-500]
   y Sch Lib - v63 - i3 - Autumn 2015 - p184(1) [51-500]
   y VOYA - v38 - i1 - April 2015 - p83(1) [51-500]

Rubin, Lawrence - *Islam in the Balance: Ideational Threats in Arab Politics*
      IJMES - v47 - i4 - Nov 2015 - p839-841 [501+]

Rubin, Miri - *The Life and Passion of William of Norwich*
      TLS - i5855 - June 19 2015 - p22(2) [501+]

Rubin, Susan Goldman - *Freedom Summer: The 1964 Struggle for Civil Rights in Mississippi*
   c BL - v111 - i9-10 - Jan 1 2015 - pS4(8) [501+]
   y SE - v79 - i3 - May-June 2015 - p145(2) [501+]
   Hot Pink: The Life and Fashions of Elsa Schiaparelli (Illus. by Rubin, Susan Goldman)
   c BL - v112 - i1 - Sept 1 2015 - p94(1) [51-500]
   c CCB-B - v69 - i2 - Oct 2015 - p109(2) [51-500]
   c KR - July 15 2015 - pNA [51-500]
   Sondheim: The Man Who Changed Musical Theater
   y VOYA - v38 - i5 - Dec 2015 - p78(1) [51-500]
   y KR - August 15 2015 - pNA [51-500]
   y PW - v262 - i34 - August 24 2015 - p83(1) [51-500]
   Stand There! She Shouted: The Invincible Photographer Julia Margaret Cameron (Illus. by Ibatoulline, Bagram)
   c HB Guide - v26 - i1 - Spring 2015 - p180(1) [51-500]

Rubini, Julie K. - *Missing Millie Benson: The Secret Case of the Nancy Drew Ghostwriter and Journalist*
   y HB - v91 - i6 - Nov-Dec 2015 - p116(2) [51-500]
   c SLJ - v61 - i12 - Dec 2015 - p146(1) [51-500]

Rubini, Rocco - *The Other Renaissance: Italian Humanism Between Hegel and Heidegger*
      RM - v69 - i2 - Dec 2015 - p405(3) [501+]

Rubinstein, Nicolai - *Studies in Italian History in the Middle Ages and the Renaissance, Volume 3: Humanists, Machiavelli, Guicciardini*
      Ren Q - v68 - i2 - Summer 2015 - p672-674 [501+]

Rubio, Gwyn Hyman - *Love and Ordinary Creatures*
      WLT - v89 - i1 - Jan-Feb 2015 - p77(1) [51-500]

Rubio, Marco - *American Dreams: Restoring Economic Opportunity for Everyone*
      NS - v144 - i5278 - Sept 4 2015 - p40(4) [501+]
      NYRB - v62 - i5 - March 19 2015 - p18(3) [501+]
      Reason - v47 - i4 - August-Sept 2015 - p58(8) [501+]

Rublack, Ulinka - *The Astronomer and the Witch: Johannes Kepler's Fight for his Mother*
      Nature - v527 - i7577 - Nov 12 2015 - p164(1) [501+]
      PW - v262 - i38 - Sept 21 2015 - p65(1) [501+]
   The First Book of Fashion: The Book of Clothes of Matthaus and Veit Konrad Schwartz of Augsburg
      Spec - v329 - i9772 - Dec 12 2015 - p78(2) [501+]

Ruble, Sarah E. - *Gospel of Freedom and Power: Protestant Missionaries in American Culture after World War II*
      Am St - v54 - i1 - Spring 2015 - p131-2 [501+]

Ruby, Laura - *Bone Gap*
   y BL - v111 - i9-10 - Jan 1 2015 - p86(1) [51-500]
   y CCB-B - v68 - i7 - March 2015 - p367(2) [51-500]
   y HB - v91 - i5 - Sept-Oct 2015 - p115(1) [51-500]
   y KR - Jan 15 2015 - pNA [51-500]
   y NYTBR - May 10 2015 - p24(L) [501+]
   y PW - v262 - i49 - Dec 2 2015 - p101(1) [51-500]
   y VOYA - v37 - i6 - Feb 2015 - p83(1) [51-500]

Rucellai, Giovanni di Pagolo - *Zibaldone*
      Ren Q - v68 - i3 - Fall 2015 - p975-977 [501+]

Ruchti, Cynthia - *Tattered and Mended: The Art of Healing the Wounded Soul*
      PW - v262 - i23 - June 8 2015 - p54(1) [51-500]

Ruchti, Lisa C. - *Catheters, Slurs, and Pickup Lines: Professional Intimacy in Hospital Nursing*
      CS - v44 - i1 - Jan 2015 - p114-115 [501+]
      SF - v93 - i3 - March 2015 - pe77(1) [501+]

Rucka, Greg - *Bravo (Read by Glouchevitch, John). Audiobook Review*
      BL - v111 - i13 - March 1 2015 - p68(1) [51-500]

Ruddell, Deborah - *The Popcorn Astronauts: And Other Biteable Rhymes (Illus. by Rankin, Joan)*
      BL - v111 - i14 - March 15 2015 - p61(1) [51-500]
   c CCB-B - v68 - i9 - May 2015 - p465(2) [51-500]
   c HB Guide - v26 - i2 - Fall 2015 - p204(1) [51-500]
   c PW - v262 - i49 - Dec 2 2015 - p55(2) [51-500]

Rudder, Christian - *Dataclysm: Love, Sex, Race, and Identity--What Our Online Lives Tell Us about Our Offline Selves*
      NYTBR - Oct 4 2015 - p28(L) [501+]

Ruddiman, John A. - *Becoming Men of Some Consequence: Youth and Military Service in the Revolutionary War*
      J Mil H - v79 - i3 - July 2015 - p819-820 [501+]
      W&M Q - v72 - i3 - July 2015 - p557-560 [501+]

Ruddy, Richard A. - *Edmund G. Ross: Soldier, Senator, Abolitionist*
      Historian - v77 - i3 - Fall 2015 - p577(3) [501+]
      JSH - v81 - i1 - Feb 2015 - p199(2) [501+]
      Roundup M - v22 - i4 - April 2015 - p26(1) [501+]
      Roundup M - v22 - i6 - August 2015 - p40(1) [501+]

Rudel, Thomas K. - *Defensive Environmentalists and the Dynamics of Global Reform*
      CS - v44 - i3 - May 2015 - p410-412 [501+]

Rudensteine, Neil L. - *Ideas of Order: A Close Reading of Shakespeare's Sonnets*
      NYTBR - Feb 1 2015 - p20(L) [501+]

Rudge, Leila - *A Perfect Place for Ted*
   c HB Guide - v26 - i1 - Spring 2015 - p44(1) [51-500]

Rudiger, Mark - *"Goldene 50er"oder "Bleierne Zeit"? Geschichtsbilder der 50er Jahre im Fernsehen der BRD, 1959-1989*
      HNet - July 2015 - pNA [501+]

Rudnick, Elizabeth - *A Frozen Heart*
   c KR - Sept 15 2015 - pNA [51-500]
   c VOYA - v38 - i4 - Oct 2015 - p78(1) [51-500]

Rudnick, Paul - *It's All Your Fault*
   y BL - v112 - i5 - Nov 1 2015 - p51(1) [51-500]
   y KR - Nov 1 2015 - pNA [51-500]
   y VOYA - v38 - i5 - Dec 2015 - p63(1) [51-500]

Rudofossi, Daniel M. - *Dealing with the Mentally Ill Person on the Street: An Assessment and Intervention Guide for Public Safety Professionals*
      RVBW - May 2015 - pNA [501+]

Rudolf, Katja - *Little Bastards in Summertime*
      Wom R Bks - v32 - i5 - Sept-Oct 2015 - p24(1) [501+]

Rudolph, Conrad - *The Mystic Ark: Hugh of Saint Victor, Art, and Thought in the Twelfth Century*
      CHR - v101 - i3 - Summer 2015 - p616(2) [501+]

Rudolph, Jessica - *Guatemala*
   c BL - v112 - i3 - Oct 1 2015 - p66(1) [51-500]
Huracan
   c SLJ - v61 - i5 - May 2015 - p132(1) [51-500]
Hurricane
   c HB Guide - v26 - i1 - Spring 2015 - p151(1) [51-500]
Tornado
   c HB Guide - v26 - i1 - Spring 2015 - p151(1) [51-500]
   c SLJ - v61 - i5 - May 2015 - p132(1) [51-500]
Zoo Clues Series
   c HB Guide - v26 - i1 - Spring 2015 - p165(1) [51-500]

Rudolph, Julia - *Common Law and Enlightenment in England, 1689-1750*
   JMH - v87 - i2 - June 2015 - p424(3) [501+]

Rudolph, Katja - *Little Bastards in Springtime*
   BL - v111 - i12 - Feb 15 2015 - p32(1) [51-500]
   KR - Feb 15 2015 - pNA [51-500]
   WLT - v89 - i6 - Nov-Dec 2015 - p65(2) [501+]

Rudolph, Shaina - *All My Stripes: A Story for Children with Autism (Illus. by Zivoin, Jennifer)*
   c CH Bwatch - May 2015 - pNA [51-500]

Rudolph, Wally - *Mighty Mighty*
   PW - v262 - i34 - August 24 2015 - p56(1) [51-500]

Rudorff, Andrea - *Frauen in den Aussenlagern des Konzentrationslagers Gross-Rosen*
   HNet - March 2015 - pNA [501+]

Rudwick, Martin J.S. - *Earth's Deep History: How It Was Discovered and Why It Matters*
   TLS - i5833 - Jan 16 2015 - p24(1) [501+]

Rudy, Jerry W. - *The Neurobiology of Learning and Memory*
   QRB - v90 - i4 - Dec 2015 - p440(2) [501+]

Rudzik, Peter - *The Complete Truly Astounding Animals*
   Am MT - v64 - i6 - June-July 2015 - p68(1) [501+]

Rue, Nancy - *Sorry I'm Not Sorry*
   c CH Bwatch - August 2015 - pNA [51-500]
You Can't Sit with Us
   c SLJ - v61 - i2 - Feb 2015 - p93(1) [51-500]

Ruebner, Tuvia - *In the Illuminated Dark: Selected Poems of Tuvia Ruebner*
   WLT - v89 - i1 - Jan-Feb 2015 - p76(2) [501+]

Ruef, Martin - *Between Slavery and Capitalism: The Legacy of Emancipation in the American South*
   BHR - v89 - i3 - Autumn 2015 - p593(3) [501+]
   CS - v44 - i6 - Nov 2015 - p767-770 [501+]
   JAH - v102 - i1 - June 2015 - p257-258 [501+]

Ruether, Rosemary Radford - *My Quests for Hope and Meaning: An Autobiography*
   Cons - v36 - i2 - Summer 2015 - p41(2) [501+]

Ruetsche, Laura - *Interpreting Quantum Theories*
   Phil R - v124 - i2 - April 2015 - p275(4) [501+]

Ruff, Jenifer - *Rothaker*
   KR - March 15 2015 - pNA [501+]

Ruff, Matt - *Lovecraft Country*
   KR - Nov 15 2015 - pNA [501+]
   PW - v262 - i48 - Nov 30 2015 - p43(1) [51-500]

Ruffin, Herbert G. - *Uninvited Neighbors: African Americans in Silicon Valley, 1769-1990*
   AHR - v120 - i1 - Feb 2015 - p227-228 [501+]
   JAH - v102 - i1 - June 2015 - p306-307 [501+]
   WHQ - v46 - i2 - Summer 2015 - p245-246 [501+]

Ruffin, Paul - *The Time the Water Rose*
   KR - Dec 1 2015 - pNA [501+]

Rufin, Jean-Christophe - *The Red Collar*
   KR - May 15 2015 - pNA [501+]
   LJ - v140 - i10 - June 1 2015 - p92(3) [501+]

Rugeley, Terry - *The River People in Flood Time: The Civil Wars in Tabasco, Spoiler of Empires*
   Ams - v72 - i3 - July 2015 - p503(505) [501+]

Rugg, Linda Haverty - *Self-Projection: The Director's Image in Art Cinema*
   Scan St - v87 - i2 - Summer 2015 - p299(5) [501+]

Ruggiero, Guido - *The Renaissance in Italy: A Social and Cultural History of the Rinascimento*
   HNet - May 2015 - pNA [501+]
   JIH - v46 - i3 - Wntr 2016 - p444-446 [501+]
   Six Ct J - v46 - i3 - Fall 2015 - p725-727 [501+]

Rugh, William A. - *Front Line Public Diplomacy: How US Embassies Communicate with Foreign Publics*
   IJMES - v47 - i3 - August 2015 - p640-641 [501+]

Ruhl, Christopher - *100 Essays I Don't Have Time to Write: On Umbrellas and Sword Fights, Parades and Dogs, Fire Alarms, Children, and Theater*
   NYTBR - Nov 29 2015 - p24(L) [501+]

Ruhlman, Michael - *In Short Measures: Three Novellas*
   KR - August 1 2015 - pNA [501+]
   PW - v262 - i32 - August 10 2015 - p32(1) [51-500]
Ruhlman's How to Braise: Foolproof Techniques and Recipes for the Home Cook
   Bwatch - May 2015 - pNA [51-500]
Ruhlman's How to Roast: Foolproof Techniques and Recipes for the Home Cook
   Bwatch - Feb 2015 - pNA [51-500]

Ruiz-Camacho, Antonio - *Barefoot Dogs: Stories*
   BL - v111 - i12 - Feb 15 2015 - p30(1) [51-500]
   KR - Jan 1 2015 - pNA [501+]
   NYTBR - April 5 2015 - p13(L) [501+]
   PW - v262 - i2 - Jan 12 2015 - p32(1) [51-500]

Ruiz, Don Miguel - *The Toltec Art of Life and Death: A Story of Discovery*
   PW - v262 - i32 - August 10 2015 - p56(1) [51-500]

Ruiz, Jason - *Americans in the Treasure House: Travel to Porfirian Mexico and the Cultural Politics of Empire*
   JAH - v101 - i4 - March 2015 - p1300-1301 [501+]

Ruiz, Julius - *The "Red Terror" and the Spanish Civil War: Revolutionary Violence in Madrid*
   AHR - v120 - i4 - Oct 2015 - p1566(1) [501+]

Ruiz, Teofilo F. - *A King Travels: Festive Traditions in Late Medieval and Early Modern Spain*
   AHR - v120 - i2 - April 2015 - p729-730 [501+]

Ruiz Zafon, Carlos - *Marina (Read by Weyman, Daniel). Audiobook Review*
   y BL - v111 - i9-10 - Jan 1 2015 - p118(1) [51-500]
Marina
   y HB Guide - v26 - i1 - Spring 2015 - p129(1) [51-500]

Rujivacharakul, Vimalin - *Architecturalized Asia: Mapping a Continent through History*
   Pac A - v88 - i3 - Sept 2015 - p683 [501+]

Rule, Adi - *The Hidden Twin*
   y KR - Jan 1 2016 - pNA [501+]

Rule, Cheryl Sternman - *Yogurt Culture: A Global Look at How to Make, Bake, Sip and Chill the World's Creamiest, Healthiest Food*
   LJ - v140 - i3 - Feb 15 2015 - p122(4) [501+]

Ruloff, Michael Christian - *Lehrerinnen und Lehrer in der Schweizer Presse*
   HNet - May 2015 - pNA [501+]

Rumer, Eugene B. - *Conflict in Ukraine: The Unwinding of the Post-Cold War Order*
   LJ - v140 - i8 - May 1 2015 - p91(1) [51-500]

Rumiz, Paolo - *The Fault Line: Traveling the Other Europe, from Finland to Ukraine*
   KR - Jan 1 2015 - pNA [501+]
   LJ - v140 - i3 - Feb 15 2015 - p119(1) [51-500]
   PW - v262 - i3 - Jan 19 2015 - p73(1) [51-500]

Rummonds, Richard-Gabriel - *Fantasies and Hard Knocks: My Life as a Printer*
   G&L Rev W - v22 - i5 - Sept-Oct 2015 - p42(1) [501+]

Rumsey, Abby Smith - *When We Are No More: How Digital Memory Is Shaping Our Future*
   KR - Dec 15 2015 - pNA [501+]

Runcie, James - *Sidney Chambers and the Forgiveness of Sins*
   BL - v111 - i13 - March 1 2015 - p25(2) [51-500]
   Ch Today - v59 - i6 - July-August 2015 - p86(1) [51-500]
   KR - March 15 2015 - pNA [501+]
   PW - v262 - i13 - March 30 2015 - p55(1) [51-500]
   RVBW - June 2015 - pNA [51-500]

Runciman, David - *The Confidence Trap: A History of Democracy in Crisis From World War I to the Present*
   Nation - v300 - i6 - Feb 9 2015 - p32(5) [501+]

Runciman, W.G. - *Very Different, But Much the Same: The Evolution of English Society since 1714*
   NS - v144 - i5247 - Jan 30 2015 - p42(2) [501+]
   TimHES - i2186 - Jan 15 2015 - p49(1) [501+]
   TLS - i5860 - July 24 2015 - p28(1) [501+]

Rundell, Katherine - *Cartwheeling in Thunderstorms (Read by Amato, Bianca). Audiobook Review*
   c BL - v111 - i19-20 - June 1 2015 - p140(1) [51-500]
   c SLJ - v61 - i6 - June 2015 - p64(2) [51-500]
Cartwheeling in Thunderstorms
   y HB Guide - v26 - i1 - Spring 2015 - p122(1) [51-500]

The Wolf Wilder
   c BL - v112 - i2 - Sept 15 2015 - p67(1) [51-500]
   c CCB-B - v69 - i1 - Sept 2015 - p50(1) [51-500]
   c HB - v91 - i6 - Nov-Dec 2015 - p91(1) [51-500]
   c KR - June 15 2015 - pNA [501+]
   y Magpies - v30 - i4 - Sept 2015 - p43(2) [501+]
   c PW - v262 - i49 - Dec 2 2015 - p69(1) [51-500]
   c Sch Lib - v63 - i4 - Winter 2015 - p232(1) [51-500]
   c SLJ - v61 - i8 - August 2015 - p90(1) [501+]
   c Spec - v328 - i9759 - Sept 12 2015 - p46(2) [501+]

Rundgren, Helen - *The World's Best Noses, Ears, and Eyes (Illus. by Arrhenius, Ingela P.)*
   c HB Guide - v26 - i1 - Spring 2015 - p157(1) [51-500]

Runia, Eelco - *Moved by the Past: Discontinuity and Historical Mutation*
   AHR - v120 - i3 - June 2015 - p963-964 [501+]

Rupke, J. - *The Individual in the Religions of the Ancient Mediterranean*
   Class R - v65 - i1 - April 2015 - p206-208 [501+]
Religion in Republican Rome. Rationalization and Ritual Change
   Class R - v65 - i1 - April 2015 - p204-206 [501+]

Rupp, Leila J. - *U.S. Lesbian, Gay, Bisexual, and Transgender History*
   G&L Rev W - v22 - i3 - May-June 2015 - p42(2) [501+]

Rupp, Stephen - *Heroic Forms: Cervantes and the Literature of War*
   J Mil H - v79 - i2 - April 2015 - p478(1) [501+]

Rusch, Arthur L. - *County Capitols: The Courthouses of South Dakota*
   Roundup M - v22 - i6 - August 2015 - p40(1) [501+]

Rusch, Elizabeth - *The Next Wave: The Quest to Harness the Power of the Oceans*
   c HB Guide - v26 - i1 - Spring 2015 - p174(2) [51-500]

Rusch, Kristine Kathryn - *Masterminds*
   PW - v262 - i16 - April 20 2015 - p58(2) [51-500]
A Murder of Clones
   Analog - v135 - i6 - June 2015 - p106(1) [501+]
The Peyti Crisis
   Analog - v135 - i6 - June 2015 - p106(1) [501+]
Search and Recovery
   Analog - v135 - i6 - June 2015 - p106(1) [501+]
Sniper
   Analog - v135 - i10 - Oct 2015 - p108(1) [501+]

Ruschemeyer, Georg - *The New Book of Optical Illusions*
   KR - Oct 1 2015 - pNA [501+]

Ruse, Michael - *Atheism: What Everyone Needs to Know*
   Comw - v142 - i8 - May 1 2015 - p22(3) [501+]
Science and Spirituality: Making Room for Faith in the Age of Science
   Dialogue - v54 - i3 - Sept 2015 - p581-583 [501+]

Rush, Lori Ericksen - *House Proud: A Social History of Atlanta Interiors, 1880-1919*
   JSH - v81 - i4 - Nov 2015 - p1004(2) [501+]

Rushby, Pamela - *Sing a Rebel Song*
   y Magpies - v30 - i4 - Sept 2015 - p36(1) [501+]

Rushdie, Salman - *Two Years Eight Months and Twenty-Eight Nights*
   NYTBR - Oct 4 2015 - p11(L) [501+]
   Atl - v316 - i2 - Sept 2015 - p34(1) [51-500]
   BL - v111 - i21 - July 1 2015 - p26(1) [51-500]
   CSM - Oct 8 2015 - pNA [51-500]
   KR - July 1 2015 - pNA [501+]
   LJ - v140 - i13 - August 1 2015 - p89(1) [51-500]
   NS - v144 - i5279 - Sept 11 2015 - p46(3) [501+]
   PW - v262 - i21 - May 25 2015 - p28(1) [501+]
   TLS - i5867 - Sept 11 2015 - p22(1) [501+]

Rushforth, Brett - *Bonds of Alliance: Indigenous and Atlantic Slaveries in New France*
   HNet - June 2015 - pNA [501+]

Rushkoff, Douglas - *Throwing Rocks at the Google Bus*
   KR - Jan 1 2016 - pNA [501+]

Rushton, Abbie - *Unspeakable*
   y Sch Lib - v63 - i1 - Spring 2015 - p57(1) [51-500]

Rushton, Julian - *Ralph Vaughan Williams: Bucolic Suite - Study Score*
   Notes - v71 - i3 - March 2015 - p573(5) [501+]
Ralph Vaughan Williams: Serenade in A Minor (1898) - Study Score
   Notes - v71 - i3 - March 2015 - p573(5) [501+]

Ruskamp, John A., Jr. - *Asiatic Echoes: The Identification of Ancient Chinese Pictograms in Pre-Columbian North American Rock Writing, 2d ed.*
   Am Ant - v80 - i3 - July 2015 - p626(2) [501+]

402 • RUSKOLA Book Review Index 2016 Cumulation

Ruskola, Teemu - *Legal Orientalism: China, the United States, and Modern Law*
HLR - v128 - i6 - April 2015 - p1677(26) [501+]
JAH - v101 - i4 - March 2015 - p1238-1239 [501+]
RAH - v43 - i2 - June 2015 - p268-273 [501+]
Rusling, Annette - *Emergency Rescue*
c KR - July 1 2015 - pNA [51-500]
Russakoff, Dale - *The Prize: Who's in Charge of America's Schools? (Read by Cross, Pete). Audiobook Review*
PW - v262 - i48 - Nov 30 2015 - p55(1) [51-500]
The Prize: Who's in Charge of America's Schools?
BL - v112 - i2 - Sept 15 2015 - p7(1) [51-500]
BooChiTr - Sept 5 2015 - p12(1) [501+]
KR - June 15 2015 - pNA [501+]
LJ - v140 - i12 - July 1 2015 - p91(2) [51-500]
NYT - August 27 2015 - pna(L) [501+]
NYTBR - August 23 2015 - p9(L) [501+]
PW - v262 - i23 - June 8 2015 - p50(1) [51-500]
Russell, Alan - *A Cold War*
BL - v112 - i1 - Sept 1 2015 - p45(1) [51-500]
KR - August 1 2015 - pNA [51-500]
PW - v262 - i35 - August 31 2015 - p64(1) [51-500]
Russell, Andrew L. - *Open Standards and the Digital Age: History, Ideology, and Networks*
AHR - v120 - i2 - April 2015 - p570-571 [501+]
BHR - v89 - i2 - Summer 2015 - p357(4) [501+]
Russell, Ann - *Little Truff and the Kereru (Illus. by Evans, Anna)*
c Magpies - v30 - i5 - Nov 2015 - pS6(1) [501+]
Russell, Ben - *James Watt: Making the World Anew*
TLS - i5841 - March 13 2015 - p11(1) [501+]
Russell, Bernadette - *Do Nice, Be Kind, Spread Happy: Acts of Kindness for Kids (Illus. by Broadbent, David)*
c KR - June 15 2015 - pNA [51-500]
c PW - v262 - i30 - July 27 2015 - p70(1) [501+]
Russell-Brown, Katheryn - *Little Melba and Her Big Trombone (Illus. by Morrison, Frank)*
c CH Bwatch - Feb 2015 - pNA [51-500]
c HB Guide - v26 - i1 - Spring 2015 - p196(1) [51-500]
Russell, Delbert W. - *Verse Saints' Lives, Written in the French of England: Saint Giles by Guillaume de Berneville, Saint George by Simund de Freine, Saint Faith of Agen by Simon of Walsingham, Saint Mary Magdalene by Guillaume Le Clerc de Normandie*
MLR - v110 - i1 - Jan 2015 - p256-257 [501+]
Russell, Douglas S. - *Churchill-Soldier: Life of a Gentleman at War*
HT - v65 - i1 - Jan 2015 - p56(2) [501+]
Russell, Gerard - *Heirs to Forgotten Kingdoms: Journeys into the Disappearing Religions of the Middle East (Read by Page, Michael). Audiobook Review*
LJ - v140 - i9 - May 15 2015 - p46(1) [51-500]
Heirs to Forgotten Kingdoms: Journeys into the Disappearing Religions of the Middle East
CC - v132 - i1 - Jan 7 2015 - p34(2) [501+]
TLS - i5850 - May 15 2015 - p28(1) [501+]
Russell, James - *The Dragon Riders (Illus. by Choi, Link)*
c Magpies - v30 - i1 - March 2015 - pS6(1) [501+]
Russell, Jan Jarboe - *The Train to Crystal City: FDR's Secret Prisoner Exchange Program and America's Only Family Internment Camp During World War II*
NYT - Jan 19 2015 - pC1(L) [501+]
NYTBR - April 26 2015 - p14(L) [501+]
TLS - i5867 - Sept 11 2015 - p5(1) [501+]
Russell, Jay - *The Lemurs' Legacy: The Evolution of Power, Sex and Love*
TimHES - i2211 - July 9 2015 - p45-46 [501+]
Russell, Kent - *I Am Sorry to Think I Have Raised a Timid Son (Read by Pratt, Sean). Audiobook Review*
LJ - v140 - i15 - Sept 15 2015 - p44(1) [51-500]
I Am Sorry to Think I Have Raised a Timid Son
BL - v111 - i13 - March 1 2015 - p15(1) [51-500]
Ent W - i1357 - April 3 2015 - p66(1) [501+]
Mac - v128 - i12 - March 30 2015 - p56(1) [501+]
NYTBR - March 29 2015 - p21(L) [501+]
TLS - i5868 - Sept 18 2015 - p29(1) [501+]
KR - Jan 1 2015 - pNA [51-500]
Russell, Leigh - *Journey to Death*
KR - Dec 15 2015 - pNA [51-500]
PW - v262 - i52 - Dec 21 2015 - p135(1) [51-500]
Russell, Mark James - *Young-hee and the Pullocho*
c BL - v111 - i16 - April 15 2015 - p50(2) [51-500]
Russell, Peter - *Prince Henry 'The Navigator': A Life*
TimHES - i2211 - July 9 2015 - p44(1) [501+]
Russell, Rachel Renee - *Tales from a Not-So-Glam TV Star*
c BL - v112 - i5 - Nov 1 2015 - p52(1) [501+]
c HB Guide - v26 - i1 - Spring 2015 - p91(1) [51-500]
Russell, Ray - *The Case against Satan*
KR - August 15 2015 - pNA [51-500]
Russell, Raymond - *The Renewal of the Kibbutz: From Reform to Transformation*
CS - v44 - i1 - Jan 2015 - p115-117 [501+]
Russell, Richard Rankin - *The Retrospect As Prospect: Seamus Heaney's Regions*
ILS - v35 - i1 - Fall 2015 - p20(2) [501+]
Russell, Robert John - *Time in Eternity: Pannenberg, Physics, and Eschatology in Creative Mutual Interaction*
TT - v72 - i2 - July 2015 - p239-240 [501+]
Russell, Romina - *Wandering Star*
y KR - Oct 1 2015 - pNA [51-500]
y VOYA - v38 - i5 - Dec 2015 - p74(1) [51-500]
Zodiac
y CCB-B - v68 - i6 - Feb 2015 - p328(1) [51-500]
y HB Guide - v26 - i1 - Spring 2015 - p122(1) [51-500]
Russell, Wendy Thomas - *Relax, It's Just God: How and Why to Talk to Your Kids about Religion When You're Not Religious*
KR - March 1 2015 - pNA [501+]
LJ - v140 - i9 - May 15 2015 - p66(2) [501+]
Russo, Alessandra - *The Untranslatable Image: A Mestizo History of the Arts in New Spain*
Ren Q - v68 - i1 - Spring 2015 - p253-255 [501+]
Russo, Lenny - *Heartland: Farm-Forward Dishes from the Great Midwest*
PW - v262 - i52 - Dec 21 2015 - p147(1) [51-500]
Russo, Marisabina - *Little Bird Takes a Bath (Illus. by Russo, Marisabina)*
c BL - v111 - i11 - Feb 1 2015 - p56(1) [51-500]
c HB Guide - v26 - i2 - Fall 2015 - p17(1) [51-500]
Russo, Monica - *Birdology: 30 Activities and Observations for Exploring the World of Birds*
c CH Bwatch - April 2015 - pNA [51-500]
Russo, Stephanie - *Women in Revolutionary Debate: Female Novelists from Burney to Austen*
MP - v112 - i4 - May 2015 - pE327(3) [501+]
Rust, Jennifer R. - *The Body in Mystery: The Political Theology of the Corpus Mysticum in the Literature of Reformation England*
Ren Q - v68 - i1 - Spring 2015 - p347-349 [501+]
Rustad, Martha E.H. - *Can You Sing "The Star-Spangled Banner"? (Illus. by Poling, Kyle)*
c HB Guide - v26 - i1 - Spring 2015 - p204(2) [51-500]
Is a Bald Eagle Really Bald? (Illus. by Conger, Holli)
c HB Guide - v26 - i1 - Spring 2015 - p204(2) [51-500]
Le temps au fil ties jours (Illus. by Enright, Amanda)
c Res Links - v20 - i3 - Feb 2015 - p50(1) [51-500]
Les recoltes - du mais aux citrouilles (Illus. by Enright, Amanda)
c Res Links - v20 - i3 - Feb 2015 - p50(2) [51-500]
Pebble Plus: Media Literacy for Kids
c HB Guide - v26 - i2 - Fall 2015 - p146(1) [51-500]
Tornadoes: Be Aware and Prepare
c HB Guide - v26 - i1 - Spring 2015 - p151(1) [51-500]
c Sci & Ch - v52 - i6 - Feb 2015 - p77 [51-500]
What Is Inside the Lincoln Memorial? (Illus. by Poling, Kyle)
c HB Guide - v26 - i1 - Spring 2015 - p204(2) [51-500]
Why Are There Stripes on the American Flag? (Illus. by Poling, Kyle)
c HB Guide - v26 - i1 - Spring 2015 - p204(2) [51-500]
Why Is the Statue of Liberty Green? (Illus. by Conger, Holli)
c HB Guide - v26 - i1 - Spring 2015 - p204(2) [51-500]
Rustad, Robert - *True Love's Kiss*
KR - August 1 2015 - pNA [501+]
Ruth, Greg - *Coming Home (Illus. by Ruth, Greg)*
c CCB-B - v68 - i5 - Jan 2015 - p245(2) [501+]
c HB Guide - v26 - i1 - Spring 2015 - p44(1) [51-500]
Ruther, Gunther - *Literatur und Politik: Ein deutsches Verhangnis?*
MLR - v110 - i1 - Jan 2015 - p305-306 [501+]
Ruther, Tobias - *Heroes: David Bowie in Berlin*
G&L Rev W - v22 - i3 - May-June 2015 - p34(2) [501+]
Rutherford, Janet Elaine - *The Beauty of God's Presence in the Fathers of the Church: The Proceedings of the Eighth International Patristic Conference, Maynooth, 2012*
Theol St - v76 - i4 - Dec 2015 - p887(1) [501+]
Rutherford, Mike - *The Living Years: The First Genesis Memoir*
Bwatch - May 2015 - pNA [51-500]
Rutherford, R.B. - *Culture in Pieces: Essays on Ancient Texts in Honour of Peter Parsons*
Class R - v65 - i2 - Oct 2015 - p319-321 [501+]
Rutherford, Ward - *Celtic Mythology: The Nature and Influence of Celtic Myth from Druidism to Arthurian Legend*
RVBW - July 2015 - pNA [51-500]
Rutherglen, Susannah - *In a New Light: Giovanni Bellini's 'St. Francis in the Desert'*
TLS - i5873 - Oct 23 2015 - p10(1) [501+]
Ruthsatz, Joanna - *The Prodigy's Cousin*
KR - Dec 15 2015 - pNA [501+]
Ruthven, Ian - *Cultural Heritage Information: Access and Management*
LJ - v140 - i10 - June 1 2015 - p118(2) [51-500]
RVBW - April 2015 - pNA [501+]
Ruti, Mari - *The Age of Scientific Sexism*
CHE - v62 - i13 - Nov 27 2015 - pB17(1) [501+]
Rutkoski, Marie - *The Winner's Crime*
y CCB-B - v68 - i6 - Feb 2015 - p329(1) [51-500]
y HB Guide - v26 - i2 - Fall 2015 - p136(1) [51-500]
y VOYA - v37 - i6 - Feb 2015 - p64(1) [51-500]
The Winner's Curse
y Sch Lib - v63 - i1 - Spring 2015 - p58(1) [51-500]
Rutledge, Fleming - *The Crucifixion: Understanding the Death of Jesus Christ*
CC - v132 - i21 - Oct 14 2015 - p32(2) [501+]
CC - v132 - i21 - Oct 14 2015 - p44(2) [501+]
Rutter, Philip - *Growing Hybrid Hazelnuts: The New Resilient Crop for a Changing Climate*
BL - v111 - i12 - Feb 15 2015 - p27(1) [51-500]
Rutz, Matthew - *Bodies of Knowledge in Ancient Mesopotamia: The Diviners of Late Bronze Age Emar and Their Tablet Collection*
JNES - v74 - i1 - April 2015 - p135(8) [501+]
Ruurs, Margriet - *A Brush Full of Colour: The World of Ted Harrison*
c CH Bwatch - July 2015 - pNA [51-500]
Families around the World (Illus. by Gordon, Jessica Rae)
c HB Guide - v26 - i1 - Spring 2015 - p137(1) [51-500]
School Days around the World (Illus. by Feagan, Alice)
c HB Guide - v26 - i2 - Fall 2015 - p154(1) [51-500]
c Res Links - v21 - i1 - Oct 2015 - p27(1) [501+]
c BL - v111 - i11 - Feb 1 2015 - p43(1) [51-500]
c KR - Feb 1 2015 - pNA [51-500]
c PW - v262 - i9 - March 2 2015 - p84(1) [501+]
Ruzzier, Sergio - *A Letter for Leo (Illus. by Ruzzier, Sergio)*
c CCB-B - v68 - i6 - Feb 2015 - p329(1) [51-500]
c HB Guide - v26 - i1 - Spring 2015 - p15(1) [51-500]
Two Mice (Illus. by Ruzzier, Sergio)
c HB - v91 - i5 - Sept-Oct 2015 - p86(1) [501+]
c KR - July 1 2015 - pNA [51-500]
c PW - v262 - i23 - June 8 2015 - p57(1) [51-500]
c SLJ - v61 - i6 - June 2015 - p74(1) [51-500]
Ryan, Annelise - *Stiff Penalty*
KR - Jan 15 2015 - pNA [51-500]
Ryan, April - *The Presidency in Black and White: My Up-Close View of Three Presidents and Race in America*
BL - v111 - i11 - Feb 1 2015 - p18(1) [51-500]
Wom R Bks - v32 - i4 - July-August 2015 - p29(3) [501+]
Ryan, Aryna - *Creativity: The Ultimate Teen Guide*
y SLJ - v61 - i6 - June 2015 - p144(1) [51-500]
Ryan, Candace - *Ewe and Aye (Illus. by Ruble, Stephanie)*
c CH Bwatch - Feb 2015 - pNA [51-500]
c HB Guide - v26 - i1 - Spring 2015 - p15(1) [51-500]
Zoo Zoom! (Illus. by Pamintuan, Macky)
c KR - Sept 1 2015 - pNA [51-500]
c PW - v262 - i36 - Sept 7 2015 - p65(1) [51-500]
Ryan, Carrie - *City of Thirst (Illus. by Harris, Todd)*
c BL - v112 - i6 - Nov 15 2015 - p53(1) [51-500]
c KR - Sept 15 2015 - pNA [51-500]
Daughter of Deep Silence (Read by Vacker, Karissa). Audiobook Review
y BL - v112 - i3 - Oct 1 2015 - p87(1) [51-500]
y SLJ - v61 - i9 - Sept 2015 - p61(3) [51-500]
Daughter of Deep Silence
y BL - v111 - i15 - April 1 2015 - p35(1) [501+]
y BL - v111 - i16 - April 15 2015 - p47(1) [51-500]
y CCB-B - v68 - i11 - July-August 2015 - p563(1) [51-500]
y HB Guide - v26 - i2 - Fall 2015 - p136(1) [51-500]
KR - April 1 2015 - pNA [51-500]
y PW - v262 - i15 - April 13 2015 - p83(1) [51-500]
y SLJ - v61 - i4 - April 2015 - p170(1) [51-500]
y VOYA - v38 - i3 - August 2015 - p68(1) [51-500]
The Map to Everywhere (Illus. by Harris, Todd)
c HB Guide - v26 - i1 - Spring 2015 - p91(1) [51-500]
c CCB-B - v68 - i6 - Feb 2015 - p330(1) [51-500]
c Sch Lib - v63 - i1 - Spring 2015 - p42(1) [51-500]

Ryan, Craig - *Sonic Wind: The Story of John Paul Stapp and How a Renegade Doctor Became the Fastest Man on Earth*
    KR - June 1 2015 - pNA [501+]
    LJ - v140 - i9 - May 15 2015 - p104(1) [51-500]
    PW - v262 - i21 - May 25 2015 - p48(1) [51-500]
    Spec - v329 - i9768 - Nov 14 2015 - p50(2) [501+]

Ryan, Damian - *Understanding Social Media: How to Create a Plan for Your Business that Works*
    RVBW - May 2015 - pNA [501+]

Ryan, David - *U.S. Foreign Policy and the Other: Transatlantic Perspectives*
    HNet - Sept 2015 - pNA [501+]

Ryan, Frank - *The Mysterious World of the Human Genome*
    KR - Dec 1 2015 - pNA [501+]

Ryan, Hank Phillippi - *Truth Be Told (Read by Sands, Xe).* Audiobook Review
    BL - v111 - i15 - April 1 2015 - p87(1) [51-500]
Truth Be Told
    RVBW - Sept 2015 - pNA [501+]
What You See
    BL - v112 - i1 - Sept 1 2015 - p51(1) [51-500]
    KR - August 15 2015 - pNA [501+]
    LJ - v140 - i14 - Sept 1 2015 - p96(2) [51-500]
    PW - v262 - i35 - August 31 2015 - p62(1) [51-500]
    RVBW - Nov 2015 - pNA [501+]

Ryan, James (b. 1985-) - *Lenin's Terror: The Ideological Origins of Early Soviet State Violence*
    HNet - Jan 2015 - pNA [501+]

Ryan, James D. - *The Spiritual Expansion of Medieval Latin Christendom: The Asian Missions*
    IBMR - v39 - i1 - Jan 2015 - p48(2) [501+]

Ryan, James R. - *Photography and Exploration*
    JRAI - v21 - i2 - June 2015 - p491(2) [501+]

Ryan, Janice Zeller - *The Modern Medallion Workbook: 11 Projects to Make, Mix & Match*
    LJ - v140 - i5 - March 15 2015 - p108(1) [51-500]

Ryan, Jeanne - *Charisma*
    y BL - v111 - i12 - Feb 15 2015 - p79(2) [51-500]
    y CCB-B - v68 - i10 - June 2015 - p513(2) [51-500]
    y VOYA - v37 - i6 - Feb 2015 - p64(1) [51-500]

Ryan, Jennifer - *At Wolf Ranch*
    BL - v111 - i11 - Feb 1 2015 - p30(1) [51-500]
Everything She Wanted
    PW - v262 - i38 - Sept 21 2015 - p59(1) [51-500]
Her Lucky Cowboy
    PW - v262 - i20 - May 18 2015 - p70(1) [51-500]
When It's Right
    PW - v262 - i3 - Jan 19 2015 - p67(1) [51-500]

Ryan, Judith - *The Cambridge Introduction to German Poetry*
    GSR - v38 - i2 - May 2015 - p239-23 [501+]

Ryan, Kay - *Erratic Facts*
    BL - v112 - i3 - Oct 1 2015 - p11(2) [51-500]
    LJ - v140 - i13 - August 1 2015 - p102(1) [51-500]
    NYTBR - Dec 27 2015 - p26(L) [501+]
    PW - v262 - i38 - Sept 21 2015 - p50(1) [51-500]

Ryan, Kelly A. - *Regulating Passion: Sexuality and Patriarchal Rule in Massachusetts, 1700-1830*
    AHR - v120 - i2 - April 2015 - p612-613 [501+]
    JAH - v102 - i2 - Sept 2015 - p547-548 [501+]
    W&M Q - v72 - i3 - July 2015 - p517-522 [501+]

Ryan, M.J. - *The Happiness Makeover: Teach Yourself to Enjoy Every Day*
    Bwatch - Feb 2015 - pNA [51-500]
The Power of Patience
    Bwatch - Jan 2015 - pNA [51-500]

Ryan, Marianne - *Baby Bod: Turn Flab to Fab in 12 Weeks Flat!*
    SPBW - July 2015 - pNA [51-500]

Ryan, Maureen - *Film and Video Budgets 6*
    RVBW - July 2015 - pNA [51-500]

Ryan, Morgan - *E.O. Wilson's Life on Earth. E-book Review*
    c Sci Teach - v82 - i7 - Oct 2015 - p82 [51-500]

Ryan, Pam Munoz - *Echo (Read by four narrators).* Audiobook Review
    c BL - v112 - i4 - Oct 15 2015 - p64(1) [501+]
    c HB - v91 - i6 - Nov-Dec 2015 - p111(1) [51-500]
    c PW - v262 - i35 - August 31 2015 - p86(2) [51-500]
    c SLJ - v61 - i8 - August 2015 - p51(1) [51-500]
Echo (Illus. by Mirtalipova, Dinara)
    y CCB-B - v68 - i7 - March 2015 - p368(1) [51-500]
    c HB - v91 - i2 - March-April 2015 - p108(1) [51-500]
    c HB Guide - v26 - i2 - Fall 2015 - p99(1) [51-500]
    c NYTBR - March 15 2015 - p17(L) [501+]
    c PW - v262 - i49 - Dec 2 2015 - p77(1) [51-500]
    y VOYA - v37 - i6 - Feb 2015 - p83(1) [51-500]
Tony Baloney: Pen Pal (Illus. by Fotheringham, Edwin)
    c SLJ - v61 - i7 - July 2015 - p70(1) [51-500]

Ryan, Patricia Twomey - *Rising Tide*
    BL - v111 - i9-10 - Jan 1 2015 - p51(1) [51-500]

Ryan, Paul - *The Way Forward: Renewing the American Idea*
    NYRB - v62 - i5 - March 19 2015 - p18(3) [501+]

Ryan, R.M. - *There's a Man with a Gun over There*
    KR - Jan 15 2015 - pNA [51-500]
    PW - v262 - i2 - Jan 12 2015 - p33(1) [51-500]

Ryan, Rob - *The Invisible Kingdom (Illus. by Ryan, Rob)*
    c KR - Oct 15 2015 - pNA [51-500]
    c PW - v262 - i42 - Oct 19 2015 - p76(2) [51-500]

Ryan, Shane - *Slaying the Tiger: A Year Inside the Ropes on the New PGA Tour*
    LJ - v140 - i12 - July 1 2015 - p89(1) [51-500]

Ryan, Shawna - *Kingdom, Book 1*
    KR - Nov 15 2015 - pNA [501+]

Ryan, Shawna Yang - *Green Island*
    KR - Nov 15 2015 - pNA [501+]

Ryan, Tom - *Peeve My Parents' Pet (Illus. by Durkin, Kenny)*
    c CH Bwatch - Jan 2015 - pNA [51-500]

Ryan, Vanessa A. - *A Palette for Murder*
    BL - v111 - i13 - March 1 2015 - p25(1) [51-500]
    KR - Feb 15 2015 - pNA [51-500]

Ryan, Yvonne - *Roy Wilkins: The Quiet Revolutionary and the NAACP*
    AHR - v120 - i1 - Feb 2015 - p291-292 [501+]
    JAH - v101 - i4 - March 2015 - p1329(1) [501+]
    JSH - v81 - i2 - May 2015 - p511(2) [501+]

Ryane, Mel - *Teaching Will*
    KR - March 15 2015 - pNA [501+]

Ryback, Timothy W. - *Hitler's First Victims: And One Man's Race for Justice*
    TimHES - i2191 - Feb 19 2015 - p53(1) [501+]
Hitler's First Victims: The Quest for Justice
    CEH - v48 - i3 - Sept 2015 - p437-439 [501+]
    Comw - v142 - i7 - April 10 2015 - p25(2) [501+]

Rybczynski, Witold - *Mysteries of the Mall and Other Essays*
    BL - v111 - i22 - August 1 2015 - p16(1) [51-500]
    KR - June 1 2015 - pNA [501+]
    Mac - v128 - i36 - Sept 14 2015 - p74(1) [501+]
    PW - v262 - i20 - May 18 2015 - p74(1) [501+]

Ryder, Dawn - *Rock Me Two Times*
    BL - v112 - i5 - Nov 1 2015 - p36(2) [51-500]

Ryding, Erik - *Gustav Mahler*
    NYRB - v62 - i20 - Dec 17 2015 - p75(3) [501+]

Rylander, Chris - *Countdown Zero*
    c HB Guide - v26 - i2 - Fall 2015 - p99(1) [51-500]

Rylant, Cynthia - *Brownie & Pearl Step Out (Illus. by Biggs, Brian)*
    c HB Guide - v26 - i1 - Spring 2015 - p55(1) [51-500]
Gooseberry Park and the Master Plan (Illus. by Howard, Arthur)
    c BL - v111 - i16 - April 15 2015 - p49(2) [51-500]
    c HB Guide - v26 - i2 - Fall 2015 - p99(1) [51-500]
    c PW - v262 - i49 - Dec 2 2015 - p64(1) [51-500]
    c SLJ - v61 - i5 - May 2015 - p97(2) [51-500]
    c KR - March 15 2015 - pNA [51-500]
Mr. Putter & Tabby Smell the Roses (Illus. by Howard, Arthur)
    c BL - v111 - i22 - August 1 2015 - p75(1) [51-500]
    c SLJ - v61 - i8 - August 2015 - p79(1) [51-500]
Mr. Putter & Tabby Turn the Page (Illus. by Howard, Arthur)
    c HB Guide - v26 - i1 - Spring 2015 - p55(1) [51-500]

Ryle, Stephen - *Erasmus and the Renaissance Republic of Letters*
    CHR - v101 - i3 - Summer 2015 - p637(3) [501+]
    Ren Q - v68 - i3 - Fall 2015 - p978-980 [501+]
    Six Ct J - v46 - i2 - Summer 2015 - p428-429 [501+]

Rylko-Bauer, Barbara - *A Polish Doctor in the Nazi Camps: My Mother's Memories of Imprisonment, Immigration, and a Life Remade*
    MAQ - v29 - i1 - March 2015 - pB36-B38 [501+]

Ryman, Kyla - *A Place to Live (Illus. by Jernigan, Case)*
    c CH Bwatch - May 2015 - pNA [51-500]

Rymes, Betsy - *Communicating beyond Language: Everyday Encounters with Diversity*
    Lang Soc - v44 - i3 - June 2015 - p450-451 [501+]

Ryner, Bradley D. - *Performing Economic Thought: English Drama and Mercantile Writing 1600-1642*
    Ren Q - v68 - i1 - Spring 2015 - p409-411 [501+]
Performing Economic Thought: English Drama and Mercantile Writing, 1600-1642
    RES - v66 - i273 - Feb 2015 - p174-176 [501+]

Rynne, Terrence J. - *Jesus Christ, Peacemaker: A New Theology of Peace*
    Theol St - v76 - i3 - Sept 2015 - p643(1) [501+]

Rynowecer, Michael B. - *Clientelligence: How Superior Client Relationships Fuel Growth and Profits*
    KR - August 1 2015 - pNA [501+]

Ryrie, Alec - *Being Protestant in Reformation Britain*
    Ren Q - v68 - i3 - Fall 2015 - p1053-1054 [501+]
    Six Ct J - v46 - i1 - Spring 2015 - p232-234 [501+]

Rzeznik, Thomas F. - *Church and Estate: Religion and Wealth in Industrial-Era Philadelphia*
    CHR - v101 - i1 - Wntr 2015 - p180(2) [501+]

Rzihacek, Andrea - *Die Urkunden Philipps von Schwaben*
    HNet - Sept 2015 - pNA [501+]

S

Saaf, Donald - *The ABC Animal Orchestra (Illus. by Saaf, Donald)*
  c SLJ - v61 - i2 - Feb 2015 - p77(1) [51-500]
  c HB Guide - v26 - i2 - Fall 2015 - p17(1) [51-500]
  c KR - Jan 1 2015 - pNA [51-500]
  c PW - v262 - i14 - April 6 2015 - p58(1) [51-500]
Sabapathy, John - *Officers and Accountability in Medieval England, 1170-1300*
    Med R - August 2015 - pNA [501+]
Sabathia, C.C. - *CC Claus: A Baseball Christmas Story (Illus. by Seeley, Laura)*
  c HB Guide - v26 - i2 - Fall 2015 - p50(1) [51-500]
Sabean, David Warren - *Space and Self in Early Modern European Cultures*
    JMH - v87 - i3 - Sept 2015 - p704(3) [501+]
Sabin, Paul - *The Bet: Paul Ehrlich, Julian Simon, and Our Gamble over Earth's Future*
    AHR - v120 - i4 - Oct 2015 - p1527-1528 [501+]
    BioSci - v65 - i7 - July 2015 - p731(3) [501+]
    JIH - v46 - i3 - Wntr 2016 - p421-433 [501+]
    PHR - v84 - i2 - May 2015 - p242(2) [501+]
Sabrow, Martin - *1989 und die Rolle der Gewalt*
    HER - v130 - i543 - April 2015 - p504(3) [501+]
Sabuda, Robert - *The Dragon and the Knight*
  c HB Guide - v26 - i2 - Fall 2015 - p100(1) [51-500]
The White House
  c KR - Dec 1 2015 - pNA [51-500]
Sacasa, Maria del Mar - *Summer Cocktails: Margaritas, Mint Juleps, Punches, Party Snacks, and More (Illus. by Striano, Tara)*
    LJ - v140 - i8 - May 1 2015 - p95(2) [51-500]
Saccardi, Marianne - *Creativity and Children's Literature: New Ways to Encourage Divergent Thinking*
    SLJ - v61 - i2 - Feb 2015 - p131(1) [51-500]
Sacco, Joe - *Bumf*
    NS - v144 - i5249 - Feb 13 2015 - p51(2) [501+]
Sachar, Louis - *Fuzzy Mud (Read by McInerney, Kathleen). Audiobook Review*
  y BL - v112 - i5 - Nov 1 2015 - p72(1) [51-500]
  c SLJ - v61 - i11 - Nov 2015 - p70(2) [51-500]
Fuzzy Mud
  c BL - v111 - i18 - May 15 2015 - p55(1) [51-500]
  c CCB-B - v69 - i1 - Sept 2015 - p50(2) [51-500]
  c HB - v91 - i4 - July-August 2015 - p143(2) [51-500]
  c KR - April 15 2015 - pNA [51-500]
  c Magpies - v30 - i3 - July 2015 - p38(1) [501+]
  c Nat Post - v17 - i230 - August 8 2015 - pWP5(1) [501+]
  c NYTBR - Nov 8 2015 - p30(L) [501+]
  c PW - v262 - i20 - May 18 2015 - p86(1) [51-500]
  c Sch Lib - v63 - i4 - Winter 2015 - p232(1) [51-500]
  c SLJ - v61 - i5 - May 2015 - p105(2) [51-500]
  y VOYA - v38 - i3 - August 2015 - p83(1) [501+]
Sachs, Aaron - *Arcadian America: The Death and Life of an Enviromental Tradition*
    Am Q - v67 - i1 - March 2015 - p267-276 [501+]
Sachs, David - *The Flood*
    KR - May 1 2015 - pNA [501+]
Sachs, Jeffrey D. - *The Age of Sustainable Development*
    BioSci - v65 - i10 - Oct 2015 - p1027(3) [501+]
    BL - v111 - i12 - Feb 15 2015 - p24(1) [51-500]
    KR - Jan 15 2015 - pNA [51-500]
    LJ - v140 - i5 - March 15 2015 - p117(1) [501+]
    Nature - v519 - i7542 - March 12 2015 - p156(1) [501+]
    New Sci - v225 - i3012 - March 14 2015 - p42(2) [501+]
    PW - v262 - i4 - Jan 26 2015 - p158(1) [51-500]
Sachs, Leon - *The Pedagogical Imagination: The Republican Legacy in Twenty-First-Century French Literature and Film*
    FS - v69 - i1 - Jan 2015 - p130-130 [501+]
    MLR - v110 - i3 - July 2015 - p877-878 [501+]
Sachsische Akademie der Kunste - *Labor der Moderne: Nachkriegsarchitektur in Europa/Laboratory of Modernism. Post-War Architecture in Europe*
    HNet - March 2015 - pNA [501+]
Sachsman, David B. - *A Press Divided: Newspaper Coverage of the Civil War*
    Bwatch - April 2015 - pNA [51-500]
Sack, Jon - *La Lucha: The Story of Lucha Castro and Human Rights in Mexico*
    TLS - i5849 - May 8 2015 - p26(1) [51-500]
Sackier, Shelley - *Dear Opl*
  c KR - June 1 2015 - pNA [51-500]
Sackner, Marvin - *The Art of Typewriting*
    LJ - v140 - i20 - Dec 1 2015 - p104(1) [51-500]
    NYTBR - Dec 6 2015 - p30(L) [501+]
Sacks, Jonathan - *Not in God's Name: Confronting Religious Violence*
    BL - v112 - i1 - Sept 1 2015 - p17(1) [51-500]
    KR - Sept 15 2015 - pNA [501+]
    LJ - v140 - i13 - August 1 2015 - p103(1) [51-500]
    NS - v144 - i5273 - July 31 2015 - p62(3) [501+]
    PW - v262 - i32 - August 10 2015 - p55(1) [51-500]
Sacks, Oliver - *Gratitude*
    KR - Nov 15 2015 - pNA [501+]
    Spec - v329 - i9772 - Dec 12 2015 - p79(3) [501+]
On the Move: A Life. Audiobook Review
    LJ - v140 - i12 - July 1 2015 - p45(1) [51-500]
On the Move: A Life (Read by Woren, Dan). Audiobook Review
    PW - v262 - i30 - July 27 2015 - p62(1) [501+]
On the Move: A Life
    BL - v111 - i17 - May 1 2015 - p67(4) [51-500]
    BL - v112 - i7 - Dec 1 2015 - p13(1) [501+]
    Ent W - i1361 - May 1 2015 - p63(1) [501+]
    Har Bus R - v93 - i12 - Dec 2015 - p124(2) [501+]
    KR - March 15 2015 - pNA [501+]
    LJ - v140 - i7 - April 15 2015 - p94(1) [51-500]
    Mac - v128 - i19-20 - May 18 2015 - p76(1) [501+]
    NS - v144 - i5262 - May 15 2015 - p45(1) [501+]
    NY - v91 - i13 - May 18 2015 - p97 [51-500]
    NYRB - v62 - i9 - May 21 2015 - p4(3) [501+]
    NYT - April 28 2015 - pC1(L) [501+]
    NYTBR - May 17 2015 - p10(L) [501+]
    PW - v262 - i12 - March 23 2015 - p66(1) [51-500]
    TLS - i5853 - June 5 2015 - p3(2) [501+]
Sackville-West, Robert - *The Disinherited: A Story of Family, Love and Betrayal*
    TLS - i5844 - April 3 2015 - p12(2) [501+]
Sada, Daniel - *One Out of Two*
    BL - v112 - i5 - Nov 1 2015 - p27(1) [51-500]
    KR - August 15 2015 - pNA [51-500]
    NYT - Nov 26 2015 - pC6(L) [501+]
    PW - v262 - i37 - Sept 14 2015 - p37(2) [51-500]
Sadan, Mandy - *Being and Becoming Kachin: Histories Beyond the State in the Borderworlds of Burma*
    AHR - v120 - i1 - Feb 2015 - p213-214 [501+]
Saddleback Educational Publishing - *Beyonce*
  y CH Bwatch - April 2015 - pNA [51-500]
  y SLJ - v61 - i9 - Sept 2015 - p151(4) [501+]
Dr. Dre
  y SLJ - v61 - i9 - Sept 2015 - p151(4) [501+]
Pharrell
  y SLJ - v61 - i9 - Sept 2015 - p151(4) [501+]
Sean Combs
  y SLJ - v61 - i9 - Sept 2015 - p151(4) [501+]

Sadler, Marilyn - *Alice from Dallas (Illus. by Hoyt, Ard)*
  c Roundup M - v22 - i5 - June 2015 - p37(2) [501+]
  c Roundup M - v22 - i6 - August 2015 - p25(1) [501+]
Charlie Piechart and the Case of the Missing Pizza Slice (Illus. by Comstock, Eric)
  c KR - July 15 2015 - pNA [51-500]
Tony Baroni Loves Macaroni (Illus. by Crovatto, Lucie)
  c SLJ - v61 - i5 - May 2015 - p91(1) [51-500]
Sadlier, Darlene J. - *Americans All: Good Neighbor Cultural Diplomacy in World War II*
    Ams - v72 - i1 - Jan 2015 - p173(2) [501+]
Sadlier, Rosemary - *Harriet Tubman: Freedom Leader, Freedom Seeker*
    CWS - v30 - i2-3 - Fall-Winter 2015 - p126(2) [501+]
Sadowski, Laurie - *The Allergy-Free Cook Makes Pies and Desserts*
    Veg J - v34 - i2 - April-June 2015 - p30(1) [51-500]
Sadra, Mulla - *The Book of Metaphysical Penetrations*
    RM - v68 - i4 - June 2015 - p861(3) [501+]
Sadur, Nina - *The Witching Hour and Other Plays*
    TLS - i5850 - May 15 2015 - p12(2) [501+]
Saeed, Aisha - *Written in the Stars*
  y HB Guide - v26 - i2 - Fall 2015 - p136(1) [51-500]
  y BL - v111 - i11 - Feb 1 2015 - p44(2) [51-500]
  y CCB-B - v68 - i9 - May 2015 - p466(1) [51-500]
  y PW - v262 - i1 - Jan 5 2015 - p75(1) [51-500]
Saenz-Lopez Perez, Sandra - *The Beatus Maps: The Revelation of the World in the Middle Ages*
    Med R - Sept 2015 - pNA [501+]
Safdarian, Davoud - *Me, Rain, and a Hired Taxi*
    KR - March 1 2015 - pNA [501+]
Safina, Carl - *Beyond Words: What Animals Think and Feel*
  y BL - v111 - i21 - July 1 2015 - p12(1) [51-500]
    Econ - v416 - i8947 - July 18 2015 - p72(US) [501+]
    KR - June 1 2015 - pNA [501+]
    LJ - v140 - i9 - May 15 2015 - p104(1) [51-500]
    New Sci - v227 - i3029 - July 11 2015 - p42(2) [501+]
    NYT - August 4 2015 - pD3(L) [501+]
    PW - v262 - i19 - May 11 2015 - p48(2) [51-500]
Safley, Thomas Max - *The History of Bankruptcy: Economic, Social and Cultural Implications in Early Modern Europe*
    JEH - v75 - i2 - June 2015 - p597-599 [501+]
Safran, Janina - *Defining Boundaries in al-Andalus: Muslims, Christians and Jews in Islamic Iberia*
    HER - v130 - i544 - June 2015 - p688(3) [501+]
Safran, Linda - *The Medieval Salento: Art and Identity in Southern Italy*
    AHR - v120 - i3 - June 2015 - p1099-1100 [501+]
    CH - v84 - i3 - Sept 2015 - p660(3) [501+]
    CHR - v101 - i4 - Autumn 2015 - p910(2) [501+]
    HNet - July 2015 - pNA [501+]
    JIH - v45 - i4 - Spring 2015 - p580-581 [501+]
    Six CJ - v46 - i3 - Fall 2015 - p807-809 [501+]
Safran, Lisa - *Cut Paste Gone*
    KR - Sept 1 2015 - pNA [501+]
Safran, Sheri - *Dinosaurs!*
  c KR - Dec 1 2015 - pNA [51-500]
Safranski, Rudiger - *Romanticism: A German Affair*
    MLN - v130 - i3 - April 2015 - p685-692 [501+]
Saft, Lauren - *Those Girls*
  y BL - v111 - i17 - May 1 2015 - p93(1) [51-500]
  y HB Guide - v26 - i2 - Fall 2015 - p136(1) [51-500]
  y KR - April 15 2015 - pNA [51-500]
  y PW - v262 - i17 - April 27 2015 - p78(2) [51-500]
  y SLJ - v61 - i2 - Feb 2015 - p107(1) [51-500]
  y VOYA - v38 - i2 - June 2015 - p67(2) [501+]

Sagar, Rahul - *Secrets and Leaks: The Dilemma of State Secrecy*
    Law&PolBR - v25 - i4 - April 2015 - p56(6) [501+]
Sagarra, Josep Maria de - *Private Life*
    PW - v262 - i30 - July 27 2015 - p41(1) [51-500]
Sage, Alison - *Sleeping Beauty (Illus. by Gibbs, Sarah)*
    c KR - August 15 2015 - pNA [51-500]
Sage, Angie - *Gargoyle Hall (Illus. by Kelly, John)*
    c SLJ - v61 - i4 - April 2015 - p149(1) [51-500]
    c BL - v111 - i17 - May 1 2015 - p55(1) [51-500]
Pathfinder: The Magykal World of Tod Hunter Moon (Illus. by Zug, Mark)
    c HB Guide - v26 - i1 - Spring 2015 - p91(1) [51-500]
    c Sch Lib - v63 - i2 - Summer 2015 - p109(1) [51-500]
Sandrider
    c KR - August 15 2015 - pNA [51-500]
    c SLJ - v61 - i8 - August 2015 - p90(2) [51-500]
Sagela, Sandra K. - *Buffalo Bill on the Silver Screen: The Films of William F. Cody*
    PHR - v84 - i2 - May 2015 - p272(2) [501+]
Sagendorph, Jean - *Icebox Cakes: Recipes for the Coolest Cakes in Town (Illus. by Donne, Tara)*
    LJ - v140 - i13 - August 1 2015 - p120(2) [51-500]
Saggioro, Fabio - *Nogara: Archeologia e storia di un villaggio medievale, scavi 2003-2008*
    Med R - June 2015 - pNA [501+]
Saguy, Abigail C. - *What's Wrong with Fat?*
    CS - v44 - i3 - May 2015 - p412-414 [501+]
Sahin, Kaya - *Empire and Power in the Reign of Suleyman: Narrating the Sixteenth-Century Ottoman World*
    AHR - v120 - i2 - April 2015 - p747-748 [501+]
    Six Ct J - v46 - i3 - Fall 2015 - p719-720 [501+]
    TLS - i5845 - April 10 2015 - p26(1) [501+]
Sahner, Christian C. - *Among the Ruins: Syria Past and Present*
    TLS - i5869 - Sept 25 2015 - p7(2) [501+]
Sahota, Sunjeev - *The Year of the Runaways*
    Lon R Bks - v37 - i20 - Oct 22 2015 - p35(1) [501+]
    NS - v144 - i5283 - Oct 9 2015 - p51(1) [501+]
    Spec - v328 - i9748 - June 27 2015 - p45(1) [501+]
Said - *The Seven Voyages of Sinbad the Sailor (Illus. by Rashin)*
    c KR - Oct 1 2015 - pNA [51-500]
Sail, Lawrence - *The Quick*
    TLS - i5872 - Oct 16 2015 - p23(1) [51-500]
Saillard, Olivier - *Impossible Wardrobes*
    NYT - Dec 6 2015 - p66(L) [51-500]
Sailor, Rachel McLean - *Meaningful Places: Landscape Photographers in the Nineteenth-Century American West*
    AHR - v120 - i1 - Feb 2015 - p260-261 [501+]
    PHR - v84 - i3 - August 2015 - p366(2) [501+]
    Roundup M - v22 - i6 - August 2015 - p40(1) [501+]
Saint James, Michael - *Bridges of Paris*
    SPBW - Feb 2015 - pNA [51-500]
Saint Mary's Press Staff - *The Catholic Children's Prayer Book (Illus. by Hale, Nathan)*
    c CH Bwatch - April 2015 - pNA [51-500]
Saint-Val, Florie - *The Little Factory of Illustration (Illus. by Saint-Val, Florie)*
    c PW - v262 - i41 - Oct 12 2015 - p69(1) [51-500]
Saintcrow, Lilith - *Blood Call*
    PW - v262 - i24 - June 15 2015 - p68(1) [51-500]
Trialer Park Fae
    PW - v262 - i16 - April 20 2015 - p59(1) [51-500]
Saintcrow, Lillith - *Roadside Magic*
    PW - v262 - i46 - Nov 16 2015 - p60(1) [51-500]
Sajdi, Dana - *The Barber of Damascus: Nouveau Literacy in the Eighteenth-Century Ottoman Levant*
    Eight-C St - v49 - i1 - Fall 2015 - p99-110 [501+]
Sajnog, Chris - *Navy SEAL Shooting*
    SPBW - Oct 2015 - pNA [51-500]
Saka, Mark Saad - *For God and Revolution: Priest, Peasant, and Agrarian Socialism in the Mexican Huasteca*
    CHR - v101 - i3 - Summer 2015 - p696(2) [501+]
    HAHR - v95 - i3 - August 2015 - p538-539 [501+]
Sakamoto, Pamela Rotner - *Midnight in Broad Daylight: A Japanese American Family Caught between Two Worlds*
    KR - Oct 1 2015 - pNA [51-500]
    PW - v262 - i41 - Oct 12 2015 - p55(2) [51-500]
Sakey, Marcus - *Written in Fire*
    KR - Oct 15 2015 - pNA [51-500]
    PW - v262 - i44 - Nov 2 2015 - p61(2) [51-500]

Sakharov, Andrei - *Reflections on Progress, Coexistence, and Intellectual Freedom*
    Nat R - v67 - i21 - Nov 19 2015 - p80(1) [501+]
Saks, Jeffrey - *To Mourn a Child: Jewish Responses to Neonatal and Childhood Death*
    Tikkun - v30 - i1 - Wntr 2015 - p51(3) [501+]
Sakudo, Akikazu - *Prions: Current Progress in Advanced Research*
    QRB - v90 - i2 - June 2015 - p225(1) [501+]
Sakuraba, Kazuki - *Red Girls: The Legend of the Akakuchibas*
    y SLJ - v61 - i8 - August 2015 - p109(2) [51-500]
Sakwa, Richard - *Frontline Ukraine: Crisis in the Borderlands*
    NS - v144 - i5267 - June 19 2015 - p42(3) [501+]
    TimHES - i2193 - March 5 2015 - p50-51 [501+]
Putin and the Oligarch: The Khodorkovsky-Yukos Affair
    E-A St - v67 - i4 - June 2015 - p678(2) [501+]
Sala, Sharon - *I'll Stand by You*
    PW - v262 - i12 - March 23 2015 - p53(2) [51-500]
Sala, Toni - *The Boys*
    KR - Sept 15 2015 - pNA [501+]
    PW - v262 - i37 - Sept 14 2015 - p40(1) [51-500]
Salaberrios, Dimas - *Street God: The Explosive True Story of a Former Drug Boss on the Run from the Hood - and the Courageous Mission That Drove Him Back*
    Ch Today - v59 - i8 - Oct 2015 - p76(1) [51-500]
Salafia, Matthew - *Slavery's Borderland: Freedom and Bondage along the Ohio River*
    Historian - v77 - i2 - Summer 2015 - p350(2) [501+]
    RAH - v43 - i3 - Sept 2015 - p498-504 [501+]
Salamon, Julie - *Cat in the City (Illus. by Weber, Jill)*
    c HB Guide - v26 - i1 - Spring 2015 - p91(1) [51-500]
Mutt's Promise (Illus. by Weber, Jill)
    c KR - Dec 15 2015 - pNA [51-500]
    c PW - v262 - i52 - Dec 21 2015 - p154(1) [51-500]
Salane, Jeffrey - *Justice*
    c BL - v111 - i18 - May 15 2015 - p66(1) [51-500]
    c HB Guide - v26 - i2 - Fall 2015 - p100(1) [51-500]
    c SLJ - v61 - i5 - May 2015 - p105(2) [51-500]
Salas, Laura Purdie - *A Rock Can Be ... (Illus. by Dabija, Violeta)*
    c HB Guide - v26 - i2 - Fall 2015 - p50(1) [51-500]
Salas, Miguel Tinker - *Venezuela: What Everyone Needs to Know*
    For Aff - v94 - i3 - May-June 2015 - pNA [501+]
    LJ - v140 - i7 - April 15 2015 - p120(2) [51-500]
Salaun, Marie - *Decoloniser l'ecole? Hawai'i, Nouvelle-Caledonie. Experiences contemporaines*
    Cont Pac - v27 - i2 - Fall 2015 - p570(3) [501+]
Salazar, Egla Martinez - *Global Coloniality of Power in Guatemala: Racism, Genocide, Citizenship*
    CWS - v30 - i2-3 - Fall-Winter 2015 - p139(2) [501+]
Salcedo, Javier - *Los montoneros del barrio*
    HAHR - v95 - i4 - Nov 2015 - p699-701 [501+]
Saldern, Adelheid von - *Amerikanismus: Kulturelle Abgrenzung von Europa und US-Nationalismus im fruhen 20. Jahrhundert*
    HNet - May 2015 - pNA [501+]
Saldivar, Jose David - *Trans-Americanity: Subaltern Modernities, Global Coloniality, and the Cultures of Greater Mexico*
    MFSF - v61 - i1 - Spring 2015 - p181-183 [501+]
Salem Press - *American Poetry of the 20th Century*
    y BL - v111 - i15 - April 1 2015 - p12(1) [51-500]
Introduction to Literary Context: Plays
    y Teach Lib - v42 - i5 - June 2015 - p10(1) [51-500]
    y BL - v111 - i19-20 - June 1 2015 - p24(1) [51-500]
Saler, Bethel - *The Settlers' Empire: Colonialism and State Formation in America's Old Northwest*
    WHQ - v46 - i4 - Winter 2015 - p504-504 [501+]
Saler, Robert C. - *Between Magisterium and Marketplace: A Constructive Account of Theology and the Church*
    CC - v132 - i19 - Sept 16 2015 - p40(3) [501+]
Salerni, Dianne K. - *The Inquisitor's Mark*
    c HB Guide - v26 - i2 - Fall 2015 - p100(1) [51-500]
Salerno, Shane - *Salinger*
    TimHES - i2218 - August 27 2015 - p43(1) [501+]
Salerno, Steven - *Wild Child (Illus. by Salerno, Steven)*
    c BL - v111 - i20 - June 15 2015 - pNA [51-500]
    c PW - v262 - i21 - May 25 2015 - p57(2) [51-500]
    c SLJ - v61 - i9 - Sept 2015 - p128(1) [51-500]
Sales, Joan - *Uncertain Glory*
    HT - v65 - i2 - Feb 2015 - p62(1) [501+]

Sales, Leila - *This Song Will Save Your Life (Read by Lowman, Rebecca). Audiobook Review*
    y HB - v91 - i4 - July-August 2015 - p168(1) [51-500]
Tonight the Streets Are Ours
    y HB - v91 - i5 - Sept-Oct 2015 - p115(2) [51-500]
    y KR - July 1 2015 - pNA [51-500]
    y PW - v262 - i27 - July 6 2015 - p74(1) [51-500]
    y SLJ - v61 - i8 - August 2015 - p110(1) [51-500]
    y VOYA - v38 - i3 - August 2015 - p68(1) [51-500]
Sales, Michael A. - *Reactor Agenda*
    KR - Nov 1 2015 - pNA [501+]
Salesses, Matthew - *The Hundred-Year Flood*
    KR - June 1 2015 - pNA [51-500]
    LJ - v140 - i17 - Oct 15 2015 - p76(1) [51-500]
    PW - v262 - i23 - June 8 2015 - p32(2) [51-500]
Salgado, Nirmala - *Buddhist Nuns and Gendered Practice: In Search of the Female Renunciant*
    JAS - v74 - i2 - May 2015 - p517-519 [501+]
Salisbury, Graham - *Hunt for the Bamboo Rat*
    y HB Guide - v26 - i1 - Spring 2015 - p122(1) [51-500]
Under the Blood-Red Sun (Read by Watanabe, Greg). Audiobook Review
    y HB - v111 - i11 - Feb 1 2015 - p62(1) [51-500]
Salisbury, Melinda - *The Sin Eater's Daughter (Read by Shields, Amy). Audiobook Review*
    y SLJ - v61 - i7 - July 2015 - p50(1) [51-500]
The Sin Eater's Daughter
    y CCB-B - v68 - i8 - April 2015 - p419(1) [51-500]
    y CH Bwatch - July 2015 - pNA [51-500]
    y HB Guide - v26 - i2 - Fall 2015 - p137(1) [51-500]
    y Magpies - v30 - i2 - May 2015 - p44(1) [51-500]
    c NYTBR - May 10 2015 - p22(L) [501+]
    y PW - v262 - i49 - Dec 2 2015 - p106(1) [51-500]
    y Sch Lib - v63 - i2 - Summer 2015 - p120(2) [51-500]
    y VOYA - v37 - i6 - Feb 2015 - p83(1) [51-500]
Salmela, Mikko - *True Emotions*
    ABR - v36 - i3 - March-April 2015 - p29(1) [501+]
Salom, Andree - *When the Anger Ogre Visits (Illus. by Salom, Ivette)*
    c CH Bwatch - June 2015 - pNA [51-500]
    c PW - v262 - i8 - Feb 23 2015 - p79(1) [51-500]
Salom, Latifah - *The Cake House*
    BL - v111 - i13 - March 1 2015 - p17(1) [51-500]
    KR - Feb 1 2015 - pNA [51-500]
Salomon, Xavier F. - *Veronese*
    Six Ct J - v46 - i3 - Fall 2015 - p831-832 [501+]
Salomons, Robert P. - *P.Cair.Preis.[sup.2&rqsb;*
    HNet - August 2015 - pNA [501+]
Salonen, Kirsi - *Entering a Clerical Career at the Roman Curia, 1458-1471*
    CHR - v101 - i4 - Autumn 2015 - p922(3) [501+]
Salonius, Pippa - *The Tree: Symbol, Allegory, and Mnemonic Device in Medieval Art and Thought*
    CHR - v101 - i4 - Autumn 2015 - p913(3) [501+]
    Med R - June 2015 - pNA [501+]
    Specu - v90 - i2 - April 2015 - p583-584 [501+]
Salter, Anastasia - *What Is Your Quest? From Adventure Games to Interactive Books*
    AL - v87 - i3 - Sept 2015 - p630-632 [501+]
Salter, James - *Life Is Meals: A Food Lover's Book of Days*
    TLS - i5834 - Jan 23 2015 - p27(1) [501+]
A Sport and a Pastime
    Esq - v163 - i6-7 - June-July 2015 - p26(2) [501+]
Salter, Ken - *Gold Fever, Part 2: San Francisco, 1851-1852*
    RVBW - Feb 2015 - pNA [51-500]
Saltsman, Amelia - *The Seasonal Jewish Kitchen: A Fresh Take on Tradition*
    BL - v112 - i3 - Oct 1 2015 - p20(1) [51-500]
    LJ - v140 - i20 - Dec 1 2015 - p129(1) [51-500]
Saltzberg, Barney - *Inside This Book (Are Three Books). (Illus. by Saltzberg, Barney)*
    c BL - v111 - i14 - March 15 2015 - p78(1) [51-500]
    c HB Guide - v26 - i2 - Fall 2015 - p17(1) [51-500]
    KR - Feb 1 2015 - pNA [51-500]
    c PW - v262 - i5 - Feb 2 2015 - p57(1) [51-500]
    c SLJ - v61 - i6 - June 2015 - p92(2) [51-500]
Saltzman, Nancy - *Radical Survivor: One Woman's Path through Life, Love, and Uncharted Tragedy*
    KR - Nov 1 2015 - pNA [51-500]
Saltzstein, Jennifer - *The Refrain and the Rise of the Vernacular in Medieval French Music and Poetry*
    FS - v69 - i2 - April 2015 - p231-2 [501+]
    MLR - v110 - i1 - Jan 2015 - p255-256 [501+]
Salvalaggio, Karin - *Burnt River*
    KR - March 1 2015 - pNA [51-500]
    PW - v262 - i7 - Feb 16 2015 - p159(1) [51-500]

Salvayre, Lydie - *Pas Pleurer*
WLT - v89 - i5 - Sept-Oct 2015 - p66(2) [501+]

Salys, Rimgaila - *The Musical Comedy Films of Grigorii Aleksandrov: Laughing Matters*
MLR - v110 - i1 - Jan 2015 - p309-310 [501+]

Salzano, Tammi - *I Love You Just the Way You Are* (Illus. by Grey, Ada)
c HB Guide - v26 - i1 - Spring 2015 - p16(1) [51-500]

Salzberg, Rosa - *Ephemeral City: Cheap Print and Urban Culture in Renaissance Venice*
HNet - March 2015 - pNA [501+]
TLS - i5870 - Oct 2 2015 - p26(2) [501+]

Salzman, Michele Renee - *The Cambridge History of Religions in the Ancient World, vol. 1: From the Bronze Age to the Hellenistic Age*
TLS - i5835 - Jan 30 2015 - p24(1) [501+]
The Cambridge History of Religions in the Ancient World, vol. 2: From the Hellenistic Age to Late Antiquity
TLS - i5835 - Jan 30 2015 - p24(1) [501+]
The Letters of Symmachus: Book 1
Class R - v65 - i1 - April 2015 - p161-163 [501+]

Salzman, Paul - *Literature and Politics in the 1620s: 'Whisper'd Counsells'*
RES - v66 - i276 - Sept 2015 - p779-780 [501+]

Salzman, Mary Elizabeth - *Aircraft*
c BL - v112 - i1 - Sept 1 2015 - p96(1) [51-500]
Automobiles
c BL - v112 - i1 - Sept 1 2015 - p96(1) [51-500]
Baby Alligators
c HB Guide - v26 - i2 - Fall 2015 - p176(1) [51-500]
Baby Animals
c HB Guide - v26 - i2 - Fall 2015 - p181(1) [51-500]
Baby Eagles
c HB Guide - v26 - i2 - Fall 2015 - p178(1) [51-500]
Biggest, Baddest Book of Flight
c HB Guide - v26 - i2 - Fall 2015 - p186(1) [51-500]
c BL - v111 - i16 - April 15 2015 - p45(1) [501+]
Camera
c BL - v112 - i1 - Sept 1 2015 - p96(1) [51-500]
Numbers 1-20 Series
c HB Guide - v26 - i1 - Spring 2015 - p149(1) [51-500]
Phonograph
c BL - v112 - i1 - Sept 1 2015 - p96(1) [51-500]

Samac, Deborah A. - *Compendium of Alfalfa Diseases and Pests*
Bwatch - April 2015 - pNA [51-500]

Samanci, Ozge - *Dare to Disappoint: Growing Up in Turkey*
BL - v112 - i6 - Nov 15 2015 - p35(1) [51-500]
y KR - Oct 15 2015 - pNA [51-500]

Samatar, Sofia - *The Winged Histories*
KR - Jan 1 2016 - pNA [51-500]

Samerski, Stefan - *Cura animarum: Seelsorge im Deutschordensland Preußen*
Med R - March 2015 - pNA(NA) [501+]

Samet, Elizabeth D. - *No Man's Land: Preparing for War and Peace in Post-9/11 America*
AM - v213 - i1 - July 6 2015 - p40(3) [501+]
AS - v84 - i1 - Wntr 2015 - p116(2) [501+]

Samit, Jay - *Disrupt You! Master Personal Transformation, Seize Opportunity, and Thrive in the Era of Endless Innovation*
PW - v262 - i21 - May 25 2015 - p49(1) [501+]

Samiuddin, Osman - *The Unquiet Ones: A History of Pakistan Cricket*
NS - v144 - i5285 - Oct 23 2015 - p51(1) [501+]

Sammons, Jeffrey T. - *Harlem's Rattlers and the Great War: The Undaunted 369th Regiment and the African American Quest for Equality*
AHR - v120 - i3 - June 2015 - p1051(1) [501+]

Samoun, Abigail - *How Penguin Says Please!* (Illus. by Watts, Sarah)
c KR - July 1 2015 - pNA [51-500]

Samoyault, Tiphaine - *Roland Barthes: Biographie*
FS - v69 - i4 - Oct 2015 - p554-555 [501+]
TLS - i5854 - June 12 2015 - p17(2) [501+]

Samphire, Patrick - *Secrets of the Dragon Tomb* (Illus. by Holmes, Jeremy)
c BL - v112 - i4 - Oct 15 2015 - p59(1) [501+]
c KR - Oct 15 2015 - pNA [51-500]
c SLJ - v61 - i10 - Oct 2015 - p94(2) [51-500]

Sampson, Fay - *The Wounded Thorn*
PW - v262 - i17 - April 27 2015 - p55(1) [501+]

Sampson, Helen - *International Seafarers and Transnationalism in the Twenty-first Century*
ERS - v38 - i8 - August 2015 - p1471(3) [501+]

Sampson, Mark - *The Secrets Men Keep*
PW - v262 - i5 - Feb 2 2015 - p34(1) [501+]

Sampson, Scott D. - *How to Raise a Wild Child: The Art and Science of Falling in Love with Nature*
PW - v262 - i5 - Feb 2 2015 - p50(1) [51-500]

Samsoe, Lene Holme - *Perfectly Feminine Knits: 25 Distinctive Designs*
LJ - v140 - i13 - August 1 2015 - p96(1) [51-500]

Samson, Polly - *The Kindness*
BL - v111 - i19-20 - June 1 2015 - p42(1) [51-500]
KR - May 15 2015 - pNA [51-500]
NYTBR - June 7 2015 - p38(L) [501+]
PW - v262 - i19 - May 11 2015 - p30(1) [51-500]
TLS - i5851 - May 22 2015 - p20(1) [501+]

Samuel, John - *What I Tell You in the Dark*
PW - v262 - i42 - Oct 19 2015 - p50(1) [51-500]

Samuel, Lawrence R. - *The American Middle Class: A Cultural History*
Historian - v77 - i3 - Fall 2015 - p579(3) [501+]
RAH - v43 - i1 - March 2015 - p168-175 [501+]

Samuel, Sigal - *The Mystics of Mile End*
y BL - v112 - i1 - Sept 1 2015 - p42(1) [51-500]
KR - August 1 2015 - pNA [51-500]
LJ - v140 - i12 - July 1 2015 - p81(2) [51-500]
Nat Post - v17 - i169 - May 23 2015 - pWP4(1) [51-500]

Samuels, Barbara - *Fred's Beds* (Illus. by Samuels, Barbara)
c HB Guide - v26 - i1 - Spring 2015 - p44(1) [51-500]

Samuels, Ellen - *Fantasies of Identification: Disability, Gender, Race*
Wom R Bks - v32 - i4 - July-August 2015 - p5(2) [501+]

Samuelson, Paul - *The Boys of Earth-180*
KR - April 15 2015 - pNA [501+]

Samuelson, Scott - *The Deepest Human Life: An Introduction to Philosophy for Everyone*
RM - v68 - i3 - March 2015 - p675(3) [501+]

Samuelsson, Marcus - *Make It Messy: My Perfectly Imperfect Life*
y BL - v111 - i19-20 - June 1 2015 - p83(1) [51-500]
y HB Guide - v26 - i2 - Fall 2015 - p211(1) [51-500]
y KR - March 1 2015 - pNA [51-500]
y SLJ - v61 - i5 - May 2015 - p142(1) [51-500]
y VOYA - v38 - i1 - April 2015 - p88(1) [51-500]

San Miguel, Guadalupe, Jr. - *Chicana/o Struggles for Education: Activism in the Community*
PHR - v84 - i1 - Feb 2015 - p124(2) [501+]
WHQ - v46 - i2 - Summer 2015 - p243-244 [501+]

Sanal, Aslihan - *New Organs within Us: Transplants and the Moral Economy*
JRAI - v21 - i1 - March 2015 - p232(2) [501+]

Sanborn, Joshua A. - *Imperial Apocalypse: The Great War and the Destruction of the Russian Empire*
J Mil H - v79 - i2 - April 2015 - p505-506 [501+]
Slav R - v74 - i3 - Fall 2015 - p600-603 [501+]

Sanchez, Anita - *Leaflets Three, Let It Be! The Story of Poison Ivy* (Illus. by Brickman, Robin)
c HB Guide - v26 - i2 - Fall 2015 - p173(1) [51-500]
c KR - Feb 1 2015 - pNA [51-500]

Sanchez, Antonio Cazorla - *Franco: The Biography of the Myth*
AHR - v120 - i1 - Feb 2015 - p344-345 [501+]

Sanchez Gazquez, Joaquin J. - *Los De Fato et Libero Arbitrio Libri Tres de Juan Gines de Sepulveda : Estudio de una obra historico-filosofico-teologica*
Six Ct J - v46 - i2 - Summer 2015 - p479-480 [501+]

Sanchez, Joseph P. - *New Mexico: A History*
Historian - v77 - i3 - Fall 2015 - p581(2) [501+]

Sanchez, Juan Reinaldo - *The Double Life of Fidel Castro: My 17 Years as Personal Bodyguard to El Lider Maximo*
LJ - v140 - i8 - May 1 2015 - p80(2) [51-500]

Sanchez, Linda - *Apache Lore and Legends of Southern New Mexico: From the Sacred Mountain*
Roundup M - v22 - i6 - August 2015 - p40(1) [501+]

Sanchez, Reuben - *Typology and Iconography in Donne, Herbert, and Milton: Fashioning the Self after Jeremiah*
Sev Cent N - v73 - i3-4 - Fall-Winter 2015 - p97(5) [501+]

Sanchez, Saul - *Rows of Memory: Journeys of a Migrant Sugar-Beet Worker*
SHQ - v118 - i4 - April 2015 - p443-445 [501+]

Sanchez-Sibony, Oscar - *Red Globalization: The Political Economy of the Soviet Cold War from Stalin to Khrushchev*
AHR - v120 - i2 - April 2015 - p745(1) [501+]
HNet - May 2015 - pNA [501+]
JIH - v46 - i1 - Summer 2015 - p120-121 [501+]
Slav R - v74 - i2 - Summer 2015 - p364-366 [501+]
TLS - i5854 - June 12 2015 - p12(1) [501+]

Sanchez-Villagra; Marcelo R. - *Issues in Palaeobiology: A Global View: Interviews and Essays*
QRB - v90 - i4 - Dec 2015 - p428(2) [501+]

Sancilio, Frederick D. - *Prevention Is the Cure! A Scientist's Guide to Extending Your Life*
RVBW - July 2015 - pNA [501+]

Sand, Alexa - *Vision, Devotion, and Self-Representation in Late Medieval Art*
Med R - August 2015 - pNA [501+]

Sand, George - *What Flowers Say: And Other Stories* (Illus. by Crabapple, Molly)
c CH Bwatch - April 2015 - pNA [501+]

Sand, Jordan - *Tokyo Vernacular: Common Spaces, Local Histories, Found Objects*
HNet - June 2015 - pNA [501+]
Pac A - v88 - i1 - March 2015 - p203 [501+]

Sandberg, Russell - *Religion, Law and Society*
J Ch St - v57 - i3 - Summer 2015 - p555-556 [501+]

Sandbrook, Dominic - *The Great British Dream Factory: The Strange History of our National Imagination*
Spec - v329 - i9761 - Sept 26 2015 - p41(1) [501+]
TimHES - i2227 - Oct 29 2015 - p51(1) [501+]

Sandbu, Martin - *Europe's Orphan: The Future of the Euro and the Politics of Debt*
PW - v262 - i35 - August 31 2015 - p78(1) [51-500]

Sandburg, Carl - *Mary Lincoln, Wife and Widow*
CSM - April 17 2015 - pNA [501+]

Sandefur, Timothy - *The Conscience of the Constitution: The Declaration of Independence and the Right to Liberty*
IndRev - v19 - i3 - Wntr 2015 - p458(4) [501+]

Sandell, David P. - *Open Your Heart: Religion and Cultural Poetics of Greater Mexico*
RVBW - July 2015 - pNA [501+]

Sandell, Marie - *The Rise of Women's Transnational Activism: Identity and Sisterhood Between the World Wars*
TimHES - i2201 - April 30 2015 - p53(1) [501+]

Sander, Robert D. - *Invasion of Laos, 1971: Lam Son 719*
NWCR - v68 - i3 - Summer 2015 - p163(3) [501+]

Sanders, Annmarie - *Spiritual Leadership for Challenging Times: Presidential Addresses from the Leadership Conference of Women Religious*
Theol St - v76 - i1 - March 2015 - p223(2) [501+]

Sanders, Ben - *American Blood*
BL - v112 - i4 - Oct 15 2015 - p17(2) [51-500]
KR - Sept 15 2015 - pNA [51-500]
LJ - v140 - i19 - Nov 15 2015 - p79(1) [51-500]
PW - v262 - i36 - Sept 7 2015 - p45(1) [51-500]

Sanders, Bernie - *Outsider in the White House*
NYRB - v62 - i17 - Nov 5 2015 - p18(3) [501+]

Sanders, Ed - *Sharon Tate: A Life*
PW - v262 - i41 - Oct 12 2015 - p57(1) [501+]
PW - Nov 1 2015 - pNA [501+]

Sanders, Ed (b. 1973-) - *Envy and Jealousy in Classical Athens: A Socio-Psychological Approach*
Class R - v65 - i2 - Oct 2015 - p364-366 [501+]

Sanders, Eli - *While the City Slept: A Love Lost to Violence and a Young Man's Descent into Madness*
KR - Dec 15 2015 - pNA [501+]
LJ - v140 - i20 - Dec 1 2015 - p119(1) [51-500]
PW - v262 - i44 - Nov 2 2015 - p74(1) [51-500]
BL - v112 - i7 - Dec 1 2015 - p8(1) [51-500]

Sanders, Ivan - *The Cinema of Istvan Szabo: Visions of Europe*
Slav R - v74 - i3 - Fall 2015 - p640-642 [501+]

Sanders, J. Aaron - *Speakers of the Dead*
KR - Jan 1 2016 - pNA [501+]
PW - v262 - i51 - Dec 14 2015 - p58(1) [51-500]

Sanders, James A. - *The Monotheizing Process: Its Origins and Development*
BTB - v45 - i3 - August 2015 - p185(1) [501+]

Sanders, Nancy I. - *A Pirate's Mother Goose*
c KR - July 15 2015 - pNA [51-500]

Sanders, Nichole - *Gender and Welfare in Mexico: The Consolidation of a Postrevolutionary State*
Ams - v72 - i2 - April 2015 - p353(2) [501+]
HAHR - v95 - i1 - Feb 2015 - p168-170 [501+]

Sanders, Robert L. - *Outer Space Bedtime Race* (Illus. by Won, Brian)
c HB Guide - v26 - i2 - Fall 2015 - p17(1) [51-500]
c SLJ - v61 - i2 - Feb 2015 - p78(1) [51-500]

Sanders, Ted - *The Box and the Dragonfly* (Illus. by Bruno, Iacopo)
c BL - v111 - i12 - Feb 15 2015 - p85(1) [51-500]
c CCB-B - v68 - i10 - June 2015 - p514(1) [51-500]
c NYTBR - May 10 2015 - p22(L) [501+]

Sanderson, Brandon - *The Bands of Mourning*
    KR - Dec 15 2015 - pNA [51-500]
    PW - v262 - i50 - Dec 7 2015 - p72(2) [51-500]
Calamity
    y KR - Jan 1 2016 - pNA [51-500]
Firefight (Read by Andrews, MacLeod). Audiobook Review
    y SLJ - v61 - i7 - July 2015 - p50(1) [51-500]
Firefight
    y BL - v111 - i9-10 - Jan 1 2015 - p88(2) [51-500]
    y CCB-B - v68 - i7 - March 2015 - p369(1) [51-500]
    y HB Guide - v26 - i2 - Fall 2015 - p137(1) [51-500]
The Hero of Ages
    Bwatch - Jan 2015 - pNA [51-500]
Mistborn
    Bwatch - Jan 2015 - pNA [51-500]
Shadows of Self
    KR - Sept 1 2015 - pNA [51-500]
    PW - v262 - i35 - August 31 2015 - p66(1) [501+]
The Well of Ascension
    Bwatch - Jan 2015 - pNA [51-500]
Sanderson, Douglas - *Cry Wolfram*
    BL - v111 - i19-20 - June 1 2015 - p56(1) [51-500]
Nights of the Horns
    BL - v111 - i19-20 - June 1 2015 - p56(1) [51-500]
Sanderson, Jimmy - *Developing Successful Social Media Plans in Sport Organizations*
    RVBW - August 2015 - pNA [51-500]
Sanderson, Ruth - *A Castle Full of Cats (Illus. by Sanderson, Ruth)*
    c HB Guide - v26 - i2 - Fall 2015 - p50(1) [51-500]
The Snow Princess (Illus. by Sanderson, Ruth)
    c HB Guide - v26 - i2 - Fall 2015 - p50(1) [51-500]
    c SLJ - v61 - i2 - Feb 2015 - p77(2) [51-500]
Sandford, John - *Deadline (Read by Conger, Eric). Audiobook Review*
    BL - v111 - i15 - April 1 2015 - p85(1) [51-500]
Deadline
    RVBW - July 2015 - pNA [51-500]
    RVBW - Nov 2015 - pNA [51-500]
Field of Prey
    RVBW - May 2015 - pNA [51-500]
Gathering Prey
    KR - April 1 2015 - pNA [51-500]
Saturn Run
    KR - August 1 2015 - pNA [501+]
    PW - v262 - i30 - July 27 2015 - p46(1) [51-500]
Uncaged (Read by Cook, Michele). Audiobook Review
    y BL - v111 - i9-10 - Jan 1 2015 - p118(1) [51-500]
Sandhaus, Louis - *Earthquakes, Mudslides, Fires and Riots: California and Graphic Design, 1936-1986*
    TLS - i5848 - May 1 2015 - p27(1) [501+]
Sandhu, Sabeen - *Asian Indian Professionals: The Culture of Success*
    CS - v44 - i1 - Jan 2015 - p146(1) [501+]
Sandler, Douglas B. - *Handbook of Postal Strikes 1890 to 2014*
    Phil Lit R - v64 - i3 - Summer 2015 - p220(2) [501+]
Sandler, Lucy Freeman - *Illuminators and Patrons in Fourteenth-Century England: The Psalter and Hours of Humphrey de Bohun and the Manuscripts of the Bohun Family*
    TLS - i5875 - Nov 6 2015 - p33(1) [501+]
Sandler, Martin W. - *Iron Rails, Iron Men, and the Race to Link the Nation: The Story of the Transcontinental Railroad*
    y BL - v112 - i1 - Sept 1 2015 - p92(1) [51-500]
    c HB - v91 - i6 - Nov-Dec 2015 - p106(1) [51-500]
    c KR - July 1 2015 - pNA [51-500]
    y SLJ - v61 - i8 - August 2015 - p129(2) [51-500]
Sandlin, Lisa - *The Do-Right*
    BL - v112 - i3 - Oct 1 2015 - p25(1) [51-500]
    KR - August 1 2015 - pNA [501+]
    PW - v262 - i31 - August 3 2015 - p34(1) [51-500]
Sandling, Molly - *Exploring America in the 1970s: Celebrating the Self*
    y VOYA - v38 - i1 - April 2015 - p89(1) [51-500]
Exploring America in the 1980s: Living in the Material World
    y VOYA - v38 - i1 - April 2015 - p89(1) [51-500]
Sandoni, Luca - *Il Sillabo di Pio IX*
    CHR - v101 - i2 - Spring 2015 - p379(2) [501+]
Sandor, Marjorie - *The Uncanny Reader: Stories from the Shadows*
    BL - v111 - i9-10 - Jan 1 2015 - p60(1) [51-500]
    Bwatch - May 2015 - pNA [51-500]

Sandoval, Summers - *Latinos at the Golden Gate: Creating Community & Identity in San Francisco*
    PHR - v84 - i3 - August 2015 - p372(3) [501+]
Sands, Kevin - *The Blackthorn Key (Read by Panthaki, Ray). Audiobook Review*
    c SLJ - v61 - i11 - Nov 2015 - p71(2) [51-500]
The Blackthorn Key
    c BL - v112 - i2 - Sept 15 2015 - p65(1) [51-500]
    c CH Bwatch - Oct 2015 - pNA [51-500]
    c KR - July 15 2015 - pNA [51-500]
    c NYTBR - Nov 8 2015 - p29(L) [501+]
    c PW - v262 - i26 - June 29 2015 - p69(1) [51-500]
    c PW - v262 - i49 - Dec 2 2015 - p79(1) [51-500]
    c PW - v262 - i51 - Dec 14 2015 - p21(6) [501+]
    c Sch Lib - v63 - i4 - Winter 2015 - p232(1) [51-500]
    c SLJ - v61 - i8 - August 2015 - p91(1) [51-500]
Sands, Lynsay - *The Highlander Takes a Bride*
    BL - v111 - i21 - July 1 2015 - p44(1) [51-500]
The Immortal Who Loved Me
    KR - Jan 15 2015 - pNA [51-500]
Sands-O'Connor, Karen - *Internationalism in Children's Series*
    Bkbird - v53 - i2 - Spring 2015 - p84(1) [501+]
Sandstrom, John - *Fundamentals of Technical Services*
    LJ - v140 - i19 - Nov 15 2015 - p97(1) [51-500]
Sandu, Anca - *Churchill's Tale of Tails (Illus. by Sandu, Anca)*
    c HB Guide - v26 - i1 - Spring 2015 - p44(1) [51-500]
Sandul, Paul J.P. - *California Dreaming: Boosterism, Memory, and Rural Suburbs in the Golden State*
    Pub Hist - v37 - i2 - May 2015 - p141(2) [501+]
    WHQ - v46 - i3 - Autumn 2015 - p391-392 [501+]
Sandwell, Ruth - *Becoming a History Teacher: Sustaining Practices in Historical Thinking and Knowing*
    Can Hist R - v96 - i2 - June 2015 - p325(3) [501+]
Sanft, Charles - *Communications and Cooperation in Early Imperial China: Publicizing the Qin Dynasty*
    AHR - v120 - i1 - Feb 2015 - p215(1) [501+]
Sangaramoorthy, Thurka - *Treating AIDS: Politics of Difference, Paradox of Prevention*
    MAQ - v29 - i2 - June 2015 - pb24-b27 [501+]
Sanger, Alice E. - *Art, Gender and Religious Devotion in Grand Ducal Tuscany*
    Ren Q - v68 - i2 - Summer 2015 - p632-634 [501+]
Sanghera, Sathnam - *Marriage Material*
    KR - Nov 1 2015 - pNA [51-500]
Sangwin, Chris - *Computer Aided Assessment of Mathematics*
    Math T - v108 - i6 - Feb 2015 - p477(1) [501+]
Sanjek, Roger - *Ethnography in Today's World: Color Full before Color Blind*
    CS - v44 - i5 - Sept 2015 - p702-704 [501+]
Sanjuan, Alejandro Garcia - *La conquista islamica de la Peninsula Iberica y la tergiversacion del pasado: Del catastrofismo al negacionismo*
    Specu - v90 - i1 - Jan 2015 - p252-253 [501+]
Sankovitch, Nina - *Signed, Sealed, Delivered: Celebrating the Joys of Letter Writing*
    CC - v132 - i10 - May 13 2015 - p41(2) [501+]
Sanna, Lucy - *The Cherry Harvest*
    LJ - v140 - i9 - May 15 2015 - p70(1) [51-500]
Sannicandro, Lisa - *I personaggi femminili del Bellum Civile di Lucano*
    Class R - v65 - i2 - Oct 2015 - p458-459 [501+]
Sansal, Boualem - *Harraga*
    NYT - Jan 29 2015 - pC6(L) [501+]
    TLS - i5843 - March 27 2015 - p20(1) [501+]
    WLT - v89 - i1 - Jan-Feb 2015 - p69(2) [501+]
Sansom, Ian - *Death in Devon*
    TLS - i5864-5865 - August 21 2015 - p23(1) [501+]
Sansone, David - *Greek Drama and the Invention of Rhetoric*
    AJP - v136 - i1 - Spring 2015 - p155-158 [501+]
Santa Cruz, Paul H. - *Making JFK Matter: Popular Memory and the Thirty-Fifth President*
    LJ - v140 - i6 - April 1 2015 - p104(2) [51-500]
Santamaria, Abigail - *Joy: Poet, Seeker, and the Woman Who Captivated C.S. Lewis*
    BL - v111 - i22 - August 1 2015 - p17(1) [51-500]
    KR - May 15 2015 - pNA [501+]
    LJ - v140 - i10 - June 1 2015 - p104(3) [51-500]
    NYTBR - August 9 2015 - p24(L) [501+]
    PW - v262 - i19 - May 11 2015 - p46(1) [51-500]
Santamaria, Daniel A. - *Extensible Processing for Archives and Special Collections: Reducing Processing Backlogs*
    Bwatch - Feb 2015 - pNA [51-500]

Santana, Carlos - *The Universal Tone: Bringing My Story to Light (Read by Davis, Jonathan). Audiobook Review*
    Bwatch - Feb 2015 - pNA [51-500]
    LJ - v140 - i7 - April 15 2015 - p49(1) [51-500]
Santasombat, Yos - *The River of Life: Changing Ecosystems of the Mekong Region*
    JAS - v74 - i2 - May 2015 - p525-526 [501+]
Santat, Dan - *The Adventures of Beekle: The Unimaginary Friend (Illus. by Santat, Dan)*
    c Magpies - v30 - i1 - March 2015 - p28(1) [501+]
Santayana, George - *The Life of Reason: Reason in Art*
    RM - v69 - i2 - Dec 2015 - p410(3) [501+]
Sante, Luc - *The Other Paris*
    KR - June 15 2015 - pNA [501+]
    Mac - v128 - i50 - Dec 21 2015 - p62(1) [501+]
    NYRB - v62 - i18 - Nov 19 2015 - p16(2) [501+]
    PW - v262 - i32 - August 10 2015 - p48(2) [51-500]
    LJ - v140 - i13 - August 1 2015 - p110(1) [51-500]
    BL - v112 - i2 - Sept 15 2015 - p21(1) [51-500]
    NYTBR - Nov 1 2015 - p16(L) [501+]
Sante Militaire, Sante Coloniale. Guerres, Maladies et Empires au long XIXe Siecle
    HNet - March 2015 - pNA [501+]
Santer, Melvin - *Confronting Contagion: Our Evolving Understanding of Disease*
    QRB - v90 - i3 - Sept 2015 - p351(2) [501+]
Santi, Federico - *The Newport Naval Training Station: A Postcard History*
    NWCR - v68 - i1 - Wntr 2015 - p145(2) [501+]
Santi, Jenny - *The Giving Way to Happiness: The Life-Changing Power of Giving*
    PW - v262 - i38 - Sept 21 2015 - p64(2) [51-500]
Santiago, Wilfred - *Michael Jordan: Bull on Parade (Illus. by Santiago, Wilfred)*
    PW - v262 - i10 - March 9 2015 - p60(1) [51-500]
Santopietro, Tom - *The Sound of Music Story: How a Beguiling Young Novice, a Handsome Austrian Captain, and Ten Singing Von Trapp Children Inspired the Most Beloved Film of All Time (Read by Summerer, Eric Michael). Audiobook Review*
    LJ - v140 - i17 - Oct 15 2015 - p53(1) [51-500]
The Sound of Music Story: How a Beguiling Young Novice, a Handsome Austrian Captain, and Ten Singing Von Trapp Children Inspired the Most Beloved Film of All Time
    BL - v111 - i12 - Feb 15 2015 - p18(1) [51-500]
    Bwatch - June 2015 - pNA [51-500]
    LJ - v140 - i6 - April 1 2015 - p96(1) [51-500]
    PW - v262 - i3 - Jan 19 2015 - p73(1) [51-500]
Santopolo, Jill - *Bad News Nails*
    c HB Guide - v26 - i2 - Fall 2015 - p100(1) [51-500]
Makeover Magic
    c HB Guide - v26 - i1 - Spring 2015 - p91(1) [51-500]
True Colors
    c HB Guide - v26 - i1 - Spring 2015 - p91(1) [51-500]
Santorum, Rick - *Bella's Gift: How One Little Girl Transformed Our Family and Inspired a Nation*
    NS - v144 - i5278 - Sept 4 2015 - p40(4) [501+]
Blue Collar Conservatives: Recommitting to an America That Works
    NYRB - v62 - i5 - March 19 2015 - p18(3) [501+]
    Reason - v47 - i4 - August-Sept 2015 - p58(8) [501+]
Santos, Care - *Dissection*
    WLT - v89 - i5 - Sept-Oct 2015 - p73(1) [51-500]
Santos-Febres, Mayra - *Solo cuento VI*
    WLT - v89 - i3-4 - May-August 2015 - p117(3) [501+]
Santos, Marisa de los - *The Precious One*
    BL - v111 - i11 - Feb 1 2015 - p23(2) [51-500]
Sanyal, Bishwapriya - *Planning Ideas That Matter: Livability, Territoriality, Governance, and Reflective Practice*
    J Urban H - v41 - i5 - Sept 2015 - p936-942 [501+]
Sanyal, Debarati - *Memory and Complicity: Migrations of Holocaust Remembrance*
    TimHES - i2215 - August 6 2015 - p46-47 [501+]
Sanzari, Felicia - *Sun Above and Blooms Below: A Springtime of Opposites (Illus. by Swan, Susan)*
    BL - v111 - i14 - March 15 2015 - p80(1) [51-500]
Sapiro, Gisele - *The French Writers' War, 1940-1953*
    TLS - i5835 - Jan 30 2015 - p26(1) [501+]
Saporta, Isabelle - *Vino Business: The Cloudy World of French Wine*
    BL - v112 - i3 - Oct 1 2015 - p14(1) [501+]
    NYTBR - Dec 6 2015 - p86(L) [501+]

Sappenfield, Heather - *Life at the Speed of Us*
  y KR - Oct 15 2015 - pNA [51-500]
  y SLJ - v61 - i11 - Nov 2015 - p121(1) [51-500]
The View from Who I Was
  y BL - v111 - i9-10 - Jan 1 2015 - p100(1) [51-500]
  y VOYA - v37 - i6 - Feb 2015 - p64(1) [51-500]
Sappington, Adam - *Heartlandia: Heritage Recipes from Portland's The Country Cat*
    LJ - v140 - i17 - Oct 15 2015 - p109(1) [51-500]
    PW - v262 - i27 - July 6 2015 - p61(1) [51-500]
Sarah, Linda - *Big Friends (Illus. by Davies, Benji)*
  c BL - v112 - i7 - Dec 1 2015 - p64(1) [51-500]
  c KR - Sept 15 2015 - pNA [51-500]
  c PW - v262 - i41 - Oct 12 2015 - p65(2) [51-500]
Mi and Museum City (Illus. by Sarah, Linda)
  c SLJ - v61 - i2 - Feb 2015 - p78(1) [51-500]
Saramago, Jos - *Skylight*
    NYTBR - Jan 18 2015 - p12(L) [501+]
Sarantis, Alexander Constantine - *War and Warfare in Late Antiquity: Current Perspectives*
    HNet - April 2015 - pNA [501+]
    Class R - v65 - i1 - April 2015 - p240-242 [501+]
Saraswati, L. Ayu - *Seeing Beauty, Sensing Race in Transnational Indonesia*
    Signs - v40 - i3 - Spring 2015 - p781(3) [501+]
Sarat, Austin - *Gruesome Spectacles: Botched Executions and America's Death Penalty*
    HLR - v128 - i5 - March 2015 - p1560(1) [1-50]
Sarat, Leah - *Fire in the Canyon: Religion, Migration, and the Mexican Dream*
    HAHR - v95 - i3 - August 2015 - p546-547 [501+]
Sarcone-Roach, Julia - *The Bear Ate Your Sandwich (Illus. by Sarcone-Roach, Julia)*
  c BL - v111 - i9-10 - Jan 1 2015 - p104(1) [51-500]
  c CCB-B - v68 - i7 - March 2015 - p369(2) [51-500]
  c HB - v91 - i1 - Jan-Feb 2015 - p72(1) [51-500]
  c HB Guide - v26 - i2 - Fall 2015 - p17(1) [51-500]
Sardanis, Andrew - *Zambia: The First 50 Years: Reflections of an Eyewitness*
    TLS - i5840 - March 6 2015 - p25(1) [501+]
Sardar, Zahid - *In and out of Paris: Gardens of Secret Delights*
    NYTBR - May 31 2015 - p36(L) [501+]
Sardar, Ziauddin - *Mecca: The Sacred City*
    Bwatch - Jan 2015 - pNA [51-500]
    TLS - i5852 - May 29 2015 - p30(1) [501+]
Sardesai, Rajdeep - *2014: The Election that Changed India*
    Lon R Bks - v37 - i17 - Sept 10 2015 - p33(2) [501+]
Sardet, Christian - *Plankton: Wonders of the Drifting World*
    LJ - v140 - i11 - June 15 2015 - p110(2) [51-500]
    Nature - v522 - i7555 - June 11 2015 - p155(1) [51-500]
    Spec - v328 - i9743 - May 23 2015 - p34(2) [501+]
Sarfati, Yusuf - *Mobilizing Religion in Middle East Politics: A Comparative Study of Israel and Turkey*
    IJMES - v47 - i1 - Feb 2015 - p212-213 [501+]
Sarfatti, Margherita Grassini - *My Fault: Mussolini as I Knew Him*
    TLS - i5855 - June 19 2015 - p31(1) [501+]
Sargam, Jennie - *Sophie*
    KR - Nov 1 2015 - pNA [501+]
Sarmiento, Kimberly - *How to Write Successful Letters of Recommendation*
    RVBW - Feb 2015 - pNA [51-500]
Sarn, Amelie - *I Love I Hate I Miss My Sister*
  y HB Guide - v26 - i1 - Spring 2015 - p122(1) [51-500]
Sarna, Jonathan D. - *Lincoln and the Jews: A History*
    PW - v262 - i2 - Jan 12 2015 - p50(1) [51-500]
Sarotte, Mary Elise - *The Collapse: The Accidental Opening of the Berlin Wall*
    CEH - v48 - i3 - Sept 2015 - p450-451 [501+]
    HNet - April 2015 - pNA [501+]
    TimHES - i2185 - Jan 8 2015 - p47-47 [501+]
Saroyan, Aram - *Still Night in L.A.*
    BL - v112 - i2 - Sept 15 2015 - p35(1) [51-500]
    LJ - v140 - i16 - Oct 1 2015 - p72(1) [51-500]
    PW - v262 - i32 - August 10 2015 - p40(2) [51-500]
    SPBW - Nov 2015 - pNA [51-500]
Sarreal, Julia - *The Guarani and Their Missions: A Socioeconomic History*
    AHR - v120 - i3 - June 2015 - p1077(1) [501+]
    HAHR - v95 - i3 - August 2015 - p524-526 [501+]
Sarris, Greg - *Grand Avenue*
    WLT - v89 - i6 - Nov-Dec 2015 - p77(1) [51-500]

Sartori, Andrew - *Liberalism in Empire: An Alternative History*
    JAS - v74 - i3 - August 2015 - p711-722 [501+]
Sartorius, David - *Ever Faithful: Race, Loyalty, and the Ends of Empire in Spanish Cuba*
    AHR - v120 - i2 - April 2015 - p676-677 [501+]
    Ams - v72 - i2 - April 2015 - p333(2) [501+]
Sartorius, Joachim - *The Geckos of Bellapais: Memories of Cyprus*
    TLS - i5843 - March 27 2015 - p31(1) [501+]
SarvenazTash - *Three Day Summer*
    PW - v262 - i14 - April 6 2015 - p61(2) [51-500]
Sarzin, Lisa Miranda - *Stories for Simon (Illus. by Briggs, Lauren)*
    Magpies - v30 - i3 - July 2015 - p30(1) [51-500]
Sasaki, S.E. - *Welcome to the Madhouse*
    KR - August 15 2015 - pNA [501+]
Sasek, Miroslav - *This Is the World: A Global Treasury*
  c HB Guide - v26 - i1 - Spring 2015 - p200(1) [51-500]
Sassaman, Kenneth E. - *Hunter-Gatherer Archaeology as Historical Process*
    Am Ant - v80 - i4 - Oct 2015 - p789(1) [501+]
Sassen, Saskia - *Expulsions: Brutality and Complexity in the Global Economy*
    Bks & Cult - v21 - i3 - May-June 2015 - p28(2) [501+]
Territory, Authority, Rights: From Medieval to Global Assemblages
    TimHES - i2211 - July 9 2015 - p46(1) [501+]
Sassi, Laura - *Goodnight, Ark (Illus. by Chapman, Jane)*
  c HB Guide - v26 - i1 - Spring 2015 - p16(1) [51-500]
Sasso, Sandy Eisenberg - *Anne Frank and the Remembering Tree (Illus. by Steiskal, Erika)*
  c PW - v262 - i3 - Jan 19 2015 - p86(1) [51-500]
Jewish Stories of Love and Marriage: Folktales, Legends, and Letters
    BL - v111 - i22 - August 1 2015 - p6(1) [51-500]
Sasson, Diane - *Yearning for the New Age: Laura Holloway-Langford and Late Victorian Spirituality*
    Am St - v54 - i1 - Spring 2015 - p133-2 [501+]
Sasson, Theodore - *The New American Zionism*
    HNet - Feb 2015 - pNA [501+]
Satie, Erik - *A Mammal's Notebook: The Writings of Erik Satie*
    Lon R Bks - v37 - i11 - June 4 2015 - p26(3) [501+]
Satlow, Michael L. - *How the Bible Became Holy*
    CH - v84 - i4 - Dec 2015 - p863(1) [51-500]
Satsuma, Shinsuke - *Britain and Colonial Maritime War in the Early Eighteenth Century: Silver, Seapower and the Atlantic*
    HNet - April 2015 - pNA [501+]
Satterfield, Steven - *Root to Leaf: A Southern Chef Cooks through the Seasons*
    CSM - March 13 2015 - pNA [501+]
    NYT - April 1 2015 - pD1(L) [501+]
    NYTBR - May 31 2015 - p24(L) [501+]
Satterlee, Thom - *The Stages*
    KR - August 1 2015 - pNA [501+]
Sattersby, Lauren - *Rock 'n' Soul*
    PW - v262 - i46 - Nov 16 2015 - p61(2) [51-500]
Sattin, Anthony - *Young Lawrence: A Portrait of the Legend as a Young Man*
    TLS - i5846 - April 17 2015 - p23(1) [501+]
The Young T.E. Lawrence
    Comw - v142 - i9 - May 15 2015 - p26(3) [501+]
    Econ - v414 - i8925 - Feb 14 2015 - p75(US) [501+]
Sattler, Jennifer - *A Chick 'n' Pug Christmas (Illus. by Sattler, Jennifer)*
  c HB Guide - v26 - i1 - Spring 2015 - p44(1) [51-500]
Chick 'n' Pug: The Love Pug (Illus. by Sattler, Jennifer)
  c KR - Oct 1 2015 - pNA [51-500]
  c PW - v262 - i41 - Oct 12 2015 - p66(2) [51-500]
  c SLJ - v61 - i8 - August 2015 - p76(1) [51-500]
Pig Kahuna: Who's That Pig? (Illus. by Sattler, Jennifer)
  c HB Guide - v26 - i2 - Fall 2015 - p50(1) [51-500]
  c SLJ - v61 - i5 - May 2015 - p91(2) [51-500]
Sattouf, Riad - *The Arab of the Future: A Childhood in the Middle East, 1978-1984*
    BL - v112 - i2 - Sept 15 2015 - p50(1) [51-500]
The Arab of the Future: A Childhood in the Middle East 1978-1984
    KR - July 15 2015 - pNA [51-500]
The Arab of the Future: A Graphic Memoir: A Childhood in the Middle East (1978-1984)
    LJ - v140 - i15 - Sept 15 2015 - p60(3) [501+]
    NYTBR - Oct 18 2015 - p9(L) [501+]
    PW - v262 - i28 - July 13 2015 - p53(1) [501+]

Satyamurti, Carole - *Mahabharata: A Modern Retelling*
    NS - v144 - i5261 - May 7 2015 - p51(1) [501+]
Saucier, Aldric J. - *Dirtbag*
    KR - June 1 2015 - pNA [501+]
Saucier, C.A.P. - *Explore the Cosmos Like Neil deGrasse Tyson: A Space Science Journey*
  y BL - v112 - i12 - Feb 15 2015 - p70(1) [51-500]
  c HB Guide - v26 - i2 - Fall 2015 - p165(1) [51-500]
Saucier, Catherine - *A Paradise of Priests: Singing the Civic and Episcopal Hagiography of Medieval Liege*
    CHR - v101 - i3 - Summer 2015 - p607(3) [501+]
Sauer, Elizabeth - *Milton, Toleration, and Nationhood*
    RES - v66 - i274 - April 2015 - p380-382 [501+]
Sauer, Tammi - *Ginny Louise and the School Showdown (Illus. by Munsinger, Lynn)*
  c CCB-B - v69 - i1 - Sept 2015 - p51(1) [51-500]
  c HB Guide - v26 - i2 - Fall 2015 - p50(1) [51-500]
  c KR - June 1 2015 - pNA [51-500]
  c SLJ - v61 - i8 - August 2015 - p61(1) [51-500]
Roar! (Illus. by Starin, Liz)
  c KR - July 15 2015 - pNA [51-500]
  c SLJ - v61 - i10 - Oct 2015 - p84(1) [51-500]
Your Alien (Illus. by Fujita, Goro)
  c KR - July 1 2015 - pNA [51-500]
  c PW - v262 - i21 - May 25 2015 - p57(1) [51-500]
  c PW - v262 - i49 - Dec 2 2015 - p19(1) [51-500]
  c SLJ - v61 - i8 - August 2015 - p76(1) [51-500]
Sauerlander, Willibald - *The Catholic Rubens: Saints and Martyrs*
    Comw - v142 - i2 - Jan 23 2015 - p24(3) [501+]
    Ren Q - v68 - i2 - Summer 2015 - p638-641 [501+]
    Theol St - v76 - i1 - March 2015 - p198(3) [501+]
Manet Paints Monet: A Summer in Argenteuil
    NYRB - v62 - i7 - April 23 2015 - p54(2) [501+]
Sauerwein, Leigh - *River Music*
  y HB Guide - v26 - i1 - Spring 2015 - p122(1) [51-500]
Saul, Scott - *Becoming Richard Pryor*
    BL - v111 - i11 - Feb 1 2015 - p16(1) [501+]
    BL - v111 - i19-20 - June 1 2015 - p30(2) [51-500]
    NW - v164 - i3 - Jan 23 2015 - pNA [501+]
Saulnier, Natasha - *Hot Dogs & Croissants*
    PW - v262 - i2 - Jan 12 2015 - p54(1) [51-500]
Saulsbury, Camilla V. - *The Chickpea Flour Cookbook: Healthy Gluten-Free and GrainFree Recipes to Power Every Meal of the Day*
    LJ - v140 - i13 - August 1 2015 - p121(1) [51-500]
Power Hungry: The Ultimate Energy Bar Cookbook
    Bwatch - May 2015 - pNA [51-500]
Saumande, Juliette - *Chop-Chop, Mad Cap! (Illus. by Cramer, Sadie)*
  c SLJ - v61 - i7 - July 2015 - p72(1) [51-500]
Saunders, Anna - *Remembering and Rethinking the GDR: Multiple Perspectives and Plural Authenticities*
    MLR - v110 - i1 - Jan 2015 - p297-298 [501+]
Saunders, Jennifer - *Bonkers: My Life in Laughs*
    LJ - v140 - i16 - Oct 1 2015 - p84(1) [51-500]
Saunders, Kate - *The Curse of the Chocolate Phoenix*
  c KR - Oct 1 2015 - pNA [51-500]
  c SLJ - v61 - i11 - Nov 2015 - p102(2) [51-500]
Five Children on the Western Front
  c Magpies - v30 - i1 - March 2015 - p14(2) [501+]
  c Sch Lib - v63 - i1 - Spring 2015 - p42(1) [51-500]
Saunders, Katie - *The Big Book of Christmas (Illus. by Saunders, Katie)*
  c PW - v262 - i37 - Sept 14 2015 - p72(2) [501+]
  c SLJ - v61 - i10 - Oct 2015 - p68(1) [51-500]
Olive Marshmallow
  c KR - Jan 15 2015 - pNA [51-500]
    PW - v262 - i2 - Jan 12 2015 - p56(1) [51-500]
Saunders, Laura - *Repositioning Reference: New Methods and New Services for a New Age*
    LJ - v140 - i5 - March 15 2015 - p119(1) [51-500]
Saunders, Richard L. - *Dale Morgan on the Mormons: Collected Works, Part 2, 1949-1970*
    Roundup M - v22 - i6 - August 2015 - p40(1) [501+]
Saunt, Claudio - *West of the Revolution: An Uncommon History of 1776*
    Historian - v77 - i3 - Fall 2015 - p582(2) [501+]
Saurer, Edith - *Liebe und Arbeit: Geschlechterbeziehungen im 19. und 20. Jahrhundert*
    HNet - Feb 2015 - pNA [501+]
Sautter, Aaron - *How to Draw Batman and His Friends and Foes (Illus. by Doescher, Erik)*
  c HB Guide - v26 - i2 - Fall 2015 - p193(1) [51-500]
How to Draw Superman and His Friends and Foes (Illus. by Doescher, Erik)
  c HB Guide - v26 - i2 - Fall 2015 - p193(1) [51-500]
How to Draw Wonder Woman, Green Lantern, and Other DC Super Heroes (Illus. by Levin, Tim)
  c Sch Lib - v63 - i3 - Autumn 2015 - p176(1) [51-500]

Sauvage, Jeanne - *Gluten-Free Wish List: Sweet and Savory Treats You've Missed the Mos*
    LJ - v140 - i19 - Nov 15 2015 - p101(1) [51-500]
Savage, Charlie - *Power Wars: Inside Obama's Post-9/11 Presidency*
    NYT - Oct 30 2015 - pC23(L) [501+]
    NYTBR - Dec 20 2015 - p16(L) [501+]
Savage, J. Scott - *Evil Twins*
  c HB Guide - v26 - i2 - Fall 2015 - p100(1) [51-500]
Fires of Invention
  c BL - v111 - i22 - August 1 2015 - p67(1) [51-500]
  c PW - v262 - i25 - June 22 2015 - p140(1) [51-500]
  c PW - v262 - i49 - Dec 2 2015 - p66(1) [51-500]
  c SLJ - v61 - i8 - August 2015 - p91(2) [51-500]
Savage, Jeff - *Super Basketball Infographics (Illus. by Schuster, Rob)*
  c HB Guide - v26 - i2 - Fall 2015 - p197(1) [51-500]
Super Hockey Infographics (Illus. by Kulihin, Vic)
  c HB Guide - v26 - i2 - Fall 2015 - p197(1) [51-500]
Savage, Jon - *1966: The Year the Decade Exploded*
    Spec - v329 - i9770 - Nov 28 2015 - p44(2) [501+]
Savage, Kim - *After the Woods*
  y KR - Nov 1 2015 - pNA [51-500]
  y SLJ - v61 - i12 - Dec 2015 - p128(1) [51-500]
Savage, Michael - *Countdown to Mecca*
    PW - v262 - i11 - March 16 2015 - p64(2) [51-500]
Identities and Social Change in Britain since 1940: The Politics of Method
    CS - v44 - i3 - May 2015 - p305-314 [501+]
Savage, Mike - *Social Class in the 21st Century*
    TimHES - i2229 - Nov 12 2015 - p50(1) [501+]
Savage, Polly - *Making Art in Africa, 1960-2010*
    HNet - July 2015 - pNA [501+]
Savage, Sam - *It Will End with Us*
    NYTBR - Jan 11 2015 - p18(L) [501+]
    PSQ - v89 - i3 - Fall 2015 - p165(3) [501+]
Savage, Stephen - *Little Tug (Illus. by Savage, Stephen)*
  c HB Guide - v26 - i2 - Fall 2015 - p17(1) [51-500]
  c SLJ - v61 - i7 - July 2015 - p57(2) [51-500]
Seven Orange Pumpkins (Illus. by Savage, Stephen)
  c KR - Jan 1 2016 - pNA [51-500]
  c SLJ - v61 - i9 - Sept 2015 - p109(2) [51-500]
Supertruck (Illus. by Savage, Stephen)
  c HB - v91 - i1 - Jan-Feb 2015 - p72(2) [501+]
  c HB Guide - v26 - i2 - Fall 2015 - p17(2) [51-500]
  c PW - v262 - i49 - Dec 2 2015 - p18(1) [51-500]
Where's Walrus? And Penguin? (Illus. by Savage, Stephen)
  c BL - v111 - i21 - July 1 2015 - p65(1) [51-500]
  c CCB-B - v69 - i2 - Oct 2015 - p110(1) [51-500]
  c HB - v91 - i5 - Sept-Oct 2015 - p87(1) [51-500]
  c KR - May 15 2015 - pNA [51-500]
  c PW - v262 - i49 - Dec 2 2015 - p19(1) [51-500]
  c SLJ - v61 - i6 - June 2015 - p93(2) [51-500]
Saval, Nikil - *Cubed: A Secret History of the Workplace*
    NYTBR - Jan 4 2015 - p24(L) [501+]
Savery, Annabel - *Brazil*
  c HB Guide - v26 - i1 - Spring 2015 - p205(1) [51-500]
Ukraine
  c HB Guide - v26 - i1 - Spring 2015 - p202(1) [51-500]
Saveur editors - *Saveur: The New Classics Cookbook*
    Bwatch - March 2015 - pNA [51-500]
Saveur: The New Classics Cookbook
    Ent W - i1346 - Jan 16 2015 - p67(1) [501+]
Saviano, Roberto - *ZeroZeroZero*
    BL - v111 - i21 - July 1 2015 - p11(1) [51-500]
    Bus W - i4436 - July 27 2015 - p71(1) [501+]
    Econ - v415 - i8944 - June 27 2015 - p72(US) [501+]
    KR - May 15 2015 - pNA [51-500]
    LJ - v140 - i12 - July 1 2015 - p97(1) [51-500]
    PW - v262 - i20 - May 18 2015 - p78(2) [51-500]
    Spec - v328 - i9751 - July 18 2015 - p39(1) [501+]
    NYTBR - July 26 2015 - p10(L) [501+]
Savignon, Jeromine - *Yves Saint Laurent's Studio: Mirror and Secrets*
    RVBW - May 2015 - pNA [51-500]
Savile, Steven - *Sunfail*
    BL - v112 - i4 - Oct 15 2015 - p28(1) [51-500]
    KR - Sept 1 2015 - pNA [51-500]
    PW - v262 - i39 - Sept 28 2015 - p71(2) [51-500]
Saville, Guy - *The Madagaskar Plan*
    BL - v111 - i18 - May 15 2015 - p38(1) [51-500]
    KR - June 1 2015 - pNA [501+]
    PW - v262 - i15 - April 13 2015 - p41(1) [51-500]
Savin, Barbara E. - *Gentle Energy Touch: The Beginner's Guide to Hands-on Healing*
    PW - v262 - i51 - Dec 14 2015 - p75(2) [51-500]

Savit, Gavriel - *Anna and the Swallow Man*
  y KR - Nov 15 2015 - pNA [51-500]
  y PW - v262 - i44 - Nov 2 2015 - p86(1) [51-500]
  y SLJ - v61 - i12 - Dec 2015 - p128(1) [51-500]
Savoy, Lauret - *Trace: Memory, History, Race, and the American Landscape*
    BL - v112 - i4 - Oct 15 2015 - p15(1) [51-500]
    KR - Oct 1 2015 - pNA [51-500]
    LJ - v140 - i12 - July 1 2015 - p108(2) [51-500]
Sawaya, Francesca - *The Difficult Art Of Giving: Patronage, Philanthropy, and the American Literary Market*
    Am St - v54 - i2 - Summer 2015 - p134-135 [501+]
    JAH - v102 - i2 - Sept 2015 - p572-572 [501+]
Sawchik, Travis - *Big Data Baseball: Math, Miracles, and the End of a 20-year Losing Streak*
  y BL - v111 - i17 - May 1 2015 - p70(1) [51-500]
    KR - April 15 2015 - pNA [51-500]
    LJ - v140 - i11 - June 15 2015 - p93(1) [51-500]
    PW - v262 - i15 - April 13 2015 - p72(2) [51-500]
Sawhill, Isabell - *Generation Unbound: Drifting into Sex and Parenthood without Marriage*
    TimHES - i2228 - Nov 5 2015 - p46(1) [501+]
Sawyer-Aitch, Anne - *Nalah Goes to Mad Mouse City*
    KR - June 1 2015 - pNA [501+]
Sawyer, Annita Perez - *Smoking Cigarettes, Eating Glass: A Psychologist's Memoir*
    LJ - v140 - i6 - April 1 2015 - p104(2) [501+]
Sawyer, Cheryl - *Murder at Cirey*
    KR - April 15 2015 - pNA [51-500]
Sawyer, Dana - *Huston Smith: Wisdomkeeper Living the World's Religions: The Authorized Biography of a 21st Century Siritual Giant*
    Parabola - v40 - i1 - Spring 2015 - p115-122 [501+]
Sax, Leonard - *The Collapse of Parenting: How We Hurt Our Kids When We Treat Them like Grown-Ups*
    BL - v112 - i6 - Nov 15 2015 - p7(1) [51-500]
    KR - Oct 15 2015 - pNA [51-500]
    PW - v262 - i42 - Oct 19 2015 - p72(1) [51-500]
Saxby, Claire - *Big Red Kangaroo (Illus. by Byrne, Graham)*
  c CCB-B - v68 - i7 - March 2015 - p370(1) [51-500]
  c HB - v91 - i2 - March-April 2015 - p124(2) [51-500]
  c HB Guide - v26 - i2 - Fall 2015 - p181(1) [51-500]
Christmas at Grandma's Beach House (Illus. by Dawson, Janine)
    Magpies - v30 - i5 - Nov 2015 - p29(1) [501+]
Emu (Illus. by Byrne, Graham)
  c BL - v111 - i18 - May 15 2015 - p48(1) [51-500]
  c CH Bwatch - June 2015 - pNA [501+]
  c HB - v91 - i4 - July-August 2015 - p162(1) [51-500]
  c SLJ - v61 - i5 - May 2015 - p136(1) [51-500]
Meet Weary Dunlop (Illus. by Lord, Jeremy)
  c Magpies - v30 - i2 - May 2015 - p23(2) [51-500]
My Name is Lizzie Flynn: A Story of the Rajah Quilt (Illus. by Newcomb, Lizzy)
    Magpies - v30 - i2 - May 2015 - p31(2) [51-500]
Saxelby, Pam - *Max and Bear (Illus. by Adams, Stephen)*
  c CH Bwatch - Jan 2015 - pNA [51-500]
Saxer, Daniela - *Die Scharfung des Quellenblicks: Forschungspraktiken in der Geschichtswissenschaft 1840-1914*
    HNet - July 2015 - pNA [501+]
Saxifrage, Carrie - *The Big Swim: Coming Ashore in a World Adrift*
    KR - Feb 15 2015 - pNA [501+]
    Nat Post - v17 - i130 - April 4 2015 - pWP4(1) [501+]
Saxonberg, Steven - *Transitions and Non-Transitions from Communism: Regime Survival in China, Cuba, North Korea, and Vietnam*
    Pac A - v88 - i1 - March 2015 - p159 [501+]
Say, Allen - *The Inker's Shadow (Illus. by Say, Allen)*
  y BL - v112 - i2 - Sept 15 2015 - p54(1) [51-500]
  c KR - August 15 2015 - pNA [51-500]
  c SLJ - v61 - i11 - Nov 2015 - p138(2) [51-500]
  c HB - v91 - i6 - Nov-Dec 2015 - p107(1) [51-500]
  y PW - v262 - i49 - Dec 2 2015 - p117(1) [51-500]
Sayeed, Asma - *Women and the Transmission of Religious Knowledge in Islam*
    JNES - v74 - i1 - April 2015 - p172(3) [501+]
Sayen, Michael S. - *The Cure for Divorce: In the Kingdom of God*
    SPBW - Oct 2015 - pNA [51-500]
Sayer, Andrew - *Why We Can't Afford the Rich*
    PW - v262 - i6 - Feb 9 2015 - p59(1) [51-500]
    TLS - i5869 - Sept 25 2015 - p4(2) [51-500]

Sayer, Derek - *Prague, Capital of the Twentieth Century: A Surrealist History*
    HNet - March 2015 - pNA [501+]
Sayers, William - *Eatymologies: Historical Notes on Culinary Terms*
    TLS - i5860 - July 24 2015 - p3(2) [51-500]
Saylor, Steven - *Wrath of the Furies*
    BL - v112 - i2 - Sept 15 2015 - p35(2) [51-500]
    KR - August 15 2015 - pNA [51-500]
    PW - v262 - i32 - August 10 2015 - p36(1) [51-500]
Sayman, Arslan - *Piraye'nin Bir Gunu (Illus. by Ucbasaran, Deniz)*
  c Bkbird - v53 - i1 - Wntr 2015 - p62(1) [501+]
Sayner, Joanne - *Reframing Antifascism: Memory, Genre and the Life Writings of Greta Kuckhoff*
    MLR - v110 - i2 - April 2015 - p601-602 [501+]
Sayre, April Pulley - *Raindrops Roll*
  c HB Guide - v26 - i2 - Fall 2015 - p167(2) [51-500]
  c PW - v262 - i49 - Dec 2 2015 - p50(2) [51-500]
Woodpecker Wham! (Illus. by Jenkins, Steve)
  c HB Guide - v26 - i2 - Fall 2015 - p178(1) [51-500]
  c BL - v111 - i15 - April 1 2015 - p38(1) [51-500]
  c HB - v91 - i3 - May-June 2015 - p131(1) [51-500]
  c KR - Feb 15 2015 - pNA [51-500]
  c PW - v262 - i20 - May 18 2015 - p85(1) [501+]
  c SLJ - v61 - i3 - March 2015 - p173(2) [51-500]
Sayre, Justin - *Husky (Read by Sayre, Justin). Audiobook Review*
  c SLJ - v61 - i11 - Nov 2015 - p71(1) [51-500]
Husky
  c BL - v111 - i22 - August 1 2015 - p67(2) [51-500]
  c KR - May 15 2015 - pNA [51-500]
  c PW - v262 - i23 - June 8 2015 - p61(1) [51-500]
  c SLJ - v61 - i8 - August 2015 - p92(1) [51-500]
  y VOYA - v38 - i4 - Oct 2015 - p61(1) [51-500]
Sayre, Kenneth M. - *Adventures in Philosophy at Notre Dame*
    CHR - v101 - i1 - Wntr 2015 - p182(2) [501+]
Sayres, Brianna Caplan - *Tiara Saurus Rex (Illus. by Boldt, Mike)*
  c HB Guide - v26 - i2 - Fall 2015 - p51(1) [51-500]
Sberlati, Francesco - *Filologia e identita nazionale: una tradizione per l'Italia unita*
    MLR - v110 - i1 - Jan 2015 - p266-268 [501+]
Scala, Elizabeth - *Desire in the Canterbury Tales*
    TimHES - i2209 - June 25 2015 - p48-49 [501+]
Scales, Helen - *Spirals in Time: The Secret Life and Curious Afterlife of Seashells*
    BL - v111 - i19-20 - June 1 2015 - p16(1) [51-500]
    Econ - v416 - i8947 - July 18 2015 - p71(US) [501+]
    KR - May 15 2015 - pNA [501+]
    LJ - v140 - i10 - June 1 2015 - p131(2) [51-500]
    Nature - v522 - i7544 - June 4 2015 - p33(1) [51-500]
    PW - v262 - i21 - May 25 2015 - p51(1) [51-500]
    Spec - v328 - i9743 - May 23 2015 - p34(2) [501+]
    TLS - i5861 - July 31 2015 - p13(1) [51-500]
Scales, Pat R. - *Books under Fire: A Hit List of Banned and Challenged Children's Books*
    BL - v111 - i13 - March 1 2015 - p50(1) [51-500]
    SLJ - v61 - i2 - Feb 2015 - p131(1) [51-500]
    VOYA - v37 - i6 - Feb 2015 - p92(1) [51-500]
Scales on Censorship: Real Life Lessons from School Library Journal
    Sch Lib - v63 - i3 - Autumn 2015 - p191(1) [51-500]
    VOYA - v38 - i3 - August 2015 - p93(1) [501+]
Scalzi, John - *The End of All Things*
    PW - v262 - i27 - July 6 2015 - p50(1) [51-500]
    KR - June 1 2015 - pNA [51-500]
Lock In
    BL - v111 - i18 - May 15 2015 - p34(1) [51-500]
    LJ - v140 - i19 - Nov 15 2015 - p110(1) [51-500]
Scandlyn, Jean - *Beyond Post-traumatic Stress: Homefront Struggles with the Wars on Terror*
    MAQ - v29 - i3 - Sept 2015 - pb-30-b-33 [501+]
Scanlon, Liz Garton - *All the World (Illus. by Frazee, Marla)*
  c SLJ - v61 - i7 - July 2015 - p57(1) [51-500]
The Great Good Summer
  c BL - v111 - i15 - April 1 2015 - p80(1) [51-500]
  c CCB-B - v69 - i1 - Sept 2015 - p51(1) [51-500]
  y HB - v91 - i3 - May-June 2015 - p117(1) [501+]
  c HB Guide - v26 - i2 - Fall 2015 - p100(1) [51-500]
  c KR - Feb 15 2015 - pNA [51-500]
  c PW - v262 - i49 - Dec 2 2015 - p70(2) [51-500]
  c SLJ - v61 - i2 - Feb 2015 - p93(2) [51-500]
  y VOYA - v38 - i1 - April 2015 - p69(1) [51-500]
In the Canyon (Illus. by Wolff, Ashley)
  c KR - June 15 2015 - pNA [51-500]
  c PW - v262 - i22 - June 1 2015 - p59(1) [51-500]
  c SLJ - v61 - i7 - July 2015 - p68(1) [51-500]

Scanlon, Sandra - *The Pro-War Movement: Domestic Support for the Vietnam War and the Making of Modern American Conservatism*
    PHR - v84 - i2 - May 2015 - p244(3) [501+]
Scanlon, Shya - *The Guild of Saint Cooper*
    KR - March 15 2015 - pNA [501+]
Scanlon, T.M. - *Being Realistic about Reasons*
    Ethics - v125 - i4 - July 2015 - p1225(6) [501+]
The Scar (Illus. by Tallec, Olivier)
    c BL - v112 - i6 - Nov 15 2015 - p48(1) [501+]
Scarantino, James R. - *The Drum Within*
    KR - Nov 15 2015 - pNA [51-500]
Scaravella, Jody - *Nonna's House: Cooking and Reminiscing with the Italian Grandmothers of Enoteca Maria*
    PW - v262 - i11 - March 16 2015 - p79(1) [51-500]
Scardamalia, Robert L. - *Aging in America*
    BL - v111 - i9-10 - Jan 1 2015 - p28(1) [51-500]
Scarry, Richard - *Best Lowly Worm Book Ever! (Illus. by Scarry, Richard)*
    c HB Guide - v26 - i1 - Spring 2015 - p16(1) [51-500]
Just Right Word Book (Illus. by Scarry, Richard)
    c SLJ - v61 - i7 - July 2015 - p56(1) [51-500]
Scattergood, Augusta - *The Way to Stay in Destiny (Read by Crouch, Michael). Audiobook Review*
    c BL - v111 - i21 - July 1 2015 - p80(1) [501+]
    c SLJ - v61 - i5 - May 2015 - p70(1) [51-500]
The Way to Stay in Destiny
    c CCB-B - v68 - i7 - March 2015 - p370(2) [51-500]
    c HB Guide - v26 - i2 - Fall 2015 - p100(1) [51-500]
Scattergood, John - *John Skelton: The Career of an Early Tudor Poet*
    Specu - v90 - i3 - July 2015 - p848-2 [501+]
Scelsa, Kate - *Fans of the Impossible Life*
    y BL - v111 - i22 - August 1 2015 - p55(2) [51-500]
    y KR - July 15 2015 - pNA [51-500]
    y PW - v262 - i26 - June 29 2015 - p70(1) [51-500]
    y PW - v262 - i49 - Dec 2 2015 - p90(2) [51-500]
    y SLJ - v61 - i8 - August 2015 - p110(1) [51-500]
    y VOYA - v38 - i3 - August 2015 - p68(1) [51-500]
Scerri, Eric - *A Tale of Seven Elements*
    Isis - v106 - i1 - March 2015 - p212(2) [51-500]
Schaad, Martin - *Dann Geh Doch Ruber - Uber die Mauer in den Osten*
    HNet - March 2015 - pNA [501+]
Die fabelhaften Bekenntnisse des Genossen Alfred Kurelia: Eine biografische Spurensuche
    Ger Q - v88 - i2 - Spring 2015 - p253(2) [501+]
Schaapman, Karina - *The Mouse Mansion*
    c CH Bwatch - Jan 2015 - pNA [51-500]
    c HB Guide - v26 - i1 - Spring 2015 - p44(1) [51-500]
Schaberg, Christopher - *The End of Airports*
    LJ - v140 - i17 - Oct 15 2015 - p110(1) [51-500]
    PW - v262 - i37 - Sept 14 2015 - p56(2) [51-500]
Schachner, Judy - *Dewey Bob (Illus. by Schachner, Judy)*
    c CH Bwatch - Oct 2015 - pNA [51-500]
    c KR - August 15 2015 - pNA [51-500]
    c PW - v262 - i24 - June 15 2015 - p81(1) [51-500]
    c SLJ - v61 - i10 - Oct 2015 - p84(1) [51-500]
Schachter, Esty - *Waiting for a Sign*
    y PW - v262 - i10 - March 9 2015 - p74(1) [51-500]
Schacker, Jennifer - *Feathers, Paws, Fins and Claws: Fairy-Tale Beasts (Illus. by Kusaite, Lina)*
    CCB-B - v69 - i2 - Oct 2015 - p122(1) [51-500]
    c KR - July 1 2015 - pNA [51-500]
    c PW - v262 - i35 - August 31 2015 - p93(1) [501+]
Schade, Susan - *Riff Raff Sails the High Cheese (Illus. by Kennedy, Anne)*
    c HB Guide - v26 - i2 - Fall 2015 - p61(1) [51-500]
Schade, Victoria - *Secrets of a Dog Trainer*
    Bwatch - March 2015 - pNA [51-500]
Schadlich, Megan E. - *Cooking Up Library Programs Teens and Tweens Will Love: Recipes for Success*
    Teach Lib - v43 - i1 - Oct 2015 - p41(3) [501+]
Schaefer, Carole Lexa - *Monkey and Elephant and a Secret Birthday Surprise (Illus. by Bernstein, Galia)*
    c HB Guide - v26 - i1 - Spring 2015 - p61(1) [51-500]
    c SLJ - v61 - i8 - August 2015 - p79(1) [51-500]
Schaefer, Lola M. - *Run for Your Life! Predators and Prey on the African Savanna (Illus. by Meisel, Paul)*
    c KR - Dec 15 2015 - pNA [51-500]
    PW - v262 - i45 - Nov 9 2015 - p58(2) [51-500]
Schaefer, Mary M. - *Women in Pastoral Office: The Story of Santa Prassede, Rome*
    Bks & Cult - v21 - i1 - Jan-Feb 2015 - p21(2) [501+]
    CH - v84 - i2 - June 2015 - p428(3) [501+]

Schaefer Riley, Naomi - *'Til Faith Do Us Part: How Interfaith Marriage Is Transforming America*
    JR - Jan 2015 - p152(2) [501+]
Schaefer, Sagi - *States of Division: Border and Boundary Formation in Cold War Rural Germany*
    HNet - June 2015 - pNA [501+]
Schaeffer, John - *Solar Living Sourcebook, 14th ed.*
    Bwatch - Feb 2015 - pNA [51-500]
Schaeffer, Merlin - *Ethnic Diversity and Social Cohesion: Immigration, Ethnic Fractionalization and Potentials for Civic Action*
    CS - v44 - i5 - Sept 2015 - p704-706 [501+]
    ERS - v38 - i8 - August 2015 - p1466(3) [501+]
Schaepdrijver, Sophie de - *Gabrielle Petit: The Death and Life of a Female Spy in the First World War*
    HT - v65 - i5 - May 2015 - p64(1) [501+]
    TimHES - i2204 - May 21 2015 - p50(1) [501+]
    TLS - i5844 - April 3 2015 - p26(1) [501+]
Schafer, Jack - *The Like Switch: An Ex-FBI Agent's Guide to Influencing, Attracting, and Winning People Over*
    BL - v111 - i12 - Feb 15 2015 - p4(1) [51-500]
Schafer, James A., Jr. - *The Business of Private Medical Practice: Doctors, Specialization, and Urban Change in Philadelphia, 1900-1940*
    JAH - v101 - i4 - March 2015 - p1295-1296 [501+]
Schallmann, Jurgen - *Arme und Armut in Gottingen 1860-1914*
    HNet - Feb 2015 - pNA [501+]
Schama, Simon - *The Face of Britain: The Nation through its Portraits*
    NS - v144 - i5283 - Oct 9 2015 - p44(3) [501+]
Rembrandt's Eyes
    NYTBR - Feb 22 2015 - p32(L) [501+]
Schanoes, Veronica - *Fairy Tales, Myth, and Psychoanalytical Theory: Feminism and Retelling the Tale*
    Bkbird - v53 - i2 - Spring 2015 - p80(2) [501+]
Schantz, Sarah Elizabeth - *Fig*
    y BL - v111 - i15 - April 1 2015 - p65(1) [51-500]
    y HB - v91 - i2 - March-April 2015 - p108(2) [51-500]
    y HB Guide - v26 - i2 - Fall 2015 - p137(1) [51-500]
    y PW - v262 - i9 - March 2 2015 - p87(1) [51-500]
    y PW - v262 - i49 - Dec 2 2015 - p91(1) [51-500]
    y VOYA - v38 - i1 - April 2015 - p69(1) [51-500]
Schaper, Donna - *Approaching the End of Life: A Practical and Spiritual Life*
    BL - v111 - i19-20 - June 1 2015 - p6(1) [51-500]
Schapiro, Ilyse - *Should I Scoop Out My Bagel? And 99 Other Answers to Your Everyday Diet and Nutrition Questions to Help You Lose Weight, Feel Great, and Live Healthy*
    PW - v262 - i52 - Dec 21 2015 - p148(2) [51-500]
Scharer, Anton - *Changing Perspectives on England and the Continent in the Early Middle Ages*
    Specu - v90 - i4 - Oct 2015 - p1165-1166 [501+]
Scharff, Virginia - *Empire and Liberty: The Civil War and the West*
    PW - v262 - i8 - Feb 23 2015 - p65(2) [501+]
Scharnhorst, Gary - *Owen Wester and the West*
    Roundup M - v23 - i1 - Oct 2015 - p35(1) [501+]
Scharr, Kurt - *Schaufeln - Schubkarren - Stacheldraht: Peter Demant - Erinnerungen eines Osterreichers an Zwangsarbeitslager und Verbannung in der Sowjetunion*
    HNet - Feb 2015 - pNA [501+]
Scharrer, Jos - *The Journalist*
    KR - Feb 15 2015 - pNA [51-500]
Schat, Karel A. - *Avian Immunology*
    QRB - v90 - i3 - Sept 2015 - p350(2) [501+]
Schatell, Brian - *Owl Boy (Illus. by Schatell, Brian)*
    c BL - v111 - i19-20 - June 1 2015 - p124(1) [51-500]
    c HB Guide - v26 - i2 - Fall 2015 - p51(1) [51-500]
    c KR - Feb 1 2015 - pNA [51-500]
Schatz, Howard - *Schatz Images: 25 Years*
    PW - v262 - i15 - April 13 2015 - p71(2) [51-500]
Schatz, Kate - *Rad American Women A-Z: Rebels, Trailblazers, and Visionaries who Shaped Our History ... and Our Future! (Illus. by Stahl, Miriam Klein)*
    c HB Guide - v26 - i2 - Fall 2015 - p213(1) [51-500]
    y KR - Feb 15 2015 - pNA [51-500]
    c PW - v262 - i4 - Jan 26 2015 - p175(1) [51-500]
Schatz, Klaus - *Geschichte der deutschen Jesuiten, 5 vols.*
    HNet - May 2015 - pNA [501+]
Schatzker, Mark - *The Dorito Effect*
    KR - April 1 2015 - pNA [501+]

The Dorito Effect: The Surprising New Truth about Food and Flavor (Read by Patton, Chris). Audiobook Review
    y BL - v112 - i3 - Oct 1 2015 - p87(1) [501+]
The Dorito Effect: The Surprising New Truth about Food and Flavor
    BL - v111 - i17 - May 1 2015 - p69(1) [51-500]
    LJ - v140 - i8 - May 1 2015 - p95(2) [51-500]
    Nat Post - v17 - i153 - May 2 2015 - pWP4(1) [501+]
    NYTBR - June 14 2015 - p13(L) [501+]
Schaufuss, Thomas - *Die politische Rolle des FDGB-Feriendienstes in der DDR: Sozialtourismus im SED-Staat*
    HER - v130 - i542 - Feb 2015 - p256(2) [501+]
Schaverien, Joy - *Boarding School Syndrome: The Psychological Trauma of the 'Privileged' Child*
    TimHES - i2222 - Sept 24 2015 - p41(1) [501+]
Schechtman, Marya - *Staying Alive: Personal Identity, Practical Concerns and the Unity of a Life*
    Lon R Bks - v37 - i12 - June 18 2015 - p39(3) [501+]
Scheck, Raffael - *French Colonial Soldiers in German Captivity during World War II*
    HNet - Sept 2015 - pNA [501+]
Scheele, Judith - *Smugglers and Saints of the Sahara: Regional Connectivity in the Twentieth Century*
    JRAI - v21 - i3 - Sept 2015 - p705(2) [501+]
Scheer, Robert - *They Know Everything about You: How Data-Collecting Corporations and Snooping Government Agencies Are Destroying Democracy*
    KR - Jan 1 2015 - pNA [501+]
    PW - v262 - i3 - Jan 19 2015 - p72(1) [501+]
Scheeren, William O. - *Technology Handbook for School Librarians*
    Teach Lib - v43 - i1 - Oct 2015 - p41(3) [501+]
Scheerger, Sarah Lynn - *Are You Still There*
    y KR - July 15 2015 - pNA [51-500]
    y SLJ - v61 - i8 - August 2015 - p110(1) [51-500]
    y VOYA - v38 - i5 - Dec 2015 - p63(1) [51-500]
Scheers, Jim - *This Is What You Want, This Is What You Get*
    y VOYA - v37 - i6 - Feb 2015 - p64(1) [51-500]
Scheff, Matt - *The Best Extreme Sports Stars of All Time*
    c HB Guide - v26 - i2 - Fall 2015 - p197(2) [51-500]
Jamie Bestwick
    c HB Guide - v26 - i1 - Spring 2015 - p184(2) [51-500]
Lyn-Z Adams Hawkins Pastrana
    c HB Guide - v26 - i1 - Spring 2015 - p184(2) [51-500]
Randy Orton
    c HB Guide - v26 - i1 - Spring 2015 - p185(1) [51-500]
The Rock
    c HB Guide - v26 - i1 - Spring 2015 - p185(1) [51-500]
SportsZone: Speed Machines
    c HB Guide - v26 - i2 - Fall 2015 - p186(1) [51-500]
Tony Hawk
    c HB Guide - v26 - i1 - Spring 2015 - p184(2) [51-500]
Torah Bright
    c HB Guide - v26 - i1 - Spring 2015 - p184(2) [51-500]
Triple H
    c HB Guide - v26 - i1 - Spring 2015 - p185(1) [51-500]
Undertaker
    c HB Guide - v26 - i1 - Spring 2015 - p185(1) [51-500]
Scheffler, Axel - *Flip Flap Safari (Illus. by Scheffler, Axel)*
    c SLJ - v61 - i6 - June 2015 - p39(2) [51-500]
Scheffler, Samuel - *Death and the Afterlife*
    Ethics - v125 - i2 - Jan 2015 - p605(6) [501+]
Scheibe, Amy - *A Fireproof Home for the Bride*
    y BL - v111 - i14 - March 15 2015 - p51(2) [51-500]
    KR - Jan 1 2015 - pNA [501+]
    LJ - v140 - i3 - Feb 15 2015 - p93(1) [51-500]
    PW - v262 - i2 - Jan 12 2015 - p2(1) [51-500]
Scheible, Jeff - *Digital Shift: The Cultural Logic of Punctuation*
    TimHES - i2213 - July 23 2015 - p46(1) [501+]
Scheier, Lawrence M. - *Handbook of Adolescent Drug Use Prevention*
    RVBW - May 2015 - pNA [501+]
Scheier, Leah - *Your Voice Is All I Hear*
    y BL - v111 - i22 - August 1 2015 - p67(1) [51-500]
    y KR - July 15 2015 - pNA [51-500]
    y PW - v262 - i24 - June 15 2015 - p86(1) [51-500]
    y SLJ - v61 - i10 - Oct 2015 - p117(1) [51-500]
    y VOYA - v38 - i4 - Oct 2015 - p61(1) [51-500]

Book Review Index 2016 Cumulation SCHMATZ • 411

Schein, S.L. - *Sophocles: Philoctetes*
Class R - v65 - i1 - April 2015 - p31-33 [501+]
Schein, Seth L. - *Sophocles: Philoctetes*
CJ - v110 - i3 - Feb-March 2015 - p382(3) [501+]
Schein, Steve - *The Alphabet House*
RVBW - Oct 2015 - pNA [51-500]
Scheipers, Sibylle - *Unlawful Combatants: A Genealogy of the Irregular Fighter*
Parameters - v45 - i2 - Summer 2015 - p127(2) [501+]
Schell, Jennifer - *"A Bold and Hardy Race of Men": The Lives and Literature of American Whalemen*
AL - v87 - i3 - Sept 2015 - p607-609 [501+]
Schell-Lambert, Theo - *The Heart of the Order*
KR - April 15 2015 - pNA [51-500]
Schell, Orville - *Wealth and Power: China's Long March to the Twenty-First Century*
JTWS - v32 - i1 - Spring 2015 - p319(2) [501+]
Schell, Patience A. - *The Sociable Sciences: Darwin and His Contemporaries in Chile*
HNet - March 2015 - pNA [501+]
Schellenberg, Betty A. - *Correspondence Primarily on "Sir Charles Grandison"*
RES - v66 - i276 - Sept 2015 - p784-786 [501+]
Scheller, Benjamin - *Die Stadt der Neuchristen: Konvertierte Juden und ihre Nachkommen im Trani des Spatmittelalters zwischen Inklusion und Exklusion*
HER - v130 - i544 - June 2015 - p706(2) [501+]
Schelly, Bill - *Harvey Kurtzman: The Man Who Created Mad and Revolutionized Humor in America*
LJ - v140 - i9 - May 15 2015 - p88(2) [51-500]
Schelske, Oliver - *Orpheus in der Spatantike. Studien und Kommentar zuden Argonautika des Orpheus: Ein literarisches, religioses und philosophisches Zeugnis*
Class R - v65 - i2 - Oct 2015 - p412-415 [501+]
Schenck, David - *Healers: Extraordinary Clinicians at Work*
Hast Cen R - v45 - i1 - Jan-Feb 2015 - p46(2) [501+]
Scheneller-McDonald, Karen - *Connecting the Drops: A Citizens' Guide to Protecting Water Resources*
New Sci - v228 - i3041 - Oct 3 2015 - p46(2) [501+]
Schenkel, Andrea Maria - *Ice Cold*
KR - April 1 2015 - pNA [51-500]
Schenkel, Susan - *An Improbable Journey: A True Story of Courage and Survival During World War II*
SPBW - May 2015 - pNA [501+]
Schepper, Anna - *The Art of Paper Weaving: 46 Colorful, Dimensional Projects*
Bwatch - Oct 2015 - pNA [51-500]
LJ - v140 - i16 - Oct 1 2015 - p82(1) [51-500]
Scherer, Andrew K. - *Embattled Bodies, Embattled Places: War in Pre-Columbian Mesoamerica and the Andes*
HAHR - v95 - i2 - May 2015 - p346-348 [501+]
Scherm, Rebecca - *Unbecoming (Read by Taber, Catherine). Audiobook Review*
LJ - v140 - i7 - April 15 2015 - p47(1) [51-500]
Unbecoming
NY - v91 - i1 - Feb 16 2015 - p71 [51-500]
NYTBR - Jan 18 2015 - p25(L) [501+]
NYTBR - Dec 6 2015 - p85(L) [501+]
Scherr, Arthur - *Thomas Jefferson's Haitian Policy: Myths and Realities*
JAH - v101 - i4 - March 2015 - p1250-1251 [501+]
Scherr, Walter J. - *Walter's Way*
RVBW - Oct 2015 - pNA [51-500]
Schertle, Alice - *Such a Little Mouse (Illus. by Yue, Stephanie)*
c BL - v111 - i11 - Feb 1 2015 - p57(1) [51-500]
c CCB-B - v68 - i9 - May 2015 - p466(2) [51-500]
c HB - v91 - i2 - March-April 2015 - p82(2) [51-500]
c HB Guide - v26 - i2 - Fall 2015 - p18(1) [51-500]
c PW - v262 - i49 - Dec 2 2015 - p18(1) [51-500]
Scherz, China - *Having People, Having Heart: Charity, Sustainable Development, and Problems of Dependence in Central Uganda*
Bks & Cult - v21 - i5 - Sept-Oct 2015 - p12(2) [501+]
Schettino, Antonio - *Quantitative Plate Tectonics: Physics of the Earth - Plate Kinematics - Geodynamics*
Phys Today - v68 - i3 - March 2015 - p51-51 [501+]
Scheuerman, Richard D. - *River Song: Naxiyamtama (Snake River-Palouse) Oral Traditions from Mary Jim, Andrew George, Gordon Fisher, and Emily Peone*
Bwatch - June 2015 - pNA [51-500]
Schiariti, Matt - *The Ghosts of Demons Past*
PW - v262 - i19 - May 11 2015 - p39(1) [51-500]
Schick, Karin - *Max Beckmann: The Still Lifes*
NYTBR - June 28 2015 - p14(L) [501+]
Schickel, Katie - *Housewitch*
BL - v111 - i9-10 - Jan 1 2015 - p38(1) [51-500]
Schickel, Richard - *Keepers: The Greatest Films--and Personal Favorites--of a Moviegoing Lifetime*
KR - March 15 2015 - pNA [51-500]
LJ - v140 - i9 - May 15 2015 - p85(2) [51-500]
NYTBR - May 31 2015 - p34(L) [501+]
PW - v262 - i17 - April 27 2015 - p62(2) [51-500]
Schieberle, Misty - *Feminized Counsel and the Literature of Advice in England, 1380-1500*
Med R - Sept 2015 - pNA [501+]
Schielke, Samuli - *Ordinary Lives and Grand Schemes: An Anthropology of Everyday Religion*
JRAI - v21 - i2 - June 2015 - p498(2) [501+]
Schiering, Marjorie S. - *Learning and Teaching Creative Cognition: The Interactive Book Report*
VOYA - v38 - i5 - Dec 2015 - p83(2) [51-500]
Schiff, Karen - *The First Supper*
KR - April 15 2015 - pNA [501+]
Schiff, Stacy - *The Witches: Salem, 1692*
Atl - v316 - i4 - Nov 2015 - p46(3) [501+]
BL - v111 - i22 - August 1 2015 - p6(1) [51-500]
BL - v112 - i1 - Sept 1 2015 - p31(1) [51-500]
Ch Today - v59 - i8 - Oct 2015 - p74(1) [51-500]
HM - v331 - i1986 - Nov 2015 - p89(6) [501+]
KR - Sept 1 2015 - pNA [501+]
LJ - v140 - i14 - Sept 1 2015 - p118(2) [51-500]
Mac - v128 - i45 - Nov 16 2015 - p57(1) [501+]
NYRB - v62 - i19 - Dec 3 2015 - p21(3) [501+]
NYT - Nov 13 2015 - pC34(L) [501+]
NYTBR - Nov 1 2015 - p14(L) [501+]
PW - v262 - i36 - Sept 7 2015 - p58(1) [51-500]
Spec - v329 - i9767 - Nov 7 2015 - p45(1) [501+]
Schiffer, Miriam B. - *Stella Brings the Family (Illus. by Clifton-Brown, Holly)*
c BL - v111 - i17 - May 1 2015 - p103(1) [51-500]
c CCB-B - v69 - i1 - Sept 2015 - p52(1) [51-500]
c HB Guide - v26 - i2 - Fall 2015 - p51(1) [51-500]
c NYTBR - July 12 2015 - p19(L) [501+]
c PW - v262 - i13 - March 30 2015 - p75(1) [51-500]
c PW - v262 - i49 - Dec 2 2015 - p32(1) [51-500]
Schiffrin, Anya - *Global Muckraking: 100 Years of Investigative Journalism from around the World*
NYRB - v62 - i10 - June 4 2015 - p43(3) [501+]
Schifino, Martin - *Paginas Criticas: Formas de leer y de narrar de Proust a "Mad Men"*
TLS - i5845 - April 10 2015 - p22(1) [501+]
Schildcrout, Jordan - *Murder Most Queer: The Homicidal Homosexual in the American Theater*
G&L Rev W - v22 - i5 - Sept-Oct 2015 - p40(2) [501+]
Schilfellite, Carmen James - *Biology after the Sociobiology Debate: What Introductory Textbooks Say About the Nature of Science and Organisms*
CS - v44 - i2 - March 2015 - p246-248 [501+]
Schillace, Brandy - *Death's Summer Coat*
KR - Oct 1 2015 - pNA [501+]
Schillebeeckx, Edward - *From North to South: Southern Scholars Engage with Edward Schillebeeckx*
Theol St - v76 - i2 - June 2015 - p387(2) [501+]
Schiller, Abbie - *When Lyla Got Lost*
c CH Bwatch - June 2015 - pNA [51-500]
c CH Bwatch - July 2015 - pNA [51-500]
Schiller, M.K. - *Unwanted Girl*
PW - v262 - i47 - Nov 23 2015 - p55(1) [51-500]
Schiller, Sophie - *Race to Tibet*
PW - v262 - i11 - March 16 2015 - p67(1) [51-500]
Schilling, Britta - *Postcolonial Germany: Memories of Empire in a Decolonized Nation*
CEH - v48 - i2 - June 2015 - p258-260 [501+]
HER - v130 - i545 - August 2015 - p1054(3) [501+]
JIH - v45 - i4 - Spring 2015 - p583-584 [501+]
Schilling, Natalie - *Sociolinguistic Fieldwork*
Lang Soc - v44 - i4 - Sept 2015 - p606-1 [501+]
Schillios, Siri - *BirdWingFeather*
c HB Guide - v26 - i1 - Spring 2015 - p45(1) [51-500]
Schindel, John - *The Babies and Doggies Book (Illus. by Woodward, Molly)*
c BL - v111 - i19-20 - June 1 2015 - p110(1) [51-500]
c KR - July 1 2015 - pNA [51-500]
Schindelbeck, Dirk - *Zigaretten-Fronten: Die politischen Kulturen des Rauchens in der Zeit des Ersten Weltkriegs*
HNet - Sept 2015 - pNA [501+]
Schindler, D.C. - *The Catholicity of Reason*
Theol St - v76 - i1 - March 2015 - p227(1) [501+]
Schindler, Holly - *Feral*
y CCB-B - v68 - i5 - Jan 2015 - p276(1) [51-500]
y HB Guide - v26 - i2 - Fall 2015 - p137(1) [51-500]
Schipper, Sebastian - *The 11th Hour*
NYT - June 12 2015 - pC8(L) [51-500]
Schlabach, Elizabeth Schroeder - *Along the Streets of Bronzeville: Black Chicago's Literary Landscape*
JAH - v101 - i4 - March 2015 - p1309(1) [501+]
Schlatter, Richard - *The Old Man and The Tree (Illus. by Schlatter, Richard)*
c CH Bwatch - Sept 2015 - pNA [51-500]
Schlee, Gunther - *Pastoralism and Politics in Northern Kenya and Southern Ethiopia*
JTWS - v32 - i1 - Spring 2015 - p327(3) [501+]
Schleiermacher, Friedrich - *On the Doctrine of Election with Special Reference to the 'Aphorisms' of Dr. Bretschneider*
Six Ct J - v46 - i3 - Fall 2015 - p826-827 [501+]
Schleifer, Ron - *Psychological Warfare in the Arab-Israeli Conflict*
Parameters - v45 - i2 - Summer 2015 - p119(2) [501+]
Schlemmer, Thomas - *Der Faschismus in Europa: Wege der Forschung*
HNet - March 2015 - pNA [501+]
Schlender, Brent - *Becoming Steve Jobs: The Evolution of a Reckless Upstart into a Visionary Leader (Read by Newbern, George). Audiobook Review*
LJ - v140 - i11 - June 15 2015 - p52(1) [51-500]
Becoming Steve Jobs: The Evolution of a Reckless Upstart into a Visionary Leader
Econ - v415 - i8932 - April 4 2015 - p77(US) [501+]
Mac - v128 - i12 - March 30 2015 - p54(1) [501+]
NYT - March 26 2015 - pC1(L) [501+]
NYT - March 26 2015 - pC1(L) [501+]
NYTBR - April 5 2015 - p21(L) [501+]
Schlereth, Eric R. - *An Age of Infidels: The Politics of Religious Controversy in the Early United States*
CHR - v101 - i3 - Summer 2015 - p675(2) [501+]
J Ch St - v57 - i2 - Spring 2015 - p388-390 [501+]
JR - v95 - i2 - April 2015 - p289(2) [501+]
RAH - v43 - i2 - June 2015 - p216-222 [501+]
Schleuning, Peter - *Vom Kaffeehaus zum Furstenhof: Johann Sebastian Bachs weltliche Kantaten*
MT - v156 - i1930 - Spring 2015 - p101-104 [501+]
Schlimm, John - *Five Years in Heaven: The Unlikely Friendship That Answered Life's Greatest Questions*
LJ - v140 - i9 - May 15 2015 - p64(2) [501+]
Schlimm, Matthew Richard - *This Strange and Sacred Scripture: Wrestling with the Old Testament and Its Oddities*
Ch Today - v59 - i4 - May 2015 - p64(1) [51-500]
Schlitz, Laura Amy - *The Hired Girl*
y BL - v111 - i21 - July 1 2015 - p55(1) [51-500]
c CCB-B - v69 - i2 - Oct 2015 - p110(2) [51-500]
y CSM - Dec 25 2015 - pNA [501+]
y HB - v91 - i5 - Sept-Oct 2015 - p116(1) [51-500]
c KR - July 15 2015 - pNA [51-500]
y NYTBR - Nov 8 2015 - p22(L) [501+]
y PW - v262 - i28 - July 13 2015 - p68(1) [51-500]
y PW - v262 - i49 - Dec 2 2015 - p115(1) [51-500]
RVBW - Sept 2015 - pNA [501+]
y SLJ - v61 - i8 - August 2015 - p98(1) [51-500]
y VOYA - v38 - i5 - Dec 2015 - p63(1) [51-500]
Schloesser, Stephen - *Visions of Amen: The Early Life and Music of Olivier Messiaen*
CC - v132 - i2 - Jan 21 2015 - p41(2) [501+]
Theol St - v76 - i4 - Dec 2015 - p848(3) [501+]
Schlogel, Karl - *Die Russische Revolution und das Schicksal der Russischen Juden: Eine Debatte in Berlin 1922/23*
HNet - June 2015 - pNA [501+]
Schlusche, Gunter - *Stadtentwicklung im Doppelten Berlin: Zeitgenossenschaft und Erinnerungsorte*
HNet - March 2015 - pNA [501+]
Schmale, Wolfgang - *Das 18. Jahrhundert*
JMH - v87 - i1 - March 2015 - p150(2) [501+]
Schmalzbauer, Leah - *The Last Best Place? Gender, Family, and Migration in the New West*
AJS - v121 - i3 - Nov 2015 - p994(3) [501+]
Schmatz, Pat - *Lizard Radio*
y BL - v111 - i22 - August 1 2015 - p60(1) [51-500]
y HB - v91 - i5 - Sept-Oct 2015 - p116(2) [51-500]
y KR - June 15 2015 - pNA [51-500]
y Magpies - v30 - i5 - Nov 2015 - p42(2) [501+]
y PW - v262 - i27 - July 6 2015 - p75(1) [51-500]
y SLJ - v61 - i7 - July 2015 - p98(1) [51-500]
y VOYA - v38 - i4 - Oct 2015 - p78(1) [501+]

Schmicker, Michael - *The Witch of Napoli*
    KR - Feb 1 2015 - pNA [501+]
    PW - v262 - i23 - June 8 2015 - p35(2) [51-500]

Schmid, Paul - *Oliver and His Egg (Illus. by Schmid, Paul)*
    c HB Guide - v26 - i1 - Spring 2015 - p16(1) [51-500]

Schmid, Sabine - *Fotografie zwischen Politik und Bild: Entwicklungen der Fotografie in der DDR*
    HNet - June 2015 - pNA [501+]

Schmid, Sonja D. - *Producing Power: The Pre-Chernobyl History of the Soviet Nuclear Industry*
    Nature - v519 - i7542 - March 12 2015 - p155(1) [51-500]

Schmid, Vernon - *Buzzard Tales: The Memoirs of a Cherokee Gunfighter*
    Roundup M - v22 - i3 - Feb 2015 - p27(1) [501+]
    Roundup M - v22 - i6 - August 2015 - p32(1) [501+]
Collected Poems, 1964-2014
    Roundup M - v22 - i6 - August 2015 - p24(1) [501+]
St. Elmo's Ghost
    Roundup M - v22 - i6 - August 2015 - p32(1) [501+]

Schmid, Wilhelm - *What We Gain as We Grow Older: On Gelassenheit*
    PW - v262 - i45 - Nov 9 2015 - p48(1) [51-500]

Schmidgall, Gary - *Containing Multitudes: Walt Whitman and the British Literary Tradition*
    TLS - i5855 - June 19 2015 - p25(1) [501+]

Schmidli, William Michael - *The Fate of Freedom Elsewhere: Human Rights and US Cold War Policy toward Argentina*
    HAHR - v95 - i4 - Nov 2015 - p723-724 [501+]

Schmidt, Aaron - *Useful, Usable, Desirable: Applying User Experience Design to Your Library*
    R&USQ - v54 - i3 - Spring 2015 - p55(2) [501+]

Schmidt, Anna - *The Drifter*
    PW - v262 - i25 - June 22 2015 - p126(1) [51-500]

Schmidt, Annie M.G. - *The Cat Who Came In off the Roof*
    c KR - Oct 1 2015 - pNA [51-500]
    c SLJ - v61 - i10 - Oct 2015 - p94(1) [51-500]

Schmidt, Benjamin - *Inventing Exoticism: Geography, Globalism, and Europe's Early Modern World*
    TimHES - v2198 - April 9 2015 - p50-51 [501+]

Schmidt-Beste, Thomas - *The Motet around 1500: On the Relationship of Imitation and Text Treatment?*
    Notes - v71 - i3 - March 2015 - p527(4) [501+]

Schmidt, Bryan Thomas - *Mission: Tomorrow*
    PW - v262 - i39 - Sept 28 2015 - p72(1) [51-500]

Schmidt, Christian - *Konnen wir der Geschichte Entkommen? Geschichtsphilosophie am Beginn des 21. Jahrhunderts*
    HNet - March 2015 - pNA [501+]

Schmidt, Elizabeth - *Foreign Intervention in Africa: From the Cold War to the War on Terror*
    AHR - v120 - i2 - April 2015 - p757-758 [501+]

Schmidt, Gary D. - *Making Americans: Children's Literature from 1930 to 1960*
    AL - v87 - i2 - June 2015 - p403-405 [501+]
Orbiting Jupiter
    y BL - v112 - i1 - Sept 1 2015 - p108(1) [51-500]
    y HB - v91 - i6 - Nov-Dec 2015 - p91(2) [51-500]
    c KR - July 15 2015 - pNA [51-500]
    c PW - v262 - i33 - August 17 2015 - p72(1) [51-500]
    c PW - v262 - i49 - Dec 2 2015 - p72(1) [51-500]
    y SLJ - v61 - i8 - August 2015 - p98(1) [51-500]
    y VOYA - v38 - i5 - Dec 2015 - p64(1) [51-500]

Schmidt, Jason - *A List of Things That Didn't Kill Me*
    y HB Guide - v26 - i2 - Fall 2015 - p211(1) [51-500]
    y SLJ - v61 - i5 - May 2015 - p142(1) [51-500]
    y VOYA - v37 - i6 - Feb 2015 - p88(1) [51-500]

Schmidt, Kristin E. - *Give Your Song a Voice (Illus. by Hare, Debra Rae)*
    c CH Bwatch - Jan 2015 - pNA [51-500]

Schmidt, Michael - *The Novel: A Biography*
    WLT - v89 - i5 - Sept-Oct 2015 - p78(2) [501+]
    Bks & Cult - v21 - i6 - Nov-Dec 2015 - p32(1) [501+]
    Sew R - v123 - i2 - Spring 2015 - p335-344 [501+]
Schwarze Flamme: Revolutionare Klassenpolitik des Anarchismus und Syndikalismus
    HNet - March 2015 - pNA [501+]

Schmidt, Ronald J, Jr. - *This Is the City: Making Model Citizens in Los Angeles*
    J Urban H - v41 - i1 - Jan 2015 - p143-9 [501+]

Schmidt, Susan - *Song of Moving Water*
    KR - June 1 2015 - pNA [501+]

Schmidt, Tiffany - *The Adventures of Black Dog (Illus. by Theophilopoulos, Andrew)*
    c KR - March 15 2015 - pNA [51-500]
Hold Me Like a Breath
    y CCB-B - v68 - i11 - July-August 2015 - p563(2) [51-500]
    y HB Guide - v26 - i2 - Fall 2015 - p137(1) [51-500]
    y KR - March 15 2015 - pNA [51-500]
    SLJ - v61 - i4 - April 2015 - p170(2) [501+]
    y VOYA - v38 - i2 - June 2015 - p68(1) [51-500]

Schmidt, Ulf - *Secret Science: A Century of Poison Warfare and Human Experiments*
    Nature - v523 - i7559 - July 9 2015 - p157(1) [51-500]

Schmiesing, Kevin - *Catholicism and Historical Narrative: A Catholic Engagement with Historical Scholarship*
    CH - v84 - i3 - Sept 2015 - p679(1) [501+]
    CHR - v101 - i1 - Wntr 2015 - p147(2) [501+]

Schmitt, Catherine - *The President's Salmon: Restoring the King of Fish and Its Home Waters*
    LJ - v140 - i11 - June 15 2015 - p111(1) [51-500]

Schmitt, Eric-Emmanuel - *Invisible Love*
    NYTBR - Jan 4 2015 - p26(L) [501+]

Schmitt, Frederick F. - *Hume's Epistemology in the Treatise: A Veritistic Interpretation*
    RM - v69 - i1 - Sept 2015 - p151(3) [501+]

Schmitt, Gavin - *The Milwaukee Mafia: Mobsters in the Heartland*
    RVBW - April 2015 - pNA [501+]

Schmitt, Gladys - *The Collected Stories of Gladys Schmitt*
    HR - v68 - i1 - Spring 2015 - p167-175 [501+]
Sonnets from an Analyst
    HR - v68 - i1 - Spring 2015 - p167-175 [501+]

Schmitt, Sarah J. - *It's a Wonderful Death*
    y BL - v112 - i4 - Oct 15 2015 - p56(1) [51-500]
    y KR - Sept 1 2015 - pNA [51-500]
    y SLJ - v61 - i11 - Nov 2015 - p121(2) [51-500]
    y VOYA - v38 - i4 - Oct 2015 - p78(2) [51-500]

Schmitz, Adriennne - *Real Estate Development: Principles and Process*
    RVBW - July 2015 - pNA [501+]

Schmitz, Beate - *How to Make Beautiful Buttons*
    BL - v111 - i15 - April 1 2015 - p12(1) [51-500]
    LJ - v140 - i6 - April 1 2015 - p92(1) [51-500]

Schmitz, David F. - *Richard Nixon and the Vietnam War: The End of the American Century*
    JAH - v101 - i4 - March 2015 - p1347-1348 [501+]

Schmitz, Winfried - *Die Griechische Gesellschaft: Eine Sozialgeschichte der Archaischen und Klassischen Zeit*
    HNet - Feb 2015 - pNA [501+]

Schmugge, Ludwig - *Marriage on Trial: Late Medieval German Couples at the Papal Court*
    CHR - v101 - i2 - Spring 2015 - p364(2) [501+]
Repertorium poenitentiariae Germanicum: Verzeichnis der in den Supplikenregistern der Ponitentiarie Kirchen, und Orte des Deutschen Reiches
    CHR - v101 - i3 - Summer 2015 - p640(2) [501+]

Schnakenberg, Robert - *The Big Bad Book of Bill Murray: A Critical Appreciation of the World's Finest Actor*
    LJ - v140 - i12 - July 1 2015 - p88(1) [51-500]

Schnapp, Alain - *World Antiquarianism: Comparative Perspectives*
    JIH - v45 - i3 - Wntr 2015 - p413-414 [501+]

Schnapp, Jeffery T. - *The Library beyond the Book*
    T&C - v56 - i4 - Oct 2015 - p957-964 [501+]

Schnee, Silke - *The Prince Who Was Just Himself (Illus. by Sistig, Heike)*
    c CH Bwatch - Oct 2015 - pNA [51-500]
    c KR - July 15 2015 - pNA [51-500]

Schneer, Jonathan - *Ministers at War: Winston Churchill and His War Cabinet*
    For Aff - v94 - i3 - May-June 2015 - pNA [501+]
    KR - Jan 1 2015 - pNA [51-500]
    NYRB - v62 - i16 - Oct 22 2015 - p28(4) [501+]
    Spec - v327 - i9735 - March 28 2015 - p40(1) [501+]

Schneid, Frederick C. - *The French-Piedmontese Campaign of 1859*
    J Mil H - v79 - i1 - Jan 2015 - p211-212 [501+]

Schneider, Anthony - *Repercussions*
    KR - Nov 15 2015 - pNA [501+]

Schneider, Antonie - *Mr. Happy & Miss Grimm (Illus. by Strasser, Susanne)*
    c HB - v91 - i3 - May-June 2015 - p97(2) [51-500]
    c HB Guide - v26 - i2 - Fall 2015 - p51(1) [51-500]
    c KR - March 1 2015 - pNA [51-500]

Schneider, Birgit - *Image Politics of Climate Change: Visualizations, Imaginations, Documentations*
    GSR - v38 - i3 - Oct 2015 - p635-652 [501+]

Schneider, Britta - *Salsa, Language and Transnationalism*
    Lang Soc - v44 - i4 - Sept 2015 - p601-1 [501+]

Schneider, David - *Crowded by Beauty: The Life and Zen of Poet Philip Whalen*
    BL - v111 - i21 - July 1 2015 - p16(2) [51-500]
    TLS - i5868 - Sept 18 2015 - p22(1) [501+]

Schneider, Josh - *Everybody Sleeps (But Not Fred). (Illus. by Schneider, Josh)*
    c CH Bwatch - May 2015 - pNA [51-500]
    c HB Guide - v26 - i2 - Fall 2015 - p51(1) [51-500]
    c KR - Jan 15 2015 - pNA [51-500]
    c PW - v262 - i49 - Dec 2 2015 - p41(1) [51-500]

Schneider, Leander - *Government of Development: Peasants and Politicians in Postcolonial Tanzania*
    IJAHS - v48 - i1 - Wntr 2015 - p158-159 [501+]

Schneider, Michael - *In der Kriegsgesellschaft: Arbeiter und Arbeiterbewegung 1939 bis 1945*
    HNet - April 2015 - pNA [501+]

Schneider, Nina - *Brazilian Propaganda: Legitimizing an Authoritarian Regime*
    JIH - v46 - i2 - Autumn 2015 - p303-305 [501+]

Schneider, Robyn - *Extraordinary Means*
    y CCB-B - v69 - i1 - Sept 2015 - p52(1) [51-500]
    c HB Guide - v26 - i2 - Fall 2015 - p137(1) [51-500]
    y KR - March 1 2015 - pNA [51-500]
    y PW - v262 - i9 - March 2 2015 - p86(1) [51-500]
    y SLJ - v61 - i3 - March 2015 - p162(1) [51-500]
    y VOYA - v38 - i1 - April 2015 - p69(1) [51-500]

Schneider, Steven Jay - *1001 Movies You Must See before You Die*
    LJ - v140 - i20 - Dec 1 2015 - p130(1) [51-500]

Schneiderhan, Erik - *The Size of Others' Burdens: Barack Obama, Jane Addams, and the Politics of Helping Others*
    KR - March 15 2015 - pNA [501+]
    PW - v262 - i17 - April 27 2015 - p66(2) [51-500]

Schneidermann, Daniel - *On n'a pas fini de rire: quelques mots a ma nouvelle famille*
    TLS - i5864-5865 - August 21 2015 - p28(2) [501+]

Schneier, Bruce - *Data and Goliath: The Hidden Battles to Collect Your Data and Control Your World*
    BL - v111 - i13 - March 1 2015 - p6(1) [51-500]
    Bwatch - May 2015 - pNA [51-500]
    Econ - v415 - i8932 - April 4 2015 - p80(US) [501+]
    KR - Feb 1 2015 - pNA [51-500]
    LJ - v140 - i11 - June 15 2015 - p111(2) [501+]
    Nature - v518 - i7540 - Feb 26 2015 - p480(2) [501+]
    New Sci - v225 - i3014 - March 28 2015 - p46(2) [501+]
    NYRB - v62 - i13 - August 13 2015 - p18(3) [501+]
    TimHES - i2204 - May 21 2015 - p51(1) [501+]

Schnell, Lisa Kahn - *High Tide for Horseshoe Crabs (Illus. by Marks, Alan)*
    BL - v111 - i14 - March 15 2015 - p62(1) [51-500]
    c HB Guide - v26 - i2 - Fall 2015 - p174(2) [51-500]
    c KR - Feb 15 2015 - pNA [51-500]

Schneller-McDonald, Karen - *Connecting the Drops: A Citizens' Guide to Protecting Water Resources*
    LJ - v140 - i14 - Sept 1 2015 - p134(1) [51-500]

Schneps, Leila - *Alexandre Grothendieck: A Mathematical Portrait*
    SIAM Rev - v57 - i1 - March 2015 - p163-164 [501+]

Schnieder, Benjamin - *Metaphysical Grounding: Understanding the Structure of Reality*
    Phil R - v124 - i3 - July 2015 - p410(6) [501+]

Schniedewind, William - *A Social History of Hebrew: Its Origins through the Rabbinic Period*
    HNet - Feb 2015 - pNA [501+]

Schnoor, Franziska - *Schafe fur die Ewigkeit: Handschriften und ihre Herstellung: Katalog zur Jahresausstellung in der Stiftsbibliothek St. Gallen*
    Med R - Feb 2015 - pNA [501+]

Schnurmann, Claudia - *Brucken aus Papier: Atlantischer Wissenstransfer in dem Briefnetzwerk des deutsch-amerikanischen Ehepaars Francis und Mathilde Lieber, 1827-1872*
    HNet - May 2015 - pNA [501+]

Schober, Anna - *The Cinema Makers: Public Life and the Exhibition of Difference in South-Eastern and Central Europe since the 1960s*
    Afterimage - v42 - i4 - Jan-Feb 2015 - p39(1) [501+]

Schoch, Rainer R. - *Amphibian Evolution: The Life of Early Land Vertebrates*
    QRB - v90 - i2 - June 2015 - p205(2) [501+]

Schocket, Andrew M. - *Fighting over the Founders: How We Remember the American Revolution*
    Pub Hist - v37 - i3 - August 2015 - p139(3) [501+]

Schoder, Angelika - *Die Vermittlung des Unbegreiflichen: Darstellungen des Holocaust im Museum*
    HNet - Sept 2015 - pNA(NA) [501+]

Schoeller, Jen - *Biggest, Baddest Book of Sea Creatures (Illus. by Schoeller, Jen)*
    c BL - v111 - i16 - April 15 2015 - p45(1) [501+]
    c HB Guide - v26 - i2 - Fall 2015 - p172(1) [51-500]
Biggest, Baddest Book of Space
    c HB Guide - v26 - i2 - Fall 2015 - p165(1) [51-500]

Schoeller, Wilfried F. - *Alfred Doblin: Eine Biographie*
    MLR - v110 - i2 - April 2015 - p594-596 [501+]

Schoeman, Karel - *This Life*
    KR - March 1 2015 - pNA [51-500]
    NYTBR - June 7 2015 - p38(L) [501+]
    PW - v262 - i11 - March 16 2015 - p57(2) [51-500]
    WLT - v89 - i3-4 - May-August 2015 - p121(1) [51-500]

Schoen, Lawrence M. - *Barsk: The Elephants' Graveyard*
    PW - v262 - i41 - Oct 12 2015 - p51(1) [51-500]

Schoene, Berthold - *The Cosmopolitan Novel*
    ABR - v36 - i5 - July-August 2015 - p8(2) [501+]

Schoene, Kerstin - *Milo Is Not a Dog Today (Illus. by Gunetsreiner, Nina)*
    c HB Guide - v26 - i2 - Fall 2015 - p18(1) [51-500]

Schoenewaldt, Pamela - *Under the Same Blue Sky*
    BL - v111 - i17 - May 1 2015 - p79(1) [51-500]

Schoenhals, Michael - *Spying for the People: Mao's Secret Agents, 1949-1967*
    Pac A - v88 - i3 - Sept 2015 - p696 [501+]

Schoeps, Julius H. - *Der Konig von Midian: Paul Friedmann und sein Traum von einem Judenstaat*
    HNet - May 2015 - pNA [501+]

Schoffman, Stuart - *The Story of Crime and Punishment (Illus. by Bougaeva, Sonja)*
    c Sch Lib - v63 - i1 - Spring 2015 - p60(1) [51-500]

Schofield, Anakana - *Martin John*
    Mac - v128 - i37 - Sept 21 2015 - p57(1) [501+]

Schofield, Don - *In Lands Imagination Favors*
    WLT - v89 - i2 - March-April 2015 - p71(1) [51-500]

Schofield, Douglas - *Time of Departure*
    KR - Oct 1 2015 - pNA [51-500]

Schofield, Malcolm - *Aristotle, Plato and Pythagoreanism in the First Century BC: New Directions for Philosophy*
    Class R - v65 - i2 - Oct 2015 - p391-393 [501+]

Schofield-Morrison, Connie - *J'ai le rythme dans la peau (Illus. by Morrison, Frank)*
    c Res Links - v20 - i5 - June 2015 - p44(1) [51-500]

Scholarship in Software - Software as Scholarship. From Genesis to Peer Review
    HNet - July 2015 - pNA [501+]

Scholastic Inc. - *Carry and Learn Shapes*
    c KR - Jan 1 2016 - pNA [51-500]
Let's Go to the Firehouse
    c KR - Jan 1 2016 - pNA [51-500]
Look Who's Talking
    c KR - Jan 1 2016 - pNA [51-500]
Touch and Feel ABC
    c KR - Jan 1 2016 - pNA [51-500]
Touch and Feel Baby Animals
    c KR - Jan 1 2016 - pNA [51-500]
Trace, Lift, and Learn
    c KR - Jan 1 2016 - pNA [51-500]

Scholder, Fritz - *Super Indian: Fritz Scholder, 1967-1980*
    BL - v112 - i1 - Sept 1 2015 - p26(1) [51-500]

Scholes, Ken - *Blue Yonders, Grateful Pies, and Other Fanciful Feasts*
    PW - v262 - i25 - June 22 2015 - p125(1) [51-500]

Scholes, Robert - *The Little Review 'Ulysses'*
    TLS - i5854 - June 12 2015 - p23(2) [501+]

Schollgen, Gregor - *Deutsche Aussenpolitik: Von 1815 bis 1945*
    HNet - June 2015 - pNA [501+]

Scholz, Hartmut - *Die mittelaterlichen Glasmalereien in Nurnberg: Sebalder Stadtseite*
    Specu - v90 - i3 - July 2015 - p849-2 [501+]

Scholz, Johannes - *Adelsbilder von der Antike bis zur Gegenwart*
    HNet - April 2015 - pNA [501+]

Scholz, Paul - *Rudy Toot Toots and His Cowboy Boots*
    c CH Bwatch - August 2015 - pNA [51-500]

Scholz, Sebastian - *Damnatio in Memoria: Deformation und Gegenkonstruktionen in der Geschichte*
    HNet - Feb 2015 - pNA [501+]

Scholz Williams, Gerhild - *Mediating Culture in the Seventeenth-Century German Novel: Eberhard Werner Happel, 1647-1690*
    Ger Q - v88 - i1 - Wntr 2015 - p112(4) [501+]

Schon, Lennart - *An Economic History of Modern Sweden*
    JEH - v75 - i1 - March 2015 - p274-276 [501+]

Schonberg, Arnold - *A Survivor from Warsaw, Opus 46 Notes* - v72 - i1 - Sept 2015 - p231(4) [501+]

Schone, Albrecht - *Der Briefschreiber Goethe*
    TLS - i5864-5865 - August 21 2015 - p33(1) [501+]

Schone-Denkinger, A. - *Corpus Vasorum Antiquorum. Deutschland. Berlin, Antikensammlung, ehemals Antiquarium. Band 15. Attisch Rotfigurige und Schwarzgefirnisste Peliken, Loutrophoren und Lebetes Gamikoi*
    Class R - v65 - i1 - April 2015 - p260-261 [501+]

Schonebaum, Andrew - *Approaches to Teaching the Story of the Stone*
    JAS - v74 - i1 - Feb 2015 - p207-208 [501+]

Schonhardt-Bailey, Cheryl - *Deliberating American Monetary Policy: A Textual Analysis*
    JEH - v75 - i1 - March 2015 - p283-284 [501+]

Schoning, Matthias - *Ernst Junger-Handbuch: Leben - Werk - Wirkung*
    HNet - April 2015 - pNA [501+]

Schonwerth, Franz Xaver von - *Original Bavarian Folktales: A Schonwerth Selection*
    TLS - i5871 - Oct 9 2015 - p26(1) [501+]
The Turnip Princess and Other Newly Discovered Fairy Tales
    c NYRB - v62 - i12 - July 9 2015 - p65(3) [501+]
    TLS - i5871 - Oct 9 2015 - p26(1) [501+]

Schoonmaker, Elizabeth - *Square Cat ABC (Illus. by Schoonmaker, Elizabeth)*
    c HB Guide - v26 - i1 - Spring 2015 - p44(2) [51-500]

Schope, Bjorn - *Der romische Kaiserhof in severischer Zeit*
    Class R - v65 - i2 - Oct 2015 - p541-543 [501+]

Schopflin, Katharine - *A Handbook for Corporate Information Professionals*
    LJ - v140 - i8 - May 1 2015 - p84(1) [501+]

Schoppa, Keith R. - *In a Sea of Bitterness: Refugees during the Sino-Japanese War*
    JAS - v74 - i3 - August 2015 - p740-742 [501+]

Schoppa, Leonard J. - *The Evolution of Japan's Party System: Politics and Policy in an Era of Institutional Change*
    JAS - v74 - i2 - May 2015 - p443-447 [501+]

Schorb, Jodi - *Reading Prisoners: Literature, Literacy, and the Transformation of American Punishment, 1700-1845*
    JAH - v102 - i2 - Sept 2015 - p536-536 [501+]

Schories, Pat - *Pants for Chuck (Illus. by Schories, Pat)*
    c HB Guide - v26 - i1 - Spring 2015 - p55(1) [51-500]
Pie for Chuck (Illus. by Schories, Pat)
    c KR - July 15 2015 - pNA [51-500]
    c SLJ - v61 - i12 - Dec 2015 - p98(1) [51-500]

Schorr, Jamie L. - *Les costeaux, ou, Les marquis frians*
    FS - v69 - i4 - Oct 2015 - p527-528 [501+]

Schorr, Melissa - *Identity Crisis*
    y KR - Nov 15 2015 - pNA [51-500]
    y SLJ - v61 - i12 - Dec 2015 - p128(1) [51-500]

Schotter, Roni - *Go, Little Green Truck! (Illus. by Kuo, Julia)*
    c KR - Dec 1 2015 - pNA [51-500]
    c PW - v262 - i46 - Nov 16 2015 - p74(1) [51-500]

Schout, Dawn - *Wanderlust*
    RVBW - March 2015 - pNA [51-500]

Schow, Betsy - *Spelled*
    y PW - v262 - i17 - April 27 2015 - p76(1) [51-500]
    y SLJ - v61 - i5 - May 2015 - p115(2) [51-500]
    y VOYA - v38 - i2 - June 2015 - p82(1) [51-500]

Schow, David J. - *DJSturbia*
    PW - v262 - i47 - Nov 23 2015 - p53(1) [51-500]

Schrad, Mark Lawrence - *Vodka Politics: Alcohol, Autocracy, and the Secret History of the Russian State*
    AHR - v120 - i1 - Feb 2015 - p359(1) [501+]
    Slav R - v74 - i1 - Spring 2015 - p187-188 [501+]

Schraer-Joiner, Lyn E. - *Music for Children with Hearing Loss: A Resource for Parents and Teachers*
    Am MT - v64 - i6 - June-July 2015 - p65(2) [501+]

Schraff, Anne - *The Life of Harriet Tubman: Moses of the Underground Railroad*
    y HB Guide - v26 - i1 - Spring 2015 - p192(1) [51-500]

Schrage, Michael - *The Innovator's Hypothesis: How Cheap Experiments are Worth More than Good Ideas*
    TimHES - i2184 - Jan 1 2015 - p65(1) [501+]

Schrager, Howard - *Chicken in the Car ... and the Car Can't Go! That's How You 'Spell' Chicago! (Illus. by Madsen, Sarah)*
    c CH Bwatch - April 2015 - pNA [51-500]

Schramm, Michael W. - *Symbolische Formung und die gesellschaftliche Konstruktion von Wirklichkeit*
    HNet - April 2015 - pNA [501+]

Schrank, Delphine - *The Rebel of Rangoon: A Tale of Defiance and Deliverance in Burma*
    BL - v111 - i19-20 - June 1 2015 - p33(2) [51-500]
    Econ - v416 - i8950 - August 8 2015 - p72(US) [501+]
    KR - May 15 2015 - pNA [501+]
    LJ - v140 - i11 - June 15 2015 - p102(1) [51-500]
    NYRB - v62 - i17 - Nov 5 2015 - p39(2) [501+]

Schrauwen, Olivier - *Arsene Schrauwen*
    ABR - v36 - i2 - Jan-Feb 2015 - p8(1) [501+]
    BL - v111 - i9-10 - Jan 1 2015 - p61(1) [51-500]
My Boy
    WLT - v89 - i2 - March-April 2015 - p10(2) [501+]

Schrefer, Eliot - *Rise and Fall*
    c CH Bwatch - July 2015 - pNA [51-500]
    c HB Guide - v26 - i2 - Fall 2015 - p100(1) [51-500]

Schreiber, Anne - *Les requins*
    c Res Links - v21 - i1 - Oct 2015 - p55(1) [51-500]

Schreiber, Daniel - *Susan Sontag: A Biography*
    Soc - v52 - i2 - April 2015 - p195(3) [501+]
    TLS - i5834 - Jan 23 2015 - p8(2) [501+]

Schreiber, Joe - *Con Academy*
    y BL - v111 - i22 - August 1 2015 - p63(1) [51-500]
    y CCB-B - v69 - i2 - Oct 2015 - p111(1) [51-500]
    y HB - v91 - i4 - July-August 2015 - p144(1) [51-500]
    y KR - June 1 2015 - pNA [51-500]
    y SLJ - v61 - i6 - June 2015 - p116(1) [51-500]

Schreiber, Michelle - *American Postfeminist Cinema: Women, Romance and Contemporary Culture*
    JGS - v24 - i3 - June 2015 - p365-366 [501+]

Schreier, Daniel - *Variation and Change in English: An Introduction*
    Lang Soc - v44 - i4 - Sept 2015 - p604-2 [501+]

Schreiter, Charlotte - *Gipsabgusse und antike Skulpturen: Prasentation un Kontext*
    Six Ct J - v46 - i3 - Fall 2015 - p775-776 [501+]

Schreuder, Deryck M. - *Universities for a New World: Making a Global Network in International Higher Education, 1913-2013*
    HNet - Feb 2015 - pNA [501+]

Schreyer, Kurt A. - *Shakespeare's Medieval Craft: Remnants of the Mysteries on the London Stage*
    Ren Q - v68 - i3 - Fall 2015 - p1142-1143 [501+]
    RES - v66 - i276 - Sept 2015 - p773-775 [501+]
    Six Ct J - v46 - i2 - Summer 2015 - p465-467 [501+]
    Specu - v90 - i3 - July 2015 - p851-852 [501+]

Schrieber, Anne - *Les pandas*
    c Res Links - v20 - i3 - Feb 2015 - p47(2) [51-500]

Schrift, Alan D. - *Poststructuralism and Critical Theory's Second Generation*
    FS - v69 - i1 - Jan 2015 - p127-128 [501+]

Schrijvers, Peter - *Those Who Hold Bastogne: The True Story of the Soldiers and Civilians Who Fought in the Biggest Battle of the Bulge*
    HNet - May 2015 - pNA [501+]
    J Mil H - v79 - i2 - April 2015 - p532-534 [501+]
    TLS - i5858 - July 10 2015 - p24(1) [501+]

Schroder, Deborah - *Exploring and Developing the Use of Art-Based Genograms in Family of Origin Therapy*
    RVBW - Sept 2015 - pNA [501+]

Schroder, Martin - *Integrating Varieties of Capitalism and Welfare State Research: A United Typology of Capitalisms*
    CS - v44 - i2 - March 2015 - p248-249 [501+]

Schrodinger, Erwin - *My View of the World*
    Nature - v526 - i7571 - Oct 1 2015 - p50(1) [51-500]

Schroeder, Abraham - *Too Many Tables (Illus. by Monkey, Micah)*
    c CH Bwatch - June 2015 - pNA [51-500]

Schroeder, Adam Lewis - *All-Day Breakfast*
    Nat Post - v17 - i107 - March 7 2015 - pWP5(1) [501+]

Schroeder, Alan - *Abe Lincoln: His Wit and Wisdom from A-Z (Illus. by O'Brien, John)*
    c HB Guide - v26 - i2 - Fall 2015 - p211(1) [51-500]

Schroeder, Alice - *The Snowball: Warren Buffett and the Business of Life*
    Forbes - v196 - i6 - Nov 2 2015 - p42(1) [501+]

Schroeder, Anne - *Cholama Moon*
    Roundup M - v22 - i3 - Feb 2015 - p27(1) [501+]
    Roundup M - v22 - i6 - August 2015 - p32(1) [501+]

Schroeder, Bernhard - *Fail Fast or Win Big: The Start-Up Plan for Starting Now*
    LJ - v140 - i2 - Feb 1 2015 - p90(3) [51-500]

Schroeder, Binette - *The Wizardling (Illus. by Schroeder, Binette)*
   c Sch Lib - v63 - i2 - Summer 2015 - p97(2) [51-500]

Schroeder, Erv - *The Memory of Stone: Meditations on the Canyons of the West (Illus. by Schroeder, Erv)*
   WLT - v89 - i3-4 - May-August 2015 - p121(1) [51-500]

Schroeder, John H. - *The Battle of Lake Champlain: A "Brilliant and Extraordinary Victory"*
   J Mil H - v79 - i3 - July 2015 - p825-826 [501+]

Schroeder, Joy A. - *Deborah's Daughters: Gender Politics and Biblical Interpretation*
   JR - v95 - i3 - July 2015 - p386(2) [501+]
   Theol St - v76 - i3 - Sept 2015 - p599(2) [501+]

Schroeder, Lisa - *All We Have Is Now*
   y BL - v111 - i19-20 - June 1 2015 - p94(1) [51-500]
   y KR - April 1 2015 - pNA [51-500]
   y SLJ - v61 - i5 - May 2015 - p124(1) [51-500]
   y VOYA - v38 - i3 - August 2015 - p83(1) [51-500]
The Bridge from Me to You
   y HB Guide - v26 - i1 - Spring 2015 - p122(1) [51-500]
The Girl in the Tower (Illus. by Ceccoli, Nicoletta)
   c KR - Dec 15 2015 - pNA [51-500]
   c SLJ - v61 - i10 - Oct 2015 - p94(2) [51-500]
The Girl in the Tower (Illus. by Ceccoli, Nicoletta)
   c PW - v262 - i51 - Dec 14 2015 - p85(1) [51-500]
My Secret Guide to Paris
   c BL - v111 - i11 - Feb 1 2015 - p52(2) [51-500]
   c HB Guide - v26 - i2 - Fall 2015 - p100(1) [51-500]
   y VOYA - v37 - i6 - Feb 2015 - p65(1) [51-500]

Schroeder, Lucinda Delaney - *Plunder of the Ancients: A True Story of Betrayal, Redemption, and an Undercover Quest to Recover Sacred Native American Artifacts*
   Roundup M - v22 - i3 - Feb 2015 - p24(2) [501+]
   Roundup M - v22 - i6 - August 2015 - p40(1) [501+]

Schroeder, Richard - *Africa after Apartheid: South Africa, Race, and Nation in Tanzania*
   ERS - v38 - i3 - March 2015 - p454(3) [501+]

Schroeder, Timothy - *In Praise of Desire*
   Ethics - v125 - i2 - Jan 2015 - p562(6) [501+]

Schroff, Laura - *An Invisible Thread Christmas Story (Illus. by Root, Barry)*
   c KR - Sept 1 2015 - pNA [51-500]
   c PW - v262 - i37 - Sept 14 2015 - p74(1) [51-500]
   c SLJ - v61 - i10 - Oct 2015 - p68(1) [51-500]

Schrum, Lynne - *Leading 21st Century Schools: Harnessing Technology for Engagement and Achievement*
   Bwatch - July 2015 - pNA [51-500]

Schuber, Frank N. - *Other Than War: The American Experience and Operations in the Post-Cold War Decade*
   APH - v62 - i2 - Summer 2015 - p52(2) [501+]

Schubert, Dirk - *Contemporary Perspectives on Jane Jacobs: Reassessing the Impacts of an Urban Visionary*
   GR - v105 - i2 - April 2015 - p258(4) [501+]
   HNet - May 2015 - pNA [501+]
Jane Jacobs und die Zukunft der Stadt: Diskurse - Perspektiven - Paradigmenwechsel
   HNet - May 2015 - pNA [501+]

Schubert, Friedrich Hermann - *Ludwig Camerarius (1573-1651): Eine Biographie*
   CEH - v48 - i1 - March 2015 - p114-115 [501+]

Schubert, Ingrid - *There Is a Crocodile under My Bed! (Illus. by Schubert, Dieter)*
   c CH Bwatch - July 2015 - pNA [51-500]
The Umbrella Book
   c Magpies - v30 - i1 - March 2015 - p27(1) [501+]

Schuchard, Ronald - *The Complete Prose of T.S. Eliot: The Critical Edition, vol. 1: Apprentice Years 1905-1918*
   HR - v68 - i1 - Spring 2015 - p125-132 [501+]
The Complete Prose of T.S. Eliot: The Critical Edition, vol. 2, The Perfect Critic 1919-1926
   HR - v68 - i1 - Spring 2015 - p125-132 [501+]

Schuck, Peter H. - *Why Government Fails so Often: And How It Can Do Better*
   IndRev - v19 - i3 - Wntr 2015 - p465(5) [501+]

Schuessler, John M. - *Deceit on the Road to War*
   Dis - v62 - i4 - Fall 2015 - p83(1) [501+]

Schuessler, Michael K. - *Foundational Arts: Mural Painting and Missionary Theater in New Spain*
   Ams - v72 - i1 - Jan 2015 - p153(2) [501+]

Schuette, Sarah L. - *Milton Hershey*
   c HB Guide - v26 - i1 - Spring 2015 - p193(1) [51-500]
So Many Shapes! A Spot-It, Learn-It Challenge
   TC Math - v21 - i9 - May 2015 - p566(2) [501+]

Schuh, Mari - *Awesome Dogs*
   c BL - v112 - i5 - Nov 1 2015 - p46(1) [51-500]
Clown Fish
   c Sch Lib - v63 - i4 - Winter 2015 - p222(1) [51-500]
Pebble Plus: Backyard Animals
   c HB Guide - v26 - i2 - Fall 2015 - p181(1) [51-500]

Schuh, Maximilian - *Aneignungen des Humanismus: Institutionelle und Individuelle Praktiken an der Universitat Ingolstadt im 15. Jahrhundert*
   CHR - v101 - i1 - Wntr 2015 - p164(2) [501+]
   HNet - July 2015 - pNA [501+]

Schuitema, Adam - *Haymaker*
   KR - Feb 15 2015 - pNA [501+]

Schuldt - *In Togo, dunkel: und andere Geschichten*
   TLS - i5872 - Oct 16 2015 - p26(1) [501+]

Schuler, Lou - *Strong: Nine Next-Level Workout Programs for Women*
   PW - v262 - i38 - Sept 21 2015 - p69(1) [51-500]

Schulhauser, Garnet - *Dancing Forever with Spirit: Astonishing Insights from Heaven*
   RVBW - May 2015 - pNA [51-500]

Schulian, John - *A Better Goodbye*
   BL - v112 - i4 - Oct 15 2015 - p18(1) [51-500]
   KR - Oct 1 2015 - pNA [51-500]
   PW - v262 - i39 - Sept 28 2015 - p62(1) [51-500]

Schull, Kent F. - *Prisons in the Late Ottoman Empire: Microcosms of Modernity*
   IJMES - v47 - i1 - Feb 2015 - p202-204 [501+]

Schulman, Bruce J. - *Making the American Century: Essays on the Political Culture of Twentieth Century America*
   JAH - v102 - i1 - June 2015 - p274-275 [501+]

Schulman, Sarah - *The Cosmopolitans*
   KR - Jan 1 2016 - pNA [51-500]
   LJ - v140 - i20 - Dec 1 2015 - p96(1) [51-500]

Schulte, Brigid - *Overwhelmed: How to Work, Love, and Play When No One Has the Time*
   y Ent W - i1358 - April 10 2015 - p66(1) [51-500]
   NYTBR - April 12 2015 - p28(L) [51-500]

Schulte, Donna Faulkner - *Santa's Search for the Perfect Child (Illus. by Chadwell, Dennis)*
   c CH Bwatch - Nov 2015 - pNA [51-500]

Schulte, Jan Erik - *Die Waffen-SS: Neue Forschungen*
   HNet - Feb 2015 - pNA [501+]
   Ger Q - v88 - i3 - Summer 2015 - p415(2) [501+]
Widerstand und Auswartiges Amt. Diplomaten gegen Hitler
   CEH - v48 - i3 - Sept 2015 - p439-441 [501+]

Schulte-Peevers, Andrea - *Berlin*
   Bwatch - May 2015 - pNA [51-500]

Schultek, Gretchen E. - *Elementary Educ 101: What They Didn't Teach You in College*
   Bwatch - April 2015 - pNA [51-500]

Schulten, Susan - *Mapping the Nation: History and Cartography in Nineteenth-Century America*
   RAH - v43 - i3 - Sept 2015 - p484-489 [501+]
   WHQ - v46 - i2 - Summer 2015 - p225-225 [501+]

Schultz, Brad - *Lombardi Dies, Orr Flies, Marshall Cries: The Sports Legacy of 1970*
   BL - v112 - i1 - Sept 1 2015 - p36(1) [51-500]
   PW - v262 - i37 - Sept 14 2015 - p58(1) [51-500]

Schultz, Duane - *Evans Carlson, Marine Raider: The Man Who Commanded America's First Special Forces*
   J Mil H - v79 - i1 - Jan 2015 - p251-252 [501+]

Schultz, Emily - *The Blondes*
   BL - v111 - i14 - March 15 2015 - p43(1) [51-500]
   Ent W - i1362 - May 8 2015 - p57(1) [51-500]
   KR - Feb 15 2015 - pNA [51-500]
   PW - v262 - i7 - Feb 16 2015 - p155(1) [51-500]

Schultz, Frances - *The Bee Cottage Story: How I Made a Muddle of Things and Decorated My Way Back to Happiness*
   PW - v262 - i18 - May 4 2015 - p115(1) [51-500]

Schultz, Gretchen - *Sapphic Fathers: Discourses of Same-Sex Desire from Nineteenth-Century France*
   TLS - i5875 - Nov 6 2015 - pNA [501+]

Schultz, Howard - *For Love of Country: What Our Veterans Can Teach Us about Citizenship, Heroism, and Sacrifice*
   NYTBR - March 15 2015 - p19(L) [501+]

Schultz, Ken - *The Complete Guide to North American Fishing*
   BL - v112 - i1 - Sept 1 2015 - p32(1) [51-500]

Schultz, Kevin M. - *Buckley and Mailer: The Difficult Friendship That Shaped the Sixties*
   BL - v111 - i16 - April 15 2015 - p14(1) [51-500]
   KR - March 15 2015 - pNA [51-500]
   LJ - v140 - i7 - April 15 2015 - p103(1) [51-500]
   Nat R - v67 - i14 - August 10 2015 - p48 [501+]
   PW - v262 - i10 - March 9 2015 - p61(1) [51-500]
   TimHES - i2223 - Oct 1 2015 - p49(1) [51-500]

Schultz Nicholson, Lorna - *Puckster Plays the Hockey Mascots*
   c Res Links - v20 - i3 - Feb 2015 - p8(1) [51-500]
Puckster's Christmas Hockey Tournament
   c Res Links - v20 - i3 - Feb 2015 - p8(2) [51-500]

Schultz, Paul H. - *Perspectives on Dodd-Frank and Finance*
   For Aff - v94 - i3 - May-June 2015 - pNA [501+]

Schultz, Peter - *Peter the Slug and the Great Forest Race (Illus. by Solyst, Ann)*
   c PW - v262 - i42 - Oct 19 2015 - p76(1) [51-500]

Schulz, Anne Markham - *The Sculpture of Tullio Lombardo*
   Apo - v181 - i629 - March 2015 - p210(2) [501+]

Schulz, Charles M. - *Peanuts: A Charlie Brown Christmas (Illus. by Jeralds, Scott)*
   c SLJ - v61 - i10 - Oct 2015 - p69(1) [51-500]

Schulz, Felix Robin - *Death in East Germany 1945-1990*
   GSR - v38 - i3 - Oct 2015 - p697-699 [501+]
   HNet - June 2015 - pNA [501+]

Schulz, Georg-Michael - *Walter Mehring*
   Ger Q - v88 - i1 - Wntr 2015 - p126(2) [501+]

Schulz, Gunther - *Regulation between Legal Norms and Economic Reality: Intentions, Effects, and Adaption - the German and American Experiences*
   HNet - Jan 2015 - pNA [501+]

Schulz, Heidi - *Hook's Daughter*
   y Sch Lib - v63 - i2 - Summer 2015 - p109(1) [51-500]
Hook's Revenge (Illus. by Hendrix, John)
   c HB Guide - v26 - i1 - Spring 2015 - p91(1) [51-500]
The Pirate Code (Illus. by Hendrix, John)
   c BL - v111 - i22 - August 1 2015 - p68(1) [51-500]
   c KR - June 15 2015 - pNA [51-500]

Schulze, Robin G. - *The Degenerate Muse: American Nature, Modernist Poetry, and the Problem of Cultural Hygiene*
   J Am St - v49 - i2 - May 2015 - p428-430 [501+]

Schumacher, Anna - *Children of the Earth*
   y BL - v111 - i19-20 - June 1 2015 - p96(1) [51-500]
   c HB Guide - v26 - i2 - Fall 2015 - p137(1) [51-500]
   y KR - April 15 2015 - pNA [51-500]
   y SLJ - v61 - i5 - May 2015 - p124(1) [51-500]
   y VOYA - v38 - i2 - June 2015 - p82(2) [51-500]

Schumacher, Hans - *Celestino Piatti's Animal ABC (Illus. by Piatti, Celestino)*
   c HB Guide - v26 - i2 - Fall 2015 - p16(1) [51-500]

Schumacher, Julie - *Dear Committee Members*
   LJ - v140 - i13 - August 1 2015 - p126(1) [51-500]
   NYTBR - Sept 20 2015 - p28(L) [501+]

Schumacher, Tony - *The British Lion*
   KR - August 15 2015 - pNA [51-500]
   PW - v262 - i32 - August 10 2015 - p37(1) [51-500]

Schuman, Michael - *Confucius: And the World He Created*
   LJ - v140 - i3 - Feb 15 2015 - p114(1) [51-500]
   PW - v262 - i1 - Jan 5 2015 - p63(1) [51-500]

Schuman, Michael A. - *The Life of Martin Luther King, Jr.: Leader for Civil Rights*
   y HB Guide - v26 - i1 - Spring 2015 - p192(1) [51-500]

Schumann, Marie, Francoise - *Salmon Maerins Gediehtsammlungen von 1538 bis 1546*
   Sev Cent N - v73 - i1-2 - Spring-Summer 2015 - p73(2) [501+]

Schurewegen, Franc - *Chateaubriand et les choses*
   FS - v69 - i2 - April 2015 - p252-2 [501+]

Schuster, David M. - *Linkers*
   KR - May 1 2015 - pNA [501+]

Schusterman, Michelle - *Dead Air (Illus. by Olesh, Stephanie)*
   c KR - June 15 2015 - pNA [51-500]
   c SLJ - v61 - i8 - August 2015 - p92(1) [51-500]

Schutte, Karen - *The Ticket*
   SPBW - Oct 2015 - pNA [51-500]

Schutte, Kimberly - *Women, Rank, and Marriage in the British Aristocracy, 1485-2000: An Open Elite?*
   Six Ct J - v46 - i2 - Summer 2015 - p515-517 [501+]

Schutten, Jan Paul - *Hello from 2030*
   c HB Guide - v26 - i1 - Spring 2015 - p174(1) [51-500]
The Mystery of Life: How Nothing Became Everything
   y KR - May 15 2015 - pNA [51-500]
The Mystery of Life: How Nothing Became Everything (Illus. by Rieder, Floor)
   c BL - v112 - i2 - Sept 15 2015 - p56(1) [51-500]
   c PW - v262 - i28 - July 13 2015 - p67(1) [51-500]
   c SLJ - v61 - i6 - June 2015 - p144(1) [51-500]

Schutz, Johannes - *Huter der Wirklichkeit: Der Dominikanerorden in der Mittelalterlichen Gesellschaft*

Skandinaviens
    HNet - June 2015 - pNA [501+]
Schutze, Sebastian - *William Blake: The Drawings for Dante's Divine Comedy*
    Apo - v181 - i629 - March 2015 - p208(2) [501+]
Schuyler, David - *The Papers of Frederick Law Olmsted, vol. IX: The Last Great Projects, 1890-1895*
    NYRB - v62 - i17 - Nov 5 2015 - p12(3) [501+]
Schwab, V.E. - *A Darker Shade of Magic (Read by Crossley, Steven). Audiobook Review*
    BL - v112 - i4 - Oct 15 2015 - p60(1) [51-500]
    LJ - v140 - i14 - Sept 1 2015 - p67(1) [51-500]
A Darker Shade of Magic
    BL - v111 - i11 - Feb 1 2015 - p32(1) [51-500]
    LJ - v140 - i9 - May 15 2015 - p74(3) [501+]
    PW - v262 - i1 - Jan 5 2015 - p56(2) [51-500]
A Gathering of Shadows
    KR - Dec 15 2015 - pNA [51-500]
    PW - v262 - i52 - Dec 21 2015 - p136(1) [51-500]
Schwabach, Karen - *The Hope Chest (Read by Mercer-Meyer, Carla). Audiobook Review*
    c SLJ - v61 - i10 - Oct 2015 - p53(2) [51-500]
Schwalbe, Michael - *Manhood Acts: Gender and the Practices of Domination*
    CS - v44 - i5 - Sept 2015 - p706-707 [501+]
Schwaller, John Frederick - *The History of the Catholic Church in Latin America: From Conquest to Revolution and Beyond*
    HNet - Sept 2015 - pNA [501+]
Schwanitz, Wolfgang G. - *Islam in Europe, Revolts in the Middle East: Islamism and Genocide from Wilhelm II and Enver Pasha through Hitler and Husseini to Arafat, Usama bin Laden, and Ahmadinejad, along with Discussions with Bernard Lewis*
    MEQ - v22 - i1 - Wntr 2015 - pNA [501+]
Schwarcz, Joe - *Monkeys, Myths, and Molecules: Separating Fact from Fiction in the Science of Everyday Life*
    LJ - v140 - i10 - June 1 2015 - p132(1) [51-500]
Schwartz, A. Brad - *Broadcast Hysteria: Orson Welles's War of the Worlds and the Art of Fake News (Read by Runnette, Sean). Audiobook Review*
    PW - v262 - i30 - July 27 2015 - p61(2) [51-500]
Broadcast Hysteria: Orson Welles's War of the Worlds and the Art of Fake News
    KR - March 15 2015 - pNA [501+]
    PW - v262 - i3 - Jan 19 2015 - p69(1) [51-500]
    BL - v111 - i13 - March 1 2015 - p12(1) [51-500]
    CSM - May 21 2015 - pNA [501+]
    LJ - v140 - i5 - March 15 2015 - p114(2) [501+]
    Reason - v47 - i3 - July 2015 - p72(3) [501+]
Schwartz, Agatha - *Gender and Modernity in Central Europe: The Austro-Hungarian Monarchy and its Legacy*
    CWS - v30 - i2-3 - Fall-Winter 2015 - p131(2) [501+]
Schwartz, Alexandra - *Come as You Are: Art of the 1990s*
    LJ - v140 - i12 - July 1 2015 - p83(1) [51-500]
    PW - v262 - i1 - Jan 5 2015 - p66(2) [51-500]
Schwartz, Amy - *100 Things That Make Me Happy*
    c HB Guide - v26 - i1 - Spring 2015 - p16(1) [51-500]
I Can't Wait! (Illus. by Schwartz, Amy)
    c HB - v91 - i6 - Nov-Dec 2015 - p74(2) [51-500]
    c KR - August 15 2015 - pNA [51-500]
    c PW - v262 - i32 - August 10 2015 - p59(1) [51-500]
    c PW - v262 - i49 - Dec 2 2015 - p27(1) [51-500]
    c SLJ - v61 - i9 - Sept 2015 - p128(1) [51-500]
Schwartz, Arthur D. - *Ethical Empowerment: Virtue beyond the Paradigms*
    SPBW - April 2015 - pNA [501+]
Schwartz, Barry - *Why We Work*
    LJ - v140 - i13 - August 1 2015 - p113(2) [51-500]
Schwartz, Benjamin E. - *Right of Boom: The Aftermath of Nuclear Terrorism*
    NYTBR - Feb 8 2015 - p13(L) [501+]
Schwartz, Betty - *Little Dinosaurs*
    c KR - Jan 1 2016 - pNA [51-500]
Schwartz, Betty Ann - *Hop, Hop Bunny (Illus. by Ng, Neiko)*
    c PW - v262 - i6 - Feb 9 2015 - p66(2) [501+]
My Barnyard!
    c KR - July 1 2015 - pNA [51-500]
My Dinosaurs!: A Read and Play Book (Illus. by Bendall-Brunello, John)
    c KR - July 1 2015 - pNA [51-500]
Run, Run Piglet (Illus. by Ng, Neiko)
    c KR - July 1 2015 - pNA [51-500]
Ten Playful Tigers: A Back-and-Forth Counting Book (Illus. by Powell, Luciana Navarro)
    c KR - July 1 2015 - pNA [51-500]

Schwartz, Casey - *In the Mind Fields: Exploring the New Science of Neuropsychoanalysis*
    KR - June 1 2015 - pNA [51-500]
    LJ - v140 - i12 - July 1 2015 - p100(1) [51-500]
    NYT - Dec 17 2015 - pC1(L) [501+]
    PW - v262 - i24 - June 15 2015 - p74(1) [51-500]
Schwartz, Corey Rosen - *Ninja Red Riding Hood (Illus. by Santat, Dan)*
    c HB Guide - v26 - i1 - Spring 2015 - p45(1) [51-500]
What about Moose? (Illus. by Yamaguchi, Keika)
    c CH Bwatch - August 2015 - pNA [51-500]
    c HB Guide - v26 - i2 - Fall 2015 - p51(1) [51-500]
    c KR - March 15 2015 - pNA [51-500]
    c SLJ - v61 - i5 - May 2015 - p92(1) [51-500]
Schwartz, D.L. - *Paideia and Cult: Christian Initiation in Theodore of Mopsuetia*
    Class R - v65 - i2 - Oct 2015 - p407-408 [501+]
Schwartz, Daniel B. - *The First Modern Jew: Spinoza and the History of an Image*
    JMH - v87 - i2 - June 2015 - p397(3) [501+]
Schwartz, Heather E. - *Bank Wisely*
    c BL - v112 - i3 - Oct 1 2015 - p44(1) [51-500]
Forced Removal: Causes and Effects of the Trail of Tears
    c HB Guide - v26 - i2 - Fall 2015 - p222(1) [51-500]
Schwartz, Jack - *The Fine Print*
    KR - August 15 2015 - pNA [51-500]
Schwartz, John - *Enchanting the Swan*
    KR - May 15 2015 - pNA [51-500]
Maarten Maartens Rediscovered
    KR - Sept 1 2015 - pNA [51-500]
Schwartz, Jordan - *The Art of LEGO Design: Creative Ways to Build Amazing Models*
    c VOYA - v37 - i6 - Feb 2015 - p88(1) [51-500]
Schwartz, Michael - *Class Divisions on the Broadway Stage: The Staging and Taming of the I.W.W.*
    Theat J - v67 - i2 - May 2015 - p371-373 [501+]
Schwartz, Michal - *Neuroimmunity: A New Science That Will Revolutionize How We Keep Our Brains Healthy and Young*
    LJ - v140 - i16 - Oct 1 2015 - p104(2) [51-500]
Schwartz, Peter - *In Defense of Selfishness: Why the Code of Self-Sacrifice Is Unjust and Destructive*
    BL - v111 - i18 - May 15 2015 - p4(1) [51-500]
    KR - March 15 2015 - pNA [51-500]
Schwartz, Samuel I. - *Street Smart: The Rise of Cities and the Fall of Cars*
    KR - August 1 2015 - pNA [51-500]
    LJ - v140 - i13 - August 1 2015 - p115(1) [51-500]
Schwartz, Seth - *The Ancient Jews from Alexander to Muhammad*
    Class R - v65 - i2 - Oct 2015 - p537-539 [501+]
    HNet - April 2015 - pNA [501+]
Schwartz, Simon - *First Man: Reimagining Matthew Henson (Illus. by Schwartz, Simon)*
    c PW - v262 - i29 - July 20 2015 - p195(1) [51-500]
    y BL - v112 - i2 - Sept 15 2015 - p52(1) [51-500]
    y KR - Sept 1 2015 - pNA [51-500]
    y SLJ - v61 - i10 - Oct 2015 - p119(2) [51-500]
The Other Side of the Wall (Illus. by Schwartz, Simon)
    y HB Guide - v26 - i2 - Fall 2015 - p212(1) [51-500]
    y KR - Jan 1 2015 - pNA [51-500]
    y VOYA - v37 - i6 - Feb 2015 - p50(2) [51-500]
    y PW - v262 - i3 - Jan 19 2015 - p87(1) [51-500]
Terrorist: Gavrilo Princip, the Assassin Who Ignited World War I
    y VOYA - v37 - i6 - Feb 2015 - p50(2) [51-500]
Schwartz, Stuart B. - *Sea of Storms: A History of Hurricanes in the Greater Caribbean from Columbus to Katrina*
    HNet - April 2015 - pNA [501+]
    Nature - v517 - i7536 - Jan 29 2015 - p551(1) [51-500]
    New Sci - v225 - i3005 - Jan 24 2015 - p47(1) [501+]
    TimHES - i2189 - Feb 5 2015 - p54-55 [501+]
Schwartzenberger, Tina - *The Canadian Shiel: From the Temperate to the Tundra*
    c Res Links - v20 - i4 - April 2015 - p14(1) [51-500]
Schwartzman, Kathleen C. - *The Chicken Trail: Following Workers, Migrants, and Corporations across the Americas*
    CS - v44 - i3 - May 2015 - p414-415 [501+]
Schwarz, Annelies - *My Bedtime Monster (Illus. by Pacovska, Kveta)*
    c KR - Oct 15 2015 - pNA [51-500]
Schwarz, Brigide - *Kurieruniversitat und Stadtromische Universitat von ca. 1300 bis 1471*
    Six Ct J - v46 - i3 - Fall 2015 - p710-713 [501+]

Schwarz, Frederick A.O., Jr. - *Democracy in the Dark: The Seduction of Government Secrecy*
    For Aff - v94 - i3 - May-June 2015 - pNA [501+]
    KR - Jan 15 2015 - pNA [501+]
    PW - v262 - i1 - Jan 5 2015 - p60(1) [51-500]
Schwarz, Jan - *Survivors and Exiles: Yiddish Culture After the Holocaust*
    RVBW - August 2015 - pNA [501+]
Schwarz, Viviane - *Is There a Dog in This Book? (Illus. by Schwarz, Viviane)*
    c HB Guide - v26 - i2 - Fall 2015 - p18(1) [51-500]
    c Magpies - v30 - i1 - March 2015 - p25(1) [51-500]
Schweer, Sebastian - *Skateboarding: Zwischen Urbaner Rebellion und Neoliberalem Selbstentwurf*
    HNet - March 2015 - pNA [501+]
Schwehn, Kaethe - *Tailings: A Memoir*
    CC - v132 - i10 - May 13 2015 - p36(1) [51-500]
Schweigart, Bill - *The Beast of Barcroft*
    PW - v262 - i39 - Sept 28 2015 - p73(1) [51-500]
Schweik, Susan M. - *The Ugly Laws: Disability in Public*
    JWH - v27 - i1 - Spring 2015 - p178(9) [501+]
Schweitzer, Sharon - *Access to Asia*
    KR - July 1 2015 - pNA [501+]
Schweizer, Bernard - *Hating God: The Untold Story of Misotheism*
    JR - v95 - i2 - April 2015 - p291(2) [501+]
Schweizer, Chris - *The Creeps: Night of the Frankenfrogs*
    c KR - May 15 2015 - pNA [51-500]
The Creeps: Night of the Frankenfrogs (Illus. by Schweizer, Chris)
    c SLJ - v61 - i6 - June 2015 - p107(1) [51-500]
    c BL - v111 - i22 - August 1 2015 - p49(1) [51-500]
Schweizer, Peter - *Clinton Cash: The Untold Story of How and Why Foreign Governments and Businesses Helped Make Bill and Hillary Rich*
    Bwatch - August 2015 - pNA [51-500]
    NYRB - v62 - i11 - June 25 2015 - p4(3) [501+]
    Prog - v79 - i9 - Sept 2015 - p44(2) [501+]
Schwyzer, Philip - *Shakespeare and the Remains of Richard III*
    Ren Q - v68 - i2 - Summer 2015 - p791-793 [501+]
Schymura, Yvonne - *Kathe Kollwitz 1867-2000: Biographie und Rezeptionsgeschichte einer Deutschen Kunstlerin*
    Ger Q - v88 - i2 - Spring 2015 - p254(3) [501+]
Scicluna, Denise - *Rock Art! Painting and Crafting with the Humble Pebble*
    LJ - v140 - i7 - April 15 2015 - p88(2) [51-500]
    PW - v262 - i11 - March 16 2015 - p81(1) [51-500]
Science in the Nation-State: Historic and Current Configurations in Global Perspective, 1800-2010
    HNet - April 2015 - pNA [501+]
Scieszka, Jon - *Frank Einstein and the Antimatter Motor (Illus. by Biggs, Brian)*
    c BL - v111 - i9-10 - Jan 1 2015 - p39(1) [501+]
    c HB Guide - v26 - i1 - Spring 2015 - p91(1) [51-500]
    c Magpies - v30 - i5 - Nov 2015 - p26(1) [501+]
Frank Einstein and the Brain Turbo (Illus. by Biggs, Brian)
    c Magpies - v30 - i5 - Nov 2015 - p26(1) [501+]
Frank Einstein and the Electro-Finger (Read by Scieszka, Jon, with Brian Biggs). Audiobook Review
    c BL - v111 - i22 - August 1 2015 - p79(2) [51-500]
    c SLJ - v61 - i6 - June 2015 - p62(1) [51-500]
Frank Einstein and the Electro-Finger (Illus. by Biggs, Brian)
    c BL - v111 - i15 - April 1 2015 - p80(1) [51-500]
    c HB Guide - v26 - i2 - Fall 2015 - p100(1) [51-500]
    c Magpies - v30 - i5 - Nov 2015 - p26(1) [501+]
    c Sch Lib - v63 - i2 - Summer 2015 - p109(2) [51-500]
Guys Read: Other Worlds
    c BL - v111 - i9-10 - Jan 1 2015 - p39(1) [501+]
Guys Read: True Stories
    c HB Guide - v26 - i2 - Fall 2015 - p202(1) [51-500]
Race from A to Z (Illus. by Shannon, David)
    c HB Guide - v26 - i2 - Fall 2015 - p18(1) [51-500]
Terrifying Tales
    c KR - May 15 2015 - pNA [51-500]
Scillian, Devin - *Memoirs of an Elf (Illus. by Bowers, Tim)*
    c HB Guide - v26 - i1 - Spring 2015 - p45(1) [51-500]
Sciolino, Elaine - *The Only Street in Paris: Life on the Rue des Martyrs*
    KR - August 15 2015 - pNA [501+]
    NYT - Dec 24 2015 - pC4(L) [501+]
    NYTBR - Dec 6 2015 - p76(L) [501+]
    BL - v112 - i2 - Sept 15 2015 - p21(1) [51-500]
    CSM - Nov 4 2015 - pNA [501+]
    LJ - v140 - i16 - Oct 1 2015 - p99(2) [51-500]
    PW - v262 - i34 - August 24 2015 - p71(1) [51-500]

Scoble, Robert - *The Corvo Cult: The History of an Obsession*
 TLS - i5877 - Nov 20 2015 - p7(1) [501+]
Raven: The Turbulent World of Baron Corvo
 TLS - i5877 - Nov 20 2015 - p7(1) [501+]
Scofield, Chris - *The Shark Curtain*
 y BL - v111 - i15 - April 1 2015 - p70(1) [51-500]
 y CCB-B - v68 - i11 - July-August 2015 - p564(1) [51-500]
 y KR - Feb 15 2015 - pNA [51-500]
 y PW - v262 - i8 - Feb 23 2015 - p77(2) [51-500]
 y SLJ - v61 - i3 - March 2015 - p162(1) [51-500]
Scogin, Gary - *Penny the Palomino Quarter Horse and Her New Shoes (Illus. by Ray, Alex)*
 c KR - Oct 1 2015 - pNA [501+]
Scolieri, Paul A. - *Dancing the New World: Aztecs, Spaniards, and the Choreography of Conquest*
 TDR - v59 - i1 - Spring 2015 - p183(2) [501+]
 Hisp R - v83 - i1 - Wntr 2015 - p113-117 [501+]
Scolik, Gabriels - *Eat! The Quick-Look Cookbook*
 BL - v111 - i22 - August 1 2015 - p13(2) [51-500]
Scollon, Bill - *Walt Disney: Drawn from Imagination*
 c HB Guide - v26 - i1 - Spring 2015 - p196(1) [51-500]
 c Sch Lib - v63 - i1 - Spring 2015 - p48(1) [51-500]
Scoppettone, Carolyn Cory - *Hold This! (Illus. by Alpaugh, Priscilla)*
 c KR - August 15 2015 - pNA [51-500]
Scotch, Allison Winn - *The Theory of Opposites (Read by Traister, Christina). Audiobook Review*
 LJ - v140 - i3 - Feb 15 2015 - p58(1) [51-500]
Scotson, James G. - *Cardboard Soldiers*
 KR - June 1 2015 - pNA [501+]
Scott, A.D. - *A Kind of Grief*
 BL - v112 - i1 - Sept 1 2015 - p48(1) [51-500]
 KR - August 1 2015 - pNA [501+]
 PW - v262 - i34 - August 24 2015 - p58(1) [51-500]
Scott, A.O. - *Better Living through Criticism: How to Think about Art, Pleasure, Beauty, and Truth*
 KR - Jan 1 2016 - pNA [501+]
 PW - v262 - i47 - Nov 23 2015 - p59(1) [51-500]
Scott-Baumann, Elizabeth - *Forms of Engagement: Women, Poetry, and Culture, 1640u-1680*
 MP - v112 - i4 - May 2015 - pE319(4) [501+]
Scott, Charlotte - *Shakespeare's Nature: From Cultivation to Culture*
 Ren Q - v68 - i1 - Spring 2015 - p400-401 [501+]
 RES - v66 - i273 - Feb 2015 - p170-172 [501+]
 Six Ct J - v46 - i3 - Fall 2015 - p763-765 [501+]
Scott, Clive - *Translating Apollinaire*
 TLS - i5859 - July 17 2015 - p25(1) [501+]
 FS - v69 - i3 - July 2015 - p429-430 [501+]
Scott, Cord A. - *Comics and Conflict: Patriotism and Propaganda from WWII through Operation Iraqi Freedom*
 JAH - v102 - i2 - Sept 2015 - p595-596 [501+]
Scott, Corinne - *Lover's Oak*
 PW - v262 - i26 - June 29 2015 - p53(1) [51-500]
Scott, Dan - *Big Buildings of the Ancient World*
 c HB Guide - v26 - i2 - Fall 2015 - p217(1) [51-500]
Big Buildings of the Modern World
 c HB Guide - v26 - i2 - Fall 2015 - p193(1) [51-500]
Blood Oath
 c KR - March 1 2015 - pNA [51-500]
 SLJ - v61 - i4 - April 2015 - p149(1) [51-500]
Scott, David (b. 1958-) - *Omens of Adversity: Tragedy, Time, Memory, Justice*
 AHR - v120 - i1 - Feb 2015 - p190(1) [501+]
 JIH - v45 - i3 - Wntr 2015 - p451-452 [501+]
 JRAI - v21 - i2 - June 2015 - p495(1) [501+]
Scott, David Meerman - *Marketing the Moon: The Selling of the Apollo Lunar Program*
 APJ - v29 - i3 - May-June 2015 - p96(3) [501+]
 T&C - v56 - i3 - July 2015 - p777-778 [501+]
Scott, Douglas D. - *Custer, Cody, and Grand Duke Alexis: Historical Archaeology of the Royal Buffalo Hunt*
 Historian - v77 - i3 - Fall 2015 - p583(2) [501+]
From These Honored Dead: Historical Archaeology of the American Civil War
 Am Ant - v80 - i2 - April 2015 - p420(2) [501+]
Scott, Elaine - *Our Moon: New Discoveries about Earth's Closest Companion*
 c KR - Dec 1 2015 - pNA [51-500]
 c PW - v262 - i47 - Nov 23 2015 - p70(1) [51-500]
Scott, Gini Graham - *Scammed: Team from the Biggest Consumer and Money Frauds How Not to Be a Victim*
 PW - v262 - i51 - Dec 14 2015 - p30(3) [51-500]
Scott, H.M. - *Modern Wars in Perspective*
 JMH - v87 - i1 - March 2015 - p151(3) [501+]

Scott, Heidi C.M. - *Chaos and Cosmos: Literary Roots of Modern Ecology in the British Nineteenth Century*
 TLS - i5841 - March 13 2015 - p25(1) [501+]
Scott, Helen C. - *New World Drama: The Performative Commons in the Atlantic World, 1649-1849*
 JAH - v102 - i2 - Sept 2015 - p524-525 [501+]
Scott, J.S. - *The Forbidden Billionaire*
 PW - v262 - i18 - May 4 2015 - p102(1) [51-500]
No Ordinary Billionaire
 PW - v262 - i6 - Feb 9 2015 - p50(1) [51-500]
Scott, James - *The Kept*
 LJ - v140 - i2 - Feb 1 2015 - p111(1) [501+]
 NYTBR - March 15 2015 - p28(L) [501+]
Target Tokyo: Jimmy Doolittle and the Raid That Avenged Pearl Harbor
 CSM - April 15 2015 - pNA [501+]
Scott, James M. - *Target Tokyo: Jimmy Doolittle and the Raid That Avenged Pearl Harbor*
 KR - Jan 1 2015 - pNA [501+]
 LJ - v140 - i3 - Feb 15 2015 - p115(1) [51-500]
Scott, Jennifer - *The Hundred Gifts*
 BL - v112 - i6 - Nov 15 2015 - p21(1) [51-500]
Scott, Jessica - *After the War*
 PW - v262 - i48 - Nov 30 2015 - p46(1) [51-500]
Before I Fall
 PW - v262 - i18 - May 4 2015 - p103(1) [51-500]
Forged in Fire
 PW - v262 - i48 - Nov 30 2015 - p46(2) [51-500]
Homefront
 PW - v262 - i47 - Nov 23 2015 - p56(1) [51-500]
It's Always Been You
 PW - v262 - i10 - March 9 2015 - p58(1) [51-500]
Scott, Jody - *Passing for Human*
 PW - v262 - i51 - Dec 14 2015 - p64(1) [51-500]
Scott, John - *Envisioning Sociology: Victor Branford, Patrick Geddes, and the Quest for Social Reconstruction*
 CS - v44 - i5 - Sept 2015 - p708-709 [501+]
Scott, Justin - *The Assassin*
 PW - v262 - i3 - Jan 19 2015 - p62(1) [51-500]
Scott, Katherine A. - *Reining in the State: Civil Society and Congress in the Vietnam and Watergate Eras*
 Historian - v77 - i1 - Spring 2015 - p141(3) [501+]
Scott, Katrina - *Tone It Up: 28 Days to Fit, Fierce, and Fabulous*
 PW - v262 - i16 - April 20 2015 - p72(1) [51-500]
Scott, Kieran - *Complete Nothing*
 y HB Guide - v26 - i1 - Spring 2015 - p122(1) [51-500]
Something True
 c HB Guide - v26 - i2 - Fall 2015 - p137(1) [51-500]
What Waits in the Woods
 y CCB-B - v68 - i10 - June 2015 - p514(2) [51-500]
 y CH Bwatch - Sept 2015 - pNA [51-500]
 c HB Guide - v26 - i2 - Fall 2015 - p137(1) [51-500]
 y KR - Jan 15 2015 - pNA [51-500]
 y VOYA - v37 - i6 - Feb 2015 - p84(1) [51-500]
Scott, Laurence - *The Four-Dimensional Human: Ways of Being in the Digital World*
 New Sci - v228 - i3045 - Oct 31 2015 - p45(1) [501+]
 NS - v144 - i5271 - July 17 2015 - p46(2) [501+]
Scott, M.J. - *The Shattered Court*
 PW - v262 - i12 - March 23 2015 - p52(1) [51-500]
Scott, Malcolm - *Chateaubriand: The Paradox of Chance*
 FS - v69 - i4 - Oct 2015 - p538-539 [501+]
Scott, Marcy - *Hummingbird Plants of the Southwest*
 RVBW - July 2015 - pNA [51-500]
Scott, Melanie - *Lawless in Leather*
 PW - v262 - i11 - March 16 2015 - p70(2) [51-500]
Playing Hard
 PW - v262 - i52 - Dec 21 2015 - p140(1) [51-500]
Scott, Michael - *Delphi: A History of the Center of the Ancient World*
 AHR - v120 - i3 - June 2015 - p1101-1102 [501+]
Scapegoats: Thirteen Victims of Military Injustice
 BL - v111 - i19-20 - June 1 2015 - p34(1) [51-500]
Scott, Michael Allan - *Grey Daze*
 KR - August 15 2015 - pNA [501+]
Scott-Moncrieff, Christina - *Complete Detox Workbook: 2-Day, 9-Day and 30-Day Makeovers to Cleanse and Revitalize Your Life*
 LJ - v140 - i6 - April 1 2015 - p111(2) [51-500]
Scott, Nancy - *The Cruising Guide to the Virgin Islands, 17th ed.*
 Bwatch - May 2015 - pNA [51-500]
Scott, Peter - *The Making of the Modern British Home: The Suburban Semi and Family Life between the Wars*
 AHR - v120 - i3 - June 2015 - p1117-1118 [501+]

Scott-Phillips, Thom - *Speaking Our Minds*
 TLS - i5851 - May 22 2015 - p28(1) [501+]
Scott, Raven - *Hard and Fast*
 PW - v262 - i47 - Nov 23 2015 - p55(1) [51-500]
Scott, Rebecca R. - *Removing Mountains: Extracting Nature and Identity in the Appalachian Coalfields*
 SF - v93 - i3 - March 2015 - pe86 [501+]
Scott, Regina - *Instant Frontier Family*
 y BL - v112 - i6 - Nov 15 2015 - p17(2) [51-500]
Scott, Ronnie - *Three Men and a Bradshaw: An Original Victorian Travel Journal*
 Spec - v328 - i9750 - July 11 2015 - p39(1) [501+]
Scott-Royce, Brenda - *Smithsonian Readers: Seriously Amazing, Level 2*
 c BL - v112 - i3 - Oct 1 2015 - p64(1) [51-500]
Scott, Russell - *The Hard Times*
 SPBW - Nov 2015 - pNA [501+]
Scott-Smith, Giles - *Western Anti-Communism and the Interdoc Network: Cold War Internationale*
 AHR - v120 - i1 - Feb 2015 - p355(1) [501+]
Scott, Steve - *Black Witch*
 RVBW - August 2015 - pNA [51-500]
Scott, Stuart - *Every Day I Fight*
 KR - March 1 2015 - pNA [501+]
Scott, Tom - *The Early Reformation in Germany: Between Secular Impact and Radical Vision*
 CH - v84 - i2 - June 2015 - p436(3) [501+]
 HER - v130 - i545 - August 2015 - p983(2) [501+]
Scott, Traer - *Nocturne: Creatures of the Night*
 c HB Guide - v26 - i1 - Spring 2015 - p157(1) [51-500]
Scott, Victoria - *Salt and Stone*
 c HB Guide - v26 - i2 - Fall 2015 - p137(1) [51-500]
 y VOYA - v38 - i1 - April 2015 - p83(1) [51-500]
The Titans
 c KR - Dec 1 2015 - pNA [51-500]
Scott, Walter - *Scott on Waterloo*
 TLS - i5854 - June 12 2015 - p27(1) [501+]
Scott, Whitney - *Embers and Flames*
 BL - v112 - i4 - Oct 15 2015 - p14(1) [51-500]
Scott, William - *The Model of Poesy*
 Six Ct J - v46 - i1 - Spring 2015 - p173(3) [501+]
Scottoline, Lisa - *Betrayed (Read by Bello, Maria). Audiobook Review*
 LJ - v140 - i6 - April 1 2015 - p48(1) [51-500]
Corrupted
 BL - v112 - i1 - Sept 1 2015 - p45(1) [51-500]
 KR - August 15 2015 - pNA [51-500]
 PW - v262 - i35 - August 31 2015 - p60(1) [51-500]
Does This Beach Make Me Look Fat? True Stories and Confessions
 BL - v111 - i19-20 - June 1 2015 - p24(1) [51-500]
 KR - May 1 2015 - pNA [501+]
 LJ - v140 - i12 - July 1 2015 - p92(1) [51-500]
 PW - v262 - i20 - May 18 2015 - p77(1) [51-500]
Every Fifteen Minutes (Read by Newbern, George). Audiobook Review
 LJ - v140 - i11 - June 15 2015 - p51(1) [51-500]
 PW - v262 - i26 - June 29 2015 - p62(2) [51-500]
Every Fifteen Minutes
 BL - v111 - i12 - Feb 15 2015 - p36(1) [51-500]
 KR - Feb 1 2015 - pNA [51-500]
 PW - v262 - i5 - Feb 2 2015 - p35(1) [51-500]
Keep Quiet
 RVBW - April 2015 - pNA [51-500]
Scotton, Christopher - *The Secret Wisdom of the Earth*
 CSM - Jan 22 2015 - pNA [501+]
 NYTBR - Jan 18 2015 - p10(L) [501+]
 SEP - v287 - i1 - Jan-Feb 2015 - p20(1) [501+]
Scotton, Rob - *Scaredy-Cat, Splat! (Illus. by Scotton, Rob)*
 c SLJ - v61 - i9 - Sept 2015 - p109(1) [51-500]
Splat the Cat and the Hotshot (Illus. by Eberz, Robert)
 c HB Guide - v26 - i2 - Fall 2015 - p61(1) [51-500]
Splat the Cat: Christmas Countdown (Illus. by Scotton, Rob)
 c PW - v262 - i37 - Sept 14 2015 - p72(2) [501+]
Splat the Cat: I Scream for Ice Cream (Illus. by Eberz, Robert)
 c HB Guide - v26 - i2 - Fall 2015 - p61(1) [51-500]
Splat the Cat: Splat and Seymour, Best Friends Forevermore (Illus. by Eberz, Robert)
 c HB Guide - v26 - i1 - Spring 2015 - p55(1) [51-500]
Scourfield, Jonathan - *Muslim Childhood: Religious Nurture in a European Context*
 JR - v95 - i2 - April 2015 - p280(3) [501+]
Scrace, Carolyn - *How to Art Doodle*
 c HB Guide - v26 - i2 - Fall 2015 - p193(1) [51-500]

Scragg, Donald - *A Conspectus of Scribal Hands Writing English, 960-1100*
    JEGP - v114 - i2 - April 2015 - p294(4) [501+]

Scranton, Laird - *Point of Origin: Gobekli Tepe and the Spiritual Matrix for the World's Cosmologies*
    Bwatch - May 2015 - pNA [51-500]

Scranton, Philip - *Reimagining Business History*
    JEH - v75 - i2 - June 2015 - p613-615 [501+]
    BHR - v89 - i1 - Spring 2015 - p155(3) [501+]

Scraton, Paul - *The Idea of a River: Walking Out of Berlin*
    TLS - i5873 - Oct 23 2015 - p30(1) [501+]

Screwvala, Ronnie - *Dream with Your Eyes Open: An Entrepreneurial Journey*
    SPBW - June 2015 - pNA [51-500]

Scribens, Sunny - *Space Song Rocket Ride (Illus. by Sim, David)*
    c HB Guide - v26 - i1 - Spring 2015 - p180(1) [51-500]

Scribner, Charity - *After the Red Army Faction: Gender, Culture, and Militancy*
    PAJ - v37 - i3 - Sept 2015 - p128-129 [501+]

Scritch Scratch Scraww Plop (Illus. by Crowther, Kitty)
    c NYTBR - Nov 8 2015 - p29(L) [501+]

Scroggs, Kirt - *It Came from beneath the Playground*
    c HB Guide - v26 - i1 - Spring 2015 - p65(2) [51-500]

Scruton, Roger - *Fools, Frauds and Firebrands: Thinkers of the New Left*
    KR - Sept 15 2015 - pNA [501+]
    PW - v262 - i31 - August 3 2015 - p45(1) [51-500]

The Meaning of Conservatism
    MA - v57 - i3 - Summer 2015 - p40(9) [501+]

Notes from Underground
    TLS - i5833 - Jan 16 2015 - p20(1) [501+]

The Soul of the World
    CC - v132 - i5 - March 4 2015 - p40(2) [501+]

Scull, Andrew - *Madness in Civilisation: A Cultural History of Insanity from the Bible to Freud, from the Madhouse to Modern Medicine*
    KR - March 1 2015 - pNA [501+]
    Nature - v520 - i7546 - April 9 2015 - p155(1) [51-500]
    NS - v144 - i5257 - April 10 2015 - p44(3) [501+]
    Spec - v327 - i9736 - April 4 2015 - p35(2) [501+]

Madness in Civilization: A Cultural History of Insanity, from the Bible to Freud, from the Madhouse to Modern Medicine
    LJ - v140 - i6 - April 1 2015 - p104(2) [501+]

Madness in Civilization: A Cultural History of Insanity from the Bible to Freud, from the Madhouse to Modern Medicine
    TLS - i5870 - Oct 2 2015 - p3(3) [501+]

Scully, Chris - *Until September*
    PW - v262 - i52 - Dec 21 2015 - p141(1) [51-500]

Scurr, Ruth - *John Aubrey: My Own Life*
    NS - v144 - i5253 - March 13 2015 - p51(1) [501+]
    Spec - v327 - i9733 - March 14 2015 - p45(2) [501+]
    TimHES - i2211 - July 9 2015 - p44(1) [501+]
    TLS - i5839 - Feb 27 2015 - p3(2) [501+]
    Econ - v415 - i8933 - April 11 2015 - p76(US) [501+]
    Lon R Bks - v37 - i19 - Oct 8 2015 - p17(2) [501+]

Sdbbe, Nina - *Love, Nina: A Nanny Writes Home*
    LJ - v140 - i13 - August 1 2015 - p126(1) [501+]

Seabrook, Jeremy - *The Song of the Shirt: The High Price of Cheap Garments, from Blackburn to Bangladesh*
    NS - v144 - i5277 - August 28 2015 - p40(1) [501+]
    TimHES - i2211 - July 9 2015 - p47(1) [501+]

Seabrook, John - *The Song Machine: Inside the Hit Factory (Read by Graham, Dion). Audiobook Review*
    LJ - v140 - i20 - Dec 1 2015 - p61(2) [51-500]

The Song Machine: Inside the Hit Factory
    BL - v112 - i3 - Oct 1 2015 - p9(1) [51-500]
    KR - July 1 2015 - pNA [501+]
    LJ - v140 - i15 - Sept 15 2015 - p79(2) [51-500]
    Mac - v128 - i43 - Nov 2 2015 - p77(1) [501+]
    Nation - v301 - i20 - Nov 16 2015 - p30(3) [501+]
    PW - v262 - i32 - August 10 2015 - p52(1) [51-500]

Seaford, Richard - *Cosmology and the Polis: The Social Construction of Space and Time in the Tragedies of Aeschylus*
    CJ - v110 - i3 - Feb-March 2015 - p374(3) [501+]

Seale, William - *The Imperial Season: America's Capital in the Time of the First Ambassadors, 1893-1918*
    JSH - v81 - i2 - May 2015 - p491(2) [501+]

Seales, Chad E. - *The Secular Spectacle: Performing Religion in a Southern Town*
    CH - v84 - i2 - June 2015 - p475(3) [501+]
    CHR - v101 - i3 - Summer 2015 - p682(2) [501+]
    JR - v95 - i4 - Oct 2015 - p581(2) [501+]
    JSH - v81 - i2 - May 2015 - p487(2) [501+]

Seals, Corinne A. - *Flexible Multilingual Education: Putting Children's Needs First*
    Lang Soc - v44 - i5 - Nov 2015 - p747-748 [501+]

Sealy, Jon - *The Whiskey Baron*
    South CR - v47 - i2 - Spring 2015 - p169-170 [501+]

Seaman, Camille - *Melting Away: A Ten-Year Journey through Our Endangered Polar Regions*
    LJ - v140 - i7 - April 15 2015 - p117(1) [51-500]
    Nature - v517 - i7536 - Jan 29 2015 - p551(1) [51-500]
    Nature - v523 - i7562 - July 30 2015 - pSB2(1) [51-500]

Seamon, John - *Memory and Movies: What Films Can Teach Us about Memory*
    Nature - v526 - i7573 - Oct 15 2015 - p321(1) [51-500]

Sear, Juliet - *Cakeology: Over 20 Sensational Step-by-Step Cake Decorating Projects*
    NYTBR - Dec 6 2015 - pNA(L) [501+]

Search Press - *A-Z of Whitework*
    LJ - v140 - i11 - June 15 2015 - p88(1) [501+]

Searcy, David - *Shame and Wonder: Essays*
    BL - v112 - i5 - Nov 1 2015 - p12(1) [51-500]
    KR - Oct 1 2015 - pNA [501+]
    LJ - v140 - i19 - Nov 15 2015 - p85(2) [51-500]
    PW - v262 - i34 - August 24 2015 - p69(1) [51-500]

Seargeant, Philip - *From Language to Creative Writing: An Introduction*
    MLR - v110 - i3 - July 2015 - p857-858 [501+]

Searle, John R. - *Seeing Things as They Are: A Theory of Perception*
    TLS - i5866 - Sept 4 2015 - p11(2) [501+]

Searle, Nicholas - *The Good Liar*
    KR - Nov 15 2015 - pNA [51-500]
    PW - v262 - i48 - Nov 30 2015 - p40(1) [501+]

Searles, Rachel - *The Lost Planet*
    c BL - v112 - i1 - Sept 1 2015 - p114(1) [51-500]

The Stolen Moon
    c HB Guide - v26 - i2 - Fall 2015 - p101(1) [51-500]

Sears, Clare - *Arresting Dress: Cross-Dressing, Law, and Fascination in Nineteenth-Century San Francisco*
    Wom R Bks - v32 - i3 - May-June 2015 - p8(2) [501+]

Sears, Michael - *Saving Jason*
    KR - Dec 1 2015 - pNA [51-500]
    PW - v262 - i50 - Dec 7 2015 - p69(1) [51-500]

Sears, Robert W. - *The Allergy Book: Solving Your Family's Nasal Allergies, Asthma, Food Sensitivities, and Related Health and Behavioral Problems*
    BL - v111 - i15 - April 1 2015 - p9(1) [51-500]
    LJ - v140 - i9 - May 15 2015 - p66(2) [51-500]

Seaton, James - *Literary Criticism from Plato to Postmodernism: The Humanistic Alternative*
    MA - v57 - i2 - Spring 2015 - p57(5) [501+]

Seaton, Jean - *'Pinkoes and Traitors': the BBC and the Nation, 1974-87*
    NS - v144 - i5251 - Feb 27 2015 - p47(1) [501+]
    Spec - v327 - i9732 - March 7 2015 - p40(1) [501+]

Pinkoes and Traitors: The BBC and the Nation, 1974-1987
    TLS - i5851 - May 22 2015 - p24(1) [501+]

Sebastiani, Silvia - *The Scottish Enlightenment: Race, Gender, and the Limits of Progress*
    Historian - v77 - i2 - Summer 2015 - p403(3) [501+]

Sebastien, Louis - *The Life of Augustine of Hippo, Part 2: The Donatist Controversy*
    Specu - v90 - i1 - Jan 2015 - p272-273 [501+]

Sebestyen, Victor - *1946: The Making of the Modern World*
    LJ - v140 - i20 - Dec 1 2015 - p117(1) [51-500]

Seccombe, Thomas - *The Problem of 'Hamlet'*
    TLS - i5866 - Sept 4 2015 - p16(1) [501+]

Secor, Laura - *Children of Paradise: The Struggle for the Soul of Iran*
    KR - Nov 15 2015 - pNA [501+]
    PW - v262 - i52 - Dec 21 2015 - p145(1) [501+]

Secrest, Meryle - *Stephen Sondheim: A Life*
    TLS - i5845 - April 10 2015 - p16(1) [501+]

Secunda, Shai - *The Iranian Talmud: Reading the Tavli in Its Sasanian Context*
    JR - Jan 2015 - p140(2) [501+]

Sedaka, Marc - *Dinosaur Pet (Illus. by Bowers, Tim)*
    c CH Bwatch - Feb 2015 - pNA [51-500]

Seddon, Angela - *Ernest Shackleton: Antarctic Explorer*
    c Sch Lib - v63 - i1 - Spring 2015 - p46(1) [51-500]

Seddon, Holly - *Try Not to Breathe*
    BL - v112 - i7 - Dec 1 2015 - p32(1) [51-500]
    KR - Nov 1 2015 - pNA [501+]
    PW - v262 - i51 - Dec 14 2015 - p59(1) [51-500]

Sedgewick, Roger - *Introduction to Programming in Python*
    Bwatch - Oct 2015 - pNA [501+]

Sedgwick, Chantele - *Love, Lucas*
    y SLJ - v61 - i5 - May 2015 - p116(1) [51-500]

Sedgwick, John - *War of Two: Alexander Hamilton, Aaron Burr, and the Duel That Stunned the Nation*
    BL - v112 - i4 - Oct 15 2015 - p15(1) [51-500]
    KR - Sept 1 2015 - pNA [501+]
    NYT - Oct 18 2015 - p3(L) [501+]
    NYTBR - Dec 13 2015 - p39(L) [501+]
    PW - v262 - i39 - Sept 28 2015 - p80(1) [501+]

Sedgwick, Julian - *The Black Dragon*
    c KR - Dec 15 2015 - pNA [51-500]

Ghosts of Shanghai
    c Sch Lib - v63 - i4 - Winter 2015 - p233(1) [51-500]

The Wheel of Life and Death: Mysterium
    y Sch Lib - v63 - i1 - Spring 2015 - p58(1) [51-500]

Sedgwick, Marcus - *The Ghosts of Heaven*
    y HB - v91 - i1 - Jan-Feb 2015 - p87(2) [51-500]
    c HB Guide - v26 - i2 - Fall 2015 - p137(2) [51-500]
    y NYTBR - Jan 18 2015 - p19(L) [501+]
    y VOYA - v37 - i6 - Feb 2015 - p65(1) [51-500]
    y CCB-B - v68 - i6 - Feb 2015 - p330(1) [51-500]
    y Sch Lib - v63 - i1 - Spring 2015 - p58(1) [51-500]

A Love Like Blood
    BL - v111 - i18 - May 15 2015 - p34(1) [51-500]

She Is Not Invisible
    y Teach Lib - v42 - i3 - Feb 2015 - p32(6) [501+]

Sedlak, David - *Water 4.0: The Past, Present, and Future of the World's Most Vital Resource*
    NYRB - v62 - i16 - Oct 22 2015 - p45(2) [501+]

Sedlmaier, Alexander - *Consumption and Violence: Radical Protest in Cold-War West Germany*
    CEH - v48 - i3 - Sept 2015 - p448-450 [501+]
    HNet - Sept 2015 - pNA [501+]

Sedor, Daniel L. - *Model Coach: A Common Sense Guide for Coaches of Youth Sports*
    RVBW - August 2015 - pNA [51-500]

Sedunary, Michael - *The Unlikely Story of Bennelong and Phillip (Illus. by Emmerichs, Bern)*
    c Magpies - v30 - i1 - March 2015 - p22(1) [501+]

Seebohm, Caroline - *Rescuing Garden: Preserving America's Historic Gardens*
    NYTBR - Dec 6 2015 - p66(L) [501+]

Seed, Andy - *Prankenstein (Illus. by Morgan, Richard)*
    c Sch Lib - v63 - i1 - Spring 2015 - p44(1) [51-500]

The Silly Book of Weird and Wacky Words (Illus. by Garrett, Scott)
    c Sch Lib - v63 - i4 - Winter 2015 - p239(1) [51-500]

Seedhouse, Erik - *Beyond Human: Engineering Our Future Evolution*
    Analog - v135 - i4 - April 2015 - p107(1) [501+]

Seefeldt, Douglas - *Cody Studies*
    WHQ - v46 - i3 - Autumn 2015 - p394-395 [501+]

Seegel, Steven - *Mapping Europe's Borderlands: Russian Cartography in the Age of Empire*
    HNet - Jan 2015 - pNA [501+]

Seeger, Christoph - *The Hepatitis B and Delta Viruses*
    RVBW - August 2015 - pNA [51-500]

Seeger, Laura Vaccaro - *Dog and Bear: Tricks and Treats*
    c HB Guide - v26 - i1 - Spring 2015 - p45(1) [51-500]

I Used to Be Afraid (Illus. by Seeger, Laura Vaccaro)
    c HB - v91 - i6 - Nov-Dec 2015 - p75(1) [51-500]
    c KR - August 15 2015 - pNA [51-500]
    c NYTBR - Oct 11 2015 - p16(L) [501+]
    c PW - v262 - i22 - June 1 2015 - p57(1) [51-500]
    c PW - v262 - i49 - Dec 2 2015 - p20(1) [51-500]
    c SLJ - v61 - i9 - Sept 2015 - p128(1) [51-500]

Seek, Amy - *God and Jetfire: Confessions of a Birth Mother*
    KR - April 1 2015 - pNA [501+]
    NY - v91 - i26 - Sept 7 2015 - p82 [51-500]
    NYTBR - July 26 2015 - p11(L) [501+]
    PW - v262 - i19 - May 11 2015 - p50(1) [51-500]

Seeley, Cathy L. - *Smarter Than We Think: More Messages about Math, Teaching, and Learning in the 21st Century*
    Math T - v109 - i1 - August 2015 - p77-77 [501+]

Seeskin, Kenneth - *Jewish Messianic Thought in an Age of Despair*
    RM - v68 - i3 - March 2015 - p677(3) [501+]

Seethaler, Robert - *A Whole Life*
    TLS - i5874 - Oct 30 2015 - p21(1) [501+]
Seevers, Boyd - *Warfare in the Old Testament: The Organization, Weapons, and Tactics of Ancient Near Eastern Armies*
    BTB - v45 - i3 - August 2015 - p184(2) [501+]
Sef, Ariela Abramovich - *Born in the Ghetto: My Triumph over Adversity*
    RVBW - March 2015 - pNA [51-500]
Seferiades, Seraphim - *Violent Protest, Contentious Politics, and the Neoliberal State*
    CS - v44 - i4 - July 2015 - p552-554 [501+]
Sefton, Maggie - *Purl Up and Die*
    Bwatch - August 2015 - pNA [51-500]
Segal, Adam - *The Hacked World Order: How Nations Fight, Trade, Maneuver, and Manipulate in the Digital Age*
    KR - Jan 1 2016 - pNA [501+]
Segal, Howard P. - *Utopias: A Brief History from Ancient Writings to Virtual Communities*
    Isis - v106 - i1 - March 2015 - p157(2) [501+]
    T&C - v56 - i4 - Oct 2015 - p972-973 [501+]
Segal, Mark - *And Then I Danced: Traveling the Road to LGBT Equality*
    BL - v112 - i1 - Sept 1 2015 - p17(1) [51-500]
    KR - August 15 2015 - pNA [501+]
    PW - v262 - i32 - August 10 2015 - p49(1) [51-500]
Segal, Mindy - *Cookie Love*
    NYT - Dec 2 2015 - pD6(L) [501+]
Segar, Michelle - *No Sweat: How the Simple Science of Motivation Can Bring You a Lifetime of Fitness*
    LJ - v140 - i7 - April 15 2015 - p109(1) [51-500]
    RVBW - Oct 2015 - pNA [51-500]
Segel, Jason - *Nightmares! (Illus. by Kwasny, Karl)*
    c Sch Lib - v63 - i1 - Spring 2015 - p44(1) [51-500]
The Sleepwalker Tonic (Read by Segel, Jason). Audiobook Review
    c SLJ - v61 - i11 - Nov 2015 - p71(2) [51-500]
The Sleepwalker Tonic
    c KR - August 15 2015 - pNA [51-500]
Segersten, Alissa - *The Elimination Diet: Discover the Foods That Are Making You Sick and Tired - and Feel Better Fast*
    PW - v262 - i7 - Feb 16 2015 - p174(1) [51-500]
Seglow, Jonathan - *Defending Associative Duties*
    Ethics - v125 - i2 - Jan 2015 - p610(5) [501+]
Segovia, Andres - *Slur Exercises, Trills, and Chromatic Octaves*
    Am MT - v64 - i4 - Feb-March 2015 - p60(2) [501+]
Segre, Chiara Valentina - *Lola and I (Illus. by Domeniconi, Paolo)*
    c KR - Nov 1 2015 - pNA [51-500]
Segundo, Jerome - *Sweet Holy Motherfucking Everloving Delusional Bastard*
    KR - July 15 2015 - pNA [51-500]
Sehat, David - *The Jefferson Rule: How the Founding Fathers Became Infallible and Our Politics Inflexible*
    CSM - May 28 2015 - pNA [51-500]
    KR - Feb 15 2015 - pNA [501+]
    LJ - v140 - i3 - Feb 15 2015 - p116(2) [51-500]
    PW - v262 - i12 - March 23 2015 - p64(1) [51-500]
Sehgal, Kabir - *Coined: The Rich Life of Money and How Its History Has Shaped Us*
    Har Bus R - v93 - i6 - June 2015 - p118(2) [501+]
    KR - Jan 1 2015 - pNA [501+]
    LJ - v140 - i3 - Feb 15 2015 - p110(1) [51-500]
    NYTBR - March 22 2015 - p23(L) [501+]
    PW - v262 - i1 - Jan 5 2015 - p63(1) [51-500]
The Wheels on the Tuk Tuk (Illus. by Golden, Jess)
    c BL - v112 - i5 - Nov 1 2015 - p44(1) [51-500]
    c PW - v262 - i34 - August 24 2015 - p79(1) [51-500]
    c SLJ - v61 - i11 - Nov 2015 - p88(1) [51-500]
Seibert, Brian - *What the Eye Hears: A History of Tap Dancing*
    BL - v112 - i4 - Oct 15 2015 - p12(1) [51-500]
    HM - v331 - i1986 - Nov 2015 - p77(3) [501+]
    KR - Sept 15 2015 - pNA [51-500]
    LJ - v140 - i16 - Oct 1 2015 - p84(1) [51-500]
    NYTBR - Dec 6 2015 - p52(L) [501+]
    PW - v262 - i37 - Sept 14 2015 - p58(1) [51-500]
Seibert, Peter - *Anne Frank: Mediengeschichten*
    HNet - March 2015 - pNA [51-500]
Seibt, Gustav - *Mit einer Art von Wut: Goethe in der Revolution*
    TLS - i5842 - March 20 2015 - p8(1) [501+]
Seichter, Sabine - *Erziehung an der Mutterbrust: Eine kritische Kulturgeschichte des Stillens*
    HNet - April 2015 - pNA [501+]

Seidel, Peter - *There Is Still Time: To Look at the Big Picture ... and Act*
    KR - August 15 2015 - pNA [501+]
    LJ - v140 - i20 - Dec 1 2015 - p128(2) [51-500]
    SPBW - Nov 2015 - pNA [51-500]
Seiden, Art - *My ABC Book (Illus. by Seiden, Art)*
    c HB Guide - v26 - i2 - Fall 2015 - p18(1) [51-500]
Seider, Aaron M. - *Memory in Vergil's Aeneid: Creating the Past*
    Class R - v65 - i1 - April 2015 - p133-135 [501+]
Seidler, Tor - *Firstborn (Read by Barber, Jenni).* Audiobook Review
    c SLJ - v61 - i5 - May 2015 - p70(1) [51-500]
Firstborn
    c BL - v111 - i12 - Feb 15 2015 - p85(1) [51-500]
    c HB Guide - v26 - i2 - Fall 2015 - p101(1) [51-500]
    c NYTBR - May 10 2015 - p17(L) [501+]
    PW - v262 - i2 - Jan 12 2015 - p60(1) [51-500]
Mean Margaret (Illus. by Agee, Jon)
    c HB Guide - v26 - i1 - Spring 2015 - p92(1) [51-500]
The Wainscott Weasel (Illus. by Marcellino, Fred)
    c HB Guide - v26 - i1 - Spring 2015 - p92(1) [51-500]
Seidlinger, Michael J. - *The Strangest*
    KR - Nov 1 2015 - pNA [501+]
Seidman, David - *What If I'm an Atheist? A Teen's Guide to Exploring a Life without Religion*
    y CCB-B - v68 - i10 - June 2015 - p515(1) [51-500]
    y HB Guide - v26 - i2 - Fall 2015 - p150(1) [51-500]
    y KR - Jan 15 2015 - pNA [51-500]
    y PW - v262 - i4 - Jan 26 2015 - p175(1) [51-500]
    y VOYA - v37 - i6 - Feb 2015 - p88(1) [51-500]
Seierstad, Asne - *One of Us: The Story of Anders Breivik and the Massacre in Norway*
    KR - Feb 15 2015 - pNA [501+]
    LJ - v140 - i6 - April 1 2015 - p108(1) [51-500]
    NS - v144 - i5253 - March 13 2015 - p48(2) [501+]
    NYRB - v62 - i4 - March 5 2015 - p55(3) [501+]
    NYT - April 10 2015 - pC21(L) [501+]
    NYTBR - April 26 2015 - p1(L) [501+]
    NYTBR - Dec 13 2015 - p12(L) [501+]
    PW - v262 - i9 - March 2 2015 - p2(1) [501+]
    Quad - v59 - i5 - May 2015 - p98(5) [501+]
    Spec - v327 - i9733 - March 14 2015 - p42(1) [501+]
Seigel, Andrea - *Everybody Knows Your Name*
    y CCB-B - v68 - i10 - June 2015 - p515(1) [51-500]
    c HB Guide - v26 - i2 - Fall 2015 - p138(1) [51-500]
    y KR - Jan 1 2015 - pNA [51-500]
    y VOYA - v37 - i6 - Feb 2015 - p66(1) [501+]
Seijas, Tatiana - *Asian Slaves in Colonial Mexico: From Chinos to Indians*
    AHR - v120 - i4 - Oct 2015 - p1531-1532 [501+]
    Ams - v72 - i3 - July 2015 - p499(2) [501+]
Seiler, Annina - *The Scripting of the Germanic Languages: A Comparative Study of "Spelling Difficulties" in Old English, Old High German and Old Saxon*
    JEGP - v114 - i3 - July 2015 - p433(3) [501+]
Seiler, Mark Daniel - *Sighing Women Tea*
    KR - March 1 2015 - pNA [501+]
Seilstad, Lorna - *As Love Blooms*
    BL - v111 - i18 - May 15 2015 - p31(1) [51-500]
Seiple, Samantha - *Lincoln's Spymaster: Allan Pinkerton, America's First Private Eye*
    c BL - v111 - i22 - August 1 2015 - p52(1) [51-500]
    c KR - July 15 2015 - pNA [51-500]
    c SLJ - v61 - i10 - Oct 2015 - p138(1) [51-500]
    y VOYA - v38 - i3 - August 2015 - p68(2) [51-500]
Seirstad, Asne - *One of Us: The Story of Anders Breivik and the Massacre in Norway*
    Bks & Cult - v21 - i5 - Sept-Oct 2015 - p38(2) [501+]
Seitz, Brian - *The Iroquois and the Athenians: A Political Ontology*
    Am Ind CRJ - v39 - i1 - Wntr 2015 - p129-131 [501+]
Selby, Hubert, Jr. - *Last Exit to Brooklyn*
    TimHES - i2210 - July 2 2015 - p47-1 [501+]
Seldon, Anthony - *Beyond Happiness: The Trap of Happiness and How to Find Deeper Meaning and Joy*
    Har Bus R - v93 - i7-8 - July-August 2015 - p130(2) [501+]
Selengut, Charles - *Our Promised Land: Faith and Militant Zionism in Israeli Settlements*
    BL - v111 - i19-20 - June 1 2015 - p12(1) [51-500]
Self, Andrew - *The Birds of London*
    TLS - i5859 - July 17 2015 - p26(1) [501+]

Self, Robert O. - *All in the Family: The Realignment of American Democracy since the 1960s*
    JWH - v27 - i1 - Spring 2015 - p161(7) [501+]
    RAH - v43 - i2 - June 2015 - p361-368 [501+]
Self, Will - *Shark*
    NYTBR - Nov 22 2015 - p36(4) [501+]
Selfors, Suzanne - *Ever After High: Next Top Villain*
    c BL - v111 - i9-10 - Jan 1 2015 - p101(1) [51-500]
The Rain Dragon Rescue (Illus. by Santat, Dan)
    c SLJ - v61 - i6 - June 2015 - p46(6) [51-500]
Selig, Paul - *The Book of Mastery*
    PW - v262 - i45 - Nov 9 2015 - p57(1) [51-500]
Seliger, Jake - *Asking Anna*
    KR - July 1 2015 - pNA [51-500]
Seligman, Adam B. - *Religious Education and the Challenge of Pluralism*
    J Ch St - v57 - i3 - Summer 2015 - p563-565 [501+]
Seligmann, Linda J. - *Broken Links, Enduring Ties: American Adoption across Race, Class, and Nation*
    CS - v44 - i5 - Sept 2015 - p709-711 [501+]
    ERS - v38 - i8 - August 2015 - p1431(3) [501+]
Seligmann, Matthew S. - *The Naval Route to the Abyss: The Anglo-German Naval Race, 1895-1914*
    J Mil H - v79 - i4 - Oct 2015 - p1153-1154 [501+]
    J Mil H - v79 - i3 - July 2015 - p851-852 [501+]
Selingo, Jeffrey J. - *College Unbound: The Future of Higher Education and What It Means for Students*
    BL - v111 - i21 - July 1 2015 - p22(2) [501+]
Sell, Roger D. - *The Ethics of Literary Communication: Genuineness, Directness, Indirectness*
    Poetics T - v36 - i1-2 - June 2015 - p141-143 [501+]
Selland, Eric - *The Guest Cat*
    WLT - v89 - i2 - March-April 2015 - p59(2) [501+]
Sellers, L.J. - *Deadly Bonds*
    RVBW - March 2015 - pNA [51-500]
Point of Control
    PW - v262 - i45 - Nov 9 2015 - p38(2) [51-500]
The Target
    RVBW - Jan 2015 - pNA [501+]
Wrongful Death
    RVBW - Nov 2015 - pNA [501+]
Sellers, Peter - *This One's Trouble*
    Nat Post - v17 - i176 - May 30 2015 - pWP5(1) [501+]
Selley, Ron - *I Won't Be Home Next Summer: Flight Lieutenant R.N. Selley DFC (1917-1941)*
    APH - v62 - i2 - Summer 2015 - p58(2) [501+]
Sellier, Marie - *My First 10 Paintings*
    c CH Bwatch - April 2015 - pNA [51-500]
Sellner, Joelle - *Punky Brewster (Illus. by Vamos, Lesley)*
    c BL - v111 - i19-20 - June 1 2015 - p67(1) [51-500]
    c KR - April 15 2015 - pNA [51-500]
    c SLJ - v61 - i6 - June 2015 - p107(1) [51-500]
Selly, Patty Born - *Connecting Animals and Children in Early Childhood*
    Sci & Ch - v52 - i8 - April-May 2015 - p28 [501+]
Seltzer, Eric - *The Long Dog (Illus. by Seltzer, Eric)*
    c CCB-B - v69 - i2 - Oct 2015 - p111(1) [51-500]
Selzer, Adam - *Play Me Backwards*
    y HB Guide - v26 - i1 - Spring 2015 - p123(1) [51-500]
Selznick, Brian - *The Marvels (Illus. by Selznick, Brian)*
    c NYTBR - Sept 13 2015 - p21(L) [501+]
    c BL - v111 - i21 - July 1 2015 - p66(1) [51-500]
    c HB - v91 - i5 - Sept-Oct 2015 - p117(1) [51-500]
    c KR - July 1 2015 - pNA [51-500]
    c Magpies - v30 - i5 - Nov 2015 - p39(1) [501+]
    y Nat Post - v17 - i266 - Sept 26 2015 - pWP5(1) [501+]
    c PW - v262 - i27 - July 6 2015 - p73(1) [51-500]
    c PW - v262 - i49 - Dec 2 2015 - p70(1) [51-500]
    c SLJ - v61 - i8 - August 2015 - p92(1) [51-500]
    y VOYA - v38 - i4 - Oct 2015 - p79(1) [501+]
Semahn, Jacob - *Goners: We All Fall Down (Illus. by Corona, Jorge)*
    y SLJ - v61 - i8 - August 2015 - p112(1) [51-500]
Sembene, Ousmane - *God's Bits of Wood*
    FS - v69 - i3 - July 2015 - p415-416 [501+]
Semken, Steven H. - *Soul External: Rediscovering The Great Blue Heron*
    SPBW - May 2015 - pNA [51-500]
Semmelhack, Elizabeth - *Out of the Box: The Rise of Sneaker Culture*
    HM - v331 - i1984 - Sept 2015 - p89(6) [501+]
Sen, Amiya P. - *Religion and Rabindranath Tagore: Select Discourses, Addresses, and Letters in Translation*
    TLS - i5868 - Sept 18 2015 - p27(1) [501+]

Sen, Chaitali - *The Pathless Sky*
   KR - August 15 2015 - pNA [51-500]
Sendker, Jan-Philipp - *Whispering Shadows*
   BL - v111 - i12 - Feb 15 2015 - p39(2) [501+]
   KR - Feb 15 2015 - pNA [51-500]
   LJ - v140 - i5 - March 15 2015 - p97(1) [501+]
   PW - v262 - i6 - Feb 9 2015 - p45(1) [51-500]
Senelick, Laurence - *The Soviet Theater: A Documentary History*
   TLS - i5850 - May 15 2015 - p11(2) [501+]
   Stanislavsky: A Life In Letters
   Theat J - v67 - i2 - May 2015 - p373-374 [501+]
Seneviratne, Samantha - *The New Sugar and Spice: A Recipe for Bolder Baking*
   LJ - v140 - i19 - Nov 15 2015 - p103(2) [51-500]
   PW - v262 - i24 - June 15 2015 - p79(1) [51-500]
Sengar, Rakesh S. - *Climate Change on Crop Productivity*
   Bwatch - June 2015 - pNA [51-500]
Sengupta, Hindol - *Recasting India: How Entrepreneurship is Revolutionising the World's Largest Democracy*
   Econ - v415 - i8934 - April 18 2015 - p78(US) [501+]
Sengupta, Sakti - *Discovering Indian Independent Cinema: The Films of Girish Kasaravall*
   KR - Dec 1 2015 - pNA [501+]
Senier, Siobhan - *Dawnland Voices: An Anthology of Indigenous Writing from New England*
   TLS - i5877 - Nov 20 2015 - p27(1) [501+]
Senior, Jennifer - *All Joy and No Fun: The Paradox of Modern Parenthood*
   NYTBR - Feb 8 2015 - p28(L) [501+]
Senior, Olive - *Anna Carries Water (Illus. by James, Laura)*
   c Bkbird - v53 - i4 - Fall 2015 - p77(1) [501+]
Senker, Cath - *Ancient Egypt in 30 Seconds: 30 Awesome Topics for Pharaoh Fanatics Explained in Half a Minute*
   c Sch Lib - v63 - i3 - Autumn 2015 - p176(1) [51-500]
   Great Britain
   c HB Guide - v26 - i1 - Spring 2015 - p202(1) [51-500]
   South Africa
   c HB Guide - v26 - i1 - Spring 2015 - p202(1) [51-500]
   Stephen Hawking
   c Sch Lib - v63 - i4 - Winter 2015 - p240(1) [51-500]
   Stories of Women in the 1960s: Fighting for Freedom
   c HB Guide - v26 - i2 - Fall 2015 - p213(1) [51-500]
Senocak, Bulent - *Shattered Dreams*
   KR - April 1 2015 - pNA [501+]
Senocak, Neslihan - *The Poor and the Perfect: The Rise of Learning in the Franciscan Order, 1209-1310*
   HER - v130 - i544 - June 2015 - p703(2) [501+]
Sensen, Oliver - *Kant on Moral Autonomy*
   Phil R - v124 - i2 - April 2015 - p263(6) [501+]
Sentier, Elen - *Gardening with the Moon and Stars*
   RVBW - August 2015 - pNA [501+]
Senzai, N.H. - *Ticket to India*
   c BL - v112 - i5 - Nov 1 2015 - p62(1) [51-500]
   c KR - Sept 15 2015 - pNA [51-500]
   c PW - v262 - i37 - Sept 14 2015 - p78(1) [51-500]
   c SLJ - v61 - i12 - Dec 2015 - p107(1) [51-500]
Seo, Kaila - *Fred (Illus. by Seo, Kaila)*
   c HB Guide - v26 - i2 - Fall 2015 - p51(1) [51-500]
Seow, C.L. - *Job 1-21: Interpretation and Commentary, vol. 1*
   Intpr - v69 - i1 - Jan 2015 - p101(2) [501+]
Sepahban, Lois - *Animal Testing: Life-Saving Research vs. Animal Welfare*
   VOYA - v38 - i2 - June 2015 - p89(1) [501+]
   Paper Wishes
   c BL - v112 - i4 - Oct 15 2015 - p59(1) [501+]
   c KR - Oct 1 2015 - pNA [51-500]
   c PW - v262 - i44 - Nov 2 2015 - p85(2) [51-500]
   c SLJ - v61 - i11 - Nov 2015 - p103(2) [51-500]
   Temple Grandin: Inspiring Animal-Behavior Scientist
   c HB Guide - v26 - i1 - Spring 2015 - p190(2) [51-500]
Sepetys, Ruta - *Salt to the Sea*
   c BL - v112 - i5 - Nov 1 2015 - p39(1) [501+]
   y BL - v112 - i7 - Dec 1 2015 - p52(1) [501+]
   y KR - Nov 15 2015 - pNA [501+]
   LJ - v140 - i20 - Dec 1 2015 - p97(1) [501+]
   y PW - v262 - i45 - Nov 9 2015 - p61(1) [501+]
   y SLJ - v61 - i12 - Dec 2015 - p128(2) [501+]
   y VOYA - v38 - i5 - Dec 2015 - p64(1) [501+]
Sepkoski, David - *Rereading the Fossil Record: The Growth of Paleobiology as an Evolutionary Discipline*
   Isis - v106 - i1 - March 2015 - p222(2) [501+]
Serafim, Leta - *The Devil Takes Half*
   KR - May 15 2015 - pNA [51-500]

When the Devil's Idle
   PW - v262 - i31 - August 3 2015 - p38(1) [51-500]
Sered, Susan Starr - *Can't Catch a Break: Gender, Jail, Drugs, and the Limits of Personal Responsibility*
   Wom R Bks - v32 - i3 - May-June 2015 - p10(3) [501+]
Serels, Steven - *Starvation and the State: Famine, Slavery, and Power in Sudan, 1883-1956*
   AHR - v120 - i2 - April 2015 - p754-755 [501+]
Sergeyev, Yaroslav D. - *Introduction to Global Optimization Exploiting Space-Filling Curves*
   SIAM Rev - v57 - i1 - March 2015 - p159-161 [501+]
SeRine, Kate - *Stop at Nothing*
   BL - v112 - i4 - Oct 15 2015 - p27(1) [51-500]
   PW - v262 - i37 - Sept 14 2015 - p49(1) [51-500]
Serle, Rebecca - *Famous in Love*
   y HB Guide - v26 - i1 - Spring 2015 - p123(1) [51-500]
Serna, Laura Isabel - *Making Cinelandia: American Films and Mexican Film Culture before the Golden Age*
   AHR - v120 - i2 - April 2015 - p679-680 [501+]
   Ams - v72 - i2 - April 2015 - p340(2) [501+]
   HAHR - v95 - i2 - May 2015 - p389-391 [501+]
   JAH - v102 - i1 - June 2015 - p277-278 [501+]
Sernovitz, Gary - *The Green and the Black*
   KR - Dec 15 2015 - pNA [51-500]
Serra, Michael - *Pirate Math: Developing Mathematical Reasoning with Games and Puzzles*
   TC Math - v21 - i8 - April 2015 - p509(2) [501+]
Serrano, Richard A. - *Last of the Blue and Gray: Old Men, Stolen Glory, and the Mystery That Outlived the Civil War*
   JSH - v81 - i1 - Feb 2015 - p211(2) [501+]
Serrell, Beverly - *Exhibit Labels: An Interpretive Approach, 2d ed.*
   y VOYA - v38 - i4 - Oct 2015 - p88(1) [51-500]
Serrier, Thomas - *Borders in the European Memories: A Typology of Remembered Borders in Today's Europe*
   HNet - August 2015 - pNA [501+]
Sertori, J.M. - *Dirty Rotten Vikings: Three Centuries of Longships, Looting and Bad Behavior (Illus. by Mazzara, Mauro)*
   c CH Bwatch - April 2015 - pNA [51-500]
Serulnikov, Sergio - *Revolution in the Andes: The Age of Tupac Amaru*
   AHR - v120 - i2 - April 2015 - p685-687 [501+]
Servacki, Kevin - *Get Mooned (Illus. by Pallace, Chris)*
   c BL - v111 - i12 - Feb 15 2015 - p86(1) [51-500]
Servadio, Gaia - *Raccogliamo le vele*
   TLS - i5835 - Jan 30 2015 - p22(1) [501+]
Service, Hugo - *Germans to Poles: Communism, Nationalism and Ethnic Cleansing after the Second World War*
   E-A St - v67 - i4 - June 2015 - p683(2) [501+]
Service, Robert - *The End of the Cold War: 1985-1991*
   CSM - Nov 12 2015 - pNA [501+]
   KR - June 15 2015 - pNA [501+]
   LJ - v140 - i11 - June 15 2015 - p100(1) [501+]
   PW - v262 - i30 - July 27 2015 - p54(1) [501+]
   Spec - v329 - i9770 - Nov 28 2015 - p42(2) [51-500]
   TimHES - i2229 - Nov 12 2015 - p48(1) [501+]
Serwacki, Kevin - *Get Mooned (Illus. by Pallace, Chris)*
   c HB Guide - v26 - i2 - Fall 2015 - p101(1) [51-500]
   c SLJ - v61 - i6 - June 2015 - p109(1) [51-500]
Serwer, Andy - *American Enterprise*
   KR - Feb 15 2015 - pNA [51-500]
Seshagiri, Urmila - *Race and the Modernist Imagination*
   MFSF - v61 - i3 - Fall 2015 - p556-559 [501+]
Seskis, Tina - *One Step Too Far*
   NYTBR - Jan 18 2015 - p26(L) [501+]
Sessa, Guido - *Molecular Plant Immunity*
   QRB - v90 - i2 - June 2015 - p232(2) [501+]
Sessions, Jennifer E. - *By Sword and Plow: France, and the Conquest of Algeria*
   J Mil H - v79 - i2 - April 2015 - p491-492 [501+]
Sessums, Kevin - *I Left It on the Mountain: A Memoir*
   BL - v111 - i12 - Feb 15 2015 - p4(1) [51-500]
   CJR - v53 - i6 - March-April 2015 - p56(2) [501+]
   G&L Rev W - v22 - i6 - Nov-Dec 2015 - p38(1) [501+]
   People - v83 - i11 - March 16 2015 - p41(NA) [501+]
Seth - *Palookaville, no. 22*
   PW - v262 - i22 - June 1 2015 - p49(1) [51-500]
Seton, Anya - *The Winthrop Woman (Read by James, Corrie). Audiobook Review*
   LJ - v140 - i3 - Feb 15 2015 - p58(2) [51-500]

Seton, Rosemary - *Western Daughters in Eastern Lands: British Missionary Women in Asia*
   JWH - v27 - i1 - Spring 2015 - p187(10) [501+]
Settis, Salvatore - *Serial/ Portable Classic: The Greek Canon and Its Mutations*
   NYRB - v62 - i13 - August 13 2015 - p12(3) [501+]
Setz, Clemens J. - *Indigo*
   NY - v90 - i43 - Jan 12 2015 - p71 [51-500]
Seubert, Xavier - *Beyond the Text: Franciscan Art and the Construction of Religion*
   Med R - May 2015 - pNA [501+]
   Theol St - v76 - i2 - June 2015 - p381(2) [501+]
Seung-U, Lee - *The Private Life of Plants*
   KR - Oct 1 2015 - pNA [501+]
Seuss, Diane - *Four-Legged Girl*
   PW - v262 - i38 - Sept 21 2015 - p50(2) [51-500]
Seuss, Dr. - *Horton and the Kwuggerbug and More Lost Stories*
   c HB Guide - v26 - i1 - Spring 2015 - p45(1) [51-500]
   Seuss-isms!
   c HB Guide - v26 - i2 - Fall 2015 - p205(1) [51-500]
Seven, John - *Frankie Liked to Sing (Illus. by Christy, Jana)*
   c BL - v111 - i19-20 - June 1 2015 - p93(1) [51-500]
   c KR - August 1 2015 - pNA [51-500]
   c SLJ - v61 - i9 - Sept 2015 - p180(1) [51-500]
   The Outlaw of Sherwood Forest
   c HB Guide - v26 - i1 - Spring 2015 - p92(1) [51-500]
   The Terror of the Tengu
   c HB Guide - v26 - i1 - Spring 2015 - p92(1) [51-500]
Sever, Shauna - *Real Sweet: More Than 80 Crave-Worthy Treats Made with Natural Sugars - Fun with Coconut Sugar, Muscovado, Turbinado, Honey, Maple Syrup, Agave Nectar, and Many More!*
   LJ - v140 - i9 - May 15 2015 - p102(2) [51-500]
Sevilla, Margarita Torres - *Kings of the Grail: Tracing the Historic Journey of the Cup of Christ from Jerusalem to Modern-Day Spain*
   KR - May 15 2015 - pNA [501+]
   PW - v262 - i23 - June 8 2015 - p56(1) [51-500]
Seward, Desmond - *Renishaw Hall: The Story of the Sitwells*
   TLS - i5874 - Oct 30 2015 - p34(1) [501+]
Sewell, Brian - *The Man Who Built the Best Car in the World (Illus. by Marjoram, Stefan)*
   Spec - v329 - i9772 - Dec 12 2015 - p87(2) [501+]
   Naked Emperors: Criticisms of English Contemporary Art
   Quad - v59 - i5 - May 2015 - p70(4) [501+]
   The White Umbrella (Illus. by Lasson, Sally Ann)
   c Spec - v327 - i9736 - April 4 2015 - p39(1) [501+]
   c TLS - i5850 - May 15 2015 - p20(1) [501+]
Sexton, Marie - *Winter Oranges*
   PW - v262 - i45 - Nov 9 2015 - p45(1) [51-500]
Sexton, Rex - *Constant Is the Rain*
   KR - April 15 2015 - pNA [501+]
Seydor, Paul - *The Authentic Death & Contentious Afterlife of Pat Garrett and Billy the Kid: The Untold Story of Peckinpah's Last Western Film*
   Si & So - v25 - i6 - June 2015 - p106(1) [501+]
   The Authentic Death & Contentious Afterlife of Pat Garrett and Billy the Kid: The Untold Storyof Peckinpah's Last Western Film
   TLS - i5862 - August 7 2015 - p23(1) [501+]
Seyler, Dorothy U. - *The Obelisk and the Englishman: The Pioneering Discoveries of Egyptologist William Bankes*
   Bwatch - August 2015 - pNA [51-500]
   KR - Feb 15 2015 - pNA [51-500]
   LJ - v140 - i7 - April 15 2015 - p95(1) [51-500]
Seymour, Deni J. - *A Fateful Day in 1698: The Remarkable Sobaipuri-O'odham Victory over the Apaches and Their Allies*
   SHQ - v118 - i4 - April 2015 - p426-427 [501+]
Seymour, Eve - *Beautiful Losers*
   KR - Jan 1 2016 - pNA [51-500]
Seymour, Gerald - *A Deniable Death*
   TimHES - i2198 - April 9 2015 - p49(1) [501+]
   The Outsiders (Read by Jackson, Gildart). Audiobook Review
   LJ - v140 - i11 - June 15 2015 - p51(1) [501+]
   The Outsiders
   BL - v111 - i11 - Feb 1 2015 - p28(1) [51-500]
   KR - Jan 1 2015 - pNA [51-500]
   The Vagabond
   KR - Nov 15 2015 - pNA [51-500]
   PW - v262 - i47 - Nov 23 2015 - p48(2) [51-500]

Seymour, Michael - *Babylon: Legend, History and the Ancient City*
    HNet - March 2015 - pNA [501+]
    HT - v65 - i6 - June 2015 - p60(2) [501+]

seymour, Nicole - *Strange Natures: Futurity, Empathy, and the Queer Ecological Imagination*
    MFSF - v61 - i1 - Spring 2015 - p168-176 [501+]

Seymour, Susan C. - *Cora Du Bois: Anthropologist, Diplomat, Agent*
    Wom R Bks - v32 - i5 - Sept-Oct 2015 - p13(2) [501+]

Sfar, Joann - *Dungeon Monstres: My Son the Killer (Illus. by Bezian)*
    y SLJ - v61 - i7 - July 2015 - p100(1) [51-500]

Shaara, Jeff - *A Blaze of Glory*
    RVBW - March 2015 - pNA [51-500]
The Fateful Lightning
    BL - v111 - i18 - May 15 2015 - p29(1) [51-500]

Shabazz, Ilyasah - *X*
    y BL - v111 - i11 - Feb 1 2015 - p45(1) [51-500]
    y BL - v111 - i16 - April 15 2015 - p57(1) [501+]
    y CCB-B - v68 - i6 - Feb 2015 - p331(1) [51-500]
    c Nat Post - v17 - i62 - Jan 10 2015 - pWP9(1) [501+]
    y NYTBR - Feb 8 2015 - p23(L) [501+]
    y VOYA - v37 - i6 - Feb 2015 - p88(2) [51-500]
    BL - v111 - i21 - July 1 2015 - p41(1) [51-500]

Shabel, Arleen - *Under Paris Rooftops*
    SPBW - August 2015 - pNA [51-500]

Shaber, Sarah R. - *Louise's Chance*
    KR - Nov 1 2015 - pNA [501+]
    PW - v262 - i46 - Nov 16 2015 - p58(1) [51-500]

Shabott, Laura - *Confessions of an Ebook Virgin: What Everyone Should Know before They Publish on the Internet*
    PW - v262 - i4 - Jan 26 2015 - p167(1) [51-500]

Shacochis, Bob - *The Woman Who Lost Her Soul*
    Spec - v327 - i9724 - Jan 10 2015 - p28(1) [51-500]

Shade, Patrick - *Freedom and Limits*
    RM - v68 - i4 - June 2015 - p859(3) [501+]

Shadmi, Koren - *The Abaddon*
    PW - v262 - i44 - Nov 2 2015 - p72(1) [51-500]

Shafak, Elif - *The Architect's Apprentice (Read by Marek, Piter). Audiobook Review*
    LJ - v140 - i15 - Sept 15 2015 - p42(1) [51-500]
The Architect's Apprentice
    CSM - April 1 2015 - pNA [501+]
    KR - Jan 15 2015 - pNA [501+]
    y NYTBR - June 14 2015 - p12(L) [501+]
    Spec - v327 - i9724 - Jan 10 2015 - p28(2) [501+]
    WLT - v89 - i2 - March-April 2015 - p62(2) [501+]

Shafer, David - *Whiskey Tango Foxtrot*
    NS - v144 - i5276 - August 21 2015 - p46(2) [501+]

Shaffer, Cynthia - *Coastal Crafts: Decorative Seaside Projects to Inspire Your Inner Beachcomber*
    LJ - v140 - i12 - July 1 2015 - p85(1) [51-500]
Simply Stitched Gifts: 21 Fun Projects Using Free-Motion Stitching
    LJ - v140 - i20 - Dec 1 2015 - p103(1) [51-500]

Shah, Aqil - *The Army and Democracy: Military Politics in Pakistan*
    NYRB - v62 - i6 - April 2 2015 - p46(3) [501+]
    Pac A - v88 - i3 - Sept 2015 - p731 [51-500]
    TLS - i5832 - Jan 9 2015 - p19(1) [501+]

Shah, Bindi V. - *Laotian Daughters: Working toward Community, Belonging, and Environmental Justice*
    CS - v44 - i3 - May 2015 - p415-417 [501+]

Shah, Nayan - *Stranger Intimacy: Contesting Race, Sexuality and the Law in the North American West*
    Am St - v54 - i2 - Summer 2015 - p59-71 [501+]

Shah, Niaz A. - *Islamic Law and the Law of Armed Conflict*
    RVBW - Oct 2015 - pNA [51-500]

Shah, Sami - *I, Migrant*
    KR - April 15 2015 - pNA [501+]

Shah, Sonia - *Pandemic: Tracking Contagions, from Cholera to Ebola and Beyond*
    BL - v112 - i7 - Dec 1 2015 - p20(1) [51-500]
    KR - Dec 15 2015 - pNA [501+]

Shah, Svati P. - *Street Corner Secrets: Sex, Work, and Migration in the City of Mumbai*
    JAS - v74 - i3 - August 2015 - p775-776 [501+]

Shahan, Sherry - *Feeding Time at the Zoo*
    c HB Guide - v26 - i1 - Spring 2015 - p157(1) [51-500]
The Little Butterfly
    c HB Guide - v26 - i2 - Fall 2015 - p175(1) [51-500]

Shaheen, Stefany - *Elle and Coach: Diabetes, the Fight for My Daughter's Life, and the Dog Who Changed Everything*
    BL - v111 - i22 - August 1 2015 - p12(1) [51-500]
    LJ - v140 - i13 - August 1 2015 - p116(1) [51-500]

Shahegh, Mahvash - *The Green Musician (Illus. by Ewart, Claire)*
    c BL - v111 - i21 - July 1 2015 - p63(1) [51-500]
    c CH Bwatch - Sept 2015 - pNA [51-500]
    c CH Bwatch - Oct 2015 - pNA [51-500]
    c KR - May 15 2015 - pNA [51-500]
    c PW - v262 - i22 - June 1 2015 - p59(1) [51-500]

Shakespeare, Nicholas - *Priscilla: The Hidden Life of an Englishwoman in Wartime France*
    NYTBR - Feb 1 2015 - p24(L) [501+]

Shakespeare, William - *Macbeth*
    Six Ct J - v46 - i1 - Spring 2015 - p215-216 [501+]
Macbeth (Illus. by Hinds, Gareth)
    y CCB-B - v68 - i8 - April 2015 - p419(2) [51-500]
MacBeth Killingit (Illus. by Carbone, Courtney)
    y KR - Nov 15 2015 - pNA [501+]
Richard III (Read by Various readers). Audiobook Review
    PW - v262 - i21 - May 25 2015 - p55(1) [51-500]
Romeo and Juliet
    y Sch Lib - v63 - i4 - Winter 2015 - p251(2) [51-500]
Romeo et Juliette (Illus. by Rovira, Francesc)
    c Res Links - v21 - i1 - Oct 2015 - p55(2) [51-500]
Srsly Hamlet
    y SLJ - v61 - i6 - June 2015 - p128(1) [51-500]
    y HB Guide - v26 - i2 - Fall 2015 - p138(1) [51-500]
YOLO Juliet
    y SLJ - v61 - i6 - June 2015 - p128(1) [51-500]
    y HB Guide - v26 - i2 - Fall 2015 - p138(1) [51-500]

Shalem, Avinoam - *The Medieval Oliphant*
    NYT - April 10 2015 - pC26(L) [501+]

Shally-Jensen, Michael - *Defining Documents in American History: The 1930s*
    y BL - v111 - i16 - April 15 2015 - p14(1) [51-500]

Shalvis, Jill - *All I Want*
    PW - v262 - i35 - August 31 2015 - p72(1) [51-500]
Second Chance Summer
    BL - v112 - i2 - Sept 15 2015 - p42(2) [501+]
    PW - v262 - i20 - May 18 2015 - p71(1) [51-500]
Still the One
    KR - Feb 15 2015 - pNA [51-500]
    PW - v262 - i9 - March 2 2015 - p72(1) [51-500]

Shamdasani, Sonu - *C.G. Jung: A Biography in Books*
    JR - v95 - i3 - July 2015 - p429(3) [501+]

Shames, Terry - *A Deadly Affair at Bobtail Ridge*
    BL - v111 - i13 - March 1 2015 - p22(1) [51-500]
    KR - Feb 1 2015 - pNA [51-500]
    PW - v262 - i6 - Feb 9 2015 - p47(1) [51-500]
The Necessary Murder of Nonie Blake
    KR - Nov 1 2015 - pNA [51-500]
    PW - v262 - i45 - Nov 9 2015 - p38(1) [51-500]

Shamir, Avner - *Christian Conceptions of Jewish Books: The Pfefferkorn Affair*
    CHR - v101 - i2 - Spring 2015 - p403(1) [501+]

Shamir, Ronen - *Current Flow: The Electrification of Palestine*
    CS - v44 - i3 - May 2015 - p417-418 [501+]
    IJMES - v47 - i2 - May 2015 - p369-381 [501+]

Shams, Mehtab - *Mantra: Karma Is a Bitch*
    SPBW - Oct 2015 - pNA [51-500]

Shan, Patrick Fuliang - *Taming China's Wilderness: Immigration, Settlement and the Shaping of the Heilongjiang Frontier, 1900-1931*
    AHR - v120 - i3 - June 2015 - p990-991 [501+]

Shanahan, Andrew - *Man v. Fat: The Weight Loss Manual*
    PW - v262 - i18 - May 4 2015 - p114(2) [51-500]

Shanahan, Murray - *The Technological Singularity*
    LJ - v140 - i14 - Sept 1 2015 - p137(1) [51-500]
    New Sci - v227 - i3038 - Sept 12 2015 - p41(1) [501+]
    TimHES - i2211 - July 9 2015 - p45-46 [501+]

Shanahan, Timothy - *Philosophy and "Blade Runner"*
    SFS - v42 - i3 - Nov 2015 - p599-601 [501+]

Shand, Jennifer - *Why Do Tractors Have Such Big Tires? (Illus. by Fabbri, Daniele)*
    c CH Bwatch - March 2015 - pNA [51-500]

Shand, Pat - *Family Pets (Illus. by Dill, Sarah)*
    c SLJ - v61 - i10 - Oct 2015 - p98(1) [51-500]

Shandler, Jeffrey - *Shtetl: A Vernacular Intellectual History*
    TLS - i5838 - Feb 20 2015 - p11(2) [501+]

Shane, Neala - *Inspired Baby Names from around the World: 6,000 International Names and the Meaning behind Them*
    LJ - v140 - i5 - March 15 2015 - p130(1) [51-500]

Shane, Rachel - *Alice in Wonderland High*
    y HB Guide - v26 - i2 - Fall 2015 - p138(1) [51-500]
    c KR - Feb 15 2015 - pNA [51-500]
    y SLJ - v61 - i6 - June 2015 - p116(1) [51-500]
    y VOYA - v38 - i2 - June 2015 - p83(1) [51-500]

Shane, Scott - *Objective Troy: A Terrorist, a President, and the Rise of the Drone*
    KR - June 15 2015 - pNA [501+]
    LJ - v140 - i13 - August 1 2015 - p111(2) [51-500]
    NYT - Sept 21 2015 - pC4(L) [501+]
    NYTBR - Sept 13 2015 - p10(L) [501+]
    PW - v262 - i30 - July 27 2015 - p52(1) [501+]

Shang, Wendy Wan-Long - *The Way Home Looks Now*
    c BL - v111 - i14 - March 15 2015 - p76(1) [51-500]
    c CCB-B - v68 - i9 - May 2015 - p467(1) [51-500]
    c HB Guide - v26 - i2 - Fall 2015 - p101(1) [51-500]
    c PW - v262 - i9 - March 2 2015 - p83(2) [51-500]
    c PW - v262 - i49 - Dec 2 2015 - p74(1) [51-500]
    c SLJ - v61 - i3 - March 2015 - p144(2) [51-500]

Shangraw, Steph - *Black Wolf*
    MFSF - v128 - i5-6 - May-June 2015 - p61(4) [501+]

Shankland, Hugh - *Out of Italy: The Story of Italians in North East England*
    HNet - May 2015 - pNA [501+]

Shankman, Andrew - *The World of the Revolutionary American Republic: Land, Labor, and the Conflict for a Continent*
    JAH - v102 - i1 - June 2015 - p232-233 [501+]

Shankman, Peter - *Zombie Loyalists: Using Great Service To Create Rabid Fans. Audiobook Review*
    LJ - v140 - i6 - April 1 2015 - p52(1) [51-500]

Shanley, Brayton - *The Many Sides of Peace: Christian Nonviolence, the Contemplative Life, and Sustainable Living*
    AM - v212 - i7 - March 2 2015 - p40(2) [501+]

Shannon, Annie - *Mastering the Art of Vegan Cooking: Over 200 Delicious Recipes and Tips to Save You Money and Stock Your Pantry*
    LJ - v140 - i13 - August 1 2015 - p119(1) [51-500]

Shannon, David (b. 1959-) - *Bugs in My Hair! (Illus. by Shannon, David) (Read by Bernstein, Jesse). Audiobook Review*
    c SLJ - v61 - i7 - July 2015 - p45(1) [51-500]
Bugs in my Hair! (Illus. by Shannon, David)
    c CH Bwatch - May 2015 - pNA [51-500]

Shannon, David T., Sr. - *George Liele's Life and Legacy: An Unsung Hero*
    JSH - v81 - i2 - May 2015 - p441(2) [501+]

Shannon, George - *Hands Say Love (Illus. by Yoo, Taeeun)*
    c HB Guide - v26 - i2 - Fall 2015 - p18(1) [51-500]
    c SLJ - v61 - i2 - Feb 2015 - p78(1) [51-500]
One Family (Illus. by Gomez, Blanca)
    c BL - v111 - i16 - April 15 2015 - p54(1) [51-500]
    c CCB-B - v68 - i11 - July-August 2015 - p564(2) [51-500]
    c HB - v91 - i3 - May-June 2015 - p98(1) [51-500]
    c HB Guide - v26 - i2 - Fall 2015 - p18(1) [51-500]
    c KR - Feb 15 2015 - pNA [51-500]
    c NYTBR - July 12 2015 - p19(L) [51-500]
    c PW - v262 - i9 - March 2 2015 - p82(1) [51-500]

Shannon, Jennifer - *The Anxiety Survival Guide for Teens: CBT Skills to Overcome Fear, Worry and Panic (Illus. by Shannon, Doug)*
    y SLJ - v61 - i12 - Dec 2015 - p146(1) [51-500]

Shannon, Laurie - *The Accommodated Animal: Cosmopolity in Shakespearean Locales*
    MP - v112 - i4 - May 2015 - pE310(6) [501+]

Shannon, Lisa J. - *Mama Koko and the Hundred Gunmen: An Ordinary Family's Extraordinary Tale of Love, Loss, and Survival in the Congo*
    BL - v111 - i9-10 - Jan 1 2015 - p24(1) [51-500]

Shannon, T. J. - *The Darkness behind Me*
    KR - July 15 2015 - pNA [501+]

Shantz-Hilkes, Chloe - *My Girlfriend's Pregnant! A Teen's Guide to Becoming a Dad (Illus. by Dawson, Willow)*
    y SLJ - v61 - i12 - Dec 2015 - p146(2) [51-500]

Shao, Qin - *Shanghai Gone: Domicide and Defiance in a Chinese Megacity*
    JAS - v74 - i3 - August 2015 - p742-743 [501+]

Shapcott, John - *Grains of Sand: Melvyn Bragg's Cumbrian Novels*
    TLS - i5833 - Jan 16 2015 - p26(2) [51-500]

Shapinsky, Peter D. - *Lords of the Sea: Pirates, Violence, and Commerce in Late Medieval Japan*
    HNet - July 2015 - pNA [501+]

Shapira, Anita - *Ben-Gurion: Father of Modern Israel*
    NYTBR - Jan 25 2015 - p15(L) [501+]
Yosef Haim Brenner: A Life
    TLS - i5855 - June 19 2015 - p28(1) [501+]

Shapira, Harel - *Waiting for Jose: The Minutemen's Pursuit of America*
CS - v44 - i2 - March 2015 - p249-251 [501+]

Shapiro, Aaron - *The Lure of the North Woods: Cultivating Tourism in the Upper Midwest*
RAH - v43 - i2 - June 2015 - p346-354 [501+]

Shapiro, B.A. - *The Muralist*
BL - v112 - i4 - Oct 15 2015 - p25(1) [51-500]
KR - Sept 1 2015 - pNA [51-500]
LJ - v140 - i19 - Nov 15 2015 - p79(2) [51-500]
PW - v262 - i38 - Sept 21 2015 - p46(1) [51-500]

Shapiro, Barbara J. - *Political Communication and Political Culture in England 1558-1688*
Six Ct J - v46 - i3 - Fall 2015 - p784-785 [501+]

Shapiro, Beth - *How to Clone a Mammoth: The Science of De-Extinction*
KR - Jan 15 2015 - pNA [501+]
LJ - v140 - i5 - March 15 2015 - p129(2) [501+]
Mac - v128 - i18 - May 11 2015 - p59(1) [501+]
Nation - v300 - i24 - June 15 2015 - p40(4) [501+]
NH - v123 - i4 - May 2015 - p47(1) [501+]
PW - v262 - i12 - March 23 2015 - p63(1) [51-500]
Spec - v328 - i9742 - May 16 2015 - p43(2) [501+]
TimHES - i2204 - May 21 2015 - p48-49 [501+]
TimHES - i2211 - July 9 2015 - p47(1) [501+]

Shapiro, Daniel - *The Red Handkerchief and Other Poems*
ABR - v36 - i5 - July-August 2015 - p17(2) [501+]

Shapiro, Gavriel - *The Tender Friendship and the Charm of Perfect Accord: Nabokov and His Father*
Slav R - v74 - i1 - Spring 2015 - p213-214 [501+]

Shapiro, Howard - *I Was Picked ... The John Challis Story*
y VOYA - v38 - i5 - Dec 2015 - p78(1) [51-500]

Shapiro, James - *1606: William Shakespeare and the Year of Lear*
NS - v144 - i5282 - Oct 2 2015 - p68(2) [501+]
Spec - v329 - i9761 - Sept 26 2015 - p36(2) [501+]
TLS - i5871 - Oct 9 2015 - p3(3) [501+]
The Year of Lear: Shakespeare in 1606
KR - June 1 2015 - pNA [501+]
LJ - v140 - i13 - August 1 2015 - p95(1) [51-500]
NYRB - v62 - i18 - Nov 19 2015 - p26(3) [501+]
y BL - v111 - i22 - August 1 2015 - p20(1) [51-500]
Comw - v142 - i17 - Oct 23 2015 - p31(2) [501+]
CSM - Oct 7 2015 - pNA [501+]
NYTBR - Dec 13 2015 - p26(L) [501+]
PW - v262 - i22 - June 1 2015 - p51(1) [501+]

Shapiro, Rami - *The Golden Rule and the Games People Play: The Ultimate Strategy for a Meaning-Filled Life*
BL - v112 - i6 - Nov 15 2015 - p14(1) [51-500]

Shapiro, Susan - *What's Never Said*
LJ - v140 - i17 - Oct 15 2015 - p76(3) [51-500]

Shapley-Box, Diane - *Tator's Swamp Fever*
c CH Bwatch - April 2015 - pNA [51-500]

Sharafeddine, Fatima - *The Amazing Discoveries of Ibn Sina (Illus. by Ali, Intelaq Mohammed)*
SLJ - v61 - i4 - April 2015 - p181(1) [51-500]
c HB Guide - v26 - i2 - Fall 2015 - p212(1) [51-500]
c Res Links - v20 - i5 - June 2015 - p21(1) [51-500]
The Amazing Travels of Ibn Battuta (Illus. by Ali, Intelaq Mohammed)
c Bkbird - v53 - i1 - Wntr 2015 - p63(1) [501+]

Sharaipotra, Sona - *Tiny Pretty Things*
y BL - v111 - i15 - April 1 2015 - p70(2) [51-500]

Sharenow, Robert - *The Girl in the Torch*
c BL - v111 - i16 - April 15 2015 - p59(2) [51-500]
c HB Guide - v26 - i2 - Fall 2015 - p101(1) [51-500]
c KR - March 1 2015 - pNA [51-500]
c SLJ - v61 - i4 - April 2015 - p149(2) [51-500]
y VOYA - v38 - i1 - April 2015 - p69(1) [51-500]

Sharer, John - *The Cockney Lad and Jim Crow*
SPBW - June 2015 - pNA [51-500]

Sharif, Malek - *Imperial Norms and Local Realities: The Ottoman Municipal Laws and the Municipality of Beirut*
HNet - June 2015 - pNA [51-500]

Sharkaway, Azza - *Question It!*
c Sci & Ch - v52 - i9 - Summer 2015 - p89 [501+]
Science Sleuths Series, 4 vols.
c Res Links - v20 - i4 - April 2015 - p21(1) [51-500]

Sharkey, Patrick - *Stuck in Place: Urban Neighborhoods and the End of Progress toward Racial Equality*
AJS - v121 - i1 - July 2015 - p288(3) [501+]

Sharma, Akhil - *Family Life*
NYTBR - March 22 2015 - p28(L) [501+]

Sharma, Mihir - *Restart: The Last Chance for the Indian Economy*
Econ - v415 - i8934 - April 18 2015 - p78(US) [501+]

Sharma, Yuyutsu - *Nine New York Poems*
WLT - v89 - i2 - March-April 2015 - p73(1) [51-500]

Sharmat, Marjorie Weinman - *Nate the Great, Where Are You? (Illus. by Wheeler, Jody)*
c HB Guide - v26 - i1 - Spring 2015 - p55(1) [51-500]

Sharone, Ofer - *Flawed System/Flawed Self: Job Searching and Unemployment Experiences*
CS - v44 - i4 - July 2015 - p463-469 [501+]
CS - v44 - i4 - July 2015 - p554-556 [501+]

Sharp, C - *The Elementalists*
KR - April 1 2015 - pNA [501+]

Sharp, Daryl - *Eros: Melodies of Love: More Jungian Notes from Underground*
RVBW - March 2015 - pNA [51-500]

Sharp, Lesley A. - *The Transplant Imaginary: Mechanical Hearts, Animal Parts, and Moral Thinking in Highly Experimental Science*
MAQ - v29 - i1 - March 2015 - p4-6 [501+]

Sharp, Susan F. - *Mean Lives, Mean Laws: Oklahoma's Women Prisoners*
Wom R Bks - v32 - i3 - May-June 2015 - p10(3) [501+]

Sharpe, Blaire - *Not Really Gone*
SPBW - Nov 2015 - pNA [51-500]

Sharpe, Kevin - *Reading Authority and Representing Rule in Early Modern England*
HER - v130 - i542 - Feb 2015 - p196(2) [501+]
Rebranding Rule: The Restoration and Revolution Monarchy, 1660-1714
JMH - v87 - i3 - Sept 2015 - p727(3) [501+]

Sharpe, Luke - *Billy Sure, Kid Entrepreneur (Illus. by Ross, Graham)*
c HB Guide - v26 - i2 - Fall 2015 - p101(1) [51-500]
c KR - March 1 2015 - pNA [51-500]
c SLJ - v61 - i3 - March 2015 - p144(1) [51-500]
c BL - v111 - i16 - April 15 2015 - p48(2) [51-500]

Sharpe, Mike - *Attack and Transport Aircraft: 1945 to Today*
c HB Guide - v26 - i1 - Spring 2015 - p137(2) [51-500]

Sharrard, Valerie - *Random Acts*
y Res Links - v20 - i3 - Feb 2015 - p35(1) [51-500]

Sharratt, Lyn - *Good to Great to Innovate: Recalculating the Route to Career Readiness, K-12+*
Bwatch - Feb 2015 - pNA [51-500]

Sharrow, Ed - *Murder in the Fifth*
KR - Sept 15 2015 - pNA [51-500]

Shashaty, Andre F. - *Rebuilding a Dream: Partnership for Sustainable Communities*
KR - March 15 2015 - pNA [501+]

Shaskan, Trisha Speed - *Punk Skunks (Illus. by Shaskan, Stephen)*
c KR - Nov 15 2015 - pNA [51-500]
c PW - v262 - i46 - Nov 16 2015 - p74(1) [51-500]

Shatkin, Laurence - *Choose Your College Major in a Day*
SPBW - Nov 2015 - pNA [51-500]

Shattuck, Shari - *Becoming Ellen*
BL - v111 - i22 - August 1 2015 - p26(1) [51-500]
KR - June 15 2015 - pNA [51-500]

Shaughnessy, Adam - *The Entirely True Story of the Unbelievable FIB*
c BL - v111 - i22 - August 1 2015 - p67(1) [51-500]
c KR - June 1 2015 - pNA [51-500]
c PW - v262 - i26 - June 29 2015 - p69(1) [51-500]
c SLJ - v61 - i7 - July 2015 - p83(1) [51-500]

Shaughnessy, Edward L. - *Unearthing the Changes: Recently Discovered Manuscripts of the Yi Jing (I Ching) and Related Texts*
JAS - v74 - i2 - May 2015 - p480-481 [501+]

Shaul, Joel - *The Conversation Train*
c Sch Lib - v63 - i4 - Winter 2015 - p254(1) [51-500]

Shaviro, Steven - *The Universe of Things: On Speculative Realism*
TLS - i5856 - June 26 2015 - p29(1) [501+]

Shavit, Ari - *My Promised Land*
NYTBR - March 22 2015 - p28(L) [501+]

Shaw, A.R. - *The China Pandemic*
KR - Jan 15 2015 - pNA [51-500]

Shaw, Adrienne - *Gaming at the Edge: Sexuality and Gender at the Margins of Gamer Culture*
CS - v44 - i5 - Sept 2015 - p747(1) [501+]
Wom R Bks - v32 - i6 - Nov-Dec 2015 - p21(2) [501+]

Shaw, Brent D. - *Bringing in the Sheaves: Economy and Metaphor in the Roman World*
Historian - v77 - i1 - Spring 2015 - p192(2) [501+]

Shaw, Bud - *Last Night in the OR: A Transplant Surgeon's Odyssey*
BL - v111 - i22 - August 1 2015 - p12(1) [51-500]
KR - July 15 2015 - pNA [501+]
LJ - v140 - i14 - Sept 1 2015 - p129(1) [51-500]

Shaw, C.A. - *Satyric Play: The Evolution of Greek Comedy and Satyr Drama*
Class R - v65 - i2 - Oct 2015 - p358-360 [501+]

Shaw, Emily - *A Historical and Etymological Dictionary of American Sign Language*
Bwatch - Oct 2015 - pNA [51-500]
RVBW - Sept 2015 - pNA [501+]

Shaw, George G. - *To the Klondike and Back 1894-1901*
RVBW - June 2015 - pNA [51-500]

Shaw, Jeff - *Concrete Evidence*
KR - Jan 1 2016 - pNA [501+]

Shaw, Jennifer L. - *Reading Claude Cahun's 'Disavowals'*
FS - v69 - i2 - April 2015 - p257-258 [501+]

Shaw, Jenny (b. 1977-) - *Everyday Life in the Early English Caribbean: Irish, Africans, and the Construction of Difference*
W&M Q - v72 - i2 - April 2015 - p377-381 [501+]

Shaw, Johnny - *Floodgate*
PW - v262 - i48 - Nov 30 2015 - p41(1) [51-500]

Shaw, Jonathan - *Narcisa*
KR - Feb 1 2015 - pNA [501+]

Shaw, Nancy - *Sheep Go to Sleep (Illus. by Apple, Margot)*
c BL - v111 - i17 - May 1 2015 - p103(1) [51-500]
c CH Bwatch - June 2015 - pNA [51-500]
c HB - v91 - i4 - July-August 2015 - p125(1) [51-500]
c KR - March 1 2015 - pNA [51-500]
c SLJ - v61 - i2 - Feb 2015 - p78(1) [51-500]

Shaw, Prue - *Reading Dante: From Here to Eternity*
NYRB - v62 - i3 - Feb 19 2015 - p36(2) [501+]

Shaw, Stephanie - *A Cookie for Santa (Illus. by Robert, Bruno)*
c HB Guide - v26 - i2 - Fall 2015 - p51(1) [51-500]
The Legend of the Beaver's Tail (Illus. by van Frankenhuyzen, Gijsbert)
c CH Bwatch - July 2015 - pNA [51-500]
c HB Guide - v26 - i2 - Fall 2015 - p160(1) [51-500]
c SLJ - v61 - i9 - Sept 2015 - p129(1) [51-500]
Under the Sleepy Stars (Illus. by Harry, Rebecca)
c KR - Jan 1 2016 - pNA [51-500]
c PW - v262 - i31 - August 3 2015 - p58(2) [501+]

Shaw, Stephanie J. - *W.E.B. Du Bois and The Souls of Black Folk*
J Am St - v49 - i1 - Feb 2015 - p200-201 [501+]

Shaw, Tucker - *Oh Yeah, Audrey!*
y HB Guide - v26 - i1 - Spring 2015 - p123(1) [51-500]

Shaw, William - *The Kings of London*
NYTBR - March 1 2015 - p29(L) [501+]
A Song for the Brokenhearted
KR - Nov 15 2015 - pNA [51-500]
PW - v262 - i47 - Nov 23 2015 - p50(1) [51-500]

Shaw, Zed A. - *Learn Ruby the Hard Way, 3d ed.*
Bwatch - May 2015 - pNA [51-500]

Shawl, Nisi - *Stories for Chip: A Tribute to Samuel R. Delany*
NYTBR - Oct 18 2015 - p18(L) [501+]
PW - v262 - i29 - July 20 2015 - p175(1) [51-500]

Shawn, Allen - *Leonard Bernstein: An American Musician*
Am Theat - v32 - i5 - May-June 2015 - p64(2) [501+]
Bks & Cult - v21 - i1 - Jan-Feb 2015 - p25(3) [501+]
TLS - i5862 - August 7 2015 - p24(1) [501+]

Shay, Shaul - *Somalia in Transition Since 2006*
Reason - v46 - i11 - April 2015 - p64(2) [501+]

Shchepakina, Elena - *Singular Pertubations: Introduction to Sysvtem Order Reduction Methods with Applications*
SIAM Rev - v57 - i2 - June 2015 - p313-313 [501+]

Shea, Bob - *Ballet Cat: The Totally Secret Secret (Illus. by Shea, Bob)*
c HB - v91 - i4 - July-August 2015 - p144(2) [51-500]
c KR - March 15 2015 - pNA [51-500]
c NYTBR - August 23 2015 - p26(L) [501+]
c PW - v262 - i49 - Dec 2 2015 - p64(1) [51-500]
c SLJ - v61 - i5 - May 2015 - p94(1) [51-500]
Dance! Dance! Underpants! (Illus. by Shea, Bob)
c KR - Nov 15 2015 - pNA [51-500]
Dinosaur vs. Mommy (Illus. by Shea, Bob)
c BL - v111 - i11 - Feb 1 2015 - p54(2) [51-500]
c CH Bwatch - May 2015 - pNA [51-500]
c HB - v91 - i2 - March-April 2015 - p83(2) [51-500]
c HB Guide - v26 - i2 - Fall 2015 - p18(1) [51-500]
c PW - v262 - i49 - Dec 2 2015 - p34(1) [51-500]
c SLJ - v61 - i2 - Feb 2015 - p78(1) [51-500]
Kid Sheriff and the Terrible Toads (Illus. by Smith, Lane)
c HB Guide - v26 - i1 - Spring 2015 - p45(1) [51-500]

The Totally Secret Secret (Illus. by Shea, Bob)
   c BL - v111 - i21 - July 1 2015 - p61(1) [51-500]
   c CCB-B - v69 - i1 - Sept 2015 - p52(2) [51-500]
Shea, Donna - *How to Make & Keep Friends: Tips for Kids to Overcome 50 Common Social Challenges*
   KR - April 1 2015 - pNA [501+]
Shea, Erin - *Seasonal Tales: Memoir*
   LJ - v140 - i12 - July 1 2015 - p5(1) [51-500]
Shea, Tom - *Unbreakable: A Navy SEAL'S Way of Life*
   LJ - v140 - i16 - Oct 1 2015 - p94(1) [501+]
Shea, William R. - *Galileo Interviewed*
   Sev Cent N - v73 - i1-2 - Spring-Summer 2015 - p44(3) [501+]
Shear, Jeff - *The Six-Degree Conspiracy, vol. 1:*
   PW - v262 - i5 - Feb 2 2015 - p39(1) [51-500]
Shearer, Alex - *The Ministry of Ghosts*
   c Sch Lib - v63 - i1 - Spring 2015 - p44(1) [51-500]
Shecter, Vicky Alvear - *Hades Speaks! A Guide to the Underworld by the Greek God of the Dead (Illus. by Larson, J.E.)*
   c HB Guide - v26 - i1 - Spring 2015 - p201(1) [51-500]
Thor Speaks! A Guide to the Realms by the Norse God of Thunder (Illus. by Larson, J.E.)
   c KR - June 1 2015 - pNA [51-500]
   c PW - v262 - i33 - August 17 2015 - p74(1) [501+]
Sheean, Olga - *Fit For Love: Find Your Self and Your Perfect Mate*
   PW - v262 - i33 - August 17 2015 - p67(1) [51-500]
Sheehan-Dean, Aaron - *A Companion to the U.S. Civil War, 2 vols.*
   JAH - v102 - i1 - June 2015 - p255-256 [501+]
   JSH - v81 - i3 - August 2015 - p731(3) [501+]
Sheehan, Jacqueline - *The Center of the World*
   LJ - v140 - i20 - Dec 1 2015 - p96(1) [501+]
Sheehan, Judy - *I Woke Up Dead at the Mall*
   y KR - Jan 1 2016 - pNA [51-500]
Sheehan, Linda Faiola - *Fore Play*
   KR - Nov 15 2015 - pNA [51-500]
Sheehan, Thomas F. - *The Nations*
   Roundup M - v22 - i6 - August 2015 - p32(1) [501+]
Sheehan, William - *Galactic Encounters: Our Majestic and Evolving Star-System, from the Big Bang to Time's End*
   Phys Today - v68 - i6 - June 2015 - p54-1 [501+]
   S&T - v129 - i4 - April 2015 - p59(1) [501+]
Sheehy, Elizabeth A. - *Sexual Assault in Canada: Law, Legal Practice and Women's Activism*
   CWS - v30 - i2-3 - Fall-Winter 2015 - p138(2) [501+]
Sheehy, Gail - *Daring: My Passage*
   Bwatch - Feb 2015 - pNA [51-500]
Sheehy, Shawn - *Welcome to the Neighborwood (Illus. by Sheehy, Shawn)*
   c BL - v111 - i16 - April 15 2015 - p52(1) [51-500]
   c HB Guide - v26 - i2 - Fall 2015 - p172(1) [51-500]
   c PW - v262 - i13 - March 30 2015 - p74(1) [51-500]
   c PW - v262 - i49 - Dec 2 2015 - p59(2) [51-500]
Sheen, Barbara - *Careers in Education*
   y SLJ - v61 - i9 - Sept 2015 - p176(1) [51-500]
Careers in Health Care
   y VOYA - v37 - i6 - Feb 2015 - p89(1) [51-500]
Careers in Sales and Marketing
   y SLJ - v61 - i9 - Sept 2015 - p176(1) [51-500]
Sheers, Owen - *I Saw a Man*
   BL - v111 - i17 - May 1 2015 - p75(1) [51-500]
   KR - March 1 2015 - pNA [51-500]
   NYT - July 13 2015 - pC1(L) [501+]
   Spec - v328 - i9745 - June 6 2015 - p38(1) [501+]
Sheetz-Nguyen, Jessica A. - *Victorian Women, Unwed Mothers and the London Foundling Hospital*
   VS - v57 - i2 - Wntr 2015 - p302(4) [501+]
Sheff, Elisabeth - *Stories from the Polycule: Real Life in Polyamorous Families*
   PW - v262 - i33 - August 17 2015 - p66(2) [51-500]
Sheff, Nic - *Harmony House*
   y KR - Dec 15 2015 - pNA [51-500]
Schizo
   y HB Guide - v26 - i1 - Spring 2015 - p123(1) [51-500]
Sheffer, Jolie A. - *The Romance of Race: Incest, Miscegenation, and Multiculturalism in the United States, 1880-1930*
   Historian - v77 - i2 - Summer 2015 - p351(2) [501+]
Shehada, Housni Alkhateeb - *Mamluks and Animals: Veterinary Medicine in Medieval Islam*
   Isis - v106 - i2 - June 2015 - p428(2) [501+]

Shehadeh, Raja - *Language of War, Language of Peace: Palestine, Israel and the Search for Justice*
   NS - v144 - i5269 - July 3 2015 - p46(3) [501+]
Sheimel, Courtney - *Zacktastic (Illus. by Crosby, Jeff)*
   c SLJ - v61 - i12 - Dec 2015 - p107(2) [51-500]
Shein, Daniel - *The Monsterjunkies*
   y KR - Sept 15 2015 - pNA [501+]
Sheinkin, Steve - *Most Dangerous: Daniel Ellsberg and the Secret History of the Vietnam War*
   y BL - v111 - i22 - August 1 2015 - p50(1) [51-500]
   y HB - v91 - i5 - Sept-Oct 2015 - p131(2) [51-500]
   y KR - July 15 2015 - pNA [51-500]
   c NYTBR - Nov 8 2015 - p25(L) [501+]
   c PW - v262 - i28 - July 13 2015 - p70(1) [51-500]
   c PW - v262 - i49 - Dec 2 2015 - p82(2) [51-500]
   y SLJ - v61 - i9 - Sept 2015 - p189(1) [51-500]
   y VOYA - v38 - i3 - August 2015 - p88(1) [51-500]
The Notorious Benedict Arnold: A True Story of Adventure, Heroism and Treachery
   y BL - v111 - i19-20 - June 1 2015 - p86(2) [501+]
The Port Chicago 50: Disaster, Mutiny, and the Fight for Civil Rights (Read by Hoffman, Dominic). Audiobook Review
   c BL - v111 - i14 - March 15 2015 - p24(2) [51-500]
The Port Chicago 50: Disaster, Mutiny, and the Fight for Civil Rights
   c HB - v91 - i1 - Jan-Feb 2015 - p27(5) [501+]
   y SE - v79 - i3 - May-June 2015 - p145(1) [501+]
Sheinmel, Alyssa - *Faceless*
   y KR - July 15 2015 - pNA [51-500]
   y SLJ - v61 - i11 - Nov 2015 - p122(1) [51-500]
   y VOYA - v38 - i4 - Oct 2015 - p61(1) [51-500]
Sheinmel, Courtney - *Edgewater*
   y CCB-B - v69 - i2 - Oct 2015 - p112(1) [51-500]
   y KR - July 15 2015 - pNA [51-500]
   y PW - v262 - i27 - July 6 2015 - p74(2) [51-500]
   y PW - v262 - i49 - Dec 2 2015 - p90(1) [51-500]
   y Sch Lib - v63 - i4 - Winter 2015 - p254(1) [51-500]
   y SLJ - v61 - i9 - Sept 2015 - p172(1) [51-500]
   y VOYA - v38 - i4 - Oct 2015 - p61(1) [51-500]
Shelbourne, Toni - *Among the Wolves: Memoirs of a Wolf Handler*
   RVBW - August 2015 - pNA [51-500]
Shelden, Michael - *Young Titan: The Making of Winston Churchill*
   Historian - v77 - i2 - Summer 2015 - p405(2) [501+]
   HT - v65 - i1 - Jan 2015 - p56(2) [51-500]
Shelden, Rachel A. - *Washington Brotherhood: Politics, Social Life, and the Coming of the Civil War*
   JSH - v81 - i2 - May 2015 - p463(2) [501+]
Sheldon, Charles - *The Wilderness of the Upper Yukon*
   Bwatch - July 2015 - pNA [51-500]
Sheldon, Dyan - *The Moon Dragons (Illus. by Blythe, Gary)*
   c HB Guide - v26 - i2 - Fall 2015 - p51(1) [51-500]
   c Sch Lib - v63 - i1 - Spring 2015 - p32(2) [51-500]
The Truth about My Success (Read by Sands, Tara). Audiobook Review
   y SLJ - v61 - i10 - Oct 2015 - p55(1) [51-500]
The Truth about My Success
   y BL - v111 - i16 - April 15 2015 - p48(1) [51-500]
   y CCB-B - v69 - i2 - Oct 2015 - p112(2) [51-500]
   y HB Guide - v26 - i2 - Fall 2015 - p138(1) [51-500]
   y KR - March 1 2015 - pNA [51-500]
   y PW - v262 - i15 - April 13 2015 - p82(1) [51-500]
   y SLJ - v61 - i5 - May 2015 - p124(1) [51-500]
   y VOYA - v38 - i1 - April 2015 - p69(2) [51-500]
Sheldon, Kathy - *'Tis the Season to Be Felt-y: Over 40 Handmade Holiday Decorations*
   LJ - v140 - i17 - Oct 15 2015 - p90(1) [51-500]
Shell, Marc - *Wampum and the Origins of American Money*
   Am Ind CRJ - v39 - i1 - Wntr 2015 - p161-163 [501+]
   Historian - v77 - i2 - Summer 2015 - p352(2) [501+]
Sheller, Mimi - *Aluminum Dreams: The Making of Light Modernity*
   AHR - v120 - i3 - June 2015 - p1064-1065 [501+]
   Isis - v106 - i2 - June 2015 - p494(2) [501+]
Citizenship from Below: Erotic Agency and Caribbean Freedom
   CS - v44 - i3 - May 2015 - p418-420 [501+]
Shelley, Fred M. - *Governments around the World: From Democracies to Theocracies*
   LJ - v140 - i14 - Sept 1 2015 - p138(2) [501+]
The World's Population: An Encyclopedia of Critical Issues, Crises, and Ever-Growing Countries
   BL - v111 - i17 - May 1 2015 - p64(1) [501+]
   R&USQ - v54 - i4 - Summer 2015 - p85(2) [501+]

Shelley, Mary - *Frankenstein (Illus. by Calero, Dennis)*
   BL - v111 - i9-10 - Jan 1 2015 - p63(1) [51-500]
   y HB Guide - v26 - i1 - Spring 2015 - p72(2) [51-500]
Shelton, Dave - *Thirteen Chairs (Illus. by Shelton, Dave)*
   y BL - v111 - i18 - May 15 2015 - p64(1) [51-500]
Thirteen Chairs
   c CCB-B - v69 - i2 - Oct 2015 - p113(1) [51-500]
Thirteen Chairs (Illus. by Shelton, Dave)
   y HB - v91 - i4 - July-August 2015 - p145(1) [51-500]
   c KR - May 1 2015 - pNA [51-500]
   y Sch Lib - v63 - i1 - Spring 2015 - p58(1) [51-500]
   y VOYA - v38 - i2 - June 2015 - p68(1) [51-500]
Shelton, J.A. - *The Women of Pliny's Letters*
   Class R - v65 - i2 - Oct 2015 - p470-472 [501+]
Shelton, Tamara Venit - *A Squatter's Republic: Land and the Politics of Monopoly in California, 1850-1900*
   AHR - v120 - i1 - Feb 2015 - p246-247 [501+]
   JAH - v101 - i4 - March 2015 - p1288-1289 [501+]
   WHQ - v46 - i1 - Spring 2015 - p87-88 [501+]
Shemer, Yaron - *Identity, Place, and Subversion in Contemporary Mizrahi Cinema in Israel*
   IJMES - v47 - i2 - May 2015 - p395-397 [501+]
Shemilt, Jane - *The Daughter*
   BL - v111 - i1 - Feb 1 2015 - p25(1) [51-500]
Shemo, Connie A. - *The Medical Ministries of Kang Cheng and Shi Meiyu, 1872-1937*
   JWH - v27 - i1 - Spring 2015 - p187(10) [501+]
Shemtov, Avi - *The Single Guy Cookbook*
   PW - v262 - i27 - July 6 2015 - p62(1) [51-500]
Shen, Grace Yen - *Unearthing the Nation: Modern Geology and Nationalism in Republican China*
   AHR - v120 - i4 - Oct 2015 - p1465-1466 [501+]
Shen, Qinna - *Beyond Alterity: German Encounters with Modern East Asia*
   CEH - v48 - i2 - June 2015 - p260-261 [501+]
Sheng, Hong - *China's State-Owned Enterprises: Nature, Performance and Reform*
   JAS - v74 - i2 - May 2015 - p482-483 [501+]
Shenk, Timothy - *Maurice Dobb: Political Economist*
   S&S - v79 - i1 - Jan 2015 - p129-132 [501+]
Shenk, Wilbert R. - *History of the American Society of Missiology, 1973-2013*
   IBMR - v39 - i2 - April 2015 - p101(1) [501+]
Shenkin, Steve - *The Port Chicago 50: Disaster, Mutiny, and the Fight for Civil Rights*
   c SLJ - v61 - i12 - Dec 2015 - p64(4) [501+]
Shenkman, Rick - *Political Animals: How Our Stone-Age Brain Gets in the Way of Smart Politics*
   BL - v112 - i5 - Nov 1 2015 - p5(1) [51-500]
   KR - Nov 1 2015 - pNA [501+]
Shenton, Caroline - *The Day Parliament Burned Down*
   Historian - v77 - i1 - Spring 2015 - p193(3) [501+]
Shepard, Aaron - *Adventures in Writing for Children*
   SPBW - March 2015 - pNA [51-500]
Shepard, Ben - *Head Hunters: The Search for a Science of the Mind*
   HT - v65 - i6 - June 2015 - p63(1) [501+]
Shepard, Geoff - *The Real Watergate Scandal: Collusion, Conspiracy, and the Plot to Bring Nixon Down*
   BL - v111 - i22 - August 1 2015 - p20(1) [51-500]
Shepard, Jim - *The Book of Aron*
   BL - v111 - i16 - April 15 2015 - p32(1) [51-500]
   KR - March 1 2015 - pNA [501+]
   Nat Post - v17 - i165 - May 16 2015 - pWP5(1) [501+]
   NY - v91 - i19 - July 6 2015 - p87 [51-500]
   NYTBR - May 24 2015 - p14(L) [501+]
   PW - v262 - i5 - Feb 2 2015 - p31(1) [51-500]
   y SLJ - v61 - i12 - Dec 2015 - p132(2) [51-500]
   Spec - v328 - i9748 - June 27 2015 - p43(2) [501+]
   TLS - i5863 - August 14 2015 - p20(1) [501+]
Shepard, Michael K. - *Asteroids: Relics of Ancient Time*
   Nature - v521 - i7553 - May 28 2015 - p421(1) [51-500]
Shepard, Neil - *Hominid Up*
   ABR - v36 - i3 - March-April 2015 - p22(2) [501+]
Shepard, Sara - *The Good Girls*
   y BL - v111 - i15 - April 1 2015 - p68(1) [51-500]
   y HB Guide - v26 - i2 - Fall 2015 - p138(1) [51-500]
   y KR - April 15 2015 - pNA [51-500]
   y VOYA - v37 - i6 - Feb 2015 - p66(1) [51-500]
The Perfectionists
   y CCB-B - v68 - i5 - Jan 2015 - p276(1) [51-500]
   y HB Guide - v26 - i1 - Spring 2015 - p123(1) [51-500]

Toxic
   y HB Guide - v26 - i1 - Spring 2015 - p123(1) [51-500]
Vicious
   c HB Guide - v26 - i2 - Fall 2015 - p138(1) [51-500]

Shepard, Wade - *Ghost Cities of China: The Story of Cities without People in the World's Most Populated Country*
     Nature - v520 - i7546 - April 9 2015 - p155(1) [51-500]
     NS - v144 - i5260 - May 1 2015 - p44(2) [501+]

Shephard, Tim - *The Routledge Companion to Music and Visual Culture: Representation in Western Music*
     PMS - v38 - i3 - July 2015 - p391(5) [501+]

Shepherd, Graham Edgar - *Ecology of Australian Temperate Reefs: The Unique South*
     QRB - v90 - i2 - June 2015 - p208(1) [501+]

Shepherd, Jessica - *Grandma*
   c HB Guide - v26 - i1 - Spring 2015 - p45(1) [51-500]

Shepherd, Jodie - *Jane Goodall*
   c BL - v112 - i4 - Oct 15 2015 - p43(1) [51-500]
Mae Jemison
   c BL - v111 - i19-20 - June 1 2015 - p93(1) [51-500]
Perseverance: I Have Grit!
   c BL - v112 - i3 - Oct 1 2015 - p66(1) [51-500]
Sacagawea
   c BL - v112 - i4 - Oct 15 2015 - p43(1) [51-500]

Shepherd, Megan - *The Cage*
   y CCB-B - v68 - i11 - July-August 2015 - p565(1) [51-500]
   c HB Guide - v26 - i2 - Fall 2015 - p138(1) [51-500]
   y KR - March 1 2015 - pNA [51-500]
   c SLJ - v61 - i2 - Feb 2015 - p107(2) [51-500]
   y VOYA - v38 - i1 - April 2015 - p83(1) [51-500]
A Cold Legacy
   c HB Guide - v26 - i2 - Fall 2015 - p138(1) [51-500]

Shepherd, Nan - *The Living Mountain*
     NS - v144 - i5278 - Sept 4 2015 - p37(1) [51-500]

Sheppard, Anne D.R. - *The Poetics of Phantasia. Imagination in Ancient Aesthetics*
     Class R - v65 - i1 - April 2015 - p68-70 [501+]

Sher, Antony - *Year of the Fat Knight: The Falstaff Diaries*
     TLS - i5864-5865 - August 21 2015 - p34(2) [501+]
     Spec - v327 - i9740 - May 2 2015 - p45(2) [501+]

Sher, Emil - *A Button Story (Illus. by Revell, Cindy)*
   c Res Links - v20 - i3 - Feb 2015 - p9(1) [51-500]
A Pebble Story
   c KR - Jan 1 2015 - pNA [51-500]
A Pebble Story (Illus. by Revell, Cindy)
   c Res Links - v20 - i3 - Feb 2015 - p9(1) [51-500]
Young Man with Camera
   y KR - July 1 2015 - pNA [51-500]
   y SLJ - v61 - i7 - July 2015 - p88(1) [51-500]
   y VOYA - v38 - i4 - Oct 2015 - p61(2) [51-500]

Sherberg, Michael - *The Governance of Friendship: Law and Gender in the Decameron*
     MLN - v130 - i1 - Jan 2015 - p145-150 [501+]

Sheridan, Frances - *Conclusion of the Memoirs of Miss Sidney Bidulph*
     TLS - i5831 - Jan 2 2015 - p23(1) [501+]

Sheridan, Mark - *Language for God in Patristic Tradition: Wrestling with Biblical Anthropomorphism*
     Theol St - v76 - i4 - Dec 2015 - p856(2) [501+]

Sherinian, Zoe C. - *Tamil Folk Music as Dalit Liberation Theology*
     IBMR - v39 - i2 - April 2015 - p105(2) [501+]

Sherkat, Darren E. - *Changing Faith: The Dynamics and Consequences of Americans' Shifting Religious Identities*
     AJS - v121 - i1 - July 2015 - p325(3) [501+]

Sherman, Daniel - *Soul, World, and Idea. An Interpretation of Plato's Republic and Phaedo*
     Class R - v65 - i1 - April 2015 - p51-53 [501+]

Sherman, Franklin - *Bridges: Documents of the Christian-Jewish Dialogue, vol. 1: The Road to Reconciliation (1945-1985)*
     Theol St - v76 - i3 - Sept 2015 - p616(3) [501+]
Bridges: Documents of the Christian-Jewish Dialogue, vol. 2: Building a New Relationship (1986-2013)
     Theol St - v76 - i3 - Sept 2015 - p616(3) [501+]

Sherman, Gisela Tobien - *The Farmerettes*
   y CH Bwatch - Oct 2015 - pNA [51-500]
   y Res Links - v20 - i4 - April 2015 - p32(1) [501+]
   y SLJ - v61 - i11 - Nov 2015 - p108(1) [51-500]
   y VOYA - v38 - i3 - August 2015 - p64(1) [51-500]

Sherman, Jacob Holsinger - *Partakers of the Divine: Contemplation and the Practice of Philosophy*
     Theol St - v76 - i4 - Dec 2015 - p877(2) [501+]

Sherman, Nancy - *Afterwar: Healing the Moral Wounds of Our Soldiers*
     ABR - v36 - i5 - July-August 2015 - p18(2) [501+]
     CC - v132 - i20 - Sept 30 2015 - p39(2) [501+]
Afterwar
     KR - Feb 1 2015 - pNA [501+]

Sherman, Randi M. - *The Truth about Caroline*
     RVBW - Oct 2015 - pNA [51-500]

Sherman, Sarah Way - *Sacramental Shopping: Louisa May Alcott, Edith Wharton, and the Spirit of Modern Consumerism*
     Nine-C Lit - v69 - i4 - March 2015 - p555(4) [501+]
     TSWL - v34 - i1 - Spring 2015 - p174-176 [501+]

Sherman, Scott - *Patience and Fortitude: Power, Real Estate, and the Fight to Save a Public Library*
     BL - v111 - i19-20 - June 1 2015 - p6(1) [51-500]
     KR - May 15 2015 - pNA [51-500]
     LJ - v140 - i11 - June 15 2015 - p101(1) [51-500]
     Mac - v128 - i25 - June 29 2015 - p55(2) [51-500]
     Nation - v300 - i29 - July 20 2015 - p43(1) [501+]
     NYT - July 12 2015 - p2(L) [501+]
     TLS - i5874 - Oct 30 2015 - p5(1) [501+]

Sherman, Suzanne - *100 Years in the Life of an American Girl*
     KR - August 1 2015 - pNA [51-500]

Shermer, Michael - *The Moral Arc: How Science and Reason lead Humanity toward Truth, Justice and Freedom*
     TimHES - i2197 - April 2 2015 - p53(1) [501+]
Skeptic: Viewing the World with a Rational Eye
     KR - Oct 1 2015 - pNA [501+]
     PW - v262 - i48 - Nov 30 2015 - p52(1) [501+]
     BL - v112 - i7 - Dec 1 2015 - p21(1) [51-500]

Sherr, Lynn - *Sally Ride: America's First Woman in Space (Read by Ward, Pam). Audiobook Review*
     BL - v111 - i9-10 - Jan 1 2015 - p116(1) [51-500]

Sherrard, Brent R. - *Fight Back*
   y KR - July 1 2015 - pNA [51-500]
   y Res Links - v20 - i5 - June 2015 - p28(1) [501+]
   y SLJ - v61 - i9 - Sept 2015 - p151(4) [501+]

Sherrard, Valerie - *Down Here (Illus. by Malenfant, Isabelle)*
   c CH Bwatch - Nov 2015 - pNA [51-500]
Rain Shadow
   y Res Links - v20 - i4 - April 2015 - p32(2) [501+]
   y VOYA - v38 - i2 - June 2015 - p68(1) [51-500]

Sherratt, Yvonne - *Hitler's Philosophers*
     CEH - v48 - i1 - March 2015 - p100-113 [501+]

Sherrod, Allen - *iOS for Game Programmers*
     Bwatch - June 2015 - pNA [51-500]

Sherrod, Egypt - *Keep Calm ... It's Just Real Estate: Your No-Stress Guide to Buying a Home*
     LJ - v140 - i6 - April 1 2015 - p101(1) [51-500]

Sherry, Kevin - *Meet the Bigfeet*
   c CH Bwatch - April 2015 - pNA [51-500]
   c HB Guide - v26 - i1 - Spring 2015 - p66(1) [51-500]
Monsters on the Run
   c KR - June 1 2015 - pNA [51-500]
Turtle Island
   c HB Guide - v26 - i1 - Spring 2015 - p45(1) [51-500]

Sherry, Maureen - *Opening Belle*
     KR - Nov 15 2015 - pNA [51-500]

Sherry, Miranda - *Black Dog Summer (Read by Bond, Jilly). Audiobook Review*
     LJ - v140 - i9 - May 15 2015 - p44(1) [51-500]
Black Dog Summer
     BL - v111 - i11 - Feb 1 2015 - p25(1) [51-500]
     LJ - v140 - i2 - Feb 1 2015 - p76(1) [51-500]

Sherry, Vincent - *Modernism and the Reinvention of Decadence*
     RES - v66 - i275 - June 2015 - p591-593 [501+]

Sherwood, Aaron - *Paul and the Restoration of Humanity in Light of Ancient Jewish Traditions*
     BTB - v45 - i1 - Feb 2015 - p60(2) [501+]

Sherwood, Jessica Holden - *Wealth, Whiteness, and the Matrix of Privilege: The View from the Country Club*
     SF - v93 - i3 - March 2015 - pe64 [501+]

Sherwood, Kate - *Sacrati*
     PW - v262 - i9 - March 2 2015 - p68(1) [51-500]

Sherwood, Marion - *Tennyson and the Fabrication of Englishness*
     VS - v57 - i3 - Spring 2015 - p549(2) [501+]

Sherwood, Timothy H. - *The Rhetorical Leadership of Fulton J. Sheen, Norman Vincent Peale, and Billy Graham in the Age of Extremes*
     CHR - v101 - i2 - Spring 2015 - p395(1) [501+]

Sherwood, Yvonne - *Biblical Blaspheming: Trials of the Sacred for a Secular Age*
     JR - v95 - i3 - July 2015 - p388(2) [501+]

Sheshunoff, Alex - *A Beginner's Guide to Paradise*
     KR - July 1 2015 - pNA [501+]

Sheth, Kashmira - *Sona and the Wedding Game (Illus. by Jaeggi, Yoshiko)*
   c CCB-B - v68 - i11 - July-August 2015 - p565(2) [51-500]
   c CH Bwatch - June 2015 - pNA [51-500]
   c HB Guide - v26 - i2 - Fall 2015 - p51(1) [51-500]
   c KR - Feb 15 2015 - pNA [51-500]

Shetreat-Klein, Maya - *The Dirt Cure: A Whole Food, Whole Planet Guide to Growing Healthy Kids in a Processed World*
     PW - v262 - i46 - Nov 16 2015 - p72(1) [51-500]

Shetterly, Susan Hand - *Swimming Home (Illus. by Raye, Rebekah)*
   c CH Bwatch - Feb 2015 - pNA [51-500]
   c CH Bwatch - April 2015 - pNA [51-500]
   c HB Guide - v26 - i1 - Spring 2015 - p45(1) [51-500]
   c Sci & Ch - v52 - i7 - March 2015 - p99 [51-500]

Shettleworth, Earle G., Jr. - *Homes Down East: Classic Maine Coastal Cottages and Town Houses*
     RVBW - April 2015 - pNA [51-500]

Shevah, Emma - *Dream On, Amber (Illus. by Crawford-White, Helen)*
   c BL - v111 - i21 - July 1 2015 - p69(2) [51-500]
   c KR - August 15 2015 - pNA [51-500]
   c NYTBR - Nov 8 2015 - p35(L) [501+]
   c PW - v262 - i32 - August 10 2015 - p59(1) [51-500]
   c PW - v262 - i49 - Dec 2 2015 - p69(2) [501+]
   c SLJ - v61 - i10 - Oct 2015 - p95(2) [51-500]

Shewring, Margaret - *Waterborne Pageants and Festivities in the Renaissance: Essays in Honour of J.R. Mulryne*
     Six Ct J - v46 - i2 - Summer 2015 - p398-399 [501+]

Shi, Li - *Rising Inequality in China: Challenges to a Harmonious Society*
     Pac A - v88 - i2 - June 2015 - p283 [501+]

Shi, Tianjian - *The Cultural Logic of Politics in Mainland China and Taiwan*
     For Aff - v94 - i1 - Jan-Feb 2015 - pNA [501+]

Shi, Yun-Bo - *Animal Metamorphosis*
     QRB - v90 - i2 - June 2015 - p227(1) [501+]

Shibahara, Taeko - *Japanese Women and the Transnational Feminist Movement before World War II*
     AHR - v120 - i4 - Oct 2015 - p1468-1469 [501+]
     PHR - v84 - i4 - Nov 2015 - p549(3) [501+]

Shidyaq, Ahmad Faris - *Leg over Leg, 4 vols.*
     TLS - i5877 - Nov 20 2015 - p28(2) [501+]
Leg over Leg
     TimHES - i2211 - July 9 2015 - p51(1) [501+]

Shiel, Walt - *Cessna Warbirds, the War Years (1941-45): The T-50 Bobcat and the Cessnas Impressed into Military Service*
     RVBW - July 2015 - pNA [501+]

Shields, A.L. - *Wilderness Rising*
     PW - v262 - i8 - Feb 23 2015 - p55(1) [51-500]

Shields, Amy - *National Geographic Kids Mon grand livre des pourquoi*
   c Res Links - v20 - i3 - Feb 2015 - p51(1) [51-500]

Shields, Carol Diggory - *After the Bell Rings: Poems about After-School Time (Illus. by Meisel, Paul)*
     BL - v111 - i14 - March 15 2015 - p60(1) [51-500]
   c HB Guide - v26 - i2 - Fall 2015 - p205(1) [51-500]

Shields, David - *I Think You're Totally Wrong: A Quarrel*
     Atl - v315 - i3 - April 2015 - p44(3) [501+]
     BL - v111 - i9-10 - Jan 1 2015 - p32(1) [51-500]
Life Is Short-Art Is Shorter: In Praise of Brevity
     PW - v262 - i6 - Feb 9 2015 - p57(1) [51-500]
War Is Beautiful: The 'New York Times' Pictorial Guide to the Glamour of Armed Conflict
     PW - v262 - i38 - Sept 21 2015 - p64(2) [51-500]

Shields, David S. - *Southern Provisions: The Creation and Revival of a Cuisine*
     BL - v111 - i15 - April 1 2015 - p10(1) [51-500]
     LJ - v140 - i2 - Feb 1 2015 - p103(1) [51-500]
     TLS - i5869 - Sept 25 2015 - p24(1) [51-500]

Shields, Gillian - *That Dog! (Illus. by Johnson-Isaacs, Cally)*
   c HB Guide - v26 - i1 - Spring 2015 - p45(1) [51-500]

Shields, Sharma - *The Sasquatch Hunter's Almanac*
     Ent W - i1348-1349 - Jan 30 2015 - p117(1) [501+]
     Nat Post - v17 - i74 - Jan 24 2015 - pWP10(1) [501+]

Shiffrin, Seana Valentine - *Speech Matters: On Lying, Morality, and the Law*
     TimHES - i2192 - Feb 26 2015 - p48(1) [501+]

Shigematsu, Setsu - *Scream from the Shadows: The Women's Liberation Movement in Japan*
     CS - v44 - i4 - July 2015 - p556-558 [501+]

Shih, Chih-Yu - *Sinicizing International Relations: Self, Civilization and Intellectual Politics in Subaltern East Asia*
    JAS - v74 - i1 - Feb 2015 - p180-181 [501+]

Shih, Clara - *The Facebook Era*
    Forbes - v196 - i6 - Nov 2 2015 - p42(1) [501+]

Shiller, Robert J. - *Irrational Exuberance*
    TimHES - i2213 - July 23 2015 - p45(1) [501+]

Shillington, Kevin - *Albert Rene: The Father of Modern Seychelles: A Biography*
    Africa T - v61 - i3 - Spring 2015 - p88(4) [501+]

Shilo, Benny - *Life's Blueprint: The Science and Art of Embryo Creation*
    BioSci - v65 - i5 - May 2015 - p526(2) [501+]
    QRB - v90 - i4 - Dec 2015 - p442(2) [501+]

Shim, Janet K. - *Heart-Sick: The Politics of Risk, Inequality, and Heart Disease*
    AJS - v120 - i6 - May 2015 - p1898(3) [501+]
    CS - v44 - i6 - Nov 2015 - p845-847 [501+]

Shimazu, Naoko - *Imagining Japan in Post-War East Asia: Identity Politics, Schooling and Popular Culture*
    Pac A - v88 - i2 - June 2015 - p317 [501+]

Shimmin, Graeme - *A Kill in the Morning*
    BL - v112 - i3 - Oct 1 2015 - p36(1) [51-500]

Shimoda, Hiraku - *Lost and Found: Recovering Regional Identity in Imperial Japan*
    AHR - v120 - i2 - April 2015 - p597-598 [501+]

Shin, Kyung-Sook - *The Girl Who Wrote Loneliness*
    BL - v112 - i2 - Sept 15 2015 - p27(1) [51-500]
    KR - July 15 2015 - pNA [501+]
    LJ - v140 - i17 - Oct 15 2015 - p81(2) [501+]

Shin, Kyung-sook - *The Girl Who Wrote Loneliness*
    NYTBR - Sept 20 2015 - p23(L) [501+]

Shin, Soon-jae - *Ruffer's Birthday Party*
    KR - April 1 2015 - pNA [51-500]

Shingu, Susumu - *Traveling Butterflies (Illus. by Shingu, Susumu)*
    c PW - v262 - i35 - August 31 2015 - p90(2) [501+]
    c HB - v91 - i6 - Nov-Dec 2015 - p107(2) [51-500]
    c BL - v112 - i4 - Oct 15 2015 - p41(1) [51-500]
    c KR - July 15 2015 - pNA [51-500]
Wandering Whale Sharks (Illus. by Shingu, Susumu)
    c HB Guide - v26 - i2 - Fall 2015 - p176(1) [51-500]
    c KR - Jan 1 2015 - pNA [51-500]
    c Res Links - v20 - i5 - June 2015 - p21(2) [51-500]

Shingu, Susumu - *Wandering Whale Sharks*
    SLJ - v61 - i3 - March 2015 - p174(1) [51-500]

Shinoda, Tomohito - *Contemporary Japanese Politics: Institutional Changes and Power Shifts*
    JAS - v74 - i2 - May 2015 - p443-447 [501+]

Shinohara, Koichi - *Spells, Images, and Mandalas: Tracing the Evolution of Esoteric Buddhist Rituals*
    JAAR - v83 - i4 - Dec 2015 - p1171-1175 [501+]

Shiomi, Chika - *Yukarism (Illus. by Shiomi, Chika)*
    y SLJ - v61 - i5 - May 2015 - p128(1) [51-500]

Shipler, David K. - *Freedom of Speech: Mightier Than the Sword*
    BL - v111 - i15 - April 1 2015 - p7(1) [51-500]
    CJR - v54 - i2 - July-August 2015 - p45(3) [501+]
    KR - March 15 2015 - pNA [501+]
    LJ - v140 - i6 - April 1 2015 - p105(1) [51-500]
    NYTBR - May 10 2015 - p16(L) [501+]
    Prog - v79 - i7-8 - July-August 2015 - p59(3) [501+]

Shipman, Pat - *The Invaders: How Humans and Their Dogs Drove Neanderthals to Extinction*
    Mac - v128 - i12 - March 30 2015 - p55(1) [501+]
    Nature - v520 - i7545 - April 2 2015 - p31(1) [51-500]
    QRB - v90 - i4 - Dec 2015 - p438(2) [501+]
    TimHES - i2200 - April 23 2015 - p50-51 [501+]
    TLS - i5848 - May 1 2015 - p8(2) [501+]

Shireen, Nadia - *Yeti and the Bird (Illus. by Shireen, Nadia)*
    c CCB-B - v68 - i9 - May 2015 - p467(2) [51-500]

Shirky, Clay - *Little Rice: Smartphones, Xiaomi, and the Chinese Dream*
    KR - August 15 2015 - pNA [501+]
    LJ - v140 - i16 - Oct 1 2015 - p105(1) [501+]

Shirley, John - *Wyatt in Wichita*
    Roundup M - v22 - i5 - June 2015 - p39(1) [501+]
    Roundup M - v22 - i6 - August 2015 - p32(1) [501+]

Shirvington, Jessica - *One Past Midnight*
    y HB Guide - v26 - i1 - Spring 2015 - p123(1) [51-500]

Shishkin, Mikhail - *Calligraphy Lesson: The Collected Stories*
    TLS - i5859 - July 17 2015 - p21(1) [501+]
    WLT - v89 - i6 - Nov-Dec 2015 - p66(2) [501+]

Shivik, John A. - *The Predator Paradox: Ending the War with Wolves, Bears, Cougars, and Coyotes*
    QRB - v90 - i3 - Sept 2015 - p329(1) [501+]

Shkandrij, Myroslav - *Ukrainian Nationalism: Politics, Ideology, and Literature, 1929-1956*
    For Aff - v94 - i3 - May-June 2015 - pNA [501+]

Shlonsky, Aron - *From Evidence to Outcomes in Child Welfare: An International Reader*
    Soc Ser R - v89 - i2 - June 2015 - p420(4) [501+]

Shnayerson, Michael - *The Contender: Andrew Cuomo, A Biography*
    NYRB - v62 - i13 - August 13 2015 - p42(4) [501+]
    NYTBR - April 5 2015 - p23(L) [501+]

Shock-Quinteros, Eva - *Eine Stadt im Krieg: Bremen 1914-1918*
    HNet - April 2015 - pNA [501+]

Shoemaker, Karen Gettert - *The Meaning of Names*
    WLT - v89 - i2 - March-April 2015 - p64(2) [501+]

Shogan, Robert - *Harry Truman and the Struggle for Racial Justice*
    Historian - v77 - i3 - Fall 2015 - p585(2) [501+]

Shoham, Liad - *Asylum City*
    RVBW - August 2015 - pNA [51-500]

Shoham-Steiner, Ephraim - *On the Margins of a Minority: Leprosy, Madness, and Disability among the Jews of Medieval Europe*
    HNet - July 2015 - pNA [501+]

Shoket, Ann - *Seventeen Ultimate Guide to College: Everything You Need to Know to Walk onto Campus and Own It!*
    y Teach Lib - v42 - i3 - Feb 2015 - p28(4) [501+]

Sholl, Betsy - *Otherwise Unseeable*
    Wom R Bks - v32 - i5 - Sept-Oct 2015 - p21(3) [501+]

Shone, Tom - *Woody Allen: A Retrospective*
    Spec - v329 - i9761 - Sept 26 2015 - p40(2) [501+]

Shooter, Jim - *Secret Wars*
    LJ - v140 - i9 - May 15 2015 - p110(1) [501+]

Shore, Debbie - *Half Yard Christmas: Easy Sewing Projects Using Left-Over Pieces of Fabric*
    LJ - v140 - i17 - Oct 15 2015 - p90(2) [501+]
Half Yard Gifts: Easy Sewing Projects Using Left-Over Pieces of Fabric
    LJ - v140 - i19 - Nov 15 2015 - p85(1) [501+]

Shore, Diane Z. - *This Is the Earth (Illus. by Minor, Wendell)*
    c KR - Nov 1 2015 - pNA [51-500]
    c PW - v262 - i47 - Nov 23 2015 - p67(1) [51-500]
    c SLJ - v61 - i10 - Oct 2015 - p130(2) [51-500]

Shore, Rebecca - *Developing Young Minds: From Conception to Kindergarten*
    PW - v262 - i42 - Oct 19 2015 - p72(1) [51-500]

Shore, Zachary - *A Sense of the Enemy: The High-Stakes History of Reading Your Rival's Mind*
    JIH - v45 - i3 - Wntr 2015 - p418-419 [501+]

Shores, Christopher - *A History of the Mediterranean Air War 1940-1945, Vol. 2: North African Desert, February 1942 - March 1943*
    APH - v62 - i1 - Spring 2015 - p57(1) [501+]

Shorr, Victoria - *Backlands*
    BL - v111 - i16 - April 15 2015 - p32(1) [51-500]
    KR - March 1 2015 - pNA [51-500]
    LJ - v140 - i8 - May 1 2015 - p66(1) [51-500]
    NYTBR - June 14 2015 - p11(L) [501+]

Short, Edward - *Newman and His Family*
    Theol St - v76 - i2 - June 2015 - p385(2) [501+]

Short, Ian - *Manual of Anglo-Norman*
    FS - v69 - i2 - April 2015 - p229-230 [501+]
    MLR - v110 - i2 - April 2015 - p539(1) [501+]

Short, John Phillip - *Magic Lantern Empire: Colonialism and Society in Germany*
    HER - v130 - i542 - Feb 2015 - p231(2) [501+]
    JMH - v87 - i1 - March 2015 - p221(4) [501+]

Short, Michael - *Correspondence of Franz Liszt and the Comtesse Marie d'Agoult*
    Notes - v71 - i3 - March 2015 - p530(3) [501+]

Shortall, Jessica - *Work. Pump. Repeat: How to Survive Breastfeeding and Going Back to Work*
    PW - v262 - i3 - Jan 19 2015 - p75(1) [501+]

Shoshkes, Ellen - *Jaqueline Tyrwhitt: A Transnational Life in Urban Planning and Design*
    HNet - April 2015 - pNA [501+]

Shostak, Sara - *Exposed Science: Genes, the Environment, and the Politics of Population Health*
    CS - v44 - i1 - Jan 2015 - p117-119 [501+]

Shoulders, Debbie - *M Is for Money: An Economics Alphabet (Illus. by Kelley, Marty)*
    SLJ - v61 - i8 - August 2015 - p124(1) [51-500]

Shoulders, Michael - *M Is for Money: An Economics Alphabet (Illus. by Kelley, Marty)*
    c CH Bwatch - Oct 2015 - pNA [51-500]

Shoulson, Jeffrey S. - *Fictions of Conversion: Jews, Christians, and Cultures of Change in Early Modern England*
    JMH - v87 - i1 - March 2015 - p167(3) [501+]
    MLR - v110 - i3 - July 2015 - p826-827 [501+]
    MP - v113 - i3 - Feb 2015 - pE224(E227) [501+]

Shoup, Jane - *Down in the Valley*
    PW - v262 - i27 - July 6 2015 - p53(1) [51-500]
Spirit of the Valley
    PW - v262 - i39 - Sept 28 2015 - p76(1) [51-500]

Showalter, Elaine - *The Civil Wars of Julia Ward Howe*
    KR - Dec 1 2015 - pNA [501+]
    LJ - v140 - i20 - Dec 1 2015 - p110(1) [51-500]

Showalter, Gena - *The Closer You Come*
    PW - v262 - i4 - Jan 26 2015 - p155(1) [51-500]
Firstlife
    y KR - Jan 1 2016 - pNA [51-500]
The Harder You Fall
    PW - v262 - i45 - Nov 9 2015 - p45(1) [51-500]
The Hotter You Burn
    PW - v262 - i24 - June 15 2015 - p70(2) [51-500]
The Queen of Zombie Hearts
    c HB Guide - v26 - i2 - Fall 2015 - p139(1) [51-500]

Showden, Carisa R. - *Choices Women Make: Agency in Domestic Violence, Assisted Reproduction, and Sex Work*
    CS - v44 - i2 - March 2015 - p251-253 [501+]

Showers, Ben - *Library Analytics and Metrics: Using Data to Drive Decisions and Services*
    LJ - v140 - i13 - August 1 2015 - p113(1) [501+]

Shown, Elizabeth - *Evidence Explained: Citing History Sources from Artifacts to Cyberspace, 3d ed.*
    BL - v112 - i6 - Nov 15 2015 - p6(1) [501+]

Shoyer, Paula - *The New Passover Menu*
    LJ - v140 - i10 - June 1 2015 - p131(1) [501+]

Shprintzen, Adam D. - *The Vegetarian Crusade: The Rise of an American Reform Movement, 1817-1921*
    AHR - v120 - i1 - Feb 2015 - p242-243 [501+]
    Historian - v77 - i2 - Summer 2015 - p354(2) [501+]
    JSH - v81 - i2 - May 2015 - p451(2) [501+]

Shraer, Maksim D. - *Bunin i Nabokov: Istoriia sopernichestva*
    Slav R - v74 - i3 - Fall 2015 - p673-674 [501+]

Shrake, Edwin - *Blessed McGill*
    Roundup M - v22 - i5 - June 2015 - p23(1) [501+]

Shraya, Vivek - *God Loves Hair (Illus. by Neufeld, Juliana)*
    Can Lit - i224 - Spring 2015 - p143 [501+]
She of the Mountains (Illus. by Biesinger, Raymond)
    Can Lit - i224 - Spring 2015 - p143 [501+]

Shreve, Susan - *The Search for Baby Ruby*
    c BL - v111 - i17 - May 1 2015 - p56(1) [51-500]
    c CCB-B - v69 - i1 - Sept 2015 - p53(1) [51-500]
    c HB Guide - v26 - i2 - Fall 2015 - p101(1) [51-500]
    c KR - March 1 2015 - pNA [51-500]
    c PW - v262 - i10 - March 9 2015 - p74(1) [51-500]
    SLJ - v61 - i4 - April 2015 - p150(1) [51-500]

Shrigley, David - *Weak Messages Create Bad Situations*
    PW - v262 - i33 - August 17 2015 - p58(1) [51-500]

Shrimpton, Nicholas - *The Warden*
    TLS - i5847 - April 24 2015 - p7(f2) [501+]

Shrum, Brianna R. - *Never Never*
    y SLJ - v61 - i11 - Nov 2015 - p122(1) [51-500]

Shteyngart, Gary - *Little Failure (Read by Todd, Jonathan)*
    BL - v111 - i9-10 - Jan 1 2015 - p120(1) [51-500]

Shue, Henry - *The American Way of Bombing: Changing Ethical and Legal Norms, from Flying Fortresses to Drones*
    HNet - August 2015 - pNA [501+]

Shufeldt, Ken - *Rage*
    PW - v262 - i27 - July 6 2015 - p51(1) [51-500]

Shugart, H.H. - *Foundations of the Earth: Global Ecological Change and the Book of Job*
    QRB - v90 - i4 - Dec 2015 - p430(1) [501+]

Shugart, Sandy - *Leadership in the Crucible of Work: Discovering the Interior Life of an Authentic Leader*
    SPBW - Feb 2015 - pNA [501+]

Shuji, Terayama - *The Crimson Thread of Abandon*
    WLT - v89 - i3-4 - May-August 2015 - p123(1) [51-500]

Shuker, David M. - *The Evolution of Insect Mating Systems*
    BioSci - v65 - i5 - May 2015 - p527(2) [501+]
    QRB - v90 - i2 - June 2015 - p222(1) [501+]

Shukla, Nikesh - *Meatspace*
 y BL - v111 - i22 - August 1 2015 - p29(1) [51-500]
 KR - July 15 2015 - pNA [51-500]
 LJ - v140 - i13 - August 1 2015 - p89(1) [51-500]
 PW - v262 - i30 - July 27 2015 - p41(1) [51-500]

Shulevitz, Uri - *Troto and the Trucks (Illus. by Shulevitz, Uri)*
 c HB - v91 - i3 - May-June 2015 - p98(2) [51-500]
 c HB Guide - v26 - i2 - Fall 2015 - p18(1) [51-500]
 c KR - Feb 15 2015 - pNA [51-500]

Shull, Megan - *The Swap*
 c HB Guide - v26 - i2 - Fall 2015 - p101(1) [51-500]

Shulman, Jeffrey - *The Constitutional Parent: Rights, Responsibilities, and the Enfranchisement of the Child*
 HLR - v128 - i4 - Feb 2015 - p1331(1) [1-50]

Shulman, Polly - *The Poe Estate*
 c KR - July 1 2015 - pNA [51-500]
 c SLJ - v61 - i8 - August 2015 - p92(2) [51-500]

Shults, F. LeRon - *Theology after the Birth of God: Atheist Conceptions in Cognition and Culture*
 Theol St - v76 - i4 - Dec 2015 - p891(1) [501+]

Shultz, Jackson Wright - *Trans/Portraits: Voices from Transgender Communities*
 BL - v111 - i22 - August 1 2015 - p23(2) [51-500]
 LJ - v140 - i14 - Sept 1 2015 - p127(2) [51-500]

Shumaker, Heather - *It's OK to Go Up the Slide: Renegade Rules for Raising Confident and Creative Kids*
 PW - v262 - i52 - Dec 21 2015 - p150(1) [51-500]

Shumsky, Ron - *The Survival Guide for School Success: Use Your Brain's Built-In Apps to Sharpen Attention, Battle Boredom, and Build Mental Muscle*
 c CH Bwatch - March 2015 - pNA [51-500]

Shumsky, Susan - *Awaken Your Third Eye: How Accessing Your Sixth Sense Can Help You Find Knowledge, Illumination, and Intuition*
 Bwatch - Sept 2015 - pNA [51-500]

Shumway, David R. - *Rock Star: The Making of Musical Icons from Elvis to Springsteen*
 JAH - v102 - i2 - Sept 2015 - p610-610 [501+]

Shupe, Joanna - *The Courtesan Duchess*
 BL - v111 - i16 - April 15 2015 - p30(1) [51-500]
 PW - v262 - i5 - Feb 2 2015 - p42(1) [51-500]
 The Harlot Countess
 PW - v262 - i12 - March 23 2015 - p55(1) [51-500]
 The Lady Hellion
 PW - v262 - i14 - April 6 2015 - p45(1) [51-500]

Shurgot, Michael W. - *Shakespeare's Sense of Character: On the Page and from the Stage*
 MLR - v110 - i3 - July 2015 - p823-824 [501+]

Shurtliff, Liesl - *Jack: The True Story of Jack & the Beanstalk (Read by Mann, Bruce). Audiobook Review*
 c BL - v112 - i3 - Oct 1 2015 - p87(1) [51-500]
 c SLJ - v61 - i7 - July 2015 - p47(1) [51-500]
 Jack: The True Story of Jack & the Beanstalk
 BL - v111 - i14 - March 15 2015 - p74(1) [51-500]
 c CCB-B - v68 - i11 - July-August 2015 - p566(1) [51-500]
 c HB Guide - v26 - i2 - Fall 2015 - p101(1) [51-500]
 c KR - Feb 1 2015 - pNA [51-500]

Shuster, Martin - *Autonomy after Auschwitz: Adorno, German Idealism, and Modernity*
 HT - v65 - i10 - Oct 2015 - p56(2) [501+]
 TLS - i5863 - August 14 2015 - p28(1) [501+]

Shusterman, Neal - *Challenger Deep (Illus. by Shusterman, Brendan)*
 y CCB-B - v68 - i10 - June 2015 - p516(1) [51-500]
 c HB Guide - v26 - i2 - Fall 2015 - p139(1) [51-500]
 y PW - v262 - i49 - Dec 2 2015 - p89(1) [51-500]
 y BL - v111 - i11 - Feb 1 2015 - p47(1) [51-500]
 y HB - v91 - i2 - March-April 2015 - p109(1) [51-500]
 y KR - Feb 1 2015 - pNA [51-500]
 y PW - v262 - i7 - Feb 16 2015 - p182(1) [51-500]
 y SLJ - v61 - i2 - Feb 2015 - p108(1) [51-500]
 y VOYA - v38 - i1 - April 2015 - p70(1) [51-500]
 Edison's Alley
 c HB - v91 - i3 - May-June 2015 - p118(2) [51-500]
 SLJ - v61 - i3 - March 2015 - p167(1) [51-500]
 Unbound
 y KR - Nov 15 2015 - pNA [51-500]
 UnDivided
 y VOYA - v37 - i6 - Feb 2015 - p83(1) [51-500]
 y HB Guide - v26 - i1 - Spring 2015 - p123(1) [51-500]

Shutan, Mary Mueller - *The Spiritual Awakening Guide: Kundalini, Psychic Abilities, and the Conditioned Layers of Reality*
 RVBW - Nov 2015 - pNA [51-500]

Shutika, Debra Lattanzi - *Beyond the Borderlands: Migration and Belonging in the United States and Mexico*
 SF - v93 - i3 - March 2015 - pe67 [501+]

Shuttlewood, Anna - *The Race to the Beach! (Illus. by Shuttlewood, Anna)*
 c Magpies - v30 - i2 - May 2015 - p27(1) [501+]
 c SLJ - v61 - i9 - Sept 2015 - p129(1) [51-500]

Shuttlewood, Craig - *Through the Town (Illus. by Shuttlewood, Craig)*
 c SLJ - v61 - i7 - July 2015 - p55(2) [51-500]

Shvidler, Eve - *Burning the Short White Coat: A Story of Becoming a Woman Doctor*
 SPBW - Oct 2015 - pNA [51-500]

Shyba, Jessica - *Naptime with Theo and Beau*
 c HB Guide - v26 - i2 - Fall 2015 - p18(1) [51-500]

Sias, Ryan - *Sniff! Sniff! (Illus. by Sias, Ryan)*
 c CH Bwatch - June 2015 - pNA [51-500]
 c HB Guide - v26 - i2 - Fall 2015 - p18(2) [51-500]
 KR - Feb 1 2015 - pNA [51-500]
 c SLJ - v61 - i5 - May 2015 - p92(1) [51-500]

Siblin, Eric - *Studio Grace: The Making of a Record*
 Nat Post - v17 - i200 - June 27 2015 - pWP5(1) [501+]

Sicard, Cheri - *Mary Jane: The Complete Marijuana Handbook for Women*
 LJ - v140 - i5 - March 15 2015 - p125(2) [51-500]

Sicher, Efraim - *Under Postcolonial Eyes: Figuring the 'Jew' in Contemporary British Writing*
 MLR - v110 - i3 - July 2015 - p855-857 [501+]

Sicius, Francis J. - *The Progressive Era*
 BL - v112 - i2 - Sept 15 2015 - p12(1) [51-500]

Sickels, Carter - *Untangling the Knot: Queer Voices on Marriage, Relationships, and Identity*
 G&L Rev W - v22 - i3 - May-June 2015 - p43(1) [501+]

Siddals, Mary McKenna - *Bringing the Outside In (Illus. by Barton, Patrice)*
 c PW - v262 - i48 - Nov 30 2015 - p57(1) [51-500]
 Shivery Shades of Halloween: A Spooky Book of Colors (Illus. by Pickering, Jimmy)
 c HB Guide - v26 - i1 - Spring 2015 - p16(1) [51-500]

Siddiqui, Mona - *Hospitality and Islam: Welcoming in God's Name*
 TimHES - i2229 - Nov 12 2015 - p46(1) [501+]

Sidebottom, Harry - *Blood & Steel*
 TLS - i5873 - Oct 23 2015 - p20(1) [501+]
 Iron & Rust
 RVBW - Jan 2015 - pNA [51-500]

Sider, Ronald J. - *Nonviolent Action: What Christian Ethics Demands But Most Christians Have Never Really Tried*
 Bwatch - May 2015 - pNA [51-500]

Sideris, Lida - *Murder and Other Unnatural Disasters*
 KR - Oct 15 2015 - pNA [501+]

Sides, Hampton - *In the Kingdom of Ice: The Grand and Terrible Polar Voyage of the USS Jeannette (Read by Morey, Arthur). Audiobook Review*
 BL - v111 - i9-10 - Jan 1 2015 - p112(1) [51-500]
 In the Kingdom of Ice: The Grand and Terrible Polar Voyage of the USS Jeannette
 NYTBR - May 31 2015 - p52(L) [501+]
 Spec - v327 - i9728 - Feb 7 2015 - p46(2) [501+]
 TLS - i5840 - March 6 2015 - p28(2) [501+]

Sidman, Joyce - *Winter Bees and Other Poems of the Cold (Illus. by Allen, Rick)*
 c BL - v111 - i9-10 - Jan 1 2015 - pS4(8) [501+]
 c NYTBR - Jan 18 2015 - p20(L) [501+]
 c HB Guide - v26 - i1 - Spring 2015 - p189(1) [51-500]

Sidransky, A.J. - *Forgiving Maximo Rothman*
 RVBW - Jan 2015 - pNA [51-500]

Sie, James - *Still Life Las Vegas (Illus. by Choi, Sungyoon)*
 y BL - v111 - i19-20 - June 1 2015 - p46(1) [51-500]
 KR - June 1 2015 - pNA [51-500]
 PW - v262 - i22 - June 1 2015 - p39(1) [51-500]

Siedentop, Larry - *Inventing the Individual: The Origins of Western Liberalism*
 AM - v213 - i3 - August 3 2015 - p32(2) [501+]
 J Ch St - v57 - i3 - Summer 2015 - p556-559 [501+]
 MA - v57 - i3 - Summer 2015 - p74(4) [501+]
 Nation - v300 - i18 - May 4 2015 - p35(4) [501+]
 RM - v68 - i3 - March 2015 - p679(2) [501+]
 Soc - v52 - i5 - Oct 2015 - p498(1) [501+]

Sieg, Wilfried - *Hilbert's Program and Beyond*
 Isis - v106 - i2 - June 2015 - p481(3) [501+]

Siegal, Ida - *Big News! (Illus. by Pena, Karla)*
 c KR - Feb 1 2015 - pNA [51-500]
 c SLJ - v61 - i2 - Feb 2015 - p78(2) [51-500]
 Emma Is on the Air: Big News! (Illus. by Pena, Karla)
 c CCB-B - v69 - i1 - Sept 2015 - p53(2) [51-500]
 c HB Guide - v26 - i2 - Fall 2015 - p71(1) [51-500]
 Party Drama!
 c KR - July 1 2015 - pNA [51-500]

Siegel, Jeremy J. - *Stocks for the Long Run: The Definitive Guide to Financial Market Returns and Long-Term Investment Strategies*
 Barron's - v95 - i32 - August 10 2015 - p40(1) [501+]

Siegel, Lee - *Groucho Marx: The Comedy of Existence*
 KR - Nov 1 2015 - pNA [501+]
 PW - v262 - i44 - Nov 2 2015 - p77(1) [51-500]
 Trance-Migrations: Stories of India, Tales of Hypnosis
 CHE - v61 - i17 - Jan 9 2015 - pNA [501+]

Siegel, Roz - *Well-Heeled: An Emily's Place Mystery*
 PW - v262 - i18 - May 4 2015 - p99(1) [51-500]

Siegel, Seth M. - *Let There Be Water: Israel's Solution for a Water-Starved World*
 KR - August 1 2015 - pNA [501+]
 LJ - v140 - i15 - Sept 15 2015 - p103(1) [51-500]

Siegelbaum, Lewis H. - *The Socialist Car: Automobility in the Eastern Bloc*
 HNet - Feb 2015 - pNA [501+]

Siegfried, Brandie R. - *God and Nature in the Thought of Margaret Cavendish*
 Sev Cent N - v73 - i1-2 - Spring-Summer 2015 - p19(3) [501+]

Sieling, Ariele - *The Wounded World*
 PW - v262 - i10 - March 9 2015 - p57(1) [51-500]

Sielsch, Leo A. - *The Cartoon Guide*
 RVBW - Oct 2015 - pNA [51-500]

Siemerling, Winfried - *The Black Atlantic Reconsidered: Black Canadian Writing, Cultural History, and the Presence of the Past*
 Can Lit - i224 - Spring 2015 - p144 [501+]

Siemon-Netto, Uwe - *Triumph of the Absurd: A Reporter's Love for the Abandoned People of Vietnam*
 SPBW - July 2015 - pNA [51-500]
 RVBW - June 2015 - pNA [51-500]

Siemsen, Michael - *Exigency*
 KR - March 15 2015 - pNA [51-500]

Siepel, Kevin H. - *Conquistador Voices: The Spanish Conquest of the Americas as Recounted Largely by the Participants, 2 vols.*
 PW - v262 - i46 - Nov 16 2015 - p70(2) [51-500]

Sierra, Javier - *The Master of the Prado*
 KR - Sept 15 2015 - pNA [51-500]
 LJ - v140 - i17 - Oct 15 2015 - p82(2) [51-500]
 PW - v262 - i37 - Sept 14 2015 - p37(1) [51-500]

Sierra, Jude - *Hush*
 PW - v262 - i11 - March 16 2015 - p70(1) [51-500]
 What It Takes
 PW - v262 - i45 - Nov 9 2015 - p44(1) [51-500]

Sierz, Aleks - *The Time Traveller's Guide to British Theatre: The First Four Hundred Years (Illus. by Illman, James)*
 Sch Lib - v63 - i4 - Winter 2015 - p252(1) [51-500]

Sietsema, Robert - *New York in a Dozen Dishes*
 LJ - v140 - i6 - April 1 2015 - p112(2) [51-500]
 PW - v262 - i18 - May 4 2015 - p108(1) [501+]

Sieve, Brian - *Ambrose Fountain (Read by Bell, Tobin). Audiobook Review*
 PW - v262 - i21 - May 25 2015 - p55(1) [51-500]

Sif, Birgitta - *Frances Dean Who Loved to Dance and Dance (Illus. by Sif, Birgitta)*
 c HB Guide - v26 - i1 - Spring 2015 - p46(1) [51-500]
 c RVBW - July 2015 - pNA [51-500]
 Where My Feet Go
 c KR - Nov 15 2015 - pNA [51-500]
 c PW - v262 - i47 - Nov 23 2015 - p65(1) [51-500]

Siff, Stephen - *Acid Hype: American News Media and the Psychedelic Experience*
 Reason - v47 - i7 - Dec 2015 - p54(1) [51-500]

Sifton, Elisabeth - *No Ordinary Men: Dietrich Bonhoeffer and Hans von Dohnanyi, Resisters Against Hitler in Church and State*
 TT - v72 - i1 - April 2015 - p123-124 [501+]

Sigel, Astrid - *Cadmium: From Toxicity to Essentiality*
 QRB - v90 - i2 - June 2015 - p225(2) [501+]

Sigel, Helmut - *Interrelations between Essential Metal Ions and Human Diseases*
 QRB - v90 - i3 - Sept 2015 - p352(2) [501+]

Sigel, Lisa Z. - *Making Modern Love: Sexual Narratives and Identities in Interwar Britain*
 Wom HR - v24 - i1 - Feb 2015 - p141-3 [501+]

Siger, Jeffrey - *Devil of Delphi*
　　BL - v112 - i2 - Sept 15 2015 - p30(1) [51-500]
　　KR - August 15 2015 - pNA [51-500]
　　PW - v262 - i31 - August 3 2015 - p35(1) [51-500]

Sigler, Scott - *Alive*
　　Ent W - i1374 - July 31 2015 - p66(1) [501+]

Sigmund, Christian - *'Konigtum' in der Politischen Kultur des Spatrepublikanischen Rom*
　　HNet - June 2015 - pNA [501+]

Sigmund, Monika - *Genuss als Politikum: Kaffeekonsum in beiden deutschen Staaten*
　　HNet - April 2015 - pNA [501+]

Signa Vides--Researching and Recording Printers' Devices: Current Activities and New Perspectives
　　HNet - June 2015 - pNA [501+]

Signer, Michael - *Becoming Madison: The Extraordinary Origins of the Least Likely Founding Father*
　　KR - Jan 15 2015 - pNA [501+]
　　LJ - v140 - i3 - Feb 15 2015 - p115(1) [501+]

Signori, Gabriela - *Das Konstanzer Konzil als Europaisches Ereignis: Begegnungen, Medien und Rituale*
　　HNet - Feb 2015 - pNA [501+]

Signori, Gabriella - *Das Schuldbuch des Basler Kaufmanns Ludwig Kilchmann*
　　Six Ct J - v46 - i3 - Fall 2015 - p785-786 [501+]

Signorile, Michelangelo - *It's Not Over: Getting beyond Tolerance, Defeating Homophobia, and Winning True Equality*
　　Advocate - i1079 - June-July 2015 - p71(2) [501+]
　　G&L Rev W - v22 - i5 - Sept-Oct 2015 - p47(2) [501+]
　　KR - March 1 2015 - pNA [501+]
　　LJ - v140 - i6 - April 1 2015 - p108(1) [501+]

Sigu, Veronique - *Medievisme et Lumieres: le Moyen Age dans la "Bibliotheque universelle des romans"*
　　MLR - v110 - i3 - July 2015 - p865-866 [501+]

Sigurdardottir, Thora - *Someone to Watch over Me*
　　KR - Jan 15 2015 - pNA [51-500]

Sigurdardottir, Yrsa - *The Silence of the Sea*
　　KR - Dec 15 2015 - pNA [51-500]
　　PW - v262 - i52 - Dec 21 2015 - p133(1) [51-500]

Siguroardottir, Steinunn - *Place of the Heart*
　　WLT - v89 - i2 - March-April 2015 - p73(1) [51-500]

Siken, Richard - *War of the Foxes*
　　BL - v111 - i17 - May 1 2015 - p73(1) [51-500]
　　LJ - v140 - i3 - Feb 15 2015 - p106(1) [51-500]
　　PW - v262 - i3 - Jan 19 2015 - p56(1) [51-500]

Siko, John - *Inside South Africa's Foreign Policy: Diplomacy in Africa from Smuts to Mbeki*
　　Africa T - v61 - i3 - Spring 2015 - p87(2) [501+]
　　For Aff - v94 - i3 - May-June 2015 - pNA [501+]

Sikora, Miroslav - *Die Waffenschmiede des "Dritten Reiches": Die deutsche Rustungsindustrie in Oberschlesien wahrend des Zweiten Weltkrieges*
　　HNet - May 2015 - pNA [501+]

Silas, Stan - *The Life of Norman, vol. 1*
　　PW - v262 - i7 - Feb 16 2015 - p166(1) [51-500]

Silbaugh, Rebecca - *Seems Like Scrappy: The Look You Love with Fat Quarters and Precuts*
　　Bwatch - Sept 2015 - pNA [51-500]

Silberklang, David - *Gates of Tears: The Holocaust in the Lublin District*
　　HNet - March 2015 - pNA [501+]

Silberman, Steve - *Neurotribes: The Legacy of Autism and How to Think Smarter about People who Think Differently*
　　New Sci - v228 - i3042 - Oct 10 2015 - p46(2) [501+]
　　New Sci - v228 - i3045 - Oct 31 2015 - p45(1) [501+]
　　Spec - v328 - i9759 - Sept 12 2015 - p38(2) [501+]

Neurotribes: The Legacy of Autism and the Future of Neurodiversity
　　Econ - v416 - i8952 - August 22 2015 - p69(US) [501+]
　　KR - June 1 2015 - pNA [501+]
　　Nature - v524 - i7565 - August 20 2015 - p288(2) [501+]
　　NYTBR - August 23 2015 - p11(L) [501+]
　　PW - v262 - i26 - June 29 2015 - p57(1) [501+]

Silberstein-Loeb, Jonathan - *The International Distribution of News: The Associated Press, Press Association, and Reuters, 1848-1947*
　　BHR - v89 - i1 - Spring 2015 - p187(3) [501+]

Silbey, Jessica - *The Eureka Myth: Creators, Innovators, and Everyday Intellectual Property*
　　Law Q Rev - v131 - Oct 2015 - p686-689 [501+]

Silbey, Joel H. - *A Companion to the Antebellum Presidents, 1837-1861*
　　JSH - v81 - i3 - August 2015 - p715(2) [501+]
　　Pres St Q - v45 - i3 - Sept 2015 - p628(2) [501+]

Silk, Michael S. - *The Classical Tradition: Art, Literature, Thought*
　　Class R - v65 - i1 - April 2015 - p275-277 [501+]
　　HNet - May 2015 - pNA [501+]

Silkey, Sarah L. - *Black Woman Reformer: Ida B. Wells, Lynching, and Transatlantic Activism*
　　HNet - July 2015 - pNA [501+]

Sill, Cathryn - *About Parrots: A Guide for Children (Illus. by Sill, John)*
　c　HB Guide - v26 - i1 - Spring 2015 - p163(1) [51-500]
Polar Regions (Illus. by Sill, John)
　c　SLJ - v61 - i9 - Sept 2015 - p181(1) [51-500]

Sillars, Stuart - *Shakespeare, Time and the Victorians: A Pictorial Exploration*
　　VS - v57 - i2 - Wntr 2015 - p319(3) [501+]

Silva-Corvalan, Carmen - *Bilingual Language Acquisition: Spanish and English in the First Six Years*
　　Lang Soc - v44 - i3 - June 2015 - p452-453 [501+]

Silva, Cristobal - *Miraculous Plagues: An Epidemiology of Early New England Narrative*
　　AL - v87 - i1 - March 2015 - p190-192 [501+]

Silva, Daniel - *The English Spy (Read by Guidall, George). Audiobook Review*
　　BL - v112 - i3 - Oct 1 2015 - p85(1) [51-500]
The English Spy
　　BL - v111 - i21 - July 1 2015 - p37(1) [51-500]
　　KR - July 1 2015 - pNA [51-500]

Silva, Jennifer M. - *Coming Up Short: Working-Class Adulthood in an Age of Uncertainty*
　　CS - v44 - i4 - July 2015 - p558-559 [501+]

Silver, Charlotte - *Bennington Girls Are Easy*
　　BL - v111 - i21 - July 1 2015 - p27(1) [51-500]
　　KR - May 1 2015 - pNA [501+]
　　LJ - v140 - i11 - June 15 2015 - p81(1) [51-500]
　　PW - v262 - i20 - May 18 2015 - p60(1) [51-500]

Silver, Eve - *Crash*
　c　HB Guide - v26 - i2 - Fall 2015 - p139(1) [51-500]
　y　Res Links - v20 - i5 - June 2015 - p28(1) [51-500]
　y　VOYA - v38 - i2 - June 2015 - p83(1) [51-500]
Push
　y　HB Guide - v26 - i1 - Spring 2015 - p123(1) [51-500]

Silver, Gail - *Peace, Bugs, and Understanding: An Adventure in Sibling Harmony (Illus. by Ly, Youme Nguyen)*
　c　CH Bwatch - June 2015 - pNA [51-500]
　c　HB Guide - v26 - i2 - Fall 2015 - p52(1) [51-500]

Silver, Larry - *Rubens, Velasquez, and the King of Spain*
　　Six Ct J - v46 - i2 - Summer 2015 - p411-412 [501+]

Silver, Nate - *The Signal and the Noise: Why So Many Predictions Fail - But Some Don't*
　　NYTBR - March 1 2015 - p28(L) [501+]

Silver, Sean - *The Mind Is a collection: Case Studies in Eighteenth Century Thought*
　　JHI - v76 - i4 - Oct 2015 - p666(1) [501+]

Silver Spoon Kitchen - *Puglia*
　　PW - v262 - i9 - March 2 2015 - p79(1) [51-500]

Silvera, Adam - *More Happy Than Not*
　y　BL - v111 - i18 - May 15 2015 - p52(1) [501+]
　y　CCB-B - v69 - i1 - Sept 2015 - p54(1) [51-500]
　c　HB Guide - v26 - i2 - Fall 2015 - p139(1) [51-500]
　c　KR - April 15 2015 - pNA [51-500]
　c　NYTBR - June 21 2015 - p18(L) [501+]
　y　PW - v262 - i15 - April 13 2015 - p83(1) [51-500]
　y　PW - v262 - i49 - Dec 2 2015 - p94(1) [51-500]
　y　SLJ - v61 - i5 - May 2015 - p124(2) [51-500]
　y　VOYA - v38 - i1 - April 2015 - p83(2) [51-500]

Silverberg, Cory - *Sex Is a Funny Word: A Book about Bodies, Feelings, and You (Illus. by Smyth, Fiona)*
　c　KR - April 15 2015 - pNA [51-500]
　c　PW - v262 - i25 - June 22 2015 - p141(1) [501+]
　c　PW - v262 - i49 - Dec 2 2015 - p84(1) [51-500]

Silverman, David - *Fighting God: An Atheist Manifesto for a Religious World*
　　BL - v112 - i6 - Nov 15 2015 - p14(1) [51-500]
　　KR - Sept 1 2015 - pNA [51-500]
　　LJ - v140 - i17 - Oct 15 2015 - p93(1) [51-500]

Silverman, David J. - *Ninigret, Sachem of the Niantics and Narragansetts: Diplomacy, War, and the Balance of Power in Seventeenth-Century New England and Indian Country*
　　W&M Q - v72 - i3 - July 2015 - p544-548 [501+]

Silverman, Erica - *Lana's World: Let's Go Fishing! (Illus. by Golden, Jess)*
　c　HB Guide - v26 - i2 - Fall 2015 - p61(1) [51-500]
　c　SLJ - v61 - i6 - June 2015 - p96(1) [51-500]
Lana's World: Let's Have a Parade! (Illus. by Golden, Jess)
　c　HB Guide - v26 - i2 - Fall 2015 - p61(1) [51-500]

Silverman, Gillian - *Bodies and Books: Reading and the Fantasy of Communion in Nineteenth-Century America*
　　MLR - v110 - i3 - July 2015 - p840-842 [501+]

Silverman, Jacob - *Terms of Service: Social Media and the Price of Constant Connection*
　　BL - v111 - i4 - March 15 2015 - p33(2) [51-500]
　　CSM - March 18 2015 - pNA [51-500]
　　KR - Feb 1 2015 - pNA [51-500]
　　LJ - v140 - i5 - March 15 2015 - p129(1) [51-500]

Silverman, Sidney B. - *The Wall, the Mount, and the Mystery of the Red Heifer*
　　KR - Oct 1 2015 - pNA [501+]

Silverman, Stephen M. - *The Catskills: Its History and How It Changed America*
　　BL - v112 - i3 - Oct 1 2015 - p13(1) [51-500]
　　KR - July 1 2015 - pNA [501+]
　　LJ - v140 - i13 - August 1 2015 - p110(1) [51-500]
　　NYTBR - Dec 6 2015 - p24(L) [501+]
　　PW - v262 - i35 - August 31 2015 - p73(1) [51-500]

Silverman, Susan - *Casting Lots*
　　KR - Jan 1 2016 - pNA [501+]

Silvermoon, Crystal - *Great Expectations (Illus. by Poon, Nokman)*
　y　SLJ - v61 - i11 - Nov 2015 - p124(1) [51-500]

Silverstein, Barry - *Let's Make Money, Honey: The Couple's Guide to Starting a Service Business*
　　RVBW - Nov 2015 - pNA [51-500]

Silverstein, Merril - *Kinship and Cohort in an Aging Society: From Generation to Generation*
　　CS - v44 - i2 - March 2015 - p253-254 [501+]

Silverstein, Robert M. - *Spectrometric Identification of Organic Compounds, 8th ed.*
　　J Chem Ed - v92 - i10 - Oct 2015 - p1602-1603 [501+]

Silverstein, Shel - *Falling Up: Poems and Drawings: Special Edition*
　y　HB Guide - v26 - i2 - Fall 2015 - p205(1) [51-500]

Silvestre, Juan Camilo Conde - *The Handbook of Historical Sociolinguistics (Read by Campoy, Juan Manuel Hernandez)*
　　Lang Soc - v44 - i5 - Nov 2015 - p745-746 [501+]

Silvey, Anita - *Untamed: The Wild Life of Jane Goodall*
　c　BL - v111 - i19-20 - June 1 2015 - p92(1) [51-500]
　c　CCB-B - v69 - i1 - Sept 2015 - p54(2) [51-500]
　c　HB - v91 - i3 - May-June 2015 - p132(2) [51-500]
　c　HB Guide - v26 - i2 - Fall 2015 - p212(1) [51-500]
　c　PW - v262 - i17 - April 27 2015 - p79(1) [51-500]
　c　PW - v262 - i49 - Dec 2 2015 - p84(1) [51-500]
　c　SLJ - v61 - i4 - April 2015 - p185(2) [51-500]

Silvia, Stephen J. - *Holding the Shop Together: German Industrial Relations in the Postwar Era*
　　GSR - v38 - i2 - May 2015 - p474-3 [501+]

Sim, David - *A Union Forever: The Irish Question and U.S. Foreign Relations in the Victorian Age*
　　AHR - v120 - i1 - Feb 2015 - p244-245 [501+]
　　JAH - v102 - i2 - Sept 2015 - p560-561 [501+]

Simak, Clifford D. - *I Am Crying All Inside and Other Stories: The Complete Short Fiction of Clifford D. Simak, vol. 1*
　　PW - v262 - i34 - August 24 2015 - p62(2) [51-500]

Simar, Candace - *Shelterbelts*
　　Roundup M - v23 - i1 - Oct 2015 - p31(1) [51-500]
　　KR - Oct 1 2015 - pNA [501+]

Simard, Remy - *Gustave (Illus. by Pratt, Pierre)*
　c　HB Guide - v26 - i1 - Spring 2015 - p46(1) [51-500]

Simberloff, Daniel - *Invasive Species: What Everyone Needs to Know*
　　QRB - v90 - i1 - March 2015 - p82(2) [501+]

Simenon, Georges - *The Saint-Fiacre Affair*
　　TLS - i5839 - Feb 27 2015 - p27(1) [501+]

Simeone, Nigel - *The Leonard Bernstein Letters*
　　Bks & Cult - v21 - i1 - Jan-Feb 2015 - p25(3) [501+]

Simic, Charles - *The Life of Images: Selected Prose*
　　BL - v111 - i14 - March 15 2015 - p27(1) [501+]
　　KR - Feb 15 2015 - pNA [51-500]
　　LJ - v140 - i5 - March 15 2015 - p106(1) [51-500]
　　NYRB - v62 - i12 - July 9 2015 - p47(2) [501+]
　　NYT - April 1 2015 - pC1(L) [501+]
　　NYTBR - Sept 6 2015 - p26(L) [501+]
　　PW - v262 - i7 - Feb 16 2015 - p168(1) [501+]

The Lunatic: Poems
    NYRB - v62 - i12 - July 9 2015 - p47(2) [501+]
    NYT - April 1 2015 - pC1(L) [501+]
    PW - v262 - i7 - Feb 16 2015 - p168(1) [501+]

Simionescu, P.A. - *Computer-Aided Graphing and Simulation Tools for AutoCAD Users*
    Bwatch - March 2015 - pNA [501+]

Simitch, Andrea - *The Language of Architecture: 26 Principles Every Architect Should Know*
    TLS - i5837 - Feb 13 2015 - p27(1) [501+]

Simmonds, Meg - *Bond by Design: The Art of the James Bond Films*
    PW - v262 - i39 - Sept 28 2015 - p83(2) [501+]

Simmons, Anthea - *The Bestest Baby! (Illus. by Birkett, Georgie)*
    c HB Guide - v26 - i2 - Fall 2015 - p19(1) [51-500]
Share! (Illus. by Birkett, Georgie)
    c HB Guide - v26 - i1 - Spring 2015 - p16(1) [51-500]

Simmons, Dan - *The Fifth Alert*
    Ent W - i1358 - April 10 2015 - p67(1) [501+]
The Fifth Heart (Read by Pittu, David). Audiobook Review
    BL - v111 - i22 - August 1 2015 - p77(1) [51-500]
    PW - v262 - i26 - June 29 2015 - p64(1) [51-500]
The Fifth Heart
    BL - v111 - i11 - Feb 1 2015 - p26(1) [51-500]
    KR - Jan 15 2015 - pNA [501+]
    LJ - v140 - i3 - Feb 15 2015 - p93(1) [51-500]
    NYTBR - April 12 2015 - p30(L) [501+]
    PW - v262 - i3 - Jan 19 2015 - p61(1) [51-500]

Simmons, Ernest L. - *The Entangled Trinity: Quantum Physics and Theology*
    Theol St - v76 - i4 - Dec 2015 - p857(2) [501+]

Simmons, Gene - *Me, Inc.*
    Kiplinger - v69 - i2 - Feb 2015 - p15(1) [501+]

Simmons, Josh - *Black River (Illus. by Simmons, Josh)*
    BL - v111 - i18 - May 15 2015 - p41(1) [51-500]

Simmons, Kristen - *The Glass Arrow (Read by Nankani, Soneela). Audiobook Review*
    y SLJ - v61 - i6 - June 2015 - p68(1) [51-500]
The Glass Arrow
    y BL - v111 - i9-10 - Jan 1 2015 - p94(1) [51-500]
    y CH Bwatch - Sept 2015 - pNA [51-500]
    c HB Guide - v26 - i2 - Fall 2015 - p139(1) [51-500]
    y VOYA - v37 - i6 - Feb 2015 - p84(1) [51-500]

Simmons, LaKisha Michelle - *Crescent City Girls: The Lives of Young Black Women in Segregated New Orleans*
    Wom R Bks - v32 - i6 - Nov-Dec 2015 - p6(3) [501+]

Simmons, Solon - *The Eclipse of America: Arguing America on Meet the Press*
    J Am St - v49 - i2 - May 2015 - p452-453 [501+]

Simmons, William Paul - *Binational Human Rights: The U.S.-Mexico Experience*
    CS - v44 - i6 - Nov 2015 - p847-848 [501+]

Simms, Brendan - *Europe: The Struggle for Supremacy, from 1453 to the Present*
    HER - v130 - i544 - June 2015 - p772(3) [501+]
    Historian - v77 - i1 - Spring 2015 - p195(2) [501+]
The Longest Afternoon: The 400 Men Who Decided the Battle of Waterloo
    HT - v65 - i7 - July 2015 - p60(1) [501+]
    Parameters - v45 - i2 - Summer 2015 - p154(2) [501+]
    TLS - i5833 - Jan 16 2015 - p12(2) [501+]

Simms, Rootie - *My Childhood Christmas*
    SPBW - June 2015 - pNA [501+]

Simms, Susan Rose - *Money Skills: Opening a Bank Account*
    c CH Bwatch - May 2015 - pNA [51-500]

Simon, Carly - *Boys in the Trees: A Memoir*
    NYT - Nov 26 2015 - pC1(L) [501+]

Simon, Clea - *Code Grey*
    BL - v111 - i21 - July 1 2015 - p35(1) [51-500]
    PW - v262 - i26 - June 29 2015 - p48(1) [51-500]
Kittens Can Kill
    BL - v111 - i9-10 - Jan 1 2015 - p50(1) [51-500]
    Bwatch - June 2015 - pNA [51-500]
    KR - Jan 15 2015 - pNA [51-500]
    PW - v262 - i1 - Jan 5 2015 - p54(1) [51-500]
When Bunnies Go Bad
    KR - Dec 1 2015 - pNA [51-500]

Simon, Coco - *Alexis, the Icing on the Cupcake*
    c HB Guide - v26 - i1 - Spring 2015 - p92[51-500]
Alexis's Cupcake Cupid
    c HB Guide - v26 - i2 - Fall 2015 - p102(1) [51-500]
Emma's Not-So-Sweet Dilemma
    c HB Guide - v26 - i2 - Fall 2015 - p102(1) [51-500]
Mia's Recipe for Disaster
    c HB Guide - v26 - i2 - Fall 2015 - p102(1) [51-500]

Simon, Joe - *The Art of the Simon and Kirby Studio (Illus. by Simon, Joe)*
    BL - v111 - i13 - March 1 2015 - p32(1) [51-500]

Simon, Jonathan - *Mass Incarceration on Trial: A Remarkable Court Decision and the Future of Prisons in America*
    HLR - v128 - i4 - Feb 2015 - p1331(2) [1-50]
    Reason - v46 - i10 - March 2015 - p71(4) [501+]

Simon, Linda - *The Greatest Shows on Earth: A History of the Circus*
    HT - v65 - i4 - April 2015 - p61(2) [501+]

Simon, Marie Jalowicz - *Underground in Berlin: A Young Woman's Extraordinary Tale of Survival in the Heart of Nazi Germany*
    KR - July 1 2015 - pNA [501+]
    LJ - v140 - i13 - August 1 2015 - p110(1) [51-500]
    Mac - v128 - i24 - June 22 2015 - p56(2) [51-500]
    NY - v91 - i34 - Nov 2 2015 - p89 [501+]
    PW - v262 - i29 - July 20 2015 - p182(1) [51-500]

Simon, Miranda K. - *Sexy Serenity: A Memoir*
    SPBW - March 2015 - pNA [51-500]

Simon, Richard - *Oskar and the Eight Blessings (Illus. by Siegel, Mark)*
    c BL - v111 - i2 - Sept 15 2015 - p69(1) [51-500]
    c HB - v91 - i6 - Nov-Dec 2015 - p60(1) [51-500]
    c KR - Sept 1 2015 - pNA [51-500]
    c PW - v262 - i37 - Sept 14 2015 - p74(1) [51-500]
    c PW - v262 - i49 - Dec 2 2015 - p62(1) [51-500]
    c SLJ - v61 - i10 - Oct 2015 - p69(1) [51-500]

Simon, Robert A. - *The Book of Eliot*
    KR - March 15 2015 - pNA [501+]

Simon, Scott - *Unforgettable: A Son, a Mother, and the Lessons of a Lifetime (Read by Simon, Scott). Audiobook Review*
    BL - v111 - i22 - August 1 2015 - p78(1) [51-500]
    LJ - v140 - i12 - July 1 2015 - p45(1) [51-500]
    PW - v262 - i21 - May 25 2015 - p56(1) [51-500]
Unforgettable: A Son, a Mother, and the Lessons of a Lifetime
    KR - Feb 1 2015 - pNA [51-500]
    NYT - June 2 2015 - pD3(L) [501+]
    People - v83 - i15 - April 13 2015 - p41(NA) [501+]
    PW - v262 - i8 - Feb 23 2015 - p68(1) [51-500]
    BL - v111 - i13 - March 1 2015 - p5(1) [51-500]

Simon, Seymour - *Frogs*
    c BL - v111 - i12 - Feb 15 2015 - p76(1) [51-500]
    c HB - v91 - i4 - July-August 2015 - p162(2) [51-500]
    c KR - Feb 1 2015 - pNA [51-500]
Our Solar System: Updated Edition
    c HB Guide - v26 - i1 - Spring 2015 - p150(1) [51-500]
The Sun: All about Solar Flares, Eclipses, Sunspots, and More!
    c SLJ - v61 - i10 - Oct 2015 - p131(1) [51-500]

Simon, Thomas W. - *Ethnic Identity and Minority Protection: Designation, Discrimination and Brutalization*
    Dialogue - v54 - i2 - June 2015 - p398-400 [501+]

Simonds, Sandra - *Steal It Back*
    PW - v262 - i46 - Nov 16 2015 - p52(2) [51-500]

Simone, Gail - *Sensation Comics Featuring Wonder Woman, vol. 1*
    PW - v262 - i16 - April 20 2015 - p63(1) [51-500]

Simonin, Louis Laurent - *An Excursion to the Poor Districts of London*
    TLS - i5831 - Jan 2 2015 - p23(1) [501+]

Simons, Paullina - *Lone Star*
    PW - v262 - i42 - Oct 19 2015 - p63(1) [51-500]

Simons, Sandi - *A Life Worth Riding*
    BL - v112 - i3 - Oct 1 2015 - p5(2) [51-500]

Simonson, Helen - *The Summer before the War*
    KR - Jan 1 2016 - pNA [51-500]

Simonson, Mary - *Body Knowledge: Performance, Intermediality, and American Entertainment at the Turn of the Twentieth Century*
    Notes - v71 - i3 - March 2015 - p522(4) [501+]

Simpson, Adam - *Energy, Governance and Security in Thailand and Myanmar (Burma): A Critical Approach to Environmental Politics in the South*
    Pac A - v88 - i3 - Sept 2015 - p737 [501+]

Simpson, Alicia - *Niketas Choniates: A Historiographical Study*
    AHR - v120 - i4 - Oct 2015 - p1542-1543 [501+]

Simpson, Audra - *Mohawk Interruptus: Political Life across the Borders of Settler States*
    Am Ind CRJ - v39 - i2 - Spring 2015 - p148-150 [501+]
Theorizing Native Studies
    WHQ - v46 - i3 - Autumn 2015 - p372-372 [501+]

Simpson, Brian P. - *Money, Banking, and the Business Cycle, 2 vols.*
    IndRev - v20 - i2 - Fall 2015 - p294(4) [501+]

Simpson, Brooks D. - *The Civil War: Told by Those Who Lived It*
    NYRB - v62 - i5 - March 19 2015 - p30(4) [501+]

Simpson, Dana - *Unicorn on a Roll: Another Phoebe and Her Unicorn Adventure (Illus. by Simpson, Dana)*
    c BL - v111 - i19-20 - June 1 2015 - p68(1) [51-500]
    c CCB-B - v68 - i10 - June 2015 - p516(2) [51-500]
Unicorn vs. Goblins
    y KR - Dec 1 2015 - pNA [51-500]

Simpson, Eileen - *Poets In Their Youth*
    Lon R Bks - v37 - i13 - July 2 2015 - p9(4) [501+]

Simpson, Helen - *Cockfosters*
    Spec - v329 - i9769 - Nov 21 2015 - p52(2) [501+]

Simpson, James - *Reynard the Fox: A New Translation*
    KR - Jan 1 2015 - pNA [501+]
    LJ - v140 - i2 - Feb 1 2015 - p84(2) [51-500]
    Lon R Bks - v37 - i21 - Nov 5 2015 - p48(2) [501+]
    TLS - i5855 - June 19 2015 - p22(2) [501+]

Simpson, Jamie - *Jamie and the Monster Bookroom (Illus. by Folnovic, Erika)*
    c Res Links - v20 - i3 - Feb 2015 - p9(2) [51-500]

Simpson, Jon Chan - *Chinkstar*
    Nat Post - v17 - i230 - August 8 2015 - pWP4(1) [501+]

Simpson, M. - *The Tattooed Arm*
    KR - Nov 1 2015 - pNA [501+]

Simpson, Mona - *Casebook*
    Wom R Bks - v32 - i4 - July-August 2015 - p15(2) [501+]

Simpson, Patricia Anne - *Religion, Reason, and Culture in the Age of Goethe*
    GSR - v38 - i1 - Feb 2015 - p166-168 [501+]

Simpson, Peter L.P. - *Political Illiberalism: A Defense of Freedom*
    RM - v68 - i4 - June 2015 - p870(2) [501+]

Simpson, Phillip W. - *Minotaur*
    y SLJ - v61 - i6 - June 2015 - p116(1) [51-500]

Sims, David - *Egypt's Desert Dreams: Development or Disasters?*
    Nation - v301 - i9-10 - August 31 2015 - p41(4) [501+]

Sims, Jessica - *Between a Vamp and a Hard Place*
    BL - v112 - i7 - Dec 1 2015 - p36(1) [51-500]
    PW - v262 - i46 - Nov 16 2015 - p63(1) [51-500]

Sims, Maynard - *Mother of Demons*
    BL - v111 - i22 - August 1 2015 - p44(1) [51-500]

Sims, Nat - *Peekaboo Barn (Illus. by Tabor, Nathan)*
    c KR - Jan 1 2015 - pNA [51-500]

Simsion, Graeme - *The Rosie Effect (Read by O'Grady, Dan). Audiobook Review*
    LJ - v140 - i3 - Feb 15 2015 - p58(2) [51-500]
The Rosie Effect
    PW - v262 - i8 - Feb 23 2015 - p70(1) [51-500]

Simukka, Salla - *As Black as Ebony (Read by McFadden, Amy). Audiobook Review*
    y SLJ - v61 - i11 - Nov 2015 - p74(1) [51-500]
As Black as Ebony
    y CCB-B - v69 - i2 - Oct 2015 - p113(1) [51-500]
    y VOYA - v38 - i3 - August 2015 - p83(2) [51-500]
    WLT - v89 - i6 - Nov-Dec 2015 - p79(1) [51-500]
As Red as Blood
    c BL - v111 - i17 - May 1 2015 - p40(1) [51-500]
    y Magpies - v30 - i1 - March 2015 - p44(1) [501+]
As White as Snow
    SLJ - v61 - i4 - April 2015 - p175(2) [51-500]
    c BL - v111 - i17 - May 1 2015 - p49(1) [51-500]
    y CCB-B - v68 - i10 - June 2015 - p517(1) [51-500]
    y Magpies - v30 - i1 - March 2015 - p44(1) [501+]

Sin-Lin - *Shattered Families, Broken Dreams: Little-Known Episodes from the History of the Persecution of Chinese Revolutionaries in Stalin's Gulag*
    NYRB - v62 - i10 - June 4 2015 - p74(3) [501+]

Sinclair, Anne - *My Grandfather's Gallery: A Family Memoir of Art and War*
    NYTBR - Nov 22 2015 - p36(L) [501+]
My Grandfather's Gallery: A Legendary Art Dealer's Escape from Vichy France
    TLS - i5838 - Feb 20 2015 - p23(1) [501+]

Sinclair, Iain - *70x70: Unlicensed Preaching: A Life Unpacked in 70 Films*
    TLS - i5851 - May 22 2015 - p26(2) [501+]
American Smoke: Journeys to the End of the Light
    WLT - v89 - i6 - Nov-Dec 2015 - p78(2) [501+]
London Overground: A Day's Walk around the Ginger Line
    Spec - v328 - i9747 - June 20 2015 - p39(1)

[501+]
    TLS - i5861 - July 31 2015 - p30(1) [501+]
Sinclair, Richard - *What Will I Be? (Illus. by Lycett-Smith, Jon)*
  c Sch Lib - v63 - i1 - Spring 2015 - p33(1) [51-500]
Sindbaek, Tea - *Usable History: Representations of Yugoslavia's Difficult Past from 1945 to 2002*
    Slav R - v74 - i1 - Spring 2015 - p176-178 [501+]
Sine, William F. - *Guardian Angel: Life and Death Adventures with Pararescue, the World's Most Powerful Commando Rescue Force*
    APH - v62 - i2 - Summer 2015 - p60(1) [501+]
Sinel, Natasha - *The Fix*
  y KR - July 15 2015 - pNA [501+]
  y SLJ - v61 - i9 - Sept 2015 - p172(2) [51-500]
  y VOYA - v38 - i4 - Oct 2015 - p62(1) [51-500]
Sinett, Todd - *3 Weeks to a Better Back: Solutions for Healing the Structural, Nutritional, and Emotional Causes of Back Pain*
    PW - v262 - i29 - July 20 2015 - p184(1) [51-500]
Singer, Barnett - *The Americanization of France: Searching for Happiness after the Algerian War*
    HT - v65 - i3 - March 2015 - p64(1) [501+]
    JMH - v87 - i3 - Sept 2015 - p742(3) [501+]
Singer, Brian C.J. - *Montesquieu and the Discovery of the Social*
    CS - v44 - i3 - May 2015 - p438-1 [501+]
Singer, Isaac Bashevis - *The Parakeet Named Dreidel (Illus. by Berkson, Suzanne Raphael)*
  c BL - v112 - i4 - Oct 15 2015 - p49(1) [51-500]
  c HB - v91 - i6 - Nov-Dec 2015 - p60(1) [51-500]
  c KR - Sept 1 2015 - pNA [51-500]
  c PW - v262 - i37 - Sept 14 2015 - p76(2) [51-500]
  c SLJ - v61 - i10 - Oct 2015 - p69(1) [51-500]
Singer, Joseph William - *No Freedom without Regulation: The Hidden Lesson of the Subprime Crisis*
    PW - v262 - i30 - July 27 2015 - p58(1) [51-500]
Singer, Marilyn - *Echo Echo: Reverso Poems about Greek Myths (Illus. by Masse, Josee)*
  c BL - v112 - i7 - Dec 1 2015 - p40(1) [51-500]
  c KR - Nov 15 2015 - pNA [51-500]
  c PW - v262 - i52 - Dec 21 2015 - p156(2) [501+]
Follow Follow: A Book of Reverso Poems (Read by Morton, Joe). Audiobook Review
    BL - v111 - i13 - March 1 2015 - p70(1) [51-500]
I'm Gonna Climb a Mountain in My Patent Leather Shoes (Illus. by Avril, Lynne)
  c HB Guide - v26 - i1 - Spring 2015 - p46(1) [51-500]
Tallulah's Tap Shoes (Illus. by Boiger, Alexandra)
  c HB Guide - v26 - i2 - Fall 2015 - p52(1) [51-500]
  c KR - Feb 1 2015 - pNA [51-500]
Singer, Merrill - *The Social Value of Drug Addicts: Uses of the Useless*
    MAQ - v29 - i1 - March 2015 - p14-16 [501+]
Singer, P.W. - *Ghost Fleet (Read by Orlow, Rich). Audiobook Review*
    PW - v262 - i35 - August 31 2015 - p83(1) [51-500]
Ghost Fleet
    Econ - v415 - i8944 - June 27 2015 - p71(US) [501+]
    KR - May 1 2015 - pNA [51-500]
    PW - v262 - i14 - April 6 2015 - p40(1) [51-500]
    TimHES - i2228 - Nov 5 2015 - p46(1) [501+]
Singer, Peter - *Famine, Affluence, and Morality*
    LJ - v140 - i16 - Oct 1 2015 - p84(2) [51-500]
    Nation - v301 - i21-22 - Nov 23 2015 - p27(4) [501+]
The Most Good You Can Do: How Effective Altruism Is Changing Ideas about Living Ethically
    NYRB - v62 - i9 - May 21 2015 - p38(3) [501+]
    TLS - i5877 - Nov 20 2015 - p3(2) [501+]
Singer, Roland - *Karpathenschlachten: Der erste und zweite Weltkrieg am oberen Karpathenbogen*
    J Mil H - v79 - i3 - July 2015 - p864-865 [501+]
Singer, Simon I. - *America's Safest City: Delinquency and Modernity in Suburbia*
    AJS - v121 - i2 - Sept 2015 - p604(3) [501+]
    Soc - v52 - i1 - Feb 2015 - p86(1) [501+]
    Soc - v52 - i4 - August 2015 - p390(4) [501+]
Singer, Tania - *Caring Economics: Conversations on Altruism and Compassion, between Scientists, Economists, and the Dalai Lama*
    KR - Feb 1 2015 - pNA [501+]
    PW - v262 - i5 - Feb 2 2015 - p45(1) [51-500]
Singer, W.W. - *When I Set Myself on Fire*
    KR - May 1 2015 - pNA [501+]
Singh, Ajit - *The Song of a Crooked River*
    KR - June 15 2015 - pNA [51-500]

Singh, Gajendra - *The Testimonies of Indian Soldiers and the Two World Wars: Between Self and Sepoy*
    AHR - v120 - i4 - Oct 2015 - p1461(1) [501+]
Singh, Nalini - *Archangel's Enigma*
    PW - v262 - i31 - August 3 2015 - p41(1) [51-500]
Shards of Hope
    KR - May 1 2015 - pNA [501+]
    PW - v262 - i15 - April 13 2015 - p64(1) [51-500]
Singh, Supriya - *Globalization and Money: A Global South Perspective*
    CS - v44 - i6 - Nov 2015 - p848-850 [501+]
Singles, Kathleen - *Alternate History: Playing with Contingency and Necessity*
    Poetics T - v36 - i1-2 - June 2015 - p143-146 [501+]
Singletary, Nancy - *It's a Sin to Be Boring*
    SPBW - Nov 2015 - pNA [51-500]
Singleton, George - *Calloustown*
    NYT - Nov 26 2015 - pC6(L) [501+]
Singleton, Glenn E. - *Courageous Conversations about Race: A Field Guide for Achieving Equity in Schools*
    Bwatch - March 2015 - pNA [501+]
Singleton, Linda Joy - *The Curious Cat Spy Club*
  c CCB-B - v68 - i10 - June 2015 - p517(1) [51-500]
  c HB Guide - v26 - i2 - Fall 2015 - p102(1) [51-500]
  c KR - Jan 15 2015 - pNA [51-500]
  c SLJ - v61 - i3 - March 2015 - p144(1) [51-500]
  y VOYA - v38 - i1 - April 2015 - p70(1) [51-500]
The Mystery of the Zorse's Mask
  c KR - July 15 2015 - pNA [51-500]
Singley, William P. - *Downbeach*
    KR - April 15 2015 - pNA [501+]
Singular, Stephen - *The Spiral Notebook: The Aurora Theater Shooter and the Epidemic of Mass Violence Committed by American Youth*
  y BL - v111 - i18 - May 15 2015 - p5(1) [501+]
    KR - May 1 2015 - pNA [501+]
    LJ - v140 - i9 - May 15 2015 - p93(1) [51-500]
    PW - v262 - i19 - May 11 2015 - p51(1) [51-500]
Sinha, Manisha - *The Slave's Cause*
    KR - Dec 15 2015 - pNA [501+]
Sinisalo, Johanna - *The Core of the Sun*
  y BL - v112 - i4 - Oct 15 2015 - p28(1) [51-500]
    KR - Oct 15 2015 - pNA [501+]
    PW - v262 - i41 - Oct 12 2015 - p44(2) [51-500]
Sinister, Bucky - *Black Hole*
    PW - v262 - i26 - June 29 2015 - p42(1) [51-500]
Sinitiere, Phillip Luke - *Protest and Propaganda: W. E. B. Du Bois, the Crisis, and American History*
    JSH - v81 - i4 - Nov 2015 - p1022(3) [501+]
Salvation with a Smile: Joel Osteen, Lakewood Church, and American Christianity
    LJ - v140 - i16 - Oct 1 2015 - p86(2) [51-500]
    PW - v262 - i37 - Sept 14 2015 - p60(2) [51-500]
Siniver, Asaf - *Abba Eban*
    KR - Sept 1 2015 - pNA [501+]
Sinnema, Donald - *Acta et Documenta Synodi Nationalis Dordrechtanae 1618-1619, vol. 1: Acta of the Synod and Dordt*
    Six Ct J - v46 - i3 - Fall 2015 - p822-823 [501+]
Sinnreich, Aram - *The Piracy Crusade: How the Music Industry's War on Sharing Destroys Markets and Erodes Civil Liberties*
    LQ - v85 - i3 - July 2015 - p339(4) [501+]
Sinor, Paul - *Wrath of the Dixie Mafia*
    SPBW - Jan 2015 - pNA [501+]
Sion, Brigitte - *Death Tourism: Disaster Sites as Recreational Landscape*
    TLS - i5872 - Oct 16 2015 - p7(1) [501+]
Sipperley, Keli - *The Old Fort at St. Augustine*
  c SLJ - v61 - i4 - April 2015 - p108(4) [501+]
Sippial, Tiffany A. - *Prostitution, Modernity, and the Making of the Cuban Republic, 1840-1920*
    Ams - v72 - i3 - July 2015 - p505(506) [501+]
Siqveland, Bob - *Simple Witness*
    SPBW - August 2015 - pNA [51-500]
Sirafi, Abu Zayd Hasan ibn Yazid - *Two Arabic Travel Books: Accounts of China and India and Mission to the Volga*
    TLS - i5877 - Nov 20 2015 - p29(1) [501+]
Sirett, Dawn - *Happy Birthday Sophie! (Illus. by Appleton, Polly)*
  c BL - v111 - i16 - April 15 2015 - p52(1) [51-500]
I'm Ready for School (Illus. by Silva, Reg)
  c KR - July 1 2015 - pNA [51-500]
Sirlin, Avi - *The Evolutionist: The Strange Tale of Alfred Russel Wallace*
    RVBW - Feb 2015 - pNA [51-500]
Sirmans, Franklin - *Basquiat and the Bayou*
    NYTBR - June 28 2015 - p27(L) [501+]

Sirois, Anne-Marie - *Riette l'assiette*
  c Res Links - v20 - i3 - Feb 2015 - p51(1) [501+]
Siroka, Eva Jana - *My Life with Berti Spranger*
    RVBW - July 2015 - pNA [51-500]
Sirott, Jonah C. - *This Is the Night*
    BL - v112 - i3 - Oct 1 2015 - p23(1) [51-500]
    KR - Sept 1 2015 - pNA [51-500]
Sirowy, Alexandra - *The Creeping*
  y CCB-B - v69 - i2 - Oct 2015 - p114(1) [51-500]
  y KR - June 15 2015 - pNA [51-500]
  y PW - v262 - i20 - May 18 2015 - p86(2) [51-500]
  y SLJ - v61 - i7 - July 2015 - p98(2) [51-500]
Sirr, Peter - *Black Wreath: The Stolen Life of James Lovett*
  y Sch Lib - v63 - i1 - Spring 2015 - p58(1) [51-500]
  y VOYA - v38 - i1 - April 2015 - p70(1) [51-500]
Sis, Peter - *Ice Cream Summer (Illus. by Sis, Peter)*
  c BL - v111 - i15 - April 1 2015 - p83(1) [51-500]
  c CCB-B - v69 - i1 - Sept 2015 - p55(1) [51-500]
  c HB - v91 - i3 - May-June 2015 - p99(2) [501+]
  c HB Guide - v26 - i2 - Fall 2015 - p52(1) [51-500]
  c KR - March 1 2015 - pNA [51-500]
  c NYTBR - June 21 2015 - p17(L) [501+]
  c NYTBR - June 21 2015 - p17(L) [501+]
  c SLJ - v61 - i5 - May 2015 - p92(2) [51-500]
The Pilot and the Little Prince: The Life of Antoine de Saint-Exupery (Illus. by Sis, Peter)
  c BL - v111 - i9-10 - Jan 1 2015 - pS4(8) [501+]
  c BL - v111 - i9-10 - Jan 1 2015 - p92(1) [501+]
Sise, Katie - *The Pretty App*
  c HB Guide - v26 - i2 - Fall 2015 - p139(1) [51-500]
  y VOYA - v37 - i6 - Feb 2015 - p66(1) [51-500]
Sisk, Christina L. - *Mexico, Nation in Transit: Contemporary Representations of Mexican Migration to the United States*
    Ams - v72 - i2 - April 2015 - p346(2) [501+]
Siskind, Jeremy - *Jazz Band Pianist: Basic Skills for the Jazz Band Pianist*
    Am MT - v64 - i4 - Feb-March 2015 - p63(1) [51-500]
Sisman, Adam - *John le Carre: The Biography*
    Atl - v316 - i5 - Dec 2015 - p28(3) [501+]
    HM - v331 - i1987 - Dec 2015 - p89(5) [501+]
    NS - v144 - i5285 - Oct 23 2015 - p46(3) [501+]
    NYT - Dec 15 2015 - pC1(L) [501+]
    NYTBR - Nov 1 2015 - p18(L) [501+]
    Spec - v329 - i9766 - Oct 31 2015 - p34(2) [501+]
Sisson, Stephanie Roth - *Star Stuff: Carl Sagan and the Mysteries of the Cosmos (Illus. by Sisson, Stephanie Roth)*
  c HB - v91 - i1 - Jan-Feb 2015 - p103(2) [51-500]
  c HB Guide - v26 - i1 - Spring 2015 - p196(1) [51-500]
Sissons, Crystal - *Queen of the Hurricanes: The fearless Elsie MacGill*
    Beav - v95 - i5 - Oct-Nov 2015 - p61(2) [501+]
Sister Souljah - *A Moment of Silence*
    LJ - v140 - i16 - Oct 1 2015 - p5(1) [51-500]
Sitney, P. Adams - *The Cinema of Poetry*
    Si & So - v25 - i6 - June 2015 - p105(1) [501+]
Sitomer, Alan Lawrence - *Daddy's Back-to-School Shopping Adventure (Illus. by Carter, Abby)*
  c HB Guide - v26 - i2 - Fall 2015 - p52(1) [51-500]
  c KR - June 1 2015 - pNA [51-500]
  c SLJ - v61 - i8 - August 2015 - p61(1) [51-500]
Noble Warrior
  y BL - v111 - i19-20 - June 1 2015 - p98(2) [51-500]
  y KR - April 15 2015 - pNA [51-500]
  y SLJ - v61 - i6 - June 2015 - p128(3) [51-500]
  y VOYA - v38 - i3 - August 2015 - p69(1) [51-500]
Sitwell, William - *A History of Food in 100 Recipes*
    LJ - v140 - i9 - May 15 2015 - p94(2) [51-500]
Six, Abigail Lee - *Gothic Terrors: Incarceration, Duplication and Bloodlust in Spanish Narrative*
    MLR - v110 - i2 - April 2015 - p574-575 [501+]
Six Sisters' Stuff - *Sweets and Treats with Six Sisters' Stuff: 100+ Desserts, Gift Ideas, and Traditions for the Whole Family*
    LJ - v140 - i15 - Sept 15 2015 - p97(1) [51-500]
Six years of re:work. A conference in Berlin
    HNet - Sept 2015 - pNA [501+]
Sixth & Spring Books - *60 Quick Knit Baby Essentials: Sweaters, Toys, Blankets, & More in Cherub from Cascade Yarns*
    LJ - v140 - i9 - May 15 2015 - p83(1) [51-500]
Siy, Alexandra - *Spidermania: Friends on the Web (Illus. by Kunkel, Dennis)*
  c BL - v112 - i5 - Nov 1 2015 - p42(2) [51-500]
  c KR - August 15 2015 - pNA [51-500]
  c SLJ - v61 - i12 - Dec 2015 - p139(1) [51-500]

Sjoberg, Fredrik - *The Fly Trap*
  NYTBR - August 2 2015 - p7(L) [501+]
  KR - April 1 2015 - pNA [501+]
  LJ - v140 - i13 - August 1 2015 - p122(1) [51-500]

Sjoberg, Laura - *Gender, War, and Conflict*
  CS - v44 - i4 - July 2015 - p579-580 [501+]

Sjoholm, Barbara - *Fossil Island*
  KR - August 1 2015 - pNA [501+]

Sjonger, Rebecca - *Biomedical Engineering and Human Body Systems*
  c BL - v112 - i4 - Oct 15 2015 - p42(1) [51-500]
Geotechnical Engineering and Earth's Materials and Processes
  c BL - v112 - i4 - Oct 15 2015 - p42(1) [51-500]

Skalka, Patricia - *Death at Gills Rock*
  BL - v111 - i17 - May 1 2015 - p28(1) [51-500]
  KR - April 15 2015 - pNA [51-500]
  PW - v262 - i17 - April 27 2015 - p54(1) [51-500]

Skambraks, Tanja - *Das Kinderbischofsfest im Mittelalter*
  HNet - Feb 2015 - pNA [501+]

Skanavis, Alex Andor - *Galaxia*
  KR - Dec 1 2015 - pNA [501+]

Skarbek, David - *The Social Order of the Underworld: How Prison Gangs Govern the American Penal System*
  IndRev - v19 - i4 - Spring 2015 - p622(4) [501+]

Skarpe, Christina - *Elephants and Savanna Woodland Ecosystems: A Study from Chobe National Park, Botswana*
  QRB - v90 - i4 - Dec 2015 - p434(2) [501+]

Skeen, Tim - *Risk*
  WLT - v89 - i3-4 - May-August 2015 - p123(2) [501+]

Skelton, Ross - *Eden Halt: An Antrim Memoir*
  ILS - v34 - i2 - Spring 2015 - p19(1) [501+]

Skenazi, Cynthia - *Aging Gracefully in the Renaissance: Stories of Later Life from Petrarch to Montaigne*
  Six Ct J - v46 - i2 - Summer 2015 - p439-440 [501+]

Skerry, Brian - *The Whale Who Won Hearts!: And More True Stories of Adventures with Animals*
  c HB Guide - v26 - i1 - Spring 2015 - p153(1) [51-500]

Skibell, Joseph - *My Father's Guitar and Other Imaginary Things*
  BL - v112 - i6 - Nov 15 2015 - p8(2) [51-500]
  KR - Sept 15 2015 - pNA [501+]

Skibsrud, Johanna - *Quartet for the End of Time*
  BL - v111 - i16 - April 15 2015 - p34(1) [51-500]
  NYTBR - Dec 13 2015 - p44(L) [501+]
  TLS - i5852 - May 29 2015 - p21(1) [501+]
Sometimes We Think You Are A Monkey (Illus. by Morstad, Julie)
  c Nat Post - v17 - i107 - March 7 2015 - pWP5(1) [501+]
  c Res Links - v20 - i5 - June 2015 - p8(1) [51-500]

Skidelsky, Robert - *Britain since 1900: A Success Story?*
  NS - v144 - i5251 - Feb 27 2015 - p48(1) [51-500]
  TLS - i5859 - July 17 2015 - p22(1) [501+]

Skidelsky, William - *Federer and Me: A Story of Obsession*
  Spec - v328 - i9746 - June 13 2015 - p37(2) [501+]
  TLS - i5854 - June 12 2015 - p12(1) [501+]
  NS - v144 - i5268 - June 26 2015 - p49(1) [501+]
  TLS - i5856 - June 26 2015 - p30(1) [51-500]

Skidmore, Lauren - *What Is Lost*
  y BL - v111 - i18 - May 15 2015 - p54(1) [51-500]

Skillen, James - *The Good of Politics: A Biblical, Historical, and Contemporary Introduction*
  J Ch St - v57 - i2 - Spring 2015 - p368-369 [501+]

Skilton, Sarah - *High & Dry*
  y HB Guide - v26 - i1 - Spring 2015 - p123(1) [51-500]

Skinner, Christopher W. - *Unity and Diversity in the Gospels and Paul: Essays in Honor of Frank J. Matera*
  Intpr - v69 - i4 - Oct 2015 - p508(1) [501+]

Skinner, David - *The Antichrist of Kokomo County*
  KR - August 1 2015 - pNA [501+]
Sailing Close to the Wind: Reminiscences
  TLS - i5839 - Feb 27 2015 - p26(1) [501+]

Skinner, Patricia - *Jews in Medieval Britain: Historical, Literary and Archaeological Perspectives*
  Specu - v90 - i4 - Oct 2015 - p1166-1167 [501+]

Skinner, Quentin - *Forensic Shakespeare*
  RES - v66 - i276 - Sept 2015 - p777-778 [501+]
  TimHES - i2186 - Jan 15 2015 - p52(1) [501+]

Skinner, Sam - *The Legend and Adventures of Bob Wire (Illus. by Skinner, Sam)*
  c CH Bwatch - April 2015 - pNA [51-500]
The Legend of Bob Wire (Illus. by Skinner, Sam)
  RVBW - May 2015 - pNA [51-500]
  SPBW - May 2015 - pNA [501+]

Skipp, John - *Book of the Dead*
  c HB Guide - v26 - i2 - Fall 2015 - p96(1) [51-500]

Sklar, Lawrence - *Philosophy and the Foundations of Dynamics*
  Phil R - v124 - i2 - April 2015 - p269(4) [501+]

Skogen, Jennifer - *The Burning*
  y SLJ - v61 - i8 - August 2015 - p110(1) [51-500]

Skole, Jacki - *Dogland: A Journey to the Heart of America's Dog Problem*
  PW - v262 - i26 - June 29 2015 - p58(1) [51-500]

Skolnick, Adam - *One Breath: Freediving, Death, and the Quest to Shatter Human Limits*
  KR - Dec 1 2015 - pNA [501+]
  LJ - v140 - i20 - Dec 1 2015 - p109(1) [51-500]

Skolnik, Jonathan - *Jewish Pasts, German Fictions: History, Memory, and Minority Culture in Germany, 1824-1955*
  CEH - v48 - i2 - June 2015 - p268-269 [501+]
  GSR - v38 - i3 - Oct 2015 - p664-666 [501+]

Skornicki, Arnault - *L'economiste, la cour, et la patrie: L'economie politique dans la France des Lumieres*
  JMH - v87 - i2 - June 2015 - p450(3) [501+]

Skovron, Jon - *This Broken Wondrous World (Read by Skovron, Jon). Audiobook Review*
  y SLJ - v61 - i12 - Dec 2015 - p80(1) [51-500]
This Broken Wondrous World
  y KR - May 1 2015 - pNA [501+]
  y Magpies - v30 - i5 - Nov 2015 - p43(1) [51-500]
  y SLJ - v61 - i6 - June 2015 - p129(1) [51-500]
  y VOYA - v38 - i2 - June 2015 - p83(1) [51-500]

Skowronek, Julia - *Biergarten Cookbook: Traditional Bavarian Recipes*
  LJ - v140 - i9 - May 15 2015 - p102(2) [51-500]

Skowronek, Russell K. - *Ceramic Production in Early Hispanic California: Craft, Economy, and Trade on the Frontier of New Spain*
  JIH - v46 - i2 - Autumn 2015 - p294-295 [501+]

Skrabec, Quentin R., Jr. - *The 100 Most Important American Financial Crises: An Encyclopedia of the Lowest Points in American Economic History*
  R&USQ - v54 - i4 - Summer 2015 - p77(2) [501+]

Skrentny, John D. - *After Civil Rights: Racial Realism in the New American Workplace*
  AJS - v120 - i4 - Jan 2015 - p1236(3) [501+]
  CS - v44 - i5 - Sept 2015 - p711-712 [501+]
  J Am St - v49 - i1 - Feb 2015 - p213-215 [501+]
  Soc Ser R - v89 - i3 - Sept 2015 - p575(5) [501+]
  Soc Ser R - v89 - i3 - Sept 2015 - p575(5) [501+]

Skrutskie, Emily - *The Abyss Surrounds Us*
  y KR - Nov 15 2015 - pNA [501+]

Skrypuch, Marsha Forchuck - *Making Bombs for Hitler*
  c Magpies - v30 - i5 - Nov 2015 - p37(2) [501+]

Skrypuch, Marsha Forchuk - *Dance of the Banished*
  y KR - Jan 15 2015 - pNA [501+]
  y Res Links - v20 - i3 - Feb 2015 - p35(2) [51-500]
  SLJ - v61 - i2 - Feb 2015 - p108(1) [51-500]

Skuncke, Marie-Christine - *Carl Peter Thunberg: Botanist and Physician*
  TLS - i5849 - May 8 2015 - p10(2) [501+]

Skuse, C.J. - *Monster*
  y Sch Lib - v63 - i4 - Winter 2015 - p250(1) [51-500]

Sky, Emma - *The Unraveling: High Hopes and Missed Opportunities in Iraq*
  BL - v111 - i15 - April 1 2015 - p22(1) [51-500]
  KR - Feb 15 2015 - pNA [51-500]
  LJ - v140 - i6 - April 1 2015 - p106(1) [51-500]
  NS - v144 - i5269 - July 3 2015 - p48(2) [51-500]
  NYTBR - July 12 2015 - p1(L) [501+]

Skye, Ione - *My Yiddish Vacation (Illus. by Menchin, Scott)*
  c HB Guide - v26 - i1 - Spring 2015 - p46(1) [51-500]

Skye, Obert - *Katfish (Illus. by Skye, Obert)*
  c HB Guide - v26 - i1 - Spring 2015 - p92(1) [51-500]
Lost & Found
  c KR - Dec 15 2015 - pNA [51-500]
Witherwood Reform School (Illus. by Thompson, Keith)
  c PW - v262 - i4 - Jan 26 2015 - p170(1) [51-500]
  c BL - v111 - i11 - Feb 1 2015 - p53(2) [51-500]
  c CCB-B - v68 - i10 - June 2015 - p518(1) [51-500]
  c VOYA - v38 - i1 - April 2015 - p84(1) [51-500]
  c HB Guide - v26 - i2 - Fall 2015 - p102(1) [51-500]

Slabosz, Trudy - *Going Veggie: The 30-Day Guide to Becoming a Healthy Vegetarian*
  Bwatch - March 2015 - pNA [51-500]

Slack, Charles - *Liberty's First Crisis: Adams, Jefferson, and the Misfits Who Saved Free Speech*
  LJ - v140 - i2 - Feb 1 2015 - p95(2) [51-500]

Slack, James D. - *Abortion, Execution, and the Consequences of Taking Life*
  Bwatch - Feb 2015 - pNA [51-500]

Slack, Michael - *Wazdot? (Illus. by Slack, Michael)*
  c HB Guide - v26 - i1 - Spring 2015 - p16(1) [51-500]

Slack, Paul - *The Invention of Improvement: Information and Material Progress in Seventeenth-Century England*
  TLS - i5859 - July 17 2015 - p12(1) [501+]

Slade, Suzanne - *Friends for Freedom: The Story of Susan B. Anthony & Frederick Douglass (Read by Mitchell, Lizan). Audiobook Review*
  c SLJ - v61 - i4 - April 2015 - p61(2) [51-500]
Friends for Freedom: The Story of Susan B. Anthony & Frederick Douglass (Illus. by Tadgell, Nicole)
  c HB Guide - v26 - i1 - Spring 2015 - p139(1) [51-500]
The Inventor's Secret: What Thomas Edison Told Henry Ford (Illus. by Reinhardt, Jennifer Black)
  c BL - v112 - i1 - Sept 1 2015 - p94(2) [51-500]
  c KR - July 1 2015 - pNA [51-500]
  c PW - v262 - i29 - July 20 2015 - p190(2) [501+]
  c SLJ - v61 - i9 - Sept 2015 - p181(2) [51-500]
With Books and Bricks: How Booker T. Washington Built a School (Illus. by Tadgell, Nicole)
  c HB Guide - v26 - i1 - Spring 2015 - p196(1) [51-500]

Slahi, Mohamedou Ould - *Guantanamo Diary*
  KR - Feb 1 2015 - pNA [501+]
  Lon R Bks - v37 - i3 - Feb 5 2015 - p40(2) [501+]
  NS - v144 - i5247 - Jan 30 2015 - p45(1) [51-500]
  NYT - Jan 26 2015 - pC1(L) [501+]
  NYTBR - Feb 1 2015 - p1(L) [501+]
  NYTBR - Dec 20 2015 - p24(L) [501+]
  VQR - v91 - i2 - Spring 2015 - p211-217 [501+]

Slanina, Frantisek - *Essentials of Econophysics Modelling*
  Phys Today - v68 - i1 - Jan 2015 - p44-45 [501+]

Slap, Stan - *Under the Hood: Fire Up and Fine-Tune Your Employee Culture*
  BL - v111 - i13 - March 1 2015 - p9(1) [51-500]
  Econ - v415 - i8934 - April 18 2015 - p77(US) [501+]

Slate, Nico - *The Prism of Race: W.E.B. Du Bois, Langston Hughes, Paul Robeson, and the Colored World of Cedric Dover*
  HNet - August 2015 - pNA [501+]

Slater, David Michael - *The Boy & the Book: A Wordless Story (Illus. by Kolar, Bob)*
  c CH Bwatch - March 2015 - pNA [51-500]
  c HB Guide - v26 - i2 - Fall 2015 - p52(1) [51-500]
  c KR - Jan 1 2015 - pNA [51-500]

Slater, Don - *New Media, Development and Globalization: Making Connections in the Global South*
  CS - v44 - i5 - Sept 2015 - p712-714 [501+]

Slater, N.W. - *Euripides: Alcestis*
  Class R - v65 - i1 - April 2015 - p34-36 [501+]

Slater, Nigel - *Eat*
  Ent W - i1346 - Jan 16 2015 - p67(1) [51-500]
The Kitchen Diaries III: A Year of Good Eating
  Spec - v329 - i9768 - Nov 14 2015 - p58(1) [501+]

Slater, Susan - *Hair of the Dog*
  BL - v111 - i19-20 - June 1 2015 - p54(1) [51-500]
  KR - May 1 2015 - pNA [51-500]
  PW - v262 - i18 - May 4 2015 - p98(1) [51-500]

Slater, Tracy - *The Good Shufu*
  KR - May 1 2015 - pNA [51-500]

Slatter, Angela - *Of Sorrow and Such*
  PW - v262 - i35 - August 31 2015 - p66(1) [51-500]

Slattery, Kathryn Lang - *Immigrant Soldier*
  KR - Jan 1 2015 - pNA [501+]

Slaughter, Anne-Marie - *Unfinished Business: Women Men Work Family*
  KR - August 15 2015 - pNA [501+]
  LJ - v140 - i14 - Sept 1 2015 - p115(1) [51-500]
  NYTBR - Sept 27 2015 - p1(L) [501+]
  PW - v262 - i34 - August 24 2015 - p76(1) [51-500]

Slaughter, Karin - *Cop Town (Read by Early, Kathleen). Audiobook Review*
  BL - v111 - i9-10 - Jan 1 2015 - p111(2) [51-500]
Pretty Girls
  BL - v111 - i22 - August 1 2015 - p36(1) [51-500]
  KR - July 15 2015 - pNA [51-500]
  LJ - v140 - i13 - August 1 2015 - p89(1) [51-500]
  NYTBR - Oct 4 2015 - p29(L) [501+]
  PW - v262 - i27 - July 6 2015 - p45(1) [51-500]

Slaughter, Mike - *The Christian Wallet: Spending, Giving, and Living with a Conscience*
    PW - v262 - i45 - Nov 9 2015 - p55(1) [51-500]

Slaughter, Thomas P. - *Independence: The Tangled Roots of the American Revolution*
    JAH - v102 - i2 - Sept 2015 - p540-541 [501+]
    JSH - v81 - i4 - Nov 2015 - p946(2) [501+]

Slavernijverleden, Gids - *Amsterdam Slavery Heritage Guide*
    Pub Hist - v37 - i1 - Feb 2015 - p127(2) [501+]

Slavik, Cory - *Building Outdoor Kitchens for Every Budget*
    LJ - v140 - i8 - May 1 2015 - p72(2) [51-500]

Slavin, Bill - *Big Star Otto (Illus. by Slavin, Bill)*
    c HB Guide - v26 - i2 - Fall 2015 - p102(1) [51-500]
    c BooChiTr - June 27 2015 - p14(1) [501+]
    c Res Links - v20 - i5 - June 2015 - p11(1) [51-500]

Slavin, Robert E. - *Proven Programs in Education: Science, Technology, and Mathematics*
    Math T - v109 - i3 - Oct 2015 - p238-238 [501+]

Slavitt, R.D. - *The Other Four Plays of Sophocles: Ajax, Women of Trachis, Electra, Philoctetes*
    Class R - v65 - i2 - Oct 2015 - p352-354 [501+]

Slayton, Rebecca - *Arguments That Count: Physics, Computing, and Missile Defense, 1949-2012*
    APJ - v29 - i3 - May-June 2015 - p95(2) [501+]

Slayton, Shonna - *Cinderella's Shoes*
    y SLJ - v61 - i12 - Dec 2015 - p128(2) [51-500]

Sleath, Eleanor - *The Orphan of the Rhine*
    TLS - i5871 - Oct 9 2015 - p26(1) [501+]

Slee, Natasha - *Design Line: History of Women's Fashion (Illus. by Mander, Sanna)*
    c CH Bwatch - August 2015 - pNA [51-500]

The Sleeper and the Spindle (Illus. by Riddell, Chris)
    c Magpies - v30 - i1 - March 2015 - p35(1) [501+]

Sleeper, Jim - *In Search of New York: A Special Issue of Dissent*
    Nation - v300 - i14 - April 6 2015 - p161(1) [501+]

Sleepy Puppy
    c KR - July 1 2015 - pNA [51-500]

Slegers, Liesbet - *Me and My Day*
    c KR - Jan 1 2015 - pNA [51-500]

Sleigh, Tom - *Station Zed*
    BL - v111 - i9-10 - Jan 1 2015 - p32(1) [51-500]

Sleight, Simon - *Young People and the Shaping of Public Space in Melbourne, 1870-1914*
    HER - v130 - i543 - April 2015 - p483(3) [501+]

Slevin, Peter - *Michelle Obama: A Life*
    BL - v111 - i12 - Feb 15 2015 - p23(1) [51-500]
    BL - v111 - i19-20 - June 1 2015 - p27(1) [51-500]
    KR - Feb 1 2015 - pNA [51-500]
    Mac - v128 - i13-14 - April 6 2015 - p74(1) [501+]
    PW - v262 - i9 - March 2 2015 - p77(1) [51-500]

Slide, Anthony - *'It's the Pictures That Got Small': Charles Brackett on Billy Wilder and Hollywood's Golden Age*
    TLS - i5853 - June 5 2015 - p30(1) [501+]

Slim, Iceberg - *Shetani's Sister*
    BL - v111 - i17 - May 1 2015 - p44(1) [51-500]
    KR - June 1 2015 - pNA [51-500]

Slipinski, Adam - *Australian Longhorn Beetles (Coleoptera: Cerambycidae)*
    QRB - v90 - i3 - Sept 2015 - p348(2) [501+]

Sloan, Holly Goldberg - *Appleblossom the Possum (Illus. by Rosen, Gary A.)*
    c KR - April 15 2015 - pNA [51-500]
    c PW - v262 - i19 - May 11 2015 - p60(2) [51-500]
    c SLJ - v61 - i5 - May 2015 - p106(1) [51-500]
    c BL - v111 - i21 - July 1 2015 - p67(1) [51-500]
    c HB - v91 - i5 - Sept-Oct 2015 - p118(1) [51-500]
    c NYTBR - Sept 13 2015 - p22(L) [501+]
Just Call My Name
    y HB Guide - v26 - i1 - Spring 2015 - p123(2) [51-500]

Sloan, Pat - *Teach Me to Applique: Fusible Applique That's Soft and Simple*
    Bwatch - July 2015 - pNA [51-500]

Sloane, William - *The Rim of Morning*
    NYTBR - Nov 1 2015 - p22(L) [501+]
    PW - v262 - i36 - Sept 7 2015 - p49(1) [51-500]

Slobodchikoff, Michael O. - *Strategic Cooperation: Overcoming the Barriers of Global Anarchy*
    E-A St - v67 - i3 - May 2015 - p510(3) [501+]

Slocum, Robert Boak - *The Anglican Imagination: Portraits and Sketches of Modern Anglican Theologians*
    TLS - i5874 - Oct 30 2015 - p13(1) [501+]

Slosberg, Mike - *A Baby to Die For*
    PW - v262 - i1 - Jan 5 2015 - p55(1) [51-500]

Sloterdijk, Peter - *In the World Interior of Capital: For a Philosophical Theory of Globalization*
    GSR - v38 - i2 - May 2015 - p476-3 [501+]
    IBMR - v39 - i1 - Jan 2015 - p48(1) [501+]

Slover, Ron - *Saving America Now: The Buffet Syndrome*
    SPBW - April 2015 - pNA [51-500]

Slowik, Michael - *After the Silents: Hollywood Film Music in the Early Sound Era, 1926-1934*
    Si & So - v25 - i4 - April 2015 - p107(1) [501+]

Sloyan, Gerard S. - *Jesus: Word Made Flesh*
    AM - v212 - i13 - April 13 2015 - p34(2) [501+]

Sloyan, Patrick J. - *The Politics of Deception: JFK's Secret Decisions on Vietnam, Civil Rights, and Cuba*
    LJ - v140 - i2 - Feb 1 2015 - p96(1) [51-500]

Sludds, Kevin - *The Incurious Seeker's Quest for Meaning: Heidegger, Mood and Christianity*
    RM - v69 - i1 - Sept 2015 - p153(3) [501+]

Sluga, Glenda - *Internationalism in the Age of Nationalism*
    JMH - v87 - i1 - March 2015 - p157(3) [501+]

Slutsch, Sergej - *Deutschland und die Sowjetunion 1933 - 1941: Dokumente. Band 1: 30. Januar 1933 - 31. Oktober 1934*
    HNet - April 2015 - pNA [501+]

Smagorinsky, Peter - *Teaching Dilemmas and Solutions in Content-Area Literacy, Grades 6-12*
    Bwatch - Feb 2015 - pNA [51-500]

Smale, Alan - *Clash of Eagles*
    KR - Jan 15 2015 - pNA [51-500]
    Analog - v135 - i9 - Sept 2015 - p108(1) [51-500]
Eagle in Exile
    PW - v262 - i47 - Nov 23 2015 - p53(1) [51-500]

Smale, Holly - *Geek Girl*
    y BL - v111 - i9-10 - Jan 1 2015 - p92(2) [51-500]
    y CCB-B - v68 - i8 - April 2015 - p420(1) [51-500]
    c HB Guide - v26 - i2 - Fall 2015 - p139(1) [51-500]
    y Sch Lib - v63 - i3 - Autumn 2015 - p184(2) [51-500]
    y VOYA - v37 - i6 - Feb 2015 - p66(1) [51-500]
Model Misfit (Read by Sobey, Katey). Audiobook Review
    y SLJ - v61 - i12 - Dec 2015 - p80(2) [51-500]
Model Misfit
    y KR - May 1 2015 - pNA [51-500]

Smaligo, Nicholas - *The Occupy Movement Explained*
    Bwatch - Jan 2015 - pNA [51-500]

Small, Andrew - *The China-Pakistan Axis: Asia's New Geopolitics*
    Econ - v414 - i8922 - Jan 24 2015 - p74(US) [501+]
    NS - v144 - i5267 - June 19 2015 - p42(3) [501+]
    TLS - i5846 - April 17 2015 - p27(1) [501+]

Small, David - *Catch That Cookie!*
    c HB Guide - v26 - i1 - Spring 2015 - p29(1) [51-500]

Small, Gary - *2 Weeks to a Younger Brain*
    LJ - v140 - i9 - May 15 2015 - p99(1) [51-500]
    RVBW - June 2015 - pNA [51-500]

Small, Helen - *The Last Chronicle of Barset*
    TLS - i5847 - April 24 2015 - p7(f2) [501+]
The Value of the Humanities
    MLR - v110 - i3 - July 2015 - p799-801 [501+]

Small, Lily - *Chloe the Kitten (Illus. by Harris-Jones, Kirsteen)*
    c PW - v262 - i3 - Jan 19 2015 - p83(1) [51-500]

Small, Marian - *Building Proportional Reasoning across Grades and Math Strands, K-8*
    Math T - v109 - i3 - Oct 2015 - p236-236 [501+]
Uncomplicating Fractions to Meet Common Core Standards in Math, K-7
    TC Math - v21 - i7 - March 2015 - p442(1) [501+]

Small, Marie White - *Stony Kill*
    LJ - v140 - i17 - Oct 15 2015 - p82(2) [51-500]

Small, Matthew - *The Wall between Us: Notes from the Holy Land*
    BL - v111 - i18 - May 15 2015 - p13(1) [51-500]

Small, Thomas - *Path of Blood: The Story of Al Qaeda's War on the House of Saud*
    PW - v262 - i4 - Jan 26 2015 - p163(1) [51-500]

Small Victories. Audiobook Review
    Bwatch - Jan 2015 - pNA [51-500]

Smallkin, Valerie Leonhart - *Springtime Dance (Illus. by Hopkins, Kimberly)*
    c CH Bwatch - Nov 2015 - pNA [51-500]

Smallman, Phyllis - *Martini Regrets*
    RVBW - June 2015 - pNA [51-500]

Smallman, Shawn - *Dangerous Spirits: The Windigo in Myth and History*
    Beav - v95 - i3 - June-July 2015 - p58(2) [51-500]

Smallman, Steve - *Cours, Petit Bonhomme, cours!*
    c Res Links - v21 - i1 - Oct 2015 - p56(1) [501+]
Hiccupotamus (Illus. by Grey, Ada)
    c HB Guide - v26 - i2 - Fall 2015 - p52(1) [51-500]
    c KR - Jan 15 2015 - pNA [51-500]
    c SLJ - v61 - i2 - Feb 2015 - p80(1) [51-500]
Mange tes legumes, Boucle d'or!
    c Res Links - v21 - i1 - Oct 2015 - p56(1) [501+]
Mouche-toi, grand mechant loup!
    c Res Links - v21 - i1 - Oct 2015 - p56(1) [501+]
Poo in the Zoo (Illus. by Grey, Ada)
    c BL - v112 - i2 - Sept 15 2015 - p69(1) [51-500]
Poo in the Zoo!
    c KR - July 1 2015 - pNA [51-500]
Scowl (Illus. by Watson, Richard)
    c HB Guide - v26 - i1 - Spring 2015 - p46(1) [51-500]
Souris Cendrillon
    c Res Links - v21 - i1 - Oct 2015 - p56(1) [501+]

Smallwood, Ashley M. - *Clovis: On the Edge of a New Understanding*
    Am Ant - v80 - i4 - Oct 2015 - p786(2) [501+]

Smallwood, Carol - *The Complete Guide to Using Google in Libraries: Instruction, Administration, and Staff Productivity, vol. 1*
    LJ - v140 - i9 - May 15 2015 - p97(1) [51-500]
Water, Earth, Air, Fire, and Picket Fences
    WLT - v89 - i1 - Jan-Feb 2015 - p77(2) [501+]
Women, Work, and the Web: How the Web Creates Entrepreneurial Opportunities
    BL - v111 - i13 - March 1 2015 - p14(1) [51-500]

Smart, Jamie - *Bunny vs. Monkey, Book 2*
    c Sch Lib - v63 - i4 - Winter 2015 - p233(1) [51-500]
Bunny vs. Monkey (Illus. by Smart, Jamie)
    c KR - Nov 1 2015 - pNA [51-500]
    c SLJ - v61 - i12 - Dec 2015 - p110(1) [51-500]

Smart, Julie - *Disability across the Developmental Life Span: For the Rehabilitation Counselor*
    J Rehab - v81 - i1 - Jan-March 2015 - p63(1) [501+]

The Smart Kid's Guide to Everyday Life Series
    c BL - v111 - i15 - April 1 2015 - p58(1) [501+]

Smart, Michal - *Kaddish: Women's Voices*
    Tikkun - v30 - i1 - Wntr 2015 - p51(3) [501+]

Smat, David R. - *The Playground Principle*
    SPBW - March 2015 - pNA [51-500]

Smeesters, Aline - *Poesie Latine a Haute Voix (1500-1700)*
    Sev Cent N - v73 - i1-2 - Spring-Summer 2015 - p82(3) [501+]

Smelcer, John - *Savage Mountain*
    c SLJ - v61 - i6 - June 2015 - p116(2) [51-500]

Smelser, Neil J. - *Getting Sociology Right: A Half-Century of Reflections*
    CS - v44 - i6 - Nov 2015 - p850-851 [501+]

Smetana, Vit - *Imposing, Maintaining, and Tearing open the Iron Curtain: The Cold War and East-Central Europe, 1945-1989*
    E-A St - v67 - i6 - August 2015 - p990(2) [501+]

Smid, Emmi - *Luna's Red Hat: An Illustrated Storybook to Help Children Cope with Loss and Suicide (Illus. by Smid, Emmi)*
    c SLJ - v61 - i11 - Nov 2015 - p133(1) [51-500]

Smidchens, Guntis - *The Power of Song: Nonviolent National Culture in the Baltic Singing Revolution*
    Slav R - v74 - i1 - Spring 2015 - p181-182 [501+]

Smil, Vaclav - *Power Density: A Key to Understanding Energy Sources and Uses*
    Nature - v523 - i7558 - July 2 2015 - p32(2) [501+]

Smilansky, Yizhar - *Khirbet Khizeh*
    Nation - v300 - i11 - March 16 2015 - p45(1) [501+]

Smiles, Terri-Lynne - *Origins*
    KR - Feb 15 2015 - pNA [501+]

Smiley, Jane - *Early Warning (Read by King, Lorelei). Audiobook Review*
    LJ - v140 - i13 - August 1 2015 - p47(1) [51-500]
Early Warning
    BL - v111 - i11 - Feb 1 2015 - p4(1) [51-500]
    BL - v111 - i13 - March 1 2015 - p27(2) [51-500]
    BL - v111 - i16 - April 15 2015 - p34(1) [501+]
    Ent W - i1362 - May 8 2015 - p57(1) [51-500]
    KR - Feb 15 2015 - pNA [501+]
    LJ - v140 - i6 - April 1 2015 - p85(1) [51-500]
    NY - v91 - i16 - June 8 2015 - p109 [51-500]
    NYTBR - June 7 2015 - p38(L) [501+]
    PW - v262 - i4 - Jan 26 2015 - p142(1) [51-500]
    TLS - i5854 - June 12 2015 - p10(1) [501+]

Every Father's Daughter: Twenty-four Women Writers Remember Their Fathers
    LJ - v140 - i12 - July 1 2015 - p83(1) [51-500]
    RVBW - August 2015 - pNA [51-500]
The Georges and the Jewels (Read by Goethals, Angela). Audiobook Review
    SLJ - v61 - i2 - Feb 2015 - p50(2) [51-500]
Golden Age
    BL - v112 - i1 - Sept 1 2015 - p39(1) [501+]
    KR - August 1 2015 - pNA [501+]
    LJ - v140 - i15 - Sept 15 2015 - p72(1) [51-500]
    NYTBR - Dec 20 2015 - p26(L) [501+]
    PW - v262 - i31 - August 3 2015 - p32(2) [51-500]
A Good Horse (Read by Goethals, Angela). Audiobook Review
    c SLJ - v61 - i6 - June 2015 - p65(1) [51-500]
Some Luck
    NYTBR - Sept 13 2015 - p32(L) [501+]
    TLS - i5834 - Jan 23 2015 - p19(1) [501+]
True Blue (Read by Goethals, Angela). Audiobook Review
    c SLJ - v61 - i8 - August 2015 - p51(1) [51-500]
Smiley, Tavis - *My Journey with Maya (Read by Smiley, Tavis). Audiobook Review*
    LJ - v140 - i10 - June 1 2015 - p62(2) [51-500]
My Journey with Maya
    KR - March 1 2015 - pNA [51-500]
Smillie, Justin - *Slow Fires: Mastering New Ways to Braise, Roast, and Grill*
    LJ - v140 - i15 - Sept 15 2015 - p102(1) [51-500]
Smilovitsky, Leonid - *Jewish Life in Belarus: The Final Decade of the Stalin Regime, 1944-1953*
    HNet - Sept 2015 - pNA [501+]
Smirl, Lisa - *Spaces of Aid: How Cars, Compounds and Hotels Shape Humanitarianism*
    TimHES - i2217 - August 20 2015 - p47-47 [501+]
Smith, A.D. - *Anselm's Other Argument*
    JR - v95 - i4 - Oct 2015 - p582(3) [501+]
Smith, Adam - *Bootleggers and Baptists: How Economic Forces and Moral Persuasion Interact to Shape Regulatory Politics*
    IndRev - v19 - i3 - Wntr 2015 - p455(4) [501+]
Smith, Alex T. - *Claude at the Beach (Illus. by Smith, Alex T.)*
    c HB Guide - v26 - i1 - Spring 2015 - p66(1) [51-500]
Claude in the Spotlight (Illus. by Smith, Alex T.)
    c SLJ - v61 - i11 - Nov 2015 - p91(2) [51-500]
Claude on the Slopes (Illus. by Smith, Alex T.)
    c HB Guide - v26 - i1 - Spring 2015 - p66(1) [51-500]
Hector et le grand mechant Chevalier
    c Res Links - v20 - i5 - June 2015 - p44(1) [51-500]
Little Red and the Very Hungry Lion
    c Sch Lib - v63 - i4 - Winter 2015 - p222(1) [51-500]
Smith, Alexander Gordon - *The Devil's Engine: Hellraisers*
    y BL - v112 - i5 - Nov 1 2015 - p54(1) [51-500]
Hellraisers
    y KR - Oct 15 2015 - pNA [51-500]
    y PW - v262 - i38 - Sept 21 2015 - p74(2) [51-500]
    y SLJ - v61 - i11 - Nov 2015 - p115(1) [51-500]
    y VOYA - v38 - i5 - Dec 2015 - p74(2) [51-500]
Smith, Alexander McCall - *The Handsome Man's De Luxe Cafe (Read by Lecat, Lisette). Audiobook Review*
    BL - v111 - i15 - April 1 2015 - p86(1) [51-500]
    LJ - v140 - i5 - March 15 2015 - p72(1) [51-500]
The Mystery of the Missing Lion (Read by Andoh, Adjoa). Audiobook Review
    c BL - v111 - i14 - March 15 2015 - p88(1) [51-500]
Precious and the Zebra Necklace
    c Magpies - v30 - i5 - Nov 2015 - p36(1) [501+]
Sunshine on Scotland Street (Read by Mackenzie, Robert Ian). Audiobook Review
    BL - v111 - i13 - March 1 2015 - p69(1) [51-500]
The Woman Who Walked in Sunshine
    BL - v112 - i3 - Oct 1 2015 - p30(1) [51-500]
    PW - v262 - i35 - August 31 2015 - p62(1) [51-500]
Smith, Alexander O. - *Malice*
    RVBW - July 2015 - pNA [51-500]
Smith, Ali - *How to Be Both (Read by Banks, John). Audiobook Review*
    LJ - v140 - i9 - May 15 2015 - p44(1) [51-500]
How to Be Both
    NY - v90 - i46 - Feb 2 2015 - p65 [51-500]
    NYTBR - Jan 4 2015 - p12(L) [501+]
    NYTBR - Oct 18 2015 - p28(L) [501+]
    Wom R Bks - v32 - i3 - May-June 2015 - p31(2) [501+]

Smith, Amanda Hilliard - *The Williamston Freedom Movement: A North Carolina Town's Struggle for Civil Rights, 1957-1970*
    JSH - v81 - i4 - Nov 2015 - p1035(2) [501+]
Smith, Amber - *The Way I Used to Be*
    y KR - Jan 1 2016 - pNA [51-500]
    y PW - v262 - i51 - Dec 14 2015 - p87(1) [51-500]
Smith, Amelia - *Scandal's Heiress*
    PW - v262 - i32 - August 10 2015 - p44(2) [51-500]
Smith, Andrew Anselmo - *100 Sideways Miles (Read by Heyborne, Kirby)*
    y BL - v112 - i7 - Dec 1 2015 - p70(1) [51-500]
100 Sideways Miles
    y HB Guide - v26 - i1 - Spring 2015 - p124(2) [51-500]
The Alex Crow (Read by Andrews, MacLeod). Audiobook Review
    c BL - v111 - i21 - July 1 2015 - p80(1) [51-500]
    y HB - v91 - i4 - July-August 2015 - p168(1) [51-500]
    PW - v262 - i17 - April 27 2015 - p72(1) [51-500]
    y SLJ - v61 - i6 - June 2015 - p68(1) [51-500]
The Alex Crow
    y CCB-B - v68 - i8 - April 2015 - p385(2) [501+]
    y HB - v91 - i3 - May-June 2015 - p119(1) [501+]
    c HB Guide - v26 - i2 - Fall 2015 - p139(1) [51-500]
    y KR - Jan 15 2015 - pNA [51-500]
    y NYTBR - April 12 2015 - p20(L) [501+]
    y PW - v262 - i49 - Dec 2 2015 - p112(1) [51-500]
    y SLJ - v61 - i2 - Feb 2015 - p108(3) [51-500]
Grasshopper Jungle
    c HB - v91 - i1 - Jan-Feb 2015 - p43(3) [501+]
Stand-Off (Illus. by Bosma, Sam)
    y BL - v111 - i22 - August 1 2015 - p66(2) [51-500]
    y PW - v262 - i49 - Dec 2 2015 - p98(1) [51-500]
Stand-Off
    y KR - July 15 2015 - pNA [51-500]
    y PW - v262 - i28 - July 13 2015 - p68(1) [51-500]
    y SLJ - v61 - i8 - August 2015 - p110(2) [51-500]
Smith, Andrew (b. 1959-) - *The Alex Crow*
    y BL - v111 - i11 - Feb 1 2015 - p47(1) [51-500]
    y PW - v262 - i3 - Jan 19 2015 - p85(1) [51-500]
Smith, Andrew (b. 1964-) - *The Victorian Gothic: An Edinburgh Companion*
    VS - v57 - i3 - Spring 2015 - p565(3) [501+]
Smith, Andrew F. - *Savoring Gotham: A Food Lover's Companion to New York City*
    NYT - Dec 27 2015 - p3(L) [501+]
Smith, Angela - *Women Drummers: A History from Rock and Jazz to Blues and Country*
    M Ed J - v102 - i1 - Sept 2015 - p21(1) [501+]
    Teach Mus - v22 - i4 - April 2015 - p69(1) [51-500]
Smith, Annabel - *Whiskey and Charlie*
    KR - Feb 1 2015 - pNA [51-500]
    BL - v111 - i12 - Feb 15 2015 - p33(2) [51-500]
Smith, Annick - *Crossing the Plains with Bruno*
    BL - v112 - i3 - Oct 1 2015 - p12(1) [51-500]
    NYTBR - Dec 6 2015 - p46(L) [501+]
    KR - August 15 2015 - pNA [51-500]
Smith, Anthony D. - *The Nation Made Real: Art and National Identity in Western Europe, 1600-1850*
    JMH - v87 - i2 - June 2015 - p411(2) [501+]
Smith, B. - *Before I Forget: Love, Hope, Help, and Acceptance in Our Fight against Alzheimer's*
    BL - v112 - i7 - Dec 1 2015 - p12(1) [51-500]
    PW - v262 - i47 - Nov 23 2015 - p63(1) [51-500]
Smith, Ben Bailey - *I Am Bear (Illus. by Akyuz, Sav)*
    c KR - Dec 15 2015 - pNA [51-500]
Smith, Benjamin T. - *The Roots of Conservatism in Mexico: Catholicism, Society, and Politics in the Mixteca Baja, 1750-1962*
    HAHR - v95 - i4 - Nov 2015 - p678-680 [501+]
Smith, Billy G. - *Ship of Death: A Voyage that Changed the Atlantic World*
    RAH - v43 - i3 - Sept 2015 - p456-461 [501+]
Smith, Brad - *Rough Justice*
    KR - Dec 1 2015 - pNA [51-500]
    PW - v262 - i50 - Dec 7 2015 - p72(1) [51-500]
Smith, Brendan - *Crisis and Survival in Late Medieval Ireland: The English of Louth and Their Neighbours, 1330-1450*
    AHR - v120 - i3 - June 2015 - p1097-1098 [501+]
    Historian - v77 - i3 - Fall 2015 - p626(2) [501+]
Smith, Briony May - *Imelda & the Goblin King (Illus. by Smith, Briony May)*
    c BL - v112 - i6 - Nov 15 2015 - p58(1) [51-500]
    c KR - Sept 15 2015 - pNA [51-500]
    c PW - v262 - i33 - August 17 2015 - p71(1) [51-500]

Smith, Bruce L.R. - *Lincoln Gordon: Architect of Cold War Foreign Policy*
    HNet - Oct 2015 - pNA [501+]
Smith, Bryan - *If Winning Isn't Everything, Why Do I Hate to Lose? (Illus. by Martin, Brian)*
    c CH Bwatch - Nov 2015 - pNA [51-500]
Is There an App for That? Hailey Discovers Happiness through Self-Acceptance (Illus. by Wish, Katia)
    c CH Bwatch - April 2015 - pNA [51-500]
Smith, C.U M. - *Brain, Mind and Consciousness in the History of Neuroscience*
    QRB - v90 - i1 - March 2015 - p94(2) [501+]
Smith, Caitlin Drake - *Franklin and the Case of the New Friend*
    c Res Links - v20 - i3 - Feb 2015 - p10(1) [51-500]
Franklin and the Radio
    c Res Links - v20 - i3 - Feb 2015 - p10(1) [51-500]
Smith, Carrie - *Silent City*
    BL - v112 - i1 - Sept 1 2015 - p50(1) [51-500]
    PW - v262 - i33 - August 17 2015 - p53(1) [51-500]
Smith, Carrie (b. 1987-) - *The Boundaries of the Literary Archive: Reclamation and Representation*
    LR - v64 - i3 - March 2015 - p268-269 [501+]
Smith, Cassandra - *U and I*
    PW - v262 - i46 - Nov 16 2015 - p54(1) [51-500]
Smith, Charles R., Jr. - *28 Days: Moments in Black History That Changed the World (Illus. by Evans, Shane W.)*
    c HB Guide - v26 - i2 - Fall 2015 - p222(1) [51-500]
Smith, Charlie - *Ginny Gall*
    KR - Dec 1 2015 - pNA [501+]
Smith, Charlotte Colding - *Images of Islam, 1453-1600: Turks in Germany and Central Europe*
    Ren Q - v68 - i3 - Fall 2015 - p1060-1062 [501+]
    Six Ct J - v46 - i1 - Spring 2015 - p135-136 [501+]
Smith, Christian - *Building Catholic Higher Education: Unofficial Reflections from the University of Notre Dame*
    Bks & Cult - v21 - i4 - July-August 2015 - p22(1) [501+]
    Theol St - v76 - i2 - June 2015 - p402(2) [501+]
The Paradox of Generosity: Giving We Receive, Grasping We Lose
    AJS - v121 - i2 - Sept 2015 - p636(3) [501+]
    CC - v132 - i8 - April 15 2015 - p36(2) [501+]
The Sacred Project of American Sociology
    Soc - v52 - i1 - Feb 2015 - p105(6) [501+]
Young Catholic America: Emerging Adults In, Out of, and Gone from the Church
    AJS - v120 - i4 - Jan 2015 - p1259(4) [501+]
    CS - v44 - i6 - Nov 2015 - p852-853 [501+]
    JR - v95 - i3 - July 2015 - p420(2) [501+]
Smith, Christopher J. - *The Creolization of American Culture: William Sidney Mount and the Roots of Blackface Minstrelsy*
    JSH - v81 - i3 - August 2015 - p720(2) [501+]
Smith, Ciete Barrett - *Magic Delivery (Illus. by Dziekan, Michal)*
    c HB Guide - v26 - i1 - Spring 2015 - p92(1) [51-500]
Smith, Claire Bidwell - *After This: When Life Is Over, Where Do We Go?*
    LJ - v140 - i9 - May 15 2015 - p93(1) [51-500]
Smith, Clark Ashton - *The Dark Eidolon and Other Fantasies*
    TLS - i5837 - Feb 13 2015 - p13(1) [501+]
Smith, Claudia - *Quarry Light*
    ABR - v36 - i2 - Jan-Feb 2015 - p19(1) [501+]
Smith, Corinne Hosfeld - *Henry David Thoreau for Kids: His Life and Ideas, with 21 Activities*
    y KR - Nov 15 2015 - pNA [51-500]
Smith, Cote - *Hurt People*
    KR - Jan 1 2016 - pNA [501+]
    PW - v262 - i51 - Dec 14 2015 - p53(2) [51-500]
Smith, Craig - *Remarkably Rexy*
    c Magpies - v30 - i4 - Sept 2015 - p28(2) [501+]
Smith, Craig A. - *A Vision of Voices: John Crosby and the Santa Fe Opera*
    ON - v80 - i2 - August 2015 - p60(1) [501+]
Smith, Curtis - *Communion*
    KR - Jan 15 2015 - pNA [51-500]
Smith, Cynthia Leitich - *Feral Nights (Read by Haberkorn, Todd, with Nick Podehl and Amy McFadden). Audiobook Review*
    BL - v111 - i13 - March 1 2015 - p71(1) [51-500]

Feral Pride (Read by four narrators). Audiobook Review
   y SLJ - v61 - i7 - July 2015 - p50(1) [51-500]
Feral Pride
   y BL - v111 - i9-10 - Jan 1 2015 - p88(1) [51-500]
   y HB - v91 - i1 - Jan-Feb 2015 - p88(1) [51-500]
   c HB Guide - v26 - i2 - Fall 2015 - p139(1) [51-500]
   y VOYA - v37 - i6 - Feb 2015 - p84(1) [51-500]

Smith, D.K. - *Mind Over Bullies*
   y KR - Sept 15 2015 - pNA [501+]

Smith, Dan (b. 1970-) - *Big Game* (Read by Bakkensen, Michael). Audiobook Review
   c SLJ - v61 - i6 - June 2015 - p65(1) [51-500]
Big Game
   c CCB-B - v68 - i9 - May 2015 - p468(2) [51-500]
   y Sch Lib - v63 - i2 - Summer 2015 - p110(1) [51-500]
   y VOYA - v37 - i6 - Feb 2015 - p66(2) [51-500]
The Darkest Heart
     BL - v111 - i22 - August 1 2015 - p32(2) [51-500]
     PW - v262 - i22 - June 1 2015 - p40(2) [51-500]
My Brother's Secret (Read by Williams, Leon). Audiobook Review
   c SLJ - v61 - i11 - Nov 2015 - p72(1) [51-500]
My Brother's Secret
   c KR - April 15 2015 - pNA [51-500]
   c SLJ - v61 - i6 - June 2015 - p104(2) [51-500]
   y VOYA - v38 - i3 - August 2015 - p69(1) [51-500]
My Friend the Enemy (Read by Williams, Leon). Audiobook Review
     SLJ - v61 - i2 - Feb 2015 - p51(1) [51-500]
My Friend the Enemy
   y CH Bwatch - March 2015 - pNA [51-500]
   c HB Guide - v26 - i1 - Spring 2015 - p92(1) [51-500]

Smith, Daniel Starza - *John Donne and the Conway Papers: Patronage and Manuscript Circulation in the Early Seventeenth Century*
     RES - v66 - i276 - Sept 2015 - p780-782 [501+]

Smith, Danna - *Arctic White* (Illus. by White, Lee)
   c KR - Oct 1 2015 - pNA [51-500]
   c PW - v262 - i47 - Nov 23 2015 - p66(1) [501+]
   c SLJ - v61 - i12 - Dec 2015 - p96(1) [51-500]
Mother Goose's Pajama Party (Illus. by Allyn, Virginia)
   c KR - August 15 2015 - pNA [51-500]
   c PW - v262 - i33 - August 17 2015 - p69(1) [51-500]
   c SLJ - v61 - i10 - Oct 2015 - p71(1) [51-500]

Smith, Darron T. - *White Parents, Black Children: Experiencing Transracial Adoption*
     SF - v93 - i3 - March 2015 - pe90 [501+]
     SF - v93 - i3 - March 2015 - pNA [501+]

Smith, David J. - *If ... A Mind-Bending New Way of Looking at Big Ideas and Numbers* (Illus. by Adams, Steve)
   c HB Guide - v26 - i1 - Spring 2015 - p148(1) [51-500]
If ... : A Mind-Bending New Way of Looking at Big Ideas and Numbers (Illus. by Adams, Steve)
     PW - v262 - i7 - Feb 16 2015 - pNA [51-500]
   c Res Links - v20 - i3 - Feb 2015 - p24(1) [501+]
If ... A Mind-Bending New Way of Looking at Big Ideas and Numbers (Illus. by Adams, Steve)
   c Magpies - v30 - i2 - May 2015 - p22(1) [501+]
Networks of Music and Culture in the Late Sixteenth and Early Seventeenth Centuries: A Collection of Essays in Celebration of Peter Philips's 450th Anniversary
     Ren Q - v68 - i1 - Spring 2015 - p362-363 [501+]

Smith, David R. - *Parody and Festivity in Early Modern Art: Essays on Comedy as Social Vision*
     Six Ct J - v46 - i1 - Spring 2015 - p138-139 [501+]

Smith, Dennis E. - *Meals in the Early Christian World: Social Formation, Experimentation, and Conflict at the Table*
     Historian - v77 - i1 - Spring 2015 - p196(2) [501+]

Smith, Donald - *The Constable's Tale*
     BL - v111 - i22 - August 1 2015 - p32(1) [51-500]
     KR - Oct 15 2015 - pNA [501+]
     NYTBR - Sept 20 2015 - p29(L) [501+]
     PW - v262 - i28 - July 13 2015 - p43(1) [51-500]

Smith, Donald B. - *Mississauga Portraits: Ojibwe Voices from Nineteenth-Century Canada*
     Can Hist R - v96 - i3 - Sept 2015 - p435(3) [501+]

Smith, Elwood H. - *How to Draw with Your Funny Bone* (Illus. by Smith, Elwood H.)
   c CCB-B - v68 - i10 - June 2015 - p518(1) [51-500]
   c HB Guide - v26 - i2 - Fall 2015 - p193(1) [51-500]
   c KR - Jan 15 2015 - pNA [51-500]

Smith, Emily Wing - *All Better Now*
   c KR - Dec 15 2015 - pNA [51-500]
     PW - v262 - i51 - Dec 14 2015 - p87(1) [51-500]

Smith, Eric - *Inked*. E-book Review
   y Sch Lib - v63 - i2 - Summer 2015 - p82(1) [51-500]

Smith, Erin A. - *What Would Jesus Read? Popular Religious Books and Everyday Life in Twentieth-Century America*
     CC - v132 - i15 - July 22 2015 - p43(1) [51-500]

Smith, Felisa A. - *Animal Body Size: Linking Pattern and Process across Space, Time, and Taxonomic Group*
     QRB - v90 - i2 - June 2015 - p210(1) [501+]
Foundations of Macroecology: Classic Papers with Commentaries
     QRB - v90 - i4 - Dec 2015 - p431(1) [501+]

Smith, Fred C. - *Trouble in Goshen: Plain Folk, Roosevelt, Jesus, and Marx in the Great Depression South*
     JAH - v102 - i1 - June 2015 - p283-284 [501+]
     JSH - v81 - i3 - August 2015 - p763(2) [501+]

Smith, Gary Scott - *Religion in the Oval Office: The Religious Lives of American Presidents*
     BL - v111 - i15 - April 1 2015 - p5(2) [51-500]

Smith, Geoffrey S. - *Guilt by Association: Heresy Catalogues in Early Christianity*
     CHR - v101 - i4 - Autumn 2015 - p902(2) [501+]

Smith, Graeme - *The Dogs Are Eating Them Now: Our War in Afghanistan*
     CSM - Jan 15 2015 - pNA [501+]

Smith, Graham - *The Major Crimes Team*
     KR - Dec 1 2015 - pNA [51-500]
     PW - v262 - i52 - Dec 21 2015 - p135(1) [51-500]

Smith, Greg - *Junior Braves of the Apocalypse: A Brave Is Brave* (Illus. by Lehner, Zach)
   y SLJ - v61 - i8 - August 2015 - p112(1) [51-500]

Smith, Greg Leitich - *Borrowed Time*
   y KR - August 1 2015 - pNA [51-500]

Smith, Harry Leslie - *Love among the Ruins: A Memoir of Life and Love in Hamburg, 1945*
     TimHES - i2227 - Oct 29 2015 - p47(1) [501+]

Smith, Hilary T. - *A Sense of the Infinite*
   y BL - v111 - i17 - May 1 2015 - p92(1) [51-500]
   y HB - v91 - i3 - May-June 2015 - p119(2) [51-500]
   c HB Guide - v26 - i2 - Fall 2015 - p139(1) [51-500]
   y KR - Feb 15 2015 - pNA [51-500]
   c Nat Post - v17 - i188 - June 13 2015 - pWP5(1) [501+]
   y PW - v262 - i11 - March 16 2015 - p86(1) [51-500]
   y VOYA - v38 - i1 - April 2015 - p70(1) [51-500]

Smith-Howard, Kendra - *Pure and Modern Milk: An Environmental History since 1900*
     JAH - v101 - i4 - March 2015 - p1296(1) [51-500]

Smith, Ian K. - *The Shred Power Cleanse: Eat Clean, Get Lean, Burn Fat*
     PW - v262 - i38 - Sept 21 2015 - p69(1) [51-500]

Smith, Icy - *Mystery of the Giant Masks of Sanxingdui* (Illus. by Roski, Gayle Garner)
   c CH Bwatch - March 2015 - pNA [51-500]
   c HB Guide - v26 - i2 - Fall 2015 - p52(1) [51-500]
   c SLJ - v61 - i7 - July 2015 - p104(1) [51-500]

Smith, J. Beverley - *Llywelyn ap Gruffudd: Prince of Wales*
     Specu - v90 - i2 - April 2015 - p586-588 [501+]

Smith, J. Douglas - *On Democracy's Doorstep: The Inside Story of How the Supreme Court Brought "One Person, One Vote" to the United States*
     HLR - v128 - i6 - April 2015 - p1896(1) [1-50]
     JSH - v81 - i4 - Nov 2015 - p1038(3) [501+]

Smith, J.L. - *The Abominators*
     SLJ - v61 - i2 - Feb 2015 - p58(1) [51-500]

Smith, James K.A. - *How (Not) to Be Secular: Reading Charles Taylor*
     CC - v132 - i13 - June 24 2015 - p42(2) [51-500]
Who's Afraid of Relativism? Community, Contingency, and Creaturehood
     CC - v132 - i5 - March 4 2015 - p33(3) [51-500]

Smith, Jane Margaret - *Australian Bushrangers Series*
   c Magpies - v30 - i2 - May 2015 - p23(1) [51-500]

Smith, Jean Edward - *Eisenhower in War and Peace*
     Pres St Q - v45 - i1 - March 2015 - p199(7) [501+]

Smith, Jeff - *Pricing Your Portraits: High-Profit Strategies for Photographers*
     Bwatch - Oct 2015 - pNA [501+]

Smith, Jeff (b. 1960-) - *Bone: Out from Boneville* (Illus. by Hamaker, Steve)
   c HB Guide - v26 - i2 - Fall 2015 - p102(1) [51-500]

Smith, Jeff (b. 1962-) - *Film Criticism, the Cold War, and the Blacklist: Reading the Hollywood Reds*
     Am St - v54 - i1 - Spring 2015 - p155-3 [501+]

Smith, Jeff (b. 1973-) - *Mr. Smith Goes to Prison: What My Year behind Bars Taught Me about America's Prison Crisis*
     BL - v112 - i2 - Sept 15 2015 - p6(1) [51-500]
     LJ - v140 - i14 - Sept 1 2015 - p127(1) [51-500]

Smith, Jennifer E. - *The Geography of You and Me*
   y Teach Lib - v42 - i3 - Feb 2015 - p28(4) [501+]
Hello, Goodbye, and Everything in Between
   y BL - v112 - i2 - Sept 15 2015 - p74(1) [51-500]
   y KR - June 15 2015 - pNA [51-500]
   y PW - v262 - i22 - June 1 2015 - p60(2) [51-500]
   y SLJ - v61 - i7 - July 2015 - p98(1) [51-500]

Smith, Jenny Leigh - *Works in Progress: Plans and Realities on Soviet Farms, 1930-1963*
     AHR - v120 - i4 - Oct 2015 - p1571-1572 [501+]
     HNet - April 2015 - pNA [501+]
     Slav R - v74 - i3 - Fall 2015 - p656-657 [501+]

Smith, Jeremy (b. 1964-) - *Red Nations: The Nationalities Experience in and after the USSR*
     AHR - v120 - i1 - Feb 2015 - p358-359 [501+]

Smith, Jeremy N. - *Epic Measures: One Doctor, Seven Billion Patients*
     BL - v111 - i14 - March 15 2015 - p32(1) [51-500]
     KR - Jan 15 2015 - pNA [501+]
     PW - v262 - i7 - Feb 16 2015 - p170(1) [51-500]

Smith, Jill Eileen - *The Crimson Cord: Rahab's Story*
     BL - v111 - i12 - Feb 15 2015 - p44(1) [51-500]

Smith, Jill Suzanne - *Berlin Coquette: Prostitution and the New German Woman, 1890-1933*
     CEH - v48 - i2 - June 2015 - p263-265 [501+]
     JIH - v46 - i1 - Summer 2015 - p119-120 [501+]

Smith, Jim - *Future Ratboy and the Attack of the Killer Robot Grannies*
   c Sch Lib - v63 - i4 - Winter 2015 - p233(1) [51-500]

Smith, Joan - *Harry McShane: No Mean Fighter*
     TimHES - i2211 - July 9 2015 - p47(1) [501+]

Smith, John David - *The Dunning School: Historians, Race, and the Meaning of Reconstruction*
     JSH - v81 - i1 - Feb 2015 - p225(3) [501+]
Lincoln and the U.S. Colored Troops
     JSH - v81 - i3 - August 2015 - p737(2) [501+]

Smith, Johnny - *Cap'n John the (Slightly) Fierce* (Illus. by Anderson, Laura Ellen)
   c Sch Lib - v63 - i3 - Autumn 2015 - p170(1) [51-500]
Sir John the (Mostly) Brave (Illus. by Anderson, Laura Ellen)
   c Sch Lib - v63 - i3 - Autumn 2015 - p170(1) [51-500]

Smith, Jonathan - *The Churchill Secret KBO*
     NS - v144 - i5267 - June 19 2015 - p50(1) [51-500]
White Hat Hacking
   y Teach Lib - v42 - i5 - June 2015 - p10(1) [51-500]
   c BL - v111 - i15 - April 1 2015 - p54(1) [51-500]

Smith, Judith E. - *Becoming Belafonte: Black Artist, Public Radical*
     Am St - v54 - i2 - Summer 2015 - p105-106 [501+]
     JAH - v102 - i2 - Sept 2015 - p617-618 [501+]
     TLS - i5841 - March 13 2015 - p27(1) [501+]

Smith, Julie (b. 1944-) - *New Orleans Noir*
     KR - Jan 1 2016 - pNA [51-500]

Smith, Julie R. - *Evaluating Instructional Leadership: Recognized Practices for Success*
     Bwatch - Sept 2015 - pNA [501+]

Smith, K.N. - *The Urban Boys*
   y KR - Jan 1 2016 - pNA [501+]

Smith, Kate - *Makery Sewing: Over 30 Projects for the Home, to Wear and to Give*
     LJ - v140 - i6 - April 1 2015 - p93(1) [51-500]

Smith, Kathryn A. - *The Taymouth Hours: Stories and the Construction of the Self in Late Medieval England*
     CHR - v101 - i1 - Wntr 2015 - p157(2) [501+]

Smith, Katy Simpson - *Free Men*
     KR - Nov 1 2015 - pNA [51-500]
     PW - v262 - i50 - Dec 7 2015 - p64(1) [51-500]
We Have Raised All of You: Motherhood in the South, 1750-1835
     AHR - v120 - i3 - June 2015 - p1011-1012 [501+]
     JSH - v81 - i2 - May 2015 - p438(2) [501+]

Smith, Kay Higuera - *Evangelical Postcolonial Conversations: Global Awakenings in Theology and Praxis*
     IBMR - v39 - i4 - Oct 2015 - p243(2) [501+]

Smith, Keith D. - *Strange Visitors: Documents in Indigenous-Settler Relations in Canada from 1876*
     Can Hist R - v96 - i3 - Sept 2015 - p437(3) [501+]

Smith, Kenneth D. - *Engaging Gifted Readers and Writers*
     RVBW - June 2015 - pNA [51-500]
     SPBW - March 2015 - pNA [501+]

Smith, Kevin (b. 1970-) - *Batman '66 Meets the Green Hornet (Illus. by Templeton, Ty)*
   y VOYA - v38 - i2 - June 2015 - p50(2) [501+]
Smith, Kevin L. - *Owning and Using Scholarship: An IP Handbook for Teachers and Researchers*
      LJ - v140 - i7 - April 15 2015 - p107(1) [51-500]
      R&USQ - v54 - i4 - Summer 2015 - p74(2) [501+]
Smith, Lachlan - *Fox Is Framed (Read by Bray, R.C.). Audiobook Review*
      PW - v262 - i21 - May 25 2015 - p53(1) [51-500]
Fox Is Framed
      BL - v111 - i11 - Feb 1 2015 - p26(2) [51-500]
      KR - Feb 1 2015 - pNA [51-500]
      PW - v262 - i7 - Feb 16 2015 - p161(1) [51-500]
Lion Plays Rough
      RVBW - March 2015 - pNA [51-500]
Smith, Lane - *Return to Augie Hobble (Illus. by Smith, Lane)*
   c BL - v111 - i17 - May 1 2015 - p100(1) [51-500]
   c CCB-B - v68 - i11 - July-August 2015 - p566(2) [51-500]
   c HB Guide - v26 - i2 - Fall 2015 - p102(1) [51-500]
   c NYTBR - June 21 2015 - p17(L) [501+]
   c PW - v262 - i49 - Dec 2 2015 - p67(2) [51-500]
   c SLJ - v61 - i3 - March 2015 - p141(1) [51-500]
Smith, Laura Harris - *The 30-Day Faith Detox: Renew Your Mind, Cleanse Your Body, Heal Your Spirit*
      PW - v262 - i41 - Oct 12 2015 - p62(1) [51-500]
Smith, Lee - *Dimestore*
      KR - Dec 15 2015 - pNA [501+]
Smith, Lesley - *The Ten Commandments: Interpreting the Bible in the Medieval World*
      Med R - June 2015 - pNA [501+]
Smith, Leslie Dorrough - *Righteous Rhetoric: Sex, Speech, and the Politics of Concerned Women for America*
      CH - v84 - i4 - Dec 2015 - p924(3) [501+]
Smith, Lindsay - *Dreamstrider*
   y KR - August 15 2015 - pNA [51-500]
   y PW - v262 - i32 - August 10 2015 - p61(2) [51-500]
   y SLJ - v61 - i9 - Sept 2015 - p173(2) [51-500]
Sekret
   y HB Guide - v26 - i1 - Spring 2015 - p124(1) [51-500]
Skandal
   y KR - Jan 15 2015 - pNA [51-500]
   y VOYA - v38 - i1 - April 2015 - p84(1) [51-500]
   y CCB-B - v68 - i11 - July-August 2015 - p567(1) [51-500]
   y HB Guide - v26 - i2 - Fall 2015 - p140(1) [51-500]
Smith-Llera, Danielle - *The Revolutionary War: A Chronology of America's Fight for Independence*
   c HB Guide - v26 - i2 - Fall 2015 - p221(1) [51-500]
Smith, Mandy - *Cabin Fever: The Sizzling Secrets of a Virgin Airlines Flight Attendant*
      KR - April 15 2015 - pNA [51-500]
Smith, Marcroy - *People of Print: Innovative, Independent Design and Illustration*
      Am Craft - v75 - i4 - August-Sept 2015 - p20(1) [501+]
Smith, Marie - *T Is for Time (Illus. by Graef, Renee)*
   c HB Guide - v26 - i2 - Fall 2015 - p166(1) [51-500]
Smith, Mark A. - *Secular Faith: Why Culture Trumps Religion in American Politics*
      BL - v112 - i1 - Sept 1 2015 - p17(1) [51-500]
Smith, Mark Allen - *The Confessor*
      PW - v262 - i20 - May 18 2015 - p64(1) [51-500]
Smith, Mark Haskell - *Naked at Lunch: A Reluctant Nudist's Adventures in the Clothing-Optional World*
      LJ - v140 - i13 - August 1 2015 - p115(1) [51-500]
      KR - April 1 2015 - pNA [51-500]
      PW - v262 - i7 - Feb 16 2015 - p167(1) [51-500]
Smith, Mark M. - *The Smell of Battle, the Taste of Siege: A Sensory History of the Civil War*
      AHR - v120 - i4 - Oct 2015 - p1492-1493 [501+]
      For Aff - v94 - i1 - Jan-Feb 2015 - pNA [51-500]
      JAH - v102 - i1 - June 2015 - p253-254 [501+]
      JSH - v81 - i4 - Nov 2015 - p993(2) [501+]
Smith, Martin Cruz - *Tatiana: An Arkady Renko Novel*
      NYTBR - Jan 11 2015 - p24(L) [501+]
Smith, Matt - *Barbarian Lord*
   y HB Guide - v26 - i1 - Spring 2015 - p124(1) [51-500]
Smith, Matthew (b. 1973-) - *Another Person's Poison: A History of Food Allergy*
      BL - v111 - i19-20 - June 1 2015 - p18(1) [51-500]
      KR - April 15 2015 - pNA [51-500]
      LJ - v140 - i7 - April 15 2015 - p114(1) [51-500]
      NYT - May 25 2015 - pC4(L) [501+]

Smith, Matthew Clark - *Small Wonders: Jean-Henri Fabre and His World of Insects (Illus. by Ferri, Giuliano)*
   c BL - v111 - i19-20 - June 1 2015 - p93(1) [51-500]
   c CCB-B - v68 - i11 - July-August 2015 - p567(2) [51-500]
   c PW - v262 - i17 - April 27 2015 - p74(1) [501+]
   c HB Guide - v26 - i2 - Fall 2015 - p212(1) [51-500]
   c KR - March 15 2015 - pNA [51-500]
   c PW - v262 - i49 - Dec 2 2015 - p50(1) [51-500]
   c SLJ - v61 - i5 - May 2015 - p136(1) [51-500]
Smith McGovern, Tessa - *London Road*
      KR - Oct 1 2015 - pNA [501+]
Smith, Merril D. - *Cultural Encyclopedia of the Breast*
      BL - v111 - i12 - Feb 15 2015 - p12(1) [51-500]
Smith, Michael - *Grasshopper Buddy (Illus. by Oliva, Octavio)*
   c HB Guide - v26 - i2 - Fall 2015 - p19(1) [51-500]
My Ducky Buddy (Illus. by Oliva, Octavio)
   c HB Guide - v26 - i2 - Fall 2015 - p19(1) [51-500]
A Smile/Una Sonrisa (Illus. by Aguiler, Manny)
   c PW - v262 - i33 - August 17 2015 - p70(1) [51-500]
Smith, Michael (b. 1946-) - *Shackleton: By Endurance We Conquer*
      TLS - i5840 - March 6 2015 - p28(2) [501+]
Smith, Michael French - *A Faraway, Familiar Place: An Anthropologist Returns to Papua New Guinea*
      JRAI - v21 - i3 - Sept 2015 - p698(1) [501+]
Smith, Michael Glover - *Flickering Empire: How Chicago Invented the U.S. Film Industry*
      RVBW - April 2015 - pNA [51-500]
Smith, Michelle - *Play On*
   y SLJ - v61 - i6 - June 2015 - p129(2) [51-500]
Smith, Mike J. - *Boko Haram: Inside Nigeria's Unholy War*
      Econ - v414 - i8931 - March 28 2015 - p85(US) [501+]
      LJ - v140 - i7 - April 15 2015 - p104(1) [51-500]
      NYRB - v62 - i12 - July 9 2015 - p22(3) [501+]
Smith, Miles Anthony - *Becoming Generation Flux: Why Traditional Career Planning Is Dead: How to Be Agile, Adapt to Ambiguity, and Develop Resilience*
      Bwatch - July 2015 - pNA [51-500]
Smith, Mitzi J. - *Teaching All Nations: Interrogating the Matthean Great Commission*
      Intpr - v69 - i1 - Jan 2015 - p124(1) [51-500]
Smith, Nathan - *Color Concrete Garden Projects: Make Your Own Planters, Furniture, and Fire Pits Using Creative Techniques and Vibrant Finishes (Illus. by Coleman, Charles)*
      LJ - v140 - i11 - June 15 2015 - p88(1) [51-500]
Smith, Neil - *Blood on Snow*
      Nat Post - v17 - i200 - June 27 2015 - pWP4(1) [501+]
      RVBW - May 2015 - pNA [51-500]
Boo
   y BL - v111 - i16 - April 15 2015 - p23(1) [51-500]
      KR - March 1 2015 - pNA [51-500]
      Mac - v128 - i21 - June 1 2015 - p56(2) [51-500]
      Nat Post - v17 - i194 - June 20 2015 - pWP5(1) [501+]
      PW - v262 - i7 - Feb 16 2015 - p163(2) [51-500]
The Room
      NS - v144 - i5248 - Feb 6 2015 - p43(1) [51-500]
Smith-Oka, Vania - *Shaping the Motherhood of Indigenous Mexico*
      HAHR - v95 - i1 - Feb 2015 - p183-185 [501+]
Smith, Page - *Tragic Encounter*
      KR - August 15 2015 - pNA [501+]
Smith, Pamela H. - *Ways of Making and Knowing: The Material Culture of Empirical Knowledge*
      Isis - v106 - i2 - June 2015 - p423(2) [501+]
      T&C - v56 - i4 - Oct 2015 - p977-978 [501+]
Smith, Patrick - *Metamorphabet (Illus. by Smith, Patrick)*
   c SLJ - v61 - i6 - June 2015 - p72(1) [51-500]
Smith, Patrick A. - *Conversations with William Gibson*
      SFS - v42 - i1 - March 2015 - p185-187 [501+]
Smith, Patti - *Collected Lyrics, 1970-2015*
   y BL - v112 - i1 - Sept 1 2015 - p29(2) [51-500]
M Train (Read by Smith, Patti). Audiobook Review
      LJ - v140 - i20 - Dec 1 2015 - p59(1) [51-500]
M Train
      BL - v112 - i1 - Sept 1 2015 - p25(1) [51-500]
      CSM - Oct 13 2015 - pNA [51-500]
      KR - August 1 2015 - pNA [51-500]
      LJ - v140 - i14 - Sept 1 2015 - p113(1) [51-500]
      Nation - v301 - i17 - Oct 26 2015 - p27(3) [501+]
      NS - v144 - i5286 - Oct 30 2015 - p45(1) [501+]
      NYRB - v62 - i16 - Oct 22 2015 - p4(2) [501+]
      NYT - Sept 20 2015 - p4(L) [501+]
      NYT - Oct 2 2015 - pC23(L) [501+]
      NYTBR - Dec 6 2015 - p29(L) [501+]
      Spec - v329 - i9768 - Nov 14 2015 - p50(1) [501+]
      PW - v262 - i32 - August 10 2015 - p53(1) [51-500]
      NYT - Oct 4 2015 - p1(L) [501+]
Patti Smith Collected Lyrics, 1970-2015
      Spec - v329 - i9768 - Nov 14 2015 - p50(1) [501+]
Smith, Paul J. - *Masters of Craft: 224 Artists in Fiber, Clay, Glass, Metal, and Wood*
      Am Craft - v75 - i4 - August-Sept 2015 - p20(1) [501+]
Smith, Paula - *Be the Change Series*
   c CH Bwatch - March 2015 - pNA [51-500]
Smith, Peter J. - *Between Two Stools: Scatology and Its Representations in English Literature, Chaucer to Swift*
      MLR - v110 - i1 - Jan 2015 - p235-237 [501+]
Diary of a Bad Year
      TimHES - i2203 - May 14 2015 - p47(1) [501+]
Smith-Prei, Carrie - *Revolting Families: Toxic Intimacy, Private Politics, and Literary Realisms in the German Sixties*
      GSR - v38 - i2 - May 2015 - p456-4 [501+]
Smith, R.R.R. - *Aphrodisias VI: The Marble Reliefs from the Julio-Claudian Sebasteion*
      TLS - i5843 - March 27 2015 - p8(2) [501+]
Smith, R. Tyson - *Fighting for Recognition: Identity, Masculinity, and the Act of Violence in Professional Wrestling*
      Theat J - v67 - i2 - May 2015 - p376-377 [501+]
Smith, Richard Norton - *On His Own Terms: A Life of Nelson Rockefeller (Read by Michael, Paul). Audiobook Review*
      BL - v111 - i19-20 - June 1 2015 - p138(1) [51-500]
On His Own Terms: A Life of Nelson Rockefeller
      BL - v111 - i19-20 - June 1 2015 - p27(1) [501+]
      Nation - v300 - i8 - Feb 23 2015 - p35(3) [501+]
Smith, Richard W. - *Bishop McIlvaine, Slavery, Britain and the Civil War*
      SPBW - July 2015 - pNA [501+]
Smith, Robert Barr - *The Outlaws: Tales of Bad Guys Who Shaped the Wild West*
      Historian - v77 - i3 - Fall 2015 - p586(2) [501+]
      Roundup M - v22 - i6 - August 2015 - p40(1) [501+]
Smith, Roger - *Between Mind and Nature: A History of Psychology*
      Historian - v77 - i2 - Summer 2015 - p417(2) [501+]
Smith, Roland - *Beneath*
   c CCB-B - v68 - i6 - Feb 2015 - p331(2) [51-500]
   c HB Guide - v26 - i2 - Fall 2015 - p102(1) [51-500]
The Edge
   y HB - v91 - i5 - Sept-Oct 2015 - p118(2) [51-500]
   y KR - August 1 2015 - pNA [51-500]
   y SLJ - v61 - i7 - July 2015 - p88(1) [51-500]
   y VOYA - v38 - i4 - Oct 2015 - p62(1) [51-500]
Mutation
   c HB Guide - v26 - i1 - Spring 2015 - p92(1) [51-500]
T Is for Time (Illus. by Graef, Renee)
   c SLJ - v61 - i6 - June 2015 - p136(1) [51-500]
Smith, Ronald L. - *Hoodoo*
   c BL - v111 - i21 - July 1 2015 - p73(1) [51-500]
   c CCB-B - v69 - i2 - Oct 2015 - p114(1) [51-500]
   c HB - v91 - i5 - Sept-Oct 2015 - p119(1) [51-500]
   c KR - June 1 2015 - pNA [51-500]
   c SLJ - v61 - i6 - June 2015 - p105(1) [501+]
Smith, Russell - *Confidence: Stories*
      PW - v262 - i21 - May 25 2015 - p32(2) [51-500]
Smith, Ryan K. - *Robert Morris's Folly: The Architectural and Financial Failures of an American Founder*
      JAH - v102 - i2 - Sept 2015 - p544-545 [501+]
Smith, S.A. - *The Oxford Handbook of the History of Communism*
      HER - v130 - i545 - August 2015 - p1034(3) [501+]
Smith, Samuel C. - *A Cautious Enthusiasm: Mystical Piety and Evangelicalism in Colonial South Carolina*
      AHR - v120 - i4 - Oct 2015 - p1478-1479 [501+]
Smith, Scott - *The Ruins*
   c LJ - v140 - i7 - April 15 2015 - p126(1) [501+]
Smith, Scott T. - *Land and Book: Literature and Land Tenure in Anglo-Saxon England*
      MLR - v110 - i3 - July 2015 - p801-802 [501+]
Smith, Seth Grahame - *The Last American Vampire*
      BL - v111 - i9-10 - Jan 1 2015 - p60(1) [501+]
Smith, Shane - *What Is Love? (Illus. by Smith, Shane)*
   c CH Bwatch - July 2015 - pNA [51-500]

Smith, Shawn Michelle - *At the Edge of Sight: Photography and the Unseen*
    Isis - v106 - i2 - June 2015 - p421(2) [501+]
    JAH - v101 - i4 - March 2015 - p1233(1) [501+]

Smith, Sheila A. - *Intimate Rivals: Japanese Domestic Politics and a Rising China*
    For Aff - v94 - i3 - May-June 2015 - pNA [501+]
    KR - Sept 15 2015 - pNA [501+]

Smith, Sherri L. - *The Toymaker's Apprentice*
  c BL - v112 - i3 - Oct 1 2015 - p80(1) [51-500]
  c KR - July 15 2015 - pNA [51-500]
  c PW - v262 - i32 - August 10 2015 - p61(1) [51-500]
  c SLJ - v61 - i9 - Sept 2015 - p146(2) [51-500]
  y VOYA - v38 - i5 - Dec 2015 - p75(1) [51-500]

Smith, Stacey L. - *Freedom's Frontier: California and the Struggle over Unfree Labor, Emancipation, and Reconstruction*
    PHR - v84 - i1 - Feb 2015 - p87(2) [501+]
    RAH - v43 - i3 - Sept 2015 - p505-511 [501+]

Smith, Stephanie - *300 Sandwiches: A Multilayered Love Story ... with Recipes*
    LJ - v140 - i8 - May 1 2015 - p96(1) [51-500]

Smith, Steven D. - *Man and Animal in Severan Rome: The Literary Imagination of Claudius Aelianus*
    AJP - v136 - i3 - Fall 2015 - p532-537 [501+]

Smith, Sydney - *Sidewalk Flowers*
  c NYTBR - July 12 2015 - p18(L) [501+]

Smith, T'ai - *Bauhaus Weaving Theory: From Feminine Craft to Mode of Design*
    Am Craft - v75 - i2 - April-May 2015 - p18(1) [501+]

Smith, Tamara Ellis - *Another Kind of Hurricane*
  y HB - v91 - i4 - July-August 2015 - p146(1) [51-500]
  c KR - May 1 2015 - pNA [51-500]
  c NYTBR - August 9 2015 - p16(L) [501+]
  c SLJ - v61 - i5 - May 2015 - p106(1) [51-500]

Smith, Tana - *DIY Bedroom Decor: 50 Awesome Ideas for Your Room*
  y LJ - v140 - i13 - August 1 2015 - p97(1) [51-500]

Smith, Tash - *Capture These Indians for the Lord: Indians, Methodists, and Oklahomans, 1844-1939*
    IBMR - v39 - i3 - July 2015 - p156(1) [501+]

Smith, Ted A. - *Weird John Brown: Divine Violence and the Limits of Ethics*
    JSH - v81 - i4 - Nov 2015 - p980(2) [501+]

Smith-Theodore, Dawn - *TuTu Thin*
    Dance - v89 - i10 - Oct 2015 - p56(1) [51-500]

Smith, Tiffany Watt - *The Book of Human Emotions: An Encyclopedia of Feeling from Anger to Wanderlust*
    TimHES - i2229 - Nov 12 2015 - p48-49 [501+]
On Flinching: Theatricality and Scientific Looking from Darwin to Shell Shock
    Theat J - v67 - i3 - Oct 2015 - p575-576 [501+]

Smith, Timothy B. - *Shiloh: Conquer or Perish*
    J Mil H - v79 - i3 - July 2015 - p840-841 [501+]

Smith, Tom Rob - *The Farm*
    RVBW - March 2015 - pNA [51-500]
    RVBW - Feb 2015 - pNA [51-500]

Smith, Tracy K. - *Ordinary Light*
    BL - v111 - i11 - Feb 1 2015 - p18(1) [51-500]
    NY - v91 - i22 - August 3 2015 - p73 [51-500]
    NYTBR - May 3 2015 - p13(L) [501+]
    PW - v262 - i9 - March 2 2015 - p77(1) [51-500]
    PW - v262 - i15 - April 13 2015 - p8(1) [51-500]

Smith, Vern E. - *The Jones Men*
    ABR - v36 - i3 - March-April 2015 - p4(2) [51-500]

Smith, Virginia - *A Kiss Is Still a Kiss*
    PW - v262 - i38 - Sept 21 2015 - p61(1) [51-500]

Smith, Wendy Hageman - *Math & Me: Embracing Success*
    Math T - v109 - i2 - Sept 2015 - p159-159 [501+]

Smith, Wilbur - *Desert God (Read by Grady, Mike). Audiobook Review*
    BL - v111 - i16 - April 15 2015 - p64(1) [51-500]
Golden Lion
    KR - Sept 15 2015 - pNA [501+]

Smith-Williams, Sunshine - *Sunny 101: The 10 Commandments of a Boss Chick*
    SPBW - June 2015 - pNA [501+]

Smither, Edward L. - *Mission in the Early Church: Themes and Reflections*
    IBMR - v39 - i2 - April 2015 - p109(1) [501+]

Smithers, Gregory D. - *The Cherokee Diaspora: An Indigenous History of Migration, Resettlement, and Identity*
    LJ - v140 - i14 - Sept 1 2015 - p119(1) [51-500]
Native Diasporas: Indigenous Identities and Settler Colonialism in the Americas
    JAH - v102 - i1 - June 2015 - p220-221 [501+]
    WHQ - v46 - i3 - Autumn 2015 - p373-373 [501+]

Slave Breeding: Sex, Violence, and Memory in African American History
    HNet - March 2015 - pNA [501+]
    HNet - April 2015 - pNA [501+]

Smithsonian - *History of the World in 1,000 Objects*
    Am Craft - v75 - i2 - April-May 2015 - p18(1) [501+]

Smolik, Jane Petrlik - *Currents*
  c BL - v111 - i16 - April 15 2015 - p59(1) [51-500]
  c KR - June 1 2015 - pNA [51-500]

Smolin, Jonathan - *Moroccan Noir: Police, Crime, and Politics in Popular Culture, Public Cultures of the Middle East and North Africa*
    AHR - v120 - i2 - April 2015 - p753-754 [501+]
    IJMES - v47 - i1 - Feb 2015 - p205-207 [501+]

Smolka, Bo - *Jackie Robinson Breaks the Color Barrier*
  c HB Guide - v26 - i2 - Fall 2015 - p200(1) [51-500]

Smoller, Laura Ackerman - *The Saint and the Chopped-Up Baby: The Cult of Vincent Ferrer in Medieval and Early Modern Europe*
    HER - v130 - i543 - April 2015 - p400(6) [501+]
    Med R - March 2015 - pNA(NA) [501+]
    AHR - v120 - i1 - Feb 2015 - p312(1) [501+]
    CH - v84 - i4 - Dec 2015 - p868(4) [501+]
    HNet - June 2015 - pNA [501+]
    Six Ct J - v46 - i2 - Summer 2015 - p463-465 [501+]

Smucker, Anna Egan - *Brother Giovanni's Little Reward: How the Pretzel Was Born (Illus. by Hall, Amanda)*
  c KR - June 15 2015 - pNA [51-500]
  c PW - v262 - i21 - May 25 2015 - p62(1) [51-500]
  c SLJ - v61 - i9 - Sept 2015 - p129(1) [51-500]

Smucker, Janneken - *Amish Quilts: Crafting and American Icon*
    JAH - v101 - i4 - March 2015 - p1246-1247 [501+]

Smucker, Marcus G. - *Spiritual Companioning: A Guide to Protestant Theology and Practice*
    CC - v132 - i21 - Oct 14 2015 - p52(2) [501+]

Smyrek, Volker - *Die Geschichte des Tonmischpults: Die technische Entwicklung der Mischpulte und der Wandel der medialen Produktionsverfahren im Tonstudio von den 1920er-Jahren bis heute*
    Isis - v106 - i2 - June 2015 - p491(2) [501+]

Smyth, Emer - *Religious Education in a Multicultural Europe: Children, Parents and Schools*
    HNet - May 2015 - pNA [501+]

Smyth, J.E. - *Fred Zinnemann and the Cinema of Resistance*
    AHR - v120 - i2 - April 2015 - p655-656 [501+]
    Roundup M - v22 - i6 - August 2015 - p40(1) [501+]

Smyth, William J. - *Toronto, the Belfast of Canada: The Orange Order and the Shaping of Municipal Culture*
    TimHES - i2216 - August 13 2015 - p46-47 [501+]

Smythe, J.P. - *Way Down Dark*
  y Magpies - v30 - i4 - Sept 2015 - p44(1) [501+]

Smythe, James - *No Harm Can Come to a Good Man*
    BL - v111 - i19-20 - June 1 2015 - p56(1) [51-500]

Snape, Michael - *The Clergy in Khaki: New Perspectives on British Army Chaplaincy in the First World War*
    CH - v84 - i1 - March 2015 - p267(4) [501+]
    HER - v130 - i542 - Feb 2015 - p234(2) [501+]

Snedden, Robert - *Materials Engineering and Exploring Properties*
  c BL - v112 - i4 - Oct 15 2015 - p42(1) [51-500]

Sneddon, Christopher - *Concrete Revolution: Large Dams, Cold War Geopolitics, and the US Bureau of Reclamation*
    Nature - v527 - i7577 - Nov 12 2015 - p163(1) [51-500]

Sneddon, Rob - *The Phantom Punch: The Story behind Boxing's Most Controversial Bout*
    LJ - v140 - i20 - Dec 1 2015 - p109(1) [51-500]

Sneed, Christine - *Paris, He Said*
    BL - v111 - i15 - April 1 2015 - p26(1) [51-500]
    KR - March 15 2015 - pNA [51-500]
    NYTBR - June 7 2015 - p17(L) [501+]

Sneideman, Joshua - *Climate Change: Discover How It Impacts Spaceship Earth (Illus. by Crosier, Mike)*
  c BL - v111 - i18 - May 15 2015 - p44(1) [51-500]
  c SLJ - v61 - i6 - June 2015 - p144(1) [51-500]

Sneider, Cary I. - *The Go-To Guide for Engineering Curricula Grades 6-8: Choosing and Using the Best Instructional Materials for your Students*
    Bwatch - May 2015 - pNA [51-500]

Snell, Danny - *Seagull*
  c Magpies - v30 - i4 - Sept 2015 - p28(1) [501+]

Snell, Heather - *Children and Cultural Memory in Texts of Childhood*
    Bkbird - v53 - i1 - Wntr 2015 - p96(2) [501+]

Snell-Rood, Claire - *No One Will Let Her Live: Women's Struggle for Well-Being in a Delhi Slum*
    TimHES - i2228 - Nov 5 2015 - p47(1) [501+]

Snesarev, Andrei Evgenievich - *Afghanistan: Preparing for the Bolshevik Incursion into Afghanistan and Attack on India, 1919-20*
    J Mil H - v79 - i2 - April 2015 - p519-520 [501+]

Snicket, Lemony - *Shouldn't You Be in School? All the Wrong Questions (Illus. by Seth)*
  c HB - v91 - i1 - Jan-Feb 2015 - p88(2) [51-500]
  c HB Guide - v26 - i1 - Spring 2015 - p92(1) [51-500]
Why Is This Night Different from All Other Nights? (Read by Aiken, Liam). Audiobook Review
  y CH Bwatch - Nov 2015 - pNA [51-500]

Sniegon, Tomas - *Vanished History: The Holocaust in Czech and Slovak Historical Culture*
    AHR - v120 - i2 - April 2015 - p741(1) [501+]

Sniegoski, Thomas E. - *A Deafening Silence in Heaven*
    PW - v262 - i37 - Sept 14 2015 - p46(1) [51-500]

Snitow, Ann - *The Feminism of Uncertainty: A Gender Diary*
    TimHES - i2221 - Sept 17 2015 - p48-49 [501+]

Snoddy, Richard - *The Soteriology of James Ussher: The Act and Object of Saving Faith*
    CH - v84 - i2 - June 2015 - p447(1) [501+]

Snodgrass, Mary Ellen - *The Encyclopedia of World Ballet*
    BL - v112 - i6 - Nov 15 2015 - p7(2) [51-500]
    LJ - v140 - i19 - Nov 15 2015 - p107(2) [51-500]

Snodgrass, Melinda - *The Edge of Dawn*
    BL - v111 - i21 - July 1 2015 - p46(1) [51-500]
    PW - v262 - i23 - June 8 2015 - p42(1) [51-500]

Snow, Carol - *The Last Place on Earth*
  y KR - Nov 15 2015 - pNA [51-500]
    PW - v262 - i48 - Nov 30 2015 - p63(1) [51-500]
  y SLJ - v61 - i12 - Dec 2015 - p116(1) [51-500]

Snow, Tiffany - *Playing Dirty*
    PW - v262 - i37 - Sept 14 2015 - p50(1) [51-500]
Power Play
    PW - v262 - i20 - May 18 2015 - p72(1) [51-500]
Shadow of a Doubt
    PW - v262 - i13 - March 30 2015 - p62(1) [51-500]

Snow, Virginia Brimhall - *Spring Walk (Illus. by Snow, Virginia Brimhall)*
  c CH Bwatch - March 2015 - pNA [51-500]

Snow White (Illus. by Bryan, Ed). E-book Review
  c SLJ - v61 - i6 - June 2015 - p72(1) [51-500]

Snowdon, Paul F. - *Persons, Animals, Ourselves*
    TimHES - i2185 - Jan 8 2015 - p49-49 [501+]
    TLS - i5839 - Feb 27 2015 - p11(1) [501+]

Snowe, Olivia - *Dandelion and the Witch (Illus. by Lamoreaux, Michelle)*
  c HB Guide - v26 - i1 - Spring 2015 - p93(1) [51-500]
The Glass Voice (Illus. by Lamoreaux, Michelle)
  c HB Guide - v26 - i1 - Spring 2015 - p93(1) [51-500]

Snyder, Betsy - *I Can Dance*
  c KR - Jan 1 2016 - pNA [51-500]

Snyder, Carla - *Sweet and Tart: 70 Irresistible Recipes with Citrus*
    LJ - v140 - i19 - Nov 15 2015 - p103(1) [51-500]
    NYTBR - Dec 6 2015 - pNA(L) [501+]

Snyder, Carrie - *The Candy Conspiracy: A Tale of Sweet Victory (Illus. by Davila, Claudia)*
  c CH Bwatch - June 2015 - pNA [51-500]
  c CH Bwatch - July 2015 - pNA [51-500]
  c HB Guide - v26 - i2 - Fall 2015 - p52(1) [51-500]
  c KR - Feb 15 2015 - pNA [51-500]
  c SLJ - v61 - i10 - Oct 2015 - p84(1) [51-500]
Girl Runner
    Wom R Bks - v32 - i6 - Nov-Dec 2015 - p19(2) [501+]

Snyder, Debra J. - *Ignite Calm: Achieving Bliss in Your Work*
    Bwatch - May 2015 - pNA [51-500]

Snyder, Elaine - *Anna & Solomon (Read by Marshall, Qarie). Audiobook Review*
    SLJ - v61 - i2 - Feb 2015 - p48(1) [51-500]

Snyder, Gail - *Stessed-Out Girl?: Girls Dealing with Feelings*
  y HB Guide - v26 - i1 - Spring 2015 - p131(1) [51-500]

Snyder, Gary - *Distant Neighbors: The Selected Letters of Wendell Berry & Gary Snyder*
    Comw - v142 - i6 - March 20 2015 - p28(3) [501+]
This Present Moment
    BL - v111 - i14 - March 15 2015 - p39(1) [51-500]
    CSM - April 24 2015 - pNA [501+]

Snyder, Laura J. - *Eye of the Beholder: Johannes Vermeer, Antoni Van Leeuwenhoek, and the Reinvention of Seeing (Read by Marston, Tamara).* Audiobook Review
    LJ - v140 - i15 - Sept 15 2015 - p44(1) [51-500]
Eye of the Beholder: Johannes Vermeer, Antoni van Leeuwenhoek, and the Reinvention of Seeing
    AS - v84 - i2 - Spring 2015 - p121(3) [501+]
    BL - v111 - i13 - March 1 2015 - p12(2) [51-500]
    New Sci - v226 - i3015 - April 4 2015 - p44(2) [501+]
    PW - v262 - i1 - Jan 5 2015 - p63(2) [51-500]

Snyder, Laurel - *Swan: The Life and Dance of Anna Pavlova (Illus. by Morstad, Julie)*
    c HB - v91 - i5 - Sept-Oct 2015 - p132(1) [51-500]
    c KR - May 1 2015 - pNA [51-500]
    c SLJ - v61 - i9 - Sept 2015 - p182(2) [51-500]

Snyder, Robert - *Crossing Broadway: Washington Heights and the Promise of New York City*
    NYT - July 12 2015 - p2(L) [501+]

Snyder, Samantha - *Attitude Is Everything*
    c SPBW - Sept 2015 - pNA [51-500]
Imagination Will Take You Everywhere, vol. 1
    SPBW - July 2015 - pNA [51-500]

Snyder, Saskia Coenen - *Building a Public Judaism: Synagogues and Jewish Identity in Nineteenth-Century Europe*
    JMH - v87 - i2 - June 2015 - p417(3) [501+]

Snyder, Scott - *Batman Eternal, Vol. 1*
    PW - v262 - i1 - Jan 5 2015 - p59(1) [51-500]
The Joker: Endgame
    PW - v262 - i38 - Sept 21 2015 - p62(1) [51-500]
Wytches (Illus. by Jock)
    BL - v112 - i2 - Sept 15 2015 - p51(2) [51-500]
    PW - v262 - i32 - August 10 2015 - p45(1) [51-500]

Snyder, Stephen - *Confessions*
    WLT - v89 - i3-4 - May-August 2015 - p112(2) [501+]

Snyder, Steve - *Shot Down: The True Story of Pilot Howard Snyder and the Crew of the B-17 Susan Ruth*
    SPBW - June 2015 - pNA [501+]

Snyder, Timothy - *Black Earth: The Holocaust as History and Warning (Read by Bramhall, Mark).* Audiobook Review
    PW - v262 - i48 - Nov 30 2015 - p55(1) [51-500]
Black Earth: The Holocaust as History and Warning
    HNet - Oct 2015 - pNA [501+]
    HT - v65 - i10 - Oct 2015 - p64(2) [501+]
    KR - July 1 2015 - pNA [501+]
    LJ - v140 - i12 - July 1 2015 - p96(1) [51-500]
    New Sci - v228 - i3045 - Oct 31 2015 - p45(1) [501+]
    NS - v144 - i5280 - Sept 18 2015 - p58(3) [501+]
    NY - v91 - i28 - Sept 21 2015 - p100 [501+]
    NYT - Sept 8 2015 - pC1(L) [501+]
    NYTBR - Sept 6 2015 - p9(L) [501+]
    PW - v262 - i26 - June 29 2015 - p58(1) [51-500]
    Spec - v328 - i9759 - Sept 12 2015 - p47(1) [501+]
    TimHES - i2220 - Sept 10 2015 - p49(1) [501+]
Stalin and Europe: Imitation and Domination, 1928-1953
    HNet - July 2015 - pNA [501+]

Snyder-Young, Dani - *Theatre of Good Intentions: Challenges and Hopes for Theatre and Social Change*
    Theat J - v67 - i3 - Oct 2015 - p579-580 [501+]

Snydr, Laurel - *Swan: The Life and Dance of Anna Pavlova (Illus. by Morstad, Julie)*
    c PW - v262 - i29 - July 20 2015 - p190(2) [501+]

Social Security Administration - *Social Security Handbook 2015: Overview of Social Security Programs*
    LJ - v140 - i14 - Sept 1 2015 - p143(1) [51-500]

Societies under Occupation in World War II: Supply, Shortage, Hunger
    HNet - June 2015 - pNA [501+]

Socken, Paul - *The Edge of the Precipice: Why Read Literature in the Digital Age?*
    MLR - v110 - i3 - July 2015 - p796-797 [501+]

Sodeman, Melissa - *Sentimental Memorials: Women and the Novel in Literary History*
    TLS - i5861 - July 31 2015 - p10(2) [501+]

Soderberg, Alexander - *The Other Son (Read by Jackson, Gildart).* Audiobook Review
    PW - v262 - i35 - August 31 2015 - p83(1) [51-500]
The Other Son
    BL - v111 - i21 - July 1 2015 - p39(1) [51-500]
    KR - May 15 2015 - pNA [51-500]
    PW - v262 - i21 - May 25 2015 - p36(1) [51-500]
    Ent W - i1373 - July 24 2015 - p67(1) [501+]

Soderberg, Erin - *The Quirks and the Quirkalicious Birthday (Illus. by Jack, Colin)*
    c HB Guide - v26 - i2 - Fall 2015 - p102(1) [51-500]

Soderholm-Difatte, Bryan - *The Golden Era of Major League Baseball: A Time of Transition and Integration*
    BL - v112 - i1 - Sept 1 2015 - p34(2) [51-500]
    PW - v262 - i39 - Sept 28 2015 - p83(1) [51-500]

Soderlund, Jean R. - *Lenape Country: Delaware Valley Society before William Penn*
    Am St - v54 - i2 - Summer 2015 - p122-123 [501+]
    JIH - v46 - i2 - Autumn 2015 - p292-294 [501+]

Soderlund, Walter C. - *The Independence of South Sudan: The Role of Mass Media in the Responsibility to Prevent*
    HNet - March 2015 - pNA [501+]

Sodha, Meera - *Made in India: Recipes from an Indian Family Kitchen*
    NYTBR - Dec 6 2015 - pNA(L) [501+]

Soehlke-Lennert, Dorothee - *How Big Is Big? How Far Is Far? (Illus. by Metcalf, Jen)*
    c SLJ - v61 - i7 - July 2015 - p104(1) [51-500]
How Big Is Big? How Far Is Far? (Illus. by Van Der Veken, Jan)
    c BL - v112 - i5 - Nov 1 2015 - p44(1) [51-500]
How Big Is Big? How Far Is Far? (Illus. by Metcalf, Jen)
    c PW - v262 - i14 - April 6 2015 - p58(1) [51-500]
How Big Is Big? How Far Is Far? (Illus. by Van Der Veken, Jan)
    c KR - May 1 2015 - pNA [51-500]

Soeren, Keil - *Multinational Federalism in Bosnia and Herzegovina*
    E-A St - v67 - i4 - June 2015 - p676(2) [501+]

Soergel, Philip M. - *Miracles and the Protestant Imagination: The Evangelical Wonder Book in Reformation Germany*
    Ren Q - v68 - i3 - Fall 2015 - p1048-1050 [501+]

Sofer, Sasson - *The Courtiers of Civilization: A Study of Diplomacy*
    HNet - Sept 2015 - pNA(NA) [501+]

Soffer, Gilad - *Duck's Vacation (Illus. by Soffer, Gilad)*
    c HB - v91 - i3 - May-June 2015 - p100(1) [51-500]
    c HB Guide - v26 - i2 - Fall 2015 - p52(1) [51-500]
    c KR - Feb 15 2015 - pNA [51-500]
    c PW - v262 - i13 - March 30 2015 - p73(1) [51-500]

Soffner, Jan - *Partizipation: Metapher, Mimesis, Musik--und die Kunst, Texte bewohnbarzu machen*
    Ger Q - v88 - i2 - Spring 2015 - p264(4) [501+]

Softer, Allison Sarnoff - *Apple Days (Illus. by McMahon, Bob)*
    c HB Guide - v26 - i1 - Spring 2015 - p46(1) [51-500]

Sohi, Seema - *Echoes of Mutiny: Race, Surveillance, and Indian Anticolonialism in North America*
    JAH - v102 - i2 - Sept 2015 - p582-583 [501+]
    JAS - v74 - i3 - August 2015 - p777-778 [501+]

Sohn, Michael - *The Good of Recognition: Phenomenology, Ethics, and Religion in the Thought of Levinas and Ricoeur*
    RVBW - March 2015 - pNA [51-500]

Sohn, Stephen Hong - *Racial Asymmetries: Asian American Fictional Worlds*
    AL - v87 - i3 - Sept 2015 - p627-629 [501+]
    J Am St - v49 - i1 - Feb 2015 - p205-208 [501+]

Soike, Lowell J. - *Busy in the Cause: Iowa, the Free-State Struggle in the West, and the Prelude to the Civil War*
    HNet - Sept 2015 - pNA(NA) [501+]
    Roundup M - v22 - i4 - April 2015 - p26(1) [501+]
    Roundup M - v22 - i6 - August 2015 - p40(1) [501+]
    WHQ - v46 - i2 - Summer 2015 - p233-234 [501+]

Sok-yong, Hwang - *Princess Bari*
    TLS - i5868 - Sept 18 2015 - p21(1) [51-500]

Sokol, Jason - *All Eyes Are Upon Us: Race and Politics from Boston to Brooklyn*
    NYTBR - Jan 11 2015 - p13(L) [501+]
    NYTBR - Jan 11 2015 - p13(L) [501+]

Solahudin - *The Roots of Terrorism in Indonesia: From Darul Islam to Jema'ah Islamiyah*
    Pac A - v88 - i4 - Dec 2015 - p966 [501+]

Solana, Michael - *Citizen Sim*
    y KR - Jan 15 2015 - pNA [51-500]

Solari, Amara - *Maya Ideologies of the Sacred: The Transfiguration of Space in Colonial Yucatan*
    HAHR - v95 - i3 - August 2015 - p511-512 [501+]

Soldatov, Andrei - *The Red Web: The Struggle between Russia's Digital Dictators and the New Online Revolutionaries*
    KR - August 1 2015 - pNA [501+]
    LJ - v140 - i15 - Sept 15 2015 - p92(2) [51-500]

Soleymaniha, Ali - *Embrace Happiness: The Art of Conflict Management*
    SPBW - August 2015 - pNA [51-500]

Solheim, Tracy - *Sleeping with the Enemy*
    PW - v262 - i29 - July 20 2015 - p175(2) [51-500]

Soli, Tatjana - *The Last Good Paradise (Read by Gilbert, Tavia).* Audiobook Review
    LJ - v140 - i8 - May 1 2015 - p41(1) [51-500]
The Last Good Paradise
    NYTBR - March 8 2015 - p25(L) [501+]

Solie, Karen - *The Road In Is Not the Same Road Out*
    BL - v111 - i16 - April 15 2015 - p13(1) [51-500]
    LJ - v140 - i8 - May 1 2015 - p78(1) [51-500]
    Nat Post - v18 - i4 - Oct 31 2015 - pWP4(1) [501+]
    PW - v262 - i16 - April 20 2015 - p51(1) [51-500]

Soliman, Wendy - *Miss Darcy's Passion*
    RVBW - August 2015 - pNA [51-500]

Soll, David - *Empire of Water: An Environmental and Political History of the New York City Water Supply*
    JEH - v75 - i1 - March 2015 - p292-293 [501+]

Soll, Jacob - *The Reckoning: Financial Accountability and the Rise and Fall of Nations*
    AR - v90 - i2 - March 2015 - p823(3) [501+]

Solomon, Asali - *Disgruntled*
    Bks & Cult - v21 - i5 - Sept-Oct 2015 - p40(2) [501+]
    LJ - v140 - i3 - Feb 15 2015 - p93(2) [51-500]
    Ms - v25 - i1 - Wntr 2015 - p56(1) [501+]

Solomon, Charles - *A Wish Your Heart Makes*
    RVBW - March 2015 - pNA [51-500]

Solomon, Marc - *Winning Marriage: The Inside Story of How Same-Sex Couples Took on the Politicians and Pundits--and Won*
    Law&PolBR - v25 - i4 - April 2015 - p50(6) [501+]

Solomon, Michael - *The Conversion Prophecy*
    SPBW - Sept 2015 - pNA [51-500]

Solomon, Noemie - *Danse: An Anthology*
    Dance RJ - v47 - i1 - April 2015 - p107-111 [501+]

Solomon, Sheldon - *The Worm at the Core: On the Role of Death in Life*
    KR - Jan 1 2015 - pNA [501+]
    LJ - v140 - i3 - Feb 15 2015 - p117(2) [51-500]
    Nature - v522 - i7544 - June 4 2015 - p33(1) [51-500]
    New Sci - v226 - i3021 - May 16 2015 - p46(1) [501+]
    NS - v144 - i5277 - August 28 2015 - p36(2) [501+]
    PW - v262 - i9 - March 2 2015 - p76(1) [51-500]
    Spec - v328 - i9743 - May 23 2015 - p36(1) [501+]
    TimHES - i2213 - July 23 2015 - p48(1) [501+]

Solomonov, Michael - *Zahav: A World of Israeli Cooking*
    LJ - v140 - i15 - Sept 15 2015 - p102(1) [51-500]
    NYT - Oct 7 2015 - pD5(L) [501+]
    NYTBR - Dec 6 2015 - p20(L) [501+]
    NYTBR - Dec 6 2015 - p20(L) [501+]
    PW - v262 - i24 - June 15 2015 - p78(2) [51-500]

Solomons, David - *My Brother Is a Superhero*
    c CCB-B - v69 - i1 - Sept 2015 - p56(1) [51-500]
    c KR - May 1 2015 - pNA [51-500]
    c Magpies - v30 - i3 - July 2015 - p38(1) [501+]
    c PW - v262 - i18 - May 4 2015 - p121(1) [51-500]
    c Sch Lib - v63 - i3 - Autumn 2015 - p170(1) [51-500]
    c SLJ - v61 - i6 - June 2015 - p105(2) [51-500]

Solomons, Jason - *Woody Allen: Film by Film*
    Spec - v329 - i9761 - Sept 26 2015 - p40(2) [501+]

Solomons, Natasha - *The Song of Hartgrove Hall*
    BL - v112 - i5 - Nov 1 2015 - p27(1) [51-500]
    KR - Sept 15 2015 - pNA [51-500]
    LJ - v140 - i20 - Dec 1 2015 - p97(1) [51-500]

Solopova, Elizabeth - *Latin Liturgical Psalters in the Bodleian Library: A Select Catalogue*
    Specu - v90 - i1 - Jan 2015 - p298-299 [501+]

Solovey, Mark - *Shaky Foundations: The Politics-Patronage-Social Science Nexus in Cold War America*
    Historian - v77 - i2 - Summer 2015 - p355(2) [501+]

Solovitch, Sara - *Playing Scared: A History and Memoir of Stage Fright*
    PW - v262 - i18 - May 4 2015 - p112(1) [51-500]
Playing Scared
    KR - April 15 2015 - pNA [501+]

Solow, Barbara - *The Economic Consequences of the Atlantic Slave Trade*
    JIH - v46 - i1 - Summer 2015 - p125-126 [501+]

Soluri, Michael - *Infinite Worlds: The People and Places of Space Exploration*
    Am Sci - v103 - i3 - May-June 2015 - p230(2) [501+]

Solway, Andrew - *From Crashing Waves to Music Download: An Energy Journey through the World of Sound*
    c BL - v111 - i15 - April 1 2015 - p60(1) [51-500]
    c HB Guide - v26 - i2 - Fall 2015 - p166(1) [51-500]
    c Sch Lib - v63 - i3 - Autumn 2015 - p176(1) [51-500]

From Sunlight to Blockbuster Movie: An Energy Journey through the World of Light
    c HB Guide - v26 - i2 - Fall 2015 - p166(1) [51-500]

Soman, David - *Ladybug Girl and the Dress-Up Dilemma (Illus. by Soman, David)*
    c HB Guide - v26 - i1 - Spring 2015 - p46(1) [51-500]

Three Bears in a Boat (Illus. by Soman, David)
    c HB Guide - v26 - i1 - Spring 2015 - p46(1) [51-500]

Somek, Alexander - *The Cosmopolitan Constitution*
    HLR - v128 - i4 - Feb 2015 - p1332(1) [1-50]

Somer, Bradley - *Fishbowl*
    KR - May 15 2015 - pNA [501+]
    PW - v262 - i26 - June 29 2015 - p41(1) [51-500]

Somers, Ian - *The Secret Gift*
    Sch Lib - v63 - i1 - Spring 2015 - p58(2) [51-500]

Somerset, Andrew J. - *Arms: The Culture and Credo of the Gun*
    Mac - v128 - i38 - Sept 28 2015 - p60(1) [501+]

Somerset, Fiona - *Feeling Like Saints: Lollard Writings after Wyclif*
    AHR - v120 - i3 - June 2015 - p1093-1094 [501+]
    MP - v113 - i1 - August 2015 - pE4(4) [501+]
    RES - v66 - i274 - April 2015 - p365-367 [501+]

Somerstein, Stephen - *Freedom Journey 1965: Photographs of the Selma to Montgomery March by Stephen Somerstein*
    Pub Hist - v37 - i3 - August 2015 - p128(9) [501+]

Somervill, Barbara A. - *South Korea*
    y VOYA - v38 - i5 - Dec 2015 - p79(1) [501+]

Somerville, Angus A. - *The Vikings and Their Age*
    JEGP - v114 - i1 - Jan 2015 - p126(2) [501+]
    Med R - August 2015 - pNA [501+]

Somerville, Charles C. - *E Is for Egypt*
    c Sch Lib - v63 - i1 - Spring 2015 - p48(1) [51-500]

Sommer, Benjamin D. - *Revelation and Authority: Sinai in Jewish Scripture and Tradition*
    PW - v262 - i19 - May 11 2015 - p54(2) [51-500]

Sommer, Bill - *A 52-Hertz Whale*
    y KR - July 1 2015 - pNA [51-500]
    y PW - v262 - i28 - July 13 2015 - p69(1) [51-500]
    y SLJ - v61 - i10 - Oct 2015 - p117(1) [51-500]

Sommers, Jackie Lea - *Truest*
    y BL - v112 - i1 - Sept 15 2015 - p75(1) [51-500]
    y KR - June 1 2015 - pNA [51-500]
    y PW - v262 - i27 - July 6 2015 - p74(1) [51-500]
    y SLJ - v61 - i6 - June 2015 - p130(1) [51-500]
    y VOYA - v38 - i4 - Oct 2015 - p62(1) [51-500]

Sommerset, Mark - *Baa Baa Smart Sheep*
    c KR - Nov 1 2015 - pNA [51-500]

Sommerstein, A.H. - *Menander: Samia*
    Class R - v65 - i2 - Oct 2015 - p387-389 [501+]

Somorjai, Adam - *The Cardinal Mindszenty Documents in American Archives*
    CHR - v101 - i2 - Spring 2015 - p342(6) [501+]

Do Not Forget This Small Honest Nation: Cardinal Mindszenty to 4 US Presidents and State Secretaries 1956-1971
    CHR - v101 - i2 - Spring 2015 - p342(6) [501+]

His Eminence Files
    CHR - v101 - i2 - Spring 2015 - p342(6) [501+]

Sancta Sedes Apostolica et Cardinalis Ioseph Mindszenty, II: Documenta 1956-1963
    CHR - v101 - i2 - Spring 2015 - p342(6) [501+]

Sancta Sedes Apostolica et Cardinalis Joseph Mindszenty, III/1.: Documenta 1963-1966
    CHR - v101 - i2 - Spring 2015 - p342(6) [501+]

Sancta Sedes Apostolica et Cardinalis Joseph Mindszenty, III/2: Documenta 1967-1971
    CHR - v101 - i2 - Spring 2015 - p342(6) [501+]

Somper, Justin - *A Conspiracy of Princes*
    y SLJ - v61 - i11 - Nov 2015 - p108(1) [51-500]

Sonderegger, Katherine - *Systematic Theology*
    Ch Today - v59 - i8 - Oct 2015 - p74(1) [501+]

Sondhaus, Lawrence - *The Great War at Sea: A Naval History of the First World War*
    HNet - April 2015 - pNA [501+]
    J Mil H - v79 - i2 - April 2015 - p506-507 [501+]
    J Mil H - v79 - i4 - Oct 2015 - p1182-1183 [501+]

Song, Eric B. - *Dominion Undeserved: Milton and the Perils of Creation*
    MLR - v110 - i3 - July 2015 - p828-830 [501+]

Song, Jesook - *Living on Your Own: Single Women, Rental Housing, and Post-Revolutionary Affect in Contemporary South Korea*
    Pac A - v88 - i3 - Sept 2015 - p721 [501+]

Song, Jiyeoun - *Inequality in the Workplace: Labor Market Reform in Japan and Korea*
    Pac A - v88 - i4 - Dec 2015 - p928 [501+]

Song, Min Hyoung - *The Children of 1965: On Writing, and Not Writing, as an Asian American*
    ERS - v38 - i3 - March 2015 - p512(2) [501+]

Song, Robert - *Covenant and Calling: Towards a Theology of Same-Sex Relationships*
    TLS - i5837 - Feb 13 2015 - p27(1) [501+]

Song, Ying - *Apricot's Revenge*
    KR - Dec 15 2015 - pNA [501+]
    PW - v262 - i51 - Dec 14 2015 - p61(2) [51-500]

Sonn, Tamara - *Islam and Democracy after the Arab Spring*
    PW - v262 - i37 - Sept 14 2015 - p62(1) [51-500]

Sonneborn, Scott - *Feet First (Illus. by Banks, Timothy)*
    c HB Guide - v26 - i1 - Spring 2015 - p93(1) [51-500]

Prisoner of the Penguin! (Illus. by Vecchio, Luciano)
    c HB Guide - v26 - i2 - Fall 2015 - p102(2) [51-500]

Sonnenburg, Justin - *The Good Gut: Taking Control of Your Weight, Your Mood and Your Long Term Health*
    KR - April 1 2015 - pNA [501+]

The Good Gut: Taking Control of Your Weight, Your Mood, and Your Long-term Health
    LJ - v140 - i8 - May 1 2015 - p96(1) [501+]

The Good Gut: Taking Control of Your Weight, Your Mood and Your Long Term Health
    New Sci - v226 - i3024 - June 6 2015 - p45(1) [501+]

The Good Gut: Taking Control of Your Weight, Your Mood and Your Long-Term Health
    Spec - v328 - i9742 - May 16 2015 - p37(1) [501+]

Sonnichsen, A.L. - *Red Butterfly (Illus. by Bates, Amy June)*
    c CCB-B - v68 - i8 - April 2015 - p420(2) [501+]
    y RVBW - June 2015 - pNA [51-500]

Red Butterfly
    c BL - v111 - i11 - Feb 1 2015 - p45(2) [51-500]

Red Butterfly (Illus. by Bates, Amy June)
    c HB Guide - v26 - i2 - Fall 2015 - p103(1) [51-500]

Red Butterfly (Illus. by June, Amy)
    c PW - v262 - i49 - Dec 2 2015 - p73(1) [51-500]

Sonnino, Paul - *The Search for the Man in the Iron Mask: A Historical Detective Story*
    PW - v262 - i48 - Nov 30 2015 - p52(1) [51-500]

Sonntag, Mary K. - *Write, If You Live to Get There*
    SPBW - Jan 2015 - pNA [51-500]

Soo, Kean - *March Grand Prix: The Fast and the Furriest (Illus. by Soo, Kean)*
    c BL - v112 - i4 - Oct 15 2015 - p37(1) [51-500]
    c CCB-B - v69 - i2 - Oct 2015 - p115(1) [51-500]
    c KR - July 15 2015 - pNA [51-500]
    c PW - v262 - i49 - Dec 2 2015 - p86(2) [51-500]

Soo, Kean Jellaby - *Jellaby: Monster in the City*
    c HB Guide - v26 - i1 - Spring 2015 - p93(1) [51-500]

Jellaby: The Lost Monster
    c HB Guide - v26 - i1 - Spring 2015 - p93(1) [51-500]

Soocher, Stan - *Baby You're a Rich Man: Suing the Beatles for Fun and Profit*
    LJ - v140 - i11 - June 15 2015 - p91(1) [51-500]

Sookhdeo, Patrick - *Dawa: The Islamic Strategy for Reshaping the Modern World*
    RVBW - June 2015 - pNA [51-500]

Soper, Steven C. - *Building a Civil Society: Associations, Public Life, and the Origins of Modern Italy*
    AHR - v120 - i1 - Feb 2015 - p347-348 [501+]
    JMH - v87 - i2 - June 2015 - p465(3) [501+]

Sorabji, John - *English Civil Justice After the Woolf and Jackson Reforms: A Critical Analysis*
    Law Q Rev - v131 - Jan 2015 - p160-162 [501+]

Sorabji, Richard - *Moral Conscience through the Ages*
    RM - v69 - i2 - Dec 2015 - p412(2) [501+]

Soranzo, Matteo - *Poetry and Identity in Quattrocento Naples*
    Ren Q - v68 - i3 - Fall 2015 - p974-975 [501+]

Sorensen, Jessica - *Nova and Quinton: No Regrets*
    BL - v111 - i15 - April 1 2015 - p32(1) [51-500]

Sorensen, Jill - *Against the Wall*
    PW - v262 - i52 - Dec 21 2015 - p140(1) [51-500]

Sorensen, Virginia - *Miracles on Maple Hill (Read by the Full Cast family). Audiobook Review*
    c SLJ - v61 - i7 - July 2015 - p47(2) [51-500]

Sorenson, Ashley - *The Very Cold, Freezing, No-Numbers Day (Illus. by Miles, David W.)*
    c KR - Jan 1 2016 - pNA [51-500]

Sorenson, Margo - *Spaghetti Smiles (Illus. by Harrington, David)*
    c HB Guide - v26 - i1 - Spring 2015 - p46(1) [51-500]

Soriano, Nancy - *The Jewelry Recipe Book: Transforming Ordinary Materials into Stylish and Distinctive Earrings, Bracelets, Necklaces, and Pins*
    PW - v262 - i11 - March 16 2015 - p80(2) [51-500]

Sormani, Philippe - *Respecifying Lab Ethnography: An Ethnomethodological Study of Experimental Physics*
    CS - v44 - i5 - Sept 2015 - p604-614 [501+]

Sorokin, Vladimir - *The Blizzard*
    HM - v331 - i1987 - Dec 2015 - p77(3) [501+]
    KR - Sept 15 2015 - pNA [501+]

Sorrentino, Christopher - *The Fugitives*
    KR - Dec 15 2015 - pNA [501+]

Sorrentino, Paul - *Stephen Crane: A Life of Fire*
    Hum - v75 - i4 - July-August 2015 - p46(2) [501+]

Sosin, Deborah - *Charlotte and the Quiet Place (Illus. by Woolley, Sara)*
    c PW - v262 - i22 - June 1 2015 - p58(1) [501+]
    c SLJ - v61 - i11 - Nov 2015 - p88(1) [51-500]

Soskin, Rupert - *Metamorphosis: Astonishing Insect Transformations*
    LJ - v140 - i20 - Dec 1 2015 - p129(1) [51-500]

Soss, Joe - *Disciplining the Poor: Neoliberal Paternalism and the Persistent Power of Race*
    SF - v93 - i3 - March 2015 - pe71 [501+]

Sotiropoulos, Karen - *Staging Race: Black Performers in Turn of the Century America*
    J Urban H - v41 - i1 - Jan 2015 - p157-8 [501+]

Sotomayor, Sonia - *My Beloved World*
    Forbes - v196 - i6 - Nov 2 2015 - p42(1) [501+]

Souders, Taryn - *Dead Possums are Fair Game*
    c KR - Sept 15 2015 - pNA [51-500]

Souhami, Diana - *Gwendolen*
    TLS - i5857 - July 3 2015 - p19(2) [501+]
    BL - v111 - i14 - March 15 2015 - p48(1) [51-500]
    KR - Jan 1 2015 - pNA [51-500]

Souhami, Jessica - *Honk Honk! Hold Tight! (Illus. by Souhami, Jessica)*
    c Sch Lib - v63 - i4 - Winter 2015 - p222(1) [51-500]
    c SLJ - v61 - i10 - Oct 2015 - p84(1) [51-500]

Souiller, Didier - *Manierisme et Litterature*
    Six Ct J - v46 - i1 - Spring 2015 - p216-217 [501+]

Soukup, Pavel - *Jan Hus: Prediger - Reformator - Martyrer*
    HNet - August 2015 - pNA [501+]

Soukup, Ruth - *Unstuffed*
    PW - v262 - i42 - Oct 19 2015 - p36(1) [51-500]

Soule, Emily Berquist - *The Bishop's Utopia: Envisioning Improvement in Colonial Peru*
    AHR - v120 - i4 - Oct 2015 - p1530-1531 [501+]
    CHR - v101 - i4 - Autumn 2015 - p961(2) [501+]
    JIH - v45 - i4 - Spring 2015 - p600-602 [501+]

Soule, Maris - *A Killer Past*
    PW - v262 - i31 - August 3 2015 - p38(1) [51-500]

Souleimanov, Emil - *Understanding Ethnopolitical Conflict: Karabakh, South Ossetia, and Abkhazia Wars Reconsidered*
    E-A St - v67 - i9 - Nov 2015 - p1514(2) [501+]

Soulieres, Robert - *Hier, tu m'aimais encore*
    y Res Links - v20 - i5 - June 2015 - p44(1) [51-500]

Soulsby, Nick - *I Found My Friends: The Oral History of Nirvana*
    BL - v111 - i11 - Feb 1 2015 - p9(1) [51-500]
    KR - Jan 15 2015 - pNA [51-500]
    LJ - v140 - i3 - Feb 15 2015 - p102(1) [501+]

Sousa, Frank - *The Tree of Young Dreamers*
    SPBW - August 2015 - pNA [51-500]

Sousanis, Nick - *Unflattening*
    NS - v144 - i5282 - Oct 2 2015 - p79(1) [501+]
    PW - v262 - i11 - March 16 2015 - p72(1) [51-500]

South, Robert - *Musica Incantans*
    Sev Cent N - v73 - i1-2 - Spring-Summer 2015 - p78(3) [501+]

South, Sheri Cobb - *Dinner Most Deadly*
    KR - August 1 2015 - pNA [501+]

Southall, Richard - *Haunted Plantations of the South*
    LJ - v140 - i9 - May 15 2015 - p93(2) [51-500]

Southard, John - *Defend and Befriend: The U.S. Marine Corps and Combined Action Platoons in Vietnam*
    AHR - v120 - i3 - June 2015 - p1072-1073 [501+]

Southard, Susan - *Nagasaki: Life after Nuclear War*
    CSM - July 30 2015 - pNA [501+]
    KR - April 15 2015 - pNA [501+]
    LJ - v140 - i9 - May 15 2015 - p92(1) [51-500]
    NY - v91 - i24 - August 24 2015 - p73 [51-500]
    NYTBR - August 2 2015 - p9(L) [501+]
    PW - v262 - i20 - May 18 2015 - p76(1) [51-500]

The Southern African Historical Society: 25th Biennial Conference "Unsettling Stories and Unstable Subjects"
    HNet - Sept 2015 - pNA [501+]

Southern, Nile - *Yours in Haste and Adoration: Selected Letters of Terry Southern*
    KR - Nov 1 2015 - pNA [501+]
    NYT - Dec 16 2015 - pC1(L) [501+]

Southon, Nicolas - *Francis Poulenc: Articles and Interviews - Notes from the Heart*
    Notes - v72 - i1 - Sept 2015 - p168(3) [501+]

Southworth, John - *Daydreams for Night (Illus. by Ouimet, David)*
    c CH Bwatch - March 2015 - pNA [51-500]
    PW - v262 - i4 - Jan 26 2015 - p171(1) [501+]
    c SLJ - v61 - i3 - March 2015 - p144(1) [501+]

Soutphommasane, Tim - *The Virtuous Citizen: Patriotism in a Multicultural Society*
    ERS - v38 - i3 - March 2015 - p538(3) [501+]

Soutter, Nicholas Lamar - *Confessions of a Sin Eater*
    KR - April 1 2015 - pNA [51-500]

Souza, George Bryan - *Portuguese, Dutch, and Chinese in Maritime Asia, c. 1585-1800*
    JEH - v75 - i2 - June 2015 - p612-613 [501+]
    Six Ct J - v46 - i2 - Summer 2015 - p396-398 [501+]

Sovacool, Benjamin K. - *Energy & Ethics: Justice and the Global Energy Challenge*
    T&C - v56 - i2 - April 2015 - p569-570 [501+]

Sowards, Steven W. - *Guide to Reference in Business and Economics*
    R&USQ - v54 - i4 - Summer 2015 - p72(1) [501+]

Sowell, Thomas - *Knowledge and Decisions*
    Nat R - v67 - i21 - Nov 19 2015 - p75(2) [501+]
Wealth, Poverty and Politics: An International Perspective
    BL - v111 - i22 - August 1 2015 - p10(1) [51-500]
    KR - June 15 2015 - pNA [501+]
    LJ - v140 - i11 - June 15 2015 - p96(2) [51-500]
    PW - v262 - i22 - June 1 2015 - p51(2) [51-500]

Soyer, Francois - *Popularizing Anti-Semitism in Early Modern Spain and Its Empire: Francisco de Torrejoncillo and the Centinela contra Judios 1674*
    Ren Q - v68 - i3 - Fall 2015 - p1056-1057 [501+]
    Six Ct J - v46 - i1 - Spring 2015 - p156-157 [501+]

Soziale Ungleichheit im Visier. Images von 'Armut' und 'Reichtum' in West und Ost nach 1945
    HNet - March 2015 - pNA [501+]

Sozialgeschichte des Todes
    HNet - Feb 2015 - pNA [501+]

Spadaro, Antonio - *A Big Heart Open to God: A Conversation with Pope Francis*
    NYRB - v62 - i3 - Feb 19 2015 - p11(3) [501+]
Cybertheology: Thinking Christianity in the Era of the Internet
    AM - v212 - i18 - May 25 2015 - p33(3) [501+]
    Bwatch - Feb 2015 - pNA [501+]

Spagna, Ana Maria - *100 Skills You'll Need for the End of the World (as We Know It)*
    Bwatch - August 2015 - pNA [51-500]

Spahr, Juliana - *That Winter the Wolf Came*
    NYTBR - August 30 2015 - p20(L) [501+]
    PW - v262 - i33 - August 17 2015 - p50(1) [51-500]

Spalding, Amy - *Kissing Ted Callahan (and Other Guys)*
    y HB Guide - v26 - i2 - Fall 2015 - p140(1) [51-500]
    y KR - Jan 15 2015 - pNA [51-500]
    y PW - v262 - i7 - Feb 16 2015 - p182(1) [51-500]
    y SLJ - v61 - i2 - Feb 2015 - p109(1) [51-500]
    y VOYA - v38 - i1 - April 2015 - p70(2) [51-500]
The New Guy (and Other Senior Year Distractions)
    y KR - Jan 1 2016 - pNA [51-500]

Spaltenstein, F. - *Commentaire des fragments dramatiques de Naevius*
    Class R - v65 - i1 - April 2015 - p110-111 [501+]

Spanagel, David I. - *DeWitt Clinton & Amos Eaton: Geology and Power in Early New York*
    AHR - v120 - i1 - Feb 2015 - p240-241 [501+]
    JAH - v102 - i1 - June 2015 - p246-247 [501+]

Spang, Rebecca L. - *Stuff and Money in the Time of the French Revolution*
    Spec - v327 - i9730 - Feb 21 2015 - p38(2) [501+]
    TLS - i5854 - June 12 2015 - p13(1) [501+]
    TLS - i5854 - June 12 2015 - p27(1) [501+]

Spaniens Stadte - Moderne Urbanitat seit 2000 Jahren (II): Mittelalter und Fruhe Neuzeit
    HNet - June 2015 - pNA [501+]

Spann, Susan - *Flask of the Drunken Master*
    KR - May 15 2015 - pNA [501+]
    PW - v262 - i21 - May 25 2015 - p37(1) [501+]

Spannenberger, Norbert - *Ein Raum im Wandel: Die Osmanisch-Habsburgische Grenzregion vom 16. bis zum 18. Jahrhundert*
    HNet - Feb 2015 - pNA [501+]
Frieden und Konfliktmanagement in interkulturellen Raumen: Das Osmanische Reich und die Habsurgermonarchie in der Fruhen Neuzeit
    Six Ct J - v46 - i3 - Fall 2015 - p839-841 [501+]

Spar, Myles O. - *Integrative Men's Health*
    LJ - v140 - i2 - Feb 1 2015 - p40(3) [501+]

Spargo, Sue - *Stitches to Savor*
    Bwatch - Oct 2015 - pNA [51-500]

Sparhawk, Bud - *Distant Seas*
    Analog - v135 - i9 - Sept 2015 - p107(2) [501+]
    PW - v262 - i10 - March 9 2015 - p56(2) [51-500]

Spark, Muriel - *The Driver's Seat*
    TimHES - i2184 - Jan 1 2015 - p63(1) [501+]

Sparkes, Ali - *Car-Jacked*
    y Sch Lib - v63 - i4 - Winter 2015 - p233(1) [51-500]

Sparks, Amber - *The Unfinished World*
    BL - v112 - i7 - Dec 1 2015 - p26(1) [51-500]
    KR - Nov 15 2015 - pNA [51-500]
    PW - v262 - i48 - Nov 30 2015 - p36(1) [51-500]

Sparks, Chris - *Heresy, Inquisition and Life Cycle in Medieval Languedoc*
    Med R - March 2015 - pNA(NA) [501+]

Sparks, Randy J. - *Where the Negroes are Masters: An African Port in the Era of the Slave Trade*
    JAH - v102 - i1 - June 2015 - p219-220 [501+]
    JSH - v81 - i2 - May 2015 - p434(3) [501+]

Sparrow, Bartholomew - *The Strategist: Brent Scowcroft and the Call of National Security*
    Parameters - v45 - i1 - Spring 2015 - p144(2) [501+]
    Nat R - v67 - i6 - April 6 2015 - p41 [501+]
    NYTBR - March 8 2015 - p24(L) [501+]

Sparrow, Leilani - *My First Day (Illus. by Taylor, Dan)*
    c KR - June 1 2015 - pNA [501+]
    c SLJ - v61 - i8 - August 2015 - p57(2) [51-500]

Spasenic, Jelena - *The Shadows of the Past: A Study of Life-World and Identity of Serbian Youth after the Milosevic Regime*
    HNet - May 2015 - pNA [501+]

Spears, Ellen Griffith - *Baptized in PCBs: Race, Pollution, and Justice in an All-American Town*
    AHR - v120 - i3 - June 2015 - p1041-1042 [501+]
    HNet - Oct 2015 - pNA [501+]
    JAH - v101 - i4 - March 2015 - p1344(1) [501+]

Spears, Kat - *Breakaway*
    y BL - v112 - i2 - Sept 15 2015 - p63(1) [51-500]
    y KR - July 15 2015 - pNA [51-500]
    y PW - v262 - i49 - Dec 2 2015 - p88(2) [51-500]
    y SLJ - v61 - i8 - August 2015 - p111(1) [51-500]
    y VOYA - v38 - i4 - Oct 2015 - p62(2) [51-500]
Sway (Read by Podehl, Nick). Audiobook Review
    c BL - v111 - i14 - March 15 2015 - p24(2) [51-500]
Sway
    y HB Guide - v26 - i1 - Spring 2015 - p124(1) [51-500]

Specht, Mary Helen - *Migratory Animals*
    NYTBR - March 15 2015 - p12(L) [501+]

Speck, Katie - *Maybelle Goes to School (Illus. by de Tagyos, Paul Ratz)*
    c BL - v111 - i19-20 - June 1 2015 - p96(1) [51-500]
    c HB Guide - v26 - i2 - Fall 2015 - p71(1) [51-500]
Maybelle Goes to School (Illus. by Tagyos, Paul Ratz)
    c SLJ - v61 - i4 - April 2015 - p139(1) [501+]

Speck, Maria - *Simply Ancient Grains: Fresh and Flavorful Whole Grain Recipes for Living Well*
    LJ - v140 - i7 - April 15 2015 - p112(1) [51-500]

Speckhardt, Roy - *Creating Change through Humanism*
    Hum - v75 - i5 - Sept-Oct 2015 - p40(2) [501+]

Spector, J. Michael - *The SAGE Encyclopedia of Educational Technology, 2 vols.*
    LJ - v140 - i10 - June 1 2015 - p133(2) [501+]

Spector, Neil - *Gone in a Heartbeat: A Physician's Search for True Healing*
    SPBW - April 2015 - pNA [501+]

Spector, Stephen - *May I Quote You on That? A Guide to Grammar and Usage*
    y BL - v111 - i21 - July 1 2015 - p11(2) [51-500]

Spector, Tim - *The Diet Myth: The Real Science behind What We Eat*
    KR - July 1 2015 - pNA [501+]
    PW - v262 - i29 - July 20 2015 - p184(2) [51-500]

Spector, Todd - *How to Pee: Potty Training for Boys (Illus. by Chung, Arree)*
    c HB Guide - v26 - i2 - Fall 2015 - p184(1) [51-500]
    c BL - v111 - i16 - April 15 2015 - p44(1) [51-500]
    c CCB-B - v68 - i11 - July-August 2015 - p568(1) [51-500]
    c HB - v91 - i2 - March-April 2015 - p126(1) [51-500]
    c KR - Feb 15 2015 - pNA [51-500]
How to Pee: Potty Training for Girls (Illus. by Chung, Arree)
    c KR - Jan 1 2016 - pNA [51-500]

Speerstra, Hylke - *Op klompen troch de dessa*
    WLT - v89 - i5 - Sept-Oct 2015 - p68(2) [501+]

Speerstra, Karen - *The Divine Art of Dying: How to Live Well While Dying*
    CC - v132 - i21 - Oct 14 2015 - p34(2) [501+]

Spellenberg, Richard - *Trees of Western North America*
    Bks & Cult - v21 - i6 - Nov-Dec 2015 - p18(2) [501+]

Spellman, Paul N. - *Old 300: Gone to Texas*
    Roundup M - v22 - i3 - Feb 2015 - p25(1) [501+]
    Roundup M - v22 - i6 - August 2015 - p40(2) [501+]

Spence, Michael - *The Bus Driver's Threnody*
    NAR - v300 - i2 - Spring 2015 - p44(1) [501+]

Spencer, Alan - *The Doorway*
    BL - v111 - i22 - August 1 2015 - p42(1) [51-500]

Spencer, Andrew M. - *Nobility and Kingship in Medieval England: The Earls and Edward I, 1272-1307*
    HER - v130 - i542 - Feb 2015 - p163(2) [501+]

Spencer, Charles - *Killers of the King: The Men Who Dared to Execute Charles I*
    TLS - i5860 - July 24 2015 - p24(1) [501+]

Spencer, Jamere A. Brown - *Manifest Destiny: The Path towards Wisdom*
    RVBW - Sept 2015 - pNA [51-500]

Spencer, Joel - *Asymptopia*
    SIAM Rev - v57 - i2 - June 2015 - p314-314 [501+]

Spencer, Leon P. - *Toward an African Church in Mozambique: Kamba Simango and the Protestant Community in Manica and Sofala, 1892-1945*
    IBMR - v39 - i3 - July 2015 - p160(1) [501+]

Spencer, Octavia - *The Sweetest Heist in History (Illus. by Spencer, Octavia). Audiobook Review*
    c SLJ - v61 - i7 - July 2015 - p48(1) [51-500]
The Sweetest Heist in History (Illus. by To, Vivienne)
    c KR - Jan 1 2015 - pNA [51-500]
    c HB Guide - v26 - i2 - Fall 2015 - p103(1) [51-500]

Spencer, Sally - *Best Served Cold*
    BL - v111 - i21 - July 1 2015 - p34(1) [51-500]
    KR - June 1 2015 - pNA [51-500]
    PW - v262 - i25 - June 22 2015 - p122(1) [51-500]
Thicker Than Water
    KR - Dec 1 2015 - pNA [51-500]
    PW - v262 - i48 - Nov 30 2015 - p42(1) [51-500]

Spencer, Sally A. - *Making the Common Core Writing Standards Accessible through Universal Design for Learning*
    Bwatch - Oct 2015 - pNA [51-500]

Spencer, Stephanie - *Alumni Voices: The Changing Experience of Higher Education*
    TimHES - i2222 - Sept 24 2015 - p41(1) [501+]

Spender, Matthew - *A House in St. John's Wood: In Search of My Parents*
    BL - v112 - i3 - Oct 1 2015 - p10(2) [51-500]
    KR - August 15 2015 - pNA [501+]
    NS - v144 - i5281 - Sept 25 2015 - p79(1) [51-500]
    TLS - i5877 - Nov 20 2015 - p10(1) [501+]

Spengler, Jessica - *White Magic: The Age of Paper*
    TimHES - i2186 - Jan 15 2015 - p53(1) [501+]

Spentzou, Efrossini - *The Roman Poetry of Love. Elegy and Politics in a Time of Revolution*
    Class R - v65 - i1 - April 2015 - p136-138 [501+]

Spera, Keith - *Groove Interrupted: Loss, Renewal, and the Music of New Orleans*
    BL - v112 - i5 - Nov 1 2015 - p18(2) [501+]

Sperb, Jason - *Disney's Most Notorious Film: Race, Convergence, and the Hidden Histories of Song of the South*
    Historian - v77 - i1 - Spring 2015 - p143(2) [501+]

Sperling, Jutta Gisela - *Medieval and Renaissance Lactations: Images, Rhetorics, Practices*
    Six Ct J - v46 - i1 - Spring 2015 - p139-3 [501+]

Sperling, Matthew - *Visionary Philology: Geoffrey Hill and the Study of Words*
    RES - v66 - i275 - June 2015 - p597-599 [501+]
Sperling, Stefan - *Reasons of Conscience: The Bioethics Debate in Germany*
    MAQ - v29 - i2 - June 2015 - pb7-b8 [501+]
Sperling, Valerie - *Sex, Politics and Putin: Political Legitimacy in Russia*
    Wom R Bks - v32 - i5 - Sept-Oct 2015 - p7(3) [501+]
Sperlinger, Tom - *Romeo and Juliet in Palestine: Teaching under Occupation*
    NS - v144 - i5269 - July 3 2015 - p46(3) [501+]
Speroni, Sperone - *Canace, 1542*
    Six Ct J - v46 - i3 - Fall 2015 - p733-734 [501+]
Sperrazza, Diana - *My Townie Heart*
    SPBW - Sept 2015 - pNA [51-500]
    SPBW - Nov 2015 - pNA [51-500]
Sperring, Mark - *How Many Sleeps 'til Christmas?*
    c   HB Guide - v26 - i1 - Spring 2015 - p46(1) [51-500]
    I'll Catch You If You Fall (Illus. by Marlow, Layn)
    c   KR - Dec 15 2015 - pNA [51-500]
    c   Sch Lib - v63 - i4 - Winter 2015 - p222(1) [51-500]
    Mabel and Me: Best of Friends (Illus. by Warburton, Sarah)
    c   BL - v111 - i16 - April 15 2015 - p51(2) [51-500]
    c   KR - Jan 15 2015 - pNA [51-500]
    Max and the Won't Go to Bed Show (Illus. by Warburton, Sarah)
    c   CH Bwatch - Jan 2015 - pNA [51-500]
    c   HB Guide - v26 - i1 - Spring 2015 - p47(1) [51-500]
    Your Hand in My Hand (Illus. by Teckentrup, Britta)
    c   BL - v112 - i6 - Nov 15 2015 - p59(1) [51-500]
    c   KR - Sept 1 2015 - pNA [51-500]
    c   PW - v262 - i29 - July 20 2015 - p192(1) [501+]
    c   SLJ - v61 - i10 - Oct 2015 - p71(1) [51-500]
Spetrino, Bill - *The Great American Dividend Machine: How an Outsider Became the Undisputed Champ of Wall Street*
    RVBW - March 2015 - pNA [501+]
Speyer, Erik - *The Adventures of Kubi (Illus. by Speyer, Erik)*
    c   KR - July 15 2015 - pNA [51-500]
Spicer, Andrew - *Lutheran Churches in Early Modern Europe*
    Six Ct J - v46 - i1 - Spring 2015 - p129-131 [501+]
Spicer, Jake - *Draw Faces in 15 Minutes*
    LJ - v140 - i13 - August 1 2015 - p94(1) [51-500]
Spickard, Paul - *Multiple Identities: Migrants, Ethnicity, and Membership*
    CS - v44 - i6 - Nov 2015 - p855-857 [501+]
    Race in Mind: Critical Essays
    PW - v262 - i39 - Sept 28 2015 - p82(1) [51-500]
Spidermania: Friends on the Web
    c   PW - v262 - i35 - August 31 2015 - p90(2) [501+]
Spiegel, Nadja - *Sometimes I Lie and Sometimes I Don't*
    KR - July 15 2015 - pNA [51-500]
Spiegel, Nina S. - *Embodying Hebrew Culture: Aesthetics, Athletics, and Dance in the Jewish Community of Mandate Palestine*
    Dance RJ - v47 - i1 - April 2015 - p111-115 [501+]
Spiegelhalter, David - *Sex by Numbers: What Statistics Can Tell Us about Sexual Behaviour*
    TimHES - i2207 - June 11 2015 - p54(1) [501+]
Spiegelman, Nadja - *Lost in NYC: A Subway Adventure (Illus. by Garcia Sanchez, Sergio)*
    c   KR - Feb 15 2015 - pNA [51-500]
    c   SLJ - v61 - i4 - April 2015 - p151(1) [51-500]
    Lost in NYC: A Subway Adventure (Illus. by Sanchez, Sergio Garcia)
    c   CCB-B - v68 - i10 - June 2015 - p477(2) [501+]
    c   HB Guide - v26 - i2 - Fall 2015 - p103(1) [51-500]
    c   PW - v262 - i49 - Dec 2 2015 - p86(1) [51-500]
    c   BL - v111 - i16 - April 15 2015 - p41(1) [51-500]
    c   HB - v91 - i4 - July-August 2015 - p146(2) [51-500]
    c   NYTBR - May 10 2015 - p21(L) [501+]
    Perdidos en NYC: Una aventura en el metro (Illus. by Moral, Lola)
    c   HB Guide - v26 - i2 - Fall 2015 - p162(1) [51-500]
Spieler, Matthew - *The U.S. House of Representatives*
    KR - Sept 15 2015 - pNA [51-500]
Spielman, David G. - *The Katrina Decade: Images of an Altered City (Illus. by Davis, Jack)*
    NYTBR - August 9 2015 - p4(L) [501+]
    LJ - v140 - i12 - July 1 2015 - p100(2) [51-500]
    New Or - v49 - i10 - July 2015 - p40(1) [501+]

Spielman, Lori Nelson - *Sweet Forgiveness*
    BL - v111 - i17 - May 1 2015 - p78(1) [51-500]
    KR - April 15 2015 - pNA [51-500]
    LJ - v140 - i9 - May 15 2015 - p77(1) [51-500]
Spier, Peter - *The Book of Jonah*
    c   HB Guide - v26 - i2 - Fall 2015 - p150(1) [51-500]
    The Fox Went Out on a Chilly Night (Illus. by Spier, Peter)
    c   HB - v91 - i3 - May-June 2015 - p140(2) [51-500]
    c   HB Guide - v26 - i2 - Fall 2015 - p194(1) [51-500]
    We the People: The Constitution of the United States
    c   HB Guide - v26 - i1 - Spring 2015 - p139(2) [51-500]
Spiers, Edward M. - *A Military History of Scotland*
    HER - v130 - i543 - Fall 2015 - p506(4) [501+]
Spillane, Joseph F. - *Coxsackie: The Life and Death of Prison Reform*
    AHR - v120 - i2 - April 2015 - p651-652 [501+]
Spillane, Mickey - *Kill Me, Darling*
    BL - v111 - i14 - March 15 2015 - p46(1) [51-500]
    PW - v262 - i4 - Jan 26 2015 - p151(1) [51-500]
    The Legend of Caleb York
    BL - v111 - i18 - May 15 2015 - p30(1) [51-500]
Spillman, Ken - *Jake's Balloon Blast (Illus. by Nixon, Chris)*
    c   CH Bwatch - Oct 2015 - pNA [51-500]
Spilman, Rick - *The Shantyman*
    KR - July 1 2015 - pNA [501+]
Spilsbury, Louise - *Oceans of the World*
    c   HB Guide - v26 - i2 - Fall 2015 - p214(1) [51-500]
    Robots in Industry
    c   BL - v112 - i6 - Nov 15 2015 - p42(1) [501+]
    Robots in Law Enforcement
    c   BL - v112 - i6 - Nov 15 2015 - p42(1) [501+]
    Robots in Space
    c   BL - v112 - i6 - Nov 15 2015 - p42(1) [501+]
Spina, Alessandro - *The Confines of the Shadow*
    Nation - v301 - i16 - Oct 19 2015 - p30(4) [501+]
    I confinni dell'ombra
    Nation - v301 - i16 - Oct 19 2015 - p30(4) [501+]
Spindler, Erica - *Magnolia Dawn*
    BL - v111 - i22 - August 1 2015 - p41(1) [51-500]
Spinelli, Eileen - *God's Amazing World (Illus. by Florian, Melanie)*
    c   CH Bwatch - Feb 2015 - pNA [51-500]
    Thankful (Illus. by Preston, Archie)
    c   KR - June 15 2015 - pNA [51-500]
    c   SLJ - v61 - i12 - Dec 2015 - p96(1) [51-500]
Spinelli, Jerry - *Mama Seeton's Whistle (Illus. by Pham, LeUyen)*
    c   CCB-B - v69 - i1 - Sept 2015 - p56(1) [51-500]
    c   HB Guide - v26 - i2 - Fall 2015 - p52(1) [51-500]
    c   PW - v262 - i49 - Dec 2 2015 - p30(2) [51-500]
Spinozzi, Paola - *'The Germ': Origins and Progenies of Pre-Raphaelite Interart Aesthetics*
    MLR - v110 - i3 - July 2015 - p845-846 [501+]
Spiotta, Dana - *Innocents and Others*
    KR - Jan 1 2016 - pNA [501+]
    PW - v262 - i51 - Dec 14 2015 - p53(1) [501+]
Spira, Timothy P. - *Waterfalls and Wildflowers in the Southern Appalachians: Thirty Great Hikes*
    LJ - v140 - i7 - April 15 2015 - p121(1) [51-500]
Spires, Ashley - *Fluffy Strikes Back*
    c   KR - Jan 1 2016 - pNA [51-500]
    Over-Scheduled Andrew (Illus. by Spires, Ashley)
    c   KR - Dec 1 2015 - pNA [51-500]
Spirito, Louis - *Gimme Shelter: A Damaged Pit Bull, an Angry Man, and How They Saved Each Other*
    PW - v262 - i24 - June 15 2015 - p78(1) [51-500]
Spiro, Anna - *Absolutely Beautiful Things: Decorating Inspiration for a Bright and Colourful Life*
    LJ - v140 - i17 - Oct 15 2015 - p91(1) [51-500]
Spiro, Gyorgy - *Captivity*
    KR - Sept 1 2015 - pNA [501+]
    LJ - v140 - i19 - Nov 15 2015 - p80(1) [51-500]
    PW - v262 - i38 - Sept 21 2015 - p51(1) [501+]
Spitler, Sue - *1,001 Delicious Soups and Stews: From Elegant Classics to Hearty One-Pot Meals, 4th ed.*
    Bwatch - March 2015 - pNA [501+]
Spittler, Gerd - *African Children at Work: Working and Learning in Growing Up for Life*
    JRAI - v21 - i1 - March 2015 - p212(2) [501+]
Spitz, Marc - *Twee: The Gentle Revolution in Music, Books, Television, Fashion, and Film*
    TLS - i5838 - Feb 20 2015 - p13(1) [501+]
Spitzer, Katja - *How Many Legs?*
    c   KR - Nov 15 2015 - pNA [51-500]
    Let's Go Outside
    c   KR - Nov 15 2015 - pNA [51-500]
    c   Sch Lib - v63 - i4 - Winter 2015 - p224(1) [51-500]

Spitzer, Mark - *Return of the Gar*
    RVBW - May 2015 - pNA [51-500]
Spitzer, Robert J. - *Guns across America: Reconciling Gun Rules and Rights*
    LJ - v140 - i8 - May 1 2015 - p91(1) [51-500]
Spivack, Kathleen - *Unspeakable Things*
    BL - v112 - i4 - Oct 15 2015 - p29(1) [501+]
    KR - Sept 15 2015 - pNA [501+]
    LJ - v140 - i17 - Oct 15 2015 - p82(2) [51-500]
    PW - v262 - i45 - Nov 9 2015 - p34(1) [51-500]
Spivakovsky, Claire - *Racialised Correctional Governance: The Mutual Constructions of Race and Criminal Justice*
    ERS - v38 - i8 - August 2015 - p1460(3) [501+]
Spivey, Donald - *Black Pearls of Wisdom: Voicing the African-American Journey for Freedom, Empowerment, and the Future*
    JSH - v81 - i4 - Nov 2015 - p1057(2) [501+]
Spjut, Stefan - *The Shapeshifters*
    BL - v111 - i19-20 - June 1 2015 - p65(1) [51-500]
    LJ - v140 - i9 - May 15 2015 - p77(1) [51-500]
    PW - v262 - i14 - April 6 2015 - p42(1) [51-500]
Spoerer, Mark - *Neue deutsche Wirtschaftsgeschichte des 20. Jahrhunderts*
    HNet - May 2015 - pNA [501+]
Spohn, Cassia - *Policing and Prosecuting Sexual Assault: Inside the Criminal Justice System*
    CS - v44 - i4 - July 2015 - p559-561 [501+]
Spohnholz, Jesse - *Exile and Religious Identity, 1500-1800*
    Six Ct J - v46 - i2 - Summer 2015 - p416-417 [501+]
Spolsky, Bernard - *The languages of the Jews: A sociolinguistic history*
    Lang Soc - v44 - i5 - Nov 2015 - p736-740 [501+]
Spong, Martha - *There's a Woman in the Pulpit: Christian Clergywomen Share Their Hard Days, Holy Moments and the Healing Power of Humor*
    BL - v111 - i18 - May 15 2015 - p4(1) [51-500]
Sponsler, Claire - *The Queen's Dumbshows: John Lydgate and the Making of Early Theater*
    AHR - v120 - i4 - Oct 2015 - p1545-1546 [501+]
    PQ - v94 - i1-2 - Wntr-Spring 2015 - p190(5) [501+]
    Ren Q - v68 - i2 - Summer 2015 - p767-769 [501+]
    RES - v66 - i275 - June 2015 - p572-573 [501+]
    Theat J - v67 - i1 - March 2015 - p147-148 [501+]
Spoo, Robert - *Without Copyrights: Piracy, Publishing, and the Public Domain*
    Clio - v44 - i2 - Spring 2015 - p288-292 [501+]
Spooner, Mary Helen - *The General's Slow Retreat: Chile after Pinochet*
    Ams - v72 - i3 - July 2015 - p516(3) [501+]
Spooner, Meagan - *Lark Ascending*
    y   HB Guide - v26 - i1 - Spring 2015 - p124(1) [51-500]
    y   Sch Lib - v63 - i1 - Spring 2015 - p59(1) [51-500]
    This Shattered World
    y   CH Bwatch - March 2015 - pNA [51-500]
Spores, Ronald - *The Mixtecs of Oaxaca: Ancient Times to the Present*
    Am Ind CRJ - v39 - i1 - Wntr 2015 - p140-142 [501+]
Spotlight on Space Science
    c   BL - v111 - i21 - July 1 2015 - p50(1) [501+]
Spoto, Donald - *A Girl's Got to Breathe: The Life of Teresa Wright*
    PW - v262 - i50 - Dec 7 2015 - p76(1) [51-500]
Spotswood, Jessica - *Sisters' Fate*
    y   HB Guide - v26 - i1 - Spring 2015 - p124(1) [51-500]
    A Tyranny of Petticoats: 15 Stories of Belles, Bank Robbers & Other Badass Girls
    y   KR - Jan 1 2016 - pNA [51-500]
    y   PW - v262 - i51 - Dec 14 2015 - p87(1) [51-500]
Spotte, Stephen - *My Watery Self: Memoirs of a Marine Scientist*
    LJ - v140 - i3 - Feb 15 2015 - p126(2) [51-500]
    SPBW - April 2015 - pNA [501+]
Spradlin, Michael P. - *Into the Killing Seas*
    c   BL - v111 - i19-20 - June 1 2015 - p105(1) [51-500]
    c   CCB-B - v69 - i1 - Sept 2015 - p56(2) [51-500]
    c   SLJ - v61 - i5 - May 2015 - p106(1) [51-500]
Spratt, R.A. - *Friday Barnes, Girl Detective (Illus. by Cosier, Phil)*
    c   KR - Oct 1 2015 - pNA [51-500]
    c   SLJ - v61 - i10 - Oct 2015 - p95(2) [51-500]
    Nanny Piggins and the Runaway Lion
    c   HB Guide - v26 - i1 - Spring 2015 - p93(1) [51-500]

Spreizer, Christa - *Discovering Women's History: German-Speaking Journalists*
    HNet - Feb 2015 - pNA [501+]

Sprigg, Christopher St. John - *Death of an Airman*
    BL - v111 - i21 - July 1 2015 - p36(1) [51-500]

Spring, Joel - *A Perfect Life*
    KR - Dec 1 2015 - pNA [501+]

Springer, Paul J. - *Cyber Warfare: A Reference Handbook*
    y BL - v111 - i17 - May 1 2015 - p62(1) [51-500]
    LJ - v140 - i9 - May 15 2015 - p105(1) [51-500]
Transforming Civil War Prisons: Lincoln, Lieber, and the Politics of Captivity
    J Mil H - v79 - i1 - Jan 2015 - p215-216 [501+]

Springer, Philipp - *Bahnhof der Tranen: Die Grenzubergangsstelle Berlin-Friedrichstrasse*
    HNet - March 2015 - pNA [501+]

Springett, Martin - *Kate & Pippin: An Unlikely Friendship (Illus. by Springett, Isobel)*
    c HB Guide - v26 - i2 - Fall 2015 - p182(1) [51-500]
    c SLJ - v61 - i5 - May 2015 - p94(1) [51-500]

Springstubb, Tricia - *Cody and the Fountain of Happiness (Read by Ross, Natalie). Audiobook Review*
    c SLJ - v61 - i9 - Sept 2015 - p58(1) [51-500]
Cody and the Fountain of Happiness (Illus. by Wheeler, Eliza)
    c BL - v111 - i12 - Feb 15 2015 - p85(1) [51-500]
    c CCB-B - v68 - i11 - July-August 2015 - p568(2) [51-500]
    c CH Bwatch - July 2015 - pNA [51-500]
    c HB - v91 - i2 - March-April 2015 - p109(2) [51-500]
    c HB Guide - v26 - i2 - Fall 2015 - p72(1) [51-500]
    c KR - Jan 15 2015 - pNA [51-500]
    c PW - v262 - i5 - Feb 2 2015 - p61(1) [51-500]
    c SLJ - v61 - i2 - Feb 2015 - p80(1) [51-500]
Moonpenny Island (Illus. by Ford, Gilbert)
    c BL - v111 - i11 - Feb 1 2015 - p52(1) [51-500]
    c CCB-B - v68 - i6 - Feb 2015 - p332(1) [51-500]
    c HB - v91 - i1 - Jan-Feb 2015 - p89(1) [51-500]
    c HB Guide - v26 - i2 - Fall 2015 - p103(1) [51-500]
    c NYTBR - Feb 8 2015 - p23(L) [501+]
    c PW - v262 - i49 - Dec 2 2015 - p72(1) [51-500]

Sprinkle, John H., Jr. - *Crafting Preservation Criteria: The National Register of Historic Places and American Historic Preservation*
    JAH - v102 - i1 - June 2015 - p207-208 [501+]

Sprout, Leslie A. - *The Musical Legacy of Wartime France*
    JMH - v87 - i3 - Sept 2015 - p740(3) [501+]
    Notes - v72 - i1 - Sept 2015 - p157(6) [501+]

Sprunk, Jon - *Storm and Steel*
    KR - May 15 2015 - pNA [51-500]
    LJ - v140 - i9 - May 15 2015 - p57(4) [51-500]

Spruytenburg, Robert - *The LaSalle Quartet: Conversations with Walter Levin*
    MT - v156 - i1930 - Spring 2015 - p111-114 [501+]

Spry, Greg - *Beyond Cloud Nine*
    PW - v262 - i9 - March 2 2015 - p69(1) [51-500]

Spude, Catherine Holder - *Saloons, Prostitutes, and Temperance in Alaska Territory*
    Reason - v47 - i3 - July 2015 - p68(4) [501+]

Spyridakis, Manos - *The Liminal Worker: An Ethnography of Work, Unemployment and Precariousness in Contemporary Greece*
    CS - v44 - i5 - Sept 2015 - p714-716 [501+]

Squailia, Gabriel - *Dead Boys*
    PW - v262 - i4 - Jan 26 2015 - p152(2) [51-500]

Squatriti, Paolo - *Landscape and Change in Early Medieval Italy: Chestnuts, Economy, and Culture*
    Specu - v90 - i3 - July 2015 - p853-854 [501+]

Squire, Ann O. - *Autism*
    c BL - v112 - i3 - Oct 1 2015 - p44(1) [51-500]

Squire, Corinne - *Living with HIV and ARVs: Three Letter Lives*
    CS - v44 - i6 - Nov 2015 - p857-859 [501+]

Squire, Michael - *The Iliad in a Nutshell. Visualizing Epic on the Roman Context*
    Class R - v65 - i2 - Oct 2015 - p566-570 [501+]

Squires, Catherine R. - *The Post-Racial Mystique: Media and Race in the Twenty-First Century*
    Am St - v54 - i1 - Spring 2015 - p172-173 [501+]

Squires, Jessica - *Building Sanctuary: The Movement to Support Vietnam War Resisters in Canada, 1965-73*
    PHR - v84 - i4 - Nov 2015 - p542(3) [501+]

Squires, Stacey - *West Indian Women's Experience in Los Angeles: The Impact of Politics and the Global Economy*
    CS - v44 - i4 - July 2015 - p580-580 [501+]

Sramek, Marsha - *The Great Grammar Book*
    SPBW - March 2015 - pNA [51-500]

Sriduangkaew, Benjanun - *Scale-Bright*
    PW - v262 - i1 - Jan 5 2015 - p57(1) [51-500]

Srinivasan, Divya - *Little Owl's Day (Illus. by Srinivasan, Divya)*
    c HB Guide - v26 - i2 - Fall 2015 - p19(1) [51-500]

Srivastava, Ashish Kumar - *Stress Biology of Cyanobacteria: Molecular Mechanisms to Cellular Responses*
    QRB - v90 - i1 - March 2015 - p99(1) [51-500]

Srivastava, Ranjana - *A Cancer Companion: An Oncologist's Advice on Diagnosis, Treatment, and Recovery*
    LJ - v140 - i15 - Sept 15 2015 - p97(1) [51-500]

Srivastava, Sanjay - *Sexuality Studies*
    JAS - v74 - i1 - Feb 2015 - p235-236 [51-500]

Srodek-Hart, Guillermo - *Stories*
    NYTBR - Dec 6 2015 - p38(L) [501+]

Srsen, Ivan - *Zagreb Noir*
    PW - v262 - i39 - Sept 28 2015 - p70(1) [51-500]

Srulovich, Itamar - *Honey & Co.: The Cookbook*
    Bwatch - Sept 2015 - pNA [51-500]
    PW - v262 - i16 - April 20 2015 - p71(1) [51-500]

St. Anthony, Jane - *Grace above All*
    y VOYA - v38 - i5 - Dec 2015 - p64(1) [51-500]
Isabelle Day Refuses to Die of a Broken Heart
    y BL - v112 - i1 - Sept 1 2015 - p104(2) [51-500]
    c KR - June 1 2015 - pNA [51-500]
    c PW - v262 - i25 - June 22 2015 - p140(1) [51-500]

St. Aubyn, Edward - *A Clue to the Exit*
    BL - v111 - i22 - August 1 2015 - p27(1) [51-500]
    KR - June 1 2015 - pNA [51-500]
    LJ - v140 - i14 - Sept 1 2015 - p96(1) [51-500]
    NYT - Sept 24 2015 - pC6(L) [501+]
    NYTBR - Sept 6 2015 - p13(L) [501+]
    PW - v262 - i24 - June 15 2015 - p57(1) [51-500]
The Complete Patrick Melrose Novels
    Ent W - i1364 - May 22 2015 - p66(1) [501+]
Lost for Words
    HR - v67 - i4 - Wntr 2015 - p685-692 [501+]
    NYTBR - May 3 2015 - p28(L) [501+]

St. Claire, Roxanne - *They All Fall Down*
    y CCB-B - v68 - i6 - Feb 2015 - p332(1) [51-500]
    y HB Guide - v26 - i1 - Spring 2015 - p122(1) [51-500]

St. James, Cassidy - *Finding a Mate: Animal Companions*
    c CH Bwatch - Feb 2015 - pNA [51-500]

St-Jean, Annie - *Le reve de Sadako*
    c Res Links - v20 - i3 - Feb 2015 - p51(1) [51-500]

St. Jean, Trina - *Blank*
    c KR - Feb 1 2015 - pNA [51-500]
    y Res Links - v20 - i3 - Feb 2015 - p36(1) [51-500]
    y VOYA - v38 - i1 - April 2015 - p71(1) [51-500]
    BL - v111 - i14 - March 15 2015 - p65(1) [51-500]

St. John, Jordon - *Lost Breweries of Toronto*
    Beav - v95 - i3 - June-July 2015 - p59(1) [51-500]

St John, Lauren - *The Glory*
    y Sch Lib - v63 - i2 - Summer 2015 - p121(1) [51-500]

St. John, Ronald Bruce - *Toledo's Peru: Vision and Reality*
    Ams - v72 - i2 - April 2015 - p355(2) [501+]

St. Mary, Robert - *The Orbit Magazine Anthology: Re-Entry*
    RVBW - Oct 2015 - pNA [501+]

Staake, Bob - *My Pet Book*
    c HB Guide - v26 - i1 - Spring 2015 - p47(1) [51-500]

Staat, Gesellschaft und Demokratisierung. Luxemburg im Kurzen 20. Jahrhundert
    HNet - Feb 2015 - pNA [501+]

Staatsaktion im Wunderland: Oper und Festspiel als Medien politischer Reprasentation, 1890-1930
    HNet - April 2015 - pNA [501+]

Stabler, David - *Kid Athletes: True Tales of Childhood from Sports Legends (Illus. by Horner, Doogie)*
    c BL - v112 - i1 - Sept 1 2015 - p98(1) [51-500]
    c KR - Sept 1 2015 - pNA [51-500]
    c CH Bwatch - Nov 2015 - pNA [51-500]
Kid Presidents: True Tales of Childhood from America's Presidents (Illus. by Horner, Doogie)
    c CH Bwatch - Jan 2015 - pNA [51-500]
    c HB Guide - v26 - i1 - Spring 2015 - p198(1) [51-500]

Stace, Lynley - *Hilda Bewildered. E-book Review*
    y SLJ - v61 - i7 - July 2015 - p52(1) [51-500]

Stacey, Shannon - *Controlled Burn. E-book Review*
    PW - v262 - i42 - Oct 19 2015 - p62(1) [51-500]
Heat Exchange
    PW - v262 - i27 - July 6 2015 - p52(1) [51-500]
Under the Lights
    PW - v262 - i14 - April 6 2015 - p46(1) [51-500]

Stach, Reiner - *Kafka: Die fruhen Jahre*
    TLS - i5856 - June 26 2015 - p8(1) [51-500]

Stack, Frank - *Foolbert Funnies: Histories and Other Fictions*
    PW - v262 - i4 - Jan 26 2015 - p157(1) [51-500]

Stack, Steven - *Suicide Movies: Social Patterns 1900-2009*
    SF - v93 - i3 - March 2015 - pe87 [51-500]
    SF - v93 - i3 - March 2015 - pNA [501+]

Stackelberg, Jurgen von - *Voltaire und Friedrich der Grosse*
    Ger Q - v88 - i2 - Spring 2015 - p242(4) [501+]

Stackhouse, John G., Jr. - *Partners in Christ: A Conservative Case for Egalitarianism*
    Ch Today - v59 - i8 - Oct 2015 - p73(1) [501+]

Stacton, David - *Kaliyuga*
    TLS - i5854 - June 12 2015 - p11(1) [501+]
Old Acquaintance
    TLS - i5854 - June 12 2015 - p11(1) [501+]
Sir Williams
    TLS - i5854 - June 12 2015 - p11(1) [501+]

Stadelmann, Amy Marie - *The Super-Smelly Moldy Blob*
    c KR - Jan 1 2016 - pNA [51-500]

Staecker, Del - *Sailor Man: The Troubled Life and Times of J.P. Nunnally, USN*
    RVBW - July 2015 - pNA [51-500]
    SPBW - June 2015 - pNA [51-500]

Stafford, Charles - *Ordinary Ethics in China*
    JRAI - v21 - i3 - Sept 2015 - p692(2) [501+]

Stafford, Tony Jason - *Shaw's Settings: Gardens and Landscapes*
    ILS - v34 - i2 - Spring 2015 - p15(1) [501+]

Stafford, William - *Ask Me: 100 Essential Poems*
    Ant R - v73 - i2 - Spring 2015 - p382(1) [51-500]
    WLT - v89 - i2 - March-April 2015 - p72(1) [501+]

Stagg, J.C.A. - *The War of 1812: Conflict for a Continent*
    HNet - Sept 2015 - pNA(NA) [501+]

Stagliano, Katie - *Katie's Cabbage (Illus. by Martin, Michelle H.)*
    c HB Guide - v26 - i2 - Fall 2015 - p53(1) [51-500]

Stahel, David - *Kiev 1941: Hitler's Battle for Supremacy in the East*
    JMH - v87 - i1 - March 2015 - p161(4) [501+]
Operation Typhoon: Hitler's March on Moscow, October 1941
    JMH - v87 - i1 - March 2015 - p161(4) [501+]

Stahl, Jerry - *OG Dad: Weird Shit Happens When You Don't Die Young*
    BL - v111 - i19-20 - June 1 2015 - p18(1) [51-500]

Stahl, Levi - *The Getaway Car: A Donald Westlake Nonfiction Miscellany*
    NYTBR - Jan 11 2015 - p26(L) [501+]

Stahl, Steve - *Shell Shock*
    BL - v111 - i17 - May 1 2015 - p44(1) [51-500]

Stainback, Kevin - *Documenting Desegregation: Racial and Gender Segregation in Private-Sector Employment since the Civil Rights Act*
    JAH - v102 - i2 - Sept 2015 - p506-508 [501+]

Stainton, Keris - *Counting Stars*
    y Sch Lib - v63 - i4 - Winter 2015 - p254(1) [51-500]
Spotlight on Sunny
    y Sch Lib - v63 - i3 - Autumn 2015 - p186(1) [51-500]

Stainton, Sue - *I Love Dogs! (Illus. by Staake, Bob)*
    c HB Guide - v26 - i1 - Spring 2015 - p16(1) [51-500]

Stakelbeck, Erick - *ISIS Exposed: Beheadings, Slavery, and the Hellish Reality of Radical Islam*
    Bwatch - May 2015 - pNA [51-500]

Staksrud, Elisabeth - *Children in the Online World: Risk, Regulation, Rights*
    CS - v44 - i2 - March 2015 - p254-256 [501+]

Staley, S.R. - *St. Nic, Inc.*
    Reason - v46 - i8 - Jan 2015 - p60(1) [51-500]

Staller, John E. - *Lightning in the Andes and Mesoamerica: Pre-Columbian, Colonial, and Contemporary Perspectives*
    Lat Ant - v26 - i3 - Sept 2015 - p428(2) [501+]

Stalter-Pace, Sunny - *Underground Movements: Modern Culture on the New York City Subway*
    T&C - v56 - i1 - Jan 2015 - p278-279 [501+]

Stamm, Peter - *All Days Are Night*
    Econ - v414 - i8926 - Feb 21 2015 - p81(US) [501+]
    NY - v91 - i4 - March 16 2015 - p83 [51-500]
    NYRB - v62 - i18 - Nov 19 2015 - p51(2) [501+]

Stamp, Emer - *The Unbelievable Top Secret Diary of Pig (Illus. by Stamp, Emer)*
    c HB Guide - v26 - i2 - Fall 2015 - p103(1) [51-500]
    c KR - Jan 1 2015 - pNA [51-500]
    c SLJ - v61 - i2 - Feb 2015 - p80(1) [51-500]

Stamp, Gavin - *Gothic for the Steam Age: An Illustrated Biography of George Gilbert Scott*
    Spec - v329 - i9761 - Sept 26 2015 - p45(1) [501+]
    TimHES - i2229 - Nov 12 2015 - p47(1) [501+]

Stampnitsky, Lisa - *Disciplining Terror: How Experts Invented "Terrorism"*
    CS - v44 - i3 - May 2015 - p420-422 [501+]

Stamps, Veda - *Flexible Wings*
    c KR - June 15 2015 - pNA [501+]

Stan, Lavinia - *Transitional Justice in Post-Communist Romania: The Politics of Memory*
    E-A St - v67 - i7 - Sept 2015 - p1155(2) [501+]

Standage, Tom - *The Victorian Internet: The Remarkable Story of the Telegraph and the Nineteenth Century's On-line Pioneers (Read by Perkins, Derek). Audiobook Review*
    LJ - v140 - i14 - Sept 1 2015 - p69(1) [51-500]

Standiford, Les - *Water to the Angels: William Mulholland, His Monumental Aqueduct, and the Rise of Los Angeles*
    KR - Jan 15 2015 - pNA [501+]
    LJ - v140 - i3 - Feb 15 2015 - p108(1) [51-500]
    NYTBR - July 5 2015 - p30(L) [501+]
    PW - v262 - i4 - Jan 26 2015 - p166(1) [51-500]

Standiford, Natalie - *The Only Girl in School*
    c KR - Nov 15 2015 - pNA [51-500]

Standish, Stephanie - *Your Personal Hang-Ups*
    Bwatch - July 2015 - pNA [51-500]

Stanfield-Mazzi, Maya - *Object and Apparition: Envisioning the Christian Divine in the Colonial Andes*
    CH - v84 - i1 - March 2015 - p242(3) [501+]
    CHR - v101 - i3 - Summer 2015 - p690(2) [501+]
    HAHR - v95 - i2 - May 2015 - p352-353 [501+]

Stanfield, Michael Edward - *Of Beasts and Beauty: Gender, Race, and Identity in Colombia*
    AHR - v120 - i1 - Feb 2015 - p303-304 [501+]
    Ams - v72 - i1 - Jan 2015 - p167(3) [501+]

Stanford, Ashley - *Asperger Syndrome and Long-Term Relationships*
    Bwatch - March 2015 - pNA [51-500]

Stanford, Frank - *Hidden Water: From the Frank Stanford Archives*
    APR - v44 - i4 - July-August 2015 - p21(7) [501+]
What about This: Collected Poems of Frank Stanford
    NY - v91 - i17 - June 22 2015 - p81 [51-500]
    PW - v262 - i11 - March 16 2015 - p62(1) [51-500]

Stanford, Peter - *Judas: The Most Hated Name in History*
    KR - Oct 15 2015 - pNA [51-500]
    PW - v262 - i45 - Nov 9 2015 - p57(1) [501+]
Judas: The Troubling History of the Renegade Apostle
    BL - v111 - i21 - July 1 2015 - p4(2) [51-500]
    NS - v144 - i5254 - March 20 2015 - p30(4) [501+]
    Spec - v327 - i9736 - April 4 2015 - p38(1) [501+]
    TLS - i5844 - April 3 2015 - p26(1) [501+]

Stangneth, Bettina - *Eichmann before Jerusalem: The Unexamined Life of a Mass Murderer*
    For Aff - v94 - i1 - Jan-Feb 2015 - pNA [501+]
    TLS - i5839 - Feb 27 2015 - p7(2) [501+]
    NYTBR - Oct 11 2015 - p28(L) [501+]

Staniford, Linda - *Clothes*
    c HB Guide - v26 - i2 - Fall 2015 - p157(1) [51-500]
Food and Drink
    c HB Guide - v26 - i2 - Fall 2015 - p189(1) [51-500]
A Place to Live
    c Sch Lib - v63 - i3 - Autumn 2015 - p160(1) [51-500]

Staniszewski, Anna - *I'm with Cupid*
    c BL - v111 - i18 - May 15 2015 - p56(1) [51-500]
    c KR - May 1 2015 - pNA [501+]
    y SLJ - v61 - i5 - May 2015 - p116(1) [51-500]
Power Down, Little Robot (Illus. by Zeltner, Tim)
    c HB Guide - v26 - i2 - Fall 2015 - p19(1) [51-500]
    c KR - Jan 1 2015 - pNA [501+]

Stanley, Brian - *The Global Diffusion of Evangelicalism: The Age of Billy Graham and John Stott*
    CH - v84 - i1 - March 2015 - p273(2) [501+]

Stanley, Diane - *The Chosen Prince (Read by Dean, Robertson). Audiobook Review*
    c SLJ - v61 - i9 - Sept 2015 - p60(1) [51-500]
The Chosen Prince
    c CCB-B - v68 - i8 - April 2015 - p421(1) [51-500]
    c HB - v91 - i1 - Jan-Feb 2015 - p89(2) [501+]
    c HB Guide - v26 - i2 - Fall 2015 - p103(1) [51-500]

Stanley, Jason - *How Propaganda Works*
    TimHES - i2218 - Nov 12 2015 - p45(1) [501+]

Stanley, Matthew - *Huxley's Church and Maxwell's Demon: From Theistic Science to Naturalistic Science*
    TimHES - i2189 - Feb 5 2015 - p56-57 [501+]

Stanley, Michael - *A Death in the Family*
    BL - v112 - i2 - Sept 15 2015 - p30(1) [51-500]
    PW - v262 - i33 - August 17 2015 - p53(2) [51-500]

Stanley, Shalanda - *Drowning Is Inevitable*
    y BL - v111 - i22 - August 1 2015 - p63(1) [51-500]
    y KR - July 1 2015 - pNA [51-500]
    y PW - v262 - i28 - July 13 2015 - p69(1) [51-500]
    y SLJ - v61 - i7 - July 2015 - p98(1) [51-500]

Stanley, Suzannah Hamlin - *DIY Wardrobe Makeovers: Alter, Refresh & Refashion Your Clothes: Step-By-Step Sewing Tutorials*
    LJ - v140 - i7 - April 15 2015 - p90(2) [51-500]

Stanley, Thomas J. - *The Millionaire Next Door*
    NYT - March 7 2015 - pB1(L) [501+]

Stannard, Neil - *The Piano Technique Demystified: Insights Into Problem Solving, 2d ed.*
    Am MT - v64 - i4 - Feb-March 2015 - p59(1) [501+]

Stanton, Andrea - *This Is Jerusalem Calling: State Radio in Mandate Palestine*
    HNet - May 2015 - pNA [501+]

Stanton, Angie - *Under the Spotlight: A Jamieson Brothers Novel*
    y VOYA - v38 - i1 - April 2015 - p71(1) [51-500]
Under the Spotlight
    y BL - v111 - i15 - April 1 2015 - p68(1) [51-500]

Stanton, Beck - *This Is a Ball (Illus. by Stanton, Beck)*
    c Magpies - v30 - i3 - July 2015 - p27(1) [501+]

Stanton, Brandon - *Humans of New York: Stories*
    LJ - v140 - i16 - Oct 1 2015 - p78(1) [501+]
    PW - v262 - i32 - August 10 2015 - p48(2) [51-500]
    KR - August 15 2015 - pNA [501+]
Little Humans
    c HB Guide - v26 - i1 - Spring 2015 - p137(1) [51-500]

Stanton, Doug - *In Harm's Way: The Sinking of the USS Indianapolis*
    CSM - Jan 26 2015 - pNA [501+]

Stanton, Richard - *A Brief History of Video Games*
    LJ - v140 - i11 - June 15 2015 - p98(2) [51-500]
    TLS - i5875 - Nov 6 2015 - p29(1) [501+]

Stanworth, Karen - *Visibly Canadian: Imaging Collective Identities in the Canadas, 1820-1910*
    Beav - v95 - i5 - Oct-Nov 2015 - p60(2) [51-500]

Stanziani, Alessandro - *Bondage: Labor and Rights in Eurasia from the Sixteenth to the Early Twentieth Centuries*
    AHR - v120 - i2 - April 2015 - p572-573 [501+]
    Slav R - v74 - i3 - Fall 2015 - p609-610 [501+]

Stapert, Calvin R. - *Playing before the Lord: The Life and Work of Joseph Haydn*
    CHR - v101 - i3 - Summer 2015 - p663(3) [501+]

Staples, Heidi - *Sew Organized for the Busy Girl: Tips to Make the Most of Your Time & Space: 23 Quick & Clever Sewing Projects You'll Love*
    LJ - v140 - i5 - March 15 2015 - p109(1) [51-500]
    PW - v262 - i7 - Feb 16 2015 - p174(2) [51-500]

Staples, James - *Leprosy and a Life in South India: Journeys with a Tamil Brahmin*
    JRAI - v21 - i3 - Sept 2015 - p699(2) [501+]

Stapleton, M.L. - *Marlowe's Ovid: The Elegies in the Marlowe Canon*
    Ren Q - v68 - i3 - Fall 2015 - p1137-1138 [501+]
    RES - v66 - i275 - June 2015 - p574-575 [501+]
    Six Ct J - v46 - i2 - Summer 2015 - p421-422 [501+]

Starbard, Ann - *The Dairy Goat Handbook: For Backyard, Homestead, and Small Farm*
    PW - v262 - i18 - May 4 2015 - p115(1) [51-500]

Starbuck, Sara - *Gardening with Young Children*
    Sci & Ch - v53 - i3 - Nov 2015 - p24 [501+]

Starck, Lindsay - *Noah's Wife*
    BL - v112 - i5 - Nov 1 2015 - p33(1) [51-500]
    KR - Nov 15 2015 - pNA [51-500]
    LJ - v140 - i19 - Nov 15 2015 - p80(1) [51-500]

Stargardt, Nicholas - *The German War: A Nation under Arms, 1939-1945*
    KR - July 1 2015 - pNA [501+]
    LJ - v140 - i15 - Sept 15 2015 - p88(1) [51-500]
    NYRB - v62 - i16 - Oct 22 2015 - p28(4) [501+]
    NYTBR - Nov 15 2015 - p16(L) [501+]
    PW - v262 - i34 - August 24 2015 - p70(1) [501+]
    Spec - v329 - i9765 - Oct 24 2015 - p34(2) [501+]
    TimHES - i2215 - Oct 22 2015 - p47(1) [501+]

Stark, Susan - *Reflection from Pope Francis: An Invitation to Journaling, Prayer, and Action*
    LJ - v140 - i2 - Feb 1 2015 - p86(1) [51-500]

Stark, Ulf - *When Dad Showed Me the Universe (Illus. by Eriksson, Eva)*
    c KR - July 15 2015 - pNA [51-500]
    c Magpies - v30 - i2 - May 2015 - p30(1) [51-500]
    c Sch Lib - v63 - i3 - Autumn 2015 - p160(2) [51-500]
    c SLJ - v61 - i7 - July 2015 - p68(1) [51-500]
The Yule Tomte and the Little Rabbits: A Christmas Story for Advent (Illus. by Eriksson, Eva)
    c HB Guide - v26 - i1 - Spring 2015 - p66(1) [51-500]

Starke, Ruth - *My Gallipoli (Illus. by Hannaford, Robert)*
    y Magpies - v30 - i1 - March 2015 - p32(1) [51-500]

Starkey, David - *Magna Carta: The True Story Behind the Charter*
    HT - v65 - i6 - June 2015 - p56(2) [501+]

Starkey, Kathryn - *A Courtier's Mirror: Cultivating Elite Identity in Thomasin von Zerclaere's Welscher Gast*
    GSR - v38 - i1 - Feb 2015 - p151-152 [501+]
    JEGP - v114 - i3 - July 2015 - p430(4) [501+]

Starkey, Scott - *Revenge of the Bully*
    c HB Guide - v26 - i1 - Spring 2015 - p93(1) [51-500]

Starkman, Dean - *The Watchdog That Didn't Bark: The Financial Crisis and the Disappearance of Investigative Journalism*
    NYRB - v62 - i10 - June 4 2015 - p43(3) [501+]

Starks, Glenn L. - *African Americans at Risk: Issues in Education, Health, Community, and Justice, 2 vols.*
    y BL - v112 - i4 - Oct 15 2015 - p5(2) [51-500]

Starks, Kyle - *Sexcastle*
    PW - v262 - i13 - March 30 2015 - p63(1) [51-500]

Starlin, Jim - *The Infinity Gauntlet*
    LJ - v140 - i9 - May 15 2015 - p110(1) [501+]

Starmer, Aaron - *The Storyteller*
    c KR - Dec 15 2015 - pNA [501+]
The Whisper (Read by Halstead, Graham). Audiobook Review
    c SLJ - v61 - i9 - Sept 2015 - p60(1) [51-500]
The Whisper
    c HB Guide - v26 - i2 - Fall 2015 - p103(1) [51-500]
    y SLJ - v61 - i2 - Feb 2015 - p94(2) [51-500]

Starmer, Clay - *Blood and Gold*
    RVBW - March 2015 - pNA [51-500]

Starnes, Cynthia Lee - *The Marriage Buyout: The Troubled Trajectory of U.S. Alimony Law*
    HLR - v128 - i3 - Jan 2015 - p1064(1) [51-500]

Starobinets, Anna - *Catlantis*
    c TLS - i5877 - Nov 20 2015 - p31(1) [501+]
The Icarus Gland: A Book of Metamorphoses
    TLS - i5844 - April 3 2015 - p21(1) [501+]

Starosielski, Nicole - *The Undersea Network*
    LJ - v140 - i3 - Feb 15 2015 - p127(1) [51-500]
    TimHES - i2193 - March 5 2015 - p48-49 [501+]

Starr, G. Gabrielle - *Feeling Beauty: The Neuroscience of Aesthetic Experience*
    MP - v112 - i4 - May 2015 - pE280(4) [501+]

Starr, Jason - *Savage Lane*
    BL - v112 - i1 - Sept 1 2015 - p49(1) [51-500]
    KR - August 1 2015 - pNA [501+]
    LJ - v140 - i16 - Oct 1 2015 - p73(1) [51-500]
    PW - v262 - i31 - August 3 2015 - p34(2) [51-500]

Starr, Michael Seth - *Black and Blue: The Redd Foxx Story*
    BL - v111 - i19-20 - June 1 2015 - p30(2) [501+]
Ringo: With a Little Help
    PW - v262 - i24 - June 15 2015 - p77(2) [51-500]

Starr, Mirabai - *Caravan of No Despair*
    KR - Oct 1 2015 - pNA [501+]

Starr, Paul - *Remedy and Reaction: The Peculiar American Struggle over Health Care Reform*
    CS - v44 - i2 - March 2015 - p256-258 [501+]

Starr, Renee - *You Are Woman, You Are Divine: The Modern Woman's Journey Back to The Goddess*
    RVBW - Oct 2015 - pNA [501+]
    RVBW - Nov 2015 - pNA [51-500]

Starr, S. Frederick - *Lost Enlightenment: Central Asia's Golden Age from the Arab Conquest to Tamerlane*
    JIH - v45 - i4 - Spring 2015 - p611-613 [501+]

Stasse, Lisa M. - *The Defiant*
    y HB Guide - v26 - i1 - Spring 2015 - p124(1) [51-500]

Statham, Leigh - *The Perilous Journey of the Not-So-Innocuous Girl*
    y SLJ - v61 - i7 - July 2015 - p88(2) [51-500]

Statiev, Alexander - *The Soviet Counterinsurgency in the Western Borderlands*
    Slav R - v74 - i1 - Spring 2015 - p153-156 [501+]

Stauart, Matthew - *Locke's Metaphysics*
    Phil R - v124 - i1 - Jan 2015 - p153(155) [501+]

Staub, Wendy Corsi - *Blood Red*
    KR - July 15 2015 - pNA [51-500]
Nine Lives
    BL - v112 - i3 - Oct 1 2015 - p27(1) [51-500]
Time Cat: The Remarkable Journeys of Jason and Gareth
    KR - Sept 1 2015 - pNA [51-500]
    PW - v262 - i33 - August 17 2015 - p50(2) [51-500]

Stauffacher, Sue - *Cassidy's Guide to Everyday Etiquette (and Obfuscation).*
    c HB Guide - v26 - i2 - Fall 2015 - p103(1) [51-500]
    c SLJ - v61 - i3 - March 2015 - p144(1) [51-500]
    y VOYA - v38 - i2 - June 2015 - p68(1) [51-500]

Stauffer, John - *Picturing Frederick Douglass: An Illustrated Biography of the Nineteenth Century's Most Photographed American*
    KR - Sept 1 2015 - pNA [501+]
    PW - v262 - i41 - Oct 12 2015 - p61(3) [51-500]
    LJ - v140 - i16 - Oct 1 2015 - p95(2) [51-500]

Staunton, Ted - *Morgan's Got Game (Illus. by Slavin, Bill)*
    Res Links - v20 - i3 - Feb 2015 - p15(1) [51-500]

Stavans, Ilan - *Latin Music: Musicians, Genres, and Themes*
    R&USQ - v54 - i3 - Spring 2015 - p63(2) [501+]
A Most Imperfect Union: A Contrarian History of the United States (Illus. by Alcaraz, Lalo)
    HNet - Feb 2015 - pNA [501+]
Quixote: The Novel and the World
    TLS - i5874 - Oct 30 2015 - p8(1) [501+]
    BL - v111 - i22 - August 1 2015 - p17(2) [51-500]
    KR - May 15 2015 - pNA [501+]
    LJ - v140 - i11 - June 15 2015 - p91(2) [51-500]
    PW - v262 - i18 - May 4 2015 - p106(1) [51-500]
Reclaiming Travel
    TLS - i5864-5865 - August 21 2015 - p34(1) [501+]

Stavridis, James - *The Accidental Admiral: A Sailor Takes Command at NATO*
    NWCR - v68 - i4 - Autumn 2015 - p117(2) [501+]
    Parameters - v45 - i2 - Summer 2015 - p147(3) [501+]

Stawrowski, Zbigniew - *The Clash of Civilizations or Civil War*
    J Ch St - v57 - i2 - Spring 2015 - p373-375 [501+]
    MA - v57 - i3 - Summer 2015 - p40(9) [501+]

Stawski, Scott - *Inflection Point: How the Convergence of Cloud, Mobility, Apps and Data Will Shape the Future of Business*
    KR - Oct 15 2015 - pNA [501+]

Stayton, Jeffrey - *This Side of the River*
    SPBW - March 2015 - pNA [51-500]
    Roundup M - v22 - i4 - April 2015 - p26(1) [501+]

Stayton, Robert Arthur - *Power Shift: From Fossil Energy to Dynamic Permanent Power*
    KR - April 15 2015 - pNA [501+]
Power Shift: From Fossil Energy to Dynamic Solar Power
    PW - v262 - i15 - April 13 2015 - p73(1) [51-500]
    y SLJ - v61 - i5 - May 2015 - p142(2) [51-500]
    SPBW - June 2015 - pNA [501+]

Stead, Philip C. - *Ideas Are All Around (Illus. by Stead, Philip C.)*
    c BL - v112 - i7 - Dec 1 2015 - p67(1) [51-500]
    c KR - Dec 15 2015 - pNA [51-500]
Lenny & Lucy (Illus. by Stead, Erin C.)
    c NYTBR - Nov 8 2015 - p34(L) [501+]
Lenny & Lucy (Illus. by Stead, Erin E.)
    c BL - v111 - i19-20 - June 1 2015 - p120(1) [51-500]
    c HB - v91 - i5 - Sept-Oct 2015 - p87(2) [51-500]
    c KR - July 1 2015 - pNA [51-500]
    c PW - v262 - i26 - June 29 2015 - p66(1) [51-500]
    c PW - v262 - i49 - Dec 2 2015 - p28(1) [51-500]
    c SLJ - v61 - i7 - July 2015 - p68(2) [51-500]
Sebastian and the Balloon (Illus. by Stead, Philip C.)
    c HB Guide - v26 - i1 - Spring 2015 - p47(1) [51-500]
A Sick Day for Amos McGee (Illus. by Stead, Erin E.)
    c BL - v112 - i4 - Oct 15 2015 - p53(1) [51-500]
Special Deliver (Illus. by Cordell, Matthew)
    c HB - v91 - i2 - March-April 2015 - p84(1) [51-500]
Special Delivery (Illus. by Cordell, Matthew)
    c BL - v111 - i11 - Feb 1 2015 - p57(1) [51-500]
    c HB Guide - v26 - i2 - Fall 2015 - p19(1) [51-500]
    c NYTBR - May 10 2015 - p18(L) [501+]

Stead, Rebecca - *Goodbye Stranger*
    c BL - v111 - i18 - May 15 2015 - p55(2) [51-500]
    c CCB-B - v69 - i1 - Sept 2015 - p57(1) [51-500]
    y HB - v91 - i4 - July-August 2015 - p147(2) [501+]
    c KR - June 1 2015 - pNA [51-500]
    y Magpies - v30 - i4 - Sept 2015 - p36(1) [501+]
    c PW - v262 - i19 - May 11 2015 - p62(1) [51-500]
    c PW - v262 - i49 - Dec 2 2015 - p70(1) [51-500]
    c Sch Lib - v63 - i4 - Winter 2015 - p233(1) [51-500]
    y SLJ - v61 - i5 - May 2015 - p116(2) [51-500]
    y VOYA - v38 - i3 - August 2015 - p69(2) [501+]

Steadman, John L. - *H.P. Lovecraft and the Black Magickal Tradition*
    RVBW - Nov 2015 - pNA [51-500]

Steadman, Ralph - *Nextinction*
    PW - v262 - i33 - August 17 2015 - p64(3) [51-500]

Stearns, James - *Sam's Big Deer (Illus. by King, Jason)*
    c CH Bwatch - Nov 2015 - pNA [51-500]

Stearns, Peter N. - *Demilitarization in the Contemporary World*
    J Mil H - v79 - i3 - July 2015 - p877-878 [501+]
The Industrial Revolution in World History
    JEH - v75 - i1 - March 2015 - p261-262 [501+]

Steavenson, Wendell - *Circling the Square: Stories from the Egyptian Revolution*
    KR - May 1 2015 - pNA [501+]
    LJ - v140 - i11 - June 15 2015 - p102(3) [501+]
    NYTBR - July 12 2015 - p22(L) [501+]
    Spec - v328 - i9756 - August 22 2015 - p38(2) [501+]

Stebelsky, Ihor - *Placing Ukraine on the Map: Stepan Rudnytsky's Nation-Building Geography*
    E-A St - v67 - i5 - July 2015 - p843(2) [501+]

Steber, Martina - *Visions of Community in Nazi Germany: Social Engineering and Private Lives*
    CEH - v48 - i2 - June 2015 - p271-273 [501+]

Stecher, Marianne T. - *The Creative Dialectic in Karen Blixen's Essays: On Gender, Nazi Germany, and Colonial Desire*
    Scan St - v87 - i2 - Summer 2015 - p292(4) [501+]

Steding, William - *Presidential Faith and Foreign Policy: Jimmy Carter the Disciple and Ronald Reagan the Alchemist*
    HT - v65 - i6 - June 2015 - p64(2) [501+]

Stedman, Gesa - *Cultural Exchange in Seventeenth-Century France and England*
    HER - v130 - i545 - August 2015 - p999(3) [501+]

Steel, Carlos - *Paganism in the Middle Ages: Threat and Fascination*
    Specu - v90 - i4 - Oct 2015 - p1167-1168 [501+]

Steel, Danielle - *Pretty Minnie in Paris (Illus. by Valiant, Kristi)*
    c HB Guide - v26 - i1 - Spring 2015 - p47(1) [51-500]

Steel, Louise - *Materiality and Consumption in the Bronze Age Mediterranean*
    Class R - v65 - i1 - April 2015 - p247-249 [501+]

Steele, Allen - *Tales of Time and Space*
    Analog - v135 - i7-8 - July-August 2015 - p188(1) [501+]
    PW - v262 - i11 - March 16 2015 - p67(2) [51-500]

Steele, David - *Radical Marriage*
    SPBW - Jan 2015 - pNA [51-500]

Steele, Ian K. - *Setting All the Captives Free: Capture, Adjustment, and Recollection in Allegheny Country*
    AHR - v120 - i1 - Feb 2015 - p233-234 [501+]
    W&M Q - v72 - i2 - April 2015 - p351-366 [501+]

Steele, Jon - *The Way of Sorrows*
    BL - v111 - i21 - July 1 2015 - p41(1) [51-500]
    KR - August 1 2015 - pNA [51-500]
    PW - v262 - i26 - June 29 2015 - p45(1) [51-500]

Steele, Michael A. - *Fresh (Illus. by Cano, Fernando)*
    c HB Guide - v26 - i1 - Spring 2015 - p80(2) [51-500]

Steele, P.M. - *A Linguistic History of Ancient Cyprus: The Non-Greek Languages, and their Relations with Greek, c. 1600-300 BC*
    Class R - v65 - i1 - April 2015 - p1-3 [501+]

Steele, Philip - *Epic Explorers: 12 Epic Journeys across Land, Sea and Space*
    c Sch Lib - v63 - i3 - Autumn 2015 - p188(1) [51-500]
Wow! I Didn't Know That: Surprising Facts About Pirates (Illus. by Aspinall, Marc)
    c HB Guide - v26 - i1 - Spring 2015 - p200(1) [51-500]

Steele-Saccio, Eva - *Dogs*
    c KR - Jan 1 2015 - pNA [51-500]

Steele, Shelby - *Shame: How America's Past Sins Have Polarized Our Country*
    Nat R - v67 - i5 - March 23 2015 - p44 [501+]
    NYTBR - March 8 2015 - p12(L) [501+]

Steele, Valerie - *Dance and Fashion*
    LJ - v140 - i5 - March 15 2015 - p102(3) [501+]

Steen, Celine - *Vegan Finger Foods*
    Veg J - v34 - i1 - Jan-March 2015 - p30(1) [51-500]

Steen, Charlie R. - *Margaret of Parma: A Life*
    JMH - v87 - i3 - Sept 2015 - p749(2) [501+]

Steen, Kathryn - *The American Synthetic Organic Chemicals Industry: War and Politics, 1910-1930*
    AHR - v120 - i4 - Oct 2015 - p1501-1502 [501+]
    HNet - March 2015 - pNA [501+]
    JAH - v102 - i2 - Sept 2015 - p586-587 [501+]

Steenburgh, Jim - *Secrets of the Greatest Snow on Earth: Weather, Climate Change, and Finding Deep Powder in Utah's Wasatch Mountains and around the World*
    Am Sci - v103 - i2 - March-April 2015 - p152(2) [501+]

Steensland, Brian - *The New Evangelical Social Engagement*
    JR - v95 - i2 - April 2015 - p284(2) [501+]
    CC - v132 - i7 - April 1 2015 - p35(3) [501+]
    CS - v44 - i5 - Sept 2015 - p716-718 [501+]

Steers, Billy - *Family Reunion (Illus. by Steers, Billy)*
    c HB Guide - v26 - i2 - Fall 2015 - p53(1) [51-500]
Farmer's Market (Illus. by Steers, Billy)
    c HB Guide - v26 - i2 - Fall 2015 - p53(1) [51-500]
New Friend
    c KR - Feb 15 2015 - pNA [51-500]
Tractor Mac Saves Christmas
    c KR - Sept 1 2015 - pNA [51-500]

Steers, Edward, Jr. - *Lincoln and Reconstruction*
    JSH - v81 - i4 - Nov 2015 - p983(3) [501+]

Steeves, Mike - *Giving Up*
    PW - v262 - i13 - March 30 2015 - p51(2) [51-500]

Stefan, Karner - *Der Kreml und die "Wende" 1989: Interne Analysen der Sowjetischen Fuhrung zum Fall der Kommunistischen Regime: Dokumente*
    HNet - March 2015 - pNA [501+]

Stefansson, Jon Kalman - *The Heart of Man*
    TLS - i5837 - Feb 13 2015 - p19(1) [501+]

Stefoff, Rebecca - *Cavnedish Square*
    c BL - v112 - i5 - Nov 1 2015 - p46(2) [51-500]

Steggall, Susan - *Colors (Illus. by Steggall, Susan)*
    c BL - v112 - i7 - Dec 1 2015 - p41(1) [51-500]
    c KR - August 15 2015 - pNA [51-500]
    c SLJ - v61 - i8 - August 2015 - p63(3) [51-500]

Stegmaier, Jamey - *A Crowdfunder's Strategy Guide: Build a Better Business by Building Community*
    Bwatch - Nov 2015 - pNA [51-500]
    LJ - v140 - i15 - Sept 15 2015 - p86(1) [51-500]

Stehle, Maria - *Ghetto Voices in Contemporary German Culture: Textscapes, Filmscapes, Soundscapes*
    MLR - v110 - i1 - Jan 2015 - p300-301 [501+]

Stehn, Carsten - *Peace Diplomacy, Global Justice and International Agency: Rethinking Human Security and Ethics in the Spirit of Dag Hammarskjold*
    HNet - March 2015 - pNA [501+]
    HNet - April 2015 - pNA [501+]

Steiger, A.J. - *Mindwalker*
    y BL - v111 - i18 - May 15 2015 - p63(1) [51-500]
    y CCB-B - v69 - i1 - Sept 2015 - p58(1) [51-500]
    y HB Guide - v26 - i2 - Fall 2015 - p140(1) [51-500]
    y SLJ - v61 - i2 - Feb 2015 - p109(1) [51-500]
    y VOYA - v38 - i2 - June 2015 - p83(1) [51-500]

Steil, Jennifer - *The Ambassador's Wife*
    NYTBR - Sept 27 2015 - p30(L) [501+]

Stein, Brynn - *Ray of Sunlight*
    SLJ - v61 - i3 - March 2015 - p162(1) [51-500]

Stein, David Ezra - *I'm My Own Dog (Illus. by Stein, David Ezra)*
    c HB Guide - v26 - i1 - Spring 2015 - p16(1) [51-500]
Tad and Dad (Illus. by Stein, David Ezra)
    c BL - v111 - i14 - March 15 2015 - p80(1) [51-500]
    c BooChiTr - June 27 2015 - p14(1) [501+]
    c HB - v91 - i3 - May-June 2015 - p101(1) [51-500]
    c HB Guide - v26 - i2 - Fall 2015 - p19(1) [51-500]
    c PW - v262 - i15 - April 13 2015 - p81(1) [501+]

Stein, Gabriele - *Sir Thomas Elyot as Lexicographer*
    Ren Q - v68 - i1 - Spring 2015 - p386-387 [501+]

Stein, Garth - *Enzo Races in the Rain! (Illus. by Alley, Zoe B.)*
    c HB Guide - v26 - i1 - Spring 2015 - p47(1) [51-500]
A Sudden Light (Read by Numrich, Seth). Audiobook Review
    y BL - v111 - i11 - Feb 1 2015 - p61(1) [51-500]

Stein-Holkeskamp, Elke - *Das archaische Griechenland: Die Stadt und das Meer*
    HNet - Sept 2015 - pNA(NA) [501+]
Stein, James D. - *L.A. Math: Romance, Crime, and Mathematics in the City of Angels*
    PW - v262 - i52 - Dec 21 2015 - p135(1) [51-500]
Stein, Jean - *West of Eden: An American Place*
    KR - Dec 15 2015 - pNA [501+]
    PW - v262 - i51 - Dec 14 2015 - p74(1) [51-500]
Stein, Lorin - *Submission*
    PW - v262 - i29 - July 20 2015 - p165(1) [51-500]
The Unprofessionals: New American Writing from The Paris Review
    Atl - v316 - i4 - Nov 2015 - p54(1) [51-500]
    KR - Sept 15 2015 - pNA [51-500]
Stein, Peter - *Little Red's Riding Hood*
    c CH Bwatch - May 2015 - pNA [501+]
Stein, Sarah Abrevaya - *Saharan Jews and the Fate of French Algeria*
    AHR - v120 - i3 - June 2015 - p1143-1144 [501+]
    IJMES - v47 - i4 - Nov 2015 - p854-856 [501+]
Stein, Triss - *Brooklyn Secrets*
    BL - v112 - i5 - Nov 1 2015 - p29(2) [51-500]
    KR - Oct 1 2015 - pNA [51-500]
Steinbaum, Keith - *The Poe Consequence*
    KR - Nov 15 2015 - pNA [501+]
Steinbeck, Thomas - *In Search of the Dark Watchers: Landscapes and Lore of Big Sur (Illus. by Brode, Benjamin)*
    PW - v262 - i5 - Feb 2 2015 - p49(2) [51-500]
Steinberg, Guido - *Saudi-Arabien: Politik, Geschichte, Religion*
    HNet - July 2015 - pNA [501+]
Steinberg, Jason - *Expanzaramadingdong (Illus. by Klein, Keith)*
    c CH Bwatch - March 2015 - pNA [51-500]
Steinberg, Jonathan - *Bismarck: A Life*
    HNet - Sept 2015 - pNA(NA) [501+]
Steinberg, Jonny - *A Man of Good Hope*
    Econ - v414 - i8922 - Jan 24 2015 - p75(US) [501+]
    Spec - v327 - i9726 - Jan 24 2015 - p43(1) [501+]
Steinberg, Justin - *Dante and the Limits of the Law*
    Med R - May 2015 - pNA [501+]
    NYRB - v62 - i3 - Feb 19 2015 - p36(2) [501+]
    Ren Q - v68 - i1 - Spring 2015 - p368-369 [501+]
    Specu - v90 - i1 - Jan 2015 - p299-301 [501+]
Steinberg, Paul F. - *Who Rules the Earth?: How Social Rules Shape Our Planet and Our Lives*
    New Sci - v225 - i3005 - Jan 24 2015 - p46(1) [501+]
Steinberg, Scott - *Make Change Work for You: 10 Ways to Future-Proof Yourself, Fearlessly Innovate, and Succeed Despite Uncertainty*
    BL - v111 - i9-10 - Jan 1 2015 - p25(1) [51-500]
Steinberg, Sheila Lakshmi - *GIS Research Methods: Incorporating Spatial Perspectives*
    Bwatch - Nov 2015 - pNA [51-500]
Steinberg, Steve - *The Colonel and Hug: The Partnership That Transformed the New York Yankees*
    KR - March 15 2015 - pNA [51-500]
    Nat R - v67 - i15 - August 24 2015 - p45 [501+]
Steinbugler, Amy C. - *Beyond Loving: Intimate Racework in Lesbian, Gay and Straight Interracial Relationships*
    CS - v44 - i1 - Jan 2015 - p119-121 [501+]
Steinem, Gloria - *My Life on the Road*
    BooChiTr - Nov 7 2015 - p12(1) [501+]
    KR - August 1 2015 - pNA [501+]
    LJ - v140 - i13 - August 1 2015 - p106(1) [51-500]
    NYTBR - Nov 15 2015 - p15(L) [501+]
    PW - v262 - i32 - August 10 2015 - p52(2) [51-500]
    Spec - v329 - i9767 - Nov 7 2015 - p41(2) [501+]
Steiner, Emily - *Reading "Piers Plowman"*
    Specu - v90 - i4 - Oct 2015 - p1169-1170 [501+]
Steiner, George - *The Idea of Europe*
    Spec - v327 - i9738 - April 18 2015 - p42(2) [501+]
Steiner, Michael C. - *Regionalists on the Left: Radical Voices from the American West*
    RAH - v43 - i1 - March 2015 - p134-142 [501+]
Steiner, Micheal C. - *Regionalists on the Left: Radical Voices from the American West*
    PHR - v84 - i2 - May 2015 - p266(3) [501+]
Steiner, Peter - *The Capitalist*
    KR - Dec 15 2015 - pNA [501+]
    PW - v262 - i51 - Dec 21 2015 - p60(1) [51-500]
Steiner, Rudolf - *Schriften zur Erkenntnisschulung: Wie Erlangt man Erkenntnisse der Hoheren Welten. Die Stufen der Hoheren Erkenntnis, hrsg. u. Kommentiert von Christian Clement*
    HNet - July 2015 - pNA [501+]
Steiner, Toni - *Jenny & Lorenzo (Illus. by Tharlet, Eve)*
    c HB Guide - v26 - i1 - Spring 2015 - p47(1) [51-500]
Steiner-Weber, Astrid - *Acta Conventus Neo-Latini Monasteriensis: Proceedings of the Fifteenth International Congress of Neo-Latin Studies*
    Sev Cent N - v73 - i3-4 - Fall-Winter 2015 - p213(4) [501+]
Steinfeld, Jemimah - *Little Emperors and Material Girls*
    TLS - i5848 - May 1 2015 - p26(1) [51-500]
Steinhart, Eric C. - *The Holocaust and the Germanization of Ukraine*
    HT - v65 - i7 - July 2015 - p62(1) [501+]
Steinhauer, Olen - *All the Old Knives (Read by Various readers). Audiobook Review*
    PW - v262 - i21 - May 25 2015 - p53(1) [51-500]
All the Old Knives
    BL - v111 - i9-10 - Jan 1 2015 - p43(2) [51-500]
    KR - Feb 1 2015 - pNA [51-500]
    LJ - v140 - i2 - Feb 1 2015 - p76(2) [51-500]
    NYT - March 2 2015 - pC1(L) [501+]
    NYTBR - April 5 2015 - p8(L) [501+]
    NYTBR - Dec 27 2015 - p24(L) [501+]
    PW - v262 - i1 - Jan 5 2015 - p52(1) [51-500]
    RVBW - Nov 2015 - pNA [51-500]
Cairo Affair
    NYTBR - Feb 15 2015 - p28(L) [501+]
    RVBW - Feb 2015 - pNA [51-500]
Steinitz, Tamar - *Translingual Identities: Language and the Self in Stefan Heym and Jakov Lind*
    MLR - v110 - i1 - Jan 2015 - p295-297 [501+]
Steinke, Ren - *Friendswood*
    NYTBR - June 21 2015 - p24(L) [501+]
Steinkellner, Teddy - *Trash Can Nights*
    y HB Guide - v26 - i1 - Spring 2015 - p124(1) [51-500]
Steinkruger, Jan-Erik - *Thematisierte Welten: Uber Darstellungspraxen in Zoologischen Garten und Vergnugungsparks*
    HNet - Feb 2015 - pNA [501+]
Steinmetz, George - *The Devil's Handwriting: Precoloniality and the German Colonial State in Qingdao, Samoa, and Southwest Africa*
    GSR - v38 - i1 - Feb 2015 - p185-187 [501+]
Sociology & Empire: The Imperial Entanglements of a Discipline
    CEH - v48 - i2 - June 2015 - p256-258 [501+]
Steinmetz, Greg - *The Richest Man Who Ever Lived: The Life and Times of Jacob Fugger*
    BL - v111 - i21 - July 1 2015 - p25(1) [51-500]
    KR - May 1 2015 - pNA [501+]
    NY - v91 - i31 - Oct 12 2015 - p103 [501+]
    NYTBR - August 2 2015 - p15(L) [501+]
    PW - v262 - i20 - May 18 2015 - p76(1) [51-500]
Stekelenburg, Jacquelien van - *The Future of Social Movement Research: Dynamics, Mechanisms, and Processes*
    CS - v44 - i5 - Sept 2015 - p724-726 [501+]
Stella, Lennon - *In the Waves (Illus. by Bjorkman, Steve)*
    c HB Guide - v26 - i2 - Fall 2015 - p53(1) [51-500]
    c KR - Feb 15 2015 - pNA [51-500]
    c Res Links - v21 - i1 - Oct 2015 - p10(1) [51-500]
Stellings, Caroline - *Gypsy's Fortune*
    c Res Links - v20 - i5 - June 2015 - p8(1) [51-500]
The Secret of the Golden Flower
    c Res Links - v20 - i3 - Feb 2015 - p36(1) [51-500]
    c BL - v111 - i17 - May 1 2015 - p56(1) [51-500]
    y CH Bwatch - May 2015 - pNA [51-500]
    SLJ - v61 - i4 - April 2015 - p158(1) [51-500]
Stelmach, Orest - *The Altar Girl*
    PW - v262 - i4 - Jan 26 2015 - p152(1) [51-500]
Stemple, Heidi E. Y. - *You Nest Here with Me (Illus. by Sweet, Melissa)*
    c HB Guide - v26 - i2 - Fall 2015 - p23(1) [51-500]
Stenger, Victor J. - *God and the Multiverse: Humanity's Expanding View of the Cosmos*
    Phys Today - v68 - i2 - Feb 2015 - p48-49 [501+]
Stenn, Kurt - *Hair: A Human History*
    KR - Dec 15 2015 - pNA [501+]
    PW - v262 - i52 - Dec 21 2015 - p145(1) [51-500]
Stent, Angela E. - *The Limits of Partnership: U.S.-Russian Relations in the Twenty-First Century*
    JTWS - v32 - i1 - Spring 2015 - p359(2) [501+]
    Slav R - v74 - i2 - Summer 2015 - p375-376 [501+]
Stenzig, Philipp - *Botschafterzeremoniell am Papsthof der Renaissance*
    CHR - v101 - i4 - Autumn 2015 - p925(4) [501+]

Stephen, Jeffrey - *Defending the Revolution: The Church of Scotland, 1689-1716*
    CH - v84 - i1 - March 2015 - p249(3) [501+]
Stephens, Bret - *America in Retreat: The New Isolationism and the Coming Global Disorder*
    CSM - Jan 23 2015 - pNA [51-500]
    NYRB - v62 - i5 - March 19 2015 - p10(24) [501+]
    Quad - v59 - i1-2 - Jan-Feb 2015 - p3(2) [501+]
Stephens, Claire Gatrell - *Library 101: A Handbook for the School Librarian, 2d ed.*
    Teach Lib - v43 - i1 - Oct 2015 - p41(3) [501+]
Stephens, John - *The Black Reckoning (Read by Dale, Jim). Audiobook Review*
    c BL - v112 - i3 - Oct 1 2015 - p86(1) [51-500]
    c SLJ - v61 - i8 - August 2015 - p51(1) [51-500]
The Black Reckoning
    c BL - v111 - i11 - Feb 1 2015 - p50(1) [51-500]
    y HB - v91 - i2 - March-April 2015 - p110(1) [51-500]
    c HB Guide - v26 - i2 - Fall 2015 - p140(1) [51-500]
    c KR - Jan 1 2015 - pNA [51-500]
    c SLJ - v61 - i5 - May 2015 - p106(1) [51-500]
The Books of Beginning: The Black Reckoning
    c CH Bwatch - Sept 2015 - pNA [51-500]
Stephens, Joshua - *The Dog Walker*
    Mac - v128 - i39 - Oct 5 2015 - p59(1) [501+]
Stephens, Kate - *College, Quicker: 24 Practical Ways to Save Money and Get Your Degree Faster*
    y VOYA - v38 - i4 - Oct 2015 - p86(1) [501+]
Stephens, Mitchell - *Beyond News: The Future of Journalism*
    NYRB - v62 - i10 - June 4 2015 - p43(3) [501+]
Stephens, Robert W. - *The Drayton Diaries*
    KR - March 15 2015 - pNA [51-500]
Stephens, S.C. - *Thoughtful*
    PW - v262 - i2 - Jan 12 2015 - p43(2) [51-500]
Stephens, Simon - *Heisenberg*
    NYT - June 30 2015 - pNA(L) [501+]
Stephens, Winifred - *The Book of France*
    Nature - v524 - i7565 - August 20 2015 - p299(1) [51-500]
Stephenson, Charles - *A Box of Sand: The Italo-Ottoman War, 1911-1912: The First Land, Sea and Air War*
    J Mil H - v79 - i4 - Oct 2015 - p1121-1126 [501+]
Stephenson, Christopher A. - *Types of Pentecostal Theology: Methods, Systems, and Spirit*
    JR - Jan 2015 - p138(3) [501+]
Stephenson, David - *Political Power in Medieval Gwynedd: Governance and the Welsh Princes*
    Med R - Jan 2015 - pNA [501+]
Stephenson, Jenn - *Performing Autobiography: Contemporary Canadian Drama*
    Theat J - v67 - i1 - March 2015 - p135-146 [501+]
Stephenson, Neal - *Seveneves (Read by Kowal, Mary Robinette). Audiobook Review*
    LJ - v140 - i13 - August 1 2015 - p47(1) [51-500]
Seveneves
    BL - v111 - i15 - April 1 2015 - p34(1) [51-500]
    Ent W - i1367 - June 12 2015 - p80(1) [501+]
    Esq - v163 - i6-7 - June-July 2015 - p26(2) [501+]
    Forbes - v196 - i6 - Nov 2 2015 - p42(1) [501+]
    KR - March 15 2015 - pNA [51-500]
    NYTBR - May 31 2015 - p15(L) [501+]
    PW - v262 - i10 - March 9 2015 - p56(1) [51-500]
Stephenson, Tom - *The Warbler Guide. E-book Review*
    y SLJ - v61 - i7 - July 2015 - p52(1) [501+]
Stephenson, Wen - *What We're Fighting for Now Is Each Other: Dispatches from the Front Lines of Climate Justice*
    y BL - v112 - i3 - Oct 1 2015 - p7(1) [51-500]
    KR - August 15 2015 - pNA [501+]
    PW - v262 - i33 - August 17 2015 - p64(1) [51-500]
Sterba, James P. - *From Rationality to Equality*
    Phil R - v124 - i3 - July 2015 - p407(3) [501+]
Sterckx, Pierre - *Tintin: Herge's Masterpiece*
    Spec - v329 - i9769 - Nov 21 2015 - p54(1) [501+]
Sterk, Andrea - *Faithful Narratives: Historians, Religion, and the Challenge of Objectivity*
    JIH - v46 - i1 - Summer 2015 - p107-109 [501+]
    Med R - Jan 2015 - pNA [501+]
    Six Ct J - v46 - i3 - Fall 2015 - p740-742 [501+]
Sterling, Bruce - *Twelve Tomorrows*
    Analog - v135 - i4 - April 2015 - p105(2) [501+]
Sterling, Cheryl - *African Roots, Brazilian Rites: Cultural and National Identity in Brazil*
    JTWS - v32 - i1 - Spring 2015 - p330(5) [501+]

Sterling Children's Books - *My First Baseball Book*
   c PW - v262 - i15 - April 13 2015 - p78(2) [501+]
My First Basketball Book
   c KR - July 1 2015 - pNA [51-500]
Sleepy Kitty
   c PW - v262 - i6 - Feb 9 2015 - p66(2) [501+]

Sterling, Eleanor J. - *Primate Ecology and Conservation: A Handbook of Techniques*
   QRB - v90 - i3 - Sept 2015 - p330(1) [501+]

Sterling Epicure - *Let's Do Brunch: Mouth-Watering Meals to Start Your Day*
   BL - v111 - i16 - April 15 2015 - p10(1) [51-500]

Sterling, Jeffrey E. - *Behind the Curtain: A Peek at Life from within the ER*
   KR - August 1 2015 - pNA [501+]

Stern, Alexandra Minna - *Telling Genes: The Story of Genetic Counseling in America*
   Isis - v106 - i1 - March 2015 - p217(2) [501+]

Stern, Ariella - *Bracha: Do You Know? (Illus. by Argoff, Patti)*
   c CH Bwatch - April 2015 - pNA [51-500]

Stern, Beth - *Yoda: The Story of a Cat and His Kittens (Illus. by Crane, Devin)*
   c HB Guide - v26 - i2 - Fall 2015 - p53(1) [51-500]

Stern, D.G. - *25 Days of Tropical Christmas (Illus. by Lane, Susan)*
   c CH Bwatch - Jan 2015 - pNA [51-500]
Hot Tea ... Cold Case
   SPBW - Jan 2015 - pNA [51-500]

Stern, David - *The Monk's Haggadah: A Fifteenth-Century Illuminated Codex from the Monastery of Tegernsee, with a Prologue by Friar Erhard von Pappenheim*
   HNet - Sept 2015 - pNA [501+]
   HNet - Sept 2015 - pNA [501+]

Stern, Jeffrey E. - *The Last Thousand: One School's Promise in a Nation at War*
   KR - Nov 1 2015 - pNA [501+]
   LJ - v140 - i20 - Dec 1 2015 - p120(1) [51-500]
   PW - v262 - i45 - Nov 9 2015 - p51(1) [51-500]

Stern, Jessica - *ISIS: The State of Terror*
   LJ - v140 - i7 - April 15 2015 - p104(1) [51-500]
   NYRB - v62 - i13 - August 13 2015 - p27(3) [501+]
   NYT - April 3 2015 - pC21(L) [501+]

Stern, Josef - *The Matter and Form of Maimonides' Guide*
   JR - v95 - i2 - April 2015 - p271(2) [501+]
   RM - v68 - i4 - June 2015 - p871(4) [501+]

Stern, Louise - *Ismael and His Sisters*
   NS - v144 - i5260 - May 1 2015 - p47(1) [51-500]

Stern, Lynn - *Improving Your Memory: How to Remember What You're Starting to Forget*
   Bwatch - March 2015 - pNA [51-500]

Stern, Nicholas - *Why Are We Waiting? The Logic, Urgency, and Promise of Tackling Climate Change*
   LJ - v140 - i12 - July 1 2015 - p109(1) [51-500]
   Lon R Bks - v37 - i18 - Sept 24 2015 - p34(3) [501+]
   NS - v144 - i5272 - July 24 2015 - p48(2) [501+]
   TimHES - i2206 - June 4 2015 - p52(1) [501+]
   TLS - i5876 - Nov 13 2015 - p22(2) [501+]

Stern, Philip J. - *Mercantilism Reimagined: Political Economy in Early Modern Britain and Its Empire*
   HNet - April 2015 - pNA [501+]
   Eight-C St - v48 - i4 - Summer 2015 - p541-542 [501+]
   JIH - v45 - i3 - Wntr 2015 - p427-428 [501+]

Stern, Robert A.M. - *Saving Place: 50 Years of New York City Landmarks*
   NYT - May 3 2015 - p5(L) [501+]

Stern, Sacha - *Time, Astronomy, and Calendars in the Jewish Tradition*
   Isis - v106 - i2 - June 2015 - p424(2) [501+]

Stern, Steve - *The Pinch*
   BL - v111 - i18 - May 15 2015 - p24(1) [51-500]
   KR - April 1 2015 - pNA [51-500]
   NYTBR - July 19 2015 - p9(L) [501+]
   PW - v262 - i16 - April 20 2015 - p46(1) [51-500]
   RVBW - Nov 2015 - pNA [51-500]

Sternberg, Eliezer J. - *NeuroLogic: The Brain's Hidden Rationale behind Our Irrational Behavior*
   KR - Nov 1 2015 - pNA [501+]
   PW - v262 - i48 - Nov 30 2015 - p52(2) [501+]

Sternberg, Giora - *Status Interaction During the Reign of Louis XIV*
   HNet - Feb 2015 - pNA [501+]

Sternberg, Julie - *Bedtime at Bessie and Lil's (Illus. by Gudeon, Adam)*
   c CCB-B - v68 - i10 - June 2015 - p519(1) [51-500]
   c HB Guide - v26 - i2 - Fall 2015 - p53(1) [51-500]
      PW - v262 - i2 - Jan 12 2015 - p56(2) [51-500]
   c SLJ - v61 - i2 - Feb 2015 - p80(1) [51-500]
Friendship Over (Illus. by Wright, Johanna)
   c HB - v91 - i1 - Jan-Feb 2015 - p90(1) [51-500]
   c HB Guide - v26 - i1 - Spring 2015 - p93(1) [51-500]
Secrets Out! (Illus. by Wright, Johanna)
   c HB - v91 - i5 - Sept-Oct 2015 - p119(2) [51-500]
   c KR - July 15 2015 - pNA [51-500]

Sternbergh, Adam - *Near Enemy*
   Mac - v128 - i2 - Jan 19 2015 - p56(2) [51-500]

Sterne, Laurence - *Tristram Shandy*
   NS - v144 - i5282 - Oct 2 2015 - p74(2) [501+]

Sternhell, Yael A. - *Routes of War: The World of Movement in the Confederate South*
   RAH - v43 - i1 - March 2015 - p77-82 [501+]

Sterrett, Andrew - *101 Careers in Mathematics*
   Math T - v109 - i1 - August 2015 - p77-78 [501+]

Stettler, Bernhard - *Bannerhandel: Ain spruch von dem langwirigen span zwuschet ainer statt zuo St. Gallen und ainem land Appenzelle, ain paner belangend*
   Six Ct J - v46 - i1 - Summer 2015 - p393-394 [501+]

Steven Chung - *Split Screen Korea: Shin Sang-ok and Postwar Cinema*
   JAS - v74 - i2 - May 2015 - p492-494 [501+]

Steven, Kenneth - *Why Dogs Have Wet Noses (Illus. by Torseter, Oyvind)*
   c KR - June 1 2015 - pNA [51-500]
   c SLJ - v61 - i11 - Nov 2015 - p88(1) [51-500]

Stevens, B.E. - *Silence in Catullus*
   Class R - v65 - i2 - Oct 2015 - p444-446 [501+]

Stevens, B.K. - *Fighting Chance*
   y BL - v112 - i1 - Sept 1 2015 - p99(2) [51-500]
   y KR - August 1 2015 - pNA [501+]

Stevens, Becca - *Letters from the Farm: A Simple Path for a Deeper Spiritual Life*
   PW - v262 - i19 - May 11 2015 - p54(1) [51-500]

Stevens, Catherine E. - *Finding Robert: What the Doctors Never Told Us about Autism Spectrum Disorder and the Hard Lessons We Learned*
   Bwatch - July 2015 - pNA [51-500]

Stevens, Chevy - *Those Girls (Read by Marie, Jorjeana). Audiobook Review*
   LJ - v140 - i17 - Oct 15 2015 - p52(1) [51-500]
Those Girls
   PW - v262 - i14 - April 6 2015 - p38(1) [51-500]
   BL - v111 - i17 - May 1 2015 - p46(1) [51-500]
   KR - May 1 2015 - pNA [51-500]
   LJ - v140 - i5 - March 15 2015 - p94(2) [51-500]

Stevens, Christopher - *Written in Stone: A Journey through the Stone Age and the Origins of Modern Language*
   KR - August 1 2015 - pNA [501+]
   LJ - v140 - i16 - Oct 1 2015 - p79(1) [51-500]
   PW - v262 - i36 - Sept 7 2015 - p58(1) [51-500]

Stevens, Courtney C. - *The Lies about Truth*
   y BL - v112 - i6 - Nov 15 2015 - p51(1) [51-500]
   y KR - Sept 15 2015 - pNA [51-500]
   y PW - v262 - i35 - August 31 2015 - p95(1) [51-500]
   y SLJ - v61 - i8 - August 2015 - p111(1) [51-500]
   y VOYA - v38 - i5 - Dec 2015 - p64(2) [51-500]

Stevens, David - *In All Respects Ready: Australia's Navy in World War One*
   J Mil H - v79 - i4 - Oct 2015 - p1184-1185 [501+]

Stevens, Elisabeth - *American Nocturne*
   KR - July 1 2015 - pNA [51-500]

Stevens, Hallam - *Life out of Sequence: A Data-Driven History of Bioinformatics*
   T&C - v56 - i1 - Jan 2015 - p301-303 [501+]

Stevens, Janice - *An Artist and a Writer Travel Highway 1 Central*
   SPBW - May 2015 - pNA [501+]

Stevens, Jeremy - *Translucence*
   KR - Nov 1 2015 - pNA [51-500]

Stevens, Kathryn - *Gorillas*
   c BL - v111 - i22 - August 1 2015 - p54(1) [51-500]
Hamsters
   c BL - v112 - i3 - Oct 1 2015 - p66(1) [51-500]

Stevens, Kevin - *Pucker Power: The Super-Powered Superpug (Illus. by Dempsey, Sheena)*
   c SLJ - v61 - i12 - Dec 2015 - p99(1) [51-500]

Stevens, Mark - *Lake of Fire*
   KR - July 1 2015 - pNA [51-500]

Stevens, Martin - *Sensory Ecology, Behaviour, and Evolution*
   QRB - v90 - i1 - March 2015 - p92(2) [501+]

Stevens, Rob - *Would the Real Stanley Carrot Please Stand Up?*
   c Sch Lib - v63 - i2 - Summer 2015 - p110(1) [51-500]

Stevens, Robert J. - *Finding Robert: What the Doctors Never Told Us about Autism Spectrum Disorder and the Hard Lessons We Learned*
   LJ - v140 - i5 - March 15 2015 - p123(2) [51-500]

Stevens, Robin - *Arsenic for Tea*
   c Sch Lib - v63 - i2 - Summer 2015 - p110(1) [51-500]
Murder Is Bad Manners
   c BL - v111 - i17 - May 1 2015 - p55(1) [51-500]
   c CCB-B - v68 - i11 - July-August 2015 - p569(1) [51-500]
   c HB Guide - v26 - i2 - Fall 2015 - p103(1) [51-500]
   c KR - Feb 1 2015 - pNA [51-500]
   c PW - v262 - i8 - Feb 23 2015 - p77(1) [51-500]
   c PW - v262 - i49 - Dec 2 2015 - p66(2) [51-500]
   y Teach Lib - v43 - i1 - Oct 2015 - p22(1) [51-500]

Stevens, Roger - *I Wish I Had a Pirate Hat (Illus. by Scobie, Lorna)*
   c Sch Lib - v63 - i4 - Winter 2015 - p241(1) [51-500]
   c SLJ - v61 - i12 - Dec 2015 - p139(2) [51-500]

Stevens, Stuart - *The Last Season: A Father, a Son, and a Lifetime of College Football*
   KR - June 15 2015 - pNA [51-500]
   PW - v262 - i28 - July 13 2015 - p57(1) [51-500]

Stevens, Taylor - *The Mask*
   BL - v111 - i17 - May 1 2015 - p31(1) [51-500]
   KR - April 15 2015 - pNA [501+]
   LJ - v140 - i11 - June 15 2015 - p81(1) [51-500]
   PW - v262 - i16 - April 20 2015 - p55(1) [51-500]

Stevens, Wendy - *Sneezes, Snorts and Sniffles: 7 Piano Pieces with Extra-musical Sounds*
   Am MT - v64 - i4 - Feb-March 2015 - p65(1) [51-500]
The Worship Piano Method Songbook
   Am MT - v64 - i5 - April-May 2015 - p52(1) [501+]

Stevenson, Augusta - *George Washington*
   c HB Guide - v26 - i1 - Spring 2015 - p196(1) [51-500]

Stevenson, Bryan - *Just Mercy: A Story of Justice and Redemption (Read by Stevenson, Bryan). Audiobook Review*
   LJ - v140 - i7 - April 15 2015 - p46(2) [51-500]
Just Mercy: A Story of Justice and Redemption
   NYTBR - Oct 11 2015 - p28(L) [501+]

Stevenson, Gregory - *A Slaughtered Lamb: Revelation and the Apocalyptic Response to Evil and Suffering*
   Intpr - v69 - i1 - Jan 2015 - p108(1) [501+]

Stevenson, Jeff C. - *Fortney Road: Life, Death, and Deception in a Christian Cult*
   SPBW - July 2015 - pNA [501+]

Stevenson, Katie - *Power and Propaganda: Scotland 1306-1488*
   Specu - v90 - i3 - July 2015 - p854-856 [501+]

Stevenson, Laura C. - *Liar from Vermont*
   ABR - v36 - i5 - July-August 2015 - p23(1) [501+]

Stevenson, Noelle - *Lumberjanes: Beware the Kitten Holy (Illus. by Allen, Brooke)*
   c SLJ - v61 - i2 - Feb 2015 - p96(1) [51-500]
Nimona. (Illus. by Stevenson, Noelle)
   y BL - v111 - i16 - April 15 2015 - p40(1) [51-500]
   y CCB-B - v68 - i11 - July-August 2015 - p569(2) [51-500]
   c NYTBR - July 12 2015 - p20(L) [501+]
      PW - v262 - i12 - March 23 2015 - p78(1) [51-500]
   y PW - v262 - i49 - Dec 2 2015 - p118(1) [51-500]
   y HB - v91 - i3 - May-June 2015 - p120(1) [51-500]
   c HB Guide - v26 - i2 - Fall 2015 - p140(1) [51-500]
   y KR - March 15 2015 - pNA [51-500]

Stevenson, Robert Louis - *The Hair Trunk or the Ideal Commonwealth: An Extravaganza*
   TLS - i5835 - Jan 30 2015 - p27(1) [501+]
The Strange Case of Dr. Jekyll and Mr. Hyde (Illus. by Ferran, Daniel)
   y HB Guide - v26 - i1 - Spring 2015 - p72(2) [51-500]

Stevenson, Robin - *The Summer We Saved the Bees*
   c KR - July 15 2015 - pNA [51-500]
   c Res Links - v21 - i1 - Oct 2015 - p21(1) [501+]
   y VOYA - v38 - i3 - August 2015 - p70(1) [51-500]
The World Without Us
   y BL - v111 - i9-10 - Jan 1 2015 - p100(2) [51-500]
   y VOYA - v38 - i1 - April 2015 - p71(1) [51-500]

Stevenson, Steven T. - *The Book of Steven*
   KR - June 15 2015 - pNA [501+]

Steward, Helen - *A Metaphysics for Freedom*
  RM - v69 - i1 - Sept 2015 - p155(2) [501+]
Steward, Samuel - *Philip Sparrow Tells All: Lost Essays by Samuel Steward, Writer, Professor, Tattoo Artist*
  PW - v262 - i39 - Sept 28 2015 - p77(1) [51-500]
Stewart, Alan - *The Oxford Francis Bacon I: Early Writings, 1584-1596*
  Six Ct J - v46 - i1 - Spring 2015 - p230-232 [501+]
Stewart, Amy - *Girl Waits with Gun*
  BL - v111 - i19-20 - June 1 2015 - p59(1) [51-500]
  KR - July 1 2015 - pNA [501+]
  LJ - v140 - i11 - June 15 2015 - p81(1) [51-500]
  NYTBR - August 30 2015 - p20(L) [51-500]
  PW - v262 - i28 - July 13 2015 - p42(1) [51-500]
Stewart, Barbara - *What We Knew*
  y BL - v111 - i21 - July 1 2015 - p60(1) [51-500]
  y SLJ - v61 - i6 - June 2015 - p130(1) [51-500]
Stewart, Ben - *Don't Trust Don't Fear Don't Beg: The Extraordinary Story of the Arctic 30*
  BL - v111 - i16 - April 15 2015 - p4(2) [51-500]
  KR - March 15 2015 - pNA [501+]
  LJ - v140 - i8 - May 1 2015 - p91(1) [51-500]
  PW - v262 - i7 - Feb 16 2015 - p167(1) [51-500]
Stewart, Brian - *Why Spy? The Art of Intelligence*
  Spec - v328 - i9752 - July 25 2015 - p31(2) [501+]
Stewart, Briony - *Here in the Garden (Illus. by Stewart, Briony)*
  c CH Bwatch - April 2015 - pNA [51-500]
  c HB Guide - v26 - i2 - Fall 2015 - p53(1) [51-500]
  c SLJ - v61 - i5 - May 2015 - p92(1) [51-500]
Stewart, Brittaney - *Journey through Life's War of the Heart*
  PW - v262 - i3 - Jan 19 2015 - p60(2) [51-500]
Stewart, Cameron - *The Batgirl of Burnside (Illus. by Tarr, Babs)*
  PW - v262 - i27 - July 6 2015 - p55(1) [51-500]
Stewart, Carla - *A Flying Affair*
  PW - v262 - i17 - April 27 2015 - p60(1) [51-500]
Stewart, Charles Anthony - *Cyprus and the Balance of Empires: Art and Archaeology from Justinian I to the Coeur de Lion*
  Med R - August 2015 - pNA [501+]
Stewart, Chuck - *Proud Heritage: People, Issues, and Documents of the LGBT Experience*
  y BL - v111 - i15 - April 1 2015 - p7(1) [501+]
Stewart, David - *Toys*
  c KR - July 1 2015 - pNA [501+]
Stewart, David O. - *Madison's Gift: Five Partnerships that Built America*
  CSM - Feb 13 2015 - pNA [501+]
The Wilson Deception
  PW - v262 - i35 - August 31 2015 - p64(1) [51-500]
Stewart, Faye - *German Feminist Queer Crime Fiction: Politics, Justice and Desire*
  Ger Q - v88 - i1 - Wntr 2015 - p127(3) [501+]
Stewart, Gail B. - *Ukraine: Then and Now*
  y VOYA - v37 - i6 - Feb 2015 - p89(1) [51-500]
Stewart, Garrett - *Closed Circuits: Screening Narrative Surveillance*
  FQ - v69 - i1 - Fall 2015 - p106(3) [501+]
Stewart, Ian - *Professor Stewart's Incredible Numbers*
  KR - Feb 1 2015 - pNA [501+]
Symmetry: A Very Short Introduction
  Math T - v108 - i7 - March 2015 - p559(1) [501+]
Stewart, Jon - *The Heibergs and the Theater: Between Vaudeville, Romantic Comedy, and National Drama*
  Scan St - v87 - i2 - Summer 2015 - p303(7) [501+]
Stewart, Jude - *Patternalia: An Unconventional History of Polka Dots, Stripes, Plaid, Camouflage, and Other Graphic Designs*
  PW - v262 - i25 - June 22 2015 - p129(1) [51-500]
Stewart, Kiera - *How to Break a Heart*
  c BL - v112 - i6 - Nov 15 2015 - p54(2) [51-500]
  c KR - Sept 15 2015 - pNA [51-500]
Stewart, Leah - *The New Neighbor*
  BL - v111 - i21 - July 1 2015 - p39(1) [51-500]
  KR - May 15 2015 - pNA [501+]
  NYTBR - July 5 2015 - p29(L) [501+]
Stewart, Mariah - *That Chesapeake Summer*
  PW - v262 - i20 - May 18 2015 - p72(1) [51-500]
Stewart, Mark - *The Boston Celtics*
  c HB Guide - v26 - i1 - Spring 2015 - p185(1) [51-500]
The Chicago Bulls
  c HB Guide - v26 - i1 - Spring 2015 - p185(1) [51-500]

The Los Angeles Lakers
  c HB Guide - v26 - i1 - Spring 2015 - p185(1) [51-500]
The Miami Heat
  c HB Guide - v26 - i1 - Spring 2015 - p185(1) [51-500]
The Oklahoma City Thunder
  c HB Guide - v26 - i1 - Spring 2015 - p185(1) [51-500]
The San Antonio Spurs
  c HB Guide - v26 - i1 - Spring 2015 - p185(1) [51-500]
Stewart, Melissa - *Does the Ear Hear?: And Other Questions about the Five Senses*
  c HB Guide - v26 - i1 - Spring 2015 - p171(1) [51-500]
Feathers: Not Just for Flying (Illus. by Brannen, Sarah S.)
  c Teach Lib - v42 - i3 - Feb 2015 - p52(1) [51-500]
How Does a Caterpillar Become a Butterfly?: And Other Questions about Butterflies
  c HB Guide - v26 - i1 - Spring 2015 - p159(1) [51-500]
How Does a Seed Sprout?: And Other Questions about Plants
  c HB Guide - v26 - i1 - Spring 2015 - p157(1) [51-500]
How Is My Brain Like a Supercomputer?: And Other Questions about the Human Body
  c HB Guide - v26 - i1 - Spring 2015 - p171(1) [51-500]
Hurricane Watch (Illus. by Morley, Taia)
  c SLJ - v61 - i12 - Dec 2015 - p140(1) [51-500]
  c BL - v111 - i22 - August 1 2015 - p74(1) [51-500]
A Place for Birds (Illus. by Bond, Higgins)
  c SLJ - v61 - i5 - May 2015 - p136(1) [51-500]
Water
  c HB Guide - v26 - i1 - Spring 2015 - p148(1) [51-500]
Why Did T. Rex Have Short Arms?: And Other Questions about Dinosaurs
  c HB Guide - v26 - i1 - Spring 2015 - p152(1) [51-500]
Stewart, Paul - *Now Then*
  TimHES - i2225 - Oct 15 2015 - p43-1 [501+]
Stewart, Todd - *See You Next Year (Illus. by Stewart, Todd)*
  c KR - Jan 15 2015 - pNA [51-500]
Stewart, Tracey - *Do unto Animals: A Friendly Guide to How Animals Live, and How We Can Make Their Lives Better*
  y BL - v112 - i3 - Oct 1 2015 - p7(1) [51-500]
Stewart, Whitney - *Meditation Is an Open Sky: Mindfulness for Kids (Illus. by Rippin, Sally)*
  c KR - Jan 15 2015 - pNA [51-500]
  c PW - v262 - i8 - Feb 23 2015 - p76(1) [501+]
  c HB Guide - v26 - i2 - Fall 2015 - p148(1) [51-500]
Stewart, Yale - *Alien Superman!*
  c HB Guide - v26 - i1 - Spring 2015 - p66(1) [51-500]
Battle of the Super Heroes!
  c HB Guide - v26 - i1 - Spring 2015 - p66(1) [51-500]
Steyn, Jan - *Orphans*
  TLS - i5844 - April 3 2015 - p21(1) [501+]
Steyn, Mark - *The (Un)Documented Mark Steyn: Don't Say You Weren't Warned*
  Spec - v327 - i9723 - Jan 3 2015 - p28(1) [501+]
Stibbe, Nina - *Man at the Helm*
  CSM - July 24 2015 - pNA [501+]
  Ent W - i1355-1356 - March 20 2015 - p105(1) [501+]
  KR - Jan 1 2015 - pNA [501+]
  NYT - April 14 2015 - pC1(L) [501+]
  NYTBR - March 8 2015 - p21(L) [501+]
  People - v83 - i11 - March 16 2015 - p41(NA) [501+]
Stickler, Matthias - *Jenseits von Aufrechnung und Verdrangung: Neue Forschungen zu Flucht, Vertreibung und Vertriebenenintegration*
  HNet - March 2015 - pNA [501+]
Stiebert, Johanna - *Fathers and Daughters in the Hebrew Bible*
  JR - Jan 2015 - p124(2) [501+]
Stiefel, Barry L. - *Jewish Sanctuary in the Atlantic World: A Social and Architectural History*
  JAH - v101 - i4 - March 2015 - p1253(1) [501+]
  Six Ct J - v46 - i3 - Fall 2015 - p810-812 [501+]

Stiefvater, Maggie - *The Anatomy of Curiosity*
  y KR - August 1 2015 - pNA [51-500]
  y SLJ - v61 - i10 - Oct 2015 - p117(2) [51-500]
  y VOYA - v38 - i5 - Dec 2015 - p75(1) [51-500]
  y BL - v112 - i2 - Sept 15 2015 - p62(1) [51-500]
Blue Lily, Lily Blue (Read by Patton, Will). Audiobook Review
  y BL - v111 - i14 - March 15 2015 - p88(1) [51-500]
Blue Lily, Lily Blue
  c CH Bwatch - April 2015 - pNA [51-500]
  y HB Guide - v26 - i1 - Spring 2015 - p124(1) [51-500]
  y VOYA - v37 - i6 - Feb 2015 - p84(1) [51-500]
Sinner
  y HB Guide - v26 - i1 - Spring 2015 - p124(1) [51-500]
Stievermann, Jan - *A Peculiar Mixture: German-Language Cultures and Identities in Eighteenth-Century North America*
  JAH - v102 - i1 - June 2015 - p229-230 [501+]
Stiftsbibliothek St. Gallen - *Der St. Galler Klosterplan: Faksimile, Begleittext, Beischriften und Ubersetzung. Mit einem Beitrag von Ernst Tremp*
  HNet - Jan 2015 - pNA [501+]
Stiftung Deutsches Historisches Museum - *Der Erste Weltkrieg in 100 Objekten*
  Ger Q - v88 - i3 - Summer 2015 - p384(9) [501+]
Kaiser und Kalifen: Karl der Grosse und die Machte am Mittelmeer um 800
  HNet - Feb 2015 - pNA [501+]
Stiftungen und Stiften im Wandel der Zeiten - Internationale Winterschule
  HNet - April 2015 - pNA [501+]
Stiglitz, Joseph E. - *Creating a Learning Society: A New Approach to Growth, Development, and Social Progress*
  Har Bus R - v93 - i3 - March 2015 - p126(2) [501+]
  NYRB - v62 - i14 - Sept 24 2015 - p32(3) [501+]
The Great Divide: Unequal Societies and What We Can Do about Them
  KR - April 1 2015 - pNA [501+]
  Nature - v522 - i7555 - June 11 2015 - p155(1) [51-500]
  NYRB - v62 - i14 - Sept 24 2015 - p32(3) [501+]
  TimHES - i2201 - April 30 2015 - p50-51 [501+]
Rewriting the Rules of the American Economy: An Agenda for Growth and Shared Prosperity
  NYRB - v62 - i14 - Sept 24 2015 - p32(3) [501+]
Stigter, Marc - *Solving the Strategy Delusion: Mobilizing People and Realizing Distinctive Strategies*
  TimHES - i2200 - April 23 2015 - p52(1) [501+]
Stihler, Cherie B. - *Wiggle Waggle Woof 1, 2, 3: A Counting Book*
  c CH Bwatch - April 2015 - pNA [51-500]
Stiles, T.J. - *Custer's Trials: A Life on the Frontier of a New America*
  KR - August 1 2015 - pNA [51-500]
  LJ - v140 - i14 - Sept 1 2015 - p113(1) [51-500]
  NYTBR - Nov 22 2015 - p26(L) [501+]
  PW - v262 - i35 - August 31 2015 - p77(1) [51-500]
  NYRB - v62 - i20 - Dec 17 2015 - p78(3) [501+]
Stilgoe, John R. - *Old Fields: Photography, Glamour, and Fantasy Landscape*
  NEQ - v88 - i1 - March 2015 - p179-182 [501+]
Stille, Ljuba - *Mia's Thumb (Illus. by Stille, Ljuba)*
  c HB - v91 - i1 - Jan-Feb 2015 - p73(2) [51-500]
  c HB Guide - v26 - i1 - Spring 2015 - p16(2) [51-500]
Stills, Caroline - *Mice Mischief: Math Facts in Action (Illus. by Rossell, Judith)*
  c HB - v91 - i1 - Jan-Feb 2015 - p106(2) [51-500]
Stilton, Geronimo - *The Enchanted Charms*
  c KR - March 15 2015 - pNA [51-500]
The Search for Treasure: The Sixth Adventure in the Kingdom of Fantasy
  c HB Guide - v26 - i1 - Spring 2015 - p93(1) [51-500]
Stilton, Thea - *The Secret of the Snow*
  c HB Guide - v26 - i1 - Spring 2015 - p93(1) [51-500]
The Treasure of the Viking Ship (Illus. by Frare, Michela)
  c HB Guide - v26 - i1 - Spring 2015 - p66(1) [51-500]
Stinchcomb, Bruce L. - *Mineral Treasures of the Ozarks*
  Bwatch - June 2015 - pNA [51-500]
Stine, Megan - *Where Is the White House? (Illus. by Groff, David)*
  c SLJ - v61 - i8 - August 2015 - p118(1) [51-500]

Stine, R.L. - *Classic Goosebumps Book #8: Say Cheese and Die (Read by Heller, Johnny). Audiobook Review*
c PW - v262 - i48 - Nov 30 2015 - p56(1) [51-500]
Don't Stay Up Late
c BL - v111 - i11 - Feb 1 2015 - p33(1) [51-500]
y BL - v111 - i12 - Feb 15 2015 - p80(1) [51-500]
c HB Guide - v26 - i2 - Fall 2015 - p140(1) [51-500]
c KR - Feb 1 2015 - pNA [51-500]
y SLJ - v61 - i8 - August 2015 - p114(2) [51-500]
It Came from Ohio! My Life as a Writer
c SLJ - v61 - i10 - Oct 2015 - p138(2) [51-500]
The Little Shop of Monsters (Read by Black, Jack). Audiobook Review
c BL - v112 - i7 - Dec 1 2015 - p71(1) [51-500]
The Little Shop of Monsters (Illus. by Brown, Marc)
c BL - v111 - i12 - Feb 15 2015 - p88(1) [51-500]
c HB - v91 - i5 - Sept-Oct 2015 - p70(1) [51-500]
c KR - August 1 2015 - pNA [51-500]
c PW - v262 - i19 - May 11 2015 - p56(1) [51-500]
c SLJ - v61 - i9 - Sept 2015 - p109(1) [51-500]
The Lost Girl
y BL - v112 - i3 - Oct 1 2015 - p73(1) [51-500]
y KR - July 15 2015 - pNA [51-500]
y SLJ - v61 - i8 - August 2015 - p114(2) [51-500]
y VOYA - v38 - i4 - Oct 2015 - p79(1) [51-500]
Party Games
y HB Guide - v26 - i1 - Spring 2015 - p125(1) [51-500]
Slappy's Tales of Horror (Illus. by Roman, Dave)
c SLJ - v61 - i9 - Sept 2015 - p149(2) [51-500]
c KR - June 15 2015 - pNA [51-500]

Sting - *There's a Little Black Spot on the Sun Today (Illus. by Volker, Sven)*
c KR - August 15 2015 - pNA [51-500]
c PW - v262 - i31 - August 3 2015 - p57(1) [51-500]
c SLJ - v61 - i12 - Dec 2015 - p96(1) [51-500]

Stirling, Jessica - *Whatever Happened to Molly Bloom?*
BL - v111 - i11 - Feb 1 2015 - p29(1) [51-500]

Stirling, S.M. - *The Change: Tales of Downfall and Rebirth*
BL - v111 - i18 - May 15 2015 - p33(1) [51-500]

Stirling, Tricia - *When My Heart Was Wicked*
y BL - v111 - i9-10 - Jan 1 2015 - p100(1) [51-500]
y CCB-B - v68 - i6 - Feb 2015 - p333(1) [51-500]
c CH Bwatch - May 2015 - pNA [501+]
c HB Guide - v26 - i2 - Fall 2015 - p140(1) [51-500]
y VOYA - v37 - i6 - Feb 2015 - p84(2) [51-500]

Stock, Doreen - *In Place of Me*
KR - Oct 1 2015 - pNA [501+]

Stock, Michael - *Penny Dora and the Wishing Box (Illus. by Grace, Sina)*
c SLJ - v61 - i11 - Nov 2015 - p105(2) [51-500]

Stockdale, Susan - *Spectacular Spots (Illus. by Stockdale, Susan)*
c BL - v111 - i15 - April 1 2015 - p38(1) [51-500]
c HB Guide - v26 - i2 - Fall 2015 - p172(1) [51-500]
c KR - Jan 15 2015 - pNA [51-500]

Stockinger, Thomas - *Dorfer und Deputierte: Die Wahlen zu den konstituierenden Parlamenten von 1848 in Niederosterreich un im Pariser Umland*
JMH - v87 - i3 - Sept 2015 - p711(3) [501+]

Stocklin-Kaldewey, Sara - *Kaiser Julians Gottesverehrung im Kontext der Spatantike*
HNet - Jan 2015 - pNA [501+]

Stockman, Daniela - *Media Commercialization and Authoritarian Rule in China*
E-A St - v67 - i1 - Jan 2015 - p149(3) [501+]

Stockwin, Julian - *Caribbee*
RVBW - Jan 2015 - pNA [51-500]

Stodghill, Ron - *Where Everybody Looks like Me: At the Crossroads of America's Black Colleges and Culture*
y BL - v112 - i1 - Sept 1 2015 - p20(1) [501+]
LJ - v140 - i14 - Sept 1 2015 - p116(1) [51-500]
PW - v262 - i30 - July 27 2015 - p58(1) [51-500]

Stoeke, Janet - *Oh No! A Fox! (Illus. by Stoeke, Janet)*
c HB Guide - v26 - i1 - Spring 2015 - p17(1) [51-500]

Stoff, Heiko - *Gift in der Nahrung: Zur Genese der Verbraucherpolitik Mitte des 20. Jahrhunderts*
HNet - Sept 2015 - pNA(NA) [501+]

Stoffers, Joy Huang - *Whasian*
y KR - Sept 1 2015 - pNA [51-500]
y SLJ - v61 - i11 - Nov 2015 - p122(1) [51-500]

Stohl, Margaret - *Dangerous Deception*
y BL - v111 - i18 - May 15 2015 - p60(2) [51-500]
y SLJ - v61 - i8 - August 2015 - p113(2) [51-500]
y VOYA - v38 - i3 - August 2015 - p77(1) [51-500]
Forever Red
y BL - v112 - i2 - Sept 15 2015 - p63(1) [51-500]
y KR - August 15 2015 - pNA [51-500]
y SLJ - v61 - i10 - Oct 2015 - p106(2) [51-500]
y VOYA - v38 - i4 - Oct 2015 - p79(1) [51-500]
Idols
y HB Guide - v26 - i1 - Spring 2015 - p125(1) [51-500]

Stojarova, Vera - *The Far Right in the Balkans*
E-A St - v67 - i5 - July 2015 - p840(3) [501+]

Stok, Barbara - *Vincent (Illus. by Stok, Barbara)*
BL - v111 - i16 - April 15 2015 - p39(2) [51-500]
PW - v262 - i10 - March 9 2015 - p60(1) [51-500]

Stoker, Bram - *Dracula (Read by Horovitch, David). Audiobook Review*
BL - v112 - i4 - Oct 15 2015 - p60(1) [51-500]
Dracula (Read by Jackson, Gildart). Audiobook Review
PW - v262 - i17 - April 27 2015 - p68(1) [51-500]

Stoker, Donald - *Clausewitz: His Life and Work*
For Aff - v94 - i1 - Jan-Feb 2015 - pNA [51-500]
HNet - June 2015 - pNA [501+]
HT - v65 - i6 - June 2015 - p62(1) [501+]

Stoker, Susan - *Protecting Caroline*
PW - v262 - i17 - April 27 2015 - p59(1) [51-500]

Stokes, Claudia - *The Altar at Home: Sentimental Literature and Nineteenth-Century American Religion*
JAH - v102 - i2 - Sept 2015 - p558-559 [501+]
MP - v113 - i2 - Nov 2015 - pE112(3) [501+]
Nine-C Lit - v70 - i2 - Sept 2015 - p282(4) [501+]

Stokes, Dale - *The Fish in the Forest: Salmon and the Web of Life*
QRB - v90 - i2 - June 2015 - p235(1) [501+]

Stokes, Melvyn - *American History through Hollywood Film: From the Revolution to the 1960s*
JSH - v81 - i2 - May 2015 - p545(1) [51-500]

Stokes, Paula - *Liars, Inc.*
c HB Guide - v26 - i2 - Fall 2015 - p140(1) [51-500]

Stokes, Peter A. - *English Vernacular Minuscule from Aethelred to Cnut, circa 990-circa 1035*
JEGP - v114 - i3 - July 2015 - p449(3) [501+]
Med R - May 2015 - pNA [501+]
RES - v66 - i276 - Sept 2015 - p766-767 [501+]

Stokes, Raymond G. - *Aus der Luft Gewonnen: Die Entwicklung der Globalen Gaseindustrie 1880-2012*
HNet - Feb 2015 - pNA [501+]

Stokes, Stacy A. - *Where the Staircase Ends*
y SLJ - v61 - i5 - May 2015 - p124(2) [51-500]

Stoknes, Per Espen - *What We Think About When We Try Not to Think about Global Warming: Toward a New Psychology of Climate Action*
LJ - v140 - i7 - April 15 2015 - p117(1) [51-500]
PW - v262 - i10 - March 9 2015 - p64(1) [51-500]

Stokoe, James - *Wonton Soup (Illus. by Stokoe, James)*
y LJ - v140 - i9 - May 15 2015 - p61(3) [501+]

Stolarz, Laurie Faria - *Welcome to the Dark House*
y HB Guide - v26 - i1 - Spring 2015 - p125(1) [51-500]

Stole, Inger L. - *Advertising at War: Business, Consumers, and Government in the 1940s*
BHR - v89 - i2 - Summer 2015 - p376(3) [501+]

Stoler, Ann Laura - *Imperial Debris: On Ruins and Ruination*
HNet - Feb 2015 - pNA [501+]

Stolker, Carel - *Rethinking the Law School: Education, Research, Outreach and Governance*
TimHES - i2195 - March 19 2015 - p52(1) [501+]

Stoll, Mark - *Inherit the Holy Mountain: Religion and the Rise of American Environmentalism*
LJ - v140 - i9 - May 15 2015 - p64(2) [501+]
PW - v262 - i15 - April 13 2015 - p73(1) [51-500]

Stollhans, Cynthia - *St. Catherine of Alexandria in Renaissance Roman Art: Case Studies in Patronage*
Ren Q - v68 - i2 - Summer 2015 - p631-632 [501+]

Stoltz, Joseph F., III - *The Gulf Theater 1813-1815*
J Mil H - v79 - i1 - Jan 2015 - p181-185 [501+]

Stoltz, Paul G. - *Grit: The New Science of What It Takes to Persevere, Flourish, Succeed*
RVBW - Feb 2015 - pNA [51-500]

Stoltzfus, Duane C.S. - *Pacifists in Chains: The Persecution of the Hutterites During the Great War*
CH - v84 - i1 - March 2015 - p266(2) [501+]

Stolz, Robert - *Bad Water: Nature, Pollution, & Politics in Japan, 1870-1950*
AHR - v120 - i2 - April 2015 - p599-600 [501+]
JIH - v46 - i1 - Summer 2015 - p151-152 [501+]

Stolzenberg, Daniel - *Egyptian Oedipus: Athanasius Kircher and the Secrets of Antiquity*
JMH - v87 - i1 - March 2015 - p146(3) [501+]

Stolzle, Astrid - *Kriegskrankenpflege im Ersten Weltkrieg. Das Pflegepersonal der freiwilligen Krankenpflege in den Etappen des deutschen Kaiserreiches*
CEH - v48 - i1 - March 2015 - p120-121 [501+]

Stone, Adam N. - *How to Succeed in the New Brand Space*
LJ - v140 - i10 - June 1 2015 - p110(2) [51-500]

Stone, Bailey - *The Anatomy of Revolution Revisited: A Comparative Analysis of England, France and Russia*
JIH - v46 - i1 - Summer 2015 - p112-113 [501+]

Stone, Brad - *The Everything Store: Jeff Bezos and the Age of Amazon*
Forbes - v196 - i6 - Nov 2 2015 - p42(1) [501+]

Stone, Charles Russell - *From Tyrant to Philosopher-King: A Literary History of Alexander the Great in Medieval and Early Modern England*
Specu - v90 - i4 - Oct 2015 - p1170-1172 [501+]

Stone, Dan - *Goodbye to All That? The Story of Europe since 1945*
AHR - v120 - i2 - April 2015 - p708-709 [501+]
CEH - v48 - i2 - June 2015 - p274-275 [501+]
The Liberation of the Camps: The End of the Holocaust and Its Aftermath
NYRB - v62 - i12 - July 9 2015 - p52(3) [501+]

Stone, David R. - *The Russian Army in the Great War: The Eastern Front, 1914-1917*
J Mil H - v79 - i4 - Oct 2015 - p1188(1) [501+]

Stone, Heather Duffy - *Over the Tracks*
y VOYA - v38 - i5 - Dec 2015 - p65(1) [501+]

Stone, Howard W. - *Defeating Depression*
KR - Jan 1 2015 - pNA [501+]

Stone, Jared - *Year of the Cow: How 420 Pounds of Beef Built a Better Life for One American Family*
KR - Jan 15 2015 - pNA [501+]
PW - v262 - i8 - Feb 23 2015 - p67(1) [501+]

Stone, Jeff - *The Day of the Jackal*
c HB Guide - v26 - i1 - Spring 2015 - p93(1) [51-500]

Stone, Joanne - *Your New Pregnancy Bible: The Experts' Guide to Pregnancy and Early Parenthood, 4th ed.*
Bwatch - Oct 2015 - pNA [51-500]

Stone, Jonathan - *The Teller*
BL - v111 - i13 - March 1 2015 - p26(1) [51-500]
KR - Feb 1 2015 - pNA [51-500]
PW - v262 - i5 - Feb 2 2015 - p38(1) [51-500]

Stone, Juliana - *Boys Like You*
y HB Guide - v26 - i1 - Spring 2015 - p25(1) [51-500]
Some Kind of Normal
y BL - v111 - i17 - May 1 2015 - p92(2) [51-500]
SLJ - v61 - i4 - April 2015 - p171(2) [51-500]
y VOYA - v38 - i2 - June 2015 - p68(2) [51-500]

Stone, Lynn - *Barn Babies!*
c CH Bwatch - April 2015 - pNA [51-500]

Stone-MacDonald, Angi - *Engaging Young Engineers: Teaching Problem Solving Skills through STEM*
RVBW - Sept 2015 - pNA [51-500]

Stone, Matthew - *Bad Judgment*
KR - July 15 2015 - pNA [501+]

Stone, Mina - *Cooking for Artists*
SPBW - August 2015 - pNA [51-500]

Stone, Nick - *The Verdict*
BL - v112 - i4 - Oct 15 2015 - p24(1) [51-500]
KR - Oct 1 2015 - pNA [51-500]
LJ - v140 - i14 - Sept 1 2015 - p96(1) [501+]
NYT - Dec 10 2015 - pC1(L) [501+]
PW - v262 - i38 - Sept 21 2015 - p54(2) [51-500]

Stone, Oliver - *The Untold History of the United States: Young Readers Edition, vol. 1: 1898-1945*
y CH Bwatch - Feb 2015 - pNA [51-500]
y HB Guide - v26 - i2 - Fall 2015 - p222(1) [51-500]

Stone, Peter - *The Canary Islands: A Cultural History*
TLS - i5846 - April 17 2015 - p27(1) [501+]

Stone, Rob - *Auditions: Architecture and Aurality*
LJ - v140 - i14 - Sept 1 2015 - p100(1) [51-500]
TimHES - i2213 - July 23 2015 - p48-49 [501+]

Stone, Rosamund Zander - *Pathways to Possibility*
PW - v262 - i42 - Oct 19 2015 - p39(1) [501+]

Stone, Tamara Ireland - *Every Last Word*
y BL - v111 - i19-20 - June 1 2015 - p95(1) [51-500]
c HB Guide - v26 - i2 - Fall 2015 - p140(1) [51-500]
y KR - April 15 2015 - pNA [51-500]
y PW - v262 - i16 - April 20 2015 - p78(1) [51-500]
y SLJ - v61 - i6 - June 2015 - p130(1) [51-500]
y VOYA - v38 - i3 - August 2015 - p70(1) [501+]

Stone, Tanya Lee - *Courage Has No Color: The True Story of the Triple Nickels, America's First Black Paratroopers*
RVBW - Feb 2015 - pNA [51-500]
The House That Jane Built: A Story about Jane Addams (Illus. by Brown, Kathryn)
c CCB-B - v69 - i1 - Sept 2015 - p58(1) [51-500]
c PW - v262 - i17 - April 27 2015 - p74(1) [501+]
c HB - v91 - i5 - Sept-Oct 2015 - p133(1) [51-500]
c PW - v262 - i49 - Dec 2 2015 - p47(1) [51-500]
c SLJ - v61 - i9 - Sept 2015 - p182(1) [51-500]

Stoneman, Richard - *The Alexander Romance in Persia and the East*
Class R - v65 - i1 - April 2015 - p91-93 [501+]
Xerxes: A Persian Life
KR - August 1 2015 - pNA [51-500]
TimHES - i2211 - July 9 2015 - p48(1) [501+]
HT - v65 - i11 - Nov 2015 - p58(1) [501+]
TimHES - i2218 - August 27 2015 - p45-46 [501+]

Stones, Alison - *Gothic Manuscripts: 1260-1320, Part 1, 2 vols.*
Med R - Jan 2015 - pNA [501+]

Stones, Brenda - *What We Eat*
   c HB Guide - v26 - i2 - Fall 2015 - p189(1) [51-500]
Stoop, Naoko - *Red Knit Cap Girl and the Reading Tree*
   c HB Guide - v26 - i1 - Spring 2015 - p47(1) [51-500]
Stoppard, Tom - *The Hard Problem*
   TLS - i5836 - Feb 6 2015 - p17(1) [501+]
Storad, Conrad J. - *Earth's Changing Surface*
   c Sci & Ch - v52 - i8 - April-May 2015 - p16 [501+]
Storer, Colin - *A Short History of the Weimar Republic*
   GSR - v38 - i2 - May 2015 - p434-3 [501+]
Storer, Jen - *Danny Best: Full On (Illus. by Vane, Mitch)*
   c Magpies - v30 - i5 - Nov 2015 - p38(1) [501+]
The Fourteenth Summer of Angus Jack (Illus. by Gifford, Lucinda)
   c Magpies - v30 - i5 - Nov 2015 - p39(1) [501+]
Stores, Bruce - *Christian Science*
   KR - April 1 2015 - pNA [51-500]
Storey, Mark - *Rural Fictions, Urban Realities: A Geography of Gilded Age American Literature*
   AL - v87 - i2 - June 2015 - p391-393 [501+]
Storey, Richard - *The Mount Athos Diet: The Mediterranean Plan to Lose Weight, Look Younger and Live Longer*
   PW - v262 - i27 - July 6 2015 - p63(2) [51-500]
Storey, Rita - *The Christmas Book*
   c HB Guide - v26 - i1 - Spring 2015 - p135(1) [51-500]
The Easter Book
   c HB Guide - v26 - i1 - Spring 2015 - p135(1) [51-500]
Plan, Prepare, Cook Series
   c HB Guide - v26 - i1 - Spring 2015 - p175(1) [51-500]
Storey, Tessa - *Healthy Living in Late Renaissance Italy*
   HER - v130 - i544 - June 2015 - p744(3) [501+]
   HNet - Jan 2015 - pNA [501+]
   Six Ct J - v46 - i1 - Spring 2015 - p228-230 [501+]
Stork, Francisco X. - *The Memory of Light*
   y BL - v112 - i5 - Nov 1 2015 - p55(2) [51-500]
   y KR - Nov 1 2015 - pNA [51-500]
Storm, Lise - *Party Politics and the Prospects for Democracy in North Africa*
   IJMES - v47 - i1 - Feb 2015 - p210-212 [501+]
Storms, G. Gilbert - *Reconnaissance on Sonora: Charles D. Poston's 1854 Exploration of Mexico and the Gadsden Purchase*
   Roundup M - v23 - i1 - Oct 2015 - p35(1) [501+]
Storrs, Landon R.Y. - *The Second Red Scare and the Unmaking of the New Deal Left*
   Historian - v77 - i1 - Spring 2015 - p144(2) [501+]
Storti, Kara - *Tripping Back Blue*
   y KR - Jan 1 2016 - pNA [51-500]
Story, James B. - *The Story: An Autobiography*
   APJ - v29 - i3 - May-June 2015 - p93(2) [501+]
The Story of the Civil Rights Movement in Photographs Series
   c BL - v111 - i15 - April 1 2015 - p58(1) [501+]
Stossel, Scott - *My Age of Anxiety: Fear, Hope, Dread, and the Search for Peace of Mind*
   NYTBR - March 8 2015 - p32(L) [501+]
Stoten, Jim - *Mr. Tweed's Good Deeds (Illus. by Stoten, Jim)*
   c Bkbird - v53 - i1 - Wntr 2015 - p63(1) [501+]
Stott, Andrew McConnell - *The Vampyre Family: Passion, Envy and the Curse of Byron*
   Clio - v44 - i2 - Spring 2015 - p217-237 [501+]
Stott, Ann - *What to Do When You're Sent to Your Room (Illus. by Gilpin, Stephen)*
   c HB Guide - v26 - i1 - Spring 2015 - p47(1) [51-500]
Stott, Libby - *Dancing with a Baptist*
   KR - August 15 2015 - pNA [501+]
Stottmeister, Jan - *Der George-Kreis und die Theosophie: Mit einem Exkurs zum Swastika-Zeichen bei Helena Blavatsky, Alfred Schuler und Stefan George*
   GSR - v38 - i2 - May 2015 - p425-3 [501+]
Stourdze, Sam - *Charlie Chaplin: The Keystone Album*
   Si & So - v25 - i7 - July 2015 - p106(1) [501+]
Stout, D.J. - *Variations on a Rectangle: Thirty Years of Graphic Design from Texas Monthly to Pentagram*
   NYTBR - Dec 6 2015 - p30(L) [501+]
Stout, Glenn - *The Selling of the Babe: The Deal That Changed Baseball and Created a Legend*
   KR - Jan 1 2016 - pNA [51-500]
Stout, Janis - *South by Southwest: Katherine Anne Porter and the Burden of Texas History*
   MFSF - v61 - i3 - Fall 2015 - p544-547 [501+]
Stout, Katie M. - *Hello, I Love You*
   y KR - March 15 2015 - pNA [51-500]
   y PW - v262 - i16 - April 20 2015 - p78(2) [51-500]
   y SLJ - v61 - i6 - June 2015 - p130(1) [51-500]
   y VOYA - v38 - i3 - August 2015 - p70(1) [51-500]

Stout, Shawn K. - *Penelope Crumb Is Mad at the Moon (Illus. by Docampo, Valeria)*
   c HB Guide - v26 - i1 - Spring 2015 - p94(1) [51-500]
A Tiny Piece of Sky
   KR - Oct 15 2015 - pNA [51-500]
Stovall, Tyler - *Transnational France: The Modern History of a Universal Nation*
   BL - v111 - i14 - March 15 2015 - p42(1) [51-500]
Stove, David - *Against the Idols of the Age*
   Nat R - v67 - i21 - Nov 19 2015 - p77(2) [501+]
Stover, Sara Avant - *The Book of She*
   RVBW - Nov 2015 - pNA [51-500]
Stower, Adam - *Troll and the Oliver (Illus. by Stower, Adam)*
   c KR - June 15 2015 - pNA [51-500]
   c SLJ - v61 - i8 - August 2015 - p76(2) [51-500]
Stowers, Sylvia C. - *Shadows of Us*
   SPBW - June 2015 - pNA [51-500]
Stoyan, Ronald - *A Paper Atlas for the Digital Age: Interstellarum Deep Sky Atlas*
   S&T - v130 - i2 - August 2015 - p57(3) [501+]
Stoykova-Klemer, Katerina - *The Season of Delicate Hunger*
   WLT - v89 - i3-4 - May-August 2015 - p123(1) [51-500]
Strachan, Hew - *The Oxford Illustrated History of the First World War*
   J Mil H - v79 - i3 - July 2015 - p855-856 [501+]
Stradal, J. Ryan - *Kitchens of the Great Midwest (Read by Ryan, Amy). Audiobook Review*
   LJ - v140 - i20 - Dec 1 2015 - p60(1) [51-500]
Kitchens of the Great Midwest
   BL - v111 - i19-20 - June 1 2015 - p44(1) [51-500]
   KR - May 15 2015 - pNA [51-500]
   LJ - v140 - i11 - June 15 2015 - p81(2) [51-500]
   NYTBR - August 9 2015 - p20(L) [501+]
   PW - v262 - i21 - May 25 2015 - p32(2) [51-500]
   SEP - v287 - i3 - May-June 2015 - p24(1) [501+]
   y SLJ - v61 - i11 - Oct 2015 - p123(1) [51-500]
Strady, Sophie - *The Memory of an Elephant: An Unforgettable Journey (Illus. by Martin, Jean-Francois)*
   c HB Guide - v26 - i1 - Spring 2015 - p47(1) [51-500]
Strahan, Michael - *Wake Up Happy: The Dream Big, Win Big Guide to Transforming Your Life*
   PW - v262 - i37 - Sept 14 2015 - p59(1) [51-500]
Strambini, Karla - *The Extraordinary Mr. Qwerty*
   c HB Guide - v26 - i1 - Spring 2015 - p47(1) [51-500]
Strand, Clark - *Waking Up to the Dark*
   KR - Feb 1 2015 - pNA [501+]
Strand, Ginger - *The Brothers Vonnegut: Science and Fiction in the House of Magic*
   BL - v112 - i1 - Sept 1 2015 - p28(2) [51-500]
   LJ - v140 - i14 - Sept 1 2015 - p102(1) [51-500]
   PW - v262 - i39 - Sept 28 2015 - p81(1) [51-500]
   KR - Sept 1 2015 - pNA [51-500]
   New R - v246 - i12 - Nov 2015 - p72(4) [501+]
Strand, Jeff - *The Greatest Zombie Movie Ever*
   y KR - Dec 15 2015 - pNA [51-500]
Strand, Mark - *Collected Poems*
   NYRB - v62 - i12 - July 9 2015 - p69(2) [501+]
Strandberg, Mats - *The Key*
   y SLJ - v61 - i8 - August 2015 - p113(1) [51-500]
Strang, Catriona - *Corked*
   Can Lit - i224 - Spring 2015 - p140 [501+]
Strang, G. Bruce - *Collision of Empires: Italy's Invasion of Ethiopia and Its International Impact*
   HNet - March 2015 - pNA [501+]
Strange, Julie-Marie - *British Family Life, 1780-1914, vol. 2: Husbands and Fathers*
   HER - v130 - i545 - August 2015 - p1015(3) [501+]
British Family Life, 1780-1914, vol. 5: Substitute Families
   HER - v130 - i545 - August 2015 - p1015(3) [501+]
Fatherhood and the British Working Class, 1865-1914
   TimHES - i2200 - April 23 2015 - p53(1) [501+]
Strangelove, Michael - *Post-TV: Piracy, Cord-cutting, and the Future of Television*
   TLS - i5868 - Sept 18 2015 - p12(2) [501+]
Strasser, Todd - *The Beast of Cretacea*
   y BL - v112 - i2 - Sept 15 2015 - p62(2) [51-500]
   y KR - August 2015 - pNA [51-500]
   y PW - v262 - i30 - July 27 2015 - p68(2) [51-500]
   y SLJ - v61 - i8 - August 2015 - p98(3) [51-500]
   y VOYA - v38 - i3 - August 2015 - p84(1) [51-500]

Stratford, Jordan - *The Case of the Girl in Grey (Illus. by Murphy, Kelly)*
   c KR - Nov 1 2015 - pNA [51-500]
   c SLJ - v61 - i12 - Dec 2015 - p108(1) [51-500]
The Case of the Missing Moonstone (Read by Barber, Nicola). Audiobook Review
   c BL - v111 - i17 - May 1 2015 - p60(1) [51-500]
   SLJ - v61 - i3 - March 2015 - p78(1) [51-500]
The Case of the Missing Moonstone (Illus. by Murphy, Kelly)
   c Res Links - v20 - i5 - June 2015 - p11(1) [51-500]
   c Sch Lib - v63 - i2 - Summer 2015 - p110(1) [51-500]
   c HB Guide - v26 - i2 - Fall 2015 - p104(1) [51-500]
The Wollenstonecraft Detective Agency
   y CH Bwatch - April 2015 - pNA [51-500]
Strathern, Paul - *Death in Florence: The Medici, Savonarola, and the Battle for the Soul of a Renaissance City*
   BL - v111 - i21 - July 1 2015 - p18(1) [51-500]
   KR - May 15 2015 - pNA [51-500]
   LJ - v140 - i10 - June 1 2015 - p116(1) [51-500]
   PW - v262 - i22 - June 1 2015 - p52(1) [51-500]
The Medici: Power, Money, and Ambition in the Italian Renaissance
   KR - Dec 1 2015 - pNA [501+]
Stratigakos, Despina - *Hitler at Home*
   NYRB - v62 - i20 - Dec 17 2015 - p36(3) [501+]
   TimHES - i2225 - Oct 15 2015 - p46-47 [501+]
Stratton, Allan - *The Dogs*
   y CCB-B - v69 - i2 - Oct 2015 - p115(1) [51-500]
   y KR - July 1 2015 - pNA [51-500]
   y Magpies - v30 - i1 - March 2015 - p44(1) [501+]
   y Res Links - v20 - i5 - June 2015 - p28(2) [501+]
   y Sch Lib - v63 - i2 - Summer 2015 - p121(1) [51-500]
   y SLJ - v61 - i7 - July 2015 - p89(2) [51-500]
   y VOYA - v38 - i4 - Oct 2015 - p63(1) [51-500]
Stratton, Billy J. - *Buried in Shades of Night: Contested Voices, Indian Captivity, and the Legacy of King Philip's War*
   Am Ind CRJ - v39 - i1 - Wntr 2015 - p116-118 [501+]
Stratton, Matthew - *The Politics of Irony in American Modernism*
   SAH - v4 - i2 - Dec 15 2015 - p296-298 [501+]
Straub, Emma - *The Vacationers*
   NYTBR - May 31 2015 - p52(L) [501+]
Straub, Peter - *Interior Darkness*
   KR - Dec 15 2015 - pNA [51-500]
Straumann, Benjamin - *Roman Law in the State of Nature*
   HT - v65 - i10 - Oct 2015 - p56(2) [501+]
Straus, Emily E. - *Death of a Suburban Dream: Race and Schools in Compton, California*
   AHR - v120 - i2 - April 2015 - p641-642 [501+]
   JAH - v101 - i4 - March 2015 - p1331-1332 [501+]
   PHR - v84 - i4 - Nov 2015 - p554(555) [501+]
   WHQ - v46 - i2 - Summer 2015 - p244-245 [501+]
Strausbaugh, John - *The Village: 400 Years of Beats and Bohemians, Radicals and Rogues: A History of Greenwich Village*
   BL - v111 - i5 - Nov 1 2015 - p18(2) [501+]
Strauss, Barry - *The Death of Caesar: The Story of History's Most Famous Assassination (Read by Dean, Robertson). Audiobook Review*
   LJ - v140 - i10 - June 1 2015 - p63(1) [51-500]
The Death of Caesar: The Story of History's Most Famous Assassination
   KR - Jan 1 2015 - pNA [501+]
   LJ - v140 - i2 - Feb 1 2015 - p96(1) [51-500]
   Mac - v128 - i10 - March 16 2015 - p57(1) [51-500]
   NYTBR - March 15 2015 - p9(L) [501+]
Strauss, Claudia - *Making Sense of Public Opinion: American Discourses about Immigration and Social Programs*
   CS - v44 - i1 - Jan 2015 - p121-123 [501+]
Strauss, Erica - *The Hands-On Home: A Seasonal Guide to Cooking, Preserving and Natural Homekeeping*
   LJ - v140 - i16 - Oct 1 2015 - p102(1) [51-500]
Strauss, Neil - *The Truth: An Uncomfortable Book about Relationships*
   BL - v112 - i3 - Oct 1 2015 - p8(1) [51-500]
   KR - Sept 1 2015 - pNA [501+]
Strawn, Brent A. - *The Oxford Encyclopedia of the Bible and Law, 2 vols.*
   BL - v111 - i21 - July 1 2015 - p4(1) [501+]
   LJ - v140 - i12 - July 1 2015 - p111(1) [51-500]
Strayed, Cheryl - *Brave Enough*
   KR - Sept 1 2015 - pNA [51-500]
Strayhorn, Willa - *The Way We Bared Our Souls*
   y CCB-B - v68 - i7 - March 2015 - p371(1) [51-500]
   c HB Guide - v26 - i2 - Fall 2015 - p140(1) [51-500]
   y VOYA - v37 - i6 - Feb 2015 - p67(1) [501+]

Book Review Index 2016 Cumulation **SUBRAMANIAN • 447**

Streb, Elizabeth - *Streb: How to Become an Extreme Action Hero*
HR - v67 - i4 - Wntr 2015 - p647-652 [501+]
Strecher, Matthew - *The Forbidden Worlds of Haruki Murakami*
HNet - Jan 2015 - pNA [501+]
Strecker, Susan - *Nowhere Girl*
KR - Jan 1 2016 - pNA [51-500]
Streeby, Shelley - *Radical Sensations: World Movements, Violence, and Visual Culture*
AL - v87 - i1 - March 2015 - p209-211 [501+]
RAH - v43 - i1 - March 2015 - p134-142 [501+]
Streelman, J. Todd - *Advances in Evolutionary Developmental Biology*
QRB - v90 - i3 - Sept 2015 - p340(2) [501+]
Street, Pat - *You're Pulling My Leg! (Illus. by Brace, Eric)*
c KR - Dec 1 2015 - pNA [51-500]
Street, Richard Steven - *Jon Lewis: Photographs of the California Grape Strike*
PHR - v84 - i1 - Feb 2015 - p102(2) [501+]
WHQ - v46 - i1 - Spring 2015 - p89-89 [501+]
Street, William - *The Tick Rider: A Story of Families, Homelands, Drugs, Redemption, and the Dividing Rio Grande*
SPBW - August 2015 - pNA [51-500]
SPBW - Sept 2015 - pNA [51-500]
Streete, Adrian - *Early Modern Drama and the Bible: Contexts and Readings, 1570-1625*
MLR - v110 - i2 - April 2015 - p525-526 [501+]
Strehle, Stephen - *The Dark Side of Church/State Separation: The French Revolution, Nazi Germany, and International Communism*
RM - v68 - i4 - June 2015 - p874(3) [501+]
Streib, Jessi - *The Power of the Past: Understanding Cross-Class Marriages*
TimHES - i2199 - April 16 2015 - p56-57 [501+]
Stresemann Workshop 2015: Illusionary Visions or Policy Options? Discontent over Cold War Security Architecture in Europe and the Search for Alternatives
HNet - Sept 2015 - pNA [501+]
Stribling, Gerry - *Buddhism for Dudes: A Jarhead's Field Guide to Mindfulness*
PW - v262 - i23 - June 8 2015 - p54(1) [51-500]
Strickland, Adrianne - *Lifeless*
y KR - May 1 2015 - pNA [51-500]
y VOYA - v38 - i3 - August 2015 - p84(1) [51-500]
Strieber, Whitley - *Underworld*
MFSF - v128 - i1-2 - Jan-Feb 2015 - p46(2) [501+]
Strietman, Elsa - *For Pleasure and Profit: Six Dutch Rhetoricians Plays, with Facing-Page Translation*
Ren Q - v68 - i3 - Fall 2015 - p1120-1121 [501+]
Strikwerda, Erik - *The Wages of Relief: Cities and the Unemployed in Prairie Canada, 1929-39*
Can Hist R - v96 - i1 - March 2015 - p133(3) [501+]
Strindberg, August - *The Defence of a Madman*
TLS - i5845 - April 10 2015 - p21(1) [501+]
Striner, Richard - *Woodrow Wilson and World War I: A Burden too Great to Bear*
J Mil H - v79 - i3 - July 2015 - p860-861 [501+]
Pres St Q - v45 - i1 - March 2015 - p215(3) [501+]
Stringer, Keith J. - *Norman Expansion: Connections, Continuities and Contrasts*
AHR - v120 - i2 - April 2015 - p700-701 [501+]
HER - v130 - i545 - August 2015 - p954(3) [501+]
Strobel, Lee - *The Case for Grace: A Journalist Explores the Evidence of Transformed Lives*
Ch Today - April 2015 - p82(1) [51-500]
Case for Grace for Kids (Illus. by Colon, Terry)
c BL - v111 - i19-20 - June 1 2015 - p76(1) [51-500]
c SLJ - v61 - i7 - July 2015 - p110(1) [51-500]
The Case for Grace Student Edition: A Journalist Explores the Evidence of Transformed Lives
y SLJ - v61 - i7 - July 2015 - p110(1) [51-500]
Stroby, Wallace - *The Devil's Share (Read by Marlo, Coleen). Audiobook Review*
BL - v112 - i2 - Sept 15 2015 - p76(1) [51-500]
The Devil's Share
BL - v111 - i18 - May 15 2015 - p27(1) [51-500]
KR - May 1 2015 - pNA [51-500]
PW - v262 - i18 - May 4 2015 - p97(1) [51-500]
Strock, Carren - *Tangled Ribbons*
PW - v262 - i8 - Feb 23 2015 - p58(1) [51-500]
Strogatz, Steven H. - *Nonlinear Dynamics and Chaos: With Applications to Physics, Biology, Chemistry, and Engineering*
Phys Today - v68 - i4 - April 2015 - p54-55 [501+]
Strohm, Paul - *Chaucer's Tale: 1386 and the Road to Canterbury*
Bks & Cult - v21 - i1 - Jan-Feb 2015 - p37(1) [501+]
Med R - August 2015 - pNA [501+]
The Poet's Tale: Chaucer and The Year That Made the Canterbury Tales
Econ - v414 - i8924 - Feb 7 2015 - p79(US) [501+]
HT - v65 - i7 - July 2015 - p61(1) [501+]
NS - v144 - i5245 - Jan 16 2015 - p47(1) [51-500]
Spec - v327 - i9725 - Jan 17 2015 - p32(2) [501+]
TimHES - i2191 - Feb 19 2015 - p52-53 [501+]
Strohn, Matthias - *World War I Companion*
HNet - May 2015 - pNA [501+]
J Mil H - v79 - i4 - Oct 2015 - p1140-1141 [501+]
Strom, Adam - *Washington's Rebuke to Bigotry: Reflections on Our First President's Famous 1790 Letter to the Hebrew Congregation In Newport, Rhode Island*
SPBW - Oct 2015 - pNA [501+]
Strong, Gordon - *Modern Homebrew Recipes: Exploring Styles and Contemporary Techniques*
Bwatch - August 2015 - pNA [51-500]
Strong, Jeremy - *A Perfectly Ordinary School (Illus. by Anderson, Scoular)*
c Sch Lib - v63 - i1 - Spring 2015 - p44(1) [51-500]
Strong, John S. - *Buddhisms: An Introduction*
LJ - v140 - i16 - Oct 1 2015 - p64(2) [501+]
Strong, Lynn Steger - *Hold Still*
KR - Jan 1 2016 - pNA [51-500]
PW - v262 - i50 - Dec 7 2015 - p62(1) [51-500]
Strong, Rowan - *Edward Bouverie Pusey and the Oxford Movement*
VS - v57 - i3 - Spring 2015 - p551(2) [501+]
Strosetzki, Christoph - *Saberes Humanisticos*
Six Ct J - v46 - i3 - Fall 2015 - p755-756 [501+]
Stroud, Carsten - *The Reckoning*
KR - June 15 2015 - pNA [501+]
PW - v262 - i24 - June 15 2015 - p64(1) [51-500]
Stroud, Dean G. - *Preaching in Hitler's Shadow: Sermons of Resistance in the Third Reich*
TT - v72 - i1 - April 2015 - p122-123 [501+]
Stroud, Jonathan - *The Hollow Boy*
c BL - v112 - i4 - Oct 15 2015 - p50(2) [51-500]
c SLJ - v61 - i12 - Dec 2015 - p108(1) [51-500]
The Whispering Skull (Read by Lyons, Katie). Audiobook Review
c BL - v111 - i14 - March 15 2015 - p24(2) [501+]
The Whispering Skull
c HB Guide - v26 - i1 - Spring 2015 - p94(1) [51-500]
Stroud, Rick - *Kidnap in Crete*
KR - Feb 1 2015 - pNA [501+]
Strouse, Ben - *Hey Boy (Illus. by Phelan, Jennifer)*
PW - v262 - i20 - May 18 2015 - p81(1) [51-500]
Strout, Elizabeth - *My Name Is Lucy Barton*
BL - v112 - i6 - Nov 15 2015 - p22(1) [51-500]
KR - Oct 15 2015 - pNA [501+]
PW - v262 - i42 - Oct 19 2015 - p48(2) [51-500]
The Stories of Frederick Busch
NYTBR - April 26 2015 - p28(L) [501+]
Strube, Sebastian - *Euer Dorf Soll Schoner Werden: Landlicher Wandel, Staatliche Planung und Demokratisierung in der Bundesrepublik Deutschland*
HNet - June 2015 - pNA [501+]
Strugatsky, Boris - *The Dead Mountaineer's Inn*
NYTBR - May 31 2015 - p38(L) [501+]
Strum, Daniel - *The Sugar Trade: Brazil, Portugal and the Netherlands (1595-1630).*
HAHR - v95 - i1 - Feb 2015 - p150-152 [501+]
JIH - v45 - i3 - Wntr 2015 - p407-412 [501+]
JMH - v87 - i3 - Sept 2015 - p707(3) [501+]
Strumwasser, Stu - *The Organ Broker*
PW - v262 - i13 - March 30 2015 - p55(2) [51-500]
RVBW - June 2015 - pNA [51-500]
Strunk, William, Jr. - *The Elements of Style*
NYT - Nov 27 2015 - pC31(L) [501+]
Strutt, Laura - *Arm Candy: Friendship Bracelets to Make and Share*
LJ - v140 - i14 - Sept 1 2015 - p104(1) [51-500]
Struzik, Edward - *Future Arctic: Field Notes from a World on the Edge*
BioSci - v65 - i8 - August 2015 - p830(2) [501+]
BioSci - v65 - i8 - August 2015 - p832(2) [501+]
BL - v111 - i12 - Feb 15 2015 - p26(2) [51-500]
Nature - v518 - i7538 - Feb 12 2015 - p165(1) [51-500]
New Sci - v226 - i3016 - April 11 2015 - p42(2) [501+]
Stuart, Alison - *Claiming the Rebel's Heart*
PW - v262 - i22 - June 1 2015 - p48(2) [51-500]
Gather the Bones. E-book Review
PW - v262 - i19 - May 11 2015 - p43(1) [51-500]
Stuart, Anne - *Consumed by Fire*
PW - v262 - i10 - March 9 2015 - p58(1) [51-500]
Stuart, David E. - *Anasazi America: Seventeen Centuries on the Road from Center Place, 2d ed.*
Roundup M - v22 - i6 - August 2015 - p41(1) [501+]
Stubbe, Henry - *Henry Stubbe and the Beginnings of Islam: The Originall & Progress of Mahometanism*
Ren Q - v68 - i1 - Spring 2015 - p357-357 [501+]
Stubbs, John - *Donne: The Reformed Soul*
TimHES - i2200 - April 23 2015 - p51(1) [501+]
Stubbs, Lisa - *Lily and Bear (Illus. by Stubbs, Lisa)*
c NYTBR - Nov 8 2015 - p33(L) [501+]
c PW - v262 - i26 - June 29 2015 - p66(1) [51-500]
c Sch Lib - v63 - i3 - Autumn 2015 - p161(1) [51-500]
c SLJ - v61 - i10 - Oct 2015 - p84(1) [51-500]
Stuchner, Joan Betty - *Bagels on Board! (Illus. by Whamond, Dave)*
c PW - v262 - i38 - Sept 21 2015 - p77(1) [501+]
c SLJ - v61 - i11 - Nov 2015 - p92(2) [51-500]
Bagels the Brave! (Illus. by Whamond, Dave)
c BL - v111 - i17 - May 1 2015 - p93(2) [51-500]
c Res Links - v20 - i4 - April 2015 - p13(1) [51-500]
Stuckey, Rachel - *Sexual Orientation and Gender Identity*
c BL - v111 - i22 - August 1 2015 - p55(1) [51-500]
Straight Talk about ... Digital Dangers
y Res Links - v21 - i1 - Oct 2015 - p45(1) [51-500]
Straight Talk about ... Sexual Orientation and Gender Identity
y Res Links - v21 - i1 - Oct 2015 - p45(1) [51-500]
Studdard, Jody - *Kiana Cruise: Apocalypse*
y KR - Nov 15 2015 - pNA [501+]
Studlar, Gaylyn - *Have Gun--Will Travel*
RVBW - August 2015 - pNA [501+]
Studner, Peter K. - *Super Job Search IV: The Complete Manual for Job Seekers and Career Changers*
SPBW - Nov 2015 - pNA [51-500]
Stuhler, Rachel - *Absolutely True Lies*
y BL - v111 - i16 - April 15 2015 - p23(1) [51-500]
KR - March 15 2015 - pNA [51-500]
LJ - v140 - i6 - April 1 2015 - p85(2) [51-500]
Stup, Sarah - *Paul and His Beast*
KR - Nov 15 2015 - pNA [501+]
Sturm, Fred - *The Art of Tuning*
Am MT - v65 - i1 - August-Sept 2015 - p8(2) [51-500]
Sturm, James - *Gryphons Aren't So Great*
c KR - July 1 2015 - pNA [51-500]
Sleepless Knight (Illus. by Sturm, James)
c CCB-B - v68 - i11 - July-August 2015 - p570(1) [51-500]
c HB - v91 - i2 - March-April 2015 - p85(1) [51-500]
c HB Guide - v26 - i2 - Fall 2015 - p19(1) [51-500]
c KR - Feb 1 2015 - pNA [51-500]
c PW - v262 - i5 - Feb 2 2015 - p57(1) [51-500]
c SLJ - v61 - i3 - March 2015 - p130(1) [51-500]
Sturma, Michael - *Fremantle's Submarines: How Allied Submariners and Western Australians Helped to Win the War in the Pacific*
RVBW - Nov 2015 - pNA [501+]
Stuttard, David - *Looking at Medea: Essays and a Translation of Euripides' Tragedy*
Class R - v65 - i2 - Oct 2015 - p354-356 [501+]
Stutzman, Ervin R. - *Joseph's Dilemma*
RVBW - Nov 2015 - pNA [51-500]
Stuyck, Karen Hanson - *Death by Dumpster*
KR - Oct 15 2015 - pNA [51-500]
Styles, Camille - *Camille Styles Entertaining: Inspired Gatherings and Effortless Style*
LJ - v140 - i3 - Feb 15 2015 - p123(1) [51-500]
Styron, William - *My Generation: Collected Nonfiction*
BL - v111 - i16 - April 15 2015 - p13(1) [51-500]
NYT - June 5 2015 - pC20(L) [501+]
NYTBR - July 5 2015 - p12(L) [501+]
KR - March 15 2015 - pNA [501+]
LJ - v140 - i7 - April 15 2015 - p88(1) [51-500]
PW - v262 - i14 - April 6 2015 - p49(1) [51-500]
Subhra, Gersh - *Billu Leaves India: Memoirs of a Boy's Journey (Illus. by MacLeod-Brudenell, Iain)*
c Sch Lib - v63 - i1 - Spring 2015 - p48(1) [51-500]
Sublett, Jesse - *Broke Not Broken: Homer Maxey's Texas Bank War*
Roundup M - v22 - i6 - August 2015 - p41(1) [501+]
Sublette, Ned - *The American Slave Coast: A History of the Slave-Breeding Industry*
KR - August 15 2015 - pNA [501+]
LJ - v140 - i14 - Sept 1 2015 - p119(1) [51-500]
Subramaniam, Arundhathi - *When God Is a Traveller*
WLT - v89 - i5 - Sept-Oct 2015 - p75(1) [51-500]
Subramanian, Meera - *A River Runs Again: India's Natural World in Crisis, from the Barren Cliffs of*

448 • SUBRAMANIAN Book Review Index 2016 Cumulation

Rajasthan to the Farmlands of Karnataka
BL - v111 - i22 - August 1 2015 - p9(1) [51-500]
CSM - August 26 2015 - pNA [501+]
KR - June 1 2015 - pNA [501+]
LJ - v140 - i13 - August 1 2015 - p122(1) [51-500]
Nature - v524 - i7564 - August 13 2015 - p159(1) [501+]
New Sci - v228 - i3041 - Oct 3 2015 - p46(2) [501+]
PW - v262 - i25 - June 22 2015 - p132(2) [51-500]
Subramanian, Narendra - *Nation and Family: Personal Law, Cultural Pluralism, and Gendered Citizenship in India*
HNet - May 2015 - pNA [501+]
Subramanian, Samanth - *This Divided Island: Stories from the Sri Lankan War*
KR - Oct 15 2015 - pNA [501+]
NYRB - v62 - i4 - March 5 2015 - p31(3) [501+]
TLS - i5844 - April 3 2015 - p28(1) [501+]
Subversive Networks: Agents of Change in International Organizations, 1920-1960
HNet - June 2015 - pNA [501+]
Suceava, Bogdan - *Miruna, a Tale*
WLT - v89 - i1 - Jan-Feb 2015 - p69(2) [501+]
Suchenski, Richard I. - *Hou Hsiao-Hsien*
HNet - Jan 2015 - pNA [501+]
Si & So - v25 - i1 - Jan 2015 - p106(1) [501+]
TLS - i5868 - Sept 18 2015 - p17(2) [501+]
Sudeikis, Jason - *Sleeping with Other People*
New York - Sept 7 2015 - pNA [501+]
New York - Sept 7 2015 - pNA [501+]
New York - Sept 7 2015 - pNA [501+]
Suderland, Maja - *Inside Concentration Camps: Social Life at the Extremes*
CS - v44 - i5 - Sept 2015 - p718-719 [501+]
Sudjic, Deyan - *Fifty Modern Buildings That Changed the World*
Bwatch - July 2015 - pNA [51-500]
Sudo, Naoto - *Nanyo-Orientalism: Japanese Representations of the Pacific*
Cont Pac - v27 - i2 - Fall 2015 - p579(5) [501+]
Suen, Anastasia - *Alternate Reality Game Designer Jane McGonigal*
c HB Guide - v26 - i1 - Spring 2015 - p196(2) [51-500]
From Accident to Hospital
c BL - v111 - i15 - April 1 2015 - p62(2) [51-500]
A Great Idea? (Illus. by Dippold, Jane)
c HB Guide - v26 - i2 - Fall 2015 - p65(1) [51-500]
iPod and Electronics Visionary Tony Fadell
c HB Guide - v26 - i1 - Spring 2015 - p196(2) [51-500]
Sugar, Alan - *Unscripted: My Ten Years in Telly*
Spec - v329 - i9768 - Nov 14 2015 - p63(1) [501+]
Sugawara no Takasue no Musume - *The Sarashina Diary: A Woman's Life in Eleventh-Century Japan*
HNet - Feb 2015 - pNA [501+]
Sugimoto, Cassidy R. - *Scholarly Metrics under the Microscope: From Citation Analysis to Academic Auditing*
LR - v64 - i6-7 - June-July 2015 - p510-512 [501+]
Sugirtharajah, R.S. - *The Bible and Asia: From the Pre-Christian Era to the Postcolonial Age*
Intpr - v69 - i4 - Oct 2015 - p496(2) [501+]
JAAR - v83 - i3 - Sept 2015 - p872-876 [501+]
Sugrue, Thomas A. - *The New Suburban History*
J Urban H - v41 - i1 - Jan 2015 - p171-10 [501+]
Suh, Serk-Bae - *Treacherous Translation: Culture, Nationalism, and Colonialism in Korea and Japan from the 1910s to the 1960s*
Pac A - v88 - i3 - Sept 2015 - p718 [501+]
Sukel, Kayt - *The Art of Risk*
KR - Jan 1 2016 - pNA [501+]
Sukhanova, Ekaterina - *Body Image and Identity in Contemporary Societies: Psychoanalytical, Social, Cultural, and Aesthetic Perspectives*
ABR - v36 - i5 - July-August 2015 - p23(2) [501+]
Sukkar, Sumia - *The Boy from Aleppo Who Painted the War*
WLT - v89 - i2 - March-April 2015 - p75(1) [51-500]
Sulak, Marcela - *Family Resemblance: An Anthology and Exploration of 8 Hybrid Literary Genres*
PW - v262 - i39 - Sept 28 2015 - p82(1) [51-500]
Sulcoski, Carol J. - *Lace Yarn Studio: Garments, Hats, and Fresh Ideas for Lace Yarn*
LJ - v140 - i8 - May 1 2015 - p73(1) [51-500]
Sullam, Simon Levis - *I carnefici italiani: Scene dal genocidio degli ebrei, 1943-1945*
TimHES - i2210 - July 2 2015 - p47-2 [501+]
TLS - i5856 - June 26 2015 - p7(1) [501+]
Sullins, D. Paul - *Keeping the Vow: The Untold Stories of Married Catholic Priests*
NYRB - v62 - i18 - Nov 19 2015 - p46(2) [501+]
Sullivan, Anna - *Secret Harbor*
PW - v262 - i3 - Jan 19 2015 - p67(1) [51-500]
Sullivan, Brendan Sean - *Irish Blood*
KR - Oct 1 2015 - pNA [501+]
Sullivan, Dan - *NoSQL for Mere Mortals*
Bwatch - Oct 2015 - pNA [501+]
Sullivan, Dana - *Kay Kay's Alphabet Safari (Illus. by Sullivan, Dana)*
c HB Guide - v26 - i2 - Fall 2015 - p53(1) [51-500]
Sullivan, Deidre - *Improper Order*
c BL - v111 - i22 - August 1 2015 - p61(1) [51-500]
Sullivan, Denis F. - *The Life of Saint Basil the Younger: Critical Edition and Annotated Translation of the Moscow Version*
CHR - v101 - i4 - Autumn 2015 - p903(2) [501+]
Med R - August 2015 - pNA [501+]
Specu - v90 - i4 - Oct 2015 - p1172-1174 [501+]
Sullivan, Derek E. - *Biggie*
y BL - v111 - i12 - Feb 15 2015 - p79(1) [51-500]
c BL - v112 - i1 - Sept 1 2015 - p99(1) [501+]
y CCB-B - v68 - i10 - June 2015 - p519(1) [51-500]
y HB - v91 - i3 - May-June 2015 - p121(1) [51-500]
c HB Guide - v26 - i2 - Fall 2015 - p141(1) [51-500]
y KR - Jan 15 2015 - pNA [51-500]
y PW - v262 - i3 - Jan 19 2015 - p84(2) [51-500]
y SLJ - v61 - i2 - Feb 2015 - p109(1) [51-500]
y VOYA - v37 - i6 - Feb 2015 - p67(1) [51-500]
Sullivan, Faith - *Good Night, Mr. Wodehouse*
BL - v112 - i1 - Sept 1 2015 - p51(1) [51-500]
KR - July 15 2015 - pNA [51-500]
PW - v262 - i29 - July 20 2015 - p162(2) [51-500]
Sullivan, James - *Seven Dirty Words: The Life and Crimes of George Carlin*
BL - v111 - i19-20 - June 1 2015 - p30(2) [501+]
Sullivan, Jazmine - *Reality Show*
People - v83 - i3 - Jan 19 2015 - p29 [501+]
People - v83 - i3 - Jan 19 2015 - p29 [501+]
People - v83 - i3 - Jan 19 2015 - p29 [501+]
People - v83 - i3 - Jan 19 2015 - p29 [501+]
People - v83 - i3 - Jan 19 2015 - p29 [501+]
Sullivan, Jem - *Karol, the Boy Who Became Pope: A Story about Saint John Paul II (Illus. by William, Maloney J.)*
c CH Bwatch - Jan 2015 - pNA [51-500]
Sullivan, Karen - *The Inner Lives of Medieval Inquisitors*
Ren Q - v68 - i2 - Summer 2015 - p710-712 [501+]
Sullivan, Kathleen - *Action for Disarmament: 10 Things You Can Do!*
BL - v111 - i9-10 - Jan 1 2015 - p64(1) [51-500]
Sullivan, Kiki - *Midnight Dolls*
y KR - July 15 2015 - pNA [51-500]
Sullivan, Margaret L. - *High Impact School Library Spaces: Envisioning New School Library Concepts*
Teach Lib - v42 - i3 - Feb 2015 - p41(1) [51-500]
Sullivan, Marnie M. - *America in the Thirties*
Am St - v54 - i2 - Summer 2015 - p102-103 [501+]
Sullivan, Martha - *If You Love Honey (Illus. by Morrison, Cathy)*
c CH Bwatch - Nov 2015 - pNA [51-500]
c KR - July 15 2015 - pNA [51-500]
Pitter and Patter (Illus. by Morrison, Cathy)
c CH Bwatch - March 2015 - pNA [51-500]
Sullivan, Mary - *Treat*
c PW - v262 - i50 - Dec 7 2015 - p84(1) [51-500]
Sullivan, Maya - *Dare to Be Your Own Boss: Follow Your Passion, Create a Niche*
KR - August 15 2015 - pNA [501+]
PW - v262 - i27 - July 6 2015 - p60(2) [51-500]
SPBW - August 2015 - pNA [501+]
Sullivan, Paul - *The Thin Green Line: The Money Secrets of the Super Wealthy*
KR - Jan 15 2015 - pNA [501+]
PW - v262 - i4 - Jan 26 2015 - p165(1) [51-500]
Sullivan, Rosemary - *Stalin's Daughter: The Extraordinary and Tumultuous Life of Svetlana Alliluyeva*
BL - v111 - i17 - May 1 2015 - p73(1) [51-500]
CSM - June 4 2015 - pNA [501+]
KR - March 15 2015 - pNA [501+]
LJ - v140 - i7 - April 15 2015 - p94(1) [51-500]
Mac - v128 - i22 - June 8 2015 - p56(1) [501+]
NYRB - v62 - i18 - Nov 19 2015 - p60(3) [501+]
NYTBR - June 14 2015 - p9(L) [501+]
PW - v262 - i14 - April 6 2015 - p50(2) [51-500]
NYT - June 10 2015 - pC1(L) [501+]
TimHES - i2211 - July 9 2015 - p45(1) [501+]
Sullivan, Shannon - *Good White People: The Problem with Middle-Class White Anti-racism*
HNet - August 2015 - pNA [501+]
Sullivan, Tara - *The Bitter Side of Sweet*
y BL - v112 - i7 - Dec 1 2015 - p53(1) [51-500]
y KR - Nov 15 2015 - pNA [51-500]
y PW - v262 - i48 - Nov 30 2015 - p61(1) [51-500]
Sully, Katherine - *My First Bible Stories (Illus. by Sanfilippo, Simona)*
c HB Guide - v26 - i2 - Fall 2015 - p150(1) [51-500]
Sultan, Tim - *Sunny's Nights: Lost and Found at a Bar on the Edge of the World*
BL - v112 - i6 - Nov 15 2015 - p7(1) [51-500]
KR - Nov 15 2015 - pNA [501+]
PW - v262 - i50 - Dec 7 2015 - p80(1) [51-500]
Sulurayok, Matilda - *Kamik's First Sled (Illus. by Leng, Qin)*
c KR - Sept 15 2015 - pNA [51-500]
c SLJ - v61 - i10 - Oct 2015 - p84(1) [51-500]
Suma, Nova Ren - *The Walls around Us (Read by King, Georgia, with Sandy Rustin). Audiobook Review*
y BL - v112 - i5 - Nov 1 2015 - p72(1) [51-500]
The Walls around Us (Read by King, Georgia). Audiobook Review
y HB - v91 - i6 - Nov-Dec 2015 - p111(1) [51-500]
The Walls around Us (Read by King, Georgia, with Sandy Rustin). Audiobook Review
y SLJ - v61 - i9 - Sept 2015 - p62(2) [51-500]
The Walls around Us
y BL - v111 - i15 - April 1 2015 - p71(1) [51-500]
y CCB-B - v68 - i10 - June 2015 - p520(1) [51-500]
y HB - v91 - i2 - March-April 2015 - p111(1) [51-500]
c HB Guide - v26 - i2 - Fall 2015 - p141(1) [51-500]
y KR - Jan 15 2015 - pNA [51-500]
y NYTBR - May 31 2015 - p54(L) [501+]
y SLJ - v61 - i3 - March 2015 - p162(3) [51-500]
y VOYA - v38 - i1 - April 2015 - p71(1) [51-500]
Sumanasara, Alubomulle - *Freedom from Anger: Understanding It, Overcoming It and Finding Joy*
PW - v262 - i15 - April 13 2015 - p73(1) [51-500]
Sumell, Matt - *Making Nice*
Ent W - i1351 - Feb 20 2015 - p63(1) [501+]
NYT - Feb 26 2015 - pC6(L) [501+]
NYTBR - July 12 2015 - p30(L) [501+]
PW - v262 - i11 - March 16 2015 - p44(2) [501+]
Summer, Mary Elizabeth - *Trust Me, I'm Lying*
y HB Guide - v26 - i1 - Spring 2015 - p125(1) [51-500]
Trust Me, I'm Trouble
y KR - August 1 2015 - pNA [51-500]
y SLJ - v61 - i9 - Sept 2015 - p173(1) [51-500]
y VOYA - v38 - i4 - Oct 2015 - p63(1) [51-500]
Summer School "Political Participation: Ideas, Forms and Modes since Antiquity"
HNet - August 2015 - pNA [501+]
Summerley, Victoria - *Longue Vue House and Gardens*
NYTBR - Dec 6 2015 - p66(L) [501+]
Summers, Courtney - *All the Rage*
y CCB-B - v68 - i11 - July-August 2015 - p570(2) [51-500]
c HB Guide - v26 - i2 - Fall 2015 - p141(1) [51-500]
y KR - Feb 1 2015 - pNA [51-500]
y PW - v262 - i9 - March 2 2015 - p87(1) [51-500]
y PW - v262 - i49 - Dec 2 2015 - p88(1) [51-500]
y SLJ - v61 - i5 - May 2015 - p125(2) [51-500]
y VOYA - v37 - i6 - Feb 2015 - p67(1) [51-500]
Summers, Gail - *Across the Inlet*
KR - June 1 2015 - pNA [501+]
Summers, Kyle - *Human Social Evolution: The Foundational Works of Richard D. Alexander*
QRB - v90 - i2 - June 2015 - p220(1) [501+]
Summers, Mark Wahlgren - *The Ordeal of the Reunion: A New History of Reconstruction*
HNet - Sept 2015 - pNA [501+]
JIH - v46 - i3 - Wntr 2016 - p462-463 [501+]
Summers, Sandra Lindemann - *Ogling Ladies: Scopophilia in Medieval German Literature*
JEGP - v114 - i2 - April 2015 - p305(4) [501+]
Summit, April R. - *Contested Waters: An Envionmental History of the Colorado River*
PHR - v84 - i2 - May 2015 - p227(5) [501+]
Summy, Barrie - *The Disappearance of Emily H.*
c BL - v111 - i17 - May 1 2015 - p55(1) [51-500]
y CCB-B - v68 - i11 - July-August 2015 - p571(1) [51-500]
c HB Guide - v26 - i2 - Fall 2015 - p104(1) [51-500]
c PW - v262 - i13 - March 30 2015 - p76(2) [51-500]
c SLJ - v61 - i2 - Feb 2015 - p94(1) [51-500]
y VOYA - v38 - i2 - June 2015 - p83(2) [51-500]
Sumner, Bernard - *Chapter and Verse: New Order, Joy Division and Me*
KR - Sept 1 2015 - pNA [501+]
NYTBR - Dec 6 2015 - p72(L) [501+]
PW - v262 - i41 - Oct 12 2015 - p60(2) [51-500]

Sumner, James - *Brewing Science: Technology and Print, 1700-1880*
T&C - v56 - i2 - April 2015 - p535-536 [501+]
Sumner, Margaret - *Collegiate Republic: Cultivating an Ideal Society in Early America*
AHR - v120 - i3 - June 2015 - p1019-1020 [501+]
Am St - v54 - i1 - Spring 2015 - p154-2 [501+]
JAH - v102 - i1 - June 2015 - p242-243 [501+]
JIH - v46 - i2 - Autumn 2015 - p296-297 [501+]
JSH - v81 - i4 - Nov 2015 - p958(2) [501+]
Sumner, Melanie - *How to Write a Novel*
KR - April 1 2015 - pNA [51-500]
LJ - v140 - i9 - May 15 2015 - p77(1) [51-500]
Sumner-Smith, Karina - *Defiant*
PW - v262 - i11 - March 16 2015 - p67(1) [51-500]
Sumption, Jonathan - *Cursed Kings: The Hundred Years War, vol. 4*
Spec - v328 - i9757 - August 29 2015 - p36(1) [501+]
Sun Yu - *Wild Rose*
Pac A - v88 - i2 - June 2015 - p294 [501+]
Pac A - v88 - i2 - June 2015 - p294 [501+]
Sundaram, Anjan - *Bad News: Last Journalists in a Dictatorship*
BL - v112 - i5 - Nov 1 2015 - p4(1) [51-500]
KR - Oct 1 2015 - pNA [501+]
Sundaram, Jomo Kwame - *Malaysia@50: Economic Development, Distribution, Disparities*
BHR - v89 - i2 - Summer 2015 - p399(3) [501+]
Sundberg, Ingrid - *All We Left Behind*
y BL - v112 - i4 - Oct 15 2015 - p56(1) [51-500]
y KR - Oct 1 2015 - pNA [51-500]
y SLJ - v61 - i11 - Nov 2015 - p122(1) [51-500]
Sundell, Joanne - *Arctic Storm*
Roundup M - v22 - i6 - August 2015 - p32(1) [501+]
Roundup M - v23 - i1 - Oct 2015 - p31(1) [501+]
Sunderland, Willard - *The Baron's Cloak: A History of the Russian Empire in War and Revolution*
AHR - v120 - i1 - Feb 2015 - p181-183 [501+]
Sundin, Sarah - *Through Waters Deep*
BL - v111 - i21 - July 1 2015 - p45(1) [51-500]
Sundquist, Josh - *We Should Hang Out Sometime: Embarrassingly, a True Story*
y CCB-B - v68 - i7 - March 2015 - p371(2) [51-500]
y HB Guide - v26 - i2 - Fall 2015 - p212(1) [51-500]
y VOYA - v37 - i6 - Feb 2015 - p67(1) [51-500]
Sundqvist, Fideli - *I Love Paper: Paper-Cutting Techniques and Templates for Amazing Toys, Sculptures, Props, and Costumes*
LJ - v140 - i8 - May 1 2015 - p72(1) [51-500]
Sundstol, Vidar - *The Ravens*
KR - March 15 2015 - pNA [51-500]
LJ - v140 - i8 - May 1 2015 - p5(1) [51-500]
Sunquist, Scott W. - *The Gospel and Pluralism Today: Reassessing Lesslie Newbigin in the 21st Century*
Ch Today - v59 - i10 - Dec 2015 - p74(1) [51-500]
Sunstein, Cass R. - *Constitutional Personae: Heroes, Soldiers, Minimalists, and Mutes*
KR - June 1 2015 - pNA [501+]
PW - v262 - i31 - August 3 2015 - p49(1) [51-500]
Simpler: The Future of Government
TimHES - i2207 - June 11 2015 - p53(1) [501+]
Valuing Life: Humanizing the Regulatory State
NYRB - v62 - i4 - March 5 2015 - p23(3) [501+]
Wiser: Getting Beyond Groupthink to Make Groups Smarter
NYRB - v62 - i4 - March 5 2015 - p23(3) [501+]
Sununu, John H. - *The Quiet Man: The Indispensable Presidency of George H.W. Bush*
LJ - v140 - i9 - May 15 2015 - p89(1) [51-500]
KR - April 15 2015 - pNA [51-500]
Suny, Ronald Grigor - *A Question of Genocide: Armenians and Turks at the End of the Ottoman Empire*
HT - v65 - i7 - July 2015 - p56(2) [501+]
"They Can Live in the Desert but Nowhere Else": A History of the Armenian Genocide
CC - v132 - i9 - April 29 2015 - p48(2) [501+]
They Can Live in the Desert but Nowhere Else: A History of the Armenian Genocide
HT - v65 - i7 - July 2015 - p56(2) [501+]
"They Can Live in the Desert But Nowhere Else": A History of the Armenian Genocide
KR - Feb 1 2015 - pNA [501+]
Lon R Bks - v37 - i11 - June 4 2015 - p6(3) [501+]
NS - v144 - i5259 - April 24 2015 - p46(3) [501+]
Suprynowicz, Vin - *The Testament of James*
SPBW - March 2015 - pNA [51-500]
Supyan, Ekaterina - *'Brautschau' auf Russisch-Judisch-Deutsch: Ein- und Ausgrenzungsprozesse des Netzwerks russisch(sprachig)er Juden in Deutschland*
Ger Q - v88 - i2 - Spring 2015 - p267(2) [501+]
Surak, Kristin - *Making Tea, Making Japan: Cultural Nationalism in Practice*
CS - v44 - i2 - March 2015 - pNA [501+]
Suresha, Ron Jackson - *The Biggest Lover: Big Boned Men's Erotica for Chubs and Chasers*
PW - v262 - i51 - Dec 14 2015 - p67(1) [51-500]
Surges, Carol S. - *Food Chains*
c HB Guide - v26 - i1 - Spring 2015 - p154(1) [51-500]
Surget, Alain - *Escape from Veracruz (Illus. by Marnat, Annette)*
c HB Guide - v26 - i2 - Fall 2015 - p71(1) [51-500]
The Pirate's Legacy (Illus. by Marnat, Annette)
c HB Guide - v26 - i2 - Fall 2015 - p71(1) [51-500]
Suri, K.C. - *Political Science, vol. 2: Indian Democracy*
Pac A - v88 - i1 - March 2015 - p139 [501+]
Surian, Adrianne - *DIY T-Shirt Crafts: From Braided Bracelets to Floor Pillows, 50 Unexpected Ways To Recycle Your Old T-Shirts*
LJ - v140 - i15 - Sept 15 2015 - p76(1) [51-500]
Surovec, Yasmine - *A Bed for Kitty (Illus. by Surovec, Yasmine)*
c HB Guide - v26 - i1 - Spring 2015 - p17(1) [51-500]
I See Kitty (Illus. by Surovec, Yasmine)
c SLJ - v61 - i7 - July 2015 - p57(1) [51-500]
My Pet Human (Illus. by Surovec, Yasmine)
c BL - v111 - i21 - July 1 2015 - p74(2) [51-500]
c CCB-B - v69 - i2 - Oct 2015 - p116(1) [51-500]
c KR - May 1 2015 - pNA [51-500]
c PW - v262 - i24 - June 15 2015 - p85(1) [501+]
c SLJ - v61 - i8 - August 2015 - p81(1) [501+]
Surrey, Janet - *The Buddha's Wife: The Path of Awakening Together*
BL - v111 - i18 - May 15 2015 - p4(1) [51-500]
PW - v262 - i19 - May 11 2015 - p55(1) [51-500]
Surrisi, C.M. - *The Maypop Kidnapping*
c KR - Dec 15 2015 - pNA [51-500]
Survivors: Politics and Semantics of a Concept
HNet - June 2015 - pNA [501+]
Surya Das, Lama - *Make Me One with Everything: Buddhist Meditations to Awaken from the Illusion of Separation*
PW - v262 - i10 - March 9 2015 - p67(1) [51-500]
Suskind, Dana - *Thirty Million Words: Building a Child's Brain*
KR - July 15 2015 - pNA [501+]
LJ - v140 - i14 - Sept 1 2015 - p132(2) [51-500]
Susskind, Richard - *The Future of the Professions: How Technology Will Transform the Work of Human Experts*
Nature - v527 - i7577 - Nov 12 2015 - p163(1) [51-500]
Sussman, Elissa - *Stray*
y HB Guide - v26 - i1 - Spring 2015 - p125(1) [51-500]
Sussman, Fiona - *Another Woman's Daughter*
BL - v112 - i5 - Nov 1 2015 - p33(1) [51-500]
Sussman, Max - *Classic Recipes for Modern People: A Collection of Culinary Favorites Reimagined*
LJ - v140 - i11 - June 15 2015 - p108(2) [501+]
Sussman, Rachel - *The Oldest Living Things in the World*
Am Sci - v103 - i1 - Jan-Feb 2015 - p69(3) [501+]
NYT - Jan 13 2015 - pD3(L) [501+]
Sussman, Robert Wald - *The Myth of Race: The Troubling Persistence of an Unscientific Idea*
BioSci - v65 - i10 - Oct 2015 - p1019(3) [501+]
JIH - v46 - i1 - Summer 2015 - p109-111 [501+]
QRB - v90 - i2 - June 2015 - p199(2) [501+]
Sustrin, Letty - *The Teacher Who Would Not Retire Loses Her Ballet Slippers (Illus. by Bone, Thomas H., III)*
c CH Bwatch - April 2015 - pNA [51-500]
Susumu, Shingu - *Traveling Butterflies (Illus. by Susumu, Shingu)*
c SLJ - v61 - i8 - August 2015 - p124(1) [51-500]
Sutcliffe, Jane - *The White House Is Burning: August 24, 1814*
c HB Guide - v26 - i1 - Spring 2015 - p205(1) [51-500]
Sutcliffe, Marcella Pellegrino - *Victorian Radicals and Italian Democrats*
HNet - August 2015 - pNA [501+]
Sutcliffe, William - *Concentr8*
y BL - v112 - i6 - Nov 15 2015 - p50(1) [51-500]
y KR - Oct 15 2015 - pNA [51-500]
y Sch Lib - v63 - i3 - Autumn 2015 - p186(1) [51-500]
y SLJ - v61 - i11 - Nov 2015 - p108(2) [51-500]
Suter, Martin - *The Last Weynfeldt*
KR - Dec 1 2015 - pNA [51-500]
PW - v262 - i50 - Dec 7 2015 - p64(1) [51-500]
Sutherland, Adam - *Being a YouTuber*
Sch Lib - v63 - i3 - Autumn 2015 - p188(1) [501+]
Sutherland, Gillian - *In Search of the New Woman: Middle-Class Women and Work in Britain*
TLS - i5873 - Oct 23 2015 - p25(1) [501+]
Sutherland-Smith, James - *Mouth*
TLS - i5861 - July 31 2015 - p23(1) [501+]
Sutherland, Stewart - *Greed: from Gordon Gekko to David Hume*
NS - v144 - i5244 - Jan 9 2015 - p34(3) [501+]
Sutherland, Suzanne - *Something Wiki*
c SLJ - v61 - i2 - Feb 2015 - p94(1) [51-500]
Under the Dusty Moon
y KR - Nov 15 2015 - pNA [51-500]
y PW - v262 - i48 - Nov 30 2015 - p63(1) [51-500]
Sutherland, Tui T. - *Against the Tide*
c CH Bwatch - April 2015 - pNA [51-500]
c HB Guide - v26 - i1 - Spring 2015 - p79(2) [51-500]
The Dragonet Prophecy
c SLJ - v61 - i6 - June 2015 - p46(6) [501+]
Krakens and Lies (Illus. by Sutherland, Kari)
y VOYA - v38 - i2 - June 2015 - p84(1) [51-500]
c HB Guide - v26 - i2 - Fall 2015 - p104(1) [51-500]
Moon Rising
c HB Guide - v26 - i2 - Fall 2015 - p104(1) [51-500]
Sutterfield, Ragan - *This Is My Body: From Obesity to Ironman, My Journey into the True Meaning of Flesh, Spirit, and Deeper Faith*
PW - v262 - i3 - Jan 19 2015 - p78(1) [51-500]
Suttill, Francis J. - *Shadows in the Fog: The True Story of Major Suttill and the Prosper French Resistance Network*
J Mil H - v79 - i2 - April 2015 - p527-529 [501+]
Sutton, Fred E. - *Hands Up: Stories of the Six-Gun Fighters of the Old Wild West*
TLS - i5862 - August 7 2015 - p16(1) [501+]
Sutton, Jenna - *All the Right Places*
BL - v111 - i18 - May 15 2015 - p31(1) [51-500]
PW - v262 - i16 - April 20 2015 - p61(1) [51-500]
Sutton, Laurie S. - *Batman: The Joker's Dozen (Illus. by Beavers, Ethen)*
c HB Guide - v26 - i2 - Fall 2015 - p104(1) [51-500]
The Ghost of the Bermuda Triangle (Illus. by Neely, Scott)
c HB Guide - v26 - i1 - Spring 2015 - p94(1) [51-500]
The Mystery of the Aztec Tomb (Illus. by Neely, Scott)
c HB Guide - v26 - i1 - Spring 2015 - p94(1) [51-500]
The Real Man of Steel (Illus. by Vecchio, Luciano)
c HB Guide - v26 - i2 - Fall 2015 - p102(2) [51-500]
Sutton, Lynn Parrish - *Animally (Illus. by Mitchell, Hazel)*
c SLJ - v61 - i11 - Nov 2015 - p88(1) [51-500]
Sutton, Mark D. - *Techniques for Virtual Palaeontology*
QRB - v90 - i3 - Sept 2015 - p323(1) [501+]
Sutton, Matthew Avery - *American Apocalypse: A History of Modern Evangelicalism*
Bks & Cult - v21 - i2 - March-April 2015 - p19(2) [501+]
Bks & Cult - v21 - i2 - March-April 2015 - p22(4) [501+]
CC - v132 - i21 - Oct 14 2015 - p33(2) [501+]
JIH - v46 - i3 - Wntr 2016 - p463-464 [501+]
NY - v91 - i8 - April 13 2015 - p72 [51-500]
TLS - i5857 - July 3 2015 - p23(1) [501+]
Sutton, Phoef - *Crush*
BL - v111 - i21 - July 1 2015 - p35(2) [51-500]
KR - May 1 2015 - pNA [51-500]
PW - v262 - i21 - May 25 2015 - p38(1) [51-500]
Sutton, Sally - *Construction (Illus. by Lovelock, Brian)*
c HB Guide - v26 - i1 - Spring 2015 - p17(1) [51-500]
c Sch Lib - v63 - i2 - Summer 2015 - p98(1) [51-500]
Zoo Train (Illus. by Parton, Daron)
c Magpies - v30 - i2 - May 2015 - p26(1) [501+]
Suurpaa, Lauri - *Death in Winterreise: Musico-Poetic Associations in Schubert's Song Cycle*
Notes - v71 - i3 - March 2015 - p532(3) [501+]
Suzanne, Lilah - *Spice*
PW - v262 - i9 - March 2 2015 - p71(1) [51-500]
Suzanne, Nicole - *Nirvana: The Angel Dream (Illus. by Johns, Sheridan)*
c CH Bwatch - April 2015 - pNA [51-500]
Suzhen, Fang - *Grandma Lives in a Perfume Village (Illus. by Danowski, Sonja)*
c SLJ - v61 - i5 - May 2015 - p92(2) [51-500]
Suzukaze, Ryo - *Attack on Titan: Kuklo Unbound (Illus. by Shibamoto, Thores)*
y SLJ - v61 - i9 - Sept 2015 - p173(1) [51-500]
Suzuki, Jeff - *Constitutional Calculus: The Math of Justice and the Myth of Common Sense*
Bwatch - August 2015 - pNA [51-500]
Svendsen, Lars - *A Philosophy of Freedom*
J Phil - v112 - i5 - May 2015 - p280-1 [501+]
Svenonius, Ian F. - *Censorship Now!!*
KR - Sept 15 2015 - pNA [501+]

Svensson, Isak - *International Mediation Bias and Peacemaking: Taking Sides in Civil Wars*
   HNet - August 2015 - pNA [501+]
Svich, Caridad - *Instructions for Breathing and Other Plays*
   WLT - v89 - i2 - March-April 2015 - p75(1) [51-500]
Svoboda, Terese - *Anything That Burns You: A Portrait of Lola Ridge, Radical Poet*
   KR - Oct 15 2015 - pNA [501+]
   PW - v262 - i46 - Nov 16 2015 - p69(2) [51-500]
Svrluga, Barry - *The Grind: Inside Baseball's Endless Season*
   Atl - v316 - i1 - July-August 2015 - p42(1) [51-500]
   BL - v111 - i19-20 - June 1 2015 - p22(1) [51-500]
   KR - May 15 2015 - pNA [51-500]
   LJ - v140 - i11 - June 15 2015 - p93(1) [51-500]
   NYTBR - Dec 6 2015 - p64(L) [51-500]
Swaab, Neil - *The Secrets to Ruling School (without Even Trying)*.
   c KR - July 15 2015 - pNA [51-500]
   c PW - v262 - i28 - July 13 2015 - p66(1) [51-500]
   The Secrets to Ruling School (without Even Trying). (Illus. by Swaab, Neil)
   c SLJ - v61 - i9 - Sept 2015 - p146(2) [51-500]
Swaby, Rachel - *Headstrong: 52 Women Who Changed Science--and the World*
   PW - v262 - i5 - Feb 2 2015 - p47(1) [51-500]
   BL - v111 - i16 - April 15 2015 - p7(2) [51-500]
   y Ent W - i1358 - April 10 2015 - p66(1) [501+]
   KR - Jan 15 2015 - pNA [501+]
   Nature - v520 - i7545 - April 2 2015 - p31(1) [51-500]
Swafford, Jan - *Beethoven: Anguish and Triumph*
   Nat R - v67 - i1 - Jan 26 2015 - p40 [501+]
   NS - v144 - i5244 - Jan 9 2015 - p36(2) [501+]
   TLS - i5856 - June 26 2015 - p3(3) [501+]
Swaim, Barton - *The Speechwriter: A Brief Education in Politics (Read by Yen, Jonathan). Audiobook Review*
   PW - v262 - i35 - August 31 2015 - p85(1) [51-500]
   The Speechwriter: A Brief Education in Politics
   NYT - July 30 2015 - pC1(L) [501+]
   TLS - i5857 - July 3 2015 - p27(1) [501+]
   Ch Today - v59 - i6 - July-August 2015 - p86(1) [51-500]
   LJ - v140 - i11 - June 15 2015 - p103(1) [51-500]
   PW - v262 - i16 - April 20 2015 - p65(1) [51-500]
   Spec - v328 - i9754 - August 8 2015 - p31(1) [501+]
   The Speechwriter
   KR - May 15 2015 - pNA [501+]
Swain, Brian - *Sistina*
   KR - March 1 2015 - pNA [501+]
Swain, Nigel - *Green Barons, Force-of-Circumstance Entrepreneurs, Impotent Mayors: Rural Change in the Early Years of Post-Socialist Capitalist Democracy*
   E-A St - v67 - i7 - Sept 2015 - p1151(2) [501+]
Swain, Susan - *First Ladies: Presidential Historians on the Lives of 45 Iconic American Women*
   BL - v111 - i14 - March 15 2015 - p32(1) [51-500]
   KR - Feb 1 2015 - pNA [501+]
   PW - v262 - i8 - Feb 23 2015 - p66(1) [51-500]
Swallow, Gerry - *Blue in the Face: A Story of Risk, Rhyme, and Rebellion*
   c KR - Oct 1 2015 - pNA [51-500]
   c SLJ - v61 - i11 - Nov 2015 - p103(2) [51-500]
Swamp, Edgar - *Glitch in the Machine*
   KR - July 15 2015 - pNA [501+]
   SPBW - July 2015 - pNA [51-500]
Swan, Bill - *Jailed for Life for Being Black: The Story of Rubin "Hurricane" Carter*
   y SLJ - v61 - i9 - Sept 2015 - p151(4) [501+]
   Real Justice: Jailed for Life for Being Black - The Story of Rubin "Hurricane" Carter
   y Res Links - v20 - i3 - Feb 2015 - p41(1) [501+]
   Real Justice: Jailed for Life for Being Black: The Story of Rubin "Hurricane" Carter
   y SLJ - v61 - i7 - July 2015 - p110(1) [51-500]
Swan, Laura - *The Wisdom of the Beguines: The Forgotten Story of a Medieval Women's Movement*
   Comw - v142 - i13 - August 14 2015 - p32(2) [501+]
Swank, Denise Grover - *Twenty-Eight and a Half Wishes*
   BL - v111 - i22 - August 1 2015 - p38(1) [51-500]
   PW - v262 - i24 - June 15 2015 - p65(2) [51-500]
   PW - v262 - i31 - August 3 2015 - p37(2) [51-500]
   RVBW - August 2015 - pNA [51-500]

Swanson, Cynthia - *The Bookseller*
   BL - v111 - i11 - Feb 1 2015 - p22(1) [51-500]
   KR - Jan 15 2015 - pNA [51-500]
   LJ - v140 - i3 - Feb 15 2015 - p94(1) [51-500]
   LJ - v140 - i6 - April 1 2015 - p119(1) [501+]
   PW - v262 - i4 - Jan 26 2015 - p146(1) [51-500]
Swanson, Doug - *Blood Aces: The Wild Ride of Benny Binion, the Texas Gangster Who Created Vegas Poker*
   Roundup M - v22 - i6 - August 2015 - p41(1) [501+]
Swanson, Drew A. - *A Golden Weed: Tobacco and Environment in the Piedmont South*
   JAH - v102 - i1 - June 2015 - p247-248 [501+]
   JSH - v81 - i4 - Nov 2015 - p975(4) [501+]
Swanson, Heidi - *Near & Far: Recipes Inspired by Home and Travel*
   LJ - v140 - i12 - July 1 2015 - p107(1) [51-500]
   NYTBR - Dec 6 2015 - pNA(L) [501+]
   PW - v262 - i27 - July 6 2015 - p61(2) [501+]
Swanson, Jennifer - *Metamorphic Rocks*
   c HB Guide - v26 - i1 - Spring 2015 - p151(1) [51-500]
Swanson, Kara W. - *Banking on the Body: The Market in Blood, Milk, and Sperm in Modern America*
   AHR - v120 - i3 - June 2015 - p1040-1041 [501+]
   BHR - v89 - i1 - Spring 2015 - p162(4) [501+]
   CS - v44 - i6 - Nov 2015 - p859-860 [501+]
Swanson, Larry W. - *Neuroanatomical Terminology: A Lexicon of Classical Origins and Historical Foundations by Larry W. Swanson*
   QRB - v90 - i2 - June 2015 - p223(2) [501+]
Swanson, Peter - *The Kind Worth Killing (Read by Heller, Johnny). Audiobook Review*
   BL - v111 - i2 - Sept 15 2015 - p78(1) [51-500]
   The Kind Worth Killing
   BL - v111 - i9-10 - Jan 1 2015 - p47(1) [51-500]
   Ent W - i1351 - Feb 20 2015 - p64(1) [501+]
   KR - Jan 1 2015 - pNA [51-500]
Swanson, Philip - *The Cambridge Companion to Gabriel Garcia Marquez*
   MLR - v110 - i2 - April 2015 - p577-578 [501+]
Swanwick, Michael - *Chasing the Phoenix*
   Analog - v135 - i9 - Sept 2015 - p107(1) [501+]
   BL - v111 - i21 - July 1 2015 - p46(1) [51-500]
   KR - June 1 2015 - pNA [51-500]
   PW - v262 - i23 - June 8 2015 - p43(1) [51-500]
Swart, Tara - *Neuroscience for Leadership: Harnessing the Brain Gain Advantage*
   TimHES - i2190 - Feb 12 2015 - p52(1) [501+]
Swarthout, Miles - *The Last Shootist*
   Roundup M - v22 - i6 - August 2015 - p32(1) [501+]
Swarts, Jonathan - *Constructing Neoliberalism: Economic Transformation in Anglo-American Democracies*
   CS - v44 - i4 - July 2015 - p561-562 [501+]
Swartz, Aaron - *The Boy Who Could Change the World: The Writings of Aaron Swartz*
   BL - v112 - i7 - Dec 1 2015 - p5(1) [51-500]
   KR - Oct 15 2015 - pNA [501+]
   LJ - v140 - i16 - Oct 1 2015 - p105(1) [51-500]
Swartz, David L. - *Symbolic Power, Politics, and Intellectuals: The Political Sociology of Pierre Bourdieu*
   CS - v44 - i5 - Sept 2015 - p720-721 [501+]
Swartz, Larry - *Dramathemes: Classroom Literacy that Will Excite, Surprise, and Stimulate Learning, 4th ed.*
   RVBW - April 2015 - pNA [501+]
Swartz, Wendy - *Early Medieval China: A Sourcebook*
   JAS - v74 - i3 - August 2015 - p743-745 [501+]
Sweatman, Jennifer L. - *The Risky Business of French Feminism: Publishing, Politics and Artistry*
   FS - v69 - i4 - Oct 2015 - p570-571 [501+]
Sweazy, Larry D. - *Escape from Hangtown*
   Roundup M - v22 - i6 - August 2015 - p33(1) [501+]
   See Also Murder
   KR - March 1 2015 - pNA [51-500]
   PW - v262 - i9 - March 2 2015 - p65(1) [51-500]
   RVBW - August 2015 - pNA [501+]
   A Thousand Falling Crows
   BL - v112 - i6 - Nov 15 2015 - p29(1) [51-500]
   KR - Nov 1 2015 - pNA [51-500]
   PW - v262 - i42 - Oct 19 2015 - p55(1) [51-500]
   Vengeance at Sundown
   Roundup M - v22 - i6 - August 2015 - p33(1) [501+]
Swedberg, Richard - *Theorizing in Social Science: The Context of Discovery*
   AJS - v121 - i1 - July 2015 - p320(3) [501+]
Swee-Hock, Saw - *Advancing Singapore-China Economic Relations*
   Pac A - v88 - i4 - Dec 2015 - p957 [501+]
Sweeney, Carole - *Michel Houellebecq and the Literature of Despair*
   FS - v69 - i1 - Jan 2015 - p115-115 [501+]

Sweeney, Cynthia - *The Nest*
   KR - Jan 1 2016 - pNA [501+]
Sweeney, Diana - *The Minnow*
   y BL - v111 - i21 - July 1 2015 - p57(1) [51-500]
   y CCB-B - v68 - i11 - July-August 2015 - p571(2) [51-500]
   y PW - v262 - i49 - Dec 2 2015 - p94(1) [51-500]
   y SLJ - v61 - i5 - May 2015 - p125(1) [51-500]
Sweeney, Edwin R. - *Cochise: Firsthand Accounts of the Chiricahua Apache Chief*
   Roundup M - v22 - i4 - April 2015 - p31(1) [501+]
   Roundup M - v22 - i6 - August 2015 - p41(1) [501+]
   SHQ - v118 - i4 - April 2015 - p433-434 [501+]
Sweeney, John - *North Korea Undercover: Inside the World's Most Secret State*
   BL - v111 - i19-20 - June 1 2015 - p25(1) [51-500]
   KR - April 15 2015 - pNA [501+]
   LJ - v140 - i10 - June 1 2015 - p122(2) [51-500]
   NYTBR - July 19 2015 - p19(L) [501+]
   PW - v262 - i16 - April 20 2015 - p65(2) [51-500]
Sweeney, Jon M. - *The Complete Francis of Assisi: His Life, the Complete Writings, and the Little Flowers*
   LJ - v140 - i16 - Oct 1 2015 - p64(2) [501+]
   When Saint Francis Saved the Church: How A Converted Medieval Troubadour Created a Spiritual Vision for the Ages
   AM - v212 - i18 - May 25 2015 - p31(3) [501+]
   CC - v132 - i12 - June 10 2015 - p37(3) [501+]
Sweeney, Linda Booth - *When the Wind Blows (Illus. by Christy, Jana)*
   c BL - v111 - i12 - Feb 15 2015 - p89(1) [51-500]
   c HB Guide - v26 - i2 - Fall 2015 - p19(1) [51-500]
   c PW - v262 - i5 - Feb 2 2015 - p58(1) [501+]
Sweeney, Marvin A. - *The Cambridge History of Religions in the Ancient World, vol. 1: From the Bronze Age to the Hellenistic Age*
   Class R - v65 - i2 - Oct 2015 - p489-492 [501+]
Sweet, Leonard - *Giving Blood: A Fresh Paradigm for Preaching*
   CC - v132 - i19 - Sept 16 2015 - p30(4) [501+]
Sweet, Melissa - *A Splash of Red: The Life and Art of Horace Pippin*
   c JE - v195 - i1 - Wntr 2015 - p52-53 [501+]
Sweetnam, Mark S. - *John Donne and Religious Authority in the Reformed English Church*
   Ren Q - v68 - i2 - Summer 2015 - p794-796 [501+]
   Six Ct J - v46 - i2 - Summer 2015 - p476-477 [501+]
   Theol St - v76 - i2 - June 2015 - p353(3) [501+]
Sweetser, Wendy - *How to Cook in 10 Easy Lessons: Learn How to Prepare Food and Cook Like a Pro*
   c BL - v112 - i3 - Oct 1 2015 - p38(1) [51-500]
   c SLJ - v61 - i12 - Dec 2015 - p147(1) [51-500]
Swendson, Shanna - *Rebel Mechanics*
   y BL - v111 - i18 - May 15 2015 - p63(1) [51-500]
   y KR - May 1 2015 - pNA [51-500]
   y SLJ - v61 - i6 - June 2015 - p118(1) [51-500]
   y VOYA - v38 - i3 - August 2015 - p84(1) [51-500]
Swensen, Cole - *Landscapes on a Train*
   PW - v262 - i42 - Oct 19 2015 - p54(1) [51-500]
Swenson, Astrid - *The Rise of Heritage: Preserving the Past in France, Germany, and England, 1789-1914*
   AHR - v120 - i4 - Oct 2015 - p1444-1445 [501+]
Swenson, Harriet K. - *Around the House: One Woman Shares How Millions Care*
   RVBW - June 2015 - pNA [51-500]
Swenson, Jamie A. - *If You Were a Dog (Illus. by Raschka, Chris)*
   c CCB-B - v68 - i5 - Jan 2015 - p277(1) [51-500]
   c HB Guide - v26 - i1 - Spring 2015 - p17(1) [51-500]
Swenson, Kirsten - *Irrational Judgments: Eva Hesse, Sol LeWitt, and 1960s New York*
   PW - v262 - i45 - Nov 9 2015 - p54(2) [51-500]
Swenson, Peter - *The Ultra Thin Man*
   LJ - v140 - i19 - Nov 15 2015 - p110(1) [51-500]
Swenson, Wallace J. - *Buell: Journey to the White Clouds*
   BL - v111 - i17 - May 1 2015 - p78(1) [51-500]
   KR - May 1 2015 - pNA [51-500]
   Roundup M - v22 - i5 - June 2015 - p39(1) [501+]
   Roundup M - v22 - i6 - August 2015 - p33(1) [501+]
   Pine Marten
   BL - v112 - i6 - Nov 15 2015 - p30(1) [51-500]
Swerts, An - *You Make Me Happy (Illus. by Bakker, Jenny)*
   c PW - v262 - i26 - June 29 2015 - p67(1) [501+]
   c SLJ - v61 - i11 - Nov 2015 - p88(1) [51-500]
Sweterlitsch, Thomas - *Tomorrow and Tomorrow*
   LJ - v140 - i2 - Feb 1 2015 - p111(1) [501+]

Swett, Pamela E. - *Selling under the Swastika: Advertising and Commercial Culture in Nazi Germany*
    AHR - v120 - i3 - June 2015 - p1134-1135 [501+]
    CEH - v48 - i1 - March 2015 - p130-132 [501+]
Swierczynski, Duane - *Canary*
  y BL - v111 - i9-10 - Jan 1 2015 - p44(2) [51-500]
    KR - Jan 1 2015 - pNA [51-500]
    LJ - v140 - i2 - Feb 1 2015 - p77(1) [51-500]
Swift, Gayle H. - *ABC, Adoption and Me (Illus. by Griffin, Paul)*
  c CH Bwatch - Jan 2015 - pNA [51-500]
Swift, Graham - *England and Other Stories*
    BL - v111 - i13 - March 1 2015 - p17(1) [51-500]
    KR - April 1 2015 - pNA [51-500]
    LJ - v140 - i8 - May 1 2015 - p68(1) [51-500]
    Mac - v128 - i21 - June 1 2015 - p57(2) [51-500]
    NYT - June 23 2015 - pC1(L) [501+]
    NYT - June 30 2015 - pNA(L) [501+]
    NYTBR - May 24 2015 - p12(L) [501+]
    PW - v262 - i9 - March 2 2015 - p62(1) [51-500]
    TLS - i5856 - June 26 2015 - p21(1) [501+]
Swift, Jessica - *The Crafter's Guide to Patterns: Create and Use Your Own Patterns for Gift Wrap, Stationery, Tiles, and More*
    BL - v111 - i18 - May 15 2015 - p10(1) [51-500]
    LJ - v140 - i11 - June 15 2015 - p86(2) [51-500]
Swift, Jonathan - *Journal to Stella: Letters to Esther Johnson and Rebecca Dingley, 1710-1713*
    TLS - i5842 - March 20 2015 - p9(1) [501+]
Swift, Lee - *Above Ground*
    PW - v262 - i23 - June 8 2015 - p43(1) [51-500]
Swift, Vivian - *Gardens of Awe and Folly: A Traveler's Journal on the Meaning of Life and Gardening*
    KR - Nov 15 2015 - pNA [501+]
    PW - v262 - i46 - Nov 16 2015 - p72(2) [51-500]
Swigger, Jessie - *History Is Bunk: Assembling the Past at Henry Ford's Greenfield Village*
    AHR - v120 - i3 - June 2015 - p1043-1044 [501+]
    Pub Hist - v37 - i1 - Feb 2015 - p129(2) [501+]
Swinburne, Richard - *Mind, Brain, and Free Will*
    Phil R - v124 - i2 - April 2015 - p255(4) [501+]
Swindall, Lindsey R. - *The Path to the Greater, Freer, Truer World: Southern Civil Rights and Anticolonialism, 1937-1955*
    AHR - v120 - i2 - April 2015 - p652-653 [501+]
    JAH - v102 - i1 - June 2015 - p302-303 [501+]
Swindell, Anthony C. - *Reforging the Bible: More Biblical Stories and Their Literary Reception*
    TLS - i5834 - Jan 23 2015 - p27(1) [501+]
Swindells, Julia - *The Oxford Handbook of the Georgian Theatre 1737-1832*
    RES - v66 - i274 - April 2015 - p384-386 [501+]
Swingen, Abigail L. - *Competing Visions of Empire: Labor, Slavery, and the Origins of the British Atlantic Empire*
    TimHES - i2197 - April 2 2015 - p54-55 [501+]
Swingle, Mari K. - *I-Minds*
    KR - May 1 2015 - pNA [501+]
Swinson, Kiki - *The Score*
    PW - v262 - i50 - Dec 7 2015 - p70(2) [51-500]
Swinton, John - *Dementia: Living in the Memories of God*
    TT - v72 - i2 - July 2015 - p247-248 [501+]
Swirski, Peter - *From Literature to Biterature: Lem, Turing, Darwin, and Explorations in Computer Literature, Philosophy of Mind, and Cultural Evolution*
    AL - v87 - i2 - June 2015 - p418-420 [501+]
Switek, Brian - *Prehistoric Predators (Illus. by Csotonyi, Julius)*
  y PW - v262 - i18 - May 4 2015 - p120(1) [51-500]
Switzer, Ronald R. - *The Steamboat Bertrand and Missouri River Commerce*
    WHQ - v46 - i1 - Spring 2015 - p83-83 [501+]
Swyler, Erika - *The Book of Speculation (Read by Fliakos, Ari). Audiobook Review*
    BL - v112 - i4 - Oct 15 2015 - p62(1) [51-500]
    LJ - v140 - i15 - Sept 15 2015 - p43(1) [51-500]
The Book of Speculation
    LJ - v140 - i7 - April 15 2015 - p80(1) [51-500]
    PW - v262 - i14 - April 6 2015 - p36(2) [51-500]
    BL - v111 - i17 - May 1 2015 - p74(1) [51-500]
    Ent W - i1369 - June 26 2015 - p66(1) [501+]
    KR - April 15 2015 - pNA [51-500]
    LJ - v140 - i6 - April 1 2015 - p119(1) [51-500]

Sydnor, Charles S. - *Slavery in Mississippi*
    JSH - v81 - i2 - May 2015 - p538(2) [51-500]
Sydor, Colleen - *Fishermen Through & Through (Illus. by Kerrigan, Brooke)*
  c Res Links - v20 - i4 - April 2015 - p8(1) [51-500]
Syer, Katherine R. - *Wagner's Visions: Poetry, Politics, and the Psyche in the Operas through Die Walkure*
    MT - v156 - i1930 - Spring 2015 - p117-120 [501+]
Syfert, Scott - *The First American Declaration of Independence? The Disputed History of the Mecklenburg Declaration of May 20, 1775*
    JSH - v81 - i2 - May 2015 - p442(2) [501+]
Syke, S.D. - *Plague Land*
    LJ - v140 - i8 - May 1 2015 - p103(1) [51-500]
Syken, Bill - *Hangman's Game*
  y BL - v111 - i19-20 - June 1 2015 - p54(1) [51-500]
    KR - June 15 2015 - pNA [51-500]
    PW - v262 - i22 - June 1 2015 - p41(1) [51-500]
Sykes, Bryan - *DNA USA: A Genetic Portrait of America*
    QRB - v90 - i1 - March 2015 - p95(2) [501+]
Sykes, Christopher Simon - *Hockney: The Biography, vol. 2: A Pilgrim's Progress*
    Apo - v181 - i627 - Jan 2015 - p94(2) [501+]
Sykes, Judith A. - *Conducting Action Research to Evaluate Your School Library*
    LQ - v85 - i1 - Jan 2015 - p123(3) [501+]
Sykes, Katharine - *Inventing Sempringham: Gilbert of Sempringham and the Origins of the Role of the Master*
    Med R - August 2015 - pNA [501+]
Sykes, Lucy - *The Knockoff (Read by Kellgren, Katherine). Audiobook Review*
    BL - v112 - i1 - Sept 1 2015 - p139(2) [51-500]
    LJ - v140 - i14 - Sept 1 2015 - p67(2) [51-500]
The Knockoff
    KR - April 1 2015 - pNA [51-500]
    LJ - v140 - i6 - April 1 2015 - p86(1) [51-500]
Sykes, S.D. - *Plague Land*
    NYTBR - March 1 2015 - p29(L) [501+]
Sykes, Sam - *The City Stained Red*
    BL - v111 - i11 - Feb 1 2015 - p32(1) [51-500]
Sykes, V.K. - *Meet Me at the Beach*
    PW - v262 - i3 - Jan 19 2015 - p67(2) [51-500]
Summer at the Shore
    PW - v262 - i21 - May 25 2015 - p43(1) [51-500]
Sylvander, Matthieu - *The Battle of the Vegetables (Illus. by Barrier, Perceval)*
  c KR - Nov 15 2015 - pNA [51-500]
  c PW - v262 - i46 - Nov 16 2015 - p76(1) [51-500]
Sylvester, Kevin - *Baseballogy: Supercool Facts You Never Knew (Illus. by Sylvester, Kevin)*
  c BL - v111 - i21 - July 1 2015 - p52(1) [51-500]
  c KR - May 1 2015 - pNA [51-500]
  c SLJ - v61 - i6 - June 2015 - p136(2) [51-500]
Minrs
  c KR - June 15 2015 - pNA [51-500]
  c PW - v262 - i23 - June 8 2015 - p61(1) [51-500]
  c SLJ - v61 - i7 - July 2015 - p83(1) [51-500]
Neil Flambe and the Bard's Banquet
  c HB Guide - v26 - i2 - Fall 2015 - p104(1) [51-500]
Sylvester, Simon - *The Visitors*
  y BL - v112 - i6 - Nov 15 2015 - p32(1) [51-500]
    KR - Sept 15 2015 - pNA [51-500]
Syme, Holger Schott - *Theatre and Testimony in Shakespeare's England: A Culture of Mediation*
    Clio - v44 - i2 - Spring 2015 - p248-252 [501+]
Syme, Janet - *Speakers' Corner at Simon Balle School*
    Sch Lib - v63 - i1 - Spring 2015 - p35(1) [51-500]
    Sch Lib - v63 - i2 - Summer 2015 - p127(1) [51-500]
Symes, Ruth - *Cornflake the Dragon: The Secret Animal Society (Illus. by Macnaughton, Tina)*
  c Sch Lib - v63 - i1 - Spring 2015 - p44(1) [51-500]
Symes, Sally - *Funny Face, Sunny Face (Illus. by Beardshaw, Rosalind)*
  c CCB-B - v68 - i10 - June 2015 - p520(1) [51-500]
  c HB Guide - v26 - i2 - Fall 2015 - p19(1) [51-500]
  c KR - Jan 15 2015 - pNA [51-500]
Symonds, Craig L. - *The Civil War at Sea*
    T&C - v56 - i2 - April 2015 - p538-540 [501+]
Symonds, Tim - *Sherlock Holmes and the Mystery of Einstein's Daughter*
    RVBW - Oct 2015 - pNA [51-500]

Symons, Allene - *Aldous Huxley's Hands*
    KR - Sept 15 2015 - pNA [501+]
Syms, Shawn - *Nothing Looks Familiar*
    Can Lit - i224 - Spring 2015 - p106 [501+]
    G&L Rev W - v22 - i5 - Sept-Oct 2015 - p42(1) [51-500]
Syson, Antonia Jane Reobone - *Fama and Fiction in Vergil's Aeneid*
    Class R - v65 - i2 - Oct 2015 - p450-452 [501+]
Syson, Lydia - *Liberty's Fire*
    Sch Lib - v63 - i3 - Autumn 2015 - p190(1) [501+]
Syutkin, Pavel - *CCCP Cookbook: True Stories of Soviet Cuisine*
    NYTBR - Dec 6 2015 - pNA(L) [501+]
Szabo, Magda - *The Door*
    NYTBR - Dec 13 2015 - p12(L) [501+]
Szalay, Michael - *Hip Figures: A Literary History of the Democratic Party*
    AL - v87 - i2 - June 2015 - p400-402 [501+]
Szaniawski, Jeremi - *The Cinema of Alexander Sokurov: Figures of Paradox*
    Slav R - v74 - i1 - Spring 2015 - p215-216 [501+]
Szarlan, Chrysler - *The Hawley Book of the Dead*
    LJ - v140 - i2 - Feb 1 2015 - p111(1) [501+]
Szczeszak-Brewer, Agata - *Empire and Pilgrimage in Conrad and Joyce*
    MFSF - v61 - i1 - Spring 2015 - p178-180 [501+]
Sze, Julie - *Fantasy Islands: Chinese Dreams and Ecological Fears in an Age of Climate Crisis*
    Nature - v517 - i7536 - Jan 29 2015 - p551(1) [51-500]
    New Sci - v225 - i3005 - Jan 24 2015 - p46(1) [501+]
Szentkuthy, Miklos - *Prae*
    TLS - i5869 - Sept 25 2015 - p12(1) [501+]
Szereto, Mitzi - *Darker Edge of Desire*
    RVBW - Feb 2015 - pNA [501+]
Szlachetko, Andrew - *The Age of Not Believing*
  c Spec - v329 - i9772 - Dec 12 2015 - p77(1) [501+]
Szpiech, Ryan - *Conversion and Narrative: Reading and Religious Authority in Medieval Polemic*
    JR - Jan 2015 - p125(3) [501+]
Szpinglas, Jeff - *X Marks the Spot (Illus. by Whamond, Dave)*
  c Res Links - v20 - i3 - Feb 2015 - p17(1) [51-500]
Sztokman, Elana Maryles - *The Men's Section: Orthodox Jewish Men in an Egalitarian World*
    CS - v44 - i3 - May 2015 - p422-423 [501+]
Szumski, Bonnie - *Careers in Biotechnology*
  y VOYA - v37 - i6 - Feb 2015 - p89(1) [51-500]
Careers in Engineering
  y VOYA - v37 - i6 - Feb 2015 - p89(1) [51-500]
Cheating
  c HB Guide - v26 - i1 - Spring 2015 - p133(1) [51-500]
Szwed, John - *Billie Holiday: The Musician and the Myth*
    KR - March 15 2015 - pNA [51-500]
    LJ - v140 - i10 - June 1 2015 - p106(1) [51-500]
    NY - v91 - i11 - May 4 2015 - p70 [51-500]
    TLS - i5851 - May 22 2015 - p27(1) [501+]
Szymanski, Stefan - *Money and Soccer: A Soccernomics Guide*
    BL - v111 - i18 - May 15 2015 - p10(2) [51-500]
    Bus W - i4429 - June 1 2015 - p66(1) [51-500]
    LJ - v140 - i9 - May 15 2015 - p85(1) [51-500]
    Mac - v128 - i25 - June 29 2015 - p54(1) [51-500]
    PW - v262 - i18 - May 4 2015 - p112(1) [51-500]
    TLS - i5860 - July 24 2015 - p30(1) [501+]
Szymborska, Wislawa - *Map: Collected and Last Poems*
    Bks & Cult - v21 - i5 - Sept-Oct 2015 - p34(2) [501+]
    BL - v111 - i14 - March 15 2015 - p39(2) [51-500]
    NYTBR - April 26 2015 - p17(L) [501+]
    PW - v262 - i11 - March 16 2015 - p61(1) [51-500]
    TLS - i5854 - June 12 2015 - p11(1) [501+]
Szymona, Marlene L. - *My Sister Beth's Pink Birthday: A Story about Sibling Relationships (Illus. by Battuz, Christine)*
  c CH Bwatch - Jan 2015 - pNA [51-500]

T

Tabak, Lawrence - *In Real Life*
    c HB Guide - v26 - i2 - Fall 2015 - p141(1) [51-500]
    c BL - v112 - i7 - Dec 1 2015 - p34(2) [501+]
Tabazadeh, Azadeh - *The Sky Detective*
    KR - Oct 15 2015 - pNA [501+]
Tabbernee, William - *Early Christianity in Contexts: An Exploration across Cultures and Continents*
    IBMR - v39 - i3 - July 2015 - p154(1) [501+]
Tabbi, Joseph - *Nobody Grew But the Business: On the Life and Work of William Gaddis*
    LJ - v140 - i8 - May 1 2015 - p73(1) [51-500]
    PW - v262 - i13 - March 30 2015 - p67(1) [51-500]
Tabery, James - *Beyond Versus: The Struggle to Understand the Interaction of Nature and Nurture*
    J Phil - v112 - i5 - May 2015 - p280-1 [501+]
    RM - v68 - i3 - March 2015 - p680(3) [501+]
Tabili, Laura - *Global Migrants, Local Culture: Natives and Newcomers in Provincial England, 1841-1939*
    VS - v57 - i3 - Spring 2015 - p559(3) [501+]
Tabouret, Francis - *Suburban Wonder: Wandering the Margins of Paris*
    TLS - i5873 - Oct 23 2015 - p30(1) [501+]
Tabucchi, Antonio - *It's Getting Later All the Time*
    NYRB - v62 - i10 - June 4 2015 - p63(3) [501+]
The Missing Head of Damasceno Monteiro
    NYRB - v62 - i10 - June 4 2015 - p63(3) [501+]
Pereira Declares: A Testimony
    NYRB - v62 - i10 - June 4 2015 - p63(3) [501+]
Requiem: A Hallucination
    NYRB - v62 - i10 - June 4 2015 - p63(3) [501+]
Time Ages in a Hurry
    KR - Feb 1 2015 - pNA [501+]
    NYRB - v62 - i10 - June 4 2015 - p63(3) [501+]
    NYT - April 30 2015 - pC6(L) [501+]
    PW - v262 - i5 - Feb 2 2015 - p31(2) [51-500]
Tristano Dies
    KR - August 1 2015 - pNA [51-500]
Tacey, David - *Religion as Metaphor: Beyond Literal Belief*
    RM - v69 - i2 - Dec 2015 - p414(2) [501+]
Tackett, Nicolas - *The Destruction of the Medieval Chinese Aristocracy*
    AHR - v120 - i4 - Oct 2015 - p1461-1462 [501+]
Tackett, Timothy - *The Coming of the Terror in the French Revolution*
    Atl - v315 - i4 - May 2015 - p54(3) [501+]
    HNet - August 2015 - pNA [501+]
    Spec - v327 - i9730 - Feb 21 2015 - p38(2) [501+]
    TLS - i5856 - June 26 2015 - p5(2) [501+]
Taddia, Irma - *The Diplomacy of Religion in Africa: The Last Manuscripts of Richard Gray*
    IJAHS - v48 - i1 - Wntr 2015 - p142-144 [501+]
Taekema, Sylvia - *Ripple Effect*
    c KR - July 1 2015 - pNA [51-500]
    c Res Links - v21 - i1 - Oct 2015 - p21(1) [51-500]
Tafdrup, Pia - *Salamander Sun*
    Sch Lib - v63 - i3 - Autumn 2015 - p178(1) [51-500]
Taft, John G. - *A Force for Good*
    KR - Jan 1 2015 - pNA [501+]
Tafuri, Nancy - *Daddy Hugs (Illus. by Tafuri, Nancy)*
    c HB Guide - v26 - i1 - Spring 2015 - p17(1) [51-500]
    c SLJ - v61 - i2 - Feb 2015 - p80(2) [51-500]
Tagg, James - *Are the Androids Dreaming Yet? Amazing Brain: Human Communication, Creativity and Free Will*
    KR - Nov 1 2015 - pNA [501+]
Tagg, Melissa - *From the Start*
    BL - v111 - i16 - April 15 2015 - p30(1) [51-500]
Tagliacozzo, Eric - *The Longest Journey: Southeast Asians and the Pilgrimage to Mecca*
    HER - v130 - i543 - April 2015 - p481(3) [501+]
    Producing Indonesia: The State of the Field of Indonesian Studies
    Pac A - v88 - i2 - June 2015 - p366 [501+]
Tagore, Rabindranath - *Chirakumar Sabha: The Bachelor's Club: A Comedy in Five Acts*
    TLS - i5868 - Sept 18 2015 - p27(1) [501+]
Tagung Lutherbilder - *Lutherbildprojektionen und ein Okumenischer Luther. Katholische und Evangelische Entwurfe Martin Luthers in Fruher Neuzeit und Moderne*
    HNet - Feb 2015 - pNA [501+]
Tahir, Sabaa - *An Ember in the Ashes (Read by Hardingham, Fiona, with Steve West). Audiobook Review*
    y BL - v112 - i2 - Sept 15 2015 - p79(2) [51-500]
    y PW - v262 - i26 - June 29 2015 - p65(1) [51-500]
    y SLJ - v61 - i7 - July 2015 - p50(2) [51-500]
An Ember in the Ashes
    c VOYA - v38 - i3 - August 2015 - p84(2) [51-500]
    y BL - v111 - i9-10 - Jan 1 2015 - p88(1) [51-500]
    y CCB-B - v68 - i10 - June 2015 - p521(1) [51-500]
    y HB Guide - v26 - i2 - Fall 2015 - p141(1) [51-500]
    y KR - Jan 15 2015 - pNA [51-500]
    y NYTBR - May 10 2015 - p25(L) [51-500]
    y PW - v262 - i5 - Feb 2 2015 - p62(2) [51-500]
    y PW - v262 - i49 - Dec 2 2015 - p101(1) [51-500]
Taillant, Jorge Daniel - *Glaciers: The Politics of Ice*
    LJ - v140 - i7 - April 15 2015 - p117(1) [51-500]
    Mac - v128 - i24 - June 22 2015 - p56(1) [51-500]
Taipale, Joona - *Phenomenology and Embodiment: Husserl and the Constitution of Subjectivity*
    RM - v69 - i2 - Dec 2015 - p415(4) [501+]
Tait, A.L. - *Prisoner of the Black Hawk*
    y Magpies - v30 - i2 - May 2015 - p39(1) [501+]
Race to the End of the World
    y Magpies - v30 - i2 - May 2015 - p39(1) [501+]
Tait, Anne - *Li Jun and the Iron Road*
    y KR - Sept 15 2015 - pNA [51-500]
    y SLJ - v61 - i1 - Nov 2015 - p122(2) [51-500]
Tait, David - *Self-Portrait with the Happiness*
    TLS - i5861 - July 31 2015 - p23(1) [501+]
Tak, Bibi Dumon - *Mikis and the Donkey (Illus. by Hopman, Philip)*
    c CCB-B - v68 - i6 - Feb 2015 - p333(1) [51-500]
Takada, Yuko - *She Wears the Pants: Easy Sew-It-Yourself Fashion with an Edgy Urban Style*
    BL - v111 - i22 - August 1 2015 - p16(2) [51-500]
Takahashi, Kimie - *Language Learning, Gender and Desire: Japanese Women on the Move*
    Lang Soc - v44 - i1 - Feb 2015 - p128-129 [501+]
Takasou, Yuki Rumine - *Cosplay Basics: A Beginners Guide to the Art of Costume Play*
    y SLJ - v61 - i7 - July 2015 - p110(1) [501+]
Takenaka, Harukata - *Failed Democratization in Prewar Japan: Breakdown of a Hybrid Regime*
    Pac A - v88 - i4 - Dec 2015 - p934 [501+]
Talbot, Christine - *A Foreign Kingdom: Mormons and Polygamy in American Political Culture, 1852-1890*
    AHR - v120 - i1 - Feb 2015 - p249(1) [501+]
    WHQ - v46 - i1 - Spring 2015 - p93-94 [501+]
Talbot, David - *The Devil's Chessboard: Allen Dulles, the CIA, and the Rise of America's Secret Government*
    KR - August 15 2015 - pNA [501+]
    LJ - v140 - i16 - Oct 1 2015 - p97(1) [501+]
Talbot, Jill Lynn - *The Way We Weren't: A Memoir*
    KR - April 1 2015 - pNA [501+]
Talde, Dale - *Asian-American: Proudly Inauthentic Recipes from the Philippines to Brooklyn*
    NYTBR - Dec 6 2015 - p20(L) [501+]
    NYTBR - Dec 6 2015 - p20(L) [501+]

Talgam, Itay - *The Ignorant Maestro: How Great Leaders Inspire Unpredictable Brilliance*
    LJ - v140 - i8 - May 1 2015 - p83(1) [51-500]
    PW - v262 - i7 - Feb 16 2015 - p167(1) [51-500]
Tall, David - *How Humans Learn to Think Mathematically: Exploring the Three Worlds of Mathematics*
    AJPsy - v128 - i3 - Fall 2015 - p407(4) [501+]
Tallack, Malachy - *Sixty Degrees North: Around the World in Search of Home*
    Nature - v524 - i7563 - August 6 2015 - p33(1) [51-500]
    TLS - i5869 - Sept 25 2015 - p23(1) [501+]
TallBear, Kim - *Native American DNA: Tribal Belonging and the False Promise of Genetic Science*
    CS - v44 - i2 - March 2015 - p260-261 [501+]
Tallec, Olivier - *Louis I, King of the Sheep (Illus. by Tallec, Olivier)*
    c KR - July 15 2015 - pNA [51-500]
    c PW - v262 - i26 - June 29 2015 - p68(1) [51-500]
    c PW - v262 - i49 - Dec 2 2015 - p35(2) [51-500]
    c SLJ - v61 - i11 - Nov 2015 - p88(1) [51-500]
Who Done It? (Illus. by Tallec, Olivier)
    c KR - August 1 2015 - pNA [51-500]
    c PW - v262 - i41 - Oct 12 2015 - p69(1) [51-500]
    c SLJ - v61 - i10 - Oct 2015 - p84(2) [51-500]
Tallent, Elizabeth - *Mendocino Fire*
    KR - August 15 2015 - pNA [51-500]
    PW - v262 - i31 - August 3 2015 - p33(1) [51-500]
Mendocino Fire: Stories
    BL - v112 - i1 - Sept 1 2015 - p42(1) [51-500]
    NYTBR - Nov 15 2015 - p21(L) [51-500]
Tallerman, David - *Patchwerk*
    PW - v262 - i48 - Nov 30 2015 - p43(1) [51-500]
Talley, Heather Laine - *Saving Face: Disfigurement and the Politics of Appearance*
    AJS - v121 - i1 - July 2015 - p334(3) [501+]
Talley, Marcia - *Daughter of Ashes*
    BL - v112 - i1 - Sept 1 2015 - p45(1) [51-500]
    PW - v262 - i27 - July 6 2015 - p48(1) [51-500]
Talley, Robin - *Lies We Tell Ourselves*
    y Sch Lib - v63 - i2 - Summer 2015 - p121(1) [501+]
    y CCB-B - v68 - i5 - Jan 2015 - p278(1) [51-500]
    y HB Guide - v26 - i1 - Spring 2015 - p125(1) [51-500]
What We Left Behind
    y BL - v111 - i22 - August 1 2015 - p61(1) [51-500]
    y KR - August 1 2015 - pNA [51-500]
    y Magpies - v30 - i5 - Nov 2015 - p44(1) [501+]
    y SLJ - v61 - i11 - Nov 2015 - p123(1) [51-500]
Talley, Sharon - *Southern Women Novelists and the Civil War: Trauma and Collective Memory in the American Literary Tradition since 1861*
    JSH - v81 - i3 - August 2015 - p728(2) [501+]
Tallis, F.R. - *The Passenger*
    BL - v112 - i7 - Dec 1 2015 - p30(2) [51-500]
    KR - Dec 15 2015 - pNA [51-500]
    PW - v262 - i50 - Dec 7 2015 - p68(1) [51-500]
The Voices (Read by Jackson, Gildart). Audiobook Review
    BL - v111 - i18 - May 15 2015 - p69(1) [51-500]
    PW - v262 - i12 - March 23 2015 - p71(1) [51-500]
Tallis, Raymond - *The Black Mirror: Fragments of an Obituary for Life*
    NS - v144 - i5277 - August 28 2015 - p36(2) [501+]
    TimHES - i2216 - August 13 2015 - p46(1) [501+]
    New Sci - v227 - i3032 - August 1 2015 - p44(2) [501+]

The Black Mirror: Looking at Life through Death
Nature - v524 - i7563 - August 6 2015 - p33(1) [51-500]
Reflections of a Metaphysical Flaneur and Other Essays
TimHES - i2211 - July 9 2015 - p47(1) [501+]
Tallitsch, Tom - *All Together Now*
Dbt - v82 - i8 - August 2015 - p93(1) [501+]
Tally, Robert T., Jr. - *Fredric Jameson: The Project of Dialectical Criticism*
ABR - v36 - i3 - March-April 2015 - p12(2) [501+]
Utopia in the Age of Globalization: Space, Representation, and the World-System
SFS - v42 - i3 - Nov 2015 - p566-573 [501+]
Talmadge, Candace L. - *The Afterlife Healing Circle: How Anyone Can Contact the Other Side*
Bwatch - August 2015 - pNA [51-500]
Talos, Emmerich - *Das austrofaschistische Herrschaftssystem: Osterreich 1933-1938, 2d ed.*
JMH - v87 - i3 - Sept 2015 - p758(3) [501+]
Talton, Jon - *High Country Nocturne*
BL - v111 - i18 - May 15 2015 - p27(1) [51-500]
KR - April 1 2015 - pNA [51-500]
Talvet, Juri - *Eesti eleegia ja teisi luuletusi, 1981-2012*
WLT - v89 - i5 - Sept-Oct 2015 - p74(1) [501+]
Tam, Patrick P.L. - *Mammalian Development: Networks, Switches, and Morphogenetic Processes*
QRB - v90 - i1 - March 2015 - p107(1) [501+]
Tamadonfar, Mehran - *Religion and Regimes: Support, Separation, and Opposition*
J Ch St - v57 - i3 - Summer 2015 - p561-563 [501+]
Tamaki, Jillian - *Super Mutant Magic Academy (Illus. by Tamaki, Jillian)*
y BL - v111 - i16 - April 15 2015 - p40(2) [51-500]
SuperMutant Magic Academy
y SLJ - v61 - i5 - May 2015 - p128(2) [51-500]
PW - v262 - i14 - April 6 2015 - p47(1) [51-500]
This One Summer
HB - v91 - i4 - July-August 2015 - p61(4) [501+]
Tamaki, Mariko - *Saving Montgomery Sole*
c SLJ - v61 - i12 - Dec 2015 - p116(1) [51-500]
This One Summer (Illus. by Tamaki, Jillian)
y Bkbird - v53 - i3 - Summer 2015 - p92(1) [501+]
Tamarkin, Annette - *Black Plus*
c KR - Dec 1 2015 - pNA [51-500]
c PW - v262 - i21 - May 25 2015 - p58(1) [501+]
Tamblyn, Amber - *Dark Sparkler*
y BL - v111 - i14 - March 15 2015 - p38(1) [51-500]
PW - v262 - i7 - Feb 16 2015 - p156(1) [51-500]
Tambor, Molly - *The Lost Wave: Women and Democracy in Postwar Italy*
AHR - v120 - i4 - Oct 2015 - p1561-1563 [501+]
Tamburini, Arianna - *Tempete*
c Res Links - v20 - i4 - April 2015 - p42(1) [51-500]
Tame, Peter D. - *Mnemosyne and Mars: Artistic and Cultural Representations of Twentieth-Century Europe at War*
FS - v69 - i1 - Jan 2015 - p126-126 [501+]
Tamen, Miguel - *What Art Is Like, in Constant Reference to the Alice Books*
VS - v57 - i2 - Wntr 2015 - p342(2) [501+]
Tamm, Henrik - *Ninja Timmy (Illus. by Tamm, Henrik)*
c BL - v112 - i5 - Nov 1 2015 - p61(1) [51-500]
c KR - Sept 1 2015 - pNA [51-500]
c PW - v262 - i39 - Sept 28 2015 - p89(2) [51-500]
Tamman, Tina - *Portrait of a Secret Agent*
TLS - i5872 - Oct 16 2015 - p26(1) [501+]
Tammela, John - *Jackie*
KR - May 15 2015 - pNA [501+]
Tammet, Daniel - *Thinking In Numbers: On Life, Love, Meaning, and Math*
Math T - v108 - i8 - April 2015 - p639(1) [501+]
Math T - v108 - i8 - April 2015 - p639(1) [501+]
Tamny, John - *Popular Economics: What the Rolling Stones, "Downton Abbey," and LeBron James Can Teach You about Economics*
Barron's - v95 - i18 - May 4 2015 - p40(1) [501+]
Tamura, Eileen H. - *In Defense of Justice: Joseph Kurihara and the Japanese American Struggle for Equality*
Pac A - v88 - i1 - March 2015 - p196 [501+]
PHR - v84 - i2 - May 2015 - p255(2) [501+]
RAH - v43 - i2 - June 2015 - p320-326 [501+]
WHQ - v46 - i1 - Spring 2015 - p91-92 [501+]
Tan, Shaun - *Rules of Summer*
c HB - v91 - i1 - Jan-Feb 2015 - p33(1) [51-500]
The Singing Bones
y Magpies - v30 - i5 - Nov 2015 - p43(1) [501+]
Sketches from a Nameless Land: The Art of The Arrival
y Sch Lib - v63 - i1 - Spring 2015 - p61(1) [51-500]

Tanabe, Shunsuke - *Japanese Perceptions of Foreigners*
Pac A - v88 - i2 - June 2015 - p310 [501+]
Tanager, H.O. - *Autograph Penis*
KR - Feb 15 2015 - pNA [501+]
Tanaka, Meca - *Meteor Prince*
y SLJ - v61 - i5 - May 2015 - p128(1) [51-500]
Tanaka, Motoko - *Apocalypse in Japanese Science Fiction*
SFS - v42 - i3 - Nov 2015 - p601-604 [501+]
Tanenbaum, Leora - *I Am Not a Slut: Slut-Shaming in the Age of the Internet*
BL - v111 - i9-10 - Jan 1 2015 - p21(2) [51-500]
Tanenbaum, Robert K. - *Fatal Conceit*
RVBW - March 2015 - pNA [501+]
RVBW - April 2015 - pNA [501+]
Trap
BL - v111 - i21 - July 1 2015 - p41(1) [51-500]
KR - June 1 2015 - pNA [51-500]
Taneti, James Elisha - *Caste, Gender, and Christianity in Colonial India: Telugu Women in Mission*
AHR - v120 - i3 - June 2015 - p986-987 [501+]
Tang, Greg - *Math for All Seasons (Illus. by Briggs, Harry)*
c JE - v195 - i1 - Wntr 2015 - p51-52 [501+]
Tangari, Nicola - *Musica e liturgia a Montecassino nel medioevo: Atti del Simposio internazionale di studi*
Specu - v90 - i1 - Jan 2015 - p301-302 [501+]
Tangredi, Sam J. - *Anti-Access Warfare: Countering A2/AD Strategies*
APJ - v29 - i3 - May-June 2015 - p90(3) [501+]
NWCR - v68 - i2 - Spring 2015 - p135(2) [501+]
Parameters - v45 - i2 - Summer 2015 - p97(11) [501+]
Tanner, Gary Rex - *The Oklahoma Gamblin' Man*
RVBW - April 2015 - pNA [51-500]
Tanner, Lian - *Icebreaker (Read by Gideon, Anne Marie). Audiobook Review*
c SLJ - v61 - i12 - Dec 2015 - p77(1) [51-500]
Icebreaker
c KR - May 15 2015 - pNA [51-500]
c PW - v262 - i19 - May 11 2015 - p61(1) [51-500]
c SLJ - v61 - i6 - June 2015 - p106(2) [51-500]
c VOYA - v38 - i3 - August 2015 - p85(1) [51-500]
Sunker's Deep
y Magpies - v30 - i1 - March 2015 - p38(1) [501+]
Tanner, Lynette Ater - *Chained to the Land: Voices from Cotton and Cane Plantations*
JSH - v81 - i4 - Nov 2015 - p1054(2) [501+]
Tanno, Kiyoto - *Migrant Workers in Contemporary Japan: An Institutional Perspective on Transnational Employment*
Pac A - v88 - i2 - June 2015 - p304 [501+]
Tanquary, Kathryn - *The Night Parade*
c KR - Oct 1 2015 - pNA [51-500]
c SLJ - v61 - i12 - Dec 2015 - p108(1) [51-500]
Tansi, Sony Labou - *L?etat honteux: Roman*
PW - v262 - i44 - Nov 2 2015 - p56(2) [51-500]
Tansley, K.C. - *The Girl Who Ignored Ghosts*
y PW - v262 - i19 - May 11 2015 - p63(1) [51-500]
y VOYA - v38 - i4 - Oct 2015 - p79(1) [51-500]
Tantillo, Sarah - *Literacy and the Common Core: Recipes for Action*
VOYA - v38 - i2 - June 2015 - p93(1) [501+]
Tanweer, Bilal - *The Scatter Here is Too Great*
TLS - i5831 - Jan 2 2015 - p18(1) [501+]
Tanzer, Molly - *Vermilion: The Adventures of Lou Merriwether, Psychopomp*
PW - v262 - i10 - March 9 2015 - p57(1) [51-500]
Taormino, Tristan - *The Feminist Porn Book: The Politics of Producing Pleasure*
Wom R Bks - v32 - i1 - Jan-Feb 2015 - p24(2) [501+]
Taplin, Oliver - *Medea*
TLS - i5870 - Oct 2 2015 - p26(1) [501+]
Sophocles: Four Tragedies: "Oedipus the King," "Aias," "Philoctetes," "Oedipus at Colonus"
TLS - i5867 - Sept 11 2015 - p13(1) [501+]
Tappy, Jose-Flore - *Oeuvres*
TLS - i5834 - Jan 23 2015 - p11(2) [501+]
Taraghi, Goli - *The Pomegranate Lady and Her Sons*
WLT - v89 - i5 - Sept-Oct 2015 - p69(3) [501+]
Taran, Leonardo - *Aristotle Poetics: Editio Maior of the Greek Text with Historical Introductions and Philological Commentaries*
Class R - v65 - i1 - April 2015 - p64-66 [501+]
Tarango, Angela - *Choosing the Jesus Way: American Indian Pentecostals and the Fight for the Indigenous Principle*
AHR - v120 - i2 - April 2015 - p645-646 [501+]
CC - v132 - i21 - Oct 14 2015 - p33(2) [501+]
CH - v84 - i3 - Sept 2015 - p693(3) [501+]
JAH - v102 - i2 - Sept 2015 - p593-594 [501+]
JSH - v81 - i3 - August 2015 - p757(2) [501+]

Tarazona, Belangela - *A Better World*
KR - Jan 1 2015 - pNA [501+]
Tarbox, A.D. - *A Prairie Food Chain*
Sci Teach - v82 - i8 - Nov 2015 - p74 [501+]
Tardi, Jacques - *Run like Crazy, Run like Hell*
PW - v262 - i9 - March 2 2015 - p73(1) [51-500]
Tardif, Benoit - *Sport-O-Rama (Illus. by Tardif, Benoit)*
c SLJ - v61 - i6 - June 2015 - p138(1) [51-500]
c BL - v111 - i12 - Feb 15 2015 - p72(1) [51-500]
c HB Guide - v26 - i2 - Fall 2015 - p200(1) [51-500]
c KR - Jan 15 2015 - pNA [51-500]
c Res Links - v21 - i1 - Oct 2015 - p27(1) [51-500]
Targoff, Ramie - *Posthumous Love: Eros and the Afterlife in Renaissance England*
MP - v113 - i2 - Nov 2015 - pE87(3) [501+]
Ren Q - v68 - i2 - Summer 2015 - p796-797 [501+]
Six Ct J - v46 - i3 - Fall 2015 - p789-791 [501+]
Tarkington, Ed - *Only Love Can Break Your Heart*
y BL - v112 - i4 - Oct 15 2015 - p33(1) [51-500]
KR - Oct 1 2015 - pNA [501+]
Tarlinskaja, Marina - *Shakespeare and the Versification of English Drama, 1561-1642*
TLS - i5861 - July 31 2015 - p24(2) [501+]
RES - v66 - i276 - Sept 2015 - p775-777 [501+]
Tarlo, Emma - *Islamic Fashion and Anti-Fashion: New Perspectives from Europe and North America*
JRAI - v21 - i3 - Sept 2015 - p694(1) [501+]
Tarpley, Todd - *Beep! Beep! Go to Sleep! (Illus. by Rocco, John)*
c BL - v111 - i22 - August 1 2015 - p70(2) [51-500]
c HB - v91 - i5 - Sept-Oct 2015 - p88(2) [51-500]
c KR - July 1 2015 - pNA [51-500]
c PW - v262 - i27 - July 6 2015 - p68(1) [51-500]
c PW - v262 - i49 - Dec 2 2015 - p41(1) [51-500]
c SLJ - v61 - i9 - Sept 2015 - p129(1) [51-500]
My Grandma's a Ninja (Illus. by Chatzikonstantinou, Danny)
c CH Bwatch - June 2015 - pNA [51-500]
c HB Guide - v26 - i2 - Fall 2015 - p53(1) [51-500]
Tarr, Judith - *Forgotten Suns*
PW - v262 - i13 - March 30 2015 - p58(2) [51-500]
Tarrow, Sidney - *Strangers at the Gates: Movements and States in Contentious Politics*
CS - v44 - i3 - May 2015 - p423-425 [501+]
Tarry, Chris - *How to Carry Bigfoot Home*
BL - v111 - i13 - March 1 2015 - p18(1) [51-500]
Tarshis, Lauren - *1916: Attaques du requin (Illus. by Dawson, Scott)*
c Res Links - v20 - i3 - Feb 2015 - p52(1) [51-500]
Five Epic Disasters
c HB Guide - v26 - i1 - Spring 2015 - p200(1) [51-500]
Les attentats du 11 septembre 2001
c Res Links - v20 - i3 - Feb 2015 - p52(1) [51-500]
Survivants - 1912: Le naufrage du Titanic (Illus. by Dawson, Scott)
y Res Links - v21 - i1 - Oct 2015 - p56(1) [501+]
Tartakoff, Paula - *Between Christian and Jew: Conversion and Inquisition in the Crown of Aragon, 1250-1391*
JR - Jan 2015 - p134(3) [501+]
Tarter, Brent - *The Grandees of Government: The Origins and Persistence of Undemocratic Politics in Virginia*
JSH - v81 - i1 - Feb 2015 - p158(3) [501+]
Tartt, Donna - *The Goldfinch*
Ant R - v73 - i1 - Wntr 2015 - p186(3) [501+]
NYTBR - April 26 2015 - p28(L) [501+]
TimHES - i2198 - April 9 2015 - p49(1) [501+]
Tarulevicz, Nicole - *Eating Her Curries and Kway: A Cultural History of Food in Singapore*
JAS - v74 - i1 - Feb 2015 - p241-244 [501+]
Taseer, Aatish - *The Way Things Were*
KR - May 1 2015 - pNA [51-500]
LJ - v140 - i10 - June 1 2015 - p96(1) [51-500]
NY - v91 - i30 - Oct 5 2015 - p82 [51-500]
PW - v262 - i18 - May 4 2015 - p2(1) [51-500]
TLS - i5866 - Sept 4 2015 - p22(1) [501+]
Tash, Sarvenaz - *Three Day Summer*
c HB Guide - v26 - i2 - Fall 2015 - p141(1) [51-500]
y KR - March 15 2015 - pNA [51-500]
y VOYA - v38 - i2 - June 2015 - p69(1) [51-500]
Tashiro, Chisato - *Five Nice Mice Build a House (Illus. by Tashiro, Chisato)*
c KR - August 15 2015 - pNA [51-500]
c PW - v262 - i39 - Sept 28 2015 - p90(2) [501+]
Tashjian, Janet - *Einstein the Class Hamster and the Very Real Game Show (Illus. by Tashjian, Jake)*
c HB Guide - v26 - i1 - Spring 2015 - p94(1) [51-500]

454 • TASKER Book Review Index 2016 Cumulation

Tasker, Yvonne - *Soldiers' Stories: Military Women in Cinema and Television since World War II*
Wom HR - v24 - i1 - Feb 2015 - p143-2 [501+]
Tassi, Paul - *The Exiled Earthborn*
PW - v262 - i38 - Sept 21 2015 - p56(1) [51-500]
The Last Exodus
PW - v262 - i27 - July 6 2015 - p50(1) [51-500]
The Sons of Sora
PW - v262 - i48 - Nov 30 2015 - p43(1) [51-500]
Tate, Don - *Poet: The Remarkable Story of George Moses Horton (Illus. by Tate, Don)*
c BL - v112 - i4 - Oct 15 2015 - p40(1) [51-500]
c HB - v91 - i5 - Sept-Oct 2015 - p133(2) [51-500]
c KR - June 1 2015 - pNA [51-500]
c PW - v262 - i29 - July 20 2015 - p190(2) [501+]
c PW - v262 - i49 - Dec 2 2015 - p50(1) [51-500]
c SLJ - v61 - i7 - July 2015 - p104(2) [51-500]
Tate, Gregory - *The Poet's Mind: The Psychology of Victorian Poetry 1830-1870*
MLR - v110 - i1 - Jan 2015 - p246-247 [501+]
Tate, James - *Dome of the Hidden Pavilion: New Poems*
LJ - v140 - i9 - May 15 2015 - p86(1) [51-500]
NYTBR - Dec 27 2015 - p11(L) [501+]
PW - v262 - i29 - July 20 2015 - p167(1) [51-500]
Tate, Karen - *Goddess Calling: Inspirational Messages and Meditations of Sacred Feminine Liberation Theology*
RVBW - June 2015 - pNA [501+]
Tate, Nikki - *Deep Roots: How Trees Sustain Our Planet*
c KR - Dec 1 2015 - pNA [51-500]
c PW - v262 - i47 - Nov 23 2015 - p70(1) [501+]
Take Shelter: At Home and Around the World
c HB Guide - v26 - i2 - Fall 2015 - p157(1) [51-500]
Tate, Nixie - *The Gypsy's Sun*
KR - Nov 15 2015 - pNA [501+]
Tatkin, Stan - *Wired for Dating: How Understanding Neurobiology and Attachment Style Can Help You Find Your Ideal Mate*
PW - v262 - i51 - Dec 14 2015 - p76(2) [501+]
Tatlock, Jason - *The Middle East: Its History and Culture*
JTWS - v32 - i1 - Spring 2015 - p344(3) [501+]
Tattersall, Ian - *A Natural History of Wine*
Nature - v582 - i7582 - Dec 17 2015 - p331(1) [501+]
The Strange Case of the Rickety Cossack and Other Cautionary Tales from Human Evolution
BL - v111 - i17 - May 1 2015 - p66(2) [51-500]
KR - April 1 2015 - pNA [501+]
Nature - v522 - i7555 - June 11 2015 - p154(2) [501+]
New Sci - v226 - i3021 - May 16 2015 - p45(1) [501+]
PW - v262 - i14 - April 6 2015 - p51(1) [51-500]
TimHES - i2214 - July 30 2015 - p46-47 [501+]
Tatulli, Mark - *Desmond Packet and the Mountain Full of Monsters*
c HB Guide - v26 - i1 - Spring 2015 - p94(1) [51-500]
Taubes, Jacob - *To Carl Schmitt: Letters and Reflections*
Dialogue - v54 - i2 - June 2015 - p380-382 [501+]
Taubhorn, Ingo - *Saul Leiter: Retrospektive*
NYRB - v62 - i12 - July 9 2015 - p10(3) [501+]
NYRB - v62 - i12 - July 9 2015 - p10(3) [501+]
Taubner, Armin - *Folded Paper German Stars: Creative Paper Crafting Ideas Inspired by Friedrich Frobel*
LJ - v140 - i13 - August 1 2015 - p95(1) [51-500]
Tausiet, Maria - *Urban Magic in Early Modern Spain: Abracadabra Omnipotens*
Six Ct J - v46 - i2 - Summer 2015 - p513-515 [501+]
Taussig, Michael - *Beauty and the Beast*
JRAI - v21 - i3 - Sept 2015 - p695(2) [501+]
Tavares, Matt - *Growing Up Pedro: How the Martinez Brothers Made It from the Dominican Republic All the Way to the Major Leagues (Illus. by Tavares, Matt)*
c CCB-B - v68 - i9 - May 2015 - p469(1) [51-500]
c HB - v91 - i1 - Jan-Feb 2015 - p104(2) [51-500]
c HB Guide - v26 - i2 - Fall 2015 - p200(1) [51-500]
c KR - March 1 2015 - pNA [51-500]
Henry Aaron's Dream (Illus. by Tavares, Matt)
c HB Guide - v26 - i2 - Fall 2015 - p200(1) [51-500]
There Goes Ted Williams: The Greatest Hitter Who Ever Lived (Illus. by Tavares, Matt)
c HB Guide - v26 - i2 - Fall 2015 - p200(1) [51-500]
Taves, Brian - *Hollywood Presents Jules Verne: The Father of Science Fiction on Screen*
SFS - v42 - i3 - Nov 2015 - p557-555 [501+]
Taw, Jennifer Morrison - *Mission Revolution: The US Military and Stability Operations*
Parameters - v45 - i2 - Summer 2015 - p131(2) [501+]
Taxation for and against Redistribution since 1945
HNet - Jan 2015 - pNA [501+]
Tayleur, Karen - *The Hush Treasure Book*
c Magpies - v30 - i4 - Sept 2015 - p29(2) [501+]
Taylor, A.J.P. - *The Struggle for Mastery in Europe, 1848-1918*
TimHES - i2211 - July 9 2015 - p44(1) [501+]
Taylor, Abbie - *The Stranger on the Train*
RVBW - Jan 2015 - pNA [51-500]
Taylor, Alan - *The Internal Enemy: Slavery and War in Virginia, 1772-1832*
Historian - v77 - i2 - Summer 2015 - p357(3) [501+]
HNet - May 2015 - pNA [501+]
Taylor, Alex - *The Marble Orchard*
BL - v111 - i9-10 - Jan 1 2015 - p48(1) [51-500]
Taylor, Andrew - *The Silent Boy*
BL - v112 - i1 - Sept 1 2015 - p49(2) [51-500]
KR - August 15 2015 - pNA [501+]
LJ - v140 - i16 - Oct 1 2015 - p73(2) [51-500]
PW - v262 - i33 - August 17 2015 - p53(1) [51-500]
Taylor, Barbara - *Slimy Spawn and Other Gruesome Life Cycles*
c CH Bwatch - Nov 2015 - pNA [51-500]
c Res Links - v20 - i3 - Feb 2015 - p18(2) [501+]
Stinky Skunks and Other Animal Adaptations
c Res Links - v20 - i3 - Feb 2015 - p18(2) [501+]
Taylor, Barbara (b. 1950-) - *The Last Asylum: A Memoir of Madness in Our Times*
TLS - i5843 - March 27 2015 - p3(3) [501+]
LJ - v140 - i6 - April 1 2015 - p104(2) [501+]
Taylor, Barbara Brown - *Learning to Walk in the Dark*
Intpr - v69 - i1 - Jan 2015 - p122(1) [51-500]
Taylor, Benjamin - *Proust: The Search*
LJ - v140 - i17 - Oct 15 2015 - p86(1) [51-500]
PW - v262 - i33 - August 17 2015 - p62(2) [51-500]
KR - August 15 2015 - pNA [51-500]
Taylor, Brad - *The Forgotten Soldier*
BL - v112 - i7 - Dec 1 2015 - p28(1) [51-500]
The Insider Threat
BL - v111 - i18 - May 15 2015 - p28(1) [51-500]
PW - v262 - i17 - April 27 2015 - p49(2) [51-500]
Taylor-Butler, Christine - *The Lost Tribes*
c KR - Jan 15 2015 - pNA [51-500]
Rosa Parks
c SLJ - v61 - i4 - April 2015 - p118(4) [501+]
Taylor, Chantell - *Rosie the Reindeer (Illus. by Tenney, Shawna J.C.)*
c CH Bwatch - Feb 2015 - pNA [51-500]
Taylor, Chloe - *Bursting at the Seams (Illus. by Zhang, Nancy)*
c HB Guide - v26 - i2 - Fall 2015 - p104(1) [51-500]
Clothes Minded (Illus. by Zhang, Nancy)
c HB Guide - v26 - i2 - Fall 2015 - p104(1) [51-500]
Sew Zoey Series (Illus. by Zhang, Nancy)
c HB Guide - v26 - i1 - Spring 2015 - p94(1) [51-500]
Taylor, Chris - *How Star Wars Conquered the Universe: The Past, Present, and Future of a Multibillion Dollar Franchise (Read by Podehl, Nick). Audiobook Review*
y BL - v111 - i18 - May 15 2015 - p71(1) [51-500]
How Star Wars Conquered the Universe: The Past, Present and Future of a Multibillion-Dollar Franchise
NS - v144 - i5264 - May 29 2015 - p80(2) [501+]
Taylor, Chris (b. 1973-) - *How Star Wars Conquered the Universe: The Past, Present, and Future of a Multibillion Dollar Franchise (Read by Podehl, Nick). Audiobook Review*
LJ - v140 - i2 - Feb 1 2015 - p47(1) [51-500]
Taylor, Chris Roy - *The Great Big Book of Aussie Inventions*
c Magpies - v30 - i1 - March 2015 - p22(1) [501+]
Taylor, Christopher A. - *Finding Her Gone*
KR - June 15 2015 - pNA [501+]
Taylor, Claire - *Heresy, Crusade and Inquisition in Medieval Quercy*
Specu - v90 - i2 - April 2015 - p588-589 [501+]
Taylor, Clark - *Seeds of Freedom: Liberating Education in Guatemala*
CS - v44 - i2 - March 2015 - p293-294 [501+]
Taylor, Craig - *Chivalry and the Ideals of Knighthood in France during the Hundred Years War*
HER - v130 - i544 - June 2015 - p722(3) [501+]
J Mil H - v79 - i2 - April 2015 - p476-477 [501+]
Taylor, D.J. - *Wrote for Luck*
Spec - v327 - i9736 - April 4 2015 - p36(1) [501+]
TLS - i5845 - April 10 2015 - p19(1) [501+]
Taylor, David - *Digital Photography Complete Course*
LJ - v140 - i16 - Oct 1 2015 - p108(2) [51-500]
Taylor, David C. - *Night Life*
BL - v111 - i12 - Feb 15 2015 - p38(1) [51-500]
KR - Feb 1 2015 - pNA [51-500]
Taylor, Elizabeth - *Mossy Trotter (Illus. by Ross, Tony)*
c TLS - i5850 - May 15 2015 - p20(1) [501+]
A View of the Harbour
Ent W - i1364 - May 22 2015 - p66(1) [501+]
Taylor, Frederick - *Coventry: November 14, 1940*
KR - August 15 2015 - pNA [501+]
LJ - v140 - i16 - Oct 1 2015 - p96(1) [51-500]
Coventry: Thursday, 14 November 1940
Spec - v329 - i9769 - Nov 21 2015 - p49(2) [501+]
The Downfall of Money: Germany's Hyperinflation and the Destruction of the Middle Class
HT - v65 - i2 - Feb 2015 - p64(2) [501+]
Taylor, Gillian F. - *Darrow's Gamble*
RVBW - Nov 2015 - pNA [51-500]
Taylor, Glenn - *A Hanging at Cinder Bottom*
KR - May 1 2015 - pNA [51-500]
Mac - v128 - i28 - July 20 2015 - p57(2) [501+]
NYTBR - August 2 2015 - p12(L) [501+]
PW - v262 - i15 - April 13 2015 - p52(1) [51-500]
Taylor, Gregory S. - *The Life and Lies of Paul Crouch: Communist, Opportunist, Cold War Snitch*
JSH - v81 - i3 - August 2015 - p771(2) [501+]
Taylor, Harry - *Pursuit*
SPBW - August 2015 - pNA [51-500]
Rogues, Riches and Retribution
SPBW - June 2015 - pNA [51-500]
Taylor, Ian - *Africa Rising? BRICS-Diversifying Dependency*
IJAHS - v48 - i1 - Wntr 2015 - p147-148 [501+]
Taylor, James - *Boardroom Scandal: The Criminalization of Company Fraud in Nineteenth-Century Britain*
HER - v130 - i543 - April 2015 - p472(3) [501+]
Taylor, Jane H.M. - *Rewriting Arthurian Romance in Renaissance France: From Manuscript to Printed Book*
FS - v69 - i1 - Jan 2015 - p88(2) [501+]
Ren Q - v68 - i3 - Fall 2015 - p1124-1126 [501+]
Taylor, Janet B. - *Into the Dim HMH*
y KR - Dec 15 2015 - pNA [51-500]
Taylor, Jeff - *The Political World of Bob Dylan: Freedom and Justice, Power and Sin*
Nat R - v67 - i24 - Dec 31 2015 - p38(2) [501+]
Taylor, Jennifer - *Architecture in the South Pacific: The Ocean of Islands*
Cont Pac - v27 - i2 - Fall 2015 - p583(4) [501+]
Taylor, Jeremy - *Body by Darwin: How Evolution Shapes Our Health and Transforms Medicine*
y BL - v112 - i4 - Oct 15 2015 - p8(2) [501+]
PW - v262 - i37 - Sept 14 2015 - p52(1) [51-500]
Taylor, Jim - *Practice Development in Sport and Performance Psychology*
RVBW - August 2015 - pNA [51-500]
Taylor, John - *The Science of Soccer: A Bouncing Ball and a Banana Kick*
y HB Guide - v26 - i1 - Spring 2015 - p185(1) [51-500]
Taylor, Katherine - *Valley Fever*
BL - v111 - i19-20 - June 1 2015 - p46(1) [51-500]
KR - April 1 2015 - pNA [501+]
NYT - June 25 2015 - pC4(L) [501+]
NYTBR - July 5 2015 - p16(L) [501+]
PW - v262 - i17 - April 27 2015 - p44(2) [51-500]
Taylor, Keith W. - *A History of the Vietnamese*
JAS - v74 - i2 - May 2015 - p449-452 [501+]
Taylor, Kimball - *The Coyote's Bicycle: The Untold Story of Seven Thousand Bicycles and the Rise of a Borderland Empire*
KR - Dec 15 2015 - pNA [501+]
PW - v262 - i47 - Nov 23 2015 - p59(1) [51-500]
Taylor, Laini - *Dreams of Gods and Monsters (Read by Hvam, Khristine). Audiobook Review*
c BL - v111 - i14 - March 15 2015 - p24(2) [501+]
Taylor, Lauren - *La pluie*
c Res Links - v21 - i1 - Oct 2015 - p56(2) [51-500]
Le soleil
c Res Links - v21 - i1 - Oct 2015 - p56(2) [51-500]
Le vent
c Res Links - v21 - i1 - Oct 2015 - p56(2) [51-500]
Taylor, Lauren Nicole - *Nora and Kettle*
y KR - Dec 1 2015 - pNA [51-500]
Taylor, Lauri - *The Accidental Truth: What My Mother's Murder Investigation Taught Me About Life*
PW - v262 - i10 - March 9 2015 - p62(1) [51-500]
Taylor, Mark C. - *Refiguring the Spiritual: Beuys, Barney, Turrell, Goldsworthy*
JR - v95 - i2 - April 2015 - p242(10) [501+]
Rewiring the Real: In Conversation with William Gaddis, Richard Powers, Mark Danielewski, and Don DeLillo
JR - v95 - i2 - April 2015 - p242(10) [501+]

Speed Limits: Where Time Went and Why We Have So Little Left
    CC - v132 - i24 - Nov 25 2015 - p36(2) [501+]
Taylor, Mark Richard - *Assassin Rabbit from the Dawn of Time*
    KR - July 15 2015 - pNA [501+]
Taylor, Mary Ellen - *The View from Prince Street*
    KR - Dec 1 2015 - pNA [501+]
Taylor, Matthew - *Goat Lips: Tales of a Lapsed Englishman*
    c BL - v112 - i3 - Oct 1 2015 - p32(2) [501+]
Taylor, Michael - *Contesting Constructed Indian-ness: The Intersection of the Frontier, Masculinity, and Whiteness in Native American Mascot Representations*
    Am Ind CRJ - v39 - i2 - Spring 2015 - p132-135 [501+]
Taylor, Miles - *The Age of Asa: Lord Briggs, Public Life and History in Britain since 1945*
    HT - v65 - i4 - April 2015 - p65(1) [501+]
The Victorian Empire and Britain's Maritime World, 1837-1901: The Sea and Global History
    HER - v130 - i543 - April 2015 - p474(2) [501+]
Taylor, Nicole M. - *Emergent Behavior*
    y SLJ - v61 - i8 - August 2015 - p114(1) [51-500]
    y VOYA - v38 - i4 - Oct 2015 - p80(1) [51-500]
Taylor, Nikki M. - *America's First Black Socialist: The Radical Life of Peter H. Clark*
    AHR - v120 - i2 - April 2015 - p621-622 [501+]
Taylor, Patrick - *An Irish Doctor in Love and at Sea*
    KR - August 15 2015 - pNA [501+]
    LJ - v140 - i15 - Sept 15 2015 - p72(1) [51-500]
Only Wounded: Stories of the Irish Troubles
    BL - v111 - i18 - May 15 2015 - p30(1) [51-500]
Taylor, Paul - *Meditations on a Heritage: Papers on the Work and Legacy of Sir Ernst Gombrich*
    Ren Q - v68 - i3 - Fall 2015 - p992-994 [501+]
Taylor, Richard - *Almost Eden*
    KR - Nov 1 2015 - pNA [501+]
Return to Eden
    KR - August 1 2015 - pNA [501+]
Taylor, S.S. - *The Expeditioners and the Secret of King Triton's Lair (Illus. by Roy, Katherine)*
    c HB Guide - v26 - i1 - Spring 2015 - p94(1) [51-500]
Taylor, Sam - *A Paris Affair*
    BL - v111 - i19-20 - June 1 2015 - p62(1) [51-500]
Taylor, Sara - *Boring Girls*
    y BL - v111 - i14 - March 15 2015 - p43(1) [51-500]
    Nat Post - v17 - i130 - April 4 2015 - pWP5(1) [501+]
    PW - v262 - i7 - Feb 16 2015 - p155(2) [51-500]
The Shore (Read by Lamia, Jenna, with MacLeod Andrews). Audiobook Review
    LJ - v140 - i16 - Oct 1 2015 - p44(1) [51-500]
The Shore
    KR - March 15 2015 - pNA [501+]
    NYTBR - Sept 13 2015 - p34(L) [501+]
    PW - v262 - i12 - March 23 2015 - p44(1) [51-500]
Taylor, Sean (b. 1965-) - *Hoot Owl, Master of Disguise (Illus. by Jullien, Jean)*
    c CCB-B - v68 - i8 - April 2015 - p421(2) [51-500]
    c HB Guide - v26 - i2 - Fall 2015 - p54(1) [51-500]
    c PW - v262 - i49 - Dec 2 2015 - p34(2) [51-500]
    c Sch Lib - v63 - i2 - Summer 2015 - p98(1) [51-500]
It's a Groovy World, Alfredo! (Illus. by Garbutt, Chris)
    c Sch Lib - v63 - i4 - Winter 2015 - p224(1) [51-500]
Where the Bugaboo Lives (Illus. by Layton, Neal)
    c Sch Lib - v63 - i4 - Winter 2015 - p224(1) [51-500]
The World-Famous Cheese Shop Break-In (Illus. by Shaw, Hannah)
    c KR - July 15 2015 - pNA [501+]
The World Famous Cheese Shop Break-In (Illus. by Shaw, Hannah)
    c Sch Lib - v63 - i4 - Winter 2015 - p224(1) [51-500]
The World-Famous Cheese Shop Break-in (Illus. by Shaw, Hannah)
    c SLJ - v61 - i11 - Nov 2015 - p88(2) [51-500]
Taylor, Sean D. - *Your Smallest Bones*
    KR - April 15 2015 - pNA [501+]
Taylor, Tony - *The Darkest Side of Saturn: Odyssey of a Reluctant Prophet of Doom*
    PW - v262 - i5 - Feb 2 2015 - p41(1) [51-500]
Taylor, Traci Leigh - *Voices from the Rainbow*
    G&L Rev W - v22 - i4 - July-August 2015 - p41(1) [51-500]

Taylor, Travis S. - *Trail of Evil*
    Analog - v135 - i11 - Nov 2015 - p106(1) [501+]
Taylor, William A. - *Every Citizen a Soldier: The Campaign for Universal Military Training after World War II*
    AHR - v120 - i4 - Oct 2015 - p1516(1) [501+]
    APJ - v29 - i6 - Nov-Dec 2015 - p94(1) [501+]
    Parameters - v45 - i1 - Spring 2015 - p155(3) [501+]
Tayne, Leslie - *Life and Debt: A Fresh Approach to Achieving Financial Wellness*
    PW - v262 - i46 - Nov 16 2015 - p71(1) [51-500]
te Loo, Sanne - *The Mermaid's Shoes*
    c HB Guide - v26 - i1 - Spring 2015 - p48(1) [51-500]
Tea, Michelle - *Girl at the Bottom of the Sea*
    y HB Guide - v26 - i2 - Fall 2015 - p141(1) [51-500]
How to Grow Up: A Memoir
    BL - v111 - i9-10 - Jan 1 2015 - p30(1) [51-500]
    G&L Rev W - v22 - i4 - July-August 2015 - p41(1) [51-500]
    LJ - v140 - i10 - June 1 2015 - p120(2) [501+]
Teachout, Zephyr - *Corruption in America: From Benjamin Franklin's Snuff Box to Citizens United*
    Dis - v62 - i1 - Wntr 2015 - p137(4) [501+]
    JAH - v102 - i2 - Sept 2015 - p523-523 [501+]
    Lon R Bks - v37 - i6 - March 19 2015 - p31(1) [501+]
Teague, Alexandra - *The Wise and Foolish Builders: Poems*
    BL - v111 - i18 - May 15 2015 - p12(1) [51-500]
    PW - v262 - i24 - June 15 2015 - p62(2) [51-500]
Teague, David - *Henry Cicada's Extraordinary Elktonium Escapade*
    c KR - Oct 1 2015 - pNA [501-500]
    c SLJ - v61 - i11 - Nov 2015 - p104(1) [51-500]
Red Hat (Illus. by Portis, Antoinette)
    c KR - Oct 1 2015 - pNA [501-500]
    c SLJ - v61 - i11 - Nov 2015 - p89(1) [51-500]
Teague, Mark - *The Sky Is Falling! (Illus. by Teague, Mark)*
    c BL - v111 - i19-20 - June 1 2015 - p124(2) [51-500]
    c HB - v91 - i4 - July-August 2015 - p125(2) [51-500]
    c KR - March 1 2015 - pNA [501+]
    c CCB-B - v69 - i2 - Oct 2015 - p116(1) [51-500]
Teasley, Ellendea Proffer - *Brodskii sredi nas*
    TLS - i5875 - Nov 6 2015 - p11(1) [501+]
Tebbetts, Chris - *Public School Superhero (Illus. by Thomas, Cory)*
    c HB Guide - v26 - i2 - Fall 2015 - p96(1) [51-500]
Tec, Nechama - *Resistance: Jews and Christians Who Defied the Nazi Terror*
    HNet - Jan 2015 - pNA [501+]
Techlin, Jonathan - *The Death You Deserve*
    KR - Nov 15 2015 - pNA [501+]
Technikstudien als Teildisziplin der Japanforschung - Japanisch-Deutsche Perspektiven der Science and Technology Studies
    HNet - July 2015 - pNA [501+]
Technologies of Spectacle - Knowledge Transfer in Early Modern Theater Cultures. Workshop
    HNet - July 2015 - pNA [501+]
TechnoSpaces: Persistence - Practices - Performance - Power
    HNet - August 2015 - pNA [501+]
Teckentrup, Britta - *Get out of My Bath! (Illus. by Teckentrup, Britta)*
    c BL - v111 - i21 - July 1 2015 - p62(1) [51-500]
    c CCB-B - v69 - i2 - Oct 2015 - p116(2) [51-500]
    c KR - June 1 2015 - pNA [51-500]
    c SLJ - v61 - i6 - June 2015 - p74(2) [51-500]
Sleep Tight, Little Bear (Illus. by Teckentrup, Britta)
    c CH Bwatch - June 2015 - pNA [51-500]
    c HB Guide - v26 - i1 - Spring 2015 - p47(1) [51-500]
Tree: A Peek-Through Picture Book (Illus. by Teckentrup, Britta)
    c PW - v262 - i44 - Nov 2 2015 - p82(1) [51-500]
    c SLJ - v61 - i11 - Nov 2015 - p81(2) [51-500]
Tree
    c KR - Dec 15 2015 - pNA [51-500]
Up & Down: A Lift-the-Flap Book
    c HB Guide - v26 - i1 - Spring 2015 - p47(1) [51-500]
Where's the Pair? A Spotting Book
    c HB Guide - v26 - i1 - Spring 2015 - p19(2) [51-500]
Where's the Pair? (Illus. by Teckentrup, Britta)
    c KR - Feb 15 2015 - pNA [51-500]
    SLJ - v61 - i4 - April 2015 - p136(1) [51-500]

Teegarden, David Arlo - *Death to Tyrants! Ancient Greek Democracy and the Struggle against Tyranny*
    Class R - v65 - i2 - Oct 2015 - p502-504 [501+]
Teege, Jennifer - *My Grandfather Would Have Shot Me: A Black Woman Discovers Her Family's Nazi Past*
    BL - v111 - i14 - March 15 2015 - p42(1) [51-500]
    LJ - v140 - i9 - May 15 2015 - p89(1) [51-500]
    Mac - v128 - i17 - May 4 2015 - p54(2) [501+]
    PW - v262 - i13 - March 30 2015 - p71(1) [51-500]
Teele, Elinor - *The Mechanical Mind of John Coggin*
    y KR - Jan 1 2016 - pNA [51-500]
Teer, Samuel - *Veda: Assembly Required*
    y SLJ - v61 - i12 - Dec 2015 - p130(1) [51-500]
Teets, Jessica C. - *Civil Society under Authoritarianism: The China Model*
    E-A St - v67 - i8 - Oct 2015 - p1343(2) [501+]
Teevan, John Addison - *Integrated Justice and Equality*
    SPBW - Jan 2015 - pNA [501+]
Tegmark, Max - *Our Mathematical Universe: My Quest for the Ultimate Nature of Reality*
    SIAM Rev - v57 - i1 - March 2015 - p153-157 [501+]
Teir, Philip - *The Winter War*
    KR - Jan 1 2016 - pNA [501+]
    Nat Post - v17 - i266 - Sept 26 2015 - pWP5(1) [501+]
    WLT - v89 - i3-4 - May-August 2015 - p118(2) [501+]
Teitel, Amy Shira - *Breaking the Chains of Gravity: The Story of Spaceflight before NASA*
    KR - Dec 1 2015 - pNA [501+]
    Nature - v527 - i7576 - Nov 5 2015 - p37(1) [51-500]
    PW - v262 - i47 - Nov 23 2015 - p61(1) [51-500]
Teitelbaum, Michael S. - *Falling Behind? Boom, Bust, and the Global Race for Scientific Talent*
    Phys Today - v68 - i3 - March 2015 - p48-50 [501+]
Tejedor, Chon - *The Early Wittgenstein on Metaphysics, Natural Science, Language and Value*
    J Phil - v112 - i5 - May 2015 - p280(1) [501+]
Tejirian, Eleanor H. - *Conflict, Conquest, and Conversion: Two Thousand Years of Christian Missions in the Middle East*
    CHR - v101 - i4 - Autumn 2015 - p891(2) [501+]
Tekavec, Heather - *Stop, Thief! (Illus. by Pratt, Pierre)*
    c HB Guide - v26 - i1 - Spring 2015 - p48(1) [51-500]
Tekiela, Stan - *Feathers: A Beautiful Look at a Bird's Most Unique Feature*
    RVBW - Jan 2015 - pNA [51-500]
Our Love of Loons
    RVBW - Jan 2015 - pNA [51-500]
Telechea, Jesus A. Solorzano - *Ser Mujer En La Ciudad Medieval Europea*
    Med R - Jan 2015 - pNA [501+]
Telelis, Ioannis - *Georgios Pachymeres, Philosophia, Book 5: Commentary in Aristotle's Meteorologica - Biblion Pempton, Ton Meteorikon*
    Med R - March 2015 - pNA(NA) [501+]
Telemann, Georg Philipp - *Chorale Settings by Telemann*
    Notes - v72 - i2 - Dec 2015 - p419(3) [501+]
Telfer, Thomas G.W. - *Ruin and Redemption: The Struggle for a Canadian Bankruptcy Law, 1867-1919*
    Can Hist R - v96 - i2 - June 2015 - p296(3) [501+]
Ruin and Redemption: The Struggle for Canadian Bankruptcy Law, 1867-1919
    BHR - v89 - i3 - Autumn 2015 - p603(2) [501+]
Telgemeier, Raina - *Saeurs*
    c Res Links - v20 - i5 - June 2015 - p44(2) [501+]
Sisters (Illus. by Lamb, Braden)
    c HB Guide - v26 - i1 - Spring 2015 - p197(1) [51-500]
Tellegen, Toon - *The Day No One Was Angry (Illus. by Boutavant, Marc)*
    c KR - Jan 15 2015 - pNA [51-500]
    c HB Guide - v26 - i2 - Fall 2015 - p54(1) [51-500]
Telles, Edward E. - *Pigmentocracies: Ethnicity, Race, and Color in Latin America*
    HAHR - v95 - i4 - Nov 2015 - p712-714 [501+]
Tello, Craig - *Yes!: My Improbable Journey to the Main Event of Wrestlemania*
    y BL - v111 - i21 - July 1 2015 - p16(1) [501+]
Telotte, J.P. - *Science Fiction TV*
    SFS - v42 - i1 - March 2015 - p187-191 [501+]
    T&C - v56 - i3 - July 2015 - p779-780 [501+]
Temin, Peter - *Keynes: Useful Economics for the World Economy*
    BHR - v89 - i2 - Summer 2015 - p347(4) [501+]
The Roman Market Economy
    AHR - v120 - i4 - Oct 2015 - p1537-1538 [501+]

456 • TEMMERMAN
Book Review Index 2016 Cumulation

Temmerman, Koen de - *Crafting Characters: Heroes and Heroines in the Ancient Greek Novel*
Class R - v65 - i2 - Oct 2015 - p393-395 [501+]
Tempest, Graham - *Casino Qaddafi*
KR - Feb 15 2015 - pNA [501+]
Tempest, Kate - *Brand New Ancients*
BL - v111 - i13 - March 1 2015 - p15(2) [501+]
y SLJ - v61 - i12 - Dec 2015 - p133(1) [51-500]
NYT - March 19 2015 - pC1(L) [501+]
Hold Your Own
y SLJ - v61 - i12 - Dec 2015 - p133(1) [51-500]
NYT - March 19 2015 - pC1(L) [501+]
PW - v262 - i7 - Feb 16 2015 - p158(1) [51-500]
Temple, Della - *Walking in Grace with Grief: Meditations for Healing after Loss*
SPBW - Oct 2015 - pNA [51-500]
SPBW - Nov 2015 - pNA [51-500]
Temple, Emily - *Juno: Queen of the Gods, Goddess of Marriage (Illus. by Young, Eric)*
c BL - v111 - i17 - May 1 2015 - p88(1) [501+]
Venus: Goddess of Love and Beauty (Illus. by Young, Eric)
c BL - v111 - i17 - May 1 2015 - p88(1) [501+]
Temple, John - *American Pain: How a Young Felon and His Ring of Doctors Unleashed America's Deadliest Drug Epidemic*
LJ - v140 - i14 - Sept 1 2015 - p123(1) [51-500]
Temple, Michael - *Decades Never Start on Time: A Richard Roud Anthology*
FQ - v68 - i3 - Spring 2015 - p100(2) [501+]
Temple, Teri - *Apollo: God of the Sun, Healing, Music, and Poetry (Illus. by Young, Eric)*
c BL - v111 - i17 - May 1 2015 - p88(1) [501+]
Neptune: God of the Sea and Earthquakes
c BL - v111 - i17 - May 1 2015 - p88(1) [501+]
Templeton, Laura - *Summer of the Oak Moon*
y SLJ - v61 - i5 - May 2015 - p125(1) [51-500]
Templin, Mary - *Panic Fiction: Women and Antebellum Economic Crisis*
JSH - v81 - i4 - Nov 2015 - p971(2) [501+]
Tennant, Bob - *Corporate Holiness: Pulpit Preaching and the Church of England Missionary Societies, 1760-1870*
JR - v95 - i3 - July 2015 - p398(2) [501+]
Tennant-Moore, Hannah - *Wreck and Order*
KR - Dec 1 2015 - pNA [501+]
PW - v262 - i47 - Nov 23 2015 - p46(1) [51-500]
TenNapel, Doug - *Nnewts: Escape from the Lizzarks (Illus. by Garner, Katherine)*
c CCB-B - v68 - i7 - March 2015 - p372(1) [51-500]
c HB Guide - v26 - i2 - Fall 2015 - p104(1) [51-500]
Tennent, Martha - *The Sea*
WLT - v89 - i5 - Sept-Oct 2015 - p59(1) [51-500]
Tennesen, Michael - *The Next Species: The Future of Evolution in the Aftermath of Man*
BL - v111 - i11 - Feb 1 2015 - p8(1) [51-500]
KR - Jan 1 2015 - pNA [51-500]
PW - v262 - i4 - Jan 26 2015 - p163(1) [51-500]
Tenzin-Dolma, Lisa - *Charlie: The Dog Who Came in from the Wild*
RVBW - Oct 2015 - pNA [51-500]
Teo, You Yenn - *Neoliberal Morality in Singapore: How Family Policies Make State and Society*
CS - v44 - i4 - July 2015 - p580-581 [501+]
Teonorio-Trillo, Mauricio - *I Speak of the City: Mexico City at the Turn of the Twentieth Century*
Historian - v77 - i1 - Spring 2015 - p146(2) [501+]
Ter Minassian, Taline - *Most Secret Agent of Empire: Reginald Teague-Jones, Master Spy of the Great Game*
Spec - v327 - i9730 - Feb 21 2015 - p43(2) [501+]
Terada, Junzo - *A Good Home for Max*
c HB Guide - v26 - i1 - Spring 2015 - p48(1) [51-500]
Teran, Andi - *Ana of California (Read by Teran, Andi). Audiobook Review*
y SLJ - v61 - i10 - Oct 2015 - p55(1) [51-500]
Ana of California
KR - April 15 2015 - pNA [51-500]
PW - v262 - i15 - April 13 2015 - p52(1) [51-500]
y SLJ - v61 - i12 - Dec 2015 - p133(1) [51-500]
Terei, Pio - *10 Goofy Geckos (Illus. by Hinde, Deborah)*
c Magpies - v30 - i4 - Sept 2015 - pS5(1) [501+]
Terey, Janos - *Atkeles Budapesten*
WLT - v89 - i6 - Nov-Dec 2015 - p75(2) [501+]
Terhune, Tori Randolph - *Land Your Dream Career: Eleven Steps to Take in College*
BL - v111 - i21 - July 1 2015 - p22(2) [501+]
TerKeurst, Lysa - *Win or Lose, I Love You (Illus. by Christy, Jana)*
c BL - v112 - i1 - Sept 1 2015 - p101(1) [51-500]
Win or Lose, I Love You! (Illus. by Christy, Jana)
c KR - July 15 2015 - pNA [51-500]
Terpstra, Nicholas - *Cultures of Charity: 'Women, Politics, and the Reform of Poor Relief in Renaissance Italy*
Historian - v77 - i1 - Spring 2015 - p197(3) [501+]
Terrall, Mary - *Catching Nature in the Act: Reaumur and the Practice of Natural History in the Eighteenth Century*
Isis - v106 - i2 - June 2015 - p448(2) [501+]
Terranova, Elaine - *Dollhouse*
Wom R Bks - v32 - i5 - Sept-Oct 2015 - p21(3) [501+]
Terras, Melissa - *Defining Digital Humanities: A Reader*
HNet - Jan 2015 - pNA [501+]
Terrell, Brandon - *Fearless (Illus. by Cano, Fernando)*
c HB Guide - v26 - i1 - Spring 2015 - p80(2) [51-500]
Terrell, Heather - *The Boundary (Illus. by Cortes, Ricardo)*
y HB Guide - v26 - i1 - Spring 2015 - p125(1) [51-500]
Terrell, Jaden - *River of Glass*
RVBW - July 2015 - pNA [51-500]
Terrell, John Edward - *A Talent for Friendship: Rediscovery of a Remarkable Trait*
Am Sci - v103 - i2 - March-April 2015 - p149(3) [501+]
Terry, Bryant - *Vegan Soul Kitchen*
Veg J - v34 - i2 - April-June 2015 - p34(1) [51-500]
Terry, Candis - *Sweet Surprise*
BL - v111 - i9-10 - Jan 1 2015 - p58(1) [51-500]
Truly Sweet
BL - v111 - i21 - July 1 2015 - p45(1) [51-500]
Terry, Clark - *Clark: The Autobiography of Clark Terry*
RVBW - Oct 2015 - pNA [51-500]
Terry, Lynn - *Tails from the Booth*
LJ - v140 - i16 - Oct 1 2015 - p100(1) [51-500]
Terry, Teri - *Mind Games*
y Sch Lib - v63 - i2 - Summer 2015 - p121(1) [51-500]
Teru, Miyamoto - *Rivers*
WLT - v89 - i5 - Sept-Oct 2015 - p71(1) [51-500]
Teruel, Jose - *Los anos norteamericanos de Luis Cernuda*
Hisp R - v83 - i2 - Spring 2015 - p231-234 [501+]
Terzian, Mary - *Politically Homeless: A Five-Year Odyssey across Three Continents*
KR - Nov 1 2015 - pNA [501+]
Terzian, Sevan G. - *Science Education and Citizenship: Fairs, Clubs and Talent Searches for Amerian Youth, 1918-1958*
Isis - v106 - i1 - March 2015 - p213(2) [501+]
Tesdeli, Diana Seeker - *Stories from the Kitchen*
BL - v112 - i3 - Oct 1 2015 - p20(1) [51-500]
Tesh, Jane - *Butterfly Waltz*
SPBW - Nov 2015 - pNA [51-500]
Teske, Roland J. - *Henry of Ghent: Summa of Ordinary Questions: Articles 35, 36, 42, and 45*
Theol St - v76 - i3 - Sept 2015 - p636(2) [501+]
Teskey, Gordon - *The Poetry of John Milton*
TimHES - i2212 - July 16 2015 - p50-51 [501+]
Tesler, Monica - *Bounders*
c KR - Oct 1 2015 - pNA [51-500]
Teslow, Tracy - *Constructing Race: The Science of Bodies and Cultures in American Anthropology*
AHR - v120 - i4 - Oct 2015 - p1502-1503 [501+]
JAH - v102 - i2 - Sept 2015 - p516-517 [501+]
Tesser, Lynn M. - *Ethnic Cleansing and the European Union: An Interdisciplinary Approach to Security, Memory and Ethnography*
E-A St - v67 - i3 - May 2015 - p507(3) [501+]
Tessicini, Dario - *Celestial Novelties on the Eve of the Scientific Revolution, 1540-1630*
Isis - v106 - i2 - June 2015 - p441(2) [501+]
Tessler, Tamar - *Abukacha's Shoes*
c KR - March 15 2015 - pNA [51-500]
c Res Links - v20 - i4 - April 2015 - p8(2) [51-500]
Testa, Judith Anne - *An Art Lover's Guide to Florence*
Ren Q - v68 - i1 - Spring 2015 - p243-244 [501+]
Testa, Maggie - *Book of Dragons (Illus. by Bialk, Andy)*
c HB Guide - v26 - i1 - Spring 2015 - p48(1) [51-500]
Testa, Rylan Jay - *The Gender Quest Workbook: A Guide for Teens and Young Adults Exploring Gender Identity*
y KR - Oct 15 2015 - pNA [51-500]
y SLJ - v61 - i12 - Dec 2015 - p147(1) [51-500]
Tetlock, Philip E. - *Superforecasting: The Art and Science of Prediction*
Har Bus R - v93 - i10 - Oct 2015 - p130(2) [501+]
KR - July 15 2015 - pNA [501+]
LJ - v140 - i14 - Sept 1 2015 - p115(1) [51-500]
Mac - v128 - i41 - Oct 19 2015 - p62(1) [501+]
NYTBR - Oct 18 2015 - p23(L) [501+]
Spec - v329 - i9762 - Oct 3 2015 - p42(2) [501+]
Tetrault, Lisa - *The Myth of Seneca Falls: Memory and the Women's Suffrage Movement, 1848-1898*
AHR - v120 - i4 - Oct 2015 - p1495-1496 [501+]
HNet - August 2015 - pNA [501+]
JAH - v102 - i2 - Sept 2015 - p559-560 [501+]
JIH - v45 - i4 - Spring 2015 - p590-591 [501+]
NEQ - v88 - i1 - March 2015 - p175-177 [501+]
Tett, Gillian - *The Silo Effect: The Peril of Expertise and the Promise of Breaking Down Barriers*
Econ - v416 - i8953 - August 29 2015 - p67(US) [501+]
Har Bus R - v93 - i9 - Sept 2015 - p122(2) [501+]
NYTBR - Sept 6 2015 - p12(L) [501+]
PW - v262 - i27 - July 6 2015 - p60(1) [51-500]
The Silo Effect: Why Putting Everything in Its Place Isn't Such a Bright Idea
NS - v144 - i5285 - Oct 23 2015 - p54(1) [501+]
Tetzeli, Rick - *Becoming Steve Jobs: The Evolution of a Reckless Upstart into a Visionary Leader*
Barron's - v95 - i14 - April 6 2015 - p37(1) [501+]
Ent W - i1357 - April 3 2015 - p66(1) [501+]
Tetzlaff, Ronald - *Recent Advances in Predicting and Preventing Epileptic Seizures*
QRB - v90 - i2 - June 2015 - p241(1) [501+]
Teufel, Annette - *Der "un-cerstandliche" Prophet: Paul Adler, ein Deutsch-Judischer Dichter*
Ger Q - v88 - i1 - Wntr 2015 - p129(2) [501+]
Teule, Jean - *The Poisoning Angel*
PW - v262 - i20 - May 18 2015 - p66(1) [51-500]
'Teutsche Liedlein' des 16. Jahrhunderts. Jahrestagung des Wolfenbutteler Arbeitskreises fur Renaissanceforschung
HNet - Feb 2015 - pNA [501+]
Tevis, Joni - *The World Is on Fire: Scrap, Treasure, and Songs of A*
LJ - v140 - i9 - May 15 2015 - p84(1) [51-500]
The World Is on Fire: Scrap, Treasure, and Songs of Apocalypse
KR - Feb 15 2015 - pNA [501+]
PW - v262 - i13 - March 30 2015 - p71(1) [51-500]
Tewell, Jeremy J. - *A Self-Evident Lie: Southern Slavery and the Threat to American Freedom*
HNet - August 2015 - pNA [501+]
Thachil, Tariq - *Elite Parties, Poor Voters: How Social Services Win Votes in India*
For Aff - v94 - i3 - May-June 2015 - pNA [501+]
Thackara, John - *How to Thrive in the Next Economy: Designing Tomorrow's World Today*
New Sci - v227 - i3039 - Sept 19 2015 - p42(2) [501+]
PW - v262 - i39 - Sept 28 2015 - p83(1) [51-500]
Thacker, Eugene - *In the Dust of the Planet*
South CR - v47 - i2 - Spring 2015 - p157-159 [501+]
Thackeray, David - *Conservatism for the Democratic Age: Conservative Cultures and the Challenge of Mass Politics in Early Twentieth Century England*
HER - v130 - i542 - Feb 2015 - p232(2) [501+]
Thackray, Arnold - *Moore's Law: The Life of Gordon Moore, Silicon Valley's Quiet Revolutionary*
KR - April 1 2015 - pNA [501+]
LJ - v140 - i8 - May 1 2015 - p98(1) [51-500]
Thai, Hung Cam - *Insufficient Funds: The Culture of Money in Low-Wage Transnational Families*
CS - v44 - i5 - Sept 2015 - p721-723 [501+]
JRAI - v21 - i3 - Sept 2015 - p706(2) [501+]
Thalassokratographie - Rezeption und Transformation Antiker Seeherrschaft
HNet - July 2015 - pNA [501+]
Thaler, Richard H. - *Misbehaving: The Making of Behavioral Economics*
BL - v111 - i18 - May 15 2015 - p7(1) [51-500]
Bwatch - July 2015 - pNA [51-500]
KR - April 1 2015 - pNA [501+]
Nature - v521 - i7550 - May 7 2015 - p31(1) [51-500]
Nature - v523 - i7562 - July 30 2015 - pSB1(1) [51-500]
NYT - May 6 2015 - pNA(L) [501+]
Misbehaving: The Making of Behavioural Economics
Econ - v415 - i8937 - May 9 2015 - p66(US) [501+]
Thalken, Jason - *Fight Like a Physicist*
KR - Sept 15 2015 - pNA [501+]
Tharp-Thee, Sandy - *The Apple Tree (Illus. by Hodson, Marlena Campbell)*
c KR - Sept 15 2015 - pNA [51-500]
That Patchwork Place - *The Quilt Calendar 2016*
Bwatch - Oct 2015 - pNA [51-500]

Thatcher, Stephanie - *Little Hoiho* (Illus. by Thatcher, Stephanie)
   c Magpies - v30 - i1 - March 2015 - pS4(2) [501+]

Thavis, John - *The Vatican Prophecies: Investigating Supernatural Signs, Apparitions, and Miracles in the Modern Age*
   KR - August 1 2015 - pNA [501+]
   LJ - v140 - i13 - August 1 2015 - p103(2) [51-500]

Thayer, James - *House of Eight Orchids*
   PW - v262 - i46 - Nov 16 2015 - p58(1) [51-500]

Thayer, John B. - *A Survivor's Tale: The Titanic 1912-2012*
   RVBW - June 2015 - pNA [51-500]

Thayer, Nancy - *The Guest Cottage*
   BL - v111 - i17 - May 1 2015 - p75(1) [51-500]
   KR - March 15 2015 - pNA [51-500]
   LJ - v140 - i7 - April 15 2015 - p80(2) [51-500]
   RVBW - July 2015 - pNA [501+]

Thayne, RaeAnne - *Redemption Bay*
   BL - v112 - i2 - Sept 15 2015 - p42(2) [501+]

Thekkumthala, Jose - *Amballore House*
   KR - Jan 1 2016 - pNA [501+]

Theobald, Ulrich - *War Finance and Logistics in Late Imperial China: A Study of the Second Jinchuan Campaign, 1771-1776*
   J Mil H - v79 - i2 - April 2015 - p485-487 [501+]

Theofilakis, Fabien - *Les prisonniers de guerre allemands, France, 1944-1949: Une captivite de guerre en temps de paix*
   AHR - v120 - i4 - Oct 2015 - p1554-1555 [501+]

Theologie und Vergangenheitsbewaltigung VI: Diskurse uber "Form," "Gestalt" und "Stil" in den 20er und 30er Jahren
   HNet - June 2015 - pNA [501+]

Theoretische und Methodische Zugriffe auf die Spatmittelalterliche Wirtschaftsgeschichte am Beispiel von Quellen zum Rechnungswesen
   HNet - March 2015 - pNA [501+]

Theotokis, Georgios - *The Norman Campaigns in the Balkans, 1081-1108*
   Med R - March 2015 - pNA(NA) [501+]

Ther, Philipp - *The Dark Side of Nation-States: Ethnic Cleansing in Modern Europe*
   Slav R - v74 - i2 - Summer 2015 - p371-372 [501+]

Die Neue Ordnung auf dem Alten Kontinent: Eine Geschichte des Neoliberalen Europa
   HNet - Jan 2015 - pNA [501+]

Thermaenius, Pehr - *The Christmas Match: Football in No Man's Land 1914*
   Mac - v128 - i40 - Oct 12 2015 - p57(1) [501+]

Theroux, Paul - *Deep South: Four Seasons on Back Roads*
   BL - v112 - i2 - Sept 15 2015 - p19(2) [51-500]
   KR - July 1 2015 - pNA [501+]
   LJ - v140 - i11 - June 15 2015 - p104(1) [51-500]
   NY - v91 - i34 - Nov 2 2015 - p90 [501+]
   NYT - Sept 20 2015 - p4(L) [501+]
   NYT - Sept 23 2015 - pC1(L) [501+]
   NYTBR - Oct 4 2015 - p17(L) [501+]
   PW - v262 - i19 - May 11 2015 - p2(1) [51-500]
   Spec - v329 - i9772 - Dec 12 2015 - p75(2) [501+]

Mr. Bones: Twenty Stories
   HR - v68 - i2 - Summer 2015 - p343-351 [501+]

Theule, Larissa - *Fat & Bones and Other Stories* (Read by Corren, Donald). Audiobook Review
   c BL - v112 - i7 - Dec 1 2015 - p70(1) [51-500]
   y SLJ - v61 - i12 - Dec 2015 - p81(1) [51-500]

Fat & Bones and Other Stories (Illus. by Doyle, Adam S.)
   y HB Guide - v26 - i1 - Spring 2015 - p1258(1) [51-500]

Theune-Vogt, Claudia - *Archaologie an Tatorten des 20. Jahrhunderts*
   HNet - Feb 2015 - pNA [501+]

Thewissen, J.G.M. - *The Walking Whales: From Land to Water in Eight Million Years*
   NH - v123 - i2 - March 2015 - p47(1) [501+]
   TimHES - i2185 - Jan 8 2015 - p52-52 [501+]
   TLS - i5843 - March 27 2015 - p28(1) [501+]

They Can Live in the Desert but Nowhere Else: A History of the Armenian Genocide
   Spec - v327 - i9738 - April 18 2015 - p34(2) [501+]

Thi Minh Tran, Phuoc - *Vietnamese Children's Favorite Stories*
   c KR - Feb 1 2015 - pNA [51-500]

Thibeault, Jason - *An Ordinary Magic*
   KR - June 15 2015 - pNA [501+]

Thiede, Todd M. - *Slashtag*
   KR - Oct 15 2015 - pNA [501+]

Thiel, Peter - *Zero to One: Notes on Startups, or How to Build the Future*
   For Aff - v94 - i1 - Jan-Feb 2015 - pNA [501+]

Thiele, Bob - *What a Wonderful World* (Illus. by Hopgood, Tim)
   c Sch Lib - v63 - i1 - Spring 2015 - p28(1) [501+]

Thiele, Jan - *Theologie in der jemenitischen Zaydiyya. Die naturphilosophischen Uberlegungen des al-Hasan ar-Rassas*
   JNES - v74 - i1 - April 2015 - p177(3) [501+]

Thielemann, Christian - *My Life with Wagner*
   Econ - v416 - i8951 - August 15 2015 - p75(US) [501+]
   Spec - v328 - i9755 - August 15 2015 - p30(2) [501+]

Thieler, Kerstin - *"Volksgemeinschaft" unter Vorbehalt: Gesinnungskontrolle und Politische Mobilisierung in der Herrschaftspraxis der NSDAP-Kreisleitung Gottingen*
   HNet - June 2015 - pNA [501+]

Thiem, Brian - *Red Line*
   BL - v111 - i19-20 - June 1 2015 - p57(1) [51-500]
   PW - v262 - i23 - June 8 2015 - p38(1) [51-500]
   SPBW - July 2015 - pNA [51-500]

Thiessen, Malte - *Infiziertes Europa: Seuchen im Langen 20. Jahrhundert*
   HNet - Feb 2015 - pNA [501+]

Thigpen, Jennifer - *Island Queens and Mission Wives: How Gender and Empire Remade Hawai'i's Pacific World*
   AHR - v120 - i4 - Oct 2015 - p1469-1470 [501+]
   WHQ - v46 - i1 - Spring 2015 - p92-93 [501+]

Thirlway, Christine E. - *Prelude to the Modernist Crisis: The "Firmin" Articles of Alfred Loisy*
   CHR - v101 - i2 - Spring 2015 - p383(3) [501+]

Thirlwell, Adam - *Lurid & Cute*
   Atl - v315 - i3 - April 2015 - p48(2) [501+]
   BL - v111 - i14 - March 15 2015 - p44(1) [51-500]
   KR - Feb 1 2015 - pNA [51-500]
   LJ - v140 - i7 - April 15 2015 - p82(1) [51-500]
   Lon R Bks - v37 - i6 - March 19 2015 - p39(2) [501+]
   NY - v91 - i15 - June 1 2015 - p75 [501+]
   NYT - May 14 2015 - pC6(L) [501+]
   NYTBR - April 26 2015 - p15(L) [501+]
   PW - v262 - i8 - Feb 23 2015 - p49(2) [51-500]
   Spec - v327 - i9726 - Jan 24 2015 - p41(2) [501+]
   TLS - i5838 - Feb 20 2015 - p20(1) [501+]

Thiselton, Anthony - *The Holy Spirit in Biblical Teaching, Through the Centuries, and Today*
   Intpr - v69 - i1 - Jan 2015 - p108(2) [501+]

Thiselton, Anthony C. - *The Thiselton Companion to Christian Theology*
   CC - v132 - i7 - April 1 2015 - p43(1) [501+]

Thistlethwaite, Susan Brooks - *Interfaith Just Peacemaking: Jewish, Christian, and Muslim Perspectives on the New Paradigm of Peace and War*
   J Ch St - v57 - i1 - Wntr 2015 - p162-164 [501+]

Thoft, Ingrid - *Brutality*
   BL - v111 - i19-20 - June 1 2015 - p48(1) [51-500]
   KR - April 15 2015 - pNA [501+]
   PW - v262 - i17 - April 27 2015 - p47(3) [501+]

Thoizet, Evelyne - *Les Mailles du filet, ou, 'Le Temps immobile' de Claude Mauriac*
   FS - v69 - i1 - Jan 2015 - p110-110 [501+]

Thom, James Alexander - *Fire in the Water*
   SPBW - Nov 2015 - pNA [51-500]

Thom, Paul - *The Logic of the Trinity: Augustine to Ockham*
   Specu - v90 - i3 - July 2015 - p856-858 [501+]

Thoma, Jesse J. - *Pedal to the Metal*
   PW - v262 - i4 - Jan 26 2015 - p156(1) [501+]

Thomas, Abigail - *What Comes Next and How to Like It*
   Econ - v415 - i8932 - April 4 2015 - p79(US) [501+]
   BL - v111 - i11 - Feb 1 2015 - p4(1) [51-500]

Thomas, Alan G. - *Best Business Practices*
   SPBW - Sept 2015 - pNA [51-500]

Thomas, Alexander R. - *Critical Rural Theory: Structure, Space, Culture*
   CS - v44 - i1 - Jan 2015 - p123-125 [501+]

Thomas, Alfred - *Shakespeare, Dissent, and the Cold War*
   Slav R - v74 - i3 - Fall 2015 - p610-611 [501+]

Thomas, Anna - *Vegan Vegetarian Omnivore: Dinner for Everyone at the Table*
   LJ - v140 - i19 - Nov 15 2015 - p103(2) [51-500]

Thomas, Ardel Haefele - *Queer Others in Victorian Gothic: Transgressing Monstrosity*
   VS - v57 - i3 - Spring 2015 - p565(3) [501+]

Thomas, Chantal - *The Exchange of Princesses*
   BL - v111 - i19-20 - June 1 2015 - p59(1) [51-500]
   KR - June 1 2015 - pNA [501+]

Thomas, Dana - *Gods and Kings: The Rise and Fall of Alexander McQueen and John Galliano*
   CSM - March 16 2015 - pNA [501+]
   Econ - v414 - i8928 - March 7 2015 - p88(US) [501+]
   NS - v144 - i5251 - Feb 27 2015 - p56(3) [501+]
   NYT - March 12 2015 - pD2(L) [501+]
   G&L Rev W - v22 - i4 - July-August 2015 - p10(3) [501+]
   New R - v246 - i4 - May 2015 - p81(3) [501+]
   NYTBR - March 8 2015 - p10(L) [501+]
   Spec - v327 - i9728 - Feb 7 2015 - p38(3) [501+]
   TLS - i5855 - June 19 2015 - p27(1) [501+]

Thomas, Debbie - *Class Act*
   c Sch Lib - v63 - i4 - Winter 2015 - p233(1) [51-500]

Thomas, Diane - *In Wilderness*
   BL - v111 - i12 - Feb 15 2015 - p31(1) [51-500]
   LJ - v140 - i3 - Feb 15 2015 - p94(1) [51-500]

Thomas, Edward - *South Sudan: A Slow Liberation*
   TLS - i5864-5865 - August 21 2015 - p35(1) [501+]

Thomas, Elizabeth Marshall - *Certain Poor Shepherds* (Illus. by Bartlett, Jonathan)
   c KR - July 1 2015 - pNA [51-500]
   c SLJ - v61 - i10 - Oct 2015 - p69(1) [51-500]

Thomas, Evan - *Being Nixon: A Man Divided*
   BooChiTr - August 8 2015 - p12(1) [501+]
   LJ - v140 - i13 - August 1 2015 - p107(1) [51-500]
   NY - v91 - i20 - July 20 2015 - p71 [51-500]
   NYT - July 2 2015 - pC1(L) [501+]
   NYTBR - July 19 2015 - p12(L) [501+]

Ike's Bluff: President Eisenhower's Secret Battle to Save the World
   Pres St Q - v45 - i1 - March 2015 - p199(7) [501+]

Thomas, Gareth - *A Welsh Dawn*
   WLT - v89 - i3-4 - May-August 2015 - p125(1) [51-500]

Thomas, George Antony - *The Politics and Poetics of Sor Juana Ines de la Cruz*
   CHR - v101 - i3 - Summer 2015 - p693(2) [501+]

Thomas, Gillian - *Because of Sex: One Law, Ten Cases, and Fifty Years That Changed American Women's Lives at Work*
   KR - Dec 15 2015 - pNA [501+]

Thomas, Hugh (b. 1931-) - *World without End: Spain, Philip II, and the First Global Empire*
   KR - June 1 2015 - pNA [501+]
   NY - v91 - i26 - Sept 7 2015 - p82 [51-500]
   NYTBR - August 9 2015 - p25(L) [501+]
   PW - v262 - i26 - June 29 2015 - p58(1) [51-500]

World without End: The Global Empire of Philip II
   TLS - i5835 - Jan 30 2015 - p3(2) [501+]

Thomas, Hugh M. - *The Secular Clergy in England, 1066-1216*
   CHR - v101 - i3 - Summer 2015 - p611(2) [501+]
   Med R - June 2015 - pNA [501+]
   TLS - i5844 - April 3 2015 - p5(1) [501+]

Thomas, Isabel - *Experiments with Electricity*
   c HB Guide - v26 - i2 - Fall 2015 - p167(1) [51-500]

Experiments with Forces
   c SLJ - v61 - i9 - Sept 2015 - p176(2) [51-500]

Experiments with Heating and Cooling
   c Sch Lib - v63 - i3 - Autumn 2015 - p176(1) [51-500]

Experiments with Magnets
   c SLJ - v61 - i9 - Sept 2015 - p176(2) [51-500]

Experiments with Materials
   c SLJ - v61 - i9 - Sept 2015 - p176(2) [51-500]

Experiments with Plants
   c SLJ - v61 - i9 - Sept 2015 - p176(2) [51-500]

Hip Hamster Projects
   c Sch Lib - v63 - i4 - Winter 2015 - p240(1) [51-500]

Number Fun: Making Numbers with Your Body
   TC Math - v22 - i2 - Sept 2015 - p117(2) [501+]

Thomas, J.C. - *Ninja Mouse: Haiku* (Illus. by Thomas, J.C.)
   c CH Bwatch - Feb 2015 - pNA [51-500]
   c PW - v262 - i5 - Feb 2 2015 - p63(1) [51-500]

Thomas, James - *Flash Fiction International: Very Short Stories from around the World*
   Econ - v415 - i8932 - April 4 2015 - p78(US) [501+]
   PW - v262 - i8 - Feb 23 2015 - p47(1) [51-500]

Thomas, Jodi - *Ask Me Why*
   PW - v262 - i21 - May 25 2015 - p42(2) [51-500]

Thomas, June Manning - *Redevelopment and Race: Planning a Finer City in Postwar Detroit*
    J Urban H - v41 - i5 - Sept 2015 - p936-942 [501+]

Thomas, Kara - *The Darkest Corners*
    y KR - Jan 1 2016 - pNA [51-500]

Thomas, Karen Kruse - *Deluxe Jim Crow: Civil Rights and American Health Policy, 1935-1954*
    JSH - v81 - i3 - August 2015 - p764(3) [501+]

Thomas, Kate - *Postal Pleasures: Sex, Scandal, and Victorian Letters*
    MLR - v110 - i3 - July 2015 - p850-851 [501+]

Thomas, Katherine Woodward - *Conscious Uncoupling: 5 Steps to Living Happily Even After*
    PW - v262 - i29 - July 20 2015 - p186(1) [51-500]

Thomas, Leah - *Because You'll Never Meet Me*
    y BL - v111 - i17 - May 1 2015 - p90(1) [51-500]
    y CCB-B - v69 - i2 - Oct 2015 - p117(1) [51-500]
    y HB - v91 - i4 - July-August 2015 - p148(1) [51-500]
    y KR - March 15 2015 - pNA [51-500]
    y Magpies - v30 - i3 - July 2015 - p44(1) [501+]
    y VOYA - v38 - i3 - August 2015 - p70(2) [501+]

Thomas, Lex - *Quarantine: The Burnouts*
    y HB Guide - v26 - i1 - Spring 2015 - p125(1) [51-500]

Thomas, Louisa - *Louisa*
    KR - Jan 1 2016 - pNA [501+]

Thomas, Lynnell L. - *Desire and Disaster in New Orleans: Tourism, Race, and Historical Memory*
    Am St - v54 - i2 - Summer 2015 - p114-115 [501+]

Thomas, Mary E. - *Multicultural Girlhood: Racism, Sexuality, and the Conflicted Spaces of American Education*
    SF - v93 - i3 - March 2015 - pe82 [501+]
    SF - v93 - i3 - March 2015 - pNA [501+]

Thomas, Matthew - *We Are Not Ourselves*
    AM - v212 - i9 - March 16 2015 - p36(3) [501+]
    RVBW - April 2015 - pNA [501+]
    RVBW - June 2015 - pNA [501+]

Thomas, Pat - *I See Things Differently: A First Look at Autism*
    c CH Bwatch - Jan 2015 - pNA [51-500]

Thomas, Paul - *Fallout*
    PW - v262 - i8 - Feb 23 2015 - p53(2) [51-500]

Thomas, Peggy - *Thomas Jefferson Grows a Nation (Illus. by Innerst, Stacy)*
    c BL - v111 - i19-20 - June 1 2015 - p92(1) [51-500]
    c SLJ - v61 - i9 - Sept 2015 - p182(2) [51-500]
    c CH Bwatch - Oct 2015 - pNA [51-500]
    c KR - June 1 2015 - pNA [51-500]
    c PW - v262 - i29 - July 20 2015 - p190(2) [51-500]

Thomas, R. William - *The Art of Gardening: Design Inspiration and Innovative Planting Techniques from Chanticleer*
    NYTBR - Dec 6 2015 - p66(L) [501+]

Thomas, Rhiannon - *Kingdom of Ashes*
    y KR - Nov 15 2015 - pNA [51-500]

A Wicked Thing
    y CCB-B - v68 - i6 - Feb 2015 - p334(1) [51-500]
    y HB Guide - v26 - i2 - Fall 2015 - p141(1) [51-500]

Thomas, Rhondda Robinson - *Claiming Exodus: A Cultural History of Afro-Atlantic Identity, 1774-1903*
    AL - v87 - i3 - Sept 2015 - p609-611 [501+]
    Historian - v77 - i1 - Spring 2015 - p205(2) [501+]

Thomas, Richard F. - *The Virgil Encyclopedia*
    Class R - v65 - i1 - April 2015 - p124-128 [501+]

Thomas, Rosie - *Daughter of the House*
    BL - v111 - i22 - August 1 2015 - p39(1) [51-500]
    KR - July 1 2015 - pNA [501+]

Thomas, Roy - *75 Years of Marvel Comics: From the Golden Age to the Silver Screen*
    NS - v144 - i5254 - March 20 2015 - p48(2) [501+]

Thomas, Samuel S. - *Creating Communities in Restoration England: Parish and Congregation in Oliver Heywood's Halifax*
    HER - v130 - i542 - Feb 2015 - p205(2) [501+]

Thomas, Sara - *Cats in Hats: 30 Knit and Crochet Patterns for Your Kitty*
    PW - v262 - i7 - Feb 16 2015 - p175(1) [51-500]

Thomas, Sarah Loudin - *Until the Harvest*
    BL - v111 - i17 - May 1 2015 - p81(1) [51-500]

Thomas, Scarlett - *The Seed Collectors*
    Spec - v328 - i9748 - June 27 2015 - p41(1) [501+]

Thomas, Scott - *Curious Creatures ABC (Illus. by Byrd, Robert)*
    c CH Bwatch - March 2015 - pNA [51-500]

Thomas, Shelley Moore - *No, No, Kitten! (Illus. by Nichols, Lori)*
    c CH Bwatch - May 2015 - pNA [501+]
    c HB Guide - v26 - i2 - Fall 2015 - p20(1) [51-500]
    c SLJ - v61 - i2 - Feb 2015 - p81(1) [51-500]

Secrets of Selkie Bay
    c BL - v111 - i21 - July 1 2015 - p77(1) [51-500]
    c CCB-B - v69 - i1 - Sept 2015 - p59(1) [51-500]
    y HB - v91 - i4 - July-August 2015 - p148(2) [51-500]
    c SLJ - v61 - i6 - June 2015 - p106(1) [51-500]
    y VOYA - v38 - i2 - June 2015 - p84(1) [51-500]

Thomas, Sherry - *The Immortal Heights*
    c HB - v91 - i5 - Sept-Oct 2015 - p120(1) [51-500]
    y KR - August 1 2015 - pNA [51-500]
    y SLJ - v61 - i9 - Sept 2015 - p173(1) [51-500]
    y VOYA - v38 - i4 - Oct 2015 - p80(1) [51-500]

The Perilous Sea
    y HB Guide - v26 - i1 - Spring 2015 - p126(1) [51-500]

Thomas, Stephen - *Cluster: Unmei*
    Analog - v136 - i1-2 - Jan-Feb 2016 - p181(2) [501+]

Thomas-Symonds, Nicklaus - *Nye: The Political Life of Aneurin Bevan*
    Lon R Bks - v37 - i9 - May 7 2015 - p24(3) [501+]
    NS - v144 - i5253 - March 13 2015 - p44(2) [501+]
    TLS - i5836 - Feb 6 2015 - p24(1) [501+]

Thomas, Wendell - *Tango*
    y KR - Feb 15 2015 - pNA [501+]

Thomas, Will - *Anatomy of Evil*
    KR - March 1 2015 - pNA [51-500]
    PW - v262 - i10 - March 9 2015 - p54(1) [51-500]

Thomason, Sarah G. - *Endangered Languages: An Introduction*
    Lang Soc - v44 - i4 - Sept 2015 - p606-1 [501+]

Thomasson, Amie L. - *Ontology Made Easy*
    TLS - i5863 - August 14 2015 - p28(1) [501+]

Thomasson, Anna - *A Curious Friendship: The Story of a Bluestocking and a Bright Young Thing*
    Spec - v327 - i9736 - April 4 2015 - p34(1) [501+]

Thome, Philippe - *Sottsass*
    TLS - i5845 - April 10 2015 - p13(1) [501+]

Thompson, Ahmir - *Somethingtofoodabout*
    KR - Jan 1 2016 - pNA [501+]

Thompson, Ann - *Macbeth: The State of Play*
    Ren Q - v68 - i2 - Summer 2015 - p788-790 [501+]

Thompson, Antonio S. - *The Routledge Handbook of American Military and Diplomatic History: 1865 to the Present*
    HNet - Jan 2015 - pNA [51-500]

Thompson, Ben - *Guts & Glory: The American Civil War (Illus. by Butzer, C.M.)*
    y HB Guide - v26 - i1 - Spring 2015 - p205(1) [51-500]

Thompson, Beverly Yuen - *Covered in Ink: Tattoos, Women and the Politics of the Body*
    UtneADi - i188 - Fall 2015 - p89(1) [501+]

Thompson, Carlene - *Can't Find My Way Home*
    BL - v111 - i9-10 - Jan 1 2015 - p45(1) [51-500]

Thompson, Carol - *Snow (Illus. by Thompson, Carol)*
    c KR - July 1 2015 - pNA [51-500]

Thompson, Charis - *Good Science: The Ethical Choreography of Stem Cell Research*
    AJS - v120 - i6 - May 2015 - p1895(4) [501+]
    CS - v44 - i6 - Nov 2015 - p861-862 [501+]

Thompson, Charles D., Jr. - *Border Odyssey*
    KR - Feb 15 2015 - pNA [501+]

Thompson, Clifford - *The Archaeologists*
    c BL - v112 - i1 - Sept 1 2015 - p97(1) [501+]

Thompson, Colin - *Fearless: Sons & Daughter (Illus. by Davis, Sarah)*
    c Magpies - v30 - i1 - March 2015 - p26(1) [501+]

Thompson, Craig - *Space Dumplins (Illus. by Thompson, Craig)*
    c BL - v111 - i22 - August 1 2015 - p48(2) [51-500]
    c PW - v262 - i49 - Dec 2 2015 - p87(1) [51-500]
    c SLJ - v61 - i8 - August 2015 - p95(1) [51-500]
    c KR - June 15 2015 - pNA [51-500]

Thompson, Curt - *The Soul of Shame: Retelling the Stories We Believe about Ourselves*
    Ch Today - v59 - i7 - Sept 2015 - p80(1) [51-500]

Thompson, Curtis L. - *God and Nature: A Theologian and a Scientist Conversing on the Divine Promise of Possibility*
    TT - v72 - i2 - July 2015 - p240-242 [501+]

Thompson, Dan - *Li'l Rip Haywire Adventures*
    c KR - Dec 15 2015 - pNA [51-500]

Thompson, Dave - *Soccer FAQ: All That's Left to Know about the Clubs, the Players, and the Rivalries*
    LJ - v140 - i9 - May 15 2015 - p85(1) [51-500]

Thompson, Des - *Nature's Conscience: The Life and Legacy of Derek Ratcliffe*
    NS - v144 - i5261 - May 7 2015 - p53(1) [501+]

Thompson, Dorothy - *The Dignity of Chartism*
    HT - v65 - i10 - Oct 2015 - p62(1) [501+]
    TLS - i5863 - August 14 2015 - p25(1) [501+]
    TimHES - i2213 - July 23 2015 - p47(1) [501+]

Thompson, Dustan - *Here at Last Is Love: Selected Poems of Dustan Thompson*
    CC - v132 - i24 - Nov 25 2015 - p42(1) [501+]

Thompson, Ethan - *How to Watch Television*
    Am St - v54 - i1 - Spring 2015 - p143-3 [501+]

Thompson, Flora - *Lark Rise to Candleford*
    CSM - June 25 2015 - pNA [501+]

Thompson, Gail L. - *Yes, You Can!*
    Bwatch - April 2015 - pNA [501+]

Thompson, Hannah - *Taboo: Corporeal Secrets in Nineteenth-Century France*
    FS - v69 - i3 - July 2015 - p403-404 [501+]

Thompson, Holly - *Falling into the Dragon's Mouth (Illus. by Huynh, Matt)*
    y SLJ - v61 - i12 - Dec 2015 - p116(1) [51-500]

Thompson, J.E. - *Disappearance at Hangman's Bluff: A Felony Bay Mystery*
    c HB Guide - v26 - i2 - Fall 2015 - p104(1) [51-500]

Thompson, J. Lee - *Never Call Retreat: Theodore Roosevelt and the Great War*
    RAH - v43 - i2 - June 2015 - p307-313 [501+]
    AHR - v120 - i1 - Feb 2015 - p277-278 [501+]
    J Mil H - v79 - i1 - Jan 2015 - p232-234 [501+]
    JAH - v101 - i4 - March 2015 - p1302(1) [501+]
    Pres St Q - v45 - i4 - Dec 2015 - p825(3) [501+]

Thompson, Janice - *Every Bride Needs a Groom*
    BL - v111 - i15 - April 1 2015 - p32(1) [51-500]
    RVBW - May 2015 - pNA [51-500]

Every Girl Gets Confused
    BL - v112 - i2 - Sept 15 2015 - p40(2) [51-500]

Thompson, Jennifer L. - *Tracing Childhood: Bioarchaeological Investigations of Early Lives in Antiquity*
    Am Ant - v80 - i2 - April 2015 - p421(2) [501+]

Thompson, John B. - *Merchants of Culture: The Publishing Business in the Twenty-First Century*
    CS - v44 - i2 - March 2015 - p261-262 [501+]

Thompson, Juan F. - *Stories I Tell Myself: Growing Up with Hunter S. Thompson*
    KR - Oct 1 2015 - pNA [51-500]
    NYT - Jan 1 2016 - pC21(L) [501+]

Thompson, Katrina Dyonne - *Ring Shout, Wheel About: The Racial Politics of Music and Dance in North American Slavery*
    AHR - v120 - i3 - June 2015 - p1024-1025 [501+]
    HNet - March 2015 - pNA [501+]
    JSH - v81 - i2 - May 2015 - p433(2) [501+]

Thompson, Ken - *The Sceptical Gardener: The Thinking Person's Guide to Good Gardening*
    Spec - v329 - i9771 - Dec 5 2015 - p44(2) [501+]

Thompson, Kevin G. - *Pacing: Individual Strategies for Optimal Performance*
    Bwatch - Feb 2015 - pNA [51-500]

Thompson, Kim - *Shadow Wrack*
    c KR - Dec 15 2015 - pNA [51-500]

Thompson, Laura - *A Different Class of Murder: The Story of Lord Lucan*
    Lon R Bks - v37 - i3 - Feb 5 2015 - p3(3) [501+]
    TLS - i5835 - Jan 30 2015 - p23(1) [501+]

Thompson, Laurie - *An Event in Autumn*
    RVBW - March 2015 - pNA [51-500]

The Second Deadly Sin
    RVBW - Jan 2015 - pNA [501+]

Thompson, Laurie Ann - *Be a Changemaker: How to Start Something That Matters*
    y HB Guide - v26 - i1 - Spring 2015 - p140(1) [51-500]

Emmanuel's Dream: The True Story of Emmanuel Ofosu Yeboah (Illus. by Qualls, Sean)
    c CCB-B - v68 - i7 - March 2015 - p372(2) [51-500]
    c HB Guide - v26 - i2 - Fall 2015 - p212(1) [51-500]
    c BL - v111 - i12 - Feb 15 2015 - p72(1) [51-500]
    c HB - v91 - i2 - March-April 2015 - p126(2) [51-500]
    SLJ - v61 - i3 - March 2015 - p174(1) [51-500]
    SLJ - v61 - i3 - March 2015 - p178(1) [51-500]

My Dog Is the Best (Illus. by Schmid, Paul)
    c BL - v111 - i19-20 - June 1 2015 - p122(1) [51-500]
    c CCB-B - v69 - i1 - Sept 2015 - p59(1) [51-500]
    c HB Guide - v26 - i2 - Fall 2015 - p20(1) [51-500]
    c KR - March 15 2015 - pNA [51-500]

Thompson, Lesley - *Ghost Girl*
    BL - v112 - i4 - Oct 15 2015 - p21(1) [51-500]

Thompson, Mark L. - *The Contest for the Delaware Valley: Allegiance, Identity, and Empire in the Seventeenth Century*
    RAH - v43 - i1 - March 2015 - p14-19 [501+]

Thompson, Mary G. - *Evil Fairies Love Hair (Illus. by Henry, Blake)*
    c HB Guide - v26 - i1 - Spring 2015 - p94(1) [51-500]

Thompson, Mike - *Wolf Point*
    Roundup M - v22 - i3 - Feb 2015 - p27(2) [501+]
    Roundup M - v22 - i6 - August 2015 - p33(1) [501+]

Thompson, Nato - *Living as Form: Socially Engaged Art from 1991-2011*
    PAJ - v37 - i2 - May 2015 - p103-110 [501+]

Thompson, Paul B. - *Lost Republic*
    y HB Guide - v26 - i1 - Spring 2015 - p126(1) [51-500]

Thompson, Peter - *State and Citizen: British America and the Early United States*
    J Am St - v49 - i1 - Feb 2015 - p187-188 [501+]
    JAH - v102 - i2 - Sept 2015 - p545-546 [501+]

Thompson, Raymond H. - *A Jesuit Missionary in Eighteenth-Century Sonora: The Family Correspondence of Philipp Segesser*
    CHR - v101 - i3 - Summer 2015 - p677(2) [501+]

Thompson, Sherwood - *Encyclopedia of Diversity and Social Justice*
    BL - v112 - i4 - Oct 15 2015 - p7(1) [51-500]

Thompson, T. - *Gods Don't Sleep*
    y KR - Feb 15 2015 - pNA [51-500]

Thompson, Tolya L. - *Fabulous Me, Piper Lee and the Peanut Butter Itch (Illus. by Gaylor, Terence)*
    c CH Bwatch - Oct 2015 - pNA [51-500]

Thompson, Vicki Lewis - *Wild about the Wrangler*
    BL - v112 - i6 - Nov 15 2015 - p31(1) [51-500]
    PW - v262 - i39 - Sept 28 2015 - p76(1) [51-500]

Thompson, Victoria - *Murder on Amsterdam Avenue*
    PW - v262 - i13 - March 30 2015 - p56(1) [51-500]
    Murder on St. Nicholas Avenue
    PW - v262 - i38 - Sept 21 2015 - p54(1) [51-500]

Thompson, William N. - *Gambling in America: An Encyclopedia of History, Issues, and Society, 2d ed.*
    BL - v111 - i16 - March 15 2015 - p12(1) [51-500]
    LJ - v140 - i7 - April 15 2015 - p118(2) [51-500]

Thompson, Wright - *The Best American Sports Writing 2015*
    BL - v112 - i1 - Sept 1 2015 - p32(1) [51-500]
    LJ - v140 - i17 - Oct 15 2015 - p93(1) [51-500]

Thomson, Bill - *The Typewriter (Illus. by Thomson, Bill)*
    c PW - v262 - i50 - Dec 7 2015 - p84(1) [51-500]

Thomson, David - *The Big Screen*
    BL - v112 - i5 - Nov 1 2015 - p18(2) [501+]
    How to Watch a Movie
    Bks & Cult - v21 - i6 - Nov-Dec 2015 - p38(1) [501+]
    BL - v112 - i3 - Oct 1 2015 - p8(2) [501+]
    KR - Sept 15 2015 - pNA [501+]
    LJ - v140 - i14 - Sept 1 2015 - p103(2) [51-500]
    Why Acting Matters
    BL - v111 - i12 - Feb 15 2015 - p20(1) [51-500]
    LJ - v140 - i3 - Feb 15 2015 - p104(2) [51-500]
    NS - v144 - i5262 - May 15 2015 - p40(3) [501+]
    NY - v91 - i4 - March 16 2015 - p83 [501+]
    TLS - i5854 - June 12 2015 - p13(1) [501+]
    TLS - i5871 - Oct 9 2015 - p7(2) [501+]

Thomson, Graeme - *George Harrison: Behind the Locked Door*
    BL - v111 - i9-10 - Jan 1 2015 - p30(1) [51-500]

Thomson, Keith - *Private Doubt, Public Dilemma: Religion and Science Since Jefferson and Darwin*
    PW - v262 - i16 - April 20 2015 - p67(1) [51-500]

Thomson, Kerr - *The Sound of Whales*
    c Sch Lib - v63 - i3 - Autumn 2015 - p170(1) [51-500]

Thomson, Mathew - *Lost Freedom: The Landscape of the Child and the British Post-War Settlement*
    AHR - v120 - i1 - Feb 2015 - p336-337 [501+]
    HER - v130 - i545 - August 2015 - p1059(3) [501+]

Thomson, Norman - *Introducing Mr. B.: The Battle Collection: Four Short Stories Inspired by Robert Burns Poems (Illus. by Lennox, Nicholas)*
    c Res Links - v20 - i3 - Feb 2015 - p17(1) [51-500]
    Introducing Mr. B.: The Farmer Collection: Four Short Stories Inspired by Robert Burns Poems (Illus. by Lennox, Nicholas)
    c Res Links - v20 - i3 - Feb 2015 - p17(1) [51-500]
    Introducing Mr. B.: The Friends Collection: Four Short Stories Inspired by Robert Burns Poems (Illus. by Lennox, Nicholas)
    c Res Links - v20 - i3 - Feb 2015 - p17(1) [51-500]

Thomson, Peter - *Kava in the Blood*
    KR - Jan 1 2016 - pNA [501+]

Thomson, Rodney M. - *Catalogue of Medieval Manuscripts of Latin Commentaries on Aristotle in British Libraries, Volume II: Cambridge*
    Med R - Sept 2015 - pNA [501+]

Thomson, Rupert - *Katherine Carlyle*
    y BL - v112 - i1 - Sept 1 2015 - p40(2) [51-500]
    KR - August 1 2015 - pNA [51-500]
    LJ - v140 - i16 - Oct 1 2015 - p74(1) [51-500]
    NYTBR - Dec 20 2015 - p19(L) [501+]
    PW - v262 - i33 - August 17 2015 - p45(1) [51-500]
    Spec - v329 - i9771 - Dec 5 2015 - p50(1) [501+]
    TLS - i5876 - Nov 13 2015 - p19(1) [501+]

Thomson, Ruth - *Photos Framed: A Fresh Look at the World's Most Memorable Photographs*
    c HB Guide - v26 - i1 - Spring 2015 - p180(1) [51-500]

Thomson, Sarah L. - *Ancient Animals: Saber-Toothed Cat (Illus. by Plant, Andrew)*
    c HB Guide - v26 - i1 - Spring 2015 - p152(1) [51-500]
    The Eureka Key
    c SLJ - v61 - i12 - Dec 2015 - p108(1) [51-500]
    Quick, Little Monkey! (Illus. by Judge, Lita)
    c KR - Dec 15 2015 - pNA [51-500]
    c PW - v262 - i50 - Dec 7 2015 - p84(1) [51-500]

Thomson, Virgil - *Virgil Thomson: Music Chronicles, 1940-1954*
    ON - v79 - i8 - Feb 2015 - p60(1) [501+]

Thon, Elsa - *If Only it Were Fiction*
    y Res Links - v20 - i4 - April 2015 - p34(1) [51-500]

Thon, Melanie Rae - *Silence and Song*
    KR - August 15 2015 - pNA [51-500]

Thonbury, Emily V. - *Becoming a Poet in Anglo-Saxon England*
    RES - v66 - i273 - Feb 2015 - p164-166 [501+]

Thondup, Gyalo - *The Noodle Maker of Kalimpong: The Untold Story of My Struggle for Tibet*
    KR - Feb 15 2015 - pNA [51-500]
    LJ - v140 - i5 - March 15 2015 - p113(2) [51-500]
    Spec - v327 - i9738 - April 18 2015 - p39(2) [501+]

Thong, Roseanne Greenfield - *Dia de Los Muertos (Illus. by Ballesteros, Carles)*
    c KR - June 1 2015 - pNA [51-500]
    c SLJ - v61 - i8 - August 2015 - p77(1) [51-500]
    Green Is a Chile Pepper. Audiobook Review
    SLJ - v61 - i2 - Feb 2015 - p48(1) [51-500]
    Noodle Magic (Illus. by So, Meilo)
    c CH Bwatch - Jan 2015 - pNA [51-500]
    c CH Bwatch - Feb 2015 - pNA [51-500]
    c HB Guide - v26 - i2 - Fall 2015 - p54(1) [51-500]
    'Twas Nochebuena (Illus. by Palacios, Sara)
    c HB Guide - v26 - i1 - Spring 2015 - p48(1) [51-500]

Thonson, Thomas - *You Don't Die of Love*
    KR - July 1 2015 - pNA [51-500]

Thor, Annika - *Deep Sea*
    y HB - v91 - i1 - Jan-Feb 2015 - p90(2) [501+]
    y HB Guide - v26 - i2 - Fall 2015 - p141(1) [51-500]
    y PW - v262 - i49 - Dec 2 2015 - p114(1) [51-500]
    y VOYA - v37 - i6 - Feb 2015 - p67(2) [51-500]

Thoresen, Kimberley A. - *The Earth beneath Our Feet*
    Sci & Ch - v52 - i5 - Jan 2015 - p87 [51-500]

Thoresen, Susan Werner - *The Yoyo and the Piggy Bank (Illus. by Eveland, Keith)*
    c CH Bwatch - July 2015 - pNA [51-500]

Thorn, Hakan - *Stad i rorelse: Stadsomvandlingen och striderna om Haga och Christiania*
    HNet - May 2015 - pNA [501+]

Thorn, Tracey - *Naked at the Albert Hall: The Inside Story of Singing*
    NS - v144 - i5259 - April 24 2015 - p51(1) [501+]
    Spec - v328 - i9742 - May 16 2015 - p43(1) [501+]

Thornberry, Neal - *Innovation Judo: Disarming Roadblocks and Blockheads on the Path to Creativity*
    RVBW - Feb 2015 - pNA [51-500]

Thornborough, Kathy - *Animals (Illus. by Petelinsek, Kathleen)*
    SLJ - v61 - i2 - Feb 2015 - p115(2) [51-500]

Thorne, Bella - *Autumn Falls (Read by Thorne, Bella). Audiobook Review*
    SLJ - v61 - i2 - Feb 2015 - p52(1) [51-500]
    Autumn Falls
    y HB Guide - v26 - i2 - Fall 2015 - p141(1) [51-500]
    y VOYA - v37 - i6 - Feb 2015 - p68(1) [51-500]
    Autumn's Kiss
    y KR - Sept 15 2015 - pNA [51-500]
    y SLJ - v61 - i10 - Oct 2015 - p106(1) [51-500]
    y VOYA - v38 - i5 - Dec 2015 - p75(1) [51-500]

Thorne, Jenn Marie - *The Wrong Side of Right*
    y BL - v111 - i11 - Feb 1 2015 - p50(1) [51-500]
    y CCB-B - v68 - i7 - March 2015 - p373(1) [51-500]
    y HB Guide - v26 - i2 - Fall 2015 - p142(1) [51-500]
    y VOYA - v37 - i6 - Feb 2015 - p68(1) [51-500]

Thorne, Kip - *The Science of Interstellar*
    NYRB - v62 - i9 - May 21 2015 - p34(3) [501+]

Thorne, T.K. - *Angels at the Gate*
    LJ - v140 - i6 - April 1 2015 - p5(1) [51-500]
    SPBW - March 2015 - pNA [51-500]

Thornhill, Jan - *Kyle Goes Alone (Illus. by Barron, Ashley)*
    c CH Bwatch - Oct 2015 - pNA [51-500]
    c KR - July 1 2015 - pNA [51-500]
    c SLJ - v61 - i10 - Oct 2015 - p85(1) [51-500]
    Winter's Coming (Illus. by Bisaillon, Josee)
    c HB Guide - v26 - i2 - Fall 2015 - p54(1) [51-500]

Thornhorn, Randy - *Wicked Temper*
    KR - Sept 1 2015 - pNA [51-500]

Thornton, Alice - *My First Booke of My Life*
    TLS - i5831 - Jan 2 2015 - p22(1) [501+]

Thornton, Betsy - *Empty Houses*
    PW - v262 - i18 - May 4 2015 - p99(1) [51-500]

Thornton, D.S. - *Scrap City*
    c BL - v112 - i3 - Oct 1 2015 - p79(1) [51-500]
    c KR - August 15 2015 - pNA [51-500]
    c SLJ - v61 - i7 - July 2015 - p83(2) [51-500]

Thornton, Dora - *A Rothschild Renaissance: Treasures from the Waddesdon Bequest*
    NYRB - v62 - i11 - June 25 2015 - p29(4) [501+]

Thornton, Ian - *The Great and Calamitous Tale of Johan Thoms*
    KR - August 15 2015 - pNA [51-500]

Thornton, Margaret - *First Impressions*
    BL - v111 - i15 - April 1 2015 - p32(1) [51-500]

Thornton, Mark R. - *Kid Moses*
    y BL - v112 - i2 - Sept 15 2015 - p27(1) [51-500]
    NYTBR - Nov 8 2015 - p37(L) [501+]
    PW - v262 - i33 - August 17 2015 - p45(1) [51-500]

Thornton, Sarah - *33 Artists in 3 Acts*
    Soc - v52 - i2 - April 2015 - p182(3) [501+]
    TLS - i5854 - June 12 2015 - p26(1) [51-500]

Thornton, T.D. - *My Adventures with Your Money: George Graham Rice and the Golden Age of the Con Artist*
    KR - Sept 15 2015 - pNA [501+]
    LJ - v140 - i16 - Oct 1 2015 - p96(2) [51-500]
    PW - v262 - i35 - August 31 2015 - p76(1) [51-500]

Thorp, James - *Dog on Stilts (Illus. by McKinnon, Angus)*
    c Sch Lib - v63 - i1 - Spring 2015 - p33(1) [51-500]

Thorpe, Adam - *The Rules of Perspective*
    TimHES - i2220 - Sept 10 2015 - p45-1 [501+]

Thorpe, Helen - *Soldier Girls: The Battles of Three Women at Home and at War (Read by Postel, Donna). Audiobook Review*
    LJ - v140 - i2 - Feb 1 2015 - p47(1) [51-500]

Thorpe, Rebecca U. - *The American Warfare State: The Domestic Politics of Military Spending*
    JAH - v101 - i4 - March 2015 - p1319-1320 [501+]

Thorpe, Will - *Incompetence*
    KR - June 15 2015 - pNA [501+]

Thorsen, T.S. - *The Cambridge Companion to Latin Love Elegy*
    Class R - v65 - i1 - April 2015 - p135-136 [501+]

Thorson, Robert M. - *Walden's Shore: Henry David Thoreau and Nineteenth Century Science*
    NEQ - v88 - i1 - March 2015 - p149-158 [501+]

Thorup, Kirsten - *The God of Chance*
    WLT - v89 - i2 - March-April 2015 - p77(1) [51-500]

Thrace - *Local Coinage and Regional Identity: Numismatic Research in the Digital Age*
    HNet - June 2015 - pNA [501+]

Thrash, Maggie - *Honor Girl: A Graphic Memoir (Illus. by Thrash, Maggie)*
    y BL - v111 - i19-20 - June 1 2015 - p67(1) [51-500]
    y KR - June 1 2015 - pNA [51-500]
    y NYTBR - August 23 2015 - p30(L) [501+]
    y PW - v262 - i22 - June 1 2015 - p62(1) [501+]
    y PW - v262 - i49 - Dec 2 2015 - p118(1) [51-500]
    y SLJ - v61 - i6 - June 2015 - p146(1) [51-500]
    y VOYA - v38 - i4 - Oct 2015 - p85(1) [51-500]

Thrasher, Shelley - *Autumn Spring*
PW - v262 - i27 - July 6 2015 - p54(1) [51-500]
Threadway, Jessica - *Lacy Eye (Read by Archer, Ellen).* Audiobook Review
LJ - v140 - i10 - June 1 2015 - p61(1) [51-500]
Threlkeld, Megan - *Pan American Women: U.S. Internationalists and Revolutionary Mexico*
Am St - v54 - i2 - Summer 2015 - p124-125 [501+]
Wom R Bks - v32 - i4 - July-August 2015 - p19(2) [501+]
Thriault, Denis - *The Peculiar Life of a Lonely Postman*
NYTBR - March 8 2015 - p34(L) [501+]
Thrift, Bryan Hardin - *Conservative Bias: How Jesse Helms Pioneered the Rise of Right-Wing Media and Realigned the Republican Party*
AHR - v120 - i2 - April 2015 - p669-670 [501+]
JSH - v81 - i2 - May 2015 - p526(2) [501+]
Throop, D. - *The Life and Times of Wilberforce Jones*
KR - April 15 2015 - pNA [501+]
Throp, Claire - *A Visit to the Space Station*
c HB Guide - v26 - i1 - Spring 2015 - p174(1) [51-500]
A Weekend with Dinosaurs
c HB Guide - v26 - i1 - Spring 2015 - p152(1) [51-500]
Thrower, Stephen - *Murderous Passions: The Delirious Cinema of Jesus Franco, vol. 1: 1959-1974*
Si & So - v25 - i9 - Sept 2015 - p104(1) [501+]
Thuesen, Sarah Caroline - *Greater Than Equal: African American Struggles for Schools and Citizenship in North Carolina, 1919-1965*
Historian - v77 - i2 - Summer 2015 - p359(2) [501+]
JSH - v81 - i1 - Feb 2015 - p230(3) [501+]
RAH - v43 - i1 - March 2015 - p177-183 [501+]
Thunder, David - *Citizenship and the Pursuit of the Worthy Life*
J Phil - v112 - i5 - May 2015 - p280(1) [501+]
Thurber, James - *The Tiger Who Would Be King (Illus. by Yoon, JooHee)*
c KR - Sept 15 2015 - pNA [51-500]
Thurber, Timothy N. - *Republicans and Race: The GOP's Frayed Relationship with African Americans, 1945-1974*
Historian - v77 - i3 - Fall 2015 - p587(2) [501+]
HNet - Feb 2015 - pNA [501+]
JSH - v81 - i4 - Nov 2015 - p1030(2) [501+]
RAH - v43 - i2 - June 2015 - p361-368 [501+]
Thurlby, Paul - *Numbers*
c Sch Lib - v63 - i1 - Spring 2015 - p33(1) [51-500]
Thurlo, David - *Grave Consequences*
KR - Feb 15 2015 - pNA [51-500]
PW - v262 - i8 - Feb 23 2015 - p52(1) [51-500]
Thurm, Marian - *The Good Life*
KR - Jan 1 2016 - pNA [501+]
Today Is Not Your Day
BL - v112 - i2 - Sept 15 2015 - p28(2) [51-500]
KR - August 1 2015 - pNA [51-500]
NYTBR - Oct 4 2015 - p10(L) [501+]
Thurman, Rob - *Nevermore*
PW - v262 - i41 - Oct 12 2015 - p51(2) [51-500]
Thurston, Bonnie - *Maverick Mark: The Untamed First Gospel*
Intpr - v69 - i1 - Jan 2015 - p106(2) [51-500]
Thussu, Daya Kishan - *Communicating India's Soft Power: Buddha to Bollywood*
Pac A - v88 - i2 - June 2015 - p345 [501+]
Thwaite, Anthony - *Going Out*
TLS - i5853 - June 5 2015 - p24(1) [501+]
Thydell, Johanna - *There's a Pig in My Class! (Illus. by Ramel, Charlotte)*
c HB Guide - v26 - i1 - Spring 2015 - p48(1) [51-500]
Thynne, Jane - *The Scent of Secrets*
KR - July 15 2015 - pNA [51-500]
Tibbott, Julie - *Members Only: Secret Societies, Sects, and Cults--Exposed!*
SLJ - v61 - i3 - March 2015 - p178(1) [51-500]
VOYA - v38 - i2 - June 2015 - p88(1) [51-500]
Tiber, Elliot - *After Woodstock: The True Story of a Belgian Movie, an Israeli Wedding, & a Manhattan Breakdown*
BL - v111 - i12 - Feb 15 2015 - p4(2) [51-500]
KR - Feb 1 2015 - pNA [51-500]
PW - v262 - i10 - March 9 2015 - p66(1) [51-500]
RVBW - Oct 2015 - pNA [501+]
Tibo, Giles - *En route, Nicolas! (Illus. by St-Aubin, Bruno)*
c Res Links - v20 - i3 - Feb 2015 - p52(1) [51-500]

Tibo, Gilles - *Le petit chevalier qui n'aimait pas la pluie (Illus. by Despres, Genevieve)*
c Res Links - v21 - i1 - Oct 2015 - p57(1) [51-500]
The Little Knight Who Battled the Rain (Illus. by Despres, Genevieve)
c Res Links - v21 - i1 - Oct 2015 - p10(2) [51-500]
Winter Break Wipeout (Illus. by St. Aubin, Bruno)
c Res Links - v20 - i3 - Feb 2015 - p10(2) [51-500]
Tichi, Cecelia - *Jack London: A Writer's Fight for a Better America*
KR - July 15 2015 - pNA [501+]
LJ - v140 - i13 - August 1 2015 - p95(2) [51-500]
Tickle, Jack - *Fish on a Dish!*
c KR - July 15 2015 - pNA [51-500]
Meet Dizzy Dinosaur!
c HB Guide - v26 - i2 - Fall 2015 - p20(1) [51-500]
Tidal, Junior - *Usability and the Mobile Web: A UTA Guide*
LJ - v140 - i9 - May 15 2015 - p97(1) [51-500]
Tidhar, Lavie - *A Man Lies Dreaming*
KR - Jan 1 2016 - pNA [51-500]
The Violent Century
PW - v262 - i2 - Jan 12 2015 - p40(1) [51-500]
BL - v111 - i11 - Feb 1 2015 - p32(1) [51-500]
Tieck, Sarah - *Aztec*
c HB Guide - v26 - i2 - Fall 2015 - p223(1) [51-500]
Big Buddy Biographies Series
c HB Guide - v26 - i2 - Fall 2015 - p212(1) [51-500]
Big Buddy Books: Native Americans
c HB Guide - v26 - i1 - Spring 2015 - p205(1) [51-500]
Blackfoot
c HB Guide - v26 - i2 - Fall 2015 - p223(1) [51-500]
Nez Perce
c HB Guide - v26 - i2 - Fall 2015 - p223(1) [51-500]
Shawnee
c HB Guide - v26 - i2 - Fall 2015 - p223(1) [51-500]
Tiede, Karen - *Knitting Fabric Rugs: 28 Colorful Designs for Crafters of Every Level*
LJ - v140 - i13 - August 1 2015 - p96(2) [51-500]
"Tiere Unserer Heimat": Auswirkungen der SED-Ideologie auf Gesellschaftliche Mensch-Tier-Verhaltnisse in der DDR
HNet - March 2015 - pNA [501+]
Tierney, Brian - *Liberty and Law: The Idea of Permissive Natural Law, 1100-1800*
AHR - v120 - i2 - April 2015 - p704-705 [501+]
MA - v57 - i3 - Summer 2015 - p61(4) [501+]
Specu - v90 - i2 - April 2015 - p590-591 [501+]
Tierney, Dominic - *The Right Way To Lose a War: America in an Age of Unwinnable Conflicts*
KR - April 15 2015 - pNA [51-500]
LJ - v140 - i9 - May 15 2015 - p96(1) [51-500]
PW - v262 - i15 - April 13 2015 - p70(1) [51-500]
Tierney, Kathleen J. - *The Social Roots of Risk: Producing Disasters, Promoting Resilience*
AJS - v121 - i2 - Sept 2015 - p646(3) [501+]
Tierney, Keith B. - *Organic Chemical Toxicology of Fishes*
QRB - v90 - i2 - June 2015 - p236(1) [51-500]
Tierney, Robert Thomas - *Tropics of Savagery: The Culture of Japanese Empire in Comparative Frame*
Cont Pac - v27 - i2 - Fall 2015 - p579(5) [501+]
Tierney, Ronald - *The Blue Dragon*
y SLJ - v61 - i9 - Sept 2015 - p151(4) [501+]
Killing Frost
KR - March 1 2015 - pNA [51-500]
PW - v262 - i13 - March 30 2015 - p57(1) [51-500]
Tierra, Lesley - *A Kid's Herb Book: For Children of All Ages*
c CH Bwatch - Nov 2015 - pNA [51-500]
Tierra, Shasta - *The Amazing Healing Power of Kitchari: Weight Loss, Detox and Rejuvenation*
SPBW - Oct 2015 - pNA [51-500]
Tiffany, Daniel - *My Silver Planet: A Secret History of Poetry and Kitsch*
MP - v113 - i1 - August 2015 - pE62(4) [501+]
Poet - v206 - i2 - May 2015 - p185(7) [501+]
Tifft, Meghan - *The Long Fire*
KR - June 1 2015 - pNA [51-500]
Tigay, Chanan - *The Lost Book of Moses: The Hunt for the World's Oldest Bible*
KR - Dec 15 2015 - pNA [501+]
PW - v262 - i51 - Dec 14 2015 - p78(1) [51-500]
Tiger Tales - *Baby Animals*
c KR - Jan 1 2015 - pNA [51-500]
Farm Puzzle and Sticker Book
c KR - Dec 1 2015 - pNA [51-500]
First Words
c KR - Jan 1 2015 - pNA [51-500]
Tildes, Phyllis Limbacher - *Baby Animals Spots & Stripes*
c KR - July 1 2015 - pNA [51-500]

Tilford, Earl H. - *Turning the Tide: The University of Alabama in the 1960s*
JSH - v81 - i3 - August 2015 - p777(2) [501+]
Tillemann, Levi - *The Great Race: The Global Quest for the Car of the Future*
Econ - v414 - i8927 - Feb 28 2015 - p76(US) [501+]
LJ - v140 - i3 - Feb 15 2015 - p110(1) [51-500]
Tillet, Salamishah - *Sites of Slavery: Citizenship and Racial Democracy in the Post-Civil Rights Imagination*
AL - v87 - i2 - June 2015 - p396-398 [501+]
Callaloo - v38 - i1 - Wntr 2015 - p228-230 [501+]
Tillman, Nancy - *The Heaven of Animals*
c HB Guide - v26 - i1 - Spring 2015 - p48(1) [51-500]
La noche en que tu naciste (Illus. by Tillman, Nancy)
c HB Guide - v26 - i2 - Fall 2015 - p162(1) [51-500]
You're Here for a Reason (Illus. by Tillman, Nancy)
c KR - July 15 2015 - pNA [51-500]
c PW - v262 - i26 - June 29 2015 - p66(1) [51-500]
c SLJ - v61 - i9 - Sept 2015 - p129(2) [51-500]
Tillotson, Richard - *What You Will on Capitol Hill*
KR - Feb 1 2015 - pNA [501+]
Timberg, Robert - *Blue-Eyed Boy: A Memoir*
NYTBR - Sept 6 2015 - p24(L) [501+]
Timberg, Scott - *Culture Crash: The Killing of the Creative Class*
Bks & Cult - v21 - i4 - July-August 2015 - p27(3) [501+]
CJR - v53 - i5 - Jan-Feb 2015 - p60(2) [501+]
Nation - v300 - i20 - May 18 2015 - p34(3) [501+]
New R - v246 - i1 - Feb 2015 - p41(5) [501+]
New Sci - v225 - i3008 - Feb 14 2015 - p46(2) [501+]
NYTBR - March 22 2015 - p17(L) [501+]
Timberlake, Richard H. - *Constitutional Money: A Review of the Supreme Court's Monetary Decisions*
IndRev - v20 - i1 - Summer 2015 - p144(4) [501+]
Timbers, Frances - *Magic and Masculinity: Ritual Magic and Gender in the Early Modern Era*
Six Ct J - v46 - i1 - Spring 2015 - p244-245 [501+]
TIME for Kids Magazine editors - *Stellar Space: 250 Facts Kids Want to Know*
c Sci & Ch - v52 - i5 - Jan 2015 - p86 [51-500]
Timmer, C. Peter - *Food Security and Scarcity: Why Ending Hunger Is So Hard*
For Aff - v94 - i3 - May-June 2015 - pNA [501+]
Timmermann, Anke - *Verse and Transmutation: A Corpus of Middle English Alchemical Poetry*
Isis - v106 - i2 - June 2015 - p432(2) [501+]
Specu - v90 - i3 - July 2015 - p858-859 [501+]
Timmers, Leo - *Franky (Illus. by Timmers, Leo)*
c PW - v262 - i51 - Dec 14 2015 - p81(1) [51-500]
Timmons, Patricia - *Gonzalo de Berceo and the Latin Miracles of the Virgin*
Specu - v90 - i3 - July 2015 - p859-861 [501+]
Timmons, Susie - *Superior Packets*
PW - v262 - i11 - March 16 2015 - p62(1) [51-500]
Timpe, Kevin - *Free Will in Philosophical Theology*
J Phil - v112 - i5 - May 2015 - p280(1) [501+]
Tiner, Billi - *Scarred Hearts*
PW - v262 - i10 - March 9 2015 - p59(1) [51-500]
Tingey, Sue - *Marked*
y BL - v112 - i5 - Nov 1 2015 - p37(1) [51-500]
Tingle, Tim - *How I Became a Ghost*
c SLJ - v61 - i12 - Dec 2015 - p64(4) [501+]
No Name
y CCB-B - v68 - i5 - Jan 2015 - p278(1) [51-500]
Tinniswood, Adrian - *The Rainborowes: One Family's Quest to Build a New England*
Historian - v77 - i2 - Summer 2015 - p360(2) [501+]
Tinsman, Heidi - *Buying into the Regime: Grapes and Consumption in Cold War Chile and the United States*
AHR - v120 - i1 - Feb 2015 - p199-201 [501+]
HAHR - v95 - i1 - Feb 2015 - p190-192 [501+]
JIH - v45 - i3 - Wntr 2015 - p448-449 [501+]
JTWS - v32 - i1 - Spring 2015 - p355(3) [501+]
Tinti, Francesca - *England and Rome in the Early Middle Ages: Pilgrimage, Art, and Politics*
Med R - August 2015 - pNA [501+]
Tinwell, Angela - *The Uncanny Valley in Games and Animation*
Bwatch - March 2015 - pNA [501+]
Tippins, Sherill - *Inside the Dream Palace: The Life and Times of New York's Legendary Chelsea Hotel*
BL - v112 - i5 - Nov 1 2015 - p18(2) [501+]
Tipton-Martin, Toni - *The Jemima Code: Two Centuries of African American Cookbooks*
NYTBR - Dec 6 2015 - p51(L) [501+]

Tirado, Linda - *Hand to Mouth: Living in Bootstrap America. Audiobook Review*
    LJ - v140 - i3 - Feb 15 2015 - p61(1) [51-500]
Tirico, Deborah Gale - *Gorgeous Wool Appliqué: A Visual Guide to Adding Dimension and Unique Embroidery*
    LJ - v140 - i16 - Oct 1 2015 - p83(2) [51-500]
Tirman, John - *Dream Chasers: Immigration and the American Backlash*
    TimHES - i2197 - April 2 2015 - p55(1) [501+]
Tirres, Christopher D. - *The Aesthetics and Ethics of Faith: A Dialogue between Liberationist and Pragmatic Thought*
    Theol St - v76 - i2 - June 2015 - p392(2) [501+]
Tischner, Lukasz - *Gombrowicza milczenie o Bogu*
    Slav R - v74 - i3 - Fall 2015 - p635-637 [501+]
Tisdale, Lenora Tubbs - *A Sermon Workbook: Exercises in the Art and Craft of Preaching*
    Intpr - v69 - i4 - Oct 2015 - p499(2) [501+]
Tisdale, Sallie - *Violation: Collected Essays*
    KR - Jan 1 2016 - pNA [501+]
Tisma, Aleksandar - *The Use of Man*
    TLS - i5841 - March 13 2015 - p20(1) [501+]
Titelbaum, Michael C. - *Quitting Certainties: A Bayesian Framework Modeling Degrees of Belief*
    J Phil - v112 - i5 - May 2015 - p280(1) [501+]
Tittensor, David - *The House of Service: The Gillen Movement and Islam's Third Way*
    IJMES - v47 - i2 - May 2015 - p402-403 [501+]
Tjelle, Kristin Fjelde - *Missionary Masculinity, 1870-1930: The Norwegian Missionaries in South-East Africa*
    AHR - v120 - i2 - April 2015 - p755-756 [501+]
    IJAHS - v48 - i1 - Wntr 2015 - p144-145 [501+]
Tkacz, Nathaniel - *Wikipedia and the Politics of Openness*
    TimHES - i2184 - Jan 1 2015 - p62-63 [501+]
Tllez, Lesley - *Eat Mexico: Recipes From Mexico City's Streets, Markets & Fondas*
    NYTBR - Dec 6 2015 - p20(L) [501+]
Toates, Frederick - *How Sexual Desire Works: The Enigmatic Urge*
    TLS - i5842 - March 20 2015 - p23(1) [501+]
Tobar, Hector - *Deep Down Dark: The Untold Stories of 33 Men Buried in a Chilean Mine, and the Miracle That Set Them Free (Read by Leyva, Henry). Audiobook Review*
    LJ - v140 - i2 - Feb 1 2015 - p47(1) [51-500]
Deep Down Dark: The Untold Stories of 33 Men Buried in a Chilean Mine, and the Miracle That Set Them Free
    NYTBR - Sept 6 2015 - p24(L) [501+]
Tobey, Elizabeth MacKenzie - *Federico Grisone: The Rules of Riding: An Edited Translation of the First Renaissance Treatise on Classical Horsemanship*
    Six Ct J - v46 - i2 - Summer 2015 - p395-396 [501+]
Tobies, Renate - *Women in Industrial Research*
    Isis - v106 - i2 - June 2015 - p485(2) [501+]
Tobin, Beth Fowkes - *The Duchess's Shells: Natural History Collecting in the Age of Cook's Voyages*
    AHR - v120 - i1 - Feb 2015 - p328-329 [501+]
Tobin, Catherine Sistrunk - *The Perfect Raisin and Pretzel Cousins Club (Illus. by Sullivan, Ellie)*
    c CH Bwatch - April 2015 - pNA [51-500]
Tobin, James - *The Man He Became: How FDR Defied Polio to Win the Presidency*
    Historian - v77 - i2 - Summer 2015 - p361(2) [501+]
Tobin, Paul - *Bandette, vol. 2: Stealers, Keepers! (Illus. by Coover, Colleen)*
    c SLJ - v61 - i10 - Oct 2015 - p120(1) [501+]
How to Capture an Invisible Cat (Illus. by Lafontaine, Thierry)
    c SLJ - v61 - i12 - Dec 2015 - p108(1) [501+]
    c KR - Dec 15 2015 - pNA [501+]
Tobin, Robert Deam - *Peripheral Desires: The German Discovery of Sex*
    JHI - v76 - i4 - Oct 2015 - p666(1) [501+]
Tobis, David - *From Pariahs to Partners: How Parents and Their Allies Changed New York City's Child Welfare System*
    CS - v44 - i2 - March 2015 - p262-264 [501+]
    Wom R Bks - v32 - i1 - Jan-Feb 2015 - p10(2) [501+]
Tobler, Stefan - *The Stream of Life*
    Nation - v301 - i21-22 - Nov 23 2015 - p31(4) [501+]
Tocco, Valeria - *Adamastor e dintorni: in ricordo di Antonio Tabucchi. Con un frammento inedito*
    MLR - v110 - i2 - April 2015 - p572-574 [501+]
Toch, Hans - *Organizational Change through Individual Empowerment: Applying Social Psychology in Prisons and Policing*
    Crim J & B - v42 - i9 - Sept 2015 - p969-971

[501+]
    CrimJR - v40 - i1 - March 2015 - p101-103 [501+]
Todaro, Julie - *Library Management for the Digital Age: A New Paradigm*
    LR - v64 - i6-7 - June-July 2015 - p508-509 [501+]
Mentoring A to Z
    LJ - v140 - i16 - Oct 1 2015 - p98(1) [51-500]
Todd, Andrew - *Military Chaplaincy in Contention: Chaplains, Churches, and the Morality of Conflict*
    Theol St - v76 - i1 - March 2015 - p203(2) [501+]
Todd, Charles - *A Fine Summer's Day*
    BL - v111 - i11 - Feb 1 2015 - p26(1) [51-500]
    NYTBR - Jan 4 2015 - p25(L) [501+]
    RVBW - Sept 2015 - pNA [51-500]
    RVBW - Oct 2015 - pNA [51-500]
Hunting Shadows
    RVBW - March 2015 - pNA [51-500]
No Shred of Evidence
    KR - Dec 15 2015 - pNA [501+]
    PW - v262 - i48 - Nov 30 2015 - p40(1) [51-500]
A Pattern of Lies (Read by Landor, Rosalyn). Audiobook Review
    BL - v112 - i6 - Nov 15 2015 - p61(1) [51-500]
A Pattern of Lies
    BL - v111 - i17 - May 1 2015 - p42(1) [51-500]
    KR - June 15 2015 - pNA [51-500]
    PW - v262 - i26 - June 29 2015 - p45(2) [51-500]
An Unwilling Accomplice
    RVBW - March 2015 - pNA [51-500]
    RVBW - June 2015 - pNA [51-500]
Todd, Emmanuel - *Qui est Charlie? Sociologie d'une crise religieuse*
    TimHES - i2211 - July 9 2015 - p50(1) [501+]
Who Is Charlie? Xenophobia and the New Middle Class
    TimHES - i2217 - August 20 2015 - p51-51 [501+]
    TLS - i5864-5865 - August 21 2015 - p28(2) [501+]
Todd, Ilima - *Remake*
    RVBW - May 2015 - pNA [51-500]
    RVBW - June 2015 - pNA [51-500]
Todd, Janet - *The Cambridge Introduction to Jane Austen, 2nd ed.*
    TLS - i5853 - June 5 2015 - p26(1) [501+]
Todd, Kim D. - *Jean Jennings Bartik, Computer Pioneer*
    c CH Bwatch - Sept 2015 - pNA [501+]
Todd, Stephen - *Leading Cases in Song*
    Law Q Rev - v131 - Jan 2015 - p166-167 [501+]
Todd, Victoria - *Marine Mammal Observer and Passive Acoustic Monitoring Handbook*
    TLS - i5866 - Sept 4 2015 - p27(1) [501+]
Todes, Daniel P. - *Ivan Pavlov: A Russian Life in Science*
    Nature - v517 - i7533 - Jan 8 2015 - p143(1) [51-500]
    TLS - i5874 - Oct 30 2015 - p3(2) [501+]
Todorova, Maria - *Remembering Communism: Private and Public Recollections of Lived Experience in Southeast Europe*
    HNet - Sept 2015 - pNA(NA) [501+]
Toews, Miriam - *All My Puny Sorrows*
    BooChiTr - Jan 10 2015 - p14(1) [501+]
    Nation - v301 - i13-14 - Sept 28 2015 - p41(4) [501+]
    NYT - Nov 27 2015 - pC31(L) [501+]
Toft, Kim Michelle - *I Can Swim a Rainbow*
    c Magpies - v30 - i4 - Sept 2015 - p28(1) [501+]
Toft, Ron - *National Birds of the World*
    c BL - v111 - i9-10 - Jan 1 2015 - p26(1) [501+]
Tognato, Carlo - *Central Bank Independence: Cultural Codes and Symbolic Performance*
    CS - v44 - i2 - March 2015 - p264-266 [501+]
Tohari, Ahmad - *The Red Bekisar*
    WLT - v89 - i6 - Nov-Dec 2015 - p67(3) [501+]
Toibin, Colm - *Nora Webster (Read by Shaw, Fiona). Audiobook Review*
    BL - v111 - i15 - April 1 2015 - p85(1) [501+]
Nora Webster
    NYRB - v62 - i1 - Jan 8 2015 - p34(2) [501+]
    NYTBR - June 7 2015 - p36(L) [501+]
On Elizabeth Bishop
    TLS - i5868 - Sept 18 2015 - p22(1) [501+]
    NYTBR - Sept 6 2015 - p26(L) [501+]
    Comw - v142 - i18 - Nov 13 2015 - p25(5) [501+]
    G&L Rev W - v22 - i5 - Sept-Oct 2015 - p32(2) [501+]
    LJ - v140 - i5 - March 15 2015 - p107(1) [501+]
    NS - v144 - i5262 - May 15 2015 - p43(1) [51-500]
    NYRB - v62 - i14 - Sept 24 2015 - p36(2) [501+]
    NYT - April 22 2015 - pC6(L) [501+]
    PW - v262 - i3 - Jan 19 2015 - p69(1) [501+]
    TimHES - i2199 - April 16 2015 - p60-2 [501+]

Tokarczuk, Olga - *Ksiegi Jakubowe*
    TLS - i5854 - June 12 2015 - p21(1) [501+]
Toksvig, Sandi - *The Tricky Art of Co-Existing: How to Behave Decently No Matter What Life Throws Your Way*
    LJ - v140 - i3 - Feb 15 2015 - p123(2) [51-500]
    PW - v262 - i5 - Feb 2 2015 - p48(1) [51-500]
Tokuda, Wendy - *Humphrey the Lost Whale, a True Story (Illus. by Wakiyama, Hanako)*
    CH Bwatch - June 2015 - pNA [51-500]
Tolan, John - *Europe and the Islamic World: A History*
    CC - v132 - i11 - May 27 2015 - p37(3) [501+]
Tolan, Sandy - *Children of the Stone: The Power of Music in a Hard Land*
    BL - v111 - i13 - March 1 2015 - p12(1) [51-500]
    KR - Jan 15 2015 - pNA [51-500]
    LJ - v140 - i7 - April 15 2015 - p104(2) [51-500]
    PW - v262 - i1 - Jan 5 2015 - p60(1) [51-500]
Tolan, Stephanie - *Wishworks, Inc. (Illus. by Bates, Amy June)*
    c Teach Lib - v42 - i5 - June 2015 - p61(1) [51-500]
Tolicetti, Raffaella - *Think! Eat! Act!*
    Veg J - v34 - i1 - Jan-March 2015 - p31(1) [51-500]
Toliver, Wendy - *Red's Untold Tale: Once upon a Time*
    y VOYA - v38 - i5 - Dec 2015 - p75(1) [51-500]
Tolkien, J.R.R. - *Beowulf: A Translation and Commentary, Together with Sellic Spell*
    NAR - v300 - i2 - Spring 2015 - p43(1) [501+]
The Lord of the Rings
    Forbes - v195 - i8 - June 15 2015 - p22(1) [501+]
Toll, Ian W. - *The Conquering Tide: War in the Pacific Islands, 1942-1944*
    KR - July 1 2015 - pNA [501+]
    LJ - v140 - i10 - June 1 2015 - p116(2) [51-500]
    NYTBR - Oct 11 2015 - p15(L) [501+]
    PW - v262 - i27 - July 6 2015 - p58(1) [51-500]
Tolley, Krystal A. - *The Biology of Chameleons*
    QRB - v90 - i1 - March 2015 - p102(1) [501+]
Tolmie, Peter - *Ethnomethodology at Play*
    CS - v44 - i4 - July 2015 - p562-564 [501+]
Tolochko, Aleksei - *Kievskaia Rus' i malorossiia v XIX veke*
    Slav R - v74 - i1 - Spring 2015 - p163-164 [501+]
Tolokonnikova, Nadya - *Comradely Greetings: The Prison Letters of Nadya and Slavoj*
    PAJ - v37 - i3 - Sept 2015 - p132-133 [501+]
Toloudis, Nicolas - *Teaching Marianne and Uncle Sam: Public Education, State Centralization, and Teacher Unionism in France and United States*
    CS - v44 - i2 - March 2015 - p266-268 [501+]
Tolsdorff, Tim - *Von der Stern-Schnuppe zum Fix-Stern: Zwei Deutsche Illustrierte und Ihre Gemeinsame Geschichte vor und nach 1945*
    HNet - Jan 2015 - pNA [501+]
Tolstikova, Dasha - *A Year without Mom (Illus. by Tolstikova, Dasha)*
    c KR - Sept 1 2015 - pNA [51-500]
    c PW - v262 - i33 - August 17 2015 - p75(1) [51-500]
    c BL - v112 - i4 - Oct 15 2015 - p37(1) [51-500]
    c Nat Post - v17 - i277 - Oct 10 2015 - pWP5(1) [501+]
    c NYTBR - Sept 13 2015 - p21(L) [501+]
    c PW - v262 - i49 - Dec 2 2015 - p87(1) [51-500]
    c SLJ - v61 - i12 - Dec 2015 - p110(1) [51-500]
Tolstoy, Leo - *Strider: The Story of a Horse*
    WLT - v89 - i5 - Sept-Oct 2015 - p77(1) [51-500]
Tolstrup, Jakob - *Russia vs. the EU: The Competition for Influence in Post-Soviet States*
    Slav R - v74 - i1 - Spring 2015 - p219-220 [501+]
Tolton, Gordon E. - *Healy's West: The Life and Times of John J. Healy*
    Roundup M - v22 - i3 - Feb 2015 - p25(1) [501+]
    Roundup M - v22 - i6 - August 2015 - p41(1) [501+]
Toltz, Steve - *Quicksand*
    LJ - v140 - i14 - Sept 1 2015 - p97(1) [51-500]
    PW - v262 - i30 - July 27 2015 - p36(2) [51-500]
    Spec - v328 - i9745 - June 6 2015 - p38(2) [501+]
    BL - v112 - i2 - Sept 15 2015 - p28(1) [51-500]
    KR - July 15 2015 - pNA [501+]
Tom, Jessica - *Food Whore*
    KR - August 15 2015 - pNA [51-500]
    LJ - v140 - i16 - Oct 1 2015 - p72(1) [51-500]
    NYTBR - Dec 6 2015 - p60(L) [501+]
Tomasello, Michael - *A Natural History of Human Thinking*
    BioSci - v65 - i4 - April 2015 - p441(4) [501+]
    RM - v69 - i1 - Sept 2015 - p156(3) [501+]
Tomasi, Peter J. - *The Mighty (Illus. by Samnee, Chris)*
    y LJ - v140 - i9 - May 15 2015 - p61(3) [501+]

Tomasik, Timothy J. - *The Most Excellent Book of Cookery*
　Ren Q - v68 - i2 - Summer 2015 - p748-749 [501+]

Tombs, Robert - *The English and Their History*
　HT - v65 - i3 - March 2015 - p60(2) [501+]
　KR - Sept 1 2015 - pNA [501+]
　LJ - v140 - i17 - Oct 15 2015 - p103(1) [501+]
　PW - v262 - i39 - Sept 28 2015 - p78(1) [51-500]
　TimHES - i2190 - Feb 12 2015 - p49(1) [501+]
　TLS - i5832 - Jan 9 2015 - p7(2) [501+]

Tomes, Nancy - *Remaking the American Patient: How Madison Avenue and Modern Medicine Turned Patients into Consumers*
　LJ - v140 - i20 - Dec 1 2015 - p123(1) [51-500]

Tomine, Adrian - *Killing and Dying: Six Stories*
　KR - August 1 2015 - pNA [501+]
　PW - v262 - i31 - August 3 2015 - p2(1) [51-500]
Killing and Dying: Six Stories (Illus. by Tomine, Adrian)
　BL - v112 - i2 - Sept 15 2015 - p50(1) [51-500]
　NS - v144 - i5282 - Oct 2 2015 - p79(1) [501+]
　NYTBR - Dec 6 2015 - p44(L) [501+]

Tomita, Yo - *Exploring Bach's B-Minor Mass*
　Notes - v72 - i1 - Sept 2015 - p173(3) [501+]

Tomkins, Paul - *The Girl on the Pier*
　KR - Oct 1 2015 - pNA [501+]

Tomley, Sarah - *Children's Book of Philosophy: An Introduction to the World's Great Thinkers and Their Big Ideas*
　c SLJ - v61 - i6 - June 2015 - p145(1) [51-500]

Tomlin, Liz - *Acts and Apparitions: Discourses on the Real in Performance Practice and Theory, 1990-2010*
　Theat J - v67 - i1 - March 2015 - p135-146 [501+]

Tomlin, T.J. - *A Divinity for All Persuasions: Almanacs and Early American Religious Life*
　JAH - v102 - i2 - Sept 2015 - p533-534 [501+]

Tomlinson, Chris - *Tomlinson Hill: The Remarkable Story of Two Families Who Share the Tomlinson Name - One White, One Black (Read by Drummond, David). Audiobook Review*
　BL - v111 - i11 - Feb 1 2015 - p60(1) [51-500]

Tomlinson, Jim - *Dundee and the Empire: Juteopolis 1850-1939*
　HER - v130 - i545 - August 2015 - p1033(2) [501+]
　HNet - July 2015 - pNA [501+]

Tomlinson, Matt - *Ritual Textuality: Pattern and Motion in Performance*
　Pac A - v88 - i3 - Sept 2015 - p755 [501+]

Tomlinson, Richard - *Amazing Grace: The Man Who Was W.G.*
　NS - v144 - i5285 - Oct 23 2015 - p50(2) [501+]
　Spec - v329 - i9763 - Oct 10 2015 - p42(1) [501+]
　TLS - i5876 - Nov 13 2015 - p10(1) [501+]

Tomlinson, Sarah - *Good Girl*
　y BL - v111 - i15 - April 1 2015 - p7(1) [51-500]

Tomlinson, Theresa - *Better Than Gold*
　c Sch Lib - v63 - i1 - Spring 2015 - p44(2) [51-500]

Tomory, Leslie - *Progressive Enlightenment: The Origins of the Gaslight Industry, 1780-1820*
　AHR - v120 - i1 - Feb 2015 - p329-330 [501+]

Tomp, Sarah - *My Best Everything*
　y BL - v111 - i11 - Feb 1 2015 - p48(1) [51-500]
　y CCB-B - v68 - i10 - June 2015 - p521(1) [51-500]
　y PW - v262 - i2 - Jan 12 2015 - p62(1) [51-500]
　y VOYA - v37 - i6 - Feb 2015 - p68(1) [51-500]

Tompkins, Cynthia - *Experimental Latin American Cinema: History and Aesthetics*
　HAHR - v95 - i1 - Feb 2015 - p182-183 [501+]

Tompkins, Daniel P. - *Caesar in the USA*
　RAH - v43 - i3 - Sept 2015 - p537-540 [501+]

Tompkins, David G. - *Composing the Party Line: Music and Politics in Early Cold War Poland and East Germany*
　CEH - v48 - i1 - March 2015 - p139-140 [501+]

Tompkins, Mark - *The Last Days of Magic*
　KR - Dec 15 2015 - pNA [51-500]

Toms, Jonathan - *Mental Hygiene and Psychiatry in Modern Britain*
　HNet - May 2015 - pNA [501+]

Tonatiuh, Duncan - *Funny Bones: Posada and His Day of the Dead Calaveras (Illus. by Tonatiuh, Duncan)*
　c BL - v111 - i21 - July 1 2015 - p52(1) [51-500]
　c CCB-B - v69 - i2 - Oct 2015 - p117(2) [51-500]
　c HB - v91 - i6 - Nov-Dec 2015 - p108(1) [51-500]
　c PW - v262 - i49 - Dec 2 2015 - p46(1) [51-500]
　c SLJ - v61 - i9 - Sept 2015 - p183(1) [51-500]
　c KR - June 15 2015 - pNA [501+]
　c PW - v262 - i29 - July 20 2015 - p190(2) [51-500]
Separate Is Never Equal: Sylvia Mendez and Her Family's Fight for Desegregation (Illus. by Tonatiuh, Duncan)
　c SE - v79 - i3 - May-June 2015 - pNA [501+]

Toncheff, Mona - *Beyond the Common Core: A Handbook for Mathematics in a PLC at Work, High School*
　Math T - v109 - i2 - Sept 2015 - p158-158 [501+]

Toner, Deborah - *Alcohol and Nationhood in Nineteenth-Century Mexico*
　TLS - i5870 - Oct 2 2015 - p9(1) [501+]

Toner, Jerry - *The Day Commodus Killed a Rhino: Understanding the Roman Games*
　HT - v65 - i4 - April 2015 - p57(1) [501+]
Homer's Turk: How Classics Shaped Ideas of the East
　JMH - v87 - i1 - March 2015 - p169(2) [501+]
Roman Disasters
　Class R - v65 - i2 - Oct 2015 - p616-617 [501+]

Toner, Tom - *The Promise of a Child*
　BL - v112 - i1 - Sept 1 2015 - p56(1) [51-500]
　PW - v262 - i29 - July 20 2015 - p174(1) [51-500]

Toney, David L. - *The Second Coming of Jesus Christ*
　KR - June 1 2015 - pNA [501+]

Tong, Tommy - *China for Children Series*
　c CH Bwatch - March 2015 - pNA [51-500]

Tonge, Jonathan - *Comparative Peace Processes*
　HNet - February 2015 - pNA [501+]

Tonias, Demetrios - *Abraham in the Works of John Chrysostom*
　Six Ct J - v46 - i3 - Fall 2015 - p744-745 [501+]

Toniolo, Gianni - *The Oxford Handbook of the Italian Economy since Unification*
　HNet - March 2015 - pNA [501+]

Tonkin, Peter - *Blind Reef*
　BL - v112 - i1 - Sept 1 2015 - p44(1) [51-500]
Mariner's Ark
　BL - v111 - i17 - May 1 2015 - p40(1) [51-500]

Tonkiss, Fran - *Cities by Design: The Social Life of Urban Form*
　AJS - v120 - i4 - Jan 2015 - p1264(3) [501+]

Tonks, Rosemary - *Bedouin of the London Evening: Collected Poems*
　Poet - v205 - i5 - Feb 2015 - p484(13) [501+]

Toohey, Peter - *Jealousy*
　Barron's - v95 - i1 - Jan 5 2015 - p18(1) [501+]
　NS - v144 - i5244 - Jan 9 2015 - p34(3) [501+]
　NYRB - v62 - i1 - Jan 8 2015 - p24(2) [501+]

Took, John - *Conversations with Kenelm: Essays on the Theology of the "Commedia"*
　MLR - v110 - i2 - April 2015 - p561-562 [501+]

Toole, Anne - *Crystal Cadets (Illus. by O'Neill, Katie)*
　c BL - v112 - i2 - Sept 15 2015 - p52(1) [51-500]
　c KR - August 1 2015 - pNA [51-500]
　c SLJ - v61 - i9 - Sept 2015 - p149(2) [51-500]

Toomey, Christine - *In Search of Buddha's Daughters*
　KR - Dec 15 2015 - pNA [501+]
　PW - v262 - i51 - Dec 14 2015 - p77(2) [51-500]
The Saffron Road: A Journey with Buddha's Daughters
　TLS - i5853 - June 5 2015 - p5(1) [501+]

Tooze, Adam - *The Deluge: The Great War, America and the Remaking of the Global Order, 1916-1931*
　AHR - v120 - i3 - June 2015 - p958-960 [501+]
The Deluge: The Great War and the Remaking of Global Order, 1916-1931
　Lon R Bks - v37 - i3 - Feb 5 2015 - p37(3) [501+]

Topik, Steven C. - *Global Markets Transformed: 1870-1945*
　JEH - v75 - i2 - June 2015 - p615-617 [501+]

Topol, Allan - *The Argentine Triangle*
　RVBW - Feb 2015 - pNA [501+]

Topol, Eric - *The Patient Will See You Now: The Future of Medicine Is in Your Hands*
　BL - v111 - i9-10 - Jan 1 2015 - p28(2) [51-500]
　NYT - Jan 6 2015 - pD5(L) [501+]
　NYTBR - Feb 15 2015 - p10(L) [501+]

Topp, Jools - *Dingle Dangle Scarecrow (Illus. by Cooper, Jenny)*
　c Magpies - v30 - i5 - Nov 2015 - pS5(1) [51-500]

Topper, Jessica - *Courtship of the Cake*
　PW - v262 - i18 - May 4 2015 - p103(1) [51-500]

Toptas, Hasan Ali - *Reckless*
　BL - v111 - i22 - August 1 2015 - p29(2) [51-500]
　KR - June 1 2015 - pNA [501+]
　TLS - i5862 - August 7 2015 - p20(1) [501+]
　WLT - v89 - i6 - Nov-Dec 2015 - p68(1) [51-500]

Tor, Magus - *My Ladybird Story*
　KR - August 1 2015 - pNA [501+]

Torchia, Joseph - *Restless Mind: "Curiositas" & the Scope of Inquiry in St. Augustine's Psychology*
　Specu - v90 - i2 - April 2015 - p591-592 [501+]

Torday, Daniel - *The Last Flight of Poxl West*
　Esq - v163 - i4 - April 2015 - p41(1) [501+]
　LJ - v140 - i2 - Feb 1 2015 - p77(1) [51-500]
　NYT - March 6 2015 - pC27(L) [501+]
　NYTBR - March 15 2015 - p1(L) [501+]
　PW - v262 - i2 - Jan 12 2015 - p32(1) [501+]

Torday, Piers - *The Dark Wild (Read by Hembrough, Oliver). Audiobook Review*
　SLJ - v61 - i4 - April 2015 - p64(1) [51-500]
The Dark Wild
　c HB Guide - v26 - i2 - Fall 2015 - p104(1) [51-500]
The Last Wild
　c HB Guide - v26 - i1 - Spring 2015 - p94(1) [51-500]

Tornio, Stacy - *Truth about Nature: A Family's Guide to 144 Common Myths about the Great Outdoors*
　BL - v111 - i11 - Feb 1 2015 - p10(1) [51-500]

Tornquist, Olle - *Assessing Dynamics of Democratisation: Transformative Politics, New Institutions, and the Case of Indonesia*
　JAS - v74 - i1 - Feb 2015 - p246-248 [501+]

Toronto Public Library - *Superbrain: The Insider's Guide to Getting Smart (Illus. by Whamond, Dave)*
　c BL - v111 - i21 - July 1 2015 - p53(1) [51-500]
　c KR - May 15 2015 - pNA [51-500]
　c SLJ - v61 - i6 - June 2015 - p145(1) [51-500]
　c Res Links - v20 - i5 - June 2015 - p22(1) [51-500]

Torpey, Jodi - *Blue Ribbon Vegetable Gardening: The Secrets to Growing the Biggest and Best Prizewinning Produce*
　PW - v262 - i36 - Sept 7 2015 - p63(1) [51-500]

Torrance, Alexis - *Individuality in Late Antiquity*
　Class R - v65 - i2 - Oct 2015 - p415-417 [501+]

Torrance, David - *Nicola Sturgeon: A Political Life*
　TLS - i5848 - May 1 2015 - p22(2) [501+]

Torre, A.R. - *The Girl in 6E*
　TLS - i5861 - July 31 2015 - p20(1) [501+]

Torrealba, Alberto Arvelo - *Florentino and the Devil*
　TLS - i5846 - April 17 2015 - p27(1) [501+]

Torres, Isabel - *Love Poetry in the Spanish Golden Age: Eros, Eris and Empire*
　MLN - v130 - i2 - March 2015 - p410-412 [501+]

Torres, J. (b. 1969-) - *Blackfire's Back! (Illus. by Nauck, Todd)*
　c HB Guide - v26 - i1 - Spring 2015 - p66(1) [51-500]
Do-Gooders (Illus. by Wagner, Justin)
　c SLJ - v61 - i8 - August 2015 - p79(1) [51-500]
Monster Zit! (Illus. by Smith, Tim, III)
　c HB Guide - v26 - i1 - Spring 2015 - p66(1) [51-500]
The Sound of Thunder (Illus. by Hicks, Faith Erin)
　c HB Guide - v26 - i1 - Spring 2015 - p95(1) [51-500]

Torres, Jennifer - *The Battle*
　c HB Guide - v26 - i1 - Spring 2015 - p95(1) [51-500]
The Disappearing
　c HB Guide - v26 - i1 - Spring 2015 - p95(1) [51-500]
Finding the Music / En pos de la musica (Illus. by Alarcao, Renato)
　c CH Bwatch - June 2015 - pNA [51-500]
　c HB Guide - v26 - i2 - Fall 2015 - p54(1) [51-500]
　c KR - March 1 2015 - pNA [51-500]
　SLJ - v61 - i4 - April 2015 - p136(1) [51-500]
The Return
　c HB Guide - v26 - i1 - Spring 2015 - p95(1) [51-500]

Torres, John Albert - *Jay-Z: Hip-Hop Mogul*
　c HB Guide - v26 - i1 - Spring 2015 - p191(1) [51-500]
Ludacris: Hip-Hop Mogul
　c HB Guide - v26 - i1 - Spring 2015 - p191(1) [51-500]

Torres, Julia - *Braver and Bolder*
　KR - July 1 2015 - pNA [501+]

Torres, Leyla - *Kitchen Dance (Illus. by Torres, Leyla)*
　c BL - v111 - i9-10 - Jan 1 2015 - pS18(5) [501+]

Torres-Roman, Steven A. - *Dragons in the Stacks: A Teen Librarian's Guide to Tabletop Role-Playing*
　SLJ - v61 - i4 - April 2015 - p187(2) [51-500]
　VOYA - v38 - i1 - April 2015 - p93(1) [51-500]

Torres-Rouff, David Samuel - *Before L.A.: Race, Space, and Municipal Power in Los Angeles, 1781-1894*
　Ams - v72 - i1 - Jan 2015 - p160(3) [501+]
　PHR - v84 - i2 - May 2015 - p257(3) [501+]
　RAH - v43 - i3 - Sept 2015 - p505-511 [501+]

Torrey, E. Fuller - *The Martyrdom of Abolitionist Charles Torrey*
　JSH - v81 - i1 - Feb 2015 - p187(2) [501+]

Torrey, Richard - *Ally-Saurus & the First Day of School (Illus. by Torrey, Richard)*
　c BL - v111 - i21 - July 1 2015 - p60(2) [51-500]
　c HB Guide - v26 - i2 - Fall 2015 - p20(1) [51-500]
　c KR - June 1 2015 - pNA [51-500]
　c PW - v262 - i49 - Dec 2 2015 - p12(1) [51-500]
　c SLJ - v61 - i8 - August 2015 - p61(1) [51-500]
The Almost Terrible Playdate
　c KR - Nov 1 2015 - pNA [51-500]
A Basketball Story
　c HB Guide - v26 - i1 - Spring 2015 - p48(1) [51-500]

A Football Story
   c HB Guide - v26 - i1 - Spring 2015 - p48(1) [51-500]
Moe Is Best (Illus. by Torrey, Richard)
   c HB Guide - v26 - i1 - Spring 2015 - p55(1) [51-500]
My Dog, Bob (Illus. by Torrey, Richard)
   c BL - v112 - i2 - Sept 15 2015 - p69(1) [51-500]
   c KR - July 15 2015 - pNA [51-500]
   c SLJ - v61 - i9 - Sept 2015 - p130(1) [51-500]

Tortora, Phyllis G. - *Survey of Historic Costume, 6th ed.*
   LJ - v140 - i14 - Sept 1 2015 - p143(3) [501+]

Tosches, Nick - *Under Tiberius*
   BL - v111 - i22 - August 1 2015 - p30(1) [51-500]
   KR - June 1 2015 - pNA [501+]
   LJ - v140 - i11 - June 15 2015 - p82(1) [51-500]
   PW - v262 - i23 - June 8 2015 - p32(1) [51-500]

Tosi, Christina - *Milk Bar Life: Recipes & Stories*
   NYTBR - May 31 2015 - p24(L) [501+]
   PW - v262 - i14 - April 6 2015 - p53(1) [51-500]

Toswell, M.J. - *The Anglo-Saxon Psalter*
   Specu - v90 - i4 - Oct 2015 - p1175-1176 [501+]

Totah, Faedah M. - *Preserving the Old City of Damascus*
   IJMES - v47 - i3 - August 2015 - p632-634 [501+]

Toten, Teresa - *Shattered Glass*
   y KR - July 15 2015 - pNA [51-500]
   y Res Links - v21 - i1 - Oct 2015 - p42(2) [501+]
   y SLJ - v61 - i11 - Nov 2015 - p116(1) [51-500]
   y VOYA - v38 - i4 - Oct 2015 - p63(2) [51-500]
The Unlikely Hero of Room 13B (Read by McClain, Jonathan). Audiobook Review
   y SLJ - v61 - i6 - June 2015 - p68(2) [51-500]
The Unlikely Hero of Room 13B
   y BL - v111 - i11 - Feb 1 2015 - p49(1) [51-500]
   y CCB-B - v68 - i10 - June 2015 - p522(1) [51-500]
   y HB Guide - v26 - i2 - Fall 2015 - p142(1) [51-500]
   y KR - Jan 15 2015 - pNA [51-500]
   y Magpies - v30 - i3 - July 2015 - p44(2) [501+]
   y Sch Lib - v63 - i2 - Summer 2015 - p121(1) [51-500]
   y Teach Lib - v43 - i1 - Oct 2015 - p23(1) [51-500]
   y VOYA - v37 - i6 - Feb 2015 - p68(1) [51-500]

Toth, Helena - *An Exiled Generation: German and Hungarian Refugees of Revolution, 1848-1871*
   HNet - July 2015 - pNA [501+]

Toth, James - *Sayyid Qutb: The Life and Legacy of a Radical Islamic Intellectual*
   J Ch St - v57 - i1 - Wntr 2015 - p157-158 [501+]

Touber, Jetze - *Law, Medicine, and Engineering in the Cult of the Saints in Counter-Reformation Rome: The Hagiographical Works of Antonio Gallonio, 1556-1605*
   Ren Q - v68 - i3 - Fall 2015 - p1040-1042 [501+]

Touchell, Dianne - *A Small Madness*
   y Magpies - v30 - i1 - March 2015 - p44(2) [501+]
   y Sch Lib - v63 - i4 - Winter 2015 - p254(1) [51-500]

Tougas, Chris - *Dojo Daytrip (Illus. by Tougas, Chris)*
   c KR - June 15 2015 - pNA [51-500]
   c SLJ - v61 - i8 - August 2015 - p63(1) [51-500]

Tougas, Joe - *The Beatles: Defining Rock 'n' Roll*
   c HB Guide - v26 - i2 - Fall 2015 - p194(1) [51-500]
Mind-Blowing Movie Stunts
   c BL - v112 - i3 - Oct 1 2015 - p60(1) [51-500]

Tougas, Shelley - *Finders Keepers*
   c BL - v112 - i1 - Sept 1 2015 - p112(2) [51-500]
   c KR - July 15 2015 - pNA [51-500]
   c SLJ - v61 - i8 - August 2015 - p93(1) [51-500]
The Graham Cracker Plot
   c HB Guide - v26 - i1 - Spring 2015 - p95(1) [51-500]

Toumani, Meline - *There Was and There Was Not: A Journey through Hate and Possibility in Turkey, Armenia, and Beyond*
   Econ - v414 - i8919 - Jan 3 2015 - p68(US) [501+]
   NYTBR - Jan 25 2015 - p14(L) [501+]

Touno, Mamare - *Log Horizon: The Beginning of Another World (Illus. by Hara, Kazuhiro)*
   y SLJ - v61 - i6 - June 2015 - p118(2) [51-500]

Tourangeau, Roger - *Hard-to-Survey Populations*
   Pub Op Q - v79 - i2 - Summer 2015 - p626(3) [501+]

Tourville, Jacqueline - *Albie's First Word: A Tale Inspired by Albert Einstein's Childhood (Illus. by Evans, Wynne)*
   c HB Guide - v26 - i1 - Spring 2015 - p48(1) [51-500]

Toussaint, Jean-Philippe - *Urgency and Patience*
   TLS - i5876 - Nov 13 2015 - p30(1) [501+]

Toussaint, Maggie - *Bubba Done It*
   KR - April 1 2015 - pNA [51-500]

Tovey, Bob - *The Last English Poachers*
   Spec - v328 - i9746 - June 13 2015 - p34(1) [501+]

Tovey, Philip - *Anglican Confirmation, 1662-1820*
   CH - v84 - i3 - Sept 2015 - p671(3) [501+]

Toward, Gary - *The Art of Being a Brilliant NQT*
   TES - i5141 - April 10 2015 - p39(1) [501+]

Towell, Katy - *Charlie and the Grandmothers*
   c BL - v111 - i21 - July 1 2015 - p68(1) [51-500]
   c CCB-B - v69 - i2 - Oct 2015 - p118(1) [51-500]
   c KR - May 1 2015 - pNA [51-500]
   c SLJ - v61 - i6 - June 2015 - p106(1) [51-500]

tower, Adam - *CrimeBiters! My Dog Is Better Than Your Dog*
   c BL - v112 - i5 - Nov 1 2015 - p59(2) [51-500]

Tower, Elizabeth A. - *Icebound Empire: Industry and Politics on the Last Frontier, 1898-1938*
   SPBW - August 2015 - pNA [51-500]

Towle, Ben - *Oyster War (Illus. by Towle, Ben)*
   y BL - v112 - i2 - Sept 15 2015 - p52(1) [51-500]
   PW - v262 - i28 - July 13 2015 - p53(1) [51-500]
   c SLJ - v61 - i10 - Oct 2015 - p98(1) [51-500]

Towler, Katherine - *The Penny Poet of Portsmouth*
   BL - v112 - i7 - Dec 1 2015 - p10(2) [51-500]
   KR - Dec 1 2015 - pNA [51-500]
   PW - v262 - i48 - Nov 30 2015 - p48(1) [51-500]

Towne, Jonathan - *Octopus Midnight*
   KR - July 15 2015 - pNA [51-500]

Townend, Jack - *A Railway ABC (Illus. by Townend, Jack)*
   c SLJ - v61 - i5 - May 2015 - p93(1) [51-500]

Townley, Roderick - *A Bitter Magic*
   c HB - v91 - i6 - Nov-Dec 2015 - p94(1) [51-500]
   c KR - Sept 15 2015 - pNA [51-500]
   c SLJ - v61 - i10 - Oct 2015 - p96(1) [51-500]

Towns, Ann E. - *Women and States: Norms and Hierarchies in International Society*
   SF - v93 - i3 - March 2015 - pNA [501+]

Townsend, Anthony - *Smart Cities: Big Data, Civic Hackers, and the Quest for a New Utopia*
   Bwatch - Feb 2015 - pNA [51-500]

Townsend, Chris - *Rattlesnakes and Bald Eagles: Hiking the Pacific Crest Trail*
   LJ - v140 - i11 - June 15 2015 - p104(1) [51-500]

Townsend, Dominique - *Shantideva: How to Wake Up a Hero (Illus. by Norbu, Tenzin)*
   c CH Bwatch - August 2015 - pNA [51-500]

Townsend, John - *Mountain Peak Peril (Illus. by Shephard, David)*
   c Sch Lib - v63 - i4 - Winter 2015 - p240(1) [51-500]

Townsend, Johnny - *Despots of Deseret*
   KR - Oct 1 2015 - pNA [501+]
Gayrabian Nights
   KR - March 15 2015 - pNA [501+]
Lying for the Lord
   KR - May 1 2015 - pNA [501+]
Missionaries Make the Best Companions
   KR - Oct 15 2015 - pNA [501+]

Townsend, Light - *On History's Trail: Speeches and Essays by the Texas State Historian, 2009-2012*
   SHQ - v118 - i4 - April 2015 - p423-424 [501+]

Townsend, Michael - *Mr. Ball: An EGG-cellent Adventure*
   c HB Guide - v26 - i1 - Spring 2015 - p66(1) [51-500]

Townsend, Robert B. - *History's Babel: Scholarship, Professionalization and the Historical Enterprise in the United States, 1880-1940*
   Isis - v106 - i1 - March 2015 - p205(2) [501+]

Townsend, Sue - *The Queen and I*
   VOYA - v38 - i3 - August 2015 - p10(2) [501+]

Townsend, Wendy - *Blue Iguana*
   y HB Guide - v26 - i1 - Spring 2015 - p126(1) [51-500]

Townshend, Charles - *The Republic: The Fight for Irish Independence*
   ILS - v35 - i1 - Fall 2015 - p11(2) [501+]

Townson, Nigel - *Is Spain Different?: A Comparative Look at the 19th & 20th Centuries*
   HNet - Sept 2015 - pNA [501+]

Toyama, Kentaro - *Geek Heresy: Rescuing Social Change from the Cult of Technology*
   KR - April 1 2015 - pNA [501+]
   LJ - v140 - i7 - April 15 2015 - p115(1) [51-500]

Toye, Richard - *Churchill's Empire: The World That Made Him and the World He Made*
   HT - v65 - i1 - Jan 2015 - p56(2) [501+]
The Roar of the Lion: The Untold Story of Churchill's World War
   HT - v65 - i1 - Jan 2015 - p56(2) [501+]

Toynbee, Arnold - *The Treatment of Armenians in the Ottoman Empire, 1915-1916: Documents Presented to Viscount Grey of Fallodon by Viscount Bryce*
   HT - v65 - i7 - July 2015 - p56(2) [501+]

Toynbee, Jason - *Black British Jazz: Ownership and Performance*
   TimHES - i2184 - Jan 1 2015 - p63(1) [501+]

Toynbee, Polly - *Cameron's Coup: How the Tories Took Britain to the Brink*
   NS - v144 - i5247 - Jan 30 2015 - p44(1) [501+]

Toyne, Simon - *The Searcher*
   BL - v112 - i4 - Oct 15 2015 - p23(1) [51-500]
   NYTBR - Oct 18 2015 - p20(L) [501+]
   PW - v262 - i34 - August 24 2015 - p59(1) [51-500]

Trabue, Alan B. - *A Life of Lies and Spies: Tales of a CIA Covert Ops Polygraph Interrogator*
   KR - April 1 2015 - pNA [501+]
   LJ - v140 - i7 - April 15 2015 - p102(1) [51-500]

Tracy, Brian - *Get Smart!*
   PW - v262 - i42 - Oct 19 2015 - p39(1) [51-500]

Tracy, Charles - *Britain's Medieval Episcopal Thrones*
   TLS - i5864-5865 - August 21 2015 - p26(2) [501+]

Tracy, James J. - *Faith, Doubt, Mystery*
   KR - Dec 1 2015 - pNA [501+]

Tracy, Jonathan - *Lucan's Egyptian Civil War*
   Class R - v65 - i2 - Oct 2015 - p460-461 [501+]

Tracy, Larissa - *Torture and Brutality in Medieval Literature: Negotiations of National Identity*
   Specu - v90 - i2 - April 2015 - p592-594 [501+]

Traflet, Janice M. - *A Nation of Small Shareholders: Marketing Wall Street after World War II*
   RAH - v43 - i1 - March 2015 - p168-175 [501+]

Traherne, Thomas - *The Works of Thomas Traherne, vol. 6*
   Sev Cent N - v73 - i3-4 - Fall-Winter 2015 - p112(5) [501+]
   TLS - i5873 - Oct 23 2015 - p22(1) [501+]

Trammell, Joel - *The CEO Tightrope: How to Master the Balancing Act of a Successful CEO*
   Bwatch - Feb 2015 - pNA [51-500]

Trampe, Stan - *Fine Art Nudes: Lighting and Posing for Black and White Photography*
   Bwatch - Oct 2015 - pNA [51-500]

Tran, Vu - *Dragonfish (Read by Taylorson, Tom, with Nancy Wu). Audiobook Review*
   LJ - v140 - i17 - Oct 15 2015 - p52(1) [51-500]
   PW - v262 - i39 - Sept 28 2015 - p85(1) [51-500]
Dragonfish
   BL - v111 - i21 - July 1 2015 - p36(1) [51-500]
   KR - June 1 2015 - pNA [501+]
   NYTBR - August 16 2015 - p10(L) [501+]
   PW - v262 - i23 - June 8 2015 - p34(1) [51-500]

Trandafoiu, Ruxandra - *Diaspora Online: Identity Politics and Romanian Migrants*
   Slav R - v74 - i2 - Summer 2015 - p392-393 [501+]

Transatlantic Theory Transfer: Missed Encounters?
   HNet - July 2015 - pNA [501+]

Transitional Justice - The Role of Historical Narrative in Times of Transitions
   HNet - July 2015 - pNA [501+]

Transnationale Praktiken der Konstruktion Europas
   HNet - Feb 2015 - pNA [501+]

The Transregional Production, Translation, and Appropriation of Knowledge: Actors, Institutions, and Discourses
   HNet - Jan 2015 - pNA [501+]

Transtromer, Tomas - *Bright Scythe: Selected Poems*
   NYTBR - Dec 27 2015 - p13(L) [501+]
   PW - v262 - i42 - Oct 19 2015 - p52(1) [51-500]
   WLT - v89 - i6 - Nov-Dec 2015 - p76(1) [501+]
Tomas Transtromer's First Poems and Notes From the Land of Lap Fever
   Bks & Cult - v21 - i2 - March-April 2015 - p32(2) [501+]

Trapani, Iza - *Old King Cole (Illus. by Trapani, Iza)*
   c KR - June 15 2015 - pNA [51-500]
   c SLJ - v61 - i9 - Sept 2015 - p112(1) [51-500]

Trapnell, David - *The Postal History of the Two-Phased Italian Occupation of South-East France 1940-1943*
   Phil Lit R - v64 - i2 - Spring 2015 - p137(2) [501+]

Trasi, Amita - *The Color of Our Sky*
   KR - July 1 2015 - pNA [501+]

Trasler, Janee - *Bathtime for Chickies (Illus. by Trasler, Janee)*
   c CCB-B - v69 - i1 - Sept 2015 - p60(1) [51-500]
   c PW - v262 - i20 - May 18 2015 - p82(2) [501+]
Mimi and Bear in the Snow (Illus. by Trasler, Janee)
   c HB Guide - v26 - i1 - Spring 2015 - p17(1) [51-500]
A New Chick for Chickies (Illus. by Trasler, Janee)
   c KR - Jan 1 2015 - pNA [51-500]

464 • TRAUB
Book Review Index 2016 Cumulation

Traub, James - *John Quincy Adams*
KR - Jan 1 2016 - pNA [501+]
Traub, Valerie - *Thinking Sex with the Early Moderns*
JHI - v76 - i4 - Oct 2015 - p666(1) [501+]
Trauschweizer, Ingo - *Failed States and Fragile Societies: A New World Disorder?*
J Mil H - v79 - i2 - April 2015 - p556-557 [501+]
Traver, N.K. - *Duplicity*
y HB Guide - v26 - i2 - Fall 2015 - p142(1) [51-500]
Travers, Ailis - *Pope Francis: The Story of Our Pope (Illus. by Carthaigh, Lir Mac)*
c BL - v111 - i19-20 - June 1 2015 - p93(1) [51-500]
Travers, P.L. - *The Fox at the Manger*
c Spec - v329 - i9772 - Dec 12 2015 - p77(1) [501+]
Mary Poppins: 80th Anniversary Collection (Illus. by Shepard, Mary)
c HB Guide - v26 - i2 - Fall 2015 - p105(1) [51-500]
Travers, Pauric - *Parnell Reconsidered*
HER - v130 - i545 - August 2015 - p1025(2) [501+]
ILS - v34 - i2 - Spring 2015 - p8(1) [501+]
Trawny, Peter - *Freedom to Fail: Heidegger's Anarchy*
TimHES - i2222 - Sept 24 2015 - p43(1) [501+]
Traynor, Killarney - *Summer Shadows*
SPBW - Feb 2015 - pNA [51-500]
Treacy, Philip - *Philip Treacy: Hat Designer*
NYT - Nov 1 2015 - p3(L) [51-500]
Treadgold, Warren - *The Middle Byzantine Historians*
HER - v130 - i544 - June 2015 - p690(2) [501+]
Specu - v90 - i1 - Jan 2015 - p302-303 [501+]
Treadway, Jessica - *Lacy Eye*
BL - v111 - i11 - Feb 1 2015 - p22(1) [51-500]
BooChiTr - March 7 2015 - p12(1) [501+]
KR - Jan 15 2015 - pNA [51-500]
PW - v262 - i4 - Jan 26 2015 - p149(1) [51-500]
Treadwell, James - *Arcadia*
KR - Dec 1 2015 - pNA [51-500]
PW - v262 - i45 - Nov 9 2015 - p40(1) [51-500]
Treasure, Geoffrey - *The Huguenots*
CHR - v101 - i4 - Autumn 2015 - p938(2) [501+]
RAH - v43 - i2 - June 2015 - p203-209 [501+]
Treat, Jeremy R. - *The Crucified King: Atonement and Kingdom in Biblical and Systematic Theology*
Theol St - v76 - i1 - March 2015 - p216(1) [501+]
Trebach, Arnold S. - *The Dream Betrayed: Racial Absurdities in Obama's America*
KR - Feb 15 2015 - pNA [501+]
Tree, Isabella - *The Living Goddess: A Journey into the Heart of Kathmandu*
RVBW - July 2015 - pNA [51-500]
TLS - i5856 - June 26 2015 - p26(1) [501+]
Tregillis, Ian - *The Mechanical*
BL - v111 - i12 - Feb 15 2015 - p45(1) [51-500]
KR - March 15 2015 - pNA [501+]
NYTBR - May 31 2015 - p38(L) [501+]
PW - v262 - i4 - Jan 26 2015 - p154(1) [51-500]
The Rising
KR - Nov 15 2015 - pNA [51-500]
PW - v262 - i45 - Nov 9 2015 - p42(1) [51-500]
Treglown, Jeremy - *Franco's Crypt: Spanish Culture and Memory since 1936*
Lon R Bks - v37 - i13 - July 2 2015 - p15(4) [501+]
Treichel, Eliot - *A Series of Small Maneuvers*
y PW - v262 - i49 - Dec 2 2015 - p96(2) [51-500]
Tremain, Rose - *The American Lover and Other Stories*
NYTBR - March 1 2015 - p10(L) [501+]
Tremayne, Peter - *The Devil's Seal: A Mystery of Ancient Ireland*
PW - v262 - i19 - May 11 2015 - p39(1) [51-500]
Tremayne, S.K. - *The Ice Twins*
KR - March 15 2015 - pNA [51-500]
LJ - v140 - i5 - March 15 2015 - p94(3) [501+]
PW - v262 - i12 - March 23 2015 - p46(1) [51-500]
Tremblay, Manon - *Quebec Women and Legislative Representations*
CWS - v30 - i2-3 - Fall-Winter 2015 - p145(2) [501+]
Tremblay, Paul - *A Head Full of Ghosts*
BL - v111 - i18 - May 15 2015 - p36(1) [51-500]
KR - May 1 2015 - pNA [51-500]
NYTBR - May 31 2015 - p42(L) [501+]
PW - v262 - i16 - April 20 2015 - p60(1) [51-500]
Trennert, Jason DeSena - *My Side of the Street: Why Wolves, Flash Boys, Quants, and Masters of the Universe Don't Represent the Real Wall Street*
Barron's - v95 - i32 - August 10 2015 - p40(1) [501+]
BL - v111 - i18 - May 15 2015 - p7(1) [51-500]
Trenow, Liz - *The Forgotten Seamstress*
TimHES - i2188 - Jan 29 2015 - p47(1) [501+]
Trenshaw, Cynthia - *Meeting in the Margins: An Invitation to Encounter Society's Invisible People*
PW - v262 - i33 - August 17 2015 - p62(1) [51-500]
Trent, Christine - *Death at the Abbey*
PW - v262 - i36 - Sept 7 2015 - p48(1) [51-500]
The Mourning Bells
KR - Feb 1 2015 - pNA [51-500]
PW - v262 - i7 - Feb 16 2015 - p162(1) [51-500]
Trent, Hank - *Narrative of James Williams, an American Slave: Annotated Edition*
JSH - v81 - i1 - Feb 2015 - p186(1) [501+]
Trent, Tererai - *The Girl Who Buried Her Dreams in a Can: A True Story (Illus. by Gilchrist, Jan Spivey)*
c BL - v112 - i2 - Sept 15 2015 - p57(2) [51-500]
c SLJ - v61 - i8 - August 2015 - p124(1) [51-500]
The Girl Who Buried Her Dreams in a Can (Illus. by Gilchrist, Jan Spivey)
c KR - August 1 2015 - pNA [51-500]
Trentham, Laura - *Caught up in the Touch*
LJ - v140 - i9 - May 15 2015 - p5(1) [51-500]
Slow and Steady Rush. E-book Review
PW - v262 - i4 - Jan 26 2015 - p156(1) [51-500]
Trentmann, Frank - *Empire of Things: How We Became a World of Consumers, from the Fifteenth Century to the Twenty-First*
KR - Jan 1 2016 - pNA [501+]
The Oxford Handbook of the History of Consumption
HER - v130 - i544 - June 2015 - p798(3) [501+]
Trepied, Benoit - *Une Mairie dans la France Coloniale: Kone, Nouvelle Caledonie*
Cont Pac - v27 - i2 - Fall 2015 - p568(3) [501+]
Tresch, John - *The Romantic Machine: Utopian Science and Technology after Napoleon*
Isis - v106 - i2 - June 2015 - p401(5) [501+]
Trest, Warren A. - *Once a Fighter Pilot: The Story of Korean War Ace Lt. Gen. Charles G. "Chick" Cleveland*
APH - v62 - i1 - Spring 2015 - p57(2) [501+]
Treuer, David - *Prudence*
BL - v111 - i9-10 - Jan 1 2015 - p53(1) [51-500]
Ent W - i1353 - March 6 2015 - p73(1) [501+]
NYTBR - April 12 2015 - p9(L) [501+]
Trevathan, Erika - *Compelled to Crave*
SPBW - April 2015 - pNA [51-500]
Trevayne, Emma - *The Accidental Afterlife of Thomas Marsden*
c BL - v111 - i18 - May 15 2015 - p65(1) [51-500]
c CCB-B - v69 - i1 - Sept 2015 - p60(1) [51-500]
y HB - v91 - i4 - July-August 2015 - p149(1) [51-500]
c KR - April 1 2015 - pNA [51-500]
c SLJ - v61 - i5 - May 2015 - p106(2) [51-500]
Flights and Chimes and Mysterious Times
c SLJ - v61 - i6 - June 2015 - p46(6) [501+]
Trevor, Adena - *Freddy and Mrs. Goodwich (Illus. by Trevor, Chelsea)*
c CH Bwatch - Oct 2015 - pNA [51-500]
Trewhitt, Philip - *Military Vehicles: 1980 to Today*
c HB Guide - v26 - i1 - Spring 2015 - p137(2) [51-500]
Trexler, David - *Becoming Dinosaurs: A Prehistoric Perspective on Climate Change Today*
Sci Teach - v82 - i2 - Feb 2015 - p66 [501+]
Trezib, Joachim - *Die Theorie der zentralen Orte in Israel und Deutschland: Zur Rezeption Walter Christallers im Kontext von Sharonplan und "Generalplan Ost"*
HNet - May 2015 - pNA [501+]
Trezise, Thomas - *Witnessing Witnessing: On the Reception of Holocaust Survivor Testimony*
HNet - March 2015 - pNA [501+]
Triandafyllidou, Anna - *Irregular Migrant Domestic Workers in Europe: Who Cares?*
CS - v44 - i1 - Jan 2015 - p125-126 [501+]
Tribbe, Matthew D. - *No Requiem for the Space Age: The Apollo Moon Landings and American Culture*
AHR - v120 - i1 - Feb 2015 - p294-295 [501+]
JAH - v102 - i1 - June 2015 - p299-300 [501+]
Trice, Linda - *Kenya's Art (Illus. by Mitchell, Hazel)*
c KR - Nov 15 2015 - pNA [51-500]
Trierweiler, Valerie - *Thank You for This Moment*
NYRB - v62 - i1 - Jan 8 2015 - p24(2) [501+]
Trifunov, David - *Ice Time*
c BL - v112 - i1 - Sept 1 2015 - p100(1) [51-500]
c Res Links - v20 - i5 - June 2015 - p29(1) [51-500]
y SLJ - v61 - i9 - Sept 2015 - p151(4) [501+]
Trigg, Mary K. - *Feminism as Life's Work: Four Modern American Women through Two World Wars*
AHR - v120 - i3 - June 2015 - p1051-1052 [501+]
HNet - May 2015 - pNA [501+]
JAH - v102 - i1 - June 2015 - p271-272 [501+]
Trigg, Roger - *Religious Diversity: Philosophical and Political Dimensions*
TLS - i5867 - Sept 11 2015 - p28(1) [501+]
Triggs, Teal - *The School of Art: Learn How to Make Great Art with 40 Simple Lessons (Illus. by Frost, Daniel)*
c Sch Lib - v63 - i4 - Winter 2015 - p240(1) [51-500]
c SLJ - v61 - i10 - Oct 2015 - p139(1) [51-500]
Trigiani, Adriana - *All the Stars in the Heavens*
BL - v112 - i1 - Sept 1 2015 - p51(1) [51-500]
KR - Sept 1 2015 - pNA [51-500]
LJ - v140 - i16 - Oct 1 2015 - p74(1) [51-500]
PW - v262 - i37 - Sept 14 2015 - p38(2) [51-500]
Trimbur, Lucia - *Come Out Swinging: The Changing World of Boxing in Gleason's Gym*
CS - v44 - i3 - May 2015 - p425-427 [501+]
Trimmer, Christian - *Mimi and Shu in I'll Race You! (Illus. by Van der Paardt, Melissa)*
c KR - Oct 1 2015 - pNA [51-500]
c SLJ - v61 - i11 - Nov 2015 - p89(1) [51-500]
Simon's New Bed (Illus. by Van der Paardt, Melissa)
c CH Bwatch - Nov 2015 - pNA [51-500]
c KR - May 1 2015 - pNA [51-500]
c PW - v262 - i19 - May 11 2015 - p60(1) [51-500]
c SLJ - v61 - i7 - July 2015 - p58(2) [51-500]
Trine, Greg - *Willy Maykit in Space (Illus. by Burks, James)*
c BL - v111 - i14 - March 15 2015 - p76(1) [51-500]
c CCB-B - v68 - i9 - May 2015 - p469(2) [51-500]
c CH Bwatch - April 2015 - pNA [51-500]
c KR - Jan 15 2015 - pNA [51-500]
Trinitapoli, Jenny - *Religion and AIDS in Africa*
CS - v44 - i5 - Sept 2015 - p591-603 [501+]
Trink, Dan - *High-Intensity 300*
Bwatch - Jan 2015 - pNA [51-500]
Triolaire, Cyril - *Le theatre en province pendant le Consulat et l'Empire*
JMH - v87 - i2 - June 2015 - p454(2) [501+]
Triolo, Pamela - *Death without Cause*
RVBW - Jan 2015 - pNA [51-500]
The Imposter
RVBW - Feb 2015 - pNA [51-500]
Tripcevich, Nicholas - *Mining and Quarrying in the Ancient Andes: Sociopolitical, Economic, and Symbolic Dimensions*
Lat Ant - v26 - i1 - March 2015 - p139(2) [501+]
Tripp, Aili Mari - *Gender, Violence, and Human Security*
AJS - v120 - i4 - Jan 2015 - p1229(3) [501+]
Tripp, Ben - *The Accidental Highwayman: Being the Tale of Kit Bristol, His Horse Midnight, a Mysterious Princess, and Sundry Magical Persons Besides*
y CCB-B - v68 - i5 - Jan 2015 - p279(1) [51-500]
y HB Guide - v26 - i1 - Spring 2015 - p126(1) [51-500]
The Fifth House of the Heart
PW - v262 - i26 - June 29 2015 - p51(1) [51-500]
Tripp, Paul David - *Awe: Why It Matters for Everything We Think, Say, and Do*
Ch Today - v59 - i9 - Nov 2015 - p76(1) [501+]
Tripp, Sebastian - *Fromm und Politisch: Christliche Anti-Apartheid-Gruppen und die Transformation des Westdeutschen Protestantismus 1970-1990*
HNet - June 2015 - pNA [501+]
Trippett, David - *Wagner's Melodies: Aesthetics and Materialism in German Musical Identity*
GSR - v38 - i3 - Oct 2015 - p667-668 [501+]
Triptow, Robert - *Class Photo*
PW - v262 - i48 - Nov 30 2015 - p47(1) [51-500]
Tristram, Anna - *Variation and Change in French Morphosyntax: The Case of Collective Nouns*
FS - v69 - i4 - Oct 2015 - p578-579 [501+]
Trittel, Katharina - *Weisskittel und Braunhemd: Der Gottinger Mediziner Rudolf Stich im Kaleidoskop*
HNet - Feb 2015 - pNA [501+]
Trivellato, Francesca - *Religion and Trade: Cross-Cultural Exchanges in World History, 1000-1900*
HNet - August 2015 - pNA [501+]
Specu - v90 - i3 - July 2015 - p878(1) [501+]
Troberg, Michelle - *Change of Object Expression in the History of French: Verbs of Helping and Hindering*
FS - v69 - i1 - Jan 2015 - p137-137 [501+]
Trochatos, Litsa - *Don't (Illus. by Johnson, Virginia)*
c HB - v91 - i1 - Jan-Feb 2015 - p74(1) [51-500]
c HB Guide - v26 - i1 - Spring 2015 - p17(1) [51-500]
c KR - Jan 1 2015 - pNA [51-500]
Trodd, Colin - *Visions of Blake: William Blake in the Art World 1830-1930*
VS - v57 - i2 - Wntr 2015 - p340(3) [501+]

Trogdon, Jo Ann - *The Unknown Travels and Dubious Pursuits of William Clark*
LJ - v140 - i11 - June 15 2015 - p100(1) [51-500]

Trohler, Daniel - *Pestalozzi and the Educationalization of the World*
HNet - Sept 2015 - pNA [501+]

Trokhimenko, Olga - *Constructing Virtue and Vice: Femininity and Laughter in Courtly Society, ca. 1150-1300*
Med R - August 2015 - pNA [501+]

Trollope, Anthony - *An Autobiography and Other Writings*
Bks & Cult - v21 - i6 - Nov-Dec 2015 - p34(2) [501+]
TLS - i5847 - April 24 2015 - p5(1) [501+]
The Duke's Children
TLS - i5847 - April 24 2015 - p3(2) [501+]
Framley Parsonage
TLS - i5847 - April 24 2015 - p7(f2) [501+]
The Way We Live Now
TimHES - i2210 - July 2 2015 - p47-1 [501+]

Trombley, Stacey - *Naked*
y SLJ - v61 - i9 - Sept 2015 - p173(1) [51-500]
y VOYA - v38 - i3 - August 2015 - p71(1) [501+]

Tromboni, Lorenza - *Inter Omnes Plato Et Aristoteles: Gli Appunti Filosofici Di Girolamo Savonarola: Introduzione, Edizione Critica E Commento*
Specu - v90 - i3 - July 2015 - p861-862 [501+]

Tromly, Benjamin - *Making the Soviet Intelligentsia: Universities and Intellectual Life under Stalin and Khrushchev*
AHR - v120 - i2 - April 2015 - p745-746 [501+]
Slav R - v74 - i3 - Fall 2015 - p665-666 [501+]

Tromly, Stephanie - *Trouble Is a Friend of Mine (Read by McInerney, Kathleen). Audiobook Review*
y PW - v262 - i48 - Nov 30 2015 - p56(1) [51-500]
y SLJ - v61 - i12 - Dec 2015 - p81(1) [51-500]
Trouble Is a Friend of Mine
y BL - v111 - i21 - July 1 2015 - p60(1) [51-500]
y CCB-B - v69 - i2 - Oct 2015 - p118(2) [51-500]
y KR - May 1 2015 - pNA [51-500]
y PW - v262 - i20 - May 18 2015 - p87(1) [51-500]
y PW - v262 - i49 - Dec 2 2015 - p99(1) [51-500]
c PW - v262 - i51 - Dec 14 2015 - p21(6) [501+]
y SLJ - v61 - i6 - June 2015 - p130(1) [51-500]
y VOYA - v38 - i3 - August 2015 - p71(2) [501+]

Tronzo, William - *Petrarch's Two Gardens: Landscape and the Image of Movement*
Specu - v90 - i1 - Jan 2015 - p304-305 [501+]

Tropes, John - *Gotcha Rhythm Right Here*
Dbt - v82 - i8 - August 2015 - p80(1) [501+]

Trosley, George - *Trosley's How to Draw Cartoon Cars*
RVBW - May 2015 - pNA [51-500]

Trosper, A.D. - *Embers at Galdrilene*
PW - v262 - i41 - Oct 12 2015 - p52(1) [51-500]

Trotta, Roberto - *The Edge of the Sky*
Astron - v43 - i2 - Feb 2015 - p17(1) [51-500]

Trotter, David - *Literature in the First Media Age: Britain between the Wars*
MP - v112 - i4 - May 2015 - pE333(3) [501+]

Trotter, Jim - *Junior Seau: The Life and Death of a Football Icon*
BL - v112 - i1 - Sept 1 2015 - p36(1) [51-500]
KR - August 1 2015 - pNA [51-500]
PW - v262 - i28 - July 13 2015 - p56(1) [51-500]

Trought, Josh - *The Community-Scale Permaculture Farm: The D Acres Model for Creating and Managing an Ecologically Designed Educational Center*
BL - v111 - i12 - Feb 15 2015 - p26(1) [51-500]
PW - v262 - i7 - Feb 16 2015 - p175(1) [51-500]

Troupe, Thomas Kingsley - *The Dark Lens*
y SLJ - v61 - i9 - Sept 2015 - p151(4) [501+]
Kitanai and Cavity Croc Brush their Teeth (Illus. by Christoph, Jamey)
c HB Guide - v26 - i2 - Fall 2015 - p184(1) [51-500]
Kitanai and Hungry Hare Eat Healthfully (Illus. by Christoph, Jamey)
c HB Guide - v26 - i2 - Fall 2015 - p190(1) [51-500]

Trovato, Bill - *Oldsmobile V-8 Engines: How to Build Max Performance*
RVBW - Oct 2015 - pNA [501+]

Trovato, Paolo - *Everything You Always Wanted to Know about Lachmann's Method: A Non-Standard Handbook of Genealogical Textual Criticism in the Age of Post-Structuralism, Cladistics and Copy-Text*
FS - v69 - i3 - July 2015 - p375(1) [501+]

Trow, M.J. - *The Blue and the Grey*
BL - v111 - i12 - Feb 15 2015 - p34(1) [51-500]
PW - v262 - i7 - Feb 16 2015 - p162(2) [51-500]
Secret World
BL - v111 - i22 - August 1 2015 - p37(1) [51-500]
PW - v262 - i28 - July 13 2015 - p47(1) [51-500]

Trowbridge, William - *Put This On, Please: New and Selected Poems*
Ga R - v69 - i1 - Spring 2015 - p133-137 [501+]

Trowler, Paul R. - *Academic Tribes and Territories: Intellectual Enquiry and the Cultures of Discipline*
TimHES - i2211 - July 9 2015 - p45(1) [501+]

Troy, Gil - *The Age of Clinton: America in the 1990s*
KR - August 15 2015 - pNA [51-500]
PW - v262 - i34 - August 24 2015 - p75(1) [51-500]

Truax, Eileen - *Dreamers: An Immigrant Generation's Fight for Their American Dream*
BL - v111 - i12 - Feb 15 2015 - p8(2) [51-500]
KR - Jan 1 2015 - pNA [51-500]
LJ - v140 - i3 - Feb 15 2015 - p118(1) [51-500]

Trubowitz, Lara - *Civil Antisemitism, Modernism, and British Culture, 1902-1939*
MFSF - v61 - i3 - Fall 2015 - p565-567 [501+]

Trubowitz, Rachel - *Nation and Nurture in Seventeenth-Century English Literature*
MP - v112 - i3 - Feb 2015 - pE247(E251) [501+]

Truc, Oliver - *Forty Days without Shadow*
BL - v111 - i12 - Feb 15 2015 - p36(1) [51-500]

Truc, Olivier - *Forty Days without Shadow*
ABR - v36 - i5 - July-August 2015 - p25(1) [501+]

True, Jacqui - *The Political Economy of Violence against Women*
CS - v44 - i1 - Jan 2015 - p127-128 [501+]

True, Sylvia - *The Wednesday Group*
BL - v111 - i11 - Feb 1 2015 - p25(1) [51-500]
KR - Jan 1 2015 - pNA [51-500]

Trueblood, Valerie - *Criminals: Love Stories*
KR - Oct 1 2015 - pNA [501+]
PW - v262 - i47 - Nov 23 2015 - p45(2) [51-500]

Trueit, Trudi - *The Sister Solution*
c KR - July 1 2015 - pNA [51-500]

Trueit, Trudi Strain - *Veterinarian*
y Teach Lib - v42 - i3 - Feb 2015 - p10(1) [51-500]
What Is Poetry?
c HB Guide - v26 - i1 - Spring 2015 - p189(1) [51-500]

Truitt, Allison J. - *Dreaming of Money in Ho Chi Minh City*
JAS - v74 - i3 - August 2015 - p791-792 [501+]

Trukhan, Ekaterina - *Me and My Cat*
c SLJ - v61 - i9 - Sept 2015 - p130(1) [51-500]

Trull, Mary - *Performing Privacy and Gender in Early Modern Literature*
Ren Q - v68 - i3 - Fall 2015 - p1129-1131 [501+]

Trumble, Dennis R. - *The Way of Science: Finding Truth and Meaning in a Scientific Worldview*
Am Bio T - v77 - i7 - Sept 2015 - p554(1) [501+]

Trumbull, Gunnar - *Consumer Lending in France and America: Credit and Welfare*
BHR - v89 - i2 - Summer 2015 - p355(3) [501+]
Strength in Numbers: The Political Power of Weak Interests
CS - v44 - i2 - March 2015 - p268-270 [501+]

Trump, Donald J. - *Time to Get Tough: Make America Great Again!*
NYRB - v62 - i14 - Sept 24 2015 - p12(3) [501+]

Trusdell, Brian - *US Women Win the World Cup*
c HB Guide - v26 - i2 - Fall 2015 - p200(1) [51-500]

Truss, Lynne - *Cat out of Hell*
KR - Jan 1 2015 - pNA [51-500]
LJ - v140 - i2 - Feb 1 2015 - p77(2) [51-500]
PW - v262 - i1 - Jan 5 2015 - p50(1) [51-500]

Trzebiatowska, Marta - *Why Are Women More Religious Than Men?*
JR - Jan 2015 - p158(3) [501+]

Tsai, Eugenie - *Kehinde Wiley: A New Republic*
LJ - v140 - i14 - Sept 1 2015 - p98(1) [51-500]

Tsai, Robert L. - *America's Forgotten Constitutions: Defiant Visions of Power and Community*
AHR - v120 - i4 - Oct 2015 - p1523-1524 [501+]
JAH - v102 - i1 - June 2015 - p215-216 [501+]
Reason - v46 - i8 - Jan 2015 - p72(3) [501+]

Tsalikoglou, Fotini - *The Secret Sister*
WLT - v89 - i6 - Nov-Dec 2015 - p68(1) [501+]

Tschechische, Slowakische und Tschechoslowakische Geschichte des 20. Jahrhunderts
HNet - June 2015 - pNA [501+]

Tschen-Emmons, James B. - *Artifacts from Ancient Rome*
BL - v111 - i12 - Feb 15 2015 - p23(1) [51-500]
R&USQ - v54 - i3 - Spring 2015 - p58(2) [51-500]
Artifacts from Medieval Europe
BL - v112 - i1 - Sept 1 2015 - p30(1) [51-500]
LJ - v140 - i10 - June 1 2015 - p134(1) [51-500]

Tse, Dorothy - *Snow and Shadow*
WLT - v89 - i1 - Jan-Feb 2015 - p70(2) [501+]

Tse, Edward - *China's Disruptors: How Alibaba, Xiaomi, Tencent, and Other Companies Are Changing the Rules of Business*
PW - v262 - i19 - May 11 2015 - p49(1) [51-500]

Tseng, Jennifer - *Mayumi and the Sea of Happiness*
BL - v111 - i17 - May 1 2015 - p76(1) [51-500]
KR - March 15 2015 - pNA [51-500]

Tsepeneag, Dumitru - *The Bulgarian Truck*
KR - Nov 15 2015 - pNA [51-500]

Tsiang, Sarah - *The Night Children (Illus. by Bodet, Delphine)*
c KR - July 15 2015 - pNA [51-500]

Tsing, Anna Lowenhaupt - *The Mushroom at the End of the World: On the Possibility of Life in Capitalist Ruins*
KR - July 15 2015 - pNA [51-500]
New Sci - v228 - i3044 - Oct 24 2015 - p44(1) [501+]
PW - v262 - i30 - July 27 2015 - p55(1) [51-500]

Ts'o, Pauline - *Whispers of the Wolf (Illus. by Ts'o, Pauline)*
c BL - v112 - i5 - Nov 1 2015 - p68(1) [51-500]
c CH Bwatch - Nov 2015 - pNA [51-500]
c SLJ - v61 - i10 - Oct 2015 - p85(1) [51-500]

Tsougarakis, Nickiphoros I. - *A Companion to Latin Greece*
Med R - Sept 2015 - pNA [501+]

Tsuchiya, Kazuyo - *Reinventing Citizenship: Black Los Angeles, Korean Kawasaki, and Community Participation*
AHR - v120 - i4 - Oct 2015 - p1455-1456 [501+]
JAH - v101 - i4 - March 2015 - p1335-1336 [501+]

Tsuge, Tadao - *Trash Market*
PW - v262 - i23 - June 8 2015 - p47(1) [51-500]

Tsui, Carmen C.M. - *Chinese Cities in a Time of Change*
J Urban H - v41 - i3 - May 2015 - p508-513 [501+]

Tsukamoto, Kenichiro - *Mesoamerican Plazas: Arenas of Community and Power*
HAHR - v95 - i2 - May 2015 - p345-346 [501+]

Tsukiori, Yoshiko - *Sewing for Your Girls: Easy Instructions for Dresses, Smocks and Frocks*
Bwatch - July 2015 - pNA [51-500]

Tubali, Shai - *Indestructible You: Building a Self That Can't be Broken*
SPBW - July 2015 - pNA [51-500]

Tuccille, Jerome - *The Roughest Riders: The Untold Story of the Black Soldiers in the Spanish American War*
PW - v262 - i29 - July 20 2015 - p182(1) [51-500]

Tuchman, Gail - *En safari*
c Res Links - v20 - i3 - Feb 2015 - p47(2) [51-500]
Safari (Read by Graham, Dion). Audiobook Review
SLJ - v61 - i4 - April 2015 - p62(1) [51-500]

Tucholke, April Genevieve - *Between the Spark and the Burn*
y HB Guide - v26 - i1 - Spring 2015 - p126(1) [51-500]
Slasher Girls and Monster Boys (Read by Daymond, Robbie). Audiobook Review
y SLJ - v61 - i12 - Dec 2015 - p81(1) [51-500]
Slasher Girls and Monster Boys
y HB - v91 - i5 - Sept-Oct 2015 - p120(2) [51-500]
y CCB-B - v69 - i2 - Oct 2015 - p119(1) [51-500]
y KR - June 15 2015 - pNA [51-500]
y PW - v262 - i20 - May 18 2015 - p87(1) [51-500]
y SLJ - v61 - i7 - July 2015 - p98(2) [51-500]
c VOYA - v38 - i3 - August 2015 - p85(1) [51-500]
Wink Poppy Midnight
y PW - v262 - i52 - Dec 21 2015 - p158(1) [51-500]

Tuck, Lily - *The Double Life of Liliane*
BL - v111 - i21 - July 1 2015 - p30(1) [51-500]
KR - July 1 2015 - pNA [51-500]
LJ - v140 - i13 - August 1 2015 - p89(2) [51-500]
NY - v91 - i35 - Nov 9 2015 - p81 [51-500]
NYT - Sept 24 2015 - pC6(L) [501+]
NYTBR - Oct 4 2015 - p20(L) [501+]
PW - v262 - i30 - July 27 2015 - p38(1) [51-500]

Tuck, Shonna - *Getting from Me to We: How to Help Young Children Fit In and Make Friends*
LJ - v140 - i15 - Sept 15 2015 - p94(2) [51-500]

Tucker, Alan - *Going Solo*
Analog - v135 - i7-8 - July-August 2015 - p187(2) [501+]

Tucker, Catlin R. - *Creatively Teach the Common Core Literacy Standards With Technology Grades 6-12*
Bwatch - Nov 2015 - pNA [51-500]

Tucker, David - *The End of Intelligence: Espionage and State Power in the Information Age*
For Aff - v94 - i1 - Jan-Feb 2015 - pNA [51-500]

Tucker, Elizabeth - *New York State Folklife Reader: Diverse Voices*
WestFolk - v74 - i1 - Wntr 2015 - p102-104 [501+]

Tucker, Garland S., III - *Conservative Heroes: Fourteen Leaders Who Shaped America, from Jefferson to Reagan*
 RVBW - August 2015 - pNA [51-500]
Tucker, Irene - *The Moment of Racial Sight: A History*
 MP - v112 - i3 - Feb 2015 - pE255(E260) [501+]
Tucker, J. Brian - *Remain in Your Calling: Paul and the Continuation of Social Identity in 1 Corinthians*
 BTB - v45 - i2 - May 2015 - p121(3) [501+]
Tucker, K.A. - *He Will Be My Ruin*
 KR - Dec 1 2015 - pNA [51-500]
 PW - v262 - i50 - Dec 7 2015 - p68(2) [51-500]
Tucker, Marilyn Evelyn - *Thomas Berry: Selected Writings on the Earth Community*
 Bwatch - Feb 2015 - pNA [51-500]
Tucker, Mark E. - *Drive or Die*
 KR - Nov 15 2015 - pNA [501+]
Tucker, Neely - *Murder, D.C.*
 BL - v111 - i18 - May 15 2015 - p28(1) [51-500]
 KR - May 15 2015 - pNA [501+]
 PW - v262 - i19 - May 11 2015 - p36(1) [51-500]
Tucker, Phillip Thomas - *Emily D. West and the "Yellow Rose of Texas" Myth*
 JSH - v81 - i2 - May 2015 - p457(2) [501+]
Tucker, Rosalyn - *Famous Pirates*
 c SLJ - v61 - i4 - April 2015 - p113(4) [501+]
Pirate Ships
 c HB Guide - v26 - i2 - Fall 2015 - p215(1) [51-500]
Pirate Treasure
 c HB Guide - v26 - i2 - Fall 2015 - p215(1) [51-500]
Ronald Reagan
 c HB Guide - v26 - i1 - Spring 2015 - p193(1) [51-500]
Tucker, Sherrie - *Dance Floor Democracy: The Social Geography of Memory at the Hollywood Canteen*
 WHQ - v46 - i3 - Autumn 2015 - p376-377 [501+]
Tucker, Spencer C. - *500 Great Military Leaders, 2 vols.*
 BL - v111 - i14 - March 15 2015 - p29(2) [51-500]
 LJ - v140 - i7 - April 15 2015 - p118(1) [51-500]
 R&USQ - v54 - i4 - Summer 2015 - p78(1) [501+]
American Civil War: A State-by State Encyclopedia, 2 vols.
 BL - v111 - i21 - July 1 2015 - p17(2) [51-500]
World War I: The Definitive Encyclopedia and Document Collection, 5 vols.
 R&USQ - v54 - i4 - Summer 2015 - p75(1) [501+]
Tuckness, Alex - *The Decline of Mercy in Public Life*
 J Phil - v112 - i5 - May 2015 - p280(1) [501+]
Tudor, Daniel - *North Korea Confidential: Private Markets, Fashion Trends, Prison Camps, Dissenters and Defectors*
 LJ - v140 - i7 - April 15 2015 - p105(1) [51-500]
 NYTBR - July 19 2015 - p19(L) [501+]
 PW - v262 - i6 - Feb 9 2015 - p58(1) [51-500]
Tudor, Maya - *The Promise of Power: The Origins of Democracy in India and Autocracy in Pakistan*
 Pac A - v88 - i1 - March 2015 - p213 [501+]
Tudor, Tasha - *1 Is One (Illus. by Tudor, Tasha)*
 c HB Guide - v26 - i2 - Fall 2015 - p20(1) [51-500]
Tueth, Michael V. - *Reeling with Laughter: American Film Comedies-from Anarchy to Mockumentary*
 SAH - v4 - i1 - Annual 2015 - p121-123 [501+]
Tuil, Karine - *The Age of Reinvention*
 KR - Sept 15 2015 - pNA [501+]
 NYT - Dec 31 2015 - pC7(L) [501+]
 PW - v262 - i42 - Oct 19 2015 - p55(1) [51-500]
Tuisl, Elisabeth - *Die Medizinische Fakultat der Universitat Wien im Mittelalter: Von der Grundung der Universitat 1365 bis zum Tod Kaiser Maximilians I. 1519*
 HNet - Feb 2015 - pNA [501+]
Tuite, Clara - *Lord Byron and Scandalous Celebrity*
 TimHES - i2194 - March 12 2015 - p53(1) [501+]
Tuite, Diane - *Brand-New and Terrific: Alex Katz in the 1950s*
 LJ - v140 - i19 - Nov 15 2015 - p83(2) [51-500]
Tulathimutte, Tony - *Private Citizens*
 y BL - v112 - i6 - Nov 15 2015 - p22(2) [51-500]
 KR - Nov 1 2015 - pNA [501+]
 PW - v262 - i48 - Nov 30 2015 - p35(2) [51-500]
Tulgan, Bruce - *Bridging the Soft Skills Gap: How to Teach the Missing Basics to Today's Young Talent*
 LJ - v140 - i14 - Sept 1 2015 - p116(1) [51-500]
Tulip, Jenny - *Which Endangered Animal Lives in Mongolia? (Illus. by Smith, Dawn)*
 c Sch Lib - v63 - i3 - Autumn 2015 - p161(1) [51-500]
Tulku, Gomo - *Seven Steps to Train Your Mind*
 RVBW - May 2015 - pNA [501+]

Tullet, Herve - *Art Workshops for Children (Illus. by Tullet, Herve)*
 c BL - v112 - i5 - Nov 1 2015 - p50(1) [51-500]
The Finger Sports Game
 c KR - Jan 1 2016 - pNA [501+]
The Game of Lines (Illus. by Tullet, Herve)
 c SLJ - v61 - i7 - July 2015 - p57(1) [51-500]
The Game of Shapes
 c KR - Jan 1 2016 - pNA [501+]
The Game of Tops and Tails (Illus. by Tullet, Herve)
 c KR - July 1 2015 - pNA [501+]
 c SLJ - v61 - i7 - July 2015 - p57(1) [51-500]
The Good Morning Game (Illus. by Tullet, Herve)
 c SLJ - v61 - i7 - July 2015 - p57(1) [51-500]
The Trail Game (Illus. by Tullet, Herve)
 c SLJ - v61 - i7 - July 2015 - p57(1) [51-500]
Tullius, Mark - *Twisted Reunion*
 KR - Jan 1 2016 - pNA [501+]
Tullson, Diane - *Foolproof*
 y Res Links - v21 - i1 - Oct 2015 - p43(1) [51-500]
 y SLJ - v61 - i9 - Sept 2015 - p151(4) [501+]
Tully, John - *The Devil's Milk: A Social History of Rubber*
 S&S - v79 - i3 - July 2015 - p480-483 [501+]
Silvertown: The Lost Story of a Strike that Shook London and Helped Modern Labour Movement
 S&S - v79 - i3 - July 2015 - p480-483 [501+]
Tuma, Refe - *What the Dinosaurs Did Last Night: A Very Messy Adventure (Illus. by Tuma, Refe)*
 c KR - July 1 2015 - pNA [501+]
 c PW - v262 - i32 - August 10 2015 - p58(1) [51-500]
 c SLJ - v61 - i9 - Sept 2015 - p130(1) [51-500]
Tumber, Catherine - *Small, Gritty and Green: The Promise of America's Smaller Industrial Cities in a Low Carbon World*
 CS - v44 - i3 - May 2015 - p427-429 [501+]
Tumbler, Terry - *Seb Cage Begins His Adventures*
 y KR - Jan 15 2015 - pNA [501+]
Tumblety, Joan - *Remaking the Male Body: Masculinity and the uses of Physical Culture in Interwar and Vichy France*
 FS - v69 - i3 - July 2015 - p433-434 [501+]
Tunnicliffe, Hannah - *Season of Salt and Honey*
 LJ - v140 - i14 - Sept 1 2015 - p97(1) [51-500]
Tunsjo, Oystein - *Security and Profit in China's Energy Policy: Hedging Against Risk*
 Pac A - v88 - i2 - June 2015 - p277 [501+]
Tuohy, Andy - *A to Z: Great Modern Artists (Illus. by Tuohy, Andy)*
 PW - v262 - i13 - March 30 2015 - p65(1) [51-500]
 y SLJ - v61 - i6 - June 2015 - p145(1) [51-500]
Tupera, Tupera - *Polar Bear's Underwear (Illus. by Tupera, Tupera)*
 c SLJ - v61 - i5 - May 2015 - p80(1) [51-500]
Tupera Tupera (firm) - *Polar Bear's Underwear*
 c HB Guide - v26 - i2 - Fall 2015 - p20(1) [51-500]
 c PW - v262 - i13 - March 30 2015 - p74(1) [51-500]
Turano, Jen - *After a Fashion*
 BL - v111 - i12 - Feb 15 2015 - p42(2) [51-500]
 PW - v262 - i2 - Jan 12 2015 - p44(1) [51-500]
In Good Company
 y BL - v111 - i21 - July 1 2015 - p44(1) [51-500]
Turchi, Peter - *A Muse and a Maze: Writing as Puzzle, Mystery, and Magic*
 RVBW - Jan 2015 - pNA [501+]
 WLT - v89 - i3-4 - May-August 2015 - p127(1) [51-500]
Turcotte, Elies - *Guyana*
 WLT - v89 - i1 - Jan-Feb 2015 - p79(1) [51-500]
Turda, Marius - *Eugenics and Nation in Early 20th Century Hungary*
 HNet - August 2015 - pNA [501+]
Turgeon, David - *La Revanche de l'ecrivaine fantome*
 Can Lit - i224 - Spring 2015 - p121 [501+]
Turgeon, Elizabeth - *La reglisse rouge (Illus. by Colpron, Pascal)*
 c Res Links - v20 - i5 - June 2015 - p45(1) [51-500]
Turing, Dermot - *Prof: Alan Turing Decoded*
 Nature - v526 - i7574 - Oct 22 2015 - p503(1) [51-500]
Turk, James - *The Money Bubble*
 SPBW - Jan 2015 - pNA [501+]
Turkel, Stanley - *Hotel Mavens: Lucius M. Boomer, George C. Boldt and Oscar of the Waldorf*
 NYT - May 3 2015 - p5(L) [501+]

Turkle, Sherry - *Reclaiming Conversation: The Power of Talk in a Digital Age*
 BL - v112 - i1 - Sept 1 2015 - p19(1) [51-500]
 BooChiTr - Oct 24 2015 - p12(1) [51-500]
 CSM - Dec 2 2015 - pNA [501+]
 KR - August 15 2015 - pNA [51-500]
 NYTBR - Oct 4 2015 - p1(L) [501+]
 PW - v262 - i32 - August 10 2015 - p51(2) [51-500]
Turley, Richard Marggraf - *The Cunning House*
 PW - v262 - i37 - Sept 14 2015 - p44(1) [51-500]
Turley, Steven E. - *Franciscan Spirituality and Mission in New Spain, 1524-1599: Conflict beneath the Sycamore Tree (Luke 19: 1-10).*
 AHR - v120 - i2 - April 2015 - p677-678 [501+]
Turnage, Sheila - *The Odds of Getting Even*
 y VOYA - v38 - i4 - Oct 2015 - p64(1) [51-500]
 c BL - v112 - i1 - Sept 1 2015 - p117(2) [51-500]
 c HB - v91 - i6 - Nov-Dec 2015 - p93(1) [51-500]
 c KR - Sept 1 2015 - pNA [51-500]
 c SLJ - v61 - i8 - August 2015 - p93(1) [51-500]
Turnbull, Alison - *Another Green World: Linn Botanic Gardens-Encounters with a Scottish Arcadia*
 TimHES - i2228 - Nov 5 2015 - p48(1) [51-500]
Turnbull, Peter - *In Vino Veritas*
 KR - Jan 1 2016 - pNA [51-500]
Turnbull, Samantha - *The Anti-Princess Club Series (Illus. by Davis, Sarah)*
 c Magpies - v30 - i2 - May 2015 - p39(1) [501+]
Turnbull, Stephanie - *Cool Stuff to Bake*
 c HB Guide - v26 - i1 - Spring 2015 - p175(2) [51-500]
Cool Stuff to Collect
 c HB Guide - v26 - i1 - Spring 2015 - p178(1) [51-500]
Cool Stuff to Grow
 c HB Guide - v26 - i1 - Spring 2015 - p175(1) [51-500]
Cool Stuff to Make with Paper
 c HB Guide - v26 - i1 - Spring 2015 - p178(1) [51-500]
Cool Stuff to Photograph
 c HB Guide - v26 - i1 - Spring 2015 - p180(1) [51-500]
Cool Stuff to Sew
 c HB Guide - v26 - i1 - Spring 2015 - p178(1) [51-500]
L'alligator
 c Res Links - v20 - i3 - Feb 2015 - p52(1) [51-500]
Racehorses
 c BL - v111 - i17 - May 1 2015 - p87(1) [51-500]
Show Horses
 c BL - v111 - i17 - May 1 2015 - p87(1) [51-500]
 c HB Guide - v26 - i2 - Fall 2015 - p182(1) [51-500]
Sports Horses
 c BL - v111 - i17 - May 1 2015 - p87(1) [51-500]
Survival Challenge
 c HB Guide - v26 - i2 - Fall 2015 - p190(1) [51-500]
Wild Horses
 c BL - v111 - i17 - May 1 2015 - p87(1) [51-500]
Turnbull, Victoria - *The Sea Tiger (Illus. by Turnbull, Victoria)*
 c BL - v112 - i4 - Oct 15 2015 - p54(1) [51-500]
 c KR - August 1 2015 - pNA [51-500]
 c PW - v262 - i35 - August 31 2015 - p88(1) [51-500]
Turner, Adair - *Between Debt and the Devil: Money, Credit, and Fixing Global Finance*
 NS - v144 - i5290 - Nov 27 2015 - p48(2) [501+]
Turner, Ann - *My Name Is Truth: The Life of Sojourner Truth (Illus. by Ransome, James E.)*
 c CCB-B - v68 - i7 - March 2015 - p373(2) [51-500]
My Name Is Truth: The Life of Sojourner Truth (Illus. by Ransome, James)
 c BL - v111 - i9-10 - Jan 1 2015 - p76(1) [51-500]
My Name Is Truth: The Life of Sojourner Truth (Illus. by Ransome, James E.)
 c HB Guide - v26 - i2 - Fall 2015 - p212(2) [51-500]
 c NYTBR - Feb 8 2015 - p22(L) [501+]
 c PW - v262 - i49 - Dec 2 2015 - p48(2) [51-500]
Turner, Brian - *My Life as a Foreign Country*
 NYTBR - Jan 11 2015 - p19(L) [501+]
 NYTBR - Dec 27 2015 - p24(L) [501+]
Turner, David - *The Old Boys: The Decline and Rise of the Public School*
 NS - v144 - i5254 - March 20 2015 - p42(3) [501+]
 Spec - v327 - i9735 - March 28 2015 - p38(1) [501+]
 TimHES - i2211 - July 9 2015 - p47(1) [501+]
 TLS - i5851 - May 22 2015 - p24(1) [501+]

Turner, Denys - *Julian of Norwich, Theologian*
    CHR - v101 - i3 - Summer 2015 - p629(2) [501+]
  Thomas Aquinas: A Portrait
    JR - v95 - i3 - July 2015 - p397(3) [501+]
Turner, Henry (b. 1962-) - *Ask the Dark (Read by Hoppe, Lincoln). Audiobook Review*
    c SLJ - v61 - i7 - July 2015 - p50(1) [51-500]
  Ask the Dark
    BL - v111 - i14 - March 15 2015 - p65(1) [51-500]
    y CCB-B - v68 - i9 - May 2015 - p470(1) [51-500]
    y HB Guide - v26 - i2 - Fall 2015 - p142(1) [51-500]
    y KR - Feb 1 2015 - pNA [51-500]
    PW - v262 - i7 - Feb 16 2015 - p181(2) [51-500]
    SLJ - v61 - i2 - Feb 2015 - p109(1) [51-500]
    y VOYA - v37 - i6 - Feb 2015 - p68(2) [51-500]
Turner, Henry S.H. - *Early Modern Theatricality*
    Six Ct J - v46 - i2 - Summer 2015 - p498-499 [501+]
    Ren Q - v68 - i1 - Spring 2015 - p389-390 [501+]
    Specu - v90 - i3 - July 2015 - p862-864 [501+]
Turner, James (b. 1946-) - *Philology: The Forgotten Origins of the Modern Humanities*
    AHR - v120 - i2 - April 2015 - p555-558 [501+]
    J Phil - v112 - i5 - May 2015 - p280(1) [501+]
    RAH - v43 - i3 - Sept 2015 - p411-419 [501+]
Turner, James Morton - *The Promise of Wilderness: American Enviromental Politics since 1964*
    Am Q - v67 - i1 - March 2015 - p267-276 [501+]
Turner, Jane - *It's Not Fair - Or Is It?*
    TES - i5158 - August 7 2015 - p35(1) [501+]
Turner, Jessica N. - *The Fringe Hours: Making Time for You*
    PW - v262 - i3 - Jan 19 2015 - p78(1) [51-500]
Turner, John D. - *Banking in Crisis: The Rise and Fall of British Banking Stability, 1800 to the Present*
    BHR - v89 - i3 - Autumn 2015 - p575(4) [501+]
Turner, John P. - *Inquisition in Early Islam: The Competition for Political and Religious Authority in the Abbasid Empire*
    AHR - v120 - i4 - Oct 2015 - p1572-1573 [501+]
Turner, Katherine Leonard - *How the Other Half Ate: A History of Working-Class Meals at the Turn of the Century*
    AHR - v120 - i1 - Feb 2015 - p263-264 [501+]
    RAH - v43 - i3 - Sept 2015 - p527-531 [501+]
Turner, Kristy - *But I Could Never Go Vegan!: 125 Recipes That Prove You Can Live without Cheese, It's Not All Rabbit Food, and Your Friends Will Still Come Over for Dinner*
    Veg J - v34 - i3 - July-Sept 2015 - p30(1) [51-500]
Turner, Marc - *When the Heavens Fall*
    KR - March 15 2015 - pNA [51-500]
    PW - v262 - i9 - March 2 2015 - p68(1) [51-500]
Turner, Mark - *The Origin of Ideas: Blending, Creativity, and the Human Spark*
    J Phil - v112 - i5 - May 2015 - p280(1) [501+]
Turner, Max - *New Order*
    y Res Links - v20 - i4 - April 2015 - p33(1) [51-500]
Turner, Pamela S. - *Samurai Rising: The Epic Life of Minamoto Yoshitsune (Illus. by Hinds, Gareth)*
    c BL - v112 - i4 - Oct 15 2015 - p40(1) [51-500]
    c KR - Nov 15 2015 - pNA [51-500]
    y SLJ - v61 - i12 - Dec 2015 - p147(2) [51-500]
Turner, Ralph V. - *Magna Carta through the Ages*
    HT - v65 - i6 - June 2015 - p56(2) [51-500]
Turner, Richard H. - *Hog: Perfect Pork Recipes from the Snout to the Squeak*
    Bwatch - June 2015 - pNA [51-500]
Turner, Sarah - *Red Stamps and Gold Stars: Fieldwork Dilemmas in Upland Socialist Asia*
    Pac A - v88 - i2 - June 2015 - p266 [501+]
Turner, Stephen L. - *The Last Trail West*
    Roundup M - v22 - i3 - Feb 2015 - p28(1) [501+]
    Roundup M - v22 - i6 - August 2015 - p33(1) [501+]
Turner, Stephen P. - *American Sociology: From Pre-Disciplinary to Post-Normal*
    CS - v44 - i1 - Jan 2015 - p146-147 [501+]
  The Politics of Expertise
    CS - v44 - i6 - Nov 2015 - p876-877 [501+]
Turner, Steve - *The Complete Beatles Songs: The Story Behind Every Beatles Song*
    LJ - v140 - i17 - Oct 15 2015 - p111(1) [51-500]
Turner, T.J. - *Lincoln's Bodyguard*
    PW - v262 - i6 - Feb 9 2015 - p48(1) [51-500]
Turner, Tom - *Palm Beach Nasty*
    RVBW - Sept 2015 - pNA [501+]

Turner, Tracey - *Deadly Snakes*
    Sci & Ch - v53 - i4 - Dec 2015 - p96 [501+]
  Hard as Nails in Ancient Rome (Illus. by Lenman, Jamie)
    c BL - v111 - i15 - April 1 2015 - p61(1) [51-500]
  How to Make a Human out of Soup (Illus. by Kindberg, Sally)
    c Sch Lib - v63 - i4 - Winter 2015 - p240(1) [51-500]
  In Ancient Egypt
    c Res Links - v21 - i1 - Oct 2015 - p27(1) [501+]
  In Ancient Greece
    c Res Links - v21 - i1 - Oct 2015 - p27(1) [501+]
  In Ancient Rome
    c Res Links - v21 - i1 - Oct 2015 - p27(1) [501+]
  Lost: Can You Survive? Series
    c Res Links - v20 - i4 - April 2015 - p13(2) [501+]
  Warriors
    c Res Links - v21 - i1 - Oct 2015 - p27(1) [501+]
Turney, Jon - *I, Superorganism: Learning to Love Your Inner Ecosystem*
    TimHES - i2198 - April 9 2015 - p52(1) [51-500]
  The Singular Universe and the Reality of Time: A Proposal in Natural Philosophy
    TimHES - i2192 - Feb 26 2015 - p51(1) [51-500]
Turnock, Julie A. - *Plastic Reality: Special Effects, Technology, and the Emergence of 1970s Blockbuster Aesthetics*
    FQ - v68 - i4 - Summer 2015 - p92(3) [501+]
Turoma, Sanna - *Empire De/Centered: New Spatial Histories of Russia and the Soviet Union*
    Slav R - v74 - i1 - Spring 2015 - p205-206 [501+]
Turrettini, Unni - *The Mystery of the Lone Wolf Killer: Anders Behring Breivik and the Threat of Terror in Plain Sight*
    KR - Sept 1 2015 - pNA [501+]
    LJ - v140 - i17 - Oct 15 2015 - p103(1) [51-500]
    PW - v262 - i35 - August 31 2015 - p78(1) [51-500]
Tursten, Helene - *The Beige Man*
    RVBW - Nov 2015 - pNA [501+]
  The Fire Dance (Illus. by Wideburg, Laura A.)
    RVBW - Jan 2015 - pNA [51-500]
  The Treacherous Net
    BL - v112 - i3 - Oct 1 2015 - p28(1) [51-500]
    KR - Oct 15 2015 - pNA [51-500]
    PW - v262 - i42 - Oct 19 2015 - p55(2) [51-500]
Turtledove, Harry - *Bombs Away*
    BL - v111 - i19-20 - June 1 2015 - p59(1) [51-500]
    KR - May 15 2015 - pNA [51-500]
    PW - v262 - i19 - May 11 2015 - p41(1) [51-500]
  We Install and Other Stories
    PW - v262 - i18 - May 4 2015 - p101(1) [51-500]
Tushnet, Eve - *Gay and Catholic: Accepting My Sexuality, Finding Community, Living My Faith*
    Comw - v142 - i3 - Feb 6 2015 - p28(3) [501+]
Tuson, Penelope - *Western Women Travelling East, 1716-1916*
    TLS - i5849 - May 8 2015 - p21(1) [501+]
Tuszynska, Agata - *Family History of Fear*
    KR - Dec 15 2015 - pNA [501+]
Tutino, Stefania - *Shadows of Doubt: Language and Truth in Post-Reformation Catholic Culture*
    CHR - v101 - i4 - Autumn 2015 - p935(3) [501+]
    HNet - Feb 2015 - pNA [501+]
    Ren Q - v68 - i2 - Summer 2015 - p671-672 [501+]
    Theol St - v76 - i3 - Sept 2015 - p608(3) [501+]
Tutka-Gwozdz, Magdalena - *Shattered Mirror: The Problem of Identity in the Post-Yugoslav Documentary*
    Slav R - v74 - i3 - Fall 2015 - p628-630 [501+]
Tutt, Rona - *Access for Everyone: Supporting Special Needs through the School Library*
    Sch Lib - v63 - i1 - Spring 2015 - p35(1) [501+]
Tuttle, Frank - *All the Paths of Shadow*
    RVBW - Nov 2015 - pNA [501+]
Tuttle, Merlin - *The Secret Lives of Bats: My Adventures with the World's Most Misunderstood Mammals*
    KR - August 1 2015 - pNA [501+]
    Nature - v527 - i7577 - Nov 12 2015 - p163(1) [51-500]
Tutu, Desmond - *In God's Hands: The Archbishop of Canterbury's Lent Book 2015*
    CC - v132 - i4 - Feb 18 2015 - p43(1) [51-500]
Tuvim, Aleksandr - *The Doors You Mark Are Your Own*
    KR - Jan 15 2015 - pNA [501+]
Tuzzo, Ralph J. - *Murder in My Corner*
    SPBW - June 2015 - pNA [51-500]
Twain, Mark - *Autobiography of Mark Twain, vol. 3*
    KR - Sept 1 2015 - pNA [501+]
  On the Wild West
    TLS - i5854 - June 12 2015 - p24(1) [501+]

Tweddell, C.H. - *Charlie's First War: South Africa, 1899-1900*
    HNet - March 2015 - pNA [501+]
    J Mil H - v79 - i2 - April 2015 - p501-502 [501+]
Tweedie, James - *The Age of New Waves: Art Cinema and the Staging of Globalization*
    J Phil - v112 - i5 - May 2015 - p280(1) [501+]
Tweedy, Damon - *Black Man in a White Coat: A Doctor's Reflections on Race and Medicine*
    BL - v112 - i7 - Dec 1 2015 - p13(1) [501+]
    BooChiTr - Oct 17 2015 - p13(1) [501+]
    KR - July 1 2015 - pNA [501+]
    LJ - v140 - i12 - July 2015 - p104(1) [51-500]
    NYT - Sept 14 2015 - pC1(L) [501+]
    NYTBR - Sept 13 2015 - p24(L) [501+]
    PW - v262 - i30 - July 27 2015 - p58(2) [501+]
    BL - v111 - i22 - August 1 2015 - p12(1) [51-500]
    Mac - v128 - i36 - Sept 14 2015 - p74(2) [501+]
Twelve Hawks, John - *Spark (Read by Brick, Scott). Audiobook Review*
    PW - v262 - i5 - Feb 2 2015 - p54(2) [51-500]
Twentieth Century Society - *100 Buildings 100 Years*
    LJ - v140 - i5 - March 15 2015 - p99(2) [501+]
Twinam, Ann - *Purchasing Whiteness: Pardos, Mulattos, and the Quest for Social Mobility in the Spanish Indies*
    JIH - v46 - i3 - Wntr 2016 - p470-471 [501+]
Twiss, Richard - *Rescuing the Gospel from the Cowboys: A Native American Expression of the Jesus Way*
    Bks & Cult - v21 - i6 - Nov-Dec 2015 - p13(2) [501+]
Twitchel, Tom - *Knack*
    y KR - Oct 15 2015 - pNA [501+]
Twohy, Mike - *Oops, Pounce, Quick, Run! (Illus. by Twohy, Mike)*
    c KR - Oct 15 2015 - pNA [51-500]
    c SLJ - v61 - i12 - Dec 2015 - p85(2) [51-500]
Twomey, Christopher P. - *The Military Lens: Doctrinal Difference and Deterrence Failure in Sino-American Relations*
    NWCR - v68 - i1 - Wntr 2015 - p139(2) [501+]
Twyman, Richard M. - *Principles of Proteomics*
    QRB - v90 - i2 - June 2015 - p228(1) [501+]
Ty, Seng - *The Years of Zero: Coming of Age under the Khmer Rouge*
    PW - v262 - i3 - Jan 19 2015 - p73(2) [501+]
Tyacke, Nicholas - *The English Revolution c.1590-1720: Politics, Religion and Communities*
    HNet - July 2015 - pNA [501+]
Tyerman, Christopher - *Chronicles of the First Crusade*
    TimHES - i2193 - March 5 2015 - p49(1) [501+]
  How to Plan a Crusade: Reason and Religious War in the Middle Ages
    Lon R Bks - v37 - i18 - Sept 24 2015 - p17(2) [501+]
    Spec - v328 - i9758 - Sept 5 2015 - p39(2) [501+]
Tyldesley, Esther - *Buy Me the Sky: The Remarkable Truth of China's One-Child Generation*
    Econ - v415 - i8941 - June 6 2015 - p75(US) [501+]
Tyldum, Morten - *The Imitation Game*
    G&L Rev W - v22 - i2 - March-April 2015 - p28(4) [501+]
    G&L Rev W - v22 - i2 - March-April 2015 - p28(4) [501+]
    NYRB - v62 - i2 - Feb 5 2015 - p19(3) [501+]
    NYRB - v62 - i2 - Feb 5 2015 - p19(3) [501+]
Tyler, Anne - *A Spool of Blue Thread (Read by Farr, Kimberly). Audiobook Review*
    BL - v111 - i21 - July 1 2015 - p79(1) [51-500]
    LJ - v140 - i8 - May 1 2015 - p41(1) [51-500]
    PW - v262 - i21 - May 25 2015 - p54(2) [51-500]
  A Spool of Blue Thread
    BooChiTr - Feb 28 2015 - p14(1) [501+]
    CC - v132 - i9 - April 29 2015 - p38(2) [501+]
    CSM - March 4 2015 - pNA [501+]
    Ent W - i1353 - March 6 2015 - p73(1) [501+]
    HR - v68 - i2 - Summer 2015 - p343-351 [501+]
    LJ - v140 - i2 - Feb 1 2015 - p78(2) [51-500]
    Mac - v128 - i9 - March 2 2015 - p61(1) [501+]
    NS - v144 - i5249 - Feb 13 2015 - p48(3) [501+]
    NY - v91 - i5 - March 23 2015 - p91 [51-500]
    NYRB - v62 - i3 - Feb 19 2015 - p21(2) [501+]
    NYT - Feb 6 2015 - pC29(L) [501+]
    NYTBR - Feb 15 2015 - p13(L) [501+]
    Spec - v327 - i9729 - Feb 14 2015 - p42(1) [501+]
    TLS - i5842 - March 20 2015 - p21(1) [501+]
Tyler, Dominick - *Uncommon Ground: A Word-lover's Guide to the British Landscape*
    Spec - v327 - i9731 - Feb 28 2015 - p36(2) [501+]
    TLS - i5854 - June 12 2015 - p11(1) [501+]
    TLS - i5871 - Oct 9 2015 - p32(1) [501+]

Tyler, John W. - *The Correspondence of Thomas Hutchinson, vol. 1: 1740-1766*
    JAH - v102 - i1 - June 2015 - p228-229 [501+]

Tyler, L.C. - *Crooked Herring*
    PW - v262 - i22 - June 1 2015 - p43(1) [51-500]

Tyler, Margaret - *The Mirror of Princely Deed and Knighthood*
    TLS - i5834 - Jan 23 2015 - p26(1) [501+]

Tyler, Paige - *Her Wild Hero*
    BL - v111 - i17 - May 1 2015 - p80(2) [51-500]
    PW - v262 - i13 - March 30 2015 - p62(1) [51-500]

  Wolf Trouble
    BL - v111 - i21 - July 1 2015 - p45(1) [501+]
    PW - v262 - i24 - June 15 2015 - p70(1) [51-500]

Tyler, Stephanie - *Vipers Rule*
    PW - v262 - i21 - May 25 2015 - p43(2) [51-500]

Tylus, Jane - *Siena: City of Secrets*
    TimHES - i2205 - May 28 2015 - p46-47 [501+]
    TLS - i5869 - Sept 25 2015 - p27(1) [501+]

Tym, Kate - *Etre genereux*
  c Res Links - v21 - i1 - Oct 2015 - p57(1) [51-500]

  Etre gentil
  c Res Links - v21 - i1 - Oct 2015 - p57(1) [51-500]

  Etre honnete
  c Res Links - v21 - i1 - Oct 2015 - p57(1) [51-500]

  Etre poli
  c Res Links - v21 - i1 - Oct 2015 - p57(1) [51-500]

Tymony, Cy - *Sneaky Math: A Graphic Primer with Projects*
    BL - v111 - i14 - March 15 2015 - p57(2) [51-500]

Tynan, Jane - *British Army Uniform and the First World War: Men in Khaki*
    TimHES - i2187 - Jan 22 2015 - p49(1) [501+]

Tynan, Katy - *Free Agent: The Independent Professional's Roadmap to Self-Employment Success*
    RVBW - June 2015 - pNA [51-500]

Tyre, Lisa Lewis - *Last in a Long Line of Rebels*
  c BL - v111 - i21 - July 1 2015 - p73(1) [51-500]
  c KR - June 15 2015 - pNA [51-500]
  c PW - v262 - i24 - June 15 2015 - p84(1) [51-500]
  c PW - v262 - i49 - Dec 2 2015 - p66(1) [51-500]
  c SLJ - v61 - i8 - August 2015 - p93(1) [51-500]

Tyrell, Chuck - *Return to Silver Creek*
    Roundup M - v22 - i6 - August 2015 - p33(1) [501+]

Tyson, Stephanie L. - *Soul Food Odyssey*
    RVBW - Oct 2015 - pNA [51-500]

Tyson, Tiffany Quay - *Three Rivers*
    BL - v111 - i19-20 - June 1 2015 - p46(1) [51-500]

Tytell, John - *The Beat Interviews: Conversations with Allen Ginsberg, William S. Burroughs, John Clellon Holmes, Herbert Huncke and Carl Solomon*
    ABR - v36 - i4 - May-June 2015 - p30(1) [501+]

Tzara, Tristan - *Vingt-Cinq poemes*
    TLS - i5851 - May 22 2015 - p16(1) [501+]

U

U.S. Military Academy - *West Point History of World War II, vol. 1*
  LJ - v140 - i20 - Dec 1 2015 - p117(1) [51-500]

U.S. Senate Select Committee on Intelligence - *Executive Summary: Committee Study of the Central Intelligence Agency's Detention and Interrogation Program*
  For Aff - v94 - i3 - May-June 2015 - pNA [501+]
Minority Views of Vice Chairman Chambliss Joined by Senators Burr, Risch, Coats, Rubio, and Coburn: Committee Study of the Central Intelligence Agency's Detention and Interrogation Program
  For Aff - v94 - i3 - May-June 2015 - pNA [501+]

Ubl, Karl - *Die Karolinger: Herrscher und Reich*
  HNet - Jan 2015 - pNA [501+]

Ubungswissen in Religion und Philosophie: Produktion, Weitergabe, Wandel
  HNet - March 2015 - pNA [501+]

Uddenberg, Nils - *The Old Man and the Cat: A Love Story*
  PW - v262 - i35 - August 31 2015 - p80(1) [51-500]

Uegaki, Chieri - *Hana Hashimoto, Sixth Violin (Illus. by Leng, Qin)*
  c HB Guide - v26 - i1 - Spring 2015 - p48(1) [51-500]
  c Res Links - v20 - i3 - Feb 2015 - p54(1) [51-500]

Ueno, Haruki - *Big Hero 6 (Illus. by Ueno, Haruki)*
  c BL - v111 - i19-20 - June 1 2015 - p68(1) [51-500]

Uesugi, Natsuya - *Grydscaen: Tribute*
  SPBW - May 2015 - pNA [51-500]

Uffelman, Minoa d. - *The Diary of Nannie Haskins Williams: A Southern Woman's Story of Rebellion and Reconstruction, 1863-1890*
  JSH - v81 - i3 - August 2015 - p730(2) [501+]

Ug, Philippe - *Robots: Watch Out, Water About! (Illus. by Hall, Cynthia)*
  c BL - v111 - i16 - April 15 2015 - p52(1) [51-500]
  c SLJ - v61 - i6 - June 2015 - p94(1) [51-500]

Uglow, Jenny - *In These Times: Living in Britain through Napoleon's Wars, 1793-1815*
  HT - v65 - i3 - March 2015 - p60(1) [501+]
  Nation - v300 - i24 - June 15 2015 - p35(5) [501+]
  NY - v90 - i47 - Feb 9 2015 - p69 [51-500]
  NYRB - v62 - i17 - Nov 5 2015 - p50(2) [501+]
  NYTBR - Feb 1 2015 - p17(L) [501+]

Uglow, Loyd - *Marksman's Trinity*
  Roundup M - v22 - i6 - August 2015 - p33(1) [501+]

Ukrainetz, Elizabeth - *The Theory of Light at Midnight*
  RVBW - Oct 2015 - pNA [51-500]

Ukraintseva, Valentina V. - *Mammoths and the Environment*
  QRB - v90 - i3 - Sept 2015 - p322(2) [501+]

Ulaby, Fawwaz T. - *Microwave Radar and Radiometric Remote Sensing*
  Bwatch - Sept 2015 - pNA [51-500]

Ulin, David L. - *Sidewalking*
  KR - Sept 1 2015 - pNA [51-500]

Ulin, Julieann Veronica - *Medieval Invasions in Modern Irish Literature*
  ILS - v34 - i2 - Spring 2015 - p4(2) [501+]

Ulitskaya, Ludmila - *The Big Green Tent*
  Atl - v316 - i5 - Dec 2015 - p42(2) [501+]
  KR - Sept 1 2015 - pNA [501+]
  NYTBR - Nov 29 2015 - p19(L) [501+]

Ullmann, Regina - *The Country Road: Stories*
  NYRB - v62 - i16 - Oct 22 2015 - p43(2) [501+]

Ullucci, Daniel - *The Christian Rejection of Animal Sacrifice*
  JR - Jan 2015 - p132(3) [501+]

Ulrich, R.B. - *A Companion to Roman Architecture*
  Class R - v65 - i1 - April 2015 - p263-266 [501+]

Ulrichsen, Kristian Coates - *The First World War in the Middle East*
  J Mil H - v79 - i4 - Oct 2015 - p1163-1164 [501+]

Ultan, Lloyd - *The Bronx: The Ultimate Guide to New York City's Beautiful Borough*
  LJ - v140 - i10 - June 1 2015 - p126(1) [51-500]

Ulturgasheva, Olga - *Narrating the Future in Siberia: Childhood, Adolescence and Autobiography among Young Eveny*
  JRAI - v21 - i1 - March 2015 - p213(2) [501+]

Ulysse, Katia D. - *Drifting*
  WLT - v89 - i1 - Jan-Feb 2015 - p71(3) [501+]

Uman, Deborah - *Staging the Blazon in Early Modern English Theater*
  Ren Q - v68 - i2 - Summer 2015 - p770-772 [501+]

Umoja, Akinyele Omowale - *This Nonviolent Stuff'll Get You Killed: How Guns Made the Civil Rights Movement Possible*
  HNet - August 2015 - pNA [501+]

Umrigar, Thrity - *The Story Hour (Read by Mathan, Sneha). Audiobook Review*
  BL - v111 - i11 - Feb 1 2015 - p60(1) [501+]

Una - *Becoming Unbecoming*
  PW - v262 - i51 - Dec 14 2015 - p69(1) [51-500]

Uncovering the Past Series
  c CH Bwatch - July 2015 - pNA [501+]

Underwood, Deborah - *Bad Bye, Good Bye (Illus. by Bean, Jonathan)*
  c BL - v111 - i9-10 - Jan 1 2015 - p92(1) [501+]
Here Comes Santa Cat (Illus. by Rueda, Claudia)
  c HB Guide - v26 - i1 - Spring 2015 - p17(1) [51-500]
Here Comes the Tooth Fairy Cat (Illus. by Rueda, Claudia)
  c CCB-B - v69 - i1 - Sept 2015 - p61(1) [51-500]
  c HB - v91 - i3 - May-June 2015 - p101(2) [501+]
  c HB Guide - v26 - i2 - Fall 2015 - p20(1) [51-500]
  c KR - March 15 2015 - pNA [51-500]
  SLJ - v61 - i4 - April 2015 - p136(2) [51-500]
Here Comes Valentine Cat (Illus. by Rueda, Claudia)
  c KR - Oct 1 2015 - pNA [51-500]
  c PW - v262 - i41 - Oct 12 2015 - p66(2) [51-500]
  c PW - v262 - i49 - Dec 2 2015 - p60(1) [51-500]
  c SLJ - v61 - i12 - Dec 2015 - p96(1) [51-500]
Interstellar Cinderella (Illus. by Hunt, Meg)
  c BL - v111 - i19-20 - June 1 2015 - p120(1) [51-500]
  c HB - v91 - i4 - July-August 2015 - p126(1) [51-500]
  c PW - v262 - i14 - April 6 2015 - p57(1) [51-500]
  c PW - v262 - i49 - Dec 2 2015 - p23(1) [51-500]
  c SLJ - v61 - i6 - June 2015 - p94(1) [51-500]

Underwood, James Lowell - *Deadly Censorship: Murder, Honor, and Freedom of the Press*
  JSH - v81 - i2 - May 2015 - p494(2) [501+]

Underwood, Michael R. - *The Shootout Solution*
  BL - v112 - i6 - Nov 15 2015 - p32(1) [51-500]

Unfried, Berthold - *Vergangenes Unrecht: Entschadigung und Restitution in einer Globalen Perspektive*
  HNet - Feb 2015 - pNA [501+]

Ungar, Barbara Louise - *Immortal Medusa*
  KR - Oct 1 2015 - pNA [51-500]

Unger, David - *The Mastermind*
  c PW - v262 - i31 - August 3 2015 - p21(1) [51-500]

Unger, Harlow Giles - *Henry Clay: America's Greatest Statesman*
  BL - v112 - i2 - Sept 15 2015 - p6(1) [51-500]
  KR - July 1 2015 - pNA [51-500]
  LJ - v140 - i14 - Sept 1 2015 - p113(1) [51-500]
  PW - v262 - i32 - August 10 2015 - p50(1) [51-500]

Unger, Nancy C. - *Beyond Nature's Housekeepers: American Women in Environmental History*
  Wom HR - v24 - i1 - Feb 2015 - p131-132 [501+]

Unger, Peter - *Empty Ideas: A Critique of Analytic Philosophy*
  J Phil - v112 - i5 - May 2015 - p280(1) [501+]
  TLS - i5833 - Jan 16 2015 - p22(2) [501+]

Unger, Roberto Mangabeira - *The Religion of the Future*
  TLS - i5836 - Feb 6 2015 - p28(1) [501+]
The Singular Universe and the Reality of Time
  Spec - v327 - i9726 - Jan 24 2015 - p46(2) [501+]

Unger, Steffen - *Der Konig von Asien: Alexander der Grosse Erobert Persien*
  HNet - March 2015 - pNA [501+]

Unger, Suanne - *Qaqamiigux: Traditional Foods and Recipes from the Aleutian and Pribilof Islands*
  LJ - v140 - i7 - April 15 2015 - p121(1) [51-500]

Ungerer, Tomi - *Snail, Where Are You? (Illus. by Ungerer, Tomi)*
  c SLJ - v61 - i6 - June 2015 - p94(2) [51-500]

United States. Department of the Navy - *How We Fight: Handbook for the Naval Warfighter*
  NWCR - v68 - i4 - Autumn 2015 - p143(2) [501+]

United States Postal Service - *The USPS 2014 Stamp Yearbook*
  Phil Lit R - v64 - i2 - Spring 2015 - p143(2) [501+]

Unkefer, Dean - *90 Church: Inside America's Notorious First Narcotics Squad*
  BL - v111 - i16 - April 15 2015 - p4(1) [51-500]
  KR - March 15 2015 - pNA [501+]
  LJ - v140 - i8 - May 1 2015 - p87(1) [51-500]
  PW - v262 - i11 - March 16 2015 - p73(1) [51-500]

Unnithan-Kumar, Maya - *Fatness and the Maternal Body: Women's Experiences of Corporeality and the Shaping of Social Policy*
  CWS - v30 - i2-3 - Fall-Winter 2015 - p135(2) [501+]

Unsworth, Emma Jane - *Animals*
  BL - v112 - i3 - Oct 1 2015 - p22(1) [51-500]
  KR - August 1 2015 - pNA [51-500]
  NYT - Sept 28 2015 - pC4(L) [501+]
  y NYTBR - Sept 20 2015 - p30(L) [501+]

Unsworth, Simon Kurt - *The Devil's Detective*
  BL - v111 - i11 - Feb 1 2015 - p25(2) [51-500]
  KR - Feb 15 2015 - pNA [51-500]
  PW - v262 - i1 - Jan 5 2015 - p56(1) [51-500]

Untermeyer, Chase - *Inside Reagan's Navy: The Pentagon Journals*
  Bwatch - June 2015 - pNA [51-500]
  NWCR - v68 - i4 - Autumn 2015 - p119(2) [501+]

Unteroberdoerster, Olaf - *Cambodia: Entering a New Phase of Growth*
  Pac A - v88 - i3 - Sept 2015 - p735 [501+]

Unterwegs auf Pilgerstrassen. Pilger aus dem Polnischen und Deutschen Raum im Spatmittelalter und der Fruhen Neuzeit
  HNet - Jan 2015 - pNA [501+]

Unterwegs im Namen der Religion II: Wege und Ziele in Vergleichender Perspektive - das Mittelalterliche Europa und Asien
  HNet - June 2015 - pNA [501+]

Untiedt, Kenneth L. - *Cowboys, Cops, Killers, and Ghosts: Legends and Lore in Texas*
  SHQ - v118 - i3 - Jan 2015 - p320-321 [501+]

Updike, John - *Selected Poems*
  NY - v91 - i34 - Nov 2 2015 - p86 [501+]
  NYRB - v62 - i20 - Dec 17 2015 - p73(2) [501+]
  NYT - Dec 23 2015 - pC1(L) [501+]

Uppal, Priscila - *Cover before Striking*
Nat Post - v17 - i74 - Jan 24 2015 - pWP9(1) [501+]

Upson, Matt - *Information Now: A Graphic Guide to Student Research*
y BL - v112 - i6 - Nov 15 2015 - p35(1) [51-500]
LJ - v140 - i19 - Nov 15 2015 - p5(1) [51-500]

Upton, Elizabeth - *Maxi the Little Taxi (Illus. by Cole, Henry)*
c KR - Jan 1 2016 - pNA [51-500]

Ur, Jason A. - *Urbanism and Cultural Landscapes in Northeastern Syria: The Tell Hamoukar Survey 1999-2001*
JNES - v74 - i1 - April 2015 - p145(6) [501+]

Ural, Susannah J. - *Don't Hurry Me Down to Hades: The Civil War in the Words of Those Who Lived It*
JSH - v81 - i1 - Feb 2015 - p204(2) [501+]

Urasek, Lauren - *Popular: The Ups and Downs of Online Dating from the Most Popular Girl in New York City*
PW - v262 - i38 - Sept 21 2015 - p70(1) [51-500]

Urbach, Karina - *Go-Betweens for Hitler*
HT - v65 - i10 - Oct 2015 - p56(2) [501+]

Urban, Hugh B. - *The Church of Scientology: A History of a New Religion*
JAH - v102 - i2 - Sept 2015 - p608-609 [501+]

Urban, Linda - *Little Red Henry (Illus. by Valentine, Madeline)*
c CH Bwatch - June 2015 - pNA [501+]
c HB - v91 - i2 - March-April 2015 - p85(2) [51-500]
c HB Guide - v26 - i2 - Fall 2015 - p20(1) [51-500]
KR - Feb 1 2015 - pNA [51-500]
c PW - v262 - i5 - Feb 2 2015 - p59(1) [51-500]
c PW - v262 - i49 - Dec 2 2015 - p30(1) [51-500]
c SLJ - v61 - i4 - April 2015 - p137(1) [51-500]
Milo Speck, Accidental Agent (Illus. by Epelbaum, Mariano)
c BL - v111 - i21 - July 1 2015 - p74(1) [51-500]
c HB - v91 - i5 - Sept-Oct 2015 - p121(1) [51-500]
Milo Speck: Accidental Agent (Illus. by Epelbaum, Mariano)
c KR - June 1 2015 - pNA [51-500]
Milo Speck, Accidental Agent (Illus. by Epelbaum, Mariano)
c PW - v262 - i22 - June 1 2015 - p60(1) [51-500]
c SLJ - v61 - i7 - July 2015 - p84(1) [51-500]
Mouse Was Mad
c CH Bwatch - August 2015 - pNA [501+]
Weekends with Max and His Dad
c KR - Jan 1 2016 - pNA [51-500]

Urbani, Ellen - *Landfall*
KR - June 15 2015 - pNA [51-500]

Urbano, A.P. - *The Philosophical Life. Biography and the Crafting of Intellectual Identity in Late Antiquity*
Class R - v65 - i1 - April 2015 - p98-99 [501+]

Urbanovic, Jackie - *Prince of a Frog (Illus. by Urbanovic, Jackie)*
c HB Guide - v26 - i2 - Fall 2015 - p20(1) [51-500]
c KR - Feb 15 2015 - pNA [51-500]

Urbanski, Charity - *Writing History for the King: Henry II and the Politics of Vernacular Historiography*
HER - v130 - i544 - June 2015 - p697(3) [501+]

Urbina, Martin Guevara - *Latino Access to Higher Education: Ethnic Realities and New Directions for the Twenty-first Century*
RVBW - Nov 2015 - pNA [501+]
Latino Police Officers in the United States: An Examination of Emerging Trends and Issues
RVBW - July 2015 - pNA [501+]

Ureneck, Lou - *The Great Fire: One American's Mission to Rescue Victims of the 20th Century's First Genocide*
Ch Today - v59 - i6 - July-August 2015 - p91(1) [51-500]
KR - March 1 2015 - pNA [51-500]
LJ - v140 - i6 - April 1 2015 - p105(1) [51-500]

Urey, Gary - *Super Schnoz and the Invasion of the Snore Snatchers (Illus. by Frawley, Keith)*
c HB Guide - v26 - i1 - Spring 2015 - p95(1) [51-500]

Urofsky, Melvin I. - *Dissent and the Supreme Court: Its Role in the Court's History and the Nation's Constitutional Dialogue*
BL - v112 - i4 - Oct 15 2015 - p7(1) [51-500]
KR - July 1 2015 - pNA [51-500]
LJ - v140 - i13 - August 1 2015 - p112(1) [501+]
NYTBR - Oct 25 2015 - p24(L) [501+]
PW - v262 - i23 - June 8 2015 - p48(1) [51-500]

Uroskie, Andrew V. - *Between the Black Box and the White Cube: Expanded Cinema and Postwar Art*
Afterimage - v42 - i5 - March-April 2015 - p35(1) [501+]

Urquhart, Emily - *Beyond the Pale: Folklore, Family and the Mystery of Our Hidden Genes*
BL - v111 - i15 - April 1 2015 - p9(1) [51-500]
KR - Feb 15 2015 - pNA [51-500]

Urquhart, Jane - *The Night Stages*
BL - v111 - i21 - July 1 2015 - p33(1) [51-500]
KR - May 15 2015 - pNA [51-500]
LJ - v140 - i11 - June 15 2015 - p82(1) [51-500]
Mac - v128 - i15 - April 20 2015 - p56(1) [51-500]
NY - v91 - i26 - Sept 7 2015 - p82 [51-500]
NYT - July 27 2015 - pC4(L) [501+]
PW - v262 - i19 - May 11 2015 - p30(2) [51-500]

Urquhart, Rachel - *The Visionist*
NYTBR - April 5 2015 - p28(L) [501+]

Urquijo-Ruiz, Rita E. - *Wild Tongues: Transnational Mexican Popular Culture*
AL - v87 - i3 - Sept 2015 - p624-627 [501+]
Aztlan - v40 - i1 - Spring 2015 - p253-257 [501+]

Urrea, Luis Alberto - *The Tijuana Book of the Dead*
BL - v111 - i11 - Feb 1 2015 - p18(1) [51-500]
LJ - v140 - i3 - Feb 15 2015 - p106(2) [51-500]
PW - v262 - i3 - Jan 19 2015 - p56(1) [51-500]
The Water Museum
KR - Feb 1 2015 - pNA [501+]
BL - v111 - i14 - March 15 2015 - p44(1) [51-500]
LJ - v140 - i6 - April 1 2015 - p87(1) [51-500]
PW - v262 - i7 - Feb 16 2015 - p152(1) [51-500]

Urschel, Joe - *The Year of Fear: Machine Gun Kelly and the Manhunt That Changed the Nation*
BL - v111 - i22 - August 1 2015 - p10(1) [51-500]
LJ - v140 - i12 - July 1 2015 - p97(2) [51-500]
PW - v262 - i28 - July 13 2015 - p58(2) [51-500]
The Year of Fear
KR - July 15 2015 - pNA [501+]

Urwand, Ben - *The Collaboration: Hollywood's Pact with Hitler*
Historian - v77 - i3 - Fall 2015 - p637(2) [501+]
JMH - v87 - i3 - Sept 2015 - p718(4) [501+]
RAH - v43 - i1 - March 2015 - p143-148 [501+]

Urza, Gabriel - *All That Followed*
BL - v111 - i19-20 - June 1 2015 - p38(1) [51-500]
KR - June 1 2015 - pNA [501+]
LJ - v140 - i11 - June 15 2015 - p82(1) [51-500]
NYTBR - August 9 2015 - p22(L) [501+]
PW - v262 - i16 - April 20 2015 - p50(1) [51-500]

Usher, David - *Let the Elephants Run: Unlock Your Creativity and Change Everything*
LJ - v140 - i11 - June 15 2015 - p104(1) [51-500]

Usher, Phillip John - *Epic Arts in Renaissance France*
MLR - v110 - i1 - Jan 2015 - p258-260 [501+]
Ren Q - v68 - i2 - Summer 2015 - p749-751 [501+]

Usher, Sam - *Il neige grand-papa!*
c Res Links - v20 - i4 - April 2015 - p42(2) [51-500]
Snow (Illus. by Usher, Sam)
c BL - v112 - i4 - Oct 15 2015 - p54(1) [51-500]
c KR - August 1 2015 - pNA [51-500]
c NYTBR - Nov 8 2015 - p31(L) [501+]
c RVBW - Oct 2015 - pNA [501+]
c SLJ - v61 - i9 - Sept 2015 - p130(1) [51-500]

Usher, Shaun - *Letters of Note: An Eclectic Collection of Correspondence Deserving of a Wider Audience*
LJ - v140 - i13 - August 1 2015 - p126(1) [501+]
More Letters of Note: Correspondence Deserving of a Wider Audience
Spec - v329 - i9765 - Oct 24 2015 - p45(1) [501+]

Usselman, Melvyn C. - *Pure Intelligence: The Life of William Hyde Wollaston*
Nature - v524 - i7563 - August 6 2015 - p33(1) [51-500]
TimHES - i2226 - Oct 22 2015 - p46-47 [501+]

Utley, Robert M. - *Wanted*
KR - Oct 1 2015 - pNA [501+]

Utopie und Alltag. Perspektiven auf Ideal und Praxis im 20. Jahrhundert
HNet - May 2015 - pNA [501+]

Utton, Dominic - *Martin Harbottle's Appreciation of Time*
LJ - v140 - i13 - August 1 2015 - p126(1) [501+]

Uttridge, Sarah - *Ocean Animals around the World*
c HB Guide - v26 - i1 - Spring 2015 - p155(1) [51-500]

Uusma, Bea - *The Expedition: A Love Story - Solving the Mystery of a Polar Tragedy*
TLS - i5840 - March 6 2015 - p28(2) [501+]

Uytanlet, Samson - *Luke-Acts and Jewish Historiography: A Study on the Theology, Literature, and Ideology of Luke-Acts*
Theol St - v76 - i3 - Sept 2015 - p602(2) [501+]

V

Vaage, Leif E. - *Borderline Exegesis*
    Theol St - v76 - i2 - June 2015 - p347(2) [501+]
Vacano, Diego A. Von - *The Color of Citizenship: Race, Modernity, and Latin American/ Hispanic Political Thought*
    HAHR - v95 - i1 - Feb 2015 - p142-144 [501+]
Vachss, Andrew - *SignWave*
    BL - v111 - i18 - May 15 2015 - p29(1) [51-500]
    KR - April 1 2015 - pNA [51-500]
    PW - v262 - i17 - April 27 2015 - p50(2) [51-500]
Vagi, Zoltan - *The Holocaust in Hungary: Evolution of a Genocide*
    HNet - April 2015 - pNA [501+]
Vahanian, Noelle - *The Rebellious No: Variations on a Secular Theology of Language*
    J Phil - v112 - i5 - May 2015 - p280(1) [501+]
Vail, Rachel - *Unfriended (Read by Allen, Corey).* Audiobook Review
    y BL - v111 - i11 - Feb 1 2015 - p62(1) [51-500]
Unfriended
    y HB Guide - v26 - i1 - Spring 2015 - p126(1) [51-500]
Vaill, Amanda - *Hotel Florida: Truth, Love, and Death in the Spanish Civil War*
    y Ent W - i1358 - April 10 2015 - p66(1) [501+]
    NYTBR - May 31 2015 - p52(L) [501+]
    NWCR - v68 - i3 - Summer 2015 - p160(2) [501+]
Vaillant, John - *The Jaguar's Children.* Audiobook Review
    LJ - v140 - i7 - April 15 2015 - p47(3) [51-500]
The Jaguar's Children
    Mac - v128 - i1 - Jan 12 2015 - p69(2) [501+]
    Nat Post - v17 - i62 - Jan 10 2015 - pWP9(1) [501+]
    NYTBR - Feb 15 2015 - p15(L) [501+]
Vailly, Joelle - *The Birth of a Genetics Policy: Social Issues of Newborn Screening*
    CS - v44 - i6 - Nov 2015 - p862-864 [501+]
Vaizey, Hester - *Born in the GDR: Living in the Shadow of the Wall*
    HT - v65 - i5 - May 2015 - p64(2) [501+]
    CSM - Jan 7 2015 - pNA [501+]
Vajpeyi, Ananya - *Righteous Republic: The Political Foundations of Modern India*
    HNet - Feb 2015 - pNA [501+]
Valckx, Catharina - *La Fete de Billy (Illus. by Valckx, Catharina)*
    c Bkbird - v53 - i1 - Wntr 2015 - p75(1) [501+]
Vale, Lawrence J. - *Purging the Poorest: Public Housing and the Design Politics of Twice-Cleared Communities*
    CS - v44 - i1 - Jan 2015 - p128-130 [501+]
Valencia, Debra - *Sewing Pretty Bags: Boutique Designs to Stitch and Love*
    LJ - v140 - i8 - May 1 2015 - p73(2) [51-500]
Valente, Catherynne M. - *The Boy Who Lost Fairyland (Illus. by Juan, Ana)*
    y HB - v91 - i3 - May-June 2015 - p121(2) [51-500]
    c HB Guide - v26 - i2 - Fall 2015 - p142(1) [51-500]
    c KR - Jan 15 2015 - pNA [51-500]
    SLJ - v61 - i3 - March 2015 - p167(1) [51-500]
Radiance
    BL - v112 - i3 - Oct 1 2015 - p36(1) [51-500]
    NYT - Oct 30 2015 - pC35(L) [501+]
    KR - June 15 2015 - pNA [51-500]
    PW - v262 - i33 - August 17 2015 - p55(1) [51-500]
Six-Gun Snow White
    KR - Sept 1 2015 - pNA [51-500]
Speak Easy
    PW - v262 - i26 - June 29 2015 - p50(1) [51-500]
Valenti, Pia - *The Garden of Monsieur Monet (Illus. by Ascari, Giancarlo)*
    c SLJ - v61 - i11 - Nov 2015 - p133(1) [51-500]

Valentin, Barbara - *False Start*
    PW - v262 - i37 - Sept 14 2015 - p48(1) [51-500]
Help Wanted
    PW - v262 - i38 - Sept 21 2015 - p61(2) [51-500]
Valentine, Genevieve - *Persona*
    PW - v262 - i2 - Jan 12 2015 - p40(1) [51-500]
Valentine, Jean - *Shirt in Heaven*
    PW - v262 - i20 - May 18 2015 - p63(1) [51-500]
    NYTBR - Dec 27 2015 - p26(L) [51-500]
Valentine, Jenny - *Fire Colour One*
    y Sch Lib - v63 - i3 - Autumn 2015 - p186(1) [51-500]
Valentine, Madeline - *George in the Dark (Illus. by Valentine, Madeline)*
    c HB Guide - v26 - i1 - Spring 2015 - p17(1) [51-500]
Valentine, Marquita - *Take the Fall*
    PW - v262 - i22 - June 1 2015 - p47(1) [51-500]
Valentine, Stephen J. - *The Lazarus Game*
    SLJ - v61 - i3 - March 2015 - p163(1) [51-500]
Valentine, Tamara - *What the Waves Know*
    KR - Dec 1 2015 - pNA [51-500]
    LJ - v140 - i20 - Dec 1 2015 - p97(1) [51-500]
Valentini, Andrea - *Le Livre des epistres du debat sus 'Le rommant de la Rose'*
    FS - v69 - i4 - Oct 2015 - p521-522 [501+]
Valentinis, Pia - *The Garden of Monsieur Monet (Illus. by Valentinis, Pia)*
    c KR - Sept 15 2015 - pNA [51-500]
Valentino, Serena - *The Beast Within: A Tale of Beauty's Prince*
    c HB Guide - v26 - i1 - Spring 2015 - p95(1) [51-500]
Valenza, A.M. - *Alexey Dyed in Red*
    PW - v262 - i39 - Sept 28 2015 - p74(1) [51-500]
Valenzuela, Luisa - *Diario de mascaras*
    WLT - v89 - i5 - Sept-Oct 2015 - p79(1) [501+]
Valerio-Jimenez, Omar S. - *River of Hope: Forging Identity and Nation in the Rio Grande Borderlands*
    HAHR - v95 - i1 - Feb 2015 - p187-188 [501+]
    PHR - v84 - i1 - Feb 2015 - p120(2) [501+]
Valiaho, Pasi - *Biopolitical Screens: Image, Power, and the Neoliberal Brain*
    Afterimage - v42 - i6 - May-June 2015 - p37(3) [501+]
Valiente, O. Ernesto - *Liberation through Reconciliation: Jon Sobrino's Christological Spirituality*
    Theol St - v76 - i4 - Dec 2015 - p879(2) [501+]
Valk, Laurens - *The LEGO Mindstorms EV3 Discovery Book: A Beginner's Guide to Building and Programming Robots*
    y VOYA - v38 - i1 - April 2015 - p88(1) [51-500]
Valkenberg, Pim - *World Religions in Dialogue: A Comparative Theological Approach*
    Theol St - v76 - i1 - March 2015 - p215(1) [501+]
Vallance, Jess - *Birdy*
    Sch Lib - v63 - i4 - Winter 2015 - p250(1) [51-500]
Valle, Laura Cristina del - *Los hijos del poder. De la elite capitular a la Revolucion de Mayo: Buenos Aires 1776-1810*
    HNet - April 2015 - pNA [501+]
Valle, Suzette - *101 Movies to See before You Grow Up*
    c BL - v112 - i6 - Nov 15 2015 - p37(1) [51-500]
Vallely, Paul - *Pope Francis: The Struggle for the Soul of Catholicism, 2d ed.*
    KR - August 1 2015 - pNA [501+]
    LJ - v140 - i6 - April 1 2015 - p108(1) [51-500]
    NS - v144 - i5278 - Sept 4 2015 - p26(4) [501+]
Valleriani, Matteo - *Metallurgy, Ballistics and Epistemic Instruments: The Nova Scientia of Nicolo Tartaglia: A New Edition*
    Isis - v106 - i1 - March 2015 - p178(2) [501+]
Vallgren, Carl-Johan - *The Merman*
    BL - v111 - i19-20 - June 1 2015 - p65(1) [51-500]
    KR - Oct 1 2015 - pNA [51-500]
Valor, Magdalena - *The Archaeology of Medieval Spain, 1100-1500*
    Specu - v90 - i3 - July 2015 - p864-865 [501+]
Vamos, Samantha R. - *Alphabet Trains (Illus. by O'Rourke, Ryan)*
    c KR - June 15 2015 - pNA [51-500]
    c SLJ - v61 - i8 - August 2015 - p77(1) [51-500]
Van Allsburg, Chris - *Just a Dream*
    c CH Bwatch - May 2015 - pNA [501+]
The Misadventures of Sweetie Pie (Illus. by Van Allsburg, Chris)
    c CCB-B - v68 - i5 - Jan 2015 - p279(1) [51-500]
    c HB Guide - v26 - i1 - Spring 2015 - p49(1) [51-500]
    c Sch Lib - v63 - i2 - Summer 2015 - p98(1) [51-500]
Van Alphen, Ernst - *The Rhetoric of Sincerity*
    TimHES - i2186 - Jan 15 2015 - p49(1) [501+]
Van Ark, Katie - *The Boy Next Door*
    y CCB-B - v68 - i7 - March 2015 - p374(1) [51-500]
Van Arsdall, Anne - *Herbs and Healers from the Ancient Mediterranean through the Medieval West: Essays in Honor of John M. Riddle*
    Isis - v106 - i1 - March 2015 - p159(2) [501+]
Van Atta, John R. - *Securing the West: Politics, Public Lands, and the Fate of the Old Republic, 1785-1850*
    AHR - v120 - i3 - June 2015 - p1014-1015 [501+]
    HNet - March 2015 - pNA [501+]
    JAH - v102 - i1 - June 2015 - p245-246 [501+]
    JSH - v81 - i4 - Nov 2015 - p955(2) [501+]
    WHQ - v46 - i4 - Winter 2015 - p503-503 [501+]
Van Beck, Sara L. - *Daffodils in American Gardens, 1733-1940*
    RVBW - August 2015 - pNA [501+]
Van Biesen, Koen - *Roger Is Reading a Book (Illus. by Van Biesen, Koen)*
    c BL - v111 - i16 - April 15 2015 - p55(1) [51-500]
    c HB - v91 - i3 - May-June 2015 - p102(2) [51-500]
    c HB Guide - v26 - i2 - Fall 2015 - p54(1) [51-500]
    c KR - Jan 15 2015 - pNA [51-500]
    c PW - v262 - i4 - Jan 26 2015 - p168(1) [51-500]
Van Booy, Simon - *Tales of Accidental Genius*
    KR - Sept 15 2015 - pNA [51-500]
Van Brakle, Josh - *The Hearts of Dragons*
    KR - Jan 1 2016 - pNA [501+]
Van Brunt, K.D. - *Win the Rings*
    y PW - v262 - i22 - June 1 2015 - p61(1) [51-500]
Van Calster, Geert - *European Private International Law*
    Law Q Rev - v131 - Jan 2015 - p165-166 [501+]
Van Cleve, George William - *A Slaveholders' Union: Slavery, Politics, and the Constitution in the Early American Republic*
    Historian - v77 - i1 - Spring 2015 - p147(2) [501+]
Van Dahl, Fiona - *Eden Green*
    PW - v262 - i45 - Nov 9 2015 - p42(2) [51-500]
van de Noort, Robert - *Climate Change in Archaeology: Building Resilience from Research in the World's Coastal Wetlands*
    Am Ant - v80 - i2 - April 2015 - p417(2) [501+]
Van de Ven, Hans - *Breaking with the Past: The Maritime Customs Service and the Global Origins of Modernity in China*
    AHR - v120 - i1 - Feb 2015 - p204-205 [501+]
    Pac A - v88 - i4 - Dec 2015 - p904 [501+]

472 • VAN DE VEN Book Review Index 2016 Cumulation

van de Ven, Hans - *Negotiating China's Destiny in World War II*
HNet - March 2015 - pNA [501+]
van de Vendel, Edward - *The Cheer-Up Bird (Illus. by Schubert, Ingrid)*
c KR - Sept 15 2015 - pNA [51-500]
The Dog That Nino Didn't Have (Illus. by Van Hertbruggen, Anton)
c KR - August 15 2015 - pNA [51-500]
c PW - v262 - i32 - August 10 2015 - p58(1) [51-500]
Van de Walle, John A. - *Teaching Student-Centered Mathematics: Developmentally Appropriate Instruction for Grades 3-5*
TC Math - v21 - i6 - Feb 2015 - p377(2) [501+]
Teaching Student-Centered Mathematics: Developmentally Appropriate Instruction for Grades Pre-K-2
TC Math - v21 - i6 - Feb 2015 - p377(1) [501+]
van den Berg, Laura - *Find Me (Read by Zeller, Emily Woo). Audiobook Review*
y BL - v111 - i22 - August 1 2015 - p77(1) [51-500]
y PW - v262 - i17 - April 27 2015 - p68(1) [51-500]
Find Me
NYTBR - March 1 2015 - p20(L) [501+]
y SLJ - v61 - i10 - Oct 2015 - p123(1) [51-500]
VQR - v91 - i1 - Wntr 2015 - p193-196 [501+]
van der Berg, Laura - *Find Me*
y HR - v68 - i1 - Spring 2015 - p151-157 [501+]
van der Heijden, Adri - *Tonio: A Requiem Memoir*
TLS - i5874 - Oct 30 2015 - p30(1) [501+]
van der Heyden, Ulrich - *Mosambikanische Vertragsarbeiter in der DDR-Wirtschaft: Hintergrund - Verlauf - Folgen*
HNet - Jan 2015 - pNA [501+]
Van der Linde, Laurel - *So, You Want To Be a Dancer? The Ultimate Guide to Exploring the Dance Industry*
BL - v111 - i14 - March 15 2015 - p59(2) [51-500]
y KR - Jan 15 2015 - pNA [51-500]
Van Der Linde, Laurel - *So, You Want to Be a Dancer? The Ultimate Guide to Exploring the Dance Industry*
c SLJ - v61 - i5 - May 2015 - p143(1) [51-500]
Van der Poel, Marc - *Neo-Latin Philology: Old Traditions, New Approaches*
Sev Cent N - v73 - i1-2 - Spring-Summer 2015 - p86(3) [501+]
Van der Post, JanGeert - *El largo y sinuoso camino: Razones por las que no ha sido construido el canal de Nicaragua*
HNet - Sept 2015 - pNA [501+]
van der Spoel, Adrian Rodriguez - *The Music of the 18th Century Codex Trujillo del Peru*
Notes - v72 - i1 - Sept 2015 - p151(3) [501+]
Van der Steen, Bart - *The City Is Ours: Squatting and Autonomous Movements in Europe from the 1970s to the Present*
HNet - June 2015 - pNA [501+]
van der Veer, Peter - *The Modern Spirit of Asia: The Spiritual and the Secular in China and India*
HNet - Sept 2015 - pNA [501+]
IBMR - v39 - i1 - Jan 2015 - p42(1) [501+]
Van Der Veer, Peter - *The Modern Spirit of Asia: The Spiritual and the Secular in China and India*
JAS - v74 - i2 - May 2015 - p456-458 [501+]
Van der Ven, Jan Pieter - *Overseas Mailers First Day Covers of Canada*
Phil Lit R - v64 - i2 - Spring 2015 - p130(2) [501+]
Van der Vlugt, Simone - *Safe as Houses*
BL - v111 - i14 - March 15 2015 - p48(1) [51-500]
Van DerStap, Sophie - *The Girl with Nine Wigs: A Memoir*
PW - v262 - i30 - July 27 2015 - p59(1) [51-500]
van Diepen, Allison - *Light of Day*
y BL - v112 - i5 - Nov 1 2015 - p55(1) [51-500]
KR - Sept 1 2015 - pNA [51-500]
KR - Sept 1 2015 - pNA [51-500]
Van Diepen, Allison - *Light of Day*
y Res Links - v21 - i1 - Oct 2015 - p43(1) [501+]
y VOYA - v38 - i5 - Dec 2015 - p65(1) [51-500]
van Diepen, Allison - *On the Edge*
y CCB-B - v68 - i6 - Feb 2015 - p334(1) [51-500]
y HB Guide - v26 - i1 - Spring 2015 - p126(1) [51-500]
van Dijk, Conrad - *John Gower and the Limits of the Law*
MLR - v110 - i3 - July 2015 - p811-812 [501+]
Specu - v90 - i2 - April 2015 - p594-595 [501+]
van Dijk, Sheri - *Relationship Skills 101 for Teens: Your Guide to Dealing with Daily Drama, Stress, and Difficult Emotions Using DBT*
SLJ - v61 - i4 - April 2015 - p185(1) [51-500]
Van Dixhorn, John - *Prisoner of Belief: One Man's Odyssey to Reclaim His Soul - From Evangelical Minister to Searching Psychologist*
SPBW - Feb 2015 - pNA [501+]
van Dokkum, Pieter - *Dragonflies: Magnificent Creatures of Water, Air, and Land (Illus. by van Dokkum, Pieter)*
Am Sci - v103 - i5 - Sept-Oct 2015 - p364(1) [51-500]
BL - v111 - i13 - March 1 2015 - p9(2) [51-500]
LJ - v140 - i3 - Feb 15 2015 - p127(2) [51-500]
Van Dolzer, Krista - *Don't Vote for Me*
y KR - May 1 2015 - pNA [51-500]
c PW - v262 - i19 - May 11 2015 - p61(2) [51-500]
c SLJ - v61 - i7 - July 2015 - p84(1) [51-500]
The Sound of Life and Everything
c CCB-B - v69 - i1 - Sept 2015 - p61(1) [51-500]
c HB Guide - v26 - i2 - Fall 2015 - p105(1) [51-500]
c KR - March 1 2015 - pNA [51-500]
c PW - v262 - i10 - March 9 2015 - p74(1) [51-500]
c SLJ - v61 - i4 - April 2015 - p150(1) [51-500]
c VOYA - v38 - i1 - April 2015 - p84(1) [51-500]
Van Doren, Adam - *The House Tells the Story: Homes of the American Presidents*
BL - v111 - i22 - August 1 2015 - p15(1) [51-500]
CSM - July 3 2015 - pNA [501+]
PW - v262 - i21 - May 25 2015 - p50(1) [51-500]
RVBW - August 2015 - pNA [51-500]
Van Draanen, Wendelin - *Sammy Keyes and the Kiss Goodbye*
c HB Guide - v26 - i1 - Spring 2015 - p95(1) [51-500]
Sammy Keyes and the Night of the Skulls (Read by Sands, Tara). Audiobook Review
SLJ - v61 - i4 - April 2015 - p64(1) [51-500]
van Duivenvoorde, Wendy - *Dutch East India Company Shipbuilding*
Bwatch - Oct 2015 - pNA [51-500]
Van Dusen, Ross - *What Makes a Rainbow?*
c CH Bwatch - August 2015 - pNA [51-500]
Van Duzer, Chet - *Sea Monsters on Medieval and Renaissance Maps*
Ren Q - v68 - i3 - Fall 2015 - p1028-1030 [501+]
Van Dyke, Dick - *Keep Moving*
KR - Sept 1 2015 - pNA [51-500]
Van Dyken, Rachel - *The Consequence of Loving Colton (Read by Podehl, Nick). Audiobook Review*
y SLJ - v61 - i7 - July 2015 - p50(1) [51-500]
van Emden, Richard - *Gallipoli: The Dardanelles Disaster in Soldiers' Words and Photographs*
Lon R Bks - v37 - i10 - May 21 2015 - p39(3) [501+]
NS - v144 - i5255 - March 27 2015 - p64(3) [501+]
Spec - v327 - i9736 - April 4 2015 - p32(2) [501+]
van Es, Bart - *Shakespeare in Company*
Six Ct J - v46 - i1 - Spring 2015 - p223-224 [501+]
Van Fleet, Matthew - *Color Dog*
c KR - Jan 1 2016 - pNA [51-500]
Van Gelder, Alex - *Mumbling Beauty Louise Bourgeois*
HM - v331 - i1986 - Nov 2015 - p77(3) [501+]
Van Gelder, Sarah - *Sustainable Happiness: Live Simply, Live Well, Make a Difference*
Bwatch - April 2015 - pNA [51-500]
van Genechten, Guido - *Gilbert the Ghost (Illus. by van Genechten, Guido)*
c KR - August 1 2015 - pNA [51-500]
c PW - v262 - i30 - July 27 2015 - p68(1) [51-500]
Little White Fish
c SLJ - v61 - i8 - August 2015 - p63(1) [51-500]
Little White Fish Has a Party
c SLJ - v61 - i8 - August 2015 - p63(1) [51-500]
Perhaps (Illus. by van Genechten, Guido)
c SLJ - v61 - i12 - Dec 2015 - p96(2) [51-500]
van Gogh, Vincent - *Ever Yours: The Essential Letters*
Lon R Bks - v37 - i15 - July 30 2015 - p7(2) [501+]
van Gorder, A. Christian - *Islam, Peace and Social Justice: A Christian Perspective*
J Ch St - v57 - i2 - Spring 2015 - p362-363 [501+]
Van Gundy, Alana - *Women, Incarceration and Human Rights Violations: Feminist Criminology and Corrections*
CS - v44 - i1 - Jan 2015 - p147 [501+]
van Haeringen, Annemarie - *Coco and the Little Black Dress (Illus. by van Haeringen, Annemarie)*
c KR - August 1 2015 - pNA [51-500]
c PW - v262 - i29 - July 20 2015 - p190(2) [501+]
c SLJ - v61 - i9 - Sept 2015 - p183(2) [51-500]
van Haeringen, Annmarie - *Coco and the Little Black Dress (Illus. by van Haeringen, Annmarie)*
c BL - v112 - i2 - Sept 15 2015 - p57(1) [51-500]
Van Havre, Jean - *La Citadelle de la Vertu ou La Veritable Tranquillite de l'Ame / Arx Virtutis Sive De Vera Animi Tranquillitate.*
Sev Cent N - v73 - i1-2 - Spring-Summer 2015 - p76(3) [501+]
Van Heekeren, Deborah - *The Shark Warrior of Alewai: A Phenomenology of Melanesian Identity*
Pac A - v88 - i4 - Dec 2015 - p973 [501+]
Van Hest, Pimm - *Weatherboy (Illus. by Devos, Kristof)*
c SLJ - v61 - i9 - Sept 2015 - p130(2) [51-500]
Van Heyningen, Elizabeth - *The Concentration Camps of the Anglo-Boer War: A Social History*
AHR - v120 - i2 - April 2015 - p760(1) [501+]
Van Hoof, Lieve - *Literature and Society in the Fourth Century AD: Performing, Constructing the Present, Presenting the Self*
HNet - June 2015 - pNA [501+]
van Hooland, Seth - *Linked Data for Libraries, Archives, and Museums: How to Clean, Link and Publish Your Metadata*
LRTS - v59 - i2 - April 2015 - p97(2) [501+]
Van Horn, Gavin - *City Creatures: Animal Encounters in the Chicago Wilderness*
LJ - v140 - i17 - Oct 15 2015 - p108(2) [51-500]
van Hout, Mies - *Pussycat, Pussycat (Illus. by van Hout, Mies)*
c KR - Sept 1 2015 - pNA [51-500]
c SLJ - v61 - i7 - July 2015 - p59(1) [51-500]
Van Hout, Mies - *Surprise (Illus. by Van Hout, Mies)*
c HB Guide - v26 - i1 - Spring 2015 - p18(1) [51-500]
van Hout, Mies - *Twinkle, Twinkle, Little Star (Illus. by Van Hout, Mies)*
c HB Guide - v26 - i1 - Spring 2015 - p145(1) [51-500]
van Houten, Therese - *Papa's War*
KR - May 15 2015 - pNA [501+]
Van Inwagen, Peter - *Existence: Essays in Ontology*
RM - v68 - i4 - June 2015 - p876(3) [501+]
J Phil - v112 - i5 - May 2015 - p280(1) [501+]
Van Koevering, Thomas E. - *Chemists*
y Teach Lib - v42 - i4 - April 2015 - p10(1) [51-500]
Van Laan, Nancy - *Forget Me Not (Illus. by Graegin, Stephanie)*
c HB Guide - v26 - i1 - Spring 2015 - p49(1) [51-500]
van Lente, Dick - *The Nuclear Age in Popular Media: A Transnational History, 1945-1965*
HNet - June 2015 - pNA [501+]
van Liere, Frans - *An Introduction to the Medieval Bible*
CH - v84 - i4 - Dec 2015 - p880(2) [501+]
CHR - v101 - i1 - Wntr 2015 - p150(2) [501+]
Med R - Jan 2015 - pNA [501+]
Six Ct J - v46 - i1 - Spring 2015 - p169(3) [501+]
Specu - v90 - i2 - April 2015 - p595-597 [501+]
van Lieshout, Elle - *Uh-Oh Octopus! (Illus. by van Hout, Mies)*
c HB Guide - v26 - i2 - Fall 2015 - p54(1) [51-500]
c KR - Feb 15 2015 - pNA [51-500]
c SLJ - v61 - i3 - March 2015 - p128(2) [51-500]
van Lieshout, Ellie - *Uh-Oh Octopus! (Illus. by van Hout, Mies)*
c CH Bwatch - July 2015 - pNA [51-500]
c CH Bwatch - Oct 2015 - pNA [51-500]
van Lieshout, Maria - *Flight 1-2-3*
c HB Guide - v26 - i2 - Fall 2015 - p20(1) [51-500]
I Use the Potty
c PW - v262 - i50 - Dec 7 2015 - p86(1) [501+]
Van Lowe, E. - *The Secrets of Love and Death*
y SLJ - v61 - i7 - July 2015 - p98(2) [51-500]
van Lunteren, Frank - *The Battle of the Bridges: The 504th Parachute Infantry Regiment in Operation Market Garden*
APH - v62 - i1 - Spring 2015 - p58(1) [501+]
van Minnen, Cornelis A. - *The U.S. South and Europe: Transatlantic Relations in the Nineteenth and Twentieth Centuries*
JSH - v81 - i1 - Feb 2015 - p189(3) [501+]
van Mourik, Pauline - *Open Education: A Study in Disruption*
TimHES - i2209 - June 25 2015 - p47(1) [501+]
Van, Muon - *In a Village by the Sea (Illus. by Chu, April)*
c CH Bwatch - April 2015 - pNA [51-500]
c CH Bwatch - June 2015 - pNA [51-500]
c KR - Feb 15 2015 - pNA [51-500]
c PW - v262 - i14 - April 6 2015 - p59(1) [51-500]
c PW - v262 - i49 - Dec 2 2015 - p27(2) [51-500]
c SLJ - v61 - i8 - August 2015 - p77(1) [51-500]
Little Tree (Illus. by Adinolfi, JoAnn)
c KR - Sept 1 2015 - pNA [51-500]
c NYTBR - Dec 20 2015 - p15(L) [501+]
c PW - v262 - i38 - Sept 21 2015 - p71(1) [51-500]
c PW - v262 - i49 - Dec 2 2015 - p30(1) [51-500]
c SLJ - v61 - i10 - Oct 2015 - p85(1) [51-500]

Van Norman, William C. - *Shade-Grown Slavery: The Lives of Slaves on Coffee Plantations in Cuba*
HNet - April 2015 - pNA [501+]
JIH - v45 - i4 - Spring 2015 - p597-598 [501+]

Van Nuffelen, Peter - *Orosius and the Rhetoric of History*
CH - v84 - i1 - March 2015 - p227(2) [501+]

Van Osselaer, Tine - *The Pious Sex: Catholic Constructions of Masculinity and Femininity in Belgium, c. 1800-1940*
CHR - v101 - i2 - Spring 2015 - p382(2) [501+]
HER - v130 - i544 - June 2015 - p775(2) [501+]

Van Pelt, James - *Pandora's Gun*
y VOYA - v38 - i4 - Oct 2015 - p80(1) [51-500]

van Pelt, Mortira Natasha - *Ancient Worlds Modern Beads: 30 Stunning Beadwork Designs Inspired by Treasures from Ancient Civilizations*
BL - v112 - i5 - Nov 1 2015 - p7(1) [51-500]
LJ - v140 - i19 - Nov 15 2015 - p82(1) [51-500]

van Poll-van de Lisdonk, M.L. - *Erasmi Opera Omnia VI-10: Annotationes in Novum Testamentum (Pars Sexta)*
Ren Q - v68 - i3 - Fall 2015 - p977-978 [501+]
Six Ct J - v46 - i2 - Summer 2015 - p437-439 [501+]

Van Praag, Menna - *The Witches of Cambridge*
BL - v112 - i7 - Dec 1 2015 - p38(1) [51-500]
PW - v262 - i46 - Nov 16 2015 - p60(2) [51-500]

Van Reybrouck, David - *Congo: The Epic History of a People*
y NYTBR - April 19 2015 - p28(L) [501+]

Van Rooyen, Suzanne - *I Heart Robot*
y SLJ - v61 - i5 - May 2015 - p125(1) [51-500]

van Sinderen, Wim - *Anton Corbijn: 1-2-3-4*
LJ - v140 - i15 - Sept 15 2015 - p81(3) [501+]

Van Slyke, Rebecca - *Mom School (Illus. by Burris, Priscilla)*
c CH Bwatch - June 2015 - pNA [51-500]
c HB Guide - v26 - i2 - Fall 2015 - p54(1) [51-500]

Van Steenwyk, Mark - *A Wolf at the Gate (Illus. by Hedstrom, Joel)*
c PW - v262 - i11 - March 16 2015 - p87(1) [51-500]
A Wolf at the Gate
KR - April 15 2015 - pNA [501+]

Van Tassel, Eloise - *Life with Howard: Howard Staats of 302 Levens Street, Dallas, Oregon*
BL - v111 - i9-10 - Jan 1 2015 - p120(1) [501+]

Van Tiem, Victoria - *Love Like the Movies*
KR - July 1 2015 - pNA [501+]

Van Tol, Alex - *Chick: Lister*
y PW - v262 - i14 - April 6 2015 - p60(1) [501+]
y Res Links - v20 - i4 - April 2015 - p33(1) [501+]
c VOYA - v38 - i1 - April 2015 - p66(2) [501+]

Van Valen, Gary - *Indigenous Agency in the Amazon: The Mojos in Liberal and Rubber-Boom Bolivia, 1842-1932*
Ams - v72 - i1 - Jan 2015 - p162(3) [501+]

Van Vleck, Jenifer - *Empire of the Air: Aviation and the American Ascendancy*
Historian - v77 - i2 - Summer 2015 - p362(3) [501+]
JAH - v101 - i4 - March 2015 - p1317-1318 [501+]

Van Vleet, Carmella - *To the Stars! The First American Woman to Walk in Space (Illus. by Wong, Nicole)*
c KR - Nov 15 2015 - pNA [501+]
c PW - v262 - i51 - Dec 14 2015 - p82(1) [501+]

Van Vorhees, Karin - *Jewelry Making 1-2-3: 45+ Simple Projects*
Bwatch - Nov 2015 - pNA [501+]

Van Waarden, J.A. - *New Approaches to Sidonius Apollinaris*
Class R - v65 - i1 - April 2015 - p163-165 [501+]

van Wagenen, Maya - *Popular: A Memoir: Vintage Wisdom for a Modern Geek*
y Teach Lib - v42 - i3 - Feb 2015 - p28(4) [501+]

van Wees, Hans - *Ships and Silver, Taxes and Tribute: A Fiscal History of Archaic Athens*
HNet - Jan 2015 - pNA [501+]

Van Wieren, Gretel - *Restored to Earth: Christianity, Environmental Ethics, and Ecological Restoration*
Theol St - v76 - i1 - March 2015 - p221(2) [501+]

Van Wright, Cornelius - *Bucky and Stu vs. the Mikanikal Man (Illus. by Van Wright, Cornelius)*
KR - April 1 2015 - pNA [501+]
c SLJ - v61 - i8 - August 2015 - p77(2) [501+]

Vanaik, Achin - *Political Science, 4 vols.*
Pac A - v88 - i1 - March 2015 - p135 [501+]

Vanamali - *The Science of the Rishis: The Spiritual and Material Discoveries of the Ancient Sages of India*
PW - v262 - i3 - Jan 19 2015 - p77(1) [501+]

Vancans, Juri - *The Bushido Element*
KR - June 15 2015 - pNA [501+]

Vance, Alexander - *Behind the Canvas*
c BL - v112 - i5 - Nov 1 2015 - p51(1) [51-500]
c KR - Oct 15 2015 - pNA [51-500]
c SLJ - v61 - i12 - Dec 2015 - p108(2) [51-500]
The Heartbreak Messenger (Read by Gebauer, Christopher). Audiobook Review
c SLJ - v61 - i12 - Dec 2015 - p77(2) [51-500]

Vance, Ashlee - *Elon Musk: How the Billionaire CEO of SpaceX and Tesla Is Shaping Our Future*
Lon R Bks - v37 - i17 - Sept 10 2015 - p3(4) [501+]
Elon Musk: Tesla, SpaceX, and the Quest for a Fantastic Future
BL - v111 - i17 - May 1 2015 - p64(2) [51-500]
Econ - v416 - i8945 - July 4 2015 - p72(US) [501+]
NYRB - v62 - i13 - August 13 2015 - p8(2) [501+]
NYT - May 13 2015 - pC1(L) [501+]
NYT - May 13 2015 - pC1(L) [501+]
KR - April 1 2015 - pNA [501+]
LJ - v140 - i7 - April 15 2015 - p114(3) [51-500]
NYTBR - May 17 2015 - p8(L) [501+]
PW - v262 - i13 - March 30 2015 - p71(1) [51-500]

Vance, Sara - *The Perfect Metabolism Plan: Restore Your Energy and Reach Your Ideal Weight*
Bwatch - June 2015 - pNA [51-500]
RVBW - March 2015 - pNA [51-500]

Vandenberg-Daves, Jodi - *Modern Motherhood: An American History*
JAH - v101 - i4 - March 2015 - p1248-1249 [501+]
Wom R Bks - v32 - i3 - May-June 2015 - p25(3) [501+]

Vandenburg, Margaret - *Home Front*
NYTBR - May 3 2015 - p30(L) [501+]
Weapons of Mass Destruction
KR - August 15 2015 - pNA [51-500]

Vander Heyden, Linda - *Mr. McGinty's Monarchs*
c KR - Dec 1 2015 - pNA [51-500]

Vanderbilt, Arthur - *The Best-Kept Boy in the World: The Short, Scandalous Life of Denny Fouts, Muse to Truman Capote, Gore Vidal, and Christopher Isherwood*
G&L Rev W - v22 - i5 - Sept-Oct 2015 - p35(2) [501+]

VanderBrug, Michael - *The Timber Press Guide to Vegetable Gardening in the Midwest*
PW - v262 - i42 - Oct 19 2015 - p72(1) [501+]

Vanderburg, Timothy W. - *Cannon Mills and Kannapolis: Persistent Paternalism in a Textile Town*
JSH - v81 - i2 - May 2015 - p488(2) [501+]

Vanderkam, Laura - *I Know How She Does It: How Successful Women Make the Most of Their Time*
BL - v111 - i18 - May 15 2015 - p6(2) [51-500]
PW - v262 - i17 - April 27 2015 - p64(2) [51-500]

VanderMeer, Ann - *Sisters of the Revolution: A Feminist Speculative Fiction Anthology*
y BL - v111 - i21 - July 1 2015 - p47(1) [51-500]
KR - June 1 2015 - pNA [51-500]

VanderMeer, Jeff - *Annihilation*
LJ - v140 - i19 - Nov 15 2015 - p110(1) [51-500]

Vanderpool, Harold Y. - *Palliative Care: The 400-Year Quest for a Good Death*
LJ - v140 - i13 - August 1 2015 - p117(1) [51-500]

Vanderputten, Steven - *Understanding Monastic Practices of Oral Communication (Western Europe, Tenth Thirteenth Centuries)*.
CHR - v101 - i2 - Spring 2015 - p354(2) [501+]

VanderVelde, Lea - *Redemption Songs: Suing for Freedom before Dred Scott*
HLR - v128 - i7 - May 2015 - p2108(1) [1-50]
JSH - v81 - i4 - Nov 2015 - p965(3) [501+]

Vanderwarker, Tony - *Ads for God*
KR - April 1 2015 - pNA [501+]

VanDerwater, Amy Ludwig - *Every Day Birds (Illus. by Metrano, Dylan)*
c KR - Nov 15 2015 - pNA [51-500]

vanDuinkerken, Wyoma - *Leading Libraries: How to Create a Service Culture*
LJ - v140 - i14 - Sept 1 2015 - p126(1) [51-500]
VOYA - v38 - i5 - Dec 2015 - p84(1) [51-500]

Vane-Wright, Dick - *Butterflies: A Complete Guide to Their Biology and Behavior, 2d ed.*
BL - v112 - i6 - Nov 15 2015 - p6(1) [51-500]

Vanhoenacker, Mark - *Skyfaring: A Journey with a Pilot*
TLS - i5852 - May 29 2015 - p29(1) [501+]
BL - v111 - i19-20 - June 1 2015 - p16(2) [51-500]
Econ - v415 - i8935 - April 25 2015 - p78(US) [501+]
KR - May 1 2015 - pNA [51-500]
LJ - v140 - i7 - April 15 2015 - p115(1) [51-500]
NYT - June 3 2015 - pC1(L) [501+]
NYTBR - July 5 2015 - p1(L) [501+]
PW - v262 - i14 - April 6 2015 - p50(1) [51-500]
Spec - v327 - i9738 - April 18 2015 - p36(1) [501+]

Vanhoozer, Kevin J. - *Faith Speaking Understanding: Performing the Drama of Doctrine*
CC - v132 - i2 - Jan 21 2015 - p37(2) [501+]

Vann, David - *Aquarium*
BL - v111 - i12 - Feb 15 2015 - p30(1) [51-500]
BooChiTr - Feb 28 2015 - p14(1) [501+]
KR - Jan 15 2015 - pNA [51-500]
NY - v91 - i10 - April 27 2015 - p77 [501+]
y NYTBR - March 8 2015 - p19(L) [501+]
PW - v262 - i2 - Jan 12 2015 - p32(1) [51-500]
Spec - v327 - i9733 - March 14 2015 - p47(1) [501+]
TLS - i5842 - March 20 2015 - p22(1) [501+]
Ent W - i1354 - March 13 2015 - p62(1) [501+]
NS - v144 - i5262 - May 15 2015 - p49(1) [501+]
A Mile Down: The True Story of a Disastrous Career at Sea
Spec - v329 - i9763 - Oct 10 2015 - p43(1) [501+]

VanSickle, Vikki - *If I Had a Gryphon (Illus. by Atkinson, Cale)*
c KR - Dec 15 2015 - pNA [51-500]
c PW - v262 - i47 - Nov 23 2015 - p67(1) [51-500]

Van't Hul, Jean - *The Artful Year: Celebrating the Seasons and Holidays with Crafts and Recipes*
RVBW - April 2015 - pNA [51-500]

Vantoch, Victoria - *The Jet Set: Airline Stewardesses and the Making of an American Icon*
JWH - v27 - i3 - Fall 2015 - p176(11) [501+]

VanVoorst, Jenny Fretland - *Animal Classification*
c HB Guide - v26 - i1 - Spring 2015 - p154(1) [51-500]
Ecosystems
c HB Guide - v26 - i1 - Spring 2015 - p154(1) [51-500]
Fretland Gems
c HB Guide - v26 - i1 - Spring 2015 - p151(1) [51-500]
What's Great about New Mexico?
c HB Guide - v26 - i1 - Spring 2015 - p203(1) [51-500]

Vapnyar, Lara - *The Scent of Pine*
NYTBR - Jan 4 2015 - p24(L) [501+]

Vaquero, Eloisa Ramirez - *El primer cartulario de los reyes de Navarra: El valor de lo escrito / Le premier cartulaire des rois de Navarre: La valeur de l'ecrit. vol. 2*
Specu - v90 - i1 - Jan 2015 - p293-294 [501+]

Varan, Sara - *Sweaterweather and Other Short Stories (Illus. by Varan, Sara)*
c PW - v262 - i46 - Nov 16 2015 - p78(1) [51-500]

Varaschin, Denis - *Histoire economique et sociale de la Savoie de 1860 a nos jours*
BHR - v89 - i3 - Autumn 2015 - p595(3) [501+]

Vargas, Deborah R. - *Dissonant Divas in Chicana Music: The Limits of La Onda*
TDR - v59 - i1 - Spring 2015 - p192(2) [501+]
Aztlan - v40 - i1 - Spring 2015 - p259-263 [501+]

Vargas, Fred - *Les Temps glaciaires*
Lon R Bks - v37 - i8 - April 23 2015 - p32(3) [501+]
TLS - i5861 - July 31 2015 - p26(1) [501+]

Vargas Llosa, Mario - *The Discreet Hero*
TLS - i5846 - April 17 2015 - p20(1) [501+]
Los cuentos de la peste
WLT - v89 - i6 - Nov-Dec 2015 - p79(1) [501+]
Notes on the Death of Culture: Essays on Spectacle and Society
TLS - i5875 - Nov 6 2015 - p15(1) [501+]

Varia, Kush - *Bollywood: Gods, Glamour, and Gossip*
Pac A - v88 - i1 - March 2015 - p220 [501+]

Varley, John - *Dark Lightning*
Analog - v135 - i4 - April 2015 - p106(2) [501+]

Varnadore, D. Gray - *Liars and Lawyers*
KR - Feb 1 2015 - pNA [501+]

Varnai, Elizabeth S. - *Good Morning Loon (Illus. by Hartley, Kate)*
c CH Bwatch - April 2015 - pNA [51-500]

Varnum, Kenneth J. - *Top Technologies Every Librarian Needs to Know: A LITA Guide*
LR - v64 - i3 - March 2015 - p269-270 [501+]

Varnum, Robin - *Alvar Nunez Cabeza de Vaca: American Trailblazer*
JAH - v102 - i2 - Sept 2015 - p523-524 [501+]
JSH - v81 - i4 - Nov 2015 - p936(3) [501+]
Roundup M - v22 - i4 - April 2015 - p31(1) [501+]
Roundup M - v22 - i6 - August 2015 - p41(1) [501+]
Six Ct J - v46 - i3 - Fall 2015 - p758-760 [501+]

Varon, Bension - *Fighting Fascism and Surviving Buchenwald: The Life and Memoir of Hans Bergas*
SPBW - Nov 2015 - pNA [51-500]

Varon, Elizabeth R. - *Appomattox: Victory, Defeat, and Freedom at the End of the Civil War*
JSH - v81 - i2 - May 2015 - p475(3) [501+]

Varon, Jeremy - *The New Life: Jewish Students of Postwar Germany*
CEH - v48 - i3 - Sept 2015 - p444-445 [501+]

Varon, Sara - *Sweatherweather and Other Short Stories (Illus. by Varon, Sara)*
c KR - Nov 15 2015 - pNA [51-500]

Varoufakis, Georgios - *Liberty Abroad: J.S. Mill on International Relations*
VS - v57 - i2 - Wntr 2015 - p289(2) [501+]

Vartanian, Oshin - *Neuroscience of Creativity*
QRB - v90 - i1 - March 2015 - p94(2) [501+]

Vartanoff, Irene - *Temporary Superheroine*
PW - v262 - i44 - Nov 2 2015 - p66(2) [501+]

Varutti, Marzia - *Museums in China: The Politics of Representation After Mao*
JRAI - v21 - i2 - June 2015 - p485(2) [501+]

Vas-Deyres, Natacha - *Les Dieux caches de la science-fiction francaise et francophone, 1950-2010*
SFS - v42 - i2 - July 2015 - p395-398 [501+]

Vasa, Monisha - *My Dearest One (Illus. by Vasa, Monisha)*
c CH Bwatch - Feb 2015 - pNA [51-500]

Vasalou, Sophia - *Schopenhauer and the Aesthetic Standpoint: Philosophy as a Practise of the Sublime*
Dialogue - v54 - i1 - March 2015 - p198-199 [501+]

Vasquez, Juan Gabriel - *The All Saints' Day Lovers*
TLS - i5860 - July 24 2015 - p20(1) [501+]
Lovers on All Saints' Day: Stories
BL - v111 - i19-20 - June 1 2015 - p44(1) [51-500]
KR - May 15 2015 - pNA [51-500]
LJ - v140 - i12 - July 1 2015 - p81(1) [51-500]
NYT - July 30 2015 - pC6(L) [501+]
PW - v262 - i18 - May 4 2015 - p94(1) [51-500]
NYTBR - Oct 4 2015 - p30(L) [501+]

Vassar, Joan - *Black*
KR - Oct 15 2015 - pNA [51-500]

Vassen, Florian - *Bibliographie Heiner Muller*
MLR - v110 - i3 - July 2015 - p911-912 [501+]

Vasset, Sophie - *Medecine and Narration in the Eighteenth Century*
FS - v69 - i2 - April 2015 - p248-249 [501+]

Vatikan und aRassendebatteo in der Zwischenkriegszeit - Stand und Perspektiven der Forschung
HNet - August 2015 - pNA [501+]

Vatter, Miguel - *Machiavelli's The Prince*
J Phil - v112 - i5 - May 2015 - p280(1) [501+]

Vauchez, Andre - *Francis of Assisi: The Life and Afterlife of a Medieval Saint*
Specu - v90 - i1 - Jan 2015 - p305-307 [501+]

Vaughan, Alden T. - *Shakespeare in America*
MLR - v110 - i1 - Jan 2015 - p241-242 [501+]

Vaughan, Betty Boudreau - *Maladies of the Mind*
KR - Dec 15 2015 - pNA [501+]

Vaughan, Blanche - *Egg: The Very Best Recipes Inspired by the Simple Egg*
Spec - v329 - i9768 - Nov 14 2015 - p58(1) [501+]

Vaughan, M.M. - *Six*
c CCB-B - v69 - i1 - Sept 2015 - p62(1) [51-500]
c KR - Feb 15 2015 - pNA [51-500]
y PW - v262 - i14 - April 6 2015 - p59(2) [51-500]

Vaughan, Sarah - *The Art of Baking Blind*
BL - v111 - i16 - April 15 2015 - p23(1) [51-500]

Vaughan, William - *Samuel Palmer: Shadows on the Wall*
Spec - v329 - i9769 - Nov 21 2015 - p49(1) [501+]

Vaughn, Bill - *Hawthorn: The Tree That Has Nourished, Healed, and Inspired through the Ages*
NH - v123 - i4 - May 2015 - p46(2) [501+]
TLS - i5866 - Sept 4 2015 - p24(1) [501+]

Vaughn, Carrie - *Kitty Saves the World*
PW - v262 - i17 - April 27 2015 - p56(1) [51-500]

Vaughn, J. Barry - *Bishops, Bourbons, and Big Mules: A History of the Episcopal Church in Alabama*
CHR - v101 - i3 - Summer 2015 - p681(2) [501+]

Vaughn, J.D. - *The Second Guard*
y CCB-B - v68 - i11 - July-August 2015 - p572(1) [51-500]
y HB Guide - v26 - i2 - Fall 2015 - p142(1) [51-500]
y KR - Feb 15 2015 - pNA [51-500]
y SLJ - v61 - i3 - March 2015 - p145(1) [51-500]

Vaughn, R.M. - *Insomnia*
Mac - v128 - i29-30 - July 27 2015 - p69(2) [501+]

Vaught, Susan - *Footer Davis Probably Is Crazy (Illus. by Reinhardt, Jennifer Black)*
c BL - v111 - i12 - Feb 15 2015 - p86(1) [51-500]
c CCB-B - v68 - i10 - June 2015 - p522(1) [51-500]
c HB - v91 - i2 - March-April 2015 - p111(2) [51-500]
c HB Guide - v26 - i2 - Fall 2015 - p105(1) [51-500]
c KR - Jan 1 2015 - pNA [51-500]
c PW - v262 - i3 - Jan 19 2015 - p84(1) [51-500]
c SLJ - v61 - i2 - Feb 2015 - p94(1) [51-500]

Vaun, Missouri - *All Things Rise*
PW - v262 - i15 - April 13 2015 - p63(1) [51-500]

Vaz, Kim Marie - *The "Baby Dolls": Breaking the Race and Gender Barriers of the New Orleans Mardi Gras Tradition*
JSH - v81 - i1 - Feb 2015 - p228(2) [501+]
Feminist Solidarity at the Crossroads: Intersectional Women's Studies for Transracial Alliance
CS - v44 - i3 - May 2015 - p429-430 [501+]

Vazsonyi, Nicholas - *The Cambridge Wagner Encyclopedia*
Notes - v71 - i4 - June 2015 - p679(9) [501+]

Veart, David - *Hello Girls and Boys! A New Zealand Toy Story*
y Magpies - v30 - i1 - March 2015 - pS8(1) [51-500]

Veatch, Robert M. - *Transplantation Ethics, 2d ed.*
Bwatch - Oct 2015 - pNA [51-500]
Cons - v36 - i2 - Summer 2015 - p44(1) [51-500]

Vecchio, Marjorie - *The Films of Claire Denis: Intimacy on the border*
FS - v69 - i4 - Oct 2015 - p572-573 [501+]

Vecchione, Michael - *Crooked Brooklyn: Taking Down Corrupt Judges, Dirty Politicians, Killers, and Body Snatchers*
KR - Sept 15 2015 - pNA [51-500]
LJ - v140 - i15 - Sept 15 2015 - p90(2) [51-500]
NYT - Nov 15 2015 - p3(L) [501+]

Vecchione, Patrice - *Step into Nature: Nurturing Imagination and Spirit in Everyday Life*
PW - v262 - i6 - Feb 9 2015 - p63(1) [51-500]

Veen, Hans-Joachim - *Denkmaler Demokratischer Umbruche nach 1945*
HNet - March 2015 - pNA [501+]

Vega, Daniella - *Survive the Night*
y Ent W - i1376 - August 14 2015 - p61(1) [51-500]

Vega, Danielle - *The Merciless*
y HB Guide - v26 - i1 - Spring 2015 - p126(1) [51-500]
Survive the Night
KR - April 1 2015 - pNA [51-500]
y SLJ - v61 - i7 - July 2015 - p99(1) [51-500]

Vegetarian Resource Group - *Vegetarian Nutrition for Teenagers*
y Veg J - v34 - i2 - April-June 2015 - p34(1) [51-500]

Vehlmann, Fabien - *The Marquis of Anaon, vol 1: The Isle of Brac*
Sch Lib - v63 - i4 - Winter 2015 - p250(1) [51-500]

Vehlow, Katja - *Abraham Ibn Daud's Dorot Olam (Generations of the Ages): A Critical Edition and Translation of Zikhron Divrey Romi, Divrey Malkhey Yisrael and the Midrash on Zechariah*
Med R - Feb 2015 - pNA [501+]

Veille, Eric - *The Bureau of Misplaced Dads (Illus. by Martin, Pauline)*
c KR - May 15 2015 - pNA [51-500]
c Nat Post - v17 - i225 - August 1 2015 - pWP5(1) [501+]
c PW - v262 - i19 - May 11 2015 - p60(1) [51-500]

Veit, Helen Zoe - *Modern Food, Moral Food: Self-Control, Science, and the Rise of Modern American Eating in the Early Twentieth Century*
HNet - Feb 2015 - pNA [501+]
Isis - v106 - i2 - June 2015 - p486(2) [501+]
RAH - v43 - i1 - March 2015 - p126-133 [501+]

Veith, Jerome - *Gadamer and the Transmission of History*
RM - v69 - i2 - Dec 2015 - p418(2) [501+]

Veith, Martin - *Unbeugsam - Ein Pionier des Rumanischen Anarchismus: Panait Musoiu*
HNet - March 2015 - pNA [501+]

Vel - *Lincoln's Story*
KR - May 1 2015 - pNA [501+]

Velasquez, Crystal - *The Circle of Lies*
c KR - Dec 1 2015 - pNA [51-500]
Hunters of Chaos
c BL - v111 - i18 - May 15 2015 - p65(2) [51-500]
c HB Guide - v26 - i2 - Fall 2015 - p105(1) [51-500]
c SLJ - v61 - i10 - Oct 2015 - p96(2) [51-500]

Velasquez, Eric - *Grandma's Records (Illus. by Velasquez, Eric)*
c BL - v111 - i9-10 - Jan 1 2015 - pS18(5) [501+]
Looking for Bongo
c KR - Jan 1 2016 - pNA [51-500]

Veldman, Meredith - *Margaret Thatcher: Shaping the New Conservatism*
TimHES - i2228 - Nov 5 2015 - p47(1) [501+]

Velkar, Aashish - *Markets and Measurements in Nineteenth-Century Britain*
HER - v130 - i542 - Feb 2015 - p225(2) [501+]

Vella, Christina - *George Washington Carver: A Life*
y BL - v112 - i2 - Sept 15 2015 - p8(1) [51-500]
LJ - v140 - i14 - Sept 1 2015 - p134(1) [51-500]
PW - v262 - i28 - July 13 2015 - p58(2) [51-500]

Velthuijs, Max - *The Kind-Hearted Monster: Two Classic Stories (Illus. by Velthuijs, Max)*
c HB Guide - v26 - i2 - Fall 2015 - p54(1) [51-500]
c SLJ - v61 - i5 - May 2015 - p93(2) [51-500]

Veltmeyer, Henry - *The Cuban Revolution as Socialist Human Development*
CS - v44 - i2 - March 2015 - p270-272 [501+]

Vendel, Edward van de - *The Dog That Nino Didn't Have (Illus. by Van Hertbruggen, Anton)*
c BL - v112 - i3 - Oct 1 2015 - p68(1) [51-500]
c NYTBR - Nov 8 2015 - p34(L) [501+]
c PW - v262 - i49 - Dec 2 2015 - p26(1) [51-500]
c SLJ - v61 - i11 - Nov 2015 - p89(1) [51-500]

Venditti, Robert - *Attack of the Alien Horde (Illus. by Higgins, Dusty)*
c CCB-B - v69 - i1 - Sept 2015 - p62(1) [51-500]
c HB Guide - v26 - i2 - Fall 2015 - p105(1) [51-500]
Miles Taylor and the Golden Cape: Attack of the Alien Horde (Illus. by Higgins, Dusty)
c SLJ - v61 - i5 - May 2015 - p107(1) [51-500]

Vendler, Helen - *The Ocean, the Bird, and the Scholar: Essays on Poets and Poetry*
Bks & Cult - v21 - i5 - Sept-Oct 2015 - p31(1) [501+]
HR - v68 - i3 - Autumn 2015 - p474-480 [501+]
NYRB - v62 - i13 - August 13 2015 - p52(3) [501+]
NYTBR - Sept 6 2015 - p26(L) [501+]
The Ocean, the Bird and the Scholar: Essays on Poets and Poetry
Spec - v328 - i9752 - July 25 2015 - p30(2) [501+]
The Ocean, the Bird, and the Scholar: Essays on Poets and Poetry
TimHES - i2208 - June 18 2015 - p46-47 [501+]
PW - v262 - i12 - March 23 2015 - p64(2) [51-500]

Venefica, Avia - *Exploring Tarot Using Radiant Rider-Waite*
RVBW - Nov 2015 - pNA [51-500]

Venet, Wendy Hamand - *A Changing Wind: Commerce and Conflict in Civil War Atlanta*
AHR - v120 - i2 - April 2015 - p629-630 [501+]
JSH - v81 - i3 - August 2015 - p741(3) [501+]

Venier, Matteo - *Platonis Gorgias Leonardo Aretino interprete*
Sev Cent N - v73 - i3-4 - Fall-Winter 2015 - p184(3) [501+]

Venkatraman, Padma - *A Time to Dance*
y Teach Lib - v42 - i3 - Feb 2015 - p28(4) [501+]

Venosa, Joseph L. - *Path toward the Nation: Islam, Community, and Early Nationalist Mobilization in Eritrea, 1941-1961*
IJAHS - v48 - i1 - Wntr 2015 - p151-152 [501+]

Venter, Eben - *Wolf, Wolf*
TLS - i5847 - April 24 2015 - p20(1) [501+]

Ventresca, Robert A. - *Soldier of Christ: The Life of Pope Pius XII*
JMH - v87 - i1 - March 2015 - p207(3) [501+]

Ventrone, Jillian - *From the Army to College: Transitioning from the Service to Higher Education*
BL - v112 - i4 - Oct 15 2015 - p8(1) [51-500]

Ventura, Marne - *Astrophysicist and Space Advocate Neil deGrasse Tys*
c HB Guide - v26 - i1 - Spring 2015 - p196(2) [51-500]
Fun Things to Do with Cardboard Tubes
c HB Guide - v26 - i1 - Spring 2015 - p178(1) [51-500]
Google Glass and Robotics Innovator Sebastian Thrun
c HB Guide - v26 - i1 - Spring 2015 - p196(2) [51-500]

Book Review Index 2016 Cumulation VIDAL • 475

Verano, M. - *Diary of a Haunting*
y CCB-B - v69 - i2 - Oct 2015 - p119(1) [51-500]
y KR - June 15 2015 - pNA [51-500]
y SLJ - v61 - i7 - July 2015 - p99(1) [51-500]
Verbeek, Peter-Paul - *Moralizing Technology: Understanding and Designing the Morality of Things*
T&C - v56 - i1 - Jan 2015 - p265-267 [501+]
Verble, Margaret - *Maud's Line*
BL - v111 - i18 - May 15 2015 - p30(1) [51-500]
KR - May 1 2015 - pNA [51-500]
Verbrugge, Martha H. - *Active Bodies: A History of Women's Physical Education in Twentieth-Century America*
JWH - v27 - i2 - Summer 2015 - p169(6) [501+]
Verday, Jessica - *Of Monsters and Madness*
y HB Guide - v26 - i1 - Spring 2015 - p126(1) [51-500]
Verde, Susan - *I Am Yoga (Illus. by Reynolds, Peter H.)*
c KR - July 15 2015 - pNA [51-500]
c SLJ - v61 - i9 - Sept 2015 - p131(1) [51-500]
You and Me (Illus. by Reynolds, Peter H.)
c HB Guide - v26 - i2 - Fall 2015 - p54(1) [51-500]
Verdeil, Chantal - *Missions chretiennes en terre d'islam, Moyen-Orient, Afrique du Nord (XVIIe--XXe siecles): Anthologie de textes missionnaires*
CHR - v101 - i4 - Autumn 2015 - p966(3) [501+]
Verdery, Katherine - *Secrets and Truths: Ethnography in the Archive of Romania's Secret Police*
HNet - March 2015 - pNA [501+]
Verdi, Jessica - *What You Left Behind*
y BL - v111 - i19-20 - June 1 2015 - p103(1) [51-500]
y KR - May 1 2015 - pNA [51-500]
y SLJ - v61 - i6 - June 2015 - p130(2) [51-500]
Verdick, Elizabeth - *Noses Are Not for Picking*
c KR - Jan 1 2015 - pNA [51-500]
Voices Are Not for Yelling (Illus. by Heinlen, Marieka)
c KR - July 1 2015 - pNA [51-500]
c SLJ - v61 - i7 - July 2015 - p57(1) [51-500]
Verdick, Mary - *No-See-Me and the Amazing Crimson Stick*
SPBW - May 2015 - pNA [51-500]
Verdon, John - *Peter Pan Must Die (Read by Fass, Robert). Audiobook Review*
BL - v111 - i12 - Feb 15 2015 - p104(1) [51-500]
Vere, Ed - *Max the Brave (Illus. by Vere, Ed)*
c KR - June 15 2015 - pNA [51-500]
c NYTBR - Oct 11 2015 - p16(L) [501+]
c PW - v262 - i25 - June 22 2015 - p136(1) [51-500]
c SLJ - v61 - i6 - June 2015 - p94(1) [51-500]
Vere-Jones, Emma - *Stan the Van Man (Illus. by Webb, Philip)*
c Magpies - v30 - i4 - Sept 2015 - pS5(1) [501+]
Verga, Giovanni - *I Malavoglia: The House by the Medlar Tree*
TLS - i5851 - May 22 2015 - p26(1) [501+]
Vergnioux, Alain - *Grandes Controverses en Education*
HNet - Feb 2015 - pNA [501+]
Vergo, Peter - *Art in Vienna, 1898-1918: Klimt, Kokoschka, Schiele, and Their Contemporaries*
LJ - v140 - i9 - May 15 2015 - p82(2) [51-500]
Verhaeghe, Paul - *What about Me? The Struggle for Identity in a Market-Based Societ*
Hum - v75 - i2 - March-April 2015 - p44(2) [501+]
Verhelst, Marlies - *The Feast for the King (Illus. by Faas, Linde)*
c CH Bwatch - July 2015 - pNA [51-500]
c HB Guide - v26 - i2 - Fall 2015 - p55(1) [51-500]
Verhille, Alexandre - *Legendary Routes of the World*
c KR - Dec 1 2015 - pNA [51-500]
Verlet, Pierre - *The Savonnerie: The James A. de Rothschild Collection at Waddesdon Manor*
NYRB - v62 - i11 - June 25 2015 - p29(4) [501+]
Vermalle, Caroline - *George's Grand Tour*
RVBW - August 2015 - pNA [51-500]
Vermes, Gabor - *Hungarian Culture and Politics in the Habsburg Monarchy, 1711-1848*
AHR - v120 - i4 - Oct 2015 - p1567-1568 [501+]
Vermes, Geza - *The True Herod*
Intpr - v69 - i1 - Jan 2015 - p125(1) [51-500]
Vermes, Timur - *Look Who's Back*
LJ - v140 - i9 - May 15 2015 - p77(1) [51-500]
NYT - April 27 2015 - pC1(L) [501+]
NYTBR - May 10 2015 - p14(L) [501+]
Vermillion, Patricia - *Hound Dawg (Illus. by Pilgrim, Cheryl)*
c PW - v262 - i28 - July 13 2015 - p65(2) [51-500]
Vermittlungspotenzial der "NS-Volksgemeinschaft" - Der Fachdidaktische Gehalt eines Wissenschaftlichen Analysekonzepts
HNet - July 2015 - pNA [501+]
Verne, Deirdre - *Drawing Blood: A Sketch in Crime Mystery*
KR - Dec 1 2015 - pNA [51-500]
Verne, Jules - *The Self-Propelled Island*
SFS - v42 - i3 - Nov 2015 - p557-555 [501+]
Vernick, Audrey - *First Grade Dropout (Illus. by Cordell, Matthew)*
c BL - v111 - i19-20 - June 1 2015 - p112(2) [51-500]
c CCB-B - v69 - i1 - Sept 2015 - p62(2) [51-500]
c CH Bwatch - August 2015 - pNA [501+]
c HB - v91 - i4 - July-August 2015 - p126(2) [501+]
c KR - June 1 2015 - pNA [51-500]
c PW - v262 - i16 - April 20 2015 - p74(1) [51-500]
c PW - v262 - i49 - Dec 2 2015 - p13(1) [51-500]
c SLJ - v61 - i8 - August 2015 - p61(1) [51-500]
The Kid from Diamond Street: The Extraordinary Story of Baseball Legend Edith Houghton (Illus. by Salerno, Steven)
c PW - v262 - i51 - Dec 14 2015 - p82(2) [501+]
Vernick-Giles, Tamara - *Global Health in Africa: Historical Perspectives on Disease Control*
IJAHS - v48 - i1 - Wntr 2015 - p150-151 [501+]
Vernon, James - *Distant Strangers: How Britain Became Modern*
AHR - v120 - i3 - June 2015 - p1115(1) [501+]
JIH - v46 - i2 - Autumn 2015 - p279-280 [501+]
Vernon, Ursula - *Castle Hangnail (Read by Sands, Tara). Audiobook Review*
c SLJ - v61 - i8 - August 2015 - p51(2) [51-500]
Castle Hangnail
BL - v111 - i14 - March 15 2015 - p73(1) [51-500]
c CCB-B - v68 - i10 - June 2015 - p523(1) [51-500]
c HB Guide - v26 - i2 - Fall 2015 - p105(1) [51-500]
c KR - Feb 1 2015 - pNA [51-500]
Hamster Princess: Harriet the Invincible (Illus. by Vernon, Ursula)
c BL - v111 - i21 - July 1 2015 - p73(1) [51-500]
c PW - v262 - i19 - May 11 2015 - p61(1) [51-500]
c PW - v262 - i49 - Dec 2 2015 - p85(2) [51-500]
c SLJ - v61 - i5 - May 2015 - p107(2) [51-500]
Harriet the Invincible
c KR - May 1 2015 - pNA [51-500]
Of Mice and Magic
c KR - Jan 1 2016 - pNA [51-500]
Veronese, Keith - *Rare: The High-Stakes Race to Satisfy Our Need for the Scarcest Metals on Earth*
Nature - v517 - i7533 - Jan 8 2015 - p142(2) [501+]
Veronico, Nicholas A. - *Hidden Warships: Finding World War II's Abandoned, Sunk, and Preserved Warships*
Bwatch - Sept 2015 - pNA [51-500]
Verroca, Rita - *Baltimore Album of Roses: Elegant Motifs to Mix & Match: Step-by-Step Techniques: Applique, Embroidery, Inking, Trapunto*
LJ - v140 - i11 - June 15 2015 - p89(1) [51-500]
Verschuuren, Gerard M. - *It's All in the Genes! Really?*
QRB - v90 - i1 - March 2015 - p97(2) [501+]
Verskin, Alan - *Oppressed in the Land? Fatwas on Muslims Living under Non-Muslim Rule from the Middle Ages to the Present*
JNES - v74 - i1 - April 2015 - p169(4) [501+]
Verso, David Rieff - *The Reproach of Hunger: Food, Justice, and Money in the Twenty-First Century*
Nature - v526 - i7573 - Oct 15 2015 - p321(1) [51-500]
Versteeg, Lizelot - *Colors Everywhere: Counting*
c PW - v262 - i23 - June 8 2015 - p58(1) [501+]
Verstraete, Larry - *Missing in Paradise*
c Res Links - v20 - i4 - April 2015 - p33(2) [51-500]
Vertesi, Janet - *Seeing Like a Rover: How Robots, Teams, and Images Craft Knowledge of Mars*
TimHES - i2213 - July 23 2015 - p50(1) [501+]
Verus, DeiAmor - *Talk to God*
SPBW - April 2015 - pNA [51-500]
Verveer, Melanne - *Fast Forward: How Women Can Achieve Power and Purpose*
KR - August 15 2015 - pNA [501+]
LJ - v140 - i15 - Sept 15 2015 - p86(1) [51-500]
PW - v262 - i31 - August 3 2015 - p50(1) [51-500]
Verzuh, Valerie K. - *Indian Country: The Art of David Bradley*
LJ - v140 - i10 - June 1 2015 - p100(1) [51-500]
Vesaas, Tarjei - *The Birds*
KR - Jan 1 2016 - pNA [501+]
Veseth, Mike - *Money, Taste, and Wine: It's Complicated!*
BL - v111 - i22 - August 1 2015 - p10(1) [51-500]
Vesole, Martin - *Sleeping Truth*
SPBW - Feb 2015 - pNA [51-500]
Vester, Matthew - *Renaissance Dynasticism and Apanage Politics: Jacques de Savoie-Nemours 1531-1585*
JMH - v87 - i1 - March 2015 - p188(2) [501+]
Vetri, Marc - *Mastering Pasta: The Art and Practice of Handmade Pasta, Gnocchi, and Risotto*
LJ - v140 - i3 - Feb 15 2015 - p122(4) [501+]
Vetsch, Erica - *The Cactus Creek Challenge*
PW - v262 - i19 - May 11 2015 - p43(1) [51-500]
Vetter, Lara - *By Avon River*
TLS - i5847 - April 24 2015 - p12(1) [501+]
Veys, Pierre - *The Machine Gunner's Ball*
c Sch Lib - v63 - i2 - Summer 2015 - p122(1) [501+]
Rain of Blood
c Sch Lib - v63 - i2 - Summer 2015 - p122(1) [501+]
Vgenopoulos, Maximos - *Primacy in the Church from Vatican I to Vatican II: An Orthodox Perspective*
CH - v84 - i2 - June 2015 - p484(2) [501+]
Viala, Kevin - *I Am a Zamboni Machine (Illus. by Migliari, Paola)*
c Res Links - v20 - i3 - Feb 2015 - p4(1) [51-500]
Viano, Hannah - *Arrow to Alaska: A Pacific Northwest Adventure (Illus. by Viano, Hannah)*
c HB Guide - v26 - i2 - Fall 2015 - p55(1) [51-500]
c KR - Jan 15 2015 - pNA [51-500]
B Is for Bear: A Natural Alphabet (Illus. by Viano, Hannah)
c KR - August 1 2015 - pNA [51-500]
c SLJ - v61 - i10 - Oct 2015 - p131(1) [51-500]
Viau, Nancy - *City Street Beat (Illus. by Bakos, Barbara)*
c HB Guide - v26 - i2 - Fall 2015 - p55(1) [51-500]
Vick, Brian E. - *The Congress of Vienna: Power and Politics after Napoleon*
HT - v65 - i10 - Oct 2015 - p56(2) [501+]
Vickers, Jason E. - *The Cambridge Companion to American Methodism*
JR - v95 - i3 - July 2015 - p422(2) [501+]
Vickers, Rebecca - *Every Person Has a History*
y HB Guide - v26 - i1 - Spring 2015 - p197(1) [51-500]
Vickers, Salley - *The Boy Who Could See Death*
Spec - v327 - i9736 - April 4 2015 - p36(1) [501+]
Vickers, Tom - *Refugees, Capitalism and the British State: Implications for Social Workers, Volunteers and Activists*
CS - v44 - i2 - March 2015 - p272-273 [501+]
ERS - v38 - i3 - March 2015 - p504(4) [501+]
Victoria, Alexandrina - *The Adventures of Alice Laselles*
Spec - v328 - i9745 - June 6 2015 - p36(2) [501+]
Vida, Vendela - *The Diver's Clothes Lie Empty (Read by Sands, Xe). Audiobook Review*
BL - v112 - i3 - Oct 1 2015 - p85(1) [51-500]
The Diver's Clothes Lie Empty
BL - v111 - i18 - May 15 2015 - p22(1) [51-500]
Ent W - i1367 - June 12 2015 - p80(1) [501+]
KR - March 15 2015 - pNA [501+]
Mac - v128 - i24 - June 22 2015 - p58(1) [501+]
NYT - June 17 2015 - pC4(L) [501+]
NYTBR - June 21 2015 - p11(L) [501+]
PW - v262 - i17 - April 27 2015 - p43(1) [51-500]
Vidal, Beatriz Martin - *Bird (Illus. by Vidal, Beatriz Martin)*
c KR - July 15 2015 - pNA [51-500]
Vidal, Cecile - *Francais? La nation en debat entre colonies et metropole, XVIe-XIXe siecle*
AHR - v120 - i3 - June 2015 - p975-976 [501+]
Louisiana: Crossroads of the Atlantic World
JSH - v81 - i2 - May 2015 - p436(3) [501+]
JAH - v102 - i2 - Sept 2015 - p528-529 [501+]
JIH - v45 - i4 - Spring 2015 - p585-586 [501+]
Vidal, Gore - *The City and the Pillar*
New R - v246 - i11 - Fall 2015 - p80(4) [501+]
Hollywood: A Novel of the Twenties
TLS - i5872 - Oct 16 2015 - p16(1) [501+]
Kalki
TLS - i5842 - March 20 2015 - p16(1) [501+]
Thieves Fall Out
NYT - April 13 2015 - pC6(L) [501+]
PW - v262 - i6 - Feb 9 2015 - p46(1) [501+]
Spec - v327 - i9739 - April 25 2015 - p43(1) [501+]
Vidal, Laurent - *Anthropology in the Making: Research in Health and Development*
MAQ - v29 - i2 - June 2015 - pb43-b45 [501+]
Vidal, Severine - *Mega Bunny (Illus. by Barroux)*
c SLJ - v61 - i12 - Dec 2015 - p97(1) [51-500]
Mega Mouse (Illus. by Barroux, Stephanie)
c KR - Oct 1 2015 - pNA [51-500]
c SLJ - v61 - i12 - Dec 2015 - p97(1) [51-500]
Mega Pig (Illus. by Barroux)
c SLJ - v61 - i12 - Dec 2015 - p97(1) [51-500]
Mega Wolf (Illus. by Barroux, Stephanie)
c SLJ - v61 - i12 - Dec 2015 - p97(1) [51-500]

Vidas, Moulie - *Tradition and the Formation of the Talmud*
　　TLS - i5838 - Feb 20 2015 - p28(1) [501+]
Vidu, Adonis - *Atonement, Law, and Justice: The Cross in Historical and Cultural Contexts*
　　CH - v84 - i4 - Dec 2015 - p930(2) [501+]
　　IBMR - v39 - i4 - Oct 2015 - p236(2) [501+]
Vidyasagar, Mathukumalli - *Hidden Markov Processes: Theory and Applications to Biology*
　　QRB - v90 - i3 - Sept 2015 - p320(2) [501+]
Vieira, Jose Luandino - *Our Musseque*
　　TLS - i5841 - March 13 2015 - p19(1) [501+]
Vieira, Linda - *Grand Canyon: A Trail Through Time (Illus. by Canyon, Christopher)*
　c　Sci & Ch - v52 - i8 - April-May 2015 - p16 [501+]
Vieira, Mark A. - *Majestic Hollywood: The Greatest Films of 1939*
　　Roundup M - v22 - i6 - August 2015 - p41(1) [501+]
Viel, Tanguy - *La disparition de Jim Sullivan*
　　FR - v89 - i2 - Dec 2015 - p66(15) [51-500]
Vienna 1815: The Making of a European Security Culture
　　HNet - Jan 2015 - pNA [501+]
Vierte Mitteldeutsche Konferenz fur Medizin- und Wissenschaftsgeschichte
　　HNet - July 2015 - pNA [501+]
Viertel, Jack - *The Secret Life of the American Musical: How Broadway Shows Are Built*
　　KR - Oct 15 2015 - pNA [501+]
　　LJ - v140 - i20 - Dec 1 2015 - p99(1) [501+]
　　PW - v262 - i45 - Nov 9 2015 - p49(1) [51-500]
Viets, Elaine - *Checked Out*
　　PW - v262 - i13 - March 30 2015 - p58(1) [51-500]
　　A Dog Gone Murder
　　RVBW - July 2015 - pNA [501+]
Viger, Lisa - *Easy, Affordable Raw: How to Go Raw on $10 a Day (or Less).*
　　Veg J - v34 - i2 - April-June 2015 - p31(1) [51-500]
Vigil, Ariana E. - *War Echoes: Gender and Militarization in U.S. Latina/o Cultural Production*
　　NWSA Jnl - v27 - i2 - Summer 2015 - p200-202 [501+]
Vigna, Paul - *The Age of Cryptocurrency: How Bitcoin and Digital Money Are Challenging the Global Economic Order*
　　Econ - v414 - i8920 - Jan 10 2015 - p77(US) [501+]
　　Har Bus R - v93 - i6 - June 2015 - p118(2) [501+]
　　NYTBR - March 22 2015 - p18(L) [501+]
　　Cryptocurrency: How Bitcoin and Digital Money are Challenging the Global Economic Order
　　New Sci - v225 - i3004 - Jan 17 2015 - p40(2) [501+]
　　TLS - i5861 - July 31 2015 - p28(1) [501+]
Vignoles, Julian - *A Delicate Wildness: The Life and Loves of David Thomson, 1914-1988*
　　TLS - i5853 - June 5 2015 - p27(1) [501+]
Viguie, Debbie - *The Rules*
　　SLJ - v61 - i4 - April 2015 - p165(1) [51-500]
　y　VOYA - v38 - i2 - June 2015 - p77(1) [51-500]
Viguie, Renan - *La traversee electrique des Pyrenees: Histoire de l'interconnexion entre la France et l'Espagne*
　　T&C - v56 - i3 - July 2015 - p769-770 [501+]
Vihvelin, Kadri - *Causes, Laws, and Free Will: Why Determinism Doesn't Matter*
　　Ethics - v125 - i4 - July 2015 - p1230(7) [501+]
Vila-Matas, Enrique - *A Brief History of Portable Literature*
　　BL - v111 - i19-20 - June 1 2015 - p38(1) [501+]
　　LJ - v140 - i10 - June 1 2015 - p92(3) [501+]
　　New R - v246 - i7-8 - July-August 2015 - p82(2) [501+]
　　NYT - August 13 2015 - pC4(L) [501+]
　　PW - v262 - i12 - March 23 2015 - p42(1) [501+]
　　TLS - i5854 - June 12 2015 - p13(1) [501+]
　　TLS - i5863 - August 14 2015 - p20(1) [501+]
　　The Illogic of Kassel
　　HR - v68 - i3 - Autumn 2015 - p510-516 [501+]
　　LJ - v140 - i9 - May 15 2015 - p77(2) [51-500]
　　New R - v246 - i7-8 - July-August 2015 - p82(2) [501+]
　　NYT - August 13 2015 - pC4(L) [501+]
　　PW - v262 - i17 - April 27 2015 - p44(1) [51-500]
　　TLS - i5854 - June 12 2015 - p13(1) [501+]
　　TLS - i5863 - August 14 2015 - p20(1) [501+]
Viladrich, Anahi - *More Than Two to Tango: Argentine Tango Immigrants in New York City*
　　CS - v44 - i6 - Nov 2015 - p864-866 [501+]

Vilaseca, David - *Queer Events: Post-Deconstructive Subjectivities in Spanish Writing and Film, 1960s to 1990s*
　　MLR - v110 - i3 - July 2015 - p887-889 [501+]
Vilcek, Jan - *Love and Science: A Memoir*
　　KR - Dec 1 2015 - pNA [501+]
Vilendrer, Nikki - *Power Play*
　　PW - v262 - i32 - August 10 2015 - p44(1) [51-500]
Villa-Flores, Javier - *Emotions and Daily Life in Colonial Mexico*
　　AHR - v120 - i3 - June 2015 - p1079-1081 [501+]
　　HAHR - v95 - i1 - Feb 2015 - p154-155 [501+]
Villaceque, N. - *Spectateurs de paroles! Deliberation democratique et theatre a Athenes a l'e'poque classique*
　　Class R - v65 - i2 - Oct 2015 - p366-368 [501+]
Villalobos, Ana - *Motherload: Making It All Better in Insecure Times*
　　TimHES - i2186 - Jan 15 2015 - p49-51 [501+]
Villani, Cedric - *Birth of a Theorem: A Mathematical Adventure*
　　New Sci - v225 - i3010 - Feb 28 2015 - p50(1) [501+]
　　PW - v262 - i8 - Feb 23 2015 - p64(2) [51-500]
　　Spec - v327 - i9731 - Feb 28 2015 - p38(1) [501+]
　　TimHES - i2192 - Feb 26 2015 - p46-47 [501+]
　　TimHES - i2211 - July 9 2015 - p46(1) [501+]
　　BL - v111 - i11 - Feb 1 2015 - p7(1) [51-500]
Villanueva, Sara - *The Angst of Adolescence: How to Parent Your Teen, and Live to Laugh About It*
　　PW - v262 - i29 - July 20 2015 - p186(1) [51-500]
Villanueva, Tino - *Asi Hablo Penelope*
　　WLT - v89 - i1 - Jan-Feb 2015 - p79(1) [51-500]
Villareal, Ray - *On the Other Side of the Bridge*
　y　CH Bwatch - Feb 2015 - pNA [501+]
Villeneuve, Anne - *Loula and Mister the Monster (Illus. by Villeneuve, Anne)*
　c　BL - v112 - i1 - Sept 1 2015 - p120(1) [51-500]
　c　KR - May 15 2015 - pNA [501+]
　c　SLJ - v61 - i12 - Dec 2015 - p97(1) [51-500]
　　Loula and the Sister Recipe
　c　HB Guide - v26 - i1 - Spring 2015 - p49(1) [51-500]
　c　Res Links - v20 - i3 - Feb 2015 - p54(1) [501+]
Villoro, Juan - *The Guilty: Stories*
　　BL - v111 - i19-20 - June 1 2015 - p40(1) [51-500]
　　The Guilty Stories
　　NYTBR - July 12 2015 - p30(L) [501+]
　　The Guilty: Stories
　　TLS - i5872 - Oct 16 2015 - p26(1) [501+]
Vilson, Jose Luis - *This Is Not a Test: A New Narrative on Race, Class, and Education*
　　HNet - August 2015 - pNA [501+]
Vince, Gaia - *Adventures in the Anthropocene: A Journey to the Heart of the Planet We Made*
　　AS - v84 - i1 - Wntr 2015 - p104(3) [501+]
Vince, Natalya - *The Republic Unsettled: Muslim French and the Contradictions of Secularism*
　　FS - v69 - i4 - Oct 2015 - p568-569 [501+]
Vincent, Constance L. - *Not Going Gently: A Psychologist Fights Back against Alzheimer's for Her Mother ... and Perhaps Herself*
　　KR - June 15 2015 - pNA [501+]
Vincent, John - *LGBT People and the UK Cultural Sector: The Response of Libraries, Museums, Archives and Heritage since 1950*
　　LR - v64 - i3 - March 2015 - p263-264 [501+]
　c　Sch Lib - v63 - i2 - Summer 2015 - p127(1) [501+]
Vincent, Nicholas - *Magna Carta: A Very Short Introduction*
　　HT - v65 - i6 - June 2015 - p56(2) [501+]
　　Magna Carta: The Foundation of Freedom 1215-2015
　　HT - v65 - i6 - June 2015 - p56(2) [501+]
　　Lon R Bks - v37 - i8 - April 23 2015 - p15(3) [501+]
　　TLS - i5868 - Sept 18 2015 - p3(2) [501+]
Vincent, Norah - *Adeline (Read by James, Corrie).*
　　Audiobook Review
　　LJ - v140 - i13 - August 1 2015 - p47(2) [51-500]
　　Adeline
　　KR - Feb 1 2015 - pNA [51-500]
　　LJ - v140 - i7 - April 15 2015 - p82(2) [51-500]
　　NS - v144 - i5261 - May 7 2015 - p46(3) [51-500]
　　NYTBR - June 14 2015 - p26(L) [501+]
　　PW - v262 - i8 - Feb 23 2015 - p50(1) [501+]
Vincent, Rachel - *Menagerie*
　　KR - August 1 2015 - pNA [51-500]
　　NYTBR - Oct 18 2015 - p18(L) [501+]
　　PW - v262 - i33 - August 17 2015 - p55(1) [51-500]

　　The Stars Never Rise
　y　CCB-B - v69 - i1 - Sept 2015 - p63(1) [51-500]
　y　HB Guide - v26 - i2 - Fall 2015 - p142(1) [51-500]
　y　KR - March 1 2015 - pNA [51-500]
　y　PW - v262 - i17 - April 27 2015 - p76(2) [51-500]
　y　SLJ - v61 - i3 - March 2015 - p163(1) [51-500]
　y　VOYA - v38 - i2 - June 2015 - p84(1) [51-500]
Vincent, Wendy - *The Complete Guide to Working With Worms: Using the Gardener's Best Friend for Organic Gardening and Composting*
　　Bwatch - Sept 2015 - pNA [51-500]
Vincenti, F.R. - *The Santero*
　　KR - Jan 1 2015 - pNA [501+]
Vincenzi, Penny - *A Perfect Heritage*
　　BL - v111 - i19-20 - June 1 2015 - p44(1) [51-500]
　　KR - May 1 2015 - pNA [501+]
　　LJ - v140 - i8 - May 1 2015 - p66(1) [51-500]
Vinchesi, M.A. - *Calpurnii Siculi: Eclogae*
　　Class R - v65 - i2 - Oct 2015 - p462-463 [501+]
Vinciguerra, Thomas - *Cast of Characters: Wolcott Gibbs, E.B. White, James Thurber, and the Golden Age of the New Yorker*
　　BL - v112 - i3 - Oct 1 2015 - p4(1) [51-500]
　　KR - Sept 1 2015 - pNA [501+]
　　LJ - v140 - i15 - Sept 15 2015 - p85(1) [51-500]
　　NYT - Nov 15 2015 - p3(L) [501+]
　　PW - v262 - i30 - July 27 2015 - p53(1) [51-500]
Vine, David - *Base Nation: How U.S. Military Bases Abroad Harm America and the World*
　　KR - June 1 2015 - pNA [501+]
　　LJ - v140 - i11 - June 15 2015 - p100(1) [51-500]
　　PW - v262 - i22 - June 1 2015 - p52(2) [51-500]
Vinel, Nicolas - *In Nicomachi arithmeticam*
　　Class R - v65 - i2 - Oct 2015 - p401-402 [501+]
Viney, William - *Waste: A Philosophy of Things*
　　J Phil - v112 - i5 - May 2015 - p280(1) [501+]
Vinogradova, Lyuba - *Defending the Motherland: The Soviet Women Who Fought Hitler's Aces*
　　NS - v144 - i5260 - May 1 2015 - p49(1) [501+]
　　Spec - v327 - i9737 - April 11 2015 - p42(1) [501+]
　　TLS - i5851 - May 22 2015 - p10(1) [501+]
Vint, Jesse Lee - *William the Conqueror vs. King Harold*
　　KR - Nov 1 2015 - pNA [501+]
Vint, Sherryl - *Science Fiction: A Guide for the Perplexed*
　　SFS - v42 - i1 - March 2015 - p191-193 [501+]
Viola, Joshua - *Nightmares Unhinged*
　　KR - Dec 15 2015 - pNA [501+]
Violante, Susan - *Tuma: The Tribe's Little Princess (Illus. by Violante, Susan)*
　c　CH Bwatch - Feb 2015 - pNA [51-500]
Violette Room - *Stylish Remakes: Upcycle Your Old T's, Sweats and Flannels into Trendy Street Fashion Pieces*
　　LJ - v140 - i13 - August 1 2015 - p97(1) [51-500]
Viorst, Judith - *Alexander, Who's Trying His Best to Be the Best Boy Ever (Illus. by Mones, Isidre)*
　c　HB Guide - v26 - i1 - Spring 2015 - p49(1) [51-500]
　　And Two Boys Booed (Illus. by Blackall, Sophie)
　c　CCB-B - v68 - i5 - Jan 2015 - p280(1) [51-500]
　c　HB Guide - v26 - i1 - Spring 2015 - p49(1) [51-500]
　　What Are You Glad About? What Are You Mad About? Poems for When a Person Needs a Poem (Illus. by White, Lee)
　c　KR - Nov 1 2015 - pNA [51-500]
　c　PW - v262 - i52 - Dec 21 2015 - p156(2) [501+]
Viraraghavan, Chitra - *The Americans*
　　KR - June 1 2015 - pNA [51-500]
Virgo, Sean - *The Shadow Mother (Illus. by Perez, Javier Serrano)*
　y　HB Guide - v26 - i1 - Spring 2015 - p126(1) [51-500]
Virjan, Emma J. - *What This Story Needs Is a Hush and a Shush (Illus. by Virjan, Emma J.)*
　c　KR - Oct 1 2015 - pNA [51-500]
　c　PW - v262 - i44 - Nov 2 2015 - p84(1) [501+]
　　What This Story Needs Is a Pig in a Wig (Illus. by Virjan, Emma J.)
　c　HB Guide - v26 - i2 - Fall 2015 - p62(1) [51-500]
　c　KR - March 15 2015 - pNA [51-500]
　c　NYTBR - August 23 2015 - p26(L) [501+]
　c　PW - v262 - i9 - March 2 2015 - p82(2) [51-500]
　c　PW - v262 - i49 - Dec 2 2015 - p39(1) [51-500]
　c　SLJ - v61 - i5 - May 2015 - p80(1) [51-500]
Viroli, Maurizio - *Redeeming "The Prince": The Meaning of Machiavelli's Masterpiece*
　　JMH - v87 - i2 - June 2015 - p461(3) [501+]
　　AHR - v120 - i4 - Oct 2015 - p1424-1426 [501+]
Virtuosen der Offentlichkeit? Friedrich von Gentz, 1764-1832: im globalen intellektuellen Kontext seiner

Zeit
 HNet - May 2015 - pNA [501+]
Visak, Tatjana - *Killing Happy Animals: Explorations in Utilitarian Ethics*
 J Phil - v112 - i5 - May 2015 - p280(1) [501+]
Visceglia, Maria Antonietta - *Morte e elezione del papa: Norme, riti e conflitti: L'Eta moderna*
 HER - v130 - i542 - Feb 2015 - p202(3) [501+]
Visconti, John D. - *Fetch More Dollars for Your Dog Training Business*
 RVBW - June 2015 - pNA [51-500]
Visits - Bilateral Relations and Personal Encounters in Israel, Germany and Beyond. International Workshop marking 50 Years of Israeli-German Diplomatic Relations 1965-2015
 HNet - August 2015 - pNA [501+]
Visscher, Roemer - *Brabbeling (1614): Een Bloemlezing*
 Ren Q - v68 - i1 - Spring 2015 - p416-417 [501+]
Visser, Arnoud S.Q. - *Reading Augustine in the Reformation: The Flexibility of Intellectual Authority in Europe, 1500-1620*
 HER - v130 - i543 - April 2015 - p439(2) [501+]
Visser, Leontine - *Governing New Guinea: An Oral History of Papuan Administrators, 1950-1990*
 Pac A - v88 - i2 - June 2015 - p375 [501+]
Vistein, Geri - *I Am Coyote*
 c KR - Sept 15 2015 - pNA [51-500]
 c SLJ - v61 - i12 - Dec 2015 - p109(1) [51-500]
Viswanath, Kaushik - *Monkeys on a Fast (Illus. by Ranade, Shilpa)*
 c KR - Jan 1 2015 - pNA [51-500]
Viswanath, Rupa - *The Pariah Problem: Caste, Religion, and the Social in Modern India*
 AHR - v120 - i3 - June 2015 - p987-988 [501+]
 For Aff - v94 - i1 - Jan-Feb 2015 - pNA [51-500]
 JAS - v74 - i3 - August 2015 - p778-780 [501+]
 Pac A - v88 - i4 - Dec 2015 - p948 [501+]
Viswanathan, Padma - *The Ever After of Ashwin Rao*
 BL - v111 - i18 - May 15 2015 - p22(1) [51-500]
 Can Lit - i224 - Spring 2015 - p111 [501+]
 KR - April 1 2015 - pNA [51-500]
 WLT - v89 - i3-4 - May-August 2015 - p119(2) [501+]
Viteritti, Joseph P. - *Summer in the City: John Lindsay, New York, and the American Dream*
 Am St - v54 - i2 - Summer 2015 - p45-55 [501+]
Viterna, Jocelyn - *Women in War: The Micro-processes of Mobilization in El Salvador*
 AJS - v120 - i5 - March 2015 - p1576(3) [501+]
Vitiello, Domenic - *Engineering Philadelphia: The Sellers Family and the Industrial Metropolis*
 T&C - v56 - i1 - Jan 2015 - p272-274 [501+]
Vitiello, Massimiliano - *Theodahad: A Platonic King at the Collapse of Ostrogothic Italy*
 Med R - June 2015 - pNA [501+]
Vito, Gennaro F. - *Practical Program Evaluation for Criminal Justice*
 CrimJR - v40 - i1 - March 2015 - p103-104 [501+]
Vitoria, Francisco de - *De actibus humanis / Sobre los actos humanos*
 Med R - August 2015 - pNA [501+]
Viva, Frank - *Outstanding in the Rain (Illus. by Viva, Frank)*
 c HB Guide - v26 - i2 - Fall 2015 - p55(1) [51-500]
 c KR - Feb 15 2015 - pNA [51-500]
 c PW - v262 - i6 - Feb 9 2015 - p64(1) [51-500]
 c Res Links - v20 - i5 - June 2015 - p8(2) [51-500]
 c SLJ - v61 - i2 - Feb 2015 - p81(1) [51-500]
Young Charlotte, Filmmaker (Illus. by Viva, Frank)
 c KR - August 15 2015 - pNA [51-500]
 c PW - v262 - i28 - July 13 2015 - p63(1) [51-500]
 c SLJ - v61 - i10 - Oct 2015 - p85(1) [51-500]
Vivancos Perez, Ricardo F. - *Radical Chicana Poetics*
 AL - v87 - i2 - June 2015 - p405-408 [501+]
Vives, Bastien - *The Chase (Illus. by Vives, Bastien)*
 y BL - v112 - i6 - Nov 15 2015 - p35(2) [51-500]
The Royal Cup (Illus. by Vives, Bastien)
 y BL - v111 - i19-20 - June 1 2015 - p67(1) [51-500]
 y SLJ - v61 - i7 - July 2015 - p100(1) [51-500]
The Stranger (Illus. by Vives, Bastien)
 y BL - v111 - i16 - April 15 2015 - p40(1) [51-500]
Vivian, H.W. - *War of Rain*
 y CH Bwatch - June 2015 - pNA [51-500]
Vivian, Siobhan - *A Little Friendly Advice*
 y CH Bwatch - May 2015 - pNA [51-500]
Vivo, Roberto - *War: A Crime against Humanity*
 KR - Oct 1 2015 - pNA [501+]
Vizenor, Gerald - *Blue Ravens*
 WLT - v89 - i2 - March-April 2015 - p79(1) [51-500]
Vizyenos, Georgios - *Moskov Selim*
 TLS - i5854 - June 12 2015 - p21(1) [501+]

Vlacos, Sophie - *Ricoeur, Literature and Imagination*
 J Phil - v112 - i5 - May 2015 - p280(1) [501+]
Vladislavic, Ivan - *The Folly*
 LJ - v140 - i17 - Oct 15 2015 - p83(1) [51-500]
 KR - June 15 2015 - pNA [51-500]
 PW - v262 - i25 - June 22 2015 - p116(1) [51-500]
The Restless Supermarket
 NS - v144 - i5244 - Jan 9 2015 - p40(2) [51-500]
Vlahos, Len - *Scar Girl*
 y KR - Dec 15 2015 - pNA [51-500]
Vlassopoulos, Kostas - *Greeks and Barbarians*
 Class R - v65 - i1 - April 2015 - p169-170 [501+]
Vnuk, Rebecca - *The Weeding Handbook: A Shelf-by-Shelf Guide*
 LJ - v140 - i15 - Sept 15 2015 - p93(1) [51-500]
 RVBW - July 2015 - pNA [51-500]
Voake, Charlotte - *Melissa's Octopus and Other Unsuitable Pets (Illus. by Voake, Charlotte)*
 c CCB-B - v68 - i11 - July-August 2015 - p572(1) [51-500]
 c CH Bwatch - July 2015 - pNA [51-500]
 c HB Guide - v26 - i2 - Fall 2015 - p21(1) [51-500]
 c Magpies - v30 - i1 - March 2015 - p26(2) [51-500]
 c Sch Lib - v63 - i1 - Spring 2015 - p33(1) [51-500]
 c SLJ - v61 - i6 - June 2015 - p94(1) [51-500]
Vodicka, Karel - *Die Prager Botschaftsfluchtlinge 1989: Geschichte und Dokumente*
 HNet - March 2015 - pNA [501+]
Vodolazkin, Eugene - *Laurus*
 BL - v112 - i3 - Oct 1 2015 - p30(1) [51-500]
 KR - August 1 2015 - pNA [501+]
Voegelin, Eric - *Philosopher of History*
 Dialogue - v54 - i3 - Sept 2015 - p541-546 [501+]
Voelkel, J&P - *The Lost City*
 c HB Guide - v26 - i2 - Fall 2015 - p105(1) [51-500]
Voelker, Andrew - *Beneath the Greater Sky*
 KR - May 1 2015 - pNA [501+]
Vogan, Travis - *ESPN: The Making of a Sports Media Empire*
 BL - v112 - i4 - Oct 15 2015 - p13(1) [51-500]
 LJ - v140 - i17 - Oct 15 2015 - p96(2) [51-500]
Vogel, Steven - *Comparative Biomechanics: Life's Physical World*
 QRB - v90 - i1 - March 2015 - p108(2) [501+]
Vogel, Vin - *The Thing about Yetis (Illus. by Vogel, Vin)*
 c BL - v112 - i5 - Nov 1 2015 - p68(1) [51-500]
 c KR - Sept 15 2015 - pNA [51-500]
 c PW - v262 - i39 - Sept 28 2015 - p88(1) [51-500]
Vogelin, Salome - *Sonic Possible Worlds: Hearing the Continuum of Sound*
 J Phil - v112 - i5 - May 2015 - p280(1) [501+]
Vogelsang, Jessica - *All Dogs Go to Kevin: Everything Three Dogs Taught Me (That I Didn't Learn in Veterinary School)*
 KR - April 15 2015 - pNA [51-500]
 PW - v262 - i19 - May 11 2015 - p48(1) [51-500]
 SEP - v287 - i3 - May-June 2015 - p24(1) [51]
Vogler, Gunter - *Die Tauferherrschaft in Munster und die Reichsstande: Die politische, religiose und militarische Dimension eines Konflikts in den Jahren 1534 bis 1536*
 Ger Q - v88 - i2 - Spring 2015 - p268(3) [501+]
Vogt, Beth K. - *Crazy Little Thing Called Love*
 KR - May 15 2015 - pNA [51-500]
 RVBW - Oct 2015 - pNA [51-500]
Vogt, Margrit - *Von Kunstworten und -werten: Die Entstehung der deutschen Kunstkritik in Periodika der Aufklarung*
 GSR - v38 - i1 - Feb 2015 - p159-161 [501+]
Vohra, Manish - *The Perceptionist*
 KR - May 1 2015 - pNA [501+]
Voigt, Cynthia - *Angus and Sadie (Read by Carter, Wendy). Audiobook Review*
 BL - v111 - i13 - March 1 2015 - p69(2) [51-500]
The Book of Kings (Illus. by Bruno, Iacopo)
 c BL - v111 - i21 - July 1 2015 - p74(1) [51-500]
 c CCB-B - v69 - i2 - Oct 2015 - p120(1) [51-500]
 c HB - v91 - i5 - Sept-Oct 2015 - p121(2) [51-500]
 c KR - July 1 2015 - pNA [51-500]
 c SLJ - v61 - i7 - July 2015 - p84(1) [51-500]
The Book of Secrets (Illus. by Bruno, Iacopo)
 c HB Guide - v26 - i1 - Spring 2015 - p95(1) [51-500]
Voigt, Deborah - *Call Me Debbie: True Confessions of a Down-to-Earth Diva*
 Bwatch - April 2015 - pNA [51-500]
 ON - v79 - i10 - April 2015 - p67(1) [51-500]
Voigt, Sebastian - *Arbeiterbewegung - Nation - Globalisierung: Bestandsaufnahmen einer alten Debatte*
 HNet - Sept 2015 - pNA [501+]
Voinov, Aleksandr - *Nightingale*
 BL - v111 - i22 - August 1 2015 - p25(1) [51-500]

Vojtech, Anna - *Surprise in the Meadow (Illus. by Vojtech, Anna)*
 c KR - Dec 15 2015 - pNA [51-500]
Vokes, Richard - *Ghosts of Kanungu: Fertility, Secrecy and Exchange in the Great Lakes of East Africa*
 JRAI - v21 - i1 - March 2015 - p242(2) [501+]
Volk, Kyle G. - *Moral Minorities and the Making of American Democracy*
 AHR - v120 - i4 - Oct 2015 - p1483-1484 [501+]
 HLR - v128 - i6 - April 2015 - p1896(1) [1-50]
 JAH - v102 - i2 - Sept 2015 - p556-557 [501+]
Volk, Toni - *Keota*
 PW - v262 - i1 - Jan 5 2015 - p50(2) [51-500]
Volkart, Silvia - *Rom am Bodensee: Die Zeit des Konstanzer Konzils*
 HNet - Feb 2015 - pNA [501+]
Volkermord zur Primetime. Der Holocaust im Fernsehen. Simon Wiesenthal Conference 2014
 HNet - March 2015 - pNA [501+]
Volland, Susan - *Mastering Sauces: The Home Cook's Guide to New Techniques for Fresh Flavors*
 LJ - v140 - i12 - July 1 2015 - p107(1) [51-500]
 PW - v262 - i18 - May 4 2015 - p113(1) [51-500]
Vollmann, William T. - *The Dying Grass*
 BL - v111 - i19-20 - June 1 2015 - p37(1) [51-500]
 CSM - July 28 2015 - pNA [501+]
 KR - May 15 2015 - pNA [501+]
 LJ - v140 - i16 - Oct 1 2015 - p5(1) [51-500]
 NS - v144 - i5275 - August 14 2015 - p43(1) [501+]
 NYTBR - August 2 2015 - p11(L) [501+]
 PW - v262 - i21 - May 25 2015 - p30(1) [51-500]
Last Stories and Other Stories
 NYTBR - Sept 13 2015 - p32(L) [501+]
Volodarsky, Boris - *Stalin's Agent: The Life and Death of Alexander Orlov*
 TLS - i5863 - August 14 2015 - p23(1) [501+]
 Spec - v327 - i9730 - Feb 21 2015 - p46(1) [501+]
Volodine, Antoine - *Post-Exoticism in Ten Lessons, Lesson Eleven*
 KR - April 15 2015 - pNA [501+]
Voloj, Julian - *Ghetto Brother: Warrior to Peacemaker (Illus. by Ahlering, Claudia)*
 y BL - v111 - i18 - May 15 2015 - p41(1) [51-500]
 PW - v262 - i19 - May 11 2015 - p44(1) [51-500]
 y SLJ - v61 - i6 - June 2015 - p146(1) [51-500]
Volponi, Paul - *Game Seven*
 c KR - Jan 1 2015 - pNA [51-500]
 y BL - v111 - i11 - Feb 1 2015 - p44(1) [51-500]
 y CCB-B - v68 - i8 - April 2015 - p422(1) [51-500]
 y HB Guide - v26 - i2 - Fall 2015 - p142(1) [51-500]
 y SLJ - v61 - i5 - May 2015 - p116(1) [51-500]
 y VOYA - v37 - i6 - Feb 2015 - p69(1) [51-500]
Voltaggio, Bryan - *Home: Recipes to Cook with Family and Friends*
 LJ - v140 - i7 - April 15 2015 - p112(1) [51-500]
 PW - v262 - i14 - April 6 2015 - p54(1) [51-500]
Voltaire - *Micromegas and Other Tales*
 TLS - i5853 - June 5 2015 - p26(2) [51-500]
Voltmer, Katrin - *The Media in Transitional Democracies*
 E-A St - v67 - i1 - Jan 2015 - p155(3) [501+]
Vom (Be-)Nutzen der Bucher. Praktiken des Buchgebrauchs in der Fruhen Neuzeit
 HNet - Feb 2015 - pNA [501+]
Von Bregenz bis Brody - von Zara bis Znojmo
 HNet - Feb 2015 - pNA [501+]
von Bulow, Ulrich - *DDR-Literatur: Eine Archivexpedition*
 HNet - Feb 2015 - pNA [501+]
Von Daten zu Erkenntnissen: Digitale Geisteswissenschaften als Mittler zwischen Information und Interpretation. DHd-Jahrestagung 2015
 HNet - July 2015 - pNA [501+]
Von Freymann, Ronald - *Gold-in-Quartz*
 SPBW - August 2015 - pNA [51-500]
von Glahn, Denise - *Music and the Skillful Listener: American Women Compose the Natural World*
 Notes - v72 - i1 - Sept 2015 - p178(4) [501+]
von Hassell, Malve - *The Falconer's Apprentice*
 y KR - April 15 2015 - pNA [501+]
 y VOYA - v38 - i3 - August 2015 - p72(1) [51-500]
Von Holleben, Jan - *That's What You Think!: A Mind-Boggling Guide to the Brain*
 SLJ - v61 - i4 - April 2015 - p185(1) [51-500]
von Kellenbach, Katharina - *The Mark of Cain: Guilt and Denial in the Post-War Lives of Nazi Perpetrators*
 CEH - v48 - i1 - March 2015 - p134-136 [501+]
Von Kuste zu Kuste - der Westliche Ostseeraum als Kontaktzone vom Fruhmittelalter bis zur Fruhen Neuzeit
 HNet - July 2015 - pNA [501+]

Von Oelhafen, Ingrid - *Hitler's Forgotten Children*
    KR - Dec 15 2015 - pNA [501+]

Von Osten, Hans - *Roundtower*
    KR - Feb 15 2015 - pNA [501+]

von Oy, Jenna - *Situation Momedy*
    BL - v112 - i2 - Sept 15 2015 - p8(1) [51-500]

Von Sholly, Pete - *Pete Von Sholly's History of Monsters*
    PW - v262 - i44 - Nov 2 2015 - p79(1) [51-500]

von Thadden, Rudolf - *Trieglaff: Balancing Church and Politics in a Pomeranian World, 1807-1948*
    CEH - v48 - i2 - June 2015 - p255-256 [501+]

Vonnegut, Kurt - *Breakfast of Champions (Read by Malkovich, John). Audiobook Review*
    NYTBR - Nov 22 2015 - p22(L) [501+]

Vora, Neha - *Impossible Citizens: Dubai's Indian Diaspora*
    IJMES - v47 - i4 - Nov 2015 - p852-854 [501+]

Vorderman, Carol - *Computer Coding for Kids*
    c Magpies - v30 - i4 - Sept 2015 - p24(1) [501+]
Help Your Kids with Music
    y SLJ - v61 - i11 - Nov 2015 - p138(2) [51-500]

Vorhaus, Robbie - *One Less, One More*
    SPBW - Jan 2015 - pNA [501+]

Vorsorgen in der Moderne. Akteure - Raume - Praktiken
    HNet - May 2015 - pNA [501+]

Vorst, Rochel Groner - *Time to Start a Brand New Year (Illus. by Scheinberg, Shepsil)*
    c CH Bwatch - Sept 2015 - pNA [51-500]

Voskuhl, Adelheid - *Androids in the Enlightenment: Mechanics, Artisans, and Cultures of the Self*
    Isis - v106 - i1 - March 2015 - p188(2) [501+]
    JMH - v87 - i1 - March 2015 - p219(3) [501+]

Voss, Hanna - *Reflexion von ethnischer Identitat(szuweisung) im deutschen Gegenwarts-theater*
    Ger Q - v88 - i3 - Summer 2015 - p395(4) [501+]

Vosse, Wilhelm - *Governing Insecurity in Japan: The Domestic Discourse and Policy Response*
    Pac A - v88 - i4 - Dec 2015 - p917 [501+]

Voth, Hans-Joachim - *Prometheus Shackled: Goldsmith Banks and England's Financial Revolution after 1700*
    T&C - v56 - i1 - Jan 2015 - p269-270 [501+]

Vout, Caroline - *The Hills of Rome: Signature of an Eternal City*
    Class R - v65 - i2 - Oct 2015 - p591-592 [501+]

Vowell, Sarah - *Lafayette in the Somewhat United States (Read by Vowell, Sarah, with eight additional readers). Audiobook Review*
    LJ - v140 - i20 - Dec 1 2015 - p61(1) [501+]
Lafayette in the Somewhat United States
    KR - July 1 2015 - pNA [501+]
    LJ - v140 - i14 - Sept 1 2015 - p119(1) [51-500]
    NYTBR - Nov 22 2015 - p31(L) [501+]
    PW - v262 - i30 - July 27 2015 - p51(1) [51-500]

Vowinckel, Annette - *Cold War Cultures: Perspectives on Eastern and Western European Societies*
    CEH - v48 - i1 - March 2015 - p142-143 [501+]

Voyer, Andrea M. - *Strangers and Neighbors: Multiculturalism, Conflict, and Community in America*
    AJS - v121 - i1 - July 2015 - p297(3) [501+]
    CS - v44 - i5 - Sept 2015 - p728-730 [501+]
    ERS - v38 - i8 - August 2015 - p1436(2) [501+]

Vrabel, Beth - *A Blind Guide to Stinkville*
    c BL - v112 - i1 - Sept 1 2015 - p112(1) [51-500]
    c KR - August 1 2015 - pNA [51-500]
    c PW - v262 - i29 - July 20 2015 - p193(1) [51-500]
    c SLJ - v61 - i8 - August 2015 - p94(1) [51-500]

Vredeveld, Margaret - *Soothe Your Soul: Meditations to Help You through Life's Painful Moments*
    KR - Feb 15 2015 - pNA [51-500]

Vreeland, Susan - *Luncheon of the Boating Party*
    CSM - Feb 23 2015 - pNA [51-500]

Vruno, Joanne - *Autumn of Elves*
    y CH Bwatch - Oct 2015 - pNA [51-500]

Vu Tran - *Dragonfish*
    LJ - v140 - i8 - May 1 2015 - p66(1) [51-500]
    NYT - August 27 2015 - pC4(L) [501+]
    WLT - v89 - i6 - Nov-Dec 2015 - p69(1) [501+]

Vvedensky, Alexander - *An Invitation for Me to Think*
    NYRB - v62 - i8 - May 7 2015 - p36(3) [501+]

W

Waber, Bernard - *Ask Me (Illus. by Lee, Suzy)*
   c HB - v91 - i3 - May-June 2015 - p103(1) [501+]
   c SLJ - v61 - i2 - Feb 2015 - p81(1) [51-500]
   c NYTBR - July 12 2015 - p18(L) [501+]
   c PW - v262 - i17 - April 27 2015 - p73(2) [501+]
   c PW - v262 - i49 - Dec 2 2015 - p25(2) [51-500]

Waberi, Abdourahman A. - *Balbala*
   FS - v69 - i3 - July 2015 - p418(1) [501+]

Wachman, Alan M. - *Why Taiwan? Geostrategic Rationales for China's Territorial Integrity*
   NWCR - v68 - i3 - Summer 2015 - p167(3) [501+]

Wachsmann, Nikolaus - *KL: A History of the Nazi Concentration Camps*
   KR - Jan 15 2015 - pNA [501+]
   Lon R Bks - v37 - i18 - Sept 24 2015 - p9(5) [501+]
   NS - v144 - i5280 - Sept 18 2015 - p58(3) [501+]
   NYRB - v62 - i12 - July 9 2015 - p52(3) [501+]
   NYTBR - July 12 2015 - p12(L) [501+]
   PW - v262 - i7 - Feb 16 2015 - p171(1) [51-500]
   TLS - i5851 - May 22 2015 - p9(2) [501+]

Wachtel, Shirley Russak - *The Music Makers*
   KR - Feb 15 2015 - pNA [501+]

Wachter, Robert - *The Digital Doctor: Hope, Hype, and Harm at the Dawn of Medicine's Computer Age*
   BL - v111 - i16 - April 15 2015 - p9(1) [501+]
   Bwatch - July 2015 - pNA [51-500]
   NYT - May 26 2015 - pD4(L) [501+]

Wacker, Eileen - *Blue Penguin and the Sensational Surf (Illus. by Low, Alan M.)*
   c CH Bwatch - Feb 2015 - pNA [51-500]
Silver Bunny and the Secret Fort Chop (Illus. by Spurging, Curt)
   c CH Bwatch - March 2015 - pNA [501+]

Wacker, Grant - *America's Pastor: Billy Graham and the Shaping of a Nation*
   CHE - v61 - i19 - Jan 23 2015 - pNA [501+]
   For Aff - v94 - i1 - Jan-Feb 2015 - pNA [51-500]
   Nation - v300 - i8 - Feb 23 2015 - p33(3) [501+]
   AM - v212 - i15 - May 4 2015 - p34(2) [501+]
   Bks & Cult - v21 - i2 - March-April 2015 - p22(4) [501+]
   Theol St - v76 - i4 - Dec 2015 - p884(2) [501+]

Wackerfuss, Andrew - *Stormtrooper Families: Homosexuality and Community in the Early Nazi Movement*
   TimHES - i2216 - August 13 2015 - p47(1) [501+]

Wacławiak, Karolina - *The Invaders*
   BL - v111 - i19-20 - June 1 2015 - p42(1) [51-500]
   KR - April 15 2015 - pNA [51-500]
   NY - v91 - i28 - Sept 21 2015 - p105 [501+]
   PW - v262 - i18 - May 4 2015 - p94(1) [51-500]

Waddell, John - *Archaeology and Celtic Myth: An Exploration*
   Med R - June 2015 - pNA [501+]
Succulent Wild Love: Six Powerful Habits for Feeling More Love More Often
   PW - v262 - i51 - Dec 14 2015 - p76(2) [501+]

Waddington, Miriam - *The Collected Poems of Miriam Waddington, vol. 1*
   Can Lit - i224 - Spring 2015 - p146 [501+]
The Collected Poems of Miriam Waddington, vol. 2
   Can Lit - i224 - Spring 2015 - p146 [501+]

Waddington, Raymond B. - *Looking into Providences: Designs and Trials in 'Paradise Lost'*
   MLR - v110 - i1 - Jan 2015 - p242-243 [501+]
Pietro Aretino: Subverting the System in Renaissance Italy
   Six Ct J - v46 - i2 - Summer 2015 - p400-402 [501+]

Wade, Becky - *A Love Like Ours (Read by Turnbull, Kate). Audiobook Review*
   BL - v112 - i6 - Nov 15 2015 - p61(1) [51-500]
A Love Like Ours
   BL - v111 - i15 - April 1 2015 - p32(1) [51-500]
   PW - v262 - i10 - March 9 2015 - p60(1) [51-500]

Wade, Mara R. - *Gender Matters: Discourses of Violence in Early Modern Literature and Arts*
   Six Ct J - v46 - i1 - Spring 2015 - p197-199 [501+]
Gender Matters: Discourses of Violence in Early Modern Literature and the Arts
   Ren Q - v68 - i3 - Fall 2015 - p1105-1106 [501+]

Wade, Nicholas - *A Troublesome Inheritance: Genes, Race and Human History*
   ERS - v38 - i8 - August 2015 - p1444(4) [501+]
   IndRev - v20 - i2 - Fall 2015 - p308(6) [501+]

Wadsworth, Nancy D. - *Ambivalent Miracles: Evangelicals and the Politics of Racial Healing*
   J Am St - v49 - i3 - August 2015 - p642-643 [501+]

Waerebeek, Ruth van - *The Taste of Belgium*
   TLS - i5864-5865 - August 21 2015 - p35(1) [501+]

Wagahara, Satoshi - *The Devil Is a Part-Timer (Illus. by Oniku)*
   y SLJ - v61 - i6 - June 2015 - p119(1) [51-500]

Wagamese, Richard - *Medicine Walk*
   KR - Feb 1 2015 - pNA [51-500]
   NYTBR - May 24 2015 - p19(L) [501+]
   PW - v262 - i10 - March 9 2015 - p50(1) [51-500]

Wagar, Chip - *The Carpathian Assignment: The True History of the Apprehension and Death of Dracula Vlad Tepes, Count and Voivode of the Principality of Transylvania*
   PW - v262 - i29 - July 20 2015 - p172(1) [501+]

Waggoner, Josephine - *Witness: A Hunkpapha Historian's Strong-Heart Song of the Lakotas*
   WHQ - v46 - i1 - Spring 2015 - p104-105 [501+]
   Roundup M - v22 - i4 - April 2015 - p31(1) [501+]
   Roundup M - v22 - i6 - August 2015 - p41(1) [501+]

Waggoner, Michael D. - *Religion in the Public Schools: Negotiating the New Commons*
   J Ch St - v57 - i3 - Summer 2015 - p580-581 [501+]

Waggoner, Robert - *Lucid Dreaming Plain and Simple: Tips and Techniques for Insight, Creativity, and Personal Growth*
   Bwatch - June 2015 - pNA [51-500]

Waggoner, Susan - *Starlight's Edge*
   y HB Guide - v26 - i1 - Spring 2015 - p127(1) [51-500]

Waggoner, Tim - *Nekropolis (Read by Jackson, Ken). Audiobook Review*
   BL - v111 - i9-10 - Jan 1 2015 - p116(1) [51-500]

Waghid, Yusef - *Dancing with Doctoral Encounters: Democratic Education in Motion*
   TimHES - i2204 - May 21 2015 - p49(1) [501+]

Wagman, Diana - *Life No. 6*
   BL - v111 - i17 - May 1 2015 - p76(1) [501+]
   KR - March 15 2015 - pNA [501+]
   NYTBR - July 5 2015 - p16(L) [501+]

Wagman-Geller, Marlene - *Behind Every Great Man: Forgotten Women behind the World's Famous and Infamous*
   BL - v111 - i13 - March 1 2015 - p16(1) [501+]
   LJ - v140 - i5 - March 15 2015 - p121(1) [51-500]

Wagner, Anke - *Help, I Don't Want a Babysitter! (Illus. by Behl, Anne-Kathrin)*
   c HB Guide - v26 - i2 - Fall 2015 - p55(1) [51-500]

Wagner, Bettina - *Worlds of Learning: The Library and World Chronicle of the Nuremberg Physician Hartmann Schedel*
   Sev Cent N - v73 - i3-4 - Fall-Winter 2015 - p187(3) [501+]

Wagner, Bruce - *I Met Someone*
   KR - Dec 15 2015 - pNA [501+]

Wagner, David P. - *Murder Most Unfortunate*
   BL - v112 - i4 - Oct 15 2015 - p22(1) [51-500]
   KR - Sept 1 2015 - pNA [51-500]
   PW - v262 - i38 - Sept 21 2015 - p54(1) [51-500]

Wagner, Frederic C., III - *The Strategy of Defeat at the Little Big Horn: A Military and Timing Analysis of the Battle*
   Roundup M - v22 - i5 - June 2015 - p36(1) [501+]
   Roundup M - v22 - i6 - August 2015 - p41(1) [501+]

Wagner, Gernot - *Climate Shock: The Economic Consequences of a Hotter Planet*
   Barron's - v95 - i36 - Sept 7 2015 - p44(1) [501+]
   For Aff - v94 - i3 - May-June 2015 - pNA [501+]
   KR - Jan 1 2015 - pNA [501+]
   Lon R Bks - v37 - i18 - Sept 24 2015 - p34(3) [501+]
   Nature - v519 - i7542 - March 12 2015 - p155(1) [51-500]
   NYRB - v62 - i10 - June 4 2015 - p36(4) [501+]
   TimHES - i2196 - March 26 2015 - p54-55 [501+]

Wagner, John A. - *Voices of the Reformation: Contemporary Accounts of Daily Life*
   BL - v112 - i2 - Sept 15 2015 - p12(1) [51-500]

Wagner, Laura Rose - *Hold Tight, Don't Let Go*
   y CCB-B - v68 - i7 - March 2015 - p374(2) [51-500]
   y HB - v91 - i1 - Jan-Feb 2015 - p91(1) [51-500]
   y HB Guide - v26 - i2 - Fall 2015 - p142(1) [51-500]
   y NYTBR - March 15 2015 - p18(L) [501+]
   y PW - v262 - i49 - Dec 2 2015 - p92(1) [51-500]

Wagner-Lawlor, Jennifer A. - *Postmodern Utopias and Feminist Fictions*
   TSWL - v34 - i1 - Spring 2015 - p187-189 [501+]

Wagner, Meike - *Theater und Öffentlichkeit im Vormarz. Berlin, Munchen und Wien als Schauplatze burgerlicher Medienpraxis*
   CEH - v48 - i3 - Sept 2015 - p427-428 [501+]

Wagner, Michael - *Why I Love Footy (Illus. by Jellett, Tom)*
   c Magpies - v30 - i2 - May 2015 - p31(1) [501+]

Wagner, Rod - *Widgets: The 12 New Rules for Managing Your Employees As If They're Real People*
   RVBW - May 2015 - pNA [51-500]

Wagner, Tony - *Most Likely to Succeed: Preparing Our Kids for the Innovation Era*
   BooChiTr - Sept 5 2015 - p14(1) [501+]
   KR - June 15 2015 - pNA [501+]
   LJ - v140 - i12 - July 1 2015 - p92(1) [51-500]
   NYTBR - August 23 2015 - p22(L) [501+]

Wahl, Charis - *Rosario's Fig Tree (Illus. by Melanson, Luc)*
   c HB Guide - v26 - i2 - Fall 2015 - p55(1) [51-500]
   c KR - Jan 15 2015 - pNA [51-500]
   c NYTBR - May 10 2015 - p23(L) [501+]
   c PW - v262 - i3 - Jan 19 2015 - p81(1) [51-500]
   c Res Links - v20 - i4 - April 2015 - p9(1) [51-500]
   c SLJ - v61 - i3 - March 2015 - p129(1) [51-500]

Wahl, Jan - *Cobweb Castle (Illus. by Gorey, Edward)*
   HB Guide - v26 - i1 - Spring 2015 - p95(1) [51-500]

I Met a Dinosaur (Illus. by Sheban, Chris)
  c HB Guide - v26 - i2 - Fall 2015 - p55(1) [51-500]
  c SLJ - v61 - i8 - August 2015 - p78(1) [51-500]
The Long Tall Journey (Illus. by Gapaillard, Laurent)
  c KR - August 15 2015 - pNA [51-500]
  c SLJ - v61 - i9 - Sept 2015 - p184(1) [51-500]
Wahl, Leslea - *The Perfect Blindside*
  y CH Bwatch - Nov 2015 - pNA [51-500]
Wahl, Phoebe - *Sonya's Chickens (Illus. by Wahl, Phoebe)*
  c KR - June 15 2015 - pNA [51-500]
    Nat Post - v17 - i240 - August 22 2015 - pWP5(1) [501+]
  c Res Links - v21 - i1 - Oct 2015 - p11(1) [501+]
  c SLJ - v61 - i10 - Oct 2015 - p85(1) [51-500]
Wahlberg, Mark - *The Gambler*
    People - v83 - i3 - Jan 19 2015 - p29 [501+]
    People - v83 - i3 - Jan 19 2015 - p29 [501+]
    People - v83 - i3 - Jan 19 2015 - p29 [501+]
    People - v83 - i3 - Jan 19 2015 - p29 [501+]
    People - v83 - i3 - Jan 19 2015 - p29 [501+]
Wahlig, Henry - *Sport im Abseits: Die Geschichte der Judischen Sportbewegung im Nationalsozialistischen Deutschland*
    HNet - June 2015 - pNA [501+]
Wahlstrom, Todd W. - *The Southern Exodus to Mexico: Migration across the Borderlands after the American Civil War*
    Roundup M - v22 - i6 - August 2015 - p41(1) [501+]
Wailoo, Keith - *Genetics and the Unsettled Past: The Collision of DNA, Race, and History*
    CS - v44 - i2 - March 2015 - p274-275 [501+]
Wainwright, Tom - *Narconomics: How to Run a Drug Cartel*
    KR - Jan 1 2016 - pNA [501+]
Wait, Lea - *Thread and Gone*
    BL - v112 - i7 - Dec 1 2015 - p32(1) [51-500]
    KR - Oct 15 2015 - pNA [501+]
Wajcman, Judy - *Pressed for Time: The Acceleration of Life in Digital Capitalism*
    Nation - v300 - i5 - Feb 2 2015 - p32(4) [501+]
    TimHES - i2187 - Jan 22 2015 - p48-49 [501+]
Wake, Peter - *Tragedy in Hegel's Early Theological Writings*
    J Phil - v112 - i5 - May 2015 - p280(1) [501+]
Wakefield, Sara - *Children of the Prison Boom: Mass Incarceration and the Future of American Inequality*
    AJS - v120 - i5 - March 2015 - p1557(3) [501+]
    CS - v44 - i5 - Sept 2015 - p730-731 [501+]
Wakefield, Stacy - *The Sunshine Crust Baking Factory*
    BL - v111 - i17 - May 1 2015 - p77(2) [51-500]
    KR - March 1 2015 - pNA [51-500]
    PW - v262 - i13 - March 30 2015 - p51(1) [51-500]
Wakefield, Vikki - *Inbetween Days*
  y Magpies - v30 - i5 - Nov 2015 - p44(1) [51-500]
Wakeham, Pauline - *Reconciling Canada: Critical Perspectives on the Culture of Redress*
    Am Ind CRJ - v39 - i1 - Wntr 2015 - p153-155 [501+]
Wakelam, Randall - *Cold War Fighters: Canadian Aircraft Procurement, 1945-54*
    APH - v62 - i1 - Spring 2015 - p58(2) [501+]
Wakelin, Daniel - *Scribal Correction and Literary Craft: English Manuscripts 1375-1510*
    RES - v66 - i276 - Sept 2015 - p767-769 [501+]
Wakeling, Edward - *Lewis Carroll: The Man and His Circle*
    Lon R Bks - v37 - i14 - July 16 2015 - p17(3) [501+]
    NS - v144 - i5255 - March 27 2015 - p68(3) [501+]
Wakin, Michele - *Otherwise Homeless: Vehicle Living and the Culture of Homelessness*
    AJS - v120 - i4 - Jan 2015 - p1283(3) [501+]
    CS - v44 - i3 - May 2015 - p439-440 [501+]
Walas, Tony - *Visions of Music: Sheet Music in the Twentieth Century*
    BL - v111 - i13 - March 1 2015 - p14(1) [51-500]
Walbert, Kate - *The Sunken Cathedral*
    BL - v111 - i18 - May 15 2015 - p25(1) [51-500]
    KR - April 1 2015 - pNA [501+]
    LJ - v140 - i7 - April 15 2015 - p82(1) [51-500]
    NYTBR - June 14 2015 - p8(L) [501+]
    PW - v262 - i11 - March 16 2015 - p60(1) [51-500]
Walby, Sylvia - *Crisis*
    TimHES - i2229 - Nov 12 2015 - p49(1) [501+]
Walcker, Yann - *Billy the Monkey, or the Prince of the Amazon (Illus. by Kenens, Sofie)*
  c CH Bwatch - Jan 2015 - pNA [51-500]

Wald, Elijah - *Dylan Goes Electric! Newport, Seeger, Dylan, and the Night That Split the Sixties*
    BL - v111 - i19-20 - June 1 2015 - p9(1) [51-500]
    KR - June 1 2015 - pNA [501+]
    LJ - v140 - i12 - July 1 2015 - p86(1) [51-500]
    NYT - July 24 2015 - pC17(L) [501+]
    Spec - v328 - i9757 - August 29 2015 - p37(1) [501+]
Wald, Gayle - *It's Been Beautiful: Soul! and Black Power Television*
    CHE - v61 - i40 - July 10 2015 - pB17(1) [501+]
Wald, Kenneth D. - *Religion and Politics in the United States, 7th ed.*
    J Ch St - v57 - i2 - Spring 2015 - p386-388 [501+]
Wald, Priscilla - *The Oxford History of the Novel in English, vol. 6: The American Novel 1870-1940*
    RES - v66 - i274 - April 2015 - p392-394 [501+]
Walde, Christine - *Neros Wirklichkeiten: Zur Rezeption einer umstrittenen Gestalt*
    Class R - v65 - i2 - Oct 2015 - p593-595 [501+]
Waldegrave, William - *A Different Kind of Weather: A Memoir*
    Spec - v328 - i9752 - July 25 2015 - p34(1) [501+]
    TLS - i5851 - May 22 2015 - p27(1) [501+]
Walden, Joshua - *Representation in Western Music*
    PMS - v38 - i3 - July 2015 - p391(5) [501+]
Walden, Mark - *H.I.V.E.: Deadlock*
  c HB Guide - v26 - i2 - Fall 2015 - p105(1) [51-500]
Retribution
  c KR - May 1 2015 - pNA [51-500]
Walder, Andrew G. - *China under Mao: A Revolution Derailed*
    HNet - May 2015 - pNA [501+]
    Spec - v328 - i9756 - August 22 2015 - p36(1) [501+]
Walder, Lajos - *Become a Message: Poems*
    PW - v262 - i33 - August 17 2015 - p48(1) [51-500]
Waldfogel, Sabra - *Slave and Sister*
    SPBW - Feb 2015 - pNA [51-500]
Waldin, Monty - *Biodynamic Gardening*
    LJ - v140 - i7 - April 15 2015 - p108(1) [51-500]
Waldman, Ayelet - *Love and Treasure*
    NYTBR - Feb 15 2015 - p28(L) [501+]
Waldman, Carl - *The Sharon Springs Timeline: A Microcosm of American History - with Dates Relating to a Remarkable Village and Neighboring Regions, from the 16th Century to Modern Times*
    RVBW - June 2015 - pNA [501+]
Waldman, Jonathan - *Rust: The Longest War*
    Atl - v315 - i2 - March 2015 - p54(2) [501+]
    BL - v111 - i12 - Feb 15 2015 - p28(1) [51-500]
    Nature - v519 - i7542 - March 12 2015 - p155(1) [51-500]
    NH - v123 - i2 - March 2015 - p46(2) [501+]
    NYT - March 10 2015 - pD5(L) [501+]
    NYTBR - April 19 2015 - p20(L) [501+]
    PW - v262 - i1 - Jan 5 2015 - p65(1) [51-500]
Waldman, Michael - *The Fight to Vote*
    KR - Dec 15 2015 - pNA [501+]
Waldman, Thomas - *War, Clausewitz, and the Trinity*
    APJ - v29 - i4 - July-August 2015 - p92(2) [501+]
Waldron, Kathleen Cook - *Between Shadows*
  c SLJ - v61 - i6 - June 2015 - p106(1) [51-500]
Waldron, Melanie - *Geography Matters in Ancient Egypt*
  c HB Guide - v26 - i2 - Fall 2015 - p217(1) [51-500]
  c Sch Lib - v63 - i3 - Autumn 2015 - p176(1) [51-500]
Geography Matters in the Inca Empire
  c HB Guide - v26 - i2 - Fall 2015 - p217(1) [51-500]
Waldstreicher, David - *A Companion to John Adams and John Quincy Adams*
    Pres St Q - v45 - i2 - June 2015 - p417(3) [501+]
Waligorska, Magdalena - *Klezmer's Afterlife: An Ethnography of the Jewish Music Revival in Poland and Germany*
    HNet - August 2015 - pNA [501+]
    HNet - August 2015 - pNA [501+]
Walker, Alison - *From Books to Bezoars: Sir Hans Sloane and His Collections*
    Ren Q - v68 - i2 - Summer 2015 - p656-658 [501+]
Walker, Anna - *Mr Huff (Illus. by Walker, Anna)*
    Magpies - v30 - i3 - July 2015 - p30(1) [501+]
Walker, Bruce - *Bruce Walker Travel Adventures*
    KR - July 15 2015 - pNA [501+]
Walker, Carol - *The Gospel of Matthew*
    KR - March 15 2015 - pNA [51-500]
Walker, Casey - *Last Days in Shanghai*
    NYTBR - Jan 25 2015 - p19(L) [501+]
    TLS - i5834 - Jan 23 2015 - p20(1) [501+]

Walker, Charles F. - *The Tupac Amaru Rebellion*
    AHR - v120 - i2 - April 2015 - p685-687 [501+]
    Eight-C St - v48 - i4 - Summer 2015 - p539-540 [501+]
    HAHR - v95 - i2 - May 2015 - p355-357 [501+]
    JIH - v46 - i1 - Summer 2015 - p141-142 [501+]
    TLS - i5831 - Jan 2 2015 - p8(1) [501+]
Walker, D.C. - *When the River Rises (Illus. by Oliveira, Bruno)*
    KR - Sept 1 2015 - pNA [501+]
  y SLJ - v61 - i10 - Oct 2015 - p120(1) [51-500]
Walker, David H. - *Migrating Voids*
    TLS - i5852 - May 29 2015 - p21(1) [501+]
Walker, Edward T. - *Grassroots for Hire: Public Affairs Consultants in American Democracy*
    AJS - v121 - i2 - Sept 2015 - p634(3) [501+]
Walker, Greg G. - *The Oxford Anthology of Tudor Drama*
    Six Ct J - v46 - i1 - Spring 2015 - p219-221 [501+]
Walker, Jeffery T. - *Legal Guide for Police: Constitutional Issues*
    RVBW - June 2015 - pNA [501+]
Walker, John - *The Clarinet in the Attic, 20 Short Recital and Study Pieces for the Intermediate Player*
    Am MT - v65 - i1 - August-Sept 2015 - p64(2) [51-500]
The Flute in the Attic, 20 Short Recital and Study Pieces for the Intermediate Player
    Am MT - v65 - i1 - August-Sept 2015 - p65(1) [501+]
The Trombone in the Attic, 20 Short Recital and Study Pieces for the Intermediate Player
    Am MT - v65 - i1 - August-Sept 2015 - p56(2) [501+]
The Trumpet in the Attic, 20 Short Recital and Study Pieces for the Intermediate Player
    Am MT - v65 - i1 - August-Sept 2015 - p56(2) [51-500]
Walker, Judy - *Turkey Trouble (Illus. by Kerber, Kathy)*
  c CH Bwatch - March 2015 - pNA [501+]
Walker, Julie Ann - *Hell or High Water*
    BL - v111 - i19-20 - June 1 2015 - p62(1) [51-500]
    PW - v262 - i18 - May 4 2015 - p102(1) [51-500]
Too Hard to Handle
    BL - v111 - i22 - August 1 2015 - p42(1) [51-500]
    PW - v262 - i31 - August 3 2015 - p42(1) [51-500]
Walker, Landry Q. - *Rebirth*
    LJ - v140 - i15 - Sept 15 2015 - p60(3) [501+]
Walker, Lawrence R. - *Landslide Ecology*
    QRB - v90 - i1 - March 2015 - p83(2) [501+]
Walker, Malcolm - *Heavenly Harmony: Organs and Organists of Exeter Cathedral*
    MT - v156 - i1931 - Summer 2015 - p120(1) [501+]
Walker, Mark - *The German Research Foundation, 1920-1970: Funding Poised between Science and Politics*
    CEH - v48 - i1 - March 2015 - p128-129 [501+]
Walker, Martin - *The Children Return*
    BL - v111 - i12 - Feb 15 2015 - p35(1) [51-500]
    KR - Feb 15 2015 - pNA [51-500]
    PW - v262 - i5 - Feb 2 2015 - p37(1) [51-500]
The Dying Season
    TimHES - i2225 - Oct 15 2015 - p43-1 [501+]
The Patriarch
    BL - v111 - i21 - July 1 2015 - p39(1) [51-500]
    KR - June 1 2015 - pNA [51-500]
    PW - v262 - i23 - June 8 2015 - p37(1) [51-500]
    NYTBR - August 16 2015 - p29(L) [501+]
Walker, Melissa - *Dust to Dust*
  y BL - v111 - i18 - May 15 2015 - p66(1) [51-500]
  y HB Guide - v26 - i2 - Fall 2015 - p142(1) [51-500]
  y KR - Feb 15 2015 - pNA [51-500]
  y SLJ - v61 - i3 - March 2015 - p163(1) [51-500]
  y VOYA - v38 - i2 - June 2015 - p84(1) [501+]
Walker, Nina - *Prism*
  y KR - Feb 15 2015 - pNA [51-500]
Walker-Nixon, Donna - *Her Texas*
    KR - March 1 2015 - pNA [501+]
Walker, Peter - *Some Here among Us*
    BL - v111 - i9-10 - Jan 1 2015 - p54(1) [51-500]
Walker, Pierre A. - *The Complete Letters of Henry James, 1878-1880, vol. 1*
    TLS - i5871 - Oct 9 2015 - p27(1) [501+]
Walker, Richard - *Utterly Amazing Human Body*
  c KR - Dec 1 2015 - pNA [51-500]
Walker, Rob - *First Words*
  c KR - July 1 2015 - pNA [51-500]
Walker, Rysa - *Time's Edge (Read by Rudd, Kate).*
Audiobook Review
    SLJ - v61 - i3 - March 2015 - p81(1) [51-500]

Walker, Sally M. - *Ghost Walls: The Story of a 17th-Century Colonial Homestead*
  y CCB-B - v68 - i5 - Jan 2015 - p280(1) [51-500]
  c HB Guide - v26 - i1 - Spring 2015 - p205(1) [51-500]
Winnie: The True Story of the Bear Who Inspired Winnie-the-Pooh (Illus. by Voss, Jonathan D.)
  c CCB-B - v68 - i7 - March 2015 - p375(1) [51-500]
  c HB - v91 - i2 - March-April 2015 - p127(2) [501+]
  c HB Guide - v26 - i2 - Fall 2015 - p181(1) [51-500]

Walker, Sarai - *Dietland (Read by Sands, Tara). Audiobook Review*
  LJ - v140 - i12 - July 1 2015 - p44(1) [51-500]
Dietland
  BL - v111 - i15 - April 1 2015 - p23(1) [51-500]
  Econ - v415 - i8940 - May 30 2015 - p82(US) [501+]
  Ent W - i1365-1366 - May 29 2015 - p109(1) [501+]
  KR - March 15 2015 - pNA [501+]
  LJ - v140 - i7 - April 15 2015 - p82(1) [51-500]
  PW - v262 - i13 - March 30 2015 - p51(1) [51-500]

Walker, Scott - *Unintimidated: A Governor's Story and a Nation's Challenge*
  NS - v144 - i5278 - Sept 4 2015 - p40(4) [501+]
  NYRB - v62 - i5 - March 19 2015 - p18(3) [501+]
  Reason - v47 - i4 - August-Sept 2015 - p58(8) [501+]

Walker, Shiloh - *Busted*
  PW - v262 - i13 - March 30 2015 - p62(1) [51-500]
Headed for Trouble
  PW - v262 - i46 - Nov 16 2015 - p62(1) [51-500]

Walker, William S. - *A Living Exhibition: The Smithsonian and the Transformation of the Universal Museum*
  RAH - v43 - i1 - March 2015 - p103-109 [501+]

Walkowitz, Daniel J. - *City Folk: English Country Dance and the Politics of the Folk in Modern America*
  J Urban H - v41 - i1 - Jan 2015 - p157-8 [501+]

Walkup, Jennifer - *This Ordinary Life*
  y SLJ - v61 - i10 - Oct 2015 - p118(1) [51-500]

Wall, Chadwick - *Water Lessons*
  KR - Jan 15 2015 - pNA [501+]

Wall, Derek - *The Commons in History: Culture, Conflict and Ecology*
  JEH - v75 - i1 - March 2015 - p270-272 [501+]

Wall, Diana Dizerega - *The Archaeology of American Cities*
  Am Ant - v80 - i2 - April 2015 - p419(2) [501+]

Wall, Laura - *Gedeon au magasin*
  c Res Links - v20 - i3 - Feb 2015 - p52(2) [501+]
Goose
  c HB Guide - v26 - i2 - Fall 2015 - p21(1) [51-500]
Goose Goes to School (Illus. by Wall, Laura)
  c BL - v111 - i21 - July 1 2015 - p62(1) [51-500]
  c KR - June 1 2015 - pNA [51-500]
  c SLJ - v61 - i8 - August 2015 - p61(1) [51-500]
Goose Goes to the Zoo (Illus. by Wall, Laura)
  c KR - Oct 15 2015 - pNA [51-500]

Wall, Mick - *Black Sabbath: Symptom of the Universe*
  BL - v111 - i13 - March 1 2015 - p12(1) [51-500]
  KR - Feb 15 2015 - pNA [501+]
Love Becomes a Funeral Pyre: A Biography of the Doors
  BL - v111 - i22 - August 1 2015 - p16(1) [51-500]
  KR - July 15 2015 - pNA [501+]
  LJ - v140 - i13 - August 1 2015 - p99(1) [51-500]

Wallace, Auralee - *Skinny Dipping with Murder*
  KR - Jan 1 2016 - pNA [51-500]

Wallace, Becky - *The Skylighter*
  y KR - Jan 1 2016 - pNA [51-500]
The Storyspinner
  y HB Guide - v26 - i2 - Fall 2015 - p143(1) [51-500]
  y PW - v262 - i4 - Jan 26 2015 - p174(1) [51-500]
  y VOYA - v37 - i6 - Feb 2015 - p85(1) [51-500]

Wallace, Brandon - *Wilder Boys*
  c BL - v111 - i16 - April 15 2015 - p50(1) [51-500]
  c HB Guide - v26 - i2 - Fall 2015 - p105(1) [51-500]
  c KR - March 1 2015 - pNA [51-500]
  c SLJ - v61 - i2 - Feb 2015 - p94(2) [51-500]

Wallace, David Foster - *The David Foster Wallace Reader*
  NW - v164 - i2 - Jan 16 2015 - pNA [501+]
  TLS - i5854 - June 12 2015 - p3(2) [501+]

Wallace, David J. - *Massive Resistance and Media Suppression: The Segregationist Response to Dissent during the Civil Rights Movement*
  JSH - v81 - i2 - May 2015 - p518(3) [501+]

Wallace, David Rains - *Mountains and Marshes: Exploring the Bay Area's Natural History*
  PW - v262 - i42 - Oct 19 2015 - p66(1) [51-500]

Wallace, Ian - *The Complete A to Z Dictionary of Dreams: Be Your Own Dream Expert*
  Bwatch - April 2015 - pNA [51-500]
The Slippers' Keeper (Illus. by Wallace, Ian)
  c CH Bwatch - March 2015 - pNA [51-500]
  BL - v111 - i14 - March 15 2015 - p62(1) [51-500]
  c Res Links - v20 - i4 - April 2015 - p21(1) [501+]
  SLJ - v61 - i4 - April 2015 - p181(1) [51-500]

Wallace, Kali - *Shallow Graves*
  y KR - Oct 1 2015 - pNA [51-500]
  y PW - v262 - i42 - Oct 19 2015 - p79(1) [51-500]

Wallace, Karen - *Snow White Sees the Light*
  c CH Bwatch - July 2015 - pNA [501+]

Wallace, Landon - *Come and Take It: Search for the Treasure of the Alamo*
  SPBW - Nov 2015 - pNA [51-500]

Wallace, Mary - *An Inuksuk Means Welcome (Illus. by Wallace, Mary)*
  c CH Bwatch - Sept 2015 - pNA [501+]
  c SLJ - v61 - i12 - Dec 2015 - p140(1) [51-500]

Wallace, Matt - *Envy of Angels*
  PW - v262 - i34 - August 24 2015 - p66(1) [51-500]
Lustlocked
  PW - v262 - i51 - Dec 14 2015 - p64(2) [51-500]

Wallace, Michael - *The Crescent Spy*
  BL - v112 - i6 - Nov 15 2015 - p25(1) [51-500]

Wallace, Miriam L. - *Re-Viewing Thomas Holcroft, 1745-1809: Essays on His Works and Life*
  MLR - v110 - i1 - Jan 2015 - p243-245 [501+]

Wallace, Nancy Elizabeth - *Water! Water! Water!*
  c HB Guide - v26 - i1 - Spring 2015 - p49(1) [51-500]

Wallace, Nancy K. - *Among Wolves*
  y VOYA - v38 - i5 - Dec 2015 - p65(1) [51-500]
Fettuccine and Four-Leaf Clovers: A Readers' Theater Script and Guide (Illus. by Mata, Nina)
  c BL - v112 - i7 - Dec 1 2015 - p43(1) [501+]
Ghosts and Gummy Worms: A Readers' Theater Script and Guide
  c BL - v112 - i7 - Dec 1 2015 - p43(1) [501+]
Groundhogs and Guinea Pigs: A Readers' Theater Script and Guide (Illus. by Mata, Nina)
  c BL - v112 - i7 - Dec 1 2015 - p43(1) [501+]
Medals and Memorials: A Readers' Theater Script and Guide (Illus. by Mata, Nina)
  c BL - v112 - i7 - Dec 1 2015 - p43(1) [501+]

Wallace, Neill - *An Unconventional Leader*
  KR - March 1 2015 - pNA [501+]

Wallace, Nicolle - *Madam President*
  BL - v111 - i16 - April 15 2015 - p26(1) [51-500]
  KR - March 15 2015 - pNA [501+]

Wallace, R. Jay - *The View from Here: On Affirmation, Attachment and the Limits of Regret*
  Ethics - v125 - i2 - Jan 2015 - p614(8) [501+]

Wallace, Rich - *The Room of Woe (Illus. by Flores, Jose Emroca)*
  c HB Guide - v26 - i2 - Fall 2015 - p65(1) [51-500]

Wallace, Sean - *The Mammoth Book of Dieselpunk*
  BL - v111 - i22 - August 1 2015 - p44(1) [51-500]
  PW - v262 - i21 - May 25 2015 - p41(1) [51-500]

Wallace, Stephen - *How My Dog Became the New Messiah*
  KR - Dec 15 2015 - pNA [501+]

Wallace, Susan Helen - *Therese of Lisieux*
  RVBW - July 2015 - pNA [51-500]

Wallach, Tommy - *Thanks for the Trouble*
  c BL - v112 - i5 - Nov 1 2015 - p39(1) [501+]
  y BL - v112 - i7 - Dec 1 2015 - p58(1) [51-500]
  y KR - Nov 15 2015 - pNA [51-500]
  y PW - v262 - i45 - Nov 9 2015 - p62(1) [51-500]
  y VOYA - v38 - i5 - Dec 2015 - p75(1) [51-500]
We All Looked Up
  y BL - v111 - i11 - Feb 1 2015 - p49(2) [51-500]
  y CCB-B - v68 - i8 - April 2015 - p422(2) [51-500]
  y HB Guide - v26 - i2 - Fall 2015 - p143(1) [51-500]
  y KR - Jan 15 2015 - pNA [501+]
  y PW - v262 - i4 - Jan 26 2015 - p174(1) [51-500]
  y PW - v262 - i49 - Dec 2 2015 - p100(1) [51-500]
  y Sch Lib - v63 - i3 - Autumn 2015 - p186(1) [51-500]
  y VOYA - v37 - i6 - Feb 2015 - p69(1) [51-500]

Wallach, Van - *Snakes of the World: A Catalogue of Living and Extinct Species*
  QRB - v90 - i1 - March 2015 - p101(2) [501+]

Wallach, Wendell - *A Dangerous Master: How to Keep Technology from Slipping beyond Our Control*
  KR - April 15 2015 - pNA [501+]
  LJ - v140 - i10 - June 1 2015 - p132(1) [51-500]
  Nature - v523 - i7559 - July 9 2015 - p157(1) [51-500]
  New Sci - v227 - i3034 - August 15 2015 - p42(2) [501+]
  PW - v262 - i14 - April 6 2015 - p48(2) [51-500]

Wallant, Edward Lewis - *The Pawnbroker*
  KR - Sept 1 2015 - pNA [501+]

Wallen, Per-Christian - *Soviet Postal Censorship during World War II*
  Phil Lit R - v64 - i1 - Wntr 2015 - p59(2) [501+]

Wallengren, Ann-Kristin - *Welcome Home, Mr. Swanson: Swedish Emigrants and Swedishness on Film*
  Scan St - v87 - i2 - Summer 2015 - p309(4) [501+]

Waller, Douglas - *Disciples: The World War II Missions of the CIA Directors Who Fought for Wild Bill Donovan*
  KR - July 15 2015 - pNA [501+]
  LJ - v140 - i14 - Sept 1 2015 - p119(2) [51-500]
  PW - v262 - i31 - August 3 2015 - p46(2) [51-500]

Waller, Gary - *Walsingham and the English Imagination*
  CHR - v101 - i4 - Autumn 2015 - p895(3) [501+]

Waller, Rebecca LLoyd - *Descartes' Temporal Dualism*
  J Phil - v112 - i5 - May 2015 - p280(1) [501+]

Waller, Sharon Biggs - *The Forbidden Orchid*
  y KR - Nov 15 2015 - pNA [501+]
  y PW - v262 - i50 - Dec 7 2015 - p87(1) [51-500]

Walliams, David - *Demon Dentist (Illus. by Ross, Tony)*
  c BL - v112 - i6 - Nov 15 2015 - p53(2) [51-500]
  c KR - Dec 1 2015 - pNA [51-500]
  c PW - v262 - i50 - Dec 7 2015 - p85(1) [51-500]
The First Hippo on the Moon (Illus. by Ross, Tony)
  c Nat Post - v17 - i74 - Jan 24 2015 - pWP9(1) [501+]

Walling, Michael G. - *Enduring Freedom, Enduring Voices: US Operations in Afghanistan*
  Mar Crp G - v99 - i5 - May 2015 - p101(2) [501+]

Wallis, Jim - *America's Original Sin: Racism, White Privilege, and the Bridge to a New America*
  LJ - v140 - i20 - Dec 1 2015 - p108(1) [51-500]

Wallis, Neill J. - *New Histories of Pre-Columbian Florida*
  Am Ant - v80 - i2 - April 2015 - p423(2) [501+]

Wallis, Rupert - *The Dark Inside*
  y Sch Lib - v63 - i1 - Spring 2015 - p59(1) [51-500]

Wallison, Peter J. - *Hidden in Plain Sight: What Really Caused the World's Worst Financial Crisis and Why It Could Happen Again*
  Barron's - v95 - i18 - May 4 2015 - p40(1) [501+]
  Nat R - v67 - i3 - Feb 23 2015 - p39 [501+]
  Reason - v47 - i1 - May 2015 - p65(3) [501+]

Wallman, James - *Stuffocation: Why We've Had Enough of Stuff and Need Experience More Than Ever*
  BL - v111 - i13 - March 1 2015 - p8(1) [51-500]
  KR - Jan 15 2015 - pNA [501+]
  LJ - v140 - i2 - Feb 1 2015 - p100(1) [51-500]

Wallmark, Laurie - *Ada Byron Lovelace and the Thinking Machine (Illus. by Chu, April)*
  c BL - v112 - i5 - Nov 1 2015 - p44(1) [51-500]
  c KR - Sept 15 2015 - pNA [51-500]
  c PW - v262 - i49 - Dec 2 2015 - p43(1) [51-500]
  c SLJ - v61 - i12 - Dec 2015 - p140(1) [51-500]

Walls, Jerry L. - *Heaven, Hell, and Purgatory: Rethinking the Things That Matter Most*
  Bwatch - April 2015 - pNA [51-500]
  Ch Today - April 2015 - p82(1) [51-500]

Walls, Seth Colter - *Gaza, Wyoming*
  KR - Oct 1 2015 - pNA [501+]

Walrath, Dana - *Like Water on Stone*
  y CCB-B - v68 - i5 - Jan 2015 - p281(1) [51-500]
  y CH Bwatch - March 2015 - pNA [51-500]
  y HB Guide - v26 - i2 - Fall 2015 - p143(1) [51-500]

Walsch, Neale Donald - *Conversations with God for Parents: Sharing the Messages with Children*
  BL - v112 - i6 - Nov 15 2015 - p12(1) [51-500]

Walser, David - *The Glass Mountain: Tales from Poland (Illus. by Pienkowski, Jan)*
  c HB Guide - v26 - i1 - Spring 2015 - p145(1) [51-500]

Walser, Robert - *Looking at Pictures*
  KR - August 1 2015 - pNA [51-500]
  PW - v262 - i30 - July 27 2015 - p53(1) [51-500]

Walsh, Aoife - *Too Close to Home*
  y Sch Lib - v63 - i3 - Autumn 2015 - p186(2) [51-500]

Walsh, Brighton - *Captive*
  PW - v262 - i4 - Jan 26 2015 - p155(1) [51-500]

Walsh, Chris - *Cowardice: A Brief History*
  AS - v84 - i1 - Wntr 2015 - p109(3) [501+]
  For Aff - v94 - i1 - Jan-Feb 2015 - pNA [51-500]
  MA - v57 - i3 - Summer 2015 - p65(3) [501+]
  NS - v144 - i5244 - Jan 9 2015 - p34(3) [501+]
  NYTBR - Jan 11 2015 - p20(L) [501+]

Walsh, Courtney - *Paper Hearts*
  BL - v111 - i11 - Feb 1 2015 - p31(1) [51-500]

Walsh, Dan - *Restoration: The Legacy*
  BL - v111 - i14 - March 15 2015 - p44(1) [51-500]
Walsh, Daniel C. - *An Air War with Cuba: The United States Radio Campaign against Castro*
  HNet - Oct 2015 - pNA [501+]
Walsh, Ellen Stoll - *Stoll Balancing Act*
  c HB Guide - v26 - i2 - Fall 2015 - p21(1) [51-500]
  Where Is Jumper? (Illus. by Walsh, Ellen Stoll)
  c KR - August 15 2015 - pNA [51-500]
  c SLJ - v61 - i10 - Oct 2015 - p71(1) [51-500]
Walsh, James D. - *Playing against the House*
  KR - Jan 1 2016 - pNA [501+]
Walsh, Jennifer - *Crooked Leg Road*
  c Sch Lib - v63 - i4 - Winter 2015 - p234(1) [51-500]
Walsh, Joanna - *Hotel*
  NYTBR - Nov 8 2015 - p10(L) [501+]
  I Love Mom (Illus. by Abbot, Judi)
  c HB Guide - v26 - i2 - Fall 2015 - p21(1) [51-500]
  c NYTBR - Feb 8 2015 - p24(L) [501+]
  Vertigo
  NYTBR - Nov 8 2015 - p10(L) [501+]
  PW - v262 - i32 - August 10 2015 - p32(2) [51-500]
  KR - August 1 2015 - pNA [51-500]
Walsh, John Patrick - *Free and French in the Caribbean: Toussaint Louverture, Aime Cesaire, and Narratives of Loyal Opposition*
  HNet - July 2015 - pNA [501+]
Walsh, Justin S.P. - *Consumerism in the Ancient World: Imports and Identity Construction*
  HNet - Feb 2015 - pNA [501+]
Walsh, Kenneth T. - *Celebrity in Chief: A History of the Presidents and the Culture of Stardom*
  LJ - v140 - i6 - April 1 2015 - p106(2) [51-500]
Walsh, Liza Gardner - *Treasure Hunter's Handbook*
  c HB Guide - v26 - i2 - Fall 2015 - p192(1) [51-500]
Walsh, M. - *The Ghost Princess*
  KR - August 1 2015 - pNA [501+]
Walsh, M.O. - *My Sunshine Away (Read by Heyborne, Kirby). Audiobook Review*
  y BL - v111 - i19-20 - June 1 2015 - p130(2) [51-500]
  My Sunshine Away
  Ent W - i1350 - Feb 13 2015 - p61(1) [501+]
  New Or - v49 - i4 - Jan 2015 - p38(1) [51-500]
Walsh, Maurice - *Bitter Freedom: Ireland in a Revolutionary World, 1918-1923*
  Spec - v327 - i9739 - April 25 2015 - p36(2) [501+]
Walsh, Michael - *The Devil's Pleasure Palace: The Cult of Critical Theory and the Subversion of the West*
  Nat R - v67 - i18 - Oct 5 2015 - p42(2) [501+]
Walsh, Michael J.K. - *Medieval and Renaissance Famagusta: Studies in Architecture, Art and History*
  HER - v130 - i543 - April 2015 - p384(16) [501+]
Walsh, Sheila - *5 Minutes with Jesus: Making Today Matter*
  PW - v262 - i27 - July 6 2015 - p66(1) [51-500]
Walsh, Thomas P. - *Tin Pan Alley and the Philippines: American Songs of War and Love, 1898-1946 - A Resource Guide*
  Notes - v72 - i1 - Sept 2015 - p153(2) [501+]
Walsh, William - *Earthburner*
  KR - Jan 1 2016 - pNA [501+]
Walsham, Alexandra - *Catholic Reformation in Protestant Britain*
  CH - v84 - i4 - Dec 2015 - p882(3) [501+]
Walshaw, Jill Maciak - *A Show of Hands for the Republic: Opinion, Information, and Repression in Eighteenth-Century Rural France*
  AHR - v120 - i3 - June 2015 - p1125-1126 [501+]
  HNet - July 2015 - pNA [501+]
Walter, Gregory - *Being Promised: Theology, Gift and Practice*
  Theol St - v76 - i1 - March 2015 - p220(1) [501+]
Walter, Jon - *Close to the Wind*
  c BL - v111 - i17 - May 1 2015 - p94(1) [51-500]
  y CCB-B - v68 - i11 - July-August 2015 - p573(1) [51-500]
  y HB - v91 - i4 - July-August 2015 - p149(2) [51-500]
  c KR - March 1 2015 - pNA [51-500]
  c SLJ - v61 - i3 - March 2015 - p145(1) [51-500]
  y VOYA - v38 - i2 - June 2015 - p69(1) [51-500]
  My Name Is Not Friday
  y KR - Oct 1 2015 - pNA [51-500]
  y SLJ - v61 - i11 - Nov 2015 - p110(2) [51-500]
  My Name's Not Friday
  y Sch Lib - v63 - i4 - Winter 2015 - p250(2) [501+]

Walter, Katie L. - *The Culture of Inquisition in Medieval England*
  CHR - v101 - i3 - Summer 2015 - p630(3) [501+]
  Reading Skin in Medieval Literature and Culture
  Specu - v90 - i4 - Oct 2015 - p1179-1180 [501+]
Walters, Angela - *Get Quilting with Angela and Cloe: 14 Projects for Kids to Sew*
  LJ - v140 - i8 - May 1 2015 - p74(1) [51-500]
Walters, Christine - *Ginny and Me: Reflections of What God Can Do*
  SPBW - Oct 2015 - pNA [501+]
Walters, Eric - *End of Days*
  y KR - July 1 2015 - pNA [51-500]
  Fight for Power
  y HB Guide - v26 - i2 - Fall 2015 - p143(1) [51-500]
  SLJ - v61 - i4 - April 2015 - p175(1) [51-500]
  y VOYA - v37 - i6 - Feb 2015 - p85(1) [51-500]
  Innocent
  y KR - July 15 2015 - pNA [51-500]
  y Res Links - v21 - i1 - Oct 2015 - p43(2) [501+]
  y SLJ - v61 - i10 - Oct 2015 - p99(1) [51-500]
  y VOYA - v38 - i4 - Oct 2015 - p64(1) [501+]
  Regenesis
  y SLJ - v61 - i12 - Dec 2015 - p116(2) [51-500]
  Say You Will
  y Res Links - v20 - i5 - June 2015 - p29(1) [501+]
  Today Is the Day (Illus. by Fernandes, Eugenie)
  c KR - August 15 2015 - pNA [51-500]
Walters, Louise - *Mrs. Sinclair's Suitcase*
  BL - v111 - i21 - July 1 2015 - p42(2) [51-500]
  KR - May 15 2015 - pNA [51-500]
  LJ - v140 - i11 - June 15 2015 - p82(1) [51-500]
Walters, Mike - *The Outlaw River Wilde: Sometimes a Man Needs to Journal*
  SPBW - July 2015 - pNA [501+]
  SPBW - Oct 2015 - pNA [501+]
Walters, Minette - *The Cellar*
  y BL - v112 - i5 - Nov 1 2015 - p30(1) [51-500]
  KR - Sept 15 2015 - pNA [51-500]
  PW - v262 - i52 - Dec 21 2015 - p131(1) [51-500]
Walters, Peter - *The Hungriest Mouth in the Sea (Illus. by Walters, Peter)*
  c PW - v262 - i35 - August 31 2015 - p90(2) [51-500]
  c CH Bwatch - Nov 2015 - pNA [51-500]
  c KR - July 15 2015 - pNA [51-500]
Walters, Suzanna Danuta - *The Tolerance Trap: How God, Genes, and Good Intentions are Sabotaging Gay Equality*
  CS - v44 - i6 - Nov 2015 - p866-867 [501+]
Walters, Terry - *Eat Clean Live Well*
  LJ - v140 - i3 - Feb 15 2015 - p122(4) [51-500]
Walters, Tom - *Your Dog and You*
  RVBW - June 2015 - pNA [51-500]
Walters, Wendy S. - *Multiply/Divide*
  KR - May 15 2015 - pNA [51-500]
Waltman, Jerold - *Congress, the Supreme Court, and Religious Liberty: The Case of City of Boerne v. Flores*
  J Ch St - v57 - i1 - Wntr 2015 - p188-190 [501+]
Waltman, Kevin - *Pull*
  y KR - August 1 2015 - pNA [51-500]
  Slump
  y HB Guide - v26 - i1 - Spring 2015 - p127(1) [51-500]
Walton, Bill - *Back from the Dead*
  KR - Jan 1 2016 - pNA [501+]
Walton, David - *Superposition*
  Analog - v135 - i6 - June 2015 - p107(1) [501+]
  KR - Feb 1 2015 - pNA [51-500]
  PW - v262 - i3 - Jan 19 2015 - p65(1) [51-500]
  Supersymmetry
  KR - July 1 2015 - pNA [501+]
  PW - v262 - i25 - June 22 2015 - p123(1) [51-500]
Walton, Jo - *The Just City*
  y SLJ - v61 - i11 - Nov 2015 - p126(2) [51-500]
  The Philosopher Kings
  BL - v111 - i18 - May 15 2015 - p38(2) [51-500]
  KR - May 15 2015 - pNA [51-500]
  LJ - v140 - i9 - May 15 2015 - p57(4) [51-500]
  PW - v262 - i20 - May 18 2015 - p69(1) [51-500]
Walton, John H. - *The Lost World of Adam and Eve: Genesis 2-3 and the Human Origins Debate*
  LJ - v140 - i9 - May 15 2015 - p64(2) [51-500]
Walton, Leslye - *The Strange and Beautiful Sorrows of Ava Lavender (Read by Campbell, Cassandra). Audiobook Review*
  y BL - v111 - i16 - April 15 2015 - p64(1) [51-500]
Walton, Nicholas - *Genoa, "La Superba": The Rise and Fall of Merchant Pirate Superpower*
  PW - v262 - i21 - May 25 2015 - p46(1) [51-500]
  TLS - i5866 - Sept 4 2015 - p30(1) [51-500]

Walton, Rick - *Girl & Gorilla (Illus. by Berger, Joe)*
  c KR - Oct 1 2015 - pNA [501+]
  c BL - v112 - i7 - Dec 1 2015 - p66(1) [51-500]
Walton, Samantha - *Guilty But Insane: Mind and Law in Golden Age Detective Fiction*
  TLS - i5873 - Oct 23 2015 - p21(1) [501+]
Walton, Will - *Anything Could Happen*
  y BL - v111 - i15 - April 1 2015 - p64(1) [51-500]
  y CCB-B - v69 - i1 - Sept 2015 - p63(2) [501+]
  y HB Guide - v26 - i2 - Fall 2015 - p143(1) [51-500]
  y KR - March 1 2015 - pNA [51-500]
  y PW - v262 - i11 - March 16 2015 - p85(2) [51-500]
  y SLJ - v61 - i5 - May 2015 - p125(2) [51-500]
  y VOYA - v38 - i3 - August 2015 - p72(1) [51-500]
Waltz, Samantha - *Blended: Writers on the Stepfamily Experience*
  KR - March 1 2015 - pNA [501+]
  LJ - v140 - i9 - May 15 2015 - p66(2) [51-500]
  PW - v262 - i8 - Feb 23 2015 - p62(1) [51-500]
Walvin, James - *Crossings: Africa, the Americas and the Atlantic Slave Trade*
  Historian - v77 - i2 - Summer 2015 - p418(2) [501+]
Walzer, Michael - *The Paradox of Liberation: Secular Revolutions and Religious Counterrevolutions*
  CC - v132 - i24 - Nov 25 2015 - p41(2) [501+]
  CHE - v61 - i35 - May 15 2015 - pB17(1) [501+]
  Nation - v301 - i23 - Dec 7 2015 - p46(7) [501+]
  NYRB - v62 - i10 - June 4 2015 - p66(3) [501+]
  TLS - i5875 - Nov 6 2015 - p14(1) [501+]
Wampole, Christy - *The Other Serious: Essays for the New American Generation*
  BL - v111 - i21 - July 1 2015 - p20(1) [51-500]
  BooChiTr - August 8 2015 - p14(1) [501+]
  HM - v331 - i1982 - July 2015 - p85(3) [501+]
  LJ - v140 - i6 - April 1 2015 - p90(1) [51-500]
  PW - v262 - i10 - March 9 2015 - p61(1) [51-500]
Wan, Amy J. - *Producing Good Citizens: Literacy Training in Anxious Times*
  Lang Soc - v44 - i5 - Nov 2015 - p741-742 [501+]
Wan, Joyce - *Are You My Mommy?*
  c KR - July 1 2015 - pNA [51-500]
  Peek-A-Boo Farm (Illus. by Wan, Joyce)
  c KR - Jan 1 2016 - pNA [51-500]
  Peek-a-Boo Zoo (Illus. by Wan, Joyce)
  c KR - July 1 2015 - pNA [51-500]
  c PW - v262 - i20 - May 18 2015 - p82(2) [51-500]
  The Whale in My Swimming Pool (Illus. by Wan, Joyce)
  c HB Guide - v26 - i2 - Fall 2015 - p21(1) [51-500]
  c KR - Jan 1 2015 - pNA [51-500]
  c NYTBR - May 31 2015 - p45(L) [501+]
Wan, Michelle - *I.O.U. Dead*
  y SLJ - v61 - i9 - Sept 2015 - p151(4) [501+]
Wan, Ming - *The China Model and Global Political Economy: Comparison, Impact, and Interaction*
  Pac A - v88 - i2 - June 2015 - p279 [501+]
Wan, Rosana Y. - *The Culinary Lives of John and Abigail Adams: A Cookbook*
  LJ - v140 - i5 - March 15 2015 - p128(1) [51-500]
Wandel, Lee Palmer - *A Companion to the Eucharist in the Reformation*
  Six Ct J - v46 - i1 - Spring 2015 - p157(3) [501+]
  Theol St - v76 - i2 - June 2015 - p364(2) [501+]
Wander, Steven H. - *The Joshua Roll*
  Med R - Sept 2015 - pNA [501+]
Wang, Andrea - *What's Great about Georgia?*
  c HB Guide - v26 - i1 - Spring 2015 - p203(1) [51-500]
  What's Great about Maine?
  c HB Guide - v26 - i2 - Fall 2015 - p220(1) [51-500]
Wang, Chi - *Obama's Challenge to China*
  KR - August 15 2015 - pNA [501+]
Wang, Chih-ming - *Transpacific Articulations: Student Migration and the Remaking of Asian America*
  JAS - v74 - i1 - Feb 2015 - p181-183 [501+]
Wang, Dorothy J. - *Thinking Its Presence: Form, Race, and Subjectivity in Contemporary Asian American Poetry*
  AL - v87 - i3 - Sept 2015 - p627-629 [501+]
Wang, Harvey - *Harvey Wang: From Darkroom to Daylight*
  LJ - v140 - i15 - Sept 15 2015 - p81(3) [501+]
Wang, Hui - *China from Empire to Nation-State*
  TLS - i5866 - Sept 4 2015 - p10(1) [501+]
Wang, Jack - *A New Hope*
  c KR - July 1 2015 - pNA [51-500]
Wang, Ping - *Ten Thousand Waves*
  WLT - v89 - i2 - March-April 2015 - p79(1) [51-500]
Wang, Q. Edward - *Chopsticks: A Cultural and Culinary History*
  TimHES - i2206 - June 4 2015 - p49(1) [501+]

Wang, Robin R. - *Yinyang: The Way of Heaven and Earth in Chinese Thought and Culture*
    Dialogue - v54 - i1 - March 2015 - p196-197 [501+]
Wang, Wensheng - *White Lotus Rebels and South China Pirates: Crisis and Reform in the Qing Empire*
    JIH - v46 - i1 - Summer 2015 - p150-151 [501+]
Wang, Yun - *The Book of Totality*
    WLT - v89 - i6 - Nov-Dec 2015 - p79(1) [51-500]
Wang, Zheng - *Never Forget National Humiliation: Historical Memory in Chinese Politics and Foreign Relations*
    AHR - v120 - i3 - June 2015 - p994-995 [501+]
Wang, Zhenping - *Tang China in Multi-Polar Asia: A History of Diplomacy and War*
    Historian - v77 - i3 - Fall 2015 - p591(2) [501+]
Wangard, Terri - *Friends and Enemies*
    PW - v262 - i45 - Nov 9 2015 - p46(1) [51-500]
Wappett, Matthew - *Emerging Perspectives on Disability Studies*
    CS - v44 - i1 - Jan 2015 - p148-149 [501+]
Wapshott, Nicholas - *The Sphinx: Franklin Roosevelt, the Isolationists, and the Road to World War II*
    TLS - i5846 - April 17 2015 - p24(1) [501+]
Warburg, Philip - *Harness the Sun*
    KR - July 1 2015 - pNA [501+]
Ward, Allyna E. - *Women and Tudor Tragedy: Feminizing Counsel and Representing Gender*
    MLR - v110 - i3 - July 2015 - p816-817 [501+]
    Six Ct J - v46 - i1 - Spring 2015 - p188-189 [501+]
Ward, Amanda Eyre - *The Same Sky*
    LJ - v140 - i3 - Feb 15 2015 - p94(2) [51-500]
    NYTBR - May 3 2015 - p30(L) [501+]
Ward, Brian - *The American South and the Atlantic World*
    J Am St - v49 - i1 - Feb 2015 - p181-185 [501+]
    JSH - v81 - i3 - August 2015 - p706(2) [501+]
    RAH - v43 - i1 - March 2015 - p26-31 [501+]
    Historian - v77 - i2 - Summer 2015 - p364(2) [501+]
Ward, Christopher - *Mac on the Road to Marseille*
    y Res Links - v20 - i3 - Feb 2015 - p36(1) [51-500]
    c SLJ - v61 - i6 - June 2015 - p109(1) [51-500]
Ward, Dan - *The Simplicity Cycle: A Field Guide to Making Things Better Without Making Them Worse*
    LJ - v140 - i8 - May 1 2015 - p83(1) [51-500]
    PW - v262 - i6 - Feb 9 2015 - p53(1) [51-500]
Ward, David - *Coleridge and the Nature of Imagination: Evolution, Engagement with the World and Poetry*
    RES - v66 - i274 - April 2015 - p386-388 [501+]
Ward, David C. - *Call Waiting*
    TLS - i5839 - Feb 27 2015 - p25(1) [501+]
Ward, Geoff K. - *The Black Child-Savers: Racial Democracy and Juvenile Justice*
    CS - v44 - i3 - May 2015 - p322-325 [501+]
Ward, Graham - *Unbelievable: Why We Believe and Why We Don't*
    TLS - i5869 - Sept 25 2015 - p28(1) [501+]
Ward, Helen - *Spots in a Box (Illus. by Ward, Helen)*
    c CH Bwatch - April 2015 - pNA [51-500]
    c HB Guide - v26 - i2 - Fall 2015 - p21(1) [51-500]
    c PW - v262 - i49 - Dec 2 2015 - p38(2) [51-500]
    c SLJ - v61 - i4 - April 2015 - p188(1) [51-500]
Ward, J.R. - *The Bourbon Kings*
    BL - v111 - i21 - July 1 2015 - p29(1) [51-500]
    PW - v262 - i25 - June 22 2015 - p126(1) [51-500]
Ward, James - *Adventures in Stationery: A Journey through Your Pencil Case*
    TLS - i5838 - Feb 20 2015 - p30(1) [501+]
The Perfection of the Paper Clip: Curious Tales of Invention, Accidental Genius, and Stationery Obsession
    BL - v111 - i15 - April 1 2015 - p7(2) [51-500]
    LJ - v140 - i7 - April 15 2015 - p115(2) [51-500]
Ward, James Mace - *Priest, Politician, Collaborator: Jozef Tiso and the Making of Fascist Slovakia*
    CHR - v101 - i1 - Wntr 2015 - p172(3) [501+]
    HER - v130 - i542 - Feb 2015 - p242(2) [501+]
    JMH - v87 - i1 - March 2015 - p231(3) [501+]
Ward, Jane - *Not Gay: Sex between Straight White Men*
    G&L Rev W - v22 - i6 - Nov-Dec 2015 - p46(1) [501+]
    TimHES - i2224 - Oct 8 2015 - p44-1 [501+]
Ward, Jennifer (b. 1963-) - *There Was an Old Martian Who Swallowed the Moon (Illus. by Gray, Steve)*
    c HB Guide - v26 - i2 - Fall 2015 - p55(1) [51-500]
There Was an Old Mummy Who Swallowed a Spider (Illus. by Gray, Steve)
    c HB - v91 - i5 - Sept-Oct 2015 - p70(1) [51-500]
    c KR - August 1 2015 - pNA [51-500]
    c PW - v262 - i30 - July 27 2015 - p67(1) [51-500]
    c SLJ - v61 - i9 - Sept 2015 - p109(1) [51-500]

Ward, Jennifer C. - *Elizabeth de Burgh, Lady of Clare (1295-1360): Household and Other Records*
    Med R - May 2015 - pNA [501+]
Ward, Jessica - *The Ultimate Disney Party Book*
    c SLJ - v61 - i9 - Sept 2015 - p184(2) [51-500]
Ward, Joseph P. - *Culture, Faith and Philanthropy: Londoners and Provincial Reform in Early Modern England*
    HER - v130 - i544 - June 2015 - p741(2) [501+]
Ward, Kaitlin - *Bleeding Earth*
    y CCB-B - v69 - i2 - Oct 2015 - p120(1) [51-500]
    y KR - Dec 1 2015 - pNA [51-500]
    y PW - v262 - i45 - Nov 9 2015 - p62(1) [51-500]
    y SLJ - v61 - i12 - Dec 2015 - p129(1) [51-500]
    c VOYA - v38 - i3 - August 2015 - p85(1) [51-500]
Ward, Lindsay - *Henry Finds His Word*
    c HB Guide - v26 - i2 - Fall 2015 - p21(1) [51-500]
The Importance of Being 3
    c KR - Nov 1 2015 - pNA [51-500]
Ward, Malachi - *From Now On*
    PW - v262 - i46 - Nov 16 2015 - p64(1) [51-500]
Ward, Matthew - *War of the World Records (Read by Crossley, Steven). Audiobook Review*
    c SLJ - v61 - i7 - July 2015 - p48(1) [51-500]
War of the World Records
    c HB Guide - v26 - i1 - Spring 2015 - p95(1) [51-500]
Ward, Michael K. - *Ghost Riders in the Sky: The Life of Stan Jones, the Singing Ranger*
    Roundup M - v22 - i6 - August 2015 - p23(1) [501+]
Ward, Nathan - *The Lost Detective: Becoming Dashiell Hammett*
    BL - v111 - i19-20 - June 1 2015 - p32(2) [51-500]
    LJ - v140 - i11 - June 15 2015 - p90(1) [51-500]
    PW - v262 - i19 - May 11 2015 - p45(1) [51-500]
    KR - May 15 2015 - pNA [501+]
Ward, Patricia - *Skinner Luce*
    KR - Nov 15 2015 - pNA [51-500]
    PW - v262 - i46 - Nov 16 2015 - p59(1) [51-500]
Ward, Peter - *A New History of Life: The Radical New Discoveries about the Origins and Evolution of Life on Earth*
    Nature - v518 - i7539 - Feb 19 2015 - p299(1) [51-500]
    New Sci - v225 - i3009 - Feb 21 2015 - p44(2) [501+]
    NYRB - v62 - i12 - July 9 2015 - p30(1) [501+]
Ward, Richard M. - *Print Culture, Crime and Justice in 18th-Century London*
    TLS - i5835 - Jan 30 2015 - p26(2) [501+]
Ward, Sarah - *Carry and Learn Numbers*
    c KR - July 1 2015 - pNA [51-500]
Colors (Illus. by Ward, Sarah)
    c KR - July 1 2015 - pNA [51-500]
In Bitter Chill
    BL - v112 - i1 - Sept 1 2015 - p47(2) [51-500]
    PW - v262 - i29 - July 20 2015 - p170(1) [51-500]
Ward, Stephanie - *Unemployment and the State in Britain: The Means Test and Protest in 1930s South Wales and North-East England*
    HER - v130 - i544 - June 2015 - p783(2) [501+]
Ward, Suzanne M. - *Rightsizing the Academic Library Collection*
    VOYA - v38 - i2 - June 2015 - p93(1) [51-500]
Ward, Terence - *The Guardian of Mercy: How an Extraordinary Painting by Caravaggio Changed an Ordinary Life Today*
    KR - Dec 15 2015 - pNA [501+]
    PW - v262 - i52 - Dec 21 2015 - p146(1) [51-500]
Wardaya, Baskara T. - *Truth Will Out: Indonesian Accounts of the 1965 Mass Violence*
    JAS - v74 - i1 - Feb 2015 - p244-246 [501+]
Warde, Mary Jane - *When the Wolf Came: The Civil War and the Indian Territory*
    JSH - v81 - i1 - Feb 2015 - p195(3) [501+]
Wardlaw, Lee - *Won Ton and Chopstick (Illus. by Yelchin, Eugene)*
    c BL - v111 - i11 - Feb 1 2015 - p57(1) [51-500]
    c CCB-B - v68 - i10 - June 2015 - p523(1) [51-500]
    c HB - v91 - i2 - March-April 2015 - p118(1) [51-500]
    c HB Guide - v26 - i2 - Fall 2015 - p205(1) [51-500]
Wardrop, Daneen - *Cyclorama*
    RVBW - May 2015 - pNA [51-500]
Ware, John A. - *A Pueblo Social History: Kinship, Sodality, and Community in the Northern Southwest*
    Am Ant - v80 - i1 - Jan 2015 - p207(2) [501+]
Ware, Robert Bruce - *The Fire Below: How the Caucasus Shaped Russia*
    E-A St - v67 - i4 - June 2015 - p681(2) [501+]

Ware, Ruth - *In a Dark, Dark Wood (Read by Church, Imogen). Audiobook Review*
    BL - v112 - i4 - Oct 15 2015 - p62(1) [51-500]
In a Dark, Dark Wood
    BL - v111 - i21 - July 1 2015 - p37(1) [51-500]
    Ent W - i1375 - August 7 2015 - p66(1) [501+]
    KR - June 15 2015 - pNA [51-500]
    Nat Post - v17 - i225 - August 1 2015 - pWP5(1) [501+]
    PW - v262 - i26 - June 29 2015 - p45(1) [51-500]
Ware, Susan - *Game, Set, Match: Billie Jean King and the Revolution in Women's Sports*
    JWH - v27 - i2 - Summer 2015 - p169(6) [501+]
Wareheim, Eric - *Tim and Eric's Zine Theory*
    Nat Post - v17 - i225 - August 1 2015 - pWP4(1) [501+]
Warga, Jasmine - *My Heart and Other Black Holes*
    y BL - v111 - i11 - Feb 1 2015 - p48(2) [51-500]
    y CCB-B - v68 - i7 - March 2015 - p375(2) [51-500]
    y HB - v91 - i1 - Jan-Feb 2015 - p91(2) [51-500]
    y HB Guide - v26 - i2 - Fall 2015 - p143(1) [51-500]
    c Nat Post - v17 - i92 - Feb 14 2015 - pWP10(1) [501+]
    y VOYA - v38 - i1 - April 2015 - p71(2) [51-500]
Wargin, Kathy-jo - *S Is for Sleeping Bear Dunes: A National Lakeshore Alphabet (Illus. by Frankenhuyzen, Gijsbert van)*
    c SLJ - v61 - i7 - July 2015 - p105(1) [51-500]
Warhol, Andy - *POPism: The Warhol Sixties*
    TLS - i5874 - Oct 30 2015 - p16(1) [51-500]
Wariner, Ruth - *The Sound of Gravel: A Memoir*
    KR - Oct 1 2015 - pNA [51-500]
    PW - v262 - i47 - Nov 23 2015 - p64(1) [51-500]
Warkentin, Germaine - *The Library of the Sydneys of Penhurst Place Circa 1665*
    TLS - i5854 - June 12 2015 - p25(1) [501+]
Pierre-Esprit Radisson: The Collected Writings, vol. 2: The Port Nelson Relations, Miscellaneous Writings, and Related Documents
    Can Hist R - v96 - i3 - Sept 2015 - p433(3) [501+]
Warman, Janice - *The World Beneath: One Boy's Struggle to Be Free*
    y Sch Lib - v63 - i1 - Spring 2015 - p59(1) [51-500]
Warman, Jessica - *The Last Good Day of the Year*
    BL - v111 - i17 - May 1 2015 - p51(1) [51-500]
    y CCB-B - v68 - i10 - June 2015 - p523(2) [51-500]
    y HB Guide - v26 - i2 - Fall 2015 - p143(1) [51-500]
    y KR - March 1 2015 - pNA [51-500]
    y SLJ - v61 - i5 - May 2015 - p126(1) [51-500]
    y VOYA - v38 - i2 - June 2015 - p69(1) [51-500]
Warmington, Paul - *Black British Intellectuals and Education: Multiculturalism's Hidden History*
    ERS - v38 - i3 - March 2015 - p497(2) [501+]
Warner, Gertrude Chandler - *The Boxcar Children: The Firehouse Mystery (Read by Gregory, Tim)*
    c CH Bwatch - April 2015 - pNA [51-500]
The Boxcar Children: The Movie Star Mystery (Read by Gregory, Tim). Audiobook Review
    c CH Bwatch - August 2015 - pNA [51-500]
The Boxcar Children: The Mystery of the Empty Safe (Read by Lilly, Aimee). Audiobook Review
    c CH Bwatch - Sept 2015 - pNA [51-500]
The Boxcar Children: The Poison Frog Mystery (Read by Gregory, Tim). Audiobook Review
    y CH Bwatch - Nov 2015 - pNA [51-500]
The Mystery of the Stolen Snowboard (Illus. by VanArsdale, Anthony)
    c HB Guide - v26 - i1 - Spring 2015 - p96(1) [51-500]
The Mystery of the Wild West Bandit (Illus. by VanArsdale, Anthony)
    c HB Guide - v26 - i1 - Spring 2015 - p96(1) [51-500]
Warner, Justin - *The Laws of Cooking and How to Break Them*
    NYTBR - Dec 6 2015 - p20(L) [501+]
    NYTBR - Dec 6 2015 - p20(L) [501+]
    PW - v262 - i31 - August 3 2015 - p51(1) [51-500]
Warner, Kathryn - *Edward II: The Unconventional King*
    Med R - June 2015 - pNA [501+]
Warner, Marina - *Once upon a Time: A Short History of Fairy Tale*
    ABR - v36 - i4 - May-June 2015 - p18(1) [501+]
    NYTBR - Jan 25 2015 - p14(L) [501+]
    TLS - i5841 - March 13 2015 - p3(3) [501+]
Warner, Michael - *The Rise and Fall of Intelligence: An International Security History*
    AHR - v120 - i3 - June 2015 - p978-979 [501+]
Warner, Penny - *The Mummy's Curse*
    c HB Guide - v26 - i2 - Fall 2015 - p105(1) [51-500]

Warner, Sally - *EllRay Jakes Is Magic! (Read by Allen, Corey). Audiobook Review*
  c SLJ - v61 - i7 - July 2015 - p45(2) [51-500]
EllRay Jakes Rocks the Holidays! (Illus. by Biggs, Brian)
  c HB Guide - v26 - i1 - Spring 2015 - p96(1) [51-500]
EllRay Jakes: The Dragon Slayer! (Illus. by Allen, Corey). Audiobook Review
  c SLJ - v61 - i3 - March 2015 - p77(1) [51-500]
EllRay Jakes: The Dragon Slayer! (Illus. by Biggs, Brian)
  c SLJ - v61 - i6 - June 2015 - p46(6) [501+]
EllRay Jakes: The Recess King! (Illus. by Biggs, Brian)
  c BL - v111 - i17 - May 1 2015 - p98(1) [51-500]
  c HB Guide - v26 - i2 - Fall 2015 - p106(1) [51-500]
  c SLJ - v61 - i5 - May 2015 - p99(2) [51-500]
Warner, William B. - *Protocols of Liberty: Communication Innovation and the American Revolution*
  Eight-C St - v48 - i3 - Spring 2015 - p359-362 [501+]
Warnes, Andrew - *American Tantalus: Horizons, Happiness, and the Impossible Pursuits of US Literature and Culture*
  TLS - i5847 - April 24 2015 - p26(2) [501+]
Warnes, Tim - *Dangerous!*
  c HB Guide - v26 - i1 - Spring 2015 - p18(1) [51-500]
The Great Cheese Robbery
  c KR - Jan 1 2015 - pNA [51-500]
The Great Cheese Robbery (Illus. by Warnes, Tim)
  c BL - v111 - i12 - Feb 15 2015 - p87(1) [51-500]
  c HB Guide - v26 - i2 - Fall 2015 - p21(1) [51-500]
Warnke, Martin - *Zeitgenossenschaft: Zum Auschwitz-Prozess 1964*
  HNet - Jan 2015 - pNA [501+]
Warraq, Ibn - *Christmas in the Koran: Luxenberg, Syriac, and the Near Eastern and Judeo-Christian Background of Islam*
  MEQ - v22 - i1 - Wntr 2015 - pNA [501+]
Warren, Andrea - *The Boy Who Became Buffalo Bill: Growing Up Billy Cody in Bleeding Kansas*
  c PW - v262 - i38 - Sept 21 2015 - p78(1) [51-500]
  c SLJ - v61 - i10 - Oct 2015 - p139(1) [51-500]
  y VOYA - v38 - i5 - Dec 2015 - p78(1) [51-500]
  c KR - Sept 15 2015 - pNA [51-500]
Warren, Elizabeth - *A Fighting Chance*
  NYTBR - April 26 2015 - p28(L) [501+]
Warren, Georgia Denton - *Winter Symphony on Lake Mattamuskeet: A Love Story*
  KR - May 1 2015 - pNA [51-500]
Warren, Jason W. - *Connecticut Unscathed: Victory in the Great Narragansett War, 1675-1676*
  NEQ - v88 - i2 - June 2015 - p327-330 [501+]
Warren, Jeremy - *Renaissance and Baroque Bronzes in and around the Peter Marino Collection*
  Ren Q - v68 - i1 - Spring 2015 - p258-259 [501+]
Warren, John - *The Nature of Crops: How We Came to Eat the Plants We Do*
  TimHES - i2211 - July 9 2015 - p46(1) [501+]
Warren, Mark R. - *Fire in the Heart: How White Activists Embrace Racial Justice*
  CS - v44 - i1 - Jan 2015 - p130-131 [501+]
Warren, Melvin L. - *Freshwater Fishes of North America*
  QRB - v90 - i2 - June 2015 - pNA [501+]
Warren, Mike - *23 Things to Do before You Are 11 1/2: A Practical Step-by-Step Guide for Things to Make in Your Backyard (Illus. by Haslam, John)*
  c PW - v262 - i30 - July 27 2015 - p70(1) [501+]
  c Sch Lib - v63 - i3 - Autumn 2015 - p177(1) [51-500]
  c SLJ - v61 - i11 - Nov 2015 - p138(1) [51-500]
Warren, Rick - *The Purpose Driven Life Devotional for Kids*
  c BL - v112 - i6 - Nov 15 2015 - p44(1) [51-500]
Warren, Rosie - *Salvage*
  NS - v144 - i5277 - August 28 2015 - p43(1) [51-500]
Warren, Sandra - *We Bought a WWII Bomber: The Untold Story of a Michigan High School, a B-17 Bomber, and the Blue Ridge Parkway!*
  PW - v262 - i42 - Oct 19 2015 - p70(1) [51-500]
Warren, Sarah - *Mikhail Larionov and the Cultural Politics of Late Imperial Russia*
  Slav R - v74 - i2 - Summer 2015 - p420-421 [501+]
Warren, Stephen - *The Worlds the Shawnees Made: Migration and Violence in Early America*
  AHR - v120 - i1 - Feb 2015 - p229-230 [501+]
  Am Ind CRJ - v39 - i2 - Spring 2015 - p172-173 [501+]
  HNet - Feb 2015 - pNA [501+]
  JAH - v101 - i4 - March 2015 - p1241-1242 [501+]
  JSH - v81 - i2 - May 2015 - p432(1) [501+]
  W&M Q - v72 - i2 - April 2015 - p351-366 [501+]
Warren, Susan May - *Always on My Mind*
  BL - v111 - i9-10 - Jan 1 2015 - p55(1) [51-500]
You're the One That I Want
  PW - v262 - i47 - Nov 23 2015 - p57(1) [51-500]
Warren, Tiffany L. - *Favorite Son*
  PW - v262 - i3 - Jan 19 2015 - p67(1) [51-500]
Warren, Tracy Anne - *The Bedding Proposal*
  PW - v262 - i5 - Feb 2 2015 - p43(1) [51-500]
Mad about the Man
  BL - v112 - i1 - Sept 15 2015 - p45(1) [51-500]
  PW - v262 - i32 - August 10 2015 - p43(1) [51-500]
Warren, Vic - *Saffron*
  PW - v262 - i9 - March 2 2015 - p69(1) [51-500]
Stairway of the Gods
  PW - v262 - i20 - May 18 2015 - p67(1) [51-500]
Warren, W.L. - *King John*
  HT - v65 - i6 - June 2015 - p56(2) [501+]
Warrick, Joby - *Black Flags: The Rise of ISIS*
  KR - August 15 2015 - pNA [501+]
  LJ - v140 - i16 - Oct 1 2015 - p97(1) [51-500]
  NYT - Dec 1 2015 - pC1(L) [501+]
  PW - v262 - i35 - August 31 2015 - p77(1) [51-500]
Warrington, Joanna - *The D Word*
  KR - August 1 2015 - pNA [501+]
Warsh, Larry - *Jean-Michel Basquiat: The Notebooks*
  PW - v262 - i19 - May 11 2015 - p49(1) [51-500]
Warwick, Claire - *Digital Humanities in Practice*
  HNet - Jan 2015 - pNA [501+]
Warwick, David R. - *The Abolition of Cash*
  KR - Oct 15 2015 - pNA [501+]
Warwick, Joe - *Where Chefs Eat: A Guide to Chefs' Favourite Restaurants*
  Econ - v414 - i8931 - March 28 2015 - p88(US) [501+]
Wascom, Kent - *Secessia*
  KR - May 1 2015 - pNA [501+]
  LJ - v140 - i11 - June 15 2015 - p82(2) [51-500]
Washburn, D.A. - *Banishment in the Later Roman Empire, 284-476 CE*
  Class R - v65 - i2 - Oct 2015 - p548-549 [501+]
Washburn, Frances - *The Red Bird All-Indian Traveling Band*
  Roundup M - v22 - i5 - June 2015 - p39(1) [501+]
  Roundup M - v22 - i6 - August 2015 - p33(1) [501+]
Washington, Harriet A. - *Infectious Madness: The Surprising Science of How We "Catch" Mental Illness*
  BL - v112 - i2 - Sept 15 2015 - p8(1) [51-500]
  KR - August 15 2015 - pNA [501+]
  LJ - v140 - i13 - August 1 2015 - p117(2) [51-500]
  PW - v262 - i32 - August 10 2015 - p50(1) [51-500]
Washington, Mary Helen - *The Other Blacklist: The African American Literary and Cultural Left of the 1950s*
  JAH - v101 - i4 - March 2015 - p1324(1) [501+]
  Wom R Bks - v32 - i1 - Jan-Feb 2015 - p14(2) [501+]
Wasmund, Shaa - *Do Less, Get More: How to Work Smart and Live Life Your Way*
  BL - v111 - i21 - July 1 2015 - p21(2) [51-500]
Wassel, Damian A. - *The Gifted: Books 1 and 2 (Illus. by Gooden, Nathan C.)*
  PW - v262 - i31 - August 3 2015 - p44(1) [51-500]
  y VOYA - v37 - i6 - Feb 2015 - p50(2) [51-500]
Wasserman, Debra - *Conveniently Vegan*
  Veg J - v34 - i2 - April-June 2015 - p33(1) [51-500]
I Love Animals and Broccoli Coloring Book
  c Veg J - v34 - i2 - April-June 2015 - p34(1) [51-500]
The Lowfat Jewish Vegetarian Cookbook: Healthy Traditions from around the World
  Veg J - v34 - i2 - April-June 2015 - p33(1) [51-500]
Meatless Meals for Working People: Quick and Easy Vegetarian Recipes
  Veg J - v34 - i2 - April-June 2015 - p33(1) [51-500]
Simply Vegan
  Veg J - v34 - i2 - April-June 2015 - p33(1) [51-500]
Vegan Handbook
  Veg J - v34 - i2 - April-June 2015 - p33(1) [51-500]
Wasserman, Robin - *Game of Flames*
  c KR - Sept 15 2015 - pNA [51-500]
Wasserstein, Bernard - *The Ambiguity of Virtue: Gertrude van Tijn and the Fate of the Dutch Jews*
  HER - v130 - i544 - June 2015 - p786(3) [501+]
Wasson, Dave - *The Big Ideas of Buster Bickles (Illus. by Wasson, Dave)*
  c HB Guide - v26 - i2 - Fall 2015 - p55(1) [51-500]
  KR - Feb 1 2015 - pNA [501+]
  c SLJ - v61 - i7 - July 2015 - p69(1) [51-500]
Watada, Terry - *The Game of 100 Ghosts*
  WLT - v89 - i3-4 - May-August 2015 - p127(1) [51-500]
Watanabe, Izumi - *Fair Value Accounting in Historical Perspective*
  AR - v90 - i2 - March 2015 - p825(4) [501+]
Watchulonis, Michael - *The Strangler Vine*
  CSM - July 24 2015 - pNA [501+]
Waterfield, Robin - *Demosthenes: Selected Speeches*
  Class R - v65 - i2 - Oct 2015 - p607-607 [501+]
Taken at the Flood: The Roman Conquest of Greece
  Class R - v65 - i2 - Oct 2015 - p615-616 [501+]
  NYRB - v62 - i4 - March 5 2015 - p40(3) [501+]
Waterhouse, Ellis - *Paintings: The James A. de Rothschild Collection at Waddesdon Manor*
  NYRB - v62 - i11 - June 25 2015 - p29(4) [501+]
Waters, Alice - *My Pantry: Homemade Ingredients That Make Simple Meals Special*
  BL - v111 - i22 - August 1 2015 - p14(1) [51-500]
Waters, Colin - *Be the First to Like This*
  WLT - v89 - i3-4 - May-August 2015 - p107(1) [51-500]
Waters, John F. - *Sharks Have Six Senses (Illus. by Barner, Bob)*
  c SLJ - v61 - i6 - June 2015 - p138(1) [51-500]
  c BL - v111 - i15 - April 1 2015 - p37(1) [51-500]
  c HB Guide - v26 - i2 - Fall 2015 - p176(1) [51-500]
  c KR - Feb 1 2015 - pNA [51-500]
Waters, Lesley - *Deliciously Dairy Free: Fresh and Simple Lactose-Free Recipes for Healthy Eating Every Day*
  Bwatch - Sept 2015 - pNA [51-500]
Waters, Luke - *NYPD Green: A Memoir*
  KR - Oct 15 2015 - pNA [501+]
  PW - v262 - i44 - Nov 2 2015 - p76(2) [51-500]
Waters, Matthew W. - *Ancient Persia: A Concise History of the Achaemenid Empire, 550-330 BCE*
  Class R - v65 - i2 - Oct 2015 - p613-614 [501+]
  Lon R Bks - v37 - i9 - May 7 2015 - p22(2) [501+]
Waters, Sarah - *The Paying Guests (Read by Stevenson, Juliet). Audiobook Review*
  BL - v111 - i15 - April 1 2015 - p85(1) [51-500]
The Paying Guests
  G&L Rev W - v22 - i4 - July-August 2015 - p42(1) [501+]
  NYTBR - Oct 11 2015 - p28(L) [501+]
Waters, Tawni - *Beauty of the Broken*
  y HB Guide - v26 - i1 - Spring 2015 - p126(1) [51-500]
Waters, Timothy William - *The Milosevic Trial: An Autopsy*
  Slav R - v74 - i1 - Spring 2015 - p157-159 [501+]
Waters, Tony - *Schooling, Childhood, and Bureaucracy: Bureaucratizing the Child*
  CS - v44 - i2 - March 2015 - p275-277 [501+]
Wathey, John C. - *The Illusion of God's Presence: The Biological Origins of Spiritual Longings*
  PW - v262 - i45 - Nov 9 2015 - p57(1) [501+]
Watkin, William - *Agamben and Indifference: A Critical Overview*
  J Phil - v112 - i5 - May 2015 - p280(1) [501+]
Watkins, Alfred - *The Old Straight Track: Its Mounds, Beacons, Moats, Sites and Mark Stones*
  TLS - i5846 - April 17 2015 - p30(1) [501+]
Watkins, Angela Farris - *Love Will See You Through: Martin Luther King Jr.'s Six Guiding Beliefs (as Told by His Niece). (Illus. by Comport, Sally Wern)*
  c CH Bwatch - April 2015 - pNA [51-500]
  c HB Guide - v26 - i2 - Fall 2015 - p154(1) [51-500]
Watkins, Charles - *Trees, Woods and Forests: A Social and Cultural History*
  Mac - v128 - i9 - March 9 2015 - p56(1) [501+]
  Nature - v517 - i7533 - Jan 8 2015 - p143(1) [51-500]
  TLS - i5846 - April 17 2015 - p21(2) [501+]
Watkins, Claire Vaye - *Gold Fame Citrus*
  BL - v111 - i22 - August 1 2015 - p27(1) [51-500]
  BooChiTr - Oct 10 2015 - p12(1) [501+]
  HM - v331 - i1984 - Sept 2015 - p79(3) [501+]
  KR - August 1 2015 - pNA [501+]
  LJ - v140 - i13 - August 1 2015 - p90(1) [51-500]
  NYTBR - Oct 4 2015 - p18(L) [501+]
  PW - v262 - i28 - July 13 2015 - p1(1) [51-500]

Watkins, Clive - *Already the Flames*
    WLT - v89 - i5 - Sept-Oct 2015 - p79(1) [51-500]

Watkins, Daniel P. - *Anna Letitia Barbauld and Eighteenth-Century Visionary Poetics*
    MLR - v110 - i2 - April 2015 - p529-531 [501+]
    TSWL - v34 - i1 - Spring 2015 - p163-165 [501+]

Watkins, John - *Mediterranean Identities in the Premodern Era: Entrepots, Islands, Empires*
    Med R - May 2015 - pNA [501+]

Watkins, Linda - *Return to Mateguas Island*
    PW - v262 - i38 - Sept 21 2015 - p56(1) [51-500]

Watkins, Ralph Basui - *The Future of the African American Church: An Invitation to Dialogue*
    CC - v132 - i21 - Oct 14 2015 - p34(2) [501+]

Watkins, Rowboat - *Rude Cakes (Illus. by Watkins, Rowboat)*
    c BL - v111 - i19-20 - June 1 2015 - p124(1) [51-500]
    c HB Guide - v26 - i2 - Fall 2015 - p21(1) [51-500]
    c NYTBR - June 21 2015 - p17(L) [501+]
    c NYTBR - June 21 2015 - p17(L) [501+]
    c PW - v262 - i15 - April 13 2015 - p77(1) [51-500]
    c PW - v262 - i49 - Dec 2 2015 - p38(1) [51-500]

Watkins, W.R. - *You. Are. Not. Alone.*
    SPBW - March 2015 - pNA [51-500]

Watry, David M. - *Diplomacy at the Brink: Eisenhower, Churchill, and Eden in the Cold War*
    HNet - March 2015 - pNA [501+]
    HNet - Sept 2015 - pNA(NA) [501+]

Watsky, Paul - *Walk-Up Music*
    KR - May 15 2015 - pNA [51-500]

Watson, Alexander - *Ring of Steel: Germany and Austria-Hungary in World War I*
    J Mil H - v79 - i1 - Jan 2015 - p234-235 [501+]
    J Mil H - v79 - i4 - Oct 2015 - p1137 [501+]

Watson, Alistair - *Playing with Scales: Piano - A Fresh Way to Practise Scales, Level One*
    Am MT - v64 - i4 - Feb-March 2015 - p64(2) [501+]

Watson, Andi - *Princess Decomposia and Count Spatula (Illus. by Watson, Andi)*
    y CCB-B - v68 - i7 - March 2015 - p376(1) [51-500]
    y HB - v91 - i3 - May-June 2015 - p122(1) [51-500]
    y HB Guide - v26 - i2 - Fall 2015 - p143(1) [51-500]

Watson, Bruce - *Light: A Radiant History from Creation to the Quantum Age*
    BL - v112 - i7 - Dec 1 2015 - p20(1) [51-500]
    KR - Nov 15 2015 - pNA [51-500]
    PW - v262 - i48 - Nov 30 2015 - p48(2) [51-500]

Watson, C.G. - *Ascending the Boneyard*
    y KR - Nov 15 2015 - pNA [51-500]

Watson, Christie - *Where Women Are Kings*
    BL - v111 - i14 - March 15 2015 - p56(1) [51-500]
    KR - Feb 15 2015 - pNA [51-500]
    NYTBR - May 10 2015 - p27(L) [501+]

Watson, Christine - *Where Women Are Kings*
    PW - v262 - i5 - Feb 2 2015 - p32(2) [51-500]

Watson, Gay - *A Philosophy of Emptiness*
    J Phil - v112 - i5 - May 2015 - p280(1) [51-500]

Watson, Jude - *Mission Titanic*
    c HB Guide - v26 - i2 - Fall 2015 - p106(1) [51-500]

Watson, Kate - *Women Writing Crime Fiction, 1860-1880: Fourteen American, British and Australian Authors*
    MLR - v110 - i2 - April 2015 - p533-535 [501+]

Watson, Kathy - *The Crossing: The Curious Story of the First Man to Swim the English Channel*
    TLS - i5864-5865 - August 21 2015 - p18(1) [501+]

Watson-Lakamp, Paula - *Marketing Moxie for Librarians: Fresh Ideas, Proven Techniques, and Innovative Approaches*
    Teach Lib - v43 - i1 - Oct 2015 - p41(3) [51-500]

Watson, Molly - *Greens + Grains: Recipes for Deliciously Healthful Meals*
    LJ - v140 - i3 - Feb 15 2015 - p122(4) [51-500]

Watson, Peter - *The German Genius: Europe's Third Renaissance*
    HT - v65 - i10 - Oct 2015 - p56(2) [501+]
Madeleine's War
    BL - v111 - i16 - April 15 2015 - p37(1) [51-500]
    LJ - v140 - i6 - April 1 2015 - p86(1) [51-500]

Watson, Renee - *This Side of Home*
    y BL - v111 - i11 - Feb 1 2015 - p44(1) [51-500]
    y CCB-B - v68 - i7 - March 2015 - p376(1) [51-500]
    y VOYA - v37 - i6 - Feb 2015 - p69(2) [51-500]

Watson, Rowan - *Word and Image: Art, Books and Design from the National Art Library*
    TLS - i5845 - April 10 2015 - p34(1) [501+]

Watson, S.J. - *Second Life*
    BL - v111 - i17 - May 1 2015 - p43(2) [51-500]
    LJ - v140 - i9 - May 15 2015 - p74(3) [51-500]
    NYTBR - July 5 2015 - p29(L) [501+]
    Obs - Feb 22 2015 - p45 [501+]
    PW - v262 - i17 - April 27 2015 - p49(1) [51-500]
    TLS - i5861 - July 31 2015 - p20(1) [51-500]
    LJ - v140 - i9 - May 15 2015 - p78(1) [51-500]
    Spec - v327 - i9729 - Feb 14 2015 - p40(2) [501+]

Watson, Samuel J. - *Peacekeepers and Conquerors: The Army Officer Corps on the American Frontier, 1821-1846*
    HNet - May 2015 - pNA [501+]

Watson, Sonja Stephenson - *The Politics of Race in Panama: Afro-Hispanic and West Indian Literary Discourses of Contention*
    HAHR - v95 - i1 - Feb 2015 - p177-178 [501+]

Watson, Stephanie - *Behold! A Baby (Illus. by Ang, Joy)*
    c HB Guide - v26 - i2 - Fall 2015 - p55(1) [51-500]
    c KR - March 15 2015 - pNA [51-500]
    c SLJ - v61 - i4 - April 2015 - p138(1) [51-500]
Bruno Mars: Pop Superstar
    y HB Guide - v26 - i1 - Spring 2015 - p193(1) [51-500]
Plan a Birthday Party. E-book Review
    c HB Guide - v26 - i1 - Spring 2015 - p142(1) [51-500]
Plan a Sleepover Party. E-book Review
    c HB Guide - v26 - i1 - Spring 2015 - p142(1) [51-500]

Watson, Sterling - *Suitcase City*
    KR - March 15 2015 - pNA [51-500]
    PW - v262 - i3 - Jan 19 2015 - p63(1) [51-500]

Watson, Tom - *Stick Cat: A Tail of Two Kitties (Illus. by Watson, Tom)*
    c SLJ - v61 - i11 - Nov 2015 - p92(2) [51-500]
Stick Dog Chases a Pizza (Illus. by Long, Ethan)
    c HB Guide - v26 - i1 - Spring 2015 - p96(1) [51-500]
Stick Dog Dreams of Ice Cream (Illus. by Watson, Tom)
    c BL - v111 - i15 - April 1 2015 - p68(1) [51-500]
    c HB Guide - v26 - i2 - Fall 2015 - p106(1) [51-500]
    c SLJ - v61 - i2 - Feb 2015 - p95(1) [51-500]

Watson, William - *The Inequality Trap: Fighting Capitalism Instead of Poverty*
    NYTBR - Dec 20 2015 - p27(L) [501+]

Watson, William E. - *Irish Americans: The History and Culture of a People*
    LJ - v140 - i5 - March 15 2015 - p130(1) [51-500]

Watt-Cloutier, Sheila - *The Right to Be Cold: One Woman's Story of Protecting Her Culture, the Arctic and the Whole Planet*
    Nat Post - v17 - i130 - April 4 2015 - pWP4(1) [501+]

Watt, Fiona - *Very First Book of Things to Spot*
    c KR - Jan 1 2016 - pNA [51-500]

Watt, Isabella M. - *Registres du Consistoire de Geneve au Temps de Calvin: Tome VIII, 25 mars 1553-1 fevrier 1554*
    Six Ct J - v46 - i2 - Summer 2015 - p467-468 [501+]

Watt, Melanie - *Bug in a Vacuum (Illus. by Watt, Melanie)*
    c BL - v112 - i1 - Sept 1 2015 - p119(1) [51-500]
    c CH Bwatch - Nov 2015 - pNA [51-500]
    c KR - June 15 2015 - pNA [51-500]
    c NYTBR - Sept 13 2015 - p21(L) [501+]
    c Res Links - v21 - i1 - Oct 2015 - p11(1) [51-500]
    c SLJ - v61 - i10 - Oct 2015 - p86(1) [51-500]

Watt, Robert N. - *Apache Warrior, 1860-86*
    Roundup M - v22 - i5 - June 2015 - p37(1) [501+]
    Roundup M - v22 - i6 - August 2015 - p41(1) [501+]

Watters, Shannon - *Lumberjanes, vol. 1: Beware the Kitten Holy (Illus. by Allen, Brooke)*
    c PW - v262 - i49 - Dec 2 2015 - p86(1) [51-500]
Lumberjanes, vol. 2: Friendship to the Max (Illus. by Allen, Brooke)
    c SLJ - v61 - i10 - Oct 2015 - p120(1) [51-500]
Peanuts: A Tribute to Charles M. Schulz
    KR - Nov 15 2015 - pNA [501+]

Watts, Bernadette - *The Bernadette Watts Collection: Stories and Fairy Tales*
    c HB Guide - v26 - i2 - Fall 2015 - p202(1) [51-500]
The Golden Plate
    c HB Guide - v26 - i1 - Spring 2015 - p49(1) [51-500]
    SLJ - v61 - i4 - April 2015 - p138(1) [51-500]
Peter's Tree (Illus. by Watts, Bernadette)
    c Sch Lib - v63 - i2 - Summer 2015 - p98(1) [51-500]
The Tortoise and the Hare: An Aesop Fable (Illus. by Watts, Bernadette)
    c BL - v111 - i17 - May 1 2015 - p86(1) [51-500]
    c CH Bwatch - April 2015 - pNA [51-500]
    c HB Guide - v26 - i2 - Fall 2015 - p160(1) [51-500]

Watts, Edward J. - *The Final Pagan Generation*
    LJ - v140 - i2 - Feb 1 2015 - p88(1) [501+]

Watts, Frances - *The Peony Lantern*
    y Magpies - v30 - i4 - Sept 2015 - p44(1) [501+]
The Secrets of Flamant Castle: The Complete Adventures of Sword Girl and Friends
    c Sch Lib - v63 - i1 - Spring 2015 - p45(1) [501+]

Watts, Merritt - *First Jobs: True Tales of Bad Bosses, Quirky Coworkers, Big Breaks, and Small Paychecks*
    LJ - v140 - i7 - April 15 2015 - p84(1) [51-500]

Watzman, Haim - *On the Margins of a Minority: Leprosy, Madness, and Disability among the Jews of Medieval Europe*
    Med R - May 2015 - pNA [501+]
    Specu - v90 - i2 - April 2015 - p584-586 [501+]

Waudby, Jeannie - *One of Us*
    y BL - v112 - i4 - Oct 15 2015 - p57(1) [51-500]
    y KR - Sept 1 2015 - pNA [51-500]
    y PW - v262 - i34 - August 24 2015 - p83(1) [51-500]
    y Sch Lib - v63 - i2 - Summer 2015 - p122(1) [51-500]
    y SLJ - v61 - i10 - Oct 2015 - p118(1) [51-500]

Waugh, John C. - *Lincoln and the War's End*
    JSH - v81 - i4 - Nov 2015 - p983(3) [501+]

Waugh, Sandra - *Lark Rising*
    y CCB-B - v68 - i5 - Jan 2015 - p281(1) [51-500]
    c CH Bwatch - Jan 2015 - pNA [501+]
    y HB Guide - v26 - i1 - Spring 2015 - p127(1) [51-500]
Silver Eve
    c KR - July 1 2015 - pNA [51-500]

Wauquelin, Jehan - *The Medieval Romance of Alexander: The Deeds and Conquests of Alexander the Great*
    Med R - Feb 2015 - pNA [501+]

Wawro, Geoffrey - *A Mad Catastrophe: The Outbreak of World War I and the Collapse of the Habsburg Empire*
    J Mil H - v79 - i4 - Oct 2015 - p1155-1156 [501+]
    Parameters - v45 - i1 - Spring 2015 - p167(4) [501+]

Wawrzinek, Christina - *In Portum Navigare: Romische Hafen an Flussen und Seen*
    HNet - Feb 2015 - pNA [501+]

Wax, Wendy - *A Week at the Lake*
    BL - v111 - i18 - May 15 2015 - p26(1) [51-500]

Waxman, Laura Hamilton - *Aerospace Engineer Aprille Ericsson*
    BL - v111 - i14 - March 15 2015 - p63(1) [501+]
    c HB Guide - v26 - i2 - Fall 2015 - p208(1) [51-500]
Computer Engineer Ruchi Sanghvi
    BL - v111 - i14 - March 15 2015 - p63(1) [501+]
    c HB Guide - v26 - i2 - Fall 2015 - p208(1) [51-500]
Genetics Expert Joanna L. Kelley
    c HB Guide - v26 - i2 - Fall 2015 - p208(1) [51-500]

Waxman, Mark S. - *The McVentures of Me, Morgan McFactoid: Hair Today, Gone Tomorrow*
    c KR - Nov 15 2015 - pNA [51-500]

Wayland, April Halprin - *More Than Enough: A Passover Story (Illus. by Kath, Katie)*
    c PW - v262 - i50 - Dec 7 2015 - p88(1) [51-500]

Waymreen, Christina - *The Seedless Trees (Illus. by Nikolouzos, John)*
    y CH Bwatch - June 2015 - pNA [51-500]
    c CH Bwatch - Oct 2015 - pNA [51-500]

Wayne, Israel - *Questions Jesus Asks: Where Divinity Meets Humanity*
    RVBW - Nov 2015 - pNA [51-500]

Wayne, Randy - *Cuba Straits (Read by Guidall, George). Audiobook Review*
    PW - v262 - i21 - May 25 2015 - p54(1) [51-500]

Wayne, Tiffany K. - *Women's Rights in the United States: A Comprehensive Encyclopedia of Issues, Events, and People, 4 vols.*
    BL - v111 - i14 - March 15 2015 - p34(1) [51-500]
    R&USQ - v54 - i4 - Summer 2015 - p84(2) [51-500]

Wayson, Billy L. - *Martha Jefferson Randolph: Republican Daughter and Plantation Mistress*
    JSH - v81 - i2 - May 2015 - p447(2) [501+]

Wazana, Nili - *All the Boundaries of the Land: The Promised Land in Biblical Thought in Light of the Ancient Near East*
    JR - v95 - i3 - July 2015 - p389(3) [501+]

Weafer, John A. - *Thirty-Three Good Men: Celibacy Obedience and Identity*
    AM - v216 - i6 - Sept 14 2015 - p42(3) [501+]

486 • WEAKLAND **Book Review Index 2016 Cumulation**

Weakland, Mark - *The Adventures of Perseus: A Graphic Retelling (Illus. by Haus, Estudio)*
c HB Guide - v26 - i2 - Fall 2015 - p158(1) [51-500]
Weather Wise Series
c BL - v111 - i15 - April 1 2015 - p58(1) [501+]
Weatherford, Carole Boston - *Freedom in Congo Square (Illus. by Christie, R. Gregory)*
c BL - v112 - i6 - Nov 15 2015 - p40(1) [51-500]
c KR - Nov 1 2015 - pNA [51-500]
c SLJ - v61 - i10 - Oct 2015 - p131(1) [51-500]
Gordon Parks: How the Photographer Captured Black and White America (Illus. by Christoph, Jamey)
c CCB-B - v68 - i9 - May 2015 - p470(2) [51-500]
c KR - Jan 1 2015 - pNA [51-500]
c HB Guide - v26 - i2 - Fall 2015 - p194(1) [51-500]
c PW - v262 - i49 - Dec 2 2015 - p47(1) [51-500]
c BL - v111 - i11 - Feb 1 2015 - p42(2) [51-500]
c HB - v91 - i3 - May-June 2015 - p133(2) [501+]
Leontyne Price: Voice of a Century (Illus. by Colon, Raul)
c CCB-B - v68 - i5 - Jan 2015 - p282(1) [51-500]
c HB - v91 - i1 - Jan-Feb 2015 - p105(1) [51-500]
c HB Guide - v26 - i1 - Spring 2015 - p197(1) [51-500]
Voice of Freedom: Fannie Lou Hamer, Spirit of the Civil Rights Movement (Illus. by Holmes, Ekua)
c BL - v111 - i21 - July 1 2015 - p53(1) [51-500]
c HB - v91 - i5 - Sept-Oct 2015 - p134(1) [501+]
Voice of Freedom: Fannie Lou Hamer, Spirit of the Civil Rights Movement (Illus. by Holmes, Ekula)
c KR - May 1 2015 - pNA [51-500]
y SLJ - v61 - i8 - August 2015 - p130(1) [51-500]
Weatherly, G. William - *Sheppard of the Argonne*
KR - Jan 15 2015 - pNA [501+]
Weaver, Alain Epp - *Mapping Exile and Return: Palestinian Dispossession and a Political Theology for a Shared Future*
JR - v95 - i4 - Oct 2015 - p584(3) [501+]
Weaver, Amanda - *A Duchess in Name*
PW - v262 - i48 - Nov 30 2015 - p45(1) [51-500]
Weaver, Ashley - *Death Wears a Mask*
BL - v112 - i2 - Sept 15 2015 - p30(1) [51-500]
KR - August 15 2015 - pNA [51-500]
PW - v262 - i30 - July 27 2015 - p42(1) [51-500]
Murder at the Brightwell (Read by Fulford-Brown, Billie). Audiobook Review
PW - v262 - i8 - Feb 23 2015 - p70(1) [51-500]
Weaver, Carol - *The Politics of the Black Sea Region: EU Neighbourhood, Conflict Zone or Future Security Community?*
Slav R - v74 - i1 - Spring 2015 - p218-219 [501+]
Weaver, Denny J. - *The Nonviolent God*
TT - v72 - i1 - April 2015 - p119-121 [501+]
Weaver, Jace - *The Red Atlantic: American Indigenes and the Making of the Modern World, 1000-1927*
AHR - v120 - i2 - April 2015 - p604-605 [501+]
HNet - May 2015 - pNA [501+]
JAH - v102 - i1 - June 2015 - p201-202 [501+]
JSH - v81 - i2 - May 2015 - p421(2) [501+]
Weaver, Jo - *Little One (Illus. by Weaver, Jo)*
c PW - v262 - i50 - Dec 7 2015 - p84(1) [51-500]
Weaver, John C. - *Sorrows of a Century: Interpreting Suicide in New Zealand, 1900-2000*
AHR - v120 - i3 - June 2015 - p1001-1002 [501+]
Weaver, Tara Austen - *Orchard House: How a Neglected Garden Taught One Family to Grow*
BL - v111 - i13 - March 1 2015 - p12(1) [51-500]
KR - Feb 1 2015 - pNA [51-500]
Weaver, William - *The Complete Cosmicomics*
Bks & Cult - v21 - i2 - March-April 2015 - p30(2) [501+]
Webb, Alban - *London Calling: Britain, the BBC World Service and the Cold War*
HNet - Feb 2015 - pNA [501+]
HT - v65 - i3 - March 2015 - p59(1) [501+]
TLS - i5870 - Oct 2 2015 - p27(1) [501+]
Webb, Betty - *The Puffin of Death*
BL - v112 - i3 - Oct 1 2015 - p27(2) [51-500]
KR - Sept 1 2015 - pNA [51-500]
PW - v262 - i32 - August 10 2015 - p36(1) [51-500]
Webb, Brandon - *The Making of a Navy SEAL: My Story of Surviving the Toughest Challenge and Training the Best*
y BL - v112 - i2 - Sept 15 2015 - p54(1) [51-500]
y SLJ - v61 - i8 - August 2015 - p130(1) [51-500]
y VOYA - v38 - i3 - August 2015 - p88(1) [51-500]
Webb, Henry - *With the Children*
KR - Nov 1 2015 - pNA [51-500]
Webb, Holly - *The Case of the Stolen Sixpence (Read by Bentinck, Anna). Audiobook Review*
SLJ - v61 - i3 - March 2015 - p78(1) [51-500]
The Case of the Stolen Sixpence (Illus. by Lindsay, Marion)
c HB Guide - v26 - i1 - Spring 2015 - p96(1) [51-500]
The Case of the Vanishing Emerald (Illus. by Lindsay, Marion)
c HB Guide - v26 - i2 - Fall 2015 - p106(1) [51-500]
c KR - Jan 1 2015 - pNA [51-500]
Little Puppy Lost (Illus. by Harry, Rebecca)
c KR - Jan 15 2015 - pNA [51-500]
c SLJ - v61 - i6 - June 2015 - p76(1) [51-500]
The Water Horse
c Sch Lib - v63 - i3 - Autumn 2015 - p170(1) [51-500]
The Winter Wolf
c Sch Lib - v63 - i1 - Spring 2015 - p45(1) [51-500]
Webb, James L.A., Jr. - *The Long Struggle against Malaria in Tropical Africa*
IJAHS - v48 - i1 - Wntr 2015 - p176-177 [501+]
JIH - v46 - i2 - Autumn 2015 - p305-307 [501+]
Webb, Mick - *The Book of Languages: Talk Your Way around the World (Illus. by Webb, Mick)*
c BL - v111 - i18 - May 15 2015 - p44(1) [51-500]
c HB Guide - v26 - i2 - Fall 2015 - p162(1) [51-500]
c KR - Feb 15 2015 - pNA [51-500]
c Res Links - v20 - i5 - June 2015 - p22(1) [501+]
c SLJ - v61 - i5 - May 2015 - p143(1) [51-500]
c PW - v262 - i9 - March 2 2015 - p84(1) [501+]
Webb, Robert H. - *Requiem for the Santa Cruz: An Environmental History of an Arizona River*
Roundup M - v22 - i6 - August 2015 - p41(1) [501+]
Webb, Steve - *City Kitty Cat (Illus. by Le Huche, Magali)*
c HB Guide - v26 - i2 - Fall 2015 - p56(1) [51-500]
c SLJ - v61 - i9 - Sept 2015 - p131(1) [51-500]
Webb, Todd - *Transatlantic Methodists: British Wesleyanism and the Formation of an Evangelical Culture in Nineteenth-Century Ontario and Quebec*
Can Hist R - v96 - i1 - March 2015 - p120(3) [501+]
CH - v84 - i2 - June 2015 - p455(3) [501+]
Webb, William - *A Dying Trade: Memoirs of a Nursing Home Proprietor*
SPBW - July 2015 - pNA [51-500]
Webber, Mark - *Aussie Grit: My Formula One Journey*
NYT - Sept 26 2015 - pNA(L) [501+]
Weber, Alan M. - *Not for Hurting (Illus. by Pate, Ashley)*
c CH Bwatch - August 2015 - pNA [51-500]
The Wedge
SPBW - Oct 2015 - pNA [51-500]
SPBW - Nov 2015 - pNA [51-500]
Weber, Benjamin - *Lutter contre les Turcs: Les formes nouvelles de la croisade pontificale au XVe siecle*
AHR - v120 - i2 - April 2015 - p702-703 [501+]
Weber, Brenda R. - *Women and Literary Celebrity in the Nineteenth Century: The Transatlantic Production of Fame and Gender*
VS - v57 - i2 - Wntr 2015 - p305(4) [501+]
Weber, Bruce - *Leap of Faith*
NYT - Dec 6 2015 - p66(L) [51-500]
Life Is a Wheel: Memoirs of a Bike-Riding Obituarist
NYTBR - May 3 2015 - p28(L) [501+]
Weber, David - *Hell's Foundations Quiver*
PW - v262 - i33 - August 17 2015 - p56(1) [51-500]
Weber, Kerry - *Mercy in the City: How to Feed the Hungry, Give Drink to the Thirsty, Visit the Imprisoned, and Keep Your Day Job*
AM - v212 - i7 - March 2 2015 - p40(2) [501+]
Weber, Mary - *Siren's Fury*
y SLJ - v61 - i8 - August 2015 - p114(2) [51-500]
Storm Siren (Read by Stevens, Christine). Audiobook Review
y BL - v111 - i9-10 - Jan 1 2015 - p118(1) [51-500]
Storm Siren
y HB Guide - v26 - i1 - Spring 2015 - p127(1) [51-500]
Weber, Mary Beth - *Rethinking Library Technical Services: Redefining Our Profession for the Future*
VOYA - v38 - i5 - Dec 2015 - p84(1) [51-500]
Weber, Max - *Asketischer Protestantismus und Kapitalismus: Schriften und Reden 1904-1911*
Theol St - v76 - i1 - March 2015 - p195(2) [501+]
Weber, Tracy - *Karma's a Killer*
KR - Oct 15 2015 - pNA [51-500]
PW - v262 - i47 - Nov 23 2015 - p52(1) [51-500]
Weber, William - *Neither Victor nor Vanquished: America and the War of 1812*
J Mil H - v79 - i1 - Jan 2015 - p205-206 [501+]
Webster, Douglas D. - *Outposts of Hope: First Peter's Christ for Culture Strategy*
Ch Today - v59 - i4 - May 2015 - p65(1) [51-500]
Webster, Jason - *The Spy with 29 Names: The Story of the Second World War's Most Audacious Double Agent*
HT - v65 - i4 - April 2015 - p62(2) [501+]
Webster, Katie - *Maple: 100 Sweet and Savory Recipes Featuring Pure Maple Syrup*
LJ - v140 - i17 - Oct 15 2015 - p109(1) [51-500]
Webster, Peter - *Archbishop Michael Ramsey: The Shape of the Church*
TLS - i5874 - Oct 30 2015 - p13(1) [501+]
Webster, Stephen - *Goldstruck: A Life Shaped by Jewellery*
NYT - Nov 23 2015 - pNA(L) [501+]
Weckel, Ulrike - *Beschamende Bilder: Deutsche Reaktionen auf Alliierte Dokumentarfilme uber Befreite Konzentrationslager*
HNet - Feb 2015 - pNA [501+]
Wedemeyer, Christian K. - *Making Sense of Tantric Buddhism: History, Semiology, and Transgression in the Indian Traditions*
HNet - March 2015 - pNA [501+]
Wedge, Hayden - *Examining Shipwrecks*
c BL - v112 - i3 - Oct 1 2015 - p52(2) [51-500]
c CH Bwatch - Oct 2015 - pNA [51-500]
Wedge, Marilyn - *A Disease Called Childhood: Why ADHD Became an American Epidemic*
KR - Jan 15 2015 - pNA [501+]
PW - v262 - i3 - Jan 19 2015 - p74(2) [51-500]
Weed, Tim - *Will Poole's Island*
y HB Guide - v26 - i2 - Fall 2015 - p143(1) [51-500]
Weeden, Jason - *The Hidden Agenda of the Political Mind: How Self-Interest Shapes Our Opinions and Why We Won't Admit It*
Reason - v46 - i9 - Feb 2015 - p65(3) [501+]
Weeks, Jessica L.P. - *Dictators at War and Peace*
For Aff - v94 - i1 - Jan-Feb 2015 - pNA [51-500]
HNet - Sept 2015 - pNA(NA) [501+]
Weeks, Nan F. - *If He Had Not Come (Illus. by Jaskiewicz, Charles)*
c CH Bwatch - Jan 2015 - pNA [51-500]
Weeks, Sarah - *Glamourpuss (Illus. by Small, David)*
c CCB-B - v68 - i7 - March 2015 - p377(1) [51-500]
c CH Bwatch - May 2015 - pNA [501+]
c HB Guide - v26 - i2 - Fall 2015 - p56(1) [51-500]
Honey (Read by Soler, Rebecca). Audiobook Review
c BL - v111 - i22 - August 1 2015 - p80(1) [51-500]
c SLJ - v61 - i6 - June 2015 - p65(1) [51-500]
Honey
c HB Guide - v26 - i2 - Fall 2015 - p106(1) [51-500]
Weems, Scott - *HA! The Science of When We Laugh and Why*
SAH - v4 - i2 - Dec 15 2015 - p285-287 [501+]
Weetman, Nova - *Frankie and Joely*
y Magpies - v30 - i3 - July 2015 - p44(2) [501+]
Wegars, Priscilla - *As Rugged as the Terrian*
PHR - v84 - i2 - May 2015 - p239(2) [501+]
Wegman, William - *Flo & Wendell Explore (Illus. by Wegman, William)*
c HB Guide - v26 - i2 - Fall 2015 - p56(1) [51-500]
Wegner, Philip E. - *Shockwaves of Possibility: Essays on Science Fiction, Globalization, and Utopia*
SFS - v42 - i3 - Nov 2015 - p566-573 [501+]
Wegwerth, A.L. - *Little Bo Peep and Her Bad, Bad Sheep (Illus. by Flowers, Luke)*
c KR - Dec 15 2015 - pNA [51-500]
Wehrey, Frederic M. - *Sectarian Politics in the Gulf: From the Iraq War to the Arab Upsprings*
IJMES - v47 - i2 - May 2015 - p403-404 [501+]
Weib, Volker - *Moderne Antimoderne: Arthur Moeller van den Bruck und der Wandel des Konservatismus*
CEH - v48 - i1 - March 2015 - p100-113 [501+]
Weiberg, Josh - *Consciousness*
J Phil - v112 - i5 - May 2015 - p280(1) [501+]
Weible, Robert - *An Irrepressible Conflict: The Empire State in the Civil War*
NYT - March 8 2015 - p3(L) [501+]
Weidenbach, Kristin - *Meet Banjo Peterson (Illus. by Hancock, James Gulliver)*
y Magpies - v30 - i1 - March 2015 - p22(2) [501+]
Weidensaul, Scott - *Peterson Reference Guide to Owls of North America and the Caribbean*
LJ - v140 - i13 - August 1 2015 - p123(1) [51-500]
Weidermann, Volker - *Ostend: Stefan Zweig, Joseph Roth, and the Summer Before the Dark*
KR - Oct 15 2015 - pNA [501+]
LJ - v140 - i20 - Dec 1 2015 - p102(2) [51-500]
PW - v262 - i44 - Nov 2 2015 - p75(2) [51-500]
Weidner, Teri - *Always Twins (Illus. by Weidner, Teri)*
c HB Guide - v26 - i2 - Fall 2015 - p21(1) [51-500]
c KR - Feb 15 2015 - pNA [51-500]
c SLJ - v61 - i8 - August 2015 - p78(1) [51-500]
Weigel, Jeff - *Dragon Girl: The Secret Valley*
c SLJ - v61 - i6 - June 2015 - p46(6) [501+]

Weightman, Gavin - *How Invention Happens*
LJ - v140 - i15 - Sept 15 2015 - p103(1) [51-500]

Weijers, Olga - *In Search of the Truth: A History of Disputation Techniques from Antiquity to Early Modern Times*
Ren Q - v68 - i2 - Summer 2015 - p667-668 [501+]

Weil, Andrew - *Fast Food, Good Food: More than 150 Quick and Easy Ways to Put Healthy, Delicious Food on the Table*
LJ - v140 - i15 - Sept 15 2015 - p102(1) [51-500]
PW - v262 - i42 - Oct 19 2015 - p71(1) [51-500]

Weil, Ann - *Betsy Ross (Illus. by Florentino, Al)*
c HB Guide - v26 - i1 - Spring 2015 - p193(1) [51-500]

Weil, Cynthia - *I'm Glad I Did (Read by Botchan, Rachel). Audiobook Review*
y SLJ - v61 - i6 - June 2015 - p68(1) [51-500]
I'm Glad I Did
y CCB-B - v68 - i7 - March 2015 - p377(2) [51-500]
y HB Guide - v26 - i2 - Fall 2015 - p143(1) [51-500]
y NYTBR - Jan 18 2015 - p19(L) [501+]
y VOYA - v37 - i6 - Feb 2015 - p70(1) [51-500]

Weil, Gordon L. - *The Good Man: The Civil War's "Christian General" and His Fight for Racial Equality*
JSH - v81 - i1 - Feb 2015 - p212(2) [501+]

Weil, Joyce - *The New Neighborhood Senior Center: Redefining Social and Service Roles for the Baby Boom Generation*
AJS - v121 - i2 - Sept 2015 - p638(3) [501+]

Weil, Rachel - *A Plague of Informers: Conspiracy and Political Trust in William III's England*
AHR - v120 - i3 - June 2015 - p1112-1113 [501+]
JIH - v45 - i3 - Wntr 2015 - p426-427 [501+]

Weil, Simone - *Simone Weil: Late Philosophical Writings*
LJ - v140 - i14 - Sept 1 2015 - p110(1) [51-500]

Weiler, Maura - *Contrition: The Art of Sibling Rivalry*
AM - v213 - i5 - August 31 2015 - p38(3) [501+]
LJ - v140 - i5 - March 15 2015 - p96(1) [501+]

Weill, Cynthia - *Mi familia calaca / My Skeleton Family (Illus. by Zarate, Jesus)*
c BL - v111 - i9-10 - Jan 1 2015 - pS18(5) [501+]

Weill-Parot, Nicolas - *Points aveugles de la nature: La rationalite scientifique medievale face a l'occulte, l'attraction magnetique et l'horreur du vide*
Isis - v106 - i2 - June 2015 - p430(3) [501+]

Weimann, Dirk - *Perspectives on English Revolutionary Republicanism*
Sev Cent N - v73 - i3-4 - Fall-Winter 2015 - p151(3) [501+]

Wein, Elizabeth - *Black Dove, White Raven*
BL - v111 - i14 - March 15 2015 - p64(1) [501+]
y BL - v111 - i16 - April 15 2015 - p57(1) [501+]
y CCB-B - v68 - i10 - June 2015 - p524(1) [51-500]
y HB - v91 - i3 - May-June 2015 - p122(2) [51-500]
y HB Guide - v26 - i2 - Fall 2015 - p144(1) [51-500]
c KR - Jan 15 2015 - pNA [51-500]
y NYTBR - May 10 2015 - p19(L) [501+]
y PW - v262 - i4 - Jan 26 2015 - p170(2) [51-500]
y PW - v262 - i49 - Dec 2 2015 - p114(1) [51-500]
y Res Links - v21 - i1 - Oct 2015 - p44(1) [51-500]
y SLJ - v61 - i3 - March 2015 - p163(2) [51-500]
y VOYA - v38 - i1 - April 2015 - p72(1) [51-500]
Rose under Fire
c HB - v91 - i1 - Jan-Feb 2015 - p40(2) [501+]

Wein, Susanne - *Antisemitismus im Reichstag: Judenfeindliche Sprache in Politik und Gesellschaft der Weimarer Republik*
HNet - July 2015 - pNA [501+]

Weinberg, Robert - *Blood Libel in Late Imperial Russia: The Ritual Murder Trial of Mendel Beilis*
Slav R - v74 - i3 - Fall 2015 - p652-653 [501+]

Weinberg, Steven - *Rex Finds an Egg! Egg! Egg!*
c HB Guide - v26 - i1 - Fall 2015 - p21(2) [51-500]
To Explain the World: The Discovery of Modern Science
Bks & Cult - v21 - i5 - Sept-Oct 2015 - p21(1) [501+]
BL - v111 - i12 - Feb 15 2015 - p16(1) [501+]
KR - Jan 15 2015 - pNA [501+]
Nature - v518 - i7539 - Feb 19 2015 - p300(1) [501+]
NY - v91 - i5 - March 23 2015 - p91 [51-500]
NYRB - v62 - i14 - Sept 24 2015 - p53(2) [501+]
NYTBR - March 8 2015 - p22(L) [501+]
Phys Today - v68 - i4 - April 2015 - p53-54 [501+]
TimHES - i2191 - Feb 19 2015 - p48-49 [501+]
TLS - i5849 - May 8 2015 - p3(2) [501+]

Weinbren, Daniel - *The Open University: A History*
TimHES - i2195 - March 19 2015 - p49(1) [501+]

Weinbrot, Howard D. - *Samuel Johnson: New Contexts for a New Century*
Biomag - v38 - i3 - Summer 2015 - p425(12) [501+]

Weiner, Dana Elizabeth - *Race and Rights: Fighting Slavery and Prejudice in the Old Northwest, 1830-1870*
RAH - v43 - i3 - Sept 2015 - p498-504 [501+]

Weiner, Eric - *The Geography of Genius: A Search for the World's Most Creative Places, from Ancient Athens to Silicon Valley*
BL - v112 - i6 - Nov 15 2015 - p4(2) [51-500]
KR - Sept 15 2015 - pNA [501+]
PW - v262 - i47 - Nov 23 2015 - p62(1) [51-500]

Weiner, Greg - *American Burke: The Uncommon Liberalism of Daniel Patrick Moynihan*
Soc - v52 - i5 - Oct 2015 - p510(3) [501+]

Weiner, Isaac - *Religion Out Loud: Religious Sound, Public Space, and American Pluralism*
CH - v84 - i2 - June 2015 - p471(3) [501+]
JAH - v101 - i4 - March 2015 - p1241-1242 [501+]

Weiner, Jennifer - *All Fall Down (Read by Chimo, Tracee). Audiobook Review*
BL - v111 - i9-10 - Jan 1 2015 - p111(1) [501+]
Who Do You Love
y BL - v111 - i22 - August 1 2015 - p30(1) [51-500]
KR - August 1 2015 - pNA [51-500]

Weiner, Nina - *Expanding Universe: Photographs from the Hubble Space Telescope*
S&T - v129 - i6 - June 2015 - p73(1) [51-500]

Weiner, Richard - *The Game for Real*
TLS - i5852 - May 29 2015 - p21(1) [501+]

Weiner, Tim - *One Man against the World: The Tragedy of Richard Nixon*
CSM - August 11 2015 - pNA [501+]
KR - June 15 2015 - pNA [501+]
NYTBR - July 19 2015 - p12(L) [501+]
PW - v262 - i24 - June 15 2015 - p2(1) [51-500]
BL - v111 - i21 - July 1 2015 - p19(1) [51-500]
BooChiTr - August 8 2015 - p12(1) [51-500]

Weinfield, Henry - *The Blank Verse Tradition from Milton to Stevens: Freethinking and the Crisis of Modernity*
MLR - v110 - i3 - July 2015 - p831-833 [501+]

Weinfurter, Stefan - *Karl der Grosse: Der Heilige Barbar*
HNet - Jan 2015 - pNA [501+]

Weingarten, Gene - *Me & Dog (Illus. by Shansby, Eric)*
c HB Guide - v26 - i1 - Spring 2015 - p49(1) [51-500]

Weingarten, Karen - *Abortion in the American Imagination: Before Life and Choice, 1880-1940*
Cons - v36 - i1 - Spring 2015 - p44(2) [501+]

Weingarten, Lynn - *Suicide Notes from Beautiful Girls*
y BL - v111 - i17 - May 1 2015 - p53(1) [51-500]
y CCB-B - v69 - i1 - Sept 2015 - p64(1) [51-500]
y KR - May 1 2015 - pNA [51-500]
c Nat Post - v17 - i220 - July 25 2015 - pWP5(1) [501+]
y SLJ - v61 - i5 - May 2015 - p126(1) [51-500]

Weinman, Sarah - *Women Crime Writers: Eight Suspense Novels of the 1940s and 1950s*
NYTBR - Nov 1 2015 - p11(L) [501+]

Weinstein, Eric - *Ruby Wizards*
c KR - Feb 15 2015 - pNA [51-500]

Weinstein, Jodi L. - *Empire and Identity in Guizhou: Local Resistance to Qing Expansion*
Historian - v77 - i3 - Fall 2015 - p592(3) [501+]

Weinstein, Philip - *Jonathan Franzen: The Comedy of Rage*
LJ - v140 - i17 - Oct 15 2015 - p86(2) [51-500]
Nation - v301 - i17 - Oct 26 2015 - p31(5) [501+]
PW - v262 - i33 - August 17 2015 - p63(1) [51-500]
TLS - i5874 - Oct 30 2015 - p19(2) [501+]

Weinstock, Jeffrey Andrew - *The Works of Tim Burton: Margins to Mainstream*
SFS - v42 - i3 - Nov 2015 - p604-606 [501+]

Weinstone, David - *Music Class Today! (Illus. by Vogel, Vin)*
c BL - v112 - i5 - Nov 1 2015 - p53(1) [51-500]
c KR - July 1 2015 - pNA [51-500]
c NYTBR - August 23 2015 - p25(L) [51-500]
c SLJ - v61 - i7 - July 2015 - p69(1) [51-500]

Weintraub, Arlene - *Heal: The Vital Role of Dogs in the Search for Cancer Cures*
PW - v262 - i37 - Sept 14 2015 - p59(1) [51-500]

Weintraub, Robert - *No Better Friend*
KR - April 1 2015 - pNA [51-500]

Weintraub, Stanley - *A Christmas Far from Home: An Epic Tale of Courage and Survival during the Korean War*
NWCR - v68 - i2 - Spring 2015 - p147(2) [501+]

Victorian Yankees at Queen Victoria's Court: American Encounters with Victoria and Albert
VS - v57 - i2 - Wntr 2015 - p357(4) [501+]

Weir, Alison - *The Lost Tudor Princess: The Life of Lady Margaret Douglas*
KR - Nov 1 2015 - pNA [501+]
LJ - v140 - i20 - Dec 1 2015 - p110(2) [51-500]
PW - v262 - i46 - Nov 16 2015 - p69(1) [51-500]
The Marriage Game (Read by Franklin, Julia). Audiobook Review
BL - v111 - i22 - August 1 2015 - p77(1) [51-500]

Weir, Andy - *The Martian (Read by Bray, R.C.). Audiobook Review*
BL - v111 - i14 - March 15 2015 - p23(2) [51-500]
The Martian
LJ - v140 - i2 - Feb 1 2015 - p111(1) [501+]
LJ - v140 - i11 - June 15 2015 - p118(1) [501+]

Weir, Howard T. - *A Paradise of Blood: The Creek War of 1813-14*
LJ - v140 - i20 - Dec 1 2015 - p117(1) [501+]

Weir, Joanne - *Kitchen Gypsy: Recipes and Stories from a Lifelong Romance with Food*
BL - v112 - i3 - Oct 1 2015 - p16(2) [51-500]
LJ - v140 - i13 - August 1 2015 - p121(1) [51-500]

Weir, Todd H. - *Secularism and Religion in Nineteenth-Century Germany: The Rise of the Fourth Confession*
JIH - v45 - i4 - Spring 2015 - p581-583 [501+]

Weis, Lois - *Class Warfare: Class, Race, and College Admissions in Top-Tier Secondary Schools*
CS - v44 - i6 - Nov 2015 - p867-869 [501+]

Weis, Rene - *The Real Traviata: The Song of Marie Duplessis*
NS - v144 - i5290 - Nov 27 2015 - p51(1) [51-500]

Weisberg, Hilda - *New on the Job: A School Librarian's Guide to Success, 2d ed.*
R&USQ - v54 - i4 - Summer 2015 - p74(1) [51-500]

Weisberg, Jacob - *Ronald Reagan*
KR - Nov 1 2015 - pNA [501+]

Weisbrode, Kenneth - *The Year of Indecision, 1946: A Tour through the Crucible of Harry Truman's America*
KR - Dec 15 2015 - pNA [501+]

Weisburd, David - *The Criminology of Place: Street Segments and Our Understanding of the Crime Problem*
CS - v44 - i2 - March 2015 - p277-278 [501+]

Weiser, Kalman - *Jewish People, Yiddish Nation: Noah Prylucki and the Folkists in Poland*
HNet - Jan 2015 - pNA [501+]

Weisman, Jonathan - *No. 4 Imperial Lane*
KR - May 15 2015 - pNA [51-500]

Weiss, Adrienne - *There Are No Solid Gold Dancers Anymore*
CWS - v30 - i2-3 - Fall-Winter 2015 - p124(1) [501+]

Weiss, George David - *What a Wonderful World (Illus. by Hopgood, Tim)*
c BL - v111 - i14 - March 15 2015 - p82(1) [51-500]
c HB Guide - v26 - i1 - Spring 2015 - p10(1) [51-500]

Weiss, Jan Merete - *A Few Drops of Blood*
RVBW - April 2015 - pNA [501+]

Weiss, Jason - *Silvina Ocampo*
HM - v330 - i1979 - April 2015 - p79(81) [501+]

Weiss, Jessica Chen - *Powerful Patriots: Nationalist Protest in China's Foreign Relations*
For Aff - v94 - i1 - Jan-Feb 2015 - pNA [51-500]

Weiss, Julian - *Locating the Middle Ages: The Spaces and Places of Medieval Culture*
JEGP - v114 - i3 - July 2015 - p441(4) [501+]
Med R - June 2015 - pNA [501+]

Weiss, Karen G. - *Party School: Crime, Campus, and Community*
CS - v44 - i4 - July 2015 - p566-567 [501+]

Weiss, Karin E. - *The Raven Watched*
KR - Sept 15 2015 - pNA [51-500]

Weiss, Kirsten - *The Perfectly Proper Paranormal Museum*
KR - Jan 1 2016 - pNA [51-500]

Weiss, Lys Ann - *The Atheist's Bible*
Med R - April 2015 - pNA [501+]

Weiss, Marion - *Public Natures: Evolutionary Infrastructures*
LJ - v140 - i14 - Sept 1 2015 - p100(1) [51-500]

Weiss, Mark - *As Luck Would Have It*
ABR - v36 - i3 - March-April 2015 - p25(1) [501+]

Weiss, Max - *In the Shadow of Sectarianism: Law, Shi'ism, and the Making of Modern Lebanon*
IJMES - v47 - i3 - August 2015 - p612-614 [501+]

Weiss, Michael - *ISIS: Inside the Army of Terror*
  Econ - v414 - i8926 - Feb 21 2015 - p80(US) [501+]
  Lon R Bks - v37 - i14 - July 16 2015 - p5(6) [501+]
  NYRB - v62 - i13 - August 13 2015 - p27(3) [501+]
  NYT - April 3 2015 - pC21(L) [501+]
  NYTBR - April 5 2015 - p11(L) [501+]
Weiss, Otto - *Kulturkatholizismus: Katholiken auf dem Weg in die Deutsche Kultur 1900-1933*
  HNet - July 2015 - pNA [501+]
Weisser, Susan Ostrov - *The Glass Slipper: Women and Love Stories*
  AL - v87 - i1 - March 2015 - p207-209 [501+]
Weissmann, Mikael - *The East Asian Peace: Conflict Prevention and Informal Peacebuilding*
  Pac A - v88 - i1 - March 2015 - p154 [501+]
Weisz, Douglas S. - *Dorothy Knapp: Philately and Family*
  Phil Lit R - v64 - i2 - Spring 2015 - p139(2) [501+]
Weitz, Chris - *The New Order (Read by Julian, Jose). Audiobook Review*
  y SLJ - v61 - i10 - Oct 2015 - p55(1) [51-500]
The Young World (Read by Julian, Jose). Audiobook Review
  y BL - v111 - i9-10 - Jan 1 2015 - p118(1) [51-500]
The Young World
  y HB Guide - v26 - i1 - Spring 2015 - p127(1) [51-500]
Weiwei, Ai - *Blog: Writings, Interviews, and Digital Rants, 2006-2009*
  TLS - i5873 - Oct 23 2015 - p16(1) [501+]
Welborn, Amy - *New Catholic Illustrated Bible (Illus. by Fredricksen, Lars)*
  CH Bwatch - April 2015 - pNA [51-500]
Welborn, L.L. - *Paul's Summons to Messianic Life: Political Theology and the Coming Awakening*
  NYRB - v62 - i17 - Nov 5 2015 - p21(3) [501+]
Welbourn, Shannon - *Be the Change in Your School*
  c CH Bwatch - March 2015 - pNA [51-500]
Welbourne, W.E. - *Cruising the Latin Tapestry*
  SPBW - June 2015 - pNA [51-500]
Welch, Edward - *Contesting Views: The Visual Economy of France and Algeria*
  MLR - v110 - i2 - April 2015 - p557-558 [501+]
Welch, H. Gilbert - *Less Medicine, More Health: 7 Assumptions That Drive Too Much Medical Care*
  BL - v111 - i11 - Feb 1 2015 - p6(1) [51-500]
  Bwatch - May 2015 - pNA [51-500]
  LJ - v140 - i2 - Feb 1 2015 - p102(2) [51-500]
Welch, Jack - *The Real-Life MBA: Your No-BS Guide to Winning the Game, Building a Team, and Growing Your Career*
  KR - Feb 15 2015 - pNA [501+]
  LJ - v140 - i8 - May 1 2015 - p83(1) [51-500]
  PW - v262 - i6 - Feb 9 2015 - p58(1) [51-500]
  BL - v111 - i15 - April 1 2015 - p8(1) [51-500]
Welch, Jenna Evans - *Love & Gelato*
  y KR - Jan 1 2016 - pNA [501+]
  y SLJ - v61 - i12 - Dec 2015 - p117(1) [51-500]
Welch, Michael - *Escape to Prison: Penal Tourism and the Pull of Punishment*
  TLS - i5872 - Oct 16 2015 - p7(1) [501+]
Weld, Kirsten - *Paper Cadavers: The Archives of Dictatorship in Guatemala*
  AHR - v120 - i2 - April 2015 - p682-683 [501+]
  Am Q - v67 - i2 - June 2015 - p505-515 [501+]
  Ams - v72 - i3 - July 2015 - p502(2) [501+]
  Archiv - i79 - Spring 2015 - p196(4) [501+]
  HAHR - v95 - i1 - Feb 2015 - p180-182 [501+]
  Nation - v300 - i11 - March 16 2015 - p39(4) [501+]
Weldon, Michele - *Escape Points*
  BL - v112 - i1 - Sept 1 2015 - p21(1) [51-500]
  KR - July 1 2015 - pNA [501+]
Welfonder, Sue-Ellen - *To Desire a Highlander*
  PW - v262 - i31 - August 3 2015 - p44(1) [51-500]
Welge, Jobst - *Genealogical Fictions: Cultural Periphery and Historical Change in the Modern Novel*
  TLS - i5848 - May 1 2015 - p27(1) [501+]
Welker, Michael - *The Depth of the Human Person: A Multidisciplinary Approach*
  Theol St - v76 - i3 - Sept 2015 - p644(2) [501+]
Welky, Ali - *A Captive Audience: Voices of Japanese American Youth in World War II Arkansas*
  BL - v112 - i6 - Nov 15 2015 - p37(1) [51-500]
Welland, Michael - *The Desert*
  Nature - v518 - i7540 - Feb 26 2015 - p482(1) [501+]

Weller, Lance - *Wilderness*
  South CR - v47 - i2 - Spring 2015 - p159-161 [501+]
Weller, Martin - *The Battle for Open: How Openness Won and Why it Dosen't Feel Like Victory*
  TimHES - i2187 - Jan 22 2015 - p50(1) [501+]
Weller, Sheila - *The News Sorority: Diane Sawyer, Katie Couric, Christiane Amanpour - and the (Ongoing, Imperfect, Complicated) Triumph of Women in TV News (Read by Hallett, Morgan). Audiobook Review*
  BL - v111 - i14 - March 15 2015 - p83(1) [51-500]
Welles, Gideon - *The Civil War Diary of Gideon Welles, Lincoln's Secretary of the Navy*
  JAH - v102 - i2 - Sept 2015 - p565-567 [501+]
Wellington, David - *The Cyclops Initiative*
  BL - v112 - i7 - Dec 1 2015 - p27(1) [51-500]
  PW - v262 - i46 - Nov 16 2015 - p55(2) [51-500]
Positive
  y BL - v111 - i13 - March 1 2015 - p31(1) [51-500]
  BL - v111 - i18 - May 15 2015 - p34(1) [501+]
  PW - v262 - i7 - Feb 16 2015 - p164(1) [51-500]
Wellington, H. Nii-Adziri - *Stones Tell Stories at Osu: Memories of a Host Community of the Danish Trans-Atlantic Slave Trade*
  Callaloo - v38 - i2 - Spring 2015 - p422-424 [501+]
Wellington, Monica - *My Leaf Book (Illus. by Wellington, Monica)*
  c KR - July 1 2015 - pNA [51-500]
  c PW - v262 - i31 - August 3 2015 - p56(1) [501+]
  c SLJ - v61 - i12 - Dec 2015 - p97(1) [51-500]
Wellman, Kathleen - *Queens and Mistresses of Renaissance France*
  Historian - v77 - i3 - Fall 2015 - p628(2) [501+]
  JMH - v87 - i1 - March 2015 - p186(2) [501+]
Wellman, Sam - *Frederick the Wise: Seen and Unseen Lives of Martin Luther's Protector*
  Six Ct J - v46 - i1 - Spring 2015 - p260-261 [501+]
Wellman, William, Jr. - *Wild Bill Wellman: Hollywood Rebel*
  KR - Feb 15 2015 - pNA [501+]
  LJ - v140 - i6 - April 1 2015 - p96(1) [51-500]
  Roundup M - v23 - i1 - Oct 2015 - p35(1) [51-500]
Wells, Barbara - *Daughters and Granddaughters of Farmworkers: Emerging from the Long Shadow of Farm Labor*
  CS - v44 - i4 - July 2015 - p581-582 [501+]
Wells, Christopher W. - *Car Country: An Environmental History*
  RAH - v43 - i2 - June 2015 - p340-345 [501+]
Wells, Dan - *Bluescreen*
  y KR - Oct 15 2015 - pNA [51-500]
  y PW - v262 - i45 - Nov 9 2015 - p62(1) [51-500]
  y SLJ - v61 - i12 - Dec 2015 - p129(1) [51-500]
The Devil's Only Friend
  y BL - v111 - i18 - May 15 2015 - p34(2) [51-500]
  PW - v262 - i15 - April 13 2015 - p61(2) [51-500]
Wells, Leslie - *Come Dancing*
  KR - Nov 15 2015 - pNA [501+]
Wells, Marcella - *Interpretive Planning for Museums: Integrating Visitor Perspectives in Decision Making*
  Pub Hist - v37 - i2 - May 2015 - p156(3) [501+]
Wells, Marcia - *Doom at Grant's Tomb*
  c KR - Jan 1 2016 - pNA [501+]
Mystery in Mayan Mexico (Illus. by Calo, Marcos)
  c HB Guide - v26 - i2 - Fall 2015 - p106(1) [51-500]
  c KR - Jan 1 2015 - pNA [501+]
Wells, Martha - *The Dead City and the Dark Earth Below: Stories of the Raksura, vol. 2*
  PW - v262 - i15 - April 13 2015 - p62(1) [51-500]
Wells, Robin - *The Wedding Tree*
  LJ - v140 - i19 - Nov 15 2015 - p80(1) [51-500]
Wells, Robison - *Dark Energy*
  y KR - Jan 1 2016 - pNA [501+]
  y PW - v262 - i50 - Dec 7 2015 - p87(1) [51-500]
Dead Zone
  y HB Guide - v26 - i1 - Spring 2015 - p127(1) [51-500]
Wells, Rosemary - *Felix Stands Tall (Illus. by Wells, Rosemary)*
  c CH Bwatch - Oct 2015 - pNA [51-500]
  c KR - July 1 2015 - pNA [501+]
  c PW - v262 - i26 - June 29 2015 - p68(1) [51-500]
  c SLJ - v61 - i7 - July 2015 - p69(2) [51-500]
Max & Ruby at the Warthogs' Wedding (Illus. by Wells, Rosemary)
  c CH Bwatch - Jan 2015 - pNA [51-500]
  c HB Guide - v26 - i1 - Spring 2015 - p18(1) [51-500]

Ten Kisses for Sophie
  c KR - Jan 1 2016 - pNA [51-500]
Use Your Words, Sophie! (Illus. by Wells, Rosemary)
  c BL - v111 - i11 - Feb 1 2015 - p57(1) [51-500]
  c CH Bwatch - June 2015 - pNA [501+]
  c HB - v91 - i2 - March-April 2015 - p86(2) [51-500]
  c HB Guide - v26 - i2 - Fall 2015 - p22(1) [51-500]
  c KR - Jan 1 2015 - pNA [501+]
  c NYTBR - March 15 2015 - p18(L) [501+]
  c NYTBR - March 15 2015 - p18(L) [501+]
  c PW - v262 - i49 - Dec 2 2015 - p33(1) [51-500]
A Visit to Dr. Duck (Illus. by Wells, Rosemary)
  c HB Guide - v26 - i1 - Spring 2015 - p18(1) [51-500]
Yoko (Illus. by Wells, Rosemary)
  c BL - v112 - i4 - Oct 15 2015 - p53(1) [51-500]
Wells, Sara - *400 Calories or Less with Our Best Bites: Tasty Choices for Healthy Families with Calorie Options for Every Appetite*
  LJ - v140 - i10 - June 1 2015 - p128(1) [51-500]
Wells, Stanley - *Great Shakespeare Actors: Burbage to Branagh*
  LJ - v140 - i8 - May 1 2015 - p77(1) [51-500]
  NS - v144 - i5262 - May 15 2015 - p40(3) [501+]
  Spec - v328 - i9742 - May 16 2015 - p38(2) [501+]
  TimHES - i2198 - April 9 2015 - p48-49 [501+]
  TLS - i5871 - Oct 9 2015 - p7(2) [501+]
The Shakespeare Book: Big Ideas Simply Explained
  c Sch Lib - v63 - i2 - Summer 2015 - p123(2) [51-500]
  y VOYA - v38 - i3 - August 2015 - p92(1) [51-500]
The Shakespeare Book
  y BL - v111 - i15 - April 1 2015 - p13(1) [501+]
  y SLJ - v61 - i6 - June 2015 - p144(2) [51-500]
Wells, Tim - *Everything Crash*
  TimHES - i2228 - Nov 5 2015 - p46(1) [501+]
Wells, William - *Detective Fiction*
  KR - Nov 15 2015 - pNA [501+]
  PW - v262 - i46 - Nov 16 2015 - p56(1) [51-500]
Welsh, Irvine - *A Decent Ride*
  KR - Dec 15 2015 - pNA [501+]
  Spec - v327 - i9737 - April 11 2015 - p40(1) [501+]
Marabou Stork Nightmares
  TimHES - i2187 - Jan 22 2015 - p49(1) [501+]
The Sex Lives of Siamese Twins
  BL - v111 - i9-10 - Jan 1 2015 - p38(2) [51-500]
  NYTBR - March 1 2015 - p21(L) [501+]
Welton, Jude - *Tomas Loves ... a Rhyming Book about Fun, Friendship--and Autism (Illus. by Telford, Jane)*
  c CH Bwatch - April 2015 - pNA [51-500]
  c CH Bwatch - May 2015 - pNA [51-500]
Welty, Eudora - *Why I Live Where I Live*
  New R - v246 - i12 - Nov 2015 - p62(5) [501+]
Welvaert, Scott R. - *The 13th Floor*
  y SLJ - v61 - i9 - Sept 2015 - p151(4) [501+]
Wenar, Leif - *Blood Oil: Tyrants, Violence, and the Rules That Run the World*
  KR - Nov 1 2015 - pNA [501+]
Wendig, Chuck - *The Harvest (Read by Podehl, Nick). Audiobook Review*
  y SLJ - v61 - i12 - Dec 2015 - p81(1) [51-500]
Mockingbird
  KR - August 15 2015 - pNA [501+]
  PW - v262 - i32 - August 10 2015 - p40(1) [51-500]
Zer0es
  KR - June 15 2015 - pNA [501+]
  PW - v262 - i20 - May 18 2015 - p67(1) [51-500]
Wendinger, Jennifer - *Unusual and Awesome Jobs Using Science: Food Taster, Human Lie Detector, and More*
  c HB Guide - v26 - i2 - Fall 2015 - p152(1) [51-500]
Wengst, Udo - *Theodor Eschenburg: Biographie einer Politischen Leitfigur 1904-1999*
  HNet - June 2015 - pNA [501+]
Weninger, Brigitte - *24 Stories for Advent (Illus. by Tharlet, Eve)*
  c PW - v262 - i37 - Sept 14 2015 - p72(2) [501+]
  c SLJ - v61 - i10 - Oct 2015 - p69(1) [51-500]
Davy Loves the Baby (Illus. by Tharlet, Eve)
  c HB Guide - v26 - i2 - Fall 2015 - p56(1) [51-500]
Happy Easter, Davy! (Illus. by Tharlet, Eve)
  c CH Bwatch - March 2015 - pNA [51-500]
Merry Christmas, Davy! (Illus. by Tharlet, Eve)
  c HB Guide - v26 - i1 - Spring 2015 - p49(1) [51-500]
"Wenn das Erbe in die Wolke Kommt": Digitalisierung und Kulturelles Erbe
  HNet - Feb 2015 - pNA [501+]

Wensheng, Wang - *White Lotus Rebels and South China Pirates: Crisis and Reform in the Qing Empire*
 JAS - v74 - i2 - May 2015 - p484-485 [501+]
Wenshi, Pan - *A Chance for Lasting Survival: Ecology and Behavior of Wild Giant Pandas*
 QRB - v90 - i2 - June 2015 - p238(2) [501+]
Wensink, Patrick - *Fake Fruit Factory*
 BL - v112 - i2 - Sept 15 2015 - p27(1) [51-500]
 KR - July 15 2015 - pNA [51-500]
Wentlent, Anna - *Alfred's IPA Made Easy: A Guidebook for the International Phonetic Alphabet*
 Teach Mus - v23 - i1 - August 2015 - p60(1) [51-500]
Wentling, Mark - *Africa's Heart*
 KR - April 15 2015 - pNA [501+]
Wentworth, Ali - *Happily Ali After: And Other Fairly True Tales*
 KR - April 1 2015 - pNA [51-500]
 LJ - v140 - i8 - May 1 2015 - p73(2) [51-500]
Wenz, Peter S. - *Functional Inefficiency: The Unexpected Benefits of Wasting Time and Money*
 PW - v262 - i17 - April 27 2015 - p66(1) [51-500]
Wenzel, Angela - *13 Art Techniques Children Should Know*
 c BL - v112 - i5 - Nov 1 2015 - p50(1) [501+]
Wenzel, Eugen - *Ein neues Lied? Ein besseres Lied? Die neuen 'Evangelien' nach Heine, Wagner und Nietzsche*
 MLR - v110 - i3 - July 2015 - p896-898 [501+]
Wenzel, Franziska - *Meisterschaft im Prozess: Der Lange Ton Frauenlobs - Texte und Studien*
 MLR - v110 - i1 - Jan 2015 - p282-284 [501+]
Wenzel, Siegfried - *The Art of Preaching: Five Medieval Texts and Translations*
 Med R - March 2015 - pNA(NA) [501+]
Werchinski-Yates, Janine - *The Secret Sock Club (Illus. by Conway, Michael P.)*
 c CH Bwatch - May 2015 - pNA [51-500]
Werkstatt Wissenschaftsgeschichte
 HNet - June 2015 - pNA [501+]
Werkstattgesprach Lehre in der Technik - und Wissenschaftsgeschichte
 HNet - May 2015 - pNA [501+]
Werlinger, Caren J. - *Cast Me Gently*
 PW - v262 - i35 - August 31 2015 - p72(1) [51-500]
Wermiel, Stephen - *Justice Brennan: Liberal Champion*
 Historian - v77 - i2 - Summer 2015 - p356(2) [501+]
Werner, Anja - *The Transatlantic World of Higher Education: Americans at German Universities, 1776-1914*
 GSR - v38 - i1 - Feb 2015 - p170-171 [501+]
Werner, Eric - *Hartwood: Bright, Wild Flavors from the Edge of the Yucatan*
 LJ - v140 - i17 - Oct 15 2015 - p109(2) [51-500]
 PW - v262 - i44 - Nov 2 2015 - p80(1) [51-500]
Werner, Markus - *Zundel's Exit*
 TLS - i5857 - July 3 2015 - p21(1) [501+]
Werner, Oliver - *Mobilisierung im Nazionalsozialismus: Institutionen und Regionen in der Kriegswirtschaft und der Verwaltung des 'Dritten Reiches' 1936 bis 1945*
 HER - v130 - i545 - August 2015 - p1042(2) [501+]
Werpehowski, William - *Virtue and the Moral Life: Theological and Philosophical Perspectives*
 Theol St - v76 - i3 - Sept 2015 - p648(1) [501+]
Werry, Philippa - *Waitangi Day: The New Zealand Story*
 c Magpies - v30 - i1 - March 2015 - pS7(2) [501+]
Wert, Michael - *Meiji Restoration Losers: Memory and Tokugawa Supporters in Modern Japan*
 AHR - v120 - i4 - Oct 2015 - p1467-1468 [501+]
Wertewandel in Wirtschaft und Arbeitswelt? Arbeit, Leistung und Fuhrung in den 1970er und 1980er Jahren in der Bundesrepublik Deutschland
 HNet - June 2015 - pNA [501+]
Werth, Leon - *33 Days*
 Atl - v316 - i1 - July-August 2015 - p46(1) [51-500]
 KR - April 1 2015 - pNA [51-500]
 TLS - i5860 - July 24 2015 - p26(2) [51-500]
Werth, Tiffany Jo - *The Fabulous Dark Cloister: Romance in England after the Reformation*
 Critm - v57 - i1 - Wntr 2015 - pNA [501+]
Wertheim, L. Jon - *The Rookie Bookie (Illus. by Swaab, Neil)*
 c CCB-B - v68 - i5 - Jan 2015 - p282(1) [51-500]
 c HB Guide - v26 - i1 - Spring 2015 - p96(1) [51-500]
 This Is Your Brain on Sports: The Science of Underdogs, the Value of Rivalry, and What We Can Learn from the T-shirt Cannon
 KR - Dec 15 2015 - pNA [51-500]
 PW - v262 - i51 - Dec 14 2015 - p74(1) [51-500]

Wertheimer, Linda K. - *Faith Ed.: Teaching about Religion in an Age of Intolerance*
 BL - v111 - i19-20 - June 1 2015 - p9(1) [51-500]
 KR - May 1 2015 - pNA [501+]
 LJ - v140 - i11 - June 15 2015 - p97(1) [51-500]
 NYTBR - August 23 2015 - p18(L) [501+]
 PW - v262 - i27 - July 6 2015 - p66(1) [51-500]
Wesline, Emmie - *Objectif Vancouver*
 y Res Links - v20 - i4 - April 2015 - p43(1) [501+]
Wessels, Marcie - *Pirate's Lullaby: Mutiny at Bedtime (Illus. by Bowers, Tim)*
 c KR - May 15 2015 - pNA [51-500]
 c SLJ - v61 - i8 - August 2015 - p78(1) [51-500]
Wessely, Christina - *Welteis: Eine Wahre Geschichte*
 HNet - June 2015 - pNA [501+]
Wessendorf, Susanne - *Second-Generation Transnationalism and Roots Migration: Cross-Border Lives*
 CS - v44 - i1 - Jan 2015 - p132-133 [501+]
West, Aaron J. - *Sting and the Police: Walking in Their Footsteps*
 PW - v262 - i32 - August 10 2015 - p54(1) [51-500]
West, Bing - *One Million Steps: A Marine Platoon at War*
 Mar Crp G - v99 - i1 - Jan 2015 - p86(1) [501+]
 Parameters - v45 - i2 - Summer 2015 - p143(2) [501+]
West-Bulford, Simon - *The Soul Continuum*
 PW - v262 - i22 - June 1 2015 - p44(1) [51-500]
West, Carly Anne - *The Bargaining*
 y BL - v111 - i9-10 - Jan 1 2015 - p87(1) [51-500]
 y CCB-B - v68 - i6 - Feb 2015 - p334(2) [51-500]
 y VOYA - v37 - i6 - Feb 2015 - p85(1) [51-500]
West, Charles - *Reframing the Feudal Revolution: Political and Social Transformation between Marne and Moselle, c.800-c.1100*
 HER - v130 - i544 - June 2015 - p692(3) [501+]
West, Chris - *A History of America in Thirty-Six Postage Stamps*
 Phil Lit R - v64 - i2 - Spring 2015 - p140(2) [501+]
West, Cornel - *Black Prophetic Fire*
 JAH - v102 - i2 - Sept 2015 - p516-517 [501+]
 HNet - March 2015 - pNA [501+]
West, Darrell M. - *Billionaires: Reflections on the Upper Crust*
 Barron's - v95 - i22 - June 1 2015 - p38(1) [51-500]
 TimHES - i2191 - Feb 19 2015 - p49(1) [501+]
West, David - *After the Dinosaurs*
 c HB Guide - v26 - i1 - Spring 2015 - p152(1) [51-500]
 Before the Dinosaurs
 c HB Guide - v26 - i1 - Spring 2015 - p152(1) [51-500]
 Diggers
 c HB Guide - v26 - i2 - Fall 2015 - p186(1) [51-500]
 Dinosaurs of the Cretaceous
 c HB Guide - v26 - i1 - Spring 2015 - p152(1) [51-500]
 Dinosaurs of the Jurassic
 c HB Guide - v26 - i1 - Spring 2015 - p152(1) [51-500]
 Dinosaurs of the Triassic
 c HB Guide - v26 - i1 - Spring 2015 - p152(1) [51-500]
 Helicopters (Illus. by West, David)
 c BL - v112 - i4 - Oct 15 2015 - p42(1) [51-500]
 Motorcycles (Illus. by West, David)
 c BL - v112 - i4 - Oct 15 2015 - p42(1) [51-500]
 The Rise of Humans
 c HB Guide - v26 - i1 - Spring 2015 - p152(1) [51-500]
 Submarines (Illus. by West, David)
 c BL - v112 - i4 - Oct 15 2015 - p42(1) [51-500]
 Tanks (Illus. by West, David)
 c BL - v112 - i4 - Oct 15 2015 - p42(1) [51-500]
 Ten of the Best God and Goddess Stories (Illus. by West, David)
 c CH Bwatch - Jan 2015 - pNA [51-500]
 Ten of the Best: Myths, Legends and Folk Stones Series, 8 vols.
 c Res Links - v20 - i4 - April 2015 - p44(1) [501+]
West, Gordon - *Jogging Round Majorca*
 TimHES - i2211 - July 9 2015 - p47(1) [501+]
West, Jacqueline - *Still Life (Illus. by Bernatene, Poly)*
 c HB Guide - v26 - i1 - Spring 2015 - p96(1) [51-500]
West, James L.W., III - *My Generation: William Styron's Collected Nonfiction*
 TLS - i5869 - Sept 25 2015 - p11(1) [501+]
West, Jerry R. - *Jerry West: The Alchemy of Memory*
 PW - v262 - i23 - June 8 2015 - p53(2) [51-500]

West, Jim - *Circulus de Potentia*
 y KR - Sept 1 2015 - pNA [501+]
West, Kasie - *The Distance between Us (Read by Marie, Jorjeana). Audiobook Review*
 SLJ - v61 - i2 - Feb 2015 - p52(1) [51-500]
 The Fill-In Boyfriend (Read by McManus, Shannon). Audiobook Review
 y SLJ - v61 - i12 - Dec 2015 - p81(1) [51-500]
 The Fill-In Boyfriend
 y BL - v111 - i15 - April 1 2015 - p65(1) [51-500]
 SLJ - v61 - i3 - March 2015 - p163(2) [51-500]
 y VOYA - v38 - i1 - April 2015 - p72(1) [51-500]
West, Kim Kardashian - *Selfish*
 NYTBR - Sept 27 2015 - p13(L) [501+]
West, Martin L. - *The Epic Cycle. A Commentary on the Lost Troy Epics*
 Class R - v65 - i1 - April 2015 - p10-11 [501+]
 The Making of the Odyssey
 TLS - i5867 - Sept 11 2015 - p10(2) [501+]
West, Martin R. - *Teachers versus the Public: What Americans Think about Schools and How to Fix Them*
 Bks & Cult - v21 - i3 - May-June 2015 - p24(2) [501+]
West, Nancy M. - *Chips: A Hometown Hero*
 KR - May 15 2015 - pNA [501+]
West, Nigel - *Double Cross in Cairo: The True Story of the Spy Who Turned the Tide of War in the Middle East*
 Spec - v327 - i9735 - March 28 2015 - p40(2) [501+]
 MI5 in the Great War
 Lon R Bks - v37 - i2 - Jan 22 2015 - p23(2) [501+]
West, Temple - *Velvet*
 y SLJ - v61 - i5 - May 2015 - p126(1) [51-500]
West, Tracey - *Rise of the Earth Dragon (Illus. by Howells, Graham)*
 y CH Bwatch - Jan 2015 - pNA [501+]
 c HB Guide - v26 - i2 - Fall 2015 - p72(1) [51-500]
 Saving the Sun Dragon (Illus. by Howells, Graham)
 c HB Guide - v26 - i2 - Fall 2015 - p72(1) [51-500]
 Secret of the Water Dragon (Illus. by Howells, Graham)
 c HB Guide - v26 - i2 - Fall 2015 - p72(1) [51-500]
Westad, Odd Arne - *Restless Empire: A Historical Atlas of Russia*
 NWCR - v68 - i1 - Wntr 2015 - p138(2) [501+]
Westall, Jennifer - *Healing Ruby*
 PW - v262 - i2 - Jan 12 2015 - p44(2) [51-500]
Westberg, Daniel A. - *Renewing Moral Theology: Christian Ethics as Action, Character and Grace*
 LJ - v140 - i9 - May 15 2015 - p64(2) [501+]
Westcott, Rebecca - *Five Things They Never Told Me*
 c Sch Lib - v63 - i3 - Autumn 2015 - p170(1) [51-500]
Westerfeld, Scott - *Afterworlds*
 y HB Guide - v26 - i1 - Spring 2015 - p127(1) [51-500]
 y Teach Lib - v42 - i3 - Feb 2015 - p28(4) [501+]
 Zeroes
 y BL - v111 - i19-20 - June 1 2015 - p103(1) [51-500]
 y KR - June 15 2015 - pNA [51-500]
 y PW - v262 - i21 - May 25 2015 - p60(2) [51-500]
 y SLJ - v61 - i7 - July 2015 - p99(1) [51-500]
Westerholm, Stephen - *Justification Reconsidered: Rethinking a Pauline Theme*
 TT - v72 - i1 - April 2015 - p112-114 [501+]
Westerlund, Kate - *If You Wish (Illus. by Ingpen, Robert)*
 c HB Guide - v26 - i1 - Spring 2015 - p49(1) [51-500]
Westerson, Jeri - *The Silence of Stones*
 KR - Dec 1 2015 - pNA [51-500]
 PW - v262 - i51 - Dec 14 2015 - p62(1) [51-500]
Westfahl, Gary - *A Day in a Working Life: 300 Trades and Professions through History, 3 vols.*
 BL - v112 - i4 - Oct 15 2015 - p6(1) [51-500]
Westheimer, Ruth K. - *The Doctor is in: Dr. Ruth on Love, Life, and Joie de Vivre*
 BL - v111 - i19-20 - June 1 2015 - p8(2) [51-500]
 KR - April 15 2015 - pNA [51-500]
 PW - v262 - i14 - April 6 2015 - p55(1) [51-500]
Westin, Julie - *Moonshadows*
 Roundup M - v23 - i1 - Oct 2015 - p31(1) [501+]
Westman, Jack C. - *The Cancer Solution: Taking Charge of Your Life with Cancer*
 SPBW - May 2015 - pNA [501+]
 SPBW - May 2015 - pNA [501+]
Weston, Carol - *Ava and Taco Cat*
 c HB Guide - v26 - i2 - Fall 2015 - p106(1) [51-500]
Weston, Danny - *The Piper*
 y Sch Lib - v63 - i1 - Spring 2015 - p59(1) [51-500]

Weston, David - *Covering Shakespeare: An Actor's Saga of Near misses and Dogged Endurance*
 TimHES - i2190 - Feb 12 2015 - p49(1) [501+]
Weston, Julie - *Moonshadows*
 BL - v111 - i19-20 - June 1 2015 - p55(1) [51-500]
 KR - June 1 2015 - pNA [51-500]
Weston, Paula - *Burn*
 y Magpies - v30 - i4 - Sept 2015 - p44(2) [501+]
 Haze
 y HB Guide - v26 - i1 - Spring 2015 - p127(1) [51-500]
Weston, Robert Paul - *Blues for Zoey*
 y VOYA - v38 - i1 - April 2015 - p72(1) [501+]
 Gobbled by Ghorks (Illus. by Lydon, Zack)
 c Res Links - v20 - i5 - June 2015 - p12(1) [51-500]
 c HB Guide - v26 - i1 - Spring 2015 - p96(1) [51-500]
Westphal, Merold - *Kierkegaard's Concept of Faith*
 Theol St - v76 - i3 - Sept 2015 - p605(2) [501+]
Westphal, Mike - *Cloud of Expectation*
 KR - Dec 1 2015 - pNA [501+]
Westphall, Allan F. - *Books and Religious Devotion: The Redemptive Reading of an Irishman in Nineteenth-Century New England*
 TLS - i5850 - May 15 2015 - p29(1) [501+]
Wetherington, Ronald K. - *Battles and Massacres on the Southwestern Frontier: Historical and Archaeological Perspectives*
 SHQ - v118 - i3 - Jan 2015 - p318-319 [501+]
 WHQ - v46 - i1 - Spring 2015 - p100-101 [501+]
 Am Ant - v80 - i1 - Jan 2015 - p209(2) [501+]
Wetmore, Alex - *Men of Feeling in Eighteenth-Century Literature: Touching Fiction*
 Eight-C St - v48 - i4 - Summer 2015 - p547-549 [501+]
Wetmore, K.J., Jr. - *Black Medea: Adaptations for Modern Plays*
 Class R - v65 - i2 - Oct 2015 - p588-590 [501+]
Wetta, Frank J. - *The Long Reconstruction: The Post-Civil War South in History, Film, and Memory*
 JSH - v81 - i2 - May 2015 - p479(2) [501+]
Wetzel, Joanne Stewart - *Playing Juliet*
 c KR - Sept 15 2015 - pNA [51-500]
 c SLJ - v61 - i11 - Nov 2015 - p104(1) [51-500]
Wetzel, Laurie - *Unclaimed*
 y PW - v262 - i25 - June 22 2015 - p142(1) [51-500]
Wexler, Barbara - *Quick Check Guide to Organic Foods*
 LJ - v140 - i5 - March 15 2015 - p130(1) [51-500]
Wexler, Django - *The Forbidden Library (Read by Morris, Cassandra). Audiobook Review*
 y HB - v91 - i4 - July-August 2015 - p168(1) [51-500]
 c SLJ - v61 - i6 - June 2015 - p65(1) [51-500]
 The Forbidden Library
 c SLJ - v61 - i6 - June 2015 - p46(6) [501+]
 The Mad Apprentice (Read by Morris, Cassandra). Audiobook Review
 c SLJ - v61 - i7 - July 2015 - p48(1) [51-500]
 The Mad Apprentice (Illus. by Jansson, Alexander)
 y HB - v91 - i2 - March-April 2015 - p112(1) [51-500]
 c HB Guide - v26 - i2 - Fall 2015 - p106(1) [51-500]
 c KR - Jan 15 2015 - pNA [51-500]
 c SLJ - v61 - i2 - Feb 2015 - p95(1) [51-500]
Wexler, Jay - *When God Isn't Green: A World-Wide Journey to Places Where Religious Practice and Environmentalism Collide*
 KR - Jan 1 2016 - pNA [501+]
Wexler, Stuart - *America's Secret Jihad: The Hidden History of Religious Terrorism in the United States*
 KR - June 1 2015 - pNA [501+]
 LJ - v140 - i13 - August 1 2015 - p111(2) [51-500]
 PW - v262 - i19 - May 11 2015 - p46(1) [51-500]
Weyland, Kurt - *Making Waves: Democratic Contention in Europe and Latin America since the Revolutions of 1848*
 JIH - v46 - i2 - Autumn 2015 - p269-270 [501+]
Weyler, Karen A. - *Empowering Words: Outsiders and Authorship in Early America*
 JAH - v101 - i4 - March 2015 - p1258-1259 [501+]
Weyn, Suzanne - *Faces of the Dead*
 y HB Guide - v26 - i1 - Spring 2015 - p127(1) [51-500]
Whalen, Brett Edward - *The Medieval Papacy*
 CHR - v101 - i1 - Wntr 2015 - p152(2) [501+]
Whaley, Diana - *Poetry from the Kings' Sagas 1: From Mythical Times to c. 1035*
 Med R - Jan 2015 - pNA [501+]
Whaley, Eileen McGuire - *Come Back Strong: A Widow's Song*
 SPBW - August 2015 - pNA [51-500]

Whaley, John Corey - *Noggin (Read by Heyborne, Kirby). Audiobook Review*
 c BL - v111 - i14 - March 15 2015 - p24(2) [501+]
Whamond, Dave - *Oddrey Joins the Team (Illus. by Whamond, Dave)*
 c HB Guide - v26 - i1 - Spring 2015 - p50(1) [51-500]
Wharton, Annabel Jane - *Architectural Agents: The Delusional, Abusive, Addictive Lives of Buildings*
 TimHES - i2204 - May 21 2015 - p52-53 [501+]
Wheatland, Thomas - *The Frankfurt School in Exile*
 CS - v44 - i3 - May 2015 - p305-314 [501+]
Wheatle, Alex - *Liccle Bit*
 y Sch Lib - v63 - i2 - Summer 2015 - p122(1) [51-500]
Wheatley, Kim - *Romantic Feuds: Transcending the 'Age of Personality'*
 MLR - v110 - i3 - July 2015 - p843-845 [501+]
Whedon, Joss - *Astonishing X-Men: Gifted*
 LJ - v140 - i13 - August 1 2015 - p48(1) [51-500]
Whedon, Zack - *Leaves on the Wind*
 LJ - v140 - i5 - March 15 2015 - p88(3) [501+]
Wheelan, Joseph - *Their Last Full Measure*
 KR - April 1 2015 - pNA [501+]
Wheeler, E.B. - *The Haunting of Springett Hall*
 y SLJ - v61 - i8 - August 2015 - p100(1) [51-500]
Wheeler, Jan Bates - *A Campaign of Quiet Persuasion: How the College Board Desegregated SAT Test Centers in the Deep South, 1960-1965*
 JSH - v81 - i1 - Feb 2015 - p245(2) [501+]
Wheeler, Jeff - *The Banished of Muirwood*
 PW - v262 - i26 - June 29 2015 - p50(2) [51-500]
Wheeler, Jill C. - *Alvin Schwartz*
 c HB Guide - v26 - i2 - Fall 2015 - p213(1) [51-500]
Wheeler, Leigh Ann - *How Sex Became a Civil Liberty*
 JWH - v27 - i1 - Spring 2015 - p161(7) [501+]
Wheeler, Lisa - *Dino-Boarding (Illus. by Gott, Barry)*
 c HB Guide - v26 - i1 - Spring 2015 - p50(1) [51-500]
 Dino-Swimming (Illus. by Gott, Barry)
 c BL - v112 - i1 - Sept 1 2015 - p101(1) [51-500]
 c SLJ - v61 - i8 - August 2015 - p78(1) [51-500]
 Uncles and Antlers (Illus. by Floca ,Brian)
 c HB Guide - v26 - i1 - Spring 2015 - p50(1) [51-500]
Wheeler, Lonnie - *Intangiball: The Subtle Things That Win Baseball Games*
 BL - v111 - i21 - July 1 2015 - p16(1) [51-500]
 KR - June 1 2015 - pNA [51-500]
 LJ - v140 - i1 - June 15 2015 - p93(1) [51-500]
 PW - v262 - i23 - June 8 2015 - p52(2) [51-500]
Wheeler, Michael - *St. John and the Victorians*
 VS - v57 - i2 - Wntr 2015 - p328(2) [501+]
Wheeler, Norton - *The Role of American NGOs in China's Modernization: Invited Influence*
 HNet - June 2015 - pNA [501+]
Wheeler, Patti - *Travels with Gannon and Wyatt: Ireland*
 SLJ - v61 - i3 - March 2015 - p167(1) [51-500]
Wheeler, Robert - *Hemingway's Paris: A Writer's City in Words and Images*
 BL - v111 - i19-20 - June 1 2015 - p28(1) [51-500]
Wheeler, Samantha - *Mister Cassowary*
 y Magpies - v30 - i5 - Nov 2015 - p39(1) [51-500]
Wheeler, Sara - *O My America! Six Women and Their Seconds Acts in a New World*
 TLS - i5835 - Jan 30 2015 - p26(1) [51-500]
Wheeler, Sean M. - *Uprise: Back Pain Liberation, by Tuning Your Body Guitar*
 PW - v262 - i29 - July 20 2015 - p185(1) [51-500]
 SPBW - July 2015 - pNA [51-500]
Wheeler, Sharon - *Walking Home: My Family and Other Rambles*
 TimHES - i2186 - Jan 15 2015 - p49(1) [501+]
Wheelwright, Hannah - *Mormon Feminism*
 PW - v262 - i37 - Sept 14 2015 - p62(1) [51-500]
Wheen, Francis - *Karl Marx: A Life*
 HT - v65 - i10 - Oct 2015 - p56(2) [51-500]
Whelan, Susan - *Don't Think about Purple Elephants (Illus. by Jones, Gwynneth)*
 c Sch Lib - v63 - i3 - Autumn 2015 - p161(1) [51-500]
Whelehan, Niall - *The Dynamiters: Irish Nationalism and Political Violence in the Wider World, 1867-1900*
 JMH - v87 - i1 - March 2015 - p179(3) [501+]
 VS - v57 - i2 - Wntr 2015 - p348(3) [501+]
Wheler, Bradford - *Inca's Death Cave*
 RVBW - June 2015 - pNA [501+]
Whelpton, Vivien - *Richard Aldington: Poet, Soldier and Lover, 1911-29*
 Lon R Bks - v37 - i2 - Jan 22 2015 - p25(3) [501+]

Whidden, James - *Monarchy and Modernity in Egypt: Politics, Islam, and Neo-Colonialism between the Wars*
 AHR - v120 - i1 - Feb 2015 - p368-369 [501+]
Whipple, Natalie - *Fish out of Water*
 c Sch Lib - v63 - i3 - Autumn 2015 - p187(1) [51-500]
Whipple, Pablo - *La gente decente de Lima y su resistencia al orden republicano: Ferarquias sociales, prensa y sistema judicial durante el siglo*
 HAHR - v95 - i1 - Feb 2015 - p160-162 [501+]
Whipple, Tom - *How to Win Games and Beat People*
 LJ - v140 - i20 - Dec 1 2015 - p109(1) [51-500]
Whistler, Rex - *An Anthology of Mine*
 Spec - v329 - i9768 - Nov 14 2015 - p60(2) [501+]
Whitaker, Alecia - *The Road to You*
 y SLJ - v61 - i11 - Nov 2015 - p123(1) [51-500]
 Wildflower
 y HB Guide - v26 - i2 - Fall 2015 - p144(1) [51-500]
Whitaker, Mark - *Cosby: His Life and Times*
 BL - v111 - i19-20 - June 1 2015 - p30(2) [501+]
Whitaker, Matthew C. - *Peace Be Still: Modern Black America from World War II to Barack Obama*
 JSH - v81 - i2 - May 2015 - p506(3) [501+]
Whitaker, Nathan - *Snap Decision*
 c HB Guide - v26 - i2 - Fall 2015 - p106(1) [51-500]
Whitby, Adele - *Betsy's Story, 1934*
 c HB Guide - v26 - i2 - Fall 2015 - p106(1) [51-500]
 Elizabeth's Story, 1848
 c HB Guide - v26 - i1 - Spring 2015 - p96(1) [51-500]
 Kate's Story, 1914
 c HB Guide - v26 - i1 - Spring 2015 - p96(1) [51-500]
 Katherine's Story, 1848
 c HB Guide - v26 - i1 - Spring 2015 - p96(1) [51-500]
 Kay's Story, 1934
 c HB Guide - v26 - i2 - Fall 2015 - p106(1) [51-500]
White, Benjamin L. - *Remembering Paul: Ancient and Modern Contests over the Image of the Apostle*
 CC - v132 - i21 - Oct 14 2015 - p32(2) [501+]
White, Betz - *Present Perfect: 25 Gifts to Sew and Bestow*
 LJ - v140 - i2 - Feb 1 2015 - p83(1) [51-500]
White Claire - *Work and Leisure in Late Nineteenth-Century French Litterature and Visual Culture: Time, Politics and Class*
 FS - v69 - i4 - Oct 2015 - p549-550 [501+]
White, Courtney - *The Age of Consequences: A Chronicle of Concern and Hope*
 BL - v111 - i9-10 - Jan 1 2015 - p21(1) [51-500]
 LJ - v140 - i2 - Feb 1 2015 - p105(1) [51-500]
 Two Percent Solutions for the Planet: 50 Low-Cost, Low-Tech, Nature-Based Practices for Combating Hunger, Drought, and Climate Change
 PW - v262 - i35 - August 31 2015 - p79(1) [51-500]
White, Daniel E. - *From Little London to Little Bengal: Religion, Print, and Modernity in Early British India, 1793-1835*
 AHR - v120 - i1 - Feb 2015 - p203(1) [501+]
White, Dave - *An Empty Hell*
 PW - v262 - i52 - Dec 21 2015 - p132(1) [51-500]
White, David V. - *Art, Science, Religion, Spirituality: Seeking Wisdom and Harmony for a Fulfilling Life*
 KR - July 15 2015 - pNA [501+]
 SPBW - August 2015 - pNA [501+]
White, Dianne - *Blue on Blue (Illus. by Krommes, Beth)*
 c HB Guide - v26 - i1 - Spring 2015 - p18(1) [51-500]
White, Edmund - *Inside a Pearl: My Years in Paris*
 NYTBR - April 5 2015 - p28(L) [501+]
 Our Young Man
 PW - v262 - i47 - Nov 23 2015 - p44(1) [51-500]
 States of Desire Revisited: Travels in Gay America
 TLS - i5833 - Jan 16 2015 - p27(1) [501+]
White, Edward - *The Tastemaker: Carl Van Vechten and Birth of Modern America*
 NYTBR - April 26 2015 - p28(L) [501+]
White, Ellen Emerson - *Webster: Tale of an Outlaw*
 c BL - v112 - i5 - Nov 1 2015 - p63(1) [51-500]
 c KR - August 15 2015 - pNA [51-500]
 c PW - v262 - i38 - Sept 21 2015 - p74(1) [51-500]
White, Eugene N. - *Housing and Mortgage Markets in Historical Perspective*
 BHR - v89 - i3 - Autumn 2015 - p626(3) [501+]
White, Gilbert - *The Natural History of Selborne*
 TimHES - i2211 - July 9 2015 - p46(1) [501+]
White, Gillian - *Lyric Shame: The 'Lyric' Subject of Contemporary American Poetry*
 RES - v66 - i276 - Sept 2015 - p803-804 [501+]

Book Review Index 2016 Cumulation WHITTALL • 491

White, Hayden - *The Practical Past*
Nation - v300 - i6 - Feb 9 2015 - p27(5) [501+]
White, Ian - *Consolidated B-24 Liberator: War paint Series No. 96*
APH - v62 - i1 - Spring 2015 - p59(1) [501+]
White, J.A. - *The Thickety: The Whispering Trees (Illus. by Offermann, Andrea)*
c PW - v262 - i4 - Jan 26 2015 - p170(1) [51-500]
c BL - v111 - i12 - Feb 15 2015 - p87(1) [51-500]
c CCB-B - v68 - i7 - March 2015 - p378(1) [51-500]
c HB Guide - v26 - i2 - Fall 2015 - p106(2) [51-500]
c PW - v262 - i49 - Dec 2 2015 - p78(2) [51-500]
c SLJ - v61 - i2 - Feb 2015 - p95(1) [51-500]
y VOYA - v38 - i2 - June 2015 - p84(2) [501+]
Well of Witches
y KR - Nov 15 2015 - pNA [51-500]
White, Jeanne - *Using Children's Literature to Teach Problem Solving in Math: Addressing the Common Core in K-2*
TC Math - v21 - i9 - May 2015 - p567(1) [501+]
White, Jen - *Survival Strategies of the Almost Brave*
c CCB-B - v69 - i2 - Oct 2015 - p121(1) [51-500]
c HB Guide - v26 - i2 - Fall 2015 - p107(1) [51-500]
c KR - March 15 2015 - pNA [51-500]
c PW - v262 - i15 - April 13 2015 - p80(1) [51-500]
c SLJ - v61 - i3 - March 2015 - p145(1) [51-500]
y VOYA - v38 - i2 - June 2015 - p69(1) [51-500]
White, Jenny B. - *Muslim Nationalism and the New Turks*
J Ch St - v57 - i1 - Wntr 2015 - p153-155 [501+]
White, Jonathan W. - *Emancipation, the Union Army, and the Reelection of Abraham Lincoln*
AHR - v120 - i2 - April 2015 - p631(1) [501+]
JAH - v101 - i4 - March 2015 - p1276(1) [501+]
White, Julie - *The Lost Diary*
y Res Links - v20 - i4 - April 2015 - p46(1) [501+]
White, Karen - *The Forgotten Room*
KR - Nov 15 2015 - pNA [501+]
The Sound of Glass
LJ - v140 - i8 - May 1 2015 - p66(2) [51-500]
White, Kate - *The Mystery Writers of America Cookbook*
LJ - v140 - i5 - March 15 2015 - p126(2) [501+]
NYTBR - Nov 1 2015 - p30(L) [501+]
The Wrong Man (Read by Bennett, Erin). Audiobook Review
LJ - v140 - i19 - Nov 15 2015 - p53(1) [51-500]
The Wrong Man
KR - May 1 2015 - pNA [51-500]
PW - v262 - i16 - April 20 2015 - p55(1) [51-500]
White, Kiersten - *Illusions of Fate*
y HB Guide - v26 - i2 - Fall 2015 - p144(1) [51-500]
White, Kristin M. - *It's the Student, Not the College: The Secrets of Succeeding at Any School--without Going Broke or Crazy*
LJ - v140 - i8 - May 1 2015 - p84(1) [51-500]
White, Lionel - *Marilyn K.: The House Next Door*
BL - v112 - i6 - Nov 15 2015 - p28(1) [51-500]
White, Louise G. - *The Calling*
KR - April 1 2015 - pNA [501+]
White, Mark - *Kennedy: A Cultural History of an American Icon*
J Am St - v49 - i2 - May 2015 - p441-444 [501+]
White, Michael - *Travels in Vermeer: A Memoir*
PW - v262 - i4 - Jan 26 2015 - p166(1) [51-500]
Vermeer in Hell: Poems
LJ - v140 - i2 - Feb 1 2015 - p88(1) [51-500]
White, Monica - *Military Saints in Byzantium and Rus, 900-1200*
AHR - v120 - i1 - Feb 2015 - p319-320 [501+]
White, Nancy - *Aviation Firefighters*
c HB Guide - v26 - i1 - Spring 2015 - p137(1) [51-500]
White, Patricia - *Women's Cinema, World Cinema: Projecting Contemporary Feminisms*
Wom R Bks - v32 - i6 - Nov-Dec 2015 - p11(3) [501+]
FQ - v69 - i1 - Fall 2015 - p99(2) [501+]
White, Paul - *Jodocus Badius Ascensius: Commentary, Commerce and Print in the Renaissance*
Ren Q - v68 - i1 - Spring 2015 - p235-237 [501+]
The Politics of Washing: Real Life in Venice
TimHES - i2203 - May 14 2015 - p47(1) [501+]
White, Philip - *Whistle Stop*
HT - v65 - i7 - July 2015 - p64(2) [501+]
White, Rachel - *Seventh. E-book Review*
PW - v262 - i19 - May 11 2015 - p42(1) [51-500]
White, Randy Wayne - *Cuba Straits*
BL - v111 - i12 - Feb 15 2015 - p29(1) [501+]
KR - Jan 15 2015 - pNA [51-500]
PW - v262 - i3 - Jan 19 2015 - p61(1) [51-500]
Haunted (Read by Raudman, Renee). Audiobook Review
BL - v111 - i12 - Feb 15 2015 - p103(1) [51-500]
White, Rob - *Youth Gangs, Violence and Social Respect*
CS - v44 - i3 - May 2015 - p440(1) [501+]
White, Roger - *C.S. Lewis and His Circle: Essays and Memoirs from the Oxford C.S. Lewis Society*
LJ - v140 - i8 - May 1 2015 - p70(1) [51-500]
White, Roseanna M. - *The Lost Heiress*
BL - v112 - i1 - Sept 1 2015 - p54(1) [51-500]
White, Sarah - *Wars Don't Happen Anymore*
ABR - v36 - i5 - July-August 2015 - p19(2) [501+]
White, Shane - *Prince of Darkness: The Untold Story of Jeremiah G. Hamilton, Wall Street's First Black Millionaire*
BL - v112 - i3 - Oct 1 2015 - p7(1) [51-500]
KR - August 1 2015 - pNA [501+]
LJ - v140 - i14 - Sept 1 2015 - p121(2) [51-500]
White, Sophie - *Wild Frenchmen and Frenchified Indians: Material Culture and Race in Colonial Louisiana*
Historian - v77 - i1 - Spring 2015 - p149(2) [501+]
JSH - v81 - i1 - Feb 2015 - p161(2) [501+]
White, Stephen - *Developments in Central and East European Politics*
E-A St - v67 - i5 - July 2015 - p835(3) [501+]
Identities and Foreign Policies in Russia, Ukraine and Belarus: The Other Europes
E-A St - v67 - i7 - Sept 2015 - p1152(2) [501+]
White, Steve - *Soldiers out of Time*
PW - v262 - i26 - June 29 2015 - p51(1) [51-500]
White, T.H. - *The Goshawk (Read by Vance, Simon). Audiobook Review*
BL - v112 - i1 - Sept 1 2015 - p140(1) [51-500]
White, Tara - *Where I Belong*
c KR - Jan 15 2015 - pNA [51-500]
y Res Links - v20 - i3 - Feb 2015 - p36(2) [51-500]
SLJ - v61 - i4 - April 2015 - p158(2) [51-500]
y VOYA - v38 - i1 - April 2015 - p72(1) [51-500]
White, Teagan - *Adventures with Barefoot Critters (Illus. by White, Teagan)*
c HB Guide - v26 - i1 - Spring 2015 - p18(1) [51-500]
White, Timothy R. - *Blue-Collar Broadway: The Craft and Industry of American Theater*
Am Theat - v32 - i2 - Feb 2015 - p58(2) [501+]
White, Virginia K. - *Warren the Honking Cat Saves the Day (Illus. by Ugang, Rosauro)*
c CH Bwatch - July 2015 - pNA [51-500]
Whitehead, Colson - *The Noble Hustle: Poker, Beef Jerky and Death*
NYTBR - April 5 2015 - p28(L) [501+]
Whitehead, Hal - *The Cultural Lives of Whales and Dolphins*
BioSci - v65 - i8 - August 2015 - p831(2) [501+]
Econ - v416 - i8947 - July 18 2015 - p72(US) [501+]
Nature - v517 - i7533 - Jan 8 2015 - p143(1) [51-500]
New Sci - v225 - i3003 - Jan 10 2015 - p43(1) [501+]
TLS - i5856 - June 26 2015 - p25(1) [501+]
Whitehead, Jason C. - *Redeeming Fear: A Constructive Theology for Living into Hope*
Intpr - v69 - i1 - Jan 2015 - p113(2) [501+]
Whitehead, Jenny - *You're a Crab! A Moody Day Book (Illus. by Whitehead, Jenny)*
c HB Guide - v26 - i2 - Fall 2015 - p22(1) [51-500]
c KR - March 15 2015 - pNA [51-500]
c PW - v262 - i22 - June 1 2015 - p58(1) [501+]
c SLJ - v61 - i6 - June 2015 - p95(1) [51-500]
Whitehead, John W. - *Battlefield America: The War on the American People*
Bwatch - June 2015 - pNA [51-500]
LJ - v140 - i9 - May 15 2015 - p96(2) [51-500]
Whitehead, Karsonya Wise - *Notes from a Colored Girl: The Civil War Pocket Diaries of Emilie Francis Davis*
JAH - v102 - i1 - June 2015 - p251-252 [501+]
Whitehead, Mark - *Environmental Transformations: A Geography of the Anthropocene*
GR - v105 - i4 - Oct 2015 - p625(4) [501+]
Whitehead, Neil L. - *Virtual War and Magical Death: Technologies and Imaginaries for Terror and Killing*
T&C - v56 - i4 - Oct 2015 - p1012-1013 [501+]
Whitehorn, Alan - *The Armenian Genocide: The Essential Reference Guide*
LJ - v140 - i14 - Sept 1 2015 - p138(1) [51-500]
BL - v112 - i3 - Oct 1 2015 - p12(2) [51-500]
Whitehouse, David - *Into the Heart of Our World: A Journey to the Center of the Earth; A Remarkable Voyage of Scientific Discovery*
BL - v112 - i7 - Dec 1 2015 - p14(1) [51-500]
KR - Nov 1 2015 - pNA [501+]
PW - v262 - i50 - Dec 7 2015 - p77(1) [51-500]
Whitelock, Anna - *Elizabeth's Bedfellows: An Intimate History of the Queen's Court*
HT - v65 - i1 - Jan 2015 - p61(1) [501+]
Whitely, Kara Richardson - *Gorge: My Journey up Kilimanjaro at 300 Pounds*
KR - Feb 15 2015 - pNA [51-500]
Whiteman, Stella - *Control Alter Delete*
PW - v262 - i42 - Oct 19 2015 - p60(1) [51-500]
Whiten, Jan - *Chooky-Doodle-Doo (Illus. by Hanley, Sinead)*
c CCB-B - v68 - i9 - May 2015 - p471(1) [51-500]
c HB Guide - v26 - i2 - Fall 2015 - p22(1) [51-500]
c SLJ - v61 - i5 - May 2015 - p80(1) [51-500]
Whitesel, Jason - *Fat Gay Men: Girth, Mirth, and the Politics of Stigma*
CS - v44 - i6 - Nov 2015 - p877-878 [501+]
JGS - v24 - i2 - April 2015 - p248-250 [501+]
Whiteside, Shaun - *Kempowski, Walter*
LJ - v140 - i3 - Feb 15 2015 - p112(1) [51-500]
Whitfield, Philip - *Firefly Encyclopedia of Animals: A Comprehensive Look at the World of Animals with Hundred of Superb Illustrations*
SLJ - v61 - i2 - Feb 2015 - p56(1) [51-500]
Whitfield, Stephen - *Omari and the People*
SPBW - Feb 2015 - pNA [51-500]
Whitfield, Teresa - *Endgame for ETA: Elusive Peace in the Basque Country*
For Aff - v94 - i1 - Jan-Feb 2015 - pNA [51-500]
TLS - i5837 - Feb 13 2015 - p12(1) [501+]
Whitford, Sara - *The Smuggler's Gambit*
y PW - v262 - i44 - Nov 2 2015 - p86(2) [51-500]
Whiting, Frances - *Walking on Trampolines*
BL - v111 - i11 - Feb 1 2015 - p24(2) [51-500]
Whiting, Jim - *Air Force Special Operations Command*
y BL - v111 - i9-10 - Jan 1 2015 - p85(1) [51-500]
FBI Hostage Rescue and SWAT Teams
y BL - v111 - i9-10 - Jan 1 2015 - p85(1) [51-500]
c HB Guide - v26 - i2 - Fall 2015 - p154(1) [51-500]
Green Berets
y BL - v111 - i9-10 - Jan 1 2015 - p85(1) [51-500]
c HB Guide - v26 - i2 - Fall 2015 - p154(1) [51-500]
Marine Corps Forces Special Operations Command
y BL - v111 - i9-10 - Jan 1 2015 - p85(1) [51-500]
Navy SEALs
c HB Guide - v26 - i2 - Fall 2015 - p154(1) [51-500]
The Story of the Los Angeles Clippers
c HB Guide - v26 - i2 - Fall 2015 - p198(1) [51-500]
Whiting, Robert - *The Reform of the English Parish Church*
Six Ct J - v46 - i3 - Fall 2015 - p727-728 [501+]
Whiting, Sue - *Platypus (Illus. by Jackson, Mark)*
Magpies - v30 - i3 - July 2015 - p22(2) [501+]
c KR - Dec 1 2015 - pNA [51-500]
Portraits of Celina
y CCB-B - v68 - i11 - July-August 2015 - p573(1) [51-500]
y HB Guide - v26 - i2 - Fall 2015 - p144(1) [51-500]
y KR - Feb 1 2015 - pNA [51-500]
y VOYA - v37 - i6 - Feb 2015 - p70(1) [501+]
Whitlatch, Jo Bell - *Guide to Reference: Essential General Reference and Library Science Sources*
R&USQ - v54 - i4 - Summer 2015 - p72(1) [501+]
Whitley, Jeremy - *Princeless: The Pirate Princess (Illus. by Higgins, Rosy)*
c SLJ - v61 - i5 - May 2015 - p110(1) [51-500]
Whitlow, Robert - *A House Divided*
PW - v262 - i25 - June 22 2015 - p127(1) [51-500]
Whitman, Walt - *Drum-Taps: The Complete 1865 Edition*
BL - v111 - i15 - April 1 2015 - p13(1) [51-500]
TLS - i5855 - June 19 2015 - p25(1) [501+]
Whitmarsh, Tim - *Battling the Gods: Atheism in the Ancient World*
BL - v112 - i3 - Oct 1 2015 - p4(1) [51-500]
KR - Sept 1 2015 - pNA [501+]
NYTBR - Nov 22 2015 - p1(L) [501+]
PW - v262 - i37 - Sept 14 2015 - p61(2) [51-500]
Whitney, Daisy - *The Fire Artist*
y HB Guide - v26 - i1 - Spring 2015 - p128(1) [51-500]
Whitson, Stephanie Grace - *Daughter of the Regiment*
PW - v262 - i6 - Feb 9 2015 - p51(1) [51-500]
Whitt, Jacqueline E. - *Bringing God to Men: American Military Chaplains and the Vietnam War*
AHR - v120 - i2 - April 2015 - p671-672 [501+]
CH - v84 - i3 - Sept 2015 - p691(3) [501+]
JAH - v101 - i4 - March 2015 - p1345-1346 [501+]
Whitta, Gary - *Abomination*
PW - v262 - i17 - April 27 2015 - p56(1) [51-500]
Whittall, Arnold - *Overture Opera Guide: "Die Meistersinger von Nurnberg"*
ON - v80 - i5 - Nov 2015 - p61(1) [501+]

492 • WHITTEMORE Book Review Index 2016 Cumulation

Whittemore, Jo - *Brooke's Not-So-Perfect Plan*
c PW - v262 - i44 - Nov 2 2015 - p85(1) [51-500]
Colonial Madness
c BL - v111 - i9-10 - Jan 1 2015 - p101(1) [51-500]
c HB Guide - v26 - i2 - Fall 2015 - p107(1) [51-500]
Whitten-Simmons, Carrie - *Nate and Shea's Adventures in South Africa*
c CH Bwatch - Oct 2015 - pNA [51-500]
Whitten-Woodring, Jenifer - *Historical Guide to World Media Freedom: A Country-by-Country Analysis*
R&USQ - v54 - i3 - Spring 2015 - p62(2) [501+]
Whittington, Hillary - *Raising Ryland: Our Story of Parenting a Transgender Child with No Strings Attached*
KR - Dec 15 2015 - pNA [501+]
PW - v262 - i52 - Dec 21 2015 - p150(1) [51-500]
Whittington, Karl - *Body-Worlds: Opicinus de Canistris and the Medieval Cartographic Imagination*
Specu - v90 - i1 - Jan 2015 - p307-309 [501+]
Whittle, Richard - *Predator: The Secret Origins of the Drone Revolution*
APJ - v29 - i6 - Nov-Dec 2015 - p92(1) [501+]
Hum - v75 - i2 - March-April 2015 - p46(2) [501+]
Whitton, Christopher - *Pliny the Younger: Epistles Book II*
Class R - v65 - i1 - April 2015 - p149-151 [501+]
Whooley, Owen - *Knowledge in the Time of Cholera: The Struggle over American Medicine in the Nineteenth Century*
CS - v44 - i4 - July 2015 - p567-569 [501+]
Isis - v106 - i1 - March 2015 - p198(2) [501+]
Whose Tools? (Illus. by Datz, Jim)
c PW - v262 - i15 - April 13 2015 - p78(2) [501+]
Whte, William - *Redbrick: A Social and Architectural History of Britain's Civic Universities*
TimHES - i2211 - July 9 2015 - p49(1) [501+]
Whybrow, Peter C. - *The Well-Tuned Brain: Neuroscience and the Life Well Lived*
BL - v111 - i16 - April 15 2015 - p9(2) [51-500]
KR - March 1 2015 - pNA [501+]
Whyte, David - *How Corrupt Is Britain?*
NS - v144 - i5265 - June 5 2015 - p44(2) [501+]
TLS - i5848 - May 1 2015 - p23(1) [501+]
Whyte, Iain Boyd - *Metropolis Berlin 1880-1940*
CEH - v48 - i1 - March 2015 - p23-24 [501+]
Whyte, Janet M. - *Shot in the Dark*
c BL - v112 - i1 - Sept 1 2015 - p101(1) [51-500]
c Res Links - v20 - i5 - June 2015 - p29(1) [51-500]
y SLJ - v61 - i9 - Sept 2015 - p151(4) [501+]
Whyte, Padraic - *Children's Literature and New York City*
Bkbird - v53 - i1 - Wntr 2015 - p92(2) [501+]
Whyte, Susan Reynolds - *Second Chances: Surviving Aids in Uganda*
MAQ - v29 - i3 - Sept 2015 - pb-27-b-29 [501+]
Whyton, Tony - *Beyond a Love Supreme: John Coltrane and the Legacy of an Album*
J Am St - v49 - i2 - May 2015 - p405-412 [501+]
Wibberley, Leonard - *The Mouse That Roared*
CSM - Feb 27 2015 - pNA [51-500]
Wick, Walter - *Can You See What I See? Christmas (Illus. by Wick, Walter)*
c SLJ - v61 - i10 - Oct 2015 - p69(1) [51-500]
Hey, Seymour! (Illus. by Wick, Walter)
c KR - May 15 2015 - pNA [51-500]
c PW - v262 - i49 - Dec 2 2015 - p58(2) [51-500]
c SLJ - v61 - i9 - Sept 2015 - p131(2) [51-500]
Wickard, Douglas - *Perfect*
KR - April 15 2015 - pNA [501+]
Wicke, Christian - *Helmut Kohl's Quest for Normality: His Representation of the German Nation and Himself*
HNet - July 2015 - pNA [501+]
Wickens, Andrew P. - *A History of the Brain: From Stone Age Surgery to Modern Neuroscience*
QRB - v90 - i4 - Dec 2015 - p439(2) [501+]
Wickham, Chris - *Framing of the Early Middle Ages*
HT - v65 - i5 - May 2015 - p56(2) [501+]
Medieval Rome: Stability and Crisis of a City, 900-1150
Med R - August 2015 - pNA [501+]
TLS - i5857 - July 3 2015 - p7(1) [501+]
Wicks, Maris - *Human Body Theater (Illus. by Wicks, Maris)*
c BL - v112 - i2 - Sept 15 2015 - p52(1) [51-500]
y KR - August 15 2015 - pNA [51-500]
c PW - v262 - i29 - July 20 2015 - p195(1) [51-500]
c SLJ - v61 - i9 - Sept 2015 - p190(1) [51-500]
Widmalm, Sven - *Neutrality in Twentieth-Century Europe: Intersections of Science, Culture, and Politics after the First World War*
Isis - v106 - i2 - June 2015 - p483(3) [501+]
Widmark, Martin - *The Diamond Mystery (Illus. by Willis, Helena)*
c HB Guide - v26 - i1 - Spring 2015 - p66(1) [51-500]
Widmer, Jeff - *Peak Season*
KR - Oct 15 2015 - pNA [51-500]
Widmer, Kurt - *Unter Zions Panier: Mormonism and Its Interaction with Germany and Its People, 1840-1990*
JAH - v101 - i4 - March 2015 - p1240-1241 [501+]
Wie Pietistisch Kann Adel Sein? Hallescher Pietismus und Adel im Langen 18. Jahrhundert. 4. Tag der Sachsen-Anhaltischen Landesgeschichte
HNet - Jan 2015 - pNA [501+]
Wiebe, Joanna - *The Wicked Awakening of Anne Merchant*
y Res Links - v20 - i3 - Feb 2015 - p37(2) [51-500]
y VOYA - v38 - i1 - April 2015 - p84(1) [51-500]
Wiebe, Rudy - *Come Back*
Can Lit - i224 - Spring 2015 - p112 [501+]
Bks & Cult - v21 - i6 - Nov-Dec 2015 - p34(3) [501+]
Wiechman, Kathy Cannon - *Empty Places*
c KR - Jan 1 2016 - pNA [51-500]
Like a River: A Civil War Novel
c CCB-B - v68 - i10 - June 2015 - p524(2) [51-500]
Like a River
c BL - v111 - i16 - April 15 2015 - p60(1) [51-500]
c CH Bwatch - May 2015 - pNA [51-500]
c HB Guide - v26 - i2 - Fall 2015 - p107(1) [51-500]
c KR - Jan 15 2015 - pNA [51-500]
c PW - v262 - i6 - Feb 9 2015 - p68(1) [51-500]
Wiederhergestellte Synagogen. Raum - Geschichte - Wandel durch Erinnerung
HNet - Sept 2015 - pNA [501+]
Wiegand, Steve - *U.S. History for Dummies, 3d ed.*
VOYA - v37 - i6 - Feb 2015 - p90(2) [501+]
Wiegand, Wayne A. - *Part of Our Lives: A People's History of the American Public Library*
BL - v112 - i6 - Nov 15 2015 - p10(1) [51-500]
LJ - v140 - i15 - Sept 15 2015 - p90(1) [51-500]
PW - v262 - i33 - August 17 2015 - p61(1) [501+]
Wiegers, Michael - *What about This: Collected Poems of Frank Stanford*
APR - v44 - i4 - July-August 2015 - p21(7) [501+]
New R - v246 - i5 - June 2015 - p82(2) [501+]
NYT - April 7 2015 - pC1(L) [501+]
NYT - Nov 27 2015 - pC31(L) [501+]
NYTBR - July 19 2015 - p14(L) [501+]
Wiehl, Lis - *A Deadly Business (Read by Laurence, Ashley). Audiobook Review*
LJ - v140 - i5 - March 15 2015 - p72(1) [51-500]
Wiehl, Lis W. - *Lethal Beauty*
KR - Jan 1 2015 - pNA [51-500]
Wieland, Karin - *Dietrich & Riefenstahl: Hollywood, Berlin, and a Century in Two Lives*
KR - August 1 2015 - pNA [501+]
LJ - v140 - i14 - Sept 1 2015 - p107(3) [51-500]
Mac - v128 - i44 - Nov 9 2015 - p126(1) [501+]
NYTBR - Dec 6 2015 - p54(L) [501+]
PW - v262 - i30 - July 27 2015 - p53(1) [51-500]
TimHES - i2226 - Oct 22 2015 - p48-49 [501+]
Wieland, Leibundgut D. - *Weihgeschenke aus dem Heiligtum der Aphrodite in Alt-Paphos. Terrakotten, Skulpturen und andere figurliche Kleinvotive*
Class R - v65 - i2 - Oct 2015 - p560-562 [501+]
Wieland, Liza - *Land of Enchantment*
BL - v111 - i13 - March 1 2015 - p20(1) [51-500]
Wielicko, Leszek A. - *Japanese Fighters in Defense of the Homeland, 1941-1944, vol. 1*
APH - v62 - i2 - Summer 2015 - p59(1) [501+]
Wielockx, Ruth - *I Won (Illus. by Wielockx, Ruth)*
c SLJ - v61 - i8 - August 2015 - p63(1) [51-500]
Wiemann, Dirk - *Perspectives on English Revolutionary Republicanism*
Six Ct J - v46 - i3 - Fall 2015 - p683-685 [501+]
Ren Q - v68 - i3 - Fall 2015 - p1085-1087 [501+]
Wiemer, Liza - *Hello?*
y SLJ - v61 - i10 - Oct 2015 - p118(1) [51-500]
Wienand, Johannes - *Contested Monarchy: Integrating the Roman Empire in the Fourth Century AD*
HNet - May 2015 - pNA [501+]
Wiener, Jon - *How We Forgot the Cold War: A Historical Journey across America*
AHR - v120 - i1 - Feb 2015 - p290-291 [501+]
JAH - v102 - i1 - June 2015 - p315-316 [501+]
Wiener, Nancy H. - *Beyond Breaking the Glass: A Spiritual Guide to Your Jewish Wedding*
RVBW - August 2015 - pNA [51-500]
Wieners, John - *Supplication: Selected Poems of John Wieners*
NY - v91 - i34 - Nov 2 2015 - p86 [501+]
PW - v262 - i38 - Sept 21 2015 - p50(1) [51-500]
Wienfort, Monika - *Verliebt, Verlobt, Verheiratet. Eine Geschichte der Ehe seit der Romantik*
GSR - v38 - i3 - Oct 2015 - p659-661 [501+]
Wieringa, Tommy - *These Are the Names*
TLS - i5838 - Feb 20 2015 - p21(1) [501+]
Wierling, Dorothee - *Eine Familie im Krieg: Leben, Sterben und Schreiben 1914-1918*
GSR - v38 - i2 - May 2015 - p428-3 [501+]
Wiersema, Robert - *Black Feathers*
PW - v262 - i26 - June 29 2015 - p49(1) [51-500]
Wiersma, Jacquelyn - *The Zodiac Recipe: An Effortless Recipe That is Certain to Help You Better Understand Your Partners, Friends and Ourselves*
RVBW - June 2015 - pNA [51-500]
Wierzbicka, Anna - *Imprisoned in English: The Hazards of English as a Default Language*
TLS - i5858 - July 10 2015 - p23(1) [501+]
Wigger, J. Bradley - *Thank You, God (Illus. by Jago)*
c HB Guide - v26 - i1 - Spring 2015 - p134(1) [51-500]
Wiggins, Sarah Woolfolk - *The Journal of Sarah Haynsworth Gayle, 1827-1835: A Substitute for Social Intercourse*
JSH - v81 - i2 - May 2015 - p456(2) [501+]
Wiggs, Susan - *Starlight on Willow Lake*
BL - v111 - i22 - August 1 2015 - p41(2) [51-500]
Wignall, Paul B. - *The Worst of Times: How Life on Earth Survived Eighty Million Years of Extinctions*
New Sci - v228 - i3042 - Oct 10 2015 - p48(1) [501+]
PW - v262 - i33 - August 17 2015 - p64(1) [51-500]
Wignell, Edel - *Bilby: Secrets of an Australian Marsupial (Illus. by Jackson, Mark)*
c CCB-B - v68 - i7 - March 2015 - p370(1) [51-500]
c HB - v91 - i2 - March-April 2015 - p122(2) [51-500]
c HB Guide - v26 - i2 - Fall 2015 - p181(1) [51-500]
Wigu Publishing - *When I Grow Up I Want to Be ... a Nurse! Amber's Accidental Journey*
c CH Bwatch - March 2015 - pNA [51-500]
Wijma, Sara M. - *Embracing the Immigrant: The Participation of Metics in Athenian Polis Religion*
HNet - Jan 2015 - pNA [501+]
WikiLeaks - *The WikiLeaks Files*
KR - June 15 2015 - pNA [501+]
Wilburn, Reginald A. - *Preaching the Gospel of Black Revolt: Appropriating Milton in Early African American Literature*
MP - v113 - i1 - August 2015 - pE47(3) [501+]
Ren Q - v68 - i3 - Fall 2015 - p1157-1158 [501+]
Wilcken, Hugo - *The Reflection*
BL - v111 - i21 - July 1 2015 - p39(1) [51-500]
KR - July 1 2015 - pNA [51-500]
LJ - v140 - i13 - August 1 2015 - p90(1) [51-500]
PW - v262 - i28 - July 13 2015 - p47(1) [51-500]
Wilcock, Lizzie - *Thirst*
y Magpies - v30 - i2 - May 2015 - p44(1) [501+]
Wilcox, Christine - *Gambling Addiction*
y BL - v111 - i15 - April 1 2015 - p54(1) [51-500]
y VOYA - v38 - i3 - August 2015 - p88(1) [51-500]
How Is Online Pornography Affecting Society?
y SLJ - v61 - i9 - Sept 2015 - p176(1) [51-500]
Is Enough Being Done to Protect Athletes from Concussions?
BL - v111 - i21 - July 1 2015 - p54(1) [51-500]
Online Privacy
y VOYA - v38 - i3 - August 2015 - p90(1) [501+]
Teens and LGBT Issues
y BL - v112 - i3 - Oct 1 2015 - p40(1) [51-500]
Wilcox, Claire - *Alexander McQueen: Savage Beauty*
TLS - i5855 - June 19 2015 - p27(1) [501+]
Wilcox, Merrie-Ellen - *What's the Buzz? Keeping Bees in Flight*
c BL - v111 - i22 - August 1 2015 - p52(1) [51-500]
c KR - July 15 2015 - pNA [51-500]
c SLJ - v61 - i7 - July 2015 - p111(1) [51-500]
Wilcox Richards, Nancy - *Entre Amis (Illus. by Goldsmith, Tom)*
c Res Links - v20 - i3 - Feb 2015 - p55(1) [1-50]
We're All Friends Here (Illus. by Goldsmith, Tom)
c Res Links - v20 - i3 - Feb 2015 - p54(1) [51-500]
Wilcox, Victoria - *The Last Decision*
KR - July 15 2015 - pNA [501+]
Wilcoxson, Troy T. - *Plexus*
KR - April 15 2015 - pNA [501+]
Wilczek, Frank - *A Beautiful Question: Finding Nature's Deep Design*
KR - May 15 2015 - pNA [501+]
Nature - v523 - i7559 - July 9 2015 - p156(2)

[501+]
 PW - v262 - i18 - May 4 2015 - p107(1) [51-500]
 Spec - v328 - i9754 - August 8 2015 - p29(1) [501+]
 TimHES - i2213 - July 23 2015 - p49(1) [501+]
 TLS - i5873 - Oct 23 2015 - p3(2) [501+]
Wilczek, Markus - *Das Artikulierte und das Inartikulierte: Eine Archaologie des Strukturalismus*
 Ger Q - v88 - i3 - Summer 2015 - p416(4) [501+]
Wild, Bryan - *Flying Blind: The Story of a Second World War Night Fighter Pilot*
 APH - v62 - i1 - Spring 2015 - p59(2) [501+]
Wild, Margaret - *Bogtrotter (Illus. by Rossell, Judith)*
 c Magpies - v30 - i2 - May 2015 - p18(1) [501+]
Nighty Night! (Illus. by Argent, Kerry)
 c CH Bwatch - Jan 2015 - pNA [51-500]
Our Baby (Illus. by Blair, Karen)
 c Magpies - v30 - i3 - July 2015 - p26(1) [501+]
This Little Piggy Went Dancing (Illus. by Niland, Deborah)
 c Sch Lib - v63 - i2 - Summer 2015 - p98(1) [51-500]
Wilde, Cecil - *A Boy Called Cin*
 PW - v262 - i19 - May 11 2015 - p42(2) [51-500]
Wilde, Fran - *Updraft*
 PW - v262 - i22 - June 1 2015 - p46(1) [51-500]
 y SLJ - v61 - i11 - Nov 2015 - p104(1) [51-500]
Wilde, James - *Hereward: End of Days: A Novel of Medieval England*
 LJ - v140 - i3 - Feb 15 2015 - p95(1) [51-500]
Wilde, Kate C. - *Autistic Logistics*
 Bwatch - April 2015 - pNA [501+]
Wilde, Lisa - *Yo Miss: A Graphic Look at High School*
 PW - v262 - i1 - Jan 5 2015 - p59(1) [51-500]
Wilde, Lori - *Back in the Game*
 BL - v111 - i12 - Feb 15 2015 - p43(1) [51-500]
Wilde, Oscar - *The Selfish Giant (Illus. by Zwerger, Lisbeth)*
 c HB Guide - v26 - i2 - Fall 2015 - p56(1) [51-500]
Wildenberg, Thomas - *Billy Mitchell's War with the Navy: The Interwar Rivalry over Air Power*
 APJ - v29 - i5 - Sept-Oct 2015 - p107(2) [501+]
 HNet - August 2015 - pNA [501+]
Wildenthal, Lora - *The Language of Human Rights in West Germany*
 JMH - v87 - i1 - March 2015 - p235(2) [501+]
Wilder, Craig Steven - *Ebony & Ivy: Race, Slavery, and the Troubled History of America's Universities*
 Am St - v54 - i1 - Spring 2015 - p141-2 [501+]
 JSH - v81 - i1 - Feb 2015 - p178(2) [501+]
Wilder, Gary - *Freedom Time: Negritude, Decolonization, and the Future of the World*
 Africa T - v61 - i4 - Summer 2015 - p104(3) [501+]
 Dis - v62 - i1 - Wntr 2015 - p145(7) [501+]
Wilder, Jasinda - *Madame X*
 PW - v262 - i35 - August 31 2015 - p67(1) [51-500]
Wilder, Laura Ingalls - *Pioneer Girl: The Annotated Autobiography of Laura Ingalls Wilder*
 Roundup M - v22 - i4 - April 2015 - p29(1) [501+]
 Wom R Bks - v32 - i3 - May-June 2015 - p18(2) [501+]
Wilder-Taylor, Stefanie - *Gummi Bears Should Not Be Organic, and Other Opinions I Can't Back Up with Facts*
 BL - v111 - i14 - March 15 2015 - p32(1) [51-500]
 KR - Feb 1 2015 - pNA [501+]
Wildman, Sarah - *Paper Love: Searching for the Girl My Grandfather Left Behind*
 CSM - Jan 30 2015 - pNA [501+]
Wilensky, Harold L. - *American Political Economy in Global Perspective*
 CS - v44 - i4 - July 2015 - p569-571 [501+]
Wilensky, Uri - *An Introduction to Agent-Based Modeling: Modeling Natural, Social, and Engineered Complex Systems with NetLogo*
 Phys Today - v68 - i8 - August 2015 - p55(1) [501+]
Wiles, Deborah - *Freedom Summer: Celebrating the 50th Anniversary of the Freedom Summer (Illus. by Lagarrigue, Jerome)*
 c HB Guide - v26 - i1 - Spring 2015 - p50(1) [51-500]
Revolution. Audiobook Review
 c BL - v111 - i14 - March 15 2015 - p24(2) [501+]
Revolution (Read by several narrators). Audiobook Review
 c HB - v91 - i2 - March-April 2015 - p131(1) [51-500]
 y SLJ - v61 - i11 - Nov 2015 - p74(1) [51-500]
Revolution
 c BL - v111 - i9-10 - Jan 1 2015 - pS4(8) [501+]
 y BL - v111 - i16 - April 15 2015 - p57(1) [501+]

Wiley, Andrea S. - *Cultures of Milk: The Biology and Meaning of Dairy Products in the United States and India*
 HNet - May 2015 - pNA [501+]
Wiley, David - *The Promise of Francis: The Man, the Pope, and the Challenge of Change*
 KR - August 15 2015 - pNA [501+]
Wiley Kids - *The Wiley Kids in the Adventure of Cottonwood Canyon. E-book Review*
 KR - July 15 2015 - pNA [501+]
Wiley, Melissa - *Inch and Roly and the Sunny Day Scare (Illus. by Jatkowska, Ag)*
 c HB Guide - v26 - i1 - Spring 2015 - p55(1) [51-500]
Wiley, Michael - *Second Skin*
 KR - Sept 15 2015 - pNA [51-500]
Wiley, Norbert - *Uprising at Bowling Green: How the Quiet Fifties Became the Political Sixties*
 CS - v44 - i5 - Sept 2015 - p732-733 [501+]
Wilhelm, Hans - *A Hole in the Wall (Illus. by Wilhelm, Hans)*
 c KR - Nov 15 2015 - pNA [51-500]
 c PW - v262 - i48 - Nov 30 2015 - p57(1) [51-500]
Wilhide, Elizabeth - *Scandinavian Home: A Comprehensive Guide to Mid-Century Modern Scandinavian Designers*
 PW - v262 - i46 - Nov 16 2015 - p72(1) [51-500]
Wilke, Daria - *Playing a Part*
 y BL - v111 - i12 - Feb 15 2015 - p83(1) [51-500]
 c CH Bwatch - June 2015 - pNA [501+]
 y HB Guide - v26 - i2 - Fall 2015 - p144(1) [51-500]
 y KR - Jan 1 2015 - pNA [51-500]
 y PW - v262 - i4 - Jan 26 2015 - p173(2) [51-500]
 y SLJ - v61 - i3 - March 2015 - p164(1) [51-500]
 y VOYA - v37 - i6 - Feb 2015 - p70(1) [51-500]
Wilker, Josh - *Benchwarmer: A Sports-Obsessed Memoir of Fatherhood*
 BL - v111 - i17 - May 1 2015 - p69(2) [51-500]
 KR - Feb 15 2015 - pNA [51-500]
 PW - v262 - i12 - March 23 2015 - p60(2) [51-500]
Wilker, Julia - *Maintaining Peace and Interstate Stability in Archaic and Classical Greece*
 HNet - June 2015 - pNA [501+]
Wilkey, Glducia Vasconcelos - *Worship and Culture: Foreign Country or Homeland?*
 IBMR - v39 - i3 - July 2015 - p158(1) [501+]
Wilkie, David J. - *A Second Shot of Coffee with Jesus (Illus. by Wilkie, David J.)*
 BL - v111 - i18 - May 15 2015 - p42(1) [51-500]
 PW - v262 - i10 - March 9 2015 - p66(2) [51-500]
Wilkin, Karen - *Willard Boepple Sculpture: The Sense of Things*
 TLS - i5833 - Jan 16 2015 - p26(1) [501+]
Wilkin, Sam - *Wealth Secrets of the One Percent: A Modern Manual to Getting Marvelously, Obscenely Rich*
 BL - v111 - i21 - July 1 2015 - p25(1) [51-500]
 KR - June 15 2015 - pNA [51-500]
 NYTBR - August 2 2015 - p17(L) [501+]
 PW - v262 - i20 - May 18 2015 - p76(1) [51-500]
Wilkins, Catherine - *Landscape Imagery, Politics, and Identity in a Divided Germany, 1968-1989*
 CEH - v48 - i2 - June 2015 - p280-281 [501+]
Wilkins, David E. - *Hollow Justice: A History of Indigenous Claims in the United States*
 AHR - v120 - i1 - Feb 2015 - p248-249 [501+]
 Am Ind CRJ - v39 - i1 - Wntr 2015 - p120-122 [501+]
 PHR - v84 - i2 - May 2015 - p261(2) [501+]
Wilkins, Joe - *The Mountain and the Fathers: Growing Up on the Big Dry*
 Bks & Cult - v21 - i1 - Jan-Feb 2015 - p14(1) [501+]
Wilkinson, Anne - *The Essential Anne Wilkinson*
 Can Lit - i224 - Spring 2015 - p146 [501+]
Wilkinson, Frances C. - *The Complete Guide to Acquisitions Management, 2d ed*
 LJ - v140 - i19 - Nov 15 2015 - p97(1) [501+]
Wilkinson, John - *Courses Matter-Woven*
 TLS - i5872 - Oct 16 2015 - p22(1) [501+]
Schedule of Unrest: Selected Poems
 TLS - i5872 - Oct 16 2015 - p22(1) [501+]
Wilkinson, Joshua Maria - *Anne Carson: Ecstatic Lyre*
 TLS - i5844 - April 3 2015 - p26(2) [501+]
Wilkinson, Kerry - *Renegade*
 y VOYA - v37 - i6 - Feb 2015 - p85(1) [501+]
Wilkinson, Lili - *Green Valentine*
 y Magpies - v30 - i4 - Sept 2015 - p45(1) [501+]
Love-Shy
 y BL - v111 - i12 - Feb 15 2015 - p82(1) [51-500]
Wilkinson, Matt - *Restless Creatures*
 KR - Dec 15 2015 - pNA [51-500]

Wilkinson, Sheena - *Grounded*
 y KR - July 15 2015 - pNA [51-500]
Still Falling
 y Sch Lib - v63 - i2 - Summer 2015 - p126(2) [51-500]
Taking Flight
 y SLJ - v61 - i7 - July 2015 - p89(1) [51-500]
 y VOYA - v38 - i3 - August 2015 - p72(1) [51-500]
Wilkinson, Steven I. - *Army and the Nation*
 HT - v65 - i7 - July 2015 - p65(1) [501+]
Wilkinson-Weber, Clare M. - *Fashioning Bollywood: The Making and Meaning of Hindi Film Costume*
 JRAI - v21 - i1 - March 2015 - p227(2) [501+]
Wilkman, Jon - *Floodpath: The Deadliest Man-Made Disaster of 20th-Century America and the Making of Los Angeles*
 BL - v112 - i5 - Nov 1 2015 - p4(1) [51-500]
 KR - Oct 1 2015 - pNA [51-500]
 PW - v262 - i45 - Nov 9 2015 - p50(1) [51-500]
Will-Weber, Mark - *Mint Juleps with Teddy Roosevelt: The Complete History of Presidential Drinking*
 Bwatch - Jan 2015 - pNA [51-500]
 RVBW - Feb 2015 - pNA [501+]
Willans, Geoffrey - *Down with Skool: A Guide to School Life for Tiny Pupils and Their Parents*
 TimHES - i2206 - June 4 2015 - p47(1) [501+]
Willard, Nancy - *The Three Mouths of Little Tom Drum (Illus. by Hawkes, Kevin)*
 c CCB-B - v68 - i8 - April 2015 - p423(1) [51-500]
 c HB Guide - v26 - i2 - Fall 2015 - p56(1) [51-500]
Willard, Ted - *The NSTA Quick-Reference Guide to the NGSS, Elementary School*
 Sci & Ch - v52 - i7 - March 2015 - p96 [501+]
The NSTA Quick-Reference Guide to the NGSS: High School
 Sci Teach - v82 - i2 - Feb 2015 - p64 [501+]
Willard, Tom - *Buffalo Soldiers*
 Roundup M - v22 - i3 - Feb 2015 - p13(1) [501+]
Willbanks, James H. - *Generals of the Army: Marshall, MacArthur, Eisenhower, Arnold, Bradley*
 HNet - Feb 2015 - pNA [501+]
A Raid Too Far: Operation Lam Son 719 and Vietnamization in Laos
 AHR - v120 - i1 - Feb 2015 - p293-294 [501+]
 JAH - v101 - i4 - March 2015 - p1345(1) [501+]
Willcocks, Leslie P. - *The Economics of Outsourcing: The International Library of Critical Writings in Economics 297*
 Bwatch - Sept 2015 - pNA [51-500]
Willeg, Lauren - *The Lure of the Moonflower (Read by Reading, Kate). Audiobook Review*
 LJ - v140 - i19 - Nov 15 2015 - p53(1) [51-500]
Willems, Mo - *I Really Like Slop! (Illus. by Willems, Mo)*
 c BL - v112 - i7 - Dec 1 2015 - p66(2) [51-500]
 c KR - Oct 15 2015 - pNA [51-500]
 c SLJ - v61 - i12 - Dec 2015 - p98(1) [51-500]
I Will Take a Nap! (Illus. by Willems, Mo)
 c BL - v111 - i19-20 - June 1 2015 - p116(1) [51-500]
 c CCB-B - v69 - i1 - Sept 2015 - p64(2) [51-500]
 c KR - April 15 2015 - pNA [51-500]
 c SLJ - v61 - i7 - July 2015 - p70(1) [51-500]
The Story of Diva and Flea (Illus. by DiTerlizzi, Tony)
 c SLJ - v61 - i9 - Sept 2015 - p136(2) [51-500]
 c PW - v262 - i33 - August 17 2015 - p71(2) [51-500]
 c BL - v112 - i1 - Sept 1 2015 - p123(1) [51-500]
 c NYTBR - Oct 11 2015 - p17(L) [501+]
 c KR - August 1 2015 - pNA [51-500]
Waiting Is Not Easy! (Illus. by Willems, Mo)
 c CH Bwatch - Jan 2015 - pNA [51-500]
 c HB Guide - v26 - i1 - Spring 2015 - p55(1) [51-500]
 c SLJ - v61 - i2 - Feb 2015 - p81(1) [51-500]
We Are in a Book!
 c JE - v195 - i2 - Spring 2015 - p55-56 [501+]
Who Flies, Cat the Cat? (Illus. by Willems, Mo)
 c HB Guide - v26 - i1 - Spring 2015 - p18(1) [51-500]
Who Sleeps, Cat the Cat? (Illus. by Willems, Mo)
 c HB Guide - v26 - i1 - Spring 2015 - p18(1) [51-500]
Willemsen, Roger - *The Ends of the Earth*
 TLS - i5855 - June 19 2015 - p30(1) [501+]
Willen, Janet - *Speak a Word for Freedom: Women against Slavery*
 y BL - v112 - i4 - Oct 15 2015 - p38(1) [51-500]
 y KR - July 15 2015 - pNA [51-500]
 c PW - v262 - i34 - August 24 2015 - p82(1) [501+]
 y Res Links - v21 - i1 - Oct 2015 - p45(2) [501+]
 y VOYA - v38 - i3 - August 2015 - p88(1) [51-500]
 y PW - v262 - i49 - Dec 2 2015 - p117(1) [51-500]

Willer, Stefan - *Erbe: Ubertragungskonzepte zwischen Natur und Kultur*
 HNet - Feb 2015 - pNA [501+]
Erbfalle: Theorie und Praxis Kultureller Ubertragung in der Moderne
 HNet - Feb 2015 - pNA [501+]
Willes, Margaret - *The Gardens of the British Working Class*
 TLS - i5861 - July 31 2015 - p12(1) [501+]
Willett, Edward - *Lake in the Clouds*
 c Res Links - v21 - i1 - Oct 2015 - p44(1) [501+]
Twist of the Blade
 y CH Bwatch - March 2015 - pNA [51-500]
 c Res Links - v20 - i3 - Feb 2015 - p54(2) [501+]
Willett, Marcia - *Postcards from the Past*
 KR - Feb 1 2015 - pNA [51-500]
 LJ - v140 - i5 - March 15 2015 - p96(2) [501+]
Willetts, Paul - *Rendezvous at the Russian Tea Rooms: The Spy Hunter, the Fashion Designer and the Man from Moscow*
 TLS - i5876 - Nov 13 2015 - p28(1) [501+]
Willey, David - *The Promise of Francis: The Man, the Pope, and the Challenge of Change*
 LJ - v140 - i14 - Sept 1 2015 - p108(1) [501+]
Willey, Margaret - *Beetle Boy*
 c CH Bwatch - Jan 2015 - pNA [51-500]
 y HB Guide - v26 - i1 - Spring 2015 - p128(1) [51-500]
 y RVBW - April 2015 - pNA [51-500]
William, Eli K.P. - *Cash Crash Jubilee*
 PW - v262 - i10 - March 9 2015 - p57(1) [51-500]
Williams, Andria - *The Longest Night*
 y BL - v112 - i4 - Oct 15 2015 - p33(1) [501+]
 KR - Dec 1 2015 - pNA [501+]
Williams, Angela W. - *Hush Now, Baby*
 KR - April 15 2015 - pNA [501+]
Williams, Barbara - *The Hope in Leaving: A Memoir*
 KR - Jan 1 2016 - pNA [501+]
Williams, Beatriz - *Along the Infinite Sea*
 BL - v112 - i2 - Sept 15 2015 - p36(1) [501+]
 KR - Sept 1 2015 - pNA [51-500]
 LJ - v140 - i14 - Sept 1 2015 - p97(1) [51-500]
 PW - v262 - i38 - Sept 21 2015 - p46(1) [501+]
The Secret Life of Violet Grant (Read by McInerney, Kathleen). Audiobook Review
 LJ - v140 - i2 - Feb 1 2015 - p45(2) [51-500]
Tiny Little Thing
 BL - v111 - i17 - May 1 2015 - p79(1) [51-500]
 KR - April 15 2015 - pNA [501+]
Williams, Bernard - *Essays and Reviews 1959-2002*
 Lon R Bks - v37 - i13 - July 2 2015 - p3(2) [501+]
 J Phil - v112 - i5 - May 2015 - p281(1) [501+]
Williams, Billy Dee - *Lady Sings the Blues*
 TimHES - i2202 - May 7 2015 - p49(1) [501+]
Williams, Bonnie - *Pete Can Fly! (Illus. by Gordon, John)*
 c HB Guide - v26 - i1 - Spring 2015 - p55(1) [51-500]
The Scoop on Ice Cream! (Illus. by Burroughs, Scott)
 c HB Guide - v26 - i1 - Spring 2015 - p175(1) [51-500]
Williams, Brenda - *Millie's Chickens (Illus. by Cis, Valeria)*
 c HB Guide - v26 - i2 - Fall 2015 - p56(1) [51-500]
 c KR - Jan 1 2015 - pNA [51-500]
 c SLJ - v61 - i3 - March 2015 - p129(1) [51-500]
Outdoor Opposites (Illus. by Oldfield, Rachel)
 c HB Guide - v26 - i2 - Fall 2015 - p194(1) [51-500]
 c KR - Feb 15 2015 - pNA [51-500]
 c PW - v262 - i14 - April 6 2015 - p58(1) [51-500]
 c SLJ - v61 - i3 - March 2015 - p129(1) [51-500]
Williams, Brendan W. - *Compromised: The Affordable Care Act and Politics of Defeat*
 KR - April 1 2015 - pNA [501+]
Williams, Brian - *Saving the Persecuted*
 c Sch Lib - v63 - i4 - Winter 2015 - p240(1) [51-500]
Williams, Brian Glyn - *Inferno in Chechnya: The Russian-Chechen Wars, the Al Qaeda Myth, and the Boston Marathon Bombings*
 PW - v262 - i33 - August 17 2015 - p63(2) [51-500]
Predators: The CIA's Drone War on al Qaeda
 APJ - v29 - i4 - July-August 2015 - p94(1) [501+]
Williams, Bunny - *On Garden Style*
 NYTBR - Dec 6 2015 - p66(L) [501+]
Williams, C.K. - *Selected Later Poems*
 NYTBR - Dec 27 2015 - p9(L) [501+]

Williams, Carol Lynch - *Never Said (Read by Arsenault, Elise). Audiobook Review*
 y SLJ - v61 - i12 - Dec 2015 - p81(1) [51-500]
Never Said
 y SLJ - v61 - i8 - August 2015 - p111(1) [51-500]
Signed, Skye Harper
 y HB Guide - v26 - i1 - Spring 2015 - p128(1) [51-500]
Williams, Charles - *African American Life and Culture in Orange Mound: Case Study of a Black Community in Memphis, Tennessee, 1890-1980*
 JSH - v81 - i1 - Feb 2015 - p217(2) [501+]
Williams, Charlotte - *Black Valley*
 BL - v111 - i18 - May 15 2015 - p26(1) [51-500]
 KR - April 15 2015 - pNA [51-500]
 PW - v262 - i14 - April 6 2015 - p42(1) [51-500]
Williams, Cindy - *Shirley, I Jest! A Storied Life*
 PW - v262 - i25 - June 22 2015 - p134(2) [51-500]
 LJ - v140 - i9 - May 15 2015 - p85(1) [51-500]
Williams, Conrad - *Dust and Desire*
 KR - Sept 1 2015 - pNA [51-500]
 PW - v262 - i36 - Sept 7 2015 - p47(1) [51-500]
Williams, D.H. - *Transformations in Biblical Literary Traditions: Incarnation, Narrative, and Ethics: Essays in Honor of David Lyle Jeffrey*
 Ch Today - v59 - i10 - Dec 2015 - p70(1) [51-500]
 Med R - August 2015 - pNA [51-500]
Williams, D.L. - *The List of Dead Smiths*
 PW - v262 - i6 - Feb 9 2015 - p48(1) [51-500]
Williams, D. Newell - *The Stone-Campbell Movement: A Global History*
 IBMR - v39 - i2 - April 2015 - p102(1) [501+]
Williams, Daniel K. - *Defenders of the Unborn: The Pro-Life Movement before Roe v. Wade*
 Ch Today - v59 - i10 - Dec 2015 - p67(3) [501+]
 PW - v262 - i45 - Nov 9 2015 - p52(2) [51-500]
Williams, Dave H. - *Small Victories*
 RVBW - April 2015 - pNA [501+]
Williams, David (b. 1959-) - *I Freed Myself: African American Self-Emancipation in the Civil War Era*
 AHR - v120 - i2 - April 2015 - p630-631 [501+]
 HNet - April 2015 - pNA [51-500]
 JSH - v81 - i3 - August 2015 - p736(2) [501+]
Williams, David (b. 1976-) - *Writing Postcommunism: Towards a Literature of the East European Ruins*
 Slav R - v74 - i2 - Summer 2015 - p391-392 [501+]
Williams, David Lay - *Rousseau's Social Contract: An Introduction*
 RM - v69 - i1 - Sept 2015 - p159(2) [501+]
Williams, Diane - *Fine, Fine, Fine, Fine, Fine*
 KR - Nov 15 2015 - pNA [51-500]
 PW - v262 - i44 - Nov 2 2015 - p58(1) [51-500]
Williams, Dinah - *Haunted Prisons*
 c HB Guide - v26 - i1 - Spring 2015 - p133(1) [51-500]
Williams, Donald E., Jr. - *Prudence Crandall's Legacy: The Fight for Equality in the 1830s, Dred Scott, and Brown v. Board of Education*
 NEQ - v88 - i3 - Sept 2015 - p530-532 [501+]
Williams, Doug - *Great Moments in Olympic Basketball*
 c HB Guide - v26 - i1 - Spring 2015 - p182(1) [51-500]
Tiger Woods Makes Masters History
 c HB Guide - v26 - i2 - Fall 2015 - p200(1) [51-500]
Williams, Dwayne D. - *An RTI Guide to Improving the Performance of African American Students*
 Bwatch - Nov 2015 - pNA [501+]
Williams, E. Freya - *Green Giants: How Smart Companies Turn Sustainability into Billion-Dollar Businesses*
 KR - June 1 2015 - pNA [501+]
 PW - v262 - i21 - May 25 2015 - p47(1) [51-500]
Williams, Emily - *The Beginning Violinist: A Companion Book for Children and Adults*
 Am MT - v64 - i6 - June-July 2015 - p70(2) [501+]
The Beginning Violinist: Piano Accompaniment
 Am MT - v64 - i6 - June-July 2015 - p70(2) [501+]
Williams, Emma - *The Story of Hurry (Illus. by Quraishi, Ibrahim)*
 c CH Bwatch - Jan 2015 - pNA [51-500]
 c HB Guide - v26 - i1 - Spring 2015 - p50(1) [51-500]
Williams, Erica Lorraine - *Sex Tourism in Bahia: Ambiguous Entanglements*
 CS - v44 - i5 - Sept 2015 - p733-734 [501+]
 ERS - v38 - i3 - March 2015 - p519(3) [501+]
Williams, Gabrielle - *The Guy, the Girl, the Artist and his Ex*
 y Magpies - v30 - i2 - May 2015 - p44(2) [501+]

Williams-Garcia, Rita - *Bottle Cap Boys Dancing on Royal Street (Illus. by Ward, Damian)*
 c CH Bwatch - August 2015 - pNA [51-500]
 c KR - August 1 2015 - pNA [51-500]
 c SLJ - v61 - i10 - Oct 2015 - p86(1) [51-500]
Gone Crazy in Alabama (Read by Johnson, Sisi A.). Audiobook Review
 c SLJ - v61 - i9 - Sept 2015 - p60(2) [51-500]
Gone Crazy in Alabama
 y BL - v111 - i16 - April 15 2015 - p57(1) [501+]
 c CCB-B - v68 - i9 - May 2015 - p435(2) [501+]
 c HB - v91 - i2 - March-April 2015 - p112(2) [51-500]
 c HB Guide - v26 - i2 - Fall 2015 - p107(2) [501+]
 c KR - Feb 1 2015 - pNA [51-500]
 c PW - v262 - i7 - Feb 16 2015 - p72(32) [51-500]
 c PW - v262 - i49 - Dec 2 2015 - p80(1) [51-500]
 c SLJ - v61 - i3 - March 2015 - p145(1) [51-500]
Williams, Gareth - *A Monstrous Commotion: The Mysteries of Loch Ness*
 Spec - v329 - i9772 - Dec 12 2015 - p77(2) [501+]
Paralysed with Fear: The Story of Polio
 HNet - July 2015 - pNA [501+]
Vikings: Life and Legend
 Med R - March 2015 - pNA(NA) [501+]
 Specu - v90 - i4 - Oct 2015 - p1180-1182 [501+]
Williams, Heather Andrea - *Help Me to Find My People: The African American Search for Family Lost in Slavery*
 HNet - Jan 2015 - pNA [51-500]
Williams, Ian - *The Bad Doctor: The Troubled Life and Times of Dr. Iwan James (Illus. by Williams, Ian)*
 BL - v111 - i19-20 - June 1 2015 - p66(1) [51-500]
 y LJ - v140 - i9 - May 15 2015 - p61(3) [501+]
 NYT - June 30 2015 - pD3(L) [501+]
 PW - v262 - i17 - April 27 2015 - p60(1) [51-500]
Williams, Isobel - *Allies and Italians under Occupation: Sicily and Southern Italy, 1943-45*
 HNet - April 2015 - pNA [501+]
Williams, J.H., III - *The Sandman: Overture*
 PW - v262 - i48 - Nov 30 2015 - p47(1) [51-500]
Williams, James W. - *Policing the Markets: Inside the Black Box of Securities Enforcement*
 CS - v44 - i3 - May 2015 - p430-432 [501+]
Williams, Jeffrey J. - *How to Be an Intellectual: Essays on Criticism, Culture, and the University*
 TimHES - i2187 - Jan 22 2015 - p52-53 [501+]
 TLS - i5851 - May 22 2015 - p12(1) [501+]
Williams, Jenny - *A Stranger in My Own Country: The 1944 Prison Diary*
 TLS - i5859 - July 17 2015 - p27(1) [501+]
Williams, John (1922-1994) - *Augustus*
 TimHES - i2211 - July 9 2015 - p47-48 [501+]
Williams, John D. - *Word Nerd: Dispatches from the Games, Grammar, and Geek Underground*
 BL - v111 - i17 - May 1 2015 - p65(1) [51-500]
 KR - April 1 2015 - pNA [501+]
 LJ - v140 - i8 - May 1 2015 - p79(1) [51-500]
 New R - v246 - i7-8 - July-August 2015 - p80(2) [501+]
 PW - v262 - i11 - March 16 2015 - p74(1) [51-500]
Williams, John H. - *Field Techniques and Tips for Nature Photographers: A Practical Guide for Quality Photo Images*
 KR - Feb 1 2015 - pNA [501+]
Williams, Joy - *The Visiting Privilege: New and Collected Stories*
 NYT - Sept 16 2015 - pC1(L) [501+]
 Bks & Cult - v21 - i5 - Sept-Oct 2015 - p40(2) [501+]
 BL - v112 - i1 - Sept 1 2015 - p44(1) [501+]
 HM - v331 - i1985 - Oct 2015 - p84(5) [501+]
 KR - July 1 2015 - pNA [51-500]
 NYTBR - Sept 27 2015 - p21(L) [501+]
Williams, Justin A. - *The Cambridge Companion to Hip-Hop*
 TLS - i5854 - June 12 2015 - p27(1) [501+]
Williams, Kate - *The Storms of War*
 KR - July 15 2015 - pNA [51-500]
 LJ - v140 - i12 - July 1 2015 - p81(1) [51-500]
Williams, Kate (b. 1974-) - *The Storms of War*
 y BL - v111 - i22 - August 1 2015 - p40(2) [51-500]
Young Elizabeth: The Making of the Queen
 CSM - Nov 17 2015 - pNA [51-500]
 KR - Sept 1 2015 - pNA [51-500]
 LJ - v140 - i17 - Oct 15 2015 - p96(2) [51-500]
 PW - v262 - i34 - August 24 2015 - p73(1) [51-500]
 BL - v112 - i3 - Oct 1 2015 - p13(1) [501+]

Williams, Katrina - *Understanding Autism: The Essential Guide for Parents*
LJ - v140 - i12 - July 1 2015 - p100(2) [51-500]

Williams, Kevin Wayne - *Everything I Know about Zombies, I Learned in Kindergarten*
RVBW - Feb 2015 - pNA [51-500]

Williams, L.C. - *Quite Happy*
KR - Oct 15 2015 - pNA [501+]

Williams, Maggie M. - *Icons of Irishness from the Middle Ages to the Modern World: The New Middle Ages*
Med R - Feb 1 2015 - pNA [51-500]

Williams, Marcia - *Les Miserables (Illus. by Williams, Marcia)*
c Sch Lib - v63 - i1 - Spring 2015 - p45(1) [51-500]
c SLJ - v61 - i2 - Feb 2015 - p87(1) [51-500]
Tales from Shakespeare (Illus. by Williams, Marcia)
c Sch Lib - v63 - i1 - Spring 2015 - p45(1) [51-500]
The Tudors: Kings, Queens, Scribes and Ferrets! (Illus. by Williams, Marcia)
c Magpies - v30 - i5 - Nov 2015 - p22(2) [501+]

Williams, Margery - *The Velveteen Rabbit (Read by Bond, Jilly). Audiobook Review*
c SLJ - v61 - i11 - Nov 2015 - p69(1) [51-500]

Williams, Mason B. - *City of Ambition*
J Urban H - v41 - i5 - Sept 2015 - p943-950 [501+]

Williams, Meg Harris - *Art and Analysis*
TimHES - i2192 - Feb 26 2015 - p47(1) [501+]

Williams, Melanie - *David Lean*
Si & So - v25 - i12 - Dec 2015 - p106(1) [51-500]

Williams, Michael - *The Trains Now Departed: Sixteen Excursions into the Lost Delights of Britain's Railways*
Spec - v328 - i9750 - July 11 2015 - p39(1) [501+]

Williams, Michael (b. 1962-) - *Diamond Boy*
y CCB-B - v68 - i6 - Feb 2015 - p335(1) [51-500]
y HB - v91 - i1 - Jan-Feb 2015 - p92(1) [51-500]
y HB Guide - v26 - i1 - Spring 2015 - p127(1) [51-500]
y Sch Lib - v63 - i2 - Summer 2015 - p122(1) [51-500]
y Teach Lib - v42 - i3 - Feb 2015 - p28(4) [501+]

Williams, Naomi J. - *Landfalls*
BL - v111 - i16 - April 15 2015 - p36(1) [51-500]
KR - June 1 2015 - pNA [501+]
NYT - August 27 2015 - pC4(L) [501+]
NYTBR - August 30 2015 - p10(L) [501+]
PW - v262 - i25 - June 22 2015 - p116(2) [51-500]
Spec - v329 - i9767 - Nov 7 2015 - p47(2) [501+]

Williams, Nathan - *The Kinfolk Home: Interiors for Slow Living*
PW - v262 - i36 - Sept 7 2015 - p63(1) [51-500]

Williams, Nigel - *R.I.P.*
Spec - v328 - i9752 - July 25 2015 - p33(2) [501+]

Williams, Oneeka - *Dr. Dee Dee Dynamo's Saturn Surprise (Illus. by Bouthyette, Valerie)*
c CH Bwatch - April 2015 - pNA [51-500]

Williams, Patricia - *Historical Texts from Medieval Wales*
MLR - v110 - i1 - Jan 2015 - p234-235 [501+]

Williams, Paul - *Mind-Bending Puzzles and Fascinating Facts: A Compendium for All Ages*
Sch Lib - v63 - i2 - Summer 2015 - p124(1) [51-500]
More Mind-Bending Puzzles and Fascinating Facts: A Compendium for All Ages
Sch Lib - v63 - i2 - Summer 2015 - p124(1) [51-500]
Yet More Mind-Bending Puzzles and Fascinating Facts
Sch Lib - v63 - i2 - Summer 2015 - p124(1) [51-500]

Williams, Paul (b. 1979-) - *Race, Ethnicity, and Nuclear War: Representations of Nuclear Weapons and Post-Apocalyptic Worlds*
AL - v87 - i1 - March 2015 - p205-206 [501+]

Williams, Pharrell - *Happy! (Illus. by Smith, Kristin)*
c BL - v112 - i6 - Nov 15 2015 - p58(1) [51-500]
c KR - Oct 1 2015 - pNA [51-500]
c SLJ - v61 - i12 - Dec 2015 - p97(1) [51-500]

Williams, Philip B. - *Thief in the Interior*
PW - v262 - i46 - Nov 16 2015 - p51(2) [51-500]

Williams, Phillip - *Empire and Holy War in the Mediterranean: The Galley and Maritime Conflict between the Habsburgs and Ottomans*
Six Ct J - v46 - i1 - Spring 2015 - p208(210) [501+]
Idolatry, Leadership, and Terrorism
KR - Dec 15 2015 - pNA [51-500]

Williams, Rachel - *Atlas of Adventures: A Collection of Natural Wonders, Exciting Experiences, and Fun Festivities from the Four Corners of the Globe (Illus. by Letherland, Lucy)*
c SLJ - v61 - i12 - Dec 2015 - p140(1) [51-500]

Williams, Raymond - *Keywords: A Vocabulary of Culture and Society*
Nation - v300 - i22 - June 1 2015 - p28(6) [501+]
Politics and Letters: Interviews with New Left Review
NS - v144 - i5252 - March 6 2015 - p42(3) [501+]

Williams, Reba White - *Bloody Royal Prints*
BL - v111 - i21 - July 1 2015 - p35(1) [51-500]
PW - v262 - i21 - May 25 2015 - p39(1) [51-500]

Williams, Ronald - *The Butterflies' Coat*
KR - Feb 1 2015 - pNA [51-500]

Williams, Rosalind - *The Triumph of Human Empire: Verne, Morris, and Stevenson at the End of the World*
JMH - v87 - i2 - June 2015 - p432(3) [501+]
T&C - v56 - i3 - July 2015 - p760-761 [501+]

Williams, Rowan - *The Edge of Words: God and the Habits of Language*
Theol St - v76 - i4 - Dec 2015 - p892(1) [501+]
TLS - i5836 - Feb 6 2015 - p28(1) [501+]
Meeting God in Mark: Reflections for the Season of Lent
CC - v132 - i4 - Feb 18 2015 - p43(1) [51-500]
TLS - i5832 - Jan 9 2015 - p23(1) [501+]
The Other Mountain
NS - v144 - i5246 - Jan 23 2015 - p42(2) [501+]

Williams, Russel - *Not I, Not Other Than I: The Life and Teachings of Russel Williams*
RVBW - Nov 2015 - pNA [501+]

Williams, Sean - *Crashland*
y HB Guide - v26 - i2 - Fall 2015 - p144(1) [51-500]
Hollowgirl
y KR - Sept 1 2015 - pNA [51-500]

Williams, Stephen N. - *The Election of Grace: A Riddle Without a Resolution?*
Bks & Cult - v21 - i5 - Sept-Oct 2015 - p18(2) [501+]

Williams, Steve - *Ace*
KR - July 1 2015 - pNA [51-500]

Williams, Taffy - *Think Agile: How Smart Entrepreneurs Adapt in Order to Succeed*
RVBW - March 2015 - pNA [51-500]

Williams, Tami - *Germaine Dulac: A Cinema of Sensations*
FQ - v68 - i3 - Spring 2015 - p91(3) [501+]

Williams, Terry - *The Con Men: Husling in New York City*
TimHES - i2226 - Oct 22 2015 - p44-45 [501+]
The Con Men: Hustling in New York City
KR - Sept 15 2015 - pNA [51-500]

Williams, Tim L. - *Skull Fragments*
BL - v111 - i11 - Feb 1 2015 - p28(1) [51-500]
PW - v262 - i3 - Jan 19 2015 - p64(1) [51-500]

Williams, Victoria - *Weird Sports and Wacky Games around the World: From Buzkashi to Zorbing*
y BL - v112 - i1 - Sept 1 2015 - p38(1) [51-500]

Williams, Walter - *The Birthday Elephant (Illus. by Williams, Walter)*
c CH Bwatch - August 2015 - pNA [51-500]

Williams, Wendy - *The Horse: The Epic History of Our Noble Companion*
BL - v111 - i21 - July 1 2015 - p12(1) [51-500]
KR - July 1 2015 - pNA [51-500]
NYTBR - Dec 13 2015 - p21(L) [501+]
PW - v262 - i27 - July 6 2015 - p57(1) [51-500]

Williams, Zoe - *Get It Together: Why We Deserve Better Politics*
TLS - i5856 - June 26 2015 - p27(1) [501+]

Williamson, Denise Gagne - *Teaching French through Drama: A Teacher Resource*
Res Links - v20 - i5 - June 2015 - p35(1) [51-500]

Williamson, Fiona - *Social Relations and Urban Space: Norwich, 1600-1700*
Sev Cent N - v73 - i3-4 - Fall-Winter 2015 - p140(4) [501+]

Williamson, Jeffrey G. - *The Cambridge History of Capitalism, 2 vols.*
For Aff - v94 - i3 - May-June 2015 - pNA [501+]
Trade and Poverty: When the Third World Fell Behind
JEH - v75 - i2 - June 2015 - p617-619 [501+]

Williamson, Jennifer A. - *Twentieth-Century Sentimentalism: Narrative Appropriation in American Literature*
AL - v87 - i1 - March 2015 - p207-209 [501+]

Williamson, Jo - *How to Be a Dog (Illus. by Williamson, Jo)*
c KR - May 15 2015 - pNA [51-500]
c Sch Lib - v63 - i4 - Winter 2015 - p224(1) [51-500]
c SLJ - v61 - i8 - August 2015 - p78(1) [51-500]

Williamson, Joshua - *Birthright, vol. 1: Homecoming (Illus. by Bressan, Andrei)*
y LJ - v140 - i9 - May 15 2015 - p61(3) [501+]
Ghosted, vol. 3: Death Wish (Illus. by Sudzuka, Goran)
BL - v111 - i13 - March 1 2015 - p36(1) [51-500]

Williamson, Marianne - *Tears to Triumph*
PW - v262 - i42 - Oct 19 2015 - p39(1) [501+]

Williamson, Michael Z. - *A Long Time until Now*
Bwatch - July 2015 - pNA [51-500]
Analog - v135 - i11 - Nov 2015 - p107(1) [501+]

Williamson, Timothy - *Tetralogue: I'm Right, You're Wrong*
TimHES - i2193 - March 5 2015 - p53(1) [501+]
TLS - i5849 - May 8 2015 - p7(2) [501+]

Willig, Lauren - *The Lure of the Moonflower*
y BL - v111 - i22 - August 1 2015 - p41(1) [51-500]
LJ - v140 - i12 - July 1 2015 - p81(1) [51-500]
The Mark of the Midnight Manzanilla (Read by Reading, Kate). Audiobook Review
BL - v111 - i9-10 - Jan 1 2015 - p114(2) [51-500]
The Other Daughter (Read by Barber, Nicola). Audiobook Review
BL - v112 - i7 - Dec 1 2015 - p69(1) [51-500]
The Other Daughter
y BL - v111 - i19-20 - June 1 2015 - p60(1) [51-500]
LJ - v140 - i11 - June 15 2015 - p83(1) [51-500]

Willingham, Theresa - *Makerspaces in Libraries*
LJ - v140 - i19 - Nov 15 2015 - p97(1) [51-500]
VOYA - v38 - i5 - Dec 2015 - p83(1) [51-500]

Willis, Connie - *The Best of Connie Willis: Award-Winning Stories*
Analog - v135 - i10 - Oct 2015 - p106(2) [51-500]

Willis, Deborah - *Envisioning Emancipation: Black Americans and the End of Slavery*
JSH - v81 - i1 - Feb 2015 - p213(2) [501+]

Willis, Elizabeth - *Alive: New and Selected Poems*
PW - v262 - i11 - March 16 2015 - p60(1) [51-500]

Willis, Emma - *Theatricality, Dark Tourism and Ethical Spectatorship: Absent Others*
Theat J - v67 - i3 - Oct 2015 - p576-578 [501+]

Willis, Gerri - *Rich Is Not a Four-Letter Word: How to Survive Obamacare, Trump Wall Street, Kick-Start Your Retirement, and Achieve Financial Success*
PW - v262 - i51 - Dec 14 2015 - p30(3) [501+]

Willis, Jeanne - *Chicken Clicking (Illus. by Ross, Tony)*
c Magpies - v30 - i4 - Sept 2015 - p30(1) [501+]
The Cow Tripped Over the Moon: A Nursery Rhyme Emergency (Illus. by Stewart, Joel)
c KR - March 15 2015 - pNA [51-500]
c Magpies - v30 - i2 - May 2015 - p28(1) [501+]
SLJ - v61 - i4 - April 2015 - p138(1) [51-500]
The Cow Tripped over the Moon (Illus. by Stewart, Joel)
c CH Bwatch - July 2015 - pNA [51-500]
The First Slodge (Illus. by Desmond, Jenni)
c HB Guide - v26 - i2 - Fall 2015 - p56(1) [51-500]
c PW - v262 - i4 - Jan 26 2015 - p168(1) [51-500]
SLJ - v61 - i4 - April 2015 - p138(1) [51-500]
Ready, Steady, Jump! (Illus. by Reynolds, Adrian)
c Sch Lib - v63 - i3 - Autumn 2015 - p161(1) [51-500]
Slug Needs a Hug! (Illus. by Ross, Tony)
c KR - July 15 2015 - pNA [51-500]
c Sch Lib - v63 - i3 - Autumn 2015 - p161(1) [51-500]
c SLJ - v61 - i9 - Sept 2015 - p132(1) [51-500]
Supercat vs. the Fry Thief (Illus. by Field, Jim)
c CCB-B - v68 - i10 - June 2015 - p525(1) [51-500]
SuperCat vs the Pesky Pirate (Illus. by Field, Jim)
c Sch Lib - v63 - i4 - Winter 2015 - p234(1) [51-500]

Willis, Jim - *1960s Counterculture: Documents Decoded*
LJ - v140 - i16 - Oct 1 2015 - p109(1) [51-500]

Willis, Meredith Sue - *Meli's Way*
y CH Bwatch - Oct 2015 - pNA [51-500]

Willis, Paul E. - *Profane Culture*
CS - v44 - i5 - Sept 2015 - p618-621 [501+]

Willis, Sam - *The Struggle for Sea Power: A Naval History of the American Revolution*
KR - Nov 15 2015 - pNA [51-500]
LJ - v140 - i20 - Dec 1 2015 - p117(1) [51-500]
PW - v262 - i46 - Nov 16 2015 - p66(1) [51-500]

Willis, Susan - *Strip Cultures: Finding America in Las Vegas*
TimHES - i2223 - Oct 1 2015 - p48-49 [501+]

Willliams, Sean - *Hollowgirl*
y BL - v112 - i5 - Nov 1 2015 - p55(1) [51-500]

Willms, Lothar - *Transgression, Tragik und Metatheater: Versuch einer Neuinterpretation des antiken Dramas*
HNet - April 2015 - pNA [501+]

Willoughby, Jennifer - *Beautiful Zero*
PW - v262 - i52 - Dec 21 2015 - p129(1) [51-500]

Willrich, Chris - *The Chart of Tomorrows*
PW - v262 - i16 - April 20 2015 - p58(1) [51-500]
c VOYA - v38 - i3 - August 2015 - p86(1) [51-500]

Wills, Brian Steel - *The River Was Dyed with Blood: Nathan Bedford Forrest and Fort Pillow*
    J Mil H - v79 - i3 - July 2015 - p842-843 [501+]
    JSH - v81 - i3 - August 2015 - p745(2) [501+]
    Roundup M - v22 - i4 - April 2015 - p26(1) [501+]

Wills, Garry - *Font of Life: Ambrose, Augustine, and the Mystery of Baptism*
    Bks & Cult - v21 - i4 - July-August 2015 - p16(1) [501+]
The Future of the Catholic Church with Pope Francis
    AM - v212 - i14 - April 27 2015 - p34(3) [501+]
    BL - v111 - i9-10 - Jan 1 2015 - p20(1) [51-500]
    Comw - v142 - i6 - March 20 2015 - p24(3) [501+]
    LJ - v140 - i2 - Feb 1 2015 - p86(1) [501+]
    PW - v262 - i3 - Jan 19 2015 - p76(1) [51-500]
Making Make-Believe Real: Politics as Theater in Shakespeare's Time
    NYRB - v62 - i5 - March 19 2015 - p41(2) [501+]

Willyerd, Karie - *Stretch: How to Future-Proof Yourself for Tomorrow's Workplace*
    LJ - v140 - i14 - Sept 1 2015 - p116(1) [51-500]

Wilmore, Elaine L. - *Making the Principal TExES Exam Real: Competency-Based Case Studies with Practice Questions*
    Bwatch - Sept 2015 - pNA [501+]

Wilner, Barry - *The Best Auto Racers of All Time*
    c HB Guide - v26 - i2 - Fall 2015 - p197(2) [51-500]
The Best NBA Dunkers of All Time
    c HB Guide - v26 - i1 - Spring 2015 - p183(1) [51-500]
On the Clock: The Story of the NFL Draft
    BL - v111 - i16 - April 15 2015 - p11(1) [51-500]
    PW - v262 - i12 - March 23 2015 - p67(1) [51-500]

Wilsdon, Christina - *Ultimate Bodypedia (Illus. by Turner, Cynthia)*
    c HB Guide - v26 - i1 - Spring 2015 - p171(1) [51-500]

Wilser, Jeff - *The Good News about What's Bad for You ... the Bad News about What's Good for You*
    KR - Sept 15 2015 - pNA [501+]
    PW - v262 - i42 - Oct 19 2015 - p71(2) [51-500]

Wilsey, John O. - *American Exceptionalism and Civil Religion: Reassessing the History of an Idea*
    BL - v112 - i6 - Nov 15 2015 - p11(1) [51-500]

Wilson, A.N. - *The Book of the People: How to Read the Bible*
    NS - v144 - i5261 - May 7 2015 - p50(2) [501+]
    Spec - v328 - i9750 - July 11 2015 - p37(2) [501+]
    TLS - i5857 - July 3 2015 - p22(1) [501+]
Victoria: A Life
    Bks & Cult - v21 - i1 - Jan-Feb 2015 - p11(1) [501+]

Wilson, Adrian - *Ritual and Conflict: The Social Relations of Childbirth in Early Modern England*
    HER - v130 - i542 - Feb 2015 - p190(2) [501+]

Wilson, Andrew - *Alexander McQueen: Blood beneath the Skin*
    NS - v144 - i5251 - Feb 27 2015 - p56(3) [501+]
    NYTBR - Nov 8 2015 - p50(L) [501+]
    PW - v262 - i27 - July 6 2015 - p57(1) [51-500]
    TLS - i5855 - June 19 2015 - p27(1) [501+]

Wilson, Andrew (b. 1967-) - *Alexander McQueen: Blood beneath the Skin*
    BL - v111 - i22 - August 1 2015 - p14(1) [51-500]
    KR - July 15 2015 - pNA [501+]
    NYT - Sept 13 2015 - p2(L) [501+]

Wilson, Anne A. - *Hover (Read by Dawe, Angela). Audiobook Review*
    LJ - v140 - i19 - Nov 15 2015 - p53(2) [501+]
Hover
    BL - v111 - i18 - May 15 2015 - p23(1) [51-500]
    KR - April 1 2015 - pNA [51-500]
    LJ - v140 - i9 - May 15 2015 - p78(1) [51-500]

Wilson, Bee - *First Bite: How We Learn to Eat*
    KR - Sept 15 2015 - pNA [501+]
    NYTBR - Dec 6 2015 - p69(L) [501+]
    PW - v262 - i41 - Oct 12 2015 - p60(1) [51-500]

Wilson, Brian C. - *Dr. John Harvey Kellogg and the Religion of Biologic Living*
    BHR - v89 - i3 - Autumn 2015 - p609(4) [501+]

Wilson, Britt - *Cat Dad, King of the Goblins*
    c Res Links - v20 - i3 - Feb 2015 - p17(2) [51-500]

Wilson, Brittany W. - *Unmanly Men: Refigurations of Masculinity in Luke-Acts*
    CC - v132 - i21 - Oct 14 2015 - p32(2) [501+]

Wilson, Carol O'Keefe - *In the Governor's Shadow: The True Story of Ma and Pa Ferguson*
    JSH - v81 - i2 - May 2015 - p499(2) [501+]
    SHQ - v118 - i3 - Jan 2015 - p330-331 [501+]

Wilson, Carter - *The Comfort of Black*
    BL - v111 - i22 - August 1 2015 - p32(1) [51-500]
    PW - v262 - i25 - June 22 2015 - p122(1) [51-500]
Final Crossing
    LJ - v140 - i14 - Sept 1 2015 - p5(1) [51-500]

Wilson, Charlie - *I Am Charlie Wilson*
    PW - v262 - i17 - April 27 2015 - p62(1) [51-500]

Wilson, Cheryl A. - *Fashioning the Silver Fork Novel*
    VS - v57 - i2 - Wntr 2015 - p312(3) [501+]

Wilson, Christopher R. - *Music in Shakespeare: A Dictionary*
    Ren Q - v68 - i2 - Summer 2015 - p779-781 [501+]

Wilson, Cintra - *Fear and Clothing: Unbuckling American Style*
    BL - v112 - i2 - Sept 15 2015 - p15(1) [501+]
    KR - July 15 2015 - pNA [501+]
    LJ - v140 - i14 - Sept 1 2015 - p100(1) [501+]
    NYTBR - Nov 8 2015 - p50(L) [501+]
    PW - v262 - i28 - July 13 2015 - p57(2) [501+]

Wilson, D. Harlan - *Battle without Honor or Humanity, vol. 1: Discombobulate & Neutralize*
    PW - v262 - i37 - Sept 14 2015 - p47(1) [501+]

Wilson, D.K. - *The Traitor's Mark*
    CSM - Dec 24 2015 - pNA [501+]
    HT - v65 - i11 - Nov 2015 - p56(2) [501+]
    KR - Sept 15 2015 - pNA [501+]
    PW - v262 - i39 - Sept 28 2015 - p64(2) [51-500]

Wilson, Daniel H. - *Popular Mechanics Robots: A New Age of Bionics, Drones and Artificial Intelligence*
    LJ - v140 - i15 - Sept 15 2015 - p103(1) [51-500]
Press Start to Play
    KR - June 15 2015 - pNA [51-500]
    PW - v262 - i24 - June 15 2015 - p68(1) [51-500]
Robogenesis
    y Ent W - i1358 - April 10 2015 - p66(1) [501+]

Wilson, David Henry - *The Night Watchman (Illus. by Fischer, Jeremie)*
    c PW - v262 - i31 - August 3 2015 - p60(1) [51-500]
You Call That Brave? (Illus. by Scharer, Kathrin)
    c CH Bwatch - July 2015 - pNA [51-500]

Wilson, David Sloan - *Does Altruism Exist? Culture, Genes, and the Welfare of Others*
    Hum - v75 - i3 - May-June 2015 - p44(2) [501+]
    Nature - v517 - i7536 - Jan 29 2015 - p550(2) [501+]
    New Sci - v225 - i3006 - Jan 31 2015 - p44(1) [501+]
    NYRB - v62 - i5 - March 19 2015 - p27(3) [501+]

Wilson, Don E. - *Wildlife of the World*
    y BL - v112 - i7 - Dec 1 2015 - p21(1) [501+]
    RVBW - July 2015 - pNA [51-500]

Wilson, Doug - *Don't Mess With These Kids!*
    c Magpies - v30 - i4 - Sept 2015 - pS6(1) [51-500]
Pudge: The Biography of Carlton Fisk
    BL - v112 - i1 - Sept 1 2015 - p36(2) [51-500]
    LJ - v140 - i13 - August 2015 - p104(1) [51-500]
    PW - v262 - i34 - August 24 2015 - p75(2) [51-500]

Wilson, Edward O. - *Half-Earth*
    KR - Jan 1 2016 - pNA [501+]
The Meaning of Human Existence (Read by Hogan, Jonathan). Audiobook Review
    LJ - v140 - i6 - April 1 2015 - p52(1) [501+]
The Meaning of Human Existence
    BioSci - v65 - i3 - March 2015 - p328(2) [501+]
    Hum - v75 - i4 - July-August 2015 - p40(2) [501+]

Wilson, Emily - *The Greatest Empire: A Life of Seneca*
    CC - v132 - i16 - August 5 2015 - p38(3) [501+]
Seneca: A Life
    Lon R Bks - v37 - i12 - June 18 2015 - p33(3) [501+]
    TLS - i5867 - Sept 11 2015 - p12(1) [501+]
    HT - v65 - i5 - May 2015 - p58(1) [501+]
    TimHES - i2201 - April 30 2015 - p52(1) [501+]

Wilson, Eric G. - *Keep It Fake: Inventing an Authentic Life*
    KR - Feb 15 2015 - pNA [501+]
    PW - v262 - i5 - Feb 2 2015 - p45(1) [501+]
    NYTBR - June 21 2015 - p15(L) [501+]

Wilson, G. Willow - *Ms. Marvel: Crushed (Illus. by Bondoc, Elmo)*
    y BL - v112 - i2 - Sept 15 2015 - p51(1) [501+]
    y SLJ - v61 - i10 - Oct 2015 - p119(1) [501+]
Ms. Marvel: Generation Why (Illus. by Wyatt, Jacob)
    y SLJ - v61 - i5 - May 2015 - p128(1) [501+]
Ms. Marvel (Illus. by Alphona, Adrian)
    y VOYA - v38 - i2 - June 2015 - p50(2) [501+]
Ms. Marvel: No Normal (Illus. by Alphona, Adrian)
    y SLJ - v61 - i5 - May 2015 - p126(2) [51-500]

Wilson, Glenis - *Dead Certainty*
    BL - v111 - i17 - May 1 2015 - p28(1) [51-500]
    PW - v262 - i17 - April 27 2015 - p54(1) [51-500]
Dead on Course
    BL - v112 - i4 - Oct 15 2015 - p20(1) [51-500]
    PW - v262 - i42 - Oct 19 2015 - p57(2) [51-500]

Wilson, Hannah - *Astronauts*
    c HB Guide - v26 - i2 - Fall 2015 - p187(1) [51-500]
Sun, Moon, and Stars
    c HB Guide - v26 - i1 - Spring 2015 - p150(1) [51-500]

Wilson, Jacqueline - *The Butterfly Club (Read by Leslay, Madeleine). Audiobook Review*
    c SLJ - v61 - i6 - June 2015 - p62(1) [51-500]
Four Children and It
    c Magpies - v30 - i1 - March 2015 - p14(2) [501+]
Katy
    c Sch Lib - v63 - i4 - Winter 2015 - p234(1) [501+]
Opal Plumstead
    c Sch Lib - v63 - i1 - Spring 2015 - p45(2) [501+]

Wilson, James Graham - *The Triumph of Improvisation: Gorbachev's Adaptability, Reagan's Engagement, and the End of the Cold War*
    AHR - v120 - i1 - Feb 2015 - p289(1) [501+]
    JAH - v101 - i4 - March 2015 - p1350(1) [501+]
    Pres St Q - v45 - i2 - June 2015 - p419(3) [501+]

Wilson, Janet - *Our Heroes: How Kids Are Making a Difference*
    c HB Guide - v26 - i1 - Spring 2015 - p140(1) [51-500]

Wilson, Jarrid - *Jesus Swagger: Break Free From Poser Christianity*
    LJ - v140 - i9 - May 15 2015 - p64(2) [501+]

Wilson, Jean Moorcroft - *Edward Thomas: From Adlestrop to Arras*
    Lon R Bks - v37 - i21 - Nov 5 2015 - p35(2) [501+]
    Spec - v328 - i9743 - May 23 2015 - p40(2) [501+]
    TLS - i5872 - Oct 16 2015 - p21(1) [501+]

Wilson, Jeff - *Mindful America: The Mutual Transformation of Buddhist Meditation and American Culture*
    HNet - March 2015 - pNA [501+]
The Model Railroader's Guide to Grain
    Bwatch - April 2015 - pNA [51-500]

Wilson, John - *Dark Terror*
    c KR - May 1 2015 - pNA [51-500]

Wilson, John F. - *Building Co-operation: A Business History of the Co-operative Group, 1863-2013*
    BHR - v89 - i3 - Autumn 2015 - p598(3) [501+]

Wilson, Jonathan R. - *God's Good World: Reclaiming the Doctrine of Creation*
    BTB - v45 - i2 - May 2015 - p124(2) [501+]

Wilson Jones, Mark - *Origins of Classical Architecture: Architecture Temples, Orders and Gifts to the Gods in Ancient Greece*
    HT - v65 - i2 - Feb 2015 - p64(1) [501+]

Wilson, Joshua C. - *The Street Politics of Abortion: Speech, Violence, and America's Culture Wars*
    HNet - June 2015 - pNA [501+]

Wilson, Kai Ashante - *The Sorcerer of the Wildeeps*
    PW - v262 - i32 - August 10 2015 - p41(1) [51-500]

Wilson, Karen - *Karen Lost and Found: Story of Undiagnosed Brain Injury and Domestic Violence*
    KR - Dec 15 2015 - pNA [51-500]

Wilson, Karma - *Bear Counts (Illus. by Chapman, Jane)*
    c BL - v111 - i17 - May 1 2015 - p100(2) [51-500]
    c HB Guide - v26 - i2 - Fall 2015 - p22(1) [51-500]
    c KR - March 1 2015 - pNA [51-500]
    c Sch Lib - v63 - i4 - Winter 2015 - p224(1) [51-500]
    c SLJ - v61 - i3 - March 2015 - p129(1) [51-500]
Bear Sees Colors (Illus. by Chapman, Jane)
    c HB Guide - v26 - i2 - Fall 2015 - p22(1) [51-500]
Duddle Puck the Puddle Duck (Illus. by Hall, Marcellus)
    c CH Bwatch - Oct 2015 - pNA [51-500]
    c KR - June 15 2015 - pNA [51-500]
    c SLJ - v61 - i9 - Sept 2015 - p132(1) [51-500]

Wilson, Lisa - *A History of Stepfamilies in Early America*
    Bks & Cult - v21 - i3 - May-June 2015 - p29(2) [501+]

Wilson, Malcolm - *Structure and Method in Aristotle's Meteorologica: A More Disorderly Nature*
    Class R - v65 - i2 - Oct 2015 - p383-384 [501+]

Wilson, Marika - *Come Count with Me!*
    c Sch Lib - v63 - i3 - Autumn 2015 - p161(1) [51-500]

Wilson, Mark - *Digger: The Dog Who Went to War*
  y Magpies - v30 - i1 - March 2015 - p32(1) [501+]
The Horse Soldier
  c Magpies - v30 - i2 - May 2015 - p32(1) [501+]
Migaloo: The White Whale
  c Magpies - v30 - i4 - Sept 2015 - p23(1) [501+]
Wilson, Marvin R. - *Exploring Our Hebraic Heritage: A Christian Theology of Roots and Renewal*
    Theol St - v76 - i3 - Sept 2015 - p612(2) [501+]
Wilson, Mary Louise - *My First Hundred Years in Show Business*
    LJ - v140 - i12 - July 1 2015 - p86(3) [51-500]
Wilson, Miranda - *Poison's Dark Works in Renaissance England*
    Ren Q - v68 - i1 - Spring 2015 - p387-389 [501+]
Wilson, N.D. - *Ninja Boy Goes to School (Illus. by Harrison, J.J.)*
  c HB Guide - v26 - i1 - Spring 2015 - p50(1) [51-500]
Wilson, Peter H. - *Heart of Europe*
    KR - Nov 15 2015 - pNA [501+]
Wilson, R. Michael - *Stagecoach Robberies in California: A Complete Record, 1856-1913*
    Roundup M - v22 - i4 - April 2015 - p31(1) [501+]
    Roundup M - v22 - i6 - August 2015 - p41(1) [501+]
Wilson, Rachel M. - *Don't Touch*
  y HB Guide - v26 - i1 - Spring 2015 - p128(1) [51-500]
Wilson, Rainn - *The Bassoon King: My Life in Art, Faith, and Idiocy*
  y BL - v112 - i5 - Nov 1 2015 - p16(1) [51-500]
    KR - Oct 1 2015 - pNA [501+]
    PW - v262 - i41 - Oct 12 2015 - p61(1) [51-500]
Wilson-Rich, Noah - *The Bee: A Natural History*
    Am Bio T - v77 - i5 - May 2015 - p393(1) [501+]
    QRB - v90 - i2 - June 2015 - p233(1) [501+]
Wilson, Richard M.S. - *The Routledge Companion to Accounting Education*
    AR - v90 - i3 - May 2015 - p1250(4) [501+]
Wilson, Robert (b. 1957-) - *You Will Never Find Me*
    BL - v111 - i13 - March 1 2015 - p26(2) [51-500]
    LJ - v140 - i5 - March 15 2015 - p97(1) [501+]
    PW - v262 - i8 - Feb 23 2015 - p52(1) [501+]
Wilson, Robert Charles - *The Affinities*
    BL - v111 - i16 - April 15 2015 - p31(1) [51-500]
    KR - March 1 2015 - pNA [501+]
    PW - v262 - i9 - March 2 2015 - p69(1) [51-500]
Wilson, Robert S. - *SoulServe*
    PW - v262 - i2 - Jan 12 2015 - p41(2) [501+]
Wilson, Sarah Hinlicky - *Woman, Women, and the Priesthood in the Trinitarian Theology of Elisabeth Behr-Sigel*
    Bks & Cult - v21 - i6 - Nov-Dec 2015 - p9(2) [501+]
    Theol St - v76 - i4 - Dec 2015 - p888(1) [501+]
Wilson, Sari - *Girl through Glass*
    BL - v112 - i4 - Oct 15 2015 - p33(1) [51-500]
    LJ - v140 - i20 - Dec 1 2015 - p97(1) [51-500]
    PW - v262 - i45 - Nov 9 2015 - p33(2) [51-500]
Wilson, Sean Michael - *Cold Mountain: The Legend of Han Shan and Shih Te, the Original Dharma Bums (Illus. by Shimojima, Akiko)*
    BL - v111 - i19-20 - June 1 2015 - p66(1) [51-500]
Wilson, Steve - *Hedgehugs (Illus. by Tapper, Lucy)*
  c KR - Oct 1 2015 - pNA [51-500]
  c PW - v262 - i41 - Oct 12 2015 - p66(2) [51-500]
Wilson, Susan - *The Dog Who Saved Me*
    KR - Jan 15 2015 - pNA [501+]
Wilson, Timothy - *Frontiers of Violence: Conflict and Identity in Ulster and Upper Silesia, 1918-1922*
    HNet - June 2015 - pNA [501+]
Wilson, Tony - *The Cow Tripped over the Moon (Illus. by Wood, Laura)*
  c Magpies - v30 - i2 - May 2015 - p28(1) [501+]
Wilson, Troy - *The Duck Says (Illus. by Boldt, Mike)*
  c Res Links - v20 - i5 - June 2015 - p9(1) [51-500]
Les cancans du canard (Illus. by Boldt, Mike)
  c Res Links - v20 - i5 - June 2015 - p45(1) [51-500]
Wilson, William Scott - *Walking the Kiso Road: A Modern-Day Exploration of Old Japan*
    NYTBR - Dec 6 2015 - p46(L) [501+]
    LJ - v140 - i15 - Sept 15 2015 - p95(1) [51-500]
    PW - v262 - i35 - August 31 2015 - p80(1) [51-500]
Wiman, Christian - *Once in the West*
    TLS - i5844 - April 3 2015 - p22(1) [501+]
    WLT - v89 - i3-4 - May-August 2015 - p124(2) [501+]

Wimbush-Bourque, Aimee - *Brown Eggs and Jam Jars: Family Recipes from the Kitchen of Simple Bites*
    LJ - v140 - i3 - Feb 15 2015 - p122(4) [501+]
Wimmer, Andreas - *Ethnic Boundary Making Institutions, Power, Networks*
    AJS - v120 - i4 - Jan 2015 - p1226(4) [501+]
Wimmer, Natasha - *Sudden Death*
    PW - v262 - i44 - Nov 2 2015 - p56(1) [501+]
Winch, Gordon - *The Last ANZAC (Illus. by Bailey, Harriet)*
  c Magpies - v30 - i1 - March 2015 - p27(1) [501+]
Winchell, Mike - *Been There, Done That: Writing Stories from Real Life*
  c PW - v262 - i36 - Sept 7 2015 - p71(1) [51-500]
  c KR - August 1 2015 - pNA [51-500]
  y VOYA - v38 - i5 - Dec 2015 - p78(1) [51-500]
  c BL - v112 - i4 - Oct 15 2015 - p50(1) [51-500]
  c SLJ - v61 - i10 - Oct 2015 - p97(1) [51-500]
Winchester, Simon - *A Crack in the Edge of the World: America ad the Great California Earthquake of 1906*
    TimHES - i2225 - Oct 15 2015 - p43-1 [501+]
Pacific: Silicon Chips and Surfboards, Coral Reefs and Atom Bombs, Brutal Dictators, Fading Empires, and the Coming Collision of the World's Superpowers (Read by Winchester, Simon). Audiobook Review
    NYTBR - Nov 22 2015 - p16(L) [501+]
Pacific: Silicon Chips and Surfboards, Coral Reefs and Atom Bombs, Brutal Dictators, Fading Empires, and the Coming Collision of the World's Superpowers
    BL - v112 - i2 - Sept 15 2015 - p21(2) [51-500]
    KR - August 1 2015 - pNA [501+]
    LJ - v140 - i14 - Sept 1 2015 - p122(1) [51-500]
    Mac - v128 - i44 - Nov 9 2015 - p125(1) [501+]
    PW - v262 - i30 - July 27 2015 - p51(2) [51-500]
The Surgeon of Crowthorne. A tale of murder, madness and the love of Words
    TimHES - i2209 - June 25 2015 - p47(1) [501+]
When the Earth Shakes: Earthquakes, Volcanoes, and Tsunamis
  c CH Bwatch - Sept 2015 - pNA [51-500]
    SLJ - v61 - i11 - Nov 2015 - p138(2) [51-500]
Winders, Jamie - *Nashville in the New Millennium: Immigrant Settlement, Urban Transformation, and Social Belonging*
    AJS - v121 - i1 - July 2015 - p299(3) [501+]
    CS - v44 - i5 - Sept 2015 - p734-736 [501+]
Wine, Mary - *Highland Spitfire*
    PW - v262 - i51 - Dec 14 2015 - p68(1) [51-500]
A Sword for His Lady
    PW - v262 - i18 - May 4 2015 - p103(1) [51-500]
Wineberg, Ronna - *On Bittersweet Place (Read by Lockford, Lesa). Audiobook Review*
    LJ - v140 - i5 - March 15 2015 - p72(1) [51-500]
Winehouse, Janis - *Loving Amy: A Mother's Story*
    KR - Jan 1 2016 - pNA [51-500]
Winfrey-Harris, Tamara L. - *The Sisters Are Alright: Changing the Broken Narrative of Black Women in America*
    LJ - v140 - i10 - June 1 2015 - p126(1) [51-500]
    PW - v262 - i20 - May 18 2015 - p78(1) [51-500]
Winfrey, Oprah - *What I Know for Sure (Read by Winfrey, Oprah). Audiobook Review*
    BL - v111 - i12 - Feb 15 2015 - p104(1) [51-500]
Wing Commander: Freedom Flight
  y SLJ - v61 - i9 - Sept 2015 - p151(4) [51-500]
Wingard-Nelson, Rebecca - *Ready for Math Series*
  c HB - v91 - i1 - Jan-Feb 2015 - p106(2) [501+]
Wingate, Lisa - *The Sea Keeper's Daughters*
    BL - v112 - i2 - Sept 15 2015 - p28(1) [51-500]
    PW - v262 - i25 - June 22 2015 - p127(2) [51-500]
Winget, Dianna Dorisi - *A Million Ways Home*
  c CH Bwatch - April 2015 - pNA [51-500]
  c HB Guide - v26 - i1 - Spring 2015 - p97(1) [51-500]
Wingfield, David - *Running with the Hounds*
    SPBW - Nov 2015 - pNA [51-500]
Wingfield, Emily - *The Trojan Legend in Medieval Scottish Literature*
    PQ - v94 - i1-2 - Wntr-Spring 2015 - p185(5) [501+]
Winick, Judd - *Hilo: The Boy Who Crashed to Earth (Illus. by Winick, Judd)*
  c BL - v112 - i4 - Oct 15 2015 - p37(1) [51-500]
  c KR - July 15 2015 - pNA [51-500]
  c PW - v262 - i27 - July 6 2015 - p75(1) [51-500]
  c SLJ - v61 - i8 - August 2015 - p95(1) [51-500]

Winik, Jay - *1944: FDR and the Year That Changed History*
    KR - August 1 2015 - pNA [501+]
    LJ - v140 - i14 - Sept 1 2015 - p120(2) [51-500]
    Nat R - v67 - i19 - Oct 19 2015 - p52(3) [501+]
    NYTBR - Nov 8 2015 - p39(L) [501+]
    PW - v262 - i34 - August 24 2015 - p74(1) [51-500]
Wink, Callan - *Dog Run Moon*
    KR - Dec 1 2015 - pNA [51-500]
    PW - v262 - i45 - Nov 9 2015 - p32(1) [51-500]
Winklareth, Robert J. - *The Battle of the Denmark Strait: A Critical Analysis of the Bismarck's Singular Triumph*
    NWCR - v68 - i4 - Autumn 2015 - p118(2) [501+]
Winkle, Kenneth J. - *Lincoln's Citadel: The Civil War in Washington, DC*
    Historian - v77 - i2 - Summer 2015 - p365(2) [501+]
    JSH - v81 - i4 - Nov 2015 - p985(2) [501+]
Winkler, Heinrich August - *The Age of Catastrophe: A History of the West 1914-1945*
    KR - Oct 1 2015 - pNA [501+]
    Lon R Bks - v37 - i22 - Nov 19 2015 - p15(3) [501+]
    NS - v144 - i5282 - Oct 2 2015 - p58(4) [501+]
Geschichte des Westens: Die Zeit der Gegenwart
    HNet - March 2015 - pNA [501+]
Geschichte des Westens: Vom Kalten Krieg zum Mauerfall
    HNet - March 2015 - pNA [501+]
Winkler, Henry - *Fake Snakes and Weird Wizards (Illus. by Garrett, Scott)*
  c HB Guide - v26 - i2 - Fall 2015 - p72(1) [51-500]
Winkler, Kathleen - *Are You Being Bullied? How to Deal with Taunting, Teasing, and Tormenting*
  y HB Guide - v26 - i1 - Spring 2015 - p132(1) [51-500]
    VOYA - v38 - i2 - June 2015 - p88(2) [51-500]
Winn, Catherine A. - *Beyond Suspicion*
  y KR - March 1 2015 - pNA [51-500]
Winn, Colette H. - *Teaching French Women Writers of the Renaissance and Reformation*
    FS - v69 - i4 - Oct 2015 - p525-526 [501+]
Winn, Don M. - *The Knighting of Sir Kaye (Illus. by Allred, Dave)*
  c PW - v262 - i13 - March 30 2015 - p76(1) [51-500]
Winn, James Anderson - *Queen Anne: Patroness of Arts*
    Sev Cent N - v73 - i3-4 - Fall-Winter 2015 - p148(3) [501+]
    TLS - i5846 - April 17 2015 - p10(2) [501+]
Winner, Lauren F. - *Wearing God: Clothing, Laughter, Fire, and Other Overlooked Ways of Meeting God*
    Bks & Cult - v21 - i3 - May-June 2015 - p9(2) [501+]
    CC - v132 - i9 - April 29 2015 - p42(2) [501+]
    Ch Today - v59 - i6 - July-August 2015 - p83(3) [501+]
    PW - v262 - i6 - Feb 9 2015 - p61(1) [51-500]
Winnerling, Tobias - *Vernunft und Imperium: Die Societas Jesu in Indien und Japan, 1542-1574*
    HNet - July 2015 - pNA [501+]
Winnette, Colin - *Haints Stay*
    KR - April 1 2015 - pNA [501+]
    PW - v262 - i14 - April 6 2015 - p35(1) [51-500]
Winningham, Geoff - *Of the Soil: Photographs of Vernacular Architecture and Stories of Changing Times in Arkansas*
    JSH - v81 - i2 - May 2015 - p543(2) [501+]
Winroth, Anders - *The Age of the Vikings*
    Med R - June 2015 - pNA [501+]
The Conversion of Scandinavia: Vikings, Merchants and Missionaries in the Remaking of Northern Europe
    HER - v130 - i542 - Feb 2015 - p153(2) [501+]
Winsbury, Rex - *Pliny the Younger: A Life in Roman Letters*
    Class R - v65 - i1 - April 2015 - p147-149 [501+]
Winslow, Don - *The Cartel*
    BL - v111 - i17 - May 1 2015 - p24(1) [501+]
    Esq - v163 - i6-7 - June-July 2015 - p26(2) [501+]
    KR - May 15 2015 - pNA [51-500]
    LJ - v140 - i10 - June 1 2015 - p96(1) [51-500]
    NYT - June 19 2015 - pC21(L) [501+]
    PW - v262 - i17 - April 27 2015 - p47(1) [51-500]
    Nat Post - v17 - i200 - June 27 2015 - pWP4(1) [501+]
Winson, Anthony - *The Industrial Diet: The Degradation of Food and the Struggle for Healthy Eating*
    CS - v44 - i4 - July 2015 - p571-572 [501+]
Winspear, Jacqueline - *The Care and Management of Lies*
    RVBW - Feb 2015 - pNA [51-500]
    RVBW - July 2015 - pNA [51-500]

A Dangerous Place
    BL - v111 - i12 - Feb 15 2015 - p35(2) [51-500]
    KR - Jan 15 2015 - pNA [51-500]
    LJ - v140 - i5 - March 15 2015 - p97(1) [501+]

Winstanley, Nicola - *The Pirate's Bed (Illus. by James, Matt)*
    c Res Links - v20 - i4 - April 2015 - p9(1) [51-500]
    c SLJ - v61 - i5 - May 2015 - p94(1) [51-500]

Winstead, J. Lloyd - *When Colleges Sang: The Story of Singing in American College Life*
    JSH - v81 - i1 - Feb 2015 - p246(2) [501+]

Winston, Sherri - *President of the Whole Sixth Grade*
    c BL - v112 - i1 - Sept 1 2015 - p118(1) [51-500]
    c KR - Sept 1 2015 - pNA [51-500]
    c SLJ - v61 - i7 - July 2015 - p84(1) [51-500]

Winstone, Martin - *The Dark Heart of Hitler's Europe: Nazi Rule in Poland under the General Government*
    HNet - July 2015 - pNA [501+]

Winstone, Ruth - *Events, Dear Boy, Events: A Political Diary of Britain from Woolf to Campbell*
    TimHES - i2209 - June 25 2015 - p46(1) [501+]

Winter, Ariel S. - *The Twenty-Year Death: Malniveau Prison*
    RVBW - Feb 2015 - pNA [501+]
The Twenty-Year Death: Police at the Funeral
    RVBW - Feb 2015 - pNA [501+]
The Twenty-Year Death: The Falling Star
    RVBW - Feb 2015 - pNA [501+]

Winter, Jay - *The First World War, vol. 1: Global War*
    J Mil H - v79 - i1 - Jan 2015 - p239-240 [501+]
    J Mil H - v79 - i4 - Oct 2015 - p1138-1140 [501+]
The First World War, vol. 2: The State
    J Mil H - v79 - i1 - Jan 2015 - p239-240 [501+]
    J Mil H - v79 - i4 - Oct 2015 - p1138-1140 [501+]
The First World War, vol. 3: Civil Society
    J Mil H - v79 - i1 - Jan 2015 - p239-240 [501+]
    J Mil H - v79 - i4 - Oct 2015 - p1138-1140 [501+]

Winter, Jeanette - *Malala, a Brave Girl from Pakistan / Iqbal, a Brave Boy from Pakistan (Illus. by Winter, Jeanette)*
    c HB Guide - v26 - i1 - Spring 2015 - p197(1) [51-500]
    c SLJ - v61 - i12 - Dec 2015 - p64(4) [501+]
Mr. Cornell's Dream Boxes
    c HB Guide - v26 - i1 - Spring 2015 - p180(1) [51-500]
Nanuk the Ice Bear (Illus. by Winter, Jeanette)
    c KR - Nov 15 2015 - pNA [51-500]
    c PW - v262 - i44 - Nov 2 2015 - p83(1) [501+]

Winter, Jerrold - *Optimal Aging*
    KR - March 1 2015 - pNA [501+]

Winter, Jonah - *The Founding Fathers! Those Horse-Ridin', Fiddle-Playin', Book-Readin', Gun-Totin' Gentlemen Who Started America (Illus. by Blitt, Barry)*
    c CCB-B - v68 - i7 - March 2015 - p378(2) [51-500]
    c HB Guide - v26 - i2 - Fall 2015 - p213(1) [51-500]
    c PW - v262 - i49 - Dec 2 2015 - p46(1) [501+]
Hillary (Illus. by Colon, Raul)
    c BL - v112 - i5 - Nov 1 2015 - p38(1) [501+]
    c KR - Nov 15 2015 - pNA [51-500]
    c PW - v262 - i42 - Oct 19 2015 - p78(1) [501+]
    c SLJ - v61 - i12 - Dec 2015 - p140(1) [501+]
How Jelly Roll Morton Invented Jazz (Illus. by Mallett, Keith)
    c CCB-B - v69 - i1 - Sept 2015 - p65(1) [501+]
    c HB Guide - v26 - i2 - Fall 2015 - p194(1) [51-500]
    c BL - v111 - i19-20 - June 1 2015 - p93(1) [51-500]
    c HB - v91 - i3 - May-June 2015 - p134(1) [51-500]
    c KR - March 15 2015 - pNA [51-500]
    c PW - v262 - i17 - April 27 2015 - p74(1) [501+]
    c SLJ - v61 - i3 - March 2015 - p175(1) [51-500]
Joltin' Joe DiMaggio (Illus. by Ransome, James E.)
    c HB Guide - v26 - i1 - Spring 2015 - p185(1) [51-500]
Lillian's Right to Vote: A Celebration of the Voting Rights Act of 1965 (Illus. by Evans, Shane W.)
    c SLJ - v61 - i6 - June 2015 - p138(1) [51-500]
    c BL - v111 - i21 - July 1 2015 - p73(1) [51-500]
    c CCB-B - v69 - i2 - Oct 2015 - p76(1) [501+]
    c HB - v91 - i5 - Sept-Oct 2015 - p89(1) [51-500]
    c KR - May 1 2015 - pNA [51-500]
    c PW - v262 - i49 - Dec 2 2015 - p28(2) [51-500]
You Never Heard of Casey Stengel?! (Illus. by Blitt, Barry)
    c PW - v262 - i51 - Dec 14 2015 - p82(2) [51-500]

Winter, Kathleen - *Boundless: Tracing Land and Dream in a New Northwest Passage*
    BL - v112 - i2 - Sept 15 2015 - p19(1) [51-500]
    KR - August 15 2015 - pNA [51-500]
    NYTBR - Dec 6 2015 - p46(L) [501+]
    TLS - i5847 - April 24 2015 - p24(1) [51-500]
The Freedom in American Songs
    Can Lit - i224 - Spring 2015 - p139 [501+]

Winter, Max - *The Afghanistan War*
    c HB Guide - v26 - i1 - Spring 2015 - p139(1) [51-500]
The Civil Rights Movement
    c HB Guide - v26 - i1 - Spring 2015 - p139(1) [51-500]

Winter, Michael - *Into the Blizzard: Walking the Fields of the Newfoundland Dead*
    Beav - v95 - i2 - April-May 2015 - p56(2) [51-500]

Winter, Stefan - *The Shiites of Lebanon under Ottoman Rule, 1516-1788*
    HNet - Sept 2015 - pNA [501+]

Winterberg, Jenna - *Light and Its Effects*
    c BL - v112 - i2 - Sept 15 2015 - p60(2) [51-500]

Winterbottom, Daniel - *Therapeutic Gardens: Design for Healing Spaces*
    BL - v111 - i18 - May 15 2015 - p9(1) [51-500]
    LJ - v140 - i8 - May 1 2015 - p93(1) [51-500]

Winters, Cat - *The Cure for Dreaming (Read by Ikeda, Jennifer). Audiobook Review*
    SLJ - v61 - i2 - Feb 2015 - p52(1) [51-500]
The Cure for Dreaming
    y HB Guide - v26 - i1 - Spring 2015 - p128(1) [51-500]
    y Sch Lib - v63 - i1 - Spring 2015 - p59(1) [51-500]
The Steep and Thorny Way
    y KR - Dec 15 2015 - pNA [51-500]
The Uninvited
    v BL - v111 - i19-20 - June 1 2015 - p61(1) [51-500]
    KR - June 1 2015 - pNA [51-500]
    LJ - v140 - i11 - June 15 2015 - p83(1) [51-500]
    PW - v262 - i26 - June 29 2015 - p43(1) [51-500]

Winters, Jamie - *Hockey Source Series, 4 vols.*
    c Res Links - v20 - i4 - April 2015 - p18(2) [501+]

Winters, Jeffrey - *Oligarchy*
    CS - v44 - i4 - July 2015 - p449-462 [501+]

Winters, Kari-Lynn - *Bad Pirate (Illus. by Griffiths, Dean)*
    c BL - v112 - i3 - Oct 1 2015 - p81(1) [51-500]
    c KR - July 1 2015 - pNA [51-500]
    c Res Links - v21 - i1 - Oct 2015 - p11(1) [51-500]
    c SLJ - v61 - i7 - July 2015 - p69(1) [51-500]
    c SLJ - v61 - i8 - August 2015 - p78(2) [51-500]
Hungry for Math: Poems to Munch On (Illus. by Collins, Peggy)
    c Res Links - v20 - i5 - June 2015 - p9(1) [51-500]
    c CH Bwatch - April 2015 - pNA [51-500]
    c HB Guide - v26 - i2 - Fall 2015 - p164(1) [51-500]

Winterson, Jeanette - *The Gap of Time: The Winter's Tale Retold*
    KR - August 15 2015 - pNA [501+]
    NS - v144 - i5282 - Oct 2 2015 - p73(1) [501+]
    NYTBR - Oct 25 2015 - p16(L) [501+]
    PW - v262 - i32 - August 10 2015 - p34(1) [51-500]
    Spec - v329 - i9762 - Oct 3 2015 - p45(1) [501+]
    TLS - i5870 - Oct 2 2015 - p20(1) [501+]
Why Be Happy When You Could Be Normal?
    TimHES - i2202 - May 7 2015 - p49(1) [501+]
    TimHES - i2207 - June 11 2015 - p53(1) [501+]

Winterstaar, A.R. - *The Child Revealed*
    KR - Dec 1 2015 - pNA [501+]The winthrop woman.(Spotlight on Historical Fiction)(Brief article)(Audiobook review) - *The Winthrop Woman (Read by James, Corrie). Audiobook Review*
    BL - v111 - i16 - April 15 2015 - p63(1) [51-500]

Wintner, Robert - *Reef Libre: Cuba-The Last, Best Reefs in the World*
    LJ - v140 - i2 - Feb 1 2015 - p105(1) [51-500]

The Wired Bunch Series. E-book Review
    c Teach Lib - v42 - i4 - April 2015 - p49(1) [51-500]

Wirestone, Max - *The Unfortunate Decisions of Dahlia Moss*
    y BL - v112 - i1 - Sept 1 2015 - p50(2) [51-500]
    KR - August 15 2015 - pNA [51-500]
    LJ - v140 - i16 - Oct 1 2015 - p74(1) [51-500]
    PW - v262 - i35 - August 31 2015 - p60(1) [51-500]

Wirten, Eva Hemmungs - *Making Marie Curie: Intellectual Property and Celebrity Culture in an Age of Information*
    RM - v69 - i1 - Sept 2015 - p160(3) [501+]
    TimHES - i2201 - April 30 2015 - p54(1) [501+]

Wirtschafter, Elise Kimerling - *Religion and Enlightenment in Catherinian Russia: The Teachings of Metropolitan Platon*
    Eight-C St - v48 - i2 - Wntr 2015 - p249-251 [501+]
    JMH - v87 - i1 - March 2015 - p238(3) [501+]

Wirtschaftsgeschichte des Ersten Weltkriegs. Okonomische Ordnung und Handeln der Unternehmen
    HNet - June 2015 - pNA [501+]

Wirtz, Kristina - *Performing Afro-Cuba: Image, Voice, Spectacle in the Making of Race and History*
    Lang Soc - v44 - i3 - June 2015 - p451-452 [501+]

Wirtz, Rita M. - *Reading Champs*
    KR - June 15 2015 - pNA [501+]

Wirzba, Norman - *From Nature to Creation: A Christian Vision for Understanding and Loving Our World*
    Ch Today - v59 - i10 - Dec 2015 - p69(1) [501+]
Way of Love
    KR - Jan 1 2016 - pNA [51-500]

Wisch, Barbara - *Acting on Faith: The Confraternity of the Gonfalone in Renaissance Rome*
    CHR - v101 - i2 - Spring 2015 - p365(2) [501+]

Wise, A.C. - *The Ultra Fabulous Glitter Squadron Saves the World Again*
    PW - v262 - i34 - August 24 2015 - p63(1) [51-500]

Wise, Rachel - *Stop the Presses!*
    c HB Guide - v26 - i1 - Spring 2015 - p97(1) [51-500]

Wise, Tim - *Under the Affluence: Shaming the Poor, Praising the Rich and Sacrificing the Future of America*
    KR - August 15 2015 - pNA [51-500]

Wiseman, Blaine - *Battle of the Plains of Abraham*
    c Res Links - v20 - i4 - April 2015 - p21(2) [51-500]
The Great Depression
    c Res Links - v20 - i4 - April 2015 - p21(2) [51-500]

Wiseman, Ellen Marie - *Coal River*
    BL - v112 - i7 - Dec 1 2015 - p33(1) [51-500]
    y VOYA - v38 - i5 - Dec 2015 - p65(1) [51-500]

Wiseman, Susan - *Early Modern Women and the Poem*
    Ren Q - v68 - i2 - Summer 2015 - p797-799 [501+]

Wiseman-Trowse, Nathan - *Nick Drake: Dreaming England*
    PMS - v38 - i2 - May 2015 - p270(4) [501+]

Wisent-Reservat und UNESCO-Welterbe. Referenzen fur den Bia?owie?a-Nationalpark
    HNet - July 2015 - pNA [501+]

Wishart, David - *Trade Secrets*
    PW - v262 - i48 - Nov 30 2015 - p41(1) [51-500]

Wishart, David J. - *The Last Days of the Rainbelt*
    PHR - v84 - i2 - May 2015 - p236(2) [501+]

Wishinsky, Frieda - *Avis Dolphin (Illus. by Dawson, Willow)*
    c CH Bwatch - May 2015 - pNA [51-500]
    y HB - v91 - i4 - July-August 2015 - p150(1) [51-500]
    c Res Links - v20 - i4 - April 2015 - p44(1) [51-500]
    c SLJ - v61 - i6 - June 2015 - p106(1) [51-500]
    c KR - Feb 15 2015 - pNA [51-500]

Wishnia, Kenneth - *Jewish Noir: Contemporary Tales of Crime and Other Dark Deeds*
    BL - v112 - i2 - Sept 15 2015 - p32(1) [51-500]
    PW - v262 - i34 - August 24 2015 - p61(1) [51-500]
    Bwatch - Nov 2015 - pNA [51-500]
    LJ - v140 - i17 - Oct 15 2015 - p84(1) [51-500]
    RVBW - Nov 2015 - pNA [51-500]

Wishon, Mark - *German Forces and the British Army: Interactions and Perceptions, 1742-1815*
    HER - v130 - i542 - Feb 2015 - p123(14) [501+]

Wisnioski, Matthew - *Engineers for Change: Competing Visions of Technology in 1960s America*
    Isis - v106 - i1 - March 2015 - p219(2) [501+]

Wisseman, Sarah - *Burnt Siena*
    KR - May 1 2015 - pNA [51-500]

Wissenschaftliches Netzwerk: Toletum. Netzwerk zur Erforschung der Iberischen Halbinsel in der Antike - Network para la Investigacion sobre la Peninsula Iberica en la Antiguedad. 5. Workshop
    HNet - Feb 2015 - pNA [501+]

Wissenschaftspolitik, Forschungspraxis und Ressourcenmobilisierung im NS-Herrschaftssystem
    HNet - July 2015 - pNA [501+]

Wissinger, Tammera Will - *There Was an Old Lady Who Gobbled a Skink*
    c KR - Dec 1 2015 - pNA [51-500]

Witek, Jo - *Brave as Can Be: A Book of Courage (Illus. by Roussey, Christine)*
    KR - August 1 2015 - pNA [51-500]
    c PW - v262 - i38 - Sept 21 2015 - p72(2) [51-500]
In My Heart: A Book of Feelings (Illus. by Roussey, Christine)
    c CH Bwatch - Feb 2015 - pNA [51-500]
    c HB Guide - v26 - i2 - Fall 2015 - p22(1) [51-500]
    c NYTBR - Feb 8 2015 - p24(L) [501+]

Witemeyer, Karen - *A Worthy Pursuit*
    PW - v262 - i15 - April 13 2015 - p65(1) [51-500]

Witherington, Ben, III - *Paul's Letter to the Philippians: A Socio-Rhetorical Commentary*
    BTB - v45 - i1 - Feb 2015 - p61(2) [501+]

Withers, Pam - *Andreo's Race*
    y KR - Feb 15 2015 - pNA [51-500]
        Res Links - v20 - i4 - April 2015 - p46(1) [51-500]
        SLJ - v61 - i3 - March 2015 - p164(1) [51-500]
    y VOYA - v38 - i2 - June 2015 - p69(1) [51-500]
First Descent
    c Sch Lib - v63 - i1 - Spring 2015 - p59(1) [51-500]

Withy, Katherine - *Heidegger on Being Uncanny*
    RM - v69 - i2 - Dec 2015 - p419(3) [501+]

Witkovsky, Matthew S. - *Sarah Charlesworth: Stills*
    LJ - v140 - i3 - Feb 15 2015 - p106(1) [51-500]

Witt, Lori A. - *The Tide of War*
    PW - v262 - i6 - Feb 9 2015 - p49(1) [51-500]

Witt, Michael - *Jean-Luc Godard, Cinema Historian*
    Nation - v300 - i11 - March 16 2015 - p35(4) [501+]

Witt, Stephen - *How Music Got Free*
    BL - v111 - i19-20 - June 1 2015 - p10(1) [51-500]
    KR - May 1 2015 - pNA [501+]
    NS - v144 - i5265 - June 5 2015 - p46(2) [501+]
How Music Got Free: The End of an Industry, the Turn of the Century, and the Patient Zero of Piracy
    CSM - August 7 2015 - pNA [501+]
    Econ - v415 - i8941 - June 6 2015 - p76(US) [501+]
    LJ - v140 - i9 - May 15 2015 - p85(2) [501+]
    NYT - June 16 2015 - pC1(L) [501+]
    NYTBR - July 26 2015 - p9(L) [501+]
    Spec - v328 - i9746 - June 13 2015 - p39(1) [501+]
How Music Got Free: What Happens When an Entire Generation Commits the Same Crime?
    TLS - i5877 - Nov 20 2015 - p25(1) [501+]

Wittenberg, David - *Time Travel: The Popular Philosophy of Narrative*
    Lon R Bks - v37 - i17 - Sept 10 2015 - p17(6) [501+]

Wittenstein, Vicki Oransky - *Reproductive Rights*
    y KR - Dec 15 2015 - pNA [51-500]

Witter, Bret - *Tuesday Tucks Me In: The Loyal Bond Between a Soldier and His Service Dog*
    c HB Guide - v26 - i1 - Spring 2015 - p169(1) [51-500]

Wittes, Benjamin - *The Future of Violence: Robots and Germs, Hackers and Drones: Confronting a New Age of Threat*
    KR - Jan 15 2015 - pNA [501+]
    LJ - v140 - i2 - Feb 1 2015 - p98(1) [51-500]
    NYRB - v62 - i13 - August 13 2015 - p18(3) [501+]

Witting, Amy - *Isobel on the Way to the Corner Shop*
    KR - Sept 1 2015 - pNA [501+]

Wittkop, Gabrielle - *Exemplary Departures*
    HM - v331 - i1985 - Oct 2015 - p73(3) [501+]
Murder Most Serene
    HM - v331 - i1985 - Oct 2015 - p73(3) [501+]

Wittler, Joan - *No Such Thing as Free Goldfish*
    y KR - Dec 1 2015 - pNA [501+]

Witton, Mark P. - *Pterosaurs: Natural History, Evolution, Anatomy*
    QRB - v90 - i2 - June 2015 - p206(2) [501+]

Wittry, Diane - *Baton Basics: Communicating Music through Gestures*
    Teach Mus - v23 - i1 - August 2015 - p61(1) [51-500]

Witwer, Michael - *Empire of Imagination: Gary Gygax and the Birth of Dungeons & Dragons*
    y BL - v112 - i2 - Sept 15 2015 - p16(1) [51-500]
    KR - June 15 2015 - pNA [501+]
    LJ - v140 - i11 - June 15 2015 - p98(2) [51-500]
    PW - v262 - i32 - August 10 2015 - p53(1) [51-500]
    SEP - v287 - i5 - Sept-Oct 2015 - p24(1) [501+]

Witze, Alexandra - *Island on Fire: The Extraordinary Story of a Forgotten Volcano That Changed the World*
    Bwatch - May 2015 - pNA [51-500]
    NH - v123 - i3 - April 2015 - p46(1) [501+]

Wiviott, Meg - *Benno and the Night of Broken Glass (Read by Berneis, Susie). Audiobook Review*
    c SLJ - v61 - i6 - June 2015 - p62(1) [51-500]
Paper Hearts
    y VOYA - v38 - i4 - Oct 2015 - p64(1) [501+]
    y KR - August 15 2015 - pNA [51-500]
    y SLJ - v61 - i9 - Sept 2015 - p162(2) [51-500]

Wizner, Jake - *Worth Writing About: Exploring Memoir with Adolescents*
    Bwatch - Nov 2015 - pNA [51-500]

Wlehl, Lis - *Lethal Beauty*
    PW - v262 - i4 - Jan 26 2015 - p151(1) [51-500]

Wodarz, Dominik - *Dynamics of Cancer: Mathematical Foundations of Oncology*
    SIAM Rev - v57 - i1 - March 2015 - p161-162 [501+]

Wodianka, Stephanie - *Metzler Lexikon Moderner Mythen: Figuren, Konzepte, Ereignisse*
    HNet - Feb 2015 - pNA [501+]

Wodicka, Tod - *The Household Spirit*
    KR - April 1 2015 - pNA [501+]
    NY - v91 - i26 - Sept 7 2015 - p82 [501+]
    NYT - June 25 2015 - pC4(L) [501+]
    PW - v262 - i15 - April 13 2015 - p55(1) [51-500]

Woelfle, Gretchen - *Mumbet's Declaration of Independence (Read by Berneis, Susie). Audiobook Review*
    c SLJ - v61 - i6 - June 2015 - p63(1) [51-500]

Woeser, Tsering - *Voices from Tibet: Selected Essays and Reportage*
    Pac A - v88 - i2 - June 2015 - p300 [501+]

Wohl, Ellen - *Wide Rivers Crossed: The South Platte and Illinois of the American Prairie*
    PHR - v84 - i2 - May 2015 - p227(5) [501+]

Wohl, Sheri Lewis - *Twisted Whispers*
    PW - v262 - i36 - Sept 7 2015 - p52(1) [51-500]

Wohlleben, Doren - *Enigmatik: Das Ratsel als Hermeneutische Grenzfigur in Mythos, Philosophie und Literatur*
    Ger Q - v88 - i1 - Wntr 2015 - p142(3) [501+]

Wohnoutka, Mike - *Dad's First Day (Illus. by Wohnoutka, Mike)*
    c BL - v111 - i19-20 - June 1 2015 - p112(1) [51-500]
    c KR - June 1 2015 - pNA [51-500]
    c SLJ - v61 - i8 - August 2015 - p61(1) [51-500]
Little Puppy and the Big Green Monster (Illus. by Wohnoutka, Mike)
    HB Guide - v26 - i1 - Spring 2015 - p18(1) [51-500]

Wojtowycz, David - *Elephant Joe, Brave Firefighter! (Illus. by Wojtowycz, David)*
    c HB Guide - v26 - i2 - Fall 2015 - p62(1) [501+]
    KR - March 1 2015 - pNA [501+]
    c SLJ - v61 - i6 - June 2015 - p96(1) [51-500]

Wolbern, Jan Philipp - *Der Haftlingsfreikauf aus der DDR 1962/63-1989: Zwischen Menschenhandel und humanitaren Aktionen*
    HNet - May 2015 - pNA [501+]

Wolever, Ruth Q. - *The Mindful Diet: How to Transform Your Relationship with Food for Lasting Weight Loss and Vibrant Health*
    BL - v111 - i13 - March 1 2015 - p10(1) [51-500]

Wolf, Allen - *Hooked*
    c BL - v112 - i3 - Oct 1 2015 - p32(2) [501+]
    KR - March 15 2015 - pNA [501+]

Wolf, Anne Marie - *Juan de Segovia and the Fight for Peace: Christians and Muslims in the Fifteenth Century*
    AHR - v120 - i4 - Oct 2015 - p1543-1544 [501+]
    CHR - v101 - i4 - Autumn 2015 - p917(3) [501+]
    Med R - June 2015 - pNA [501+]
    Ren Q - v68 - i3 - Fall 2015 - p1057-1059 [501+]
    Six Ct J - v46 - i3 - Fall 2015 - p794-796 [501+]
    Specu - v90 - i4 - Oct 2015 - p1182-1183 [501+]

Wolf, Ben - *Blood for Blood*
    PW - v262 - i12 - March 23 2015 - p56(1) [51-500]

Wolf, Christa - *Moskauer Tagebucher: Wer Wir Sind und Wer Wir Waren*
    Ger Q - v88 - i1 - Wntr 2015 - p130(2) [501+]

Wolf, Dick - *The Ultimatum*
    BL - v111 - i17 - May 1 2015 - p47(1) [51-500]
    KR - April 15 2015 - pNA [51-500]
    PW - v262 - i15 - April 13 2015 - p57(2) [51-500]

Wolf, Fay - *New Order*
    PW - v262 - i42 - Oct 19 2015 - p36(1) [51-500]

Wolf, Gita - *Visit the Bhil Carnival (Illus. by Amaliyar, Subhash)*
    c HB Guide - v26 - i2 - Fall 2015 - p56(1) [51-500]
    c KR - Feb 15 2015 - pNA [51-500]
    c PW - v262 - i8 - Feb 23 2015 - p74(2) [51-500]
    c Sch Lib - v63 - i1 - Spring 2015 - p46(1) [51-500]
    SLJ - v61 - i4 - April 2015 - p138(1) [51-500]

Wolf, Hubert - *The Nuns of Sant'Ambrogio: The True Story of a Convent in Scandal (Read by Boehmer, Paul). Audiobook Review*
    PW - v262 - i21 - May 25 2015 - p56(1) [51-500]
The Nuns of Sant'Ambrogio: The True Story of a Convent in Scandal
    Mac - v128 - i2 - Jan 19 2015 - p56(1) [51-500]
    NYTBR - March 15 2015 - p30(L) [501+]

The Nuns of Sant'Ambrogio: The True Story of a Convent Scandal
    HT - v65 - i8 - August 2015 - p64(2) [501+]

Wolf, Kordula - *"Guerra santa" e conquiste islamiche nel Mediterraneo*
    HNet - Sept 2015 - pNA [501+]

Wolf, Martin - *The Shifts and the Shocks: What We've Learned - and Have Still to Learn - from the Financial Crisis*
    For Aff - v94 - i4 - July-August 2015 - pNA [501+]
    TLS - i5831 - Jan 2 2015 - p9(1) [501+]

Wolf-Meyer, Matthew J. - *The Slumbering Masses: Sleep, Medicine, and Modern American Life*
    CS - v44 - i2 - March 2015 - p280-282 [501+]
    MAQ - v29 - i1 - March 2015 - pB52-B54 [501+]

Wolf, Michaela - *Die vielsprachige Seele Kakaniens: Ubersetzen und Dolmetschen in der Habsburgermonarchie 1848 bis 1918*
    GSR - v38 - i1 - Feb 2015 - p179-181 [501+]

Wolf, Nicholas M. - *An Irish-Speaking Island: State, Religion, Community, and the Linguistic Landscape in Ireland, 1770-1870*
    ILS - v35 - i1 - Fall 2015 - p3(1) [501+]

Wolf, Spencer - *After Mind*
    KR - May 15 2015 - pNA [501+]

Wolf, Susan - *The Variety of Values: Essays on Morality, Meaning, and Love*
    TimHES - i2202 - May 7 2015 - p53(1) [501+]

Wolf, Uwe - *Gottfried August Homilius: Thematisches Verzeichnis der musikalischen Werke*
    Notes - v72 - i2 - Dec 2015 - p380(3) [501+]

Wolfe, Alan - *At Home in Exile: Why Diaspora Is Good for the Jews*
    Comw - v142 - i4 - Feb 20 2015 - p20(3) [501+]

Wolfe, Ethan J. - *The Last Ride*
    Roundup M - v22 - i6 - August 2015 - p33(1) [501+]
The Range War of '82
    BL - v111 - i19-20 - June 1 2015 - p60(1) [51-500]
    KR - July 1 2015 - pNA [51-500]
The Regulator
    BL - v111 - i12 - Feb 15 2015 - p41(1) [51-500]
    Roundup M - v22 - i4 - April 2015 - p34(1) [501+]
    Roundup M - v22 - i6 - August 2015 - p33(1) [501+]

Wolfe, Gene - *A Borrowed Man*
    BL - v112 - i3 - Oct 1 2015 - p36(1) [51-500]
    PW - v262 - i34 - August 24 2015 - p64(1) [51-500]

Wolfe, Jeremy M. - *Sensation & Perception*
    QRB - v90 - i4 - Dec 2015 - p441(2) [501+]

Wolfe, Michele - *The Three Graces*
    KR - Nov 1 2015 - pNA [501+]

Wolfe, Suzanne M. - *The Confessions of X*
    PW - v262 - i52 - Dec 21 2015 - p141(1) [51-500]

Wolfe, Tom - *The Bonfire of the Vanities*
    Nation - v300 - i14 - April 6 2015 - p161(1) [501+]
Radical Chic and Mau Mauing the Flak Catchers
    Nat R - v67 - i21 - Nov 19 2015 - p74(1) [501+]

Wolff, Ariana - *Khan Academy and Salman Khan*
    c SLJ - v61 - i4 - April 2015 - p118(4) [51-500]

Wolff, Isabel - *Shadows over Paradise*
    BL - v111 - i9-10 - Jan 1 2015 - p54(1) [51-500]
    LJ - v140 - i2 - Feb 1 2015 - p78(1) [51-500]

Wolff, Joshua D. - *Western Union and the Creation of the American Corporate Order, 1848-1893*
    RAH - v43 - i2 - June 2015 - p245-248 [501+]

Wolff, Larry - *Paolina's Innocence: Child Abuse in Casanova's Venice*
    Eight-C St - v48 - i2 - Wntr 2015 - p246-248 [501+]

Wolff, Michael - *Television Is the New Television: The Unexpected Triumph of Old Media in the Digital Age*
    Barron's - v95 - i27 - July 6 2015 - p35(1) [501+]
    Mac - v128 - i26-27 - July 6 2015 - p66(1) [501+]
    NYRB - v62 - i15 - Oct 8 2015 - p17(3) [501+]
    NYT - June 26 2015 - pNA(L) [501+]

Wolff, Perry - *Allied Air Power 1942-1945: A Newsreel History of Allied Air Force Operations in World War II*
    APH - v42 - i2 - Summer 2015 - p53(2) [51-500]

Wolff-Poweska, Anna - *Memory as Burden and Liberation: Germans and their Nazi Past (1945-2010).*
    HNet - July 2015 - pNA [501+]

Wolff, Rebecca - *One Morning*
    LJ - v140 - i12 - July 1 2015 - p88(1) [51-500]
    PW - v262 - i33 - August 17 2015 - p49(1) [51-500]

Wolff, Sandra - *Die "Konstanzer Chronik" Gebhart Dachers: "By des Byschoffs zyten Volgiengen disz Nachgeschriben ding vnd Sachen ... ". Codex Sangallensis 646: Edition und Kommentar*
    HNet - Feb 2015 - pNA [501+]

Wolff, Susan - *Quackers Wants to Fly (Illus. by Currie, Justin)*
    c CH Bwatch - Nov 2015 - pNA [51-500]

Wolffe, John - *Protestant-Catholic Conflict from the Reformation to the 21st Century: The Dynamics of Religious Difference*
    HER - v130 - i545 - August 2015 - p1065(3) [501+]

Wolfman, Marv - *Crisis on Infinite Earths*
    LJ - v140 - i9 - May 15 2015 - p110(1) [501+]
    New Teen Titans, vol. 2 (Illus. by Romeo, George Perez)
    y SLJ - v61 - i7 - July 2015 - p100(1) [51-500]

Wolfreys, Julian - *Dickens's London: Perception, Subjectivity and Phenomenal Urban Multiplicity*
    VS - v57 - i2 - Wntr 2015 - p323(3) [501+]

Wolfson, Ron - *The Best Boy in the United States of America: A Memoir of Blessing and Kisses*
    PW - v262 - i27 - July 6 2015 - p67(1) [51-500]

Wolitzer, Meg - *Belzhar*
    y HB Guide - v26 - i1 - Spring 2015 - p128(1) [51-500]
    y Sch Lib - v63 - i1 - Spring 2015 - p59(2) [51-500]

Wolk, Alan - *Over the Top: How the Internet Is (Slowly but Surely) Changing the Television Industry*
    NYRB - v62 - i15 - Oct 8 2015 - p17(3) [501+]

Wolkenhauer, Jan - *Senecas Schrift und der Wandel im Romischen Benefizienwesen*
    HNet - July 2015 - pNA [501+]

Woll, Cornelia - *The Power of Inaction: Bank Bailouts in Comparison*
    AJS - v121 - i1 - July 2015 - p313(3) [501+]
    For Aff - v94 - i3 - May-June 2015 - pNA [501+]

Woll, Kris - *Nelson Mandela: South African President and Civil Rights Activist*
    c BL - v111 - i19-20 - June 1 2015 - p90(1) [51-500]

Wollard, Kathy - *How Come? Every Kid's Science Questions Explained*
    Am Bio T - v77 - i7 - Sept 2015 - p555(1) [501+]

Wollny, Peter - *J.S. Bach's Chamber Music for Violin*
    Notes - v72 - i2 - Dec 2015 - p415(5) [501+]

Wolny, Philip - *Isaac Asimov*
    y Teach Lib - v42 - i4 - April 2015 - p10(1) [51-500]

Wolters, Cleary - *Out of Orange: A Memoir*
    BL - v111 - i17 - May 1 2015 - p63(2) [51-500]
    LJ - v140 - i9 - May 15 2015 - p93(1) [51-500]

Wolterstorff, Nicholas P. - *Journey toward Justice: Personal Encounters in the Global South*
    BTB - v45 - i2 - May 2015 - p126(2) [501+]

Wolverton, Barry - *The Vanishing Island*
    c KR - June 15 2015 - pNA [51-500]
    c PW - v262 - i26 - June 29 2015 - p69(1) [51-500]
    c SLJ - v61 - i9 - Sept 2015 - p147(2) [51-500]

Wolverton, Basil - *Creeping Death from Neptune: The Life and Comics of Basil Wolverton (Illus. by Wolverton, Basil)*
    BL - v111 - i13 - March 1 2015 - p32(1) [51-500]

Womack, Gwendolyn - *The Memory Painter*
    BL - v111 - i13 - March 1 2015 - p24(1) [51-500]
    KR - March 1 2015 - pNA [51-500]
    LJ - v140 - i2 - Feb 1 2015 - p78(1) [51-500]

Womack, Kenneth - *The Beatles Encyclopedia: Everything Fab Four*
    R&USQ - v54 - i3 - Spring 2015 - p59(1) [501+]

Wombacher, Michael - *Good Dog, Happy Baby: Preparing Your Dog for the Arrival of Your Child*
    LJ - v140 - i8 - May 1 2015 - p93(1) [51-500]

Womersley, David - *Gulliver's Travels*
    MLR - v110 - i2 - April 2015 - p528-529 [501+]
    James II: The Last Catholic King
    TLS - i5859 - July 17 2015 - p23(1) [501+]

Won, Brian - *Hooray for Hat!*
    c Sch Lib - v63 - i1 - Spring 2015 - p33(1) [51-500]

Wondriska, William - *Puff*
    c HB Guide - v26 - i2 - Fall 2015 - p56(1) [51-500]

Wong, Andrew - *A Wong: The Cookbook*
    Spec - v329 - i9768 - Nov 14 2015 - p58(1) [501+]

Wong, Bill - *A Year in China: Bill Wong's Diaries in His Father's Home Village 1936-37*
    Can Lit - i224 - Spring 2015 - p148 [501+]

Wong, Cecily - *Diamond Head*
    BL - v111 - i13 - March 1 2015 - p27(1) [51-500]
    KR - Feb 1 2015 - pNA [51-500]
    LJ - v140 - i2 - Feb 1 2015 - p78(1) [51-500]
    PW - v262 - i8 - Feb 23 2015 - p50(1) [51-500]

Wong, David - *Futuristic Violence and Fancy Suits*
    BL - v112 - i1 - Sept 1 2015 - p56(1) [51-500]
    KR - August 1 2015 - pNA [501+]
    NYTBR - Oct 18 2015 - p18(L) [501+]
    PW - v262 - i31 - August 3 2015 - p39(1) [51-500]

Wong, Raymond F.L. - *In Search of Words*
    y KR - Sept 1 2015 - pNA [501+]

Wong, Rita - *Undercurrent*
    Can Lit - i224 - Spring 2015 - p140 [501+]

Wong, Roberto - *Paris D.F.*
    WLT - v89 - i6 - Nov-Dec 2015 - p69(2) [501+]

Wonnell, Donn - *290: A Novel of the American Civil War*
    KR - June 1 2015 - pNA [51-500]

Woo, Sung Ju - *Love Love*
    y BL - v111 - i22 - August 1 2015 - p28(2) [51-500]
    KR - July 1 2015 - pNA [51-500]
    LJ - v140 - i17 - Oct 15 2015 - p83(2) [51-500]
    PW - v262 - i30 - July 27 2015 - p36(1) [51-500]

Wood, Alix - *Art Installations (Illus. by Stevens, Gareth)*
    c BL - v111 - i15 - April 1 2015 - p60(1) [51-500]

Wood, Andy - *The Memory of the People: Custom and Popular Senses of the Past in Early Modern England*
    HER - v130 - i544 - June 2015 - p735(3) [501+]

Wood, Audrey - *The Full Moon at the Napping House (Illus. by Wood, Don)*
    c KR - July 15 2015 - pNA [51-500]
    c NYTBR - Nov 8 2015 - p29(L) [51-500]
    PW - v262 - i27 - July 6 2015 - p72(1) [51-500]
    c SLJ - v61 - i10 - Oct 2015 - p86(1) [51-500]

Wood, Benjamin - *The Ecliptic*
    Spec - v328 - i9755 - August 15 2015 - p32(1) [501+]

Wood, Claire - *Dickens and the Business of Death*
    TimHES - i2205 - May 28 2015 - p49(1) [51-500]

Wood, Darlene R. - *The Trouble with Peer Pressure: A Simple "My ADHD Story" for Young Teens (Illus. by Guiza, Victor)*
    y CH Bwatch - Feb 2015 - pNA [51-500]

Wood, Douglas - *When a Grandpa Says "I Love You" (Illus. by Bell, Jennifer A.)*
    c HB Guide - v26 - i2 - Fall 2015 - p22(1) [51-500]

Wood, Douglas J. - *Presidential Declarations*
    KR - June 1 2015 - pNA [501+]

Wood, Fiona - *Six Impossible Things*
    y BL - v111 - i19-20 - June 1 2015 - p100(2) [51-500]
    y HB - v91 - i5 - Sept-Oct 2015 - p122(1) [51-500]
    y KR - June 15 2015 - pNA [51-500]
    y PW - v262 - i19 - May 11 2015 - p63(1) [51-500]
    y VOYA - v38 - i3 - August 2015 - p72(1) [51-500]
    Wildlife
    y HB Guide - v26 - i1 - Spring 2015 - p128(1) [51-500]
    y Teach Lib - v42 - i3 - Feb 2015 - p28(4) [501+]

Wood, Gillen D'Arcy - *Tambora: The Eruption That Changed the World*
    HNet - May 2015 - pNA [501+]
    Lon R Bks - v37 - i3 - Feb 5 2015 - p27(2) [501+]

Wood, Ian - *The Modern Origins of the Early Middle Ages*
    AHR - v120 - i1 - Feb 2015 - p309-310 [501+]
    HER - v130 - i542 - Feb 2015 - p138(2) [501+]
    HNet - Jan 2015 - pNA [501+]
    HT - v65 - i5 - May 2015 - p56(2) [501+]

Wood, James - *The Fun Stuff and Other Essays*
    HM - v330 - i1977 - Feb 2015 - p84(6) [501+]
    The Nearest Thing to Life
    LJ - v140 - i8 - May 1 2015 - p74(1) [51-500]
    NS - v144 - i5275 - August 14 2015 - p38(3) [501+]
    TLS - i5870 - Oct 2 2015 - p24(1) [501+]
    NYTBR - August 23 2015 - p38(L) [501+]
    PW - v262 - i12 - March 23 2015 - p58(1) [51-500]
    Spec - v327 - i9738 - April 18 2015 - p41(1) [501+]
    TLS - i5854 - June 12 2015 - p11(1) [501+]

Wood, Jason - *Last Words: Considering Contemporary Cinema*
    Si & So - v25 - i6 - June 2015 - p106(1) [501+]
    The Making of a Cultural Landscape: The English Lake District as Tourist Destination, 1750-2010
    HER - v130 - i544 - June 2015 - p791(3) [501+]

Wood, Laura - *Poppy Pym and the Pharaoh's Curse*
    c Sch Lib - v63 - i4 - Winter 2015 - p236(1) [51-500]

Wood, Lesley J. - *Direct Action, Deliberation, and Diffusion: Collective Action After the WTO Protests in Seattle*
    CS - v44 - i2 - March 2015 - p282-284 [501+]

Wood, Levison - *Walking the Nile*
    PW - v262 - i51 - Dec 14 2015 - p72(2) [51-500]
    KR - Nov 1 2015 - pNA [501+]

Wood, Lucy - *Weathering*
    KR - Sept 15 2015 - pNA [501+]
    BL - v111 - i11 - Feb 1 2015 - p25(1) [51-500]

Wood, Luke J. - *Black Males in Postsecondary Education: Examining Their Experiences in Diverse Institutional Contexts*
    JNE - v84 - i1 - Wntr 2015 - p96-98 [501+]

Wood, Martin - *Liberty Style*
    LJ - v140 - i5 - March 15 2015 - p102(3) [501+]

Wood, Michael - *Alfred Hitchcock: The Man Who Knew Too Much*
    Econ - v414 - i8929 - March 14 2015 - p85(US) [501+]
    KR - Jan 15 2015 - pNA [501+]
    LJ - v140 - i3 - Feb 15 2015 - p97(1) [501+]
    Lon R Bks - v37 - i11 - June 4 2015 - p19(4) [501+]
    NS - v144 - i5258 - April 17 2015 - p60(2) [501+]
    NYTBR - May 31 2015 - p34(L) [501+]
    Spec - v327 - i9738 - April 18 2015 - p45(1) [501+]

Wood, Philip - *The Chronicle of Seert: Christian Historical Imagination in Late Antique Iraq*
    AHR - v120 - i4 - Oct 2015 - p1573-1574 [501+]

Wood, Robert E. - *Hegel's Introduction to the System: Encyclopaedia Phenomenology and Psychology*
    RM - v69 - i2 - Dec 2015 - p421(3) [501+]

Wood, Sherri Lynn - *The Improv Handbook for Modern Quilters: A Guide to Creating, Quilting and Living Courageously*
    LJ - v140 - i9 - May 15 2015 - p83(1) [51-500]

Wood, Wally - *The Girl in the Photo*
    SPBW - June 2015 - pNA [51-500]

Wood, William - *Blaise Pascal on Duplicity, Sin, and the Fall: The Secret Instinct*
    JR - v95 - i2 - April 2015 - p269(2) [501+]
    Rel St - v51 - i2 - June 2015 - p271-275 [501+]

Woodacre, Elena - *The Queens Regnant of Navarre: Succession, Politics, and Partnership, 1274-1512*
    HNet - March 2015 - pNA [501+]

Woodall, Brian - *Growing Democracy in Japan: The Parliamentary Cabinet System since 1868*
    Pac A - v88 - i4 - Dec 2015 - p922 [501+]

Woodard, Vincent - *Delectable Negro: Human Consumption and Homoeroticism within US Slave Culture*
    AHR - v120 - i4 - Oct 2015 - p1489-1490 [501+]

Woodbridge, John D. - *Church History, vol. 2: From Pre-Reformation to the Present Day: The Rise and Growth of the Church in Its Cultural, Intellectual, and Political Context*
    Six Ct J - v46 - i2 - Summer 2015 - p484-485 [501+]

Woodcock, Jon - *Coding Games in Scratch*
    c KR - Nov 1 2015 - pNA [51-500]

Woodford, Chris - *Atoms Under the Floorboards: The Surprising Science Hidden in Your Home*
    y BL - v111 - i18 - May 15 2015 - p7(2) [51-500]
    LJ - v140 - i8 - May 1 2015 - p98(1) [51-500]
    c Sci Teach - v82 - i8 - Nov 2015 - p72 [51-500]

Woodhead, Christine - *The Ottoman World*
    HER - v130 - i543 - April 2015 - p453(3) [501+]

Woodier, Olwen - *The Apple Cookbook: 125 Freshly Picked Recipes*
    LJ - v140 - i12 - July 1 2015 - p107(1) [51-500]

Wooding, Chris - *Velocity*
    y Sch Lib - v63 - i4 - Winter 2015 - p251(1) [51-500]

Wooding, Lucy - *The Tudor Discovery of Ireland*
    TimHES - i2224 - Oct 8 2015 - p47(1) [51-500]

Woodley, Frank - *Kizmet and the Case of the Tassie Tiger*
    c Magpies - v30 - i4 - Sept 2015 - p38(1) [501+]

Woodley, Jenny - *Art for Equality: The NAACP's Cultural Campaign for Civil Rights*
    JAH - v101 - i4 - March 2015 - p1303-1304 [501+]
    JSH - v81 - i3 - August 2015 - p759(3) [501+]

Woodman, A.J. - *From Poetry to History. Selected Papers*
    Class R - v65 - i1 - April 2015 - p116-118 [501+]

Woodman, Ned - *Game On*
    c Teach Lib - v42 - i3 - Feb 2015 - p55(1) [51-500]

Woodroof, Martha - *Small Blessings (Read by King, Lorelei). Audiobook Review*
    BL - v111 - i13 - March 1 2015 - p69(1) [51-500]

Woodrow, Allan - *Class Dismissed*
    c BL - v112 - i5 - Nov 1 2015 - p59(1) [51-500]
    c KR - August 1 2015 - pNA [51-500]
    c SLJ - v61 - i10 - Oct 2015 - p97(2) [51-500]

Woods, C.J. - *Travellers' Accounts as Source-Material for Irish Historians*
    ILS - v34 - i2 - Spring 2015 - p11(1) [501+]
Woods, Chris - *Sudden Justice: America's Secret Drone Wars*
    AM - v213 - i14 - Nov 9 2015 - p40(3) [501+]
    KR - March 1 2015 - pNA [501+]
    PW - v262 - i10 - March 9 2015 - p64(2) [51-500]
Woods, Michael E. - *Emotional and Sectional Conflict in the Antebellum United States*
    AHR - v120 - i3 - June 2015 - p1026-1027 [501+]
    JAH - v102 - i2 - Sept 2015 - p563-564 [501+]
    JSH - v81 - i4 - Nov 2015 - p978(2) [501+]
Woods, Rich - *Yahweh to Hell: Why We Need Jesus Out of Politics!*
    RVBW - Nov 2015 - pNA [51-500]
    SPBW - Oct 2015 - pNA [51-500]
Woods, Robert - *Mrs Stone and Dr Smellie: Eighteenth Century Midwives and their Patients*
    HT - v65 - i5 - May 2015 - p60(1) [501+]
Woods, Sarah - *On a Wing and a Prayer: One Woman's Adventure into the Heart of the Rainforest*
    LJ - v140 - i13 - August 1 2015 - p122(1) [51-500]
Woods, Sherryl - *Dogwood Hill*
    BL - v112 - i2 - Sept 15 2015 - p42(2) [501+]
Willow Brook Road
    BL - v112 - i2 - Sept 15 2015 - p48(1) [51-500]
    PW - v262 - i33 - August 17 2015 - p56(2) [51-500]
Woods, Stuart - *Foreign Affairs*
    BL - v112 - i1 - Sept 1 2015 - p46(1) [51-500]
    KR - August 15 2015 - pNA [51-500]
    PW - v262 - i29 - July 20 2015 - p168(1) [51-500]
Hot Pursuit
    BL - v111 - i12 - Feb 15 2015 - p37(2) [51-500]
    KR - Feb 1 2015 - pNA [51-500]
    PW - v262 - i5 - Feb 2 2015 - p36(2) [51-500]
Naked Greed
    BL - v111 - i19-20 - June 1 2015 - p56(1) [51-500]
    KR - June 1 2015 - pNA [51-500]
    PW - v262 - i19 - May 11 2015 - p34(2) [51-500]
Scandalous Behavior
    BL - v112 - i7 - Dec 1 2015 - p31(1) [51-500]
    KR - Nov 1 2015 - pNA [51-500]
    PW - v262 - i45 - Nov 9 2015 - p36(1) [51-500]
Woods, William F. - *The Medieval Filmscape: Reflections of Fear and Desire in a Cinematic Mirror*
    Med R - May 2015 - pNA [501+]
    Specu - v90 - i4 - Oct 2015 - p1183-1185 [501+]
Woodson, Jacqueline - *Brown Girl Dreaming (Read by Woodson, Jacqueline). Audiobook Review*
    c BL - v111 - i9-10 - Jan 1 2015 - p117(1) [51-500]
    c SLJ - v61 - i2 - Feb 2015 - p38(3) [501+]
Brown Girl Dreaming
    c HB Guide - v26 - i1 - Spring 2015 - p197(1) [51-500]
    c BL - v111 - i9-10 - Jan 1 2015 - pS4(8) [501+]
This Is the Rope: A Story from the Great Migration (Read by Waites, Channie). Audiobook Review
    SLJ - v61 - i3 - March 2015 - p77(1) [51-500]
Woodward, Bob - *The Last of the President's Men*
    LJ - v140 - i20 - Dec 1 2015 - p111(1) [51-500]
    NYT - Oct 16 2015 - pC23(L) [501+]
Woodward, David R. - *The American Army and the First World War*
    HNet - March 2015 - pNA [501+]
    J Mil H - v79 - i2 - April 2015 - p515-516 [501+]
    J Mil H - v79 - i4 - Oct 2015 - p1173-1174 [501+]
Woodward, Ella - *Deliciously Ella: 100+ Easy, Healthy, and Delicious Plant-Based, Gluten-Free Recipes*
    NYTBR - May 31 2015 - p24(L) [501+]
    PW - v262 - i9 - March 2 2015 - p78(2) [51-500]
Woodward, Gerard - *Vanishing*
    BL - v111 - i16 - April 15 2015 - p38(1) [51-500]
    KR - March 15 2015 - pNA [501+]
    NYTBR - June 28 2015 - p28(L) [501+]
Woodward, John - *Ocean: A Visual Encyclopedia*
    c SLJ - v61 - i10 - Oct 2015 - p57(1) [51-500]
Shark Wars: Creatures of the Deep Go Head to Head
    c SLJ - v61 - i7 - July 2015 - p105(1) [51-500]
Shark Wars: Creatures of the Deep Go Head-to-Head
    c CH Bwatch - April 2015 - pNA [51-500]
Woodward, Kerry C. - *Pimping the Welfare System: Empowering Participants with Economic, Social, and Cultural Capital*
    CS - v44 - i4 - July 2015 - p572-574 [501+]
Woodworth, Marc - *How to Write about Music: Excerpts from the 33.3 Series, Magazines, Books and Blogs with Advice from Industry-leading Writers*
    TimHES - i2211 - July 9 2015 - p49(1) [501+]

Woodworth, Steven E. - *The Vicksburg Campaign, March 29-May 18, 1863*
    JSH - v81 - i2 - May 2015 - p469(3) [501+]
Woody, Robert H. - *Social Psychology of Musicianship*
    M Ed J - v101 - i3 - March 2015 - p17(1) [501+]
Woog, Adam - *The Baltic States: Then and Now*
    y VOYA - v37 - i6 - Feb 2015 - p89(1) [51-500]
Woolard, Jim R. - *Raiding with Morgan*
    Roundup M - v22 - i6 - August 2015 - p33(1) [501+]
Woolf, Alex - *Children of the Holocaust*
    c HB Guide - v26 - i1 - Spring 2015 - p201(2) [51-500]
Dread Eagle
    c Sch Lib - v63 - i1 - Spring 2015 - p60(1) [51-500]
Meteor: Perspectives on Asteroid Strikes
    y VOYA - v38 - i1 - April 2015 - p89(1) [51-500]
My Life in India
    c Sch Lib - v63 - i3 - Autumn 2015 - p177(1) [51-500]
My Life in Indonesia
    c BL - v111 - i16 - April 15 2015 - p45(2) [51-500]
My Life in Kenya
    c BL - v111 - i16 - April 15 2015 - p45(2) [51-500]
Woolf, Karen McCarthy - *Ten: The New Wave*
    c Sch Lib - v63 - i1 - Spring 2015 - p49(1) [51-500]
Woolf, Oleg - *Bessarabian Stamps*
    WLT - v89 - i6 - Nov-Dec 2015 - p70(2) [501+]
Woolf, Virginia - *Jacob's Room (Read by Stevenson, Juliet). Audiobook Review*
    LJ - v140 - i8 - May 1 2015 - p41(2) [51-500]
On Being Ill
    TimHES - i2218 - August 27 2015 - p43-1 [501+]
Woolford, Andrew - *Colonial Genocide in Indigenous North America*
    WHQ - v46 - i3 - Autumn 2015 - p366-366 [501+]
Woollacott, Alfred, III - *The Immigrant*
    KR - Jan 1 2015 - pNA [501+]
Woollard, Elli - *The Giant of Jum (Illus. by Davies, Benji)*
    c Sch Lib - v63 - i3 - Autumn 2015 - p161(1) [51-500]
Woollett, Laura A. - *Big Top Burning: The True Story of an Arsonist, a Missing Girl, and the Greatest Show on Earth*
    c BL - v111 - i19-20 - June 1 2015 - p72(2) [51-500]
    c CCB-B - v69 - i1 - Sept 2015 - p65(2) [51-500]
    c HB Guide - v26 - i2 - Fall 2015 - p222(1) [51-500]
    c KR - April 15 2015 - pNA [51-500]
    c SLJ - v61 - i6 - June 2015 - p145(1) [51-500]
Woolley, Peter - *Hills and Mountains in Watercolour*
    LJ - v140 - i10 - June 1 2015 - p102(1) [51-500]
Woolpert, Rose Ann - *Big Bill and His Little Mixer Truck*
    c CH Bwatch - March 2015 - pNA [51-500]
Woolsey, Robert J. - *The General's Briefer*
    KR - Jan 1 2016 - pNA [51-500]
Woolston, Blythe - *MARTians*
    y BL - v112 - i1 - Sept 1 2015 - p105(1) [51-500]
    y KR - August 15 2015 - pNA [51-500]
    y PW - v262 - i32 - August 10 2015 - p62(1) [51-500]
    y PW - v262 - i49 - Dec 2 2015 - p110(1) [51-500]
    c SLJ - v61 - i9 - Sept 2015 - p162(2) [51-500]
Wooster, Patricia - *Flickr Cofounder and Web Community Creator Caterina Fake*
    c HB Guide - v26 - i1 - Spring 2015 - p196(2) [51-500]
So, You Want to Work in Fashion? How to Break into the World of Fashion and Design
    c HB Guide - v26 - i2 - Fall 2015 - p152(1) [51-500]
YouTube Founders Steve Chen, Chad Hurley, and Jawed Karim
    c HB Guide - v26 - i1 - Spring 2015 - p196(2) [51-500]
Wootten, William - *The Alvarez Generation: Thom Gunn, Geoffrey Hill, Ted Hughes, Sylvia Plath, and Peter Porter*
    TimHES - i2202 - May 7 2015 - p52-53 [501+]
    TLS - i5875 - Nov 6 2015 - p8(1) [501+]
Wootton, David - *The Invention of Science: A New History of the Scientific Revolution*
    BL - v112 - i6 - Nov 15 2015 - p5(2) [51-500]
    CSM - Dec 9 2015 - pNA [501+]
    KR - Oct 15 2015 - pNA [501+]
    LJ - v140 - i19 - Nov 15 2015 - p101(3) [51-500]
    Nature - v524 - i7566 - August 27 2015 - p412(2) [501+]
    PW - v262 - i42 - Oct 19 2015 - p66(1) [501+]
    TimHES - i2220 - Sept 10 2015 - p44-2 [501+]
The Word Wizard Series
    c CH Bwatch - August 2015 - pNA [51-500]
Work, Henry H. - *Wood, Whiskey and Wine: A History of Barrels*
    TLS - i5845 - April 10 2015 - p29(1) [501+]

Working with Nineteenth-Century Medical and Health Periodicals
    HNet - July 2015 - pNA [501+]
Workman, David L. - *Letter from Alabama: The Inspiring True Story of Strangers Who Saved a Child and Changed a Family Forever*
    SPBW - August 2015 - pNA [51-500]
Workman, Katie - *Dinner Solved! 100 Ingenious Recipes That Make the Whole Family Happy, Including You!*
    LJ - v140 - i12 - July 1 2015 - p107(1) [51-500]
    PW - v262 - i22 - June 1 2015 - p55(1) [51-500]
Workshop Biographie-Forschung
    HNet - March 2015 - pNA [501+]
Workshop Historisch-Biographisches Informationssystem
    HNet - March 2015 - pNA [501+]
Workshop: Public History in Studium und Ausbildung
    HNet - June 2015 - pNA [501+]
World Book - *Enigmas of History, 8 vols.*
    y VOYA - v38 - i4 - Oct 2015 - p85(1) [51-500]
Worrall, Di - *The Personal Accountability Code: The Step-by-Step Guide to a Winning Strategy That Transforms Your Goals into Reality with the New Science of Accountability*
    SPBW - August 2015 - pNA [501+]
Worringer, Renee - *Ottomans Imagining Japan: East, Middle East, and Non-Western Modernity at the Turn of the Twentieth Century*
    AHR - v120 - i2 - April 2015 - p583-584 [501+]
Worsley, Lucy - *The Art of the English Murder: From Jack the Ripper and Sherlock Holmes to Agatha Christie and Alfred Hitchcock (Read by Flosnik, Anne). Audiobook Review*
    LJ - v140 - i7 - April 15 2015 - p49(1) [51-500]
    PW - v262 - i8 - Feb 23 2015 - p72(1) [51-500]
Worster, Donald - *Shrinking the Earth: The Rise and Decline of American Abundance*
    KR - Dec 15 2015 - pNA [501+]
    PW - v262 - i50 - Dec 7 2015 - p78(2) [501+]
Wort, Oliver - *John Bale and Religious Conversion in Reformation England*
    HER - v130 - i542 - Feb 2015 - p179(2) [501+]
Worte - Konzepte - Bedeutungen. Welche Historische Semantik fur das Mittelalter? Abschlusstagung des Leibniz-Projekts "Politische Sprache im Mittelalter. Semantische Zugange"
    HNet - May 2015 - pNA [501+]
Worth, Bonnie - *Once upon a Mastodon: All about Prehistoric Mammals (Illus. by Ruiz, Aristides)*
    c HB Guide - v26 - i2 - Fall 2015 - p168(2) [51-500]
Worth, John E. - *Discovering Florida: First-Contact Narratives from Spanish Expeditions along the Lower Gulf Coast*
    Am St - v54 - i2 - Summer 2015 - p111-112 [501+]
    JSH - v81 - i4 - Nov 2015 - p934(2) [501+]
Wortham, Reavis Z. - *Dark Places*
    KR - July 1 2015 - pNA [51-500]
    PW - v262 - i30 - July 27 2015 - p44(1) [51-500]
Wortham, Simon Morgan - *The Poetics of Sleep: From Aristole to Nancy*
    FS - v69 - i2 - April 2015 - p279(1) [501+]
Worthen, John - *The Life of William Wordsworth: A Critical Biography*
    RES - v66 - i274 - April 2015 - p388-389 [501+]
    TLS - i5875 - Nov 6 2015 - p3(2) [501+]
Worthen, Johnny - *Celeste*
    y SLJ - v61 - i11 - Nov 2015 - p110(1) [51-500]
Worthen, Molly - *Apostles of Reason: The Crisis of Authority in American Evangelicalism*
    CH - v84 - i1 - March 2015 - p276(3) [501+]
    JSH - v81 - i2 - May 2015 - p512(3) [501+]
Worthen, William B. - *Shakespeare Performance Studies*
    Ren Q - v68 - i3 - Fall 2015 - p1145-1147 [501+]
Worthington, I. - *Alexander the Great: A Reader*
    Class R - v65 - i1 - April 2015 - p179-181 [501+]
Worthington, Ian - *By the Spear: Philip II, Alexander the Great, and the Rise and Fall of the Macedonian Empire*
    Bks & Cult - v21 - i2 - March-April 2015 - p27(1) [501+]
    Class R - v65 - i2 - Oct 2015 - p506-508 [501+]
    NYRB - v62 - i4 - March 5 2015 - p40(3) [501+]
Worthington, Michelle - *Noah Chases the Wind (Illus. by Cowman, Joseph)*
    c KR - Feb 15 2015 - pNA [51-500]
Wortman, Richard - *Russian Monarchy: Representation and Rule: Collected Articles*
    Slav R - v74 - i1 - Spring 2015 - p188-189 [501+]
Wortsman, Peter - *Selected Tales of the Brothers Grimm*
    c NYRB - v62 - i12 - July 9 2015 - p65(3) [501+]
Woshinsky, Barbara R. - *Imagining Women's Conventual Spaces in France, 1600-1800: The Cloister Disclosed*
    CHR - v101 - i2 - Spring 2015 - p376(2) [501+]

Wosk, Julie - *My Fair Ladies: Female Robots, Androids, and Other Artificial Eves*
  LJ - v140 - i10 - June 1 2015 - p106(1) [51-500]
Wotton, Roger S. - *Walking with Gosse: Natural History, Creation and Religious Conflicts*
  Isis - v106 - i1 - March 2015 - p194(2) [501+]
Wouk, Herman - *Sailor and Fiddler*
  KR - Dec 15 2015 - pNA [501+]
Wowtscherk, Christoph - *Was wird, wenn die Zeitbombe hochgeht? Eine sozialgeschichtliche Analyse der fremdenfeindlichen Ausschreitungen in Hoyerswerda im September 1991*
  GSR - v38 - i3 - Oct 2015 - p707-708 [501+]
Woycicka, Zofia - *Arrested Mourning: Memory of the Nazi Camps in Poland, 1944-1950*
  AHR - v120 - i2 - April 2015 - p738-739 [501+]
Wray, John - *The Lost Time Accidents*
  KR - Nov 1 2015 - pNA [501+]
  PW - v262 - i44 - Nov 2 2015 - p56(1) [51-500]
Wren, Tegan - *Inconceivable!*
  y VOYA - v38 - i5 - Dec 2015 - p65(2) [51-500]
Wright, Aneurin - *Things to Do in a Retirement Home Trailer Park ... When You're 29 and Unemployed*
  PW - v262 - i45 - Nov 9 2015 - p46(1) [51-500]
Wright, Angus - *The Oresteia*
  TLS - i5856 - June 26 2015 - p17(2) [501+]
Wright, Anna - *A Tower of Giraffes: Animals in Groups (Illus. by Wright, Anna)*
  c PW - v262 - i35 - August 31 2015 - p90(2) [501+]
  c KR - August 15 2015 - pNA [51-500]
  c SLJ - v61 - i9 - Sept 2015 - p185(1) [51-500]
Wright, Ben - *Apocalypse and the Millennium in the American Civil War Era*
  JSH - v81 - i2 - May 2015 - p464(3) [501+]
Wright, C.D. - *The Poet, the Lion, Talking Pictures, El Farolito, a Wedding in St. Roch, the Big Box Store, the Warp in the Mirror, Spring, Midnights, Fire & All*
  PW - v262 - i46 - Nov 16 2015 - p51(1) [51-500]
Wright, Caroline - *Mix + Match Cakes: A Batter, a Syrup, a Frosting = a New Way to Bake*
  PW - v262 - i52 - Dec 21 2015 - p147(1) [51-500]
Wright, Christopher - *The Echo of Things: The Lives of Photographs in the Solomon Islands*
  Pac A - v88 - i2 - June 2015 - p379 [501+]
Wright, Clare - *We Are the Rebels: The Women and Women Who Made Eureka*
  y Magpies - v30 - i5 - Nov 2015 - p23(1) [501+]
Wright, Danielle - *My Village: Rhymes from around the World (Illus. by Moriuchi, Mique)*
  c Sch Lib - v63 - i2 - Summer 2015 - p113(1) [51-500]
Wright, Dawn - *Ocean Solutions, Earth Solutions*
  Bwatch - Oct 2015 - pNA [51-500]
  RVBW - Sept 2015 - pNA [51-500]
Wright, Denis - *Nanotech*
  y Magpies - v30 - i4 - Sept 2015 - pS7(1) [501+]
Wright, Donald P. - *On Point II: Transition to the New Campaign; The United States Army in Operation IRAQI FREEDOM, May 2003-January*
  APJ - v29 - i2 - March-April 2015 - p175(2) [501+]
Wright, Elizabeth R. - *The Battle of Lepanto*
  Six Ct J - v46 - i3 - Fall 2015 - p834-836 [501+]
Wright, Elle - *Forbidden Man*
  PW - v262 - i27 - July 6 2015 - p54(1) [51-500]
Wright, Erica - *The Granite Moth*
  KR - Sept 15 2015 - pNA [501+]
  PW - v262 - i36 - Sept 7 2015 - p46(1) [51-500]
Wright, James F. - *Nutmeg (Illus. by Crofts, Jackie)*
  y SLJ - v61 - i6 - June 2015 - p131(1) [51-500]
Wright, Jennifer - *It Ended Badly: 13 of the Worst Breakups in History*
  BL - v112 - i1 - Sept 1 2015 - p18(1) [51-500]
  LJ - v140 - i16 - Oct 1 2015 - p96(1) [51-500]
  PW - v262 - i22 - June 1 2015 - p56(1) [51-500]
Wright, Johanna - *The Orchestra Pit*
  c HB Guide - v26 - i1 - Spring 2015 - p50(1) [51-500]
Wright, John - *A History of Libya*
  HNet - June 2015 - pNA [501+]
Wright, John C. - *The Architect of Aeons*
  BL - v111 - i15 - April 1 2015 - p33(2) [51-500]
  KR - Feb 15 2015 - pNA [51-500]
  PW - v262 - i9 - March 2 2015 - p68(1) [51-500]
Wright, Kim - *The Canterbury Sisters*
  BL - v111 - i18 - May 15 2015 - p22(1) [51-500]
Wright, Kit - *Ode to Didcot Power Station*
  TLS - i5839 - Feb 27 2015 - p24(1) [51-500]
Wright, Laura - *Bonded*
  PW - v262 - i32 - August 10 2015 - p44(1) [51-500]

Brash
  PW - v262 - i3 - Jan 19 2015 - p68(1) [51-500]
Wright, Lawrence - *Thirteen Days in September: Carter, Begin, and Sadat at Camp David (Read by Bramhall, Mark). Audiobook Review*
  BL - v111 - i16 - April 15 2015 - p62(1) [51-500]
Thirteen Days in September: The Dramatic Story of the Struggle for Peace
  CC - v132 - i12 - June 10 2015 - p36(2) [51-500]
  NYTBR - May 17 2015 - p32(L) [501+]
Wright, Maureen - *Elizabeth Wolstenholme Elmy and the Victorian Feminist Movement: The Biography of an Insurgent Woman*
  HER - v130 - i542 - Feb 2015 - p229(2) [501+]
Go to Sleep, Maddie! (Illus. by Schlossberg, Elisabeth)
  c HB Guide - v26 - i2 - Fall 2015 - p22(1) [51-500]
Wright, N.T. - *Paul and the Faithfulness of God*
  AM - v212 - i1 - Jan 6 2015 - p37 [501+]
Pauline Perspectives: Essays on Paul, 1978-2013
  TLS - i5853 - June 5 2015 - p29(1) [501+]
Wright, Patrick - *On Living in an Old Country*
  TimHES - i2184 - Jan 1 2015 - p63(1) [501+]
Wright, Rebecca Hu-Van - *The Three Billy Goats Gruff/Ttizi Chqqh Chq'i Taa'ii (Illus. by Hu, Ying-Hwa)*
  c CH Bwatch - Oct 2015 - pNA [51-500]
Wright, Richard B. - *A Life with Words: A Writer's Memoir*
  Mac - v128 - i40 - Oct 12 2015 - p56(2) [51-500]
Wright, Robert E. - *Corporation Nation*
  JEH - v75 - i1 - March 2015 - p285-286 [501+]
Wright, Robin M. - *Mysteries of the Jaguar Shamans of the Northwest Amazon*
  Ams - v72 - i1 - Jan 2015 - p164(3) [501+]
Wright, Ronald - *The Gold Eaters*
  BL - v112 - i2 - Sept 15 2015 - p36(2) [51-500]
  KR - Sept 1 2015 - pNA [501+]
  LJ - v140 - i16 - Oct 1 2015 - p74(1) [51-500]
  Mac - v128 - i39 - Oct 5 2015 - p59(1) [51-500]
  NYTBR - Nov 15 2015 - p19(L) [501+]
  PW - v262 - i36 - Sept 7 2015 - p44(1) [51-500]
Wright, Scott - *Student's Essential Studies for Clarinet: A Sequential Collection of 40 Standard Etudes for the Advancing Student*
  Am MT - v64 - i4 - Feb-March 2015 - p65(2) [501+]
Wright, Shelley - *Our Ice Is Vanishing/Sikuvut Nunguliqtuq: A History of Inuit, Newcomers, and Climate Change*
  HNet - Sept 2015 - pNA(NA) [501+]
Wright, Susan Elliot - *The Secrets We Left Behind*
  BL - v111 - i14 - March 15 2015 - p53(2) [51-500]
  LJ - v140 - i10 - June 1 2015 - p90(1) [501+]
Wright, Tom - *Blackbird*
  BL - v111 - i17 - May 1 2015 - p20(1) [51-500]
  Esq - v163 - i6-7 - June-July 2015 - p26(2) [51-500]
  KR - April 15 2015 - pNA [51-500]
  NYTBR - July 5 2015 - p29(L) [501+]
  PW - v262 - i16 - April 20 2015 - p57(1) [51-500]
Surprised by Scripture: Engaging with Contemporary Issues
  TLS - i5834 - Jan 23 2015 - p25(1) [501+]
Wright, Tom F. - *The Cosmopolitan Lyceum: Lecture Culture and the Globe in Nineteenth-Century America*
  J Am St - v49 - i2 - May 2015 - p422-423 [501+]
Wrigley, Annabel - *We Love to Craft: Christmas Fun Stuff for Kids: 17 Handmade Fabric and Paper Projects*
  c PW - v262 - i37 - Sept 14 2015 - p72(2) [51-500]
Wrobel, David M. - *Global West, American Frontier: Travel, Empire, and Exceptionalism from Manifest Destiny to the Great Depression*
  PHR - v84 - i2 - May 2015 - p268(2) [501+]
  WHQ - v46 - i2 - Summer 2015 - p226-227 [501+]
Wrong, Michela - *Borderlines*
  NS - v144 - i5277 - August 28 2015 - p43(1) [51-500]
  Spec - v328 - i9757 - August 29 2015 - p37(2) [501+]
Wu, Ellen D. - *The Color of Success: Asian Americans and the Origins of the Model Minority*
  ERS - v38 - i8 - August 2015 - p1422(2) [501+]
  JAH - v101 - i4 - March 2015 - p1336-1337 [501+]
  PHR - v84 - i4 - Nov 2015 - p551(553) [501+]
  WHQ - v46 - i1 - Spring 2015 - p90-91 [501+]
Wu, Judy Tzu-Chun - *Radicals on the Road: Internationalism, Orientalism, and Feminism during the Vietnam Era*
  PHR - v84 - i1 - Feb 2015 - p110(3) [501+]

Wu, Mike - *Ellie (Illus. by Wu, Mike)*
  c HB Guide - v26 - i2 - Fall 2015 - p57(1) [51-500]
  c KR - March 1 2015 - pNA [501+]
  c Nat Post - v17 - i200 - June 27 2015 - pWP5(1) [501+]
  c PW - v262 - i10 - March 9 2015 - p70(1) [51-500]
  c SLJ - v61 - i5 - May 2015 - p94(1) [51-500]
Wu, Yiching - *The Cultural Revolution at the Margins: Chinese Socialism in Crisis*
  AHR - v120 - i3 - June 2015 - p994(1) [501+]
  HNet - Oct 2015 - pNA [501+]
WuDunn, Sheryl - *A Path Appears: Transforming Lives, Creating Opportunity*
  NYTBR - Oct 4 2015 - p28(L) [501+]
Wujastyk, Dagmar - *Well-Mannered Medicine: Medical Ethics and Etiquette in Classical Ayurveda*
  Isis - v106 - i1 - March 2015 - p158(2) [501+]
Wukovits, John - *Hell from the Heavens*
  KR - Feb 15 2015 - pNA [501+]
Wulf, Andrea - *The Invention of Nature: Alexander von Humboldt's New World*
  LJ - v140 - i19 - Nov 15 2015 - p105(1) [51-500]
  NY - v91 - i33 - Oct 26 2015 - p80 [501+]
  NYRB - v62 - i16 - Oct 22 2015 - p37(3) [501+]
  BL - v112 - i2 - Sept 15 2015 - p7(2) [51-500]
  BL - v112 - i7 - Dec 1 2015 - p13(1) [501+]
  KR - July 15 2015 - pNA [501+]
  Nature - v525 - i7567 - Sept 3 2015 - p31(1) [51-500]
  NYTBR - Sept 27 2015 - p19(L) [501+]
  NYTBR - Dec 13 2015 - p12(L) [501+]
  PW - v262 - i29 - July 20 2015 - p180(1) [51-500]
The Invention of Nature: The Adventures of Alexander von Humboldt, the Lost Hero of Science
  New Sci - v227 - i3037 - Sept 5 2015 - p44(2) [501+]
  TLS - i5876 - Nov 13 2015 - p23(1) [501+]
Wulfinghoff, Donald R. - *Super House: Design Your Dream Home for Super Energy Efficiency, Total Comfort, Dazzling Beauty, Awesome Strength, and Economy*
  PW - v262 - i3 - Jan 19 2015 - p75(1) [51-500]
  SPBW - Oct 2015 - pNA [51-500]
Wunderli, Stephen - *Little Boo (Illus. by Zeltner, Tim)*
  c HB Guide - v26 - i2 - Fall 2015 - p22(1) [51-500]
Wunsch, Carsten - *Handbuch Medienrezeption*
  HNet - July 2015 - pNA [501+]
Wunschmann, Kim - *Before Auschwitz: Jewish Prisoners in the Prewar Concentration Camps*
  JIH - v46 - i3 - Wntr 2016 - p446-448 [501+]
  NYRB - v62 - i12 - July 9 2015 - p52(3) [501+]
  TimHES - i2201 - April 30 2015 - p55(1) [501+]
Wurster, Charles F. - *DDT Wars: Rescuing Our National Bird, Preventing Cancer, and Creating the Environmental Defense Fund*
  PW - v262 - i18 - May 4 2015 - p109(1) [51-500]
Wuthnow, Robert - *Inventing American Religion: Polls, Surveys, and the Tenuous Quest for a Nation's Faith*
  LJ - v140 - i16 - Oct 1 2015 - p64(2) [501+]
  PW - v262 - i32 - August 10 2015 - p56(1) [51-500]
Red State Religion: Faith and Politics in America's Heartland
  Bks & Cult - v21 - i2 - March-April 2015 - p25(3) [501+]
Remaking the Heartland: Middle America since the 1950s
  CS - v44 - i4 - July 2015 - p574-576 [501+]
Rough Country: How Texas Became America's Most Powerful Bible-Belt State
  Bks & Cult - v21 - i2 - March-April 2015 - p25(3) [501+]
  CC - v132 - i1 - Jan 7 2015 - p30(3) [501+]
  CS - v44 - i3 - May 2015 - p325-329 [501+]
  J Ch St - v57 - i2 - Spring 2015 - p390-392 [501+]
  JAH - v102 - i1 - June 2015 - p314-315 [501+]
  JSH - v81 - i4 - Nov 2015 - p974(2) [501+]
Small-Town America: Finding Community, Shaping the Future
  Bks & Cult - v21 - i2 - March-April 2015 - p25(3) [501+]
Wyatt-Brown, Bertram - *A Warring Nation: Honor, Race, and Humiliation in America and Abroad*
  AHR - v120 - i2 - April 2015 - p619(1) [501+]
  JAH - v101 - i4 - March 2015 - p1234(1) [501+]
  JSH - v81 - i4 - Nov 2015 - p1052(2) [501+]
Wyatt, Michael - *The Cambridge Companion to the Italian Renaissance*
  TLS - i5859 - July 17 2015 - p24(1) [501+]
Wyckoff, William - *How to Read the American West: A Field Guide*
  GR - v105 - i2 - April 2015 - p245(4) [501+]

Wyk, Ben-Erik van - *Phytomedicines, Herbal Drugs, and Poisons*
    New Sci - v227 - i3031 - July 25 2015 - p42(1) [501+]

Wyld, Evie - *All the Birds, Singing*
    NYTBR - Feb 22 2015 - p32(L) [501+]

Wyle, Dirk - *Yucatan Is Murder*
    KR - August 15 2015 - pNA [51-500]

Wylie, Philip - *Very Late Diagnosis of Asperger Syndrome, Autism Spectrum Disorder: How Seeking a Diagnosis in Adulthood Can Change Your Life*
    Bwatch - July 2015 - pNA [51-500]

Wyma, Kay Wills - *I'm Happy for You (Sort of ... Not Really): Finding Contentment in a Culture of Comparison (Read by Brunjes, Tracy). Audiobook Review*
    LJ - v140 - i16 - Oct 1 2015 - p45(1) [51-500]

Wynd, Viktor - *Viktor Wynd's Cabinet of Wonders*
    TLS - i5836 - Feb 6 2015 - p27(1) [501+]

Wynn, Patricia - *Acts of Faith*
    KR - Jan 15 2015 - pNA [501+]

Wynn, Phillip - *Augustine on War and Military Service*
    CHR - v101 - i3 - Summer 2015 - p603(2) [501+]

Wynn, Thomas - *How to Think Like a Neandertal*
    QRB - v90 - i2 - June 2015 - p221(1) [501+]

Wynn, Todd - *The Trespasser*
    KR - June 1 2015 - pNA [501+]

Wynn, Tom - *Representing Violence in France 1760-1820*
    FS - v69 - i3 - July 2015 - p397-398 [501+]

Wynne, Anthony - *Murder of a Lady*
    KR - Dec 15 2015 - pNA [51-500]
    PW - v262 - i48 - Nov 30 2015 - p42(1) [51-500]

Wynne, Ben - *In Tune: Charley Patton, Jimmie Rodgers, and the Roots of American Music*
    JSH - v81 - i4 - Nov 2015 - p1015(2) [501+]

Wynne, Dawn - *The Miracle Mitzvah Moose (Illus. by Pineiro, Gloria)*
    c CH Bwatch - Nov 2015 - pNA [51-500]

Wynne-Jones, Tim - *The Emperor of Any Place*
    y BL - v112 - i2 - Sept 15 2015 - p63(2) [51-500]
    y HB - v91 - i6 - Nov-Dec 2015 - p94(1) [51-500]
    c KR - Sept 1 2015 - pNA [51-500]
    y PW - v262 - i29 - July 20 2015 - p194(1) [51-500]
    y PW - v262 - i49 - Dec 2 2015 - p114(2) [51-500]
    y SLJ - v61 - i10 - Oct 2015 - p118(1) [51-500]
    y Teach Lib - v43 - i1 - Oct 2015 - p23(1) [51-500]
    c VOYA - v38 - i3 - August 2015 - p86(1) [501+]

Wyrick, Jason - *Vegan Tacos*
    Veg J - v34 - i2 - April-June 2015 - p31(1) [51-500]

Wyss, Marco - *Peacekeeping in Africa: The Evolving Security Architecture*
    HNet - June 2015 - pNA [501+]

X Y Z

Xhama, Bardhyl - *Djali me tre brire*
    Bkbird - v53 - i1 - Wntr 2015 - p75(1) [501+]
Xi, Jinping - *The Governance of China*
    NYRB - v62 - i13 - August 13 2015 - p32(3) [501+]
Xiang, Biao - *Return: Nationalizing Transnational Mobility in Asia*
    Pac A - v88 - i2 - June 2015 - p259 [501+]
Xiao, Hui Faye - *Family Revolution: Marital Strife in Contemporary Chinese Literature and Visual Culture*
    HNet - August 2015 - pNA [501+]
    JAS - v74 - i2 - May 2015 - p485-486 [501+]
Xiao, Liu - *Contemporary Jewelry Design: Thoughts on Inspiration and Expression*
    Am Craft - v75 - i5 - Oct-Nov 2015 - p24(1) [501+]
Xiaolong, Qiu - *Shanghai Redemption*
    BL - v111 - i22 - August 1 2015 - p37(1) [501+]
Xinjiang, Rong - *Eighteen Lectures on Dunhuang*
    JAS - v74 - i1 - Feb 2015 - p217-218 [501+]
Xinran - *Buy Me the Sky: The Remarkable Truth of China's One-Child Generations*
    Spec - v328 - i9746 - June 13 2015 - p36(2) [501+]
Xiong, Ge - *A World without Boundaries*
    RVBW - August 2015 - pNA [501+]
Xu, Xiaoqun - *Cosmopolitanism, Nationalism, and Individualism in Modern China: The Chenbao Fukan and the New Culture Era, 1918-1928*
    AHR - v120 - i4 - Oct 2015 - p1462-1464 [501+]
Xue, Can - *The Last Lover*
    TLS - i5834 - Jan 23 2015 - p20(1) [501+]
Yaccarino, Dan - *Billy and Goat at the State Fair (Read by Heyborne, Kirby). Audiobook Review*
    c SLJ - v61 - i10 - Oct 2015 - p50(1) [51-500]
Billy and Goat at the State Fair (Illus. by Yaccarino, Dan)
    c BL - v111 - i21 - July 1 2015 - p61(1) [51-500]
    c HB Guide - v26 - i2 - Fall 2015 - p57(1) [51-500]
    c KR - April 15 2015 - pNA [51-500]
        PW - v262 - i15 - April 13 2015 - p77(1) [51-500]
    c SLJ - v61 - i6 - June 2015 - p95(1) [51-500]
Doug Unplugs on the Farm
    c HB Guide - v26 - i1 - Spring 2015 - p50(1) [51-500]
Zorgoochi Intergalactic Pizza: Delivery of Doom
    c HB Guide - v26 - i2 - Fall 2015 - p107(1) [51-500]
Yack, Bernard - *Nationalism and the Moral Psychology of Community*
    CS - v44 - i3 - May 2015 - p432-434 [501+]
Yacovissi, Jennifer Bort - *Up the Hill to Home*
    BL - v111 - i16 - April 15 2015 - p38(1) [51-500]
Yacowitz, Caryn - *I Know an Old Lady Who Swallowed a Dreidel (Illus. by Slonim, David)*
    c HB Guide - v26 - i1 - Spring 2015 - p50(1) [51-500]
Yaeko, Nogami - *The Labyrinth*
    TLS - i5832 - Jan 9 2015 - p18(1) [501+]
Yafa, Stephen. - *Grain of Truth: The Real Case For and Against Wheat and Gluten*
    LJ - v140 - i7 - April 15 2015 - p114(1) [51-500]
Yafa, Stephen - *Grain of Truth: The Real Case for and against Wheat and Gluten*
    PW - v262 - i12 - March 23 2015 - p62(2) [51-500]
Yafasova, Dina - *Don't Call Me a Victim!*
    WLT - v89 - i2 - March-April 2015 - p79(1) [501+]
Yager, Robert E. - *Exemplary STEM Programs: Designs for Success*
    Sci & Ch - v52 - i5 - Jan 2015 - p82 [501+]
    Sci Teach - v82 - i1 - Jan 2015 - p66 [51-500]

Yagoda, Ben - *The B-Side*
    Reason - v47 - i4 - August-Sept 2015 - p68(1) [51-500]
The B Side: The Death of Tin Pan Alley and the Rebirth of the Great American Song
    Ent W - i1350 - Feb 13 2015 - p61(1) [501+]
    NY - v91 - i3 - March 9 2015 - p95 [51-500]
    NYTBR - Feb 15 2015 - p11(L) [501+]
Yahgulanaas, Michael Nicoll - *Red: A Haida Manga*
    Bwatch - June 2015 - pNA [51-500]
Yakich, Mark - *Poetry: A Survivor's Guide*
    PW - v262 - i38 - Sept 21 2015 - p66(1) [51-500]
Yakimov, Radka - *Cafe "The Blue Danube"*
    KR - Feb 1 2015 - pNA [501+]
Dreams and Shadows
    KR - May 15 2015 - pNA [501+]
Yallop, Jacqueline - *Dreamstreets: A Journey through Britain's Village Utopias*
    TLS - i5867 - Sept 11 2015 - p27(1) [501+]
Yalom, Irvin D. - *Creatures of a Day: And Other Tales of Psychotherapy*
    TimHES - i2197 - April 2 2015 - p54(1) [501+]
Yalom, Marilyn - *The Social Sex: A History of Female Friendship*
    y BL - v112 - i1 - Sept 1 2015 - p20(1) [51-500]
        LJ - v140 - i10 - June 1 2015 - p117(1) [51-500]
        NYTBR - Sept 20 2015 - p11(L) [501+]
        PW - v262 - i24 - June 15 2015 - p73(1) [51-500]
Yamada, Koun - *Zen: The Authentic Gate*
    PW - v262 - i19 - May 11 2015 - p53(1) [51-500]
Yamagishi, Takakazu - *War and Health Insurance Policy in Japan and the United States: World War II to Postwar Reconstruction*
    JAS - v74 - i3 - August 2015 - p758-759 [501+]
Yamane, David - *Becoming Catholic: Finding Rome in the American Religious Landscape*
    AJS - v120 - i6 - May 2015 - p1884(3) [501+]
Yambert, Karl - *The Contemporary Middle East: A Westview Reader*
    JTWS - v32 - i1 - Spring 2015 - p341(3) [501+]
Yamkdag, Yucel - *Healing the Nation: Prisoners of War, Medicine and Nationalism in Turkey, 1914-1939*
    Historian - v77 - i3 - Fall 2015 - p629(2) [501+]
Yan, Kin Sheung Chiaretto - *Evangelization in China: Challenges and Prospects*
    CC - v132 - i21 - Oct 14 2015 - p33(2) [501+]
    IBMR - v39 - i2 - April 2015 - p100(2) [501+]
    Theol St - v76 - i2 - June 2015 - p386(1) [501+]
Yan, Lianke - *The Four Books*
    TLS - i5862 - August 7 2015 - p20(1) [501+]
Yanagihara, Hanya - *A Little Life*
    BL - v111 - i12 - Feb 15 2015 - p32(1) [51-500]
    Econ - v416 - i8951 - August 15 2015 - p74(US) [501+]
    Ent W - i1355-1356 - March 20 2015 - p102(1) [501+]
    KR - Jan 1 2015 - pNA [51-500]
    Lon R Bks - v37 - i18 - Sept 24 2015 - p32(2) [501+]
    NS - v144 - i5283 - Oct 9 2015 - p50(2) [501+]
    NW - v164 - i15 - April 17 2015 - pNA [501+]
    NY - v91 - i14 - May 25 2015 - p73 [51-500]
    NYRB - v62 - i19 - Dec 3 2015 - p18(3) [501+]
    NYT - Oct 1 2015 - pC1(L) [501+]
    NYTBR - April 5 2015 - p9(L) [501+]
    Spec - v328 - i9755 - August 15 2015 - p36(1) [501+]
    TLS - i5854 - June 12 2015 - p10(1) [501+]
    TLS - i5859 - July 17 2015 - p20(1) [501+]
Yanai, Itai - *The Society of Genes*
    PW - v262 - i42 - Oct 19 2015 - p65(1) [51-500]

Yancey, Rick - *The Infinite Sea (Read by Strole, Phoebe, with Ben Yannette). Audiobook Review*
    SLJ - v61 - i3 - March 2015 - p81(1) [51-500]
The Infinite Sea
    y HB Guide - v26 - i1 - Spring 2015 - p128(1) [51-500]
Yanez, Anthony - *A Wild Ride on the Water Cycle (Illus. by Guillory, Mike)*
    c CH Bwatch - Feb 2015 - pNA [51-500]
Yang, Belle - *Hurry Home, Hedgehog! (Illus. by Yang, Belle)*
    c KR - July 1 2015 - pNA [51-500]
Yang, Gene Luen - *Secret Coders (Illus. by Holmes, Mike)*
    c KR - June 1 2015 - pNA [51-500]
    c SLJ - v61 - i9 - Sept 2015 - p150(1) [51-500]
    c HB - v91 - i6 - Nov-Dec 2015 - p94(2) [51-500]
    c PW - v262 - i24 - June 15 2015 - p87(1) [51-500]
    c BL - v111 - i22 - August 1 2015 - p49(1) [51-500]
The Shadow Hero
    y HB Guide - v26 - i1 - Spring 2015 - p128(1) [51-500]
Yang, Huilin - *China, Christianity, and the Question of Culture*
    IBMR - v39 - i2 - April 2015 - p104(2) [501+]
Yang, J. Michael - *Spectrum of Mind: An Inquiry into the Principles of the Mind and the Meaning of Life*
    KR - August 15 2015 - pNA [501+]
Yang, Ziheng - *Molecular Evolution: A Statistical Approach*
    QRB - v90 - i1 - March 2015 - p89(2) [501+]
Yankelevich, Matvei - *Today I Wrote Nothing: The Selected Writings of Daniil Kharms*
    NYRB - v62 - i8 - May 7 2015 - p36(3) [501+]
Yankey, Lindsey - *Sun and Moon (Illus. by Yankey, Lindsey)*
    c BL - v111 - i19-20 - June 1 2015 - p125(1) [51-500]
    c KR - April 15 2015 - pNA [51-500]
    c SLJ - v61 - i6 - June 2015 - p95(1) [51-500]
Yano, Christine R. - *Pink Globalization: Hello Kitty's Trek Across the Pacific*
    JRAI - v21 - i1 - March 2015 - p228(2) [501+]
    Pac A - v88 - i1 - March 2015 - p207 [501+]
Yansky, Brian - *Utopia, Iowa*
    y CCB-B - v68 - i6 - Feb 2015 - p335(2) [51-500]
    y HB Guide - v26 - i2 - Fall 2015 - p144(1) [51-500]
    y VOYA - v37 - i6 - Feb 2015 - p85(2) [51-500]
Yao, Stephen G. - *Foreign Accents: Chinese American Verse from Exclusion to Postethnicity*
    AL - v87 - i3 - Sept 2015 - p627-629 [501+]
Yap, Dalton - *A Matter of Conduct: The True Story of a Man Who Battled a Bank and Won*
    KR - June 15 2015 - pNA [501+]
Yapa, Sunil - *Your Heart Is a Muscle the Size of a Fist*
    BL - v111 - i5 - Nov 1 2015 - p29(1) [51-500]
    KR - Nov 1 2015 - pNA [501+]
    LJ - v140 - i17 - Oct 15 2015 - p84(1) [51-500]
    PW - v262 - i41 - Oct 12 2015 - p44(1) [51-500]
Yaqub, Aladdin M. - *Al-Ghazali's Moderation in Belief*
    Med R - Sept 2015 - pNA [501+]
Yarbough, Oliver Larry - *Passion: Contemporary Writers on the Story of Calvary*
    Bwatch - June 2015 - pNA [501+]
Yarbrough, Oliver Larry - *Engaging the Passion: Perspectives on the Death of Jesus*
    CC - v132 - i21 - Oct 14 2015 - p32(2) [501+]
Yardi, Robin - *The Midnight War of Mateo Martinez*
    c KR - Dec 15 2015 - pNA [51-500]
They Just Know (Illus. by Klein, Laurie Allen)
    c KR - July 15 2015 - pNA [51-500]

Yarlett, Emma - *Orion and the Dark (Illus. by Yarlett, Emma)*
   c HB Guide - v26 - i2 - Fall 2015 - p57(1) [51-500]
   c KR - Feb 15 2015 - pNA [51-500]
   c SLJ - v61 - i9 - Sept 2015 - p132(1) [51-500]

Yarrow, Andrew L. - *Thrift: The History of an American Cultural Movement*
   NYTBR - March 22 2015 - p16(L) [501+]

Yarrow, Kit - *Decoding the New Consumer Mind: How and Why We Shop and Buy*
   Har Bus R - v93 - i4 - April 2015 - p110(2) [501+]

Yasuda, Anita - *Astronomy: Cool Women in Space (Illus. by Chandhok, Lena)*
   c BL - v111 - i22 - August 1 2015 - p54(1) [51-500]
Explore Norse Myths! With 25 Great Projects (Illus. by Stone, Bryan)
   BL - v112 - i7 - Dec 1 2015 - p40(2) [51-500]
   c PW - v262 - i33 - August 17 2015 - p74(1) [501+]
Gibbons
   c BL - v112 - i6 - Nov 15 2015 - p42(1) [51-500]
Native Nations of the Northwest Coast
   c CH Bwatch - Oct 2015 - pNA [51-500]
Native Nations of the Plains
   c CH Bwatch - Oct 2015 - pNA [51-500]
Stephen Harper
   c Res Links - v20 - i3 - Feb 2015 - p24(2) [51-500]
What's Great about Mississippi?
   c HB Guide - v26 - i2 - Fall 2015 - p220(1) [51-500]

Yasutomo, Dennis T. - *Japan's Civil-Military Diplomacy: The Banks of the Rubicon*
   Pac A - v88 - i4 - Dec 2015 - p917 [501+]

Yates, Alexander - *The Winter Place*
   y BL - v112 - i3 - Oct 1 2015 - p76(2) [51-500]
   y KR - August 15 2015 - pNA [51-500]
   y SLJ - v61 - i9 - Sept 2015 - p173(2) [51-500]
   y VOYA - v38 - i5 - Dec 2015 - p76(1) [51-500]

Yates, Bill - *Dreams Rewritten*
   SPBW - July 2015 - pNA [51-500]

Yates, Christopher J. - *Black Chalk*
   BL - v111 - i22 - August 1 2015 - p31(1) [51-500]
   KR - June 15 2015 - pNA [51-500]

Yates, David - *Hope for Winter: The True Story of a Remarkable Dolphin Friendship*
   c CH Bwatch - March 2015 - pNA [51-500]
   c HB Guide - v26 - i1 - Spring 2015 - p167(1) [51-500]

Yates, Maisy - *Bad News Cowboy*
   PW - v262 - i26 - June 29 2015 - p52(1) [51-500]

Yates, Marie - *Reggie & Me*
   RVBW - Oct 2015 - pNA [51-500]

Yatzek, Richard - *Russia in Private*
   CSM - Jan 20 2015 - pNA [51-500]

Yavuz, M. Hakan - *War and Nationalism: The Balkan Wars, 1912-1913, and Their Sociopolitical Implications*
   HNet - April 2015 - pNA [501+]

Yavuz, R. Isil - *The Outsider Entrepreneurs*
   AJS - v120 - i4 - Jan 2015 - p1245(3) [501+]

Yawein, Oleg - *The Hermitage XXI: The New Art Museum in the General Staff Building*
   LJ - v140 - i8 - May 1 2015 - p69(2) [51-500]

Yazbek, Samar - *The Crossing: My Journey to the Shattered Heart of Syria*
   Econ - v416 - i8946 - July 11 2015 - p73(US) [501+]
   TLS - i5869 - Sept 25 2015 - p7(2) [501+]

Yearwood, Trisha - *Trisha's Table: My Feel-Good Favorites for a Balanced Life*
   PW - v262 - i9 - March 2 2015 - p79(1) [51-500]

Yeatts, Tabatha - *Wiesel, Wiesenthal, Klarsfeld: The Holocaust Survivors*
   y HB Guide - v26 - i1 - Spring 2015 - p201(1) [51-500]

Yeazell, Ruth Bernard - *Picture Titles: How and Why Western Paintings Acquired Their Names*
   TimHES - i2224 - Oct 8 2015 - p44-45 [501+]

Yee, Kristina - *Miss Todd and Her Wonderful Flying Machine (Illus. by Yee, Kristina)*
   c SLJ - v61 - i11 - Nov 2015 - p133(1) [51-500]

Yee, Lisa - *The Kidney Hypothetical, or, How to Ruin Your Life in Seven Days (Read by de Ocampo, Ramon). Audiobook Review*
   y BL - v112 - i5 - Nov 1 2015 - p72(1) [51-500]
   y SLJ - v61 - i9 - Sept 2015 - p62(1) [51-500]
The Kidney Hypothetical, or, How to Ruin Your Life in Seven Days
   y BL - v111 - i12 - Feb 15 2015 - p82(1) [51-500]
   y CCB-B - v68 - i8 - April 2015 - p423(2) [51-500]
   y HB - v91 - i3 - May-June 2015 - p123(1) [501+]
   y HB Guide - v26 - i2 - Fall 2015 - p144(1) [51-500]
   y KR - Jan 1 2015 - pNA [51-500]
   y PW - v262 - i4 - Jan 26 2015 - p172(1) [51-500]
   y Teach Lib - v42 - i4 - April 2015 - p28(1) [51-500]
   y VOYA - v37 - i6 - Feb 2015 - p70(2) [51-500]

Yee, Lydia - *Magnificent Obsessions: The Artist as Collector*
   LJ - v140 - i11 - June 15 2015 - p85(1) [51-500]

Yee, Paul - *Chinese Fairy Tale Feasts: A Literary Cookbook (Illus. by Wang, Shaoli)*
   c HB Guide - v26 - i2 - Fall 2015 - p160(1) [51-500]
      PW - v262 - i4 - Jan 26 2015 - p171(1) [501+]
   c Res Links - v20 - i3 - Feb 2015 - p25(1) [51-500]
A Superior Man
   LJ - v140 - i17 - Oct 15 2015 - p84(1) [51-500]

Yee, Shirley J. - *An Immigrant Neighborhood: Interethnic and Interracial Encounters in New York before 1930*
   HNet - June 2015 - pNA [501+]

Yee, Wong Herbert - *My Autumn Book (Illus. by Yee, Wong Herbert)*
   c HB - v91 - i5 - Sept-Oct 2015 - p89(2) [51-500]
   c KR - June 15 2015 - pNA [51-500]
   c PW - v262 - i31 - August 3 2015 - p56(1) [51-500]
   c SLJ - v61 - i6 - June 2015 - p95(2) [51-500]

Yeh, Emily T. - *Mapping Shangrila: Contested Landscapes in the Sino-Tibetan Borderlands*
   GR - v105 - i3 - July 2015 - p388(3) [501+]
Taming Tibet: Landscape Transformation and the Gift of Chinese Development
   Pac A - v88 - i1 - March 2015 - p192 [501+]

Yeh, Kat - *The Truth about Twinkie Pie*
   c BL - v111 - i9-10 - Jan 1 2015 - p104(1) [51-500]
   c HB Guide - v26 - i2 - Fall 2015 - p107(1) [51-500]
   y VOYA - v37 - i6 - Feb 2015 - p71(1) [51-500]

Yeh, Wen-Hsin - *Mobile Horizons: Dynamics across the Taiwan Strait*
   Pac A - v88 - i4 - Dec 2015 - p915 [501+]
Mobile Subjects: Boundaries and Identities in the Modern Korean Diaspora
   JAS - v74 - i3 - August 2015 - p770-771 [501+]

Yelavich, Brando - *Wildboy: An Epic Trek Around the Coast of New Zealand*
   y Magpies - v30 - i4 - Sept 2015 - pS8(1) [501+]

Yelchin, Eugene - *Arcady's Goal*
   c HB Guide - v26 - i1 - Spring 2015 - p97(1) [51-500]

Yelich-Koth, Christa - *Illusion*
   PW - v262 - i30 - July 27 2015 - p47(1) [51-500]

Yellen, Sherman - *Cousin Bella: The Whore of Minsk*
   PW - v262 - i4 - Jan 26 2015 - p167(1) [51-500]

Yellin, Eric S. - *Racism in the Nation's Service: Government Workers and the Color Line in Woodrow Wilson's America*
   AHR - v120 - i3 - June 2015 - p1048-1049 [501+]

Yelton, Barry D. - *Season of the Crow*
   RVBW - Nov 2015 - pNA [51-500]

Yenne, Bill - *Hit the Target: Eight Men Who Led the Eighth Air Force to Victory over the Luftwaffe*
   LJ - v140 - i12 - July 1 2015 - p96(1) [51-500]
Operation Long Jump
   Ch Today - v59 - i6 - July-August 2015 - p86(1) [51-500]
US Guided Missiles: The Definitive Reference Guide
   APJ - v29 - i5 - Sept-Oct 2015 - p108(2) [501+]

Yenson, Mark L. - *Existence as Prayer: The Consciousness of Christ in the Theology of Hans Urs von Balthasar*
   Theol St - v76 - i1 - March 2015 - p190(3) [501+]

Yeo, Matthew - *The Acquisition of Books by Chetham's Library, 1655-1700*
   BSA-P - v109 - i3 - Sept 2015 - p425-428 [501+]

Yeo, Richard - *Notebooks, English Virtuosi, and Early Modern Science*
   AHR - v120 - i2 - April 2015 - p714-715 [501+]
   RM - v68 - i3 - March 2015 - p682(3) [501+]

Yeomans, Rory - *Faschismus, Religion und Gewalt in Sudosteuropa: Die Legion Erzengel und die Ustasa im historischen Vergleich*
   Slav R - v74 - i1 - Spring 2015 - p167-168 [501+]

Yep, Laurence - *A Dragon's Guide to Making Your Human Smarter*
   c KR - Dec 15 2015 - pNA [51-500]
A Dragon's Guide to the Care and Feeding of Humans (Read by Denaker, Susan). Audiobook Review
   c BL - v111 - i18 - May 15 2015 - p70(1) [51-500]
   c SLJ - v61 - i6 - June 2015 - p65(1) [51-500]
A Dragon's Guide to the Care and Feeding of Humans (Illus. by GrandPre, Mary)
   c BL - v111 - i12 - Feb 15 2015 - p85(1) [51-500]
   c CCB-B - v68 - i8 - April 2015 - p424(1) [51-500]
   c CH Bwatch - April 2015 - pNA [51-500]
   c CH Bwatch - May 2015 - pNA [51-500]
   c HB - v91 - i3 - March-April 2015 - p113(1) [501+]
   c HB Guide - v26 - i2 - Fall 2015 - p107(1) [51-500]
   c PW - v262 - i3 - Jan 19 2015 - p82(1) [51-500]
   c SLJ - v61 - i6 - June 2015 - p46(6) [501+]

Yep, Ray - *Negotiating Autonomy in Greater China: Hong Kong and Its Sovereign before and after 1997*
   Pac A - v88 - i2 - June 2015 - p298 [501+]

Yeshaya, Joachim J.M.S. - *Poetry and Memory in Karaite Prayer: The Liturgical Poetry of the Karaite Poet Moses ben Abraham Dar'I*
   Med R - Sept 2015 - pNA [501+]
   Specu - v90 - i1 - Jan 2015 - p309-311 [501+]

Yglesias, Rafael - *The Wisdom of Perversity*
   BL - v111 - i9-10 - Jan 1 2015 - p43(1) [51-500]
   KR - Jan 15 2015 - pNA [51-500]
   NYTBR - April 5 2015 - p16(L) [501+]
   PW - v262 - i1 - Jan 5 2015 - p50(1) [51-500]

Yi, A. - *A Perfect Crime*
   y BL - v111 - i17 - May 1 2015 - p42(1) [51-500]
   TLS - i5853 - June 5 2015 - p27(1) [501+]

Yi-Chong, Xu - *The Political Economy of State-Owned Enterprises in China and India*
   JAS - v74 - i2 - May 2015 - p486-488 [501+]

Yilmaz, Hale - *Becoming Turkish: Nationalist Reforms and Cultural Negotiations in Early Republican Turkey, 1923-1945*
   JIH - v45 - i3 - Wntr 2015 - p438-439 [501+]

Ying Ying - *Starting with Max: How a Wise Stray Dog Gave Me Strength and Inspiration*
   LJ - v140 - i3 - Feb 15 2015 - p120(1) [51-500]

Yip, Andrew Kam-Tuck - *Religious and Sexual Identities: A Multi-faith Exploration of Young Adults*
   CS - v44 - i5 - Sept 2015 - p736-737 [501+]

Yizhar, S. - *Khirbet Khizeh*
   NYTBR - Feb 22 2015 - p26(L) [501+]

Ylvisaker, Anne - *The Curse of the Buttons*
   c HB Guide - v26 - i1 - Spring 2015 - p97(1) [51-500]

Yntema, Douwe - *The Archaeology of South-East Italy in the First Millennium BC: Greek and Native Societies of Apulia and Lucania between the 10th and the 1st century BC*
   HNet - August 2015 - pNA [501+]

Yocum, Demetrio S. - *Petrarch's Humanist Writing and Carthusian Monasticism: The Secret Language of the Self*
   Specu - v90 - i3 - July 2015 - p867-868 [501+]

Yoder, Jennifer A. - *Crafting Democracy: Regional Politics in Post-Communist Europe*
   E-A St - v67 - i4 - June 2015 - p684(2) [501+]

Yoder, Joella G. - *A Catalogue of the Manuscripts of Christiaan Huygens, Including a Concordance with His Oeuvres Completes*
   Isis - v106 - i2 - June 2015 - p446(2) [501+]

Yoder, Joshua - *Representatives of Roman Rule: Roman Provincial Governors in Luke-Acts*
   HNet - May 2015 - pNA [501+]

Yoffie, David B. - *Strategy Rules: Five Timeless Lessons from Bill Gates, Andy Grove, and Steve Jobs*
   Econ - v415 - i8934 - April 18 2015 - p80(US) [501+]
   KR - Feb 1 2015 - pNA [501+]

Yohalem, Eve - *Cast Off: The Strange Adventures of Petra De Winter and Bram Broen*
   c BL - v111 - i16 - April 15 2015 - p59(1) [51-500]
   c KR - March 15 2015 - pNA [51-500]
   c PW - v262 - i14 - April 6 2015 - p61(1) [51-500]
   c CCB-B - v68 - i11 - July-August 2015 - p574(1) [51-500]
   c HB Guide - v26 - i2 - Fall 2015 - p107(1) [51-500]
   c SLJ - v61 - i5 - May 2015 - p107(1) [51-500]
   y VOYA - v38 - i2 - June 2015 - p69(2) [51-500]

Yoho, R.G. - *The Evil Day*
   Roundup M - v22 - i5 - June 2015 - p39(1) [501+]
   Roundup M - v22 - i6 - August 2015 - p33(1) [501+]

Yokota, Masao - *Japanese Animation: East Asian Perspectives*
   JAS - v74 - i2 - May 2015 - p433-436 [501+]

Yokoyama, Koitsu - *An Intelligent Life: Buddhist Psychology of Self-Transformation*
   PW - v262 - i23 - June 8 2015 - p54(1) [51-500]

Yolen, Jane - *Animal Stories: Heartwarming True Tales from the Animal Kingdom (Illus. by Ishida, Jui)*
   c HB Guide - v26 - i1 - Spring 2015 - p157(1) [51-500]
Bad Girls: Sirens, Jezebels, Murderesses, Thieves & Other Female Villains (Read by Rosenblat, Barbara). Audiobook Review
   y BL - v111 - i16 - April 15 2015 - p63(1) [51-500]
Centaur Rising
   c CCB-B - v68 - i5 - Jan 2015 - p283(1) [51-500]
   c HB Guide - v26 - i1 - Spring 2015 - p97(1) [51-500]

How Do Dinosaurs Stay Friends? (Illus. by Teague, Mark)
c KR - Dec 1 2015 - pNA [51-500]
How Do Dinosaurs Stay Safe? (Illus. by Teague, Mark)
c HB Guide - v26 - i2 - Fall 2015 - p22(1) [51-500]
The Last Changeling
c HB Guide - v26 - i1 - Spring 2015 - p97(1) [51-500]
A Plague of Unicorns
c CCB-B - v68 - i6 - Feb 2015 - p336(1) [51-500]
c HB Guide - v26 - i1 - Spring 2015 - p97(1) [51-500]
Sing a Season Song (Illus. by Ashlock, Lisel Jane)
c KR - July 15 2015 - pNA [51-500]
c PW - v262 - i29 - July 20 2015 - p192(1) [501+]
c SLJ - v61 - i9 - Sept 2015 - p132(2) [51-500]
c PW - v262 - i49 - Dec 2 2015 - p56(1) [51-500]
Stone Angel (Read by Botchan, Rachel). Audiobook Review
c SLJ - v61 - i8 - August 2015 - p48(1) [51-500]
Stone Angel (Illus. by Green, Katie May)
c BL - v111 - i12 - Feb 15 2015 - p88(2) [51-500]
c CCB-B - v68 - i10 - June 2015 - p525(2) [51-500]
c KR - Jan 1 2015 - pNA [51-500]
The Stranded Whale (Illus. by Cataldo, Melanie)
c KR - May 15 2015 - pNA [51-500]
c SLJ - v61 - i6 - June 2015 - p96(1) [51-500]
Trash Mountain (Illus. by Monroe, Chris)
c BL - v111 - i12 - Feb 15 2015 - p77(1) [51-500]
c HB Guide - v26 - i2 - Fall 2015 - p107(1) [51-500]
c KR - Jan 15 2015 - pNA [51-500]
You Nest Here with Me (Illus. by Sweet, Melissa)
c BL - v111 - i14 - March 15 2015 - p82(1) [51-500]
c CH Bwatch - April 2015 - pNA [51-500]
c HB - v91 - i2 - March-April 2015 - p87(1) [51-500]
c NYTBR - March 15 2015 - p16(L) [501+]
c PW - v262 - i3 - Jan 19 2015 - p81(1) [51-500]
c SLJ - v61 - i2 - Feb 2015 - p81(1) [51-500]
Yom, Bun - *Tomorrow I'm Dead*
SPBW - Oct 2015 - pNA [51-500]
Yomtov, Nel - *Colin Kaepernick*
c HB Guide - v26 - i1 - Spring 2015 - p183(1) [51-500]
Enchantment of the World Series
c BL - v111 - i21 - July 1 2015 - p54(1) [51-500]
Neil Armstrong Walks on the Moon
c BL - v112 - i3 - Oct 1 2015 - p60(1) [51-500]
Robert Griffin III
c HB Guide - v26 - i1 - Spring 2015 - p183(1) [51-500]
Titanic Disaster! Nickolas Flux and the Sinking of the Great Ship (Illus. by Simmons, Mark)
c BL - v111 - i16 - April 15 2015 - p46(1) [51-500]
c HB Guide - v26 - i2 - Fall 2015 - p218(1) [51-500]
Trapped in Antarctica! Nickolas Flux and the Shackleton Expedition (Illus. by Simmons, Mark)
c BL - v111 - i16 - April 15 2015 - p46(1) [51-500]
c HB Guide - v26 - i2 - Fall 2015 - p215(1) [51-500]
Yonezu, Yusuke - *Circles*
c PW - v262 - i6 - Feb 9 2015 - p66(2) [501+]
Moving Blocks (Illus. by Yonezu, Yusuke)
c KR - July 1 2015 - pNA [51-500]
c SLJ - v61 - i7 - July 2015 - p57(2) [51-500]
Squares (Illus. by Yonezu, Yusuke)
c KR - July 1 2015 - pNA [51-500]
c SLJ - v61 - i7 - July 2015 - p57(2) [51-500]
Triangles
c KR - Jan 1 2016 - pNA [51-500]
Yong, Amos - *The Future of Evangelical Theology: Soundings from the Asian American Diaspora*
IBMR - v39 - i3 - July 2015 - p155(2) [501+]
Yoo, Grace J. - *Caring across Generations: The Linked Lives of Korean American Families*
CS - v44 - i3 - May 2015 - p440-441 [501+]
Soc - v52 - i2 - April 2015 - p193(2) [501+]
Yoo, Paula - *Lily's New Home (Illus. by Ng-Benitez, Shirley)*
c KR - Dec 15 2015 - pNA [51-500]
Twenty-two Cents: Muhammad Yunus and the Village Bank (Illus. by Akib, Jamel)
c HB Guide - v26 - i1 - Spring 2015 - p197(1) [51-500]
c SLJ - v61 - i12 - Dec 2015 - p64(4) [501+]
Want to Play? (Illus. by Ng-Benitez, Shirley)
c KR - Dec 15 2015 - pNA [51-500]
Yood, Charles N. - *Hybrid Zone: Computers and Science at Argonne National Laboratory, 1946-1992*
T&C - v56 - i1 - Jan 2015 - p295-296 [501+]
Yoon, Ae-hae - *Who Eats First? (Illus. by Yang, Hae-won)*
c KR - Feb 15 2015 - pNA [51-500]
Yoon, JooHee - *Beastly Verse (Illus. by Yoon, JooHee)*
c BL - v111 - i18 - May 15 2015 - p46(2) [51-500]
c HB - v91 - i4 - July-August 2015 - p151(2) [51-500]
c SLJ - v61 - i5 - May 2015 - p136(1) [51-500]
c KR - March 1 2015 - pNA [51-500]
c NYTBR - April 12 2015 - p18(L) [501+]
c PW - v262 - i49 - Dec 2 2015 - p54(1) [51-500]
Yoon, Nicola - *Everything, Everything (Read by Turpin, Bahni, with Robbie Daymond). Audiobook Review*
y SLJ - v61 - i11 - Nov 2015 - p74(1) [51-500]
Everything, Everything (Illus. by Yoon, David)
y BL - v112 - i2 - Sept 15 2015 - p74(1) [51-500]
y Ent W - i1377 - August 21 2015 - p108(1) [501+]
y HB - v91 - i6 - Nov-Dec 2015 - p95(1) [51-500]
y KR - July 15 2015 - pNA [51-500]
y Magpies - v30 - i5 - Nov 2015 - p44(2) [501+]
y NYTBR - Nov 8 2015 - p33(L) [501+]
y PW - v262 - i24 - June 15 2015 - p84(1) [51-500]
c PW - v262 - i51 - Dec 14 2015 - p21(6) [501+]
y SLJ - v61 - i8 - August 2015 - p111(2) [51-500]
Yoon, Paul - *Snow Hunters*
NYTBR - Jan 11 2015 - p24(L) [501+]
Yoon, Salina - *Be a Friend (Illus. by Yoon, Salina)*
c BL - v112 - i6 - Nov 15 2015 - p56(1) [51-500]
c KR - Oct 15 2015 - pNA [51-500]
Penguin and Pumpkin (Illus. by Yoon, Salina)
c HB Guide - v26 - i1 - Spring 2015 - p18(1) [51-500]
Penguin's Big Adventure (Illus. by Yoon, Salina)
c KR - June 15 2015 - pNA [51-500]
c SLJ - v61 - i6 - June 2015 - p96(1) [51-500]
Stormy Night
c HB Guide - v26 - i2 - Fall 2015 - p23(1) [51-500]
Tap to Play!
c HB Guide - v26 - i2 - Fall 2015 - p23(1) [51-500]
York, A.J. - *Delilah Dusticle*
y SPBW - April 2015 - pNA [51-500]
Eliza Bluebell
c SPBW - April 2015 - pNA [51-500]
York, Kelley - *Modern Monsters*
y VOYA - v38 - i3 - August 2015 - p72(2) [501+]
York, Raani - *Dragonbride*
y PW - v262 - i4 - Jan 26 2015 - p174(1) [51-500]
York, Sabrina - *Hannah and the Highlander*
PW - v262 - i29 - July 20 2015 - p176(1) [51-500]
Susana and the Scot
PW - v262 - i50 - Dec 7 2015 - p74(2) [51-500]
York, Sara - *Pray the Gay Away*
KR - Feb 15 2015 - pNA [501+]
Yosef, Benjamin - *Inner Messiah, Divine Character: Narrative Approaches to Be beyond Best*
RVBW - Feb 2015 - pNA [51-500]
Yoshida, Takashi - *From Cultures of War to Cultures of Peace: War and Peace Museums in Japan, China, and South Korea and Embattled Memories: Contested Meanings in Korean War Memorials*
Pub Hist - v37 - i2 - May 2015 - p152(3) [501+]
From Cultures of War to Cultures of Peace: War and Peace Museums in Japan, China, and South Korea
Pac A - v88 - i4 - Dec 2015 - p930 [501+]
Yoshikawa, Saeko - *William Wordsworth and the Invention of Tourism, 1820-1900*
RES - v66 - i274 - April 2015 - p390-391 [501+]
Yoshimatsu, Hidetaka - *Comparing Institution-Building in East Asia: Power Politics, Governance, and Critical Junctures*
Pac A - v88 - i3 - Sept 2015 - p679 [501+]
Yoshimi, Yoshiaki - *Grassroots Fascism: The War Experience of the Japanese People*
HNet - June 2015 - pNA [501+]
Yoshino, Kenji - *Speak Now: Marriage Equality on Trial: The Story of Hollingsworth v. Perry*
KR - Feb 15 2015 - pNA [51-500]
LJ - v140 - i6 - April 1 2015 - p105(3) [51-500]
NY - v91 - i13 - May 18 2015 - p97 [51-500]
NYTBR - May 10 2015 - p28(L) [501+]
Yoshitake, Shinsuke - *It Might Be an Apple*
c Magpies - v30 - i2 - May 2015 - p30(1) [501+]
Yosmaoglu, Ipek - *Blood Ties: Religion, Violence, and the Politics of Nationhood in Ottoman Macedonia, 1878-1908*
AHR - v120 - i2 - April 2015 - p749-750 [501+]
IJMES - v47 - i1 - Feb 2015 - p200-202 [501+]
JIH - v45 - i3 - Wntr 2015 - p436-438 [501+]
Slav R - v74 - i1 - Spring 2015 - p164-165 [501+]
Yoss - *A Planet for Rent*
ABR - v36 - i4 - May-June 2015 - p26(2) [501+]
Nation - v301 - i11-12 - Sept 14 2015 - p37(1) [501+]
Yost, Ann - *A Stitch in Crime*
BL - v111 - i13 - March 1 2015 - p26(1) [51-500]
KR - Feb 15 2015 - pNA [51-500]
Yost, Daniel - *Never Foul a Jump Shooter: A Guide to Basketball Lingo, Lessons and Laughs*
SPBW - May 2015 - pNA [51-500]
Youmans, Marly - *Maze of Blood*
Ch Today - v59 - i10 - Dec 2015 - p70(1) [51-500]
Young, Barbara - *The Persona of Ingmar Bergman: Conquering Demons through Film*
PW - v262 - i32 - August 10 2015 - p53(1) [51-500]
Young Bear, Ray - *Manifestation Wolverine*
BL - v112 - i5 - Nov 1 2015 - p14(1) [51-500]
Young, Brian - *Patrician Families and the Making of Quebec: The Taschereaus and McCords*
Can Hist R - v96 - i3 - Sept 2015 - p445(3) [501+]
Young, Carol - *The Adventures of Chloe Zoe Young: Chloe's Surfing Adventure*
c CH Bwatch - August 2015 - pNA [51-500]
Young, Celeste - *Baby & Me Knits: 20 Timeless Designs for Baby & Mom*
LJ - v140 - i14 - Sept 1 2015 - p106(1) [51-500]
Young, Charles S. - *Name, Rank, and Serial Number: Exploiting Korean War POWs at Home and Abroad*
AHR - v120 - i1 - Feb 2015 - p285-286 [501+]
JAH - v102 - i1 - June 2015 - p294-295 [501+]
Young, Cybele - *Nancy Knows (Illus. by Young, Cybele)*
c HB Guide - v26 - i1 - Spring 2015 - p18(2) [51-500]
The Queen's Shadow: A Story about How Animals See
c HB Guide - v26 - i2 - Fall 2015 - p57(1) [51-500]
The Queen's Shadow: A Story about How Animals See (Illus. by Young, Cybele)
c KR - Jan 1 2015 - pNA [51-500]
c Nat Post - v17 - i101 - Feb 28 2015 - pWP5(1) [501+]
c Res Links - v20 - i5 - June 2015 - p22(1) [51-500]
y SLJ - v61 - i3 - March 2015 - p175(1) [51-500]
Some Things I've Lost (Illus. by Young, Cybele)
c BL - v112 - i5 - Nov 1 2015 - p53(1) [51-500]
c KR - July 15 2015 - pNA [51-500]
y Nat Post - v17 - i266 - Sept 26 2015 - pWP5(1) [501+]
c PW - v262 - i28 - July 13 2015 - p63(2) [51-500]
c PW - v262 - i49 - Dec 2 2015 - p22(1) [51-500]
c SLJ - v61 - i10 - Oct 2015 - p86(1) [51-500]
Young, Damon - *My Pop is a Pirate (Illus. by Carnavas, Peter)*
c Magpies - v30 - i3 - July 2015 - p27(1) [501+]
Young, Dean - *Shock by Shock*
LJ - v140 - i12 - July 1 2015 - p88(2) [51-500]
PW - v262 - i33 - August 17 2015 - p49(2) [51-500]
Young, Ed - *Should You Be a River: A Poem about Love*
c PW - v262 - i49 - Dec 2 2015 - p32(1) [51-500]
c PW - v262 - i7 - Feb 16 2015 - pNA [51-500]
c HB Guide - v26 - i2 - Fall 2015 - p57(1) [51-500]
Young, Edward M. - *Death from Above: The 7th Bombardment Group in World War II*
APH - v62 - i1 - Spring 2015 - p60(1) [501+]
Young, Elliott - *Alien Nation: Chinese Migration in the Americas from the Coolie Era through World War II*
HNet - March 2015 - pNA [501+]
Young, Ernest P. - *Ecclesiastical Colony: China's Catholic Church and the French Religious Protectorate*
JAS - v74 - i1 - Feb 2015 - p210-212 [501+]
Young, Ethan - *Nanjing: The Burning City*
PW - v262 - i38 - Sept 21 2015 - p62(1) [51-500]
Young, Francis - *English Catholics and the Supernatural, 1553-1829*
HER - v130 - i544 - June 2015 - p750(2) [501+]
Historian - v77 - i3 - Fall 2015 - p630(2) [501+]
Young, Hester - *The Gates of Evangeline*
New Or - v49 - i10 - July 2015 - p40(1) [501+]
KR - July 1 2015 - pNA [501+]
PW - v262 - i27 - July 6 2015 - p44(2) [51-500]
Young, J.R. - *The Tale of Nottingswood*
KR - Feb 15 2015 - pNA [501+]
Young, Jack - *Hail, Cigaros!*
KR - Dec 15 2015 - pNA [501+]
Young, James - *Acts of War*
SPBW - April 2015 - pNA [501+]
Young, Jessica - *All Paws on Deck (Illus. by Burks, James)*
c KR - Nov 1 2015 - pNA [51-500]
c PW - v262 - i45 - Nov 9 2015 - p60(1) [501+]
Digging for Dinos (Illus. by Burks, James)
c KR - Dec 15 2015 - pNA [51-500]
Original Recipe (Illus. by Scheret, Jessica)
c HB Guide - v26 - i2 - Fall 2015 - p72(1) [51-500]
Spy Guy: The Not-So-Secret Agent (Illus. by Santoso, Charles)
c BL - v111 - i17 - May 1 2015 - p56(1) [51-500]
c CH Bwatch - June 2015 - pNA [51-500]
c HB Guide - v26 - i2 - Fall 2015 - p57(1) [51-500]
c KR - Feb 15 2015 - pNA [51-500]
c PW - v262 - i9 - March 2 2015 - p82(1) [51-500]
c SLJ - v61 - i2 - Feb 2015 - p81(1) [51-500]

Young, John - *Winston Churchill's Last Campaign: Britain and the Cold War, 1951-55*
    HT - v65 - i1 - Jan 2015 - p56(2) [501+]
Young, Josa - *Sail upon the Land*
    KR - April 15 2015 - pNA [501+]
Young, Josephine - *Marty the Masked Marvel: Dragonasaurus Tales (Illus. by Young, Josephine)*
    c CH Bwatch - Jan 2015 - pNA [51-500]
Young, Judy (b. 1956-) - *Digger and Daisy Go to the City (Illus. by Sullivan, Dana)*
    c HB Guide - v26 - i2 - Fall 2015 - p62(1) [51-500]
    c KR - Jan 1 2015 - pNA [51-500]
    Digger and Daisy Go to the Doctor (Illus. by Sullivan, Dana)
    c HB Guide - v26 - i2 - Fall 2015 - p62(1) [51-500]
    Promise
    c BL - v111 - i21 - July 1 2015 - p76(1) [51-500]
    c KR - May 15 2015 - pNA [51-500]
    Sleepy Snoozy Cozy Coozy: A Book of Animal Beds (Illus. by Monroe, Michael Glenn)
    c SLJ - v61 - i9 - Sept 2015 - p185(1) [51-500]
    Sleepy Snoozy, Cozy Coozy (Illus. by Monroe, Michael Glenn)
    c CH Bwatch - May 2015 - pNA [51-500]
    Sleepy Snoozy Cozy Coozy (Illus. by Monroe, Michael Glenn)
    c CH Bwatch - July 2015 - pNA [51-500]
Young, Karen Romano - *Space Junk: The Dangers of Polluting Earth's Orbit*
    y BL - v112 - i7 - Dec 1 2015 - p48(1) [51-500]
    y KR - Oct 15 2015 - pNA [51-500]
    c SLJ - v61 - i12 - Dec 2015 - p147(1) [51-500]
    Try This! 50 Fun Experiments for the Mad Scientist in You
    c HB Guide - v26 - i2 - Fall 2015 - p163(1) [51-500]
Young, Louisa - *The Heroes' Welcome*
    BL - v111 - i12 - Feb 15 2015 - p40(2) [51-500]
    KR - Jan 15 2015 - pNA [51-500]
Young, Mary - *The Baul Tradition: Sahaj Vision East and West*
    RVBW - Jan 2015 - pNA [501+]
Young, Moira - *Raging Star (Read by Lind, Heather). Audiobook Review*
    c BL - v111 - i14 - March 15 2015 - p24(2) [501+]
    Raging Star
    y HB Guide - v26 - i1 - Spring 2015 - p129(1) [51-500]
Young, Neil - *Special Deluxe: A Memoir of Life and Cars (Read by Young, Neil). Audiobook Review*
    Bwatch - Feb 2015 - pNA [51-500]
Young, Neil J. - *We Gather Together: The Religious Right and the Problem of Interfaith Politics*
    LJ - v140 - i16 - Oct 1 2015 - p64(2) [501+]
Young, Nicholas D. - *Educational Entrepreneurship: Promoting Public-Private Partnerships for the 21st Century*
    y VOYA - v38 - i5 - Dec 2015 - p84(1) [501+]
Young, Ralph - *Dissent: The History of an American Idea*
    KR - March 15 2015 - pNA [501+]
    LJ - v140 - i6 - April 1 2015 - p105(1) [51-500]
    PW - v262 - i9 - March 2 2015 - p74(1) [51-500]
    RVBW - August 2015 - pNA [501+]
Young, Rebecca - *Teacup (Illus. by Ottley, Matt)*
    y Magpies - v30 - i1 - March 2015 - p33(1) [501+]
Young, Samantha - *Moonlight on Nightingale Way*
    PW - v262 - i16 - April 20 2015 - p62(1) [51-500]
Young, Sherban - *Double Cover*
    PW - v262 - i9 - March 2 2015 - p66(2) [51-500]
    Fleeting Chance
    PW - v262 - i9 - March 2 2015 - p67(2) [51-500]
    Fleeting Promise
    KR - Nov 15 2015 - pNA [501+]
Young, Simon N.M. - *Hong Kong's Court of Final Appeal: The Development of the Law in China's Hong Kong*
    Pac A - v88 - i2 - June 2015 - p296 [501+]
Young-Stone, Michele - *Above Us Only Sky*
    BL - v111 - i11 - Feb 1 2015 - p20(1) [51-500]
Young, Suzanne - *Hotel Ruby*
    y BL - v112 - i4 - Oct 15 2015 - p45(1) [51-500]
    y KR - August 15 2015 - pNA [51-500]
    y SLJ - v61 - i11 - Nov 2015 - p123(1) [51-500]
    y VOYA - v38 - i5 - Dec 2015 - p76(1) [51-500]
    The Remedy
    y BL - v111 - i15 - April 1 2015 - p70(1) [51-500]
    y HB Guide - v26 - i2 - Fall 2015 - p144(1) [51-500]
    y KR - Feb 1 2015 - pNA [51-500]
    y SLJ - v61 - i3 - March 2015 - p164(1) [51-500]
    y VOYA - v38 - i1 - April 2015 - p84(2) [51-500]
Young, Timothy - *The Angry Little Puffin*
    c HB Guide - v26 - i2 - Fall 2015 - p57(1) [51-500]

Young, Tom - *The Hunters*
    BL - v111 - i21 - July 1 2015 - p37(1) [51-500]
    PW - v262 - i20 - May 18 2015 - p65(1) [51-500]
Young, Vershawn Ashanti - *From Bourgeouis to Boojie: Black Middle Class Performances*
    Callaloo - v38 - i1 - Wntr 2015 - p219-222 [501+]
Youngblood, Kevin J. - *Jonah: God's Scandalous Mercy*
    BTB - v45 - i2 - May 2015 - p117(2) [501+]
Younge-Ullman, Danielle - *Lola Carlyle's 12-Step Romance*
    y KR - March 1 2015 - pNA [51-500]
    y SLJ - v61 - i3 - March 2015 - p164(1) [51-500]
    y VOYA - v38 - i1 - April 2015 - p72(2) [501+]
Younger, Daniel - *Zen and the Art of Cannibalism*
    PW - v262 - i28 - July 13 2015 - p50(1) [51-500]
Youngs, Richard - *The Uncertain Legacy of Crisis: European Foreign Policy Faces the Future*
    For Aff - v94 - i3 - May-June 2015 - pNA [501+]
Yourgrau, Barry - *Mess: One Man's Struggle to Clean up His House and His Act (Read by Brooke, Peter). Audiobook Review*
    LJ - v140 - i17 - Oct 15 2015 - p54(1) [51-500]
    Mess: One Man's Struggle to Clean up His House and His Act
    BL - v111 - i19-20 - June 1 2015 - p33(1) [51-500]
    KR - May 15 2015 - pNA [51-500]
    Nature - v524 - i7564 - August 13 2015 - p159(1) [501+]
    NYTBR - Nov 15 2015 - p30(L) [501+]
    PW - v262 - i13 - March 30 2015 - p64(1) [51-500]
Yousafzai, Malala - *I Am Malala: How One Girl Stood Up for Education and Changed the World*
    c HB Guide - v26 - i1 - Spring 2015 - p197(1) [51-500]
Yousif, Keri - *Balzac, Grandville, and the Rise of Book Illustration*
    MLR - v110 - i3 - July 2015 - p866-867 [501+]
Yousufi, Mushtaq Ahmed - *Mirages of the Mind*
    KR - June 15 2015 - pNA [501+]
    PW - v262 - i21 - May 25 2015 - p30(1) [51-500]
Yow, Cheun Hoe - *Guangdong and Chinese Diaspora: The Changing Landscape of Qiaoxiang*
    Pac A - v88 - i4 - Dec 2015 - p909 [501+]
YoYo - *Return of the Queen (Illus. by YoYo)*
    BL - v111 - i13 - March 1 2015 - p44(1) [51-500]
Yu, Hua - *China in Ten Words*
    CSM - Jan 16 2015 - pNA [51-500]
    The Seventh Day
    NYTBR - March 22 2015 - p22(L) [501+]
Yu Huang, Ann - *White Sails*
    RVBW - July 2015 - pNA [51-500]
Yu, LiAnne - *Consumption in China: How China's New Consumer Ideology Is Shaping the Nation*
    Pac A - v88 - i4 - Dec 2015 - p913 [501+]
Yuan, Haiwang - *Tibetan Folktales*
    Teach Lib - v42 - i3 - Feb 2015 - p42(1) [51-500]
Yuan, Qian - *Macaroni Isn't the Same without Cheese (Illus. by Rotter, Phoebe)*
    c KR - Oct 1 2015 - pNA [501+]
Yuchi, Seirai - *Ground Zero, Nagasaki*
    WLT - v89 - i5 - Sept-Oct 2015 - p67(2) [501+]
Yudell, Michael - *Race Unmasked: Biology and Race in the Twentieth Century*
    Am St - v54 - i2 - Summer 2015 - p128-129 [501+]
    BioSci - v65 - i10 - Oct 2015 - p1019(3) [501+]
    QRB - v90 - i4 - Dec 2015 - p423(2) [501+]
Yudina, Anna - *Furnitecture: Funiture That Transforms Space*
    LJ - v140 - i5 - March 15 2015 - p109(1) [51-500]
Yue, Yuan - *A Changing China: Day to Day Life in the New Century*
    RVBW - August 2015 - pNA [51-500]
Yueh, Linda - *China's Growth: The Making of an Economic Superpower*
    E-A St - v67 - i7 - Sept 2015 - p1163(2) [501+]
    Pac A - v88 - i1 - March 2015 - p163 [501+]
Yufeng Wu - *ReCombinatorics: The Algorithmics of Ancestral Recombination Graphs and Explicit Phylogenetic Networks*
    QRB - v90 - i3 - Sept 2015 - p344(2) [501+]
Yukich, Grace - *One Family under God: Immigration Politics and Progressive Religion in America*
    CS - v44 - i5 - Sept 2015 - p737-738 [501+]
Yukiko, Ivy - *Henshin*
    PW - v262 - i8 - Feb 23 2015 - p60(1) [51-500]
Yuknavitch, Lidia - *The Small Backs of Children*
    KR - May 1 2015 - pNA [501+]
    LJ - v140 - i9 - May 15 2015 - p79(1) [51-500]
    PW - v262 - i21 - May 25 2015 - p31(1) [51-500]

Yuly, Toni - *Cat Nap (Illus. by Yuly, Toni)*
    c BL - v112 - i7 - Dec 1 2015 - p66(1) [51-500]
    c KR - Oct 15 2015 - pNA [51-500]
    c PW - v262 - i44 - Nov 2 2015 - p84(1) [51-500]
    c SLJ - v61 - i12 - Dec 2015 - p86(1) [51-500]
    Early Bird (Illus. by Yuly, Toni)
    c SLJ - v61 - i7 - July 2015 - p57(2) [51-500]
    Night Owl (Illus. by Yuly, Toni)
    c BL - v111 - i9-10 - Jan 1 2015 - p106(2) [51-500]
    c HB Guide - v26 - i2 - Fall 2015 - p23(1) [51-500]
Yum, Hyewon - *Puddle (Illus. by Yum, Hyewon)*
    c KR - Dec 15 2015 - pNA [51-500]
    c PW - v262 - i51 - Dec 14 2015 - p81(2) [51-500]
    The Tzvin's Little Sister
    c HB Guide - v26 - i1 - Spring 2015 - p19(1) [51-500]
Yumiko, Hana da - *Isolated Connected Kyushu Island*
    KR - May 1 2015 - pNA [501+]
Yun, Jung - *Shelter*
    KR - Jan 1 2016 - pNA [51-500]
Yusaf, Shundana - *Broadcasting Buildings: Architecture on the Wireless, 1927-1945*
    TLS - i5855 - June 19 2015 - p10(1) [501+]
Yusagi, Aneko - *The Rising of the Shield Hero (Illus. by Minami, Seira)*
    y SLJ - v61 - i12 - Dec 2015 - p117(1) [51-500]
Yusuf, Moeed - *Insurgency and Counterinsurgency in South Asia: Through a Peacebuilding Lens*
    HNet - Feb 2015 - pNA [501+]
Yuval, Israel Jacob - *Conflict and Religious Conversation in Latin Christendom: Studies in Honour of Ora Limor*
    Specu - v90 - i4 - Oct 2015 - p1185-1187 [501+]
Yuwiler, Janice M. - *What Is Self-Injury Disorder?*
    y VOYA - v38 - i5 - Dec 2015 - p80(1) [51-500]
Yvonne, Collette - *The Perils of Pauline*
    SPBW - March 2015 - pNA [51-500]
Zabawa, Mark Allen - *A Restful Mind*
    RVBW - March 2015 - pNA [501+]
Zabecki, David T. - *Germany at War: 400 Years of Military History*
    BL - v111 - i9-10 - Jan 1 2015 - p21(1) [501+]
Zaccaria, Massimo - *Anch'io per la tua bandiera: Il V Battaglione Ascari in missione sul fronte libico*
    J Mil H - v79 - i4 - Oct 2015 - p1121-1126 [501+]
Zacchi, Romana - *Richard Rowlands Verstegan: A Versatile Man in an Age of Turmoil*
    Ren Q - v68 - i1 - Spring 2015 - p352-353 [501+]
Zachhuber, Johannes - *Theology as Science in Nineteenth-Century Germany*
    CH - v84 - i1 - March 2015 - p258(3) [501+]
    Theol St - v76 - i1 - March 2015 - p179(3) [501+]
Zachter, Mort - *Gil Hodges: A Hall of Fame Life*
    LJ - v140 - i3 - Feb 15 2015 - p103(2) [501+]
Zack, Ian - *Say No to the Devil: The Life and Musical Genius of Rev. Gary Davis*
    LJ - v140 - i5 - March 15 2015 - p108(1) [51-500]
    TLS - i5844 - April 3 2015 - p27(1) [501+]
Zackheim, Victoria - *Faith: Essays from Believers, Agnostics, and Atheists*
    LJ - v140 - i3 - Feb 15 2015 - p107(1) [51-500]
Zadoff, Allen - *The Traitor: Boy Nobody*
    y Sch Lib - v63 - i3 - Autumn 2015 - p187(1) [51-500]
Zadoff, Mirjam - *Der Rote Hiob: Das Leben des Werner Scholem*
    HNet - Jan 2015 - pNA [501+]
Zafirovski, Milan - *Modernity and Terrorism: From Anti-Modernity to Modern Global Terror*
    CS - v44 - i5 - Sept 2015 - p739-740 [501+]
Zafzaf, Muhammad - *Monarch of the Square: An Anthology of Muhammad Zafzaf's Short Stories*
    WLT - v89 - i5 - Sept-Oct 2015 - p70(1) [501+]
Zagami, Leo Lyon - *Pope Francis: The Last Pope? Money, Masons and Occultism in the Decline of the Catholic Church*
    SPBW - May 2015 - pNA [501+]
Zaganczyk-Neufeld, Agnieszka - *Die Gegluckte Revolution: Das Politische und der Umbruch in Polen 1976-1997*
    HNet - July 2015 - pNA [501+]
Zagano, Phyllis - *Ordination of Women to the Diaconate in the Eastern Churches: Essays by Cipriano Vagaggini*
    Theol St - v76 - i4 - Dec 2015 - p882(2) [501+]
Zagarenski, Pamela - *The Whisper (Illus. by Zagarenski, Pamela)*
    c BL - v112 - i1 - Sept 1 2015 - p123(1) [51-500]
    c HB - v91 - i5 - Sept-Oct 2015 - p90(1) [51-500]
    c KR - August 1 2015 - pNA [51-500]
    c PW - v262 - i31 - August 3 2015 - p60(1) [51-500]
    c SLJ - v61 - i7 - July 2015 - p70(2) [51-500]

Zager, Deane May - *The Highest Rung of the Ladder: Achieving the American Dream*
  SPBW - August 2015 - pNA [51-500]

Zagzebski, Linda - *Epistemic Authority: A Theory of Trust, Authority, and Autonomy in Belief*
  Phil R - v124 - i1 - Jan 2015 - p159(4) [501+]

Zaharieva, Virginia - *Nine Rabbits*
  WLT - v89 - i2 - March-April 2015 - p66(1) [501+]

Zahavi, Hellen - *Dirty Weekend*
  TimHES - i2226 - Oct 22 2015 - p45(1) [501+]

Zahler, Diane - *Baker's Magic*
  c KR - Dec 1 2015 - pNA [51-500]
  c PW - v262 - i48 - Nov 30 2015 - p61(1) [51-500]
  Princess of the Wild Swans
  c Teach Lib - v43 - i1 - Oct 2015 - p42(1) [51-500]
  Sleeping Beauty's Daughters
  c Teach Lib - v43 - i1 - Oct 2015 - p42(1) [51-500]

Zahler, Reuben - *Ambitious Rebels: Remaking Honor, Law, and Liberalism in Venezuela, 1780-1850*
  Ams - v72 - i3 - July 2015 - p507(508) [501+]

Zahn, Timothy - *Pawn's Gambit*
  KR - Oct 15 2015 - pNA [51-500]
  PW - v262 - i41 - Oct 12 2015 - p51(1) [51-500]
  Soulminder
  Analog - v135 - i4 - April 2015 - p106(1) [501+]

Zahnarzte und Dentisten vor, wahrend und nach der Zeit des Nationalsozialismus
  HNet - May 2015 - pNA [501+]

Zahniser, J.D. - *Alice Paul: Claiming Power*
  HNet - Jan 2015 - pNA [501+]
  Wom R Bks - v32 - i1 - Jan-Feb 2015 - p18(3) [501+]
  AHR - v120 - i3 - June 2015 - p1035-1036 [501+]

Zahradnik, Rich - *Drop Dead Punk*
  PW - v262 - i25 - June 22 2015 - p123(1) [51-500]

Zaidman, Harriet - *Sherman and the Sheep Shape Contest (Illus. by Nadeau, Sonia)*
  c Res Links - v20 - i4 - April 2015 - p9(1) [51-500]

Zail, Suzy - *Playing for the Commandant (Read by Foster, Emily). Audiobook Review*
  SLJ - v61 - i2 - Feb 2015 - p52(1) [51-500]
  Playing for the Commandant
  y HB Guide - v26 - i1 - Spring 2015 - p129(1) [51-500]

Zajko, Vanda - *Classical Myth and Psychoanalysis: Ancient and Stories of the Self*
  Class R - v65 - i2 - Oct 2015 - p601-603 [501+]

Zakaria, Fareed - *In Defense of a Liberal Education (Read by Zakaria, Fareed). Audiobook Review*
  PW - v262 - i26 - June 29 2015 - p65(1) [51-500]
  In Defense of a Liberal Education
  Comw - v142 - i14 - Sept 11 2015 - p32(3) [501+]
  KR - March 15 2015 - pNA [501+]
  PW - v262 - i15 - April 13 2015 - p13(1) [501+]
  TimHES - i2210 - July 2 2015 - p47-1 [501+]

Zakaria, Rafia - *The Upstairs Wife: An Intimate History of Pakistan*
  Ms - v25 - i1 - Wntr 2015 - p57(1) [501+]
  Nation - v301 - i13-14 - Sept 28 2015 - p45(1) [501+]
  CSM - Feb 5 2015 - pNA [501+]
  NYTBR - March 29 2015 - p20(L) [501+]

Zakarian, Geoffrey - *My Perfect Pantry: 150 Easy Recipes from 50 Essential Ingredients*
  BL - v111 - i9-10 - Jan 1 2015 - p29(1) [501+]

Zaleski, Philip - *The Fellowship: The Literary Lives of the Inklings: J. R. R. Tolkien and C. S. Lewis, Owen Barfield, Charles Williams*
  BL - v111 - i17 - May 1 2015 - p71(1) [501+]
  The Fellowship: The Literary Lives of the Inklings: J.R.R. Tolkien, C.S. Lewis, Owen Barfield, Charles Williams
  CSM - June 2 2015 - pNA [501+]
  HM - v330 - i1981 - June 2015 - p77(3) [501+]
  KR - March 15 2015 - pNA [501+]
  LJ - v140 - i5 - March 15 2015 - p107(2) [501+]
  Nat R - v67 - i12 - July 6 2015 - p40 [501+]
  NYTBR - May 31 2015 - p38(L) [501+]
  PW - v262 - i10 - March 9 2015 - p61(1) [501+]
  AM - v213 - i8 - Sept 28 2015 - p44(2) [501+]
  NY - v91 - i29 - Sept 28 2015 - p72 [501+]

Zalloua, Zahi - *Reading Unruly: Interpretation and its Ethical Demands*
  MLR - v110 - i3 - July 2015 - p858-859 [501+]

Zaman, Nashat - *The Scorch of a Skilten*
  y KR - Oct 1 2015 - pNA [51-500]

Zambra, Alejandro - *Bonsai*
  NY - v91 - i17 - June 22 2015 - p77 [501+]
  My Documents
  BL - v111 - i12 - Feb 15 2015 - p32(1) [51-500]
  Ent W - i1352 - Feb 27 2015 - p61(1) [501+]
  NYT - Feb 26 2015 - pC6(L) [501+]
  Ways of Going Home
  NY - v91 - i17 - June 22 2015 - p77 [501+]

Zamir, Shamoon - *The Gift of the Face: Portraiture and Time in Edward S. Curtis's "The North American Indian"*
  WHQ - v46 - i3 - Autumn 2015 - p371-371 [501+]

Zamir, Tzachi - *Acts: Theater, Philosophy, and the Performing Self*
  Theat J - v67 - i2 - May 2015 - p362-363 [501+]

Zamora, Emilio - *The World War I Diary of Jose de la Luz Saenz*
  SHQ - v118 - i3 - Jan 2015 - p332-333 [501+]

Zamoyski, Adam - *Phantom Terror: Political Paranoia and the Creation of the Modern State, 1789-1848*
  Atl - v315 - i4 - May 2015 - p54(3) [501+]
  NYRB - v62 - i14 - Sept 24 2015 - p69(2) [501+]
  Phantom Terror: The Threat of Revolution and the Repression of Liberty 1789-1848
  TLS - i5837 - Feb 13 2015 - p8(1) [501+]

Zamperini, Louis - *Devil at My Heels: A Heroic Olympian's Astonishing Story of Survival as a Japanese POW in World War II*
  y JAH - v102 - i1 - June 2015 - p317-321 [501+]

Zancan, Caroline - *Local Girls*
  y BL - v111 - i18 - May 15 2015 - p23(2) [51-500]
  KR - May 15 2015 - pNA [51-500]
  NYTBR - July 26 2015 - p26(L) [501+]

Zander, Bianca - *The Predictions*
  y BL - v111 - i18 - May 15 2015 - p24(1) [51-500]

Zander, Joakim - *The Swimmer*
  LJ - v140 - i3 - Feb 15 2015 - p95(1) [51-500]
  NYTBR - May 31 2015 - p16(L) [501+]

Zandri, Vincent - *Orchard Grove*
  PW - v262 - i45 - Nov 9 2015 - p38(1) [51-500]

Zane, J. Peder - *Off the Books*
  KR - Feb 15 2015 - pNA [51-500]

Zanes, Warren - *Petty: The Biography*
  BL - v112 - i3 - Oct 1 2015 - p9(1) [51-500]
  KR - Sept 1 2015 - pNA [51-500]
  LJ - v140 - i17 - Oct 15 2015 - p87(2) [51-500]
  PW - v262 - i37 - Sept 14 2015 - p58(1) [51-500]

Zanetti, Rebecca - *Mercury Striking*
  PW - v262 - i52 - Dec 21 2015 - p140(2) [51-500]

Zanish-Belcher, Tanya - *Perspectives on Women's Archive*
  Signs - v40 - i2 - Wntr 2015 - p515(7) [501+]

Zanker, Paul - *Die romische Stadt: Eine kurze Geschichte*
  Class R - v65 - i2 - Oct 2015 - p617-618 [501+]

Zanobi, Alessandra - *Seneca's Tragedies and the Aesthetics of Pantomime*
  Class R - v65 - i1 - April 2015 - p143-145 [501+]

Zanoni, Elena - *Scienza, patria, religione: Antonio Stoppani e la cultura italiana dell'Ottocento*
  Isis - v106 - i2 - June 2015 - p464(2) [501+]

Zantonyi, Maura - *Vidi et intellexi: Die Schrifthermeneutik in der Visionstrilogie Hildegards von Bingen*
  Specu - v90 - i3 - July 2015 - p868-869 [501+]

Zantovsky, Michael - *Havel: A Life*
  AM - v212 - i20 - June 22 2015 - p34(3) [501+]
  BL - v111 - i19-20 - June 1 2015 - p27(1) [501+]
  NYRB - v62 - i7 - April 23 2015 - p25(3) [501+]
  Soc - v52 - i5 - Oct 2015 - p507(3) [501+]

Zappa, Marcia - *Chicago Bears*
  c HB Guide - v26 - i1 - Spring 2015 - p185(1) [51-500]
  Dallas Cowboys
  c HB Guide - v26 - i1 - Spring 2015 - p185(1) [51-500]
  Denver Broncos
  c HB Guide - v26 - i2 - Fall 2015 - p200(1) [51-500]
  Echidnas
  c BL - v112 - i3 - Oct 1 2015 - p52(1) [51-500]
  Green Bay Packers
  c HB Guide - v26 - i1 - Spring 2015 - p185(1) [51-500]
  Miami Dolphins
  c HB Guide - v26 - i1 - Spring 2015 - p185(1) [51-500]
  New Orleans Saints
  c HB Guide - v26 - i2 - Fall 2015 - p200(1) [51-500]
  Seattle Seahawks
  c HB Guide - v26 - i2 - Fall 2015 - p200(1) [51-500]
  Washington Redskins
  c HB Guide - v26 - i2 - Fall 2015 - p200(1) [51-500]

Zappa, Shana Muldoon - *Libby and the Class Election*
  c KR - July 15 2015 - pNA [51-500]
  c SLJ - v61 - i10 - Oct 2015 - p98(1) [51-500]
  Sage and the Journey to Wishworld
  c KR - July 15 2015 - pNA [51-500]
  c SLJ - v61 - i10 - Oct 2015 - p98(1) [51-500]

Zappia, Francesca - *Made You Up*
  y BL - v111 - i15 - April 1 2015 - p67(1) [51-500]
  y CCB-B - v68 - i11 - July-August 2015 - p574(2) [51-500]
  y HB Guide - v26 - i2 - Fall 2015 - p144(1) [51-500]
  y KR - Feb 15 2015 - pNA [51-500]
  y PW - v262 - i13 - March 30 2015 - p77(2) [51-500]
  y SLJ - v61 - i3 - March 2015 - p164(1) [51-500]
  y VOYA - v38 - i2 - June 2015 - p70(1) [51-500]

Zappia, Natale A. - *Traders and Raiders: The Indigenous World of the Colorado Basin, 1540-1859*
  Eight-C St - v48 - i3 - Spring 2015 - p353-356 [501+]
  HNet - Feb 2015 - pNA [501+]
  JAH - v102 - i1 - June 2015 - p221-222 [501+]
  W&M Q - v72 - i3 - July 2015 - p499-508 [501+]

Zaraska, Marta - *Meathooked*
  KR - Nov 15 2015 - pNA [51-500]

Zarate, Oscar - *Hysteria*
  BL - v112 - i6 - Nov 15 2015 - p34(1) [51-500]

Zarate, Ricardo - *The Fire of Peru: Recipes and Stories from My Peruvian Kitchen*
  PW - v262 - i29 - July 20 2015 - p183(1) [51-500]

Zarecki, Jonathan - *Cicero's Ideal Statesman in Theory and Practice*
  Class R - v65 - i2 - Oct 2015 - p430-432 [501+]

Zaretsky, Robert - *Boswell's Enlightenment*
  CC - v132 - i7 - April 1 2015 - p43(1) [501+]
  NYRB - v62 - i10 - June 4 2015 - p49(2) [501+]
  TLS - i5871 - Oct 9 2015 - p10(2) [501+]
  CSM - March 25 2015 - pNA [501+]
  HNet - June 2015 - pNA [501+]
  KR - Jan 1 2015 - pNA [501+]
  PW - v262 - i4 - Jan 26 2015 - p159(1) [501+]
  Life Worth Living: Albert Camus and the Quest for Meaning
  Historian - v77 - i3 - Fall 2015 - p632(2) [501+]

Zarsadiaz, James - *Dreams of Los Angeles: Traversing Power, Navigating Space, and Recovering the Everyday*
  J Urban H - v41 - i3 - May 2015 - p514-520 [501+]

Zartman, I. William - *Banning the Bang or the Bomb? Negotiating the Nuclear Test Ban Regime*
  HNet - May 2015 - pNA [501+]

Zarycki, Tomasz - *Ideologies of Eastness in Central and Eastern Europe*
  E-A St - v67 - i9 - Nov 2015 - p1498(2) [501+]

Zavala, Adriana - *Frida Kahlo's Garden*
  LJ - v140 - i15 - Sept 15 2015 - p73(1) [51-500]

Zavan, Laura - *Venice: Cult Recipes*
  TLS - i5841 - March 13 2015 - p30(1) [501+]

Zavella, Patricia - *I'm Neither Here nor There: Mexicans' Quotidian Struggles with Migration and Poverty*
  CS - v44 - i2 - March 2015 - p284-285 [501+]

Zawidzki, Tadeusz Wieslaw - *Mindshaping: A New Framework for Understanding Human Social Cognition*
  RM - v69 - i1 - Sept 2015 - p162(3) [501+]

Zawistoski, Ann Gwinn - *Glasses (Illus. by Woodworth, Heidi M.)*
  c PW - v262 - i6 - Feb 9 2015 - p66(2) [51-500]

Zayarny, Jack - *Hurricanes*
  c Res Links - v20 - i3 - Feb 2015 - p25(1) [51-500]

Zayas, Luis H. - *Forgotten Citizens: Deportation, Children, and the Making of American Exiles and Orphans*
  KR - Feb 15 2015 - pNA [51-500]
  LJ - v140 - i8 - May 1 2015 - p92(1) [51-500]

Zchomelidse, Nino M. - *Art, Ritual, and Civic Identity in Medieval Southern Italy*
  Med R - August 2015 - pNA [51-500]
  Ren Q - v68 - i2 - Summer 2015 - p647-649 [501+]

Zdarsky, Chip - *Howard the Duck: What the Duck (Illus. by Quinones, Joe)*
  y BL - v112 - i6 - Nov 15 2015 - p35(1) [51-500]

Zecchini, Laetitia - *Arun Kolatkar and Literary Modernism in India: Moving Lines*
  TLS - i5845 - April 10 2015 - p31(1) [501+]

Zee, Joe - *That's What Fashion Is*
  KR - June 1 2015 - pNA [51-500]

Zei, Alke - *Me molivi Faber noumero dyo*
  WLT - v89 - i1 - Jan-Feb 2015 - p72(1) [501+]

Zeiger, Jennifer - *Mammoth and Mastodon*
  c BL - v112 - i2 - Sept 15 2015 - p59(1) [501+]
  Pterosaur
  c BL - v112 - i2 - Sept 15 2015 - p59(1) [501+]
  Saber-Toothed Cat
  c BL - v112 - i2 - Sept 15 2015 - p59(1) [501+]

Zeigler, Alan - *Short: An International Anthology of Five Centuries of Short-Stories Prose Poems, Brief Essays, &*

Other Short Prose Forms
    ABR - v36 - i3 - March-April 2015 - p19(1) [501+]

Zeigler, David - *Evolution: Components and Mechanisms*
    QRB - v90 - i2 - June 2015 - p216(2) [501+]

Zeisler, Avital - *Weapons of Fitness: The Women's Ultimate Guide to Fitness, Self-Defense, and Empowerment*
    PW - v262 - i7 - Feb 16 2015 - p174(1) [51-500]

Zeiss, Joyce Burns - *Out of the Dragon's Mouth*
    y BL - v111 - i11 - Feb 1 2015 - p44(1) [51-500]
    y VOYA - v38 - i1 - April 2015 - p73(1) [51-500]

Zeitlin, Meredith - *Sophomore Year Is Greek to Me*
    y HB Guide - v26 - i2 - Fall 2015 - p145(1) [51-500]
    y VOYA - v37 - i6 - Feb 2015 - p71(1) [51-500]

Zelden, Charles L. - *Thurgood Marshall: Race, Rights, and the Struggle for a More Perfect Union*
    HNet - Feb 2015 - pNA [501+]

Zeldin, Theodore - *The Hidden Pleasures of Life: A New Way of Remembering the Past and Imagining the Future*
    TLS - i5864-5865 - August 21 2015 - p36(1) [501+]

Zelizer, Julian E. - *The Fierce Urgency of Now: Lyndon Johnson, Congress, and the Battle for the Great Society*
    Dis - v62 - i4 - Fall 2015 - p170(6) [501+]
    LJ - v140 - i2 - Feb 1 2015 - p96(1) [51-500]
    Nat R - v67 - i4 - March 9 2015 - p42 [501+]

Zelko, Frank - *Make It a Green Peace! The Rise of Countercultural Environmentalism*
    JAH - v101 - i4 - March 2015 - p1340-1341 [501+]

Zellentin, Holger Michael - *The Qur'an's Legal Culture: The Didascalia Apostolorum as a Point of Departure*
    Theol St - v76 - i1 - March 2015 - p172(2) [501+]

Zeltser, David - *Lug: Dawn of the Ice Age (Illus. by Gerardi, Jan)*
    c HB Guide - v26 - i1 - Spring 2015 - p97(1) [51-500]
Ninja Baby (Illus. by Goode, Diane)
    c BL - v112 - i5 - Nov 1 2015 - p66(1) [51-500]
    c KR - August 15 2015 - pNA [51-500]
    c PW - v262 - i34 - August 24 2015 - p78(1) [51-500]
    c PW - v262 - i49 - Dec 2 2015 - p36(1) [51-500]
    c SLJ - v61 - i10 - Oct 2015 - p86(1) [51-500]

Zeman, M.Y. - *Snowball: Chronicles of a Wererabbit*
    KR - Nov 1 2015 - pNA [51-500]

Zeman, Nicholas Bernhardt - *Essential Skills for 3D Modeling, Rendering, and Animation*
    Bwatch - March 2015 - pNA [501+]
    Bwatch - June 2015 - pNA [501+]

Zembrzycki, Stacey - *According to Baba: A Collaborative Oral History of Sudbury's Ukrainian Community*
    Can Hist R - v96 - i1 - March 2015 - p145(4) [501+]

Zemeckis, Leslie - *Goddess of Love Incarnate: The Life of Stripteuse Lili St. Cyr*
    BL - v112 - i1 - Sept 15 2015 - p14(1) [51-500]
    KR - July 1 2015 - pNA [51-500]
    LJ - v140 - i14 - Sept 1 2015 - p109(1) [51-500]

Zemke, Deborah - *My Life in Pictures (Illus. by Zemke, Deborah)*
    c KR - Dec 15 2015 - pNA [51-500]

Zemler, Jeffrey Allen - *James Madison, the South, and the Trans-Appalachian West, 1783-1803*
    JSH - v81 - i2 - May 2015 - p446(2) [501+]

Zemmour, Eric - *Le Suicide francais*
    NYRB - v62 - i5 - March 19 2015 - p43(2) [501+]
    TLS - i5852 - May 29 2015 - p10(2) [501+]

Zeng, Joddie - *The Popularity Project*
    y KR - July 1 2015 - pNA [51-500]

Zenith, Richard - *Multitudinous Heart: Selected Poems*
    NYT - July 3 2015 - pC17(L) [501+]

Zenko, Micah - *Red Team: How to Succeed by Thinking like the Enemy*
    BL - v112 - i4 - Oct 15 2015 - p8(1) [51-500]
    Har Bus R - v93 - i10 - Oct 2015 - p130(2) [501+]
    PW - v262 - i39 - Sept 28 2015 - p83(1) [51-500]

Zenner, Brandon - *The Experiment of Dreams*
    KR - May 15 2015 - pNA [51-500]

Zentner, Jeff - *The Serpent King*
    y BL - v112 - i6 - Nov 15 2015 - p49(1) [51-500]
    y KR - Dec 15 2015 - pNA [51-500]
    y PW - v262 - i51 - Dec 14 2015 - p86(1) [51-500]

Zentrum Revisited. Bilanz und Perspektiven der Forschung zum Politischen Katholizismus im Kaiserreich
    HNet - March 2015 - pNA [501+]

Zepeda, Gwendolyn - *Monsters, Zombies and Addicts*
    BL - v111 - i14 - March 15 2015 - p39(1) [51-500]

Zerbe, Britt - *The Birth of the Royal Marines, 1664-1802*
    J Mil H - v79 - i2 - April 2015 - p479-480 [501+]

Zerr, J.J. - *The Junior Officer Bunkroom*
    KR - Dec 15 2015 - pNA [51-500]

Zervigon, Andres Mario - *John Heartfield and the Agitated Image: Photography, Persuasion, and the Rise of Avant-Garde Photomontage*
    HNet - July 2015 - pNA [501+]

Zettel, Sarah - *The Assassin's Masque*
    y VOYA - v38 - i5 - Dec 2015 - p66(1) [51-500]
The Assassins's Masque
    y KR - Oct 1 2015 - pNA [51-500]
Dangerous Deceptions
    y HB Guide - v26 - i2 - Fall 2015 - p145(1) [51-500]

Zeuske, Michael - *Amistad: A Hidden Network of Slavers and Merchants*
    HNet - April 2015 - pNA [501+]

Zewde, Bahru - *The Quest for Socialist Utopia: The Ethiopian Student Movement, c. 1960-1974*
    AHR - v120 - i1 - Feb 2015 - p375-376 [501+]
    IJAHS - v48 - i1 - Wntr 2015 - p118-120 [501+]

Zhang, Amy - *Falling into Place*
    y HB Guide - v26 - i1 - Spring 2015 - p129(1) [51-500]
This Is Where the World Ends
    y KR - Dec 15 2015 - pNA [51-500]
    y PW - v262 - i51 - Dec 14 2015 - p86(2) [51-500]

Zhang, Guochang - *Accounting Information and Equity Valuation: Theory, Evidence, and Applications*
    AR - v90 - i3 - May 2015 - p1253(4) [501+]

Zhang, Jinghong - *Puer Tea: Ancient Caravans and Urban Chic*
    JRAI - v21 - i3 - Sept 2015 - p696(2) [501+]

Zhang, Kat - *Echoes of Us*
    y HB Guide - v26 - i2 - Fall 2015 - p145(1) [51-500]

Zhang, Li-Fang - *The Malleability of Intellectual Styles*
    AJPsy - v128 - i1 - Spring 2015 - p115(8) [501+]

Zhao, Linda Shuo - *Financing Illegal Migration: Chinese Underground Banks and Human Smuggling in New York City*
    CS - v44 - i3 - May 2015 - p441(1) [501+]

Zhao, Yong - *Who's Afraid of the Big Bad Dragon: Why China Has the Best (and Worst) Education System in the World*
    y VOYA - v37 - i6 - Feb 2015 - p89(1) [51-500]

Zhen, Lian Quan - *Chinese Watercolor Journeys*
    Bwatch - May 2015 - pNA [51-500]

Zheng, Yaling - *Create Classic Sudoku*
    KR - Jan 1 2016 - pNA [501+]

Zhenyun, Liu - *The Cook, the Crook, and the Real Estate Tycoon*
    KR - June 1 2015 - pNA [501+]
    LJ - v140 - i15 - Sept 15 2015 - p65(1) [51-500]
    PW - v262 - i26 - June 29 2015 - p42(1) [51-500]

Zheutlin, Peter - *Rescue Road: One Man, Thirty Thousand Dogs, and a Million Miles on the Last Hope Highway*
    BL - v112 - i4 - Oct 15 2015 - p9(1) [51-500]
    KR - July 1 2015 - pNA [501+]
    LJ - v140 - i14 - Sept 1 2015 - p128(1) [51-500]

Zhou, Xun - *Forgotten Voices of Mao's Great Famine, 1958-1962: An Oral History*
    Historian - v77 - i3 - Fall 2015 - p594(2) [501+]

Zhu, Dandan - *1956: Mao's China and the Hungarian Crisis*
    Pac A - v88 - i1 - March 2015 - p184 [501+]

Zhu, Liping - *The Road to Chinese Exclusion: The Denver Riot, 1880 Election and the Rise of the West*
    PHR - v84 - i3 - August 2015 - p365(1) [501+]

Zhu, Youlan - *Derivative Securities and Difference Methods*
    SIAM Rev - v57 - i1 - March 2015 - p162-163 [501+]

Zhuang, Henry - *The Mind inside Tai Chi*
    Bwatch - Sept 2015 - pNA [51-500]

Ziarek, Ewa Plonowska - *Feminist Aesthetics and the Politics of Modernism*
    MFSF - v61 - i1 - Spring 2015 - p200-203 [501+]
    TSWL - v34 - i1 - Spring 2015 - p185-187 [501+]

Ziarek, Krzysztof - *Language after Heidegger*
    RM - v68 - i3 - March 2015 - p684(3) [501+]

Zickermann, Kathrin - *Across the German Sea: Early Modern Scottish Connections with the Wider Elbe-Weser Region*
    Six Ct J - v46 - i2 - Summer 2015 - p433-434 [501+]

Zieba, Maciej - *Papal Economics: The Catholic Church on Democratic Capitalism from 'Rerum Novarum' to 'Caritas in Veritate'*
    J Ch St - v57 - i2 - Spring 2015 - p380-382 [501+]

Ziebell, Donn G. - *Conceal Carry: Pause: The Pursuit of Trained Readiness with a Goal to Avoid a 3-Second-Long Gun Fight*
    RVBW - Oct 2015 - pNA [501+]

Ziefert, Harriet - *101 Ways to Be a Good Granny (Illus. by Kath, Katie)*
    c PW - v262 - i26 - June 29 2015 - p67(1) [501+]
Can You Whoo, Too? (Illus. by Fatus, Sophie)
    c KR - August 1 2015 - pNA [51-500]
    c SLJ - v61 - i10 - Oct 2015 - p86(1) [51-500]
Sleepy Dog, Wake Up! (Illus. by Gorbaty, Norman)
    c HB Guide - v26 - i2 - Fall 2015 - p62(1) [51-500]
Think About Series (Illus. by Bolam, Emily)
    c HB Guide - v26 - i1 - Spring 2015 - p130(1) [51-500]
What Ship Is Not a Ship? (Illus. by Masse, Josee)
    c HB Guide - v26 - i2 - Fall 2015 - p195(1) [51-500]
Where Is the Rocket?
    c HB Guide - v26 - i1 - Spring 2015 - p19(1) [51-500]

Ziegler, Dieter - *Rohstoffgewinnung im Strukturwandel: Der Deutsche Bergbau im 20. Jahrhundert*
    HNet - March 2015 - pNA [501+]

Ziegler, Dominic - *Black Dragon River: A Journey down the Amur River at the Borderlands of Empires*
    BL - v112 - i2 - Sept 15 2015 - p19(1) [51-500]
    KR - Sept 15 2015 - pNA [501+]
    LJ - v140 - i17 - Oct 15 2015 - p106(1) [51-500]
    NYTBR - Dec 6 2015 - p46(L) [501+]
    PW - v262 - i39 - Sept 28 2015 - p79(2) [51-500]

Ziegler, Edith M. - *Harlots, Hussies, and Poor Unfortunate Women: Crime, Transportation, and the Servitude of Female Convicts*
    JAH - v102 - i1 - June 2015 - p225-225 [501+]
    Wom R Bks - v32 - i4 - July-August 2015 - p10(2) [501+]

Ziegler, Gunter M. - *Do I Count?: Stories from Mathematics*
    Math T - v108 - i7 - March 2015 - p559(1) [501+]

Ziegler, Jennifer - *Revenge of the Angels*
    c PW - v262 - i37 - Sept 14 2015 - p75(1) [501+]

Ziegler, Mary - *After Roe: The Lost History of the Abortion Debate*
    Econ - v415 - i8943 - June 20 2015 - p81(US) [501+]

Ziegler, Philip - *Diana Cooper*
    NYRB - v62 - i10 - June 4 2015 - p33(3) [501+]
Edward Health: The Authorised Biography
    TimHES - i2224 - Oct 8 2015 - p43(1) [501+]
George VI: The Dutiful King
    TLS - i5841 - March 13 2015 - p10(2) [501+]

Zielregion Ostmitteleuropa - Migration im 20. Jahrhundert
    HNet - Feb 2015 - pNA [501+]

Ziemkiewicz, Rafal A. - *Michnikowszczyzna: Zapis choroby*
    Nation - v300 - i1 - Jan 5 2015 - p27(10) [501+]

Zientara, Sharon - *Quick Crocheted Accessories*
    LJ - v140 - i12 - July 1 2015 - p87(1) [51-500]

Ziff, John - *American Revolution*
    y BL - v112 - i6 - Nov 15 2015 - p43(1) [51-500]

Ziff, Marsha - *The Reconstruction of the South after the Civil War*
    y HB Guide - v26 - i1 - Spring 2015 - p203(1) [51-500]

Ziglar, Christy - *Whatever Wanda! (Illus. by Billin-Frye, Paige)*
    c CH Bwatch - June 2015 - pNA [51-500]

Zilberg, Elana - *Space of Detention: The Making of a Transnational Gang Grisis between Los Angeles and San Salvador*
    CS - v44 - i1 - Jan 2015 - p133-135 [501+]

Zilelian, Aida - *The Legacy of Lost Things*
    KR - April 1 2015 - pNA [51-500]

Zimbalist, Andrew - *Circus Maximus: The Economic Gamble behind Hosting the Olympics and the World Cup*
    Econ - v414 - i8927 - Feb 28 2015 - p74(US) [501+]

Zimmer, Catherine - *Surveillance Cinema*
    FQ - v69 - i1 - Fall 2015 - p106(3) [501+]
    TimHES - i2216 - August 13 2015 - p44-45 [501+]

Zimmer, Marc - *Bioluminescence: Nature and Science at Work*
    y BL - v112 - i4 - Oct 15 2015 - p38(1) [51-500]
    y KR - July 15 2015 - pNA [51-500]
    y Sci Teach - v82 - i8 - Nov 2015 - p73 [51-500]
    y SLJ - v61 - i8 - August 2015 - p131(1) [51-500]

Zimmer, Michael - *Miami Gundown*
    Roundup M - v22 - i6 - August 2015 - p33(1) [501+]

Zimmer, Oliver - *Remaking the Rhythms of Life: German Communities in the Age of the Nation-State*
    HER - v130 - i545 - August 2015 - p1027(3) [501+]
    Historian - v77 - i1 - Spring 2015 - p199(2) [501+]
    JMH - v87 - i2 - June 2015 - p486(3) [501+]

Zimmer, Stephen - *Horses and Cattle, and a Double-Rigged Saddle*
  Roundup M - v22 - i6 - August 2015 - p41(1) [501+]

Zimmerman, Jane - *Essential Movement Only*
  KR - Jan 15 2015 - pNA [501+]

Zimmerman, Jereme - *Make Mead Like a Viking: Traditional Techniques for Brewing Natural, Wild-Fermented, Honey-Based Wines and Beers*
  BL - v112 - i3 - Oct 1 2015 - p18(1) [51-500]

Zimmerman, Jonathan - *Too Hot to Handle: A Global History of Sex Education*
  For Aff - v94 - i4 - July-August 2015 - pNA [501+]
  LJ - v140 - i3 - Feb 15 2015 - p111(1) [51-500]
  Soc - v52 - i3 - June 2015 - p283(1) [501+]

Zimmerman, Michael J. - *Ignorance and Moral Obligation*
  Ethics - v125 - i4 - July 2015 - p1236(6) [501+]

Zimmerman, Minerva - *Take on Me*
  PW - v262 - i34 - August 24 2015 - p66(1) [51-500]

Zimmerman, Virginia - *The Rosemary Spell*
  c PW - v262 - i39 - Sept 28 2015 - p93(1) [51-500]
  c BL - v112 - i4 - Oct 15 2015 - p59(1) [51-500]
  y KR - Oct 1 2015 - pNA [51-500]
  c PW - v262 - i49 - Dec 2 2015 - p78(1) [51-500]
  c SLJ - v61 - i11 - Nov 2015 - p110(1) [51-500]

Zimmerman, Yvonne C. - *Other Dreams of Freedom: Religion, Sex, and Human Trafficking*
  J Am St - v49 - i2 - May 2015 - p454-456 [501+]
  J Ch St - v57 - i1 - Wntr 2015 - p177-179 [501+]

Zimring, Carl A. - *Clean and White: A History of Environmental Racism in the United States*
  LJ - v140 - i19 - Nov 15 2015 - p99(2) [51-500]
  PW - v262 - i47 - Nov 23 2015 - p61(1) [51-500]

Zink, Eren - *Hot Science, High Water: Assembling Nature, Society and Environmental Policy in Contemporary Vietnam*
  Pac A - v88 - i1 - March 2015 - p224 [501+]

Zink, Michel - *Ille Journee d'etudes anglo-normades: Adaptation, parodie et autres emplois*
  Specu - v90 - i4 - Oct 2015 - p1195(1) [501+]

Zink, Michelle - *Lies I Told*
  y HB Guide - v26 - i2 - Fall 2015 - p145(1) [51-500]
  y KR - Jan 1 2015 - pNA [51-500]
  y PW - v262 - i9 - March 2 2015 - p86(2) [51-500]
  y VOYA - v37 - i6 - Feb 2015 - p71(1) [51-500]
  Promises I Made
  y KR - August 15 2015 - pNA [51-500]
  y SLJ - v61 - i9 - Sept 2015 - p174(1) [51-500]

Zink, Nell - *Mislaid (Read by Campbell, Cassandra). Audiobook Review*
  LJ - v140 - i13 - August 1 2015 - p48(1) [51-500]
  Mislaid
  HM - v330 - i1980 - May 2015 - p79(3) [501+]
  KR - March 1 2015 - pNA [51-500]
  LJ - v140 - i6 - April 1 2015 - p86(2) [51-500]
  New York - May 18 2015 - pNA [501+]
  NYT - May 20 2015 - pC1(L) [501+]
  NYTBR - June 7 2015 - p12(L) [501+]
  PW - v262 - i13 - March 30 2015 - p49(1) [51-500]
  Mislaid & the Wallcreeper--the Neil Zink Collection. E-book Review
  Lon R Bks - v37 - i14 - July 16 2015 - p25(2) [501+]
  Mislaid & the Wallcreeper--the Neil Zink Collection
  NS - v144 - i5269 - July 3 2015 - p53(1) [501+]
  The Wallcreeper
  Nation - v300 - i18 - May 4 2015 - p45(1) [501+]

Zinoman, Peter - *Vietnamese Colonial Republican: The Political Vision of Vu Trong Phung*
  AHR - v120 - i1 - Feb 2015 - p214-215 [501+]
  JAS - v74 - i1 - Feb 2015 - p248-250 [501+]

Zinovieff, Sofka - *The Mad Boy, Lord Berners, My Grandmother and Me: An Aristocratic Family, a High-Society Scandal and an Extraordinary Legacy*
  Econ - v414 - i8930 - March 21 2015 - p74(US) [501+]
  KR - Jan 1 2015 - pNA [501+]
  LJ - v140 - i3 - Feb 15 2015 - p108(1) [51-500]
  G&L Rev W - v22 - i5 - Sept-Oct 2015 - p50(1) [501+]
  NYRB - v62 - i7 - April 23 2015 - p16(3) [501+]
  NYTBR - April 26 2015 - p11(L) [501+]

Zinsli, Samuel Christian - *Kommentar zur Vita Heliogabali der Historia Augusta*
  HNet - March 2015 - pNA [501+]

Ziolkowski, Margaret - *Soviet Heroic Poetry in Context: Folklore or Fakelore*
  MLR - v110 - i1 - Jan 2015 - p308-309 [501+]

Zion, Gene - *Harry the Dirty Dog (Illus. by Graham, Margaret Bloy)*
  c BL - v112 - i4 - Oct 15 2015 - p53(1) [51-500]

Zipes, Jack - *Grimm Legacies: The Magic Spell of the Grimms' Folk and Fairy Tales*
  c NYRB - v62 - i12 - July 9 2015 - p65(3) [501+]
  The Original Folk and Fairy Tales of the Brothers Grimm: The Complete First Edition (Illus. by Dezso, Andrea)
  MFSF - v128 - i5-6 - May-June 2015 - p59(2) [501+]
  The Original Folk and Fairy Tales of the Brothers Grimm: The Complete First Edition (Illus. by Grimm, Jacob)
  HT - v65 - i4 - April 2015 - p62(1) [501+]

Ziser, Michael - *Environmental Practice and Early American Literature*
  AL - v87 - i3 - Sept 2015 - p605-607 [501+]

Ziskin, James W. - *Stone Cold Dead*
  PW - v262 - i10 - March 9 2015 - p55(1) [51-500]

Zito, Greg - *History of Street Cops*
  SPBW - March 2015 - pNA [51-500]

Zizek, Slavoj - *Absolute Recoil: Towards a New Foundation of Dialectical Materialism*
  NS - v144 - i5253 - March 13 2015 - p52(2) [501+]
  Trouble in Paradise: From the End of History to the End of Capitalism
  NS - v144 - i5253 - March 13 2015 - p52(2) [501+]

Zobal, Silas Dent - *The Inconvenience of the Wings*
  KR - July 1 2015 - pNA [501+]

Zobel, Melissa Tantaquidgeon - *Wakanabi Blues*
  y KR - March 15 2015 - pNA [51-500]

Zoboli, Giovanna - *Animal Supermarket (Illus. by Mulazzani, Simona)*
  c KR - Feb 15 2015 - pNA [51-500]
  c SLJ - v61 - i7 - July 2015 - p70(1) [51-500]

Zoehfeld, Kathleen Weidner - *Prehistoric Mammals (Illus. by Tempesta, Franco)*
  c BL - v111 - i22 - August 1 2015 - p75(1) [51-500]
  c HB Guide - v26 - i2 - Fall 2015 - p169(1) [51-500]

Zoellner, Tom - *Train: Riding the Rails That Created the Modern World - from the Trans-Siberian to the 'Southwest Chief'*
  TLS - i5845 - April 10 2015 - p32(1) [501+]

Zoepf, Katherine - *Excellent Daughters: The Secret Lives of Young Women Who Are Transforming the Arab World*
  BL - v112 - i7 - Dec 1 2015 - p6(1) [51-500]
  KR - Oct 15 2015 - pNA [501+]
  PW - v262 - i41 - Oct 12 2015 - p56(2) [51-500]

Zogg, Fabian - *Lust am Lesen: Literarische Anspielungen im Frieden des Aristophanes*
  Class R - v65 - i2 - Oct 2015 - p363-364 [501+]

Zoglin, Richard - *Hope: Entertainer of the Century*
  Bks & Cult - v21 - i3 - May-June 2015 - p8(2) [501+]
  BL - v111 - i19-20 - June 1 2015 - p30(2) [501+]
  NYRB - v62 - i5 - March 19 2015 - p21(2) [501+]
  Reason - v47 - i2 - June 2015 - p65(3) [501+]
  Si & So - v25 - i3 - March 2015 - p104(2) [501+]

Zohar, Gil - *Israel and the Arab World*
  y BL - v112 - i3 - Oct 1 2015 - p40(1) [51-500]

Zohar, Zvi - *Rabbinic Creativity in the Modern Middle East*
  Tikkun - v30 - i1 - Wntr 2015 - p53(2) [501+]

Zola, Emile - *The Conquest of Plassans*
  MLR - v110 - i3 - July 2015 - p869-870 [501+]

Zollars, Mimi - *Benediction for a Black Swan*
  KR - August 15 2015 - pNA [501+]

Zolotow, Charlotte - *Changes: A Child's First Poetry Collection (Illus. by Beeke, Tiphanie)*
  BL - v111 - i14 - March 15 2015 - p60(1) [51-500]
  c HB Guide - v26 - i2 - Fall 2015 - p205(1) [51-500]
  c KR - Feb 15 2015 - pNA [51-500]
  c PW - v262 - i2 - Jan 12 2015 - p58(1) [501+]
  Say It! (Illus. by Stevenson, James)
  c KR - August 1 2015 - pNA [51-500]

Zommer, Yuval - *The Big Blue Thing on the Hill (Illus. by Zommer, Yuval)*
  c CCB-B - v68 - i8 - April 2015 - p424(2) [51-500]
  One Hundred Bones
  c KR - Jan 1 2016 - pNA [51-500]

Zonana, Linda Howard - *Vertigo! When the World Spins out of Control*
  SPBW - May 2015 - pNA [501+]

Zook, Melinda S. - *Protestantism, Politics, and Women in Britain, 1660-1714*
  JMH - v87 - i2 - June 2015 - p423(2) [501+]

Zoref, Lior - *Mindsharing: The Art of Crowdsourcing Everything*
  KR - Feb 15 2015 - pNA [51-500]
  PW - v262 - i5 - Feb 2 2015 - p48(1) [51-500]

Zori, Davide - *Viking Archaeology in Iceland: Mosfell Archaeological Project*
  Med R - June 2015 - pNA [501+]

Zornberg, Avivah Gottlieb - *Bewilderments: Reflections on the Book of Numbers*
  BL - v111 - i13 - March 1 2015 - p5(2) [501+]

Zourkova, Krassi - *Wildalone*
  LJ - v140 - i6 - April 1 2015 - p119(1) [501+]

Zuchora-Walske, Christine - *Key Discoveries in Earth and Space Science*
  y HB Guide - v26 - i2 - Fall 2015 - p164(1) [51-500]
  Key Discoveries in Engineering and Design
  y HB Guide - v26 - i2 - Fall 2015 - p186(1) [51-500]
  Key Discoveries in Life Science
  y HB Guide - v26 - i2 - Fall 2015 - p172(1) [51-500]
  Lightning Bolt Books: Robots Everywhere! Series
  c HB Guide - v26 - i1 - Spring 2015 - p173(1) [51-500]
  Science Gets It Wrong Series
  c HB Guide - v26 - i1 - Spring 2015 - p148(1) [51-500]
  Your Head Shape Reveals Your Personality: Science's Biggest Mistakes about the Human Body
  c HB Guide - v26 - i1 - Spring 2015 - p172(1) [51-500]

Zucker, Jonny - *Supersonic*
  c Teach Lib - v42 - i3 - Feb 2015 - p55(1) [51-500]

Zucker, Stefan - *Franco Corelli and a Revolution in Singing: Fifty-Four Tenors Spanning 200 Years*
  KR - April 15 2015 - pNA [51-500]
  LJ - v140 - i9 - May 15 2015 - p86(1) [51-500]

Zuckerman, Ethan - *Rewire: Digital Cosmopolitans in the Age of Connection*
  CS - v44 - i2 - March 2015 - p285-287 [501+]

Zuckerman, Linda - *The Day Is Waiting (Illus. by Freeman, Don)*
  c SLJ - v61 - i10 - Oct 2015 - p86(1) [51-500]

Zuckerman, Phil - *Living the Secular Life: New Answers to Old Questions*
  NYTBR - Dec 20 2015 - p24(L) [501+]

Zuckert, Catherine H. - *Leo Strauss and the Problem of Political Philosophy*
  Pers PS - v44 - i4 - Oct-Dec 2015 - p257-260 [501+]

Zucketman, Gregory - *The Frackers: The Outrageous Inside Story of the New Billionaire*
  En Jnl - v36 - i3 - July 2015 - p359(3) [501+]

Zuckoff, Allan - *Finding Your Way to Change: How the Power of Motivational Interviewing Can Reveal What You Want and Help You Get There*
  LJ - v140 - i9 - May 15 2015 - p98(1) [51-500]

Zucman, Gabriel - *The Hidden Wealth of Nations: The Scourge of Tax Havens*
  LJ - v140 - i15 - Sept 15 2015 - p86(2) [51-500]

Zuercher, Gary - *The Glow of Paris: The Bridges of Paris at Night*
  KR - Feb 1 2015 - pNA [501+]
  SPBW - Jan 2015 - pNA [501+]

Zukowsky, John - *Why on Earth Would Anyone Build That: Modern Architecture Explained*
  RVBW - Nov 2015 - pNA [501+]
  Why You Can Build it Like That: Modern Architecture Explained
  Nature - v525 - i7568 - Sept 10 2015 - p185(1) [51-500]

Zulaika, Joseba - *That Old Bilbao Moon: The Passion and Resurrection of a City*
  SPBW - August 2015 - pNA [501+]

Zulauf, Sander - *Basho in America*
  KR - Jan 1 2015 - pNA [501+]

Zullo, Allan - *10 True Tales: Battle Heroes*
  c BL - v111 - i18 - May 15 2015 - p44(1) [51-500]
  10 True Tales: FBI Heroes
  BL - v111 - i17 - May 1 2015 - p82(1) [51-500]
  10 True Tales: Heroes of 9/11
  c BL - v111 - i19-20 - June 1 2015 - p72(1) [51-500]
  c SLJ - v61 - i6 - June 2015 - p145(1) [51-500]
  10 True Tales: World War I Heroes
  c BL - v112 - i6 - Nov 15 2015 - p37(1) [51-500]

Zullo, Germano - *Jumping Jack (Illus. by Albertine)*
  c HB Guide - v26 - i1 - Spring 2015 - p50(1) [51-500]

Zunde, Romy Sai - *Release the Beast (Illus. by Merkens, Cinzah)*
  c Magpies - v30 - i2 - May 2015 - pS5(1) [501+]

Zunic, Nikolaj - *Distinctions of Being: Philosophical Approaches to Reality*
  RM - v69 - i1 - Sept 2015 - p127(4) [501+]

Zuniga, Elisabeth - *A Friend for Bo (Illus. by Zuniga, Elisabeth)*
  c KR - Nov 1 2015 - pNA [51-500]
  c PW - v262 - i41 - Oct 12 2015 - p65(1) [51-500]
  c SLJ - v61 - i11 - Nov 2015 - p77(1) [51-500]

Zupan, Kim - *The Ploughmen*
  NYTBR - Jan 4 2015 - p18(L) [501+]
  Roundup M - v22 - i3 - Feb 2015 - p28(1) [501+]
  Roundup M - v22 - i6 - August 2015 - p33(1) [501+]

Zurcher, Frederic - *Idolatry of Blood: Religion for a Post-Modern World*
  SPBW - Nov 2015 - pNA [501+]

Zurcher Werkstatt Historische Bildungsforschung
  HNet - May 2015 - pNA [501+]

Zurita, Raul - *The Country of Planks/ El Pais de Tablas*
  PW - v262 - i20 - May 18 2015 - p62(2) [51-500]

Zuromskis, Catherine - *The Factory: Photography and the Warhol Community*
  Afterimage - v42 - i6 - May-June 2015 - p39(3) [501+]

Snapshot Photography: The Lives of Images
  Biomag - v38 - i3 - Summer 2015 - p436(3) [501+]

Zusak, Markus - *I Am the Messenger*
  y Sch Lib - v63 - i2 - Summer 2015 - p127(1) [51-500]

The Underdogs (Read by Wemyss, Stig). Audiobook Review
  y SLJ - v61 - i6 - June 2015 - p68(1) [51-500]

Zweig, Eric - *Dominant Defensemen*
  c Res Links - v20 - i3 - Feb 2015 - p25(1) [51-500]

Great Goalies
  c Res Links - v20 - i3 - Feb 2015 - p25(1) [51-500]

Super Scorers
  c Res Links - v20 - i3 - Feb 2015 - p25(1) [51-500]

Zweig, Jason - *The Devil's Financial Dictionary*
  Barron's - v95 - i40 - Oct 5 2015 - p34(1) [501+]

Zweig, Stefan - *Montaigne*
  LJ - v140 - i20 - Dec 1 2015 - p105(1) [51-500]

The Society of the Crossed Keys
  TLS - i5841 - March 13 2015 - p12(1) [501+]

Zwicky, Jan - *Chamber Music: The Poetry of Jan Zwicky*
  Can Lit - i224 - Spring 2015 - p133 [51-500]

Vittoria Colonna: Selections from the Rime Spirituali (Illus. by Moody, Robert)
  Can Lit - i224 - Spring 2015 - p128 [501+]

Zwierlein - *Ignorance, Nescience, Nonknowledge: Late Medieval and early modern coping with Unknowns*
  HNet - August 2015 - pNA [501+]

Zwies, Sebastian - *Das Kloster Fulda und seine Urkunden: Moderne archivische Erschliessung und ihre Perspektiven fur die historische Forschung*
  HNet - April 2015 - pNA [501+]

Zwischen Utopie und Apokalypse. Nukleare technopolitics in der Sowjetunion
  HNet - Sept 2015 - pNA(NA) [501+]

A

c 0-20 (Illus. by Hawcock, David) — *Hawcock, David*
c 1.000 Animals (Illus. by Dyson, Nikki) — *Greenwell, Jessica*
c 1-2-3 A Calmer Me: Helping Children Cope When Emotions Get Out of Control (Illus. by Keay, Claire) — *Patterson, Colleen A.*
c 1-2-3 ZooBorns! — *Bleiman, Andrew*
c 1 Cookie, 2 Chairs, 3 Pears: Numbers Everywhere — *Brocket, Jane*
c 1 Is One (Illus. by Tudor, Tasha) — *Tudor, Tasha*
$2.00 a Day: Living on Almost Nothing in America (Read by Johnson, Allyson). Audiobook Review — *Edin, Kathryn J.*
$2.00 a Day: Living on Almost Nothing in America — *Edin, Kathryn J.*
y 2 a.m. at the Cat's Pajamas (Read by Goethals, Angela). Audiobook Review — *Bertino, Marie-Helene*
y 2 Billion under 20: How Millennial Are Breaking Down Age Barriers and Changing the World — *Ferreira, Stacey*
2. Dresdner Nachwuchskolloquium zur Geschlechterforschung
2. Korinther — *Arzt-Grabner, Peter*
2 Weeks to a Younger Brain — *Small, Gary*
c 3, 2, 1, Go! (Illus. by McCully, Emily Arnold) — *McCully, Emily Arnold*
3D Printing: A Powerful New Curriculum Tool for Your School Library — *Cano, Lesley M.*
c 3 Falafels in My Pita (Illus. by Mack, Steve) — *Friedman, Maya*
The 3rd Woman — *Freedland, Jonathan*
3. Treffen des "Arbeitskreis Moulagen"
c The 3 W Boys: A Children's Book of Short Stories (Illus. by Ouano, Lucent) — *Costolo, Raebeth*
3 Weeks to a Better Back: Solutions for Healing the Structural, Nutritional, and Emotional Causes of Back Pain — *Sinett, Todd*
The 4PS Framework — *Rana, Yadvinder S.*
4. Tagung des Zentralinstituts "Anthropologie der Religion(en)"
4th Century Karia. Defining a Karian Identity under the Hekatomnids — *Henry, Olivier*
4. ZeitgeschichtsTage Pragser Wildsee
5@55: The 5 Essential Legal Documents You Need by Age 55 — *Grimaldi, Judith D.*
c 5 Minute Bedtime Stories
c 5 Minute Christmas Stories
5 Minutes with Jesus: Making Today Matter — *Walsh, Sheila*
c The 5 Misfits (Illus. by Alemagna, Beatrice) — *Alemagna, Beatrice*
5 Practices for Orchestrating Task-Based Discussions in Science — *Cartier, Jennifer*
c 5 Seconds of Summer: Hey, Let's Make a Band! — *5 Seconds of Summer*
y 5 to 1 — *Bodger, Holly*
The 6:41 to Paris — *Blondel, Jean-Philippe*
y The 6 Voyages of Lone Sloane (Illus. by Druillet, Philippe) — *Druillet, Philippe*
c 7 Days — *Ainsworth, Eve*
7 Easy Ways to Show Your Employees You Care! A Booklet for Hotel Managers and Others — *Hiller, Jokima*
7 Women: And the Secret of Their Greatness — *Metaxas, Eric*
c 8: An Animal Alphabet (Illus. by Cooper, Elisha) — *Cooper, Elisha*
c 8-Bit Baseball (Illus. by Ferrara, Eduardo) — *Bowen, Carl*
8 Keys to Old School Parenting for Modern-Day Families — *Mascolo, Michael F.*
8 Keys to Practicing Mindfulness: Practical Strategies for Emotional Health and Well-Being — *Reeds, Manuela Mischke*
8 Keys to Raising the Quirky Child: How to Help a Kid Who Doesn't Quite Fit In — *Bowers, Mark*
The 8th Circle — *Cain, Sarah*
9 1/2 Narrow: My Life in Shoes — *Morrisroe, Patricia*
9/11 als Bildereignis: Zur Visuellen Bewaltigung des Anschlags — *Becker, Anne*
10:04 (Read by Summerer, Eric Michael). Audiobook Review — *Lerner, Ben*
10:04 — *Lerner, Ben*
c 10 Goofy Geckos (Illus. by Hinde, Deborah) — *Terei, Pio*
10 Percent Human: How Your Body's Microbes Hold the Key to Health and Happiness — *Collen, Alanna*
c 10 Rivers That Shaped The World (Illus. by Rosen, Kim) — *Peters, Marilee*
c 10 True Tales: Battle Heroes — *Zullo, Allan*
10 True Tales: FBI Heroes — *Zullo, Allan*
c 10 True Tales: Heroes of 9/11 — *Zullo, Allan*
c 10 True Tales: World War I Heroes — *Zullo, Allan*
The 11th Hour — *Schipper, Sebastian*
12 Amazing Franchise Opportunities for 2015 — *Hayes, John P.*
c The 12 Days o' Yule: A Scots Christmas Rhyme (Illus. by Land, Matthew) — *Rennie, Susan*
The 12 Drop Rule: Getting the Most out of Wine and Life — *Drinan, Patrick*
c The 12 Labors of Hercules: A Graphic Retelling (Illus. by Haus, Estudio) — *Hoena, Blake*
c 12 Things to Know about Fracking — *Felix, Rebecca*
c 13 Architects Children Should Know — *Heine, Florian*
c 13 Art Techniques Children Should Know — *Wenzel, Angela*
y 13 Hours — *Dhami, Narinder*
c The 13-Storey Treehouse (Read by Wemyss, Stig). Audiobook Review — *Griffiths, Andy*
c The 13-Storey Treehouse (Illus. by Denton, Terry) — *Griffiths, Andy*
y The 13th Floor — *Welvaert, Scott R.*
13 Ways of Looking at a Fat Girl — *Awad, Mona*
14/18: Der Weg nach Versailles — *Friedrich, Jorg*
14 Characteristic Pieces for the Intermediate Pianist — *Clark, Larry*
15 Minutes to Fit: The Simple 30-Day Guide to Total Fitness, 15 Minutes at a Time — *Light, Zuzka*
The 15 Miracles of Love — *Hoffman, Spencer*
c 15 Things Not to Do with a Baby (Illus. by Sterling, Holly) — *McAllister, Margaret*
17 Carnations: The Royals, the Nazis, and the Biggest Cover-up in History — *Morton, Andrew*
18th-Century English Organ Music: A Graded Anthology, 4 vols. — *Patrick, David*
18 Wheels of Horror — *Miller, Eric*
21 Days of a Neurasthenic — *Mirbeau, Octave*
21 Songs in 6 Days: Learn Ukulele the Easy Way — *Peters, Jenny*
21st Century Ellis: Operational Art and Strategic Prophecy for the Modern Era — *Friedman, Brent A.*
21st Century Sims: Innovation, Education, and Leadership for the Modern Era — *Armstrong, Benjamin E.*
c 23 Things to Do before You Are 11 1/2: A Practical Step-by-Step Guide for Things to Make in Your Backyard (Illus. by Haslam, John) — *Warren, Mike*
24/7: Schlaflos im Spatkapitalismus — *Crary, Jonathan*
24 Hours at Waterloo: 18 June 1815 — *Kershaw, Robert*
24 Pages and Other Poems — *Fishman, Lisa*
c 24 Stories for Advent (Illus. by Tharlet, Eve) — *Weninger, Brigitte*
y 25 10-Minute Plays for Teens — *Harbison, Lawrence*
c 25 Days of Tropical Christmas (Illus. by Lane, Susan) — *Stern, D.G.*
25 Jahre Aufarbeitung der Geschichte der sowjetischen Speziallager
c 25 Roses — *Faris, Stephanie*
25th Street Confidential: Drama, Decadence, and Dissipation along Ogden's Rowdiest Road — *Holley, Val*
25 Women: Essays on Their Art — *Hickey, Dave*
c The 26-Storey Treehouse (Read by Wemyss, Stig). Audiobook Review — *Griffiths, Andy*
c 28 Days: Moments in Black History That Changed the World (Illus. by Evans, Shane W.) — *Smith, Charles R., Jr.*
28. Jahrestagung des Schwerter Arbeitskreises Katholizismusforschung
30 April 1945 — *Kluge, Alexander*
The 30-Day Faith Detox: Renew Your Mind, Cleanse Your Body, Heal Your Spirit — *Smith, Laura Harris*
The 30-Day Sobriety Solution: How to Cut Back or Quit Drinking in the Privacy of Your Own Home — *Canfield, Jack*
The 30-Day Sobriety Solution: How to Quit or Cut Back Drinking in the Privacy of Your Own Home — *Canfield, Jack*
The 30-Day Vegan Challenge — *Patrick-Goudreau, Colleen*
30 Days — *D'Abo, Christine*
30 Great Myths about the Romantics — *Blackwell, Wiley*
30 Illegal Years to the Strip: The Untold Stories of the Gangsters Who Built the Early Las Vegas Strip — *Friedman, Bill*
30-Second Shakespeare: 50 Key Aspects of His Works, Life and Legacy, Each Explained in Half a Minute — *Barber, Rose*
30 Slippers to Knit and Felt: Fabulous Projects You Can Make, Wear, and Share — *Nerjordet, Arne*
30 Years After: Issues and Representations of the Falklands War — *Berberi, Carine*
33 Artists in 3 Acts — *Thornton, Sarah*
33 Days — *Werth, Leon*
y The 39 Clues: Unstoppable Book 4: Flashpoint — *Korman, Gordon*
c The 39-Storey Treehouse (Read by Wemyss, Stig). Audiobook Review — *Griffiths, Andy*
39th Annual Conference on the Political Economy of the World-System: Global Inequalities: Hegemonic Shifts and Regional Differentiations
y The 39th Clues — *Korman, Gordon*
40/40 Vision: Clarifying Your Mission in Midlife — *Greer, Peter*
40 Days with the Holy Spirit — *Levison, Jack*
c 40 Fun Fables: Tales That Trick, Tickle and Teach (Illus. by Hoffmire, F. Baird) — *Hamilton, Martha*
c 40 Fun Fables: Tales That Trick, Tickle and Teach (Illus. by Hoffmeier, F. Baird) — *Hamilton, Martha*
41: A Portrait of My Father (Read by Bush, George W.). Audiobook Review — *Bush, George W.*
41: A Portrait of My Father — *Bush, George W.*
c 43 Old Cemetery Road: The Loch Ness Punster (Illus. by Klise, M. Sarah) — *Klise, Kate*
y 44 Hours or Strike! — *Dublin, Anne*
45: Die Welt am Wendepunkt — *Buruma, Ian*
c 50 Cent: Hip-Hop Mogul — *Burlingame, Jeff*
50 Great American Places — *Glass, Brent D.*
y 50 Impressive Kids and Their Amazing (and True!) Stories — *Mitchell, Saundra*

50 Jahre Unabhangigkeit in Afrika: Kontinuitaten, Bruche, Perspektiven — *Bierschenk, Thomas*
50 More Ways to Soothe Yourself without Food: Mindfulness Strategies to Cope with Stress and End Emotional Eating — *Albers, Susan*
50 Politics Classics — *Butler-Bowdon, Tom*
The 50s: The Story of a Decade — *Finder, Harry*
c **The 50 States: Explore the U.S.A with 50 Fact-Filled Maps! (Illus. by Linero, Sol)** — *Balkan, Gabrielle*
c **The 50 States: Explore the U.S.A. with 50 Fact-Filled Maps! (Illus. by Linero, Sol)** — *Balkan, Gabrielle*
c **The 50 States: Explore the U.S.A. with 50 Fact-Filled Maps! (Illus. by Linero, Sol)** — *Balkan, Gabrielle*
c **50 Unbelievable Women and Their Fascinating (and True!) Stories (Illus. by Petrus, Cara)** — *Mitchell, Saundra*
50 Ways to Ruin a Rake — *Lee, Jade*
The 51 Day War: Ruin and Resistance in Gaza — *Blumenthal, Max*
y **A 52-Hertz Whale** — *Sommer, Bill*
52 Men — *Leonard, Louise Wareham*
y **The 52nd** — *Dela*
52 Ways to Get Unstuck: Exercises to Break through Writer's Block — *Mandeville, Chris*
59 Reasons to Write: Mini-Lessons, Prompts, and Inspiration for Teachers — *Messner, Kate*
60 Quick Knit Baby Essentials: Sweaters, Toys, Blankets, & More in Cherub from Cascade Yarns — *Sixth & Spring Books*
c **The 65-Storey Treehouse (Illus. by Denton, Terry)** — *Griffiths, Andy*
68. Baltisches Historikertreffen
70x70: Unlicensed Preaching: A Life Unpacked in 70 Films — *Sinclair, Iain*
y **'74 and Sunny** — *Benza, A.J.*
75 Fun Fat-Quarter Quilts: 13 Quilts + 62 Innovative Variations — *Cerda, Roxane*
75 Masterpieces Every Christian Should Know: The Fascinating Stories behind Great Works of Art, Literature, Music, and Film — *Glaspey, Terry*
75 Years of Marvel Comics: From the Golden Age to the Silver Screen — *Thomas, Roy*
77 Dream Songs — *Berryman, John*
77 Dream Songs — *Cole, Henri*
81 Days below Zero: The Incredible Survival Story of a World War II Pilot in Alaska's Frozen Wilderness — *Murphy, Brian*
88 Days to Kandahar: A CIA Diary — *Grenier, Robert L.*
c **88 Lime Street: The Way In** — *Kirby, Denise*
y **'89 Walls** — *Pierson, Katie*
90 Church: Inside America's Notorious First Narcotics Squad — *Unkefer, Dean*
y **99 Days** — *Cotugno, Katie*
99 Keys to a Creative Life: Spiritual, Intuitive and Awareness Practices for Personal Fulfillment — *Harris, Melissa*
100 Books Every Blues Fan Should Own — *Komara, Edward*
100 Buildings 100 Years — *Twentieth Century Society*
100 Days — *Hale, Mimsy*
100 Deadly Skills: The SEAL Operative's Guide to Eluding Pursuers, Evading Capture, and Surviving Any Dangerous Situation — *Emerson, Clint*
100 Essays I Don't Have Time to Write: On Umbrellas and Sword Fights, Parades and Dogs, Fire Alarms, Children, and Theater — *Ruhl, Sarah*
100 Essential Things You Didn't Know You Didn't Know about Math and the Arts — *Barrow, John D.*
The 100 Greatest Silent Film Comedians — *Roots, James*
100 Million Years of Food: What Our Ancestors Ate and Why It Matters Today — *Le, Stephen*
The 100 Most Important American Financial Crises: An Encyclopedia of the Lowest Points in American Economic History — *Skrabec, Quentin R., Jr.*
c **100 Pablo Picassos (Illus. by Lemay, Violet)**
100 Painters of Tomorrow — *Beers, Kurt*
100 Recipes: The Absolute Best Ways to Make the True Essentials — *America's Test Kitchen*
y **100 Sideways Miles (Read by Heyborne, Kirby)** — *Smith, Andrew Anselmo*
y **100 Sideways Miles** — *Smith, Andrew Anselmo*
100 Skills You'll Need for the End of the World (as We Know It). — *Spagna, Ana Maria*
100 Things I Learned in Heaven — *Bauer, Karen*
c **100 Things That Make Me Happy** — *Schwartz, Amy*
c **100 Trillion Good Bacteria Living in the Human Body (Illus. by Ruffle, Mark)** — *Rockett, Paul*
100 Years in the Life of an American Girl — *Sherman, Suzanne*

100 Years of the Best American Short Stories — *Moore, Lorrie*
101 Careers in Mathematics — *Sterrett, Andrew*
c **101 Movies to See before You Grow Up** — *Valle, Suzette*
101 Outstanding Graphic Novels, 4th ed. — *Fingeroth, Daniel J.*
c **101 Things to Do before You Grow Up: Fun Activities for You to Check off Your List (Illus. by Bramall, Dan)** — *Dower, Laura*
c **101 Ways to Amaze & Entertain: Amazing Magic and Hilarious Jokes to Try on Your Friends and Family** — *Gross, Peter*
c **101 Ways to Be a Good Granny (Illus. by Kath, Katie)** — *Ziefert, Harriet*
102 Days of War: How Osama Bin Laden, Al Qaeda & The Taliban Survived 2001 — *Barzilai, Yaniv*
121 First Dates: How to Succeed at Online Dating, Fall in Love, and Live Happily Ever After — *Newman, Wendy*
c **125 Cool Inventions: Supersmart Machines and Wacky Gadgets You Never Knew You Wanted!** — *National Geographic Kids*
150 Best Mini Interior Ideas — *Mola, Francesc Zamora*
150 Jahre Italien: Themen, Wege, offene Fragen — *Griessner, Florika*
The 228 Legacy — *Chow, Jennifer J.*
y **250 Hours** — *Nelson, Colleen*
290: A Novel of the American Civil War — *Wonnell, Donn*
c **300 Minutes of Danger** — *Heath, Jack*
300 Sandwiches: A Multilayered Love Story ... with Recipes — *Smith, Stephanie*
c **365 Days of Wonder: Mr. Browne's Book of Precepts** — *Palacio, R.J.*
365 Ways to Develop Your Psychic Ability: Simple Tools to Increase Your Intuition and Clairvoyance — *Chauran, Alexandra*
400 Calories or Less with Our Best Bites: Tasty Choices for Healthy Families with Calorie Options for Every Appetite — *Wells, Sara*
438 Days: An Extraordinary True Story of Survival at Sea — *Franklin, Jonathan*
500 Crochet Stitches: The Ultimate Crochet Stitch Bible — *Knight, Erika*
500 Great Military Leaders, 2 vols. — *Tucker, Spencer C.*
The 613 — *Rand, Archie*
750 Knitting Stitches: The Ultimate Knit Stitch Bible — *Pavilion Books*
750 Years in Paris — *Mahe, Vincent*
800 Jahre "Welscher Gast". Neue Fragen zu einer alten Verhaltenslehre in Wort und Bild
817 - Die Urkundliche Ersterwahnung von Villingen und Schwenningen. Alemannien und das Reich in der Zeit Kaiser Ludwigs des Frommen
850 Intriguing Questions about Judaism: True, False, or in Between — *Eisenberg, Ronald L.*
c **999 Frogs and a Little Brother (Illus. by Murakami, Yasunari)** — *Kimura, Ken*
c **1,000 Facts about the Bible** — *Currie, Robin*
1,001 Delicious Soups and Stews: From Elegant Classics to Hearty One-Pot Meals, 4th ed. — *Spitler, Sue*
1001 Movies You Must See before You Die — *Schneider, Steven Jay*
1177 B.C.: The Year Civilization Collapsed — *Cline, Eric H.*
1215: The Year of Magna Carta — *Gillingham, John*
1381: The Year of the Peasants' Revolt — *Barker, Juliet*
1,411 Quite Interesting Facts to Knock You Sideways — *Lloyd, John*
y **1493 for Young People: From Columbus's Voyage to Globalization** — *Mann, Charles C.*
1511-2011: Philippe de Commynes. Droit, ecriture: Deux piliers de la souverainete — *Blanchard, Joel*
1606: William Shakespeare and the Year of Lear — *Shapiro, James*
1635: A Parcel of Rogues — *Dennis, Andrew*
The 1711 Expedition to Quebec: Politics and the Limitations of British Global Strategy — *Lyons, Adam*
1716 - Leibniz' Letztes Lebensjahr: Unbekanntes zu einem Bekannten Universalgenie
y **1776: The Illustrated Edition** — *McCullough, David*
1808: The Flight of the Emperor — *Gomes, Laurentino*
1813: Napoleon, Metternich und das Weltgeschichtliche Duell von Dresden — *Muchler, Gunter*

1820: Disorder and Stability in the United Kingdom — *Chase, Malcolm*
y **1854: Do You Dare? Eureka Boys** — *Matthews, Penny*
1864: The Forgotten War That Shaped Modern Europe — *Buk-Swienty, Tom*
1882: Custer in Chains — *Conroy, Robert*
The 1910 Slocum Massacre: An Act of Genocide in East Texas — *Bills, E.R.*
1914: The Avant-Gardes at War — *Kunst- und Ausstellungshalle der Bundesrepublik Deutschland*
y **1915: Do You Dare? Jimmy's War** — *Clark, Sherryl*
1915: Wounds of War — *Menefy, Diana*
1916: A Global History — *Jeffery, Keith*
c **1916: Attaques du requin (Illus. by Dawson, Scott)** — *Tarshis, Lauren*
The 1918 Flu Pandemic: Core Events of a Worldwide Outbreak — *Micklos, John., Jr.*
1920: The Year That Made the Decade Roar — *Burns, Eric*
1924 — *Range, Peter Ross*
1929: Mapping the Jewish World — *Diner, Hasia R.*
1932: The Rise of Hitler & FDR: Two Tales of Politics, Betrayal, and Unlikely Destiny — *Pietrusza, David*
1944: FDR and the Year That Changed History — *Winik, Jay*
1946: The Making of the Modern World — *Sebestyen, Victor*
1956: Mao's China and the Hungarian Crisis — *Zhu, Dandan*
1960s Counterculture: Documents Decoded — *Willis, Jim*
1965: The Most Revolutionary Year in Music — *Jackson, Andrew Grant*
1966: The Year the Decade Exploded — *Savage, Jon*
1971: A Global History of the Creation of Bangladesh — *Raghavan, Srinath*
1984
The 1989 Revolutions in Central and Eastern Europe: From Communism to Pluralism — *McDermott, Kevin*
1989 und die Rolle der Gewalt — *Sabrow, Martin*
1995: The Year the Future Began — *Campbell, W. Joseph*
2001 and Counting: Kubrick, Nietzsche, and Anthropology — *Kapferer, Bruce*
2014 Official First Day Cover Collection
The 2014 Postal Service Guide to U.S. Stamps
2014: The Election that Changed India — *Sardesai, Rajdeep*
2015 Brookman — *Macdonald, David S.*
2020: The Fall of Islamic States — *Chamanara, Sohrab*
2,100 Asanas: The Complete Yoga Poses — *Lacerda, Daniel*
c **5,000 Awesome Facts (about Everything!) 2** — *Beer, Julie*
c **The $25,000 Flight: How Lindbergh Set a Daring Record... (Illus. by Lowe, Wesley)** — *Houran, Lori Haskins*
A, B, C: Three Short Novels — *Delany, Samuel R.*
c **A+ for Big Ben (Illus. by LaFave, Kim)** — *Ellis, Sarah*
c **An A from Miss Keller (Illus. by Polacco, Patricia)** — *Polacco, Patricia*
A Is for Arsenic: The Poisons of Agatha Christie — *Harkup, Kathryn*
c **A Is for Australia: A Factastic Tour** — *Lessac, Frane*
The A Swing: The Alternative Approach to Great Golf — *Leadbetter, David*
y **A to Z: Great Modern Artists (Illus. by Tuohy, Andy)** — *Tuohy, Andy*
A-Z of Bird Portraits: An Illustrated Guide to Painting Beautiful Birds in Acrylics — *Forkner, Andrew*
A-Z of Embroidery Stitches 2
A-Z of Heirloom Sewing — *Country Bumpkin*
A-Z of Whitework — *Search Press*
The A26 — *Garnier, Pascal*
c **Aa-Zz: A Pop-Up Alphabet (Illus. by Hawcock, David)** — *Hawcock, David*
c **Aaron and Alexander: The Most Famous Duel in American History (Illus. by Brown, Don)** — *Brown, Don*
c **Aaron Has a Lazy Day** — *Eastman, P.D.*
Aaron Henry of Mississippi: Inside Agitator — *Morrison, Minion K.C.*
c **Aaron Loves Apples and Pumpkins (Illus. by Eastman, P.D.)** — *Eastman, P.D.*
The Abaddon — *Shadmi, Koren*
Abba Eban — *Siniver, Asaf*
The Abbey — *Martin, James (b. 1960-)*

The Abbots of Wearmouth and Jarrow — Grocock, Christopher
c Abbreviations — Murray, Kara
c ABC, Adoption and Me (Illus. by Griffin, Paul) — Swift, Gayle H.
c The ABC Animal Orchestra (Illus. by Saaf, Donald) — Saaf, Donald
c ABC Dream — Krans, Kim
c ABC Insects — American Museum of Natural History
c The ABC of Fantastic Princes (Illus. by Puchner, Willy) — Puchner, Willy
c ABC School's for Me! (Illus. by Munsinger, Lynn) — Katz, Susan B.
ABCDEEG — Holton, John
c ABC's Down on the Farm (Illus. by Munro, Eileen) — Munro, Eileen
ABCs of Beautiful Light: A Complete Course in Lighting for Photographers — Olson, Rosanne
The ABCs of Success: The Essential Principles from America's Greatest Prosperity Teacher — Proctor, Bob
c ABCs on Wings (Illus. by Olivera, Ramon) — Olivera, Ramon
Abducting a General — Fermor, Patrick Leigh
Abe & Fido: Lincoln's Love of Animals and the Touching Story of His Favorite Canine Companion — Algeo, Matthew
c Abe Lincoln and the Selfie That Saved the Union — Potter, David (b. 1955-)
Abe Lincoln: His Wit and Wisdom from A-Z (Illus. by O'Brien, John) — Schroeder, Alan
Abelard in Four Dimensions: A Twelfth-Century Philosopher in His Context and Ours — Marenbon, John
"Aber eines lugt er nicht: Echtheit" - Perspektiven auf Hubert Fichte — Gillett, Robert
Abgrenzung und Hoffnung: gt;gt;Europa<< in der deutschen, britischen und amerikanischen Presse 1945-1980 — Brill, Ariane
Aboard Cabrillo's Galleon — Echeverria Bender, Christine
Abolishing the Taboo: Dwight D. Eisenhower and American Nuclear Doctrine, 1945-1961 — Jones, Brian Madison
The Abolition of Cash — Warwick, David R.
The Abolition of Man — Lewis, C.S.
The Abolition of Slavery in Ottoman Tunisia — Montana, Ismael M.
The Abolitionist Imagination — Delbanco, Andrew
Abominable Science! Origins of the Yeti, Nessie, and Other Famous Cryptids — Loxton, Daniel
Abomination — Whitta, Gary
The Abominators — Smith, J.L.
Aboriginal and Visible Minority Librarians: Oral Histories from Canada — Lee, Deborah
Abortion, Execution, and the Consequences of Taking Life — Slack, James D.
Abortion in the American Imagination: Before Life and Choice, 1880-1940 — Weingarten, Karen
Abortion Law in Transnational Perspective: Cases and Controversies — Cook, Rebecca J.
Abounding in Kindness: Writing for the People of God — Johnson, Elizabeth A.
y About a Girl — McCarry, Sarah
c About Parrots: A Guide for Children (Illus. by Sill, John) — Sill, Cathryn
About That Fling — Fenske, Tawna
About Women: Conversations between a Writer and a Painter — Alther, Lisa
Above Ground — Swift, Lee
y Above the Dreamless Dead: World War I in Poetry and Comics — Duffy, Chris
Above the Line — MacLaine, Shirley
y Above the Waterfall — Rash, Ron
Above Us Only Sky — Young-Stone, Michele
c Abracadabra! It's Spring! (Illus. by Gal, Susan) — O'Brien, Anne Sibley
c Abracadabra: The Story of Magic through the Ages (Illus. by Ivanov, Aleksey) — Newquist, H.P.
c Abracazebra (Illus. by Docherty, Thomas) — Docherty, Helen
Abraham Ibn Daud's Dorot Olam (Generations of the Ages): A Critical Edition and Translation of Zikhron Divrey Romi, Divrey Malkhey Yisrael and the Midrash on Zechariah — Vehlow, Katja
Abraham in the Works of John Chrysostom — Tonias, Demetrios
Abraham Joshua Heschel: The Call of Transcendence — Held, Shai
Abraham Kuyper: Modern Calvinist, Christian Democrat — Bratt, James D.

Abraham Lincoln and White America — Dirck, Brian R.
c Abraham Lincoln: The 16th President — Gregory, Josh
Abraham: The World's First (But Certainly Not Last) Jewish Lawyer — Dershowitz, Alan M.
Abroad at Home: The 600 Best International Travel Experiences in North America — National Geographic Society (U.S.)
Abroad — Crouch, Katie
The Abrupt Physics of Dying — Hardisty, Paul E.
Abschlusstagung des DFG-Netzwerks "ZeitenWelten. Zur Verschrankung von Weltdeutung und Zeitwahrnehmung im Fruhen und Hohen Mittelalter"
c ABSee (Illus. by Doyle, Elizabeth) — Doyle, Elizabeth
Absolute Music: The History of an Idea — Bonds, Mark Evan
Absolute Recoil: Towards a New Foundation of Dialectical Materialism — Zizek, Slavoj
Absolutely Beautiful Things: Decorating Inspiration for a Bright and Colourful Life — Spiro, Anna
Absolutely One Thing — Child, Lauren
y Absolutely True Lies — Stuhler, Rachel
c Absolutely Truly (Read by Rubinate, Amy). Audiobook Review — Frederick, Heather Vogel
c Absolutely Truly — Frederick, Heather Vogel
Absolution: A Palestinian Israeli Love Story — Georgy, R.F.
The Absolution — Holt, Jonathan
The Absolution of Roberto Acestes Laing — Rombes, Nicholas
Abstraction and Reality: The Sculpture of Ivor Roberts-Jones — Black, Jonathan
c Abuela (Illus. by Kleven, Elisa) — Dorros, Arthur
c Abukacha's Shoes — Tessler, Tamar
Abundance from the Desert: Classical Arabic Poetry — Farrin, Raymond
The Abundance: Narrative Essays Old and New — Dillard, Annie
y The Abyss Surrounds Us — Skrutskie, Emily
The Academic Library Administrator's Field Guide — Nelson, Bryce
Academic Tribes and Territories: Intellectual Enquiry and the Cultures of Discipline — Trowler, Paul R.
The Academy — Payne, J.T.
Academy Gothic — Hill, James Tate
Academy Street — Costello, Mary
c The Acadians — Mitchell, Sara
Accent on Two Pianos: Intermediate to Advanced Level — Gillock, William
Accepting the Disaster — Mehigan, Joshua
Access for Everyone: Supporting Special Needs through the School Library — Tutt, Rona
Access to Asia — Schweitzer, Sharon
The Accessibility of Music: Participation, Reception, and Contact — Eisentraut, Jochen
Accessible Citizenships: Disability, Nation, and the Cultural Politics of Greater Mexico — Minich, Julie Avril
Accessing the Future — Allan, Kathryn
Accidence Will Happen: The Non-Pedantic Guide to English Usage — Kamm, Oliver
y The Accident — Freeman, Shannon
The Accident — Pavone, Chris
y The Accident Season (Read by Minifie, Colby). Audiobook Review — Fowley-Doyle, Moira
y The Accident Season — Fowley-Doyle, Moira
The Accidental Admiral: A Sailor Takes Command at NATO — Stavridis, James
y The Accidental Afterlife of Thomas Marsden — Trevayne, Emma
The Accidental Alchemist — Pandian, Gigi
Accidental Brownie: A Childhood Memoir — Froiland, Paul
The Accidental Caregiver — Collins, Gregor
y The Accidental Data Scientist — Affelt, Amy
The Accidental Diarist: A History of the Daily Planner in America — McCarthy, Molly
Accidental Empress — Pataki, Allison
c Accidental Genius (Illus. by Miller, Antonia) — Murray, Tamsyn
y The Accidental Highwayman: Being the Tale of Kit Bistrol, His Horse Midnight, a Mysterious Princess, and Sundry Magical Persons Besides — Tripp, Ben
The Accidental Indexer — Badgett, Nan
c The Accidental Prime Minister — McLaughlin, Tom
The Accidental Prime Minister: The Making and Unmaking of Manmohan Singh — Baru, Sanjaya
The Accidental Revolutionary: George Whitefield and the Creation of America — Mahaffey, Jerome D.

Accidental Saints: Finding God in All the Wrong People — Bolz-Weber, Nadia
The Accidental Truth: What My Mother's Murder Investigation Taught Me About Life — Taylor, Lauri
c Accidentally Evil — Chapman, Lara
Accidents of Providence — Brown, Stacia M.
The Accommodated Animal: Cosmopolity in Shakespearean Locales — Shannon, Laurie
Accomplishing NAGPRA: Perspectives on the Intent, Impact, and Future of the Native American Graves Protection and Repatriation Act — Chari, Sangita
According to Baba: A Collaborative Oral History of Sudbury's Ukrainian Community — Zembrzycki, Stacey
An Account of the Decline of the Great Auk, According to One Who Saw It — Greengrass, Jessie
Accounting for Non-Accountants, 10th ed. — Horner, David
Accounting Information and Equity Valuation: Theory, Evidence, and Applications — Zhang, Guochang
The Accounts of Godfrey of Crowland, Abbot of Peterborough 1299-1321 — Raban, Sandra
c Accuracy in Media — Fromm, Megan
Accused: My Fight for Truth, Justice, and the Strength to Forgive — Craft, Tonya
Ace — Williams, Steve
c Ace Dragon Ltd. (Illus. by Blake, Quentin) — Hoban, Russell
Achebe and Friends at Umuahia: The Making of a Literary Elite — Ochiagha, Terri
The Achievement Habit: Stop Wishing, Start Doing, and Take Command of Your Life — Roth, Bernard
c Acid. Audiobook Review — Pass, Emma
Acid Hype: American News Media and the Psychedelic Experience — Siff, Stephen
Acid Rain and the Rise of the Environmental Chemist in Nineteenth-Century Britain: The Life and Work of Robert Angus Smith — Reed, Peter
Acknowledged Legislator: Critical Essays on the Poetry of Martin Espada — Carvaljo, Edward J.
The Acolyte — Cutter, Nick
The Acquisition of Books by Chetham's Library, 1655-1700 — Yeo, Matthew
The Acquisition of Sociolinguistic Competence in a Lingua Franca Context — Durham, Mercedes
Across Borders: Latin Perspectives in the Americas Reshaping Religion, Theology, and Life — Rieger, Byoerg
Across That Bridge — Lewis, John
Across the Bloody Chasm: The Culture of Commemoration among Civil War Veterans — Harris, M. Keith
Across the Cheyenne River — Nesbitt, John D.
Across the German Sea: Early Modern Scottish Connections with the Wider Elbe-Weser Region — Zickermann, Kathrin
Across the Inlet — Summers, Gail
Across the Pond — McCormick, Michael
Across the World with the Johnsons: Visual Culture and American Empire in the Twentieth Century — Ahrens, Prue
c Acrostic Poems (Illus. by Petelinsek, Kathleen) — Bolt, Lisa M.
Act Like a Leader, Think Like a Leader — Ibarra, Herminia
Act of God — Ciment, Jill
Acta Conventus Neo-Latini Monasteriensis: Proceedings of the Fifteenth International Congress of Neo-Latin Studies — Steiner-Weber, Astrid
Acta et Documenta Synodi Nationalis Dordrechtanae 1618-1619, vol. 1: Acta of the Synod and Dordt — Sinnema, Donald
Acting Like It Matters: John Malpede and the Los Angeles Poverty Department — McEnteer, James
Acting on Faith: The Confraternity of the Gonfalone in Renaissance Rome — Wisch, Barbara
Acting White?: Rethinking Race in "Post-Racial" America — Carbado, Devon W.
c The Action Bible 1: The Battle Begins: The Story of Creation (Illus. by Cariello, Sergio) — Cook, David C.
Action for Disarmament: 10 Things You Can Do! — Sullivan, Kathleen
Action, Knowledge, and Will — Hyman, John
c Action Movie Kid (Illus. by Fabbretti, Valerio) — Hashimoto, Daniel
Active Bodies: A History of Women's Physical Education in Twentieth-Century America — Verbrugge, Martha H.

An Activity-Based Approach to Early Intervention, 4th ed. — Johnson, JoAnn
An Actor's Companion — Barrish, Seth
The Actor's Secret: Techniques for Transforming Habitual Patterns and Improving Performance — Polatin, Betsy
Acts and Apparitions: Discourses on the Real in Performance Practice and Theory, 1990-2010 — Tomlin, Liz
Acts of Faith — Wynn, Patricia
Acts of War — Young, James
Acts: Theater, Philosophy, and the Performing Self — Zamir, Tzachi
c The Actual & Truthful Adventures of Becky Thatcher (Read by Gilbert, Tavia). Audiobook Review — Lawson, Jessica
c The Actual & Truthful Adventures of Becky Thatcher — Lawson, Jessica
Ad Nauseam — Koob, Jeff
c Ada Byron Lovelace and the Thinking Machine (Illus. by Chu, April) — Wallmark, Laurie
Adak: The Rescue of Alfa Foxtrot 586 — Jampoler, Andrew C. A.
Adam Ferguson in the Scottish Enlightenment: The Roman Past and Europe's Future — McDaniel, Iain
c Adam & Thomas (Illus. by Dumas, Philippe) — Appelfeld, Aharon
Adam Usk's Secret — Justice, Steven
Adamastor e dintorni: in ricordo di Antonio Tabucchi. Con un frammento inedito — Tocco, Valeria
y Adaptation — Lo, Malinda
Adapting to Alzheimer's: Support for When Your Parent Becomes Your Child — Harris, Sherry Lynn
Adapting to Climate Change: Lessons from Natural Hazards Planning — Glavovic, Bruce C.
Addendum to a Photo Album — Otroshenko, Vladislav
Addicted.pregnant.poor — Knight, Kelly Ray
Addiction and Self-Control: Perspectives from Philosophy, Psychology and Neuroscience — Levy, Neil
Addiction Trajectories — Raikhel, Eugene
The Addictocarb Diet: Avoid the 9 Highly Addictive Carbs While Eating Anything Else You Want — Roseman, Bruce
Adeline (Read by James, Corrie). Audiobook Review — Vincent, Norah
Adeline — Vincent, Norah
Adelsbilder von der Antike bis zur Gegenwart — Scholz, Johannes
The ADHD Advantage: What You Thought Was a Diagnosis May Be Your Greatest Strength — Archer, Dale
Adios, America! The Left's Plan to Turn Our Country into a Third World Hellhole — Coulter, Ann
Adios Nino: The Gangs of Guatemala City and the Politics of Death — Levenson, Deborah T.
Adjudication in Action: An Ethnomethodology of Law, Morality and Justice — Dupret, Baudouin
Admen, Mad Men, and the Real World of Advertising: Essential Lessons for Business and Life — Marinaccio, Dave
Admirable Evasions: How Psychology Undermines Morality — Dalrymple, Theodore
y The Admissions — Moore, Meg Mitchell
The Adobe Photoshop Lightroom CC / Lightroom 6 Book: The Complete Guide for Photographers — Evening, Martin
Adonis: The Myth of the Dying God in the Italian Renaissance — Caruso, Carlo
Adopted Territory: Transnational Korean Adoptees and the Politics of Belonging — Kim, Eleana J.
Adorno and the Ends of Philosophy — Bowie, Andrew
Adrenaline — Hoffman, Brian B.
c Adrenaline Crush — Crompton, Laurie Boyle
y Adrian and the Tree of Secrets (Illus. by Caillou, Marie) — Homel, David
y Adrian and the Tree of Secrets (Illus. by Caillou, Marie) — Hubert
y Adrift — Griffin, Paul
Ads for God — Vanderwarker, Tony
Adult Onset — MacDonald, Ann-Marie
Advanced Chain Maille Jewelry Workshop: Weaving with Rings and Scale Maille — Karon, Karen
Advanced Math for Young Students: A First Course in Algebra — Keller, Philip
The Advancement of Music in Enlightenment England: Benjamin Cooke and the Academy of Ancient Music — Eggington, Tim
Advances in Evolutionary Developmental Biology — Streelman, J. Todd

Advances in Positive Organizational Psychology — Bakker, Arnold B.
Advancing Singapore-China Economic Relations — Swee-Hock, Saw
Advent in Narnia: Reflections for the Season — Haverkamp, Heidi
The Adventure of Being Human: Lessons on Soulful Living from the Heart of the Urantia Revelation — Francis, Gavin
The Adventure of the Busts of Eva Peron — Gamerro, Carlos
The Adventure of the Plated Spoon and Other Tales of Sherlock Holmes — Estleman, Loren D.
c The Adventurers — Elliot, Rachel
c The Adventures and Life Lessons of Wolfy (Illus. by Escalona, Earlene Gayle) — Franks, Lane
c Adventures in Famous Places — Lonely Planet
c Adventures in Flatfrost (Illus. by McPhillips, Robert) — Quinn, Jordan
Adventures in Human Being: A Grand Tour from the Cranium to the Calcaneum — Francis, Gavin
Adventures in Muniland: A Guide to Municipal Bond Investing in the Post-Crisis Era — Comes, Michael F.
Adventures in Philosophy at Notre Dame — Sayre, Kenneth M.
Adventures in Saying Yes: A Journey from Fear to Faith — Medearis, Carl
Adventures in Stationery: A Journey through Your Pencil Case — Ward, James
Adventures in the Anthropocene: A Journey to the Heart of the Planet We Made — Vince, Gaia
Adventures in the Lives of Others: Ethical Dilemmas in Factual Filmmaking — Quinn, James
Adventures in Writing for Children — Shepard, Aaron
The Adventures of Alice Laselles — Victoria, Alexandrina
c The Adventures of Beekle: The Unimaginary Friend (Illus. by Santat, Dan) — Santat, Dan
c The Adventures of Black Dog (Illus. by Theophilopoulos, Andrew) — Schmidt, Tiffany
c The Adventures of Blue Ocean Bob: A Challenging Job (Illus. by Keele, Kevin) — Olbrys, Brooks
The Adventures of Brusanus, Prince of Hungaria — Riche, Barnabe
The Adventures of Brusanus, Prince of Hungaria — Khoury, Joseph
c The Adventures of Chloe Zoe Young: Chloe's Surfing Adventure — Young, Carol
The Adventures of Emery Jones, Boy Science Wonder: The Hard Problems — Johnson, Charles
The Adventures of Holly White and the Incredible Sex Machine — Kneen, Krissy
The Adventures Of Jon Paul Chavalier — Lee, Niclaus
c The Adventures of Kubi (Illus. by Speyer, Erik) — Speyer, Erik
c The Adventures of Lettie Peppercorn (Illus. by Bernatene, Poly) — Gayton, Sam
c The Adventures of Long Arm (Illus. by Bitskoff, Aleksei) — Nixon, Sam
c The Adventures of Marlin the Monkey — Newcomer, Ron
c The Adventures of Max the Minnow (Illus. by Sullivan, Don) — Boniface, William
c The Adventures of Miss Petitfour (Illus. by Block, Emma) — Michaels, Anne
c The Adventures of Mr. Toad (Illus. by Roberts, David) — Moorhouse, Tom
c The Adventures of Perseus: A Graphic Retelling (Illus. by Haus, Estudio) — Weakland, Mark
c The Adventures of Piratess Tilly (Illus. by Watson, Karen) — Lorayne, Elizabeth
y The Adventures of Radisson 2: Back to the New World — Fournier, Martin
y The Adventures of Radisson 2: Back to the New World — McCambridge, Peter
c The Adventures of Rainbow Fish (Illus. by Pfister, Marcus) — Pfister, Marcus
The Adventures of Sir Thomas Browne in the 21st Century — Aldersey-Williams, Hugh
Adventures of the Symbolic: Post-Marxism and Radical Democracy — Breckman, Warren
c Adventures with Barefoot Critters (Illus. by White, Teagan) — White, Teagan
c Adventures with Mr. Wugigdem — Chapman, Allan Westcott
c Adventures with Waffles (Read by Daniels, Luke). Audiobook Review — Parr, Maria
c Adventures with Waffles (Illus. by Forrester, Kate) — Parr, Maria
The Adventuress — Alexander, Tasha

Advertising at War: Business, Consumers, and Government in the 1940s — Stole, Inger L.
Advice to Single Women — Brown, Haydn
Advise and Consent — Drury, Allen
Aeneid 6: A Commentary, 2 vols. — Horsfall, Nicholas
y The Aeronaut's Windlass — Butcher, Jim
Aerospace Engineer Aprille Ericsson — Waxman, Laura Hamilton
Aeschylus: Suppliant Women — Bowen, Anthony J.
The Aesthetics and Ethics of Faith: A Dialogue between Liberationist and Pragmatic Thought — Tirres, Christopher D.
The Aesthetics of Design — Forsey, Jane
Aesthetics of Sorrow: The Wailing Culture of Yemenite Jewish Women — Gamliel, Tovah
The Aesthetics of Strangeness: Eccentricity and Madness in Early Modern Japan — Brecher, W. Puck
An Affair Downstairs — Browning, Sherri
c An Affectionate Farewell: The Story of Old Bob and Old Abe (Illus. by Dodson, Bert) — Krisher, Trudy
c Affenpinschers — Petrie, Kristin
The Affinities — Wilson, Robert Charles
Affirming: Letters, 1975-1997 — Berlin, Isaiah
Affluence and Influence: Economic Inequality and Political Power in America — Gilens, Martin
c Affordable Art Projects for Kids — Feterl, Amanda
Afghan Modern — Crews, Robert D.
Afghanistan: Preparing for the Bolshevik Incursion into Afghanistan and Attack on India, 1919-20 — Snesarev, Andrei Evgenievich
c The Afghanistan War — Winter, Max
Africa, 4th ed. — Grosz-Ngate, Maria
Africa 39 — Allfrey, Ellah Wakatama
y Africa — Harris, Tim
Africa after Apartheid: South Africa, Race, and Nation in Tanzania — Schroeder, Richard
Africa, Asia, and the History of Philosophy: Racism in the Formation of the Philosophical Canon, 1780-1830 — Park, Peter K.J.
Africa in Florida: Five Hundred Years of African Presence in the Sunshine State — Carlson, Amanda B.
Africa in the World: Capitalism, Empire, Nation-State — Cooper, Frederick
Africa Rising? BRICS-Diversifying Dependency — Taylor, Ian
Africa: Why Economists Get It Wrong — Jerven, Morten
The African AIDS Epidemic: A History — Iliffe, John
c African-American Culture — Bailer, Darice
African American Felon Disenfranchisement: Case Studies in Modern Racism and Political Exclusion — Pinkard, John E.
African American Leadership: A Concise Reference Guide — King-Meadows, Tyson D.
African American Life and Culture in Orange Mound: Case Study of a Black Community in Memphis, Tennessee, 1890-1980 — Williams, Charles
The African American Press in World War II: Toward Victory at Home and Abroad — Alkebulan, Paul
African American Slavery and Disability: Bodies, Property, and Power in the Antebellum South, 1800-1860 — Boster, Dea H.
African American Voices: A Documentary Reader from Emancipation to the Present — Brown, Leslie
African Americans against the Bomb: Nuclear Weapons, Colonialism, and the Black Freedom Movement — Intondi, Vincent J.
African Americans and Criminal Justice: An Encyclopedia — Jones-Brown, Delores D.
y African Americans at Risk: Issues in Education, Health, Community, and Justice, 2 vols. — Starks, Glenn L.
African Americans in U.S. Foreign Policy: From the Era of Frederick Douglass to the Age of Obama — Heywood, Linda
African Art and Agency in the Workshop — Kasfir, Sidney Littlefield
African Art as Philosophy: Senghor, Bergson and the Idea of Negritude — Diagne, Souleymane Bachir
African-Atlantic Cultures and the South Carolina Lowcountry — Brown, Ras Michael
African-Brazilian Culture and Regional Identity in Bahia, Brazil — Ickes, Scott
African Canadians in Union Blue: Enlisting for the Cause in the Civil War — Reid, Richard M.
African Canadians in Union Blue: Volunteering for the Cause in the Civil War — Reid, Richard M.

African-Centered Research Methodologies: From Ancient Times to the Present — Bangura, Abdul Karim
African Children at Work: Working and Learning in Growing Up for Life — Spittler, Gerd
African Dance Trends — Gagne, Tammy
The African Equation — Khadra, Yasmina
c An African Princess: From African Orphan to Queen Victoria's Favourite — Myers, Walter Dean
The African Project Manager — Davies, H. 'Tomi
African Roots, Brazilian Rites: Cultural and National Identity in Brazil — Sterling, Cheryl
c African Savanna — Llewellyn, Claire
An African Slaving Port and the Atlantic World: Benguela and Its Hinterland — Candido, Mariana P.
African Titanics — Khaal, Abu Bakr
African Video Movies and Global Desires: A Ghanaian History — Garritano, Carmela
African Women: A Historical Panorama — Romero, Patricia W.
Africans to Spanish America: Expanding the Diaspora — Bryant, Sherwin K.
Africa's Heart — Wentling, Mark
Afrikanerinnen in Deutschland: Lebenslagen, Eifahrungen und Erwartungen — Nestvogel, Renate
Afro-Cuban Costumbrismo: From Plantations to the Slums — Ocasio, Rafael
After a Fashion — Turano, Jen
After a While You Just Get Used to It: A Tale of Family Clutter — Knapp, Gwendolyn
After Abel and Other Stories — Lemberger, Michal
After Alexander: The Time of the Diadochi (323-281 BC). — Alonso Troncoso, Victor
y After Alice — Maguire, Gregory
After and Before — Alexander, Ted M.
After Appomattox: Military Occupation and the Ends of War — Downs, Gregory P.
After Arundel: Religious Writing in Fifteenth-Century England — Gillespie, Vincent
After Birth — Albert, Elisa
After Buddhism: Rethinking the Dharma for a Secular Age — Batchelor, Stephen
After Civic Humanism: Learning and Politics in Renaissance Italy — Baker, Nicholas Scott
After Civil Rights: Racial Realism in the New American Workplace — Skrentny, John D.
After Cloven Tongues of Fire: Protestant Liberalism in Modern American History — Hollinger, David A.
c After Dark — Leck, James
After Django: Making Jazz in Postwar France — Perchard, Tom
After Expulsion: 1492 and the Making of Sephardic Jewry — Ray, Jonathan
After Hitler: The Last Days of the Second World War in Europe — Jones, Michael
After Hitler: The Last Days of World War II in Europe — Jones, Michael
y After Hours — Kennedy, Claire
After Mahler: Britten, Weill, Henze, and Romantic Redemption — Downes, Stephen
After Mind — Wolf, Spencer
After Montaigne: Contemporary Essayists Cover the 'Essays' — Lazar, David
After Nature: A Politics for the Anthropocene — Purdy, Jedediah
After Newspeak: Language Culture and Politics in Russia from Gorbachev to Putin — Gorham, Michael S.
After Occupy: Economic Democracy for the 21st Century — Malleson, Tom
After Phrenology: Neural Reuse and the Interactive Brain — Anderson, Michael L.
After Preservation: Saving American Nature in the Age of Humans — Minteer, Ben A.
After Roe: The Lost History of the Abortion Debate — Ziegler, Mary
y The After-Room — Meloy, Maile
After She's Gone — Jackson, Lisa
After Slavery: Race, Labor, and Citizenship in the Reconstruction South — Baker, Bruce E.
After Snowden: Privacy, Secrecy, and Security in the Information Age — Goldfarb, Ronald
After Tamerlane: The Global History of Empire Since 1405 — Darwin, John
After the Ancestors: An Anthropologist's Story — Beatty, Andrew
c After the Ashes — Joiner, Sara K.
After the Beautiful: Hegel and the Philosophy of Pictorial Modernism — Pippin, Robert B.
After the Bell Rings: Poems about After-School Time (Illus. by Meisel, Paul) — Shields, Carol Diggory

After the Circus — Modiano, Patrick
After the Civil War: Making Memory and Re-making Spain since 1936 — Richards, Michael
After the Crash — Bussi, Michel
After the Dance: My Life with Marvin Gaye — Gaye, Jan
c After the Dinosaurs — West, David
After the Holodomor: The Enduring Impact of the Great Famine on Ukraine — Graziosi, Andrea
After the Monkey Trial: Evangelical Scientists and a New Creationism — Rios, Christopher M.
After the New Order: Space, Politics and Jakarta — Kusno, Abidin
After the Parade — Ostlund, Lori
After the Red Army Faction: Gender, Culture, and Militancy — Scribner, Charity
y After the Red Rain — Lyga, Barry
After the Revolution: Youth, Democracy, and the Politics of Disappointment in Serbia — Greenberg, Jessica
After the Ruin — Goodchild, Harriet
After the Silents: Hollywood Film Music in the Early Sound Era, 1926-1934 — Slowik, Michael
After the Storm (Read by McInerney, Kathleen). Audiobook Review — Castillo, Linda
After the Storm — Castillo, Linda
After the Tall Timber: Collected Nonfiction — Adler, Renata
After the Titanic: A Life of Derek Mahon — Enniss, Stephen
After the War — Scott, Jessica
c After the Wind: 1996 Everest Tragedy: One Survivor's Story — Kasischke, Lou
y After the Woods — Savage, Kim
After the Wrath of God: AIDS, Sexuality, and American Religion — Petro, Anthony M.
After They Closed the Gates: Jewish Illegal Immigration to the United States, 1921-1965 — Garland, Libby
After This: Survivors of the Holocaust Speak — Nelson, Alice
After This: When Life Is Over, Where Do We Go? — Smith, Claire Bidwell
After Translation: The Transfer and Circulation of Modern Poetics across the Atlantic — Infante, Ignacio
y After Us — Hart, Amber
After Wagner: Histories of Modernist Music Drama from Parsifal to Nono — Berry, Mark
After We Fall — Kavanagh, Emma
After Woodstock: The True Story of a Belgian Movie, an Israeli Wedding, & a Manhattan Breakdown — Tiber, Elliot
After Yorktown: The Final Struggle for American Independence — Glickstein, Don
After You Hear It's Cancer: A Guide to Navigating the Difficult Journey Ahead — Leifer, John
After You Left/They Took It Apart — Mottalini, Chris
After You — Moyes, Jojo
After Yugoslavia: The Cultural Spaces of a Vanished Land — Gorup, Radmila Jovanovic
Afterimage — Kowallis, J.
Afterimage of the Revolution: Cumann na Ngaedheal and Irish Politics, 1922-1932 — Knirck, Jason
c The Afterlife Academy — Cole, Frank L.
The Afterlife Healing Circle: How Anyone Can Contact the Other Side — Talmadge, Candace L.
The Afterlife of Austria-Hungary: The Image of the Habsburg Monarchy in Interwar Europe — Kozuchowski, Adam
The Afterlife of 'Little Women' — Clark, Beverly Lyon
Afterlife with Archie — Francavilla, Francesco
y Afterlight — Lim, Rebecca
Aftermath Lounge — McMullan, Margaret
y Aftermath — Goldsworthy, Sandy
The Aftermath of the Global Crisis in the European Union — Farkas, Beata
Aftershock — Donlay, Philip
Aftershock: The Untold Story of Surviving Peace — Green, Matthew
Afterwar: Healing the Moral Wounds of Our Soldiers — Sherman, Nancy
Afterwar — Sherman, Nancy
y Afterworlds — Westerfeld, Scott
Again and Again — Bravo, Ellen
Against a Brightening Sky — Moyer, Jamie Lee
Against Autobiography: Albert Memmi and the Production of Theory — Brozgal, Lia Nicole
Against Equality: Queer Revolution, Not Mere Inclusion — Conrad, Ryan
Against Football: One Fan's Reluctant Manifesto — Almond, Steve

Against Immediate Evil: American Internationalists and the Four Freedoms on the Eve of World War II — Johnstone, Andrew
Against Individualism: A Confucian Rethinking of the Foundations of Morality, Politics, Family, and Religion — Rosemont, Henry
Against Nature — Espedal, Tomas
Against Security: How We Go Wrong at Airports, Subways, and Other Sites of Ambiguous Danger — Molotch, Harvey
Against the Closet: Black Political Longing and the Erotics of Race — Abdur-Rahman, Aliyyah I.
y Against the Country — Metcalf, Ben
Against the Flow: The Inspiration of Daniel in an Age of Relativism — Lennox, John C.
Against the Idols of the Age — Stove, David
Against the Profit Motive: The Salary Revolution in American Government, 1780-1940 — Parrillo, Nicholas R.
Against the Ropes — Murray, Jeanette
Against the Rules — Howard, Linda
c Against the Tide — Sutherland, Tui T.
Against the Tide: Rickover's Leadership Principles and the Rise of the Nuclear Navy — Oliver, Dave
Against the Troika: Crisis and Austerity in the Eurozone — Flassbeck, Heiner
Against the Wall — Sorensen, Jill
Against Wind and Tide: The African American Struggle against the Colonization Movement — Power-Greene, Ousmane K.
Agamben and Indifference: A Critical Overview — Watkin, William
c Agatha (Illus. by Pignataro, Anna) — Pignataro, Anna
The Age of Acquiescence: The Life and Death of American Resistance to Organised Wealth and Power — Fraser, Steve
The Age of Acquiescence: The Life and Death of American Resistance to Organized Wealth and Power — Fraser, Steve
Age of Ambition: Chasing Fortune, Truth, and Faith in the New China — Osnos, Evan
The Age of Asa: Lord Briggs, Public Life and History in Britain since 1945 — Taylor, Miles
The Age of Aspiration: Power, Wealth, and Conflict in Globalizing India — Hiro, Dilip
The Age of Attila: Fifth-Century Byzantium and the Barbarians — Gordon, Colin Douglas
The Age of Catastrophe: A History of the West 1914-1945 — Winkler, Heinrich August
The Age of Clinton: America in the 1990s — Troy, Gil
The Age of Consequences: A Chronicle of Concern and Hope — White, Courtney
The Age of Cryptocurrency: How Bitcoin and Digital Money Are Challenging the Global Economic Order — Vigna, Paul
The Age of Dignity: Preparing for the Elder Boom in a Changing America — Poo, Ai-jen
The Age of Earthquakes: A Guide to the Extreme Present — Coupland, Douglas
The Age of Ecology: A Global History — Radkau, Joachim
The Age of Edison: Electric Light and the Invention of Modern America — Freeberg, Ernest
The Age of Evangelicalism: America's Born-Again Years — Miller, Steven P.
The Age of Genius — Grayling, A.C
An Age of Infidels: The Politics of Religious Controversy in the Early United States — Schlereth, Eric R.
The Age of Jackson and the Art of American Power, 1815-1848 — Nester, William
An Age of Neutrals: Great Power Politics, 1815-1914 — Abbenhuis, Maartje
The Age of New Waves: Art Cinema and the Staging of Globalization — Tweedie, James
c The Age of Not Believing — Szlachetko, Andrew
The Age of Reinvention — Tuil, Karine
The Age of Scientific Naturalism: Tyndall and His Contemporaries — Lightman, Bernard
The Age of Scientific Sexism — Ruti, Mari
The Age of Selfishness: Ayn Rand, Morality, and the Financial Crisis (Illus. by Cunningham, Darryl) — Cunningham, Darryl
The Age of Stagnation: Why Perpetual Growth Is Unattainable and the Global Economy is in Peril — Das, Satyajit
The Age of Sustainable Development — Sachs, Jeffrey D.
The Age of the Battleship, 1890-1922 — Harris, Brayton
The Age of the Crisis of Man: Thought and Fiction in America, 1933-1973 — Greif, Mark

The Age of the Successors and the Creation of the Hellenistic Kingdoms — Hauben, Hans
The Age of the Vikings — Winroth, Anders
Ageing Selves and Everyday Life in the North of England: Years in the Making — Degnen, Cathrine
The Agency of Children: From Family to Global Human Rights — Oswell, David
Agent Ex — Robinson, Gina
Agents of Babylon: What the Prophecies of Daniel Tell Us about the End of Days — Jeremiah, David
Agents of Empire: Knights, Corsairs, Jesuits and Spies in the Sixteenth-Century Mediterranean World — Malcolm, Noel
Agents of the Internet Apocalypse — Gladstone, Wayne
The Agility Shift: Creating Agile and Effective Leaders, Teams, and Organizations — Meyer, Pamela
Agincourt: The Fight for France — Fiennes, Ranulph
Aging and Loss: Mourning and Maturity in Contemporary Japan — Danely, Jason
Aging and Working in the New Economy: Changing Career Structures in Small IT Firms — McMullin, Julie Ann
Aging Gracefully in the Renaissance: Stories of Later Life from Petrarch to Montaigne — Skenazi, Cynthia
Aging in America — Scardamalia, Robert L.
c Agnes and Clarabelle (Illus. by Palacios, Sara) — Griffin, Adele
Agnes Martin — Morris, Frances
Agnes Martin: Her Life and Art — Princenthal, Nancy
Agostino — Moore, Michael F.
An Agrarian Republic: Farming, Antislavery Politics, and Nature Parks in the Civil War Era — Dean, Adam Wesley
c Agricultural Engineering and Feeding the Future — Rooney, Anne
c Ah! (Illus. by Spagnol, Estelle Billon) — Collet, Geraldine
The Aha! Factor: The Intuitive Guide to Getting What You Desire and Deserve — Cooper, Mariana M.
Aha! Moments of Insight That Shape Our World — Irvine, William B.
Ai Weiwei Architecture — Klein, Caroline
AIDS: Between Science and Politics — Piot, Peter
Aim at the Centaur Stealing Your Wife — Nelson, Jennifer
Aimless Love — Collins, Billy
Ain't Got No Home: America's Great Migrations and the Making of an Interracial Left — Battat, Erin Royston
Ain't No Trust: How Bosses, Boyfriends, and Bureaucrats Fail Low-Income Mothers and Why It Matters — Levine, Judith A.
Aiol: A Chanson de Geste: Modern Edition and First English Translation — Malicote, Sandra
c Air — Lawrence, Ellen
Air and Darkness — Drake, David
Air and Sea Power in World War I: Combat Experience in the Royal Flying Corps and the Royal Navy — Philpott, Maryam
An Air Fighter's Scrapbook — Jones, Ira
y Air Force Special Operations Command — Whiting, Jim
Air Power in UN Operations: Wings for Peace — Dorn, A. Walter
y Air Travel: Science, Technology, Engineering — Otfinoski, Steven
An Air War with Cuba: The United States Radio Campaign against Castro — Walsh, Daniel C.
c Aircraft — Salzmann, Mary Elizabeth
c Aisha the Navigator Trains a Leader! (Illus. by Hilley, Thomas) — Makin, Amir
y Aisle 17 — Bowman, Robert
y Akarnae: The Medoran Chronicles Begin — Noni, Lynette
Akira Kurosawa and I — Hashimoto, Shinobu
Akten zur Auswartigen Politik der Bundesrepublik Deutschland 1983 — Institut fur Zeitgeschichte Munchen - Berlin im Auftrag des Auswartigen Amts
Akten zur Auswartigen Politik der Bundesrepublik Deutschland 1984 — Institut fur Zeitgeschichte Munchen - Berlin im Auftrag des Auswartigen Amts
Akteure Mittelalterlicher Aussenpolitik. Das Beispiel Ostmitteleuropas
Akteure, Tiere, Dinge: Verfahrensweisen der Naturgeschichte

Aktuelle Forschungen zu Postsozialistischen Stadten Ostmitteleuropas: Transformation Offentlicher Urbaner Raume nach 1989 - Akteure, Praxen und Strategien
Al Crocevia della Storia: Poesia, Religione e Politica in Vittoria Colonna
Al-Ghazali's Moderation in Belief — Yaqub, Aladdin M.
Al-Jahiz: In Praise of Books — Montgomery, James E.
Al Qaeda, the Islamic State, and the Global Jihadist Movement: What Everyone Needs to Know — Byman, Daniel
Al Seruizio della Repubblica di Venezia: Le lettere di Massimiliano Buzzaccarini Gonzaga, Commendatore di Malta, inviate alia Magistratura dei Cinque Savii alia Mercanzia 1754-1776 — Mallia-Milanes, Victor
Al-Shabaab in Somalia: The History and Ideology of a Militant Islamist Group, 2005-2012 — Hansen, Stig Jarle
Alabama Studio Sewing Patterns: A Guide to Customizing a HandStitched Alabama Chanin Wardrobe — Chanin, Natalie
c Alabaster Shadows (Illus. by Doucet, Rashad) — Gardner, Matt
c Aladdin (Illus. by Rossi, Francesca) — Francia, Giada
Alain Prost — Hamilton, Maurice
c The Alamo: Would You Join the Fight? — Landau, Elaine
Alan Jay Lerner: A Father's Letters — McHugh, Dominic
Alan S. Milward and a Century of European Change — Guirao, Fernando
Alan Turing: Pioneer of the Information Age
Alan Turing: The Enigma — Hodges, Andrew
c Alan's Big, Scary Teeth — Jarvis
Alaska's Snow White and Her Seven Sled Dogs — Dwyer, Mindy
c Alaska's Three Little Pigs — Laverde, Arlene
c Albert Adds Up! (Illus. by Melmon, Deborah) — May, Eleanor
c Albert and Little Henry — Alborough, Jez
Albert Cammu's 'The New Mediterranean Culture': A Text and its Contexts — Foxlee, Neil
y Albert Einstein: Forging the Path of Modern Physics — Dakers, Diane
c Albert Einstein: Revolutionary Physicist — Anderson, Jennifer Joline
Albert Is Not Scared (Illus. by Melmon, Deborah) — May, Eleanor
Albert Rene: The Father of Modern Seychelles: A Biography — Shillington, Kevin
c Albert Starts School (Illus. by Melmon, Deborah) — May, Eleanor
c Albert the Muffin-Maker (Illus. by Melmon, Deborah) — May, Eleanor
c Alberto Del Rio — Markegard, Blake
c Albie's First Word: A Tale Inspired by Albert Einstein's Childhood (Illus. by Evans, Wynne) — Tourville, Jacqueline
The Albino's Treasure — Douglas, Stuart
Albrecht Durer nelle fonti Italiane antiche, 1508-1686 — Fara, Giovanni Maria
Alchemical Belief: Occultism in the Religious Culture of Early Modern England — Janacek, Bruce
The Alchemist's Daughter — Lawrence, Mary
The Alchemy of Chaos — Maresca, Marshall Ryan
y Alchemy's Daughter — Osborne, Mary A.
Alcohol: A History — Phillips, Rod
Alcohol and Nationhood in Nineteenth-Century Mexico — Toner, Deborah
Alcohol and Violence: The Nature of the Relationship and the Promise of Prevention — Parker, Robert Nash
Alcohol in Latin America: A Social and Cultural History — Pierce, Gretchen
Aldous Huxley's Hands — Symons, Allene
c Alef Is for Abba / Alef Is for Ima (Illus. by Basaluzzo, Constanza) — Kafka, Rebecca
Alehouses and Good Fellowship in Early Modern England — Hailwood, Mark
Alert (Read by Leyva, Henry, with Danny Mastrogiorigio). Audiobook Review — Patterson, James
Alessandro Grandi: Il primo libro de motetti a due, tre, quattro, cinque, and otto voci, con una Messa a Quattro — Collins, Dennis
The Aleut Internments of World War II: Islanders Removed from Their Homes by Japan and the United States — Estlack, Russell W.
y The Alex Crow (Read by Andrews, MacLeod). Audiobook Review — Smith, Andrew Anselmo

y The Alex Crow — Smith, Andrew Anselmo
y The Alex Crow — Smith, Andrew (b. 1959-)
Alex Haley: And the Books That Changed a Nation — Norrell, Robert J.
Alex Haley's Roots: An Author's Odyssey — Henig, Adam
c Alex Morgan — Jokulsson, Illugi
c Alexander and the Wind-Up Mouse (Illus. by Lionni, Leo) — Lionni, Leo
c Alexander Graham Bell: Inventeur de genie — Raimbault, Alain
Alexander Hamilton — Chernow, Ron
Alexander McQueen: Blood beneath the Skin — Wilson, Andrew
Alexander McQueen: Blood beneath the Skin — Wilson, Andrew (b. 1967-)
Alexander McQueen: Savage Beauty — Wilcox, Claire
c Alexander Ovechkin — Frederick, Shane
The Alexander Romance in Persia and the East — Stoneman, Richard
Alexander the Great: A Reader — Worthington, I.
Alexander the Great: A Very Short Introduction — Bowden, Hugh
Alexander the Great. The Story of an Ancient Life — Martin, Thomas R.
c Alexander, Who's Trying His Best to Be the Best Boy Ever (Illus. by Mones, Isidre) — Viorst, Judith
Alexander Wilson: The Scot Who Founded American Ornithology — Burtt, Edward H., Jr.
c Alexander's Army (Read by Corkhill, Raphael). Audiobook Review — D'Lacey, Chris
c Alexander's Army — d'Lacey, Chris
y Alexander's Army — D'Lacey, Chris
Alexander's Heirs: The Age of the Successors — Anson, Edward M.
Alexandre Grothendieck: A Mathematical Portrait — Schneps, Leila
Alexandrian Cosmopolitanism: An Archive — Halim, Hala
Alexandrian Summer — Goren, Yitzhak Gormezano
Alexandrian Summer — Gormezano Goren, Yitzhak
Alexey Dyed in Red — Valenza, A.M.
c Alexis, the Icing on the Cupcake — Simon, Coco
c Alexis's Cupcake Cupid — Simon, Coco
Alfie Bloom and the Secrets of Hexbridge Castle — Kent, Gabrielle
c Alfie in the Garden (Illus. by Gliori, Debi) — Gliori, Debi
Alfred Andersch Desertiert: Fahnenflucht und Literatur (1944-1952). — Doring, Jorg
Alfred Doblin: Eine Biographie — Schoeller, Wilfried F.
Alfred Hitchcock — Ackroyd, Peter
Alfred Hitchcock: The Man Who Knew Too Much — Wood, Michael
c Alfred Ollivant's Bob, Son of Battle: The Last Gray Dog of Kenmuir (Illus. by Kirmse, Marguerite) — Davis, Lydia
Alfred the Great — Horspool, David
Alfred's IPA Made Easy: A Guidebook for the International Phonetic Alphabet — Wentlent, Anna
Algerian Diary — Davis, Gerald
The Algonquin Round Table New York: A Historical Guide — Fitzpatrick, Kevin C.
y Algonquin Spring — Revelle, Rick
c Ali: An American Champion — Denenberg, Barry
Alibaba's World: How a Remarkable Chinese Company Is Changing the Face of Global Business — Erisman, Porter
Alibis of Empire: Henry Maine and the Ends of Liberal Imperialism — Mantena, Karuna
Alice and the Fly — Rice, James
Alice + Freda Forever: A Murder in Memphis (Illus. by Klann, Sally) — Coe, Alexia
c Alice from Dallas (Illus. by Hoyt, Ard) — Sadler, Marilyn
Alice in Bed — Hooper, Judith
Alice in Chains — de Sola, David
Alice in Shandehland: Scandal and Scorn in the Edelsonj-Horowitz Murder Case — Halpern, Monda
Alice in Wonderland: Down the Rabbit Hole (Illus. by Puybaret, Eric) — Carroll, Lewis
c Alice in Wonderland: Down the Rabbit Hole (Illus. by Puybaret, Eric) — Rhatigan, Joe
Alice in Wonderland — Carroll, Lewis
y Alice in Wonderland (Illus. by Ferran, Daniel) — Carroll, Lewis
y Alice in Wonderland High — Shane, Rachel
c Alice in Wonderland: With Three Dimensional Pop-Up Scenes (Illus. by Taylor, Maria) — Carroll, Lewis

c Alice-Miranda in Paris — *Harvey, Jacqueline*
Alice Paul: Claiming Power — *Zahniser, J.D.*
Alice Waters and the Trip to Delicious (Read by Hamilton, Laura). Audiobook Review — *Martin, Jacqueline Briggs*
Alice's Adventures in Wonderland: 150th Anniversary ed. — *Burstein, Mark*
Alice's Adventures in Wonderland Decoded: The Full Text of Lewis Carroll's Novel with Its Many Hidden Meanings Revealed — *Day, David*
c Alicia's Misadventures in Computer Land — *Garcia, Belinda Vasquez*
c Alien Invasion in My Backyard (Illus. by Boiling, Ruben) — *Bolling, Ruben*
c Alien Invasion in My Backyard — *Bolling, Ruben*
Alien Nation: Chinese Migration in the Americas from the Coolie Era through World War II — *Young, Elliott*
Alien Rule — *Hechter, Michael*
c Alien Superman! — *Stewart, Yale*
Alienating Labour: Workers on the Road from Socialism to Capitalism in East Germany and Hungary — *Bartha, Eszter*
Alienation — *Jaeggi, Rahel*
c Alison's Little Brother (Illus. by Patterson, Josh) — *Chapleau, Heather*
y Alistair Grim's Odditorium (Illus. by To, Vivienne) — *Funaro, Gregory*
y Alive — *Baker, Chandler*
Alive — *Sigler, Scott*
Alive, Alive Oh! And Other Things That Matter — *Athill, Diana*
y Alive and Kicking — *Lynch, Chris*
Alive: New and Selected Poems — *Willis, Elizabeth*
y Alive — *Baker, Chandler*
All Aboard! (Illus. by Lowery, Mike) — *Dotlich, Rebecca Kai*
c All about Animals Close Up — *Kalman, Bobbie*
c All about Baseball — *Doeden, Matt*
c All about China: Stories, Songs, Crafts and More for Kids (Illus. by Wang, Lin) — *Branscombe, Allison*
c All about Football — *Doeden, Matt*
c All about Hockey — *Doeden, Matt*
y All about the Green: The Teens' Guide to Finding Work and Making Money — *McGuire, Kara*
c All about the Philippines: Stories, Songs, Crafts and Games for Kids (Illus. by Dandan-Albano, Corazon) — *Jimenez, Gidget Roceles*
y All American Boys — *Reynolds, Jason*
All Backs Were Turned — *Hlasko, Marek*
c All Better Now — *Smith, Emily Wing*
All Canada in the Hands of the British: General Jeffery Amherst and the 1760 Campaign to Conquer New France — *Cubbison, Douglas R.*
All Day and a Night — *Burke, Alafair*
All-Day Breakfast — *Schroeder, Adam Lewis*
All Day Long: A Portrait of Britain at Work — *Biggs, Joanna*
All Days Are Night — *Stamm, Peter*
All Dogs Go to Kevin: Everything Three Dogs Taught Me (That I Didn't Learn in Veterinary School). — *Vogelsang, Jessica*
All Dressed in White — *Burke, Alafair*
All Dressed in White — *Clark, Mary Higgins*
All Eyes Are Upon Us: Race and Politics from Boston to Brooklyn — *Sokol, Jason*
y All Fall Down (Read by Stevens, Eileen). Audiobook Review — *Carter, Ally*
All Fall Down (Read by Chimo, Tracee). Audiobook Review — *Weiner, Jennifer*
y All Fall Down — *Carter, Ally*
c All for a Dime — *Hillenbrand, Will*
All for Nothing: Hamlet's Negativity — *Cutrofello, Andrew*
All for the King's Shilling: The British Soldier under Wellington, 1808-1814 — *Coss, Edward J.*
All for You — *Florand, Laura*
y All Four Stars — *Dairman, Tara*
c All I Want For Christmas Is You (Illus. by Madden, Colleen) — *Carey, Mariah*
All I Want Is a Job: Unemployed Women Navigating the Public Workforce System — *Gatta, Mary*
All I Want — *Shalvis, Jill*
All In: How Our Work-First Culture Fails Dads, Families, and Businesses--and How We Can Fix It Together — *Levs, Josh*
c All in One Day (Illus. by Cowman, Joseph) — *Huber, Mike*
All in the Family: The Realignment of American Democracy since the 1960s — *Self, Robert O.*

The All-India Muslim League, 1906-1947: A Study of Leadership in the Evolution of a Nation — *Becker, Mary Louise*
All Involved — *Gattis, Ryan*
All Is Not Yet Lost — *Fagin, Betsy*
All Joking Aside: American Humor and Its Discontents — *Krefting, Rebecca*
All Joy and No Fun: The Paradox of Modern Parenthood — *Senior, Jennifer*
All Lies: A Story of the Portland Spies — *Macpherson, David*
All Men Fear Me — *Casey, Donis*
All Men Free and Brethren: Essays on the History of African American Freemasonry — *Hinks, Peter P.*
c All Mine! — *Hicks, Zehra*
All Monsters Must Die — *Bartas, Magnus*
All My Puny Sorrows — *Toews, Miriam*
c All My Stripes: A Story for Children with Autism (Illus. by Zivoin, Jennifer) — *Rudolph, Shaina*
y All-New Ultimates Vol. 1: Power for Power (Illus. by Pinna, Amilcar) — *Fiffe, Michel*
All of Me — *Moran, Kelly*
y All of the Above — *Dawson, James*
All of Us and Everything — *Asher, Bridget*
All One Breath — *Burnside, John*
All Our Names — *Mengestu, Dinaw*
c All Paws on Deck (Illus. by Burks, James) — *Young, Jessica*
All Points Patchwork: English Paper Piecing beyond the Hexagon for Quilts & Small Projects — *Gilleland, Diane*
c All Rise for the Honorable Perry T. Cook — *Connor, Leslie*
The All Saints' Day Lovers — *Vasquez, Juan Gabriel*
All Saints — *Miller, K.D.*
c All Shook Up! — *Crozon, Alain*
All Simple Things But Time — *Bernstein, Howard*
All That Followed — *Urza, Gabriel*
All That You've Seen Here Is God — *Doerries, Bryan*
c All the Answers — *Messner, Kate*
All the Beautiful Brides — *Herron, Rita*
All the Birds in the Sky — *Anders, Charlie Jane*
All the Birds, Singing — *Wyld, Evie*
All the Boundaries of the Land: The Promised Land in Biblical Thought in Light of the Ancient Near East — *Wazana, Nili*
y All the Bright Places (Read by Heyborne, Kirby, with Ari Meyers). Audiobook Review — *Niven, Jennifer*
y All the Bright Places (Read by Heyborne, Kirby). Audiobook Review — *Niven, Jennifer*
y All the Bright Places — *Niven, Jennifer*
All the Broken Places — *Eden, Anise*
All The Days and Nights — *Govinden, Niven*
All the Houses — *Olsson, Karen*
All the King's Men: The British Redcoat in the Era of Sword and Musket — *David, Saul*
All the King's Men: The British Soldier from the Restoration to Waterloo — *David, Saul*
All the Light We Cannot See — *Doerr, Anthony*
All the Lights On: Reimagining Theater with Ten Thousand Things — *Hensley, Michelle*
c All the Lost Things (Illus. by Canby, Kelly) — *Canby, Kelly*
y All the Major Constellations — *Cranse, Pratima*
All the Old Knives (Read by Various readers). Audiobook Review — *Steinhauer, Olen*
All the Old Knives — *Steinhauer, Olen*
All the Paths of Shadow — *Tuttle, Frank*
All the Places to Go: How Will You Know? — *Ortberg, John*
All the Pretty Horses — *McCarthy, Cormac*
y All the Rage — *Summers, Courtney*
All the Right Places — *Sutton, Jenna*
All the Stars in the Heavens — *Trigiani, Adriana*
All the Things We Never Knew: Chasing the Chaos of Mental Illness — *Hamilton, Sheila*
All the Tricks of the Trade: Everything You Need to Know about Comedy — *Blumenfeld, Robert*
All the Truth Is Out: The Week Politics Went Tabloid — *Bai, Matt*
All the Ways We Kill and Die — *Castner, Brian*
All the Wild That Remains: Edward Abbey, Wallace Stegner, and the American West — *Gessner, David*
All the Wild That Remains — *Gessner, David*
All the Winters After — *Halverson, Sere Prince*
c All the World (Illus. by Frazee, Marla) — *Scanlon, Liz Garton*
All The Wrong Places: A Life Lost and Found (Read by Verner, Adam). Audiobook Review — *Connors, Philip*
All the Wrong Places: A Life Lost and Found — *Connors, Philip*

All the Wrong Places — *Lieberman, Lisa*
All Things Cease to Appear — *Brundage, Elizabeth*
All Things Julius Caesar: An Encyclopedia of Caesar's World and Legacy — *Lovano, Michael*
All Things Possible: Setbacks and Success in Politics and Life — *Cuomo, Andrew M.*
All Things Quilting with Alex Anderson: From First Step to Last Stitch — *Anderson, Alex*
All Things Rise — *Vaun, Missouri*
All Things Tending towards the Eternal — *Lee, Kathleen*
y All This Life — *Mohr, Joshua*
All Those Strangers: The Art and Lives of James Baldwin — *Field, Douglas*
All Those Vanished Engines — *Park, Paul*
y All Together Now — *Hornby, Gill*
All Together Now — *Tallitsch, Tom*
y All We Have Is Now — *Schroeder, Lisa*
y All We Left Behind — *Sundberg, Ingrid*
All Who Go Do Not Return — *Deen, Shulem*
c All Year Round (Illus. by Ojala, Eiko) — *Katz, Susan B.*
c All Year Round (Illus. by Leduc, Emilie) — *Leduc, Emilie*
y All You Are — *Karre, Elizabeth*
All You Can Pay: How Companies Use Our Data to Empty Our Wallet — *Bernasek, Ann*
Allegorizing History: The Venerable Bede, Figural Exegesis, and Historical Theory — *Furry, Timothy J.*
An Allegory of Divine Love: The Netherlands Blockbook 'Canticum Canticorum' — *Lavin, Marilyn Aronberg*
Allelopoiese - Konzepte zur Beschreibung Kulturellen Wandels. Jahrestagung 2014 des SFB 644 "Tranformationen der Antike"
Allen Dulles, the OSS, and Nazi War Criminals: The Dynamics of Selective Prosecution — *Lingen, Kerstin von*
Allen Klein: The Man Who Bailed Out the Beatles, Made the Stones, and Transformed Rock and Roll — *Goodman, Fred*
c Allergies — *Levine, Michelle*
The Allergy Book: Solving Your Family's Nasal Allergies, Asthma, Food Sensitivities, and Related Health and Behavioral Problems — *Sears, Robert W.*
The Allergy-Free Cook Makes Pies and Desserts — *Sadowski, Laurie*
Alliance and Landscape: On Perry Mesa in the Fourteenth Century — *Abbott, David R.*
c Allie, First at Last — *Cervantes, Angela*
Allied Air Power 1942-1945: A Newsreel History of Allied Air Force Operations in World War II — *Wolff, Perry*
The Allied Air War and Urban Memory: The Legacy of Strategic Bombing in Germany — *Arnold, Jorg*
Allied Power: Mobilizing Hydro-electricity during Canada's Second World War — *Evenden, Matthew*
Allies and Italians under Occupation: Sicily and Southern Italy, 1943-45 — *Williams, Isobel*
Alligator Candy: A Memoir — *Kushner, David*
c Alligators and Crocodiles — *Marsh, Laura*
Allingham: The Long Journey Home — *Horst, John C.*
Allowing for Exceptions: A Theory of Defences and Defeasibility — *d'Almeida, Luis Duarte*
The Allure of Order: High Hopes, Dashed Expectations, and the Troubled Quest to Remake American Schooling — *Mehta, Jal*
The Allure of the Archives — *Farge, Arlette*
y Ally Hughes Has Sex Sometimes — *Moulin, Jules*
Ally: My Journey across the American-Israeli Divide (Read by Oren, Michael B.). Audiobook Review — *Oren, Michael B.*
Ally: My Journey across the American-Israeli Divide — *Oren, Michael B.*
c Ally-Saurus & the First Day of School (Illus. by Torrey, Richard) — *Torrey, Richard*
The Almanac of American Education, 2014-2015 — *Gaquin, Deirdre A.*
Almost Crimson — *Kelly, Dasha*
Almost Eden — *Taylor, Richard*
Almost Everything Very Fast — *Kloeble, Christopher*
Almost Famous Women: Stories (Read by Lockford, Lesa). Audiobook Review — *Bergman, Megan Mayhew*
Almost Famous Women: Stories — *Bergman, Megan Mayhew*
y Almost Grace — *Rowell, Rosie*
y Almost Midnight — *Hunter, C.C.*

The Almost Nearly Perfect People: Behind the Myth of the Scandinavian Utopia — Booth, Michael
Almost Sleeping My Way to Timbuktu: West Africa on a Shoestring by Public Transport with No French — Khumalo, Sihle
c The Almost Terrible Playdate — Torrey, Richard
Alone and Not Alone — Padgett, Ron
Alone Atop the Hill: The Autobiography of Alice Dunnigan, Pioneer of the National Black Press — Booker, Carol McCabe
Alone atop the Hill: The Autobiography of Alice Dunnigan, Pioneer of the National Black Press — Dunnigan, Alice
Alone in the Dark — Rose, Karen
Alone on the Wall — Honnold, Alex
c Alone Together (Illus. by Bloom, Suzanne) — Bloom, Suzanne
Along the Broken Road — Burch, Heather
Along the Infinite Sea — Williams, Beatriz
Along the Streets of Bronzeville: Black Chicago's Literary Landscape — Schlabach, Elizabeth Schroeder
y Along the Way — Kolosov, Jacqueline
c Alpha (Illus. by Arsenault, Isabelle) — Arsenault, Isabelle
Alpha Docs: The Making of a Cardiologist — Munoz, Daniel
Alpha God: The Psychology of Religious Violence and Oppression — Garcia, Hector A.
c Alpha (Illus. by Arsenault, Isabelle) — Arsenault, Isabelle
c Alphabet Al's ABC Book of Words and Rhymes — Caudle, Melissa
The Alphabet House (Read by Malcolm, Graeme). Audiobook Review — Adler-Olsen, Jussi
The Alphabet House — Schein, Steve
The Alphabet of Birds — Naude, S.J.
c The Alphabet of Bugs: An ABC Book (Illus. by Cutting, Ann) — Gates, Valerie
y Alphabet of Dreams — Fletcher, Susan
c The Alphabet — Down, Reg
c Alphabet School (Illus. by Johnson, Stephen T.) — Johnson, Stephen T.
c Alphabet Trains (Illus. by O'Rourke, Ryan) — Vamos, Samantha R.
c Alphabetabum: An Alphabet Album — Raschka, Chris
Alphabetical: How Every Letter Tells a Story — Rosen, Michael
The Alpine Zen — Daheim, Mary
Already the Flames — Watkins, Clive
Als das Dorf noch Zukunft war: Agrarismus und Expertise zwischen Zarenreich und Sowjetunion — Bruisch, Katja
The ALTA Project — Chen, David
The Altar at Home: Sentimental Literature and Nineteenth-Century American Religion — Stokes, Claudia
The Altar Girl — Stelmach, Orest
Altar'd: Faith Building Evidence Leading to New Life — Cavaiani, Jay
Alter-Nations: Nationalisms, Terror and the State in Nineteenth-Century Britain and Ireland — Martin, Amy E.
Alternate History: Playing with Contingency and Necessity — Singles, Kathleen
c Alternate Reality Game Designer Jane McGonigal — Suen, Anastasia
Alternative Filmmusik zu einem Ausschnitt aus The Grapes of Wrath — Eisler, Hanns
The Alternative Jukebox: 500 Extraordinary Tracks That Tell a Story of Alternative Music
Alternative Theories of Competition: Challenges to the Orthodoxy — Moudud, Jamee K.
y Althea & Oliver — Moracho, Cristina
Altman — Altman, Kathryn Reed
Altruism — Ricard, Matthieu
The Altruistic Brain: How We Are Naturally Good — Pfaff, Donald W.
Aluminum Dreams: The Making of Light Modernity — Sheller, Mimi
Alumni Voices: The Changing Experience of Higher Education — Spencer, Stephanie
Alvar Nunez Cabeza de Vaca: American Trailblazer — Varnum, Robin
The Alvarez Generation: Thom Gunn, Geoffrey Hill, Ted Hughes, Sylvia Plath, and Peter Porter — Wootten, William
c Alvin Ho: Allergic to the Great Wall, the Forbidden Palace, and Other Tourist Attractions (Illus. by Pham, LeUyen) — Look, Lenore
c Alvin Schwartz — Wheeler, Jill C.

Alvin York: A New Biography of the Hero of the Argonne — Mastriano, Douglas V.
y Always a Catch — Richmond, Peter
y Always, Abigail — Cavanaugh, Nancy J.
y Always Emily — MacColl, Michaela
y Always Faithful — Jones, Patrick
c Always Mom, Forever Dad (Illus. by Weber, Penny) — Rowland, Joanna
Always on My Mind — Warren, Susan May
Always Pack a Party Dress — Brooks, Amanda
c Always (Illus. by Dodd, Emma) — Dodd, Emma
c Always Remember (Illus. by Jago) — Meng, Cece
c Always Twins (Illus. by Weidner, Teri) — Weidner, Teri
Am Fluss — Kinsky, Esther
Am I My Genes? Confronting Fate and Family Secrets in the Age of Genetic Testing — Klitzman, Robert L.
y Am I Normal Yet? — Bourne, Holly
Amarres Perros — Castaneda, Jorge
Amaskan's Blood — Oak, Raven
c Amazing Aaron to Zero Zippers: An Introduction to Baseball History — Nadel, Matt
c The Amazing Age of John Roy Lynch (Illus. by Tate, Don) — Barton, Chris
c Amazing America Series — Rowell, Rebecca
c Amazing Animal Communications — Gray, Leon
c Amazing Animal Senses (Illus. by Llewellyn, Claire) — Llewellyn, Claire
c Amazing Animals: A Collection of Creatures Great and Small — de la Bedoyere, Camilla
c Amazing Animals (Illus. by Channing, Margot) — Channing, Margot
c Amazing Animals Series — Riggs, Kate
c Amazing Applications and Perfect Programs — Gifford, Clive
c Amazing Brain Mysteries — O'Brien, Cynthia
y The Amazing C on Science — deBoer, Robin
c The Amazing Discoveries of Ibn Sina (Illus. by Ali, Intelaq Mohammed) — Sharafeddine, Fatima
c The Amazing Erik (Illus. by Cowman, Joseph) — Huber, Mike
y Amazing Fantastic Incredible: A Marvelous Memoir (Illus. by Doran, Colleen) — Lee, Stan
y Amazing Feats of Biological Engineering — Abramovitz, Melissa
Amazing Grace: The Man Who Was W.G. — Tomlinson, Richard
c The Amazing Hamweenie Escapes! (Illus. by Bowman, Patty) — Bowman, Patty
The Amazing Healing Power of Kitchari: Weight Loss, Detox and Rejuvenation — Tierra, Shasta
c Amazing Places (Illus. by Hale, Christy) — Hopkins, Lee Bennett
c Amazing Places (Illus. by Soentpiet, Chris) — Hopkins, Lee Bennett
c Amazing Plant Powers: How Plants Fly, Fight, Hide, Hunt, and Change the World — Leedy, Loreen
c Amazing Reptiles Series — Bell, Samantha
c Amazing Robots Series: Robots in Industry
c The Amazing Spider-Man: Edge of Spider-Verse (Illus. by Isanove, Richard) — Hine, David
c The Amazing Travels of Ibn Battuta (Illus. by Ali, Intelaq Mohammed) — Sharafeddine, Fatima
The Amazing True Story of How Babies Are Made — Katauskas, Fiona
c The Amazing Wilmer Dooley: A Mumpley Middle School Mystery (Illus. by Montalvo, Rodolfo) — DeWitt, Fowler
The Amazing World of Flyingfish — Howell, Steve N.G.
Amazonian Routes: Indigenous Mobility and Colonial Communities in Northern Brazil — Roller, Heather F
The Amazons: Lives and Legends of Warrior Women Across the Ancient World — Mayor, Adrienne
Amazons, Wives, Nuns & Witches: Women and the Catholic Church in Colonial Brazil, 1500-1822 — Myscofski, Carole A.
Amballore House — Thekkumthala, Jose
The Ambassador — Avner, Yehuda
c Ambassador — Alexander, William
The Ambassador's Wife — Steil, Jennifer
c Amber Brown Is Tickled Pink (Read by Lubotsky, Dana). Audiobook Review — Coville, Bruce
y Amber Smoke — Cast, Kristin
The Ambidextrous Universe — Gardner, Martin
Ambiguitat und Gesellschaftliche Ordnung im Mittelalter. 21. Tagung des Brackweder Arbeitskreises fur Mittelalterforschung
The Ambiguity of Virtue: Gertrude van Tijn and the Fate of the Dutch Jews — Wasserstein, Bernard

Ambiguous Anniversary: The Bicentennial of the International Slave Trade Bans — Gleeson, David T.
The Ambiguous Nation: Case Studies from Southeastern Europe in the 20th Century — Brunnbauer, Ulf
Ambition & Anxiety: Courts and Courtly Discourse, c. 700-1600 — Gasper, Giles E.M.
Ambitious Rebels: Remaking Honor, Law, and Liberalism in Venezuela, 1780-1850 — Zahler, Reuben
Ambivalent Miracles: Evangelicals and the Politics of Racial Healing — Wadsworth, Nancy D.
Ambrose Fountain (Read by Bell, Tobin). Audiobook Review — Sieve, Brian
c An Ambush of Tigers: A Wild Gathering of Collective Nouns (Illus. by Jago) — Rosenthal, Betsy R.
c Amelia Bedelia Chalks One Up (Illus. by Avril, Lynne) — Parish, Herman
c Amelia Bedelia Is for the Birds (Illus. by Avril, Lynne) — Parish, Herman
c Amelia Bedelia Shapes Up (Illus. by Avril, Lynne) — Parish, Herman
c Amelia Bedelia's First Day of School (Illus. by Avril, Lynne) — Parish, Herman
c Amelia, the Moochins and the Sapphire Palace (Illus. by Blanchard, Evonne) — Blanchard, Evonne
c Amelia's Middle-School Graduation Yearbook — Moss, Marissa
Amelioration and Empire: Progress and Slavery in the Plantation Americas — Dierksheide, Christa
America, 1844: Religious Fervor, Westward Expansion, and the Presidential Election That Transformed the Nation — Bicknell, John
America and Britain: Was There Ever a Special Relationship? — Arnold, Guy
America Ascendant: A Revolutionary Nation's Path to Addressing Its Deepest Problems and Leading the 21st Century — Greenberg, Stanley B.
America Dancing: From the Cakewalk to the Moonwalk — Pugh, Megan
America in Retreat: The New Isolationism and the Coming Global Disorder — Stephens, Bret
America in the Thirties — Sullivan, Marnie M.
America Invades — Kelly, Christopher
America is Elsewhere: The Noir Tradition in the Age of Consumer Culture — Dussere, Erik
America Is Not Broke: Four Multi-Trillion Dollar Paths to a Thriving America — Baker, Scott
America Needs Talent: Attracting, Educating and Deploying the 21st-Century Workforce — Merisotis, Jamie
America: The Black Point of View: An Investigation and Study of the White People of America and Western Europe and the Autobiography of an American Ghetto Boy, the 1950s and 1960s — Rose, Tony
y American Ace — Nelson, Marilyn
c American Alligators: Armored Roaring Reptiles — Hirsch, Rebecca E.
American Apocalypse: A History of Modern Evangelicalism — Sutton, Matthew Avery
American Apostles: When Evangelicals Entered the World of Islam — Heyrman, Christine Leigh
American Arabesque: Arabs, Islams, and the Nineteenth-Century Imaginary — Berman, Jacob Rama
The American Army and the First World War — Woodward, David R.
American Arsenal: A Century of Waging War — Coffey, Patrick
American Big Business in Britain and Germany: A Comparative History of Two "Special Relationships" in the 20th Century — Berghahn, Volker R.
American Blood — Sanders, Ben
American Blood: The Ends of the Family in American Literature, 1850-1900 — Jackson, Holly
American Bomber Aircraft Development in World War II — Norton, Bill
The American Book of Days, 5th ed. — Le Rouge, Mary
American Boys: The True Story of the Lost 74 of the Vietnam War — Esola, Louise
American Burke: The Uncommon Liberalism of Daniel Patrick Moynihan — Weiner, Greg
American Capitals: A Historical Geography — Montes, Christian
American Carnage: Wounded Knee, 1890 — Greene, Jerome A.
American Carnage: Wounded Knee, 1890 — Powers, Thomas

American Catch: The Fight for Our Local Seafood — Greenberg, Paul
American Catholics in Transition — D'Antonio, William V.
American Christian Support for Israel: Standing with the Chosen People, 1948-1975 — Crouse, Eric R.
American Christianity: The Continuing Revolution — Cox, Stephen
American Civil Religion: What Americans Hold Sacred — Gardella, Peter
American Civil War: A State-by State Encyclopedia, 2 vols. — Tucker, Spencer C.
The American Civil War and the Shaping of British Democracy — Kinser, Brent E.
American Classics Reinvented — Ahern, Shauna James
The American Constitution and Religion — Regan, Richard J.
American Copper — Ray, Shann
c American Crows — Petrie, Kristin
American Crucifixion: The Murder of Joseph Smith and the Fate of the Mormon Church — Beam, Alex
c American Curl Cats — Finne, Stephanie
American Dance: The Complete Illustrated History — Fuhrer, Margaret
American Democracy: From Tocqueville to Town Halls to Twitter — Perrin, Andrew J.
An American Diplomat in Bolshevik Russia — Poole, De Witt Clinton
American Dreamers: How the Left Changed a Nation — Kazin, Michael
American Dreams: Restoring Economic Opportunity for Everyone — Rubio, Marco
American Economic History: A Dictionary and Chronology — Olson, James S.
American Energy Policy in the 1970s — Lifset, Robert
American Enterprise — Serwer, Andy
American Epics: Thomas Hart Benton and Hollywood — Bailly, Austen Barron
American Evangelicalism: George Marsden and the State of American Religious History — Dochuk, Darren
American Exceptionalism and Civil Religion: Reassessing the History of an Idea — Wilsey, John O.
American Food — Gilbert, Sara
American Foodie: Taste, Art and the Cultural Revolution — Furrow, Dwight
American Force: Dangers, Delusions, and Dilemmas in National Security — Betts, Richard K.
American Foreign Policy and Its Thinkers — Anderson, Perry
American Founding Son: John Bingham and the Invention of the Fourteenth Amendment — Magliocca, Gerard N.
c American Fun Facts (Illus. by Dewalle, Medhi) — Bright, J.E.
American Fun: Four Centuries of Joyous Revolt — Beckman, John
American Gandhi: A.J. Muste and the History of Radicalism in the Twentieth Century — Danielson, Leilah
American Geographers and Geography: Toward Geographic Science — Martin, Geoffrey
American Ghost: A Family's Haunted Past in the Desert Southwest (Read by Sands, Xe). Audiobook Review — Nordhaus, Hannah
American Ghost: A Family's Haunted Past in the Desert Southwest — Nordhaus, Hannah
American Grand Strategy in the Mediterranean during World War II — Buchanan, Andrew
American Guy: Masculinity in American Law and Literature — Levmore, Saul
American Heathens: Religion, Race, and Reconstruction in California — Paddison, Joshua
American Hero: The Marquis Lafayette Reconsidered — Auricchio, Laura
American History, 1493-1945 — Matthew, Adam
American History through Hollywood Film: From the Revolution to the 1960s — Stokes, Melvyn
American Housewife — Ellis, Helen
The American Idea of England, 1776-1840: Transatlantic Writing — Clark, Jennifer
American Identity and the Politics of Multiculturalism — Citrin, Jack
American Immunity: War Crimes and the Limits of International Law — Hagopian, Patrick
The American Imperial Gothic: Popular Culture, Empire, Violence — Hoglund, John
An American in Scotland — Ranney, Karen
American Indian Women — Deval, Patrick
American Indians in U.S. History, 2d ed. — Nichols, Roger L.

American Insecurity: Why Our Economic Fears Lead to Political Inaction — Levine, Adam Seth
The American Isherwood — Berg, James J.
The American Jewish Story through Cinema — Goldman, Eric A.
American Justice 2014: Nine Clashing Visions on the Supreme Court — Epps, Garrett
American Labor and Economic Citizenship: New Capitalism from World War I to the Great Depression — Hendrickson, Mark
The American Lover and Other Stories — Tremain, Rose
American Made: Why Making Things Will Return Us to Greatness — DiMicco, Dan
y American Meteor (Read by Bramhall, Mark). Audiobook Review — Lock, Norman
American Meteor — Lock, Norman
The American Middle Class: A Cultural History — Samuel, Lawrence R.
American Military History: A Survey from Colonial Times to the Present — Allison, William T.
American Mojo: Lost and Found: Restoring Our Middle Class before the Wind Blows By — Kiernan, Peter D.
American Musicals: The Complete Books and Lyrics of 16 Broadway Classics, 1927-1969 — Green, Stanley
American Mythmaker: Walter Noble Burns and the Legends of Billy the Kid, Wyatt Earp, and Joaquin Murrieta — Dworkin, Mark J.
American Nietzsche: A History of an Icon and His Ideas — Ratner-Rosenhagen, Jennifer
American Nocturne — Stevens, Elisabeth
The American Non-Dilemma: Racial Inequality Without Racism — DiTomaso, Nancy
American Pain: How a Young Felon and His Ring of Doctors Unleashed America's Deadliest Drug Epidemic — Temple, John
American Paper Mills, 1690-1832: A Directory of the Paper Trade with Notes on Products, Watermarks, Distribution Methods, and Manufacturing Techniques — Bidwell, John
American Passage: The Communications Frontier in Early New England — Grandjean, Katherine
The American People, vol. 1: Search for My Heart — Kramer, Larry
American Phoenix: John Quincy and Louisa Adams, the War of 1812, and the Exile That Saved American Independence — Cook, Jane Hampton
y American Poetry of the 20th Century — Salem Press
American Political Economy in Global Perspective — Wilensky, Harold L.
American Postfeminist Cinema: Women, Romance and Contemporary Culture — Schreiber, Michelle
American Power after the Financial Crisis — Kirshner, Jonathan
The American President: From Teddy Roosevelt to Bill Clinton — Leuchtenburg, William E.
American Protestants and the Debate over the Vietnam War: Evil Was Loose in the World — Bogaski, George
American Public Opinion, Advocacy, and Policy in Congress: What the Public Wants and What It Gets — Burstein, Paul
American Pulp: How Paperbacks Brought Modernism to Main Street — Rabinowitz, Paula
American Queen: The Rise and Fall of Kate Chase Sprague, Civil War "Belle of the North" and Gilded Age Woman of Scandal — Oller, John
American Railroads: Decline and Renaissance in the Twentieth Century — Gallamore, Robert E.
American Reckoning: The Vietnam War and Our National Identity — Appy, Christian G.
American Reference Books Annual, vol. 46 — Hysell, Shannon G.
American Religion: Contemporary Trends — Marler, Penny Long
y The American Revolution by the Numbers — Lanser, Amanda
y American Revolution — Ziff, John
The American Revolution through British Eyes: A Documentary Collection, 2 vols. — Barnes, James J.
American Revolutionary: The Evolution of Grace Lee Boggs — Lee, Grace
American Sampler — Duran, Jane
The American Sea: A Natural History of the Gulf of Mexico — Darnell, Rezneat Milton
The American Search for Economic Justice — McClelland, Peter
American Settler Colonialism: A History — Hixson, Walter L.

The American Slave Coast: A History of the Slave-Breeding Industry — Sublette, Ned
American Smoke: Journeys to the End of the Light — Sinclair, Iain
American Sniper — McEwen, Scott
American Sociology: From Pre-Disciplinary to Post-Normal — Turner, Stephen P.
American Sons — Boyce, Christopher
The American South and the Atlantic World — Ward, Brian
American Spring: Lexington, Concord, and the Road to Revolution — Borneman, Walter R.
American Studies: Disziplingeschichte und Geschlecht — Harders, Levke
American Studies, Ecocriticism, and Citizenship: Thinking and Acting in the Local and Global Commons — Adamson, Joni
American Sweepstakes: How One Small State Bucked the Church, the Feds, and the Mob to Usher in the Lottery Age — Flynn, Kevin
The American Synthetic Organic Chemicals Industry: War and Politics, 1910-1930 — Steen, Kathryn
American Tantalus: Horizons, Happiness, and the Impossible Pursuits of US Literature and Culture — Warnes, Andrew
American Tax Resisters — Huret, Romain D.
American Travelers on the Nile: Early US Visitors to Egypt, 1774-1839 — Oliver, Andrew
American Umpire — Cobbs Hoffman, Elizabeth
American "Unculture" in French Drama: Homo Americanus and the Post-1960 French Resistance — Essif, Les
American Value: Migrants, Money, and Meaning in El Salvador and the United States — Pedersen, David
American Vandal: Mark Twain Abroad — Morris, Roy, Jr.
The American Warfare State: The Domestic Politics of Military Spending — Thorpe, Rebecca U.
American Warlord: A True Story — Dwyer, Johnny
American Warlords: How Roosevelt's High Command Led America to Victory in World War II — Jordan, Jonathan W.
The American Way of Bombing: Changing Ethical and Legal Norms, From Flying Fortresses to Drones — Evangelista, Matthew
The American Way of Bombing: Changing Ethical and Legal Norms, from Flying Fortresses to Drones — Shue, Henry
American Wine: A Coming of Age Story — Acitelli, Tom
American Zoo: A Sociological Safari — Grazian, David
c Americanine: A Haute Dog in New York (Illus. by Kebbi, Yann) — Kebbi, Yann
The Americanization of France: Searching for Happiness after the Algerian War — Singer, Barnett
The Americanization of Narcissism — Lunbeck, Elizabeth
The Americans — Viraraghavan, Chitra
Americans against the City: Anti-urbanism in the Twentieth Century — Conn, Steven
Americans All: Good Neighbor Cultural Diplomacy in World War II — Sadlier, Darlene J.
Americans in the Treasure House: Travel to Porfirian Mexico and the Cultural Politics of Empire — Ruiz, Jason
America's Assembly Line — Nye, David E.
America's Bank: The Epic Struggle to Create the Federal Reserve — Lowenstein, Roger
America's Bitter Pill: Money, Politics, Backroom Deals, and the Fight to Fix Our Broken Healthcare System — Brill, Steven
America's Church: The National Shrine and Catholic Presence in the Nation's Capital — Llywelyn, Dorian
America's Corporal: James Tanner in War and Peace — Marten, James
America's Darwin: Darwinian Theory and U.S. Literary Culture — Gianquitto, Tina
America's Dirty Wars: Irregular Warfare from 1776 to the War on Terror — Crandall, Russell
America's Dreyfus: The Case Nixon Rigged — Brady, Joan
America's England: Antebellum Literature and Atlantic Sectionalism — Hanlon, Christopher
America's Favorite Holidays: Candid Histories — Forbes, Bruce David
America's First Black Socialist: The Radical Life of Peter H. Clark — Taylor, Nikki M.
America's First Chaplain: The Life and Times of Reverend Jacob Duche — Dellape, Kevin J.
America's First Daughter — Dray, Stephanie

America's Forgotten Constitutions: Defiant Visions of Power and Community — *Tsai, Robert L.*
America's Founding and the Struggle Over Economic Inequality — *Fatovic, Clement*
America's Mayor: John V. Lindsay and the Reinvention of New York — *Roberts, Sam*
America's Moment: Creating Opportunity in the Connected Age — *Baird, Zoe*
America's Moment: Creating Opportunity in the Connected Age — *Rework America*
America's Original Sin: Racism, White Privilege, and the Bridge to a New America — *Wallis, Jim*
America's Pastor: Billy Graham and the Shaping of a Nation — *Wacker, Grant*
America's Safest City: Delinquency and Modernity in Suburbia — *Singer, Simon I.*
America's Secret Jihad: The Hidden History of Religious Terrorism in the United States — *Wexler, Stuart*
America's U-boats: Terror Trophies of World War I — *Dubbs, Chris*
America's Unwritten Constitution: The Precendents and Principles We Live By — *Amar, Akhil, Reed*
America's War Machine: Vested Interests, Endless Conflicts — *McCartney, James*
Americo Paredes: Culture and Critique — *Limon, Jose E.*
Amerikanismus: Kulturelle Abgrenzung von Europa und US-Nationalismus im fruhen 20. Jahrhundert — *Saldern, Adelheid von*
Ametora: How Japan Saved American Style — *Marx, W. David*
Amherst — *Nicholson, William*
c Ami y Perlita (Illus. by Temperini, Eliana Judith) — *Barrios, Enrique*
Amigas y Amantes: Sexually Nonconforming Latinas Negotiate Family — *Acosta, Katie L.*
y Amina — *Powers, J.L.*
Amiri Baraka & Edward Dorn: The Collected Letters — *Pisano, Claudia Moreno*
The Amish Clockmaker — *Clark, Mindy Starns*
The Amish Heart of Ice Mountain — *Long, Kelly*
An Amish Man of Ice Mountain — *Long, Kelly*
Amish Quilts: Crafting and American Icon — *Smucker, Janneken*
Amistad: A Hidden Network of Slavers and Merchants — *Zeuske, Michael*
The Amistad Rebellion: An Atlantic Odyssey of Slavery and Freedom — *Rediker, Marcus*
y Amity — *Ostow, Micol*
Amlethus — *Melanson, Carl*
Ammiano Marcellino XXVIII e XXIX: Problemi storici e storiografici — *Bocci, Stefano*
Amnesia — *Carey, Peter*
c Among a Thousand Fireflies (Illus. by Lieder, Rick) — *Frost, Helen*
Among Murderers: Life after Prison — *Heinlein, Sabine*
Among the Ruins: Syria Past and Present — *Sahner, Christian C.*
Among the Ten Thousand Things — *Pierpont, Julia*
Among the Wolves: Memoirs of a Wolf Handler — *Shelbourne, Toni*
Among Unknown Tribes: Rediscovering the Photographs of Explorer Carl Lumholtz — *Broyles, Bill*
y Among Wolves — *Wallace, Nancy K.*
Amor che move: linguaggio del corpo e forma del desiderio in Dante, Pasolini e Morante — *Gragnolati, Manuele*
'Amor' sans 'desonor': une pragmatique pour Tristan et Yseult — *Grigoriu, Brindusa*
Amp Up Your Sales — *Paul, Andy*
Amphibian Evolution: The Life of Early Land Vertebrates — *Schoch, Rainer R.*
c Amphibians and Reptiles: A Compare and Contrast Book — *Hall, Katharine*
c Amphibians and Reptiles — *Hall, Katharine*
Amsterdam — *McEwan, Ian*
Amsterdam Slavery Heritage Guide — *Slavernijverleden, Gids*
Amulet Keepers — *Northrop, Michael*
c Amusing Animal Jokes to Tickle Your Funny Bone — *LaRoche, Amelia*
Amusing Ourselves to Death — *Postman, Neil*
c Amy Namey in Ace Reporter (Illus. by Madrid, Erwin) — *McDonald, Megan*
c Amy's Very Merry Christmas (Illus. by Riti, Marsha) — *Barkley, Callie*
y Ana of California (Read by Teran, Andi). Audiobook Review — *Teran, Andi*
y Ana of California — *Teran, Andi*

Anaconda Choke — *Brown, Jeremy*
Anadarko: A Kiowa Country Mystery — *Holm, Tom*
The Analogical Turn: Rethinking Modernity with Nicholas of Cusa — *Hoff, Johannes*
Analogie et recit de voyage: voir, mesurer, interpreter le monde — *Guyot, Alain*
Analysing Social Work Communication: Discourse in Practice — *Hall, Christopher*
Analytical Psychology in Exile: The Correspondence of C.G. Jung and Erich Neumann — *Liebscher, Martin*
Analyze and Define the Assignment — *Bodden, Valerie*
Anarchic Solidarity: Autonomy, Equality, and Fellowship in Southeast Asia — *Gibson, Thomas*
Anasazi America: Seventeen Centuries on the Road from Center Place, 2d ed. — *Stuart, David E.*
y Anastasia and Her Sisters — *Meyer, Carolyn*
y The Anatomical Shape of a Heart — *Bennett, Jenn*
Anatomies: Stories — *McCarty, Susan*
Anatomy in Diagnostic Imaging, 3d ed. — *Fleckenstein, Peter*
The Anatomy of a Calling: A Doctor's Journey from the Head to the Heart and a Prescription for Finding Your Life's Purpose — *Rankin, Lissa*
Anatomy of a Kidnapping: A Doctor's Story — *Berk, Steven L.*
y Anatomy of a Misfit — *Portes, Andrea*
Anatomy of a Robot: Literature, Cinema, and the Cultural Work of Artificial People — *Kakoudaki, Despina*
The Anatomy of Addiction — *Mohammad, Akikur*
The Anatomy of Bloom: Harold Bloom and the Study of Influence and Anxiety — *Heys, Alistair*
An Anatomy of Chinese: Rhythm, Metaphor, Politics — *Link, Perry*
y The Anatomy of Curiosity — *Stiefvater, Maggie*
Anatomy of Delusion — *Kellerman, Henry*
Anatomy of Evil — *Thomas, Will*
Anatomy of Love: A Natural History of Mating, Marriage, and Why We Stray — *Fisher, Helen*
The Anatomy of Revolution Revisited: A Comparative Analysis of England, France and Russia — *Stone, Bailey*
The Anatomy of Terror: Political Violence under Stalin — *Harris, James*
Anay's Will to Learn: A Woman's Education in the Shadow of the Maquiladoras — *Hampton, Elaine*
Ancestors and Antiretrovirals: The Biopolitics of HIV/AIDS in Post-Apartheid South Africa — *Decoteau, Claire Laurier*
Ancestors and Antiretrovirals: The Biopolitics of HIV/AIDS in Postapartheid South Africa — *Decoteau, Claire Laurier*
Ancestors in Our Genome: The New Science of Human Evolution — *Harris, Eugene E.*
The Ancestors of Christ Windows at Canterbury Cathedral — *Caviness, Madeline H.*
Ancestral Fault in Ancient Greece — *Gagne, Renaud*
Ancestral Machines — *Cobley, Michael*
Anch'io per la tua bandiera: Il V Battaglione Ascari in missione sul fronte libico — *Zaccaria, Massimo*
Anchor and Flares: A Memoir of Motherhood, Hope and Service — *Braestrup, Kate*
Anchored: Finding Hope in the Unexpected — *Aimee, Kayla*
y The Anchoress — *Cadwallader, Robyn*
Anchoritism in the Middle Ages: Texts and Traditions — *Innes-Parker, Catherine*
The Ancient Alien Question: A New Inquiry into the Existence, Evidence, and Influence of Ancient Visitors — *Coppens, Philip*
c Ancient Animals: Saber-Toothed Cat (Illus. by Plant, Andrew) — *Thomson, Sarah L.*
y Ancient Appetites — *McGann, Oisin*
The Ancient Art of Growing Old — *Payne, Tom*
c Ancient Aztecs — *Kenney, Karen Latchana*
Ancient Christian Martyrdom: Diverse Practices, Theologies, and Traditions — *Moss, Candida R.*
Ancient Christian Worship: Early Church Practices in Social, Historical, and Theological Perspective — *McGowan, Andrew B.*
c Ancient Egypt (Illus. by Lowery, Mike) — *Jennings, Ken*
c Ancient Egypt: An Interactive History Adventure — *Adamson, Heather*
Ancient Egypt in 30 Seconds: 30 Awesome Topics for Pharaoh Fanatics Explained in Half a Minute — *Senker, Cath*
Ancient Egyptian Administration — *Garcia, Juan Carlos Moreno*
c The Ancient Egyptians — *Cooke, Tim*

Ancient Ethnography: New Approaches — *Almagor, Eran*
The Ancient Giants Who Ruled America: The Missing Skeletons and the Great Smithsonian Cover-Up — *Dewhurst, Richard J.*
Ancient Greek Women in Film — *Nikoloutsos, K.P.*
Ancient Israel: The Former Prophets Joshua, Judges, Samuel, and Kings: A Translation with Commentary — *Alter, Robert*
The Ancient Jews from Alexander to Muhammad — *Schwartz, Seth*
y Ancient Maya — *Edwards, Sue*
Ancient Maya Political Dynamics — *Foias, Antonia E.*
The Ancient Mediterranean Environment between Science and History — *Harris, William V.*
The Ancient Near East: History, Society and Economy — *Liverani, Mario*
Ancient Oceans of Central Kentucky — *Nahm, David Connerley*
Ancient Persia: A Concise History of the Achaemenid Empire, 550-330 BCE — *Waters, Matthew W.*
The Ancient Quarrel between Philosophy and Poetry — *Barfield, Raymond*
Ancient Rome: From Romulus to Justinian — *Martin, Thomas R.*
The Ancient Sailing Season — *Beresford, James*
Ancient Sex: New Essays — *Blondell, Ruby*
c Ancient Sumer — *Kelly, Tracey*
Ancient Worlds Modern Beads: 30 Stunning Beadwork Designs Inspired by Treasures from Ancient Civilizations — *van Pelt, Mortira Natasha*
Ancillary Mercy — *Leckie, Ann*
And after Many Days — *Ile, Jowhor*
And Again — *Chiarella, Jessica*
c And Away We Go! (Illus. by Migy) — *Migy*
And I Love Her — *Force, Marie*
And Is There Honey Still for Tea? — *Murphy, Peter*
c And Nick (Illus. by Gore, Leonid) — *Gore, Emily*
And Only to Deceive (Read by Reading, Kate). Audiobook Review — *Alexander, Tasha*
And So Is the Bus — *Birstein, Yossel*
And Sometimes I Wonder about You (Read by Onayemi, Prentice). Audiobook Review — *Mosley, Walter*
And Sometimes I Wonder about You — *Mosley, Walter*
And Still I Rise: Black America since MLK — *Gates, Henry Louis, Jr.*
c And Tango Makes Three (Illus. by Cole, Henry) — *Richardson, Justin*
y And the Band Played Waltzing Matilda (Illus. by Whatley, Bruce) — *Bogle, Eric*
c And the Cow Said (Illus. by Gausden, Vicki) — *Cotton, Katie*
And the Dark Sacred Night — *Glass, Julia*
And the Good News Is ... : Lessons and Advice from the Bright Side — *Perino, Dana*
And the Mountains Echoed (Read by Hosseini, Khaled). Audiobook Review — *Hosseini, Khaled*
c And Then Another Sheep Turned Up (Illus. by Adele, Amy) — *Gehl, Laura*
c And Then Comes Christmas (Illus. by Christy, Jana) — *Brenner, Tom*
And Then He Kissed Me — *Amos, Kim*
And Then I Danced: Traveling the Road to LGBT Equality — *Segal, Mark*
And Then the Hawk Said ... — *Morris, D.C.*
"And Touching Our Society": Fashioning Jesuit Identity in Elizabethan England — *McCoog, Thomas M.*
c And Two Boys Booed (Illus. by Blackall, Sophie) — *Viorst, Judith*
y And We Stay — *Hubbard, Jenny*
y And West Is West — *Childress, Ron*
c And What If I Won't? (Illus. by Davila, Claudia) — *Fergus, Maureen*
c And What If I Won't? (Illus. by Leng, Qin) — *Fergus, Maureen*
And Yet ... — *Hitchens, Christopher*
The Andean Science of Weaving: Structures and Techniques of Warp-Faced Weaves — *Arnold, Denise Y.*
y Anders and the Comet — *Mackay, Gregory*
Anders Breivik and the Rise of Islamophobia — *Bangstad, Sindre*
Andersonville (Read by Gardner, Grover). Audiobook Review — *Kantor, MacKinlay*
Andersonville — *Erdelac, Edward M.*
Andre Bazin's New Media — *Andrew, Dudley*
Andre the Giant: Closer to Heaven — *Easton, Brandon*
Andrea del Sarto: The Renaissance Workshop in Action — *Brooks, Julian*

Andrea Pozzo and Video Art — *Burda-Stengel, Felix*
y Andreo's Race — *Withers, Pam*
c Andrew Draws — *McPhail, David*
Andrew Jackson, Southerner — *Cheathem, Mark R.*
c Andrew Luck — *Gregory, Josh*
Andrew Marvell's Liminal Lyrics: The Space Between — *Faust, Joan*
Andrew Melville (1545-1622): Writings, Reception, and Reputation — *Mason, Roger A.*
Andrew Melville and Humanism in Renaissance Scotland, 1545-1622 — *Holloway, Ernest R., III*
Andrews on Civil Processes, vol. 1: Court Proceedings and Principles — *Andrews, Neil*
Andrews on Civil Processes, vol. 2: Arbitration and Mediation — *Andrews, Neil*
Androids and Intelligent Networks in Early Modern Literature and Culture: Artificial Slaves — *LaGrandeur, Kevin*
Androids in the Enlightenment: Mechanics, Artisans, and Cultures of the Self — *Voskuhl, Adelheid*
Andromeda's War — *Deitz, William C.*
Andronicus Camaterus — *Bucossi, Alessandra*
c Andy, Also (Illus. by Eaton, Maxwell, III) — *Eaton, Maxwell, III*
Andy & Don: The Making of a Friendship and a Classic American TV Show — *de Vise, Daniel*
Andy Warhol: The Complete Commissioned Record Covers, 1949-1987, 2d ed. — *Marechal, Paul*
Andy Warhol Was a Hoarder: Inside the Minds of History's Great Personalities — *Kalb, Claudia*
An Anecdotal Death — *Roby, Kinley*
Aneignungen des Humanismus: Institutionelle und Individuelle Praktiken an der Universitat Ingolstadt im 15. Jahrhundert — *Schuh, Maximilian*
Angel in Aisle 3: The True Story of a Mysterious Vagrant, a Convicted Banker, and the Unlikely Friendship That Saved Both Their Lives — *Edwards, Frederick*
c Angel Island: Gateway to Gold Mountain — *Freedman, Russell*
Angel of Eden — *McIntosh, D.J.*
Angel of Storms — *Canavan, Trudi*
c Angel of Venice — *Hoffman, Mary*
Angel Patriots: The Crash of United Flight 93 and the Myth of America — *Riley, Alexander T.*
c The Angel Tree — *Benedis-Grab, Daphne*
An Angel Walks through the Stage and Other Essays — *Fosse, Jon*
Angela's Decision: Outsmarting My Cancer Genes and Determining My Fate — *Fishbaugh, Angela Schmidt*
The Angelic Mother and the Predatory Seductress: Poor White Women in Southern Literature of the Great Depression — *Lancaster, Ashley Craig*
Angelica's Smile — *Camilleri, Andrea*
c Angelina's Big City Ballet (Illus. by Craig, Helen) — *Holabird, Katharine*
c Angelina's Cinderella (Illus. by Craig, Helen) — *Holabird, Katharine*
Angels at the Gate — *Thorne, T.K.*
Angels Burning — *O'Dell, Tawni*
Angels, Demons and the New World — *Cervantes, Fernando*
Angels of Light?: Sanctity and the Discernment of Spirits in the Early Modern Period — *Copeland, Clare*
Angels of the Underground — *Kaminski, Theresa*
The Angel's Share — *Ellis, Garfield*
Angels: The Definitive Guide to Angels from around the World — *Faugerolas, Marie-Ange*
Angels Three: The Karen Perry Story — *Napoleon, Landon J.*
Angels with Dirty Faces — *Imarisha, Walidah*
Angelus — *Benulis, Sabrina*
Anger and Racial Politics: The Emotional Foundation of Racial Attitudes in America — *Banks, Antoine J.*
Anger Is an Energy: My Life Uncensored (Read by Perkins, Derek). Audiobook Review — *Lydon, John*
Anger Is an Energy: My Life Uncensored — *Lydon, John*
The Anger Meridian — *Jones, Kaylie*
Angewandte Geschichte: Neue Perspektiven auf Geschichte in der Offentlichkeit — *Niesser, Jacqueline*
Anglican Confirmation, 1662-1820 — *Tovey, Philip*
The Anglican Imagination: Portraits and Sketches of Modern Anglican Theologians — *Slocum, Robert Boak*
Anglo-American Connections in Japanese Chemistry: The Lab as Contact Zone — *Kikuchi, Yoshiyuki*

Anglo-German Relations and the Protestant Cause: Elizabethan Foreign Policy and Pan-Protestantism — *Gehring, David Scott*
Anglo-Norman Studies, XXXVI: Proceedings of the Battle Conference 2013 — *Bates, David*
Anglo-Saxon Farms and Farming — *Banham, Debby*
Anglo-Saxon Keywords — *Frantzen, Allen J.*
The Anglo-Saxon Literature Handbook — *Amodio, Mark C.*
Anglo-Saxon Manuscripts: A Bibliographic Handlist of Manuscripts and Manuscript Fragments Written or Owned in England up to 1100 — *Gneuss, Helmut*
The Anglo-Saxon Psalter — *Toswell, M.J.*
The Anglo-Saxon World — *Higham, Nicholas J.*
c The Angry Little Puffin — *Young, Timothy*
Angry Optimist: The Life and Times of Jon Stewart — *Rogak, Lisa*
The Angst of Adolescence: How to Parent Your Teen, and Live to Laugh About It — *Villanueva, Sara*
Anguish, Anger, and Folkways in Soviet Russia — *Rittersporn, Gabor T.*
Angular Unconformity: Collected Poems, 1970-2014 — *McKay, Don*
Angus and Sadie (Read by Carter, Wendy). Audiobook Review — *Voigt, Cynthia*
Animal Acts: Performing Species Today — *Chaudhuri, Una*
c Animal Beauty (Illus. by Roskifte, Kristin) — *Roskifte, Kristin*
Animal Behavior — *Midthun, Joseph*
Animal Body Size: Linking Pattern and Process across Space, Time, and Taxonomic Group — *Smith, Felisa A.*
c The Animal Book: A Collection of the Fastest, Fiercest, Toughest, Cleverest, Shyest - And Most Surprising-Animals on Earth — *Jenkins, Steve*
c Animal Brainiacs — *Franchino, Vicky*
c Animal Classification — *VanVoorst, Jenny Fretland*
c Animal Colors — *Feldman, Thea*
c Animal Eyes — *Holland, Mary*
c Animal Faces — *Arlon, Penelope*
c Animal Friends — *Brook-Piper, Holly*
c Animal Helpers: Raptor Centers — *Curtis, Jennifer Keats*
c Animal Hospital: Rescuing Urban Wildlife — *Coey, Julia*
Animal Infographics — *Oxlade, Chris*
c Animal Kingdom Series — *Levine, Michelle*
Animal Knits for Kids: 30 Cute Knitted Projects They'll Love — *Berry, Amanda*
Animal Metamorphosis — *Shi, Yun-Bo*
Animal Models for the Study of Human Disease — *Conn, P. Michael*
Animal Movement across Scales — *Hansson, Lars-Anders*
Animal Oppression and Human Violence: Domesecration, Capitalism, and Global Conflict — *Nibert, David A.*
c Animal Partners (Illus. by Bersani, Shennen) — *Cohn, Scotti*
c Animal Pollinators — *Boothroyd, Jennifer*
c Animal Rescue — *George, Patrick*
c Animal School: What Class Are You? (Illus. by Garland, Michael) — *Lord, Michelle*
c Animal Senses — *Buchanan, Shelly C.*
Animal Shenanigans: 24 Creative, Interactive Story Programs for Preschoolers — *Reid, Rob*
Animal Social Networks — *Krause, Jens*
c Animal Sounds — *Davenport, Maxine*
c Animal Stories: Heartwarming True Tales from the Animal Kingdom (Illus. by Ishida, Jui) — *Yolen, Jane*
Animal Suffering and the Problem of Evil — *Creegan, Nicola Hoggard*
c Animal Supermarket (Illus. by Mulazzani, Simona) — *Zoboli, Giovanna*
c Animal Superstars and More True Stories of Amazing Animal Talents (Read by Heller, Johnny). Audiobook Review — *Newman, Aline Alexander*
c Animal Teachers (Illus. by Hudson, Katy) — *Halfmann, Janet*
Animal Testing: Life-Saving Research vs. Animal Welfare — *Sephaban, Lois*
The Animal Too Big to Kill — *McCrae, Shane*
Animal, Vegetable, Mineral? How Eighteenth-Century Science Disrupted the Natural Order — *Gibson, Susannah*
Animal Weapons: The Evolution of Battle — *Emlen, Douglas J.*
c Animales: Descubre la fascinante diversidad de la naturaleza
c Animalium (Illus. by Scott, Katie) — *Broom, Jenny*

c Animally (Illus. by Mitchell, Hazel) — *Sutton, Lynn Parrish*
c Animals: A Visual Encyclopedia — *Buckley, James, Jr.*
Animals (Illus. by Petelinsek, Kathleen) — *Thornborough, Kathy*
The Animals — *Kiefer, Christian*
y Animals — *Unsworth, Emma Jane*
c Animals — *de la Bedoyere, Camilla*
Animals and Early Modern Identity — *Cuneo, Pia F.*
Animals and Inequality in the Ancient World — *Arbuckle, Benjamin S.*
Animals Don't Blush — *Gross, David R.*
Animals Have Feelings Too: Eight Original Piano Solos — *Linn, Jennifer*
c Animals Helping to Detect Diseases — *Gray, Susan H.*
Animals in Photographs — *Kovacs, Arpad*
Animals in the Classical World: Ethical Perspectives from Greek and Roman Texts — *Harden, Alastair*
c Animals of Alaska: A Coloring and Activity Book (Illus. by Rhodes, Lisa) — *Rhodes, Lisa*
c The Animals' Santa (Illus. by Brett, Jan) — *Brett, Jan*
c Animals That Make Me Say Ewww! — *Cusick, Dawn*
c Animals That Make Me Say Ouch! — *Cusick, Dawn*
c Animals That Make Me Say Wow! — *Cusick, Dawn*
c Animals Work — *Lewin, Ted*
c Anime and Manga — *Allen, John*
The Anime Encyclopedia: A Century of Japanese Animation, 3rd ed. — *Clements, Jonathan*
c Ann Olly Explores: 7 Wonders of the Chesapeake Bay — *Allen, Elaine*
Ann Tenna — *Marchetto, Marisa Acocella*
Anna: A Doctor's Quest into the Unknown — *Derechin, Michael*
y Anna and the Swallow Man — *Savit, Gavriel*
c Anna Banana and the Chocolate Explosion! (Illus. by Dormal, Alexis) — *Roques, Dominique*
c Anna, Banana, and the Friendship Split (Illus. by Park, Meg) — *Rissi, Anica Mrose*
c Anna, Banana, and the Monkey in the Middle (Illus. by Park, Meg) — *Rissi, Anica Mrose*
c Anna Carries Water (Illus. by James, Laura) — *Senior, Olive*
Anna & Froga: Thrills, Spills and Gooseberries — *Ricard, Anouk*
Anna Howard Shaw: The Work of Woman Suffrage — *Franzen, Trisha*
Anna Karenina — *Bartlett, Rosamund*
Anna Letitia Barbauld and Eighteenth-Century Visionary Poetics — *Watkins, Daniel P.*
Anna & Solomon (Read by Marshall, Qarie). Audiobook Review — *Snyder, Elaine*
Annals of the Deep Sky: A Survey of Galactic and Extragalactic Objects — *Kanipe, Jeff*
Anna's Crossing — *Fisher, Suzanne Woods*
c Anna's Heaven — *Hole, Stian*
Anne Carson: Ecstatic Lyre — *Wilkinson, Joshua Maria*
Anne Frank 80 Years: A Memorial Tour in Current Images — *Jansen, Ronald Wilfred*
c Anne Frank and the Remembering Tree (Illus. by Steiskal, Erika) — *Sasso, Sandy Eisenberg*
Anne Frank: Mediengeschichten — *Seibert, Peter*
Anne Frank Remembered: The Story of the Woman Who Helped to Hide the Frank Family (Read by Rosenblat, Barbara). Audiobook Review — *Gies, Miep*
y Anne & Henry — *Ius, Dawn*
c Anne of Green Gables (Read by Frasier, Shelly). Audiobook Review — *Montgomery, Lucy Maud*
Annihilation — *VanderMeer, Jeff*
The Annihilation of Nature: Human Extinction of Birds and Mammals — *Ceballos, Gerardo*
The Annotated Alice: 150th Anniversary Deluxe ed. — *Carroll, Lewis*
The Annotated Little Women — *Alcott, Louisa May*
The Annotated Wuthering Heights — *Bronte, Emily*
c The Annoying Crush (Illus. by Kraft, Jason) — *O'Ryan, Ray*
Annual Review of Applied Linguistics — *Mackey, Alison*
Annual Review of Cultural Heritage Informatics 2012-2013 — *Hastings, Samantha K.*
Anodea Judith's Chakra Yoga — *Judith, Anodea*
Anomalous Cognition: Remote Viewing Research and Theory — *May, Edwin C.*
y Anomaly — *Kuper, Tonya*
Anonymous Soldiers: The Struggle for Israel, 1917-1947 — *Hoffman, Bruce*
y Another Day (Read by McInerney, Kathleen). Audiobook Review — *Levithan, David*
y Another Day — *Levithan, David*

Another Green World: Linn Botanic Gardens-Encounters with a Scottish Arcadia — Turnbull, Alison
y Another Kind of Hurricane — Smith, Tamara Ellis
y Another Little Piece of My Heart: My Life of Rock and Revolution in the '60s — Goldstein, Richard
Another Man's War: The Story of Burma Boy in Britain's Forgotten African Army — Phillips, Barnaby
Another Mother's Son — Davey, Janet
Another Person's Poison: A History of Food Allergy — Smith, Matthew (b. 1973-)
Another Woman's Daughter — Sussman, Fiona
Another Year in Oman — Heines, Matthew D.
Anselm's Other Argument — Smith, A.D.
Answerable Style: The Idea of the Literary in Medieval England — Grady, Frank
Answering the Call: Popular Islamic Activism in Sadat's Egypt — al-Arian, Abdullah
The Antagonist Principle: John Henry Newman and the Paradox of Personality — Poston, Lawrence
Antarctica and the Arctic Circle: A Geographic Encyclopedia of the Earth's Polar Regions — Hund, Andrew J.
Antarctica in Fiction: Imaginative Narratives of the Far South — Leane, Elizabeth
Anthem: Social Movements and the Sound of Solidarity in the African Diaspora — Redmond, Shana L.
Anthology of Easier Classical Piano: 174 Favorite Piano Pieces by 44 Composers — Hal Leonard Publishing Corporation
An Anthology of Mine — Whistler, Rex
y The Anthropologist's Daughter — Jackson, Vanessa Furse
Anthropology and Anthropologists: The British School in the Twentieth Century — Kuper, Adam
Anthropology in the Making: Research in Health and Development — Vidal, Laurent
An Anthropology of Architecture — Buchli, Victor
The Anthropology of Citizenship: A Reader — Lazar, Sian
The Anthropology of Ignorance: An Ethnographic Approach — High, Casey
The Anthropology of Performance: A Reader — Korom, Frank J.
Anti-Access Warfare: Countering A2/AD Strategies — Tangredi, Sam J.
Anti-Judaism: The History of a Way of Thinking — Nirenberg, David
Anti-Judaism: The Western Tradition — Nirenberg, David
Anti-Liberal Europe: A Neglected Story of Europeanization — Gosewinkel, Dieter
c The Anti-Princess Club Series (Illus. by Davis, Sarah) — Turnbull, Samantha
y Anti-Semitism and the "Final Solution": The Holocaust Overview — Byers, Ann
The Anti-Witch — Favret-Saada, Jeanne
Antibodies: A Laboratory Manual — Greenfield, Edward A.
The Anticancer Diet: Reduce Cancer Risk through the Foods You Eat — Khayat, David
The Antichrist of Kokomo County — Skinner, David
The Anticipatory Corpse: Medicine, Power, and the Care of the Dying — Bishop, Jeffrey P.
Antidote for Night — De la O, Marsha
Antidote to Venom — Crofts, Freeman Wills
Antigone, Interrupted — Honig, Bonnie
Antike Wirtschaft — Reden, Sitta von
The Antimodern Condition: An Argument against Progress — King, Peter
Antipodean America: Australasia and the Constitution of U.S. Literature — Giles, Paul
Antiques Swap — Allan, Barbara
The Antiquity of the Italian Nation: The Cultural Origins of a Political Myth in Modern Italy — De Francesco, A.
Antisemitischer Alltag und Holocaust - Rekonstruktion und Erinnerung
Antisemitism and the American Far Left — Noorwood, Stephan H.
Antisemitism in an Era of Transition: Continuities and Impact in Post-Communist Poland and Hungary — Guesnet , Francois
Antisemitismus im Reichstag: Judenfeindliche Sprache in Politik und Gesellschaft der Weimarer Republik — Wein, Susanne
Antisemitismus in Galizien: Agitation, Gewalt und Politik gegen Juden in der Habsburgermonarchie um 1900 — Buchen, Tim

Antisemitismus und Rassismus- Verflechtungen? 5. Tagung: Blickwinkel. Antisemitismuskritisches Forum fur Bildung und Wissenschaft
Antiwar Dissent and Peace Activism in World War I America — Bennett, Scott H.
c Anton and Cecil: Cats on Track (Illus. by Murphy, Kelly) — Martin, Lisa
Anton Corbijn: 1-2-3-4 — van Sinderen, Wim
Anton Friedrich Justus Thibaut (1772-1840): Ein Heidelberger Professor zwischen Wissenschaft und Politik — Kaufmann, Dorte
The Antonio II Badile Album of Drawings: The Origins of Collecting Drawings in Early Modern Northern Italy — Karet, Evelyn
Antony and Cleopatra (Read by Crossley, Steven). Audiobook Review — Goldsworthy, Adrian
c Ants — Hansen, Grace
c Anxiety: Deal with it before it Ties You Up in Knots (Illus. by Heeley, Ted) — Mandel, Joey
y The Anxiety Survival Guide for Teens: CBT Skills to Overcome Fear, Worry and Panic (Illus. by Shannon, Doug) — Shannon, Jennifer
The Anxiety Toolkit: Strategies for Fine-Tuning Your Mind and Moving Past Your Stuck Points — Boyes, Alice
Anxious: The Modern Mind in the Age of Anxiety — LeDoux, Joseph
Anxious: Using the Brain to Understand and Treat Fear and Anxiety — LeDoux, Joseph
Any Mummers 'lowed in?: Christmas Mummering Traditions — Jarvis, Dale
Any Other Name — Johnson, Craig
c Any Questions? (Illus. by Gay, Marie-Louise) — Gay, Marie-Louise
c Anybody Shining (Read by Jackson, Suzy). Audiobook Review — Dowell, Frances O'Rourke
c Anybody Shining — Dowell, Frances O'Roark
c Anyone but Ivy Pocket (Illus. by Cantini, Barbara) — Krisp, Caleb
y Anything Could Happen — Walton, Will
Anything for You — Higgins, Kristan
Anything That Burns You: A Portrait of Lola Ridge, Radical Poet — Svoboda, Terese
y Anything That Isn't This — Priestley, Chris
c Anywhere but Paradise — Bustard, Anne
Anzac and Its Enemies: The History War on Australia's National Identity — Bendle, Mervyn F.
c Anzac Boys (Illus. by Cuthbertson, Ollie) — Bradman, Tony
c Anzac Sons: Young Peoples Edition — Paterson, Allison Marlow
c Anzac Ted (Illus. by Landsberry, Belinda) — Landsberry, Belinda
Anzac's Long Shadow: The Cost of Our National Obsession — Brown, James
c Anzard — Conroy, Christopher
c Aoleon the Martian Girl — Levasseur, Brent
APA Dictionary of Psychology, 2d ed. — American Psychological Association
Apache Lore and Legends of Southern New Mexico: From the Sacred Mountain — Sanchez, Linda
c Apache Resistance: Causes and Effects of Geronimo's Campaign — Dell, Pamela
Apache Warrior, 1860-86 — Watt, Robert N.
c Apatosaurus — Lennie, Charles
APE: Author, Publisher, Entrepreneur - How To Publish a Book — Kawasaki, Guy
c Apes a-Go-Go! (Illus. by Allen, A. Richard) — Milisic, Roman
Apex — Naam, Ramez
Aphrodisiacs, Fertility and Medicine in Early Modern England — Evans, Jennifer
Aphrodisias VI: The Marble Reliefs from the Julio-Claudian Sebasteion — Smith, R.R.R.
c Aphrodite the Fair — Holub, Joan
Apocalypse and the Millennium in the American Civil War Era — Wright, Ben
Apocalypse Baby — Despentes, Virginie
c Apocalypse Bow Wow (Illus. by Proimos, James, Jr.) — Proimos, James, III
Apocalypse in Japanese Science Fiction — Tanaka, Motoko
The Apocalypse in the Early Middle Ages — Palmer, James T.
Apocalyptic Discourse in Contemporary Culture: Post-Millennial Perspectives on the End of the World — Germana, Monica
ApocalyptiGirl: An Aria for the End Times — MacLean, Andrew
The Apocrypha: Core Biblical Studies — deSilva, David

Apollinaire in the Great War, 1914-1918 — Hunter, David
c Apollo — O'Connor, George
c Apollo: God of the Sun, Healing, Music, and Poetry (Illus. by Young, Eric) — Temple, Teri
Apollo in the Grass: Selected Poems — Kushner, Aleksandr
Apostle: Travels among the Tombs of the Twelve — Bissell, Tom
Apostles of Reason: The Crisis of Authority in American Evangelicalism — Worthen, Molly
The Apostles of Satan — Kimmich, F. Scott
Apostolic Iconography and Florentine Confraternities in the Age of Reform — Dow, Douglas N.
The App Generation: How Today's Youth Navigate Identity, Intimacy, and Imagination in the Digital World — Gardner, Howard
The Appalachian — Robinson, Kirk Ward
Apparition Island — LeClair, Jenifer
Apparitions: Architecture That Has Disappeared from Our Cities — Hughes, T. John
y The Appearance of Annie Van Sinderen (Read by Bernstein, Jesse). Audiobook Review — Howe, Katherine
y The Appearance of Annie Van Sinderen — Howe, Katherine
The Appetite Solution: Lose Weight Effortlessly and Never be Hungry Again — Colella, Joseph
Appetites for Thought: Philosophers and Food — Onfray, Michel
c Apple — Bodden, Valerie
y Apple and Rain — Crossan, Sarah
The Apple Cookbook: 125 Freshly Picked Recipes — Woodier, Olwen
c Apple Days (Illus. by McMahon, Bob) — Softer, Allison Sarnoff
c Apple — Green, Sara
c The Apple Tree (Illus. by Hodson, Marlena Campbell) — Tharp-Thee, Sandy
c Appleblossom the Possum (Illus. by Rosen, Gary A.) — Sloan, Holly Goldberg
The Appleman and the Poet — Butler, Hubert
c Apples and Pumpkins (Illus. by Rockwell, Lizzy) — Rockwell, Anne
Appletopia: Media Technology and the Religious Imagination of Steve Jobs — Robinson, Brett T.
Application for Release from the Dream: Poems — Hoagland, Tony
Applications of Mathematics in Economics — Page, Warren
Applied Minds: How Engineers Think — Madhavan, Guru
Applied Psycholinguistics — Crago, Martha
Applique: The Basics & Beyond — Pittman, Janet
Applying the Wisdom of the World's Greatest Management Thinker — Cohen, William A.
Appomattox: Victory, Defeat, and Freedom at the End of the Civil War — Varon, Elizabeth R.
Apportionment of Blame — Redfern, Keith
Approaches to Teaching Milton's 'Paradise Lost' — Herman, Peter C.
Approaches to Teaching the Story of the Stone — Schonebaum, Andrew
Approaches to Teaching the Works of Carmen Martin Gaite — Brown, Joan L.
Approaches to the Byzantine Family — Brubaker, Leslie
Approaching Ali: A Reclamation in Three Acts — Miller, Davis
Approaching the End: Eschatological Reflections on Church, Politics, and Life — Hauerwas, Stanley
Approaching the End of Life: A Practical and Spiritual Life — Schaper, Donna
Apps for Librarians: Using the Best Mobile Technology to Educate, Create, and Engage — Hennig, Nicole
y Apps: From Concept to Consumer — Gregory, Josh
Apres la Grande Guerre: Comment les Amerindiens des Etats-Unis sont devenus patriotes — Grillot, Thomas
Apricot's Revenge — Song, Ying
Apuleius' Platonism: The Impersonation of Philosophy — Fletcher, Richard
c Aqualicious — Kann, Victoria
y Aquarion Evol (Illus. by Aogiri) — Kawamori, Shoji
y Aquarium — Vann, David
Aquatic Entomology — Lancaster, Jill
Aquinas and Calvin on Romans: God's Justification and Our Participation — Raith, Charles, II
Arab Art Histories: The Khalid Shoman Collection — Rogers, Sarah A.

Arab-Israeli Conflict: The Essential Reference Guide — Roberts, Priscilla
Arab Jazz — Gordon, Sam
The Arab of the Future: A Childhood in the Middle East, 1978-1984 — Sattouf, Riad
The Arab of the Future: A Childhood in the Middle East 1978-1984 — Sattouf, Riad
The Arab of the Future: A Graphic Memoir: A Childhood in the Middle East (1978-1984). — Sattouf, Riad
Arab Responses to Fascism and Nazism: Attraction and Repulsion — Gershoni, Israel
The Arab Uprisings Explained: New Contentious Politics in the Middle East — Lynch, Marc
Arab World Research Source — EBSCO Publishing
The Arabian Nights: An Anthology — Ouyang, Wen-chin
The Arabs of the Ottoman Empire, 1516-1918: A Social and Cultural History — Masters, Bruce
Aratus and the Astronomical Tradition — Gee, Emma
Arbeit an der Literatur: Zur Mythizitat der Artusromane Hartmanns von Aue — Hoffmann, Ulrich
Arbeit: Eine Globalhistorische Perspektive. 13. bis 21. Jahrhundert — Komlosy, Andrea
Arbeiterbewegung - Nation - Globalisierung: Bestandsaufnahmen einer alten Debatte — Voigt, Sebastian
Arbeits- und Lebensalltag Evangelischer Krankenpflege: Organisation, Soziale Praxis und Biographische Erfahrungen, 1945-1980 — Kreutzer, Susanne
Arbitrary Rule: Slavery, Tyranny, and the Power of Life and Death — Nyquist, Mary
The Arc of the Swallow — Gazan, Sissel-Jo
y Arcadia — Pears, Iain
Arcadia — Treadwell, James
Arcadia Britannica: A Modern British Folklore Portrait — Bourne, Henry
Arcadian America: The Death and Life of an Enviromental Tradition — Sachs, Aaron
The Arcadian Library: Bindings and Provenance — Mandelbrote, Giles
c Arcady's Goal — Yelchin, Eugene
c The Archaeologists — Thompson, Clifford
Archaeology and Architecture of the Military Orders: New Studies — Piana, Mathias
Archaeology and Celtic Myth: An Exploration — Waddell, John
The Archaeology and Ethnography of Central Africa — Denbow, James
Archaeology and Language in the Andes: A Cross-Disciplinary Exploration of Prehistory — Heggarty, Paul
The Archaeology of American Cities — Rothschild, Nan A.
The Archaeology of American Cities — Wall, Diana Dizerega
An Archaeology of Asian Transnationalism — Ross, Douglas E.
The Archaeology of Cyprus: From Earliest Prehistory through the Bronze Age — Knapp, A. Bernard
The Archaeology of Greek and Roman Troy — Rose, Charles Brian
The Archaeology of Israelite Society in Iron Age II — Faust, Avraham
The Archaeology of Medieval Spain, 1100-1500 — Gutierrez, Avelino
The Archaeology of Medieval Spain, 1100-1500 — Valor, Magdalena
The Archaeology of Sanitation in Roman Italy: Toilets, Sewers, and Water Systems — Koloski-Ostrow, Ann Olga
The Archaeology of Smoking and Tobacco — Fox, Georgia L.
The Archaeology of South-East Italy in the First Millennium BC: Greek and Native Societies of Apulia and Lucania between the 10th and the 1st century BC — Yntema, Douwe
Archaic Style in English Literature, 1590-1674 — Munro, Lucy
Archangel — Reed, Marguerite
Archangel's Enigma — Singh, Nalini
Archaologie an Tatorten des 20. Jahrhunderts — Theune-Vogt, Claudia
Archaologie und Bodendenkmalpflege in der Rheinprovinz 1920-1945 — Kunow, Jurgen
Archaologie und Krieg. Ein Neues Arbeitsfeld
Archbishop Michael Ramsey: The Shape of the Church — Webster, Peter
y Archie Archives: Prom Pranks and Other Stories — Montana, Bob

Archie Greene and the Magician's Secret — Everest, D.D.
c Archie the Daredevil Penguin (Illus. by Rash, Andy) — Rash, Andy
Archie vs. Sharknado — Ferrante, Anthony
c Archimedes and the Door of Science — Bendick, Jeanne
Archipelago — Anedda, Antonella
The Architect of Aeons — Wright, John C.
The Architect's Apprentice (Read by Marek, Piter). Audiobook Review — Shafak, Elif
y The Architect's Apprentice — Shafak, Elif
Architects of Austerity: International Finance and the Politics of Growth — Major, Aaron
Architects of Growth? Sub-national Governments and Industrialization in Asia — Hutchinson, Francis E.
Architectural Agents: The Delusional, Abusive, Addictive Lives of Buildings — Wharton, Annabel Jane
Architecturalized Asia: Mapping a Continent through History — Rujivacharakul, Vimalin
Architecture and Panelling: The James A. de Rothschild Bequest at Waddesdon Manor — Pons, Bruno
Architecture, Art and Identity in Venice and Its Territories, 1450-1750: Essays in Honour of Deborah Howard — Avcioglu, Nebahat
Architecture at the End of the Earth: Photographing the Russian North — Brumfield, William
Architecture in the South Pacific: The Ocean of Islands — Taylor, Jennifer
The Architecture of Concepts: The Historical Formation of Human Rights — de Bolla, Peter
The Architecture of Freedom: How to Free Your Soul — Cross, Tim
The Architecture of Paul Rudolph — Rohan, Timothy M.
Architecture, Politics and Identity in Divided Berlin — Pugh, Emily
Architectures de papier: La France et l'Europe — Lemerle, Frederique
Architektur der Diplomatie: Reprasentation in europaischen Botschaftsbauten, 1800-1920. Konstantinopel - Rom - Wien - St. Petersburg — Hort, Jakob
The Archival Turn in Feminism: Outrage in Order — Eichhorn, Kate
The Archive Thief: The Man Who Salvaged French Jewish History in the Wake of the Holocaust — Left, Lisa Moses
Archives and Societal Provenance: Australian Essays — Piggott, Michael
Archives of Origins: Sanskrit, Philology, Anthropology in Nineteenth Century Germany — Rabault-Feuerhahn, Pascale
Archiving the Unspeakable: Silence, Memory, and the Photographic Record in Cambodia — Caswell, Michelle
Archiving the Unspeakable: Silence, Memory, and the Photographic Record in Cambodia — Michelle, Caswell
y Archivist Wasp — Kornher-Stace, Nicole
y Arclight — McQuein, Joisin L.
c Arctic Animals — Carpenter, Tad
c Arctic Animals — Inhabit Media
y The Arctic Code — Kirby, Matthew J.
Arctic Lights, Arctic Nights — Miller, Debbie S.
Arctic Storm — Sundell, Joanne
Arctic Summer — Galgut, Damon
y Arctic Thaw: Climate Change and the Global Race for Energy — McPherson, Stephanie Sammartino
c Arctic White (Illus. by White, Lee) — Smith, Danna
Ardennes 1944: Hitler's Last Gamble — Beevor, Antony
Ardennes 1944: The Battle of the Bulge — Beevor, Antony
Ardenness 1944: The Battle of the Bulge — Beevor, Antony
Ardor — Calasso, Roberto
c Are Crop Circles Real? — Lassieur, Allison
Are Dolphins Really Smart? — Gregg, Justin
c Are Humans Damaging the Atmosphere? — Chambers, Catherine
Are Libraries Obsolete? An Argument for Relevance in the Digital Age — Herring, Mark Y.
Are Non-Christians Saved? Joseph Ratzinger's Thoughts on Religious Pluralism — Mong, Ambrose
Are the Androids Dreaming Yet? Amazing Brain: Human Communication, Creativity and Free Will — Tagg, James
Are We All Scientific Experts Now? — Collins, Harry

Are We Having Fun Yet? The Cooking and Partying Handbook — Hagar, Sammy
c Are We There, Yeti? (Illus. by Anstee, Ashlyn) — Anstee, Ashlyn
c Are We There Yeti? (Illus. by Freshley, Taylor) — Morris, Kerry
c Are You a Ewe? — Felix, Rebecca
y Are You at Risk for Food Allergies? Peanut Butter, Milk, and Other Deadly Threats — Gordon, Sherri Mabry
y Are You Being Bullied? How to Deal with Taunting, Teasing, and Tormenting — Winkler, Kathleen
y Are You Doing Risky Things? Cutting, Bingeing, Snorting, and Other Dangers — Rebman, Renee
Are You Doing Risky Things? Cutting, Bingeing, Snorting, and Other Dangers — Rebman, Renee C.
y Are You Downloading Copyrighted Stuff? Stealing or Fair Use — Gordon, Sherri Mabry
Are You Empowered??? The Basics — Lynn, Cynthia
y Are You Fat? The Obesity Issue for Teens — Gay, Kathlyn
y Are You Misusing Other People's Words? What Plagiarism Is and How to Avoid It — Francis, Barbara
c Are You My Daddy? (Illus. by Parker-Rees, Guy) — Oliver, Ilanit
c Are You My Mommy? (Illus. by Murphy, Mary) — Murphy, Mary
c Are You My Mommy? — Wan, Joyce
y Are You Seeing Me? — Groth, Darren
y Are You Still There — Scheerger, Sarah Lynn
c Are You the Pirate Captain? (Illus. by Parsons, Garry) — Jones, Gareth P.
c Are You What You Eat? A Guide to What's on Your Plate and Why — Baggaley, Ann
c Are You What You Eat? A Guide to What's on Your Plate and Why! — DK Publishing
y Area 51 — Haney, Jill
c Area 51 — Karst, Ken
y Arena 13 — Delaney, Joseph
Arendt and America — King, Richard H.
c Ares and the Spear of Fear (Illus. by Phillips, Craig) — Holub, Joan
c Ares: Bringer of War (Illus. by O'Connor, George) — O'Connor, George
c Arf! Arf! (Illus. by Braun, Sebastien) — Nosy Crow
y Argentina — Blashfield, Jean F.
The Argentine Silent Majority: Middle Classes, Politics, Violence, and Memory in the Seventies — Carassai, Sebastian
The Argentine Triangle — Topol, Allan
The Argonauts — Nelson, Maggie
Arguedas/Vargas Liosa: Dilemas y ensamblajes — Morana, Mabel
An Argument Open to All: Reading The Federalist in the Twenty-First Century — Levinson, Sanford
Arguments That Count: Physics, Computing, and Missile Defense, 1949-2012 — Slayton, Rebecca
Arguments with Silence: Writing the History of Roman Women — Richlin, Amy
The Ariadne Objective: The Underground War to Rescue Crete from the Nazis — Davis, Wes
Ariadne's Thread: In Memory of W.G. Sebald — Comber, Philippa
Arianism: Roman Heresy and Barbarian Creed — Berndt, Guido M.
Ariel's Ecology: Plantations, Personhood, and Colonialism in the American Tropics — Allewaert, Monique
Aristocratic Families in Republican France, 1870-1940 — MacKnight, Elizabeth C.
Aristocratic Vice: The Attack on Duelling, Suicide, Adultery, and Gambling in Eighteenth-Century England — Andrew, Donna T.
Aristophanes' Frogs — Griffith, Mark
An Aristotelian Realist Philosophy of Mathematics: Mathematics as the Science of Quantity and Structure — Franklin, James
Aristotelianism in the First Century B.C.E.: Xenarchus of Seleucia — Falcon, Andrea
Aristotle and the Virtues — Curzer, Howard
Aristotle as Teacher: His Introduction to a Philosophic Science — Bruell, Christopher
Aristotle on Perceiving Objects — Marmodoro, Anna
Aristotle, Plato and Pythagoreanism in the First Century BC: New Directions for Philosophy — Schofield, Malcolm
Aristotle Poetics: Editio Maior of the Greek Text with Historical Introductions and Philological Commentaries — Taran, Leonardo
Aristotle's Empiricism: Experience and Mechanics in the 4th Century BC — De Groot, Jean

Aristotle's Empiricism — De Groot, Jean
Arizona Dream: A True Story from a Real-Life "Ocean's Eleven" — Alisic, Adnan
Arlene Shechet: All at Once — Porter, Janelle
Arm Candy: Friendship Bracelets to Make and Share — Strutt, Laura
Arm Knitting — Bassetti, Amanda
The Arma Christi in Medieval and Early Modern Material Culture — Cooper, Lisa H.
y Armada (Read by Wheaton, Wil). Audiobook Review — Cline, Ernest
y Armada — Cline, Ernest
c An Armadillo in Paris — Kraulis, Julie
Arme und Armut in Gottingen 1860-1914 — Schallmann, Jurgen
The Armenian Genocide: A Complete History — Kevorkian, Raymond
The Armenian Genocide: The Essential Reference Guide — Whitehorn, Alan
The Armenians in the Medieval Islamic World: Paradigms of Interaction, Seventh to Fourteenth Centuries, vol. 3: Medieval Cosmopolitanism and the Images of Islam, Thirteenth to Fourteenth Centuries — Dadoyan, Seta B.
Arming Mother Nature: The Birth of Catastrophic Environmentalism — Hamblin, Joseph Darwin
Arming the Nation for War: Mobilization, Supply, and the American War Effort in World War II — Patterson, Robert P.
Armor Hunters — Kindt, Matt
Arms and the Dudes: How Three Stoners from Miami Beach Became the Most Unlikely Gunrunners in History — Lawson, Guy
Arms: The Culture and Credo of the Gun — Somerset, Andrew J.
Armsbearing and the Clergy in the History and Canon Law of Western Christianity — Duggan, Lawrence C.
Armut im geteilten Deutschland: Die Wahrnehmung sozialer Randlagen in der Bundesrepublik und der DDR — Lorke, Christoph
Armut in der Renaissance — Bergdolt, Klaus
Armut und Fursorge: Einfuhrung in die Geschichte der Sozialen Arbeit von der Antike bis zur Gegenwart — Rathmayr, Bernhard
The Army and Democracy: Military Politics in Pakistan — Shah, Aqil
Army and the Nation — Wilkinson, Steven I.
An Army Doctor on the Western Frontier: Journals and Letters of John Vance Lauderdale, 1864-1890 — Lauderdale, John Vance
Army Film and the Avent Garde: Cinema and Experiment in the Czechoslovak Millitary — Lovejoy, Alice
The Army in Cromwellian England, 1649-1660 — Reece, Henry
The Army Surveys of Gold Rush California: Reports of the Topographical Engineers — Anderson, Laura Lee
Arnas Magnaeus Philologus, 1663-1730 — Jonsson, Mar
Arnold Schoenberg's A Survivor from Warsaw in Postwar Europe — Calico, Joy H.
c Around the Clock — Chast, Roz
Around the House: One Woman Shares How Millions Care — Swenson, Harriet K.
c Around the World: A Colorful Atlas for Kids (Illus. by Corr, Christopher) — Ganeri, Anita
Around the World in 50 Years: My Adventure to Every Country on Earth — Podell, Albert
c Around the World (Illus. by Shuttlewood, Craig) — Haworth, Katie
Arqueologia Alto Amazonica: Los Origenes de la Civilizacion en el Peru — Nunez, Quirino Olivera
Arras Hanging: The Textile that Determined Early Modern Literature and Drama — Olson, Rebecca
Arrested Justice: Black Women, Violence, and America's Prison Nation — Richie, Beth E.
Arrested Mounting: Memory of the Nazi Camps in Poland, 1944-1950 — Woycicka, Zofia
Arresting Citizenship: The Democratic Consequences of American Crime Control — Lerman, Amy E.
Arresting Dress: Cross-Dressing, Law, and Fascination in Nineteenth-Century San Francisco — Sears, Clare
Arrian: Alexander the Great — Hammond, Martin
c Arrow to Alaska: A Pacific Northwest Adventure (Illus. by Viano, Hannah) — Viano, Hannah
Arrow's Hell — Fernando, Chantal
y Arrows — Gorzelanczyk, Melissa
Arrows of Rain — Ndibe, Okey

The Arrows of the Sun: Armed Forces in Sippar in the First Millennium BC — MacGinnis, John
The Arrows of Time — Egan, Greg
Ars Dictaminis: Briefsteller und verbale Kommunikation in den italienischen Stadtkommunen des 11. Bis 13. Jahrhunderts — Hartmann, Florian
Arsenal of Democracy: The American Automobile Industry in World War II — Hyde, Charles K.
Arsene Schrauwen — Schrauwen, Olivier
Arsenic and Old Books — James, Miranda
c Arsenic for Tea — Stevens, Robin
Arsinoe of Egypt and Macedon: A Royal Life — Carney, Elizabeth Donnelly
y The Arsonist — Miller, Sue
Art: A Visual History — Cumming, Robert
Art and Analysis — Williams, Meg Harris
Art and Architecture in Mexico — Oles, James
Art and Murder — Easton, Don
Art and Religious Image in El Greco's Italy — Casper, Andrew R.
Art and Social Movements: Cultural Politics in Mexico — McCaughan, Edward J.
Art and Truth after Plato — Rockmore, Tom
Art before Breakfast: A Zillion Ways to Be More Creative No Matter How Busy You Are — Gregory, Danny
The Art Book Tradition in Twentieth-Century Europe — Brown, Kathryn
Art Deco Mailboxes: An Illustrated Design History — Greene, Karen
Art + Fashion: Collaborations and Connections between Icons — Cutler, E.P.
Art for Equality: The NAACP's Cultural Campaign for Civil Rights — Woodley, Jenny
Art from a Fractured Past: Memory and Truth-Telling in Post-Shining Path Peru — Milton, Cynthia E.
Art, Gender and Religious Devotion in Grand Ducal Tuscany — Sanger, Alice E.
Art in History: 600 BC to 2000 AD — Kemp, Martin
Art in Sixteenth-Century Venice: Context, Practices, Developments — Grabski, Jozef
Art in the Blood — MacBird, Bonnie
Art in Time: A World History of Styles and Movements — Banai, Noit
Art in Vienna, 1898-1918: Klimt, Kokoschka, Schiele, and Their Contemporaries — Vergo, Peter
c Art Installations (Illus. by Stevens, Gareth) — Wood, Alix
An Art Lover's Guide to Florence — Testa, Judith Anne
Art, Music, and Spectacle in the Age of Rubens: The Pompa Introitus Ferdinandi — Knaap, Anna C.
Art Nouveau Fashion — Rose, Clare
The Art of Arguing in the World of Renaissance Humanism — Laureys, Marc
The Art of Arts Integration: Theoretical Perspectives and Practical Guidelines — Chemi, Tatiana
The Art of Asking, or, How I Learned to Stop Worrying and Let People Help (Read by Palmer, Amanda). Audiobook Review — Palmer, Amanda
The Art of Audit: Eight Remarkable Government Auditors on Stage — Janssen, Roel
The Art of Baking Blind — Vaughan, Sarah
The Art of Being a Brilliant NQT — Toward, Gary
The Art of Charlie Chan Hock Chye — Liew, Sonny
The Art of Comic Book Writing: The Definitive Guide to Outlining, Scripting, and Pitching Your Sequential Art Stories — Kneece, Mark
The Art of Controversy: Political Cartoons and Their Enduring Power — Navasky, Victor S.
The Art of Conversion — Fromont, Cecile
The Art of Crash Landing — DeCarlo, Melissa
The Art of David Jones: Vision and Memory — Bankes, Ariane
The Art of Empathy: The Mother of Sorrows in Northern Renaissance Art and Devotion — Areford, David S.
The Art of Forgery: The Minds, Motives and Methods of the Master Forgers — Charney, Noah
The Art of Gardening: Design Inspiration and Innovative Planting Techniques from Chanticleer — Thomas, R. William
The Art of Grace: On Moving Well through Life — Kaufman, Sarah L.
The Art of Insight in Science and Engineering: Mastering Complexity — Mahajan, Sanjoy
The Art of Invective: Selected Non-Fiction, 1953-94 — Potter, Dennis
The Art of Kozu — Edgecombe, James

The Art of Language Invention: From Horse-Lords to Dark Elves, the Words Behind World-Building — Peterson, David J.
c The Art of LEGO Design: Creative Ways to Build Amazing Models — Schwartz, Jordan
The Art of Listening in the Early Church — Harrison, Carol
The Art of Making Vegetarian Sausages — Marianski, Stanley
The Art of Memoir — Karr, Mary
The Art of Natural Cheesemaking: Using Traditional, Non-Industrial Methods and Raw Ingredients to Make the World's Best Cheeses — Asher, David
The Art of Nick Cave: New Critical Essays — Baker, John Haydn
y The Art of Not Breathing — Alexander, Sarah
The Art of Paper Weaving: 46 Colorful, Dimensional Projects — Schepper, Anna
The Art of Papercutting — Palmer, Jessica
The Art of Perspective — Castellani, Christopher
The Art of Play: Recess and the Practice of Invention — Beresin, Anna R.
The Art of Preaching: Five Medieval Texts and Translations — Wenzel, Siegfried
The Art of Professing in Bourbon Mexico: Crowned-Nun Portraits and Reform in the Convent — Cordova, James M.
The Art of Risk — Sukel, Kayt
The Art of Scalability: Scalable Web Architecture, Processes, and Organizations for the Modern Enterprise — Abbott, Martin L.
The Art of Sinning — Jeffries, Sabrina
The Art of Space — Miller, Ron
The Art of Sumi-E: Beautiful Ink Painting Using Japanese Brushwork — Okamoto, Naomi
The Art of Taming a Rake — Jordan, Nicole
The Art of the Burger: More Than 50 Recipes to Elevate the Burger to Perfection — Fischer, Jens
The Art of the Con: The Most Notorious Fakes, Frauds, and Forgeries in the Art World — Amore, Anthony M.
The Art of the English Murder: From Jack the Ripper and Sherlock Holmes to Agatha Christie and Alfred Hitchcock (Read by Flosnik, Anne). Audiobook Review — Worsley, Lucy
The Art of the Pimp — Hof, Dennis
c The Art of the Possible: An Everyday Guide to Politics (Illus. by McLaughlin, Julie) — Keenan, Edward
The Art of the Publisher — Calasso, Roberto
The Art of the Simon and Kirby Studio (Illus. by Simon, Joe) — Simon, Joe
The Art of the Start 2.0: The Time-Tested, Battle-Hardened Guide for Anyone Starting Anything — Kawasaki, Guy
The Art of Thomas Bewick — Donald, Diana
The Art of Tuning — Sturm, Fred
The Art of Typewriting — Sackner, Marvin
The Art of Veiled Speech: Self-Censorship from Aristophanes to Hobbes — Baltussen, Han
The Art of War — Coonts, Stephen
The Art of X-Ray Reading — Clark, Roy Peter
Art outside the Lines: New Perspectives on GDR Art Culture — Kelly, Elaine
Art Quilts of the Midwest — McCray, Linzee Kull
Art, Ritual, and Civic Identity in Medieval Southern Italy — Zchomelidse, Nino M.
Art & Science: A Curriculum for K-12 Teachers from the J. Paul Getty Museum — J. Paul Getty Museum Science Department
Art, Science, Religion, Spirituality: Seeking Wisdom and Harmony for a Fulfilling Life — White, David V.
Art Students League of New York on Painting: Lessons and Meditations on Mediums, Styles, and Methods — McElhinney, James L.
Art Therapy with Neurological Conditions — Liebmann, Marion
Art Therapy with Physical Conditions — Liebmann, Marion
c Art Workshops for Children (Illus. by Tullet, Herve) — Tullet, Herve
The Artemis Connection — Di Paolo, David
y Artemis Fowl: The Opal Deception: The Graphic Novel (Illus. by Rigano, Giovanni) — Colfer, Eoin
Artemisia Gentileschi: The Language of Painting — Locker, Jesse M.
The Artful Year: Celebrating the Seasons and Holidays with Crafts and Recipes — Van't Hul, Jean
Arthur and George — Barnes, Julian

Arthur Ashe: Tennis and Justice in the Civil Rights Era — *Hall, Eric Allen*
Arthur Elgort: The Big Picture — *Elgort, Arthur*
Arthur Richard Weber. Ein norddeutscher Kaufmann in Japan zur Zeit der Meiji-Restauration — *Janocha, Peter*
Arthur Schnitzler und die Musik — *Aumhammer, Achim*
Arthur's Men — *Gamache, Dan*
The Artichoke Queen — *Duffy, Owen*
Articles and Interviews: Notes from the Heart — *Poulenc, Francis*
c Artie's Party (Featuring the Vita-Men!). (Illus. by Bonin, Anna) — *Noble, Justin*
Artifact & Artifice: Classical Archaeology and the Ancient Historian — *Hall, Jonathan M.*
Artifact (Read by Ryan, Allyson). Audiobook Review — *Pandian, Gigi*
Artifacts and Allegiances: How Museums Put the Nation and the World on Display — *Levitt, Peggy*
Artifacts from Ancient Rome — *Tschen-Emmons, James B.*
Artifacts from Medieval Europe — *Tschen-Emmons, James B.*
Artificial Absolutes — *Fan, Mary*
Artificial Hells: Participatory Art and the Politics of Spectatorship — *Bishop, Claire*
Artisan/Practitioners and the Rise of the New Sciences, 1400-1600 — *Long, Pamela*
y The Artisans — *Reece, Julie*
An Artist and a Writer Travel Highway 1 Central — *Stevens, Janice*
Artistic Experimentation in Music: An Anthology — *Crispin, Darla*
Artistic Practice as Research in Music: Theory, Criticism, Practice — *Digantan-Dack, Mine*
The Artist's Garden: American Impressionism and the Garden Movement — *Marley, Anna O.*
An Artist's Journey through Wonderland — *Fowler, Katie*
Artists of Sedona, 1930-1999 — *Garrison, Gene K.*
Artists Unframed: Snapshots from the Smithsonian's Archives of American Art — *Foresta, Merry A.*
c Arto's Big Move (Illus. by Arnaldo, Monica) — *Arnaldo, Monica*
Arts and Crafts Furniture Projects: A Skill-Building Guide Featuring 9 Beautiful Projects — *Paolini, Gregory*
c Arts and Crafts — *McDowell, Pamela*
Artwash: Big Oil and the Arts — *Evans, Mel*
Arun Kolatkar and Literary Modernism in India: Moving Lines — *Zecchini, Laetitia*
Arvida — *Archibald, Samuel*
Aryan Papers — *Dynin, George*
c As an Oak Tree Grows — *Karas, G. Brian*
c As Big as You — *Acton, Sara*
y As Black as Ebony (Read by McFadden, Amy). Audiobook Review — *Simukka, Salla*
y As Black as Ebony — *Simukka, Salla*
As Chimney Sweepers Come to Dust (Read by Entwistle, Jayne). Audiobook Review — *Bradley, Alan*
y As Chimney Sweepers Come to Dust — *Bradley, Alan*
As Close to Us as Breathing — *Poliner, Elizabeth*
As Country as It Gets: Short Stories from Appalachia — *Roberts, Cas*
As Good as Dead — *Evans, Elizabeth*
As If! The Oral History of "Clueless" as Told by Amy Heckerling and the Cast and Crew (Read by Marie, Jorjeana). Audiobook Review — *Chaney, Jen*
As If! The Oral History of "Clueless" as Told by Amy Heckerling and the Cast and Crew — *Chaney, Jen*
As Long as We Both Shall Love: The White Wedding in Postwar America — *Dunak, Karen M.*
As Love Blooms — *Seilstad, Lorna*
As Luck Would Have It — *Weiss, Mark*
As Near as I Can Get — *Ableman, Paul*
As Night Falls (Read by Berneis, Susie). Audiobook Review — *Milchman, Jenny*
As Night Falls — *Milchman, Jenny*
y As Red as Blood — *Simukka, Salla*
As Rugged as the Terrian — *Wegars, Priscilla*
y As the Lilacs Bloomed — *Hegedus, Anna Molnar*
As the Poppies Bloomed — *Boyadjian, Maral*
As Trains Pass By — *Bang, Herman*
y As White as Snow — *Simukka, Salla*
Asa — *Crownover, Jay*
Asanas for Autism and Special Needs — *Hardy, Shawnee Thornton*

AsapScience: Answers to the World's Weirdest Questions, Most Persistent Rumors, and Unexplained Phenomena — *Moffit, Mitchell*
Ascendance — *Birmingham, John*
y Ascending the Boneyard — *Watson, C.G.*
Ascetic Culture: Essays in Honor of Philip Rousseau — *Leyerle, Blake*
Ascetic Pneumatology from John Cassian to Gregory the Great — *Humphries, Thomas L., Jr.*
y Ash: A Destined Novel — *Petroff, Shani*
The Ash and the Thorn: God on Trial? — *Roller, Leonard H.*
y Ash & Bramble — *Prineas, Sarah*
The Ash Tree — *Rackham, Oliver*
Ashes: A Firefighter's Tale — *Candelaria, Mario*
Ashes in My Mouth, Sand in My Shoes: Stories — *Petterson, Per*
Ashes in the Wind — *Bland, Christopher*
Ashes of Eden — *Everson, Seven*
Ashes to Ashes — *Duffy, Margaret*
c Ashes to Ashes — *Han, Jenny*
The Ashgate Research Companion in Popular Culture in Early Modern England — *Hadfield, Andrew*
The Ashgate Research Companion to Byzantine Hagiography, vol. 2: Genres and Contexts — *Efthymiadis, Stephanos*
The Ashgate Research Companion to Giorgio Vasari — *Cast, David J.*
The Ashgate Research Companion to Religion and Conflict Resolution — *Marsden, Lee*
The Ashgate Research Companion to the Counter-Reformation — *Bamji, Alexandra*
The Ashgate Research Companion to the Korean War — *Matray, James I.*
The Ashgate Research Companion to the Thirty Years' War — *Asbach, Olaf*
y Ashley Bell — *Koontz, Dean*
c Ashley Bryan's Puppets: Making Something from Everything — *Bryan, Ashley*
Ashley's War: The Untold Story of a Team of Women Soldiers on the Special Ops Battlefield — *Lemmon, Gayle Tzemach*
Ashoka in Ancient India — *Lahiri, Nayanjot*
The Ashtabula Hat Trick — *Roberts, Les*
Asi empieza lo malo — *Marias, Javier*
Asi Hablo Penelope — *Villanueva, Tino*
Asia en la Espana del siglo XIX: literatos, viajeros, intelectuales y diplomaticos ante Oriente — *Joan, Torres-Pou*
Asia, Europe and the Emergence of Modern Science: Knowledge Crossing Boundaries — *Bala, Arun*
The Asian American Avant-Garde: Universalist Aspirations in Modernist Literature and Art — *Clark, Audrey Wu*
Asian-American: Proudly Inauthentic Recipes from the Philippines to Brooklyn — *Talde, Dale*
Asian American Sexual Politics: The Construction of Race, Gender and Sexuality — *Chou, Rosalind S.*
Asian Americans in Dixie: Race and Migration in the South — *Joshi, Khyati Y.*
Asian and Pacific Regional Cooperation: Turning Zones of Conflict into Arenas of Peace — *Haas, Michael*
Asian Comics — *Lent, John A.*
Asian Indian Professionals: The Culture of Success — *Sandhu, Sabeen*
Asian Maritime Strategies: Navigating Troubled Waters — *Cole, Bernard D.*
The Asian Mediterranean: Port Cities and Trading Networks in China, Japan and Southeast Asia, 13th-21st Century — *Gipouloux, Francois*
Asian Slaves in Colonial Mexico: From Chinos to Indians — *Seijas, Tatiana*
Asia's Cauldron: The South China Sea and the End of a Stable Pacific — *Kaplan, Robert D.*
Asia's Unknown Uprisings, Vol. 2: People Power in the Philippines, Burma, Tibet, China, Taiwan, Bangladesh, Nepal, Thailand, and Indonesia — *Katsiaficas, George*
Asiatic Echoes: The Identification of Ancient Chinese Pictograms in Pre-Columbian North American Rock Writing, 2d ed. — *Ruskamp, John A., Jr.*
Ask Him Why — *Hyde, Catherine Ryan*
c Ask Me (Illus. by Lee, Suzy) — *Waber, Bernard*
Ask Me: 100 Essential Poems — *Stafford, William*
c Ask Me (Illus. by Lee, Suzy) — *Waber, Bernard*
Ask Me Why — *Thomas, Jodi*
Ask the Beasts: Darwin and the God of Love — *Johnson, Elizabeth A.*
c Ask the Dark (Read by Hoppe, Lincoln). Audiobook Review — *Turner, Henry (b. 1962-)*
y Ask the Dark — *Turner, Henry (b. 1962-)*

Ask the Moon: New and Collected Poems 1948-2014 — *Abse, Dannie*
Asketischer Protestantismus und Kapitalismus: Schriften und Reden 1904-1911 — *Weber, Max*
Asking Anna — *Seliger, Jake*
Asking for It — *Pace, Lilah*
Asking for It: The Alarming Rise of Rape Culture--and What We Can Do about It — *Harding, Kate*
c Asking Questions about How the News Is Created — *Mooney, Carla*
c ASL Tales: Annie's Tails (Illus. by Pierleoni, Gina) — *Murphy, Stacy Anne*
y Asp of Ascension: A Nefertari Hughes Mystery — *Myers, B.R.*
Aspects of Dostoevskii: Art, Ethics and Faith — *Reid, Robert*
Aspects of Psychologism — *Crane, Tim*
Aspects of Violence in Renaissance Europe — *Davies, Jonathan*
Asperger Syndrome and Long-Term Relationships — *Stanford, Ashley*
An Asperger's Guide to Entrepreneurship: Setting Up Your Own Business for Professionals with Autism Spectrum Disorder — *Bergemann, Rosalind A.*
Asperger's Teens: Understanding High School for Students on the Autism Spectrum — *Grossberg, Blythe*
The Aspirational Investor: Taming the Markets to Achieve Your Life's Goals — *Chhabra, Ashvin B.*
Aspiring Adults Adrift: Tentative Transitions of College Graduates — *Arum, Richard*
Aspiring Adults Adrift: Tentative Transitions of College Graduates — *Roksa, Josipa*
Aspiring to Fullness in a Secular Age: Essays on Religion and Theology in the Work of Charles Taylor — *Colorado, Carlos D.*
Aspiring to Greatness: West Virginia University Since World War II — *Lewis, Ronald L.*
The Assassin — *Cussler, Clive*
The Assassin — *Scott, Justin*
The Assassin Lotus — *Angsten, David*
Assassin Rabbit from the Dawn of Time — *Taylor, Mark Richard*
Assassin Trail — *Jons, Hal*
The Assassination of Margaret Thatcher: Stories (Read by Carr, Jane). Audiobook Review — *Mantel, Hilary*
The Assassination of Margaret Thatcher: Stories — *Mantel, Hilary*
Assassinations, Threats, and the American Presidency: From Andrew Jackson to Barack Obama — *Feinman, Ronald L.*
Assassins — *Deva, Mukul*
The Assassins — *Lynds, Gayle*
y Assassin's Heart — *Ahiers, Sarah*
y The Assassin's Masque — *Zettel, Sarah*
Assassin's Wall. E-book Review — *Dubin, Amanda S.*
y The Assassins's Masque — *Zettel, Sarah*
Assault with a Deadly Lie — *Raphael, Lev*
Assembling Flann O'Brien — *Long, Maebh*
Assessing Bilingual Children in Context: An Integrated Approach — *Clinton, Amanda B.*
Assessing Dynamics of Democratisation: Transformative Politics, New Institutions, and the Case of Indonesia — *Tornquist, Olle*
Assessing Liaison Librarians: Documenting Impact for Positive Change — *Mack, Daniel C.*
Assessing Service Quality: Satisfying the Expectations of Library Customers, 3d ed. — *Hernon, Peter*
Assimilate: A Critical History of Industrial Music — *Reed, S. Alexander*
Assimilated Jews in the Warsaw Ghetto, 1940-1943 — *Person, Katarzyna*
Assimilating Seoul: Japanese Rule and the Politics of Public Space in Colonial Korea, 1910-1945 — *Henry, Todd A.*
The Assistant — *Malamud, Bernard*
The Association of Small Bombs — *Mahajan, Karan*
c Asteroid Hunters — *Owen, Ruth*
c Asteroids — *Riggs, Kate*
c Asteroids and Comets — *Graham, Ian*
Asteroids: Relics of Ancient Time — *Shepard, Michael K.*
c Astonishing Animals (Illus. by Dogi, Fiammetta) — *Ganeri, Anita*
y The Astonishing Life of Octavian Nothing, Traitor to the Nation, vol. 1: The Pox Party — *Anderson, M.T.*
Astonishing X-Men: Gifted — *Whedon, Joss*
c The Astounding Broccoli Boy — *Boyce, Frank Cottrell*
c The Astounding Broccoli Boy — *Cottrell Boyce, Frank*
y Astray — *Parker, Amy Christine*

c Astrid the Fly (Illus. by Jonsson, Maria) — Jonsson, Maria
y The Astrologer's Daughter — Lim, Rebecca
Astrology in Ancient Mesopotamia — Baigent, Michael
c Astronauts! — Kelley, K.C.
c Astronauts — Wilson, Hannah
The Astronomer and the Witch: Johannes Kepler's Fight for his Mother — Rublack, Ulinka
c Astronomy: Cool Women in Space (Illus. by Chandhok, Lena) — Yasuda, Anita
c Astrophysicist and Space Advocate Neil deGrasse Tys — Ventura, Marne
c Astrotwins: Project Blastoff — Kelly, Mark
Asylum — de Beauvoir, Jeannette
Asylum City — Shoham, Liad
Asylum — de Beauvoir, Jeannette
Asylum Doctor: James Woods Babcock and the Red Plague of Pellagra — Bryan, Charles S.
Asymptopia — Spencer, Joel
c At Battle in the Civil War: An Interactive Battlefield Adventure — Lassieur, Allison
c At Battle in World War II: An Interactive Battlefield Adventure — Doeden, Matt
At Death's Window — Kelly, Jim
y At Ease — Ross, Jeff
At Eternity's Sunrise: The Imaginative World of William Blake — Damrosch, Leo
At Freddie's — Callow, Simon
At Freedoms Limit: Islam and the Postcolonial Predicament — Abbas, Sadia
At Hawthorn Time — Harrison, Melissa
At His Command: Historical Romance Version — Kaufman, Ruth
At His Service — Rock, Suzanne
At Home in Exile: Why Diaspora Is Good for the Jews — Wolfe, Alan
c At Home In Her Tomb (Illus. by Brannen, Sarah S.) — LiuPerkins, Christine
At Home in Last Chance — Armstrong, Cathleen
At Home in Persimmon Hollow — Bauer, Gerri
c At Home With...Series — Cooke, Tim
At Night We Walk in Circles — Alarcon, Daniel
At Pyramid Lake — Mergen, Bernard
At Swim-Two-Birds — O'Brien, Flann
c At the Beach (Illus. by Rockwell, Harlow) — Rockwell, Anne
At The Bottom of the Everything — Dolnick, Ben
At the Crossroads between War and Peace: The London Naval Conference of 1930 — Maurer, John H.
At the Drop of a Hat — McKinlay, Jenn
y At the Edge of Empire — Kraus, Daniel
At the Edge of Sight: Photography and the Unseen — Smith, Shawn Michelle
At the Edge of the Orchard — Chevalier, Tracy
At the Edge of the Sea — Cox, Karen M.
At the Edge of Uncertainty: 11 Discoveries Taking Science by Surprise — Brooks, Michael
At the Edges of States: Dynamics of State Formation in the Indonesian Borderlands — Michael, Eilenberg
At the Existentialist Cafe — Bakewell, Sarah
At the Limits of the Secular: Reflections on Faith and Public Life — Barbieri, William A., Jr.
At the Margins of Victorian Britain: Politics, Immorality and Britishness in the Nineteenth Century — Grube, Dennis
c At the Marsh in the Meadow (Illus. by Guerlais, Gerald) — Mebane, Jeanie
At the Point of a Cutlass: The Pirate Capture, Bold Escape, and Lonely Exile of Philip Ashton — Flemming, Gregory N.
At the Water's Edge (Read by Eyre, Justine). Audiobook Review — Gruen, Sara
At the Water's Edge — Gruen, Sara
y At the World's End — Fisher, Catherine
At the Writing Desk — Kofler, Werner
At Vanity Fair: From Bunyan to Thackeray — Milne, Kirsty
At War in Distant Waters: British Colonial Defense in the Great War — Pattee, Phillip G.
At War on the Gothic Line — Jennings, Christian
At Wolf Ranch — Ryan, Jennifer
Ataturk in the Nazi Imagination — Ihrig, Stefan
Atavisms — Bock, Raymond
Atelier Crenn: Metamorphosis of Taste (Illus. by Anderson, Ed) — Crenn, Dominique
The Atheism That Saved Me — Morlan, Robert
Atheism: What Everyone Needs to Know — Ruse, Michael
The Atheist Who Didn't Exist — Bannister, Andy
The Atheist's Bible — Weiss, Lys Ann

y Athena the Proud — Holub, Joan
The Athenian Amnesty and Reconstructing the Law — Carawan, Edwin,
The Athletic Aesthetic — Black, Kojo
Atkeles Budapesten — Terey, Janos
Atlanta, Cradle of the New South: Race and Remembering in the Civil War's Aftermath — Link, William A.
Atlanta's Living Legacy: A History of Grady Memorial Hospital and Its People — Moran, Martin
y Atlantia — Condie, Ally
c Atlantis — Karst, Ken
y Atlantis in Peril — Barron, T.A.
Atlantis Rising — Craw, Gloria
c Atlas of Adventures: A Collection of Natural Wonders, Exciting Experiences, and Fun Festivities from the Four Corners of the Globe (Illus. by Letherland, Lucy) — Williams, Rachel
c Atlas of Adventures — Letherland, Lucy
Atlas of Crustacean Larvae — Martin, Joel W.
Atlas of Knowledge: Anyone Can Map — Borner, Katy
Atlas of the Functional City: CIAM 4 and Comparative Urban Analysis — Es, Evelien van
Atlas of the Human Body (Illus. by Mecchubot, Kanitta) — Jessop, Vanessa
c Atlas of the World, 21st ed. — National Geographic Society (U.S.)
Atmosphere of Hope: Searching for Solutions to the Climate Crisis — Flannery, Tim
y Atoms Under the Floorboards: The Surprising Science Hidden in Your Home — Woodford, Chris
Atonement, Law, and Justice: The Cross in Historical and Cultural Contexts — Vidu, Adonis
Attachment — Noiville, Florence
Attachments — Rowell, Rainbow
c Attack and Transport Aircraft: 1945 to Today — Sharpe, Mike
c Attack of the Alien Horde (Illus. by Higgins, Dusty) — Venditti, Robert
c Attack of the Zombie Clones — McCreely, Havelock
y Attack on Titan: Kuklo Unbound (Illus. by Shibamoto, Thores) — Suzukaze, Ryo
y Attack on Titan: The Harsh Mistress of the City, Part 1 (Illus. by Murata, Range) — Kawakami, Ryo
y Attack on Titan: The Harsh Mistress of the City, Part 2 (Illus. by Murata, Range) — Isayama, Hajime
Atthis: The Ancient Histories of Athens — Rhodes, Peter J.
Attilio Grisafi — Romani, Ludovico
c Attitude Is Everything — Snyder, Samantha
Attrition: Fighting the First World War — Philpott, William
c Au coeur de la jungle (Illus. by Lavoie, Camille) — Moore, Carole
Au Jour le jour 5 — De Roux, Paul
Au Naturel: Naturism, Nudism, and Tourism in Twentieth-Century France — Harp, Stephen L.
Auctor et Auctoritas in Latinis Medii Aevi Litteris — D'Angelo, Edoardo
The Audacious Ascetic: What Bin Laden Sound Archive Reveals about al-Qa'ida — Miller, Flagg
The Audacious Ascetic: What Obama Bin Laden's Sound Archive Reveals about al-Qa'ida — Miller, Flagg
The Audacious Crimes of Colonel Blood — Hutchinson, Robert
c Audacity Jones to the Rescue — Larson, Kirby
y Audacity — Crowder, Melanie
The Audition Bible — Powell, Holly
Auditions: Architecture and Aurality — Stone, Rob
Audrey and Bill: A Romantic Biography of Audrey Hepburn & William Holden — Epstein, Edward Z.
c Audrey (Cow): An Oral Account of a Most Faring Escape, Based More or Less on a True Story (Illus. by Mai-Wyss, Tatjana) — Bar-El, Dan
Audrey's Tree House (Illus. by Bentley, Jonathan) — Hughes, Jenny
Auf dem Weg zu einer Geschichte der Sensibilitat. Empfindsamkeit und Sorge fur Katastrophenopfer
Auf dem Weg zu einer transnationalen Erinnerungskultur? Konvergenzen, Interferenzen und Differenzen der Erinnerung an den Ersten Weltkrieg im Jubilaumsjahr 2014
Auf der Suche nach der Okonomie: Historische Annaherungen — Dejung, Christof
Auftrag: Menschenraub - Entfuhrungen von Westberlinern und Bundesburgern durch das Ministerium fur Staatssicherheit der DDR — Muhle, Susanne
Augenzeuge des Konstanzer Konzils: Die Chronik des Ulrich Richental — Gerlach, Henry

c Auggie and Me: Three Wonder Stories — Palacio, R.J.
y The August 5 — Helland, Jenna
The August Gales: The Tragic Loss of Fishing Schooners in the North Atlantic, 1926 and 1927 — Hallowell, Gerald
August, October — Barba, Andres
August: Osage County (Read by Various readers). Audiobook Review — Letts, Tracy
August: Osage County (Read by a full cast of performers). Audiobook Review — Letts, Tracy
August Weismann: Development, Heredity, and Evolution — Churchill, Frederick B.
Auguste Comte: Die Macht der Zeichen — Lepenies, Wolf
Augustin, philosophe et predicateur: Hommage a Goulven Madec; Actes du colloque international organise a Paris les 8 et 9 septembre 2011 — Bochet, Isabelle
Augustine and Apocalyptic — Doody, John
Augustine: Conversions to Confessions — Fox, Robin Lane
Augustine on War and Military Service — Wynn, Phillip
Augustine's Confessions: Philosophy in Autobiography — Mann, William E.
Augustine's Manichean Dilemma, vol. 2: Making a "Catholic" Self, 388-401 C.E. — BeDuhn, Jason David
Augustine's Virgilian Retreat: Reading the Auctores at Cassiciacum — Pucci, Joseph Michael
Augustus — Williams, John (1922-1994)
Augustus: First Emperor of Rome — Goldsworthy, Adrian
Augustus: The Biography — Bleicken, Jochen
Aundy — Hatfield, Shanna
Aunt Dimity and the Summer King — Atherton, Nancy
c Aunty Edna of Duck Creek Pond (Illus. by Allen, Lisa) — Gray, Nigel
Aurality: Listening and Knowledge in Nineteenth-Century Colombia — Gautier, Ana Maria Ochoa
Aurora — Robinson, Kim Stanley
Aurora (Morgen Rote im Auffgang, 1612) and Fundamental Report (Grundlicher Bericht, Mysterium Pansophicum, 1620). — Boehme, Jacob
Aurora — Robinson, Kim Stanley
Aus den Giftschranken des Kommunismus. Methodische Fragen zum Umgang mit den Uberwachungsakten in Sudost- und Mitteleuropa
Aus der Luft Gewonnen: Die Entwicklung der Globalen Gaseindustrie 1880-2012 — Stokes, Raymond G.
Auschwitz as World Heritage: UNESCO, Poland, and History Politics
y Auschzvitz, Bergen-Belsen, Treblinka: The Holocaust Camps — Byers, Ann
Auslandische Zwangsarbeiterinnen und Zwangsarbeiter und die Berliner Justiz, 1939-1945
Auslese fur die Siedlergesellschaft: Die Einbeziehung Volksdeutscher in die NS-Erbgesundheitspolitik im Kontext der Umsiedlungen 1939-1945 — Fiebrandt, Maria
Ausnahmezustande: Entgrenzungen und Regulierungen in Europa Wahrend des Kalten Krieges — Rauh, Cornelia
Ausreise per Antrag: Der Lange Weg nach Druben - Eine Studie uber Herrschaft und Alltag in der DDR-Provinz — Hurtgen, Renate
Aussenpolitik und Offentlichkeit: Massenmedien, Meinungsforschung und Arkanpolitik in den deutsch-amerikanischen Beziehungen von Erhard bis Brandt — Hoeres, Peter
Aussie Grit: My Formula One Journey — Webber, Mark
c An Aussie Year: Twelve Months in the Life of Australian Kids — McCartney, Tania
c Austin, Lost in America (Illus. by Czekaj, Jef) — Czekaj, Jef
c Austin Mahone: Famous Pop Singer and Songwriter — Diver, Lucas
y Australia and Southeast Asia — Harris, Tim
Australia and the War in the Air — Molkentin, Michael
y Australia to Zimbabwe: A Rhyming Romp around the World to 24 Countries — Fitts, Ruth
Australian Beetles: Morphology, Classification and Keys — Lawrence, John F.
c Australian Bushrangers Series — Smith, Jane Margaret

Australian Dictionary of Biography, 19 vols. — *Australian National University*
c Australian Kids through the Years (Illus. by Joyner, Andrew) — *McCartney, Tania*
Australian Longhorn Beetles (Coleoptera: Cerambycidae). — *Slipinski, Adam*
y Australia's Great War: 1915 — *Murphy, Sally*
y Australia's Greatest Landmarks and Locations — *Grant, Virginia*
Austro-Hungarian War Aims in the Balkans during World War I — *Fried, Marvin Benjamin*
The Authentic Death & Contentious Afterlife of Pat Garrett and Billy the Kid: The Untold Story of Peckinpah's Last Western Film — *Seydor, Paul*
The Authentic Death & Contentious Afterlife of Pat Garrett and Billy the Kid: The Untold Storyof Peckinpah's Last Western Film — *Seydor, Paul*
Authentic Learning in the Digital Age: Engaging Students through Inquiry — *Pahomov, Larissa*
Authentic Portuguese Cooking — *Ortiz, Ana Patuieia*
The Authentic Sale: A Goddess's Guide to Business — *Cohen-First, Rena*
Authentic: The Politics of Ambivalence in a Brand Culture — *Banet-Weiser, Sarah*
Authenticity and Victimhood in 20th Century History and Commemorative Culture
c Author — *Mahaney, Ian F.*
Authoring the Past: History, Autobiography and Politics in Medieval Catalonia — *Aurell, Jaume*
Authoritarian El Salvador: Politics and the Origins of the Military Regimes, 1880-1940 — *Ching, Erik*
Authorities and Adaptations: The Reworking and Transmission of Textual Sources in Medieval Ireland — *Boyle, Elizabeth*
Authority and Diplomacy from Dante to Shakespeare — *Powell, Jason*
Authority and Imitation: A Study of the Cosmographia of Bernard Silvestris — *Kauntze, Mark*
Authority in Byzantium — *Armstrong, Pamela*
Authority in European Book Culture 1400-1600 — *Bromilow, Pollie*
The Author's Hand and the Printer's Mind — *Chartier, Roger*
The Author's Voice in Classical and Late Antiquity — *Marmorodo, Anna*
Authorship in the Long Eighteenth Century — *Griffin, Dustin*
c Autism — *Squire, Ann O.*
Autism and Gender: From Refrigerator Mothers to Computer Geeks — *Jack, Jordynn*
Autism Causes, Prevention and Treatment — *Cannell, John*
The Autism Discussion Page on Anxiety, Behavior, School, and Parenting Strategies: A Toolbox for Helping Children with Autism Feel Safe, Accepted and Competent — *Nason, Bill*
The Autism Discussion Page on the Core Challenges of Autism: A Toolbox for Helping Children with Autism Feel Safe, Accepted, and Competent — *Nason, Bill*
The Autism Job Club: The Neurodiverse Workforce in the New Normal of Employment — *Bernick, Michael*

The Autism Parents' Guide to Reclaiming Your Life: How to Build the Best Life While Successfully Raising A Child with Autism — *Picon, Deanna*
Autistic Logistics — *Wilde, Kate C.*
Autobiography — *Morrissey*
An Autobiography and Other Writings — *Trollope, Anthony*
Autobiography in Black and Brown: Ethnic Identity in Richard Wright and Richard Rodriguez — *Garcia, Michael Nieto*
The Autobiography of Eleanor Roosevelt (Read by Gilbert, Tavia). Audiobook Review — *Roosevelt, Eleanor*
The Autobiography of James T. Kirk — *Goodman, David A.*
Autobiography of Mark Twain, vol. 3 — *Twain, Mark*
Autobiography: The Rainbow Comes and Goes, The Light of Common Day, Trumpets from the Steep — *Cooper, Diana*
Autograph Penis — *Tanager, H.O.*
The Automation — *Gabbler, G.B.*
The Automaton in English Renaissance Literature — *Hyman, Wendy Beth*
The Automobile Club of Egypt — *Al Aswany, Alaa*
The Automobile Club of Egypt — *Aswany, Alaa Al*
c Automobiles — *Salzmann, Mary Elizabeth*
Autonomy after Auschwitz: Adorno, German Idealism, and Modernity — *Shuster, Martin*
Autoritat und Krise. der Verlust der Eindeutigkeit und Seine Folgen am Beispiel der Mittelalterlichen Gegenpapste
The Autumn Crush — *Anselmi, Andrew Eustace*
The Autumn Dead / The Night Remembers — *Gorman, Ed*
Autumn Falls (Read by Thorne, Bella). Audiobook Review — *Thorne, Bella*
y Autumn Falls — *Thorne, Bella*
Autumn Killing — *Kallentoft, Mons*
c Autumn: Leaves Fall From the Trees! (Illus. by Brooks, Emily) — *Bell, Lisa*
y Autumn of Elves — *Vruno, Joanne*
The Autumn Republic — *McClellan, Brian*
Autumn Spring — *Thrasher, Shelley*
The Autumnlands, vol. 1: Tooth and Claw — *Busiek, Kurt*
y Autumn's Kiss — *Thorne, Bella*
c Autumn's Secret Gift (Illus. by Pooler, Paige) — *Allen, Elise*
c Ava and Taco Cat — *Weston, Carol*
Ava Helen Pauling: Partner, Activist, Visionary — *Carson, Mina*
c Ava the Monster Slayer (Illus. by Felten, Ross) — *Maggiore, Lisa*
c Avalanches — *Merrick, Patrick*
c Avalon — *Arnett, Mindee*
y Avalon Rising — *Rose, Kathryn*
The Avant-Garde and the Popular in Modern China: Tian Han and the Intersection of Performance and Politics — *Luo, Liang*
c Ava's Adventure (Illus. by Weber, Penny) — *Pedersen, Laura*
Avelynn — *Campbell, Marissa*
Aventures de l'analyse de Fermat a Borel: Melanges en l'honneur de Christian Gilain — *Fery, Suzanne*
Avenue of Mysteries — *Irving, John*

Avenue of Spies: A True Story of Terror, Espionage, and One American Family's Heroic Resistance in Nazi-Occupied Paris — *Kershaw, Alex*
The Average Girl — *Goode, Angelina*
Average Is Over: Powering America beyond the Age of the Great Stagnation — *Cowen, Tyler*
Avian Immunology — *Schat, Karel A.*
c Aviation Firefighters — *White, Nancy*
The Aviators: Eddie Rickenbacker, Jimmy Doolittle, Charles Lindbergh, and the Epic Age of Flight — *Groom, Winston*
y Avis Dolphin (Illus. by Dawson, Willow) — *Wishinsky, Frieda*
c Aw, Nuts! (Illus. by McClurkan, Rob) — *McClurkan, Rob*
y Awake — *Preston, Natasha*
c Awake Beautiful Child (Illus. by Lam, Gracia) — *Rosenthal, Amy Krouse*
Awake Chimera — *Graykin, Justine*
Awaken from the Darkness — *Harker, Kevin M.*
Awaken: Letters of a Spiritual Father to This Generation — *Nance, Terry*
Awaken Your Third Eye: How Accessing Your Sixth Sense Can Help You Find Knowledge, Illumination, and Intuition — *Shumsky, Susan*
Awakening Higher Consciousness: Guidance from Ancient Egypt and Sumer — *Dickie, Lloyd M.*
Away in a Manger — *Bowen, Rhys*
c Away She Goes Riding into Women's History (Illus. by Belloni, Valentina) — *Coleman, Wim*
y Away We Go — *Ostrovski, Emil*
Awe: Why It Matters for Everything We Think, Say, and Do — *Tripp, Paul David*
c Awesome African Animals Series — *Amstutz, Lisa J.*
c Awesome Algorithms and Creative Coding — *Gifford, Clive*
c Awesome Animal Stories for Kids (Illus. by Hart, James) — *Darlinson, Aleesah*
c Awesome Dogs — *Schuh, Mari*
y The Awesome — *Darrows, Eva*
c Awesome Special Effects — *Hammelef, Danielle S*
c Awkward (Illus. by Chmakova, Svetlana) — *Chmakova, Svetlana*
The Axeman — *Celestin, Ray*
The Ayahuasca Test Pilots Handbook — *Kilham, Chris*
c Ayala's Dreams — *Jespersen, Debbie*
Ayoade on Ayoade: A Cinematic Odyssey — *Ayoade, Richard*
Ayurveda Made Modern: Political Histories of Indigenous Medicine in North India, 1900-1955 — *Berger, Rachel*
Ayya's Accounts: A Ledger of Hope in Modern India — *Pandian, Anand*
c Aztec — *Tieck, Sarah*
c Aztec Empire — *Bodden, Valerie*
Aztec Goddesses and Christian Madonnas: Images of the Divine Feminine in Mexico — *Kroger, Joseph*
Aztec Philosophy: Understanding a World in Motion — *Maffie, James*
c Aztec Warriors — *Bodden, Valerie*
Aztecs on Stage: Religious Theater in Colonial Mexico — *Burkhart, Louise M.*
Aztlan and Arcadia: Religion, Ethnicity, and the Creation of Place — *Lint Sagarena, Roberto Ramon*
Aztlan Arizona: Mexican American Educational Empowerment, 1968-1978 — *Echeverria, Darius V.*
c Azzi in Between (Illus. by Garland, Sarah) — *Garland, Sarah*

B

c B. Bear & Lolly: Off to School — *Livingston, A.A.*
c B in the World (Illus. by Schlott, Stephen) — *Mentyka, Sharon*
c B Is for Bear: A Natural Alphabet (Illus. by Viano, Hannah) — *Viano, Hannah*
c B Is for Bedtime (Illus. by Pignataro, Anna) — *Hamilton, Margaret*
c B Is for Box: The Happy Little Yellow Box (Illus. by Carter, David A.) — *Carter, David A.*
B & Me: A True Story of Literary Arousal — *Hallman, J.C.*
c A B See — *Doyle, Elizabeth*
The B-Side — *Yagoda, Ben*
The B Side: The Death of Tin Pan Alley and the Rebirth of the Great American Song — *Yagoda, Ben*
c Baa, Baa, Black Sheep (Illus. by Cabrera, Jane) — *Cabrera, Jane*
c Baa Baa Smart Sheep — *Sommerset, Mark*
Baal's Priests: The Loyalist Clergy and the English Revolution — *McCall, Fiona*
y Baba Yaga's Assistant (Illus. by Carroll, Emily) — *McCoola, Marika*
c The Babies and Doggies Book (Illus. by Woodward, Molly) — *Schindel, John*
Babies without Borders: Adoption and Migration across the Americas — *Dubinsky, Karen*
c Baboons — *Roumanis, Alexis*
c Baby Alligators — *Salzmann, Mary Elizabeth*
c Baby Animals — *Salzmann, Mary Elizabeth*
c Baby Animals — *Tiger Tales*
c Baby Animals Spots & Stripes — *Tildes, Phyllis Limbacher*
c Baby Bear — *Nelson, Kadir*
c Baby Bedtime (Illus. by Quay, Emma) — *Fox, Mem*
Baby Bod: Turn Flab to Fab in 12 Weeks Flat! — *Ryan, Marianne*
Baby Boomers and Generational Conflict — *Bristow, Jennie*
Baby Brights: 30 Colorful Crochet Accessories — *McCafferty, Kathleen*
The "Baby Dolls": Breaking the Race and Gender Barriers of the New Orleans Mardi Gras Tradition — *Vaz, Kim Marie*
c Baby Eagles — *Salzmann, Mary Elizabeth*
c Baby Foxes — *Borgert-Spaniol, Megan*
c Baby Giraffes — *Borgert-Spaniol, Megan*
c Baby Hedgehogs — *Borgert-Spaniol, Megan*
c Baby Hippos — *Borgert-Spaniol, Megan*
c Baby Koalas — *Borgert-Spaniol, Megan*
c Baby Lady's Scary Night: A Ladybug Story (Illus. by Triplett, Ginger) — *Davydov, Marina*
c Baby Love (Illus. by Hughes, Brooke Boynton) — *DiTerlizzi Angela*
c Baby Loves Sports: A High-Contrast Action Book (Illus. by Rojas, R.D.)
c Baby Loves to Party! (Illus. by Kirwan, Wednesday) — *Kirwan, Wednesday*
Baby & Me Knits: 20 Timeless Designs for Baby & Mom — *Young, Celeste*
y The Baby — *Drakeford, Lisa*
c Baby Party (Illus. by Poole, Susie) — *O'Connell, Rebecca*
c Baby Pig Pig Walks (Illus. by McPhail, David) — *McPhail, David*
Baby Poop: What Your Pediatrician May Not Tell You — *Palmer, Linda F.*
c Baby Santa and the Gift of Giving (Illus. by Wilson, Phil) — *DeLand, M. Maitland*
c Baby Squirrels — *Borgert-Spaniol, Megan*
c The Baby Swap (Illus. by Joyner, Andrew) — *Ormerod, Jan*

c Baby Talk — *Blackstone, Stella*
A Baby to Die For — *Slosberg, Mike*
Baby, You Are My Religion: Women, Gay Bars, and Theology Before Stonewall — *Cartier, Marie*
Baby You're a Rich Man: Suing the Beatles for Fun and Profit — *Soocher, Stan*
Babylon: Legend, History and the Ancient City — *Seymour, Michael*
Babylon's Ark: The Incredible Wartime Rescue of the Baghdad Zoo (Read by Vance, Simon). Audiobook Review — *Anthony, Lawrence*
c Babymouse: Bad Babysitter (Illus. by Holm, Matthew) — *Holm, Jennifer L.*
c Baby's First ABC — *Davenport, Maxine*
c A Baby's Guide to Surviving Dad (Illus. by Americo, Tiago) — *Bird, Benjamin*
Bacchus (Illus. by Campbell, Eddie) — *Campbell, Eddie*
Bach: Music in the Castle of Heaven — *Gardiner, John Eliot*
Back Blast — *Greaney, Mark*
Back Channel (Read by Turpin, Bahni). Audiobook Review — *Carter, Stephen L.*
Back Channel to Cuba: The Hidden History of Negotiations Between Washington and Havana — *LeoGrande, William M.*
Back from Afghanistan: Workshop on the Experiences of Veterans from the War in Afghanistan in Tajikistan, Ukraine, Belarus, Russia, Lithuania and Germany
Back from the Dead — *Walton, Bill*
Back in Play — *Aicher, Linda*
Back in the Game — *Wilde, Lori*
Back in the USSR: Heroic Adventures in Transnistria (Illus. by Danziger, Nick) — *MacLean, Rory*
y Back That Thing — *Moore, Stephanie Perry*
Back to the Future of Socialism — *Hain, Peter*
Back to the Garden: Nature and the Mediterranean World from Prehistory to the Present — *McGregor, James H. S.*
Back to Vietnam — *Head, Elaine*
Backcast — *McMan, Ann*
Background Modeling and Foreground Detection for Video Surveillance — *Bouwmans, Thierry*
Backhand Smash — *Gregson, J.M.*
c Backhoe Joe (Illus. by Cameron, Craig) — *Alexander, Lori*
Backing Up the Beast — *Anderson, Josh*
Backlands — *McGarrity, Michael*
Backlands — *Shorr, Victoria*
y Backlash — *Littman, Sarah Darer*
A Backpack, a Bear, and Eight Crates of Vodka — *Golinkin, Lev*
Backpacking with the Saints: Wilderness Hiking as Spiritual Practice — *Lane, Belden C.*
Backroads Pragmatists: Mexico's Melting Pot and Civil Rights in the United States — *Flores, Ruben*
The Backwards Birthday Party (Illus. by Groenink, Chuck) — *Chapin, Tom*
c Backwards Moon — *Losure, Mary*
Backwater Blues: The Mississippi Flood of 1927 in the African American Imagination — *Mizelle, Richard M., Jr.*
Backyard Biodiesel: How to Brew Your Own Fuel — *Estill, Lyle*
c Backyard Camp-Out (Illus. by Henninger, Michelle) — *Nolen, Jerdine*
The Backyard Homestead Book of Kitchen Know-How — *Chesman, Andrea*
c Backyard Witch: Sadie's Story (Illus. by Marcero, Deborah) — *Heppermann, Christine*

Bacteriology in British India: Laboratory Medicine and the Tropics — *Chakrabarti, Pratik*
The Bad Actor — *Ebisch, Glen*
Bad Angels — *Danvers, Dennis*
c Bad Apple's Perfect Day — *Hemingway, Edward*
y Bad Business — *Dakers, Diane*
c Bad Bye, Good Bye (Illus. by Bean, Jonathan) — *Underwood, Deborah*
A Bad Character — *Kapoor, Deepti*
Bad Company and Burnt Powder: Justice and Injustice in the Old Southwest — *Alexander, Bob*
Bad Country — *McKenzie, C.B.*
Bad Days in History — *Farquhar, Michael*
y The Bad Doctor: The Troubled Life and Times of Dr. Iwan James (Illus. by Williams, Ian) — *Williams, Ian*
c Bad Dog Flash — *Paul, Ruth*
Bad Dyke: Salacious Stories from a Queer Life — *Moon, Alison*
Bad Faith: When Religious Belief Undermines Modern Medicine — *Offit, Paul A.*
c Bad for You — *Glines, Abbi*
y Bad Girls: Sirens, Jezebels, Murderesses, Thieves & Other Female Villains (Read by Rosenblat, Barbara). Audiobook Review — *Yolen, Jane*
Bad Girls: Young Women, Sex, and Rebellion before the Sixties — *Littauer, Amanda H.*
c The Bad Guys Episode 1 — *Blabey, Aaron*
c Bad Hair Day — *Mlynowski, Sarah*
Bad Judgment — *Stone, Matthew*
y Bad Kid: A Memoir — *Crabb, David*
c Bad Kitty Goes to the Vet (Illus. by Bruel, Nick) — *Bruel, Nick*
c Bad Kitty: Puppy's Big Day — *Bruel, Nick*
c Bad Luck — *Bosch, Pseudonymous*
y Bad Magic (Illus. by Ford, Gilbert) — *Bosch, Pseudonymous*
Bad New Days: Art, Criticism, Emergency — *Foster, Hal*
Bad News Cowboy — *Yates, Maisy*
Bad News: Last Journalists in a Dictatorship — *Sundaram, Anjan*
c Bad News Nails — *Santopolo, Jill*
c Bad Pirate (Illus. by Griffiths, Dean) — *Winters, Kari-Lynn*
Bad Sex — *Martin, Clancy*
Bad Souls, Madness and Responsibility in Modern Greece — *Davis, Elizabeth Anne*
Bad Water: Nature, Pollution, & Politics in Japan, 1870-1950 — *Stolz, Robert*
The Badass Body Diet: The Breakthrough Diet and Workout for a Tight Booty, Sexy Abs, and Lean Legs — *Abbott, Christmas*
y Baddawi (Illus. by Abdelrazaq, Leila) — *Abdelrazaq, Leila*
The Badger Knight (Read by Halstead, Graham). Audiobook Review — *Erskine, Kathryn*
c The Badger Knight — *Erskine, Kathryn*
The Badger: The Life of Bernard Hinault and the Legacy of French Cycling — *Fotheringham, William*
Badlands — *Box, C.J.*
Badlands — *Kroetsch, Robert*
c Bagels on Board! (Illus. by Whamond, Dave) — *Stuchner, Joan Betty*
c Bagels the Brave! (Illus. by Whamond, Dave) — *Stuchner, Joan Betty*
Baggage — *Redling, S.G.*
Baghdad Blues — *Hajdu, Laszlo*
The Baghdad Lawyer: Fighting for Justice in Saddam's Iraq — *Aris, Sabah*
Bagmen — *Lashner, William*

Bah! Said the Baby (Illus. by Plecas, Jennifer) — Plecas, Jennifer
Bahnhof der Tranen: Die Grenzubergangsstelle Berlin-Friedrichstrasse — Springer, Philipp
Bain de lune — Lahens, Yanick
Bake Happy: 100 Playful Desserts with Rainbow Layers, Hidden Fillings, Billowy Frostings, and More — Fertig, Judith
y The Bakehouse — Cowley, Joy
c Baker's Magic — Zahler, Diane
The Baker's Tale — Hauser, Thomas
The Baker's Tale: Ruby Spriggs and the Legacy of Charles Dickens — Hauser, Thomas
Baking Chez Moi: Recipes From My Paris Home to Your Home Anywhere — Greenspan, Dorie
c Baking Day at Grandma's (Illus. by Denise, Christopher) — Denise, Anika
c The Baking Life of Amelie Day — Curtis, Vanessa
Baking with the Brass Sisters: Over 125 Recipes for Classic Cakes, Pies, Cookies, Breads, Desserts, and Savories from America's Favorite Home Bakers (Illus. by Ryan, Andy) — Brass, Marilyn
Baking You Happy: Gluten-Free Recipes from Sweet Freedom Bakery (100 Percent Vegan). — Lubert, Allison
Baksheesh (Bribes). — Kane, D.S.
c Balaclava Boy (Illus. by Mitchell, Sandy) — Robson, Jenny
The Balance of Nature and Human Impact — Rohde, Klaus
y Balancing Act: Chloe by Design (Illus. by Hagel, Brooke) — Gurevich, Margaret
c Balancing Act — Gurevich, Margaret
Balancing on a Planet: The Future of Food and Agriculture — Cleveland, David A.
Balbala — Waberi, Abdourahman A.
Bald, Fat & Crazy: How I Beat Cancer While Pregnant with One Daughter and Adopting Another — Hosford, Stephanie
Bald Is Better with Earrings: A Survivor's Guide to Getting through Breast Cancer — Hutton, Andrea
c A Bale of Turtles (Illus. by Rothermel, Mary) — Clancey, Lee
Balkan Smoke: Tobacco and the Making of Modern Bulgaria — Neuburger, Mary C.
The Balkan Trilogy — Manning, Olivia
Ball — Ison, Tara
c Ball Game Math — Marsico, Katie
Ball of Fire: The Tumultuous Life and Comic Art of Lucille Ball — Kanfer, Stefan
Ball — Ison, Tara
The Ballad of a Small Player — Osborne, Lawrence
The Ballad of Black Tom — LaValle, Victor
The Ballad of David and Israel — Palmer, Roderick Byron
Ballad of the Black and Blue Mind — Roiphe, Anne
c Ballerina Gets Ready (Illus. by Stock, Catherine) — Kent, Allegra
c Ballet Cat: The Totally Secret Secret (Illus. by Shea, Bob) — Shea, Bob
The Ballet Lover's Companion — Anderson, Zoe
Ballet Spectacular: A Young Ballet Lover's Guide and an Insight into a Magical World — Miles, Lisa
Ballistic — Mortimer, Adam Egypt
c The Balloon Is Doomed (Illus. by Mundt, A.M.) — Eyton, Christopher
Ballots, Bullets, and Bargains: American Foreign Policy and Presidential Elections — Armacost, Michael H.
Balm — Perkins-Valdez, Dolen
Balthasar Hubmaier and the Clarity of Scripture: A Critical Response Issue — Chatfield, Graeme R.
Balthasar on the Spiritual Senses: Perceiving Splendor — McInroy, Mark
Balthasar on the Spiritual Senses: Perceiving Splendour — McInroy, Mark
y The Baltic States: Then and Now — Woog, Adam
Baltimore Album of Roses: Elegant Motifs to Mix & Match: Step-by-Step Techniques: Applique, Embroidery, Inking, Trapunto — Verroca, Rita
Balto's Story — Blake, Kevin
Balzac et Bianchon — Mikhaelevitch, Alexandre
Balzac, Grandville, and the Rise of Book Illustration — Yousif, Keri
Bamboo & Fern — Brown, Ava
The Bamboo Stalk — Alsanousi, Saud
y The Bamboo Sword — Preus, Margi
c Bamboozled, 21st Anniversary ed. — Legge, David
Ban en Banlieue — Kapil, Bhanu
c Band Instruments — Boncens, Christophe
c Bandette, vol. 2: Stealers, Keepers! (Illus. by Coover, Colleen) — Tobin, Paul

c Bandit — Miles, Ellen
The Bands of Mourning — Sanderson, Brandon
c The Bane Chronicles — Clare, Cassandra
y Bang! Tango (Illus. by Sibar, Adrian) — Kelly, Joe
The Bangkok Asset — Burdett, John
The Banished Lands — Mester, Benjamin
The Banished of Muirwood — Wheeler, Jeff
Banishment in the Later Roman Empire, 284-476 CE — Washburn, D.A.
y Banjo Paterson (Illus. by Lumsden, Glen) — Drummond, Allan
c Bank Wisely — Schwartz, Heather E.
Banking in Crisis: The Rise and Fall of British Banking Stability, 1800 to the Present — Turner, John D.
Banking in Oklahoma before Statehood — Hightower, Michael J.
Banking on Confidence: A Guidebook to Financial Literacy — Cline, Dale K.
Banking on the Body: The Market in Blood, Milk, and Sperm in Modern America — Swanson, Kara W.
Banksia Lady: Celia Rosser, Botanical Artist — Landon, Carolyn
Bannerhandel: Ain spruch von dem langwirigen span zwuschet ainer statt zuo St. Gallen und ainem land Appenzell, ain paner belangend — Stettler, Bernhard
Banning the Bang or the Bomb? Negotiating the Nuclear Test Ban Regime — Zartman, I. William
A Banquet of Consequences — George, Elizabeth
The Bantam and the Soldier (Illus. by Belton, Robyn) — Beck, Jennifer
Baptism, Brotherhood, and Belief in Reformation Germany: Anabaptism and Lutheranism, 1525-1585 — Hill, Kat
Baptists in America: A History — Kidd, Thomas S.
Baptized in PCBs: Race, Pollution, and Justice in an All-American Town — Spears, Ellen Griffith
Bar Nights — Matthes, Dave
Bar Tartine: Techniques and Recipes — Balla, Nicolaus
Barbara Gonzaga: Die Briefe / Le Lettere — Antenhofer, Christina
Barbara Pym: A Passionate Force — Allestree, Ann
Barbara the Slut and Other People — Holmes, Lauren
Barbarian Days: A Surfing Life — Finnegan, William
y Barbarian Lord — Smith, Matt
Barbarian Spring — Luscher, Jonas
Barbarians and Brothers: Anglo-American Warfare, 1500-1865 — Lee, Wayne E.
The Barbecue Lover's Big Book of BBQ Sauces: 225 Extraordinary Sauces, Rubs, Marinades, Mops, Bastes, Pastes, and Salsas, for Smoke-Cooking or Grilling — Jamison, Cheryl
The Barber of Damascus: Nouveau Literacy in the Eighteenth-Century Ottoman Levant — Sajdi, Dana
Barcelona: Visual Culture, Space and Power — Buffery, Helena
Barchester Towers — Bowen, John
The Bare Bones: An Unconventional Evolutionary History of the Skeleton — Bonnan, Matthew F.
Barefoot at the Lake: A Boyhood Summer in Cottage Country — Fogle, Bruce
Barefoot at the Lake: A Memoir of Summer People and Water Creatures — Fogle, Bruce
Barefoot Doctors and Western Medicine in China — Fang, Xiaoping
Barefoot Dogs: Stories — Ruiz-Camacho, Antonio
The Barefoot Lawyer: A Blind Man's Fight for Justice and Freedom in China — Guangcheng, Chen
Barefoot to Avalon: A Brother's Story — Payne, David
Barely Composed — Fulton, Alice
y The Bargaining — West, Carly Anne
The Bark before Christmas — Berenson, Laurien
Bark: Stories — Moore, Lorrie
Barlaam and Josaphat: A Christian Tale of the Buddha — de Cambrai, Gui
Barlow by the Book — McAllister, John
c Barn Babies! — Stone, Lynn
Barn Find Road Trip — Cotter, Tom
Barocke Baustellen in Bayern. Akteure, Ablaufe und Wirtschaftliche Bedeutung
The Baron's Cloak: A History of the Russian Empire in War and Revolution — Sunderland, Willard
Baroque Science — Gal, Ofer
Baroque Sovereignty: Carlos De Siguenza Y Gongora and the Creole Archive of Colonial Mexico — More, Anna
Barren Branches — Richards, Laurie
c Barrier — Jones, Patrick

A Barrow Boy's Cadenza — Adams, Pete
Barsk: The Elephants' Graveyard — Schoen, Lawrence M.
Bartholomeus Spranger: Splendor and Eminence in Imperial Prague — Metzler, Sally
Bartolomeo Marchionni "Homem de grossa fazend" (ca. 1450-1530): Un mercante fiorentino a Lisbona e l'Impero portoghese — Bruscoli, Francesco Guidi
Base Nation: How U.S. Military Bases Abroad Harm America and the World — Vine, David
Baseball Dads — Hiley, Matthew S.
c Baseball: Great Moments, Records, and Facts — Borth, Teddy
Baseball Maverick: How Sandy Alderson Revolutionized Baseball and Revived the Mets — Kettmann, Steve
c The Baseball Player and the Walrus (Illus. by Latimer, Alex) — Loory, Ben
c Baseballogy: Supercool Facts You Never Knew (Illus. by Sylvester, Kevin) — Sylvester, Kevin
c Basher History: States and Capitals: United We Stand! — Green, Dan
Basho in America — Zulauf, Sander
Basic Marquetry and Beyond: Expert Techniques for Crafting Beautiful Images with Veneer and Inlay — Horner, Ken
The Basics of Data Literacy: Helping Your Students (and You!) Make Sense of Data - PB343X — Bowen, Michael
The Basics of Winning Lotto/Lottery — Jones, Prof.
The Basilica of St. Francis in Assisi — Malafarina, Gianfranco
Basketball History for Kids — Panchyk, Richard
c A Basketball Story — Torrey, Richard
Basquiat and the Bayou — Sirmans, Franklin
Basquiat: The Unknown Notebooks — Buchhart, Dieter
y The Bassoon King: My Life in Art, Faith, and Idiocy — Wilson, Rainn
Bastards: A Memoir (Read by Delaine, Christina). Audiobook Review — King, Mary Anna
Bastards: A Memoir — King, Mary Anna
Bastards of the Reagan Era — Betts, Reginald Dwayne
Bastards of Utopia: Living Radical Politics After Socialism — Razsa, Maple
c A Bat Cannot Bat, a Stair Cannot Stare: More about Homonyms and Homophones (Illus. by Goneau, Martin) — Cleary, Brian P.
Bat Conservation: Global Evidence for the Effects of Interventions — Berthinussen, Anna
y The Batgirl of Burnside (Illus. by Tarr, Babs) — Fletcher, Brenden
The Batgirl of Burnside (Illus. by Tarr, Babs) — Stewart, Cameron
Bathroom — Penner, Barbara
Bathsheba: Reluctant Beauty — Hunt, Angela
c Bathtime (Illus. by Dicmas, Courtney) — Dicmas, Courtney
c Bathtime for Chickies (Illus. by Trasler, Janee) — Trasler, Janee
y Batman '66 Meets the Green Hornet (Illus. by Templeton, Ty) — Smith, Kevin (b. 1970-)
y Batman '66, vol. 1 (Illus. by Case, Jonathan) — Parker, Jeff
c Batman beyond 2.0, vol. 1: Rewired (Illus. by Wight, Eric) — Higgins, Kyle
Batman Eternal, Vol. 1 — Snyder, Scott
c Batman: The Jiro Kuwata Batmanga, vol. 2 (Illus. by Kuwata, Jiro) — Kuwata, Jiro
c Batman: The Joker's Dozen (Illus. by Beavers, Ethen) — Sutton, Laurie S.
c Batman's Dark Secret (Illus. by Muth, Jon J.) — Puckett, Kelley
Baton Basics: Communicating Music through Gestures — Wittry, Diane
c Bats in the Band — Lies, Brian
Bats of the Republic — Dodson, Zachary Thomas
c The Battle — Torres, Jennifer
The Battle against Anarchist Terrorism: An International History, 1878-1934 — Jensen, Richard Bach
The Battle Belongs to the Lord: Overcoming Life's Struggles through Worship (Read by Carlisle, Jodi). Audiobook Review — Meyer, Joyce
c Battle Bunny (Illus. by Myers, Matthew, III) — Barnett, Mac
c Battle for a New Nation: Causes and Effects of the Revolutionary War — Radomski, Kassandra
The Battle for Darracia — Cash, Michael Phillip
Battle for Ground Zero: Inside the Political Struggle to Rebuild the World Trade Center — Greenspan, Elizabeth

The Battle for Mozambique: The Frelimo-Renamo Struggle, 1977-1992 — *Emerson, Stephen A.*
The Battle for Open: How Openness Won and Why it Doesn't Feel Like Victory — *Weller, Martin*
The Battle for Paradise — *Evans, Jeremy*
The Battle for Room 314: My Year of Hope and Despair in a New York City High School — *Boland, Ed*
c Battle for the Nether — *Cheverton, Mark*
y Battle Lines: A Graphic History of the Civil War (Illus. by Fetter-Vorm, Jonathan) — *Fetter-Vorm, Jonathan*
y Battle Lines: A Graphic History of the Civil War (Illus. by Kelman, Ari) — *Fetter-Vorm, Jonathan*
y Battle Lines: A Graphic History of the Civil War (Illus. by Fetter-Vorm, Jonathan) — *Kelman, Ari*
y Battle Lines: A Graphic History of the Civil War (Illus. by Fetter-Vorm, Jonathan) — *Fetter-Vorm, Jonathan*
c The Battle of Bayport — *Dixon, Franklin W.*
y Battle of Britain — *Holland, James*
c The Battle of Darcy Lane — *Altebrando, Tara*
The Battle of Ezra Church and the Struggle for Atlanta — *Hess, Earl J.*
The Battle of Jericho: A Detective Jericho Novel — *Marks, Walter*
The Battle of Lake Champlain: A "Brilliant and Extraordinary Victory" — *Schroeder, John H.*
The Battle of Lepanto — *Wright, Elizabeth R.*
y The Battle of Little Bighorn in United States History — *Ferrell, Nancy*
c Battle of Little Bighorn — *Hamilton, John*
The Battle of Marathon in Scholarship: Research, Theories and Controversies since 1850 — *Fink, Dennis L.*
The Battle of Oriskany and General Nicholas Herkimer — *Boehlert, Paul A.*
The Battle of the Atlantic: How the Allies Won the War — *Dimbleby, Jonathan*
c Battle of the Bots — *Richards, C.J.*
The Battle of the Bridges: The 504th Parachute Infantry Regiment in Operation Market Garden — *van Lunteren, Frank*
y Battle of the Bulge — *Atkinson, Rick*
The Battle of the Denmark Strait: A Critical Analysis of the Bismarck's Singular Triumph — *Winklareth, Robert J.*
c Battle of the Plains of Abraham — *Wiseman, Blaine*
The Battle of the Sexes in French Cinema, 1930-1956 — *Burch, Noel*
c Battle of the Super Heroes! — *Stewart, Yale*
c The Battle of the Vegetables (Illus. by Barrier, Perceval) — *Sylvander, Matthieu*
The Battle of Versailles: The Night American Fashion Stumbled into the Spotlight and Made History — *Givhan, Robin*
The Battle over Marriage: Gay Rights Activism through the Media — *Moscowitz, Leigh*
c The Battle over Slavery: Causes and Effects of the U.S. Civil War — *Capek, Michael*
Battle without Honor or Humanity, vol. 1: Discombobulate & Neutralize — *Wilson, D. Harlan*
Battlefield America: The War on the American People — *Whitehead, John W.*
Battlemage — *Aryan, Stephen*
Battles and Massacres on the Southwestern Frontier: Historical and Archaeological Perspectives — *Wetherington, Ronald K.*
Battles and Massacres on the Southwestern Frontier: Historical and Archaeological Perspectives — *Levine, Frances*
Battles and Massacres on the Southwestern Frontier: Historical and Archaeological Perspectives — *Wetherington, Ronald K.*
y Battlesaurus: Rampage at Waterloo — *Falkner, Brian*
c Battling for Victory: The Coolest Robot Competitions — *Clay, Kathryn*
Battling the Gods: Atheism in the Ancient World — *Whitmarsh, Tim*
Baudelaire's Media Aesthetics: The Gaze of the Flaneur and 19th-Century Media — *Grotta, Marit*
Bauhaus on the Swan: Elise Blumann, an Emigre Artist in Western Australia, 1938-1948 — *Quin, Sally*
Bauhaus Weaving Theory: From Feminine Craft to Mode of Design — *Smith, T'ai*
The Baul Tradition: Sahaj Vision East and West — *Young, Mary*
Bayerische Romer - Romische Bayern. Lebensgeschichten aus Vor- und Fruhmoderne

The Bayeux Tapestry, Bayeux MediathEque Municipale: MS 1 - A Sourcebook — *Brown, Shirley Ann*
c Bayou Magic (Read by Turpin, Bahni). Audiobook Review — *Rhodes, Jewell Parker*
Bayou Magic — *Rhodes, Jewell Parker*
The Bazaar of Bad Dreams — *King, Stephen*
Bazin on Global Cinema 1948-1958 — *Cardullo, Bert*
BBQ Bistro: Simple, Sophisticated French Recipes for Your Grill — *Adler, Karen*
BDSM in American Science Fiction and Fantasy — *Call, Lewis*
y Be a Changemaker: How to Start Something That Matters — *Thompson, Laurie Ann*
c Be a Friend (Illus. by Yoon, Salina) — *Yoon, Salina*
c Be a Star! — *Alexander, Heather*
c Be a Survivor (Illus. by Sassin, Eva) — *Oxlade, Chris*
c Be a Zoologist — *Belton, Blair*
c Be Careful, Icarus! (Illus. by Patricelli, Leslie) — *Holub, Joan*
Be Frank with Me — *Johnson, Julia Claiborne*
Be Good and Do Good: Thinking through Moral Theology — *Brady, Bernard V.*
y Be Not Afraid — *Galante, Cecilia*
c Be Patient, Pandora! (Illus. by Patricelli, Leslie) — *Holub, Joan*
Be Positive, No Matter What — *Nolan, Karen J.*
c Be Safe around Fire (Illus. by Baroncelli, Silvia) — *Heos, Bridget*
c Be Safe around Strangers (Illus. by Baroncelli, Silvia) — *Heos, Bridget*
c Be Safe around Water — *Heos, Bridget*
Be Safe I Love You — *Hoffman, Cara*
Be Safe, Love Mom — *Brye, Elaine Lowry*
c Be Safe on the Internet (Illus. by Baroncelli, Silvia) — *Heos, Bridget*
c Be Safe on the Playground (Illus. by Baroncelli, Silvia) — *Heos, Bridget*
c Be Safe on Your Bike (Illus. by Baroncelli, Silvia) — *Heos, Bridget*
Be Sand, Not Oil: The Life and Work of Amos Vogel — *Cronin, Paul*
y Be Smart about Credit: Credit and Debit Management — *Kowalski, Kathiann M.*
y Be Smart about Investing: Planning, Saving, and the Stock Market — *Kowalski, Kathiann M.*
y Be Smart about Money: Money Management and Budgeting — *Gordon, Sherri Mabry*
y Be Smart about Shopping: The Critical Consumer and Civic Financial Responsibility — *Kowalski, Kathiann M.*
y Be Smart about Your Career: College, Income, and Careers — *Graham, Amy*
y Be Smart about Your Future: Risk Management and Insurance — *Graham, Amy*
c Be the Change in Your School — *Welbourn, Shannon*
c Be the Change Series — *Kopp, Megan*
c Be the Change Series — *Smith, Paula*
Be the First to Like This — *Waters, Colin*
c Bea in The Nutcracker (Illus. by Isadora, Rachel) — *Isadora, Rachel*
A Beach for Albert (Illus. by Melmon, Deborah) — *May, Eleanor*
c The Beach House (Illus. by Bates, Amy June) — *Caswell, Deanna*
Beach Town (Read by McInerney, Kathleen). Audiobook Review — *Andrews, Mary Kay*
Beach Town — *Andrews, Mary Kay*
Bead and Wire Fashion Jewelry: A Collection of Stunning Statement Pieces to Make — *Rose, Jessica*
Beaded Jewelry: Wirework Techniques — *Eddy, Carson*
Beaded Lace Knitting: Techniques and 25 Beaded Lace Designs for Shawls, Scarves, and More — *Allis, Anniken*
c Beagles — *Finne, Stephanie*
Beale Street Dynasty: Sex, Song, and the Struggle for the Soul of Memphis — *Lauterbach, Preston*
A Beam of Light — *Camilleri, Andrea*
c A Bean, a Stalk and a Boy Named Jack (Illus. by Callicutt, Kenny) — *Joyce, William*
c Bean — *Murray, Laura K.*
c A Bean and Cheese Taco Birthday / Un Cumpleanos Con Tacos de Frijoles Con Queso (Illus. by Trujillo, Robert) — *Bertrand, Diane Gonzales*
c Bear and Bunny (Illus. by Hillenbrand, Will) — *Pinkwater, Daniel*
c Bear and Duck (Illus. by Hudson, Katy) — *Hudson, Katy*
c Bear and Squirrel Are Friends ... Yes, Really! (Illus. by Pilutti, Deb) — *Pilutti, Deb*

c The Bear Ate Your Sandwich (Illus. by Sarcone-Roach, Julia) — *Sarcone-Roach, Julia*
c A Bear Called Paddington (Read by Fry, Stephen). Audiobook Review — *Bond, Michael (b. 1926-)*
c Bear Can Dance! (Illus. by Bloom, Suzanne) — *Bloom, Suzanne*
c Bear Can't Sleep! (Illus. by Julian, Sean) — *McGee, Marni*
c Bear Counts (Illus. by Chapman, Jane) — *Wilson, Karma*
c Bear & Hare Go Fishing (Illus. by Gravett, Emily) — *Gravett, Emily*
c Bear & Hare: Snow! (Illus. by Gravett, Emily) — *Gravett, Emily*
c Bear Hug (Illus. by McEwen, Katharine) — *McEwen, Katharine*
c Bear Hugging and Cancer Crushing (Illus. by Hogan, Steve) — *Gilcris, Eric*
c Bear Is Not Tired — *Gavin, Ciara*
c Bear on the Home Front (Illus. by Deines, Brian) — *Innes, Stephanie*
c The Bear Report (Illus. by Heder, Thyra) — *Heder, Thyra*
c Bear Sees Colors (Illus. by Chapman, Jane) — *Wilson, Karma*
c Bearded Dragons — *Raum, Elizabeth*
Bearing the Unbearable: Trauma, Gospel, and Pastoral Care — *Hunsinger, Deborah van Deusen*
c Bears and a Birthday (Illus. by Walker, David) — *Parenteau, Shirley*
c Bears Don't Read! (Illus. by Chichester Clark, Emma) — *Chichester Clark, Emma*
c Bears Make the Best Reading Buddies — *Oliver, Carmen*
c The Bear's Sea Escape (Illus. by Chaud, Benjamin) — *Chaud, Benjamin*
c The Bear's Surprise (Illus. by Chaud, Benjamin) — *Chaud, Benjamin*
c The Bear's Surprise — *Chaud, Benjamin*
c Bear's Truck Is Stuck! (Illus. by Truong, Tom) — *Hegarty, Patricia*
c A Bear's Year (Illus. by Turley, Gerry) — *Duval, Kathy*
y Beast: Blood, Struggle, and Dreams at the Heart of Mixed Martial Arts — *Merlino, Doug*
c The Beast in My Belly (Illus. by Kozlowski, Tomasz) — *Kasdepke, Grzegorz*
c Beast Keeper (Illus. by Bean, Brett) — *Coats, Lucy*
The Beast of Barcroft — *Schweigart, Bill*
y The Beast of Cretacea — *Strasser, Todd*
c The Beast Within: A Tale of Beauty's Prince — *Valentino, Serena*
y Beastkeeper — *Hellisen, Cat*
c Beastly Babies (Illus. by Wenzel, Brendan) — *Jackson, Ellen*
y Beastly Bones — *Ritter, William*
c Beastly Verse (Illus. by Yoon, JooHee) — *Yoon, JooHee*
y Beasts & Children: Stories — *Parker, Amy*
c Beasts of Olympus: Beast Keeper (Illus. by Roberts, David) — *Coats, Lucy*
The Beat Goes On: The Complete Rebus Stories — *Rankin, Ian*
The Beat Interviews: Conversations with Allen Ginsberg, William S. Burroughs, John Clellon Holmes, Herbert Huncke and Carl Solomon — *Tytell, John*
y Beat the Odds — *Atwood, Megan*
Beatific Enjoyment in Medieval Scholastic Debates: The Complex Legacy of Saint Augustine and Peter Lombard — *Kitanov, Severin Valentinov*
Beating Autism: How Alternative Medicine Cured My Child — *Evans, Anne M.*
Beatlebone — *Barry, Kevin*
Beatleness — *Leonard, Candy*
The Beatles and Me on Tour — *Davis, Ivor*
c The Beatles: Defining Rock 'n' Roll — *Tougas, Joe*
The Beatles Encyclopedia: Everything Fab Four — *Womack, Kenneth*
Beaton: Photographs — *Holborn, Mark*
Beatrice and Benedick — *Fiorato, Marina*
Beatrice and the Basilisk — *McCandless, Bruce, III*
c Beatrice More Moves In (Illus. by Flook, Helen) — *Hughes, Alison*
Beatrix Potter and Her Paint Box (Illus. by McPhail, David) — *McPhail, David*
c Beatrix Potter and the Unfortunate Tale of a Borrowed Guinea Pig (Illus. by Voake, Charlotte) — *Hopkinson, Deborah*
The Beatus Maps: The Revelation of the World in the Middle Ages — *Saenz-Lopez Perez, Sandra*

The Beau Monde: Fashionable Society in Georgian London — *Greig, Hannah*
The Beautiful Anxiety — *Jones, Jill*
c Beautiful Beasts: A Collection of Creatures Past and Present — *de la Bedoyere, Camilla*
c Beautiful Birds (Illus. by Walker, Emmanuelle) — *Roussen, Jean*
Beautiful Braiding Made Easy: Using Kumihimo Disks and Plates, rev. ed. — *Deighan, Helen*
The Beautiful Bureaucrat — *Phillips, Helen*
Beautiful Chaos: A Life in the Theater — *Perloff, Carey*
Beautiful Data: A History of Vision and Reason since 1945 — *Halpern, Orit*
Beautiful Designs with SuperDuos and Twin Beads — *Cave, Carolyn*
Beautiful Geometry — *Jost, Eugen*
y Beautiful Girl — *Philips, Fleur*
c Beautiful Hands (Illus. by Otoshi, Kathryn) — *Baumgarten, Bret*
c Beautiful Hands (Illus. by Otoshi, Kathryn) — *Otoshi, Kathryn*
Beautiful Hero: How We Survived the Khmer Rouge — *Lau, Jenny*
The Beautiful Librarians — *O'Brien, Sean*
Beautiful Losers — *Seymour, Eve*
c Beautiful Moon: A Child's Prayer (Illus. by Velasquez, Eric) — *Bolden, Tonya*
c Beautiful Moon / Bella Luna (Illus. by Leick, Bonnie) — *Jeffers, Dawn*
Beautiful Mutants and Swallowing Geography: Two Early Novels — *Levy, Deborah*
The Beautiful One — *Greenwood, Emily*
Beautiful Paper Cutting: 30 Creative Projects For Cards, Gifts, Decor, and Jewelry — *Deakin, Ellen*
The Beautiful Possible — *Gottlieb, Amy*
A Beautiful Question: Finding Nature's Deep Design — *Wilczek, Frank*
The Beautiful Unseen: Variations on Fog and Forgetting — *Boelte, Kyle*
Beautiful Wall — *Gonzalez, Ray*
The Beautiful Way Of Life — *Feusi, Rene*
c Beautiful Yetta's Hanukkah Kitten (Illus. by Pinkwater, Jill) — *Pinkwater, Daniel*
Beautiful Zero — *Willoughby, Jennifer*
y Beauty (Read by Parry, Charlotte). Audiobook Review — *McKinley, Robin*
The Beauty — *Hirshfield, Jane*
Beauty and the Beast — *Taussig, Michael*
Beauty Is a Wound — *Kurniawan, Eka*
y The Beauty Is in the Walking — *Moloney, James*
The Beauty of God's Presence in the Fathers of the Church: The Proceedings of the Eighth International Patristic Conference, Maynooth, 2012 — *Rutherford, Janet Elaine*
y Beauty of the Broken — *Waters, Tawni*
The Beauty of What Remains: Family Lost, Family Found — *Hadler, Susan Johnson*
The Beauty — *Hirshfield, Jane*
c Beauty Queen — *Mylnowski, Sarah*
c Beauty Queens (Read by Bray, Libba). Audiobook Review — *Bray, Libba*
Beauty, Spirit, Matter: Icons in the Modern World — *Hart, Aidan*
Beauty: The Fortunes of an Ancient Greek Idea — *Konstan, David*
Beauty's Kingdom (Read by Campbell, Cassandra). Audiobook Review — *Anne Rice,*
Beauty's Kingdom — *Rice, Anne*
c Beavers — *Gish, Melissa*
c Beavers — *Riggs, Kate*
c Bebe Goes Shopping (Illus. by Salerno, Steven) — *Elya, Susan Middleton*
Because — *Langedijk, Jack A.*
c Because I Am a Girl I Can Change the World — *McCarney, Rosemary*
Because of Sex: One Law, Ten Cases, and Fifty Years That Changed American Women's Lives at Work — *Thomas, Gillian*
y Because They Marched: The People's Campaign for Voting Rights That Changed America — *Freedman, Russell*
Because We Say So — *Chomsky, Noah*
y Because You'll Never Meet Me — *Thomas, Leah*
c Because Your Grandparents Love You (Illus. by Alley, R.W.) — *Clements, Andrew*
c Becca and the Prisoner's Cross (Read by DeLisle, Arielle). Audiobook Review — *Abbott, Tony*
Become a Message: Poems — *Walder, Lajos*
Become Your Own Boss in 12 Months: A Month-by-Month Guide to a Business That Works — *Emerson, Melinda F.*

Becoming a History Teacher: Sustaining Practices in Historical Thinking and Knowing — *Sandwell, Ruth*
Becoming a Mountain — *Alter, Stephen*
Becoming a Poet in Anglo-Saxon England — *Thonbury, Emily V.*
Becoming a Professor: A Guide to a Career in Higher Education — *Iding, Marie*
Becoming a School Principal: Learning to Lead, Leading to Learn — *Fiarman, Sarah E.*
Becoming a Woman in the Age of Letters — *Goodman, Dena*
Becoming an Embedded Librarian: Making Connections in the Classroom — *Reale, Michelle*
Becoming Belafonte: Black Artist, Public Radical — *Smith, Judith E.*
Becoming Bureaucrats: Socialization at the Front Lines of Government Service — *Oberfield, Zachary W.*
Becoming Catholic: Finding Rome in the American Religious Landscape — *Yamane, David*
Becoming Christian: Race, Reformation, and Early Modern English Romance — *Britton, Dennis Austin*
Becoming Confederates: Paths to a New National Loyalty — *Gallagher, Gary W.*
Becoming Criminal: The Socio-Cultural Origins of Law, Transgression, and Deviance — *Crewe, Don*
y Becoming Darkness — *Brambles, Lindsay Francis*
Becoming Dinosaurs: A Prehistoric Perspective on Climate Change Today — *Trexler, David*
Becoming Ellen — *Shattuck, Shari*
Becoming Fluent: How Cognitive Science Can Help Adults Learn a Foreign Language — *Roberts, Richard*
Becoming Freud: The Making of a Psychoanalyst — *Phillips, Adam*
Becoming Frum: How Newcomers Learn the Language and Culture of Orthodox Judaism — *Benor, Sarah B.*
Becoming Generation Flux: Why Traditional Career Planning Is Dead: How to Be Agile, Adapt to Ambiguity, and Develop Resilience — *Smith, Miles Anthony*
Becoming Heinrich Schenker: Music Theory and Ideology — *Morgan, Robert P.*
Becoming Holy in Early Canada — *Pearson, Timothy G.*
Becoming Human: The Matter of the Medieval Child — *Mitchell, J. Allan*
y Becoming Jinn — *Goldstein, Lori*
Becoming Madison: The Extraordinary Origins of the Least Likely Founding Father — *Signer, Michael*
y Becoming Maria: Love and Chaos in the South Bronx — *Manzano, Sonia*
Becoming Mead: The Social Process of Academic Knowledge — *Huebner, Daniel*
Becoming Men of Some Consequence: Youth and Military Service in the Revolutionary War — *Ruddiman, John A.*
Becoming New York's Finest: Race, Gender, and the Integration of the NYPD, 1935-1980 — *Darien, Andrew T.*
Becoming Nicole: The Transformation of an American Family — *Nutt, Amy Ellis*
The Becoming of the Body: Contemporary Women's Writing in French — *Damle, Amaleena*
Becoming Ottomans: Sephardi Jews and Imperial Citizenship in the Modern Era — *Cohen, Julia Phillips*
Becoming Richard Pryor — *Saul, Scott*
Becoming Right: How Campuses Shape Young Conservatives — *Binder, Amy J.*
Becoming Steve Jobs: The Evolution of a Reckless Upstart into a Visionary Leader (Read by Newbern, George). Audiobook Review — *Schlender, Brent*
Becoming Steve Jobs: The Evolution of a Reckless Upstart into a Visionary Leader — *Schlender, Brent*
Becoming Steve Jobs: The Evolution of a Reckless Upstart into a Visionary Leader — *Tetzeli, Rick*
Becoming Steve Jobs: The Evolution of a Reckless Upstart into a Visionary Leader — *Schlender, Brent*
Becoming the Beach Boys, 1961-1963 — *Murphy, James B.*
Becoming the Tupamaros: Solidarity and Transnational Revolutionaries in Uruguay and the United States — *Churchill, Lindsey*
Becoming Turkish: Nationalist Reforms and Cultural Negotiations in Early Republican Turkey, 1923-1945 — *Yilmaz, Hale*
Becoming Un-Orthodox: Stories of Ex-Hasidic Jews — *Davidman, Lynn*
Becoming Unbecoming — *Una*

Becoming Vegan: The Complete Reference to Plant-Based Nutrition — *Davis, Brenda*
Becoming Westerly: Surf Champion Peter Drouyn's Transformation into Westerly Windina — *Brisick, Jamie*
Becoming Winston Churchill — *McMenamin, Michael*
c A Bed for Bear (Illus. by McFarland, Clive) — *McFarland, Clive*
c A Bed for Kitty (Illus. by Surovec, Yasmine) — *Surovec, Yasmine*
A Bed of Scorpions — *Flanders, Judith*
Beda: A Journey through the Seven Kingdoms in the Age of Bede — *Leyser, Henrietta*
The Bedding Proposal — *Warren, Tracy Anne*
Bede and the Future — *Darby, Peter*
Bedeviled: Lewis, Tolkien and the Shadow of Evil — *Duriez, Colin*
Bedouin of the London Evening: Collected Poems — *Tonks, Rosemary*
c Bedtime at Bessie and Lil's (Illus. by Gudeon, Adam) — *Sternberg, Julie*
c Bedtime Blastoff! — *Reynolds, Luke*
c Bedtime Kisses (Illus. by Nielson, Ginger) — *Larson, Karin*
c Bedtime Math 2: This Time It's Personal (Illus. by Paillot, Jim) — *Overdeck, Laura*
c Bedtime Math: The Truth Comes Out (Illus. by Paillot, Jim) — *Overdeck, Laura*
The Bee: A Natural History — *Wilson-Rich, Noah*
The Bee Cottage Story: How I Made a Muddle of Things and Decorated My Way Back to Happiness — *Schultz, Frances*
c Bee Dance (Illus. by Chrustowski, Rick) — *Chrustowski, Rick*
c The Bee Who Spoke: The Wonderful World of Belle and the Bee (Illus. by Gibbon, Rebecca) — *MacCuish, Al*
c Beebear Board (Illus. by Sievers, Lee) — *Follett, Ross C.*
Beef with Tomato — *Haspiel, Dean*
The Beekeeper's Daughter — *Montefiore, Santa*
A Beeline to Murder — *Lester, Meera*
Been There, Done That: Family Wisdom for Modern Times — *Roker, Al*
y Been There, Done That: Writing Stories from Real Life — *Winchell, Mike*
c Beep! Beep! Go to Sleep! (Illus. by Rocco, John) — *Tarpley, Todd*
The Beer Bible — *Alworth, Jeff*
Beer Terrain: From Field to Glass — *Cook, Jonathan (b. 1970-)*
Bees: A Natural History — *O'Toole, Christopher*
The Bees (Read by Cassidy, Orlagh). Audiobook Review — *Pauli, Laline*
c Bees — *Frisch, Aaron*
Beeswax Alchemy: How to Make Your Own Candles, Soap, Balms, Salves, and Home Decor from the Hive — *Ahnert, Petra*
Beethoven: Anguish and Triumph — *Swafford, Jan*
Beethoven's Symphonies: An Artistic Vision — *Lockwood, Lewis*
y Beethoven's Tenth — *Harvey, Brian*
Beethoven's Theatrical Quartets: Opp. 59, 74 and 95 — *November, Nancy*
c Beetle Boy — *Leonard, M.G.*
y Beetle Boy — *Willey, Margaret*
c Beetle Busters: A Rogue Insect and the People Who Track It (Illus. by Harasimowicz, Ellen) — *Burns, Loree Griffin*
The Beetlebung Farm Cookbook — *Fischer, Chris*
Beetles of Eastern North America — *Evans, Arthur V.*
c Before After (Illus. by Ramstein, Anne-Margot) — *Ramstein, Anne-Margot*
c Before After (Illus. by Ramstein, Anne-Margot) — *Aregui, Matthias*
Before and after Muhammad: The First Millennium Refocused — *Fowden, Garth*
Before and During — *Ready, Oliver*
Before Auschwitz: Jewish Prisoners in the Prewar Concentration Camps — *Wunschmann, Kim*
Before, During, After (Read by Shah, Neil). Audiobook Review — *Bausch, Richard*
y Before Goodbye — *Cross, Mimi*
y Before He Finds Her (Illus. by Whelan, Julia). Audiobook Review — *Kardos, Michael*
y Before He Finds Her — *Kardos, Michael*
Before I Fall — *Scott, Jessica*
Before I Forget: Love, Hope, Help, and Acceptance in Our Fight against Alzheimer's — *Smith, B.*
c Before I Leave (Illus. by Bagley, Jessixa) — *Bagley, Jessixa*

c Before I Sleep I Say Thank You (Illus. by Rojas, Mary) — *Ekster, Carol Gordon*
Before Jutland: The Naval War in Northern European Waters, August 1914-February 1915 — *Goldrick, James*
Before L.A.: Race, Space, and Municipal Power in Los Angeles, 1781-1894 — *Torres-Rouff, David Samuel*
Before Orientalism: Asian Peoples and Cultures in European Travel Writing, 1245-1510 — *Phillips, Kim M.*
Before Sliced Bread — *Kerr, Jeannette*
c Before the Dinosaurs — *West, David*
Before the Door of God: An Anthology of Devotional Poetry — *Hopler, Jay*
Before the West Was West: Critical Essays on Pre-1800 Literature of the American Frontiers — *Hamilton, Amy T.*
Before the Windrush: Race Relations in Twentieth-Century Liverpool — *Belchem, John*
y Before Tomorrowland (Illus. by Case, Jonathan) — *Jensen, Jeff*
y Before Tomorrowland (Illus. by Case, Jonathon) — *Jensen, Jeff*
Beg For Mercy — *Felony, Miles*
Beggar Thy Neighbor: A History of Usury and Debt — *Geisst, Charles R.*
Begging for It — *Pace, Lilah*
The Beginner's Book of Meditation — *Orosz, Attila*
A Beginner's Guide to Bear Spotting (Illus. by Roberts, David) — *Robinson, Michelle*
c A Beginner's Guide to Immortality: From Alchemy to Avatars (Illus. by Holinaty, Josh) — *Birmingham, Maria*
Beginner's Guide to Mosaic — *Massey, Peter*
A Beginner's Guide to Paradise — *Sheshunoff, Alex*
c The Beginner's Guide to Rugby — *Cruden, Aaron*
A Beginner's Life: The Adventures of Tom Phillips — *Phillips, Tom*
The Beginning and End of Rape: Confronting Sexual Violence in Native America — *Deer, Sarah*
A Beginning-Intermediate Grammar of Hellenistic Greek — *Funk, Robert W.*
The Beginning of Scandinavian Settlement in England: The Viking 'Great Army' and Early Settlers, c. 865-900 — *McLeod, Shane*
c Beginning-to-Read: Dear Dragon (Illus. by Schimmell, David) — *Hillert, Margaret*
The Beginning Translator's Workbook — *Jones, Michele H.*
The Beginning Violinist: A Companion Book for Children and Adults — *Williams, Emily*
The Beginning Violinist: Piano Accompaniment — *Williams, Emily*
Beginning with the Mirror: Ten Stories about Love, Desire and Moving between Worlds — *Dube, Peter*
The Beginnings of University English: Extramural Study, 1885-1910 — *Lawrie, Alexandra*
The Beguines of Medieval Paris: Gender, Patronage, and Spiritual Authority — *Miller, Tanya Stabler*
Behave — *Romano-Lax, Andromeda*
Behavioral Genetics of the Fly — *Dubnau, Josh*
y Behind Closed Doors — *Haynes, Elizabeth*
Behind Every Great Man: Forgotten Women behind the World's Famous and Infamous — *Wagman-Geller, Marlene*
Behind God's Back — *Nykanen, Harri*
c Behind the Badge: Crimefighters through History (Illus. by Williams, Gareth) — *Butts, Ed*
Behind the Binoculars: Interviews with Acclaimed Birdwatchers — *Avery, Mark*
c Behind the Canvas — *Vance, Alexander*
Behind the Curtain: A Peek at Life from within the ER — *Sterling, Jeffrey E.*
Behind the Curve: Science and the Politics of Global Warming — *Howe, Joshua P.*
Behind the Front: British Soldiers and French Civilians, 1914-1918 — *Gibson, Craig*
Behind the Gas Mask: The U.S. Chemical Warfare Service in War and Peace — *Faith, Thomas I.*
c Behind the Lines: WWI's Little-Known Story of German Occupation, Belgian Resistance, and the Band of Yanks Who Helped Save Millions from Starvation — *Miller, Jeffrey B.*
Behind the Mask: The Life of Vita Sackville-West — *Dennison, Matthew*
Behind the Smile: A Story of Carol Moseley Braun's Historic Senate Campaign — *Morris, Jeannie*
Behind the Walls: A City Beseiged — *Pierce, Nicola*
c Behold! A Baby (Illus. by Ang, Joy) — *Watson, Stephanie*

Behold the Black Caiman: A Chronicle of Ayorgeo Life — *Bessire, Lucas*
y Behold the Bones — *Parker, Natalie C.*
The Beige Man — *Tursten, Helene*
Beijing Xingwei: Contemporary Chinese Time-Based Art — *Meiling Cheng*
y Being a Girl — *Long, Hayley*
c Being a Good Citizen: A Kids' Guide to Community Involvement (Illus. by Haggerty, Tim) — *Kreisman, Rachelle*
Being a Historian: An Introduction to the Professional World of History — *Banner, James M., Jr.*
Being a State and States of Being in Highland Georgia — *Muhlfried, Florian*
Being a YouTuber — *Sutherland, Adam*
Being American in Europe, 1750-1860 — *Kilbride, Daniel*
Being and Becoming Kachin: Histories Beyond the State in the Borderworlds of Burma — *Sadan, Mandy*
y Being Audrey Hepburn — *Kriegman, Mitchell*
Being Berlusconi: The Rise and Fall from Cosa Nostra to Bunga Bunga — *Day, Michael*
Being Christian in Late Antiquity: A Festschrift for Gillian Clark — *Harrison, Carol*
Being Danish: Paradoxes of Identity in Everyday Life — *Jenkins, Richard*
c Being Fit — *Bodden, Valerie*
Being German, Becoming Muslim: Race, Religion, and Conversion in the New Europe — *Ozyurek, Esra*
Being Human: Human Being, Manifesto for a New Psychology — *Cromwell, Rue L.*
Being Malay in Indonesia: Histories, Hopes and Citizenship in the Riau Archipelago — *Long, Nicholas J.*
Being Maori in the City: Indigenous Everyday Life in Auckland — *Gagne, Natacha*
Being Mortal: Illness, Medicine and What Matters in the End — *Gawande, Atul*
Being Mortal: Medicine and What Matters in the End (Read by Petkoff, Robert). Audiobook Review — *Gawande, Atul*
Being Mortal: Medicine and What Matters in the End — *Gawande, Atul*
Being Nixon: A Man Divided — *Thomas, Evan*
Being Nuclear: Africans and the Global Uranium Trade — *Hecht, Gabrielle*
Being Promised: Theology, Gift and Practice — *Walter, Gregory*
Being Protestant in Reformation Britain — *Ryrie, Alec*
Being Realistic about Reasons — *Scanlon, T.M.*
Beings: Contemporary Peruvian Short Stories — *Heath, Anna*
Beirut, Beirut — *Ibrahim, Sonallah*
Beirut Noir — *Humaydan, Iman*
Bela Bartok — *Cooper, David*
c Belches, Burps, and Farts Oh My! (Illus. by Naujokaitis, Pranas T.) — *Bennett, Artie*
Belgrad zwischen Sozialistischem Herrschaftsanspruch und Gesellschaftlichem Eigensinn: Die Jugoslawische Hauptstadt als Entwurf und Urbane Erfahrung — *Munnich, Nicole*
y Believarexic — *Johnson, J.J.*
Believe and Destroy: Intellectuals in the SS War Machine — *Ingrao, Christian*
c Believe It or Not, My Brother Has a Monster! (Illus. by Slonim, David) — *Nesbitt, Kenn*
Believe No One — *Garrett, A.D.*
Believer: My Forty Years in Politics (Read by Axelrod, David). Audiobook Review — *Axelrod, David*
Believer: My Forty Years in Politics — *Axelrod, David*
y The Bell Between Worlds: The Mirror Chronicles — *Johnstone, Ian*
The Bell Curve: Intelligence and Class Structure in American Life — *Herrnstein, Richard J.*
The Bell Tolls for No One — *Bukowski, Charles*
Bell Weather — *Mahoney, Dennis*
c Bella's Best of All (Illus. by Harper, Jamie) — *Harper, Jamie*
c Bella's Birthday Unicorn (Illus. by Ying, Victoria) — *Burkhart, Jessica*
Bella's Gift: How One Little Girl Transformed Our Family and Inspired a Nation — *Santorum, Rick*
The Belle of Charleston — *Hines, Jerri*
Belle: the True Story of Dido Belle — *Byrne, Paula*
Belles and Whistles: Five Journeys through Time on Britain's Train — *Martin, Andrew*
c Belles baleines — *Charlesworth, Liza*
The Belles of Williamsburg — *Maillard, Mary*

Belligerent Muse: Five Northern Writers and How They Shaped Our Understanding of the Civil War — *Cushman, Stephen*
The Bells of Memory — *Boullata, Issa J.*
c Belly Up — *Gibbs, Stuart*
Belonging: Solidarity and Division in Modern Societies — *Guibernau, Montserrat*
The Beloved — *Rattle, Alison*
Below the Belt — *Murray, Jeanette*
c Below Your Belt: A Pelvic Health Handbook for Girls (Illus. by Ihm, Jeni Donatelli) — *Lavender, Missy*
The Beltway Beast — *Moon, Munir*
y Belzhar — *Wolitzer, Meg*
Ben and Ellen Harper: A House Is a Home — *Harper, Ben*
Ben Draws Trouble — *Davies, Matt*
c Ben Franklin's Big Splash: The Mostly True Story of His First Invention (Read by Berneis, Susie). Audiobook Review — *Rosenstock, Barb*
c Ben Franklin's Big Splash: The Mostly True Story of His First Invention (Illus. by Schindler, S.D.) — *Rosenstock, Barb*
Ben-Gurion: Father of Modern Israel — *Shapira, Anita*
c Ben Says Goodbye (Illus. by LaFave, Kim) — *Ellis, Sarah*
Ben & Zip: Two Short Friends (Illus. by Goldsmith, Tom) — *Linden, Joanne*
Benazir Bhutto: Favored Daughter — *Allen, Brooke*
Benchere in Wonderland — *Gillis, Steven*
Benchmarking Muslim Well-Being in Europe: Reducing Disparities and Polarizations — *Jackson, Pamela Irving*
Benchwarmer: A Sports-Obsessed Memoir of Fatherhood — *Wilker, Josh*
Bending Adversity: Japan and the Art of Survival — *Pilling, David*
Bending toward Justice: The Voting Rights Act and the Transformation of American Democracy — *May, Gary*
c Beneath — *Smith, Roland*
Beneath His Wings — *Pruitt, Jenny*
Beneath the Bonfire — *Butler, Nickolas*
Beneath the Greater Sky — *Voelker, Andrew*
c Beneath the Stone Forest (Illus. by McPhillips, Robert) — *Quinn, Jordan*
Beneath the Surface: Killer Whales, SeaWorld, and the Truth beyond Blackfish — *Hargrove, John*
Beneath the Tor — *Milton, Nina*
Benediction for a Black Swan — *Zollars, Mimi*
Benefit of the Doubt — *Griffin, Neal*
Bengali Harlem and the Lost Histories of South Asian America — *Bald, Vivek*
c Benjamin Bear in Brain Storms! (Illus. by Coudray, Philippe) — *Coudray, Philippe*
Benjamin Disraeli Letters, vol. IX: 1865-1867 — *Pharand, Michel W.*
c Benjamin Franklin: Huge Pain in My ... (Illus. by Zweibel, Alan) — *Mansbach, Adam*
Benjamin Franklin in London — *Goodwin, George*
Bennington Girls Are Easy — *Silver, Charlotte*
c Benno and the Night of Broken Glass (Read by Berneis, Susie). Audiobook Review — *Wiviott, Meg*
c Benny and Penny in Lost and Found! — *Hayes, Geoffrey*
Bensheimer Gesprache: Financiers und Staatsfinanzen (Teil 2).
Beowulf: A Translation and Commentary, Together with Sellic Spell — *Tolkien, J.R.R.*
Beowulf on Film: Adaptations and Variations — *Haydock, Nickolas*
Berenice II and the Golden Age of Ptolemaic Egypt — *Clayman, Dee L.*
c The Berenstain Bears' Please and Thank You Book (Illus. by Berenstain, Mike) — *Berenstain, Mike*
c The Berenstain Bears: The Biggest Brag (Illus. by Berenstain, Mike) — *Berenstain, Mike*
Berg — *Quin, Ann*
Bergung von Kulturgut im Nationalsozialismus. Mythen - Hintergrunde - Auswirkungen
Bericht zur VII. Nachwuchstagung der Konferenz fur Geschichtsdidaktik
Berkeley's Puzzle: What Does Experience Teach Us? — *Campbell, John (b. 1956-)*
Berkshire beyond Buffett: The Enduring Value of Values — *Cunningham, Lawrence A.*
Berlin — *Schulte-Peevers, Andrea*
Berlin Airlift: Air Bridge to Freedom: A Photographic History of the Great Airlift — *McAllister, Bruce*
Berlin Coquette: Prostitution and the New German Woman, 1890-1933 — *Smith, Jill Suzanne*

Berlin im Nationalsozialismus: Politik und Gesellschaft, 1933-1945 — *Hachtmann, Rudiger*
Berlin: Imagine a City — *MacLean, Rory*
Berliner Friedenspfarrer und der Erste Weltkrieg: Ein Lesebuch — *Lipp, Karlheinz*
c The Bernadette Watts Collection: Stories and Fairy Tales — *Watts, Bernadette*
c Bernard — *Jones, Rob*
Bernard Berenson: Formation and Heritage — *Connors, Joseph*
Bernard Kops: Fantasist, London Jew, Apocalyptic Humorist — *Baker, William (b. 1944-)*
c Bernice Gets Carried Away (Illus. by Harrison, Hannah E.) — *Harrison, Hannah E.*
Bernie — *Rall, Ted*
Bernstein Meets Broadway: Collaborative Art in a Time of War — *Oja, Carol J.*
The Bernward Gospels: Art, Memory and the Episcopate in Medieval Germany — *Kingsley, Jennifer P.*
Berryman's Sonnets — *Bernard, April*
Berryman's Sonnets — *Berryman, John*
Bertha of the Big Foot: A Thirteenth-Century Epic — *le Roi, Adenet*
The Berthouville Silver Treasure and Roman Luxury — *Lapatin, Kenneth*
Bertie's Guide to Life and Mothers — *McCall Smith, Alexander*
Bertolt Brecht: A Literary Life — *Parker, Stephen*
Besatzungskinder und Wehrmachtskinder - Auf der Suche nach Identitat und Resilienz
Beschamende Bilder: Deutsche Reaktionen auf Alliierte Dokumentarfilme uber Befreite Konzentrationslager — *Weckel, Ulrike*
Beschreibungsversuche der Judenfeindschaft: Zur Geschichte der Antisemitismusforschung vor 1944 — *Hahn, Hans-Joachim*
Besh Big Easy — *Besh, John*
Beside Myself — *Morgan, Ann*
The Beslan Massacre: Myths & Facts — *Burakov, Alexander*
Bessarabian Stamps — *Woolf, Oleg*
c Bessie Coleman — *Flynn, Riley*
The Best American Comics 2015 — *Lethem, Jonathan*
The Best American Essays 2015 — *Levy, Ariel*
The Best American Infographics 2015 — *Cook, Gareth*
The Best American Mystery Stories 2015 — *Patterson, James*
y The Best American Nonrequired Reading, 2015 — *Johnson, Adam*
The Best American Science Fiction and Fantasy 2015 — *Hill, Joe*
The Best American Short Stories 2015 — *Boyle, T.C.*
The Best American Sports Writing 2015 — *Thompson, Wright*
The Best American Travel Writing, 2015 — *McCarthy, Andrew*
c The Best Auto Racers of All Time — *Wilner, Barry*
c The Best Bat (Illus. by Madrid, Erwin) — *Howard, Ryan*
c The Best Birthday Present Ever! — *Mantle, Ben*
Best Boy (Read by Pinchot, Bronson). Audiobook Review — *Gottlieb, Eli*
The Best Boy in the United States of America: A Memoir of Blessing and Kisses — *Wolfson, Ron*
Best Boy — *Gottlieb, Eli*
Best Business Practices — *Thomas, Alan G.*
Best European Fiction 2015 — *Camel, West*
Best European Fiction 2016 — *Fosse, Jon*
c The Best Extreme Sports Stars of All Time — *Scheff, Matt*
Best Food Writing 2015 — *Hughes, Holly*
c The Best Friend Battle (Illus. by Santoso, Charles) — *Eyre, Lindsay*
c Best Friend Next Door (Read by Sands, Tara, with Cassandra Morris). Audiobook Review — *Mackler, Carolyn*
y Best Friend Next Door — *Mackler, Carolyn*
c Best Friend Trouble (Illus. by Despres, Genevieve) — *Itani, Frances*
Best Friends Forever — *Roby, Kimberla Lawson*
y Best Friends through Eternity — *McNicoll, Sylvia*
c The Best Golfers of All Time — *Daniel, P.K.*
c Best Grandma in the World — *Livanios, Eleni*
c The Best Grandpa in the World! (Illus. by Lutje, Susanne) — *Livanios, Eleni*
c The Best Hockey Players of All Time — *Graves, Will*
The Best Homemade Kids' Snacks on the Planet: More Than 200 Healthy Homemade Snacks You and Your Kids Will Love — *Fuentes, Laura*
The Best Horror of the Year, vol. 7 — *Datlow, Ellen*

The Best-Kept Boy in the World: The Short, Scandalous Life of Denny Fouts, Muse to Truman Capote, Gore Vidal, and Christopher Isherwood — *Vanderbilt, Arthur*
The Best Laid Wedding Plans — *Austin, Lynnette*
Best Lesbian Erotica — *Antoniou, Laura*
c Best Lowly Worm Book Ever! (Illus. by Scarry, Richard) — *Scarry, Richard*
The Best Natural Homemade Skin and Hair Care Products — *Gomez, Mar*
c The Best NBA Centers of All Time — *Donnelly, Patrick*
c The Best NBA Dunkers of All Time — *Wilner, Barry*
c The Best NBA Forwards of All Time — *Donnelly, Patrick*
c The Best NBA Guards of All Time — *Graves, Will*
The Best of Both Rogues — *Grace, Samantha*
The Best of Carol Klose: Fifteen Original Piano Solos — *Klose, Carol*
The Best of Connie Willis: Award-Winning Stories — *Willis, Connie*
The Best of 'Dear Bill': The Collected Letters of Denis Thatcher — *Ingrams, Richard*
The Best of Enemies — *Lancaster, Jen*
The Best of Gregory Benford — *Benford, Gregory*
The Best of Me — *Barrett, Elisabeth*
The Best of Nancy Kress — *Kress, Nancy*
c Best Paper — *Eaddy, Susan*
c The Best Part of the Day (Illus. by Edelson, Wendy) — *Breathnach, Sarah Ban*
c The Best Parts of Christmas (Illus. by Murguia, Bethanie Deeney) — *Murguia, Bethanie Deeney*
Best Practices: Mobile Library Services — *Harmon, Charles*
Best Served Cold — *Spencer, Sally*
c The Best Soccer Players of All Time — *McDougall, Chros*
Best STEM Resources for Nextgen Scientists: The Essential Selection and User's Guide — *Hopwood, Jennifer L.*
y The Best Summer Programs for Teens, 2016-2017 — *Berger, Sandra L.*
c The Best Sweater (Illus. by Gill, Sarah) — *Garner, Lynna*
The Best Team Money Can Buy: The Los Angeles Dodgers' Wild Struggle to Build a Baseball Powerhouse — *Knight, Molly*
c The Best Tennis Players of All Time — *Gitlin, Marty*
The Best Writing on Mathematics 2013 — *Pitici, Mircea*
The Best Writing on Mathematics 2014 — *Pitici, Mircea*
The Best Writing on Mathematics 2015 — *Pitici, Mircea*
c The Bestest Baby! (Illus. by Birkett, Georgie) — *Simmons, Anthea*
A Bestiary of East Tennessee: Illustrated in Felt — *Keffer, David J.*
c Besties, Sleepovers, and Drama Queens: Questions and Answers about Friends (Illus. by Mora, Julissa) — *Loewen, Nancy*
The Bet: Paul Ehrlich, Julian Simon, and Our Gamble over Earth's Future — *Sabin, Paul*
y Bet Your Life — *Casey, Jane*
Beta-Life — *Amos, Martyn*
The Betrayal: The 1919 World Series and the Birth of Modern Baseball — *Fountain, Charles*
Betrayed (Read by Bello, Maria). Audiobook Review — *Scottoline, Lisa*
The Betrothed — *Manzoni, Alessandro*
c Betsy Ross (Illus. by Florentino, Al) — *Weil, Ann*
c Betsy's Story, 1934 — *Whitby, Adele*
A Better Goodbye — *Schulian, John*
Better Homes and Corpses — *Bridge, Kathleen*
Better: How I Let Go of Control, Held on to Hope, and Found Joy in My Darkest Hour — *Robach, Amy*
y Better Left Buried — *Haughton, Emma*
Better Living through Criticism: How to Think about Art, Pleasure, Beauty, and Truth — *Scott, A.O.*
c Better Nate Than Ever — *Federle, Tim*
Better on Toast: Happiness on a Slice of Bread — *Donenfeld, Jill*
A Better Place — *Flax, Mike*
Better Than Before: Mastering the Habits of Our Everyday Lives (Read by Rubin, Gretchen). Audiobook Review — *Rubin, Gretchen*
Better than Before: Mastering the Habits of Our Everyday Lives — *Rubin, Gretchen*
Better Than Fiction 2: More True Travel Tales From Great Fiction Writers — *George, Don*
c Better Than Gold — *Tomlinson, Theresa*

y Better Than Perfect — *Kantor, Melissa*
Better When He's Bold — *Crownover, Jay*
Better When He's Brave — *Crownover, Jay*
A Better World — *Tarazona, Belangela*
c BetterNot! And the Tale of Bratsville: Teaching Morals and Manners (Illus. by Fong, Roderick) — *Del Vecchio, Gene*
y Betting Game — *O'Connor, Heather M.*
Betting on the Africans: John F. Kennedy's Courting of African Nationalist Leaders — *Muehlenbeck, Philip E.*
Betting the Farm on a Drought: Stories from the Front Lines of Climate Change — *McGraw, Seamus*
Bettler, Diebe, Unterwelt: Leonaert Bramer illustriert spanische Romane — *Riether, Achim*
Betty Boo — *Pineiro, Claudia*
c Betty Bunny Didn't Do It (Read by Kellgren, Katherine). Audiobook Review — *Kaplan, Michael B.*
c Betty Bunny Loves Easter (Illus. by Jorisch, Stephane) — *Kaplan, Michael B.*
c Betty Goes Bananas in Her Pyjamas (Illus. by Antony, Steve) — *Antony, Steve*
c Betty Goes Bananas (Illus. by Antony, Steve) — *Antony, Steve*
c Betty Q Investigates (Illus. by McClellan, Maddy) — *Gorman, Karyn*
Bettyville: A Memoir (Read by Woodman, Jeff). Audiobook Review — *Hodgman, George*
Bettyville: A Memoir — *Hodgman, George*
Between a Vamp and a Hard Place — *Sims, Jessica*
Between — *Abdou, Angie*
Between Birth and Death: Female Infanticide in Nineteenth-Century China — *King, Michelle T.*
Between Christian and Jew: Conversion and Inquisition in the Crown of Aragon, 1250-1391 — *Tartakoff, Paula*
Between Constantinople and Rome: An Illuminated Byzantine Gospel Book (Paris gr. 54) and the Union of Churches — *Maxwell, Kathleen*
Between Debt and the Devil: Money, Credit, and Fixing Global Finance — *Turner, Adair*
Between Earth and Heaven: Liminality and the Ascencion of Christ in Anglo-Saxon Literature — *Kramer, Johanna*
Between Flesh and Steel: A History of Military Medicine from the Middle Ages to the War in Afghanistan — *Gabriel, Richard*
Between Gods: A Memoir — *Pick, Alison*
Between Here and Gone — *Ferrer, Barbara*
Between Here and the Yellow Sea (Read by Heyborne, Kirby). Audiobook Review — *Pizzolatto, Nic*
Between Jewish Tradition and Modernity: Rethinking an Old Opposition: Essays in Honor of David Ellenson — *Meyer, Michael A.*
Between Land and Sea: The Atlantic Coast and the Transformation of New England — *Pastore, Christopher L.*
Between Magisterium and Marketplace: A Constructive Account of Theology and the Church — *Saler, Robert C.*
Between Mao and McCarthy: Chinese American Politics in the Cold War Years — *Brooks, Charlotte*
Between Mind and Nature: A History of Psychology — *Smith, Roger*
Between Monopoly and Free Trade: The English East India Company, 1600-1757 — *Erikson, Emily*
Between Pagan and Christian — *Jones, Christopher P.*
Between Past and Future: Eight Exercises in Political Thought — *Arendt, Hannah*
Between Personal and Institutional Religion: Self, Doctrine, and Practice in Late Antique Eastern Christianity — *Bitton-Ashkelony, Brouria*
Between Philosophy and Literature: Bakhtin and the Question of the Subject — *Erdinast-Vulcan, Daphna*
Between Politics and Culture: New Perspectives on the History of the Bohemian Lands and the First Czechoslovak Republic
Between Raid and Rebellion: The Irish in Buffalo and Toronto, 1867-1916 — *Jenkins, William*
Between River and Sea: Encounters in Israel and Palestine — *Murphy, Dervla*
c Between Shadows — *Waldron, Kathleen Cook*
Between Slavery and Capitalism: The Legacy of Emancipation in the American South — *Ruef, Martin*
Between State and Synagogue: The Secularization of Contemporary Israel — *Ben-Porat, Guy*
Between Text and Patient: The Medical Enterprise in Medieval and Early Modern Europe — *Glaze, Florence Eliza*

Between the Black Box and the White Cube: Expanded Cinema and Postwar Art — *Uroskie, Andrew V.*
Between the Brown and the Red — *Kunicki, Mikolaj Stanislaw*
Between the Dark and the Daylight: Embracing the Contradictions of Life — *Chittister, Joan*
Between the Living and the Dead — *Crider, Bill*
y Between the Notes — *Roat, Sharon Huss*
y Between the Spark and the Burn — *Tucholke, April Genevieve*
Between the Tides — *Marren, Susannah*
Between the World and Me (Read by Coates, Ta-Nehisi). Audiobook Review — *Coates, Ta-Nehisi*
y Between the World and Me — *Coates, Ta-Nehisi*
Between the World and Me (Read by Coates, Ta-Nehisi). Audiobook Review — *Coates, Ta-Nehisi*
Between the World and Me — *Coates, Ta-Nehisi*
Between These Walls — *Herrick, John*
Between Two Stools: Scatology and Its Representations in English Literature, Chaucer to Swift — *Smith, Peter J.*
y Between Two Worlds — *Kirkpatrick, Katherine*
Between Two Worlds: How the English Became Americans — *Gaskill, Malcolm*
y Between Us and the Moon — *Maizel, Rebecca*
Between Worlds: An Anthology of Contemporart Fiction and Criticism — *Poe, Deborah*
Between Worlds: The Travels of Yusuf Khan Kambalposh — *Hasan, Mushirul*
Between Yesterday and Tomorrow: German Visions of Europe, 1926-1950 — *Bailey, Christian*
Between You and Me: Confessions of a Comma Queen (Read by Norris, Mary). Audiobook Review — *Norris, Mary*
Between You and Me: Confessions of a Comma Queen — *Norris, Mary*
Between You and Me: Confessions of a Comma Queen — *Morris, Mary*
Between You and Me — *Nadelson, Scott*
Between You & Me: Confessions of a Comma Queen (Read by Norris, Mary). Audiobook Review — *Norris, Mary*
Between You & Me: Confessions of a Comma Queen — *Norris, Mary*
Beveled Edges and Mitered Corners: Poems — *Lee, Mary Elizabeth*
y Beware the Little White Rabbit: An Alice in Wonderland-Inspired Anthology — *Delany, Shannon*
c Beware the Power of the Dark Side (Illus. by McQuarrie, Ralph) — *Angleberger, Tom*
y Beware the Wild — *Parker, Natalie C.*
Bewegung/en - 5. Jahrestagung der Fachgesellschaft Geschlechterstudien/Gender Studies Association
Bewilderments: Reflections on the Book of Numbers — *Zornberg, Avivah Gottlieb*
c Bewitched in Oz — *Burns, Laura J.*
c The Bewundering World of Bewilderbeests (Illus. by Fort, Bailey) — *Fort, Bailey*
y Beyonce — *Saddleback Educational Publishing*
Beyond a Love Supreme: John Coltrane and the Legacy of an Album — *Whyton, Tony*
Beyond Ainu Studies: Changing Academic and Public Perspectives — *Hudson, Mark J.*
Beyond Air-Sea Battle: The Debate over US Military Strategy in Asia — *Friedberg, Aaron L.*
Beyond Alterity: German Encounters with Modern East Asia — *Shen, Qinna*
Beyond Biofatalism: Human Nature for an Evolving World — *Barker, Gillian*
Beyond Book Sales: The Complete Guide to Raising Real Money for Your Library — *Dowd, Susan*
Beyond Breaking the Glass: A Spiritual Guide to Your Jewish Wedding — *Wiener, Nancy H.*
Beyond Bullying: Breaking the Cycle of Shame, Bullying, and Violence — *Fast, Jonathan*
Beyond Caring Labour to Provisioning Work — *Neysmith, Sheila M.*
Beyond Caste: Identity and Power in South Asia, Past and Present — *Guha, Sumit*
Beyond Championships: A Playbook for Winning at Life — *Joyce, Dru, II*
y Beyond Championships, Teen Edition: A Playbook for Winning at Life — *Joyce, James Dru, II*
Beyond Civilization and Barbarism: Culture and Politics in Postrevolutionary Argentina — *Brendan, Lanctot*
Beyond Cloud Nine — *Spry, Greg*
y Beyond Clueless — *Alsenas, Linas*
y Beyond Crazy — *Loughead, Deb*

Beyond Democracy in Cambodia: Political Reconstruction in a Post-Conflict Society — *Ojendal, Joakim*
Beyond Discrimination: Racial Inequality in a Postracist Era — *Harris, Fredrick*
Beyond Expectations: Out of the Surf — *Montgomery, Thaddaeus U.*
Beyond Gatsby: How Fitzgerald, Hemingway, and Writers of the 1920s Shaped American Culture — *McParland, Robert*
Beyond Goals: Effective Strategies for Coaching and Mentoring — *David, Susan*
Beyond Happiness: The Trap of Happiness and How to Find Deeper Meaning and Joy — *Seldon, Anthony*
Beyond Happiness: The Upside of Feeling Down — *Hutson, Matthew*
Beyond Hercules — *Roffe, Stephen*
Beyond Human: Engineering Our Future Evolution — *Seedhouse, Erik*
Beyond Loving: Intimate Racework in Lesbian, Gay and Straight Interracial Relationships — *Steinbugler, Amy C.*
y Beyond Magenta: Transgender Teens Speak Out (Read by Eby, Tanya). Audiobook Review — *Kuklin, Susan*
Beyond Magna Carta: A Constitution for the United Kingdom — *Blick, Andrew*
Beyond Measure: Rescuing an Overscheduled, Overtested, Underestimated Generation — *Abeles, Vicki*
Beyond Modernity. Transepochal Perspectives on Spaces, Actors, and Structures
Beyond Mothers, Monsters, Whores: Thinking about Women's Violence in Global Politics — *Gentry, Caron E.*
c Beyond My Dreams — *Marmureanu, Peter*
Beyond Nature's Housekeepers: American Women in Environmental History — *Unger, Nancy C.*
Beyond News: The Future of Journalism — *Stephens, Mitchell*
Beyond NGO-ization: The Development of Social Movements in Central and Eastern Europe — *Jacobsson, Kerstin*
Beyond: Our Future in Space — *Impey, Chris*
Beyond Partition: Gender, Violence, and Representation in Postcolonial India — *Misri, Deepti*
Beyond Post-traumatic Stress: Homefront Struggles with the Wars on Terror — *Scandlyn, Jean*
Beyond Redemption — *Fletcher, Michael R.*
Beyond Redemption: Race, Violence, and the American South after the Civil War — *Emberton, Carole*
Beyond Rosie: A Documentary History of Women and World War II — *Brock, Julia*
Beyond Scylla and Charybdis — *Johannsen, Birgitte Beggild*
Beyond Shangri-La: America and Tibet's Move into the Twenty-First Century — *Knaus, John Kenneth*
Beyond Sinology: Chinese Writing and Scripts of Culture — *Bachner, Andrea*
y Beyond Suspicion — *Winn, Catherine A.*
Beyond SWAT: History, Society and Economy along the Afghanistan-Pakistan Frontier — *Hopkins, Benjamin D.*
Beyond Territorial Disputes in the South China Sea: Legal Frameworks for the Joint Development of Hydrocarbon Resources — *Beckman, Robert*
Beyond the Abortion Wars: A Way Forward for a New Generation — *Camosy, Charles C.*
Beyond the Arab Spring: The Evolving Ruling Bargain in the Middle East — *Kamrava, Mehran*
Beyond the Balance of Power: France and the Politics of National Security in the Era of the First World War — *Jackson, Peter*
Beyond the Borderlands: Migration and Belonging in the United States and Mexico — *Shutika, Debra Lattanzi*
Beyond the Burghal Hidage: Anglo-Saxon Civil Defence in the Viking Age — *Baker, John Timothy*
Beyond the Cold War: Lyndon Johnson and the New Global Challenges of the 1960s — *Gavin, Francis J.*
Beyond the Common Core: A Handbook for Mathematics in a PLC at Work, Grades K-5 — *Dixon, Juli K.*
Beyond the Common Core: A Handbook for Mathematics in a PLC at Work, High School — *Toncheff, Mona*
Beyond the Eagle's Shadow: New Histories of Latin America's Cold War — *Garrard-Burnett, Virginia*
Beyond the Great Water — *Kuri, Frederick*

Beyond the Horizon — *Ireland, Ryan*
c Beyond the Kingdoms (Read by Colfer, Chris). Audiobook Review — *Colfer, Chris*
c Beyond the Laughing Sky (Illus. by Morstad, Julie) — *Cuevas, Michelle*
Beyond the Pale: Folklore, Family and the Mystery of Our Hidden Genes — *Urquhart, Emily*
c Beyond the Pond (Illus. by Kuefler, Joseph) — *Kuefler, Joseph*
Beyond the Sunrise (Read by Landor, Rosalyn). Audiobook Review — *Balogh, Mary*
Beyond the Text: Franciscan Art and the Construction of Religion — *Seubert, Xavier*
Beyond the War on Invasive Species: A Permaculture Approach to Ecosystem Restoration — *Orion, Tao*
c Beyond the Western Deep (Illus. by Bennett, Rachel) — *Kain, Alex*
Beyond Versus: The Struggle to Understand the Interaction of Nature and Nurture — *Tabery, James*
Beyond Willpower: The Secret Principle to Achieving Success in Life, Love, and Happiness (Read by Singer, Erik). Audiobook Review — *Loyd, Alexander*
Beyond Willpower: The Secret Principle to Achieving Success in Life, Love, and Happiness — *Loyd, Alexander*
y Beyond Words: What Animals Think and Feel — *Safina, Carl*
c The Bezert (Illus. by Knier, Maria) — *Knier, Maria*
Bhangra and Asian Underground: South Asian Music and the Politics of Belonging in Britain — *Bakrania, Falu*
Bias in the Booth: An Insider Exposes How Sports Media Distort the News — *Gwinn, Dylan*
The Bias of Temperament in American Politics, 2d ed. — *Kremi, William P.*
The Bible and Asia: From the Pre-Christian Era to the Postcolonial Age — *Sugirtharajah, R.S.*
The Bible and Posthumanism — *Koosed, Jennifer L.*
Bible, Borders, Belonging(s): Engaging Readings from Oceania — *Havea, Jione*
The Bible Doesn't Say That — *Hoffman, Joel M.*
Bible, Gender, Sexuality: Reframing the Church's Debate on Same-Sex Relationships — *Brownson, James V.*
The Bible in Medieval Tradition: The Letter to the Romans — *Levy, Ian Christopher*
Bible in Mission — *Hoggarth, Pauline*
The Bible in Shakespeare — *Hamlin, Hannibal*
The Bible in the Public Square: Its Enduring Influence in American Life — *Chancey, Mark A.*
Biblical Blaspheming: Trials of the Sacred for a Secular Age — *Sherwood, Yvonne*
Biblical Economic Ethics: Sacred Scripture's Teachings on Economic Life — *Barrera, Albino*
Biblical Essays in Honor of Daniel J. Harrington, SJ, and Richard J. Clifford, SJ: Opportunity for No Little Instruction — *Frechette, Christopher G.*
Biblical Interpretation and Philosophical Hermeneutics — *McLean, B.H.*
Biblical Prophecy: Perspectives for Christian Theology, Discipleship, and Ministry — *Davis, Ellen F.*
BiblioCraft: The Modern Crafter's Guide to Using Library Resources to Jumpstart Creative Projects — *Pigza, Jessica*
Bibliographie critique des ouvrages et traductions de Gabriel Chappuys — *Dechaud, Jean-Marc*
Bibliographie Heiner Muller — *Vassen, Florian*
BiblioTech: Why Libraries Matter More Than Ever in the Age of Google (Read by Zingarelli, Tom). Audiobook Review — *Palfrey, John*
BiblioTech: Why Libraries Matter More Than Ever in the Age of Google — *Palfrey, John*
Bibliotheca Fictiva: A Collection of Books and Manuscripts Relating to Literary Forgery — *Freeman, Arthur*
Bicycle Design: An Illustrated History — *Hadland, Tony*
Biddy Debeau for His Life — *Hilton, Dan G.*
Bieganski: The Brute Polak Stereotype in Polish-Jewish Relations and American Popular Culture — *Goska, Danusha V.*
Bielefeld und die Welt: Pragungen und Impulse — *Buschenfeld, Jurgen*
Bien Cuit: The Art of Bread — *Golper, Zachary*
Biergarten Cookbook: Traditional Bavarian Recipes — *Skowronek, Julia*
Bifes Mal Passados: Passeios e outras catastrofes por terra de Sua Majestade — *Magueijo, Joao*
c The Big Adventure — *Ellis, Elina*

c Big and Small (Illus. by Chapman, Jane) — Bennett, Elizabeth
c Big-Animal Vets! — Rich, Mari
The Big Bad Book of Bill Murray: A Critical Appreciation of the World's Finest Actor — Schnakenberg, Robert
c Big Bad Detective Agency (Illus. by Hale, Bruce) — Hale, Bruce
c The Big Bad Wolf and the Robot Pig (Illus. by Cross, Kevin) — North, Laura
Big Band Drumming Fill-osophy — Fidyk, Steve
c Big Battles of World War II — Benoit, Peter
c Big Bear Little Chair (Illus. by Boyd, Lizi) — Boyd, Lizi
c Big, Bigger, Biggest — Felix, Rebecca
c Big Bill and His Little Mixer Truck — Woolpert, Rose Ann
The Big Bitch — Lang, John Patrick
The Big Blue Thing on the Hill (Illus. by Zommer, Yuval) — Zommer, Yuval
c The Big Book of Animals of the World (Illus. by Konnecke, Ole) — Konnecke, Ole
c The Big Book of Australian History, 2d ed. — Macinnis, Peter
The Big Book of Bacon: Savory Flirtations, Dalliances, and Indulgences with the Underbelly of the Pig — Pearsall, Jennifer L.S.
c The Big Book of Christmas (Illus. by Saunders, Katie) — Saunders, Katie
c The Big Book of Happy (Illus. by Marshall, Natalie) — Marshall, Natalie
The Big Book of Mod Podge: Decoupage Made Easy — Inc. Plaid Enterprises
The Big Book of Sherlock Holmes Stories — Penzler, Otto
c The Big Book of Silly (Illus. by Marshall, Natalie) — Marshall, Natalie
c The Big Book of Superheroes (Illus. by Paprocki, Greg) — King, Bart
c Big Book of the Boy — Lacey, Minna
The Big Book of Wooden Locks: Complete Plans for Nine Working Wooden Locks — Detweiler, Tim
c Big Bot, Small Bot: A Book of Robot Opposites (Illus. by Rosenthal, Marc) — Rosenthal, Marc
The Big Bout — Lister, Michael
c Big Buddy Biographies Series — Tieck, Sarah
c Big Buddy Books: Native Americans — Tieck, Sarah
c Big Buildings of the Ancient World — Scott, Dan
c Big Buildings of the Modern World — Scott, Dan
c Big Cat (Illus. by Long, Ethan) — Long, Ethan
c Big Cats, Little Cats — McKay, Sindy
c Big Cats Series — Archer, Claire
c Big Dad Bubble (Illus. by Salmieri, Daniel) — Rubin, Adam
c The Big Dark — Philbrick, Rodman
Big Data: Analysen zum Digitalen Wandel von Wissen, Macht und Okonomie — Reichert, Ramon
y Big Data Baseball: Math, Miracles, and the End of a 20-year Losing Streak — Sawchik, Travis
Big Data in a Transdisciplinary Perspective: Herrenhauser Konferenz
Big Data, Little Data, No Data: Scholarship in the Networked World — Borgman, Christine L.
c A Big Day for Migs! — Hodgkinson, Jo
c Big Dog and Little Dog (Illus. by Pilkey, Dav) — Pilkey, Dav
c Big Dog Decisions (Illus. by Montalto, Luisa) — Jakubowski, Michele
y A Big Dose of Lucky — Jocelyn, Marthe
The Big Drift — Dearen, Patrick
The Big Drugstore — Irelan, Patrick
A Big Enough Lie — Bennett, Eric
The Big Fear — Case, Andrew
The Big Fix — Grimes, Linda
y Big Freedia: God Save the Queen Diva! — Big Freedia
c Big Friends (Illus. by Davies, Benji) — Sarah, Linda
c Big Game (Read by Bakkensen, Michael). Audiobook Review — Smith, Dan (b. 1970-)
c Big Game — Gibbs, Stuart
y Big Game — Smith, Dan (b. 1970-)
Big Gay Ice Cream: Saucy Stories and Frozen Treats: Going All the Way With Ice Cream — Petroff, Bryan
Big Girl: How I Gave Up Dieting and Got a Life — Miller, Kelsey
The Big Green Tent — Ulitskaya, Ludmila
A Big Heart Open to God: A Conversation with Pope Francis — Spadaro, Antonio
c Big Hero 6 (Illus. by Ueno, Haruki) — Ueno, Haruki
c The Big Ideas of Buster Bickles (Illus. by Wasson, Dave) — Wasson, Dave

The Big Jones Cookbook: Recipes for Savoring the Heritage of Regional Southern Cooking — Fehribach, Paul
y The Big Lie — Mayhew, Julie
Big Little Felt Fun: 60+ Projects That Jump, Swim, Roll, Sprout and Roar — Lim, Jeanette
Big Little Lies (Read by Lee, Caroline). Audiobook Review — Moriarty, Liane
Big Magic: Creative Living beyond Fear (Read by Gilbert, Elizabeth). Audiobook Review — Gilbert, Elizabeth
Big Magic: Creative Living beyond Fear — Gilbert, Elizabeth
The Big Midweek: Life Inside the Fall — Hanley, Steve
c Big Nate Lives It Up — Peirce, Lincoln
c Big News! (Illus. by Pena, Karla) — Siegal, Ida
Big Porn Inc: Exposing the Harms of the Global Pornography Industry — Reist, Melinda Tankard
c The Big Princess (Illus. by Miura, Taro) — Miura, Taro
The Big Question: Why We Can't Stop Talking about Science, Faith, and God — McGrath, Alister
The Big Question: Why We Can't Stop Talking about Science, Faith, and God — McGrath, Alister E.
c Big Red Kangaroo (Illus. by Byrne, Graham) — Saxby, Claire
The Big Rewind — Cudmore, Libby
Big Science: Ernest Lawrence and the Invention That Launched the Military-Industrial Complex (Read by Souer, Bob). Audiobook Review — Hiltzik, Michael
Big Science: Ernest Lawrence and the Invention that Launched the Military-Industrial Complex — Hiltzik, Michael
The Big Screen — Thomson, David
c The Big Secret: The Whole and Honest Truth About Santa Claus (Illus. by Boorn, D.W.) — Boorn, D.W.
The Big Seven — Harrison, Jim
The Big Show: The Greatest Pilot's Story of World War II — Clostermann, Pierre
c Big Star Otto (Illus. by Slavin, Bill) — Slavin, Bill
c A Big Surprise for Little Card (Illus. by Raff, Anna) — Harper, Charise Mericle
The Big Swim: Coming Ashore in a World Adrift — Saxifrage, Carrie
c Big Time Series — Bodden, Valerie
c Big Top Burning: The True Story of an Arsonist, a Missing Girl, and the Greatest Show on Earth — Woollett, Laura A.
Big Tractor (Illus. by Clement, Nathan) — Clement, Nathan
c Big Tractors (Illus. by Nunn, Paul E.) — Dufek, Holly
The Big Trip: Your Ultimate Guide to Gap Years and Overseas Adventures, 3d ed.
Big Trophies, Epic Hunts — Boone and Crockett Club
Big Weed: An Entrepreneur's High-Stakes Adventures in Budding Legal Marijuana Business — Hageseth, Christian
Big Weed: An Entrepreneur's High-Stakes Adventures in the Budding Legal Marijuana Business — Hageseth, Christian
The Big Whatever — Doyle, Peter
Big Yoga for Less Stress — Kerr, Meera Patricia
Bigamy and Christian Identity in Late Medieval Champagne — McDougall, Sara
y The Bigfoot Book: The Encyclopedia of Sasquatch, Yeti, and Cryptid Primates — Redfern, Nick
c Bigfoot Does Not Like Birthday Parties (Illus. by Temairik, Jamie) — Ode, Eric
c Bigfoot Is Missing! (Illus. by MinaLima) — Lewis, J. Patrick
c Biggest, Baddest Book of Caves — Kuskowski, Alex
c Biggest, Baddest Book of Flight — Salzmann, Mary Elizabeth
c Biggest, Baddest Book of Ghosts — Deyoe, Aaron
c Biggest, Baddest Book of Sea Creatures (Illus. by Schoeller, Jen) — Schoeller, Jen
c Biggest, Baddest Book of Space — Schoeller, Jen
The Biggest Lover: Big Boned Men's Erotica for Chubs and Chasers — Suresha, Ron Jackson
c The Biggest Pumpkin (Illus. by Stone-Barker, Holly) — Horning, Sandra
c The Biggest Story: How the Snake Crusher Brings Us Back to the Garden (Illus. by Clark, Don) — DeYoung, Kevin
c Biggety Bat: Chow Down, Biggety! (Illus. by Zenz, Aaron) — Ingalls, Ann
y Biggie — Sullivan, Derek E.
The Bigness of the World — Ostlund, Lori

The Bigs: The Secrets Nobody Tells Students and Young Professionals About How to Find a Great Job — Carpenter, Ben
c Bijou Needs a Home (Illus. by Franson, Leanne) — Hughes, Susan
c Bike On, Bear! (Illus. by Litten, Kristyna) — Liu, Cynthea
c Bikers Are Animals 3: On the Road : A Children's Book on Motorcycling (Illus. by Jamiol, Paul) — Jamiol, Paul
c Bilby: Secrets of an Australian Marsupial (Illus. by Jackson, Mark) — Wignell, Edel
Bild: Ein Interdisziplinares Handbuch — Gunzel, Stephan
Bilder von Europa im Mittelalter — Oschema, Klaus
Bildungsreisende und Arbeitsmigrantinnen: Auslandserfahrungen Deutscher Lehrerinnen zwischen Nationaler und Internationaler Orientierung — Gippert, Wolfgang
Bilingual Development and Literacy Learning: East Asian and International Perspectives — Francis, Norbert
Bilingual Language Acquisition: Spanish and English in the First Six Years — Silva-Corvalan, Carmen
Bilingual Public Schooling in the United States: A History of America's "Polyglot Boardinghouse". — Ramsey, Paul J.
c Bill Gates: Microsoft Founder and Philanthropist — Kjelle, Marylou Morano
c Bill Gates — Harbo, Christopher L.
The Bill of Rights: James Madison and the Politics of the People's Parchment Barrier — Berkin, Carol
The Bill of Rights: The Fight To Secure America's Liberties — Berkin, Carol
The Bill of the Century — Risen, Clay
Bill O'Reilly's Legends and Lies: The Real West — O'Reilly, Bill
Billie — Gavalda, Anna
Billie Holiday: The Musician and the Myth — Szwed, John
c Billie's Great Desert Adventure (Illus. by Coburn, Alisa) — Rippin, Sally
Billion-Dollar Ball: A Journey through the Big-Money Culture of College Football — Gaul, Gilbert M.
The Billion Dollar Spy: A True Story of Cold War Espionage and Betrayal (Read by Woren, Dan). Audiobook Review — Hoffman, David E.
The Billion Dollar Spy: A True Story of Cold War Espionage and Betrayal — Hoffman, David E.
A Billion Ways to Die — Knopf, Chris
Billionaires: Reflections on the Upper Crust — West, Darrell M.
Billions to Bust--and Back: How I Made, Lost and Rebuilt a Fortune, and What I Learned on the Way — Bjorgolfsson, Thor
c Billu Leaves India: Memoirs of a Boy's Journey (Illus. by MacLeod-Brudenell, Iain) — Subhra, Gersh
c Billy and Goat at the State Fair (Read by Heyborne, Kirby). Audiobook Review — Yaccarino, Dan
c Billy and Goat at the State Fair (Illus. by Yaccarino, Dan) — Yaccarino, Dan
Billy Martin: Baseball's Flawed Genius — Pennington, Bill
Billy Mitchell's War with the Navy: The Interwar Rivalry over Air Power — Wildenberg, Thomas
Billy Name--the Silver Age: Black & White Photographs from Andy Warhol's Factory — Name, Billy
c Billy Sure, Kid Entrepreneur (Illus. by Ross, Graham) — Sharpe, Luke
c Billy the Bully (Illus. by Vasquez, Romney) — Palmer, Lacretia
c Billy the Monkey, or the Prince of the Amazon (Illus. by Kenens, Sofie) — Walcker, Yann
c Billy's Booger (Illus. by Joyce, William) — Joyce, William
Binary Star — Gerard, Sarah
Binational Human Rights: The U.S.-Mexico Experience — Simmons, William Paul
The Bind — Goldsmith, William
Binge (Read by Oakley, Tyler). Audiobook Review — Oakley, Tyler
c Binny in Secret (Illus. by Player, Micah) — McKay, Hilary
Binoculars: Masquerading as a Sighted Person — DiMeo, Philip F.
c Binoculars — Koontz, Robin
Bio-Young: Get Younger at a Cellular and Hormonal Level — Dillon, Roxy
Biocode: The New Age of Genomics — Field, Dawn
Biodiversity Conservation and Environmental Change — Gillson, Lindsey

Biodiversity Monitoring and Conservation: Bridging the Gap between Global Commitment and Local Action — Collen, Ben
Biodynamic Gardening — Waldin, Monty
Bioethics and the Human Goods: An Introduction to Natural Law Bioethics — Gomez-Lobo, Alfonso
Biogeography of Australasia: A Molecular Analysis — Heads, Michael
Biographia Literaria: Or, Biographical Sketches of My Literary Life and Opinions — Coleridge, Samuel Taylor
Biographie and Politique: Vie publique, vie privee, de l'Ancien Regime a la Restauration — Ferret, Olivier
Biographisches Handbuch des Deutschen Auswartigen Dienstes 1871-1945, vol. 5: T-Z — Isphording, Bernd
Biography and the Black Atlantic — Lindsay, Lisa A.
Biography of a Hacienda: Work and Revolution in Rural Mexico — Newman, Elizabeth Terese
A Biography of Paul Berg: The Recombinant DNA: Controversy Revisited — Friedberg, Errol C.
A Biography of the Spirit — Haughey, John
Biological Autonomy: A Philosophical and Theoretical Inquiry — Moreno, Alvaro
Biological Relatives: IVF, Stem Cells, and the Future of Kinship — Franklin, Sarah
The Biologist's Imagination: Innovation in the Biosciences — Hoffman, William
Biology after the Sociobiology Debate: What Introductory Textbooks Say About the Nature of Science and Organisms — Schilfellite, Carmen James
The Biology and Ecology of Tintinnid Ciliates: Models for Marine Plankton — Dolan, John R.
The Biology Book: From the Origin of Life to Epigenics, 250 Milestones in the History of Biology — Gerald, Michael C
The Biology of Chameleons — Tolley, Krystal A.
The Biology of Desire: Why Addiction Is Not a Disease — Lewis, Marc
y Bioluminescence: Nature and Science at Work — Zimmer, Marc
c Biomedical Engineering and Human Body Systems — Sjonger, Rebecca
Biometrics State: The Global Politics of Identification and Surveillance in South Africa, 1850 to the Present — Breckenridge, Keith
Biophilia — Marley, Christopher
Biopolitical Screens: Image, Power, and the Neoliberal Brain — Valiaho, Pasi
Biopolitik und Sittlichkeitsreform: Kampagnen Gegen Alkohol, Drogen und Prostitution 1880-1950 — Grosse, Judith
Biosocial Becomings: Integrating Social and Biological Anthropology — Ingold, Tim
Biracial in America: Forming and Performing Racial Identity — Khanna, Nikki
Bird — Holland, Noy
c Bird (Illus. by Vidal, Beatriz Martin) — Vidal, Beatriz Martin
c Bird and Bear (Illus. by James, Ann) — James, Ann
c Bird & Diz (Illus. by Young, Ed) — Golio, Gary
c Bird-Eating Spiders — Archer, Claire
A Bird in the Hand: Chicken Recipes for Every Day and Every Mood — Henry, Diana
c A Bird Is a Bird (Illus. by Rockwell, Lizzy) — Rockwell, Lizzy
c Bird & Squirrel on the Edge! (Illus. by Burks, James) — Burks, James
c BirdCatDog: A Graphic Novel (Illus. by Bosch, Meritxell) — Nordling, Lee
c Birdie's Big-Girl School Day (Illus. by Rim, Sujean) — Rim, Sujean
c Birdie's First Day of School (Illus. by Rim, Sujean) — Rim, Sujean
Birding by Impression: A Different Approach to Knowing and Identifying Birds — Karlson, Kevin T.
Birdmen: The Wright Brothers, Glenn Curtiss, and the Battle to Control the Skies — Goldstone, Lawrence
c Birdology: 30 Activities and Observations for Exploring the World of Birds — Russo, Monica
The Birds — Vesaas, Tarjei
Birds and Climate Change: Impacts and Conservation Responses — Pearce-Higgins, James W.
Birds and Frogs: Selected Papers, 1990-2014 — Dyson, Freeman J.
Birds and Frogs: Selected Papers, 1990-2014 — Dyson, Freeman J.
Bird's Flight — Murphy, Audrey
c Birds — Murray, Julie
c Birds — Royston, Angela

The Birds of London — Self, Andrew
c Birds — Arlon, Penelope
c Birds — Morey, Allan
Birds without Wings — Bernieres, Louis de
c BirdWingFeather — Schillios, Siri
Birdy — Vallance, Jess
c The Birdy Snatchers (Illus. by Marko, Cyndi) — Marko, Cyndi
Birrung: The Secret Friend — French, Jackie
Birth of a Bridge — de Kerangal, Maylis
The Birth of a Genetics Policy: Social Issues of Newborn Screening — Vailly, Joelle
The Birth of a Nation: How a Legendary Filmmaker and a Crusading Editor Reignited America's Civil War — Lehr, Dick
The Birth of a Nation — McEwan, Paul
Birth of a Theorem: A Mathematical Adventure — Villani, Cedric
The Birth of American Law: An Italian Philosopher and the American Revolution — Bessler, John D.
The Birth of Chinese Feminism: Essential Texts in Transnational Theory — Liu, Lydia H.
The Birth of Insight: Meditation, Modern Buddhism, and the Burmese Monk Ledi Sayadaw — Braun, Erik
y The Birth of Modern India — Dunn, John M.
The Birth of New Criticism: Conflict and Conciliation in the Early Works of William Empson, I.A. Richards, Robert Graves and Laura Riding — Childs, Donald J.
The Birth of Territory — Elden, Stuart
The Birth of the New Justice: The Internationalization of Crime and Punishment, 1919-1950 — Lewis, Mark
The Birth of the Pill: How Four Crusaders Reinvented Sex and Launched a Revolution — Eig, Jonathan
The Birth of the Royal Air Force: An Encyclopedia of British Air Power Before and During the Great War 1914 to 1918 — Philpott, Ian M.
The Birth of the Royal Marines, 1664-1802 — Zerbe, Britt
The Birth of Theory — Cole, Andrew
c A Birthday Basket for Tia (Illus. by Lang, Cecily) — Mora, Pat
c A Birthday Cake for George Washington (Illus. by Brantley-Newton, Vanessa) — Ganeshram, Ramin
c The Birthday Cake: The Adventures of Pettson and Findus (Illus. by Nordqvist, Sven) — Nordqvist, Sven
c The Birthday Elephant (Illus. by Williams, Walter) — Williams, Walter
The Birthday Lunch — Clark, Joan
c Birthday Mice! (Illus. by Cushman, Doug) — Roberts, Bethany
c Birthday Party SBD (Illus. by Badon, Joe) — Passo, Elizabeth
c Birthday Vicious — de la Cruz, Melissa
Birthright — Jones, Mike
y Birthright, vol. 1: Homecoming (Illus. by Bressan, Andrei) — Williamson, Joshua
Bischofsbild und Bischofssitz: Geistige und geistliche Impulse aus regionalen Zentren des Hochmittelalters — Neuheuser, Hanns Peter
Bishop McIlvaine, Slavery, Britain and the Civil War — Smith, Richard W.
Bishops, Bourbons, and Big Mules: A History of the Episcopal Church in Alabama — Vaughn, J. Barry
Bishops, Clerks, and Diocesan Governance in Thirteenth-Century England: Reward and Punishment — Burger, Michael
Bishops on the Border: Pastoral Responses to Immigration — Adams, Mark
The Bishop's Utopia: Envisioning Improvement in Colonial Peru — Soule, Emily Berquist
y The Bishop's Wife (Read by Potter, Kirsten). Audiobook Review — Harrison, Mette Ivie
Bismarck: A Life — Steinberg, Jonathan
Bismarck: Grosse - Grenzen - Leistungen — Kraus, Hans-Christof
Bison — Morris, Desmond
Bitch Planet, bk.1: Extraordinary Machine (Illus. by De Landro, Valentine) — DeConnick, Kelly Sue
Bitch Planet, vol. 1 — DeConnick, Kelly Sue
Bite at First Sight — Ann, Brooklyn
Bite the Biscuit — Johnston, Linda O.
y Bits and Pieces — Maberry, Jonathan
c Bitsy Bee Goes to School — Carter, David A.
Bitter Bite — Estep, Jennifer
Bitter Bronx — Charyn, Jerome
Bitter Bronx: Thirteen Stories — Charyn, Jerome
Bitter Creek — Bowen, Peter

Bitter Freedom: Ireland in a Revolutionary World, 1918-1923 — Walsh, Maurice
c A Bitter Magic — Townley, Roderick
Bitter Roots: The Search for Healing Plants in Africa — Osseo-Asare, Abena Dove
Bitter Rose — Delvaux, Martine
The Bitter Season — Hoag, Tami
y The Bitter Side of Sweet — Sullivan, Tara
Bitter Waters — Hurd, Brian
Bittersweet — Albert, Susan Wittig
Bittersweet Creek — Kilpatrick, Sally
c Bizarre mais vrai! 300fets renversants — National Geographic Kids
Bizet — Macdonald, Hugh
c Bizzy Bear: Knights' Castle (Illus. by Davis, Benjie) — Davis, Benjie
c Bizzy Bear's Big Building Book (Illus. by Davies, Benji) — Davies, Benji
c Blabbering Bethann — Britt, Chris
Black — Vassar, Joan
Black against Empire: The History and Politics of the Black Panther Party — Martin, Waldo E.
The Black Album: Il noir tra cronaca e romanzo — Amici, Marco
Black and Blue: The Redd Foxx Story — Starr, Michael Seth
Black and Brown in Los Angeles: Beyond Conflict and Coalition — Kun, Josh
Black and Brown Planets: The Politics of Race in Science Fiction — Lavender, Isiah, III
Black and White and Dead All Over — Castle, Anna
c Black and White in Winter — Carole, Bonnie
c Black and White Nighty-Night — Jones, Sarah
c Black and White (Illus. by Ipcar, Dahlov) — Ipcar, Dahlov
c Black and White — Macaulay, David
Black Asset Poverty and the Enduring Racial Divide — Martin, Lori Latrice
The Black Atlantic Reconsidered: Black Canadian Writing, Cultural History, and the Presence of the Past — Siemerling, Winfried
Black Bart Reborn — Bartholomew, Steve
Black Baseball, Black Business: Race Enterprise and the Fate of the Segregated Dollar — Newman, Roberta J.
c Black Bears — Borgert-Spaniol, Megan
The Black Body in Ecstasy: Reading Race, Reading Pornography — Nash, Jennifer C.
The Black Box Society: The Secret Algorithms That Control Money and Information — Pasquale, Frank
Black British Intellectuals and Education: Multiculturalism's Hidden History — Warmington, Paul
Black British Jazz: Ownership and Performance — Toynbee, Jason
Black Broadway: African Americans on the Great White Way — Lane, Stewart F.
Black-Brown Solidarity: Racial Politics in the New Gulf South — Marquez, John D.
y Black Cairn Point — McFall, Claire
The Black Calhouns: From Civil War to Civil Rights with One African American Family — Buckley, Gail Lumet
Black Canyon — Bates, Jeremy
The Black Carriage — Crutchley, Edward B.
Black Cat Bone: Poems — Burnside, John
c Black Cat, White Cat (Illus. by Borando, Silvia) — Borando, Silvia
Black Chalk — Yates, Christopher J.
The Black Child-Savers: Racial Democracy and Juvenile Justice — Ward, Geoff K.
Black Citizenship and Authenticity in the Civil Rights Movement — Hoble, Randooph
Black City Saint — Knaak, Richard A.
Black Citymakers: How The Philadelphia Negro Changed Urban America — Hunter, Marcus Anthony
Black Country — Berry, Liz
Black Creek — Lamberson, Gregory
y The Black Crow Conspiracy — Edge, Christopher
Black Dawn — Harber, Cristin
Black Deutschland — Pinckney, Darryl
Black Diamond — Mda, Zakes
Black Dog Summer (Read by Bond, Jilly). Audiobook Review — Sherry, Miranda
Black Dog Summer — Sherry, Miranda
y Black Dove, White Raven — Wein, Elizabeth
c The Black Dragon — Sedgwick, Julian
Black Dragon River: A Journey down the Amur River at the Borderlands of Empires — Ziegler, Dominic

Black Earth: The Holocaust as History and Warning (Read by Bramhall, Mark). Audiobook Review — Snyder, Timothy
Black Earth: The Holocaust as History and Warning — Snyder, Timothy
Black Ethnics: Race, Immigration, and the Pursuit of the American Dream — Greer, Christina M.
The Black-Eyed Blonde — Black, Benjamin
Black Eyed Susans (Read by Dykhouse, Whitney). Audiobook Review — Heaberlin, Julia
Black-Eyed Susans — Heaberlin, Julia
Black Faculty in the Academy: Narratives for Negotiating Identity and Achieving Career Success — Bonner, Fred A., III
Black Feathers — Wiersema, Robert
Black Flags: The Rise of ISIS — Warrick, Joby
Black Folklore and the Politics of Racial Representation — Moody-Turner, Shirley
The Black Fountain Goddess — Moynahan, Jean
Black France/France Noire: The History and Politics of Blackness — Keaton, Trica Danielle
Black Freedom, White Resistance, and Red Menace: Civil Rights and Anticommunism in the Jim Crow South — Katagiri, Yasuhiro
Black Genesis: The Prehistoric Origins of Ancient Egypt — Bauval, Robert
Black Girl Dangerous: On Race, Queerness, Class, and Gender — McKenzie, Mia
Black Glass — Fowler, Karen Joy
Black Hole: How an Idea Abandoned by Newtonians, Hated by Einstein, and Gambled on by Hawking Became Loved — Bartusiak, Marcia
Black Hole — Sinister, Bucky
c Black Horizon — Harris, M.G.
The Black House — May, Peter
y Black Ice — Fitzpatrick, Becca
Black Ice — Morgan, Max
Black Inked Pearl — Finnegan, Ruth
Black Internationalist Feminism: Woman Writers of the Black Left, 1945-1995 — Higashida, Cheryl
Black Intersectionalities: A Critique for the 21st Century — Michlin, Monica
Black Iris — Raeder, Leah
Black Is Not a Color — Gaston, Rozsa
Black Jews in Africa and the Americas — Parfitt, Tudor
The Black Jews of Africa: History, Religion, Identity — Bruder, Edith
y Black Knight — Pike, Christopher
Black Legacies: Race and the European Middle Ages — Ramey, Lynn T.
Black Life in Old New Orleans — Medley, Keith Weldon
y The Black Lotus — Fanning, Kieran
Black Males in Postsecondary Education: Examining Their Experiences in Diverse Institutional Contexts — Wood, Luke J.
c Black Mambas — Franchino, Vicky
Black Man in a White Coat: A Doctor's Reflections on Race and Medicine — Tweedy, Damon
Black Market Britain, 1939-1955 — Roodhouse, Mark
Black Medea: Adaptations for Modern Plays — Wetmore, K.J., Jr.
The Black Mirror: Fragments of an Obituary for Life — Tallis, Raymond
The Black Mirror: Looking at Life through Death — Tallis, Raymond
Black Morocco: A History of Slavery, Race, and Islam — Hamel, Chouki el
The Black Musician and the White City: Race and Music in Chicago, 1900-1967 — Absher, Amy
The Black Officer Corps: A History of Black Military Advancement from Integration through Vietnam — Hampton, Isaac
Black Panthers for Beginners (Illus. by Tooks, Lance) — Boyd, Herb
Black Pearls of Wisdom: Voicing the African-American Journey for Freedom, Empowerment, and the Future — Spivey, Donald
Black Performance Theory — DeFrantz, Thomas F.
c Black Plus — Tamarkin, Annette
Black Poet — Ali, Cassius
Black Power in the Caribbean — Quinn, Kate
The Black Power Movement and American Social Work — Bell, Joyce M.
c The Black Power Movement — Rissman, Rebecca
The Black Presidency — Dyson, Michael Eric
Black Print with a White Carnation: Mildred Brown and the Omaha Star Newspaper, 1938-1989 — Forss, Amy Helene
Black Prophetic Fire — West, Cornel
Black Rabbit Hall — Chase, Eve

c The Black Reckoning (Read by Dale, Jim). Audiobook Review — Stephens, John
y The Black Reckoning — Stephens, John
Black Regions of the Imagination: African American Writers between the Nation and the World — Dunbar, Eve
Black River (Read by Newbern, George). Audiobook Review — Hulse, S.M.
Black River (Illus. by Simmons, Josh) — Simmons, Josh
Black Run — Manzini, Antonio
Black Sabbath: Symptom of the Universe — Wall, Mick
Black Scorpion: The Tyrant Reborn — Land, Jon
Black Silent Majority: The Rockefeller Drug Laws and the Politics of Punishment — Fortner, Michael Javen
Black Skin, White Coats: Nigerian Psychiatrists, Decolonization, and the Globalization of Psychiatry — Heaton, Matthew M.
The Black Snow — Lynch, Paul
Black Sparta — Mitchison, Naomi
Black Spokane: The Civil Rights Struggle in the Inland Northwest — Mack, Dwayne A.
Black Star: Britain's Asian Youth Movements — Ranamurthy, Anandi
Black Star, Crescent Moon: The Muslim International and Black Freedom beyond America — Daulatzai, Sohail
y The Black Stars — Krokos, Dan
Black Stars — Ngo Tu Lap
Black Sun Descending — Legault, Stephen
Black Tide Rising — McMillen, R.J.
Black Valley — Williams, Charlotte
Black Vodka: Ten Stories — Levy, Deborah
Black, White, and Red All Over: A Cultural History of the Radical Press in Its Heyday, 1900-1917 — Lumsden, Linda J.
Black & White Cinema: A Short History — Dixon, Wheeler Winston
Black Widow Spiders — Hesper, Sam
Black Witch — Scott, Steve
Black Wolf — Shangraw, Steph
Black Wolves — Elliott, Kate
Black Woman Reformer: Ida B. Wells, Lynching, and Transatlantic Activism — Silkey, Sarah L.
Black Women against the Land Grab: The Fight for Racial Justice in Brazil — Perry, Keisha-Khan Y.
Black Women and Politics in New York City — Gallagher, Julie A.
y Black Wreath: The Stolen Life of James Lovett — Sirr, Peter
Blackass — Barrett, A. Igoni
Blackballed: The Black Vote and U.S. Democracy — Pinckney, Darryl
Blackballed: The Black & White Politics of Race on America's Campuses — Ross, Lawrence
c Blackbeard — Gagne, Tammy
c Blackbird — Carey, Anna
Blackbird — Wright, Tom
c Blackbird Fly — Kelly, Erin Entrada
c Blackfire's Back! (Illus. by Nauck, Todd) — Torres, J. (b. 1969-)
c Blackfoot — Tieck, Sarah
y Blackhearts — Castroman, Nicole
Black'Mor Chronicles: The Cursed; Welcome to the Park of Chimeras — Black'Mor, Elian
c Blackout — Black, Peter Jay
Blackout — Rosenfelt, David
Blackout: Remembering the Things I Drank to Forget (Read by Hepola, Sarah). Audiobook Review — Hepola, Sarah
Blackout: Remembering the Things I Drank to Forget — Hepola, Sarah
c The Blackthorn Key (Read by Panthaki, Ray). Audiobook Review — Sands, Kevin
c The Blackthorn Key — Sands, Kevin
y Blade Singer — De Orive, Aaron
Blair Inc.: The Man behind the Mask — Beckett, Francis
Blaise Pascal on Duplicity, Sin, and the Fall: The Secret Instinct — Wood, William
c Blake Griffin — Gregory, Josh
c Blake the Baker: Develop Understanding of Fractions and Numbers — Quinlivan, Ada
The Blameless Victim — Rhodes, Harold
c Blanche Hates the Night (Illus. by Delacroix, Sibylle) — Delacroix, Sibylle
y Blank — St. Jean, Trina
The Blank Verse Tradition from Milton to Stevens: Freethinking and the Crisis of Modernity — Weinfield, Henry

c A Blanket Quite Rare (Illus. by Ikegami, Lisa Geotus) — Ikegami, Lisa Geotus
Blaze Away — James, Bill
A Blaze of Glory — Shaara, Jeff
c Blazing Courage — Halls, Kelly Milner
c The Blazing Star — Hunter, Erin
The Blazing World — Hustvedt, Siri
y Bleed Like Me — Desir, Christa
y Bleeding Earth — Ward, Kaitlin
Bleeding Kansas, Bleeding Missouri: The Long Civil War on the Border — Earle, Jonathan
Bleeding Talent: How the U.S. Military Mismanages Great Leaders and Why It's Time for a Revolution — Kane, Tim
Bleedovers — Rose, William Todd
Blended: Writers on the Stepfamily Experience — Waltz, Samantha
Blender for Animation and Film-Based Production — Manrique, Michelangelo
Blessed McGill — Shrake, Edwin
The Blessing of Movement — Konrad, Deborah
A Blessing Well Disguised: A Blinded Artist's Inner Journey out of the Dark — Burlingame, Lloyd
c The Blessings of Friendship Treasury (Illus. by Engelbreit, Mary) — Engelbreit, Mary
The Bletchley Girls — Dunlop, Tessa
y Blind — DeWoskin, Rachel
c The Blind Boy & the Loon (Illus. by Arnaquq-Baril, Alethea) — Arnaquq-Baril, Alethea
Blind Eye — Gorman, Jane
c A Blind Guide to Stinkville — Vrabel, Beth
Blind Reef — Tonkin, Peter
y A Blind Spot for Boys — Chen, Justina
Blind to Sameness: Sexpectations and the Social Construction of Male and Female Bodies — Friedman, Asia
Blinded by Sight: Seeing Race through the Eyes of the Blind — Obasogie, Osagie K.
y Blinded by the Light (Illus. by Rocafort, Kenneth) — Pfeifer, Will
Blinders, Blunders, and Wars: What America and China Can Learn — Gompert, David C.
y Blindside — Chambers, Aidan
Blindsided by God: Disappointment, Suffering, and the Untamable Goodness of God — Chin, Peter
y A Blink of the Screen: Collected Shorter Fiction — Pratchett, Terry
y Bliss — Mitchell, Shay
c The Blitz Next Door — Forde, Cathy
c Blizzard — Markovics, Joyce
The Blizzard — Gambrell, Jamey
The Blizzard — Sorokin, Vladimir
c Blizzard (Illus. by Rocco, John) — Rocco, John
c Blizzard: Colorado, 1886 — Duey, Kathleen
c Block Party Surprise (Illus. by Henninger, Michelle) — Nolen, Jerdine
Blog: Writings, Interviews, and Digital Rants, 2006-2009 — Weiwei, Ai
y Blonde Eskimo — Hunt, Kristen
The Blondes — Schultz, Emily
Blood: A Critique of Christianity — Anidjar, Gil
Blood Aces: The Wild Ride of Benny Binion, the Texas Gangster Who Created Vegas Poker — Swanson, Doug
Blood and Earth: Modern Slavery, Ecocide, and the Secret to Saving the World — Bales, Kevin
Blood and Gold — Starmer, Clay
c Blood and Guts and Rats' Tail Pizza (Illus. by Fisher, Chris) — French, Vivian
Blood and Home in Early Modern Drama: Domestic Identity on the Renaissance Stage — Balizet, Ariane M.
Blood and Ink: Ignacio Ellacuria, Jon Sobrino, and the Jesuit Martyrs of the University of Central America — Lassalle-Klein, Robert
Blood and Rain. E-book Review — Rolfe, Glenn
y Blood and Salt — Liggett, Kim
Blood Brothers — Haffner, Ernst
Blood Brothers: The Fatal Friendship between Muhammad Ali and Malcolm X — Roberts, Randy
Blood Call — Saintcrow, Lilith
Blood Cries Afar: The Forgotten Invasion of England, 1216 — McGlynn, Sean
Blood-Drenched Beard — Galera, Daniel
Blood Father — Dawn, Tessa
Blood Foam — DuBois, Brendan
Blood for Blood — Wolf, Ben
Blood in Her Veins: Nineteen Stories from the World of Jane Yellowrock — Hunter, Faith
Blood Libel in Late Imperial Russia: The Ritual Murder Trial of Mendel Beilis — Weinberg, Robert
Blood Lyrics — Ford, Katie

Blood Money — Lister, Michael
Blood Moon — Lister, Michael
c Blood Oath — Scott, Dan
y Blood of My Blood — Lyga, Barry
Blood of My Fathers — Bornstein, Bernard
y The Blood of Olympus — Riordan, Rick
Blood of the Cosmos — Anderson, Kevin J.
Blood Oil: Tyrants, Violence, and the Rules That Run the World — Wenar, Leif
Blood on Snow (Read by Smith, Patti). Audiobook Review — Nesbo, Jo
Blood on Snow — Nesbo, Jo
Blood on Snow — Smith, Neil
Blood on the Stage, 480 B.C. to 1600 A.D.: Milestone Plays of Murder, Mystery, and Mayhem - An Annotated Repertoire — Kabatchnik, Amnon
Blood on the Tides: The Ozidi Saga and Oral Epic Narratology — Okpewho, Isidore
y Blood Passage — Demetrios, Heather
Blood Ransom: Stories from the Front Line in the War against Somali Piracy — Boyle, John
Blood Red — Staub, Wendy Corsi
Blood Runs Green: The Murder That Transfixed Gilded Age Chicago — O'Brien, Gillian
Blood, Salt, Water — Mina, Denise
Blood Sisters — Masterton, Graham
Blood Sisters: The Women behind the Wars of the Roses — Gristwood, Sarah
Blood Sisters: Vampire Stories — Guran, Paula
Blood & Steel — Sidebottom, Harry
The Blood Strand — Ould, Chris
Blood Sweep — Havill, Steven F.
Blood Ties — Guild, Nicholas
Blood Ties: Religion, Violence, and the Politics of Nationhood in Ottoman Macedonia, 1878-1908 — Yosmaoglu, Ipek
Blood Vengeance — Dawn, Tessa
Blood Will Tell — Dams, Jeanne M.
y Blood Will Tell — Henry, April
Blood Wizard Chronicles — Erickson, Jay
The Blooding — McGee, James
y Bloodkin — Atwater-Rhodes, Amelia
Bloodshot Reborn: Colorado — Lemire, Jeff
Bloodspell — Dini, Paul
y Bloodstone: Legend of Ironheart (Illus. by van Deelan, Fred) — Boroughs, Allan
The Bloody Chamber and Other Stories — Carter, Angela
Bloody Lowndes: Civil Rights and Black Power in Alabama's Black Belt — Jeffries, Hasan Kwame
Bloody Royal Prints — Williams, Reba White
Bloody Sunday — Johnstone, J.A.
c Bloom (Illus. by Small, David) — Cronin, Doreen
The Bloomsbury Anthology of Contemporary Jewish American Poetry — Ager, Deborah
The Bloomsbury Group Memoir Club — Rosenbaum, S.P.
The Bloomsbury Introduction to Creative Writing — Mokhtari, Tara
The Bloomsbury Introduction to Popular Fiction — Berberich, Christine
Bloomsbury's Outsider: A Life of David Garnett — Knights, Sarah
A Blossom of Bright Light — Chazin, Suzanne
The Blossoms of Sixty-Four Sunsets — Durga Lai Shrestha
Blowing the Roof off the Twenty-First Century — McChesney, Robert W.
c Blown Away (Illus. by Biddulph, Rob) — Biddulph, Rob
Blue — Domanick, Joe
y Blue — Glass, Lisa
The Blue and the Grey — Trow, M.J.
c Blue and Yellow in Summer — Carole, Bonnie
c Blue Animals — Borth, Teddy
c Blue Balloons and Rabbit Ears — Offen, Hilda
The Blue Between Sky and Water — Abulhawa, Susan
y Blue Birds — Rose, Caroline Starr
Blue Book of Gun Values, 36th ed. — Fjestad, S.P.
c Blue Bottle Mystery — Hoopmann, Kathy
The Blue — Clarke, Lucy
Blue-Collar Broadway: The Craft and Industry of American Theater — White, Timothy R.
Blue Collar Conservatives: Recommitting to an America That Works — Santorum, Rick
Blue Darker Than Black — Jenne, Mike
y The Blue Dragon — Tierney, Ronald
Blue-Eyed Boy: A Memoir — Timberg, Robert
Blue-Eyed Stranger — Beecroft, Alex
Blue Fasa — Mackey, Nathaniel
The Blue Flower — McWilliam, Candia
The Blue Folio — McMahon, Matt

c The Blue Forest (Illus. by Young, Stephanie) — Fischer, Luke
Blue Future: Protecting Water for People and the Planet Forever — Barlow, Maude
Blue Gemini — Jenne, Mike
The Blue Guitar — Banville, John
Blue Hanuman — Larkin, Joan
Blue Horses: Poems — Oliver, Mary
The Blue Hour — Kennedy, Douglas
y Blue Iguana — Townsend, Wendy
Blue in a Red State — Krebs, Justin
c Blue in the Face: A Story of Risk, Rhyme, and Rebellion — Swallow, Gerry
Blue Ink — Liang, David
Blue Is the Warmest Color — Maroh, Julie
Blue Labour: Forging a New Politics — Geary, Ian
Blue Labyrinth (Read by Auberjonois, Rene). Audiobook Review — Preston, Douglas
y Blue Lily, Lily Blue (Read by Patton, Will). Audiobook Review — Stiefvater, Maggie
y Blue Lily, Lily Blue — Stiefvater, Maggie
The Blue Line — Betancourt, Ingrid
Blue Mondays: The Complete Series — Dubberley, Emily
c Blue Moon (Illus. by Oktober, Tricia) — Oktober, Tricia
c Blue Mountain — Leavitt, Martine
Blue Ocean Strategy: How to Create Uncontested Market Space and Make the Competition Irrelevant — Kim, W. Chan
c Blue on Blue (Illus. by Krommes, Beth) — White, Dianne
c Blue Penguin and the Sensational Surf (Illus. by Low, Alan M.) — Wacker, Eileen
Blue Ravens — Vizenor, Gerald
Blue Ribbon Canning: Spreads, Sauces and More — Amendt, Linda J.
c Blue Ribbon Summer — Hapka, Catherine
Blue Ribbon Vegetable Gardening: The Secrets to Growing the Biggest and Best Prizewinning Produce — Torpey, Jodi
Blue Sky — Kindall, Brian
Blue Stars — Gray, Emily
Blue Sun, Yellow Sky — Hoang, Jamie Jo
Blue: The LAPD and the Battle to Redeem American Policing — Domanick, Joe
Blue, Too: More Writing by (for or about) Working-Class Queers — Ricketts, Wendell
The Blue Touch Paper: A Memoir — Hare, David
c The Blue Vase (Illus. by Bisaillon, Josee) — Jovanovic, Katarina
y Blue Voyage — Renn, Diana
c Blue Whale Blues (Illus. by Carnavas, Peter) — Carnavas, Peter
c The Blue Whale (Illus. by Desmond, Jenni) — Desmond, Jenni
c The Blue Whale — Desmond, Jenni
y The Blue Woods — Maggi, Nicole
Blue Yodel — Elkins, Ansel
Blue Yonders, Grateful Pies, and Other Fanciful Feasts — Scholes, Ken
The Blue Zones Solution: Eating and Living Like the World's Healthiest People — Buettner, Dan
Blueberry Boys — North, Vanessa
Blueprint for Tomorrow: Redesigning Schools for Student-Centered Learning — Nair, Prakash
Blueprints — Delinsky, Barbara
Blues for folkhemmet: Noranalyse af Arne Dahls Europa Blues — Kirkegaard, Peter
y Blues for Zoey — Weston, Robert Paul
y Bluescreen — Wells, Dan
Bluestone: New and Selected Poems — Lasdun, James
The Blumhouse Book of Nightmares: The Haunted City — Blum, Jason
The Blunders of Our Governments — King, Anthony
c BMX Champion — Nixon, James
c BMX — Hamilton, John
y Bo at Iditarod Creek (Illus. by Pham, LeUyen) — Hill, Kirkpatrick
c Boa Constrictors: Prey-Crushing Reptiles — Hirsch, Rebecca E.
y Boarding School Girls — Eve, Helen
Boarding School Syndrome: The Psychological Trauma of the 'Privileged' Child — Schaverien, Joy
Boardroom Scandal: The Criminalization of Company Fraud in Nineteenth-Century Britain — Taylor, James
y The Boardwalk — Coleman, Reed Farrel
c Boas — McDonald, Mary Ann
The Boatmaker — Benditt, John
c Boats — Murray, Julie
Boats and Harbours in Acrylic — Evans, Charles

c Boats Float! (Illus. by Wiggins, Mick) — Lyon, George Ella
c Boats for Papa (Illus. by Bagley, Jessixa) — Bagley, Jessixa
c Boats Go (Illus. by Light, Steve) — Light, Steve
c Bob and Flo (Illus. by Ashdown, Rebecca) — Ashdown, Rebecca
Bob Dylan: All the Songs: The Story behind Every Track — Margotin, Philippe
c Bob Is a Unicorn (Illus. by Nelson-Schmidt, Michelle) — Nelson-Schmidt, Michelle
Bob the Railway Dog (Illus. by McLean, Andrew) — Fenton, Corinne
c Bobby and Mandee's Too Safe for Strangers (Illus. by Cotton, Sue Lynn) — Kahn, Robert
Bobby Wonderful: An Imperfect Son Buries His Parents — Morris, Bob
Boccaccio: A Critical Guide to the Complete Works — Kirkham, Victoria
Boccaccio umanista: Studi su Boccaccio e Apuleio — Candido, Igor
Boccaccio's Fabliaux: Medieval Short Stories and the Function of Reversal — Brown, Katherine A.
c Bodie: The Town That Belongs to Ghosts — Blake, Kevin
Bodies and Books: Reading and the Fantasy of Communion in Nineteenth-Century America — Silverman, Gillian
Bodies and Things in Nineteenth-Century Literature and Culture — Boehm, Katharina
Bodies beyond Borders: The Circulation of Anatomical Knowledge, 1750-1950
Bodies in Balance: The Art of Tibetan Medicine — Hofer, Theresia
Bodies of Knowledge in Ancient Mesopotamia: The Diviners of Late Bronze Age Emar and Their Tablet Collection — Rutz, Matthew
Bodies of Light — Moss, Sarah
Bodies on the Line: Performance and the Sixties Poetry Reading — Allison, Raphael
y The Bodies We Wear — Roberts, Jeyn
Body and Nation: The Global Realm of U.S. Body Politics in the Twentieth Century — Rosenberg, Emily S.
c Body Bones (Illus. by Rotner, Shelley) — Rotner, Shelley
y Body by Darwin: How Evolution Shapes Our Health and Transforms Medicine — Taylor, Jeremy
Body by Weimar: Athletes, Gender and German Modernity — Jensen, Erik N.
Body Counts: The Vietnam War and Militarized Refugees — Espiritu, Yen Le
Body, Dress, and Identity in Ancient Greece — Lee, Mireille M.
Body Electric — Revis, Beth
Body Fuel: Calorie-Cycle Your Way to Reduced Body Fat and Greater Muscle Definition — Lauren, Mark
Body Image and Identity in Contemporary Societies: Psychoanalytical, Social, Cultural, and Aesthetic Perspectives — Sukhanova, Ekaterina
The Body in Mystery: The Political Theology of the Corpus Mysticum in the Literature of Reformation England — Rust, Jennifer R.
The Body in the Belfry (Read by Eby, Tanya). Audiobook Review — Page, Katherine Hall
The Body in the Birches: A Faith Fairchild Mystery — Page, Katherine Hall
The Body in the Birches — Page, Katherine Hall
y The Body Institute — Riggs, Carol
Body Intelligence: Harness Your Body's Energies for Your Best Life — Cardillo, Joseph
Body Knowledge: Performance, Intermediality, and American Entertainment at the Turn of the Twentieth Century — Simonson, Mary
The Body of Faith: A Biological History of Religion in America — Fuller, Robert C.
Body of Truth: How Science, History, and Culture Drive Our Obsession with Weight--and What We Can Do about It — Brown, Harriet
A Body Politic to Govern: The Political Humanism of Elizabeth I — Booth, Ted
Body Shots — Rainey, Anne
The Body Snatcher — Landers, Clifford E.
A Body to Spare — Jaffarian, Sue Ann
A Body, Undone — Crosby, Christina
The Body Where I Was Born — Nettel, Guadalupe
Body-Worlds: Opicinus de Canistris and the Medieval Cartographic Imagination — Whittington, Karl
A Body You Have Prepared for Me: The Spirituality of the Letter to the Hebrews — McCruden, Kevin
A Bodyguard of Lies — Eich, Raymond

Boethius as a Paradigm of Late Ancient Thought — Kirchner, Andreas
Bog Bodies Uncovered: Solving Europe's Ancient Mystery — Aldhouse-Green, Miranda
Bogie and Bacall: Love Lessons from a Legendary Romance — de la Hoz, Cindy
c Bogtrotter (Illus. by Rossell, Judith) — Wild, Margaret
Bohemian Gospel — Carpenter, Dana Chamblee
Bohemians, Bootleggers, Flappers, and Swells — Carter, Graydon
Bohemians, Bootleggers, Flappers and Swells: The Best of Early Vanity Fair — Carter, Graydon
Boho Crochet: 30 Hip and Happy Projects — Eriksson, Hazel
y Boitamemoire — Des Roches, Roger
Boko Haram: Inside Nigeria's Unholy War — Smith, Mike J.
Boko Haram: Nigeria's Islamist Insurgency — Comolli, Virginia
Bolano: A Biography in Conversations — Maristain, Monica
Bolano traducido: Nueva literatura mundial — Corral, Will H.
Bold — Diamandis, Peter H.
"A Bold and Hardy Race of Men": The Lives and Literature of American Whalemen — Schell, Jennifer
Bold: How to Go Big, Create Wealth, and Impact the World (Read by Kotler, Steven). Audiobook Review — Diamandis, Peter H.
c The Bolds (Illus. by Roberts, David) — Clary, Julian
The Bollywood Bride — Dev, Sonali
Bollywood: Gods, Glamour, and Gossip — Varia, Kush
The Bolt from the Blue: Air Power in the Cycle of Strategies — Kainikara, Sanu
The Bomb Maker's Son — Rotstein, Robert
c Bomb Squad Technician — Perritano, John
Bombay Blues — Hidier, Tanuja Desai
Bombay Velvet — Kashyap, Anurag
y Bomber — Dowswell, Paul
Bomber Aircraft of 305 Squadron — Musialkowski, Lechostaw
The Bombers and the Bombed: Allied Air War over Europe, 1940-1945 — Overy, Richard
Bombs Away — Turtledove, Harry
Bon Appetit: The Food Lover's Cleanse; 140 Delicious, Nourishing Recipes That Will Tempt You Back into Healthful Eating — Dickerman, Sara
Bon usage et variation sociolinguistique: Perspectives diachroniques et traditions nationales — Ayres-Bennett, Wendy
Bonanzas & Borrascas: Copper Kings and Stock Frenzies, 1885-1918 — Lingenfelter, Richard E.
Bonanzas & Borrascas: Gold Lust and Silver Sharks, 1848-1884 — Lingenfelter, Richard E.
Bonaparte: 1769-1802 — Gueniffey, Patrice
Bond by Design: The Art of the James Bond Films — Simmonds, Meg
The Bond of Time: An Epic Love Poem — Pule, John Puhiatau
Bondage: Labor and Rights in Eurasia from the Sixteenth to the Early Twentieth Centuries — Stanziani, Alessandro
Bonded — Wright, Laura
Bonds of Alliance: Indigenous and Atlantic Slaveries in New France — Rushforth, Brett
Bonds of Love & Blood — MacDonald, Marylee
The Bone Clocks (Read by Various readers). Audiobook Review — Mitchell, David
y The Bone Clocks — Mitchell, David
The Bone Clocks — Mitchell, David Stephen
c Bone Collection: Dinosaurs and Other Prehistoric Animals — Colson, Rob
c Bone Collection: Skulls (Illus. by Doyle, Sandra) — de la Bedoyere, Camilla
Bone Deep Broth: Healing Recipes with Bone Broth — Chen, Taylor
Bone Digger — Hirt, Douglas
y Bone, Fog, Ash & Star — Egan, Catherine
y Bone Gap — Ruby, Laura
Bone Girl — Drake, Annette
The Bone Labyrinth — Rollins, James
The Bone Orchard — Doiron, Paul
c Bone: Out from Boneville (Illus. by Hamaker, Steve) — Smith, Jeff (b. 1960-)
Bone Swans — Cooney, Claire S.E.
Bone to be Wild — Haines, Carolyn
y A Bone to Pick. Audiobook Review — Bittman, Mark
A Bone to Pick (Read by Fass, Robert). Audiobook Review — Bittman, Mark
A Bone to Pick — Bittman, Mark
c A Bone to Pick — McMurchy-Barber, Gina

The Bone Tree — Iles, Greg
Bones and All — DeAngelis, Camille
The Bones of You — Howells, Debbie
The Bones Will Speak — Parks, Carrie Stuart
The Bonfire of the Vanities — Wolfe, Tom
y Bonhoeffer: Pastor, Martyr, Prophet, Spy (Read by Hillgartner, Malcolm). Audiobook Review — Metaxas, Eric
y Bonhoeffer: Pastor, Martyr, Prophet, Spy, student ed. — Metaxas, Eric
Bonhoeffer the Assassin? Challenging the Myth, Recovering His Call to Peacemaking — Nation, Mark Thiessen
c Bonhomme de neige (Illus. by Williams, Sam) — Rollins, Jack
Bonita Avenue — Buwalda, Peter
c Bonjour Camille (Illus. by Aguilar, Laia) — Cano, Felipe
Bonkers: My Life in Laughs — Saunders, Jennifer
Bonn 1314 - Kronung, Krieg und Kompromiss
c Bonny Grows Her Feathers and Learns to Fly — Robertson-Buchanan, Angela
Bonsai — Zambra, Alejandro
c Boo! A Book of Spooky Surprises (Illus. by Galloway, Fhiona) — Litton, Jonathan
y Boo — Smith, Neil
c Boo! (Illus. by Patricelli, Leslie) — Patricelli, Leslie
c Boo-La-La Witch Spa (Illus. by Roxas, Isabel) — Berger, Samantha
c Book (Illus. by Hoopes, Natalie) — Miles, David
Book Destruction from the Medieval to the Contemporary — Partington, Gill
Book Fairs For Authors — DeKay, Larry
Book in Honor of Augustus (Liber ad Honorem Augusti). — da Eboli, Pietro
Book in Honor of Augustus — Hood, Gwyneth
c The Book Itch: Freedom, Truth & Harlem's Greatest Bookstore (Illus. by Christie, R. Gregory) — Nelson, Vaunda Micheaux
Book M: A London Widow's Life Writings — Austen, Katherine
y Book: My Autobiography (Illus. by Packer, Neil) — Agard, John
c Book-o-Beards: A Wearable Book (Illus. by Nassner, Alyssa) — Lemke, Donald
c Book-o-Beards: A Wearable Book (Illus. by Lentz, Bob) — Lempke, Donald
y The Book of Aron — Shepard, Jim
y The Book of Bad Things — Poblocki, Dan
The Book of Barkley: Love and Life through the Eyes of a Labrador Retriever — Johnson, L.B.
The Book of Beetles: A Life-Size Guide to Six Hundred of Nature's Gems — Bouchard, Patrice
The Book of Broadway: The 150 Definitive Plays and Musicals — Grode, Eric
The Book of Colors — Barfield, Raymond
The Book of Common Prayer: A Biography — Jacobs, Alan
c The Book of Dares for Lost Friends — Kelley, Jane
c Book of Dragons (Illus. by Bialk, Andy) — Testa, Maggie
The Book of Eliot — Simon, Robert A.
c A Book of Feelings (Illus. by Rubbino, Salvatore) — McCardie, Amanda
The Book of France — Stephens, Winifred
The Book of Human Emotions: An Encyclopedia of Feeling from Anger to Wanderlust. — Smith, Tiffany Watt
The Book of I — Armenteros, Jorge
The Book of Isaiah: Enduring Questions Answered Anew: Essays Honoring Joseph Blenkinsopp and His Contribution to the Study of Isaiah — Bautch, Richard J.
The Book of Ivy — Engel, Amy
The Book of Joan: Tales of Mirth, Mischief, and Manipulation (Read by Rivers, Melissa). Audiobook Review — Rivers, Melissa
The Book of Job: A Biography — Larrimore, Mark
c The Book of Jonah — Spier, Peter
c The Book of Kings (Illus. by Bruno, Iacopo) — Voigt, Cynthia
c The Book of Kringle: Legend of the North Pole (Illus. by Wenzel, David) — Partridge, Derek Velez
y The Book of Laney — Collins, Myfanwy
c The Book of Languages: Talk Your Way around the World (Illus. by Webb, Mick) — Webb, Mick
The Book of Life — Harkness, Deborah
The Book of Lost and Found — Foley, Lucy
The Book of Love: Improvisations on a Crazy Little Thing — Rosenblatt, Roger
The Book of Magic: From Antiquity to the Enlightenment — Copenhaver, Brian

The Book of Margery Kempe — Bale, Anthony
The Book of Margery Kempe — Kempe, Margery
The Book of Mastery — Selig, Paul
The Book of Memory — Gappah, Petina
The Book of Metaphysical Penetrations — Sadra, Mulla
c Book of Nature Poetry — Lewis, J. Patrick
The Book of Night Women (Read by Miles, Robin). Audiobook Review — James, Marlon
Book of Numbers — Cohen, Joshua
The Book of Phoenix — Okorafor, Nnedi
c The Book of Secrets (Illus. by Bruno, Iacopo) — Voigt, Cynthia
The Book of She — Stover, Sara Avant
The Book of Speculation (Read by Fliakos, Ari). Audiobook Review — Swyler, Erika
The Book of Speculation — Swyler, Erika
y A Book of Spirits and Thieves — Rhodes, Morgan
The Book of Steven — Stevenson, Steven T.
The Book of Stone — Papernick, Jonathan
c The Book of Storms — Hatfield, Ruth
The Book of Strange New Things (Read by Cohen, Josh). Audiobook Review — Faber, Michel
y The Book of Strange New Things — Faber, Michel
c Book of the Dead (Read by De Ocampo, Ramon). Audiobook Review — Northrop, Michael
c Book of the Dead — Skipp, John
y Book of the Dead — Northrop, Michael
The Book of the People: How to Read the Bible — Wilson, A.N.
c The Book of Three — Alexander, Lloyd
The Book of Tokyo: A City in Short Fiction — Emmerich, Michael
The Book of Tokyo — Emmerich, Michael
The Book of Totality — Wang, Yun
The Book of Trees: Visualizing Branches of Knowledge — Lima, Manuel
Book of Tripe — Reynaud, Stephane
y The Book of Unknown Americans (Read by Avila, Christine). Audiobook Review — Henriquez, Cristina
y The Book of Unknown Americans — Henriquez, Cristina
The Book of Wanderings: A Mother-Daughter Pilgrimage — Meyer, Kimberly
c The Book of Wisdom — Falcon, Jeremy
The Book of Yokai: Mysterious Creatures of Japanese Folklore — Foster, Michael Dylan
y Book Scavenger (Illus. by Watts, Sarah) — Bertman, Jennifer Chambliss
c The Book That Proves Time Travel Happens — Clark, Henry
y The Book That Proves Time Travel Happens (Illus. by Holmes, Jeremy) — Clark, Henry
c The Book That Proves Time Travel Happens — Clark, Henry
The Book Trade in the Italian Renaissance — Nuovo, Angela
Book Was There — Piper, Andrew
c The Book with No Pictures — Novak, B.J.
The Booke of Ovyde Named Methamorphose — Caxton, William
The Bookish Riddarasogur: Writing Romance in Late Mediaeval Iceland — Barnes, Geraldine
Bookmarked: Reading My Way from Hollywood to Brooklyn — Fairey, Wendy
Books and Religious Devotion: The Redemptive Reading of an Irishman in Nineteenth-Century New England — Westphall, Allan F.
c Books for Me! (Illus. by Laughead, Mike) — Fliess, Sue
Books in Bloom: Discovering the Plant Biology in Great Children's Literature — Bang-Jensen, Valerie
c The Books of Beginning: The Black Reckoning — Stephens, John
The Books of Jonathan: Four Men, One God — Levinson, Gary
The Books That Changed my Life — Patrick, Bethanne
Books That Cook: The Making of a Literary Meal — Goldthwaite, Melissa A.
The Books That Define Ireland — Fanning, Bryan
Books under Fire: A Hit List of Banned and Challenged Children's Books — Scales, Pat R.
Bookscape: Geographies of Printing and Publishing in London before 1800 — Raven, James
The Bookseller — Swanson, Cynthia
Boolean Functions Complexity: Advances and Frontiers — Jukna, Stasys
c Boom Boom (Illus. by Chodos-Irvine, Margaret) — Naberhaus, Sarvinder

Boom, Bust and Crisis: Labour, Corporate Power and Politics in Canada — Peters, John (b. 1963-)
c Boom Snot Twitty (Read by Gilbert, Tavia). Audiobook Review — Cronin, Doreen
c Boom Snot Twitty This Way That Way (Illus. by Liwska, Renata) — Cronin, Doreen
c Boom Snot Twitty: This Way That Way (Illus. by Liwska, Renata) — Cronin, Doreen
c Boom Snot Twitty This Way That Way (Illus. by Liwska, Renata) — Cronin, Doreen
c Boombin and Lama: A Story of Friendship, Investigation and Adventure! (Illus. by Guthrie, Damon) — Chema, Boona
Boone and Crockett Club Collection
c Boo's Beard (Illus. by Straker, Bethany) — Mannering, Rose
Bootleggers and Baptists: How Economic Forces and Moral Persuasion Interact to Shape Regulatory Politics — Smith, Adam
Bootleggers and Borders: The Paradox of Prohibition on a Canada-U.S. Borderland — Moore, Stephen T.
The Bootlegger's Legacy — Clifton, Ted
Boots and Burgers: An Arizona Handbook for Hungry Hikers — Naylor, Roger
Bootstrapping Democracy: Transforming Local Governance and Civil Society in Brazil — Baiocchi, Gianpaolo
Borb — Little, Jason
y The Borden Murders: Lizzie Borden & the Trial of the Century — Miller, Sarah Elizabeth
The Border — McCammon, Robert
y Border Disputes: A Global Encyclopedia — Brunet-Jailly, Emmanuel
Border Law: The First Seminole War and American Nationhood — Rosen, Deborah
Border Odyssey — Thompson, Charles D., Jr.
Border Patrol Nation: Dispatches from the Front Lines of Homeland Security — Miller, Todd
Border Work: Spatial Lives of the State in Rural Central Asia — Reeves, Madeleine
Borderland Lives in Northern South Asia — Gellner, David N.
Borderland on the Isthmus: Race, Culture, and the Struggle for the Canal Zone — Donoghue, Michael E.
Borderlands Saints: Secular Sanctity in Chicano/a and Mexican Culture — Martin, Desiree A.
Borderline — Marklund, Liza
Borderline Exegesis — Vaage, Leif E.
Borderline — Block, Lawrence
Borderline — Herzberg, Bob
Borderline — Marklund, Liza
Borderlines — Wrong, Michela
Borders in the European Memories: A Typology of Remembered Borders in Today's Europe — Serrier, Thomas
The Borders of Race in Colonial South Africa: The Kat River Settlement, 1829-1856 — Ross, Robert
y Boring Girls — Taylor, Sara
c Born! A Foal, Five Kittens and Confederation (Illus. by Jones, Brenda) — Kessler, Deirdre
Born Bad: Original Sin and the Making of the Western World — Boyce, James
c Born for Greatness: Me, You, and the Dalai Lama (Illus. by Roberts, Monica) — Ray, Alice
Born Free and Equal? A Philosophical Inquiry into the Nature of Discrimination — Lippert-Rasmussen, Kasper
y The Born Frees: Writing with the Girls of Gugulethu — Burge, Kimberly
Born from the Gaze of God: The Tibhirine Journal of a Martyr Monk — Lebreton, Christophe
Born in a Burial Gown — Craven, Mike
Born in the GDR: Living in the Shadow of the Wall — Vaizey, Hester
Born in the Ghetto: My Triumph over Adversity — Sef, Ariela Abramovich
c Born in the Wild: Baby Mammals and Their Parents (Illus. by Judge, Lita) — Judge, Lita
Born of Defiance (Read by Berman, Fred). Audiobook Review — Kenyon, Sherrilyn
Born on the Bayou: A Memoir — Lourd, Blaine
y Born Survivors: Three Young Mothers and Their Extraordinary Story of Courage, Defiance, and Hope — Holden, Wendy
Born to Be King — Mayer, Catherine
Born to be Wild — McBee, Randy D.
Born to Drum: The Truth about the World's Greatest Drummers--from John Bonham and Keith Moon to Sheila E. and Dave Grohl — Barrell, Tony
Born under Auschwitz: Melancholy Traditions in Postwar German Literature — Cosgrove, Mary

Born with Teeth: A Memoir (Read by Mulgrew, Kate). Audiobook Review — Mulgrew, Kate
Born with Teeth: A Memoir — Mulgrew, Kate
Borrowed Forms: The Music and Ethics of Transnational Fiction — Lachman, Kathryn
A Borrowed Man — Wolfe, Gene
y Borrowed Time — Smith, Greg Leitich
Bosnia-Herzegovina since Dayton: Civic and Uncivic Values — Ramet, Sabrina P.
The Bosnian Muslims in the Second World War: A History — Hoare, Marko Attila
Boss Life: Surviving My Own Small Business — Downs, Paul
c Bossing the Bronx Bombers at Yankee Stadium — Aretha, David
Bossypants — Fey, Tina
c The Boston Celtics — Stewart, Mark
The Boston Girl (Read by Lavin, Linda). Audiobook Review — Diamant, Anita
The Boston Girl — Diamant, Anita
c The Boston Tea Party: Would You Join the Revolution? — Landau, Elaine
The Boston Trader — Flanders, Jefferson
Boswell's Enlightenment — Zaretsky, Robert
Bosworth 1485: A Battlefield Rediscovered — Foard, Glenn
Bosworth 1485: The Battle That Transformed England — Jones, Michael
Both of Me — Friesen, Jonathan
Both Sides of the Sunset: Photographing Los Angeles — Brown, Jane
Botschafterzeremoniell am Papsthof der Renaissance — Stenzig, Philipp
c Bottle Cap Boys Dancing on Royal Street (Illus. by Ward, Damian) — Williams-Garcia, Rita
Bottled: A Mom's Guide to Early Recovery — Bowman, Dana
The Bottom — Owen, Howard
The Bottom of Your Heart: The Inferno for Commissario Ricciardi — de Giovanni, Maurizio
Bottomland — Hoover, Michelle
Boudica's Odyssey in Early Modern England — Frenee-Hutchins, Samantha
Boudoir Lighting: Simple Techniques for Dramatic Photography — Owen, Robin
Bough Down — Green, Karen
The Boulder Brothers: Meet Mo and Jo (Illus. by Collet-Derby, Pierre) — Lynn, Sarah
c Bounce Back: How to Be a Resilient Kid — Moss, Wendy L.
The Bounce, Vol. 1 — Casey, Joe
Bound by Sin — Frank, Jacquelyn
Bound: Over 20 Artful Handmade Books — Ekrem, Erica
Bound to Emancipate: Working Women and Urban Citizenship in Early Twentieth-Century China and Hong Kong — Chin, Angelina
Bound with Love — Mury, Megan
The Boundaries of Desire: A Century of Bad Laws, Good Sex, and Changing Identities — Berkowitz, Eric
The Boundaries of the Literary Archive: Reclamation and Representation — Smith, Carrie (b. 1987-)
Boundaries Undermined: The Ruins of Progress on the Bangladesh-India Border — Hussain, Delwar
y The Boundary (Illus. by Cortes, Ricardo) — Terrell, Heather
Boundary Problems — Bechtel, Greg
c Bounders — Tesler, Monica
c The Boundless (Read by Podehl, Nick). Audiobook Review — Oppel, Kenneth
y The Boundless — Oppel, Kenneth
Boundless: Tracing Land and Dream in a New Northwest Passage — Winter, Kathleen
Bourbon Empire: The Past and Future of America's Whiskey — Mitenbuler, Reid
The Bourbon Kings — Ward, J.R.
Bourbon Street: A History — Campanella, Richard
Boutique Bags: Classic Style for Modern Living — Kim, Sue
c Bow-Tie Pasta: Acrostic Poems (Illus. by Rowland, Andy) — Cleary, Brian P.
c Bow-Wow! Dog Helpers — Markovics, Joyce
c Bow-Wow's Nightmare Neighbors (Illus. by Newgarden, Mark) — Cash, Megan Montague
y Bowie on Bowie: Interviews and Encounters with David Bowie — Egan, Sean
A Bowl Full of Nails — Degelman, Charles
Bowl of Fruit (1907). — Cacoyannis, Panayotis
Bowled Over: The Bowling Greens of Britain — Hornby, Hugh

c The Box and the Dragonfly (Illus. by Bruno, Iacopo) — Sanders, Ted
Box of Cigar Bands — McComb Sinclair, James C., II
A Box of Sand: The Italo-Ottoman War, 1911-1912: The First Land, Sea and Air War — Stephenson, Charles
The Box Wine Sailors: Misadventures of a Broke Young Couple at Sea — McCullough, Amy
c The Boxcar Children Guide to Adventure: A How-to for Mystery Solving, Make-It-Yourself Projects, and More — Boxcar Children
c The Boxcar Children: The Firehouse Mystery (Read by Gregory, Tim) — Warner, Gertrude Chandler
c The Boxcar Children: The Movie Star Mystery (Read by Gregory, Tim). Audiobook Review — Warner, Gertrude Chandler
c The Boxcar Children: The Mystery of the Empty Safe (Read by Lilly, Aimee). Audiobook Review — Warner, Gertrude Chandler
y The Boxcar Children: The Poison Frog Mystery (Read by Gregory, Tim). Audiobook Review — Warner, Gertrude Chandler
c Boxers & Saints (Illus. by Pien, Lark) — Leun Yang, Gene
Boxes — Gamier, Pascal
A Boy Asked the Wind — Nickel, Barbara
c The Boy at the Top of the Mountain — Boyne, John
A Boy Called Cin — Wilde, Cecil
The Boy from Aleppo Who Painted the War — Sukkar, Sumia
y The Boy I Love — de Gramont, Nina
c The Boy in Number Four (Illus. by Thomson, Regan) — Kootstra, Kara
y The Boy in the Black Suit (Read by Allen, Corey). Audiobook Review — Reynolds, Jason
y The Boy in the Black Suit — Reynolds, Jason
Boy Lost in Wild — Hasiuk, Brenda
y The Boy Meets Girl Massacre — Hogarth, Ainslie
y The Boy Most Likely To (Read by Andrews, MacLeod). Audiobook Review — Fitzpatrick, Huntley
y The Boy Most Likely To — Fitzpatrick, Huntley
The Boy Next Door — Lopez, Jennifer
y The Boy Next Door — Van Ark, Katie
Boy of the Border — Bontemps, Arna
c The Boy on the Page (Illus. by Carnavas, Peter) — Carnavas, Peter
The Boy Problem: Educating Boys in Urban America, 1870-1970 — Grant, Julia
Boy, Snow, Bird — Oyeyemi, Helen
c The Boy & the Book: A Wordless Story (Illus. by Kolar, Bob) — Slater, David Michael
c Boy, Were We Wrong about the Human Body! (Illus. by Tilley, Debbie) — Kudlinski, Kathleen V.
c Boy, Were We Wrong about the Weather! (Illus. by Serra, Sebastia) — Kudlinski, Kathleen V.
y The Boy Who Became Buffalo Bill: Growing Up Billy Cody in Bleeding Kansas — Warren, Andrea
The Boy Who Carried Bricks: A True Story — Carter, Alton
The Boy Who Could Change the World: The Writings of Aaron Swartz — Swartz, Aaron
The Boy Who Could See Death — Vickers, Salley
c The Boy Who Cried Shark (Illus. by Blecha, Aaron) — Ocean, Davy
y The Boy Who Dared — Bartoletti, Susan Campbell
The Boy Who Fell off the Mayflower, or, John Howland's Good Fortune (Illus. by Lynch, Patrick James) — Lynch, Patrick James
The Boy Who Harnessed the Wind (Read by Jackson, Korey). Audiobook Review — Kamkwamba, William
c The Boy Who Harnessed the Wind (Illus. by Hymas, Anna) — Kamkwamba, William
The Boy Who Knew Everything — Forester, Victoria
y The Boy Who Lost Fairyland (Illus. by Juan, Ana) — Valente, Catherynne M.
The Boy Who Lost His Bumble (Illus. by Esberger, Trudi) — Esberger, Trudi
c The Boy Who Loved Math: The Improbable Life of Paul Erdos (Illus. by LeUyen, Pham) — Heiligman, Deborah
c The Boy Who Loved the Moon (Illus. by Alaimo, Rino) — Alaimo, Rino
y The Boy Who Played with Fusion: Extreme Science, Extreme Parenting, and How to Make a Star — Clynes, Tom
The Boy Who Stole Attila's Horse — Repila, Ivan
c The Boy Who Stopped Time (Illus. by Joharapurkar, Pritali) — Massa, Michael A.
The Boy with the Porcelain Blade — Patrick, Den
c The Boy with the Sweet-Treat Touch (Illus. by Chapman, Neil) — North, Laura

Boy with Thorn — *Laurentiis, Rickey*
y The Boy with Two Heads — *Mulligan, Andy*
Boycott — *Place, Vanessa*
The Boys — *Sala, Toni*
y Boy's Best Friend — *Banks, Kate*
c The Boy's Book of Inventions — *Baker, Ray Stannard*
A Boy's Book of Nervous Breakdowns — *Paine, Tom*
y Boys Don't Knit (in Public). — *Easton, T.S.*
y Boys Don't Knit — *Easton, Tom*
y The Boys in the Boat (Read by Bramhall, Mark). Audiobook Review — *Brown, Daniel James*
y The Boys in the Boat — *Brown, Daniel James*
y The Boys in the Boat — *Brown, Daniel James (b. 1951-)*
c The Boys in the Boat — *Brown, Daniel James*
Boys in the Trees: A Memoir — *Simon, Carly*
y Boys Like You — *Stone, Juliana*
The Boys of Earth-180 — *Samuelson, Paul*
y The Boys of Fire and Ash — *McIsaac, Meaghan*
y The Boys School Girls: Abby's Shadow — *Chase, Lil*
y The Boys Who Challenged Hitler: Knud Pedersen and the Churchill Club (Read by Hoose, Phillip). Audiobook Review — *Hoose, Phillip*
y The Boys Who Challenged Hitler: Knud Pedersen and the Churchill Club (Read by Braun, Michael). Audiobook Review — *Hoose, Phillip*
y The Boys Who Challenged Hitler: Knud Pedersen and the Churchill Club — *Hoose, Phillip*
Brabbeling (1614): Een Bloemlezing — *Visscher, Roemer*
y Brace Mouth, False Teeth — *Brahmachari, Sita*
c Bracha: Do You Know? (Illus. by Argoff, Patti) — *Stern, Ariella*
c Brachio (Illus. by Fitzgibbon, Terry) — *Eggleton, Jill*
c Brachiosaurus — *Gregory, Josh*
Bradstreet Gate — *Kirman, Robin*
Brady vs Manning: The Untold Story of the Rivalry That Transformed the NFL — *Myers, Gary*
The Brain: An Illustrated History of Neuroscience — *Jackson, Tom*
The Brain Electric: The Dramatic High-Tech Race to Merge Minds and Machines — *Gay, Malcolm*
y The Brain: Journey through the Universe Inside Your Head (Illus. by Casteel, Tom) — *Mooney, Carla*
c Brain Launch & Other Perfectly Awesome Stories — *Chris, Jerry*
Brain, Mind and Consciousness in the History of Neuroscience — *Smith, C.U M.*
Brain Storms: The Race to Unlock the Mysteries of Parkinson's Disease — *Palfreman, Jon*
The Brain, the Nervous System, and Their Diseases — *Hellier, Jennifer L.*
The Brain: The Story of You — *Eagleman, David*
Brains, Buddhas, and Believing: The Problem of Intentionality in Classical Buddhist and Cognitive-Scientific Philosophy of Mind — *Arnold, Daniel Anderson*
The Brain's Way of Healing — *Doidge, Norman*
The Brain's Way of Healing: Remarkable Discoveries and Recoveries from the Frontiers of Neuroplasticity (Read by Newbern, George). Audiobook Review — *Doidge, Norman*
The Brain's Way of Healing: Remarkable Discoveries and Recoveries from the Frontiers of Neuroplasticity — *Doidge, Norman*
y Bram Stoker's Dracula: A Graphic Novel (Illus. by Alfonso, Jose) — *Burgin, Michael*
c Bramble and Maggie: Spooky Season — *Friend, Alison*
c Brambleheart: A Story about Finding Treasure and the Unexpected Magic of Friendship (Illus. by Cole, Henry) — *Cole, Henry*
c Brambleheart (Illus. by Cole, Henry) — *Cole, Henry*
c Brambleheart — *Cole, Henry*
Branching Out — *March, Kerstin*
Brand Luther: How an Unheralded Monk Turned His Small Town into a Center of Publishing, Made Himself the Most Famous Man in Europe--and Started the Protestant Reformation — *Pettegree, Andrew*
y Brand New Ancients — *Tempest, Kate*
Brand-New and Terrific: Alex Katz in the 1950s — *Tuite, Diane*
c A Brand New Day: A Banana Split Story (Illus. by Bossio, Paula). E-book Review — *Chung, A.S.*
Branded — *Masters, Ben*
Brando's Smile: His Life, Thought, and Work — *Mizruchi, Susan L.*
Brash — *Wright, Laura*
Brass Bands of the World: Militarism, Colonial Legacies, and Local Music Making — *Reily, Suzel Ana*

'Brautschau' auf Russisch-Judisch-Deutsch: Ein- und Ausgrenzungsprozesse des Netzwerks russisch(sprachig)er Juden in Deutschland — *Supyan, Ekaterina*
Brave as Can Be: A Book of Courage (Illus. by Roussey, Christine) — *Witek, Jo*
c Brave Chicken Little (Illus. by Byrd, Robert) — *Byrd, Robert*
Brave Companions (Read by McCullough, David). Audiobook Review — *McCullough, David*
Brave Enough — *Strayed, Cheryl*
c Brave Girl: Clara and the Shirtwaist Makers' Strike of 1909 (Read by Lockford, Lesa). Audiobook Review — *Markel, Michelle*
Brave Girls: Raising Young Women with Passion and Purpose to Become Powerful Leaders — *Radin, Stacey*
c Brave Hearts — *Goldish, Meish*
Brave the Heat — *Humphreys, Sara*
Braver and Bolder — *Torres, Julia*
Bravo (Read by Glouchevitch, John). Audiobook Review — *Rucka, Greg*
c Bravo, Chico Canta! Bravo! (Illus. by Carling, Amelia Lau) — *Mora, Pat*
c Brazil — *Savery, Annabel*
Brazil: The Troubled Rise of a Global Power — *Reid, Michael*
Brazilian Propaganda: Legitimizing an Authoritarian Regime — *Schneider, Nina*
Brazil's Living Museum: Race, Reform, and Tradition in Bahia — *Romo, Anadelia A.*
Breach of Power — *Barrett, Chuck*
Bread — *Brettschneider, Dean*
Bread upon the Waters: The St. Petersburg Grain Trade and the Russian Economy, 1703-1811 — *Jones, Robert E.*
Breadline Britain: The Rise of Mass Poverty — *Lansley, Stewart*
Break Free — *Lewis, Robert E.*
Break the Norms: Questioning Everything You Think You Know about God and Truth, Life and Death, Love and Sex — *Bhardwaj, Chandresh*
Break Your Heart — *Helms, Rhonda*
y Breakaway — *Spears, Kat*
y Breakaway: Beyond the Goal — *Morgan, Alex*
y The BreakBeat Poets: New American Poetry in the Age of Hip-Hop — *Coval, Kevin*
Breakfast of Champions (Read by Malkovich, John). Audiobook Review — *Vonnegut, Kurt*
y Breakfast Served Anytime — *Combs, Sarah*
y Breaking Butterflies — *Anjelais, M.*
y Breaking Democracy's Spell — *Dunn, John*
Breaking Free — *Lubitz, Rob*
The Breaking Hour — *Crossley-Holland, Kevin*
c Breaking News: Bear Alert — *Biedrzycki, David*
The Breaking Point — *Bass, Jefferson*
y Breaking Sky — *McCarthy, Cori*
Breaking the Chains of Gravity: The Story of Spaceflight before NASA — *Teitel, Amy Shira*
c Breaking the Ice — *Nall, Gail*
Breaking the Male Code: Unlocking the Power of Friendship — *Garfield, Robert*
Breaking the Ties that Bound: The Politics of Marital Strife in Late Imperial Russia — *Engel, Barbara Alpern*
Breaking Up Is Hard to Do — *Coleman, Sue*
Breaking Wild — *Les Becquets, Diane*
Breaking with the Past: The Maritime Customs Service and the Global Origins of Modernity in China — *Van de Ven, Hans*
Breaking Women: Gender, Race, and the New Politics of Imprisonment — *McCorkel, Jill A.*
Breakneck — *Arcan, Nelly*
y Breakout (Read by Berman, Fred). Audiobook Review — *Emerson, Kevin*
y Breakout — *Emerson, Kevin*
Breakthrough! 100 Astronomical Images That Changed the World — *Gendler, Robert*
y Breakthrough: How One Teen Innovator Is Changing the World — *Andraka, Jack*
c Breakthrough! How Three People Saved "Blue Babies" and Changed Medicine Forever — *Murphy, Jim (b. 1947-)*
Breakthrough: The Making of America's First Woman President — *Cohen, Nancy L.*
c Bream Gives Me Hiccups and Other Stories — *Eisenberg, Jesse*
Breast Cancer at 35: A Memoir — *Burns, Amy*
Breath of Dragons: Vanished — *Randolph, Tina M.*
A Breath of Life — *Lorenz, Johnny*
y Breathe, Annie, Breathe — *Kennealy, Miranda*

Breathing Race into the Machine: The Surprising Career of the Spirometer from Plantation to Genetics — *Braun, Lundy*
Breathing Space: The Natural and Unnatural History of Air — *Everard, Mark*
Breathturn into Timestead — *Celan, Paul*
Breezeway: New Poems — *Ashbery, John*
The Brethren — *Merle, Robert*
"The Breviary of Britain" (1573), with Selections from "The History of Cambria" (1584). — *Llwyd, Humphrey*
Brewed in Japan: The Evolution of the Japanese Beer Industry — *Alexander, Jeffrey W.*
Brewing Identities: Globalisation, Guinness and the Production of Irishness — *Murphy, Brenda*
Brewing Science: Technology and Print, 1700-1880 — *Sumner, James*
Brexit: How Britain Will Leave Europe — *MacShane, Denis*
Brian Boru and the Battle of Clontarf — *Duffy, Sean*
Brian Froud's Faeries' Tales — *Froud, Brian*
Brian May's Red Special — *May, Brian*
y Briar Queen — *Harbour, Katherine*
y Briar Rose — *Oliver, Jana*
The Bridal Chair — *Goldreich, Gloria*
The Bride of Christ Goes to Hell: Metaphor and Embodiment in the Lives of Pious Women, 200-1500 — *Elliott, Dyan*
c Bride of Slug Man — *Mata, Julie*
A Bridge across the Ocean: The United States and the Holy See between the Two World Wars — *Castagna, Luca*
The Bridge Builder: The Life and Continuing Legacy of Rabbi Yechiel Eckstein — *Chafets, Zev*
y The Bridge from Me to You — *Schroeder, Lisa*
y The Bridgeport Poltergeist: True Tales of a Haunted House — *Hall, William J.*
Bridges: Documents of the Christian-Jewish Dialogue, vol. 1: The Road to Reconciliation (1945-1985). — *Sherman, Franklin*
Bridges: Documents of the Christian-Jewish Dialogue, vol. 2: Building a New Relationship (1986-2013). — *Sherman, Franklin*
Bridges of Paris — *Saint James, Michael*
y Bridget: A New Australian — *Moloney, James*
c Bridget Wilder: Spy-in-Training — *Bernstein, Jonathan*
Bridging the Soft Skills Gap: How to Teach the Missing Basics to Today's Young Talent — *Tulgan, Bruce*
Bridging Traditions: Alchemy, Chemistry, and Paracelsian Practices in the Early Modern Era — *Parshall, Karen Hunger*
Bridging Troubled Waters: China, Japan, and Maritime Order in the East China Sea — *Manicom, James*
Brief Candle in the Dark: My Life in Science — *Dawkins, Richard*
Brief Encounters: A Collection of Contemporary Nonfiction — *Kitchen, Judith*
A Brief History of Creation: Science and the Search for the Origin of Life — *Mesler, Bill*
A Brief History of Portable Literature — *Vila-Matas, Enrique*
A Brief History of Seven Killings — *James, Marlon*
A Brief History of Video Games — *Stanton, Richard*
A Brief History of Women in Quebec — *Baillargeon, Denyse*
'Brief Lives' with 'An Apparatus for the Lives of Our English Mathematical Writers' — *Aubrey, John*
Brief Loves That Live Forever — *Makine, Andrei*
Brief Stop on the Road from Auschwitz — *Rosenberg, Goran*
y Bright Coin Moon — *Lopresti, Kirsten*
The Bright Continent: Breaking Rules and Making Change in Modern Africa — *Olopade, Dayo*
Bright Dead Things — *Limon, Ada*
y Bright Lights, Dark Nights (Illus. by Emond, Stephen) — *Emond, Stephen*
Bright Lights in the Dark Ages: The Thaw Collection of Early Medieval Ornaments — *Adams, Noel*
Bright Lines — *Islam, Tanwi Nandini*
A Bright Moon for Fools — *Gibson, Jasper*
Bright Morning Star — *Coffey, Tom*
Bright Scythe: Selected Poems — *Transtromer, Tomas*
Bright Shards of Someplace Else — *McFawn, Monica*
c Bright Sky, Starry City (Illus. by Sicuro, Aimee) — *Krishnaswami, Uma*
Brilla, mar del Eden — *Ibanez, Andres*
c Brilliant (Illus. by Hughes, Emily) — *Doyle, Roddy*
Brilliant Discourse: Pictures and Readers in Early Modern Rome — *Lincoln, Evelyn*

Brilliant Green: The Surprising History and Science of Plant Intelligence — Mancuso, Stefano
y The Brilliant History of Color in Art — Finlay, Victoria
y The Brilliant Light of Amber Sunrise — Crow, Matthew
c The Brilliant World of Tom Gates — Pichon, Liz
Brill's Encyclopaedia of the Neo-Latin World — Ford, Philip
Bring On the Dusk — Buchman, M.L.
c Bringing Down the Mouse — Mezrich, Ben
Bringing Fossils to Life: An Introduction to Paleobiology — Prothero, Donald R.
Bringing God to Men: American Military Chaplains and the Vietnam War — Whitt, Jacqueline E.
Bringing in the Sheaves: Economy and Metaphor in the Roman World — Shaw, Brent D.
Bringing Math Students into the Formative Assessment Equation: Tools and Strategies for the Middle Grades — Creighton, Susan Janssen
c Bringing the Outside In (Illus. by Barton, Patrice) — Siddals, Mary McKenna
The Brink — Bunn, Austin
c Bristly Hair and I Don't Care! (Illus. by Budde, Nadia) — Budde, Nadia
Britain against Napoleon: The Organization of Victory 1793-1815 — Knight, Roger
Britain and Colonial Maritime War in the Early Eighteenth Century: Silver, Seapower and the Atlantic — Satsuma, Shinsuke
Britain and the Bomb: Nuclear Diplomacy, 1964-1970 — Gill, David James
Britain and Wellington's Army: Recruitment, Society and Tradition, 1807-13 — Linch, Kevin
Britain since 1900: A Success Story? — Skidelsky, Robert
Britain's Black Debt: Reparations for Caribbean Slavery and Genocide — Beckles, Hillary McD.
Britain's Future in Europe: Reform, Renegotiation, Repatriation or Secession? — Emerson, Michael
Britain's Medieval Episcopal Thrones — Tracy, Charles
Britain's Two World Wars against Germany: Myth, Memory and the Distortions of Hindsight — Bond, Brian
Britannia and the Bear: The Anglo-Russian Intelligence Wars, 1917-1929 — Madeira, Victor
Britannia Obscura: Mapping Hidden Britain — Parker, Joanne
The British Aesthetic Tradition: From Shaftesbury to Wittgenstein — Costelloe, Timothy M.
British Army Uniform and the First World War: Men in Khaki — Tynan, Jane
British Ethical Theorists from Sidgwick to Ewing — Hurka, Thomas
British Family Life, 1780-1914, vol. 1: Growing Up — Nelson, Claudia
British Family Life, 1780-1914, vol. 2: Husbands and Fathers — Strange, Julie-Marie
British Family Life, 1780-1914, vol. 3: Wives and Mothers — Egenolf, Susan B.
British Family Life, 1780-1914, vol. 4: Extended Families — Egenolf, Susan B.
British Family Life, 1780-1914, vol. 5: Substitute Families — Strange, Julie-Marie
The British Imperial Army in the Middle East: Morale and Military Identity in the Sinai and Palestine Campaigns, 1916-1918 — Kitchen, James E.
British-Islamic Identity: Third-Generation Bangladeshis from East London — Hoque, Aminul
British Jewry since Emancipation — Alderman, Geoffrey
The British Lion — Schumacher, Tony
British Literature and Print Culture — Jung, Sandro
c British Mammals — Collinson, Clare
British Miscalculations: The Rise of Muslim Nationalism, 1918-1925 — Friedman, Isaiah
British North America in the Seventeenth and Eighteenth Centuries — Foster, Stephen
British Pirates and Society, 1680-1730 — Lincoln, Margarette
The British Soldier in the Peninsular War — Daly, Gavin
British Story: A Romance — Nath, Michael
British Tank Production and the War Economy, 1934-1945 — Coombs, Benjamin
c British Trees — Munson, Victoria
British Untouchables: A Study of Dalit Identity and Education — Ghuman, Paul
British Weather and the Climate of Enlightenment — Golinski, Jan

British Women Writers and the Short Story, 1850-1930: Reclaiming Social Space — Krueger, Kate
British Women's Life Writing: 1760-1840 — Culley, Amy
British Women's Travel to Greece, 1840-1914: Travels in the Palimpsest — Mahn, Churnjeet
The Broad Fork: Recipes for the Wide World of Vegetables and Fruits — Acheson, Hugh
Broad Influence — Newton-Small, Jay
Broadcast Hysteria: Orson Welles's War of the Worlds and the Art of Fake News (Read by Runnette, Sean). Audiobook Review — Schwartz, A. Brad
Broadcast Hysteria: Orson Welles's War of the Worlds and the Art of Fake News — Schwartz, A. Brad
Broadcasting Buildings: Architecture on the Wireless, 1927-1945 — Yusaf, Shundana
Broadcasting Empire: The BBC and the British World, 1922-1970 — Potter, Simon J.
Broadcasting Happiness: The Science of Igniting and Sustaining Positive Change — Gielan, Michelle
Broadcasting in the Modernist Era — Feldman, Matthew
Broadside Ballads from the Pepys Collection: A Selection of Texts, Approaches, and Recordings — Fumerton, Patricia
Broadway Musicals Show by Show, 8th ed. — Green, Stanley
c The Brockenspectre (Illus. by Smy, Pam) — Newbery, Linda
The Brockhurst File — Kramer, Lynne Adair
Brodskii sredi nas — Teasley, Ellendea Proffer
Brodsky Translating Brodsky: Poetry in Self-Translation — Berlina, Alexandra
Brody: Eine Galizische Grenzstadt im Langen 19. Jahrhundert — Kuzmany, Borries
Broke Not Broken: Homer Maxey's Texas Bank War — Sublett, Jesse
y Broken — Curley, Marianne
Broken — Edwards, Tanille
Broken Angels — Heath, Russell
The Broken Compass: Parental Involvement with Children's Education — Robinson, Keith
y Broken Crowns — DeStefano, Lauren
Broken Harmony: Shakespeare and the Politics of Music — Ortiz, Joseph M.
The Broken House — La Farge, Tom
Broken Juliet — Rayven, Leisa
Broken Links, Enduring Ties: American Adoption across Race, Class, and Nation — Seligmann, Linda J.
Broken Mirrors — Khoury, Elias
Broken Promise — Barclay, Linwood
Broken Ranks — King, Hiram
The Broken Road: From the Iron Gates to Mount Athos — Fermor, Patrick Leigh
Broken Sleep — Bauman, Bruce
y Broken Strings — Farrer, Maria
y The Broken Sun: Book III in the Jack Mason Adventures — Pitt, Darrell
Broken Vows — Carlson, N.O.
The Bronte Cabinet: Three Lives in Nine Objects — Lutz, Deborah
y The Bronte Plot — Reay, Katherine
y The Bronte Sisters — Reef, Catherine
Bronx Faces and Voices — Hill, Emita Brady
The Bronx: The Ultimate Guide to New York City's Beautiful Borough — Ultan, Lloyd
y Brood (Read by Rodgers, Elisabeth S.). Audiobook Review — Novak, Chase
c Brooke's Not-So-Perfect Plan — Whittemore, Jo
Brooklyn: A Personal Memoir: With the Lost Photographs of David Attie (Illus. by Attie, David) — Capote, Truman
c Brooklyn ABC: A Scrapbook of Everyone's Favorite Borough — Poluchowicz, Krzysztof
Brooklyn on Fire — Levy, Lawrence H.
Brooklyn Secrets — Stein, Triss
The Broom of God — Bragg, John
c The Broomstick Bike — Bennett, Veronica
Brother — Ahlborn, Ania
c Brother Giovanni's Little Reward: How the Pretzel Was Born (Illus. by Hall, Amanda) — Smucker, Anna Egan
Brother, I'm Dying — Danticat, Edwidge
c Brother vs. Brother (Illus. by Kunkel, Mike) — Kunkel, Mike
y The Brotherhood and the Shield: The Three Thorns — Gibney, Michael

Brotherly Love: Freemasonry and Male Friendship in Enlightenment France — Loiselle, Kenneth
Brothers — Mohrbacher, Paul
c Brothers — McPhail, David
Brothers Armed: Military Aspects of the Crisis in Ukraine — Howard, Colby
Brothers Armed: Military Aspects of the Crisis in Ukraine — Pukhov, Ruslan
The Brothers — Gessen, Masha
A Brother's Cold Case — Herrick, Dennis
Brothers in Arms: Chinese Aid to the Khmer Rouge, 1975-1979 — Mertha, Andrew
Brothers in Arms, Partners in Trade: Dutch-Indigenous Alliances in the Atlantic World, 1595-1674 — Meuwese, Mark
The Brothers' Keepers — Horton, N.L.B.
y Brothers of the Buffalo — Bruchac, Joseph
Brothers, Rivals, Victors: Eisenhower, Patton, Bradley and the Partnership That Drove the Allied Conquest in Europe — Jordan, Jonathan W.
The Brothers: The Road to an American Tragedy — Gessen, Masha
The Brothers Vonnegut: Science and Fiction in the House of Magic — Strand, Ginger
c Brown and Orange in Fall — Carole, Bonnie
c Brown Bear, Brown Bear, What Do You See? (Illus. by Carle, Eric) — Martin, Bill, Jr.
Brown Boys and Rice Queens: Spell-Binding Performance in the Asias — Eng-Beng Lim
Brown Boys and Rice Queens: Spellbinding Performance in the Asias — Eng-Beng Lim
Brown Eggs and Jam Jars: Family Recipes from the Kitchen of Simple Bites — Wimbush-Bourque, Aimee
Brown-Eyed Girl — Kleypas, Lisa
c Brown Girl Dreaming (Read by Woodson, Jacqueline). Audiobook Review — Woodson, Jacqueline
c Brown Girl Dreaming — Woodson, Jacqueline
c Brown Horse Escape Artist! and More True Stories of Animals — Blewett, Ashlee Brown
Brown Is the New White — Phillips, Steve
Browned Off Bloody-Minded: The British Soldier Goes to War 1939-1945 — Allport, Alan
c Brownie & Pearl Step Out (Illus. by Biggs, Brian) — Rylant, Cynthia
Browsings: A Year of Reading, Collecting, and Living with Books (Read by Lescault, John). Audiobook Review — Dirda, Michael
Browsings: A Year of Reading, Collecting, and Living with Books — Dirda, Michael
Bruce Springsteen and the E Street Band 1975: Photographs — Pyle, Barbara
Bruce Walker Travel Adventures — Walker, Bruce
Brucken aus Papier: Atlantischer Wissenstransfer in dem Briefnetzwerk des deutsch-amerikanischen Ehepaars Francis und Mathilde Lieber, 1827-1872 — Schnurmann, Claudia
The Brueghel Moon — Chiladze, Tamaz
Brunch at Bobby's: 140 Recipes for the Best Part of the Weekend — Flay, Bobby
c Bruno and Titch: A Tale of a Boy and His Guinea Pig — Dempsey, Sheena
y Bruno Mars: Pop Superstar — Watson, Stephanie
y Brunt Boggart: A Tapestry of Tales — Greygoose, David
Brush Back (Read by Peakes, Karen). Audiobook Review — Paretsky, Sara
Brush Back — Paretsky, Sara
c A Brush Full of Colour: The World of Ted Harrison — Ruurs, Margriet
A Brush with Danger — Frost, Adam
c Brush Your Hair, Medusa! (Illus. by Patricelli, Leslie) — Holub, Joan
Brutality — Thoft, Ingrid
Bryant & May and the Burning Man — Fowler, Christopher
BSAVA Manual of Canine and Feline Ophthalmology, 3d ed. — Gould, David
The BSCS 5E Instructional Model — Bybee, Rodger W.
Bubba Done It — Toussaint, Maggie
c Bubbe's Belated Bat Mitzvah (Illus. by Cis, Valeria) — Pinson, Isabel
c Bubble Trouble — Percival, Tom
y The Bubble Wrap Boy — Earle, Phil
c Bucket Filling from A to Z: The Key to Being Happy (Illus. by Zimmer, Glenn) — McCloud, Carol
c Buckle and Squash: The Perilous Princess Plot (Illus. by Courtauld, Sarah) — Courtauld, Sarah
Buckley and Mailer: The Difficult Friendship That Shaped the Sixties — Schultz, Kevin M.
c Buck's Tooth (Illus. by Kredensor, Diane) — Kredensor, Diane

Buck's Tooth — Kredensor, Diane
Bucky and Stu vs. the Mikanikal Man (Illus. by Van Wright, Cornelius) — Van Wright, Cornelius
Budapest Romance — Gaston, Rozsa
Buddha's Table — Mingkwan, Chat
The Buddha's Wife: The Path of Awakening Together — Surrey, Janet
Buddhism for Couples: A Calm Approach to Relationships — Napthali, Sarah
Buddhism for Dudes: A Jarhead's Field Guide to Mindfulness — Stribling, Gerry
Buddhism in a Dark Age: Cambodian Monks under Pol Pot — Harris, Ian
Buddhism, Unitarianism, and the Meiji Competition for Universality — Mohr, Michel
Buddhisms: An Introduction — Strong, John S.
Buddhist Biology: Ancient Eastern Wisdom Meets Modern Western Science — Barash, David P.
Buddhist Nuns and Gendered Practice: In Search of the Female Renunciant — Salgado, Nirmala
Buddhists: Understanding Buddhism through the Lives of Practitioners — Lewis, Todd
c Buddy and Earl Go Exploring (Illus. by Sookocheff, Carey) — Fergus, Maureen
c Buddy and Earl (Illus. by Sookocheff, Carey) — Fergus, Maureen
Buddy Holly: Is Alive and Well on Ganymede (Read by Heyborne, Kirby). Audiobook Review — Denton, Bradley
c Budgeting, Spending, and Saving — Kemper, Bitsy
Buell: Journey to the White Clouds — Swenson, Wallace J.
Buenos Aires — Gardner, James
Buffalo Bill on the Silver Screen: The Films of William F. Cody — Sagela, Sandra K.
Buffalo Noir — Park, Ed
The Buffalo Soldiers — Prebble, John
Buffalo Soldiers — Willard, Tom
Buffalo Trail — Guinn, Jeff
Buffoon Men: Classic Hollywood Comedians and Queered Masculinity — Balcerzak, Scott
Bug Book — Baker, Nick
c Bug Detective: Amazing Facts, Myths, and Quirks of Nature (Illus. by Rossi, Francesca) — Li, Maggie
c Bug in a Vacuum (Illus. by Watt, Melanie) — Watt, Melanie
Bug Music: How Insects Gave us Rhythm and Noise — Rothenberg, David
c Bug on a Bike (Illus. by Monroe, Chris) — Monroe, Chris
c Bugs in My Hair! (Illus. by Shannon, David) (Read by Bernstein, Jesse). Audiobook Review — Shannon, David (b. 1959-)
c Bugs in my Hair! (Illus. by Shannon, David) — Shannon, David (b. 1959-)
c Build, Beaver, Build!: Life at the Longest Beaver Dam — Markle, Sandra
y Build Your Own Website: A Comic Guide to HTML, CSS, and WordPress (Illus. by Gee, Kim) — Cooper, Nate
c Builder Mouse — Eldarova, Sofia
The Builders — Polansky, Daniel
Builders of a New South: Merchants, Capital, and the Remaking of Natchez, 1865-1914 — Anderson, Aaron D.
Building a Better Teacher: How Teaching Works (and How to Teach it to Everyone). — Green, Elizabeth
Building a Civil Society: Associations, Public Life, and the Origins of Modern Italy — Soper, Steven C.
Building a Core Print Collection for Preschoolers — Bailey, Alan R.
Building a Latino Civil Rights Movement: Puerto Ricans, African Americans, and the Pursuit of Racial Justice in New York City — Lee, Sonia Song-Ha
Building a Public Judaism: Synagogues and Jewish Identity in Nineteenth-Century Europe — Snyder, Saskia Coenen
Building a Sacred Mountain: The Buddhist Architecture of China's Mount Wutai — Lin, Wei-Cheng
Building a Timeless House in an Instant Age — Hull, Brent
Building Art: The Life and Work of Frank Gehry — Goldberger, Paul
Building Catholic Higher Education: Unofficial Reflections from the University of Notre Dame — Smith, Christian
Building Co-operation: A Business History of the Co-operative Group, 1863-2013 — Wilson, John F.
Building Europe on Expertise: Innovators, Organizers, Networkers — Kohlrausch, Martin

Building for the Arts: The Strategic Design of Cultural Facilities — Frumkin, Peter
Building Fortress Europe: The Polish-Ukrainian Frontier — Follis, Karolina S.
Building: Letters, 1960-1975 — Berlin, Isaiah
Building Outdoor Kitchens for Every Budget — Cory, Steve
Building Outdoor Kitchens for Every Budget — Slavik, Cory
Building Proportional Reasoning across Grades and Math Strands, K-8 — Small, Marian
Building Resilience: Social Capital in Post-Disaster Recovery — Aldrich, Daniel P.
Building Sanctuary: The Movement to Support Vietnam War Resisters in Canada, 1965-73 — Squires, Jessica
Building the Beloved Community: Philadelphia's Interracial Civil Rights Organizations and Race Relations, 1930-1970 — Arnold, Stanley Keith
Building the H Bomb: A Personal History — Ford, Kenneth W.
Building the Land of Dreams: New Orleans and the Transformation of Early America — Faber, Eberhard L.
Building the Modern Church: Roman Catholic Church Architecture in Britain, 1955 to 1975 — Proctor, Robert (b. 1973-)
Building the Most Complex Structure on Earth: An Epigenetic Narrative of Development and Evolution of Animals — Cabej, Nelson R.
Building the Old Time Religion: Women Evangelists in the Progressive Era — Pope-Levison, Priscilla
Building the State: Architecture, Politics and State Formation in Post-War Central Europe — Molnar, Virag
c Building the White House — Proudfit, Benjamin
Buildings of Empire — Jackson, Ashley
c Buildings on the Farm — Borth, Teddy
Built: Saints of Denver — Crownover, Jay
c The Buk Buk Buk Festival (Illus. by Auch, Mary Jane) — Auch, Mary Jane
Bukharan Jews and the Dynamics of Global Judaism — Cooper, Alanna E.
The Bulgarian Truck — Tsepeneag, Dumitru
Bull Mountain (Read by Troxell, Brian). Audiobook Review — Panowich, Brian
Bull Mountain — Panowich, Brian
Bullarium Cyprium, vol. 3: Lettres papales relatives a Chypre, 1316-1378 — Perrat, Charles
c Bulldogs — Barnes, Nico
c Bulldozer's Big Day (Illus. by Rohmann, Eric) — Fleming, Candace
c Bulldozers — Lennie, Charles
The Bullet — Kelly, Mary Louise
y The Bullet Catch — Axelrod, Amy
Bullet Catcher — Bradford, Chris
Bullets, Badges, and Bridles: Horse Thieves and the Societies That Pursued Them — Burchill, John K.
The Bullfight — Inoue, Yasushi
The Bullied Anthology: Stories of Success — Kaushik, Bhavya
y Bullied Kids Speak Out: We Survived--How You Can Too — Blanco, Jodee
Bullies: A Friendship — Abramovich, Alex
y The Bullies of Wall Street — Bair, Sheila
Bullpen — Morreale, P.
Bulls before Breakfast: Running with the Bulls and Celebrating Fiesta de San Fermin in Pamplona, Spain — Milligan, Peter N.
c The Bully Bug (Illus. by Calo, Marcos) — Lubar, David
Bully Nation: Why America's Approach to Childhood Aggression Is Bad for Everyone — Porter, Susan Eva
The Bully of Order — Hart, Brian
The Bully Pulpit: Theodore Roosevelt, William Howard Taft, and the Golden Age of Journalism — Goodwin, Doris Kearns
Bullying beyond the Schoolyard — Hinduja, Sameer
y Bullying — Perdew, Laura
Bum Rap — Levine, Paul
Bumf — Sacco, Joe
c Bums and Tums (Illus. by Foot, Mandy)
c Bun Bun and Milby Go Walkabout — Kirk, Joe
Bundnisse. Politische und Intellektuelle Allianzen im Jahrhundert der Aufklarung
Bunin i Nabokov: Istoriia sopernichestva — Shraer, Maksim D.
y The Bunker Diary — Brooks, Kevin
Bunker Hill: A City, a Siege, a Revolution — Philbrick, Nathaniel

Bunkers: Atlantvoldens perspektiver i Danmark — Hansen, Lulu Anne
Bunnies (Illus. by Anderson, Laura Ellen) — Anderson, Laura Ellen
c Bunnies!!! (Illus. by Atteberry, Kevan) — Atteberry, Kevan
c Bunny Dreams (Illus. by McCarty, Peter) — McCarty, Peter
c Bunny Hopwell's First Spring (Illus. by Dixon, Rachel) — Fritz, Jean
c Bunny Roo, I Love You (Illus. by White, Teagan) — Marr, Melissa
c Bunny the Brave War Horse: Based on a True Story (Illus. by Lafance, Marie) — MacLeod, Elizabeth
c Bunny vs. Monkey, Book 2 — Smart, Jamie
c Bunny vs. Monkey (Illus. by Smart, Jamie) — Smart, Jamie
c Bunny's First Spring (Illus. by McPhail, David) — Lloyd-Jones, Sally
The Bunraku Puppet Theatre of Japan: Honor, Vengeance, and Love in Four Plays of the 18th and 19th Centuries — Jones, Stanleigh H.
BurdaStyle Modern Sewing: Wardrobe Essentials — BurdaStyle, Inc.
The Burden of Memory — Cole, Welcome
The Burdens of Empire: 1539 to the Present — Pagden, Anthony
c The Bureau of Misplaced Dads (Illus. by Martin, Pauline) — Veille, Eric
The Burglar Who Counted the Spoons — Block, Lawrence
A Burglar's Guide to the City — Manaugh, Geoff
Burgos in the Peninsular War, 1808-1814: Occupation, Siege, Aftermath — Freeman, Philip
The Buried Giant (Read by Horovitch, David). Audiobook Review — Ishiguro, Kazuo
The Buried Giant — Ishiguro, Kazuo
Buried Glory: Portraits of Soviet Scientists — Hargittai, Istvan
Buried in Beignets — Ripley, J.R.
Buried in Shades of Night: Contested Voices, Indian Captivity, and the Legacy of King Philip's War — Stratton, Billy J.
Buried Secrets — Hannon, Irene
c Buried Sunlight: How Fossil Fuels Have Change the Earth (Illus. by Bang, Molly) — Bang, Molly
c Buried Sunlight: How Fossil Fuels Have Changed the Earth (Illus. by Bang, Molly) — Bang, Molly
c Buried Sunlight: How Fossil Fuels Have Changed the Earth (Illus. by Bang, Molly) — Chisholm, Penny
Buried Treasure: Overlooked, Forgotten and Uncrowned Classic Albums — Hegarty, Dan
The Burma Spring: Aung San Suu Kyi and the New Struggle for the Soul of a Nation — Pederson, Rena
Burma's Economy in the Twentieth Century — Brown, Ian
Burn — Jury, Walter
y Burn — Weston, Paula
y Burn Girl — Mikulencak, Mandy
Burn It Down — Byrum, Katie
Burn It Up — McKenna, Cara
y Burned — Deen, Natasha
The Burned Bridges of Ward, Nebraska — Curtright, Eileen
Burned Deep — Fox, Calista
y Burning — Rollins, Danielle
y The Burning — Skogen, Jennifer
The Burning Answer: A User's Guide to the Solar Revolution — Barnham, Keith
The Burning Answer: The Solar Revolution: A Quest for Sustainable Power — Barnham, Keith
Burning Down George Orwell's House — Ervin, Andrew
Burning Down the House: The End of Youth Prison — Bernstein, Nell
y Burning Glass — Purdie, Kathryn
Burning Heat — Burnsworth, David
c The Burning Horizon — Hunter, Erin
y Burning Kingdoms — DeStefano, Lauren
Burning Man: Art on Fire — Raiser, Jennifer
y Burning Midnight — McIntosh, Will
y Burning Nation — Reedy, Trent
The Burning Room (Read by Welliver, Titus). Audiobook Review — Connelly, Michael
The Burning Room — Connelly, Michael
y The Burning Sea — Collins, Paul
The Burning Shore: How Hitler's U-Boats Brought World War II to America — Offley, Ed
Burning the Grass: At the Heart of Change in South Africa, 1990-2011 — Jagielski, Wojciech
Burning the Short White Coat: A Story of Becoming a Woman Doctor — Shvidler, Eve

Burnout to Brilliance: Strategies for Sustainable Success — Morris, Jayne
A Burnt Child — Dagerman, Stig
Burnt Cork: Traditions and Legacies of Blackface Minstrelsy — Johnson, Stephen Burge
Burnt River — Salvalaggio, Karin
Burnt Siena — Wisseman, Sarah
Burnt Toast Makes You Sing Good (Read by Campbell, Cassandra). Audiobook Review — Flinn, Kathleen
Burqa of Skin — Arcan, Nelly
c Bursting at the Seams (Illus. by Zhang, Nancy) — Taylor, Chloe
Bury St Edmunds and the Norman Conquest — Licence, Tom
Burying Ben — Kirschman, Ellen
The Burying Ground — Kellough, Janet
Burying the Ex — Dante, Joe
The Bus Driver's Threnody — Spence, Michael
The Bus Is for Us! (Illus. by Tyler, Gillian) — Rosen, Michael
c The Bus Ride (Illus. by Dubuc, Marianne) — Dubuc, Marianne
c The Bus Ride — Dubuc, Marianne
The Bushido Element — Vancans, Juri
Bushmaster: Raymond Ditmars and the Hunt for the World's Largest Viper — Eatherley, Dan
Business Goals and Social Commitment: Shaping Organizational Capabilities--Colombia's Fundacion Social, 1984-2011 — Davila, Jose Camilo
A Business History of the Swatch Group: The Rebirth of Swiss Watchmaking and the Globalization of the Luxury Industry — Donze, Pierre-Yves
Business in the Age of Extremes: Essays in Modern German and Austrian Economic History — Berghoff, Hartmut
The Business of Identity: Jews, Muslims, and Economic Life in Medieval Egypt — Ackerman-Lieberman, Phillip I.
The Business of Private Medical Practice: Doctors, Specialization, and Urban Change in Philadelphia, 1900-1940 — Schafer, James A., Jr.
The Business Romantic: Give Everything, Quantify Nothing, and Create Something Greater Than Yourself — Leberecht, Tim
Busker's Holiday — Gussow, Adam
Busted — Walker, Shiloh
c Buster the Little Garbage Truck (Illus. by Zimmer, Kevin) — Berneger, Marcia
Buster: The Military Dog Who Saved a Thousand Lives — Barrow, Will
c Buster the Very Shy Dog Finds a Kitten — Bechtold, Lisze
c Busy Baby: Friends (Illus. by Gillingham, Sara) — Gillingham, Sara
Busy: How to Thrive in a World of Too Much — Crabbe, Tony
Busy in the Cause: Iowa, the Free-State Struggle in the West, and the Prelude to the Civil War — Soike, Lowell J.
c Busy Trucks on the Go (Illus. by Culotta, Kent) — Ode, Eric
c But! — Hamilton, Tim

But Enough about Me: A Memoir — Reynolds, Burt
But I Could Never Go Vegan!: 125 Recipes That Prove You Can Live without Cheese, It's Not All Rabbit Food, and Your Friends Will Still Come Over for Dinner — Turner, Kristy
c But It's Not My Fault (Illus. by DuFalla, Anita) — Cook, Julia
Butcher a Hog — O'Sullivan, Brian
The Butcher — Hillier, Jennifer
The Butcher's Daughter — McMillin, Mark M.
The Butcher's Sons — Hess, Scott Alexander
The Butcher's Trail: How the Search for Balkan War Criminals Became the World's Most Successful Manhunt — Borger, Julian
Butter Baked Goods: Nostalgic Recipes from a Little Neighborhood Bakery — Daykin, Rosie
Butterfield's Byway: America's First Overland Mail Route across the West — Groves, Melody
Butterflies — Marent, Thomas
Butterflies: A Complete Guide to Their Biology and Behavior, 2d ed. — Vane-Wright, Dick
The Butterflies' Coat — Williams, Ronald
Butterflies in November — FitzGibbon, Brian
The Butterflies of North America, Diurnal Lepidoptera: Whence They Come, Where They Go, and What They Do — Peale, Titian Ramsay, II
c Butterflies — Delano, Marfe Ferguson
c The Butterfly Club (Read by Leslay, Madeleine). Audiobook Review — Wilson, Jacqueline
c Butterfly Counting (Illus. by Bersani, Shennen) — Pallotta, Jerry
Butterfly in the Typewriter: The Tragic Life of John Kennedy Toole and the Remarkable Story of a Confederacy of Dunces — MacLauchlin, Cory
A Butterfly Journey: Maria Sibylla Merian, Artist and Scientist — Friedewald, Boris
Butterfly Kills — Chapman, Brenda
c Butterfly Park (Illus. by MacKay, Elly) — MacKay, Elly
Butterfly Waltz — Tesh, Jane
c The Buttermilk Biscuit Boy (Illus. by Klein, Laurie) — Nelson, Amanda S.
y Button Hill — Bradford, Michael
c Button Nose the Sad Little Bear (Illus. by Wilder, Brittany) — LoBiondo, Gina
c A Button Story (Illus. by Revell, Cindy) — Sher, Emil
Buy Me the Sky: The Remarkable Truth of China's One-Child Generation — Tyldesley, Esther
Buy Me the Sky: The Remarkable Truth of China's One-Child Generations — Xinran
Buying a Better World: George Soros and Billionaire Philanthropy — Porter, Anna
Buying into Fair Trade: Culture, Morality, and Consumption — Brown, Keith R.
Buying into the Regime: Grapes and Consumption in Cold War Chile and the United States — Tinsman, Heidi
Buying the Vote: A History of Campaign Finance Reform — Mutch, Robert E.
A Buzz in the Meadow: The Natural History of a French Farm — Goulson, Dave
Buzz Kill (Read by Moon, Erin). Audiobook Review — Fantaskey, Beth

Buzzard Tales: The Memoirs of a Cherokee Gunfighter — Schmid, Vernon
Buzzing Hemisphere/Rumor Hemisferico — Noel, Urayoan
c Buzzy Bee's Birthday Party (Illus. by Holt, Richard) — Cowley, Joy
c Buzzy Bee's Food Shapes (Illus. by Holt, Richard) — Cowley, Joy
By All Accounts: General Stores and Community Life in Texas and Indian Territory — English, Linda
By All Means Necessary: How China's Resource Quest Is Changing the World — Economy, Elizabeth
By Avon River — Vetter, Lara
c By Day, By Night (Illus. by So, Meilo) — Gibson, Amy
By Its Cover — Leon, Donna
c By Mouse & Frog (Ilus. by Freedman, Deborah) — Freedman, Deborah
c By Mouse & Frog (Illus. by Freeman, Deborah) — Freeman, Deborah
By Night the Mountain Burns — Laurel, Juan Tomas Avila
By Royal Appointment: Tales from the Privy Council--the Unknown Arm of Government — Rogers, David
By Sword and Plow: France, and the Conquest of Algeria — Sessions, Jennifer E.
By the People: Rebuilding Liberty without Permission — Murray, Charles
By the Rivers of Water: A Nineteenth-Century Atlantic Odyssey — Clarke, Erskine
By the Spear: Philip II, Alexander the Great, and the Rise and Fall of the Macedonian Empire — Worthington, Ian
By the Sweat of your Brow: Roman Slavery in its Socio-Economic Setting — Roth, Ulrike
c By Trolley Past Thimbledon Bridge (Illus. by Bileck, Marvin) — Bryan, Ashley
By What Is Sure to Follow — Burton, Donald N.
By Your Side — Calvert, Candace
c Bye-Bye Grumpy Fly (Illus. by Paul, Ruth) — Paul, Ruth
Bye, Bye Love — Larsen, K.J.
Byrd — McCarthy, Kerry
Byron and the Discourses of History — Pomare, Carla
Byron in Geneva: That Summer of 1816 — Ellis, David
Byron's Romantic Politics: The Problem of Metahistory — Cochran, Peter
Bystander, Rescuer or Perpetrators? The Neutral Countries and the Shoah
Byzantine Art and Diplomacy in an Age of Decline — Hilsdale, Cecily J.
Byzantine Images and Their Afterlives: Essays in Honor of Annemarie Weyl Carr — Jones, Lynn
The Byzantine-Islamic Transition in Palestine: An Archeological Approach — Avni, Gideon
Byzantine Matters — Cameron, Averil
Byzantium and the Turks in the Thirteenth Century — Korobeinikov, Dimitri
y BZRK Apocalypse (Read by Evers-Swindell, Nico). Audiobook Review — Grant, Michael
y BZRK Apocalypse — Grant, Michael

C

C.G. Jung: A Biography in Books — *Shamdasini, Sonu*
A C.H. Sisson Reader — *Louth, Charlie*
c C Is for Chickasaw (Illus. by Long, Aaron) — *Barnes, Wiley*
y C.O.W.L., vol. 2: Principles of Power (Illus. by Reis, Rod) — *Higgins, Kyle*
y C.O.W.L., vol. 2: The Greater Good (Illus. by Reis, Rod) — *Higgins, Kyle*
C.S. Lewis and His Circle: Essays and Memoirs from the Oxford C.S. Lewis Society — *White, Roger*
The Cabaret of Plants: Botany and the Imagination — *Mabey, Richard*
The Cabaret of Plants: Forty Thousand Years of Plant Life and the Human Imagination — *Mabey, Richard*
Cabin Fever: The Sizzling Secrets of a Virgin Airlines Flight Attendant — *Smith, Mandy*
Cabin Lessons: A Nail-by-Nail Tale: Building Our Dream Cottage from 2x4s, Blisters, and Love — *Carlsen, Spike*
c The Cabinet of Curiosities: 36 Tales Brief and Sinister (Illus. by Jansson, Alexander) — *Bachmann, Stefan*
Cabinet of Mathematical Curiosities at Teachers College: David Eugene Smith's Collection — *Murray, Diane M.*
Cable Guys: Television and Masculinities in the Twenty-First Century — *Lotz, Amanda*
Cables, Crises, and the Press: The Geopolitics of the New International Information System in the Americas, 1866-1903 — *Britton, John A.*
The Cactus Creek Challenge — *Vetsch, Erica*
Cadence to Glory — *Dearmon, Mary Beth*
Cadmium: From Toxicity to Essentiality — *Sigel, Astrid*
Caesar in the City of Amun: Egyptian Temple Construction and Theology in Roman Thebes — *Klotz, David*
Caesar in the USA — *Tompkins, Daniel P.*
Cafe Europa — *Ifkovic, Ed*
Cafe Noir — *Hardy, Ross C.*
The Cafe Spice Cookbook: 84 Quick and Easy Indian Recipes for Everyday Meals — *Nayak, Hari*
Cafe "The Blue Danube" — *Yakimov, Radka*
y The Cage — *Shepherd, Megan*
The Cage-Busting Teacher — *Hess, Frederick M.*
c A Cage of Rotos — *Griffin, Matt*
Caging the Robin — *Crawford, Tom*
c Cailyn and Chloe Learn about Conjunctions (Illus. by Haus, Estudio) — *Atwood, Megan*
Cairo Affair — *Steinhauer, Olen*
c Cajun 'Ti Beau and the Cocodries (Illus. by D'Antoni, Colleen) — *Gibson, Cay*
c The Cake (Illus. by de Monfreid, Dorothee) — *de Monfreid, Dorothee*
The Cake House — *Salom, Latifah*
The Cake Therapist — *Fertig, Judith*
Cakeology: Over 20 Sensational Step-by-Step Cake Decorating Projects — *Sear, Juliet*
Cakes, Custard and Category Theory: Easy Recipes for Understanding Complex Maths — *Eugenia Cheng*
c Cakes in Space (Illus. by McIntyre, Sarah) — *Reeve, Philip*
Calabria: The Other Italy — *Haid, Karen*
Calamities and the Economy in Renaissance Italy: The Grand Tour of the Horsemen of the Apocalypse — *Alfani, Guido*
y Calamity — *Sanderson, Brandon*
Calculations in Chemistry: An Introduction — *Nelson, Eric A.*
A Calculus of Color: The Integration of Baseball's American League — *McGregor, Robert Kuhn*

Calculus without Derivatives — *Pemnot, Jean Paul*
c Caleb Davis Bradham: Pepsi-Cola Inventor — *Lianas, Sheila Griffin*
Calf: A Novel — *Kleine, Andrea*
Calico Cats — *Dash, Meredith*
Califia Women: Feminist Education against Sexism, Classism, and Racism — *Pomerleau, Clark A.*
y California — *Lepucki, Edan*
California Bones — *Eekhout, Greg van*
California Dreaming: Boosterism, Memory, and Rural Suburbs in the Golden State — *Sandul, Paul J.P.*
The Caliph's Splendor — *Bobrick, Benson*
Call and Response — *Kincaid, Paul*
Call for Change: The Medicine Way of American Indian History, Ethos, and Reality — *Fixico, Donald L.*
A Call from Spooner Street — *Ascher, Carol*
y Call Me Athena: Greek Goddess of Wisdom — *Bridges, Shirin Yim*
Call Me Burroughs: A Life — *Miles, Barry*
Call Me Debbie: True Confessions of a Down-to-Earth Diva — *Voigt, Deborah*
Call Me Home — *Kruse, Megan*
y Call Me Isis: Egyptian Goddess of Magic (Illus. by Bridges, Shirin Yim) — *Maurer, Gretchen*
y Call Me Ixchel: Mayan Goddess of the Moon (Illus. by Bridges, Shirin Yim) — *Havemeyer, Janie*
c Call Me Tree / Llamame Arbol — *Gonzalez, Maya Christina*
The Call of Bilal: Islam in the African Diaspora — *Curtis, Edward E.*
y The Call of the Osprey (Illus. by Munoz, William) — *Patent, Dorothy Hinshaw*
Call on Me — *Loren, Roni*
A Call to Arms: Mobilizing America for World War II — *Klein, Maury*
A Call to Arms — *Pope, Thomas*
Call Waiting — *Ward, David C.*
Called for Life: How Loving Our Neighbor Led Us into the Heart of the Ebola Epidemic — *Brantly, Kent*
y The Caller — *Marillier, Juliet*
Calligraphy Lesson: The Collected Stories — *Shishkin, Mikhail*
Callimachus in Context: From Plato to the Augustan Poets — *Acosta-Hughes, Benjamin*
The Calling — *White, Louise G.*
c Calling All Cars (Illus. by Beise, Sarah) — *Fliess, Sue*
Calling and Clarity: Discovering What God Wants for Your Life — *Koskela, Doug*
y Calling Maggie May — *Anonymous*
y Calling the Shots — *Karre, Elizabeth*
Calling the Shots! Using Film Techniques to Inspire Brilliant Creative Writing — *Handel, Nick*
Calling Tower — *Leone, Josh*
Calloustown — *Singleton, George*
Calm Baby Gently — *Hutton, John*
c Calm Girl: Yoga for Stress Relief — *Rissman, Rebecca*
The Calm Ocean — *Roth, Gerhard*
The Caloris Rim Project — *Mac Donald, Glenn P.*
Calpurnii Siculi: Eclogae — *Vinchesi, M.A.*
y Calvin — *Leavitt, Martine*
Calvin Institute of Christian Worship Liturgical Series — *Bauer, Michael J.*
c Calvin Johnson — *Bodden, Valerie*
c Calvin, Look Out!: A Bookworm Birdie Gets Glasses (Illus. by Bendis, Keith) — *Berne, Jennifer*
Calvin Meets Voltaire: The Clergy of Geneva in the Age of Enlightenment, 1685-1798 — *McNutt, Jennifer Powell*
Calvinism: A History — *Hart, Darryl G.*

Cambodia: Entering a New Phase of Growth — *Unteroberdoerster, Olaf*
c The Cambodian Dancer: Sophany's Gift of Hope (Illus. by Hale, Christy) — *Reicherter, Daryn*
c Cambodian Dancer: Sophany's Gift of Hope (Illus. by Hale, Christy) — *Reicherter, Daryn*
The Cambrian Explosion: The Construction of Animal Biodiversity. — *Erwin, Douglas H.*
Cambrian Ocean World: Ancient Sea Life of North America — *Foster, John*
Cambridge — *Kaysen, Susanna*
The Cambridge Companion to American Civil Rights Literature — *Armstrong, Julie Buckner*
The Cambridge Companion to American Methodism — *Vickers, Jason E.*
The Cambridge Companion to American Science Fiction — *Link, Eric Carl*
The Cambridge Companion to Aristotle's Politics — *Deslauriers, Marguerite*
The Cambridge Companion to Gabriel Garcia Marquez — *Swanson, Philip*
The Cambridge Companion to Hip-Hop — *Williams, Justin A.*
The Cambridge Companion to James Baldwin — *Elam, Michele*
The Cambridge Companion to Latin Love Elegy — *Thorsen, T.S.*
The Cambridge Companion to Michael Tippett — *Gloag, Kenneth*
The Cambridge Companion to Muhammad — *Brockopp, Jonathan E.*
The Cambridge Companion to Pentecostalism — *Robeck, Cecil M., Jr.*
The Cambridge Companion to Rudyard Kipling — *Booth, Howard J.*
The Cambridge Companion to Sensation Fiction — *Mangham, Andrew*
A Cambridge Companion to Textual Scholarship — *Fraistat, Neil*
The Cambridge Companion to the Age of Attila — *Maas, Michael*
The Cambridge Companion to the Bloomsbury Group — *Rosner, Victoria*
The Cambridge Companion to the French Enlightenment — *Brewer, Daniel*
The Cambridge Companion to the Italian Renaissance — *Wyatt, Michael*
The Cambridge Companion to the Literature of Paris — *Milne, Anna-Louise*
The Cambridge Companion to the Literature of the American South — *Monteith, Sharon*
The Cambridge Companion to the Symphony — *Horton, Julian*
The Cambridge Companion to "To the Lighthouse" — *Pease, Allison*
The Cambridge Companion to "Ulysses" — *Latham, Sean*
The Cambridge Edition of the Works of F. Scott Fitzgerald, 14 vols. — *Fitzgerald, F. Scott*
The Cambridge History of Capitalism, 2 vols. — *Williamson, Jeffrey G.*
The Cambridge History of Early Medieval English Literature — *Lees, Clare A.*
The Cambridge History of Gay and Lesbian Literature — *McCallum, E.L.*
The Cambridge History of Painting in the Classical World — *Pollitt, J.J.*
The Cambridge History of Religions in the Ancient World, vol. 1: From the Bronze Age to the Hellenistic Age — *Sweeney, Marvin A.*

The Cambridge History of Religions in the Ancient World, vol. 1: From the Bronze Age to the Hellenistic Age — *Salzman, Michele Renee*
The Cambridge History of Religions in the Ancient World, vol. 2: From the Hellenistic Age to Late Antiquity — *Adler, William*
The Cambridge History of Religions in the Ancient World, vol. 2: From the Hellenistic Age to Late Antiquity — *Salzman, Michele Renee*
The Cambridge Introduction to George Orwell — *Rodden, John*
The Cambridge Introduction to German Poetry — *Ryan, Judith*
The Cambridge Introduction to Jane Austen, 2nd ed. — *Todd, Janet*
The Cambridge Introduction to Theatre Directing — *Innes, Christopher*
The Cambridge Wagner Encyclopedia — *Vazsonyi, Nicholas*
Cambridgeshire — *Bradley, Simon*
Came Men on Horses: The Conquistador Expeditions of Francisco Vazquez de Coronado and Don Juan de Onate — *Hoig, Stan*
Camelot's Court: Inside the Kennedy White House — *Dallek, Robert*
c Camels — *Riggs, Kate*
c Camels Are Awesome! — *Morey, Allan*
c Camera — *Salzmann, Mary Elizabeth*
Cameron's Coup: How the Tories Took Britain to the Brink — *Toynbee, Polly*
Camille — *Lemaitre, Pierre*
Camille Styles Entertaining: Inspired Gatherings and Effortless Style — *Styles, Camille*
The Campaign of 1812 — *Rauch, Steven J.*
A Campaign of Quiet Persuasion: How the College Board Desegregated SAT Test Centers in the Deep South, 1960-1965 — *Wheeler, Jan Bates*
Campo de guerra: Premio Anagrama de Ensayo — *Rodriguez, Sergio Gonzales*
Camus et l'imposible treve civile: suivi d'une correspondance avec Amar Ouzegane — *Poncet, Charles*
Can a Renewal Movement Be Renewed?: Questions for the Future of Ecumenism — *Kinnamon, Michael*
Can and Can'tankerous — *Ellison, Harlan*
Can Democracy Be Saved? Participation, Deliberation and Social Movements — *Della Porta, Donatella*
Can Financial Markets be Controlled — *Davies, Howard*
c Can I Bring Saber to New York City, Ms. Mayor? (Illus. by Love, Judy) — *Grambling, Lois G.*
c Can I Come Too? (Illus. by Bayley, Nicola) — *Patten, Brian*
Can I Go Now? The Life of Sue Mengers, Hollywood's First Superagent — *Kellow, Brian*
Can Russia Modernise?: 'Sistema,' Power Networks and Informal Governance — *Ledeneva, Alena*
Can Singapore Survive? — *Mahbubani, Kishore*
c Can We Help? Kids Volunteering to Help Their Communities (Illus. by Ancona, George) — *Ancona, George*
c Can You Say It, Too? Jingle! Jingle! (Illus. by Braun, Sebastian) — *Braun, Sebastien*
c Can You Say It, Too? Jingle! Jingle! (Illus. by Braun, Sebastien) — *Braun, Sebastien*
c Can You Say It, Too? Quack! Quack! (Illus. by Braun, Sebastien) — *Braun, Sebastien*
c Can You See What I See? Christmas (Illus. by Wick, Walter) — *Wick, Walter*
Can You Sing "The Star-Spangled Banner"? (Illus. by Poling, Kyle) — *Rustad, Martha E.H.*
c Can You Whoo, Too? (Illus. by Fatus, Sophie) — *Ziefert, Harriet*
Canace, 1542 — *Speroni, Sperone*
c Canada en une journee — *Gurth, Per-Henrik*
Canada in the Great Power Game, 1914-2014 — *Dyer, Gwynne*
Canada the Good: A Short History of Vice since 1500 — *Martel, Marcel*
Canada Transformed: The Speeches of Sir John A. Macdonald: A Bicentennial Celebration — *Gibson, Sarah Katherine*
Canada's Bastions of Empire: Haliflax, Victoria and the Royal Navy 1749-1918 — *Elson, Bryan*
Canadian Churches and the First World War — *Heath, Gordon L.*
c Canadian Coins — *Crewe, Sabrina*
The Canadian Law of Unjust Enrichment and Restitution — *McInnes, Mitchell*
c Canadian Mounties — *Crewe, Sabrina*
c The Canadian Shiel: From the Temperate to the Tundra — *Schwartzenberger, Tina*

The Canadian Theater 1813 — *Barbuto, Richard*
The Canadian Theatre 1814 — *Barbuto, Richard*
Canadians and Their Pasts — *Conrad, Margaret*
y Canary — *Swierczynski, Duane*
The Canary Islands: A Cultural History — *Stone, Peter*
A Cancer Companion: An Oncologist's Advice on Diagnosis, Treatment, and Recovery — *Srivastava, Ranjana*
A Cancer in the Family — *Ross, Theodora*
The Cancer Solution: Taking Charge of Your Life with Cancer — *Westman, Jack C.*
The Cancer Survivors Club: A Collection of Inspirational and Uplifting Survival Stories — *Geiger, Chris*
Cancer Virus: The Story of Epstein-Barr Virus — *Crawford, Dorothy H.*
Cancerlandia! — *Alvarado Valdivia, Juan*
Candidate — *Ewens, Tracy*
c The Candy Conspiracy: A Tale of Sweet Victory (Illus. by Davila, Claudia) — *Snyder, Carrie*
Candy Corn Murder — *Meier, Leslie*
The Candy Store — *Poague, Michele*
Cane and Abe — *Grippando, James*
The Cane Creek Regulators — *Boggs, Johnny D.*
The Cannabis Encyclopedia: The Definitive Guide to Cultivation and Consumption of Medical Marijuana — *Cervantes, Jorge*
y Canned and Crushed — *Belford, Bibi*
Cannon Mills and Kannapolis: Persistent Paternalism in a Textile Town — *Vanderburg, Timothy W.*
Cannonbridge — *Barnes, Jonathan*
Cannot Stay: Essays on Travel — *Oderman, Kevin*
Canon Law, Religion, and Politics: Liber Amicorum Robert Somerville — *Blumenthal, Uta-Renate*
Can't Catch a Break: Gender, Jail, Drugs, and the Limits of Personal Responsibility — *Sered, Susan Starr*
Can't Find My Way Home — *Thompson, Carlene*
y Can't Look Away — *Cooner, Donna*
Can't We Talk about Something More Pleasant? — *Chast, Roz*
The Canterbury Sisters — *Wright, Kim*
Canto General, Canto II, The Heights of Macchu Picchu — *Morin, Tomas Q.*
Canto Hondo / Deep Song — *Alarcon, Francisco X.*
The Canyon — *Crawford, Stanley*
Canyon in the Body — *Lan Lan*
Canyon of Dreams: Stories from Grand Canyon History — *Lago, Don*
Cape Deception — *Nordstrom, Eugene*
Capital — *Lanchester, John*
Capital and Corporal Punishment in Anglo-Saxon England — *Gates, Jay Paul*
Capital as Will and Imagination: Schumpeter's Guide to the Postwar Japanese Miracle — *Metzler, Mark*
Capital Culture: J. Carter Brown, the National Gallery of Art, and the Reinvention of the Museum Experience — *Harris, Neil*
Capital Dames: The Civil War and the Women of Washington, 1848-1868 — *Roberts, Cokie*
c Capital Days: Michael Shiner's Journal and the Growth of Our Nation's Capital — *Bolden, Tonya*
Capital Failure: Rebuilding Trust in Financial Services — *Morris, Nicholas*
Capital in the Twenty-First Century — *Piketty, Thomas*
Capital: New York, Capital of the 20th Century — *Goldsmith, Kenneth*
Capital of the World: The Race to Host the United Nations — *Mires, Charlene*
Capital, the State and War: Class Conflict and Geopolitics in the Thirty Years' Crisis, 1914-1945 — *Anievas, Alexander*
Capitalism from Below: Markets and Institutional Change in China — *Nee, Victor*
Capitalism: Money, Morals and Markets — *Plender, John*
The Capitalism Papers: Fatal Flaws of an Obsolete System — *Mander, Jerry*
Capitalism v. Democracy: Money in Politics and the Free Market Constitution — *Kuhner, Timothy K.*
Capitalist Development in India's Informal Economy — *Basile, Elisabetta*
The Capitalist — *Steiner, Peter*
The Capitalist Transformation of State Socialism: The Making and Breaking of State Social Society, and What Followed — *Lane, David*
Capitalizing on Crisis: The Political Origins of the Rise of Finance — *Krippner, Greta R.*
c Cap'n John the (Slightly) Fierce (Illus. by Anderson, Laura Ellen) — *Smith, Johnny*

Capone, the Cobbs, and Me — *Burwell, Rex*
y Captain — *Angus, Sam*
The Captain and "The Cannibal": An Epic Story of Exploration, Kidnapping, and the Broadway Stage — *Fairhead, James*
c Captain Awesome and the Easter Egg Bandit (Illus. by O'Connor, George) — *Kirby, Stan*
c Captain Awesome Gets a Hole-in-One (Illus. by O'Connor, George) — *Kirby, Stan*
c Captain Awesome vs. the Evil Babysitter (Illus. by O'Connor, George) — *Kirby, Stan*
c Captain Beastlie's Pirate Party (Illus. by Mould, Chris) — *Coats, Lucy*
y Captain Coconut & the Case of the Missing Bananas (Illus. by Sundram, Priya) — *Ravishankar, Anushka*
Captain in Calico — *Fraser, George MacDonald*
c Captain Jack and the Pirates (Illus. by Oxenbury, Helen) — *Bently, Peter*
c Captain Marvel: Higher, Further, Faster, More (Illus. by Lopez, David) — *Deconnick, Kelly Sue*
y Captain Marvel: Stay Fly (Illus. by Lopez, David) — *Deconnick, Kelly Sue*
c Captain No Beard and the Aurora Borealis (Illus. by Roman, Carole P.) — *Roman, Carole P.*
c Captain Underpants and the Sensational Saga of Sir Stinks-a-Lot (Illus. by Pilkey, Dav) — *Pilkey, Dav*
c Captain Underpants and the Tyrannical Retaliation of the Turbo Toilet 2000 (Illus. by Pilkey, Dav) — *Pilkey, Dav*
The Captain's Bluestocking Mistress — *Ridley, Erica*
c Captive — *Carter, Aimee*
y Captive — *Grainger, A.J.*
Captive — *Walsh, Brighton*
A Captive Audience: Voices of Japanese American Youth in World War II Arkansas — *Welky, Ali*
The Captive Condition — *Keating, Kevin P.*
Captive Prince — *Pacat, C.S.*
The Captive Stage: Performance and the Proslavery Imagination of the Antebellum North — *Jones, Douglas A., Jr.*
Captives — *Manea, Norman*
Captives in Blue: The Civil War Prisons of the Confederacy — *Pickenpaugh, Roger*
Captivity — *Spiro, Gyorgy*
y The Capture — *Isbell, Tom*
Capture These Indians for the Lord: Indians, Methodists, and Oklahomans, 1844-1939 — *Smith, Tash*
Captured: From the Frontier Diary of Infant Danny Duly — *Lalire, Gregory J.*
Capturing Contemporary Japan: Differentiation and Uncertainty — *Kawano, Satsuki*
Capturing Music: The Story of Notation — *Kelly, Thomas Forrest*
Car Country: An Environmental History — *Wells, Christopher W.*
Car Crazy: The Battle for Supremacy between Ford and Olds and the Dawn of the Automobile Age — *Miller, G. Wayne*
y Car-Jacked — *Sparkes, Ali*
Car Safety Wars: One Hundred Years of Technology, Politics, and Death — *Lemov, Michael R.*
Car Wars: The Rise, the Fall, and the Resurgence of the Electric Car — *Fialka, John J.*
Caravaggio: Reflections and Refractions — *Pericolo, Lorenzo*
Caravan of No Despair — *Starr, Mirabai*
Carbide Tipped Pens — *Choi, Eric*
Carbon — *Boyd, Daniel*
c The Carbon Cycle — *Dakers, Diane*
Carbon Democracy: Political Power in the Age of Oil — *Mitchell, Timothy*
Carbon Nation: Fossil Fuels in the Making of American Culture — *Johnson, Bob*
The Carbon Rush: The Truth Behind the Carbon Market Smokescreen — *Miller, Amy*
c Carcass Chewers of the Animal World — *Rake, Jody Sullivan*
Cardboard Soldiers — *Scotson, James G.*
The Cardinal Mindszenty Documents in American Archives — *Somorjai, Adam*
Cardinal Rules — *Delinsky, Barbara*
The Cardinal's Sin — *Lane, Robert*
The Cardinals Way: How One Team Embraced Tradition and Moneyball at the Same Time — *Megdal, Howard*
Cards That Wow with Sizzix: Techniques and Ideas for Using Die-Cutting and Embossing Machines — *Barnard, Stephanie*
The Care and Management of Lies — *Winspear, Jacqueline*
Care Giver — *Blanchard, Richard*

Career of Evil — Galbraith, Robert
y Careers for Tech Girls in Video Game Development — La Bella, Laura
y Careers in Biotechnology — Szumski, Bonnie
y Careers in Education — Sheen, Barbara
y Careers in Engineering — Szumski, Bonnie
y Careers in Finance — Mattern, Joanne
y Careers in Health Care — Sheen, Barbara
Careers in Music Librarianship III: Reality and Reinvention — Cleveland, Susannah
y Careers in Sales and Marketing — Sheen, Barbara
y Careers: The Graphic Guide to Finding the Perfect Job for You — DK
Careless People: Murder, Mayhem, and the Invention of The Great Gatsby — Churchwell, Sarah
Caribbee — Stockwin, Julian
Caring across Generations: The Linked Lives of Korean American Families — Yoo, Grace J.
Caring Economics: Conversations on Altruism and Compassion, between Scientists, Economists, and the Dalai Lama — Ricard, Matthieu
Caring Economics: Conversations on Altruism and Compassion, between Scientists, Economists, and the Dalai Lama — Singer, Tania
Caring Economics: Conversations on Altruism and Compassion Between Scientists, Economists, and the Dalai Lama — Dalai Lama XIV
Caring for Our Own: Why There Is No Political Demand for New American Social Welfare Rights — Levitsky, Sandra R.
Carl Peter Thunberg: Botanist and Physician — Skuncke, Marie-Christine
Carl Schmitt - Ernst Rudolf Huber: Briefwechsel 1926-1981 — Grothe, Ewald
Carl von Siemens, 1829-1906: Ein Leben zwischen Familie und Weltfirma — Lutz, Martin
A Carlin Home Companion: Growing Up with George — Carlin, Kelly
c Carlos le carlin — Blabey, Aaron
c Carl's Halloween (Illus. by Day, Alexandra) — Day, Alexandra
c Carmelo Anthony — Jackson, Aurelia
Carmina — Catullus
y The Carnival at Bray (Read by Moon, Erin). Audiobook Review — Foley, Jessie Ann
y The Carnival at Bray — Foley, Jessie Ann
c A Carnival of Cats (Illus. by Bridgeman, Kristi) — Ghigna, Charles
c The Carnival (Illus. by Tharlet, Eve) — Luciani, Brigitte
c Carnivores (Illus. by Benefield, James) — Benefield, James
c Carol Carnage: Malicious Mishearings of Your Yuletide Favourites — Rowson, Martin
Carolina Israelite: How Harry Golden Made Us Care about Jews, the South, and Civil Rights — Hartnett, Kimberly Marlowe
Carolina Planters on the Alabama Frontier: The Spencer-Robeson-McKenzie Family Papers — Pattillo, Edward
Caroline — Hunter, Rebecca
Caroline of Lichtfield — Montolieu, Isabelle de
The Carolingian Debate over Sacred Space — Collins, Samuel W.
y Carousel — Ritchie, Brendan
The Carpathian Assignment: The True History of the Apprehension and Death of Dracula Vlad Tepes, Count and Voivode of the Principality of Transylvania — Wagar, Chip
Carpets of the Art Deco Era — Day, Susan
The Carrot Purple and Other Curious Stories of the Food We Eat — Denker, Joel S.
c Carrots Like Peas: And Other Fun Facts (Illus. by Spurgeon, Aaron) — Eliot, Hannah
c Carry and Learn Numbers — Ward, Sarah
c Carry and Learn Shapes — Scholastic Inc.
Carry Me — Behrens, Peter
y Carry On: The Rise and Fall of Simon Snow — Rowell, Rainbow
Carrying Off the Palaces: John Ruskin's Lost Daguerreotypes — Jacobson, Ken
c Cars — Murray, Julie
The Cartaker of the Cosmos: Living Responsibly in an Unfinished World — Lachman, Gary
c Cartboy Goes to Camp — Campbell, L.A.
The Cartel — Winslow, Don
c Carter Finally Gets It (Read by Podehl, Nick). Audiobook Review — Crawford, Brent
Carter & Lovecraft — Howard, Jonathan L.
Cartoon Faces: How to Draw Faces, Features & Expressions — Hart, Christopher
The Cartoon Guide — Sielsch, Leo A.

y The Cartoon Guide to Algebra (Illus. by Gonick, Larry) — Gonick, Larry
The Cartoon Introduction to Philosophy — Patton, Michael F.
The Cartoon Introduction to Statistics — Klein, Grady
Cartoons for Victory — Bernard, Warren
c Cartwheeling in Thunderstorms (Read by Amato, Bianca). Audiobook Review — Rundell, Katherine
c Cartwheeling in Thunderstorms — Rundell, Katherine
Casada: A History of an Italian Village and Its People — Comis, Anna
Casanova — Fraction, Matt
Cascade Falls — Ferber, Bruce
The Case against Satan — Russell, Ray
The Case Against the Supreme Court — Chemerinsky, Erwin
A Case for Character: Towards a Lutheran Virtue Ethics — Biermann, Joel D.
The Case for Grace: A Journalist Explores the Evidence of Transformed Lives — Strobel, Lee
c Case for Grace for Kids (Illus. by Colon, Terry) — Strobel, Lee
y The Case for Grace Student Edition: A Journalist Explores the Evidence of Transformed Lives — Strobel, Lee
c The Case for Loving: The Fight for Interracial Marriage (Illus. by Alko, Selina) — Alko, Selina
c The Case for Loving: The Fight for Interracial Marriage (Illus. by Qualls, Sean) — Alko, Selina
The Case of Lisandra P. — Gremillon, Helene
c The Case of the Battling Bots — O'Donnell, Liam
c The Case of the Bogus Detective — Lawrence, Caroline
c The Case of the Buried Bones (Illus. by Wummer, Amy) — Montgomery, Lewis B.
c The Case of the Deadly Desperados — Lawrence, Caroline
The Case of the Dotty Dowager — Ace, Cathy
The Case of the Fickle Mermaid — Brackston, P.J.
c The Case of the Girl in Grey (Illus. by Murphy, Kelly) — Stratford, Jordan
c The Case of the Good-Looking Corpse — Lawrence, Caroline
y The Case of the Lonely One (Illus. by Allison, John) — Allison, John
c The Case of the Missing Carrot Cake (Illus. by Zemke, Deborah) — Newman, Robin
The Case of the Missing Madonna — Anderson, Lin
c The Case of the Missing Moonstone (Read by Barber, Nicola). Audiobook Review — Stratford, Jordan
c The Case of the Missing Moonstone (Illus. by Murphy, Kelly) — Stratford, Jordan
The Case of the Missing Morris Dancer — Ace, Cathy
c The Case of the Pistol-Packing Widows — Lawrence, Caroline
The Case of the Red-Handed Thesus — Powell, Jessie Bishop
The Case of the Sin City Sister — Hinton, Lynne
c The Case of the Slime Stampede (Illus. by Deas, Mike) — O'Donnell, Liam
c The Case of the Snack Snatcher (Illus. by Grand, Aurelie) — O'Donnell, Liam
The Case of the Stolen Sixpence (Read by Bentinck, Anna). Audiobook Review — Webb, Holly
c The Case of the Stolen Sixpence (Illus. by Lindsay, Marion) — Webb, Holly
c The Case of the Vanishing Emerald (Illus. by Lindsay, Marion) — Webb, Holly
c The Case of the Vanishing Little Brown Bats: A Scientific Mystery — Markle, Sandra
c The Case of the Weird Blue Chicken: The Next Misadventure (Read by Crupper, Adam). Audiobook Review — Cronin, Doreen
c The Case of the Weird Blue Chicken: The Next Misadventure (Illus. by Cornell, Kevin) — Cronin, Doreen
The Case of the Yellow Diamond — Brookins, Carl
Case Studies in Bayesian Statistical Modelling and Analysis — Alston, Clair L.
Casebook — Simpson, Mona
Cash Crash Jubilee — William, Eli K.P.
Cash Flow Forever — Johnson, Jeff K
Cash Landing — Grippando, James
Casino Qaddafi — Tempest, Graham
Cassey Ho's Hot Body Year-Round: The Pop Pilates to Get Slim, Eat Clean, and Live Happy through Every Season. — Harmony, Cassey Ho.
Cassidy's Guide to Everyday Etiquette (and Obfuscation). — Stauffacher, Sue
c Cast Away on the Letter A (Illus. by Fred) — Fred
Cast Me Gently — Werlinger, Caren J.

Cast of Characters: Wolcott Gibbs, E.B. White, James Thurber, and the Golden Age of the New Yorker — Vinciguerra, Thomas
y Cast Off: The Strange Adventures of Petra De Winter and Bram Broen — Yohalem, Eve
The Castaway Lounge — Boilard, Jon
Castaway Planet: A Crash Course in Survival — Flint, Eric
c The Castaways — Keene, Brian
Caste, Gender, and Christianity in Colonial India: Telugu Women in Mission — Taneti, James Elisha
Casting Lots — Silverman, Susan
c Castle — Keenan, Sheila
c A Castle Full of Cats (Illus. by Sanderson, Ruth) — Sanderson, Ruth
c Castle Hangnail (Read by Sands, Tara). Audiobook Review — Vernon, Ursula
Castle Hangnail — Vernon, Ursula
y Castle in Danger — Rautenberg, Karen Rita
c Castle (Illus. by McCall, Henrietta) — Bergin, Mark
Castlereagh: A Life — Bew, John
The Castrato: Reflections on Natures and Kinds — Feldman, Martha
Casualties — Marro, Elizabeth
The Casualties — Holdstock, Nick
Casualties of History: Wounded Japanese Servicemen and the Second World War — Pennington, Lee
c Cat and the Beanstalk (Illus. by Beacon, Dawn) — Guillain, Charlotte
c The Cat at the Wall — Ellis, Deborah
c Cat & Bunny (Illus. by Lundquist, Mary) — Lundquist, Mary
c Cat Dad, King of the Goblins — Wilson, Britt
c Cat & Dog — Foreman, Michael
c Cat Got a Lot (Illus. by Henry, Steve) — Henry, Steve
Cat in a Zebra Zoot Suit: A Midnight Louie Mystery — Douglas, Carole Nelson
c Cat in the City (Illus. by Weber, Jill) — Salamon, Julie
Cat Is Art Spelled Wrong — Casey, Caroline
A Cat Is Chasing Me through This Book! (Illus. by Perez, Carmen) — Bird, Benjamin
c Cat Nap (Illus. by Yuly, Toni) — Yuly, Toni
Cat out of Hell — Truss, Lynne
The Cat Sitter's Whiskers — Clement, Blaize
The Cat Sitter's Whiskers — Clement, John
c The Cat, the Dog, Little Red, the Exploding Eggs, the Wolf, and Grandma (Illus. by Fox, Christyan) — Fox, Diane
c The Cat, the Dog, Little Red, the Exploding Eggs, the Wolf and Grandma's Wardrobe (Illus. by Fox, Christyan) — Fox, Diane
Cat Town — Hagiwara, Sakutaro
c The Cat Who Came In off the Roof — Schmidt, Annie M.G.
c The Cat Who Tamed the West — Huckins, Holly
c Cat Whys — Prap, Lila
c The Cat with the Coloured Tail (Illus. by Dabarera, Dinalie) — Mears, Gillian
y Catacomb — Roux, Madeleine
The Catalain Book of Secrets — Lourey, Jessica
Cataloging for School Librarians — Kelsey, Marie
Catalogue of Medieval Manuscripts of Latin Commentaries on Aristotle in British Libraries, Volume II: Cambridge — Thomson, Rodney M.
A Catalogue of the Manuscripts of Christiaan Huygens, Including a Concordance with His Oeuvres Completes — Yoder, Joella G.
Catalogus Translationum et Commentariorum: Medieval and Renaissance Latin Translations and Commentaries — Dinkova-Bruun, Greti
y Catalyst — Kang, Lydia
Catalyst Architecture: Rio de Janeiro, New York, Tokyo, Copenhagen — Kiib, Hans
y Catalyst — Kang, Lydia
y Catalyst — Kincaid, S.J.
Catarina's Ring — McGuinness, Lisa
Catastrophe 1914: Europe Goes to War — Hastings, Max
Catch a Falling Heiress — Guhrke, Laura Lee
c Catch That Cookie! (Illus. by Chou, Joey) — Livingston, A.A.
c Catch That Cookie! — Small, David
c Catch the Volt — Gwynne, Phillip
Catch Up: Developing Countries in the World Economy — Nayyar, Deepak
y Catch Us If You Can — Feinstein, Marc
c Catch You Later, Traitor (Read by Turetsky, Mark). Audiobook Review — Avi
y Catch You Later, Traitor — Avi
y Catch Your Death — Child, Lauren

Catching Nature in the Act: Reaumur and the Practice of Natural History in the Eighteenth Century — Terrall, Mary
Catching the Sky: Two Brothers, One Family, and Our Dream to Fly — Moore, Colten
A Catechism for Business: Tough Ethical Questions and Insights from Catholic Teaching — Abela, Andrew V.
c The Categorical Universe of Candice Phee — Jonsberg, Barry
Category Mistakes — Magidor, Ofra
A Catered Mother's Day — Crawford, Isis
c Caterina and the Best Beach Day — Kono, Erin Eitter
Caterva — Filloy, Juan
Catherine of Siena: The Creation of a Cult — Hamburger, Jeffrey F.
The Catherine Wheel — Harrower, Elizabeth
Catheters, Slurs, and Pickup Lines: Professional Intimacy in Hospital Nursing — Ruchti, Lisa C.
Catholic Borderlands: Mapping Catholicism onto American Empire, 1905-1935 — Martinez, Anne M.
c The Catholic Children's Prayer Book (Illus. by Hale, Nathan) — Saint Mary's Press Staff
The Catholic Church and Argentina's Dirty War — Morello, Gustavo
Catholic History for Today's Church: How Our Past Illuminates Our Present — O'Malley, John W.
The Catholic Labyrinth: Power, Apathy, and a Passion for Reform in the American Church — McDonough, Peter
Catholic Moral Theology and Social Ethics: A New Method — Astorga, Christina A.
Catholic Progressives in England After Vatican II — Corrin, Jay P.
Catholic Reformation in Protestant Britain — Walsham, Alexandra
The Catholic Rubens: Saints and Martyrs — Sauerlander, Willibald
The Catholic Studies Reader — Fisher, James T.
Catholic Vietnam: A Church from Empire to Nation — Keith, Charles
Catholic Women's Movements in Liberal and Fascist Italy — Dawes, Helena
Catholicism and Historical Narrative: A Catholic Engagement with Historical Scholarship — Schmiesing, Kevin
The Catholicisms of Coutances: Varieties of Religion in Early Modern France, 1350-1789 — Hayden, J. Michael
The Catholicity of Reason — Schindler, D.C.
Catholiques au defi de la Reforme: La coexistence confessionnelle a Utrecht au XVIIe siecle — Forclaz, Bertrand
c Catlantis — Starobinets, Anna
c Cats — Murray, Julie
c Cats Are Cats — Gorbachev, Valeri
c Cats Get Famous (Illus. by Barrett, Ron) — Barrett, Ron
c Cats Got Talent — Barrett, Ron
Cats in Hats: 30 Knit and Crochet Patterns for Your Kitty — Thomas, Sara
Cats on the Job: 50 Fabulous Felines Who Purr, Mouse, and Even Sing for Their Supper — Rogak, Lisa
The Catskills: Its History and How It Changed America — Silverman, Stephen M.
Catullus: Poems, Books, Readers — Du Quesnay, Ian M.
c Catwoman Gets Busted by the Batman (Illus. by Jones, Christopher) — Matheny, Bill
The Caucasus: A History — Forsyth, James
Cauchemar — Grigorescu, Alexandra
Caught on Camera: Film in the Courtroom from the Nuremberg Trials to the Trials of the Khmer Rouge — Delage, Christian
Caught: The Prison State and the Lockdown of American Politics — Gottschalk, Marie
Caught up in the Touch — Trentham, Laura
Cauldron of Resistance: Ngo Dinh Diem, the United States, and 1950s Southern Vietnam — Chapman, Jessica M.
The Causal Angel — Rajaniemi, Hannu
y Cause and Effect: The French Revolution — Green, Robert
Cause for Thought: An Essay in Metaphysics — Burbridge, John
The Cause of All Nations: An International History of the American Civil War — Doyle, Don H.
The Causes and Consequences of Group Violence: From Bullies to Terrorists — Hawdon, James
Causes, Laws, and Free Will: Why Determinism Doesn't Matter — Vihvelin, Kadri

A Cautious Enthusiasm: Mystical Piety and Evangelicalism in Colonial South Carolina — Smith, Samuel C.
The Cave — Montgomery, Michela
Cave and Cosmos — Harner, Michael
The Caveman — Horst, Jorn Lier
The Cavendon Women — Bradford, Barbara Taylor
c Cavnedish Square — Stefoff, Rebecca
c CC Claus: A Baseball Christmas Story (Illus. by Seeley, Laura) — Sabathia, C.C.
CCCP Cookbook: True Stories of Soviet Cuisine — Syutkin, Pavel
CCTV: A Technology under the Radar? — Kroener, Inga
c Ce livre a mange mon chien! — Byrne, Richard
c Ce n'est pas mon chapeau (Illus. by Klassen, Jon) — Klassen, Jon
c Ceci est un orignal (Illus. by Lichtenheld, Tom) — Morris, Richard T.
c Cecilia and Miguel Are Best Friends (Illus. by Muraida, Thelma) — Bertrand, Diane Gonzales
y Celebrating Australia — Marwood, Lorraine
y Celebrating Islamic Festivals — Miles, Liz
Celebrating Life — Asterino, Brenda M.
c Celebrating North Carolina (Illus. by Canga, C.B.) — Bauer, Marion Dane
Celebrating Pennsylvania: 50 States to Celebrate (Illus. by Canga, C.B.) — Kurtz, Jane
c Celebrating Washington State (Illus. by Canga, C.B.) — Bauer, Marion Dane
c Celebrations and Special Days — Lawrence, Ellen
Celebrity Cast — Groome, Harry
Celebrity in Chief: A History of the Presidents and the Culture of Stardom — Walsh, Kenneth T.
y Celeste — Worthen, Johnny
Celestial Novelties on the Eve of the Scientific Revolution, 1540-1630 — Tessicini, Dario
Celestial Wonders in Reformation Germany — Kurihara, Ken
Celestino Galiani e la Sacra Scrittura: Alle radici del pensiero napoletano del Settecento — Costa, Gustavo
c Celestino Piatti's Animal ABC (Illus. by Piatti, Celestino) — Schumacher, Hans
c Cell Phones and Society Series
y The Cellar — Walters, Minette
c Cells — Duke, Shirley
Celtic Influences in Germanic Religion: A Survey — Egeler, Matthias
Celtic Mythology: The Nature and Influence of Celtic Myth from Druidism to Arthurian Legend — Rutherford, Ward
The Celtic Myths: A Guide to the Ancient Gods and Legends — Aldhouse-Green, Miranda
Celts and Their Cultures at Home and Abroad: A Festschrift for Malcolm Broun — Ahlqvist, Anders
y The Cemetery Boys — Brewer, Heather
Censors at Work: How States Shaped Literature — Darnton, Robert
Censorship and the Limits of the Literary: A Global View — Moore, Nicole
Censorship Now!! — Svenonius, Ian F.
c Centaur Rising — Yolen, Jane
Center and Periphery: Studies on Power in the Medieval World in Honor of William Chester Jordan — Jansen, Katherine L.
Center of Gravity — McNeill, Laura
The Center of the World — Sheehan, Jacqueline
Centering Animals in Latin American History — Few, Martha
Central Bank Independence: Cultural Codes and Symbolic Performance — Tognato, Carlo
Central Europe in the High Middle Ages: Bohemia, Hungary and Poland, c. 900-c.1300 — Berend, Nora
Centralia — Dellosso, Mike
Centuries of Change: Which Century Saw the Most Change and What It Matters to Us — Mortimer, Ian
A Century of British Cooking — Patten, Marguerite
A Century of Service: The U.S. Navy on Cape Henlopen, Lewes, Delaware, 1898-1996 — Manthorpe, William H.J., Jr.
A Century of War, a Century of Debate: Historians Debate German History
The CEO Buys In — Herkness, Nancy
The CEO Tightrope: How to Master the Balancing Act of a Successful CEO — Trammell, Joel
Ceramic Production in Early Hispanic California: Craft, Economy, and Trade on the Frontier of New Spain — Skowronek, Russell K.
Ceremonial Entries in Early Modern Europe: The Iconography of Power — Mulryne, J.R.
c Ceremonies and Celebrations — McDowell, Pamela

c Certain Poor Shepherds (Illus. by Bartlett, Jonathan) — Thomas, Elizabeth Marshall
y Certain Signals — Karre, Elizabeth
Certainty — Bevine, Victor
Cervantes' "Don Quixote" — Echevarria, Roberto Gonzalez
Cesaree Maritime: Ville fortifiee du Proche-Orient — Mesqui, Jean
Cess — Lish, Gordon
Cessna Warbirds, the War Years (1941-45): The T-50 Bobcat and the Cessnas Impressed into Military Service — Shiel, Walt
c C'est la fete des Peres! — Pelletier, Dominique
c C'est Noel! — Pelletier, Dominique
c C'est Paques! — Pelletier, Dominique
y C'etait un 8 aout — Bergeron, Alain M.
y Chaco Canyon — Eboch, Chris
Chad — Chapman, Gary
The Chagos Islanders and International Law — Allen, Stephen
The Chain: Farm, Factory, and the Fate of Our Food — Genoways, Ted
Chained to the Land: Voices from Cotton and Cane Plantations — Tanner, Lynette Ater
The Challenge of Linear Time: Nationhood and the Politics of History in East Asia — Murthy, Viren
The Challenge of Things: Thinking through Troubled Times — Grayling, A.C.
y Challenger Deep (Illus. by Shusterman, Brendan) — Shusterman, Neal
The Challenges of Being a Rural Gay Man: Coping with Stigma — Preston, Deborah Bray
The Challenges of Nuclear Non-Proliferation — Burns, Richard D.
Challenges on the Emmaus Road: Episcopal Bishops Confront Slavery, Civil War, and Emancipation — Dorn, T. Felder
Challenging the Bard: Dostoevsky and Pushkin. A Study of a Literary Relationship — Rosenshield, Gary
Chamber Music: An Extensive Guide for Listeners — Murray, Lucy Miller
Chamber Music: The Poetry of Jan Zwicky — Zwicky, Jan
The Chambers Dictionary, 13th ed.
Chameleon: The True Story of an Impostor's Remarkable Odyssey — Brandt, Robert
c Chameleons — Murray, Peter (b. 1952-)
Champion of the Scarlet Wolf, Book 1 — Hale, Ginn
Champion of the Scarlet Wolf, Book 2 — Hale, Ginn
c The Championship! (Illus. by Ryser, Nicolas) — Richard, Laurent
Chan Heart, Chan Mind: A Meditation on Serenity and Growth — Guo, Jun
Chance — Nunn, Kem
A Chance for Lasting Survival: Ecology and Behavior of Wild Giant Pandas — Wenshi, Pan
Chance Harbor — Robinson, Holly
c Chance of a Lifetime — Folau, Israel
Chance of a Lifetime — Pappano, Marilyn
c The Chance You Won't Return — Cardi, Annie
Change and Conflict in the U.S. Army Chaplain Corps since 1945 — Loveland, Anne C.
A Change in Worlds on the Sino-Tibetan Borderlands: Politics, Economics, and Environments in Northern Sichuan — Hayes, Jack Patrick
Change of Heart: Justice, Mercy, and Making Peace with My Sister's Killer — Bishop, Jeanne
Change of Heart — Jebber, Molly
Change of Object Expression in the History of French: Verbs of Helping and Hindering — Troberg, Michelle
The Change: Tales of Downfall and Rebirth — Stirling, S.M.
Change Your Mind, Change Your Health — Ludovici, Anne Marie
c Changement de ligne — Mack, W.C.
Changes: A Child's First Poetry Collection (Illus. by Beeke, Tiphanie) — Zolotow, Charlotte
Changing Behaviors: On the Rise of the Psychological State — Jones, Rhys
A Changing China: Day to Day Life in the New Century — Yue, Yuan
The Changing Face of World Cities: Young Adult Children of Immigrants in Europe and the United States — Crul, Maurice
Changing Faith: The Dynamics and Consequences of Americans' Shifting Religious Identities — Sherkat, Darren E.
Changing Homelands: Hindu Politics and the Partition of India — Nair, Neeti
The Changing Nature of Citizenship

Changing Perspectives on England and the Continent in the Early Middle Ages — Scharer, Anton
The Changing Politics of Education: Privatization and the Dispossessed Lives Left Behind — Fabricant, Michael
Changing Spaces — King, Nancy
Changing Subjects: Digressions in Modern American Poetry — Reddy, Srikanth
Changing the Game: Women at Work in Las Vegas, 1940-1990 — Goodwin, Joanne L.
Changing the Questions: Explorations in Christian Ethics — Farley, Margaret A.
Changing the Subject: Art and Attention in the Internet Age — Birkerts, Sven
A Changing Wind: Commerce and Conflict in Civil War Atlanta — Venet, Wendy Hamand
The Changs Next Door to the Diazes: Remapping Race in Suburban California — Cheng, Wendy
Channel 37: Season One! — Lagasse, Paul
Channel Shore: From the White Cliffs to Land's End — Fort, Tom
Channelling Mobilities: Migration and Globalisation in the Suez Canal Region and Beyond, 1869-1914 — Huber, Valeska
y Chantarelle — Morgan, G.A.
Chanter sur le livre a la Renaissance: Les traites de contrepoint de Vicente Lusitano — Canguilhem, Philippe
y Chantress Fury — Greenfield, Amy Butler
y Chaos — Bross, Lanie
Chaos and Cosmos: Literary Roots of Modern Ecology in the British Nineteenth Century — Scott, Heidi C.M.
Chaos Unleashed — Karpyshyn, Drew
The Chapel — Downing, Michael
Chapelwood — Priest, Cherie
Chapter and Verse: New Order, Joy Division and Me — Sumner, Bernard
Chapter One — Henderson, Ella
Character and the Individual Personality in English Renaissance Drama: Tragedy, History and Tragicomedy — Curran, John E., Jr.
Character as Moral Fiction — Alfano, Mark
y Character, Driven — Lubar, David
Characteristically American: Memorial Architecture, National Identity, and the Egyptian Revival — Giguere, Joy M.
Chariots and Other Wheeled Vehicles in Italy before the Roman Empire — Crouwel, Joost H.
y Charisma — Ryan, Jeanne
Charity Detox: What Charity Would Look Like If We Cared about Results — Lupton, Robert D.
Charity & Sylvia: A Same-Sex Marriage in Early America — Cleves, Rachel Hope
Charlemagne's Early Campaigns (768-777): A Diplomatic and Military Analysis — Bachrach, Bernard
Charlemagne's Survey of the Holy Land: Wealth, Personnel, and Buildings of a Mediterranean Church between Antiquity and the Middle Ages, with a Critical Edition and Translation of the Original Text — McCormick, Michael
y Charles Darwin and the Theory of Natural Selection — Hesse, Alan J.
Charles Dickens' Favorite Daughter: The Life, Loves, And Art Of Katey Dickens Perugini — Hawksley, Lucinda
Charles Dickens's Great Expectations: A Cultural Life, 1860-2012 — Hammond, Mary
Charles I: An Abbreviated Life — Kishlansky, Mark
Charles I and the People of England — Cressy, David
Charles Ives in the Mirror: American Histories of an Iconic Composer — Paul, David C.
Charles Marville: Photographer of Paris — Kennel, Sarah
Charles O'Conor of Ballinagare: Life and Works — Gibbons, Luke
Charles: The Heart of a King — Mayer, Catherine
Charles Walters: The Director Who Made Hollywood Dance — Phillips, Brent
Charles Williams: The Third Inkling — Lindop, Grevel
Charleston in Black and White: Race and Power in the South after the Civil Rights Movement — Estes, Steve
c Charley Harper's Count the Birds (Illus. by Harper, Charley) — Burke, Zoe
c Charley Harper's What's in the Coral Reef?: A Nature Discovery Book (Illus. by Harper, Charley) — Burke, Zoe
c Charlie and the Blanket Toss (Illus. by Martinsen, Sarah) — Brown, Tricia

c Charlie and the Grandmothers — Towell, Katy
c Charlie and the New Baby (Illus. by deGroat, Diane) — Drummond, Ree
A Charlie Brown Religion — Lind, Stephen J.
c Charlie Bumpers vs. The Perfect Little Turkey (Read by Harley, Bill). Audiobook Review — Harley, Bill
c Charlie Bumpers vs. the Perfect Little Turkey (Illus. by Gustavson, Adam) — Harley, Bill
c Charlie Bumpers vs. the Squeaking Skull (Illus. by Gustavson, Adam) — Harley, Bill
The Charlie Chaplin Archives — Duncan, Paul
Charlie Chaplin: The Keystone Album — Stourdze, Sam
c Charlie Joe Jackson's Guide to Making Money (Illus. by Coovert, J.P.) — Greenwald, Tommy
c Charlie Joe Jackson's Guide to Planet Girl (Read by Andrews, MacLeod). Audiobook Review — Greenwald, Tommy
c Charlie Joe Jackson's Guide to Planet Girl (Illus. by Coovert, J.P.) — Greenwald, Tommy
c Charlie le chien du ranch (Illus. by de Groat, Diane) — Drummond, Ree
Charlie Martz and Other Stories: The Unpublished Stories — Leonard, Elmore
Charlie Mike: A True Story of Heroes Who Brought Their Mission Home — Klein, Joe
Charlie Munger: The Complete Investor — Griffin, Tren
Charlie Palmer's American Fare: Everyday Recipes from My Kitchen to Yours — Palmer, Charlie
c Charlie Piechart and the Case of the Missing Pizza Slice (Illus. by Comstock, Eric) — Comstock, Eric
c Charlie Piechart and the Case of the Missing Pizza Slice (Illus. by Comstock, Eric) — Sadler, Marilyn
c Charlie Plays Ball (Illus. by deGroat, Diane) — Drummond, Ree
y Charlie, Presumed Dead — Heltzel, Anne
Charlie: The Dog Who Came in from the Wild — Tenzin-Dolma, Lisa
Charlie the Ranch Dog (Illus. by deGroat, Diane) — Drummond, Ree
c Charlie's Birthday Wish (Illus. by Sauer, Scott) — Micka, Rene
c Charlie's Dirt Day (Illus. by Hudon-Verrelli, Jacqueline) — Larsen, Andrew
Charlie's First War: South Africa, 1899-1900 — Tweddell, C.H.
c Charlotte and the Quiet Place (Illus. by Woolley, Sara) — Sosin, Deborah
Charlotte's Story — Benedict, Laura
Charm Love Friendship Bracelets: 35 Unique Designs with Polymer Clay, Macrame, Knotting, and Braiding — Haab, Sherri
y Charmed (Read by Ricci, Tai Alexandra). Audiobook Review — Krys, Michelle
y Charmed — Krys, Michelle
Charmed and Dangerous: Ten Tales of Gay Paranormal Romance and Urban Fantasy — Price, Jordan Castillo
y The Charmed Children of Rookskill Castle — Fox, Janet
Charmed Particles — Kolaya, Chrissy
Charny's Men-at-Arms: Questions Concerning the Joust, Tournaments, and War — Muhlberger, Steven
The Chart of Tomorrows — Willrich, Chris
Charters of Christ Church Canterbury, 2 vols. — Brooks, Nicholas P.
The Chartist Imaginary: Literary Form in Working-Class Political Theory and Practice — Loose, Margaret A.
y The Chase (Illus. by Vives, Bastien) — Vives, Bastien
Chase Me — Bailey, Tessa
Chase Your Shadow: The Trials of Oscar Pistorius — Carlin, John
Chasing Arizona: One Man's Yearlong Obsession with the Grand Canyon State — Lamberton, Ken
y Chasing Before — Appelhans, Lenore
Chasing Dragons: An Uncommon Memoir in Photographs — Hayward, Bill
c Chasing Freedom: The Life Journeys of Harriet Tubman and Susan B. Anthony, Inspired by Historical Facts (Read by Mitchell, Lizan). Audiobook Review — Grimes, Nikki
c Chasing Freedom: The Life Journeys of Harriet Tubman and Susan B. Anthony, Inspired by Historical Facts (Illus. by Wood, Michele) — Grimes, Nikki
Chasing Ghosts: A Memoir of a Father, Gone to War — DeSalvo, Louise
c Chasing Gold — Hapka, Catherine
Chasing Justice — Griffin, H. Terrell

Chasing Lost Time: The Life of C.K. Scott Moncrieff: Soldier, Spy, and Translator — Findlay, Jean
y Chasing Perfection: The Principles Behind Winning Football the De La Salle Way — Ladouceur, Bob
y Chasing Power — Durst, Sarah Beth
c Chasing Secrets (Read by Vacker, Karissa). Audiobook Review — Choldenko, Gennifer
y Chasing Secrets — Choldenko, Gennifer
Chasing Shadows: The Nixon Tapes, the Chennault Affair, and the Origins of Watergate — Hughes, Ken
Chasing Sound: Technology, Culture, and the Art of Studio Recording from Edison to the LP — Horning, Susan Schmidt
Chasing Sunsets — Kingsbury, Karen
c Chasing the Moon (Illus. by Chatterjee, Somnath) — Massey, Tyler James
Chasing the Phoenix — Swanwick, Michael
Chasing the Red Queen: The Evolutionary Race between Agricultural Pests and Poisons — Dyer, Andy
Chasing the Santa Fe Ring: Power and Privilege in Territorial New Mexico — Caffey, David L.
Chasing the Scream: The First and Last Days of the War on Drugs — Hari, Johann
y Chasing the Storm: Tornadoes, Meteorology, and Weather Watching — Miller, Ron
y Chasing the Valley — Melki-Wegner, Skye
Chasing Weather: Tornadoes, Tempests, and Thunderous Skies in Word and Image — Mirriam-Goldberg, Caryn
Chasm — Miller, Susan Cummins
The Chastened Heart — Crooke, Robert
Chateaubriand et les choses — Schurewegen, Franc
Chateaubriand: The Paradox of Chance — Scott, Malcolm
Chattanooga, 1865-1900: A City Set Down in Dixie — Ezzell, Tim
Chaucer and Array: Patterns of Costume and Fabric Rhetoric in the Canterbury Tales, Troilus and Criseyde and Other Works — Hodges, Laura F.
Chaucer, Gower, and the Vernacular Rising: Poetry and the Problem of the Populace after 1381 — Arner, Lynn
Chaucer's (Anti-)Eroticisms and the Queer Middle Ages — Pugh, Tison
Chaucer's Tale: 1386 and the Road to Canterbury — Strohm, Paul
c Cheating — Szumski, Bonnie
y Cheating for the Chicken Man — Cummings, Priscilla
Checked Out — Viets, Elaine
Checking the Courts: Law, Ideology, and Contingent Discretion — Randazzo, Kirk A.
Cheddar: A Journey to the Heart of America's Most Iconic Cheese — Edgar, Gordon
c The Cheer-Up Bird (Illus. by Schubert, Ingrid) — van de Vendel, Edward
The Cheese and the Worms: The Cosmos of a Sixteenth-Century Miller — Ginzburg, Carlo
The Cheese Lover's Cookbook — Chambers, Emily
A Cheese of Some Importance — Giesser, Mark R.
y Cheesie Mack Is Sort of Freaked Out (Illus. by Holgate, Douglas) — Cotler, Steve
Chefs' Easy Weeknight Dinners — Cowin, Dana
Chelsea Girls — Myles, Eileen
The Chemical History of Color — Orna, Mary Virginia
Chemical Reactions — National Science Teachers Association
Chemistry in Context: Applying Chemistry to Society, 8th ed. — Middlecamp, Catherine H.
The Chemistry of Alchemy: From Dragon's Blood to Donkey Dung: How Chemistry Was Forged — Cobb, Cathy
Chemistry of Sustainable Energy — Carpenter, Nancy E.
y Chemists — Van Koevering, Thomas E.
Cherishing Antiquity: The Cultural Construction of an Ancient Chinese Kingdom — Milburn, Olivia
y Chernobyl's Wild Kingdom: Life in the Dead Zone — Johnson, Rebecca L.
c The Cherokee — Craats, Rennay
The Cherokee Diaspora: An Indigenous History of Migration, Resettlement, and Identity — Smithers, Gregory D.
Cherokee Newspaper, 1828-1906: Tribal Voice of a People in Transition — Holland, Cullen Joe
The Cherokee Rose — Miles, Tiya
Cherokee Sister: The Collected Writings of Catharine Brown, 1818-1823 — Gaul, Theresa Strouth
c Cherry Blossom Baseball — Maruno, Jennifer
The Cherry Harvest — Sanna, Lucy
c The Cherry Thief — Galindo, Renata

The Chesapeake Campaign 1813-1814 — *Niemeyer, Charles P.*
The Chess Player's Bible: Illustrated Strategies for Staying Ahead of the Game, 2d ed. — *Eade, James*
y The Chess Queen Enigma — *Gleason, Colleen*
The Chessman — *Gordon-Smith, Dolores*
c Chester the Cedar Christmas Tree (Illus. by Houston, Bobbie) — *Keith, Pat*
The Chevalier of Touches — *D'Aurevilly, Jules Barbey*
Chewing Gum — *Bushnaf, Mansour*
y Chi di zhi lian — *Chang, Eileen*
Chicago: A Comix Memoir — *Head, Glenn*
c Chicago Bears — *Zappa, Marcia*
c Chicago Blackhawks — *Butler, Erin*
c The Chicago Bulls — *Stewart, Mark*
Chicago Hustle and Flow: Gangs, Gangsta Rap, and Social Class — *Harkness, Geoff*
Chicago Hustle and Flow: Gangs, Gangsta Rap, and Social Class — *Harkness, Geoffrey*
Chicago Law: A Trial Lawyer's Journey — *Garofalo, Joseph*
Chicago Noir: The Classics — *Meno, Joe*
The Chicago School Diaspora: Epistemology and Substance — *Low, Jacqueline*
Chicago Street Cop — *McCarthy, Pat*
Chicagoland: Illusions of the Literal — *Gubin, Steve*
Chicagonomics: The Evolution of Chicago Free Market Economics — *Ebenstein, Lanny*
Chicana/o Struggles for Education: Activism in the Community — *San Miguel, Guadalupe, Jr.*
The Chicano Movement: Perspectives from the Twenty-First Century — *Garcia, Mario T.*
A Chick in the Cockpit: My Life Up in the Air — *Armstrong, Erika*
y Chick: Lister — *Van Tol, Alex*
c A Chick 'n' Pug Christmas (Illus. by Sattler, Jennifer) — *Sattler, Jennifer*
c Chick 'n' Pug: The Love Pug (Illus. by Sattler, Jennifer) — *Sattler, Jennifer*
c Chicken Clicking (Illus. by Ross, Tony) — *Willis, Jeanne*
c A Chicken Followed Me Home! Questions and Answers about a Familiar Fowl (Illus. by Page, Robin) — *Page, Robin*
c Chicken House — *Lee, Ingrid*
c Chicken in the Car ... and the Car Can't Go! That's How You 'Spell' Chicago! (Illus. by Madsen, Sarah) — *Schrager, Howard*
Chicken in the Mango Tree: Food and Life in a Thai-Khmer Village — *Alford, Jeffrey*
The Chicken Keeper's Problem Solver: 100 Common Problems Explored and Explained — *Graham, Chris.*
c Chicken Lily (Illus. by Crittenden, Nina Victor) — *Mortensen, Lori*
c The Chicken Squad: The First Misadventure (Read by Grupper, Adam). Audiobook Review — *Cronin, Doreen*
The Chicken Trail: Following Workers, Migrants, and Corporations across the Americas — *Schwartzman, Kathleen C.*
c The Chicken Who Had a Toothache (Illus. by Guettier, Benedicte) — *Guettier, Benedicte*
c Chickens — *Murray, Julie*
The Chickpea Flour Cookbook: Healthy Gluten-Free and GrainFree Recipes to Power Every Meal of the Day — *Saulsbury, Camilla V.*
Chief Customer Officer 2.0: How to Build Your Customer-Driven Growth Engine — *Bliss, Jeanne*
Chief Executive to Chief Justice: Taft betwixt the White House and Supreme Court — *Gould, Lewis L.*
Chief of Thieves — *Kohlhagen, Steven W.*
Chiefs and Challengers: Indian Resistance and Cooperation in Southern California, 1769-1906 — *Phillips, George Harwood*
Chiesa Cattolica e Minoranze in Italia nella Prima Meta del Novecento: Il Caso Veneto a Confronto — *Perin, Raffaella*
c Chik Chak Shabbat (Illus. by Brooker, Kyrsten) — *Rockliff, Mara*
The Child Cases: How America's Religious Exemption Laws Harm Children — *Rogers, Alan*
Child, Church, and Compassion: Towards Child Theology in Romania — *Prevette, Bill*
c Child Convicts — *Brennan, Net*
The Child Garden
The Child Garden — *McPherson, Catriona*
A Child of One's Own: Parental Stories — *Bowlby, Rachel*
Child of the Covenant — *Gravell, Kim*

Child, Please: How Mama's Old-School Lessons Helped Me Check Myself before I Wreck Myself — *Caviness, Ylonda Gault*
Child, Please: How Mama's Old-School Lessons Helped Me Check Myself before I Wrecked Myself — *Caviness, Ylonda Gault*
The Child Poet — *Aridjis, Homero*
The Child Revealed — *Winterstaar, A.R.*
A Child Shall Lead Them: Martin Luther King Jr., Young People, and the Movement — *Burrow, Rufus, Jr.*
c Child Soldier: When Boys and Girls Are Used in War (Illus. by Davila, Claudia) — *Chikwanine, Michel*
c Child Soldier: When Boys and Girls Are Used in War (Illus. by Chikwanine, Michel) — *Humphreys, Jessica Dee*
c Child Soldier: When Boys and Girls Are Used in War (Illus. by Davila, Claudia) — *Humphreys, Jessica Dee*
Child Workers and Industrial Health in Britain, 1780-1850 — *Kirby, Peter*
A Childhood — *Oberski, Jona*
Childhood and Emotion: Across Cultures, 1450-1800 — *Jarzebowski, Claudia*
Childhood and Emotion: Across Cultures, 1450-1800 — *Kopelson, Heather Miyano*
Childhood Fears. E-book Review — *D'Auria, Don*
Childhood Obesity in America: Biography of an Epidemic — *Dawes, Laura*
Childness and the Writing of the German Past: Tropes of Childhood in Contemporary German Literature — *Maguire, Nora*
The Children Act — *McEwan, Ian*
Children and Cultural Memory in Texts of Childhood — *Snell, Heather*
Children and the Politics of Cultural Belonging — *Hearst, Alice*
Children and Youth during the Gilded Age and Progressive Era — *Marten, James*
The Children Bob Moses Led: A Novel of Freedom Summer — *Heath, William*
c Children Growing Up with War — *Matthews, Jenny*
Children in the Online World: Risk, Regulation, Rights — *Staksrud, Elisabeth*
Children into Swans: Fairy Tales and the Pagan Imagination — *Beveridge, Jan*
The Children of 1965: On Writing, and Not Writing, as an Asian American — *Song, Min Hyoung*
The Children of Darkness — *Litwack, David*
The Children of Henry VIII — *Guy, John*
The Children of Immigrants at School: A Comparative Look at Integration in the United States and Western Europe — *Alba, Richard*
Children of Immigrants in a Globalized World: A Generational Experience — *Colombo, Enzo*
Children of Katrina — *Fothergill, Alice*
Children of Monsters: An Inquiry into the Sons and Daughters of Dictators — *Nordlinger, Jay*
Children of Paradise: The Struggle for the Soul of Iran — *Secor, Laura*
Children of Rus': Right-Bank Ukraine and the Invention of a Russian Nation — *Hillis, Faith*
Children of the Comet — *Moffitt, Donald*
Children of the Dictatorship: Student Resistance, Cultural Politics, and the "Long 1960s" in Greece — *Kornetis, Kostis*
y Children of the Earth — *Schumacher, Anna*
c Children of the Holocaust — *Woolf, Alex*
Children of the Prison Boom: Mass Incarceration and the Future of American Inequality — *Wakefield, Sara*
Children of the Revolution — *Robinson, Peter*
Children of the Stone: The Power of Music in a Hard Land — *Tolan, Sandy*
Children of the Tide: A Victorian Detective Story — *Redfern, Jon*
The Children Return — *Walker, Martin*
Children, War and Propaganda — *Collins, Ross F.*
c Children's Book of Philosophy: An Introduction to the World's Great Thinkers and Their Big Ideas — *Tomley, Sarah*
The Children's Crusade (Read by Smith, Cotter). Audiobook Review — *Packer, Ann*
The Children's Crusade — *Packer, Ann*
c A Children's Guide to Arctic Birds (Illus. by Christopher, Danny) — *Pelletier, Mia*
The Children's Home — *Lambert, Charles*
Children's Literature and New York City — *Whyte, Padraic*
Children's Services Today: A Practical Guide for Librarians — *Larson, Jeanette*
y Chili Queen: Mi Historia — *Martinello, Marian*

Chilled: How Refrigeration Changed the World and Might Do So Again — *Jackson, Tom*
Chimera — *Grant, Mira*
The Chimera Murders — *Maldonado, Frank E.*
The Chimera Sanction — *Baby, Andre K.*
The Chimp and the River: How AIDS Emerged from an African Forest — *Quammen, David*
c The Chimpanzee Children of Gombe: 50 Years with Jane Goodall at Gombe National Park (Illus. by Neugebauer, Michael) — *Goodall, Jane*
c Chimpanzees — *Friesen, Helen Lepp*
c Chimpanzees Are Awesome! — *Peterson, Megan Cooley*
c China — *Bodden, Valerie*
China 1945: Mao's Revolution and America's Fateful Choice — *Bernstein, Richard*
c China — *Powell, Jillian*
China and Europe in 21st Century Global Politics: Partnership, Competition or Co-Evolution — *Austermann, Frauke*
The China Boom: Why China Will Not Rule the World — *Hung, Ho-Fung*
The China Challenge: Shaping the Choices of a Rising Power — *Christensen, Thomas J.*
China, Christianity, and the Question of Culture — *Yang, Huilin*
The China Collector: America's Century-Long Hunt for Asian Art Treasures — *Meyer, Karl E.*
The China Collectors: America's Century-Long Hunt for Asian Art Treasures — *Meyer, Karl*
The China Collectors: America's Century-Long Hunt for Asian Art Treasures — *Meyer, Karl E.*
China Constructing Capitalism: Economic Life and Urban Change — *Keith, Michael*
c China for Children Series — *Tong, Tommy*
China from Empire to Nation-State — *Wang, Hui*
China in Ten Words — *Yu, Hua*
The China Mirage: The Hidden History of American Disaster in Asia — *Bradley, James*
The China Model and Global Political Economy: Comparison, Impact, and Interaction — *Wan, Ming*
The China Model: Political Meritocracy and the Limits of Democracy — *Bell, Daniel A.*
The China-Pakistan Axis: Asia's New Geopolitics — *Small, Andrew*
The China Pandemic — *Shaw, A.R.*
The China Path to Economic Transition and Development — *Hong, Yinxing*
China Rich Girlfriend (Read by Look, Lydia). Audiobook Review — *Kwan, Kevin*
China Rich Girlfriend — *Kwan, Kevin*
The China Triangle: Latin America's China Boom and the Fate of the Washington Consensus — *Gallagher, Kevin P.*
China under Mao: A Revolution Derailed — *Walder, Andrew G.*
China's Battle for Korea: The 1951 Spring Offensive — *Li, Xiaobing*
China's Disruptors: How Alibaba, Xiaomi, Tencent, and Other Companies Are Changing the Rules of Business — *Tse, Edward*
China's Forgotten People — *Holdstock, Nick*
China's Growth: The Making of an Economic Superpower — *Yueh, Linda*
China's Reforming Churches: Mission, Polity, and Ministry in the Next Christendom — *Baugus, Bruce P.*
China's Regional Relations: Evolving Foreign Policy Dynamics — *Beeson, Mark*
China's Road to Greater Financial Stability: Some Policy Perspectives — *Das, Udaibir S.*
China's Saints: Catholic Martyrdom during the Qing (1644-1911). — *Clark, Anthony E.*
China's Second Continent: How a Million Migrants Are Building a New Empire in Africa — *French, Howard*
China's Second Continent: How a Million Migrants Are Building a New Empire in Africa — *French, Howard A.*
China's State-Owned Enterprises: Nature, Performance and Reform — *Sheng, Hong*
Chinatown Kitchen: From Noodles to Nuoc Cham: Delicious Dishes from Southeast Asian Ingredients — *Mabbott, Lizzie*
Chine-Algerie: Une Relation Singuliere en Afrique — *Pairault, Thierry*
Chinese Brush Painting: Flowers — *Lok, Joan*
Chinese Cities in a Time of Change — *Tsui, Carmen C.M.*
Chinese Comfort Women: Testimonies from Imperial Japan's Sex Slaves — *Qiu, Peipei*

Chinese Cubans: A Transnational History — Lopez, Kathleen
c Chinese Fairy Tale Feasts: A Literary Cookbook (Illus. by Wang, Shaoli) — Yee, Paul
y The Chinese Head Tax and Anti-Chinese Immigration Policies in the Twentieth Century — Chan, Arlene
Chinese Industrial Espionage: Technology Acquisition and Military Modernization — Hannas, William C.
Chinese Lives: The People Who Made a Civilization — Mair, Victor H.
Chinese Money in Global Context: Historic Junctures between 600 BCE and 2012 — Horesh, Niv
Chinese Politics in the Era of Xi Jinping: Renaissance, Reform, or Retrogression? — Lam, Willy Wo-Lap
Chinese Turkestan: A Photographic Journey through an Ancient Civilization (Illus. by Pyle, Ryan) — Pyle, Ryan
Chinese Watercolor Journeys — Zhen, Lian Quan
Chinkstar — Simpson, Jon Chan
Chinookan Peoples of the Lower Columbia — Boyd, Robert T.
c Chippy Chipmunk: Friends in the Garden — Miller, Kathy M.
Chips: A Hometown Hero — West, Nancy M.
c Chips and Cheese and Nana's Knees: What Is Alliteration? (Illus. by Goneau, Martin) — Cleary, Brian P.
Chirakumar Sabha: The Bachelor's Club: A Comedy in Five Acts — Tagore, Rabindranath
c The Chirping Band (Illus. by Jang, EunJoo) — Lee, WonKyeong
c Chitty-Chitty Bang-Bang: The Magical Car (Illus. by Burningham, John) — Fleming, Ian
The Chivalric Folk Tradition in Sicily: A History of Storytelling, Puppetry, Painted Carts and Other Arts — Croce, Marcella
Chivalry and the Ideals of Knighthood in France during the Hundred Years War — Taylor, Craig
c Chloe in India — Darnton, Kate
c Chloe the Kitten (Illus. by Harris-Jones, Kirsteen) — Small, Lily
Choco Revisited: New Research on the Prehistory of Chaco Canyon, New Mexico — Heitman, Carrie C.
The Chocolate Clown Corpse — Carl, JoAnna
Chocolate Islands: Cocoa, Slavery, and Colonial Africa — Higgs, Catherine
c Chocolate Milk, Por Favor: Celebrating Diversity with Empathy (Illus. by Farrell, Donna) — Dismondy, Maria
y Chocolate: Sweet Science and Dark Secrets of the World's Favorite Treat — Frydenborg, Kay
Chocolate: Sweet Science & Dark Secrets of the World's Favorite Treat — Frydenborg, Kay
c Chocolate's Dream (Illus. by Coco, Cha) — Blasco, Elisabet
Choctaw Resurgence in Mississippi: Race, Class, and Nation Building in the Jim Crow South, 1830-1977 — Osburn, Katherine M.B.
c The Choice — Clark, Kathy
Choice — Orbach, Hilary
y The Choice — Clark, Kathy
Choices Women Make: Agency in Domestic Violence, Assisted Reproduction, and Sex Work — Showden, Carisa R.
Choked Up — Mack, Janey
Cholama Moon — Schroeder, Anne
Chomp, Chomp, Chomp — Hansen, Aliena
c Choo-Choo Boogie — Grill, Joyce
c Choo Choo — Child's Play
c Chooky-Doodle-Doo (Illus. by Hanley, Sinead) — Whiten, Jan
Choose Your College Major in a Day — Shatkin, Laurence
Choose Your Own Misery: The Office Adventure — Macdonald, Mike
y Choosing Courage: Inspiring Stories of What It Means to Be a Hero — Collier, Peter
Choosing Homes, Choosing Schools: Residential Segregation and the Search for a Good School — Lareau, Annette
Choosing Hope: Moving Forward from Life's Darkest Hours — Roig-DeBellis, Kaitlin
c Choosing News: What Gets Reported and Why — Palser, Barb
The Choosing — Dekker, Rachelle
Choosing Peace: New Ways to Communicate to Reduce Stress, Create Connection, and Resolve Conflict — Lasater, Ike
Choosing Terror: Virtue, Friendship, and Authenticity in the French Revolution — Linton, Marisa

Choosing the Jesus Way: American Indian Pentecostals and the Fight for the Indigenous Principle — Tarango, Angela
c Chop-Chop, Mad Cap! (Illus. by Cramer, Sadie) — Saumande, Juliette
Chop Suey, USA: The Story of Chinese Food in America — Chen, Yong
Chopsticks: A Cultural and Culinary History — Wang, Q. Edward
Chopsticks and Gambling — Lam, Desmond
The Chora of Metaponto 4: The Late Roman Farmhouse at San Biagio — Lapadula, Erminia
Choral Error Detection: Exercises for Developing Musicianship — Hondorp, Paul
Choral Mediations in Greek Tragedy — Gagne, Renaud
Chorale Settings by Telemann — Telemann, Georg Philipp
Chord — Barot, Rick
A Chorus of Innocents — Chisholm, P.F.
Choruses, Ancient and Modern — Billings, Joshua
Chosen Capital: The Jewish Encounter with American Capitalism — Kobrin, Rebecca
A Chosen Exile: A History of Racial Passing in America — Hobbs, Allyson
c The Chosen Prince (Read by Dean, Robertson). Audiobook Review — Stanley, Diane
c The Chosen Prince — Stanley, Diane
Choucas — Nalkowska, Zofia
Chowderland: Hearty Soups and Stews with Sides and Salads to Match — Dojny, Brooke
Christ Absent and Present: A Study in Pauline Christology — Orr, Peter
Christ and Analogy: The Christocentric Metaphysics of Hans Urs von Balthasar — Johnson, Junius
Christ and Community: The Gospel Witness to Jesus — Henderson, Suzanne Watts
Christ and Reconciliation — Kdrkkdinen, Veli-Matti
Christ Child: Cultural Memories of a Young Jesus — Davis, Stephen J.
The Christ Child in Medieval Culture: Alpha es et O! — Dzon, Mary
Christ in the Life and Teaching of Gregory of Nazianzus — Hofer, Andrew
Christ Meets Me Everywhere: Augustine's Early Figurative Exegesis — Cameron, Michael
Christ Transformed into a Virgin Woman: Lucia Brocadelli, Heinrich Institoris, and the Defense of the Faith — Herzig, Tamar
y Christa's Luck — Grais, Jennifer
The Christian Century and the Rise of the Protestant Mainline — Coffman, Elesha J.
The Christian Century and the Rise of the Protestant Mainline — Coffman, Elisha J.
Christian Conceptions of Jewish Books: The Pfefferkorn Affair — Shamir, Avner
Christian Democrat Internationalism: Its Action in Europe and Worldwide from post World War II until the 1990s — Durand, Jean-Dominique
Christian Economic Ethics: History and Implications — Finn, Daniel K.
Christian Faith and the Earth: Current Paths and Emerging Horizons in Ecotheology — Conradie, Ernst M.
Christian Higher Education: A Global Reconnaissance — Carpenter, Joel
Christian Hits for Teens, 3 vols. — Bober, Melody
Christian Human Rights — Moyn, Samuel
Christian Political Witness — Kalantzis, George
Christian Prophecies as a Reflex to Competing Concepts of Order
Christian Reconstruction: R.J. Rushdoony and American Religious Conservatism — McVicar, Michael J.
The Christian Rejection of Animal Sacrifice — Ullucci, Daniel
Christian Science — Stores, Bruce
Christian Theology in Practice: Discovering a Discipline — Miller-McLemore, E. Rhodes
The Christian Wallet: Spending, Giving, and Living with a Conscience — Slaughter, Mike
Christianity in Roman Africa: The Development of Its Practices and Beliefs — Burns, J. Patout, Jr.
Christianity in Stained Glass — Kogel, Lynne Alcott
Christianity, Islam, and the Negro Race — Blyden, Edward W.
Christianity, Latinity, and Culture: Two Studies on Lorenzo Valla — Camporeale, Salvatore I.
Christians and Jews in Angevin England: The York Massacre of 1190, Narratives and Contexts — Jones, Sarah Rees

Christians in an Age of Wealth: A Biblical Theology of Stewardship — Blomberg, Craig L.
Christina Rossetti and the Bible — Ludlow, Elizabeth
Christine de Pizan and the Fight for France — Adams, Tracy
Christliche Weltgeschichte im 12: Jahrhundert - Themen, Variationen und Kontraste - Untersuchungen zu Hugo von Fleury, Ordericus Vitalis, und Otto von Freising — Megier, Elisabeth
c Christmas (Illus. by Ho, Jannie) — Dahl, Michael
c Christmas and New Year's Eve (Illus. by Nguyen, Dustin) — Nguyen, Dustin
c Christmas at Grandma's Beach House (Illus. by Dawson, Janine) — Saxby, Claire
c Christmas at Last! (Illus. by Dann, Penny) — Hearn, Sam
Christmas Bells — Chiaverini, Jennifer
c The Christmas Book — Storey, Rita
c A Christmas Carol — Dickens, Charles
c A Christmas Carol (Illus. by Kelley, Gerald) — Dickens, Charles
c The Christmas Coal Man (Illus. by Kulka, Joe) — Kulka, Joe
c Christmas Fairy Magic (Illus. by Collingridge, Catharine) — McNamara, Margaret
A Christmas Far from Home: An Epic Tale of Courage and Survival during the Korean War — Weintraub, Stanley
c Christmas in New York City! (Illus. by Lucco, Kristine) — Manzione, Lisa
Christmas in the Koran: Luxenberg, Syriac, and the Near Eastern and Judeo-Christian Background of Islam — Warraq, Ibn
Christmas Is for Bad Girls — Alynn, Jess
The Christmas Match: Football in No Man's Land 1914 — Thermaenius, Pehr
c Christmas Mice! (Illus. by Cushman, Doug) — Roberts, Bethany
c The Christmas Show — Patterson, Rebecca
c The Christmas Stick (Illus. by Yilmaz, Necdet) — Myers, Tim J.
The Christmas Truce: Myth, Memory, and the First World War — Crocker, Terri Blom
c A Christmas Wish for Corduroy (Illus. by Wheeler, Jody) — Hennessy, B.G.
c Christmastime in New York City — Munro, Roxie
c Christopher Columbus — Rajczak, Michael
Christopher Marlowe at 450 — Deats, Sara Munson
Christ's First Theologian: The Shape of Paul's Thought — Keck, Leander
A Chronicle of Intimacies — Raynor, John S.
The Chronicle of Seert: Christian Historical Imagination in Late Antique Iraq — Wood, Philip
c Chronicles from Chateau Moines — Holingue, Evelyne
Chronicles of Majnun Layla and Selected Poems — Haddad, Qassim
Chronicles of the First Crusade — Tyerman, Christopher
Chronicles of the Investiture Contest: Frutolf of Michelsberg and His Continuato — McCarthy, Thomas J.H.
Chronicles of the Investiture Contest: Frutolf of Michelsberg and His Continuators — McCarthy, T.J.H.
Chronicon: Medieval Narrative Sources, A Chronological Guide with Introductory Essays — Bak, Janos M.
c Chubby Wubbles: A Ferret's Tale — Abrams, M.J.
c Chuck and Woodchuck (Illus. by Bell, Cece) — Bell, Cece
c Chukfi Rabbit's Big, Bad Bellyache: A Trickster Tale (Illus. by Widener, Leslie Stall) — Rodgers, Greg
A Church, a School: Pulitzer Prize-Winning Civil Rights Editorials from the Atlanta Constitution — McGill, Ralph
Church and Estate: Religion and Wealth in Industrial-Era Philadelphia — Rzeznik, Thomas F.
The Church and the Left — Michnik, Adam
Church History, vol. 2: From Pre-Reformation to the Present Day: The Rise and Growth of the Church in Its Cultural, Intellectual, and Political Context — Woodbridge, John D.
The Church in Devon, 400-1560 — Orme, Nicholas
Church of Marvels — Parry, Leslie
The Church of Scientology: A History of a New Religion — Urban, Hugh B.
Church of Spies: The Pope's Secret War against Hitler — Riebling, Mark
Church of the Adagio — Dacey, Philip
Church Resistance to Nazism in Norway: 1940-1945 — Hassing, Arne

Church-State Relations in the Early American Republic, 1787-1846 — *Kabala, James S.*
A Church with the Soul of a Nation: Making and Remaking the United Church of Canada — *Airhart, Phyllis D.*
Churchill and America — *Gilbert, Martin*
Churchill and Empire: Portrait of an Imperialist — *James, Lawrence*
Churchill and the Archangel Fiasco — *Kettle, Martin*
Churchill and the Islamic World: Orientalism, Empire and Diplomacy in the Middle East — *Dockter, Warren*
Churchill and the Jews: A Lifelong Friendship — *Gilbert, Martin*
y The Churchill Club: Knud Pedersen and the Boys Who Challenged Hitler — *Hoose, Phillip*
The Churchill Factor: How One Man Made History (Read by Shepherd, Simon). Audiobook Review — *Johnson, Boris*
The Churchill Factor: How One Man Made History — *Johnson, Boris*
Churchill on the Home Front, 1900-55 — *Addison, Paul*
The Churchill Secret KBO — *Smith, Jonathan*
Churchill-Soldier: Life of a Gentleman at War — *Russell, Douglas S.*
Churchill, Strategy and History — *Ben-Moshe, Tuvia*
Churchill: The Prophetic Statesman — *Humes, James C.*
Churchill's Bomb: How the United States Overtook Britain in the First Nuclear Arms Race — *Farmelo, Graham*
Churchill's Cookbook — *Landemare, Georgina*
Churchill's Crusade: The British Invasion of Russia, 1918-20 — *Kinvig, Douglas*
Churchill's Empire: The World That Made Him and the World He Made — *Toye, Richard*
Churchill's Secret War: The British Empire and the Ravaging of India during World War II — *Mukerjee, Madhusree*
c Churchill's Tale of Tails (Illus. by Sandu, Anca) — *Sandu, Anca*
Churchill's 'World Crisis' as History — *Prior, Robin*
Churchmen and Urban Government in Late Medieval Italy, c. 1200-c. 1450: Cases and Contexts — *Andrews, Frances*
y Chu's Day at the Beach (Illus. by Rex, Adam) — *Gaiman, Neil*
c Chu's First Day of School (Illus. by Rex, Adam) — *Gaiman, Neil*
Ciao Biscotti: Sweet and Savory Recipes Celebrating Italy's Favorite Cookie — *Marchetti, Domenica*
Ciao, Carpaccio! An Infatuation — *Morris, Jan*
CIA's June 2013 Response to the SSCI Study on the Former Detention and Interrogation Program — *Central Intelligence Agency*
Cicero on Politics and the Limits of Reason: The Republic and Laws — *Atkins, Jed W.*
Cicero's De Provinciis Consularibus Oratio: Introduction and Commentary — *Grillo, Luca*
Cicero's Ideal Statesman in Theory and Practice — *Zarecki, Jonathan*
Cicero's Pro L. Murena Oratio — *Fantham, Elaine*
The Cigar Factory — *Moore, Michele*
Cilia and Flagella-Ciliates and Flagellates: Ultrastructure and Cell Biology, Function and Systematics, Symbiosis and Biodiversity — *Hausmann, Klaus*
Cinco Becknell — *Maynard, Lee*
c Cinco de Mouse-O! (Read by Heybome, Kirby). Audiobook Review — *Cox, Judy*
c Cinderella: A Paper-Cut Book (Illus. by Dennis, Sarah) — *Dennis, Sarah*
Cinderella Girl — *Gerhardsen, Carin*
The Cinderella Murder — *Burke, Alafair*
The Cinderella Murder — *Clark, Mary Higgins*
c Cinderella: The Terrible Truth (Illus. by Dreidemy, Joelle) — *North, Laura*
y Cinderella's Shoes — *Slayton, Shonna*
c Cinderella's Stepsister and the Big Bad Wolf (Illus. by Blanco, Migy) — *Carey, Lorraine*
The Cinema and Its Shadow: Race and Technology in Early Cinema — *Maurice, Alice*
Cinema and the Republic: Filming on the Margins in Comtemporary France — *Ervine, Jonathan*
The Cinema Makers: Public Life and the Exhibition of Difference in South-Eastern and Central Europe since the 1960s — *Schober, Anna*
Cinema of Actuality: Japanese Avant-Garde Filmmaking in the Season of Image Politics — *Furuhata, Yuriko*

The Cinema of Alexander Sokurov: Figures of Paradox — *Szaniawski, Jeremi*
The Cinema of Istvan Szabo: Visions of Europe — *Sanders, Ivan*
The Cinema of Poetry — *Sitney, P. Adams*
Cinematic Appeals: The Experience of New Movie Technologies — *Rogers, Ariel*
Cinnamon Toasted — *Oust, Gail*
Cinquante ans apres Vatican II: Que reste-t-il a mettre en oeuvre? — *Routhier, Gilles*
y The Cipher — *Ford, John C.*
The Circle — *Anderson, Alison*
The Circle — *Minier, Bernard*
The Circle — *Eggers, Dave*
Circle of Eight: Creating Magic for Your Place on Earth — *Meredith, Jane*
y Circle of Fire — *Dennis, H.L.*
c The Circle of Lies — *Velasquez, Crystal*
y Circle of Stones — *Fisher, Catherine*
c Circle, Square, Moose (Illus. by Zelinsky, Paul O.) — *Bingham, Kelly*
c Circles — *Yonezu, Yusuke*
Circling the Square: Stories from the Egyptian Revolution — *Steavenson, Wendell*
Circling the Sun (Read by McEwan, Katharine). Audiobook Review — *McLain, Paula*
Circling the Sun — *McLain, Paula*
Circular Statistics in R — *Pewsey, Arthur*
The Circulation of (Post)Colonial Knowledge: A Transpacific History, 1800-1980
y Circulus de Potentia — *West, Jim*
c The Circus Goes to Sea (Illus. by Klise, M. Sarah) — *Klise, Kari Allente*
Circus Maximus: The Economic Gamble behind Hosting the Olympics and the World Cup — *Zimbalist, Andrew*
c Circus Mirandus (Read by Pinchot, Bronson). Audiobook Review — *Beasley, Cassie*
y Circus Mirandus (Illus. by Sudyka, Diana) — *Beasley, Cassie*
c Circus Train (Illus. by Matthews, Melanie) — *Judd, Jennifer Cole*
The Cistercian Order in Medieval Europe, 1090-1500 — *Jamroziak, Emilia*
Citation, Intertextuality and Memory in the Middle Ages and Renaissance, vol. 2: Cross-Disciplinary Perspectives on Medieval Culture — *Di Bacco, Guiliano*
Citation, Intertextuality and Memory in the Middle Ages and Renaissance, vol. 2: Cross-Disciplinary Perspectives on Medieval Cultures — *Di Bacco, Guiliano*
Cites humanistes, cites politiques, 1400-1600 — *Crouzet-Pavan, Elisabeth*
Cities and Citizenship — *Hoiston, James*
Cities and River Environments: A Versatile Relationship: Conflicts between Local, National and Transnational Patterns of Governance in East Central Europe and Beyond
Cities and Science: Urban History and the History of Science in the Study of Early Modern and Modern Europe
Cities by Design: The Social Life of Urban Form — *Tonkiss, Fran*
Cities from Scratch: Poverty and Informality in Urban Latin America — *Fischer, Brodwyn*
Cities Full of Symbols: A Theory of Urban Space and Culture — *Nas, Peter J. M.*
Cities in Civilization — *Hall, Peter Geoffrey*
Cities I've Never Lived In: Stories — *Majka, Sara*
Cities of Commerce: The Institutional Foundations of International Trade in the Low Countries, 1250-1650 — *Gelderblom, Oscar*
Cities of Empire: The British Colonies and the Creation of the Urban World — *Hunt, Tristram*
Citizen: An American Lyric (Read by Johnson, Allyson). Audiobook Review — *Rankine, Claudia*
Citizen: An American Lyric — *Rankine, Claudia*
Citizen Coke: The Making of Coca-Cola Capitalism — *Elmore, Bartow J.*
y Citizen Sim — *Solana, Michael*
Citizen Strangers: Palestinians and the Birth of Israel's Liberal Settler State — *Robinson, Shira*
Citizens Divided: Campaign Finance Reform and the Constitution — *Post, Robert C.*
Citizens in the Present: Youth Civic Engagement in the Americas — *De los Angeles Torres, Maria*
Citizens in the Present: Youth Civic Engagement in the Americas — *De Los Angeles Torres, Maria*
Citizens of Asian America: Democracy and Race during the Cold War — *Cheng, Cindy I-Fen*

Citizenship and Governance in a Changing City: Somerville, MA — *Ostrander, Susan A.*
Citizenship and Its Discontents: An Indian History — *Jayal, Niraja Gopal*
Citizenship and the Pursuit of the Worthy Life — *Thunder, David*
Citizenship between Empire and Nation: Remaking France and French Africa, 1945-1960 — *Cooper, Frederick*
Citizenship from Below: Erotic Agency and Caribbean Freedom — *Sheller, Mimi*
Citizenship in Cold War America: The National Security State and the Possibilities of Dissent — *Friedman, Andrea*
Citrus: Sweet & Savory Sun-Kissed Recipes — *Aikman-Smith, Valerie*
y City 1 — *Rosenblum, Gregg*
The City and American Environmentalism — *Gioielli, Robert*
The City and the Fields — *Breiger, Marek*
The City and the Pillar — *Vidal, Gore*
The City at Three P.M.: Writing, Reading, and Traveling — *LaSalle, Peter*
c City Atlas — *Cherry, Georgia*
The City (Read by Jackson, Korey). Audiobook Review — *Koontz, Dean*
City Beasts: Fourteen Stories of Uninvited Wildlife — *Kurlansky, Mark*
c City Birds (Illus. by Norman, Dean) — *Norman, Dean*
City by City: Dispatches from the American Metropolis — *Gessen, Keith*
A City Called Heaven: Chicago and the Birth of Gospel Music — *Marovich, Robert M.*
City, Chant, and the Topography of Early Music: In Honor of Thomas Forrest Kelly — *Cuthbert, Michael Scott*
City Creatures: Animal Encounters in the Chicago Wilderness — *Van Horn, Gavin*
c City Firefighters — *Goldish, Meish*
City Folk: English Country Dance and the Politics of the Folk in Modern America — *Walkowitz, Daniel J.*
A City for Children: Women, Architecture, and the Charitable Landscapes of Oakland, 1850-1950 — *Gutman, Marta*
The City Is Ours: Squatting and Autonomous Movements in Europe from the 1970s to the Present — *Van der Steen, Bart*
City Kaiju — *Rapacz, Mark*
c City Kitty Cat (Illus. by Le Huche, Magali) — *Webb, Steve*
The City Lost and Found: Capturing New York, Chicago, and Los Angeles, 1960-1980 — *Bussard, Katherine A.*
y City Love — *Colasanti, Susane*
City of Ambition — *Williams, Mason B.*
City of Blades — *Bennett, Robert Jackson*
City of Clowns — *Alarcon, Daniel*
City of Darkness and Light — *Bowen, Rhys*
City of Dis — *Butler, David (b. 1964-)*
City of Echoes — *Ellis, Robert*
City of Fae. E-book Review — *Da Costa, Pippa*
y City of Halves — *Inglis, Lucy*
City of Knowledge in Twentieth-Century Iran: Shiraz, History and Poetry — *Manoukian, Setrag*
City of Ladies — *Kennedy, Sarah*
City of Lies: Love, Sex, Death and the Search for Truth in Tehran (Read by Lisle, Sylvia). Audiobook Review — *Navai, Ramita*
City of Rose — *Hart, Rob*
y City of Savages — *Kelly, Lee*
City of the Iron Fish — *Ings, Simon*
c City of Thirst (Illus. by Harris, Todd) — *Ryan, Carrie*
y City of Thorns: Nine Lives in the World's Largest Refugee Camp — *Rawlence, Ben*
City of Wisdom and Blood — *Merle, Robert*
City on a Grid: How New York Became New York — *Koeppel, Gerard*
City on a Hill — *Neill, Ted*
City on Fire — *Hallberg, Garth Risk*
City Spaces: Filling in Berlin's Gaps — *Groschner, Annett*
The City Stained Red — *Sykes, Sam*
c City Street Beat (Illus. by Bakos, Barbara) — *Viau, Nancy*
A City That Sings: Cincinnati's Choral Tradition 1800-2012 — *Roma, Catherine*
City versus Countryside in Mao's China: Negotiating the Divide — *Brown, Jeremy (b. 1976-)*
Civic Agency in Africa: Arts of Resistance in the 21st Century — *Obadare, Ebenezer*

Civic Engagement, Digital Networks, and Political Reform in Africa — *Mudhai, Okoth F.*
The Civic Imagination: Making a Difference in American Political Life — *Baiocchi, Gianpaolo*
c Civic Unrest: Investigate the Struggle for Social Change (Illus. by Chandhok, Lena) — *Lusted, Marcia Amidon*
Civil Antisemitism, Modernism, and British Culture, 1902-1939 — *Trubowitz, Lara*
Civil Disagreement: Personal Integrity in a Pluralistic Society — *Langerak, Edward*
Civil Rights and the Making of the Modern American State — *Francis, Megan Ming*
Civil Rights in the White Literary Imagination: Innocence by Association — *Gray, Jonathan W.*
The Civil Rights Movement in America: From Black Nationalism to the Women's Political Council — *Levy, Peter B.*
The Civil Rights Movement in Mississippi — *Ownby, Ted*
c The Civil Rights Movement — *Winter, Max*
c Civil Rights — *Ataton, Hilaire*
Civil Society in Putin's Russia — *Chebankova, Elena*
Civil Society under Authoritarianism: The China Model — *Teets, Jessica C.*
Civil Uprisings in Modern Sudan: The 'Khartoum Springs' of 1964 and 1985 — *Berridge, W.J.*
The Civil War and American Art — *Harvey, Eleanor J.*
The Civil War as Global Conflict: Transnational Meanings of the American Civil War — *Gleeson, David T.*
The Civil War at Sea — *Symonds, Craig L.*
y The Civil War by the Numbers — *Lanser, Amanda*
Civil War — *Millar, Mark*
The Civil War Diary of Gideon Welles, Lincoln's Secretary of the Navy — *Welles, Gideon*
Civil War Dynasty: The Ewing Family of Ohio — *Heineman, Kenneth J.*
The Civil War Guerilla: Unfolding the Black Flag in History, Memory, and Myth — *Beilein, Joseph M., Jr.*
The Civil War in 50 Objects — *Holzer, Harold*
The Civil War in Popular Culture: Memory and Meaning — *Kreiser, Lawrence A.*
The Civil War in Southern Appalachian Methodism — *Dunn, Durwood*
The Civil War in the Border South — *Phillips, Christopher*
The Civil War in the Jackson Purchase, 1861-1862: The Pro-Confederate Struggle and Defeat in Southwest Kentucky — *Lee, Dan*
Civil War in the North Carolina Quaker Belt: The Confederate Campaign against Peace Agitators, Deserters, and Draft Dodgers — *Auman, William T.*
Civil War — *Ackroyd, Peter*
The Civil War: Told by Those Who Lived It — *Simpson, Brooks D.*
The Civil Wars of Julia Ward Howe — *Showalter, Elaine*
The Civilian Conservation Corps in Southern Illinois, 1933-1942 — *Ripplemeyer, Kay*
A Civilized Woman: M.L. Boonlua Debyasuvarn and the Thai Twentieth Century — *Kepner, Susan Fulop*
The Civilizing Machine: A Cultural History of Mexican Railroads, 1876-1910 — *Matthews, Michael*
The Civilizing Mission in the Metropole: Algerian Families and the French Welfare State during Decolonization — *Lyons, Amelia H.*
Cixous's Semi-Fictions: Thinking at the Borders of Fiction — *Hanrahan, Mairead*
Clade — *Bradley, James*
Claimed — *Kennedy, Elle*
Claiming Exodus: A Cultural History of Afro-Atlantic Identity, 1774-1903 — *Thomas, Rhondda Robinson*
Claiming Society for God: Religious Movements & Social Welfare — *Davis, Nancy J.*
Claiming the Rebel's Heart — *Stuart, Alison*
Claiming the Union: Citizenship in the Post-Civil War South — *Lee, Susanna Michele*
Clandestine — *Janes, J. Robert*
y Clariel (Read by Malcolm, Graeme). Audiobook Review — *Nix, Garth*
y Clariel — *Nix, Garth*
The Clarinet in the Attic, 20 Short Recital and Study Pieces for the Intermediate Player — *Walker, John*
Clarion Call of the Last Kallus — *Krass, Peter*
c Clark in the Deep Sea (Illus. by Alley, R.W.) — *Alley, R.W.*
Clark: The Autobiography of Clark Terry — *Terry, Clark*

c Clark the Shark Takes Heart (Illus. by Francis, Guy) — *Hale, Bruce*
c Clark the Shark: Tooth Trouble (Illus. by Francis, Guy) — *Hale, Bruce*
The Clash of Civilizations or Civil War — *Stawrowski, Zbigniew*
Clash of Eagles — *Smale, Alan*
Clash of the Couples: A Humorous Collection of Completely Absurd Lovers' Squabbles and Relationship Spats — *Ponti, Crystal*
c Clash of the Dinosaurs (Illus. by Croucher, Barry) — *Johnson, Jinny*
The Clasp — *Crosley, Sloane*
c Class Act — *Thomas, Debbie*
Class and Colonialism in Antarctic Exploration, 1750-1920 — *Maddison, Ben*
c Class Dismissed — *Woodrow, Allan*
Class Divisions on the Broadway Stage: the Staging and Taming of the I.W.W. — *Schwartz, Michael*
Class in Soweto — *Alexander, Peter*
The Class of '65: A Student, a Divided Town, and the Long Road to Forgiveness — *Auchmutey, Jim*
Class Photo — *Triptow, Robert*
c Class Stories Series
Class Warfare: Class, Race, and College Admissions in Top-Tier Secondary Schools — *Weis, Lois*
Classic Cashes In — *Myers, Amy*
Classic Cookies with Modern Twists: 100 Best Recipes for Old and New Favorites — *Jackson, Ellen*
c Classic Goosebumps Book #8: Say Cheese and Die (Read by Heller, Johnny). Audiobook Review — *Stine, R.L.*
Classic in the Dock — *Myers, Amy*
Classic Recipes for Modern People; A Collection of Culinary Favorites Reimagined — *Sussman, Max*
The Classical Liberal Constitution: The Uncertain Quest for Limited Government — *Epstein, Richard A.*
Classical Literature: A Very Short Introduction — *Allan, William*
Classical Literature — *Jenkyns, Richard*
Classical Masculinity and the Spectacular Body on Film: the Mighty Sons of Hercules — *O'Brien, Daniel (b. 1967-)*
The Classical Mexican Cinema: The Poetics of the Exceptional Golden Age Films — *Berg, Charles Ramirez*
Classical Myth and Psychoanalysis: Ancient and Modern Stories of the Self — *Zajko, Vanda*
The Classical Tradition: Art, Literature, Thought — *Silk, Michael S.*
Classical Traditions in Science Fiction — *Rogers, Brett M.*
Classical Victorians. Scholars, Scoundrels and Generals in Pursuit of Antiquity — *Richardson, Edmund*
The Classification of Sex: Alfred Kinsey and the Organization of Knowledge — *Drucker, Donna J.*
c Classified: Spies at Work — *Hyde, Natalie*
Classroom Routines for Real Learning: Daily Management Exercises That Empower and Engage Students — *Harper, Jennifer*
Classrooms and Clinics: Urban Schools and the Protection and Promotion of Child Health, 1870-1930 — *Meckel, Richard A.*
y The Classy Crooks Club — *Cherry, Alison*
c Claude at the Beach (Illus. by Smith, Alex T.) — *Smith, Alex T.*
c Claude in the Spotlight (Illus. by Smith, Alex T.) — *Smith, Alex T.*
c Claude on the Slopes (Illus. by Smith, Alex T.) — *Smith, Alex T.*
Claude Vivier: A Composer's Life — *Gilmore, Bob*
Clausewitz: His Life and Work — *Stoker, Donald*
Clausewitz's Timeless Trinity: A Framework for Modern War — *Fleming, Colin M.*
Clay Water Brick: Finding Inspiration from Entrepreneurs Who Do the Most with the Least — *Jackley, Jessica*
Clayfeld Holds On — *Pack, Robert*
c Clayton Stone, at Your Service — *Jones, Ena*
Clean Air Handbook, 4th ed. — *Hunton and Williams*
Clean and White: A History of Environmental Racism in the United States — *Zimring, Carl A.*
A Clean Break: My Story — *Bassons, Christophe*
Clean Eating Freezer Meals — *McCauley, Tiffany*
Clear by Fire — *Hood, Joshua*
Clearer Skies over China: Reconciling Air Quality, Climate, and Economic Goals — *Nielsen, Chris P.*
Cleavage, Connection and Conflict in Rural, Urban and Contemporary Asia — *Bunnell, Tim*
c Clementine for Christmas — *Benedis-Grab, Daphne*

Clementine: The Life of Mrs. Winston Churchill — *Purnell, Sonia*
c Cleo (Illus. by Pineiro, Azul) — *Jurado, Anabel*
c Cleo Edison Oliver, Playground Millionaire (Illus. by Meyer, Jennifer L.) — *Frazier, Sundee T.*
Cleopatra's Shadows — *Holleman, Emily*
The Clergy in Khaki: New Perspectives on British Army Chaplaincy in the First World War — *Snape, Michael*
The Clergy Sex Abuse Crisis and the Legal Responses — *O'Reilly, James T.*
Clerical Celibacy in the West: c. 1100-1700 — *Parish, Helen*
The Clerics of Islam: Religious Authority and Political Power in Saudi Arabia — *Mouline, Nabil*
c Click! (Illus. by Ebbeler, Jeffrey) — *Ebbeler, Jeffrey*
c Click, Clack, Ho! Ho! Ho! (Illus. by Lewin, Betsy) — *Cronin, Doreen*
c Click, Clack, Peep! (Illus. by Lewin, Betsy) — *Cronin, Doreen*
c Click! (Illus. by Ebbeler, Jeffrey) — *Ebbeler, Jeffrey*
c Click! (Illus. by Ebbeler, Jeffrey) — *Ebbeler, Jeffrey*
Clientelligence: How Superior Client Relationships Fuel Growth and Profits — *Rynowecer, Michael B.*
c Clifford Celebrates Hanukkah — *Bridwell, Norman*
y Climate Change — *Nakaya, Andrea C.*
Climate Change and Global Warming of Inland Waters: Impacts and Mitigation for Ecosystems and Societies — *Goldman, Charles R.*
Climate Change and the Course of Global History: A Rough Journey — *Brooke, John L.*
c Climate Change: Discover How It Impacts Spaceship Earth (Illus. by Crosier, Mike) — *Sneideman, Joshua*
Climate Change in Archaeology: Building Resilience from Research in the World's Coastal Wetlands — *van de Noort, Robert*
y Climate Change (Illus. by Basher, Simon) — *Green, Dan*
Climate Change on Crop Productivity — *Sengar, Rakesh S.*
Climate Insurgency: A Strategy for Survival — *Brecher, Jeremy*
Climate Modeling for Scientists and Engineers — *Darke, John B.*
A Climate of Crisis: America in the Age of Environmentalism — *Allitt, Patrick*
Climate Shock: The Economic Consequences of a Hotter Planet — *Wagner, Gernot*
Climate Smart & Energy Wise: Advancing Science Literacy, Knowledge, and Know-How — *McCaffrey, Mark S.*
c Climbing Everest (Illus. by Amatrula, Michele) — *Herman, Gail*
Climbing Mount Laurel: The Struggle for Affordable Housing and Social Mobility in an American Suburb — *Massey, Douglas S.*
Climbing the Charts: What Radio Airplay Tells Us about the Diffusion of Innovation — *Rossman, Gabriel*
Clinical Labor: Tissue Donors and Research Subjects in the Global Bioeconomy — *Cooper, Melinda*
Clinical Psychopharmacology: A Practical Approach — *Marin, Humberto*
The Clint Eastwood Westerns — *Neibaur, James L.*
Clinton Cash: The Untold Story of How and Why Foreign Governments and Businesses Helped Make Bill and Hillary Rich — *Schweizer, Peter*
Clio among the Muses: Essays on History and the Humanities — *Hoffer, Peter Charles*
c Clockwork City (Illus. by McClaren, Meredith) — *McClaren, Meredith*
The Clockwork Crown — *Cato, Beth*
The Clockwork Dagger — *Cato, Beth*
Clockwork Lives — *Anderson, Kevin J.*
A Clockwork Orange — *Burgess, Anthony*
y Cloning — *Henneberg, Susan*
Cloning Noah — *Ross, Cheri Barton*
c Close Encounters of the Nerd Kind — *Miller, Jeff*
Close Kin and Distant Relatives: The Paradox of Respectability in Black Women's Literature — *Morris, Susana M.*
Close Quarters — *Magson, Adrian*
Close to Hugh — *Endicott, Marina*
y Close to the Wind — *Walter, Jon*
y Close Your Eyes, Hold Hands (Read by Blewer, Grace). Audiobook Review — *Bohjalian, Chris*
Closed Circuits: Screening Narrative Surveillance — *Stewart, Garrett*
c The Closer — *Rivera, Mariano*
The Closer You Come — *Showalter, Gena*

556 • CLOSET/Title Index

Closet Queens: Some 20th Century British Politicians — *Bloch, Michael*
Closing the Distance — *Dowson, Jeff*
Closing Time: Prohibition, Rum-Runners, and Border Wars — *Francis, Daniel*
Closure: The Rush to End Grief and What It Costs Us — *Berns, Nancy*
Closure: The Rush to End Grief and What It Costs Us — *Ken, Ivy*
c **Cloth Lullaby: The Woven Life of Louise Bourgeois (Illus. by Arsenault, Isabelle)** — *Novesky, Amy*
c **Clothes** — *Staniford, Linda*
Clothes, Clothes, Clothes. Music, Music, Music. Boys, Boys, Boys — *Albertine, Viv*
c **Clothes Minded (Illus. by Zhang, Nancy)** — *Taylor, Chloe*
c **The Clothes We Wear** — *Lawrence, Ellen*
c **Clothesline Clues to Sports People Play (Illus. by Davies, Andy Robert)** — *Heling, Kathryn*
c **Clothing** — *McDowell, Pamela*
Clothing Poverty: The Hidden World of Fast Fashion and Second-Hand Clothes — *Brooks, Andrew*
Clothing the Clergy: Virtue and Power in Medieval Europe, c. 800-1200 — *Miller, Maureen C.*
Clothing the Poor in Nineteenth-Century England — *Richmond, Vivienne*
y **Cloud 9** — *Campbell, Alex*
The Cloud Collector — *Freemantle, Brian*
Cloud Computing and Electronic Discovery — *Martin, James P.*
c **Cloud Country (Illus. by Klocek, Noah)** — *Becker, Bonny*
Cloud of Expectation — *Westphal, Mike*
Cloud of the Impossible: Negative Theology and Planetary Entanglement — *Keller, Catherine*
c **Clouds: A Compare and Contrast Book** — *Hall, Katharine*
c **Clouds** — *Delano, Marfe Ferguson*
c **The Cloudspotter (Illus. by McLaughlin, Tom)** — *McLaughlin, Tom*
y **Clover's Luck (Illus. by Boiger, Alexandra)** — *George, Kallie*
Clovis Caches: Recent Discoveries and New Research — *Huckell, Bruce B.*
Clovis: On the Edge of a New Understanding — *Smallwood, Ashley M.*
c **Clown Fish** — *Schuh, Mari*
Clownfellas: Tales of the Bozo Family — *Mellick, Carlton, III*
c **Clownfish/ Peces Payaso** — *Naglehout, Ryan*
Clowning and Authorship in Early Modern Theatre — *Preiss, Richard*
y **Club and Prescription Drug Abuse** — *Bodden, Valerie*
Club Red: Vacation Travel and the Soviet Dream — *Koenker, Diane P.*
A Clue to the Exit — *St. Aubyn, Edward*
Cluster: Unmei — *Thomas, Stephen*
The Coaching Solution — *Robertson, Renee*
y **Coal Power** — *Bailey, Diane*
y **Coal River** — *Wiseman, Ellen Marie*
Coal Wars — *Martin, Richard*
Coal Wars: Unions, Strikes, and Violence in Depression-Era Central Washington — *Bullock, David*
Coastal Crafts: Decorative Seaside Projects to Inspire Your Inner Beachcomber — *Shaffer, Cynthia*
Coastlines: The Story of Our Shore — *Barkham, Patrick*
Cobra — *Meyer, Deon*
Cobweb Castle (Illus. by Gorey, Edward) — *Wahl, Jan*
Cochise: Firsthand Accounts of the Chiricahua Apache Chief — *Sweeney, Edwin R.*
c **Cock-a-Doodle-Doo-Bop! (Illus. by Myers, Matt)** — *Black, Michael Ian*
c **Cockatoo, Too (Illus. by Murguia, Bethanie Deeney)** — *Murguia, Bethanie Deeney*
Cockfosters — *Simpson, Helen*
The Cockney Lad and Jim Crow — *Sharer, John*
The Cockney Who Sold the Alps: Albert Smith and the Ascent of Mont Blanc — *McNee, Alan*
Cocktail Noir: From Gangsters and Gin Joints to Gumshoes and Gimlets — *Deitche, Scott M.*
c **Coco and the Little Black Dress (Illus. by van Haeringen, Annemarie)** — *van Haeringen, Annemarie*
c **Coco and the Little Black Dress (Illus. by van Haeringen, Annmarie)** — *van Haeringen, Annmarie*
Coconut Cowboy — *Dorsey, Tim*
Cod: A Biography of the Fish That Changed the World — *Kurlansky, Mark*
Code Black — *Moss, Tina*
Code Grey — *Simon, Clea*

Code Name: Tracker — *Blum, Art*
Code of Disjointed Letters — *Alkan, Oktay*
Code of Honor — *Johnson, Missy*
y **Code of Honor** — *Gratz, Alan*
Codename Xenophon — *Kanaris, Leo*
The Codex Canadensis and the Writings of Louis Nicolas — *Nicolas, Louis*
Codex Sinaiticus: New Perspectives on the Ancient Biblical Manuscript — *McKendrick, Scot*
Codifying Contract Law: International and Consumer Law Perspectives — *Keyes, Mary*
c **Coding Games in Scratch** — *Woodcock, Jon*
c **Cody and the Fountain of Happiness (Read by Ross, Natalie). Audiobook Review** — *Springstubb, Tricia*
c **Cody and the Fountain of Happiness (Illus. by Wheeler, Eliza)** — *Springstubb, Tricia*
c **Cody Secret of the Mountain Dog** — *Kimmel, Elizabeth*
Cody Studies — *Seefeldt, Douglas*
Coffee, Tea and Chocolate: Fueling Modernity: Athenaeum Lecture and Workshop
Coffin Riders — *Bodden, James W.*
Cognitive Approaches to Old English Poetry — *Harbus, Antonina*
The Cognitive Neurosciences — *Gazzanign, Michael S.*
Coin-Operated Americans: Rebooting Boyhood at the Video Game Arcade — *Kocurek, Carly A.*
The Coincidence of Coconut Cake — *Reichert, Amy E.*
Coined: The Rich Life of Money and How Its History Has Shaped Us — *Sehgal, Kabir*
c **Cold as Ice** — *Mlynowski, Sarah*
Cold Betrayal (Read by Ziemba, Karen). Audiobook Review — *Jance, J.A.*
Cold Betrayal — *Jance, J.A.*
y **Cold Burn of Magic** — *Estep, Jennifer*
Cold Cold Heart (Read by Whelan, Julia). Audiobook Review — *Hoag, Tami*
Cold Cold Heart — *Hoag, Tami*
The Cold Cold Sea — *Huber, Linda*
Cold Feet — *FitzHenry, Amy*
Cold Frame — *Deutermann, P.T.*
Cold-Hearted Rake — *Kleypas, Lisa*
Cold Iron — *Leicht, Stina*
c **A Cold Legacy** — *Shepherd, Megan*
Cold Morning — *Ifkovic, Ed*
Cold Mountain: The Legend of Han Shan and Shih Te, the Original Dharma Bums (Illus. by Shimojima, Akiko) — *Wilson, Sean Michael*
Cold Pastoral — *Duley, Margaret*
Cold Shot — *Pettrey, Dani*
y **Cold Spell** — *Pearce, Jackson*
Cold Spring — *McGinley, Patrick*
Cold Trail — *Dawson, Janet*
The Cold War and Soviet Distrust of Churchill's Pursuit of Detente, 1951-55 — *Bar-Noi, Uri*
Cold War Christians and the Spectre of Nuclear Deterrence, 1945-1959 — *Gorry, Jonathan*
Cold War Comforts: Canadian Women, Child Safety, and Global Insecurity — *Brookfield, Tarah*
Cold War Crossings: International Travel and Exchange across the Soviet Bloc, 1940s-1960s — *Babiracki, Patryk*
Cold War Crucible: The Korean Conflict and the Postwar World — *Hajimu, Masuda*
Cold War Cultures: Perspectives on Eastern and Western European Societies — *Vowinckel, Annette*
Cold War Dixie: Militarization and Modernization in the American South — *Frederickson, Kari A.*
Cold War Fighters: Canadian Aircraft Procurement, 1945-54 — *Wakelam, Randall*
Cold War Kids: Politics and Childhood in Postwar America, 1945-1960 — *Holt, Marilyn Irvin*
A Cold War — *Russell, Alan*
c **Cold War on Maplewood Street (Read by Rubinate, Amy). Audiobook Review** — *Rosengren, Gayle*
y **Cold War on Maplewood Street** — *Rosengren, Gayle*
Cold War Progressives: Women's Interracial Organizing for Peace and Freedom — *Castledine, Jacqueline*
Cold War Rivalry and the Perception of the American West — *Goral, Pawel*
A Cold War — *Russell, Alan*
c **The Cold War: Secrets, Special Missions, and Hidden Facts about the CIA, KGB, and M16** — *Bearce, Stephanie*
c **The Cold War: Secrets, Special Missions, and Hidden Facts about the CIA, KGB, and MI6** — *Bearce, Stephanie*
Cold War Social Science: Knowledge Production, Liberal Democracy, and Human Nature — *Cravens, Hamilton*
c **Cold War Spies** — *Goodman, Michael E.*

A Cold War State of Mind: Brainwashing and Postwar American Society — *Dunne, Matthew W.*
A Cold White Fear — *Harlick, R.J.*
Coleridge and the Nature of Imagination: Evolution, Engagement with the World and Poetry — *Ward, David*
c **Colin Kaepernick** — *Yomtov, Nel*
Collaboration Begins with You — *Blanchard, Ken*
The Collaboration: Hollywood's Pact with Hitler — *Urwand, Ben*
Collaborative Intelligence — *Markova, Dawna*
Collage Paint Draw: Explore Mixed Media Techniques & Materials — *Pelletier, Sue*
A Collapse of Horses: Stories — *Evenson, Brian*
The Collapse of Parenting: How We Hurt Our Kids When We Treat Them like Grown-Ups — *Sax, Leonard*
The Collapse of Western Civilization: A View from the Future — *Oreskes, Naomi*
The Collapse: The Accidental Opening of the Berlin Wall — *Sarotte, Mary Elise*
Collapsed World — *Nobit, John*
Collar Robber — *Locke, Hillary Bell*
c **Collared Lizard** — *Ang, Karen*
y **Collateral Damage** — *Chartier, Brent*
y **Collateral Damage** — *Jones, Patrick*
Collect and Record! Jewish Holocaust Documentation in Early Postwar Europe — *Jockusch, Laura*
Collected Essays on War, Holocaust and the Crisis of Communism — *Gross, Jan Tomasz*
The Collected Letters of Robinson Jeffers, with Selected Letters of Una Jeffers, vol. 2 and 3 — *Jeffers, Robinson*
y **Collected Lyrics, 1970-2015** — *Smith, Patti*
The Collected Papers of Albert Einstein, vol. 12: The Berlin Years: Correspondence, January-December 1921 — *Einstein, Albert*
The Collected Papers of Albert Einstein: vol. 13: The Berlin Years: Writings and Correspondence, January 1922-March 1923 — *Einstein, Albert*
Collected Papers on Alexander the Great — *Badian, Ernst*
Collected Papers on English Legal History — *Baker, John Hamilton*
Collected Poems, 1964-2014 — *Schmid, Vernon*
Collected Poems: 1969-2014 — *Mehrotra, Arvind Krishna*
The Collected Poems — *Beckett, Samuel*
The Collected Poems of James Laughlin — *Glassgold, Peter*
The Collected Poems of James Laughlin — *Laughlin, James*
The Collected Poems of John Crowe Ransom — *Mazer, Ben*
The Collected Poems of Miriam Waddington, vol. 1 — *Waddington, Miriam*
The Collected Poems of Miriam Waddington, vol. 2 — *Waddington, Miriam*
The Collected Poems of Philip Lamantia — *Caples, Garrett*
Collected Poems — *Duffy, Carol Ann*
Collected Poems — *Strand, Mark*
The Collected Prose of Elizabeth Bishop — *Bishop, Elizabeth*
The Collected Sermons of Walter Brueggemann, vol. 2 — *Brueggemann, Walter*
The Collected Short Stories — *Healy, Dermot*
The Collected Stories of Gladys Schmitt — *Schmitt, Gladys*
The Collected Stories of John Cheever — *Cheever, John*
Collected Stories of William Faulkner — *Barth, John*
Collected Stories of William Faulkner
y **The Collected Stories of Winnie the Pooh (Read by Dench, Judi). Audiobook Review** — *Milne, A.A.*
Collected Stories — *Barth, John*
Collected Stories — *Lispector, Clarice*
Collected Works of Erasmus, vols. 37-38: Apophthegmata — *Knott, Betty I.*
The Collected Writings, vol. 2: The Port Nelson Relations — *Radisson, Pierre-Esprit*
c **Collecting and Understanding the Wonders of the Natural World** — *Grice, Gordon*
Collecting Easter Island Stamps and Postal History — *Pendleton, Steve*
Collecting Old Maps — *Manasek, F.J.*
Collecting Shakespeare: The Story of Henry and Emily Folger — *Grant, Stephen H.*
Collection Canada 2014
Collection Evaluation in Academic Libraries: A Practical Guide for Librarians — *Kohn, Karen C.*
Collection of Sand: Essays — *Calvino, Italo*

The Collection Program in Schools: Concepts and Practices, 5th ed. — Bishop, Kay
The Collection's at the Core: Revitalizing Your Library with Innovative Resources for the Common Cores and STEM — Mardis, Marcia
Collective Courage: A History of African American Cooperative Economic Thought and Practice — Nembhard, Jessica Gordon
The Collective Legacy — Menard, Lawrence
The Collectivistic Premise — Merchant, Eli
Collector of Secrets — Goodfellow, Richard
Collector's Guide to the Zeolite Group — Lauf, Robert J.
College Disrupted: The Great Unbundling of Higher Education — Craig, Ryan
c The College Football Championship: The Fight for the Top Spot — Doeden, Matt
y College, Quicker: 24 Practical Ways to Save Money and Get Your Degree Faster — Stephens, Kate
College Unbound: The Future of Higher Education and What It Means for Students — Selingo, Jeffrey J.
Collegiate Republic: Cultivating an Ideal Society in Early America — Sumner, Margaret
Collier's Guide to Night Photography in the Great Outdoors — Collier, Grant
An Collins and the Historical Imagination — Howard, W. Scott
Collins English Dictionary, 12th ed. — Forsyth, Mark
Collision — Cohen, William S.
Collision of Empires: Italy's Invasion of Ethiopia and Its International Impact — Strang, G. Bruce
Colombia and World War I: The Experience of a Neutral Latin American Nation during the Great War and Its Aftermath, 1914-1921 — Rausch, Jane M.
The Colonel and Hug: The Partnership That Transformed the New York Yankees — Steinberg, Steve
Colonel House: A Biography of Woodrow Wilson's Silent Partner — Neu, Charles E.
c Colonel Theodore Roosevelt — Adler, David A.
Colonial Comics: New England, 1620-1750 — Rodriguez, Jason
Colonial Genocide in Indigenous North America — Woolford, Andrew
c Colonial Madness — Whittemore, Jo
Colonial Mediascapes: Sensory Worlds of the Early Americas — Cohen, Matt
Colonial Pathologies, Environment, and Western Medicine in Saint-Louis-du-Senegal, 1867-1920 — Ngalamulume, Kalala
Colonial Rule and Social Change in Korea, 1910-1945 — Lee, Hong Yung
Colonialism by Proxy: Hausa Imperial Agents and Middle Belt Consciousness in Nigeria — Ochonu, Moses E.
Colonialism, Maasina Rule, and the Origins of Malaitan Kastom — Akin, David W.
Coloniality, Religion, and the Law in the Early Iberian World — Arias, Santas
Colonies — Rozycki, Tomasz
Colonization and the Origins of Humanitarian Governance: Protecting Aborigines across the Nineteenth-Century British Empire — Lester, Alan
A Colony Sprung from Hell: Pittsburgh and the Struggle for Authority on the Western Pennsylvania Frontier, 1744-1794 — Barr, Daniel P.
Color Concrete Garden Projects: Make Your Own Planters, Furniture, and Fire Pits Using Creative Techniques and Vibrant Finishes (Illus. by Coleman, Charles) — Smith, Nathan
c Color Dog — Van Fleet, Matthew
Color Lab for Mixed-Media Artists: 52 Exercises for Exploring Color Concepts through Paint, Collage, Paper, and More — Forman, Deborah
c The Color Monster: A Pop-Up Book of Feelings (Illus. by Llenas, Anna) — Llenas, Anna
The Color of Citizenship: Race, Modernity, and Latin American/ Hispanic Political Thought — Vacano, Diego A. Von
The Color of Food: Stories of Race, Resilience and Farming — Bowens, Natasha
c A Color of His Own: Spanish-English Bilingual Edition (Illus. by Lionni, Leo) — Mlawer, Teresa
The Color of Our Sky — Trasi, Amita
The Color of Smoke — Lakatos, Menyhert
The Color of Sound: Race, Religion, and Music in Brazil — Burdick, John
The Color of Success: Asian Americans and the Origins of the Model Minority — Wu, Ellen D.

Color + Pattern: 50 Playful Exercises for Exploring Pattern Design — Howell, Khristian A.
c The Color Thief: A Family's Story of Depression (Illus. by Littlewood, Karin) — Peters, Andrew Fusek
Colorado: A Historical Atlas — Noel, Thomas J.
Colorful Crochet Lace: 22 Chic Garments and Accessories — Hall, Mary Jane
A Colorful History of Popular Delusions — Bartholomew, Robert E.
c Coloring Animal Mandalas — Piersall, Wendy
Coloring Book — Quinn, Colin
Colorless Tsukuru Tazaki and His Years of Pilgrimage (Read by Locke, Bruce). Audiobook Review — Murakami, Haruki
Colorless Tsukuru Tazaki and His Years of Pilgrimage (Illus. by Locke, Bruce) (Read by Locke, Bruce). Audiobook Review — Murakami, Haruki
Colorless Tsukuru Tazaki and His Years of Pilgrimage (Read by Locke, Bruce). Audiobook Review — Murakami, Haruki
Colorless Tsukuru Tazaki and His Years of Pilgrimage — Murakami, Haruki
c Colors — Graire, Virginie
c Colors (Illus. by Steggall, Susan) — Steggall, Susan
c Colors (Illus. by Ward, Sarah) — Ward, Sarah
c Colors Everywhere: Counting — Versteeg, Lizelot
c The Colors of Israel — Raz, Rachel
c Colors of the Wind: The Story of Blind Artist and Champion Runner George Mendoza (Illus. by Mendoza, George) — Powers, J.L.
c Colors, Shapes & Counting: A Point & Name Book of Rhymes — Caudle, Melissa
c Colors versus Shapes — Boldt, Mike
c The Colour Thief: A Family's Story of Depression (Illus. by Littlewood, Karin) — Peters, Andrew Fusek
Colouring In — Huth, Angela
The Colours of Reality — McEwen, Rory
The Columbia Anthology of Modern Japanese Drama — Rimer, J. Thomas
The Columbia Anthology of Yuan Drama — Hsia, Chih-tsing
The Columbia Antology of Japanese Essays: "Zuihitsu" from the Tenth to the Twenty-First Century — Carter, Steven D.
The Columbia River: A Historical Travel Guide — Roe, Joann
c Columbus Day — Dash, Meredith
Columns of Vengeance: Soldiers, Sioux, and the Punitive Expeditions, 1863-1864 — Beck, Paul N.
Coma (Read by LaVoy, January). Audiobook Review — Cook, Robin
The Comanche Fights Again — Harrison, D.M.
Combat-Ready Kitchen — de Salcedo, Anastada Marx
The Combat Soldier: Infantry Tactics and Cohesion in the Twentieth and Twenty-First Centuries — King, Anthony
y Combat Zone — Jones, Patrick
Combating Climate Change: An Agricultural Perspective — Kang, Manjit S.
Combating Jihadism: American Hegemony and Interstate Cooperation in the War on Terrorism — Mendelsohn, Barak
Combating Mountaintop Removal: New Directions in the Fight against Big Coal — McNeil, Bryan T.
Come and Take It: Search for the Treasure of the Alamo — Wallace, Landon
Come as You Are: Art of the 1990s — Schwartz, Alexandra
Come as You Are: The Surprising New Science That Will Transform Your Sex Life — Nagoski, Emily
Come Away with Me — Brown, Karma
Come Back — Wiebe, Rudy
Come Back Strong: A Widow's Song — Whaley, Eileen McGuire
y Come Back to Me — Gray, Mila
c Come Count with Me! — Wilson, Marika
Come Dancing — Wells, Leslie
Come Hell or Highball — Chance, Maia
Come Out Swinging: The Changing World of Boxing in Gleason's Gym — Trimbur, Lucia
Come Rain or Come Shine — Karon, Jan
Come the Revolution — Chadwick, Frank
Come to Harm — McPherson, Catriona
c Come with Me to Paris (Illus. by Heo, Min) — Fowler, Gloria
The Comedians: Drunks, Thieves, Scoundrels, and the History of American Comedy — Nesteroff, Kliph
y A Comedy and a Tragedy: A Memoir of Learning How to Read and Write — Culley, Travis Hugh

Comedy and the Feminine Middlebrow Novel: Elizabeth Von Arnim and Elizabeth Taylor — Brown, Erica
Comedy, Caricature and The Social Order, 1820-50 — Maidment, Brian
Comedy Writing Self-Taught: The Professional Skill-Building Course in Writing Stand-Up, Sketch, and Situation Comedy — Perret, Gene
c The Comet of Doom (Illus. by Laughead, Mike) — Perritano, John
c Comets — Riggs, Kate
Comfort: A Novel of the Reverse Underground Railroad — Maxon, H.A.
Comfort and Joy: Cooking for Two: Small Batch Meals for Every Occasion — Lane, Christina
The Comfort of Black — Wilson, Carter
The Comfort of Little Things: An Educator's Guide to Second Chances — Bruno, Holly Elissa
The Comfort of Strangers — McEwan, Ian
Comic Book Crime: Truth, Justice, and the American Way — Phillips, Nickie D.
Comic Book Geographies — Dittmer, Jason
The Comic Book Story of Beer: The World's Favorite Beverage from 7000 BC to Today's Craft Brewing Revolution (Illus. by McConnell, Aaron) — Hennessey, Jonathan
Comic, Curious and Quirky: News Stories from Centuries Past — Levin, Rona
Comic Japan: Best of Zero Gravity Cartoons from The Japan Times — Dahl, Roger
Comic Medievalism: Laughing at the Middle Ages — D'Arcens, Louise
A Comic Vision of Great Constancy: Stories about Unlocking the Wisdom of Everyman — Griesinger, Alan
Comics and Conflict: Patriotism and Propaganda from WWII through Operation Iraqi Freedom — Scott, Cord A.
Comics Art — Gravett, Paul
c Comics Squad: Lunch! — Holm, Jennifer L.
c Comics Squad: Recess! — Holm, Jennifer L.
Comics through Time: A History of Icons, Idols, and Ideas, 4 vols. — Booker, M. Keith
Comin' Right at Ya — Benson, Ray
Coming Back to Life: The Updated Guide to The Work That Reconnects — Macy, Joanna
Coming for to Carry Me Home: Race in America from Abolitionism to Jim Crow — Martinez, J. Michael
c Coming Home (Illus. by Ruth, Greg) — Ruth, Greg
Coming into the Country — McPhee, John
y Coming of Age at the End of Days — LaPlante, Alice
Coming of Age in Nineteenth-Century India: The Girl-Child and the Art of Playfulness — Lal, Ruby
Coming of Political Age: American Schools and the Civic Development of Immigrant Youth — Callahan, Rebecca M.
The Coming of the Terror in the French Revolution — Tackett, Timothy
Coming Out Christian in the Roman World: How the Followers of Jesus Made a Place in Caesar's Empire — Boin, Douglas
Coming Out: The New Dynamics — Guittar, Nicholas A.
Coming Up Short: Working-Class Adulthood in an Age of Uncertainty — Silva, Jennifer M.
Commanders and Command in the Roman Republic and Early Empire — Drogula, Fred K.
y Comme un tour de magie — Larouche, Nadya
Commemoration in America: Essays on Monuments, Memorialization, and Memory — Gobel, David
Commentaire des fragments dramatiques de Naevius — Spaltenstein, F.
c Commentarii de Inepto Puero — Kinney, Jeff
Commerce with the Universe: Africa, India, and the Afrasian Imagination — Desai, Gaurav
Commercial Agriculture, the Slave Trade, and Slavery in Atlantic Africa — Law, Robin
Commercial Poultry Production on Maryland's Lower Eastern Shore: The Role of African Americans, 1930s to 1990s — Omo-Osagie, Solomon Iyobosa, II
A Commercial Republic: America's Enduring Debate over Democratic Capitalism — O'Connor, Mike
Commercial Visions: Science, Trade, and Visual Culture in the Dutch Golden Age — Margocsy, Daniel
Commitment and Compassion: Essays on Georg Buchner. Festschrift for Gerhard P. Knapp — Fortmann, Patrick
Committed Styles: Modernism, Politics, and Left-Wing Literature in the 1930s — Kohlmann, Benjamin

Commodities and Colonialism: The Story of Big Sugar in Indonesia, 1880-1942 — *Knight, G. Roger*
The Common Cause: Postcolonial Ethics and the Practice of Democracy, 1900-1955 — *Gandhi, Leela*
The Common Core in Action: Ready to Use Lesson Plans for K-6 Librarians — *Jesseman, Deborah J.*
Common Ground at the Nexus of Information Literacy and Scholarly Communication — *Davis-Kahl, Stephanie*
Common Ground — *Cowen, Rob*
Common Law and Enlightenment in England, 1689-1750 — *Rudolph, Julia*
The Common Law in Colonial America, vol. 2: The Middle Colonies and the Carolinas, 1660-1730 — *Nelson, William E.*
Common People: In Pursuit of My Ancestors — *Light, Alison*
Common People: The History of an English Family — *Light, Alison*
A Common Strangeness: Contemporary Poetry, Cross-Cultural Encounter, Comparative Literature — *Edmond, Jacob*
Common Things: Romance and the Aesthetics of Belonging in Atlantic Modernity — *Lilley, James D.*
Common Threads: A Cultural History of Clothing in American Catholicism — *Dwyer-McNulty, Sally*
The Commons in History: Culture, Conflict and Ecology — *Wall, Derek*
Commonwealth of Letters: British Literary Culture and the Emergence of Postcolonial Aesthetics — *Kalliney, Peter J.*
The Communal Idea in the 21st Century — *Ben-Rafael, Eliezer*
Communal Luxury: The Political Imaginary of the Paris Commune — *Ross, Kristin*
Communicating beyond Language: Everyday Encounters with Diversity — *Rymes, Betsy*
Communicating India's Soft Power: Buddha to Bollywood — *Thussu, Daya Kishan*
Communicating Observations in Early Modern Letters (1500-1675): Epistolography and Epistemology in the Age of the Scientific Revolution — *Miert, Dirk van*
Communication, Public Opinion, and Globalization in Urban China — *Lee, Francis L.F.*
Communications and Cooperation in Early Imperial China: Publicizing the Qin Dynasty — *Sanft, Charles*
Communications, Media and the Imperial Experience: Britain and India in the Twentieth Century — *Kaul, Chandrika*
Communing with Music: Practicing the Art of Conscious Listening — *Cantello, Matthew*
Communion — *Smith, Curtis*
Communism, Nationalism and Ethnicity in Poland, 1944-1950 — *Fleming, Michael*
Communism on Tomorrow Street: Mass Housing and Everyday Life after Stalin — *Harris, Steven E.*
Communities of Faith in Africa and the African Diaspora: In Honor of Dr. Tite Tienou, with Additional Essays on World Christianity — *Essamuah, Casely B.*
The Community and Homo Criticus: Performance in the Age of Neoliberalism — *Hunka, George*
Community by Design: The Olmsted Form and the Development of Brookline, Massachusetts — *Morgan, Keith N.*
The Community College Advantage: Your Guide to a Low-Cost, High-Reward College Experience — *Melville, Diane*
c Community Helpers Series
Community Lost: The State, Civil Society, and Displaced Survivors of Hurricane Katrina — *Angel, Ronald J.*
The Community-Scale Permaculture Farm: The D Acres Model for Creating and Managing an Ecologically Designed Educational Center — *Trought, Josh*
Como la sombra que se va — *Molina, Antonio Munoz*
Companeras: Zapatista Women's Stories — *Klein, Hilary*
A Companion to Astrology in the Renaissance — *Dooley, Brendan*
A Companion to Boethius in the Middle Ages — *Kaylor, Noel Harold, Jr.*
A Companion to Bonaventure — *Hammond, Jay M.*
A Companion to Early Modern Hispanic Theater — *Kallendorf, Hilaire*
A Companion to Fifteenth-Century English Poetry — *Edwards, Anthony Stockwell Garfield*
A Companion to Fifteenth-Century English Poetry — *Boffey, Julia*

A Companion to Greek and Roman Sexualities — *Hubbard, Thomas K.*
A Companion to John Adams and John Quincy Adams — *Waldstreicher, David*
A Companion to John of Ruusbroec — *Arblaster, John*
A Companion to Latin Greece — *Tsougarakis, Nickiphoros I.*
A Companion to Livy — *Mineo, Bernard*
A Companion to Luis de Molina — *Kaufmann, Matthias*
A Companion to Medieval Palermo: The History of a Mediterranean City from 600 to 1500 — *Nef, Annliese*
A Companion to Mediterranean History — *Horden, Peregrine*
A Companion to Rawls — *Mandle, Jon*
A Companion to Rawls — *Reidy, David A.*
A Companion to Roman Architecture — *Ulrich, R.B.*
A Companion to Ronald Reagan — *Johns, Andrew L.*
A Companion to Terence — *Augoustakis, Antony*
A Companion to the Ancient Novel — *Cueva, Edmund P.*
A Companion to the Antebellum Presidents, 1837-1861 — *Silbey, Joel H.*
A Companion to the Archaeology of the Roman Republic — *Evans, Jane DeRose*
A Companion to the Early Modern Printed Book in Britain, 1476-1558 — *Gillespie, Vincent*
A Companion to the Early Printed Book in Britain, 1476-1558 — *Gillespie, Vincent*
A Companion to the Eucharist in the Reformation — *Wandel, Lee Palmer*
A Companion to the Latin Medieval Commentaries on Aristotle's Metaphysics — *Amerini, Fabrizio*
A Companion to the U.S. Civil War, 2 vols. — *Sheehan-Dean, Aaron*
A Companion to the Works of Max Frisch — *Berwald, Olaf*
The Company and the Shogun: The Dutch Encounter with Tokugawa Japan — *Clulow, Adam*
A Company Man: The Remarkable French-Atlantic Voyage of a Clerk for the Company of the Indies — *Caillot, Marc-Antoine*
A Company of One: Insecurity, Independence and the New World of White Collar Unemployment — *Lane, Carrie*
The Company of Trees: A Year in a Lifetime's Quest — *Pakenham, Thomas*
The Company She Kept — *Mayor, Archer*
Comparative Biomechanics: Life's Physical World — *Vogel, Steven*
Comparative Matters: The Renaissance of Comparative Constitutional Law — *Hirschl, Ran*
Comparative Peace Processes — *Tonge, Jonathan*
c Comparative Religion: Investigate the World through Religious Tradition (Illus. by Chandhok, Lena) — *Mooney, Carla*
Comparative Study of Child Soldiering on Myanmar-China Border: Evolutions, Challenges and Countermeasures — *Chen, Kai*
c Comparing Animal Traits — *Hirsch, Rebecca E.*
Comparing Institution-Building in East Asia: Power Politics, Governance, and Critical Junctures — *Yoshimatsu, Hidetaka*
Compass and a Camera — *Burchik, Steven*
c Compass of Dreams (Illus. by Bruno, Iacopo) — *Baccalario, Pierdomenico*
Compassionate Confinement: A Year in the Life of Unit C — *Abrams, Laura S.*
Compassionate Stranger: Asenath Nicholson and the Great Irish Famine — *Murphy, Maureen O'Rourke*
The Compatibility Gene: How Our Bodies Fight Disease, Attract Others, and Define Our Selves — *Davis, Daniel M.*
Compelled to Crave — *Trevathan, Erika*
The Compelling Ideal: Thought Reform and the Prison in China, 1901-1956 — *Kiely, Jan*
Compendium of Alfalfa Diseases and Pests — *Samac, Deborah A.*
Competing Visions of Empire: Labor, Slavery, and the Origins of the British Atlantic Empire — *Swingen, Abigail L.*
The Competition: A Rachel Knight Novel — *Clark, Marcia*
The Competition — *Clark, Marcia*
The Compilation of Knowledge in the Middle Ages — *Munoz, Maria Jose*
Compleat Gentleman, 1634 — *Peacham, Henry*
The Complete A to Z Dictionary of Dreams: Be Your Own Dream Expert — *Wallace, Ian*
c The Complete Adventures of Johnny Mutton — *Proimos, James*

The Complete Beatles Songs: The Story Behind Every Beatles Song — *Turner, Steve*
The Complete Book of 1940s Broadway Musicals — *Dietz, Dan*
The Complete Book of 1950s Broadway Musicals — *Dietz, Dan*
y The Complete Bostock and Harris — *Garfield, Leon*
c The Complete Chi's Sweet Home, vol. 1 (Illus. by Kanata, Konami) — *Kanata, Konami*
The Complete Cosmicomics — *Weaver, William*
Complete Detox Workbook; 2-Day, 9-Day and 30-Day Makeovers to Cleanse and Revitalize Your Life — *Scott-Moncrieff, Christina*
c The Complete First Edition: The Original Folk and Fairy Tales of the Brothers Grimm — *Grimm, Jacob*
The Complete Francis of Assisi: His Life, the Complete Writings, and the Little Flowers — *Sweeney, Jon M.*
c The Complete Guide to a Dog's Best Friend (Illus. by West, David) — *Gardner, Felicity*
The Complete Guide to Acquisitions Management, 2d ed. — *Wilkinson, Frances C.*
The Complete Guide to Companion Planting: Everything You Need to Know to Make Your Garden Successful — *Mayer, Dale*
The Complete Guide to Creating Oils, Soaps, Creams, and Herbal Gels for Your Mind and Body: 101 Natural Body Care Recipes — *Jones, Marlene*
The Complete Guide to Drying Foods at Home — *Paajanen, Terri*
The Complete Guide to Even More Vegan Food Substitutions: The Latest and Greatest Methods for Veganizing Anything Using More Natural, Plant-Based Ingredients — *Newman, Joni Marie*
The Complete Guide to Growing Tomatoes: Everything You Need to Know Explained Simply: Including Heirloom Tomatoes — *Everhart, Cherie H.*
The Complete Guide to Hunting, Butchering, and Cooking Wild Game, vol. 1: Big Game — *Rinella, Steven*
The Complete Guide to Hunting, Butchering, and Cooking Wild Game, vol. 2: Small Game and Fowl — *Rinella, Steven*
The Complete Guide to Making Wire Jewelry: Techniques, Projects, and Jig Patterns from Beginner to Advanced — *Devenney, Wing Mun*
The Complete Guide to North American Fishing — *Schultz, Ken*
The Complete Guide to Using Google in Libraries: Instruction, Administration, and Staff Productivity, vol. 1 — *Smallwood, Carol*
The Complete Guide to Working With Worms: Using the Gardener's Best Friend for Organic Gardening and Composting — *Vincent, Wendy*
A Complete Identity: The Youthful Hero in the Work of G.A. Henty and George MacDonald — *Johnson, Rachel E.*
The Complete Idiot's Guide Music Dictionary — *Felix, Stanford*
The Complete Journals of L.M. Montgomery: The PEI Years, 1889-1900 — *Montgomery, L.M.*
The Complete Letters of Henry James, 1878-1880, vol. 1 — *Walker, Pierre A.*
y Complete Nothing — *Scott, Kieran*
The Complete Patrick Melrose Novels — *St. Aubyn, Edward*
c Complete Photo Guide to Bead Crafts — *Kopperude, Amy*
Complete Photo Guide to Crochet — *Burger, Deborah*
c Complete Photo Guide to Sewing — *Bergeron, Janith*
Complete Poems of Emily Dickinson — *Dickinson, Emily*
The Complete Poems of James Dickey — *Bigs, Ward*
The Complete Poems of William Barnes, vol. 1: Poems in the Broad Form of the Dorset Dialect — *Burton, Tom L.*
Complete Poetical Works and Selected Prose — *Bacovia, George*
The Complete Poetry of Robert Herrick, 2 vols. — *Cain, Tom*
The Complete Prose of T.S. Eliot: The Critical Edition, vol. 1: Apprentice Years 1905-1918 — *Schuchard, Ronald*
The Complete Prose of T.S. Eliot: The Critical Edition, vol. 2, The Perfect Critic 1919-1926 — *Schuchard, Ronald*
The Complete Stories — *Lispector, Clarice*
The Complete Stories — *Malamud, Bernard*
The Complete Stories — *Butts, Mary*
The Complete Stories — *Lispector, Clarice*

The Complete Truly Astounding Animals — Rudzik, Peter
The Complete Works of John Milton, vol. 6: Vernacular Regicide and Republican Writings — Keeble, Neil Howard
The Complete Works of Primo Levi — Goldstein, Ann
The Complete Works of Primo Levi — Levi, Primo
The Complete Works of Rosa Luxemburg: Economic Writings 1, vol. 1 — Hudis, Peter
The Complete Works of W.H. Auden: Prose, vol. 5: 1963-1968 — Auden, W.H.
The Complete Works of W.H. Auden: Prose, vol. 6: 1969-1973 — Auden, W.H.
The Complete Works of W.H. Auden: Prose, vol. 6, 1969-1973 — Mendelson, Edward
The Complete Works of W.H. Auden: Prose, vols. 5-6 — Auden, W.H.
Complete Works — Lafayette, Madame de
c Completely Clementine (Read by Almasy, Jessica). Audiobook Review — Pennypacker, Sara
c Completely Clementine (Illus. by Frazee, Marla) — Pennypacker, Sara
A Complex Fate: William L. Shirer and the American Century — Cuthbertson, Ken
The Complexity Paradox: The More Answers We Find, the More Questions We Have — Mossman, Kenneth L.
Complicated Grief — Mullen, Laura
Complicity, Censorship and Criticism: Negotiating Space in the GDR Literary Sphere — Jones, Sara (b. 1980-)
Complicity in the Holocaust: Churches and Universities in Nazi Germany — Ericksen, Robert P.
Composer Showcase: An Awesome Adventure, Eight Original Piano Solos — Lybeck-Robinson, Lynda
Composer Songs: Meet 12 Famous Composers through Song — Albrecht, Sally K.
A Composer's Guide to Game Music — Phillips, Winifred
The Composer's Landscape: The Pianist as Explorer, Interpreting the Scores of Eight Masters — Montparker, Carol
Composing for the Red Screen: Prokofiev and Soviet Film — Bartig, Kevin
Composing the Party Line: Music and Politics in Early Cold War Poland and East Germany — Tompkins, David G.
Compromised: The Affordable Care Act and Politics of Defeat — Williams, Brendan W.
c Compulsion — Boone, Martina
Compulsion — Brennan, Allison
Compulsion — Levin, Meyer
Computer Aided Assessment of Mathematics — Sangwin, Chris
Computer-Aided Graphing and Simulation Tools for AutoCAD Users — Simionescu, P.A.
c Computer Coding for Kids — Vorderman, Carol
Computer Engineer Ruchi Sanghvi — Waxman, Laura Hamilton
c Computer Networks — Gifford, Clive
The Computing Universe: A Journey Through a Revolution — Hey, Tony
Computing with Quantum Cats: From Colossus to Qubits — Gribbin, John
Comradely Greetings: The Prison Letters of Nadya and Slavoj — Tolokonnikova, Nadya
Comrades-in-Arms — Oakes, Rita
y Con Academy — Schreiber, Joe
The Con Men: Husling in New York City — Williams, Terry
The Con Men: Hustling in New York City — Williams, Terry
Conceal Carry; Pause: The Pursuit of Trained Readiness with a Goal to Avoid a 3-Second-Long Gun Fight — Ziebell, Donn G.
Conceived in Doubt: Religion and Politics in the New American Nation — Porterfield, Amanda
Conceiving Citizens: Women and the Politics of Motherhood in Iran — Kashani-Sabet, Firoozeh
Conceiving Cuba: Reproduction, Women, and the State in the Post-Soviet Era — Andaya, Elise
Conceiving Freedom: Women of Color, Gender, and the Abolition of Slavery in Havana and Rio De Janeiro — Cowling, Camillia
Conceiving Masculinity: Male Infertility, Medicine, and Identity — Barnes, Liberty Walther
y Concentr8 — Sutcliffe, William
The Concentration Camps of the Anglo-Boer War: A Social History — Van Heyningen, Elizabeth
The Concept of the World Economy: Intellectual Histories

Conceptions of Chinese Democracy: Reading Sun Yat-sen, Chiang Kai-shek, and Chiang Ching-kuo — Lorenzo, David J.
Concepts of Creativity in Seventeenth-Century England — Herissone, Rebecca
Conceptual Breakthroughs in Evolutionary Genetics: A Brief History of Shifting Paradigms — Avise, John C.
The Conceptual Link from Physical to Mental — Kirk, Robert
The Concerned Women of Buduburam — Holzer, Elizabeth
Concho — Holmes, Denzel
Conciliarism and Church Law in the Fifteenth Century: Studies on Franciscus Zabarella and the Council of Constance — Morrissey, Thomas E.
The Concise Guide to Hip-Hop Music: A Fresh Look at the Art of Hip Hop, from Old School Beats to Freestyle Rap — Edwards, Paul
The Concise History of the Crusades — Madden, Thomas
Concise Pun-ishing Dictionary for English Speakers — Dominiguez, Pablo
Conclave Conspiracy — Philbrook, Burnham
Conclusion of the Memoirs of Miss Sidney Bidulph — Sheridan, Frances
A Concordance to the Rhymes of the Faerie Queene — Brown, Richard Danson
Concorde: The Rise and Fall of the Supersonic Airliner — Glancey, Jonathan
Concrete and Culture: A Material History — Forty, Adrian
Concrete Angel — Abbott, Patricia
Concrete Evidence — Shaw, Jeff
Concrete Jungle: New York City and Our Last Best Hope for a Sustainable Future — Eldredge, Niles
Concrete Park, vol 1: You Send Me (Illus. by Puryear, Tony) — Puryear, Tony
Concrete Revolution: Large Dams, Cold War Geopolitics, and the US Bureau of Reclamation — Sneddon, Christopher
Concussion — Laskas, Jeanne Marie
Condemned to Death — Harrison, Cora
Conditions on the Ground — Hooyman, Kevin
Condos and Condoms — Alexander, Evam
Conducting Action Research to Evaluate Your School Library — Sykes, Judith A.
Conductors, Semiconductors, Superconductors: An Introduction to Solid State Physics — Huebener, Rudolf P.
A Coney Island Reader — Parascandola, Louis J.
A Coney Island Reader: Through Dizzy Gates of Illusion — Baker, Kevin
Coney Island: Visions of an American Dreamland, 1861-2008 — Frank, Robin Jaffee
Confederate Bushwacker: Mark Twain in the Shadow of the Civil War — Loving, Jerome
Confederate Combat Commander: The Remarkable Life of Brigadier General Alfred Jefferson Vaughan Jr. — Peterson, Lawrence K.
Confederate Generals in the Trans-Mississippi: Essaya on America's Civil War — Hewitt, Lawrence Lee
Confederate Slave Impressment in the Upper South — Martinez, Jaime Amanda
Confederate Visions: Nationalism, Symbolism, and the Imagined South in the Civil War — Binnington, Ian
Confession of the Lioness — Brookshaw, David
Confession of the Lioness — Couto, Mia
Confessions — Snyder, Stephen
Confessions of a Camo Queen: Living with an Outdoorsman — Berube, Kristen
Confessions of a Headmaster — Cummins, Paul F.
Confessions of a Hollywood Nobody — Bronson, Dan
The Confessions of a Number One Son: The Great Chinese American Novel — Chin, Frank
Confessions of a Sin Eater — Soutter, Nicholas Lamar
Confessions of a Time Traveler — Raham, R. Gary
Confessions of an Ebook Virgin: What Everyone Should Know before They Publish on the Internet — Shabott, Laura
c Confessions of an Imaginary Friend: A Memoir by Jacques Papier (Illus. by Cuevas, Michelle) — Cuevas, Michelle
Confessions of an Italian — Nievo, Ippolito
Confessions of Faith in Early Modern England — Conti, Brooke
The Confessions of X — Wolfe, Suzanne M.
The Confessor — Smith, Mark Allen
The Confessors' Club — Fredrickson, Jack
Confidence — Landman, Seth
The Confidence Effect: Every Woman's Guide to the Attitude that Attracts Success — Killelea, Grace

The Confidence Game: Why We Fall for It...Every Time — Konnikova, Maria
The Confidence Game: Why We Fall for ItaEvery Time — Konnikova, Maria
The Confidence Myth: Why Women Undervalue Their Skills and How To Get Over It — Lerner, Helene
Confidence: Stories — Smith, Russell
The Confidence Trap: A History of Democracy in Crisis From World War I to the Present — Runciman, David
The Confidential Guide to Golf Courses — Doak, Tom
The Confines of the Shadow — Spina, Alessandro
Conflict and Command — Hubbell, John T.
Conflict and Conversion: Catholicism in Southeast Asia, 1500-1700 — Alberts, Tara
Conflict and Conversion in Sixteenth Century Central Mexico: The Augustinian War on and Beyond the Chichimeca Frontier — Jackson, Robert H.
Conflict and Religious Conversation in Latin Christendom: Studies in Honour of Ora Limor — Yuval, Israel Jacob
Conflict, Conquest, and Conversion: Two Thousand Years of Christian Missions in the Middle East — Tejirian, Eleanor H.
Conflict, Crime, and the State in Postcommunist Eurasia — Cornell, Svante
Conflict, Democratization, and the Kurds in the Middle East: Turkey, Iran, Iraq, and Syria — Gurses, Mehmet
Conflict in Ukraine: The Unwinding of the Post-Cold War Order — Rumer, Eugene B.
Conflict Resolution for Holy Beings: Poems — Harjo, Joy
Conflicted Mission: Faith, Disputes, and Deception on the Dakota Frontier — Clemmons, Linda M.
Conflicting Webs — Quinn, Darlene
y The Conformity — Jacobs, John Hornor
Confronting Capitalism: Real Solutions for a Troubled Economic System — Kotler, Philip
Confronting Contagion: Our Evolving Understanding of Disease — Santer, Melvin
Confronting Decline: The Political Economy of Deindustrialization in Twentieth-Century New England — Koistinen, David
Confronting Memories of World War II: European and Asian Legacies — Chirot, Daniel
Confucius: And the World He Created — Schuman, Michael
Confucius Jane — Lynch, Katie
y Congo: The Epic History of a People — Van Reybrouck, David
The Congress — Folman, Ari
The Congress of Vienna: Power and Politics after Napoleon — Vick, Brian E.
Congress, the Supreme Court, and Religious Liberty: The Case of City of Boerne v. Flores — Waltman, Jerold
Conjurer la Guerre: Violence et Pouvoir a Houailou — Naepels, Michel
y The Conjurer's Riddle — Cremer, Andrea
Conjuring Casanova — Rea, Melissa
Conkers: British Twins in Nazi Germany — Lambert, Ken
Connect: How Companies Succeed by Engaging Radically with Society — Browne, John
c Connect the Stars — de los Santos, Marisa
c Connect with Text — Guillain, Charlotte
Connected: How Trains, Genes, Pineapples, Piano Keys, and a Few Disasters Transformed Americans at the Dawn of the Twentieth Century — Cassedy, Steven
Connected in Cairo: Growing Up Cosmopolitan in the Modern Middle East — Peterson, Mark Allen
Connecticut Unscathed: Victory in the Great Narragansett War, 1675-1676 — Warren, Jason W.
Connecting Animals and Children in Early Childhood — Selly, Patty Born
y Connecting Dots — Jennings, Sharon
Connecting the Drops: A Citizens' Guide to Protecting Water Resources — Scheneller-McDonald, Karen
Connecting the Drops: A Citizens' Guide to Protecting Water Resources — Schneller-McDonald, Karen
The Connicle Curse: A Colin Pendragon Mystery — Harris, Gregory
The Conquering Tide: War in the Pacific Islands, 1942-1944 — Toll, Ian W.
The Conquering Writer: Llewelyn Powys: A Consumptive's Diary, 1910 — Foss, Peter J.
Conquerors: How Portugal Forged the First Global Empire — Crowley, Roger

Conquerors: How Portugal Seized the Indian Ocean and Forged the First Global Empire — Crowley, Roger
The Conquest of Plassans — Zola, Emile
The Conquest of the Russian Arctic — Josephson, Paul R.
Conquistador Voices: The Spanish Conquest of the Americas as Recounted Largely by the Participants, 2 vols. — Siepel, Kevin H.
Conran on Color — Conran, Terence
Conscience and Its Enemies: Confronting the Dogmas of Liberal Secularism — George, Robert P.
The Conscience of the Constitution: The Declaration of Independence and the Right to Liberty — Sandefur, Timothy
The Conscious Brain: How Attention Engenders Experience — Prinz, Jesse
Conscious Uncoupling: 5 Steps to Living Happily Even After — Thomas, Katherine Woodward
Consciousness — Weiberg, Josh
Consciousness, Attention, and Conscious Attention — Haladjian, Haroutioun
Consciousness in Action — Hurley, Susan
y Consent — Ohlin, Nancy
y The Consequence of Loving Colton (Read by Podehl, Nick). Audiobook Review — Van Dyken, Rachel
The Conservatarian Manifesto: Libertarians, Conservatives, and the Fight for the Right's Future — Cooke, Charles C.W.
Conservation for Cities: How to Plan and Build Natural Infrastructure — McDonald, Robert I.
Conservatism for the Democratic Age: Conservative Cultures and the Challenge of Mass Politics in Early Twentieth Century England — Thackeray, David
Conservative Bias: How Jesse Helms Pioneered the Rise of Right-Wing Media and Realigned the Republican Party — Thrift, Bryan Hardin
The Conservative Heart: How to Build a Fairer, Happier, and More Prosperous America — Brooks, Arthur C.
Conservative Heroes: Fourteen Leaders Who Shaped America, from Jefferson to Reagan — Tucker, Garland S., III
The Conservative Intellectual Movement in America since 1945 — Nash, George H.
Conservatives versus Wildcats: A Sociology of Financial Conflict — Polillo, Simone
Consolidated B-24 Liberator: War paint Series No. 96 — White, Ian
A Conspectus of Scribal Hands Writing English, 960-1100 — Scragg, Donald
y Conspiracy of Blood and Smoke (Read by Wilds, Heather). Audiobook Review — Blankman, Anne
y Conspiracy of Blood and Smoke — Blankman, Anne
y A Conspiracy of Princes — Somper, Justin
y The Conspiracy of Us (Read by Whelan, Julia). Audiobook Review — Hall, Maggie
y The Conspiracy of Us — Hall, Maggie
Conspiracy Theory in America — DeHaven-Smith, Lance
The Constable's Tale — Smith, Donald
Constance Fenimore Woolson: Portrait of a Lady Novelist — Rioux, Anne Boyd
Constant Fear (Read by Berkrot, Peter). Audiobook Review — Palmer, Daniel
y Constant Fear — Palmer, Daniel
Constant Is the Rain — Sexton, Rex
Constant Lambert: Beyond the Rio Grande — Lloyd, Stephen
Constantin von Neurath: Eine Politische Biographie — Ludicke, Lars
Constantine of Rhodes, On Constantinople and the Church of the Holy Apostles — James, Liz
Constantine Porphyrogennetos: The Book of Ceremonies, with the Greek Edition of the Corpus Scriptorum Historiae Byzantinae: Bonn, 1829 — Moffatt, Ann
Constantine the Emperor — Potter, David S. (b. 1957-)
Constantinople Quilts: 8 Stunning Applique Projects Inspired by Turkish Iznik Tiles — Harvey, Tamsin
Constituting Old Age in Early Modern English Literature, from Queen Elizabeth to 'King Lear' — Martin, Christopher
The Constitution: An Introduction — Paulsen, Michael Stokes
The Constitution Before the Judgment Seat: The Prehistory and Ratification of the American Constitution, 1787-1791 — Heideking, Jurgen
The Constitution of the United States of America: Modern Edition — Bain, Henry

Constitutional Calculus: The Math of Justice and the Myth of Common Sense — Suzuki, Jeff
Constitutional Change and Democracy in Indonesia: Problems of International Politics — Horowitz, Donald
Constitutional Law of Scotland — Page, Alan
Constitutional Money: A Review of the Supreme Court's Monetary Decisions — Timberlake, Richard H.
The Constitutional Parent: Rights, Responsibilities, and the Enfranchisement of the Child — Shulman, Jeffrey
Constitutional Personae: Heroes, Soldiers, Minimalists, and Mutes — Sunstein, Cass R.
Constitutive Visions: Indigeneity and Commonplaces of National Identity in Republican Ecuador — Olson, Christa J.
Constructing a German Diaspora: The "Greater German Empire," 1871-1914 — Manz, Stefan
Constructing Capitalisms: Transforming Business Systems in Central and Eastern Europe — Martin, Roderick
Constructing Gender in Medieval Ireland — Dooley, Ann
Constructing Neoliberalism: Economic Transformation in Anglo-American Democracies — Swarts, Jonathan
Constructing Race: The Science of Bodies and Cultures in American Anthropology — Teslow, Tracy
Constructing Survey Data: An Interactional Approach — Gobo, Giampietro
Constructing the World — Chalmers, David J.
Constructing Urban Space with Sounds and Music — Belgiojoso, Ricciarda
Constructing Virtue and Vice: Femininity and Laughter in Courtly Society, ca. 1150-1300 — Trokhimenko, Olga
Constructing Worlds: Photography and Architecture in the Modern Age — Pardo, Alona
c Construction (Illus. by Lovelock, Brian) — Sutton, Sally
The Construction of National Identity in Taiwan's Media, 1896-2012 — Hsu, Chien-Jung
The Construction of the Heavens: William Herschel's Cosmology — Hoskin, Michael
c A Construction Worker's Tools — McFadden, Jesse
Constructive Illusions: Misperceiving the Origins of International Cooperation — Grynaviski, Eric
Constructivism in Ethics — Bagnoli, Carla
The Consultant — Little, Bentley
Consultation and Cultural Heritage: Let Us Reason Together — Nissley, Claudia
Consumed — Cronenberg, David
Consumed (Read by Hurt, William). Audiobook Review — Cronenberg, David
Consumed by Fire — Stuart, Anne
Consumer Engineering: Mid-Century Mass Consumption between Planning Euphoria and the Limits of Growth, 1930s-1970s
Consumer Lending in France and America: Credit and Welfare — Trumbull, Gunnar
y Consumer Nation Series, 4 vols. — Colson, Mary
Consumerism in the Ancient World: Imports and Identity Construction — Walsh, Justin S.P.
Consumers, Tinkerers, Rebels: The People Who Shaped Europe — Oldenziel, Ruth
Consuming Desires: Family Crisis and the State in the Middle East — Hasso, Frances S.
Consumption and Culture in Sixteenth-Century Ireland: Saffron, Stockings and Silk — Flavin, Susan
Consumption and Violence: Radical Protest in Cold-War West Germany — Sedlmaier, Alexander
Consumption in China: How China's New Consumer Ideology Is Shaping the Nation — Yu, LiAnne
c Contact (Illus. by Fisher-Johnson, Paul) — Blackman, Malorie
Contacts with the Gods from Space — King, George
Contagious Communities: Medicine, Migration, and the NHS in Post War Britain — Bivins, Roberta
The Container Principle: How a Box Changes the Way We Think — Klose, Alexander
Container Theme Gardens: 42 Combinations, Each Using 5 Perfectly Matched Plants (Illus. by Cardillo, Rob) — Ondra, Nancy J.
Containing Multitudes: Walt Whitman and the British Literary Tradition — Schmidgall, Gary
Contemporary American Print Makers — Rooney, E. Ashley

Contemporary Arab-American Literature: Transnational Reconfigurations of Citizenship and Belonging — Fadda-Conrey, Carol
Contemporary Challenges to the Laws of War: Essays in Honour of Professor Peter Rowe — Harvey, Caroline
Contemporary Dystopian Fiction for Young Adults: Brave New Teenagers — Basu, Balaka
Contemporary Environmental History of the Soviet Union and the Successor States, 1970-2000: Ecological Globalization and Regional Dynamics (EcoGlobReg) - Arbeitstreffen
The Contemporary Francophone African Intellectual — Edwards, Natalie
y Contemporary Immigration in America: A State-by-State Encyclopedia, 2 vols. — Arnold, Kathleen A.
Contemporary India: Society and Its Governance — Premchand, A.
Contemporary Iranian Art: From the Street to the Studio — Grigor, Talinn
Contemporary Japanese Politics: Institutional Changes and Power Shifts — Shinoda, Tomohito
Contemporary Jewelry Design: Thoughts on Inspiration and Expression — Xiao, Liu
Contemporary Korean Art: Tansaekhwa and the Urgency of Method — Kee, Joan
The Contemporary Middle East: A Westview Reader — Yambert, Karl
Contemporary Perspectives on Jane Jacobs: Reassessing the Impacts of an Urban Visionary — Schubert, Dirk
Contemporary Women Playwrights: Into the Twenty-First Century — Farfan, Penny
The Contender: Andrew Cuomo, A Biography — Shnayerson, Michael
Contentious Activism and Inter-Korean Relations — Chubb, Danielle L.
Contes a Cristaux: Memoires d'un Cristallier Savoisien — Ducarre, Claude Julien
Contest for California: From Spanish Colonization to the American Conquest — Hyslop, Stephen G.
The Contest for the Delaware Valley: Allegiance, Identity, and Empire in the Seventeenth Century — Thompson, Mark L.
Contest Winners for Three: Piano Trios from the Alfred, Belwin and Myklas Libraries, 5 vols. — Alfred Publishing
Contestation and Adaptation: The Politics of National Identity in China — Han, Enze
Contested Frontiers in the Syria-Lebanon-Israel Region: Cartography, Sovereignty, and Conflict — Kaufman, Asher
Contested Monarchy: Integrating the Roman Empire in the Fourth Century AD — Wienand, Johannes
Contested Spaces of Early America — Barr, Juliana
Contested Water: The Struggle against Water Privatization in the United States and Canada — Robinson, Joanna L.
Contested Waters: An Environmental History of the Colorado River — Summit, April R.
Contesting Catholicity: Theology for Other Baptists — Freeman, Curtis W.
Contesting Colonial Authority: Medicine and Indigenous Responses in Nineteenth- and Twentieth-Century India — Bala, Poonam
Contesting Constructed Indian-ness: The Intersection of the Frontier, Masculinity, and Whiteness in Native American Mascot Representations — Taylor, Michael
Contesting History: Narratives of Public History — Black, Jeremy
Contesting Symbolic Landscape in Jerusalem: Jewish/Islamic Conflict over the Museum of Tolerance at Mamilla Cemetery — Reiter, Yitzhak
Contesting the Moral High Ground: Popular Moralists in Mid-Twentieth-Century Britain — Phillips, Paul T.
Contesting the Postwar City: Working-Class and Growth in 1940s Milwaukee — Fure-Slocum, Eric
Contesting Views: The Visual Economy of France and Algeria — Welch, Edward
Continental Crucible: Big Business, Workers and Unions in the Transformation of North America — Roman, Richard
Continental Drift — Gaffield, Nancy
Continental Strangers: German Exile Cinema, 1933-1951 — Gemunden, Gerd
Contingent Maps: Rethinking Western Women's History and the North American West — Gray, Susan E.

Continuation to Sidney's Arcadia, 1607-1867, 4 vols. — Mitchell, Marea
Continuing Encounters between Past and Present — Caldwell, Dorigen
Continuity despite Change: The Politics of Labor Regulation in Latin America — Carnes, Matthew E.
A Continuous Revolution: Making Sense of Cultural Revolution Culture — Mittler, Barbara
The Contours of Mass Violence in Indonesia, 1965-68 — Kammen, Douglas
Contra vitam monasticam epistula: Andrea Alciato's Letter against Monastic Life — Alciati, Andrea
Contraband: Louis Mandrin and the Making of a Global Underground — Kwass, Michael
Contraband: Smuggling and the Birth of the American Century — Cohen, Andrew Wender
y Contract City — Falkin, Mark
c The Contract — Jeter, Derek
Contract Theory in Continuous-Time Models — Cvitanic, Jaksa
The Contractor State and its Implications, 1659-1815 — Harding, Richard
Contrary Motion — Mozina, Andy
Contrastive Register Variation: A Quantitative Approach to the Comparison of English and German — Neumann, Stella
Contrition: The Art of Sibling Rivalry — Weiler, Maura
Control Alter Delete — Whiteman, Stella
The Control of Nature — McPhee, John
Controlled Burn. E-book Review — Stacey, Shannon
Controlling Paris: Armed Forces and Counter-Revolution, 1789-1848 — House, Jonathan M.
Controlling the Message: New Media in American Political Campaigns. — Farrar-Myers, Victoria A.
Controversial New Religions — Lewis, James R.
Conus of the Southeastern United States and Caribbean — Kohn, Alan J.
Conveniently Vegan — Wasserman, Debra
y Convergence (Illus. by Tong, Andie) — Lee, Stan
Convergence: A Voyage through French Polynesia — Rodgers, Sally-Christine
A Convergence of Two Minds — Croxton, Randolph R.
c The Conversation Train — Shaul, Joel
Conversations with a Brazilian Drug Dealer — Gay, Robert
Conversations with Architects: In the Age of Celebrity — Belogolovsky, Vladimir
Conversations with Beethoven — Friedman, Sanford
Conversations with God for Parents: Sharing the Messages with Children — Walsch, Neale Donald
Conversations with Kenelm: Essays on the Theology of the "Commedia" — Took, John
Conversations with the Conroys: Interviews with Pat Conroy and His Family — Edgar, Walter
Conversations with Toni Cade Bambara — Lewis, Thabiti
Conversations with William Gibson — Smith, Patrick A.
y Conversion — Howe, Katherine
Conversion and Identity in the Viking Age — Garipzanov, Ildar
Conversion and Narrative: Reading and Religious Authority in Medieval Polemic — Szpiech, Ryan
The Conversion of Scandinavia: Vikings, Merchants and Missionaries in the Remaking of Northern Europe — Winroth, Anders
The Conversion Prophecy — Solomon, Michael
Converts to Judaism: Stories from Biblical Times to Today — Epstein, Lawrence J.
y Conviction — Gilbert, Kelly Loy
The Convictions of John Delahunt — Hughes, Andrew
Cook County ICU: 30 Years of Unforgettable Patients and Odd Cases — Franklin, Cory
Cook It in Cast Iron: Kitchen-Tested Recipes for the One Pan That Does it All — America's Test Kitchen
The Cook, the Crook, and the Real Estate Tycoon — Zhenyun, Liu
The Cookbook for Children with Special Needs: Learning a Life Skill with Fun, Tasty, Healthy Recipes — French, Deborah
The Cooke Sisters: Education, Piety and Politics in Early Modern England — Allen, Gemma
Cooked Up: Food Fiction from around the World — Chiew, Elaine
The Cookers: Time and Time Again
Cookie Craft: Baking and Decorating Techniques for Fun and Festive Occasions — Peterson, Valerie
The Cookie Doctor — Pugliese, Peter T.
c A Cookie for Santa (Illus. by Robert, Bruno) — Shaw, Stephanie

Cookie Love — Segal, Mindy
c Cookie Meets Peanut (Illus. by Roode, Daniel) — Frankel, Bethenny
Cooking and Dining in Tudor and Early Stuart England — Brears, Peter
Cooking and Eating in Renaissance Italy: From Kitchen to Table — McIver, Katherine A.
y Cooking as Fast as I Can: A Chef's Story of Family, Food, and Forgiveness — Cora, Cat
y Cooking Class: 50 Fun Recipes Kids Will Love to Make (and Eat)! (Illus. by Bidwell, Julie) — Cook, Deanna F
c Cooking Class: 50 Fun Recipes Kids Will Love to Make (and Eat)! (Illus. by Bidwell, Julie) — Cook, Deanna F.
Cooking for Artists — Stone, Mina
Cooking Like a Master Chef: 100 Recipes to Make the Everyday Extraordinary — Elliot, Graham
c Cooking School — Gilbert, Sara
Cooking Up a Storm: Recipes Lost and Found from the Times-Picayune of New Orleans — Bienvenu, Marcelle
Cooking Up Library Programs Teens and Tweens Will Love: Recipes for Success — Schadlich, Megan E.
c Cook's Coloring Book: Simple Recipes for Beginners (Illus. by Lewis, Rachel) — Lewis, Rachel
Cook's Country Eats Local: 150 Regional Recipes You Should Be Making No Matter Where You Live — America's Test Kitchen
The Cooks — Facas, Charles
c Cool Breads & Biscuits: Easy & Fun Comfort Food — Kuskowski, Alex
c Cool Cake Mix Cupcakes: Fun & Easy Baking Recipes for Kids! — Kuskowski, Alex
c Cool Creations in 101 Pieces — Kenney, Sean
c Cool Crocheting for Kids: A Fun and Creative Introduction to Fiber Art — Kuskowski, Alex
Cool Down and Work Through Anger/Calmate y supera la ira — Meiners, Cheri J.
c Cool Embroidery for Kids: A Fun and Creative Introduction to Fiber Art — Kuskowski, Alex
Cool: How Air Conditioning Changed Everything — Basile, Salvatore
Cool: How the Brain's Hidden Quest for Cool Drives Our Economy and Shapes Our World — Quartz, Steven
Cool Japan Guide: Fun in the Land of Manga, Lucky Cats and Ramen — Denson, Abby
Cool Jazz Spy — Bartusiak, Paul J.
c Cool Jump-Rope Tricks You Can Do! — Fisher, David
c Cool Punch Needle for Kids: A Fun and Creative Introduction to Fiber Art — Kuskowski, Alex
c Cool Sewing for Kids: A Fun and Creative Introduction to Fiber Art — Kuskowski, Alex
c Cool Stuff to Bake — Turnbull, Stephanie
c Cool Stuff to Collect — Turnbull, Stephanie
c Cool Stuff to Grow — Turnbull, Stephanie
c Cool Stuff to Make with Paper — Turnbull, Stephanie
c Cool Stuff to Photograph — Turnbull, Stephanie
c Cool Stuff to Sew — Turnbull, Stephanie
Coolie Woman: The Odyssey of Indenture — Bahadur, Gaiutra
Cop Job — Knopf, Chris
Cop Town (Read by Early, Kathleen). Audiobook Review — Slaughter, Karin
y COPD — Abramovitz, Melissa
Copenhagen Tales — Constantine, Helen
The Copernican Revolution: Planetary Astronomy in the Development of Western Thought — Kuhn, Thomas S.
Coping with Crisis: The Resilience and Vulnerability of Pre-Industrial Settlements — Curtis, Daniel R.
Coping with Immeasurable Losses: Population of the European Cities and World War I
c The Copper Gauntlet (Illus. by Fischer, Scott) — Black, Holly
c The Copper Gauntlet (Illus. by Fischer, Scott) — Clare, Cassandra
c Copper Magic — Gibson, Julia Mary
Coproducing Asia: Locating Japanese-Chinese Regional Film and Media — DeBoer, Stephanie
The Copts of Egypt: The Challenges of Modernisation and Identity — Ibrahim, Vivian
Copygirl — Mitchael, Anna
Copyright for Archivists and Records Managers, 5th ed. — Padfield, Tim
Copyright: Interpreting the Law for Libraries, Archives and Information Services, 6th ed. — Cornish, Graham P.
The Copyright Wars: Three Centuries of Trans-Atlantic Battle — Baldwin, Peter

Cora Du Bois: Anthropologist, Diplomat, Agent — Seymour, Susan C.
c Cora, tu veux une crepe? (Illus. by Bond, Felicia) — Numeroff, Laura
y The Core of the Sun — Sinisalo, Johanna
The Coregasm Workout: The Revolutionary Method for Better Sex Through Exercise. — Herbenick, Debby
Coretta Scott King Award Books Discussion Guide: Pathways to Democracy — Phelps, Adelaide Poniatowski
c Coretta Scott King (Illus. by Freeman, Laura) — Krull, Kathleen
The Corinthia and the Northeast Peloponnese: Topography and History from Prehistoric Times until the End of Antiquityq — Kissas, Konstantinos
Corita Kent: Art and Soul: The Biography — Dammann, April
c Cork and Fuzz: Merry Merry Holly Holly (Illus. by McCue, Lisa) — Chaconas, Dori
c Cork and Fuzz: Spring Cleaning (Illus. by McCue, Lisa) — Chaconas, Dori
Corked — Strang, Catriona
A Corkscrew Life — Coulson, Richard
c Corn — Murray, Laura K.
The Corn King and the Spring Queen — Mitchison, Naomi
Cornbread Nation 7: The Best of Southern Food Writing — Lam, Francis
Cornelius von Ayrenhoff: Ein Wiener Theaterdichter — Mansky, Matthias
A Corner of the World — Fernandez-Pintado, Mylene
c Cornflake the Dragon: The Secret Animal Society (Illus. by Macnaughton, Tina) — Symes, Ruth
Coronado's Well-Equipped Army: The Spanish Invasion of the American Southwest — Hutchins, John M.
The Coronation Chair and Stone of Scone: History, Archaeology and Conservation — Rodwell, Warwick
Corporate Holiness: Pulpit Preaching and the Church of England Missionary Societies, 1760-1870 — Tennant, Bob
Corporate Humanities in Higher Education: Moving Beyond the Neoliberal Academy — Di Leo, Jeffrey
Corporation Nation — Wright, Robert E.
The Corpse Bridge — Booth, Stephen
The Corpse Washer — Antoon, Sinan
A Corpus of Syriac Incantation Bowls: Syriac Magical Texts from Late-Antique Mesopotamia — Moriggi, Marco
Corpus Vasorum Antiquorum. Deutschland. Berlin, Antikensammlung, ehemals Antiquarium. Band 15. Attisch Rotfigurige und Schwarzgefirnisste Peliken, Loutrophoren und Lebetes Gamikoi — Schone-Denkinger, A.
y Corr Syl the Terrible — Rogers, Garry
Corrado de Hirsau e il "Dialogus de cruce": Per la recostruzione del profilo di un autore monastico del XII secolo — Rainini, Marco
Correspondance de Theodore de Beze, vol. 38 — Dufour, Alain
Correspondance litteraire — Grimm, Friedrich Melchior
The Correspondence of Charles Darwin — Burkhardt, Frederick
Correspondence of Franz Liszt and the Comtesse Marie d'Agoult — Short, Michael
The Correspondence of Thomas Hutchinson, vol. 1: 1740-1766 — Tyler, John W.
Correspondence Primarily on "Sir Charles Grandison" — Schellenberg, Betty A.
Correspondence with Sarah Wescomb, Frances Grainger and Laetitia Pilkington — Dussinger, John A.
Corridors of the Night — Perry, Anne
Corrupted — Scottoline, Lisa
Corrupted Memory — Daniel, Ray
Corruption: A Very Short Introduction — Holmes, Leslie
Corruption as a Last Resort: Adapting to the Market in Central Asia — McMann, Kelly M.
Corruption in America: From Benjamin Franklin's Snuff Box to Citizens United — Teachout, Zephyr
Corsair — Cambias, James L.
Cortes Connection — Mateland, Vanessa
Corto Maltese: Under the Sign of Capricorn — Pratt, Hugo
Corvette: Seven Generations of American High Performance — Leffingwell, Randy
The Corvo Cult: The History of an Obsession — Scoble, Robert
Cosby: His Life and Times — Whitaker, Mark

The Cosmic Script: Sacred Geometry and the Science of Arabic Penmanship, 2 vols. — Moustafa, Ahmed
The Cosmic Web: Mysterious Architecture of the Universe — Gott, J. Richard
Cosmigraphics: Picturing Space through Time — Benson, Michael
Cosmo Lang: Archbishop in War and Crisis — Beaken, Robert
c Cosmoe's Wiener Getaway (Read by Martella, Vincent). Audiobook Review — Brallier, Max
c Cosmoe's Wiener Getaway (Illus. by Maguire, Rachel) — Brallier, Max
Cosmology and the Polis: The Social Construction of Space and Time in the Tragedies of Aeschylus — Seaford, Richard
Cosmopolitan Attachment: Pluralism and Civic Identity in Late Ottoman Cities — Ersoy, Ahmet
The Cosmopolitan Constitution — Somek, Alexander
The Cosmopolitan Lyceum: Lecture Culture and the Globe in Nineteenth-Century America — Wright, Tom F.
The Cosmopolitan Novel — Schoene, Berthold
Cosmopolitan Sexualities: Hope and the Humanist Imagination — Plummer, Ken
Cosmopolitanism and Nationhood in the Age of Jefferson — Nicolaisen, Peter
Cosmopolitanism in Mexican Visual Culture — Fernandez, Maria
Cosmopolitanism, Nationalism, and Individualism in Modern China: The Chenbao Fukan and the New Culture Era, 1918-1928 — Xu, Xiaoqun
The Cosmopolitans — Schulman, Sarah
The Cosmopolites: The Coming of the Global Citizen — Abrahamian, Atossa Araxia
Cosmos: The Infographic Book of Space — Lowe, Stuart
Cosmosapiens: How We Are Evolving from the Origin of the Universe — Hands, John
Cosmosis — Pryce, Thomas
Cosmosis — Rey, Rainer
y Cosplay Basics: A Beginners Guide to the Art of Costume Play — Takasou, Yuki Rumine
y The Cost of All Things — Lehrman, Maggie
The Cost of Courage — Kaiser, Charles
Costa Rica: A Journey Through Nature — Hepworth, Adrian
The Costs and Consequences of Living in a World Shaped by Leisure Culture: New Literature on Tourism and Urban Recreation in America — Guillen, Nalleli
Costume en Face: A Primer of Darkness for Young Boys and Girls — Hijikata, Tatsumi
Costume in the Comedies of Aristophanes — Compton-Engle, Gwendolyn
y The Cottage in the Woods — Coville, Katherine
Cotton's Inferno — Dunlap, Phil
c Cottontail Rabbits — Petrie, Kristin
Couched in Death: Klinai and Identity in Anatolia and Beyond — Baughan, Elizabeth P.
c Could a Penguin Ride a Bike? ... and Other Questions (Illus. by Bitskoff, Aleksei) — de la Bedoyere, Camilla
c Could a Shark Do Gymnastics? (Illus. by Bitskoff, Aleksei) — de la Bedoyere, Camilla
c Could a Whale Swim to the Moon? (Illus. by Bitskoff, Aleksei) — de la Bedoyere, Camilla
c Could an Octopus Climb a Skyscraper? ... and Other Questions (Illus. by Bitskoff, Aleksei) — de la Bedoyere, Camilla
Could Be a Crowd — Munoz, C.J.
c "Could You Lift Up Your Bottom?" (Illus. by Chung, Sung-hwa) — Chang, Hee-jung
A Council for the Global Church: Receiving Vatican II in History — Faggioli, Massimo
A Council That Will Never End: "Lumen Gentium" and the Church Today — Lakeland, Paul
Count the Waves: Poems — Beasley, Sandra
c Count with Maisy, Cheep, Cheep, Cheep! (Illus. by Cousins, Lucy) — Cousins, Lucy
c Countablock (Illus. by Peskimo) — Franceschelli, Christopher
Countdown — Cannon, Julie
Countdown to Mecca — Savage, Michael
Countdown to Zero Hour — Rosso, Nico
c Countdown Zero — Rylander, Chris
The Counter-Revolution of 1776: Slave Resistance and the Origins of the United States of America — Horne, Gerald
Counternarratives: Stories and Novellas — Keene, John
c Counting Change (Illus. by Longhi, Katya) — Heos, Bridget

c Counting Crows (Illus. by Dunlavey, Rob) — Appelt, Kathi
c Counting Dogs (Illus. by Barclay, Eric) — Barclay, Eric
Counting Down The Rolling Stones: Their 100 Finest Songs — Beviglia, Jim
c Counting Lions: Portraits from the Wild (Illus. by Walton, Stephen) — Cotton, Katie
Counting Money — Alaina, Maria
c Counting on Community (Illus. by Nagara, Innosanto) — Nagara, Innosanto
Counting People: A DIY Manual for Local and Family Historians — Moore, John S.
y Counting Stars — Stainton, Keris
c Countries: Mack's World of Wonder (Illus. by Mack) — Mack
A Country Called Childhood: Children and the Exuberant World — Griffiths, Jay
A Country Called Prison: Mass Incarceration and the Making of a New Nation — Looman, Mary D.
The Country House Ideal: Recent Work by ADAM Architecture — Musson, Jeremy
A Country in Mind — Beudel, Saskia
Country Living American Style: Decorate, Create, Celebrate — Country Living Magazine
Country Living Porches and Outdoor Spaces — Cavender, Cathy
Country Living Smart Storage Solutions: Creative Closets, Stylish Shelves and More — Rains, Valerie
y The Country of Ice Cream Star — Newman, Sandra
The Country of Planks/ El Pais de Tablas — Zurita, Raul
The Country Road: Stories — Ullmann, Regina
Country Soul — Hughes, Charles L.
Country Wines — Aylett, Mary
y Countryside: The Book of the Wise — Cope, J.T., IV
County and City Extra: Special Historical Edition — Gaquin, Deirdre A.
County Capitols: The Courthouses of South Dakota — Rusch, Arthur L.
The Coup at Catholic University: The 1968 Revolution in American Catholic Education — Mitchell, Peter M.
Coup de Foudre — Kalfus, Ken
Couple Mechanics — Alard, Nelly
y Courage and Defiance: Stories of Spies, Saboteurs, and Survivors in World War II Denmark — Hopkinson, Deborah
c Courage for Beginners — Harrington, Karen
Courage Has No Color: The True Story of the Triple Nickels, America's First Black Paratroopers — Stone, Tanya Lee
Courage in the Democratic Polis: Ideology and Critique in Classical Athens — Balot, Ryan K.
y The Courage of Cat Campbell — Lowe, Natasha
The Courage to Act: A Memoir of a Crisis and Its Aftermath — Bernanke, Ben S.
y The Courage to Compete: Living with Cerebral Palsy and Following My Dreams — Curran, Abbey
The Courage to Try — Popovich, C.A.
Courageous Conversations about Race: A Field Guide for Achieving Equity in Schools — Singleton, Glenn E.
Courier — Irving, Terry
c Cours, Petit Bonhomme, cours! — Smallman, Steve
Course Correction: A Story of Rowing and Resilience in the Wake of Title IX — Gilder, Ginny
Course Correction — Gilder, Ginny
The Course of Nature: A Book of Drawings on Natural Selection and Its Consequences — Pollack, Amy
Courses Matter-Woven — Wilkinson, John
The Court and the World: American Law and the New Global Realities — Breyer, Stephen
Court Ceremonies and Rituals of Power in Byzantium and the Medieval Mediterranean: Comparative Perspectives — Beihammer, Alexander
Court Ceremonies and the Rituals of Power in Byzantium and the Medieval Mediterranean: Comparative Perspectives — Parani, Maria
The Court Journals and Letters of Frances Burney, vols. 3 and 4: 1788 — Clark, Lorna
The Court Journals and Letters of Frances Burney, vols. 3 and 4: 1788 — Clark, Lorna J.
The Court of Appeal for Ontario: Defining the Right of Appeal, 1792- 2013 — Moore, Christopher
y Court of Fives — Elliott, Kate
Court of the Dragon — Javier, Paolo
y A Court of Thorns and Roses — Maas, Sarah J.
The Courtesan — Curry, Alexandra
The Courtesan Duchess — Shupe, Joanna

Courtesans, Concubines, and the Cult of Female Fidelity — Bossier, Beverly
A Courtier's Mirror: Cultivating Elite Identity in Thomasin von Zerclaere's Welscher Gast — Starkey, Kathryn
The Courtiers of Civilization: A Study of Diplomacy — Sofer, Sasson
Courting Democracy in Bosnia and Herzegovina: The Hague Tribunal's Impact in a Postwar State — Nettelfield, Lara J.
Courting Kids: Inside an Experimental Youth Court — Barrett, Carla J.
Courting the Cop. E-book Review — Kwan, Coleen
The Courtly and Commercial Art of the Wycliffite Bible — Kennedy, Kathleen E.
Courtroom to Revolutionary Stage: Performance and Ideology in Weimar Political Trials — Grunwald, Henning
Courtship of the Cake — Topper, Jessica
Cousin Bella: The Whore of Minsk — Yellen, Sherman
The Covenant: A Jackie Lyons Mystery — Crook, Jeff
Covenant and Calling: Towards a Theology of Same-Sex Relationships — Song, Robert
The Covenant Kitchen: Food and Wine for the New Jewish Table — Morgan, Jeff
y Covenant's End — Marmell, Ari
Coventry: Medieval Art, Architecture and Archaeology in the City and Its Vicinity — Monckton, Linda
Coventry: November 14, 1940 — Taylor, Frederick
Coventry: Thursday, 14 November 1940 — Taylor, Frederick
Cover — Mendelsund, Peter
Cover before Striking — Uppal, Priscila
Covered in Ink: Tattoos, Women and the Politics of the Body — Thompson, Beverly Yuen
Covering Shakespeare: An Actor's Saga of Near misses and Dogged Endurance — Weston, David
Covering the United States Supreme Court in the Digital Age — Davis, Richard
The Cow-Hunter — Hudson, Charles
c The Cow Tripped Over the Moon: A Nursery Rhyme Emergency (Illus. by Stewart, Joel) — Willis, Jeanne
c The Cow Tripped over the Moon (Illus. by Stewart, Joel) — Willis, Jeanne
c The Cow Tripped over the Moon (Illus. by Wood, Laura) — Wilson, Tony
c The Cow Who Climbed a Tree (Illus. by Merino, Gemma) — Merino, Gemma
Coward (Illus. by Phillips, Sean) — Brubaker, Ed
Cowardice: A Brief History — Walsh, Chris
c The Cowboy — Muller, Hildegard
The Cowboy and the Canal: How Theodore Roosevelt Cheated Colombia, Stole Panama, and Bamboozled America — Carlisle, J.M.
Cowboy Heaven — Brooks, Cheryl
Cowboy Take Me Away — Lane, Soraya
Cowboys and Indies: The Epic History of the Record Industry — Murphy, Gareth
The Cowboy's Cookbook: Recipes and Tales from Campfires, Cookouts, and Chuck Wagons — Monahan, Sherry
Cowboys, Cops, Killers, and Ghosts: Legends and Lore in Texas — Untiedt, Kenneth L.
Cowed: The Hidden Impact of 93 Million Cows on America's Health, Economy, Politics, Culture, and Environment — Hayes, Denis
c Cows — Murray, Julie
c The Cow's Girl: The Making of a Real Cowgirl — Caldwell, Charlotte
The Cowshed — Ji, Xianlin
Coxsackie: The Life and Death of Prison Reform — Spillane, Joseph F.
The Coyote's Bicycle: The Untold Story of Seven Thousand Bicycles and the Rise of a Borderland Empire — Taylor, Kimball
CP Cats: A Complete Guide to Drawing Cats in Colored Pencil — Gyling, Gemma
CP Horses: A Complete Guide to Drawing Horses in Colored Pencil — Knox, Cynthia
Crack Cocaine Users: High Society and Low Life in South London — Briggs, Daniel
y A Crack in Everything — Long, Ruth Frances
A Crack in the Edge of the World: America ad the Great California Earthquake of 1906 — Winchester, Simon
Crack99: The Takedown of a $100 Million Chinese Software Pirate — Hall, David Locke
Cracked — Leslie, Barbra
Cracking the Sky — Cooper, Brenda

Cradle to Grave (Read by Berneis, Susie). Audiobook Review — *Kuhns, Eleanor*
The Crafter's Guide to Patterns: Create and Use Your Own Patterns for Gift Wrap, Stationery, Tiles, and More — *Swift, Jessica*
Crafting a Colorful Home: A Room-by-Room Guide to Personalizing Your Space with Color — *Nicholas, Kristin*
Crafting Characters: Heroes and Heroines in the Ancient Greek Novel — *Temmerman, Koen de*
Crafting Democracy: Regional Politics in Post-Communist Europe — *Yoder, Jennifer A.*
Crafting Lives: African American Artisans in New Bern, North Carolina, 1770-1900 — *Bishir, Catherine W.*
Crafting Preservation Criteria: The National Register of Historic Places and American Historic Preservation — *Sprinkle, John H., Jr.*
Crafting 'The Indian': Knowledge, Desire, and Play in Indianist Reenactment — *Kalshoven, Petra T.*
Craigie Aitchison: A Life in Colour — *Haste, Cate*
Cranach-Werke am Ort Ihrer Bestimmung
c Crane Boy (Illus. by Landowne, Youme) — *Cohn, Diana*
c Crankenstein (Illus. by Santat, Dan) — *Berger, Samantha*
y Crash — *Silver, Eve*
Crash Course in Marketing for Libraries 2d ed. — *Alman, Susan*
Crash Course in Readers' Advisory — *Orr, Cynthia*
c A Crash of Rhinos (Illus. by Lomp, Stephan) — *Danylyshyn, Greg*
y Crashland — *Williams, Sean*
Crave — *Cannady, Laurie Jean*
The Crawford County Sketchbook — *Janikowski, Tom*
y Crazy — *Phillips, Linda Vigen*
c Crazy about Hockey! (Illus. by Rasmussen, Gerry) — *Lesynski, Loris*
c Crazy Classrooms (Illus. by Wells, Steve) — *Cookson, Paul*
Crazy Dumplings — *Roberts, Amanda*
c Crazy for Science with Carmelo the Science Fellow (Illus. by Geran, Chad) — *Piazza, Carmelo*
Crazy Little Thing Called Love — *Vogt, Beth K.*
Crazy Mountain Kiss — *McCafferty, Keith*
Create a Happy Business: How to Be a Successful SoloPreneur — *Merlo, Carol*
Create Classic Sudoku — *Zheng, Yaling*
Created and Led by the Spirit: Planting Missional Congregations — *Dreier, Mary Sue Dehmlow*
Creating a Beautiful Mess: Ten Essential Play Experiences for a Joyous Childhood — *Gadzikowski, Ann*
Creating a College That Works: Audrey Cohen and Metropolitan College of New York — *Roosevelt, Grace G.*
Creating a Common Polity: Religion, Economy, and Politics in the Making of the Greek Koinon — *Mackil, Emily*
Creating a Learning Society: A New Approach to Growth, Development, and Social Progress — *Stiglitz, Joseph E.*
Creating and Contesting Carolina: Proprietary Era Histories — *LeMaster, Michelle*
Creating Aztlan: Chicano Art, Indigenous Sovereignty, and Lowriding Across Turtle — *Miner, Dylan A.T.*
Creating Books for the Young in the New South Africa: Essays on Authors and Illustrators of Children's and Young Adult Literature — *Lehman, Barbara A.*
Creating Business Agility: How Convergence of Cloud, Social, Mobile, Video, and Big Data Enables Competitive Advantage — *Heisterberg, Rodney*
Creating Change through Humanism — *Speckhardt, Roy*
Creating Cistercian Nuns: The Women's Religious Movement and Its Reform in Thirteenth-Century Champagne — *Lester, Anne E.*
Creating Citizenship in the Nineteenth-Century South — *Link, William A.*
Creating Communities in Restoration England: Parish and Congregation in Oliver Heywood's Halifax — *Thomas, Samuel S.*
Creating Conservatism: Postwar Words That Made an American Movement — *Lee, Michael J.*
Creating Holy People and Places on the Periphery: A Study on the Emergence of Cults of Native Saints in the Ecclesiastical Provinces of Lund and Uppsala from the Eleventh to the Thirteenth Centuries — *Ellis Nilsson, Sara E.*
c Creating Horror Comics — *Belmonte, David*

Creating Magnificence in Renaissance Florence — *Howard, Peter*
Creating Mexican Consumer Culture in the Age of Porfirio Diaz — *Bunker, Steven B.*
Creating Symmetry: The Artful Mathematics of Wallpaper Patterns — *Farris, Frank A.*
Creating Texas: A Brief History of the Revolution — *Dane, Jeffrey*
Creating the American West: Boundaries and Borderlands — *Everett, Derek R.*
Creating the British Atlantic: Essays on Transportation, Adaptation, and Continuity — *Greene, Jack P.*
Creating the Future: Art and Los Angeles in the 1970s — *Fallon, Michael*
Creating the Illusion: A Fashionable History of Hollywood Costume Designers — *Jorgensen, Jay*
Creation — *Fergusson, David*
Creative Anarchy — *Bosler, Denise*
The Creative Dialectic in Karen Blixen's Essays: On Gender, Nazi Germany, and Colonial Desire — *Stecher, Marianne T.*
Creative Schools: The Grassroots Revolution That's Transforming Education — *Robinson, Ken*
Creative Soldered Jewelry and Accessories: 20+ Earrings, Necklaces, Bracelets and More (Illus. by Bluhm, Lisa) — *Bluhm, Lisa*
y Creative, Successful, Dyslexic: 23 High Achievers Share Their Stories — *Rooke, Margaret*
The Creative Tarot: A Modern Guide to an Inspired Life — *Crispin, Jessa*
Creatively Teach the Common Core Literacy Standards With Technology Grades 6-12 — *Tucker, Catlin R.*
Creativity and Children's Literature: New Ways to Encourage Divergent Thinking — *Saccardi, Marianne*
The Creativity Cure: How to Build Happiness with Your Own Two hands — *Barron, Carrie*
y Creativity: The Ultimate Teen Guide — *Ryan, Aryna*
Creator God, Evolving World — *Crysdale, Cynthia*
c Creature Features: 25 Animals Explain Why They Look the Way They Do (Illus. by Jenkins, Steve) — *Jenkins, Steve*
c Creature Keepers and the Hijacked Hydro-Hide (Illus. by Rohitash Rao) — *Nelson, Peter*
c Creature Keepers and the Swindled Soil-Soles — *Nelson, Peter*
c A Creature of Moonlight — *Hahn, Rebecca*
c Creaturepedia: Welcome to the Greatest Show on Earth (Illus. by Barman, Adrienne) — *Barman, Adrienne*
Creatures of a Day: And Other Tales of Psychotherapy — *Yalom, Irvin D.*
c Creatures of the Deep — *de la Bedoyere, Camilla*
c Creatures of the Deep (Illus. by Mendez, Simon) — *Rake, Matthew*
Creatures of the Night — *Bedoyere, Camilla de la*
Credit, Fashion, Sex: Economies of Regard in Old Regime France — *Crowston, Clare Haru*
The Creek War 1813-1815 — *Blackmon, Richard D.*
Creeping Death from Neptune: The Life and Comics of Basil Wolverton (Illus. by Wolverton, Basil) — *Wolverton, Basil*
y The Creeping — *Sirowy, Alexandra*
c The Creeps: Night of the Frankenfrogs — *Schweizer, Chris*
c The Creeps: Night of the Frankenfrogs (Illus. by Schweizer, Chris) — *Schweizer, Chris*
c Creepy Carrots. Audiobook Review — *Reynolds, Aaron*
Creepy Crawlies and the Scientific Method: More Than 100 Hands-On Science Experiments for Children — *Kneidel, Sally*
c Creepy, Crawly Creatures (Illus. by Mendez, Simon) — *Rake, Matthew*
y Crenshaw — *Applegate, Katherine*
The Creolization of American Culture: William Sidney Mount and the Roots of Blackface Minstrelsy — *Smith, Christopher J.*
Crescent City Girls: The Lives of Young Black Women in Segregated New Orleans — *Simmons, LaKisha Michelle*
Crescent Moon over Carolina: William Moultrie and American Liberty — *Bragg, C.L.*
The Crescent Spy — *Wallace, Michael*
Crib — *Petrucci, Mario*
c Cricket Song — *Hunter, Anne*
c Cricket's Close Call (Illus. by Franson, Leanne) — *Hughes, Susan*
Cries for Help, Various: Stories — *Powell, Padgett*

Crime and Punishment in Early Modern Germany — *Boes, Maria R.*
The Crime and the Silence: A Quest for the Truth of a Wartime Massacre — *Bikont, Anna*
The Crime and the Silence: Confronting the Massacre of Jews in Wartime Jedwabne — *Bikont, Anna*
The Crime and the Silence — *Bikont, Anna*
Crime News in Modern Britain: Press Reporting and Responsibility, 1820-2010 — *Rowbotham, Judith*
The Crime of All Crimes: Toward a Criminology of Genocide — *Rafter, Nicole*
Crime Seen — *Lines, Kate*
c CrimeBiters! My Dog Is Better Than Your Dog — *tower, Adam*
Crimes of Peace: Mediterranean Migrations at the World's Deadliest Border — *Albahari, Maurizio*
c Criminal Destiny — *Korman, Gordon*
Criminal Law and Emotions in European Legal Cultures: From the 16th Century to the Present
A Criminal Magic — *Kelly, Lee*
Criminal Resistance?: The Politics of Kidnapping Oil Workers — *Oriola, Temitope B.*
Criminal That I Am: A Memoir — *Ridha, Jennifer*
The Criminal Underworld in a Medieval Islamic Society: Narratives from Cairo and Damascus under the Mamluks — *Petry, Carl F.*
Criminals: Love Stories — *Trueblood, Valerie*
The Criminology of Place: Street Segments and Our Understanding of the Crime Problem — *Weisburd, David*
y Crimson Bound — *Hodge, Rosamund*
The Crimson Cord: Rahab's Story — *Smith, Jill Eileen*
The Crimson Emperor: A Tale of Imperial Byzantium — *Baren, Wim*
y The Crimson Gate — *Miller, Whitney A.*
The Crimson Petal and the White — *Faber, Michel*
Crimson Shore — *Child, Lincoln*
Crimson Shore — *Preston, Douglas*
The Crimson Thread of Abandon — *Shuji, Terayama*
c Crinkle, Crackle, Crack: It's Spring! (Illus. by Shelley, John) — *Bauer, Marion Dane*
Crises in Early Modern Times: Scenarios - Experiences - Management - Coping
Crisis — *Walby, Sylvia*
Crisis and Survival in Late Medieval Ireland: The English of Louth and Their Neighbours, 1330-1450 — *Smith, Brendan*
Crisis at Work: Identity and the End of Career — *Potter, Jesse*
Crisis Cities: Disaster and Redevelopment in New York and New Orleans — *Gotham, Kevin Fox*
Crisis in the Mediterranean: Naval Competition and Great Power Politics, 1904-1914 — *Hendrickson, Jon K.*
A Crisis of Community: The Trials and Transformation of a New England Town, 1815-1848 — *Fuhrer, Mary Babson*
The Crisis of Confidence in the Catholic Church — *Helmick, Raymond G.*
The Crisis of Genocide, vol. 1, Devastation: The European Rimlands, 1912-1938 — *Levene, Mark*
The Crisis of Genocide, vol. 2, Annihilation: The European Rimlands, 1939-1953 — *Levene, Mark*
The Crisis of German Historicism — *Keedus, Liisi*
The Crisis of Modernity — *Del Noce, Augusto*
Crisis on Infinite Earths — *Wolfman, Marv*
Crisis Point: Why We Must--and How We Can--Overcome Our Broken Politics in Washington and across America — *Lott, Trent*
c Cristiano Ronaldo: International Soccer Star — *Logothetis, Paul*
Critical Insights: American Creative Nonfiction — *Ellis, Jay*
Critical Insights: Magical Realism — *Calvo, Ignacio Lopez*
Critical Perspectives on Roman Baroque Sculpture — *Colantuono, Anthony*
Critical Reflections on Ownership — *Elgar, Edward*
Critical Rural Theory: Structure, Space, Culture — *Thomas, Alexander R.*
A Critical Theory of Creativity: Utopia, Aesthetics, Atheism and Design — *Howells, Richard*
c Critter Colors — *G., Ashley*
Croc by the Rock (Illus. by Gordon, Mike) — *Robinson, Hilary*
Crochet for Christmas: 29 Patterns for Handmade Holiday Decorations and Gifts — *Baca, Salena*
Crochet So Lovely: 21 Carefree Lace Designs — *Omdahl, Kristin*

Crochet the Perfect Gift: Designs Just Right for Giving and Ideas for Every Occasion — *Goldin, Kat*

The Crocheter's Skill-Building Workshop: Essential Techniques for Becoming a More Versatile — *Ohrenstein, Dora*

c Crocodile Encounters! And More True Stories of Adventures with Animals — *Barr, Brady*

c Crocodile or Alligator? — *Kralovansky, Susan*

c The Crocodile Tomb — *Paver, Michelle*

c The Crocodile Under the Bed (Illus. by Kerr, Judith) — *Kerr, Judith*

c The Crocodolly — *McKenna, Martin*

c Crocs at Work (Illus. by Mate, Rae) — *Heidbreder, Robert*

Cronicling the West of Harper's: Coast to Coast with Frenzeny and Tavernier in 1873-1874 — *Chalmers, Claudine*

c Cronus and the Threads of Dread (Illus. by Phillips, Craig) — *Holub, Joan*

Crooked — *Grossman, Austin*

Crooked Brooklyn: Taking Down Corrupt Judges, Dirty Politicians, Killers, and Body Snatchers — *Vecchione, Michael*

Crooked Heart — *Evans, Lissa*

The Crooked Heart of Mercy — *Livingston, Billie*

Crooked Herring — *Tyler, L.C.*

The Crooked House — *Kent, Christobel*

c Crooked Leg Road — *Walsh, Jennifer*

Crooked Paths to Allotment: The Fight over Federal Indian Policy after the Civil War — *Genetin-Pilawa, C. Joseph*

Cross and Kremlin: A Brief History of the Orthodox Church in Russia — *Bremer, Thomas*

Cross and Scepter: The Rise of the Scandinavian Kingdoms from the Vikings to the Reformation — *Bagge, Sverre*

Cross-Cultural Connections in Crime Fictions — *Miller, Vivien*

Cross-Cultural Exchange in the Atlantic World: Angola and Brazil during the Era of the Slave Trade — *Ferreira, Roquinaldo*

Cross Dog Blues — *Brock, Richard M.*

The Cross of War: Christian Nationalism and U.S. Expansion in the Spanish-American War — *McCullough, Matthew*

c Cross-Pollination — *Ransom, Candice*

The Crossing — *Connelly, Michael*

The Crossing — *Miller, Andrew*

Crossing Borders, Claiming a Nation: A History of Argentine Jewish Women, 1880-1955 — *Deutsch, Sandra McGee*

Crossing Boundaries in Tokugawa Society: Suzuki Bokushi, a Rural Elite Commoner — *Moriyama, Takeshi*

Crossing Broadway: Washington Heights and the Promise of New York City — *Snyder, Robert*

Crossing in Time: The First Disaster — *Orton, D.L.*

y Crossing into Brooklyn — *McGuigan, Mary Ann*

The Crossing: My Journey to the Shattered Heart of Syria — *Yazbek, Samar*

The Crossing of Antarctica: Original Photographs from the Epic Journey That Fulfilled Shackleton's Dream — *Lowe, George*

Crossing the Bay of Bengal: The Furies of Nature and the Fortunes of Migrants — *Amrith, Sunil S.*

The Crossing: The Curious Story of the First Man to Swim the English Channel — *Watson, Kathy*

Crossing the Ice — *Comeaux, Jennifer*

Crossing the Line — *Armistead, Caitlyn*

Crossing the Line: Women's Interracial Activism in South Carolina during and after World War II — *Jones-Branch, Cherisse*

Crossing the Plains with Bruno — *Smith, Annick*

Crossing the River: A Life in Brazil — *Ragsdale, Amy*

Crossing the Water and Keeping the Faith: Haitian Religion in Miami — *Rey, Terry*

Crossings: Africa, the Americas and the Atlantic Slave Trade — *Walvin, James*

y The Crossover — *Alexander, Kwame*

Crossover — *Proffet, Paul*

c The Crossover (Read by Allen, Corey). Audiobook Review — *Alexander, Kwame*

y The Crossover — *Alexander, Kwame*

Crossroads: Extraordinary Recipes from the Restaurant That Is Reinventing Vegan Cuisine — *Ronnen, Tal*

Crossroads: Women Coming of Age in Today's Uganda — *Conte, Christopher*

Crosstown Crush — *McKenna, Cara*

Crouching Tiger: What China's Militarism Means for the World — *Navarro, Peter*

Crow Fair: Stories — *McGuane, Thomas*

c Crow Made a Friend (Illus. by Peot, Margaret) — *Peot, Margaret*

y Crow Mountain — *Inglis, Lucy*

c A Crow of His Own (Illus. by Costello, David Hyde) — *Lambert, Megan Dowd*

c A Crow of His Own (Illus. by Costello, David Hyde) — *Lambert, Megan Dowd. A Crow of His Own.(Brief article)(Book review)(Children's review)*

Crowded by Beauty: The Life and Zen of Poet Philip Whalen — *Schneider, David*

Crowded Orbits: Conflict and Cooperation in Space — *Moltz, James Clay*

A Crowdfunder's Strategy Guide: Build a Better Business by Building Community — *Stegmaier, Jamey*

Crowdsourcing Our Cultural Heritage — *Ridge, Mia*

c The Crowham Martyrs — *McLoughlin, Jane*

The Crown — *Oakes, Colleen*

c The Crown Affair: From the Files of a Hard-Boiled Detective (Illus. by Axelsen, Stephen) — *Ransom, Jeanie Franz*

c The Crown Affair: From the Files of a Hard-Boiled Detective (Illus. by Axelsen, Stephen) — *Ransom, Jeanie Franz*

c The Crown Affair (Illus. by Axelsen, Stephen) — *Ramsom, Jeanie Franz*

A Crown for Cold Silver — *Marshall, Alex*

c Crown of the Cowibbean (Illus. by Litwin, Mike) — *Litwin, Mike*

y Crown of Three — *Blackthorn, J.D.*

y Crown of Three — *Rinehart, J.D.*

c The Crow's Tale (Illus. by Howarth, Naomi) — *Howarth, Naomi*

Crucible of Command: Ulysses S. Grant and Robert E. Lee: The War They Fought, the Peace They Forged (Read by Burns, Traber). Audiobook Review — *Davis, William C.*

Crucible of Command: Ulysses S. Grant and Robert E. Lee--the War They Fought, the Peace They Forged — *Davis, William C.*

Crucible of Command: Ulysses S. Grant and Robert E. Lee - the War They Fought, the Peace They Forged — *Davis, William C.*

y A Crucible of Souls: Book One of the Sorcery Ascendant Sequence — *Hogan, Mitchell*

Crucible Zero — *Monk, Devon*

Crucibles of Black Empowerment: Chicago's Neighborhood Politics from the New Deal to Harold Washington — *Helgeson, Jeffrey*

The Crucified King: Atonement and Kingdom in Biblical and Systematic Theology — *Treat, Jeremy R.*

Crucifixion Creek — *Maitland, Barry*

The Crucifixion: Understanding the Death of Jesus Christ — *Rutledge, Fleming*

A Crude Look at the Whole: The Science of Complex Systems in Business, Life, and Society — *Miller, John H.*

Cruel Modernity — *Franco, Jean*

The Cruising Guide to the Virgin Islands, 17th ed. — *Scott, Nancy*

Cruising the Latin Tapestry — *Welbourne, W.E.*

Cruising with Kate: A Parvenu in Xanadu — *Connors, Bernard*

Cruising with Kate: A Parvenu in Xanadu — *Conners, Bernard F.*

c Crunch! (Illus. by Rabei, Carolina) — *Rabei, Carolina*

The Crusade for Equality in the Workplace: The Griggs v. Duke Power Story — *Belton, Robert*

The Crusade Indulgence: Spiritual Rewards and the Theology of Crusades, c. 1095-1216 — *Bysted, Ane L.*

Crusader Castles of Cyprus: The Fortifications of Cyprus under the Lusignans, 1191-1489 — *Petre, James*

The Crusades: A Reader — *Allen, Susan Jane*

The Crusades and the Near East: Cultural Histories — *Kostick, Conor*

The Crusades of Cesar Chavez: A Biography — *Pawel, Miriam*

Crusading and the Ottoman Threat, 1453-1505 — *Housley, Norman*

Crusading and Warfare in the Middle Ages: Realities and Representations, Essays I nHonour of John France — *John, Simon*

Crush — *Sutton, Phoef*

y Crushed (AA) Novel — *Blake, Kasi*

Crutched Friars and Croisiers: The Canons Regular of the Order of the Holy Cross in England and France — *Hayden, Michael J.*

The Cry of Tamar: Violence Against Women and the Church's Response — *Cooper-White, Pamela*

Cry of Wonder — *Hughes, Gerard W.*

Cry Uncle — *McLean, Russel D.*

Cry Wolf — *Gregorio, Michael*

Cry Wolfram — *Sanderson, Douglas*

c Crybaby (Illus. by Yelchin, Eugene) — *Beaumont, Karen*

Cryptocurrency: How Bitcoin and Digital Money are Challenging the Global Economic Order — *Vigna, Paul*

y Crystal (Read by Johnson, Sisi Aisha). Audiobook Review — *Myers, Walter Dean*

c Crystal and Breanna: The Secret of Blackridge Farm (Illus. by Fletcher, Christina) — *Mowry, Barbara*

c Crystal Cadets (Illus. by O'Neill, Katie) — *Toole, Anne*

y Crystal Force — *Ducie, Joe*

c Crystal Keepers (Read by Nobbs, Keith). Audiobook Review — *Mull, Brandon*

c Crystal Keepers — *Mull, Brandon*

c Crystal Kingdom — *Hocking, Amanda*

y The Crystal Navigator: A Perilous Journey through Time — *Lodge, Nancy Kunhardt*

c Crystals — *Hirsch, Rebecca E.*

c Cub Reporter Meets Famous Americans Series (Illus. by Jones, Doug) — *Barton, Jen*

Cuba and its Neighbors: Democracy in Motion — *August, Arnold*

Cuba & Angola: Fighting for Africa's Freedom and Our Own — *Castro, Fidel*

Cuba Straits (Read by Guidall, George). Audiobook Review — *Wayne, Randy*

Cuba Straits — *White, Randy Wayne*

Cuban Cocktails: 100 Classic and Modern Drinks — *DeRossi, Ravi*

Cuban Color in Tourism and La Lucha: An Ethnography of Racial Meanings — *Roland, L. Kaifa*

Cuban Identity and the Angolan Experience — *Peters, Christabelle*

Cuban Revelations: Behind the Scenes in Havana — *Frank, Marc*

The Cuban Revolution as Socialist Human Development — *Veltmeyer, Henry*

Cubed: A Secret History of the Workplace — *Saval, Nikil*

Cubism: The Leonard A. Lauder Collection — *Braun, Emily*

c Cub's Journey Home (Illus. by Graham, Georgia) — *Graham, Georgia*

Cuckoo: Cheating by Nature — *Davies, Nick*

y Cuckoo Song — *Hardinge, Frances*

c Cueillette au verger (Je lis avec Mademoiselle Nancy). (Illus. by Glasser, Robin Preiss) — *O'Connor, Jane*

The Culinary Imagination — *Gilbert, Sandra M.*

The Culinary Lives of John and Abigail Adams: A Cookbook — *Wan, Rosana Y.*

Culling: New and Selected Nature Poems — *Held, George*

Culling the Masses: The Democratic Origins of Racist Immigration Policy in the Americas — *FitzGerald, David Scott*

Cult, Myth, and Occasion in Pindar's Victory Odes: A Study of Isthmian 4, Pythian 5, Olympian 1, and Olympian 3 — *Krummen, Eveline*

The Cult of St. Clare of Assisi in Early Modern Italy — *Debby, Ben-Aryeh Nirit*

The Cult of St. Clare of Assisi in Early Modern Italy — *Debby, Nirti Ben-Aryeh*

The Cult of the Duce: Mussolini and the Italians — *Gundle, Stephen*

Cult Places and Cult Personnel in the Roman Empire — *Fishwick, Duncan*

Cultivating Chaos: How to Enrich Landscapes with Self-Seeding Plants — *Becker, Jurgen*

Cultivating Connections: The Making of Chinese Prairie Canada — *Marshall, Alison R.*

Cultivating the Nile: The Everyday Politics of Water in Egypt — *Barnes, Jessica*

The Cultivation of Taste: Chefs and the Organization of Fine Dining — *Lane, Christel*

Cultural Capital: The Rise and Fall of Creative Britain — *Hewison, Robert*

Cultural Cues: Joe Day, Adib Cure and Carie Penabad, Tom Wiscombe — *Rappaport, Nina*

Cultural Difference and Material Culture in Middle English Romance: Normans and Saxons — *Battles, Dominique*

Cultural Encyclopedia of the Breast — *Smith, Merril D.*

Cultural Encyclopedia of the Penis — *Kimmel, Michael*

Cultural Encyclopedia of the Penis — *Kimmel, Michael S.*

Cultural Exchange in Seventeenth-Century France and England — *Stedman, Gesa*

Cultural Heritage Information: Access and Management — *Ruthven, Ian*

A Cultural History of Firearms in the Age of Empire — *Jones, Karen*

A Cultural History of the Senses, 6 vols. — *Classen, Constance*

The Cultural Lives of Whales and Dolphins — Whitehead, Hal
The Cultural Logic of Politics in Mainland China and Taiwan — Shi, Tianjian
The Cultural Matrix: Understanding Black Youth — Patterson, Orlando
Cultural Mediation: Creativity, Performance, Display
y The Cultural Monuments of Tibet — Henss, Michael
Cultural Negotiations: The Role of Women in the Founding of Americanist Archaeology — Browman, David L.
Cultural Renewal: Restoring the Liberal and Fine Arts — Pontynen, Arthur
The Cultural Revolution at the Margins: Chinese Socialism in Crisis — Wu, Yiching
Cultural Struggles: Performance, Ethnography, Praxis — Conquergood, Dwight
Cultural Traditions in Germany — Peppas, Lynn
Cultural Traditions in Iran — Peppas, Lynn
Cultural Traditions in Jamaica — Peppas, Lynn
Cultural Traditions in Kenya — Burns, Kelly
c Cultural Traditions in My World Series
Cultural Traditions in Sweden — Hyde, Natalie
Culture and Liberty in the Age of the American Revolution — Rozbicki, Michal Jan
Culture and the Death of Cod — Eagleton, Terry
Culture Crash: The Killing of the Creative Class — Timberg, Scott
Culture, Faith and Philanthropy: Londoners and Provincial Reform in Early Modern England — Ward, Joseph P.
Culture in Conflict: Irregular Warfare, Culture Policy, and the Marine Corps — Holmes-Eber, Paula
Culture in Pieces: Essays on Ancient Texts in Honour of Peter Parsons — Rutherford, R.B.
Culture, Interaction and Person Reference in an Australian Language — Garde, Murray
Culture Makers: Urban Performance and Literature in the 1920s — Koritz, Amy
Culture Monitoring — Liautaud, Martine
The Culture of Disaster — Huet, Marie-Helene
The Culture of Inquisition in Medieval England — Walter, Katie L.
The Culture of Inquisition in Medieval England — Flannery, Mary C.
The Culture of Mental Illness and Psychiatric Practice in Africa — Akyeampong, Emmanuel
Culture, Power, and Authoritarianism in the Indonesian State: Cultural Policy across the Twentieth-Century to the Reform Era — Jones, Tod
Culture, Suicide, and the Human Condition — Honkasalo, Marja-Liisa
c Cultures and Customs Series — Ganeri, Anita
Cultures of Charity: 'Women, Politics, and the Reform of Poor Relief in Renaissance Italy — Terpstra, Nicholas
Cultures of Milk: The Biology and Meaning of Dairy Products in the United States and India — Wiley, Andrea S.
Cultures of Religious Reading in the Late Middle Ages: Instructing the Soul, Feeding the Spirit, and Awakening the Passion — Corbellini, Sabrina
Cumbia!: Scenes of a Migrant Latin American Music Genre — Fernandez l'Hoeste, Hector D.
Cunegonde's Kidnapping: A Story of Religious Conflict in the Age of Enlightenment — Kaplan, Benjamin J.
Cuneiform — Finkel, Irving
The Cunning House — Turley, Richard Marggraf
The Cunning of Uncertainty — Nowotny, Helga
A Cup of Redemption — Bumpus, Carole
A Cup of Water under My Bed: A Memoir — Hernandez, Daisy
Cups and Saucers: Paper-Pieced Kitchen Designs — Bakker, Maaike
Cups, Sticks & Nibbles: Unlock Your Inner Hosting Confidence with Stress-Free Tips & Recipes — Meyer, Nicole L.
Cura animarum: Seelsorge im Deutschordensland Preuben — Samerski, Stefan
Curationism: How Curating Took Over the Art World and Everything Else — Balzer, David
Curationism: How Curating Took Over the Art World — Balzer, David
The Curatorial Avant-Garde: Surrealism and Exhibition Practise in France, 1925-1941 — Jolles, Adam
The Curator's Handbook — George, Adrian

Cure: A Journey into the Science of Mind over Body — Marchant, Jo
The Cure for Divorce: In the Kingdom of God — Sayen, Michael S.
The Cure for Dreaming (Read by Ikeda, Jennifer). Audiobook Review — Winters, Cat
y The Cure for Dreaming — Winters, Cat
A Cure for Suicide — Ball, Jesse
c Curieux de nature: Les oiseaux — Arpin, Mylene
Curing Medicare — Lazris, Andy
Curing Queers: Mental Nurses and Their Patients, 1935-74 — Dickinson, Tommy
The Curiosities — Reid, Christopher
Curiosity — Manguel, Alberto
The Curious Autobiography of Elaine Jakes — Jakes, H.R.
A Curious Beginning — Raybourn, Deanna
The Curious Case of H.P. Lovecraft — Roland, Paul
y The Curious Cat Spy Club — Singleton, Linda Joy
c Curious Creatures ABC (Illus. by Byrd, Robert) — Thomas, Scott
c Curious Critters: Marine (Illus. by FitzSimmons, David) — FitzSimmons, David
c Curious Critters: Michigan (Illus. by FitzSimmons, David) — FitzSimmons, David
A Curious Friendship: The Story of a Bluestocking and a Bright Young Thing — Thomasson, Anna
c Curious George Discovers Space — Perez, Monica
c Curious George Discovers the Ocean — Freitas, Bethany V.
c Curious George Discovers the Sun — Meier, Anna
c Curious George: Gymnastics Fun — Calvo, Carlos E.
c Curious George Makes Maple Syrup (Illus. by Rey, Hans Augusto) — Rey, Hans Augusto
The Curious Map Book — Baynton-Williams, Ashley
A Curious Mind: The Secret to a Bigger Life (Read by Butz, Norbert Leo). Audiobook Review — Grazer, Brian
A Curious Mind: The Secret to a Bigger Life — Fishman, Charles
A Curious Mind: The Secret to a Bigger Life — Grazer, Brian
c A Curious Tale of the In-Between — DeStefano, Lauren
c The Curious Tale of the In-Between — DeStefano, Lauren
y A Curious Tale of the In-Between — DeStefano, Lauren
c A Curious Tale of the In-Between — Destefano, Lauren
y The Curious Tale of the Lady Caraboo — Johnson, Catherine (b. 1962-)
Curious: The Desire to Know and Why Your Future Depends on It — Leslie, Ian
c The Curious World of Calpurnia Tate (Read by Ross, Natalie). Audiobook Review — Kelly, Jacqueline
c The Curious World of Calpurnia Tate — Kelly, Jacqueline
The Currency of Paper — Kovacs, Alex
Current Flow: The Electrification of Palestine — Shamir, Ronen
Current Medical Diagnosis and Treament 2015 — Papadakis, Maxine A.
Current Medical Diagnosis and Treatment Study Guide — Quinn, Gene R.
Current Research at Kultepe-Kanesh: An Interdisciplinary and Integrative Approach to Trade Networks, Internationalism, and Identity — Atici, Levent
c Currents — Smolik, Jane Petrlik
The Currents of War: A New History of American-Japanese Relations, 1899-1941 — Pash, Sidney
Curriculum-Based Library Instruction: From Cultivating Faculty Relationships to Assessment — Blevins, Amy
c A Curry for Murray (Illus. by Masciullo, Lucia) — Hunter, Kate
The Curse of Anne Boleyn — Humphreys, C.C.
The Curse of Crow Hollow — Coffey, Billy
The Curse of Jacob Tracy — Messinger, Holly
c The Curse of the Baskervilles (Illus. by Breyer, Mark) — Bergmann, Daniel
c The Curse of the Buttons — Ylvisaker, Anne
c The Curse of the Chocolate Phoenix — Saunders, Kate
c Curse of the Iris — Fry, Jason
c The Curse of the King (Illus. by Norstrand, Torstein) — Lerangis, Peter
Curse of the King — Pye, Omari

Cursed Are You! The Phenomenology of Cursing in Cuneiform and Hebrew Texts — Kitz, Anne Marie
Cursed by Fire — Frank, Jacquelyn
Cursed by Ice — Frank, Jacquelyn
Cursed Kings: The Hundred Years War, vol. 4 — Sumption, Jonathan
Cursed Victory: A History of Israel and the Occupied Territories — Bregman, Ahron
Curtain Call — Quinn, Anthony
Curtain Calls — Ponepinto, Joseph
Curtains? The Future of the Arts in America — Kaiser, Michael M.
c Curtsies and Conspiracies (Read by Quick, Moira). Audiobook Review — Carriger, Gail
The Curve of Time (Read by Henderson, Heather). Audiobook Review — Blanchet, M. Wylie
Curvology: The Origins and Power of Female Body Shape — Bainbridge, David
Curvology: The Origins and Power of the Female Body Shape — Bainbridge, David
c The Curvy Tree (Illus. by Dorman, Brandon) — Colfer, Chris
Cusco: Urbanism and Archaeology in the Inka World — Farrington, Ian
Cusp: Word Sonnets (Illus. by Frye, Sebastian) — Mayne, Seymour
Custer, Cody, and Grand Duke Alexis: Historical Archaeology of the Royal Buffalo Hunt — Scott, Douglas D.
Custer's Gold — Lubetkin, M. John
Custer's Trials: A Life on the Frontier of a New America — Stiles, T.J.
c Custom Confections: Delicious Desserts You Can Create and Enjoy — Besel, Jen
Customer-Based Collection Development: An Overview — Bridges, Karl
Customize Your Crochet: Adjust to Fit; Embellish To Taste — Hubert, Margaret
y Cut Both Ways — Mesrobian, Carrie
Cut It Out: The C-Section Epidemic in America — Morris, Theresa
y Cut Me Free — Johansson, J.R.
Cut Me In — McBain, Ed
The Cut of the Whip/Bring Me Another Corpse/Time Enough to Die — Babe, Peter
c Cut Off — Bastedo, Jamie
y The Cut Out — Heath, Jack
Cut Paste Gone — Safran, Lisa
y A Cut Too Far — Brown, Herman
c Cutie Pie Looks for the Easter Bunny: A Tiny Tab Book (Illus. by Ho, Jannie) — Crow, Nosy
Cut'n Paste the Body. Korper und Geschlecht in Zeiten Ihrer Technologischen (Re)Produzierbarkeit
Cutting along the Color Line: Black Barbers and Barber Shops in America — Mills, Quincy T.
Cy Twombly: Late Paintings, 2003-2011 — Pavlouskova, Nela
Cy Twombly's Things — Nesin, Kate
y Cyber Attack — Gitlin, Martin
Cyber Realm — McDonald, Wren
c Cyber Spy Hunters! — Rich, Mari
y Cyber Warfare: A Reference Handbook — Springer, Paul J.
The Cybernetics Moment: Or Why We Call Our Age the Information Age — Kline, Ronald R.
Cyberphobia: Identity, Trust, Security and the Internet — Lucas, Edward
Cybertheology: Thinking Christianity in the Era of the Internet — Spadaro, Antonio
Cycle of Fear: Syria's Alawites in War and Peace — Goldsmith, Leon
The Cycling City: Bicycles & Urban America in the 1890s — Friss, Evan
Cycling the Mekong — Daly, Gerry
The Cyclops Initiative — Wellington, David
Cyclorama — Wardrop, Daneen
Cynthia: A Companion to the Text of Propertius — Heyworth, Stephen J.
Cypro-Minoan Inscriptions, vol. 2: The Corpus — Ferrara, Silvia
Cyprus and the Balance of Empires: Art and Archaeology from Justinian I to the Coeur de Lion — Stewart, Charles Anthony
Czech-Jewish and Polish-Jewish Studies: (Dis) Similarities
The Czecho-Slovak Struggle for Independence, 1914-1920 — Mueggenberg, Brent
Czechs, Slovaks, and the Jews, 1938-48: Beyond Idealisation and Condemnation — Lanicek, Jan

D

c D-Day — *Atkinson, Rick*
D-Day in History and Memory: The Normandy Landings in International Remembrance and Commemoration — *Dolski, Michael*
D-Day through French Eyes: Normandy 1944 — *Roberts, Mary Louise*
D.I.Y. Magic: A Strange and Whimsical Guide to Creativity — *Alvarado, Anthony*
c D Is for Duck Calls (Illus. by Hanson, Sydney) — *Robertson, Kay*
The D Word — *Warrington, Joanna*
Da santa Chiara a suor Francesca Farnese: Il francescanesimo femminile e il monastero di Fara in Sabina — *Gajano, Boesch Sofia*
Da shi dai li de xiao za zhi : "Xin er tong" ban yue kan, 1941-1949 — *Leung, For-Hing*
y Da Vinci's Tiger — *Elliott, Laura*
y Da Vinci's Tiger — *Elliott, Laura Malone*
Dachau and the SS: A Schooling in Violence — *Dillon, Christopher*
The Dad Report: Fathers, Sons, and Baseball Families — *Cook, Kevin*
c The Dad with 10 Children (Illus. by Guettier, Benedicte) — *Guettier, Benedicte*
The Daddy Diaries — *Braff, Joshua*
c Daddy Hugs (Illus. by Tafuri, Nancy) — *Tafuri, Nancy*
Daddy Said a Word I Never Heard — *Cohn, Scott M.*
c Daddy Sat on a Duck (Illus. by Cohn, Scott M.) — *Cohn, Scott M.*
c Daddy Sat on a Duck — *Cohn, Scott M.*
c Daddy's Back-to-School Shopping Adventure (Illus. by Carter, Abby) — *Sitomer, Alan Lawrence*
c Dad's First Day (Illus. by Wohnoutka, Mike) — *Wohnoutka, Mike*
Dad's War Photos: Adventures in the South Pacific — *Bertrand, Neal*
The Daemon Knows: Literary Greatness and the American Sublime — *Bloom, Harold*
Daffodils in American Gardens, 1733-1940 — *Van Beck, Sara L.*
The Daily Breath: Transform Your Life One Breath at a Time — *Morofsky, Scott A.*
c Daily Life in Ancient Egypt — *Nardo, Don*
Daily Life in the Hellenistic Age: From Alexander to Cleopatra — *Evans, James Allan*
c Daily Life in the Islamic Golden Age — *Nardo, Don*
c Daily Life in U.S. History Series — *Onsgard, Bethany*
Daily Zen Doodles: 365 Tangle Creations for Inspiration, Relaxation and Mindfulness — *Patel, Meera Lee*
c Dairy — *Bodden, Valerie*
The Dairy Goat Handbook: For Backyard, Homestead, and Small Farm — *Starbard, Ann*
c Daisy Malone and the Blue Glowing Stone — *O'Loghlin, James*
c Daisy Saves the Day (Illus. by Hughes, Shirley) — *Hughes, Shirley*
Daisy Turner's Kin: An African American Family Saga — *Beck, Jane C.*
The Dakota: A History of the World's Best-Known Apartment Building — *Alpern, Andrew*
Dale Morgan on the Mormons: Collected Works, Part 2, 1949-1970 — *Saunders, Richard L.*
Dalit Assertion — *Pai, Sudha*
c Dallas Cowboys — *Zappa, Marcia*
c The Daltons' Amnesia (Illus. by Morris) — *Fauche, Xavier*
Damage Day — *Asher, Dylan Edward*
y Damage Done — *Panitch, Amanda*
y Damaged — *Reed, Amy*

Damnatio in Memoria: Deformation und Gegenkonstruktionen in der Geschichte — *Scholz, Sebastian*
The Damned — *Pyper, Andrew*
Damned Nation: Hell in America from the Revolution to Reconstruction — *Lum, Kathryn Gin*
The Damned: The Darkest Hand Trilogy — *Richardson, Tarn*
Danach - Der Holocaust als Erfahrungsgeschichte 1945 - 1949. 5. Internationale Konferenz zur Holocaustforschung
Dance and Fashion — *Steele, Valerie*
c Dance! Dance! Underpants! (Illus. by Shea, Bob) — *Shea, Bob*
Dance Floor Democracy: The Social Geography of Memory at the Hollywood Canteen — *Tucker, Sherrie*
Dance in Handel's London Operas — *McCleave, Sarah*
A Dance in the Woods: A Mother's Insight — *Brennan, Janet K.*
A Dance of Assassins: Performing Early Colonial Hegemony in the Congo — *Roberts, Allen F.*
y Dance of the Banished — *Skrypuch, Marsha Forchuk*
Dance of the Bones — *Jance, J.A.*
Dance on Its Own Terms: Histories and Methodologies — *Bales, Melanie*
The Dance Theatre of Jean Cocteau — *Ries, Frank W.D.*
A Dance to the Music of Time — *Powell, Anthony*
Dance to the Piper — *de Mille, Agnes*
Dance with the Devil, Book 1: The Devil's Own — *March, J.D.*
Dancin' in Anson — *Carlson, Paul H.*
Dancing for Fun — *Greathouse, Mark L.*
Dancing Forever with Spirit: Astonishing Insights from Heaven — *Schulhauser, Garnet*
Dancing in the Dark — *Knausgaard, Karl Ove*
Dancing in the Dark — *Knausgaard, Karl Ove*
Dancing Jewish: Jewish Identity in American Modern and Postmodern Dance — *Rossen, Rebecca*
Dancing Tango, Passionate Encounters in a Globalizing World — *Davis, Kathy*
Dancing Tango: Passionate Encounters in a Globalizing World — *Davis, Kathy*
Dancing the New World: Aztecs, Spaniards, and the Choreography of Conquest — *Scolieri, Paul A.*
Dancing through Life — *Bure, Candace Cameron*
Dancing to the Precipice: Lucie De La Tour Du Pin and the French Revolution — *Moorehead, Caroline*
Dancing with a Baptist — *Stott, Libby*
Dancing with Doctoral Encounters: Democratic Education in Motion — *Waghid, Yusef*
Dancing with Mermaids — *Gibson, Miles*
y Dancing with Molly — *Horowitz, Lena*
Dancing with the Devil in the City of God: Rio De Janeiro on the Brink — *Barbassa, Juliana*
c Dandelion and the Witch (Illus. by Lamoreaux, Michelle) — *Snowe, Olivia*
c The Dandelion Seed's Big Dream (Illus. by Arbo, Cris) — *Anthony, Joseph*
c Dandelions (Illus. by Lonergan, Kirrili) — *McKelvey, Katrina*
Dando razones de nuestra esperanza: La pregunta acerca del mal — *Aste, Gerardo*
c Danger in Ancient Rome — *Messner, Kate*
Danger in the Darkest Hour (Read by Osborne, Mary Pope). Audiobook Review — *Osborne, Mary Pope*
c Danger in the Darkest Hour: Super Edition (Illus. by Murducca, Sal) — *Osborne, Mary Pope*

c Danger Is Everywhere: A Handbook for Avoiding Danger (Illus. by Judge, Chris) — *O'Doherty, David*
c Dangerous! — *Warnes, Tim*
c Dangerous Deception — *Kehret, Peg*
y Dangerous Deception — *Stohl, Margaret*
y Dangerous Deceptions — *Zettel, Sarah*
Dangerous Digestion: The Politics of American Dietary Advice — *DuPuis, E. Melanie*
Dangerous Games: What the Moral Panic over Role-Playing Games Says about Play, Religion, and Imagined Worlds — *Laycock, Joseph P.*
Dangerous Guests: Enemy Captives and Revolutionary Communities during the War for Independence — *Miller, Ken*
Dangerous Jeeps and Me — *Embrey, Jenelle R.*
y Dangerous Lies — *Fitzpatrick, Becca*
A Dangerous Master: How to Keep Technology from Slipping beyond Our Control — *Wallach, Wendell*
Dangerous Others, Insecure Societies: Fear and Social Division — *Lianos, Michalis*
A Dangerous Place — *Dobbs, Maisie*
A Dangerous Place — *Winspear, Jacqueline*
Dangerous Pregnancies: Mothers, Disabilities, and Abortion in Modern America — *Reagan, Leslie J.*
Dangerous Rhythm: Why Movie Musicals Matter — *Barrios, Richard*
Dangerous Spirits: The Windigo in Myth and History — *Smallman, Shawn*
y The Dangerous Summer of Jesse Turner — *Reep, D.C.*
The Dangerous Type — *Rhoads, Loren*
Dangerous When Wet — *Brickhouse, Jamie*
Dangerously Broken — *Branley, Eden*
Dangerously Sleepy: Overworked Americans and the Cult of Manly Wakefulness — *Derickson, Alan*
c Danica Patrick — *Anderson, Jameson*
c Daniel Finds a Poem (Illus. by Archer, Micha) — *Archer, Micha*
c Daniel O'Dowd Was Ever So Loud, Ever So (Illus. by Ellis, Elina) — *Fulton, Julie*
c Daniel X: Lights Out (Read by Landon, Aaron). Audiobook Review — *Patterson, James*
Daniel's True Desire — *Burrowes, Grace*
Dann Geh Doch Ruber - Uber die Mauer in den Osten — *Schaad, Martin*
c Danny (Illus. by Bee, Yann Le) — *Bee, Yann Le*
c Danny — *Le Bec, Yann*
c Danny and the Dinosaur and the New Puppy — *Hale, Bruce*
c Danny Best: Full On (Illus. by Vane, Mitch) — *Storer, Jen*
c Danny's Doodles: The Squirting Donuts — *Adler, David A.*
Danse: An Anthology — *Solomon, Noemie*
Dante: A Very Short Introduction — *Hainsworth, Peter*
Dante and the Limits of the Law — *Steinberg, Justin*
c Dante of the Maury River (Read by Jackson, J.D.). Audiobook Review — *Amateau, Gigi*
c Dante of the Maury River — *Amateau, Gigi*
Dantean Dialogues: Engaging with the Legacy of Amilcare Iannucci — *Lombardi, Elena*
Dante's Dilemma — *Raimondo, Lynne*
Dante's Lyric Poetry: Poems of Youth and of the "Vita Nuova" — *Barolini, Teodolinda*
Danubius Danubia — *Kabdebo, Tamas*
c Dappled Annie and the Tigrish (Illus. by Hayward, Annie) — *McCallum, Mary*
Darcus Howe: a Political Biography — *Howe, Darcus*
Dare I Believe — *Holland, Laura*

Dare to Be Your Own Boss: Follow Your Passion, Create a Niche — *Sullivan, Maya*
y Dare to Disappoint: Growing Up in Turkey — *Samanci, Ozge*
Dare to Pair: The Ultimate Guide to Chocolate and Wine Pairing — *Pech, Julie*
Dare to Run — *McLaughlin, Jen*
Dare to Serve: How to Drive Superior Results by Serving Others — *Bachelder, Cheryl*
Dare We Speak of Hope — *Boesak, Allan Aubrey*
y Daredevil — *Hinton, Nigel*
c Daredevil Duck (Illus. by Adler, Charlie) — *Adler, Charlie*
c Daredevil Duck (Illus. by Adler, Charlie) — *Alder, Charlie*
c Daredevil Duck (Illus. by Alder, Charlie) — *Alder, Charlie*
Daredevil: The Daring Life of Betty Skelton. Audiobook Review — *McCarthy, Meghan*
The Daredevils — *Amdahl, Gary*
c Darien and the Lost Paints of Telinoria (Illus. by Kunce, Craig) — *Kunce, Jeanna*
c Darien and the Seed of Obreget (Illus. by Kunce, Craig) — *Kunce, Jeanna*
c Daring (Illus. by Cano, Fernando) — *Hoena, Blake*
The Daring Exploits of a Runaway Heiress — *Alexander, Victoria*
Daring Greatly — *Brown, Brene*
Daring: My Passage — *Sheehy, Gail*
c The Daring Prince Dashing (Illus. by West, Karl) — *Reeder, Marilou T.*
Daring to Date Again — *Evans, Ann Anderson*
c Dario and the Whale (Illus. by Masseva, Bistra) — *Malone, Cheryl Lawton*
Darius in the Shadow of Alexander — *Briant, Pierre*
The Darjeeling Distinction: Labor and Justice on Fair-Trade Tea Plantations in India — *Besky, Sarah*
Darjeeling: The Colorful History and Precarious Fate of the World's Greatest Tea — *Koehler, Jeff*
Dark Age Liguria: Regional Identity and Local Power, c. 400-1020 — *Balzaretti, Ross*
y Dark Agent (Illus. by Tortosa, Wilson) — *Bowen, Carl*
Dark Alchemy — *Bickle, Laura*
A Dark and Twisted Tide — *Bolton, Sharon*
Dark Angel — *Nunnally, Tiina*
The Dark Art: My Undercover Life in Global Narco-Terrorism — *Follis, Edward*
Dark City Lights: New York Stories — *Block, Lawrence*
y Dark Company — *Ghent, Natale*
Dark Corners — *Rendell, Ruth*
y The Dark Days Club — *Goodman, Alison*
Dark Debt — *Neill, Chloe*
The Dark Eidolon and Other Fantasies — *Smith, Clark Ashton*
y Dark Energy — *Wells, Robison*
Dark Energy — *Morgan, Robert*
Dark Engine, vol. 1: The Art of Destruction — *Burton, Ryan*
The Dark Forest — *Liu, Cixin*
The Dark Forest — *Martinsen, Joel*
Dark Green — *Hunt, Emily*
The Dark Heart of Hitler's Europe: Nazi Rule in Poland under the General Government — *Winstone, Martin*
y The Dark Inside — *Wallis, Rupert*
Dark Intelligence — *Asher, Neal*
c The Dark Island — *Chantler, Scott*
Dark Knight III: The Master Race — *Miller, Frank*
y The Dark Lens — *Troupe, Thomas Kingsley*
Dark Light of Love — *Dunne, John S.*
Dark Lightning — *Varley, John*
Dark Matter and the Dinosaurs: The Astounding Interconnectedness of the Universe — *Randall, Lisa*
The Dark — *Carr, Forrest*
Dark Mirror: The Medieval Origins of Anti-Jewish Iconography — *Lipton, Sara*
Dark Money, Stiper PACs, and the 2012 Election — *Powell, Larry*
The Dark Net: Inside the Digital Underworld — *Bartlett, Jamie*
Dark Orbit — *Gilman, Carolyn Ives*
Dark Places — *Wortham, Reavis Z.*
Dark Places of the Earth: The Voyage of the Slave Ship Antelope — *Bryant, Jonathan M.*
Dark Prayer — *Mostert, Natasha*
Dark Prince, Heed Thy Queen — *K., Kathleen*
The Dark Prince — *Leech, Emma V.*
Dark Reservations — *Fortunato, John*
Dark Road, Dead End — *Cioffari, Philip*
The Dark Road to Mercy (Read by Bergmann, Erik). Audiobook Review — *Cash, Wiley*

Dark Rooms — *Anolik, Lili*
Dark Screams, vol. 1 (Read by Daniels, Luke). Audiobook Review — *Freeman, Brian James*
Dark Screams, vol. 4 — *Freeman, Brian James*
Dark Screams, vol. 5 — *Freeman, Brian James*
y Dark Shimmer — *Napoli, Donna Jo*
The Dark Side of Church/State Separation: The French Revolution, Nazi Germany, and International Communism — *Strehle, Stephen*
The Dark Side of Nation-States: Ethnic Cleansing in Modern Europe — *Ther, Philipp*
The Dark Side of the Crescent Moon — *Gounev, Georgy*
The Dark Side of the Enlightenment: Wizards, Alchemists, and Spiritual Seekers in the Age of Reason — *Fleming, John V.*
The Dark Side of the Road — *Green, Simon R.*
y Dark Sparkler — *Tamblyn, Amber*
Dark Sparring: Poems — *Marsh, Selina Tusitala*
Dark Spies (Read by Orlow, Rich). Audiobook Review — *Dunn, Matthew*
Dark, Sweet: New and Selected Poems — *Hogan, Linda*
c Dark Terror — *Wilson, John*
Dark Tides — *Ewan, Chris*
y Dark Turns — *Holahan, Cate*
Dark Victory — *DuBois, Brendan*
y The Dark Water — *Fishman, Seth*
Dark Waters — *Goff, Chris*
The Dark Wild (Read by Hembrough, Oliver). Audiobook Review — *Torday, Piers*
c The Dark Wild — *Torday, Piers*
The Darkening Trapeze: Last Poems — *Levis, Larry*
Darker Edge of Desire — *Szereto, Mitzi*
A Darker Shade of Magic (Read by Crossley, Steven). Audiobook Review — *Schwab, V.E.*
A Darker Shade of Magic — *Schwab, V.E.*
The Darker Side of Western Modernity — *Mignolo, Walter D.*
Darker the Release — *Kent, Claire*
Darkest before Dawn — *Banks, Maya*
y The Darkest Corners — *Thomas, Kara*
The Darkest Days: The Truth behind Britain's Rush to War, 1914 — *Newton, Douglas*
The Darkest Heart — *Smith, Dan (b. 1970-)*
y The Darkest Part of the Forest (Read by Fortgang, Lauren). Audiobook Review — *Black, Holly*
y The Darkest Part of the Forest — *Black, Holly*
The Darkest Period: The Kanza Indians and Their Last Homeland, 1846-1873 — *Parks, Ronald D.*
The Darkest Side of Saturn: Odyssey of a Reluctant Prophet of Doom — *Taylor, Tony*
The Darkling Child — *Brooks, Terry*
A Darkling Sea (Read by Lowlor, Patrick). Audiobook Review — *Cambias, James L.*
y Darkmouth — *Hegarty, Shane*
c Darkmouth: The Legends Begin (Illus. by de la Rue, James) — *Hegarty, Shane*
Darkmouth: The Legends Begin (Illus. by Rue, James de la) — *Hegarty, Shane*
Darkness at Noon — *Koestler, Arthur*
The Darkness behind Me — *Shannon, T. J.*
Darkness, Darkness — *Harvey, John*
y Darkness Hidden — *Marriott, Zoe*
The Darkness of the Present: Poetics, Anachronism, and the Anomaly — *McCaffery, Steve*
Darkness on His Bones — *Hambly, Barbara*
The Darkness Rolling — *Blevins, Win*
Darkness Sticks to Everything — *Hennen, Tom*
The Darkness That Divides Us — *Dorrestein, Renate*
Darkness the Color of Snow — *Cobb, Thomas*
y Darkthaw — *Boorman, Kate A.*
The Darling Dahlias and the Eleven O'Clock Lady — *Albert, Susan Wittig*
Darling Monster: The Letters of Lady Diana Cooper to Her Son John Julius Norwich, 1939-1952 — *Norwich, John Julius*
Darrow's Gamble — *Taylor, Gillian F.*
c Darth Vader and Friends (Illus. by Brown, Jeffrey) — *Brown, Jeffrey*
Darwin and His Children: His Other Legacy — *Berra, Tim M.*
Darwin and Theories of Aesthetics and Cultural History — *Larson, Barbara*
Darwin Becomes Art: Aesthetic Vision in the Wake of Darwin, 1870-1920 — *Ridley, Hugh*
Darwin Deleted: Imagining a World without Darwin — *Bowler, Peter J.*
Darwinistas: The Construction of Evolutionary Thought in Nineteenth Century Argentina — *Levine, Alex*

Darwin's Dice: The Idea of Chance in the Thought of Charles Darwin — *Johnson, Curtis*
y Darwin's Watch: The Science of Discworld III — *Pratchett, Terry*
Das 18. Jahrhundert — *Schmale, Wolfgang*
Das archaische Griechenland: Die Stadt und das Meer — *Stein-Holkeskamp, Elke*
Das Archiv für Religionswissenschaft in den Jahren 1919 bis 1939: Dargestellt auf der Grundlage des Briefwechsels zwischen Otto Weinrich und Martin P:n Nilsson — *Durkop, Martina*
Das Artikulierte und das Inartikulierte: Eine Archaeologie des Strukturalismus — *Wilczek, Markus*
Das austrofaschistische Herrschaftssystem: Osterreich 1933-1938, 2d ed. — *Talos, Emmerich*
Das Beginenwesen in frankischen und bayerischen Bischofsstadten — *Hien, Hannah*
Das begrenzte Papsttum: Spielraumepapstlkhen Handels - Legaten: Delegierte Richter Grenzen — *Herbers, Klaus*
Das Briefbuch Abt Wibalds von Stablo und Corvey, 3 vols. — *Hartmann, Martina*
Das Buch Witsch: Das schwindelerregende Leben des Verlegers Joseph Caspar Witsch — *Moller, Frank*
Das Deutsche Volk und die Politik
Das Ende des Holocaust — *Rosenfeld, Alvin H.*
Das Ende des Konigreichs Hannover und Preussen: Die Jahre 1865 und 1866 — *Koster, Fredy*
Das Geschlecht der Diplomatie: Geschlechterrollen in den Aussenbeziehungen vom Spatmittelalter bis zum 20. Jahrhundert — *Bastian, Corina*
Das Imaginare des Kalten Krieges: Beitrage zu einer Kulturgeschichte des Ost-West-Konfliktes in Europa — *Eugster, David*
Das Kapital im 21. Jahrhundert — *Piketty, Thomas*
Das Kinderbischofsfest im Mittelalter — *Skambraks, Tanja*
Das Kloster Fulda und seine Urkunden: Moderne archivische Erschliessung und ihre Perspektiven fur die historische Forschung — *Zwies, Sebastian*
Das Konstanzer Konzil 1414-1418: Weltereignis des Mittelalters: Essays — *Braun, Karl-Heinz*
Das Konstanzer Konzil 1414-1418: Weltereignis des Mittelalters. Katalog zur Grossen Landesausstellung Baden-Wurttemberg in Konstanz vom 27. April bis zum 21. September 2014 — *Landesmuseum, Badisches*
Das Konstanzer Konzil als Europaisches Ereignis: Begegnungen, Medien und Rituale — *Signori, Gabriela*
Das Konstanzer Konzil: Kirchenpolitik - Weltgeschehen - Alltagsleben — *Buck, Thomas M.*
Das Kosmoskop: Karten und ihre Benutzer in der Pflanzengeographie des 19. Jahrhunderts — *Guttler, Nils*
"Das Leben ist eine Rutschbahn ... " Albert Steinruck: Eine Biographie des Schauspielers, Malers und Bohemiens — *Heymann, Margret*
Das Mittelalter im 19. Jahrhundert: Ein Beitrag zur Kompositionsgeschichte in Frankreich — *Morent, Stefan*
"Das Nibelungenlied" und "Die Klage," nach der Handschrift 857 der Stiftsbibliothek St. Gallen — *Heinzle, Joachim*
Das Publikum macht die Musik: Musikleben in Berlin, London und Wien im 19. Jahrhundert — *Muller, Sven Oliver*
Das Reboot: How German Soccer Reinvented Itself and Conquered the World — *Honigstein, Raphael*
Das Recht der "Soldatenkaiser": Rechtliche Stabilitat in Zeiten Politischen Umbruchs? — *Babusiaux, Ulrike*
Das romische Spielwesen in der Spatantike — *Puk, Alexander*
Das Schuldbuch des Basler Kaufmanns Ludwig Kilchmann — *Signori, Gabriella*
Das Tauferreich von Munster: Ursprunge und Merkmale eines religiosen Aufbruchs — *Lutterbach, Hubertus*
c Dash (Illus. by Jessell, Tim) — *Klimo, Kate*
c Dash — *Larson, Kirby*
c The Dastardly Deed (Illus. by Portillo, Josie) — *Grant, Holly*
Data and Goliath: The Hidden Battles to Collect Your Data and Control Your World — *Schneier, Bruce*
Data-ism: Inside the Big Data Revolution — *Lohr, Steve*
Data-ism: The Revolution Transforming Decision Making, Consumer Behavior, and Almost Everything Else — *Lohr, Steve*
Database of Dreams — *Lemov, Rebecca*

Dataclysm: Love, Sex, Race, and Identity--What Our Online Lives Tell Us about Our Offline Selves — *Rudder, Christian*
Date Night In: More than 120 Recipes to Nourish Your Relationship — *Rodriguez, Ashley*
Date-Onomics: How Dating Became a Lopsided Numbers Game — *Birger, Jon*
y Date with a Rockstar — *Gagnon, Sarah*
y Dating Down — *Lyons, Stefanie*
The Dating of Beowulf: A Reassessment — *Neidorf, Leonard*
The Daughter — *Shemilt, Jane*
The Daughter of an Earl — *Morgan, Victoria*
Daughter of Ashes — *Talley, Marcia*
Daughter of Blood — *Lowe, Helen*
y Daughter of Chaos — *McConnel, Jen*
y Daughter of Deep Silence (Read by Vacker, Karissa). Audiobook Review — *Ryan, Carrie*
y Daughter of Deep Silence — *Ryan, Carrie*
y Daughter of Dusk (Read by Amato, Bianca). Audiobook Review — *Blackburne, Livia*
y Daughter of Dusk — *Blackburne, Livia*
Daughter of Gods and Shadows — *Brooks, Jayde*
Daughter of Good Fortune: A Twentieth-Century Chinese Peasant Memoir — *Huiqin, Chen*
A Daughter of No Nation — *Dellamonica, A.M.*
Daughter of the House — *Thomas, Rosie*
Daughter of the Regiment — *Whitson, Stephanie Grace*
Daughters and Granddaughters of Farmworkers: Emerging from the Long Shadow of Farm Labor — *Wells, Barbara*
The Daughters — *Celt, Adrienne*
Daughters of Charity: Women, Religious Mission, and Hospital Care in Los Angeles, 1856-1927 — *Gunnell, Kristine Ashton*
Daughters of Divorce: Overcome the Legacy of Your Parents' Breakup and Enjoy a Happy, Long-Lasting Relationship — *Gaspard, Terry*
Daughters of Frankenstein: Lesbian Mad Scientists! — *Berman, Steve*
Daughters of Parvati: Women and Madness in Contemporary India — *Pinto, Sarah*
Daughters of the Samurai: A Journey from East to West and Back — *Nimura, Janice P.*
Daughters of the Samurai: A Journey from East to West and Back — *Janice P. Nimura*
y Daughters of the Samurai: A Journey from East to West and Back — *Nimura, Janice P.*
y Daughters unto Devils — *Lukavics, Amy*
David Bellamy's Winter Landscapes in Watercolour — *Bellamy, David*
David Foster Wallace and 'The Long Thing' — *Boswell, Marshall*
The David Foster Wallace Reader — *Wallace, David Foster*
David Lean — *Williams, Melanie*
David & Lee Roy: A Vietnam Story — *Nelson, David L.*
David Lynch: The Factory Photographs — *Giloy-Hirtz, Petra*
David Lynch: The Man from Another Place — *Lim, Dennis*
David Lynch: The Unified Field — *Cozzolino, Robert*
c Davy Loves the Baby (Illus. by Tharlet, Eve) — *Weninger, Brigitte*
Dawa: The Islamic Strategy for Reshaping the Modern World — *Sookhdeo, Patrick*
Dawkins, Redux: Nathaniel Comfort TakesIssue with the Second Instalment of the Evolutionary Biologist's Autobiography — *Dawkins, Richard*
Dawn and Sunset: Insight into the Mystery of the Early Mesopotamian Civilization — *Baizerman, Michael*
The Dawn of Canada's Century: Hidden Histories — *Darroch, Gordon*
c The Dawn of Planet Earth — *Rake, Matthew*
The Dawn of Technicolor 1915-1935 — *Layton, James*
Dawn of the Deb — *Moore, Laurie*
Dawn of the Neuron: The Early Struggles to Trace the Origin of Nervous Systems — *Anctil, Michel*
The Dawning Moon of the Mind: Unlocking the Pyramid Texts — *Morrow, Susan Brind*
Dawnland Voices: An Anthology of Indigenous Writing from New England — *Senier, Siobhan F.*
y Day 21 — *Morgan, Kass*
c A Day and Night in the Desert (Illus. by Arnold, Caroline) — *Arnold, Caroline*
c A Day and Night in the Rain Forest (Illus. by Arnold, Caroline) — *Arnold, Caroline*
c A Day at Grandma's (Illus. by Choi, Yangsook) — *Lee, Mi-ae*

The Day Commodus Killed a Rhino: Understanding the Roman Games — *Toner, Jerry*
c The Day Everything Went Wrong (Illus. by Jackowski, Amelie) — *Petz, Moritz*
Day Four (Read by Rawlins, Penelope). Audiobook Review — *Lotz, Sarah*
Day Four — *Lotz, Sarah*
A Day in a Working Life: 300 Trades and Professions through History, 3 vols. — *Westfahl, Gary*
A Day in Canada (Illus. by Gurth, Per-Henrik) — *Gurth, Per-Henrik*
Day in the Life of the English Language: A Microcosmic Usage Handbook — *Cioffi, Frank L.*
c The Day Is Waiting (Illus. by Freeman, Don) — *Zuckerman, Linda*
c The Day No One Was Angry (Illus. by Boutavant, Marc) — *Tellegen, Toon*
The Day of Atonement (Read by Roukin, Samuel). Audiobook Review — *Liss, David*
Day of Independence — *Johnstone, William W.*
y Day of Infamy: The Story of the Attack on Pearl Harbor — *Otfinoski, Steven*
c Day of the Dead — *Murray, Julie*
Day of the Dragonking — *Irving, Terry*
c The Day of the Jackal — *Stone, Jeff*
The Day Parliament Burned Down — *Shenton, Caroline*
Day Shift — *Harris, Charlaine*
c The Day the Crayons Came Home (Illus. by Jeffers, Oliver) — *Daywalt, Drew*
c The Day the Crayons Came Home — *Daywalt, Drew*
c The Day the Crayons Came Home (Illus. by Jeffers, Oliver) — *Daywalt, Drew*
c The Day the Mustache Took Over (Illus. by Easler, Kris) — *Katz, Alan*
The Day the Renaissance Was Saved: The Battle of Anghiari and da Vinci's Lost Masterpiece — *Capponi, Niccolo*
c The Day the Sun Did Not Rise and Shine (Illus. by Rauwerda, Peter-Paul) — *Enzerink, Mirjam*
The Day We Met — *Coleman, Rowan*
c A Day with Bonefish Joe (Illus. by Wege, Diana) — *Howard, Elizabeth*
c A Day with Cinderella — *Cooper, Gemma*
c A Day with Monster — *Gleiner, Kelli*
DayBlack — *Cross, Keef*
Daydreamers — *Harper, Jonathan*
c Daydreams for Night (Illus. by Ouimet, David) — *Southworth, John*
Daydreams of Angels — *O'Neill, Heather*
Daydreams of Angels: Stories — *O'Neill, Heather*
The Daylight Marriage — *Pitlor, Heidi*
c Daylight Starlight Wildlife (Illus. by Minor, Wendell) — *Minor, Wendell*
The Days Between — *Falk, Marcia*
Days of Awe — *Fox, Lauren*
Days of Rage: America's Radical Underground, the FBI, and the Forgotten Age of Revolutionary Violence (Read by Porter, Ray). Audiobook Review — *Burrough, Bryan*
Days of Rage: America's Radical Underground, the FBI, and the Forgotten Age of Revolutionary Violence — *Burrough, Bryan*
Days of Revolution: Political Unrest in an Iranian Village — *Hegland, Mary Elaine*
Days of Shame & Failure — *Knox, Jennifer L.*
Days of the Giants — *Petrella, R.J.*
c Days of the Knights (Illus. by Neubecker, Robert) — *Neubecker, Robert*
The Days Trilogy, Expanded Edition — *Rodgers, Marion Elizabeth*
c Daytime Nighttime (Illus. by Low, William) — *Low, William*
DC Trip — *Benincasa, Sara*
DCC Projects and Applications — *Grivno, Cody*
DDR-Literatur: Eine Archivexpedition — *von Bulow, Ulrich*
DDT Wars: Rescuing Our National Bird, Preventing Cancer, and Creating the Environmental Defense Fund — *Wurster, Charles F.*
De actibus humanis / Sobre los actos humanos — *Vitoria, Francisco de*
De Bow's Review: The Antebellum Vision of a New South — *Kvach, John F.*
The de cosmos enigma — *Hawkins, Gordon*
"De itinere navali": A German Third Crusader's Chronicle of His Voyage and the Siege of Almohad Silves, 1189 AD/Muwahid Xelb, 585 AH — *Cushing, Dana*
De nobilitate animi, ed. and trans — *Aragonia, Guillelmus de*

De Obitu Lohannis Stoefler Lustingani Mathematici Tubingensis elegia (Augsburg 1531): Ein Gedicht auf den Tod des Tubinger Astronomen Johannes Stoffler — *Reysmann, Theodor*
De-Stalinization Reconsidered: Persistence and Change in the Soviet Union — *Bohn, Thomas M.*
De Terremotu — *Manetti, Giannozzo*
De triennen fan cheetah: 27 Fryske ferhalen — *Feddema, Anne*
Deacon's Winter — *Burgraff, Roger*
c Dead Air (Illus. by Olesh, Stephanie) — *Schusterman, Michelle*
The Dead Assassin — *Entwistle, Vaughn*
The Dead Assassin: The Paranormal Casebooks of Sir Arthur Conan Doyle — *Entwistle, Vaughn*
c The Dead Bird (Illus. by Robinson, Christian) — *Brown, Margaret Wise*
Dead Birds — *Grissom, Eric*
c Dead Boy — *Gale, Laurel*
Dead Boys — *Squailia, Gabriel*
Dead Certainty — *Wilson, Glenis*
The Dead City and the Dark Earth Below: Stories of the Raksura, vol. 2 — *Wells, Martha*
The Dead Duke, His Secret Wife, and the Missing Corpse: An Extraordinary Edwardian Case of Deception and Intrigue — *Eatwell, Piu Marie*
The Dead Duke, His Secret Wife and the Missing Corpse — *Eatwell, Piu Marie*
Dead Girl Walking — *Brookmyre, Christopher*
y The Dead Girls of Hysteria Hall — *Alender, Katie*
The Dead Ground — *McGowan, Claire*
Dead Heading — *Aird, Catherine*
c The Dead House (Illus. by McMorris, Kelley) — *Johnson, Allen, Jr.*
y The Dead House — *Kurtagich, Dawn*
y The Dead I Know — *Gardner, Scot*
y The Dead I Know — *Gardner, Scott*
y Dead in the Water — *Lynch, Chris*
y Dead Investigation — *Price, Charlie*
The Dead Key — *Pulley, D.M.*
The Dead Ladies Project: Exiles, Expats, and Ex-Countries — *Crispin, Jessa*
The Dead Lands (Read by Graham, Holter). Audiobook Review — *Percy, Benjamin*
y The Dead Lands — *Percy, Benjamin*
Dead Letter Office — *Hue*
Dead Man's Fancy — *McCafferty, Keith*
Dead Man's Float — *Harrison, Jim*
Dead Man's Reach — *Jackson, D.B.*
The Dead Man's Treasure — *Bock, Kris*
Dead Men — *Foster, John C.*
The Dead Mountaineer's Inn — *Strugatsky, Boris*
The Dead of August — *Cacoyannis, Panayotis*
y Dead of Winter: The Arcana Chronicles — *Cole, Kresley*
Dead on Course — *Wilson, Glenis*
c Dead or Alive? Discover the Most Amazing Animal Survivors (Illus. by Horne, Sarah) — *Gifford, Clive*
c Dead Possums are Fair Game — *Souders, Taryn*
Dead Presidents: An American Adventure into the Strange Deaths and Surprising Afterlives of Our Nation's Leaders — *Carlson, Brady*
The Dead Rabbit Drinks Manual: Secret Recipes and Barroom Tales from Two Belfast Boys Who Conquered the Cocktail World — *Muldoon, Sean*
Dead Red — *O'Mara, Tim*
Dead Repunzel — *Houston, Victoria*
y Dead Ringer — *Belleau, Heidi*
Dead Ringer — *Cone, William*
Dead Ringer — *Fox, Sarah*
Dead Soon Enough — *Cha, Steph*
Dead Spots — *Frater, Rhiannon*
The Dead Student — *Katzenbach, John*
y Dead to Me — *McCoy, Mary*
Dead to the World — *Cooper, Susan Rogers*
y Dead upon a Time — *Paulson, Elizabeth*
Dead Wake: The Last Crossing of the Lusitania (Read by Brick, Scott). Audiobook Review — *Larson, Erik*
Dead Wake: The Last Crossing of the Lusitania — *Larson, Erik*
The Dead Wife's Handbook — *Beckerman, Hannah*
The Dead Will Tell (Read by McInerney, Kathleen). Audiobook Review — *Castillo, Linda*
Dead Women Talking: Figures of Injustice in American Literature — *Norman, Brian*
The Dead Won't Die — *McKinney, Joe*
y Dead Zones: Why Earth's Waters Are Losing Oxygen — *Hand, Carol*
Dead Zonew — *Wells, Robison*
The Dead Zoo — *Berry, Ciaran*
y Deadfall — *Carey, Anna*
Deadlands: Ghostwalkers — *Maberry, Jonathan*

Deadlight Hall — Rayne, Sarah
Deadline (Read by Conger, Eric). Audiobook Review — Sandford, John
Deadline — Sandford, John
c The Deadly 7 (Illus. by Jennings, Garth) — Jennings, Garth
A Deadly Affair at Bobtail Ridge — Shames, Terry
Deadly Assets — Griffin, W.E.B.
Deadly Bonds — Sellers, L.J.
A Deadly Business (Read by Laurence, Ashley). Audiobook Review — Wiehl, Lis
Deadly Censorship: Murder, Honor, and Freedom of the Press — Underwood, James Lowell
y Deadly Design — Dockter, Debra
Deadly Desires at Honeychurch Hall — Dennison, Hannah
Deadly Election — Davis, Lindsey
c Deadly Pole to Pole Diaries — Backshall, Steve
Deadly Secret of the Lusitania — Light, Ivan
Deadly Snakes — Turner, Tracey
A Deadly Tail — Lyle, Dixie
Deadly Virtues — Bannister, Jo
A Deadly Wandering: A Mystery, a Landmark Investigation, and the Astonishing Science of Attention in the Digital Age — Richtel, Matt
Deadly Words: Witchcraft in the Bocage — Favret-Saada, Jeanne
Deadout — McGoran, Jon
A Deafening Silence in Heaven — Sniegoski, Thomas E.
Deal: My Three Decades of Drumming, Jams, and Drugs with the Grateful Dead — Eisen, Benjy
Deal: My Three Decades of Drumming, Jams, and Drugs with the Grateful Dead — Kreutzmann, Bill
Dealing with China: An Insider Unmasks the New Economic Superpower (Read by Stillwell, Kevin). Audiobook Review — Paulson, Henry M., Jr.
Dealing with Darwin: Place, Politics, and Rhetoric in Religious Engagements with Evolution — Livingstone, David N.
Dealing with the Mentally Ill Person on the Street: An Assessment and Intervention Guide for Public Safety Professionals — Rudofossi, Daniel M.
c Dear Bunny — Cotton, Katie
Dear Chairman: Boardroom Battles and the Rise of Shareholder Activism — Gramm, Jeff
Dear Committee Members — Schumacher, Julie
c Dear Dragon Flies a Kite (Illus. by Pullan, Jack) — Hillert, Margaret
c Dear Dragon Goes to Grandpa's Farm (Illus. by Pullan, Jack) — Hillert, Margaret
c Dear Dragon Goes to the Aquarium (Illus. by Pullan, Jack) — Hillert, Margaret
c Dear Dragon Goes to the Police Station (Illus. by Pullan, Jack) — Hillert, Margaret
Dear Elizabeth; A Play in Letters from Elizabeth Bishop to Robert Lowell and Back Again (Read by Williams, JoBeth). Audiobook Review — Buhl, Sarah
Dear Emma — Heaney, Katie
c Dear Hank Williams — Holt, Kimberly Willis
Dear Hannah: A Geek's Life in Self-Improvement — Dhingra, Philip
Dear Jeff — Gough, Kerry
c Dear Malala, We Stand with You — McCarney, Rosemary
Dear Mendl, Dear Reyzl: Yiddish Letter Manuals from Russia and America — Nakhimovsky, Alice
Dear Mister Essay Writer Guy: Advice and Confessions on Writing, Love, and Cannibals — Moore, Dinty W.
Dear Mom and Dad — McGowen, Georgia Lee
c Dear Mr. Washington (Illus. by Carpenter, Nancy) — Cullen, Lynn
Dear Mr. You — Parker, Mary-Louise
c Dear Opl — Sackier, Shelley
c Dear Panda — Latimer, Miriam
Dear Prudence — Farrow Bruns, Prudence
Dear Reader — Fournel, Paul
Dear Santa: Children's Christmas Letters and Wish Lists, 1870-1920 — Harrell-Sesniak, Mary
c Dear Santa, Love, Rachel Rosenstein (Illus. by Davenier, Christine) — Feet, Amanda
c Dear Santa, Love, Rachel Rosenstein (Illus. by Davenier, Christine) — Peet, Amanda
Dear Thief — Harvey, Samantha
c Dear Tomato: An International Crop of Food and Agriculture Poems (Illus. by Wasserman, Norie) — Hoyte, Carol Ann
c Dear Wandering Wildebeest and Other Poems from the Water Hole (Illus. by Wadham, Anna) — Latham, Irene

Dear White Christians: For Those Still Longing for Racial Reconciliation — Harvey, Jennifer
c Dear Yeti (Illus. by Kwan, James) — Kwan, James
y Dearest — Kontis, Alethea
Dearest Margarita: An Edwardian Love Story in Postcards — Gordon, Eleo
Dearest Rogue — Hoyt, Elizabeth
Dearly Departed — Conrad, Hy
Death and a Cup of Tea — Faraday, Jess
Death and a Maiden: Infanticide and the Tragical History of Grethe Schmidt — Myers, William David
The Death and Afterlife of the North American Martyrs — Anderson, Emma
y The Death and Life of Zebulon Finch: At the Edge of Empire — Kraus, Daniel
y The Death and Life of Zebulon Finch, vol. 1: At the Edge of Empire — Kraus, Daniel
Death and Mr. Pickwick — Jarvis, Stephen
Death and the Afterlife — Scheffler, Samuel
Death and the Brewmaster's Widow — Ross, Loretta
Death at Dovecote Hatch — Cannell, Dorothy
Death at Gills Rock — Skalka, Patricia
Death at Tammany Hall — O'Brien, Charles
Death at the Abbey — Trent, Christine
Death at the Black Bull — Hayes, Frank
Death by Arbitrage, or, Live Low Die High — Barthel, Urno
Death by Dumpster — Stuyck, Karen Hanson
Death by Effigy: A Case from the Mexican Inquisition — Corteguera, Luis R.
Death by Tea — Erickson, Alex
y Death by Toilet Paper — Gephart, Donna
Death by Video Game: Tales of Obsession from the Virtual Frontline — Parkin, Simon
Death by Water — Oe, Kenzaburo
The Death Camps of Croatia: Visions and Revisions, 1941-1945 — Israeli, Raphael
y The Death Code — Cummings, Lindsay
Death Comes to Kurland Hall — Lloyd, Catherine
y Death Coming up the Hill — Crowe, Chris
Death Ex Machina — Corby, Gary
Death for Dinner: The Benders of (Old) Kansas: The Biography of a Family of Mass Killers — De La Garza, Phyllis
Death from Above: The 7th Bombardment Group in World War II — Young, Edward M.
Death Fugue — Keyi, Sheng
Death in Brittany — Bannalec, Jean-Luc
Death in Brittany — McDonagh, Sorcha
Death in Devon — Sansom, Ian
Death in East Germany 1945-1990 — Schulz, Felix Robin
Death in Eden — Heald, Paul
Death in Florence: The Medici, Savonarola, and the Battle for the Soul of a Renaissance City — Strathern, Paul
A Death In Geneva — Clift, A. Denis
Death in Salem (Read by Berneis, Susie). Audiobook Review — Kuhns, Eleanor
Death in Salem — Kuhns, Eleanor
Death in the Congo: Murdering Patrice Lumumba — Gerard, Emmanuel
A Death in the Family — Stanley, Michael
Death in the Pines — Hartmann, Thom
Death in the Shape of a Young Girl: Women's Political Violence in the Red Army Faction — Melzer, Patricia
Death in Veracruz — Camin, Hector Aguilar
Death in Winterreise: Musico-Poetic Associations in Schubert's Song Cycle — Suurpaa, Lauri
Death Invites You — Halter, Paul
Death, Life, and Religious Change in Scottish Towns, c. 1350-1560 — Cowan, Mairi
y Death Marked — Cypess, Leah
Death Money — Chang, Henry
Death, Mourning, and the Afterlife in Korea: From Ancient to Contemporary Times — Horlyck, Charlotte
Death of a Bride and Groom — Emerson, Allan J.
Death of a Century: A Novel of the Lost Generation — Robinson, Daniel
Death of a Chimney Sweep (Read by Malcolm, Graeme). Audiobook Review — Beaton, M.C.
Death of a Liar — Beaton, M.C.
Death of a Nightingale — Friis, Agnete
Death of a Nurse — Beaton, M.C.
Death of a Policeman — Beaton, M.C.
Death of a Suburban Dream: Race and Schools in Compton, California — Straus, Emily E.
Death of a Texas Ranger: A True Story of Murder and Vengeance on the Texas Frontier — Massey, Cynthia L.

The Death of Adam — Robinson, Marilynne
Death of an Airman — Sprigg, Christopher St. John
Death of an Alchemist — Lawrence, Mary
The Death of Caesar: The Story of History's Most Famous Assassination (Read by Dean, Robertson). Audiobook Review — Strauss, Barry
The Death of Caesar: The Story of History's Most Famous Assassination — Strauss, Barry
The Death of Cancer: After Fifty Years on the Front Lines of Medicine, a Pioneering Oncologist Reveals Why the War on Cancer Is Winnable--and How We Can Get There — DeVita, Vincent T., Jr.
The Death of Cancer: After Fifty Years on the Front Lines of Medicine, a Pioneering Oncologist Reveals Why the War on Cancer Is Winnable-and How We Can Get There — DeVita, Vincent T.
The Death of Cancer: After Fifty Years on the Front Lines of Medicine, a Pioneering Oncologist Reveals Why the War on Cancer Is Winnable - and How We Can Get There — DeVita, Vincent T.
The Death of Cancer: After Fifty Years on the Front Lines of Medicine, a Pioneering Oncologist Reveals Why the War on Cancer is Winnable and How We Can Get There — DeVita, Vincent T.
The Death of Captain America (Read by Rohan, Richard). Audiobook Review — Hama, Larry
The Death of Captain America. Audiobook Review — Hama, Larry
The Death of Captain America: Civil War Aftermath (Read by Rohan, Richard). Audiobook Review — Kama, Larry
The Death of Magic — Black, Daniel
The Death of Money: The Coming Collapse of the International Monetary System — Rickards, James
The Death of Rex Nhongo — George, C.B.
Death of Riley — Bowen, Rhys
Death of the Artist — Fransman, Karrie
The Death of the Big Men and the Rise of the Big Shots: Custom and Conflict in East New Britain — Martin, Keir
c The Death of the Hat: A Brief History of Poetry in 50 Objects (Illus. by Raschka, Chris) — Janeczko, Paul B.
The Death of the Messiah and the Birth of the New Covenant: A (Not So) New Model of the Atonement — Gorman, Michael J. (b. 1955-)
Death on Demand — Kelly, Jim
A Death on Diamond Mountain: A True Story of Obsession, Madness, and the Path to Enlightenment — Carney, Scott
Death on the High Lonesome — Hayes, Frank
Death on the Prairie — Ernst, Kathleen
The Death Penalty, vol. 1 — Derrida, Jacques
c Death Poem — McClements, Richard
The Death Ritual at Cluny in the Central Middle Ages / Le rituel de la mort a Cluny au Moyen Age central — Paxton, Frederick S.
The Death Row All Stars: A Story of Baseball, Corruption, and Murder — Kazanjian, Howard
Death Steppe — Bruce, Judy
Death to Tyrants! Ancient Greek Democracy and the Struggle against Tyranny — Teegarden, David Arlo
Death Tourism: Disaster Sites as Recreational Landscape — Sion, Brigitte
Death Valley National Park: A History — Miller, Char
Death Valley National Park: A History — Rothman, Hal K.
Death Wave — Bova, Ben
Death Wears a Beauty Mask and Other Stories (Read by Maxwell, Jan, with Robert Petkoff). Audiobook Review — Clark, Mary Higgins
Death Wears a Mask — Weaver, Ashley
Death without Cause — Triolo, Pamela
The Death You Deserve — Techlin, Jonathan
The Death's Head Chess Club — Donoghue, John
Deaths in Venice: The Cases of Gustav von Aschenbach — Kitcher, Philip
Death's Summer Coat — Schillace, Brandy
c The Deavys — Foster, Alan Dean
Debates in the Digital Humanities — Gold, Matthew K.
Debating American Identity: Southwestern Statehood and Mexican Immigration — Noel, Linda C.
Debating Democratization in Myanmar — Cheesman, Nick
Debating Multiculturalism in the Nordic Welfare States — Kivisto, Peter
Debating War in Chinese History — Lorge, Peter A.
Deborah's Daughters: Gender Politics and Biblical Interpretation — Schroeder, Joy A.
Debris — Hardeastle, Kevin

Debt-Free U: How I Paid for an Outstanding College Education without Loans, Scholarships, or Mooching off My Parents — Bissonnette, Zac
The Debt of Tamar — Dweck, Nicole
Debt: The First 5,000 Years — Graeber, David
Debt to Society: Accounting for Life under Capitalism — Joseph, Miranda
The Debtor Class — Goldman, Ivan G.
Debtor Nation: The History of America In Red America — Hyman, Louis
y Debunk It!: How to Stay Sane in a World of Misinformation — Grant, John
Debunking Darwin — Anderson, Joseph
Decades Never Start on Time: A Richard Roud Anthology — Temple, Michael
The Decagon House Murders — Ayatsuji, Yukito
Decameron — Boccaccio, Giovanni
The Decameron Third Day in Perspective — Ciabattoni, Francesco
Decapitating the Union: Jefferson Davis, Judah Benjamin and the Plot to Assassinate Lincoln — Fazio, John C.
Deceit on the Road to War — Schuessler, John M.
c December Dog (Illus. by Gurney, John Steven) — Roy, Ron
The Decent Proposal — Donovan, Kemper
A Decent Ride — Welsh, Irvine
Decentring the Avant-Garde — Backstrom, Per
Deception Island — Kell, Brynn
y Deception of a Highlander — Martin, Madeline
c Deception on the Set — Dixon, Franklin W.
Deceptions — Armstrong, Kelley
Deceptions — Kelly, Linda Armstrong
y Deception's Pawn — Friesner, Esther
y Deceptive — Lloyd-Jones, Emily
The Deceptive Fibionary — Kasper, Leagan E.
A Deceptive Homecoming — Loan-Wilsey, Anna
Decimi Magni Ausonii: Ludus septem sapientum — Cazzuffi, Elena
Deciphering the New Antisemitism — Rosenfeld, Alvin H.
The Decision — Brunstetter, Wanda E.
The Decision-Maker's Guide to Long-Term Financing — Ohle, Kathrin
Decision Taking, Confidence and Risk Management in Banks in the 19th and 20th Century
The Decision — Brunstetter, Wanda E.
A Decisive Decade: An Insider's View of the Civil Rights Movement during the 1960s — McKersie, Robert B.
Decks Complete: Expert Advice from Start to Finish — Grice, Scott
The Decline and Fall of the Dukes of Leinster, 1872-1948: Love, War, Debt and Madness — Dooley, Terence
The Decline of Mercy in Public Life — Tuckness, Alex
The Decline of Serfdom in Late Medieval England: From Bondage to Freedom — Bailey, Mark
Decline of the Animal Kingdom — Clarke, Laura
Decoded — Mai Jia
Decoding the New Consumer Mind: How and Why We Shop and Buy — Yarrow, Kit
Decoding Vatican II: Interpretation and Ongoing Reception — Clifford, Catherine E.
Decoloniser l'ecole? Hawai'i, Nouvelle-Caledonie. Experiences contemporaines — Salaun, Marie
Decolonising the Intellectual: Politics, Culture, and Humanism at the End of the French Empire — Harrison, Olivia C.
Decolonization and the Evolution of International Human Rights — Burke, Roland
Decolonizing Knowledge: Figures, Narratives, and Practices
The Deconstructed Church: Understanding Emerging Christianity — Marti, Gerardo
c Decorated Horses (Illus. by Brett, Jeannie) — Patent, Dorothy Hinshaw
Decorating with the Five Elements of Feng Shui — Morris, Tisha
Decreation: The Last Things of All Creatures — Griffiths Paul J.
Dedicated to God: An Oral History of Cloistered Nuns — Reese, Abbie
Dedicated: Training Your Children to Trust and Follow Jesus — Houser, Jason
Deeds Done beyond the Sea: Essays on William of Tyre, Cyprus and the Military Orders Presented to Peter Edbury — Edgington, Susan B.
c Deeney I Feel Five! — Murguia, Bethanie
The Deep — Cutter, Nick
c The Deep Dark Wood (Illus. by Pye, Ali) — Hall, Algy Craig

c Deep Deep Sea (Illus. by Preston-Gannon, Frann) — Preston-Gannon, Frann
c The Deep Dish on Pizza! (Illus. by Guidera, Daniel) — Krensky, Stephen
Deep Down Dark: The Untold Stories of 33 Men Buried in a Chilean Mine, and the Miracle That Set Them Free (Read by Leyva, Henry). Audiobook Review — Tobar, Hector
Deep Down Dark: The Untold Stories of 33 Men Buried in a Chilean Mine, and the Miracle That Set Them Free — Tobar, Hector
The Deep End — Kearns, J.M.
The Deep End — Kong, Debra Purdy
Deep Ends: The J.G. Ballard Anthology 2014 — McGrath, Rick
Deep Lane — Doty, Mark
Deep Lane: Poems — Doty, Mark
Deep Lane — Doty, Mark
Deep Map Country: Literary Cartography of the Great Plains — Maher, Naramore Susan
c Deep Roots: How Trees Sustain Our Planet — Tate, Nikki
y Deep-Sea Exploration — Mara, Wil
y Deep Sea — Thor, Annika
c Deep Snow (Illus. by Martchenko, Michael) — Munsch, Robert
Deep South: Four Seasons on Back Roads — Theroux, Paul
The Deep State: The Fall of the Constitution and the Rise of a Shadow Government — Lofgren, Mike
Deep Violence: Military Violence, War Play, and the Social Life of Weapons — Bourke, Joanna
Deep Work: Rules for Focused Success in a Distracted World — Newport, Cal
A Deeper Cut — Haymore, Sheri Wren
The Deeper Genome: Why There Is More to the Human Genome Than Meets the Eye — Parrington, John
Deeper Than Indigo: Tracing Thomas Machell, Forgotten Explorer — Balfour-Paul, Jenny
The Deepest Human Life: An Introduction to Philosophy for Everyone — Samuelson, Scott
Deer — Fletcher, John
Deer Island — Ansell, Neil
c The Deer with the Purple Nose (Illus. by Brillhart, Wayne L.) — Brillhart, Wayne L.
The Defeat of Solidarity: Anger and Politics in Postcommunist Europe — Ost, David
Defeating Depression — Stone, Howard W.
Defeating Lee: A History of the Second Corps, Army of the Potomac — Kreiser, Lawrence A.
The Defence of a Madman — Strindberg, August
Defend and Befriend: The U.S. Marine Corps and Combined Action Platoons in Vietnam — Southard, John
y Defend or Die: The Siege of Hong Kong — Chan, Gillian
The Defender: How the Legendary Black Newspaper Changed America — Michael, Ethan
The Defender: How the Legendary Black Newspaper Changed America — Michaeli, Ethan
c The Defenders: Bully Patrol (Illus. by Butler, Tad) — Carter, Monika
Defenders of the Unborn: The Pro-Life Movement before Roe v. Wade — Williams, Daniel K.
Defending a New Nation, 1783-1811 — Maas, John R.
Defending Associative Duties — Seglow, Jonathan
Defending Beef: The Case for Sustainable Meat Production — Niman, Nicolette Hahn
Defending the History of Economic Thought — Kates, Steven
Defending the Motherland: The Soviet Women Who Fought Hitler's Aces — Vinogradova, Lyuba
Defending the Revolution: The Church of Scotland, 1689-1716 — Stephen, Jeffrey
Defensive Environmentalists and the Dynamics of Global Reform — Rudel, Thomas K.
c The Defiant — Quint, M.
y The Defiant — Stasse, Lisa M.
Defiant — Sumner-Smith, Karina
Defiant Diplomat: George Platt Waller, American Consul in Nazi-Occupied Luxembourg, 1939-1941 — Fletcher, Willard Allen
The Defiant Life of Vera Figner: Surviving the Russian Revolution — Hartnett, Lynne Ann
c Define Normal (Read by Lakin, Christine). Audiobook Review — Peters, Julie Anne
Defining Beauty: The Body in Ancient Greek Art — Jenkins, Ian
Defining Boundaries in al-Andalus: Muslims, Christians and Jews in Islamic Iberia — Safran, Janina

Defining Deutschtum: Political Ideology, German Identity, and Music-Critical Discourse in Liberal Vienna — Brodbeck, David
Defining Digital Humanities: A Reader — Terras, Melissa
y Defining Documents in American History: American West, 1836-1900
y Defining Documents in American History: The 1930s — Shally-Jensen, Michael
Defining Greek Narrative — Cairns, Douglas L.
Defining Student Success: The Role of School and Culture — Nunn, Lisa M.
Definitely, Maybe, Yours — Reed, Lissa
The Definitive Personal Assistant and Secretarial Handbook — France, Sue
Defizitare Souverane? Fruhneuzeitliche Rechtfertigungsnarrative im Konflikt/Deficient Monarchs? Legitimation in Conflict
Defying Convention: U.S. Resistance to the UN Treaty on Women's Rights — Baldez, Lisa
The Degenerate Muse: American Nature, Modernist Poetry, and the Problem of Cultural Hygiene — Schulze, Robin G.
Degraded Work: The Struggle at the Bottom of the Labor Market — Doussard, Marc
Degrees of Freedom: The Origins of Civil Rights in Minnesota, 1865-1912 — Green, William D.
Degrees of Inequality: How the Politics of Higher Education Sabotaged the American Dream — Mettler, Suzanne
Delectable Negro: Human Consumption and Homoeroticism within US Slave Culture — Woodard, Vincent
Delete: A Design History of Computer Vapourware — Atkinson, Paul
Deliberating American Monetary Policy: A Textual Analysis — Schonhardt-Bailey, Cheryl
The Delicate Fire — Mitchison, Naomi
y Delicate Monsters — Kuehn, Stephanie
A Delicate Wildness: The Life and Loves of David Thomson, 1914-1988 — Vignoles, Julian
Delicious Decadence: The Rediscovery of French Eighteenth-Century Painting in the Nineteenth Century — Faroult, Guillaume
Delicious Foods (Read by Hannaham, James). Audiobook Review — Hannaham, James
Delicious Foods — Hannaham, James
Deliciously Dairy Free: Fresh and Simple Lactose-Free Recipes for Healthy Eating Every Day — Waters, Lesley
Deliciously Ella: 100+ Easy, Healthy, and Delicious Plant-Based, Gluten-Free Recipes — Woodward, Ella
y Delilah Dusticle — York, A.J.
Delinquent Palaces — Chapman, Danielle
The Delinquents — Asmus, James
The Delirium of Hope — Remender, Rick
Delius and His Music — Lee-Brownie, Martin
y Deliverance — Redwine, C.J.
The Deliverance of Others: Reading Literature in a Global Age — Palumbo-Liu, David
Delphi: A History of the Center of the Ancient World — Scott, Michael
The Deluge: The Great War, America and the Remaking of the Global Order, 1916-1931 — Tooze, Adam
The Deluge: The Great War and the Remaking of Global Order, 1916-1931 — Tooze, Adam
y Delusion Road — Aker, Don
The Deluxe Food Lover's Companion, 2d ed. — Herbst, Ron
Deluxe Jim Crow: Civil Rights and American Health Policy, 1935-1954 — Thomas, Karen Kruse
Dem Dry Bones: Preaching, Death, and Hope — Powery, Luke A.
The Dema and the Christ: My Engagement and Inner Dialogue with the Cultures and Religions of Melanesia — Mantovani, Ennio
Demand the Impossible: Science Fiction and the Utopian Imagination — Moylan, Tom
Dementia: Living in the Memories of God — Swinton, John
Demeter, Isis, Vestra, and Cybele. Studies in Greek and Roman Religion in Honour of Giulia Sfameni Gasparro — Mastrocinque, A.
Demilitarization in the Contemporary World — Stearns, Peter N.
The Demise of Virtue in Virtual America: The Moral Origins of the Great Recession — Bosworth, David
y Democracy (Illus. by Di Donna, Annie) — Papadatos, Alecos

Democracy (Illus. by Papadatos, Alecos) — *Papadatos, Alecos*
Democracy and Justice: Collected Writings — *Reiner, Desiree Ramos*
Democracy Assistance from the Third Wave: Polish Engagement in Belarus and Ukraine — *Pospieszna, Paulina*
Democracy Declassified: Oversight and the Secrecy Dilemma in Liberal States — *Colaresi, Michael P.*
Democracy, Gender and Social Policy in Russia: A Wayward Society — *Chandler, Andrea*
Democracy in Black: How Race Still Enslaves the American Soul — *Glaude, Eddie S., Jr.*
Democracy in the Dark: The Seduction of Government Secrecy — *Schwarz, Frederick A.O., Jr.*
Democracy in the Making: How Activist Groups Form — *Blee, Kathleen M.*
Democracy of Sound: Music Piracy and the Remaking of American Copyright in the Twentieth Century — *Cummings, Alex Sayf*
Democracy Prevention: The Politics of the US-Egyptian Alliance — *Brownlee, Jason*
Democracy without Justice in Spain: The Politics of Forgetting — *Encarnacioon, Omar G.*
Democratic by Design: How Carsharing, Co-Ops and Community Land Trusts Are Reinventing America — *Metcalf, Gabriel*
Democratic Institutions and Authoritarian Rule in Southeast Europe — *Dolenec, Danijela*
Democratic Renewal and the Mutual Aid Legacy of US Mexicans — *Pycior, Julie Leininger*
Democratic Uprisings in the New Middle East: Youth, Technology, Human Rights, and US Foreign Policy — *Monshipouri, Mahmood*
Democratization and Authoritarianism in the Arab World — *Diamond, Larry*
Democratizing Texas Politics: Race, Identity, and Mexican American Empowerment, 1945-2002 — *Marquez, Benjamin*
Demokratie in der Geschichte - Herausforderungen in der Gegenwart
c Demolition Dad (Illus. by Ogilvie, Sara) — *Earle, Phil*
c Demolition Dad — *Earle, Phil*
y The Demon Conspiracy — *Gemmill, R.L.*
c The Demon Curse — *Nicholson, Simon*
c Demon Dentist (Illus. by Ross, Tony) — *Walliams, David*
c Demon Derby — *Harris, Carrie*
A Demon Summer (Read by Page, Michael). Audiobook Review — *Malliet, G.M.*
Demonizing the Jews: Luther and the Protestant Church in Nazi Germany — *Probst, Christopher J.*
c Demons and Dragons (Illus. by Chilvers, Nigel) — *Peebles, Alice*
Demons and Spirits of the Land: Ancestral Lore and Practices — *Lecouteux, Claude*
Demosthenes: Selected Speeches — *Waterfield, Robin*
Den Krieg Denken: Kriegswahrnehmung und Kriegsdeutung in Mitteleuropa in der Ersten Halfte des 17. Jahrhunderts
Den Protest Regieren. Staatliches Handeln, Neue Soziale Bewegungen und Linke Organisationen in den 1970er- und 1980er-Jahren
Deng Xiaoping: A Revolutionary Life — *Pantsov, Alexander V.*
A Deniable Death — *Seymour, Gerald*
Denial of Violence: Ottoman Past, Turkish Present, and Collective Violence against the Armenians, 1789-2009 — *Gocek, Fatma Muge*
Denkmal Film, vol. 1: Der Film als Kulturerbe — *Bohn, Anna*
Denkmaler Demokratischer Umbruche nach 1945 — *Veen, Hans-Joachim*
y Denton Little's Deathdate (Read by Rubin, Lance). Audiobook Review — *Rubin, Lance*
y Denton Little's Deathdate — *Rubin, Lance*
c Denver Broncos — *Zappa, Marcia*
Departure — *Riddle, A.G.*
Deploying Orientalism in Culture and History: From Germany to Central and Eastern Europe — *Hodkinson, James*
Deportiraneto na evreite ot Vardarska Makedoniia, Belomorska Trakiia i Pirot, mart 1943 g. Dokumenti ot b'lgarskite arkhivi — *Danova, Nadia*
Depraved Heart — *Cornwell, Patricia*
Depth — *Rosen, Lev AC*
The Depth of the Human Person: A Multidisciplinary Approach — *Welker, Michael*
Der Antikommunismus in seiner Epoche. Weltanschauung, Bewegung, Regierende Partei

Der Arbeitende Korper im Spannungsfeld von Krankheit und Gesundheit. Neue Perspektiven auf die Gewerkschaftsgeschichte V
Der Aufbruch zur Demokratie in Ostmitteleuropa zwischen den Kriegen. Notwendige Bausteine fur ein Gesamtbild Europaischer Demokratiegeschichte
Der Ausstellungsraum im Kunstmarkt
Der Bildhauer Hans Juncker: Wunderkind zwischen Spatrenaissance und Barock — *Richter, Thomas*
Der Bombenkrieg: Europa 1939-1945 — *Overy, Richard*
Der Briefschreiber Goethe — *Schone, Albrecht*
Der Deutsche Film im Kalten Krieg/Cinema Allemand et Guerre Froid — *Niemeyer, Christin*
Der Dollfuss-Mythos: Eine Biographie des Posthumen — *Dreidemy, Lucile*
Der Erste Weltkrieg in 100 Objekten — *Stiftung Deutsches Historisches Museum*
Der Erste Weltkrieg und die Christenheit: Ein Globaler Uberblick — *Greschat, Martin*
Der Europagedanke westeuropaischer faschistischer Bewegungen 1940-1945 — *Grunert, Robert*
"Der Farbfilm Marschiert!" Fruhe Farbfilmverfahren und NS-Propaganda 1933-1945 — *Alt, Dirk*
Der Faschismus in Europa: Wege der Forschung — *Schlemmer, Thomas*
Der George-Kreis und die Theosophie: Mit einem Exkurs zum Swastika-Zeichen bei Helena Blavatsky, Alfred Schuler und Stefan George — *Stottmeister, Jan*
Der Haftlingsfreikauf aus der DDR 1962/63-1989: Zwischen Menschenhandel und humanitaren Aktionen — *Wolbern, Jan Philipp*
Der Jansenismus--eine "katholische Haresie"? Das Ringen um Gnade, Rechtfertigung und die Autoritat Augustins in der fruhen Neuzeit — *Burkard, Dominik*
Der Kaiser schickt Soldaten aus: Ein Sarajevo-Roman — *Ferk, Janko*
Der Kapitalismus Entdeckt das Volk: Wie die Deutschen Grossbanken in den 1950er und 1960er Jahren zu Ihrer Privaten Kundschaft Kamen — *Gonser, Simon*
Der Klang des Gulag: Musik und Musiker in den Sowjetischen Zwangsarbeitslagern der 1920er- bis 1950er-Jahre — *Klause, Inna*
Der Konig von Asien: Alexander der Grosse Erobert Persien — *Unger, Steffen*
Der Konig von Midian: Paul Friedmann und sein Traum von einem Judenstaat — *Schoeps, Julius H.*
Der Kreml und die "Wende" 1989: Interne Analysen der Sowjetischen Fuhrung zum Fall der Kommunistischen Regime: Dokumente — *Stefan, Karner*
Der Krieg ist vorbei. Heimkehr - Trauma - Weiterleben
Der Lange Sommer der Theorie: Geschichte einer Revolte 1960-1990 — *Felsch, Philipp*
"Der Letzte der Ungerechten": Der "Judenalteste" Benjamin Murmelstein in Filmen 1942-1975 — *Loewy, Ronny*
Der letzte Gegenpapst: Felix V. Studien zu Herrschaftspraxis und Legitimationsstrategien, 1434-1451 — *Giessmann, Ursula*
Der Liber Ordinarius Hallensis 1532 (Staatsbibliothek Bamberg, Msc. Lit. 119): Liturgische Reformen am Neuen Stift in Halle an der Saale unter Albrecht Kardinal von Brandenburg — *Hamann, Matthias*
Der liebe und werthe Fried: Kriegskonzepte und Neutralitatsvorstellungen in der Fruhen Neuzeit — *Gotthard, Axel*
Der Militarisch-Medizinische Komplex in der Fruhen Neuzeit: Zum Verhaltnis von Militar, Medizin, Gesellschaft und Staat
Der offentliche Autor: Uber die Selbstinszenierung von Schriftstellern — *John-Wenndorf, Carolin*
Der Putsch gegen Gorbatschow und das Ende der Sowjetunion — *Lozo, Ignaz*
Der romische Kaiserhof in severischer Zeit — *Schope, Bjorn*
Der Rote Hiob: Das Leben des Werner Scholem — *Zadoff, Mirjam*
Der Schatten des grossen Konigs: Friedrich II und die Literatur — *De Bruyn, Wolfgang*
"Der Schimmelreiter": Novelle von Theodor Storm. Historisch-kritische Edition — *Eversberg, Gerd*
Der St. Galler Klosterplan: Faksimile, Begleittext, Beischriften und Ubersetzung. Mit einem Beitrag von Ernst Tremp — *Stiftsbibliothek St. Gallen*
Der "un-cerstandliche" Prophet: Paul Adler, ein Deutsch-Judischer Dichter — *Teufel, Annette*

Der "Unterricht der Visitatoren" und die Durchsetzung der Reformation in Kursachsen
Der verbannte Stratege: Xenophon und der Tod des Thukydides — *Nickel, Rainer*
Der verlorene Himmel: Glaube in Deutschland seit 1945 — *Grossbolting, Thomas*
Der Wiener Kongress: Die Neugestaltung Europas 1814/15 — *Duchhardt, Heinz*
Der Wiener Kongress: Die neugestaltung Europas 1814-1815 — *Duchhardt, Heinz*
Der Wille zum Wesen: Weltanschauungskultur, Charakterologisches Denken und Judenfeindschaft in Deutschland 1890-1940 — *Leo, Per*
Der Zweite Weltkrieg. Kulturtourismus und Politik
Derailing Democracy in Afghanistan: Elections in an Unstable Political Landscape — *Coburn, Noah*
y Derapages — *East, Genevieve*
c Derek Jeter's Ultimate Baseball Guide 2015 (Illus. by Jones, Damien) — *Dobrow, Larry*
Derek Roshier: Rethink/Re-entry — *Hockney, David*
Derivative Securities and Difference Methods — *Zhu, Youlan*
Derrida and Our Animal Others: Derrida's Final Seminar, 'The Beast and the Sovereign' — *Krell, David Farrell*
Des Apophtegmes a la Polyanthee: Erasme et le Genre des Dits Memorables — *Lobbes, Louis*
Des comptes d'apothicaires: Les epices dans la comptabilite de la Maison de Savoie — *Abbott, Fanny*
Descartes n'a pas dit [...&rqsb; Un repertoire des fausses idees sur l'auteur da Discours de la mathods, avec les elements utiles et une esquisse d'apologie — *Kambouchner, Denis*
Descartes' Temporal Dualism — *Waller, Rebecca LLoyd*
Descent (Read by Bray, R.C., with Sands, Xe). Audiobook Review — *Johnston, Tim*
The Descent — *Algonquin, Tim Johnston*
The Desert — *Welland, Michael*
Desert City Diva — *Fayman, Corey Lynn*
Desert God (Read by Grady, Mike). Audiobook Review — *Smith, Wilbur*
Desert Rising — *Grant, Kelley*
c Deserts — *Gray, Leon*
y Design a Skyscraper (Illus. by Aleksic, Vladimir) — *Koll, Hilary*
c Design a Skyscraper (You Do the Math). (Illus. by Aleksic, Vladimir) — *Koll, Hilary*
The Design and Statistical Analysis of Animal Experiments — *Bate, Simon T.*
Design by IKEA: A Cultural History — *Kristofferson, Sara*
y Design Diva (Illus. by Hagel, Brooke) — *Gurevich, Margaret*
c Design Line: History of Women's Fashion (Illus. by Mander, Sanna) — *Slee, Natasha*
Design Mom: How to Live with Kids: A Room-by-Room Guide — *Blair, Gabrielle Stanley*
The Design of Everyday Things — *Norman, Donald*
Design to Grow: How Coca-Cola Learned to Combine Scale & Agility (and How You Can Too). — *Butler, David*
Designer Crochet: 32 Patterns to Elevate Your Style, Sizes Small to 5X — *Mullett-Bowlsby, Shannon*
Designing Dixie: Tourism, Memory, and Urban Space in the New South — *Hillyer, Reiko*
Designing Fictions: Literature Confronts Advertising — *Ross, Michael*
Designing Here/Now: A Global Selection of Objects, Concepts and Spaces for the Future — *Chochinov, Allan*
Designing Online Information Literacy Games Students Want to Play — *Markey, Karen*
Designing Schools for Meaningful Professional Learning — *Bradley, Janice*
Designing the New American University — *Crow, Michael M.*
Designing Tito's Capital: Urban Planning, Modernism, and Socialism in Belgrade — *Le Normand, Brigitte*
Designing Training — *Hawks, Melanie*
Desire and Disaster in New Orleans: Tourism, Race, and Historical Memory — *Thomas, Lynnell L.*
Desire in the Canterbury Tales — *Scala, Elizabeth*
c Desmond Packet and the Mountain Full of Monsters — *Tatulli, Mark*
c Desolation Canyon — *London, Jonathan*
Desolation Sound — *Heston, Fraser C.*
Desordres createurs : L'invention politique a la faveur des troubles — *Mesnil, Emmanuelle Tixier du*

Despatches from the Front: Matthew Halton, Canada's Voice at War — Halton, David
Desperado — Bingham, Lisa
y Desperate Characters — Fox, Paula
Desperate Clarity: Chronicles of Intellectual Life, 1942 — Holland, Michael
A Desperate Fortune — Kearsley, Susanna
Desperate Magic: The Moral Economy of Witchcraft in Seventeenth-Century Russia — Kivelson, Valerie
Desperate Measures — Bannister, Jo
Desperate Shop Girls — Gersh, David L.
Desperation Passes — Hutcheon, Phil
Despots of Deseret — Townsend, Johnny
The Desserts of Jordi Roca: More Than 80 Sweet Recipes — Roca, Jordi
c Dessine-moi un Martien (Illus. by Lamontagne, Jacques) — Cote, Denis
Destination Dixie: Tourism and Southern History — Cox, Karen L.
Destination Hope: A Guidethrough Life's Unexpected Journeys — Nichol, Shellie
Destiny and Power: The American Odyssey of George Herbert Walker Bush — Meacham, Jon
Destiny: Step into Your Purpose — Jakes, T.D.
Destiny's Captive — Jenkins, Beverly
Destroyer Angel — Barr, Nevada
Destruction and Sorrow beneath the Heavens — Krasznahorkai, Laszlo
The Destruction of Da Derga's Hostel: Kingship and Narrative Artistry in a Mediaeval Irish Saga — O'Connor, Ralph
The Destruction of the Medieval Chinese Aristocracy — Tackett, Nicolas
Destruction Was My Beatrice: Dada and the Unmaking of the Twentieth Century — Rasula, Jed
Destructive and Terrorist Cults: A New Kind Slavery — Banisadr, Masoud
Detained and Deported: Stories of Immigrant Families Under Fire — Regan, Margaret
Detained: Emails and Musings from a Spiritual Journey through Abu Ghraib, Kandahar, and Other Garden Spots — Rees, Brian
Detective Fiction — Wells, William
c Detective Gordon: The First Case (Illus. by Spee, Gitte) — Nilsson, Ulf
c The Detective's Assistant — Hannigan, Kate
Determined Spirits: Eugenics, Heredity and Racial Regeneration in Anglo-American Spiritualist Writing, 1848-1930 — Ferguson, Christine
Determining the Shakespeare Canon: Arden of Faversham and A Lover's Complaint — Jackson, MacDonald P.
y The Detour — Bodeen, S.A.
Detour: Hollywood — Dickerson, William
y Detroit — Moussavi, Sam
Detroit Country Music: Mountaineers, Cowboys, and Rockabillies — Maki, Craig
Detroit Is Our Beat: Tales of the Four Horsemen — Estleman, Loren
Detroit Is Our Beat: Tales of the Four Horsemen — Estleman, Loren D.
Detroit: Race Riots, Racial Conflicts, and Efforts to Bridge the Racial Divide — Darden, Joe T.
Detroit Speed's How to Build a Pro Touring Car — Byrd, Tommy Lee
Deuteronomy-Kings as Emerging Authoritative Books: A Conversation — Edelman, Diana V.
Deutsch-Israelische Fussballfreundschaft. 8. Sporthistorische Konferenz Irsee
Deutsch-Polnische-Ukrainische Sommerakademie
Deutsch-Russische Arbeitsgesprache zu mittelalterlichen Handschriften und Drucken aus Halberstadt in russischen Bibliotheken — Bentzinger, Rudolf
Deutsche Altertumswissenschaftler im Amerikanischen Exil: Eine Rekonstruktion — Obermayer, Hans Peter
Deutsche Aussenpolitik: Von 1815 bis 1945 — Schollgen, Gregor
Deutsche Frauen in den Sudsee-Kolonien des Kaiserreichs: Alltag und Beziehungen zur indigenen Bevolkerung, 1884-1919 — Loosen, Livia
Deutsche Sportwissenschaft in der Weimarer Republik und im Nationalsozialismus, vol. 2: Die Geschichte der Deutschen Hochschule fur Leibesubungen 1919-1925 — Court, Jurgen
Deutschland - Russland: Stationen gemeinsamer Geschichte, Orte der Erinnerung: Band 3: Das 20. Jahrhundert — Altricher, Helmut
Deutschland und die Sowjetunion 1933 - 1941: Dokumente. Band 1: 30. Januar 1933 - 31. Oktober 1934 — Slutsch, Sergej

Devadatta's Poems — Beveridge, Judith
Develop Your Medical Intuition: Activate Your Natural Wisdom for Optimum Health and Well-being — Dillard, Sherrie
Developing Essential Understanding of Geometry and Measurement, Grades 3-5 — Dougherty, Barbara J.
Developing Essential Understanding of Geometry and Measurement, Pre-K-Grade 2 — Godenberg, E. Paul
Developing Excellent Care for People Living with Dementia in Care Homes — Baker, Caroline
Developing Minds — LaPoma, Jonathan
Developing Successful Social Media Plans in Sport Organizations — Sanderson, Jimmy
Developing Young Minds: From Conception to Kindergarten — Shore, Rebecca
The Development of Ethics: A Historical and Critical Study — Irwin, Terence
Development, Power, and the Environment — Islam, Md Saidul
Developmental Biology — Gilbert, Scott F.
Developments in Central and East European Politics — White, Stephen
Deviance and Risk on Holiday: An Ethnography of British Tourists in Ibiza — Briggs, Daniel
y Deviate — Clark, Tracy
The Devil: A New Biography — Almond, Philip C.
The Devil and the Doctor — Keller, David H.
y The Devil and Winnie Flynn (Illus. by Ostow, David) — Ostow, Micol
The Devil at Genesee Junction: The Murders of Kathy Bernhard and George-Ann Formicola, 6/66 — Benson, Michael
y Devil at My Heels: A Heroic Olympian's Astonishing Story of Survival as a Japanese POW in World War II — Zamperini, Louis
The Devil in Jerusalem — Ragen, Naomi
The Devil in the Valley — Freeman, Castle
y The Devil Is a Part-Timer (Illus. by Oniku) — Wagahara, Satoshi
The Devil Is Here in These Hills: West Virginia's Coal Miners and Their Battle for Freedom — Green, James
Devil of Delphi — Siger, Jeffrey
The Devil Takes a Bride — London, Julia
The Devil Takes Half — Serafim, Leta
The Devil That Never Dies: The Rise and Threat of Global Antisemitism — Goldhagen, Daniel Jonah
The Devil Wears Spurs — Lane, Soraya
The Devil Will Come — Cooper, Glenn
The Devil Wins: A History of Lying from the Garden of Eden to the Enlightenment — Denery, Dallas G.
The Devil Wins: A History of Lying from the Garden of Eden to the Enlightenment — Denery, Dallas G., II
The Devil Wins: A History of Lying from the Garden of Eden to the Enlightenment — Denery, Dallas G., II
The Devil Within: Possession and Exorcism in the Christian West — Levack, Brian P.
y The Devil You Know — Doller, Trish
The Devil You Know. Audiobook Review — de Mariaffi, Elisabeth
y The Devil You Know — de Mariaffi, Elisabeth
c The Devil You Know — Dollar, Trish
y The Devil You Know — Doller, Trish
y Devil You Know — MacPhail, Catherine
The Devils' Alliance: Hitler's Pact with Stalin, 1939-1941 — Moorhouse, Roger
Devils and Dust — Rhoades, J.D.
y The Devil's Angel — Brooks, Kevin
The Devil's Bag Man — Mansbach, Adam
Devil's Bridge — Fairstein, Linda
The Devil's Chessboard: Allen Dulles, the CIA, and the Rise of America's Secret Government — Talbot, David
Devil's Daughter — Michele, Hope Schenk-de
The Devil's Detective — Unsworth, Simon Kurt
y The Devil's Dreamcatcher — Hosie, Donna
y The Devil's Engine: Hellraisers — Smith, Alexander Gordon
The Devil's Financial Dictionary — Zweig, Jason
The Devil's Game — Chercover, Sean
The Devil's Handwriting: Precoloniality and the German Colonial State in Qingdao, Samoa, and Southwest Africa — Steinmetz, George
Devil's Harbor — Gilly, Alex
y The Devil's Intern — Hosie, Donna
The Devil's Making — Haldane, Sean
The Devil's Making — Hatdane, Sean
The Devil's Milk: A Social History of Rubber — Tully, John

The Devil's Monk — Fraser, Sara
y The Devil's Only Friend — Wells, Dan
The Devil's Own — Brown, Sandra
The Devil's Pleasure Palace: The Cult of Critical Theory and the Subversion of the West — Walsh, Michael
y Devil's Pocket — Dixon, John
The Devil's Seal: A Mystery of Ancient Ireland — Tremayne, Peter
The Devil's Share (Read by Marlo, Coleen). Audiobook Review — Stroby, Wallace
The Devil's Share — Stroby, Wallace
c Devin Rhodes Is Dead — Kam, Jennifer
The Devine Within: Selectrd Writings on Enligtenment. — Huxley, Aldous
y Devon Day and the Sweetwater Kid: Down the Owlhoot Trail — Hays, J.E.S.
c Devon: The Wild Adventures of Devon and Friends — Marcus, Elena N.
The Devonshire Manuscript: A Women's Book of Courtly Poetry — Douglas, Lady Margaret
DevOps: A Software Architect's Perspective — Bass, Len
y Devoted (Read by Grace, Jennifer). Audiobook Review — Mathieu, Jennifer
y Devoted — Mathieu, Jennifer
Devoted in Death — Robb, J.D.
Devotion — Barber, Ros
Devotion: An Epic Story of Heroism, Friendship, and Sacrifice — Makos, Adam
Dewdrops — Morris, Jessica L.
c Dewey Bob (Illus. by Schachner, Judy) — Schachner, Judy
DeWitt Clinton & Amos Eaton: Geology and Power in Early New York — Spangael, David I.
Dexter Is Dead — Lindsay, Jeff
c Dexter the Courageous Koala — Blackadder, Jesse
c Dia de Los Muertos (Illus. by Ballesteros, Carles) — Thong, Roseanne Greenfield
Diaboliques: Six Tales of Decadence — Barbey d'Aurevilly, Jules
The Diachrony of Negation — Mosegaard Hansen, Maj-Britt
Diakonia Studies: Critical Issues in Ministry — Collins, John N.
Dialect in Film and Literature — Hodson, Jane
Dialog und Debatte in der Spatantike — Cameron, Averil
Dialogic Aspects of the Cuban Novel of the 1990s — Dorado-Otero, Angela
Dialysis — Frieden, Lisa
Diamond — Elyot, Justine
y Diamond Boy — Williams, Michael (b. 1962-)
The Diamond Caper — Mayle, Peter
Diamond Grove Slave Tree — Cavazos, Xavier
Diamond Head — Wong, Cecily
c The Diamond Mystery (Illus. by Willis, Helena) — Widmark, Martin
Diamond of Jeru. Audiobook Review — L'Amour, Louis
y The Diamond Thief — Gosling, Sharon
Diamonds and Pirates — Labriola, Jerry
Diamonds for Death — Randall, Gregory C.
Diamonds in the Rough: A History of Alabama's Cahaba Coal Field — Day, James Sanders
Diana Cooper — Ziegler, Philip
Diane von Furstenberg: A Life Unwrapped — Diliberto, Gioia
The Diaries of John Gregory Bourke, vol. 5: May 23, 1881-August 26, 1881 — Robinson, Charles M., III
Diario de mascaras — Valenzuela, Luisa
Diary af a Deadhead: A Wild Magical Ride into the World of Sound and Vibration — Carson, Candace D.
Diary and Autobiographical Writings of Louisa Catherine Adams, 2 vols. — Graham, Judith S.
Diary of a Bad Year — Smith, Peter J.
y Diary of a Basketball Hero (Illus. by Heinrich, Sally) — Flint, Shamini
y Diary of a Golf Pro (Illus. by Heinrich, Sally) — Flint, Shamini
y Diary of a Haunting — Verano, M.
Diary of a Jackwagon — Hawkins, Tim
c Diary of a Mad Brownie (Read by Full cast). Audiobook Review — Coville, Bruce
c Diary of a Mad Brownie (Illus. by Kidby, Paul) — Coville, Bruce
Diary of a Southern Refugee during the War — Robertson, James I., Jr.
The Diary of a Suicidal Artist — Pfundt, Andreas Peter
The Diary of a Teenage Girl — Heller, Marielle

c Diary of a Time Traveler (Illus. by Stevenson, Nicholas) — *Long, David*
c Diary of a Time Traveller (Illus. by Stevenson, Nicholas) — *Long, David*
y Diary of a Waitress: The Not-So-Glamorous Life of a Harvey Girl — *Meyer, Carolyn*
c Diary of a Wimpy Kid: The Long Haul — *Kinney, Jeff*
Diary of an Accidental Wallflower — *McQuiston, Jennifer*
Diary of an Airdale — *Ericson, P.J.*
c The Diary of Dennis the Menace: Bash Street Bandit! — *Butler, Steve*
Diary of General Patrick Gordon of Auchleuchries, 1635-99, vol. 3-5 — *Fedosov, Dmitry*
The Diary of Nannie Haskins Williams: A Southern Woman's Story of Rebellion and Reconstruction, 1863-1890 — *Uffelman, Minoa d.*
The Diary of Samuel Pepys, 1660-1669, 3 vols. (Read by Pugh, Leighton). Audiobook Review — *Pepys, Samuel*
Diary of the Fall — *Laub, Michel*
Diaspo/Renga — *Flacker, Marilyn*
Diaspora Online: Identity Politics and Romanian Migrants — *Trandafoiu, Ruxandra*
Diasporas of the Mind: Jewish and Postcolonial Writing and the Nightmare of History — *Cheyette, Bryan*
Diasporic Chineseness after the Rise of China: Communities and Cultural Production — *Kuehn, Julia*
The Dice Cup — *Fuller, John*
Dick Dowling: Galway's Hero of Confederate Texas — *Collins, Timothy*
Dick Francis's Damage — *Francis, Felix*
Dickens and the Business of Death — *Wood, Claire*
Dickens, His Parables, and His Reader — *Lewis, Linda M.*
y The Dickens Mirror — *Bick, Ilsa J.*
Dickens's London: Perception, Subjectivity and Phenomenal Urban Multiplicity — *Wolfreys, Julian*
Dictablanda: Politics, Work, and Culture in Mexico, 1938-1968 — *Gillingham, Paul*
Dictablanda: Politics, Work, and Culture in Mexico — *Gillingham, Paul*
Dictator — *Harris, Robert*
Dictators at War and Peace — *Weeks, Jessica L.P.*
Dictatorships and Democracy in African Development: The Political Economy of Public Goods Provision in Nigeria — *LeVan, A. Carl*
c Dictionary for Kids: The Essential Guide to Math Terms, 4th ed. — *Fitzgerald, Theresa R.*
A Dictionary for the Modern Trumpet Player — *Koehler, Elisa*
A Dictionary of Law, 8th ed. — *Law, Jonathan*
Dictionary of Music Education — *Ely, Mark C.*
A Dictionary of Mutual Understanding — *Copleton, Jackie*
Dictionary of Non-Philosophy — *Laruelle, Francois*
The Dictionary of Science for Gardeners: 6000 Scientific Terms Explored and Explained — *Allaby, Michael*
The Dictionary of Science for Gardens: 6000 Scientific Terms for Explored and Explained — *Allaby, Michael*
Dictionary of the American West — *Blevins, Win*
Dictionary of Untranslatables: A Philosophical Lexicon — *Cassin, Barbara*
Dictionnaire des Gens de Couleur dans la France Moderne (Debut XVIe s.-1792), vol. 2: La Bretagne — *Noel, Erick*
Dictionnaire du livre de jeunesse: la litterature d'enfance et de jeunesse en France — *Nieres-Chevrel, Isabelle*
c Did Christopher Columbus Really Discover America?: And Other Questions about the New World — *Berne, Emma Carlson*
Did God Really Command Genocide? — *Copan, Paul*
y Did I Mention I Love You? — *Maskame, Estelle*
Did You Ever Have a Family — *Clegg, Bill*
Did You Ever See a Dream Walking? American Conservative Thought in the Twentieth Century — *Buckley, William F., Jr.*
c Did You Know That I Love You? (Illus. by Pierce, Christa)
c Did You Know That I Love You? (Illus. by Pierce, Christa) — *Pierce, Christa*
Didache: The Teaching of the Twelve Apostles — *Jefford, Clayton N.*
Die Again Tomorrow — *Peikoff, Kira*
Die Ahnen der hochmittelalterlichen deutschen Konigen, Kaiser und ihrer Gemahlinnen: Ein kommentiertes Tafelwerk, vol. 3: 1198-1250 — *Hlawitschka, Eduard*
Die allgemeine Altersrentenversorgung in der — *Mucke, Lukas*
Die Ambivalenz des Guten: Menschenrechte in der Internationalen Politik seit den 1940ern — *Eckel, Jan*
Die amerikanische Reeducation-Politik nach 1945: Interdisziplinare Perspektiven auf "America's Germany" — *Gerund, Katharina*
"Die Arbeiterfrage soll mit Hilfe von KZ-Haftlingen Gelost Werden": Zwangsarbeit in KZ-Aussenlagern auf dem Gebiet der Heutigen Tschechischen Republik — *Adam, Alfons*
Die Autonomie der Routine: Wie im 12. Jahrhundert das Englische Schatzamt Entstand — *Kypta, Ulla*
Die Belasteten: 'Euthanasie' 1939-1945: Eine Gesellschaftsgeschichte — *Aly, Gotz*
Die Bildung der Geisteswissenschaften: Zur Genese einer Sozialen Konstruktion zwischen Diskurs und Feld — *Hamann, Julian*
Die bohmischen Lander in den Wiener Zeitschriften und Almanachen des Vormarz, 1805-1848 — *Marinelli-Konig, Gertraud*
Die Bombe als Option: Motive fur den Aufbau einer atomtechnischen Infrastruktur in der Bundesrepublik bis 1963 — *Hanel, Tilmann*
Die Buchse der Pandora: Geschichte des Ersten Weltkrieges — *Leonhard, Jorn*
Die "Cantiones Sacrae" (1625) von Heinrich Schutz - Entstehungsbedingungen im konfessionellen Kontext des fruhen 17. Jahrhunderts
Die Darstellung des Inkommensurablen in der Geschichtskultur des 19. Jahrhunderts
Die Deportation der Juden aus Berlin: Die nationalsozialistische Vernichtungspolitik und das Sammellager Grosse Hamburger Strasse — *Jah, Akim*
Die Deutschen Dominikaner und Dominikanerinnen 1221-1515
Die Donau von 1740 bis 1875: Eine kulturwissenschaftliche Untersuchung — *Qian, Kefei*
Die Entdeckung der Dritten Welt: Dekolonisierung und Neue Radikale Linke in Frankreich — *Kalter, Christoph*
Die Erfindung der Reinheit: Eine andere Geschichte der fruhen Neuzeit — *Burschel, Peter*
Die Etrusker — *Bubenheimer-Erhart, Friederike*
Die Externsteine. Ein Denkmal als Objekt wissenschaftlicher Forschung und Projektionsflache volkischer Vorstellungen
Die fabelhaften Bekenntnisse des Genossen Alfred Kurelia: Eine biografische Spurensuche — *Schaad, Martin*
Die Farben hofischer Korper: Farbattribuierung und hofische Identitat in mittelhochdeutschen Artus- und Tristanromane — *Oster, Carolin*
Die Fremde als Heimat: Heimatkunst, Kolonialismus, Expeditionen — *Parr, Rolf*
Die Gegluckte Revolution: Das Politische und der Umbruch in Polen 1976-1997 — *Zaganczyk-Neufeld, Agnieszka*
Die Geschichte der Schweiz — *Kreis, Georg*
Die Geschichte des Tonmischpults: Die technische Entwicklung der Mischpulte und der Wandel der medialen Produktionsverfahren im Tonstudio von den 1920er-Jahren bis heute — *Smyrek, Volker*
Die Geschwindigkeitsfabrik: Eine Fragmentarische Kulturgeschichte des Autounfalls — *Bickenbach, Matthias*
Die gregorianischen Gesange des Essener Liber ordinarius: Transkription und vergleichende Untersuchungen zu den Gesangen aus den Handschriften Essen Hs. 19 und Dusseldorf Ms. C 47 — *Becker, Wolfgang*
Die Griechische Gesellschaft: Eine Sozialgeschichte der Archaischen und Klassischen Zeit — *Schmitz, Winfried*
Die Grosse Depression: Die Weltwirtschaftskrise 1929-1939 — *Hesse, Jan-Otmar*
Die Herausforderungen des "Kurzen Jahrhunderts": Die Deutsche und Italienische Geschichte und Geschichtswissenschaft zwischen Krieg, Diktatur und Demokratie
Die I Will Not — *Rizzolo, S.K.*
Die Interaktion von Herrschern und Eliten in imperialen Ordnungen
Die Internationale der Konservativen: Transnationale Elitenzirkel und private Aussenpolitik in Westeuropa seit 1945 — *Grossmann, Johannes*
Die Kampfgruppe Gegen Unmenschlichkeit (KgU): Widerstand und Spionage im Kalten Krieg 1948-1959 — *Heitzer, Enrico*
Die Karolinger: Herrscher und Reich — *Ubl, Karl*
Die Katholische Kirche im Ersten Weltkrieg: Zwischen Nationalismus und Friedenswillen — *Latzel, Martin*
Die Kirchliche Krise des Spatmittelalters: Schisma, Konziliarismus und Konzilien — *Muller, Heribert*
Die Klage des Kunstlers
Die Konfessionalisierungparadigma: Leistungen, Probleme, Grenzen — *Brockmann, Thomas*
Die "Konstanzer Chronik" Gebhart Dachers: "By des Byschoffs zyten Volgiengen disz Nachgeschriben ding vnd Sachen ... ". Codex Sangallensis 646: Edition und Kommentar — *Wolff, Sandra*
Die Konsumentenstadt - Konsumenten in der Stadt des Mittelalters
Die Konzilien der karolingischen Teilreiche 875-911/Concilia aevi Karolini DCCCLXXV-DCCCCXI — *Hartmann, Wilfried*
Die Kunst Gehort dem Volke? Volkskunst in der Fruhen DDR zwischen Politischer Lenkung und Asthetischer Praxis — *Kuhn, Cornelia*
Die Medizinische Fakultat der Universitat Wien im Mittelalter: Von der Grundung bis zum Tod Kaiser Maximilians I. 1519 — *Tuisl, Elisabeth*
Die Metaphorik der Autobahn: Literatur, Kunst, Film und Architektur nach 1945 — *Rohnert, Jan*
Die mittelalterliche Sakramentsnische auf Gotland (Schweden): Kunst und Liturgie — *Kroesen, Justin*
Die mittelalterlichen Glasmalereien in Nurnberg: Sebalder Stadtseite — *Scholz, Hartmut*
Die Napoleonischen Kriege als Europaischer Erinnerungsort?
Die Neue Ordnung auf dem Alten Kontinent: Eine Geschichte des Neoliberalen Europa — *Ther, Philipp*
Die Papste und die Einheit der Lateinischen Welt
Die Politik des Traumas: Gewalterfahrungen und Psychisches Leid in den USA, in Deutschland und im Israel/Palastina-Konflikt — *Brunner, Jose*
Die politische Rolle des FDGB-Feriendienstes in der DDR: Sozialtourismus im SED-Staat — *Schaufuss, Thomas*
Die Prager Botschaftsfluchtlinge 1989: Geschichte und Dokumente — *Vodicka, Karel*
Die Presse in der Julikrise 1914: Die Internationale Berichterstattung und der Weg in den Ersten Weltkrieg — *Geiss, Peter*
Die Rehabilitierung des Opfers: Zum Dialog zwischen Rene Girard und Raymund Schwager um die Angemessenheit der Rede vom Opfer im christlichen Kontext — *Moosbrugger, Mathias*
Die Reisetagebucher — *Fontane, Theodor*
Die romische Stadt: Eine kurze Geschichte — *Zanker, Paul*
Die Russische Revolution und das Schicksal der Russischen Juden: Eine Debatte in Berlin 1922/23 — *Schlogel, Karl*
Die Scharfung des Quellenblicks: Forschungspraktiken in der Geschichtswissenschaft 1840-1914 — *Saxer, Daniela*
Die SED in der Ara Honecker: Machtstrukturen, Entscheidungsmechanismen und Konfliktfelder in der Staatspartei 1971 bis 1989 — *Malycha, Andreas*
Die Sicherheit des Westens: Entstehung und Funktion der G7-Gipfel — *Bohm, Enrico*
Die Siegel der lateinischen Konige von Jerusalem — *Mayer, Hans Eberhard*
Die Stadt der Neuchristen: Konvertierte Juden und ihre Nachkommen im Trani des Spatmittelalters zwischen Inklusion und Exklusion — *Scheller, Benjamin*
Die Sterbe- und Ewigkeitslieder in Deutschen Lutherischen Gesangbuchern des 17. Jahrhunderts — *Lorbeer, Lukas*
Die Stuhlbruder des Speyerer Domstifts: Betbruder, Kirchendiener und Almosener des Reichs — *Gutermann, Sven*
Die Stunde der Frauen: Zwischen Monarchie, Weltkrieg und Wahlrecht 1913-1919 — *Meiners, Antonia*
Die Tagebucher I (1792-1801), vols. 1-5 — *Hatje, Frank*
Die Tauferherrschaft in Munster und die Reichsstande: Die politische, religiose und militarische Dimension eines Konflikts in den Jahren 1534 bis 1536 — *Vogler, Gunter*

Die Theorie der zentralen Orte in Israel und Deutschland: Zur Rezeption Walter Christallers im Kontext von Sharonplan und "Generalplan Ost" — Trezib, Joachim

Die Thule-Gesellschaft und die Kokuryukai: Geheimgesellschaften im Global-Historischen Vergleich — Jacob, Frank

Die Tondi mit Kaiserbildern in Venedig und Washington, D.C.

Die Transformation des Kirchenbegriffs in der Fruhaufklarung — Lehmann, Roland

Die Universitaten der DDR und der Mauerbau 1961 — Kratzner, Anita

"Die Unsichtbaren": Hilfsberufe in der Medizin und den Naturwissenschaften

Die Urkunden Philipps von Schwaben — Rzihacek, Andrea

Die Vereinigte Stahlwerke AG im Nationalsozialismus: Konzernpolitik zwischen Marktwirtschaft und Staatswirtschaft — Donges, Alexander

Die Vereinigten Staaten von Europa Sind Unser Ziel: Arbeiterbewegung und Europa im Fruhen 20. Jahrhundert — Buschak, Willy

Die Vermittlung des Unbegreiflichen: Darstellungen des Holocaust im Museum — Schoder, Angelika

Die versöhnten Burger: Der Zweite Weltkrieg in deutsch-niederlandischen Begegnungen 1945-2000 — Gundermann, Christine

Die vielsprachige Seele Kakaniens: Ubersetzen und Dolmetschen in der Habsburgermonarchie 1848 bis 1918 — Wolf, Michaela

Die Waffen-SS: Neue Forschungen — Schulte, Jan Erik

Die Waffenschmiede des "Dritten Reiches": Die deutsche Rustungsindustrie in Oberschlesien wahrend des Zweiten Weltkrieges — Sikora, Miroslav

Die Wahrsagekunst im Alten Orient: Zeichen des Himmels und der Erde — Maul, Stefan M.

"Die Wehrmacht der Deutschen Republik ist die Reichswehr": Die Deutsche Armee 1918-1921 — Keller, Peter

Die Welt in Bildern: Erfahrung und Evidenz in Friedrich J. Bertuchs "Bilderbuch fur Kinder" — Chakkalakal, Silvy

Die Wikinger und das Frankische Reich: Identitaten zwischen Konfrontation und Annaherung — Hofmann, Kerstin P.

Die Wirklichkeit der Geschichte: Wissenschaftstheoretische, Mediale und Lebensweltliche Aspekte eines (Post-)Konstruktivistischen Wirklichkeitsbegriffes in den Kulturwissenschaften — Haas, Stefan

Die Zweite Philippica als Flugschrift in der Spaten Republik — Ott, Frank-Thomas

y Diego's Crossing — Hough, Robert

Dienst, Verdienst und Distinktion: Furstliche Selbstbehauptungsstrategien der Hohenzollern im 15. Jahrhundert — Bourree, Katrin

The Diet Myth: The Real Science behind What We Eat — Spector, Tim

y Dietary Supplements: Harmless, Helpful, or Hurtful? — Goldsmith, Connie

Dietland (Read by Sands, Tara). Audiobook Review — Walker, Sarai

Dietland — Walker, Sarai

Dietrich & Riefenstahl: Hollywood, Berlin, and a Century in Two Lives — Wieland, Karin

Dieu, la nature et l'homme: L'originalite de l'Occident — Blay, Michel

Difference of a Different Kind: Jewish Constructions of Race during the Long Eighteenth Century — Idelson-Shein, Iris

A Different Class of Murder: The Story of Lord Lucan — Thompson, Laura

Different Every Time: The Authorised Biography of Robert Wyatt — O'Dair, Marcus

A Different Kind of Weather: A Memoir — Waldegrave, William

A Different Lie — Haas, Derek

c A Different Me — Blumenthal, Deborah

Differential Equations: Theory, Technique, and Practice. Second Edition — Krantz, Steven G.

The Difficult Art Of Giving: Patronage, Philanthropy, and the American Literary Market — Sawaya, Francesca

Difficult Decisions: Closing and Merging Academic Libraries — Holder, Sara

c Dig In! (Illus. by Peterson, Mary) — Jenson-Elliott, Cindy

The Dig — Jones, Cynan

Dig Two Graves — Powers, Kim

c Digby O'Day and the Great Diamond Robbery (Illus. by Vulliamy, Clara) — Hughes, Shirley

c Digby O'day in the Fast Lane (Illus. by Vulliamy, Clara) — Hughes, Shirley

c Digger and Daisy Go to the City (Illus. by Sullivan, Dana) — Young, Judy (b. 1956-)

c Digger and Daisy Go to the Doctor (Illus. by Sullivan, Dana) — Young, Judy (b. 1956-)

y Digger: The Dog Who Went to War — Wilson, Mark

c Diggers — West, David

c Digging a Hole to Heaven: Coal Miner Boys — Nelson, S. D.

c Digging a Hole to Heaven — Nelson, S.D.

c Digging for Dinos (Illus. by Burks, James) — Young, Jessica

c Digging for Stegosaurus: A Discovery Timeline — Holtz, Thomas R., Jr.

c Digging for Tyrannosaurus Rex: A Discovery Timeline — Holtz, Thomas R., Jr.

c Digging for Tyrannosaurus Rex: A Discovery Timeline (Illus. by Skrepnick, Michael) — Holtz, Thomas R., Jr.

The Digital Apocalypse — Groves, David

Digital Disconnect: How Capitalism Is Turning the Internet against Democracy — McChesney, Robert W.

The Digital Doctor: Hope, Hype, and Harm at the Dawn of Medicine's Computer Age — Wachter, Robert

Digital Gold: Bitcoin and the Inside Story of the Misfits and Millionaires Trying to Reinvent Money — Popper, Nathaniel

Digital Gold — Popper, Nathaniel

Digital Handmade: Craftsmanship and the New Industrial Revolution — Johnston, Lucy

Digital Humanities in Practice — Warwick, Claire

Digital Humanities in the Library: Challenges and Opportunities for Subject Specialists — Hartsell-Gundy, Arianne

Digital Is Destroying Everything: What the Tech Giants Won't Tell You about How Robots, Big Data and Algorithms Are Radically Remaking Your Future — Edwards, Andrew V.

Digital Memory and the Archive — Ernst, Wolfgang

Digital Modernism: Making it New in New Media — Pressman, Jessica

Digital Photography Complete Course — Taylor, David

Digital Shift: The Cultural Logic of Punctuation — Scheible, Jeff

Digital State: The Story of Minnesota's Computing Industry — Misa, Thomas J.

c Digital Technology — Jackson, Tom

Digital to the Core: Remastering Leadership for Your Industry, Your Enterprise, and Yourself — Raskino, Mark

Digitally Enabled Social Change: Activism in the Internet Age — Earl, Jennifer

Digitizing Medieval and Early Modern Material Culture — Nelson, Brent

Dignity and Destiny: Humanity in the Image of God — Kilner, John F.

The Dignity of Chartism — Thompson, Dorothy

Dilemmas of Adulthood: Japanese Women and the Nuances of Long-Term Resistance — Rosenberger, Nancy

c Dill & Bizzy: An Odd Duck and a Strange Bird (Illus. by Ericson, Lisa) — Ericson, Nora

c Dilly Dally Daisy — Fearing, Mark

y Dime — Frank, E.R.

Dime Stories — Fitzpatrick, Tony

The Dimension of Color: Robert Grosseteste's "De colore" — Grosseteste, Robert

The Dimensions of Consequentialism — Peterson, Martin

Dimestore — Smith, Lee

c Dindy and the Elephant — Laird, Elizabeth

Dine Perspectives: Revitalizing and Reclaiming Navajo Thought — Lee, Lloyd L.

c Dingle Dangle Scarecrow (Illus. by Cooper, Jenny) — Topp, Jools

c The Dining and Social Club for Time Travellers (Illus. by Feaver, Doug) — Kishimoto, Elyse

c Dining with ... Monsters! — Baruzzi, Agnese

Dining with the Georgians: A Delicious History — Kay, Emma

Dinner — Aira, Cesar

Dinner Most Deadly — South, Sheri Cobb

Dinner — Aira, Cesar

The Dinner Party: Judy Chicago and the Power of Popular Feminism, 1970-2007 — Gerhard, Jane F.

Dinner Pies: From Shepherd's Pies and Pot Pies to Turnovers, Quiches, Hand Pies, and More — Haedrich, Ken

Dinner Solved! 100 Ingenious Recipes That Make the Whole Family Happy, Including You! — Workman, Katie

c The Dinner That Cooked Itself — Hsyu, J.C.

Dinner with Buddha — Merullo, Roland

c Dino-Boarding (Illus. by Gott, Barry) — Wheeler, Lisa

c Dino-Dinners (Illus. by Granstrom, Brita) — Manning, Mick

c Dino-Mike and the T. Rex Attack — Aureliani, Franco

c Dino-Swimming (Illus. by Gott, Barry) — Wheeler, Lisa

c Dino Treasures (Illus. by Morrison, Cathy) — Donald, Rhonda Lucas

c Dinoblock (Illus. by Peskimo) — Franceschelli, Christopher

c Dinosaur Boy — Oakes, Cary Putman

c Dinosaur Boy Saves Mars — Oakes, Cory Putman

c Dinosaur Disco (Illus. by Parton, Daron) — Kelly, Deborah

The Dinosaur Lords — Milan, Victor

c Dinosaur Parade (Illus. by Halpern, Shari) — Halpern, Shari

c Dinosaur Pet (Illus. by Bowers, Tim) — Sedaka, Marc

c Dinosaur Police — McIntyre, Sarah

c Dinosaur Poo! (Illus. by Fox, Diane) — Fox, Christyan

c Dinosaur Rocket! (Illus. by Dale, Penny) — Dale, Penny

c Dinosaur Safari — Nosy Crow

c Dinosaur vs. Mommy (Illus. by Shea, Bob) — Shea, Bob

c Dinosaurs?! (Illus. by Prap, Lila) — Prap, Lila

c Dinosaurs! — Safran, Sheri

c Dinosaurs and Other Prehistoric Creatures (Illus. by Scrace, Carolyn) — Channing, Margot

Dinosaurs and Other Reptiles from the Mesozoic of Mexico — Rivera-Sylva, Hector E.

c The Dinosaurs Are Having a Party! (Illus. by Parsons, Garry) — Jones, Gareth P.

c Dinosaurs around the World — Alderton, David

c Dinosaurs from Head to Tail (Illus. by Moriya, Kwanchai) — Roderick, Stacey

c Dinosaurs Live On! And Other Fun Facts (Illus. by Spurgeon, Aaron) — DiSiena, Laura Lyn

c Dinosaurs Live On! And Other Fun Facts (Illus. by Spurgeon, Aaron) — Disiena, Laura Lyn

c Dinosaurs Living in My Hair (Illus. by Matsick, Anni) — Rose-Vallee, Jayne M.

c Dinosaurs of the Cretaceous — West, David

c Dinosaurs of the Jurassic — West, David

c Dinosaurs of the Triassic — West, David

c Dinosaurs! Pop-Up Paper Designs — Hawcock, David

c Dinosaurs Rule (Illus. by Minister, Peter) — Rake, Matthew

c Dinotrux Dig the Beach (Illus. by Gall, Chris) — Gall, Chris

Dionysus Resurrected: Perfrmances of Euripides' The Bacchae in a Globalizing World — Fischer-Lichte, Erika

The Diorama — Bendix, Sebastian

Diotima's Children: German Aesthetic Rationalism from Leibniz to Lessing — Beiser, Frederick

Dipingere coi colori adatti: 'I Malavoglia' e il romanzo moderno — Baldini, Alessio

Diplomacy at the Brink: Eisenhower, Churchill, and Eden in the Cold War — Watry, David M.

Diplomacy in Black and White: John Adams, Toussaint Louverture, and Their Atlantic World Alliance — Johnson, Ronald Angelo

The Diplomacy of Religion in Africa: The Last Manuscripts of Richard Gray — Taddia, Irma

Diplomacy's Value: Creating Security in 1920s Europe and the Contemporary Middle East — Rathbun, Brian C.

The Diplomatic Education of Franklin D. Roosevelt, 1882-1933 — Cross, Graham

Diplomatic Games: Sport, Statecraft, and International Relations since 1945 — Dichter, Heather L.

Diplomatie mit Gefuhl: Vertrauen, Misstrauen und die Aussenpolitik der Bundesrepublik Deutschland — Kreis, Reinhild

Dire le social dans le roman francophone contemporain — Bisanswa, Justin K.

Direct Action, Deliberation, and Diffusion: Collective Action After the WTO Protests in Seattle — Wood, Lesley J.

Diriger une grande entreprise au XXe siecle: L'elite industrielle francaise — Joly, Herve

The Dirt Cure: A Whole Food, Whole Planet Guide to Growing Healthy Kids in a Processed World — Shetreat-Klein, Maya
Dirtbag — Saucier, Aldric J.
c Dirty Air — Lawrence, Ellen
Dirty Blvd.: The Life and Music of Lou Reed — Levy, Aidan
Dirty Blvd: The Life and Music of Lou Reed — Levy, Aidan
Dirty Deals? An Encyclopedia of Lobbying, Political Influence, and Corruption — Handlin, Amy
The Dirty Dozen: 12 Nasty Fighting Techniques for Any Self-Defense Situation — Jordan, Larry
The Dirty Dust: Cre na Cille — O Cadhain, Mairtin
Dirty Old London: The Victorian Fight against Filth — Jackson, Lee
Dirty Rats? — Gustavson, Adam
c Dirty Rats? (Illus. by Gustavson, Adam) — Lunde, Darrin P.
c Dirty Rotten Vikings: Three Centuries of Longships, Looting, and Bad Behavior (Illus. by Mazzara, Mauro) — Clements, Jonathan
c Dirty Rotten Vikings: Three Centuries of Longships, Looting and Bad Behavior (Illus. by Mazzara, Mauro) — Sertori, J.M.
y Dirty Rush — Bell, Taylor
c The Dirty Trick (Illus. by Smith, Kim) — Falcone, L.M.
Dirty Weekend — Zahavi, Hellen
y Dirty Wings — McCarry, Sarah
Dirty Words and Filthy Pictures — Geltzer, Jeremy
Disability across the Developmental Life Span: For the Rehabilitation Counselor — Smart, Julie
Disability and Identity: Negotiating Self in a Changing Society — Darling, Rosalyn Benjamin
Disability and Justice: The Capabilities Approach in Practice — Riddle, Christopher A.
Disability and Passing: Blurring the Lines of Identity — Brune, Jeffrey A.
A Disability History of the United States — Nielsen, Kim E.
Disability in Eastern Europe and the Former Soviet Union: History, Policy and Everyday Life — Iarskaia-Smirnova, Elena
Disability Incarcerated: Imprisonment and Disability in the United States and Canada — Ben-Moshe, Liat
Disagreement — Frances, Bryan
y Disappear Home — Hurwitz, Laura
c Disappearance at Hangman's Bluff: A Felony Bay Mystery — Thompson, J.E.
The Disappearance Boy — Bartlett, Neil
y The Disappearance of Emily H. — Summy, Barrie
c The Disappearance of Tom Pile — Beck, Ian
The Disappeared — Ohlsson, Kristina
c The Disappearing — Torres, Jennifer
y Disappearing Act — Gaetz, Dayle Campbell
c The Disappearing Dolphins (Read by Swaim, Michael) — Kelman, Jennifer
The Disappearing Mestizo: Configuring Difference in the Colonial New Kingdom of Granada — Rappaport, Joanne
The Disarmed Heart — McCaslin, Susan
Disaster Drawn: Visual Witness, Comics, and Documentary Form — Chute, Hillary L.
The Disaster Profiteers: How Natural Disasters Make the Rich Richer and the Poor Even Poorer — Mutter, John C.
The Disaster Profiteers — Mutter, John C.
c Disaster Science Series
Disaster Writing: The Cultural Politics of Catastrophe in Latin America — Anderson, Mark D.
Disasters and the American State — Roberts, Patrick S.
The Disasters of Violence, War and Extremism
The Discerning Gentleman's Guidebook to Britain's American Colonies: The 1770's Edition — Rotherham, Lee
The Disciples According to Mark: Markan Redaction in Current Debate — Black, C. Clifton
Disciples: The World War II Missions of the CIA Directors Who Fought for Wild Bill Donovan — Waller, Douglas
Discipline and Indulgence: College Football, Media, and the American Way of Life during the Cold War — Montez de Oca, Jeffrey
Disciplining Terror: How Experts Invented "Terrorism" — Stampnitsky, Lisa
Disciplining the Poor: Neoliberal Paternalism and the Persistent Power of Race — Soss, Joe
Disclaimer — Knight, Renee

The Disclosure of Politics: Struggles over the Semantics of Secularization — Lara, Maria Pia
The Discomfort Zone: How Leaders Turn Difficult Conversations Into Breakthroughs — Reynolds, Marcia
Discontent and Its Civilizations: Dispatches from Lahore, New York, and London — Hamid, Mohsin
Discount — Gray, Casey
Discourse, Politics and Media in Contemporary China — Cao, Qing
Discourses of Discipline: An Anthropology of Corporal Punishment in Japan's Schools and Sports — Miller, Aaron L.
Discourses of Empire: The Gospel of Mark from a Postcolonial Perspective — Leander, Hans
c Discover Jellyfish — Gray, Susan H.
c Discovering a New World: Would You Sail with Columbus? — Landau, Elaine
Discovering Confederation: A Canadian's Story — Ajzenstat, Janet
Discovering Florida: First-Contact Narratives from Spanish Expeditions along the Lower Gulf Coast — Worth, John E.
Discovering Forgiveness — Dunn, Larry A.
Discovering Imperialism: Social Democracy to World War I — Day, Richard B.
Discovering Indian Independent Cinema: The Films of Girish Kasaravall — Sengupta, Sakti
Discovering Music from the Inside: An Autobiography — Gordon, Edwin E.
Discovering New Zealand Trees — Morris, Sandra
Discovering Texas History — Glasrud, Bruce A.
Discovering the Human Person: In Conversation with John Paul II — Grygiel, Stanislaw
Discovering the Impressionists: Paul Durand-Ruel and the New Painting — Patry, Sylvie
Discovering the Olmecs: An Unconventional History — Grove, David C.
Discovering Tuberculosis: A Global History, 1900 to the Present — McMillen, Christian W.
Discovering Vintage New York: A Guide to the City's Timeless Shops, Bars, Delis and More — Broder, Mitch
Discovering Women's History: German-Speaking Journalists — Spreizer, Christa
The Discovery of Mankind: Atlantic Encounters in the Age of Columbus — Abulafia, David
The Discreet Hero — Llosa, Mario Vargas
The Discreet Hero — Vargas Llosa, Mario
Discrete or Continuous?: The Quest for Fundamental Length in Modern Physics — Hagar, Amit
A Disease Called Childhood: Why ADHD Became an American Epidemic — Wedge, Marilyn
A Disease in the Public Mind: A New Understanding of Why We Fought the Civil War — Fleming, Thomas
Disease, Resistance, and Lies: The Demise of the Transatlantic Slave Trade to Brazil and Cuba — Graden, Dale T.
Disease, War, and the Imperial State: The Welfare of the British Armed Forces during the Seven Years' War — Charters, Erica
Disengaged — Hiller, Mischa
Disgraced — Florio, Gwen
Disgruntled — Solomon, Asali
c Disgusting & Dreadful Science Series — Claybourne, Anna
Dishing the Dirt — Beaton, M.C.
Disinformation — Leviston, Frances
The Disinherited: A Story of Family, Love and Betrayal — Sackville-West, Robert
Disinherited: How Washington Is Betraying America's Young — Furchtgott-Roth, Diana
Disknowledge: Literature, Alchemy, and the End of Humanism in Renaissance England — Eggert, Katherine
The Dismantling — DeLeeuw, Brian
Dismember Remember: Das Anatomische Theater von Lina Saneh und Rabih Mroue — Bellan, Monique
Dismembering the American Dream: The Life and Fiction of Richard Yates — Charlton-Jones, Kate
c The Disney Book: A Celebration of the World of Disney — Fanning, Jim
c Disney Frozen, Special Edition: Junior Novelization — Nathan, Sarah
c Disney Lands — Pearson, Ridley
c Disney Mickey and Friends: Mickey's Birthday — Risco, Elle D.
Disney's Most Notorious Film: Race, Convergence, and the Hidden Histories of Song of the South — Sperb, Jason

Dispatches from Dystopia: Histories of Places Not Yet Forgotten — Brown, Kathryn L.
Dispatches from Pluto: Lost and Found in the Mississippi Delta — Grant, Richard
Dispersed but Not Destroyed: A History of the Seventeenth-Century Wendat People — Labelle, Kathryn Magee
Displacement (Illus. by Knisley, Lucy) — Knisley, Lucy
Display of Art in the Roman Palace, 1550-1750 — Feigenbaum, Gail
Disposable Asset — Altman, John
Disposable Heroes: The Betrayal of African American Veterans — Fleury-Steiner, Benjamin
The Dispossessed — Le Guin, Ursula K.
Dispossession: The Plundering of German Jewry, 1933-1945 and Beyond
y The Disreputable History of Frankie Landau-Banks — Lockhart, E.
Disrupt You! Master Personal Transformation, Seize Opportunity, and Thrive in the Era of Endless innovation — Samit, Jay
Disrupt Yourself: Disruptive Innovation to Work — Johnson, Whitney
Disruptive Power: The Crisis of the State in the Digital Age — Owen, Taylor
Dissection — Santos, Care
Dissent and the Bible in Britain, c. 1650-1950 — Mandelbrote, Scott
Dissent and the Supreme Court: Its Role in the Court's History and the Nation's Constitutional Dialogue — Urofsky, Melvin I.
Dissent on the Margins: How Soviet Jehovah's Witnesses Defied Communism and Lived to Preach about It — Baran, Emily B.
Dissent: The History of an American Idea — Young, Ralph
y Dissonance — O'Rourke, Erica
Dissonant Divas in Chicana Music: The Limits of La Onda — Vargas, Deborah R.
y The Distance between Lost and Found — Holmes, Kathryn
The Distance between Us (Read by Marie, Jorjeana). Audiobook Review — West, Kasie
y The Distance from Me to You — Gessner, Marina
Distance in Preaching: Room to Speak, Space to Listen — Brothers, Michael
A Distant Dream — Bruce, Valerie
Distant Light — Moresco, Antonio
Distant Markets, Distant Harms: Economic Complicity and Christian Ethics — Finn, Daniel K.
y The Distant Marvels — Acevedo, Chantel
Distant Neighbors: The Selected Letters of Wendell Berry & Gary Snyder — Snyder, Gary
Distant Reading — Moretti, Franco
Distant Seas — Sparhawk, Bud
Distant Strangers: Ethics, Psychology, and Global Poverty — Lichtenberg, Judith
Distant Strangers: How Britain Became Modern — Vernon, James
Distant Wars Visible: The Ambivalence of Witnessing — Kozol, Wendy
Distilled: From Absinthe and Brandy to Vodka and Whiskey, the World's Finest Artisan Spirits Unearthed, Explained and Enjoyed — Harrison, Joel
Distilling Ideas: An Introduction to Mathematical Thinking — Katz, Brian P.
Distinctions of Being: Philosophical Approaches to Reality — Zunic, Nikolaj
Distribution Revolution: Conversations about the Digital Future of Film and Television — Curtin, Michael
Distrust That Particular Flavor — Gibson, William
Disturbing Practices: History, Sexuality, and Women's Experience of Modern War — Doan, Laura
Dithyramb in Context — Kowalzig, Barbara
Divergent Paths: The Academy and the Judiciary — Posner, Richard A.
The Diver's Clothes Lie Empty (Read by Sands, Xe). Audiobook Review — Vida, Vendela
The Diver's Clothes Lie Empty — Vida, Vendela
Diversity in Diaspora: Hmong Americans in the Twenty-First Century — Pfeifer, Mark Edward
c Divided — Chapman, Elsie
Divided Friends: Portraits of the Roman Catholic Modernist Crisis in the United States — Portier, William L.
Divided Nations and European Integration — Mabry, Tristan James
Divided Rule: Sovereignty and Empire in French Tunisia, 1881-1938 — Lewis, Mary Dewhurst

c Divided We Fall (Read by Eiden, Andrew). Audiobook Review — Reedy, Trent
The Dividing Line Histories of William Byrd II of Westover — Berland, Kevin Joel
The Dividing Line Histories of William Byrd II of Westover — Byrd, William, II
Dividing the Nile: Egypt's Economic Nationalists in the Sudan 1918-56 — Mills, David E.
The Divine Art of Dying: How to Live Well While Dying — Speerstra, Karen
Divine Callings: Understanding the Call to Ministry in Black Pentecostalism — Pitt, Richard
Divine Collision: An African Boy, an American Lawyer, and Their Remarkable Battle for Freedom — Gash, Jim
Divine Enticement: Theological Seductions — MacKendrick, Karmen
Divine Fury: A History of Genius — McMahon, Darrin M.
y The Divine (Illus. by Hanuka, Asaf) — Lavie, Boaz
The Divine
Divine Men and Women in the History and Society of Late Hellenism — Dzielska, Maria
Divine Names: The 99 Healing Names of the One Love — Al-Rawi, Rosina-Fawzia
The Divine Office in Anglo-Saxon England, 597-c. 1000 — Billett, Jesse D.
y The Divine One — Mani, Danielle R.
Divine Punishment — Ramirez, Sergio
Divine Roosters and Angry Clowns — Crimi, Frank
Divine Sex: A Compelling Vision for Christian Relationships in a Hypersexualized Age — Grant, John
A Divinity for All Persuasions: Almanacs and Early American Religious Life — Tomlin, T.J.
The Divinization of Caesar and Augustus: Precedents, Consequences, Implications — Koortbojian, Michael
c Divorce Is the Worst (Illus. by Higginbotham, Anastasia) — Higginbotham, Anastasia
Divorce Turkish Style: A Kati Hirschel Mystery — Aykol, Esmahan
c The Diwali Gift (Illus. by Koan, Anna) — Chopra, Shweta
Diwata — Reyes, Barbara Jane
c Dix petits orteils (Illus. by Church, Caroline Jayne) — Church, Caroline Jayne
c Dixie and the Best Day Ever (Illus. by Rogers, Jacqueline) — Gilman, Grace
Dixie Highway: Road Building and the Making of the Modern South, 1900-1930 — Ingram, Tammy
Dixie Redux: Essays in Honor of Sheldon Hackney — Arsenault, Raymond
Dixie Redux: Essays in Honor of Sheldon Hackney — Raymond Arsenault
y DIY Bedroom Decor: 50 Awesome Ideas for Your Room — Smith, Tana
DIY Nut Milks, Nut Butters, And More — King, Melissa
DIY Succulents: From Placecards to Wreaths, 35+ Ideas for Creative Projects with Succulents — Daigle, Tawni
DIY T-Shirt Crafts: From Braided Bracelets to Floor Pillows, 50 Unexpected Ways To Recycle Your Old T-Shirts — Surian, Adrianne
DIY Wardrobe Makeovers: Alter, Refresh & Refashion Your Clothes; Step-By-Step Sewing Tutorials — Stanley, Suzannah Hamlin
c Dizvali — Murray, Julie
DJ Culture in the Mix: Power, Technology, and Social Change in Electronic Dance Music — Attias, Bernardo Alexander
Djali me tre brire — Xhama, Bardhyl
DJSturbia — Schow, David J.
DMZ Crossing: Performing Emotional Citizenship along the Korean Border — Kim, Suk-Young
DNA USA: A Genetic Portrait of America — Sykes, Bryan
y Do Aliens Exist? — Kallen, Stuart A.
Do Babies Matter? Gender and Family in the Ivory Tower — Mason, Mary Ann
c Do-Gooders (Illus. by Wagner, Justin) — Torres, J. (b. 1969-)
Do Guns Make Us Free? Democracy and the Armed Society — DeBrabander, Firmin
y Do Haunted Houses Exist? — MacKay, Jenny
Do I Count?: Stories from Mathematics — Ziegler, Gunter M.
Do I Have to Say Hello? Aunt Delia's Manners Quiz (Illus. by Koren, Edward) — Ephron, Delia
c Do I Need It? (And What If I Do?): Answers to All Your Questions about Plastic Surgery — Camp, Francesca

Do It Like a Woman — Criado-Perez, Caroline
Do Less, Get More: How to Work Smart and Live Life Your Way — Wasmund, Shaa
c Do Nice, Be Kind, Spread Happy: Acts of Kindness for Kids (Illus. by Broadbent, David) — Russell, Bernadette
c Do Nice. Be Kind. Spread Happy
Do No Harm: Stories of Life, Death, and Brain Surgery (Read by Barclay, Jim). Audiobook Review — Marsh, Henry
Do No Harm: Stories of Life, Death, and Brain Surgery — Marsh, Henry
c Do Not Disturb the Dragon (Illus. by Schoenmaker, Patrick) — Guy, David
Do Not Find Me — Novak, Kathleen
Do Not Forget This Small Honest Nation: Cardinal Mindszenty to 4 US Presidents and State Secretaries 1956-1971 — Somorjai, Adam
Do Not Forsake Me — Bittner, Rosanne
c Do Not Open until Christmas — Little, Jean
Do Not Sell at Any Price: The Wild, Obsessive Hunt for the World's Rarest 78 rpm Records — Petrusich, Amanda
The Do-Over — Ossip, Kathleen
Do Over: Rescue Monday, Reinvent Your Work, and Never Get Stuck — Acuff, Jon
The Do-Right — Sandlin, Lisa
c Do Something for Others: The Kids' Book of Citizenship — Hanson, Anders
Do the Balkans Begin in Vienna? The Geopolitical and Imaginary Borders between the Balkans and Europe — Foteva, Ana
Do the Kind Thing: Think Boundlessly, Work Purposefully, Live Passionately — Lubetzky, Daniel
c Do Trees Sneeze? (Illus. by Lawton, Val) — Freeman, Jean
y Do unto Animals: A Friendly Guide to How Animals Live, and How We Can Make Their Lives Better — Stewart, Tracey
y Do Witches Exist? — Netzley, Patricia D.
c Do You Know Pippi Longstocking? — Nyman, Ingrid
c Do You Know? Series (Illus. by Sampar) — Bergeron, Alain M.
c Do You Know the Rhinoceros? (Illus. by Sampar) — Bergeron, Alain M.
c Do You Know the Rhinoceros? (Illus. by Sampar) — Bergeron, Alain
c Do You Know? Tigers
c Do You Know Tigers? (Illus. by Sampar) — Bergeron, Alain M.
c Do You Love Dogs? — Hume, Clair
c Do You Really Want a Guinea Pig? (Illus. by Longhi, Katya) — Heos, Bridget
c Do You Really Want a Lizard? (Illus. by Longhi, Katya) — Heos, Bridget
c Do You Really Want a Snake? (Illus. by Longhi, Katya) — Heos, Bridget
c Do You Really Want a Turtle? (Illus. by Longhi, Katya) — Heos, Bridget
c Do You Really Want to Meet a Crocodile? (Illus. by Fabbri, Daniele) — Meister, Cari
c Do You Really Want to Meet a Swan? (Illus. by Fabbri, Daniele) — Meister, Cari
c Do You Really Want to Meet ... ? (Illus. by Fabbri, Daniele) — Aboff, Marcie
c Do You Really Want to Visit a Coral Reef? (Illus. by Fabbri, Daniele) — Heos, Bridget
c Do You Really Want to Visit a Desert? (Illus. by Fabbri, Daniele) — Heos, Bridget
c Do You Really Want to Visit a Prairie? (Illus. by Fabbri, Daniele) — Heos, Bridget
c Do You Really Want to Visit a Rainforest? (Illus. by Fabbri, Daniele) — Heos, Bridget
c Do You Really Want to Visit a Temperate Forest? (Illus. by Fabbri, Daniele) — Heos, Bridget
c Do You Really Want to Visit a Wetland? (Illus. by Fabbri, Daniele) — Heos, Bridget
c Do You Want to Be a Medieval Knight? (Illus. by Bergin, Mark) — MacDonald, Fiona
c Do You Want to Build a Snowman? (Illus. by Mosqueda, Olga T.) — Glass, Calliope
c Do Your Ears Hang Low? (Illus. by Doss, Andrea) — Bell, Lucy
Do Your Om Thing: Bending Yoga Tradition to Fit Your Modern Life — Pacheco, Rebecca
Doc Holiday in Film and Literature — Linder, Shirley Ayn
Doc Holliday in Film and Literature — Linder, Shirley Ayn
c Doc McStuffins Doctor's Helper — Higginson, Sheila Sweeny
The Doctor and Mr. Dylan. — Novak, Rick

Doctor Benjamin Franklin's Dream America — Ober, Damien
Doctor Death (Read by Barber, Nicola). Audiobook Review — Kaaberbol, Lene
Doctor Death — Kaaberbol, Lene
c Doctor Dolittle (Illus. by Chwast, Seymour) — Chwast, Seymour
c Doctor Dolittle (Illus. by Chwast, Seymour) — Lofting, Hugh
c Doctor Grundy's Undies (Illus. by Kinnaird, Ross) — McMillan, Dawn
The Doctor is in: Dr. Ruth on Love, Life, and Joie de Vivre — Westheimer, Ruth K.
c Doctor Nice (Illus. by Gorbachev, Valeri) — Gorbachev, Valeri
c Doctor Proctor's Fart Powder (Read by Dufris, William). Audiobook Review — Nesbo, Jo
Doctor Thorne — Dentith, Simon
The Doctors Are In: The Essential and Unofficial Guide to Doctor Who's Greatest Time Lord — Burk, Graeme
A Doctor's Case for Medical Marijuana — Casarett, David
Doctors Dissected — Haynes, Jane
The Doctor's Kidney Diets: A Nutritional Guide to Managing and Slowing the Progression of Chronic Kidney Disease — Kang, Mandip S.
Doctors without Borders: Humanitarian Quests, Impossible Dreams of Medecins Sans Frontieres — Fox, Renee C.
Doctrinal Controversy and Lay Religiosity in Late Reformation Germany: The Case of Mansfeld — Christman, Robert J.
Doctrine, Strategy and Military Culture: Military-Strategic Doctrine Development in Australia, Canada and New Zealand, 1987-2007 — Jackson, Aaron P.
Documentary Culture and the Laity in the Early Middle Ages — Brown, Warren C.
Documentary Trial Plays in Contemporary American Theater — O'Connor, Jacqueline
Documenting Desegregation: Racial and Gender Segregation in Private-Sector Employment since the Civil Rights Act — Stainback, Kevin
Documents Concerning Cyprus from the Hospitallers' Rhodian Archives: 1409-1459 — Borchardt, Karl
y Dodger (Read by Briggs, Stephen). Audiobook Review — Pratchett, Terry
Dodging Extinction: Power, Food, Money, and the Future of Life on Earth — Barnosky, Anthony D.
Does Altruism Exist? Culture, Genes, and the Welfare of Others — Wilson, David Sloan
Does Science Need a Global Language? English and the Future of Research — Montgomery, Scott L.
c Does the Ear Hear?: And Other Questions about the Five Senses — Stewart, Melissa
Does This Beach Make Me Look Fat? True Stories and Confessions — Scottoline, Lisa
The Dog — O'Neill, Joseph
c Dog and Bear: Tricks and Treats — Seeger, Laura Vaccaro
c Dog and Mouse (Illus. by Nelson-Schmidt, Michelle) — Nelson-Schmidt, Michelle
y Dog Beach Unleashed — Greenwald, Lisa
Dog Bites Caesar! A Reading of Juvenal's Satire 5 — Nadeau, Yvan
The Dog Called Hitler Lena — Domanski, Walerian
Dog Company: The Boys of Pointe du Hoc: The Rangers Who Accomplished D-Day's Toughest Mission and Led the Way Across Europe — O'Donnell, Patrick K.
Dog Crazy: A Novel of Love Lost and Found — Donohue, Meg
c A Dog Day for Susan — Fergus, Maureen
c A Dog Day (Illus. by Rand, Emily) — Rand, Emily
c Dog Days for Delaney — Jones, Jen
Dog Ear — Johnstone, Jim
c Dog Ears — Booth, Anne
c Dog Eat Dog — Marciotte, Jake
A Dog Gone Murder — Viets, Elaine
c The Dog Lover's Guide — Head, Honor
The Dog Master — Cameron, W. Bruce
Dog Medicine: How My Dog Saved Me from Myself — Barton, Julie
c A Dog Named Zero and the Apple with No Name (Illus. by Bartlett, T.C.) — Bartlett, T.C.
c Dog on Stilts (Illus. by McKinnon, Angus) — Thorp, James
c The Dog, Ray — Coggin, Linda
Dog Run Moon — Wink, Callan
The Dog: Stories — Livings, Jack

c The Dog That Nino Didn't Have (Illus. by Van Hertbruggen, Anton) — van de Vendel, Edward
c The Dog That Nino Didn't Have (Illus. by Van Hertbruggen, Anton) — Vendel, Edward van de
The Dog Thief — Kearney, Jill
Dog Training the American Male — Knight, L.A.
The Dog Walker — Stephens, Joshua
c A Dog Wearing Shoes (Illus. by Ko, Sangmi) — Ko, Sangmi
The Dog Who Saved Me — Wilson, Susan
Dog Years: Faithful Friends, Then and Now — Jones, Amanda
The Dogist: Photographic Encounters with 1,000 Dogs — Friedman, Elias Weiss
Dogland: A Journey to the Heart of America's Dog Problem — Skole, Jacki
c Dogs — Steele-Saccio, Eva
y The Dogs — Stratton, Allan
Dogs and Underdogs: Finding Happiness at Both Ends of the Leash — Abbott, Elizabeth
The Dogs Are Eating Them Now: Our War in Afghanistan — Smith, Graeme
c Dogs Are People, Too: A Collection of Cartoons to Make Your Tail Wag (Illus. by Coverly, Dave) — Coverly, Dave
c A Dog's Breakfast (Illus. by McElhinney, Glenn) — Graves, Annie
y Dogs Don't Talk — May, Nancy
A Dog's Gift — Drury, Bob
A Dog's Gift: The Inspirational Story of Veterans and Children Healed by Man's Best Friend — Drury, Bob
Dogs of Courage: When Britain's Pets Went to War — Campbell, Christy
y The Dogs of Littlefield — Berne, Suzanne
The Dogs of the Sinai — Fortini, Franco
c Dogs — Furstinger, Nancy
Dogwatch: Poems — Gwynn, R.S.
Dogwood Hill — Woods, Sherryl
Doing Anthropological Research: A Practical Guide — Konopinski, Natalie
Doing Emotions History — Matt, Susan J.
Doing Good Better: Effective Altruism and A Radical New Way to Make A Difference — MacAskill, William
Doing Good Better: Effective Altruism and How You Can Make a Difference — MacAskill, William
Doing Good: Racial Tensions and Workplace Inequalities at a Community Clinic in El Nuevo South — Deeb-Sossa, Natalia
Doing Harder Time? The Experiences of an Ageing Male Prison Population in England and Wales — Mann, Natalie
y Doing Right — Jones, Patrick
Doing the Devil's Work — Loehfelm, Bill
Doing the Math of Mission: Fruits, Faithfulness, and Metrics — Rendle, Gil
c Dojo Daytrip (Illus. by Tougas, Chris) — Tougas, Chris
Doktoranden-Kolloquium "FUER Geschichtsbewusstsein"
Dolce Far Niente in Arabia: Georg August Wallin and His Travels in the 1840s — Edgren-Henrichson, Nina
c The Doldrums (Illus. by Gannon, Nicholas) — Gannon, Nicholas
The Doll Collection — Datlow, Ellen
c A Doll for Marie (Illus. by Duvoisin, Roger) — Fatio, Louise
The Doll Maker — Montanari, Richard
c The Doll People Set Sail (Illus. by Helquist, Brett) — Martin, Ann M.
c Dolley Madison (Illus. by Johnson, Steve) — Krull, Kathleen
Dollhouse — Terranova, Elaine
The Doll's House — Phillips, Louise
c Dolls of Hope — Parenteau, Shirley
Dolores del Rio: Beauty in Light and Shade — Hallett, Hilary A.
Dolphin — Rauch, Alan
c Dolphins (Illus. by Keimig, Candice) — Baltzer, Rochelle
c Dolphins: Ocean Life — Hansen, Grace
Dome of the Hidden Pavilion: New Poems — Tate, James
Domesday: Book of Judgement — Harvey, Sally
A Domestic Animal — King, Francis
Domestic Frontiers: Gender, Reform, and American Interventions in the Ottoman Balkans and the Near East, 1831-1908 — Reeves-Ellington, Barbara
Domestic Intimacies: Incest and the Liberal Subject in Nineteenth-Century America — Connolly, Brian

Domestic Negotiations: Gender, Nation, and Self-Fashioning in US Mexicana and Chicana Literature and Art — McMahon, Marci R.
Domestic Violence and the Islamic Tradition — Esack, Farid
Domesticated: Evolution in a Man-Made World — Francis, Richard C.
Domesticating Ibsen for Italy: Enrico and Icilio Polese's Ibsen Campaign — D'Amico, Giuliano
Domesticity and Consumer Culture in Iran: Interior Revolutions of the Modern Era — Karimi, Pamela
c Dominant Defensemen — Zweig, Eric
Dominatrix: Gender, Eroticism and Control in the Dungeon — Lindemann, Danielle J.
Dominican Baseball: New Pride, Old Prejudice — King-White, Ryan
Dominican Baseball: New Pride, Old Prejudice — Klein, Alan
Dominion Undeserved: Milton and the Perils of Creation — Song, Eric B.
The Domino Diaries: My Decade Boxing with Olympic Champions and Chasing Hemingway's Ghost in the Last Days of Castro's Cuba — Butler, Brin-Jonathan
Don Paterson: Contemporary Critical Essays — Pollard, Natalie
Donabe: Classic and Modern Japanese Clay Pot Cooking — Moore, Naoko Takei
Donaugrenzen in Literatur und Film. Internationale Tagung
Done in One — Jerkins, Grant
c The Donkey Lady Fights La Llorona and Other Stories / La Senora Asno Se Enfrenta a La Llorona Y Otros Cuentos — Garza, Xavier
c The Donkey Lady Fights La Llorona and Other Stories/La Senora Asno se enfrenta a La Llorona y otros cuentos — Garza, Xavier
c Donkey's Kite: A Horse Valley Adventure (Illus. by Allen, Liana-Melissa) — Allen, Liana-Melissa
Donne del Rinascimento a Roma e dintorni — Esposito, Anna
Donne: The Reformed Soul — Stubbs, John
c Donny's Inferno — Catanese, P.W.
Donovan's Devils: OSS Commandos behind Enemy Lines: Europe, World War II — Lulushi, Albert
c Don't (Illus. by Johnson, Virginia) — Trochatos, Litsa
Don't Be a Stranger — Nesbitt, John D.
Don't Call Me a Victim! — Yafasova, Dina
c Don't Call Me Grandma (Illus. by Zunon, Elizabeth) — Nelson, Vaunda Micheaux
y Don't Call Me Kit Kat — Farnham, K.J.
Don't Eat This If You're Taking That: The Hidden Risks of Mixing Food and Medicine — Fernstrom, Madelyn Hirsch
y Don't Ever Change — Bloom, M. Beth
Don't Ever Look Back — Friedman, Daniel
Don't Ever Whisper: Darlene Keju, Pacific Health Pioneer, Champion for Nuclear Survivors — Johnson, Giff
y Don't Fail Me Now (Read by Ojo, Adenrele). Audiobook Review — LaMarche, Una
y Don't Fail Me Now — LaMarche, Una
c Don't Feed the Geckos! — English, Karen
c Don't Forget Tiggs! (Illus. by Ross, Tony) — Rosen, Michael
Don't Get Me Wrong — Kavanagh, Marianne
c Don't Give This Book a Bowl of Milk! (Illus. by Perez, Carmen) — Bird, Benjamin
Don't Go Home (Read by Reading, Kate). Audiobook Review — Hart, Carolyn
Don't Go Home — Hart, Carolyn
Don't Hurry Me Down to Hades: The Civil War in the Words of Those Who Lived It — Ural, Susannah J.
Don't Just Sit There — Bowman, Katy
c Don't Kick Up a Fuss, Gus! (Illus. by Meserve, Adria) — Meserve, Adria
Don't Know Where, Don't Know When — Laing, Annette
Don't Leave Yet: How My Mother's Alzheimer's Opened My Heart — Hanstedt, Constance
y Don't Let Go — Gagnon, Michelle
Don't Let My Baby Do Rodeo — Fishman, Boris
Don't Look Back — Hurwitz, Gregg
Don't Look, Don't Touch, Don't Eat: The Science behind Revulsion — Curtis, Valerie
Don't Look Now — Gagnon, Michelle
Don't Lose Her — King, Jonathon
Don't Lose Her — Ktna, Jonathon
Don't Mean Nuthin' — Lealos, Ron
c Don't Mess With These Kids! — Wilson, Doug
y Don't Stay Up Late — Stine, R.L.

c Don't Stick Sticks Up Your Nose! Don't Stuff Stuff In Your Ears! — Altman, Jerald S.
Don't Suck, Don't Die: Giving Up Vic Chesnutt — Hersh, Kristin
Don't Tell Her to Relax: 22 Ways to Support Your Infertile Loved One — El Kouri, Zahie
Don't Tell Her to Relax: 22 Ways to Support Your Infertile Loved One through Diagnosis, Treatment, and Beyond — El Kourl, Zahie
Don't Tell Me to Wait: How the Fight for Gay Rights Changed America and Transformed Obama's Presidency — Eleveld, Kerry
Don't Tell Me to Wait — Eleveld, Kerry
c Don't Think about Purple Elephants (Illus. by Jones, Gwynneth) — Whelan, Susan
c Don't Throw It to Mo! (Illus. by Ricks, Sam) — Adler, David A.
c Don't Throw It to Mo! (Illus. by Ricks, Sam) — Don't Throw It to Mo!
Don't Throw the Book at Them: Communicating the Christian Message to People Who Don't Read — Box, Harry
y Don't Touch — Wilson, Rachel M.
c Don't Trip, Pip! (Illus. by Cartwright, Amy) — Powell, Marie
Don't Trust Don't Fear Don't Beg: The Extraordinary Story of the Arctic 30 — Stewart, Ben
Don't Try This At Home — Readman, Angela
y Don't Vote for Me — Van Dolzer, Krista
c Doom at Grant's Tomb — Wells, Marcia
Doomed by Hope: Essays on Arab Theatre — Houssami, Eyad
Doomed to Succeed: The U.S.-Israel Relationship from Truman to Obama — Ross, Dennis
The Doomsday Equation — Richtel, Matt
The Door — Rix, Len
The Door — Szabo, Magda
The Door Ajar: False Closure in Greek and Roman Literature and Art — Grewing, Farouk
c The Door by the Staircase (Illus. by Murphy, Kelly) — Marsh, Katherine
y The Door in the Moon — Fisher, Catherine
The Door of the Sad People — Blackburn, Alexander
y The Door That Lead to Where — Gardner, Sally
y The Door That Led to Where — Gardner, Sally
The Doors You Mark Are Your Own — Elliott, Okla
The Doors You Mark Are Your Own — Tuvim, Aleksandr
The Doorway — Spencer, Alan
Doped: The Real Life Story of the 1960s Racehorse Doping Gang — Reid, Jamie
Dorfer und Deputierte: Die Wahlen zu den konstituierenden Parlamenten von 1848 in Niederosterreich un im Pariser Umland — Stockinger, Thomas
The Dorito Effect — Schatzker, Mark
y The Dorito Effect: The Surprising New Truth about Food and Flavor (Read by Patton, Chris). Audiobook Review — Schatzker, Mark
The Dorito Effect: The Surprising New Truth about Food and Flavor — Schatzker, Mark
Dork Diaries 9: Tales from a Not-So-Dorky Drama Queen — Renee, Rachel
c Dorothea's Eyes: Dorothea Lange Photographs the Truth (Illus. by DuBois, Gerard) — Rosenstock, Barb
Dorothy Knapp: Philately and Family — Weisz, Douglas S.
Dorothy Must Die Stories: No Place Like Oz — Paige, Danielle
c Dory and the Real True Friend (Illus. by Hanlon, Abby) — Hanlon, Abby
c Dory and the Real True Friend — Hanlon, Abby
c Dory Fantasmagory (Read by Jackson, Suzy). Audiobook Review — Hanlon, Abby
c Dory Fantasmagory — Hanlon, Abby
Dostoevskii's Overcoat: Influence, Comparison, and Transposition — Andrew, Joe
Dostoevsky and the Catholic Underground — Blake, Elizabeth A.
y Dotwav — Lancaster, Mike A.
Double Agents: Espionage, Literature, and Liminal Citizens — Carlston, Erin G.
Double Cover — Young, Sherban
Double Cross in Cairo: The True Story of the Spy Who Turned the Tide of War in the Middle East — West, Nigel
c Double Cross — Gibbs, Stuart
Double Cross Trail Drive — Cunningham, Chet
Double-Diffusive Convection — Radko, Timour
Double Double: How to Double Your Revenue and Profit in 3 Years or Less — Herold, Cameron

y Double Exposure — Birdsall, Bridget
Double Fudge Brownie Murder (Read by Toren, Susan). Audiobook Review — Fluke, Joanne
Double Fudge Brownie Murder — Fluke, Joanne
c Double Happiness (Illus. by Chau, Alina) — Ling, Nancy Tupper
Double Jinx — Reddy, Nancy
The Double Life of Fidel Castro: My 17 Years as Personal Bodyguard to El Lider Maximo — Sanchez, Juan Reinaldo
The Double Life of Laurence Oliphant — Casey, Bart
The Double Life of Liliane — Tuck, Lily
The Double Life of Paul de Man — Barish, Evelyn
y Double or Nothing — Payton, Belle
c Double Reverse — Bowen, Fred
A Double Sorrow: A Version of Troilus and Criseyde — Greenlaw, Lavinia
Double Switch — Monday, T.T.
c Double Trouble for Anna Hibiscus! (Illus. by Tobia, Lauren) — Atinuke
y Double Vision — Bradley, F.T.
Double Vision — Marshall, Colby
y Doubleborn — Forward, Toby
y The Doublecross (and Other Skills I Learned as a Superspy). — Pearce, Jackson
y The Doubt Factory — Bacigalupi, Paolo
A Doubter's Almanac — Canin, Ethan
c Doug Unplugs on the Farm — Yaccarino, Dan
Doughboys on the Great War: How American Soldiers Viewed Their Military Experience — Gutierrez, Edward A.
Douglas MacAgy and the Foundations of Modern Art Curatorship — Beasley, David
y Dove Arising — Bao, Karen
y Dove Exiled — Bao, Karen
Down — Blue, Ally
Down among the Dead Men — Lovesey, Peter
Down and Out in Los Angeles and Berlin: The Sociospatial Exclusion of Homeless People — Mahs, Jurgen von
Down Don't Bother Me — Miller, Jason
y Down from the Mountain — Fixmer, Elizabeth
c Down Here (Illus. by Malenfant, Isabelle) — Sherrard, Valerie
Down in the Chapel: Religious Life in American Prison — Dubler, Joshua
Down in the Chapel: Religious Life in an American Prison — Dubler, Joshua
Down in the Valley — Shoup, Jane
Down Stream: A History and Celebration of Swimming the River Thames — Davies, Caitlin
Down the Rabbit Hole — Robb, J.D.
Down to the Crossroads: Civil Rights, Black Power, and the Meredith March against Fear — Goudsouzian, Aram
Down with Skool: A Guide to School Life for Tiny Pupils and Their Parents — Willans, Geoffrey
Downbeach — Singley, William P.
The Downfall of Money: Germany's Hyperinflation and the Destruction of the Middle Class — Taylor, Frederick
Downtown Film and TV Culture: 1975-2001 — Hawkins, Joan
Downtown Italian: Recipes Inspired by Italy, Created in New York's West Village — Campanale, Joe
Downward Facing Death — Kelly, Michelle
Downwind: A People's History of the Nuclear West — Fox, Sarah Alisabeth
c Doyli to the Rescue: Saving Baby Monkeys in the Amazon (Illus. by Burnham, Cathleen) — Burnham, Cathleen
c Doyli to the Rescue: Saving Baby Monkeys in the Amazon — Burnham, Cathleen
c A Dozen Cousins (Illus. by Usher, Sam) — Houran, Lori Haskins
c Dozer's Run: A True Story of a Dog and His Race (Illus. by Panza, Rosana) — Levy, Debbie
c Dozi the Alligator Finds a New Home (Illus. by Sammarco, Nicola) — Boris, Daniel
c Dr. Critchlore's School for Minions (Illus. by Sutphin, Joe) — Grau, Sheila
c Dr. Dee Dee Dynamo's Saturn Surprise (Illus. by Bouthyette, Valerie) — Williams, Oneeka
y Dr. Dre — Saddleback Educational Publishing
Dr Fischer of Geneva — Greene, Graham
Dr. John Harvey Kellogg and the Religion of Biologic Living — Wilson, Brian C.
Dr. John Moore, 1792-1802: A Life in Medicine, Travel, and Revolution — Fulton, Henry L.
c Dr Karl's Biggest Book of Science Stuff and Nonsense (Illus. by Jeffery, Russell) — Kruszelnicki, Karl

Dr. Kellyann's Bone Broth Diet: Lose up to 15 Pounds, 4 Inches, and Your Wrinkles in Just 21 Days — Petrucci, Kellyann
c Dr. KittyCat Is Ready to Rescue Posy the Puppy — Clarke, Jane
c Dr. Seuss (Illus. by Krull, Kathleen) — Klimo, Kate
Dr. Stephanie's Relationship Repair for Couples: A Customer Service Approach for Minimizing Conflict and Creating Lasting Love in Your Relationships — Knarr, Stephanie Weiland
Dr. Strangelove, or, How I Learned to Stop Worrying and Love the Bomb — Kramer, Peter
Dr. Susan Love's Breast Book, 6th ed — Love, Susan M.
Dracula (Read by Horovitch, David). Audiobook Review — Stoker, Bram
Dracula (Read by Jackson, Gildart). Audiobook Review — Stoker, Bram
Dracula and Philosophy — Michaud, Nicolas
The Drafter — Harrison, Kim
c Drag Racing — Monnig, Alex
c Dragon and Captain (Illus. by Turnbloom, Lucas) — Allabach, P.R.
c The Dragon and the Knight — Sabuda, Robert
Dragon Coast — Greg van Eekhout
Dragon Day — Brackmann, Lisa
c Dragon Girl: The Secret Valley — Weigel, Jeff
Dragon Heart — Holland, Cecelia
Dragon in Exile — Miller, Steve (b. 1950-)
c Dragon Jelly (Illus. by Hendra, Sue) — Freedman, Claire
y The Dragon Lantern: A League of Seven
y The Dragon Lantern: A League of Seven (Illus. by Helquist, Brett) — Gratz, Alan
y The Dragon Lantern: A League of Seven Novel (Illus. by Helquist, Brett) — Gratz, Alan
The Dragon of Handale — Clark, Cassandra
Dragon of the Stars — Cavanaugh, Alex J.
Dragon Queen — Deas, Stephen
c The Dragon Riders (Illus. by Choi, Link) — Russell, James
The Dragon Ring — Coleman, C. Craig
c Dragon Shield — Fletcher, Charlie
c The Dragon Stoorworm (Illus. by Land, Matthew) — Breslin, Theresa
c Dragonario: Un catalogo de dragonas y dragones (Illus. by Gu, Raquel) — Gu, Raquel
y Dragonbride — York, Raani
c The Dragonet Prophecy — Sutherland, Tui T.
Dragonfish (Read by Taylorson, Tom, with Nancy Wu). Audiobook Review — Tran, Vu
Dragonfish — Tran, Vu
Dragonfish — Vu Tran
Dragonflies: Magnificent Creatures of Water, Air, and Land (Illus. by van Dokkum, Pieter) — van Dokkum, Pieter
c The Dragonfly Club: A Friend In Need — Ringness, Mari
c The Dragonfly Effect — Korman, Gordon
c Dragonquest (Illus. by Harris, Wayne) — Baillie, Allan
c Dragons and Hot Sauce and Other Imaginations (Illus. by Young, Andy) — Moore, Mike
Dragons at Crumbling Castle and Other Tales (Read by Rhind-Tutt, Julian). Audiobook Review — Pratchett, Terry
c Dragons at Crumbling Castle and Other Tales (Illus. by Beech, Mark) — Pratchett, Terry
c Dragons Beware! (Illus. by Rosado, Rafael) — Aguirre, Jorge
c Dragons Beware! (Illus. by Rosado, Rafael) — Jorge, Aguirre
c Dragons Can't Swim (Illus. by Melling, David) — French, Vivian
c Dragon's Extraordinary Egg (Illus. by Gliori, Debi) — Gliori, Debi
c Dragon's Extraordinary Egg — Gliori, Debi
c A Dragon's Guide to Making Your Human Smarter — Yep, Laurence
c A Dragon's Guide to the Care and Feeding of Humans (Read by Denaker, Susan). Audiobook Review — Yep, Laurence
y A Dragon's Guide to the Care and Feeding of Humans (Illus. by GrandPre, Mary) — Yep, Laurence
Dragons in the Stacks: A Teen Librarian's Guide to Tabletop Role-Playing — Torres-Roman, Steven A.
A Dragon's Mage — Lietz, Cecilia
Dragons, Serpents, and Slayers in the Classical and Early Christian Worlds: A Sourcebook — Ogden, Daniel
c The Dragon's Toothache — Besant, Annie

c Dragons vs Dinos (Illus. by Redlich, Ben) — Pearson, Maggie
y Dragons vs. Drones — King, Wesley
c The Dragonsitter (Illus. by Parsons, Garry) — Lacey, Josh
c Drake Makes a Splash (Illus. by Jack, Colin) — O'Ryan, Ray
The Drama of Living: Becoming Wise in the Spirit — Ford, David
The Drama of Reform: Theology and Theatricality, 1461-1553 — Atkin, Tamara
Dramathemes: Classroom Literacy that Will Excite, Surprise, and Stimulate Learning, 4th ed. — Swartz, Larry
c Draw! (Illus. by Colon, Raul) — Colon, Raul
Draw Faces in 15 Minutes — Spicer, Jake
c Draw What You See: The Life and Art of Benny Andrews (Illus. by Andrews, Benny) — Benson, Kathleen
Drawing Blood: A Memoir — Crabapple, Molly
Drawing Blood: A Sketch in Crime Mystery — Verne, Deirdre
Drawing Fire: Cold Case Justice — Cantore, Janice
c Drawing Ocean Animals (Illus. by Calle, Juan) — Colich, Abby
Drawing the Line: The Father Reimagined in Faulkner, Wright, O'Connor, and Morrison — Fowler, Doreen
c Drawing Wild Animals (Illus. by Juta, Jason) — Colich, Abby
Drawing with Mark: Let's Go to the Zoo!/Zoo Stories
Drawings for Architecture Design and Ornament: The James A. de Rothschild Bequest at Waddesdon Manor, 2 vols. — Laing, Alastair
Drawn and Quarterly: Twenty-Five Years of Contemporary Cartooning, Comics and Graphic Novels — Devlin, Tom
Drawn from Water: An American Poet, An Ethiopian Family, an Israeli Story — Elenbogen, Dina
The Drayton Diaries — Stephens, Robert W.
c Dread Eagle — Woolf, Alex
c The Dreaded Ogress of the Tundra (Illus. by MacDougall, Larry) — Christopher, Neil
A Dreadful Deceit: The Myth of Race from the Colonial Era to Obama's America — Jones, Jacqueline
y The Dreadful Fate of Jonathan York: A Yarn for the Strange at Heart — Merritt, Kory
y Dream a Little Dream — Gier, Kerstin
The Dream Betrayed: Racial Absurdities in Obama's America — Trebach, Arnold S.
y The Dream Carvers — Clark, Joan
Dream Chasers: Immigration and the American Backlash — Tirman, John
Dream Cities: Seven Urban Ideas That Shape the World — Graham, Wade
Dream Cities: Utopia and Prose by Poets in Nineteenth-Century France — Kerr, Greg
c The Dream Doctor: A Lighthearted Journey to Help the Children in Your Life Discover Dreams Have Something to Teach Us (Illus. by Beening, Kathleen) — Anaries, Kathryn
Dream House — Armsden, Catherine
Dream Interpretation for Beginners: Understand the Wisdom of Your Sleeping Mind — Brandon, Diane
The Dream Lover (Read by Sutton-Smith, Emily). Audiobook Review — Berg, Elizabeth
The Dream Lover — Berg, Elizabeth
The Dream of a Democratic Culture: Mortimer J. Adler and the Great Books Idea — Lacy, Tim
The Dream of My Return — Moya, Horacio Castellanos
The Dream of the Great American Novel — Buell, Lawrence
c Dream On, Amber (Illus. by Crawford-White, Helen) — Shevah, Emma
c Dream On — Mlynowski, Sarah
The Dream Songs — Berryman, John
The Dream Songs — Hofmann, Michael
y Dream Things True — Marquardt, Marie
y Dream Warriors. E-book Review — Pease, D. Robert
Dream West: Politics and Religion in Cowboy Movies — Brode, Douglas
Dream with Your Eyes Open: An Entrepreneurial Journey — Screwvala, Ronnie
Dream Wrecks — Heimbold, Dick
c Dreamcatcher — Curtin, Ann
Dreamers: An Immigrant Generation's Fight for Their American Dream — Truax, Eileen
The DREAMers: How the Undocumented Youth Movement Transformed the Immigrant Rights Debate — Nicholls, Walter J.

y Dreamfever — *Alloway, Kit*
y Dreamfire — *Alloway, Kit*
Dreamhouse: Interiors by Penny Drue Baird — *Baird, Penny Drue*
y Dreaming in Indian: Contemporary Native American Voices — *Charleybov, Lisa*
Dreaming of Dry Land: Environmental Transformation in Colonial Mexico City — *Candiani, Vera*
Dreaming of Money in Ho Chi Minh City — *Truitt, Allison J.*
y Dreamland — *Anderson, Robert L.*
Dreamland of Humanists: Warburg, Cassirer, Panofsky, and the Hamburg School — *Levine, Emily J.*
Dreamland: The True Tale of America's Opiate Epidemic — *Quinones, Sam*
Dreamless — *Brekke, Jergen*
Dreams and Shadows — *Yakimov, Radka*
Dreams and the Invisible World in Colonial New England: Indians, Colonists, and the Seventeenth Century — *Plane, Ann Marie*
Dreams Are Made for Children (Illus. by Green Ilya) — *Michel, Misja Fitzgerald*
Dreams, Dreamers and Visions: The Early Modern Atlantic World — *Plane, Ann Marie*
Dreams of Dreams and the Last Three Days of Fernando Pessoa — *Peters, Nancy J.*
Dreams of Earth and Sky — *Dyson, Freeman*
c Dreams of Freedom in Words and Pictures — *Amnesty International UK*
c Dreams of Freedom: In Words and Pictures — *Amnesty International UK*
c Dreams of Freedom in Words and Pictures — *Amnesty International UK*
c Dreams of Gods and Monsters (Read by Hvam, Khristine). Audiobook Review — *Taylor, Laini*
Dreams of Los Angeles: Traversing Power, Navigating Space, and Recovering the Everyday — *Zarsadiaz, James*
Dreams of My Mothers: A Story of Love Transcendent — *Peterson, Joel L.*
Dreams of Shreds & Tatters — *Downum, Amanda*
Dreams of the Good Life: The Life of Flora Thompson and the Creation of 'Lake Rise to Candleford' — *Mabey, Richard*
Dreams of the Red Phoenix — *Pye, Virginia*
Dreams Rewritten — *Yates, Bill*
Dreams to Remember: Otis Redding, Stax Records, and the Transformation of Southern Soul — *Ribowsky, Mark*
Dreamstreets: A Journey through Britain's Village Utopias — *Yallop, Jacqueline*
y Dreamstrider — *Smith, Lindsay*
c Dreamwood — *Mackey, Heather*
Dreamy Quilts: 14 Timeless Projects to Welcome You Home — *Nelson, Lydia Loretta*
Dreimal Deutschland und Zuruck — *Mueller-Stahl, Annin*
The Dress: 100 Ideas That Changed Fashion Forever — *Fogg, Marnie*
Dress Casual: How College Students Redefined American Style — *Clemente, Deirdre*
Dress Code: The Naked Truth about Fashion — *Arntzen, Mari Grinde*
Dressed for War: Uniform, Civilian Clothing and Trappings, 1914 to 1918 — *Edwards, Nina*
Dressing (Illus. by DeForge, Michael) — *DeForge, Michael*
Dressing Up for Halloween — *Griswold, Cliff*
The Dressmaker — *Ham, Rosalie*
The Dressmaker's War — *Chamberlain, Mary*
y Drew — *Cooper, T.*
c Drew the Screw (Illus. by Cerato, Mattia) — *Cerato, Mattia*
The Dreyfus Affair and the Rise of the French Public Intellectual — *Conner, Tom*
y Drift — *Hutchins, M.K.*
y Drift & Dagger — *Kulper, Kendall*
Drifter — *Brandon, Ivan*
The Drifter — *Petrie, Nicholas*
The Drifter — *Schmidt, Anna*
Drifting — *Ulysse, Katia D.*
Drifting among Rivers and Lakes: Southern Song Dynasty Poetry and the Problem of Literary History — *Fuller, Michael A.*
Drinking in America: Our Secret History — *Cheever, Susan*
Drinking Smoke: The Tobacco Syndemic in Oceania — *Marshall, Mac*
Drinking the Devil's Acre: A Love Letter from San Francisco and Her Cocktails — *McDonnell, Duggan*

Drinking with the Saints: The Sinner's Guide to a Holy Happy Hour — *Foley, Michael P.*
Dritter Workshop zur Jugendbewegungsforschung
c Drive: A Look at Roadside Opposites (Illus. by Hatanaka, Kellen) — *Hatanaka, Kellen*
c Drive: A Look at Roadside Opposites — *Hatanaka, Kellen*
Drive: A Look Roadside Opposites — *Hatanaka, Kellen*
y Drive Me Crazy — *McVoy, Terra Elan*
Drive or Die — *Tucker, Mark E.*
Driven — *Armstrong, Kelley*
Driven from New Orleans: How Nonprofits Betray Public Housing and Promote Privatization — *Arena, John*
The Driver's Seat — *Spark, Muriel*
Driving after Class: Anxious Times in an American Suburb — *Heiman, Rachel*
Driving Demand — *Hidalgo, Carlos*
Driving Hungry — *Mosler, Layne*
Driving Hungry: A Memoir — *Mosler, Layne*
Driving Hungry — *Mosler, Layne*
Driving Lessons — *Hesik, Annameekee*
Driving the Future: Combating Climate Change with Cleaner, Smarter Cars — *Oge, Margo*
Driving the King — *Howard, Ravi*
y Driving with the Top Down (Read by Cassidy, Orlagh). Audiobook Review — *Harbison, Beth*
Drone — *Rothstein, Adam*
Drone Command — *Maden, Mike*
The Drone Eats With Me: Diaries from a City Under Fire — *Abu Saif, Atef*
Drone Theory — *Chamayou, Gregoire*
Drone Wars: Transforming Conflict, Law, and Policy — *Bergen, Peter L.*
y Drones — *Henneberg, Susan*
Drones and Targeted Killing: Legal, Moral and Geopolitical Issues — *Cohn, Marjorie*
Drop Dead Punk — *Zahradnik, Rich*
c Drop It, Rocket! — *Hills, Tad*
y Drop — *Everson, Katie*
y A Drop of Night — *Bachmann, Stefan*
y Dropping In — *Havel, Geoff*
The Drosten's Curse — *Kennedy, A.L.*
Drought-Adapted Vine — *Revell, Donald*
y Drowned — *Reilly, Nichola*
The Drowned Boy — *Fossum, Karin*
y Drowned City: Hurricane Katrina and New Orleans (Illus. by Brown, Don) — *Brown, Don*
The Drowning — *Lackberg, Camilla*
The Drowning Eyes — *Foster, Emily*
The Drowning Ground — *Marrison, James*
y Drowning Is Inevitable — *Stanley, Shalanda*
Drugs for Life: How Pharmaceutical Companies Define Our Health — *Dumit, Joseph*
y Drugs in American Society: An Encyclopedia of History, Politics, Culture, and the Law — *Marion, Nancy E.*
c Drum Dream Girl: How One Girl's Courage Changed Music (Illus. by Lopez, Rafael) — *Engle, Margarita*
Drum-Taps: The Complete 1865 Edition — *Whitman, Walt*
The Drum Tower — *Moshiri, Farnoosh*
The Drum Within — *Scarantino, James R.*
c The Drummer Boy (Illus. by Nille, Peggy) — *Min, SooHyeon*
The Drummond Girls — *Link, Mardi Jo*
Drunken Fireworks (Read by Sample, Tim). Audiobook Review — *King, Stephen*
The Drunken Monkey: Why We Drink and Abuse Alcohol — *Dudley, Robert*
The Drunken Spelunker's Guide to Plato — *Giuffre, Kathy*
c Druthers (Illus. by Phelan, Matt) — *Phelan, Matt*
The Druze: A New Cultural and Historical Appreciation — *Halabi, Abbas*
Dry Bones — *Johnson, Craig*
y Dryland — *Jaffe, Sara*
"Du Hattest es Besser als Ich": 2 Bruder im 20. Jahrhundert — *Nonnenmacher, Frank*
Du spiritualisme et de quelques-unes de ses consequences — *Aubert, Albert*
Duane's Depressed — *McMurtry, Larry*
Dublin: The Making of a Capital City — *Dickson, David*
A Duchess in Name — *Weaver, Amanda*
The Duchess's Shells: Natural History Collecting in the Age of Cook's Voyages — *Tobin, Beth Fowkes*
c Duck, Death and the Tulip (Illus. by Erlbruch, Wolf) — *Erlbruch, Wolf*
c Duck, Duck, Dinosaur (Illus. by Vidal, Oriol) — *George, Kallie*

c Duck Duck Moose (Illus. by Jones, Noah Z.) — *Bardhan-Quallen, Sudipta*
c Duck & Goose: Colors! (Illus. by Hills, Tad) — *Hills, Tad*
c Duck in the Fridge (Illus. by Mack, Jeff) — *Mack, Jeff*
c The Duck Says (Illus. by Boldt, Mike) — *Wilson, Troy*
c Ducks to Water (Illus. by Dawson, Janine) — *Avison, Brett*
c Duck's Vacation (Illus. by Soffer, Gilad) — *Soffer, Gilad*
Duct Tape: 101 Adventurous Ideas for Art, Jewelry, Flowers, Wallets and More — *Davis, Forest Walker*
c Duddle Puck the Puddle Duck (Illus. by Hall, Marcellus) — *Wilson, Karma*
Dude Making a Difference — *Greenfield, Rob*
c Dude, Where's My Saxophone? (Illus. by Cattish, Anna) — *Cobb, Amy*
Duel of Shadows — *Hall, Billy*
The Duesenberg Caper — *Corea, Roger*
Duet in Beirut — *Ben-David, Mishka*
Duff Bakes: Think and Bake Like a Pro at Home — *Goldman, Duff*
The Duff Cooper Diaries — *Norwich, John Julius*
Duff Cooper: The Authorized Biography — *Charmley, John*
The Duke and the Lady in Red — *Heath, Lorraine*
A Duke But No Gentleman — *Hawkins, Alexandra*
The Duke Can Go to the Devil — *Knightley, Erin*
Duke Ellington as Pianist: A Study of Styles — *Cooper, Matthew J.*
Dukes Are Forever — *Harrington, Anna*
The Duke's Children — *Trollope, Anthony*
The Duke's Disaster — *Burrowes, Grace*
Dukes Prefer Blondes — *Chase, Loretta*
y Dumb Chocolate Eyes (Illus. by Shoard, Emma) — *Brooks, Kevin*
Dumped: Stories of Women Unfriending Women — *Gaby, Nina*
y Dumplin' (Read by Stevens, Eileen). Audiobook Review — *Murphy, Julie*
y Dumplin' — *Murphy, Julie*
c Duncan the Story Dragon (Illus. by Driscoll, Amanda) — *Driscoll, Amanda*
c Dunces Rock — *Jaimet, Kate*
Dundee and the Empire: Juteopolis 1850-1939 — *Tomlinson, Jim*
Dune — *Herbert, Frank*
The Dungeon House — *Edwards, Martin*
y Dungeon Monstres: My Son the Killer (Illus. by Bezian) — *Sfar, Joann*
c The Dungeoneers — *Anderson, John David*
Dunmore's New World: The Extraordinary Life of a Royal Governor in Revolutionary America--with Jacobites, Counterfeiters, Land Schemes, Shipwrecks, Scalping, Indian Politics, Runaway Slaves, and Two Illegal Royal Weddings — *David, James Corbett*
The Dunning School: Historians, Race, and the Meaning of Reconstruction — *Smith, John David*
y Duplicity — *Traver, N.K.*
A Durable Fire: The Letters of Duff and Diana Cooper, 1913-1950 — *Cooper, Artemis*
y Durarara!! (Illus. by Yasuda, Suzuhito) — *Narita, Ryohgo*
Durchkreuzte Zeit: Zur asthetischen Temporalitat der spaten Gedichte von Nelly Sachs und Paul Celan — *Neumann, Annja*
Durham Cathedral: History, Fabric and Culture — *Brown, David (b. 1948-)*
Durham Priory Manorial Accounts, 1277-1310 — *Britnell, Richard*
Dust — *Owuor, Yvonne Adhiambo*
Dust and Desire — *Williams, Conrad*
Dust Bound for Heaven: Explorations in the Theology of Thomas Aquinas — *Hutter, Reinhard*
The Dust That Falls from Dreams (Read by Jay, Avita). Audiobook Review — *de Bernieres, Louis*
The Dust That Falls from Dreams — *de Bernieres, Louis*
y Dust to Dust — *Walker, Melissa*
Dutch East India Company Shipbuilding — *van Duivenvoorde, Wendy*
Duty — *Gates, Robert M.*
Duveen: The Story of the Most Spectacular Art Dealer of All Time — *Behrman, Samuel Nathaniel*
Dvostruke manjine u Srbiji: O posebnostima u religiji i etnicitetu Rumuna u Vojvodini — *Djuric-Milovanovic, Aleksandra*
Dwayne Wade — *Jackson, Aurelia*
Dying Every Day: Seneca at the Court of Nero — *Romm, James*

Dying for Ideas: The Dangerous Lives of the Philosophers — *Bradatan, Costica*
The Dying Grass — *Vollmann, William T.*
Dying Modern: A Meditation on Elegy — *Fuss, Diana*
The Dying Season — *Walker, Martin*
Dying to Forget — *Gendzier, Irene L.*
Dying to Tell — *O'Connor, T.J.*
A Dying Trade: Memoirs of a Nursing Home Proprietor — *Webb, William*
Dying Unneeded: The Cultural Context of the Russian Mortality Crisis — *Parsons, Michelle A.*
Dylan: Disc by Disc — *Bream, Jon*
Dylan Goes Electric! Newport, Seeger, Dylan, and the Night That Split the Sixties — *Wald, Elijah*

Dylan: The Biography — *McDougal, Dennis*
c **Dylan the Villain (Illus. by Campbell, K.G.)** — *Campbell, K.G.*
Dylan Thomas: A Centenary Celebration — *Ellis, Hannah*
The Dylanologists: Adventures in the Land of Bob — *Kinney, David*
The Dynamics of Auction: Social Interaction and the Sale of Fine Art and Antiques — *Heath, Christian*
Dynamics of Cancer: Mathematical Foundations of Oncology — *Wodarz, Dominik*
Dynamics of Innovation: The Expansion of Technology in Modern Times — *Caron, Francois*

Dynamics of Neo-Latin and the Vernacular: Language and Poetics, Translation and Transfer — *Deneire, Tom*
Dynamiques du monde rural dans la conjoncture de 1300: Echanges, prelevements et consommation en Mediterranee occidentale — *Bourin, Monique*
The Dynamite Room — *Hewitt, Jason*
The Dynamiters: Irish Nationalism and Political Violence in the Wider World, 1867-1900 — *Whelehan, Niall*
Dynastic Marriages 1612/1615: A Celebration of the Habsburg and Bourbon Unions — *McGowan, Margaret M.*
Dynasty: The Rise and Fall of the House of Caesar — *Holland, Tom*

E

E.E. Cummings: Complete Poems, 1904-1962 — *Cummings, E.E.*
c E.E. Cummings (Illus. by Eidrigevicius, Stasys) — *Berry, S.L.*
c E Is for Egypt — *Somerville, Charles C.*
c E.O. Wilson's Life on Earth. E-book Review — *Ryan, Morgan*
Each Thing Unblurred Is Broken — *Baker, Andrea*
Eager to Love: The Alternative Way of Francis of Assisi — *Rohr, Richard*
c Eagle — *Bodden, Valerie*
The Eagle and the Dragon: Globalization and European Dreams of Conquest in China and America in the Sixteenth Century — *Gruzinski, Serge*
Eagle in Exile — *Smale, Alan*
The Eagle in Splendour: Inside the Court of Napoleon — *Mansel, Philip*
c The Eagle Inside (Illus. by Bancroft, Bronwyn) — *Bancroft, Jack Manning*
y Eagle Talons — *Murphy, Robert Lee*
c Eagles — *Riggs, Kate*
c The Eagles are Back (Read by Minor, Wendell). Audiobook Review — *George, Jean Craighead*
An Eames Anthology — *Eames, Charles*
Eamon de Valera: A Will to Power — *Fanning, Ronan*
c Earclaw and Eddie — *Miller, Daniel Jude*
The Earl Claims a Bride — *Grey, Amelia*
The Earl of Brass — *Jorgenson, Kara*
The Earliest Christian Meeting Places: Almost Exclusively Houses? — *Adams, Edward*
The Earliest Instrument: Ritual Power and Fertility Magic of the Flute in Upper Paleolithic Culture — *Neal, Lana*
Earls Colne's Early Modern Landscapes — *MacKinnon, Dolly*
The Earl's Complete Surrender — *Barnes, Sophie*
The Earl's Defiant Wallflower — *Ridley, Erica*
Earls Just Want to Have Fun — *Galen, Shana*
The Early Anglo-Saxon Kingdoms of Southern Britain AD 450-650: Beneath the Tribal Hidage — *Harrington, Sue*
c Early Bird (Illus. by Yuly, Toni) — *Yuly, Toni*
Early Christianity in Contexts: An Exploration across Cultures and Continents — *Tabbernee, William*
Early Commentaries on the Rule of the Friars Minor, vol. 1: The 1242 Commentary, Hugh of Digne, David of Augsburg, John of Wales — *Flood, David*
c The Early Cretaceous: Notes, Drawings, and Observations from Prehistory (Illus. by Alonso, Juan Carlos) — *Alonso, Juan Carlos*
Early Greek Mythography, vol. 1: Text and Introduction — *Fowler, Robert L.*
Early Greek Mythography, vol. 2: Commentary — *Fowler, Robert L.*
Early History of the Southwest through the Eyes of German-Speaking Jesuit Missionaries: A Transcultural Experience in the Eighteenth Century — *Classen, Albrecht*
Early Islam: A Critical Reconstruction Based on Contemporary Sources — *Ohlig, Karl-Heinz*
The Early Laps of Stock Car Racing: A History of the Sport and Business Through 1974 — *Ellison, Betty Boles*
The Early Luther: Stages in a Reformation Reorientation — *Hamm, Berndt*
Early Medieval China: A Sourcebook — *Swartz, Wendy*
Early Medieval Europe, 300-1050: The Birth of Western Society — *Rollason, David*

Early Medieval Monasticism in the North Sea Zone: A Conference Examining New Research and Fresh Perspectives
Early Modern Cultures of Translation — *Newman, Karen*
Early Modern Drama and the Bible: Contexts and Readings, 1570-1625 — *Streete, Adrian*
Early Modern Habsburg Women: Transnational Contexts, Cultural Conflicts, Dynastic Continuities — *Cruz, Anne J.*
The Early Modern Italian Domestic Interior, 1400-1700: Objects, Spaces, Domesticities — *Campbell, Erin J.*
Early Modern Jesuits between Obedience and Conscience during the Generalate of Claudio Acquaviva (1581-1615). — *Mostaccio, Silvia*
Early Modern Theatricality — *Turner, Henry S.H.*
Early Modern Things: Objects and Their Histories, 1500-1800 — *Findlen, Paula*
Early Modern Women and the Poem — *Wiseman, Susan*
Early Modern Writing and the Privatisation of Experience — *Davis, Nick*
The Early Morning of War: Bull Run, 1861 — *Longacre, Edward G.*
Early Music Editing: Principles, Historiography, Future Directions — *Dumitrescu, Theodor*
Early One Morning — *Baily, Virginia*
The Early Prophets: Joshua, Judges, Samuel and Kings — *Fox, Everett*
The Early Reformation in Germany: Between Secular Impact and Radical Vision — *Scott, Tom*
Early Rymes of Robyn Hood: An Edition of the Texts, ca. 1425 to ca. 1600 — *Ohlgren, Thomas H.*
The Early Stories of Truman Capote — *Capote, Truman*
The Early Textual History of Lucretius' De Rerum Natura — *Butterfield, David J.*
The Early Textual History of Lucretius' De rerum natura — *David, Butterfield*
Early Warning (Read by King, Lorelei). Audiobook Review — *Smiley, Jane*
Early Warning — *Smiley, Jane*
The Early Wittgenstein on Metaphysics, Natural Science, Language and Value — *Tejedor, Chon*
Early Yiddish Epic — *Frakes, Jerold J.*
c Earmuffs for Everyone! How Chester Greenwood Became Known as the Inventor of Earmuffs (Illus. by McCarthy, Meghan) — *McCarthy, Meghan*
Earnhardt Nation: The Full-Throttle Saga of NASCAR's First Family — *Busbee, Jay*
c The Earth (Illus. by Bonilla, Rocio) — *Roca, Nuria*
y Earth and Sky (Read by Dykhouse, Whitney). Audiobook Review — *Crewe, Megan*
The Earth beneath Our Feet — *Thoresen, Kimberley A.*
c Earth Day — *Murray, Julie*
y Earth Flight — *Edwards, Janet*
Earth Hour — *Malouf, David*
y The Earth is Singing — *Curtis, Vanessa*
Earth Memories — *Powys, Llewelyn*
c Earth: No Place Like Home — *Markovics, Joyce*
Earth Politics: Religion, Decolonization, and Bolivia's Indigenous Intellectuals — *Ari, Waskar*
Earth Science Success, 2d ed.: 55 Table-Ready, Notebook-Based Lessons — *Oates-Bockenstedt, Catherine*
y Earth & Sky — *Crewe, Megan*
c Earth Space Moon Base — *Price, Ben Joel*
Earthburner — *Walsh, William*
Earthman Jack vs. the Secret Army — *Kadish, Matthew*

c Earthquake — *Markovics, Joyce*
y Earthquake — *Pike, Aprilynne*
y Earthquake: Perspectives on Earthquake Disasters — *Rooney, Anne*
c Earthquake: San Francisco, 1906 — *Duey, Kathleen*
Earthquakes, Mudslides, Fires and Riots: California and Graphic Design, 1936-1986 — *Sandhaus, Louis*
y Earthrise: My Adventures as an Apollo 14 Astronaut — *Mitchell, Edgar*
c Earth's Changing Surface — *Storad, Conrad J.*
Earth's Cycles in Action Series — *Dakers, Diane*
Earth's Cycles — *Dakers, Diane*
Earth's Deep History: How It Was Discovered and Why It Matters — *Rudwick, Martin J.S.*
Earth's Imagined Corners — *Linse, Tamara*
c Earth's Water Cycle — *Dakers, Diane*
Easiest if I Had a Gun — *Gerhard Martin*
Easily Distracted — *Coogan, Steve*
East African Hip Hop: Youth Culture and Globalization — *Ntarangwi, Mwenda*
East Asian Development: Foundations and Strategies — *Perkins, Dwight H.*
The East Asian Peace: Conflict Prevention and Informal Peacebuilding — *Weissmann, Mikael*
East German Cinema: DEFA and Film History — *Heiduschke, Sebastian*
The East India Company and Religion, 1698-1858 — *Carson, Penelope*
c The Easter Book — *Storey, Rita*
c Easter Bunnies — *Merrick, Patrick*
c Easter: The King James Version (Illus. by Pienkowski, Jan) — *Pienkowski, Jan*
Eastern European Railways in Transition: Nineteenth to Twenty-First Centuries — *Roth, Ralf*
Eastern Mediterranean — *Meleagrou, Ivi*
Eastern Orthodox Encounters of Identity and Otherness: Values, Self-Reflection, Dialogue — *Krawchuk, Andrii*
Easy, Affordable Raw: How to Go Raw on $10 a Day (or Less). — *Viger, Lisa*
Easy Studies for Acoustic and Electric Guitar — *Oser, Stefan*
The Easy Vegan Cookbook: Make Healthy Home Cooking Practically Effortless — *Hester, Kathy*
Eat — *Slater, Nigel*
Eat, Chew, Live: 4 Revolutionary Ideas to Prevent Diabetes, Lose Weight and Enjoy Food — *Poothullil, John M.*
Eat Clean Live Well — *Walters, Terry*
Eat, Drink, and be Wary: How Unsafe Is Our Food? — *Duncan, Charles M.*
c Eat, Eat, Eat! Cheese, Cheese, Cheese! (Illus. by Bartlett, T.C.) — *Bartlett, T.C.*
Eat It Later: Mastering Self Control and the Slimming Power of Postponement — *Alvear, Michael*
c Eat, Leo! Eat! (Illus. by Bisaillon, Josee) — *Adderson, Caroline*
y Eat Like a Champion — *Castle, Jill*
The Eat Like a Man Guide to Feeding a Crowd: How to Cook for Family, Friends, and Spontaneous Parties — *D'Agostino, Ryan*
Eat Local for Less: The Ultimate Guide to Opting Out of Our Broken Industrial Food System — *Castillo, Julie*
Eat Mexico: Recipes From Mexico City's Streets, Markets & Fondas — *Tllez, Lesley*
Eat My Heart Out — *Pilger, Zoe*
Eat! The Quick-Look Cookbook — *Scolik, Gabriels*
y Eat the Sky, Drink the Ocean — *Murray, Kirsty*
Eat Your Greens: The Surprising Power of Homegrown Leaf Crops — *Kennedy, David*

c Eat Your Science Homework: Recipes for Inquiring Minds (Illus. by Hernandez, Leeza) — McCallum, Ann
c Eat Your U.S. History Homework: Recipies for Revolutionary Minds (Illus. by Hernandez, Leeza) — McCallum, Ann
Eating Asian America: A Food Studies Reader — Ku, Robert Ji-Song
Eating Culture: An Anthropological Guide to Food — Crowther, Gillian
Eating Earth: Environmental Ethics and Dietary Choice — Kemmerer, Lisa
c Eating Ethically — Felix, Rebecca
Eating Her Curries and Kway: A Cultural History of Food in Singapore — Tarulevicz, Nicole
Eating People Is Wrong, and Other Essays on Famine, Its Past, and Its Future — Grada, Cormac O.
Eating Puerto Rico: A History of Food, Culture, and Identity — Ortiz Cuadra, Cruz Miguel
Eating Rome: Living the Good Life in the Eternal City — Minchilli, Elizabeth
Eating Together: Food, Friendship, and Inequality — Julier, Alice P.
Eating Viet Nam: Dispatches from a Blue Plastic Table — Holliday, Graham
Eating Words: A Norton Anthology of Food Writing — Gilbert, Sandra M.
Eaton's: The Trans-Canada Store — Kopytek, Bruce Allen
Eatymologies: Historical Notes on Culinary Terms — Sayers, William
Ebola '76 — Elsir, Amir Tag
y The Ebola Epidemic: The Fight, the Future — Goldsmith, Connie
y Ebola: Fears and Facts — Newman, Patricia
Ebola: Stigma and Western Conspiracy — Davieson, Adrian A.
Ebony & Ivy: Race, Slavery, and the Troubled History of America's Universities — Wilder, Craig Steven
The EC Archives: The Haunt of Fear, vol. 2
Ecclesiastical Colony: China's Catholic Church and the French Religious Protectorate — Young, Ernest P.
c Echidnas — Zappa, Marcia
c Echo (Read by four narrators). Audiobook Review — Ryan, Pam Munoz
y Echo (Illus. by Mirtalipova, Dinara) — Ryan, Pam Munoz
c Echo Echo: Reverso Poems about Greek Myths (Illus. by Masse, Josee) — Singer, Marilyn
Echo Lake — Neggers, Carla
The Echo of Things: The Lives of Photographs in the Solomon Islands — Wright, Christopher
Echoes in the Well — Dhanoa, Belinder
Echoes of Mutiny: Race, Surveillance, and Indian Anticolonialism in North America — Sohi, Seema
y Echoes of Us — Zhang, Kat
Echo's Bones — Nixon, Mark
Echo's Bones — Beckett, Samuel
Echo's Voice: The Theatres of Sarrante, Duras, Cixous and Renaude — Noonan, Mary
Eclats d'Autriche: vingt etudes sur l'image de la culture autrichienne aux XXe et XXIe siecles — de Daran, Valerie
The Eclipse of America: Arguing America on Meet the Press — Simmons, Solon
The Ecliptic — Wood, Benjamin
Eco-Business: A Big-Brand Takeover of Sustainability — Dauvergne, Peter
Eco-Joyce: The Environmental Imagination of James Joyce — Brazeau, Robert
y Eco Warrior — Roy, Philip
Ecocritical Theory: New European Approaches — Goodbody, Axel
The Ecological Genomics of Fungi — Martin, Francis
Ecological Statistics: Contemporary Theory and Application — Fox, Gordon A.
Ecology — Cain, Michael L.
Ecology and Religion — James, George Alfred
Ecology is Permanent Economy: The Activism and Environmental Philosophy of Sunderlal Bahuguna — James, George Alfred
Ecology of Australian Temperate Reefs: The Unique South — Shepherd, Graham Edgar
The Ecology of British Romantic Conservatism, 1790-1837 — Castellano, Katey
Ecology of Climate Change: The Importance of Biotic Interactions — Post, Eric
The Ecology of Tropical East Asia — Corlett, Richard T.
Ecology or Catastrophe: The Life of Murray Bookchin — Biehl, Janet

The Economic and Social History of Brazil since 1889 — Luna, Francisco Vidal
Economic Cataracts, vol. 1 — Love, Preston, Jr.
The Economic Consequences of the Atlantic Slave Trade — Solow, Barbara
Economic Equality and Direct Democracy in Ancient Athens — Patriquin, Larry
An Economic History of Modern Sweden — Schon, Lennart
An Economic History of Nineteenth-Century Europe: Diversity and Industrialization — Berend, Ivan
An Economic History of Twentieth-Century Europe: Economic Regimes from Laissez-Faire to Globalization — Berend, Ivan
Economic Shalom: A Reformed Primer on Faith, Work, and Human Flourishing — Bolt, John
Economic Theory and the Ancient Mediterranean — Jones, Donald W.
Economic Women: Essays on Desire and Dispossession in Nineteenth-Century British Culture — Dalley, Lana L.
The Economics of Creativity: Art and Achievement Under Uncertainty — Menger, Pierre-Michel
The Economics of Inequality — Piketty, Thomas
The Economics of Outsourcing: The International Library of Critical Writings in Economics 297 — Willcocks, Leslie P.
Economics Rules: The Rights and Wrongs of the Dismal Science — Rodrik, Dani
c Economics through Infographics (Illus. by Stankiewicz, Steven) — Kenney, Karen Latchana
Economists and the State: What Went Wrong — Roth, Timothy P.
The Economists
The Economy of Glory: From Ancien Regime France to the Fall of Napoleon — Morrissey, Robert
Ecosickness in Contemporary U.S. Fiction: Environment and Affect — Houser, Heather
c Ecosystems — VanVoorst, Jenny Fretland
c Ecosystems Inside Out Series — Bow, James
The Ecumenical Legacy of Johannes Cardinal Willebrands — Denaux, Adelbert
Ecumenical Perspectives on the Filioque for the Twenty-First Century — Habets, Myk
Ecumenism, Memory and German Nationalism, 1817-1917 — Landry, Stan M.
Ed Bacon: Planning, Politics, and the Building of Modern Philadelphia — Heller, Gregory L.
c Edda: A Little Valkyrie's First Day at School (Read by Berneis, Susie). Audiobook Review — Auerbach, Adam
c Edda: A Little Valkyrie's First Day of School (Illus. by Auerbach, Adam) — Auerbach, Adam
Eddic, Skaldic, and Beyond: Poetic Variety in Medieval Iceland and Norway — Chase, Martin
c Eddie's Tent and How to Go Camping — Garland, Sarah
y Eden — Nadin, Joanna
Eden Green — Van Dahl, Fiona
Eden Halt: An Antrim Memoir — Skelton, Ross
Eden — Fox, Candice
y Eden West (Read by Haberkorn, Todd). Audiobook Review — Hautman, Pete
y Eden West — Hautman, Pete
c Eden's Wish — Crowl, M. Tara
Edgar Allan Poe — Cafiero, Giuseppe
c Edgar Allan Poe (Illus. by Kelley, Gary) — Frisch, Aaron
Edge — Oldham, Nick
y The Edge — Smith, Roland
The Edge Becomes the Center: An Oral History of Gentrification in the Twenty-First Century — Gibson, D.W.
The Edge Becomes the Center: An Oral History of Gentrification in the Twenty-First Century — Gibson, David William
y Edge: Collected Stories — Kerr, M.E.
The Edge is Where the Centre Is: David Rudkin and Penda's Fen - A Conversation — Evans, Gareth
Edge of Dark — Cooper, Brenda
The Edge of Dawn — Snodgrass, Melinda
The Edge of Dreams — Bowen, Rhys
y The Edge of Forever — Hurst, Melissa E.
The Edge of Islam: Personhood, and Ethnoreligious Boundaries on the Kenya Coast — McIntosh, Janet
y Edge of Lost — McMorris, Kristina
y The Edge of Me — Brittan, Jane
The Edge of the Precipice: Why Read Literature in the Digital Age? — Socken, Paul
y The Edge of the Shadows — George, Elizabeth
The Edge of the Sky — Trotta, Roberto

The Edge of the World: A Cultural History of the North Sea and the Transformation of Europe — Pye, Michael
The Edge of Words: God and the Habits of Language — Williams, Rowan
y Edgewater — Sheinmel, Courtney
c Edible Colors — Bass, Jennifer Vogel
Edible Memory: The Lure of Heirloom Tomatoes and Other Forgotten Foods — Jordan, Jennifer A.
c Edible Numbers — Bass, Jennifer Vogel
The Edible South: The Power of Food and the Making of an American Region — Ferris, Marcie Cohen
Edible Wild Plants and Herbs: A Compendium of Recipes and Remedies — Michael, Pamela
The Edinburgh Companion to the Bible and the Arts — Prickett, Stephen
y Edison's Alley — Elfman, Eric
c Edison's Alley — Shusterman, Neal
Edith Kermit Roosevelt: Creating the Modern First Lady — Gould, Lewis L.
Editionen! Wozu? Wie? Und wie Viele? Zum Stand der Historischen 'Edition' in der Schweiz im Digitalen Zeitalter
c Edmond, the Moonlit Party (Illus. by Boutavant, Marc) — Desbordes, Astrid
c Edmond: The Moonlit Party (Illus. by Boutavant, Marc) — Desbordes, Astrid
c Edmond, the Moonlit Party (Illus. by Boutavant, Marc) — Desbordes, Astrid
c Edmonds Beginner's Cookbook — Goodman, Fielder
Edmund Burke in America: The Contested Career of the Father of Modern Conservatism — Maciag, Drew
Edmund Burke: The First Conservative — Norman, Jesse
Edmund Campion: A Scholarly Life — Kilroy, Gerard
Edmund G. Ross: Soldier, Senator, Abolitionist — Ruddy, Richard A.
c Edmund Unravels (Read by Poe, Richard). Audiobook Review — Kolb, Andrew
c Edmund Unravels (Illus. by Kolb, Andrew) — Kolb, Andrew
Edna Andrade — Balken, Debra Bricker
Eduardo Paolozzi at New Worlds: Science Fiction and Art in the Sixties — Brittain, David
Eduardo Paolozzi — Collins, Judith
Educate Your Brain: Use Mind-Body Balance to Learn Faster, Work Smarter and Move More Easily through Life — Brown, Kathy
The Educated Eye: Visual Culture and Pedagogy in the Life Sciences — Anderson, Nancy
Educating America's Military — Johnson-Freese, Joan
Educating Ireland: Schooling and Social Change, 1700-2000 — Raftery, Deirder
Education — Hankiewicz, John
Education and Immigration — Kao, Grace
Education and the State in Modern Peru: Primary Schooling in Lima, 1821-c. 1921 — Espinoza, G. Antonio
Education Essential for Global Competitiveness: A Critical Pedagogy of Resistance: 34 Pedagogues We Need to Know — Kirylo, James D.
Education in Prison: Studying through Distance Learning — Hughes, Emma
y The Education of a Poker Player — McManus, James
The Education of a Traitor — Grobman, Svetlana
The Education of David Martin: The Making of an Unlikely Sociologist — Martin, David (b. 1929-)
y The Education of Ivy Blake — Airgood, Ellen
The Education of Kevin Powell: A Boy's Journey into Manhood — Powell, Kevin (b. 1966-)
c Education through the Years: How Going to School Has Changed in Living Memory — Lewis, Clare
y Educational Entrepreneurship: Promoting Public-Private Partnerships for the 21st Century — Young, Nicholas D.
Educations in Ethnic Violence: Identity, Educational Bubbles, and Resource Mobilization — Lange, Matthew
Educators Resource Directory, 11th ed. — Grey House Publishing
Edward Bouverie Pusey and the Oxford Movement — Strong, Rowan
Edward Gorey: His Book Cover Art and Design — Heller, Steven
Edward Health: The Authorised Biography — Ziegler, Philip
c Edward Hopper Paints His World (Illus. by Minor, Wendell) — Burleigh, Robert
Edward II: The Unconventional King — Warner, Kathryn

Edward III and the Triumph of England: The Battle of Crecy and the Company of the Garter — *Barber, Richard*
Edward S. Curtis: One Hundred Masterworks — *Cardozo, Christopher*
Edward Thomas: From Adlestrop to Arras — *Wilson, Jean Moorcroft*
Edward Upward and Left-Wing Literary Culture in Britain — *Kohlmann, Benjamin*
Edward VI: The Last Boy King — *Alford, Stephen*
y Edward Wynkoop: Soldier and Indian Agent — *Oswald, Nancy*
Een land van waan en wijs: Geschiedens van de Nederlandse jeugdliteratuur — *Ghesquiere, Rita*
c Eeny, Meeny, Miney, Mo and Flo! (Illus. by Molk, Laurel) — *Molk, Laurel*
Eeny Meeny — *Arlidge, M.J.*
c Eerie Inns — *Lunis, Natalie*
Eesti eleegia ja teisi luuletusi, 1981-2012 — *Talvet, Juri*
Effective Discipling in Muslim Communities: Scripture, History, and Seasoned Practices — *Little, Don*
Effective Intercultural Communication: A Christian Perspective — *Moreau, A. Scott*
EFI Conversions: How to Swap Your Carb for Electronic Fuel Injection — *Candela, Tony*
The Egg and I (Read by Henderson, Heather). Audiobook Review — *MacDonald, Betty*
Egg Heaven — *Parks, Robin*
c Egg: Nature's Perfect Package (Illus. by Jenkins, Steve) — *Jenkins, Steve*
y Egg & Spoon — *Maguire, Gregory*
Egg: The Very Best Recipes Inspired by the Simple Egg — *Vaughan, Blanche*
Egidio da Viterbo: Cardinale Agostiniano tra Roma e l'Europa del Rinascimento - Atti del Convegno, Viterbo, 22-23 setiembre 2012--Roma, 26-28 setiembre 2012 — *Chiabo, Myriam*
c Egypt — *Bodden, Valerie*
c Egypt — *Powell, Jillian*
Egypt and the Limits of Hellenism — *Moyer, Ian S.*
c The Egyptian Cat Mystery (Illus. by Elkerton, Andy) — *Dolan, Penny*
Egyptian Oedipus: Athanasius Kircher and the Secrets of Antiquity — *Stolzenberg, Daniel*
c The Egyptian Prophecy (Illus. by Laughead, Mike) — *Perritano, John*
c Egyptian Pyramids — *Raum, Elizabeth*
Egypt's Desert Dreams: Development or Disasters? — *Sims, David*
Ehrenburger der Nation: Die Kriegsbeschadigten des Ersten Weltkriegs in Politik und Propaganda des Nationalsozialismus — *Loffelbein, Nils*
Eichmann before Jerusalem: The Unexamined Life of a Mass Murderer — *Stangneth, Bettina*
Eichmann in Jerusalem: A Report on the Banality of Evil — *Arendt, Hannah*
The Eight-Bit Bard — *Rath, Aaron*
Eight Hundred Grapes — *Dave, Laura*
c Eight Jolly Reindeer (Illus. by Rogers, Jacqueline) — *Oliver, Ilanit*
Eighteen Lectures on Dunhuang — *Xinjiang, Rong*
Eighteenth-Century Fiction and the Reinvention of Wonder — *Kareem, Sarah Tindal*
Eighty-Eight Years: The Long Death of Slavery in the United States, 1777-1865 — *Rael, Patrick*
Eileen — *Moshfegh, Ottessa*
Eileen Gray: Her Work and Her World — *Goff, Jennifer*
Eileen — *Moshfegh, Ottessa*
Ein Feentempel der Mode oder Eine vergessene Familie, ein ausgeloschter Ort: Die Familie Freudenberg und das Modehaus "Herrmann Gerson" — *Kessemeier, Gesa*
Ein Land unterwegs: Kulturgeschichte Polens seit 1945 — *Krzoska, Markus*
Ein neues Lied? Ein besseres Lied? Die neuen 'Evangelien' nach Heine, Wagner und Nietzsche — *Wenzel, Eugen*
Ein Raum im Wandel: Die Osmanisch-Habsburgische Grenzregion vom 16. bis zum 18. Jahrhundert — *Spannenberger, Norbert*
"Ein Wunderwerk der Technik": Fruhe Computernutzung in der Schweiz — *Egger, Josef*
"Eine Familie im Krieg: Leben, Sterben und Schreiben 1914-1918 — *Wierling, Dorothee*
Eine Stadt im Krieg: Bremen 1914-1918 — *Shock-Quinteros, Eva*
Eine Stadt im Krieg: Bremen 1914-1918: Szenische Lesung: Auswahl und Zusammenstellung der Originaldokumente — *Luchinger, Peter*

Eine unbekannte Konzilssynopse aus dem Ende des 9. Jahrhunderts — *Hoffman, Lars M.*
Einfach Vornehm: Die Hausleute der Nordwestdeutschen Kustenmarsch in der Fruhen Neuzeit — *Cronshagen, Jessica*
An Einstein Encyclopedia — *Calaprice, Alice*
Einstein: His Space and Times — *Gimbel, Steven*
The Einstein Prophecy — *Masello, Robert*
The Einstein Proxy — *Dimodica, Steve*
c Einstein the Class Hamster and the Very Real Game Show (Illus. by Tashjian, Jake) — *Tashjian, Janet*
Einstein's Beach House — *Appel, Jacob M.*
Einstein's Berlin: In the Footsteps of a Genius — *Hoffmann, Dieter*
Einstein's Dice and Schrodinger's Cat: How Two Great Minds Battled Quantum Randomness to Create a Unified Theory of Physics — *Halpern, Paul*
Eisenhower: A Life — *Johnson, Paul*
Eisenhower and the Cold War Arms Race: "Open Skies" and the Military-Industrial Complex — *Bury, Helen*
Eisenhower and the Cold War Economy — *McClenahan, William, Jr.*
Eisenhower in War and Peace — *Smith, Jean Edward*
Eisenhower: The White House Years — *Newton, Jim*
Eisenhower's Armies — *Bar, Niall*
Eisenhower's Guerrillas: The Jedburghs, the Maquis, and the Liberation of France — *Jones, Benjamin*
Eisenhower's Sputnik Moment: The Race for Space and World Prestige — *Mieczkowski, Yanek*
y Either the Beginning or the End of the World — *Farish, Terry*
El Barroco, marco de agua de la narrativa hispanoamericana — *Cevellos, Santiago*
c El Deafo (Illus. by Bell, Cece) — *Bell, Cece*
El dinero en la obra de Quevedo: la crisis de identidad en la sociedad feudal espanola a principios del siglo XVII — *Eberhard, Geisler*
c El edificio (Illus. by Rabanal, Daniel) — *Buitrago, Jairo*
El "Facet," una "ars amandi" medieval: Edicio i estudi — *Cantavella, Rosanna*
El largo y sinuoso camino: Razones por las que no ha sido construido el canal de Nicaragua — *Van der Post, JanGeert*
El mundo de afuera — *Franco, Jorge*
El Pantano y Otros Sitios del Formativo Medio en el Valle de Mascota, Jalisco — *Mountjoy, Joseph*
El Paso Twilight — *DeMarinis, Rick*
El Paso's Muckraker: The Life of Owen Payne White — *Christian, Garna L.*
c El pequeno mago (Illus. by Kohara, Kazuno) — *Kohara, Kazuno*
c El Perro con Sombrero: A Bilingual Doggy Tale (Illus. by Henry, Jed) — *Kent, Derek Taylor*
El primer cartulario de los reyes de Navarra: El valor de lo escrito / Le premier cartulaire des rois de Navarre: La valeur de l'ecrit. vol. 2 — *Vaquero, Eloisa Ramirez*
El Rio Mapocho y sus riberas: Espacio public e intervencion urbana en Santiago de Chile (1855-1918). — *Castillo Fernandez, Simon*
El Sistema: Orchestrating Venezuela's Youth — *Baker, Geoffrey*
El Vaticano II como software de la Iglesia actual — *Hunermann, Peter*
Elaine de Kooning: Portraits — *Fortune, Brandon*
Elaine's: The Rise of One of New York's Most Legendary Restaurants from Those Who Were There — *Penn, Amy Phillips*
c Elan in Deep — *McVoy, Terra*
Elder Brother and the Law of the People: Contemporary Kinship and Cowessess First Nation — *Innis, Robert Alexander*
Elder Northfield's Home, or, Sacrificed on the Mormon Altar: A Story of the Blighting Curse of Polygamy — *Bartlett, A. Jennie*
Eldership and the Mission of God: Equipping Teams for Faithful Church Leadership — *Briggs, J.R.*
Eleanor — *Gurley, Jason*
Eleanor Marx: A Life — *Holmes, Rachel*
Eleanor of Castille: The Shadow Queen — *Cockerill, Sara*
Eleanor & Park — *Rowell, Rainbow*
c The Election (Illus. by Jagucki, Marek) — *Levenson, Eleanor*
Election Notebook: The Inside Story of the Battle over Britain's Future and My Personal Battle to Report It — *Robinson, Nick*
The Election of 1860 Reconsidered — *Fuller, A. James*

The Election of Grace: A Riddle Without a Resolution? — *Williams, Stephen N.*
Electric City: General Electric in Schenectady — *Blackwelder, Julia Kirk*
Electric Shock: From the Gramophone to the iPhone: 125 Years of Pop Music — *Doggett, Peter*
Electrifying India: Regional Political Economies of Development — *Kale, Sunila S.*
Electronic Iran: The Cultural Politics of an Online Evolution — *Akhavan, Niki*
Electronic Publishing : Politics and Pragmatics — *Egan, Gabriel*
Electronics for Artists: Adding Light, Motion, and Sound to Your Artwork — *Field, Simon Quellen*
Elegia — *da Settimello, Arrigo*
Elegy for a Broken Machine — *Phillips, Patrick*
Elegy: The First Day on the Somme — *Roberts, Andrew*
Elektra: Bloodlines (Illus. by Del Mundo, Michael) — *Blackman, W. Haden*
The Element of Power: Gadgets, Guns, and the Struggle for a Sustainable Future in the Rare Metal Age — *Abraham, David S.*
The Elementalists — *Sharp, C*
Elementary Educ 101: What They Didn't Teach You in College — *Schultek, Gretchen E.*
The Elements of Eloquence: How to Turn the Perfect English Phrase — *Forsyth, Mark*
The Elements of Style — *Strunk, William, Jr.*
The Elements: The New Guide to the Building Blocks of Our Universe — *Challoner, Jack*
y Elena Vanishing: A Memoir — *Dunkle, Elena*
Elena Vanishing — *Dunkle, Elena*
The Elephant Chaser's Daughter — *Raj, Shilpa Anthony*
Elephant Complex: Travels in Sri Lanka — *Gimlette, John*
Elephant Don: The Politics of a Pachyderm Posse — *O'Connell, Caitlin*
Elephant House (Illus. by Blau, Dick) — *Rothfels, Nigel*
c Elephant in the Dark (Illus. by Yelchin, Eugene) — *Javaherbin, Mina*
c Elephant Joe, Brave Firefighter! (Illus. by Wojtowycz, David) — *Wojtowycz, David*
c Elephant Man (Illus. by Hodnefjeld, Hilde) — *Di Fiore, Mariangela*
c The Elephant Who Liked to Smash Small Cars (Illus. by Solbert, Ronni) — *Merrill, Jean*
c Elephantastic! (Illus. by Tourlonias, Joelle) — *Engler, Michael*
c The Elephantom (Illus. by Collins, Ross) — *Collins, Ross*
Elephants and Savanna Woodland Ecosystems: A Study from Chobe National Park, Botswana — *Skarpe, Christina*
c The Elevator Ghost (Illus. by Innerst, Stacy) — *Huser, Glen*
Elevator — *Fay, Emma*
Eleven Prague Corpses: Stories — *Kobrin, Kirill*
y The Eleventh Doctor: After Life (Illus. by Fraser, Simon) — *Ewing, Al*
The Eleventh Hour: How Great Britain, the Soviet Union, and the U.S. Brokered an Unlikely Deal That Won the War — *Keeney, L. Douglas*
Elfquest — *Pini, Richard*
Elgin Baylor: The Man Who Changed Basketball — *Bayne, Bijan C.*
Eli Reed: A Long Walk Home — *Reed, Eli*
Elimination — *Gorman, Ed*
The Elimination Diet: Discover the Foods That Are Making You Sick and Tired - and Feel Better Fast — *Segersten, Alissa*
The Eliot Girls — *Bridge, Krista*
c Eliot Ness — *Gagne, Tammy*
Elisha Forerunner of Jesus Christ — *Arnold, Daniel*
Elite Parties, Poor Voters: How Social Services Win Votes in India — *Thachil, Tariq*
Elites: A General Model — *Milner, Murray, Jr.*
c Eliza Bluebell — *York, A.J.*
Elizabeth Bishop: The North Haven Journal, 1974-1979 — *McPeck, Eleanor M.*
Elizabeth de Burgh, Lady of Clare (1295-1360): Household and Other Records — *Ward, Jennifer C.*
Elizabeth I and Her Circle — *Doran, Susan*
Elizabeth Is Missing — *Healey, Emma*
Elizabeth Patterson Bonaparte: An American Aristocrat in the Early Republic — *Lewis, Charlene M. Boyer*
Elizabeth: Renaissance Prince — *Hilton, Lisa*
Elizabeth Singer Rowe and the Development of the English Novel — *Backscheider, Paula R.*

584 • ELIZABETH/Title Index

c Elizabeth Started All the Trouble — *Rappaport, Doreen*
Elizabeth Wolstenholme Elmy and the Victorian Feminist Movement: The Biography of an Insurgent Woman — *Wright, Maureen*
Elizabethan Naval Administration — *Knighton, Charles S.*
The Elizabethan New Year's Gift Exchanges, 1559-1603 — *Lawson, Jane A.*
Elizabethan Seneca: Three Tragedies — *Ker, James*
Elizabeth's Bedfellows: An Intimate History of the Queen's Court — *Whitelock, Anna*
c Elizabeth's Story, 1848 — *Whitby, Adele*
c Ella (Illus. by Chin, Marcos) — *Kasdan, Mallory*
c Ella and Penguin Stick Together
c Ella and Penguin Stick Together (Illus. by Bonnet, Rosalinde) — *Maynor, Megan*
c Ella Bella Ballerina and A Midsummer Night's Dream (Illus. by Mayhew, James) — *Mayhew, James*
Ella's Kitchen: The First Foods Book: The Purple One — *Hamlyn*
Elle — *Mars, Emma*
Elle and Coach: Diabetes, the Fight for My Daughter's Life, and the Dog Who Changed Everything — *Shaheen, Stefany*
Ellen: A Collection of Stories and Essays in Honor of Ellen Gray Massey — *Law, Steven*
Ellen Harmon White: American Prophet — *Aamodt, Terrie Dopp*
c Ellie (Illus. by Wu, Mike) — *Wu, Mike*
c Ellie and the Good-Luck Pig (Illus. by Riti, Marsha) — *Barkley, Callie*
The Ellie McDoodle Diaries: Ellie for President — *Barshaw, Ruth McNally*
c Ellie Needs to Go — *Reynolds, Kate E.*
y Ellie's Story (Illus. by Cowdrey, Richard) — *Cameron, W. Bruce*
c Elliot's Arctic Surprise (Illus. by Chessa, Francesca) — *Barr, Catherine*
c Elliott the Otter: The Totally Untrue Story of Elliott, Boss of the Bay (Illus. by Skewes, John) — *Ode, Eric*
Ellis Island Nation: Immigration Policy and American Identity in the Twentieth Century — *Fleegler, Robert L.*
c EllRay Jakes Is Magic! (Read by Allen, Corey). Audiobook Review — *Warner, Sally*
c EllRay Jakes Rocks the Holidays! (Illus. by Biggs, Brian) — *Warner, Sally*
c EllRay Jakes: The Dragon Slayer! (Illus. by Allen, Corey). Audiobook Review — *Warner, Sally*
c EllRay Jakes: The Dragon Slayer! (Illus. by Biggs, Brian) — *Warner, Sally*
c EllRay Jakes: The Recess King! (Illus. by Biggs, Brian) — *Warner, Sally*
c Elmer — *McKee, David*
c Elmer and Butterfly (Illus. by McKee, David) — *McKee, David*
c Elmer and the Flood (Illus. by McKee, David) — *McKee, David*
c Elmer and the Monster (Illus. by McKee, David) — *McKee, David*
Eloge du blasphème — *Fourest, Caroline*
Elon Musk: How the Billionaire CEO of SpaceX and Tesla Is Shaping Our Future — *Vance, Ashlee*
Elon Musk: Tesla, SpaceX, and the Quest for a Fantastic Future — *Vance, Ashlee*
Eloquent Wisdom: Rhetoric, Cosmology and Delight in the Theology of Augustine of Hippo — *Clavier, Mark F.M.*
Elsewhere — *Rabinovici, Doron*
c The Elves and the Trendy Shoes — *Foster, Evelyn*
c Elvis: The Story of the Rock and Roll King (Illus. by Christensen, Bonnie) — *Christensen, Bonnie*
c Elwood Bigfoot (Illus. by Wragg, Nate) — *Esbaum, Jill*
Emails from India — *Harper, Janis*
Emanations: Foray into Forever — *Kaplan, Carter*
y The Emancipated — *Reyes, M.G.*
y Emancipation Proclamation — *Bolden, Tonya*
Emancipation, the Union Army, and the Reelection of Abraham Lincoln — *White, Jonathan W.*
c Embassy Row — *Carter, Ally*
Embattled Bodies, Embattled Places: War in Pre-Columbian Mesoamerica and the Andes — *Scherer, Andrew K.*
Embattled Memories: Contested Meanings in Korean War Memorials — *Choi, Suhi*
Embattled Rebel: Jefferson Davis as Commander in Chief — *McPherson, James M.*
The Embedded Librarian's Cookbook — *Calkins, Kaijsa*

y An Ember in the Ashes (Read by Hardingham, Fiona, with Steve West). Audiobook Review — *Tahir, Sabaa*
y An Ember in the Ashes — *Tahir, Sabaa*
Embers — *Hopkins, Karen Ann*
Embers and Flames — *Scott, Whitney*
y Embers & Ash — *Goeglein, T. M.*
Embers at Galdrilene — *Trosper, A.D.*
Emblems of the Passing World: Poems after Photographs by August Sander — *Kirsch, Adam*
Embodied Narratives: Connecting Stories, Bodies, Cultures and Ecologies — *Formenti, Laura*
Embodied Words, Spoken Signs: Sacramentality and the Word in Rahner and Chauvet — *Beaton, Rhodora E.*
Embodying Hebrew Culture: Aesthetics, Athletics, and Dance in the Jewish Community of Mandate Palestine — *Spiegel, Nina S.*
Embrace Happiness: The Art of Conflict Management — *Soleymaniha, Ali*
Embracing Cuba — *Motley, Bryan*
Embracing the Divine: Passion and Politics in the Christian Middle East — *Khater, Akram Fouad*
Embracing the Immigrant: The Participation of Metics in Athenian Polis Religion — *Wijma, Sara M.*
Embracing the Wild in Your Dog — *Bailey, Bryan*
Embroidery: A Step-by-Step Guide to More Than 200 Stitches — *Ganderton, Lucinda*
Embryos under the Microscope: The Diverging Meanings of Life — *Maienschein, Jane*
c The Emerald Berries (Illus. by Bell, Jennifer A.) — *Green, Poppy*
c The Emerald Dragon (Illus. by McMorris, Kelly) — *Fields, Jan*
The Emerald Light in the Air — *Antrim, Donald*
Emergence: Labeled Autistic — *Grandin, Temple*
The Emergence of British Power in India, 1600-1784: A Grand Strategic Interpretation — *Bryant, Gerald James*
The Emergence of Impartiality — *Murphy, Kathryn*
The Emergence of Modern Shiism: Islamic Reform in Iraq and Iran — *Heern, Zackery*
The Emergence of Tropical Medicine in France — *Osborne, Michael A.*
The Emergence of Video Processing Tools: Television Becoming Unglued — *High, Kathy*
c Emergency Aid — *Leavitt, Amie*
Emergency Preparedness and Disaster Recovery in School Libraries: Creating a Safe Haven — *Kaaland, Christie*
c Emergency Rescue — *Rusling, Annette*
c Emergency Vehicles (Illus. by Biesty, Stephen) — *Green, Rod*
y Emergent Behavior — *Taylor, Nicole M.*
c Emergent — *Cohn, Rachel*
Emerging German-Language Novelists of the Twenty-First Century
Emerging German-Language Novelists of the Twenty-First Century — *Marven, Lyn*
The Emerging Middle Class in Africa — *Ncube, Mthuli*
Emerging Perspectives on Disability Studies — *Wappett, Matthew*
Emerging Technologies: A Primer for Librarians — *Koerber, Jennifer*
Emigration Nations: Policies and Ideologies of Emigrant Engagement — *Collyer, Michael*
Emigres: The Transformation of Art Publishing in Britain — *Nyburg, Anna*
Emil Brunner: A Reappraisal — *McGrath, Alister E.*
Emil du Bois-Reymond: Neuroscience, Self, and Society in Nineteenth-Century Germany — *Finkelstein, Gabriel*
Emily D. West and the "Yellow Rose of Texas" Myth — *Tucker, Phillip Thomas*
c Emily Dickinson (Illus. by Stermer, Dugald) — *Berry, S.L.*
y Emily Sparkes and the Friendship Fiasco — *Fitzgerald, Ruth*
c Eminem: Hip-Hop Mogul — *Burlingame, Jeff*
Eminent Victorians on American Democracy: The View from Albion — *Prochaska, Frank*
Emma: A Modern Retelling — *McCall Smith, Alexander*
y Emma (Illus. by Tse, Po) — *Emma*
c Emma and Julia Love Ballet (Illus. by McClintock, Barbara) — *McClintock, Barbara*
c Emma and the Blue Genie (Illus. by Meyer, Kerstin) — *Funke, Cornelia*
y Emma G. Loves Boyz — *Meyer, Taro*

c Emma Is on the Air: Big News! (Illus. by Pena, Karla) — *Siegal, Ida*
Emmanuel Levinas and the Limits to Ethics: A Critique and a Re-Appropriation — *Botwinick, Aryeh*
c Emmanuel's Dream: The True Story of Emmanuel Ofosu Yeboah (Illus. by Qualls, Sean) — *Thompson, Laurie Ann*
c Emma's Not-So-Sweet Dilemma — *Simon, Coco*
Emmett Till: The Murder That Shocked the World and Propelled the Civil Rights Movement — *Anderson, Devery S.*
y Emmy & Oliver — *Benway, Robin*
Emotion and Healing in the Energy Body: A Handbook of Subtle Energies in Massage and Yoga — *Henderson, Robert*
Emotional and Sectional Conflict in the Antebellum United States — *Woods, Michael E.*
Emotional Excess on the Shakespearean Stage: Passion's Slaves — *Escolme, Bridget*
Emotional Insight: The Epistemic Role of Emotional Experience — *Brady, Michael*
Emotions and Daily Life in Colonial Mexico — *Villa-Flores, Javier*
Empathy and Morality — *Maibom, Heidi L.*
Empathy: Philosophical and Psychological Perspectives — *Coplan, Amy*
Emperor Huizong — *Ebrey, Patricia Buckley*
y The Emperor of Any Place — *Wynne-Jones, Tim*
The Emperor of Ice-Cream — *Duggan, Christopher*
Emperor of Liberty: Thomas Jefferson's Foreign Policy — *Cogliano, Francis D.*
The Emperor of Water Clocks — *Komunyakaa, Yusef*
c The Emperor Penguin's New Clothes (Illus. by Beacon, Dawn) — *Guillain, Charlotte*
c Emperor Pickletine Rides the Bus — *Angleberger, Tom*
Emperor Sigismund and the Orthodox World — *Mitsiou, Ekaterini*
The Emperor's Last Island: A Journey to St Helena — *Blackburn, Julia*
c The Emperor's New Uniform — *Kennedy, Kelly*
Empire — *Ridyard, Jennifer*
Empire — *Connolly, John*
The Empire Abroad and the Empire at Home: African American Literature and the Era of Overseas Expansion — *Gruesser, John Cullen*
Empire and Co-operation: How the British Empire Used Co-Operatives in Its Development Strategies 1900-1970 — *Rhodes, Rita*
Empire and Holy War in the Mediterranean: The Galley and Maritime Conflict between the Habsburgs and Ottomans — *Williams, Phillip*
Empire and Identity in Guizhou: Local Resistance to Qing Expansion — *Weinstein, Jodi L.*
Empire and Liberty: The Civil War and the West — *Scharff, Virginia*
Empire and Pilgrimage in Conrad and Joyce — *Szczeszak-Brewer, Agata*
Empire and Power in the Reign of Suleyman: Narrating the Sixteenth-Century Ottoman World — *Sahin, Kaya*
Empire and the Animal Body: Violence, Identity and Ecology in Victorian Adventure Fiction — *Miller, John*
Empire by Treaty: Negotiating European Expansion, 1600-1900 — *Belmessous, Saliha*
Empire De/Centered: New Spatial Histories of Russia and the Soviet Union — *Turoma, Sanna*
Empire in Waves: A Political History of Surfing — *Laderman, Scott*
Empire of Chance: The Napoleonic Wars and the Disorder of Things — *Engberg-Pedersen, Anders*
Empire of Cotton: A Global History (Read by Frangione, Jim). Audiobook Review — *Beckert, Sven*
Empire of Cotton: A Global History — *Beckert, Sven*
Empire of Cotton: A New History of Global Capitalism — *Beckert, Sven*
Empire of Deception: The Incredible Story of a Master Swindler Who Seduced a City and Captivated the Nation (Read by Berkrot, Peter). Audiobook Review — *Jobb, Dean*
Empire of Deception: The Incredible Story of a Master Swindler Who Seduced a City and Captivated the Nation — *Jobb, Dean*
Empire of Fear: Inside the Islamic State — *Hosken, Andrew*
"An Empire of Ideals": The Chimeric Imagination of Ronald Reagan — *Garrison, Justin D.*
y Empire of Imagination: Gary Gygax and the Birth of Dungeons & Dragons — *Witwer, Michael*

An Empire of Memory: The Legend of Charlemagne, the Franks, and Jerusalem Before the First Crusade — Gabriele, Matthew
The Empire of Necessity: Slavery, Freedom, and Deception in the New World — Grandin, Greg
The Empire of Necessity: The Untold History of a Slave Rebellion in the Age of Liberty — Grandin, Greg
y Empire of Night — Armstrong, Kelley
An Empire of Others: Creating Ethnographic Knowledge in Imperial Russia and the USSR — Cvetkovski, Roland
Empire of Religion: Imperialism and Comparative Religion — Chidester, David
Empire of Scholars: Universities, Networks, and the British Academic World, 1850-1939 — Pietsch, Tamson
Empire of Self: A Life of Gore Vidal — Parini, Jay
y Empire of Shadows — Forster, Miriam
Empire of Sin: A Story of Sex, Jazz, Murder, and the Battle for New Orleans (Read by Dean, Robertson). Audiobook Review — Krist, Gary
Empire of Sin: A Story of Sex, Jazz, Murder, and the Battle for New Orleans — Krist, Gary
Empire of Tea: The Asian Leaf That Conquered the World — Ellis, Markman
Empire of Tea: The Asian Leaf That Conquered the World — Mauger, Matthew
Empire of the Air: Aviation and the American Ascendancy — Van Vleck, Jenifer
An Empire of the East: Travels in Indonesia — Lewis, Norman
The Empire of the Senses (Read by Lane, Christopher). Audiobook Review — Landau, Alexis
The Empire of the Senses — Landau, Alexis
c Empire of the Waves: Voyage of the Moon Child — Richardson, Christopher
Empire of Things: How We Became a World of Consumers, from the Fifteenth Century to the Twenty-First — Trentmann, Frank
Empire of Vines: Wine Culture in America — Hannickel, Erica
Empire of Water: An Environmental and Political History of the New York City Water Supply — Soll, David
Empire on Display: San Francisco's Panama-Pacific International Exposition of 1915 — Moore, Sarah J.
An Empire on the Edge: How Britain Came to Fight America — Bunker, Nick
Empire, Religion and Revolution in Early Virginia, 1607-1786 — Bell, James B.
Empire Rising — Campbell, Rick
Empire, Technology and Seapower: Royal Navy Crisis in the Age of Palmerston — Fuller, Howard J.
Empires at War, 1911-1923 — Gerwarth, Robert
Empire's Children: Child Emigration, Welfare, and the Decline of the British World, 1869-1967 — Boucher, Ellen
Empire's Crossroads: A History of the Caribbean from Columbus to the Present Day — Gibson, Carrie
Empire's End — Jenkins, Jerry B.
Empires of Love: Europe, Asia and the Making of Early Modern Identity — Nocentelli, Carmen
Employee Risk Management: How to Protect Your Business Reputation and Reduce Your Legal Liability — Rideout, Helen
The Empowered Empath: Owning, Embracing, and Managing Your Special Gifts — Rosetree, Rose
Empowering the People of God: Catholic Action before and after Vatican II — Bonner, Jeremy
Empowering Words: Outsiders and Authorship in Early America — Weyler, Karen A.
Empress Dowager Cixi: The Concubine Who Launched Modern China — Chang, Jung
The Empress Game — Mason, Rhonda
The Empress of Art — Jaques, Susan
The Empress of Mars — Baker, Kage
Empress San Francisco: The Pacific Rim, the Great West, & California at the Panama-Pacific International Exposition — Markwyn, Abigail M.
Emptiness: Feeling Christian in America — Corrigan, John
Empty Bottle of Gin — Parks, Conon
Empty Chairs — Liu, Xia
The Empty Church: Theater, Theology, and Bodily Hope — Craigo-Snell, Shannon
y Empty Cup — Costigan, Suzanne
Empty Hands: A Memoir — Ntleko, Abegail
An Empty Hell — White, Dave
Empty Houses — Thornton, Betsy

Empty Ideas: A Critique of Analytic Philosophy — Unger, Peter
Empty Labor: Idleness and Workplace Resistance — Paulsen, Roland
The Empty Loom — Gibb, Robert
Empty Nest, What's Next? Parenting Adult Children without Losing Your Mind — Howe, Michele
c Empty Places — Wiechman, Kathy Cannon
Empty Rooms — Mariotte, Jeffrey J.
c Emu (Illus. by Byrne, Graham) — Saxby, Claire
y En Recuerdo de: The Dying Art of Mexican Cemeteries in the Southwest — Jordan, Bruce F.
c En route, Nicolas! (Illus. by St-Aubin, Bruno) — Tibo, Giles
c En safari — Tuchman, Gail
Enabling Acts: The Hidden Story of How the Americans with Disabilities Act Gave the Largest U.S. Minority Its Rights — Davis, Lennard J.
Enabling Acts: The Hidden Story of How the Americans with Disabilities Act Gave the Largest US Minority Its Rights — Davis, Lennard J.
Enacting Power: The Criminalization of Obeah in the Anglophone Caribbean 1760-2011 — Handler, Jerome S.
y Enchanted Air: Two Cultures, Two Wings: A Memoir (Illus. by Rodriguez, Edel) — Engle, Margarita
Enchanted August — Bowen, Brenda
c The Enchanted Charms — Stilton, Geronimo
c The Enchanted Egg — George, Kallie
Enchanting the Swan — Schwartz, John
y Enchantment Lake — Preus, Margi
Enchantment of a Highlander — Martin, Madeline
c Enchantment of the World Series — Yomtov, Nel
Enchantress of Paris — Jefferson, Marci
Encore — Koetting, Alexis
y Encore to an Empty Room — Emerson, Kevin
Encounter on the Great Plains: Scandinavian Settlers and the Dispossession of Dakota Indians, 1890-1930 — Hansen, Karen V.
Encountering God in Tyrannical Texts: Reflections on Paul, Women, and the Authority of Scripture — Gench, Frances Taylor
Encountering Jesus, Encountering Scripture — Crump, David
Encountering Modernity: Christianity in East Asia and Asian America — Park, Albert L.
Encountering Religion: Responsibility and Criticism after Secularism — Roberts, Tyler
Encountering the Pacific in the Age of the Enlightenment — Gascoigne, John
Encounters at the Heart of the World: A History of the Mandan People — Fenn, Elizabeth A.
Encounters in Avalanche Country: A History of Survival in the Mountain West, 1820-1920 — Di Stefano, Diana L.
Encounters in Modern Jewish Thought: The Works of Eva Jospe, vol. 1: Martin Buber — Jospe, Raphael
Encounters: My Life in Publishing — Braziller, George
Encyclical on Climate Change and Inequality: On Care for Our Common Home — Francis I, Pope
The Encyclopaedia of the Dead — Kis, Danilo
Encyclopaedism from Antiquity to the Renaissance — Konig, Jason
Encyclopedia of Aesthetics, 2d ed. — Kelly, Michael
y Encyclopedia of Careers and Vocational Guidance, 16th ed., 5 vols. — Ferguson Publishing
Encyclopedia of Christian Education, 3 vols. — Kurian, George Thomas
Encyclopedia of Diversity and Social Justice — Thompson, Sherwood
The Encyclopedia of Drawing Techniques — Harrison, Hazel
Encyclopedia of Education Economics and Finance — Brewer, Dominic J.
The Encyclopedia of European Migration and Minorities: From the Seventeenth Century to the Present — Bade, Klaus J.
The Encyclopedia of Film Composers — Hischak, Thomas S.
The Encyclopedia of Greek Tragedy, 3 vols. — Roisman, Hanna
Encyclopedia of Humor Studies — Attardo, Salvatore
Encyclopedia of Pop Music Aliases, 1950-2000 — Leszczak, Bob
Encyclopedia of the FIFA World Cup — Dunmore, Tom
The Encyclopedia of the Industrial Revolution in World History — Hendrickson, Kenneth E., III
Encyclopedia of the Zombie: The Walking Dead in Popular Culture and Myth — Pulliam, June Michele

The Encyclopedia of World Ballet — Snodgrass, Mary Ellen
The End Game — Coulter, Catherine
End Game: Tipping Point for Planet Earth — Barnosky, Anthony D.
End Games in Bordeaux — Massie, Allan
The End of a Global Pox: America and the Eradication of Smallpox in the Cold War Era — Reinhardt, Bob H.
The End of Absence: Reclaiming What We've Lost in a World of Constant Connection — Harris, Michael
The End of Airports — Schaberg, Christopher
The End of All Things — Scalzi, John
The End of American World Order — Acharya, Amitav
The End of Apartheid: Diary of a Revolution — Renwick, Robin
The End of Average: How We Succeed in a World That Values Sameness — Rose, Todd
The End of Banking: Money, Credit, and the Digital Revolution — McMillan, Jonathan
The End of Cinema? A Medium in Crisis in the Digital Age — Gaudreault, Andre
y The End of College: Creating the Future of Learning and the University of Everywhere — Carey, Kevin
The End of Days — Bernofsky, Susan
The End of Days — Erpenbeck, Jenny
The End of Days
y End of Days — Ee, Susan
y End of Days — Walters, Eric
End of Discussion: How the Left's Outrage Industry Shuts Down Debate, Manipulates Voters, and Makes America Less Free and Fun — Ham, Mary Katharine
The End of Doom: Environmental Renewal in the Twenty-First Century — Bailey, Ronald
The End of Healing — Bailey, Jim
The End of Hope - the Beginning: Narratives of Hope in the Face of Death and Trauma — McCarroll, Pamela R.
The End of Intelligence: Espionage and State Power in the Information Age — Tucker, David
The End of Me: Where Real Life in the Upside-Down Ways of Jesus Begins — Idleman, Kyle
The End of Memory: A Natural History of Aging and Alzheimer's — Ingram, Jay
The End of Normal: The Great Crisis and the Future of Growth — Galbraith, James K.
The End of Plenty: The Race to Feed a Crowded World — Bourne, Joel K., Jr.
The End of Power: From Boardrooms to Battlefields and Churches to States, Why Being in Charge Isn't What It Used to Be — Naim, Moises
The End of Satisfaction: Drama and Repentance in the Age of Shakespeare — Hirschfeld, Heather
The End of Self Help: Discovering Peace and Happiness Right at the Heart of Your Messy, Scary Brilliant Life — Brenner, Gail
The End of the Cold War: 1985-1991 — Service, Robert
c The End of the Line — McKay, Sharon E.
The End of the Rainbow: How Educating for Happiness - Not Money - Would Transform Our Schools — Engel, Susan
c The End of the Rainbow (Illus. by Donnelly, Liza) — Donnelly, Liza
The End of the Rainbow — Donnelly, Liza
The End of the Rainy Season: Discovering My Family's Hidden Past in Brazil — Lindberg, Marian E.
The End of the World and Other Teachable Moments : Jacques Derrida's Final Seminar — Naas, Michael
The End of the World Is Rye — Cottrell, Brett
The End of Traditional Religion and the Rise of Christianity — O'Donell, James J.
The End of Tsarist Russia: The March to World War I and Revolution — Lieven, Dominic
End Time — Korman, Keith
End Unemployment Now: How to Eliminate Joblessness, Debt, and Poverty Despite Congress — Batra, Ravi
Endangered (Read by Chandler, David). Audiobook Review — Box, C.J.
Endangered — Box, C.J.
y Endangered — Giles, Lamar
y Endangered — Jaimet, Kate
c Endangered and Extinct Amphibians — Ransom, Candice
c Endangered and Extinct Birds — Boothroyd, Jennifer
c Endangered and Extinct Fish — Boothroyd, Jennifer

c Endangered and Extinct Invertebrates — Boothroyd, Jennifer
c Endangered and Extinct Mammals — Boothroyd, Jennifer
c Endangered and Extinct Reptiles — Boothroyd, Jennifer
Endangered Edens: Exploring the Arctic National Wildlife Refuge, Costa Rica, the Everglades, and Puerto Rico — Essen, Marty
c Endangered Energy: Investigating the Scarcity of Fossil Fuels — Iyer, Rani
y Endangered — Jaimet, Kate
Endangered Languages: An Introduction — Thomason, Sarah G.
c Endangered Rivers: Investigating Rivers in Crisis — Iyer, Rani
Endgame for ETA: Elusive Peace in the Basque Country — Whitfield, Teresa
y Endgame: The Calling — Johnson-Shelton, Nils
y Endgame: The Complete Training Diaries, vols. 1-3 — Frey, James
Ending Medical Reversal — Prasad, Vinayak K.
Ending Terrorism in Italy — Bull, Anna Cento
c Endless — Brian, Kate
c The Endless Lake — Hunter, Erin
Endless Spanish/Infinity Espanol. E-book Review — Originator
Ends of Enlightenment — Bender, John
The Ends of the Body: Identity and Community in Medieval Culture — Akbari, Suzanne Conklin
The Ends of the Earth — Willemsen, Roger
c Ends of the Earth (Illus. by Dorman, Brandon) — Hale, Bruce
c Endurance — Ganeri, Anita
y Endure — Larson, Sara B.
Enduring Courage: Ace Pilot Eddie Rickenbacker and the Dawn of the Age of Speed (Read by Herrmann, Edward). Audiobook Review — Ross, John F.
Enduring Freedom, Enduring Voices: US Operations in Afghanistan — Walling, Michael G.
c Enduring Mysteries Series
Enemy in the East: Hitler's Secret Plans to Invade the Soviet Union — Muller, Rolf-Dieter
The Enemy Inside: A Paul Madriani Novel — Martini, Steve
Energized — Behre, Mary
Energy and Electricity in Industrial Nations: The Sociology and Technology of Energy — Mazur, Allan
Energy Capitals: Local Impact, Global Influence — Pratt, Joseph A.
Energy & Ethics: Justice and the Global Energy Challenge — Sovacool, Benjamin K.
Energy, Governance and Security in Thailand and Myanmar (Burma): A Critical Approach to Environmental Politics in the South — Simpson, Adam
c Energy in Action — Barchers, Suzanne
Energy Revolution: The Physics and the Promise of Efficient Technology — Prentiss, Mara
Enforcing Order: An Ethnography of Urban Policing — Fassin, Didier
Engage — Griesel, Dian
Engage the Fox: A Business Fable about Thinking Critically and Motivating Your Team — Lawrence, Jen
Engaging Bodies: The Politics and Poetics of Corporeality — Albright, Ann Cooper
Engaging China: Myth, Aspiration, and Strategy in Canadian Policy from Trudeau to Harper — Evans, Paul M.
Engaging Gifted Readers and Writers — Smith, Kenneth J.
Engaging Musical Practices: A Sourcebook for Middle School General Music — Burton, Suzanne L.
Engaging Strangers: Civil Rites, Civic Capitalism, and Public Order in Boston — Monti, Daniel J., Jr.
Engaging Strangers: Civil Rites, Civil Capitalism, and Public Order in Boston — Monti, Daniel J., Jr.
Engaging the Passion: Perspectives on the Death of Jesus — Yarbrough, Oliver Larry
Engaging the World: Christian Communities in Contemporary Global Societies — Adogame, Afe
Engaging Young Engineers: Teaching Problem Solving Skills through STEM — Stone-MacDonald, Angi
Engel der Effizienz: Eine Mediengeschichte der Unternehmensberatung — Hoof, Florian
Engel's England: Thirty-Nine Counties, One Capital and One Man — Engel, Matthew
c Engibear's Bridge (Illus. by Johnston, Benjamin) — King, Andrew

The Engine of Complexity: Evolution as Computation — Mayfield, John E.
c Engineer Ari and the Passover Rush (Illus. by Kober, Shahar) — Cohen, Deborah Bodin
y Engineering — Newcomb, Tim
The Engineering Book: From the Catapult to the Curiosity Rover, 250 Milestones in the History of Engineering — Brain, Marshall
Engineering Philadelphia: The Sellers Family and the Industrial Metropolis — Vitiello, Domenic
Engineering War and Peace in Modern Japan, 1868-1964 — Nishiyama, Takashi
Engineers and the Making of the Francoist Regime — Camprubi, Lino
Engineers for Change: Competing Visions of Technology in 1960s America — Wisnioski, Matthew
England and Other Stories — Swift, Graham
England and Rome in the Early Middle Ages: Pilgrimage, Art, and Politics — Tinti, Francesca
England, Arise: The People, the King and the Great Revolt of 1381 — Barker, Juliet
The English and Their History — Tombs, Robert
The English Boccaccio: A History in Books — Armstrong, Guyda
English Catholic Exiles in Late Sixteenth-Century Paris — Gibbons, Katy
English Catholics and the Supernatural, 1553-1829 — Young, Francis
English Civil Justice After the Woolf and Jackson Reforms: A Critical Analysis — Sorabji, John
English Episcopal Acta 42: Ely 1198-1256 — Karn, Nicholas
The English in Love: The Intimate Story of an Emotional Revolution — Langhamer, Claire
The English Martyr from Reformation to Revolution — Dailey, Alice
English Nuns and the Law in the Middle Ages: Cloistered Nuns and their Lawyers, 1293-1540 — Makowski, Elizabeth
The English Poems of Richard Crashaw — Crashaw, Richard
English Poetry and Old Norse Myth: A History — O'Donoghue, Heather
English Poets in the Late Middle Ages: Chaucer, Langland and Others — Burrow, John A.
English Renaissance Translation Theory — Rhodes, Neil
The English Revolution c.1590-1720: Politics, Religion and Communities — Tyacke, Nicholas
An English Spring: Memoirs — Murphy-O'Connor, Cormac
The English Spy (Read by Guidall, George). Audiobook Review — Silva, Daniel
The English Spy — Silva, Daniel
English Students at Leiden University, 1575-1650: Advancing Your Abilities in Learning and Bettering Your Understanding of the World and State Affairs — Progler, Daniela
English Traits — Emerson, Ralph Waldo
English Vernacular Minuscule from Aethelred to Cnut, circa 990-circa 1035 — Stokes, Peter A.
An English Year: Twelve Months in the Life of England's Kids — McCartney, Tania
The Englishness of English Art — Pevsner, Nikolaus
Englishness: Politics and Culture, 1880-1920, 2d ed. — Dodd, Philip
Engraving Virtue: The Printing History of a Premodern Korean Moral Primer — Oh, Young Kyun
y Enhancing Teaching and Learning in the 21st-Century Academic Library — Eden, Bradford L.
The Enigma Always — Breakfield, Charles V.
The Enigma Stolen — Burkey, Roxanne E.
Enigmas of Health and Disease: How Epidemiology Helps Unravel Scientific Mysteries — Morabia, Alfredo
y Enigmas of History, 8 vols. — World Book
Enigmatik: Das Ratsel als Hermeneutische Grenzfigur in Mythos, Philosophie und Literatur — Wohlleben, Doren
An Enlightened Duke: The Life of Archibald Campbell, 1682-1761, Earl of Ilay, 3rd Duke of Argyll — Emerson, Roger L.
Enlightened Metropolis: Constructing Imperial Moscow, 1762-1855 — Martin, Alexander M.
Enlightened Sentiments: Judgement and Antonomy in the Age of Sensibility — Nazar, Hina
Enlightened World Appropriations. Imperial Actors and Scenarios of Change
Enlightened Zeal: The Hudson's Bay Company and Scientific Networks, 1670-1870 — Binnema, Ted

Enlightening Symbols: A Short History of Mathematical Notation and Its Hidden Powers — Mazur, Joseph
Enlightenment and Revolution: The Making of Modern Greece — Kitromilides, Paschalis M.
The Enlightenment: History of an Idea — Ferrone, Vincenzo
y The Enlightenment — Allman, Toney
The Enlightenment of Nina Findlay — Gillies, Andrea
Enlightenment's Frontier: The Scottish Highlands and the Origins of Environmentalism — Jonsson, Fredrik Albritton
Ennius and the Architecture of the Annales — Elliott, J.
c Enormous Smallness: A Story of E.E. Cummings (Illus. by Di Giacomo, Kris) — Burgess, Matthew
c Enormous Smallness: A Story of E. E. Cummings (Illus. by Di Giacomo, Kris) — Burgess, Matthew
c Enormous Smallness: A Story of E.E. Cummings (Illus. by Di Giacomo, Kris) — Burgess, Matthew
Enough Already: Create Success on Your Own Terms — Iamele, Mike
Enough Already: Create Success on Your Own Terms — Lamele, Mike
y Enslavement — Friesen, Melinda
y Ensnared — Howard, A.G.
y Entangled — Capetta, Amy Rose
Entangled Roots: The Mystery of Peterborough's Headless Corpse — Lundahl, Bev
The Entangled State: Sorcery, State Control, and Violence in Indonesia — Herriman, Nicholas
The Entangled Trinity: Quantum Physics and Theology — Simmons, Ernest L.
Enter Pale Death (Read by Brenher, Matthew). Audiobook Review — Cleverly, Barbara
Entering a Clerical Career at the Roman Curia, 1458-1471 — Salonen, Kirsi
Entering Uncharted Waters? ASEAN and the South China Sea — Chachavalpongpun, Pavin
Entering Your Own Heart: A Guide to Developing Self Love, Inner Peace and Happiness — Morton, Carole J.
c The Entertainer (Illus. by Dodd, Emma) — Dodd, Emma
Entertaining Elephants: Animal Agency and the Business of the American Circus — Nance, Susan
Entertaining Judgement: The Afterlife in Popular Imagination — Garrett, Greg
Entertaining Judgment: The Afterlife in Popular Imagination — Garrett, Greg
c The Entirely True Story of the Unbelievable FIB — Shaughnessy, Adam
Entnazifizierte Zone? Zum Umgang mit der Zeit des Nationalsozialismus in ostdeutschen Stadt- und Regionalmuseen — Museumsverband des Landes Brandenburg
c Entombed — Krovatin, Christopher
c Entre Amis (Illus. by Goldsmith, Tom) — Wilcox Richards, Nancy
Entre la Renaissance et les Lumieres, le 'Theophrastus redivivus' (1659). — Genoux, Nicole
Entre stabilite et itinerance: Livres et Culture des Ordres Mendiants — Beriou, Nicole
Entrelac 2: New Techniques for Interlace Knitting — Drysdale, Rosemary
Entrepreneurial Litigation: It's Rise, Fall, and Future — Coffee, John C., Jr.
Entrepreneurial Selves: Neoliberal Respectability and the Making of a Caribbean Middle Class — Freeman, Carla
The Entrepreneurial State: Debunking Public vs. Private Sector Myths — Mazzucato, Mariana
Entrepreneurship and Multinationals: Global Business and the Making of the Modern World — Jones, Geoffrey
Entrepreneurship: Create Your Own Business (Illus. by Crosier, Mike) — Kahan, Alex
Entrepreneurship for the Rest of Us: How to Create Innovation and Opportunity Everywhere — Brown, Paul B.
Entrevoir — Katsaropoulos, Chris
Entrevoir suivi de Le front contre la vitre et de La halte obscure — De Roux, Paul
The Entropy of Bones — Jama-Everett, Ayize
y Entrusted — Gray, Allegra
Entry Island — May, Peter
Entstehung des Nibelungenstoffes im 8: Jahrhundert — Bleck, Reinhard
Environmental Activism and the Urban Crisis: Baltimore, St. Louis, Chicago — Gioielli, Robert R.
An Environmental History of Russia — Josephson, Paul

An Environmental History of the Middle Ages: The Crucible of Nature — Aberth, John
Environmental Practice and Early American Literature — Ziser, Michael
c Environmental Protection — Bankston, John
Environmental Transformations: A Geography of the Anthropocene — Whitehead, Mark
Envisioning Christ on the Cross: Ireland and the Early Medieval West — Mullins, Juliet
Envisioning Emancipation: Black Americans and the End of Slavery — Willis, Deborah
Envisioning Freedom: Cinema and the Building of Modern Black Life — Caddoo, Cara
Envisioning Howard Finster: The Religion and Art of a Stranger from Another World — Girardot, Norman
Envisioning Islam: Syriac Christians and the Early Muslim World — Penn, Michael Philip
Envisioning Socialism: Television and the Cold War in the German Democratic Republic — Gumbert, Heather
Envisioning Socialism: Television and the Cold War in the German Democratic Republic — Gumbert, Heather L.
Envisioning Sociology: Victor Branford, Patrick Geddes, and the Quest for Social Reconstruction — Scott, John
Envisioning the Bishop: Images and the Episcopacy in the Middle Ages — Danielson, Sigrid
Envy and Jealousy in Classical Athens: A Socio-Psychological Approach — Sanders, Ed (b. 1973-)
Envy of Angels — Wallace, Matt
Envy Up, Scorn Down: How Status Divides Us — Fiske, Susan T.
c Enzo Races in the Rain! (Illus. by Alley, Zoe B.) — Stein, Garth
Ephemeral City: Cheap Print and Urban Culture in Renaissance Venice — Salzberg, Rosa
Epic Arts in Renaissance France — Usher, Phillip John
The Epic Cycle. A Commentary on the Lost Troy Epics — West, Martin L.
c Epic Explorers: 12 Epic Journeys across Land, Sea and Space — Steele, Philip
Epic Game — Kowalski, William
Epic Measures: One Doctor, Seven Billion Patients — Smith, Jeremy N.
c Epic Stunts — Hammelef, Danielle S.
Epic Tomatoes: How to Select and Grow the Best Varieties of All Time — LeHoullier, Craig
Epic Visions: Visuality in Greek and Latin Epic and its Reception — Lovatt, Helen
Epictete: Sentences et fragments — d'Jeranian, Olivier
Epidemic City: The Politics of Public Health in New York — Colgrove, James
y Epidemiology: The Fight against Ebola and Other Diseases — Hand, Carol
y Epidemiology: The Fight Against Ebola & Other Diseases — Lokere, Jillian
Epigenetic Regulation and Epigenomics — Meyers, Robert A.
Epigenetics and Development — Heard, Edith
Epigenetics, Environment, and Genes — Kang, Sun Woo
Epilogue — Boast, Will
Epinets: The Epistemic Structure and Dynamics of Social Networks — Moldoveanu, Mihnea C.
Episcopal Appointments in England, c.1214-1344: From Episcopal Election to Papal Provision — Harvey, Katherine
An Episode of Sparrows — Godden, Rumer
The Episodic Career: How to Thrive at Work in the Age of Disruption — Chideya, Farai
Episodic Poetics: Politics and Literary Form after the Constitution — Garrett, Matthew
Epistemic Authority: A Theory of Trust, Authority, and Autonomy in Belief — Zagzebski, Linda
Epistemologies of In-Betweenness: East Central Europe and the World History of Social Science, 1890-1945
Epistemologies of the South: Justice against Epistemicide — de Sousa Santos, Boaventura
Epistolarum Iuvenilium Libri Octo Petri Candidi Decembrii — Petrucci, Federico
Equal Security: Europe and the SALT Process, 1969-1976 — Dietl, Ralph L.
Equal Time, Equal Value: Community Currencies and Time Banking in the US — Collom, Ed
Equinox — Cantrell, Christian
Era of Experimentation: American Political Practices in the Early Republic — Peart, Daniel

An Era without Memories: Chinese Contemporary Photography on Urban Transformation — Jiang, Jiehong
Erased from Space and Consciousness: Israel and the Depopulated Palestinian Villages of 1948 — Kadman, Noga
Erasmi Opera Omnia VI-10: Annotationes in Novum Testamentum (Pars Sexta). — van Poll-van de Lisdonk, M.L.
Erasmus and the Renaissance Republic of Letters — Ryle, Stephen
Erasmus of Rotterdam: Advocate of a New Christianity — Christ-Von Wedel, Christine
Erbe: Ubertragungskonzepte zwischen Natur und Kultur — Willer, Stefan
Erbfalle: Theorie und Praxis Kultureller Ubertragung in der Moderne — Willer, Stefan
y Eren — Clark, Simon P.
Erfahrungsbruch und Generationsbehauptung: Die gt;Kriegsjugendgeneration< in den beiden deutschen Nachkriegsgesellschaften — Mockel, Benjamin
Eric Rohmer: Biographie — De Baecque, Antoine
c Eric Vale, Epic Fail (Illus. by Bauer, Joe) — Bauer, Michael Gerard
Eric Walrond: A Life in the Harlem Renaissance and the Transatlantic Caribbean — Davis, James C.
Erich Graf--Musician, Flutist, Advocate — Graf, Erich
Erinnerungen: Emma Furstin zu Castell-Rudenhausen — Dohna, Jesko Graf zu
c Ernest Shackleton: Antarctic Explorer — Seddon, Angela
Ernst Bloch and His Contemporaries: Locating Utopian Messianism — Boldyrev, Ivan
Ernst Haas: On Set — Haas, Ernst
Ernst Junger-Handbuch: Leben - Werk - Wirkung — Schoning, Matthias
Ernst Troeltsch: Kritische Gesamtausgabe, vol. 2 — Graf, Friedrich Wilhelm
Eros and Sexuality in Islamic Art — Leoni, Francesca
Eros and Tragedy: Jewish Male Fantasies and the Masculine Revolution of Zionism — Nur, Ofer Nordheimer
Eros: Melodies of Love: More Jungian Notes from Underground — Sharp, Daryl
Erotic Cultures of Renaissance Italy — Matthews-Grieco, Sara F.
Erotic Exchanges: The World of Elite Prostitution in Eighteenth-Century Paris — Kushner, Nina
Erotic Infidelities: Love and Enchantment in Angela Carter's The Bloody Chamber — Lau, Kimberly
Erratic Facts — Ryan, Kay
"Erst stirbt der Wald, dann du!": Das Waldsterben als westdeutsches Politikum — Metzger, Birgit
Eruption: The Untold Story of Mount St. Helens — Olson, Steve
Erziehung als Wissenschaft: Ovide Decroly und sein Weg vom Arzt zum Padagogen — Blichmann, Annika
Erziehung an der Mutterbrust: Eine kritische Kulturgeschichte des Stillens — Seichter, Sabine
Es gibt kein Himmelreich auf Erden: Heinrich Margulies - ein sakularer Zionist — Rohl, Vera Regine
Es gilt das Gesprochene Wort: Oral History und Zeitgeschichte Heute — Andresen, Knud
Es gilt das gesprochene Wort. Oral History und Zeitgeschichte heute. Tagung zu Ehren von Dorothee Wierling
The Escape (Read by McLarty, Ron). Audiobook Review — Baldacci, David
Escape from Baghdad! — Hossain, Saad
c Escape from Baxters' Barn (Illus. by Bond, Rebecca) — Bond, Rebecca
Escape from Baxter's Barn (Illus. by Bond, Rebecca) — Bond, Rebecca
c Escape from Baxters' Barn (Illus. by Bond, Rebecca) — Bond, Rebecca
Escape from Dorkville — Ammerman, Dean
Escape from Hangtown — Sweazy, Larry D.
c Escape from Mr. Lemoncello's Library (Read by Bernstein, Jesse). Audiobook Review — Grabenstein, Chris
Escape from Netherworld — Kuklis, David
y Escape from the Past: The Duke's Wrath — Oppenlander, Annette
y Escape from Tibet: A True Story — Gray, Nick
c Escape from Veracruz (Illus. by Marnat, Annette) — Surget, Alain
c Escape in Time (Illus. by McGaw, Laurie) — Lowenstein-Malz, Ronit
The Escape — Baldacci, David

y The Escape — Jayne, Hannah
Escape Points — Weldon, Michele
c Escape to California (Illus. by Pamintuan, Macky) — Brown, Jeff
Escape to Prison: Penal Tourism and the Pull of Punishment — Welch, Michael
y Escaping Perfect — Harrison, Emma
Escaping Yesterday — Nowak, Pamela
Eschatological Subjects: Divine and Literary Judgment in Fourteenth-Century French Poetry — Moreau, J.M.
"Eschez d'amours": A Critical Edition of the Poem and its Latin Glosses — Heyworth, Gregory
The Escort — Altom, Laura Marie
c Escrito y Dibujado por Enriqueta (Illus. by Liniers) — Liniers
Eshen: An American Colony — Davison, Michael H.
Eshu: Yoruba God, Powers, and the Imaginative Frontiers — Falola, Toyin
Esoteric Egypt: The Sacred Science of the Land of Khem — Gordonm, J.S.
ESP Wars — May, Edwin C.
Espen Ash Lad: Folk Tales from Norway — Gambles, Robert
ESPN: The Making of a Sports Media Empire — Vogan, Travis
Essais d'histoire de la traduction: avatars de Janus — D'Hulst, Lieven
Essais philosophiques: Du credo ancien a l'homme technologique — Jonas, Hans
Essay: A Critical Memoir — Revell, Donald
Essays after Eighty — Hall, Donald
Essays and Reviews 1959-2002 — Williams, Bernard
Essays in Honour of Wole Soyinka at Eighty — Agyeman-Duah, Ivor
Essays in Russian Social and Economic History — Hoch, Steven L.
Essays on Alfredo Bryce Echenique, Peruvian Literature and Culture — Hart, Stephen M.
Essays on Church, State and Politics — Hunter, Ian
Essays on the Poetry of Trevor Joyce — O'Mahony, Niamh
The Essential Anne Wilkinson — Wilkinson, Anne
y Essential Articles 2015: Understanding Our World: Articles, Opinions, Arguments, Personal Accounts, Opposing Viewpoints — Kershaw, Anne Louise
The Essential Cy Twombly — Del Roscio, Nicola
Essential Dynamics and Relativity — O'Donnell, Peter J.
The Essential Ellen Willis — Aronowitz, Nona Willis
Essential Emeril: Favorite Recipes and Hard-Won Wisdom from My Life in the Kitchen — Lagasse, Emeril
The Essential Ginsberg — Ginsberg, Allen
The Essential Goethe — Goethe, Johann Wolfgang von
The Essential Lapsit Guide: A Multimedia How-To-Do-It Manual and Programming Guide for Stimulating Literacy Development from 12 to 24 Months — Ernst, Linda L.
Essential MATLAB and Octave — Rogel-Salazar, Jesus
Essential Movement Only — Zimmerman, Jane
The Essential Photographer Workbook: The Beginner's Guide to Creating Impressive Digital Photos — Dantzig, Stephen
Essential Readings in Evolutionary Biology — Ayala, Francisco J.
Essential Skills for 3D Modeling, Rendering, and Animation — Zeman, Nicholas Bernhardt
The Essential W.P. Kinsella — Kinsella, W.P.
Essentials of Conservation Biology — Primack, Richard B.
Essentials of Econophysics Modelling — Slanina, Frantisek
The Essentials of Ibadi Islam — Hoffman, Valerie
Essex: The Cultural Impact of an Elizabethan Courtier — Connolly, Annaliese
Essie's Roses — Muriel, Michelle
c Est-ce que les girafes dansent? (Illus. by Parker-Rees, Guy) — Andreae, Giles
Establishing Religious Freedom: Jefferson's Statute in Virginia — Buckley, Thomas E.
The Establishment: And How They Get Away with It — Jones, Owen
c Estas manos: Manitas de mi familia/These Hands: My Family's Hands (Illus. by Costello, Shawn) — Caraballo, Samuel
Esther — Kanner, Rebecca
c Esther's Rainbow (Illus. by Acton, Sara) — Kane, Kim
Estimating — Alaina, Maria

Etablierung in der Fremde: Vertriebene Wissenschaftler in den USA nach 1933 — *Fleck, Christian*
Eterlimus — *Hamza, Aziz*
The Eterna Files — *Hieber, Leanna Renee*
y Eternal — *Hunter, C.C.*
y The Eternal City — *Morris, Paula*
The Eternal Criminal Record — *Jacobs, James B.*
Eternal Ephemera: Adaptation and the Origin of Species from the Nineteenth Century through Punctuated Equilibria and Beyond — *Eldredge, Niles*
The Eternal Nazi: From Mauthausen to Cairo, the Relentless Pursuit of SS Doctor Aribert Heim — *Mekhennet, Souad*
Eternal Ravenna: From the Etruscans to the Venetians — *David, Massimiliano*
Eternal Sunshine of the Spotless Mind — *Butler, Andrew M.*
The Eternal War: A Psychological Perspective on the Arab-Israeli Conflict — *Abraham, Antoine J.*
The Eternal World — *Farnsworth, Christopher*
Eternidad — *Harwood, B. Thomas*
y Eternity — *de la Pena, Matt*
y The Eternity Key: Into the Dark, Book 2 — *Despain, Bree*
y The Eternity Key — *Despain, Bree*
Eternity Street: Violence and Justice in Frontier Los Angeles — *Faragher, John Mack*
Eternity's Sunrise: The Imaginative World of William Blake — *Damrosch, Leo*
y Eternity's Wheel — *Gaiman, Neil*
y Etherworld — *Gabel, Claudia*
Ethical Approaches in Contemporary German-Language Literature and Culture — *Jeremiah, Emily*
Ethical Eating in the Postsocialist and Socialist World — *Jung, Yuson*
Ethical Empowerment: Virtue beyond the Paradigms — *Schwartz, Arthur D.*
Ethical Perspectives on Animals in the Renaissance and Early Modern Period — *Muratori, Cecilia*
Ethics and Children's Literature — *Mills, Claudia*
Ethics and Enjoyment in Late Medieval Poetry: Love after Aristotle — *Rosenfeld, Jessica*
Ethics and Spirituality — *Curran, Charles E.*
Ethics as a Work of Charity: Thomas Aquinas and Pagan Virtue — *Decosimo, David*
Ethics in Ancient Israel — *Barton, John*
The Ethics of Embryonic Stem Cell Research — *Devolder, Katrien*
The Ethics of Everyday Life: Moral Theology, Social Anthropology, and the Imagination of the Human — *Banner, Michael*
The Ethics of Immigration — *Carens, Joseph H.*
The Ethics of Information — *Floridi, Luciano*
The Ethics of Insurgency: A Critical Guide to Just Guerrilla Warfare — *Gross, Michael L.*
The Ethics of Literary Communication: Genuineness, Directness, Indirectness — *Sell, Roger D.*
The Ethics of Preventive War — *Chatterjee, Deen K.*
The Ethics of Swagger: Prizewinning African American Novels, 1977-1993 — *Hill, Michael DeRell*
The Ethics Police: The Struggle to Make Human Research Safe — *Klitzman, Robert L.*
Ethnic American Food Today — *Long, Lucy M.*
y Ethnic American Literature: An Encyclopedia for Students — *Nelson, Emmanuel S.*
Ethnic Boundary Making Institutions, Power, Networks — *Wimmer, Andreas*
Ethnic Cleansing and the European Union: An Interdisciplinary Approach to Security, Memory and Ethnography — *Tesser, Lynn M.*
Ethnic Cleansing and the Indian: The Crime That Should Haunt America — *Anderson, Gary Clayton*
Ethnic Conflict and War Crimes in the Balkans: The Narratives of Denial in Post-Conflict Serbia — *Obradovic-Wochnik, Jelena*
Ethnic Diversity and Social Cohesion: Immigration, Ethnic Fractionalization and Potentials for Civic Action — *Schaeffer, Merlin*
Ethnic Historians and the Mainstream: Shaping American's Immigration Story — *Kraut, Alan M.*
Ethnic Humor in Multiethnic America — *Gillota, David*
Ethnic Identity and Minority Protection: Designation, Discrimination and Brutalization — *Simon, Thomas W.*
Ethnic Minorities of Central and Eastern Europe in the Internet Space: A Computer-Assisted Content Analysis — *Alexeeva, Olga*

Ethnic Patriotism and the East Africa Revival: A History of Dissent 1935-1972 — *Peterson, Derek R.*
Ethnicity, Borders, and the Grassroots Interface with the State: Studies on Southeast Asia in Honor of Charles F. Keyes — *Marston, John A.*
Ethnographic Encounters in Israel: Poetics and Ethics of Fieldwork — *Markowitz, Fran*
Ethnographies of Reason — *Livingston, Eric*
Ethnography after Antiquity: Foreign Lands and Peoples in Byzantine Literature — *Kaldellis, Anthony*
Ethnography in Today's World: Color Full before Color Blind — *Sanjek, Roger*
Ethnomethodology at Play — *Tolmie, Peter*
Ethnomethodology's Program: Working out Durkheim's Aphorism — *Garfinkel, Harold*
Ethnonationalist Conflict in Postcommunist States: Varieties of Governance in Bulgaria, Macedonia, and Kosovo: National and Ethnic Conflict in the Twenty-First Century — *Koinova, Maria*
c Etre genereux — *Tym, Kate*
c Etre gentil — *Tym, Kate*
c Etre honnete — *Tym, Kate*
c Etre poli — *Tym, Kate*
Etta and Otto and Russell and James — *Hooper, Emma*
c Ettore Boiardi: Chef Boyar dee Manufacturer — *Lianas, Sheila Griffin*
Etymology and the Invention of English in Early Modern Literature — *Crawforth, Hannah*
Eucharist as Meaning: Critical Metaphysics and Contemporary Sacramental Theology — *Mudd, Joseph C.*
The Eudemian Ethics on the Voluntary, Friendship, and Luck: The Sixth S.V. Keeling Colloquium in Ancient Philosophy — *Leigh, Fiona*
Euer Dorf Soll Schoner Werden: Landlicher Wandel, Staatliche Planung und Demokratisierung in der Bundesrepublik Deutschland — *Strube, Sebastian*
Eugene Braumwald and the Rise of Modern Medicine — *Lee, Thomas H.*
Eugene O'Neill: A Life in Four Acts — *Dowling, Robert M.*
Eugenics and Nation in Early 20th Century Hungary — *Turda, Marius*
Euphoria — *King, Lily*
Eure Namen sind im Buch des Lebens geschrieben: Antike und mittelalterliche Quellen als Grundlage moderner prosopographischer Forschung — *Berndt, Rainer*
Eureka! Discovering Your Inner Scientist — *Orzel, Chad*
The Eureka Factor: Aha Moments, Creative Insight, and the Brain — *Kounios, John*
c The Eureka Key — *Thomson, Sarah L.*
Eureka Man — *Middleton, Patrick*
The Eureka Myth: Creators, Innovators, and Everyday Intellectual Property — *Silbey, Jessica*
c Eureka! The Most Amazing Scientific Discoveries of All Time — *Goldsmith, Mike*
Euripides: Alcestis — *Slater, N.W.*
Europa, das Meer und die Welt. Akteure, Agenten, Abenteurer
Europa der Regionen - Nordrhein-Westfalen und seine Grenzraume
Europa Postale: L'opera di Ottavio Codogno luogotenente dei Tasso nella Milano Seicentesca — *Fedele, Clemente*
Europa w obliczu konca — *Krol, Marcin*
Europabild - Kulturwissenschaften - Staatsbegriff: Die Revista de Occidente (1923-1936) und der deutsch-spanische Kulturtransfer der Zwischenkriegszeit — *Antonius, Carl*
Europas Einigung: Eine Unvollendete Geschichte — *Loth, Wilfried*
y Europe — *Harris, Tim*
Europe and the Islamic World: A History — *Tolan, John*
Europe and the Maritime World: A Twentieth-Century History — *Miller, Michael B.*
Europe Entrapped — *Offe, Claus*
Europe Meets China: China Meets Europe: The Beginnings of European-Chinese Scientific Exchange in the Seventeenth Century — *Deiwiks, Shu-Jyuan*
A Europe of Courts, a Europe of Factions
Europe on Trial: The Story of Collaboration, Resistance, and Retribution During World War II — *Deak, Istvan*
Europe: The Struggle for Supremacy, from 1453 to the Present — *Simms, Brendan*
European Colonialism since 1700 — *Lehning, James R.*

The European Economy Since 1914, 5th ed. — *Aldcroft, Derek H.*
European Integration and the Atlantic Community in the 1980s — *Patel, Kiran Klaus*
European Muslim Antisemitism: Why Young Urban Males Say They Don't Like Jews — *Jikell, Gunther*
European National Identities. Elements, Transitions, Conflicts — *Leutzsch, Andreas*
European Portrait Photography since 1990 — *Gierstberg, Frits*
European Private International Law — *Van Calster, Geert*
European Resistance in the Second World War — *Cooke, Philip E.*
The European Retail Trade and the Clothing Industry in Historical Perspective
Europeanization of Foreign Policies: International Socialization in Intergovernmental Policy Fields and the Example of the EPC/CSFP
Europeans Engaging the Atlantic: Knowledge and Trade, 1500-1800 — *Lachenicht Susanne*
Europe's Green Revolution and Others Since: The Rise and Fall of Peasant-Friendly Plant Breeding — *Harwood, Jonathan*
Europe's Orphan: The Future of the Euro and the Politics of Debt — *Sandbu, Martin*
Europica varietas — *Csombor, Marton Szepsi*
Euryhaline Fishes — *McCormick, Stephen D.*
Eusebius — *Johnson, Aaron P.*
y Euthanasia — *Nakaya, Andrea C.*
y The Euthanist — *Dolan, Alex*
c Eva and Sadie and the Best Classroom Ever! (Illus. by Allen, Elanna) — *Cohen, Jeff*
c Eva Sees a Ghost (Illus. by Elliott, Rebecca) — *Elliott, Rebecca*
Evaluating Empire and Confronting Colonialism in Eighteenth-Century Britain — *Greene, Jack P.*
Evaluating Instructional Leadership: Recognized Practices for Success — *Smith, Julie R.*
Evaluation et contre-pouvoir: Portee ethique et politique du jugement de valeur dans le stoicisme romain — *Alexandre, Sandrine*
The Evangelical Origins of the Living Constitution — *Compton, John W.*
Evangelical Postcolonial Conversations: Global Awakenings in Theology and Praxis — *Smith, Kay Higuera*
Evangelical versus Liturgical? Defying a Dichotomy — *Ross, Melanie C.*
Evangeline — *Adams, Clint*
Evangelization in China: Challenges and Prospects — *Yan, Kin Sheung Chiaretto*
Evans Carlson, Marine Raider: The Man Who Commanded America's First Special Forces — *Schultz, Duane*
c Eva's Treetop Festival (Illus. by Elliott, Rebecca) — *Elliott, Rebecca*
Eve Arnold — *Di Giovanni, Janine*
The Eve of Destruction: How 1965 Transformed America — *Patterson, James T.*
Evel Knievel Jumps the Snake River Canyon — *Jones, Kelly (b. 1948-)*
Even Dogs in the Wild — *Rankin, Ian*
y Even in Paradise — *Philpot, Chelsey*
c Even Monsters Say Good Night (Illus. by Marts, Doreen Mulryan) — *Marts, Doreen Mulryan*
Even the Dead — *Black, Benjamin*
c Even the Score — *Payton, Belle*
Even This I Get to Experience (Read by Lear, Norman). Audiobook Review — *Lear, Norman*
Even Vampires Get the Blues — *Hill, Sandra*
y Even When You Lie to Me — *Alcott, Jessica*
The Evening Chorus — *Humphreys, Helen*
Evening News: Optics, Astronomy, and Journalism in Early Modern Europe — *Reeves, Eileen*
The Evening Spider — *Arsenault, Emily*
Evening's Empires — *McAuley, Paul*
An Event in Autumn — *Thompson, Laurie*
Events, Dear Boy, Events: A Political Diary of Britain from Woolf to Campbell — *Winstone, Ruth*
y Eventual Poppy Day — *Hathorn, Libby*
c Eventually Everything Connects (Illus. by Lora, Loris) — *Lora, Loris*
Ever After — *Deveraux, Jude*
Ever After (Read by Potter, Kirsten). Audiobook Review — *Deveraux, Jude*
c Ever After High: Next Top Villain — *Selfors, Suzanne*
Ever After — *Deveraux, Jude*
Ever After — *Lacey, Rachel*
The Ever After of Ashwin Rao — *Viswanathan, Padma*
Ever Faithful: Race, Loyalty, and the Ends of Empire in Spanish Cuba — *Sartorius, David*

Ever Yours: The Essential Letters — *van Gogh, Vincent*
c Everblaze — *Messenger, Shannon*
The Everett Interpretation of Quantum Mechanics: Collected Works, 1955-1980, with Commentary — *Everett, Hugh, III*
Evergreen Falls — *Freeman, Kimberley*
Everland — *Hunt, Rebecca*
Everlast — *Bard, Richard*
c Evermore Dragon (Illus. by Cecil, Randy) — *Joosse, Barbara*
c Evermore (Illus. by Reed, Daniel) — *Carmody, Isobelle*
c The Evertree — *Lu, Marie*
y Evertrue: An Everneath Novel — *Ashton, Brodi*
Every Able Body — *Reichart, David*
Every Anxious Wave — *Daviau, Mo*
y Every Breath — *Marney, Ellie*
c Every Breath We Take — *Ajmera, Maya*
Every Bride Needs a Groom — *Thompson, Janice*
Every Citizen a Soldier: The Campaign for Universal Military Training after World War II — *Taylor, William A.*
c Every Day Birds (Illus. by Metrano, Dylan) — *VanDerwater, Amy Ludwig*
Every Day but Tuesday — *Freeman, Barbara Claire*
Every Day I Fight — *Platt, Larry*
Every Day I Fight — *Scott, Stuart*
Every Day Is for the Thief — *Cole, Teju*
Every Father's Daughter: Twenty-four Women Writers Remember Their Fathers — *Smiley, Jane*
Every Father's Daughter: Twenty-Four Women Writers Remember Their Fathers — *McMullan, Margaret*
Every Father's Daughter: Twenty-four Women Writers Remember Their Fathers — *Smiley, Jane*
Every Fifteen Minutes (Read by Newbern, George). Audiobook Review — *Scottoline, Lisa*
Every Fifteen Minutes — *Scottoline, Lisa*
Every Gift Matters: How Your Passion Can Change the World — *Morgridge, Carrie*
Every Girl Gets Confused — *Thompson, Janice*
Every Heart a Doorway — *McGuire, Seanan*
Every Landlord's Guide to Managing Property: Best Practices, From Move-In to Move-Out — *Boyer, Michael*
y Every Last Promise — *Halbrook, Kristin*
Every Last Tie — *Kaczynski, David*
y Every Last Word — *Stone, Tamara Ireland*
Every Leaf a Mirror: A Jim Wayne Miller Reader — *Grubbs, Morris Allen*
Every Little Kiss — *Amos, Kim*
Every Little Kiss — *Castle, Kendra Leigh*
c Every Little Thing (Illus. by Brantley-Newton, Vanessa) — *Marley, Cedella*
y Every Person Has a History — *Vickers, Rebecca*
y Every Place Has a History — *Langley, Andrew*
y Every Second Counts — *McKenzie, Sophie*
Every Secret Thing — *Bartley, Christopher*
Every Song Ever: Twenty Ways to Listen in an Age of Musical Plenty — *Ratliff, Ben*
Every Soul — *Collins, L.K.*
Every Soul Is Free — *Massey, Edward*
Every Time a Friend Succeeds Something inside Me Dies: The Life of Gore Vidal — *Parini, Jay*
Every Time I Find the Meaning of Life, They Change It: Wisdom of the Great Philosophers on How to Live — *Klein, Daniel*
Every Town Is a Sports Town: Business Leadership at ESPN, from the Mailroom to the Boardroom (Read by Bodenheimer, George). Audiobook Review — *Bodenheimer, George*
Every Town Is a Sports Town: Business Leadership at ESPN, from the Mailroom to the Boardroom — *Bodenheimer, George*
y Every Word — *Marney, Ellie*
Everybody Else: Adoption and the Politics of Domestic Diversity in Postwar America — *Potter, Sarah*
Everybody Goes to Jimmy's — *Mayo, Michael*
y Everybody Knows Your Name — *Seigel, Andrea*
Everybody Matters: The Extraordinary Power of Caring for Your People Like Family — *Chapman, Bob*
Everybody Rise (Read by Kellgren, Katherine). Audiobook Review — *Clifford, Stephanie*
Everybody Rise — *Clifford, Stephanie*
c Everybody Says Shalom (Illus. by Shipman, Talitha) — *Kimmelman, Leslie*
c Everybody Sleeps (But Not Fred). (Illus. by Schneider, Josh) — *Schneider, Josh*

Everybody Wants to Rule the World (Read by Full cast). Audiobook Review — *Abnett, Dan*
y Everyday Ambassador — *Otto, Kate*
Everyday Easy — *Pascale, Lorraine*
Everyday Ethics: Voices from the Front Line of Community Psychiatry — *Brodwin, Paul*
Everyday Heroism in the United States, Britain, and Germany from the 19th to the 21st Century
Everyday Illegal: When Policies Undermine Immigrant Families — *Dreby, Joanna*
Everyday Life in Joseon-Era Korea: Economy and Society — *The Organization of Korean Historians*
Everyday Life in the Early English Caribbean: Irish, Africans, and the Construction of Difference — *Shaw, Jenny (b. 1977-)*
Everyday Life in Viking-Age Towns: Social Approaches to Towns in England and Ireland, c. 800-1100 — *Hadley, Dawn M.*
Everyday Mercies — *Miller, Evie Yoder*
The Everyday of Memory: Between Communism and Post-Communism — *Rabikowska, Marta*
Everyday Products in the Middle Ages: Crafts, Consumption and the Individual in Northern Europe c. AD 800-1600 — *Hansen, Gitte*
The Everyday Rice Cooker: Soups, Sides, Grains, Mains, and More (Illus. by Causey, Jennifer) — *Phillips, Diane*
Everyday Technology: Machines and the Making of India's Modernity — *Arnold, David (b. 1946-)*
Everyday Vegan Eats — *Dever, Zsu*
Everyday Witchcraft: Making Time for Spirit in a Too-Busy World — *Blake, Deborah*
Everyone Is African: How Science Explodes the Myth of Race — *Fairbanks, Daniel J.*
c Everyone Is Equal: The Kids' Book of Tolerance — *Hanson, Anders*
Everyone Is Italian on Sunday! — *Ray, Rachael*
c Everyone Loves Bacon (Illus. by Wight, Eric) — *DiPucchio, Kelly*
c Everyone Loves Bacon (Illus. by Wright, Eric) — *Dipucchio, Kelly*
Everyone's a Winner: Life in Our Congratulatory Culture — *Best, Joel*
c Everything (Illus. by Dodd, Emma) — *Dodd, Emma*
c Everything — *Dodd, Emma*
Everything at Last — *Lang, Kimberly*
c Everything Birds of Prey — *Hoena, Blake*
The Everything Box — *Kadrey, Richard*
Everything Broken Up Dances — *Byrne, James*
y Everything But the Truth — *Hubbard, Mandy*
Everything Crash — *Wells, Tim*
y Everything, Everything (Read by Turpin, Bahni, with Robbie Daymond). Audiobook Review — *Yoon, Nicola*
y Everything, Everything (Illus. by Yoon, David) — *Yoon, Nicola*
Everything I Know about Zombies, I Learned in Kindergarten — *Williams, Kevin Wayne*
Everything I Left Unsaid — *O'Keefe, M.*
Everything I Never Told You — *Ng, Celeste*
Everything in Its Right Place: Spinoza and Life by the Light of Nature — *Almog, Joseph*
c Everything Insects — *Gleason, Carrie*
c Everything Is a Poem: The Best of J. Patrick Lewis (Illus. by Pritelli, Maria Cristina) — *Lewis, J. Patrick*
Everything Is Connected to Everything Else: 101 Stories about 21st Century Geography — *Lee, Carl*
Everything is Happening: Journey into a Painting — *Jacobs, Michael*
Everything Mind — *Grosso, Chris*
Everything She Forgot — *Ballantyne, Lisa*
Everything She Wanted — *Ryan, Jennifer*
c Everything Soccer — *Hoena, Blake*
The Everything Store: Jeff Bezos and the Age of Amazon — *Stone, Brad*
y Everything That Makes You — *McStay, Moriah*
Everything to Nothing: The Poetry of the Great War, Revolution and the Transformation of Europe — *Buelens, Geert*
c Everything Vikings: All the Incredible Facts and Fierce Fun You Can Plunder — *Higgins, Nadia*
Everything You Always Wanted to Know about Lachmann's Method: A Non-Standard Handbook of Genealogical Textual Criticism in the Age of Post-Structuralism, Cladistics and Copy-Text — *Trovato, Paolo*
Everything You Ever Wanted: A Memoir — *Lauren, Jillian*
Eve's Hollywood — *Babitz, Eve*
c Evette's Invitation (Illus. by Cowman, Joseph) — *Huber, Mike*

Evgenij Polivanov (1891-1938): Penser le langage au temps de Staline — *Archaimbault, Sylvie*
Evicted — *Desmond, Matthew*
The Evidence Enigma: Correctional Boot Camps and Other Failures in Evidence-Based Policymaking — *Bergin, Tiffany*
Evidence Explained: Citing History Sources from Artifacts to Cyberspace, 3d ed. — *Shown, Elizabeth*
Evidence from Earth Observation Satellites: Emerging Legal Issues — *Purdy, Ray*
Evidence of Editing: Growth and Change of Texts in the Hebrew Bible — *Muller, Reinhard*
y Evidence of Things Not Seen — *Lane, Lindsey*
The Evidence Room — *Harvey, Cameron*
Evidentialism and the Will to Believe — *Aikin, Scott F.*
Evidentiality in interaction — *Nuckolls, Janis*
c Evie Brooks Is Marooned in Manhattan — *Agnew, Sheila*
Evie's War — *Mackenzie, Anna*
Evil: A History in Modern French Literature and Thought — *Catani, Damian*
The Evil Day — *Yoho, R.G.*
c Evil Fairies Love Hair (Illus. by Henry, Blake) — *Thompson, Mary G.*
The Evil Hours: A Biography of Post-Traumatic Stress Disorder (Read by Chamberlain, Mike). Audiobook Review — *Morris, David J.*
The Evil Hours: A Biography of Post-Traumatic Stress Disorder — *Morris, David J.*
Evil in Modern thought: An Alternative histoty of Philosophy — *Neiman, Susan*
y Evil Librarian (Read by Foster, Emily). Audiobook Review — *Knudsen, Michelle*
y Evil Librarian. Audiobook Review — *Knudsen, Michelle*
y Evil Librarian — *Knudsen, Michelle*
Evil Men — *Dawes, James*
An Evil Mind — *Carter, Chris*
The Evil Necessity: British Naval Impressment in the Eighteenth-Century Atlantic World — *Brunsman, Denver*
The Evil of Oz — *Fuller, Ryan*
c Evil Spy School (Read by Frazier, Gibson). Audiobook Review — *Gibbs, Stuart*
y Evil Spy School — *Gibbs, Stuart*
c Evil Twins — *Savage, J. Scott*
Evita, Inevitably: Performing Argentina's Female Icons before and after Eva Peron — *Graham-Jones, Jean*
Evolution 2.0: Breaking the Deadlock between Darwin and Design — *Marshall, Perry*
Evolution and the Mechanisms of Decision Making — *Hammerstein, Peter*
Evolution: Components and Mechanisms — *Zeigler, David*
Evolution, Games, and God: The Principle of Cooperation — *Nowak, Martin A.*
The Evolution Myth: or, The Genes Cry Out Their Urgent Song, Mister Darwin Got It Wrong — *Mejsnar, Jiri A.*
The Evolution of Everything: How New Ideas Emerge — *Ridley, Matt*
The Evolution of Inquiry: Controlled, Guided, Modeled, and Free — *Callison, Daniel*
The Evolution of Insect Mating Systems — *Shuker, David M.*
The Evolution of Japan's Party System: Politics and Policy in an Era of Institutional Change — *Schoppa, Leonard J.*
The Evolution of Mann: Herbie Mann and the Flute in Jazz — *Ginell, Cary*
The Evolution of Sex Determination — *Beukeboom, Leo W.*
The Evolution of Social Communication in Primates: A Multidisciplinary Approach — *Pina, Marco*
y Evolution: The Whole Story — *Parker, Steve*
The Evolutionary Interpretation of Treaties — *Bjorge, Eirik*
The Evolutionist: The Strange Tale of Alfred Russel Wallace — *Sirlin, Avi*
The Evolving Citizen: American Youth and the Changing Norms of Democratic Engagement — *Childers, Jay P.*
The Evolving God: Charles Darwin on the Naturalness of Religion — *Pleins, J. David*
Evo's Bolivia: Continuity and Change — *Farthing, Linda C.*
c Ewe and Aye (Illus. by Ruble, Stephanie) — *Ryan, Candace*
Ex-Combatants, Religion and Peace in Northern Ireland: The Role of Religion in Transitional Justice — *Brewer, John D.*

The Ex — Burke, Alafair
The Ex-Prisoner's Dilemma: How Women Negotiate Competing Narratives of Reentry and Desistance — Leverentz, Andrea M.
The Exact Unknown and Other Tales of Modern China — Cook, Isham
An Exaggerated Murder — Cook, Josh
c Examining Shipwrecks — Wedge, Hayden
Excavating the Sky — Kulakov, Konstantin
Excavations at Zeugma: Conducted by Oxford Archaeology — Aylward, William
Excellent Daughters: The Secret Lives of Young Women Who Are Transforming the Arab World — Zoepf, Katherine
Excellent Sheep: The Miseducation of the American Elite and the Way to a Meaningful Life (Read by Foster, Mel). Audiobook Review — Deresiewicz, William
Excellent Sheep: The Miseducation of the American Elite and the Way to a Meaningful Life — Deresiewicz, William
Exceptional (Read by Durante, Emily). Audiobook Review — Petosa, Jess
Exceptional: Why the World Needs a Powerful America — Cheney, Dick
Excerpts from a Secret Prophecy — Klink, Joanna
The Exchange of Princesses — Thomas, Chantal
Exchanges in Exoticism: Cross-Cultural Marriage and the Making of the Mediterranean in Old French Romance — Moore, Megan
Excisions — Best, Clare
Excited to Learn: Motivation and Culturally Responsive Teaching — Ginsberg, Margery B.
Excluded Ancestors, Inventible Traditions: Essays Toward a More Inclusive History of Anthropology — Handler, Richard
An Excursion to the Poor Districts of London — Simonin, Louis Laurent
Executing God: Rethinking Everything You've Been Taught about Salvation and the Cross — Baker, Sharon
Executing Lean Improvements: A Practical Guide with Real-World Healthcare Case Studies — Delisle, Dennis R.
y The Executioner's Daughter — Hardstaff, Jane
Executive Summary: Committee Study of the Central Intelligence Agency's Detention and Interrogation Program — U.S. Senate Select Committee on Intelligence
Exegesis del "error": una reinterpretacion de la praxis de escritura en Libro de la vida, Novelas ejemplares y Desenganos amorosos — Elena, Rodriguez-Guridi
Exemplary Ambivalence in Late Nineteenth-Century Spanish America: Narrating Creole Subjectivity — Austin, Elisabeth L.
Exemplary Departures — Wittkop, Gabrielle
Exemplary STEM Programs: Designs for Success — Yager, Robert E.
Exercises in Criticism: The Theory and Practice of Literary Constraint — Brury, Louis
Exercises in Programming Style — Lopes, Cristina Videira
y Exhibit Labels: An Interpretive Approach, 2d ed. — Serrell, Beverly
Exhibiting Animals in Nineteenth-Century Britain: Empathy, Education, Entertainment — Cowie, Helen
Exhibiting Madness in Museums: Remembering Psychiatry through Collection and Display — Coleborne, Catharine
Exhibiting the Past: Historical Memory and the Politics of Museums in Postsocialist China — Denton, Kirk A.
Exhuming Loss: Memory, Materiality and Mass Graves of the Spanish Civil War — Renshaw, Layla
Exigency — Siemsen, Michael
The Exile — Adams, C.T.
Exile and Nomadism in French and Hispanic Women's Writing — Averis, Kate
Exile and Religious Identity, 1500-1800 — Spohnholz, Jesse
Exile and Revolution: Jose' D. Poyo, Key West, and Cuban Independence — Poyo, Gerald E.
Exile at Dawn — Fox, Stuart
The Exiled Earthborn — Tassi, Paul
An Exiled Generation: German and Hungarian Refugees of Revolution, 1848-1871 — Toth, Helena
The Exiled Generations: Legacies of the Southern Baptist Convention Holy Wars — Kell, Carl L.

Existence as Prayer: The Consciousness of Christ in the Theology of Hans Urs von Balthasar — Yenson, Mark L.
Existence: Essays in Ontology — Van Inwagen, Peter
Existentialism: An Introduction — Aho, Kevin
Existentialism and Contemporary Cinema: A Beauvoirian Perspective — Boule, Jean-Pierre
Existenzweisen: Eine Anthropologie der Modernen — Latour, Bruno
Exit — Arcan, Nelly
Exit — Boote, Julian
y Exit, Pursued by a Bear — Johnston, E.K.
Exit Right: The People Who Left the Left and Reshaped the American Century — Oppenheimer, Daniel
Exit Stage Left — Ison, Graham
Exit Strategy — Diaz, Lena
Exo — Gould, Steven
Exodus and Liberation: Deliverance Politics from John Calvin to Martin Luther King Jr. — Coffey, John
Exotic Gems, vols. 2 and 3 — Newman, Renee
Expanding Universe: Photographs from the Hubble Space Telescope — Weiner, Nina
c Expanzaramadingdong (Illus. by Klein, Keith) — Steinberg, Jason
The Expatriates — Lee, Janice Y.K.
The Expectant Father: The Ultimate Guide for Dads-to-Be, 4th ed. — Brott, Armin A.
The Expedition: A Love Story - Solving the Mystery of a Polar Tragedy — Uusma, Bea
The Expedition to the Baobab Tree — Coetzee, J.M.
The Expeditionary Force Marines Sourcebook — Jackson, Irvin
c The Expeditioners and the Secret of King Triton's Lair (Illus. by Roy, Katherine) — Taylor, S.S.
The Expeditions: An Early Biography of Muhammad — Rashid, Maemar Ibn
Expendable — Fischer, Peter S.
Experience and Experimental Writing: Literary Pragmatism from Emerson to the Jameses — Grimstad, Paul
Experience and Teleology in Ancient Historiography: "Futures Past" from Herodotus to Augustine — Grethlein, Jonas
The Experience of God: Being, Consciousness, Bliss — Hart, David Bentley
y Experiencing America's Story through Fiction: Historical Novels for Grades 7-12 — Crew, Hilary Susan
Experiencing Byzantium — Nesbitt, Claire
Experiencing Globalization: Religion in Contemporary Contexts — Hault, Derrick
Experiencing Stravinsky: A Listener's Companion — Maconie, Robin
Experiencing the French Revolution — Andress, David
The Experiment of Dreams — Zenner, Brandon
c Experiment with a Plant's Living Environment — Higgins, Nadia
c Experiment with What a Plant Needs to Grow — Higgins, Nadia
Experimental Buddhism: Innovation and Activism in Contemporary Japan — Nelson, John K.
Experimental Homebrewing: Mad Science in the Pursuit of Great Beer — Beechum, Drew
Experimental Latin American Cinema: History and Aesthetics — Tompkins, Cynthia
Experimental Life: Vitalism in Romantic Science and Literature — Mitchell, Robert
Experimenter — Almereyda, Michael
The Experimenters: Chance and Design at Black Mountain College — Diaz, Eva
c Experiments with Electricity — Thomas, Isabel
c Experiments with Forces — Thomas, Isabel
c Experiments with Heating and Cooling — Thomas, Isabel
c Experiments with Magnets — Thomas, Isabel
c Experiments with Materials — Thomas, Isabel
c Experiments with Plants — Thomas, Isabel
The Expert Expert Witness: More Maxims and Guidelines for Testifying in Court, 2d ed. — Brodsky, Stanley L.
Experten der Vernichtung: Das T4-Reinhardt-Netzwerk in den Lagern Belzec, Sobibor und Treblinka — Berger, Sara
Expiration Date — Kilpatrick, Nancy
y Expiration Day — Powell, William Campbell
Explaining Norms — Brennan, Geoffrey
Explanationes symboli aevi carolini — Keefe, Susan
Exploding the Reading: Building a World of Responses from One Small Story, 50 Interactive Strategies for Increasing Comprehension — Booth, David
Exploiting Africa: The Influence of Maoist China in Algeria, Ghana, and Tanzania — Chau, Donovan C.
c Explorations of Commander Josh, Book 1: In Space (Illus. by Servetnik, Anton) — LeBlanc, Donna
Explorations of Jesuit Practices in Italy and North America — Celenza, Harwell Anna
c Explore 360: Pompeii (Illus. by Vongprachanh, Somchith) — Chrisp, Peter
c Explore 360: Pompeii — Chrisp, Peter
c Explore 360: Pompeii (Illus. by Vongprachanh, Somchith) — Chrisp, Peter
c Explore Fossils! With 25 Great Projects (Illus. by Stone, Bryan) — Brown, Cynthia Light
c Explore Honey Bees! With 25 Great Projects (Illus. by Stone, Bryan) — Blobaum, Cindy
c Explore My World: Penguins — Esbaum, Jill
c Explore Norse Myths! With 25 Great Projects (Illus. by Stone, Bryan) — Yasuda, Anita
c Explore Poetry! With 25 Great Projects (Illus. by Stone, Bryan) — Diehn, Andi
c Explore Soil! With 25 Great Projects — Reilly, Kathleen M.
c Explore Solids and Liquids! With 25 Great Projects — Reilly, Kathleen M.
y Explore the Cosmos Like Neil deGrasse Tyson: A Space Science Journey — Saucier, C.A.P.
y Explorer: The Hidden Doors: Seven Graphic Stories — Kibuishi, Kazu
The Explorers Guild, vol. 1: A Passage to Shambhalla — Baird, Jon
The Explorer's Roadmap to National-Socialism: Sven Hedin, Geography and the Path to Genocide — Danielsson, Sarah K.
y Exploring America in the 1970s: Celebrating the Self — Sandling, Molly
y Exploring America in the 1980s: Living in the Material World — Sandling, Molly
Exploring and Developing the Use of Art-Based Genograms in Family of Origin Therapy — Schroder, Deborah
Exploring Bach's B-Minor Mass — Tomita, Yo
Exploring Color Photography: From Film to Pixels — Hirsch, Robert
Exploring Disability Identity and Disability Rights through Narratives: Finding a Voice of Their Own — Malhotra, Ravi
Exploring English Castles — Morris, Edd
Exploring Intercultural Communication: Language in Action — Hua, Zhu
Exploring Lincoln: Great Historians Reappraise Our Greatest President — Holzer, Harold
y Exploring Nature's Pattern Magic — Pigneguy, Dee
Exploring Our Hebraic Heritage: A Christian Theology of Roots and Renewal — Wilson, Marvin R.
Exploring Practices of Ministry — Cooper-White, Pamela
Exploring Tarot Using Radiant Rider-Waite — Venefica, Avia
Exploring the Dilemma of Domesticity — Essbaum, Jill Alexander
Exploring the Dutch Empire: Agents, Networks and Institutions, 1600-2000 — Antunes, Catia
Exploring Victorian Travel Literature: Disease, Race and Climate — Howell, Jessica
Expo 58 (Read by Rvan, Nannlenn). Audiobook Review — Coe, Jonathan
y Exposed — Graves, Judith
Exposed: Desire and Disobedience in the Digital Age — Harcourt, Bernard E.
Exposed Science: Genes, the Environment, and the Politics of Population Health — Shostak, Sara
y Exposing Crime and Corruption — Doeden, Matt Whistle-Blowers
Exposing the Third Reich: Colonel Truman Smith in Hitler's Germany — Gole, Henry G.
y Exposing Torture: Centuries of Cruelty — Marcovitz, Hal
Expressivism, Pragmatism and Representationalism — Price, Huw
The Expulsion of the Moriscos from Spain: A Mediterranean Diaspora — Garcia-Arenal, Mercedes
Expulsions: Brutality and Complexity in the Global Economy — Sassen, Saskia
c Exquisite Captive — Demetrios, Heather
y Exquisite Corpse (Illus. by Bagieu, Penelope) — Bagieu, Penelope
Exquisite Folly — Carriel, Jonathan

Extensible Processing for Archives and Special Collections: Reducing Processing Backlogs — Santamaria, Daniel A.
Extinction — Molles, D.J.
Extinction and Evolution: What Fossils Reveal about the History of Life — Eldredge, Niles
c The Extincts (Illus. by Muradov, Roman) — Cossanteli, Veronica
Extra Ecclesiam ... : Zur Institution und Kritik von Kirche — Klingen, Henning
y Extra Life — Nikitas, Derek
Extra Math Practice: Grade 4 Workbook — McArdle, Sean
Extra Math Practice: K Workbook — McArdle, Sean
Extra Yarn (Read by Barber, Nicole). Audiobook Review — Barnett, Mac
Extracting the Stone of Madness: Poems 1962-1972 — Pizarnik, Alejandra
y Extraction — Diaz, Stephanie
c Extraordinary — Franklin, Miriam Spitzer
The Extraordinary Journey of the Fakir Who Got Trapped in Ikea Wardrobe — Purtolas, Romain
y Extraordinary Means — Schneider, Robyn
c The Extraordinary Mr. Qwerty — Strambini, Karla
y Extraordinary People: A Semi-Comprehensive Guide to Some of the World's Most Fascinating Individuals (Illus. by Scamihorn, Aaron) — Hearst, Michael
Extraordinary Rendition — Freeman, Ru
c Extraordinary Warren Saves the Day (Illus. by Dillard, Sarah) — Dillard, Sarah

c Extreme Earth — Reynolds, Toby
The Extreme Life of the Sea — Palumbi, Stephen R.
Extreme Medicine: How Exploration Transformed Medicine in the Twentieth Century — Fong, Kevin
c Extreme Supercars — Harrison, Paul
c Extreme Weather: Surviving Tornadoes, Sandstorms, Hailstorms, Blizzards, Hurricanes, and More! — Kostigen, Thomas M.
Extreme: Why Some People Thrive at the Limits — Barrett, Emma
Extremist for Love: Martin Luther King Jr., Man of Ideas and Nonviolent Social Action — Burrow, Rufus, Jr.
Exuberance of Meaning: The Art Patronage of Catherine the Great — Kirin, Asen
An Eye for an Eye: A Global History of Crime and Punishment — Roth, Mitchel P.
c Eye: How It Works — Keenan, Sheila
c The Eye of Midnight — Brumbach, Andrew
Eye of Newt and Toe of Frog, Adder's Fork and Lizard's Leg: The Lore and Mythology of Amphibians and Reptiles — Crump, Marty
Eye of the Beholder: Johannes Vermeer, Antoni Van Leeuwenhoek, and the Reinvention of Seeing (Read by Marston, Tamara). Audiobook Review — Snyder, Laura J.
Eye of the Beholder: Johannes Vermeer, Antoni van Leeuwenhoek, and the Reinvention of Seeing — Snyder, Laura J.
y The Eye of the Falcon — Paver, Michelle
y The Eye of Zoltar — Fforde, Jasper

Eye on the Struggle: Ethel Payne, the First Lady of the Black Press — Morris, James McGrath
c Eye Sore — Jackson, Melanie
c Eye to Eye (Illus. by Base, Graeme) — Base, Graeme
Eyes — Gass, William H.
Eyes Full of Empty — Guez, Jeremie
Eyes: Novellas & Stories — Gass, William H.
y Eyes Wide Open: Going behind the Environmental Headlines (Read by Parks, Tom). Audiobook Review — Fleischman, Paul
y Eyes Wide Open: Going behind the Environmental Headlines — Fleischman, Paul
Ez egy ilyen csucs: A nagy Sziv Erno fuzet — Darvasi, Laszlo
Ezra Pound: Poet: A Portrait of the Man and His Work, 2 vols. — Moody, A. David
Ezra Pound: Poet: A Portrait of the Man and His Work, vol. 2, The Epic Years, 1921-1939 — Moody, A. David
Ezra Pound: Poet, A Portrait of the Man and His Work, vol. 2, The Epic Years, 1921-1939 — Moody, A. David
Ezra Pound: Poet: A Portrait of the Man and His Work, vol. 2: The Epic Years, 1921-1939 — Moody, A. David
Ezra Pound: Poet: A Portrait of the Man and His Work, vol. 2, The Epic Years, 1921-1939 — Moody, A. David
Ezra Pound: Poet: A Portrait of the Man and His Work, vol. 3: The Tragic Years — Moody, A. David
Ezra Pound's Eriugena — Byron, Mark

F

F — *Kehlmann, Daniel*
F.B. Eyes: How J. Edgar Hoover's Ghostreaders Framed African American Literature — *Maxwell, William J.*
c F Is for Feelings (Illus. by Mitchell, Flazel) — *Millar, Goldie*
c F is for Football (Illus. by Somerville, Charles C.) — *Elliott, Ned*
F — *Kehlmann, Daniel*
y F. Scott Fitzgerald and the Jazz Age — *Morretta, Alison*
F. Scott Fitzgerald's Fiction: "An Almost Theatrical Innocence" — *Irwin, John T.*
c Fab Four Friends: The Boys Who Became the Beatles (Illus. by Gustavson, Adam) — *Reich, Susanna*
c Fable Comics — *Duffy, Chris*
Fabled Fifteen, The Pacific War Saga of Carrier Air Group 15 — *Cleaver, Thomas McKelvey*
Fabric of Space: Water, Modernity, and the Urban Imagination — *Gandy, Matthew*
The Fabric of Space: Water, Modernity, and the Urban Imagination — *Gandy, Matthew*
The Fabulous Dark Cloister: Romance in England after the Reformation — *Werth, Tiffany Jo*
c Fabulous Frogs (Illus. by Hopgood, Tim) — *Jenkins, Martin*
c Fabulous Me, Piper Lee and the Peanut Butter Itch (Illus. by Gaylor, Terence) — *Thompson, Tolya L.*
The Fabulous Shadow — *Herter, Philip*
The Face: A Time Code — *Ozeki, Ruth*
The Face in the Glass: And Other Gothic Tales — *Braddon, Maria Elizabeth*
The Face of Britain: The Nation through its Portraits — *Schama, Simon*
The Face of Mammon: The Matter of Money in English Renaissance Literature — *Landreth, David*
The Face That Changed It All: A Memoir — *Johnson, Beverly*
Face to Face: Interviews with Artists — *Cork, Richard*
The Facebook Era — *Shih, Clara*
Faceless — *Grant, Cathryn*
y Faceless — *Sheinmel, Alyssa*
Faceoff — *Baldacci, David*
y Faces of the Dead — *Weyn, Suzanne*
The Faces of the Other: Religious Rivalry and Ethnic Encounters in the Later Roman World — *Kahlos, Maijastina*
c Facing a Frenemy (Illus. by Bishop, Tracy) — *Fields, Jan*
Facing Climate Change — *Kiehl, Jeffrey T.*
Facing Eugenics: Reproduction, Sterilization, and the Politics of Choice — *Dyck, Erika*
Facing Fearful Odds: My Father's Story of Captivity, Escape and Resistance 1940-45 — *Jay, John*
Facing Fire — *Dimon, HelenKay*
Facing the Challenge of Emancipation: A Study of the Ministry of William Hart Coleridge, First Bishop of Barbados, 1824-1842 — *Goodridge, Sehon S.*
Facsimile of the Henry VIII Book — *Fallows, David*
Factions, Friends and Feasts: Anthropological Perspectives on the Mediterranean — *Boissevain, Jeremy*
The Factory: Photography and the Warhol Community — *Zuromskis, Catherine*
The Fade Out (Illus. by Phillips, Sean) — *Brubaker, Ed*
Fade to Black — *Duff, Sue*
Fading into Focus — *Kantor, Joan*
Fado Resounding: Affective Politics and Urban Life — *Gray, Lila Ellen*
c Faerieground (Illus. by Sawyer, Odessa) — *Bracken, Beth*

c Faery Swap — *Quinn, Susan Kaye*
Fail, Fail Again, Fail Better: Wise Advice for Leaning into the Unknown — *Chodron, Pema*
Fail Fast or Win Big: The Start-Up Plan for Starting Now — *Schroeder, Bernhard*
FAILE: Works on Wood: Process, Paintings and Sculpture
Failed Democratization in Prewar Japan: Breakdown of a Hybrid Regime — *Takenaka, Harukata*
Failed States and Fragile Societies: A New World Disorder? — *Trauschweizer, Ingo*
Failing Our Brightest Kids: The Global Challenge of Educating High-Ability Students — *Finn, Chester E., Jr.*
Failing Our Veterans: The G.I. Bill and the Vietnam Generation — *Boulton, Mark*
Failure and the American Writer: A Literary History — *Jones, Gavin*
The Failure to Prevent World War I: The Unexpected Armageddon — *Gardner, Hall*
Failure: Why Science Is So Successful — *Firestein, Stuart*
The Fair Fight — *Freeman, Anna*
Fair Trade: Eine global-lokale Geschichte am Beispiel des Kaffees — *Quaas, Ruben*
Fair Value Accounting in Historical Perspective — *Watanabe, Izumi*
Faire court: L'esthetique de la brievete dans la litterature du Moyen Age — *Croizy-Naquet, Catherine*
Faire l'idiot: La politique de Deleuze — *Mengue, Philippe*
y Fairest (Read by Soler, Rebecca). Audiobook Review — *Meyer, Marissa*
y Fairest — *Meyer, Marissa*
c Fairy Tale Adventures (Illus. by Rossi, Francesca) — *Francia, Giada*
y Fairy Tale Baking: More Than 50 Enchanting Cakes, Bakes, and Decorations — *Khan, Ramla*
The Fairy Tale Girl — *Branch, Susan*
c The Fairy-Tale Handbook (Illus. by Tomic, Tomislav) — *Hamilton, Libby*
c The Fairy-Tale Matchmaker — *Baker, E.D.*
A Fairy Tale — *Bengtsson, Jonas T.*
Fairy Tales and True Stories: The History of Russian Literature for Children and Young People — *Hellman, Ben*
c Fairy Tales for Little Folks (Illus. by Moses, Will) — *Moses, Will*
c Fairy Tales from the Brothers Grimm — *Grimm, Wilhelm*
Fairy Tales, Myth, and Psychoanalytical Theory: Feminism and Retelling the Tale — *Schanoes, Veronica*
Fairy Tales Transformed? Twenty-First-Century Adaptations and the Politics of Wonder — *Bacchilega, Cristina*
c Fairytales for Mr. Barker (Illus. by Ahlberg, Jessica) — *Ahlberg, Jessica*
Faisal of Iraq — *Allawi, Ali A.*
Faith and Leadership: The Papacy and the Roman Catholic Church — *Riccards, Michael P.*
Faith and the Founders of the American Republic — *Dreisbach, Daniel L.*
Faith and the State: A History of Islamic Philanthropy in Indonesia — *Fauzia, Amelia*
Faith and Wisdom in Science — *McLeish, Tom*
Faith as an Option: Possible Futures for Christianity — *Joas, Hans*
Faith-Based Policy: A Litmus Test for Understanding Contemporary America — *Chandler, John*
Faith, Doubt, Mystery — *Tracy, James J.*

Faith Ed.: Teaching about Religion in an Age of Intolerance — *Wertheimer, Linda K.*
Faith: Essays from Believers, Agnostics, and Atheists — *Zackheim, Victoria*
Faith, Family, and Filipino American Community Life — *Cherry, Stephen M.*
Faith, Fiction, and Force in Medieval Baptism Debates — *Colish, Marcia L.*
Faith in Empire: Religion, Politics, and Colonial Rule in French Senegal, 1880-1940 — *Foster, Elizabeth*
Faith in the Face of Empire: The Bible through Palestinian Eyes — *Raheb, Mitri*
Faith on the Avenue: Religion on a City Street — *Day, Katie*
Faith Speaking Understanding: Performing the Drama of Doctrine — *Vanhoozer, Kevin J.*
Faith vs. Fact: Why Science and Religion Are Incompatible — *Coyne, Jerry A.*
Faithful and Virtuous Night — *Gluck, Louise*
Faithful Bodies: Performing Religion and Race in the Puritan Atlantic — *Kopelson, Heather Miyano*
The Faithful Couple — *Miller, A.D.*
The Faithful Executioner: Life and Death, Honor and Shame in the Turbulent Sixteenth Century — *Harrington, Joel F.*
A Faithful Farewell: Living Your Last Chapter with Love — *McEntyre, Marilyn Chandler*
Faithful Labourers: A Reception History of Paradise Lost, 1667-1970 — *Leonard, John*
Faithful Narratives: Historians, Religion, and the Challenge of Objectivity — *Sterk, Andrea*
Faithful Place (Read by Reynolds, Tim Gerard). Audiobook Review — *French, Tana*
Faithful Translators: Authorship, Gender, and Religion in Early Modern England — *Goodrich, Jaime*
The Faiths of the Postwar Presidents: From Truman to Obama — *Holmes, David L.*
Fake Fruit Factory — *Wensink, Patrick*
y Fake ID — *Giles, Lamar*
Fake Missed Connections — *Lauer, Brett Fletcher*
c Fake Snakes and Weird Wizards (Illus. by Garrett, Scott) — *Winkler, Henry*
Fakes!? Hoaxes, Counterfeits, and Deceptions in Early Modern Science — *Beretta, Marco*
y Faking Perfect — *Phillips, Rebecca*
Falafel: A National Icon — *Raviv, Yael*
Falcon — *Kendig, Rome*
y The Falconer's Apprentice — *von Hassell, Malve*
y The Fall — *Preller, James*
The Fall: A Father's Memoir in 424 Steps — *Mainardi, Diogo*
The Fall (Read by Colacci, David). Audiobook Review — *Lescroart, John*
The Fall — *Lescroart, John*
The Fall — *Pineiro, R.J.*
Fall In, Fall Out: The Dogface Years — *Crew, Joseph*
c Fall Is Here! (Illus. by Galloway, Fhiona) — *Jones, Frankie*
c Fall Leaves (Illus. by MacKay, Elly) — *Holland, Loretta*
y The Fall — *Griffin, Bethany*
c Fall of Heroes — *Kraatz, Jeramey*
The Fall of Language in the Age of English — *Mizumura, Minae*
The Fall of Moscow Station — *Henshaw, Mark*
Fall of Night — *Moberry, Jonathan*
The Fall of Princes — *Goolrick, Robert*
The Fall of the Faculty: The Rise of the All-Administrative University and Why It Matters — *Ginsberg, Benjamin*

Fall of the Flying Dragon: South Vietnamese Air Force 1973-75 — *Grandolini, Albert*
y The Fall of the House of West (Illus. by Rubin, David) — *Pope, Paul*
The Fall of the Ottomans: The Great War in the Middle East — *Rogan, Eugene*
The Fall of Tsarism: Untold Stories of the February 1917 Revolution — *Lyandres, Semion*
Fall with Me — *Armentrout, Jennifer L.*
Fallen Forests: Emotion, Embodiment and Ethics in American Women's Environmental Writing, 1781-1924 — *Kilcup, Karen L.*
Fallen Glory: The Lives and Deaths of Twenty Lost Buildings from the Tower of Babel to the Twin Towers — *Crawford, James*
y The Fallen — *Higson, Charlie*
Fallen Land — *Brown, Taylor*
Fallen Leaves: Last Words on Life, Love, War and God — *Durant, Will*
Fallen Sparrow — *Keeley, D.A.*
Falling after 9/11: Crisis in American Art and Literature — *Pozorski, Aimee*
Falling Back: Incarceration and Transitions to Adulthood among Urban Youth — *Fader Jamie J.*
Falling Behind? Boom, Bust, and the Global Race for Scientific Talent — *Teitelbaum, Michael S.*
The Falling Down Dance — *Martin, Chris*
Falling for Prince Charles — *Baratz-Logsted, Lauren*
Falling for You — *Mansell, Jill*
Falling Hard — *Dimon, HelenKay*
Falling in Love — *Leon, Donna*
Falling in Love with Hominids — *Hopkinson, Nalo*
Falling into Bed with a Duke — *Heath, Lorraine*
y Falling into Place — *Zhang, Amy*
y Falling into the Dragon's Mouth (Illus. by Huynh, Matt) — *Thompson, Holly*
Falling Like Snowflakes — *Hunter, Denise*
Falling Off Broadway — *Black, David*
Falling out of Time — *Cohen, Jessica*
c Falling Rock (Illus. by Robertson, Joyce) — *Heller, Rebecca*
Falling Short: The Coming Retirement Crisis and What to Do about It — *Ellis, Charles D.*
y Falling Up: Poems and Drawings: Special Edition — *Silverstein, Shel*
Falling Up: The Days and Nights of Carlisle Floyd: The Authorized Biography — *Holliday, Thomas*
y Fallout — *Bond, Gwenda*
Fallout — *Thomas, Paul*
y Fallout — *Bond, Gwenda*
y Falls the Shadow — *Gaither, Stefanie*
Fallujah Awakens: Marines, Sheikhs, and the Battle against Al-Qaeda — *Ardolino, Bill*
Fallujah Redux: The Anbar Awakening and the Struggle with Al-Qaeda — *Green, Daniel R.*
Falschung und Fake: Zur diskurskritischen Dimension des Tauschens — *Doll, Martin*
The False Apocalypse: From Stalinism to Capitalism — *Lubonja, Fatos*
y False Future — *Krokos, Dan*
False Impression — *Heley, Veronica*
False Positive — *Grant, Andrew*
False Start — *Valentin, Barbara*
False Tongues — *Charles, Kate*
Fama and Fiction in Vergil's Aeneid — *Syson, Antonia Jane Reobone*
Fame Attack: The Inflation of Celebrity and Its Consequences — *Rojek, Chris*
The Fame Game: A Superstar's Guide to Getting Rich and Famous — *Knazev, Sergey*
The Familiar: One Rainy Day in May — *Danielewski, Mark*
The Familiar: One Rainy Day in May — *Danielewski, Mark Z.*
The Familiar, vol. 1: One Rainy Day in May — *Danielewski, Mark Z.*
The Familiar, vol. 2: Into the Forest — *Danielewski, Mark Z.*
Familiensache Kirche? Die Fugger und die Konfessionalisierung
c Families (Illus. by Rotner, Shelley) — *Rotner, Shelley*
Families and Faith: How Religion Is Passed Down across Generations — *Bengston, Vern L.*
c Families around the World (Illus. by Gordon, Jessica Rae) — *Ruurs, Margriet*
c Families, Families, Families! (Illus. by Lang, Max) — *Lang, Suzanne*
Family and Intimate Mobilities — *Holdsworth, Clare*
Family and Life: Pastoral Reflections — *Francis I, Pope*
Family Business: The Essentials — *Leach, Peter*

The Family Calendar Cookbook: From Birthdays to Bake Sales, Good Food to Carry You through the Year — *Banfield, Kelsey*
Family-Centered Early Intervention: Supporting Infants and Toddlers in Natural Environments — *Raver, Sharon A.*
c Family Changes: Explaining Divorce to Children (Illus. by Lovsin, Polona) — *Maker, Azmaira H.*
Family Furnishings: Selected Stories, 1995-2014 — *Munro, Alice*
Family History of Fear — *Tuszynska, Agata*
Family Life — *Sharma, Akhil*
Family Matters: Puerto Rican Women Authors on the Island and the Mainland — *Moreno, Marisel C.*
Family Money: Property, Race, and Literature in the Nineteenth Century — *Clymer, Jeffory A.*
The Family of Abraham: Jewish, Christian and Muslim Interpretations — *Bakhos, Carol*
A Family of No Prominence: The Descendants of Pak Tokhwa and the Birth of Modern Korea — *Park, Eugene Y.*
c Family Pets (Illus. by Dill, Sarah) — *Shand, Pat*
Family Politics: Domestic Life, Devastation and Survival, 1900-1950 — *Ginsborg, Paul*
Family Resemblance: An Anthology and Exploration of 8 Hybrid Literary Genres — *Sulak, Marcela*
c Family Reunion (Illus. by Steers, Billy) — *Steers, Billy*
Family Revolution: Marital Strife in Contemporary Chinese Literature and Visual Culture — *Xiao, Hui Faye*
y The Family Romanov: Murder, Rebellion, and the Fall of Imperial Russia — *Fleming, Candace*
c Family Ties (Read by Bernstein, Jesse). Audiobook Review — *Paulsen, Gary*
y Family Ties — *Paulsen, Gary*
The Family Tooth — *Avery, Ellis*
The Family Tree: A Kinship Lynching in Georgia, a Legacy of Secrets, and My Search for the Truth — *Branan, Karen*
Family Values: The Ethics of Parent-Child Relationships — *Brighouse, Harry*
Famine, Affluence, and Morality — *Singer, Peter*
Famines during the 'Little Ice Age,' 1300-1800: Socio-Natural Entanglements in Premodern Societies
Famous Assassinations in World History: An Encyclopedia — *Newton, Michael*
Famous First Facts: A Record of First Happenings, Discoveries, and Inventions in American History, 7th ed. — *Kane, Joseph Nathan*
c Famous Graveyards — *Rajczak, Kristen*
y Famous in Love — *Serle, Rebecca*
y Famous Last Words — *Alender, Katie*
c Famous Phonies: Legends, Fakes, and Frauds Who Changed History — *DuMont, Brianna*
c Famous Pirates — *Tucker, Rosalyn*
Famous Trees of Texas — *Riley, Gretchen*
Famous Works of Art--and How They Got That Way — *Nici, John B.*
Fanaticus: Mischief and Madness in the Modern Sports Fan — *Gubar, Justine*
Fancy — *Davies, Jeremy M.*
c Fancy Nancy and the Wedding of the Century (Illus. by Glasser, Robin Preiss) — *O'Connor, Jane*
c Fancy Nancy's Fabulous Fall Storybook Collection (Illus. by Glasser, Robin Preiss) — *O'Connor, Jane*
Fanfares and Finesse: A Performer's Guide to Trumpet History and Literature — *Koehler, Elisa*
y The Fangirl's Guide to the Galaxy: A Handbook for Girl Geeks — *Maggs, Sam*
c Fangs a Lot: Final Notes from a Totally Lame Vampire (Illus. by Pinder, Andrew) — *Collins, Tim*
Fannie Barrier Williams: Crossing the Borders of Region and Race — *Hendricks, Wanda A.*
Fannie Hardy Eckstorm and Her Quest for Local Knowledge, 1865-1946 — *MacDougall, Pauleena M.'*
Fanny Says — *Brown, Nickole*
y Fans of the Impossible Life — *Scelsa, Kate*
Fantasia of Color in Early Cinema — *Gunning, Tom*
Fantasies and Hard Knocks: My Life as a Printer — *Rummonds, Richard-Gabriel*
Fantasies of Identification: Disability, Gender, Race — *Samuels, Ellen*
c The Fantastic Ferris Wheel: The Story of Inventor George Ferris (Illus. by Salerno, Steven) — *Kraft, Betsy Harvey*
c Fantastic Fugitives — *DuMont, Brianna*
The Fantastic in Holocaust Literature and Film: Critical Perspectives — *Kerman, Judith B.*

Fantastic Planets, Forbidden Zones, and Lost Continents: The 100 Greatest Science-Fiction Films — *Brode, Douglas*
Fantastical: Tales of Bears, Beer and Hemophilia — *Bulatovic, Marija*
Fantasy Islands: Chinese Dreams and Ecological Fears in an Age of Climate Crisis — *Sze, Julie*
c Fantasy League — *Lupica, Mike*
A Fantasy Medley 3 — *Hearne, Kevin*
c The Fantasy Soccer Wall (Illus. by Kennedy, Kelly) — *Bryant, Anne*
c Fantasy Sports — *Bosma, Sam*
c Fantasy Sports No. 1 (Illus. by Bosma, Sam) — *Bosma, Sam*
Fantomas versus the Multinational Vampires: An Attainable Utopia — *Cortazar, Julio*
Far as the Eye Can See — *Bausch, Robert*
The Far End of Happy — *Craft, Kathryn*
Far-Fetched — *Johnston, Devin*
c Far from Fair — *Arnold, Elana K.*
c Far from Home: The Sisters of Street Child — *Doherty, Berlie*
The Far Reaches: Phenomenology, Ethics, and Social Renewal in Central Europe — *Gubser, Michael*
The Far Right in the Balkans — *Stojarova, Vera*
Faraday, Maxwell, and the Electromagnetic Field: How Two Men Revolutionized Physics — *Forbes, Nancy*
A Faraway, Familiar Place: An Anthropologist Returns to Papua New Guinea — *Smith, Michael French*
c Faraway Father (Illus. by Hill, Eva) — *Hill, Eva*
c Faraway Friends (Illus. by Cox, Russ) — *Cox, Russ*
c Farewell Floppy (Illus. by Chaud, Benjamin) — *Chaud, Benjamin*
Farewell Kabul: From Afghanistan to a More Dangerous World — *Lamb, Christina*
Farewell to Prosperity: Wealth, Identity, and Conflict in Postwar America — *Rose, Lisle A.*
Farewell to the World: A History of Suicide — *Barbagil, Marzio*
A Farewell to Windemere — *Mooers, John*
Fargo's Legacy — *Hatch, Tylor*
c Farley Farts — *Muller, Birte*
The Farm — *Smith, Tom Rob*
c Farm Animals — *La Coccinella*
c Farm: Barnyard Fun — *Litton, Jonathan*
Farm for Mutes — *Anastasopoulos, Dimitri*
The Farm Novel in North America: Genre and Nation in the United States, English Canada, and French Canada, 1845-1945 — *Freitag, Florian*
c Farm Puzzle and Sticker Book — *Tiger Tales*
The Farm — *Smith, Tom Rob*
Farmed and Dangerous — *Maxwell, Edith*
c The Farmer and the Clown — *Frazee, Marla*
c Farmer David: The Dunster Show (Illus. by McLoughlin, Zack) — *Crane, Stuart*
The Farmer in England, 1650-1980 — *Hoyle, Richard W.*
c Farmer Kobi's Hanukkah Match (Illus. by Decker, C.B.) — *Rostoker-Gruber, Karen*
c Farmer Will Allen and the Growing Table (Illus. by Larkin, Eric-Shabazz) — *Martin, Jacqueline Briggs*
y The Farmerettes — *Sherman, Gisela Tobien*
c Farmer's Market (Illus. by Steers, Billy) — *Steers, Billy*
Farms, Factories, and Families: Italian American Women of Connecticut — *Riccio, Anthony V.*
Farryn's War — *Meierz, Christie*
c Fart Squad (Illus. by Gilpin, Stephen) — *Pilger, Seamus*
Farthest Field: An Indian Story of the Second World War — *Karnad, Raghu*
Faschismus, Religion und Gewalt in Sudosteuropa: Die Legion Erzengel und die Ustasa im historischen Vergleich — *Yeomans, Rory*
The Fascist Party and Popular Opinion in Mussolini's Italy — *Corner, Paul*
Fascist Voices: An Intimate History of Mussolini's Italy — *Duggan, Christopher*
Fashion and Museums: Theory and Practice — *Melchior, Riegels*
The Fashion Encyclopedia: A Visual Resource for Terms, Techniques, and Styles — *Angus, Emily*
Fashion Germany — *Rink, Martina*
Fashion Lives: Fashion Icons with Fern Mallis — *Mallis, Fern*
Fashion Victims: Dress at the Court of Louis XVI and Marie-Antoinette — *Chrisman-Campbell, Kimberly*
Fashion Victims: The Dangers of Dress Past and Present — *David, Alison Matthews*
A Fashionable Indulgence — *Charles, K.J.*

Fashioning Bollywood: The Making and Meaning of Hindi Film Costume — Wilkinson-Weber, Clare M.
Fashioning the Body: An Intimate History of the Silhouette — Bruna, Denis
Fashioning the Silver Fork Novel — Wilson, Cheryl A.
c **Fast and Furry Racers: The Silver Serpent Cup** — Emmett, Jonathan
c **Fast Break** — Lupica, Mike
Fast Food, Good Food: More than 150 Quick and Easy Ways to Put Healthy, Delicious Food on the Table — Weil, Andrew
Fast Food Maniac — Hein, John
Fast Forward: How Women Can Achieve Power and Purpose — Verveer, Melanne
c **Fast Freddy (Illus. by Sharp, Dan)** — Mancini, Lee Ann
Fast into the Night: A Woman, Her Dogs, and Their Journey North on the Iditarod Trail — Moderow, Debbie Clarke
Fast-Piece Applique: Easy, Artful Quilts by Machine — Hughes, Rose
Fast Shuffle — Black, David
The Faster Redder Road: The Best UnAmerican Stories of Stephen Graham Jones — Jones, Stephen Graham
Faster Road Racing: 5K to Half Marathon — Pfitzinger, Pete
Fastest Things on Wings: Rescuing Hummingbirds in Hollywood — Masear, Terry
Fasti Austriae 1736: Ein naulateinisches Gedicht in funfzehn europaischen Sprachen — Romer, Franz
Fat Blame: How the War on Obesity Victimizes Women and Children — Herndon, April Michelle
y **Fat & Bones and Other Stories (Read by Corren, Donald). Audiobook Review** — Theule, Larissa
y **Fat & Bones and Other Stories (Illus. by Doyle, Adam S.)** — Theule, Larissa
c **Fat Boy vs. the Cheerleaders (Read by Podehl, Nick). Audiobook Review** — Herbach, Geoff
Fat Gay Men: Girth, Mirth, and the Politics of Stigma — Whitesel, Jason
Fat Girl Walking: Sex, Food, Love, and Being Comfortable in Your Skin ... Every Inch of It — Gibbons, Brittany
Fat Quarters: Small Fabrics, More Than 50 Big Ideas — Lark Crafts
Fata Morgana — Basara, Svetislav
Fatal Catch — Rowson, Pauline
y **A Fatal Chapter** — Barrett, Lorna
Fatal Conceit — Tanenbaum, Robert K.
y **Fatal Faults: The Story of the Challenger Explosion** — Braun, Eric
y **Fatal Fever: Tracking Down Typhoid Mary** — Jarrow, Gail
The Fatal Flame — Faye, Lyndsay
Fatal Flaws: How a Misfolded Protein Baffled Scientists and Changed the Way We Look at the Brain — Ingram, Jay
Fatal Glamour: The Life of Rupert Brooke — Delany, Paul
Fatal Reaction — Frisch, Belinda
Fatal Redemption — Kilzer, Lou
Fatal Retribution — Graves, Diana
Fatal Revolutions: Natural History, West Indian Slavery and the Routes of American Literature — Iannini, Christopher P.
Fatal Rivalry, Flodden 1513: Henry VIII, James IV and the Battle for Renaissance Britain — Goodwin, George
The Fatal Shore — Hughes, Robert
The Fatal Sin of Love — Chen, G.X.
Fatale — Manchette, Jean-Patrick
Fate, Glory, and Love in Early Modern Gallery Decoration: Visualizing Supreme Power — Lagerlof, Margaretha Rossholm
The Fate of Freedom Elsewhere: Human Rights and US Cold War Policy toward Argentina — Schmidli, William Michael
The Fate of Ideas: Seductions, Betrayals, Appraisals — Boyers, Robert
The Fate of Reason — Beiser, Frederick
A Fateful Day in 1698: The Remarkable Sobaipuri-O'odham Victory over the Apaches and Their Allies — Seymour, Deni J.
The Fateful Day — Rowe, Rosemary
The Fateful Lightning — Shaara, Jeff
Fateful Ties: A History of America's Preoccupation with China — Chang, Gordon H.
Fateful Transitions: How Democracies Manage Rising Powers, from the Eve of World War I to China's Ascendance — Kliman, Daniel

Fates and Furies (Read by Damron, Will, with Julia Whelan). Audiobook Review — Groff, Lauren
Fates and Furies (Read by Damron, Will, with Julia Whelan) — Groff, Lauren
Fates and Furies — Groff, Lauren
Father and Daughter: Patriarchy, Gender and Social Science — Oakley, Ann
Father Comes Home from the Wars — Parks, Suzan-Lori
The Father-Daughter Club — Ragsdale, Alison
A Father for Lilja — Merey, Ryszard I.
Father Ghost — Green, B.
The Father of Modern Landmarkism: The Life of Ben M. Bogard — Pratt, J. Kristian
Father of Route 66: The Story of Cy Avery — Kelly, Susan Croce
The Father of the Arrow is the Thought — DeWeese, Christopher
Father, Son, Stone — Goodman, Allan H.
Fatherhood and Its Representations in Middle English Texts — Moss, Rachel E.
Fatherhood and the British Working Class, 1865-1914 — Strange, Julie-Marie
Fatherland: A Family History (Illus. by Bunjevac, Nina) — Bunjevac, Nina
Fathers and Daughters in the Hebrew Bible — Stiebert, Johanna
y **FatherSonFather** — Jacobs, Evan
y **Fathomless** — Pillsworth, Anne M.
Fatizen 24602 (Illus. by Arrigo, Mason) — Barragan, Philip C., III
Fatness and the Maternal Body: Women's Experiences of Corporeality and the Shaping of Social Policy — Unnithan-Kumar, Maya
Fauji Banta Singh and Other Stories — Binning, Sadhu
y **The Fault in Our Stars** — Green, John
The Fault Line: Traveling the Other Europe, from Finland to Ukraine — Rumiz, Paolo
Fault Lines — Pryce-Jones, David
y **Fault Lines** — Perritano, John
y **Fault Lines** — Ortega, Brenda
Faulty Predictions — Greenberg, Karin-Lin
Faustina I and II: Imperial Women of the Golden Age — Levick, Barbara M.
Faux Pas — Esposito, Shannon
Favela: Four Decades of Living on the Edge in Rio de Janeiro — Perlman, Janice
The Favor of Friends: Intercession and Aristocratic Politics in Carolingian and Ottonian Europe — Gilsdorf, Sean
Favorite Bedtime Stories — Fitzgerald, John M.
Favorite Son — Warren, Tiffany L.
Faxed: The Rise and Fall of the Fax Machine — Coopersmith, Jonathan
y **FBI Hostage Rescue and SWAT Teams** — Whiting, Jim
F*ck Feelings — Bennett, Michael I.
y **FDR and the American Crisis** — Marrin, Albert
FDR and the Holocaust: A Breach of Faith — Medoff, Rafael
Fear and Clothing: Unbuckling American Style — Wilson, Cintra
Fear and the Muse Kept Watch: The Russian Masters--from Akhmatova and Pasternak to Shostakovich and Eisenstein--under Stalin — McSmith, Andy
Fear Itself: The New Deal and the Origins of Our Time — Katznelson, Ira
Fear of Crime in the United States: Causes, Consequences, and Contradictions — Lane, Jodi
Fear of Dying — Jong, Erica
Fear of Fifty — Jong, Erica
Fear of Flying — Jong, Erica
The Fear of French Negroes: Transcolonial Collaboration in the Revolutionary Americas — Johnson, Sarah E.
The Fear of Islam — Green, Todd H.
Fear the Darkness (Read by Toren, Suzanne). Audiobook Review — Masterman, Becky
Fear the Darkness (Illus. by Masterman, Becky) — Masterman, Becky
Fearful Spirits, Reasoned Follies: The Boundaries of Superstition in Late Medieval Europe — Bailey, Michael D.
Fearless — James, Elliott
y **The Fearless** — Pass, Emma
c **Fearless (Illus. by Cano, Fernando)** — Terrell, Brandon
c **Fearless Flyer: Ruth Law and Her Flying Machine (Illus. by Colon, Raul)** — Lang, Heather

Fearless Genius: The Digital Revolution in Silicon Valley, 1985-2000 — Menuez, Doug
c **Fearless: Sons & Daughter (Illus. by Davis, Sarah)** — Thompson, Colin
Fearsome Creatures of the Lumberwoods: 20 Chilling Tales from the Wilderness (Illus. by Mead, Tom) — Johnson, Hal
The Feast and the Pulpit: Sermons and the Cult of St. Elizabeth of Hungary, 1235-ca. 1500 — Gecser, Otto
A Feast for the Eyes: Art, Performance, and the Late Medieval Banquet — Normore, Christina
c **The Feast for the King (Illus. by Faas, Linde)** — Verhelst, Marlies
Feast of the Innocents — Rosero, Evelio
Feasting on the Gospels: Mark — Jarvis, Cynthia A.
Feasting on the Word: Guide to Children's Sermons — Bartlett, David L.
c **Feathered Dinosaurs (Illus. by Low, William)** — Guiberson, Brenda Z.
A Feathered River across the Sky: The Passenger Pigeon's Flight to Extinction — Greenberg, Joel
Feathers: A Beautiful Look at a Bird's Most Unique Feature — Tekiela, Stan
c **Feathers: Not Just for Flying (Illus. by Brannen, Sarah S.)** — Stewart, Melissa
Feathers, Paws, Fins and Claws: Fairy-Tale Beasts (Illus. by Kusaite, Lina) — Schacker, Jennifer
February Fever — Lourey, Jess
Fed, White, and Blue: Finding America with My Fork — Majumdar, Simon
Federer and Me: A Story of Obsession — Skidelsky, William
Federico Grisone: The Rules of Riding: An Edited Translation of the First Renaissance Treatise on Classical Horsemanship — Tobey, Elizabeth MacKenzie
Feeding the Fire: Recipes and Strategies for Better Barbecue and Grilling — Carroll, Joe
c **Feeding the Flying Fanellis: And Other Poems from a Circus Chef (Illus. by Kawa, Cosei)** — Hosford, Kate
c **Feeding Time at the Zoo** — Shahan, Sherry
The Feel of the City: Experiences of Urban Transformation — Kenny, Nicholas
y **Feel Real Good** — Moore, Stephanie Perry
The Feel Rich Project: Reinventing Your Understanding of True Wealth to Find True Happiness — Kay, Michael F.
Feeling Beauty: The Neuroscience of Aesthetic Experience — Starr, G. Gabrielle
Feeling Great: Creating a Life of Optimism, Enthusiasm and Contentment — Janki, Dadi
Feeling Like Saints: Lollard Writings after Wyclif — Somerset, Fiona
Feeling Mediated: A History of Media Technology and Emotion in America — Malin, Brenton J.
Feeling Pleasures: The Sense of Touch in Renaissance England — Moshenska, Joe
y **Feeling Unloved? Girls Dealing with Feelings** — Kavanaugh, Dorothy
Feeling Women's Liberation — Hesford, Victoria
c **Feelings (Illus. by Knight, Paula)** — Law, Felicia
c **Feet First (Illus. by Banks, Timothy)** — Sonneborn, Scott
c **Feet, Go to Sleep (Illus. by Smith, Maggie)** — Bottner, Barbara
Feinde, Freunde, Fremde? Deutsche Perspektiven auf die USA
Felicity: Poems — Oliver, Mary
c **Felix Stands Tall (Illus. by Wells, Rosemary)** — Wells, Rosemary
y **Fell of Dark** — Downes, Patrick
Fellini: The Sixties — Bowman, Manoah
The Fellowship: The Literary Lives of the Inklings: J. R. R. Tolkien and C. S. Lewis, Owen Barfield, Charles Williams — Zaleski, Philip
The Fellowship: The Literary Lives of the Inklings: J.R.R. Tolkien, C.S. Lewis, Owen Barfield, Charles Williams — Zaleski, Philip
Felt and Fibre Art: A Practical Guide to Making Beautiful Felted Artworks — Hughes, Val
Female Alliances: Gender, Identity, and Friendship in Early Modern Britain — Herbert, Amanda E.
Female Circumcision and Clitoridectomy in the United States: A History of a Medical Treatment — Rodriguez, Sarah B.
The Female Complaint: Tales of Unruly Women — Kearns, Rosalie Morales
y **Female Genital Cutting** — Meyer, Terry Teague
Female Rebellion in Young Adult Dystopian Fiction — Day, Sara K.

Female SS Guards and Workaday Violence: The Majdanek Concentration Camp, 1942-1944 — *Mailander, Elissa*
Femininity and Authorship in the Novels of Elizabeth Von Arnim: At Her Most Radiant Moment — *Romhild, Juliane*
Femininity, Crime and Self-Defence in Victorian Literature and Society: From Dagger-Fans to Suffragettes — *Godfrey, Emelyne*
Feminism as Life's Work: Four Modern American Women through Two World Wars — *Trigg, Mary K.*
The Feminism of Uncertainty: A Gender Diary — *Snitow, Ann*
y Feminism: Reinventing the F Word — *Higgins, Nadia Abushanab*
Feminist Aesthetics and the Politics of Modernism — *Ziarek, Ewa Plonowska*
Feminist Catholic Theological Ethics: Conversations in the World Church — *Hogan, Linda*
Feminist Constitutionalism: Global Perspectives — *Baines, Beverley*
Feminist Edges of the Qur'an — *Hidayatullah, Aysha A.*
Feminist Film Theory and 'Cleo from 5 to 7' — *Neroni, Hilary*
Feminist Pedagogy for Library Instruction — *Accardi, Maria T.*
The Feminist Porn Book: The Politics of Producing Pleasure — *Taormino, Tristan*
Feminist, Queer, Crip — *Kafer, Alison*
Feminist Solidarity at the Crossroads: Intersectional Women's Studies for Transracial Alliance — *Vaz, Kim Marie*
The Feminist Utopia Project: Fifty-Seven Visions of a Wildly Better Future — *Brodsky, Alexandra*
Feminized Counsel and the Literature of Advice in England, 1380-1500 — *Schieberle, Misty*
y Femme — *Bach, Mette*
Femmes et Exils: Forms et figures — *Bourque, Dominique*
c Fenway and Hattie — *Coe, Victoria J.*
y Feral — *Schindler, Holly*
Feral Cities: Adventures with Animals in the Urban Jungle — *Donovan, Tristan*
Feral Nights (Read by Haberkorn, Todd, with Nick Podehl and Amy McFadden). Audiobook Review — *Smith, Cynthia Leitich*
y Feral Pride (Read by four narrators). Audiobook Review — *Smith, Cynthia Leitich*
y Feral Pride — *Smith, Cynthia Leitich*
y Ferals — *Grey, Jacob*
Ferdinand II: Counter-Reformation Emperor, 1578-1637 — *Bireley, Robert*
Ferdinand Raimund: Samtliche Werke - Historisch-kritische Ausgabe, vol. i: Der Barometermacher auf der Zauberinsel; Der Diamant des Geisterkonigs — *Hein, Jurgen*
Ferguson and Faith: Sparking Leadership and Awakening Community — *Francis, Leah Gunning*
Fermented: A Beginner's Guide to Making Your Own Sourdough, Yogurt, Sauerkraut, Kefir, Kimchi, and More — *Pike, Charlotte*
Ferocious Reality: Documentary according to Werner Herzog — *Ames, Eric*
y Ferrari — *Paine, Jed*
c Ferret Fun in the Sun (Illus. by de Tagyos, Paul Ratz) — *Rostoker-Gruber, Karen*
Fertile Bonds: Bedouin Class, Kinship, and Gender in the Bekaa Valley — *Joseph, Suzanne E.*
Fertile Disorder: Spirit Possession and Its Provocation of the Modern — *Ram, Kalpana*
Fervent Charity — *Callen, Paulette*
Festival Classics for Alto Saxophone: 21 Solo Pieces with Piano Accompaniment — *Clark, Larry*
Festival Classics for Violin: 13 Solo Pieces with Piano Accompaniment — *Clark, Larry*
The Festival of Insignificance — *Kundera, Milan*
Festive in Death — *Robb, J.D.*
c Fetch (Illus. by Hurley, Jorey) — *Hurley, Jorey*
Fetch More Dollars for Your Dog Training Business — *Visconti, John D.*
c Fetch! With Ruff Ruffman: Ruff Ruffman's 44 Favorite Science Activities (Illus. by WGBH Educational Foundation)
c Fettuccine and Four-Leaf Clovers: A Readers' Theater Script and Guide (Illus. by Mata, Nina) — *Wallace, Nancy K.*
The Fever of 1721: The Epidemic That Revolutionized Medicine and American Politics — *Coss, Stephen*

Fevered Measures: Public Health and Race at the Texas-Mexico Border, 1848-1942 — *Mckiernan-Gonzalez, John*
Few and Far Between: On the Trail of Britain's Rarest Animals — *Elder, Charlie*
A Few Drops of Blood — *Weiss, Jan Merete*
Fiber: Sculpture 1960-Present — *Porter, Jenelle*
The Fibonacci Murders — *Lehman, Dale E.*
c Fibonacci Zoo (Illus. by Wald, Christina) — *Robinson, Tom*
Fichte's Vocation of Man: New Interpretive and Critical Essays — *Breazeale, Daniel*
Ficino in Spain — *Byrne, Susan*
Fictions Inc.: The Corporation in Postmodern Fiction, Film and Popular Culture — *Clare, Ralph*
Fictions nationales: Cinema, empire et nation en Ouzbekistan — *Drieu, Cloe*
Fictions of Conversion: Jews, Christians, and Cultures of Change in Early Modern England — *Shoulson, Jeffrey S.*
Fictions of Fact and Value: The Erasure of Logical Positivism in American Literature, 1945-1975 — *LeMahieu, Michael*
Fictive Kinship: Family Reunification and the Meaning of Race and Nation in American Immigration — *Lee, Catherine*
c Fiddle Dee Dee (Illus. by Berndt, Jackie) — *Gilbert, Faye Alison*
Fidel Castro — *Caistor, Nick*
Field & Feast: Sublime Food from a Brave New Farm — *Carlson, Dean*
y A Field Guide to Awkward Silences — *Petri, Alexandra*
A Field Guide to Gettysburg: Experiencing the Battlefield through Its History, Places, and People — *Reardon, Carol*
The Field Guide to Peppers — *DeWitt, Dave*
A Field Guide to the Natural Communities of Michigan — *Cohen, Joshua G.*
The Field of Cloth of Gold — *Richardson, Glenn*
Field of Prey — *Sandford, John*
The Field of the Cloth of Gold — *Mills, Magnus*
A Field Philosopher's Guide to Fracking: How One Texas Town Stood Up to Big Oil and Gas — *Briggle, Adam*
Field Techniques and Tips for Nature Photographers: A Practical Guide for Quality Photo Images — *Williams, John H.*
c Field-Trip Fiasco (Illus. by Love, Judy) — *Danneberg, Julie*
c Field Trip — *Paulsen, Gary*
Fields of Blood: Religion and the History of Violence (Read by Armstrong, Karen). Audiobook Review — *Armstrong, Karen*
Fields of Blood: Religion and the History of Violence — *Armstrong, Karen*
Fields of Play: An Ethnography of Children's Sports — *Dyke, Noel*
Fields of Wrath — *Reichert, Mickey Zucker*
Fierce Convictions: The Extraordinary Life of Hannah More — *Prior, Karen Swallow*
Fierce Patriot: The Tangled Lives of William Tecumseh Sherman — *O'Connell, Robert L.*
The Fierce Urgency of Now: Lyndon Johnson, Congress, and the Battle for the Great Society — *Zelizer, Julian E.*
Fiercombe Manor — *Riordan, Kate*
c Fiesta! (Illus. by Moreno, Rene King) — *Ginger Foglesong Guy*
"Fievres d'Afrique", suivi de trois recits inedits: "La Recluse", "La Duchesse" et "Minne Water: Lac d'Amour" — *Charbonneau, Louis*
c The Fifolet (Illus. by Lindsley, Jennifer) — *Downing, Johnette*
Fifteen Dogs — *Alexis, Andre*
c Fifteen Dollars and Thirty-five Cents: A Story about Choices (Illus. by Cole, Kathryn) — *Cole, Kathryn*
c Fifteen Dollars and Thirty-five Cents: A Story about Choices (Illus. by Leng, Qin) — *Cole, Kathryn*
The Fifth Alert — *Simmons, Dan*
The Fifth Gospel (Read by Davenport, Jack). Audiobook Review — *Caldwell, Ian*
The Fifth Gospel — *Caldwell, Ian*
The Fifth Heart (Read by Pittu, David). Audiobook Review — *Simmons, Dan*
The Fifth Heart — *Simmons, Dan*
The Fifth House of the Heart — *Tripp, Ben*
The Fifth Season: The Broken Earth, Bk. 1 — *Jemisin, N.K.*
Fifties Ethnicities: The Ethnic Novel and Mass Culture at Midcentury — *Floreani, Tracy*

Fifty Fashion Designers That Changed the World — *The Design Museum*
Fifty-Fifty O'Brien: A U.S. Marine Sniper in One Hell of a War with One Shot to Survive. Audiobook Review — *Hubbard, L. Ron*
Fifty Modern Buildings That Changed the World — *Sudjic, Deyan*
Fifty Yards and Holding — *Barnes, David-Matthew*
A Fifty-Year Silence: Love, War, and a Ruined House in France — *Mouillot, Miranda Richmond*
Fifty Years of Revolution: Perspectives on Cuba, the United States, and the World — *Marino, Soraya M. Castro*
y Fig — *Schantz, Sarah Elizabeth*
The Figaro Murders — *Lebow, Laura*
The Fight: A Secret Service Agent's Inside Account of Security Failings and the Political Machine — *Bongino, Dan*
y Fight Back — *Sherrard, Brent R.*
The Fight for Immortality — *Arthur, Peter*
y Fight for Power — *Walters, Eric*
The Fight for Status and Privilege in Late Medieval and Early Modern Castile, 1465-1598 — *Crawford, Michael J.*
The Fight for the Four Freedoms: What Made FDR and the Greatest Generation Truly Great — *Kaye, Harvey J.*
y Fight Like a Girl: Learning Curve (Illus. by Lee, Soo) — *Pinckney, David*
Fight Like a Physicist — *Thalken, Jason*
The Fight to Save Juarez: Life in the Heart of Mexico's Drug War — *Ainslie, Ricardo C.*
The Fight to Vote — *Waldman, Michael*
The Fighter and the Fallen Woman — *Cayne, Pamela*
Fighter Pilot's Daughter: Growing up in the Sixties and the Cold War — *Lawlor, Mary*
Fighters in the Shadows: A New History of the French Resistance — *Gildea, Robert*
Fighting Chance (Read by Colacci, David). Audiobook Review — *Haddam, Jane*
A Fighting Chance — *Warren, Elizabeth*
y A Fighting Chance — *Melendez Salinas, Claudia*
y Fighting Chance — *Stevens, B.K.*
Fighting Dirty — *Halston, Sidney*
Fighting Fascism and Surviving Buchenwald: The Life and Memoir of Hans Bergas — *Varon, Bension*
Fighting for Recognition: Identity, Masculinity, and the Act of Violence in Professional Wrestling — *Smith, R. Tyson*
Fighting for the Soul of Germany: The Catholic Struggle for Inclusion after Unification — *Bennette, Rebecca Ayako*
Fighting God: An Atheist Manifesto for a Religious World — *Silverman, David*
Fighting Jim Crow in the County of Kings: The Congress of Racial Equality in Brooklyn — *Purnell, Brian*
Fighting over the Founders: How We Remember the American Revolution — *Schocket, Andrew M.*
Fighting Shadows in Vietnam: A Combat Memoir — *Moynihan, Michael P., Jr.*
Fighting the Cold War: A Soldier's Memoir — *Galvin, John R.*
Fighting the Great War at Sea: Strategy, Tactics and Technology — *Friedman, Norman*
Fighting the Retreat from Arabia and the Gulf: The Collected Essays and Reviews of J.B. Kelly — *Kelly, John B.*
Fighting Westway: Environmental Law, Citizen Activism, and the Regulatory War That Transformed New York City — *Buzbee, William W.*
Figure Drawing Studio: Drawing and Painting the Nude Figure from Pose Photos — *Krieger, Butch*
Figures of Fear — *Masterton, Graham*
Figures of Southeast Asian Modernity — *Barker, Joshua*
Figures publiques: L'Invention de la celebrite, 1750-1850 — *Lilti, Antoine*
Figuring Out Figurative Art — *Freeman, Damien*
Figuring Style: The Legacy of Renaissance Rhetoric — *Christiansen, Nancy L.*
Fiji Random Garage Maid Special 01-- Preparation — *Raimey, Jusin*
y The Fill-In Boyfriend (Read by McManus, Shannon). Audiobook Review — *West, Kasie*
y The Fill-In Boyfriend — *West, Kasie*
Filled with All the Fullness of God: An Introduction to Catholic Spirituality — *McDermott, Thomas*
Film and Video Budgets 6 — *Ryan, Maureen*
Film as Film: The Collected Writings of Gregory J. Markopoulos — *Markopoulos, Gregory J.*

Film Criticism, the Cold War, and the Blacklist: Reading the Hollywood Reds — *Smith, Jeff (b. 1962-)*
Film Rhythm after Sound: Technology, Music, and Performance — *Jacobs, Lea*
Filming the Body in Crisis: Trauma, Healing and Hopefulness — *Quinlivan, Davina*
y Filmish: A Graphic Journey through Film (Illus. by Ross, Edward) — *Ross, Edward*
The Films of Claire Denis: Intimacy on the border — *Vecchio, Marjorie*
The Films of Eric Rohmer: French New Wave to Old Master — *Anderst, Leah*
Filologia e identita nazionale: una tradizione per l'Italia unita — *Sberlati, Francesco*
Filthy Rich — *DePaul, Virna*
The Final Crisis of the Stuart Monarchy: The Revolutions of 1688-91 in their British, Atlantic and European Contexts — *Harris, Tim*
Final Crossing — *Wilson, Carter*
y The Final Four: The Pursuit of College Basketball Glory — *Deoden, Matt*
Final Judgment: The Last Law Lords and the Supreme Court — *Paterson, Alan*
The Final Mission of Bottoms Up: A World War II Pilot's Story — *Okerstrom, Dennis R.*
The Final Pagan Generation — *Watts, Edward J.*
Final Passages: The Intercolonial Slave Trade of British America, 1619-1807 — *O'Malley, Gregory E.*
The Final Recollections of Charles Dickens — *Hauser, Thomas*
The Final Reveille — *Flower, Amanda*
The Final Silence — *Neville, Stuart*
Final Theory — *Cassidy, Bonny*
Final Words — *O'Donnell, Patrick Ian*
Finale — *Mallon, Thomas*
The Financial Decline of a Great Power: War, Influence, and Money in Louis XIV's France — *Rowlands, Guy*
Financial Inclusion at the Bottom of the Pyramid — *Realini, Carol*
Financial Reporting Disclosures: Market and Regulatory Failures — *Institute of Chartered Accountants in England and Wales*
Financing Illegal Migration: Chinese Underground Banks and Human Smuggling in New York City — *Zhao, Linda Shuo*
Finanzierung des Bildungswesens in der Helvetischen Republik: Vielfalt - Entwicklungen - Herausforderungen — *Bruhwiler, Ingrid*
Finches of Mars — *Aldiss, Brian W.*
Find a Way: One Wild and Precious Life — *Nyad, Diana*
Find Her — *Gardner, Lisa*
c The Find It Book (Illus. by Sheehan, Lisa) — *Brown, Margaret Wise*
Find It, File It, Flog It: Pharma's Crippling Addiction and How to Cure it — *Rees, Hedley*
Find It in the Talmud: An Encyclopedia of Jewish Ethics and Conduct — *Judovits, Mordechai*
y Find Me (Read by Zeller, Emily Woo). Audiobook Review — *van den Berg, Laura*
y Find Me — *van der Berg, Laura*
y Find Me — *van der Berg, Laura*
y Find Me Unafraid: Love, Loss, and Hope in an African Slum — *Odede, Kennedy*
Find the Good: Unexpected Life Lessons from a Small-Town Obituary Writer (Read by Lende, Heather). Audiobook Review — *Lende, Heather*
Find the Good: Unexpected Life Lessons from a Small-Town Obituary Writer — *Lende, Heather*
c Finder, Coal Mine Dog — *Hart, Alison*
Finders Keepers (Read by Patton, Will). Audiobook Review — *King, Stephen*
Finders Keepers — *King, Stephen*
c Finders Keepers — *Tougas, Shelley*
c Finders Keepers (Illus. by Kasza, Keiko) — *Kasza, Keiko*
c Finding a Mate: Animal Companions — *St. James, Cassidy*
Finding Abbey: The Search for Edward Abbey and His Hidden Desert Grave — *Prentiss, Sean*
Finding Amos — *Mason, J.D.*
Finding and Seeking — *O'Donovan, Oliver*
y Finding Audrey (Read by Whelan, Gemma). Audiobook Review — *Kinsella, Sophie*
y Finding Audrey — *Kinsella, Sophie*
Finding Equilibrium: Arrow, Debreu, McKenzie, and the Problem of Scientific Credit — *Duppe, Till*
y Finding Forever — *Baker, Ken*
c Finding Fortune (Illus. by Ray, Delia) — *Ray, Delia*
Finding Glory — *Arden, Sara*

Finding God in the Verbs: Crafting a Fresh Language of Prayer — *Isbell, Jennie*
Finding Her Gone — *Taylor, Christopher A.*
Finding Home — *Finch, Michael*
Finding Home: Real Stories of Migrant Britain — *Dugan, Emily*
Finding Inspiration at the Top of the World — *Dinerstein, Rebecca*
y Finding Jake — *Reardon, Bryan*
Finding McLuhan: The Mind/The Man/The Message — *Rogers, Jaqueline McLeod*
Finding Me — *Cushman, Kathryn*
c Finding Monkey Moon (Illus. by Wilkinson, Kate) — *Pulford, Elizabeth*
y Finding Mr. Brightside — *Clark, Jay*
Finding Ourselves at the Movies: Philosophy for a New Generation — *Kahn, Paul W.*
y Finding Paris — *Preble, Joy*
y The Finding Place — *Hartley, Julie*
y Finding Promise — *Dunn, Scarlett*
Finding Robert: What the Doctors Never Told Us about Autism Spectrum Disorder and the Hard Lessons We Learned — *Stevens, Robert J.*
Finding Robert: What the Doctors Never Told Us about Autism Spectrum Disorder and the Hard Lessons We Learned — *Stevens, Catherine E.*
y Finding Ruby Starling — *Rivers, Karen*
Finding Samuel Lowe: China, Jamaica, Harlem — *Madison, Paula Williams*
c Finding Serendipity (Illus. by Lewis, Stevie) — *Banks, Angelica*
y Finding Someplace — *Patrick, Denise Lewis*
c Finding Spring (Illus. by Berger, Carin) — *Berger, Carin*
c Finding the Music / En pos de la musica (Illus. by Alarcao, Renato) — *Torres, Jennifer*
Finding the Rainbow — *Borum, Traci*
c Finding the Worm (Read by Plew, Everette). Audiobook Review — *Goldblatt, Mark*
y Finding the Worm — *Goldblatt, Mark*
Finding Their Voice: Northeastern Villagers and the Thai State — *Keyes, Charles*
Finding Them Gone: Visiting China's Poets of the Past — *Red Pine*
c Finding Winnie: The True Story of the World's Most Famous Bear (Illus. by Blackall, Sophie) — *Mattick, Lindsay*
Finding You In Fertility — *Arredondo, Francisco*
Finding Your Way to Change: How the Power of Motivational Interviewing Can Reveal What You Want and Help You Get There — *Zuckoff, Allan*
Finding Zero: A Mathematician's Odyssey to Uncover the Origins of Numbers — *Aczel, Amir*
Finding Zero: A Mathematician's Odyssey to Uncover the Origins of Numbers — *Aczel, Amir D.*
Findings — *Jamie, Kathleen*
c Findus Disappears! (Illus. by Nordqvist, Sven) — *Nordqvist, Sven*
Fine Art Nudes: Lighting and Posing for Black and White Photography — *Trampe, Stan*
The Fine Art of Fashion Illustration — *Robinson, Julian*
The Fine Art of Fucking Up — *Dicharry, Cate*
The Fine Art of Murder — *Barnes, Emily*
Fine Art Portrait Photography: Lighting, Posing & Postproduction from Concept to Completion — *Bruleigh, Nylora*
A Fine Body of Men: The Orleans Light Horse Louisiana Cavalry, 1861-1865 — *Moriarty, Donald Peter, II*
c A Fine Dessert: Four Centuries, Four Families, One Delicious Treat (Illus. by Blackall, Sophie) — *Jenkins, Emily*
Fine, Fine, Fine, Fine, Fine — *Williams, Diane*
The Fine Print — *Schwartz, Jack*
A Fine Romance (Read by Bergen, Candice). Audiobook Review — *Bergen, Candice*
A Fine Romance — *Bergen, Candice*
A Fine Romance (Read by Bergen, Candice). Audiobook Review — *Bergen, Candice*
A Fine Romance — *Bergen, Candice*
A Fine Summer's Day — *Todd, Charles*
A Finely Knit Murder — *Goldenbaum, Sally*
c The Finger Sports Game — *Tullet, Herve*
Fingerprints of the Gods: The Evidence of Earth's Lost Civilization — *Hancock, Graham*
Finn — *Brookhouse, Christopher*
y Finn Fancy Necromancy (Read by Haberkorn, Todd). Audiobook Review — *Henderson, Randy*
Finn Fancy Necromancy — *Henderson, Randy*
The Finnish Girl — *Frahmann, Dennis*

c The Fintastic Fishsitter (Illus. by Jagucki, Marek) — *O'Hara, Mo*
y Fiona — *Moore, Meredith*
c Fiona's Lace — *Polacco, Patricia*
c Fire! (Illus. by Bixley, Donovan) — *Mewburn, Kyle*
Fire and Forget: Short Stories from the Long War — *Gallagher, Matt*
c Fire and Ice — *Hale, Shannon*
Fire and Ice: Soot, Solidarity, and Survival on the Roof of the World — *Mingle, Jonathan*
y The Fire Artist — *Whitney, Daisy*
The Fire Below: How the Caucasus Shaped Russia — *Ware, Robert Bruce*
c Fire Birds: Valuing Natural Wildfires and Burned Forests (Illus. by Collard, Braden G.) — *Collard, Sneed B., III*
y The Fire Children — *Roy, Lauren*
y Fire Colour One — *Valentine, Jenny*
The Fire Dance (Illus. by Wideburg, Laura A.) — *Tursten, Helene*
c Fire Engine No. 9 (Illus. by Austin, Mike) — *Austin, Mike*
y Fire Fight — *Guest, Jacqueline*
Fire Flowers — *Byrne, Ben*
y Fire Girl — *Ralphs, Matt*
Fire + Ice: Classic Nordic Cooking — *Goldstein, Darra*
Fire in the Canyon: Religion, Migration, and the Mexican Dream — *Sarat, Leah*
Fire in the Heart: How White Activists Embrace Racial Justice — *Warren, Mark R.*
Fire in the Water — *Thom, James Alexander*
The Fire of Peru: Recipes and Stories from My Peruvian Kitchen — *Zarate, Ricardo*
Fire on the Water: China, America, and the Future of the Pacific — *Haddick, Robert*
y The Fire Sermon — *Haig, Francesca*
Fire Shut Up in My Bones: A Memoir — *Blow, Charles M.*
Fire Songs — *Harsent, David*
c Fire Trucks — *Riggs, Kate*
Fire War — *Michael, T.T.*
y The Fire Wish — *Lough, Amber*
c Firebird: Ballerina Misty Copeland Shows a Young Girl How to Dance Like the Firebird (Illus. by Myers, Christopher) — *Copeland, Misty*
c Firebrand — *Barnhart, Aaron*
The Firebrand and the First Lady: Portrait of a Friendship: Pauli Murray, Eleanor Roosevelt, and the Struggle for Social Justice — *Bell-Scott, Patricia*
Firebreak — *Fields, Tricia*
Firebug (Read by Ahn, Ali). Audiobook Review — *McBride, Lish*
y Firebug — *McBride, Lish*
y The Firebug of Balrog County — *Oppegaard, David*
y Firefight (Read by Andrews, MacLeod). Audiobook Review — *Sanderson, Brandon*
y Firefight — *Sanderson, Brandon*
Firefight: The Century-Long Battle to Integrate New York's Bravest — *Otis, Ginger Adams*
Fireflies at Twilight: Letters from Pat Adams — *Adams, Cate*
Firefly Encyclopedia of Animals: A Comprehensive Look at the World of Animals with Hundred of Superb Illustrations — *Whitfield, Philip*
Firefly Encyclopedia of Dinosaurs and Prehistoric Animals — *Palmer, Douglas*
c Firefly Hollow (Illus. by Denise, Christopher) — *McGhee, Alison*
c Firefly July (Illus. by Sweet, Melissa) — *Janeczko, Paul B.*
y A Fireproof Home for the Bride — *Scheibe, Amy*
The Fires of Autumn — *Nemirovsky, Irene*
y The Fires of Calderon — *Cummings, Lindsay*
c Fires of Invention — *Savage, J. Scott*
Firesmoke — *Janmohamed, Sheniz*
y Firewalker — *Angelini, Josephine*
First Aid in the Laboratory and Workshop — *Eldridge, Arthur A.*
First Aid, Survival, and CPR: Home and Field Pocket Guide — *Jones, Shirley A.*
The First American Declaration of Independence? The Disputed History of the Mecklenburg Declaration of May 20, 1775 — *Syfert, Scott*
The First American Evangelical: A Short Life of Cotton Mather — *Kennedy, Rick*
The First American Grand Prix: The Savannah Auto Races, 1908-1911 — *Bailey, Tanya A.*
The First Anglo-Afghan Wars: A Reader — *Burton, Antoinette*

The First Bad Man (Read by July, Miranda). Audiobook Review — July, Miranda
The First Bad Man — July, Miranda
First Bite: How We Learn to Eat — Wilson, Bee
c First Bites: Tidbits of American History for the Young and Young at Heart — Moss, Dixie
The First Bohemians: Life and Art in London's Golden Age — Gatrell, Vic
The First Book of Fashion: The Book of Clothes of Matthaus and Veit Konrad Schwartz of Augsburg — Rublack, Ulinka
c The First Christmas: The King James Version (Illus. by Pienkowski, Jan) — Pienkowski, Jan
The First Civil Right: How Liberals Built Prison America — Murakawa, Naomi
The First Clash: The Miraculous Greek Victory at Marathon - and Its Impact on the Western Civilization — Lacey, Jim
The First Collection of Criticism by a Living Female Rock Critic — Hopper, Jessica
The First Congress: How James Madison, George Washington, and a Group of Extraordinary Men Invented the Government — Bordewich, Fergus M.
c First Contact (Illus. by Spaziante, Patrick) — Lewman, David
A First Course in the Calculus of Variations — Kot, Mark
First Creatures: A Journey through Grief — Liberati, Tami
c First Day at Zoo School — Dillard, Sarah
First Day Covers of Canada's 1976 Olympic Games Issues — Dickinson, Gary
The First Days of August — Froning, Alan
c First Descent — Withers, Pam
First Entrepreneur — Lengel, Edward G.
The First Epoch: The Eighteenth Century and the Russian Cultural Imagination — Golburt, Luba
c First Facts: Your Body Systems — Brett, Flora
c First Flight around the World: The Adventures of the American Fliers Who Won the Race — Grove, Tim
c The First Flute / Whowhoahyayzo Tohkohya (Illus. by Oelze, Don) — Bouchard, David
c The First Flute / Whowhoahyayzo Tohkohya — Bouchard, David
The First French Reformation: Church Reform and the Origins of the Old Regime — Lange, Tyler
First Frost (Read by Ericksen, Susan). Audiobook Review — Allen, Sarah Addison
First Global Humanitarianism Research Academy (GHRA) 2015
c First Grade Dropout (Illus. by Cordell, Matthew) — Vernick, Audrey
c First Grade, Here I Come! (Illus. by Walker, David) — Johnston, Tony
c The First Hippo on the Moon (Illus. by Ross, Tony) — Walliams, David
c First Hockey Words — Giirth, Per-Henrik
First Impressions — Thornton, Margaret
The First Islamic Reviver: Abu Hamid al-Ghazali and His Revival of the Religious Sciences — Garden, Kenneth
First Jobs: True Tales of Bad Bosses, Quirky Coworkers, Big Breaks, and Small Paychecks — Watts, Merritt
First, Kill All the Marriage Counselors: Modern-Day Secrets to Being Desired, Cherished, and Adored for Life — Doyle, Laura
The First King of Hollywood — Goessel, Tracey
The First King of Hollywood: The Life of Douglas Fairbanks — Goessel, Tracey
The First Knowledge Economy: Human Capital and the European Economy, 1750-1850 — Jacob, Margaret C.
First Ladies: NPR American Chronicles (Read by Roberts, Cokie). Audiobook Review
First Ladies of Gardening: Designers, Dreamers and Divas — Howcroft, Heidi
First Ladies: Presidential Historians on the Lives of 45 Iconic American Women — Swain, Susan
The First Letter from New Spain: The Lost Petition of Cortes and His Company, June 20, 1519 — Nader, Helen
y First Man: Reimagining Matthew Henson (Illus. by Schwartz, Simon) — Schwartz, Simon
The First Modern Jew: Spinoza and the History of an Image — Schwartz, Daniel B.
First Nations, Museums, Narrations: Stories of the 1929 Franklin Motor Expedition to the Canadian Prairies — Brown, Alison K.
The First Nazi — Brownell, Will
The First Order — Abbott, Jeff

First Over There: The Attack on Cantigny, America's First Battle of World War I — Davenport, Matthew J.
The First President: A Life of John L. Dube, Founding President of the ANC — Hughes, Heather
The First Presidential Contest: 1796 and the Founding of American Democracy — Pasley, Jeffrey L.
c First Robotics — Gilby, Nancy Benovich
c The First Slodge (Illus. by Desmond, Jenni) — Willis, Jeanne
c First Snow (Illus. by McCarty, Peter) — McCarty, Peter
c The First Snowfall — Rockwell, Anne
First Son: The Biography of Richard M. Daley — Koeneman, Keith
c The First Step: How One Girl Put Segregation on Trial (Illus. by Lewis, E.B.) — Goodman, Susan E.
The First Supper — Schiff, Karen
c First Team — Green, Tim
The First Thanksgiving: What the Real Story Tells Us about Loving God and Learning from History — McKenzie, Robert Tracy
First the Kingdom of God: Global Voices on Global Mission — Darko, Daniel K.
First, the 'Saturday People', and Then the.... — Portnoy, Bruce
y First & Then — Mills, Emma
y First There Was Forever — Romano, Juliana
First Time in Forever — Morgan, Sarah
The First Time She Drowned — Kletter, Kerry
First Time with a Highlander — Cready, Gwyn
First to Fly: The Story of the Lafayette Escadrille: The American Heroes Who Flew for France in World War I — Flood, Charles Bracelen
c First to the Top: Sir Edmund Hillary's Amazing Everest Adventure (Illus. by Morris, Phoebe) — Hill, David
First Touch — Paige, Laurelin
The First Treatise on Museums: Samuel Quiccheberg's "Inscriptiones," 1565 — Quiccheberg, Samuel
y The First Twenty — Lavoie, Jennifer
First Week Blues (Illus. by Evans, Anna) — Greensdale, Jesse
c First Words — Tiger Tales
c First Words — Walker, Rob
y First World War for Dummies — Lang, Sean
The First World War in 100 Objects — Doyle, Peter
The First World War in Computer Games — Kempshall, Chris
The First World War in the Middle East — Ulrichsen, Kristian Coates
The First World War — Purdue, A.W.
The First World War, vol. 1: Global War — Winter, Jay
The First World War, vol. 2: The State — Winter, Jay
The First World War, vol. 3: Civil Society — Winter, Jay
First Year Healthy — DeForge, Michael
The First Year of Teaching: Classroom Research to Increase Student Learning — Mahiri, Jabari
c First, You Explore: The Story of the Young Charles Townes (Illus. by Cook, Trahem) — Haynie, Rachel
c First, You Explore: The Story of Young Charles Townes (Illus. by Cook, Trahem) — Haynie, Rachel
c Firstborn (Read by Barber, Jenni). Audiobook Review — Seidler, Tor
c Firstborn — Seidler, Tor
y Firstlife — Showalter, Gena
y Firsts — Flynn, Laurie Elizabeth
c Fish — Murray, Julie
c Fish — Levine, Michelle
Fish and Chips: A History — Panayi, Panikos
c Fish-FishFish (Illus. by Bosch, Meritxell) — Nordling, Lee
c Fish Food (Illus. by Lohlein, Henning) — Mansfield, Andy
y Fish in a Tree (Read by McInerney, Kathleen). Audiobook Review — Hunt, Lynda Mullaly
y Fish in a Tree — Hunt, Lynda Mullaly
c The Fish in the Bathtub: Little Gems (Illus. by Bailey, Peter) — Colfer, Eoin
The Fish in the Forest: Salmon and the Web of Life — Stokes, Dale
c Fish Jam — Howarth, Kylie
The Fish Ladder: A Journey Upstream — Norbury, Katharine
c Fish on a Dish! — Tickle, Jack
c Fish out of Water — Whipple, Natalie
A Fish out of Water? From Contemplative Solitude to Carthusian Involvement in Pastoral Care and Reform Activity — Molvarec, Stephen J.

c A Fish to Feed (Illus. by Hu, Ying-Hwa) — Mayer, Ellen
Fishbowl — Somer, Bradley
The Fisherman's Ball — Dutra, Janice J.
The Fishermen — Obioma, Chigozie
c Fishermen Through & Through (Illus. by Kerrigan, Brooke) — Sydor, Colleen
Fishers and Plunderers: Theft, Slavery and Violence at Sea — Couper, Alastair
Fishes: A Guide to Their Diversity — Hastings, Philip A.
The Fishing Fleet: Husband-Hunting in the Raj — de Courcy, Anne
Fishing for Fairness: Poverty, Morality and Marine Resource Regulation in the Philippines — Fabinyi, Michael
Fishing with RayAnne — Finch, Ava
Fishtown: A Jack Regan/Izzy Ichowitz Novel — Goldstein, Neal
Fit For Love: Find Your Self and Your Perfect Mate — Sheean, Olga
Fit Not Healthy: How One Woman's Obsession to Be the Best Nearly Killed Her — Alford, Vanessa
Fitness Running: 78 Workouts from the Mile to the Marathon — Brown, Richard L.
Five Brides — Everson, Eva Marie
Five Came Back: A Story of Hollywood and the Second World War — Harris, Mark
c Five Children and It — Nesbit, E.
c Five Children on the Western Front — Saunders, Kate
Five Days — Micros, Matt
Five Dollars and a Pork Chop Sandwich — Berry, Mary Frances
c Five Epic Disasters — Tarshis, Lauren
c Five Little Ducklings Go to School (Illus. by Julian, Sean) — Roth, Carol
c Five Little Monkeys — Marshall, Natalie
c Five Nice Mice Build a House (Illus. by Tashiro, Chisato) — Tashiro, Chisato
Five Nights in Paris: After Dark in the City of Light — Baxter, John
c The Five of Us (Illus. by Blake, Quentin) — Blake, Quentin
c Five, Six, Seven, Nate! (Read by Federle, Tim). Audiobook Review — Federle, Tim
y The Five Stages of Andrew Brawley (Illus. by Larsen, Christine) — Hutchinson, Shaun David
c Five Stories — Alter, Anna
y Five Summers (Read by Revasch, Abigail). Audiobook Review — LaMarche, Una
c Five Things They Never Told Me — Westcott, Rebecca
The Five Times I Met Myself — Rubart, James L.
Five Words: Critical Semantics in the Age of Shakespeare and Cervantes — Greene, Roland
Five Year Mission: the Labour Party under Ed Miliband — Bale, Tim
Five Years in Heaven: The Unlikely Friendship That Answered Life's Greatest Questions — Schlimm, John
Fives and Twenty-Fives (Read by five participants). Audiobook Review — Pitre, Michael
Fives and Twenty-Fives — Pitre, Michael
y The Fix — Sinel, Natasha
The Fixer (Read by Kearney, Steven). Audiobook Review — Finder, Joseph
y The Fixer — Barnes, Jennifer Lynn
The Fixer — Finder, Joseph
The Fixer (Read by Kearney, Steven). Audiobook Review — Finder, Joseph
y The Fixer — Barnes, Jennifer Lynn
The Fixer — Finder, Joseph
y The Fixer — Barnes, Jennifer Lynn
The Fixer — Finder, Joseph
The Fixer (Read by Kearny, Steven). Audiobook Review — Finder, Joseph
c Fizzlebert Stump: The Boy Who Cried Fish (Illus. by Horne, Sarah) — Harrold, A.F.
Flags and Faces: The Visual Culture of America's First World War — Lubin, David M.
c Flags over America: A Star-Spangled Story (Illus. by Harness, Cheryl) — Harness, Cheryl
c Flame and Ashes: The Great Fire Diary of Triffie Winsor — McNaughton, Janet
The Flame In The Cauldron — Foxwood, Orion
Flame Out — Cooley, M.P.
Flame Tree Road — Patal, Shona
Flame Tree Road — Patel, Shona
Flann O'Brien and Modernism — Murphet, Julian
Flann O'Brien: Contesting Legacies — Borg, Ruben
Flannery O'Connor: Fiction Fired by Faith — O'Donnell, Angela Alaimo

Flannery O'Connor: Writing a Theology of Disabled Humanity — *Basselin, Timothy J.*
Flappers: Six Women of a Dangerous Generation — *Mackrell, Judith*
Flash — *Ball, Donna*
y Flash Boys: A Wall Street Revolt — *Lewis, Michael M.*
Flash Fiction International: Very Short Stories from around the World — *Thomas, James*
y A Flash of Blue — *Farrer, Maria*
Flash: The Homeless Donkey Who Taught Me about Life, Faith and Second Chances — *Ridge, Rachel Anne*
c Flashback Four: The Lincoln Project — *Gutman, Dan*
y Flashes — *O'Rourke, Tim*
c Flashlight (Illus. by Boyd, Lizi) — *Boyd, Lizi*
Flashpoints: The Emerging Crisis in Europe (Read by Turk, Bruce). Audiobook Review — *Friedman, George*
Flask of the Drunken Master — *Spann, Susan*
c The Flat Rabbit (Illus. by Oskarsson, Bardur) — *Oskarsson, Bardur*
c Flat Stanley and the Very Big Cookie (Illus. by Pamintuan, Macky) — *Brown, Jeff*
The Flat White Economy — *McWilliams, Douglas*
Flat World Navigation: Collaboration and Networking in the Global Digital Economy — *McDonald, Kim Chanlder*
Flavian Poetry and its Greek Past — *Augoustakis, Antony*
Flavorful: 150 Irresistible Desserts in All-Time Favorite Flavors — *Boyle, Tish*
Flavors of Aloha: Cooking with Tommy Bahama — *Rodgers, Rick*
y Flawd: How to Stop Hating on Yourself, Others, and the Things That Make You Who You Are (Read by Rigal, Emily-Anne). Audiobook Review — *Rigal, Emily-Anne*
Flawed System/Flawed Self: Job Searching and Unemployment Experiences — *Sharone, Ofer*
The Flea Market in Valparaiso — *Rosenstock, Gabriel*
c Fleabrain Loves Franny — *Rocklin, Joanne*
Fleas, Flies, and Friars: Children's Poetry from the Middle Ages — *Orme, Nicholas*
c Fleeced — *Irving, Ellie*
The Fleet Book of the Alaska Packers Association, 1893-1945: An Historical Overview and List — *Dyal, Donald H.*
Fleeting Chance — *Young, Sherban*
Fleeting Promise — *Young, Sherban*
The Fleeting Years — *Monk, Connie*
y Flesh and Bone — *Alton, William L.*
Flesh and Wires — *Hatton, Jackie*
Fleshing the Spirit: Spirituality and Activism in Chicana, Latina, and Indigenous Women's Lives — *Facio, Elisa*
Flexible Multilingual Education: Putting Children's Needs First — *Seals, Corinne A.*
c Flexible Wings — *Stamps, Veda*
y The Flicker Men — *Kosmatka, Ted*
Flickering Empire: How Chicago Invented the U.S. Film Industry — *Smith, Michael Glover*
c Flickr Cofounder and Web Community Creator Caterina Fake — *Wooster, Patricia*
c Flight 1-2-3 — *van Lieshout, Maria*
Flight 232: A Story of Disaster and Survival — *Gonzales, Laurence*
Flight from Death — *Galenorn, Yasmine*
Flight of Dreams — *Lawhon, Ariel*
c Flight of the King — *Grey, C.R.*
Flight Plan Africa: Portuguese Airpower in Counterinsurgency, 1961-1974 — *Cann, John P.*
Flight to Canada — *Reed, Ishmael*
A Flight without Wings: My Experience with Heaven — *McLaughlin, Brian A.*
c Flights and Chimes and Mysterious Times — *Trevayne, Emma*
Flights of Imagination: Aviation, Landscape, Design — *Dumpelmann, Sonja*
c The Flinkwater Factor — *Hautman, Pete*
The Flip — *Phillip, Michael*
Flip and Fuse Quilts: 12 Fun Projects: Easy Foolproof Technique: Transform Your Applique! — *Harmening, Marcia*
c Flip Flap Safari (Illus. by Scheffler, Axel) — *Scheffler, Axel*
Flipped for Murder — *Day, Maddie*
c Flippy Floppy Ocean Animals (Illus. by Touliatou, Sophia) — *Poitier, Anton*
y Flirty Dancing — *McLachlan, Jenny*
c Flo & Wendell Explore (Illus. by Wegman, William) — *Wegman, William*
c Float (Illus. by Miyares, Daniel) — *Miyares, Daniel*

Floating Collections: A Collection Development Model for Long-Term Success — *Barlett, Wendy K.*
c Floating on Mama's Song / Flotando en la cancion de mama (Illus. by Morales, Yuyi) — *Lacamara, Laura*
c Flood — *Greenlaw, M. Jean*
The Flood — *Sachs, David*
The Flood Girls — *Fifield, Richard*
The Flood — *Hewson, David*
Flood of Fire — *Ghosh, Amitav*
Floodgate — *Shaw, Johnny*
Floodpath: The Deadliest Man-Made Disaster of 20th-Century America and the Making of Los Angeles — *Wilkman, Jon*
c Floods: Be Aware and Prepare — *Gray-Wilburn, Renee*
c Flop to the Top! (Illus. by Davis, Eleanor) — *Davis, Eleanor*
c Flop to the Top! (Illus. by Weing, Drew) — *Davis, Eleanor*
c Flora and the Penguin — *Idle, Molly*
Flora Illustrata: Great Works from the LuEsther T. Mertz Library of the New York Botanical Garden — *Fraser, Susan M.*
Flora Lyndsay: Or, Passages in an Eventful Life — *Moodie, Susanna*
c Florabelle (Illus. by Barrager, Brigette) — *Quinton, Sasha*
FloraBunda Style: Super Simple Art Doodles to Color, Craft and Draw — *McNeill, Suzanne*
Florence Gordon — *Morton, Brian*
c Florence Nightingale — *Alexander, Carol*
Florence: The Paintings and Frescoes, 1250-1743 — *King, Ross*
The Florentine Deception — *Nachenberg, Carey*
Florentino and the Devil — *Torrealba, Alberto Arvelo*
Florenz! — *Horst, Baader von*
The Florida Edition of the World of Laurence Sterne, vol. 9: The Miscellaneous Writings and Sterne's Subscribers, an Identification List — *Gerard, William Blake*
c Florida's Burmese Pythons: Squeezing the Everglades — *Aronin, Miriam*
Florynce "Flo" Kennedy: The Life of a Black Feminist Radical — *Randolph, Sherie M.*
Flourishing: Health, Disease, and Bioethics in Theological Perspective — *Messer, Neil*
The Flower Farmer's Year: How to Grow Cut Flowers for Pleasure and Profit. — *Newbery, Georgie*
Flower of Iowa — *Ringel, Lance*
The Flower Workshop: Lessons in Arranging Blooms, Branches, Fruit, and Foraged Materials — *Chezar, Ariella*
c Flowers Are Calling (Illus. by Pak, Kenard) — *Gray, Rita*
Fluchtlinge und Vertriebene in der DDR-Aufbaugeneration: Sozial- und Biographiegeschichtliche Studien — *Konig, Christian*
Fluchtlingslager im Nachkriegsdeutschland: Migration, Politik, Erinnerung — *Bispinck, Henrik*
Fluent Selves: Autobiography, Person, and History in Lowland South America — *Oakdale, Suzanne*
c Fluff and Other Stuff (Illus. by Blow, Dreda) — *Merz, Bruno*
c Fluff Dragon — *Clark, Platte F.*
c Fluffy Strikes Back — *Spires, Ashley*
Fluid New York: Cosmopolitan Urbanism and the Green Imagination — *Joseph, May*
c Flunked (Read by Condon, Kristin). Audiobook Review — *Calonita, Jen*
c Flunked — *Calonita, Jen*
Flut und Boden: Roman einer Familie — *Leo, Per*
The Flute in the Attic, 20 Short Recital and Study Pieces for the Intermediate Player — *Walker, John*
c Flutter & Hum: Animal Poems / Aleteo y Zumbido: Poemas de Animales (Illus. by Paschkis, Julie) — *Paschkis, Julie*
c Flutterby Butterfly (Illus. by Parrish, Emma) — *Parrish, Emma*
y Fly a Jet Fighter (Illus. by Mills, Steve) — *Koll, Hilary*
c Fly! (Illus. by Edwards, Karl Newsom) — *Edwards, Karl Newsom*
Fly! — *Edwards, Karl Newsom*
Fly Away Free — *Coppola, Anne Turner*
Fly Away, Pigeon — *Abonji, Melinda Nadj*
c Fly Fishing — *Hamilton, S.L.*
c Fly Guy Presents: Bats (Illus. by Arnold, Tedd) — *Arnold, Tedd*
c Fly Guy Presents: Insects (Illus. by Arnold, Tedd) — *Arnold, Tedd*
c Fly Guy's Amazing Tricks — *Arnold, Tedd*

c Fly-in Fly-out Dad (Illus. by Dawson, Janine) — *Murphy, Sally*
Fly! — *Edwards, Karl Newsom*
c The Fly (Illus. by Horacek, Petr) — *Horacek, Petr*
Fly the Wild Echoes — *Bailey, Elizabeth*
The Fly Trap — *Sjoberg, Fredrik*
A Flying Affair — *Stewart, Carla*
c The Flying Beaver Brothers and the Crazy Critter Race (Illus. by Eaton, Maxwell, III) — *Eaton, Maxwell, III*
c The Flying Beaver Brothers and the Hot-Air Baboons — *Eaton, Maxwell, III*
c The Flying Birds (Illus. by Kim, Ju-kyoung) — *Han, Eun-sun*
Flying Blind: The Story of a Second World War Night Fighter Pilot — *Wild, Bryan*
c Flying Cars: The True Story — *Glass, Andrew*
The Flying Circus — *Crandall, Susan*
The Flying Classroom (Illus. by Trier, Walter) — *Bell, Anthea*
Flying Dinosaurs: How Fearsome Reptiles Became Birds — *Pickrell, John*
c Flying Free: Stories and Where They Come From: A Book for Curious Children — *Frater, Adrienne M.*
c The Flying Hand of Marco B. (Illus. by Kober, Shahar) — *Leiter, Richard*
c Flying High (Illus. by Smith, Craig) — *Morgan, Sally*
Flying Home: Seven Stories of the Secret City — *Nicholson, David*
Flying Hung-Over — *Oard, Brian*
y The Flywheel — *Gough, Erin*
Focus on Me — *Erickson, Megan*
y The Fog Diver — *Ross, Joel*
Fog Island Mountains (Read by Ikeda, Jennifer). Audiobook Review — *Bailat-Jones, Michelle*
Fokus Handwerk: Aktuelle Perspektiven einer Interdisziplinaren Handwerksforschung. Themen, Fragestellungen, Quellen und Methoden
The Fold — *Clines, Peter*
The Folded Clock: A Diary (Read by Gilbert, Tavia). Audiobook Review — *Julavits, Heidi*
The Folded Clock: A Diary — *Julavits, Heidi*
Folded Paper German Stars: Creative Paper Crafting Ideas Inspired by Friedrich Frobel — *Taubner, Armin*
Folk City: New York and the American Folk Music Revival — *Cohen, Ronald D.*
Folk City: New York and the American Folk Musical Revival — *Cohen, Ronald D.*
Folk Culture in the Digital Age: The Emergent Dynamics of Human Interaction — *Blank, Trevor J.*
Folk Healing and Health Care Practices in Britain and Ireland: Stethoscopes, Wands and Crystals — *Moore, Ronnie*
The Folklore of the Freeway: Race and Revolt in the Modernist City — *Avila, Eric*
Folklore Rules: A Fun, Quick, and Useful Introduction to the Field of Academic Folklore Studies — *McNeill, Lynne S.*
Folksongs of Another America: Field Recordings from the Upper Midwest, 1937-1946 — *Leary, James P.*
Follies of God: Tennessee Williams and the Women of the Fog — *Grissom, James*
Follow Follow: A Book of Reverso Poems (Read by Morton, Joe). Audiobook Review — *Singer, Marilyn*
c Follow the Drinking Gourd: Come Along the Underground Railroad (Illus. by Martin, Courtney A.) — *Coleman, Wim*
Follow Your Gut: The Enormous Impact of Tiny Microbes — *Knight, Rob*
Follow Your Heart — *Kaufman, Ruth*
Following Farage: On the Trail of the People's Army — *Bennett, Owen*
Following His Heart — *Fasano, Donna*
Following Oil: Four Decades of Cycle-Testing Experiences and What They Foretell about U.S. Energy Independence — *Petrie, Thomas*
Following the Leader: Ruling China, from Deng Xiaoping to Xi Jinping — *Lampton, David M.*
Following Zwingli: Applying the Past in Reformation Zurich — *Baschera, Luca*
Folly — *Cameron, Stella*
The Folly — *Vladislavic, Ivan*
Font of Life: Ambrose, Augustine, and the Mystery of Baptism — *Wills, Garry*
The Font of Life — *Ibn Gabirol, Solomon*
Fontane-Studien: Gesammelte Aufsatze zu Romanen, Gedichten und Reportagen — *Chambers, Helen*
Food: A Love Story (Read by Gaffigan, Jim). Audiobook Review — *Gaffigan, Jim*
The Food Activist Handbook — *Berlow, Ali*
c Food and Drink — *Staniford, Linda*

Food and French — Bourgeois, Pam
Food and the Self: Consumption, Production and Material Culture — de Solier, Isabelle
The Food Babe Way: Break Free from the Hidden Toxins in Your Food and Lose Weight, Look Years Younger, and Get Healthy in Just 21 Days! — Hari, Vani
c Food Chains — Surges, Carol S.
Food Co-ops in America: Communities, Consumption, and Economic Democracy — Knupfer, Anne Meis
Food, Eating and Identity in Early Medieval England — Frantzen, Allen J.
Food, Farms, and Solidarity: French Farmers Challenge Industrial Agriculture and Genetically Modified Crops — Heller, Chaia
Food Gift Love: More Than 100 Recipes to Make, Wrap, and Share — Battista, Maggie
c Food in Schools — Allman, Toney
Food in Time and Place: The American Historical Association Companion to Food History — Freedman, Paul
The Food Lab: Better Home Cooking through Science — Lopez-Alt, J. Kenji
The Food Lab: Better Home Cooking through Science — Lopez-Alt, J. Kenji
The Food Lab: Better Home Cooking through Science — Lopez-Alt, J. Kenji
The Food Lover's Anthology — Hunt, Peter
The Food of Taiwan: Recipes from the Beautiful Island — Erway, Cathy
y Food Science: You Are What You Eat — Lanser, Amanda
Food Security and Scarcity: Why Ending Hunger Is So Hard — Timmer, C. Peter
Food Webs and Biodiversity: Foundations, Models, Data — Rossberg, Axel G.
Food Whore — Tom, Jessica
Food52 Baking: 60 Sensational Treats You Can Pull Off in a Snap — Hesser, Amanda
Food52 Genius Recipes: 100 Recipes That Will Change the Way You Cook — Miglore, Kristen
Food52 Vegan: 60 Vegetable-Driven Recipes for Any Kitchen — Hamshaw, Gena
c Foodprints: The Story of What We Eat (Illus. by Kinnaird, Ross) — Ayer, Paula
c Foodprints: The Story of What We Eat (Illus. by Olenina, Ira) — Ayer, Paula
c Foodprints: The Story of What we Eat (Illus. by Kinnaird, Ross) — Ayer, Paula
Foods That Changed History: How Foods Shaped Civilization from the Ancient World to the Present — Cumo, Christopher
A Fool for a Client — Hall, Parnell
Fool Me Once — Hockensmith, Steve
Foolbert Funnies: Histories and Other Fictions — Stack, Frank
Fooling Around with Cinderella — Juba, Stacy
y Foolproof — Tullson, Diane
Foolproof: Why Safety Can Be Dangerous and How Danger Makes Us Safe — Ip, Greg
Fools, Frauds and Firebrands: Thinkers of the New Left — Scruton, Roger
y Fool's Gold — Gregory, Philippa
Fool's Quest — Hobb, Robin
Fool's Talk: Recovering the Art of Christian Persuasion — Guinness, Os
A Foot in the River: Why Our Lives Change--and the Limits of Evolution — Fernandez-Armesto, Felipe
c Football (Illus. by Humphrey, Booby) — Nixon, James
Football Cliches: Decoding the Oddball Phrases, Colorful Gestures, and Unwritten Rules of Soccer across the Pond — Hurrey, Adam
c Football: Great Moments, Records, and Facts — Borth, Teddy
c A Football Story — Torrey, Richard
y Footer Davis Probably Is Crazy (Illus. by Reinhardt, Jennifer Black) — Vaught, Susan
c Footpath Flowers (Illus. by Smith, Sydney) — Lawson, JonArno
Footprints in the Desert — Akhtar, Maha
For a Little While — Bass, Rick
For a New West: Essays, 1919-1958 — Polanyi, Karl
For God and Ireland: The Fight for Moral Superiority in Ireland 1922-1932 — McCabe, M.P.
For God and Kaiser: The Imperial Austrian Army from 1619-1918 — Bassett, Richard
For God and Revolution: Priest, Peasant, and Agrarian Socialism in the Mexican Huasteca — Saka, Mark Saad
For Keeps: Meaningful Patchwork for Everyday Living — Gibson, Amy

For Love and Money: Care Provision in the United States — Folbre, Nancy
For Love of Animals: Christian Ethics, Consistent Action — Camosy, Charles C.
For Love of Country: What Our Veterans Can Teach Us about Citizenship, Heroism, and Sacrifice (Read by Chandrasekaran, Rajiv). Audiobook Review — Chandrasekaran, Rajiv
For Love of Country: What Our Veterans Can Teach Us about Citizenship, Heroism, and Sacrifice — Schultz, Howard
For Love or Magic — March, Lucy
For Pleasure and Profit: Six Dutch Rhetoricians Plays, with Facing-Page Translation — Strietman, Elsa
y For Real — Cherry, Alison
For Real — Hall, Alexis
For Sale--American Paradise: How Our Nation Was Sold an Impossible Dream in Florida — Drye, Willie
c For Soccer-Crazy Girls Only — Downing, Erin
For the Common Defense: A Military History of the United States from 1607 to 2012 — Millett, Alan R.
For the Dead — Hallinan, Timothy
For the Dignified Dead — Genelin, Michael
For the Love of Cake — Dutton, Erin
For the Love of Reading: Guide to K-8 Reading Promotions — Baumann, Nancy L.
For the Record — Focht, Eric
y For the Record — Huang, Charlotte
c For the Right to Learn: Malala Yousafzai's Story (Illus. by Bock, Janna) — Langston-George, Rebecca
For Today I Am a Boy — Fu, Kim
For White Folks Who Teach in the Hood ... and the Rest of Y'all Too — Emdin, Christopher
For You Were Strangers — Pirrone, D.M.
For Your Love — Jenkins, Beverly
Foragers, Farmers, and Fossil Fuels: How Human Values Evolve — Morris, Ian
y Forbidden — Bunting, Eve
Forbidden — Clamp, Cathy
y Forbidden — Little, Kimberley Griffiths
The Forbidden Billionaire — Scott, J.S.
c The Forbidden City — McNally, John
Forbidden Fashions: Invisible Luxuries in Early Venetian — Campagnol, Isabella
c The Forbidden Flats — Eddleman, Peggy
The Forbidden Fruit — Flowers, Tamsin
y The Forbidden Library (Read by Morris, Cassandra). Audiobook Review — Wexler, Django
c The Forbidden Library — Wexler, Django
Forbidden Man — Wright, Elle
y The Forbidden Orchid — Waller, Sharon Biggs
y The Forbidden Wish — Khoury, Jessica
The Forbidden Worlds of Haruki Murakami — Strecher, Matthew
A Force for Good — Taft, John G.
A Force for Good: The Dalai Lama's Vision for Our World — Goleman, Daniel
Force of Attraction — Ayres, D.D.
c Forced Removal: Causes and Effects of the Trail of Tears — Schwartz, Heather E.
Forced to Flee: Visual Stories by Refugee Youth from Burma — Berg, Erika
Forcing the Spring: Inside the Fight for Marriage Equality — Becker, Jo
Fore Play — Sheehan, Linda Faiola
y Forecast — Costelloe, Sarah
Foreign Accents: Chinese American Verse from Exclusion to Postethnicity — Yao, Stephen G.
Foreign Affairs — Woods, Stuart
Foreign Aid and the Legacy of Harry S. Truman — Geselbracht, Raymond H.
The Foreign Consuls among Us — Hofstadter, Cami
Foreign Fighters: Transnational Identity in Civil Conflicts — Malet, David
Foreign Gods, Inc. — Ndibe, Okey
Foreign Intervention in Africa: From the Cold War to the War on Terror — Schmidt, Elizabeth
A Foreign Kingdom: Mormons and Polygamy in American Political Culture, 1852-1890 — Talbot, Christine
Foreign Modernism: Cosmopolitanism, Identity, and Style in Paris — Junyk, Ihor
The Foreign Office Mind: The Making of British Foreign Policy, 1865-1914 — Otte, T.G.
The Foreign Policies of Post-Yugoslav States: From Yugoslavia to Europe — Keil, Soeren
Foreign Relations: American Immigration in Global Perspective — Gabaccia, Donna R.
Foreign Relations Law — McLachlan, Campbell

Foreign Rule in Western Europe: Towards a Comparative History of Military Occupations 1940-1949
Foreigners and Their Food: Constructing Otherness in Jewish, Christian, and Islamic Law — Freidenreich, David
Forensic Medicine and Death Investigation in Medieval England — Butler, Sara M.
y Forensic Science: In Pursuit of Justice — Carmichael, L.E.
Forensic Shakespeare — Skinner, Quentin
Forensics: The Anatomy of Crime — McDermid, Val
c Forensics: The Scene of the Crime — Peppas, Lynn
Forensics: What Bugs, Burns, Prints, DNA, and More Tell Us about Crime — McDermid, Val
c A Forest Divided — Hunter, Erin
The Forest Garden Greenhouse: How to Design and Manage an Indoor Permaculture Oasis — Osentowski, Jerome
c Forest of Wonders (Illus. by Madsen, Jim) — Park, Linda Sue
Forests and Global Change — Coomes, David A.
c Forests Inside Out — Bow, James
Forever Evil — Finch, David
y Forever for a Year — Gottfred, B.T.
Forever His Texas Bride — Broday, Linda
Forever in Vein — LaGreca, Jody R.
y Forever Red — Stohl, Margaret
c Forever Smurfette — Peyo
Forever This Time — McGinnis, Maggie
Forever Vietnam: How a Divisive War Changed American Public Memory — Kieran, David
Forever with You — Armentrout, Jennifer L.
Forever Your Earl — Leigh, Eva
y Forged — Bowman, Erin
Forged in Fire — Scott, Jessica
The Forgers — Morrow, Bradford
y Forget Me — Harrington, Kim
c Forget Me Not (Illus. by Graegin, Stephanie) — Van Laan, Nancy
c The Forget-Me-Not Summer (Illus. by Kim, Ji-Hyuk) — Howland, Leila
Forget Tomorrow — Dunn, Pintip
y The Forgetting Time — Guskin, Sharon
Forging Authenticity: Bastianini and the Neo-Renaissance in Nineteenth-Century Florence — Moskowitz, Anita Fiderer
Forging Capitalism: Rogues, Swindlers, Frauds and the Rise of Modern Finance — Klaus, Ian
Forgiveness 4 You — Bauer, Ann
Forgiving Effie Beck — Fitzjerrell, Karen Casey
Forgiving Maximo Rothman — Sidransky, A.J.
c Forgotten Bones: Uncovering a Slave Cemetery — Huey, Lois Miner
Forgotten Citizens: Deportation, Children, and the Making of American Exiles and Orphans — Zayas, Luis H.
Forgotten Dead: Mob Violence against Mexicans in the United States, 1848-1928 — Carrigan, William D.
The Forgotten Depression, 1921: The Crash That Cured Itself — Grant, James
The Forgotten First: B-1 and the Integration of the Modern Navy — Albright, Alex
The Forgotten Flapper — Giles, Laini
Forgotten Foundations of Bretton Woods: International Development and the Making of the Postwar Order — Helleiner, Eric
The Forgotten Girls — Blaedel, Sara
The Forgotten Presidents: Their Untold Constitutional Legacy — Gerhardt, Michael J.
y The Forgotten Recipe — Clipston, Amy
The Forgotten Room (Read by McClain, Johnathan). Audiobook Review — Child, Lincoln
The Forgotten Room — Child, Lincoln
The Forgotten Room — White, Karen
The Forgotten Seamstress — Trenow, Liz
c The Forgotten Sisters — Hale, Shannon
The Forgotten Soldier — Taylor, Brad
Forgotten Suns — Tarr, Judith
Forgotten: The Untold Story of D-Day's Black Heroes, at Home and at War — Hervieux, Linda
Forgotten Trials of the Holocaust — Bazyler, Michael J.
Forgotten Voices — Adams, Jane A.
Forgotten Voices of Mao's Great Famine, 1958-1962: An Oral History — Zhou, Xun
y Fork-Tongue Charmers — Durham, Paul
Forked — Jayaraman, Saru
Form and Dialectic in Georg Simmel's Sociology: A New Interpretation — Jary, David
Form and Function in Roman Oratory — Berry, D.H.

Formal Causes: Definition, Explanation, and Primacy in Socratic and Aristotelian Thought — *Ferejohn, Michael T.*
Formal Matters: Reading the Materials of English Renaissance Literature — *Deutermann, Allison K.*
The Formation of Candomble: Vodun History and Ritual in Brazil — *Pares, Luis Nicolau*
The Formation of the Child in Early Modern Spain — *Coolidge, Grace E.*
Formationen des Politischen: Anthropologie politischer Felder — *Adam, Jens*
Formative Assessment in the New Balanced Literacy Classroom — *Policastro, Margaret M.*
Formative Fictions: Nationalism, Cosmopolitanism, and the Bildungsroman — *Boes, Tobias*
Formidable Lord Quentin — *Rice, Patricia*
Forms of Engagement: Women, Poetry, and Culture, 1640u-1680 — *Scott-Baumann, Elizabeth*
The Forms of the Affects — *Brinkema, Eugenie*
Forms of Thought: A Study in Philosophical Logic — *Lowe, E.J.*
Forms: Whole, Rhythm, Hierarchy, Network — *Levine, Caroline*
Formula One and Beyond: The Autobiography — *Mosley, Max*
c Formula One Racing — *James, Brant*
The Forsaken — *Atkins, Ace*
Forsaken — *Barker, J.D.*
Forsaken — *Howell, Ross, Jr.*
y Fort — *DeFelice, Cynthia*
Fort Marion Prisoners and the Trauma of Native Education — *Glancy, Diane*
y Fort — *DeFelice, Cynthia*
c The Fort — *DeFelice, Cynthia*
c Fort — *DeFelice, Cynthia*
Fort Worth: Outpost, Cowtown, Boomtown — *Rich, Harold*
Fortify Your Life: Your Guide to Vitamins, Minerals, and More — *Dog, Tieraona Low*
Fortney Road: Life, Death, and Deception in a Christian Cult — *Stevenson, Jeff C.*
The Fortress of Solitude — *Moses, Itamar*
A Fortunate Blizzard — *Chase, L.C.*
A Fortunate Man: The Story of a Country Doctor — *Berger, John*
Fortunate Son — *Fogerty, John*
c Fortune Falls — *Goebel, Jenny*
Fortune Hunters — *Masters, Riley*
Fortune Smiles: Stories — *Johnson, Adam*
Fortune Tellers: The Story of America's First Economic Forecasters — *Friedman, Walter A.*
Fortune's Fool: The Life of John Wilkes Booth — *Alford, Terry*
The Fortunes of Africa: A 5,000-Year History of Wealth, Greed and Endeavour — *Meredith, Martin*
The Fortunes of Francis Barber: The True Story of the Jamaican Slave Who Became Samuel Johnson's Heir — *Bundock, Michael*
Forty Days without Shadow — *Truc, Oliver*
Forty Days without Shadow — *Truc, Olivier*
y Forty Dreaming — *Hyde, Michael*
Forty Rooms — *Grushin, Olga*
Forty Thieves — *Perry, Thomas*
Fossil Island — *Sjoholm, Barbara*
Fossils of the Carpathian Region — *Fozy, Istvan*
The Foster Factory — *Learmont, David*
Fostering Algebraic Thinking with Casio Technology: Investigations for the PRISM Graphing Calculator — *Goerdt, Sonja L.*
Fostering Children's Number Sense in Grades K-2: Turning Math Inside Out — *Nelson, Greg*
Foster's Market Favorites: 25th Anniversary Collection — *Foster, Sara*
Fotografia e Imperio: paisagens para um Brasil moderno — *Brizuela, Natalia*
Fotografie im Dienst der Wissenschaft
Fotografie zwischen Politik und Bild: Entwicklungen der Fotografie in der DDR — *Schmid, Sabine*
Fouilles executees a Malia. Le Quartier Mu V. Vie quotidienne at techniques au Minoen Moyen II — *Poursat, J.C.*
c Foul Ball Frame-Up at Wrigley Field — *Aretha, David*
y Foulsham — *Carey, Edward*
y Found (Read by Podehl, Nick). Audiobook Review — *Coben, Harlan*
y Found — *Coben, Harlan*
c Found All Around: A Show-and-Tell of Found Poetry (Illus. by Heathwood, Karen) — *Dalal, Krishna*
Found, Near Water — *Hayton, Katherine*
Found Theology: History, Imagination and the Holy Spirit — *Quash, Ben*
c Found Things — *Hilton, Marilyn*

Foundational Arts: Mural Painting and Missionary Theater in New Spain — *Schuessler, Michael K.*
Foundations of Macroecology: Classic Papers with Commentaries — *Smith, Felisa A.*
The Foundations of Medieval Papal Legation — *Rennie, Kriston R.*
Foundations of the Earth: Global Ecological Change and the Book of Job — *Shugart, H.H.*
The Founders and Finance: How Hamilton, Gallatin, and Other Immigrants Forged a New Economy — *McCraw, Thomas K.*
Founders as Fathers: The Private Lives and Politics of the American Revolutionaries — *Glover, Lorri*
Founder's Son: A Life of Abraham Lincoln — *Brookhiser, Richard*
The Founders: The Origins of the ANC and the Struggle for Democracy in South Africa — *Odendaal, Andre*
The Founding Conservatives: How a Group of Unsung Heroes Saved the American Revolution — *Lefer, David*
c The Founding Fathers! Those Horse-Ridin', Fiddle-Playin', Book-Readin', Gun-Totin' Gentlemen Who Started America (Illus. by Blitt, Barry) — *Winter, Jonah*
Founding Grammars: How Early America's War over Words Shaped Today's Language — *Ostler, Rosemarie*
Founding the Fathers: Early Church History and Protestant Professors in Nineteenth Century America — *Clark, Elizabeth A.*
The Foundling's War — *Deon, Michel*
The Four Books — *Lianke, Yan*
The Four Books — *Rojas, Carlos*
The Four Books — *Yan, Lianke*
c Four Children and It — *Wilson, Jacqueline*
Four Classic Mormon Village Studies — *Bahr, Howard M.*
The Four Deaths of Acorn Whistler: Telling Stories in Colonial America — *Piker, Joshua*
Four Decades On: Vietnam, the United States, and the Legacies of the Second Indochina War — *Laderman, Scott*
Four Degrees of Global Warming: Australia in a Hot World — *Christoff, Peter*
The Four-Dimensional Human: Ways of Being in the Digital World — *Scott, Laurence*
Four Fields — *Dee, Tim*
The Four Horsemen of the Investor's Apocalypse — *Klosterman, Robert J.*
The Four Intelligences of the Business Mind: How to Rewire Your Brain and Your Business for Success — *Nazemoff, Valeh*
Four Last Songs: Aging and Creativity in Verdi, Strauss, Messiaen, and Britten — *Hutcheon, Linda*
Four-Legged Girl — *Seuss, Diane*
Four Nights with the Duke — *James, Eloisa*
Four Novels of the 1970s: Fifty-Two Pickup, Swag, Unknown Man No. 89, The Switch — *Leonard, Elmore*
Four Novels of the 1980s: City Primeval, LaBrava, Glitz, Freaky Deaky — *Leonard, Elmore*
Four Revolutions in the Earth Sciences: From Heresy to Truth — *Powell, James Lawrence*
Four Seats — *Cooley, Aaron*
Four Square Leagues: Pueblo Indian Land in New Mexico — *Ebright, Malcolm*
Four Steeples Over the City Streets: Religion and Society in New York's Early Republic Congregations — *Bulthuis, Kyle T.*
The Four Words For Home — *Chuang, Angie*
Four Years in the Mountains of Kurdistan: An Armenian Boy's Memoir of Survival — *Haigaz, Aram*
Four Years in the Mountains of Kurdistan: An Armenian Boy's Memoir of Survival (Read by Chekenian, Iris Haigaz) — *Haigaz, Aram*
Four Years in the Mountains of Kurdistan: An Armenian Boy's Memoir of Survival — *Haigaz, Aram*
Fourteen Stories That Inspired Satyajit Ray — *Chattopadhyay, Bhaskar*
c The Fourteenth Goldfish (Read by Perna, Georgette). Audiobook Review — *Holm, Jennifer L.*
c The Fourteenth Goldfish — *Holm, Jennifer L.*
c The Fourteenth Summer of Angus Jack (Illus. by Gifford, Lucinda) — *Storer, Jen*
The Fourth Horseman — *Hagberg, David*
y Fourth of July Creek — *Henderson, Smith*
The Fourth Pig — *Mitchison, Naomi*
y The Fourth Wish — *Ribar, Lindsay*
c Fowl Play (Illus. by Nichols, Travis) — *Nichols, Travis*

Fowler's Dictionary of Modern English Usage, 4th ed. — *Butterfield, Jeremy*
c Fox and Squirrel Make a Friend — *Ohi, Ruth*
c The Fox at the Manger — *Travers, P.L.*
c The Fox Chase (Illus. by Nordqvist, Sven) — *Nordqvist, Sven*
The Fox-Hunting Controversy, 1781-2004 — *May, Allyson N.*
Fox Is Framed (Read by Bray, R.C.). Audiobook Review — *Smith, Lachlan*
Fox Is Framed — *Smith, Lachlan*
c Fox on the Loose! (Illus. by Porter, Matthew) — *Porter, Matthew*
c The Fox (Illus. by Bertolucci, Federico) — *Brremaud, Frederic*
c Fox Talk — *Carmichael, L.E.*
Fox Tooth Heart — *McManus, John*
Fox Tooth Heart: Stories — *McManus, John*
Fox Tossing and Other Forgotten and Dangerous Sports, Pastimes, and Games — *Brooke-Hitching, Edward*
Fox Tossing, Octopus Wrestling and Other Forgotten Sports — *Brooke-Hitching, Edward*
c The Fox Went Out on a Chilly Night (Illus. by Spier, Peter) — *Spier, Peter*
c Foxcraft: The Taken — *Iserles, Inbali*
c Fox's Garden — *Camcam, Princesse*
c Foxtrot (Illus. by Moor, Becka) — *Moor, Becka*
The Frackers: The Outrageous Inside Story of the New Billionaire — *Zucketman, Gregory*
y Fracking: A Reference Handbook — *Newton, David E.*
Fracking Justice — *Fitzgerald, Michael J.*
Fractions — *Alaina, Maria*
Fracture: Barack Obama, the Clintons, and the Racial Divide — *Reid, Joy-Ann*
Fracture: Life and Culture in the West, 1918-1938 — *Blom, Philipp*
Fracture: Life & Culture in the West, 1918-1938 — *Blom, Philipp*
Fractured Days — *Roland, Rebecca*
The Fracturing of the American Corporate Elite — *Mizruchi, Mark*
y Fragile Bones: Harrison & Anna — *Nicholson, Lorna Schultz*
Fragile by Design: The Political Origins of Banking Crises and Scarce Credit — *Calomiris, Charles W.*
Fragile Empire: How Russia Fell in and out of Love with Vladimir Putin — *Judah, Ben*
Fragile Majorities and Education: Belgium, Catalonia, Northern Ireland and Quebec — *Mcandrew, Marie*
Fragments and Assemblages: Forming Compilations of Medieval London — *Bahr, Arthur*
Fragments of a Lost Homeland: Remembering Armenia — *Marsoobian, Armen T.*
Fragments of Horror (Illus. by Ito, Junji) — *Ito, Junji*
y The Frail Days — *Prendergast, Gabrielle*
Fram — *Himmer, Steve*
Framed Butterflies — *Rahman, Raad*
c Framed in France (Illus. by Pamintuan, Macky) — *Brown, Jeff*
Framing Chief Leschi: Narratives and the Politics of Historical Justice — *Blee, Lisa*
Framing Floors, Walls and Ceilings
Framing of the Early Middle Ages — *Wickham, Chris*
Framley Parsonage — *Trollope, Anthony*
Francais? La nation en debat entre colonies et metropole, XVIe-XIXe siecle — *Vidal, Cecile*
c France — *Lynch, Annabelle*
France and the Age of Revolution: Regimes Old and New from Louis XIV to Napoleon Bonaparte — *Doyle, William*
France since 1815 — *Evans, Martin*
France under Fire: German Invasion, Civilian Flight, and Family Survival during World War II — *Risser, Nicole Dombrowski*
Frances Burney and Narrative Prior to Ideology — *McCrea, Brian*
c Frances Dean Who Loved to Dance and Dance (Illus. by Sif, Birgitta) — *Sif, Birgitta*
Frances Ha: A Noah Baumbach Picture — *Baumbach, Noah*
Francia et Germania: Studies in Strengleikar and Pidreks saga af Bern — *Johansson, Karl G.*
c Francine Poulet Meets the Ghost Raccoon (Read by McInerney, Kathleen). Audiobook Review — *DiCamillo, Kate*
c Francine Poulet Meets the Ghost Raccoon (Read by McInerney, Kathleen). Audiobook Review — *DiCamillo, Kate*
c Francine Poulet Meets the Ghost Raccoon (Illus. by Van Dusen, Chris) — *DiCamillo, Kate*

c Francine Poulet Meets the Ghost Raccoon: Tales from Deckawoo Drive, vol. 2 (Illus. by Van Dusen, Chris) — DiCamillo, Kate
Francis: A New World Pope — Cool, Michel
Francis Bacon in Your Blood: A Memoir — Peppiatt, Michael
The Francis Effect: A Radical Pope's Challenge to the American Catholic Church — Gehring, John
The Francis Miracle — Allen, John L., Jr.
Francis of Assisi and His Canticle of Brother Sun Reassessed — Moloney, Brian
Francis of Assisi: The Life and Afterlife of a Medieval Saint — Vauchez, Andre
Francis: Pope of Good Promise — Burns, Jimmy
Francis Poulenc: Articles and Interviews - Notes from the Heart — Southon, Nicolas
Francis Poulenc: His Life & Work with Authoritative Text and Selected Music — Lung, Sam
Francis Watkins and the Dollond Telescope Patent Controversy — Gee, Brain
The Franciscan Heart of Thomas Merton: A New Look at the Spiritual Inspiration of His Life, Thought, and Writing — Horan, Daniel P.
Franciscan Spirituality and Mission in New Spain, 1524-1599: Conflict beneath the Sycamore Tree (Luke 19: 1-10). — Turley, Steven E.
Franciscanos eminentes en territorios de fronteras — Cabranes, Amaya
c Francisco's Kites / Las cometas de Francisco (Illus. by Undercuffler, Gary) — Klepeis, Alicia Z.
c Francisco's Kites/Las cometas de Francisco (Illus. by Undercuffler, Gary) — Klepeis, Alicia Z.
Franco: A Personal and Political Biography — Payne, Stanley G.
Franco Corelli and a Revolution in Singing: Fifty-Four Tenors Spanning 200 Years — Zucker, Stefan
Franco Sells Spain to America: Hollywood, Tourism, and Public Relations as Postwar Spanish Soft Power — Rosendorf, Neal M.
Franco: The Biography of the Myth — Sanchez, Antonio Cazorla
Francophone Cultures and Geographies of Identity — Murdoch, H. Adlai
Franco's Crypt: Spanish Culture and Memory since 1936 — Treglown, Jeremy
y The Frangipani Hotel — Kupersmith, Violet
Frank: A Life in Politics from the Great Society to Same-Sex Marriage (Read by Frank, Barney). Audiobook Review — Frank, Barney
Frank: A Life in Politics from the Great Society to Same-Sex Marriage — Frank, Barney
c Frank! — Brecon, Connah
Frank Auerbach: Speaking and Painting — Lampert, Catherine
Frank & Ava: In Love and War — Brady, John
Frank Cioffi: The Philosopher in Shirt-Sleeves — Ellis, David
c Frank Einstein and the Antimatter Motor (Illus. by Biggs, Brian) — Scieszka, Jon
c Frank Einstein and the Brain Turbo (Illus. by Biggs, Brian) — Scieszka, Jon
c Frank Einstein and the Electro-Finger (Read by Scieszka, Jon, with Brian Biggs). Audiobook Review — Scieszka, Jon
c Frank Einstein and the Electro-Finger (Illus. by Biggs, Brian) — Scieszka, Jon
Frank Gehry — Lemonier, Aurelien
Frank Jacobs (Illus. by Davis, Jack) — Jacobs, Frank
Frank Lloyd Wright and his Manner of Thought — Klinkowitz, Jerome
c Frank Pearl in the Awful Waffle Kerfuffle (Illus. by Madrid, Erwin) — McDonald, Megan
Frank Sinatra: An Extraordinary Life — Leigh, Spencer
Frank Stella: A Retrospective — Auping, Michael
Frank Underhill and the Politics of Ideas — Dewar, Kenneth C.
c Frankencrayon (Illus. by Hall, Michael) — Hall, Michael
y Frankenstein (Illus. by Calero, Dennis) — Shelley, Mary
The Frankenstein of 1790 and Other Lost Chapters from Revolutionary France — Douthwaite, Julia V.
c Frankenstein's Fright before Christmas (Illus. by Walton, Rick) — Bemonster, Ludworst
c Frankenstink! Garbage Gone Bad (Illus. by Lightburn, Ron) — Lightburn, Ron
The Frankfurt School in Exile — Wheatland, Thomas
y Frankie and Joely — Weetman, Nova

Frankie Avalon's Italian Family Cookbook: From Mom's Kitchen to Mine and Yours — Avalon, Frankie
y Frankie Fox Girl Spy: Ready Set Spy — Poshoglian, Yvette
c Frankie Liked to Sing (Illus. by Christy, Jana) — Seven, John
Frankie Styne and the Silver Man — Page, Kathy
c Franklin and the Case of the New Friend — Smith, Caitlin Drake
c Franklin and the Radio — Smith, Caitlin Drake
Franklin Barbecue: A Meat-Smoking Manifesto — Franklin, Aaron
Franklin Barbecue: A Meat-Smoking Manifesto — Mackay, Jordan
Franklin D. Roosevelt: Road to the New Deal, 1882-1939 — Daniels, Roger
c Franklin D. Roosevelt: The 32nd President — Gregory, Josh
c Franky (Illus. by Timmers, Leo) — Timmers, Leo
Franz Ferdinand: Der eigensinnige Thronfolger — Grabmayr, Susanna
Franz Kafka: The Poet of Shame and Guilt — Friedlander, Saul
Franz Rosenzweig's Conversions: World Denial and World Redemption — Pollock, Benjamin
Franz Schubert and His World — Gibbs, Christopher H.
Franz Schubert: The Complete Songs — Johnson, Graham
The Fraternity Of The Soul Eater — Lerner, Scott
The Fraud — Parks, Brad
Fraud, Corruption and Sport — Brooks, Graham
Frauen in den Aussenlagern des Konzentrationslagers Gross-Rosen — Rudorff, Andrea
Frauenstimmen in der Spatmittelalterlichen Stadt? Testamente von Frauen aus Luneburg, Hamburg und Wien als Soziale Kommunikation — Pajcic, Kathrin
The Freach and Keen Murders: The True Story of the Crime That Shocked and Changed a Community Forever — Munleyand, Kathleen P.
Freaks I've Met — Jans, Donald
y Freaks of Nature — Brotherlin, Wendy
c Freckleface Strawberry: Backpacks! (Illus. by Pham, LeUyen) — Moore, Julianne
c Freckleface Strawberry: Loose Tooth! (Illus. by Pham, LeUyen) — Moore, Julianne
c Freckleface Strawberry: Lunch, or What's That? (Illus. by Pham, LeUyen) — Moore, Julianne
c Fred (Illus. by Seo, Kaila) — Seo, Kaila
Fred Pinsocket Loves Bananas — Apel, Peter
Fred Sanger: Double Nobel Laureate: A Biography — Brownlee, George G.
Fred Zinnemann and the Cinema of Resistance — Smyth, J.E.
c Freddie and Gingersnap Find a Cloud to Keep — Kirsch, Vincent X.
c Freddy and Frito and the Clubhouse Rules (Illus. by Friend, Alison) — Friend, Alison
Freddy and Frito and the Clubhouse Rules — Friend, Alison
c Freddy and Mrs. Goodwich (Illus. by Trevor, Chelsea) — Trevor, Adena
c Freddy Tangles: Champ or Chicken (Illus. by Jellett, Tom) — Brand, Jack
c Freddy Tangles: Legend or Loser (Illus. by Jellett, Tom) — Brand, Jack
Freddy the Frogcaster and the Big Blizzard — Dean, Janice
c Freddy the Frogcaster and the Huge Hurricane — Dean, Janice
c Freddy the Penny (Illus. by Genelza, Novella) — Begun, Gabrielle
c Frederick (Illus. by Lionni, Leo) — Lionni, Leo
Frederick Douglass in Ireland: The Black O'Connell — Fenton, Laurence
Frederick Law Olmsted: Plans and Views of Public Parks — Beveridge, Charles E.
Frederick Law Olmsted: Writings on Landscape, Culture, and Society — Beveridge, Charles E.
Frederick the Great: King of Prussia — Blanning, Tim
Frederick the Wise: Seen and Unseen Lives of Martin Luther's Protector — Wellman, Sam
c Frederick's Journey: The Life of Frederick Douglass (Illus. by Ladd, London) — Rappaport, Doreen
Fredric Jameson: The Project of Dialectical Criticism — Tally, Robert T., Jr.
c Fred's Beds (Illus. by Samuels, Barbara) — Samuels, Barbara
Free Agent: The Independent Professional's Roadmap to Self-Employment Success — Tynan, Katy

Free and French in the Caribbean: Toussaint Louverture, Aime Cesaire, and Narratives of Loyal Opposition — Walsh, John Patrick
Free Black Communities and the Underground Railroad: The Geography of Resistance — LaRoche, Cheryl Janifer
Free Electricity — Rhodes, Ryan
Free Jazz/Black Power — Carles, Philippe
A Free Man — Basilieres, Michel
Free Market Tuberculosis: Managing Epidemics in Post-Soviet Georgia — Koch, Erin
Free Men — Smith, Katy Simpson
Free-Motion Quilting for Beginners: And Those Who Think They Can't — Hanson, Molly
Free Range Triangle Quilts — Marston, Gwen
Free Refills — Grinspoon, Peter
A Free-Spirited Woman: The London Diaries of Gladys Langford, 1938-1940 — Malcolmson, Patricia
A Free State — Piazza, Tom
Free Technology for Libraries — Deschenes, Amy
c Free Verse — Dooley, Sarah
Free: Why Science Hasn't Disproved Free Will — Mele, Alfred R.
Free Will in Philosophical Theology — Timpe, Kevin
Free Your Mind: An African American Guide to Meditation and Freedom — Rainey, Cortez R.
Freedom and Limits — Shade, Patrick
Freedom and the Self: Essays on the Philosophy of David Foster Wallace — Cahn, Steven M.
Freedom Burning: Anti-slavery and Empire in Victorian Britain — Huzzey, Richard
Freedom from Anger: Understanding It, Overcoming It and Finding Joy — Sumanasara, Alubomulle
The Freedom in American Songs — Winter, Kathleen
c Freedom in Congo Square (Illus. by Christie, R. Gregory) — Weatherford, Carole Boston
Freedom Journey 1965: Photographs of the Selma to Montgomery March by Stephen Somerstein — Somerstein, Stephen
Freedom of Speech: Mightier Than the Sword — Shipler, David K.
Freedom Regained: the Possibility of Free Will — Baggini, Julian
y Freedom Ride — Lawson, Sue
c Freedom Summer: Celebrating the 50th Anniversary of the Freedom Summer (Illus. by Lagarrigue, Jerome) — Wiles, Deborah
y Freedom Summer: The 1964 Struggle for Civil Rights in Mississippi — Rubin, Susan Goldman
Freedom Time: Negritude, Decolonization, and the Future of the World — Wilder, Gary
Freedom to Fail: Heidegger's Anarchy — Trawny, Peter
The Freedom to Kill — Nicholas, J.W.
Freedom's Ballot: African American Political Struggles in Chicago from Abolition to the Great Migration — Garb, Margaret
Freedom's Child — Miller, Jax
Freedom's Debt: The Royal African Company and the Politics of the Atlantic Slave Trade, 1672-1752 — Pettigrew, William A.
Freedom's Delay: America's Struggle for Emancipation, 1776-1865 — Carden, Allen
Freedom's Forge: How American Business Produced Victory in World War II — Herman, Arthur
Freedom's Frontier: California and the Struggle over Unfree Labor, Emancipation, and Reconstruction — Smith, Stacey L.
Freedom's Mirror: Cuba and Haiti in the Age of Revolution — Ferrer, Ada
Freedom's Pragmatist: Lyndon Johnson and Civil Rights — Ellis, Sylvia
c Freedom's Price — MacColl, Michaela
Freedom's Price: Serfdom, Subjection, and Reform in Prussia, 1648-1848 — Eddie, Sean A.
c Freedom's School (Illus. by Ransome, James E.) — Cline-Ransome, Lesa
Freedom's Seekers: Essays on Comparative Emancipation — Kerr-Ritchie, Jeffrey R.
Freeform Wire Art Jewelry: Techniques for Designing with Wire, Beads and Gems — Bird, Gayle
Freeman's: The Best New Writing on Arrival — Freeman, John
c Freeze-land: A New Beginning — Ayaz, Huda
Freie Anerkennung ubergeschichtlicher Bindungen: Katholische Geschichtswahrnehmung im deutschsprachigen Raum des 20 Jahrhutiderts — Pittrof, Thomas
c Freight Train (Illus. by Crews, Donald) — Crews, Donald

Freiheit, Menschenwurde, Solidaritat. Das Erbe der Revolutionen von 1989
Fremantle's Submarines: How Allied Submariners and Western Australians Helped to Win the War in the Pacific — *Sturma, Michael*
Fremde Gemeinschaft: Deutsch-judische Literatur der Moderne — *Liska, Vivian*
c The French — *Mitchell, Sara*
The French Anarchists in London, 1880-1914: Exile and Transnationalism in the First Globalisation — *Bantman, Constance*
The French and Indian War and the Conquest of New France — *Nester, William R.*
The French and Indian War in North Carolina: The Spreading Flames of War — *Maass, John R.*
French Art Deco — *Goss, Jared*
French Baroque Music of New Orleans: Spiritual Songs from the Ursuline Convent — *Lemmon, Alfred E.*
French Books of Hours: Making an Archive of Prayer, c.1400-1600 — *Reinburg, Virginia*
French Coast — *Hughes, Anita*
French Colonial Fascism: The Extreme Right in Algeria, 1919-1939 — *Kalman, Samuel*
The French Colonial Imagination: Writing the Indian Uprisings, 1857-1858, from Second Empire to Third Republic — *Frith, Nicola*
French Colonial Soldiers in German Captivity during World War II — *Scheck, Raffael*
French Comedy on Screen: A Cinematic History — *Fournier, Lanzoni Remi*
French Concession — *Bai, Xiao*
c French Food — *Gilbert, Sara*
French General: A Year of Jewelry; 36 Projects with Vintage Beads — *Meng, Kaari*
The French-Piedmontese Campaign of 1859 — *Schneid, Frederick C.*
The French Prize — *Nelson, James L.*
French Reflections on the Shakespearean Tragic: Three Case Studies — *Hillman, Richard*
The French Republic: History, Values, Debates — *Berenson, Edward*
The French Revolution and the Birth of Electoral Democracy — *Edelstein, Melvin*
The French Revolution Debate and the British Novel, 1790-1814: The Struggle for History's Authority — *Rooney, Morgan*
French Visitors to Newfoundland: An Anthology of Nineteenth-Century Travel Writing — *Jamieson, Scott*
French Women and the Empire: The Case of Indochina — *Ha, Marie-Paul*
The French Writers' War, 1940-1953 — *Sapiro, Gisele*
A Frenchwoman's Imperial Story: Madame Luce in Nineteenth-Century Algeria — *Rogers, Rebecca*
Frend — *Miller, Jonathan R.*
c Fresh (Illus. by Cano, Fernando) — *Steele, Michael A.*
c Fresh Delicious: Poems from the Farmers' Market (Illus. by Moriuchi, Mique) — *Latham, Irene*
Fresh Fruit, Broken Bodies: Migrant Farmworkers in the United States — *Holmes, Seth M.*
Fresh Hell — *Johnson, Rachel*
A Fresh Look at Fear: Encountering Jesus in Our Weakness — *Baumann, Dan*
Fresh Prints: 25 Easy and Enticing Printing Projects to Make at Home — *Leech, Christine*
Freshwater Fishes of North America — *Warren, Melvin L.*
Freshwater Passages: The Trade and Travels of Peter Pond — *Chapin, David*
Fresno Growing Up: A City Comes of Age: 1945-1985 — *Provost, Stephen H.*
c Fretland Gems — *VanVoorst, Jenny Fretland*
Freunde Roms und Volker der Finsternis: Die papstliche Konstruktion von Anderen im 8. und 9. Jahrhundert — *Gantner, Clemens*
The Friars in Ireland, 1224-1540 — *O Clabaigh, Colman*
c Fribbet the Frog and the Tadpoles (Illus. by Roman, Carole P.) — *Roman, Carole P.*
c Frida and Bear — *Browne, Anthony*
y Frida and Diego: Art, Love, Life — *Reef, Catherine*
Frida Kahlo: The Gisle Freund Photographs — *Freund, Gisle*
Frida Kahlo's Garden — *Zavala, Adriana*
c Friday Barnes, Girl Detective (Illus. by Cosier, Phil) — *Spratt, R.A.*
Frieden und Konfliktmanagement in interkulturellen Raumen: Das Osmanische Reich und die Habsburgermonarchie in der Fruhen Neuzeit — *Spannenberger, Norbert*

Friedensethik im fruhen Mittalalter: Theologie zwischen Kritik und Legitimation von Gewalt — *Beestermoller, Gerhard*
Friedensordnungen in Geschichtswissenschaftlicher und Geschichtsdidaktischer Perspektive
Friedrich Max Muller and His Asian Interlocutors: Academic Knowledge about 'Oriental Religions' in Late Nineteenth-Century Europe
Friedrich Ohly: Vergegenwartigung eines grossen Philologen — *Harms, Wolfgang*
Friend and Foe: When to Cooperate, When to Compete, and How to Succeed at Both — *Galinsky, Adam*
Friend & Foe — *Galinsky, Adam*
c A Friend for Bo (Illus. by Zuniga, Elisabeth) — *Zuniga, Elisabeth*
c A Friend for Lakota: The Incredible True Story of a Wolf Who Braved Bullying (Illus. by Dutcher, Jim) — *Dutcher, Jamie*
c A Friend for Lakota: The Incredible True Story of a Wolf Who Braved Bullying (Illus. by Dutcher, Jim) — *Dutcher, Jim*
c A Friend in Need (Illus. by Pankhurst, Kate) — *Jarman, Julia*
A Friend of Mr. Lincoln — *Harrigan, Stephen*
c Friend or Foe: The Whole Truth about Animals People Love to Hate (Illus. by Anderson, David) — *Kaner, Etta*
y Friend or Foe: Which Side Are You On? — *Gallagher, Brian*
c Friends (Illus. by Ikegami, Aiko) — *Ikegami, Aiko*
Friends and Enemies — *Wangard, Terri*
Friends Disappear: The Battle for Racial Equality in Evanston — *Barr, Mary*
c Friends for Freedom: The Story of Susan B. Anthony & Frederick Douglass (Read by Mitchell, Lizan). Audiobook Review — *Slade, Suzanne*
c Friends for Freedom: The Story of Susan B. Anthony & Frederick Douglass (Illus. by Tadgell, Nicole) — *Slade, Suzanne*
y Friends for Life — *Norriss, Andrew*
Friends in High Places — *Peacock, Caro*
Friends of Alice Wheeldon: The Anti-War Activist Accused of Plotting to Kill Lloyd George — *Rowbotham, Sheila*
Friends, Patrons, Clients. Final Conference of the PhD Research Group Graduiertenkolleg 1288
c Friendshape: An Uplifting Celebration of Friendship (Illus. by Lichtenheld, Tom) — *Rosenthal, Amy Krouse*
Friendship — *Gould, Emily*
Friendship and Politics in Post-Revolutionary France — *Horowitz, Sarah*
Friendship and Sociability in Premodern Europe: Contexts, Concepts and Expressions — *Gill, Amyrose McCue*
Friendship and Sociability in Premodern Europe: Contexts, Concepts, and Expressions — *Gill, Amyrose McCue*
Friendship as Sacred Knowing: Overcoming Isolation — *Kimbriel, Samuel*
c A Friendship for Today — *McKissack, Patricia C.*
c Friendship Is like a Seesaw (Illus. by Agocs, Irisz) — *Innes, Shona*
The Friendship of Criminals — *Glinski, Robert*
c Friendship Over (Illus. by Wright, Johanna) — *Sternberg, Julie*
c Friendship Quilt (Illus. by Jeong, Hajin) — *Kim, Cecil*
c The Friendship Riddle (Read by Rustin, Sandy). Audiobook Review — *Blakemore, Megan Frazer*
c The Friendship Riddle — *Blakemore, Megan Frazer*
Friendswood — *Steinke, Ren*
c Fright Club (Illus. by Long, Ethan) — *Long, Ethan*
c Frightfully Friendly Ghosties: Ghostly Holler-Day (Illus. by Roberts, David) — *King, Daren*
The Fringe Hours: Making Time for You — *Turner, Jessica N.*
c Fripon le curieux (Illus. by Franson, Leanne) — *Hughes, Susan*
Frisk Me — *Layne, Lauren*
Frog — *Goldblatt, Howard*
Frog — *Mo, Yan*
c Frog and Friends Celebrate Thanksgiving, Christmas, and New Year's Eve — *Bunting, Eve*
Frog Music — *Donoghue, Emma*
c Frog on a Log? (Illus. by Field, Jim) — *Gray, Kes*
c Frog or Toad? — *Kralovansky, Susan*
c Froggy Goes to the Library (Illus. by Remkiewicz, Frank) — *London, Jonathan*
c Froggy's Birthday Wish (Read by McDonough, John). Audiobook Review — *London, Jonathan*

c Froggy's Birthday Wish (Illus. by Remkiewicz, Frank) — *London, Jonathan*
c Frogs — *Bishop, Nic*
c Frogs — *Simon, Seymour*
c Frogs — *Delano, Marfe*
c Frogs — *Frisch, Aaron*
c Frogs Play Cellos: And Other Fun Facts (Illus. by Oswald, Pete) — *DiSiena, Laura Lyn*
Froi of the Exiles (Read by Cartwright, Grant). Audiobook Review — *Marchetta, Melina*
y From a Distant Star (Read by Rudd, Kate). Audiobook Review — *McQuestion, Karen*
y From a Distant Star — *McQuestion, Karen*
From a Drood to a Kill — *Green, Simon R.*
From a Nation Torn: Decolonizing French Colonial Art and Representation in France, 1945-1962 — *Feldman, Hannah*
From Accident to Hospital — *Suen, Anastasia*
From Acorns to Warehouses: Historical Political Economy of Southern California's Inland Empire — *Patterson, Thomas C.*
From Akhenaten to Moses — *Assmann, Jan*
From Antiquities to Heritage: Transformations of Cultural Memory — *Eriksen, Anne*
c From Apple Trees to Cider, Please! (Illus. by Patton, Julia) — *Chernesky, Felicia Sanzari*
From Bad Boys to New Men? Masculinity, Sexuality, and Violence in the Work of Eric Jourdan — *Heathcote, Owen*
From Bad to Wurst — *Hunter, Maddy*
From Battlefields Rising: How the Civil War Transformed American Literature — *Fuller, Randall*
From Books to Bezoars: Sir Hans Sloane and His Collections — *Walker, Alison*
From Bourgeouis to Boojie: Black Middle Class Performances — *Young, Vershawn Ashanti*
From Brown to Meredith: The Long Struggle for School Desegration in Louisville, Kentucky, 1954-2007 — *K'Meyer, Tracy E.*
From Bruges with Love — *Aspe, Pieter*
c From Bulb to Tulip — *Owings, Lisa*
From Cahokia to Larson to Moundville — *Byers, A. Martin*
From Camelot to Obamalot: Essays on Medieval and Modern Arthurian Literature — *Fichte, Byjoerg O.*
From Chicken Feet to Crystal Baths: An Englishman's Travels throughout China — *Mote, Ian*
From Classroom to Battlefield: Victoria High School and the First World War — *Gough, Barry*
From Command to Consent: The Representation and Interpretation of Power in the Late Medieval Eurasian World
From Copperas to Cleanup: The History of Vermont's Elizabeth Copper Mine — *Kierstead, Matt*
c From Crashing Waves to Music Download: An Energy Journey through the World of Sound — *Solway, Andrew*
From Cuba with Love: Sex and Money in the Twenty-First Century — *Daigle, Megan*
From Cultures of War to Cultures of Peace: War and Peace Museums in Japan, China, and South Korea and Embattled Memories: Contested Meanings in Korean War Memorials — *Yoshida, Takashi*
From Cultures of War to Cultures of Peace: War and Peace Museums in Japan, China, and South Korea — *Yoshida, Takashi*
From Darkness into Light: Perspectives on Film Preservation and Restoration — *Devraj, Rajesh*
From Deep State to Islamic State: The Arab Counter-Revolution and its Jihadi Legacy — *Filiu, Jean-Pierre*
From Development to Dictatorship: Bolivia and the Alliance for Progress in the Kennedy Era — *Field, Thomas C., Jr.*
From Dust to Life: The Origin and Evolution of Our Solar System — *Chambers, John*
From Eden to Eternity: Creations of Paradise in the Later Middle Ages — *Minnis, Alastair*
From Elsewhere — *Carson, Ciaran*
From Empire to Republic: Turkish Nationalism and the Armenian Genocide — *Ackam, Taner*
From Enemy to Friend: Jewish Wisdom and the Pursuit of Peace — *Eilberg, Amy*
From England to France: Felony and Exile in the High Middle Ages — *Jordan, William Chester*
From Eve to Evolution: Darwin, Science, and Women's Rights in Gilded Age America — *Hamlin, Kimberly A.*

From Every Tribe and Nation: A Historian's Discovery of the Global Christian Story — Noll, Mark A.

From Evidence to Outcomes in Child Welfare: An International Reader — Shlonsky, Aron

From Fake to Forever — Cantrell, Kat

c From Farm to Restaurant (Illus. by Hord, Colleen) — Hord, Colleen

From France with Love: Gender and Identity in French Romantic Comedy — Harrod, Mary

From Francophonie to World Literature in French: Ethics, Poetics, and Politics — Migraine-George, Therese

From Frank: Desk Notes to Make Humans Smile — Greetings from Frank L.L.C.

From Guernica to Human Rights: Essays on the Spanish Civil War — Carroll, Peter N.

From Hand to Handle: The First Industrial Revolution — Barham, Lawrence

From House of Lords to Supreme Court, Judges, Jurists and the Process of Judging — Lee, James

From India: Over 100 Recipes to Celebrate Food, Family & Tradition — Mahadevan, Kumar

From Knowledge to Beatitude: St. Victor, Twelfth-Century Schools, and Beyond: Essays in Honor of Grover A. Zinn, Jr. — Matter, E. Ann

c From Korea to California: Our Journey to America (Illus. by Kim, Arnold) — Cha, Grace

From Kutch to Tashkent: The Indo-Pakistan War of 1965 — Bajwa, Farooq

From Language to Creative Writing: An Introduction — Seargeant, Philip

From Lenin to Castro, 1917-1939: Early Encounters between Moscow and Havana — Bain, Mervyn J.

From Literature to Biterature: Lem, Turing, Darwin, and Explorations in Computer Literature, Philosophy of Mind, and Cultural Evolution — Swirski, Peter

From Little London to Little Bengal: Religion, Print, and Modernity in Early British India, 1793-1835 — White, Daniel E.

From Logos to Trinity: The Evolution of Religious Beliefs from Pythagoras to Tertullian — Hillar, Marian

From Main Street to Mall: The Rise and Fall of the American Department Store — Howard, Vicki

From Middle Class Society to an Age of Inequality? Social Change and Changing Concepts of Inequality in Germany and Great Britain after 1945

From Mother to Son: The Selected Letters of Marie de l'Incarnation to Claude Martin — Dunn, Mary

From Mutual Observation to Propaganda War: Premodern Revolts in Their Transnational Representations — Griesse, Malte

From Nature to Creation: A Christian Vision for Understanding and Loving Our World — Wirzba, Norman

From North to South: Southern Scholars Engage with Edward Schillebeeckx — Schillebeeckx, Edward

From Nothing: A Theology of Creation — McFarland, Ian A.

From Now On — Ward, Malachi

From Oikonomia to Political Economy: Constructing Economic Knowledge from the Renaissance to the Scientific Revolution — Maifreda, Germano

From Orphan to Adoptee: U.S. Empire and Genealogies of Korean Adoption — Pate, SooJin

From Pariahs to Partners: How Parents and Their Allies Changed New York City's Child Welfare System — Tobis, David

From Plantations to University Campus: The Social History of Cave Hill, Barbados — Marshall, Woodville K.

From Plato to Platonism — Gerson, Lloyd P.

From Poetry to History. Selected Papers — Woodman, A.J.

From Prehistoric Villages to Cities: Settlement Aggregation and Community Transformation — Lindeman, Michael

From Rationality to Equality — Sterba, James P.

From Scratch. E-book Review — Goodman, Rachel

c From Sea to Shining Sea (Illus. by Arciero, Susan) — Gingrich, Callista

From Selma to Montgomery: The Long March to Freedom — Combs, Barbara Harris

From Shame to Sin: The Christian Transformation of Sexual Morality in Late Antiquity — Harper, Kyle

From Slavery to the Cooperative Common Wealth: Labor and Republican Liberty in the Nineteenth Century — Gourevitch, Alex

From Small Screen to Vinyl: A Guide to Television Stars Who Made Records, 1950-2000 — Leszczak, Bob

From Social Movement to Moral Market: How the Circuit Riders Sparked an IT Revolution and Created a Technology Market — McInerney, Paul-Brian

From Solidarity to Sellout: The Restoration of Capitalism in Poland — Kowalik, Tadeusz

From Solidarity to Sellout: The Restoration of Capitalism in Poland — Lewandowska, Eliza

From Stilettos to the Stock Exchange: Inside the Life of a Serial Entrepreneur — Aldatz, Tina

From Storefront to Monument: Tracing the Public History of the Black Museum Movement — Burns, Andrea A.

From Sugar to Revolution: Women's Visions of Haiti, Cuba, and the Dominican Republic — Chancy, Myriam J.A.

c From Sunlight to Blockbuster Movie: An Energy Journey through the World of Light — Solway, Andrew

From Teilhard to Omega: Co-creating an Unfinished Universe — Delio, Ilia

From the Army to College: Transitioning from the Service to Higher Education — Ventrone, Jillian

From the Author's Private Collection — Amling, Eric

From the Dead — Billingham, Mark

From the Forest to the Sea: Emily Carr in British Columbia — Milroy, Sarah

From the Great Wall to the Great Collider: China and the Quest to Uncover the Inner Workings of the Universe — Nadis, Steve

From the Molecular World: A Nineteenth-Century Science Fantasy — Kopp, Hermann

From the Mouths of Dogs: What Our Pets Teach Us about Life, Death, and Being Human — Hollars, B.J.

From the New World: Poems 1976-2014 — Graham, Jorie

c From the Notebooks of a Middle School Princess (Read by McInerney, Kathleen). Audiobook Review — Cabot, Meg

c From the Notebooks of a Middle School Princess (Illus. by Cabot, Meg) — Cabot, Meg

From the Other Side of the World: Extraordinary Entrepreneurs, Unlikely Places — Bayrasli, Elmira

From the Outside In: Suburban Elites, Third-Sector Organizations, and the Reshaping of Philadelphia — Adams, Carolyn T.

From the Outside In: Suburban Elites, Third Sector Organizations, and the Reshaping of Philadelphia — Adams, Carolyn T.

From the Poplars — Nicholson, Cecily

From the Score to the Stage: An Illustrated History of Continental Opera Production and Staging — Baker, Evan

From the Source: Italy: Authentic Recipes from the People That Know Them Best — Lonely Planet

From the Start — Tagg, Melissa

From the West Coast to the Western Front: British Columbians and the Great War — Forsythe, Mark

From the Yoga Mat to the Corner Office — Furth, Yvonne James

From These Hands: A Journey along the Coffee Trail — McCurry, Steve

From These Honored Dead: Historical Archaeology of the American Civil War — Geier, Clarence R.

From These Honored Dead: Historical Archaeology of the American Civil War — Scott, Douglas D.

y From This Moment — Barnholdt, Lauren

From Tyrant to Philosopher-King: A Literary History of Alexander the Great in Medieval and Early Modern England — Stone, Charles Russell

From Vatican II to Pope Francis — Crowley, Paul

From War to Post-War. Reflections on the End of the Second World War

y From Where I Watch You — Grogan, Shannon

From Willow Creek to Sacred Heart: Rekindling My Love for Catholicism — Haw, Chris

From Words to Deeds: The Effectiveness of Preaching in the Late Middle Ages — Muzzarelli, Maria Giuseppina

From Working to Wisdom: The Adventures and Dreams of Older Americans — Hare, Brendan

Fromm und Politisch: Christliche Anti-Apartheid-Gruppen und die Transformation des Westdeutschen Protestantismus 1970-1990 — Tripp, Sebastian

Front Line Public Diplomacy: How US Embassies Communicate with Foreign Publics — Rugh, William A.

y Front Lines — Grant, Michael

Front Porch Politics: The Forgotten Heyday of American Activism in the 1970s and 1980s — Foley, Michael Stewart

Front Runner — Francis, Felix

The Front Seat Passenger — Garnier, Pascal

Frontier Boosters: Port Townsend and the Culture of Development in the American West, 1850-1895 — Naylor, Elaine

Frontier Doctors and Snake Oil Peddlers: A Journal of Early Medical Procedures — Pryor, Alton

Frontier Seaport: Detroit's Transformation into an Atlantic Entrepot — Cangany, Catherine

Frontiers of Possession: Spain and Portugal in Europe and the Americas — Herzog, Tamar

Frontiers of Violence: Conflict and Identity in Ulster and Upper Silesia, 1918-1922 — Wilson, Timothy

Frontline Ukraine: Crisis in the Borderlands — Sakwa, Richard

Fronto: Selected Letters — Davenport, Caillan

Frost: That Was the Life That Was: The Authorised Biography — Hegarty, Neil

y Frostborn (Read by Tassone, Fabio). Audiobook Review — Anders, Lou

c Frostborn (Illus. by Gerard, Justin) — Anders, Lou

Frosted Cowboy — Ross, Charlene

y Frosted Kisses — Hepler, Heather

y Frostfire — Hocking, Amanda

c Frozen Charlotte — Bell, Alex

c Frozen Floppies (Illus. by Adams, Mark Wayne) — Hope, John

c A Frozen Heart — Rudnick, Elizabeth

Frozen in Amber — Ames, Phyllis

y Frozen in Time: Clarence Birdseye's Outrageous Idea about Frozen Food — Kurlansky, Mark

c Frozen Solid by Mr. Freeze! (Illus. by Jones, Christopher) — Matheny, Bill

y Frozen: The Junior Novelization (Read by Arndt, Andi). Audiobook Review

c Frozen Treats (Illus. by Water, Erica-Jane) — Perelman, Helen

c Frozen Wild: How Animals Survive in the Coldest Places on Earth (Illus. by Arnosky, Jim) — Arnosky, Jim

Fruhneuzeitliche Bildungssysteme im Interkonfessionellen Vergleich. Inhalte - Infrastrukturen - Netzwerke

The Fruit of Liberty: Political Culture in the Florentine Renaissance, 1480-1550 — Baker, Nicholas Scott

c Fruits — Lassieur, Allison

c The Fruits We Eat (Illus. by Gibbons, Gail) — Gibbons, Gail

The Fruits We Eat — Gibbons, Gail

Fu-Go: The Curious History of Japan's Balloon Bomb Attack on America — Coen, Ross

Fu-go: The Curious History of Japan's Balloon Bomb Attack on America — Coen, Ross Allen

Fuckology: Critical Essays on John Money's Diagnostic Concepts — Downing, Lisa

y Fuel under Fire — Goldstein, Margaret J.

y Fuel under Fire: Petroleum and Its Perils — Goldstein, Margaret J.

Fueled by Failure: Using Detours and Defeats to Power Progress — Bloom, Jeremy

Fueling the Gilded Age: Railroads, Miners, and Disorder in Pennsylvania Coal Country — Arnold, Andrew B.

c The Fugitive (Read by Thomas, Richard). Audiobook Review — Grisham, John

The Fugitives — Sorrentino, Christopher

Full Belly: Good Eats for a Healthy Pregnancy — Desmond, Tara Mataraza

Full-Body Fitness for Runners — McLaurin, Thad H.

The Full Catastrophe: Travels among the New Greek Ruins — Angelos, James

c Full Cicada Moon — Hilton, Marilyn

Full Contact — Castille, Sarah

Full-Court Quest: The Girls from Fort Shaw Indian School, Basketball Champions of the World — Peavy, Linda

Full Force and Effect (Read by Brick, Scott). Audiobook Review — Greaney, Mark

Full Force and Effect — Greaney, Mark

A Full Life: Reflections at Ninety (Illus. by Carter, Jimmy) (Read by Carter, Jimmy). Audiobook Review — Carter, Jimmy

A Full Life: Reflections at Ninety — Carter, Jimmy

c The Full Moon at the Napping House (Illus. by Wood, Don) — Wood, Audrey

Full Moon Stages: Personal Notes from 50 Years of The Living Theatre — Malina, Judith

c Full Speed Ahead! How Fast Things Go (Illus. by Cruschiform) — *Cruschiform*
c Fun and Festive Fall Crafts: Leaf Rubbings, Dancing Scarecrows, and Pinecone Turkeys — *McGee, Randel*
c Fun and Festive Spring Crafts: Flower Puppets, Bunny Masks, and Mother's Day Pop-Up Cards — *McGee, Randel*
c Fun and Festive Summer Crafts: Tie-Dyed Shirts, Bug Cages, and Sand Castles — *McGee, Randel*
c Fun and Festive Winter Crafts: Snow Globes, Groundhog Puppets, and Fairy Masks — *McGee, Randel*
Fun and Fruit (Illus. by Pijpers, Edie) — *Barahona, Maria Teresa*
c The Fun Book of Scary Stuff (Illus. by Yum, Hyewon) — *Jenkins, Emily*
Fun City: John Lindsay, Joe Namath, and How Sports Saved New York in the 1960s — *Deveney, Sean*
c Fun in the Sun (Illus. by Catrow, David) — *Catrow, David*
The Fun Stuff and Other Essays — *Wood, James*
c Fun Things to Do with Cardboard Tubes — *Ventura, Marne*
c Fun Things to Do with Paper Cups and Plates — *Laughlin, Kara L.*
c Fun with Ed and Fred (Illus. by Hodson, Ben) — *Bolger, Kevin*
Functional Behavior Assessment for People with Autism: Making Sense of Seemingly Senseless Behavior, 2d ed. — *Glasberg, Beth A.*
Functional Inefficiency: The Unexpected Benefits of Wasting Time and Money — *Wenz, Peter S.*
Fundamentals of Collection Development and Management, 3rd ed. — *Johnson, Peggy*
Fundamentals of Technical Services — *Sandstrom, John*
The Funding of State and Local Pensions: 2014-2018 — *Munnell, Alicia H.*
Fundraiser A: My Fight for Freedom and Justice — *Blagojevich, Robert*
Funeral Games in Honor of Arthur Vincent Lourie — *Moricz, Klara*
Funeral Hotdish — *Bommersbach, Jana*
The Funerary Speech for John Chrysostom — *Barnes, Timothy David*
Funf Monate in Berlin: Briefe von Edgar N. Johnson aus dem Jahre 1946 — *Breunig, Werner*
c The FunGkins: The Battle for Halladon — *Gray, C. Raymond*
c Funky Little Monkey (Illus. by Davis, Christopher) — *Buttar, Debbie*
c Funniest Bone Animal Jokes Series (Illus. by Mitchell, Susan K.) — *LaRoche, Amelia*
The Funniest One in the Room: The Lives and Legends of Del Close — *Johnson, Kim*
c Funny Bones: Posada and His Day of the Dead Calaveras (Illus. by Tonatiuh, Duncan) — *Tonatiuh, Duncan*

c Funny Face, Sunny Face (Illus. by Beardshaw, Rosalind) — *Symes, Sally*
c Funny Families — *Norman, Mark*
Funny Girl (Read by Fielding, Emma). Audiobook Review — *Hornby, Nick*
Funny Girl — *Hornby, Nick*
y Funny Ha-Ha Funny Peculiar — *Astley, Neil*
Funny-Hahas — *Gudlat, Ted*
Funny on Purpose: The Definitive Guide to an Unpredictable Career in Comedy — *Randazzo, Joe*
c A Funny Thing Happened on the Way to School ... (Illus. by Chaud, Benjamin) — *Cali, Davide*
Funnybooks: The Improbable Glories of the Best American Comic Books — *Barrier, Michael*
Fur den christlichen und sozialen Volksstaat: Die Badische Zentrumspartei in der Weimarer Republik — *Kitzing, Michael*
c Fur, Fins, and Feathers: Abraham Dee Bartlett and the Invention of the Modern Zoo (Illus. by Maxwell, Cassandre) — *Maxwell, Cassandre*
Furious Cool: Richard Pryor and the World That Made Him (Read by Graham, Dion). Audiobook Review — *Henry, Joe*
Furiously Happy: A Funny Book about Horrible Things (Read by Lawson, Jenny). Audiobook Review — *Lawson, Jenny*
Furiously Happy: A Funny Book about Horrible Things — *Lawson, Jenny*
Furnitecture: Funiture That Transforms Space — *Yudina, Anna*
c Furs, Fins, and Feathers: Abraham Dee Bartlett and the Invention of the Modern Zoo (Illus. by Maxwell, Cassandre) — *Maxwell, Cassandre*
Furst und Furstin als Kunstler. Herrschaftliches Kunstlertum zwischen Habitus, Norm und Neigung Furstliche Erziehung und Ausbildung im Spatmittelalterlichen Reich — *Musegades, Benjamin*
y Fury — *James, Steven*
The Fury (Read by Dean, Robertson). Audiobook Review — *Gericke, Shane*
y Fury (Read by Podehl, Nick). Audiobook Review — *James, Steven*
A Fury in the Words: Love and Embarrassment in Shakespeare's Venice — *Berger, Harry, Jr.*
The Fury — *Gericke, Shane*
Fusarium: Genomics, Molecular and Cellular Biology — *Brown, Daren W.*
c The Future Architect's Handbook — *Beck, Barbara*
Future Arctic: Field Notes from a World on the Edge — *Struzik, Edward*
Future Crimes: Everything is Connected, Everyone is Vulnerable and What We Can Do About It — *Goodman, Marc*
Future Crimes: Everything is Connected, Everyone is Vulnerable and What We Can Do About It (Read by Dean, Robertson). Audiobook Review — *Goodman, Marc*

Future Crimes: Everything is Connected, Everyone is Vulnerable and What We Can Do About It — *Goodman, Marc*
The Future Falls — *Huff, Tanya*
The Future for Creative Writing — *Harper, Graeme*
Future Imperfect — *Chambers, M. Scott*
The Future Is Not What It Used To Be: Climate Change and Energy Scarcity — *Friedrichs, Jorg*
The Future of Evangelical Theology: Soundings from the Asian American Diaspora — *Yong, Amos*
The Future of Illusion: Political Theology and Early Modern Texts — *Kahn, Victoria*
The Future of Social Movement Research: Dynamics, Mechanisms, and Processes — *Stekelenburg, Jacquelien van*
The Future of the African American Church: An Invitation to Dialogue — *Watkins, Ralph Basui*
The Future of the Brain: Essays by the World's Leading Neuroscientists — *Marcus, Gary*
The Future of the Catholic Church with Pope Francis — *Wills, Garry*
The Future of the Mind: The Scientific Quest to Understand, Enhance, and Empower the Mind (Read by Chin, Feodor). Audiobook Review — *Kaku, Michio*
The Future of the Music Business: How to Succeed with the New Digital Technologies — *Gordon, Steve*
The Future of the Professions: How Technology Will Transform the Work of Human Experts — *Susskind, Richard*
The Future of the World Trading System: Asian Perspectives — *Baldwin, Richard E.*
The Future of Trauma Theory: Contemporary Literary and Cultural Criticism — *Buelens, Gert*
The Future of Violence: Robots and Germs, Hackers and Drones: Confronting a New Age of Threat — *Wittes, Benjamin*
y Future Perfect — *Larsen, Jen*
Future Promotheus II: Revolution, Successions & Resurrections — *Erickson, J.M.*
c Future Ratboy and the Attack of the Killer Robot Grannies — *Smith, Jim*
Future War: The Re-Enchantment of War in the Twenty-First Century — *Coker, Christopher*
The Future We Want: Radical Ideas for the New Century — *Leonard, Sarah*
Futures of Modernity: Challenges for Cosmopolitical Thought and Practice — *Heinlein, Michael*
Futures of Surrealism: Myth, Science Fiction and Fantastic Art in France, 1936-1969 — *Parkinson, Gavin*
Futures Past: 1926: The Birth of Modern Science Fiction — *Emerson, Jim*
Futuristic Violence and Fancy Suits — *Wong, David*
Futuro Esquecido: A Recepcao da Ficcao Cyberpunk na America Latina. E-book Review — *Londero, Rudolfo Rurato*
y Fuzzy Forensics: DNA Fingerprinting Gets Wild — *Carmichael, L.E.*
y Fuzzy Mud (Read by McInerney, Kathleen). Audiobook Review — *Sachar, Louis*
y Fuzzy Mud — *Sachar, Louis*

G

c **Gabby Duran and the Unsittables (Illus. by Conners, Daryle)** — *Allen, Elise*
c **Gabby Duran and the Unsittables (Illus. by Connors, Daryle)** — *Allen, Elise*
c **Gabby Duran and the Unsittables** — *Allen, Elise*
c **Gabe: The Dog Who Sniffs Out Danger** — *Feldman, Thea*
y **Gabi: A Girl in Pieces** — *Quintero, Isabel*
Gabriel: A Poem — *Hirsch, Edward*
c **Gabriel Finley and the Raven's Riddle (Read by Goldstrom, Michael). Audiobook Review** — *Hagen, George*
c **Gabriel Finley and the Raven's Riddle (Illus. by Bakal, Scott)** — *Hagen, George*
c **Gabriel Finley and the Raven's Riddle** — *Hagen, George*
Gabrielle Petit: The Death and Life of a Female Spy in the First World War — *Schaepdrijver, Sophie de*
y **Gabriel's Clock** — *Pashley, Hilton*
Gadamer and the Transmission of History — *Veith, Jerome*
c **Gadzooks! A Comically Quirky Audio Book (Read by several narrators). Audiobook Review** — *Park, Adele*
Gaga Feminism: Sex, Gender, and the End of Normal — *Halberstam, J. Jack*
Galactic Encounters: Our Majestic and Evolving Star-System, from the Big Bang to Time's End — *Sheehan, William*
Galadria: Peter Huddleston & The Mists of the Three Lakes — *Leon, Miguel Lopez de*
c **Galapagos Tortoises: Long-Lived Giant Reptiles** — *Hirsch, Rebecca E.*
Galatians — *Moo, Douglas J.*
Galatians — *Oakes, Peter*
Galaxia — *Skanavis, Alex Andor*
c **Galaxies** — *Riggs, Kate*
c **Galaxies and Stars** — *Graham, Ian*
The Galaxy Game — *Lord, Karen*
The Galaxy Pirates: Hunt for the Pyxis — *Ferraris, Zoe*
c **Galaxy's Most Wanted (Illus. by Edwards, Nick)** — *Kloepfer, John*
y **Galgorithm** — *Karo, Aaron*
Galileo Interviewed — *Shea, William R.*
Galileo: Science and Faith — *Carroll, William*
Galileo's Middle Finger: Heretics, Activists, and the Search for Justice in Science — *Dreger, Alice*
Galileo's Reading — *Hall, Crystal*
Galileo's Telescope: A European Story — *Camerota, Michele*
Galileo's Telescope — *Bucciantini, Massimo*
The Gallery of Lost Species — *Berkhout, Nina*
Gallic War — *Edwards, H.J.*
Gallipoli 1915 — *Murray, Joseph*
Gallipoli: A Soldier's Story — *Beecroft, Arthur*
Gallipoli — *FitzSimons, Peter*
Gallipoli — *Moorehead, Alan*
Gallipoli: The Dardanelles Disaster in Soldiers' Words and Photographs — *van Emden, Richard*
y **Gallipoli: The Landing (Illus. by Gardiner, Mal)** — *Dolan, Hugh*
c **Galloping through History: Amazing True Horse Stories** — *MacLeod, Elizabeth*
The Gambler — *Wahlberg, Mark*
y **Gambling Addiction** — *Wilcox, Christine*
Gambling in America: An Encyclopedia of History, Issues, and Society, 2d ed. — *Thompson, William N.*
Gambling on Ore: The Nature of Metal Mining in the United States, 1860-1910 — *Curtis, Kent A.*
Gambrelli and the Prosecutor — *Giliotti, Laurence*
y **The Game** — *McGill, Leslie*

c **Game Changer: John McLendon and the Secret Game (Illus. by DuBurke, Randy)** — *Coy, John*
y **Game Changer** — *Bowler, Tim*
c **Game-Day Youth: Learning Football's Lingo** — *Bohnert, Suzy Beamer*
The Game for Real — *Weiner, Richard*
The Game: Inside the Secret World of Major League Baseball's Power Brokers — *Pessah, Jon*
The Game Must Go On: Hank Greenberg, Pete Gray, and the Great Days of Baseball on the Home Front in WWII — *Klima, John*
The Game of 100 Ghosts — *Watada, Terry*
c **Game of Flames** — *Wasserman, Robin*
c **The Game of Lines (Illus. by Tullet, Herve)** — *Tullet, Herve*
y **The Game of Lives** — *Dashner, James*
y **The Game of Love and Death** — *Brockenbrough, Martha*
Game of Mirrors — *Camilleri, Andrea*
The Game of Probability: Literature and Calculation from Pascal to Kleist — *Campe, Rudiger*
y **Game of Queens** — *Edghill, India*
c **The Game of Shapes** — *Tullet, Herve*
A Game of Their Own: Voices of Contemporary Women in Baseball — *Ring, Jennifer*
A Game of Thrones, 5 vols. (Read by Dotrice, Roy). Audiobook Review — *Martin, George R.R.*
c **The Game of Tops and Tails (Illus. by Tullet, Herve)** — *Tullet, Herve*
c **Game On** — *Woodman, Ned*
Game, Set and Match: Secret Weapons of the World's Top Tennis Players — *Hodgkinson, Mark*
Game, Set, Match: Billie Jean King and the Revolution in Women's Sports — *Ware, Susan*
y **Game Seven** — *Volponi, Paul*
y **Game Time, Mallory! (Illus. by Kalis, Jennifer)** — *Friedman, Laurie*
Gamelife: A Memoir — *Clune, Michael W.*
y **The Gamers** — *Little, Shauna Sare*
The Game's Not Over: In Defense of Football — *Easterbrook, Gregg*
y **The Games of Lives** — *Dashner, James*
y **Games Wizards Play** — *Duane, Diane*
Gaming at the Edge: Sexuality and Gender at the Margins of Gamer Culture — *Shaw, Adrienne*
Gandhi before India — *Guha, Ramachandra*
Gandhian Nonviolent Struggle and Untouchability in South India: The 1924-25 Vykom Satyagraha and Mechanisms of Change — *King, Mary Elizabeth*
c **Ganesha: The Curse on the Moon (Illus. by Nagulakonda, Rajesh)** — *Dutta, Sourav*
Gang Life in Two Cities: An Insider's Journey — *Duran, Robert J.*
Gangland Chicago: Criminality and Lawlessness in the Windy City — *Lindberg, Richard*
Gangs of Shadow — *O'Neill, Michael*
Gangster Warlords: Drug Dollars, Killing Fields, and the New Politics of Latin America — *Grillo, Ioan*
Gangsterismo: The United States, Cuba, and the Mafia; 1933 to 1966 — *Colhoun, Jack*
Gangsterland (Read by Heller, Johnny). Audiobook Review — *Goldberg, Tod*
Gangsterland — *Goldberg, Tod*
The Gap of Time: The Winter's Tale Retold — *Winterson, Jeanette*
Gap Year Girl: A Baby Boomer Adventure across 21 Countries — *Bohr, Marianne C.*
Gap Year: How Delaying College Changes People in Ways the World Needs — *O'Shea, Joseph*
The Garage: Automobile and Building Innovation in America's Early Auto Age — *Jakle, John A.*
Garbageman — *Dean, Erik*

Garbo's Last Stand — *Miller, Jon James*
Garden City: Work, Rest, and the Art of Being Human — *Comer, John Mark*
Garden Inspirations — *Moss, Charlotte*
c **The Garden Monster (Illus. by Palmisciano, Diane)** — *Giff, Patricia Reilly*
Garden of Dreams and Desires — *Painter, Kristen*
Garden of Lies (Read by Underwood, Louise Jane). Audiobook Review — *Quick, Amanda*
Garden of Lies — *Quick, Amanda*
c **The Garden of Monsieur Monet (Illus. by Ascari, Giancarlo)** — *Valenti, Pia*
c **The Garden of Monsieur Monet (Illus. by Valentinis, Pia)** — *Valentinis, Pia*
The Gardener — *Brykczynski, Jan*
The Gardener's Garden — *Cox, Madison*
The Gardener's Guide to Weather and Climate: How to Understand the Weather and Make It Work for You — *Allaby, Michael*
Gardening with Less Water: Low-Tech, Low-Cost Techniques: Use Up to 90 Percent Less Water in Your Garden — *Bainbridge, David A.*
Gardening with the Moon and Stars — *Sentier, Elen*
Gardening with Young Children — *Starbuck, Sara*
Gardens of Awe and Folly: A Traveler's Journal on the Meaning of Life and Gardening — *Swift, Vivian*
Gardens of Eden: Long Island's Early Twentieth-Century Planned Communities — *MacKay, Robert B.*
The Gardens of the British Working Class — *Willes, Margaret*
c **Gargoyle Hall (Illus. by Kelly, John)** — *Sage, Angie*
c **Gargoyles Gone AWOL (Illus. by Horne, Sarah)** — *Beauvais, Clementine*
Garibaldi — *Possieri, Andrea*
c **Garter Snakes** — *Petrie, Kristin*
Gary Sees History: A Child's Journey — *Hooker Jr., Gary*
y **Gasp** — *McMann, Lisa*
Gatecrashing Paradise: Misadventures in the Real Maldives — *Chesshyre, Tom*
The Gatekeeper's Son — *Fladmark, C.R.*
The Gates of Europe: A History of Ukraine — *Plokhy, Serhii*
The Gates of Evangeline — *Young, Hester*
Gates of Fire — *Pressfield, Steven*
Gates of Tears: The Holocaust in the Lublin District — *Silberklang, David*
The Gates of the Alamo — *Harrigan, Stephen*
c **The Gateway 1: The Four Fingered Man** — *Jones, Cerberus*
c **The Gateway 2: The Warriors of Brin-Hask** — *Jones, Cerberus*
Gateway to Freedom: The Hidden History of the Underground Railroad (Read by Jackson, J.D.). Audiobook Review — *Foner, Eric*
Gateway to Freedom: The Hidden History of the Underground Railroad — *Foner, Eric*
Gateway to the Confederacy: New Perspectives on the Chickamauga and Chattanooga Campaigns, 1862-1863 — *Jones, Evan C.*
The Gateways Haggadah: A Seder for the Whole FamilyThe Gateways Haggadah: A Seder for the Whole Family — *Redner, Rebecca*
Gather the Bones. E-book Review — *Stuart, Alison*
Gathering Carrageen: A Return to Donegal — *Connell, Monica*
y **Gathering Darkness** — *Rhodes, Morgan*
Gathering Deep — *Maxwell, Lisa*
Gathering Evidence — *Hughes, Caoilinn*
y **Gathering Frost** — *Davis, Kaitlyn*
A Gathering of Shadows — *Schwab, V.E.*

Gathering Prey — Sandford, John
Gathering Together: The Shawnee People through Diaspora and Nationhood, 1600-1870 — Lakomaki, Sami
Gay and Catholic: Accepting My Sexuality, Finding Community, Living My Faith — Tushnet, Eve
Gay Berlin: Birthplace of a Modern Identity — Beachy, Robert
Gay Directors, Gay Films? Pedro Almodovar, Terence Davies, Todd Haynes, Gus Van Sant, John Waters — Levy, Emanuel
Gay Is Good: The Life and Letters of Gay Rights Pioneer Franklin Kameny — Long, Michael G.
y Gay & Lesbian History for Kids: The Century-Long Struggle for LGBT Rights, with 21 Activities — Pohlen, Jerome
Gay Novels of Britain, Ireland and the Commonwealth, 1881-1981: A Reader's Guide — Gunn, Drewey Wayne
The Gay Revolution: The Story of the Struggle — Faderman, Lillian
Gayrabian Nights — Townsend, Johnny
Gaza: A History — Filiu, Jean-Pierre
Gaza, Wyoming — Walls, Seth Colter
GBH — Lewis, Ted
Gdansk: Miasto od Nowa — Perkowski, Piotr
y Gearhead — McGill, Leslie
Gearing Up for Learning beyond K-12 — Alexander, Bryan
The Geckos of Bellapais: Memories of Cyprus — Sartorius, Joachim
c Geckos — Riggs, Kate
Gedenken und (k)ein Ende - Was bleibt vom Jahr 2014? Das Gedenkjahr 1914/2014 und sein historiografisches Vermachtnis
c Gedeon au magasin — Wall, Laura
y Geek Girl — Smale, Holly
Geek Heresy: Rescuing Social Change from the Cult of Technology — Toyama, Kentaro
Geek Knits: Over 30 Projects for Fantasy Fanatics, Science Fiction Fiends, and Knitting Nerds — Carr, Toni
Geek Physics: Surprising Answers to the Planet's Most Interesting Questions, 2d ed. — Allain, Rhett
Geek Sublime: The Beauty of Code, the Code of Beauty (Read by Shah, Neil). Audiobook Review — Chandra, Vikram
Gegenstucke: Populares Wissen im transatlantischen Vergleich — Heumann, Ina
Geheimdienste: Netzwerke, Seilschaften und Patronage in Nachrichtendienstlichen Institutionen Geis — O'Reilly, Caitriona
Geldlose Zeiten und Uberfullte Kassen: Sparen, Leihen und Vererben in der Landlichen Gesellschaft Westfalens (1830-1866). — Bracht, Johannes
Gemeinschaftsdenken in Europa: Das Gesellschaftskonzept 'Volksheim' im Vergleich 1900-1938 — Lehnert, Detlef
c Gemma & Gus (Illus. by Dunrea, Olivier) — Dunrea, Olivier
Gems & Crystals: From One of the World's Great Collections, rev. ed. — Harlow, George E.
Gender and Authority in Medieval Society
Gender and Genre: German Women Write the French Revolution — Hilger, Stephanie M.
Gender and Global Justice — Jaggar, Alison M.
Gender and Justice: Violence, Intimacy, and Community in Fin-de-Siecle Paris — Ferguson, Eliza Earle
Gender and Law in the Japanese Imperium — Burns, Susan L.
Gender and Modernity in Central Europe: The Austro-Hungarian Monarchy and its Legacy — Schwartz, Agatha
Gender and Race in Antebellum Popular Culture — Roth, Sarah N.
Gender and Song in Early Modern England — Dunn, Leslie C.
Gender and the Long Postwar: The United States and the Two Germanys, 1945-1989 — Hagemann, Karen
Gender and Ventriloquism in Victorian and Neo-Victorian Fiction: Passionate Puppets — Davies, Helen
Gender and Welfare in Mexico: The Consolidation of a Postrevolutionary State — Sanders, Nichole
Gender Bias in Mystery and Romance Novel Publishing: Mimicking Masculinity and Femininity — Faktorovich, Anna
Gender Hurts: A Feminist Analysis of the Politics of Transgenderism — Jeffreys, Sheila
Gender in Chinese Music — Harris, Rachel

Gender in Geschichtsdidaktik und Geschichtsunterricht. Einig in der Kontroverse
Gender, Manumission, and the Roman Freedwoman — Perry, M.J.
Gender Matters: Discourses of Violence in Early Modern Literature and Arts — Wade, Mara R.
Gender Matters: Discourses of Violence in Early Modern Literature and the Arts — Wade, Mara R.
Gender, Nation and the Formation of the Twentieth-Century Mexican Literary Canon — Bowskill, Sarah
Gender - Nation - Emancipation. Women and Families in the 'Long' Nineteenth Century in Italy and Germany
Gender on the Edge: Transgender, Gay, and Other Pacific Islanders — Besnier, Niko
The Gender Politics of the Namibian Liberation Struggle — Akawa, Martha
y The Gender Quest Workbook: A Guide for Teens and Young Adults Exploring Gender Identity — Testa, Rylan Jay
Gender Uberall!? Beitrage zur Interdisziplinaren Geschlechterforschung — Fellner, Astrid M.
Gender, Violence, and Human Security — Tripp, Aili Mari
Gender, War, and Conflict — Sjoberg, Laura
Gendered Commodity Chains: Seeing Women's Work and Households in Global Production — Dunaway, Wilma A.
Gendered Identities in Bernard of Clairvaux's Sermons on The Song of Songs: Performing the Bride — Engh, Line Cecilie
Gendered Perceptions of Florentine Last Supper Frescoes, c. 1350-1490 — Hiller, Diana
Gendered Resistance: Women, Slavery, and the Legacy of Margaret Garner — Frederickson, Mary E.
"Gendered Voices" - Neue Perspektiven auf Digitale Zeitzeug_Innen-Archive
Gendering Science Fiction Films: Invaders from the Suburbs — George, Susan A.
Gene Jockeys: Life Science and the Rise of Biotech Enterprise — Rasmussen, Nicolas
Gene Mapper — Fujii, Taiyo
Gene.sys: Magigate Returns — Gourgey, Bill
The Gene, the Clinic and the Family: Diagnosing Dysmorphology, Reviving Medical Dominance — Latimer, Joanna
Genealogical Fictions: Cultural Periphery and Historical Change in the Modern Novel — Welge, Jobst
Genealogies Philosophique, Politique, et Imaginaire de la Technoscience — Hottois, Gilbert
The Genealogy of a Gene: Patents, HIV/AIDS, and Race — Jackson, Myles W.
Genealogy of the Tragic: Greek Tragedy and German Philosophy — Billings, Joshua
The General and the Genius: Groves and Oppenheimer: The Unlikely Partnership That Built the Atom Bomb — Kunetka, James W.
The General and the Politician: Dwight Eisenhower, Richard Nixon, and American Politics — Malsberger, John W.
The General Councils of Latin Christendom: From Constantinople IV (869/870) to Lateran V (1512-1517). — Istituto per le scienze religiose Bologna
General Gordon Granger: The Savior of Chickamauga and the Man behind "Juneteenth" — Conner, Robert C.
General Paul von Lettow-Vorbeck: My Life — Pierce, James
General Percy Kirke and the Later Stuart Army — Childs, John
A General Theory of Oblivion — Agualusa, Jose Eduardo
The General's Briefer — Woolsey, Robert J.
y Generals Die in Bed — Harrison, Charles Yale
Generals of the Army: Marshall, MacArthur, Eisenhower, Arnold, Bradley — Willbanks, James H.
The Generals: Patton, MacArthur, Marshall, and the Winning of World War II — Groom, Winston
The General's Slow Retreat: Chile after Pinochet — Spooner, Mary Helen
Generation — McGrath, Paula
A Generation Removed: The Fostering and Adoption of Indigenous Children in the Postwar World — Jacobs, Margaret D.
Generation Unbound: Drifting into Sex and Parenthood without Marriage — Sawhill, Isabell
Generation und Medizin. Generationen in der Sozialgeschichte der Medizin

Generation Vet: Composition, Student Veterans, and the Post-9/11 University — Doe, Sue
Generation Z: Their Voices, Their Lives — Combi, Chloe
Generational Conflict and University Reform: Oxford in the Age of Revolution — Ellis, Heather
Generic Histories of German Cinema: Genre and Its Deviations — Fisher, Jaimey
A Generous and Merciful Enemy: Life for German Prisoners of War during the American Revolution — Krebs, Daniel
The Generous Dead — Mann, Sandra
Genes et l'outre-mer: Actes notaries de Famagouste et d'autres localites du Proche-Orient, XIVe-XVe s. — Balard, Michel
Genesis: In the Beginning — Bergant, Dianne
Genesis of the Salk Institute: The Epic of Its Founders. — Bourgeois, Suzanne
Genesis: Truman, American Jews, and the Origins of the Arab/Israeli Conflict — Judis, John B.
Genetic Explanations: Sense and Nonsense — Krimsky, Sheldon
Genetics and Philosophy: An Introduction — Griffiths, Paul
Genetics and the Unsettled Past: The Collision of DNA, Race, and History — Wailoo, Keith
c Genetics Expert Joanna L. Kelley — Waxman, Laura Hamilton
Genghis Khan: His Conquests, His Empire, His Legacy — McLynn, Frank
Genghis Khan: The Man Who Conquered the World — McLynn, Frank
Genius at Play: The Curious Mind of John Horton Conway — Roberts, Siobhan
Genius in France: An Idea and its Uses — Jefferson, Ann
The Genius of Democracy: Fictions of Gender and Citizenship in the United States, 1860-1945 — Olwell, Victoria
The Genius of Earth Day: How a 1970 Teach-In Unexpectedly Made the First Green Generation — Rome, Adam
Genius, Power and Magic: A Cultural History of Germany from Goethe to Wagner — Cavaliero, Roderick
y Genius! The Most Astonishing Inventions of All Time — Kespert, Deborah
Genius, vol. 1: Siege (Illus. by Richardson, Afua) — Bernardin, Marc
Genoa — Metcalf, Paul
Genoa, "La Superba": The Rise and Fall of Merchant Pirate Superpower — Walton, Nicholas
Genocide on the Drina River — Becirevic, Edina
Genova y la Monarquia Hispanica (1528-1713). — Herrero Sanchez, Manuel
The Gentle Art of Murder: A Dorothy Martin Mystery — Dams, Jeanne M.
The Gentle Art of Murder — Dams, Jeanne M.
Gentle Energy Touch: The Beginner's Guide to Hands-on Healing — Savin, Barbara E.
Gentleman Jole and the Red Queen — Bujold, Lois McMaster
A Gentleman's Game — Romain, Theresa
y Genuine Sweet — Harkey, Faith
Genuss als Politikum: Kaffeekonsum in beiden deutschen Staaten — Sigmund, Monika
Geo Power: Stay Warm, Keep Cool and Save Money with Geothermal Heating and Cooling — Lloyd, Donal Blaise
Geographical Knowledge and Imperial Culture in the Early Modern Ottoman Empire — Emiralioglu, Pinar
The Geographical Unconscious — Loukaki, Argyro
Geographies of Liberation: The Making of an Afro-Arab Political Imaginary — Lubin, Alex
Geographies of the Holocaust — Knowles, Anne Kelly
Geographies of the Romantic North: Science, Antiquarianism, and Travel, 1790-1830 — Byrne, Angela
Geography and the Classical World: Unearthing Historical Geography's Forgotten Past — Koelsch, William A.
c Geography Matters in Ancient Egypt — Waldron, Melanie
c Geography Matters in the Inca Empire — Waldron, Melanie
The Geography of Genius: A Search for the World's Most Creative Places, from Ancient Athens to Silicon Valley — Weiner, Eric
Geography of Shame — Feola, Maryann
The Geography of Strabo: An English Translation, with Introduction and Notes — Roller, Duane W.

y   The Geography of You and Me — *Smith, Jennifer E.*
    The Geology of New Hampshire's White Mountains
        — *Eusden, J. Dykstra*
    The Geomancer — *Griffith, Clay*
    Geometric Knitting Patterns: A Sourcebook of Classic
        to Contemporary Designs — *Barrett, Tina*
    The Geometry of Desert — *Kagan, Shelly*
    Geopolitical Economy: After U.S. Hegemony,
        Globalization and Empire — *Desai, Radhika*
c   George (Read by Clayton, Jamie). Audiobook Review
        — *Clayton, Jamie*
c   George — *Gino, Alex*
    George Condo — *Baker, Simon*
    George Eliot and Intoxication — *McCormack, Kathleen*
    George Eliot in Society: Travels Abroad and Sundays
        at the Priory — *McCormack, Kathleen*
    George Frederick Bodley: And the Later Gothic
        Revival in Britain and America — *Hall, Michael*
    George Frideric Handel: A Life with Friends
        — *Harris, Ellen T.*
    George Harrison: Behind the Locked Door
        — *Thomson, Graeme*
c   George in the Dark (Illus. by Valentine, Madeline)
        — *Valentine, Madeline*
    George Liele's Life and Legacy: An Unsung Hero
        — *Shannon, David T., Sr.*
    George & Martha Washington: A Revolutionary
        Marriage — *Fraser, Flora*
    George Moore: Across Borders — *Huguet, Christine*
    George Moore: Dublin, Paris, Hollywood
        — *Montague, Conor*
    George Owen Squier: U.S. Army Major General,
        Inventor, Aviation Pioneer, Founder of Muzak
        — *Clark, Paul W.*
    George the Dog, John the Artist: A Rescue Story
        — *Dolan, John*
    George the Dog, John the Artist — *Dolan, John*
    George V: The Unexpected King — *Cannadine, David*
    George VI: The Dutiful King — *Ziegler, Philip*
    George W. Bush — *Mann, James*
    George Washington and the Half-King Chief
        Tanacharison: An Alliance That Began the French
        and Indian War — *Misencik, Paul R.*
y   George Washington Carver: A Life — *Vella, Christina*
c   George Washington — *Stevenson, Augusta*
    George Washington Written upon the Land — *Levy, Philip*
    George Washington's Journey: The President Forges a
        New Nation — *Breen, T.H.*
    George Whitefield: America's Spiritual Founding
        Father — *Kidd, Thomas S.*
    The Georges and the Jewels (Read by Goethals,
        Angela). Audiobook Review — *Smiley, Jane*
    Georges Florovsky and the Russian Religious
        Renaissance — *Gavriluyk, Paul L.*
    George's Grand Tour — *Vermalle, Caroline*
    Georges Seurat: The Art of Vision — *Foa, Michelle*
    The Georgetown Set: Friends and Rivals in Cold War
        Washington — *Herken, Gregg*
    Georgia Women: Their Lives and Times, vol. 2
        — *Clark, Kathleen Ann*
    Georgialina: A Southland as We Knew It — *Poland, Tom*
    Georgios Pachymeres, Philosophia, Book 5:
        Commentary in Aristotle's Meteorologica - Biblion
        Pempton, Ton Meteorikon — *Telelis, Ioannis*
c   Geotechnical Engineering and Earth's Materials and
        Processes — *Sjonger, Rebecca*
c   Gerbil, Uncurled (Illus. by Del Rizzo, Suzanne)
        — *Hughes, Alison*
    Gerholm Scholem in Deutschland: Zwischen
        Seelenverwandtschaft und Sprachlosigkeit
        — *Morgenstern, Matthias*
    'The Germ': Origins and Progenies of Pre-Raphaelite
        Interart Aesthetics — *Spinozzi, Paola*
    Germaine Dulac: A Cinema of Sensations — *Williams, Tami*
    German Autumn — *Dagerman, Stig*
    German Colonialism in a Global Age — *Naranch, Bradley*
    German Expansionism, Imperial Liberalism and the
        United States, 1776-1945 — *Guettel, Jens-Uwe*
    German Feminist Queer Crime Fiction: Politics,
        Justice and Desire — *Stewart, Faye*
    German Forces and the British Army: Interactions
        and Perceptions, 1742-1815 — *Wishon, Mark*
    The German Friend — *Larson, John W.*
    The German Genius: Europe's Third Renaissance
        — *Watson, Peter*
    The German Gothic Novel in Anglo-German
        Perspective — *Bridgwater, Patrick*

    German Immigrants, Race, and Citizenship in the
        Civil War Era — *Efford, Alison Clark*
    German Intellectuals and the Challenge of Democratic
        Renewal: Culture and Politics after 1945 — *Forner, Sean A.*
    German Literature as World Literature — *Beebee, Thomas Oliver*
    German Literature in a New Century: Trends,
        Traditions, Transitions, Transformations
        — *Gerstenberger, Katharina*
    German Philosophy, 1760-1860 — *Pinkard, Terry*
    German POWs, Der Ruf, and the Genesis of Group
        47: The Political Journey of Alfred Andersch and
        Hans Werner Richter — *Horton, Aaron D.*
    German Professionals in the United States: A
        Gendered Analysis of the Migration Decision of
        Highly Skilled Families — *Eich-Krohm, Astrid*
    The German Research Foundation, 1920-1970:
        Funding Poised between Science and Politics
        — *Walker, Mark*
    The German Right in the Weimar Republic: Studies
        in the History of German Conservatism,
        Nationalism, and Antisemitism — *Jones, Larry Eugen*
    German Romance V: Hartmann von Aue, Erec
        — *Edwards, Cyril*
    The German Roots of Nineteenth-Century American
        Theology — *Aubert, Annette G.*
    German through English Eyes: A History of Language
        Teaching and Learning in Britain 1500-2000
        — *McLelland, Nicola*
    German Visions of India, 1871-1918: Commandeering
        the Holy Ganges during the Kaiserreich — *Myers, Perry*
    The German War: A Nation under Arms, 1939-1945
        — *Stargardt, Nicholas*
    Germanica — *Conroy, Robert*
    Germans to Poles: Communism, Nationalism and
        Ethnic Cleansing after the Second World War
        — *Service, Hugo*
    Germany and the Black Diaspora: Points of Contact,
        1250-1914 — *Honeck, Mischa*
    Germany at War: 400 Years of Military History
        — *Zabecki, David T.*
    Germany: Memories of a Nation — *MacGregor, Neil*
    Germs Are Us: Collaborating for Life — *Benarde, Melvin A.*
    Gerrard Winstanley: The Digger's Life and Legacy
        — *Gurney, John*
    Geschichte als Politikum: Offentliche und Private
        Kontroversen um die Deutung der
        DDR-Vergangenheit — *Hess, Pamela*
    Geschichte der deutschen Jesuiten, 5 vols. — *Schatz, Klaus*
    Geschichte der Medienokonomie: Eine Einfuhrung in
        die Traditionelle Medienwirtschaft von 1750 bis
        2000 — *Muhl-Benninghaus, Wolfgang*
    Geschichte des Bergischen Landes: Band 1: Bis zum
        Ende des Herzogtums 1806 — *Gorissen, Stefan*
    Geschichte des Westens: Die Zeit der Gegenwart
        — *Winkler, Heinrich August*
    Geschichte des Westens: Vom Kalten Krieg zum
        Mauerfall — *Winkler, Heinrich August*
    Geschichte Deutschlands im 20. Jahrhundert
        — *Herbert, Ulrich*
    Geschichte schreiben im osmanischen Sudosteuropa:
        Eine Kulturgeschichte orthodoxer Historiographie
        des 16. und 17. Jahrhunderts — *Petrovszky, Konrad*
    Geschichtsbewusstsein und Zukunftserwartung in
        Pietismus und Erweckungsbewegung — *Breul, Wolfgang*
    Geschichtsmythen in Europa - Chancen und
        Herausforderungen im Geschichtsunterricht
    Geschlecht in der Geschichte: Integriert oder
        Separiert? Gender als Historische
        Forschungskategorie — *Bothe, Alina*
    Geschlecht und Gewaltgemeinschaften
    Gesellschaft in der europaischen Integration seit den
        1950er Jahren: Migration - Konsum - Sozialpolitik
        - Representationen — *Bauerkamper, Arnd*
    Gesta sanctae ac universalis octavae synodi quae
        Constantinopoli congregata est Anastasio
        bibliothecario interprete — *Anastasius the Librarian*
    The Gestapo: The Myth and Reality of Hitler's Secret
        Polic — *McDonough, Frank*
c   Get a Good Night's Sleep! (Illus. by Marsico, Katie)
        — *Marsico, Katie*
c   Get a Hit, Mo! (Illus. by Ricks, Sam) — *Adler, David A.*
c   Get a Job at a Business (Illus. by Cannell, Jon)
        — *Jacobson, Ryan*

c   Get a Job Helping Others (Illus. by Cannell, Jon)
        — *Jacobson, Ryan*
c   Get a Job Making Stuff to Sell (Illus. by Cannell, Jon)
        — *Jacobson, Ryan*
c   Get a Summer Adventure Job (Illus. by Cannell, Jon)
        — *Jacobson, Ryan*
y   Get Dirty — *McNeil, Gretchen*
c   Get Ella to the Apollo (Illus. by Bernard, Courtney)
        — *Mullarkey, Lisa*
y   Get Even — *McNeil, Gretchen*
    Get Fit with Video Workouts — *Potts, Sue Davis*
y   Get Happy — *Amato, Mary*
    Get in Trouble: Stories (Read by several narrators).
        Audiobook Review — *Link, Kelly*
    Get in Trouble: Stories — *Link, Kelly*
c   Get into Art Animals: Enjoy Great Art: Then Create
        Your Own! (Illus. by Brooks, Susie) — *Brooks, Susie*
c   Get into Art Places: Discover Great Art and Create
        Your Own! (Illus. by Brooks, Susie) — *Brooks, Susie*
c   Get into Art: Telling Stories (Illus. by Brooks, Susie)
        — *Brooks, Susie*
    Get It Together: Why We Deserve Better Politics
        — *Williams, Zoe*
c   Get Lost, Odysseus! — *McMullan, Kate*
c   Get Mooned (Illus. by Pallace, Chris) — *Pallace, Chris*
c   Get Mooned (Illus. by Pallace, Chris) — *Servacki, Kevin*
c   Get Mooned (Illus. by Pallace, Chris) — *Serwacki, Kevin*
c   Get out of My Bath! (Illus. by Teckentrup, Britta)
        — *Teckentrup, Britta*
    Get Quilting with Angela and Cloe: 14 Projects for
        Kids to Sew — *Walters, Angela*
c   Get Reel: Produce Your Own Life — *Kajuth, Nancy Mramor*
    Get Smart! — *Tracy, Brian*
    Get Started Quilting: The Complete Beginner Guide
        — *Alexandrakis, Jessica*
c   Get the Scoop on Animal Puke! From Zombie Ants to
        Vampire Bats, 251 Cool Facts about Vomit,
        Regurgitation, & More! (Illus. by Cusick, Dawn)
        — *Cusick, Dawn*
    Get the Truth: Former CIA Officers Teach You How
        to Persuade Anyoneto Tell All. Audiobook Review
        — *Houston, Philip*
c   Get to Know Chameleons — *Brett, Flora*
c   Get to Know Komodo Dragons — *Brett, Flora*
c   Get to Know Reptiles — *Brett, Flora*
c   Get Wet! (Illus. by Cartwright, Amy) — *Powell, Marie*
    Get What's Yours: The Secrets to Maxing Out Your
        Social Security (Read by Cumming, Jeff).
        Audiobook Review — *Kotlikoff, Laurence J.*
    Get What's Yours: The Secrets to Maxing Out Your
        Social Security — *Kotlikoff, Laurence J.*
    Get Your Bake On: Sweet and Savory Recipes from
        My Home to Yours — *Emmett, Brian*
    Get Your Hopes Up! Expect Something Good to
        Happen to You Every Day — *Meyer, Joyce*
    The Getaway Car: A Donald Westlake Nonfiction
        Miscellany — *Stahl, Levi*
    Getting beyond Better: How Social Entrepreneurship
        Works — *Martin, Roger L.*
    Getting By: Estates, Class and Culture in Austerity
        Britain — *Mckenzie, Lisa*
    Getting from Me to We: How to Help Young Children
        Fit In and Make Friends — *Tuck, Shonna*
    Getting Gamers: The Psychology of Video Games and
        Their Impact on the People Who Play Them
        — *Madigan, Jamie*
    Getting High: Marijuana Through the Ages
        — *Chasteen, John Charles*
    Getting It Right — *Arthur, A.M.*
    Getting More for Less: The Gravity of America's
        Choices — *LaRoque, George, III*
    Getting (More of) What You Want: How the Secrets
        of Economics and Psychology Can Help You
        Negotiate Anything, in Business and in Life
        — *Neale, Margaret A.*
    Getting Physical: The Rise of Fitness Culture in
        America — *McKenzie, Shelly*
    Getting Real — *Carlson, Gretchen*
    Getting Sociology Right: A Half-Century of
        Reflections — *Smelser, Neil J.*
    Getting Started with Demand-Driven Acquisitions for
        E-books: A LITA Guide — *Arndt, Theresa S.*
    Getting the Holy Ghost: Urban Ethnography in a
        Brooklyn Pentecostal Tongue-Speaking Church
        — *Marina, Peter*

Getting the Word Out: Academic Libraries as Scholarly Publishers — Bonn, Maria
c Getting through My Parents' Divorce — Baker, Amy J.L.
Getting to Grey Owl — Caswell, Kurt
Getting to Know Jesus: An Invitation to Walk with the Lord Day by Day — Kampmann, Eric
Gettysburg — Guelzo, Allen C.
y The Gettysburg Address: Perspectives on Lincoln's Greatest Speech — Conant, Sean
Gettysburg Religion: Refinement, Diversity, and Race in the Antebellum and Civil War Border North — Longenecker, Steve
Gewaltkulturen von den Kolonialkriegen bis zur Gegenwart
Gewerkschaftspolitik in den Langen 1970er Jahren. Ein Workshop zur Edition "Quellen zur Geschichte der Deutschen Gewerkschaftsbewegung im 20. Jahrhundert"
The Ghastly McNastys: The Lost Treasure of Little Snoring (Illus. by Asquith, Ros) — Gardner, Lyn
y Ghetto Brother: Warrior to Peacemaker (Illus. by Ahlering, Claudia) — Voloj, Julian
Ghetto Voices in Contemporary German Culture: Textscapes, Filmscapes, Soundscapes — Stehle, Maria
Ghettoside: A True Story of Murder in America (Read by Lowman, Rebecca). Audiobook Review — Leovy, Jill
Ghettoside: A True Story of Murder in America (Read by Lowman, Rebecca). Audiobook Review — Leovy, Jill
Ghettoside: A True Story of Murder in America — Leovy, Jill
Ghettoside: Investigating a Homicide Epidemic — Leovy, Jill
The Ghost Box — Duran, Mike
Ghost Cities of China: The Story of Cities without People in the World's Most Populated Country — Shepard, Wade
The Ghost Fields: A Ruth Galloway Mystery — Griffiths, Elly
Ghost Finders: Ghost of a Chance. Audiobook Review — Green, Simon R.
Ghost Fleet (Read by Orlow, Rich). Audiobook Review — Singer, P.W.
Ghost Fleet — Singer, P.W.
Ghost Girl — Thompson, Lesley
y Ghost House — Adornetto, Alexandra
y Ghost Hunting — Hamilton, S.L.
Ghost Image — Crosby, Ellen
The Ghost in My Brain: How a Concussion Stole My Life and How the New Science of Brain Plasticity Helped Me Get It Back — Elliott, Clark
The Ghost in the Electric Blue Suit (Read by Jackson, Gildart). Audiobook Review — Joyce, Graham
The Ghost, Josephine — Rau, Brad
c Ghost Light Burning (Illus. by Fabbretti, Valerio) — Fields, Jan
Ghost Month — Lin, Ed
y Ghost Most Foul — Grayson, Patti
The Ghost Network — Disabato, Catie
c The Ghost of Donley Farm (Illus. by Klein, Laurie Allen) — Johnson, Jaime Gardner
y The Ghost of Karl Marx (Illus. by Mary, Donatien) — de Calan, Ronan
c The Ghost of the Bermuda Triangle (Illus. by Neely, Scott) — Sutton, Laurie S.
The Ghost of the Mary Celeste — Martin, Valerie
The Ghost Princess — Walsh, M.
Ghost Riders in the Sky: The Life of Stan Jones, the Singing Ranger — Ward, Michael K.
c Ghost Ships — Owings, Lisa
Ghost Summer: Stories — Due, Tananarive
y Ghost Walls: The Story of a 17th-Century Colonial Homestead — Walker, Sally M.
Ghost Wanted — Hart, Carolyn
The Ghost Warriors — Katz, Samuel M
Ghosted, vol. 3: Death Wish (Illus. by Sudzuka, Goran) — Williamson, Joshua
Ghostheart — Ellory, R.J.
c Ghostlight — Gensler, Sonia
Ghostly: A Collection of Ghost Stories — Niffenegger, Audrey
Ghostly Adventures of Sherlock Holmes — Gold, Marv
Ghostly Apparitions: German Idealism, the Gothic Novel, and Optical Media — Andriopoulos, Stefan
y Ghostly Evidence: Exploring the Paranormal — Halls, Kelly Milner
Ghostly Figures: Memory and Belatedness in Postwar American Poetry — Keniston, Ann

c Ghostly Thief of Time — Bolling, Ruben
Ghosts: A Haunted History — Morton, Lisa
c Ghosts and Gummy Worms: A Readers' Theater Script and Guide — Wallace, Nancy K.
c The Ghosts Go Haunting (Illus. by Record, Adam) — Ketteman, Helen
c The Ghosts Go Spooking (Illus. by Storms, Patricia) — Bozik, Chrissy
The Ghosts of Demons Past — Schiariti, Matt
y The Ghosts of Heaven — Sedgwick, Marcus
The Ghosts of K2 — Conefrey, Mick
Ghosts of Kanungu: Fertility, Secrecy and Exchange in the Great Lakes of East Africa — Vokes, Richard
Ghosts of My Life: Writings on Depression, Hauntology and Lost Futures — Fisher, Mark
c Ghosts of Shanghai — Sedgwick, Julian
c The Ghosts of Tarawera — Copsey, Sue
The Ghosts of the Avant-Garde(s): Exorcising Experimental Theater and Performance — Harding, James M.
Ghosts of the New City: Spirits, Urbanity, and the Ruins of Progress in Chiang Mai — Johnson, Andrew Alan
c The Ghosts Who Danced — Pirotta, Saviour
The Ghosts Who Travel with Me: A Literary Pilgrimage Through Brautigan's America — Green, Allison
Giallo Fantastique: Tales of Crime and Terror — Lockhart, Ross E.
Giambattista Bodoni: His Life and His World — Lester, Valerie
c The Giant of Jum (Illus. by Davies, Benji) — Woollard, Elli
c Giant Vehicles (Illus. by Biesty, Stephen) — Green, Rod
Giants among Men: Y.A., L.T., the Big Tuna, and Other New York Giants Stories — Berkow, Ira
c Giants and Trolls (Illus. by Chilvers, Nigel) — Peebles, Alice
c Gibbons — Yasuda, Anita
Gideon Smith and the Mask of the Ripper — Barnett, David
The Gift (Read by Gallagher, Rebecca). Audiobook Review — Brunstetter, Wanda E.
c A Gift for Matthew (Illus. by Lobastov, Masha) — Muzekari, Nick
Gift in der Nahrung: Zur Genese der Verbraucherpolitik Mitte des 20. Jahrhunderts — Stoff, Heiko
The Gift of a Charm — Hill, Melissa
The Gift of Caring: Saving Our Parents from the Perils of Modern Healthcare — Houle, Marcy Cottrell
The Gift of Failure: How the Best Parents Learn to Let Go So Their Children Can Succeed — Lahey, Jessica
Gift of Sydney — Richards, D. Manning
The Gift of the Face: Portraiture and Time in Edward S. Curtis's "The North American Indian" — Zamir, Shamoon
Gift: The Art of David Flores — Flores, David
y Gifted — Hounam, Donald
y The Gifted: Books 1 and 2 (Illus. by Gooden, Nathan C.) — Wassel, Damian A.
Gifted Hands: The Ben Carson Story — Carson, Ben
Gifts from the Thunder Beings: Indigenous Archery and European Firearms in the Northern Plains and the Central Subarctic, 1670-1870 — Bohr, Roland
c Gigantosaurus (Illus. by Duddle, Jonny) — Duddle, Jonny
Gil Hodges: A Hall of Fame Life — Zachter, Mort
c Gilbert the Ghost (Illus. by van Genechten, Guido) — van Genechten, Guido
Gilbert: The Last Years of W.G. Grace — Connelly, Charlie
The Gilded Hour — Donati, Sara
The Gilded Life of Matilda Duplaine — Brunkhorst, Alex
y The Gilded Life of Matilda Duplaine — Duplaine, Matilda
The Gilded Razor: A Memoir — Lansky, Sam
Gilliamesque: A Pre-posthumous Memoir — Gilliam, Terry
Gilliamesque — Gilliam, Terry
Gimme Shelter: A Damaged Pit Bull, an Angry Man, and How They Saved Each Other — Spirito, Louis
Gin: The Manual — Broom, Dave
c Gina's Wheels (Illus. by Greenhorn, Diane L.) — Bishop, Mary Harelkin
Ginger Snaps: A Jack Patterson Thriller — Hubbell, Webb

c Gingerbread for Liberty! How a German Baker Helped Win the American Revolution (Illus. by Kirsch, Vincent X.) — Rockliff, Mara
c The Gingerbread Man Loose at Christmas (Illus. by Lowery, Mike) — Murray, Laura (b. 1970-)
Ginny and Me: Reflections of What God Can Do — Walters, Christine
Ginny Gall — Smith, Charlie
c Ginny Louise and the School Showdown (Illus. by Munsinger, Lynn) — Sauer, Tammi
Giordano Bruno: An Introduction — Blum, Raul Richard
Giorgio de Chirico and the Metaphysical City: Nietzsche, Modernism, Paris — Merjian, Ara H.
Giorgio de Chirico and the Metaphysical City: Nietzsche, Modernism — Merijian, Ara H.
Giovanni Paolo Colonna: Oratorii — Lora, Francesco
Gipsabgusse und antike Skulpturen: Prasentation un Kontext — Schreiter, Charlotte
Giraffe: Biology, Behaviour and Conservation — Dagg, Anne Innis
c Giraffe Meets Bird (Illus. by Bender, Rebecca) — Bender, Rebecca
A Girl and Her Greens: Hearty Meals from the Garden — Bloomfield, April
y The Girl at Midnight (Read by Whelan, Julia). Audiobook Review — Grey, Melissa
y The Girl at Midnight — Grey, Melissa
y Girl at the Bottom of the Sea — Tea, Michelle
y The Girl at the Center of the World — Aslan, Austin
Girl at War — Novic, Sara
The Girl behind the Door: A Father's Quest to Understand His Daughter's Suicide — Brooks, John
y Girl Defective — Howell, Simmone
y The Girl from Everywhere — Heilig, Heidi
The Girl from Human Street: Ghosts of Memory in a Jewish Family — Cohen, Roger
The Girl from Human's Street: Ghosts of Memory in a Jewish Family — Cohen, Roger
The Girl from Krakow — Rosenberg, Alex
The Girl from the Garden — Foroutan, Parnaz
c The Girl from the Great Sandy Desert (Illus. by Street, Mervyn) — Chuguna, Jukuna Mona
The Girl from the North — Bruno, Cat
y The Girl from the Tar Paper School: Barbara Rose Johns and the Advent of the Civil Rights Movement — Kanefield, Teri
The Girl from the Train — Joubert, Irma
c Girl & Gorilla (Illus. by Berger, Joe) — Walton, Rick
The Girl in 6E — Torre, A.R.
Girl in a Band: A Memoir (Read by Gordon, Kim). Audiobook Review — Gordon, Kim
Girl in a Band: A Memoir — Gordon, Kim
Girl in a Band — Gordon, Kim
y Girl in Dior (Illus. by Goetzinger, Annie) — Goetzinger, Annie
Girl in Dior — Goetzinger, Annie
Girl in Glass: How My "Distressed Baby" Defied the Odds, Shamed a CEO, and Taught Me the Essence of Love, Heartbreak, and Miracles — Fei, Deanna
Girl in the Blue Coat — Hesse, Monica
Girl in the Dark: A Memoir (Read by Curtis, Hannah). Audiobook Review — Lyndsey, Anna
Girl in the Dark: A Memoir — Lyndsey, Anna
Girl in the Dark — Pauw, Marion
The Girl in the Ice — Hammer, Lotte
Girl in the Moonlight — Dubow, Charles
The Girl in the Photo — Wood, Wally
y The Girl in the Red Coat — Hamer, Kate
The Girl in the Spider's Web (Read by Vance, Simon). Audiobook Review — Lagercrantz, David
The Girl in the Spider's Web — Lagercrantz, David
y The Girl in the Torch — Sharenow, Robert
c The Girl in the Tower (Illus. by Ceccoli, Nicoletta) — Schroeder, Lisa
c The Girl in the Tower (Illus. by Ceccoli, Nicoletta) — Schroeder, Lisa
c The Girl in the Well Is Me — Rivers, Karen
y Girl in the Woods: A Memoir — Matis, Aspen
y Girl Last Seen — Anastasiu, Heather
The Girl on the Pier — Tomkins, Paul
The Girl on the Swing and At Night in Crumbling Voices — Grandbois, Peter
The Girl on the Train (Read by Corbett, Clare). Audiobook Review — Hawkins, Paula
The Girl on the Train — Hawkins, Paula
c Girl Power 5-Minute Stories
Girl Runner — Snyder, Carrie
Girl Sent Away — Griffin, Lynne
y Girl Singer — Carlon, Mick
Girl through Glass — Wilson, Sari

Girl Underwater (Read by Whelan, Julia). Audiobook Review — *Kells, Claire*
y Girl Underwater — *Kells, Claire*
y A Girl Undone — *Linka, Catherine*
Girl Waits with Gun — *Stewart, Amy*
c The Girl Who Buried Her Dreams in a Can: A True Story (Illus. by Gilchrist, Jan Spivey) — *Trent, Tererai*
c The Girl Who Buried Her Dreams in a Can (Illus. by Gilchrist, Jan Spivey) — *Trent, Tererai*
y The Girl Who Could Not Dream — *Durst, Sarah Beth*
The Girl Who Couldn't Read (Read by Roberts, William). Audiobook Review — *Harding, John*
The Girl Who Couldn't Stop Arguing — *Kite, Melissa*
y The Girl Who Fell — *Parker, S.M.*
y The Girl Who Ignored Ghosts — *Tansley, K.C.*
c The Girl Who Rode the Wind — *Gregg, Stacy*
y The Girl Who Slept with God — *Brelinski, Val*
The Girl Who Stole My Holocaust — *Chayut, Noam*
The Girl Who Was Saturday Night — *O'Neill, Heather*
The Girl Who Wrote in Silk (Read by Zeller, Emily Woo). Audiobook Review — *Estes, Kelli*
The Girl Who Wrote in Silk — *Estes, Kelli*
The Girl Who Wrote Loneliness — *Shin, Kyung-Sook*
The Girl Who Wrote Loneliness — *Shin, Kyung-sook*
y The Girl with All the Gifts — *Carey, Mike*
The Girl with Nine Wigs: A Memoir — *Van DerStap, Sophie*
The Girl with Seven Names: A North Korean Defector's Story — *Lee, Hyeonseo*
The Girl with the Deep Blue Eyes — *Block, Lawrence*
c The Girl with the Glass Bird — *Kerr, Esme*
c The Girl with the Parrot on Her Head — *Hirst, Daisy*
c The Girl with the Sunshine Smile (Illus. by Brett, Cathy) — *McCombie, Karen*
y The Girl with the Wrong Name — *Miller, Barnabas*
y Girl World: How to Ditch the Drama and Find Your Inner Amazing — *Ottaviano, Patricia*
Girls and Sex: Navigating the Complicated New Landscape — *Orenstein, Peggy*
Girls Coming to Tech! A History of American Engineering Education for Women — *Bix, Amy Sue*
A Girl's Got to Breathe: The Life of Teresa Wright — *Spoto, Donald*
Girl's Guide to DIY Fashion: Design & Sew 5 Complete Outfits — *Low, Rachel*
Girls in Justice — *Ross, Richard*
c The Girls of Gettysburg — *Miller, Bobbi*
The Girls of Mischief Bay (Read by Eby, Tanya). Audiobook Review — *Mallery, Susan*
The Girls of Mischief Bay — *Mallery, Susan*
The Girls She Left Behind — *Graves, Sarah*
y Girls vs. Guys: Surprising Differences between the Sexes — *Rosen, Michael J.*
Girls Will Be Boys: Cross-Dressed Women, Lesbians, and American Cinema, 1908-1934 — *Horak, Laura*
Girls Will Be Girls: Dressing Up, Playing Parts and Daring to Act Differently — *O'Toole, Emer*
Gironimo! Riding the Very Terrible 1914 Tour of Italy — *Moore, Tim*
Girrrl — *Govaere, Devin*
GIs in Germany: The Social, Economic, Cultural, and Political History of the American Military Presence — *Maulucci, Thomas W. Jr.*
GIS Research Methods: Incorporating Spatial Perspectives — *Steinberg, Sheila Lakshmi*
c Give and Take — *Raschka, Chris*
Give It All — *McKenna, Cara*
y Give It Up — *Moore, Stephanie Perry*
Give Me Liberty or Give Me Obama-care — *Ramirez, Michael*
y Give Me Wings: How a Choir of Former Slaves Took on the World — *Lowinger, Kathy*
Give Us the Ballot: The Modern Struggle for Voting Rights in America — *Berman, Ari*
Give Your Heart to the Hawks: A Tribute to the Mountain Men — *Blevins, Win*
c Give Your Song a Voice (Illus. by Hare, Debra Rae) — *Schmidt, Kristin E.*
The Given World — *Palaia, Marian*
The Givenness of Things: Essays — *Robinson, Marilynne*
c Giving a Presentation (Illus. by Williams, Nate) — *Bodden, Valerie*
Giving Blood: A Fresh Paradigm for Preaching — *Sweet, Leonard*
Giving Up — *Steeves, Mike*
The Giving Way to Happiness: The Life-Changing Power of Giving — *Santi, Jenny*
c Gizmo the Lonely Robucket (Illus. by Forbus, Tiffanie) — *Lloyd, Ann*

Gizzi's Healthy Appetite: Food to Nourish the Body and Feed the Soul — *Erskine, Gizzi*
Gjelina: Cooking from Venice, California — *Lett, Travis*
Glaciers: The Politics of Ice — *Taillant, Jorge Daniel*
Gladstone: Ireland and Beyond — *Daly, Mary E.*
c Glamorous Garbage (Illus. by Newman, Barbara Johansen) — *Newman, Barbara Johansen*
c Glamorous Garbage (Illus. by Newman, Barbara Johnson) — *Newman, Barbara Johansen*
c Glamourpuss (Illus. by Small, David) — *Weeks, Sarah*
y A Glance Backward (Illus. by Sandoval, Tony) — *Paquet, Pierre*
y The Glass Arrow (Read by Nankani, Soneela). Audiobook Review — *Simmons, Kristen*
y The Glass Arrow — *Simmons, Kristen*
The Glass Cage: Automation and Us — *Carr, Nicholas*
The Glass Cage: Where Automation Is Taking Us — *Carr, Nicholas*
Glass Ceilings and Dirt Floors: Women, Work, and the Global Economy — *Hinze, Christine Firer*
c The Glass Children — *Ohlsson, Kristina*
The Glass City: Toledo and the Industry That Built It — *Floyd, Barbara L.*
Glass Half Full: The Decline and Rebirth of the Legal Profession — *Barton, Benjamin H.*
The Glass Kitchen (Read by Whelan, Julia). Audiobook Review — *Lee, Linda Francis*
c The Glass Mountain: Tales from Poland (Illus. by Pienkowski, Jan) — *Walser, David*
Glass on the Chimney and Other Poems — *Grant, Jamie*
y The Glass Sentence — *Grove, S.E.*
The Glass Slipper: Women and Love Stories — *Weisser, Susan Ostrov*
y Glass Sword — *Aveyard, Victoria*
c The Glass Voice (Illus. by Lamoreaux, Michelle) — *Snowe, Olivia*
c Glasses (Illus. by Woodworth, Heidi M.) — *Zawistoski, Ann Gwinn*
c Glasses to Go — *Eliot, Hannah*
Glaubensheil: Wegweisung ins Christentum gemass der Lehre Hildegards von Bingen — *Berndt, Rainer*
Glimpses of Gauguin — *D'Agincourt, Maryann*
Glimpses of Wilderness — *Proescholdt, Kevin*
c The Glimpsing Book — *Loe, Steve*
Glitch in the Machine — *Swamp, Edgar*
y The Glittering World — *Levy, Robert*
Global Appetites: American Power and the Literature of Food — *Carruth, Allison*
c Global Baby Bedtimes — *Global Fund for Children*
c Global Baby Bedtimes — *Global Fund For Children*
c Global Baby Boys — *Ajmera, Maya*
The Global Code: How a New Culture of Universal Values Is Reshaping Business and Marketing — *Rapaille, Clotaire*
Global Coloniality of Power in Guatemala: Racism, Genocide, Citizenship — *Salazar, Egla Martinez*
Global Communication Electric: Business, News, and Politics in the World of Telegraphy — *Hampf, M. Michaela*
Global Crisis: War, Climate Change and Catastrophe in the Seventeenth Century — *Parker, Geoffrey*
The Global Decline of the Mandatory Death Penalty: Constitutional Jurisprudence and Legislative Reform in Africa, Asia, and the Caribbean — *Novak, Andrew*
Global Diasporas and Mission — *Im, Chandler H.*
Global Diasporas in the Age of High Imperialism
The Global Diffusion of Evangelicalism: The Age of Billy Graham and John Stott — *Stanley, Brian*
Global Economic History: A Very Short Introduction — *Allen, Robert C.*
Global Families: A History of Asian International Adoption in America — *Choy, Catherine Ceniza*
The Global Gospel: Achieving Missional Impact in Our Multicultural World — *Mischke, Werner*
Global Health in Africa: Historical Perspectives on Disease Control — *Vernick-Giles, Tamara*
A Global History of Sexuality: The Modern Era — *Buffington, Robert M.*
Global Intellectual History — *Moyn, Samuel*
Global Interdependence: The World after 1945 — *Iriye, Akira*
Global Islamophobia: Muslims and Moral Panic in the West — *Morgan, George*
Global Markets Transformed: 1870-1945 — *Topik, Steven C.*
Global Migrants, Local Culture: Natives and Newcomers in Provincial England, 1841-1939 — *Tabili, Laura*

Global Migration Issues: Old Assumptions, New Dynamics — *Arcarazo, Diego Acosta*
Global Muckraking: 100 Years of Investigative Journalism from around the World — *Schiffrin, Anya*
Global Muslims in the Age of Steam and Print — *Gelvin, James L.*
The Global Offensive: The United States, the Palestine Liberation Organization, and the Making of the Post-Cold War Order — *Chamberlin, Paul Thomas*
Global Philosophy: What Philosophy Ought to Be — *Maxwell, Nicholas*
The Global Pigeon — *Jerolmack, Colin*
Global Population: History, Geopolitics, and Life on Earth — *Bashford, Alison*
The Global President: International Media and the US Government — *Farnsworth, Stephen J.*
The Global Republic: America's Inadvertent Rise to World Power — *Ninkovich, Frank*
The Global Revolution: A History of International Communism 1917-1991 — *Pons, Silvio*
The Global Right Wing and the Clash of World Politics — *Bob, Clifford*
Global Rivalries: Standards Wars and the Transnational Cotton Trade — *Quark, Amy A.*
Global Rome: Changing Faces of the Eternal City — *Marinaro, Isabella Clough*
Global Rules: America, Britain and a Disordered World — *Cronin, James E.*
The Global Seven Years War, 1754-1763: Britain and France in a Great Power Contest — *Baugh, Daniel*
Global Street Art: The Street Artists and Trends Taking Over the World — *Bofkin, Lee*
Global Unions, Local Power: The New Spirit of Transnational Labor Organizing — *McCallum, Jamie K.*
The Global Village Myth: Distance, War, and the Limits of Power — *Porter, Patrick*
The Global War for Internet Governance — *DeNardis, Laura*
Global West, American Frontier: Travel, Empire, and Exceptionalism from Manifest Destiny to the Great Depression — *Wrobel, David M.*
Globales Geschichtsbewusstsein: Die Entstehung der Multipolaren Welt vom 18. Jahrhundert bis in die Gegenwart — *Heuer, Andreas*
Globalisierung der Kirchen: Der Okumenische Rat der Kirchen und die Entdeckung der Dritten Welt in den 1960er und 1970er Jahren — *Kunter, Katharina*
Globalization and Culture: Global Melange — *Pieterse, Jan Nederveen*
Globalization and Development in East Asia — *Pieterse, Jan Nederveen*
Globalization and Money: A Global South Perspective — *Singh, Supriya*
The Globalization of Inequality — *Bourguignon, Francois*
The Globalization of Supermax Prisons — *Ross, Jeffrey Ian*
Globalizing Oil: Firms and Oil Market Governance in France, Japan, and the United states — *Hughes, Llewelyn*
Globe: Life in Shakespeare's London — *Arnold, Catharine*
Glocal Affairs: Art Biennials in Context
c The Gloomy Ghost (Illus. by Calo, Marcos) — *Lubar, David*
Glorious: A Novel of the American West — *Guinn, Jeff*
Glorious Catastrophe: Jack Smith, Performance and Visual Culture — *Johnson, Dominic*
The Glorious Heresies — *McInerney, Lisa*
Glorious Misadventures: Nikolai Rezanov and the Dream of a Russian America — *Matthews, Owen*
The Glorious Revolution and the Continuity Law — *Kay, Richard*
c The Glorkian Warrior Eats Adventure Pie (Illus. by Kochalka, James) — *Kochalka, James*
y The Glory — *St John, Lauren*
The Glory Gets — *Jeffers, Honoree Fanonne*
c Glory O'Brien's History of the Future (Read by Lakin, Christine). Audiobook Review — *King, A.S.*
y Glory O'Brien's History of the Future — *King, A.S.*
The Glory of Life — *Kumpfmuller, Michael*
Glosae super Iohannem — *Anselm of Laon*
Glossaire j'y serre mes gloses — *Masson, Andre*
Glow — *Beauman, Ned*
c Glow: Animals with Their Own Night-Lights (Illus. by Beck, W.H.) — *Beck, W.H.*
c Glow: Animals with Their Own Night-Lights — *Beck, W.H.*

c Glow: Animals with Their Own Night-Lights (Illus. by Beck, W.H.) — Beck, W.H.
c Glow-in-the-Dark Creatures — Hyde, Natalie
The Glow of Paris: The Bridges of Paris at Night — Zuercher, Gary
Gluten-Free Classic Snacks: 100 Recipes for the Brand-Name Treats You Love — Hunn, Nicole
The Gluten-Free Vegetarian Family Cookbook: 150 Healthy Recipes for Meals, Snacks, Sides, Desserts, and More — O'Brien, Susan
Gluten-Free Wish List: Sweet and Savory Treats You've Missed the Mos — Sauvage, Jeanne
Glyphbinder — Bakutis, T. Eric
y GMO Food — Newton, David E.
The Gnome Project: One Woman's Wild and Woolly Adventure — Peill-Meninghaus, Jessica
Gnostic Mysteries of Sex: Sophia the Wild One and Erotic Christianity — Churton, Tobias
Go and Bury Your Dead — Brooks, Bill
Go-Betweens for Hitler — Urbach, Karina
Go Big, Go Bold--Large-Scale Modern Quilts: 10 Projects, Quick to Cut, Fast to Sew — Cain, Barbara
Go Blended! A Handbook for Blending Technology in Schools — Arney, Liz
c Go, Cub! — Neuman, Susan B.
Go Down Hard — Buck, Craig Faustus
c Go Fast, Goo — Murphy, Todd
c Go! Fight! Twin! — Payton, Belle
Go Figure! New Perspectives on Guston — Miller, Peter Benson
c Go! Go! Go! Stop! (Illus. by Harper, Charise Mericle) — Harper, Charise Mericle
Go, Green Gecko! (Illus. by Tolland, Margaret) — Hay, Gay
c Go Home Flash (Illus. by Paul, Ruth) — Paul, Ruth
c Go Home, Little One! — James, Cate
c Go-Kart Racing — Hamilton, John
c Go, Little Green Truck! (Illus. by Kuo, Julia) — Schotter, Roni
Go Nation: Chinese Masculinities and the Game of Weiqi in China — Moskowitz, Marc L.
c Go Packers Activity Book — Hall, Darla
c Go, Pea, Go! (Illus. by Sonnenburg, Chris) — Moshier, Joe
Go See the Eclipse and Take a Kid with You — Percival, Chap
Go Set a Watchman (Read by Witherspoon, Reese). Audiobook Review — Lee, Harper
Go Set a Watchman — Lee, Harper
c Go, Shapes, Go! (Illus. by Fleming, Denise) — Fleming, Denise
The Go-To Guide for Engineering Curricula Grades 6-8: Choosing and Using the Best Instructional Materials for your Students — Sneider, Cary I.
c Go to School, Little Monster (Illus. by Leick, Bonnie) — Ketteman, Helen
c Go to Sleep, Groundhog! (Read by Berneis, Susie). Audiobook Review — Cox, Judy
Go to Sleep, Little Farm (Read by Cabezas, Maria). Audiobook Review — Ray, Mary Lyn
c Go to Sleep, Little Farm (Illus. by Neal, Christopher Silas) — Ray, Mary Lyn
c Go to Sleep, Maddie! (Illus. by Schlossberg, Elisabeth) — Wright, Maureen
c Go to Sleep, Monty! (Illus. by Geyer, Kim) — Geyer, Kim
Go Your Own Way — Riley, Zane
c Goat Lips: Tales of a Lapsed Englishman — Taylor, Matthew
c Goatilocks and the Three Bears (Illus. by Howard, Arthur) — Perl, Erica S.
c Goats — Murray, Julie
c Gobble, Gobble, Tucker! — McGuirk, Leslie
c Gobbled by Ghorks (Illus. by Lydon, Zack) — Weston, Robert Paul
Gobekli Tepe: Genesis of the Gods: The Temple of the Watchers and the Discovery of Eden — Collins, Andrew
Goblins — Bernstein, David
c Goblins on the Prowl — Coville, Bruce
c The Goblin's Puzzle: Being the Adventures of a Boy with No Name and Two Girls Called Alice (Illus. by Eckwall, Jensine) — Chilton, Andrew S.
God and Government: Twenty-Five Years of Fighting for Equality, Secularism, and Freedom of Conscience — Lynn, Barry W.
God and Jetfire: Confessions of a Birth Mother — Seek, Amy
God and Nature: A Theologian and a Scientist Conversing on the Divine Promise of Possibility — Thompson, Curtis L.

God and Nature in the Thought of Margaret Cavendish — Siegfried, Brandie R.
God and the Multiverse: Humanity's Expanding View of the Cosmos — Stenger, Victor J.
God as Love: The Concept and Spiritual Aspect of Agape in Modern Russian Religious Thought — Oravecz, Johannes Miroslav
God at the Margins: Making Theological Sense of Religious Plurality — Light, Aimee Upjohn
y God Awful Loser — Acevedo, Silvia
God Does No Wrong — Howse, Jan Wooden
God, Faith and Identity from the Ashes: Reflections of Children and Grandchildren of Holocaust Survivors — Rosensaft, Menachem
God for the Rest of Us: Experience Unbelievable Love, Unlimited Hope, and Uncommon Grace — Antonucci, Vince
God, Guns, Grits, and Gravy — Huckabee, Mike
God Has Begun a Great Work in Us: Embodied Love in Consecrated Life and Ecclesial Movements — King, Jason
God Has No Grandchildren — Kim, Gyeong-Uk
God Help the Child (Read by Morrison, Toni). Audiobook Review — Morrison, Toni
God Help the Child — Morrison, Toni
A God in Ruins (Read by Jennings, Alex). Audiobook Review — Atkinson, Kate
A God in Ruins — Atkinson, Kate
God Is Not Here: A Soldier's Struggle with Torture, Trauma, and the Moral Injuries of War — Edmonds, Bill Russell
God Loves Hair (Illus. by Neufeld, Juliana) — Shraya, Vivek
God Loves Haiti — Leger, Dimitry Elias
God Mocks: A History of Religious Satire from the Hebrew Prophets to Stephen Colbert — Lindvall, Terry
God & Mrs Thatcher: The Battle for Britain's Soul — Filby, Eliza
The God of Chance — Thorup, Kirsten
The God of Small Things — Roy, Arundhati
God of Speed — Davies, Luke
The God Problem: How a Godless Cosmos Creates — Bloom, Howard
God Speaks: What He Says, What He Means — Evans, Craig A.
A God That Could Be Real: Spirituality, Science, and the Future of Our Planet — Abrams, Nancy Ellen
God, Value, and Nature — Ellis, Fiona
God War — Black, Daniel
The Goddaughter Caper — Campbell, Melodie
y Goddess — Gardiner, Kelly
Goddess Calling: Inspirational Messages and Meditations of Sacred Feminine Liberation Theology — Tate, Karen
The Goddess' Daughter — Pi, M. Naresh
The Goddess of Buttercups and Daisies — Millar, Martin
Goddess of Fire — Kirchner, Bharti
Goddess of Love Incarnate: The Life of Stripteuse Lili St. Cyr — Zemeckis, Leslie
The Goddess Pose — Goldberg, Michelle
The Goddess Pose: The Audacious Life of Indra Devi, the Woman Who Helped Bring Yoga to the West — Goldberg, Michelle
Goddesses Never Age: The Secret Prescription for Radiance, Vitality, and Well-Being — Northrup, Christiane
Godkiller, vol. 1 (Illus. by Wieszczyk, Anna) — Pizzolo, Matt
Godless Country — Hunt, Alaric
c God's Amazing World (Illus. by Florian, Melanie) — Spinelli, Eileen
Gods and Kings: The Rise and Fall of Alexander McQueen and John Galliano — Thomas, Dana
God's Bankers: A History of Money & Power at the Vatican — Posner, Gerald
God's Bits of Wood — Sembene, Ousmane
God's Dog — Marani, Diego
y Gods Don't Sleep — Thompson, T.
The God's Eye View — Eisler, Barry
God's Gangs: Barrio Ministry, Masculinity, and Gang Recovery — Flores, Edward Orozco
God's Good World: Reclaiming the Doctrine of Creation — Wilson, Jonathan R.
Gods in Dwellings: Temples and Divine Presence in the Ancient Near East — Hundley, Michael B.
God's Kingdom — Mosher, Howard Frank
God's Laboratory: Assisted Conception in the Andes. — Roberts, Elizabeth F.S.
The Gods of H.P. Lovecraft — French, Aaron J.
The Gods of Tango — De Robertis, Carolina

Gods of the Morning: A Bird's-Eye View of a Changing World — Lister-Kaye, John
Gods of the Morning: A Bird's-Eye View of a Changing Year — Lister-Kaye, John
God's Planet — Gingerich, Owen
God's Saving Grace: A Pauline Theology — Matera, Frank J.
God's Traitors: Terror and Faith in Elizabethan England — Childs, Jessie
Goebbels: A Biography — Longerich, Peter
Goethe's Allegories of Identity — Brown, Jane K.
Goethes Freunde in Gotha und Weimar — Damm, Sigrid
Goethe's Ghosts: Reading and the Persistence of Literature — Richter, Simon
GoGo Juice — Cleary, Jon
Goin' Crazy with Sam Peckinpah and All Our Friends — Evans, Max
Going Ape: Florida's Battles over Evolution in the Classroom — Haught, Brandon
Going for a Song: An Anthology of Poems about Antiques — Hillier, Bevis
Going for Broke: Japanese American Soldiers in the War against Nazi Germany — McCaffrey, James M.
Going Home for Apples and Other Stories — O'Meara, Richard Michael
Going into the City: Portrait of a Critic as a Young Man — Christgau, Robert
Going Out — Thwaite, Anthony
Going Places — Berla, Kathryn
Going Solo — Tucker, Alan
Going to Pot: Why the Rush to Legalize Marijuana Is Harming America — Bennett, William J.
Going to the Palais: A Social and Cultural History of Dancing and Dance Halls in Britain, 1918-1960 — Fowler, David
Going Veggie: The 30-Day Guide to Becoming a Healthy Vegetarian — Slabosz, Trudy
y Going Where It's Dark — Naylor, Phyllis Reynolds
The Gold Eaters — Wright, Ronald
Gold Fame Citrus — Watkins, Claire Vaye
Gold Fever — Boggan, Steve
Gold Fever, Part 2: San Francisco, 1851-1852 — Salter, Ken
Gold-in-Quartz — Von Freymann, Ronald
c Gold Rush Dog (Illus. by Montgomery, Michael G.) — Hart, Alison
Gold Throne in Shadow — Planck, M.C.
Golda Meir: True Grit — Atkins, Ann
Golda Slept Here — Amiry, Suad
Golden Age — Smiley, Jane
Golden Age
The Golden Age of Murder: The Mystery of the Writers Who Invented the Modern Detective Story — Edwards, Martin
The Golden Age of Pantomime: Slapstick, Spectacle and Subversion in Victorian England — Richards, Jeffrey
The Golden Age of Shtetl: A New History of Jewish Life in Eastern Europe — Petrovsky-Shtern, Yohanan
The Golden Arrow — Richardson, Lloyd
The Golden Bowl — James, Henry
y The Golden Braid — Dickerson, Melanie
y The Golden Compass: The Graphic Novel, vol. 1 (Illus. by Oubrerie, Clement) — Pullman, Philip
Golden Earrings — Alexandra, Belinda
The Golden Era of Major League Baseball: A Time of Transition and Integration — Soderholm-Difatte, Bryan
The Golden Game: The Story of California Baseball — Nelson, Kevin
y Golden Girl — Mancusi, Mari
The Golden Lad: The Haunting Story of Quentin and Theodore Roosevelt — Burns, Eric
The Golden Lands: Cambodia, Indonesia, Laos, Myanmar, Thailand and Vietnam — Lall, Vikram
Golden Lion — Smith, Wilbur
c The Golden Plate — Watts, Bernadette
The Golden Rule and the Games People Play: The Ultimate Strategy for a Meaning-Filled Life — Shapiro, Rami
Golden Son
Golden Son — Brown, Pierce
The Golden Son — Gowda, Shilpi Somaya
y The Golden Specific (Read by Campbell, Cassandra). Audiobook Review — Grove, S.E.
y The Golden Specific — Grove, S.E.
c The Golden Spike: How a Photograph Celebrated the Transcontinental Railroad — Nardo, Don
Golden State — Kegan, Stephanie
c The Golden Touch — Huser, Glen

The Golden Wave: Culture and Politics after Sri Lanka's Tsunami Disaster — *Gamburd, Michele Ruth*
A Golden Weed: Tobacco and Environment in the Piedmont South — *Swanson, Drew A.*
"Goldene 50er"oder "Bleierne Zeit"? Geschichtsbilder der 50er Jahre im Fernsehen der BRD, 1959-1989 — *Rudiger, Mark*
Goldeneye: Where Bond Was Born: Ian Fleming's Jamaica — *Parker, Matthew*
The Goldfinch — *Tartt, Donna*
Goldfrank's Toxicologic Emergencies, 10th ed. — *Hoffman, Robert S.*
c Goldie Takes a Stand! Golda Meir's First Crusade (Illus. by Garrity-Riley, Kelsey) — *Krasner, Barbara*
c Goldilocks: A Pop-Up Book — *O'Leary, John*
c Goldilocks and the Three Bears (Illus. by Daubney, Kate) — *Alperin, Mara*
c Goldilocks and the Three Bears — *Gorbachev, Valeri*
Goldstruck: A Life Shaped by Jewellery — *Webster, Stephen*
The Golem of Paris — *Kellerman, Jonathan*
The Golem Redux: From Prague to Post-Holocaust Fiction — *Baer, Elizabeth R.*
c Golemchik (Illus. by Exley, William) — *Exley, William*
Golf Ball — *Brown, Harry*
c The Gollywhopper Games: Friend of Foe (Illus. by Jamieson, Victoria) — *Feldman, Jody*
c The Gollywhopper Games: Friend or Foe (Illus. by Jamieson, Victoria) — *Feldman, Jody*
c Gollywood Here I Come! (Illus. by Cerato, Mattia) — *Barto, Terry John*
Gombrowicza milczenie o Bogu — *Tischner, Lukasz*
c Gon, the Little Fox (Illus. by Mita, Genjirou) — *Niimi, Nankichi*
The Gondi: Family Strategy and Survival in Early Modern France — *Milstein, Joanna*
Gone-Away World — *Harkaway, Nick*
Gone Cold — *Corleone, Douglas*
c Gone Crazy in Alabama (Read by Johnson, Sisi A.). Audiobook Review — *Williams-Garcia, Rita*
y Gone Crazy in Alabama — *Williams-Garcia, Rita*
Gone Girl — *Flynn, Gillian*
Gone in a Heartbeat: A Physician's Search for True Healing — *Spector, Neil*
Gone with the Mind — *Leyner, Mark*
y Goners: We All Fall Down (Illus. by Corona, Jorge) — *Semahn, Jacob*
Gonzalo de Berceo and the Latin Miracles of the Virgin — *Timmons, Patricia*
Gonzo Girl — *Della Pietra, Cheryl*
Gonzo Girl — *Pietra, Cheryl Della*
Good and Cheap: Eat Well on $4/Day — *Brown, Leanne*
The Good Book: Writers Reflect on Favorite Bible Passages — *Blauner, Andrew*
Good-Bye Hegemony!: Power and Influence in the Global System — *Reich, Simon*
Good Catholics: The Battle over Abortion in the Catholic Church — *Miller, Patricia*
Good Cheap Eats: Dinner in 30 Minutes (or Less!). — *Fisher, Jessica*
Good Cheap Eats: Everyday Dinners and Fantastic Feasts for $10 (or Less). — *Fisher, Jessica*
The Good Death: An Exploration of Dying in America — *Neumann, Ann*
Good Decisions...Most of the Time: Because Life Is Too Short Not to Eat Chocolate — *Brooks, Danielle*
Good Dog, Happy Baby: Preparing Your Dog for the Arrival of Your Child — *Wombacher, Michael*
c Good Dog Lion (Illus. by Dean, David) — *McCall Smith, Alexander*
c The Good Dog (Illus. by Olson, Jennifer Gray) — *Kessler, Todd*
c Good Dragon, Bad Dragon (Illus. by Rassmus, Jens) — *Nostlinger, Christine*
c Good Dream, Bad Dream: The World's Heroes Save the Night! — *Calle, Juan*
Good Earl Gone Bad — *Collins, Manda*
c Good Enough for a Sheep Station — *Cox, David*
A Good Family — *Fassnacht, Erik*
A Good Family — *Hajin, Seo*
Good Food: Grounded Practical Theology — *Ayres, Jennifer*
y Good Girl — *Tomlinson, Sarah*
Good Girls, Good Germans: Girls' Education and Emotional Nationalism in Wilhelmine Germany — *Askey, Jennifer Drake*
Good Girls — *Hirshberg, Glen*
y The Good Girls — *Shepard, Sara*
The Good Goodbye — *Buckley, Carla*

The Good Gut: Taking Control of Your Weight, Your Mood and Your Long Term Health — *Sonnenburg, Justin*
The Good Gut: Taking Control of Your Weight, Your Mood, and Your Long-term Health — *Sonnenburg, Justin*
The Good Gut: Taking Control of Your Weight, Your Mood and Your Long Term Health — *Sonnenburg, Justin*
The Good Gut: Taking Control of Your Weight, Your Mood and Your Long-Term Health — *Sonnenburg, Justin*
c A Good Home for Max — *Terada, Junzo*
c A Good Horse (Read by Goethals, Angela). Audiobook Review — *Smiley, Jane*
Good Housekeeping Grilling
Good Jobs, Bad Jobs: The Rise of Polarized and Precarious Employment Systems in the United States, 1970s-2000s — *Kalleberg, Arne*
The Good Karma Diet: Eat Gently, Feel Amazing, Age in Slow Motion — *Moran, Victoria*
A Good Killing — *Leotta, Allison*
The Good Liar — *Searle, Nicholas*
The Good Life — *Thurm, Marian*
c The Good Little Book (Illus. by Arbona, Marion) — *Maclear, Kyo*
The Good Man: The Civil War's "Christian General" and His Fight for Racial Equality — *Weil, Gordon L.*
c Good Morning, Canada (Illus. by Beck, Andrea Lynn) — *Beck, Andrea Lynn*
c The Good Morning Game (Illus. by Tullet, Herve) — *Tullet, Herve*
c Good Morning Loon (Illus. by Hartley, Kate) — *Varnai, Elizabeth S.*
c Good Morning to Me! (Illus. by Judge, Lita) — *Judge, Lita*
Good Mother, Bad Mother — *Ford, Gina*
Good Mourning: A Memoir — *Meyer, Elizabeth*
The Good Neighbor — *Nathan, Amy Sue*
Good Neighbours — *Hersant, Beth*
The Good News about What's Bad for You ... the Bad News about What's Good for You — *Wilser, Jeff*
c Good Night! — *Long, Ethan*
c Good Night, Firefly (Illus. by Alborozo, Gabriel) — *Alborozo, Gabriel*
c Good Night, Firefly (Illus. by Alborozo, Gabriel) — *Aldorozo, Gabriel*
c Good Night, Knight (Illus. by Lewin, Betsy) — *Lewin, Betsy*
c Good Night Like This — *Murphy, Mary*
Good Night, Mr. Kissinger and Other Stories — *Ahmed, K. Anis*
Good Night, Mr. Wodehouse — *Sullivan, Faith*
c Good! Night! — *Long, Ethan*
c Good Night, Truck (Illus. by McKenzie, Heath) — *Odgers, Sally*
c Good Night Yoga: A Pose-by-Pose Bedtime Story (Illus. by Hinder, Sarah Jane) — *Gates, Mariam*
The Good of Politics: A Biblical, Historical, and Contemporary Introduction — *Skillen, James*
The Good of Recognition: Phenomenology, Ethics, and Religion in the Thought of Levinas and Ricoeur — *Sohn, Michael*
c Good Ogre — *Clark, Platte F.*
Good on Paper — *Cantor, Rachel*
Good People — *Lopez, Robert*
Good Pharma: The Public-Health Model of the Mario Negri Institute — *Light, Donald W.*
A Good Place to Hide: How One French Village Saved Thousands of Lives during World War II. — *Grose, Peter*
Good Posture Made Easy: Look and Feel Your Best for Life — *Mayes, Carrie*
A Good Rake Is Hard to Find — *Collins, Manda*
Good Rogue Is Hard to Find — *Bowen, Kelly*
Good Science: The Ethical Choreography of Stem Cell Research — *Thompson, Charis*
The Good Shufu — *Slater, Tracy*
c The Good Sister — *Kain, Jamie*
The Good Spy — *Bird, Kai*
The Good Story: Exchanges on Truth, Fiction and Psychotherapy — *Coetzee, J.M.*
y The Good, the Bad, and the Beagle — *Burns, Catherine Lloyd*
The Good, the Bad, and the Furry: Life With the World's Most Melancholy Cat — *Cox, Tom*
The Good, the Bad and the Smug — *Holt, Tom*
The Good, the Bad, and the Vampire — *Humphreys, Sara*

Good Thinking: What You Need to Know to Be Smarter, Safer, Wealthier, and Wiser — *Harrison, Guy P.*
Good to Great to Innovate: Recalculating the Route to Career Readiness, K-12+ — *Sharratt, Lyn*
The Good War: Why We Couldn't Win the War or the Peace in Afghanistan — *Fairweather, Jack*
A Good Way to Go — *Helton, Peter*
Good White People: The Problem with Middle-Class White Anti-racism — *Sullivan, Shannon*
The Good Years! Historical Trajectories 1980-2010
c The Goodbye Book (Illus. by Parr, Todd) — *Parr, Todd*
Goodbye, Miss Emily — *George, Martha Sibley*
Goodbye Parkinson's, Hello Life! The Gyro-Kinetic Method for Eliminating Symptoms and Reclaiming Your Good Health — *Kerten, Alex*
y Goodbye Stranger — *Stead, Rebecca*
Goodbye to All That? The Story of Europe since 1945 — *Stone, Dan*
Goodbye to the Dead — *Freeman, Brian*
c Goodnight Already! (Illus. by Davies, Benji) — *John, Jory*
c Goodnight, Ark (Illus. by Chapman, Jane) — *Sassi, Laura*
c Goodnight Football (Illus. by Forshay, Christina) — *Dahl, Michael*
Goodnight Goes Riding and Other Poems — *Miller, Rod*
c Goodnight, Good Dog (Illus. by Malone, Rebecca) — *Ray, Mary Lyn*
c Goodnight, Grizzle Grump! (Illus. by Blecha, Aaron) — *Blecha, Aaron*
c Goodnight Moon / Buenas Noches, Luna (Illus. by Hurd, Clement) — *Brown, Margaret Wise*
c Goodnight Santa: The Perfect Bedtime Book (Illus. by East, Nick) — *Robinson, Michelle*
c Goodnight Selfie (Illus. by Collet-Derby, Pierre) — *Menchin, Scott*
c Goodnight Songs: A Celebration of the Seasons (Illus. by Brown, Peter) — *Brown, Margaret Wise*
c Goodnight, You (Illus. by Cote, Genevieve) — *Cote, Genevieve*
c Google Glass and Robotics Innovator Sebastian Thrun — *Ventura, Marne*
The Google Guys: Inside the Brilliant Minds of Google Founders Larry Page and Sergey Brin — *Brandt, Richard L.*
Google Search Secrets — *Burns, Christa*
Googolplex — *Johansson, Kjell-Gunnar*
y Goose — *O'Porter, Dawn*
c Goose — *Wall, Laura*
c Goose Goes to School (Illus. by Wall, Laura) — *Wall, Laura*
c Goose Goes to the Zoo (Illus. by Wall, Laura) — *Wall, Laura*
c Gooseberry Park and the Master Plan (Illus. by Howard, Arthur) — *Rylant, Cynthia*
c GoPro Inventor Nick Woodman — *Doeden, Matt*
c Gordon Parks: How the Photographer Captured Black and White America (Illus. by Christoph, Jamey) — *Weatherford, Carole Boston*
Gorge: My Journey up Kilimanjaro at 300 Pounds — *Whitely, Kara Richardson*
Gorgeous Wool Applique: A Visual Guide to Adding Dimension and Unique Embroidery — *Tirico, Deborah Gale*
c Gorilla Dawn — *Lewis, Gill*
c Gorilla Journal — *Franklin, Carolyn*
y Gorilla Tactics — *Grau, Sheila*
c Gorillas — *McDowell, Pamela*
c Gorillas — *Stevens, Kathryn*
c Gorillas in Our Midst (Illus. by Fairgray, Richard) — *Fairgray, Richard*
Gorsky — *Goldsworthy, Vesna*
The Goshawk (Read by Vance, Simon). Audiobook Review — *White, T.H.*
Gospel According to the Klan: The KKK's Appeal to Protestant America, 1915-1930 — *Baker, Kelly J.*
The Gospel and Pluralism Today: Reassessing Lesslie Newbigin in the 21st Century — *Sunquist, Scott W.*
The Gospel in Culture: Contextualization Issues through Asian Eyes — *Maggay, Melba Padilla*
Gospel of Freedom and Power: Protestant Missionaries in American Culture after World War II — *Ruble, Sarah E.*
The Gospel of Loki (Read by Corduner, Allan). Audiobook Review — *Harris, Joanne M.*
The Gospel of Loki — *Harris, Joanne M.*
The Gospel of Matthew — *Walker, Carol*

Gospel of the Family: Going beyond Cardinal Kasper's Proposal in the Debate on Marriage, Civil Re-Marriage, and Communion in the Church — Perez-Soba, J.J.
The Gospel of the Family — Kasper, Walter
The Gospel of the Lord: How the Early Church Wrote the Story of Jesus — Bird, Michael F.
The Gospel of the Twin — Cooper, Ron
y The Gospel Truth — Pignat, Caroline
Got Milked? The Great Dairy Deception and Why You'll Thrive without Milk — Hamilton, Alissa
Gotcha Rhythm Right Here — Tropes, John
c Goth Girl and the Fete Worse than Death — Riddell, Chris
y Gotham Academy: Welcome to Gotham Academy — Cloonan, Becky
Gothic for the Steam Age: An Illustrated Biography of George Gilbert Scott — Stamp, Gavin
Gothic Manuscripts: 1260-1320, Part 1, 2 vols. — Stones, Alison
Gothic Subjects: The Transformation of Individualism in American Fiction, 1790-1861 — Roberts, Sian Silyn
Gothic Terrors: Incarceration, Duplication and Bloodlust in Spanish Narrative — Six, Abigail Lee
Gothic Wonder: Art, Artifice and the Decorated Style, 1290-1350 — Binski, Paul
Gotta Go, Gotta Flow: Life, Love, and Lust on Chicago's South Side from the Seventies — Abramson, Michael
Gottfried August Homilius: Thematisches Verzeichnis der musikalischen Werke — Wolf, Uwe
Gotthold Ephraim Lessing: His Life, Works, and Thought — Nisbet, H.B.
Gottlicher Zorn und Menschliches Mass: Religiose Abweichung in Fruhneuzeitlichen Stadtgemeinschaften — Kastner, Alexander
Governance, and Law in Ancient India: Kautuilya's Arthasastra — Olivelle, Patrick
The Governance of China — Xi, Jinping
The Governance of Friendship: Law and Gender in the Decameron — Sherberg, Michael
Governed by a Spirit of Opposition: The Origins of American Political Practice in Colonial Philadelphia — Roney, Jessica Choppin
Governing Indigenous Territories: Enacting Sovereignty in the Ecuadorian Amazon — Juliet S. Erazo
Governing Insecurity in Japan: The Domestic Discourse and Policy Response — Vosse, Wilhelm
Governing New Guinea: An Oral History of Papuan Administrators, 1950-1990 — Visser, Leontine
Government against Itself: Public Union Power and its Consequences — DiSalvo, Daniel
Government and Community in the English Provinces, 1700-1870 — Eastwood, David
Government and the Economy — Dieterle, David A.
Government Budgeting: A Practical Guidebook — Guess, George M.
Government of Development: Peasants and Politicians in Postcolonial Tanzania — Schneider, Leander
The Government of Mistrust: Illegibility and Bureaucratic Power in Socialist Vietnam — MacLean, Ken
Government of Paper: The Materiality of Bureaucracy in Urban Pakistan — Hull, Matthew S.
Governments around the World: From Democracies to Theocracies — Shelley, Fred M.
The Governor's Wife (Read by Hoye, Stephen). Audiobook Review — Harvey, Michael
The Governor's Wife — Harvey, Michael
The Governor's Wife — Kelly, Michael
Gowanus — Alexiou, Joseph
GPS Declassified: From Smart Bombs to Smartphones — Easton, Richard D.
GQ Drinks: The Cocktail Collection for Discerning Drinkers — Henderson, Paul
c Grace (Illus. by Parkinson, Kate) — Parkinson, Kate
y Grace above All — St. Anthony, Jane
Grace and Style: The Art of Pretending You Have It — Helbig, Grace
y Grace and the Guiltless — Johnson, Erin
Grace Cries Uncle — Hyzy, Julie
Grace Kelly: Film Stills — Dreier, Daniel
Grace — Baker, Calvin
The Grace of Kings — Liu, Ken
c Graceful (Read by McInerney, Kathleen). Audiobook Review — Mass, Wendy
y Graceful — Mass, Wendy
c Gracefully Grayson — Polonsky, Ami
y The Gracekeepers — Logan, Kirsty

The Graduate School Mess: What Caused It and How We Can Fix It — Cassuto, Leonard
c Graduation Day — Charbonneau, Joelle
Graff — Graff, Laurence
Graft — Hill, Matt
c The Graham Cracker Plot — Tougas, Shelley
Grain of Truth: The Real Case For and Against Wheat and Gluten — Yafa, Stephen.
Grain of Truth: The Real Case for and against Wheat and Gluten — Yafa, Stephen
Grains of Gold: Tales of a Cosmopolitan Traveler — Chopel, Gendun
Grains of Sand: Melvyn Bragg's Cumbrian Novels — Shapcott, John
The Grammar of God: A Journey into the Words and Worlds of the Bible (Read by Kushner, Aviya). Audiobook Review — Kushner, Aviya
The Grammar of God: A Journey into the Words and Worlds of the Bible — Kushner, Aviya
The Grammar of Good Friday: Macaronic Sermons of Late Medieval England — Johnson, Holly
A Grammar of Justice: The Legacy of Ignacio Ellacuria — Ashley, J. Matthew
The Grammie Guide: Activities and Answers for Grandparenting Today — Eby, Jan
c Gran on a Fan (Illus. by Hodson, Ben) — Bolger, Kevin
Granada: A Pomegranate in the Hand of God — Nightingale, Steven
Grand Avenue — Sarris, Greg
c Grand Canyon: A Trail Through Time (Illus. by Canyon, Christopher) — Vieira, Linda
Grand Crusades: The Early Jack Vance, vol. 5 — Dowling, Terry
Grand Menteur — Ah-Sen, Jean Marc
Grand Prix Circuits — Hamilton, Maurice
Grand Strategy in Theory and Practice: The Need for an Effective American Foreign Policy — Martel, William C.
c Grandad's Island (Illus. by Davies, Benji) — Davies, Benji
Grandbaby Cakes: Modern Recipes, Vintage Charm, Soulful Memories — Adams, Jocelyn Delk
The Grandchildren of Solano Lopez: Frontier and Nation in Paraguay — Chesterton, Bridget Maria
c Granddaddy's Turn: A Journey to the Ballot Box (Illus. by Ransome, James E.) — Bandy, Michael S.
The Grandees of Government: The Origins and Persistence of Undemocratic Politics in Virginia — Tarter, Brent
Grandes Controverses en Education — Vergnioux, Alain
c Grandma — Shepherd, Jessica
c Grandma and Her Chocolate Labrador (Illus. by Nguyen, Cindy) — Fischer, P.J.
Grandma Gatewood's Walk: The Inspiring Story of the Woman Who Saved the Appalachian Trail (Read by Lawlor, Patrick). Audiobook Review — Montgomery, Ben
c Grandma in Blue with Red Hat (Illus. by Bliss, Harry) — Menchin, Scott
c Grandma Is a Slowpoke (Illus. by Coxon, Michele) — Halfmann, Janet
c Grandma Lives in a Perfume Village (Illus. by Danowski, Sonja) — Fang, Suzhen
c Grandma Lives in a Perfume Village (Illus. by Danowski, Sonja) — Suzhen, Fang
c "Grandma, What Is a Soul?" (Illus. by Herrick, Karen E.) — Herrick, Karen E.
c Grandma's Christmas Wish (Illus. by Brown, Petra) — James, Helen Foster
c Grandma's House (Illus. by Melvin, Alice) — Melvin, Alice
c Grandma's Records (Illus. by Velasquez, Eric) — Velasquez, Eric
Grandmothers at Work: Juggling Families and Jobs — Meyer, Madonna Harrington
c Grandpa Loves You! (Illus. by Brown, Petra) — James, Helen Foster
Grandpa's Third Drawer — Kopelman, Judy Tal
Grandpa's Wisdom: Secrets to the Good Life — Blasiman, Jayme
Grani russkogo raskola: Zametki o nashei istorii ot XVII veka do 1917 goda — Pyzhikov, A.V.
y Granite — Robson, Jenny
The Granite Moth — Wright, Erica
Granma Nineteen and the Soviet's Secret — Ondjaki
c Grant and Tillie Go Walking (Illus. by Smith, Sydney) — Kulling, Monica
Grant of Immunity — Holms, Garret
Grant Park — Pitts, Leonard, Jr.

Grant under Fire: An Expose of Generalship and Character in the American Civil War — Rose, Joseph A.
Granta 127: Japan — Motoya, Yukiko
Grantville Gazette VII — Flint, Eric
c Granuaile: Queen of Storms (Illus. by Pizzari, Luca) — Hendrick, Dave
y The Graphic Canon of Children's Literature: The World's Greatest Kids' Lit as Comics and Visuals — Kick, Russ
y The Graphic Canon of Children's Literature: The World's Greatest Kid's Lit as Comics and Visuals — Kick, Russ
Graphic Clay: Ceramic Surfaces and Printed Image Transfer Techniques — Burnett, Jason Bige
Graphic Medicine Manifesto — Czerwiec, MK
c The Grasshopper and the Ants (Illus. by Pinkney, Jerry) — Pinkney, Jerry
Grasshopper Buddy (Illus. by Oliva, Octavio) — Smith, Michael
c Grasshopper Jungle — Smith, Andrew Anselmo
y Grasshopper Jungle (Read by Smith, Andrew)
c The Grasshopper & the Ants (Illus. by Pinkney, Jerry) — Pinkney, Jerry
c Grasshoppers Dance (Illus. by Rycroft, Nina) — MacIver, Juliette
Grassroots Asian Theology: Thinking the Faith from the Ground Up — Chan, Simon
Grassroots Fascism: The War Experience of the Japanese People — Yoshimi, Yoshiaki
Grassroots for Hire: Public Affairs Consultants in American Democracy — Walker, Edward T.
Grateful Dead and the Art of Rock Improvisation — Malvinni, David
The Grateful Life: The Secret to Happiness, and the Science of Contentment — Lesowitz, Nina
c Grateful — Mutala, Marion
Gratitude — Sacks, Oliver
The Gratitude Diaries: How a Year Looking on the Bright Side Transformed My Life — Kaplan, Janice
Grave Consequences — Thurlo, David
Grave on Grand Avenue — Hirahara, Naomi
Grave Phantoms — Bennett, Jenn
The Grave Soul — Hart, Ellen
Graves' Retreat / Night of Shadows — Gorman, Ed
y The Graveyard Book (Read by Jacobi, Derek). Audiobook Review — Gaiman, Neil
y The Graveyard Book Graphic Novel, vol. 1 (Illus. by Scott, Steve) — Gaiman, Neil
y The Graveyard Book Graphic Novel, vol. 2 (Illus. by LaFuente, David) — Gaiman, Neil
y The Graveyard Book Graphic Novel, vol. 2 (Illus. by Russell, P. Craig) — Gaiman, Neil
Graveyard of Empires — Cole, Lincoln
Graveyard Poetry: Religion, Aesthetics and the Mid-Eighteenth-Century Poetic Condition — Parisot, Eric
y Graveyard Quest — Green, K.C.
c Gravity-Defying Animals — Lunis, Natalie
Gravity: Newtonian, Post-Newtonian, Relativistic — Poisson, Eric
Gravity's Ghost and Big Dog: Scientific Discovery and Social Analysis in the Twenty-Firt Century — Collins, Harry
The Gray Notebook — Pla, Josep
c Gray Wolves: Howling Pack Mammals — Hirsch, Rebecca E.
GrayNet — Kane, D.S.
The Great Age of Mission: Some Historical Studies in Mission History — Nemer, Lawrence
The Great American Dividend Machine: How an Outsider Became the Undisputed Champ of Wall Street — Spetrino, Bill
The Great American Health Hoax — Francis, Raymond
The Great American Mosaic: An Exploration of Diversity in Primary Documents — Okihiro, Gary Y.
Great American Railroad Stories
The Great American Scaffold: Intertextuality and Identity in American Presidential Discourse — Austermuhl, Frank
y The Great American Whatever — Federle, Tim
The Great and Calamitous Tale of Johan Thoms — Thornton, Ian
The Great and Holy War: How World War I Became a Religious Crusade — Jenkins, Philip
c The Great and Mighty Nikko! A Bilingual Counting Book (Illus. by Garza, Xavier) — Garza, Xavier
c The Great and Mighty Nikko! (Illus. by Garza, Xavier) — Garza, Xavier

c The Great and Powerful (Illus. by Isik, Krystal) — Phillips, Ruby Ann
A Great and Terrible King: Edward I and the Forging of Britain — Morris, Marc
c The Great and the Grand (Illus. by Robbins, Elizabeth) — Fox, Benjamin
A Great and Wretched City: Promise and Failure in Machiavelli's Florentine Political Thought — Jurdjevic, Mark
The Great Archaeologists — Fagan, Brian
A Great Aridness: Climate Change and the Future of the American Southwest — deBuys, William
c Great Ball of Light (Illus. by Holmes, Jeremy) — Kuhlman, Evan
c Great Ball of Light — Kuhlman, Evan
The Great Beanie Baby Bubble: Mass Delusion and the Dark Side of Cute — Bissonnette, Zac
Great Bear Wild: Dispatches from a Northern Rainforest — McAllister, Ian
c The Great Big Book of Aussie Inventions — Taylor, Chris Roy
c A Great Big Cuddle: Poems for the Very Young (Illus. by Riddell, Chris) — Rosen, Michael
c The Great Big Dinosaur Treasury: Tales of Adventure and Discovery — Carrick, Carol
c The Great Big Green Book (Illus. by Asquith, Ros) — Hoffman, Mary
c Great Britain — Senker, Cath
The Great British Dream Factory: The Strange History of our National Imagination — Sandbrook, Dominic
c Great Building Designs, 1900-Today — Graham, Ian
Great Catastrophe: Armenians and Turks in the Shadow of Genocide — de Waal, Thomas
c The Great Cheese Robbery — Warnes, Tim
c The Great Cheese Robbery (Illus. by Warnes, Tim) — Warnes, Tim
The Great Christ Comet: Revealing the True Star of Bethlehem — Nicholl, Colin
The Great Civilized Conversation: Education for a World Community — De Bary, William Theodore
The Great Cook: Essential Techniques and Inspired Flavors to Make Every Dish Better — Briscione, James
The Great Debate: Edmund Burke, Thomas Paine, and the Birth of Right and Left — Levin, Yuval
y The Great Depression for Kids: Hardship and Hope in 1930s America, with 21 Activities — Mullenbach, Cheryl
c The Great Depression — Wiseman, Blaine
The Great Depression of the 1930s: Lessons for Today — Crafts, Nicholas
The Great Detective — Dundas, Zach
The Great Detective: The Amazing Rise and Immortal Life of Sherlock Holmes — Dundas, Zach
The Great Disconnect in Early Childhood Education — Gramling, Michael
The Great Divide — Grace, Stephen
The Great Divide: The Conflict between Washington and Jefferson That Defined a Nation — Fleming, Thomas
The Great Divide: Unequal Societies and What We Can Do about Them — Stiglitz, Joseph E.
The Great Dominion: Winston Churchill in Canada, 1900-1954 — Dilks, David
c Great Electronic Gadget Designs 1900-Today — Graham, Ian
c The Great Escape (Illus. by Wight, Eric) — Egan, Kate
The Great Estate — Browning, Sherri
The Great Exhibition: A Documentary History, 4 vols. — Cantor, Geoffrey
y Great Expectations (Illus. by Poon, Nokman) — Silvermoon, Crystal
y Great Expectations: Manga Classics (Illus. by Poon, Nokman) — Dickens, Charles
Great Expectations (Illus. by Poon, Nokman) — Dickens, Charles
The Great Explosion: Gunpowder, the Great War, and a Disaster on the Kent Marshes — Dillon, Brian
The Great Fire: One American's Mission to Rescue Victims of the 20th Century's First Genocide — Ureneck, Lou
The Great Forgetting — Renner, James
Great Game East: India, China, and the Struggle for Asia's Most Volatile Frontier — Lintner, Bertil
The Great Game of Genocide: Imperialism, Nationalism and the Destruction of the Ottoman Armenians — Bloxham, Donald
c Great Goalies — Zweig, Eric
y The Great Good Summer — Scanlon, Liz Garton
c The Great Googly Moogly — Dicmas, Courtney

The Great Grammar Book — Sramek, Marsha
c Great Horned Owls — Leaf, Christina
y The Great Hunt — Higgins, Wendy
c A Great Idea? (Illus. by Dippold, Jane) — Suen, Anastasia
The Great Indian Phone Book: How Cheap Mobile Phones Change Business, Politics and Daily Life — Doron, Assa
The Great Indian Phone Book: How the Cheap Cell Phone Changes Business, Politics, and Daily Life — Doron, Assa
Great Is the Truth: Secrecy, Scandal, and the Quest for Justice at the Horace Mann School — Kamil, Amos
Great Lakes Creoles: A French-Indian Community on the Northern Borderlands, Prairie Du Chien, 1750-1860 — Murphy, Lucy Eldersveld
The Great Latin American Novel — Riley, Brendan
The Great Leader and the Fighter Pilot: The True Story of the Tyrant Who Created North Korea and the Young Lieutenant Who Stole His Way to Freedom — Harden, Blaine
The Great Loop Experience-From Concept to Completion — Hospodar, George
The Great Maya Droughts in Cultural Context: Case Studies in Resilience and Vulnerability — Iannone, Gyles
Great Men Die Twice: The Selected Works of Mark Kram — Kram, Mark, Jr.
c Great Moments in Olympic Basketball — Williams, Doug
c Great Moments in Olympic Gymnastics — Lawrence, Blythe
c Great Moments in Olympic Skating — Barnas, Jo-Ann
c Great Moments in Olympic Snowboarding — Howell, Brian
c The Great Monkey Rescue: Saving the Golden Lion Tamarins — Markle, Sandra
The Great Mortdecai Moustache Mystery — Bonfiglioli, Kyril
The Great Mother Bible — Cromwell, Mare
Great New Ways with Granny Squares — P., Rosa
Great North Road — Hamilton, Peter F.
The Great Ocean: Pacific Worlds from Captain Cook to the Gold Rush — Igler, David
The Great Parade: Broadway's Astonishing, Never-to-Be-Forgotten 1963-1964 Season — Filichia, Peter
c The Great Pirate Christmas Battle (Illus. by Jaskiel, Stan) — Lewis, Michael G.
The Great Powers and the International System: Systemic Theory in Empirical Perspective — Braumoeller, Bear F.
The Great Race: The Global Quest for the Car of the Future — Tillemann, Levi
The Great Rebirth — Aslund, Anders
The Great Reformer: Francis and the Making of a Radical Pope — Ivereigh, Austen
The Great Reformer: Francis and the Making of a Radical Pope — Ivereigh, Austen
The Great Reformer: Francis and the Making of a Radical Pope
The Great Rent Wars: New York, 1917-1929 — Fogelson, Robert M.
Great Shakespeare Actors: Burbage to Branagh — Wells, Stanley
Great Shakespeareans Set III, vol. II: Berlioz, Verdi, Wagner, Britten — Albright, Daniel
y Great Showdowns: The Revenge (Illus. by Campbell, Scott) — Campbell, Scott
The Great Silent Majority: Nixon's 1969 Speech on Vietnamization — Campbell, Karlyn Kohrs
Great Soul of Siberia: Passion, Obsession, and One Man's Quest for the World's Most Elusive Tiger — Park, Sooyong
The Great Surge: The Ascent of the Developing World — Radelet, Steven
The Great Swindle — Lemaitre, Pierre
c The Great Thanksgiving Escape — Fearing, Mark
Great Tide Rising — Moore, Kathleen Dean
The Great Transformation of Japanese Capitalism — Lechevalier, Sebastien
The Great Transition: Shifting from Fossil Fuels to Solar and Wind Energy — Brown, Lester R.
c Great Wall of China — Raum, Elizabeth
The Great War and the Origins of Humanitarianism, 1918-1924 — Cabanes, Bruno
The Great War at Sea: A Naval History of the First World War — Sondhaus, Lawrence
The Great War Dawning: Germany and Its Army at the Start of World War I — Buchholz, Frank
The Great War for Peace — Mulligan, William

The Great War — Gatalica, Aleksandar
The Great War of Our Time: The CIA's Fight against Terrorism from al Qa'ida to ISIS — Morell, Michael
c The Great War — Kay, Jim
c The Great War: Stories Inspired by Items from the First World War. Audiobook Review
y The Great War: Stories Inspired by Items from the First World War (Illus. by Kay, Jim) — Almond, David
c The Great White Man-Eating Shark (Illus. by Allen, Jonathan) — Mahy, Margaret
The Great White Way: Race and the Broadway Musical — Hoffman, Warren
The Great Work: Self-Knowledge and Healing through the Wheel of the Year — Lazic, Tiffany
Greater Than Equal: African American Struggles for Schools and Citizenship in North Carolina, 1919-1965 — Thuesen, Sarah Caroline
Greater Than Gold — Aanensen, Gayle Eggen
The Greater War: Other Combatants and Other Fronts, 1914-1918 — Krause, Jonathan
The Greatest Books You'll Never Read
The Greatest Books You'll Never Read: Unpublished Masterpieces by the World's Greatest Writers — Richards, Bernard
The Greatest Empire: A Life of Seneca — Wilson, Emily
The Greatest Gatsby: A Visual Book of Grammar — Riddle, Tohby
The Greatest Knight: The Remarkable Life of William Marshal, the Power Behind Five English Thrones — Asbridge, Thomas
The Greatest Knight: The Remarkable Life of William Marshall, the Power Behind Five English Thrones — Asbridge, Thomas
c Greatest Movie Monsters Series — Roza, Greg
The "Greatest Problem": Religion and State Formation in Meiji Japan — Maxey, Trent E.
The Greatest Prospector in the World — Dunn, Ken
The Greatest Shows on Earth: A History of the Circus — Simon, Linda
The Greatest Victory: Canada's One Hundred Days, 1918 — Granatstein, J.L.
y The Greatest Zombie Movie Ever — Strand, Jeff
Greco-Roman Culture and the New Testament: Studies Commemorating the Centennial of the Pontifical Biblical Institute — Aune, David E.
Greco-Scythian Art and the Birth of Eurasia: From Classical Antiquity to Russian Modernity — Meyer, Hans-Caspar
c Greece — Bodden, Valerie
Greece — Murray, Julie
Greece and Mesopotamia. Dialogues in Literature — Haubold, Johannes
Greece and Rome at the Crystal Palace: Classical Sculpture and Modern Britain, 1854-1936 — Nichols, Kate
Greed and Grievance: Ex-Militants' Perspectives on the Conflict in Solomon Islands, 1998-2003 — Allen, Matthew G.
Greed: from Gordon Gekko to David Hume — Sutherland, Stewart
c The Greedy Rainbow — Chandler, Susan
Greek-American Relations from Monroe to Truman — Repousis, Angelo
Greek Drama and the Invention of Rhetoric — Sansone, David
Greek Drama IV: Texts, Contexts, Performance — Rosenbloom, David Scott
Greek Epigram in Reception. J.A. Symonds, Oscar Wilde, and the Invention of Desire, 1805-1929 — Nisbet, Gideon
Greek into Latin from Antiquity until the Nineteenth Century — Glucker, John
Greek Models of Mind and Self — Long, A.A.
Greek Tragedy on Screen — Michelakis, Pantelis
Greeks and Barbarians — Vlassopoulos, Kostas
The Greeks in Asia — Boardman, John
Green and Pleasant Land — Cutler, Judith
The Green and the Black — Sernovitz, Gary
The Green and the Gray: The Irish in the Confederate States of America — Gleeson, David T.
c Green Animals — Borth, Teddy
Green Barons, Force-of-Circumstance Entrepreneurs, Impotent Mayors: Rural Change in the Early Years of Post-Socialist Capitalist Democracy — Swain, Nigel
c Green Bay Packers — Zappa, Marcia
y Green Berets — Whiting, Jim
c The Green Bicycle — Al Mansour, Haifaa

c The Green Box League of Nutritious Justice
    — Kantor, Keith
   The Green Eyed Girl — Chew, J.W.
   Green Giants: How Smart Companies Turn
    Sustainability into Billion-Dollar Businesses
    — Williams, E. Freya
   Green Glowing Skull — Corbett, Gavin
   Green Gold: Alabama's Forests and Forest Industries
    — Fickle, James E.
   Green Hell — Bruen, Ken
   Green Hills of Africa — Hemingway, Ernest
   Green Home Building: Money-Saving Strategies for
    an Affordable, Healthy, High-Performance Home
    — Cook, Miki
   Green Is a Chile Pepper. Audiobook Review — Thong,
    Roseanne Greenfield
   Green Island — Ryan, Shawna Yang
c Green Lizards vs. Red Rectangles (Illus. by Antony,
    Steve) — Antony, Steve
c The Green Musician (Illus. by Ewart, Claire)
    — Shahegh, Mahvash
   Green on Blue — Ackerman, Elliot
c Green Queen (Illus. by Mourning, Tuesday)
    — Peschke, Marci
   The Green Road — Enright, Anne
   The Green Room — Enright, Anne
c The Green Sea Turtle — Muller, Isabel
   Green Speculations: Science Fiction and
    Transformative Environmentalism — Otto, Eric C.
y The Green Teen Cookbook: Recipes for All Seasons
    — Marchive, Laurane
c Green Thumbs-Up! (Illus. by Chatelain, Eva)
    — Meyerhoff, Jenny
y Green Valentine — Wilkinson, Lili
   Greenback Dollar: The Incredible Rise of the
    Kingston Trio — Bush, William J.
   Greenbeaux — Bergheim, David
c Greenglass House (Read by Coffey, Chris Henry).
    Audiobook Review — Milford, Kate
c Greenglass House (Illus. by Zollars, Jaime) — Milford,
    Kate
   Greening Death: Reclaiming Burial Practices and
    Restoring Our Tie to the Earth — Kelly, Suzanne
   The Greening of Asia: The Business Case for Solving
    Asia's Environmental Emergency — Clifford, Mark
c Greenling (Illus. by Pinfold, Levi) — Pinfold, Levi
   Greenmantle — Buchan, John
   Greens 24/7: More Than 100 Quick, Easy, and
    Delicious Recipes for Eating Leafy Greens and
    Other Green Vegetables, at Every Meal — Nadel,
    Jessica
   Greens + Grains: Recipes for Deliciously Healthful
    Meals — Watson, Molly
   Greetings from My Girlie Leisure Place — Mesmer,
    Sharon
   Greg Egan — Burnham, Karen
   Gregorius: An Incestuous Saint in Medieval Europe
    and Beyond — Murdoch, Brian
   Gregory the Great, Moral Reflections on the Book of
    Job, vol. 1: Preface and Books 1-5 — Kerns, Brian
   Grendel's Game — Mauritzson, Erik
   Grendel's Mother — Morrison, Susan Signe
   Grenzen der Pluralisierung? Zur Konflikthaftigkeit
    Religioser Identitatsbildung und Erinnerungskultur
    in Europa seit der Fruhen Neuzeit
   Grenzraume - Raumgrenzen: Landliche Lebenswelten
    aus Kulturwissenschaftlicher Sicht
c Gretchen over the Beach — Alley, R.W.
   Gretel and the Case of the Missing Frog Prints
    — Brackston, P.J.
   Grey — James, E.L.
   Grey (Read by Webber, Zachary). Audiobook Review
    — James, E.L.
   Grey Daze — Scott, Michael Allan
c Gridiron Showdown — Maddox, Jake
   Grief, Folly, Love: Searching for Truth in War
    — Martin, Timothy
   Grief Is the Thing with Feathers — Porter, Max
   The Grierson Effect: Tracing Documentary's
    International Movement — Druick, Zoe
c The Griffin and the Dinosaur: How Adrienne Mayor
    Discovered a Fascinating Link between Myth and
    Science (Read by Rowar, Graham). Audiobook
    Review — Mayor, Adrienne
   Griffith Stadium — Ambros, Robert
   Grill Nation: 200 Surefire Recipes, Tips, and
    Techniques to Grill Like a Pro — Guas, David
   Grilled Pizza the Right Way: The Best Technique for
    Cooking Incredible Tasting Pizza Flatbread on
    Your Barbecue Page Street — Delpha, John
c The Grimjinx Rebellion (Illus. by Helquist, Brett)
    — Farrey, Brian

c Grimm Legacies: The Magic Spell of the Grimms'
    Folk and Fairy Tales — Zipes, Jack
c The Grimstones: Hatched — Asphyxia
y The Grin in the Dark (Illus. by Evergreen, Nelson)
    — Darke, J.A.
   The Grind: Inside Baseball's Endless Season
    — Svrluga, Barry
c The Grindle Witch — Myers, Benjamin J.
   Grit in Your Craw — Luckadoo, Robert
   Grit, Noise and Revolution: The Birth of Detroit Rock
    'n' Roll — Carson, David A.
   Grit: The Life and Politics of Paul Martin Sr
    — Donaghy, Greg
   Grit: The New Science of What It Takes to Persevere,
    Flourish, Succeed — Stoltz, Paul G.
c Grizzly Bears of Alaska: Explore the Wild World of
    Bears (Illus. by Endres, Patrick J.) — Miller,
    Debbie S.
   A Grizzly in the Mail and Other Adventures in
    American History — Grove, Tim
c Grognonstein (Illus. by Santat, Dan) — Berger,
    Samantha
c Gronk: A Monster's Story (Illus. by Cook, Katie)
    — Cook, Katie
   Groove Interrupted: Loss, Renewal, and the Music of
    New Orleans — Spera, Keith
c Groovy Graphing: Quadrant One and Beyond
    — Arias, Lisa
   Groucho Marx: The Comedy of Existence — Siegel,
    Lee
   Groucho: The Life and Times of Julius Henry Marx
    — Kanfer, Stefan
c The Ground Squirrels Take Glacier, Maybe... (Illus.
    by Johnson, Sandra) — Johnson, Sandra
   Ground Zero, Nagasaki — Yuchi, Seirai
y Grounded — Wilkinson, Sheena
   Grounded: Finding God in the World: A Spiritual
    Revolution — Bass, Diana Butler
y Grounded: The Adventures of Rapunzel — Morrison,
    Megan
c Groundhog Day — Murray, Julie
c Groundhogs and Guinea Pigs: A Readers' Theater
    Script and Guide (Illus. by Mata, Nina) — Wallace,
    Nancy K.
c Groundhog's Day Off (Illus. by Helquist, Brett)
    — Pearlman, Robb
c Groundhog's Dilemma (Illus. by Faulkner, Matt)
    — Remenar, Kristen
   Grounds of Judgment: Extraterritoriality and
    Imperial Power in Nineteenth-Century China and
    Japan — Cassel, Par Kristoffer
   The Group Theater: Passion, Politics, and
    Performance in the Depression Era — Chinoy,
    Helen Krich
   The Grove Dictionary of American Music, 2d ed., 8
    vols. — Garrett, Charles Hiroshi
   Grow a Little Fruit Tree — Ralph, Ann
   Grow a Living Wall: Create Vertical Gardens with
    Purpose — Coronado, Shawna
   Grow All You Can Eat in 3 Square Feet — Johnsen,
    Kate
   Grow Your Own Wedding Flowers: How to Grow and
    Arrange Your Own Rowers for All Special
    Occasions — Newbery, Georgie
   Grow Your Value: Living and Working to Your Full
    Potential — Brzezinski, Mika
   Growing Democracy in Japan: The Parliamentary
    Cabinet System since 1868 — Woodall, Brian
   Growing Hybrid Hazelnuts: The New Resilient Crop
    for a Changing Climate — Rutter, Philip
   Growing Space: A History of the Allotment Movement
    — Acton, Lesley
c Growing Together across the Autism Spectrum
    — Marks, Elizabeth
   Growing Tomorrow: A Farm-to-Table Journey in
    Photos and Recipes: Behind the Scenes with 18
    Extraordinary Sustainable Farmers Who Are
    Changing the Way We Eat — Pritchard, Forrest
c The Growing Up Book for Boys: What Boys on the
    Autism Spectrum Need to Know! (Illus. by Suggs,
    Margaret Anne) — Hartan, Davida
c The Growing Up Guide for Girls: What Girls on the
    Autism Spectrum Need to Know! (Illus. by Suggs,
    Margaret Anne) — Hartan, Davida
   Growing Up in 20th Century European
    Borderlands/Kindheit in europaischen
    Grenzregionen im 20. Jahrhundert
   Growing Up Jewish in Alexandria: The Story of a
    Sephardic Family's Exodus from Egypt — Carasso,
    Lucienne
c The Growing Up of Princess Eva (Illus. by Rangala,
    Gopinath) — Feuer, Rhoda

c Growing Up Pedro: How the Martinez Brothers Made
    It from the Dominican Republic All the Way to the
    Major Leagues (Illus. by Tavares, Matt) — Tavares,
    Matt
   Growing Up Superheroes: The Extraordinary
    Adventures of Deihlia Nye — Fraser, Diane
c Growing Up without My Daddy (Illus. by Shorter,
    Susan) — Adley, Angel
c Growl! Growl! (Illus. by Braun, Sebastien) — Nosy
    Crow
   The Grown Ups — Antalek, Robin
c Grown-Ups, the World, and Me! (Illus. by Pare,
    Roger) — Lazar, Judith
   The Growth of Non-Western Cities: Primary and
    Secondary Urban Networking, c. 900-1900 — Hall,
    Kenneth R.
c Grub in Love (Illus. by Warburton, Sarah)
    — Burlingham, Abi
c The Grudge Keeper (Read by McDonough, John).
    Audiobook Review — Rockliff, Mara
   Gruesome Spectacles: Botched Executions and
    America's Death Penalty — Sarat, Austin
   Grumpmuffin across the Pond — Greer, Neville
   Grun-Tu-Molani — Ravinthiran, Vidyan
y Grunge Gods and Graveyards — Giarratano,
    Kimberly G.
   Grydscaen: Tribute — Uesugi, Natsuya
y Gryphons Aren't So Great — Sturm, James
   Guangdong and Chinese Diaspora: The Changing
    Landscape of Qiaoxiang — Yow, Cheun Hoe
   Guano and the Opening of the Pacific World: A
    Global Ecological History — Cushman, Gregory T.
   Guantanamo Diary — Slahi, Mohamedou Ould
   Guapa — Haddad, Saleem
   The Guarani and Their Missions: A Socioeconomic
    History — Sarreal, Julia
   Guaranteed Heroes — Lashner, William
   Guaranteed Pure: The Moody Bible Institute,
    Business, and the Making of Modern
    Evangelicalism — Gloege, Timothy E.W.
   Guaranteed to Bleed — Mulhern, Julie
y Guardian — Deen, Natasha
   Guardian Angel: Life and Death Adventures with
    Pararescue, the World's Most Powerful Commando
    Rescue Force — Sine, William F.
c The Guardian Dragon (Illus. by Lucas, Diane)
    — Breen, U.M.
   The Guardian of Mercy: How an Extraordinary
    Painting by Caravaggio Changed an Ordinary Life
    Today — Ward, Terence
   Guardian of Paradise — Lawrence, W.E
   Guardian of the Golden Gate — Briggs, Kevin
   The Guardian Stones — Reed, Eric
y Guardians — Kim, Susan
   Guardians of the Galaxy: Rocket Raccoon and Groot
    Steal the Galaxy! (Read by Full cast). Audiobook
    Review — Abnett, Dan
   The Guardians: The League of Nations and the Crisis
    of Empire — Pedersen, Susan
   The Guardianship of Best Interests: Institutional Care
    for the Children of the Poor in Halifax, 1850-1960
    — Lafferty, Renee N.
   Guarding Eden: Champions of Climate Action
    — Hart, Deborah
y Guarding Secrets — Jones, Patrick
   Guarding the Air — Harding, Gunnar
c Guatemala — Rudolph, Jessica
   Gubbeen: The Story of a Working Farm and Its
    Foods — Ferguson, Giana
   Guerilla Furniture Design: How to Build Lean,
    Modern Furniture with Salvaged Materials
    — Holman, Will
   The Guernsey Literary and Potato Pie Society
    — Barrows, Annie
   "Guerra santa" e conquiste islamiche nel Mediterraneo
    — Wolf, Kordula
   Guerre et deplacements de populations. Regards
    croises sur l'Europe aux XIXe et XXe siecles
   Guerreros y traidores: De la Guerra de Espana a la
    Guerra fria — Reverte, Jorge M.
   Guerrilla Auditors: The Politics of Transparency in
    Neoliberal Paraguay — Hetherington, Kregg
c Guess Who, Haiku (Illus. by Shea, Bob) — Caswell,
    Deanna
c Guess Who's My Pet — Mumme, Sarah
   A Guest at the Shooters' Banquet: My Grandfather's
    SS Past, My Jewish Family, a Search for the Truth
    — Gabis, Rita
   The Guest Cat — Selland, Eric
   The Guest Cottage — Thayer, Nancy
   The Guest Room — Bohjalian, Chris

Guest Workers and Resistance to U.S. Corporate Despotism — *Ness, Immanuel*
Guida ai Fondi Manoscritti, Numismatici, a Stampa della Biblioteca Vaticana, vol. 1: Dipartimento Manoscritti — *D'Aiuto, Francesco*
Guida ai Fondi Manoscritti, Numismatici, a Stampa della Biblioteca Vaticana, vol 2: Dipartimento Stampati--Dipartimento del Gabinetto Numismatico--Ufficio della Prefettura — *D'Aiuto, Francesco*
Guide Bleu — *Ortlieb, Gilles*
A Guide Book of Mercury Dimes, Standing Liberty Quarters, and Liberty Walking Half Dollars — *Bowers, David*
Guide de la Recherche en Histoire Antillaise et Guyanaise — *Begot, Danielle*
The Guide for the Perplexed — *Cronin, Paul*
A Guide to Functional Analysis — *Krantz, Steven G.*
Guide to Implementing the Next Generation Science Standards — *National Research Council*
Guide to Natural Mental Health: Anxiety, Bipolar, Depression, Schizophrenia, and Digital Addiction — *Jiang, William*
Guide to Reference: Essential General Reference and Library Science Sources — *Whitlatch, Jo Bell*
Guide to Reference in Business and Economics — *Sowards, Steven W.*
c **A Guide to Sisters (Illus. by Barton, Suzanne)** — *Metcalf, Paula*
Guide to the Aqueducts of Ancient Rome — *Aicher, Peter J.*
The Guild and Guild Buildings of Shakespeare's Stratford: Society: Religion, Education and Stage — *Mulryne, J.R.*
The Guild of Saint Cooper — *Scanlon, Shya*
y **Guile** — *Cooper, Constance*
Guillaume Apollinaire — *Campa, Laurence*
Guillaume de Machaut: Secretary, Poet, Musician — *Leach, Elizabeth Eva*
Guilt by Association: Heresy Catalogues in Early Christianity — *Smith, Geoffrey S.*
Guilty as Sin — *Cutler, Judith*
Guilty But Insane: Mind and Law in Golden Age Detective Fiction — *Walton, Samantha*
c **Guilty? Crime, Punishment, and the Changing Face of Justice** — *Kanefield, Teri*
The Guilty One (Read by Eby, Tanya). Audiobook Review — *Littlefield, Sophie*
The Guilty One — *Littlefield, Sophie*
The Guilty: Stories — *Villoro, Juan*
The Guilty Stories — *Villoro, Juan*

The Guilty: Stories — *Villoro, Juan*
Guilty Waters — *Masters, Priscilla*
c **Guinea Dog 3** — *Jennings, Patrick*
c **Guinea Pig Killer (Illus. by McElhinney, Glenn)** — *Graves, Annie*
c **Guion the Lion: A Colorful World (Illus. by Morales, Joseba)** — *Macsovits, Rebecca Wilson*
The Guise of Another — *Eskens, Allen*
Guitar Hero — *Lee, Day's*
Guitar Makers: The Endurance of Artisanal Values in North America — *Dudley, Kathryn Marie*
Guittard Chocolate Cookbook: Decadent Recipes from San Francisco's Premium Bean-to-Bar Chocolate Company — *Guittard, Amy*
Gulag Town, Company Town: Forced Labor and Its Legacy in Vorkuta — *Barenberg, Alan*
The Gulf Theater 1813-1815 — *Stoltz, Joseph F., III*
Gulliver's Travels — *Womersley, David*
Gulp: Adventures on the Alimentary Canal — *Roach, Mary*
c **Gumballs (Illus. by Baker, Keith)** — *Baker, Keith*
Gumbo — *Curry, Dale*
Gumiguru — *Muzanenhamo, Togara*
Gummi Bears Should Not Be Organic, and Other Opinions I Can't Back Up with Facts — *Wilder-Taylor, Stefanie*
Gumption: Relighting the Torch of Freedom with America's Gutsiest Troublemakers (Read by Offerman, Nick). Audiobook Review — *Offerman, Nick*
Gumption: Relighting the Torch of Freedom with America's Gutsiest Troublemakers — *Offerman, Nick*
Gumshoe — *Leininger, Rob*
The Gun — *Nakamura, Fuminori*
Gun Baby Gun: A Bloody Journey into the World of the Gun — *Overton, Iain*
Gun, Needle, Spoon: A Memoir — *O'Neil, Patrick*
Gun Street Girl — *McKinty, Adrian*
Gun Violence and Public Life — *Luke, Timothy W.*
The Gunman — *Manchette, Jean-Patrick*
Gunnar Aslund's Gothenburg: The Transformation of Public Architecture in Interwar Europe — *Adams, Nicholas*
A Gunner in Lee's Army: The Civil War Letters of Thomas Henry Carter — *Dozier, Graham T.*
The Gunpowder Age — *Andrade, Tonio*
Guns across America: Reconciling Gun Rules and Rights — *Spitzer, Robert J.*
c **Gunslingers and Cowboys** — *Nolan, Frederick*
Gunsmoke Bonanza — *Martin, Chuck*

The Gurkha's Daughter — *Parajuly, Prajwal*
Gurunanda's Happy Breath Yoga: Wall Street Yoga — *Gurunanda*
c **Gus** — *Dunrea, Olivier*
c **Gus & Me: The Story of My Granddad and My First Guitar (Illus. by Richards, Theodora)** — *Richards, Keith*
c **Gus (Illus. by Dunrea, Olivier)** — *Dunrea, Olivier*
Gustav Adolph Comaro Riecke: Schulpolitik und Schulpadagogik zur Zeit des Vormarz, und der Revolution von 1848/49 — *Metzger, Folker*
Gustav Mahler — *Ryding, Erik*
Gustav Mahler's Symphonic Landscapes — *Peattie, Thomas*
c **Gustave (Illus. by Pratt, Pierre)** — *Simard, Remy*
Gusto for Things: A History of Objects in Seventeenth-Century Rome — *Ago, Renata*
The Gut Balance Revolution: Boost Your Metabolism, Restore Your Inner Ecology, and Lose the Weight for Good! — *Mullin, Gerard E.*
Gut: The Inside Story of Our Body's Most Underrated Organ — *Enders, Giulia*
Gutenberg's Apprentice — *Christie, Alix*
y **Guts & Glory: The American Civil War (Illus. by Butzer, C.M.)** — *Thompson, Ben*
The Guts — *Doyle, Roddy*
Gutshot: Stories — *Gray, Amelia*
y **The Guy, the Girl, the Artist and his Ex** — *Williams, Gabrielle*
The Guy Wolf Dancing — *Cook-Lynn, Elizabeth*
Guyana — *Turcotte, Elies*
y **Guy's Guide** — *Clark, Travis*
Guys Like Me — *Fabre, Dominique*
c **Guys Read: Other Worlds** — *Scieszka, Jon*
c **Guys Read: True Stories** — *Scieszka, Jon*
Gwendolen — *Souhami, Diana*
Gwendolen
Gwendolen — *Souhami, Diana*
c **Gwendolyn Grace (Illus. by Hannigan, Katherine)** — *Hannigan, Katherine*
Gwendolyn's Sword — *Haltom, E.A.*
Gymnasium im Strukturellen Wandel: Befunde und Perspektiven von den Preussischen Reformen bis zur Reform der Gymnasialen Oberstufe — *Ritzi, Christian*
c **Gymnastics: Great Moments, Records, and Facts** — *Borth, Teddy*
y **Gyo (Illus. by Ito, Junji)** — *Ito, Junji*
y **Gypsy Girl** — *James, Kathryn*
c **Gypsy's Fortune** — *Stellings, Caroline*
The Gypsy's Sun — *Tate, Nixie*

H

y H.E.A.R. — *Epstein, Robin*
c H.I.V.E.: Deadlock — *Walden, Mark*
  H Is for Hawk (Read by Macdonald, Helen). Audiobook Review — *Macdonald, Helen*
  H Is for Hawk — *Macdonald, Helen*
c H Is for Holy (Illus. by Hayward, Heather) — *Boyd, Nika*
c H.O.R.S.E.: A Game of Basketball and Imagination (Read by Graham, Dion). Audiobook Review — *Myers, Christopher*
  H.P. Lovecraft and the Black Magickal Tradition — *Steadman, John L.*
  H.P. Lovecraft's Collected Fiction: A Variorum Edition, 3 vols. — *Joshi, Sunand T.*
y H2O — *Bergin, Virginia*
  HA! The Science of When We Laugh and Why — *Weems, Scott*
c Haatchi & Little B: The Inspiring True Story of One Boy and His Dog — *Holden, Wendy*
  Habermas and Religion — *Calhoun, Craig*
  Habitus und Politik in Karnten: Soziogenetische und Psychogenetische Grundlagen des Systems Jorg Haider — *Dorner-Horig, Christian*
  The Habsburgs: Dynasty, Culture and Politics — *Fichtner, Paula Sutter*
  Hacienda — *Charlier, Marj*
  Hack Attack: The Inside Story of How the Truth Caught Up with Rupert Murdoch — *Davies, Nick*
  The Hacked World Order: How Nations Fight, Trade, Maneuver, and Manipulate in the Digital Age — *Segal, Adam*
  Hacker, Hoaxer, Whistleblower, Spy: The Many Faces of Anonymous — *Coleman, Gabriella*
c Hacking Fashion: Fleece — *Fontichiaro, Kristin*
  Had I Known: A Memoir of Survival (Read by Lunden, Joan). Audiobook Review — *Lunden, Joan*
  Had I Known: A Memoir of Survival — *Lunden, Joan*
  The Hadal Zone: Life in the Deepest Oceans — *Jamieson, Alan*
c Hades Speaks! A Guide to the Underworld by the Greek God of the Dead (Illus. by Larson, J.E.) — *Shecter, Vicky Alvear*
  Haeckel's Embryos: Images, Evolution, and Fraud — *Hopwood, Nick*
  Hail, Cigaros! — *Young, Jack*
  Hail of Fire: A Man and His Family Face Natural Disaster — *Fritz, Randy*
  Hail to the Redskins — *Lazarus, Adam*
  Haints: American Ghosts, Millennial Passions, and Contemporary Gothic Fictions — *Redding, Arthur*
  Haints Stay — *Winnette, Colin*
  Hair: A Human History — *Stenn, Kurt*
  Hair of the Dog — *Slater, Susan*
  The Hair Trunk or the Ideal Commonwealth: An Extravaganza — *Stevenson, Robert Louis*
  The Hairdresser of Harare — *Huchu, Tendai*
c Hairs / Pelitos (Illus. by Ybanez, Terry) — *Cisneros, Sandra*
c Hairy Harold and His Extraordinary Trip to New York — *Quintero, Andres*
  Haitian Graves — *Delany, Vicki*
  The Haitian Revolution: A Documentary History — *Geggus, David*
  The Haitian Revolution in the Literary Imagination: Radical Horizons, Conservative Constraints — *Kaisary, Philip*
c The Halcyon Bird — *Beyer, Kat*
y Half a Creature from the Sea: A Life in Stories (Illus. by Taylor, Eleanor) — *Almond, David*
  Half a King (Read by Keating, John). Audiobook Review — *Abercrombie, Joe*
  Half a Lifelong Romance — *Chang, Eileen*

c Half a Man (Illus. by O'Callaghan, Gemma) — *Morpurgo, Michael*
  Half a War (Read by Keating, John). Audiobook Review — *Abercrombie, Joe*
  Half a War — *Abercrombie, Joe*
c Half a World Away — *Kadohata, Cynthia*
  Half an Inch of Water: Stories — *Everett, Percival*
y Half Bad (Read by Prekopp, Carl). Audiobook Review — *Green, Sally*
  The Half Brother — *LeCraw, Holly*
  Half-Earth — *Wilson, Edward O.*
  The Half Has Never Been Told: Slavery and the Making of American Capitalism — *Baptist, Edward E.*
y Half in Love with Death — *Ross, Emily*
y The Half Life of Molly Pierce — *Leno, Katrina*
  Half-Life: The Divided Life of Bruno Pontecorvo, Physicist or Spy — *Close, Frank*
  Half Life: The Divided Life of Bruno Pontecorvo, Physicist or Spy — *Close, Frank*
y Half Lost — *Green, Sally*
c Half Magic (Illus. by Bodecker, N.M.) — *Eager, Edward*
c Half My Facebook Friends Are Ferrets — *Buckle, J.A.*
  Half of a Yellow Sun: A Novel — *Adichie, Chimamanda Ngozi*
y The Half That's Never Been Told: The Real-Life Reggae Adventures of Doctor Dread — *Doctor Dread*
  Half the World (Read by Keating, John). Audiobook Review — *Abercrombie, Joe*
y Half the World — *Abercrombie, Joe*
y Half Wild — *Green, Sally*
  Half Yard Christmas: Easy Sewing Projects Using Left-Over Pieces of Fabric — *Shore, Debbie*
  Half Yard Gifts: Easy Sewing Projects Using Left-Over Pieces of Fabric — *Shore, Debbie*
y Halfway Perfect — *Cross, Julie*
c A Hall Lot of Trouble at Cooperstown — *Aretha, David*
  Hall of Mirrors: The Great Depression, the Great Recession, and the Uses--and Misuses--of History — *Eichengreen, Barry*
  Hall of Small Mammals — *Pierce, Thomas*
y Halley — *Gibbons, Faye*
  Hallow This Ground — *Rafferty, Colin*
c Halloween and Thanksgiving (Illus. by Nguyen, Dustin) — *Nguyen, Dustin*
  Halo Found Hope: A Memoir — *Matzelle, Helo*
  Hamlet after Q1: An Uncanny History of the Shakespearean Text — *Lesser, Zachary*
  Hamlet — *Lehmann, Alan W.*
c Hamlet (Illus. by Shimony, Yaniv) — *Knapman, Timothy*
  Hammer Head: The Making of a Carpenter — *MacLaughlin, Nina*
c Hamster Monster (Illus. by Lohlein, Henning) — *Lohlein, Susanne*
c Hamster Princess: Harriet the Invincible (Illus. by Vernon, Ursula) — *Vernon, Ursula*
c Hamsters — *Murray, Julie*
c Hamsters — *Stevens, Kathryn*
  The Han Commanderies in Early Korean History — *Byington, Mark E.*
c Hana Hashimoto, Sixth Violin (Illus. by Leng, Qin) — *Uegaki, Chieri*
  Hand Drawn Jokes for Smart, Attractive People — *Diffee, Matthew*
  The Hand on the Mirror: A True Story of Life Beyond Death. — *Durham, Janis Heaphy*
  The Hand on the Mirror — *Durham, Janis Heaphy*

  A Hand Reached Down to Guide Me: Stories and a Novella — *Gates, David*
  The Hand That Feeds You — *Rich, A.J.*
  Hand to Mouth: Living in Bootstrap America. Audiobook Review — *Tirado, Linda*
  A Handbook for Corporate Information Professionals — *Schopflin, Katharine*
c Handbook For Dragon Slayers — *Haskell, Merrie*
  Handbook of Adolescent Drug Use Prevention — *Scheier, Lawrence M.*
  The Handbook of Historical Sociolinguistics (Read by Campoy, Juan Manuel Hernandez) — *Silvestre, Juan Camilo Conde*
  A Handbook of Korean Zen Practice: A Mirror on the Son School of Buddhism (Son'ga kwigam). — *Jorgensen, John*
  Handbook of Medieval Studies: Terms-Methods-Trends, 3 vols — *Classen, Albrecht*
  Handbook of Postal Strikes 1890 to 2014 — *Sandler, Douglas B.*
  Handbook of Religion: A Christian Engagement with Traditions, Teachings, and Practices — *Muck, Terry C.*
  The Handbook of Religions in Ancient Europe — *Christensen, Lisbeth Bredholt*
  Handbook of Research in Education Finance and Policy — *Ladd, Helen F.*
  Handbook of Sociology and Human Rights — *Brunsman, David L.*
  Handbook of Vance Space — *Andre-Driussi, Michael*
  Handbook of Work-Life Integration among Professionals: Challenges and Opportunities — *Major, Debra A.*
  Handbuch Medienrezeption — *Wunsch, Carsten*
c A Handful of Stars (Read by Cabezas, Maria). Audiobook Review — *Lord, Cynthia*
c A Handful of Stars — *Lord, Cynthia*
  Handlanger der SS: Die Rolle der Trawniki-Manner im Holocaust — *Benz, Angelika*
c Handmade Crafts: By Children for Children (Illus. by Montero, Manuela) — *Rodriguez, Guadalupe*
  Handmade Interiors: Create Your Own Soft Furnishings from Cushions to Curtains — *DK Publishing, Inc.*
  Handmade Soap Book: Easy Soapmaking with Natural Ingredients, 2d ed. — *Coss, Melinda*
  The Hands of Peace: A Holocaust Survivor's Fight for Civil Rights in the American South — *Ingram, Marione*
  The Hands-On Home: A Seasonal Guide to Cooking, Preserving and Natural Homekeeping — *Strauss, Erica*
c Hands Say Love (Illus. by Yoo, Taeeun) — *Shannon, George*
  Hands Up: Stories of the Six-Gun Fighters of the Old Wild West — *Sutton, Fred E.*
  The Handsome Man's De Luxe Cafe (Read by Lecat, Lisette). Audiobook Review — *Smith, Alexander McCall*
  Handwriting Analysis: Discover Your Own Vocational/Career Potential — *DeWitt, David J.*
y The Handy American History Answer Book — *Hudson, David L., Jr.*
  The Handy English Grammar Answer Book — *Hult, Christine A.*
  The Handy Hockey Answer Book — *Fischler, Stan*
y The Handy Islam Answer Book — *Renard, John*
y The Handy Military Answer Book — *Crompton, Samuel Willard*
  The Handy Mythology Answer Book — *Leeming, David A.*

The Handy Nutrition Answer Book — *Barnes-Svarney, Patricia*
c Hang On, Monkey! — *Neuman, Susan B.*
The Hanged Man — *Elrod, P.N.*
A Hanging at Cinder Bottom — *Taylor, Glenn*
The Hanging Girl — *Adler-Olsen, Jussi*
Hanging Mary — *Higginbotham, Susan*
A Hanging Offence — *Cummer, Don*
y Hangman's Game — *Syken, Bill*
c Hank Has a Dream — *Dudley, Rebecca*
c Hanna, My Holocaust Story — *Alexander, Goldie*
Hannah and the Highlander — *York, Sabrina*
Hannah Arendt: A Life in Dark Times — *Heller, Anne C.*
Hannah Arendt, Totalitarianism, and the Social Sciences — *Baehr, Peter*
c Hannah Is a Big Sister (Illus. by Stott, Dorothy) — *Capucilli, Alyssa Satin*
Hannah Mary Tabbs and the Disembodied Torso — *Gross, Kali Nicole*
Hannibal: A Hellenistic Life — *MacDonald, Eve*
Hanoi's Road to the Vietnam War, 1954-1965 — *Asselin, Pierre*
Hanoi's War: An International History of the War for Peace in Vietnam — *Nguyen, Lien-Hang T.*
Hanok: The Korean House (Illus. by Lee, Jongkeun) — *Park, Nani*
Hans Buchenbacher: Erinnerungen 1933-1949 - Zugleich eine Studie zur Geschichte der Anthroposophie im Nationalsozialismus — *Buchenbacher, Hans*
Hans-Dietrich Genscher, das Auswartige Amt, und die deutsche Vereinigung — *Ritter, Gerhard A.*
Hans Schmithals (1878-1964): Malerei zwischen Jugendstil und Abstraktion — *Richter, Andrea*
Hans Sigrist Symposium: Women and Precarity: Historical Perspectives
c Hansel and Gretel: A Fairy Tale with a Down Syndrome Twist (Illus. by Lenart, Claudia Maria) — *Kats, Jewel*
c Hansel and Gretel and the Green Witch — *North, Laura*
c Hansel and Gretel (Illus. by Mattotti, Lorenzo) — *Gaiman, Neil*
c Hansel & Gretel (Illus. by Mattotti, Lorenzo) — *Gaiman, Neil*
c Hansel & Gretel (Illus. by Hobbie, Holly) — *Hobbie, Holly*
Hansische Identitaten
c Hanukkah Cookies with Sprinkles (Illus. by Ebbeler, Jeffrey) — *Adler, David A.*
Hanukkah in America: A History — *Ashton, Dianne*
c Hanukkah Is Coming! (Illus. by Garofoli, Viviana) — *Newman, Tracy*
The Happiest People in the World — *Clarke, Brock*
Happily Ali After: And Other Fairly True Tales — *Wentworth, Ali*
Happiness: A Philosopher's Guide — *Lenoir, Frederic*
Happiness and Goodness: Philosophical Reflections on Living Well — *Cahn, Steven M.*
Happiness as an Enterprise: An Essay on Neoliberal Life — *Binkley, Sam*
Happiness for Beginners — *Center, Katherine*
The Happiness Industry: How the Government and Big Business Sold Us Well-Being — *Davies, William*
The Happiness Industry — *Davies, William*
Happiness Is a Warm Carcass: Assorted Sordid Stories from the Photographer in the Midst — *Peterson, David*
c Happiness Is ... (Illus. by Pfister, Marcus) — *Pfister, Marcus*
The Happiness Makeover: Teach Yourself to Enjoy Every Day — *Ryan, M.J.*
Happiness: Ten Years of n+1 — *nplusone*
c Happy! (Illus. by Dodd, Emma) — *Dodd, Emma*
c Happy! (Illus. by Smith, Kristin) — *Williams, Pharrell*
Happy Are the Happy — *Reza, Yasmina*
c Happy Birthday, Cupcake! — *Border, Terry*
c Happy Birthday, Elephant! — *La Coccinella*
c Happy Birthday, Madame Chapeau (Illus. by Roberts, David) — *Beaty, Andrea*
c Happy Birthday, Mr. Croc! (Illus. by Lodge, Jo) — *Lodge, Jo*
c Happy Birthday, Mr Croc! (Illus. by Lodge, Jo) — *Lodge, Jo*
c Happy Birthday, Mr. Croc! (Illus. by Lodge, Jo) — *Lodge, Jo*
c Happy Birthday Sophie! (Illus. by Appleton, Polly) — *Sirett, Dawn*
c Happy Birthday, Superman! (Illus. by Bone, J.) — *Fisch, Sholly*

The Happy Christian: Ten Ways To Be a Joyful Believer in a Gloomy World — *Murray, David*
c Happy Easter, Davy! (Illus. by Tharlet, Eve) — *Weninger, Brigitte*
c Happy Halloween, Witch's Cat! (Illus. by Muncaster, Harriet) — *Muncaster, Harriet*
Happy Healthy Vegan Kitchen — *Patalsky, Kathy*
c Happy in Our Skin (Illus. by Tobia, Lauren) — *Manushkin, Fran*
The Happy Kid Handbook: How to Raise Joyful Children in a Stressful World — *Hurley, Katie*
Happy Stories about Well Adjusted People — *Ollmann, Joe*
Harbour Street — *Cleeves, Ann*
Hard and Fast — *Scott, Raven*
A Hard and Heavy Thing — *Hefti, Matthew J.*
c Hard as Nails in Ancient Rome (Illus. by Lenman, Jamie) — *Turner, Tracey*
Hard Beat — *Bromberg, K.*
Hard Charger — *Fobes, Tracy*
Hard Choices (Read by Chalfant, Kathleen). Audiobook Review — *Clinton, Hillary Rodham*
Hard Choices — *Clinton, Hillary Rodham*
Hard Core Romance: Fifty Shades of Grey, Best-Sellers, and Society — *Illouz, Eva*
Hard Latitudes — *Birtcher, Baron R.*
The Hard Problem — *Stoppard, Tom*
Hard Times in the Marvelous City: From Dictatorship to Democracy in the Favelas of Rio de Janeiro — *McCann, Bryan*
Hard Times: Inequality, Recession, Aftermath — *Clark, Tom*
The Hard Times — *Scott, Russell*
Hard to Let Go — *Kaye, Laura*
Hard-to-Survey Populations — *Tourangeau, Roger*
Hard-to-Teach Biology Concepts, 2d ed. — *Koba, Susan*
Hardcastle's Collector — *Ison, Graham*
The Harder They Come — *Boyle, T.C.*
The Harder You Fall — *Showalter, Gena*
y Hardwired — *Currie, Lindsay*
c Hardwired — *Leaver, Trisha*
c Hare and Tortoise Race across Israel (Illus. by Goodreau, Sarah) — *Gehl, Laura*
c Harlem Hellfighters (Illus. by Kelley, Gary) — *Lewis, J. Patrick*
Harlem Nocturne: Women Artists and Progressive Politics during World War II — *Griffin, Farah Jasmine*
c Harlem Renaissance Party (Illus. by Ringgold, Faith) — *Ringgold, Faith*
Harlem: The Four Hundred Year History from Dutch Village to Capital of Black America — *Gill, Jonathan*
Harlem's Rattlers and the Great War: The Undaunted 369th Regiment and the African American Quest for Equality — *Sammons, Jeffrey T.*
The Harlot Countess — *Shupe, Joanna*
Harlots, Hussies, and Poor Unfortunate Women: Crime, Transportation, and the Servitude of Female Convicts — *Ziegler, Edith M.*
Harmattan: A Philosophical Fiction — *Jackson, Michael*
Harmony House — *Sheff, Nic*
Harness the Sun — *Warburg, Philip*
c Harold and the Purple Crayon (Illus. by Johnson, Crockett) — *Johnson, Crockett*
Harold Town — *Nowell, Iris*
The Harpsichord and Clavichord: An Encyclopaedia, 2d ed. — *Kipnis, Igor*
Harraga — *Sansal, Boualem*
Harriet Beecher Stowe: A Spiritual Life — *Koester, Nancy*
y Harriet Beecher Stowe and the Abolitionist Movement — *Moretta, Alison*
c Harriet Can Carry It (Illus. by Vonthron-Laver, Sarah) — *Mueller, Kirk Jay*
c Harriet the Invincible — *Vernon, Ursula*
Harriet Tubman: Freedom Leader, Freedom Seeker — *Sadlier, Rosemary*
Harriet Wolf's Seventh Book of Wonders — *Baggott, Julianna*
Harriman vs. Hill: Wall Street's Great Railroad War — *Haeg, Larry*
Harrison Squared — *Gregory, Daryl*
c Harry and Hope — *Lean, Sarah*
Harry Gruyaert — *Gruyaert, Harry*
Harry Gruyaert — *Hebel, Francois*
Harry Gruyaert (Illus. by Gruyaert, Harry) — *Hebel, Francois*
Harry Harrison, Harry Harrison — *Harrison, Harry*
Harry McShane: No Mean Fighter — *Smith, Joan*

Harry Mount's Odyssey: Ancient Greece in the Footsteps of Odysseus — *Mount, Harry*
Harry Partch: Hobo Composer — *Granade, S. Andrew*
y Harry Potter and the Sorcerer's Stone (Illus. by Kay, Jim) — *Rowling, J.K.*
c Harry the Dirty Dog (Illus. by Graham, Margaret Bloy) — *Zion, Gene*
Harry Truman and the Struggle for Racial Justice — *Shogan, Robert*
c Harry's Secret — *Heiss, Anita*
Hartwood: Bright, Wild Flavors from the Edge of the Yucatan — *Werner, Eric*
y The Harvest (Read by Podehl, Nick). Audiobook Review — *Wendig, Chuck*
The Harvest Man: a Novel of Scotland Yard's Murder Squad — *Grecian, Alex*
The Harvest Man — *Gracian, Alex*
Harvest of Blessings — *Hubbard, Charlotte*
Harvest Your Own Lumber: How to Fell, Saw, Dry and Mill Wood — *English, John*
Harvey Kurtzman: The Man Who Created Mad and Revolutionized Humor in America — *Schelly, Bill*
y Harvey Milk: Pioneering Gay Politician — *Grinapol, Corinne*
Harvey Wang: From Darkroom to Daylight — *Wang, Harvey*
c Has Anyone Seen Jessica Jenkins? — *Kessler, Liz*
Has Anyone Seen My Pants? — *Colonna, Sarah*
y Has to Be Love — *Perry, Jolene*
Hasidism Incarnate: Hasidism, Christianity, and the Construction of Modern Judaism — *Magid, Shaul*
y Hassled Girl? Girls Dealing with Feelings — *Kavanaugh, Dorothy*
c Hatch, Little Egg (Illus. by Manceau, Edouard) — *Manceau, Edouard*
Hate Crimes in Cyberspace — *Citron, Danielle Keats*
Hate Thy Neighbor: Move-In Violence and the Persistence of Racial Segregation in American Housing — *Bell, Jeannine*
Hating God: The Untold Story of Misotheism — *Schweizer, Bernard*
Hauerwas: A (Very) Critical Introduction — *Healy, Nicholas M.*
Haunted (Read by Raudman, Renee). Audiobook Review — *White, Randy Wayne*
The Haunted House Diaries: The True Story of a Quiet Connecticut Town in the Center of a Paranormal Mystery — *Hall, William J.*
c The Haunted Library (Illus. by Damant, Aurore) — *Butler, Dori Hillestad*
y Haunted — *Carthage, Lynn*
Haunted Plantations of the South — *Southall, Richard*
c Haunted Prisons — *Williams, Dinah*
The Haunted Season — *Malliet, G.M.*
Haunting Images: A Cultural Account of Selective Reproduction in Vietnam — *Gammeltoft, Tine M.*
Haunting Mr. Darcy: A Spirited Courtship — *Mackrory, KaraLynne*
y The Haunting of Springett Hall — *Wheeler, E.B.*
y The Haunting of Sunshine Girl (Read by McKenzie, Paige). Audiobook Review — *McKenzie, Paige*
y The Haunting of Sunshine Girl — *McKenzie, Paige*
The Haunting of the Mexican Border — *Ferguson, Kathryn*
Hauntings: Dispelling the Ghosts Who Run Our Lives — *Hollis, James*
Hausfrau (Read by Marno, Mozhan). Audiobook Review — *Essbaum, Jill Alexander*
Hausfrau — *Essbaum, Jill Alexander*
Havana Hardball: Spring Training, Jackie Robinson, and The Cuban League — *Brioso, Cesar*
Have Gun--Will Travel — *Studlar, Gaylyn*
c Have You Heard the Nesting Bird? (Illus. by Pak, Kenard) — *Gray, Rita*
c Have You Seen My Dragon? (Illus. by Light, Steve) — *Light, Steve*
Have You Seen My Monster? (Illus. by Light, Steve) — *Light, Steve*
Havel: A Life — *Zantovsky, Michael*
Having People, Having Heart: Charity, Sustainable Development, and Problems of Dependence in Central Uganda — *Scherz, China*
Havisham — *Frame, Ronald*
y Havoc — *Higgins, Jane*
Hawai'i Nights — *Andreo, Rogelio Bernal*
The Hawkeye (Illus. by Pulido, Javier) — *Fraction, Matt*
The Hawkins Ranch in Texas: From Plantation Times to the Present — *Furse, Margaret Lewis*
The Hawley Book of the Dead — *Szarlan, Chrysler*
y Hawthorn — *Goodman, Carol*

Hawthorn: The Tree That Has Nourished, Healed, and Inspired through the Ages — *Vaughn, Bill*
Haydee Santamaria, Cuban Revolutionary: She Led by Transgression — *Randall, Margaret*
Hayek on Mill: The Mill-Taylor Friendship and Other Writings — *Hayek, Friedrich*
Hayek on Mill: The Mill-Taylor Friendship and Related Writings — *Hayek, Friedrich*
Haymaker — *Schuitema, Adam*
y Haze — *Weston, Paula*
Hazelet's Journal — *Clark, John H.*
he Assimilated Cuban's Guide to Quantum Santeria — *Hernandez, Carlos*
He Drinks Poison — *Cunningham, Laine*
c He Laughed with His Other Mouths — *Anderson, M.T.*
he Myth of Mirror Neurons: The Real Neuroscience of Communication and Cognition — *Hickok, Gregory*
He Runs, She Runs: Why Gender Stereotypes Do Not Harm Women Candidates — *Brooks, Deborah Jordan*
He Wanted the Moon: The Madness and Medical Genius of Dr. Perry Baird, and His Daughter's Quest to Know Him — *Baird, Mimi*
He Will Be My Ruin — *Tucker, K.A.*
Head Case: My Brain and Other Wonders — *Cohen, Cole*
Head Cases: Julia Kristeva on Philosophy and Art in Depressed Times — *Miller, Elaine P.*
A Head Full of Ghosts — *Tremblay, Paul*
Head Hunters: The Search for a Science of the Mind — *Shepard, Ben*
c Head Lice (Illus. by Gravel, Elise) — *Gravel, Elise*
y Head of the River — *Harry, Pip*
The Head of the Saint — *Acioli, Socorro*
Head of the State: A Political Entertainment — *Marr, Andrew*
The Headache Godfather: The Story of Dr. Seymour Diamond and How He Revolutionized the Treatment of Headaches — *Diamond, Seymour*
Headaches among the Overtones: Music in Beckett/Beckett in Music — *Laws, Catherine*
Headed for Trouble — *Walker, Shiloh*
Headhunting and Other Sports Poems — *Raisor, Philip*
Headline Murder — *Bartram, Peter*
The Headmaster's Darlings — *Clark, Catherine*
Heads or Hearts — *Johnston, Paul*
The Headscarf Debates: Conflicts of National Belonging — *Korteweg, Anna*
Headscarves and Hymens: Why The Midde East Needs a Sexual Revolution — *Eltahawy, Mona*
Headscarves and Hymens: Why the Middle East Needs a Sexual Revolution — *Eltahawy, Mona*
y Headstrong: 52 Women Who Changed Science--and the World — *Swaby, Rachel*
Heal: The Vital Role of Dogs in the Search for Cancer Cures — *Weintraub, Arlene*
The Healer — *Primm, Beny J.*
Healers: Extraordinary Clinicians at Work — *Schenck, David*
Healing from Incest: Intimate Conversations with My Therapist — *Henderson, Geri*
Healing Gotham: New York City's Public Health Policies for the Twenty-First Century — *Berg, Bruce F.*
The Healing I Took Birth For: Practicing the Art of Compassion — *Levine, Ondrea*
The Healing Light of Angels: Transforming Your Past, Present, and Future with Divine Energy — *Keyes, Raven*
Healing Ruby — *Westall, Jennifer*
Healing Secular Life: Loss and Devotion in Modern Turkey — *Dole, Christopher*
Healing the Nation: Prisoners of War, Medicine and Nationalism in Turkey, 1914-1939 — *Yamkdag, Yucel*
Health and Girlhood in Britain, 1874-1920 — *Marland, Hilary*
Health Care as a Social Good: Religious Values and American Democracy — *Craig, David M.*
The Health Gap: The Challenge of an Unequal World — *Marmot, Michael*
Health Trackers: How Technology Is Helping Us Monitor and Improve Our Health — *MacManus, Richard*
Health under Fire: Medical Care during America's Wars — *Arnold, James R.*
Health, Wellbeing, Competence and Aging — *Leung, Ping-Chung*
Healthcare Reform in America, 2d ed. — *Kronenfeld, Jennie Jacobs*

Healthy Latin Eating: Our Favorite Family Recipes Remixed — *Martinez, Angie*
Healthy Living in Late Renaissance Italy — *Storey, Tessa*
Healthy Pasta: The Sexy, Skinny, and Smart Way to Eat Your Favorite Food — *Bastianich, Joseph*
Healy's West: The Life and Times of John J. Healy — *Tolton, Gordon E.*
y Heap House — *Carey, Edward*
y Hear — *Epstein, Robin*
Hear My Sad Story: The True Tales That Inspired "Stagolee," "John Henry," and Other Traditional American Folk Songs — *Polenberg, Richard*
Hear the Wind Sing — *Goossen, Ted*
Hearing and the Hospital: Sound, Listening, Knowledge, and Experience — *Rice, Tom*
Hearing Loss: Facts and Fiction — *Frantz, Timothy*
The Hearing-Loss Guide: Useful Information and Advice for Patients and Families — *Burkey, John M.*
The Heart — *de Kerangal, Maylis*
Heart and Soul in the Kitchen — *Pepin, Jacques*
y The Heart at War — *Banner, Catherine*
The Heart Goes Last — *Atwood, Margaret*
The Heart Healers: The Misfits, Mavericks, and Rebels Who Created the Greatest Medical Breakthrough of Our Lives — *Forrester, James*
The Heart Is Strange: New Selected Poems — *Berryman, John*
The Heart Is Strange — *Berryman, John*
Heart Land: A Place Called Ockley Green — *Miller, Caroline*
y A Heart Like Ringo Starr — *High, Linda Oatman*
y Heart of a Samurai — *Preus, Margi*
y The Heart of Betrayal (Read by Lee, Ann Marie). Audiobook Review — *Pearson, Mary E.*
y The Heart of Betrayal — *Pearson, Mary E.*
The Heart of Biblical Theology: Providence Experienced — *Elliott, Mark W.*
Heart of Europe — *Wilson, Peter H.*
The Heart of Human Rights — *Buchanan, Allen*
The Heart of Man — *Stefansson, Jon Kalman*
Heart of the Liliko'i — *Hankins, Dena*
Heart of the Order: Baseball Poems — *Fried, Gabriel*
The Heart of the Order — *Schell-Lambert, Theo*
A Heart Once Broken — *Eicher, Jerry S.*
A Heart Revealed — *Kilpack, Josi S.*
Heart-Sick: The Politics of Risk, Inequality, and Heart Disease — *Shim, Janet K.*
The Heart You Carry Home — *Miller, Jennifer*
y Heartache and Other Natural Shocks — *Leznoff, Glenda*
Heartbreak Hotel — *Moggach, Deborah*
c The Heartbreak Messenger (Read by Gebauer, Christopher). Audiobook Review — *Vance, Alexander*
y The Heartbreakers — *Novak, Ali*
Heartfelt Memorial Services: Your Guide for Planning Meaningful Funerals, Celebrations of Life and Times of Remembrance — *Molander, Beverly*
Heartificial Intelligence — *Havens, John C.*
Heartland: Farm-Forward Dishes from the Great Midwest — *Russo, Lenny*
Heartland Tobacco War — *Givel, Michael S.*
Heartlandia: Heritage Recipes from Portland's The Country Cat — *Sappington, Adam*
Hearts Made Whole — *Hedlund, Jody*
The Hearts of Dragons — *Van Brakle, Josh*
Hearts of Pine: Songs in the Lives of Three Korean Survivors of the Japanese "Comfort Women" — *Pilzer, Joshua D.*
Heartsong Cottage — *March, Emily*
Heat Exchange — *Stacey, Shannon*
The Heat Is On — *Rose, Katie*
The Heat of Betrayal — *Kennedy, Douglas*
y Heat of the Moment — *Barnholdt, Lauren*
Heat of the Moment — *Handerland, Lori*
The Heathen School: A Story of Hope and Betrayal in the Age of the Early Republic — *Demos, John*
c Heather Has Two Mommies (Illus. by Cornell, Laura) — *Newman, Leslea*
Heatstroke: Nature in an Age of Global Warming — *Barnosky, Anthony D.*
Heaven Adores You — *Rossi, Nickolas*
Heaven and Earth in Anglo-Saxon England: Theology and Society in an Age of Faith — *Forbes, Helen Foxhall*
Heaven Can Wait: Purgatory in Catholic Devotional and Popular Culture — *Pasulka, Diana Walsh*
Heaven, Hell, and Purgatory: Rethinking the Things That Matter Most — *Walls, Jerry L.*

Heaven in Conflict: Franciscans and the Boxer Uprising in Shanxi — *Clark, Anthony E.*
Heaven Is Beautiful — *Panagore, Peter Baldwin*
c The Heaven of Animals — *Tillman, Nancy*
Heaven: Poems — *Phillips, Rowan Ricardo*
Heavenly Harmony: Organs and Organists of Exeter Cathedral — *Walker, Malcolm*
Heaven's Bankers: Inside the Hidden World of Islamic Finance — *Irfan, Harris*
Heaven's Consciousness: A Near-Death Experience with Relevant Poetry — *Dooley, Rhonda Nell*
Heaven's Fall — *Goyer, David S.*
c Heaven's Flower — *Anna, Dawn*
Heavenward and Worldly: Church and Religious Orders in (Post) Secular Society — *Dienberg, Thomas*
Heavy Weather — *Fischer, Normandie*
The Hebrew Prophets after the Shoah: A Mandate for Change — *Gossai, Hemchand*
c Hector and Hummingbird (Illus. by Frith, Nicholas John) — *Frith, Nicholas John*
c Hector et le grand mechant Chevalier — *Smith, Alex T.*
c Hedgehogs — *Gregory, Josh*
c Hedgehugs (Illus. by Tapper, Lucy) — *Wilson, Steve*
A Hedonist Manifesto — *Onfray, Michel*
Hegel — *Fritzman, Hegel J.M.*
Hegel — *Heidegger, Martin*
Hegel and the Metaphysics of Absolute Negativity — *Bowman, Brady*
Hegel, the End of History, and the Future — *Dale, Eric M.*
Hegel, the End of History, and the Future — *Dale, Eric Michael*
Hegel's Introduction to the System: Encyclopaedia Phenomenology and Psychology — *Wood, Robert E.*
Hegel's Theory of Responsibility — *Alznauer, Mark*
The Heibergs and the Theater: Between Vaudeville, Romantic Comedy, and National Drama — *Stewart, Jon*
Heidegger in France — *Janicaud, Dominique*
Heidegger on Being Uncanny — *Withy, Katherine*
Heidegger: Thinking of Being — *Braver, Lee*
Heideggers Testament: Der Philosoph, der Spiegel und die SS — *Hachmeister, Lutz*
c Heidi Heckelbeck and the Tie-Dyed Bunny — *Coven, Wanda*
c Heidi Heckelbeck Gets the Sniffles (Illus. by Burris, Priscilla) — *Coven, Wanda*
c Heidi Heckelbeck Is a Flower Girl (Illus. by Burris, Priscilla) — *Coven, Wanda*
c Heidi Heckelbeck Is Not a Thief! (Illus. by Burris, Priscilla) — *Coven, Wanda*
Heilige und geheiligte Dinge. Formen und Funktionen
Heilstheater: Figur des barocken Trauerspiels zwischen Gryphius und Kleist — *Harst, Joachim*
Heinrich Cla beta 1868-1953: Die politische Biographie eines Alldeutschen — *Leicht, Johannes*
Heinrich Himmler: A Life — *Longerich, Peter*
Heinrich von Kleist and Jean-Jacques Rousseau: Violence, Identity, Nation — *Howe, Steven*
Heinrich von Kleist and Modernity — *Fischer, Bernd*
Heinrich von Kleist: Artistic and Political Legacies — *High, Jeffrey L.*
y The Heir — *Cass, Kiera*
y The Heir and the Spare — *Albright, Emily*
y Heir of Fire (Read by Evans, Elizabeth). Audiobook Review — *Maas, Sarah J.*
y Heir of Fire — *Maas, Sarah J.*
Heir to the Duke — *Ashford, Jane*
Heir to the Empire City: New York and the Making of Theodore Roosevelt — *Kohn, Edward P.*
y Heir to the Jedi: Star Wars (Read by Thompson, Marc). Audiobook Review — *Hearne, Kevin*
Heirs and Assigns — *Eccles, Marjorie*
Heirs to Forgotten Kingdoms: Journeys into the Disappearing Religions of the Middle East (Read by Page, Michael). Audiobook Review — *Russell, Gerard*
Heirs to Forgotten Kingdoms: Journeys into the Disappearing Religions of the Middle East — *Russell, Gerard*
Heisenberg — *Stephens, Simon*
Heist: The Oddball Crew behind the $17 Million Loomis Fargo Theft — *Diamant, Jeff*
Helen Andelin and the Fascinating Womanhood Movement — *Neuffer, Julie Debra*
Helen Waddell and Maude Clarke: Irishwomen, Friends, and Scholars — *FitzGerald, Jennifer*
Helen Waddell Reassessed: New Readings — *FitzGerald, Jennifer*
Helena Rubinstein: Beauty is Power — *Klein, Mason*

Helene Schweitzer: A Life of Her Own — *Marxsen, Patti M.*
c **Helicopters** — *Riggs, Kate*
c **Helicopters (Illus. by West, David)** — *West, David*
c **Helicopters** — *Confalone, Nick*
Heliopause — *Christie, Heather*
The Helios Disaster — *Knausgaard, Linda Bostrom*
Hell and Good Company: The Spanish Civil War and the World It Made — *Rhodes, Richard*
Hell from the Heavens — *Wukovits, John*
Hell Is a Very Small Place: Voices from Solitary Confinement — *Casella, Jean*
Hell or High Water — *Walker, Julie Ann*
Hell to Pay — *Disher, Garry*
Hellenistic and Biblical Greek: A Graduated Reader — *McLean, B.H.*
The Hellenistic Far East: Archaeology, Language, and Identity in Greek Central Asia — *Mairs, Rachel*
y **Hellhole** — *Damico, Gina*
y **Hello?** — *Wiemer, Liza*
c **Hello Animals, What Makes You Special? (Illus. by Botman, Loes)** — *Botman, Loes*
c **Hello from 2030** — *Schutten, Jan Paul*
y **Hello Girls and Boys! A New Zealand Toy Story** — *Veart, David*
y **Hello, Goodbye, and Everything in Between** — *Smith, Jennifer E.*
y **Hello, I Love You** — *Stout, Katie M.*
c **Hello, I'm Johnny Cash (Illus. by Ford, A.G.)** — *Neri, G.*
Hello Kitty: It's about Time — *McGinty, Ian*
c **Hello Kitty Summertime Fun** — *Jones, Frankie*
Hello Life! — *Butler, Marcus*
c **Hello, Ocean Friends: A High-Contrast Book (Illus. by Lemay, Violet)**
c **Hello Ruby** — *Liukas, Linda*
c **Hello World! (Illus. by Beavis, Paul)** — *Beavis, Paul*
y **Hellraisers** — *Smith, Alexander Gordon*
Hell's Bounty — *Lansdale, Joe R.*
c **Hell's Foundations Quiver** — *Weber, David*
Hell's Gate — *Crompton, Richard*
Helmut Kohl's Quest for Normality: His Representation of the German Nation and Himself — *Wicke, Christian*
c **Help, I Don't Want a Babysitter! (Illus. by Behl, Anne-Kathrin)** — *Wagner, Anke*
Help in Our Time and Manet's Genre Paintings of Everyday Light — *Byrne, Ryan P.*
Help Me to Find My People: The African American Search for Family Lost in Slavery — *Williams, Heather Andrea*
c **Help! My Brother's a Zombie (Illus. by McElhinney, Glenn)** — *Graves, Annie*
c **Help! The Wolf Is Coming! (Illus. by Bourgeau, Vincent)** — *Ramadier, Cedric*
Help Wanted — *Valentin, Barbara*
y **Help Your Kids with Music** — *Vorderman, Carol*
c **Helping Children with Life-Threatening Medical Issues** — *Mattern, Joanne*
c **Helping the Community Series**
Hemingway in Love: His Own Story — *Hotchner, A.E.*
Hemingway's Paris: A Writer's City in Words and Images — *Wheeler, Robert*
y **Henni (Illus. by Lasko-Gross, Miss)** — *Lasko-Gross, Miss*
Henri Duchemin and His Shadows — *Bove, Emmanuel*
Henricus Glareanus's (1488-1563) Chronologia of the Ancient World: A Facsimile Edition of a Heavily Annotated Copy Held in Princeton University Library — *Grafton, Anthony T.*
c **Henry Aaron's Dream (Illus. by Tavares, Matt)** — *Tavares, Matt*
c **Henry Cicada's Extraordinary Elktonium Escapade** — *Teague, David*
Henry Clay: America's Greatest Statesman — *Unger, Harlow Giles*
y **Henry David Thoreau for Kids: His Life and Ideas, with 21 Activities** — *Smith, Corinne Hosfeld*
Henry David Thoreau: Spiritual and Prophetic Writings — *Flinders, Tim*
c **Henry Finds His Word** — *Ward, Lindsay*
Henry Ford — *Curcio, Vincent*
y **Henry Ford for Kids: His Life and Ideas, with 21 Activities** — *Reis, Ronald A.*
Henry George and the Crisis of Inequality: Progress and Poverty in the Gilded Age — *O'Donnell, Edward T.*
c **Henry Holton Takes the Ice (Illus. by Palacios, Sara)** — *Bradley, Sandra*
c **Henry Hubble's Book of Troubles (Illus. by Myer, Andy)** — *Myer, Andy*

c **Henry Hyena, Why Won't You Laugh? (Illus. by Claude, Jean)** — *Jantzen, Doug*
Henry II: A Prince among Princes — *Barber, Richard*
c **Henry Is a Big Brother (Illus. by Stott, Dorothy)** — *Capucilli, Alyssa Satin*
Henry James and the Culture of Consumption — *El-Ravess, Miranda*
Henry James's Enigmas: Turning the Screw of Eternity? — *Perrot, Jean*
Henry of Ghent: Summa of Ordinary Questions: Articles 35, 36, 42, and 45 — *Teske, Roland J.*
Henry Stubbe and the Beginnings of Islam: The Originall & Progress of Mahometanism — *Stubbe, Henry*
Henry VIII and the Anabaptists — *Pleysier, Elizabeth*
The Henry VIII Book — *Fallows, David*
Henry VIII: The Quest for Fame — *Guy, John*
c **Henry Wants More! (Illus. by Hughes, Brooke Boynton)** — *Ashman, Linda*
c **Henry's Stars (Illus. by Elliot, David)** — *Elliot, David*
c **Hens for Friends (Illus. by Hansen, Amelia)** — *De Lisle, Sandy*
Henshin (Illus. by Niimura, Ken) — *Niimura, Ken*
Henshin — *Yukiko, Ivy*
The Hepatitis B and Delta Viruses — *Seeger, Christoph*
Her — *Lane, Harriet*
Her Appearing — *Hanway, Donald*
y **Her Cold Revenge** — *Johnson, Erin*
Her Final Breath — *Dugoni, Robert*
Her Idea (Illus. by Alexander, Rilla) — *Alexander, Rilla*
Her Lucky Cowboy — *Ryan, Jennifer*
Her Majesty's Mischief — *Herring, Peg*
Her Name Is Rose — *Breen, Christine*
c **Her Pink Hair (Illus. by Dana, Jill)** — *Dana, Jill*
Her Texas — *Walker-Nixon, Donna*
Her Wild Hero — *Tyler, Paige*
Heraclix and Pomp: A Novel of the Fabricated and the Fey — *Aguirre, Forrest*
The Herald of Hell — *Doherty, Paul*
Heraldique et numismatique I: Moyen Age - Temps modernes — *Loskoutoff, Yvan*
Heralds and Heraldry in Shakespeare's England — *Ramsay, Nigel*
The Herbal Apothecary: 100 Medicinal Herbs and How to Use Them — *Pursell, J.J.*
The "Herbal" of al-Ghafiq?: A Facsimile Edition with Critical Essays — *Ragep, F. Jamil*
Herbert Hensley Henson: A Biography — *Peart-Binns, Byjohn S.*
Herbie Hancock: Possibilities (Read by Hancock, Herbie). Audiobook Review — *Hancock, Herbie*
Herbie Hancock: Possibilities — *Hancock, Herbie*
Herbie's Game — *Hallinan, Timothy*
c **Herbivores (Illus. by Benefield, James)** — *Benefield, James*
Herbs and Healers from the Ancient Mediterranean through the Medieval West: Essays in Honor of John M. Riddle — *Van Arsdall, Anne*
Herbs & Spices: The Cook's Reference — *Norman, Jill*
c **Hercufleas (Illus. by Cottrill, Peter)** — *Gayton, Sam*
A Hercules in the Cradle: War, Money, and the American State, 1783-1867 — *Edling, Max M.*
Herding Hemingway's Cats: Understanding How Our Genes Work — *Arney, Kat*
Here (Illus. by McGuire, Richard) — *McGuire, Richard*
c **The Here and Now** — *Brashares, Ann*
y **Here and There: Leaving Hasidism, Keeping My Family** — *Deitsch, Chaya*
Here and There — *Dalin, Karen*
Here and There: Reading Pennsylvania's Working Landscapes — *Conlogue, Bill*
Here Are the Young Men — *Doyle, Rob*
Here at Last Is Love: Selected Poems of Dustan Thompson — *Thompson, Dustan*
Here by the Bloods — *Boyce, Brandon*
Here Come the Dogs — *Musa, Omar*
c **Here Comes Santa Cat (Illus. by Rueda, Claudia)** — *Underwood, Deborah*
c **Here Comes the Parade! (Illus. by Newton, Vanessa Brantley)** — *Dungy, Tony*
c **Here Comes the Tooth Fairy Cat (Illus. by Rueda, Claudia)** — *Underwood, Deborah*
c **Here Comes Valentine Cat (Illus. by Rueda, Claudia)** — *Underwood, Deborah*
c **Here I Am (Illus. by Sanchez, Sonia)** — *Kim, Patti*
c **Here in the Garden (Illus. by Stewart, Briony)** — *Stewart, Briony*

c **Here Is Big Bunny (Illus. by Henry, Steve)** — *Henry, Steve*
c **Here Is the Baby (Illus. by Yoo, Taeeun)** — *Kanevsky, Polly*
Here Is the World: A Year of Jewish Holidays (Illus. by Gal, Susan) — *Newman, Leslea*
Here on the Edge: How a Small Group of World War II Conscientious Objectors Took Art and Peace from the Margins to the Mainstream — *McQuiddy, Steve*
c **Here She Is! (Illus. by Tharlet, Eve)** — *Leblanc, Catherine*
Here There Is No Why — *Roth, Rachel*
Heresy, Crusade and Inquisition in Medieval Quercy — *Taylor, Claire*
Heresy, Inquisition and Life Cycle in Medieval Languedoc — *Sparks, Chris*
Heresy Trials and English Women Writers, 1400-1670 — *Gertz, Genelle*
Heretic: Why Islam Needs a Reformation Now — *Ali, Ayaan Hirsi*
Heretic: Why Islam Needs a Reformation Now — *Hirsi Ali, Ayaan*
c **Hereville: How Mirka Caught a Fish (Illus. by Deutsch, Barry)** — *Deutsch, Barry*
Hereward: End of Days; A Novel of Medieval England — *Wilde, James*
Heritage Management in Korea and Japan: The Politics of Antiquity and Identity — *Pai, Hyung Il*
Heritage Politics: Shuri Castle and Okinawa's Incorporation into Modern Japan, 1879-2000 — *Loo, Tze May*
Hermann Bahr: Osterreichischer Kritiker europaischer Avantgarden — *Muller, Martin Anton*
Hermann Broch und die Romantik — *Lutzeler, Paul Michael*
Hermann Henselmann in seiner Berliner Zeit (1949-1995). Der Architekt, die Macht und die Baukunst. 11. Hermann-Henselmann-Kolloquium
c **Herman's Letter (Illus. by Percival, Tom)** — *Percival, Tom*
c **Herman's Vacation (Illus. by Percival, Tom)** — *Percival, Tom*
c **Hermelin the Detective Mouse (Illus. by Grey, Mini)** — *Grey, Mini*
c **Hermit Crabs** — *Murray, Julie*
The Hermitage XXI: The New Art Museum in the General Staff Building — *Yawein, Oleg*
The Hermit's Hut: Architecture and Asceticism in India — *Ashraf, Kazi K.*
Hernani — *Janc, John J.*
Herndon on Lincoln: Letters — *Herndon, William H.*
c **Hero** — *Lean, Sarah*
The Hero — *Rubin, David*
y **Hero Complex** — *Froley, Margaux*
c **The Hero in You (Illus. by Padron, Angela)** — *Paul, Ellis*
The Hero of Ages — *Sanderson, Brandon*
Hero of Fort Schuyler: Selected Revolutionary War Correspondence of Brigadier General Peter Gansevoort, Jr. — *Ranzan, David A.*
The Hero of Italy: Odoardo Farnese, Duke of Parma, His Soldiers and His Subjects in the Thirty Years' War — *Hanlon, Gregory*
Hero or Tyrant? Henry III, King of France, 1574-89 — *Knecht, Robert J.*
Hero or Tyrant?: Henry III, King of France, 1574-89 — *Knecht, Robert J.*
c **The Hero Twins: A Navajo-English Story of the Monster Slayers (Illus. by James, Nolan Karras)** — *Kristofic, Jim*
c **The Hero Two Doors Down: Based on the True Story of Friendship Between a Boy and a Baseball Legend** — *Robinson, Sharon*
Herodotus and Hellenistic Culture: Literary Studies in the Reception of "Histories" — *Priestley, Jessica*
Heroes: David Bowie in Berlin — *Ruther, Tobias*
c **Heroes of History (Illus. by Stanton, Joe Todd)** — *Ganeri, Anita*
c **Heroes of the Wild: The Whale Who Saved (Illus. by Wright, Annabel)** — *Davies, Nicola*
c **Heroes on the Side** — *Marko, Cyndi*
The Heroes' Welcome — *Young, Louisa*
Heroic Forms: Cervantes and the Literature of War — *Rupp, Stephen*
Heroin, Organized Crime, and the Making of Modern Turkey — *Gingeras, Ryan*
The Heroine Next Door — *Nackerdien, Zeena*
Heroines of the French Epic: A Second Selection of Chansons de geste — *Newth, Michael A.H.*
Heroism and Gender in War Films — *Ritzenhoff, Karen A.*

c The Hero's Guide to Being an Outlaw — Healy, Christopher
Herring Tales: How the Silver Darlings Shaped Human Taste and History — Murray, Donald S.
Herrschaft durch Esoterik in der intellektuellen Kultur der Weimarer Republik
Herrschaftserzahlungen. Wilhelm II. in der Kulturgeschichte
c Hershel and the Hanukkah Goblins: 25th Anniversary Edition (Illus. by Hyman, Trina Schart) — Kimmel, Eric A.
Herta Muller — Haines, Brigid
Herzl's Vision: Theodor Herzl and the Foundation of the Jewish State — Avineri, Shlomo
Hesiodic Voices: Studies in the Ancient Reception of Hesiod's Work and Days — Hunter, Richard
Hesiodic Voices: Studies in the Ancient Reception of Hesiod's Works and Days — Hunter, Richard
Hesitation Wounds — Koppelman, Amy
y Hester on the Run — Byler, Linda
Hexagon Happenings — Forster, Carolyn
y Hexed — Krys, Michelle
y Hexed — Nelson, Michael Alan
Hexerei und Offentlichkeit
Hey Boy (Illus. by Phelan, Jennifer) — Strouse, Ben
c Hey Charleston! The True Story of the Jenkins Orphanage Band (Illus. by Bootman, Colin) — Rockwell, Anne
c Hey, Charlie! (Illus. by Crank, Donny) — Kruse, Donald W.
c Hey Diddle Diddle (Illus. by Melmon, Deborah) — Melmon, Deborah
c Hey Jack! The Star of the Week — Rippin, Sally
c Hey, Seymour! (Illus. by Wick, Walter) — Wick, Walter
c Hi! (Illus. by Long, Ethan) — Long, Ethan
Hi Hitler! How the Nazi Past Is Being Normalized in Contemporary Culture — Rosenfeld, Gavriel D.
c Hiawatha and the Peacemaker (Illus. by Shannon, David) — Robertson, Robbie
c Hiccupotamus (Illus. by Grey, Ada) — Smallman, Steve
c Hickory, Dickory, Dock (Illus. by Galloway, Fhiona) — Galloway, Fhiona
c Hickory Dickory Dog — Murray, Alison
Hidato Fun 10 — Benedek, Gyora
y Hidden — Napoli, Donna Jo
Hidden — Olson, Karen E.
The Hidden Agenda of the Political Mind: How Self-Interest Shapes Our Opinions and Why We Won't Admit It — Weeden, Jason
c Hidden: An Irish Princess' Tale — Napoli, Donna Jo
Hidden Bodies — Kepnes, Caroline
Hidden But Now Revealed: A Biblical Theology of Mystery — Beale, G.K.
The Hidden Child — Lackberg, Camilla
The Hidden — Christopher, Neil
Hidden Folk: Icelandic Fantasies — Arnason, Eleanor
c The Hidden Forest (Illus. by Baker, Alan) — Jensen, Daintry
y Hidden Gold: A True Story of the Holocaust — Burakowski, Ella
The Hidden Half of Nature: The Microbial Roots of Life and Health — Montgomery, David R.
The Hidden History of America at War: Untold Tales from Yorktown to Fallujah — Davis, Kenneth C.
Hidden Hunger: Gender and the Politics of Smarter Foods — Kimura, Aya Hirata
Hidden Impact — Neff, Charles
Hidden in Plain Sight: What Really Caused the World's Worst Financial Crisis and Why It Could Happen Again — Wallison, Peter J.
Hidden in the Mix: The African American Presence in Country Music — Pecknold, Diane
Hidden Inheritance: Family Secrets, Memory, and Faith — Neumark, Heidi B.
Hidden Islam — Degiorgis, Nicolo
Hidden Kerry: The Keys to the Kingdom — Joy, Breda
The Hidden Man — Blake, Robin
The Hidden Man — Cumming, Charles
The Hidden Man — Blake, Robin
Hidden Markov Processes: Theory and Applications to Biology — Vidyasagar, Mathukumalli
Hidden Natural Histories: Herbs — Hurst, Kim
Hidden Natural Histories: Trees — Kingsbury, Noel
The Hidden Perspective: The Military Conversations 1906-1914 — Owen, David (b. 1938-)
The Hidden Pleasures of Life: A New Way of Remembering the Past and Imagining the Future — Zeldin, Theodore

Hidden Religion: The Greatest Mysteries and Symbols of the World's Religious Beliefs — Issitt, Micah L.
y The Hidden Things, vol. 9 — Bracken, Beth
c The Hidden Treasure (Illus. by Ying, Victoria) — Burkhart, Jessica
Hidden: True Stories of Children Who Survived World War II — Prins, Marcel
y The Hidden Twin — Rule, Adi
Hidden Vices — Carpenter, C.J.
Hidden Warships: Finding World War II's Abandoned, Sunk, and Preserved Warships — Veronico, Nicholas A.
Hidden Water: From the Frank Stanford Archives — Stanford, Frank
The Hidden Wealth of Nations: The Scourge of Tax Havens — Zucman, Gabriel
Hide — Griffin, Matthew
c The Hide-and-Scare Bear (Illus. by Bates, Ivan) — Bates, Ivan
c Hide and Seek Harry at the Playground (Illus. by Harrison, Kenny) — Harrison, Kenny
c Hide and Seek: Kiwi Critters (Illus. by Shaw, Rupert) — Blaber, Donna
y Hide and Seek — Casey, Jane
Hide — Griffin, Matthew
y Hider Seeker Secret Keeper — Kiem, Elizabeth
c Hiding Dinosaurs (Illus. by Moynihan, Dan) — Moynihan, Dan
Hiding in Plain Sight (Read by Miles, Robin). Audiobook Review — Farah, Nuruddin
Hiding in Plain Sight — Farah, Nuruddin
y Hier, tu m'aimais encore — Soulieres, Robert
Hieroglyph: Stories & Visions for a Better Future — Finn, Ed
High as the Horses' Bridles — Chesire, Scott
High Command: British Military Leadership in the Iraq and Afghanistan Wars — Elliott, Christopher L.
High Country Nocturne — Talton, Jon
High Dive — Lee, Jonathan
The High Divide — Enger, Lin
y High & Dry — Skilton, Sarah
High Holiday Porn — Bayme, Eytan
High Impact School Library Spaces: Envisioning New School Library Concepts — Sullivan, Margaret L.
High-Intensity 300 — Trink, Dan
The High King's Golden Tongue — Derr, Megan
The High Line — James Corner Field
The High Line — James Corner Field Operations
The High Mountains of Portugal — Martel, Yann
High-Ranking Widows in Medieval Iceland and Yorkshire: Property, Power, Marriage and Identity in the Twelfth and Thirteenth Centuries — Ricketts, Philadelphia
High Rider — Gallaher, Bill
The High Seminaiy, vol. 2: A History of Clemson University, 1964-2000 — Reel, Jerome V.
High Society Dinners: Dining in Tsarist Russia — Lotman, Yuri
High Speed Trains — Clapper, Nikki Bruno
High Stakes — McEvoy, John
High Tide for Horseshoe Crabs (Illus. by Marks, Alan) — Schnell, Lisa Kahn
High Title of a Communist: Postwar Party Discipline and the Values of the Soviet Regime — Cohn, Edward
High-Yield Routines for Grades K-8 — McCoy, Ann
High-Yield Vegetable Gardening: Grow More of What You Want in the Space You Have — McCrate, Colin
A Higher Call — Alexande, Larry
Higher Ed — McWatt, Tessa
Higher Education in the American West: Regional History and State Contexts — Goodchild, Lester F.
Higher Education, Leadership and Women Vice Chancellors: Fitting in to Communities of Practice of Masculinities — Burkinshaw, Paula
A Higher Form of Killing: Six Weeks in World War I That Forever Changed the Nature of Warfare — Preston, Diana
A Higher Standard: Leadership Strategies from America's First Female Four-Star General — Dunwoody, Ann
The Highest Poverty: Monastic Rules and Form-of-Life — Agamben, Giorgio
The Highest Rung of the Ladder: Achieving the American Dream — Zager, Deane May
Highgrove: An English Country Garden — Guinness, Bunny
Highland Guard — Howell, Hannah

Highland Park and River Oaks: The Origins of Garden Suburban Community Planning in Texas — Ferguson, Cheryl Caldwell
Highland Spitfire — Wine, Mary
The Highlander Takes a Bride — Sands, Lynsay
Highlander Undone — Brockway, Connie
The Highlander's Bride — Forester, Amanda
The Highwayman — Byrne, Kerrigan
c Hilarious Huge Animal Jokes to Tickle Your Funny Bone — Niven, Felicia Lowenstein
Hilbert's Lectures on the Foundations of Arithmetic and Logic, 1917-1933 — Ewald, Wiliam
Hilbert's Program and Beyond — Sieg, Wilfried
c Hilda and the Black Hound (Illus. by Pearson, Luke) — Pearson, Luke
y Hilda Bewildered. E-book Review — Stace, Lynley
y The Hill of the Red Fox — McLean, Allan Campbell
c Hillary (Illus. by Colon, Raul) — Winter, Jonah
The Hillary Doctrine: Sex and American Foreign Policy — Hudson, Valerie M.
y Hillary Rodham Clinton: A Woman Living History — Blumenthal, Karen
y Hillary Rodham Clinton: Do All the Good You Can — Levinson, Cynthia
c Hillary Rodham Clinton: Dreams Taking Flight (Illus. by Bates, Amy June) — Krull, Kathleen
Hillary Rodham Clinton: On the Couch: Inside the Mind and Life of Hillary Clinton — Bond, Alma H.
c Hillary Rodham Clinton: Some Girls Are Born to Lead (Illus. by Pham, LeUyen) — Markel, Michelle
Hills and Mountains in Watercolour — Woolley, Peter
The Hills of Rome: Signature of an Eternal City — Vout, Caroline
The Hilltop (Read by Fass, Robert). Audiobook Review — Gavron, Assaf
The Hilltop — Gavron, Assaf
c Hilo: The Boy Who Crashed to Earth (Illus. by Winick, Judd) — Winick, Judd
Himmlers Lehrer: Die Weltanschauliche Schulung in der SS 1933-1945 — Harten, Hans-Christian
Hindsight in Greek and Roman History — Powell, Anton
Hindu Theology and Biology: the Bhagavata Purana and Contemporary Theory — Edelmann, Jonathan B.
Hinter der Front. Der Erste Weltkrieg in Westfalen. 22. Tagung "Fragen der Regionalgeschichte"
Hip Figures: A Literary History of the Democratic Party — Szalay, Michael
Hip Hamster Projects — Thomas, Isabel
Hip Hop Family Tree, vol. 3: 1983-1984 (Illus. by Piskor, Ed) — Piskor, Ed
c A Hippo in Our Yard (Illus. by Donnelly, Liza) — Donnelly, Liza
c HippoDuck: Trouble at the Airport (Illus. by Haufiller, Gaston) — Magura, Sandra
c Hippos Are Huge! (Illus. by Trueman, Matthew) — London, Jonathan
c Hipster le chat: Chroniques de la faune urbaine — Demers, Guillaume
y The Hired Girl — Schlitz, Laura Amy
The Hired Man — Forna, Aminatta
Hirohito's War: The Pacific War, 1941-1945 — Pike, Francis
The Hirschfeld Century: Portrait of an Artist and His Age (Illus. by Hirschfeld, Al) — Hirschfeld, Al
The Hirschfeld Century: Portrait of an Artist and His Age — Hirschfeld, Al
The Hirschfeld Century: Portrait of an Artist and His Age (Illus. by Hirschfeld, Al) — Hirschfeld, Al
The Hirsel Excavations — Cramp, Rosemary
His Eminence Files — Somorjai, Adam
His Father's Eyes — Coe, David B.
His First and Last — Osburn, Terri
His Hiding Place Is Darkness: A Hindu-Catholic Theopoetics of Divine Absence — Clooney, Francis X.
His Kind of Trouble — Austin, Terri L.
His Own Man — Ribeiro, Edgard Telles
His Right Hand — Harrison, Mette Ivie
His Steadfast Love and Other Stories — Brownsey, Paul
His to Take — Black, Shayla
His Whole Life — Hay, Elizabeth
His Wicked Reputation — Hunter, Madeline
Hispanic Caribbean Literature of Migration: Narratives of Displacement — Rosario, Vanessa Perez
Hissing Cousins: The Untold Story of Eleanor Roosevelt and Alice Roosevelt Longworth — Peyser, Marc

c Hissy Fitz (Illus. by Austin, Michael Allen) — Jennings, Patrick
Histoire Auguste, vol. 3, part 2: Vie d'Alexandre Severe — Bertrand-Dagenbach, Cecile
Histoire de l'Europe editee d'apres les carnets de captivite, 1916-1918 — Devroey, Henri
Histoire economique et sociale de la Savoie de 1860 a nos jours — Varaschin, Denis
Histoire litteraire des benedictins de Saint-Maur, Tome Quatrieme (1724-1787). — Lenain, Philippe
The Historia Ierosolimitana of Baldric of Bourgueil — Biddlecombe, Steven
An Historian in Peace and War: The Diaries of Harold Temperley — Otte, T.G.
Historians across Borders: Writing American History in a Global Age — Barreyre, Nicolas
Historians and Nationalism: East-Central Europe in the Nineteenth Century — Baar, Monika
Historians Debate the Rise of the West — Daly, Jonathan W.
Historic Heston — Blumenthal, Heston
An Historical Account of the Black Empire of Hayti — Rainsford, Marcus
A Historical and Etymological Dictionary of American Sign Language — Shaw, Emily
y Historical Animals: The Dogs, Cats, Horses, Snakes, Goats, Rats, Dragons, Bears, Elephants, Rabbits, and Other Creatures That Changed the World (Illus. by Jeff Albrecht Studios) — Moberg, Julia
Historical Atlas of Ancient Christianity — Di Berardino, Angelo
Historical Atlas of Northeast Asia, 1590-2010: Korea, Manchuria, Mongolia, Eastern Siberia — Narangoa, Li
Historical Collections — Barber, Jon Warner
Historical Dictionary of American Theater: Beginnings — Fisher, James
Historical Dictionary of the American Frontier — Buckley, Jay H.
Historical Dictionary of the British Empire — Panton, Kenneth J.
Historical GIS Research in Canada — Bonnell, Jennifer
A Historical Guide to F. Scott Fitzgerald — Curnutt, Kirk
Historical Guide to World Media Freedom: A Country-by-Country Analysis — Whitten-Woodring, Jenifer
Historical Legacies of Communism in Russia and Eastern Europe — Kotkin, Stephen
The Historical Origins of Terrorism in America, 1644-1880 — Kumamoto, Robert
Historical Texts from Medieval Wales — Williams, Patricia
The Historical Uncanny: Disability, Ethnicity, and the Politics of Holocaust Memory — Knittel, Susanne C.
Histories Book V — Herodotus
Histories of 1914. Debates and Use of Origins of World War One in Southeastern Europe
Histories of American Foodways: Annual Meeting of the Historians in the DGfA
Histories of Archaeological Practices: Reflections on Methods, Strategies and Social Organization in Past Fieldwork — Jensen, Ola Wolfhechel
Historiography and History Education in the South Slavic and Albanian Speaking Regions
Historiography, Empire and the Rule of Law: Imagined Constitutions, Remembered Legalities — Duncanson, Ian
Historiography in Saudi Arabia: Globalization and the State in the Middle East — Determann, Jorg Matthias
c Historium (Illus. by Wilkinson, Richard) — Nelson, Jo
The History — Attaleiates, Michael
History and Popular Memory: The Power of Story in Moments of Crisis — Cohen, Paul A.
The History and Present State of Virginia — Parrish, Susan Scott
History, Ideology, and Bible Interpretation in the Dead Sea Scrolls: Collected Studies — Dimant, Devorah
A History in Sum: 150 Years of Mathematics at Harvard (1825-1975). — Nadis, Steve
History Is Bunk: Assembling the Past at Henry Ford's Greenfield Village — Swigger, Jessie
History, Literature, Critical Theory — LaCapra, Dominick
The History Manifesto — Guldi, Jo
History, Memory and Politics in Central and Eastern Europe: Memory Games — Mink, George
The History of Akbar, vol. 1 — Fazl, Abu'l

History of America in 50 Documents — Matthew, Adam
A History of America in Thirty-Six Postage Stamps — West, Chris
The History of American Higher Education: Learning and Culture from the Founding to World War II — Geiger, Roger L.
A History of Architecture in 100 Buildings — Cruickshank, Dan
The History of Argentina. 2d ed. — Lewis, Daniel
The History of Arsaces, Prince of Betlis — Johnston, Charles
y History of Asian Americans: Exploring Diverse Roots — Lee, Jonathan H.X.
A History of Balance, 1250-1375: The Emergence of a New Model of Equilibrium and Its Impact on Medieval Thought — Kaye, Joel
The History of Bankruptcy: Economic, Social and Cultural Implications in Early Modern Europe — Safley, Thomas Max
A History of Baseball in 100 Objects: A Tour through the Bats, Balls, Uniforms, Awards, Documents, and Other Artifacts That Tell the Story of the National Pastime — Leventhal, Josh
The History of Bhutan — Phuntsho, Karma
The History of British Women's Writing, 1920-1945: Vol. 8 — Joannou, Maroula
The History of Cartography: Cartography in the Twentieth Century, 2 vols. — Monmonier, Mark
c A History of Civilization in 50 Disasters — Eaton, Gale
History of Cognitive Neuroscience — Bennett, Maxwell R.
The History of Emotions: An Introduction — Plamper, Jan
A History of Family Planning in Twentieth-Century Peru — Lopez, Raul Necochea
c A History of Film — Eboch, M.M.
A History of Food in 100 Recipes — Sitwell, William
y A History of Glitter and Blood (Illus. by Johnson, Cathy G.) — Moskowitz, Hannah
y A History of Glitter and Blood (Illus. by Johnson, Cathy G.) — Moskowitz, Hannah
y A History of Glitter and Blood (Illus. by Johnson, Cathy G.) — Moskowitz, Hannah
A History of Heists: Bank Robbery in America — Clark, Jerry
History of Heralds in Europe
c The History of Independence Day — Donaghey, Reese
History of International Fashion — Grumbach, Didier
A History of Ireland in 100 Objects — O'Toole, Fintan
A History of Japanese Political Thought, 1600-1901 — Hiroshi, Watanabe
A History of Libya — Wright, John
A History of Loneliness (Read by Doyle, Gerard). Audiobook Review — Boyne, John
A History of Loneliness — Boyne, John
A History of Modern Aesthetics, 3 vols. — Guyer, Paul
The History of Modern France: From the Revolution to the Present Day — Fenby, Jonathan
A History of Modern Librarianship: Constructing the Heritage of Western Cultures — Richards, Pamela Spence
y The History of Modern Music — Anniss, Matt
A History of Modern Tibet, Volume 3: The Storm Clouds Descend, 1955-1957 — Goldstein, Melvyn C.
c The History of Money: From Bartering to Banking (Illus. by Kitamura, Satoshi) — Jenkins, Martin
A History of Money — Pauls, Alan
History of Nebraska, 4th ed. — Naugle, Ronald C.
A History of New York in 101 Objects — Roberts, Sam
y The History of Nursing — Craig, Elizabeth
The History of Oxford University Press — Gadd, Ian
The History of Professional Nursing in North Carolina, 1902-2002 — Pollitt, Phoebe
History of Rock 'n' Roll in Ten Songs — Marcus, Greil
History of Rocketry and Astronautics: AAS History Series, Vol. 40 — Rothmund, Christophe
History of Rocketry and Astronautics: AAS History Series, vol. 41 — Dougherty, Kerrie
A History of Stepfamilies in Early America — Wilson, Lisa
History of Street Cops — Zito, Greg
A History of the All-India Muslim League, 1906-1947 — Afzal, Rafique
History of the American Society of Missiology, 1973-2013 — Shenk, Wilbert R.
The History of the Book in 100 Books — Cave, Roderick
A History of the Brain: From Stone Age Surgery to Modern Neuroscience — Wickens, Andrew P.

The History of the Catholic Church in Latin America: From Conquest to Revolution and Beyond — Schwaller, John Frederick
A History of the Electron: J.J. and G.P. Thomson — Navarro, Jaume
A History of the French in London: Liberty, Equality, Opportunity — Kelly, Debra
A History of the Mediterranean Air War 1940-1945, Vol. 2: North African Desert, February 1942 - March 1943 — Shores, Christopher
The History of the National Encuentros: Hispanic Americans in the One Catholic Church — Paredes, Mario J.
A History of the Pakistan Army: Wars and Insurrection — Cloughley, Brian
A History of the Vietnamese — Taylor, Keith W.
A History of the World Cup: 1930-2014 — Lisi, Clemente A.
A History of the World in 100 Objects — MacGregor, Neil
History of the World in 1,000 Objects — DK Publishing, Inc.
History of the World in 1,000 Objects — Smithsonian
A History of U.S. Nuclear Testing and Its Influence on Nuclear Thought, 1945-1963 — Blades, David M.
y The History of Video Games — Bjornlund, Lydia
A History of Violence — Martinez, Oscar
A History of War in 100 Battles — Overy, Richard
A History of Zimbabwe — Mlambo, Alois S.
Historyblogosphere: Bloggen in den Geschichtswissenschaften — Haber, Peter
c History's All-Stars (Illus. by Henderson, Meryl) — Kudlinski, Kathleen V.
History's Babel: Scholarship, Professionalization and the Historical Enterprise in the United States, 1880-1940 — Townsend, Robert B.
c History's Mysteries Series — Levy, Janey
History's People: Personalities and the Past — MacMillan, Margaret
y The Hit (Read by Roukin, Samuel). Audiobook Review — Burgess, Melvin
y The Hit — Burgess, Melvin
y Hit — Dawson, Delilah S.
y Hit and Miss — Jeter, Derek
y Hit Count — Lynch, Chris
y Hit & Miss (Read by Williams, Jesse). Audiobook Review — Jeter, Derek
y Hit — Dawson, Delilah S.
Hit the Target: Eight Men Who Led the Eighth Air Force to Victory over the Luftwaffe — Yenne, Bill
c A Hitch at the Fairmont (Illus. by Bertozzi, Nick) — Averbeck, Jim
Hitchcock a la Carte — Olsson, Jan
Hitchcock Lost and Found: The Forgotten Films — Kerzoncuf, Alain
Hitchcock on Hitchcock: Selected Writings and Interviews, vol. 2 — Hitchcock, Alfred
Hitler at Home — Stratigakos, Despina
y Hitler, Goebbels, Himmler: The Nazi Holocaust Masterminds — Altman, Linda Jacobs
Hitler und Humor - Geht Das? Der "Fuhrer" als Zielscheibe von Satire und Karikatur
Hitler's Art Thief: Hildebrand Gurlitt, the Nazis and the Looting of Europe's Treasures — Ronald, Susan
Hitler's Berlin: Abused City — Friedrich, Thomas
Hitler's First Victims: And One Man's Race for Justice — Ryback, Timothy W.
Hitler's First Victims: The Quest for Justice — Ryback, Timothy W.
Hitler's Forgotten Children — Von Oelhafen, Ingrid
y Hitler's Last Days: The Death of the Nazi Regime and the World's Most Notorious Dictator — O'Reilly, Bill
Hitler's Philosophers — Sherratt, Yvonne
Hitler's Shadow Empire: Nazi Economics and the Spanish Civil War — Barbieri, Pierpaolo
Hitler's Uranium Club: The Secret Recordings at Farm Hall — Bernstein, Jeremy
y Hitlist — Rawson, K.
HIV Exceptionalism: Development through Disease in Sierra Leone — Benton, Adia
The Hive Construct — Maskill, Alexander
The Hoarders — Hering, Scott
A Hoarse Half-Human Cheer — Kennedy, X.J.
Hobbes, the Scriblerians and the History of Philosophy — Condren, Conal
A Hobbit, a Wardrobe, and a Great War: How J.R.R. Tolkien and C.S. Lewis Rediscovered Faith, Friendship, and Heroism in the Cataclysm of 1914-1918 — Loconte, Joseph

Hochkultur in der Sowjetunion und in ihren Nachfolgestaaten im 20. Jahrhundert in kulturgeschichtlicher Perspektive

c Hockey: Great Moments, Records, and Facts — *Borth, Teddy*

c Hockey Hero (Illus. by Pullen, Zachary) — *Hyman, Zachary*

c Hockey Source Series, 4 vols. — *Winters, Jamie*

Hockney: The Biography, vol. 2: A Pilgrim's Progress — *Sykes, Christopher Simon*

Hoe, Heaven & Hell — *Garcia, Nasario*

Hofkapelle und Kaplane im Konigreich Sizilien (1130-1266). — *Geis, Lioba*

Hog: Perfect Pork Recipes from the Snout to the Squeak — *Turner, Richard H.*

The Hoggs of Texas: Letters and Memoirs of an Extraordinary Family, 1887-1906 — *Bernhard, Virginia*

The Hog's Back Mystery — *Crofts, Freeman Wills*

c Hoiho Paku (Illus. by Roberts, Ngaere) — *Roberts, Ngaere*

c Hokey Dowa Gerda and the Snowflake Girl — *Matheson, M.J.*

Hokusai's Great Wave: A Global Icon — *Guth, Christine M.E.*

Holacracy: The New Management System for a Rapidly Changing World — *Robertson, Brian J.*

Hold Me Close — *Hart, Megan*

y Hold Me Closer: The Tiny Cooper Story — *Levithan, David*

y Hold Me Like a Breath — *Schmidt, Tiffany*

y Hold on Tight — *Glines, Abbi*

Hold Still — *Strong, Lynn Steger*

y Hold Still: A Memoir with Photographs — *Mann, Sally*

c Hold This! (Illus. by Alpaugh, Priscilla) — *Scoppettone, Carolyn Cory*

y Hold Tight, Don't Let Go — *Wagner, Laura Rose*

y Hold Your Own — *Tempest, Kate*

Holderlin's Hymns: "Germania" and "The Rhine" — *Heidegger, Martin*

Holding Fast to Dreams: Empowering Youth from the Civil Rights Crusade to STEM Achievement — *Hrabowski, Freeman A., III*

Holding On Upside Down: The Life and Work of Marianne Moore — *Leavell, Linda*

Holding the Shop Together: German Industrial Relations in the Postwar Era — *Silvia, Stephen J.*

c A Hole in the Wall (Illus. by Wilhelm, Hans) — *Wilhelm, Hans*

c The Hole to China — *Rex, Michael*

c Holey Moley (Illus. by Ehler, Lois) — *Ehler, Lois*

c Holey Moley (Illus. by Ehlert, Lois) — *Ehlert, Lois*

y Holidays, Festivals, and Celebrations of the World Dictionary, 5th ed. — *Pearline, Jaikumar*

The Holistic Cat: A Complete Guide to Natural Health Care — *Mash, Holly*

Holland's Golden Age in America: Collecting the Arts of Rembrandt, Vermeer, and Hals — *Quodbach, Esmee*

Holloman Air Force Base, Images of America — *Page, Joseph T., II*

c The Hollow Boy — *Stroud, Jonathan*

c Hollow City (Read by Heyborne, Kirby). Audiobook Review — *Riggs, Ransom*

The Hollow Girl — *Coleman, Reed Farrel*

Hollow Heart — *Di Grado, Viola*

Hollow Justice: A History of Indigenous Claims in the United States — *Wilkins, David E.*

The Hollow Land — *Gardam, Jane*

Hollow Man — *Pryor, Mark*

The Hollow of the Hand — *Harvey, Polly Jean*

The Hollow Queen — *Haydon, Elizabeth*

Hollowed Out: Why the Economy Doesn't Work without a Middle Class — *Madland, David*

y Hollowgirl — *Williams, Sean*

y Hollowgirl — *Williiams, Sean*

Hollywood: A Novel of the Twenties — *Vidal, Gore*

Hollywood — *Bachardy, Don*

Hollywood and Hitler, 1933-1939 — *Doherty, Thomas*

Hollywood Babylon — *Anger, Kenneth*

Hollywood Clown: An Inside Look into the Competitive and Political World of Children's Birthday Parties of Hollywood's Rich and Famous — *Lassen, Jason*

Hollywood Exiles in Europe: The Blacklist and Cold War Film Culture — *Prime, Rebecca*

Hollywood Frame by Frame: The Unseen Silver Screen in Contact Sheets, 1951-1997 — *Longworth, Karina*

Hollywood Presents Jules Verne: The Father of Science Fiction on Screen — *Taves, Brian*

Hollywood Stunt Performers, 1910s-1970s: A Biographical Dictionary — *Freese, Gene Scott*

Hollywood Vault: Film Libraries before Home Video — *Hoyt, Eric*

Hollywoods Kriege: Geschichte einer Heimsuchung — *Bronfen, Elisabeth*

The Holocaust and European Societies. Social Processes and Social Dynamics

The Holocaust and the Germanization of Ukraine — *Steinhart, Eric C.*

The Holocaust and the Revival of Psychological History — *Hughes, Judith M.*

The Holocaust and the West German Historians: Historical Interpretations and Autobiographical Memory — *Berg, Nicolas*

The Holocaust Averted: An Alternate History of American Jewry, 1938-1967 — *Gurock, Jeffrey*

Holocaust Consciousness in Contemporary Britain — *Pearce, Andy*

The Holocaust in Greece: Genocide and Its Aftermath

The Holocaust in Hungary: Evolution of a Genocide — *Vagi, Zoltan*

The Holocaust in the East: Local Perpetrators and Soviet Responses — *David-Fox, Michael*

Holocaust Mothers and Daughters: Family, History, and Trauma — *Clementi, Federica K.*

c The Holocaust — *Peppas, Lynn Leslie*

y Holocaust Resistance — *Blohm, Craig E.*

The Hologenome Concept: Human, Animal and Plant Microbiota — *Rosenberg, Eugene*

The Holy Innocents and Other Stories — *Bird, Joan Carol*

The Holy Mark — *Alexander, Gregory*

Holy Matter: Changing Perceptions of the Material World in Late Medieval Christianity — *Ritchey, Sara*

Holy Nation: The Transatlantic Quaker Ministry in an Age of Revolution — *Crabtree, Sarah*

The Holy Spirit in Biblical Teaching, Through the Centuries, and Today — *Thiselton, Anthony*

Holy Spirit: Inner Fire, Giver of Life and Comforter of the Poor — *Boff, Leonardo*

Holy Treasure and Sacred Song: Relic Cults and Their Liturgies in Medieval Tuscany — *Brand, Benjamin*

The Holy Trinity in the Life of the Church — *Anatolios, Khaled*

Holy War and Rapprochement: Studies in the Relations between the Mamluk Sultanate and the Mongol Ilkhanate, 1260-1335 — *Amitai, Reuven*

Holy War, Martyrdom, and Terror: Christianity, Violence, and the West, ca. 70 C. E. to the Iraq War — *Buc, Philippe*

Holy Warriors: The Religious Ideology of Chivalry — *Kaeuper, Richard W.*

Homage to a Broken Man — *Mommsen, Peter*

Homage to Catalonia — *Orwell, George*

Homage to New Orleans — *Morris, Leon*

Home — *Allen, John S.*

c Home (Illus. by Ellis, Carson) — *Ellis, Carson*

c Home — *Ellis, Carson*

c Home Alone: The Classic Illustrated Storybook (Illus. by Smith, Kim)

c Home and Away: A World War II Christmas Story — *Hughes, Dean*

Home by Nightfall — *Finch, Charles*

Home: Chronicles of a North Country Life — *Powning, Beth*

Home Cooking 101: How to Make Everything Taste Better — *Moulton, Sara*

Home Fires: How Americans Kept Warm in the 19th Century — *Adams, Sean Patrick*

Home Fires — *Kirscht, Judith*

Home for Dinner: Mixing Food, Fun, and Conversation for a Happier Family and Healthier Kids — *Fishel, Anne K.*

c A Home for Mr. Emerson (Illus. by Fotheringham, Edwin) — *Kerley, Barbara*

c A Home for Shimmer — *Hopkins, Cathy*

The Home Front in Britain: Images, Myths and Forgotten Experiences Since 1914 — *Andrews, Maggie*

Home Front — *Vandenburg, Margaret*

Home Is Burning: A Memoir — *Marshall, Dan*

Home Is the Place (Read by Siegfried, Mandy, with Lorna Raver). Audiobook Review — *Martin, Ann M.*

y Home Is the Place — *Martin, Ann M.*

Home Is Where the School Is: The Logic of Homeschooling and the Emotional Labor of Mothering — *Lois, Jennifer*

Home Is Where Your Boots Are — *Lloyd, Kalan Chapman*

The Home Place (Read by Nichols, Andrus). Audiobook Review — *La Suer, Carrie*

Home: Recipes to Cook with Family and Friends — *Voltaggio, Bryan*

The Home Reference to Holistic Health & Healing: Easy-To-Use Natural Remedies, Herbs, Flower Essences, Essential Oils, Supplements, and Therapeutic Practices for Health, Happiness, and Well-Being. — *Mars, Brigitte*

The Home Rule Crisis, 1912-14 — *Doherty, Gabriel*

c Home Run — *Green, Tim*

Home Squadron: The U.S. Navy on the North Atlantic Station — *Rentfrow, James C.*

c Home Tweet Home — *Dicmas, Courtney*

Home, Uprooted: Oral Histories of India's Partition — *Chawla, Devika*

Home with Henry: A Memoir — *Kaier, Anne*

Homefront — *Scott, Jessica*

Homefront 911: How Families of Veterans Are Wounded by Our Wars — *Bannerman, Stacy*

Homefront — *Magner, Scott James*

Homegrown Terror: Benedict Arnold and the Burning of New London — *Lehman, Eric D.*

c The Homemade Cake Contest — *Basho, Midori*

The Homemade Kitchen: Recipes for Cooking with Pleasure — *Chernila, Alana*

Homemade Men in Postwar Austrian Cinema: Nationhood, Genre and Masculinity — *Fritsche, Maria*

c A Homemade Together Christmas (Illus. by Cocca-Leffler, Maryann) — *Cocca-Leffler, Maryann*

c Homer Henry Hudson's Curio Museum (Illus. by Rock, Zack) — *Rock, Zack*

Homer: Iliad Book XXII — *de Jong, I.J.F.*

Homer: Odyssey Books XIII and XIV — *Bowie, Angus M.*

Homer: The Odyssey — *Hammond, Martin*

Homeric Effects in Vergil's Narrative — *Barchiesi, Alessandro*

Homeric Speech and the Origins of Rhetoric — *Knudsen, Rachel Ahern*

Homer's Turk: How Classics Shaped Ideas of the East — *Toner, Jerry*

Homes Down East: Classic Maine Coastal Cottages and Town Houses — *Shettleworth, Earle G., Jr.*

c Homesick Penguin (Illus. by Palen, Debbie) — *Bowser, Ken*

Homespun Gospel: The Triumph of Sentimentality in Contemporary American Evangelicalism — *Brenneman, Todd M.*

Homicide in Pre-Famine and Famine Ireland — *McMahon, Richard*

The Homing Instinct: Meaning and Mystery in Animal Migration — *Heinrich, Bernd*

y The Homing Instinct — *Heinrich, Bernd*

Hominid Up — *Shepard, Neil*

Homo Imperii: A History of Physical Anthropology in Russia — *Mogilner, Marina*

The Homoerotics of Orientalism — *Boone, Joseph Allen*

The Honest Truth about Dishonesty: How We Lie to Everyone--Especially Ourselves — *Ariely, Dan*

y The Honest Truth — *Gemeinhart, Dan*

c Honey (Read by Soler, Rebecca). Audiobook Review — *Weeks, Sarah*

c Honey — *Weeks, Sarah*

Honey & Co.: Food from the Middle East — *Packer, Sarit*

Honey & Co.: The Cookbook — *Srulovich, Itamar*

Honey from the Lion — *Null, Matthew Neill*

y Honey Girl — *Freeman, Lisa*

Honeydew: Stories — *Pearlman, Edith*

c Honeyky Hanukah (Illus. by Horowitz, Dave) — *Guthrie, Woody*

Honeymoon — *Modiano, Patrick*

Hong Kong's Court of Final Appeal: The Development of the Law in China's Hong Kong — *Young, Simon N.M.*

Hong Kong's War Crimes Trials — *Linton, Suzannah*

c Honk Honk! Hold Tight! (Illus. by Souhami, Jessica) — *Souhami, Jessica*

Honky Tonk Samurai — *Lansdale, Joe R.*

Honor above All — *Bard-Collins, J.*

y Honor Girl: A Graphic Memoir (Illus. by Thrash, Maggie) — *Thrash, Maggie*

Honor, History, and Relationship: Essays in Second-Personal Ethics, vol. 2 — *Darwall, Stephen*

Honour, Exchange and Violence in Beowulf — *Baker, Peter S.*

Honourable Friends? Parliament and the Fight for Change — Lucas, Caroline
c Honouring the Buffalo: A Plains Cree Legend (Illus. by Keepness, Mike) — Lavallee, Ray
Hoo-Doo Cowboys and Bronze Buckaroos: Conceptions of the African American West — Johnson, Michael K
c Hoodoo — Smith, Ronald L.
c Hooked — Wolf, Allen
Hooked: How to Build Habit-Forming Products — Eyal, Nir
y Hook's Daughter — Schulz, Heidi
c Hook's Revenge (Illus. by Hendrix, John) — Schulz, Heidi
c Hooray for Hat! — Won, Brian
c Hooray for Hoppy! — Hopgood, Tim
c Hooray for Kids — Lang, Suzanne
Hoosiers: A New History of Indiana — Madison, James H.
c Hoot — Litton, Jonathan
c Hoot and Peep (Illus. by Judge, Lita) — Judge, Lita
c Hoot! Hoot! — Nosy Crow
c Hoot Owl, Master of Disguise (Illus. by Jullien, Jean) — Taylor, Sean (b. 1965-)
c Hop (Illus. by Hurley, Jorey) — Hurley, Jorey
c Hop, Bunny!: Explore the Forest — Neuman, Susan B.
The Hop Grower's Handbook: The Essential Guide for Sustainable, Small-Scale Production for Home and Market — Gehring, Dietrich
c Hop, Hop Bunny (Illus. by Ng, Neiko) — Schwartz, Betty Ann
c Hop! Hop! (Illus. by Patricelli, Leslie) — Patricelli, Leslie
c Hop Up! Wriggle Over! (Illus. by Honey, Elizabeth) — Honey, Elizabeth
y Hope: A Memoir of Survival in Cleveland — DeJesus, Gina
Hope: A School, a Team, a Dream — Reynolds, Bill
c The Hope Chest (Read by Mercer-Meyer, Carla). Audiobook Review — Schwabach, Karen
Hope: Entertainer of the Century — Zoglin, Richard
Hope for a Cool Pillow — Overton, Margaret
Hope for the Caregiver — Rosenberger, Peter
c Hope for Winter: The True Story of a Remarkable Dolphin Friendship — Yates, David
Hope Harbor (Read by Plummer, Therese). Audiobook Review — Hannon, Irene
Hope Harbor — Hannon, Irene
y Hope in a Ballet Shoe — DePrince, Michaela
Hope in Action: Subversive Eschatology in the Theology of Edward Schillebeeckx and Johann Baptist Metz — Rodenborn, Steven M.
The Hope in Leaving: A Memoir — Williams, Barbara
Hope, Make, Heal: 20 Crafts to Mend the Heart — Donenfeld, Maya Pagan
Hope Makes Love — Cole, Trevor
Hope on Earth: A Conversation — Ehrlich, Paul R.
Hope Sings, So Beautiful: Graced Encounters across the Color Line — Pramuk, Christopher
Hope to Die (Read by Boatman, Michael, with Scott Sowers). Audiobook Review — Patterson, James
The Hopeful — O'Neill, Tracy
Hopelessly Hollywood — Lewis, David H.
Hopes for Better Spouses: Protestant Marriage and Church Renewal in Early Modern Europe, India, and North America — Roeber, A.G.
c Hoppelpopp and the Best Bunny (Illus. by Kaufmann, Angelika) — Lobe, Mira
c The Hoppernots — Dempsey, Deborah Blake
c Hopper's Destiny (Illus. by To, Vivienne) — Fiedler, Lisa
Horace and Housman — Gaskin, Richard
Horace: Odes Book I — Mayer, Roland
The Hormone Reset Diet: Heal Your Metabolism to Lose Up to 15 Pounds in 21 Days — Gottfried, Sara
The Horn of Africa — Mengisteab, Kidane
The Horrell Wars: Feuding in Texas and New Mexico — Johnson, David
c Horrible Harry and the Hallway Bully (Read by Heller, Johnny). Audiobook Review — Kline, Suzy
Horror Hospital Unplugged — Cooper, Dennis
c Horror House (Illus. by Monnier, Ron) — Larry, H.I.
The Horror of It All: One Moviegoer's Love Affair with Masked Maniacs, Frightened Virgins, and the Living Dead — Rockoff, Adam
Horror Stories: Classic Tales from Hoffmann to Hodgson — Jones, Darryl
The Horrors of Trauma in Cinema: Violence Void Visualization — Elm, Michael
c A Horse Called Hero — Angus, Sam
The Horse Healer: A Novel — Giner, Gonzalo
The Horse in Early Modern English Culture: Bridled, Curbed, and Tamed — Ornellas, Kevin De

Horse Nations: The Worldwide Impact of the Horse on Indigenous Societies — Mitchell, Peter (b. 1962-)
c Horse Raid: The Making of a Warrior (Illus. by Goble, Paul) — Goble, Paul
c The Horse Soldier — Wilson, Mark
The Horse: The Epic History of Our Noble Companion — Williams, Wendy
Horsefever — Hope, Lee
c Horses — Murray, Julie
Horses and Cattle, and a Double-Rigged Saddle — Zimmer, Stephen
c Horses around the World — Jackson, Tom (b. 1972-)
Horses at Work: Harnessing Power in Industrial America — Greene, Ann Norton
Horses That Buck: The Story of Champion Bronc Rider Bill Smith — Kahn, Margot
c Horton and the Kwuggerbug and More Lost Stories (Read by Cox, Chris, with Charles Cohen). Audiobook Review
c Horton and the Kwuggerbug and More Lost Stories — Seuss, Dr.
Hospice — Howard, Gregory
Hospitality and Islam: Welcoming in God's Name — Siddiqui, Mona
Host — Cook, Robin
Host of Memories — Lighte, Peter Rupert
Hostage — Delargy, Marlaine
Hostage — Ohlsson, Kristina
y Hostage Run — Klavan, Andrew
Hostage Taker (Read by Eby, Tanya). Audiobook Review — Pintoff, Stefanie
Hostage Taker — Pintoff, Stefanie
Hostile Takeover — Kuhn, Shane
Hostile Witness — Adams, Leigh
The Hot Bread Kitchen Cookbook: Artisanal Baking from Around the World — Rodriguez, Jessamyn Waldman
Hot Copy: Classic Gay Erotica from the Magazine Era — Chase, Dale
The Hot Countries — Hallinan, Timothy
Hot Dogs & Croissants — Saulnier, Natasha
A Hot Glue Gun Mess: Funny Stories, Pretty DIY Projects — Maroun, Taren
Hot Head — Ings, Simon
Hot Knots: Fresh Macrame Ideas for Jewelry, Home, and Fashion — Hartmann, Kat
c Hot Pink: The Life and Fashions of Elsa Schiaparelli (Illus. by Rubin, Susan Goldman) — Rubin, Susan Goldman
Hot Point — Buchman, M.L.
y Hot Pterodactyl Boyfriend — Cumyn, Alan
Hot Pursuit — Woods, Stuart
Hot Rod Gallery: A Nostalgic Look at Hot Rodding's Golden Years: 1930-1960 — Ganahl, Pat
c Hot Rod Hamster and the Awesome ATV Adventure! (Illus. by Anderson, Derek) — Lord, Cynthia
c Hot Rod Hamster and the Haunted Halloween Party! (Illus. by Anderson, Derek) — Lord, Cynthia
c Hot Rod Hamster and the Wacky Whatever Race! (Illus. by Paprocki, Greg) — Lord, Cynthia
Hot Science, High Water: Assembling Nature, Society and Environmental Policy in Contemporary Vietnam — Zink, Eren
Hot Tea ... Cold Case — Stern, D.G.
The Hot Zone (Read by Rosenblat, Barbara). Audiobook Review — Castle, Jayne
Hotel — Walsh, Joanna
y Hotel Florida: Truth, Love, and Death in the Spanish Civil War — Vaill, Amanda
Hotel Life: The Story of a Place Where Anything Can Happen — Levander, Caroline Field
Hotel Living — Pappos, Ioannis
Hotel Mavens: Lucius M. Boomer, George C. Boldt and Oscar of the Waldorf — Turkel, Stanley
Hotel Moscow — Carner, Talia
y Hotel Ruby — Young, Suzanne
c Hotel Strange: Wake Up, Spring (Illus. by Ferrier, Katherine) — Ferrier, Katherine
The Hotel Years — Roth, Joseph
Hotels of North America — Moody, Rick
c Hotshots — Goldish, Meish
The Hotter You Burn — Showalter, Gena
Hou Hsiao-Hsien — Suchenski, Richard I.
c Hound Dawg (Illus. by Pilgrim, Cheryl) — Vermillion, Patricia
The Hound of the Baskervilles (Read by Klinger, Leslie). Audiobook Review — Doyle, Arthur Conan
y The Hound of the Baskervilles (Illus. by Ferran, Daniel) — Doyle, Arthur Conan
Hounded — Rosenfelt, David
c Hour of the Bees — Eager, Lindsay
The Hour of the Star — Lispector, Clarice
Hour of the Wolf — Nesser, Hakan
y The Hourglass Factory — Ribchester, Lucy
The Hours Count — Cantor, Jillian

y The House — Lauren, Christina
c House Arrest — Holt, K.A.
The House at Ujazdowskie 16: Jewish Families in Warsaw after the Holocaust — Auerbach, Karen
House Beautiful Pink — Cregan, Lisa
The House by the Lake: A Story of Germany — Harding, Thomas
A House Divided — Whitlow, Robert
c A House for Hermit Crab — Carle, Eric
House Guests, House Pests: A Natural History of Animals in the Home — Jones, Richard
The House in Smyrna — Levy, Tatiana Salem
A House in St. John's Wood: In Search of My Parents — Spender, Matthew
The House is Full of Yogis — Hodgkinson, Will
The House of Commons: An Anthropology of Mps at Work — Crewe, Emma
c The House of Commons — Rose, Simon
House of Echoes — Duffy, Brendan
House of Eight Orchids — Thayer, James
The House of Eyes — Elliott, Patricia
House of Harwood — Pritzker, Olivia Batker
The House of Hawthorne — Robuck, Erika
The House of Medici: Inheritance of Power — Charles, Edward
y A House of My Own: Stories from My Life — Cisneros, Sandra
The House of Owls — Angell, Tony
House of Robots (Read by Patterson, Jack). Audiobook Review — Patterson, James
y House of Secrets: Battle of the Beasts (Illus. by Call, Greg) — Columbus, Chris
The House of Service: The Gillen Movement and Islam's Third Way — Tittensor, David
The House of Shattered Wings — de Bodard, Aliette
The House of Small Shadows — Novdl, Adam
The House of the Deaf Man — Kristufek, Peter
House of the Rising Sun — Burke, James Lee
House of Thieves — Belfoure, Charles
The House of Twenty Thousand Books — Abramsky, Sasha
y House of Windows — Casale, Alexia
The House of Wolfe: A Border Noir (Read by DeSantos, David). Audiobook Review — Blake, James Carlos
The House of Wolfe: A Border Noir — Blake, James Carlos
y The House on Stone's Throw Island — Poblocki, Dan
House Proud: A Social History of Atlanta Interiors, 1880-1919 — Rush, Lori Ericksen
House Rivals — Lawson, Mike
The House Tells the Story: Homes of the American Presidents — Van Doren, Adam
c The House That Jane Built: A Story about Jane Addams (Illus. by Brown, Kathryn) — Stone, Tanya Lee
The House That Kills — Pugmire, John
c The House That Zack Built (Illus. by Murray, Alison) — Murray, Alison
c The House That's Your Home (Illus. by Dyer, Jane) — Lloyd-Jones, Sally
The House They Couldn't Build — Mamatha, B.
Housebreaking — Pope, Dan
The Household Spirit — Wodicka, Tod
Household Workers Unite: The Untold Story of African American Women Who Built a Movement — Nadasen, Premilla
Houses for a New World: Builders and Buyers in American Suburbs, 1945-1965 — Lane, Barbara Miller
Housewitch — Schickel, Katie
Housing and Mortgage Markets in Historical Perspective — White, Eugene N.
Houston, We Have a Narrative: Why Science Needs Story — Olson, Randy
Houston's Hermann Park: A Century of Community — Bradley, Barrie Scardino
Hover (Read by Dawe, Angela). Audiobook Review — Wilson, Anne A.
Hover — Wilson, Anne A.
How about Never--Is Never Good for You?: My Life in Cartoons — Mankoff, Bob
How Adam Smith Can Change Your Life: An Unexpected Guide to Human Nature and Happiness — Roberts, Russ
How Americans Make Race: Stories, Institutions, Spaces — Hayward, Clarissa Rile
How an Unheralded Monk Turned His Small Town into a Center of Publishing, Made Himself the Most Famous Man in Europe--and Started the Protestant Reformation — Pettegree, Andrew
c How and What Do Animals Eat? — Kalman, Bobbie
c How and What Do Animals Learn? — Kalman, Bobbie
c How and Why Do Animals Adapt? — Kalman, Bobbie

c How and Why Do Animals Build Homes? — Kalman, Bobbie
c How and Why Do Animals Change? — Kalman, Bobbie
c How and Why Do Animals Communicate? — Kalman, Bobbie
c How and Why Do Animals Move? — Kalman, Bobbie
c How and Why Do People Copy Animals? — Kalman, Bobbie
   How and Why God Evolved — Khan, Babar Shah
   How Are Digital Devices Impacting Society? — Abramovitz, Melissa
c How Big Is Big? How Far Is Far? (Illus. by Metcalf, Jen) — Soehlke-Lennert, Dorothee
c How Big Is Big? How Far Is Far? (Illus. by Van Der Veken, Jan) — Soehlke-Lennert, Dorothee
c How Big Is Big? How Far Is Far? (Illus. by Metcalf, Jen) — Soehlke-Lennert, Dorothee
c How Big Is Big? How Far Is Far? (Illus. by Van Der Veken, Jan) — Soehlke-Lennert, Dorothee
   How Brands Grow: Part 2 — Romaniuk, Jenni
   How Champions Think: In Sports and in Life — Rotella, Bob
   How College Works — Chambliss, Daniel F.
   How Come? Every Kid's Science Questions Explained — Wollard, Kathy
   How Corrupt Is Britain? — Whyte, David
   How Could This Happen: Explaining the Holocaust — McMillan, Dan
   How Dante Can Save Your Life: The Life-Changing Wisdom of History's Greatest Poem — Dreher, Rod
   How Did I Get Here?: Making Peace with the Road Not Taken — Browner, Jesse
y How Do Cell Phones Affect Health? — Nakaya, Andrea C.
y How Do Cell Phones Affect Society? — Nakaya, Andrea C.
c How Do Dinosaurs Stay Friends? (Illus. by Teague, Mark) — Yolen, Jane
c How Do Dinosaurs Stay Safe? (Illus. by Teague, Mark) — Yolen, Jane
   How Do I Keep My Employees Motivated?:The Practice of Empathy-Based Management — Langelett, George
c How Does a Caterpillar Become a Butterfly?: And Other Questions about Butterflies — Stewart, Melissa
c How Does a Seed Sprout?: And Other Questions about Plants — Stewart, Melissa
   How Does a Single Blade of Grass Thank the Sun? — Lau, Doretta
c How Does Weather Change? — Boothroyd, Jennifer
c How Effective Is Recycling? — Chambers, Catherine
   How English Became the Global Language — Northrup, David
   How Finance Is Shaping the Economies of China, Japan, and Korea — Park, Yung Chul
   How Free Will Works: A Dualist Theory of Human Action — Duncan, Natalia
   How Glass Changed the World: The History and Chemistry of Glass from Antiquity to the 13th Century — Rasmussen, Seth C.
   How "God" Works — Brain, Marshall
   How Good We Can Be: Ending the Mercenary Society and Building a Great Country — Hutton, Will
   How Google Works — Rosenberg, Jonathan
   How Humans Learn to Think Mathematically: Exploring the Three Worlds of Mathematics — Tall, David
c How I Alienated My Grandma (Illus. by Williamson, Fraser) — Main, Suzanne
c How I Became a Ghost — Tingle, Tim
   How I Look: From Upstate New York to Downtown Manhattan, Adventures in American Style — Boehlert, Bart
   How I Met My Countess — Boyle, Elizabeth
   How I Shed My Skin: Unlearning the Racist Lessons of a Southern Childhood (Read by Leyva, Henry). Audiobook Review — Grimsley, Jim
   How I Shed My Skin: Unlearning the Racist Lessons of a Southern Childhood — Grimsley, Jim
   How Immigrants Impact Their Homelands — Eckstein, Susan Eva
   How India Became Territorial: Foreign Policy, Diaspora, Geopolitics — Abraham, Itty
   How Invention Happens — Weightman, Gavin
c How Is My Brain Like a Supercomputer?: And Other Questions about the Human Body — Stewart, Melissa
y How Is Online Pornography Affecting Society? — Wilcox, Christine
   How Israel Became a People — Hawkins, Ralph K.
   How It Feels to Be Free: Black Women Entertainers and the Civil Rights Movement — Feldstein, Ruth
y How It Went Down (Read by several narrators). Audiobook Review — Magoon, Kekla

y How It Went Down — Magoon, Kekla
   How It Works: Recovering Citizens in Post-Welfare Philadelphia — Fairbanks, Robert P., II
c How Jelly Roll Morton Invented Jazz (Illus. by Mallett, Keith) — Winter, Jonah
   How Jesus Became God: The Exaltation of a Jewish Preacher from Galilee — Ehrman, Bart D.
   How Labour Governments Fall: From Ramsay MacDonald to Gordon Brown — Heppell, Timothy
   How Languages Work: Art Introduction to Language Linguistics. — Genetti, Carol
   How Literature Plays with the Brain: The Neuroscience of Reading and Art — Armstrong, Paul B.
   How Long Will South Africa Survive? The Looming Crisis — Johnson, Richard William
c How Lunchbox Jones Saved Me From Robots, Traitors, and Missy the Cruel — Brown, Jennifer
c How Machines Work: Zoo Break! (Illus. by Macaulay, David) — Macaulay, David
   How Many Is Too Many? The Progressive Argument for Reducing Immigration into the United States — Cafaro, Philip
c How Many Legs? (Illus. by Field, Jim) — Gray, Kes
c How Many Legs? — Spitzer, Katja
c How Many Sleeps 'til Christmas? — Sperring, Mark
   How Memory Works--and How to Make It Work for You — Madigan, Robert
c How Mirka Caught a Fish — Deutsch, Barry
   How Music Got Free — Witt, Stephen
   How Music Got Free: The End of an Industry, the Turn of the Century, and the Patient Zero of Piracy — Witt, Stephen
   How Music Got Free: What Happens When an Entire Generation Commits the Same Crime? — Witt, Stephen
   How My Dog Became the New Messiah — Wallace, Stephen
   How (Not) to Be Secular: Reading Charles Taylor — Smith, James K.A.
   How Not to Be Wrong: The Hidden Maths of Everyday Life — Ellenberg, Jordan
   How Not to Be Wrong: The Power of Mathematical Thinking — Ellenberg, Jordan
y How (Not) to Fall in Love — Roberts, Lisa Brown
   How Our Days Became Numbered: Risk and the Rise of the Statistical Individual — Bouk, Dan
   How Paris Became Paris: The Invention of the Modern City — DeJean, Joan
c How Penguin Says Please! (Illus. by Watts, Sarah) — Samoun, Abigail
   How Plants Work: The Science behind the Amazing Things Plants Do — Chalker-Scott, Linda
   How Politics Makes Us Sick: Neoliberal Epidemics — Macmillan, Palgrave
   How Propaganda Works — Stanley, Jason
   How Race Is Made in America: Immigration, Citizenship, and the Historical Power of Racial Scripts — Molina, Natalia
   How Reason Almost Lost Its Mind: The Strange Career of Cold War Rationality — Erickson, Paul
c How Recycling Works — Barker, Geoff
   How Rome Fell (Read by Perkins, Derek). Audiobook Review — Goldsworthy, Adrian
y How Serious a Problem Is Synthetic Drug Use? — Parks, Peggy
   How Sex Became a Civil Liberty — Wheeler, Leigh Ann
   How Sexual Desire Works: The Enigmatic Urge — Toates, Frederick
   How Should We Live? A Practical Approach to Everyday Morality — Kekes, John
   How Snakes Work: Structure, Function, and Behavior of the World's Snakes — Lillywhite, Harvey B.
   How Soon Is Now? Medieval Texts, Amateur Readers, and the Queerness of Time — Dinshaw, Carolyn
y How Star Wars Conquered the Universe: The Past, Present, and Future of a Multibillion Dollar Franchise (Read by Podehl, Nick). Audiobook Review — Taylor, Chris
   How Star Wars Conquered the Universe: The Past, Present, and Future of a Multibillion Dollar Franchise (Read by Podehl, Nick). Audiobook Review — Taylor, Chris (b. 1973-)
   How Star Wars Conquered the Universe: The Past, Present and Future of a Multibillion-Dollar Franchise — Taylor, Chris
c How Strong Is an Ant?: And Other Questions about Bugs and Insects — Carson, Mary Kay
   How the Beowulf Poet Employs Biblical Typology: His Christian Portrayal of Heroism — Helder, William
   How the Bible Became Holy — Satlow, Michael L.
   How the Earth Turned Green; A Brief 3.8-Billion-Year History of Plants — Armstrong, Joseph E.

   How The Earth Turned Green: A Brief 3.8-Billion-Year History of Plants — Armstrong, Joseph E.
c How the Elephant Got Her Trunk (Illus. by Tjornehoj, T.G.) — Kipling, Rudyard
   How the French Think: An Affectionate Portrait of an Intellectual People — Hazareesingh, Sudhir
   How the Gringos Stole Tequila — Martineau, Chantal
   How the Internet Became Commercial — Greenstein, Shane
c How the Library (Not the Prince) Saved Rapunzel (Illus. by Ashdown, Rebecca) — Meddour, Wendy
   How the Other Half Ate: A History of Working-Class Meals at the Turn of the Century — Turner, Katherine Leonard
   How the Other Half Banks: Exclusion, Exploitation, and the Threat to Democracy — Baradaran, Mehrsa
   How the Other Half Banks — Baradaran, Mehrsa
c How the Sun Got to Coco's House (Illus. by Graham, Bob) — Graham, Bob
c How the Trees Got Their Voices (Illus. by Lion, Susan Andra) — Lion, Susan Andra
c How the US Security Agencies Work — Cobb, Allan B.
   How The War Was Won: Air-Sea Power and Allied Victory in World War II — O'Brien, Payson
   How the World Moves: The Odyssey of an American Indian Family — Nabokov, Peter
   How the World Was Won: The Americanization of Everywhere — Conrad, Peter
   How Things Came to Be: Inuit Stories of Creation (Illus. by Fiegenschuh, Emily) — Qitsualik-Tinsley, Rachel
c How Things Work: Facts and Fun, Questions and Answers, Things to Make and Do — Dauvois, Sophie
   How to Act Like a Grown-Up — DuPre, Mark
c How to Art Doodle — Scrace, Carolyn
   How to Avoid Bag Lady Syndrome — Drucker, Lance
c How to Babysit a Leopard: And Other True Stories from Our Travels across Six Continents (Illus. by Lewin, Betsy) — Lewin, Ted
c How to Babysit a Leopard and Other True Stories from Our Travels across Six Continents (Illus. by Lewin, Betsy) — Lewin, Ted
   How to Babysit a Leopard: And Other True Stories from Our Travels across Six Continents (Illus. by Lewin, Betsy) — Lewin, Ted
c How to Babysit a Leopard and Other True Stories from Our Travels across Six Continents (Illus. by Lewin, Ted) — Lewin, Ted
c How to Bake a Book (Illus. by Burfoot, Ella) — Burfoot, Ella
   How to Bake Pi: An Edible Exploration of the Mathematics of Mathematics (Read by Gilbert, Tavia). Audiobook Review — Cheng, Eugenia
   How to Bake Pi: An Edible Exploration of the Mathematics of Mathematics — Cheng, Eugenia
   How to Be a Bad Bitch — Rose, Amber
c How to Be a Dog (Illus. by Williamson, Jo) — Williamson, Jo
y How to Be a Girl: The Common Sense Guide to Girlhood — Naik, Anita
   How to Be a Good Mommy When You're Sick: A Guide to Motherhood with Chronic Illness — Graves, Emily
   How to Be a Grown-Up — Kraus, Nicola
   How to Be a Grown-Up — McLaughlin, Emma
   How to Be a Heroine, or, What I've Learned from Reading Too Much — Ellis, Samantha
   How to Be a Husband — Dowling, Tim
c How to Be a Space Explorer — Brake, Mark
   How to Be a Superhero — Edlitz, Mark
   How to Be a Tudor: A Dawn-to-Dusk Guide to Tudor Life — Goodman, Ruth
   How to Be Alive: A Guide to the Kind of Happiness That Helps the World — Beavan, Colin
   How to Be an Intellectual: Essays on Criticism, Culture, and the University — Williams, Jeffrey J.
y How to Be Bad — Lockhart, E.
   How to Be Both (Read by Banks, John). Audiobook Review — Smith, Ali
   How to Be Both — Smith, Ali
y How to Be Brave — Kottaras, E. Katherine
   How to Be Drawn — Hayes, Terrance
y How to be Happy — Burton, David
   How to Be Happy (or at Least Less Sad). — Crutchley, Lee
   How to Be: Six Simple Rules for Being the Best Kid You Can Be — Leaf, Munroe
c How to Behave at a Dog Show (Illus. by Ross, Heather) — Rosenberg, Madelyn
c How to Behave at a Tea Party (Illus. by Ross, Heather) — Rosenberg, Madelyn

c How to Break a Heart — Stewart, Kiera
c How to Build a Car — Lacey, Saskia
How to Build Chicken Coops: Everything You Need To Know — Johnson, Samantha
c How to Camp like a Pro — Burlingame, Jeff
c How to Canoe and Kayak like a Pro — Norris, Ashley P. Watson
c How to Capture an Invisible Cat (Illus. by Lafontaine, Thierry) — Tobin, Paul
How to Carry Bigfoot Home — Tarry, Chris
c How to Catch a Mouse (Illus. by Leathers, Philippa) — Leathers, Philippa
How to Catch a Prince — Hauck, Rachel
How to Catch a Russian Spy: The True Story of an American Civilian Turned Double Agent — Jamali, Naveed
c How to Catch Santa (Illus. by Wildish, Lee) — Reagan, Jean
How to Clone a Mammoth: The Science of De-Extinction — Shapiro, Beth
c How to Code in 10 Easy Lessons: Learn How to Design and Code Your Very Own Computer Game (Illus. by Foster, Walter, Jr.) — McManus, Sean
How to Conceive Naturally: And Have a Healthy Pregnancy after 30 — Orecchio, Christa
How to Cook a Moose: A Culinary Memoir — Christensen, Kate
c How to Cook in 10 Easy Lessons: Learn How to Prepare Food and Cook Like a Pro — Sweetser, Wendy
How to Create the Perfect Wife: Britain's Most Ineligible Bachelor and His Enlightened Quest to Train the Ideal Mate — Moore, Wendy
c How to Deal with Bullies Superhero Style (Illus. by Palen, Debbie) — Blevins, Wiley
How to Do Ecology: A Concise Handbook — Karban, Richard
How to Do Everything: Genealogy, 4th ed. — Morgan, George G.
How to Do Things with Pornography — Bauer, Nancy
How to Do Things with Words — Austin, John Langshaw
c How to Draw a Dragon (Illus. by Florian, Douglas) — Florian, Douglas
c How to Draw Batman and His Friends and Foes (Illus. by Doescher, Erik) — Sautter, Aaron
How to Draw Manga Boys: In Simple Steps — Li, Yishan
How to Draw Manga Girls: In Simple Steps — Li, Yishan
How to Draw Reptiles and Mammals: An Educational Guide — Phelps, Earl R.
c How to Draw Superman and His Friends and Foes (Illus. by Doescher, Erik) — Sautter, Aaron
How to Draw with Your Funny Bone (Illus. by Smith, Elwood H.) — Smith, Elwood H.
How to Draw Wonder Woman, Green Lantern, and Other DC Super Heroes (Illus. by Levin, Tim) — Sautter, Aaron
c How to Dress a Dragon (Illus. by Barclay, Eric) — Godin, Thelma Lynne
c How to Fall — Casey, Jane
c How to Find Magical Creatures — Hamilton, Libby
How to Fly a Horse: The Secret History of Creation, Invention, and Discovery — Ashton, Kevin
How to Fly a Horse: The Secret History of Creation, Invention, and Discovery — Kevin Ashton
c How to Fly with Broken Wings — Elson, Jane
c How to Freshwater Fish like a Pro — Burlingame, Jeff
How To Get into a Military Service Academy: A Step-by-Step Guide to Getting Qualified, Nominated, and Appointed — Dobson, Michael Singer
How to Grow Up: A Memoir — Tea, Michelle
c How to Hike like a Pro — Norris, Ashley P. Watson
How to Innovate: The Essential Guide for Fearless School Leaders — Brown, Mary Moss
How to Juggle without Balls — Haddon, Karen
How to Knit Socks That Fit: Techniques for Toe-Up and Cuff-Down Styles — Druchunas, Donna
c How to Live Like a Roman Gladiator (Illus. by Epelbaum, Mariano) — Ganeri, Anita
c How to Live Like a Viking Warrior (Illus. by Epelbaum, Mariano) — Ganeri, Anita
How to Live on Other Planets: A Handbook for Aspiring Aliens — Merriam, Joanne
c How to Look After Your Kitten — Piers, Helen
c How to Make a Human out of Soup (Illus. by Kindberg, Sally) — Turner, Tracey
y How to Make a Movie in 10 Easy Lessons — Blofield, Robert
How to Make Beautiful Buttons — Schmitz, Beate
How to Make & Keep Friends: Tips for Kids to Overcome 50 Common Social Challenges — Shea, Donna

How to Make Slipcovers: Designing, Measuring, and Sewing Perfect-Fit Slipcovers for Chairs, Sofas, and Ottomans — Hoskins, Patricia
How to Make Your Money Last: The Indispensable Retirement Guide — Quinn, Jane Bryant
How to Manage Stress — Hird, Suzanne
c How to Mend a Heart (Illus. by Gillingham, Sara) — Gillingham, Sara
c How to Outfox Your Friends When You Don't Have a Clue — Keating, Jess
How to Overcome Once-Easy Tasks That are Now Pains in the You-Know-What!, 3d ed. — Latimer, Helen
How to Pass as Human — Kelman, Nic
c How to Pee: Potty Training for Boys (Illus. by Chung, Arree) — Spector, Todd
c How to Pee: Potty Training for Girls (Illus. by Chung, Arree) — Spector, Todd
How to Plan a Crusade: Reason and Religious War in the Middle Ages — Tyerman, Christopher
How to Prepare for Old Age: Without Taking the Fun Out of Life — Otis, Bernard S.
c How to Put Your Parents to Bed (Illus. by Cole, Babette) — Larsen, Mylisa
How to Raise a Wild Child: The Art and Science of Falling in Love with Nature — Sampson, Scott D.
How to Raise an Adult: Break Free of the Overparenting Trap and Prepare Your Kid for Success — Lythcott-Haims, Julie
How to Read a Latin Poem: If You Can't Read Latin Yet — Fitzgerald, William
c How to Read a Story (Illus. by Siegel, Mark) — Messner, Kate
How to Read Islamic Carpets — Denny, Walter B.
How to Read the American West: A Field Guide — Wyckoff, William
How to Read the Bible — Cox, Harvey
How to Read the Bible and Still Be a Christian: Struggling with Divine Violence from Genesis through Revelation — Crossan, John Dominic
How to Read the Bible — Cox, Harvey
How to Relax — Hanh, Tich Nhat
How to Rescue a Rake — Fresina, Jayne
How to Retire with Enough Money: And How to Know What Enough Is — Ghilarducci, Teresa
How to Run a Government So that Citizens Benefit and Taxpayers Don't Go Crazy — Barber, Michael
c How to Save a Species — Baillie, Marilyn
y How to Say I Love You Out Loud — Cozzo, Karole
How to Seduce a Billionaire — Da Costa, Portia
How to Seduce a Scot — English, Christy
c How to Share with a Bear (Illus. by Graegin, Stephanie) — Pinder, Eric
How to Skin a Lion: A Treasury of Outmoded Advice — Cock-Starkey, Claire
How to Solar Power Your Home: Everything You Need to Know Explained Simply — Maeda, Martha
c How to Speak Cat: A Guide to Decoding Cat Language — Newman, Aline Alexander
c How to Speak Dolphin — Rorby, Ginny
c How to Spy on a Shark (Illus. by Marquez, Francisca) — Houran, Lori Haskins
How to Start a Fire — Lutz, Lisa
How to Study Math: 80 Ways to Make the Grade — Golpalkrishna, Sara Lynn
How to Study Math: 80 Ways to Make the Grade — Gopalkrishna, Sara Lynn
How to Succeed in the New Brand Space — Stone, Adam N.
c How to Surprise a Dad (Illus. by Wildish, Lee) — Reagan, Jean
How to Survive Your Sisters — Campbell, Ellie
c How to Swallow a Pig: Step-by-Step Advice from the Animal Kingdom (Illus. by Jenkins, Steve) — Jenkins, Steve
How to Talk about Places You've Never Been: On the Importance of Armchair Travel — Bayard, Pierre
How to Teach: A Practical Guide for Librarians — Crane, Beverly E.
How to Think Like a Neandertal — Wynn, Thomas
How to Thrive in the Next Economy: Designing Tomorrow's World Today — Thackara, John
y How to Train Your Dragon (Read by Tennant, David). Audiobook Review — Cowell, Cressida
c How to Train Your Dragon — Cowell, Cressida
How to Use Graphic Design to Sell Things, Explain Things, Make Things Look Better, Make People Laugh, Make People Cry, and (Every Once in a While) Change the World — Bierut, Michael
How to Walk Away — Birman, Lisa
How to Watch a Movie — Thomson, David
How to Watch Television — Thompson, Ethan
How to Wed a Warrior — English, Christy
y How to Win at High School — Matthews, Owen
How to Win Friends and Influence People — Carnegie, Dale

How to Win Games and Beat People — Whipple, Tom
c How to Write a Drama — Kopp, Megan
c How to Write a Fantasy Story — Hyde, Natalie
How to Write a Novel — Sumner, Melanie
How to Write a Thesis — Eco, Umberto
How to Write about Music: Excerpts from the 33.3 Series, Magazines, Books and Blogs with Advice from Industry-leading Writers — Woodworth, Marc
c How to Write an Adventure Story — Hyde, Natalie
c How to Write Realistic Fiction — Flatt, Lizann
How to Write Successful Letters of Recommendation — Sarmiento, Kimberly
c How to Write Your Best Story Ever! — Edge, Christopher
c How to Zap Zombies (Illus. by Garrigue, Roland) — Leblanc, Catherine
How UFOs Conquered the World: The History of a Modern Myth — Clarke, David
How Universities Work — Lombardi, John V.
How We Are, How We Break, and How We Mend — Deary, Vincent
How We Die Now: Intimacy and the Work of Dying — Erickson, Karla A.
c How We Fall — Brauning, Kate
How We Fight: Handbook for the Naval Warfighter — United States. Department of the Navy
How We Forgot the Cold War: A Historical Journey across America — Wiener, Jon
How We Got to Now: Six Innovations That Made the Modern World (Read by Newbern, George). Audiobook Review — Johnson, Steven
How We Got to Now: Six innovations That Made the Modern World. Audiobook Review
How We Hope: A Moral Psychology — Martin, Adrienne M.
How We Live Now: Redefining Home and Family in the 21st Century — DePaulo, Bella
y How Wendy Redbird Dancing Survived the Dark Ages of Nought — Hawks, Lyn Fairchild
How You Were Born — Cayley, Kate
c Howard B. Wigglebottom Listens to a Friend (Illus. by Cutting, David A.) — Binkow, Ana Howard
y Howard the Duck: What the Duck (Illus. by Quinones, Joe) — Zdarsky, Chip
However Long the Night: Molly Melching's journey to Help Millions of African Women and Girls Triumph — Molloy, Aimee
Howl: Of Woman and Wolf — Bird, Susan Imhoff
c The Howling Ghost — Pike, Christopher
How's Your Faith? An Unlikely Spiritual Journey — Gregory, David
y HPV — Parks, Peggy J.
HRC: State Secrets and the Rebirth of Hillary Clinton — Allen, Jonathan
HT 2014: "Gewinner oder Verlierer?" - Das Historische Urteil im Geschichtsunterricht als Qualitatsmerkmal und Desiderat
HT 2014: Gewinner und Verlierer: Das Jahr 1914 im Geschichtsunterricht und Geschichtsbewusstsein aus Internationaler Perspektive
HT 2014: Herrschaft und Ihre Mittlerinstanzen. Lokale Administrationen und Akteure in den im Zweiten Weltkrieg von der Wehrmacht Besetzten Gebieten
HT 2014: Jenseits von Gewinn und Verlust: Entscheidungsfindung in der Fruhen Neuzeit
HT 2014: Reichtum - Zur Geschichte einer Umstrittenen Sozialfigur
HT 2014: The Biggest Loser. Gewinnen und Verlieren durch Diaten in Deutschland und den USA zwischen 1860 und 2004
HT 2014: Veni, Vidi, Vici: (Re)prasentationen von Sieghaftigkeit in der Antike
HT 2014: Verlorenes und Gewonnenes. Geschlechterverhaltnisse und der Wandel des Politischen in der 'Langen Geschichte der Wende' in Ostdeutschland 1980 bis 2000
HT 2014: Wikipedia und Geschichtswissenschaft. Eine Zwischenbilanz
Hubris: The Tragedy of War in the Twentieth Century — Horne, Alistair
Hubris: Why Economists Failed to Predict the Crisis and How to Avoid the Next One — Desai, Meghnad
Hubs of Empire: The Southeastern Lowcountry and British Caribbean — Mulcahy, Matthew
Huck Finn's America: Mark Twain and the Era That Shaped His Masterpiece — Levy, Andrew
Huckabee: The Authorized Biography — Lamb, Scott
Huckleberry Hearts — Beckstrand, Jennifer
c Hudson in Provence: A Paris-Chien Adventure — Mancuso, Jackie Clark
c The Hueys: in What's the Opposite? (Illus. by Jeffers, Oliver) — Jeffers, Oliver
c Huff and Puff Have Too Much Stuff (Illus. by Guile, Gill) — Rabe, Tish

c Hug Machine (Illus. by Campbell, Scott) — Campbell, Scott
c The Huge Hair Scare — Pankhurst, Kate
Hugo & Rose — Foley, Bridget
The Huguenots in Later Stuart Britain, Volume I — Gwynn, Robin
The Huguenots — Treasure, Geoffrey
c The Hula-Hoopin' Queen (Illus. by Brantley-Newton, Vanessa) — Godin, Thelma Lynne
The Human Age: The World Shaped By Us (Read by Caruso, Barbara). Audiobook Review — Ackerman, Diane
The Human Age: The World Shaped By Us — Ackerman, Diane
c The Human Body in 30 Seconds (Illus. by Robins, Wesley) — Claybourne, Anna
c The Human Body (Illus. by Lowery, Mike) — Jennings, Ken
c The Human Body: The Story of How We Protect, Repair, and Make Ourselves Stronger — Newquist, H.P.
y Human Body Theater (Illus. by Wicks, Maris) — Wicks, Maris
Human Dignity in Contemporary Ethics — Kirchhoffer, David G.
The Human Equations — Creek, Dave
Human Evolution: Genes, Genealogies and Phylogenies — Finlay, Graeme
Human Expansion — Holgate, Steve
Human Identity and Identification — Gowland, Rebecca
Human Kindness and the Smell of Warm Croissants: An Introduction to Ethics — Ogien, Ruwen
Human Monsters — Lamberson, Gregory
Human Nature and Jewish Thought: Judaism's Case for Why Persons Matter — Mittleman, Alan L.
Human Race — Mortimer, Ian
Human Rights and Democracy: The Precarious Rights of Ideals — Landman, Todd
Human Rights and Humanitarian Interventions
Human Rights and the Uses of History — Moyn, Samuel
Human Rights in Our Own Backyard: Injustice and Resistance in the United States — Armaline, William T.
Human Rights: The Hard Questions — Holder, Cindy
Human Social Evolution: The Foundational Works of Richard D. Alexander — Summers, Kyle
Human Wildlife Conflict: Complexity in the Marine Environment — Draheim, Megan
Human Work — Borodale, Sean
Humane Insight: Looking at Images of African American Suffering and Death — Baker, Courtney R.
Humanistic Scholarship and the Anthropocene: Approaching China from a Sustainability Paradigm
A Humanitarian Past — Anggard, Adele
Humanitarian Violence: The US Deployment of Diversity — Atanasoski, Neda
The Humanities "Crisis" and the Future of Literary Studies — Jay, Paul
The Humanities, Higher Education, and Academic Freedom: Three Necessary Arguments — Berube, Michael
Humankind: How Biology and Geography Shape Human Diversity — Harcourt, Alexander H.
The Humans — Karam, Stephen
Humans Need Not Apply: A Guide to Wealth and Work in the Age of Artificial Intelligence — Kaplan, Jerry
Humans of New York: Stories — Stanton, Brandon
Humble Confidence: Spiritual and Pastoral Guidance from Karl Rahner — Bacik, James J.
Humboldt and Jefferson: A Transatlantic Friendship of the Enlightenment — Rebok, Sandra
The Humbug Murders: An Ebenezer Scrooge Mystery — Oliver, L. J.
Hume: An Intellectual Biography — Harris, James A.
Hume's Epistemology in the Treatise: A Veritistic Interpretation — Schmitt, Frederick F.
Hummelo: A Journey through a Plantsman's Life — Oudolf, Piet

The Hummingbird — Hiekkapelto, Kati
The Hummingbird — Kiernan, Stephen P.
Hummingbird Plants of the Southwest — Scott, Marcy
c Hummingbirds — Riggs, Kate
c Hummingbirds — Petrie, Kristin
The Hummingbird's Cage — Dietrich, Tamara
Hummingbirds — Orenstein, John M.
The Humor Code: A Global Search for What Makes Things Funny — McGraw, Peter
c Humorous Small Critter Jokes to Tickle Your Funny Bone — Mitchell, Susan K.
c Humphrey Audio Collection, bks. 8-11. Audiobook Review — Birney, Betty G.
Humphrey the Lost Whale, a True Story (Illus. by Wakiyama, Hanako) — Tokuda, Wendy
c Humphrey's Creepy-Crawly Camping Adventure (Illus. by Burris, Priscilla) — Birney, Betty G.
c Humphrey's Playful Puppy Problem (Illus. by Burris, Priscilla) — Birney, Betty G.
c Humphrey's Really Wheely Racing Day (Illus. by Burris, Priscilla) — Birney, Betty G.
c Humpty Dumpty (Illus. by Chatzikonstantinou, Danny) — Harbo, Christopher
Hundred Days: The Campaign That Ended World War I — Lloyd, Nick
The Hundred Gifts — Scott, Jennifer
The Hundred-Year Flood — Salesses, Matthew
The Hundred-Year House — Makkai, Rebecca
The Hundred-Year Marathon: China's Secret Strategy to Replace America as the Global Superpower — Pillsbury, Michael
The Hundred-Year Walk: An Armenian Odyssey — MacKeen, Dawn Anahid
The Hundred Years War: A People's History — Green, David
The Hundred Years' War: Modern War Poems — Astley, Neil
Hungarian Culture and Politics in the Habsburg Monarchy, 1711-1848 — Vermes, Gabor
Hunger Makes Me a Modern Girl: A Memoir — Brownstein, Carrie
The Hunger of the Wolf — Marche, Stephen
Hunger Strike: Margaret Thatcher's Battle with the IRA, 1980-1981 — Hennessey, Thomas
c The Hungriest Mouth in the Sea (Illus. by Walters, Peter) — Walters, Peter
Hungry Bengal: War, Famine and the End of Empire — Mukherjee, Janam
c Hungry Coyote (Illus. by Caple, Laurie) — Blackford, Cheryl
c Hungry for Math: Poems to Munch On (Illus. by Collins, Peggy) — Winters, Kari-Lynn
Hungry Ghosts — Blair, Peggy
c Hungry Johnny (Illus. by Ballinger, Wesley) — Minnema, Cheryl
c A Hungry Lion, or A Dwindling Assortment of Animals (Illus. by Cummins, Lucy) — Cummins, Lucy
c A Hungry Lion, or a Dwindling Assortment of Animals (Illus. by Cummins, Lucy Ruth) — Cummins, Lucy Ruth
The Hungry Mind: The Origins of Curiosity in Childhood — Engel, Susan
c Hungry Roscoe (Illus. by Plant, David J.) — Plant, David J.
The Hunt for Hitler's Warship — Bishop, Patrick
y Hunt for the Bamboo Rat — Salisbury, Graham
c Hunt for the Hydra — Fry, Jason
The Hunt for Vulcan: And How Albert Einstein Destroyed a Planet, Discovered Relativity, and Deciphered the Universe — Levenson, Thomas
y The Hunted — de la Pena, Matt
y The Hunted — Hart, C.J.
y Hunter — Lackey, Mercedes
y The Hunter Awakens — Roper, J.R.
Hunter-Gatherer Archaeology as Historical Process — Sassaman, Kenneth E.
Hunter Killer: Inside America's Unmanned Air War — McCurley, T. Mark
The Hunter Killers: The Extraordinary Story of the First Wild Weasels, the Band of Maverick Aviators Who Flew the Most Dangerous Missions of the Vietnam War — Hampton, Dan

c Hunter Moran Digs Deep — Giff, Patricia Reilly
Hunter S. Thompson's Fear and Loathing in Las Vegas — Little, Troy
The Hunters — Young, Tom
Hunters in the Dark — Osborne, Lawrence
y Hunter's Moon — Mason, Sophie
c Hunters of Chaos — Velasquez, Crystal
c Hunters of the Great Forest — Nolan, Dennis
The Hunter's Promise: An Abenaki Tale (Illus. by Farnsworth, Bill) — Bruchac, Joseph
Hunter's Trail — Olson, Melissa F.
The Hunting Gun — Inoue, Yasushi
Hunting Nazis in Franco's Spain — Messenger, David A.
y The Hunting of Sunshine Girl — McKenzie, Paige
Hunting Shadows — Todd, Charles
The Hunting Trip — Butterworth, William E., III
c Huracan — Rudolph, Jessica
c Hurricane — Rudolph, Jessica
Hurricane Katrina and the Forgotten Coast of Mississippi — Cutter, Susan L.
y Hurricane: Perspectives on Storm Disasters — Langley, Andrew
c Hurricane Watch (Illus. by Morley, Taia) — Stewart, Melissa
c Hurricanes — Zayarny, Jack
c Hurry Home, Hedgehog! (Illus. by Yang, Belle) — Yang, Belle
Hurry Please I Want to Know: Stories — Griner, Paul
c Hurry Up and Wait (Illus. by Kalman, Maira) — Handler, Daniel
c Hurry Up, Ilua! (Illus. by Hicks, Nola Helen) — Hicks, Nola Helen
Hurt People — Smith, Cote
A Hurting Sport: Another Year inside the Sweet Science — Hauser, Thomas
The Husband Swap: A True Story of Unconventional Love — Leontiades, Louisa
Hush — Marshall-Ball, Sara
c Hush : A Kiwi Lullaby (Illus. by Burdan, Andrew) — Cowley, Joy
y The Hush — Melki-Wegner, Skye
Hush — Sierra, Jude
Hush, Hush (Read by Maxwell, Jan). Audiobook Review — Lippman, Laura
Hush, Hush — Monaghan, Tess
Hush Hush — Lippman, Laura
Hush Now, Baby — Williams, Angela W.
c The Hush Treasure Book — Tayleur, Karen
c Husky (Read by Sayre, Justin). Audiobook Review — Sayre, Justin
y Husky — Sayre, Justin
Huston Smith: Wisdomkeeper Living the World's Religions: The Authorized Biography of a 21st Century Siritual Giant — Sawyer, Dana
Huter der Wirklichkeit: Der Dominikanerorden in der Mittelalterlichen Gesellschaft Skandinaviens — Schutz, Johannes
Huxley's Church and Maxwell's Demon: From Theistic Science to Naturalistic Science — Stanley, Matthew
Hyacinth Girls (Read by Hamilton, Laura. with Emily Sutton-Smith). Audiobook Review — Frankel, Lauren
y Hyacinth Girls — Frankel, Lauren
Hybrid Zone: Computers and Science at Argonne National Laboratory, 1946-1992 — Yood, Charles N.
A Hymn before Battle — Ringo, John
Hyper Nature — Martin, Philippe
y Hypercar — Jubermann, David
Hypersexuality and Headscarves: Race, Sex, and Citizenship in the New Germany — Partridge, Damani J.
Hypnos: Notes from the French Resistance, 1943-44 — Char, Rene
c Hypnotize a Tiger: Poems about Just about Everything (Illus. by Brown, Calef) — Brown, Calef
Hysteria — Zarate, Oscar
Hysteric — Arcan, Nelly
c Hysterical Dog Jokes to Tickle Your Funny Bone — Niven, Felicia Lowenstein
The Hystery App — Davy, V.T.

I

I-8 Ordinis primi tomus octavus: Iusus Exclusus, De civilitate morum puerilium, Conflictus Thaliae et Barbariei — *Menchi, Silvana Seidel*
I Always Cry at Weddings — *Goff, Sara*
c I Am a Bear (Illus. by Dumont, Jean-Francois) — *Dumont, Jean-Francois*
c I Am a Bear — *Dumont, Jean-Francois*
c I Am a Big Brother — *Church, Caroline Jayne*
"I Am a Phenomenon Quite out of the Ordinary": The Notebooks, Diaries, and Letters of Daniil Kharms — *Anemone, Anthony*
c I Am a Witch's Cat — *Muncaster, Harriet*
c I Am a Zamboni Machine (Illus. by Migliari, Paola) — *Viala, Kevin*
c I Am Albert Einstein (Illus. by Eliopoulos, Christopher) — *Meltzer, Brad*
c I Am an Aspie Girl: A Book for Young Girls with Autism Spectrum Conditions (Illus. by Ferguson, Teresa) — *Bulhak-Paterson, Danuta*
I Am Barbarella: Stories — *Gilstrap, Beth*
c I Am Bear (Illus. by Akyuz, Sav) — *Smith, Ben Bailey*
I Am Because You Are — *Lief, Jacob*
"I Am Busy Drawing Pictures": The Civil War Art and Letters of Private John Jacob Omenhausser, CSA — *Musick, Michael P.*
I Am Charlie Wilson — *Wilson, Charlie*
c I Am Coyote — *Vistein, Geri*
I Am Crying All Inside and Other Stories: The Complete Short Fiction of Clifford D. Simak, vol. 1 — *Simak, Clifford D.*
c I am Doodle Cat (Illus. by Marriott, Lauren) — *Patrick, Kat*
y I Am Drums — *Grosso, Mike*
I Am Evelyn Amony — *Amony, Evelyn*
c I Am Henry Finch (Illus. by Schwarz, Viviane) — *Deacon, Alexis*
y I Am Her Revenge — *Moore, Meredith*
c I Am Jackie Robinson (Illus. by Eliopoulos, Christopher) — *Meltzer, Brad*
c I Am Jazz (Illus. by McNicholas, Shelagh) — *Jennings, Jazz*
c I Am Malala: How One Girl Stood Up for Education and Changed the World — *Yousafzai, Malala*
c I Am Not a Minority! I'm Part of the Majority! — *Christopher, Valerie*
I Am Not a Slut: Slut-Shaming in the Age of the Internet — *Tanenbaum, Leora*
I am not Esther — *Beale, Fleur*
y I Am Princess X (Illus. by Ciesemier, Kali) — *Priest, Cherie*
I Am Radar — *Larsen, Reif*
c I am Rosa Parks (Illus. by Eliopoulos, Christopher) — *Meltzer, Brad*
c I Am So Brave! (Illus. by Gillingham, Sara) — *Krensky, Stephen*
I Am Sorry to Think I Have Raised a Timid Son (Read by Pratt, Sean). Audiobook Review — *Russell, Kent*
I Am Sorry to Think I Have Raised a Timid Son — *Russell, Kent*
I am the Beggar of the World: Landays from contemporary Afghanistan — *Murphy, Seamus*
y I Am the Messenger — *Zusak, Markus*
c I Am the Wolf ... and Here I Come! (Illus. by Guettier, Benedicte) — *Guettier, Benedicte*
I Am with You Always (Illus. by Duckworth, Jeffrey) — *O'Quinn, Lynne Robertson*
c I Am Yoga (Illus. by Reynolds, Peter H.) — *Verde, Susan*
I Am Your Judge — *Neuhaus, Nele*
c I Ate a Cicada Today (Illus. by Crossan, Jeff) — *Crossan, Jeff*

c I Ate a Cicada Today — *Crossan, Jeff*
I Blame Dennis Hopper: And Other Stories from a Life Lived in and out of the Movies — *Douglas, Illeana*
c I Broke My Arm — *Herrington, Lisa M.*
I Called Him Necktie — *Flasar, Milena Michiko*
c I Can Dance — *Snyder, Betsy*
c I Can Do It! (Illus. by Pedler, Caroline) — *Corderoy, Tracey*
I Can Do It Myself (Illus. by Fisher, Valorie) — *Fisher, Valorie*
c I Can Give You Anything but Love — *Indiana, Gary*
c I Can Help! (Illus. by Anderson, Peggy Perry) — *Anderson, Peggy Perry*
c I Can Roar! (Illus. by Asch, Frank) — *Asch, Frank*
I Can See in the Dark — *Anderson, James*
c I Can Swim a Rainbow — *Toft, Kim Michelle*
c I Can't Believe You Said That!: My Story about Using My Social Filter...or Not! (Illus. by DuFalla, Anita) — *Cook, Julia*
I Can't Eat Peanuts — *Marisco, Katie*
c I Can't Wait! (Illus. by Schwartz, Amy) — *Schwartz, Amy*
I carnefici italiani: Scene dal genocidio degli ebrei, 1943-1945 — *Sullam, Simon Levis*
c I Carry Your Heart with Me — *Cummings, E.E.*
I Centri Minori Della Toscana Nel Medioevo — *Pinto, Giuliano*
I confinni dell'ombra — *Spina, Alessandro*
y I Crawl through It (Read by King, A.S.). Audiobook Review — *King, A.S.*
y I Crawl through It — *King, A.S.*
c I Declare, Charlie Brown! (Illus. by Brannon, Tom) — *Reeves, Diane Lindsey*
c I Didn't Do My Homework Because ... (Illus. by Chaud, Benjamin) — *Cali, Davide*
I Do Wish This Cruel War Was Over: First-Person Accounts of Civil War Arkansas from the Arkansas Historical Quarterly — *Christ, Mark K.*
I Documenti diplomatici italiani. Terza Serie: 1896-1907. Vol. IX: 29 marzo 1905-28 maggio 1906 — *D'Ovidio, Francesco Lefebvre*
I Don't Have a Happy Place: Cheerful Stories of Despondency and Gloom — *Korson, Kim*
c I Don't Know How the Story Ends — *Cheaney, J.B.*
c I Don't Like Cheese (Illus. by Merrick, Lauren) — *Chandler, Hannah*
c I Don't Like Koala (Illus. by Santoso, Charles) — *Ferrell, Sean*
c I (Don't) Like Snakes (Illus. by Lozano, Luciano) — *Davies, Nicola*
I Don't Live Here Anymore — *Kreslehner, Gabi*
c I Don't Want to Be a Frog (Illus. by Boldt, Mike) — *Petty, Dev*
c I Don't Want to Go to School! — *Blake, Stephanie*
I Feel Like Going On: Life, Game, and Glory — *Paisner, Daniel*
c I Feel Sick! (Illus. by Ross, Tony) — *Ross, Tony*
c I, Fly: The Buzz about Flies and How Awesome They Are (Illus. by Plecas, Jennifer) — *Heos, Bridget*
I Found My Friends: The Oral History of Nirvana — *Soulsby, Nick*
I Freed Myself: African American Self-Emancipation in the Civil War Era — *Williams, David (b. 1959-)*
c I Get Dressed (Illus. by McPhail, David) — *McPhail, David*
I Get Sunburned — *Marisco, Katie*
I Greet You at the Beginning of a Great Career: The Selected Correspondence of Lawrence Ferlinghetti and Allen Ginsberg, 1955-1997 — *Ferlinghetti, Lawrence*

I Greet You at the Beginning of a Great Career: The Selected Correspondence of Lawrence Ferlinghetti and Allen Ginsberg, 1955-1997 — *Morgan, Bill*
I Greet You at the Beginning of a Great Career: The Selected Correspondence of Lawrence Ferlinghetti and Allen Ginsberg, 1955-1997 — *Ferlinghetti, Lawrence*
c I Had a Favorite Dress (Read by Turpin, Bahni). Audiobook Review — *Ashburn, Boni*
c I Had a Favorite Hat (Illus. by Ng, Robyn) — *Ashburn, Boni*
I Had Jelly on My Nose and a Hole in My Breeches — *McNally, Robert*
I Had to Survive — *Canessa, Roberto*
I Hate Pinatas: Surviving Life's Unexpected Surprises — *Maloy, Heather*
c I Hear a Pickle: And Smell, See, Touch, and Taste It, Too! (Illus. by Isadora, Rachel) — *Isadora, Rachel*
"I Hear America Singing": Folk Music and National Identity — *Donaldson, Rachel Clare*
I Heard a Rumor — *Hodges, Cheris*
y I Heart Robot — *Van Rooyen, Suzanne*
c I Know a Bear — *Johnson, Mariana Ruiz*
c I Know an Old Lady Who Swallowed a Dreidel (Illus. by Slonim, David) — *Yacowitz, Caryn*
I Know How She Does It: How Successful Women Make the Most of Their Time — *Vanderkam, Laura*
c I Know Sasquatch — *Bradley, Jess*
I Left It on the Mountain: A Memoir — *Sessums, Kevin*
c I Like Animals — *Ipcar, Dahlov*
c I Like to Draw! — *Baltzer, Rochelle*
c I Like to Squeak! How Do You Speak? (Illus. by Galloway, Fhiona) — *Litton, Jonathan*
c I Lost a Tooth — *Herrington, Lisa M.*
c I Love Animals and Broccoli Coloring Book — *Wasserman, Debra*
c I Love Dogs! (Illus. by Staake, Bob) — *Stainton, Sue*
c I Love Grass (Illus. by Boston, Maria) — *Boston, Maria*
c I Love Hugs — *de la Bedoyere, Camilla*
y I Love I Hate I Miss My Sister — *Sarn, Amelie*
c I Love Kisses — *de la Bedoyere, Camilla*
c I Love Mom (Illus. by Abbot, Judi) — *Walsh, Joanna*
c I Love My Puppy — *Church, Caroline Jayne*
c I Love My Robot — *Church, Caroline Jayne*
I Love Paper: Paper-Cutting Techniques and Templates for Amazing Toys, Sculptures, Props, and Costumes — *Sundqvist, Fideli*
c I Love This Tree: Discover the Life, Beauty and Importance of Trees — *Claybourne, Anna*
I Love to Paint! — *Lipsey, Jennifer*
c I Love You Already! (Illus. by Davies, Benji) — *John, Jory*
c I Love You, Baby (Illus. by Dodd, Emma) — *Andreae, Giles*
c I Love You Forever (Illus. by McNicholas, Shelagh) — *Bridges, Margaret Park*
c I Love You Just the Way You Are (Illus. by Grey, Ada) — *Salzano, Tammi*
c I Love You More Than Moldy Ham (Illus. by Armstrong-Ellis, Carey F.) — *Armstrong-Ellis, Carey F.*
c I Love You Near and Far (Illus. by Henry, Jed) — *Parker, Marjorie Blain*
c I Love You, One to Ten (Illus. by Leist, Christina) — *Adderson, Caroline*
c I Love You (Illus. by Cottingham, Tracy)
c I Love You to Pieces! — *Keith, Barbara Benson*
c I Love You Very Muchly ... : The Story of the Brave Little Girl — *Marino, Rick*

I Malavoglia: The House by the Medlar Tree — Verga, Giovanni
c I Met a Dinosaur (Illus. by Sheban, Chris) — Wahl, Jan
I Met Lucky People: The Story of the Romani Gypsies — Matras, Yaron
I Met Someone — Wagner, Bruce
I, Migrant — Shah, Sami
I-Minds — Swingle, Mari K.
c I Miss You Very Muchly: City of the Cats: Nika's Trek to Find Big Brother (Illus. by Contento, Dindo) — Marino, Rick
I Must Be Living Twice: New and Selected Poems 1975-2014 — Myles, Eileen
c I Never Liked Wednesdays (Illus. by Broad, Michael) — McGough, Roger
y I.O.U. Dead — Wan, Michelle
I padroni dei libri: Il controllo sulla stampa nella prima eta moderna — Infelise, Mario
I personaggi femminili del Bellum Civile di Lucano — Sannicandro, Lisa
I Pity the Poor Immigrant — Lazar, Zachary
c I Play (Illus. by McPhail, David) — McPhail, David
c I Pledge Allegiance (Illus. by Barton, Patrice) — Mora, Pat
I pronostici di Domenico Maria da Novara — Bonoli, Fabrizio
I Put a Spell on You — Burnside, John
c I Really Like Slop! (Illus. by Willems, Mo) — Willems, Mo
I Refuse — Petterson, Per
I Refuse — Bartlett, Don
I Refuse — Pettersen, Per
I Refuse — Petterson, Per
I Regret Everything — Greenland, Seth
I Regret Nothing: A Memoir — Lancaster, Jen
y I Remember Beirut (Illus. by Abirached, Zeina) — Abirached, Zeina
y I Remember You (Read by Rankin, Emily). Audiobook Review — Bell, Cathleen Davitt
y I Remember You — Bell, Cathleen Davitt
I, Ripper — Hunter, Stephen
I Saw a Man — Sheers, Owen
I Saw Her That Night — Jancar, Drago
I Saw the Blues — Payne, Jackie
c I Say Shehechiyanu (Illus. by Filipina, Monika) — Rocklin, Joanne
c I See a Pattern Here (Illus. by Goldstone, Bruce) — Goldstone, Bruce
c I See and See (Illus. by Lewin, Ted) — Lewin, Ted
I See Falling Stars — Orr, Tamar B.
c I See Kitty (Illus. by Surovec, Yasmine) — Surovec, Yasmine
c I See Rainbows — Beaton, Kathryn
y I See Reality: Twelve Short Stories about Real Life — Kendall, Grace
c I See the Promised Land: A Life of Martin Luther King Jr. (Illus. by Chitrakar, Manu) — Flowers, Arthur
c I See Things Differently: A First Look at Autism — Thomas, Pat
I Speak of the City: Mexico City at the Turn of the Twentieth Century — Teonorio-Trillo, Mauricio
I Spor Jons Laerda — Guttormsson, Hjorleifur
c I Stink (Illus. by McMullan, Jim) — McMullan, Kate
I Suck at Relationships So You Don't Have To — Frankel, Bethenny
I, Superorganism: Learning to Love Your Inner Ecosystem — Turney, Jon
y I Take You (Read by Whelan, Julia). Audiobook Review — Kennedy, Eliza
y I Take You — Kennedy, Eliza
I Tasso e le Poste d'Europa - The Tassis Family and the European Postal Service - First International Symposium — Cattani, Adriano
y I Text Dead People — Cooper, Rose
I Think You're Totally Wrong: A Quarrel — Powell, Caleb
I Think You're Totally Wrong: A Quarrel — Shields, David
c I Thought This Was a Bear Book (Illus. by Davies, Benji) — Lazar, Tara
I Too Have Some Dreams: N. M. Rashed and Modernism in Urdu Poetry — Pue, A. Sean
I Totally Funniest (Read by Seratch, Frankie). Audiobook Review — Patterson, James
I Ulu I Ke Kumu — Nogelmeier, Puakea
c I Use the Potty — van Lieshout, Maria
c I Used to Be Afraid (Illus. by Seeger, Laura Vaccaro) — Seeger, Laura Vaccaro
c I Wanna Go Home (Illus. by Catrow, David) — Orloff, Karen Kaufman

c I Want a Cat: My Opinion Essay (Illus. by O'Neill, Ewa) — Pattison, Darcy
c I Want a Dog: My Opinion Essay (Illus. by O'Neill, Ewa) — Pattison, Darcy
c I Want a Monster! — Gravel, Elise
c I Want My Daddy! (Illus. by Edgson, Alison) — Corderoy, Tracey
c I Want to Be a Ballerina (Illus. by Coh, Smiljana) — Membrino, Anna
c I Want to Be a Witch (Illus. by Cunliffe, Ian) — Cunliffe, Ian
c I Want to Eat Your Books (Illus. by Parker, Tyler) — Lefranc, Karin
c I Want to Go Home! (Illus. by Ross, Tony) — Ross, Tony
I Want You to Want Me — Kelly, Erika
I Was a Child — Kaplan, Bruce Eric
I Was a Revolutionary: Stories — Milward, Andrew Malan
I Was Blind (Dating), but Now I See: My Misadventures in Dating, Waiting, and Stumbling into Love — Rische, Stephanie
y I Was Here (Read by Marie, Jorjeana). Audiobook Review — Forman, Gayle
y I Was Here — Forman, Gayle
I Was Only Nineteen: A Memoir — Harlum, Raewyn
y I Was Picked ... The John Challis Story — Shapiro, Howard
I Was There: 1066 (Illus. by Garton, Michael) — Eldridge, Jim
y I Will Always Write Back: How One Letter Changed Two Lives — Alifirenka, Caitlin
c I Will Chomp You! (Illus. by Shea, Bob) — John, Jory
c I Will Fight Monsters for You (Illus. by Lyona) — Balmes, Santi
I Will Find You: A Reporter Investigates the Life of the Man Who Raped Her — Connors, Joanna
I Will Love You For the Rest of My Life: Breakup Stories — Czyzniejewski, Michael
I Will Never Forget: A Daughter's Story of Her Mother's Arduous and Humorous Journey through Dementia — Pereira, Elaine C.
c I Will Never Get a Star on Mrs. Benson's Blackboard (Illus. by Mann, Jennifer K.) — Mann, Jennifer K.
c I Will Not (Illus. by Eitan, Ora) — Farouky, Naila
c I Will Take a Nap! (Illus. by Willems, Mo) — Willems, Mo
c I Wish I Could Draw — Fagan, Cary
c I Wish I Had a Pirate Hat (Illus. by Scobie, Lorna) — Stevens, Roger
c I Wish You More (Illus. by Lichtenheld, Tom) — Rosenthal, Amy Krouse
y I Woke Up Dead at the Mall — Sheehan, Judy
c I Won (Illus. by Wielockx, Ruth) — Wielockx, Ruth
I Won't Be Home Next Summer: Flight Lieutenant R.N. Selley DFC (1917-1941). — Selley, Ron
c I Yam a Donkey! (Illus. by Bell, Cece) — Bell, Cece
y Ian Quicksilver: The Warrior's Return — Peterson, Alyson
Icarus Falling: The True Story of a Nightclub Bouncer Who Wanted to Be a Fucking Movie Star But Settled for Being a Fucking Man — Meyer, Christopher Paul
The Icarus Gland: A Book of Metamorphoses — Starobinets, Anna
Icarus — Meyer, Deon
Ice Chest — Rhoades, J.D.
The Ice Child and Other Stories — Arden, Leon
Ice Cold — Bell, Anthea
Ice Cold — Schenkel, Andrea Maria
The Ice Cream Blonde: The Whirlwind Life and Mysterious Death of Screwball Comedienne Thelma Todd — Morgan, Michelle
c Ice Cream Summer (Illus. by Sis, Peter) — Sis, Peter
c Ice Cream Work (Illus. by Naoshi) — Naoshi
The Ice Dragon (Illus. by Royo, Luis) — Martin, George R.R.
c Ice Fishing — Hamilton, S.L.
c Ice in the Jungle (Illus. by Hofmann-Maniyar, Ariane) — Hofmann-Maniyar, Ariane
The Ice is Melting: Ethics in the Arctic — Helgesen, Leif Magne
y Ice Kissed — Hocking, Amanda
y Ice Like Fire — Raasch, Sara
Ice Pops! 50 Delicious, Fresh, and Fabulous Icy Treats — Roden, Nadia
Ice Time — Trifunov, David
The Ice Twins — Tremayne, S.K.
y Ice War — Falkner, Brian
The Iceberg — Courts, Marion
The Iceberg — Coutts, Marion

Icebound Empire: Industry and Politics on the Last Frontier, 1898-1938 — Tower, Elizabeth A.
c Icebox Cakes: Recipes for the Coolest Cakes in Town (Illus. by Donne, Tara) — Sagendorph, Jean
c Icebreaker (Read by Gideon, Anne Marie). Audiobook Review — Tanner, Lian
c Icebreaker — Tanner, Lian
Icefall — Philip, Gillian
Ich Erschreibe mich Selbst: (Autor)Biografisches Schreiben bei Horst Bienek — Pietrek, Daniel
"Ich habe mich nur an das geltende Recht gehalten": Herkunft, Arbeitsweise und Mentalitat der Warter und Vernehmer der Stasi-Untersuchungshaftanstalt Berlin-Hohenschonhausen — Martin, Elisabeth
Ich und Karl der Grosse: Das Leben des Hoflings Einhard — Patzold, Steffen
c The Icing on the Cake — Levine, Deborah A.
Iconoclasm from Antiquity to Modernity — Kolrud, Kristine
The Iconography of Malcolm X — Abernethy, Graeme
Icons of Irishness from the Middle Ages to the Modern World: The New Middle Ages — Williams, Maggie M.
Icons of Style: Sneakers
Icons of Style: T-Shirts — Daily Street, The
c Icy Comets Sometimes Have Tails — Glaser, Chaya
I'd Walk with My Friends if I Could Find Them — Goolsby, Jesse
c Ida, Always (Illus. by Santoso, Charles) — Levis, Caron
y Ida M. Tarbell: The Woman Who Challenged Big Business--and Won! — McCully, Emily Arnold
Ida McKinley: The Turn-of-the-Century First Lady through War, Assassination, and Secret Disability — Anthony, Carl Sferrazza
c Ida's Present (Illus. by Kim, IhHyeon) — Lee, HaeDa
The Idea of a River: Walking Out of Berlin — Scraton, Paul
The Idea of Europe — Steiner, George
The Idea of Hegel's Science of Logic — Rosen, Stanley
The Idea of Liberty in Canada during the Age of Atlantic Revolutions, 1776-1838 — Ducharme, Michel
The Idea of Love — Henry, Patti Callahan
The Ideal in the West — Beardsley, David A.
The Ideal Refugees: Gender, Islam, and the Sahrawi Politics of Survival, Gender, Culture, and Politics in the Middle East (Gender, Culture, and Politics in the Middle East). — Fiddian-Qasmiyeh, Elena
Ideal: The Novel and the Play — Rand, Ayn
The Idealist: Aaron Swartz and the Rise of Free Culture on the Internet — Peters, Justin
c Ideas Are All Around (Illus. by Stead, Philip C.) — Stead, Philip C.
Ideas of Liberty in Early Modern Europe: From Machiavelli to Milton — Gatti, Hilary
Ideas of Order: A Close Reading of Shakespeare's Sonnets — Rudenstine, Neil L.
Ideas of Power in the Late Middle Ages, 1296-1417 — Canning, Joseph
Identification and Evaluation of Learning Disabilities — Johnson, Evelyn S.
Identities and Foreign Policies in Russia, Ukraine and Belarus: The Other Europes — White, Stephen
Identities and Social Change in Britain since 1940: The Politics of Method — Savage, Michael
The Identity and the Life of the Church: John Calvin's Ecclesiology in the Perspective of His Anthropology — Kim, Yosep
y Identity Crisis — Schorr, Melissa
Identity: Fragments, Frankness — Nancy, Jean-Luc
The Identity of Jesus: Nordic Voices — Byrkskog, Samuel
Identity, Place, and Subversion in Contemporary Mizrahi Cinema in Israel — Shemer, Yaron
Ideologias, practicas y discursos. La construccion cultural del mundo social, siglos XVII-XIX — Piere, Jaime
An Ideological Death: Suicide in Israeli Literature — Harris, Rachel S.
Ideologies of Eastness in Central and Eastern Europe — Zarycki, Tomasz
Idiopathy — Byers, Sam
Idolatry, Leadership, and Terrorism — Williams, Phillip
Idolatry of Blood: Religion for a Post-Modern World — Zurcher, Frederic
y Idols — Stohl, Margaret
Idyll Threats — Gayle, Stephanie
c If ... A Mind-Bending New Way of Looking at Big Ideas and Numbers (Illus. by Adams, Steve) — Smith, David J.

If ... : A Mind-Bending New Way of Looking at Big Ideas and Numbers (Illus. by Adams, Steve) — Smith, David J.
c If ... A Mind-Bending New Way of Looking at Big Ideas and Numbers (Illus. by Adams, Steve) — Smith, David J.
c If An Elephant Went to School (Illus. by Wood, Laura) — Fischer, Ellen
If Anything Should Happen — Hill, Bonnie Hearn
If at Birth You Don't Succeed: My Adventures with Disaster and Destiny — Anner, Zach
y If, by Miracle — Kutz, Michael
If Elvis Presley Is King Who Is James Brown, God? — Baraka, Amiri
If Ever You Go: A Map of Dublin in Poetry and Song — Boran, Pat
y If Everyone Knew Every Plant and Tree — Johnston, Julia
c If Everything Were Pink (Illus. by Lalalimola) — Eliot, Hannah
c If He Had Not Come (Illus. by Jaskiewicz, Charles) — Weeks, Nan F.
If He's Noble — Howell, Hannah
If I Could Turn Back Time (Read by Cassidy, Orlagh). Audiobook Review — Harbison, Beth
y If I Could Turn Back Time — Harbison, Beth
y If I Ever Get Out of Here (Read by Gansworth, Eric). Audiobook Review — Gansworth, Eric
If I Fall, If I Die — Christie, Michael
c If I Had a Gryphon (Illus. by Atkinson, Cale) — VanSickle, Vikki
c If I Had a Triceratops (Illus. by O'Connor, George) — O'Connor, George
If I Plug My Ears, God Can't Tell Me What to Do: And Other Ways We Miss Out on God's Adventures — Clemence, Jessie
If I Should Die — Frank, Matthew
c If I Went to the Moon (Illus. by Romanenko, Vasiliza) — Blau, Sara
y If I Were You — Margolis, Leslie
If Jack Had — Rappaport, Steve
c If Kids Ran the World (Illus. by Dillon, Diane) — Dillon, Leo
c If Kids Ruled the World (Illus. by Huyck, David) — Bailey, Linda
If Memory Serves: Gay Men, AIDS, and the Promise of the Queer Past — Castiglia, Christopher
c If My Dad Were an Animal (Illus. by Robaard, Jedda) — Robaard, Jedda
c If My Mom Were a Bird (Illus. by Robaard, Jedda) — Robaard, Jedda
y If Only it Were Fiction — Thon, Elsa
c If Picasso Went to the Zoo: An Illustrated Introduction to Art History for Children by Art Teachers — Gibbons, Eric
If the Oceans Were Ink: An Unlikely Friendship and a Journey to the Heart of the Qur'an — Power, Carla
If the Raindrops United: Drawings and Cartoons — Friedlander, Judah
If the Tabloids Are True What Are You? — Harvey, Matthea
If the Viscount Falls — Jeffries, Sabrina
c If Winning Isn't Everything, Why Do I Hate to Lose? (Illus. by Martin, Brian) — Smith, Bryan
If You Can Tell — McMichael, James
c If You Could Be Mine — Farizan, Sara
If You Ever Want to Bring an Alligator to School, Don't! (Illus. by Parsley, Elise) — Parsley, Elise
c If You Find This — Baker, Matthew
If You Find This Letter: My Journey to Find Purpose through Hundreds of Letters to Strangers — Brencher, Hannah
c If You Find This — Baker, Matthew
c If You Love Honey (Illus. by Morrison, Cathy) — Sullivan, Martha
If You Love Me, Take Me Now — Cox, Steve
If You Only Knew (Read by Rubinate, Amy). Audiobook Review — Higgins, Kristan
If You Only Knew — Higgins, Kristan
c If You Plant a Seed (Illus. by Nelson, Kadir) — Nelson, Kadir
c If You See a Cow — Larranaga, Ana
If You Steal — Jason
If You Want to Know Who We Are: The Rathmines and Rathgar Musical Society 1913-2013 — Dungan, Myles
c If You Were a Dog (Illus. by Raschka, Chris) — Swenson, Jamie A.
c If You Were a Panda Bear (Read by Stechschulte, Tom). Audiobook Review — Minor, Florence

If You Were Me and Lived in ... Greece — Roman, Carole P.
c If You Were Me and Lived in ... Scotland (Illus. by Roman, Carole P.) — Roman, Carole P.
y If You Were Me — Hepburn, Sam
c If You Wish (Illus. by Ingpen, Robert) — Westerlund, Kate
y If You Wrong Us — Klehr, Dawn
c If You're a Robot and You Know It (Illus. by Musical Robot) — Carter, David A.
c If You're Happy and You Know It (Illus. by Krummer, Mark) — Everett, Melissa
y If You're Lucky — Prinz, Yvonne
y If You're Reading This — Reedy, Trent
c The Ifs Return (Illus. by Walls, Frank) — Pooker, J.D.
c Iginla Sparks the Flames (Illus. by McLaughlin, Gary) — Leonetti, Mike
Ignacio de Loyola — Garcia Hernan, Enrique
c Igneous Rocks — Owings, Lisa
y Ignite — Larson, Sara B.
Ignite Calm: Achieving Bliss in Your Work — Snyder, Debra J.
Igniting the American Revolution: 1773-1775 — Beck, Derek W.
Ignorance and Moral Obligation — Zimmerman, Michael J.
Ignorance, Nescience, Nonknowledge: Late Medieval and early modern coping with Unknowns — Zwierlein
The Ignorant Maestro: How Great Leaders Inspire Unpredictable Brilliance — Talgam, Itay
Ignoring Nature No More: The Case for Compassionate Conservation — Bekoff, Marc
Il carme 67 di Catullo — Portuese, Orazio
c Il neige grand-papa! — Usher, Sam
Ike's Bluff: President Eisenhower's Secret Battle to Save the World — Thomas, Evan
Il Beato P. Gabriele M. Allegra: Dall'Italia alla Cina — De Marco, Vittorio
Il commissario distrettuale nel Veneto asburgico: Un funzionario dell' Impero tra mediazione politica e controllo sociale — Rossetto, Luca
Il existe d'autres mondes — Bayard, Pierre
Il fascismo in provincia: Articolazioni e gestione del potere tra centro e periferia — Corner, Paul
Il liber di Catullo: Tradizione, modelli e fortleben — Biondi, Giuseppe Gilberto
Il mondo del vaso Chigi: Pittura, guerra e societa a Corinto alla meta del VII secolo a.C — D'Acunto, Matteo
Il Novellario - Enciclatalogo della Posta in Italia, vol. II: Una Posta Belle Epoque 1889-1921 — Filanci, Franco
Il novus libellus di Catullo: Transmissione del testo, problematicita della grafia e dell'interpunzione — Bonvicini, Mariella
Il Poeta e il suo pubblico: Lettura e commento dei testi lirici nel Cinquecento Convegno internazionale di Studi — Leporatti, Roberto
Il Professorino: Giuseppe Dossetti tra Crisi del Fascismo e Costruzione della Democrazia, 1940-1948 — Galavotti, Enrico
Il Servizio Prioritario: storia, francobolli, tariffe ed aspetti collezionistici — Cipriani, Nicola Luciano
Il Sillabo di Pio IX — Sandoni, Luca
The Iliad: A New Translation — Green, Peter
The Iliad. Audiobook Review
c The Iliad (Illus. by Packer, Neil) — Cross, Gillian
The Iliad in a Nutshell. Visualizing Epic on the Roman Context — Squire, Michael
y The Iliad (Illus. by Packer, Neil) — Cross, Gillian
The Iliad — Homer
I'll Always Be with You — Armour, Violetta
I'll Be There — Chase, Samantha
y I'll Be There — Goldberg, Holly
c I'll Catch You If You Fall (Illus. by Marlow, Layn) — Sperring, Mark
y I'll Give You the Sun (Read by Whelan, Julia, with Jesse Bernstein). Audiobook Review — Nelson, Jandy
y I'll Give You the Sun — Nelson, Jandy
c I'll Haunt You! Meet a Ghost (Illus. by Buccheri, Chiara) — Knudsen, Shannon
I'll Have What She's Having: My Adventures in Celebrity Dieting — Harrington, Rebecca
y I'll Meet You There — Demetrios, Heather
I'll Never Write My Memoirs — Jones, Grace
I'll See You in Paris — Gable, Michelle
I'll Stand by You — Sala, Sharon
I'll Tell You Mine: Thirty Years of Essays from the Iowa Nonfiction Writing Program — Edelman, Hope

Ille Journee d'etudes anglo-normades: Adaptation, parodie et autres emplois — Zink, Michel
The Illegal — Hill, Lawrence
Illegal: Reflections of an Undocumented Immigrant — N., Jose Angel
Illegality, Inc: Clandestine Migration and the Business of Bordering Europe — Andersson, Ruben
illiam Cameron Menzies: The Shape of Films to Come — Cortis, James
The Illiterate — Kristof, Agota
Illocality — Massey, Joseph
The Illogic of Kassel — Vila-Matas, Enrique
y Illuminae — Kaufman, Amie
Illuminating the Word: The Making of the Saint John's Bible — Calderhead, Christopher
The Illuminations — O'Hagan, Andrew
Illuminations — Benjamin, Walter
Illuminators and Patrons in Fourteenth-Century England: The Psalter and Hours of Humphrey de Bohun and the Manuscripts of the Bohun Family — Sandler, Lucy Freeman
Illusion — Yelich-Koth, Christa
The Illusion of God's Presence: The Biological Origins of Spiritual Longings — Wathey, John C.
y Illusionarium — Dixon, Heather
y Illusions of Fate — White, Kiersten
y Illusive — Lloyd-Jones, Emily
An Illustrated Guide to Mobile Technology — Date, Sachin
Illustrated Religious Texts in the North of Europe, 1500-1800 — Dietz, Feike
An Illustrated Treasury of Scottish Mythical Creatures (Illus. by Leiper, Kate) — Breslin, Theresa
Illustrating the Phaenomena: Celestial Cartography in Antiquity and the Middle Ages — Dekker, Elly
c I'm a Big Girl: A Story for Dads and Daughters (Illus. by Wells, Lea) — Pope, Greg
I'm a Different Type of Apple — Elliott, Kevin D., Sr.
c I'm a Dirty Dinosaur (Illus. by James, Ann) — Brian, Janeen
c I'm a Hungry Dinosaur (Illus. by James, Ann) — Brian, Janeen
c I'm a Midnight Snacker! Meet a Vampire (Illus. by Buccheri, Chiara) — Bullard, Lisa
I'm Already Disturbed Please Come In: Parasites, Social Media and Other Planetary Disturbances (a Memoir, of Sorts). — Glancy, Gabrielle
c I'm an Alien and I Want to Go Home! (Illus. by Kelley, Marty) — Franklin, Jo
Im Bilde. Visualisierung Vormoderner Geschichte in Modernen Medien
c I'm Brave (Read by Banks, Jonathan). Audiobook Review — McMullan, Kate
c I'm Cool! (Illus. by McMullan, Jim) — McMullan, Kate
Im Dienste der nationalsozialistischen Volkstumspolitik in Lothringen: Auf den Spuren meines Gro[sz&rqsb;vaters — Gehrig, Astrid
c I'm Fearsome and Furry! Meet a Werewolf (Illus. by Moran, Mike) — Bullard, Lisa
y I'm from Nowhere — Myers, Suzanne
I'm Glad about You — Rebeck, Theresa
y I'm Glad I Did (Read by Botchan, Rachel). Audiobook Review — Weil, Cynthia
y I'm Glad I Did — Weil, Cynthia
c I'm Going to Catch My Tail! — Matison, Jimbo
c I'm Gonna Climb a Mountain in My Patent Leather Shoes (Illus. by Avril, Lynne) — Singer, Marilyn
I'm Happy for You (Sort of ... Not Really): Finding Contentment in a Culture of Comparison (Read by Brunjes, Tracy). Audiobook Review — Wyma, Kay Wills
I'm Jack — Blacklock, Mark
c I'm My Own Dog (Illus. by Stein, David Ezra) — Stein, David Ezra
I'm Neither Here nor There: Mexicans' Quotidian Struggles with Migration and Poverty — Zavella, Patricia
c I'm New Here (Illus. by O'Brien, Anne Sibley) — O'Brien, Anne Sibley
I'm Not a Celebrity, I am a Muslim: One Woman's Journey to a World of Faith — Patel, Sahera
I'm Not a Terrorist, But I've Played One on TV: Memoirs of a Middle Eastern Funny Man — Jobrani, Maz
c I'm Not Hatching — Gehl, Laura
c I'm Not Moving (Illus. by Cerato, Mattia) — Blevins, Wiley
c I'm Ready for School (Illus. by Silva, Reg) — Sirett, Dawn

c I'm Right Here (Illus. by Duzakin, Akin)
— Orbeck-Nilssen, Constance
Im Schatten des Weltkriegs: Massengewalt der Ustasa gegen Serben, Juden und Roma in Kroatien 1941-1945 — Korb, Alexander
Im Sog der Katastrophe: Lateinamerika und der Erste Weltkrieg — Rinke, Stefan
I'm Special: And Other Lies We Tell Ourselves to Get through Our Twenties — O'Connell, Ryan
I'm Traveling Alone — Bjork, Samuel
c I'm Trying to Love Spiders (Illus. by Barton, Bethany) — Barton, Bethany
c I'm Undead and Hungry! Meet a Zombie (Illus. by Buccheri, Chiara) — Knudsen, Shannon
I'm Very into You: Correspondence 1995-1996 — Acker, Kathy
y I'm with Cupid — Staniszewski, Anna
The Image and its Prohibition in Jewish Antiquity — Pearce, Sarah
Image, Identity, and the Forming of the Augustinian Soul — Drever, Matthew
Image in Outline: Reading Lou Andreas-Salome — Brinker-Gabler, Gisela
An Image of God: The Catholic Struggle with Eugenics — Leon, Sharon M.
The Image of the Black in Western Art, Vol. 5: The Twentieth Century; The Rise of Black Artists — Bindman, David
The Image of Venice: Fialetti's View and Sir Henry Wotton — Howard, Deborah
Image Politics of Climate Change: Visualizations, Imaginations, Documentations — Schneider, Birgit
Images and Words — Hovaguimian, Vroni
Images from the Arsenal of Democracy — Hyde, Charles K.
Images of Islam, 1453-1600: Turks in Germany and Central Europe — Smith, Charlotte Colding
Images of the Pagan Gods: Papers of a Conference in Memory of Jean Seznec — Duits, Rembrandt
c The Imaginary (Illus. by Gravett, Emily) — Harrold, A.F.
c Imaginary Fred (Illus. by Jeffers, Oliver) — Colfer, Eoin
c Imagination According to Humphrey — Birney, Betty G.
c The Imagination Box — Ford, Martyn
Imagination, Meditation, and Cognition in the Middle Ages — Karnes, Michelle
Imagination Will Take You Everywhere, vol. 1 — Snyder, Samantha
Imaginations and Configurations of Polish Society - From the Middle Ages through the 20th Century
Imaginative Card Play — Reese, Terence
c Imagine a World — Gonsalves, Rob
c Imagine a World (Illus. by Sonsalves, Rob) — Gonsalves, Rob
Imagined Communities: Reflections on the Origin and Spread of Nationalism — Anderson, Benedict
Imagined Liberation: Xenophobia, Citizenship, and Identity in South Africa, Germany, and Canada — Adam, Heribert
Imaging Marine Life: Macrophotography and Microscopy Approaches for Marine Biology — Reynaud, Emmanuel G.
Imagining Germany Imagining Asia: Essays in Asian-German Studies — Fuechtner, Veronika
Imagining Geronimo: An Apache Icon in Popular Culture — Clements, William M.
Imagining Hoover Dam: The Making of a Cultural Icon — Childers, Carr Leisl
Imagining Japan in Post-War East Asia: Identity Politics, Schooling and Popular Culture — Shimazu, Naoko
Imagining Methodism in Eighteenth-Century Britain: Enthusiasm, Belief, and the Borders of the Self — Anderson, Misty G.
Imagining Women's Conventual Spaces in France, 1600-1800: The Cloister Disclosed — Woshinsky, Barbara R.
Imagining Xerxes: Ancient Perspectives on a Persian King — Bridges, Emma
Imago Exegetica: Visual Images as Exegetical Instruments, 1400-1700 — Clifton, James
Imago Exegetica: Visual Images as Exegetical Instruments, 1400-1700 — Melion, Walter S.
c Imani's Moon (Read by Boafo, MaameYaa). Audiobook Review — Brown-Wood, JaNay
c Imani's Moon (Illus. by Mitchell, Hazel) — Brown-Wood, JaNay
Imbeciles: The Supreme Court, American Eugenics, and the Sterilization of Carrie Buck — Cohen, Adam

c Imelda & the Goblin King (Illus. by Smith, Briony May) — Smith, Briony May
Imigrant Narratives: Orientalism and Cultural Translation in Arab American and Arab British Literature — Hassan, Wail S.
Imitatio Christi: The Poetics of Piety in Early Modern England — Perry, Nandra
The Imitation Game — Tyldum, Morten
The Imjin and Kapyong Battles, Korea, 1951 — MacKenzie, S.P.
y Immaculate — Detweiler, Katelyn
Immersive Theatres: Intimacy and Immediacy in Contemporary Performance — Machon, Josephine
The Immigrant — Woollacott, Alfred, III
Immigrant Exclusion and Insecurity in Africa: Coethnic Strangers — Adida, Claire
The Immigrant Expert — Macala, Robert M.
Immigrant Model — Moscaliuc, Mihaela
An Immigrant Neighborhood: Interethnic and Interracial Encounters in New York before 1930 — Yee, Shirley J.
Immigrant Soldier — Slattery, Kathryn Lang
Immigrant Women Workers in the Neoliberal Age — Flores-Gonzalez, Nilda
Immigrants and Crime in the New Destinations — Ferraro, Vincent A.
An Immigrant's Journey into the Cosmos — Misconi, N.Y.
c Immigration — Flatt, Lizann
Immigration and National Identities in Latin America — Foote, Nicola
The Immigration Crucible: Transforming Race, Nation and the Limits of the Law — Kretsedemas, Philip
Immigration, Ethnicity, and National Identity in Brazil, 1808 to the Present — Lesser, Jeffrey
c Immigration — Flatt, Lizann
Immigration Outside the Law — Motomura, Hiroshi
Immigration, Poverty, and Socioeconomic Inequality — Card, David
The Immortal Evening: A Legendary Dinner with Keats, Wordsworth and Lamb — Plumly, Stanley
y The Immortal Heights — Thomas, Sherry
The Immortal Irishman: The Irish Revolutionary Who Became an American Hero — Egan, Timothy
y Immortal Max — Clifton, Lutricia
Immortal Medusa — Ungar, Barbara Louise
The Immortal Who Loved Me — Sands, Lynsay
The Immortals — Brodsky, Jordanna Max
The Immune System — Larson, Nathan
Immunity — Antrim, Taylor
Immunity and Tolerance — OEGarra, Anne
Immunity — Antrim, Taylor
Impact Investment — Allman, Keith A.
The Impact of Idealism: The Legacy of Post-Kantian German Thought — Boyle, Nicholas
y The Impact of Technology in Sport — Anniss, Matt
The Impact of the First World War on U.S. Policymakers: American Strategic and Foreign Policy Formulation, 1938-1942 — Carew, Michael G.
Impact Player — Richardson, Bobby
y Impact: The Story of the September 11 Terrorist Attacks — Doeden, Matt
Impasse — Buckingham, Royce Scott
An Impatient Life: A Memoir — Bensaid, Daniel
Imperatives of Culture: Selected Essays on Korean History, Literature, and Society from the Japanese Colonial Era — Hanscom, Christopher P.
Imperator et Pontifex: Forschungen zum Verhaltnis von Kaiserlicher und Romischer Kurie im Zeitalter der Konfessionalisierung — Roller, Alexander
Imperator und Pontifex: Forschungen zum Verhaltnis von Kaiserlicher und romischer Kurie im Zeitalter der Konfessionalisierung, 1555-1648 — Koller, Alexander
Imperfect Sword — Campbell, Jack
Imperial Ambition in the Early Modern Mediterranean: Genoese Merchants and the Spanish Crown — Dauverd, Celine
Imperial Apocalypse: The Great War and the Destruction of the Russian Empire — Sanborn, Joshua A.
Imperial Blues: Geographies of Race and Sex in Jazz Age New York — Ngo, Fiona I.B.
Imperial Citizen: Marriage and Citizenship in the Ottoman Frontier Provinces of Iraq — Kern, Karen M.
Imperial Contagions: Medicine, Hygiene, and Cultures of Planning in Asia — Peckham, Robert
Imperial Debris: On Ruins and Ruination — Stoler, Ann Laura

Imperial Eclipse: Japan's Strategic Thinking about Continental Asia before August 1945 — Koshiro, Yukiko
Imperial from the Beginning: The Constitution of the Original Executive — Prakash, Saikrishna Bangalore
Imperial Gothic: Religious Architecture and High Anglican Culture in the British Empire, c. 1840-1870 — Bremner, G.A.
Imperial Norms and Local Realities: The Ottoman Municipal Laws and the Municipality of Beirut — Sharif, Malek
Imperial Portugal in the Age of Atlantic Revolutions: The Luso-Brazilian World, c. 1770-1850 — Paquette, Gabriel B.
Imperial Rome AD 284 to 363: The New Empire — Harries, Jill
The Imperial Season: America's Capital in the Time of the First Ambassadors, 1893-1918 — Seale, William
Imperial Spaces: Placing the Irish and Scots in Colonial Australia — Proudfoot, Lindsay J.
Imperial Technoscience: Transnational Histories of MRI in the United States, Britain, and India — Prasad, Amit
The Imperial University: Academic Repression and Scholarly Dissent — Chatterjee, Piya
"Imperiale Emotionen" Zur Konzeptualisierung ost-westlicher Affektkulturen angesichts der Ukraine-Krise
Imperialism and Capitalism in the Twenty-First Century: A System in Crisis — Petras, James
Imperialism and the Origins of Mexican Culture — MacLachlan, Colin M.
Imperio e informacion: funciones del saber en el dominio colonial espanol — Brendecke, Arndt
Imperium: A Fiction of the South Seas — Kracht, Christian
Impersonal Enunciation, or the Place of Film — Metz, Christian
The Implacable Absence: A Non-Idiomatic Improvisational Duet — Gorton, Henry E.
Implementing the Common Core State Standards through Mathematical Problem Solving, Grades 3-5 — Foote, Mary Q.
Implicit Functions and Solution Mappings: A View from Variational Analysis, 2d ed. — Dontchev, Asen L.
c The Importance of Being 3 — Ward, Lindsay
The Importance of Being Civil: The Struggle for Political Decency — Hall, John A.
The Importance of Being Little: What Preschoolers Really Need from Grownups — Christakis, Erika
The Importance of Elsewhere: Philip Larkin's Photographs — Bradford, Richard
The Importance of Place in Contemporary Italian Crime Fiction: A Bloody Journey — Pezzotti, Barbara
Imposing, Maintaining, and Tearing open the Iron Curtain: The Cold War and East-Central Europe, 1945-1989 — Smetana, Vit
c Impossible! — Magorian, Michelle
Impossible Bottle: Poems — Emerson, Claudia
Impossible Citizens: Dubai's Indian Diaspora — Vora, Neha
The Impossible Craft: Literary Biography — Donaldson, Scott
The Impossible Exile: Stefan Zweig at the End of the World — Prochnik, George
c The Impossible Knife of Memory (Read by Whelan, Julia). Audiobook Review — Anderson, Laurie Halse
c The Impossible Quest: The Beast of Blackmoor Bog — Forsyth, Kate
c The Impossible Quest: Wolves of the Witchwood — Forsyth, Kate
c The Impossible Voyage of Kon-Tiki (Illus. by Ray, Deborah Kogan) — Ray, Deborah Kogan
Impossible Wardrobes — Saillard, Olivier
y Imposter — John, Antony
The Imposter — Triolo, Pamela
y The Impostor Queen — Fine, Sarah
c Impressionism: 13 Artists Children Should Know — Heine, Florian
Impressionism in Canada: A Journey of Rediscovery — Prakash, A.K.
y Impressionism — Gunderson, Jessica
Impressions — Koch, Aidan
The Imprint of Another Life: Adoption Narratives and Human Possibility — Homans, Margaret
Imprison'd Wranglers: The Rhetorical Culture of the House of Commons, 1760-1800 — Reid, Christopher

Imprisoned in English: The Hazards of English as a Default Language — Wierzbicka, Anna
The Improbability of Love — Rothschild, Hannah
An Improbable Friendship: The Remarkable Lives of Israeli Ruth Dayan and Palestinian Raymonda Tawil and Their Forty-Year Peace Mission — David, Anthony
Improbable Future — Biederman, Edwin W., Jr.
An Improbable Journey: A True Story of Courage and Survival During World War II — Schenkel, Susan
Improbable Libraries: A Visual Journey to the World's Most Unusual Libraries — Johnson, Alex
y The Improbable Theory of Ana & Zak — Katcher, Brian
The Improbable War: China, the United States, and the Logic of Great Power Conflict — Coker, Christopher
y The Improbable Wonders of Moojie Littleman — Gregory, Robin
An Improper Arrangement — Michaels, Kasey
c Improper Order — Sullivan, Deirdre
The Improv Handbook for Modern Quilters: A Guide to Creating, Quilting and Living Courageously — Wood, Sherri Lynn
Improving Your Memory: How to Remember What You're Starting to Forget — Stern, Lynn
Improvise: Unconventional Career Advice from an Unlikely CEO — Cook, Fred
Imprudent King: A New Life of Philip II — Parker, Geoffrey
The Impulsive, Disorganized Child: Solutions for Parenting Kids with Executive Functioning Difficulties — Forgan, James W.
c In (Illus. by McClure, Nikki) — McClure, Nikki
c In a Cloud of Dust (Illus. by Deines, Brian) — Fullerton, Alma
In a Dark, Dark Wood (Read by Church, Imogen). Audiobook Review — Ware, Ruth
In a Dark, Dark Wood — Ware, Ruth
In a Dark Wood: What Dante Taught Me about Grief, Healing, and the Mysteries of Love — Luzzi, Joseph
In a Different Key: The Story of Autism — Donvan, John
In a French Kitchen: Tales and Traditions of Everyday Home Cooking in France — Loomis, Susan Herrmann
y In a Handful of Dust — McGinnis, Mindy
In a New Light: Giovanni Bellini's 'St. Francis in the Desert' — Rutherglen, Susannah
In a Sea of Bitterness: Refugees during the Sino-Japanese War — Schoppa, Keith R.
(In a Sense) Lost and Found — Muradov, Roman
y In a Split Second — McKenzie, Sophie
In a Vertigo of Silence — Polli, Miriam
c In a Village by the Sea (Illus. by Chu, April) — Van, Muon
y In a World Just Right — Brooks, Jen
In Absence of Fear — Chaney, Celeste
In All Respects Ready: Australia's Navy in World War One — Stevens, David
In America: Travels with John Steinbeck — Mak, Geert
c In Ancient Egypt — Turner, Tracey
c In Ancient Greece — Turner, Tracey
c In Ancient Rome — Turner, Tracey
In and out of Paris: Gardens of Secret Delights — Sardar, Zahid
In Another Country: Selected Stories — Constantine, David
In Another Life — Johnson, Julie Christine
In Bed with a Spy — Alexander, Alyssa
In Between Dreams — Rooks, Erin Kerr
In Bitter Chill — Ward, Sarah
In Certain Circles — Harrower, Elizabeth
In Character: Opera Portraiture — Martin, John F.
In Command of History: Churchill Fighting and Writing the Second — Reynolds, David
c In Darkling Wood — Carroll, Emma
In Defence of War — Biggar, Nigel
In Defense of a Liberal Education (Read by Zakaria, Fareed). Audiobook Review — Zakaria, Fareed
In Defense of a Liberal Education — Zakaria, Fareed
In Defense of Disciplines: Interdisciplinarity and Specialization in the Research University — Jacobs, Jerry A.
In Defense of Justice: Joseph Kurihara and the Japanese American Struggle for Equality — Tamura, Eileen H.
In Defense of Read-Aloud: Sustaining Best Practice — Layne, Steven L.

In Defense of Selfishness: Why the Code of Self-Sacrifice Is Unjust and Destructive — Schwartz, Peter
In der Kriegsgesellschaft: Arbeiter und Arbeiterbewegung 1939 bis 1945 — Schneider, Michael
In Europe's Shadow: Two Cold Wars and a Thirty-Year Journey Through Romania and Beyond — Kaplan, Robert D.
In Every Way — Brown, Nic
In Every Way That Matters — Cheevers, William
In Firefly Valley — Cabot, Amanda
In Foreign Fields: The Politics and Experiences of Transnational Sport Migration — Carter, Thomas F.
In Gallup, Greed — Lowe, Tower
In God's Hands: The Archbishop of Canterbury's Lent Book 2015 — Tutu, Desmond
In God's Path: The Arab Conquests and the Creation of an Islamic Empire — Hoyland, Robert G.
y In Good Company — Turano, Jen
In Harm's Way: The Sinking of the USS Indianapolis — Stanton, Doug
y In Hiding — Quddus, Marguerite Elias
In Lands Imagination Favors — Schofield, Don
In Light of Another's Word: European Ethnography in the Middle Ages — Khanmohamadi, Shirin A.
In Manchuria: a Village Called Wasteland and the Transformation of Rural China — Meyer, Michael
c In Mary's Garden (Illus. by Kugler, Tina) — Kugler, Tina
In Montmartre: Picasso, Matisse and Modernism in Paris, 1900-1910 — Roe, Sue
In Montmartre: Picasso, Matisse and the Birth of Modernist Art (Read by Bering, Emma). Audiobook Review — Roe, Sue
In Montmartre: Picasso, Matisse and the Birth of Modernist Art — Roe, Sue
In Motion, at Rest: The Event of the Athletic Body — Farred, Grant
In My Heart: A Book of Feelings (Illus. by Roussey, Christine) — Witek, Jo
Nicomachi arithmeticam — Vinel, Nicolas
In Night's City — Nelson, Dorothy
In No Great Hurry: 13 Lessons in Life with Saul Leiter — Leach, Tomas
In One Yard: Close to Nature — Hatch, Warren A.
In Order to Live: A North Korean Girl's Journey to Freedom — Park, Yeonmi
In Other Words — Lahiri, Jhumpa
In Our Backyard: Human Trafficking in America and What We Can Do to Stop It (Read by Zanzarella, Nicol). Audiobook Review — Belles, Nita
In Our Hands: The Struggle for U.S. Child Care Policy — Palley, Elizabeth
y In Our Village: San Francisco's Tenderloin through the Eyes of Its Youth — Cervone, Barbara
c In, Over and On! (the Farm). (Illus. by Long, Ethan) — Long, Ethan
In Paradise — Matthiessen, Peter
In Peace and Freedom: My Journey in Selma — Johnson, Kathryn Lee
In Place of Me — Stock, Doreen
In Portum Navigare: Romische Hafen an Flussen und Seen — Wawrzinek, Christina
In Poseidons Reich XX, "Land Unter!"
In Praise of Desire — Schroeder, Timothy
"In principio erat Verbum": Philosophy and Theology in the Commentaries on the Gospel of John — Amerini, Fabrizio
In Pursuit of Butterflies: A Fifty-Year Affair — Oates, Matthew
In Pursuit of Early Mammals — Jaworowska, Zofia Kielan
y In Real Life — Love, Jessica
c In Real Life — Tabak, Lawrence
In Real Life: Searching for Connection in High-Tech Times — Mitchell, Jon
In Remembrance of Emmett Till: Regional Stories and Media Responses to the Black Freedom Struggle — Mace, Darryl
In Response to the Religious Other: Ricoeur and the Fragility of Interreligious Encounters — Moyaert, Marianne
In Retrospect: From the Pill to the Pen — Djerassi, Carl
In Retrospect — Larson, Ellen
In Search of a Legacy — Batson, Jon
In Search of Buddha's Daughters — Toomey, Christine
In Search of Cell History: The Evolution of Life's Building Blocks — Harold, Franklin M.
In Search of First Contact: The Vikings of Vinland, the Peoples of the Dawnland, and the Anglo-American Anxiety of Discovery — Kolodny, Annette
In Search of 'La Grande Illusion': A Critical Appreciation of Jean Renoir's Elusive Masterpiece — MacDonald, Nicholas
In Search of New York: A Special Issue of Dissent — Sleeper, Jim
y In Search of Pharrell Williams — Lester, Paul
In Search of Sacred Time: Jacobus de Voragine and the Golden Legend — Le Goff, Jacques
y In Search of Sam — Butcher, Kristin
In Search of Scandal — Lord, Susanne
In Search of Sir Thomas Browne: The Life and Afterlife of the Seventeenth Century's Most Inquiring Mind (Read by Vance, Simon). Audiobook Review — Aldersey-Williams, Hugh
In Search of Sir Thomas Browne: The Life and Afterlife of the Seventeenth Century's Most Inquiring Mind — Aldersey-Williams, Hugh
In Search of the Amazon: Brazil, the United States, and the Nature of a Region — Garfield, Seth
In Search of the Christian Buddha: How an Asian Sage Became a Medieval Saint — Lopez, Donald S., Jr.
In Search of the Dark Watchers: Landscapes and Lore of Big Sur (Illus. by Brode, Benjamin) — Steinbeck, Thomas
In Search of the First Venetians: Prosopography of Early Medieval Venice — Berto, Luigi Andrea
In Search of the Good: A Life in Bioethics — Callahan, Daniel
c In Search of the Little Prince: The Story of Antoine de Saint-Exupery (Illus. by Landmann, Bimba) — Landmann, Bimba
In Search of the Movement — Hedin, Benjamin
In Search of the New Woman: Middle-Class Women and Work in Britain — Sutherland, Gillian
In Search of the Truth: A History of Disputation Techniques from Antiquity to Early Modern Times — Weijers, Olga
y In Search of Words — Wong, Raymond F.L.
In Search of Your German Roots: A Complete Guide to Tracing Your Ancestors in the Germanic Areas of Europe, 5th ed. — Baxter, Angus
In Short Measures: Three Novellas — Ruhlman, Michael
In Silence and Dignity: The Single Mother Story — Okoli, Kate
In Some Other World, Maybe — Goldhagen, Shari
y In the Afterlight — Bracken, Alexandra
In the Air Tonight — Handeland, Lori
In the All-Night Cafe: A Memoir of Belle and Sebastian's Formative Year — David, Stuart
In the Ballast to the White Sea: A Scholarly Edition — Lowry, Malcolm
In the Beginning: The Martin Luther King Jr. International Chapel at Morehouse College — Nix, Echol, Jr.
In the Beginning Was the Word: The Bible in American Public Life, 1492-1783 — Noll, Mark A.
In the Cafe of Lost Youth — Modiano, Patrick
c In the Canyon (Illus. by Wolff, Ashley) — Scanlon, Liz Garton
In the Cause of Freedom: Radical Black Internationalism from Harlem to London, 1917-1939 — Makalani, Minkah
In the City of Gold and Silver: The Story of Begum Hazrat Mahal — Mourad, Kenize
In the Company of Legends — Kramer, Joan
In the Company of Sherlock Holmes: Stories Inspired by the Holmes Canon — King, Laurie R.
In the Country: Stories — Alvar, Mia
In the Dark — Moggach, Deborah
In the Dark Places — Robinson, Peter
c In the Deep Dark Deep (Illus. by Price, Ben Joel) — Price, Ben Joel
In the Distance — Michaels, Nikka
In the Dust of the Planet — Thacker, Eugene
y In the End — Lunetta, Demitria
In the Evil Day: Violence Comes to One Small Town — Carey, Richard Adams
y In the Fields and the Trenches: The Famous and the Forgotten on the Battlefields of World War I — Hollihan, Kerrie Logan
y In the Footsteps of Crazy Horse (Illus. by Yellowhawk, Jim) — Marshall III, Joseph M.
y In the Footsteps of Crazy Horse (Illus. by Yellowhawk, Jim) — Marshall, Joseph, III
c In the Forbidden City — Chiu, Kwong Chin
In the Godfather Garden: The Long Life and Times of Richie "the Boot" Boiardo — Linnett, Richard

In the Governor's Shadow: The True Story of Ma and Pa Ferguson — Wilson, Carol O'Keefe
In the Illuminated Dark: Selected Poems of Tuvia Ruebner — Ruebner, Tuvia
In the Kingdom of Ice: The Grand and Terrible Polar Voyage of the USS Jeannette (Read by Morey, Arthur). Audiobook Review — Sides, Hampton
In the Kingdom of Ice: The Grand and Terrible Polar Voyage of the USS Jeannette — Sides, Hampton
In the Land of the Eastern Queendom: The Politics of Gender and Ethnicity on the Sino-Tibetan Border — Jinba, Tenzin
In the Language of Miracles — Hassib, Rajia
In the Light of Science: Our Ancient Quest for Knowledge and the Measure of Modern Physics — Nicolaides, Demetris
In the Light of What We Know — Rahman, Zia Haider
In the Mind Fields: Exploring the New Science of Neuropsychoanalysis — Schwartz, Casey
In the Mouth of the Whale — McAuley, Paul
y In the Mouth of the Wolf — Maggi, Nicole
In the Murmurs of the Rotten Carcass Economy — Borcutzky, Daniel
In the Museum of Man: Race, Anthropology, and Empire in France, 1850-1950 — Conklin, Alice L.
In the Name of Oil: Anglo-American Relations in the Middle East, 1950-1958 — Pearson, Ivan L. G.
c In the New World: A Family in Two Centuries (Illus. by Holtei, Christa) — Raidt, Gerda
In the Night of Time — Grossman, Edith
c In the Rainforest (Illus. by Duke, Kate) — Duke, Kate
c In the Rainforest — Feldman, Llewellyn
In the Saguaro Forest — Amorose, Mark
In the Service of His Korean Majesty: William Nelson Lovatt, the Pusan Customs, and Sino-Korea Relations, 1876-1888 — Patterson, Wayne
In the Shadow of Edgar Allan Poe: Classic Tales of Terror 1816-1914 — Klinger, Leslie S.
In the Shadow of Hitler: Alabama's Jews, the Second World War, and the Holocaust — Puckett, Dan J.
In the Shadow of Kinzua: The Seneca Nation of Indians since World War II — Hauptman, Laurence Marc
In the Shadow of Sectarianism: Law, Shi'ism, and the Making of Modern Lebanon — Weiss, Max
y In the Shadow of the Ark — Provoost, Anne
In the Shadow of the Greatest Generation: The Americans Who Fought the Korean War — Pash, Melinda L.
In the Shadow of the Towers: Speculative Fiction in a Post-9/11 World — Lain, Douglas
In the Shadow of Zion: Promised Lands Before Israel — Rovner, Adam
In the Skin of a Jihadist: A Young Journalist Enters the ISIS Recruitment Network — Erelle, Anna
y In the Skin of a Monster — Barker, Kathryn
In the Slender Margin — Joseph, Eve
In the Society of Fascists: Acclimation, Acquiescence, and Agency in Mussolini's Italy — Albanese, Giulia
In the Spirit of a New People: The Cultural Politics of the Chicano Movement — Ontiveros, Randy J.
y In the Time of Dragon Moon — Carey, Janet Lee
c In the Tree Top: A New Lullaby (Illus. by Emery, Steve) — Jones, Candide
y In the Unlikely Event (Read by McInerney, Kathleen). Audiobook Review — Blume, Judy
y In the Unlikely Event — Blume, Judy
In the Wake of the Templars: Kill by Numbers — Rhoads, Loren
c In the Waves (Illus. by Bjorkman, Steve) — Stella, Lennon
In the Woods — Jones, Merry
In the World Interior of Capital: For a Philosophical Theory of Globalization — Sloterdijk, Peter
In Their Own Hands — Ashe, Jeffrey
c In Their Shoes: Fairy Tales and Folktales — Nicholson, Julia
In Their Voices: Black Americans on Transracial Adoption — Roorda, Rhonda M.
In These Times: Living in Britain through Napoleon's Wars, 1793-1815 — Uglow, Jenny
c In This Book (Illus. by Jolivet, Joelle) — Marceau, Fani
In Time We Shall Know Ourselves — King, Richard H.
y In Todd We Trust — Galveston, Louise
In Togo, dunkel: und andere Geschichten — Schuldt
In Too Deep — Davenport, Bea
In Trace of TR: A Montana Hunter's Journey — Aadland, Dan

In Transit: The Formation of the Colonial East Asian Cultural Sphere — Kleeman, Faye Yuan
In Tune: Charley Patton, Jimmie Rodgers, and the Roots of American Music — Wynne, Ben
In Vino Veritas — Turnbull, Peter
In Walt We Trust: How a Queer Socialist Poet Can Save America From Itself — Marsh, John
In Wilderness — Thomas, Diane
In Your Crib — Clarke, Austin
In-Your-Face Politics: The Consequences of Uncivil Media — Mutz, Diana C.
y In Your Face: The Culture of Beauty and You (Illus. by Klassen, Karen) — Graydon, Shari
Ina Coolbrith: The Bittersweet Song of California's First Poet Laureate — George, Aleta
Inattention and Inertia in Household Finance: Evidence from the Danish Mortgage Market — Andersen, Steffen
y Inbetween Days — Wakefield, Vikki
Inca Sacred Space: Landscape, Site and Symbol in the Andes — Meddens, Frank
Incarcerated: Letters from Inmate 92510 — Iversen, Inger
Incarceration Nations: A Journey to Justice in Prisons around the World — Dreisinger, Baz
The Incarnate Being Phenomenon in African Culture: Anthropological Perspectives on the Igala of North-Central Nigeria — Miachi, Tom A.
Incarnate Grace: Poems — Linehan, Moira
The Incarnations — Barker, Susan
Inca's Death Cave — Wheler, Bradford
Incendies — Coissard, Francoise
c Inch and Roly and the Sunny Day Scare (Illus. by Jatkowska, Ag) — Wiley, Melissa
Incident at the Otterville Station: A Civil War Story of Slavery and Rescue — Christgau, John
Incidents in the Night, Book 2 — B., David
Incidents of Travel in Poetry: New and Selected Poems — Lima, Frank
Inclusion Strategies That Work! Research-Based Methods for the Classroom — Karten, Toby J.
The Inclusive Toolbox: Strategies and Techniques for All Teachers — Megan, Gross
Incoming: Collected Stories — Amato, Vic
c Incommunicado — Platt, Randall
The Incomparables — Legat, Alexandra
Incompetence — Thorpe, Will
Incomplete Works — Horrocks, Dylan
Inconceivable Beasts: The Wonders of the East in the Beowulf Manuscript — Mittman, Asa Simon
y Inconceivable! — Wren, Tegan
The Inconvenience of the Wings — Zobal, Silas Dent
An Inconvenient Genocide: Who Now Remembers the Armenians? — Robertson, Geoffrey
The Inconvenient Indian — King, Thomas
Incorrect Merciful Impulses — Rankine, Camille
Increase, Decrease: 99 Step-by-Step Methods: Find the Perfect Technique for Shaping Every Knitting Project — Durant, Judith
c Incredible Creatures (Illus. by Scrace, Carolyn) — Channing, Margot
The Incredible Herb Trimpe — Cassell, Dewey
y The Incredible Plate Tectonics Comic (Illus. by Wallenta, Adam) — Lee, Kanani K.M.
c The Incredible Space Raiders from Space! — King, Wesley
c The Incredible Twisting Arm (Illus. by Wight, Eric) — Egan, Kate
The Incredibly Spaced-Out Adventures of Jupiter Jackson — Herman, Eric
The "Incumberances": British Women in India 1615-1856 — Gaughan, Joan Mickelson
An Incurable Past: Nasser's Egypt Then and Now — Belli, Meriam N.
The Incurables — Bassoff, Jon
The Incurious Seeker's Quest for Meaning: Heidegger, Mood and Christianity — Sludds, Kevin
Indelible Ink — Betts, Matt
Independence Day — Coes, Ben
Independence Lost: Lives on the Edge of the American Revolution — DuVal, Kathleen
The Independence of South Sudan: The Role of Mass Media in the Responsibility to Prevent — Soderlund, Walter C.
Independence: The Tangled Roots of the American Revolution — Slaughter, Thomas P.
Independent Chinese Documentary: From the Studio to the Street — Robinson, Luke
The Independent Director: The Non-Executive Director's Guide to Effective Board Presence — Brown, Gerry

Independent Ed: Inside a Career of Big Dreams, Little Movies, and the Twelve Best Days of My Life — Burns, Edward
Independent Stardom: Freelance Women in the Hollywood Studio System — Carman, Emily
y Independent Study — Charbonneau, Joelle
The Indestructible Houseplant: 200 Beautiful Plants That Everyone Can Grow — Martin, Tovah
Indestructible You: Building a Self That Can't be Broken — Tubali, Shai
The Index Card: Why Personal Finance Doesn't Have to be Complicated — Olen, Helaine
Indexing — McGuire, Seanan
c Indi Surfs — Gorman, Chris
c India — Powell, Jillian
India and Europe in the Global Eighteenth Century — Davies, Simon
India and the Nuclear Non-Proliferation Regime: The Perennial Outlier — Kumar, A. Vinod
India at War: The Subcontinent and the Second World War — Khan, Yasmin
India: Future Tense — Richards, Peter
India in the Chinese Imagination: Myth, Religion, and Thought — Kieschinick, John
The Indian Army and the End of the Raj — Marston, Daniel
The Indian — Gnarr, Jon
Indian Buddhist Philosophy — Carpenter, Amber
The Indian Corps on the Western Front: A Handbook and Battlefield Guide — Doherty, Simon
Indian Country: The Art of David Bradley — Verzuh, Valerie K.
Indian English and the Fiction of Natural Literature — George, Rosemary Marangoly
Indian Nocturne — Parks, Tim
The Indian Ocean and US Grand Strategy: Ensuring Access and Promoting Security — Dombrowski, Peter
The Indian Ocean in World History — Alpers, Edward A.
Indian Play: Indigenous Identities at Bacone College — Neuman, Lisa K.
Indian Resilience and Rebuilding: Indigenous Nations in the Modern American West — Fixico, Donald L.
Indian Rope Trick — Jasay, Anthony de
An Indian Social Democracy: Integrating Markets, Democracy and Social Justice, 2 vols. — Khilnani, Sunil
Indians and the Political Economy of Colonial Central America, 1670-1810 — Patch, Robert W.
India's Human Security: Lost Debates, Forgotten People, Intractable Challenges — Miklian, Jason
India's Ocean: The Story of India's Bid for Regional Leadership — Brewster, David
The Indicted South: Public Criticism, Southern Inferiority, and the Politics of Whiteness — Maxwell, Angie
The Indies and the Medieval West: Thought, Report, Imagination — O'Doherty, Marianne
Indigenous Agency in the Amazon: The Mojos in Liberal and Rubber-Boom Bolivia, 1842-1932 — Van Valen, Gary
Indigenous Encounters with Neoliberalism: Place, Women, and the Environment in Canada and Mexico — Altamirano-Jimenez, Isabel
Indigenous Intellectuals: Knowledge, Power, and Colonial Culture in Mexico and the Andes — Ramos, Gabriela
Indigenous Landscapes and Spanish Missions: New Perspectives from Archaeology and Ethnohistory — Panich, Lee
Indigenous Landscapes and Spanish Missions: New Perspectives from Archaeology and Ethnohistory — Panich, Lee M.
An Indigenous Peoples' History of the United States (Read by Merlington, Laural). Audiobook Review — Dunbar-Ortiz, Roxanne
An Indigenous Peoples' History of the United States — Dunbar-Ortiz, Roxanne
Indigenous Women, Work, and History, 1940-1980 — McCallum, Mary Fane Logan
Indigo — Setz, Clemens J.
The Indistinct Human in Renaissance Literature — Feerick, Jean E.
The Individual in the Religions of the Ancient Mediterranean — Rupke, J.
Individuality and Modernity in Berlin: Self and Society from Weimar to the Wall — Follmer, Moritz
Individuality in Late Antiquity — Torrance, Alexis
Individuals and Society in Mycenaean Pylos — Nakassis, Dimitri

Indonesia Etc.: Exploring the Improbable Nation
— Pisani, Elizabeth
The Indrawn Heart: An Estonian Journey — Boyle, Max
The Industrial Diet: The Degradation of Food and the Struggle for Healthy Eating — Winson, Anthony
y The Industrial Revolution in United States History — McCormick, Anita Louise
The Industrial Revolution in World History — Stearns, Peter N.
The Industrial Revolution: Key Themes and Documents — Olson, James S.
The Industries of the Future — Ross, Alec
An Industrious Mind: The Worlds of Sir Simonds D'Ewes — McGee, J. Sears
c Indy Car Racing — Daniel, P.K.
Indy Writes Books: A Book Lovers Anthology — Green, John
Inequality and the 1 Per Cent — Dorling, Danny
Inequality, Education and Social Power
Inequality in the Promised Land: Race, Resources and Suburban Schooling — Lewis-McCoy, R. L'Heureux
Inequality in the Workplace: Labor Market Reform in Japan and Korea — Jiyeoun Song
Inequality in the Workplace: Labor Market Reform in Japan and Korea — Song, Jiyeoun
The Inequality Trap: Fighting Capitalism Instead of Poverty — Watson, William
Inequality: What Can Be Done? — Atkinson, Anthony
Inequality: What Can Be Done? — Atkinson, Anthony B.
An Infamous Army — Heyer, Georgette
Infamy: The Shocking Story of the Japanese American Internment in World War II — Reeves, Richard
y Infandous — Arnold, Elana K.
y Infected — Littlefield, Sophie
Infectious Madness: The Surprising Science of How We "Catch" Mental Illness — Washington, Harriet A.
The Infernal — Doten, Mark
y Inferno — Macauley, Jo
Inferno: An Anatomy of American Punishment — Ferguson, Robert A.
Inferno in Chechnya: The Russian-Chechen Wars, the Al Qaeda Myth, and the Boston Marathon Bombings — Williams, Brian Glyn
Infested: How the Bed Bug Infiltrated Our Bedrooms and Took Over the World — Borel, Brooke
Infidel Kings and Unholy Warriors: Faith, Power, and Violence in the Age of Crusade and Jihad — Catlos, Brian A.
The Infidel Stain — Carter, M.J.
The Infidel Stain — Carter, Miranda J.
The Infiltrator — Mazur, Robert
Infinite Home (Read by Lewis, Christa). Audiobook Review — Alcott, Kathleen
Infinite Home — Alcott, Kathleen
y Infinite in Between (Read by Yuen, Erin). Audiobook Review — Mackler, Carolyn
y Infinite in Between — Mackler, Carolyn
y An Infinite Number of Parallel Universes — Ribay, Randy
The Infinite Sea (Read by Strole, Phoebe, with Ben Yannette). Audiobook Review — Yancey, Rick
y The Infinite Sea — Yancey, Rick
Infinite Worlds: The People and Places of Space Exploration — Soluri, Michael
Infinitesimal: How a Dangerous Mathematical Theory Shaped the Modern World — Alexander, Amir
Infinity Bell — Monk, Devon
y Infinity Coil — Chan, Marty
The Infinity Gauntlet — Starlin, Jim
y Infinity Lost — Harrison, S.
Infiziertes Europa: Seuchen im Langen 20. Jahrhundert — Thiessen, Malte
Inflection Point: How the Convergence of Cloud, Mobility, Apps and Data Will Shape the Future of Business — Stawski, Scott
The Influence Machine: The U.S. Chamber of Commerce and the Corporate Capture of American Life — Katz, Alyssa
Infomaniac: Become an Expert in an Hour (Illus. by Derrick, Stuart)
The Informal and Underground Economy of the South Texas Border — Richardson, Chad
Informal Labor, Formal Politics, and Dignified Discontent in India — Agarwala, Rina
The Informal Post-Socialist Economy: Embedded Practices and Livelihoods — Morris, Jeremy

Information 2.0: New Models of Information Production, Distribution and Consumption — de Saulles, Martin
Information and Intrigue: From Index Cards to Dewey Decimals to Alger Hiss — Burke, Colin B.
Information et opinion publique a toulouse a la fin du moyen age — Nadrigny, Xavier
Information Experience: Approaches to Theory and Practice
Information Governance and Assurance: Reducing Risk, Promoting Policy — MacLennan, Alan
Information Graphics: Space (Illus. by Daniel, Jennifer) — Rogers, Simon
y Information Insecurity: Privacy under Siege — January, Brendan
Information Management for Development Organisations — Powell, Mike
Information Needs Analysis: Principles and Practice in Information Organizations — Dorner, Daniel G.
y Information Now: A Graphic Guide to Student Research — Upson, Matt
Infrared Astronomy--Seeing the Heat: From William Herschel to the Herschel Space Observatory — Clements, David L.
Infrastructure for Asian Connectivity — Bhattacharyay, Biswa Nath
Inga Tells All — Inga
Ingenious Machinists: Two Inventive Lives from the American Industrial Revolution — Connors, Anthony J.
The Ingenious Mr. Pyke: Inventor, Fugitive, Spy — Hemming, Henry
Ingredients: A Visual Exploration of 75 Additives and 25 Food Products — Eschliman, Dwight
y Inherit Midnight — Myers, Kate Kae
Inherit the Holy Mountain: Religion and the Rise of American Environmentalism — Stoll, Mark
y Inherit the Stars — Elwood, Tessa
Inherit the Stars — Peak, Tony
y Inheritance — Forrest, Lisa
y Inheritance — Lo, Malinda
Inheritance: How Our Genes Change Our Lives and Our Lives Change Our Genes — Moalem, Sharon
y An Inheritance of Ashes — Bobet, Leah
Inheritances: Stories — Black, William
The Inheritors — Golding, William
Inhuman Citizenship: Traumatic Enjoyment and Asian American Literature — Chang, Juliana
Inhuman Nature — Cohen, Jeffrey Jerome
The Initiatory Path in Fairy Tales: The Alchemical Secrets of Mother Goose — Roger, Bernard
Injustice — Goodman, Lee
Injustice: Why Social Inequality Still Persists — Dorling, Danny
Injustices: The Supreme Court's History of Comforting the Comfortable and Afflicting the Afflicted — Millhiser, Ian
y Ink and Ashes — Maetani, Valynne E.
y Ink and Bone — Caine, Rachel
c Inkblot: Drip, Splat, and Squish Your Way to Creativity (Illus. by Peot, Margaret) — Peot, Margaret
y Inked. E-book Review — Smith, Eric
y The Inker's Shadow (Illus. by Say, Allen) — Say, Allen
Inking the Borders of Heaven and Hell: The Art of Ramon Maiden — Maiden, Ramon
y Inland — Rosenfield, Kat
c Inline Skating — Hamilton, John
The Inn at Ocean's Edge — Coble, Colleen
c The Inn Between — Cohen, Marina
Innenansichten - Deutschland 1945
Inner City Romance — Colwell, Guy
The Inner Lives of Medieval Inquisitors — Sullivan, Karen
Inner Messiah, Divine Character: Narrative Approaches to Be beyond Best — Yosef, Benjamin
Innocence — Barnes, Julian
Innocence, or, Murder on Steep Street — Kovaly, Heda Margolius
y Innocent — Walters, Eric
The Innocent and the Criminal Justice System: A Sociological Analysis of Miscarriages of Justice — Naughton, Michael
Innocent Blood — Lister, Michael
Innocent Damage — Lewis, Robert K.
The Innocent Eye: Why Vision Is Not a Cognitive Process — Orlandi, Nico
The Innocent — Gabhart, Ann H.
Innocent Weapons: The Soviet and American Politics of Childhood in the Cold War — Peacock, Margaret

Innocents and Others — Spiotta, Dana
Innovating Minds: Rethinking Creativity to Inspire Change — Koutstaal, Wilma
Innovating Out of Crisis: How Fujifilm Survived (and Thrived) as Its Core Business Was Vanishing — Komori, Shigetaka
Innovation Judo: Disarming Roadblocks and Blockheads on the Path to Creativity — Thornberry, Neal
Innovations in Refugee Protection: A Compendium of UNHCR's 60 Years. Including Case Studies on IT Communities, Vietnamese Boatpeople, Chilean Exile and Namibian Repatriation — Druke, Luise
Innovative Methods of Marine Ecosystem Restoration — Goreau, Thomas J.
The Innovators: How a Group of Hackers, Geniuses, and Geeks Created the Digital Revolution (Read by Boutsikaris, Dennis). Audiobook Review — Isaacson, Walter
The Innovators: How a Group of Hackers, Geniuses, and Geeks Created the Digital Revolution — Isaacson, Walter
The Innovator's Hypothesis: How Cheap Experiments are Worth More than Good Ideas — Schrage, Michael
Inquisition in Early Islam: The Competition for Political and Religious Authority in the Abbasid Empire — Turner, John P.
The Inquisitor in the Hat Shop: Inquisition, Forbidden Books and Unbelief in Early Modern Venice — Barbierato, Federico
Inquisitoren-Handbuher: Papsturkunden und juristische Gutachten aus dem 13. Jahrhundert mit Edition des Consilium von Guido Fulcodii — Bivolarov, Vasil
c The Inquisitor's Mark — Salerni, Dianne K.
The Insect Farm — Prebble, Stuart
Insect Molecular Genetics: An Introduction to Principles and Applications — Hoy, Marjorie A.
Insect Resistance Management: Biology, Economics, and Prediction — Onstad, David W.
c Insects — Morey, Allan
c Insects Close Up Series
Inside a Pearl: My Years in Paris — White, Edmund
Inside a Silver Box — Mosley, Walter
y Inside Biosphere 2: Earth Science under Glass (Illus. by Uhlman, Tom) — Carson, Mary Kay
Inside Concentration Camps: Social Life at the Extremes — Suderland, Maja
Inside My Own Skin — Fonclare, Guillaume de
Inside Newark: Decline, Rebellion, and the Search for Transformation — Curvin, Robert
c Inside of a Dog — Horowitz, Alexandra
Inside Out — Riley, Lia
c Inside Out Series — Brow, James
The Inside-Outside Book of London — Munro, Roxie
Inside Paradise Lost: Reading the Designs of Milton's Epic — Quint, David
Inside Reagan's Navy: The Pentagon Journals — Untermeyer, Chase
Inside South Africa's Foreign Policy: Diplomacy in Africa from Smuts to Mbeki — Siko, John
Inside Syria — Erlich, Reese
Inside the Bloody Chamber: Aspects of Angela Carter — Frayling, Christopher
Inside the Brotherhood — Kandil, Hazem
Inside the Cell: The Dark Side of Forensic DNA — Murphy, Erin E.
Inside the Cell: The Dark Side of Forensic DNA (Illus. by Murphy, Erin E.) — Murphy, Erin E.
Inside the Crystal Ball: How to Make and Use Forecasts — Harris, Maury
Inside the Dream Palace: The Life and Times of New York's Legendary Chelsea Hotel — Tippins, Sherill
Inside the Head of Bruno Schulz — Biller, Maxim
Inside the Jesuits: How Pope Francis is Changing the Church and the World — Kaiser, Robert Blair
Inside the Machine: Art and Invention in the Electronic Age — Prelinger, Megan
Inside the Miracle: Enduring Suffering, Approaching Wholeness — Nepo, Mark
Inside the O'Briens (Read by Sudduth, Skipp). Audiobook Review — Genova, Lisa
Inside the O'Briens — Genova, Lisa
Inside the Rise of HBO: A Personal History of the Company That Transformed Television — Mesce, Bill, Jr.
c Inside This Book (Are Three Books). (Illus. by Saltzberg, Barney) — Saltzberg, Barney
The Insider Threat — Taylor, Brad
Insights: How Expert Principals Make Difficult Decisions — McLaughlin, Dionne V.

Insignia of Rank in the Nahua World: From the Fifteenth to the Seventeenth Century — *Olko, Justyna*
The Insistence of God: A Theology of Perhaps — *Caputo, John D.*
Insomnia — *Vaughn, R.M.*
Insomnia: Poems — *Pastan, Linda*
Inspector Abberline and the Gods of Rome — *Clark, Simon (b. 1958-)*
y Inspector of the Dead — *Morrell, David*
The Inspiration and Interpretation of Scripture: What the Early Church Can Teach Us — *Graves, Michael*
Inspired Baby Names from around the World: 6,000 International Names and the Meaning behind Them — *Shane, Neala*
Inspired: The Holy Spirit and the Mind of Faith — *Levison, Jack*
Inspiring Teaching: Preparing Teachers to Succeed in Mission-Driven Schools — *Feiman-Nemser, Sharon*
y Instant Frontier Family — *Scott, Regina*
y Instinct — *Kenyon, Sherrilyn*
Institutional Trust and Economic Policy: Lessons from the History of the Euro — *Gyorffy, Dora*
Institutionen der Erinnerung
Instructions for Breathing and Other Plays — *Svich, Caridad*
y Instructions for the End of the World — *Kain, Jamie*
Instrumental: A Memoir of Madness, Medication and Music — *Rhodes, James*
Insufficient Funds: The Culture of Money in Low-Wage Transnational Families — *Thai, Hung Cam*
Insurgency and Counterinsurgency in South Asia: Through a Peacebuilding Lens — *Yusuf, Moeed*
The Insurgency Trap: Labor Politics in Postsocialist China — *Friedman, Eli*
Insuring the City: The Prudential Center and the Postwar Urban Landscap — *Rubin, Elihu*
Intacti saltus: Studi sull III libro delle Georgiche — *Pieri, Bruna*
Intangiball: The Subtle Things That Win Baseball Games — *Wheeler, Lonnie*
Integrated Justice and Equality — *Teevan, John Addison*
Integrating Pedagogy and Technology: Improving Teaching and Learning in Higher Education — *Bernauer, James A.*
Integrating Varieties of Capitalism and Welfare State Research: A United Typology of Capitalisms — *Schroder, Martin*
Integration in Ireland: The Everyday Lives of African Migrants — *Murphy, Fiona*
Integration Nation: Immigrants, Refugees, and America at Its Best — *Eaton, Susan E.*
Integration: The Power of Being Co-Active in Work and Life — *Betz, Ann*
Integrative Men's Health — *Spar, Myles O.*
Integrative Organismal Biology — *Martin, Lynn B.*
Intellectual Authority and Literary Culture in the U.S., 1790-1900 — *Leypoldt, Gunter*
Intellectual Freedom for Teens: A Practical Guide for Young Adult and School Librarians — *Fletcher-Spear, Kristen*
Intellectual Freedom Manual, 9th ed. — *Magi, Trina*
Intellectual History: Traditions and Perspectives
The Intellectual Journey of Thomas Berry: Imagining the Earth Community — *Eaton, Heather*
The Intellectual Life of Edmund Burke: From the Sublime and Beautiful to American Independence — *Bromwich, David*
Intellectual Traditions at the Medieval University: The Use of Philosophical Psychology in Trinitarian Theology among the Franciscans and Dominicans, 1250-1350, 2 vols. — *Friedman, Russell L.*
Intellectuals Journey: The Translation of Ideas in Enlightenment England, France and Ireland
Intellettuali in esilio: Dall'inquisizione romana al fascismo — *Caravale, Giorgio*
Intelligence in the Flesh: Why Your Mind Needs Your Body Much More Than it Thinks — *Claxton, Guy*
An Intelligent Life: Buddhist Psychology of Self-Transformation — *Yokoyama, Koitsu*
An Intelligent Person's Guide to Education — *Little, Tony*
Intelligent Sentient? — *Ramsey, Luke*
Intelligently Designed: How Creationists Built the Campaign against Evolution — *Caudill, Edward*
Intende, Lector: Echoes of Myth, Religion and Ritual in the Ancient Novel — *Pinheiro, Futre*
Intentional — *Arbor, Lynn*

Intentional Talk: How to Structure and Lead Productive Mathematical Discussions — *Kazemi, Elham*
Inter Omnes Plato Et Aristoteles: Gli Appunti Filosofici Di Girolamo Savonarola: Introduzione, Edizione Critica E Commento — *Tromboni, Lorenza*
Interacting with History: Teaching with Primary Sources — *Lehman, Katherine*
Interacting with Informational Text for Close and Critical Reading — *Erfourth, Jill*
Interactions of Monetary Policy and Central Bank Governance: Modern Monetary Policy and Central Bank Governance — *Eijffinger, Sylvester C.W.*
Interactions with a Violent Past: Reading Post-Conflict Landscapes in Cambodia, Lao, and Vietnam — *Pholsena, Vatthana*
Intercept: The Secret History of Computers and Spies — *Corera, Gordon*
Interconnections: Gender and Race in American History — *Faulkner, Carol*
Interculturalism: The New Era of Cohesion and Diversity — *Cantle, Ted*
Interdisciplinarity: Reconfigurations of the Social and Natural Sciences — *Barry, Andrew*
Interdisciplinary Interpretation: Paul Ricoeur and the Hermeneutics of Theology and Science — *Reynhout, Kenneth A.*
Interesting: My Autobiography — *Davis, Steve*
Interfaith Just Peacemaking: Jewish, Christian, and Muslim Perspectives on the New Paradigm of Peace and War — *Thistlethwaite, Susan Brooks*
Interior Darkness — *Straub, Peter*
Interior Landmarks: Treasures of New York — *Gura, Judith*
Interlock: Art, Conspiracy, and the Shadow Worlds of Mark Lombardi — *Goldstone, Patricia*
Interlopers of Empire: The Lebanese Diaspora in Colonial French West Africa — *Arsan, Andrew*
Internal Colonization: Russia's Imperial Experience — *Etkind, Alexander*
The Internal Enemy: Slavery and War in Virginia, 1772-1832 — *Taylor, Alan*
Internal Medicine — *Holt, Terrence*
International Bohemia: Scenes of Nineteenth-Century Life — *Cottom, Daniel*
International Business Expansion: A Step-by-Step Guide to Launch Your Company into Other Countries — *Gioeli, Anthony*
International Congresses and World History: CISH and NOGWHISTO, August 2015
International Crime in the 20th Century: The League of Nations Era, 1919-1939 — *Knepper, Paul*
The International Distribution of News: The Associated Press, Press Association, and Reuters, 1848-1947 — *Silberstein-Loeb, Jonathan*
The International Encyclopedia of Digital Communication and Society, 3 vols. — *Mansell, Robina*
International Legitimacy and the Politics of Security: The Strategic Deployment of Lawmakers in the Israeli Military — *Craig, Alan*
International Mediation Bias and Peacemaking: Taking Sides in Civil Wars — *Svensson, Isak*
The International Novel — *Patterson, Annabel*
International Organizations and Internal Conditionality: Making Norms Matter — *Fawn, Rick*
International Perspectives on Accounting and Corporate Behavior — *Ito, Kuno*
International Relations since the End of the Cold War: New and Old Dimensions — *Lundestad, Geir*
International Seafarers and Transnationalism in the Twenty-first Century — *Sampson, Helen*
International Security, Political Crime, and Resistance: The Transnationalisation of Normative Orders and the Formation of Criminal Law Regimes in the 19th and 20th Century
International Symposium Multidisciplinary Methods in Archaeology: Latest Updates and Outlook
Internationale Tagung: Der Brief in Seinem Umfeld
Internationalism in Children's Series — *Sands-O'Connor, Karen*
Internationalism in the Age of Nationalism — *Sluga, Glenda*
The Internet in China: Cultural, Political, and Social Dimensions, 1980s-2000s — *Esarey, Ashley*
The Internet Is Not the Answer — *Keen, Andrew*
Internet Literature in China — *Hockx, Michel*
The Internet of Things — *Greengard, Samuel*
The Internet of Us — *Lynch, Michael Patrick*
Interpreting AristotleEs Posterior Analytics in Late Antiquity and Beyond — *Haas, Frans A.J. de*

Interpreting Clifford Geertz: Cultural Investigation in the Social Sciences — *Alexander, Jeffrey C.*
Interpreting Dante: Essays on the Traditions of Dante Commentary — *Nasti, Paola*
Interpreting LGBT History at Museums and Historic Sites — *Ferentinos, Susan*
Interpreting Proclus: From Antiquity to the Renaissance — *Gersh, Stephen*
Interpreting Quantum Theories — *Ruetsche, Laura*
Interpreting the Ancien Regime — *Bien, David*
Interpreting the English Village: Landscape and Community at Shapwick, Somerset — *Aston, Mick*
Interpreting the Peace: Peace Operations, Conflict and Language in Bosnia-Herzegovina — *Kelly, Michael*
Interpreting the Prophets: Reading, Understanding, and Preaching from the Worlds of the Prophets — *Chalmers, Aaron*
Interpretive Planning for Museums: Integrating Visitor Perspectives in Decision Making — *Wells, Marcella*
Interrelations between Essential Metal Ions and Human Diseases — *Sigel, Helmut*
Interreligious Hermeneutics and the Pursuit of Truth — *Hustwit, J.R.*
The Interstellar Age: Inside the Forty-Year Voyager Mission. — *Bell, Jim*
c Interstellar Cinderella (Illus. by Hunt, Meg) — *Underwood, Deborah*
The Intervals of Cinema — *Ranciere, Jacques*
The Interwoven Lives of Sigmund, Anna and W. Ernest Freud: Three Generations of Psychoanalysis — *Benveniste, Daniel*
Intimacies: A New World of Relational Life — *Frank, Alan*
Intimacy Idiot — *Oliver, Isaac*
Intimate — *Douglas, Kate*
Intimate Activism: The Struggle for Sexual Rights in Postrevolutionary Nicaragua — *Howe, Cymene*
The Intimate Bond: How Animals Shaped Human History — *Fagan, Brian*
Intimate Indigeneities: Race, Sex, and History in the Small Spaces of Andean Life — *Canessa, Andrew*
Intimate Reconstructions: Children in Postemancipation Virginia — *Jones, Catherine A.*
Intimate Rivals: Japanese Domestic Politics and a Rising China — *Smith, Sheila A.*
y Into a Million Pieces — *Cook, Angela V.*
Into Daylight — *Harrison, Jeffrey*
Into Disaster: Chronicles of Intellectual Life, 1941 — *Holland, Michael*
Into Focus: An Exhibitionist's Show & Tell-All — *Arrow, Cameron*
Into New Territory: American Historians and the Concept of US Imperialism — *Morgan, James G.*
Into Oblivion — *Indridason, Arnaldur*
Into the Blizzard: Walking the Fields of the Newfoundland Dead — *Winter, Michael*
y Into the Dangerous World (Illus. by Sovak, Jean-Marc Superville) — *Chibbaro, Julie*
y Into the Dark — *Patti, Caroline T.*
y Into the Dim HMH — *Taylor, Janet B.*
c Into the Dorkness (Illus. by Edwards, Nick) — *Kloepfer, John*
Into the Fire: Disaster and the Remaking of Gender — *Pacholok, Shelley*
Into the Forest — *Danielewski, Mark Z.*
Into the Fury — *Martin, Kat*
y Into the Grey — *Kierman, Celine*
Into the Heart of Our World: A Journey to the Center of the Earth; A Remarkable Voyage of Scientific Discovery — *Whitehouse, David*
c Into the Killing Seas — *Spradlin, Michael P.*
Into the Maelstrom — *Drake, David*
Into the Magic Shop: A Neurosurgeon's Quest to Discover the Mysteries of the Brain and the Secrets of the Heart — *Doty, James R.*
Into the Nest: Intimate Views of the Courting, Parenting, and Family Lives of Familiar Birds — *Erickson, Laura*
Into the Night: Tales of Nocturnal Wildlife Expeditions — *Adams, Rick A.*
Into the Open: 1990 - The First Year of Transition
Into the Realm of Time — *Prill, Scott Douglas*
Into the Savage Country — *Burke, Shannon*
c Into the Snow (Illus. by Saito, Masamitsu) — *Kaneko, Yuki*
Into the Valley — *Galm, Ruth*
y Into the Wasteland — *Choyce, Lesley*
Intro to Alien Invasion (Illus. by Ahn, Nancy) — *King, Owen*
Intro to Alien Invasion — *King, Owen*

Introducing Christian Mission Today: Scripture, History, and Issues — *Goheen, Michael W.*
Introducing English Medieval Book History: Manuscripts, their Producers and their Readers — *Hanna, Ralph*
c Introducing Mr. B.: The Battle Collection: Four Short Stories Inspired by Robert Burns Poems (Illus. by Lennox, Nicholas) — *Thomson, Norman*
c Introducing Mr. B.: The Farmer Collection: Four Short Stories Inspired by Robert Burns Poems (Illus. by Lennox, Nicholas) — *Thomson, Norman*
c Introducing Mr. B.: The Friends Collection: Four Short Stories Inspired by Robert Burns Poems (Illus. by Lennox, Nicholas) — *Thomson, Norman*
Introducing the Ancient Greeks: From Bronze Age Seafarers to Navigators of the Western Mind — *Hall, Edith*
Introducing World Religions: A Christian Engagement — *Farhadian, Charles E.*
Introduction to a True History of Cinema and Television — *Godard, Jean-Luc*
An Introduction to Agent-Based Modeling: Modeling Natural, Social, and Engineered Complex Systems with NetLogo — *Wilensky, Uri*
An Introduction to Design Arguments — *Jantzen, Benjamin C.*
Introduction to Finite and Spectral Element Methods Using MATLAB — *Pozrikidis, Constantine*
Introduction to General Relativity, Black Holes, and Cosmology — *Choquet-Bruhat, Yvonne*
Introduction to Global Missions — *Pratt, Zane*
Introduction to Global Optimization Exploiting Space-Filling Curves — *Sergeyev, Yaroslav D.*
An Introduction to International Migration Studies: European Perspectives — *Martiniello, Marco*
Introduction to Islam: Beliefs and Practices in Historical Perspective — *Hillenbrand, Carole*
An Introduction to Lightning — *Cooray, Vernon*
y Introduction to Literary Context: Plays — *Salem Press*
An Introduction to Military Ethics: A Reference Handbook — *Rhodes, Bill*
Introduction to Mycology in the Tropics — *Piepenbring, Meike*
An Introduction to Phytoplanktons: Diversity and Ecology — *Pal, Ruma*
Introduction to Policing: The Pillar of Democracy — *Haberfeld, M.R.*
An Introduction to Practical Laboratory Optics — *James, John Francis*
Introduction to Probability and Statistics for Ecosystem Managers: Simulation and Resampling — *Haas, Timothy C.*
Introduction to Programming in Python — *Sedgewick, Roger*
Introduction to Research and Medical Literature, 4th ed. — *Forister, J. Glenn*
An Introduction to the Chansons de Geste: New Perspectives on Medieval Literature--Authors and Traditions — *Jones, Catherine M.*
An Introduction to the Chansons de Geste — *Jones, Catherine M.*
An Introduction to the Medieval Bible — *van Liere, Frans*
An Introduction to the Philosophy of Art — *Eldridge, Richard*
The Introvert Entrepreneur: Amplify Your Strengths and Create Success On Your Own Terms — *Buelow, Beth L.*
The Intruder — *Norlen, Paul*
The Intruder — *Ostlundh, Hakan*
The Intuitive Parent: Why the Best Thing for Your Child Is You — *Camarata, Stephen*
c An Inuksuk Means Welcome (Illus. by Wallace, Mary) — *Wallace, Mary*
c Inundacion — *Greenlaw, M. Jean*
y Invaded — *Landers, Melissa*
The Invaded: How Latin Americans and their Allies Fought and Ended U.S. Occupations — *McPherson, Alan L.*
The Invaders — *Waclawiak, Karolina*
The Invaders: How Humans and Their Dogs Drove Neanderthals to Extinction — *Shipman, Pat*
Invasion of Laos, 1971: Lam Son 719 — *Sander, Robert D.*
Invasion of Privacy (Read by Michael, Paul). Audiobook Review — *Reich, Christopher*
Invasion of Privacy — *Reich, Christopher*
c Invasion of the Overworld — *Cheverton, Mark*
Invasion of the Tearling (Read by Porter, Davina). Audiobook Review — *Johansen, Erika*
The Invasion of the Tearling — *Johansen, Erika*

Invasive Species in a Globalized World: Ecological, Social and Legal Perspectives on Policy — *Keller, Reuben P.*
Invasive Species: What Everyone Needs to Know — *Simberloff, Daniel*
Invented by Law: Alexander Graham Bell and the Patent That Changed America — *Beauchamp, Christopher*
Inventing a Christian America: The Myth of the Religious Founding — *Green, Steven K.*
Inventing a Path: Studies in Medieval Rhetoric in Honour of Mary Carruthers — *Iseppi De Filippis, Laura*
Inventing American Religion: Polls, Surveys, and the Tenuous Quest for a Nation's Faith — *Wuthnow, Robert*
Inventing Custer: The Making of an American Legend — *Caudill, Edward*
Inventing Eden: Primitivism, Millennialism, and the Making of New England — *Hutchins, Zachary McLeod*
Inventing Eleanor: The Medieval and Post-Medieval Image of Eleanor of Aquitaine — *Evans, Michael R.*
Inventing Ethan Allen — *Duffy, John J.*
Inventing Exoticism: Geography, Globalism, and Europe's Early Modern World — *Schmidt, Benjamin*
Inventing Late Night: Steve Allen and the Original Tonight Show — *Alba, Ben*
Inventing Sempringham: Gilbert of Sempringham and the Origins of the Role of the Master — *Sykes, Katharine*
Inventing Stanley Park: An Environmental History — *Kheraj, Sean*
Inventing the Individual: The Origins of Western Liberalism — *Siedentop, Larry*
Inventing the Spectator: Subjectivity and the Theatrical Experience in Early Modern France — *Harris, Joseph*
Inventing the Way of the Samurai: Nationalism, Internationalism, and Bushido in Modern Japan — *Benesch, Oleg*
The Invention of a European Development Aid Bureaucracy: Recycling Empire — *Dimier, Veronique*
The Invention of Fire — *Holsinger, Bruce*
The Invention of God — *Romer, Thomas*
The Invention of Improvement: Information and Material Progress in Seventeenth-Century England — *Slack, Paul*
The Invention of Nature: Alexander von Humboldt's New World — *Wulf, Andrea*
The Invention of Nature: The Adventures of Alexander von Humboldt, the Lost Hero of Science — *Wulf, Andrea*
The Invention of News: How the World Came to Know about Itself — *Pettegree, Andrew*
The Invention of Peter: Apostolic Discourse and Papal Authority in Late Antiquity — *Demacopoulos, George E.*
The Invention of Religion in Japan — *Josephson, Jason*
The Invention of Science: A New History of the Scientific Revolution — *Wootton, David*
Invention of Space: City Travel Literature — *Enric, Bou*
The Invention of Wings (Read by Lamia, Jenna). Audiobook Review — *Kidd, Sue Monk*
y Inventions and Discoveries of People of Color: Prehistoric to Today — *Gilchrist, Kelvin K.*
c Inventions That Could Have Changed the World ... But Didn't! (Illus. by Owsley, Anthony) — *Rhatigan, Joe*
Inventive Weaving on a Little Loom: Discover the Full Potential of the Rigid-Heddle Loom, for Beginners and Beyond — *Mitchell, Syne*
Inventology: How We Dream Up Things That Change the World — *Kennedy, Pagan*
c The Inventor's Secret: What Thomas Edison Told Henry Ford (Illus. by Reinhardt, Jennifer Black) — *Slade, Suzanne*
Inverse Infrastructures: Disrupting Networks from Below — *Egyedi, Tineke M.*
y Investigate Alcohol — *Ambrose, Marylou*
y Investigate Club Drugs — *Eldridge, Alison*
y Investigate Cocaine and Crack — *Ambrose, Marylou*
y Investigate Methamphetamine — *Ambrose, Marylou*
y Investigate Steroids and Performance Drugs — *Latta, Sara L.*
Investigating Adolescent Health Communication: A Corpus Linguistics Approach — *Harvey, Kevin*

y Investigating Ghosts and the Spirit World — *Henneberg, Susan*
The Investigation — *Kim, Chi-Young*
The Investigation — *Lee, J.M.*
An Investigation into Early Desert Pastoralism: Excavations at the Camel Site, Negev — *Rosen, Steven A.*
y Invincible — *Reed, Amy*
c The Invinsible — *Kahaney, Amelia*
c InvisiBill (Illus. by Petricic, Dusan) — *Fergus, Maureen*
Invisible Beasts: Tales of the Animals That Go Unseen among Us — *Muir, Sharona*
The Invisible Bridge (Read by de Vries, David). Audiobook Review — *Perlstein, Rick*
The Invisible Bridge — *Perlstein, Rick*
Invisible Chains: Overcoming Coercive Control in Your Intimate Relationship — *Fontes, Lisa Aronson*
Invisible City — *Dahl, Julia*
y Invisible Girl — *Hemingway, Mariel*
The Invisible History of the Human Race: How DNA and History Shape Our Identities and Our Futures — *Kenneally, Christine*
Invisible Immigrants: The English in Canada since 1945 — *Barber, Marilyn*
Invisible in Austin: Life and Labor in an American City — *Auyero, Javier*
Invisible Ink: My Mother's Secret Love Affair with a Famous Cartoonist — *Griffith, Bill*
c The Invisible Kingdom (Illus. by Ryan, Rob) — *Ryan, Rob*
Invisible Love — *Schmitt, Eric-Emmanuel*
Invisible Men: Mass Incarceration and the Myth of Black Progress — *Pettit, Becky*
y Invisible Monsters — *McCune, Joshua*
Invisible Population: The Place of the Dead in East Asian Megacities — *Aveline-Dubach, Natacha*
Invisible Streets — *Ball, Toby*
Invisible: The Dangerous Allure of the Unseen — *Ball, Philip*
c An Invisible Thread Christmas Story (Illus. by Root, Barry) — *Schroff, Laura*
Invisible Threads — *Beresford, Lucy*
The Invisibles — *Holland, Jesse J.*
y The Invisibles — *Galante, Cecilia*
An Invitation for Me to Think — *Vvedensky, Alexander*
The Invitation-Only Zone: The True Story of North Korea's Abduction Project — *Boynton, Robert S.*
Invitation to the Psalms: A Reader's Guide for Discovery and Engagement — *Jacobson, Rolf A.*
An Invitation to Think and Feel Differently in the New Millennium — *Bury, Harry J.*
Invitations from Afar — *King, Linda A.W.*
iOS for Game Programmers — *Sherrod, Allen*
iPad for Dummies — *Baig, Edward C.*
y iPad in Education for Dummies — *Gliksman, Sam*
The iPhone Photographer: How to Take Professional Photographs with Your iPhone — *Fagans, Michael*
iPhoneOnly — *Calverley, Julian*
c iPod and Electronics Visionary Tony Fadell — *Suen, Anastasia*
Iran: A Very Short Introduction — *Ansari, Ali*
Iran between Islamic Nationalism and Secularism: The Constitutional Revolution of 1906 — *Martin, Vanessa*
Iran-Contra: Reagan's Scandal and the Unchecked Abuse of Presidential Power — *Byrne, Malcolm*
The Iran-Iraq War: A Military and Strategic History — *Murray, Williamson*
The Iranian Talmud: Reading the Tavli in Its Sasanian Context — *Secunda, Shai*
Iraq: A History — *Robertson, John*
Iraq in Wartime: Soldiering, Martyrdom, and Remembrance — *Khoury, Dina Rizk*
The Iraqi Novel: Key Writers, Key Texts — *Cobham, Catherine*
c Ira's Shakespeare Dream (Illus. by Cooper, Floyd) — *Armand, Glenda*
c The Ire of Iron Claw (Illus. by Hamilton, James) — *Hamilton, Kersten*
Ireland, Africa, and the End of Empire: Small State Identity in the Cold War, 1955-75 — *O'Sullivan, Kevin*
Ireland and the Irish in Interwar England — *Moulton, Mo*
Ireland in Official Print Culture, 1800-1850: A New Reading of the Poor Inquiry — *O Ciosain, Niall*
Ireland in the Medieval World AD 400-1000: Landscape, Kingship, and Religion — *Bhreathnach, Edel*

Ireland in the Virginian Sea: Colonialism in the British Atlantic — Horning, Audrey
Ireland's Western Islands: Inishbofin, the Aran Islands, Inishturk, Inishark, Clare and Turbot Islands — Carlos, John
Irenaeus of Lyons: Identifying Christianity — Behr, John
c Irene's Wish (Illus. by Ford, A.G.) — Nolen, Jerdine
c The Iridescence of Birds: A Book about Henri Matisse (Illus. by Hooper, Hadley) — MacLachlan, Patricia
The Iris Fan (Read by Dunnem, Bernadette). Audiobook Review — Rowland, Laura Jon
y Iris the Colorful — Holub, Joan
Irish Americans: The History and Culture of a People — Watson, William E.
Irish Blood — Sullivan, Brendan Sean
The Irish Brotherhood: John F. Kennedy, His Inner Circle and the Improbable Rise to the Presidency — O'Donnell, Helen
Irish Catholicism and Science: From Godless Colleges to the Celtic Tiger — O'Leary, Don
Irish Classrooms and British Empire: Imperial Contexts in the Origins of Modern Education — Dickson, David
The Irish Countrywomen's Association Book of Crafts: 40 Projects To Make at Home — Irish Countrywomen's Association
An Irish Doctor in Love and at Sea — Taylor, Patrick
The Irish Garden — Powers, Jane
The Irish Hand: Scribes and their Manuscripts from the Earliest Times — O'Neill, Timothy
The Irish in the Spanish Armies in the Seventeenth Century — de Mesa, Eduardo
Irish London: Middle-Class Migration in the Global Eighteenth Century — Bailey, Craig
The Irish New Woman — O'Toole, Tina
Irish Officers in the British Forces, 1922-1945 — O'Connor, Steven
The Irish Parliamentary Party and the Third Home Rule Crisis — McConnel, James
Irish Political Prisoners, 1920-1962: Pilgrimage of Desolation — McConville, Sean
Irish Socialist Republicanism, 1906-36 — Grant, Adrian
An Irish-Speaking Island: State, Religion, Community, and the Linguistic Landscape in Ireland, 1770-1870 — Wolf, Nicholas M.
The Irish Times: 150 Years of Influence — Brown, Terence
Irish Women Dramatists, 1908-2001 — Kearney, Eileen
Irish Women's Fiction: From Edgeworth to Enright — Ingman, Heather
Iron Age America before Columbus — Conner, William D.
The Iron Assassin — Greenwood, Ed
y The Iron Golem — Page, Christian
c Iron Hearted Violet — Barnhill, Kelly
Iron Lazar: A Political Biography of Lazar Kaganovich — Rees, E.A.
The Iron Princess: Amalia Elisabeth and the Thirty Years War — Helfferich, Tryntje
y Iron Rails, Iron Men, and the Race to Link the Nation: The Story of the Transcontinental Railroad — Sandler, Martin W.
Iron & Rust — Sidebottom, Harry
The Iron Sickle — Limon, Martin
The Iron Trial (Read by Boehmer, Paul). Audiobook Review — Black, Holly
y The Iron Trial (Illus. by Fischer, Scott) — Black, Holly
Iron Wolf — Brown, Dale
y Irona 700 — Duncan, Dave
c The Iroquois — Lomberg, Michelle
The Iroquois and the Athenians: A Political Ontology — Seitz, Brian
Irrational Exuberance — Shiller, Robert J.
Irrational Judgments: Eva Hesse, Sol LeWitt, and 1960s New York — Swenson, Kirsten
Irregular Migrant Domestic Workers in Europe: Who Cares? — Triandafyllidou, Anna
Irregular Migration and Invisible Welfare — Ambrosini, Maurizio
Irrelationship: How We Use Dysfunctional Relationships to Hide From Intimacy — Borg, Mark B.
An Irrepressible Conflict: The Empire State in the Civil War — Weible, Robert
Irrepressible: The Jazz Age Life of Henrietta Bingham — Bingham, Emily
The Irresistible Rogue — Bowman, Valerie

Irritable Hearts: A PTSD Love Story — McClelland, Mac
c Is a Bald Eagle Really Bald? (Illus. by Conger, Holli) — Rustad, Martha E.H.
c Is Atlantis Real? — Lassieur, Allison
Is Enough Being Done to Protect Athletes from Concussions? — Wilcox, Christine
Is Fat Bob Dead Yet? — Dobyns, Stephen
Is Gwyneth Paltrow Wrong about Everything?: How the Famous Sell Us Exilers of Health, Beauty & Happiness — Caulfield, Timothy
c Is It Hanukkah Yet? (Illus. by Psacharopulo, Alessandra) — Barash, Chris
Is It My Body? Selected Texts — Gordon, Kim
c Is It Passover Yet? (Illus. by Psacharopulo, Alessandra) — Barash, Chris
Is Legalized Marijuana Good for Society? — Netzley, Patricia D.
c Is Mommy? (Illus. by Frazee, Marla) — Chang, Victoria
Is Shame Necessary? New Uses for an Old Tool
Is Shame Necessary? New Uses for an Old Tool — Jacquet, Jennifer
Is Spain Different?: A Comparative Look at the 19th & 20th Centuries — Townson, Nigel
c Is That a Cat? (Illus. by Hamilton, Tim) — Hamilton, Tim
Is That All There Is?: The Strange Life of Peggy Lee — Gavin, James
Is the American Century Over? — Nye, Joseph S.
c Is the Bermuda Triangle Real? — Lassieur, Allison
c Is the Loch Ness Monster Real? — Lassieur, Allison
c Is There a Dog in This Book? (Illus. by Schwarz, Viviane) — Schwarz, Viviane
c Is There an App for That? Hailey Discovers Happiness through Self-Acceptance (Illus. by Wish, Katia) — Smith, Bryan
Is This America? Katrina as Cultural Trauma — Eyerman, Ron
y Isaac Asimov — Wolny, Philip
Isaac Beeckman on Matter and Motion: Mechanical Philosophy in the Making — Berkel, Klaas van
c Isaac Newton: Genius Mathematician and Physicist — Mooney, Carla
Isabel Allende's House of the Spirits Trilogy: Narrative Geographies — Martin, Karen Wooley
c Isabel Feeney: Star Reporter — Fantaskey, Beth
y Isabelle Day Refuses to Die of a Broken Heart — St. Anthony, Jane
c Ishmael: The Shepherd Boy of Bethlehem — d'Abbadie, Joelle
Ishmael's Oranges — Hjaj, Claire
ISIS Exposed: Beheadings, Slavery, and the Hellish Reality of Radical Islam — Stakelbeck, Erick
ISIS: Inside the Army of Terror — Weiss, Michael
ISIS: The State of Terror — Berger, J.M.
ISIS: The State of Terror — Stern, Jessica
y Isla and the Happily Ever After — Perkins, Stephanie
Islam and Assisted Reproductive Technologies: Sunni and Shia Perspectives — Inhorn, Marcia C.
Islam and Democracy after the Arab Spring — Sonn, Tamara
Islam and Literalism: Literal Meaning and Interpretation in Islamic Legal Theory — Gleave, Robert
Islam and Nazi Germany's War — Motadel, David
Islam and Public Controversy in Europe — Gole, Nilufer
Islam and the Fate of Others: The Salvation Question — Khalil, Mohammad Hassan
Islam and the Future of Tolerance: A Dialogue — Harris, Sam
Islam and the Making of the Nation: Kartosuwiryo and Political Islam in 20th Century Indonesia — Formichi, Chiara
Islam, Christianity, and the Making of Czech Identity, 1453-1683 — Lisy-Wagner, Laura
Islam in Europe, Revolts in the Middle East: Islamism and Genocide from Wilhelm II and Enver Pasha through Hitler and Husseini to Arafat, Usama bin Laden, and Ahmadinejad, along with Discussions with Bernard Lewis — Schwanitz, Wolfgang G.
Islam in the Balance: Ideational Threats in Arab Politics — Rubin, Lawrence
Islam Is a Foreign Country: American Muslims and the Global Crisis of Authority — Grewal, Zareena
Islam Is a Foreign Country — Chaudhry, Ayesha S.
Islam, Peace and Social Justice: A Christian Perspective — van Gorder, A. Christian
Islamic Fashion and Anti-Fashion: New Perspectives from Europe and North America — Tarlo, Emma

Islamic Law and the Law of Armed Conflict — Shah, Niaz A.
Islamic Legal Thought: A Compendium of Muslim Jurists — Arabi, Oussama
Islamic State: The Digital Caliphate — Atwan, Abdel Bari
The Islamist Phoenix: The Islamic State and the Redrawing of the Middle East — Napoleoni, Loretta
Islamophobia in the West: Measuring and Explaining Individual Attitudes — Helbling, Marc
The Islamophobia Industry: How the Right Manufactures Fear of Muslims — Lean, Nathan
The Island — Lee, Nancy
c Island Birthday (Illus. by Hogan, Jamie) — Murray, Eva
y Island Fire — Neal, Toby
The Island of Dr. Libris (Read by Heyborne, Kirby). Audiobook Review — Grabenstein, Chris
c The Island of Dr. Libris — Grabenstein, Chris
c The Island of Excess Love — Block, Francesca Lia
The Island of Knowledge: The Limits of Science and the Search for Meaning. — Gleiser, Marcelo
c Island of Legends — McMann, Lisa
c An Island of Our Own — Nicholls, Sally
y Island of Shipwrecks — McMann, Lisa
Island of the Doomed — Le Clezio, J.M.G.
Island on Fire: The Extraordinary Story of a Forgotten Volcano That Changed the World — Witze, Alexandra
Island Park — Keck, Edward
Island Queens and Mission Wives: How Gender and Empire Remade Hawai'i's Pacific World — Thigpen, Jennifer
c Island Treasures: Growing Up in Cuba (Illus. by Martorell, Antonio) — Ada, Alma
c Island Treasures: Growing Up in Cuba (Illus. by Martorell, Antonio) — Ada, Alma Flor
The Islanders — Gamier, Pascal
Islanders in the Empire: Filipino and Puerto Rican Laborers in Hawai'i — Poblete, Joanna
Islands and the Military Orders, c. 1291-c. 1798 — Buttigieg, Emanuel
Islands at Risk? Environments, Economies and Contemporary Change — Connell, John (b. 1946-)
y The Islands at the End of the World — Aslan, Austin
Islands of Empire: Pop Culture and U.S. Power — Fojas, Camilla
Islands of Privacy — Nippert-Eng, Christena
y The Isle — Frankel, Jordana
The Isle of Stone — Nicastro, Nick
y The Isle of the Lost (Read by Carson, Sofia). Audiobook Review — de la Cruz, Melissa
y The Isle of the Lost — de la Cruz, Melissa
Ismael and His Sisters — Stern, Louise
Isn't That Rich — Kirshenbaum, Richard
c The Isobel Journal: Just a Girl from Where Nothing Really Happens — Harrop, Isobel
Isobel on the Way to the Corner Shop — Witting, Amy
Isolated Connected Kyushu Island — Yumiko, Hana da
Isolation — Evans, Mary Anna
y Israel and the Arab World — Zohar, Gil
Israel and the Cold War from the War of Independence to the Six Days War: The United States, the Soviet Union, the Arab-Israeli Conflict, and the Question of Soviet Jewry — Heller, Yoseph
The Israeli Mind: How the Israeli National Character Shapes Our World — Gratch, Alon
Israel's Silent Defender: An Inside Look at Sixty Years of Israeli Intelligence — Gilboa, Amos
Issac Asimov's I, Robot: To Obey — Reichert, Mickey Zucker
Issues in Palaeobiology: A Global View: Interviews and Essays — Sanchez-Villagra; Marcelo R.
c Issues in Sports Series
y Issues That Concern You — Furey, Hester
c Issun Boshi: The One-Inch Boy (Illus. by Icinori) — Icinori
Istanbul — Maxwell, Virginia
Isthmus — LaSalle, Gerard
It Began with Babbage: The Genesis of Computer Science — Dasgupta, Subrata
c It Came from beneath the Playground — Scroggs, Kirt
c It Came from Ohio! My Life as a Writer — Stine, R.L.
It Couldn't Have Been the Pay: A Life of Teaching and Learning in Public Schools — Rothstein, Irving
It Ended Badly: 13 of the Worst Breakups in History — Wright, Jennifer
It Had to Be Him — Baumann, Tamra

It Happened in Boston? (Read by Fass, Robert). Audiobook Review — *Greenan, Russell H.*
It Happened on Broadway: An Oral History of the Great White Way — *Frommer, Myrna katz*
y It Happens: A Guide to Contemporary Realistic Fiction for the YA Reader — *Jensen, Kelly*
c It Might Be an Apple — *Yoshitake, Shinsuke*
c It Must Have Been You! (Illus. by Mian, Fatima) — *Mian, Zanib*
It Only Comes Out at Night and Other Stories — *Etchison, Dennis*
It Only Hurts When I Can't Run: One Girl's Story — *Parker, Gewanda J.*
It Runs in the Family — *Berrigan, Frida*
It Seems Like a Mighty Long Time — *Jackson, Angela*
It Shouldn't Have Been Beautiful — *Purpura, Lia*
It Started with Copernicus: Vital Questions about Science — *Parsons, Keith*
It Started with Paris — *Kelly, Cathy*
It Starts with Trouble — *Davis, Clark*
It Was Me All Along: A Memoir (Read by Mitchell, Andie). Audiobook Review — *Mitchell, Andie*
It Was Me All Along: A Memoir — *Mitchell, Andie*
It Will End with Us — *Savage, Sam*
It Won't Always Be This Great — *Mehlman, Peter*
The Italian American Table: Food, Family, and Community in New York City — *Cinotto, Simone*
The Italian Army and the First World War — *Gooch, John*
Italian Crime Fiction — *Pieri, Giuliana*
Italian Fascism's Empire — *Ben-Ghiat, Ruth*
Italian Survival Guide: The Language and Culture You Need to Travel with Confidence in Italy — *Bingham, Elizabeth*
Italian Venice: A History — *Bosworth, R.J.B.*
An Italian Wife — *Furnivall, Kate*
Italian Women and International Cold War Politics, 1944-1968 — *Pojmann, Wendy*
The Italians — *Hooper, John*
The Italic People of Ancient Apulia: New Evidence from Pottery for Workshops, Markets and Customs — *Carpenter, Thomas H.*
Italy's Margins: Social Exclusion and Nation Formation since 1861 — *Forgacs, David*
Iterative Methods for Linear Systems and Applications — *Olshanskii, Maxim A.*
c It's a Groovy World, Alfredo! (Illus. by Garbutt, Chris) — *Taylor, Sean (b. 1965-)*
It's a Long Story: My Life (Read by Grant, Ryan Christopher). Audiobook Review — *Ritz, David*
It's a Long Story: My Life (Illus. by Ritz, David) — *Nelson, Willie*
It's a Long Story: My Life — *Ritz, David*
It's a Minefield — *Horn, Robert*
c It's a Seashell Day (Illus. by Kreloff, Elliot) — *Ochiltree, Dianne*
It's a Sin to Be Boring — *Singletary, Nancy*
y It's a Wonderful Death — *Schmitt, Sarah J.*
y It's about Love — *Camden, Steven*
It's All in the Genes! Really? — *Verschuuren, Gerard M.*
y It's All Your Fault — *Rudnick, Paul*
c It's Alright to Look Different (Illus. by Ferrando, Salva) — *Coulter, Benedict*

It's Always Been You — *Scott, Jessica*
It's Always Sunny and Philosophy — *Hunt, Roger*
c It's an Orange Aardvark — *Hall, Michael*
It's Been Beautiful: Soul! and Black Power Television — *Wald, Gayle*
c It's Called Kibud Av Va'Eim! A Story about Honoring Parents (Illus. by Ebert, Len) — *Rosenfeld, Dina*
c It's Easter, Little Bunny! (Illus. by Boyer, Robin) — *Jaeger, Elizabeth*
c It's Getting Hot in Here: The Past, Present, and Future of Climate Change — *Heos, Bridget*
It's Getting Later All the Time — *Tabucchi, Antonio*
It's Good to Be Gronk — *Gronkowski, Rob*
It's in His Heart — *Alexander, Shelly*
It's My Life: My Struggle with Mental Illness — *Desjardins-Kelly, Irma*
It's. Nice. Outside — *Kokoris, Jim*
It's No Good — *Medvedev, Kirill*
It's Not about Perfect: Competing for My Country and Fighting for My Life — *Miller, Shannon*
It's Not about the Dog — *Chehak, Susan Taylor*
It's Not Always Racist ... But Sometimes It Is — *Poulton, Dionne Wright*
c It's Not Easy Being Number Three (Illus. by Dernavich, Drew) — *Dernavich, Drew*
It's Not Fair - Or Is It? — *Turner, Jane*
It's Not Me It's You — *McFarlane, Mhairi*
It's Not Over: Getting beyond Tolerance, Defeating Homophobia, and Winning True Equality — *Signorile, Michelangelo*
It's Not What You Think: Why Christianity Is so Much More Than Going to Heaven When You Die — *Bethke, Jefferson*
It's OK to Go Up the Slide: Renegade Rules for Raising Confident and Creative Kids — *Shumaker, Heather*
c It's Okay to Make Mistakes — *Parr, Todd*
It's One for the Money: The Song Snatchers Who Carved Up a Century of Pop and Sparked a Musical Revolution — *Heylin, Clinton*
It's Only Love — *Force, Marie*
c It's Only Stanley (Read by Newbern, George). Audiobook Review — *Agee, Jon*
c It's Only Stanley (Illus. by Agee, Jon) — *Agee, Jon*
c It's Only Stanley (Illus. by Newbern, George) — *Agee, Jon*
c It's Perfectly Normal: Changing Bodies, Growing Up, Sex, and Sexual Health (Illus. by Emberley, Michael) — *Harris, Robbie H.*
c It's Raining Bats and Frogs (Illus. by Henry, Steven) — *Colby, Rebecca*
c It's Raining Bats & Frogs (Illus. by Henry, Steven) — *Colby, Rebecca*
c It's Ramadan, Curious George (Illus. by Young, Mary O'Keefe) — *Rey, H.A.*
c It's Snow Day (Illus. by Cobb, Rebecca) — *Curtis, Richard*
c It's So Amazing!: A Book about Eggs, Sperm, Birth, Babies, and Families (Illus. by Emberley, Michael) — *Harris, Robie H.*
It's the Economy, Stupid — *Pryce, Vicky*
c It's the Great Pumpkin, Charlie Brown (Illus. by Jeralds, Scott) — *McMahon, Kara*

'It's the Pictures That Got Small': Charles Brackett on Billy Wilder and Hollywood's Golden Age — *Slide, Anthony*
It's the Student, Not the College: The Secrets of Succeeding at Any School--without Going Broke or Crazy — *White, Kristin M.*
c It's Tough to Lose Your Balloon (Illus. by Krosoczka, Jarrett J.) — *Krosoczka, Jarrett J.*
c It's Up to Charlie Hardin — *Ing, Dean*
It's What I Do: A Photographer's Life of Love and War — *Addario, Lynsey*
It's You — *Porter, Jane*
It's Your Move: My Million Dollar Method for Taking Risks with Confidence and Succeeding at Work and Life — *Altman, Josh*
c It's Your World: Get Informed, Get Inspired, and Get Going! — *Clinton, Chelsea*
c It's Your World: Get Informed, Get Inspired and Get Going! — *Clinton, Chelsea*
c It's Your World: Get Informed, Get Inspired & Get Going! (Read by Clinton, Chelsea). Audiobook Review — *Clinton, Chelsea*
c It's Your World: Get Informed, Get Inspired & Get Going! — *Clinton, Chelsea*
Itself — *Armantrout, Rae*
c The Itsy Bitsy Snowman (Illus. by Rescek, Sanja) — *Burton, Jeffrey*
c Itsy Bitsy Spider and Other Rhymes (Illus. by Meredith, Samantha) — *Meredith, Samantha*
c Itsy Bitsy Spider — *Emberley, Ed*
c Itty Bitty Kitty and the Rainy Play Day (Illus. by Burks, James) — *Holub, Joan*
c Itty Bitty Kitty (Illus. by Burks, James) — *Holub, Joan*
IV Encuentro Interdisciplinario sobre Estudios de Memoria
IV ENIUGH Congress "Encounters, Circulations and Conflicts": Conflicts and War
IV ENIUGH Congress "Encounters, Circulations and Conflicts": Gender
IV ENIUGH Congress "Encounters, Circulations and Conflicts": Higher Education
IV ENIUGH Congress "Encounters, Circulations and Conflicts": The Histories of Humanitarianism
IV ENIUGH Congress "Encounters, Circulations and Conflicts": The Ottoman Empire in World and Global History
IV ENIUGH Congress "Encounters, Circulations and Conflicts": Zentrum und Peripherie
Ivan Pavlov: A Russian Life in Science — *Todes, Daniel P.*
c Ivan: The Remarkable True Story of the Shopping Mall Gorilla (Illus. by Karas, G. Brian) — *Applegate, Katherine*
Ivan's Legacy — *Collis, Kathryn*
I've Got a Time Bomb — *Lamb, Sybil*
I've Got You Under My Skin — *Clark, Mary Higgins*
Ivory — *Park, Tony*
Ivory Vikings: The Mystery of the Most Famous Chessmen in the World and the Woman Who Made Them — *Brown, Nancy Marie*
Iz ognia da v polymia: Rossiiskaia politika posle — *GelEman, Vladimir*
c Izzy Barr, Running Star (Illus. by Shepperson, Rob) — *Mills, Claudia*
c Izzy & Oscar (Illus. by Dockray, Tracy) — *Estes, Allison*

J

J: A Novel — *Jacobson, Howard*
c J Is for Jazz (Illus. by Maidagan, Maria Corte) — *Ingalls, Ann*
J.M. Coetzee and the Life of Writing: Face-to-Face with Time — *Attwell, David*
J.M.W. Turner: Painting Set Free — *Brown, David Blayney*
c J.P. and the Bossy Dinosaur (Illus. by Sirotich, Erica) — *Crespo, Ana*
c J.P. and the Giant Octopus (Illus. by Sirotich, Erica) — *Crespo, Ana*
J.S. Bach's Chamber Music for Violin — *Wollny, Peter*
J.S. Bach's Johannine Theology: The St. John Passion and the Cantatas for Spring 1725 — *Chafe, Eric*
c Jack (Illus. by dePaola, Tomie) — *dePaola, Tomie*
Jack and the Beanstalk. E-book Review — *Nosy Crow*
c Jack and the Beanstalk (Illus. by Chambers, Mark) — *Alperin, Mara*
c Jack and the Hurricane (Illus. by Goudie, Craig) — *Goudie, Joshua*
c Jack and the Jelly Bean Stalk (Illus. by Pichon, Liz) — *Mortimer, Rachel*
c Jack and the Wild Life (Illus. by Stevanovic, Ivica) — *Doan, Lisa*
c Jack at the Helm (Illus. by Stevanovic, Ivica) — *Doan, Lisa*
c Jack Frost (Illus. by Joyce, William) — *Joyce, William*
Jack Kemp: The Bleeding-Heart Conservative Who Changed America — *Barnes, Fred*
Jack Kemp: The Bleeding-Heart Conservative Who Changed America — *Kondracke, Morton*
Jack London: A Writer's Fight for a Better America — *Tichi, Cecelia*
Jack London: An American Life — *Labor, Earle*
y Jack & Louisa: Act 1 (Illus. by Wetherhead, Kate) — *Keenan-Bolger, Andrew*
y Jack & Louisa: Act 2 — *Keenan-Bolger, Andrew*
Jack Maggs — *Carey, Peter*
The Jack of Souls — *Merlino, Stephen C.*
Jack of Spades (Read by Barrett, Joe). Audiobook Review — *Oates, Joyce Carol*
Jack of Spades — *Oates, Joyce Carol*
Jack of Spies — *Downing, David*
Jack Pine — *Hazelgrove, William*
c Jack: The True Story of Jack & the Beanstalk (Read by Mann, Bruce). Audiobook Review — *Shurtliff, Liesl*
Jack: The True Story of Jack & the Beanstalk — *Shurtliff, Liesl*
Jackaby (Read by Barber, Nicola). Audiobook Review — *Ritter, William*
Jackaby — *Ritter, William*
c Jackdaw and the Randoms — *David, Stuart*
c The Jacket (Illus. by Tolstikova, Dasha) — *Hall, Kirsten*
Jackie — *Tammela, John*
c Jackie Robinson: Baseball Legend — *Hansen, Grace*
c Jackie Robinson Breaks the Color Barrier — *Smolka, Bo*
c Jackie Robinson (Illus. by Henderson, Meryl) — *Dunn, Herb*
c Jackrabbit McCabe and the Electric Telegraph (Illus. by Espinosa, Leo) — *Rozier, Lucy Margaret*
Jacksonland: President Andrew Jackson, Cherokee Chief John Ross, and a Great American Land Grab (Read by Inskeep, Steve). Audiobook Review — *Inskeep, Steve*
Jacksonland: President Andrew Jackson, Cherokee Chief John Ross, and a Great American Land Grab — *Inskeep, Steve*
Jacob Jump — *Morris, Eric*

Jacob Lawrence: The Migration Series — *Dickerman, Leah*
c Jacob's Little Sister — *Cohen, Miriam*
Jacob's Room (Read by Stevenson, Juliet). Audiobook Review — *Woolf, Virginia*
Jacqueline Bouvier Kennedy Onassis: The Untold Story — *Leaming, Barbara*
Jade Dragon Mountain (Read by Shih, David). Audiobook Review — *Hart, Elsa*
Jade Dragon Mountain — *Hart, Elsa*
c J'adore les calins — *de la Bedoyere, Camilla*
The Jaguar's Children. Audiobook Review — *Vaillant, John*
The Jaguar's Children — *Vaillant, John*
c J'ai le rythme dans la peau (Illus. by Morrison, Frank) — *Schofield-Morrison, Connie*
y Jailed for Life for Being Black: The Story of Rubin "Hurricane" Carter — *Swan, Bill*
Jake Makes a World: Jacob Lawrence, a Young Artist in Harlem (Illus. by Myers, Christopher) — *Rhodes-Pitts, Sharifa*
Jake's Balloon Blast (Illus. by Nixon, Chris) — *Spillman, Ken*
c Jala and the Wolves — *Dumas, Marti*
Jalos, USA: Transnational Community and Identity — *Mirande, Alfredo*
c The Jam Doughnut That Ruined My Life (Illus. by Shaw, Hannah) — *Lowery, Mark*
c Jam for Nana (Illus. by Stewart, Lisa) — *Kelly, Deborah*
Jam on the Vine — *Barnett, LaShonda Katrice*
Jamaal's Journey — *McCormack, John*
Jamaat-e-Islami Women in Pakistan: Vanguard of a New Modernity? — *Jamal, Amina*
y Jamaica — *Bjorklund, Ruth*
Jamaica's Difficult Subjects — *Harrison, Sheri-Marie*
James and Esther Cooper Jackson: Love and Courage in the Black Freedom Movement — *Haviland, Sara Rzeszutek*
James Baldwin and the Queer Imagination — *Brim, Matt*
James Baldwin: The Last Interview: And Other Conversations — *Baldwin, James*
James Buchanan and the Coming of the Civil War — *Quist, John W.*
James: Diaspora Rhetoric of a Friend of God — *Aymer, Margaret*
James II: The Last Catholic King — *Womersley, David*
James K. McGuire: Boy Mayor and Irish Nationalist — *Fahey, Joseph E.*
James Madison: A Life Reconsidered — *Cheney, Lynne*
James Madison, the South, and the Trans-Appalachian West, 1783-1803 — *Zemler, Jeffrey Allen*
James McHenry, Forgotten Federalist — *Robbins, Karen E.*
James Merrill: Life and Art — *Hammer, Langdon*
The James Plays — *Munro, Rona*
c James to the Rescue (Illus. by Murphy, Kelly) — *Broach, Elise*
James Watt: Making the World Anew — *Russell, Ben*
James Welling: The Mind on Fire — *McFadden, Jane*
c Jamie and the Monster Bookroom (Illus. by Folnovic, Erika) — *Simpson, Jamie*
Jamie Bestwick — *Scheff, Matt*
c Jampires (Illus. by O'Connell, David) — *McIntyre, Sarah*
Jan Hus: Prediger - Reformator - Martyrer — *Soukup, Pavel*
Jan Patocka and the Heritage of Phenomenology — *Chavtik, Ivan*

Jan Sluijters Oorlogprenten, 1915-1919: Politieke Oorlogsprenten uit de Nieuwe Amsterdammer — *Kruft, Anton*
Jane and the Waterloo Map — *Barron, Stephanie*
Jane Austen's Cults and Cultures — *Johnson, Claudia L.*
Jane Austen's Erotic Advice — *Raff, Sarah*
Jane Austen's Names: Riddles, Persons, Places — *Doody, Margaret*
Jane Eyre's Sisters: How Women Live and Write the Heroine's Story — *Bower, Jody Gentian*
c Jane Foster's 123 (Illus. by Foster, Jane) — *Foster, Jane*
c Jane Foster's ABC (Illus. by Foster, Jane) — *Foster, Jane*
c Jane Goodall — *Shepherd, Jodie*
c Jane Goodall: Chimpanzee Expert & Activist — *Hansen, Grace*
Jane Jacobs und die Zukunft der Stadt: Diskurse - Perspektiven - Paradigmenwechsel — *Schubert, Dirk*
Jane Means Appleton Pierce: U.S. First Lady, 1853-1857: Her Family, Life, and Times — *Covell, Ann*
c Janine (Illus. by Cocca-Leffler, Maryann) — *Cocca-Leffler, Maryann*
January 1973 — *Robenalt, James*
c Janusz Korczak and the Orphans of the Warsaw Ghetto — *Cohen-Janca, Irene*
c Japan — *Centore, Michael*
Japan and the Shackles of the Past — *Murphy, Taggart*
Japan at Nature's Edge: The Environmental Context of a Global Power — *Miller, Ian Jared*
Japan Journeys: Famous Woodblock Prints of Cultural Sights in Japan — *Marks, Andreas*
Japan Restored: How Japan Can Reinvent Itself and Why This Is Important for America and the World — *Prestowitz, Clyde*
The Japan-South Korea Identity Clash: East Asian Security and the United States — *Glosserman, Brad*
Japan: The Paradox of Harmony — *Hirata, Keiko*
The Japanese American Cases: The Rule of Law in Time of War — *Daniels, Roger*
The Japanese-American Cases: The Rule of Law in Time of War — *Daniels, Roger*
y Japanese-American Internment during World War II — *Becker, Peggy Daniels*
Japanese Animation: East Asian Perspectives — *Yokota, Masao*
Japanese Architecture — *Locher, Mira*
Japanese Buddhist Pilgrimage — *Pye, Michael*
Japanese Fighters in Defense of the Homeland, 1941-1944, vol. 1 — *Wielicko, Leszek A.*
Japanese Historiography and the Gold Seal of 57 C.E.: Relic, Text, Object, Fake — *Fogel, Joshua A.*
The Japanese House Reinvented — *Jodidio, Philip*
The Japanese Lover — *Allende, Isabel*
The Japanese Lover (Illus. by Caistor, Nick) — *Allende, Isabel*
The Japanese Lover — *Allende, Isabel*
Japanese Perceptions of Foreigners — *Tanabe, Shunsuke*
Japanese Tree Burial: Ecology, Kinship and the Culture of Death — *Boret, Sebastien Penmellen*
Japanese Women and the Transnational Feminist Movement before World War II — *Shibahara, Taeko*
Japanische Unternehmen in Deutschland. Ein Aufeinandertreffen verschiedener Kulturen — *Albers, Meike Michele*

Japanoise: Music at the Edge of Circulation — Novak, David
Japan's Civil-Military Diplomacy: The Banks of the Rubicon — Yasutomo, Dennis T.
Jaqueline Tyrwhitt: A Transnational Life in Urban Planning and Design — Shoshkes, Ellen
c The Jar of Happiness (Illus. by Burrows, Ailsa) — Burrows, Ailsa
c Jars of Hope: How One Woman Helped Save 2,500 Children during the Holocaust (Illus. by Owenson, Meg) — Roy, Jennifer
y Jasmine and Maddie — Pakkala, Christina
y Jasmine Skies — Brahmachari, Sita
c Jason and the Golden Fleece (Illus. by Hartas, Leo)
c Jaspar Tristram — Clarke, A.W.
c Jasper and the Magpie: Enjoying Special Interests Together (Illus. by Merry, Alex) — Mayfield, Dan
c Jasper and Willie: Wildfire — Fleming, Bryn
c Jasper John Dooley: Lost and Found (Illus. by Shiell, Mike) — Adderson, Caroline
c Jasper John Dooley: You're in Trouble (Illus. by Clanton, Ben) — Adderson, Caroline
The Java Tutorial: A Short Course on the Basics, 6th ed. — Gallardo, Raymond
c Jay-Z: Hip-Hop Mogul — Torres, John Albert
Jazz: America's Gift: From Its Birth to George Gershwin's Rhapsody in Blue and Beyond — Gerber, Richie
Jazz: America's Gift — Gerber, Richie
Jazz and Machine-Age Imperialism: Music, "Race," and Intellectuals in France, 1918-1945 — Lane, Jeremy F.
Jazz Band Pianist: Basic Skills for the Jazz Band Pianist — Siskind, Jeremy
Jazz Diasporas — Braggs, Rashida K.
The Jazz Palace — Morris, Mary
Jazz-Rock Piano Chops: Firing Up Your Technique — Harrison, Mark
JD: A Novel — Merlis, Mark
Je me souviens? Le passe du Quebec dans la conscience de sa jeunesse — Letourneau, Jocelyn
c Je porte mes lunettes magiques — Dean, Kimberly
c Je suis capable! Series — Pelletier, Dominique
Jealousy — Toohey, Peter
Jean-Claude Grumberg: Three Plays — Grumberg, Jean-Claude
"Jean de Saintre": A Late Medieval Education in Love and Chivalry — de La Sale, Antoine
Jean de Vauzelles et le creuset lyonnais: Un humaniste catholique au service de Marguerite de Navarre entre France, Italie et Allemagne — Kammerer, Elsa
Jean de Vauzelles et le creuset lyonnais: Un humaniste catholique au service de Marguerite de Navarre entre France, Italie et Allemagne, 1520-1550 — Kammerer, Elsa
c Jean Jennings Bartik, Computer Pioneer — Todd, Kim D.
Jean-Luc Godard, Cinema Historian — Witt, Michael
Jean-Marie Leclair: Concertos pour violon et orchestre op. VII — Castelain, Louis
Jean-Michel Basquiat: Now's the Time — Buchhart, Dieter
Jean-Michel Basquiat: The Notebooks — Warsh, Larry
Jean Paton and the Struggle to Reform American Adoption — Carp, E. Wayne
Jean-Paul Sartre: Key Concepts — Churchill, Steven
c Jeanne Mance: Cofondatrice de Montreal — Plouffe, Manon
Jebel Marra — Green, Michelle
Jeeves and the Wedding Bells (Read by Rhind-Tutt, Julian). Audiobook Review — Faulks, Sebastian
c Jeff and George and the Totem Pole (Illus. by Anastasopoulos, Julia) — Child, Emily
The Jefferson Rule: How the Founding Fathers Became Infallible and Our Politics Inflexible — Sehat, David
c Jellaby: Monster in the City — Soo, Kean Jellaby
c Jellaby: The Lost Monster — Soo, Kean Jellaby
c Jelly Bean (Illus. by McGuire, Erin) — Lord, Cynthia
c Jelly Has a Wobble — Guard, Candy
c Jellybean Mouse (Illus. by Balsara, Andrea Torrey) — Roy, Philip
c Jellyfish — Hansen, Grace
Jellyfish — Galloway, Janice
The Jemima Code: Two Centuries of African American Cookbooks — Tipton-Martin, Toni
c Jennie Jenkins (Illus. by Ashley, Maurer) — Feierabend, John M.
Jennifer's Journal: The Life of a Suburban Girl, vol. 1 — Crute, Jennifer
c Jenny & Lorenzo (Illus. by Tharlet, Eve) — Steiner, Toni

Jenseits von Aufrechnung und Verdrangung: Neue Forschungen zu Flucht, Vertreibung und Vertriebeneninintegration — Stickler, Matthias
c Jeremiah Lucky and the Guardian Angel (Illus. by Hammond, Eric) — Freeman, Jane Ellen
Jeremiah: Pain and Promise — O'Connor, Kathleen M.
Jeremiah's Scribes: Creating Sermon Literature in Puritan New England — Neuman, Meredith Marie
Jeremias Drexel's 'Christian Zodiac — Crowe, Nicholas J.
Jeremy Hutchinson's Case Histories: From Lady Chatterley's Lover to Howard Marks — Grant, Thomas
Jeremy Thorpe — Bloch, Michael
Jernigan — Gates, David
Jerry Lee Lewis: His Own Story — Bragg, Rick
Jerry West: The Alchemy of Memory — West, Jerry R.
Jeru's Journey — Josephson, Sanford
Jerusalem as Narrative Space / Erzahlraum Jerusalem — Hoffman, Annette
Jesse — Burke, Glen Alan
y Jesse's Girl — Kenneally, Miranda
c Jessica's Box (Illus. by Carnavas, Peter) — Carnavas, Peter
c Jessica's Ghost — Norriss, Andrew
c Jessie Elliot Is a Big Chicken — Gravel, Elise
c Jessie's Island (Illus. by Lott, Sheena) — McFarlane, Sheryl
Jesuit Accounts of the Colonial Americas: Intercultural Transfers, Intellectual Transfers, intellectual Disutes, and Textualities — Donato, Clorinda
A Jesuit Missionary in Eighteenth-Century Sonora: The Family Correspondence of Philipp Segesser — Thompson, Raymond H.
Jesuit Student Groups, the Universidad Iberoamericana, and Political Resistance in Mexico, 1913-1979 — Espinosa, David
Jesuits and Fortifications: The Contribution of the Jesuits to Military Architecture in the Baroque Age — De Lucca, Denis
Jesus against the Scribal Elite: The Origins of the Conflict — Keith, Chris
Jesus and Magic: Freeing the Gospel Stories from Modern Misconceptions — Horsley, Richard A.
The Jesus and Mary Chain — Hayne, Zoe
Jesus as a Figure in History: How Modern Historians View the Man from Galilee — Powell, Mark Allan
Jesus Christ, Peacemaker: A New Theology of Peace — Rynne, Terrence J.
The Jesus Cow — Perry, Michael
Jesus, Debt, and the Lord's Prayer: First-Century Debt and Jesus' Intentions — Oakman, Douglas E.
The Jesus Dialogues: Jesus Speaks with Religious Founders and Leaders — Hill, Brennan R.
Jesus in History, Legend, Scripture, and Tradition: A World Encyclopedia — Houlden, Leslie
The Jesus Movement and Its Expansion: Meaning and Mission — Freyne, Sean
Jesus: One Man, Two Faiths: A Dialough between Christians & Muslims — Messier, Ron
Jesus Swagger: Break Free From Poser Christianity — Wilson, Jarrid
Jesus Was a Migrant — Cornell, Deirdre
Jesus without Borders: Christology in the Majority World — Green, Gene L.
Jesus: Word Made Flesh — Sloyan, Gerard S.
y Jet Black Heart — Flavin, Teresa
c Jet Plane — Macaulay, David
The Jet Sex: Airline Stewardesses and the Making of an American Icon — Vantoch, Victoria
Jewel City: Art from San Francisco's Panama-Pacific International Exposition — Ganz, James A.
y The Jewel — Ewing, Amy
Jewelry Making 1-2-3: 45+ Simple Projects — Van Vorhees, Karin
The Jewelry Recipe Book: Transforming Ordinary Materials into Stylish and Distinctive Earrings, Bracelets, Necklaces, and Pins — Soriano, Nancy
Jewels of Allah: The Untold Story of Women in Iran — Ansary, Nina
Jewish Culture in Early Modern Europe: Essays in Honor of David B. Ruderman — Cohen, Richard I.
y The Jewish Dog — Kravitz, Asher
Jewish Identities in Postcommunist Russia and Ukraine: An Uncertain Ethnicity — Gitelman, Zvi
Jewish Identity: The Challenge of Peoplehood Today — Popkin, Ruth Shamir
Jewish Life in Belarus: The Final Decade of the Stalin Regime, 1944-1953 — Smilovitsky, Leonid
Jewish Life in Nazi Germany: Dilemmas and Responses — Nicosia, Francis R.

Jewish Masculinities: German Jews, Gender, and History — Baader, Benjamin Maria
Jewish Messianic Thought in an Age of Despair — Seeskin, Kenneth
Jewish Noir: Contemporary Tales of Crime and Other Dark Deeds — Wishnia, Kenneth
The Jewish Olympics — Kaplan, Ron
Jewish Pasts, German Fictions: History, Memory, and Minority Culture in Germany, 1824-1955 — Skolnik, Jonathan
Jewish People, Yiddish Nation: Noah Prylucki and the Folkists in Poland — Weiser, Kalman
Jewish Poland Revisited: Heritage Tourism in Unquiet Places — Lehrer, Erica T.
'Jewish Questions' in International Politics - Diplomacy, Rights and Intervention
Jewish Sanctuary in the Atlantic World: A Social and Architectural History — Stiefel, Barry L.
Jewish Spain: A Mediterranean Memory — Linhard, Tabea Alexa
Jewish Stories of Love and Marriage: Folktales, Legends, and Letters — Sasso, Sandy Eisenberg
Jewish War under Trajan and Hadrian — Horbury, William
Jewish Wisdom for Growing Older — Friedman, Dayle A.
Jews and Genes: The Genetic Future in Contemporary Jewish Thought — Dorff, Elliot N.
Jews and Samaritans. The Origins and History of Their Early Relations — Knoppers, Gary N.
Jews and the Military: A History — Penslar, Derek J.
Jews, Christians and Muslims in Medieval and Early Modern Times: A Festschrift in Honor of Mark R. Cohen — Franklin, Arnold E.
Jews, Christians, and the Abode of Islam: Modern Scholarship, Medieval Realities — Lassner, Jacob
Jews, Christians, and the Roman Empire: The Poetics of Power in Late Antiquity — Dohrmann, Natalie B.
Jews in Medieval Britain: Historical, Literary and Archaeological Perspectives — Skinner, Patricia
Jews in the Early Modern English Imagination: A Scattered Nation — Holmberg, Eva Johanna
The Jezebel Remedy — Clark, Martin
JFK and LBJ: The Last Two Great Presidents — Hodgson, Godfrey
Jigsaw Man — Forbes, Elena
The Jihadis Return: ISIS and the New Sunni Uprising — Cockburn, Patrick
Jill Bash — Jackson, Maurice
y Jillian Cade: (Fake) Paranormal Investigator — Klein, Jen
Jilting the Duke — Miles, Rachael
c Jim Arnosky's Wild World — Arnosky, Jim
Jim Crow: A Historical Encyclopedia of the American Mosaic — Brown, Nikki L.M.
Jim Crow Wisdom: Memory and Identity in Black America since 1940 — Holloway, Jonathan Scott
c Jim Morgan and the Door at the Edge of the World — Raney, James Matlack
Jimfish — Hope, Christopher
Jimmy Bluefeather — Heacox, Kim
c Jimmy Handstand (Illus. by Cowen, Linda) — Karalis, Sylvia
Jimmy: Toughest. Dog. Ever. — Mills, Sally Hill
Jimmy Van Heusen: Swinging on a Star — Coppula, Christopher A.
Jimmy's Blues and Other Poems — Baldwin, James
c Jim's Lion (Illus. by Deacon, Alexis) — Hoban, Russell
c Jingle Bells (Illus. by Howarth, Jill) — Howarth, Jill
c Jingle Bells: A Magical Cut-Paper Edition (Illus. by Puttapipat, Niroot) — Pierpont, James Lord
c Jingle Bells (Illus. by Sanderson, Ruth) — Hapka, Catherine
Jinn and Juice — Peeler, Nicole
y Jinx's Fire — Blackwood, Sage
c JJ Goes to Puppy Class — Rose-Solomon, Diane
Joan Littlewood: Dreams and Realities: The Official Biography — Rankin, Peter
Joan of Arc: A History (Read by Flosnik, Anne). Audiobook Review — Castor, Helen
Joan of Arc: A History — Castor, Helen
Joan of Arc: A Life Transfigured — Harrison, Kathryn
Job 1-21: Interpretation and Commentary, vol. 1 — Seow, C.L.
The Job — Evanovich, Janet
The Job (Read by Brick, Scott). Audiobook Review — Evanovich, Janet
The Job Pirate: An Entertaining Tale of My Job-Hopping Journey in America — Christopher, Brandon

The Job: True Tales from the Life of a New York City Cop (Read by Osborne, Steve). Audiobook Review — Osborne, Steve
The Job: True Tales from the Life of a New York City Cop — Osborne, Steve
c Job Wanted (Illus. by Sheban, Chris) — Bateman, Teresa
c Jobs in My School Series
Jocasta — Aldiss, Brian
c Jodie's Shabbat Surprise (Illus. by Topaz, Ksenia) — Levine, Anna
Jodocus Badius Ascensius: Commentary, Commerce and Print in the Renaissance — White, Paul
y Joe All Alone — Nadin, Joanna
Joe Black: More Than a Dodger — Black, Martha Jo
Joe, the Slave Who Became an Alamo Legend — Jackson, Ron J., Jr.
c Joelito's Big Decision/La gran decision de Joelito (Illus. by Camacho, Daniel) — Berlak, Ann
c Joey and the Giant Box (Illus. by Byrne, Mike) — Lakritz, Deborah
y Joey and the Magic Map — Anderson, Tory C.
Jogging Round Majorca — West, Gordon
Johann Adolph Scheibe: Passions-Cantata "Vor Harpe er bleven til Sorrig" — Ewald, Johannes
Johannes Haller (1865-1947): Briefe eines Historikers — Hasselhorn, Benjamin
Johannes Hevelius and His World: Astronomer, Cartographer, Philosopher, and Correspondent — Kremer, Richard L.
Johannes Popitz (1884-1945): Gorings Finanzminister und Verschworer Gegen Hitler: Eine Biographie — Nagel, Anne C.
John and George: The Dog Who Saved My Life — Dolan, John
John Ashbery and English Poetry — Hickman, Ben
John Aubrey: My Own Life — Scurr, Ruth
John Bale and Religious Conversion in Reformation England — Wort, Oliver
John Ball's In the Heat of the Night. Audiobook Review — Pelfrey, Matt
John Birch: A Life — Lautz, Terry
John Cage Was — Klosty, James
John Calvin as Sixteenth-Century Prophet — Balserak, Jon
c John Cena — Markegard, Blake
John Donne and Religious Authority in the Reformed English Church — Sweetnam, Mark S.
John Donne and the Conway Papers: Patronage and Manuscript Circulation in the Early Seventeenth Century — Smith, Daniel Starza
John F. Kennedy — Ling, Peter J.
John Gower and the Limits of the Law — van Dijk, Conrad
John Gower, Poetry and Propaganda in Fourteenth-Century England — Carlson, David R.
c John Green: Star Author, Vlogbrother, and Nerdfighter — Braun, Eric
y John Green: Teen Whisperer: Studies in Young Adult Literature — Deakin, Kathleen
John Heartfield and the Agitated Image: Photography, Persuasion, and the Rise of Avant-Garde Photomontage — Zervigon, Andres Mario
John Heartfield: Ein politisches Leben — Coles, Anthony
John Hughes: A Life in Film: The Genius behind Ferris Bueller, The Breakfast Club, Home Alone, and More — Honeycutt, Kirk
John, Jesus, and the Renewal of Israel — Horsley, Richard A.
c John Joe's Tune: How New Zealand Got its National Anthem (Illus. by Ross, Christine) — Atkinson, Tania
John Kemble's Gibraltar Journal: The Spanish Expedition of the Cambridge Apostles, 1830-1831 — Nye, Eric
John Knox — Dawson, Jane
John le Carre: The Biography — Sisman, Adam
c John Lincoln Clem: Civil War Drummer Boy (Illus. by Noble, Steve) — Abbott, E.F.
John Mayall: The Blues Crusader — Logoz, Dinu
John Maynard Keynes — Barnett, Vincent
The John Michell Reader: Writings and Rants of a Radical Traditionalist — Godwin, Joscelyn
John Milton: An Annotated Bibliography, 1989-1999 — Huckabay, Calvin
c John Muir Wrestles a Waterfall (Illus. by Hogan, Jamie) — Danneberg, Julie
c John Muir Wrestles a Waterfall (Illus. by Hogan, Jamie) — Daneberg, Julie
c John Muir Wrestles a Waterfall (Illus. by Hogan, Jamie) — Danneberg, Julie

John Mullan: The Tumultuous Life of a Western Road Builder — Petersen, Keith C.
John Nichols's The Progresses and Public Processions of Queen Elizabeth I: A New Edition of the Early Modern Sources — Goldring, Elizabeth
John P. McGovern: A Lifetime in Stories — Boutwell, Bryant
c John Pemberton: Coca-Cola Developer — Lianas, Sheila Griffin
John Prine: In Spite of Himself — Huffman, Eddie
John Quincy Adams — Traub, James
John Skelton: The Career of an Early Tudor Poet — Scattergood, John
John the Baptist's Prayer or The Descent into Hell from the Exeter Book: Text, Translation and Critical Study — Rambaran-Olm, M.R.
John the Pupil — Flusfeder, David
John V. Lindsay: 50th Anniversary Commemoration — Kriegel, Jay L.
John Wayne — Eyman, Scott
John Wayne: The Life and Legend — Eyman, Scott
John Wayne's Way: Life Lessons from the Duke — Brody, Douglas
John Wayne's World: Transnational Masculinity in the Fifties — Meeuf, Russell
John Wesley and Universalism — Ellison, James A.
John Wesley in America: Restoring Primitive Christianity — Hammond, Geordan
John Williams's Film Music: Jaws, Star Wars, Raiders of the Lost Ark, and the Return of the Classical Hollywood Music Style — Audissino, Emilio
John Woolman's Path to the Peaceable Kingdom: A Quaker in the British Empire — Plank, Geoffrey
John Wyclif on War and Peace — Cox, Rory
John XXIII: The Medicine of Mercy — Faggioli, Massimo
Johnny Carson — Bushkin, Henry
c Johnny Danger DIY Spy: Failure Is Not an Option — Millett, Peter
Johnny Mercer: Southern Songwriter for the World — Eskew, Glenn T.
Johnson and Boswell: A Biography of a Friendship — Radner, John B.
Joining the Dots: A Fresh Approach to Piano Sight-Reading, vols. 6-8 — Bullard, Alan
c JoJo and the Big Day (Illus. by Duran, Leslie) — Duran, Leslie
Jojo's Bizarre Adventure, Part 1: Phantom Blood, Vol. 1 — Araki, Hirohiko
The Joker: A Memoir — Hudgins, Andrew
The Joker: Endgame — Snyder, Scott
c The Jolly Dodgers! Pirates Who Pretended (Illus. by Louden, Janette) — Griffiths, Neil
Jolly Lad — Doran, John
c Jolly Snow — Hissey, Jane
c Joltin' Joe DiMaggio (Illus. by Ransome, James E.) — Winter, Jonah
Jon Fixx — Fluck, Jason Squire
Jon Lewis: Photographs of the California Grape Strike — Street, Richard Steven
c Jon-Lorond Saves the Day (Illus. by Flowers, Luke) — Rasco, Hanna
Jonah: God's Scandalous Mercy — Youngblood, Kevin J.
Jonah, Tobit, Judith — Nowell, Irene
Jonas in Frames — Hutchinson, Chris
Jonas Salk: A Life — Jacobs, Charlotte DeCroes
Jonathan Edwards and the Church — Bezzant, Rhys S.
Jonathan Edwards and the Psalms: A Redemptive-Historical Vision of Scripture — Barshinger, David P.
Jonathan Franzen: The Comedy of Rage — Weinstein, Philip
Jonathan Strange & Mr. Norrell — Clarke, Susanna
Jonathan Swift: His Life and His World — Damrosch, Leo
Jones' After the Smoke Clears: Surviving the Police Shooting--an Analysis of the Post Officer-Involved Shooting Trauma — Pasciak, Adam
The Jones Men — Smith, Vern E.
y Jonesbridge: Echoes of Hinterland — Parker, M.E.
Joni Mitchell: In Her Own Words — Marom, Malka
c Jonny Jakes Investigates the Hamburgers of Doom — Judge, Malcolm
c Jorge el Curioso: Se Divierte Haciendo Gimnasia / Curious George: Gymnastics Fun — Calvo, Carlos E.
Jornalero: Being a Day Laborer in the USA — Ordonez, Juan Thomas

c Jose Pablo & Jane and the Hot Air Contraption (Illus. by Domingo, Jose) — Domingo, Jose
Joseph Cornell: Wanderlust — Lea, Sarah
Joseph Smith and The Latter-day Saints — Dewey, Richard Lloyd
Josephine Baker and the Rainbow Tribe — Guterl, Matthew Pratt
c Josephine: The Dazzling Life of Josephine Baker (Illus. by Robinson, Christian) — Powell, Patricia Hruby
Joseph's Dilemma — Stutzman, Ervin R.
Joseph's Temples: The Dynamic Relationship between Freemasonry and Mormonism — Homer, Michael W.
Josephus Daniels: His Life and Times — Craig, Lee A.
Josephus, the Emperors, and the City of Rome: From Hostage to Historian — Den Hollander, William
Josette — Bittner, Kathleen
Josette — Roth, Kathleen Bittner
c Josh Baxter Levels Up — Brown, Gavin
Joshua Chamberlain and the Civil War: At Every Hazard — Cost, Matthew
The Joshua Roll — Wander, Steven H.
Joshua Takano Chambers-Letson, a Race So Different: Performance and Law in Asian America — Chambers-Letson, Joshua Takano
y The Journal — Donovan, Lois
The Journal of Sarah Haynsworth Gayle, 1827-1835: A Substitute for Social Intercourse — Wiggins, Sarah Woolfolk
The Journal of Vincent Du Maurier — Ambroziak, K.P.
The Journal of Vincent du Maurier
Journal to Stella: Letters to Esther Johnson and Rebecca Dingley, 1710-1713 — Swift, Jonathan
The Journalist — Scharrer, Jos
c Journee pyjama (Illus. by Martchenko, Michael) — Munsch, Robert
Journey beyond Hardship: A Practical, Hopeful Guide for Getting through Tough Times — Pacini, Greg
Journey by Moonlight — Rix, Len
The Journey Home: My Life in Pinstripes — Posada, Jorge
A Journey into Russia — Muhling, Jens
Journey of an American Son — Hazen, John
y The Journey of Lewis and Clark in United States History — Edwards, Judith
Journey through Life's War of the Heart — Stewart, Brittaney
A Journey Through Philosophy in 101 Anecdotes — Rescher, Nicholas
A Journey Through the Big-Money Culture of College Football — Gaul, Gilbert M.
c A Journey through the Human Body — Parker, Steve
Journey to Colonus — Debrot, Franklin
Journey to Death — Russell, Leigh
The Journey to the Arab Spring: The Ideological Roots of the Middle East Upheaval in Arab Liberal Thought — Govrin, David
c Journey to the Moon: A Pop-Up Lunar Adventure — Mansfield, Andy
Journey to the Sun: Junipero Serra's Dream and the Founding of California — Orfalea, Gregory
Journey toward Justice: Personal Encounters in the Global South — Wolterstorff, Nicholas P.
c Journey's End (Illus. by Allen, Douglas) — Holt, Christopher
Journeys Home: Inspiring Stories, Plus Tips and Strategies to Find Your Family History — McCarthy, Andrew
Journeys into Madness: Mapping Mental Illness in the Austro-Hungarian Empire — Blackshaw, Gemma
Journeys into the Past: History as a Tourist Attraction in the 19th and 20th Centuries
Joy in the Journey: Finding Abundance in the Shadow of Death — Hayner, Steve
The Joy of Financial Security — Cygan, Donna Skeels
The Joy of Killing — MacLean, Harry N.
The Joy of Tax — Murphy, Richard
Joy: Poet, Seeker, and the Woman Who Captivated C.S. Lewis — Santamaria, Abigail
Joy Ride: Show People and their Shows — Lahr, John
Joy to the Worlds: Mysterious Speculative Fiction for the Holidays — Chance, Maia
The Joyful Table — Joy, Susan
y Joyride — Banks, Anna
Joyriding in Riyadh: Oil, Urbanism, and Road Revolt — Menoret, Pascal
Juan Boutista de Anza: The King's Governor in New Mexico — Herrera, Carlos R.

Juan de Segovia and the Fight for Peace: Christians and Muslims in the Fifteenth Century — *Wolf, Anne Marie*
Juan Gregorio Palechor: The Story of My Life — *Jimeno, Myriam*
y Juba! — *Myers, Walter Dean*
Jubal Early: Robert E. Lee's "Bad Old Man" — *Cooling, Benjamin Franklin, III*
y Jubilee Manor — *Hagen, Bethany*
Judah in the Neo-Babylonian Period: The Archaeology of Desolation — *Faust, Avraham*
The Judas Dilemma — *Heath, Robert*
Judas — *Davies, Damian Walford*
Judas: The Most Hated Name in History — *Stanford, Peter*
Judas: The Troubling History of the Renegade Apostle — *Stanford, Peter*
The Judges of Hades: and Other Simon Ark Stories — *Hoch, Edward D.*
Judging Positivism — *Martin, Margaret*
Judging the Boy Scouts of America: Gay Rights, Freedom of Association, and the Dale Case — *Ellis, Richard J.*
Judgment at Istanbul: The Armenian Genocide Trials — *Dadrian, Vahakn N.*
Judicial Decision-Making in a Globalized World: A Comparative Analysis of the Changing Practices of Western Highest Courts — *Mak, Elaine*
Judische Klagen Gegen Reichsadelige: Prozesse am Reichshofrat in den Herrschaftsjahren Rudolfs II. und Franz I. Stephans — *Griemert, Andre*
y Judith Kerr's Creatures (Illus. by Kerr, Judith) — *Kerr, Judith*
Judith Scott: Bound and Unbound — *Morris, Catherine*
Judy & Liza & Robert & Freddie & David & Sue & Me ... : A Memoir — *Phillips, Stevie*
c Judy Moody, Mood Martian (Read by Rosenblat, Barbara). Audiobook Review — *McDonald, Megan*
c Judy Moody, Mood Martian (Illus. by Reynolds, Peter H.) — *McDonald, Megan*
Jugenddelinquenz: Die Produktivitat eines Problems in den USA der Spaten 1940er bis 1960er Jahre — *Mackert, Nina*
Juggernaut — *Gormley, Amelia C.*
Juggling with Knives: Smart Investing in the Coming Age of Volatility — *Jubak, Jim*
Jugoslawien in den 1960er Jahren: Auf dem Weg zu einem (a)Normalen Staat? — *Grandits, Hannes*
Jules Ferry: La liberte et la tradition — *Ozouf, Mona*
Jules Verne inedit: les manuscrits dechiffres — *Butcher, William*
y Jules Verne's 20,000 Leagues under the Sea: A Graphic Novel (Illus. by Ruiz, Alfonso) — *Bowen, Carl*
c Julia and the Art of Practical Travel (Illus. by Blume, Lesley M.M.) — *Blume, Lesley M.M.*
Julia Child: An Extraordinary Life in Words and Pictures (Illus. by Gorham, Joanna) — *Hagar, Erin*
c Julia, Child (Illus. by Morstad, Julie) — *Maclear, Kyo*
Julia, Skydaughter — *Dunn, Robin Wyatt*
y Julian — *Bell, William*
Julian of Norwich, Theologian — *Turner, Denys*
Julian's Gospel: Illuminating the Life and Revelations of Julian of Norwich — *Rolf, Veronica Mary*
c Julia's House for Lost Creatures (Illus. by Hatke, Ben) — *Hatke, Ben*
c Julia's Magic Putter (Illus. by Lindt, Peggy) — *Jasinski, Page O'Brien*
Juliette a Barcelone — *Brasset, Rose-Line*
y Juliette a la Havane (Illus. by Charette, Geraldine) — *Brasset, Rose-Line*
Juliette and the Monday ManDates — *Doughty, Becky*
c Juliette Kinzie: Frontier Storyteller — *Conn, Kathe Crowley*
c The Jumbies (Read by Miles, Robin). Audiobook Review — *Baptiste, Tracey*
y The Jumbies — *Baptiste, Tracey*
c Jump Back, Paul: The Life and Poems of Paul Laurence Dunbar — *Derby, Sally*

c Jump Back, Paul: The Life and Poems of Paul Laurence Dunbar (Illus. by Qualls, Sean) — *Derby, Sally*
Jump Cut — *Hellmann, Libby Fischer*
c Jump, Pup! — *Neuman, Susan B.*
c Jumping Jack (Illus. by Albertine) — *Zullo, Germano*
c Jumping Off Library Shelves: A Book of Poems (Illus. by Manning, Jane) — *Hopkins, Lee Bennett*
c Jumping Spiders — *Archer, Claire*
c Juna's Jar (Illus. by Hoshino, Felicia) — *Bahk, Jane*
c Junction — *Jurevicius, Nathan*
Junction True — *Fawkes, Ray*
June — *Bakker, Gerbrand*
A June of Ordinary Murders — *Brady, Conor*
c Juneteenth for Mazie (Illus. by Cooper, Floyd) — *Cooper, Floyd*
Jungle Animals around the World — *Alderton, David*
c The Jungle Book — *Kipling, Rudyard*
y Junior Braves of the Apocalypse: A Brave Is Brave (Illus. by Lehner, Zach) — *Smith, Greg*
Junior Leadership in Afghanistan, 2006-2010 — *Groen, Jos M.H.*
The Junior Officer Bunkroom — *Zerr, J.J.*
Junior Seau: The Life and Death of a Football Icon — *Trotter, Jim*
y Juniors — *Hemmings, Kaui Hart*
Junipero Serra: California, Indians, and the Transformation of a Missionary — *Beebe, Rose Marie*
Junipero Serra: California's Founding Father — *Hackel, Steven W.*
Junk DNA: A Jouney through the Dark Matter of the Genome — *Carey, Nessa*
Junk DNA: A Journey through the Dark Matter of the Genome — *Carey, Nessa*
c Junk Drawer Chemistry: 50 Awesome Experiments That Don't Cost a Thing — *Mercer, Bobby*
c Junk Food, Yes or No — *Carole, Bonnie*
c The Junkyard Bot (Illus. by Fujita, Goro) — *Richards, C.J.*
c Juno: Queen of the Gods, Goddess of Marriage (Illus. by Young, Eric) — *Temple, Emily*
c Jupiter — *Bloom, J.P.*
Jupiter's Legacy — *Millar, Mark*
Jurassic Park (Read by Brick, Scott). Audiobook Review — *Crichton, Michael*
Jurassic Park — *Crichton, Michael*
Jurgen Moltmann: Collected Readings — *Kohl, Margaret*
Jurgen Ponto: Bankier und Burger — *Ahrens, Ralf*
c Just a Dream — *Van Allsburg, Chris*
y Just a Drop of Water — *Cerra, Kerry O'Malley*
c Just a Duck? (Illus. by Bramsen, Carin) — *Bramsen, Carin*
Just a Little Kiss — *Pizzitola, Renita*
Just a Little Love (Illus. by Mayer, Mercer) — *Mayer, Mercer*
y Just a Queen — *Caro, Jane*
y Just a Special Thanksgiving — *Mayer, Mercer*
Just a Summer Fling — *Cameron, Cate*
A Just and Generous Nation: Abraham Lincoln and the Fight for American Opportunity — *Holzer, Harold*
Just Another Southern Town: Mary Church Terrell and the Struggle for Racial Justice in the Nation's Capita — *Quigley, Joan*
Just Be a Dad: Things My Father Never Told Me — *Cave, George*
c Just Because I Am: A Child's Book of Affirmation (Illus. by Iwai, Melissa) — *Payne, Lauren Murphy*
c Just Breathe (Illus. by Bailey, Melissa) — *Rivlin-Gutman, Annette*
Just Call Me Superhero — *Bronsky, Alina*
Just Call Me Superhero — *Mohr, Tim*
y Just Call My Name — *Sloan, Holly Goldberg*
y The Just City — *Walton, Jo*
c Just for Today (Illus. by Landmann, Bimba) — *John XXIII, St.*
c Just Grace Gets Crafty — *Harper, Charise Mericle*
c Just Imagine (Illus. by Sharratt, Nick) — *Goodhart, Pippa*
Just in Time for a Highlander — *Cready, Gwyn*

c Just Itzy (Illus. by Pizzoli, Greg) — *Krumwiede, Lana*
Just Jake: Dog Eat Dog (Illus. by Villa, Victor Rivas) — *Marcionette, Jake*
c Just Joking 6: 300 Hilarious Jokes about Everything, Including Tongue Twisters, Riddles, and More! — *Pattison, Rosie Gowsell*
c Just Joking: Animal Riddles — *Lewis, J. Patrick*
Just Keep Breathing: A Shocking Expose of Letters You Never Imagined a Generation Would Write — *Dabbs, Reggie*
Just Kids from the Bronx: Telling It the Way It Was: An Oral History (Read by Alda, Arlene). Audiobook Review — *Alda, Arlene*
Just Kids from the Bronx: Telling It the Way It Was: An Oral History — *Alda, Arlene*
c Just Like Daddy (Illus. by Nedelcu, Ovi) — *Nedelcu, Ovi*
c Just Like I Wanted (Illus. by Gordon-Noy, Aya) — *Keller, Elinoar*
c Just Like Me, Climbing a Tree: Exploring Trees around the World (Illus. by Bernhard, Durga Yael) — *Bernhard, Durga Yael*
y Just Like the Movies — *Fiore, Kelly*
Just Married: Same-Sex Couples, Monogamy & the Future of Marriage — *Macedo, Stephen*
Just Medicine — *Matthew, Dayna Bowen*
Just Mercy: A Story of Justice and Redemption (Read by Stevenson, Bryan). Audiobook Review — *Stevenson, Bryan*
Just Mercy: A Story of Justice and Redemption — *Stevenson, Bryan*
y Just My Luck — *McGovern, Cammie*
c Just My Rotten Luck (Read by Kennedy, Bryan). Audiobook Review — *Patterson, James*
y Just My Type: Understanding Personality Profiles — *Rosen, Michael J.*
c Just One Apple (Illus. by Janosch) — *Janosch*
Just over the Horizon — *Bear, Greg*
Just Queer Folks: Gender and Sexuality in Rural America — *Johnson, Colin R.*
c Just Right for Two (Illus. by Beardshaw, Rosalind) — *Corderoy, Tracey*
c Just Right Word Book (Illus. by Scarry, Richard) — *Scarry, Richard*
Just Say Yes — *Hayley, Elizabeth*
Just So Happens — *Obata, Fumio*
c Just So Stories for Little Children, vol. 2 (Illus. by Wallace, Ian) — *Kipling, Rudyard*
A Just Society for Ireland? 1964-1987 — *Meehan, Ciara*
Just Sustainablility: Technology, Ecology, and Resource Extraction — *Peppard, Christiana Z.*
y Just Visiting — *Adler, Dahlia*
Just War: Authority, Tradition, and Practice — *Lang, Anthony F., Jr.*
Just Water: Theology, Ethics, and the Global Water Crisis — *Peppard, Christiana Z.*
Just Who Loses?: Discrimination in the United States, vol. 2 — *Lucas, Samuel Roundfield*
c Justice — *Salane, Jeffrey*
Justice among Nations: A History of International Law — *Neff, Stephen C.*
Justice at Redwillow — *Nesbitt, John D.*
Justice Brennan: Liberal Champion — *Wermiel, Stephen*
Justice Calling — *Bellet, Annie*
The Justice Calling: Where Passion Meets Perseverance — *Hoang, Bethany Hanke*
Justice, Dissent, and the Sublime — *Canuel, Mark*
Justice for None — *Harvey, J.M.*
Justice Is for the Lonely — *Clark, Steve*
Justification Reconsidered: Rethinking a Pauline Theme — *Westerholm, Stephen*
Justifier en mathematiques — *Nabonnand, Philippe*
Justifying Genocide — *Ihrig, Stefan*
Justine et autres romans — *De Sade, D.A.F.*
Justus Moser 1720-1794 — *Heese, Thorsten*
Juvenile Nation: Youth, Emotions and the Making of the Modern British Citizen, 1880-1914 — *Olsen, Stephanie*
The Juvenilization of American Christianity — *Bergler, Thomas E.*
Juventud — *Blakeslee, Vanessa*
Juxtaposition and the Elisha Cycle — *Gilmour, Rachelle*

K

K.L. Reich — *Amat-Piniella, Joaquim*
Kabbalah: A Neurocognitive Approach to Mystical Experiences — *Arzy, Shahar*
Kabbalistic Revolution: Reimagining Judaism in Medieval Spain — *Lachter, Hartley*
Kaddish: Women's Voices — *Smart, Michal*
Kafamda Bir Tuhaflik — *Pamuk, Orhan*
Kafka: Die fruhen Jahre — *Stach, Reiner*
Kafka's Law: The Trial and American Criminal Justice — *Burns, Robert P.*
Kaijumax: Terror and Respect — *Cannon, Zander*
Kaiser Julians Gottesverehrung im Kontext der Spatantike — *Stocklin-Kaldewey, Sara*
Kaiser und Kalifen: Karl der Grosse und die Machte am Mittelmeer um 800 — *Stiftung Deutsches Historisches Museum*
Kaiser Wilhelm II — *Rohl, John C.*
y Kalahari — *Khoury, Jessica*
Kaleidoscope City: A Year in Varanasi — *Ede, Piers Moore*
Kaliyuga — *Stacton, David*
Kalki — *Vidal, Gore*
Kamal Jann — *Edde, Dominique*
c Kamik's First Sled (Illus. by Leng, Qin) — *Sulurayok, Matilda*
y Kammie on First: Baseball's Dottie Kamenshek — *Houts, Michelle*
Kampf um die Ressourcen - Relevanz der Energiepreise fur deutsche Unternehmen
The Kanak Awakening: The Rise of Nationalism in New Caledonia — *Chappell, David A.*
Kandinsky als Padagoge — *Graeff, Alexander*
Kansas City: A Food Biography — *Broomfield, Andrea L.*
Kansas Trail Guide: The Best Hiking, Biking, and Riding in the Sunflower State — *Conard, Jonathan*
Kant and Rational Psychology — *Dyck, Corey W.*
Kant and the Creation of Freedom: A Theological Problem — *Insole, Christopher J.*
Kant on Moral Autonomy — *Sensen, Oliver*
Kant's Organicism: Epigenesis and the Development of Critical Philosophy — *Mensch, Jennifer*
Kant's Religion within the Boundaries of Mere Reason: A Critical Guide — *Michalson, Gordon E.*
y Kanye West: God and Monster — *Beaumont, Mark*
c Kanye West: Hip-Hop Mogul — *Burlingame, Jeff*
Karachi: Ordered Disorder and the Struggle for the City — *Gayer, Laurent*
Karate Chop/Minna Needs Rehearsal Space — *Nors, Dorthe*
Karen Lost and Found: Story of Undiagnosed Brain Injury and Domestic Violence — *Wilson, Karen*
Karen Memory — *Bear, Elizabeth*
Karl Barth's Emergency Homiletic, 1932-1933: A Summons to Prophetic Witness at the Dawn of the Third Reich — *Hancock, Angela Dienhart*
Karl der Grosse: Der Heilige Barbar — *Weinfurter, Stefan*
Karl der Grosse: Gewalt und Glaube — *Fried, Johannes*
Karl Gutzkow: Erinnerungen, Berichte und Urteile seiner Zeitgenossen. Eine Dokumentation — *Rasch, Wolfgang*
Karl Marx: A Life — *Wheen, Francis*
Karl Marx: An Intellectual Biography — *Hosfeld, Rolf*
Karl Rahner's Theological Aesthetics — *Fritz, Peter Joseph*
Karma's a Killer — *Weber, Tracy*
c Karol, the Boy Who Became Pope: A Story about Saint John Paul II (Illus. by William, Maloney J.) — *Sullivan, Jem*

Karpathenschlachten: Der erste und zweite Weltkrieg am oberen Karpathenbogen — *Singer, Roland*
c Kate & Pippin: An Unlikely Friendship (Illus. by Springett, Isobel) — *Springett, Martin*
c Kate the Great: Except When She's Not (Illus. by Becker, Suzy) — *Becker, Suzy*
y Kate Triumph — *Arnold, Shari*
y Kate Walden Directs: Bride of Slug Man — *Mata, Julie*
c Kate's Story, 1914 — *Whitby, Adele*
c Katfish (Illus. by Skye, Obert) — *Skye, Obert*
Kathe Kollwitz 1867-2000: Biographie und Rezeptionsgeschichte einer Deutschen Kunstlerin — *Schymura, Yvonne*
y Katherine Carlyle — *Thomson, Rupert*
c Katherine's Story, 1848 — *Whitby, Adele*
Katholische Missionsschulen in Deutschland 1887-1940 — *Gast, Holger*
Katholischer Historismus? Zum historischen Denken in der Deutschsprachigen Kirchengeschichte um 1900 Heinrich Schrors - Albert Ehrhard - Joseph Schnitzer — *Klapczynski, Gregor*
c Katie and the Fancy Substitute (Illus. by Lyon, Tammie) — *Manushkin, Fran*
y Katie Friedman Gives Up Texting! (Illus. by Coovert, J.P.) — *Greenwald, Tommy*
y Katie Friedman Gives Up Texting! (and Lives to Tell about It). (Illus. by Coovert, J.P.) — *Greenwald, Tommy*
c Katie Fry, Private Eye: The Lost Kitten (Illus. by Newton, Vanessa Brantley) — *Cox, Katherine*
Katie Gale: A Coast Salish Woman's Life on Oyster Bay — *De Danaan, Llyn*
c Katie Mcginty Wants a Pet (Illus. by Simpson, Finn) — *Harrington, Jenna*
c Katie's Cabbage (Illus. by Martin, Michelle H.) — *Stagliano, Katie*
Katrina: After the Flood — *Rivlin, Gary*
The Katrina Decade: Images of an Altered City (Illus. by Davis, Jack) — *Spielman, David G.*
c Katy — *Wilson, Jacqueline*
c Katy Duck's Happy Halloween (Illus. by Cole, Henry) — *Capucilli, Alyssa Satin*
c Katy Perry: Chart-Topping Superstar — *Owings, Lisa*
c Katy Perry: Famous Pop Singer and Songwriter — *Diver, Lucas*
Katya — *Martell, Jon*
y The Kaurava Empire: The Vengeance of Ashwatthama (Illus. by Nagar, Sachin) — *Quinn, Jason*
Kava in the Blood — *Thomson, Peter*
c Kay Kay's Alphabet Safari (Illus. by Sullivan, Dana) — *Sullivan, Dana*
Kay WalkingStick: An American Artist — *Ash-Milby, Kathleen*
c Kaya's Journey Begins, 2 vols. (Illus. by Myers, Morgan Rae) — *Crowder, Drew*
c Kayla and Kugel (Illus. by Koffsky, Ann D.) — *Koffsky, Ann D.*
c Kayla and Kugel (Illus. by Koffsky, Ann D) — *Koffsky, Ann D.*
c Kay's Story, 1934 — *Whitby, Adele*
Kazakh Oneri: 5 Tomdyk — *Mukhamediev, Konyr*
Kazakhskoie igrovoie kino: Ekranno-follornie traditsii i obraz geroia — *Nogerbek, Bauyrzhan*
c KeeKee's Big Adventures in Athens, Greece (Illus. by Uhelski, Casey) — *Jones, Shannon*
Keelic and the Space Pirates — *Edlund, Alexander*
c The Keep — *Egan, Jennifer*
Keep Calm ... It's Just Real Estate: Your No-Stress Guide to Buying a Home — *Sherrod, Egypt*
Keep Calm — *Binder, Mike*

c Keep Dancing, Katie (Illus. by Lyon, Tammie) — *Manushkin, Fran*
Keep Hold — *Grubb, Michelle*
Keep It Fake: Inventing an Authentic Life — *Wilson, Eric G.*
Keep Moving — *Van Dyke, Dick*
Keep On Loving You — *Ridgway, Christie*
Keep on Walkin', Keep on Talkin': An Oral History of the Greensboro Civil Rights Movement — *Pfaff, Eugene E.*
Keep Out of Reach of Children: Reye's Syndrome, Aspirin, and the Politics of Public Health — *Largent, Mark A.*
Keep Quiet — *Scottoline, Lisa*
Keep Your Friends Close — *Daly, Paula*
The Keeper: A Life of Saving Goals and Achieving Them — *Howard, Tim*
y The Keeper — *Baldacci, David*
y The Keeper — *Martin, Darragh*
y The Keeper of the Mist — *Neumeier, Rachel*
c The Keeper: The Unguarded Story of Tim Howard — *Howard, Tim*
y Keepers of the Labyrinth — *Moulton, Erin E.*
Keeper's Reach — *Neggers, Carla*
Keepers: The Greatest Films--and Personal Favorites--of a Moviegoing Lifetime — *Schickel, Richard*
Keeping an Eye Open: Essays on Art — *Barnes, Julian*
Keeping Fit from A to Z / Mantente en forma de la A a la Z — *Maze, Stephanie*
Keeping Mother's Secrets — *May, Tracy*
Keeping the Immigrant Bargain: The Costs and Rewards of Success in America — *Louie, Vivian*
c Keeping the Peace: The Kids' Book of Peacemaking — *Hanson, Anders*
Keeping the Vow: The Untold Stories of Married Catholic Priests — *Sullins, D. Paul*
Keeping Time: An Introduction to Archival Best Practices for Music Librarians — *Hooper, Lisa*
Kehinde Wiley: A New Republic — *Tsai, Eugenie*
Kei — *Aladjai, Erni*
c Kell and the Detectives (Illus. by Davis, Rich) — *Pattison, Darcy*
Kem Weber: Designer and Architect — *Long, Christopher*
Kempowski, Walter — *Whiteside, Shaun*
Kendo: Culture of the Sword — *Bennett, Alexander C.*
The Kennan Diaries — *Kennan, George F.*
Kennedy: A Cultural History of an American Icon — *White, Mark*
Kennesaw Mountain: Sherman, Johnston, and the Atlanta Campaign — *Hess, Earl J.*
Kennewick Man: The Scientific Investigation of an Ancient American Skeleton — *Owsley, Douglas M.*
Kentucky Confederates: Secession, Civil War, and the Jackson Purchase — *Craig, Berry*
c Kenya's Art (Illus. by Mitchell, Hazel) — *Trice, Linda*
Keota — *Volk, Toni*
Kepler and the Universe: How One Man Revolutionized Astronomy — *Love, David K.*
The Kept — *Scott, James*
c Kerenza: A New Australian — *Hawke, Rosanne*
Kerrigan in Copenhagen: A Love Story, by Thomas E. Kennedy — *Kennedy, Thomas E.*
c Ketzel, the Cat Who Composed (Illus. by Bates, Amy June) — *Newman, Leslea*
c Kevin Durant — *Bodden, Valerie*
y The Key — *Elfgren, Sara B.*
y The Key — *Strandberg, Mats*
y Key Discoveries in Earth and Space Science — *Zuchora-Walske, Christine*

y Key Discoveries in Engineering and Design — Zuchora-Walske, Christine
y Key Discoveries in Life Science — Zuchora-Walske, Christine
y Key Discoveries in Physical Science — Marsico, Katie
c The Key That Swallowed Joey Pigza (Read by Gantos, Jack). Audiobook Review — Gantos, Jack
c The Key that Swallowed Joey Pigza. Audiobook Review — Gantos, Jack
c The Key That Swallowed Joey Pigza — Gantos, Jack
c The Key That Swallowed Joey Pigza (Illus. by Tazzyman, David) — Gantos, Jack
   Key Topics in Conservation Biology 2 — Macdonald, David W.
   Keynes: Useful Economics for the World Economy — Temin, Peter
c Keys (Illus. by Morgan, Josh) — Cotter, Sacha
   Keywords: A Vocabulary of Culture and Society — Williams, Raymond
c Khan Academy and Salman Khan — Wolff, Ariana
   Khirbet Khizeh — Smilansky, Yizhar
   Khirbet Khizeh — Yizhar, S.
   Khodorchur 100 Years Later — Gianighian, Raphael
   Khomeini: Life of a Ayatollah — Moin, Baqer
y Kiana Cruise: Apocalypse — Studdard, Jody
   Kick-Back — Cain, Chelsea
   Kick Her Again; She's Irish — O'Reiley, Mary
c Kickboxing and MMA: Winning Ways — Johnson, Nathan
c Kid Athletes: True Tales of Childhood from Sports Legends (Illus. by Horner, Doogie) — Stabler, David
   The Kid — Brandlee, Ben, Jr.
   The Kid from Diamond Street: The Extraordinary Story of Baseball Legend Edith Houghton (Illus. by Salerno, Steven) — Vernick, Audrey
   Kid Gloves: a Voyage Round My Father — Mars-Jones, Adam
   Kid Me Not: An Anthology by Child-Free Women of the '60s, Now in Their 60s — Hughes, Aralyn
y Kid Moses — Thornton, Mark R.
c Kid Owner — Green, Tim
c Kid President's Guide to Being Awesome — Novak, Robby
c Kid Presidents: True Tales of Childhood from America's Presidents (Illus. by Horner, Doogie) — Stabler, David
c Kid Sheriff and the Terrible Toads (Illus. by Smith, Lane) — Shea, Bob
c Kidding around NYC — Roche, Suzanne
   Kidnap in Crete — Stroud, Rick
   The Kidnapping of Jamaica's Homeland Security: The Adventures of the Expeditor — Davis, Joe S.
y The Kidney Hypothetical, or, How to Ruin Your Life in Seven Days (Read by de Ocampo, Ramon). Audiobook Review — Yee, Lisa
y The Kidney Hypothetical, or, How to Ruin Your Life in Seven Days — Yee, Lisa
   The Kids' Book of Simple Machines: Cool Projects and Activities That Make Science Fun! — Doudna, Kelly
c Kids Cook French — Pepin, Claudine
   Kids, Cops, and Confessions: Inside the Interrogation Room — Feld, Barry C.
c A Kid's Guide to Keeping Chickens — Caughey, Melissa
c The Kids' Guide to Staying Awesome and in Control: Simple Stuff to Help Children Regulate Their Emotions and Sense (Illus. by Apsley) — Brukner, Lauren
c A Kid's Guide to the Middle East Series — Perdew, Laura
c A Kid's Herb Book: For Children of All Ages — Tierra, Lesley
c A Kid's Life during the American Civil War — Machajewski, Sarah
   Kids on YouTube: Technical Identities and Digital Literacies — Lange, Patricia A.
c Kids Top 10 Pet Cats — Rau, Dana Meachen
   Kiel und die Marine 1865-2015: 150 Jahre Gemeinsame Geschichte
   Kierkegaard, Eve and Metaphors of Birth — Assiter, Alison
   Kierkegaard: Exposition and Critique — Hampson, Daphne
   Kierkegaard's Concept of Faith — Westphal, Merold
   Kierkegaard's Existentialism — Leone, George
   Kierkegaard's Journals and Notebooks — Kierkegaard, Soren
   Kierkegaard's Journals and Notebooks, vol. 7 — Cappelorn, Niels Jorgen

   Kiev 1941: Hitler's Battle for Supremacy in the East — Stahel, David
   Kievskaia Rus' i malorossiia v XIX veke — Tolochko, Aleksei
c Kiki and Jacques — Ross, Susan
c Kiki Kokt: La leyenda encantada del coqui (Illus. by Rodriguez, Ed) — Rodriguez, Ed
   The Kill — Casey, Jane
   Kill Again — Baer, Neal
   Kill Chain: The Rise of High-Tech Assassins — Cockburn, Andrew
   Kill Chain: The Rise of the High-Tech Assassins — Cockburn, Andrew
   A Kill in the Morning — Shimmin, Graeme
   Kill Me, Darling — Spillane, Mickey
   Kill My Mother — Feiffer, Jules
   Kill Shot — Bunn, Bill
y Kill the Boy Band — Moldavsky, Goldy
y Kill the Silence: A Survivor's Life Reclaimed — Korra, Monika
   Kill without Mercy — Ivy, Alexandra
   Killer — Kellerman, Jonathan
   Killer Apes, Naked Apes, and Just Plain Nasty People: The Misuse and Abuse of Science in Political Discourse — Perry, Richard J.
   Killer Care — Lieber, James B.
   Killer, Come Hither — Begley, Louis
c Killer Game — McKay, Kirsty
   Killer Gourmet — McKevett, G.A.
y Killer Instinct — Barnes, Jennifer Lynn
   The Killer Next Door (Read by Church, Imogen). Audiobook Review — Marwood, Alex
   The Killer Next Door — Marwood, Alex
   The Killer of Cancer Rising — O'Rorke, Torena
c Killer of Enemies — Bruchac, Joseph
   A Killer Past — Soule, Maris
c Killer Plants and Other Green Gunk — Claybourne, Anna
   Killer Weed: Marijuana Grow Ops, Media, and Justice — Boyd, Susan C.
y Killer Within — Green, S.E.
   Killer Year: Stories to Die For (Read by Devries, David). Audiobook Review — Child, Lee
   The Killers: A Narrative of Real Life in Philadelphia — Lippard, George
   Killers of the King: The Men Who Dared to Execute Charles I — Spencer, Charles
   Killing a King: The Assassination of Yitzhak Rabin and the Remaking of Israel — Ephron, Dan
   Killing and Dying: Six Stories — Tomine, Adrian
   Killing and Dying: Six Stories (Illus. by Tomine, Adrian) — Tomine, Adrian
   Killing Auntie — Bursa, Andrzej
   The Killing Forest — Blaedel, Sara
   Killing from the Inside Out: Moral Injury and Just War — Meagher, Robert Emmett
   Killing Frost — Tierney, Ronald
   Killing Happy Animals: Explorations in Utilitarian Ethics — Visak, Tatjana
   The Killing II — Hewson, David
   The Killing III: Based on the BAFTA Award-Winning TV Series Written by Soren Sveistrup — Hewson, David
   A Killing in Zion — Hunt, Andrew
y The Killing Jar — Bosworth, Jennifer
   Killing Jesus — Dugard, Martin
   The Killing Kind — Holm, Chris
   The Killing Lessons — Black, Saul
   Killing Lincoln: The Shocking Assassination That Changed America — O'Reilly, Bill
   Killing Maine — Bond, Mike
   Killing Monica (Read by Plummer, Therese). Audiobook Review — Bushnell, Candace
   Killing Monica — Bushnell, Candace
   A Killing on Ring Jaw Bluff: The Great Recession and the Death of Small Town Georgia — Rawlings, William
   Killing Patton: The Strange Death of World War II's Most Audacious General — Dugard, Martin
   Killing Pilgrim — Mattich, Alen
   Killing Pretty — Kadrey, Richard
   Killing Reagan: The Violent Assault That Changed a Presidency — O'Reilly, Bill
   The Killing Room: A Mystery in Florence — Kent, Christobel
   Killing the Messenger — Brock, David
y Killing Time in Crystal City — Lynch, Chris
   Killing Time in Saudi Araba — Heines, Matthew D.
   Killing Titan — Bear, Greg
   Killing Trail — Mizushima, Margaret
   A Killing Winter — Callaghan, Tom

c The Killing Woods (Read by Hardingham, Fiona). Audiobook Review — Christopher, Lucy
   Kilts and Daggers — Roberts, Victoria
   A Kim Jong-Il Production: The Extraordinary True Story of a Kidnapped Filmmaker, His Star Actress, and a Young Dictator's Rise to Power (Read by Park, Stephen). Audiobook Review — Fischer, Paul
   A Kim Jong-Il Production: The Extraordinary True Story of a Kidnapped Filmmaker, His Star Actress, and a Young Dictator's Rise to Power — Fischer, Paul
   Kim Kardashian's Marriage — Riviere, Sam
c The Kind-Hearted Monster: Two Classic Stories (Illus. by Velthuijs, Max) — Velthuijs, Max
   A Kind of Grief — Scott, A.D.
   The Kind Worth Killing (Read by Heller, Johnny). Audiobook Review — Swanson, Peter
   The Kind Worth Killing — Swanson, Peter
y Kinda Like Brothers — Booth, Coe
   Kinder Than Solitude — Li, Yiyun
   Kinder und Krieg. Epochenubergreifende Analysen zu Kriegskindheiten im Wandel
c Kindergarten Luck (Illus. by Godbout, Genevieve) — Borden, Louise
   Kindfulness Meditation — Brahm, Ajahn
   The Kindness — Samson, Polly
y The Kindness of Enemies — Aboulela, Leila
   Kindred by Choice: Germans and American Indians since 1800 — Penny, H. Glenn
   The Kinfolk Home: Interiors for Slow Living — Williams, Nathan
y King — Oh, Ellen
   King Alfred's Book of Laws: A Study of the Domboc and Its Influence on English Identity — Preston, Todd
   The King and Queen of Malibu — Randall, David K.
c The King and the Magician (Illus. by Gusti) — Bucay, Jorge
c The King and the Sea: 21 Extremely Short Stories (Illus. by Erlbruch, Wolf) — Janisch, Heinz
c King Burue Changes the Rules (Illus. by Beheshti, Amene) — Bajlo, Natalija
c The King Cat (Illus. by Altes, Marta) — Altes, Marta
c King Cobras: Hooded Venomous Reptiles — Hirsch, Rebecca E.
y King Dork Approximately — Portman, Frank
   King James Bible across Borders and Centuries — Duran, Angelica
   King John — Warren, W.L.
   King John: And the Road to Magna Carta — Church, Stephen
   King John: England, Magna Carta and the Making of a Tyrant — Church, Stephen
   King John: Treachery and Tyranny in Medieval England: The Road to Magna Carta — Morris, Marc
   King John: Treachery, Tyranny and the Road to Magna Carta — Morris, Marc
   The King of Fear — Chapman, Drew
   King of Kings: The Triumph and Tragedy of Emperor Haile Selassie I of Ethiopia — Asserate, Asfa-Wossen
   King of Kings: Triumph and Tragedy of Emperor Haile Selassie I of Ethiopia — Asserate, Asfa-Wossen
   The King of Little Things (Illus. by Wenzel, David T.) — Lepp, Bil
   King of the Comics: One Hundred Years of King Features Syndicate — Mullaney, Dean
   King of the Cracksmen — O'Flaherty, Dennis
   King of the Gypsies — Myka, Lenore
   King of the Lions and other Animal Stories — Feinland, Stephen
   The King of the Sea Monkeys — Cull, Mark E.
   King of Yiddish — Leviant, Curt
c King Red and the White Snow: And Other Tales for Children (Illus. by Down, Reg) — Down, Reg
c A King Salmon Journey (Illus. by Van Zyle, Jon) — Miller, Debbie S.
   King Sigismund Chapel at Cracow Cathedral, 1515-1533 — Mossakowski, Stanislaw
c King Thrushbeard (Illus. by Dobrescu, Irina) — Grimm, Jacob
   A King Travels: Festive Traditions in Late Medieval and Early Modern Spain — Ruiz, Teofilo F.
y King Tut's Tomb — Moore, Shannon Baker
   A King Undone — Davis, Cooper
   Kingdom, Book 1 — Ryan, Shawna
   Kingdom Come — Jensen, Jane
y Kingdom of Ashes — Thomas, Rhiannon

The Kingdom of Insignificance: Miron Bialoszewski and the Quotidian, the Queer, and the Traumatic — Nizynska, Joanna
A Kingdom of Souls — Hodorova, Daniela
Kingdom of Speculation — Goldberg, Barbara
c The Kingdom of the Sun and Moon — Press, Lowell H.
Kingdoms of God — Hart, Kevin
Kingfisher — McKillip, Patricia A.
c The Kingfisher Soccer Encyclopedia — Gifford, Clive
Kings and Emperors — Lambdin, Dewey
The King's Bed: Sex, Power and the Court of Charles II — Jordan, Don
The King's Body: Burial and Succession in Late Anglo-Saxon England — Marafioti, Nicole
King's College Chapel 1515-2015: Art, Music and Religion in Cambridge — Massing, J.M.
The King's Justice: Two Novellas — Donaldson, Stephen R.
Kings, Lords, and Men in Scotland and Britain, 1300-1625: Essays in Honour of Jenny Wormald — Godfrey, Mark
Kings of Fortune — Cheung, Roderick
The Kings of London — Shaw, William
Kings of the Grail: Tracing the Historic Journey of the Cup of Christ from Jerusalem to Modern-Day Spain — Sevilla, Margarita Torres
Kingship and Consent in Anglo-Saxon England, 871-978: Assemblies and the State in the Early Middle Ages — Roach, Levi
Kingship and Masculinity in Late Medieval England — Lewis, Katherine J.
Kingship, Legislation and Power in Anglo-Saxon England — Owen-Crocker, Gale R.
Kinshasa: Tales of the Invisible City — De Boeck, Filip
Kinship across Borders: A Christian Ethic of Immigration — Heyer, Kristin E.
Kinship and Cohort in an Aging Society: From Generation to Generation — Silverstein, Merril
Kinship and Performance in the Black and Green Atlantic — Gough, Kathleen M.
Kinship in Thucydides: Intercommunal Ties and Historical Narrative — Fragoulaki, Maria
Kinski — Hardman, Gabriel
Kipling and Trix — Hamer, Mary
c Kirby's Journal: Backyard Butterfly Magic — Caldwell, Charlotte
Kirche, Krieg und Katholiken: Geschichte und Gedachtnis im 20 Jahrhundert — Hummel, Karl-Joseph
Kirche vor Ort: Pfarreikulturen im vormodernen Europa
y Kirin Rise: The Cast of Shadows — Cruz, Ed
Kirtland Temple: The Biography of a Shared Mormon Sacred Space — Howlett, David J.
The Kiskadee of Death — Dunlap, Jan
A Kiss Is Still a Kiss — Smith, Virginia
y Kiss Kill Vanish — Martinez, Jessica
c Kiss, Kiss (Illus. by Laplante, Jacques) — Couelle, Jennifer
c Kiss, Kiss, Pout-Pout Fish (Illus. by Hanna, Dan) — Diesen, Deborah
Kiss Me Hello — Burrowes, Grace
y Kiss of Broken Glass — Kuderick, Madeleine
y The Kiss of Deception — Pearson, Mary E.
The Kiss on Castle Road — Christopher, Lauren
Kiss the Earl — Lamm, Gina
c Kisses and Cuddles (Illus. by Galloway, Fhiona) — Fronis, Aly
Kissing in America — Rabb, Margo
y Kissing Ted Callahan (and Other Guys). — Spalding, Amy
Kissinger: The Idealist, 1923-1968 — Ferguson, Niall
Kissinger's Shadow: The Long Reach of America's Most Controversial Statesman — Grandin, Greg
Kit Carson and the First Battle of Adobe Walls: A Tale of Two Journeys — Lynn, Alvin R.
c Kitanai and Cavity Croc Brush their Teeth (Illus. by Christoph, Jamey) — Troupe, Thomas Kingsley
c Kitanai and Hungry Hare Eat Healthfully (Illus. by Christoph, Jamey) — Troupe, Thomas Kingsley
c Kitchen Chaos — Levine, Deborah A.
Kitchen Creamery: Making Yogurt, Butter and Cheese at Home — Hill, Louella
c Kitchen Dance (Illus. by Torres, Leyla) — Torres, Leyla
The Kitchen Diaries III: A Year of Good Eating — Slater, Nigel
Kitchen Gypsy: Recipes and Stories from a Lifelong Romance with Food — Weir, Joanne
c Kitchen Science Lab for Kids — Heinecke, Liz

Kitchens of the Great Midwest (Read by Ryan, Amy). Audiobook Review — Stradal, J. Ryan
y Kitchens of the Great Midwest — Stradal, J. Ryan
Kith, Kin, and Neighbors: Communities and Confessions in Seventeenth-Century Wilno — Frick, David
c Kitten Tale (Illus. by Rohmann, Eric) — Rohmann, Eric
Kittens Can Kill — Simon, Clea
c Kitty and Me — Kane, Sharon Smith
Kitty Genovese: The Murder, the Bystanders, the Crime That Changed America — Cook, Kevin
Kitty Saves the World — Vaughn, Carrie
Kiya: Hope of the Pharaoh — Hamstead, Katie
c Kizmet and the Case of the Tassie Tiger — Woodley, Frank
The Kizuna Coast — Massey, Sujata
KL: A History of the Nazi Concentration Camps — Wachsmann, Nikolaus
Klandestine: How a Klan Lawyer and a Checkbook Journalist Helped James Earl Ray Cover Up His Crime — McMichael, Pate
c KLassie Come-Home: An Adaptation of Eric Knight's Classic Story (Illus. by Ivanov, Olga) — Knight, Eric
Klaus — Massle, Allan
Kleine Erinnerungen: Raume, Praktiken und Akteure landlicher Erinnerungen
Klezmer's Afterlife: An Ethnography of the Jewish Music Revival in Poland and Germany — Waligorska, Magdalena
c Klickitat — Rock, Peter
y Knack — Twitchel, Tom
The Knife — Ritchell, Ross
Knife Fights: A Memoir of Modern War in Theory and Practice — Nagl, John A.
A Knight of the Seven Kingdoms — Martin, George R.R.
The Knight of the Swords — Moorcock, Michael
Knight Writings: Three Tragedies and a Romance — Pierce, Cahterine J.
c The Knighting of Sir Kaye (Illus. by Allred, Dave) — Winn, Don M.
y Knightley and Son: K-9 — Gavin, Rohan
c Knightmare: Rotten Luck! (Illus. by Blunt, Fred) — Bently, Peter
c The Knights Before Christmas (Illus. by Magoon, Scott) — Holub, Joan
The Knights Errant of Anarchy: London and the Italian Anarchist Diaspora — Di Paola, Pietro
c Knights at 2nd Earth: Tears of an Honorable King (Illus. by Raimey, Justin) — Raimey, Terry L.
c Knit-Knotters: A Branches Book (Illus. by Tran, Turine) — Hay, Sam
Knit the Sky: Cultivate Your Creativity with a Playful Way of Knitting — Redmond, Lea
c Knit Together (Illus. by Dominguez, Angela) — Dominguez, Angela
Knit Wear Love: Foolproof Instructions for Knitting Your Best-Fitting Sweaters Ever in the Styles You Love to Wear — Herzog, Amy
Knit Your Own Pet: Easy-to-Follow Patterns for a Cat, Mouse, Guinea Pig, Pony, and More Adorable Companions — Muir, Sally
Knitless: 50 No-Knit, Stash-Busting Yarn Projects — McFadden, Laura
Knitting Fabric Rugs: 28 Colorful Designs for Crafters of Every Level — Tiede, Karen
Knitting Fresh Brioche: Creating Two-Color Twists and Turns — Marchant, Nancy
Knitting Pearls: Writers Writing about Knitting — Hood, Ann
Knock at the Door of Opportunity: Black Migration to Chicago, 1900-1919 — Reed, Christopher Robert
c Knock Knock: My Dad's Dream for Me (Illus. by Collier, Bryan) — Beaty, Daniel
Knock on Wood — Johnston, Linda O.
c Knockabout Cricket: A Story of Sporting Legend Johnny Mullagh (Illus. by Walters, Ainsley) — McMullin, Neridah
The Knockoff (Read by Kellgren, Katherine). Audiobook Review — Sykes, Lucy
The Knockoff — Sykes, Lucy
y Knockout Games — Neri, G.
KnockOut — Jodzio, Jim
Know the Night: A Memoir of Survival in the Small Hours — Mutch, Maria
y Know Your Beholder — Rapp, Adam
c The Knowing Book (Illus. by Cordell, Matthew) — Dotlich, Rebecca Kai
Knowing Things: Circulations and Transitions of Objects in Natural History

Knowing Who You Are: Eight Surprising Images of Christian Identity — Gill, Malcolm
The Knowledge — Peake, Robert
Knowledge and Decisions — Sowell, Thomas
Knowledge and Evidence: Investigating Technologies in Practice — Berner, Boel
Knowledge in the Time of Cholera: The Struggle over American Medicine in the Nineteenth Century — Whooley, Owen
Knuckleball: The History of the Unhittable Pitch — Freedman, Lew
The Knute Rockne Kid — Bruno, Frank J.
c Koala Hospital — Eszterhas, Suzi
c Koalas — Esbaum, Jill
"Kollektive Akteure" und Gewalt. Macht und Ohnmacht im 20. Jahrhundert
Koloniales Spektakel in 9x14: Bildpostkarten im Deutschen Kaiserreich — Axster, Felix
Kombinirani izborni sustavi u Europi 1945-2014: Parne komparacije Njemacke i Italije, Bugarske i Hrvatske — Kasapovic, Mirjana
Kommentar zur Vita Heliogabali der Historia Augusta — Zinsli, Samuel Christian
Kommunisten Gegen Hitler und Stalin: Die Linke Opposition der KPD in der Weimarer Republik. Eine Gesamtdarstellung — Bois, Marcel
c Komodo Dragons: Deadly Hunting Reptiles — Hirsch, Rebecca E.
Kongo: Power and Majesty — LaGamma, Alisa
'Konigtum' in der Politischen Kultur des Spatrepublikanischen Rom — Sigmund, Christian
Konnen wir der Geschichte entkommen? Geschichtsphilosophie am Beginn des 21. Jahrhunderts — Schmidt, Christian
Konrad Morgen: The Conscience of a Nazi Judge — Pauer-Studer, Herlinde
Konstantin der Grosse: Kaiser zwischen Machtpolitik und Religion — Rosen, Klaus
Konstanz 1414-1418: Eine Stadt und ihr Konzil — Keupp, Jan
Konstitutionalismus in Europa: Entwicklung und Interpretation — Lehnert, Detlef
Konstrukteure der Nation: Geschichtsprofessoren als Politische Akteure in Vormarz und Revolution 1848/49 — Lenhard-Schramm, Niklas
Konzepte des Authentischen - Prozesse der Authentisierung
Konzeptionelle Uberlegungen zur Edition von Rechnungen und Amtsbuchern des Spaten Mittelalters
c Kookoo Kookaburra (Illus. by Dreise, Gregg) — Dreise, Gregg
KooKooLand — Norris, Gloria
Kooperation statt Klassenkampf? Zur Bedeutung kooperativer wirtschaftlicher Leitbilder fur die Arbeitszeitsenkung in Kaiserreich und Bundesrepublik — Franz, Albrecht
Korean Horror Cinema — Peirse, Alison
The Korean Popular Culture Reader — Kim, Kyung Hyun
Koreans in North America: Their Twenty-First Century Experiences — Min, Pyong Gap
Korea's Great Buddhist-Confucian Debate: The Treatises of Chong Tojon (Sambong) and Hamho Tukt'ong — Muller, Charles
Koreatown — Hong, Deuki
Kosher: Private Regulation in the Age of Industrial Food — Lytton, Timothy D.
y Krabat & the Sorcerer's Mill — Bell, Anthea
Kraft der Symbole: Wie Wir Uns Von Der Gesellschaft Leiten Lassen und Dabei die Wirklichkeit Selbst Mitgestalten — Beetz, Michael
Kraftwerk: Publikation — Buckley, David
y Krakens and Lies (Illus. by Sutherland, Kari) — Sutherland, Tui T.
Krazy Kodak Moments — Albright, James M.
Kreditgeld in der romischen Antike: Ursprunge, Entstehung, Ubertragung und Verbreitung — Bange, Matthias
The Kree/Skrull War — Buscema, Sal
The Kreutzer Sonata Variations: Lev Tolstoy's Novella and Counterstories by Sofiya Tolstaya and Lev Lvovich Tolstoy — Katz, Michael R.
Kreuzzug und Regionale Herrschaft: Die Alteren Grafen von Berg 1147-1225 — Berner, Alexander
Krieg der Welten: Wissenschaftliche Tagung zur Geschichte des Kalten Krieges
Krieg! Juden zwischen den Fronten 1914-1918 — Heikaus, Ulrike
Kriege im 21. Jahrhundert: Neue Herausforderungen der Friedensbewegung — Bauer, Rudolph
Kriegserfahrungen erzahlen

Kriegskrankenpflege im Ersten Weltkrieg. Das Pflegepersonal der freiwilligen Krankenpflege in den Etappen des deutschen Kaiserreiches — *Stolzle, Astrid*

Kriegslandschaften. Gewalt, Zerstorung und Erinnerung

Kriegswirtschaft und Arbeitseinsatz bei der Auto Union AG Chemnitz im Zweiten Weltkrieg — *Kukowski, Martin*

Krimtataren in Geschichte und Gegenwart

Krippe, Kuche, Kombinat - Frauen im Kommunismus. 7. Hohenschonhausen-Forum

Kris Kristofferson: Country Highwayman — *Hurd, Mary G.*

c Kristen Stewart — *Bodden, Valerie*

Krupp: A History of the Legendary German Firm — *James, Harold*

Ksiegi Jakubowe — *Tokarczuk, Olga*

Kuca secanja i zaborava — *David, Filip*

Kuche, Kuhlschrank, Kilowatt: Zur Geschichte des Privaten Energiekonsums in Deutschland 1945-1990 — *Gerber, Sophie*

c The Kudzu Cookbook: Cooking Up a Storm with That Wild and Crazy Vine That Grows in Miles-Per-Hour! (Illus. by French, Kristen) — *Longmeyer, Carole Marsh*

Kulturelle Phanomene des Altertums zwischen Regularitat, Distinktion und Devianz

Kulturkatholizismus: Katholiken auf dem Weg in die Deutsche Kultur 1900-1933 — *Weiss, Otto*

Kulturtransfer am Furstenhof: Hofische Austauschprozesse und Ihre Medien im Zeitalter Kaiser Maximilians I — *Muller, Matthias*

c Kung Fu Kitty: Laying Down the Law (Illus. by Gentile, Michael) — *Bortz, Lauri*

Kunst im Deutschen Orden

c Kunu's Basket: A Story From Indian Island (Illus. by Drucker, Susan) — *Francis, Lee DeCora*

c The Kurdles (Illus. by Goodin, Robert) — *Goodin, Robert*

Kurienuniversitat und Stadtromische Universitat von ca. 1300 bis 1471 — *Schwarz, Brigide*

Kurt Cobain: The Last Session — *Frohman, Jesse*

Kvachi — *Javakhishvili, Mikheil*

Kwajalein: An Island Like No Other — *Jacobson, Lynn A.*

Kyiv, Ukraine: The City of Domes and Demons from the Collapse of Socialism to the Mass Uprising of 2013-2014 — *Cybriwsky, Roman Adrian*

c Kyle Goes Alone (Illus. by Barron, Ashley) — *Thornhill, Jan*

c Kylie, Aaron: Canadian Geographic Biggest and Best of Canada: 1000 Facts and Figures — *Kylie, Aaron*

Kyoto Gardens: Masterworks of the Japanese Gardener's Art — *Clancy, Judith*

Kyotofu: Uniquely Delicious Japanese Desserts — *Bermensolo, Nicole*

L

L.A. Math: Romance, Crime, and Mathematics in the City of Angels — *Stein, James D.*
L.A. Plays itself / Boys in the Sand — *Patton, Cindy*
The L.M. Montgomery Reader, vol. 3: A Legacy in Review — *Lefebvre, Benjamin*
La bibilioteca di Pietro Crinito: Manoscritti e libri a stampa della raccolta libraria di un umanista fiorentino (Textes et Etudes du Moyen Age 60.) Porto: federation international des instituts d'etudes medievales — *Marchiaro, Michaelangiola*
c La chasse aux bestioles — *Charlesworth, Liza*
La Citadelle de la Vertu ou La Veritable Tranquillite de l'Ame / Arx Virtutis Sive De Vera Animi Tranquillitate. — *Van Havre, Jean*
La citta del Seicento — *Pesco, Daniela del*
La comptabilite fondamentale — *Okamba, Emmanuel*
La Comunicazione Epistolare da e per Torino, Volume II - Vittorio Amedeo II e le prime Tariffe per la Posta delle Lettere — *Robetti, Italo*
La Congiura dei Pazzi: I Documenti del Conflitto fra Lorenzo de' Medici e Sisto IV: Le Bolle di Scomunica, la "Florentina synodus," e la "Dissentio" Insoria tra la Santita del Papa e i Fiorentini — *Daniels, Tobias*
La congiura dei Pazzi: I documenti del conflitto fra Lorenzo de' Medici e Sisto IV: Le bolle di scomunica, la "Florentina synodus," e la "Dissentio" insorta tra la Santita del Papa e i Fiorentini. Edizione critica e comment — *Daniels, Tobias*
La conquete du Roussillon par Pierre le Ceremonieux — *Claverie, Pierre-Vincent*
La conquista islamica de la Peninsula Iberica y la tergiversacion del pasado: Del catastrofismo al negacionismo — *Sanjuan, Alejandro Garcia*
La Conquistadora: The Virgin Mary at War and Peace in the Old and New Worlds — *Remensnyder, Amy G.*
La cruzada en tiempos de Alfonso X — *Rodriguez Garcia, Jose Manuel*
La danse des ombres — *Dadsetan, Mehdi*
La dea di Erice e la sua diffusione nel Mediterraneo. Un culto tra Fenici, Greci e Romani — *Leitz, Beatrice*
La defensa del imperio.: JuliauN De Arriaga En La Armada — *Kuethe, Allan J.*
La Defense de la Syrie-Palestine des Achemenides aux Lagides: Histoire et Archeologie des Fortifications a l'Ouest du Jourdain de 532 a 199 Avant J.-C. — *Balandier, Claire*
La disparition de Jim Sullivan — *Viel, Tanguy*
La Fauconnerie a la Renaissance: Le "Hieracosophion" (1582-1584) de Jacques Auguste de Thou — *de Smet, Ingrid A.R.*
c La Fete de Billy (Illus. by Valckx, Catharina) — *Valckx, Catharina*
La Fete de l'insignificance — *Kundera, Milan*
y La forme floue ties fantomes — *Bouchard, Camille*
La France peripherique — *Guilluy, Christophe*
La Frontera: Forests and Ecological Conflict in Chile's Frontier Territory — *Klubock, Thomas Miller*
La gente decente de Lima y su resistencia al orden republicano: Ferarquias sociales, prensa y sistema judicial durante el siglo — *Whipple, Pablo*
La Guerre Apres la Guerre: L'Echo de la Grande Guerre dans la Caricature — *Gardes, Jean-Claude*
c La lecon de trombone (Illus. by Eid, Jean-Paul) — *Lemieux, Genevieve*
La Litterature de Montaigne: Proceedings of the Tenth Cambridge French Renaissance Colloquium 1-4 September 2008 — *Ford, Philip*
y La LNH, un reve impossible — *Gelinas, Luc*

La Lucha: The Story of Lucha Castro and Human Rights in Mexico — *Sack, Jon*
La lune aux XVIIe et XVIIIe siecles — *Grell, Chantal*
y La machine a mesurer l'amour — *Mercier, Johanne*
La Marche des lemmings: la deuxieme mort de Charlie Hebdo — *Federbusch, Serge*
La Mort de Napoleon — *Leys, Simon*
c La mysterieuse boutique de Monsieur Bottom (Illus. by Ben, Magali) — *Hurtut, Caroline*
c La noche en que tu naciste (Illus. by Tillman, Nancy) — *Tillman, Nancy*
La Oculta — *Faciolince, Hector Abad*
La Passione di Felice Martire, vescovo di Nola (BHL): Edizione critica e traduzione — *Manfredonia, Rosa*
La Pena Maxima — *Roncagliolo, Santiago*
La piece et le geste: Artisans, marchands et savoir technique a Londres au XVIIIe siecle — *Hilaire-Perez, Liliane*
c La pluie — *Taylor, Lauren*
La Plume et la tribune, II: Discours et correspondance — *De L'Hospital, Michel*
La presa di potere dell'Inquizitione romana, 1550-1553 — *Firpo, Massimo*
c La reglisse rouge (Illus. by Colpron, Pascal) — *Turgeon, Elizabeth*
y La Reine Margot — *Laframboise, Michele*
La Republique des lettres — *Fumaroli, Marc*
La Revanche de l'ecrivaine fantome — *Turgeon, David*
La rivista 'Commerce' e Marguerite Caetani, vol. 2: Giuseppe Ungaretti - lettere a Marguerite Caetani — *Levie, Sophie*
La Seigneurie collective: Pairs, pariers, paratge; les coseigneurs du XIe au XIIIe siecle — *Debax, Helene*
La Semilla Y La Cizana — *Barca, Pedro Calderon de la*
La sociabilite epistolaire chez Ciceron — *Bernard, Jacques-Emmanuel*
La Sollecitudine Ecclesiale di Monsignor Roncalli in Bulgaria (1925-1934). — *Kartaloff, Kiril Plamen*
La traversee electrique des Pyrenees: Histoire de l'interconnexion entre la France et l'Espagne — *Viguie, Renan*
La Venus hottentote: Entre Barnum et Museum — *Blanckaert, Claude*
La Vie d'Edouard le Confesseur, by a Nun of Barking Abbey — *Bliss, Jane*
L'abbaye cistercienne de Begard des origines a 1476: Histoire et chartes — *Evans, Claude*
Labels and Libels: Naming Beguines in Northern Medieval Europe — *Bohringer, Letha*
c Labor Day — *Dash, Meredith*
Labor der Moderne: Nachkriegsarchitektur in Europa/Laboratory of Modernism. Post-War Architecture in Europe — *Sachsische Akademie der Kunste*
Labor Disorders in Neoliberal Italy: Mobbing, Well-being, and the Workplace — *Mole, Noelle J.*
Laboratory of Learning: HBCU Laboratory Schools and Alabama State College Lab High in the Era of Jim Crow — *Pierson, Sharon Gay*
Laboratory Techniques in Organic Chemistry: Supporting Inquiry-Driven Experiments, 4th ed. — *Mohrig, Jerry R.*
Labors of Love: Nursing Homes and the Structures of Care Work — *Rodriguez, Jason*
Labour and the Caucus: Working-Class Radicalism and Organised Liberalism in England, 1868-88 — *Owen, James*
Labour Markets and Identity on the Post-Industrial Assembly Line — *Lloyd, Anthony*

Labyrinth: A Journey through London's Underground — *Coysh, Louise*
The Labyrinth — *Yaeko, Nogami*
Lacan on Madness: Madness, Yes You Can't — *Gherovici, Patricia*
Lace Yarn Studio: Garments, Hats, and Fresh Ideas for Lace Yarn — *Sulcoski, Carol J.*
Lactivism: How Feminists and Fundamentalists, Hippies and Yuppies, and Physicians and Politicians Made Breastfeeding Big Business and Bad Policy — *Jung, Courtney*
Lacy Eye (Read by Archer, Ellen). Audiobook Review — *Threadway, Jessica*
Lacy Eye — *Treadway, Jessica*
y The Ladies of Managua — *Gage, Eleni N.*
Ladies of the Canyons: A League of Extraordinary Women and Their Adventures in the American Southwest — *Poling-Kempes, Lesley*
The Lady Agnes Mystery, vol. 1 — *Japp, Andrea*
The Lady Agnes Mystery, vol. 2 — *Japp, Andrea*
Lady Be Good — *Duran, Meredith*
Lady Bird and Lyndon: The Hidden Story of a Marriage That Made a President — *Caroli, Betty Boyd*
Lady Bridget's Diary — *Rodale, Maya*
Lady Byron and Her Daughters — *Markus, Julia*
Lady Constance Lytton: Aristocrat, Suffragette, Martyr — *Jenkins, Lyndsey*
Lady Emily's Exotic Journey — *Marek, Lillian*
The Lady from Zagreb (Read by Lee, John). Audiobook Review — *Kerr, Philip*
The Lady from Zagreb — *Kerr, Philip*
The Lady Hellion — *Shupe, Joanna*
c Lady Liberty: A Biography (Illus. by Tavares, Matt) — *Rappaport, Doreen*
The Lady Meets Her Match — *Conkle, Gina*
A Lady of Good Family — *Mackin, Jeanne*
The Lady of Misrule — *Dunn, Suzannah*
c Lady Pancake & Sir French Toast (Illus. by Kearney, Brendan) — *Funk, Josh*
Lady Sings the Blues — *Williams, Billy Dee*
The Lady with the Borzoi: Blanche Knopf, Literary Tastemaker Extraordinaire — *Claridge, Laura*
The Ladybird Story: Children's Books for Everyone — *Johnson, Lorraine*
c Ladybug Girl and the Best Ever Playdate (Illus. by Soman, David) — *Davis, Jacky*
c Ladybug Girl and the Dress-Up Dilemma (Illus. by Soman, David) — *Soman, David*
The Lady's Command — *Laurens, Stephanie*
Lafayette: His Extraordinary Life and Legacy — *Miller, Donald (b. 1934-)*
Lafayette in the Somewhat United States (Read by Vowell, Sarah, with eight additional readers). Audiobook Review — *Vowell, Sarah*
Lafayette in the Somewhat United States — *Vowell, Sarah*
LaFosse and Alexander's Origami Jewelry: Easy-to-Make Paper Pendants, Bracelets, Necklaces and Earrings — *LaFosse, Michael G.*
The Lagoon: How Aristotle Invented Science — *Leroi, Armand Marie*
Laibach und NSK: Die Inquisitionsmaschine im Kreuzverhor — *Monroe, Alexei*
y Lailah — *Kelly, Nikki*
c Lailah's Lunchbox (Illus. by Lyon, Lea) — *Faruqi, Reem*
y Lair of Dreams — *Bray, Libba*
y Lair of Dreams (Read by LaVoy, January). Audiobook Review — *Bray, Libba*
y Lair of Dreams — *Bray, Libba*

Lake Effect: Tales of Large Lakes, Arctic Winds, and Recurrent Snows — Monmonier, Mark
The Lake House — Morton, Kate
c Lake in the Clouds — Willett, Edward
Lake Methodism: Polite Literature and Popular Religion in England, 1780-1830 — Cragwall, Jasper
The Lake of Far: Stories — Lilly, Paul R.
Lake of Fire — Stevens, Mark
Lake of Two Mountains — Pare, Arleen
L'Album multicolore — Dupre, Louise
c L'alligator — Turnbull, Stephanie
Lamastu: An Edition of the Canonical Series of Lamastu Incantations and Rituals and Related Texts from the Second and First Millennia B.C — Farber, Walter
Lamaze: An International History — Michaels, Paula A.
L'America nell' "Occidente": Storia della dottrina Monroe — Mariano, Marco
L'amour et les forets — Reinhardt, Eric
Lamp Black, Wolf Grey — Brackston, Paula
c Lana's World: Let's Go Fishing! (Illus. by Golden, Jess) — Silverman, Erica
c Lana's World: Let's Have a Parade! (Illus. by Golden, Jess) — Silverman, Erica
Land Access and Resettlement: A Guide to Best Practice — Reddy, Gerry
Land and Book: Literature and Land Tenure in Anglo-Saxon England — Smith, Scott T.
The Land Ballot — Adcock, Fleur
The Land Breakers — Ehle, John
Land, Livelihood, and Civility in Southern Mexico: Oaxaca Valley Communities in History — Cook, Scott
A Land of Aching Hearts: The Middle East in the Great War — Fawaz, Leila Tarazi
Land of Enchantment — Wieland, Liza
y The Land of Forgotten Girls — Kelly, Erin Entrada
The Land of Gold — Barker, Sebastian
c The Land of Line (Illus. by Hussenot, Victor) — Hussenot, Victor
c The Land of Lines (Illus. by Hussenot, Victor) — Hussenot, Victor
c Land of Or (Illus. by Allen, Toby) — Mullaly, Katie
The Land of Rain Shadow: Horned Toad, Texas — Roach, Joyce Gibson
Land of Shadows — Royal, Priscilla
The Land of the Elephant Kings: Space, Territory, and Ideology in the Seleucid Empire — Kosmin, Paul J.
c Land of the Free: The Kids' Book of Freedom — Hanson, Anders
The Land of the Green Man: A Journey through the Supernatural Landscapes of the British Isles — Larrington, Carolyne
c Land of the Legend — Ghodrati, Esfandiar
Land of the Turquoise Mountains: Journeys Across Iran — Massoudi, Cyrus
The Land of Too Much: American Abundance and the Paradox of Poverty — Prasad, Monica
The Land Shall Be Deluged in Blood: A New History of the Nat Turner Revolt — Breen, Patrick H.
c Land Shark (Illus. by Mantle, Ben) — Ferry, Beth
Land Your Dream Career: Eleven Steps to Take in College — Terhune, Tori Randolph
Landfall — Urbani, Ellen
Landfalls — Williams, Naomi J.
Landgartha: A Tragicomedy by Henry Burnell — Rankin, Deana
Landmarks — Macfarlane, Robert
Landmarks Revisited: The Vekhi Symposium 100 Years On — Aizelwood, Robin
Landor's Cleanness: A Study of Walter Savage Landor — Roberts, Adam
Landscape and Change in Early Medieval Italy: Chestnuts, Economy, and Culture — Squatriti, Paolo
Landscape and Society in Contemporary Ireland — McGrath, Brendan
Landscape Imagery, Politics, and Identity in a Divided Germany, 1968-1989 — Wilkins, Catherine
The Landscape of Imagination: Collected Essays of James Corner 1990-2010 — Corner, James
Landscapes for the People: George Alexander Grant, First Chief Photographer of the National Park Service — Davis, Ren
Landscapes of Communism: A History through Buildings — Hatherley, Owen
Landscapes of War and Memory: The Two World Wars in Canadian Literature and the Arts, 1977-2007 — Grace, Sherrill
Landscapes on a Train — Swensen, Cole

Landslide Ecology — Walker, Lawrence R.
"Landwirtschaft und Dorfgesellschaft im Ausgehenden Mittelalter." Herbsttagung des Konstanzer Arbeitskreises fur Mittelalterliche Geschichte e.V
Langland and the Rokele Family: The Gentry Background to Piers Plowman — Adams, Robert
c Langston Hughes — Berry, S.L.
Language! 500 Years of the Vulgar Tongue — Green, Jonathon
Language after Heidegger — Ziarek, Krzysztof
Language and Enlightenment: The Berlin Debates of the Eighteenth Century — Lifschitz, Avi
Language and Identity in Modern Egypt — Bassiouney, Reem
Language and Literary Form in French Caribbean Writing — Britton, Celia
Language and Muslim Immigrant Childhoods: The Politics of Belonging — Garcia-Sanchez, Inmaculada Ma
Language Arts (Read by Gilbert, Tavia). Audiobook Review — Kallos, Stephanie
Language Arts — Kallos, Stephanie
Language Arts (Read by Gilbert, Tavia). Audiobook Review — Kallos, Stephanie
Language Arts — Kallos, Stephanie
Language as the Site of Revolt in Medieval and Early Modern England: Speaking as a Woman — Bodden, Mary-Catherine
Language for God in Patristic Tradition: Wrestling with Biblical Anthropomorphism — Sheridan, Mark
The Language Hoax: Why the World Looks the Same in Any Language — McWhorter, John H.
Language Learner Narrative: An Exploration of 'Mundigkeit' in Intercultural Literature — O'Sullivan, Helen
Language Learning, Gender and Desire: Japanese Women on the Move — Takahashi, Kimie
Language, Madness, and Desire: On Literature — Foucault, Michel
The Language of Architecture: 26 Principles Every Architect Should Know — Simitch, Andrea
The Language of Byzantine Learned Literature — Hinterberger, Martin
The Language of Food: A Linguist Reads the Menu — Jurafsky, Dan
The Language of Houses: How Buildings Speak to Us — Lurie, Alison
The Language of Human Rights in West Germany — Wildenthal, Lora
The Language of Law — Marmor, Andrei
The language of life and death: The transformation of experience in oral narrative — Labov, William
The Language of Paradise — Moss, Barbara Klein
The Language of Salvation: Discovering the Riches of What It Means to Be Saved — Kuligin, Victor
The Language of Secrets — Khan, Ausma Zehanat
The Language of Secular Islam: Urdu Nationalism and Colonial India — Datla, Kavita Saraswathi
The Language of the Dead: A World War II Mystery — Kelly, Stephen
Language of War, Language of Peace: Palestine, Israel and the Search for Justice — Shehadeh, Raja
Language Policy and the Discourse on Languages in Ukraine under President Viktor Yanukovych — Moser, Michael
Language Variation: European Perspectives IV — Auer, Peter
Languages of Politics in Nineteenth Century Britain — Craig, David
The languages of the Jews: A sociolinguistic history — Spolsky, Bernard
Lantern Fish — Howell, Sara
c Lantern Sam and the Blue Streak Bandits — Beil, Michael D.
Lanterne Rouge: The Last Man in the Tour de France — Leonard, Max
Laotian Daughters: Working toward Community, Belonging, and Environmental Justice — Shah, Bindi V.
LAPD '53 — Ellroy, James
c Lara of Newtown — McKimmie, Chris
The Larder: Food Studies Methods from the American South — Edge, John T.
The Larder: Food Studies Methods from the American South — Engelhardt, Elizabeth
Large Animal Veterinarian — Edgar, Sherra G.
Large Carnivore Conservation: Integrating Science and Policy in the North American West — Clark, Susan G.
Large Us the Smallest We've Got: A Jigsaw Puzzle — Hamilton, Jed
y Lark Ascending — Spooner, Meagan

Lark Rise to Candleford — Thompson, Flora
y Lark Rising — Waugh, Sandra
The Larousse Book of Bread: 80 Recipes to Make at Home — Kayser, Eric
y Larp! To Geek or Not to Geek (Illus. by Gunter, Gray) — Jolley, Dan
c Larry Gets Lost under the Sea (Illus. by Skewes, John) — Ode, Eric
c Larry the Little Orphan Dog — Kaladeen, Jean
L'Artillerie de Campagne de l'Armee Imperiale Allemande, 5 vols. — Delsert, Bernard
Las musas rameras: Oficio dramatico y conciencia profesional en Lope de Vega — Reidy, Alejandro Garcia
Las razones del censor: Control ideologico y censura de libros en la primera Edad Moderna — Esteve, Cesc
c Las zanahorias maleficas (Illus. by Brown, Peter) — Reynolds, Aaron
The LaSalle Quartet: Conversations with Walter Levin — Spruytenburg, Robert
Lassalles "Sudliche Avantgarde": Protokollbuch des Allgemeinen Deutschen Arbeitervereins der Gemeinde Augsburg (1864-1867). — Murr, Karl Borromaus
c Lassie Come-Home — Hill, Susan
The Last Act of Love: The Story of My Brother and His Sister — Rentzenbrink, Cathy
The Last Afrikaner Leaders: A Supreme Test of Power — Giliomee, Hermann
The Last Aloha — Kocol, Cleo Fellers
The Last American Vampire (Read by Andrews, MacLeod). Audiobook Review — Grahame-Smith, Seth
The Last American Vampire — Smith, Seth Grahame
c The Last ANZAC (Illus. by Bailey, Harriet) — Winch, Gordon
The Last Armada: Queen Elizabeth, Juan del Aguila, and the 100-Day Spanish Invasion of England — Ekin, Des
The Last Asylum: A Memoir of Madness in Our Times — Taylor, Barbara (b. 1950-)
c The Last Bargain — Aiyer, Samita
c Last Battle: Causes and Effects of the Massacre at Wounded Knee — Dell, Pamela
The Last Battle: When U.S. and German Soldiers Joined Forces in the Waning Hours of World War II in Europe — Harding, Stephen
The Last Best Lie — Quinn, Kennedy
The Last Best Place? Gender, Family, and Migration in the New West — Schmalzbauer, Leah
The Last Blank Spaces: Exploring Africa and Australia — Kennedy, Dane
Last Boat to Yokohama: The Life and Legacy of Beate Sirota Gordon — Azimi, Nassrine
c The Last Bogler — Jinks, Catherine
The Last Bohemia: Scenes from the Life of Williamsburg, Brooklyn — Anasi, Robert
The Last Book — Gerritsen, Reinier
The Last Book Ever Written — Kruvant, Jonah
The Last Bookaneer (Read by Vance, Simon). Audiobook Review — Pearl, Matthew
The Last Bookaneer — Pearl, Matthew
c The Last Boy at St. Edith's — Malone, Lee Gjertsen
Last Bus to Wisdom — Doig, Ivan
c Last-but-Not-Least: Lola and the Cupcake Queens (Illus. by Hoppe, Paul) — Pakkala, Christine
c Last-but-Not-Least Lola and the Wild Chicken (Illus. by Hoppe, Paul) — Pakkala, Christine
The Last Campaign: How Presidents Rewrite History, Run for Posterity & Enshrine Their Legacies — Clark, Anthony
The Last Caribbean Frontier, 1795-1815 — Candlin, Kit
Last Chance Hero — Armstrong, Cathleen
Last Chance Hero — Ramsey, Hope
Last Chance Llama Ranch — Fields, Hilary
Last Chance Mustang: The Story of One Horse, One Horseman, and One Final Shot at Redemption — Bornstein, Mitchell
c The Last Changeling — Yolen, Jane
Last Child in the Woods: Saving Our Children from Nature-Deficit Disorder — Louv, Richard
c The Last Chocolate Chip Cookie (Illus. by Elsom, Clare) — Rix, Jamie
c The Last Christmas Tree (Illus. by Campion, Pascal) — Krensky, Stephen
The Last Chronicle of Barset — Small, Helen
The Last Comanche Moon — Peterson, Troy Everett
The Last Confession of Thomas Hawkins — Hodgson, Antonia

The Last Crusade in the West: Castile and the Conquest of Granada — O'Callaghan, Joseph F.
The Last Dawn — Gannon, Joe
Last Day of the Year: Selected Poems — Kruger, Michael
Last Days in Shanghai — Walker, Casey
Last Days in Vietnam — Kennedy, Rory
The Last Days of California — Miller, Mary
c The Last Days of Jesus: His Life and Times — O'Reilly, Bill
The Last Days of Magic — Tompkins, Mark
The Last Days of Rabbit Hayes — McPartlin, Anna
Last Days of the Condor — Grady, James
The Last Days of the Rainbelt — Wishart, David J.
The Last Days of Video — Hawkins, Jeremy
The Last Decision — Wilcox, Victoria
The Last Dream Keeper — Benson, Amber
The Last Dreamer — Josselsohn, Barbara Solomon
The Last Dreamgirl — Hayes, Shane
The Last Drop: The Politics of Water — Gonzales, Mike
The Last Drop: The Politics of Water — Gonzalez, Mike
The Last Election — Collins, Gary H.
The Last Empire: The Final Days of the Soviet Union — Plokhy, Serhii
y The Last Encampment: A Novel — Freed, Jenn
The Last English Poachers — Tovey, Bob
y The Last Ever After — Chainani, Soman
Last Exit to Brooklyn — Selby, Hubert, Jr.
The Last Exodus — Tassi, Paul
y The Last Faerie Queen — Pitcher, Chelsea
Last First Snow — Gladstone, Max
The Last Flight of Poxl West — Daniel Torday
The Last Flight of Poxl West — Torday, Daniel
Last Folio — Dojc, Yuri
y The Last Forever — Caletti, Deb
The Last Four Days of Paddy Buckley — Massey, Jeremy
y The Last Generation — Robertson, Ben
y The Last Good Day of the Year — Warman, Jessica
The Last Good Paradise (Read by Gilbert, Tavia). Audiobook Review — Soli, Tatjana
The Last Good Paradise — Soli, Tatjana
The Last Good Place — Burcell, Robin
The Last Illusion — Khakpour, Porochista
c Last in a Long Line of Rebels — Tyre, Lisa Lewis
The Last Incantations — Mura, David
Last Indian Summer — Davis, Richard
c The Last Kids on Earth (Illus. by Holgate, Douglas) — Brallier, Max
The Last Kind Words Saloon: A Novel — McMurtry, Larry
c The Last King of Angkor Wat — Base, Graeme
The Last Laugh: Folk Humor, Celebrity Culture, and Mass-Mediated Disasters in the Digital Age — Blank, Trevor J.
y The Last Leaves Falling — Benwell, Sarah
The Last Love Song: A Biography of Joan Didion — Daugherty, Tracy
The Last Love Song — Daugherty, Tracy
The Last Love Song: The Biography of Joan Didion — Daugherty, Tracy
The Last Lover — Xue, Can
The Last Lynching — Pitch, Anthony S.
The Last Magazine — Hastings, Michael
Last Man Off — Lewis, Matt
The Last Midwife — Dallas, Sandra
c Last Minute Science Projects with Biomes (Illus. by LaBaff, Tom) — Gardner, Robert
c The Last Musketeer — Gibbs, Stuart
y Last Night at the Circle Cinema — Franklin, Emily
Last Night in the OR: A Transplant Surgeon's Odyssey — Shaw, Bud
The Last of Our Kind — McFarland, Gerald W.
Last of the Blue and Gray: Old Men, Stolen Glory, and the Mystery That Outlived the Civil War — Serrano, Richard A.
The Last of the Light: About Twilight — Davidson, Peter
Last of the Living Blue: A Year of Living and Dying Among the Trees — Getz, Gin
The Last of the President's Men. — Woodward, Bob
Last of the Sandwalkers (Illus. by Hosier, Jay) — Hosier, Jay
c Last of the Sandwalkers (Illus. by Hosler, Jay) — Hosler, Jay
c Last of the Spirits — Priestley, Chris
Last of the Tasburai — Khan, Rehan
The Last of the Wine — Renault, Mary
The Last Pagans of Rome — Cameron, Alan
c Last Panda Standing — Krosoczka, Jarrett J.

The Last Pilot — Johncock, Benjamin
y The Last Place on Earth — Snow, Carol
The Last Professors: The Corporate University and the Fate of the Humanities — Donoghue, Frank
The Last Projector — Keaton, David James
Last Ragged Breath — Keller, Julia
The Last Ride — Wolfe, Ethan J.
The Last Season: A Father, a Son, and a Lifetime of College Football — Stevens, Stuart
y The Last September — de Gramont, Nina
The Last September — De Gramont, Nina
The Last Shootist — Swarthout, Miles
y The Last Sister — McKinney-Whitaker, Courtney
c The Last Soldier — Gray, Keith
The Last Soldiers of the Cold War: The Story of the Cuban Five — Morais, Fernando
Last Song before Night — Myer, Ilana C.
The Last Stalinist: The Life of Santiago Carrillo — Preston, Paul
c Last Stand: Causes and Effects of the Battle of the Little Bighorn — Higgins, Nadia
The Last Stand of the Tin Can Sailors — Hornfischer, James D.
c Last Stop on Market Street (Read by Mitchell, Lizan). Audiobook Review — De la Pena, Matt
c Last Stop on Market Street (Illus. by Robinson, Christian) — de la Pena, Matt
c Last Stop on Market Street — Robinson, Christian
Last Stories and Other Stories — Vollmann, William T.
The Last Summer at Chelsea Beach — Jenoff, Pam
The Last Summer of the Water Strider — Lott, Tim
y The Last Summer of Us — Harcourt, Maggie
y The Last Supper — Dickson, Allison, M.
c The Last Sword — Powell, Huw
y The Last Thirteen: Book Thirteen: 1 — Phelan, James
y The Last Thirteen — Phelan, James
The Last Thousand: One School's Promise in a Nation at War — Stern, Jeffrey E.
y The Last Time We Say Goodbye — Hand, Cynthia
Last to Die: A Defeated Empire, a Forgotten Mission, and the Last American Killed in World War II — Harding, Stephen
The Last to Fall: The 1922 March, Battles, and Deaths of U.S. Marines at Gettysburg — Fulton, Richard D.L.
Last to Join the Fight: The 66th Georgia Infantry — Cone, Daniel
The Last Trail West — Turner, Stephen L.
The Last Trojan Hero: A Cultural History of Virgil's "Aeneid" — Hardie, Philip
The Last Two Seconds — Bang, Mary Jo
The Last Unicorn: A Search for One of Earth's Fairest Creatures — deBuys, William
The Last Unicorn: A Search for One of Earth's Rarest Creatures — deBuys, William
The Last Unicorn: A Search for One of Earth's Rarest Creatures — DeBuys, William
The Last Unicorn: A Search for One of Earth's Rarest Creatures — deBuys, William
The Last Unicorn — DeBuys, William
The Last Volcano: A Man, a Romance, and the Quest to Understand Nature's Most Magnificent Fury — Dvorak, John
The Last Volcano — Dvorak, John
The Last Warrior: Andrew Marshall and the Shaping of Modern American Defense Strategy — Krepinevich, Andrew F.
The Last Weynfeldt — Suter, Martin
c The Last Wild — Torday, Piers
Last Winter, We Parted — Nakamura, Fuminori
Last Winter, We Parted — Powell, Allison Markin
The Last Witness — Meyrick, Denzil
The Last Witness — Parker, K.J.
The Last Word — Kureishi, Hanif
Last Words — Koryta, Michael
Last Words (Read by Petkoff, Robert). Audiobook Review — Koryta, Michael
Last Words: Considering Contemporary Cinema — Wood, Jason
Last Words from Montmartre — Heinrich, Ari Larissa
Last Words of the Holy Ghost — Cashion, Matt
y Last Year's Mistake — Ciocca, Gina
The Last Years op' Saint Therese: Doubt and Darkness: 1895-1897 — Nevin, Thomas R.
The Late Child and Other Animals — Cook, Marguerite Van
A Late Encounter with the Civil War — Kreyling, Michael
A Late Fifteenth-Century Dominical Sermon Cycle — Morrison, Stephen
Late Fragments — Gross, Kate

Late Medieval and Early Modern Ritual: Studies in Italian Urban Culture — Cohn, Samuel, Jr.
The Late Parade: Poems — Fitzgerald, Adam
The Late Poetry of the Lake Poets: Romanticism Revised — Fulford, Tim
Late Shakespeare, 1608-1613 — Power, Andrew J.
Late Victorian Crime Fiction in the Shadow of Sherlock — clarke, Clare
Latest Readings — James, Clive
Latin: A Linguistic Introduction — Oniga, Renato
Latin America in a Global Context
Latin American Cinema — Hart, Stephen M.
The Latin Church in Cyprus, 1313-1378 — Coureas, Nicholas
Latin-into-Hebrew: Texts and Studies, vol. 2: Texts in Context — Fidora, Alexander
Latin Liturgical Psalters in the Bodleian Library: A Select Catalogue — Solopova, Elizabeth
Latin Love Poetry — McCoskey, Denise Eileen
Latin Music: Musicians, Genres, and Themes — Stavans, Ilan
Latin: Story of a World Language — Leonhardt, Jurgen
Latino Access to Higher Education: Ethnic Realities and New Directions for the Twenty-first Century — Urbina, Martin Guevara
Latino America: How America's Most Dynamic Population Is Poised to Transform the Politics of the Nation — Barreto, Matt
The Latino Generation: Voices of the New America — Garcia, Mario T.
Latino Mennonites: Civil Rights, Faith, and Evangelical Culture — Hinojosa, Felipe
Latino Mennonites: Civil Rights, Faith, and Evangelical Culture
Latino Pentecostals in America: Faith and Politics in Action — Espinosa, Gaston
Latino Police Officers in the United States: An Examination of Emerging Trends and Issues — Urbina, Martin Guevara
Latino Stats: American Hispanics by the Numbers — Malave, Idelisse
Latino Urbanism: The Politics of Planning, Policy, and Redevelopment — Diaz, David R.
Latinos and Latinas at Risk: Issues in Education, Health, Community, and Justice, 2 vols. — Gutierrez, Gabriel
Latinos at the Golden Gate: Creating Community & Identity in San Francisco — Sandoval, Summers
Latinos Facing Racism: Discrimination, Resistance, and Endurance — Feagin, Joe R.
y Latitude Zero — Renn, Diana
c Latke, the Lucky Dog (Illus. by Beeke, Tiphanie) — Fischer, Ellen
Latter-Day Lore: Mormon Folklore Studies — Eliason, Eric A.
Laudato Si': On Care for Our Common Home — Francis I, Pope
The Laudians and the Elizabethan Church: Conformity and Religious Identity in Post-Reformation England — Lane, Calvin
c Laugh-Along Lessons: 5 Minute Stories (Illus. by Munsinger, Lynn) — Lester, Helen
c Laugh Your Head Off: Funny Stories for All Kinds of Kids (Illus. by Hart, James) — Darlinson, Aleesah
y Laughing at My Nightmare — Burcaw, Shane
The Laughing Monsters — Johnson, Denis
Laughter in Ancient Rome: On Joking, Tickling, and Cracking Up — Beard, Mary
y Launch a Rocket into Space — Koll, Hilary
y Launch a Rocket into Space (Illus. by Aleksic, Vladimir) — Koll, Hilary
c Launch a Rocket into Space (Illus. by Aleksic, Vladimir) — Mills, Steve
c Lauren Ipsum: A Story about Computer Science and Other Improbable Things (Illus. by Lipovaca, Miran) — Bueno, Carlos
Laurus — Vodolazkin, Eugene
The Lausanne Movement: A Range of Perspectives — Dahle, Margunn Serigstad
c L'autobus magic presente series: La Terre — Jackson, Tom
c L'autobus magic presente series: Les creatures marines — Jackson, Tom
c L'autruche et l'ours polaire (Illus. by Perreault, Guillaume) — De Blois, Helene
The Lavender Lane Lothario — Handler, David
Lavina — Marcus, Mary
c L'avion de Julie (Illus. by Martchenko, Michael) — Munsch, Robert
Law and Custom in Korea: Comparative Legal History — Kim, Marie Seong-Hak

Law and History in Cervantes'Don Quixote — *Byrne, Susan*
Law and Islamization of Morocco under the Almoravids: The Fatwas of Ibn Rushd al-Jadd to the Far Maghrib — *Gomez-Rivas, Camilo*
Law and Piety in Medieval Islam — *Reid, Megan H.*
Law and Religion in the Eastern Mediterranean: From Antiquity to Early Islam — *Hagedorn, Anselm C.*
Law and Revolution in South Africa: uBuntu, Dignity, and the Struggle for Constitutional Transformation — *Cornell, Drucilla*
Law and the Gay Rights Story: The Long Search for Equal Justice in a Divided Democracy — *Frank, Walter*
The Law Book: From Hammurabi to the International Criminal Court, 250 Milestones in the History of Law — *Roffer, Michael H.*
Law & Equity: Approaches in Roman Law and Common Law — *Koops, Egbert*
Law, Medicine, and Engineering in the Cult of the Saints in Counter-Reformation Rome: The Hagiographical Works of Antonio Gallonio, 1556-1605 — *Touber, Jetze*
The Law of Contract Damages — *Kramer, Adam*
The Law of Kinship: Anthropology, Pyschoanalysis, and the Family in France — *Robcis, Camille*
The Law of Loving Others (Read by Cooper-Novack, Hallie). Audiobook Review — *Axelrod, Kate*
y The Law of Loving Others — *Axelrod, Kate*
The Law of the Land: A Grand Tour of Our Constitutional Republic — *Amar, Akhil Reed*
Law, Rights and Ideology in Russia: Landmarks in the Destiny of a Great Power — *Bowring, Bill*
The Law School of University College Dublin: A History — *Osborough, W.N.*
Lawfare: Law as a Weapon of War — *Kittrie, Orde F.*
Lawless Guns — *Duggan, M.*
Lawless in Leather — *Scott, Melanie*
Law's Dominion: Medieval Studies for Paul Hyams — *Escobar-Vargas, M. Carolina*
The Laws of Average — *Dodge, Trevor*
The Laws of Cooking and How to Break Them — *Warner, Justin*
The Laws of Late Medieval Italy (1000-1500): Foundations for a European Legal System — *Ascheri, Mario*
The Laws of Medicine: Field Notes from an Uncertain Science (Read by Fontana, Santino). Audiobook Review — *Mukherjee, Siddhartha*
The Laws of Medicine: Field Notes from an Uncertain Science — *Mukherjee, Siddhartha*
The Laws of Murder (Read by Langton, James). Audiobook Review — *Finch, Charles*
Laws, Outlaws, and Terrorists: Lessons from the War on Terrorism — *Blum, Gabriella*
Law's Virtues: Fostering Autonomy and Solidarity in American Society — *Kaveny, M. Cathleen*
Lawyer for the Dog — *Robinson, Lee*
Lawyer Up — *Allure, Kate*
Lawyering for the Rule of Law: Government Lawyers and the Rise of Judicial Power in Israel — *Dotan, Yoav*
Lay Death at Her Door — *Buhmann, Elizabeth*
Lay Down Your Weary Tune — *Belcher, W.B.*
Layer, Paint and Stitch — *Dolan, Wendy*
Laying the Children's Ghosts to Rest: Canada's Home Children in the West — *Joyce, Sean Arthur*
The Lazarus Game — *Valentine, Stephen J.*
c Lazy Bear, Crazy Bear (Illus. by Hodson, Ben) — *Bolger, Kevin*
c Lazy Dave (Illus. by Jarvis) — *Jarvis*
c Lazy Dave (Illus. by Jarvis, Peter) — *Jarvis*
LBJ and Grassroots Federalism: Congressman Bob Poage, Race, and Change in Texas — *Duke, Robert Harold*
Le Armate Francesi in Italia, 1792-1814: Storia Postale e Catalogazione — *Giribone, Pietro*
Le Blanc qui s'etait fait negre — *Guillot, Rene*
Le Bucoliche — *Cucchiarelli, Andrea*
Le Cardinal Jean du Bellay: Diplomatie et culture dans l'Europe de la Renaissance — *Michon, Cedric*
Le Cinquiesme Tome des 'Histoires tragiques' — *Campagne, Herve-Thomas*
Le collezioni mineralogiche del Museo di Storia Naturale dell'Universita di Firenze dalle origini a oggi — *Cipriani, Curzio*
Le Condottiere — *Perec, Georges*
Le cour politique des meres: Analyse du mouvement des meres de soldats en Russie — *Lebedev, Anna Colin*

c Le Defi de Dominic (Illus. by Sampar) — *Bergeron, Alain M.*
c Le defile des fantomes (Illus. by Storms, Patricia) — *Bozik, Chrissy*
Le destin douloureux de Walther Ritz (1878-1909): Physicien theoricien de genie — *Pont, Jean-Claude*
le Donei des amanz — *Holden, Anthony J.*
Le fatiche di Benedetto XIV: Origine ed evoluzione dei trattati di Prospero Lambertini — *Fattori, MariaTeresa*
c Le gout — *Ganeri, Anita*
Le Grand Meaulnes — *Fournier, Alain*
c Le hamster et la gerbille — *Johnson, Jinny*
Le jardin dans l'Antiquite: Introduction et huit exposes suivis de discussions — *Coleman, Kathleen*
c Le lac aux mysteres — *Nelson, Suzanne*
Le Livre blanc — *Pic, Anne-Sophie*
Le livre de raison de Paul de Sade (Avignon, 1390-1394). — *Bresc, Henri*
Le Livre d'Elise — *Musomandera, Elise Rida*
Le Livre des epistres du debat sus 'Le rommant de la Rose' — *Valentini, Andrea*
Le Meridional — *Lopes, Henri*
Le origini chimiche della vita: Legami tra la rivoluzione di Lavoisier e la biologia di Lamarck — *Bandinelli, Angela*
c Le Papa de David (Illus. by Martchenko, Michael) — *Munsch, Robert*
Le parti huguenot: Chronique d'une desillusion, 1557-1572 — *Daussy, Hugues*
c Le petit chevalier qui n'aimait pas la pluie (Illus. by Despres, Genevieve) — *Tibo, Gilles*
c Le Pit a Papa (Illus. by Trudel, Jean-Luc) — *Comeau, Marie-France*
Le Postcolonial compare: anglophonie, francophonie — *Joubert, Claire*
Le Pouvoir Absolu: Naissance de l'Imaginaire Politique de la Royaute — *Jouanna, Arlette*
Le Prince Eugene de Savoie et le Sud-Est Europeen (1683-1736). — *Nouzille, Jean*
Le Prince, son peuple et le bien commun de l'Antiquite tardive a la fin du Moyen Age — *Picard, Jean-Michel*
c Le reve de Sadako — *St-Jean, Annie*
Le roi, la cour, l'Etat: De la Renaissance a l'absolutisme — *Le Roux, Nicolas*
Le Roman sans aventure — *Daunais, Isabelle*
c Le soleil — *Taylor, Lauren*
y Le souverain dans l'ombre — *Nielsen, Jennifer A.*
Le Sublime et le grotesque — *Miernowski, Jan*
Le Suicide francais — *Zemmour, Eric*
c Le temps au fil ties jours (Illus. by Enright, Amanda) — *Rustad, Martha E.H.*
Le theatre en province pendant le Consulat et l'Empire — *Triolaire, Cyril*
Le Tourisme Comme Facteur de Transformations Economiques, Techniques et Sociales (XIXe-Xxe Siecles): Tourism as a Factor of Economic, Technical and Social Transformations (XIXth-XXth Centuries). — *Gigase, Marc*
c Le trefle a quatre feuilles (Illus. by Glasser, Robin Preiss) — *O'Connor, Jane*
c Le tresor de Memramcook (Illus. by Cormiere, Maurice) — *Langlois, Dominic*
Le Triangle d'hiver — *Deck, Julia*
c Le vent — *Taylor, Lauren*
c Le verbe Aimer au present de l'indicatif — *Pelletier, Dominique*
c Le verbe Avoir au present de Vindicatif — *Pelletier, Dominique*
c Le verbe Etre au present de l'indicatif — *Pelletier, Dominique*
c Le verbe Finir au present de l'indicatif — *Pelletier, Dominique*
c Le veritable abominable homme des neiges — *Mendicino, Valentina*
c Le voilier d'Olivier: Une aventure en anagrammes — *Messier, Mireille*
Leadership BS: Fixing Workplaces and Careers One Truth at a Time — *Pfeffer, Jeffrey*
Leadership Coaching for Educators — *Reiss, Karla*
Leadership in Balance: New Habits of the Mind — *Kucia, John F.*
Leadership in the Crucible of Work: Discovering the Interior Life of an Authentic Leader — *Shugart, Sandy*
Leadership Psychology: How the Best Leaders Inspire Their People — *Cutler, Alan*
Leading 21st Century Schools: Harnessing Technology for Engagement and Achievement — *Schrum, Lynne*
Leading Cases in Song — *Todd, Stephen*

Leading Libraries: How to Create a Service Culture — *vanDuinkerken, Wyoma*
y Leading Lines: A Pippa Greene Novel — *Guertin, Chantel*
Leading Small Groups in the Way of Jesus — *Boren, M. Scott*
Leading with Purpose: How to Engage, Empower and Encourage Your People to Reach Their Full Potential — *Koehler, Marc*
y Leaf (Illus. by Ma, Daishu) — *Ma, Daishu*
c Leaflets Three, Let It Be! The Story of Poison Ivy (Illus. by Brickman, Robin) — *Sanchez, Anita*
c The League of Beastly Dreadfuls (Read by Landor, Rosalyn). Audiobook Review — *Grant, Holly*
c The League of Beastly Dreadfuls, book 1 (Illus. by Portillo, Josie) — *Grant, Holly*
c The League of Beastly Dreadfuls (Illus. by Portillo, Josie) — *Grant, Holly*
The League of Outsider Baseball: An Illustrated History of Baseball's Forgotten Heores (Illus. by Cieradkowski, Gary Joseph) — *Cieradkowski, Gary Joseph*
The League of Outsider Baseball: An Illustrated History of Baseball's Forgotten Heroes (Illus. by Cieradkowski, Gary Joseph) — *Cieradkowski, Gary Joseph*
y The League of Seven (Illus. by Helquist, Brett) — *Gratz, Alan*
The League of Unexceptional Children (Illus. by Lancett, James) — *Daneshvari, Gitty*
c The League of Unexceptional Children — *Daneshvari, Gitty*
Leak: Why Mark Felt Became Deep Throat — *Holland, Max*
c The Leaky Battery Sets Sail — *Jones, Gareth P.*
The Lean Farm: How to Minimize Waste, Increase Efficiency, and Maximize Value and Profits with Less Work — *Hartman, Ben*
A Lean Third — *Kelman, James*
Leaning into Love: A Spiritual Journey through Grief — *Mansfield, Elaine*
Leap of Faith — *Weber, Bruce*
c Leaps and Bounce (Illus. by Cordell, Matthew) — *Hood, Susan*
Learn Ruby the Hard Way, 3d ed. — *Shaw, Zed A.*
c Learn to Draw Cats and Kittens: Step-by-Step Instructions for More Than 25 Favorite Feline Friends (Illus. by Cuddy, Robin) — *Osle, Janessa*
c Learn to Draw Forest Animals: Step-by-Step Instructions for MoreThan 25 Woodland Creatures (Illus. by Cuddy, Robbin) — *Gilbert, Elizabeth T.*
Learn to Paint in Acrylics with 50 Small Paintings: Pick Up the Skills, Put on the Paint, Hang Up Your Art — *Nelson, Mark Daniel*
Learn to Quilt-as-You-Go: 14 Projects You Can Finish Fast — *Erla, Gudrun*
Learn to Write Badly: How to Succeed in the Social Sciences — *Billig, Michael*
The Learned Ones: Nahua Intellectuals in Postconquest Mexico — *McDonough, Kelly S.*
The Learned Ones: Nahua Intellectuals in Postconquest Mexico (Illus. by McDonough, Kelly S.) — *McDonough, Kelly S.*
c Learning about Plagiarism — *Clapper, Nikki Bruno*
Learning about Primary Sources — *Clapper, Nikki Bruno*
c Learning about South America — *Adamson, Thomas K.*
c Learning about World War I and World War II with Arts and Crafts — *Challen, Paul*
Learning and Teaching Creative Cognition: The Interactive Book Report — *Schiering, Marjorie S.*
Learning and Teaching Healthy Piano Technique: Training as an Instructor in the Taubman Approach — *Milanovic, Therese*
Learning by Doing — *Bessen, James*
Learning Cyrillic — *Albahari, David*
Learning from the Wounded: The Civil War and the Rise of American Medical Science — *Devine, Shauna*
Learning How to Feel: Children's Literature and Emotional Socialization, 1870-1970 — *Frevert, Ute*
Learning in the Fast Lane: 8 Ways to Put ALL Students on the Road to Academic Success — *Rollins, Suzy Pepper*
Learning Modern Algebra: From Early Attempts to Prove Fermat's Last Theorem — *Cuoco, Al*
c Learning Outdoors with the Meek Family — *Meek, Tim*
Learning the Hard Way: Masculinity, Place, and the Gender Gap in Education — *Morris, Edward W.*
y Learning the Ropes — *Polak, Monique*

Learning to Become a Professional in a Textually-Mediated World: A Text-Oriented Study of Placement Practices — *Lau, Ken*
Learning to Die in London, 1380-1540 — *Appleford, Amy*
Learning to Eat along the Way — *Bendet, Margaret*
Learning to See Creatively: Design, Color, and Composition in Photography, 3d ed. — *Peterson, Bryan*
Learning to See Invisible Children: Inclusion of Children with Disabilities in Central Asia — *Rouse, Martyn*
Learning to Walk in the Dark — *Taylor, Barbara Brown*
The Least Likely Man: Marshall Nirenberg and the Discovery of the Genetic Code — *Portugal, Franklin H.*
c Leatherback Sea Turtles: Ancient Swimming Reptiles — *Hirsch, Rebecca E.*
Leave the Dogs at Home — *Arbogast, Claire S.*
Leaves on the Wind — *Whedon, Zack*
Leaving before the Rains Come (Read by Fuller, Alexandra). Audiobook Review — *Fuller, Alexandra*
Leaving before the Rains Come — *Fuller, Alexandra*
Leaving Berlin (Read by Brill, Corey). Audiobook Review — *Kanon, Joseph*
Leaving Berlin — *Kanon, Joseph*
Leaving Orbit — *Dean, Margaret Lazarus*
Leaving Orbit: Notes from the Last Days of American Spaceflight — *Dean, Margaret Lazarus*
Leaving Orbit: Notes from the Last Days of American Spaceflight — *Dean, Margaret Lazarus.*
Leaving Orbit: Notes from the Last Days of American Spaceflight — *Dean, Margaret Lazarus*
Leaving Prostitution: Getting Out and Staying Out of Sex Work — *Oselin, Sharon S.*
y The Leaving Season — *Jordan, Cat*
Leaving the Atocha Station — *Lerner, Ben*
Leaving the Jewish Fold: Conversion and Radical Assimilation in Modern Jewish History — *Endelman, Todd M.*
y Leaving Waden — *Rider, Jordan C.*
Lebanon Adrift: From Battleground to Playground — *Khalaf, Samir*
Leben fur die Sache: Vera Figner, Vera Zasulic und das radikale Milieu im spaten Zarenreich — *Rindlisbacher, Stephan*
The Lebensborn Experiment — *Grant, Scott*
c Lebron James — *Gregory, Josh*
c LeBron James — *Jackson, Aurelia*
y LeBron James: Champion Basketball Star — *Bodden, Valerie*
L'echange - Der Austausch. 7. Interdisziplinarer deutsch-franzosischer Workshop fur Nachwuchswissenschaftler/innen
L'economiste, la cour, et la patrie: L'economie politique dans la France des Lumieres — *Skornicki, Arnault*
Lectures de Charles d'Orleans: Les Ballades — *Hue, Denis*
Lectures on the History of Moral and Political Philosophy — *Cohen, Gerald A.*
Lectures on the Philosophy of Art: The Hotho Transcript of the 1823 Berlin Lectures — *Hegel, Georg Wilhelm Friedrich*
Lee Miller: A Woman's War — *Roberts, Hilary*
c Leeches — *Marsico, Katie*
c Leeching the Sirens — *Prince, T.M.*
Leena Krohn: Collected Fiction — *Krohn, Leena*
c The Left Behinds: The iPhone That Saved George Washington (Read by Heyborne, Kirby). Audiobook Review — *Potter, David*
The Left Behinds: The iPhone That Saved George Washington (Read by Heyborne, Kirby). Audiobook Review — *Potter, David (B. 1955-)*
c The Left Behinds: The iPhone That Saved George Washington — *Potter, David*
c The Left Behinds: The iPhone That Saved George Washington — *Potter, David (B. 1955-)*
y The Left Behinds: The iPhone That Saved George Washington — *Potter, David (b. 1955-)*
The Left-Hand Way — *Doyle, Tom*
Left of the Bang — *Lowdon, Claire*
The Left Side of History: World War II and the Unfulfilled Promise of Communism in Eastern Europe — *Ghodsee, Kristen Rogheh*
Left to Chance: Hurricane Katrina and the Story of Two New Orleans Neighborhoods — *Kroll-Smith, Steve*
Leftover Women — *Hong Fincher, Leta*
Leg over Leg, 4 vols. — *Shidyaq, Ahmad Faris*
Leg over Leg — *Shidyaq, Ahmad Faris*

The Legacies of Jean-Luc Godard
Legacies of the War on Poverty — *Bailey, Martha J.*
Legacies of Violence: Eastern Europe's First World War — *Bohler, Jochen*
A Legacy in Arms: American Firearm Manufacture, Design, and Artistry, 1800-1900 — *Rattenbury, Richard C.*
The Legacy of Christopher Columbus in the Americas: New Nations and a Transatlantic Discourse of Empire — *Bartosik-Velez, Elise*
The Legacy of David Foster Wallace — *Cohen, Samuel*
The Legacy of Johann Strauss — *Lang, Zoe Alexis*
y Legacy of Kings — *Herman, Eleanor*
The Legacy of Lost Things — *Zilelian, Aida*
The Legacy of Ruth Bader Ginsburg — *Dodson, Scott*
A Legacy of Sephardic, Mediterranean and American Recipes — *Almeleh, Rachel*
y Legacy of the Claw — *Grey, C.R.*
Legacy: The Hidden Keys to Optimizing Your Family Wealth Decisions — *Orlando, Richard J.*
Legal Challenges in the Global Financial Crisis: Bail-outs, the Euro and Regulation — *Ringe, Wolf-Georg*
y Legal Drug: A Drugstore with Medicine and a Danger — *CLAMP (Mangaka writing/artist group)*
Legal Guide for Police: Constitutional Issues — *Walker, Jeffery T.*
A Legal History of the Civil War and Reconstruction: A Nation of Rights — *Edwards, Laura F.*
Legal Integration of Islam: A Transatlantic Comparison — *Joppke, Christian*
The Legal Language of Scottish Burghs: Standardization and Lexical Bundles — *Kopaczyk, Joanna*
Legal Orientalism: China, the United States, and Modern Law — *Ruskola, Teemu*
Legal Pluralism and Empires, 1500-1850 — *Benton, Lauren*
Legal Professional Privilege for Corporations: A Guide to Four Major Common Law Jurisdictions — *Higgins, Andrew A.*
Legal Reference for Librarians: How and Where to Find the Answers — *Healey, Paul D.*
Legal Rights: The Guide for Deaf and Hard of Hearing People, 6th ed. — *National Association of the Deaf*
y Legalizing Marijuana — *Allen, John*
Legally Tied — *Dorsette, Chelsea*
Legend: A Harrowing Story from the Vietnam War of One Green Beret's Heroic Mission to Rescue a Special Forces Team Caught Behind Enemy Lines — *Blehm, Eric*
c The Legend and Adventures of Bob Wire (Illus. by Skinner, Sam) — *Skinner, Sam*
The Legend of Bob Wire (Illus. by Skinner, Sam) — *Skinner, Sam*
The Legend of Caleb York — *Spillane, Mickey*
The Legend of Devil's Creek — *Alexander, D.C.*
The Legend of Jake Jackson: The Last of the Great Gunfighters and Comanche Warriors — *Joiner, William H., Jr.*
The Legend of Lyon Redmond — *Long, Julie Anne*
c The Legend of Saint Nicholas (Illus. by Ferri, Giuliano) — *Grun, Anselm*
The Legend of Sheba — *Lee, Tosca*
c The Legend of the Beaver's Tail (Illus. by van Frankenhuyzen, Gijsbert) — *Shaw, Stephanie*
A Legend of the Future — *Rojas, Agustin de*
c The Legend of Zelda: A Link to the Past (Illus. by Ishinomori, Shotaro) — *Ishinomori, Shotaro*
y Legend: The Graphic Novel (Illus. by Kaari) — *Dragoon, Leigh*
Legenda maior sive Legenda admirabilis virginis Catherine de Senis — *da Capua, Raimondo*
c Legendary Routes of the World — *Verhille, Alexandre*
The Legendary Sagas: Origins and Development — *Lassen, Annette*
Legendary Star-Lord: Face It, I Rule (Illus. by Medina, Paco) — *Humphries, Sam*
c The Legends Begin (Illus. by de la Rue, James) — *Hegarty, Shane*
The Legends Begin — *Hegarty, Shane*
c Legends: The Best Players, Games, and Teams in Baseball — *Bryant, Howard*
c Legends: The Best Players, Games, and Teams in Football — *Bryant, Howard*
Legion's Lawyers — *Aiello, Vince*
Legitimization in World Society — *Mascareno, Aldo*
c Lego Chain Reactions — *Murphy, Pat*
y The LEGO Mindstorms EV3 Discovery Book: A Beginner's Guide to Building and Programming Robots — *Valk, Laurens*

Lehrerinnen und Lehrer in der Schweizer Presse — *Ruloff, Michael Christian*
Leibniz — *Arthur, Richard T.W.*
Leibniz's Principle of Identity of Indiscernibles — *Rodriguez-Pereyra, Gonzalo*
"Leidenschaften". 20. Fachtagung des Arbeitskreises Geschlechtergeschichte der Fruhen Neuzeit
c Leif the Lucky — *d'Aulaire, Ingri*
y Leif's Journey — *Hokenson, Terry*
The Leipzig Affair — *Rintoul, Fiona*
Leisured Resistance: Villas, Literature and Politics in the Roman World — *Dewar, Michael*
Leisurely Islam: Negotiating Geography and Morality in Shi'ite South Beirut — *Deeb, Lara*
Lekturen der Erinnerung: Lessing, Kant, Hegel — *Gilgen, Peter*
c Lelani and the Plastic Kingdom — *Johnston, Robb N.*
Lemnos: Cultura, storia, archeologia, topografia di un'isola del nord-Egeo — *Ficuciello, Laura*
Lemon Blossoms — *Romano, Nina*
c The Lemonade Hurricane: A Story about Mindfulness and Meditation (Illus. by Morris, Jennifer E.) — *Morelli, Licia*
Lempad of Bali: The Illuminating Line — *Carpernter, Bruce W.*
The Lemurs' Legacy: The Evolution of Power, Sex and Love — *Russell, Jay*
A Lenape among the Quakers: The Life of Hannah Freeman — *Marsh, Dawn G.*
Lenape Country: Delaware Valley Society before William Penn — *Soderlund, Jean R.*
c Lend a Hand: Poems about Giving (Illus. by Ladd, London) — *Frank, John*
Lending to the Borrower from Hell: Debt, Taxes, and Default in the Age of Philip II — *Drelichman, Mauricio*
Lenin Lives Next Door: Marriage, Martinis, and Mayhem in Moscow — *Eremeeva, Jennifer*
Leningrad: Siege and Symphony — *Moynahan, Brian*
Lenin's Terror: The Ideological Origins of Early Soviet State Violence — *Ryan, James (b. 1985-)*
y Lennie the Legend: Solo to Sydney by Pony — *Reeder, Stephanie Owen*
c Lenny & Lucy (Illus. by Stead, Erin C.) — *Stead, Philip C.*
c Lenny & Lucy (Illus. by Stead, Erin E.) — *Stead, Philip C.*
L'enquete TRA, histoire d'un outil, outil pour l'histoire. Tome 1: 1793-1902 — *Bourdieu, Jerome*
Lens of War: Exploring Iconic Photographs of the Civil War — *Gallman, J. Matthew*
Lenten Reflections: From the Desert to the Resurrection — *Lopes, Milton E.*
c Leo: A Ghost Story (Illus. by Robinson, Christian) — *Barnett, Mac*
c Leo Da Vinci vs the Ice-Cream Domination League (Illus. by Faber, Jules) — *Pryor, Michael*
Leo Strauss and Anglo-American Democracy: A Conservative Critique — *Havers, Grant N.*
Leo Strauss and the Problem of Political Philosophy — *Zuckert, Catherine H.*
Leon Battista Alberti and Nicholas Cusanus: Towards an Epistemology of Vision for Italian Renaissance Art and Culture — *Carman, Charles H.*
Leon Blum: Prime Minister, Socialist, Zionist — *Birnbaum, Pierre*
Leon Patterson — *Haslam, Gerald W.*
Leon Trotsky — *Le Blanc, Paul*
Leonard Bernstein: An American Musician — *Shawn, Allen*
The Leonard Bernstein Letters — *Simeone, Nigel*
Leonard de Vinci, l'homme de Guerre — *Brioist, Pascal*
Leonardo Da Vinci: The Resurrection of the Gods — *Merezhkovsky, Dmitry*
Leonardo da Vinci: Vorbild Natur - Zeichnungen und Modelle — *Boucheron, Patrick*
Leonardo, Michelangelo, and the Art of the Figure — *Cole, Michael W.*
Leonora — *Poniatowska, Elena*
c Leontyne Price: Voice of a Century (Illus. by Colon, Raul) — *Weatherford, Carole Boston*
The Leopard — *Lampedusa, Giuseppe Tomasi di*
Leopardi's Nymphs: Grace, Melancholy, and the Uncanny — *Camilletti, Fabio A.*
c Leopardpox! (Illus. by Hoffman, Omer) — *Landau, Orna*
c Leopardpox! (Illus. by Hoffmann, Omer) — *Landau, Orna*
y The Leopard's Tail — *Davies, Nicola*
c Leopold the Lion (Illus. by Barshaw, Ruth McNally) — *Brennan-Nelson, Denise*

y L'Epopee de Petit-Jules — *Rouy, Maryse*
y L'Epreuve de fer (Illus. by Fisher, Scott) — *Black, Holly*
Leprosy and a Life in South India: Journeys with a Tamil Brahmin — *Staples, James*
c Leroy Ninker Saddles Up (Read by Morey, Arthur). Audiobook Review — *DiCamillo, Kate*
c Leroy Ninker Saddles Up (Illus. by Van Dusen, Chris) — *DiCamillo, Kate*
c Les abeilles — *Charlesworth, Liza*
c Les amis qui ne pensaient qu'a gagner — *Oldland, Nicholas*
Les Annees 40 sont de retour: petite lecon d'histoire pour comprendre les crises du present — *Dely, Renaud*
c Les attentats du 11 septembre 2001 — *Tarshis, Lauren*
Les Banques centrales a l'echelle du monde — *Feiertag, Olivier*
c Les cancans du canard (Illus. by Boldt, Mike) — *Wilson, Troy*
c Les cochons — *Charlesworth, Liza*
Les costeaux, ou, Les marquis frians — *De Vise, Jean Donneau*
Les costeaux, ou, Les marquis frians — *Schorr, Jame L.*
c Les crabes — *Charlesworth, Liza*
Les Dieux caches de la science-fiction francaise et francophone, 1950-2010 — *Vas-Deyres, Natacha*
c Les escargots — *Charlesworth, Liza*
Les fabuleuses histoires de madame B. — *Beaudoin, Claire*
Les filles de saint Bruno au Moyen Age: Les moniales cartusiennes et l'exemple de Premol — *Rochet, Quentin*
c Les grenouilles — *Charlesworth, Liza*
Les groupes de Lie dans l'oeuvre de Hermann Weyl — *Eckes, Christopher*
Les Guise et leur paraitre — *Meiss-Even, Marjorie*
Les Guise et paraitre — *Meiss-Even, Marjorie*
Les Mailles du filet, ou, 'Le Temps immobile' de Claude Mauriac — *Thoizet, Evelyne*
Les Mineraux de Sainte-Marie-Aux-Mines — *Martaud, Alain*
c Les Miserables (Illus. by Williams, Marcia) — *Williams, Marcia*
c Les Miserables (Illus. by Williams, Marcia) — *Hugo, Victor*
Les Muses secretes: Kabbale, alchimie et litterature a la Renaissance — *Camos, Rosanna Gorris*
Les Obus miaulaient: Six lettres a Albert Dupont avec dix dessins de Olivier Jung — *Apollinaire, Guillaume*
c Les oeufs de la poule — *Charlesworth, Liza*
Les Organisations Internationales Africaines et le Maintien de la Paix : L'exemple de la CEDEAO, Liberia, Sierra Leone, Guinee-Bissau, Cote d'Ivoire — *Ndiaye, Papa Samba*
c Les pandas — *Schrieber, Anne*
Les Peaux noires: scenes de la vie des esclaves — *Eyma, Xavier*
c Les phoques — *Charlesworth, Liza*
c Les pirates de la cote d'argent — *Chantler, Scott*
c Les poneys — *Marsh, Laura*
c Les princesses ne portent pas de jeans (Illus. by Franson, Leanne) — *Bellingham, Brenda*
Les prisonniers de guerre allemands, France, 1944-1949: Une captivite de guerre en temps de paix — *Theofilakis, Fabien*
c Les recoltes - du mais aux citrouilles (Illus. by Enright, Amanda) — *Rustad, Martha E.H.*
Les registres des consistoires des Eglises Reformees de France, XVIe-XVIIe siecles: Un inventaire — *Mentzer, Raymond A.*
c Les requins — *Schreiber, Anne*
c Les sauterelles — *Charlesworth, Liza*
Les savoirs magiques et leur transmission de l'antiquite a la Renaissance — *Dasen, Veronique*
c Les serpents — *Charlesworth, Liza*
Les strategies matrimoniales, IXe-XIIIe siecle — *Aurell, Martin*
Les Temps glaciares — *Vargas, Fred*
Les theologiens jesuites: Un courant uniforme? — *Fedou, Michel*
Les tranches de vie de Felix Tome 4: Un ninja sous le soleil — *Dubreuil, Annie*
Les Tyrannicides d'Athenes: Vie et mort de deux statues — *Azoulay, Vincent*
Les Voies romaines en Gaule — *Coulon, Gerard*
Lesley Blanch: On the Wilder Shores of Love — *Chamberet, Georgia de*

L'Esploratore del Duce: Le avventure di Giuseppe Tucci e la politica Italiana in Oriente da Mussolini a Andreotti; con il carteggio di Giulio Andreotti — *Garzilli, Enrica*
A Less Green and Pleasant Land: Our Threatened Wildlife — *Maclean, Norman*
Less Medicine, More Health: 7 Assumptions That Drive Too Much Medical Care — *Welch, H. Gilbert*
A Less Perfect Union: The Case for States' Rights — *Freedman, Adam*
Less Than Hero — *Browne, S.G.*
The Less We Touch — *Duin, Steve*
Lesser Beasts: A Snout-to-Tail History of the Humble Pig — *Essig, Mark*
Lesser Beasts: A Snout-to-Tail-History of the Humble Pig — *Essig, Mark*
Lesser Beasts: A Snout-to-Tail History of the Humble Pig — *Essig, Mark*
Lesser Evils — *Flanagan, Joe*
Lessing and the German Enlightenment — *Robertson, Ritchie*
Lessing's Hamburg Dramaturgy: A New and Complete Translation — *Lessing, Gotthold Ephraim*
Lessings Kiste: Nicolais Plan und das Grimm'sche Worterbuch — *Kappeler, Manfred*
c Lesson for the Wolf (Illus. by Cook, Alan) — *Qitsualik-Tinsley, Rachel*
Lessons for Survivors — *Cochrane, Charlie*
Lessons from Tara: Life Advice from the World's Most Brilliant Dog — *Rosenfelt, David*
Lessons in Contempt: Poul Raeff's Translation and Publication in 1516 of Johannes Pfefferkorn's The Confession of the Jews — *Adams, Jonathan*
Lessons in Relationship Dyads — *Mirolla, Michael*
Lessons of Hope: How to Fix Our Schools — *Klein, Joel*
Lessons of Lifelong Intimacy: Building a Stronger Marriage Without Losing Yourself - The 9 Principles of a Balanced and Happy Relationship — *Gurian, Michael*
Lessons of Lifelong Intimacy: Building a Stronger Marriage Without Losing Yourself; The 9 Principles of a Balanced and Happy Relationship — *Gurian, Michael*
c Lest We Forget (Illus. by Knowles, Isobel) — *Brown, Kerry*
Let God Arise: The War and Rebellion of the Camisards — *Monahan, W. Gregory*
Let Me Be Frank with You — *Ford, Richard*
y Let Me Die in His Footsteps — *Roy, Lori*
Let Me Explain You — *Liontas, Annie*
Let Me Heal: The Opportunity to Preserve Excellence in American Medicine — *Ludmerer, Kenneth M.*
Let Me See It — *Magruder, James*
Let Me Tell You: New Stories, Essays, and Other Writings — *Jackson, Shirley*
Let Scholarships Pay the Way — *Andrews, Eve-Marie*
c Let Sleeping Dogs Lie — *Becker, Helaine*
Let the Elephants Run: Unlock Your Creativity and Change Everything — *Usher, David*
c Let the Games Begin! (Illus. by McPhillips, Robert) — *Quinn, Jordan*
Let the People In — *Reid, Jan*
Let the People Rule: Theodore Roosevelt and the Birth of the Presidential Primary — *Cowan, Geoffrey*
Let There Be Water: Israel's Solution for a Water-Starved World — *Siegel, Seth M.*
Let Us Fight as Free Men: Black Soldiers and Civil Rights — *Knauer, Christine*
Let Us Now Praise Famous Men — *Evans, Walker*
L?etat honteux: Roman — *Tansi, Sony Labou*
Lethal Beauty — *Wiehl, Lis W.*
Lethal Beauty — *Wlehl, Lis*
Let's Be Less Stupid: An Attempt to Maintain My Mental Faculties — *Marx, Patricia*
c Let's Catch That Rainbow (Illus. by Keane, Ann) — *Keane, Ann*
c Let's Celebrate Columbus Day — *deRubertis, Barbara*
c Let's Celebrate Constitution Day — *DeRubertis, Barbaara*
c Let's Celebrate Earth Day — *deRubertis, Barbara*
c Let's Celebrate Earth Day — *DeRubertis, Barbara*
c Let's Celebrate Labor Day — *DeRubertis, Barbara*
c Let's Celebrate Presidents' Day — *deRubertis, Barbara*
c Let's Celebrate Veterans Day — *deRubertis, Barbara*
Let's Do Brunch: Mouth-Watering Meals to Start Your Day — *Sterling Epicure*
y Let's Get Lost — *Alsaid, Adi*
c Let's Go Outside — *Spitzer, Katja*
c Let's Go to the Firehouse — *Scholastic Inc.*

c Let's Go to the Hardware Store (Illus. by Iwai, Melissa) — *Rockwell, Anne*
Let's Let That Are Not Yet: Inferno — *Pavlic, Ed*
c Let's Make Faces (Illus. by Piven, Hanoch) — *Piven, Hanoch*
Let's Make Money, Honey: The Couple's Guide to Starting a Service Business — *Silverstein, Barry*
c Let's Play!: Discover and Explore the Everyday World with Your Child — *Hertzog, Nancy B.*
c Let's Play (Illus. by Alborozo, Gabriel) — *Alborozo, Gabriel*
c Let's Rock! — *Berk, Sheryl*
Let's Split! A Complete Guide to Separatist Movements and Aspirant Nations, from Abkhazia to Zanzibar — *Roth, Christopher F.*
Let's Stay Together — *Murray, J.J.*
Let's Talk about Death: Asking the Questions That Profoundly Change the Way We Live and Die — *Gordon, Steve*
c Let's Talk about Dinosaurs (Illus. by Teckentrup, Britta) — *Blackford, Harriet*
c Let's Visit England — *Lynch, Anabelle*
The Letter Bearer — *Allison, Robert*
The Letter Collection of Peter Abelard and Heloise — *Abelard, Peter*
c A Letter for Leo (Illus. by Ruzzier, Sergio) — *Ruzzier, Sergio*
y The Letter for the King — *Dragt, Tonke*
Letter from Alabama: The Inspiring True Story of Strangers Who Saved a Child and Changed a Family Forever — *Workman, David L.*
Letter to a Future Lover: Marginalia, Errata, Secrets, Inscriptions, and Other Ephemera Found in Libraries — *Monson, Ander*
Letter to Jimmy: On the Twentieth Anniversary of Your Death — *Mabanckou, Alain*
A Letter to My Mom — *Erspamer, Lisa*
Letters and Epistolary Culture in Early Medieval China — *Richter, Antje*
c Letters Are for Learning — *Neyer, Andrew*
c Letters from a Southern Mother (Illus. by Martin, Danny) — *Beene, Alex Anthony*
Letters from Galveston — *Rowe, Karen Paysse*
Letters from My Father's Murderer: A Journey of Forgiveness — *Coombs, Laurie A.*
Letters from the Farm: A Simple Path for a Deeper Spiritual Life — *Stevens, Becca*
Letters from the Road — *Davis, G Gordon*
Letters of Conrad Russell, 1897-1947 — *Blakiston, Georgiana*
The Letters of Ernest Hemingway, vol. 3: 1926-1929 — *Hemingway, Ernest*
The Letters of Evelyn Waugh and Diana Cooper — *Cooper, Artemis*
The Letters of James Agee to Father Flye — *Phelps, Robert*
The Letters of Lady Anne Bacon — *Bacon, Anne Cooke*
Letters of Note: An Eclectic Collection of Correspondence Deserving of a Wider Audience — *Usher, Shaun*
The Letters of Samuel Beckett: 1957-1965 — *Craig, George*
The Letters of Samuel Beckett, vol. 3: 1957-1965 — *Beckett, Samuel*
The Letters of Sarah Scott — *Pohl, Nicole*
The Letters of Symmachus: Book 1 — *Salzman, Michele Renee*
The Letters of T. S. Eliot, vol. 5: 1930-1931 — *Eliot, T.S.*
Letters to His Children from an Uncommon Attorney — *Roberts, David*
Letters to Poseidon — *Nooteboom, Cees*
Letters to Santa Claus — *Elves, The*
Letters to Santa Claus: The Elves — *Koch, Pat*
Letters to the Lost — *Grey, Iona*
Letters to the Poet from His Brother — *Montoya, Maceo*
Letters to Vera — *Nabokov, Vladimir*
y Letters to Zell — *Griep, Camielle*
Letters to Zell — *Griep, Camille*
Letting and Hiring in Roman Legal Thought: 27 BCE-284 CE — *Du Plessis, Paul J.*
Letting Go of Legacy Services: Library Case Studies — *Evangeliste, Mary*
Letting Them Die: Why AIDS Prevention Programmes Fail — *Campbell, Catherine*
L'Europe Coloniale et le Grand Tournant de la Conference de Berlin — *de Gemeaux, Christine*
The Levant Trilogy — *Manning, Olivia*

Level 4: Virus Hunters of the CDC: Tracking Ebola and the World's Deadliest Viruses — McCormick, Joseph B.
y The Leveller — Durango, Julia
The Levellers: Radical Political Thought in the English Revolution — Foxley, Rachel
Leverage Leadership — Bambrick-Santoyo, Paul
Leviathan — Campbell, Jack
Leviathans at the Gold Mine: Creating Indigenous and Corporate Actors in Papua New Guinea — Golub, Alex
Lewis and Clark among the Nez Perce: Strangers in the Land of the Nimiipuu — Hoxie, Frederick E.
Lewis and Clark among the Nez Perce: Strangers in the Land of the Nimiipuu — Pinkham, Allen V.
Lewis Carroll — Cohen, Morton
Lewis Carroll: The Man and His Circle — Wakeling, Edward
The Lewis Man — May, Peter
Lexical Variation and Attrition in the Scottish Fishing Communities — Millar, Robert McColl
Lexikon of the Hispanic Baroque: Transatlantic Exchange and Transformation — Levy, Evonne
The LGBT and Modern Family Money Manual: Financial Strategies for You and Your Loved Ones — Hanson, Holly
LGBT People and the UK Cultural Sector: The Response of Libraries, Museums, Archives and Heritage since 1950 — Vincent, John
L'Historiographie medievale normande et ses sources antiques (Xe-XIIe siecle): Actes du colloque de Cerisy-la-Salle et du Scriptorial d'Avranches — Bauduin, Pierre
L'honneur du soldat: ethique martiale et discipline guerriere dans la France des Lumieres — Guinier, Arnaud
L'Humain et l'animal dans la France Medievale — Fabry-Tehranchi, Irene
y Li Jun and the Iron Road — Bourgeois, Paulette
y Li Jun and the Iron Road — Tait, Anne
y Liam Darcy, I Loathe You — Doxey, Heidi Jo
Liar: A Memoir — Roberge, Rob
The Liar (Read by LaVoy, January). Audiobook Review — Roberts, Nora
The Liar — Roberts, Nora
Liar from Vermont — Stevenson, Laura C.
Liars and Lawyers — Varnadore, D. Gray
Liar's Bench — Richardson, Kim Michele
c Liars, Inc. — Stokes, Paula
The Liar's Wife. (Read by Podehl, Nick). Audiobook Review — Gordon, Mary
The Liar's Wife: Four Novellas — Gordon, Mary
Libanios: Zeuge einer schwindenden Welt — Nesselrath, Heinz-Günther
Libanius the Sophist: Rhetoric, Reality, and Religion in the Fourth Century — Cribiore, Raffaella
c Libby and the Class Election — Zappa, Shana Muldoon
"Liber instrumentorum iconographicus": Ein illustriertes Maschinenbuch — Fontana, Johannes
Liberal Arts at the Brink — Ferrall, Victor E., Jr.
The Liberal Unionist Party: A History — Cawood, Ian
Liberalism and Empire: A Study in Nineteenth-Century British Liberal Thought — Mehta, Uday Singh
Liberalism in Empire: An Alternative History — Sartori, Andrew
Liberalism: The Life of an Idea — Fawcett, Edmund
Liberalismus und Bismarck. Liberale Wahrnehmungen des "Eisernen Kanzlers" in zwei Jahrhunderten
Liberated Threads: Black Women, Style, and the Global Politics of Soul — Ford, Tanisha C.
The Liberation of the Camps: The End of the Holocaust and Its Aftermath — Stone, Dan
Liberation Theology for Armchair Theologians — De La Torre, Miguel A.
Liberation through Reconciliation: Jon Sobrino's Christological Spirituality — Valiente, O. Ernesto
Liberty Abroad: J.S. Mill on International Relations — Varouxakis, Georgios
Liberty and Law: The Idea of Permissive Natural Law, 1100-1800 — Tierney, Brian
Liberty and Other Stories. E-book Review — Hall, Alexis
Liberty Bazaar — Chadwick, David
Liberty of the Imagination: Aesthetic Theory, Literary Form, and Politics in the Early United States — Cahill, Edward
Liberty Style — Wood, Martin
Liberty's Dawn: A People's History of the Industrial Revolution — Griffin, Emma
Liberty's Fire — Syson, Lydia
Liberty's First Crisis: Adams, Jefferson, and the Misfits Who Saved Free Speech — Slack, Charles
Libra Road — Hargreaves, Paul
The Librarian — Elizarov, Mikhail
The Librarian's Guide to Micropublishing: Helping Patrons and Communities Use Free and Low-Cost Publishing Tools To Tell Their Stories — Crawford, Walt
Librarian's Guide to Online Searching: Cultivating Database Skills for Research and Instruction, 4th ed. — Bell, Suzanne S.
Libraries and the Affordable Care ACT: Helping the Community Understand Health-Care Options — Goldsmith, Francisca
Library 101: A Handbook for the School Librarian, 2d ed. — Stephens, Claire Gatrell
Library Analytics and Metrics: Using Data to Drive Decisions and Services — Showers, Ben
Library as Safe Haven: Disaster Planning, Response, and Recovery — Halsted, Deborah D.
The Library at Mount Char — Hawkins, Scott
y The Library at Mount Char (Read by Huber, Hillary). Audiobook Review — Hawkins, Scott
The Library at Mount Char — Hawkins, Scott
The Library beyond the Book — Schnapp, Jeffery T.
c A Library Book for Bear (Illus. by Denton, Kady MacDonald) — Becker, Bonny
y Library Consortia: Models for Collaboration and Sustainability — Horton, Valerie
c Library Day (Illus. by Rockwell, Lizzy) — Rockwell, Anne
c A Library Field Trip — Martin, Isabel
The Library Innovation Toolkit: Ideas, Strategies, and Programs — Molaro, Anthony
Library Management for the Digital Age: A New Paradigm — Todaro, Julie
y Library of Souls — Riggs, Ransom
The Library of the Badia Fiesolana: Intellectual History and Education under the Medici — Dressen, Angela
The Library of the Sydneys of Penhurst Place Circa 1665 — Warkentin, Germaine
Library Programs and Services: The Fundamentals. 8th ed. — Evans, G. Edward
Library Security: Better Communication, Safer Facilities — Albrecht, Steve
Libro segundo del Espejo del perfecto principe cristiano — de Monzon, Francisco
The Libyan Revolution and Its Aftermath — Cole, Peter
y Liccle Bit — Wheatle, Alex
License to Quill — della Quercia, Jacopo
y License to Spill: A Pretenders Novel — Harrison, Lisi
c License to Thrill — Gutman, Dan
License to Wed: What Legal Marriage Means to Same-Sex Couples — Richman, Kimberly D.
Licensed to Practice: The Supreme Court Defines the American Medical Profession — Mohr, James C.
c Lidia's Egg-Citing Farm Adventure (Illus. by Graef, Renee) — Bastianich, Lidia
Lidia's Mastering the Art of Italian Cuisine: Everything You Need to Know to Be a Great Italian Cook — Bastianich, Lidia Matticchio
The Lie and the Lady — Noble, Kate
The Lie of You — Lythell, Jane
y The Lie Tree — Hardinge, Frances
Liebe und Arbeit: Geschlechterbeziehungen im 19. und 20. Jahrhundert — Saurer, Edith
Liem Sioe Liong's Salim Group: The Business Pillar of Suharto's Indonesia — Borsuk, Richard
The Lies about Truth — Stevens, Courtney C.
Lies, First Person — Hareven, Gail
y Lies I Told — Zink, Michelle
y Lies in the Dust: A Tale of Remorse from the Salem Witch Trials (Illus. by Decker, Timothy) — Crane, Jakob
Lies That Bind — Barbieri, Maggie
y The Lies We Tell — Carter, Meg
y Lies We Tell Ourselves — Talley, Robin
The Lieutenant Don't Know: One Marine's Story of Warfare and Combat Logistics in Afghanistan — Clement, Jeff
Life after Dark: A History of British Nightclubs and Music Venues — Haslam, Dave
Life after Faith: The Case for Secular Humanism — Kitcher, Philip
Life among the Savages (Read by Lockford, Lesa) Audiobook Review — Jackson, Shirley
Life and Death in the Andes: On the Trail of Bandits, Heroes, and Revolutionaries — MacQuarrie, Kim
The Life and Death of Sophie Stark (Read by Dolan, Amanda). Audiobook Review — North, Anna
The Life and Death of Sophie Stark — North, Anna
The Life and Death of the Paris Commune — Merriman, John
Life and Debt: A Fresh Approach to Achieving Financial Wellness — Tayne, Leslie
Life and Ideas: The Anarchist Writings of Errico Malatesta — Malatesta, Errico
The Life and Legends of Calamity Jane — Etulain, Richard W.
The Life and Lies of Paul Crouch: Communist, Opportunist, Cold War Snitch — Taylor, Gregory S.
Life and Other Near-Death Experiences — Pagan, Camille
The Life and Passion of William of Norwich — Rubin, Miri
The Life and Pontificate of Pope Pius XII: Between History and Controversy — Coppa, Frank J.
The Life and the Adventures of a Haunted Convict — Reed, Austin
Life and Times of a Big River: An Uncommon Natural History of Alaska's Upper Yukon — Marchand, Peter J.
c The Life and Times of Benny Alvarez — Johnson, Peter
The Life and Times of Bob Cratchit — Distler, Dixie
The Life and Times of Frederick Douglass (Read by Allen, Richard). Audiobook Review — Douglass, Frederick
The Life and Times of General China: Mau Mau and the End of Empire in Kenya — Osborne, Myles
The Life and Times of Halycon Sage: Or the Last Book Ever Published — Bushnell, Karima Vargas
The Life and Times of Mickey Rooney — Lertzman, Richard A.
The Life and Times of Wilberforce Jones — Throop, D.
The Life and Work of Gunther Anders: Emigre, Iconoclast, Philosopher, Man of Letters — Bischof, Gunter
The Life and Writings of Luisa de Carvajal y Mendoza — Carvajal y Mendoza, Luisa de
The Life and Writings of Luisa De Carvajal y Mendoza — Cruz, Anne J.
A Life at the Chalkface: The Memoir of a London Headteacher — Kent, Mike
y Life at the Speed of Us — Sappenfield, Heather
Life Atomic: A History of Radioisotopes in Science and Medicine — Creager, Angela N.H.
The Life Balance Playbook — Landau, Laura
The Life-Changing Magic of Not Giving a F*ck: How to Stop Spending Time You Don't Have with People You Don't Like Doing Things You Don't Want to Do — Knight, Sarah
The Life-Changing Magic of Tidying Up: The Japanese Art of Decluttering and Organizing. Audiobook Review — Kondo, Marie
Life-Course Perspectives on Military Services — Moore, Brenda L.
y Life Cycle of a Lie — Olsen, Sylvia
c Life Cycles — Riley, Peter
A Life Dedicated to the Republic: Vavro Srobar's Slovak Czechoslovakism — Baer, Josette
Life Drawing — Black, Robin
c Life during the Great Depression — Lanier, Wendy H.
c Life during the Industrial Revolution — Garstecki, Julia
y Life during the Renaissance — Marcovit, Hal
c Life during the Revolutionary War — Hinman, Bonnie
Life Embitters — Pla, Josep
Life, End Of — Brooke-Rose, Christine
A Life for a Life — Muir, T. Frank
Life for a Life — Muir, T. Frank
Life from Scratch: A Memoir of Food, Family, and Forgiveness — Martin, Sasha
A Life Ignited — Kinard, Rhonda
Life in a Corner: Cultural Episodes in Southeastern Utah, 1880-1950 — McPherson, Robert S.
c Life in America: Comparing Immigrant Experiences — Baker, Brynn
y Life in Ancient Egypt — Nardo, Don
y Life in Ancient Greece — Nardo, Don
c Life in Colonial Australia — Littlejohn, Marion
Life in Crisis: The Ethical Journey of Doctors without Borders — Redfield, Peter
y Life in Nazi Germany — Marcovitz, Hal
Life in New York: How I Learned to Love Squeegee Men, Token Suckers, Trash Twisters, and Subway Sharks — Pedersen, Laura
A Life in Red — Beasley, David
Life in Squares

y Life in the Time of Shakespeare — Marcovitz, Hal
c Life in the War — Cooke, Tim
Life in Words: Essays on Chaucer, the Gawain-Poet, and Malory — Mann, Jill
The Life Informatic: Newsmaking in the Digital Era — Boyer, Dominic
Life Interrupted: Trafficking into Forced Labor in the United States — Abend, Gabriel
Life Interrupted: Trafficking into Forced Labor in the United States — Brennan, Denise
Life Is a Gift: A Book for Thankful Hearts — Paraclete Press
Life Is a Wheel: Memoirs of a Bike-Riding Obituarist — Weber, Bruce
c Life Is like the Wind (Illus. by Agocs, Irisz) — Innes, Shona
Life Is Meals: A Food Lover's Book of Days — Salter, James
Life Is Short--Art Is Shorter: In Praise of Brevity — Shields, David
Life-Like — Litt, Toby
life.love.beauty — Allen, Keegan
Life Moves Pretty Fast: The Lessons We Learned from 1980s Movies (and Why We Don't Learn Them from Movies Any More). — Freeman, Hadley
The Life Negroni — Banks, Leigh
Life No. 6 — Wagman, Diana
Life of a Counterfeiter — Inoue, Yasushi
The Life of Augustine of Hippo, Part 2: The Donatist Controversy — Sebastien, Louis
y The Life of Carter G. Woodson: Father of African-American History — Durden, Robert F.
The Life of Catalina de Erauso, the Lieutenant Nun: An Early Modern Autobiography — Perez-Villanueva, Sonia
The Life of Elves — Barbery, Muriel
The Life of George Eliot — Henry, Nancy
y The Life of Harriet Tubman: Moses of the Underground Railroad — Schraff, Anne
The Life of Images: Selected Prose — Simic, Charles
A Life of Lies and Spies: Tales of a CIA Covert Ops Polygraph Interrogator — Trabue, Alan B.
y The Life of Martin Luther King, Jr.: Leader for Civil Rights — Schuman, Michael A.
The Life of Norman, vol. 1 — Silas, Stan
The Life of Patriarch Ignatius — David, Nicetas
y The Life of Paul Laurence Dunbar: Portrait of a Poet — Reef, Catherine
The Life of R. H. Tawney: Socialism and History — Goldman, Lawrence
The Life of Reason: Reason in Art — Santayana, George
The Life of Roman Republicanism — Connolly, Joy
The Life of Saint Basil the Younger: Critical Edition and Annotated Translation of the Moscow Version — Sullivan, Denis F.
The Life of Saul Bellow: To Fame and Fortune, 1915-1964 — Leader, Zachary
The Life of the Longhouse: An Archaeology of Ethnicity — Metcalf, Peter
c The Life of Ty: Friends of a Feather (Illus. by Henry, Jed) — Myracle, Lauren
The Life of William Apess, Pequot — Gura, Philip F.
The Life of William Wordsworth: A Critical Biography — Worthen, John
c Life of Zarf: The Trouble with Weasels. Audiobook Review — Harrell, Rob
c Life of Zarf: The Trouble with Weasels — Harrell, Rob
Life on Display: Revolutionizing U.S. Museums of Science and Natural History in the Twentieth Century — Rader, Karen A.
c Life on Mars — Brown, Jennifer
Life on the Edge: The Coming of Age of Quantum Biology — Al-Khalili, Jim
Life on the Edge: The Coming of Age of Quantum Biology — McFadden, Johnjoe
c Life on the Frontier — Onsgard, Bethany
Life, Only Better — Gavalda, Anna
Life or Death — Robotham, Michael
Life out of Sequence: A Data-Driven History of Bioinformatics — Stevens, Hallam
Life Reimagined — Hagerty, Barbara Bradley
The Life Sciences in Early Modern Philosophy — Nachtomy, Ohad
y Life Unaware — Gibsen, Cole
Life Unfolding: How the Human Body Creates Itself — Davies, Jamie A.
Life, War, Earth: Deleuze and the Sciences — Protevi, John
Life with Howard: Howard Staats of 302 Levens Street, Dallas, Oregon — Van Tassel, Eloise

A Life with Words: A Writer's Memoir — Wright, Richard B.
c Life without Nico (Illus. by Olea, Francisco Javier) — Maturana, Andrea
Life Worth Living: Albert Camus and the Quest for Meaning — Zaretsky, Robert
A Life Worth Riding — Simons, Sandi
Lifeblood: Oil, Freedom, and the Forces of Capital — Huber, Matthew T.
y The Lifeboat Clique — Parks, Kathy
The Lifecycle of Software Objects — Chiang, Ted
c Lifeguard Dogs — Lunis, Natalie
y Lifeless — Strickland, Adrianne
Life's Blueprint: The Science and Art of Embryo Creation — Shilo, Benny
Life's Engines: How Microbes Made Earth Habitable — Falkowski, Paul G.
Life's Greatest Secret — Cobb, Matthew
Life's Greatest Secret: The Race to Crack the Genetic Code — Cobb, Matthew
Life's Greatest Secret: The Story of the Race to Crack the Genetic Code — Cobb, Matthew
Life's Too Short to Pretend You're Not Religious — Dark, David
c Lifesize Ocean (Illus. by Jackson-Carter, Stuart) — Ganeri, Anita
c Lifesize Rainforest (Illus. by Jackson-Carter, Stuart) — Ganeri, Anita
y Lifespan of Starlight — Kalkipsakis, Thalia
Lifted: A Cultural History of the Elevator — Bernard, Andreas
Lifted by the Great Nothing — Dimechkie, Karim
Lifted to the Wind — Gardner, Susan
Lifting My Voice — Hendricks, Barbara
Light: A Radiant History from Creation to the Quantum Age — Watson, Bruce
c Light — Lawrence, Ellen
Light and Its Effects — Winterberg, Jenna
Light Atonement — Ariyana
The Light Between Us: Stories from Heaven, Lessons for the Living — Jackson, Laura Lynne
y Light & Dark: The Awakening of the Mageknight — Fife, D. M
c Light Helps Me See — Boothroyd, Jennifer
The Light in Cuban Eyes: Lake Forest College's Madeleine P. Plonsker Collection of Contemporary Cuban Photography — Plonsker, Madeleine
Light in Germany: Scenes from an Unknown Enlightenment — Reed, T.J.
A Light in the Wilderness — Kirkpatrick, Jane
c Light Makes Colors — Boothroyd, Jennifer
y Light of Day — van Diepen, Allison
y Light of Day — Van Diepen, Allison
The Light of Hidden Flowers — Handford, Jennifer
The Light of the World — Alexander, Elizabeth
c Light & Sound Waves Close-Up Series — Johnson, Robin
y The Light That Gets Lost — Carthew, Natasha
Light: The Visible Spectrum and Beyond — Arcand, Kimberly
The Lighthouse of Souls — Almada, Ariel A.
Lighthouses — McVety, Allison
Lighting Design for Commercial Portrait Photography — Emery, Jennifer
Lighting the World: Transforming Our Energy Future by Bringing Electricity to Everyone — Rogers, Jim E.
Lighting Up: The Rise of Social Smoking on College Campuses — Nichter, Mimi
The Lightkeepers — Geni, Abby
Lightless — Higgins, C.A.
The Lightless Sky — Passarlay, Gulwali
y Lightning — Calhoun, Bonnie S.
c Lightning Bolt Books: Robots Everywhere! Series — Zuchora-Walske, Christine
c The Lightning Catcher (Illus. by Jamieson, Victoria) — Cameron, Anne
Lightning in the Andes and Mesoamerica: Pre-Columbian, Colonial, and Contemporary Perspectives — Staller, John E.
y The Lightning Queen — Resau, Laura
The Lightning Stones — Du Brul, Jack
Lights, Camera, Murder! — Celine, Marie
c The Lights Go On Again — Pearson, Kit
The Lights of Pointe-Noire — Mabanckou, Alain
Lights Out: A Cyberattack, a Nation Unprepared, Surviving the Aftermath — Koppel, Ted
Like a Bomb Going Off: Leonid Yakobson and Ballet as Resistance in Soviet Russia — Ross, Janice
c Like a River: A Civil War Novel — Wiechman, Kathy Cannon
c Like a River — Wiechman, Kathy Cannon

c Like A Wolf (Illus. by Guilloppe, Antoine) — Elschner, Geraldine
Like a Woman — Busman, Debra
Like Branches to Wind: Poems 2008 — Milazzo, Richard
Like Family — Giordano, Paolo
y Like It Never Happened — Adrian, Emily
y Like No Other (Read by Odom, Leslie, with Phoebe Strole). Audiobook Review — LaMarche, Una
y Like No Other — LaMarche, Una
The Like Switch: An Ex-FBI Agent's Guide to Influencing, Attracting, and Winning People Over — Schafer, Jack
Like Water, Like Bread — Kohler, Joyce Webb
y Like Water on Stone — Walrath, Dana
Likenesses: Translation, Illustration, Interpretation — Reynolds, Matthew
c Li'l Rip Haywire Adventures — Thompson, Dan
Lila — Robinson, Marilynne
Lila's Hamsa — Kurtis, Arlene
c Lili Tutti-Frutti (Illus. by Richard, Serge V.) — Bourget, Edith
c Lillian's Right to Vote: A Celebration of the Voting Rights Act of 1965 (Illus. by Evans, Shane W.) — Winter, Jonah
c Lilliput — Gayton, Sam
c Lilliput (Illus. by Ratterree, Alice) — Gayton, Sam
y Lilli's Quest — Perl, Lila
c Lily and Bear (Illus. by Stubbs, Lisa) — Stubbs, Lisa
The Lily and the Thistle: The French Tradition and the Older Literature of Scotland — Calin, William
c The Lily-Livered Prince: Tales from Schwartzgarten, vol. 3 — Hill, Christopher William
c Lily the Elf: The Elf Flute (Illus. by Coutts, Lisa) — Bradford, Anna
c Lily the Elf: The Wishing Seed (Illus. by Coutts, Lisa) — Bradford, Anna
c Lily's New Home (Illus. by Ng-Benitez, Shirley) — Yoo, Paula
Limber — Pelster, Angela
Limbo — Mazzuco, Melania G.
The Liminal War — Jama-Everett, Ayize
The Liminal Worker: An Ethnography of Work, Unemployment and Precariousness in Contemporary Greece — Spyridakis, Manos
The Limits of Partnership: U.S.-Russian Relations in the Twenty-First Century — Stent, Angela E.
Limonov: The Outrageous Adventures of the Radical Soviet Poet Who Became a Bum in New York, a Sensation in France and a Political Antihero in Russia — Carrere, Emmanuel
Lin Shu, Inc.: Translation and the Making of Modern Chinese Culture — Hill, Michael Gibbs
Lincoln and Oregon Country Politics in the Civil War Era — Etulain, Richard W.
Lincoln and Reconstruction — Rodrigue, John C.
Lincoln and Reconstruction — Steers, Edward, Jr.
Lincoln and the Jews: A History — Sarna, Jonathan D.
Lincoln and the Military — Marszalek, John F.
Lincoln and the Power of the Press: The War for Public Opinion — Holzer, Harold
Lincoln and the Triumph of the Nation: Constitutional Conflict in the American Civil War — Neely, Mark E., Jr.
Lincoln and the U.S. Colored Troops — Smith, John David
Lincoln and the War's End — Waugh, John C.
A Lincoln Dialogue — Rawley, James A.
Lincoln Gordon: Architect of Cold War Foreign Policy — Smith, Bruce L.R.
Lincoln's Autocrat: The Life of Edwin Stanton — Marvel, William
Lincoln's Billy — LeClair, Tom
Lincoln's Body: A Cultural History (Read by Larkin, Pete). Audiobook Review — Fox, Richard Wightman
Lincoln's Body: A Cultural History — Fox, Richard Wightman
Lincoln's Bodyguard — Turner, T.J.
Lincoln's Citadel: The Civil War in Washington, DC — Winkle, Kenneth J.
Lincoln's Ethics — Carson, Thomas L.
Lincoln's Greatest Case: The River, the Bridge, and the Making of America — McGinty, Brian
Lincoln's Last Speech: Wartime Reconstruction and the Crisis of Reunion — Masur, Louis P.
Lincoln's Political Thought — Kateb, George
y Lincoln's Spymaster: Allan Pinkerton, America's First Private Eye — Seiple, Samantha
Lincoln's Story — Vel
Lincoln's Tragic Pragmatism: Lincoln, Douglas, and Moral Conflict — Burt, John

c A Line Can Be (Illus. by Ljungkvist, Laura)
— Ljungkvist, Laura
Line Dances around the World — Kjelle, Marylou Morano
A Line of Blood — McPherson, Ben
c Line Up, Please! — Ohmura, Tomoko
c Ling & Ting: Twice as Silly (Illus. by Lin, Grace) — Lin, Grace
Lingo: Around Europe in Sixty Languages — Dorren, Gaston
Lingo — Dorren, Gaston
Lingua e identita a 150 anni dall'Unita d'Italia — Brera, Matteo
Lingua Spagnola e cultura Ispanica a Napoli fra rinascimento e barocco: Testimonianze a stampa — Garcia, Encarnacion Sanchez
A Linguistic History of Ancient Cyprus: The Non-Greek Languages, and their Relations with Greek, c. 1600-300 BC — Steele, P.M.
Linked Data for Libraries, Archives, and Museums: How to Clean, Link and Publish Your Metadata — van Hooland, Seth
Linkers — Schuster, David M.
Linnets and Valerians — Goudge, Elizabeth
L'Intention du poete: Clement Marot "autheur" — Berthon, Guillaume
c The Lion and the Bird (Illus. by Dubuc, Marianne) — Dubuc, Marianne
c Lion and Tiger and Bear: Tag! You're It! (Illus. by Long, Ethan) — Long, Ethan
y Lion Heart: A Scarlet Novel — Gaughen, A.C.
y Lion Heart — Gaughen, A.C.
c The Lion Inside (Illus. by Field, Jim) — Bright, Rachel
c Lion, Lion (Illus. by Day, Larry) — Busch, Miriam
Lion of Rora (Illus. by Lewis, Jackie) — Gage, Ruth
The Lion of Sabray: The Afghani Warrior Who Defied the Taliban and Saved the Life of Navy SEAL Marcus Luttrell — Robinson, Patrick
Lion of the Senate: When Ted Kennedy Rallied the Democrats in a GOP Congress — Littlefield, Nick
Lion Plays Rough — Smith, Lachlan
c Lion Practice — Carlisle, Emma
Lion Songs — Eyre, Banning
c The Lion & the Mouse (Illus. by Pinkney, Jerry) — Pinkney, Jerry
c Lionel and Molly: Colors (Illus. by Racklyeft, Jess) — Lake, Joanna
c Lionel Messi: Soccer Sensation — Logothetis, Paul
The Lioness in Winter: Writing an Old Woman's Life — Burack-Weiss, Ann
c Lionheart (Illus. by Collingridge, Richard) — Collingridge, Richard
Lionheart: The Diaries of Richard I — Manson, Chris
The Lion's Gate: on the Front Lines of the Six Day War — Pressfield, Steven
Lions in the Balance: Man-Eaters, Manes, and Men with Guns — Packer, Craig
The Lion's Mouth — Holt, Anne
Liquid Intelligence: The Art and Science of the Perfect Cocktail — Arnold, Dave (b. 1971-)
Liquidated: An Ethnography of Wall Street — Ho, Karen
Lire, choisir, ecrire: La vulgarisation des savoirs du Moyen Age a la Renaissance — Giacomotto-Charra, Violaine
L'isola esile: Studi sull'Inno a Delo di Callimaco — Giuseppetti, M.
c List for Santa, List for Life — Corner, T.E.
The List — Calhoun, Anne
The List of Dead Smiths — Williams, D.L.
List of the Lost — Morrissey
y A List of Things That Didn't Kill Me — Schmidt, Jason
y Listed — Freeman, Shannon
y Listen, Slowly (Read by Lam, Lulu). Audiobook Review — Lai, Thanhha
y Listen, Slowly — Lai, Thanhha
Listen ... till You Disappear — Kettelhut, Martin
c Listen to Our World (Illus. by Sweet, Melissa) — Martin, Bill, Jr.
Listen to the Lambs — Daniel, Black
y Listen to the Moon — Morpurgo, Michael
Listen to Your Mother: What She Said Then, What We're Saying Now — Imig, Ann
The Listener — Basch, Rachel
The Listening Life: Embracing Attentiveness in a World of Distraction — McHugh, Adam
Listening to Killers: Lessons Learned from My Twenty Years as a Psychological Expert Witness in Murder Cases — Garbarino, James

Listening to Sea Lions: Currents of Change from Galapagos to Patagonia — Meltzoff, Sarah Keene
Listening to Stone: The Art and Life of Isamu Noguchi — Herrera, Hayden
Listening to the Bible: The Art of Faithful Biblical Interpretation — Bryan, Christopher
Listening to the French New Wave: The Film Music and Composers of Postwar French Art Cinema — McMahon, Orlene Denice
Liszt's Final Decade — Pesce, Dolores
Lit Up: One Reporter, Three Schools, and Twenty-Four Books That Can Change Lives — Denby, David
L'Italia e la guerra di Libia cent'anni dopo — Micheletta, Luca
Literacy and Intellectual Life in the Cherokee Nation: 1820-1906 — Parins, James W.
Literacy and the Common Core: Recipes for Action — Tantillo, Sarah
Literarische Deutschlandreisen nach 1989 — Bruckner, Leslie
Literary and Visual Ralegh — Armitage, Christopher M.
The Literary Churchill: Author, Reader, Actor — Rose, Jonathan
Literary Criticism from Plato to Postmodernism: The Humanistic Alternative — Seaton, James
The Literary Criticism of Matthew Arnold: Letters to Clough, the 1853 Preface, and Some Essays — Olsen, Flemming
Literary Folios and Ideas of the Book in Early Modern England — Connor, Francis X.
Literary Half-Lives: Doris Lessing, Clancy Sigal, and Roman a Clef — Rubenstein, Roberta
Literary Knowing in Neoclassical France: From Poetics to Aesthetics — Delehanty, Ann T.
Literary Rivals: Feuds and Antagonisms in the World of Books — Bradford, Richard
The Literary Thing: History, Poetry and the Making of Modern Cultural Sphere — Chaudhuri, Rosinka
A Literary Tour of Italy — Parks, Tim
Literatur und Politik: Ein deutsches Verhangnis? — Ruther, Gunther
Literatur und Zeitgeschichte: Zwischen Historisierung und Musealisierung — Golec, Janusz
Literaturaustausch im Geteilten Deutschland 1945-1972 — Frohn, Julia
Literature and Landscape in East Devon — Nasmyth, Peter
Literature and Liberty: Essays in Libertarian Literary Criticism — Mendenhall, Allen P.
Literature and Politics in the 1620s: 'Whisper'd Counsells' — Salzman, Paul
Literature and Society in the Fourth Century AD: Performing, Constructing the Present, Presenting the Self — Van Hoof, Lieve
Literature and the Encounter with God in Post-Reformation England — Martin, Michael
Literature, Commerce, and the Spectacle of Modernity, 1750u-1800 — Keen, Paul
Literature in the First Media Age: Britain between the Wars. — Trotter, David
Literature, Modernism, and Dance — Jones, Susan
The Literature of the Lebanese Diaspora: Representations of Place and Transnational Identity — Bayeh, Jumana
Literatur en observantie: De "Spieghel der volcomenheit" van Hendrik Herp en de dynamiek van laatmiddeleeuwse tekstverspreiding — Dlabacova, Anna
"Literchoor Is My Beat": A Life of James Laughlin, Publisher of New Directions — MacNiven, Ian S.
Litterature, Geography, and the Postmodern Poetics of Place — Prieto, Eric
c A Little ABC Book — Palmer, Jenny
c Little Author in the Big Woods: A Biography of Laura Ingalls Wilder (Illus. by Thermes, Jennifer) — McDonough, Yona Zeldis
c Little Baby Buttercup (Illus. by Byun, You) — Ashman, Linda
Little Bastards in Springtime — Rudolph, Katja
Little Bastards in Summertime — Rudolf, Katja
Little Beach Street Bakery — Colgan, Jenny
c Little Bean's Funderwear Day! (Illus. by Zobel, David) — Noone, Roni
Little Beasts — McGevna, Matthew
c Little Bell and the Moon (Illus. by Deppe, Iris) — Paley-Phillips, Giles
c Little Big Boubo (Illus. by Alemagna, Beatrice) — Alemagna, Beatrice
c Little Big (Illus. by Bentley, Jonathan) — Bentley, Jonathan

c Little Bird Takes a Bath (Illus. by Russo, Marisabina) — Russo, Marisabina
c The Little Bird Who Lost His Song — Robaard, Jedda
c Little Bird's Bad Word (Illus. by Grant, Jacob) — Grant, Jacob
y A Little Bit Langston — Demcak, Andrew
A Little Bit of Spectacular — Phillips, Gin
c Little Bitty Friends (Illus. by Barton, Patrice) — McPike, Elizabeth
Little Black Lies — Block, Sandra
Little Black Lies — Bolton, Sharon
c Little Bo Peep and Her Bad, Bad Sheep (Illus. by Flowers, Luke) — Wegwerth, A.L.
c Little Boo (Illus. by Zeltner, Tim) — Wunderli, Stephen
c The Little Book of Big Fears (Illus. by Arnaldo, Monica) — Arnaldo, Monica
c The Little Bookshop and the Origami Army — Foreman, Michael
Little Boy Needs Ride — Bower, Chris
The Little Brother — Patterson, Victoria
c Little Bubba Looks For His Elephant — Ho, Jannie
c Little Butterfly — Logan, Laura
c The Little Butterfly — Shahan, Sherry
c Little Cat's Luck — Bauer, Marion Dane
c Little Celeste — McNiff, Dawn
c Little Chanclas (Illus. by Crosthwaite, Luis Humberto) — Lozano, Jose
c Little Chanclas (Illus. by Lozano, Jose) — Lozano, Jose
c Little Dinosaurs — Schwartz, Betty
Little Dreams in Glass and Metal: Enameling in America — Nelson, Harold B.
The Little Edges — Moten, Fred
c Little Elephant's Blocked Trunk — Archer, Dosh
c Little Elfie One (Illus. by Manning, Jane) — Jane, Pamela
c Little Elliot, Big City (Illus. by Curato, Mike) — Curato, Mike
c Little Elliot, Big Family (Illus. by Curato, Mike) — Curato, Mike
Little Emperors and Material Girls — Steinfeld, Jemimah
c The Little Factory of Illustration (Illus. by Saint-Val, Florie) — Saint-Val, Florie
Little Failure (Read by Todd, Jonathan) — Shteyngart, Gary
The Little Free Library Book — Aldrich, Margret
y A Little Friendly Advice — Vivian, Siobhan
c The Little Gardener (Illus. by Hughes, Emily) — Hughes, Emily
Little Gem: 15 Paper-Pieced Miniature Quilts — Kauffman, Connie
The Little Girl Who Fought the Great Depression: Shirley Temple and 1930s America — Kasson, John F.
Little Girls — Malfi, Ronald
c Little Golden Bear (Illus. by Terrano, Doina Cociuba) — King, K.L.
c Little Gray's Great Migration (Illus. by Gabriel, Andrea) — Lindsey, Marta
A Little Greek Reader — Morwood, James
c Little Green Peas: A Big Book of Colors (Illus. by Baker, Keith) — Baker, Keith
A Little Guide to the 15th Arrondissement for the Use of Phantoms — Caillois, Roger
c The Little Hippo: A Children's Book Inspired by Egyptian Art (Illus. by Klauss, Anja) — Elschner, Geraldine
A Little History of the United States — Davidson, James West
c Little Hoiho (Illus. by Thatcher, Stephanie) — Thatcher, Stephanie
Little House Living: The Make-Your-Own Guide to a Frugal, Simple, and Self-Sufficient Life — Alink, Melissa
c Little Humans — Stanton, Brandon
y A Little in Love — Fletcher, Susan
c Little Jessie's Beach Fun — Nat, Gowri
c Little Kids First Big Book of Bugs — Hughes, Catherine D.
c Little Kids First Big Book of How — Esbaum, Jill
c Little Kids First Big Book of Who — Esbaum, Jill
c The Little Kids' Table (Illus. by Uhles, Mary) — Riehle, Mary Ann McCabe
c The Little Kids' Table (Illus. by Uhles, Mary Reaves) — Riehle, Mary Ann McCabe
c The Little Knight Who Battled the Rain (Illus. by Despres, Genevieve) — Tibo, Gilles
c Little Kunoichi, The Ninja Girl (Illus. by Ishida, Sanae) — Ishida, Sanae
A Little Life — Yanagihara, Hanya

c Little Lucy Goes to School (Illus. by Kanzler, John) — Cooper, Ilene
A Little Lumpen Novelita — Bolano, Roberto
Little Manila Is in the Heart: The Making of the Filipina/o American Community in Stockton, California — Mabalon, Dawn Bohulano
c Little Melba and Her Big Trombone (Illus. by Morrison, Frank) — Russell-Brown, Katheryn
Little Men, Big World / Vanity Row — Burnett, W.R.
Little Miss, Big Sis (Illus. by Reynolds, Peter H.) — Rosenthal, Amy Krouse
c Little Miss Evil — Leung, Bryce
Little Miss Sure Shot — Marshall, Jeffrey
c The Little Moon Raven — Pfister, Marcus
c The Little Moose Who Couldn't Go to Sleep (Illus. by Stimson, James) — Claflin, Willy
A Little More Free — McFetridge, John
c The Little Mouse Santi (Illus. by Germano, Santiago) — Ray, David Eugene
Little Nemo: Dream another Dream — O'Neill, Joshua
y Little Nemo's Big New Dreams — O'Neill, Josh
c Little Nino's Pizzaria — Barbour, Karen
c Little One (Illus. by Weaver, Jo) — Weaver, Jo
c Little Owl's Day (Illus. by Srinivasan, Divya) — Srinivasan, Divya
The Little Paris Bookshop (Read by West, Steve). Audiobook Review — George, Nina
The Little Paris Bookshop — George, Nina
The Little Paris Bookshop — Pare, Simon
c The Little Parrot and the Angel's Tears — Narasimhan, M. Amu
c Little Pea (Illus. by Corace, Jen) — Rosenthal, Amy Krouse
y Little Peach — Kern, Peggy
c Little Penguin Gets the Hiccups (Illus. by Bentley, Tadgh) — Bentley, Tadgh
Little Pretty Things — Rader-Day, Lori
c The Little Prince (Illus. by Saint-Exupery, Antoine de) — Norminton, Gregory
c Little Puffin's First Flight (Illus. by Van Zyle, Jon) — London, Jonathan
Little Puppy and the Big Green Monster (Illus. by Wohnoutka, Mike) — Wohnoutka, Mike
c Little Puppy Lost (Illus. by Harry, Rebecca) — Webb, Holly
Little Quilts and Gifts from Jelly Roll Scraps: 30 Gorgeous Projects for Using up Your Left-Over Fabric — Forster, Carolyn
c Little Red and the Very Hungry Lion — Smith, Alex T.
The Little Red Chairs — O'Brien, Edna
c Little Red Gliding Hood (Illus. by Cummings, Troy) — Lazar, Tara
c Little Red Henry (Illus. by Valentine, Madeline) — Urban, Linda
c Little Red Quacking Hood — Jones, Noah Z.
Little Red Readings: Historical Materialist Perspectives on Children's Literature — Hubler, Angela E.
c Little Red Riding Hood/Caperucita Roja (Illus. by Cuellar, Olga) — Mlawer, Teresa
c Little Red Riding Hood: Not Quite (Illus. by Bixley, Donovan) — Morrison, Yvonne
c Little Red Riding Hood (Illus. by Schauer, Loretta) — Alperin, Mara
c Little Red Riding Hood (Illus. by Rossi, Francesca) — Francia, Giada
c Little Red Riding Hood (Illus. by Schenker, Sybille) — Grimm, Jacob
Little "Red Scares": Anti-Communism and Political Repression in the United States, 1921-1946 — Goldstein, Robert Justin
c Little Red's Riding Hood — Stein, Peter
The Little Review 'Ulysses' — Scholes, Robert
Little Rice: Smartphones, Xiaomi, and the Chinese Dream — Shirky, Clay
c Little Robot (Illus. by Hatke, Ben) — Hatke, Ben
c Little Shaq (Illus. by Taylor, Theodore, III) — O'Neal, Shaquille
c The Little Shop of Monsters (Read by Black, Jack). Audiobook Review — Stine, R.L.
c The Little Shop of Monsters (Illus. by Brown, Marc) — Stine, R.L.
The Little Silver Book - Interviewing — Berdiev, Neil
Little Sister Death — Gay, William
Little Sister Death — Gray, William
c Little Sleepyhead (Illus. by Barton, Patrice) — McPike, Elizabeth
c The Little Snowplow (Illus. by Parker, Jake) — Koehler, Lora
The Little Spark: 30 Ways to Ignite Your Creativity — Bloomston, Carrie

c Little Tree (Illus. by Long, Loren) — Long, Loren
c Little Tree (Illus. by Adinolfi, JoAnn) — Van, Muon
c The Little Tree That Would Not Share (Illus. by Costa, Nicoletta) — Costa, Nicoletta
c Little Truff and the Kereru (Illus. by Evans, Anna) — Russell, Ann
c Little Tug (Illus. by Savage, Stephen) — Savage, Stephen
Little Victories — Gay, Jason
Little Victories: Perfect Rules for Imperfect Living — Gay, Jason
The Little Washer of Sorrows — Fawcett, Katherine
Little White Bull: British Fiction in the 50s and 60s — Muckle, John
c Little White Fish — van Genechten, Guido
c Little White Fish Has a Party — van Genechten, Guido
y Little White Lies — Baker, Brianna
y Little White Lies — Dale, Katie
Little Woman in Blue — Atkins, Jeannine
Little Women (Read by Berneis, Susie). Audiobook Review — Alcott, Louisa May
c A Little Women Christmas (Illus. by Ibatoulline, Bagram) — Frederick, Heather Vogel
c Littleland: Around the World (Illus. by Billet, Marion) — Billet, Marion
c The Littlest Bird (Illus. by Ellis, Elina) — Edwards, Gareth
c The Littlest Bunny in Canada: An Easter Adventure (Illus. by Dunn, Robert) — Jacobs, Lily
c The Littlest Giant: The Story of Vamana (Illus. by Moore, Emma V.) — Greene, Joshua M.
Litt's Drug Eruption and Reaction Manual, 21st ed. — Litt, Jerome Z.
Liturgical Subjects: Christian Ritual, Biblical Narrative, and the Formation of the Self in Byzantium — Krueger, Derek
Liturgy and Society in Early Medieval Rome — Romano, John F.
Liturgy as a Way of Life: Embodying the Arts in Christian Worship — Benson, Bruce Ellis
Liturgy in Postcolonial Perspectives: Only One Is Holy — Carvalhaes, Claudio
Liturgy of Liberation: A Christian Commentary on Shankara's "Upadesasahasri" — Locklin, Reid B.
The Liturgy of Life: The Interrelationship of Sunday Eucharist and Everyday Worship Practices — Manalo, Ricky
Live and Die Like a Man: Gender Dynamics in Urban Egypt — Ghannam, Farha
Live Art in LA: Performance in Southern California, 1970-1983 — Phelan, Peggy
Live at the Fillmore East and West: Getting Backstage and Personal with Rock's Greatest Legends (Read by Berkrot, Peter). Audiobook Review — Glatt, John
Live Bait — Genovesi, Fabio
Live, Eat, Cook Healthy: Simple, Fresh and Delicious Recipes for Balanced Living — Khanna, Rachel
Live Long and Prosper: How Black Megachurches Address HIV/AIDS and Poverty in the Age of Prosperity Theology — Barnes, Sandra L.
Live Right and Find Happiness (Although Beer Is Much Faster): Life Lessons and Other Ravings from Dave Barry — Barry, Dave
Lively Capital: Biotechnologies, Ethics, and Governance in Global Markets — Rajan, Kaushik Sunder
The Liverpool Companion to World Science Fiction Film — Fritzsche, Sonja
Lives in Common: Arabs and Jews in Jerusalem, Jaffa and Hebron — Klein, Menachem
Lives in Ruins: Archaeologists and the Seductive Lure of Human Rubble — Johnson, Marilyn
Lives in Ruins: Archaeologists and the Seductive Lure of Human Rubble (Read by Huber, Hillary). Audiobook Review — Johnson, Marilyn
Lives in Writing: Essays — Lodge, David
The Lives of Erich Fromm: Love's Prophet — Friedman, Lawrence J.
The Lives of Frederick Douglass — Levine, Robert S.
Lives of Girls and Women — Munro, Alice
The Lives of Muhammad — Ali, Kecia
The Lives of Others — Mukherjee, Neel
The Lives of Robert Ryan — Jones, J.R.
Lives of the Artists, Lives of the Architects — Obrist, Hans Ulrich
c Lives of the Explorers: Discoveries, Disasters (and What the Neighbors Thought). (Illus. by Hewitt, Kathryn) — Krull, Kathleen
Lives of the Family: Stories of Fate and Circumstances — Chong, Denise

Lives of-the Great Photographers — Hacking, Juliet
Living a Big War in a Small Place: Spartanburg, South Carolina, during the Confederacy — Racine, Philip N.
Living Alone: Globalization, Identity, and Belonging — Jamieson, Lynn
Living Art in Papua New Guinea — Cochrane, Susan
Living as Form: Socially Engaged Art from 1991-2011 — Thompson, Nato
Living Beings: Perspectives on Interspecies Engagements — Dransart, Penelope
c Living beside a River — Labrecque, Ellen
Living Black: Social Life in an African American Neighborhood — Fleisher, Mark S.
Living Dead in the Pacific: Contested Sovereignty and Racism in Genetic Research on Taiwan Aborigines — Munsterhjelm, Mark
A Living Exhibition: The Smithsonian and the Transformation of the Universal Museum — Walker, William S.
c Living Fossils: Clues to the Past (Illus. by Plant, Andrew) — Arnold, Caroline
The Living Goddess: A Journey into the Heart of Kathmandu — Tree, Isabella
Living Hell: The Dark Side of the Civil War — Adams, Michael C.C.
Living History: On the Front Lines for Israel and the Jews 2003-2015 — Chesler, Phyllis
The Living Icon in Byzantium and Italy: The Vita Image, Eleventh to Thirteenth Centuries — Chatterjee, Paroma
c Living in a City — Labrecque, Ellen
c Living in a Desert — Labrecque, Ellen
Living in Balance — Levey, Joel
Living in European Borderlands
Living in Infamy: Felon Disenfranchisement and the History of American Citizenship — Holloway, Pippa
Living in Squares, Loving in Triangles: The Lives and Loves of Virginia Woolf and the Bloomsbury Group — Licence, Amy
Living in the Crossfire: Favela Residents, Drug Dealers and Police Violence in Rio de Janeiro — Alve, Maria Helena Moreira
Living in the Crosshairs: The Untold Stories of Anti-Abortion Terrorism — Cohen, David S.
Living in the Land of Limbo: Fiction and Poetry about Family Caregiving — Levine, Carol
Living Intersections: Transnational Migrant Identifications in Asia — Pluss, Caroline
Living Karma: The Religious Practices of Ouyi Zhixu — McGuire, Beverley Foulks
Living Large: Wilna Hervey and Nan Mason — Eckhardt, Joseph P.
Living Luxe Gluten Free — Lee, Michelle
Living Mindfully: At Home, at Work, and in the World — David, Deborah Schoeberlein
The Living Mountain — Shepherd, Nan
Living Oil: Petroleum Culture in the American Century — LeMenager, Stephanie
c Living on a Mountain — Labrecque, Ellen
Living on Paper: Letters from Iris Murdoch, 1934-1995 — Horner, Avril
Living on Paper: Letters from Iris Murdoch 1934-1995 — Murdoch, Iris
Living on Your Own: Single Women, Rental Housing, and Post-Revolutionary Affect in Contemporary South Korea — Song, Jesook
Living Passionately — Blon, Maria
Living Recovery: Youth Speak Out on "Owning" Mental Illness — Leavey, JoAnn Elizabeth
Living the Dream: New Immigration Policies and the Lives of Undocumented Latino Youth — Chavez, Maria
Living the Secular Life: New Answers to Old Questions — Zuckerman, Phil
Living Translation: Language and the Search for Resonance in U.S. Chinese Medicine — Pritzker, Sonya E.
Living Well in Renaissance Italy: The Virtues of Humanism and the Irony of Leon Battista Alberti — Kircher, Timothy
c Living Wild Series — Gish, Melissa
Living with HIV and ARVs: Three Letter Lives — Squire, Corinne
Living with HIV and Dying with AIDS: Diversity, Inequality and Human Rights in the Global Pandemic — Doyal, Lesley
Living with Intent: My Somewhat Messy Journey to Purpose, Peace, and Joy — Chopra, Mallika
Living with Time to Think: The Goddaughter Letters — Kline, Nancy

Living without a Why: Meister Eckhart's Critique of the Medieval Concept of Will — *Connolly, John M.*
The Living Years: The First Genesis Memoir — *Rutherford, Mike*
The Livres-Souvenirs of Colette: Genre and the Telling of Time — *Freadman, Anne*
c Lizard from the Park (Illus. by Pett, Mark) — *Pett, Mark*
y The Lizard Princess — *Davies, Tod*
y Lizard Radio — *Schmatz, Pat*
c The Lizard War — *Patton, Jack*
Liza's England — *Barker, Pat*
c Lizzie! (Illus. by Gilbert, Elliott) — *Kumin, Maxine*
c Lizzie and the Last Day of School (Illus. by McLeod, Kris Aro) — *Noble, Trinka Hakes*
y Lizzie and the Lost Baby — *Blackford, Cheryl*
Lizzie Borden on Trial: Murder, Ethnicity, and Gender — *Conforti, Joseph A.*
c Llama Llama Gram and Grandpa (Illus. by Dewdney, Anna) — *Dewdney, Anna*
c Llama Llama Gram and Grandpa — *Dewdney, Anna*
c Llama Llama Sand and Sun (Illus. by Dewdney, Anna) — *Dewdney, Anna*
c Llama Llama Trick or Treat — *Dewdney, Anna*
Llewellyn's Complete Book of Chakras: Your Definitive Source of Energy Center Knowledge for Health, Happiness, and Spiritual Evolution — *Dale, Cyndi*
Llewellyn's Complete Dictionary of Dreams: Over 1,000 Dream Symbols and Their Universal Meanings — *Lennox, Michael*
c Lloyd Llama (Illus. by Jones, Sarah) — *Jones, Sarah*
Llywelyn ap Gruffudd: Prince of Wales — *Smith, J. Beverley*
Lo! Jacaranda: A Spanish Gypsy's Cante Jondo — *Freiermuth, Harry*
Lo studio dell' antichita: Giorgio Pasquali e i filologi classici — *Giordano, Fausto*
Lo sviluppo sospeso: Il Mezzogiorno e l'impresa pubblica, 1948-1973 — *De Benedetti, Augusto*
Lo 'Zibaldone' di Leopardi come ipertesto: Atti del Convegno internazionale Barcellona, Universitat de Barcelona, 26-27 ottobre 2012 — *Muniz, Maria de las Nieves Muniz*
Load Poems Like Guns: Women's Poetry from Herat, Afghanistan — *Marie, Farzana*
A Loaded Gun: Emily Dickinson for the 21st Century — *Charyn, Jerome*
Loathing Lincoln: An American Tradition from the Civil War to the Present — *Barr, John McKee*
y Local Girls — *Zancan, Caroline*
A Local Habitation and a Name: Imagining Histories in the Italian Renaissance — *Ascoli, Albert Russell*
Local History Reference Collections for Public Libraries — *Marquis, Kathy*
Local Story: The Massie-Kahahawai Case and the Culture of History — *Rosa, John P.*
Locally Laid — *Amundsen, Lucie B.*
Locating Neoliberalism in East Asia: Neoliberalizing Spaces in Developmental States — *Park, Bae-gyoon*
Locating the Middle Ages: The Spaces and Places of Medieval Culture — *Weiss, Julian*
Location Filming in Arizona: The Screen Legacy of the Grand Canyon State — *DeBarbieri, Lili*
c The Loch Ness Monster (Illus. by Billau, Lois) — *Chambers, Catherine*
The Lock and Key of Medicine: Monoclonal Antibodies and the Transformation of Healthcare — *Marks, Lara*
Lock In — *Scalzi, John*
y Lock & Mori — *Petty, Heather W.*
Lockdown on Rikers: Shocking Stories of Abuse and Injustice at New York's Notorious Jail — *Buser, Mary E.*
c The Locker Ate Lucy! (Illus. by Ricks, Sam) — *Chabert, Jack*
The Locker — *Magson, Adrian*
Locke's Metaphysics — *Stauart, Matthew*
Locke's Moral Man — *LoLordo, Antonia*
The Locket — *Rowlands, Jennifer L.*
Locus Amoenus — *Alexander, Victoria N.*
Locus of Authority: The Evolution of Faculty Roles in the Governance of Higher Education — *Bowen, William G.*
y Log Horizon: The Beginning of Another World (Illus. by Hara, Kazuhiro) — *Touno, Mamare*
c Logan Pryce Makes a Mess (Illus. by Brown, Petra) — *Gilmore, Grace*
Logan: The Honorable Life and Scandalous Death of a Western Lawman — *Boor, Jackie*
The Logic Bomb — *Lord, Scott Richard*

The Logic of the Trinity: Augustine to Ockham — *Thom, Paul*
Logos — *Neeleman, John*
Loitering: New and Collected Essays — *D'Ambrosio, Charles*
Lokale Geschichte(n), (Macht-)Politik und die Suche nach Historischer Authentizitat
Loki, Agent of Asgard, vol. 2 — *Garbett, Lee*
Loki Schmidt: Die Biographie — *Lehberger, Reiner*
c Lola and I (Illus. by Domeniconi, Paolo) — *Segre, Chiara Valentina*
c Lola and the Tattletale Zeke — *Goldman, Marcia*
y Lola Carlyle's 12-Step Romance — *Younge-Ullman, Danielle*
c Lola Levine Is Not Mean! (Illus. by Dominguez, Angela) — *Brown, Monica*
c Lola Plants a Garden (Illus. by Beardshaw, Rosalind) — *McQuinn, Anna*
c Lola's Toybox: The Patchwork Picnic (Illus. by Shield, Guy) — *Parker, Danny*
Lolita — *Nabokov, Vladimir*
c The Lollipop Monster's Christmas — *Krackow, Eric T.*
Lombardi Dies, Orr Flies, Marshall Cries: The Sports Legacy of 1970 — *Schultz, Brad*
London: A Visitor's Guide — *Cross, Craig*
London Calling: Britain, the BBC World Service and the Cold War — *Webb, Alban*
London Fog: The Biography — *Corton, Christine L.*
London for Lovers: Romantic Days and Nights out in the City — *Hodges, Sam*
London Overground: A Day's Walk around the Ginger Line — *Sinclair, Iain*
London/ Pittsburgh — *Neville, Mark*
London Road — *Smith McGovern, Tessa*
London: The Selden Map and the Making of a Global City, 1549-1689 — *Batchelor, Robert K.*
London War Notes — *Panter-Downes, Mollie*
London Zoo and the Victorians: 1828-1859 — *Ito, Takashi*
Lone Rider — *Daniels, B.J.*
Lone Star: A History of Texas and the Texans — *Fehrenbach, T.R.*
Lone Star — *Simons, Paullina*
The Loneliest Boy in the World: The Last Child of the Great Blasket Island — *O Cathain, Gearoid Cheaist*
Loneliness and Its Opposite: Sex, Disability, and the Ethics of Engagement — *Kullck, Don*
c The Lonely Planet Kids Travel Book: Mind-Blowing Stuff on Every Country in the World — *Lonely Planet Kids*
Lonely Planet's Ultimate Travel: Our List of the 500 Best Places on the Planet - Ranked — *Noble, Karyn*
Lonely Trumpet — *Boggs, Johnny D.*
c The Lonely Typewriter (Illus. by Dalton, Max) — *Ackerman, Peter*
The Lonely War: One Woman's Account of the Struggle for Modern Iran — *Fathi, Nazila*
Lonesome Dove — *McMurtry, Larry*
The Lonesome Trials of Johnny Riles — *Hill, Gregory*
The Lonesome Trials of Johnny Riles — *Hills, Gregory*
The Loney — *Hurley, Andrew Michael*
y Long Ago and Far Away — *Joseph, Robert*
The Long and Faraway Gone — *Berney, Lou*
c Long Ben (Henry Every). — *Bankston, John*
Long Black Curl — *Bledsoe, Alex*
Long Change — *Gillmor, Don*
c The Long Dog (Illus. by Seltzer, Eric) — *Seltzer, Eric*
The Long Emancipation: The Demise of Slavery in the United States — *Berlin, Ira*
The Long Fire — *Tifft, Meghan*
The Long Hello: Memory, My Mother and Me — *Borrie, Cathie*
The Long High Noon — *Estleman, Loren D.*
A Long High Whistle: Selected Columns on Poetry — *Biespiel, David*
The Long, Hot Summer of 1967: Urban Rebellion in America — *McLaughlin, Malcolm*
Long Live Grover Cleveland — *Klose, Robert*
The Long March of Pop: Art, Music, and Design, 1930-1995 — *Crow, Thomas*
Long Mile Home: Boston under Attack, the City's Courageous Recovery, and the Epic Hunt for Justice — *Helman, Scott*
Long Night of the Tankers: Hitler's War against Caribbean Oil — *Herwig, Holger H.*
The Long Reconstruction: The Post-Civil War South in History, Film, and Memory — *Wetta, Frank J.*
The Long Rifle Season — *Murray, James*
The Long Shadow of Lincoln's Gettysburg Address — *Peatman, Jared*
The Long Song — *Levy, Andrea*

Long Story Short: The Only Storytelling Guide You'll Ever Need — *Leitman, Margot*
The Long Struggle against Malaria in Tropical Africa — *Webb, James L.A., Jr.*
c Long Tail Kitty: Come Out and Play (Illus. by Pien, Lark) — *Pien, Lark*
c The Long Tall Journey (Illus. by Gapaillard, Laurent) — *Wahl, Jan*
A Long Time until Now — *Williamson, Michael Z.*
Long upon the Land — *Maron, Margaret*
The Long Utopia — *Baxter, Stephen*
Long Wars and the Constitution — *Griffin, Stephen M.*
The Long Way Back — *Prewitt, J. Everett*
A Long Way from Paris — *Murray, E.C.*
A Long way from the Armstrong Beer Parlour: A Life in Rare Books - Essays by Richard Landon — *Korey, Marie Elena*
The Long Way Home (Read by Cosham, Ralph). Audiobook Review — *Penny, Louise*
The Long Way Home — *Penny, Louise*
y Longbow Girl — *Davies, Linda*
The Longest Afternoon: The 400 Men Who Decided the Battle of Waterloo — *Simms, Brendan*
The Longest August: The Unflinching Rivalry Between India and Pakistan — *Hiro, Dilip*
The Longest Journey: Southeast Asians and the Pilgrimage to Mecca — *Tagliacozzo, Eric*
The Longest Kill: The Story of Maverick 41, One of the World's Greatest Snipers — *Harrison, Craig*
y The Longest Night — *Williams, Andria*
The Longest Trail: Writings on American Indian History, Culture, and Politics — *Josephy, Alvin M.*
The Longest Year: America at War and at Home in 1944 — *Brooks, Victor*
Longing for Community: Church, Ummah, or Somewhere in Between? — *Greenlee, David*
Longing for the Bomb: Oak Ridge and Atomic Nostalgia — *Freeman, Lindsey A.*
The Longue Duree and World-Systems Analysis — *Lee, Richard E.*
Longue Vue House and Gardens — *Summerley, Victoria*
Lonnie Gentry — *Brandvold, Peter*
c Look! (Illus. by Mack, Jeff) — *Mack, Jeff*
c Look! (Illus. by Manceau, Edouard) — *Manceau, Edouard*
c Look and Be Grateful (Illus. by De Paola, Tomie) — *De Paola, Tomie*
c Look and Be Grateful (Illus. by dePaola, Tomie) — *dePaola, Tomie*
c Look and Be Grateful (Illus. by dePaola, Tomie) — *Depaola, Tomie*
Look Back in Laughter: Oxford's Postwar Golden Age — *Johnson, R.W.*
c Look Back! (Illus. by Binch, Caroline) — *Cooke, Trish*
Look Both Ways — *Perry, Carol J.*
y Look Both Ways in the Barrio Blanco — *Robbins Rose, Judith*
c Look Both Ways in the Barrio Blanco — *Rose, Judith Robbins*
c Look Both Ways in the Barrio Blanco (Illus. by Rose, Judith Robbins) — *Rose, Judith Robbins*
c Look Both Ways in the Barrio Blanco — *Rose, Judith Robbins*
Look Out for Bugs — *Prokopowicz, Jen*
c Look Out, Mouse! — *Bjorkman, Steve*
c Look Where We Live! A First Book of Community Building (Illus. by Ritchie, Scot) — *Ritchie, Scot*
Look Who's Back — *Vermes, Timur*
c Look Who's Talking — *Scholastic Inc.*
Looking at Medea: Essays and a Translation of Euripides' Tragedy — *Stuttard, David*
Looking at Mindfulness: Twenty-Five Ways to Live in the Moment Through Art — *Andre, Christophe*
Looking at Pictures — *Walser, Robert*
c Looking at the Moon — *Pearson, Kit*
Looking beyond Suppression: Community Strategies to Reduce Gang Violence — *Gebo, Erika*
Looking for Balance: China, the United States, and Power Balancing in East Asia — *Chan, Steve*
c Looking for Bongo — *Velasquez, Eric*
Looking for Leroy: Illegible Black Masculinities — *Neal, Mark Anthony*
y Looking for Redfeather — *Collison, Linda*
c Looking Glass Girl — *Cassidy, Cathy*
Looking into Providences: Designs and Trials in 'Paradise Lost' — *Waddington, Raymond B.*
Looking Like the Enemy: Japanese Mexicans, the Mexican State, and US Hegemony, 1897-1945 — *Garcia, Jerry*
c Looks Like Daylight — *Ellis, Deborah*
c The Looney Experiment — *Reynolds, Luke*

c Loop Loom Bracelets — *Johnson, Anne Akers*
y Loop — *Akins, Karen*
c Loos, Poos, and Number Twos: A Disgusting Journey through the Bowels of History (Illus. by Morgan-Jones, Tom) — *Hepplewhite, Peter*
Loose Connections: From Narva Maantee to Great Russell Street — *Menell, Esther*
c Loose Strands. E-book Review — *Darned Sock Productions*
Loose Strife — *Barry, Quan*
Loosed upon the World — *Adams, John Joseph*
The Looting Machine — *Burgis, Tom*
The Looting Machine: Warlords, Tycoons, Smugglers and the Systematic Theft of Africa's Wealth — *Burgis, Tom*
Loquela — *Labbe, Carlos*
y Lorali — *Dockrill, Laura*
Lord Byron and Scandalous Celebrity — *Tuite, Clara*
Lord Byron's Prophecy — *Eads, Sean*
Lord Fear — *Mann, Lucas*
y Lord Fenton's Folly — *Kilpack, Josi S.*
Lord Jim (Read by Jerrom, Ric). Audiobook Review — *Conrad, Joseph*
Lord Lyons: A Diplomat in an Age of Nationalism and War — *Jenkins, Brian*
Lord Mansfield: Justice in the Age of Reason — *Poser, Norman*
Lord of Janissaries — *Pournelle, Jerry*
Lord of Scoundrels (Read by Reading, Kate). Audiobook Review — *Chase, Loretta*
Lord of Strange Deaths: The Fiendish World of Sax Rohmer — *Baker, Phil*
Lord of the Flies — *Golding, William*
The Lord of the Psalms — *Miller, Patrick D.*
The Lord of the Rings — *Tolkien, J.R.R.*
Lord of the Swallows — *de Villiers, Gerard*
Lord of the Wings (Read by Dunne, Bernadette). Audiobook Review — *Andrews, Donna*
Lord of the Wings — *Andrews, Donna*
Lord of War — *Chandler, A.K.*
Lord Strange's Men and Their Plays — *Manley, Lawrence*
Lord Taciturn — *de Assis, Machado*
Lord Taciturn — *Machado de Assis, Joaquim Maria*
Lords of Secrecy: The National Security Elite and America's Stealth Warfare — *Horton, Scott*
Lords of the Sea: Pirates, Violence, and Commerce in Late Medieval Japan — *Shapinsky, Peter D.*
Loren Miller: Civil Rights Attorney and Journalist — *Hassan, Amina*
Lorena Garcia's New Taco Classics — *Garcia, Lorena*
Lorenzo di Filippo Strozzi and Niccolo Machiavelli: Patron, Client, and the Pistola fatta per la peste / An Epistle Written Concerning the Plague — *Landon, William J.*
c The Los Angeles Lakers — *Stewart, Mark*
Los Angeles Sketchbook — *Florczyk, Piotr*
Los anos norteamericanos de Luis Cernuda — *Teruel, Jose*
Los cuentos de la peste — *Vargas Llosa, Mario*
Los De Fato et Libero Arbitrio Libri Tres de Juan Gines de Sepulveda : Estudio de una obra historico-filosofico-teologica — *Sanchez Gazquez, Joaquin J.*
Los hijos del poder. De la elite capitular a la Revolucion de Mayo: Buenos Aires 1776-1810 — *Valle, Laura Cristina del*
Los Incas en la colonia: Estudios sobre los siglos XVI, XVII y XVIII en los Andes — *Pease Garcia-Yrigoyen, Franklin*
Los Lobos: Dream in Blue — *Morris, Chris*
Los montoneros del barrio — *Salcedo, Javier*
y Losers Take All — *Klass, David*
Losing Faith — *Mitzner, Adam*
Losing Me — *Margolis, Sue*
Losing Our Religion: How Unaffiliated Parents Are Raising Their Children — *Manning, Christel*
Losing the Center: The Decline of American Liberalism, 1968-1992 — *Bloodworth, Jeffrey*
Losing the Light — *Dunlop, Andrea*
Loss Angeles: Stories — *Cailler, Mathieu*
c Lost — *Bodeen, S.A.*
The Lost — *McCade, Cole*
Lost among the Baining: Adventure, Marriage, and Other Fieldwork — *Pool, Gail*
Lost and Found (Read by Carrington, Nigel). Audiobook Review — *Davis, Brooke*
Lost and Found: Recovering Regional Identity in Imperial Japan — *Shimoda, Hiraku*
The Lost and the Blind — *Burke, Declan*
Lost Animals: Extinction and the Photographic Record — *Fuller, Errol*

The Lost Art of Dress: The Women Who Once Made America Stylish — *Przybyszewski, Linda*
The Lost Art of Reading Nature's Signs: Use Outdoor Clues to Find Your Way, Predict the Weather, Locate Water, Track Animals - and Other Forgotten Skills — *Gooley, Tristan*
The Lost Book of Moses: The Hunt for the World's Oldest Bible — *Tigay, Chanan*
c Lost Boy — *Green, Tim*
The Lost Boys Symphony — *Ferguson, Mark Andrew*
Lost Breweries of Toronto — *St. John, Jordon*
c Lost: Can You Survive? Series — *Turner, Tracey*
Lost Canyon — *Revoyr, Nina*
The Lost Carving: A Journey to the Heart of Making — *Esterly, David*
The Lost Child — *Phillips, Caryl*
Lost Chords and Christian Soldiers: The Sacred Music of Sir Arthur Sullivan — *Bradley, Ian C.*
c The Lost City — *Voelkel, J&P*
Lost Classroom, Lost Community: Catholic Schools' Importance in Urban America — *brinig, Margaret F.*
The Lost Codex: An OPSIG Team Black Novel — *Jacobson, Alan*
The Lost Colonies of Ancient America: A Comprehensive Guide to the Pre-Columbian Visitors Who Really Discovered America — *Joseph, Frank*
The Lost Concerto — *Mario, Helaine*
Lost Destiny: Joe Kennedy Jr. and the Doomed WWII Mission to Save London — *Axelrod, Alan*
The Lost Detective: Becoming Dashiell Hammett — *Ward, Nathan*
y The Lost Diary — *White, Julie*
c Lost Dog (Illus. by Garland, Michael) — *Garland, Michael*
c Lost Dog — *Garland, Michael*
The Lost Elements: The Periodic Table's Shadow Side — *Fontani, Marco*
Lost Enlightenment: Central Asia's Golden Age from the Arab Conquest to Tamerlane — *Starr, S. Frederick*
Lost for Words — *St. Aubyn, Edward*
c Lost & Found — *Skye, Obert*
c Lost. Found. (Illus. by Cordell, Matthew) — *Arnold, Marsha Diane*
c Lost. Found. (Illus. by Cordell, Matthew) — *Diane, Marsha*
Lost Freedom: The Landscape of the Child and the British Post-War Settlement — *Thomson, Mathew*
The Lost Garden — *Ang, Li*
The Lost Generation: The Rustication of China's Educated Youth (1968-1980). — *Bonnin, Michel*
c The Lost Generation: The Young Person's Guide to World War I — *Barr, Martyn*
y The Lost Girl — *Bianca, Mari*
y The Lost Girl — *Stine, R.L.*
The Lost Girls — *Glatt, John*
The Lost Girls: The True Story of the Cleveland Abductions and the Incredible Rescue of Michelle Knight, Amanda Berry, and Gina DeJesus — *Glatt, John*
The Lost Gospel: Decoding the Ancient Texts that Reveals Jesus' Marriage to Mary the Magdalene — *Jacobovici, Simcha*
Lost Ground — *Jordan, Ulla*
The Lost Heiress — *White, Roseanna M.*
y The Lost Hero: The Graphic Novel (Illus. by Powell, Nate) — *Riordan, Rick*
Lost Hierarchy — *Arman, Khurram*
The Lost Identity Casualties — *Ekemar, Kim*
The Lost Imperialist: Lord Dufferin, Memory and Myth-Making in an Age of Celebrity — *Gailey, Andrew*
The Lost Imperialist: Lord Dufferin, Memory and Mythmaking in an Age of Celebrity — *Gailey, Andrew*
Lost in His Eyes — *Neiderman, Andrew*
c Lost in London — *Callaghan, Cindy*
c Lost in NYC: A Subway Adventure (Illus. by Garcia Sanchez, Sergio) — *Spiegelman, Nadja*
c Lost in NYC: A Subway Adventure (Illus. by Sanchez, Sergio Garcia) — *Spiegelman, Nadja*
c Lost in Paris — *Callaghan, Cindy*
c Lost in the Backyard — *Hughes, Alison*
c Lost in the Mouseum (Illus. by Melmon, Deborah) — *May, Eleanor*
c Lost in the Sun (Read by De Ocampo, Ramon). Audiobook Review — *Graff, Lisa*
c Lost in the Sun — *Graff, Lisa*
y Lost in Thought — *Bertrand, Cara*

Lost in Transition: Hong Kong Culture in the Age of China — *Chu, Yiu-Wai*
The Lost Journals of Sylvia Plath — *Knutsen, Kimberly*
The Lost Landscape: A Writer's Coming of Age — *Oates, Joyce Carol*
y The Lost Marble Notebook of Forgotten Girl & Random Boy — *Jaskulka, Marie*
Lost Near Eternity — *Bowman, D.E.*
c The Lost Planet — *Searles, Rachel*
Lost Plays in Shakespeare's England — *McInnis, David*
c The Lost Prince — *Myklusch, Matt*
c Lost Property (Illus. by Poyiadgi, Andy) — *Poyiadgi, Andy*
The Lost Region: Toward a Revival of Midwestern History — *Lauck, Jon K.*
y Lost Republic — *Thompson, Paul B.*
Lost Souls — *Patrick, Seth*
c The Lost Sword — *Pitt, Darrell*
The Lost Time Accidents — *Wray, John*
c The Lost Track of Time (Read by Jiles, Jennifer). Audiobook Review — *Britt, Paige*
c The Lost Track of Time (Illus. by White, Lee) — *Britt, Paige*
c Lost Treasures — *O'Brien, Cynthia*
c The Lost Tribes — *Taylor-Butler, Christine*
The Lost Tribes of Tierra del Fuego: Selk'nam, Yamana, Kawsqar — *Gusinde, Martin*
The Lost Tudor Princess: The Life of Lady Margaret Douglas — *Weir, Alison*
The Lost Wave: Women and Democracy in Postwar Italy — *Tambor, Molly*
The Lost White Tribe — *Robinson, Michael F.*
Lost Words — *Gardini, Nicola*
The Lost World of Adam and Eve: Genesis 2-3 and the Human Origins Debate — *Walton, John H.*
Lost World of the Golden King: In Search of Ancient Afghanistan — *Holt, Frank L.*
The Lost World of the Old Ones: Discoveries in the Ancient Southwest — *Roberts, David*
Lotions, Potions, Pills, and Magic: Health Care in Early America — *Breslaw, Elaine G.*
c Lots of Bots (Illus. by Fujita, Goro) — *Richards, C.J.*
c Lots of Kisses — *Crozier, Lorna*
y Lottery Boy — *Byrne, Michael*
The Lotus Cross — *Anderson, Ray*
c Loud Lula (Illus. by Boldt, Mike) — *Duffield, Katy S.*
Louder Than Words: Harness the Power of Your Authentic Voice — *Henry, Todd*
y The Loudness — *Courage, Nick*
Louis Armstrong: Master of Modernism — *Brothers, Thomas*
Louis Armstrong's New Orleans — *Brothers, Thomas*
Louis Ginzberg's "Legends of the Jews": Ancient Jewish Folk Literature Reconsidered — *Hasan-Rokem, Galit*
c Louis I, King of the Sheep (Illus. by Tallec, Olivier) — *Tallec, Olivier*
Louis L'Amour on Film and Television — *Andreychuk, Ed*
Louis Raemaekers 'Armed with Pen and Pencil': How a Dutch Cartoonist Became World Famous during the First World War — *de Ranitz, Ariane*
c Louis Riel: Combattant metis — *Noel-Maw, Marline*
Louis van Gaal: The Biography — *Meijer, Maarten*
Louis XIV's Assault on Privilege: Nicolas Desmaretz and the Tax on Wealth — *McCollim, Gary B.*
Louisa — *Thomas, Louisa*
Louisa Catherine: The Other Mrs. Adams — *Heffron, Margery M.*
Louisa May Alcott: Work, Eight Cousins, Rose in Bloom, Stories and Other Writings — *Alcott, Louisa May*
Louisa Meets Bear — *Gornick, Lisa*
Louise Bourgeois: Structures of Existence - The Cells — *Lorz, Julienne*
Louise Brooks: Detective — *Geary, Rick*
c Louise Loves Art (Illus. by Light, Kelly) — *Light, Kelly*
Louise Talma: A Life in Composition — *Leonard, Kendra Preston*
c Louise Trapeze Did Not Lose the Juggling Chickens — *Ostow, Micol*
c Louise Trapeze Is Totally 100 Percent Fearless (Illus. by Barrager, Brigette) — *Ostow, Micol*
Louise's Chance — *Shaber, Sarah R.*
Louisiana: Crossroads of the Atlantic World — *Vidal, Cecile*
Louisiana Saves the Library — *Cogburn, Emily Beck*
c Louisiana, the Jewel of the Deep South (Illus. by Marshall, Julia) — *Downing, Johnette*

The Louisville, Cincinnati and Charleston Rail Road: Dreams of Linking North and South — *Grant, H. Roger*
c Loula and Mister the Monster (Illus. by Villeneuve, Anne) — *Villeneuve, Anne*
c Loula and the Sister Recipe — *Villeneuve, Anne*
c L'ours brun — *Johnson, Jinny*
Lousy Sex: Creating Self in an Infectious World — *Gerald N. Callahan*
Lovable, Livable Home: How to Add Beauty, Get Organized, and Make Your House Work for You — *Petersik, John*
Lovable Livable Home: How to Add Beauty, Get Organized, and Make Your House Work for You — *Petersik, Sherry*
c Love (Illus. by Bertolucci, Federico) — *Brremaud, Frederic*
Love — *Carter, Angela*
Love — *Kasper, Leagan E.*
The Love Affairs of Lord Byron — *Gribble, Francis Henry*
Love, Again: The Wisdom of Unexpected Romance — *Pell, Eve*
Love, Alba — *Burnham, Sophy*
c Love Always Everywhere (Illus. by Massini, Sarah) — *Massini, Sarah*
Love among the Ruins: A Memoir of Life and Love in Hamburg, 1945 — *Smith, Harry Leslie*
Love and Friendship and Other Youthful Writings — *Austen, Jane*
Love and Justice as Competences: Three Essays on the Sociology of Action — *Boltanski, Luc*
The Love and Lemons Cookbook: An Apple-to-Zucchini Celebration of Impromptu Cooking — *Donofrio, Jeanine*
Love and Liberation: Autobiographical Writings of the Tibetan Buddhist Visionary Sera Khandro — *Jacoby, Sarah H.*
Love and Lies: An Essay on Truthfulness, Deceit, and the Growth and Care of Erotic Love — *Martin, Clancy*
Love and Math: The Heart of Hidden Reality — *Frenkel, Edward*
Love and Miss Communication — *Friedland, Elyssa*
Love and Ordinary Creatures — *Rubio, Gwyn Hyman*
y Love and Other Perishable Items — *Buzo, Laura*
y Love and Other Theories — *Bass, Alexis*
Love and Other Unknown Variables — *Alexander, Shannon Lee*
Love and Other Ways of Dying: Essays — *Paterniti, Michael*
Love and Other Wounds — *Harper, Jordan*
Love and Power: Caribbean Discourses on Gender — *Barriteau, V. Eudine*
y Love and Profanity: A Collection of True, Tortured, Wild, Hilarious, Concise, and Intense Tales of Teenage Life — *Healy, Nick*
y Love and Profanity. — *Healy, Nick*
Love and Providence: Recognition in Ancient Novel — *Montiglio, Silvia*
Love and Rockets, vol. 7 — *Hernandez, Gilbert*
Love and Science: A Memoir — *Vilcek, Jan*
Love and Treasure — *Waldman, Ayelet*
Love and War: How Militarism Shapes Sexuality and Romance — *Digby, Tom*
Love Becomes a Funeral Pyre: A Biography of the Doors — *Wall, Mick*
y Love Bomb — *McLachlan, Jenny*
The Love Darg — *Batchelor, Paul*
Love Everyone: The Transcendent Wisdom of Neem Karoii Baba Told through the Stories of the Westerners Whose Lives He Transformed — *Markus, Parvati*
The Love Fight — *Ferretti, Tony*
y Love Fortunes and Other Disasters — *Karalius, Kimberly*
c Love from a Star (Illus. by Gazzetta, Katherine Cutchin) — *Gazzetta, Katherine Cutchin*
c Love from Paddington (Illus. by Fortnum, Peggy) — *Bond, Michael (b. 1926-)*
Love: From the Big Screen to My Life Scene — *Bell, Reginald, Jr.*
y Love & Gelato — *Welch, Jenna Evans*
Love Her, Love Her Not: The Hillary Paradox — *Bamberger, Joanne Cronrath*
Love in Lowercase — *Miralles, Francesc*
Love in Print in the Sixteenth Century: The Popularization of Romance — *Moulton, Ian Frederick*
Love in the Antropocene — *Jamieson, Dale*

Love in the Elephant Tent: How Running Away with the Circus Brought Me Home — *Cremonesi, Kathleen*
Love in the Time of Communism: Intimacy and Sexuality in the GDR — *McLellan, Josie*
Love in the Time of Revolution: Transatlantic Literary Radicalism and Historical Change, 1793-1818 — *Cayton, Andrew*
Love in the Time of Scandal — *Linden, Caroline*
Love in Vain: The Story of the Ruts and Ruts DC — *Link, Roland*
c Love Is Forever (Illus. by Balsaitis, Rachael) — *Rislov, Casey*
Love Is in the Air — *Destiny, A.*
c Love Is My Favorite Thing (Illus. by Chichester Clark, Emma) — *Chichester Clark, Emma*
Love Is Red (Read by Boehmer, Paul, with Emily Durante). Audiobook Review — *Jaff, Sophie*
Love Is Red — *Jaff, Sophie*
y Love Is the Drug — *Johnson, Alaya Dawn*
c A Love Letter from God (Illus. by Watson, Laura) — *Hallinan, P.K.*
Love Letters from Mount Rushmore: The Story of a Marriage, a Monument, and a Moment in History — *Cerasani, Richard*
Love Letters in the Sand — *Francis, June*
c Love Letters to the Dead (Read by Whelan, Julia). Audiobook Review — *Dellaira, Ava*
y Love Lies Beneath — *Hopkins, Ellen*
A Love Like Blood — *Sedgwick, Marcus*
A Love Like Ours (Read by Turnbull, Kate). Audiobook Review — *Wade, Becky*
A Love Like Ours — *Wade, Becky*
Love Like the Movies — *Van Tiem, Victoria*
y Love Love — *Woo, Sung J.*
y Love, Lucas — *Sedgwick, Chantele*
y Love, Lucy — *Lindner, April*
Love May Fail — *Quick, Matthew*
Love Me If You Dare — *Blake, Toni*
Love, Money, and HIV: Becoming a Modern African Woman in the Age of AIDS — *Mojola, Sanyu A.*
c Love Monster and the Last Chocolate (Illus. by Bright, Rachel) — *Bright, Rachel*
c Love Monster and the Perfect Present (Illus. by Bright, Rachel) — *Bright, Rachel*
Love, Nina: A Nanny Writes Home — *Sdbbe, Nina*
The Love Object: Selected Stories — *O'Brien, Edna*
The Love of God: Divine Gift, Human Gratitude, and Mutual Faithfulness in Judaism — *Levenson, Jon D.*
Love on the Rocks — *Costa, Catie*
c Love or Something Like It — *Friedman, Laurie*
y Love or Something Like It — *Friedman, Laurie B.*
Love, or, the Witches of Windward Circle — *McFadden, C. A.*
Love, Paul Gambaccini: My Year under the Yewtree — *Gambaccini, Paul*
Love Poems — *Brecht, Bertolt*
Love Poetry in the Spanish Golden Age: Eros, Eris and Empire — *Isabel, Torres*
Love Poetry in the Spanish Golden Age: Eros, Eris and Empire — *Torres, Isabel*
Love, Sex and Other Foreign Policy Goals — *Armstrong, Jesse*
The Love She Left Behind — *Coe, Amanda*
y Love-Shy — *Wilkinson, Lili*
Love Somebody Like You — *Fox, Susan*
The Love Song of Miss Queenie Hennessy — *Joyce, Rachel*
Love Songs: The Hidden History — *Gioia, Ted*
Love Sonnets and Elegies — *Labe, Louise*
y Love Spell — *Kerick, Mia*
Love Struck — *McGee, Laurelin*
Love Style Life — *Dore, Garance*
y The Love That Split the World — *Henry, Emily*
Love: The Psychology of Attraction — *Becker-Phelps, Leslie*
Love under Repair: How to Save Your Marriage and Survive Couples Therapy — *Miller, Keith A.*
c Love Will See You Through: Martin Luther King Jr.'s Six Guiding Beliefs (as Told by His Niece). (Illus. by Comport, Sally Wern) — *Watkins, Angela Farris*
Love Your Job: The New Rules for Career Happiness — *Harnon, Kerry*
Love Your Job: The New Rules of Career Happiness — *Hannon, Kerry*
Lovecraft and a World in Transition: Collected Essays on H.P. Lovecraft — *Joshi, Sunand T.*
Lovecraft Country — *Ruff, Matt*
The Loved Ones — *Hughes, Mary-Beth*
c Lovely Old Lion (Illus. by Varley, Susan) — *Jarman, Julia*

Lover in the Nobody — *Harnisch, Jonathan*
The Lovers: Afghanistan's Romeo and Juliet: The True Story of How They Defied Their Families and Escaped an Honor Killing — *Nordland, Rod*
The Lovers: Afghanistan's Romeo and Juliet: The True Story of How They Defied Their Families and Escaped an Honor Killing — *Nordland, Rod: The Lovers.(Book review)*
Lovers at the Chameleon Club, Paris 1932 — *Prose, Francine*
A Lover's Discourse: Fragments — *Barthes, Roland*
Lover's Oak — *Scott, Corinne*
The Lovers of Amherst — *Nicholson, William*
Lovers on All Saints' Day: Stories — *Vasquez, Juan Gabriel*
Love's Alchemy — *Crockett, Bryan*
y Love's Rescue — *Johnson, Christine*
Love's Sweet Sorrow — *Brawer, Richard*
Lovesick — *Driggers, James*
Lovewell's Fight: War, Death, and Memory in Borderland New England — *Cray, Robert E.*
c Lovey Bunny — *Lombardi, Kristine A.*
Loving Amy: A Mother's Story — *Winehouse, Janis*
Loving Dallas — *Quinn, Caisey*
Loving Day — *Johnson, Mat*
Loving Eleanor — *Albert, Susan Wittig*
Loving Learning: How Progressive Education Can Save America's Schools — *Little, Tom*
Loving Learning — *Little, Tom*
Loving Literature: A Cultural History — *Lynch, Deidre Shauna*
Loving Nature, Fearing the State: Environmentalism and Antigovernment Politics before Reagan — *Darke, Brian Allan*
Loving Nature, Fearing the State: Environmentalism and Antigovernment Politics before Reagan — *Drake, Brian Allen*
Loving Our Addicted Daughters Back to Life; A Guidebook for Parents — *Dahl, Linda*
Loving Our Enemies: Reflections on the Hardest Commandment — *Forest, Jim*
Loving the Chase — *Lovelace, Sharia*
Loving the Poor, Saving the Rich: Wealth, Poverty, and Early Christian Formation — *Rhee, Helen*
The Low Glycal Diet — *Dunham's, Jeffrey S.*
A Low-Visibility Force Multiplier: Assessing China's Cruise Missile Ambitions. E-book Review — *Gormley, Dennis M.*
The Lower Quarter — *Blackwell, Elise*
The Lowfat Jewish Vegetarian Cookbook: Healthy Traditions from around the World — *Wasserman, Debra*
The Lowland — *Lahiri, Jhumpa*
y Lowriders in Space (Illus. by Raul the Third) — *Camper, Cathy*
Loyal Enemies: British Converts to Islam, 1850-1950 — *Gilham, Jamie*
Loyal Sons: Jews in the German Army in the Great War — *Appelbaum, Peter C.*
y Loyalist to a Fault — *Munday, Evan*
Loyalty and Liberty: American Countersubversion from World War I to the McCarthy Era — *Goodall, Alex*
Loyalty Betrayed: Jewish Chaplains in the German Army during the First World War — *Appelbaum, Peter C.*
The Luba Poems — *Inez, Colette*
c Lucado Treasury of Bedtime Prayers (Read by Garver, Kathy). Audiobook Review — *Lucado, Denalyn*
Lucan's Egyptian Civil War — *Tracy, Jonathan*
c The Luchair Stones — *Ogilvie, Isabel*
Lucid Dreaming Plain and Simple: Tips and Techniques for Insight, Creativity, and Personal Growth — *Waggoner, Robert*
The Luck Archive: Exploring Belief, Superstition, and Tradition — *Menjivar, Mark*
Luck Be a Lady — *Duran, Meredith*
The Luck Uglies: Fork-Tongue Charmers (Illus. by Antonsson, Petur) — *Durham, Paul*
c The Luck Uglies: Fork-Tongue Charmers — *Durham, Paul*
The Luckiest — *McWarren, Mila*
Luckiest Girl Alive — *Knoll, Jessica*
c Lucky — *Hill, Chris*
c Lucky (Illus. by Mackintosh, David) — *Mackintosh, David*
Lucky Alan and Other Stories — *Lethem, Jonathan*
c A Lucky Author Has a Dog (Illus. by Henry, Steven) — *Ray, Mary Lyn*
Lucky Jim — *Amis, Kingsley*

A Lucky Life Interrupted (Read by Bramhall, Mark). Audiobook Review — Brokaw, Tom
A Lucky Life Interrupted — Brokaw, Tom
c The Lucky Litter — Curtis, Jennifer Keats
Lucky Peach Presents: 101 Easy Asian Recipes — Meehan, Peter
y Lucky Penny (Illus. by Ota, Yuko) — Hirsh, Ananth
Lucky Rice — Chang, Danielle
c Lucky Rocks — Richter, Murray
c The Lucky Seven Show (Illus. by Kinra, Richa) — Johnston, Mary Jo Wisneski
Lucky Shot — Daniels, B.J.
y Lucky Strike — Pyron, Bobbie
Lucky Us — Bloom, Amy
c The Lucky Wheel, Book 2 (Illus. by Brown, Petra) — Gilmore, Grace
c The Lucky Wheel (Illus. by Brown, Petra) — Gilmore, Grace
The Lucky Years — Agus, David B.
Lucretia Mott's Heresy: Abolition and Women's Rights in Nineteenth-Century America — Faulkner, Carol
Lucretius and His Sources: A Study of Lucretius, De Rerum Natura I 635-920 — Montarese, Francesco
c Lucy in the City: A Story about Developing Spatial Thinking Skills (Illus. by Wood, Laura) — Dillemuth, Julie
c Lucy Lick-Me-Not and the Greedy Gubbins — Carmel, Claudine
Lucy Longwhiskers Gets Lost — Meadows, Daisy
Lucy Stone: An Unapologetic Life — McMillen, Sally G.
c Lucy Tries Luge (Illus. by Hearne, James) — Bowes, Lisa
c Lucy's Holiday Surprise (Illus. by Fitzgerald, Royce) — Cooper, Ilene
c Lucy's Light (Illus. by Alvarez, Silvia) — Del Mazo, Margarita
Lucy's Light — Mazo, Margarita del
c Ludacris: Hip-Hop Mogul — Torres, John Albert
Ludolf und Wansleben - Orientalistik, Politik und Geschichte zwischen Gotha und Afrika 1650-1700
Ludwig Camerarius (1573-1651): Eine Biographie — Schubert, Friedrich Hermann
Ludwig Wittgenstein: Ein biographisches Album — Nedo, Michael
Ludwigstein: Annaherungen an die Geschichte der Burg im 20. Jahrhundert. Archivtagung im Archiv der Deutschen Jugendbewegung
The Lufthansa Heist: Behind the Six-Million Dollar Cash Haul That Shook the World — Hill, Henry
c Lug: Dawn of the Ice Age (Illus. by Gerardi, Jan) — Zeltser, David
c Luigi and the Barefoot Races (Illus. by Boyd, Aaron) — Paley, Dan

Luke-Acts and Jewish Historiography: A Study on the Theology, Literature, and Ideology of Luke-Acts — Uytanlet, Samson
c Luke and the Little Seed (Illus. by Ferri, Giuliano) — Ferri, Giuliano
Luke Jensen Bounty Hunter: Bloody Sunday — Johnstone, William W.
Luke Skywalker Can't Read: And Other Geeky Truths — Britt, Ryan
y Lullaby — Beckett, Bernard
c Lullaby (Illus. by Bubar, Lorraine) — Friedman, Debbie
c Lullaby and Kisses Sweet: Poems to Love With Your Baby (Illus. by Nassner, Alyssa) — Hopkins, Lee Bennett
c Lullaby and Kisses Sweet: Poems to Love with Your Baby — Hopkins, Lee Bennett
c A Lullaby for Little One (Illus. by Fuge, Charles) — Casey, Dawn
c Lulu and the Hamster in the Night (Illus. by Lamont, Priscilla) — McKay, Hilary
c Lulu and the Witch Baby (Illus. by Sinclair, Bella) — O'Connor, Jane
y Lulu Anew (Illus. by Davodeau, Etienne) — Davodeau, Etienne
Lulu Anew — Davodeau, Etienne
c Lulu la tres chic — May, Kayla
c Lulu Loves Flowers (Illus. by Beardshaw, Rosalind) — McQuinn, Anna
c Lulu's Party (Illus. by Chase, Kit) — Chase, Kit
c Lumberjanes: Beware the Kitten Holy (Illus. by Allen, Brooke) — Stevenson, Noelle
c Lumberjanes, vol. 1: Beware the Kitten Holy (Illus. by Allen, Brooke) — Watters, Shannon
c Lumberjanes, vol. 2: Friendship to the Max (Illus. by Allen, Brooke) — Watters, Shannon
y Lumiere — Garlick, Jacqueline E.
c Luna & Me: The True Story of a Girl Who Lived in a Tree to Save a Forest — Kostecki-Shaw, Jenny Sue
c Luna & Me: The True Story of a Girl Who Lived in a Tree to Save a Forest (Illus. by Kostecki-Shaw, Jenny Sue) — Kostecki-Shaw, Jenny Sue
c Luna & Me: The True Story of Girl Who Lived in a Tree to Save a Forest (Illus. by Kostecki-Shaw, Jenny Sue) — Kostecki-Shaw, Jenny Sue
Luna: New Moon — McDonald, Ian
c Luna's Red Hat: An Illustrated Storybook to Help Children Cope with Loss and Suicide (Illus. by Smid, Emmi) — Smid, Emmi
The Lunatic: Poems — Simic, Charles
The Lunatic
c Lunch Lady and the Schoolwide Scuffle — Krosoczka, Jarrett J.
Lunch Poems — O'Hara, Frank
y The Lunch Witch (Illus. by Lucke, Deb) — Lucke, Deb

Lunch with a Bigot — Kumar, Amitava
Luncheon of the Boating Party — Vreeland, Susan
y Lungdon (Illus. by Carey, Edward) — Carey, Edward
y The Lure — Ewing, Lynne
The Lure of Technocracy — Habermas, Jurgen
The Lure of the Moonflower (Read by Reading, Kate). Audiobook Review — Willeg, Lauren
y The Lure of the Moonflower — Willig, Lauren
The Lure of the North Woods: Cultivating Tourism in the Upper Midwest — Shapiro, Aaron
Lurid & Cute — Thirlwell, Adam
Lusitania: An Epic Tragedy — Preston, Diana
Lusitania: Triumph, Tragedy, and the End of the Edwardian Age — King, Greg
Lust am Lesen: Literarische Anspielungen im Frieden des Aristophanes — Zogg, Fabian
Lust & Wonder — Burroughs, Augusten
Lusting for London: Australian Expatriate Writers at the Hub of Empire, 1870-1950 — Morton, Peter
Lustlocked — Wallace, Matt
Lutheran Churches in Early Modern Europe — Spicer, Andrew
A Lutheran Plague: Murdering to Die in the Eighteenth Century — Krogh, Tyge
Luther's Fortress: Martin Luther and His Reformation under Siege — Reston, James, Jr.
Luther's Works, vol. 75: Church Postil I — Mayes, Benjamin T.G.
Luther's Works, vol. 76: Church Postil II — Mayes, Benjamin T.G.
Lutter contre les Turcs: Les formes nouvelles de la croisade pontificale au XVe siecle — Weber, Benjamin
c The Luvya Tree (Illus. by Thinkstock) — Robinson, D'Wayne
Luwian Identities. Culture, Language and Religion between Anatolia and the Aegean — Mouton, Alice
A Luxury of the Understanding: On the Value of the True Belief — Hazlet, Allan
The Luzern Photograph — Bayer, William
Lycurgan Athens and the Making of Classical Tragedy — Hanink, Johanna
Lying for the Lord — Townsend, Johnny
y Lying Out Loud — Keplinger, Kody
Lyme Disease: Why It's Spreading, How It Makes You Sick, and What to Do about It — Barbour, Alan G.
c Lyn-Z Adams Hawkins Pastrana — Scheff, Matt
Lynching beyond Dixie: American Mob Violence outside the South — Pfeifer, Michael J.
Lynchings in Kansas, 1850s-1932 — Frazier, Harriet C.
Lynette Yiadom-Boakye — Beckwith, Naomi
The Lyre of Orpheus: Popular Music, the Sacred, & the Profane — Partridge, Christopher
Lyric Shame: The 'Lyric' Subject of Contemporary American Poetry — White, Gillian

M

c M Is for Manger (Illus. by Keay, Claire) — *Bowman, Crystal*
c M Is for Money: An Economics Alphabet (Illus. by Kelley, Marty) — *Shoulders, Michael*
c M Is for Money: An Economics Alphabet (Illus. by Kelley, Marty) — *Shoulders, Debbie*
c M Is for Monster: A Fantastic Creatures Alphabet (Illus. by Kelley, Gerald) — *Lewis, J. Patrick*
  M Train (Read by Smith, Patti). Audiobook Review — *Smith, Patti*
  M Train — *Smith, Patti*
c Ma grande famille — *Petricic, Dusan*
c Ma MacDonald Flees the Farm (Illus. by Mark, Alycia) — *Beckstrand, Karl*
  Maangchi's Real Korean Cooking: Authentic Dishes for the Home Cook — *Chattman, Lauren*
  Maangchi's Real Korean Cooking: Authentic Dishes for the Home Cook — *Maangchi*
  Maarten Maartens Rediscovered — *Schwartz, John*
c Mabel and Me: Best of Friends (Illus. by Warburton, Sarah) — *Sperring, Mark*
c Mabel Jones and the Forbidden City — *Mabbitt, Will*
  Mabiki: Infanticide and Population Growth in Eastern Japan, 1660-1950 — *Drixler, Fabian*
y Mac on the Road to Marseille — *Ward, Christopher*
c Macanudo No. 2 (Illus. by Liniers) — *Liniers*
c Macaroni Isn't the Same without Cheese (Illus. by Rotter, Phoebe) — *Yuan, Qian*
c Macarooned on a Dessert Island (Illus. by Wald, Christina) — *Downing, Johnette*
  Macaulay and Son: Architects of Imperial Britain — *Hall, Catherine*
y Macbeth: A Play by William Shakespeare (Illus. by Hinds, Gareth) — *Hinds, Gareth*
  Macbeth — *Shakespeare, William*
y Macbeth (Illus. by Hinds, Gareth) — *Shakespeare, William*
y MacBeth Killingit (Illus. by Carbone, Courtney) — *Shakespeare, William*
  Macbeth: The State of Play — *Thompson, Ann*
  Macdonald at 200: New Reflections and Legacies — *Dutil, Patrice*
  Macedonia: The Political, Social, Economic and Cultural Foundations of a Balkan State — *De Munck, Viktor C.*
  Machado de Assis: A Literary Life — *Jackson, K. David*
  Machaut and the Medieval Apprenticeship Tradition: Truth, Fiction and Poetic Craft — *Kelly, Douglas*
  Machiavelli: A Portrait — *Celenza, Christopher A.*
  Machiavelli — *Black, Robert*
  Machiavelli's The Prince — *Vatter, Miguel*
  The Machine and the Ghost: Technology and Spiritualism in Nineteenth-to Twenty-First-Century Art and Culture — *Matheson, Neil*
  The Machine Awakes — *Christopher, Adam*
c The Machine Gunner's Ball — *Veys, Pierre*
  Machine Made: Tammany Hall and the Creation of Modern American Politics — *Golway, Terry*
  Machines of Loving Grace: The Quest for Common Ground between Humans and Robots — *Markoff, John*
y Machu Picchu — *Meinking, Mary*
c Machu Picchu — *Raum, Elizabeth*
  Macroanalysis: Digital Methods and Literary History — *Jockers, Matthew L.*
c Mad about Monkeys (Illus. by Davey, Owen) — *Davey, Owen*
  Mad about the Man — *Warren, Tracy Anne*
  The Mad and the Bad — *Manchette, Jean-Patrick*
c The Mad Apprentice (Read by Morris, Cassandra). Audiobook Review — *Wexler, Django*

y The Mad Apprentice (Illus. by Jansson, Alexander) — *Wexler, Django*
y Mad as Hell: The Making of Network and the Fateful Vision of the Angriest Man in Movies — *Itzkoff, Dave*
  The Mad Boy, Lord Berners, My Grandmother and Me: An Aristocratic Family, a High-Society Scandal and an Extraordinary Legacy — *Zinovieff, Sofka*
  A Mad Catastrophe: The Outbreak of World War I and the Collapse of the Habsburg Empire — *Wawro, Geoffrey*
c Mad Dogs — *Gumnut, I.B.*
  The Mad Feast: An Ecstatic Tour through America's Food — *Frank, Matthew Gavin*
  The Mad Feast — *Frank, Matthew*
  Mad Genius: A Manifesto for Entrepreneurs — *Gage, Randy*
  Mad Honey Symposium — *Mao, Sally Wen*
  Mad Matters: A Critical Reader in Canadian Mad Studies — *LeFrancois, Brenda A.*
  Mad Men and Bad Men: What Happened When British Politics Met Advertising — *Delaney, Sam*
  Mad Men and Politics: Nostalgia and the Remaking of Modern America — *Beail, Linda*
  Mad Men Unzipped: Fans on Sex, Love, and the Sixties on TV — *Dill-Shackleford, Karen E.*
  Mad Miss Mimic — *Henstra, Sarah*
y Mad Music: Charles Ives, the Nostalgic Rebel — *Budiansky, Stephen*
  Mad Random — *Miller, Donna*
c Mad Scientist Academy: The Dinosaur Disaster (Illus. by McElligott, Matthew) — *McElligott, Matthew*
c The Mad Scientist Next Door (Illus. by Walker, Rory) — *De Marco, Clare*
  Mad Tuscans and Their Families: A History of Mental Disorder in Early Modern Italy — *Mellyn, Elizabeth W.*
  The Madagaskar Plan — *Saville, Guy*
  Madam Ambassador: Three Years of Diplomacy, Dinner Parties, and Democracy in Budapest — *Kounalakis, Eleni*
c Madam and Nun and 1001 (Illus. by Gable, Brian) — *Cleary, Brian P.*
c Madam Eiffle: The Love Story of the Eiffel Tower (Illus. by Csil) — *Briere-Haquet, Alice*
  Madam President — *Wallace, Nicolle*
c Madame Eiffel: The Love Story of the Eiffel Tower (Illus. by Csil) — *Briere-Haquet, Alice*
  Madame Frankenstein — *Rich, Jamie*
c Madame Martine Breaks the Rules (Illus. by Brannen, Sarah S.) — *Brannen, Sarah S.*
c Madame Martine (Illus. by Brannen, Sarah S.) — *Brannen, Sarah S.*
  Madame Picasso. Audiobook Review — *Girard, Anne*
c Madame Sonia Delaunay — *Monaco, Gerard Lo*
c Madame Sonia Delaunay — *Lo Monaco, Gerard*
y Madame Tussaud's Apprentice — *Duble, Kathleen Benner*
  Madame X — *Wilder, Jasinda*
c Maddie's Dream — *Hapka, Catherine*
c Maddi's Fridge (Illus. by Vogel, Vin) — *Brandt, Lois*
  Maddoc — *Nelson, B.C.*
  Maddy Kettle: The Adventure of the Thimblewitch (Illus. by Orchard, Eric) — *Orchard, Eric*
  Maddy Patti and the Great Curiosity: Helping Children Understand Diabetes (Illus. by Dey, Lorraine) — *Abel, Mary Bilderback*
c Maddy West and the Tongue Taker (Illus. by Bixley, Donovan) — *Falkner, Brian*
  Made Flesh: Sacrament and Poetics in Post-Reformation England — *Johnson, Kimberly*
  Made for Us — *Chase, Samantha*

y Made for You — *Marr, Melissa*
  Made in America: A Modern Collection of Classic Recipes — *Garrelts, Colby*
  Made in Detroit: Poems — *Piercy, Marge*
  Made in India: Recipes from an Indian Family Kitchen — *Sodha, Meera*
  Made to Kill — *Christopher, Adam*
y Made You Up — *Zappia, Francesca*
  Madeleine's War — *Watson, Peter*
c Madeline (Illus. by Bemelmans, Ludwig) — *Bemelmans, Ludwig*
  Madeline Kahn: Being the Music: A Life — *Madison, William V.*
  Mademoiselle Chanel — *Gortner, C.W.*
  Mademoiselle: Coco Chanel and the Pulse of History (Read by Gilbert, Tavia). Audiobook Review — *Garelick, Rhonda K.*
  Mademoiselle: Coco Chanel and the Pulse of History — *Garelick, Rhonda K.*
c Madison and the New Neighbors (Illus. by Brown, Jonathan) — *Braver, Vanita*
  Madison's Gift: Five Partnerships that Built America — *Stewart, David O.*
  Madison's Music: On Reading the First Amendment — *Neuborne, Burt*
  Madison's Song — *Amsden, Christine*
y Madly — *Alward, Amy*
  The Madman and the Assassin — *Martelle, Scott*
  Madman at Kilifi — *Gachagua, Clifton*
c The Madman of Piney Woods (Read by Heyborne, Kirby, with J.D. Jackson). Audiobook Review — *Curtis, Christopher Paul*
y The Madman of Piney Woods — *Curtis, Christopher Paul*
  Madness in Civilisation: A Cultural History of Insanity from the Bible to Freud, from the Madhouse to Modern Medicine — *Scull, Andrew*
  Madness in Civilization: A Cultural History of Insanity from the Bible to Freud, from the Madhouse to Modern Medicine — *Scull, Andrew*
  Madness in Civilization: A Cultural History of Insanity from the Bible to Freud, from the Madhouse to Modern Medicine — *Scull, Andrew*
  Madness in Solidar — *Modesitt, L.E., Jr.*
c The Madness of Captain Cyclops (Illus. by Laughead, Mike) — *Perritano, John*
y A Madness So Discreet — *McGinnis, Mindy*
  The Madwoman Upstairs — *Lowell, Catherine*
c Mae and the Moon (Illus. by Gigot, Jami) — *Gigot, Jami*
c Mae Jemison — *Shepherd, Jodie*
c Mae Jemison — *Colins, Luke*
  Maestra. Film. — *Murphy, Catherine*
  The Maestro, the Magistrate & the Mathematician — *Huchu, Tendai*
  Maeve's Times: In Her Own Words (Read by Binchy, Kate). Audiobook Review — *Binchy, Maeve*
  Magazines, Travel, and Middlebrow Culture: Canadian Periodicals in English and French, 1925-1960 — *Hammill, Faye*
c Magdalena's Picnic/El Picnic de Magdalena (Illus. by Deahl, Gretchen) — *Morrissey, Patricia Aguilar*
y The Mage of Trelian — *Knudsen, Michelle*
  Mage's Blood (Read by Podehl, Nick). Audiobook Review — *Hair, David*
c Maggie: A Girl of the Streets — *Maxwell, Marie*
c Maggie and Milly and Molly and May (Illus. by Perry, Marcia) — *Cummings, E.E.*
c Maggie and Wendel: Imagine Everything! (Illus. by Doerrfeld, Cori) — *Doerrfeld, Cori*
  Maggie Bright: A Novel of Dunkirk — *Groot, Tracy*
  Maggie Smith: A Biography — *Coveney, Michael*

The Maghreb Conspiracy: The Third Spy Story in Croft's — *Croft, Roger*
c Magic and Illusions — *Cooke, Tim*
Magic and Kingship in Medieval Iceland: The Construction of a Discourse of Political Resistance — *Meylan, Nicolas*
Magic and Masculinity: Ritual Magic and Gender in the Early Modern Era — *Timbers, Frances*
c The Magic Box (Illus. by Smith, Kim) — *Falcone, L.M.*
c Magic Delivery (Illus. by Dziekan, Michal) — *Smith, Ciete Barrett*
Magic in the Cloister: Pious Motives, Illicit Interests, and Occult Approaches to the Medieval Universe — *Page, Sophie*
c Magic in the Mix — *Barrows, Annie*
Magic Lantern Empire: Colonialism and Society in Germany — *Short, John Phillip*
c Magic Little Words (Illus. by Gauthier, Manon) — *Delaunois, Angele*
c Magic Little Words ... to Help You through Your Day (Illus. by Gauthier, Manon) — *Delaunois, Angele*
Magic Mushroom Explorer: Psilocybin and the Awakening Earth — *Powell, Simon G.*
The Magic of Math: Solving for x and Figuring out Why — *Benjamin, Arthur*
c The Magic of Maxwell and His Tail — *Kanefield, Maureen Stolar*
c Magic Science Series
c The Magic Scooter (Illus. by Hearn, Sam) — *Jarman, Julia*
The Magic Screen: A History of Regent Street Cinema — *Penn, Elaine*
Magic Shifts — *Andrews, Ilona*
c The Magic Stones (Illus. by Vincent-Sy, Jan Michael) — *Nor, Grandma*
The Magic Strings of Frankie Presto — *Albom, Mitch*
c The Magic Thief: Home (Illus. by Caparo, Antonio Javier) — *Prineas, Sarah*
c Magic Tree House Survival Guide (Illus. by Murdocca, Sal) — *Osborne, Mary Pope*
c Magic vs. Bird in the NCAA Final — *Daniel, P.K.*
c Magic Words! (Illus. by Kunkel, Mike) — *Kunkel, Mike*
c The Magical Fantastical Fridge (Illus. by Tinari, Leah) — *Coben, Harlan*
c The Magical Fantastical Fridge (Illus. by Tinari, Leah) — *Harlan Coben*
Magical Shetland Lace Shawls to Knit: Feather Soft and Incredibly Light: 15 Great Patterns and Full Instructions — *Lovick, Elizabeth*
c The Magical Snow Garden (Illus. by Chapman, Jane) — *Corderoy, Tracey*
The Magical World of Moss Gardening — *Martin, Annie*
The Magician — *Pupa, D.A.*
c The Magician of Auschwitz (Illus. by Newland, Gillian) — *Kacer, Kathy*
The Magician's Daughter — *Janeway, Judith*
y The Magician's Dream: An Oona Crate Mystery — *Odyssey, Shawn Thomas*
y The Magician's Fire — *Nicholson, Simon*
The Magician's Land (Read by Bramhall, Mark). Audiobook Review — *Grossman, Lev*
The Magician's Land — *Grossman, Lev*
The Magician's Lie (Read by Podehl, Nick). Audiobook Review — *Macallister, Greer*
The Magician's Lie — *Macallister, Greer*
Magicians of the Gods — *Hancock, Graham*
y The Magician's Secret — *Keene, Carolyn*
Magistra Doctissima: Essays in Honor of Bonnie Wheeler — *Armstrong, Dorsey*
Magna Carta: A Very Short Introduction — *Vincent, Nicholas*
Magna Carta — *Carpenter, David*
y Magna Carta and Its Gifts to Canada — *Harris, Carolyn*
Magna Carta: Law, Liberty, Legacy — *Breay, Claire*
Magna Carta — *Carpenter, David*
Magna Carta: The Birth of Liberty — *Jones, Dan*
Magna Carta: The Foundation of Freedom 1215-2015 — *Vincent, Nicholas*
Magna Carta: The Making and Legacy of the Great Charter — *Jones, Dan*
Magna Carta: The True Story Behind the Charter — *Starkey, David*
Magna Carta through the Ages — *Turner, Ralph V.*
Magna Carta Uncovered — *Arlidge, Anthony*
Magnetic North — *Maynard, Lee*
c The Magnificent Lizzie Brown and the Devil's Hound — *Lockwood, Vicki*

y The Magnificent Lizzie Brown and the Mysterious Phantom — *Lockwood, Vicki*
y Magnificent Minds: 16 Pioneering Women in Science & Medicine — *Noyce, Pendred E.*
Magnificent Mistakes in Mathematics — *Posamentier, Alfred S.*
Magnificent Obsessions: The Artist as Collector — *Yee, Lydia*
Magnificent Principia: Exploring Isaac Newton's Masterpiece — *Pask, Colin*
Magno Girl — *Canzano, Joe*
Magnolia Dawn — *Spindler, Erica*
c Magnolia — *Cook, Kristi*
c Magnus Chase and the Gods of Asgard: The Sword of Summer — *Riordan, Rick*
y Magonia — *Headley, Maria Dahvana*
c Magpie Learns a Lesson (Illus. by Erzinger, Tania) — *Morgan, Sally*
Magpie: Sweets and Savories from Philadelphia's Favorite Pie Boutique — *Ricciardi, Holly*
Magpies, Homebodies, and Nomads: A Modern Knitter's Guide to Discovering and Exploring Style (Illus. by Flood, Jared) — *Rose, Cirilia*
Mahabharata: A Modern Retelling — *Satyamurti, Carole*
c Mahalia Jackson: Walking with Kings and Queens (Illus. by Holyfield, John) — *Nolan, Nina*
Mahler's Symphonic Sonatas — *Monahan, Seth*
y Maid of Deception — *McGowan, Jennifer*
y Maid of Wonder — *McGowan, Jennifer*
y Maid-Sama!, 2 vols. (Illus. by Fujiwara, Hiro) — *Fujiwara, Hiro*
Maiden Lane — *Januska, Michael*
Maiden Voyage: The Senzaimaru and the Creation of Modern Sino-Japanese Relations — *Fogel, Joshua A.*
y Mailbox — *Freund, Nancy*
The Main Event: Boxing in Nevada from the Mining Camps to the Las Vegas Strip — *Davies, Richard O.*
Main Street Oklahoma: Stories of Twentieth-Century America — *Reese, Linda W.*
c The Maine Coon's Haiku: And Other Poems for Cat Lovers (Illus. by White, Lee) — *Rosen, Michael J.*
Mainstreaming Torture: Ethical Approaches in the Post-9/11 United States — *Gordon, Rebecca*
Maintaining Peace and Interstate Stability in Archaic and Classical Greece — *Wilker, Julia*
The Maintenance of Headway — *Mills, Magnus*
The Maisky Diaries: Red Ambassador to the Court of Sir Jame's, 1932-1943 — *Gorodetsky, Gabriel*
The Maisky Diaries: Red Ambassador to the Court of St. James's, 1932-1943 — *Gorodetsky, Gabriel*
The Maisky Diaries: Red Ambassador to the Court of St. James's, 1932-1943 — *Maisky, Ivan*
Maison Goossens: Haute Couture Jewelry — *Mauries, Patrick*
c Maisy Goes on a Plane — *Cousins, Lucy*
c Maisy Goes to London — *Cousins, Lucy*
c Maisy's Christmas Tree (Illus. by Cousins, Lucy) — *Cousins, Lucy*
c Maisy's Digger — *Cousins, Lucy*
c Maisy's Pirate Ship — *Cousins, Lucy*
c Maisy's Tractor (Illus. by Cousins, Lucy) — *Cousins, Lucy*
Maize for the Gods: Unearthing the 9,000-Year History of Corn — *Blake, Michael*
Majestic Hollywood: The Greatest Films of 1939 — *Vieira, Mark A.*
The Majesty of the People: Popular Sovereignty and the Role of the Writer in the 1790s — *Green, Georgina*
The Major Crimes Team — *Smith, Graham*
Major-General Thomas Harrison: Millenarianism, Fifth Monarchism and the English Revolution 1616-1660 — *Farr, David*
Major Misconduct — *Jamieson, Kelly*
Major Works on Religion and Politics — *Niebuhr, Reinhold*
c Make a Wish, Midas! (Illus. by Patricelli, Leslie) — *Holub, Joan*
Make Change Work for You: 10 Ways to Future-Proof Yourself, Fearlessly Innovate, and Succeed Despite Uncertainty — *Steinberg, Scott*
Make 'Em Laugh: Short-Term Memories of Longtime Friends — *Reynolds, Debbie*
c Make Friends, Break Friends (Illus. by Pankhurst, Kate) — *Jarman, Julia*
Make It a Green Peace! The Rise of Countercultural Environmentalism — *Zelko, Frank*
c Make It Here: Inciting Creativity and Innovation in Your Library — *Hamilton, Matthew*

y Make It Messy: My Perfectly Imperfect Life — *Samuelsson, Marcus*
Make Me Lose Control — *Ridgway, Christie*
y Make Me — *Child, Lee*
Make Me One with Everything: Buddhist Meditations to Awaken from the Illusion of Separation — *Surya Das, Lama*
Make Me Stay — *Burton, Jaci*
Make Mead Like a Viking: Traditional Techniques for Brewing Natural, Wild-Fermented, Honey-Based Wines and Beers — *Zimmerman, Jereme*
c Make Money Choices — *Reina, Mary*
Make Peace before the Sun Goes Down: The Long Encounter of Thomas Merton and His Abbot, James Fox — *Lipsey, Roger*
Make Something Up: Stories You Can't Unread — *Palahniuk, Chuck*
Make You Burn — *Crane, Megan*
Make You Mine — *Ashenden, Jackie*
y Make Your Home Among Strangers — *Crucet, Jennine Capo*
y Makena's Shadow — *Lee, Monica K.K.*
c Makeover Magic — *Santopolo, Jill*
Makers and Users of Medieval Books: Essays in Honour of A.S.G. Edwards — *Meale, Carol M.*
Makerspaces in Libraries — *Willingham, Theresa*
Makerspaces: Top Trailblazing Projects — *Bagley, Caitlin A.*
Makery Sewing: Over 30 Projects for the Home, to Wear and to Give — *Smith, Kate*
c Making a Friend (Read by Berneis, Susie). Audiobook Review — *McGhee, Alison*
Making a Global Immigrant Neighborhood: Brooklyn's Sunset Park — *Hum, Tarry*
Making a Life in Multiethnic Miami: Immigration and the Rise of a Global City — *Aranda, Elizabeth M.*
Making a Life in Multiethnic Miami: Immigration and the Rise of a Global City — *Elizabeth M. Aranda,*
Making a Living, Making a Life — *Rose, Daniel*
Making a Point: The Persnickety Story of English Punctuation — *Crystal, David*
Making Americans: Children's Literature from 1930 to 1960 — *Schmidt, Gary D.*
Making Americans: Jews and the Broadway Musical — *Most, Andrea*
The Making and Breaking of Soviet Lithuania: Memory and Modernity in the Wake of War — *Davioliute, Violeta*
Making and Breaking the Gods: Christian Reponses to Pagan Sculpture in Late Antiquity — *Kristensen, Troels Myrup*
The Making and Unmaking of a Saint: Hagiography and Memory in the Cult of Gerald of Aurillac — *Kuefler, Mathew*
The Making and Unmaking ofa Saint: Hagiography and Memory in the Cult of Gerald of Aurillac — *Kuefler, Mathew*
Making and Unmaking Public Health in Africa: Ethnographic and Historical Perspectives — *Prince, Ruth J.*
Making Art in Africa, 1960-2010 — *Savage, Polly*
Making Aztlan: Ideology and Culture of the Chicana and Chicano Movement, 1966-1977 — *Gomez-Quinones, Juan*
c Making Bombs for Hitler — *Skrypuch, Marsha Forchuck*
Making Chinese Australia: Urban Elites, Newspapers and the Formation of Chinese-Australian Identity, 1892-1912 — *Kuo, Mei-Fen*
Making Cinelandia: American Films and Mexican Film Culture before the Golden Age — *Serna, Laura Isabel*
Making David into Goliath: How the World Turned against Israel — *Muravchik, Joshua*
Making Democratic Governance Work: How Regimes Shape Prosperity, Welfare and Peace — *Norris, Pippa*
Making Do in Damascus: Navigating a Generation of Change in Family and Work, Contemporary Issues in the Middle East — *Gallagher, Sally K.*
Making England Western: Occidentalism, Race, and Imperial Culture — *Makdisi, Saree*
Making Freedom: The Underground Railroad and the Politics of Slavery — *Blackett, R.J.M.*
The Making Friends Program: Supporting Acceptance in Your K-2 Classroom — *Favazza, Paddy C.*
Making Good Neighbors: Civil Rights, Liberalism, and Integration in Postwar Philadelphia — *Perkiss, Abigail*

Making Hispanics: How Activists, Bureaucrats, and Media Constructed a New American — Mora, G. Cristina

Making History New: Modernism and Historical Narrative — O'Malley, Seamus

c Making It Home — Roche, Suzanne

Making JFK Matter: Popular Memory and the Thirty-Fifth President — Santa Cruz, Paul H.

c Making Machines with Pulleys — Oxlade, Chris

c Making Machines with Ramps and Wedges — Oxlade, Chris

c Making Machines with Springs — Oxlade, Chris

Making Make-Believe Real: Politics as Theater in Shakespeare's Time — Wills, Garry

Making Marie Curie: Intellectual Property and Celebrity Culture in an Age of Information — Hemmungs, Eva

Making Marie Curie: Intellectual Property and Celebrity Culture in an Age of Information — Joyner, Richard

Making Marie Curie: Intellectual Property and Celebrity Culture in an Age of Information — Wirten, Eva Hemmungs

Making Marriage: Husbands, Wives and the American State in Dakota and Ojibwe Country — Denial, Catherine J.

Making Micronesia: A Political Biography of Tosiwo Nakayama — Hanlon, David

Making Modern Love: Sexual Narratives and Identities in Interwar Britain — Sigel, Lisa Z.

Making Modernism Soviet: The Russian Avant-Garde in the Early Soviet Era, 1918-1928 — Kachurin, Pamela

Making Money: Coin, Currency and the Coming of Capitalism — Desan, Christine

Making Monte Carlo: A History of Speculation and Spectacle — Braude, Mark

Making Moros: Imperial Historism and American Military Rule in the Philippines' Muslim South — Hawkins, Michael C.

Making Movies into Art: Picture Craft from the Magic Lantern to Early Hollywood — Askari, Kaveh

Making National News: A History of Canadian Press — Allen, Gene

Making Nature: The History of a Scientific Journal. — Baldwin, Melinda

Making Nice — Sumell, Matt

The Making of a Cultural Landscape: The English Lake District as Tourist Destination, 1750-2010 — Wood, Jason

The Making of a Healer: Teachings of My Oneida Grandmother — FourEagles, Russell

The Making Of A Mystic — Fievet, Paddy

y The Making of a Navy SEAL: My Story of Surviving the Toughest Challenge and Training the Best — Webb, Brandon

The Making of a New Rural Order in South China, vol. 1: Village, Land, and Lineage in Huizhou, 900-1600 — McDermott, Joseph P.

The Making of a Southern Democracy: North Carolina Politics from Kerr Scott to Pat McCrory — Eamon, Tom

The Making of an Abolitionist — Brennan, Denis

The Making of Asian America: A History — Lee, Erika

The Making of Assisi: The Pope, the Franciscans and the Painting of the Basilica — Cooper, Donal

The Making of Europe: A Geological History — Park, Graham

The Making of Home: The 500-Year Story of How Our Houses Became Our Homes — Flanders, Judith

The Making of Medieval Antifraternalism: Polemic, Violence, Deviance, and Remembrance — Geltner, Guy

The Making of Middle Classes: Social Mobility and Boundary Work in Global Perspective

The Making of Modern Chinese Medicine, 1850-1960 — Andrews, Bridie

The Making of Romantic Love: Longing and Sexuality in Europe, South Asia, and Japan, 900-1200 CE — Reddy, William M.

The Making of the American Essay — D'Agata, John

The Making of the First Korean President: Syngman Rhee's Quest for Independence, 1875-1948 — Lew, Young Ick

The Making of the Middle Sea: A History of the Mediterranean from the Beginning to the Emergency of the Classical World — Broodbank, Cyprian

The Making of the Modern British Home: The Suburban Semi and Family Life between the Wars — Scott, Peter

The Making of the Modern Police, 1780-1914 — Lawrence, Paul

The Making of the Modern Refugee — Gatrell, Peter

The Making of the New Negro: Black Authorship, Masculinity, and Sexuality in the Harlem Renaissance — Pochmara, Ana

The Making of the Odyssey — West, Martin L.

The Making of Zombie Wars — Hemon, Aleksandar

y Making Pretty — Haydu, Corey Ann

Making Rocky Mountain National Park: The Environmental History of an American Treasure — Frank, Jerry J.

Making Samba: A New History of Race and Music in Brazil — Hertzman, Marc A.

Making Seafood Sustainable: American Experiences in Global Perspective — Blackford, Mansel

Making Sense of American Liberalism — Bell, Jonathan

Making Sense of Constitutional Monarchism in Post-Napoleonic France and Germany — Prutsch, Markus J.

Making Sense of Micronesia: The Logic of Pacific Island Culture — Hezel, Francis X.

Making Sense of Public Opinion: American Discourses about Immigration and Social Programs — Strauss, Claudia

Making Sense of Tantric Buddhism: History, Semiology, and Transgression in the Indian Traditions — Wedemeyer, Christian K.

Making Sense of the City: Local Government, Civic Culture, and Community Life in Urban America — Fairbanks, Robert B.

Making Space: How the Brain Knows Where Things Are — Groh, Jennifer M.

Making Tea, Making Japan: Cultural Nationalism in Practice — Surak, Kristin

Making the American Body: The Remarkable Saga of the Men and Women Whose Feats, Feuds, and Passions Shaped Fitness History — Black, Jonathan

Making the American Century: Essays on the Political Culture of Twentieth Century America — Schulman, Bruce J.

Making the Common Core Writing Standards Accessible through Universal Design for Learning — Spencer, Sally A.

Making the Modern American Fiscal State: Law, Politics, and the Rise of Progressive Taxation, 1877-1929 — Mehrotra, Ajay K.

Making the Modern American Fiscal State: Law, Politics, and the Rise of Progressive Taxation, 1877-1929 — Mehrotta, Ajay K.

Making the Principal TExES Exam Real: Competency-Based Case Studies with Practice Questions — Wilmore, Elaine L.

Making the Soviet Intelligentsia: Universities and Intellectual Life under Stalin and Khrushchev — Tromly, Benjamin

Making the World Safe for Workers: Labor, the Left, and Wilsonian Internationalism — McKillen, Elizabeth

Making Toronto Modern: Architecture and Design, 1895-1975 — Armstrong, Christopher

Making Waves: Democratic Contention in Europe and Latin America since the Revolutions of 1848 — Weyland, Kurt

Maladies of the Mind — Vaughan, Betty Boudreau

c Malaika's Costume (Illus. by Luxbacher, Irene) — Hohn, Nadia L.

c Malala, a Brave Girl from Pakistan / Iqbal, a Brave Boy from Pakistan (Illus. by Winter, Jeanette) — Winter, Jeanette

c Malala Yousafzai and the Girls of Pakistan — Aretha, David

c Malala Yousafzai — Doak, Robin S.

c Malala Yousafzai: Shot by the Taliban, Still Fighting for Equal Education — Doeden, Matt

Malanga Chasing Vallejo: Selected Poems of Cesar Vallejo: New Translations and Notes — Malanga, Gerard

Malaysia@50: Economic Development, Distribution, Disparities — Sundaram, Jomo Kwame

c Malcolm under the Stars (Illus. by Lies, Brian) — Beck, W.H.

Malcolm X: A Life of Reinvention — Marable, Manning

Malcolm X at Oxford Union: Racial Politics in a Global Era — Ambar, Saladin

The Maldives: Islamic Republic, Tropical Autocracy — Robinson, J.J.

Male Beauty: Postwar Masculinity in Theater, Film, and Physique Magazines — Krauss, Kenneth

Male Rape Is a Feminist Issue: Feminism, Governmentality and Male Rape — Cohen, Claire

Male Sex Work and Society — Minichiello, Victor

Malee: A Tear in the Ocean — McAllister, William V.M., III

Malestrom: Manhood Swept into the Currents of a Changing World — James, Carolyn Custis

Malevolent Muse: The Life of Alma Mahler — Arthur, Donald

Malfunctioning Democracy in Japan: Quantitative Analysis in a Civil Society — Kobayashi, Yoshiaki

Malice — Higashino, Keigo

Malice — Smith, Alexander O.

Malignant: How Cancer Becomes Us — Jain, S. Lochlann

Malignant Metaphor: Finding the Hidden Meaning of Cancer — Mitchell, Alanna

Malinche, Pocahontas, and Sacagawea: Indian Women as Cultural Intermediaries and National Symbols — Jager, Rebecca Kay

The Malleability of Intellectual Styles — Zhang, Li-Fang

c Mallory McDonald, Baby Expert (Illus. by Kalis, Jennifer) — Friedman, Laurie

c The Maloneys' Magical Weatherbox — Quinlan, Nigel

Malory and Christianity: Essay on Sir Thomas Malory's " Morte Darthur" — Hanks, Thomas D.

Malory and His European Contemporaries: Adapting Late Arthurian Romance — Edlich-Muth, Miriam

The Maltby Brothers' Civil War — Delaney, Norman C.

Malthus: The Life and Legacies of an Untimely Prophet — Mayhew, Robert J.

Mama and the Hungry HOle — DeBiase, Johanna

c Mama Bird Papa Bird (Illus. by Thomas, Faith) — Obermeier, Wanda

Mama Koko and the Hundred Gunmen: An Ordinary Family's Extraordinary Tale of Love, Loss, and Survival in the Congo — Shannon, Lisa J.

c Mama Seeton's Whistle (Illus. by Pham, LeUyen) — Spinelli, Jerry

Mama Tried — Flake, Emily

Mama Used to Say: Change Your Thinking, Change Your Life — Digby Nelson, Joyce

c Maman, je t'aime tant! (Illus. by Fleming, Kim) — Mitchell, Laine

c Mama's Nightingale: A Story of Immigration and Separation (Illus. by Staub, Leslie) — Danticat, Edwidge

c Mama's Nightingale (Illus. by Staub, Leslie) — Danticat, Edwidge

c Mama's Right Here (Illus. by Corke, Estelle) — Kerner, Susan

Mambu et son amour — Charbonneau, Louis

Mamluks and Animals: Veterinary Medicine in Medieval Islam — Shehada, Housni Alkhateeb

Mammalian Development: Networks, Switches, and Morphogenetic Processes — Tam, Patrick P.L.

c Mammals — Levine, Michelle

c Mammals — Royston, Angela

c Mammals around the World — Alderton, David

A Mammal's Notebook: The Writings of Erik Satie — Satie, Erik

c Mammoth and Mastodon — Zeiger, Jennifer

The Mammoth Book of Dieselpunk — Wallace, Sean

The Mammoth Book of Madonna — Morgan, Michelle

The Mammoth Book of Sherlock Holmes Abroad — Clark, Simon

Mammoths and the Environment — Ukraintseva, Valentina V.

A MAMo State of Mind: Kanaka Maoli Arts and the Review of Three Concurrent Exhibitions — Kahanu, Noelle M.K.Y.

Mamushka: A Cookbook: Recipes from Ukraine & Eastern Europe — Hercules, Olia

Man and Animal in Severan Rome: The Literary Imagination of Claudius Aelianus — Smith, Steven D.

A Man Apart: Bill Coperthwaite's Radical Experiment in Living — Forbes, Peter

Man at the Helm — Stibbe, Nina

Man Enough: How Jesus Redefines Manhood — Pyle, Nate

The Man He Became: How FDR Defied Polio to Win the Presidency — Tobin, James

The Man in a Hurry — Morand, Paul

Man in Profile: Joseph Mitchell of The New Yorker — Kunkel, Thomas

The Man in the Monster: An Intimate Portrait of a Serial Killer — Elliott, Martha

The Man in the Monster — Elliott, Martha
A Man Lies Dreaming — Tidhar, Lavie
Man Made Murder: The Blood Road Trilogy — Rider, Z.
c The Man Made of Stars — Clark, M.H.
A Man Most Driven: Captain John Smith, Pocahontas and the Founding of America — Firstbrook, Peter
Man of Destiny: FDR and the Making of the American Century — Hamby, Alonzo L.
A Man of Good Hope — Steinberg, Jonny
A Man of His Word — Monso, Imma
Man of the Century: Winston Churchill and His Legend since 1945 — Ramsden, John
Man on Fire — Kelman, Stephen
The Man That Got Away: The Life and Songs of Harold Arlen — Rimler, Walter
Man Tiger — Kurniawan, Eka
Man to Man: Desire, Homosociality, and Authority in Late-Roman Manhood — Masterson, Mark
Man v. Fat: The Weight Loss Manual — Shanahan, Andrew
Man v. Nature: Stories — Cook, Diane
y Man Walks on the Moon — Bodden, Valerie
The Man Who Built the Best Car in the World (Illus. by Marjoram, Stefan) — Sewell, Brian
The Man Who Closed the Asylums: Franco Basaglia and the Revolution in Mental Health Care — Foot, John
The Man Who Couldn't Stop: OCD and the True Story of a Life Lost in Thought — Adam, David
The Man Who Fell from the Sky — Coel, Margaret
The Man Who Invented Fiction: How Cervantes Ushered in the Modern World — Egginton, William
The Man Who Painted the Universe: The Story of a Planetarium in the Heart of the North Woods — Legro, Ron
The Man Who Saved Henry Morgan — Hough, Robert
The Man Who Snapped His Fingers — Hachtroudi, Fariba
The Man Who Spoke Snakish — Kivirahk, Andrus
The Man Who Stalked Einstein: How Nazi Scientist Philipp Lenard Changed the Course of History — Hillman, Bruce J.
The Man Who Thought He Was Napoleon: Towards a Political History of Madness — Murat, Laure
The Man Who Touched His Own Heart: True Tales of Science, Surgery, and Mystery — Dunn, Rob
The Man Who Walked Away — Casey, Maud
The Man Who Was Norris: The Life of Gerald Hamilton — Cullen, Tom
The Man Who Wasn't There: Investigations into the Strange New Science of the Self — Ananthaswamy, Anil
The Man Who Wasn't There: Investigations into the Strange New Science of the Self — Ananthaswamy, Anil
The Man Who Would Not Be Washington: Robert E. Lee's Civil War and His Decision That Changed American History. Audiobook Review — Horn, Jonathan
The Man Who Would Not Be Washington: Robert E. Lee's Civil War and His Decision That Changed American History — Horn, Jonathan
c The Man with Messy Hair — Allen, Pamela
The Man with the Golden Typewriter: Ian Fleming's James Bond Letters — Fleming, Fergus
The Man with the Golden Typewriter: Ian Fleming's James Bond Letters — Fleming, Ian
The Man Without A Face: The Unlikely Rise of Vladimir Putin — Gessen, Masha
The Man without a Shadow — Oates, Joyce Carol
The Managed Heart: Commercialization of Human Feeling — Hochschild, Arlie Russell
The Management of Insects in Recreation and Tourism. — Lemelin, Harvey Raynald
The Management of Luxury: A Practitioner's Handbook — Berghaus, Benjamin
Managing Bubbie — Lazega, Russel
Managing Children's Services in Libraries, 4th ed. — Fasick, Adele M.
Managing Conflict in a World Adrift — Crocker, Chester A.
Managing Copyright in Higher Education: A Guidebook — Ferullo, Donna L.
Managing Madness in the Community: The Challenge of Contemporary Mental Health Care — Dobransky, Kerry Michael
Managing Mass Culture: Serialization, Standardization and Modernity, 1880-1940
Managing Prostate Cancer: A Guide for Living Better — Roth, Andrew J.

Managing the Cycle of Acting-Out Behavior in the Classroom — Colvin, Geoff
Managing with Data: Using ACRLMetrics and PLAmetrics — Hernon, Peter
Managing Your Business with 7 Key Numbers — Prager, Jeffrey Kenneth
Managing Your Child's Chronic Pain — Palermo, Tonya M.
Manana — Hjortsberg, William
c Manatee Rescue (Illus. by Wright, Annabel) — Davies, Nicola
Manchu Princess, Japanese Spy: The Story of Kawashima Yoshiko, the Cross-Dressing Spy Who Commanded Her Own Army — Birnbaum, Phyllis
Mandate of Heaven and the Great Ming Code — Jiang, Younglin
Mandated Reporter — Koretsky, J. Lea
Mandela's Kinsmen: Nationalist Elites and Apartheid's First Bantustan — Gibbs, Timothy
Manet Paints Monet: A Summer in Argenteuil — Sauerlander, Willibald
Manga Crash Course: Drawing Manga Characters and Scenes from Start to Finish — Petrovic, Mina
c Mange tes legumes, Boucle d'or! — Smallman, Steve
c Manger (Illus. by Cann, Helen) — Hopkins, Lee Bennett
Mangle Boards of Northern Europe: A Definitive Guide to the Geographic Origins of Mangle Boards — Raymond, Jay
c Mango, Abuela, and Me (Illus. by Dominguez, Angela) — Medina, Meg
c Mango and Bambang, the Not-a-Pig — Faber, Polly
Manhattan in Miniature — Grace, Margaret
y Manhattan Mayhem: New Crime Stories from Mystery Writers of America — Clark, Mary Higgins
The Manhattan Project — Kishik, David
Manhattan to Minisink: American Indian Place Names in Greater New York and Vicinity — Grumet, Robert S.
Manhattan Transfer — Passos, John Dos
Manhood Acts: Gender and the Practices of Domination — Schwalbe, Michael
c Manhunt — Messner, Kate
y Mania — Johansson, J.R.
Manierisme et Litterature — Souiller, Didier
Manifest Destinations: Cities and Tourists in the Nineteenth-Centuary American West — Gruen, J. Philip
Manifest Destiny: The Path towards Wisdom — Spencer, Jamere A. Brown
Manifestation Wolverine — Young Bear, Ray
Maninbo: Peace & War — Ko, Un
The Manly Art of Knitting — Fougner, Dave
Mann des gedruckten Wortes: Helmut Schmidt und die Medien — Birkner, Thomas
y A Manner of Being: Writers on Their Mentors — Liontas, Annie
Manon Lescaut — Puccini, Giacomo
The Man's Guide to Women: Scientifically Proven Secrets from the "Love Lab" about What Women Really Want — Gottman, John
A Man's World: The Double Life of Emile Griffith — Mcrae, Donald
Mantissa Veleiate — Criniti, Nicola
The Mantle of Command: FDR at War, 1941-1942 — Hamilton, Nigel
Mantra: Karma Is a Bitch — Shams, Mehtab
A Manual for Cleaning Women: Selected Stories — Berlin, Lucia
A Manual for Cleaning Women: Selected Stories — Emerson, Stephen
c A Manual for Marco (Illus. by Tejpar, Iman) — Abdullah, Shaila
Manual of Anglo-Norman — Short, Ian
Manual of Psychomagic: The Practice of Shamanic Psychotherapy — Jodorowsky, Alejandro
Manufacturing Middle Ages: Entangled History of Medievalism in Nineteenth-Century Europe — Geary, Patrick J.
Manufacturing Morals: The Values of Silence in Business School Education — Anteby, Michel
Manufacturing the Modern Patron in Victorian California: Cultural Philanthropy, Industrial Capital, and Social Authority — Ott, John
Manuscript and Print in London c. 1475-1530 — Boffey, Julia
Manuscript Miscellanies in Early Modern England — Eckhardt, Joshua
Manuscripta Illuminata: Approaches to Understanding Medieval and Renaissance Manuscripts — Hourihane, Colum

Manuscripts and Printed Books in Europe 1350-1550 — Cayley, Emma
Manuscrits et pratiques autographes chez les ecrivains francais de la fin du Moyen Age: L'exemple de Christine de Pizan — Delsaux, Olivier
The Many Altars of Modernity: Toward a Paradigm for Religion in a Pluralist Age — Berger, Peter L.
The Many Faces of Beauty — Hosle, Vittorio
The Many Faces of Christ: Portraying the Holy in the East and West, 300-1300 — Bacci, Michele
The Many Faces of Christ: The Thousand-Year Story of the Survival and Influence of the Lost Gospels — Jenkins, Philip
The Many Faces of Josephine Baker: Dancer, Activist, Spy — Caravantes, Peggy
The Many-Headed Muse: Tradition and Innovation in Late Classical Greek Lyric Poetry — LeVen, Pauline A.
The Many-Headed Muse. Tradition and Innovation in Late Classical Greek Lyric Poetry — LeVen, Pauline A.
y The Many Lives of John Stone — Buckley-Archer, Linda
The Many Sides of Peace: Christian Nonviolence, the Contemplative Life, and Sustainable Living — Shanley, Brayton
The Manzoni Family — Ginzburg, Natalia
Mao: The Real Story — Pantsov, Alexander V.
c Maori Art for Kids — Noanoa, Julie
Mao's Little Red Book: A Global History — Cook, Alexander C.
Map: Collected and Last Poems — Szymborska, Wislawa
Map: Exploring the World — Hessler, John
A Map of Betrayal. Audiobook Review — Ha Jin
A Map of Betrayal — Ha Jin
A Map of Betrayal — Jin, Ha
The Map of Chaos — Palma, Felix J.
y Map of Fates — Hall, Maggie
c The Map to Everywhere (Illus. by Harris, Todd) — Ryan, Carrie
y The Map Trap — Clements, Andrew
The Map Turtle and Sawback Atlas: Ecology, Evolution, Distribution, and Conservation — Lindeman, Peter V.
Mapa dibujado por un espia — Infante, Guillermo Cabrera
Maple: 100 Sweet and Savory Recipes Featuring Pure Maple Syrup — Webster, Katie
c Maple (Read by Nielsen, Stina). Audiobook Review — Nichols, Lori
c Maple & Willow Apart (Illus. by Nichols, Lori) — Nichols, Lori
c Maple & Willow Together — Nichols, Lori
Maplecroft (Read by Parker, Johanna) — Priest, Cherie
y Mapmaker (Read by Moon, Erin). Audiobook Review — Bomback, Mark
y Mapmaker — Bomback, Mark
Mapmaker — Galaxy Craze
y The Mapmaker's Children — McCoy, Sarah
c Mapping a Village — Green, Jen
Mapping Europe's Borderlands: Russian Cartography in the Age of Empire — Seegel, Steven
Mapping Exile and Return: Palestinian Dispossession and a Political Theology for a Shared Future — Weaver, Alain Epp
Mapping Malory: Regional Identities and National Geographies in Le Morte Darthur — Armstrong, Dorsey
Mapping National Anxieties: Thailand's Southern Conflict — McCargo, Duncan
Mapping "Race": Critical Approaches to Health Disparities Research — Gomez, Laura
Mapping Race: Critical Approaches to Health Disparities Research — Gomez, Laura E.
Mapping Shangrila: Contested Landscapes in the Sino-Tibetan Borderlands — Yeh, Emily T.
Mapping the Cold War: Cartography and the Framing of America's International Power — Barney, Timothy
Mapping the End of Empire: American and British Strategic Visions in the Postwar World — Husain, Aiyaz
Mapping the Nation: History and Cartography in Nineteenth-Century America — Schulten, Susan
The Mapuche in Modern Chile: A Cultural History — Crow, Joanna
Marabou Stork Nightmares — Welsh, Irvine
Marathon Fighters and Men of Maple: Ancient Acharnai — Kellogg, Danielle L.
y The Marauders — Cooper, Tom

Marbeck and the Gunpowder Plot — *Pilkington, John*
The Marble Orchard — *Taylor, Alex*
Marc-Antoine Muret: Des "Isles Fortunees" au Rivage Romain — *Girot, Jean-Eudes*
Marc Chagall: Grenzgange zwischen Literatur und Malerei — *Koller, Sabine*
Marcas autoriales de segmentacion en las comedias autografas de Lope de Vega: Estudio y analisis — *Crivellari, Daniele*
c Marcel the Shell: The Most Surprised I've Ever Been (Illus. by Lind, Amy) — *Fleischer-Camp, Dean*
c Marcello — *Lacombe, Jean*
y March, Book 2 (Illus. by Powell, Nate) — *Lewis, John*
c March Grand Prix: The Fast and the Furriest (Illus. by Soo, Kean) — *Soo, Kean*
March of the Crabs, vol. 1: The Crabby Condition — *Pins, Arthur de*
The March on Washington: Jobs, Freedom, and the Forgotten History of Civil Rights — *Jones, William P.*
c Marcher dans le ciel (Illus. by Boulanger, Annie) — *Cotten, Sonia*
Marching Home: Union Veterans and Their Unending Civil War — *Jordan, Brian Matthew*
Marching into Darkness: The Wehrmacht and the Holocaust in Belarus — *Beorn, Waitman W.*
Marching into Darkness: The Wehrmacht and the Holocaust in Belarus — *Beorn, Waitman Wade*
Marching to the Canon: The Life of Schubert's Marche Militaire — *Messing, Scott*
Marco and Devil's Bargain — *Kelly, Carla*
The Marco Effect — *Adler-Olsen, Jussi*
Marco Polo: The Journey That Changed the World (Read by Vance, Simon). Audiobook Review — *Man, John*
y The Mare — *Gaitskill, Mary*
c Maren Loves Luke Lewis — *Jones, Jen*
Margaret of Anjou — *Iggulden, Conn*
Margaret of Parma: A Life — *Steen, Charlie R.*
Margaret Thatcher: Shaping the New Conservatism — *Veldman, Meredith*
Margaret Thatcher: The Authorised Biography, vol. 2: Everything She Wants — *Moore, Charles*
c Margaret Wise Brown's The Golden Bunny: And 17 Other Stories and Poems (Illus. by Weisgard, Leonard) — *Brown, Margaret Wise*
Margery & Pamela — *Huber, Laurel Davis*
Marginal Modernity: The Aesthetics of Dependency from Kierkegaard to Joyce — *Lisi, Leonardo F.*
Margot Asquith's Great War Diary, 1914-16: The View from Downing Street — *Brock, Michael*
Margot at War: Love and Betrayal in Downing Street, 1912-16 — *de Courcy, Anne*
c Margret and H.A. Rey's Curious George Goes to a Bookstore (Illus. by Young, Mary O'Keefe) — *Bartynski, Julie M.*
c Marguerite's Christmas (Illus. by Blanchet, Pascal) — *Desjardins, India*
c Marguerite's Fountain — *Elliot, Rachel*
Mari Magno, Dipsychus and Other Poems — *Clough, Arthur Hugh*
Mariama: Different But Just the Same (Illus. by Uya, Nivola) — *Cornelles, Jeronimo*
c Mariam's Easter Parade (Illus. by Wasielewski, Margaret Markarian) — *Markarian, Marianne*
c Marie Curie — *Edison, Erin*
Marie NDiaye: Blankness and Recognition — *Asibong, Andrew*
Marie von Clausewitz: The Woman Behind the Making of On War — *Bellinger, Vanya Eftimova*
Marilyn K.: The House Next Door — *White, Lionel*
Marilyn Minter: Pretty/Dirty — *Arning, Bill*
Marilyn Monroe Day by Day: A Timeline of People, Places, and Events — *Rollyson, Carol*
c Marilyn's Monster (Illus. by Phelan, Matt) — *Knudsen, Michelle*
y Marina (Read by Weyman, Daniel). Audiobook Review — *Ruiz Zafon, Carlos*
y Marina — *Ruiz Zafon, Carlos*
Marine Conservation: Science, Policy, and Management — *Ray, G. Carleton*
y Marine Corps Forces Special Operations Command — *Whiting, Jim*
c Marine Firefighters — *Goldish, Meish*
Marine Mammal Observer and Passive Acoustic Monitoring Handbook — *Todd, Victoria*
Marine Sergeant Freddy Gonzalez, Vietnam War Hero — *Flores, John W.*
Mariner's Ark — *Tonkin, Peter*
Marinetti Dines with the High Command — *Cavell, Richard*

Mario Lanza: Singing to the Gods — *Mannering, Derek*
c Marion Strikes a Pose — *Riti, Marsha*
y Mariposa U — *Gonzalez, Rigoberto*
Marissa Mayer and the Fight to Save Yahoo! — *Carlson, Nicholas*
The Maritain Factor: Taking Religion into Interwar Modernism — *Hynickx, Rajsh*
A Maritime Archaeology of Ships: Innovation and Social Change in Medieval and Early Modern Europe — *Adams, Jonathan*
Marivaudage: theories et pratiques d'un discours — *Gallouet, Catherine*
Marivaux et la science du caractere — *Benharrech, Sarah*
Marjorie Harris Carr: Defender of Florida's Environment — *Macdonald, Peggy*
The Mark and the Void — *Murray, Paul*
Mark Bittman's Kitchen Matrix — *Bittman, Mark*
Mark Bittman's Kitchen Matrix: Visual Recipes to Make Cooking Easier than Ever — *Bittman, Mark*
Mark & Empire: Feminist Reflections — *Cobb, Laurel K.*
Mark My Words: Native Women Mapping Our Nations — *Goeman, Mishuana*
The Mark of Cain: Guilt and Denial in the Post-War Lives of Nazi Perpetrator — *Kellenbach, Katharina von*
The Mark of Cain: Guilt and Denial in the Post-War Lives of Nazi Perpetrators — *von Kellenbach, Katharina*
y The Mark of the Dragonfly — *Johnson, Jaleigh*
The Mark of the Midnight Manzanilla (Read by Reading, Kate). Audiobook Review — *Willig, Lauren*
c Mark of the Thief (Read by Andrews, Macleod). Audiobook Review — *Nielsen, Jennifer A.*
y Mark of the Thief — *Nielsen, Jennifer A.*
The Mark on Eve — *Fox, Joel*
Mark Rothko — *Rothko, Christopher*
Mark Rothko — *Cohen-Solal, Annie*
Mark Rothko: Toward the Light in the Chapel — *Cohen-Solal, Annie*
Mark Rothko: Towards the Light in the Chapel — *Cohen-Solal, Annie*
Mark Twain's America: A Celebration in Words and Images — *Katz, Harry L.*
y Marked (Illus. by Cantirino, Sally) — *McCaffrey, Laura Williams*
y Marked — *Tingey, Sue*
Marked Off — *Cameron, Don*
Market Madness: A Century of Oil Panics, Crises, and Crashes — *Clayton, Blake C.*
c Market Maze (Illus. by Munro, Roxie) — *Munro, Roxie*
The Market Preparation of Carolina Rice: An Illustrated History of Innovations in the Lowcountry Rice Kingdom — *Porcher, Richard Dwight, Jr.*
Marketing above the Noise: Achieve Strategic Advantage with Marketing That Matters — *Popky, Linda J.*
Marketing and Social Media: A Guide for Libraries, Archives, and Museums — *Koontz, Christie*
Marketing for Tomorrow, Not Yesterday — *Raj, Zain*
Marketing Literature and Posthumous Legacies: The Symbolic Capital of Leonid Andreev and Vladimir Nabokov — *Leving, Yuri*
Marketing Moxie for Librarians: Fresh Ideas, Proven Techniques, and Innovative Approaches — *Watson-Lakamp, Paula*
Marketing Schools, Marketing Cities: Who Wins and Who Loses When Schools Become Urban Amenities — *Cucchiara, Maia Bloomfield*
Marketing the Moon: The Selling of the Apollo Lunar Program — *Scott, David Meerman*
The Marketplace of Ideas: Reform and Resistance in the American University — *Menand, Louis*
Markets and Measurements in Nineteenth-Century Britain — *Velkar, Aashish*
Markets in the Name of Socialism: The Left-Wing Origins of Neoliberalism — *Bockman, Johanna*
Markets of Sorrow, Labors of Faith: New Orleans in the Wake of Katrina — *Adams, Vincanne*
Markets over Mao: The Rise of Private Business in China — *Lardy, Nicholas R.*
Marking Modern Times: A History of Clocks, Watches, and Other Timekeepers in American Life — *McCrossen, Alexis*
Marking Time: Derrida, Blanchot, Beckett, des Forets, Klossowski, Laporte — *Maclachlan, Ian*

Marks of an Absolute Witch: Evidentiary Dilemmas in Early Modern England — *Darr, Orna Alyagon*
Marksman's Trinity — *Uglow, Loyd*
c Markus "Notch" Persson — *Orr, Tamra*
c Marlene and Sofia: A Double Love Story — *Barrento, Pedro*
c Marlene, Marlene, Queen of Mean (Illus. by Tusa, Tricia) — *Lynch, Jane*
Marlowe's Ovid: The Elegies in the Marlowe Canon — *Stapleton, M.L.*
c Marooned in the Arctic: The True Story of Ada Blackjack, the "Female Robinson Crusoe" — *Caravante, Peggy*
The Marquis — *Auricchio, Laura*
The Marquis of Anaon, vol 1: The Isle of Brac — *Vehlmann, Fabien*
Marrakech Express — *Millar, Peter*
The Marriage Act — *Everett, Alyssa*
Marriage Boot Camp: Defeat the Top Ten Marriage Killers and Build a Rock-Solid Relationship — *Carroll, Jim*
The Marriage Buyout: The Troubled Trajectory of U.S. Alimony Law — *Starnes, Cynthia Lee*
Marriage Can Be Hazardous to Your Health — *Kane, Arnold*
The Marriage Game (Read by Franklin, Julia). Audiobook Review — *Weir, Alison*
Marriage Markets: How Inequality Is Remaking the American Family — *Carbone, June*
Marriage Material — *Sanghera, Sathnam*
Marriage of Inconvenience — *Macomber, Debbie*
c The Marriage of Miss Jane Austen — *Hemingway, Collins*
The Marriage of Opposites (Read by Reuben, Gloria). Audiobook Review — *Hoffman, Alice*
The Marriage of Opposites — *Hoffman, Alice*
The Marriage of True Minds — *Field, L.L.*
Marriage on the Mend: Healing Your Relationship After Crisis, Separation, or Divorce — *Bragg, Clint*
Marriage on Trial: Late Medieval German Couples at the Papal Court — *Schmugge, Ludwig*
The Marriage Pact — *Pullen, M.J.*
The Marriage Recital — *Grant, Katharine*
Married Sex — *Kornbluth, Jesse*
Married to a Perfect Stranger — *Ashford, Jane*
y Marry, Kiss, Kill — *Flett-Giordano, Anne*
The Marrying Kind? Debating Same-Sex Marriage within the Lesbian and Gay Movement — *Bernstein, Mary*
c Mars — *Bloom, J.P.*
c Mars — *Carney, Elizabeth*
y Mars Evacuees — *McDougall, Sophia*
c Mars: Red Rocks and Dust — *Markovics, Joyce*
Marseille Noir — *Fabre, Cedric*
y The Marsh Demon (Illus. by Evergreen, Nelson) — *Hulme-Cross, Benjamin*
c The Marsh Road Mysteries: Diamonds and Daggers (Illus. by Reed, Nathan) — *Caldecott, Elen*
Marshlands — *Olshan, Matthew*
The Marshmallow Test: Mastering Self-Control — *Mischel, Walter*
The Marshmallow Test: Understanding Self-Control and How to Master It — *Mischel, Walter*
Marsilio Ficino: Index Rerum — *Kugelmeier, Christoph*
c Marston, Elsa (Illus. by Ewart, Claire) — *Marston, Ewart, Claire*
Martha Jefferson Randolph: Republican Daughter and Plantation Mistress — *Wayson, Billy L.*
Martial Bliss: The Story of The Military Bookman — *Colt, Margaretta Barton*
The Martian (Read by Bray, R.C.). Audiobook Review — *Weir, Andy*
The Martian — *Weir, Andy*
The Martian Chronicles — *Bradbury, Ray*
The Martian — *Weir, Andy*
y MARTians — *Woolston, Blythe*
Martin Delrio: Demonology and Scholarship in the Counter-Reformation — *Machielsen, Jan*
Martin Harbottle's Appreciation of Time — *Utton, Dominic*
Martin John — *Schofield, Anakana*
Martin Luther, 2d ed. — *Mullett, Michael A.*
c Martin Luther King, Jr. Day — *Dash, Meredith*
Martin Luther King Jr., Heroism, and African American Literature — *Harris, Trudier*
Martin Luther: Visionary Reformer — *Hendrix, Scott H.*
Martin Luther's Anti-Semitism: Against His Better Judgment — *Gritsch, Eric W.*
y Martin Marten — *Doyle, Brian*

y Martin Marten (Illus. by van Dusen, Katrina) — Doyle, Brian
y Martin Marten — Doyle, Brian
   Martin Ramirez: Framing His Life and Art — Espinosa, Victor M.
   Martini Regrets — Smallman, Phyllis
   The Martini Shot: A Novella and Stories (Read by Graham, Dion). Audiobook Review — Pelecanos, George
   The Martini Shot: A Novella and Stories — Pelecanos, George
   The Martini Shot and Other Stories — Pelecanos, George
c Marty the Masked Marvel: Dragonasaurus Tales (Illus. by Young, Josephine) — Young, Josephine
   The Martyrdom of Abolitionist Charles Torrey — Torrey, E. Fuller
y Marvel and a Wonder — Meno, Joe
c The Marvellous Fluffy Squishy Itty Bitty (Illus. by Alemagna, Beatrice) — Alemagna, Beatrice
   The Marvelous Clouds: Toward a Philosophy of Elemental Media — Peters, John Durham
c Marvelous Cornelius: Hurricane Katrina and the Spirit of New Orleans (Illus. by Parra, John) — Bildner, Phil
   Marvelous Things Overheard — Mlinko, Ange
y The Marvels (Illus. by Selznick, Brian) — Selznick, Brian
   Marvin Miller: Baseball Revolutionary — Burk, Robert F.
   Marx and Nature: A Red and Green Perspective — Burkett, Paul
   Marxism and the Making of China: A Doctrinal History — Gregor, A. James
   Marxistische Geschichtskulturen und soziale Bewegungen wahrend des Kalten Krieges in Westeuropa
   Mary Ann Carroll: First Lady of the Highwaymen — Monroe, Gary
   Mary Butts and British Neo-Romanticism: The Enchantment of Place — Radford, Andrew
c Mary Cassatt: Extraordinary Impressionist Painter (Illus. by Swiatkowska, Gabi) — Herkert, Barbara
   Mary Ellen Mark: Tiny, Streetwise Revisited — Mark, Mary Ellen
   Mary Jane: The Complete Marijuana Handbook for Women — Sicard, Cheri
   Mary Lincoln, Wife and Widow — Sandburg, Carl
   Mary Magdalene and Her Sister Martha: An Edition and Translation of the Medieval Welsh Lives — Cartwright, Jane
   Mary McGrory: The First Queen of Journalism — Norris, John
c Mary Molds a Monster (Illus. by Bernard, Courtney) — Mullarkey, Lisa
   Mary Pickford: Canada's Silent Siren, America's Sweetheart — Leavey, Peggy Dymond
c Mary Poppins: 80th Anniversary Collection (Illus. by Shepard, Mary) — Travers, P.L.
c Mary: The Summoning — Monahan, Hillary
c Mary Todd Lincoln (Illus. by Baddley, Elizabeth) — Krull, Kathleen
   Mary Tudor — Hugo, Victor
   Mary Wollstonecraft and Feminist Republicanism — Halldenius, Lena
c Mary's Wild Winter Feast (Illus. by Koch, Nobu) — Lindoff, Hannah
   MAS: The Modern Architecture Symposia, 1962-1966 — Bletter, Rosemarie Haag
   Masculindians: Conversations about Indigenous Manhood — McKegney, Sam
   Masculinities in Chinese History — Hinsch, Bret
   Masculinity after Trujillo: The Politics of Gender in Dominican Literature — Horn, Maja
   Masculinity and Sexuality in Modern Mexico — Macias-Gonzalez, Victor M.
   Masculinity and the Hunt: Wyatt to Spenser — Bates, Catherine
   Masculinity and the New Imperialism: Rewriting Manhood in British Popular Literature, 1870-1914 — Deane, Bradley
   Masculinity in the Contemporary Romantic Comedy: Gender as Genre — Alberti, John
   Masculinity in the Reformation Era — Hendrix, Scott H.
   Mashi: The Unfulfilled Baseball Dreams of Masanori Murakami, the First Japanese Major Leaguer — Fitts, Robert K.
   The Mask — Stevens, Taylor
   Mask of the Verdoy — Lecomber, Phil
   Masked: The Life of Anna Leonowens, Schoolmistress at the Court of Siam — Habegger, Alfred

y The Masked Truth — Armstrong, Kelley
c Mason Jar Crafts for Kids — Braden, Linda Z.
   Mason, Paul
y The Masque of a Murderer — Calkins, Susanna
   The Masquerading Magician — Pandian, Gigi
   Mass Flourishing: How Grassroots Innovation Created Jobs, Challenge, and Change — Phelps, Edmund S.
   Mass Incarceration on Trial: A Remarkable Court Decision and the Future of Prisons in America — Simon, Jonathan
   The Mass Observers: A History, 1937-1949 — Hinton, James
   Massacre at Point of Rocks — Hocking, Doug
   Massacre Gun — Hasebe, Yasuharu
   A Massacre in Memphis: The Race Riot That Shook the Nation One Year After the Civil War — Ash, Stephen V.
y Massacre of the Miners — Anderson, T. Neill
   Massacre on the Merrimack: Hannah Duston's Captivity and Revenge in Colonial America — Atkinson, Jay
   Massacre: The Life and Death of the Paris Commune — Merriman, John
   Massive Pissed Love — Hell, Richard
   Massive Resistance and Media Suppression: The Segregationist Response to Dissent during the Civil Rights Movement — Wallace, David J.
   The Master — Me, Tara Sue
   The Master Algorithm: How the Quest for the Ultimate Learning Machine Will Remake Our World — Domingos, Pedro
   The Master Algorithm — Domingos, Pedro
   The Master Communicator's Handbook — Erickson, Teresa
   The Master of Confessions: The Making of a Khmer Rouge Torturer (Illus. by Gilly, Alex) — Cruvellier, Thierry
   Master of Shadows — Oliver, Neil
   The Master of the Prado — Sierra, Javier
   Master of Thin Air: Life and Death on the World's Highest Peaks — Lock, Andrew
y A Master Plan for Rescue — Newman, Janis Cooke
   Master Thieves: The Boston Gangsters Who Pulled Off the World's Greatest Art Heist — Kurkjian, Stephen
   Master Thieves: The Boston Gangsters Who Pulled Off the World's Greatest Art Heist (Read by Chamberlain, Mike). Audiobook Review — Kurkjian, Stephen
   Master Thieves: The Boston Gangsters Who Pulled Off the World's Greatest Art Heist — Kurkjian, Stephen
   Master Thomas Aquinas and the Fullness of Life — Boyle, John F. (b. 1958-)
   The Master Yeshua: The Undiscovered Gospel of Joseph — Luck, Joyce
   Master Your Brain: Training Your Mind for Success in Life — Adcock, Phillip
   Mastering Chaos: The Metafictional Worlds of Evgeny Popov — Morris, Jeremy
   Mastering Iron: The Struggle to Modernize an American Iron Industry, 1800-1868 — Knowles, Anne Kelly
   Mastering "Metrics": The Path from Cause to Effect — Angrist, Joshua D.
   Mastering Negative Impulsive Thoughts — MacIntosh, Harold J.
   Mastering Pasta: The Art and Practice of Handmade Pasta, Gnocchi, and Risotto — Vetri, Marc
   Mastering Sauces: The Home Cook's Guide to New Techniques for Fresh Flavors — Volland, Susan
   Mastering the Art of Vegan Cooking: Over 200 Delicious Recipes and Tips to Save You Money and Stock Your Pantry — Shannon, Annie
   Mastering the Niger: James MacQueen's African Geography and the Struggle over Atlantic Slavery — Lambert, David
c The Mastermind — Unger, David
c Masterminds — Korman, Gordon
   Masterminds — Rusch, Kristine Kathryn
c Masterminds — Korman, Gordon
   The Masters at Home: Recipes, Stories and Photographs — Bloomsbury Publishing
   Masters' Mysterium — Reynolds, R.R.
   Masters of Craft: 224 Artists in Fiber, Clay, Glass, Metal, and Wood — Smith, Paul J.
c Masters of Disguise — Johnson, Rebecca L.
   Masters of Empire: Great Lakes Indians and the Making of America — McDonnell, Michael A.
   Masters, Slaves, and Exchange: Power's Purchase in the Old South — Hillard, Kathleen M.

   Masters, Slaves, and Exchange: Power's Purchase in the Old South — Hilliard, Kathleen M.
   The Masters Workshop Collection — Cornelius, James Bryan
c The Matawehi Fables: Arohanui: Revenge of the Fey — Pearse-Otene, Helen
c The Matawehi Fables: Meariki: The Quest for Truth — Pearse-Otene, Helen
   A Match for Marcus Cynster — Laurens, Stephanie
   The Match Girl and the Heiress — Koven, Seth
   The Match of the Century: Marrying the Duke — Maxwell, Cathy
   A Match to Die For — Mathews, Ellen
   Matchbox Theatre: Thirty Short Entertainments — Frayn, Michael
   The Matchmaker (Read by Bennett, Erin). Audiobook Review — Hilderbrand, Elin
   Mate Bond — Ashley, Jennifer
   Material Culture and Authenticity: Fake Branded Fashion in Europe — Craciun, Magdalena
   The Material Gene: Gender, Race, and Heredity After the Human Genome Project — Happe, Kelley E.
y Material Girls — Dimopoulos, Elaine
   Material Relations: The Marriage Figurines of Prehispanic Honduras — Hendon, Julia A.
   A Materialism for the Masses: Saint Paul and the Philosophy of Undying Life — Blanton, Ward
   Materiality and Consumption in the Bronze Age Mediterranean — Steel, Louise
   The Materiality of the Past: History and Representation in Sikh Tradition — Murphy, Anne
   Materially Crafted: A DIY Primer for the Design-Obsessed — Hudgins, Victoria
c Materials Engineering and Exploring Properties — Snedden, Robert
   Maternal Megalomania. Julia Domna and the Imperial Politics of Motherhood — Langford, Julie
   Maternity Leave — Halpern, Julie
y Math — Buckley, James, Jr.
c Math at the Art Museum (Illus. by Kim, Yun-ju) — Group Majoongmul
   Math Bytes: Google Bombs, Chocolate-Covered Pi, and Other Cool Bits in Computing — Chartier, Tim
c Math for All Seasons (Illus. by Briggs, Harry) — Tang, Greg
   Math Is a Verb: Activities and Lessons from Cultures around the World — Barkley, Cathy
c A Math Journey through Planet Earth — Rooney, Anne
c A Math Journey through Space — Rooney, Anne
c A Math Journey through the Animal Kingdom — Rooney, Anne
c A Math Journey through the Human Body — Rooney, Anne
c A Math Journey through the Planet Earth — Rooney, Anne
   Math & Me: Embracing Success — Smith, Wendy Hageman
   The Math Myth — Hacker, Andrew
c Math on the Move — Marsico, Katie
c Math World Series (Illus. by Longhi, Katya) — Heos, Bridget
   Mathematical Couriosities: A Treasure Trove of Unexpected Entertainments — Posamentier, Alfred S.
   Mathematical Models for Teaching Reasoning without Memorization — Kajander, Ann
   Mathematical Theologies: Nicholas of Cusa and the Legacy of Thierry of Chartres — Albertson, David
   Mathematical Tools for Understanding Infectious Disease Dynamics — Diekmann, Odo
   A Mathematician's Lament: How School Cheats Us Out of Our Most Fascinating and Imaginative Art Form — Lockhart, Paul
   Mathematicians on Creativity — Borwein, Peter B.
   The Mathematician's Shiva — Rojstczer, Stuart
   Mathematics and the Real World: The Remarkable Role of Evolution in the Making of Mathematics — Artstein, Zvi
   Mathematics for Equity: A Framework for Successful Practice — Nasir, Na'ilah Suad
   Mathematics for the Liberal Arts — Brown, Jason I.
c Mathematics Lessons Learned from across the World, Prekindergarten-Grade 8 — Lott, Johnny W.
   Mathematics without Apologies: Porteait of a Problematic vocation — Harris, Michael
   Mathematics without Apologies: Portrait of a Problematic Vocation — Harris, Michael
   Mathematizing: An Emergent Math Curriculum Approach for Young Children — Rosales, Allen C.

The Matheny Manifesto: A Young Manager's Old-School Views on Success in Sports and Life — Matheny, Mike
Matiere de France oder Matiere des Francs? Die germanische Heldenepik und die Anfange der Chanson de Geste — Borgmann, Nils
Matisse in the Barnes Foundation — Bois, Yve-Alain
c Matisse's Garden (Illus. by Amodeo, Cristina) — Friedman, Samantha
The Matiushin Case — Pavlov, Oleg
The Matriarch of Ruins — McDaniels, Edison
The Matter and Form of Maimonides' Guide — Stern, Josef
Matter and Method in the Long Chemical Revolution: Laws of Another Order — Boantza, Victor D.
The Matter Factory: A History of the Chemistry Laboratory — Morris, Peter J.T.
A Matter of Conduct: The True Story of a Man Who Battled a Bank and Won — Yap, Dalton
A Matter of Grave Concern (Read by Page, Michael). Audiobook Review — Novak, Brenda
y A Matter of Heart — Dominy, Amy Fellner
Matthew Boulton: Enterprising Industrialist of the Enlightenment — Quickenden, Kenneth
Matthew Boulton: Enterprising Industrialist of the Enlightenment — Baggott, Sally
Matthew Fontaine Maury, Father of Oceanography: A Biography, 1806-1873 — Grady, John
A Mattress Maker's Daughter: The Renaissance Romance of Don Giovanni de' Medici and Livia Vernazza — Dooley, Brendan
Mature Themes — Durbin, Andrew
Maud's Line — Verble, Margaret
Maureen O'Hara: The Biography — Malone, Aubrey
Maurice Dobb: Political Economist — Shenk, Timothy
Maverick Mark: The Untamed First Gospel — Thurston, Bonnie
c Max and Bear (Illus. by Adams, Stephen) — Saxelby, Pam
c Max and Marla (Illus. by Boiger, Alexandra) — Boiger, Alexandra
c Max and the Won't Go to Bed Show (Illus. by Warburton, Sarah) — Sperring, Mark
c Max and Voltaire: Getting to Know You (Illus. by Choquette, Gabriel) — Bail, Mina Mauerstein
Max Beckmann: The Still Lives — Schick, Karin
c Max Goes to the Space Station (Illus. by Carroll, Michael) — Bennett, Jeffrey
c Max Helsing and the Thirteenth Curse — Jobling, Curtis
Max Hildebert Boehm: Radikales Ordnungsdenken vom Ersten Weltkrieg bis in die Bundesrepublik — Prehn, Ulrich
c Max & Ruby at the Warthogs' Wedding (Illus. by Wells, Rosemary) — Wells, Rosemary
c Max the Brave (Illus. by Vere, Ed) — Vere, Ed
Max Weber and 'The Protestant Ethic': Twin Histories — Ghosh, Peter
Max Weber and the Protestant Ethic: Twin Histories — Ghosh, Peter
Max Weber: Ein Leben zwischen den Epochen — Kaube, Jurgen
Max Weber in Politics and Social Thought: From Charisma to Canonization — Derman, Joshua
Max Weber: Preusse, Denker, Muttersohn, Eine Biographie — Kaesler, Dirk
Max Weber's Theory of Personality: Individuation, Politics and Orientalism in the Sociology of Religion — Farris, Sara R.
c Maxi and the Magical Money Tree — Hall, Tiffany
c Maxi the Little Taxi (Illus. by Cole, Henry) — Upton, Elizabeth
Maximilian and Carlota: Europe's Last Empire in Mexico — Amberson, Mary Margaret McAllen
Maximizing Profits: A Practical Guide for Portrait Photographers — Nordstrom, Lori
Maximus — Black, Richard L.
c Max's Math (Illus. by Kulikov, Boris) — Banks, Kate
c Maxx Airborne and the Legends of Rucker Park — Barnett, Scot
y May I Quote You on That? A Guide to Grammar and Usage — Spector, Stephen
Maya after War: Conflict, Power and Politics in Guatemala — Burrell, Jennifer L.
Maya Art and Architecture, 2d ed. — Miller, Mary Ellen
Maya Creation Myths: Words and Worlds of the Chilam Balam — Knowlton, Timothy W.
Maya Deren: Incomplete Control — Keller, Sarah
c Maya et Mitaine: De Saint-Jean a Paris (Illus. by Roy, Rejean) — Duguay, Joanie

Maya Ideologies of the Sacred: The Transfiguration of Space in Colonial Yucatan — Solari, Amara
Maya Lords and Lordship: The Formation of Colonial Society in Yucatan, 1350-1600 — Quezada, Sergio
c Maya Moore: WNBA Champion — Ervin, Phil
Maya Pilgrimage to Natural Landscapes: Insights from Archaeology, History, and Ethnography — Palka, Joel W.
Mayakovsky: A Biography — Jangfeldt, Bengt
c Maya's Blanket / La Manta de Maya (Illus. by Diaz, David) — Brown, Monica
c Maya's Blanket/La manta de Maya (Illus. by Diaz, David) — Brown, Monica
c Maybe a Fox — Appelt, Kathi
Maybe in Another Life — Reid, Taylor
Maybe in Another Life — Reid, Taylor Jenkins
y Maybe One Day — Kantor, Melissa
c Maybe Something Beautiful: How Art Transformed a Neighborhood (Illus. by Lopez, Rafael) — Campoy, F. Isabel
c Maybelle Goes to School (Illus. by de Tagyos, Paul Ratz) — Speck, Katie
c Maybelle Goes to School (Illus. by Tagyos, Paul Ratz) — Speck, Katie
c The Mayflower (Illus. by Lessac, Frane) — Greenwood, Mark
c Mayhem — Pinborough, Sarah
Mayhem at Buffalo Bill's Wild West: A Jemmy McBustle Mystery — Amis, Fedora
c The Maypop Kidnapping — Surrisi, C.M.
Mayumi and the Sea of Happiness — Tseng, Jennifer
Maze of Blood — Youmans, Marly
The Maze Runner Collector's Edition: The Scorch Trials — Dashner, James
c Mazel Tov! It's a Boy/Mazel Tov! It's a Girl — Korngold, Jamie
c Mazel Tov! It's a Boy/Mazel Tov! It's a Girl (Illus. by Finkelstein, Jeff) — Korngold, Jamie
c Mazel Tov! It's a Boy/Mazel Tov! It's a Girl — Korngold, Jamie
McCann — Benacre, John
c McToad Mows Tiny Island (Illus. by Hendrix, John) — Angleberger, Tom
c The McVentures of Me, Morgan McFactoid: Hair Today, Gone Tomorrow — Waxman, Mark S.
y Me and Earl and the Dying Girl (Read by Various readers). Audiobook Review — Andrews, Jesse
y Me and Earl and the Dying Girl — Andrews, Jesse
c Me and My Cat — Trukhan, Ekaterina
c Me and My Dad! (Illus. by Edgson, Alison) — Ritchie, Alison
Me and My Daddy Listen to Bob Marley: Novellas & Stories — Pancake, Ann
c Me and My Day — Slegers, Liesbet
c Me and My Dragon: Christmas Spirit (Illus. by Biedrzycki, David) — Biedrzycki, David
c Me and My Dragon (Illus. by Biedrzycki, David) — Biedrzycki, David
y Me Being Me Is Exactly as Insane as You Being You — Hasak-Lowy, Todd
c Me & Dog (Illus. by Shansby, Eric) — Weingarten, Gene
Me, Inc. — Simmons, Gene
Me ... Jane (Read by Kellgren, Katherine). Audiobook Review — McDonnell, Patrick
Me, Margarita — Kordzaia-Samadashvili, Ana
The Me, Me, Me Epidemic: A Step-by-Step Guide to Raising Capable, Grateful Kids in an Over-Entitled World — McCready, Amy
Me molivi Faber noumero dyo — Zei, Alke
y Me, My Hair, and I: Twenty-Seven Women Untangle an Obsession — Benedict, Elizabeth
Me, Rain, and a Hired Taxi — Safdarian, Davoud
c Me, Too! (Illus. by Smith, Lori Joy) — Dunklee, Annika
y Meadowlands — Jeffrey, Elizabeth
Meadowlark Economics — Eggert, James
Meals in the Early Christian World: Social Formation, Experimentation, and Conflict at the Table — Smith, Dennis E.
c The Mean Girl Meltdown (Illus. by Hanson, Sydney) — Eyre, Lindsay
c The Mean Girl Meltdown — Eyre, Lindsay
Mean Lives, Mean Laws: Oklahoma's Women Prisoners — Sharp, Susan F.
c Mean Margaret (Illus. by Agee, Jon) — Seidler, Tor
Meaning in Life: An Analytic Study — Metz, Thaddeus
The Meaning of Conservatism — Scruton, Roger
The Meaning of Freedom: And Other Difficult Dialogues — Davis, Angela Y.

The Meaning of Human Existence (Read by Hogan, Jonathan). Audiobook Review — Wilson, Edward O.
The Meaning of Human Existence — Wilson, Edward O.
The Meaning of Names — Shoemaker, Karen Gettert
The Meaning of Science: An Introduction to the Philosophy of Science — Lewens, Tim
The Meaning of the Library: A Cultural History — Crawford, Alice
Meaningful Metrics: A 21st Century Librarian's Guide to Bibliometrics, Altmetrics, and Research Impact — Roemer, Robin Chin
Meaningful Places: Landscape Photographers in the Nineteenth-Century American West — Sailor, Rachel McLean
Meant for You — Chase, Samantha
Meant to Be — James, Jessica
Meanwhile There Are Letters: The Correspondence of Eudora Welty and Ross Macdonald — Marrs, Suzanne
Measure of a Man: From Auschwitz Survivor to Presidents' Tailor — Greenfield, Martin
A Measure of the Earth: The Cole-Ware Collection of American Baskets — Bell, Nicholas R.
Measure Yourself against the Earth: Essays — Kingwell, Mark
Measures of Astonishment: Poets on Poetry — Atwood, Margaret
Measuring — Alaina, Maria
The Meat Racket: The Secret Takeover of America's Food Business — Leonard, Christopher
Meathooked — Zaraska, Marta
Meatless in Cowtown: A Vegetarian Guide to Food and Wine, Texas Style — Meyn, Laura Samuel
Meatless Meals for Working People: Quick and Easy Vegetarian Recipes — Wasserman, Debra
y Meatspace — Shukla, Nikesh
Mecca: The Sacred City — Sardar, Ziauddin
y Mechanica — Cornwell, Betsy
The Mechanical — Tregillis, Ian
c Mechanical Marvels (Illus. by Connell, Tom) — Litton, Jonathan
y The Mechanical Mind of John Coggin — Teele, Elinor
Mechanisms of Morphogenesis — Davies, Jamie A.
c Mechant Minou: Quelle journee! — Bruel, Nick
c Medals and Memorials: A Readers' Theater Script and Guide (Illus. by Mata, Nina) — Wallace, Nancy K.
Medea — Taplin, Oliver
Medecine and Narration in the Eighteenth Century — Vasset, Sophie
Medecine, astrologie et magie entre Moyen Age et Renaissance: Autour de Pietro d'Abano — Boudet, Jean-Patrice
Medecine et religion: Collaborations, competitions, conflits (XIIe-Xxe siecle). — Donato, Maria Pia
Medecine et religion: Competitions, collaborations, conflits - XII-XX siecles — Donato, Maria Pia
Media and the Cold War, 1975-1991
Media Commercialization and Authoritarian Rule in China — Stockman, Daniela
Media, Erotics, and Transnational Asia — Mankekar, Purnima
The Media in Transitional Democracies — Voltmer, Katrin
Mediating Cultural Diversity in a Globalised Public Space — Rigoni, Isabelle
Mediating Culture in the Seventeenth-Century German Novel: Eberhard Werner Happel, 1647-1690 — Scholz Williams, Gerhild
The Mediating Nation: Late American Realism, Globalization, and the Progressive State — Cadle, Nathaniel
Mediating the Global: Expatria's Forms and Consequences in Kathmandu — Hindman, Heather
Mediatrix: Women, Politics, & Literary Production in Early Modern England — Crawford, Julie
The Medical Ministries of Kang Cheng and Shi Meiyu, 1872-1937 — Shemo, Connie A.
Medical Monopoly: Intellectual Property Rights and the Origins of the Modern Pharmaceutical Industry — Gabriel, Joseph M.
Medical, Psychosocial and Vocational Aspects of Disability, 4th ed. — Brodwin, Martin G.
Medical Saints: Cosmas and Damian in a Postmodern World — Duffin, Jacalyn
The Medicean Succession: Monarchy and Sacral Politics in Duke Cosimo dei Medici's Florence — Murry, Gregory
The Medici: Power, Money, and Ambition in the Italian Renaissance — Strathern, Paul

Medicine and Compassion: A Tibetan Lama and an American Doctor on How to Provide Care with Compassion and Wisdom — *Rinpoche, Chokyi Nyima*
Medicine and Religion: A Historical Introduction — *Ferngren, Gary B.*
Medicine and the Saints: Science, Islam, and the Colonial Encounter in Morocco, 1877-1956 — *Amster, Ellen J.*
Medicine between Science and Religion: Explorations on Tibetan Grounds — *Adams, Vincanne*
Medicine in Iran: Profession, Practice, and Politics, 1800-1925 — *Ebrahimnejad, Hormoz*
Medicine Walk — *Wagamese, Richard*
Medicis Daughter — *Perinot, Sophie*
Medieval and Monastic Derry: Sixth Century to 1600 — *Lacey, Brian*
Medieval and Renaissance Famagusta: Studies in Architecture, Art and History — *Walsh, Michael J.K.*
Medieval and Renaissance Lactations: Images, Rhetorics, Practices — *Sperling, Jutta Gisela*
Medieval Childhood: Archaeological Approaches — *Hadley, Dawn M.*
Medieval Christianity: A New History (Read by Larkin, Pete). Audiobook Review — *Madigan, Kevin*
Medieval Christianity: A New History — *Madigan, Kevin*
Medieval Crossover: Reading the Secular against the Sacred — *Newman, Barbara*
The Medieval Culture of Disputation: Pedagogy, Practice, and Performance — *Novikoff, Alex J.*
Medieval European Coinage, vol. 6: The Iberian Peninsula — *Crusafont, Miquel*
The Medieval Filmscape: Reflections of Fear and Desire in a Cinematic Mirror — *Woods, William F.*
Medieval Hackers — *Kennedy, Kathleen E.*
Medieval Invasions in Modern Irish Literature — *Ulin, Julieann Veronica*
The Medieval Kirk, Cemetery and Hospice at Kirk Ness, North Berwick: The Scottish Seabird Center Excavations 1999-2006 — *Romankiewicz, Tanja*
The Medieval Kirk, Cemetery and Hospice at Kirk Ness, North Berwick: The Scottish Seabird Centre Excavations 1999-2006 — *Addyman, Thomas*
A Medieval Latin Miscellany: An Intermediate Reader — *Robson, Art*
The Medieval Manuscripts at Maynooth: Explorations in the Unknown — *Lucas, Peter J.*
The Medieval Motion Picture: The Politics of Adaptation — *Johnston, Andrew James*
Medieval Mythography, vol. 3: The Emergence of Italian Humanism, 1321-1475 — *Chance, Jane*
The Medieval Oliphant — *Shalem, Avinoam*
Medieval Oral Literature — *Reichl, Karl*
The Medieval Papacy — *Whalen, Brett Edward*
Medieval Romance and Material Culture — *Perkins, Nicholas*
The Medieval Romance of Alexander: The Deeds and Conquests of Alexander the Great — *Wauquelin, Jehan*
Medieval Rome: Stability and Crisis of a City, 900-1150 — *Wickham, Chris*
The Medieval Salento: Art and Identity in Southern Italy — *Safran, Linda*
The Medieval Shepherd: Jean de Brie's Le Bon Berger, 1379 — *Carroll, Carleton W.*
Medieval Tastes: Food, Cooking, and the Table — *Montanari, Massimo*
Medievalism: A Critical History — *Matthews, David*
Medievalism: Key Critical Terms — *Emery, Elizabeth*
Medievisme et Lumieres: le Moyen Age dans la "Bibliotheque universelle des romans" — *Sigu, Veronique*
Meditation as a Way of Life: Philosophy and Practice — *Pritz, Alan L.*
c Meditation Is an Open Sky: Mindfulness for Kids (Illus. by Rippin, Sally) — *Stewart, Whitney*
Meditations — *Marcus Aurelius*
Meditations on a Heritage: Papers on the Work and Legacy of Sir Ernst Gombrich — *Taylor, Paul*
MeditationSwerve: Your Very Own Jackass Sweetheart Meditation Companion — *Li, Larry*
The Mediterranean Air War: Airpower and Allied Victory in World War II — *Ehlers, Jr., Robert S.*
The Mediterranean Family Table: 125 Simple, Everyday Recipes Made with the Most Delicious and Healthiest Food on Earth — *Acquista, Angelo*
Mediterranean Identities in the Premodern Era: Entrepots, Islands, Empires — *Watkins, John*
Mediterranean Journey — *Eyerman, Ann*

Mediterranes Kaisertum und imperiale Ordnungen: Das lateinische Kaiserreich von Konstantinopel — *Burkhardt, Stefan*
Medizin und Religion, Heilkunde und Seelsorge. Jahrestagung 2015 des Vereins fur Sozialgeschichte der Medizin - Geschichte(n) von Gesundheit und Krankheit
Medizinische Belehrung fur das Burgertum: Medikale Kulturen in der Zeitschrift "Die Gartenlaube" — *Mildenberger, Florian*
Medusa's Web — *Powers, Tim*
c Meerkat's Burrow — *Phillips, Dee*
y Meet Banjo Peterson (Illus. by Hancock, James Gulliver) — *Weidenbach, Kristin*
c Meet Dizzy Dinosaur! — *Tickle, Jack*
Meet Me at the Beach — *Sykes, V.K.*
Meet Me Halfway: Milwaukee Stories — *Morales, Jennifer*
Meet Me in Atlantis: My Obsessive Quest to Find the Sunken City (Read by Garman, Andrew). Audiobook Review — *Adams, Mark*
Meet Me in Atlantis: My Obsessive Quest to Find the Sunken City — *Adams, Mark*
y Meet Me in Venice: A Chinese Immigrant's Journey from the Far East to the Faraway West — *Ma, Suzanne*
c Meet the Ancient Egyptians — *Abbott, Simon*
c Meet the Bigfeet — *Sherry, Kevin*
c Meet the Dullards (Illus. by Salmieri, Daniel) — *Pennypacker, Sara*
c Meet the Incredible Romans — *Abbott, Simon*
c Meet Weary Dunlop (Illus. by Lord, Jeremy) — *Saxby, Claire*
Meeting China Halfway: How to Defuse the Emerging US-China Rivalry — *Goldstein, Lyle J.*
Meeting God in Mark: Reflections for the Season of Lent — *Williams, Rowan*
Meeting in the Margins: An Invitation to Encounter Society's Invisible People — *Trenshaw, Cynthia*
Meeting the English — *Clanchy, Kate*
c Meg Goldberg on Parade (Illus. by Lyles, Christopher) — *Rosenbaum, Andrea*
c Meg Goldberg on Parade (Illus. by Lyles, Christopher) — *Rosenbaum, Andria*
c Mega Bunny (Illus. by Barroux) — *Vidal, Severine*
c Mega Mouse (Illus. by Barroux, Stephanie) — *Vidal, Severine*
c Mega Pig (Illus. by Barroux) — *Vidal, Severine*
c Mega Wolf (Illus. by Barroux, Stephanie) — *Vidal, Severine*
c Megafast Trucks — *Farndon, John*
c Megan Owlet (Illus. by Maresca, Beth Anne) — *Maresca, Beth Anne*
Mehrsprachigkeit in der Fruhen Neuzeit — *Gluck, Helmut*
Meiji Restoration Losers: Memory and Tokugawa Supporters in Modern Japan — *Wert, Michael*
Meisterschaft im Prozess: Der Lange Ton Frauenlobs - Texte und Studien — *Wenzel, Franziska*
Melancholy II — *Fosse, Jon*
Melancholy Manor — *DeFarr, Ellie*
y Meli's Way — *Willis, Meredith Sue*
c Melissa's Octopus and Other Unsuitable Pets (Illus. by Voake, Charlotte) — *Voake, Charlotte*
Melody: Story of a Nude Dancer (Illus. by Rancourt, Sylvie) — *Rancourt, Sylvie*
The Melon Capital of the World — *Allmendinger, Blake*
c Melonhead and the Later Gator Plan (Illus. by Johnson, Gillian) — *Kelly, Katy*
Meltdown in Haditha: The Killing of 24 Iraqi Civilians by US Marines and the Failure of Military Justice — *Englade, Kenneth F.*
Melting Away: A Ten-Year Journey through Our Endangered Polar Regions — *Seaman, Camille*
Melville: Fashioning in Modernity — *Matterson, Stephen*
c Melvis and Elvis (Illus. by Tankard, Jeremy) — *Lee, Dennis*
Members Only: Secret Societies, Sects, and Cults--Exposed! — *Tibbott, Julie*
Memento Mori: The Dead among Us — *Koudounaris, Paul*
Memoires sur le XVIIIe siecle et sur la Revolution — *Morellet, Andre*
Memoirs of a Ghost: One Sheet Away — *Cagan, Andrea*
c Memoirs of a Neurotic Zombie, 2: Escape from Camp — *Norton, Jeff*
c Memoirs of a Neurotic Zombie: Escape from Camp
c Memoirs of an Elf (Illus. by Bowers, Tim) — *Scillian, Devin*

Memoirs of Casanova — *Casanova, Giacomo*
MemoRandom — *de la Motte, Anders*
Memoria Romana: Memory in Rome and Rome in Memory — *Galinsky, Karl*
The Memorial Art and Architecture of Vicksburg National Military Park — *Panhorst, Michael W.*
Memoriale: Edizione critica — *Foligno, Angela of*
Memories — *Partridge, Frances*
Memories of Absence: How Muslims Remember Jews in Morocco — *Boum, Aomar*
Memories of London — *De Amicis, Edmondo*
Memories of Mount Qilai — *Mu, Yang*
Memories of Thompson Orphanage: Charlotte, North Carolina — *Batson, Stella Henson Griggs*
Memory and Complicity: Migrations of Holocaust Remembrance — *Sanyal, Debarati*
Memory and Covenant: The Role of Israel's and God's Memory in Sustaining the Deuteronomic and Priestly Covenants — *Ellman, Barat*
Memory and Movies: What Films Can Teach Us about Memory — *Seamon, John*
Memory and Myths of the Norman Conquest — *Brownlie, Siobhan*
Memory and Religious Experience in the Greco-Roman World — *Cusumano, Nicola*
Memory as Burden and Liberation: Germans and their Nazi Past (1945-2010). — *Wolff-Poweska, Anna*
Memory Hold-the-Door: The Autobiography of John Buchan — *Buchan, John*
Memory in Vergil's Aeneid: Creating the Past — *Seider, Aaron M.*
y The Memory Key — *Liu, Liana*
Memory Man (Read by McLarty, Ron). Audiobook Review — *Baldacci, David*
Memory Man — *Baldacci, David*
c Memory Maze — *Korman, Gordon*
c The Memory of an Elephant: An Unforgettable Journey (Illus. by Martin, Jean-Francois) — *Strady, Sophie*
y The Memory of Light — *Francisco X*
y The Memory of Light — *Stork, Francisco X.*
The Memory of Stone: Meditations on the Canyons of the West (Illus. by Schroeder, Erv) — *Schroeder, Erv*
The Memory of the People: Custom and Popular Senses of the Past in Early Modern England — *Wood, Andy*
The Memory of Time: Contemporary Photographs at the National Gallery of Art — *Greenough, Sarah*
A Memory of Violets — *Gaynor, Hazel*
The Memory Painter — *Womack, Gwendolyn*
c The Memory Shed (Illus. by Smith, Craig) — *Morgan, Sally*
c The Memory Singer — *King, T. Jackson*
Memory Theater — *Critchley, Simon*
Memory Theatre — *Critchley, Simon*
The Memory Weaver — *Kirkpatrick, Jane*
Memphis Noir — *Cantwell, Laureen P.*
Men at the Center: Redemptive Governance under Louis IX — *Jordan, William Chester*
Men in Green — *Bamberger, Michael*
Men: Notes from an Ongoing Investigation — *Kipnis, Laura*
Men of Bronze: Hoplite Warfare in Classical Greece — *Kagan, Donald*
Men of Feeling in Eighteenth-Century Literature: Touching Fiction — *Wetmore, Alex*
Men of Violence: A John Henry Cole Story — *Brooks, Bill*
Men of War: The American Soldier in Combat at Bunker Hill, Gettysburg, and Iwo Jima — *Rose, Alexander*
Men to Devils, Devils to Men: Japanese War Crimes and Chinese Justice — *Kushner, Barak*
The Men Who Made the Yankees: The Odyssey of the World's Greatest Team from Baltimore to the Bronx — *Nikola-Lisa, W.*
The Men with the Movie Camera: The Poetics of Visual Style in Soviet Avant-Garde Cinema of the 1920s — *Cavendish, Philip*
Menagerie — *Vincent, Rachel*
Menander: Samia — *Sommerstein, A.H.*
Mendicants and Merchants in the Medieval Mediterranean — *Chubb, Taryn E.L.*
y Mending Horses — *Barker, M.P.*
Mendocino Fire — *Tallent, Elizabeth*
Mendocino Fire: Stories — *Tallent, Elizabeth*
y Meningitis — *Craig, Lizabeth*
c The Menino: A Story Based on Real Events (Illus. by Isol) — *Isol*
The Men's Section: Orthodox Jewish Men in an Egalitarian World — *Sztokman, Elana Maryles*

Menstruation and the Female Body in Early Modern England — Read, Sara
Mental (Dis)Order in Later Medieval Europe — Katajala-Peltomaa, Sari
Mental Hygiene and Psychiatry in Modern Britain — Toms, Jonathan
Mentoring A to Z — Todaro, Julie
The Menzies Era: The Years that Shaped Modern Australia — Howard, John
Mercantilism Reimagined: Political Economy in Early Modern Britain and Its Empire — Stern, Philip J.
Mercenari: Il mestiere delle armi nel mondo greco antico — Bettalli, Marco
The Merchants' Capital: New Orleans and the Political Economy of the Nineteenth-Century South — Marler, Scott P.
Merchants of Culture: The Publishing Business in the Twenty-First Century — Thompson, John B.
Merchants of Independence: International Trade on the Santa Fe Trail, 1827-1860 — O'Brien, William Patrick
y The Merciless — Vega, Danielle
Mercurino di Gattinara and the Creation of the Spanish Empire — Boone, Rebecca Ard
Mercury and the Making of California: Mining, Landscape, and Race, 1840-1890 — Johnston, Andrew Scott
Mercury Retrograde. E-book Review — Bickle, Laura
Mercury Striking — Zanetti, Rebecca
Mercy in the City: How to Feed the Hungry, Give Drink to the Thirsty, Visit the Imprisoned, and Keep Your Day Job — Weber, Kerry
y Mercy Mode — Garner, Em
Mercy of a Rude Stream: The Complete Novels — Roth, Henry
The Mercy of the Night — Corbett, David
The Mercy of the Sky: The Story of a Tornado — Bailey, Holly
The Mercy Seat — Price, Wayne
Mercy: The Essence of the Gospel and the Key to Christian Life — Kasper, Walter
Mergers and Alliances: The Wider View, the Operational View and Cases — Penniman, W. David
y Meridian — McQuein, Joisin L.
y The Merit Birds — Powell, Kelley
Merit: The History of a Founding Ideal from the American Revolution to the Twenty-First Century — Kett, Joseph F.
Merkantilismus: Wiederaufnahme einer Debatte — Moritz, Isenmann
c Mermaid (Illus. by Anderson, Laura Ellen) — Burnell, Cerrie
The Mermaid Chair — Kidd, Sue Monk
The Mermaid Collector — Marks, Erika
Mermaid Moon — Coble, Colleen
Mermaids — Kingshill, Sophia
y The Mermaid's Child — Baker, Jo
c The Mermaid's Gift (Illus. by Wagoner, Traci Van) — McAdam, Claudia Cangilla
Mermaids in Paradise (Read by Campbell, Cassandra). Audiobook Review — Millet, Lydia
Mermaids in Paradise — Millet, Lydia
Mermaids — Kingshill, Sophia
c The Mermaid's Shoes — te Loo, Sanne
y The Mermaid's Sister — Noble, Carrie Anne
The Merman — Vallgren, Carl-Johan
c Merry Christmas, Bugs! — Carter, David A.
c Merry Christmas, Davy! (Illus. by Tharlet, Eve) — Weninger, Brigitte
c Merry Christmas, Mr. Mouse (Illus. by Buehner, Mark) — Buehner, Caralyn
c Merry Christmas, Squirrels! (Illus. by Rose, Nancy) — Rose, Nancy
The Merry-Go-Round — Fasano, Donna
The Mersault Investigation — Daoud, Kamel
c Mes premiers petits livres series C, 20 vols. — Charlesworth, Liza
Mesa of Sorrows: A History of the Awat'ovi Massacre — Brooks, James F.
c Mesmerized: How Ben Franklin Solved a Mystery That Baffled All of France (Illus. by Bruno, Iacopo) — Rockliff, Mara
Mesoamerican Plazas: Arenas of Community and Power — Tsukamoto, Kenichiro
Mesomedes: Inno a phi nu sigma iota sigma — Lanna, Sara
Mess: One Man's Struggle to Clean up His House and His Act (Read by Brooke, Peter). Audiobook Review — Yourgrau, Barry
Mess: One Man's Struggle to Clean up His House and His Act — Yourgrau, Barry
Message from the Memoirist — Pines, Paul

y Messenger of Fear — Grant, Michael
c Messenger: The Legend of Joan of Arc (Illus. by Hart, Sam) — Grant, Michael
y Messenger: The Legend of Joan of Arc (Illus. by Hart, Sam) — Lee, Tony
y The Messengers — Hogan, Edward
c Messy Jesse (Illus. by Bowles, Paula) — Bowles, Paula
Met Her on the Mountain: A Forty-Year Quest to Solve the Appalachian Cold-Case Murder of Nancy Morgan — Pinsky, Mark I.
Metaliteracy: Reinventing Information Literacy to Empower Learners — Mackey, Thomas P.
Metallomics and the Cell — Banci, Lucia
Metallurgy, Ballistics and Epistemic Instruments: The Nova Scientia of Nicolo Tartaglia: A New Edition — Valleriani, Matteo
Metals, Culture, and Capitalism: An Essay on the Origins of the Modern World — Goody, Jack
c Metamorphabet (Illus. by Smith, Patrick) — Smith, Patrick
c Metamorphic Rocks — Swanson, Jennifer
Metamorphoses — Mosley, Nicholas
Metamorphoses of the City: On the Western Dynamic — Manent, Pierre
Metamorphosis: Astonishing Insect Transformations — Soskin, Rupert
The Metamorphosis — Bernofsky, Susan
The Metaphor Deception — Adams, Birch
Metaphor — Donoghue, Denis
Metaphysical Grounding: Understanding the Structure of Reality — Schnieder, Benjamin
Metaphysical Odyssey into the Mexican Revolution — Mayo, C.M.
Metaphysics and Grammar — Charlton, William
Metaphysics and the Tri-Personal God — Hasker, William
A Metaphysics for Freedom — Steward, Helen
y Meteor: Perspectives on Asteroid Strikes — Woolf, Alex
y Meteor Prince — Tanaka, Meca
The Methampehetamine Industry in America: Transnational Cartels and Local Entrepreneurs — Brownstein, Henry H.
The Methamphetamine Industry in America: Transnational Cartels and Local Entrepreneurs — Brownstein, Henry H.
Method 15/33 — Kirk, Shannon
Method for the Easy Comprehension of History — Bodin, Jean
Methodism in the American Forest — Richey, Russell E.
Methodists and Their Missionary Societies, 1760-1900 — Pritchard, John
Methods of Molecular Analysis in the Life Sciences — Hofmann, Andreas
Methods of Murder: Beccarian Introspection and Lombrosian Vivisection in Italian Crime Fiction — Past, Elena
The Methuselah Project — Barry, Rick
The Methuselarity Transformation — Moskovitz, Rick
Metis in Canada: History, Identity, Law and Politics — Adams, Christopher
"Metis": Race, Recognition, and the Struggle for Indigenous Peoplehood — Andersen, Chris
Metis: Race, Recognition, and the Struggle for Indigenous Peoplehood — Andersen, Chris
The Metrics of Human Consciousness — Barrett, Richard
Metropole, Provinz und Welt: Raum und Mobilitat in der Literatur des Realismus — Berbig, Roland
Metropolen der Moderne: Eine europaische Stadtgeschichte seit 1850 — Lenger, Friedrich
Metropolis Berlin 1880-1940 — Whyte, Iain Boyd
Metropolis: Mapping the City — Black, Jeremy
Metropolitan Temporalities
Metzler Lexikon Moderner Mythen: Figuren, Konzepte, Ereignisse — Wodianka, Stephanie
Meursault, Contre-Enquete — Daoud, Kamel
The Meursault Investigation — Cullen, John
The Meursault Investigation — Daoud, Kamel
Mex-Cine: Mexican Filmmaking, Production, and Consumption in the Twenty-First Century — Aldama, Frederick Luis
Mexican Americans and the Question of Race — Dowling, Julie A.
Mexican Inclusion: The Origins of Anti-Discrimination Policy in Texas and the Southwest — Gritter, Matthew
The Mexican Revolution: Conflict and Consolidation, 1910-1940 — Richmond, Douglas W.
Mexicans in the Making of America — Foley, Neil

Mexico at War: From the Struggle for Independence to 21st Century Drug Wars — Marley, David F.
Mexico from the Inside Out — Olvera, Enrique
Mexico, Nation in Transit: Contemporary Representations of Mexican Migration to the United States — Sisk, Christina L.
Mexico20: New Voices, Old Traitors — Pierre, D.B.C.
Mexico's Once and Future Revolution: Social Upheaval and the Challenge of Rule since the Late Nineteenth Century — Joseph, Gilbert M.
c Mi and Museum City (Illus. by Sarah, Linda) — Sarah, Linda
c Mi familia calaca / My Skeleton Family (Illus. by Zarate, Jesus) — Weill, Cynthia
Mi ricordo — Capriolo, Paola
MI5 in the Great War — West, Nigel
c Miami Dolphins — Zappa, Marcia
Miami Gundown — Zimmer, Michael
c The Miami Heat — Stewart, Mark
c Mia's Recipe for Disaster — Simon, Coco
c Mia's Thumb (Illus. by Stille, Ljuba) — Stille, Ljuba
c Mice and Spider and Webs...Oh My! (Illus. by KJ of Kalpart) — Cannon, Sherrill S.
c Mice Mischief: Math Facts in Action (Illus. by Rossell, Judith) — Stills, Caroline
Michael Attaleiates and the Politics of Imperial Decline in Eleventh-Century — Krallis, Dimitris
c Michael Bird-Boy (Illus. by dePaola, Tomie) — dePaola, Tomie
Michael Costa: England's First Conductor: The Revolution in Musical Performance in England, 1830-1880 — Goulden, John
Michael G. Coney: SF Gateway Omnibus — Coney, Michael G.
Michael Jordan: Bull on Parade (Illus. by Santiago, Wilfred) — Santiago, Wilfred
Michael Jordan: The Life — Lazenby, Roland
y Michael & Maria — Layne, Shannon
Michael Polanyi and His Generation: Origins of the Social Construction of Science — Nye, Mary Jo
y Michael Vey: Hunt for Jade Dragon — Evans, Richard Paul
Michel Houellebecq and the Literature of Despair — Sweeney, Carole
Michel Stuelers Gedenkbuch (1629-1649): Alltagsleben in Bohmen zur Zeit des Dreissigjahrigen Krieges — Kilian, Jan
Michelangelo's Christian Mysticism: Spirituality, Poetry and Art in Sixteenth-Century Italy — Prodan, Sarah Rolfe
Michelle Obama: A Life — Slevin, Peter
Michnikowszczyzna: Zapis choroby — Ziemkiewicz, Rafal A.
c Microbes: Discover an Unseen World with 25 Projects (Illus. by Casteel, Tom) — Burillo-Kirch, Christine
The Microbiome Solution: A Radical New Way to Heal Your Body from the Inside Out — Chutkan, Robynne
Microfarming for Profit: From Garden to Glory — Dewitt, Dave
Micromegas and Other Tales — Voltaire
The Micronutrient Miracle: The 28-Day Plan to Lose Weight, Increase Your Energy, and Reduce Disease — Calton, Jayson
Microshelters: 59 Creative Cabins, Tiny Houses, Tree Houses, and Other Small Structures — Diedricksen, Derek
Microsoft Powerpoint 2013 Pocket Primer — Richardson, Theodor
Microwave Radar and Radiometric Remote Sensing — Ulaby, Fawwaz T.
The Middle Ages in Children's Literature — Bradford, Clare
The Middle Ages — Fried, Johannes
The Middle Ages without Feudalism: Essays in Criticism and Comparison on the Medieval West — Reynolds, Susan
The Middle Byzantine Historians — Treadgold, Warren
Middle East Authoritarianisms: Governance, Contestation and Regime Resilience in Syria and Iran — Heydemann, Steven
The Middle East: Its History and Culture — Tatlock, Jason
The Middle English Life of Christ: Academic Discourse, Translation, and Vernacular Theology — Johnson, Ian
The Middle of the Journey — Engel, Monroe
Middle Passage — Johnson, Charles
c The Middle School Rules of Brian Urlacher — Jensen, Sean
Middle Waters — Clarke, John

Middlebrow Queer: Christopher Isherwood in America — *Harker, Jaime*
Midian Unmade: Tales of Clive Barker's Nightbreed — *Howison, Del*
Midmen — *Ochs, Steve*
c Midnight: A True Story of Loyalty in World War I (Illus. by Lessac, Frane) — *Greenwood, Mark*
The Midnight Assassin: Panic, Scandal, and the Hunt for America's First Serial Killer — *Hollandsworth, Skip*
Midnight at the Pera Palace: The Birth of Modern Istanbul — *King, Charles*
Midnight Blind — *Brookes, Adam*
y Midnight Dolls — *Sullivan, Kiki*
Midnight in Broad Daylight: A Japanese American Family Caught between Two Worlds — *Sakamoto, Pamela Rotner*
Midnight in Siberia: A Train Journey into the Heart of Russia (Read by Greene, David). Audiobook Review — *Greene, David*
Midnight in Siberia: A Train Journey into the Heart of Russia — *Greene, David*
Midnight in St. Petersburg — *Bennett, Vanora*
The Midnight Letterbox: Selected Letters 1950-2010 — *Morgan, Edwin*
c Midnight Madness at the Zoo (Illus. by Jones, Karen) — *Craig, Sherryn*
c The Midnight Owl (Illus. by Coutts, Lisa) — *Branford, Anna*
Midnight Ride — *Johnson, Cat*
The Midnight Spy — *Hamilton, Kiki*
Midnight Sun — *Nesbo, Jo*
Midnight Taxi Tango — *Older, Daniel Jose*
y Midnight Thief (Read by Amato, Bianca). Audiobook Review — *Blackburne, Livia*
c Midnight Thief — *Blackburne, Livia*
c The Midnight Visitors (Illus. by Parry, Jo) — *David, Juliet*
c The Midnight War of Mateo Martinez — *Yardi, Robin*
Midnight Wrangler — *Johnson, Cat*
Midnight's Furies: The Deadly Legacy of India's Partition — *Hajari, Nisid*
Midnightstown — *French, Tom*
A Midsummer's Equation — *Higashino, Keigo*
Midwest Foraging: 115 Wild and Flavorful Edibles from Burdock to Wild Peach — *Rose, Lisa M.*
Midwest Maize: How Corn Shaped the U.S. Heartland — *Clampitt, Cynthia*
The Midwife Factor — *Gossett, GiGi*
c The Midwife of Bethlehem (Illus. by Lucas, Diane) — *Driggs, Shad*
The Midwife's Choice — *Parr, Delia*
The Midwife's Tale — *Parr, Delia*
c Migaloo: The White Whale — *Wilson, Mark*
Mightier Than the Sword — *Archer, Jeffrey*
y The Mighty (Illus. by Samnee, Chris) — *Tomasi, Peter J.*
Mighty Mighty — *Rudolph, Wally*
c Mighty Mo (Illus. by Brown, Alison) — *Brown, Alison*
c Mighty Mole and Super Soil (Illus. by Wallace, Chad) — *Quattlebaum, Mary*
A Mighty Purpose: How Jim Grant Sold the World on Saving its Children — *Fifield, Adam*
c Mighty Robot vs. The Stupid Stinkbugs from Saturn — *Ricotta, Ricky*
Mighty Star and the Castle of the Cancatervater — *Degen, A.*
c Migloo's Day (Illus. by Bee, William) — *Bee, William*
c Migrant (Illus. by Pedro, Javier Martinez) — *Mateo, Jose Manuel*
c Migrant (Illus. by Pedro, Javier Martinez) — *Ready, Emmy Smith*
Migrant Imaginaries: Figures in Italian Migration Literature — *Burns, Jennifer*
Migrant Workers in Contemporary Japan: An Institutional Perspective on Transnational Employment — *Tanno, Kiyoto*
Migrants and Cities: The Accommodation of Migrant Organizations in Europe — *Fauser, Margit*
c Migrants and Refugees — *Carr, Aaron*
Migrants in Translation: Caring and the Logics of Difference in Contemporary Italy — *Giordano, Cristiana*
Migrating Voids — *Walker, David H.*
Migration, Citizenship and Intercultural Relations: Looking through the Lens of Social Inclusion — *Mansouri, Fethi*
Migration in and out of East and Southeast Europe: Values, Networks, Well-Being
y Migration Nation: Animals on the Go from Coast to Coast — *O'Sullivan, Joanne*

c Migration Nation: Animals on the Go from Coast to Coast — *O'Sullivan, Joanne*: Migration Nation.(Children's review)(Brief article)(Book review)
Migration: The Biology of Life on the Move by Hugh Dingle — *Dingle, Hughp*
Migration und Familie
Migratory Animals — *Specht, Mary Helen*
c Miguel Cabrera: MVP and Triple Crown Winner — *Flynn, Brendan*
c Mike Mulligan and His Steam Shovel — *Burton, Virginia Lee*
y Mike's Place: A True Story of Love, Blues, and Terror in Tel Aviv — *Baxter, Jack*
Mikhail Larionov and the Cultural Politics of Late Imperial Russia — *Warren, Sarah*
c Mikis and the Donkey (Illus. by Hopman, Philip) — *Tak, Bibi Dumon*
c Mikis and the Donkey (Illus. by Hopman, Philip) — *Dumon Tak, Bibi*
Mikkeller's Book of Beer: Includes 25 Original Mikkeller Brewing Recipes — *Bjergso, Mikkel Borg*
Mikrokosmos und Makrokosmos. Meistersinger als mentalitats- und ideengeschichtlicher Ausdruck der Stadt im spaten Mittelalter und Fruher Neuzeit
Milano guelfa, 1302-1310 — *Grillo, Paolo*
y Milayna — *Pickett, Michelle K.*
Mildreds: The Cookbook — *Mildred's*
A Mile Down: The True Story of a Disastrous Career at Sea — *Vann, David*
A Mile North of Good and Evil — *Hayes, Charles D.*
y Miles from Nowhere — *Clipston, Amy*
c Miles Morales: The Ultimate Spider-Man (Illus. by Marquez, David) — *Bendis, Brian Michael*
c Miles Taylor and the Golden Cape: Attack of the Alien Horde (Illus. by Higgins, Dusty) — *Venditti, Robert*
Miles to Go before We Sleep: Well-Worn Paths and New Directions for Educational Historians — *Alvarez, Rene Luis*
Miley Cyrus and Her Dead Petz — *Cyrus, Miley*
y Miley Cyrus: Pop Princess — *Anderson, Jennifer Joline*
Militarhistorische Sammlungen in Bibliotheken - Bewahren, Erschliessen, Prasentieren
Militarism in a Global Age: Naval Ambitions in Germany and the United States before World War I — *Bonker, Dirk*
The Military and Colonial Destruction of the Roman Landscape of North Africa, 1830-1900 — *Greenhalgh, Michael*
Military Chaplaincy in Contention: Chaplains, Churches, and the Morality of Conflict — *Todd, Andrew*
Military Chaplains in Afghanistan, Iraq, and Beyond — *Patterson, Eric*
Military Culture and Popular Patriotism in Late Imperial Austria — *Cole, Laurence*
A Military History of Scotland — *Spiers, Edward M.*
The Military Lens: Doctrinal Difference and Deterrence Failure in Sino-American Relations — *Twomey, Christopher P.*
Military Saints in Byzantium and Rus, 900-1200 — *White, Monica*
Military Transition in Early Modern Asia, 1400-1750: Cavalry, Guns, Government and Ships — *Roy, Kaushik*
c Military Vehicles: 1980 to Today — *Trewhitt, Philip*
Milk Bar Life: Recipes & Stories — *Tosi, Christina*
Milked — *Doyle, Lisa*
c The Milkshake Detectives — *Butler, Heather*
Mill Power: The Origin and Impact of Lowell National Historical Park — *Marion, Paul*
Millennials with Kids: Marketing to This Powerful and Surprisingly Different Generation of Parents — *Fromm, Jeff*
Millennium — *Nolane, Richard D.*
Miller's Valley — *Quindlen, Anna*
The Milli Vanilli Condition: Essays on Culture in the New Millennium — *Espina, Eduardo*
c Millie the Octopus Learns to Hula Dance (Illus. by Thompson, Leslie) — *Makhlouf, Jack*
c Millie's Chickens (Illus. by Cis, Valeria) — *Williams, Brenda*
Million Dollar Women: Raise Capital and Take Your Business Further, Faster — *Pimsleur, Julia*
y A Million Miles Away — *Avery, Lara*
y A Million Times Goodnight — *McBride, Kristina*
c A Million Ways Home — *Winget, Dianna Dorisi*
A Million Windows — *Murnane, Gerald*
The Millionaire and the Bard: Henry Folger's Obsessive Hunt for Shakespeare's First Folio — *Mays, Andrea*

The Millionaire in the Next Cubicle: A Corporate Everyman's Blueprint to Financial Independence — *Mendez, Chip*
The Millionaire Next Door — *Stanley, Thomas J.*
The Millionaire's Cross — *Nudo, Sal*
The Millionaires' Squadron: The Remarkable Story of 601 Squadron and the Flying Sword — *Moulson, Tom*
c Milo and Millie — *Robaard, Jedda*
c Milo and the Mysterious Island — *Pfister, Marcus*
c Milo Is Not a Dog Today (Illus. by Gunetsreiner, Nina) — *Schoene, Kerstin*
c Milo Speck, Accidental Agent (Illus. by Epelbaum, Mariano) — *Urban, Linda*
c Milo Speck, Accidental Agent (Illus. by Epelbaum, Mariano) — *Urban, Linda*
c Milo Speck, Accidental Agent (Illus. by Epelbaum, Mariano) — *Urban, Linda*
c Milo's Hat Trick (Read by Newbern, George). Audiobook Review — *Agee, John*
The Milosevic Trial: An Autopsy — *Waters, Timothy William*
Milosz et la France — *Delaperriere, Maria*
Milt Gross' New York (Illus. by Gross, Milt) — *Gross, Milt*
Milton and Questions of History: Essays by Canadians Past and Present — *Mohamed, Feisal G.*
Milton and the People — *Hammond, Paul*
Milton and the Politics of Public Speech — *Lynch, Helen*
c Milton Hershey — *Schuette, Sarah L.*
Milton, Toleration, and Nationhood — *Sauer, Elizabeth*
The Milwaukee Mafia: Mobsters in the Heartland — *Schmitt, Gavin*
Milwaukee Mayhem: Murder and Mystery in the Cream City's First Century — *Prigge, Matthew J.*
c Mimi and Bear in the Snow (Illus. by Trasler, Janee) — *Trasler, Janee*
c Mimi and Shu in I'll Race You! (Illus. by Van der Paardt, Melissa) — *Trimmer, Christian*
Mimi's Trapese — *Rosser, J. Allyn*
c Mina's White Canvas (Illus. by Lee, Hyeon-Ju) — *Lee, Hyeon-Ju*
Mind-Bending Puzzles and Fascinating Facts: A Compendium for All Ages — *Williams, Paul*
c Mind-Blowing Movie Stunts — *Tougas, Joe*
The Mind-Body Stage: Passion and Interaction In the Cartesian Theater — *Gobert, R. Darren*
Mind, Brain, and Free Will — *Swinburne, Richard*
y Mind Games — *Terry, Teri*
Mind Hacking: How to Change Your Mind for Good in 21 Days — *Hargrave, John*
The Mind inside Tai Chi — *Zhuang, Henry*
The Mind Is a collection: Case Studies in Eighteenth Century Thought — *Silver, Sean*
c Mind Muddlers: What You See Is Not What You Get! — *Bowles, Anna*
The Mind of the African Strongman: Conversations with Dictators, Statesmen, and Father Figures — *Cohen, Herman J.*
The Mind of the Nation: Volkerpsychologie in Germany, 1851-1955 — *Klautke, Egbert*
y Mind Over Bullies — *Smith, D.K.*
Mind-set Adjustments — *Kenyeres, Nick*
c Mind Your Monsters (Illus. by Vidal, Oriol) — *Bailey, Catherine*
Mindful America: The Mutual Transformation of Buddhist Meditation and American Culture — *Wilson, Jeff*
The Mindful Diet: How to Transform Your Relationship with Food for Lasting Weight Loss and Vibrant Health — *Wolever, Ruth Q.*
The Mindful Home: The Secrets to Making Your Home a Place of Harmony, Beauty, Wisdom and True Happiness — *Hassed, Craig*
The Mindful Parent: Strategies from Peaceful Cultures to Raise Compassionate, Well-Balanced Kids — *Peterson, Charlotte*
The Mindful School Leader: Practices to Transform Your Leadership and School — *Brown, Valerie*
Mindful Work: How Meditation Is Changing Business from the Inside Out — *Gelles, David*
Minding the Modern: Human Agency, Intellectual Traditions, and Responsible Knowledge — *Pfau, Thomas*
Mind's Eye: Stories from Whapmagoostui — *Marshall, Susan*
Minds on Mathematics: Using Math Workshop to Develop Deep Understanding in Grades 4-8 — *Hoffer, Wendy Ward*

Mindshaping: A New Framework for Understanding Human Social Cognition — Zawidzki, Tadeusz Wieslaw
Mindsharing: The Art of Crowdsourcing Everything — Zoref, Lior
y Mindwalker — Steiger, A.J.
Mindware: Tools for Smart Thinking — Nisbett, Richard E.
Mine — Dimon, HelenKay
c Mine! (Illus. by Heap, Sue) — Heap, Sue
c Mine! (Illus. by Jin, Susie Lee) — Jin, Susie Lee
y Minecraft Combat Handbook — Milton, Stephanie
Mineral Treasures of the Ozarks — Stinchcomb, Bruce L.
Mineralogische Sammlung Deutschland: Das Krugerhaus in Freiberg — Richter, Uwe
Ming Tea Murder — Childs, Laura
c Ming's Adventure with Confucius in Qufu, A Story in English and Chinese (Illus. by Jian, Li) — Jian, Li
Miniature Needle Painting Embroidery: Vintage Portraits, Florals and Birds — Burr, Trish
Miniatures in Style: Six Original Piano Solos in Baroque, Classical, Romantic, Impressionist, and Contemporary Styles — Rejino, Mona
Minimum Income Protection in FLux — Marx, Ive
Mining and Quarrying in the Ancient Andes: Sociopolitical, Economic, and Symbolic Dimensions — Tripcevich, Nicholas
Mining, Monies, and Culture in Early Modern Societies: East Asian and Global Perspectives — Nagase-Reimer, Keiko
c Minion — Anderson, John David
Ministerialitat, Ritterschaft und landstandischer Adel im Rheinland, 11.-19. Jahrhundert
Ministers at War: Winston Churchill and His War Cabinet — Schneer, Jonathan
Minister's Shoes — Mariotti, Celine Rose
c The Ministry of Ghosts — Shearer, Alex
The Ministry of Guidance Invites You to Not Stay — Majd, Hooman
c Minna's Patchwork Coat (Illus. by Mills, Lauren A.) — Mills, Lauren A.
Minni and Muninn: Memory in Medieval Nordic Culture — Hermann, Pernille
c Minnie in Paris (Illus. by Wall, Mike) — Higginson, Sheila Sweeny
Minnow — McTeer, James E., II
Minnow — Oakes, Stephanie
y The Minnow — Sweeney, Diana
The Minor Clergy of Exeter Cathedral: Biographies, 1250-1548 — Orme, Nicholas
Minor White: Manifestations of the Spirit — J. Martineau Paul
Minor White: Manifestations of the Spirit — Martineau, Paul
Minority Languages in the Linguistic Landscape — Gorter, Durk
Minority Views of Vice Chairman Chambliss Joined by Senators Burr, Risch, Coats, Rubio, and Coburn: Committee Study of the Central Intelligence Agency's Detention and Interrogation Program — U.S. Senate Select Committee on Intelligence
y Minotaur — Rock, J.A.
y Minotaur — Simpson, Phillip W.
c Minrs — Sylvester, Kevin
Mint Juleps with Teddy Roosevelt: The Complete History of Presidential Drinking — Will-Weber, Mark
y Minus Me — Rossland, Ingelin
Minute Zero — Moss, Todd
c Mira donde vivo! / Look Where I Live! (Illus. by Comfort, Louise) — Bruzzone, Catherine
Miracle at the Higher Ground Cafe — Lucado, Max
The Miracle Girl — Roe, Andrew
c The Miracle Mitzvah Moose (Illus. by Pineiro, Gloria) — Wynne, Dawn
c Miracle on 133rd Street (Illus. by Priceman, Marjorie) — Manzano, Sonia
Miracle on Voodoo Mountain: A Young Woman's Remarkable Story of Pushing Back the Darkness for the Children of Haiti — Boudreaux, Megan
Miracles and Conundrums of the Secondary Planets — Appel, Jacob M.
Miracles and the Protestant Imagination: The Evangelical Wonder Book in Reformation Germany — Soergel, Philip M.
c Miracles on Maple Hill (Read by the Full Cast family). Audiobook Review — Sorensen, Virginia
Miracles: What They Are, Why They Happen, and How They Can Change Your Life (Read by Sanders, Fred). Audiobook Review — Metaxas, Eric

The Miraculous Conformist: Valentine Greatrakes, the Body Politic and the Politics of Healing in Restoration Britain — Elmer, Peter
The Miraculous Conformist: Valentine Greatrakes, the Body Politic, and the Politics of Healing in Restoration Britain — Elmer, Peter
Miraculous Plagues: An Epidemiology of Early New England Narrative — Silva, Cristobal
Miraculous Silence: A Journey to Illumination and Healing through Prayer — Rahbar, Mitra
Mirage — Anonymous
Mirages of the Mind — Yousufi, Mushtaq Ahmed
Miranda's Book — Corn, Alfred
Mircea Eliade: From Magic to Myth — Idel, Moshe
y The Mirror Chronicles: The Bell Between Worlds — Johnstone, Ian
Mirror Image, Charisma, Brontomek! — Coney, Michael G.
The Mirror of Princely Deed and Knighthood — Tyler, Margaret
Mirror on the Floor — Bowering, George
y Mirrored — Flinn, Alex
c Mirrored (Illus. by McElhinney, Glenn) — Graves, Annie
Miruna, a Tale — Suceava, Bogdan
The Misadventures of Awkward Black Girl — Rae, Issa
c The Misadventures of Salem Hyde: Cookie Catastrophe (Illus. by Cammuso, Frank) — Cammuso, Frank
c The Misadventures of Salem Hyde: Dinosaur Dilemma (Illus. by Cammuso, Frank) — Cammuso, Frank
c The Misadventures of Sweetie Pie (Illus. by Van Allsburg, Chris) — Van Allsburg, Chris
c The Misadventures of the Family Fletcher (Read by Woren, Dan). Audiobook Review — Alison, Dana
c The Misadventures of the Family Fletcher — Levy, Dana Alison
Misalliance: Ngo Dinh Diem, the United States, and the Fate of South Vietnam — Miller, Edward Garvey
c Misbehaving — Glines, Abbi
Misbehaving: The Making of Behavioral Economics — Thaler, Richard H.
Misbehaving: The Making of Behavioural Economics — Thaler, Richard H.
c Mischief and Malice — Amoss, Berthe
c Mischief Season — Marciano, John Bemelmans
y Misdirected — Berman, Ari
Mise en Scene and Film Style: From Classical Hollywood to New Media Art — Martin, Adrian
Miserere Mei: The Penitential Psalms in Late Medieval and Early Modern England — King'oo, Clare Costley
Miseryland — Roberts, Keller
The Misfit Economy: Lessons in Creativity from Pirates, Hackers, Gangsters and Other Informal Entrepreneurs — Clay, Alexa
The Misfit Economy: Lessons in Creativity from Pirates, Hackers, Gangsters, and Other Informal Entrepreneurs — Clay, Alexa
The Misfit Economy — Clay, Alexa
Misfits — Leigh, Garrett
Mislaid (Read by Campbell, Cassandra). Audiobook Review — Zink, Nell
Mislaid — Zink, Nell
Mislaid & the Wallcreeper--the Neil Zink Collection. E-book Review — Zink, Nell
Mislaid & the Wallcreeper--the Neil Zink Collection — Zink, Nell
Misled by Nature: Contemporary Art and the Baroque — Crowston, Catherine
A Misplaced Massacre: Struggling over the Memory of Sand Creek — Kelman, Ari
c Miss Brooks' Story Nook (Where Tales Are Told and Ogres Are Welcome). (Illus. by Emberley, Michael) — Bottner, Barbara
Miss Carter's War — Hancock, Sheila
Miss Darcy's Passion — Soliman, Wendy
Miss Dreamsville and the Lost Heiress of Collier County — Hearth, Amy Hill
Miss Emily — O'Connor, Nuala
c Miss Emily (Illus. by Matt Phelan,) — Muten, Burleigh
c Miss Hazeltine's Home for Shy and Fearful Cats (Illus. by Sif, Birgitta) — Potter, Alicia
Miss Jessie's: Creating a Successful Business from Scratch--Naturally — Branch, Miko
Miss Julia Lays down the Law — Ross, Ann B.
c Miss Mary Mack — Bell, Lucy
c Miss Mary Reporting: The True Story of Sportswriter Mary Garber (Illus. by Payne, C.F.) — Macy, Sue
Miss Match — McGee, Laurelin

y Miss Mayhem — Hawkins, Rachel
c Miss Moon: Wise Words from a Dog Governess — Hill, Janet
Miss Ruffles Inherits Everything — Martin, Nancy
y Miss Solitude — Girard, Edith
c Miss Suki Is Kooky! (Read by Goldsmith, Jared). Audiobook Review — Gutman, Dan
c Miss Todd and Her Wonderful Flying Machine (Illus. by Yee, Kristina) — Poletti, Frances
c Miss Todd and Her Wonderful Flying Machine (Illus. by Yee, Kristina) — Yee, Kristina
Missed Approach — Adams, Mack
y The Misshapes: Annihilation Day — Flynn, Alex
c Missile Mouse: The Star Crusher (Illus. by Parker, Jake) — Parker, Jake
The Missing — O'Hagan, Andrew
c Missing! — Dicker, Katie
Missing — Adamov, Bob
Missing — Hawken, Sam
c Missing! — Dicker, Katie
The Missing and the Dead — MacBride, Stuart
c The Missing Dog Is Spotted — Kerrin, Jessica Scott
The Missing Head of Damasceno Monteiro — Tabucchi, Antonio
c Missing in Paradise — Verstraete, Larry
Missing Insects — Rosenthal, Naomi M.
The Missing Kennedy: Rosemary Kennedy and the Secret Bonds of Four Women — Koehler-Pentacoff, Elizabeth
Missing Links: Practical and Surprisingly Effective Tools for Self-Transformation ... and Behavior Modification — Petra, Daniel
Missing Microbes: How the Overuse of Antibiotics Is Fueling Our Modern Plagues (Read by Lawlor, Patrick G.). Audiobook Review — Blaser, Martin J.
Missing Microbes: How the Overuse of Antibiotics Is Fueling Our Modern Plagues — Blaser, Martin J.
y Missing Millie Benson: The Secret Case of the Nancy Drew Ghostwriter and Journalist — Rubini, Julie K.
The Missing Piece — Egan, Kevin
Missing Pieces — Gudenkauf, Heather
The Missing Woman and Other Stories — Burns, Carole
Missing You — Coben, Harlan
c The Missing Zucchini — Falcone, L.M.
c The Missing Zucchini (Illus. by Smith, Kim) — Falcone, L.M.
Mission Accomplished? The Crisis of International Intervention — Jenkins, Simon
The Mission Chinese Food Cookbook — Bowien, Danny
Mission High: One School, How Experts Tried to Fail It, and the Students and Teachers Who Made It Triumph — Rizga, Kristina
Mission in the Early Church: Themes and Reflections — Smither, Edward L.
c Mission Mumbai — Narsimhan, Mahtab
c Mission: New Baby: Top-Secret Info for Big Brothers and Sisters (Illus. by Lundquist, Mary) — Hood, Susan
The Mission of Preaching: Equipping the Community for Faithful Witness — Johnson, Patrick W.T.
c Mission Ouaouaron (Illus. by Cormier, France) — Bergeron, Alain M.
Mission Revolution: The US Military and Stability Operations — Taw, Jennifer Morrison
Mission Station Christianity: Norwegian Missionaries in Colonial Natal and Zululand, Southern Africa, 1850-1890 — Hovland, Ingie
c Mission Titanic — Watson, Jude
Mission: Tomorrow — Schmidt, Bryan Thomas
c Mission: Wolf Rescue: All about Wolves and How to Save Them — Jazynka, Kitson
Missional Worship, Worshipful Mission: Gathering as God's People, Going Out in God's Name — Meyers, Ruth A.
Missionaries Make the Best Companions — Townsend, Johnny
Missionaries of Republicanism: A Religious History of the Mexican-American War — Pinheiro, John C.
Missionary Bishop: Jean-Marie Odin in Galveston and New Orleans — Foley, Patrick
Missionary Discourses of Difference: Negotiating Otherness in the British Empire, 1840-1900 — Cleall, Esme
Missionary Families: Race, Gender, and Generation on the Spiritual Frontier — Manktelow, Emily J.
Missionary Masculinity, 1870-1930: The Norwegian Missionaries in South-East Africa — Tjelle, Kristin Fjelde

The Missionary Strategies of the Jesuits in Ethiopia, 1555-1632 — Cohen, Leonardo
The Missionary's Curse and Other Tales from a Chinese Catholic Village — Harrison, Henrietta
Missions chretiennes en terre d'islam, Moyen-Orient, Afrique du Nord (XVIIe--XXe siecles): Anthologie de textes missionnaires — Verdeil, Chantal
y Missions Impossible: Extraordinary Stories of Daring and Courage — Flynn, Hazel
Missionspharmazie: Konzepte, Praxis, Organisation und wissenschaftliche Ausstrahlung — Anagnostou, Sabine
Mississauga Portraits: Ojibwe Voices from Nineteenth-Century Canada — Smith, Donald B.
Mississippi Eyes: The Story and Photography of the Southern Documentary Project — Herron, Matt
Mississippi Praying: Southern White Evangelicals and the Civil Rights Movement, 1945-1975 — Dupont, Carolyn Renee
Mississippi River Tragedies: A Century of Unnatural Disaster — Klein, Christine A.
Missoula: Rape and the Justice System in a College Town (Read by Marno, Mozhan). Audiobook Review — Krakauer, Jon
Missoula: Rape and the Justice System in a College Town (Read by Brick, Scott). Audiobook Review — Marno, Mozhan
y Missoula: Rape and the Justice System in a College Town — Krakauer, Jon
The Mistake I Made — Daly, Paula
y Mistake Wisconsin — Niebruegge, Kersti
Mistborn — Sanderson, Brandon
Mister Black — Michelle, P.T.
y Mister Cassowary — Wheeler, Samantha
c Mister Doctor: Janusz Korczak and the Orphans of the Warsaw Ghetto (Illus. by Quarello, Maurizio A.C.) — Janea, Irene Cohen
y Mister Doctor: Janusz Korczak and the Orphans of the Warsaw (Illus. by Quarello, Maurizio) — Cohen-Janca, Irene
c Mister H (Illus. by Lozano, Luciano) — Nesquens, Daniel
c Mister Horizontal & Miss Vertical (Illus. by Zagnoli, Olimpia) — Bedrick, Claudia
c Mister Spears and His Hairy Ears (Illus. by Kinnaird, Ross) — McMillan, Dawn
y Mistletoe and Mr. Right — Payne, Lyla
Mistress of Melody — Lawson, Anthea
The Mistress of Tall Acre — Frantz, Laura
The Mistresses of Cliveden: Three Centuries of Scandal, Power and Intrigue — Livingstone, Natalie
c Misty (Illus. by Meserve, Jessica) — Dencer, Christine
c Misty Copeland: Power and Grace — Corman, Richard
c Misty (Illus. by Meserve, Jessica) — Dencer, Christine
Mit den Toten und fur die Toten: Zur Konfessionalisierung der Sepulkralkultur im Munsterland — Brademann, Jan
Mit der Antike Schule Machen? Das Integrative Potenzial der Alten Geschichte fur das Historische Lernen
Mit einer Art von Wut: Goethe in der Revolution — Seibt, Gustav
Mit Zitaten kommunizieren: Untersuchungen zur Zitierweise in der Korrespondenz des Marcus Tullius Cicero — Behrendt, Anja
c Mitchell Video Games — Haugen, Hayley
c Mitford at the Fashion Zoo — Robertson, Donald
Mittelalterliche Bibelhandschriften am Niederrhein — Karpp, Gerhard
Mittelhochdeutsches Worterbuch, Band 2, Doppellieferung 1/2: Lieferung 1: evuegerin - gemeilic: Lieferung 2: gemeinde-gevaerlich — Gartner, Kurt
Mitten in Europa: Verflechtung und Abgrenzung in der Schweizer Geschichte — Holenstein, Andre
c The Mitten String (Illus. by Swarner, Kristina) — Rosner, Jennifer
c Mix It Up! (Illus. by Tullet, Herve) — Franceschelli, Christopher
Mix + Match Cakes: A Batter, a Syrup, a Frosting: a New Way to Bake — Wright, Caroline
Mixed Matches: Transgressive Unions in Germany from the Reformation to the Enlightenment — Luebke, David M.
c Mixed Me! (Illus. by Evans, Shane) — Diggs, Taye
c Mixed Me! (Illus. by Evans, Shane W.) — Diggs, Taye
Mixed Messages: Cultural and Genetic Inheritance in the Constitution of Human Society — Paul, Robert A.
Mixed Race Identities — Aspinall, Peter
Mixed Signals. E-book Review — Cole, Alyssa

The Mixtecs of Oaxaca: Ancient Times to the Present — Spores, Ronald
The Mixture as Before — Harris, Rosie
MJ: The Genius of Michael Jackson — Knopper, Steve
Mnemosyne and Mars: Artistic and Cultural Representations of Twentieth-Century Europe at War — Tame, Peter D.
c Mo and Beau (Illus. by Nastanlieva, Vanya) — Nastanlieva, Vanya
Moab, Utah by Day & Night (Illus. by Collier, Grant) — Collier, Grant
The Mob and the City: The Hidden History of How the Mafia Captured New York — Hortis, C. Alexander
Mob Cop: My Life of Crime in the Chicago Police Department — Pascente, Fred
Mobile Horizons: Dynamics across the Taiwan Strait — Yeh, Wen-Hsin
Mobile Pastoralism and the Formation of Near Eastern Civilizations: Weaving Together Society — Porter, Anne
Mobile Subjects: Boundaries and Identities in the Modern Korean Diaspora — Yeh, Wen-Hsin
Mobilisierung der Sinne: Der Hollywood-Kriegsfilm zwischen Genrekino und Historie — Kappelhoff, Hermann
Mobilisierung im Nazionalsozialismus: Institutionen und Regionen in der Kriegswirtschaft und der Verwaltung des 'Dritten Reiches' 1936 bis 1945 — Werner, Oliver
Mobilitat und Umwelt
Mobilities in Socialist and Post-Socialist States: Societies on the Move — Horschelmann, Kathrin
Mobilizing Democracy: Globalization and Citizenship Protest — Almeida, Paul
Mobilizing Piety: Islam and Feminism in Indonesia — Rinaldo, Rachel
Mobilizing Religion in Middle East Politics: A Comparative Study of Israel and Turkey — Sarfati, Yusuf
Mobius Dick — Crumey, Andrew
c Mocha Dick: The Legend and Fury (Illus. by Enos, Randall) — Heinz, Brian
Mochi's War: The Tragedy of Sand Creek — Enss, Chris
Mock Modernism: An Anthology of Parodies, Travesties, Frauds, 1910-1935 — Diepeveen, Leonard
The Mockingbird Next Door: Life with Harper Lee — Mills, Marja
Mockingbird — Wendig, Chuck
Moctezuma. Apogeo y caida del imperio azteca — Graulich, Michel
Model Coach: A Common Sense Guide for Coaches of Youth Sports — Sedor, Daniel L.
y Model Misfit (Read by Sobey, Katey). Audiobook Review — Smale, Holly
y Model Misfit — Smale, Holly
The Model of Poesy — Scott, William
The Model Railroader's Guide to Grain — Wilson, Jeff
Model Railroads Go to War — Kempinski, Bernard
Model Woman: Eileen Ford and the Business of Beauty — Lacey, Robert
Modern Albania: From Dictatorship to Democracy in Europe — Abrahams, Fred C.
The Modern American Military — Kennedy, David M.
c Modern Art Adventures: 36 Creative, Hands-on Projects Inspired by Artists from Monet to Banksy — Pitamic, Maja
The Modern Castrato: Gaetano Guadagni and the Coming of a New Operatic Age — Howard, Patricia
Modern Country Knits: 30 Designs from Juniper Moon Farm — Gibbs, Susan
Modern Curriculum for Gifted and Advanced Academic Students — Kettler, Todd
Modern Dublin: Urban Change and the Irish Past, 1957-1973 — Hanna, Erika
Modern Families: Parents and Children in New Family Forms — Golombok, Susan
Modern Families: Stories of Extraordinary Journeys to Kinship — Gamson, Joshua
The Modern Family Cookbook — Modern Family
Modern Food, Moral Food: Self-Control, Science, and the Rise of Modern American Eating in the Early Twentieth Century — Veit, Helen Zoe
Modern Genocide: The Definitive Resource and Document Collection — Bartrop, Paul R.
Modern German Midwifery, 1885-1960 — Fallwell, Lynne
Modern Homebrew Recipes: Exploring Styles and Contemporary Techniques — Strong, Gordon

Modern India in German Archives, 1706-1989: Inaugural Project Workshop
Modern Islamic Thought in a Radical Age: Religious Authority and Internal Criticism — Moosa, Ebrahim
Modern Jewish Cooking: Recipes and Customs for Today's Kitchen — Koenig, Leah
The Modern Kosher Kitchen: More Than 125 Inspired Recipes for a New Generation of Kosher Cooks — Fein, Ronnie
A Modern Look at the Hoof — Craig, Monique
Modern Love, and Other Poems — Mitchell, Rebecca
Modern Man — Flint, Anthony
The Modern Medallion Workbook: 11 Projects to Make, Mix & Match — Ryan, Janice Zeller
The Modern Mercenary: Private Armies and What They Mean for World Order — McFate, Sean
Modern Military Aircraft: The World's Great Weapons — Newdick, Thomas
y Modern Monsters — York, Kelley
Modern Motherhood: An American History — Vandenberg-Daves, Jodi
Modern Occultism in Late Imperial Russia — Mannherz, Julia
The Modern Origins of the Early Middle Ages — Wood, Ian
y Modern Romance: An Investigation (Read by Ansari, Aziz). Audiobook Review — Ansari, Aziz
y Modern Romance: An Investigation — Ansari, Aziz
Modern Romance — Klinenberg, Eric
The Modern Savage: Our Unthinking Decision to Eat Animals — McWilliams, James
The Modern Spirit of Asia: The Spiritual and the Secular in China and India — van der Veer, Peter
The Modern Spirit of Asia: The Spiritual and the Secular in China and India — Van Der Veer, Peter
A Modern Twist: Create Quilts with a Colorful Spin — Barnes, Natalie
Modern Wars in Perspective — Scott, H.M.
A Modern Way to Eat: 200+ Satisfying Vegetarian Recipes (That Will Make You Feel Amazing). — Jones, Anna
Modern Women on Trial: Sexual Transgression in the Age of the Flapper — Bland, Lucy
Moderne Antimoderne: Arthur Moeller van den Bruck und der Wandel des Konservatismus — Weib, Volker
Moderne. Weltkrieg. Irrenhaus. 1900-1930 — Goldmann, Renate
Modernism and Autobiography — DiBattista, Maria
Modernism and Cosmology: Absurd Lights — Ebury, Katherine
Modernism and the Cult of Mountains: Music, Opera, Cinema — Morris, Christopher
Modernism and the New Spain: Britain, Cosmopolitan Europe, and Literary History — Rogers, Gayle
Modernism and the Reinvention of Decadence — Sherry, Vincent
Modernism at the Barricades: Aesthetics, Politics, Utopia — Bronner, Stephen Eric
Modernism, Feminism and the Culture of Boredom — Pease, Allison
Modernism: Keywords — Cuddy-Keane, Melba
Modernism, Middlebrow and the Literary Canon — Jaillant, Lise
Modernist Fiction and Vagueness: Philosophy, Form, and Language — Quigley, Megan
The Modernist Masquerade: Stylizing Life, Literature, and Costumes in Russia — McQuillen, Colleen
Modernity and Terrorism: From Anti-Modernity to Modern Global Terror — Zafirovski, Milan
Modernity Britain, 1957-1962 — Kynaston, David
The Modernity of Others: Jewish Anti-Catholicism in Germany and France — Joskowicz, Ari
Modernizing the Nation: Spain during the Reign of Alfonso XIII, 1902-1931 — Moreno-Luzon, Javier
The Modi Effect: Inside Narendra Modi's Campaign to Transform India — Price, Lance
c Moe Is Best (Illus. by Torrey, Richard) — Torrey, Richard
Mohawk Interruptus: Political Life across the Borders of Settler States — Simpson, Audra
Moi Muzh Daniil Kharms — Durnovo, Marina
Moines et demons: Autobiographie et individualite au Moyen Age, VIIe-XIIIe siecle — Barthelemy, Dominique
Moira de Erasmo Roterodamo: A Critical Edition of the Early Modern Spanish Translation of Erasmus's 'Encomium Moriae' — Ledo, Jorge
Mojo Triangle: Birthplace of Country, Blues, Jazz and Rock 'n' Roll — Dickerson, James L.

Mojo Workin': The Old African American Hoodoo System — Hazzard-Donald, Katrina
Molecular Evolution: A Statistical Approach — Yang, Ziheng
Molecular Plant Immunity — Sessa, Guido
Molecules: The Elements and Architecture of Everything — Gray, Theodore
c Moletown (Illus. by Kuhlmann, Torben) — Kuhlmann, Torben
y Molina: The Story of the Father Who Raised an Unlikely Baseball Dynasty — Molina, Bengie
Mollicutes: Molecular Biology and Pathogensis — Browning, Glenn F.
c Molly and Pim and the Millions of Stars — Murray, Martine
c Molly and the Bully (Illus. by Sekulic, Britt) — Payne, Ed
c Mom School (Illus. by Burris, Priscilla) — Van Slyke, Rebecca
c Mom, There's a Bear at the Door (Illus. by Olten, Manuela) — Lipan, Sabine
y The Moment — Hammond, Kristie
The Moment of Racial Sight: A History — Tucker, Irene
A Moment of Silence — Sister Souljah
c The Moment You Were Born: A Story for You and Your Premature Baby (Illus. by Hehenberger, Shelly) — Lane, Sandra M.
c Mommy and Daddy Love You (Illus. by Ladecka, Anna) — Kim, Cecil
c Mommy Goes to the Office — Mesara-Dogan, Gulden
c Mommy Is a Worrywart (Illus. by Kaye, Jenni) — Kaye, Jenni
c Mommy, You're Special to Me (Illus. by Fleming, Kim) — Mitchell, Laine
c Mommy's Little Sunflowers (Illus. by Edgson, Alison) — McAllister, Angela
c Mom's Big Catch — McKenna, Marla
c Mom's the Word (Illus. by Littler, Jamie) — Knapman, Timothy
c Momster (Illus. by Mahr, Peter) — Jensen-Kimball, Laura
c Mon guide du del et des etoiles — Prinja, Raman
c Mona — Miles, Ellen
Monarch of the Square: An Anthology of Muhammad Zafzaf's Short Stories — Zafzaf, Muhammad
Monarchy and Modernity in Egypt: Politics, Islam, and Neo-Colonialism between the Wars — Whidden, James
Monarchy and the End of Empire: The House of Windsor, the British Government, and the Postwar Commonwealth — Murphy, Philip
A Monarchy of Letters: Royal Correspondence and English Diplomacy in the Reign of Elizabeth I — Allinson, Rayne
Monasteries on the Borders of Medieval Europe: Conflict and Cultural Interaction — Jamroziak, Emilia
A Monastery in Time: The Making of Mongolian Buddhism — Humphrey, Caroline
Monastic Women and Religious Orders in Late Medieval Bologna — Johnson, Sherri Franks
Monday, Monday — Crook, Elizabeth
c Monday Morning Leadership (Illus. by Loughmiller, Matt) — Addis, Evelyn
Mondo Nano: Fun and Games in the World of Digital Matter — Milburn, Colin
Monet and the Birth of Impressionism — Kramer, Felix
c Monet Changes Mediums (Illus. by Bernard, Courtney) — Mullarkey, Lisa
The Monet Murders — Mort, Terry
Money and Political Economy in the Enlightenment — Carey, Daniel
Money and Soccer: A Soccernomics Guide — Szymanski, Stefan
Money, Banking, and the Business Cycle, 2 vols. — Simpson, Brian P.
The Money Bubble — Turk, James
The Money Compass: Where Your Money Went and How to Get It Back — Grinmaldi, Mark A.
Money, Family, Murder — Patten, Timothy
Money for the Asking: Fundraising in Music Libraries — Munstedt, Peter
The Money Makers: How Roosevelt and Keynes Ended the Depression, Defeated Fascism, and Secured a Prosperous Peace — Rauchway, Eric
Money Money Money Water Water Water — Mead, Jane
Money, Oil and Empire in the Middle East: Sterling amd Postwar Imperialism, 1944-1971 — Galpern, Steven G.

c Money Skills: Opening a Bank Account — Simms, Susan Rose
Money, Taste, and Wine: It's Complicated! — Veseth, Mike
Money: The Unauthorized Biography--from Coinage to Cryptocurrencies — Martin, Felix
The Money Trader — Anderson, Jerry
Money, Trains, and Guillotines: Art and Revolution in 1960s Japan — Marotti, William
The Mongol Empire: Genghis Khan, His Heirs and the Founding of Modern China — Man, John
The Mongols and the Black Sea Trade in the Thirteenth and Fourteenth Centuries — Ciociltan, Virgil
y The Mongoose: XIII Mystery, vol. 1 (Illus. by Meyer, Ralph) — Dorison, Xavier
Mongrels or Marvels: The Levantine Writings of Jacqueline Shohet Kabarnoff — Manning, Olivia
Monk Dawson — Read, Piers Paul
c Monkey (Illus. by Brown, Marc) — Brown, Marc
c Monkey and Duck Quack Up! (Illus. by Fotheringham, Edwin) — Hamburg, Jennifer
Monkey and Elephant and a Secret Birthday Surprise (Illus. by Bernstein, Galia) — Schaefer, Carole Lexa
c The Monkey and the Bee (Illus. by Raymundo, Peter) — Bloom, C.P.
c The Monkey and the Bee (Illus. by Bloom, C.P.) — Raymundo, Peter
c Monkey and the Little One (Illus. by Alexander, Claire) — Alexander, Claire
y Monkey Business — Margolis, Leslie
c Monkey Me and the New Neighbor — Roland, Timothy
y Monkey Me and the School Ghost — Roland, Timothy
c Monkey: Not Ready for Kindergarten (Illus. by Brown, Marc) — Brown, Marc
c Monkey or Ape? — Kralovansky, Susan
y Monkey Wars — Kurti, Richard
The Monkey's Mask: Identity, Memory, Narrative and Voice — Kearney, Chris
Monkeys, Myths, and Molecules: Separating Fact from Fiction in the Science of Everyday Life — Schwarcz, Joe
c Monkeys on a Fast (Illus. by Ranade, Shilpa) — Viswanath, Kaushik
c The Monkey's Secret — Choldenko, Gennifer
The Monk's Haggadah: A Fifteenth-Century Illuminated Codex from the Monastery of Tegernsee, with a Prologue by Friar Erhard von Pappenheim — Stern, David
The Monks of Saint Pancras: Lewes Priory, England's Premier Cluniac Monastery and its Dependencies, 1076-1537 — Mayhew, Graham
Mono Lake: From Dead Sea to Environmental Treasure — Hoffman, Abraham
Monolith — Hutson, Shaun
Monologue: What Makes America Laugh before Bed (Read by Heller, Johnny). Audiobook Review — Macks, Jon
Monologue: What Makes America Laugh before Bed — Macks, Jon
The Monopolists: Obsession, Fury, and the Scandal behind the World's Favorite Board Game — Pilon, Mary
Monopolizing the Master: Henry James and the Politics of Literary Scholarship — Anesko, Michael
The Monotheizing Process: Its Origins and Development — Sanders, James A.
Monseigneur Darboy (1813-1871): Archeveque de Paris entre Pie IX et Napoleon III — Boudon, Jacques-Olivier
Monsieur Jean: From Bachelor to Father — Berberian, Charles
y Monster (Illus. by Anyabwile, Dawud) — Myers, Walter Dean
y Monster — Skuse, C.J.
The Monster Book of Manga Steampunk — Balaguer, Jorge
c Monster Book — Hoogstad, Alice
Monster Busters — Funke, Cornelia
Monster Goose Nursery Rhymes (Illus. by Larson, Abigail) — Henry, Josh
c Monster Goose Nursery Rhymes (Illus. by Larson, Abigail) — Herz, Henry
c Monster Goose Nursery Rhymes (Illus. by Larson, Abigail) — Herz, Josh
Monster Hunters: On the Trail with Ghost Hunters, Bigfooters, Ufologists, and Other Paranormal Investigators — Krulos, Tea
c Monster Hunters (Illus. by Brundage, Scott) — Fields, Jan

c A Monster Moved In! (Illus. by Schauer, Loretta) — Knapman, Timothy
c Monster Needs a Christmas Tree (Illus. by Grieb, Wendy) — Czajak, Paul
c Monster Needs a Party (Illus. by Grieb, Wendy) — Czajak, Paul
c Monster Needs Your Vote (Illus. by Grieb, Wendy) — Czajak, Paul
c Monster on the Hill (Illus. by Harrell, Rob) — Harrell, Rob
c Monster Party! (Illus. by Bach, Annie) — Bach, Annie
c Monster School: The Spooky Sleepover — Keane, Dave
c Monster Trouble! (Illus. by Robertson, Michael) — Fredrickson, Lane
c The Monster Under My Web (Illus. by Gresham, Charlene) — Gresham, Charlene
y The Monster Within — Pitt, Darrell
c Monster Zit! (Illus. by Smith, Tim, III) — Torres, J. (b. 1969-)
c The Monsterator — Graves, Keith
c The Monsterjunkies — Shein, Daniel
y Monsterland — Cash, Michael Phillip
Monsters and Monstrosity from the Fin de Siecle to the Millennium — Brown, Rebecca A.
c Monsters Love School — Austin, Mike
y Monsters of the Deep — Perritano, John
y Monsters on Land — Perritano, John
c Monsters on the Run — Sherry, Kevin
Monsters: The Hindenburg Disaster and the Birth of Pathological Technology — Regis, Ed
Monsters, Zombies and Addicts — Zepeda, Gwendolyn
c Monstrous (Illus. by Young, Skottie) — Connolly, MarcyKate
y Monstrous Affections: An Anthology of Beastly Tales — Link, Kelly
A Monstrous Commotion: The Mysteries of Loch Ness — Williams, Gareth
c Monstrous — Connolly, MarcyKate
c Monstrous (Illus. by Young, Skottie) — Connolly, MarcyKate
The Monstrous — Datlow, Ellen
Montaigne et les livres — Gray, Floyd
Montaigne — Zweig, Stefan
Montaigne: une anthropologie des passions — Ferrari, Emiliano
Montaigne's English Journey: Reading the Essays in Shakespeare's Day — Hamlin, William M.
Montalbano's First Case and Other Stories — Camilleri, Andrea
Montana Cherries — Law, Kim
Montana: The Biography of Football's Joe Cool — Dunnavant, Keith
The Montana Vigilantes, 1863-1870: Gold, Guns, and Gallows — Dillon, Mark C.
The Montana Vigilantes, 1863-1870: Golds, Guns, and Gallows — Dillon, Mark C.
Montana Winter — Roberts, M.J.
Montcalm & Wolfe: Two Men Who Forever Changed the Course of Canadian History — Carrier, Roch
Monte Cassino: Ten Armies in Hell — Caddick-Adams, Peter
Monterey — Milk Carton Kids
Montesquieu and the Discovery of the Social — Singer, Brian C.J.
c Montessori Map Work (Illus. by Nassner, Alyssa) — George, Bobby
c The Montgomery Bus Boycott: A Primary Source Exploration of the Protest for Equal Treatment — Kimmel, Allison Crotzer
Montgomery Ward & Co. Catalogue & Buyers' Guide 1895 — Montgomery Ward
The Month That Changed The World: July 2014 — Martel, Gordon
Montpelier Tomorrow — MacDonald, Marylee
c Monty's Magnificent Mane (Illus. by O'Neill, Gemma) — O'Neill, Gemma
Monty's Men: The British Army and the Liberation of Europe, 1944-5 — Buckley, John
Monuments and Monumentality across Medieval and Early Modern Europe: Proceedings of the 2011 Stirling Conference — Penman, Michael
The Mood Guide to Fabric and Fashion: The Essential Guide from the World's Most Famous Fabric Store — Miller, Johnny
Moods — Hoffmann, Yoel
Moody Bitches: The Truth about the Drugs You're Taking, the Sleep You're Missing, the Sex You're Not Having, and What's Really Making You Crazy (Read by Campbell, Cassandra). Audiobook Review — Holland, Julie

Moody Bitches: The Truth about the Drugs You're Taking, the Sleep You're Missing, the Sex You're Not Having, and What's Really Making You Crazy — *Holland, Julie*
Moody Bitches: The Truth about the Drugs, You're Taking, the Sleep You're Missing, the Sex You're Not Having, and What's Really Making You Crazy — *Holland, Julie*
y Moon at Nine — *Ellis, Deborah*
Moon Baboon Canoe — *Barwin, Gary*
c Moon Bear (Illus. by Gottardo, Alessandro) — *Lewis, Gill*
c Moon Bears (Illus. by Newman, Mark) — *Newman, Mark*
Moon Country — *Arnott, Peter*
c The Moon Dragons (Illus. by Blythe, Gary) — *Sheldon, Dyan*
Moon in a Dead Eye — *Garnier, Pascal*
The Moon in the Palace — *Randel, Weina Dai*
c The Moon Is Going to Addy's House (Illus. by Pearle, Ida) — *Pearle, Ida*
c Moon Rising — *Sutherland, Tui T.*
y Moon Tears — *Frische, M.M.*
Moondance Beach — *Donovan, Susan*
Moone Boy: The Blunder Years (Read by O'Dowd, Chris, and Nick V. Murphy). Audiobook Review — *O'Dowd, Chris*
y Moone Boy: The Blunder Years (Illus. by Giampaglia, Walter) — *O'Dowd, Chris*
c Moonfin: Through the Watery Door — *Mintie, L.L.*
Moonlight on Butternut Lake — *McNear, Mary*
Moonlight on Nightingale Way — *Young, Samantha*
Moonlight over Paris — *Robson, Jennifer*
The Moonlit Door — *Lake, Deryn*
c The Moonlit Party (Illus. by Boutavant, Marc) — *Desbordes, Astrid*
c Moonman (Illus. by Barraud, Ned) — *Barraud, Ned*
c Moonpenny Island (Illus. by Ford, Gilbert) — *Springstubb, Tricia*
Moonraker (Read by Nighy, Bill). Audiobook Review — *Fleming, Ian*
Moonrise — *Bova, Ben*
c Moons — *Riggs, Kate*
Moonshadows — *Westin, Julie*
Moonshadows — *Weston, Julie*
c Moonshot: The Indigenous Comics Collection — *Nicholson, Hope*
The Moonstone (Read by Pickup, Ronald). Audiobook Review — *Collins, Wilkie*
Moonstruck: How Lunar Cycles Affect Life — *Naylor, Ernest*
c Moore Zombies: The Search for Gargoy (Illus. by Allen, Brian) — *Knuth, Wendy*
Moore's Law: The Life of Gordon Moore, Silicon Valley's Quiet Revolutionary — *Thackray, Arnold*
The Moor's Account — *Lalami, Laila*
Moral Agents: Eight Twentieth-Century American Writers — *Mendelson, Edward*
Moral als Kapital in Antiken Gesellschaften
The Moral Arc: How Science and Reason lead Humanity toward Truth, Justice and Freedom — *Shermer, Michael*
Moral Authority, Men of Science, and the Victorian Novel — *DeWitt, Anne*
Moral Blindness: The Loss of Sensitivity in Liquid Modernity — *Bauman, Zygmunt*
The Moral Case for Fossil Fuels — *Epstein, Alex*
The Moral Complexities of Eating Meat — *Bramble, Ben*
Moral Conscience through the Ages — *Sorabji, Richard*
The Moral Economy: Poverty, Credit, and Trust in Early Modern Europe — *Fontaine, Laurence*
The Moral Economy: Poverty, Credit, and Trust in Early Modern Europe — *Henderickson, Jon K.*
Moral Error Theory: History, Critique, Defence — *Olson, Jonas*
Moral Imagination — *Bromwich, David*
Moral Minorities and the Making of American Democracy — *Volk, Kyle G.*
Moral Nation: Modern Japan and Narcotics in Global History — *Kingsberg, Miriam*
Moral Perception — *Audi, Robert*
Moral Reason — *Markovits, Julia*
Moral Time — *Black, Donald*
Morality and War: Can War Be Just in the Twenty-First Century? — *Fisher, David*
The Morality of Private War — *Pattison, James*
Morality: Truly Christian, Truly African: Foundational, Methodological, and Theological Considerations — *Odozor, Paulinus Ikechukwu*

Moralizing Technology: Understanding and Designing the Morality of Things — *Verbeek, Peter-Paul*
c More! (Illus. by Warnes, Tim) — *Corderoy, Tracey*
c More about Paddington (Illus. by Fortnum, Peggy) — *Bond, Michael (b. 1926-)*
More American Than Southern: Kentucky, Slavery, and the War for an American Ideology, 1828-1861 — *Mattehews, Gary R.*
c More and More (Illus. by Dodd, Emma) — *Dodd, Emma*
More Awesome Than Money: Four Boys and Their Heroic Quest to Save Your Privacy from Facebook — *Dwyer, Jim*
More Awesome Than Money: Four Boys, Three Years, and a Chronicle of Ideals and Ambition in Silicon Valley — *Dwyer, Jim*
c More Blueberries! (Illus. by Melo, Esperanca) — *Musgrave, Susan*
More Classics to Moderns, Books 1-6, Second Series — *Agay, Denes*
More Creative Lettering: Techniques and Tips from Top Artists — *Doh, Jenny*
More Fallacies, Flaws, and Flimflam — *Barbeau, Edward*
More Fool Me: A Memoir — *Fry, Stephen*
More Fool Me — *Fry, Stephen*
y More Happy Than Not — *Silvera, Adam*
More Human: Designing a World Where People Come First — *Hilton, Steve*
More Important than the Music: A History of Jazz Discography — *Epperson, Bruce D.*
More Letters of Note: Correspondence Deserving of a Wider Audience — *Usher, Shaun*
More Library Mashups: Exploring New Ways to Deliver Library Data — *Engard, Nicole C.*
More Lives than One: The Extraordinary Life of Felix Dennis — *Byrne, Fergus*
More Mexican Everyday: Simple, Seasonal, Celebratory — *Bayless, Rick*
More Mind-Bending Puzzles and Fascinating Facts: A Compendium for All Ages — *Williams, Paul*
More Money Than God — *Michelson, Richard*
More Monster Knits for Little Monsters; 20 Super-Cute Animal-Themed Hat and Mitten Sets to Knit — *Khegay, Nuriya*
More Perfect Unions: The American Search for Marital Bliss — *Davis, Rebecca L.*
More Studies in Ethnomethodology — *Liberman, Kenneth*
More Than Conquerors: A Memoir of Lost Arguments — *Hustad, Megan*
c More Than Enough: A Passover Story (Illus. by Kath, Katie) — *Wayland, April Halprin*
More Than Happy: The Wisdom of Amish Parenting — *Miller, Serena B.*
More Than Hot: A Short History of Fever — *Hamlin, Christopher*
More Than Just War: Narratives of the Just War Tradition and Military Life — *Jones, Charles A.*
More Than Nature Needs: Language, Mind, and Evolution — *Bickerton, Derek*
More Than Shelter: Activism and Community in San Francisco Public Housing — *Howard, Amy L.*
More Than Two to Tango: Argentine Tango Immigrants in New York City — *Viladrich, Anahi*
More Than Words — *Kove, T.T.*
More Than You Know — *Gracen, Jennifer*
Morgan le Fay, Shapeshifter — *Hebert, Jill M.*
c Morgan's Boat Ride (Illus. by Bald, Anna) — *MacDonald, Hugh*
Morgan's Got Game (Illus. by Slavin, Bill) — *Staunton, Ted*
Moriarty — *Horowitz, Anthony*
Mormon Feminism — *Wheelwright, Hannah*
The Mormon Tabernacle Choir: A Biography — *Hicks, Michael*
Morning and Evening — *Fosse, Jon*
Morning Briefings — *Digiacomo, Christine*
Morning Sea — *Mazzantini, Margaret*
Morning Star — *Brown, Pierce*
c A Morning to Polish and Keep (Illus. by Lott, Sheena) — *Lawson, Julie*
c A Morning with Grandpa (Illus. by Forshay, Christina) — *Liu, Sylvia*
Moroccan Noir: Police, Crime, and Politics in Popular Culture, Public Cultures of the Middle East and North Africa — *Smolin, Jonathan*
The Moroccan Women's Rights Movement — *Evrard, Amy Young*
Morocco on a Plate: Breads, Entrees and Desserts with Authentic Spice — *Hofberg, Caroline*

c Morris Micklewhite and the Tangerine Dress (Illus. by Malenfant, Isabelle) — *Baldacchino, Christine*
Mort(e): A Novel (Read by Pinchot, Bronson). Audiobook Review — *Repino, Robert*
Mort(e). — *Repino, Robert*
Mortal Blessings: A Sacramental Farewell — *O'Donnell, Angela Alaimo*
y Mortal Danger — *Aguirre, Ann*
y Mortal Gods — *Blake, Kendare*
y Mortal Heart (Read by Grace, Jennifer). Audiobook Review — *LaFevers, Robin*
y Mortal Heart — *LaFevers, Robin*
Mortal Thoughts: Religion, Secularity and Identity in Shakespeare and Early Modern Culture — *Cummings, Brian*
Morte e elezione del papa: Norme, riti e conflitti: Il medioevo — *Paravicini-Bagliani, Agostino*
Morte e elezione del papa: Norme, riti e conflitti: L'Eta moderna — *Visceglia, Maria Antonietta*
Mortgage Matters — *Gutierrez, Sylvia M.*
c Mortimer Keene: Dino Danger (Illus. by Mould, Chris) — *Healey, Tim*
Mosaic Garden Projects: Add Color to Your Garden with Tables, Fountains, Bird Baths, and More — *Brody, Mark*
Mosaic Garden Projects: Add Color to Your Garden with Tables, Fountains, Birdbaths, and More — *Brody, Mark*
Mosambikanische Vertragsarbeiter in der DDR-Wirtschaft: Hintergrund - Verlauf - Folgen — *van der Heyden, Ulrich*
Moscow in Movement: Power and Opposition in Putin's Russia — *Greene, Samuel A.*
Moses Finley and Politics — *Harris, William V.*
c Moses: The True Story of an Elephant Baby — *Perepeczko, Jenny*
Moskauer Tagebucher: Wer Wir Sind und Wer Wir Waren — *Wolf, Christa*
Moskov Selim — *Vizyenos, Georgios*
c The Mosquito Brothers (Illus. by Salcedo, Erica) — *Ondaatje, Griffin*
Mosquito Trails: Ecology, Health, and the Politics of Entanglement — *Nading, Alex*
y Mosquitoland (Read by Strole, Phoebe). Audiobook Review — *Arnold, David (b. 1981-)*
y Mosquitoland — *Arnold, David (b. 1981-)*
Moss: Stories from the Edge of Nature — *Keane, Marc Peter*
c Mossy Trotter (Illus. by Ross, Tony) — *Taylor, Elizabeth*
The Most Adorable Animals in the World — *Gagne, Tammy*
The Most Amazing Creature in the Sea (Illus. by Spirin, Gennady) — *Guiberson, Brenda Z.*
y The Most Beautiful Bully — *Freeman, Shannon*
A Most Beautiful Deception — *Lacroix, Melissa Morelli*
The Most Dangerous Book: The Battle for James Joyce's Ulysses — *Birmingham, Kevin*
y Most Dangerous: Daniel Ellsberg and the Secret History of the Vietnam War — *Sheinkin, Steve*
The Most Defiant Devil: William Temple Hornaday and His Controversial Crusade to Save American Wildlife — *Dehler, Gregory J.*
c The Most Endangered Animals in the World — *Gagne, Tammy*
The Most Excellent Book of Cookery — *Tomasik, Timothy J.*
The Most Good You Can Do: How Effective Altruism Is Changing Ideas about Living Ethically — *Singer, Peter*
A Most Imperfect Union: A Contrarian History of the United States (Illus. by Alcaraz, Lalo) — *Stavans, Ilan*
y Most Likely to Succeed — *Echols, Jennifer*
Most Likely to Succeed: Preparing Our Kids for the Innovation Era — *Wagner, Tony*
c The Most Powerful Thing in the World (Illus. by Barrett, Angela) — *French, Vivian*
Most Secret Agent of Empire: Reginald Teague-Jones, Master Spy of the Great Game — *Ter Minassian, Taline*
A Most Uncertain Crusade: The United States, the United Nations, and Human Rights, 1941-1953 — *Brucken, Rowland M.*
The Most Wanted Man in China: My Journey from Scientist to Enemy of the State — *Fang, Lizhi*
The Most Wanted Man in China: My Journey from Scientist to Enemy of the State — *Lizhi, Fang*
Most Wanted Particle: The Inside Story of the Hunt for the Higgs, the Heart of the Future of Physics — *Butterworth, Jon*

c The Most Wonderful Thing in the World (Illus. by Barrett, Angela) — French, Vivian
The Motet around 1500: On the Relationship of Imitation and Text Treatment? — Schmidt-Beste, Thomas
c Moth or Butterfly? — Kralovansky, Susan
The Moth Snowstorm: Nature and Joy — McCarthy, Michael
c Mother Bruce (Illus. by Higgins, Ryan T.) — Higgins, Ryan T.
c Mother Goose's Pajama Party (Illus. by Allyn, Virginia) — Smith, Danna
The Mother of All Booklists: The 500 Most Recommended Nonfiction Reads for Ages 3 to 103 — Martin, William Patrick
Mother of Demons — Sims, Maynard
y Mother of Eden — Beckett, Chris
Motherhood and Infertility in Ireland: Understanding the Presence of Absence — Allison, Jill
Motherhood and Patriarchal Masculinities in Sixteenth-Century Italian Comedy — Manes, Yael
Mothering the Fatherland: A Protestant Sisterhood Repents for the Holocaust — Faithful, George
y Motherland: Growing Up with the Holocaust — Goldberg, Rita
The Motherless Child in the Novels of Pauline Hopkins — Bergman, Jill
Motherless Child — Hirshberg, Glen
y The Motherless Child Project — McQueen, Janie
Motherload: Making It All Better in Insecure Times — Villalobos, Ana
Mothers, Tell Your Daughters (Read by Delaine, Christina). Audiobook Review — Campbell, Bonnie Jo
Mothers, Tell Your Daughters — Campbell, Bonnie Jo
Motherwit — Pawar, Urmila
c Mothman's Curse (Illus. by Hindle, James K.) — Hayes, Christine
c Motiti Blue and the Oil Spill — McCauley, Debbie
Motive — Kellerman, Jonathan
Motive und Rollen des Autors in Vergils Eklogen, den Oden des Horaz und den Elegien des Properz — Kimmel, Meike
c Motocross — Hamilton, John
c Motorcycles (Illus. by West, David) — West, David
Motorcycles I've Loved: A Memoir — Brooks-Dalton, Lily
Motorcycles I've Loved: A Memoir — Dalton, Lily Brooks
Motorcycles I've Loved: A Memoir — Brooks-Dalton, Lily
Motoring West, vol. 1: Automobile Pioneers, 1900-1909 — Blodgett, Peter J.
c Mouche-toi, grand mechant loup! — Smallman, Steve
The Mount Athos Diet: The Mediterranean Plan to Lose Weight, Look Younger and Live Longer — Storey, Richard
Mount Terminus — Grand, David
The Mountain and the Fathers: Growing Up on the Big Dry — Wilkins, Joe
The Mountain and the Wall — Ganieva, Alisa
The Mountain Can Wait — Leipciger, Sarah
Mountain City Girls — McGarrigle, Anna
c The Mountain Jews and the Mirror (Illus. by Kosec, Polona) — Feuerman, Ruchama King
c The Mountain Jews and the Mirror (Illus. by Calderon, Polona) — Feuerman, Ruchama Kinger
The Mountain Midwife — Eakes, Laurie Alice
c Mountain Peak Peril (Illus. by Shephard, David) — Townsend, John
Mountain Rampage — Graham, Scott
The Mountain Shadow — Roberts, Gregory David
y The Mountain Story — Lansens, Lori
Mountains and Marshes: Exploring the Bay Area's Natural History — Wallace, David Rains
Mounting Frustration: The Art Museum in the Age of Black Power — Cahan, Susan E.
c Mountwood School for Ghosts — Ibbotson, Toby
y Mourner's Bench — Faye, Sanderia
The Mourning Bells — Trent, Christine
Mourning Headband for Hue: An Account of the Battle for Hue, Vietnam 1968 — Ca, Nha
Mourning Lincoln — Hodes, Martha
c The Mouse Mansion — Schaapman, Karina
Mouse Models of Cancer: A Laboratory Manual — Abate-Shen, Cory
c Mouse Scouts: Make a Difference (Illus. by Dillard, Sarah) — Dillard, Sarah
c Mouse Scouts (Illus. by Dillard, Sarah) — Dillard, Sarah
c A Mouse So Small (Illus. by Pedler, Caroline) — McAllister, Angela

The Mouse That Roared — Wibberley, Leonard
c Mouse Was Mad — Urban, Linda
c The Mouse Who Ate the Moon — Horacek, Petr
c Mouse's First Night at Moonlight School (Illus. by Pye, Ali) — Puttock, Simon
c Mousetropolis (Illus. by Christie, R. Gregory) — Christie, R. Gregory
c A Mousy Mess (Illus. by Melmon, Deborah) — Driscoll, Laura
Mouth — Sutherland-Smith, James
The Mouth of the Crocodile — Pearce, Michael
Move: Putting America's Infrastructure Back in the Lead — Kanter, Rosabeth Moss
Move Up: Why Some Cultures Advance While Others Don't — Rapaille, Clotaire
Move Your Blooming Corpse — Ireland, D.E.
Moved by the Past: Discontinuity and Historical Mutation — Runia, Eelco
Movie Freak: My Life Watching Movies — Gleiberman, Owen
Movie Star by Lizzie Pepper — Liftin, Hilary
c Movies and TV Top Tens — Donovan, Sandy
c Movila mano / I Moved My Hand (Illus. by Sadat, Mandana) — Lujan, Jorge
c Moving Blocks (Illus. by Yonezu, Yusuke) — Yonezu, Yusuke
Moving Images: Nineteenth-Century Reading and Screen Practices — Groth, Helen
Moving in the Shadows: Violence in the Lives of Minority Women and Children — Rehman, Yasmin
Moving Matters: Paths of Serial Migration — Ossman, Susan
y Moving Target — Gonzalez, Christina Diaz
Mozart: A Life — Johnson, Paul
Mozos: A Decade Running with the Bulls of Spain — Hillman, Bill
Mr. and Mrs. Disraeli: A Strange Romance — Hay, Daisy
Mr. and Mrs. Doctor — Iromuanya, Julie
c Mr. Ball: An EGG-cellent Adventure — Townsend, Michael
Mr. Bones: Twenty Stories — Theroux, Paul
c Mr. Brown's Fantastic Hat — Imai, Ayano
Mr. Campion's Fox — Ripley, Mike
Mr Churchill's Profession: Statesman, Orator, Writer — Clarke, Peter
c Mr. Cornell's Dream Boxes — Winter, Jeanette
c Mr. Ferris and His Wheel (Illus. by Ford, Gilbert) — Davis, Kathryn Gibbs
Mr. Flagler's St. Augustine — Graham, Thomas (b. 1943-)
c Mr. Frank (Illus. by Luxbacher, Irene) — Luxbacher, Irene
c Mr. Goat's Valentine (Illus. by Zimmer, Kevin) — Bunting, Eve
c Mr. Happy & Miss Grimm (Illus. by Strasser, Susanne) — Schneider, Antonie
Mr Huff (Illus. by Walker, Anna) — Walker, Anna
c Mr. Jacobson's Window — Froese, Deborah
Mr. Kafka: And Other Tales from the Time of the Cult — Hrabal, Bohumil
c Mr. Lemoncello's Library Olympics — Grabenstein, Chris
Mr. Mac and Me — Freud, Esther
c Mr. McGinty's Monarchs — Vander Heyden, Linda
c The Mr. Men Collection, vol. 1 (Read by Dale, Jim). Audiobook Review — Hargreaves, Roger
Mr. Mercedes — King, Stephen
c Mr. Mistoffelees (Illus. by Robins, Arthur) — Eliot, T.S.
Mr. Mojo: A Biography of Jim Morrison — Jones, Dylan
c Mr. Okra Sells Fresh Fruits and Vegetables (Illus. by Henriquez, Emile) — Daley, Lashon
Mr. Osborne's Economic Experiment: Austerity 1945-51 and 2010 — Keegan, William
Mr. P.C.: The Life and Music of Paul Chambers — Palmer, Rob
c Mr. Pants: It's Go Time! — McCormick, Scott
c Mr. Pants: Slacks, Camera, Action! (Illus. by Lazzell, R.H.) — McCormick, Scott
c Mr. Pants: Trick or Feet! (Illus. by Lazzell, R.H.) — McCormick, Scott
c Mr. Postmouse's Rounds (Illus. by Dubuc, Marianne) — Dubuc, Marianne
c Mr. Postmouse's Rounds — Dubuc, Marianne
c Mr. Puffball: Stunt Cat to the Stars (Illus. by Lombardo, Constance) — Lombardo, Constance
Mr. Putin: Operative in the Kremlin — Hill, Fiona
c Mr. Putter & Tabby Smell the Roses (Illus. by Howard, Arthur) — Rylant, Cynthia

c Mr. Putter & Tabby Turn the Page (Illus. by Howard, Arthur) — Rylant, Cynthia
c Mr. Reaper (Illus. by Miyanishi, Tatsuya) — Miyanishi, Tatsuya
Mr. Robot — Malek, Rami
Mr. Selden's Map of China: Decoding the Secrets of a Vanished Cartographer — Brook, Timothy
Mr Smiley: My Last Pill and Testament — Marks, Howard
Mr. Smith Goes to Prison: What My Year behind Bars Taught Me about America's Prison Crisis — Smith, Jeff (b. 1973-)
Mr. Splitfoot — Hunt, Samantha
c Mr. Squirrel and the Moon (Illus. by Meschenmoser, Sebastian) — Meschenmoser, Sebastian
Mr. Suicide — Cushing, Nicole
c Mr. Tiger Goes Wild — Brown, Peter (b. 1979-)
c Mr. Tweed's Good Deeds (Illus. by Stoten, Jim) — Stoten, Jim
c Mr. Wayne's Masterpiece (Illus. by Polacco, Patricia) — Polacco, Patricia
Mr. West — Blake, Sarah
Mr. Wrigley's Ball Club: Chicago and the Cubs during the Jazz Age — Ehrgott, Roberts
c Mr. Wugidgem and the Dark Journey — Chapman, Allan Westcott
c Mr. Wugidgem and the Faces of Freedom — Chapman, Allan Westcott
c Mr. Wugidgem and the Phoenix Journey — Chapman, Allan Westcott
c Mr. Wugidgem and the Snow Queen — Chapman, Allan Westcott
c Mrs. Carter's Butterfly Garden — Rich, Steve
Mrs. Engels — McCrea, Gavin
Mrs. Grant and Madame Jule — Chiaverini, Jennifer
Mrs. Houdini — Kelly, Victoria
Mrs. Hudson In New York — Brown, Barry S.
Mrs. Lee's Rose Garden: The True Story of the Founding of Arlington National Cemetery — DeVito, Carlo
c Mrs. Mo's Monster — Beavis, Paul
c Mrs. Noodlekugel and Drooly the Bear (Illus. by Stower, Adam) — Pinkwater, Daniel
Mrs. Pargeter's Principle — Brett, Simon
Mrs. Queen Takes the Train — Kuhn, William
Mrs. Roosevelt's Confidante — MacNeal, Susan Elia
Mrs. Sinclair's Suitcase — Walters, Louise
Mrs Stone and Dr Smellie: Eighteenth Century Midwives and their Patients — Woods, Robert
Mrs. Valentine's Revenge — Ginsberg, Al
Mrs. Wheelbarrow's Practical Pantry: Recipes and Techniques for Year-Round Preserving — Barrow, Cathy
c Mrs. Yonkers is Bonkers! (Read by Goldsmith, Jared). Audiobook Review — Gutman, Dan
c Ms. Coco Is Loco (Read by Goldsmith, Jared). Audiobook Review — Gutman, Dan
y Ms. Marvel: Crushed (Illus. by Bondoc, Elmo) — Wilson, G. Willow
y Ms. Marvel: Generation Why (Illus. by Wyatt, Jacob) — Wilson, G. Willow
y Ms. Marvel (Illus. by Alphona, Adrian) — Wilson, G. Willow
y Ms. Marvel: No Normal (Illus. by Alphona, Adrian) — Wilson, G. Willow
c Ms. Rapscott's Girls (Read by Kellgren, Katherine). Audiobook Review — Primavera, Elise
c Ms. Rapscott's Girls (Illus. by Primavera, Elise) — Primavera, Elise
c Ms. Spell (Illus. by Long, Ethan) — Long, Ethan
Mu Shiying: China's Lost Modernist — Field, Andrew David
c Muddle & Mo — Robinson, Nikki Slade
Muddy Jungle Rivers: A River Assault Boat Cox'n's Memory Journey of His War in Vietnam and Return Home — Affield, Wendell
Muhammad in History, Thought, and Culture: An Encyclopedia of the Prophet of God — Fitzpatrick, Coeli
Mujeres en el cambio social en el siglo XX mexicano — Aceves, Maria Teresa Fernandez
Mujeres epicas espanolas: silencios, olvidos e ideologias — Ratcliffe, Marjorie
The Mulatto Republic: Class, Race, and Dominican National Identity — Mayes, April J.
The Mulberry Bush — McCarry, Charles
Mules — Muldoon, Paul
Mulieres Religiosae: Shaping Female Spiritual Authority in the Medieval and Early Modern Periods — Fraeters, Veerle
c Mullaly Fish in a Tree — Hunt, Lynda

Multicultural Girlhood: Racism, Sexuality, and the Conflicted Spaces of American Education — Thomas, Mary E.
Multinational Federalism in Bosnia and Herzegovina — Soeren, Keil
Multiple Identities: Migrants, Ethnicity, and Membership — Spickard, Paul
Multiple Listings — McMillan, Tracy
Multiple Modernities and Postsecular Societies — Rosati, Massimo
Multiples in Pre-Modern Art — Cupperi, Walter
Multiply/Divide — Walters, Wendy S.
The Multisensory Museum: Cross-Disciplinary Perspectives on Touch, Sounds, Smell, Memory, and Space — Levant, Nina
Multitudinous Heart: Selected Poems: A Bilingual Edition — de Andrade, Carlos Drummond
Multitudinous Heart: Selected Poems: A Bilingual Edition — Drummond, Carlos
Multitudinous Heart: Selected Poems — Zenith, Richard
c Mum Goes to Work (Illus. by Rudge, Leila) — Gleeson, Libby
c Mumbet's Declaration of Independence (Read by Berneis, Susie). Audiobook Review — Woelfle, Gretchen
Mumbling Beauty Louise Bourgeois — Van Gelder, Alex
Mumbling Reality Louise Bourgeois — Gelder, Alex Van
Mummies around the World: An Encyclopedia of Mummies in History, Religion, and Popular Culture — Cardin, Matt
c Mummy Cat (Illus. by Brown, Lisa) — Ewert, Marcus
c The Mummy's Curse — Warner, Penny
c Mummy's Home! (Illus. by Yarlett, Emma) — MacGregor, Christopher
c Muncha! Muncha! Muncha! (Illus. by Karas, G. Brian) — Fleming, Candace
Munich Airport — Baxter, Greg
The Muralist — Shapiro, B.A.
Murder 101 — Kellerman, Faye
Murder and Mendelssohn — Greenwood, Kerry
Murder and Other Unnatural Disasters — Sideris, Lida
Murder at Barclay Meadow — Eckel, Wendy Sand
Murder at Beechwood — Maxwell, Alyssa
Murder at Camp Delta: A Staff Sergeant's Pursuit of Truth about Guantanamo Bay — Hickman, Joseph
Murder at Cape Three Points — Quartey, Kwei
Murder at Cirey — Sawyer, Cheryl
Murder at San Quentin — George, Edward
Murder at the Brightwell (Read by Fulford-Brown, Billie). Audiobook Review — Weaver, Ashley
Murder at the Manor: Country House Mysteries — Edwards, Martin
The Murder Bag (Read by Mace, Colin). Audiobook Review — Parsons, Tony
The Murder, Betrayal, and Slaughter of the Glorious Charles, Count of Flanders. — Galbert of Bruges
Murder by Candlelight: The Gruesome Crimes Behind Our Romance with the Macabre — Beran, Michael Knox
Murder by Kindness: The Gift Quilt — Graham, Barbara
Murder by Suspicion — Heley, Veronica
Murder Comes Calling — Challinor, C.S.
y The Murder Complex — Cummings, Lindsay
Murder, D.C. — Tucker, Neely
Murder Freshly Baked (Read by Ertl, Renee). Audiobook Review — Chapman, Vannetta
Murder Freshly Baked — Chapman, Vannetta
Murder in Ely — Nelson, D-L
Murder in Hindsight — Cleeland, Anne
Murder in Megara — Reed, Mary
Murder in Memphis — Porch, Dorris D.
Murder in My Corner — Tuzzo, Ralph J.
Murder in Pigalle — Black, Cara
Murder in the Fifth — Sharrow, Ed
Murder in the Merchant's Hall — Emerson, Kathy Lynn
Murder in the Paperback Parlor — Adams, Ellery
Murder in the Queen's Wardrobe — Emerson, Kathy Lynn
y Murder Is Bad Manners — Stevens, Robin
Murder, Mayhem and Music Hall: The Dark Side of Victorian London — Anthony, Barry
Murder Most Malicious — Maxwell, Alyssa
Murder Most Queer: The Homicidal Homosexual in the American Theater — Schildcrout, Jordan
Murder Most Serene — Wittkop, Gabrielle
Murder Most Unfortunate — Wagner, David P.

Murder New York Style: Family Matters — Page, Anita
Murder of a Lady — Wynne, Anthony
A Murder of Clones — Rusch, Kristine Kathryn
Murder of Crows — Bellet, Annie
The Murder of Halland — Juul, Pia
The Murder of Harriet Krohn — Fossum, Karin
The Murder of King James I — Bellany, Alistair
A Murder of Magpies (Read by Duerden, Susan). Audiobook Review — Flanders, Judith
A Murder of Magpies — Flanders, Judith
The Murder of William of Norwich: The Origins of the Blood Libel in Medieval Europe — Rose, E.M.
Murder on a Summer's Day — Brody, Frances
Murder on Amsterdam Avenue — Thompson, Victoria
Murder on Easter Island — Conrad, Gary D.
Murder on St. Nicholas Avenue — Thompson, Victoria
Murder on the Bucket List — Perona, Elizabeth
Murder on the Champ de Mars — Black, Cara
Murder on the Last Frontier — Pegau, Cathy
Murder on the Minneapolis — Davison, Anita
Murder on the Switzerland Trail — Befeler, Mike
A Murder over a Girl: Justice, Gender, Junior High — Corbett, Ken
The Murder Road — Booth, Stephen
Murder She Wrote: The Ghost and Mrs. Fletcher — Paley-Bain, Renee
Murder State: California's Native American Genocide, 1846-1873 — Lindsay, Brendan C.
Murder under the Bridge — Raphael, Kate Jessica
Murder with a Twist — Kiely, Tracy
Murder with Fried Chicken and Waffles — Herbert, A.L.
Murdered on the Streets of Tombstone — Aros, Joyce
The Murderer's Daughter — Kellerman, Jonathan
A Murderous Mind — Adams, Jane A.
Murderous Passions: The Delirious Cinema of Jesus Franco, vol. 1: 1959-1974 — Thrower, Stephen
y The Murdstone Trilogy — Peet, Mal
c Murilla Gorilla and the Hammock Problem (Illus. by Lee, Jacqui) — Lloyd, Jennifer
c The Murk — Lettrick, Robert
c Murphy in the City (Illus. by Provensen, Alice) — Provensen, Alice
Murty Classical Library of India — Pollock, Sheldon
Muse: A Novel — Galassi, Jonathan
Muse — Galassi, Jonathan
A Muse and a Maze: Writing as Puzzle, Mystery, and Magic — Turchi, Peter
Muse — Galassi, Jonathan
The Muses and Their Afterlife in Post-Classical Europe — Christian, Kathleen W.
Museum Masterpieces: Piano Solos Inspired by Great Works of Art, 4 vols. — Rollin, Catherine
A Museum of One's Own: Private Collecting, Public Gift — Higonnet, Anne
Museums in China: The Politics of Representation After Mao — Varutti, Marzia
The Mushroom at the End of the World: On the Possibility of Life in Capitalist Ruins — Tsing, Anna Lowenhaupt
Music along the Rapidan: Civil War Soldiers, Music, and Community during Winter Quarters — Davis, James A.
Music along the Rapidan — Davis, James A.
c Music and Dance — McDowell, Pamela
Music and Levels of Narration in Film: Steps across the Border — Heldt, Guido
Music and the British Military in the Long Nineteenth Century — Herbert, Trevor
Music and the Making of Modern Science — Pesic, Peter
Music and the Myth of Arcadia in Renaissance Italy — Gerbino, Giuseppe
Music and the Skillful Listener: American Women Compose the Natural World — von Glahn, Denise
c Music and Theater Top Tens — Donovan, Sandy
Music and Ultra-Modernism in France: A Fragile Consensus, 1913-1939 — Kelly, Barbara L.
Music as Cultural Mission: Explorations of Jesuit Practices in Italy and North America — Celenza, Anna Harwell
Music at Midnight: The Life and Poetry of George Herbert — Drury, John
Music behind Barbed Wire: A Diary of Summer 1940 — Gal, Hans
c Music Class Today! (Illus. by Vogel, Vin) — Weinstone, David
Music, Dance and Society: Medieval and Renaissance Studies in Memory of Ingrid G. Brainard — Buckley, Ann

Music for Children with Hearing Loss: A Resource for Parents and Teachers, — Schraer-Joiner, Lyn E.
Music for the Melodramatic Theater in Nineteenth-Century London and New York — Pisani, Michael V.
Music for Wartime: Stories — Makkai, Rebecca
Music in Kenya Christianity: Logooli Religious Song — Kidula, Jean Ngoya
Music in Shakespeare: A Dictionary — Wilson, Christopher R.
Music in the Baroque — Heller, Wendy
y The Music Industry — Anniss, Matt
Music Lab: We Rock!: A Fun Family Guide for Exploring Rock Music History — Hanley, Jason
The Music Makers — Wachtel, Shirley Russak
Music, Modernity, and God: Essays in Listening — Begbie, Jeremy
The Music of Herbert Howells — Cooke, Phillip A.
The Music of the 18th Century Codex Trujillo del Peru — van der Spoel, Adrian Rodriguez
The Music Parent's Survival Guide — Nathan, Amy
Music, Piety, and Propaganda: The Soundscapes of Counter-Reformation Bavaria — Fisher, Alexander J.
Music Room Posters Set 1: Sousa, Vaughan Williams, Holst, Grainger — Olson, Maria
Music, Style, and Aging: Growing Old Disgracefully? — Bennett, Andy
Music Theory Secrets: 94 Strategies for the Starting Musician — Coppenbarger, Brent
Music to Silence to Music: A Biography of Henry Grimes — Frenz, Barbara
The Music Treatises of Thomas Ravenscroft: 'Treatise of Practicall Musick' and A Briefe Discourse — Duffin, Ross W.
Musica e liturgia a Montecassino nel medioevo: Atti del Simposio internazionale di studi — Tangari, Nicola
Musica Incantans — South, Robert
The Musical Brain - and Other Stories — Andrews, Chris
The Musical Brain and Other Stories — Aira, Cesar
Musical Chairs — Levin, Sheila
The Musical Comedy Films of Grigorii Aleksandrov: Laughing Matters — Salys, Rimgaila
The Musical Experience: Rethinking Music Teaching and Learning — Barrett, Janet R.
The Musical Iconography of Power in Seventeenth-Century Spain and Her Territories — Gonzalez, Sara
The Musical Legacy of Wartime France — Sprout, Leslie A.
A Musical Life in Two Worlds: The Autobiography of Hugo Leichtentritt — Leichtentritt, Hugo
Musicals: The Definitive Illustrated Story — DK Publishing
A Musician Divided: Andre Tchaikowsky in His Own Words — Belina-Johnson, Anastasia
Musik in neuzeitlichen Konfessionskulturen (16. bis 19. Jahrhundert): Raume - Medien - Funktionen — Fischer, Michael
Musik und Melancholie im Werk Heimito von Doderers — Brinkmann, Martin
Musik und Tod im Mittelalter: Imaginationsraume der Transzendenz — Bruggisser-Lanker, Therese
Musik und Vergnugen am Hohen Ufer. Fest- und Kulturtransfer von Venedig nach Hannover in der Fruhen Neuzeit
Musikalische Skalen bei Naturwissenschaftlern der fruhen Neuzeit: Eine elementarmathematische Analyse — Buhler, Walter
Musikphilosophie zur Einfuhrung — Klein, Richard
Musikwissenschaft: Generationen, Netzwerke, Denkstrukturen
Muslim and Christian Contact in the Middle Ages — Rodriguez, Jarbel
The Muslim Brotherhood in Europe — Meijer, Roel
Muslim Childhood: Religious Nurture in a European Context — Scourfield, Jonathan
Muslim-Christian Dialogue in Postcolonial Northern Nigeria: The Challenges of Inclusive Cultural and Religious Pluralism — Iwuchukwu, Marinus C.
Muslim-Christian Relations Observed: Comparative Studies from Indonesia and the Netherlands — Kuster, Volker
Muslim Nationalism and the New Turks — White, Jenny B.
Muslim Zion: Pakistan as a Political Idea — Devji, Faisal
Muslims and Crusaders: Christianity's Wars in the Middle East, 1095-1382, from the Islamic Sources — Christie, Niall

Muslims and Jews in France: History of a Conflict — Mandel, Maud S.
Muslims of Medieval Latin Christendom, c. 1050-1614 — Catlos, Brian A.
Mussolini's Death March: Eyewitness Accounts of Italian Soldiers on the Eastern Front — Revelli, Nuto
Mussolini's Policemen: Behaviour, Ideology and Institutional Culture in Representation and Practice — Dunnage, Jonathan
Mussolini's Policemen: Behaviour, Ideology, and Institutional Culture in Representation and Practice — Dunnage, Jonathan
Must Love Otters (Read by Nordlinger, Romy). Audiobook Review — Gordon, Eliza
c Must. Push. Buttons (Illus. by Krosoczka, Jarrett J.) — Good, Jason
Must We Divide History into Periods? — Goff, Jacques Le
Must We Divide History into Periods? — Le Goff, Jacques
c Mustache Baby Meets His Match (Illus. by Ang, Joy) — Heos, Bridget
Mustang Spring — McCall, Deanna Dickinson
The Musubi Murder — Bow, Frankie
c Mutation — Smith, Roland
c Mutt's Promise (Illus. by Weber, Jill) — Salamon, Julie
c My ABC Book (Illus. by Seiden, Art) — Seiden, Art
c My Abuelita (Illus. by Morales, Yuyi) — Johnston, Tony
My Adventures with Your Money: George Graham Rice and the Golden Age of the Con Artist — Thornton, T.D.
My Age of Anxiety: Fear, Hope, Dread, and the Search for Peace of Mind — Stossel, Scott
c My Alien and Me (Illus. by McLaughlin, Tom) — Prasadam-Halls, Smriti
c My Amazing Body (Illus. by Sanders, Allan) — Martin, Ruth
My American Duchess — James, Eloisa
c My Australian Story: Vietnam — Challinor, Deborah
My Autistic Awakening: Unlocking the Potential for a Life Well Lived — Harris, Rachael Lee
c My Autumn Book (Illus. by Yee, Wong Herbert) — Yee, Wong Herbert
My Avant-Garde Education — Cooper, Bernard
My Badass Book of Saints: Courageous Women Who Showed Me How to Live — Johnson, Maria Morera
c My Barnyard! — Schwartz, Betty Ann
c My Bedtime Monster (Illus. by Pacovska, Kveta) — Schwarz, Annelies
My Beloved World — Sotomayor, Sonia
c My Best Buddy (Illus. by Tanco, Miguel) — Kim, YeShil
y My Best Everything — Tomp, Sarah
c My Bibi Always Remembers (Illus. by Wohnoutka, Mike) — Buzzeo, Toni
c My Big Barefoot Book of Wonderful Words — Fatus, Sophie
c My Big Brother's Birthday (Illus. by Asher, John J.) — Asher, John J.
c My Big Fat Zombie Goldfish (Read by Gebauer, Christopher). Audiobook Review — O'Hara, Mo
c My Big Fat Zombie Goldfish: Fins of Fury (Illus. by Jagucki, Marek) — O'Hara, Mo
c My Big, Wonderful Barefoot Book of Words — Fatus, Sophie
c My Bike — Blaine, Victor
c My Bike (Illus. by Barton, Byron) — Barton, Byron
c My Body Needs Exercise — Gleisner, Jenna Lee
My Boy — Schrauwen, Olivier
My Brain on Fire — Pitt, Leonard
My Brilliant Friend — Ferrante, Elena
My Brother in Arms — Forester, Thad
c My Brother Is a Superhero — Solomons, David
c My Brother's Secret (Read by Williams, Leon). Audiobook Review — Smith, Dan (b. 1970-)
y My Brother's Secret — Smith, Dan (b. 1970-)
y My Brother's Shadow — Avery, Tom
c My Brother's Story (Illus. by McMorris, Kelley) — Johnson, Allen, Jr.
c My Brother's War — Hill, David
My Captivity: A Pioneer Woman's Story of Her Life among the Sioux — Kelly, Fanny
My Childhood Christmas — Simms, Rootie
My Chinese America — Gee, Allen
My Christian Journey with Zen — Ericsson, Gustav
c My Clothes, Your Clothes (Illus. by Kurilla, Renee) — Bullard, Lisa

c My Colors, My World / Mis colores, mi mundo (Illus. by González, Maya Christina) — Gonzalez, Maya Christina
My Confection — Kotin, Lisa
My Cool Kitchen: A Style Guide to Unique and Inspirational Kitchens (Illus. by Maxted, Richard) — Field-Lewis, Jane
c My Cousin Momo (Illus. by OHora, Zachariah) — Ohora, Zachariah
c My Cousin Momo (Illus. by OHora, Zachariah) — OHora, Zachariah
c My Cousin's Keeper — French, Simon
c My Crazy Dog: My Narrative Essay (Illus. by O'Neill, Ewa) — Pattison, Darcy
c My Dad Is a Giraffe (Illus. by King, Stephen Michael) — King, Stephen Michael
My Daughter, Her Suicide, and God — Antus, Marjorie
My Dear BB: The Letters of Bernard Berenson and Kenneth Clark, 1925-1959 — Berenson, Bernard
My Dear BB: The Letters of Bernard Berenson and Kenneth Clark, 1925-1959 — Camming, Robert
c My Dearest One (Illus. by Vasa, Monisha) — Vasa, Monisha
c My Diary from the Edge of the World — Anderson, Jodi Lynn
c My Dinosaur is More Awesome! (Illus. by Coster, Simon) — Coster, Simon
c My Dinosaurs!: A Read and Play Book (Illus. by Bendall-Brunello, John) — Schwartz, Betty Ann
My Documents — McDowell, Megan
My Documents — Zambra, Alejandro
My Dog Always Eats First: Homeless People and Their Animals — Irvine, Leslie
c My Dog, Bob (Illus. by Torrey, Richard) — Torrey, Richard
c My Dog Is Better Than Your Dog (Illus. by Stower, Adam) — Greenwald, Tommy
c My Dog Is the Best (Illus. by Schmid, Paul) — Thompson, Laurie Ann
c My Dog's a Chicken (Illus. by Wilsdorf, Anne) — Montanari, Susan McElroy
c My Ducky Buddy (Illus. by Oliva, Octavio) — Smith, Michael
My Exodus: Leaving the Slavery of Religion, Loving the Image of God in Everyone — Chambers, Alan
My Eyes Looking Back at Me: Insight into a Survivor's Soul — Meinstein, Menucha
My Fair Gentleman — Allen, Nancy Campbell
My Fair Ladies: Female Robots, Androids, and Other Artificial Eves — Wosk, Julie
c My Family Is a Zoo — Gerrard, K.A.
c My Family Tree and Me (Illus. by Petricic, Dusan) — Petricic, Dusan
c My Family, Your Family (Illus. by Kurilla, Renee) — Bullard, Lisa
My Fat Dad — Lerman, Dawn
My Father, the Pornographer: A Memoir — Offutt, Chris
My Father's Guitar and Other Imaginary Things — Skibell, Joseph
My Father's Wives — Greenberg, Mike
My Fault: Mussolini as I Knew Him — Sarfatti, Margherita Grassini
My Feelings: Poems — Flynn, Nick
My Fight for a New Taiwan: One Woman's Journey from Prison to Power — Hsiu-Lien, Lu
c My First 10 Paintings — Sellier, Marie
c My First Baseball Book — Sterling Children's Books
c My First Basketball Book — Sterling Children's Books
c My First Bible Stories (Illus. by Sanfilippo, Simona) — Sully, Katherine
c My First Book of Football (Illus. by Hinds, Bill) — Bugler, Beth
c My First Book of Funny Animals — Rhatigan, Joe
c My First Book of Mandarin Chinese Words — Kudela, Katy R.
My First Booke of My Life — Thornton, Alice
c My First Busy Book — Carle, Eric
c My First Counting Book (Illus. by Williams, Garth) — Moore, Lilian
c My First Day (Illus. by Taylor, Dan) — Sparrow, Leilani
c My First Guide to Magic Tricks (Illus. by Charney, Steve) — Barnhart, Norm
c My First Guide to Paper Airplanes — Harbo, Christopher
My First Hundred Years in Show Business — Wilson, Mary Louise
c My First Trucks — Davis, Sarah
c My Food, Your Food (Illus. by Schneider, Christine M.) — Bullard, Lisa

c My Friend Is Buddhist — Orr, Tamra
c My Friend Is Hindu — Ejaz, Khadija
My Friend the Enemy (Read by Williams, Leon). Audiobook Review — Smith, Dan (b. 1970-)
y My Friend the Enemy — Smith, Dan (b. 1970-)
y My Gallipoli (Illus. by Hannaford, Robert) — Starke, Ruth
My Generation: Collected Nonfiction — Styron, William
My Generation: William Styron's Collected Nonfiction — West, James L.W., III
My Ghanaian Odyssey — Agyeman-Duah, Baffour
y My Girlfriend's Pregnant! A Teen's Guide to Becoming a Dad (Illus. by Dawson, Willow) — Shantz-Hilkes, Chloe
My Grandfather Would Have Shot Me: A Black Woman Discovers Her Family's Nazi Past — Teege, Jennifer
c My Grandfather's Coat (Illus. by McClintock, Barbara) — Aylesworth, Jim
My Grandfather's Gallery: A Family Memoir of Art and War — Sinclair, Anne
My Grandfather's Gallery: A Legendary Art Dealer's Escape from Vichy France — Sinclair, Anne
c My Grandma's a Ninja (Illus. by Chatzikonstantinou, Danny) — Tarpley, Todd
My Grandmother Asked Me to Tell You She's Sorry — Backman, Fredrik
y My Heart and Other Black Holes — Warga, Jasmine
My Heart Is a Drunken Compass: A Memoir — Martinez, Domingo
c My Heart Is Laughing (Illus. by Eriksson, Eva) — Lagercrantz, Rose
My Hermitage: How the Hermitage Survived Tsars, Wars, and Revolution to Become the Greatest Museum in the World — Piotrovsky, Mikhail
y My Hero Academia (Illus. by Horikoshi, Kohei) — Horikoshi, Kohei
My Highland Bride — Greyson, Maeve
My Highland Spy — Roberts, Victoria
y My Hiroshima — Morimoto, Junko
My History: A Memoir of Growing Up — Fraser, Antonia
c My Home, Your Home (Illus. by Becker, Paula) — Bullard, Lisa
c My Hot Air Balloon (Illus. by Drzycimski, Leigh) — Carr, Karen
c My House (Illus. by Barton, Byron) — Barton, Byron
c My House Is Alive! — Ritchie, Scot
c My Humongous Hamster Goes to School (Illus. by Freytag, Lorna) — Freytag, Lorna
My Impending Death — Laser, Michael
My Journey — Karan, Donna
My Journey at the Nuclear Brink — Perry, William J.
My Journey through War and Peace: Explorations of a Young Filmmaker, Feminist and Spiritual Seeker — Burch, Melissa
My Journey with Maya (Read by Smiley, Tavis). Audiobook Review — Smiley, Tavis
My Journey with Maya — Smiley, Tavis
My Kind of Justice — Bury, Col
c My Kiss Won't Miss! (Illus. by Tufan, Mirela) — Dahlseng, Lesley
c My Kiss Won't Miss (Illus. by Tufan, Mirela) — Dahlseng, Lesley
My Kitchen Year: 136 Recipes That Saved My Life (Illus. by Vang, Mikel) — Reichl, Ruth
My Lady Gloriana — Halliday, Sylvia
My Ladybird Story — Tor , Magus
c My Language, Your Language — Bullard, Lisa
c My Leaf Book (Illus. by Wellington, Monica) — Wellington, Monica
My Leaky Body: Tales from the Gurney — Devaney, Julie
My Life — Maxim, Hiram S.
My Life and the Beautiful Music — Hotten, Jon
My Life as a Foreign Country — Turner, Brian
My Life as a Mermaid and Other Stories — Grow, Jen
My Life as Athena — Ignatius, Daphne
y My Life before Me — McClintock, Norah
My Life before the World War, 1860-1917: A Memoir — Pershing, John J.
c My Life in Dioramas (Illus. by Bonaddio, T.L.) — Altebrando, Tara
c My Life in France — Coster, Patience
My Life in Houses — Forster, Margaret
c My Life in India — Woolf, Alex
c My Life in Indonesia — Woolf, Alex
c My Life in Jamaica — Coster, Patience
c My Life in Kenya — Woolf, Alex
My Life in Middlemarch — Mead, Rebecca

c My Life in Pictures (Illus. by Zemke, Deborah) — Zemke, Deborah
My Life on the Road — Steinem, Gloria
My Life with Berti Spranger — Siroka, Eva Jana
c My Life with Liars — Carter, Caela
My Life with Wagner — Thielemann, Christian
c My Light (Illus. by Bang, Molly) — Chisholm, Penny
c My Little Book of Big Trucks — Head, Honor
c My Little Book of Sharks — de la Bedoyere, Camilla
c My Little Book of Volcanoes and Earthquakes — Martin, Claudia
My Loaded Gun, My Lonely Heart — Rose, Martin
My Mad Russian — Meyers, Steven Key
c My Magic Glasses — Gray, Virginia Butler
c My Military Mom (Illus. by Persico, Zoe) — Harrington, Claudia
c My Misadventures as a Teenage Rock Star — Raskin, Joyce
My Mistake: A Memoir — Menaker, Daniel
c My Mom Is Having Surgery: A Kidney Story (Illus. by Contento, Dindo) — Cortez, Brenda E.
c My Mommy, M.S. and Me (Illus. by Jakosalem, Lyle) — Garcia, Stephanie
c My Mother Always Tells Me (Illus. by Nadeau, Sonia) — Kinsman, Sharla
c My Name Is Aviva (Illus. by Jatkowska, Ag) — Newman, Leslea
c My Name Is Bob (Illus. by Kelley, Gerald) — Jenkins, Bowen
My Name is Lizzie Flynn: A Story of the Rajah Quilt (Illus. by Newcomb, Lizzy) — Saxby, Claire
My Name Is Lucy Barton — Strout, Elizabeth
My Name Is Mahtob: The Story That Began in the Global Phenomenon 'Not without My Daughter' Continues — Mahmoody, Mahtob
y My Name Is Not Friday — Walter, Jon
c My Name Is River — Dunham, Wendy
c My Name Is Truth: The Life of Sojourner Truth (Illus. by Ransome, James E.) — Turner, Ann
My Name Is Truth: The Life of Sojourner Truth (Illus. by Ransome, James) — Turner, Ann
My Name Is Truth: The Life of Sojourner Truth (Illus. by Ransome, James E.) — Turner, Ann
y My Name's Not Friday — Walter, Jon
My Native Land A4 — Blandiana, Ana
y My Near-Death Adventures — DeCamp, Alison
c My New Team (Illus. by Madrid, Erwin) — Howard, Ryan
c My New Zealand 123 Book — Brown, James
c My New Zealand ABC Book — Brown, James
c My New Zealand Colours Book — Brown, James
My October — Rothman, Claire Holden
My Old Dog: Rescued Pets with Remarkable Second Acts (Illus. by Fusaro, Lori) —,Coffey, Laura T.
My Old Dog: Rescued Pets with Remarkable Second Acts — Coffey, Laura T.
My Organic Life: How a Pioneering Chef Helped Shape the Way We Eat Today — Pouillon, Nora
My Own Pioneers, 3 vols. — Kappler, Kathryn J.
My Own Special Way (Illus. by Fidawi, Maya) — AlKhayyat, Mithaa
My Pantry: Homemade Ingredients That Make Simple Meals Special — Waters, Alice
My Paris Dream: An Education in Style, Slang, and Seduction in the Great City on the Seine — Betts, Kate
My Paris Market Cookbook: A Culinary Tour of French Flavors and Seasonal Recipes — Dilling, Emily
c My Pen (Illus. by Myers, Christopher) — Myers, Christopher
My Perfect Pantry: 150 Easy Recipes from 50 Essential Ingredients — Zakarian, Geoffrey
c My Pet Book — Staake, Bob
c My Pet Human (Illus. by Surovec, Yasmine) — Surovec, Yasmine
c My Pet Rattlesnake (Illus. by Castro L., Antonio) — Hayes, Joe
c My Pop is a Pirate (Illus. by Carnavas, Peter) — Young, Damon
My Promised Land — Shavit, Ari
My Pulse is an Earthquake — FitzPatrick, Kristin
c My Puppy Gave to Me (Illus. by Rremsner, Cynthia) — Dannenbring, Cheryl
My Quests for Hope and Meaning: An Autobiography — Ruether, Rosemary Radford
"My Rare Wit Killing Sin": Poems of a Restoration Courtier — Killigrew, Anne
My Reincarnations: Time Traveler — Hanna, Earle W., Sr.
c My Religion, Your Religion (Illus. by Conger, Holli) — Bullard, Lisa

c My Rotten Friend (Illus. by Epelbaum, Mariano) — Blake, Stephanie J.
c My Rules for Being a Pretty Princess (Illus. by McKenzie, Heath) — McKenzie, Heath
My Salinger Year — Rakoff, Joanna
c My School Yard Garden — Rich, Steve
y My Second Life — Bird, Faye
c My Secret Guide to Paris — Schroeder, Lisa
y My Secret to Tell — Richards, Natalie D.
y My Seneca Village — Nelson, Marilyn
My Side of the Street: Why Wolves, Flash Boys, Quants, and Masters of the Universe Don't Represent the Real Wall Street — Trennert, Jason DeSena
My Silver Planet: A Secret History of Poetry and Kitsch — Tiffany, Daniel
c My Sister Beth's Pink Birthday: A Story about Sibling Relationships (Illus. by Battuz, Christine) — Szymona, Marlene L.
y My Smoky Bacon Crisp Obsession — Buckle, J.A.
My Soul Immortal — Printy, Jen
c My Spring Robin (Illus. by Rockwell, Harlow) — Rockwell, Anne
My Story — Gillard, Julia
c My Story, My Dance: Robert Battle's Journey to Alvin Ailey (Illus. by Ransome, James E.) — Cline-Ransome, Lesa
c My Story, My Dance: Robert Battle's Journey to Alvin Ailey (Illus. by Ransome, James E.) — Cline-Ranson, Lesa
c My Story, My Dance: Robert Battle's Journey to Alvin Ailey — Cline-Ransome, Lesa
My Struggle, bk. 3 — Knausgaard, Karl Ove
My Struggle Book Four — Knausgaard, Karl Ove
My Struggle: Book Four — Knausgaard, Karl Ove
My Struggle: Book One (Read by Ballerini, Edoardo). Audiobook Review — Knausgaard, Karl Ove
My Struggle: Boyhood — Knausgaard, Karl Ove
y My Sunshine Away (Read by Heyborne, Kirby). Audiobook Review — Walsh, M.O.
My Sunshine Away — Walsh, M.O.
c My Super-Spy Diary (Illus. by Dreidemy, Joelle) — Gale, Emily
My T-Shirt and Other Clothes: Well Made, Fair Trade — Greathead, Helen
c My Tata's Remedies / Los remedios de mi Tata (Illus. by Castro, Antonio) — Rivera-Ashford, Roni Capin
y My Teacher Flunked the Planet — Coville, Bruce
y My Teacher Glows in the Dark — Coville, Bruce
c My Teacher Is a Monster! (No, I Am Not). (Illus. by Brown, Peter) — Brown, Peter (b. 1979-)
c My Teacher Is an Idiom — Gilson, Jamie
c My Teacher Is an Idiom (Illus. by Meisel, Paul) — Gilson, Jamie
c My Three Best Friends and Me, Zulay (Illus. by Brantley-Newton, Vanessa) — Best, Cari
My Tibetan Childhood: When Ice Shattered Stone — Nulo, Naktsang
My Townie Heart — Sperrazza, Diana
y My True Love Gave to Me: Twelve Holiday Stories — Perkins, Stephanie
c My Two Blankets (Illus. by Blackwood, Freya) — Kobald, Irena
c My Two Homes (Illus. by Persico, Zoe) — Harrington, Claudia
My Two Italies — Luzzi, Joseph
My Unsentimental Education — Monroe, Debra
c My Very First Dinosaurs Book (Illus. by Frith, Alex) — Frith, Alex
My View of the World — Schrodinger, Erwin
c My Village: Rhymes from around the World (Illus. by Moriuchi, Mique) — Wright, Danielle
My Voice Is My Weapon: Music, Nationalism, and the Poetics of Palestinian Resistance — McDonald, David A.
My Watery Self: Memoirs of a Marine Scientist — Spotte, Stephen
My Wife Wants You to Know I'm Happily Married — Franklin, Joey
c My Wild Family (Illus. by Moreau, Laurent) — Moreau, Laurent
c My Wilderness: An Alaskan Adventure (Illus. by McGehee, Claudia) — McGehee, Claudia
c My Wilderness (Illus. by McGehee, Claudia) — McGehee, Claudia
y My World Is Over: The Day it All Went Dark — Budig, Bridget Hoolihan
My Year in Oman — Heines, Matthew D.
c My Year of Epic Rock — Pyros, Andrea
My Year of Running Dangerously: A Dad, a Daughter, and a Ridiculous Plan — Foreman, Tom

c My Yiddish Vacation (Illus. by Menchin, Scott) — Skye, Ione
c My Zombie Hamster — McCreely, Havelock
Mycroft Holmes — Abdul-Jabbar, Kareem
c Myles and the Monster Outside — Dowding, Philippa
The Myriad Carnival — Bright, Matthew
Myrrh — Griffiths, K.
c Mystere a la montagne du Diable — Paradis, Odile
The Mysteries of Artemis of Ephesos: Cult, Polis, and Change in the Graeco-Roman World — Rogers, Guy MacLean
Mysteries of the Jaguar Shamans of the Northwest Amazon — Wright, Robin M.
Mysteries of the Mall and Other Essays — Rybczynski, Witold
The Mysteries of the Marco Polo Maps — Olshin, Benjamin B.
Mysterieuse Madame de Pompadour — Muchembled, Robert
c Mysterious Creatures — Dicker, Katie
c A Mysterious Egg (Illus. by Boldt, Mike) — McAnulty, Stacy
A Mysterious Life and Calling: From Slavery to Ministry in South Carolina — Riley, Charlotte S.
c Mysterious Places — Dicker, Katie
The Mysterious World of the Human Genome — Ryan, Frank
c The Mystery across the Secret Bridge (Illus. by Calo, Marcos) — Paris, Harper
The Mystery and Agency of God: Divine Being and Action in the World — Kirkpatrick, Frank G.
The Mystery at Sag Bridge — Camalliere, Pat
c Mystery Files Series — O'Brien, Cynthia
c Mystery in Mayan Mexico (Illus. by Calo, Marcos) — Wells, Marcia
c The Mystery in the Forbidden City (Illus. by Calo, Marcos) — Paris, Harper
y Mystery in the Frozen Lands — Godfrey, Martyn
Mystery of Chaco Canyon: Dan y Roque — Hocking, Doug
y The Mystery of Hollow Places — Podos, Rebecca
y The Mystery of Life: How Nothing Became Everything — Schutten, Jan Paul
c The Mystery of Life: How Nothing Became Everything (Illus. by Rieder, Floor) — Schutten, Jan Paul
c The Mystery of the Aztec Tomb (Illus. by Neely, Scott) — Sutton, Laurie S.
Mystery of the Church, People of God: Yves Conger's Total Ecclesiology as a Path to Vatican II — Beal, Rose M.
c The Mystery Of the Cursed Poodle — Pankhurst, Kate
c Mystery of the Giant Masks of Sanxingdui (Illus. by Roski, Gayle Garner) — Smith, Icy
The Mystery of the Lone Wolf Killer: Anders Behring Breivik and the Threat of Terror in Plain Sight — Turrettini, Unni
The Mystery of the Lost Cezanne — Longworth, M.L.
c Mystery of the Map — Chabert, Jack
The Mystery of the Missing Lion (Read by Andoh, Adjoa). Audiobook Review — McCall Smith, Alexander
The Mystery of the Missing Lion (Read by Andoh, Adjoa). Audiobook Review — Smith, Alexander McCall
c The Mystery of the Stolen Snowboard (Illus. by VanArsdale, Anthony) — Warner, Gertrude Chandler
c The Mystery of the Suspicious Spices (Illus. by Calo, Marcos) — Paris, Harper
The Mystery of the Venus Island Fetish — Flannery, Tim
c The Mystery of the Wild West Bandit (Illus. by VanArsdale, Anthony) — Warner, Gertrude Chandler
c The Mystery of the Zorse's Mask — Singleton, Linda Joy
The Mystery Writers of America Cookbook — White, Kate
The Mystic Ark: Hugh of Saint Victor, Art, and Thought in the Twelfth Century — Rudolph, Conrad
The Mystic Marriage — Jones, Heather Rose
Mystic — Denzel, Jason
The Mystical as Political: Democracy and Non-Radical Orthodoxy — Papanikolaou, Aristotle
The Mystical Backpacker: How to Discover Your Destiny in the Modern World — Papp, Hannah
Mystical Science and Practical Religion: Muslim, Hindu, and Sikh Discourse on Science and Technology — Cimino, Richard

Mysticism and Spirituality, Part I: Mysticism, Fullness of Life — *Panikkar, Raimon*
y The Mystics of Mile End — *Samuel, Sigal*
Myth, Memory, Trauma: Rethinking the Stalinist Past in the Soviet Union, 1953-70 — *Jones, Polly*
The Myth of Brilliant Summers — *Collings, Austin*
The Myth of Emptiness and the New American Literature of Place — *Harding, Wendy*
A Myth of Innocence: Mark and Christian Origins — *Mack, Burton L.*
The Myth of Liberal Ascendancy: Corporate Dominance from the Great Depression to the Great Recession — *Domhoff, G. William*
The Myth of Morgan la Fey — *Perez, Kristina*
The Myth of Race: The Troubling Persistence of an Unscientific Idea — *Sussman, Robert Wald*

The Myth of Seneca Falls: Memory and the Women's Suffrage Movement, 1848-1898 — *Tetrault, Lisa*
The Myth of the Press Gang: Volunteers, Impressment and the Naval Manpower Problem in the Late Eighteenth Century — *Dancy, J. Ross*
Mythborn II: Bane of the Warforged — *Lakshman, Vijay*
Mythical — *Martin, C.E.*
Mythologies of the Prophet Muhammad in Early Modern English Culture — *Dimmock, Matthew*
Mythologizing Jesus: From Jewish Teacher to Epic Hero — *MacDonald, Dennis R.*
y Mythology of the Egyptians — *Nardo, Don*
The Mythology of Work: How Capitalism Persists Despite Itself — *Fleming, Peter*
c Mythology: Oh My! Gods and Goddesses — *Budzik, Mary*

Mythos and Cosmos: Mind and Meaning in the Oral Age — *Lundwall, John Knight*
Mythos Kreuzzuge: Selbst- und Fremdbilder in historischen Romanen — *Hinz, Felix*
c Myths and Legends of Africa — *Leonard, Scott A.*
c Myths and Legends of Australia, New Zealand, and Pacific Islands — *Croy, Anita*
c Myths and Legends of Scandinavia — *Leonard, Scott A.*
c Myths and Legends of South Asia and Southeast Asia — *Leonard, Scott A.*
Myths and Mortals: Family Business Leadership and Succession Planning — *Keyt, Andrew*
The Myths of Happiness: What Should Make You Happy, but Doesn't, What Shouldn't Make You Happy, but Does — *Lyubomirsky, Sonja*

N

Nabokov in America: On the Road to Lolita — *Roper, Robert*
Nach dem Konstruktivismus? Aktuelle Strategien der Kontextualisierung in der Neuen Ideengeschichte
Nach der Natur. Das Artensterben und die modern Kulter — *Heise, Ursula K.*
Nacht uber Europa: Kulturgeschichte des Ersten Weltkrieges — *Piper, Ernst*
Nachwuchssymposium "An die Arbeit! Minderheiten und Erwerbserfarhungen im 19. und 20. Jahrhundert"
c Nadine, My Funny and Trusty Guide Dog (Illus. by Ford, Stephanie) — *Fleischman, Carol Chiodo*
Nagasaki: Life after Nuclear War — *Southard, Susan*
Nahua and Maya Catholicisms: Texts and Religion in Colonial Central Mexico and Yucatan — *Christensen, Mark Z.*
Nairn's London — *Nairn, Ian*
The Naive Guys: A Memoir of Friendship, Love and Tech in the Early 1990s — *Patz, Harry, Jr.*
The Naive Guys — *Patz, Harry, Jr.*
Nakamura Reality — *Austin, Alex*
Naked: A Cultural History of American Nudism — *Hoffman, Brian*
Naked — *Redgold, Eliza*
y Naked — *Trombley, Stacey*
Naked at Lunch: A Reluctant Nudist's Adventures in the Clothing-Optional World — *Smith, Mark Haskell*
Naked at the Albert Hall: The Inside Story of Singing — *Thorn, Tracey*
Naked Earth — *Chang, Eileen*
Naked Emperors: Criticisms of English Contemporary Art — *Sewell, Brian*
The Naked Eye — *Johansen, Roy*
Naked Greed — *Woods, Stuart*
c Naked Trevor — *Elliott, Rebecca*
y The Nakeds — *Glatt, Lisa*
Nalah Goes to Mad Mouse City — *Sawyer-Aitch, Anne*
The Nalini Method: 7 Workouts for 7 Moods — *Mehta, Rupa*
y The Name of the Blade — *Marriott, Zoe*
Name of the Devil — *Mayne, Andrew*
The Name of the Game — *Dawson, Jennifer*
Name, Rank, and Serial Number: Exploiting Korean War POWs at Home and Abroad — *Young, Charles S.*
Nameless — *John, David*
The Nameless Dark: A Collection — *Grau, T.E.*
Names, Ethnicity and Populations: Tracing Identity in Space — *Mateos, Pablo*
Namibia's Rainbow Project: Gay Rights in an African Nation — *Lorway, Robert*
Naming God: Avinu Malkeinu, Our Father, Our King — *Hoffman, Lawrence A.*
Naming Monsters — *Eaton, Hannah*
Nan-Core — *Numata, Mahokaru*
c Nana in the City (Read by Gebauer, Christopher). Audiobook Review — *Castillo, Lauren*
c Nana in the City (Illus. by Castillo, Lauren) — *Castillo, Lauren*
c Nancy Clancy, Secret of the Silver Key (Illus. by Glasser, Robin Preiss) — *O'Connor, Jane*
c Nancy Clancy, Star of Stage and Screen (Illus. by Glasser, Robin Preiss) — *O'Connor, Jane*
y Nancy Drew Diaries (Read by Marie, Jorjeana). Audiobook Review — *Keene, Carolyn*
c Nancy Drew: Identity Revealed — *Keene, Carolyn*
c Nancy Drew: Identity Theft — *Keene, Carolyn*
c Nancy Drew: Secret Identity — *Keene, Carolyn*

c Nancy Drew: The Clue at Black Creek Farm (Read by Marie, Jorjeana). Audiobook Review — *Keene, Carolyn*
c Nancy Knows (Illus. by Young, Cybele) — *Young, Cybele*
Nancy Love and the WASP Ferry Pilots of World War II — *Rickman, Sarah Byrn*
Nancy Loves Slugqo: Complete Dailies 1949-1951 — *Bushmiller, Ernie*
Nanise', A Navajo Herbal — *Mayes, Vernon O.*
Nanjing: The Burning City — *Young, Ethan*
c Nanny and Me (Illus. by Kruger, Sydni) — *Romano, Florence Ann*
c Nanny Piggins and the Runaway Lion — *Spratt, R.A.*
c Nanny X (Illus. by Donnelly, Karen) — *Rosenberg, Madelyn*
c Nanny X Returns — *Rosenberg, Madelyn*
y Nanotech — *Wright, Denis*
c The Nantucket Lightship Basket Mystery (Illus. by Bell, Samantha) — *Carmody, Carolyn*
c Nanuk the Ice Bear (Illus. by Winter, Jeanette) — *Winter, Jeanette*
Nanyo-Orientalism: Japanese Representations of the Pacific — *Sudo, Naoto*
Naoko — *Higashino, Keigo*
Naomi and Her Friends — *Morrison-Topping, Alan*
c Nap-A-Roo (Illus. by Parker, Tyler) — *Kurjan, Kristy*
Napalm: An American Biography — *Neer, Robert M.*
Napoleon: A Life (Read by Lee, John Rafter). Audiobook Review — *Roberts, Andrew*
Napoleon: A Life — *Roberts, Andrew*
Napoleon and the Struggle for Germany: The Franco-Prussian War of 1813, 2 vols. — *Leggiere, Michael V.*
Napoleon in Italy: The Sieges of Mantua, 1796-1799 — *Cuccia, Phillip R.*
Napoleon on War — *Colson, Bruno*
Napoleon: Soldier of Destiny — *Broers, Michael*
Napoleon the Great — *Roberts, Andrew*
c Naptime (Illus. by de Mouy, Iris) — *de Mouy, Iris*
c Naptime with Theo and Beau — *Shyba, Jessica*
Narcisa — *Shaw, Jonathan*
The Narcissist You Know: Defending Yourself against Extreme Narcissists in an All-about-Me Age — *Burgo, Joseph*
Narcissus: The Last Days of Lord Byron — *Ahola, Robert Joseph*
A Narco-History: How the United States and Mexico Jointly Created the "Mexican Drug War" — *Boullosa, Carmen*
Narconomics: How to Run a Drug Cartel — *Wainwright, Tom*
Narrating the Future in Siberia: Childhood, Adolescence and Autobiography among Young Eveny — *Ulturgasheva, Olga*
Narrations d'un nouveau siecle: romans et ecrits francais — *Blanckeman, Bruno*
Narrative of James Williams, an American Slave: Annotated Edition — *Trent, Hank*
Narrative Responses to the Trauma of the French Revolution — *Astbury, Katherine*
The Narrative Shape of Truth: Veridiction in Modern European Literature — *Kliger, Ilya*
Narratives of Child Neglect in Romantic and Victorian Culture — *Benziman, Galia*
Narratives of Europe and European Integration. 11th Annual Conference of the History of European Integration Research Society
Narratives of Free Trade: The Commercial Cultures of Early US-China Relations — *Johnson, Kendall*

Narratives of War: Military and Civilian Experience in Britain and Ireland, 1793-1815 — *Kennedy, Catriona*
Narratology and Classics: A Practical Guide — *De Jong, Irene J.F.*
The Narrators of Barbarian History — *Goffart, Walter*
The Narrow Door: A Memoir of Friendship — *Lisicky, Paul*
The Narrow Edge: A Tiny Bird, an Ancient Crab, and an Epic Journey — *Cramer, Deborah*
The Narrow Path to War — *Frizzell, D.L.*
The Narrow Road to the Deep North — *Flanagan, Richard*
Narvla's Celtic New Year — *Gilardi, Therese*
NASA's First A: Aeronautics from 1958 to 2008. E-book Review — *Ferguson, Robert G.*
c NASCAR Racing — *Long, Dustin*
Nashida Kitaro's Chiasmatic Chorology: Palce of Dialectic, Dialectic of Palce — *Krummel, John W.M.*
Nashville in the New Millennium: Immigrant Settlement, Urban Transformation, and Social Belonging — *Winders, Jamie*
The Nashville Sound: Bright Lights and Country Music — *Hemphill, Paul*
Nashville's Lower Broad — *Rouda, Bill*
c Nat the Cat Can Sleep Like That (Illus. by Anderson, Tara) — *Allenby, Victoria*
Nat Turner and the Rising in Southampton County — *Allmendinger, David F., Jr.*
c Natalie and the Night Sky (Illus. by McAllister, Kent) — *Dibb, Carolyn*
c Nate and Shea's Adventures in South Africa — *Whitten-Simmons, Carrie*
c Nate Likes to Skate — *Degen, Bruce*
c Nate the Great, Where Are You? (Illus. by Wheeler, Jody) — *Sharmat, Marjorie Weinman*
c Nathan Hale's Hazardous Tales: The Underground Abductor (Illus. by Hale, Nathan) — *Hale, Nathan*
The Nation: A Biography: The First 150 Years — *Guttenplan, D.D.*
Nation and Family: Personal Law, Cultural Pluralism, and Gendered Citizenship in India — *Subramanian, Narendra*
A Nation and Not a Rabble: The Irish Revolution, 1913-1923 — *Ferriter, Diarmaid*
Nation and Nurture in Seventeenth-Century English Literature — *Trubowitz, Rachel*
Nation Builder: John Quincy Adams and the Grand Strategy of the Republic — *Edel, Charles N.*
Nation Building: Craft and Contemporary American Culture — *Bell, Nicholas R.*
A Nation Can Rise No Higher Than Its Women: African American Muslim Women in the Movement for Black Self-Determination, 1950-1975 — *Jeffries, Bayyinah S.*
The Nation Made Real: Art and National Identity in Western Europe, 1600-1850 — *Smith, Anthony D.*
Nation/Nazione: Irish Nationalism and the Italian Risorgimento — *Barr, Colin*
A Nation of Nations: A Great American Immigration Story — *Gjelten, Tom*
A Nation of Small Shareholders: Marketing Wall Street after World War II — *Traflet, Janice M.*
Nation on the Take: How Big Money Corrupts Our Democracy and What We Can Do about It — *Potter, Wendell*
A Nation Rising: Hawaiian Movements for Life, Land, and Sovereignty — *Goodyear-Ka'opua, Noelani*
Nation-States and the Global Environment: New Approaches to International Environmental History — *Bsumek, Erika Marie*

Nation within a Nation: The American South and the Federal Government — Feldman, Glenn
The Nation Writ Small: African Fictions and Feminisms 1958-1988 — Andrade, Susan Z.
c National Birds of the World — Toft, Ron
The National Council on Indian Opportunity: Quiet Champion of Self-Determination — Britten, Thomas A.
A National Force: The Evolution of Canada's Army, 1950-2000 — Kasurak, Peter
c National Geographic Book of Nature Poetry: More Than 200 Poems with Photographs That Float, Zoom, and Bloom! — Lewis, J. Patrick
c National Geographic Kids Almanac 2016 — National Geographic
y National Geographic Kids Guide to Photography: Tips and Tricks on How to Be a Great Photographer from the Pros and Your Pals at My Shot — Honovich, Nancy
c National Geographic Kids Mission — Blewett, Ashlee Brown
c National Geographic Kids Mon grand livre des pourquoi — Shields, Amy
c National Geographic Kids Weird but True! Ripped from the Headlines: Real-Life Stories You Have to Read to Believe — National Geographic Kids
c National Geographic Readers: Barack Obama — Gilpin, Caroline Crosson
c National Geographic Readers: Nelson Mandela — Kramer, Barbara
The National Home Maintenance Manual: The Complete Guide to Caring for Your Home — MacLellan, David E.
National Minorities in the Soviet Bloc after 1945
The National Origins of Policy Ideas: Knowledge Regimes in the United States, France, Germany, and Denmark — Campbell, John L.
National Prayers: Special Worship since the Reformation, vol. 1: Special Prayers, Fasts and Thanksgivings in the British Isles, 1533-1688 — Mears, Natalie
National Security and Double Government — Glennon, Michael J.
Nationalism and the Cinema in France: Political Mythologies and Film Events, 1945-1995 — Frey, Hugo
Nationalism and the Moral Psychology of Community — Yack, Bernard
Nationalism and War — Hall, John A.
Nationalists Passions — Kaufman, Stuart J.
Nationhood, Providence, and Witness: Israel in Modern Theology and Social Theory — Moseley, Carys
The Nations — Sheehan, Thomas F.
Nations Divided: American Jews and the Struggle over Apartheid — Feld, Marjorie N.
Nations Divided: American Jews and the Struggle over Apartheid — Field, Marjorie N.
Nations under God: How Churches Use Moral Authority to Influence Policy — Grzymala-Busse, Anna
Native American DNA: Tribal Belonging and the False Promise of Genetic Science — TallBear, Kim
The Native American Renaissance: Literary Imagination and Achievement — Lee, A. Robert
Native Americans in Early North Carolina: A Documentary History — Isenbarger, Dennis L.
Native Brazil: Beyond the Convert and the Cannibal, 1500-1900 — Langfur, Hal
Native Diasporas: Indigenous Identities and Settler Colonialism in the Americas — Smithers, Gregory D.
Native: Dispatches from an Israeli-Palestinian Life — Kashua, Sayed
Native Evangelism in Central America — Nutini, Hugo G.
c Native Nations of California — Naber, Therese
c Native Nations of the Arctic and Subarctic — Powell, Marie
c Native Nations of the Great Basin and Plateau — Krasner, Barbara
c Native Nations of the Northeast — Krasner, Barbara
c Native Nations of the Northwest Coast — Yasuda, Anita
c Native Nations of the Plains — Yasuda, Anita
c Native Nations of the Southeast — Naber, Therese
c Native Nations of the Southwest — Krasner, Barbara
Native Recognition: Indigenous Cinema and the Western — Hearne, Joanna
Native Tongue Stranger Talk: The Arabic and French Literary Landscapes of Lebanon — Hartman, Michelle

c The Nativity (Illus. by di Bondone, Giotto) — Elschner, Geraldine
c The Nativity (Illus. by Giotto) — Elschner, Geraldine
Natur und Industrie im Sozialismus: Eine Umweltgeschichte der DDR — Huff, Tobias
The Natural Beauty Solution: Break Free from Commercial Beauty Products Using Simple Recipes and Natural Ingredients — Leonard, Mary Helen
Natural Born Heroes: How a Daring Band of Misfits Mastered the Lost Secrets of Strength and Endurance (Read by Smith, Nicholas Guy). Audiobook Review — McDougall, Christopher
Natural Born Heroes: How a Daring Band of Misfits Mastered the Lost Secrets of Strength and Endurance — McDougall, Christopher
Natural Capital: Valuing the Planet — Helm, Dieter
Natural Deduction: An Introduction to Logic with Real Arguments, a Little History, and Some Humour — Arthur, Richard T.W.
A Natural History of English Gardening, 1650-1800 — Laird, Mark
A Natural History of Human Thinking — Tomasello, Michael
The Natural History of Selborne — White, Gilbert
A Natural History of Wine — Tattersall, Ian
Natural Law in Theories the Early Enlightenment — Hochstrasser, Tim
The Natural Psychic: Ellen Dugan's Personal Guide to the Psychic Realm — Dugan, Ellen
Natural Stories — Nettel, Guadalupe
Natural to Knockout Makeup, Beauty & You: Techniques for Straight Corrective Makeup — Brown, Carl
c The Natural World of North America — Daly, Ruth
Naturalism and the First-Person Perspective — Baker, Lynne Rudder
A Naturalist Goes Fishing: Casting in Fragile Waters from the Gulf of Mexico to New Zealand's South Island — McClintock, James
Naturalists in Paradise: Wallace, Bates and Spruce in the Amazon — Hemming, John
y Nature Anatomy: The Curious Parts and Pieces of the Natural World — Rothman, Julia
Nature and Wealth: Overcoming Environmental Scarcity and Inequality — Barbier, Edward B.
The Nature of Asian Politics — Gilley, Bruce
The Nature of Childhood: An Environmental History of Growing Up in America since 1865 — Riney-Kehrberg, Pamela
The Nature of Crops: How We Came to Eat the Plants We Do — Warren, John
The Nature of the Beast (Read by Bathurst, Robert). Audiobook Review — Penny, Louise
The Nature of the Beast — Penny, Louise
The Nature of the Beasts: Empire and Exhibition at the Tokyo Imperial Zoo — Miller, Ian Jared
The Nature of Trauma in American Novels — Balaev, Michelle
Nature Protection, Environmental Policy, and Social Movements in Communist and Capitalist Countries during the Cold War
Nature's Civil War: Common Soldiers and the Environment in 1862 Virginia — Meier, Kathryn Shively
Nature's Conscience: The Life and Legacy of Derek Ratcliffe — Thompson, Des
c Nature's Day: Discover the World of Wonder on Your Doorstep (Illus. by Kroll, Danielle) — Maguire, Kay
Nature's Entrepot: Philadelphia's Urban Sphere and Its Environmental Thresholds — Black, Brian C.
Nature's Fortune: How Business and Society Thrive by Investing in Nature — Adams, Jonathan S.
Nature's Housekeeper — Gurnow, Michael
Nature's Larder: Cooking with the Senses — De la Falaise, Daniel
Nature's Noblemen: Transatlantic Masculinities and the Nineteenth-Century American West — Rico, Monica
Naughtier Than Nice — Dickey, Eric Jerome
c The Naughtiest Reindeer at the Zoo (Illus. by Greenberg, Nicki) — Greenberg, Nicki
c The Naughty List (Illus. by Fry, Michael) — Fry, Michael
c The Naughty List — Fry, Michael
c Naughty Mabel (Illus. by Krall, Dan) — Elliott, Devlin
c Naughty Mabel (Illus. by Krall, Dan) — Lane, Nathan
Nautical Chic — Butchart, Amber Jane
c The Navajo — Craats, Rennay
Naval Resistance to Britain's Growing Power in India, 1600-1800: The Saffron Banner and the Tiger of Mysore — MacDougall, Phillip

Naval Resistance to Britain's Growing Power in India, 1660-1800: The Saffron Banner and the Tiger of Mysore — MacDougall, Philip
The Naval Route to the Abyss: The Anglo-German Naval Race, 1895-1914 — Seligmann, Matthew S.
y Naveed: Through My Eyes — Heffernan, John
Navel Gazing; True Tales of Bodies, Mostly Mine (but Also My Mom's, Which I Know Sounds Weird). — Black, Michael Ian
c Navid's Story (Illus. by Topf, Jonathan) — Glynne, Andy
Navigating Gendered Terrain: Stereotypes and Strategy in Political Campaigns — Dittmar, Kelly
Navigating Life with Multiple Sclerosis — Costello, Kathleen
Navigating the Future with Scenario Planning: A Guidebook for Librarians — Giesecke, Joan
Navigating the Spanish Lake: The Pacific in the Iberian World, 1521-1898 — Buschmann, Rainer F.
Navy Priest: The Life of Captain Jake Laboon, S.J. — Gribble, Richard
Navy SEAL Dogs: My Tale of Training Canines for Combat (Read by Kramer, Michael). Audiobook Review — Ritland, Mike
Navy SEAL Shooting — Sajnog, Chris
c Navy SEALs — Whiting, Jim
Navy SEALs: Their Untold Story — Couch, Dick
c The Navy's Night Before Christmas (Illus. by Manders, John) — Ford, Christine
The Nay Science: A History of German Indology — Adluri, Vishwa
Nazi Policy on the Eastern Front, 1941: Total War, Genocide, and Radicalization — Kay, Alex J.
y Nazi War Criminals — Nardo, Don
Nazira Zeineddine: A Pioneer of Islamic Feminism — Cooke, Miriam
Near and Distant Neighbors: A New History of Soviet Intelligence — Haslam, Jonathan
Near Death — Cooper, Glenn
Near Enemy — Sternbergh, Adam
Near & Far: Recipes Inspired by Home and Travel — Swanson, Heidi
Near to the Wild Heart — Entrekin, Alison
c A Nearer Moon — Crowder, Melanie
The Nearest Thing to Life — Wood, James
y Nearly Found — Cosimano, Elle
Nearly Orthodox: On Being a Modern Woman in an Ancient Tradition — Carlson, Angela Doll
The Nearness of Others: Searching for Tact and Contact in the Age of HIV — Caron, David
Nebula Awards Showcase 2013 — Asaro, Catherine
Nebula Awards Showcase 2015 — Bear, Greg
The Necessary Death of Lewis Winter — Mackay, Malcolm
A Necessary End — Brown, Holly
The Necessary Murder of Nonie Blake — Shames, Terry
The Necessary War, vol. 1: Canadians Fighting the Second World War, 1939-1943 — Cook, Tim
The Necklace and Other Stories: Maupassant for Modern Times — Maupassant, Guy de
Nectar of the Gods — Miller, L.S.
y Need — Charbonneau, Joelle
Need Big Love - Need it Now — Jackson, Sharley
y Need — Charbonneau, Joel
y Need — Charbonneau, Joelle
Need You for Always — Adair, Marina
The Needlepoint Book: New, Revised, and Updated Third Edition — Christensen, Jo Ippolito
Negociando la obediencia: Gestion y reforma de los virreinatos americanos en tiempos del conde-duque de Olivares — Amadori, Arrigo
Negocier la defense: Plaider pour les criminels au siecle des Lumieres a Geneve — Briegel, Francoise
A Negotiated Landscape: The Transformation of San Francisco's Waterfront Since 1950 — Rubin, Jasper
Negotiated Power: The State, Elites, and Local Governance in Twelfth- to Fourteenth-Century China — Lee, Sukhee
Negotiating a River: Canada, the US, and the Creation of the St. Lawrence Seaway — Macfarlane, Daniel
Negotiating Autonomy in Greater China: Hong Kong and Its Sovereign before and after 1997 — Yep, Ray
Negotiating China's Destiny in World War II — van de Ven, Hans
Negotiating in Civil Conflict: Constitutional Construction and Imperfect Bargaining in Iraq — Hamoudi, Haider Ala
Negotiating Political Identities: Multiethnic Schools and Youth in Europe — Faas, Daniel

Negotiating the Landscape: Environment and Monastic Identity in the Medieval Ardennes — *Arnold, Ellen F.*
The Negotiator: A Memoir — *Mitchell, George*
Negro Comrades of the Crown: African-Americans and the British Empire Fight the U.S. Before Emancipation — *Horne, Gerald*
Negroes and the Gun: The Black Tradition of Arms — *Johnson, Nicholas*
Negroland: A Memoir — *Jefferson, Margo*
The Neighborhood in the Internet: Design Research Projects in Community Informatics — *Carroll, John Millar*
c Neighborhood Sharks: Hunting with the Great Whites of California's Farallon Islands (Illus. by Roy, Katherine) — *Roy, Katherine*
Neighboring Faiths: Christianity, Islam, and Judaism in the Middle Ages and Today — *Nirenberg, David*
Neighborly Adversaries: Readings in U.S.-Latin American Relations, 3d ed. — *LaRosa, Michael J.*
Neighbors: The Destruction of the Jewish Community in Jedwabne, Poland — *Gross, Jan T.*
c Neighbors: The Water Critters (Illus. by Kim, Joung un) — *Held, George*
c Neighbors: The Water Critters (Illus. by Kim, Joung un) — *Held, George*
Neighbours and Successors of Rome: Traditions of Glass Production and Use in Europe and the Middle East in the Later First Millennium AD — *Keller, Daniel*
Neighing with Fire — *O'Sullivan, Kathryn*
Neil Armstrong: A Life of Flight (Read by Prichard, Michael). Audiobook Review — *Barbree, Jay*
c Neil Armstrong: First Man on the Moon (Fact Cat). — *Bingham, Jane*
c Neil Armstrong Walks on the Moon — *Yomtov, Nel*
c Neil deGrasse Tyson — *Diprimio, Pete*
c Neil Flambe and the Bard's Banquet — *Sylvester, Kevin*
Neil Gaiman in the 21st Century: Essays on the Novels, Children's Stories, Online Writings, Comics and Other Works — *Prescott, Tara*
Neither Victor nor Vanquished: America and the War of 1812 — *Weber, William*
Nekropolis (Read by Jackson, Ken). Audiobook Review — *Waggoner, Tim*
Nel laboratorio della storia: Una guida alle fonti dell'eta' moderna — *Paoli, Maria Pia*
c Nellie Belle (Illus. by Austin, Mike) — *Fox, Mem*
c Nellie Bly and Investigative Journalism for Kids: Mighty Muckrakers from the Golden Age to Today, with 21 Activities — *Mahoney, Ellen*
Nelly and the Quest for Captain Peabody — *Chambers, Roland*
Nelly Dean: A Return to Wuthering Heights — *Case, Alison*
Nels Anderson's World War I Diary — *Powell, Allen Kent*
c Nelson Mandela — *Ridley, Frances*
c Nelson Mandela: South African President and Civil Rights Activist — *Woll, Kris*
c Nelson Mandela: South African Revolutionary — *Gormley, Beatrice*
c Nelson Mandela: World Leader for Human Rights — *Doeden, Matt*
Nemesis — *Gienny, Misha*
Nemesis Games (Read by Mays, Jefferson). Audiobook Review — *Corey, James S.A.*
Nemesis Games — *Corey, James S.A.*
Nemesis — *Coulter, Catherine*
Nemesis — *Roth, Philip*
Nemesis: One Man and the Battle for Rio — *Glenny, Misha*
Neo-Latin and the Humanities: Essays in Honour of Charles E. Fantazzi — *Deitz, Luc*
Neo-Latin and the Humanities: Essays in Honour of Charles E. Fantazzi — *Kircher, Timothy*
Neo-Latin Commentaries and the Management of Knowledge in the Late Middle Ages and the Early Modern Period (1400-1700). — *Enenkel, Karl*
Neo-Latin Philology: Old Traditions, New Approaches — *Van der Poel, Marc*
Neocybernetics and Narrative — *Clarke, Bruce*
Neoliberal Bonds: Undoing Memory in Chilean Art and Literature — *Blanco, Fernando A.*
Neoliberal Morality in Singapore: How Family Policies Make State and Society — *Teo, You Yenn*
c Neon Aliens Ate My Homework and Other Poems — *Cannon, Nick*
Neorassismus im Spannungsfeld der Kulturen - (k)ein Bildungsproblem!?
Neotropical Insect Galls — *Fernandes, Wilson Geraldo*

c Neptune — *Bloom, J.P.*
c Neptune: God of the Sea and Earthquakes — *Temple, Teri*
Nequa, 3d ed. — *Adams, Jack*
c Nerdy Birdy (Illus. by Davies, Matt) — *Reynolds, Aaron*
Neron en Occident: Une figure de l'histoire — *Grau, Donatien*
Neros Wirklichkeiten: Zur Rezeption einer umstrittenen Gestalt — *Walde, Christine*
The Nerve of It: Poems New and Selected — *Emanuel, Lynn*
c Nest (Read by Lamia, Jenna). Audiobook Review — *Ehrlich, Esther*
c The Nest (Illus. by Klassen, Jon) — *Oppel, Kenneth*
The Nest — *Sweeney, Cynthia*
c Nest (Read by Lamia, Jenna). Audiobook Review — *Ehrlich, Esther*
c Nest — *Ehrlich, Esther*
c A Nest Is Noisy (Illus. by Long, Sylvia) — *Aston, Dianna Hutts*
c A Nest of Snakes (Illus. by McMorris, Kelley) — *Johnson, Allen, Jr.*
Nest of Worlds — *Huberath, Marek S.*
c Nest — *Hurley, Jorey*
c The Nesting Quilt (Illus. by Falwell, Cathryn) — *Falwell, Cathryn*
The Net Is Dark and Full of Terrors — *Reagle, Joseph M., Jr.*
Nettle King — *Harbour, Katherine*
The Network Reshapes the Library: Lorcan Dempsey on Libraries, Services, and Networks — *Dempsey, Lorcan*
The Network Reshapes the Library — *Dempsey, Lorcan*
Networks of Music and Culture in the Late Sixteenth and Early Seventeenth Centuries: A Collection of Essays in Celebration of Peter Philips's 450th Anniversary — *Smith, David J.*
Netzwerke der Entnazifizierung: Kontinuitaten im Deutschen Musikleben am Beispiel von Werner Egk, Hilde und Heinrich Strobel — *Custodis, Michael*
Neue deutsche Wirtschaftsgeschichte des 20. Jahrhunderts — *Spoerer, Mark*
Neue Forschungen zu Spatmittelalterlichen Landtransfers und Bodenmarkten zwischen Rhein und Alpen
Neue Nachbarschaft: Deutschland und die Niederlande, Bildformung und Beziehungen seit 1990 — *Jurgens, Hanco*
Neue Nachbarschaft: Deutschland und die Niederlande, Bildformung und Beziehungen seit 1990 — *Pekelder, Jacco*
Neue Soziale Bewegungen in der 'Provinz' 1970-1990
Neue Tendenzen der Italienforschung zu Mittelalter und Renaissance
Neue Vielfalt. Medienpluralitat und -konkurrenz in historischer Perspektive
Neuere Forschungen zur Frauen - und Geschlechtergeschichte
Neuere Tendenzen in der Historiographiegeschichte
Neuroanatomical Terminology: A Lexicon of Classical Origins and Historical Foundations by Larry W. Swanson — *Swanson, Larry W.*
The Neurobiology of Learning and Memory — *Rudy, Jerry W.*
Neurobiology of Monotremes: Brain Evolution in Our Distant Mammalian Cousins — *Ashwell, Ken*
Neuroimmunity: A New Science That Will Revolutionize How We Keep Our Brains Healthy and Young — *Schwartz, Michal*
NeuroLogic: The Brain's Hidden Rationale behind Our Irrational Behavior — *Sternberg, Eliezer J.*
The Neurological Patient in History — *Jacyna, L. Stephen*
Neuromancer — *Gibson, William*
Neuroscience: A Historical Introduction — *Glickstein, Mitchell*
Neuroscience for Leadership: Harnessing the Brain Gain Advantage — *Swart, Tara*
Neuroscience of Creativity — *Vartanian, Oshin*
Neurotribes: The Legacy of Autism and How to Think Smarter about People who Think Differently — *Silberman, Steve*
Neurotribes: The Legacy of Autism and the Future of Neurodiversity — *Silberman, Steve*
Neutral Accent: How Language, Labor, and Life Became Global — *Aneesh, A.*
Neutrality in Twentieth-Century Europe: Intersections of Science, Culture, and Politics after the First World War — *Widmalm, Sven*

y Never Always Sometimes — *Alsaid, Adi*
Never Argue with a Dead Person: True and Unbelievable Stories from the Other Side — *John, Thomas*
c Never Ask a Dinosaur to Dinner (Illus. by Parker-Rees, Guy) — *Edwards, Gareth*
Never Broken: Songs Are Only Half the Story — *Jewel*
Never Call Retreat: Theodore Roosevelt and the Great War — *Thompson, J. Lee*
y Never Ending — *Bedford, Martyn*
Never Enough: Donald Trump and the Pursuit of Success — *D'Antonio, Michael*
Never Forget National Humiliation: Historical Memory in Chinese Politics and Foreign Relations — *Wang, Zheng*
Never Foul a Jump Shooter: A Guide to Basketball Lingo, Lessons and Laughs — *Yost, Daniel*
c Never Give Up: A Story about Self-Esteem (Illus. by Leng, Qin) — *Cole, Kathryn*
Never Goodnight — *Moodysson, Coco*
c Never Insult a Killer Zucchini (Illus. by Clark, David) — *Azose, Elana*
Never Let Me Leave — *Brozek, Jennifer*
y Never Look Down — *Easley, Warren C.*
y Never Never — *Shrum, Brianna R.*
The Never-Open Desert Diner — *Anderson, James*
Never Resist a Rake — *Marlowe, Mia*
Never Safe, Always Fun! — *Mitchell, Graham*
y Never Said (Read by Arsenault, Elise). Audiobook Review — *Williams, Carol Lynch*
y Never Said — *Williams, Carol Lynch*
Never Say Die — *Gerritsen, Tess*
Never Tear Us Apart — *Murphy, Monica*
c Never Tickle a Tiger (Illus. by Boutavant, Marc) — *Butchart, Pamela*
Never Too Late to Go Vegan — *Messina, Virginia*
Never Trust a Skinny Italian Chef — *Bottura, Massimo*
c Never Was a Grump Grumpier (Illus. by Bartlett, T.C.) — *Bartlett, T.C.*
c Never Wear Red Lipstick on Picture Day: And Other Lessons I've Learned (Illus. by Lewis, Stevie) — *Gutknecht, Allison*
Never Wholly Other: A Muslima Theology of Religious Pluralism — *Lamptey, Jerusha Tanner*
Neverending Beginnings — *Escobar, Mary Chris*
Neverhome — *Hunt, Laird*
y Neverland — *Arnold, Shari*
Nevermore — *Thurman, Rob*
y Nevermore! Tales of Murder, Mystery and the Macabre: Neo-Gothic Fiction Inspired by the Imagination of Edgar Allan Poe — *Kilpatrick, Nancy*
New American Stories — *Marcus, Ben*
The New American Zionism — *Sasson, Theodore*
The New and Improved Romie Futch — *Elliott, Julia*
The New Annotated H.P. Lovecraft — *Klinger, Leslie S.*
The New Anti-Semitism — *Chesler, Phyllis*
New Approaches to Sidonius Apollinaris — *Van Waarden, J.A.*
The New Arab Man: Emergent Masculinities, Technologies, and Islam in the Middle East — *Ritchie, Jason*
The New Arabs: How the Millennial Generation Is Changing the Middle East — *Cole, Juan*
c A New Arrival — *Alter, Anna*
New Art City: Manhattan at Mid-Century — *Perl, Jed*
The New Artisans II — *Dupon, Olivier*
New Avengers: Breakout. Audiobook Review — *Kwitney, Alisa*
New Babylonians: A History of Jews in Modern Iraq — *Bashkin, Orit*
A New Birth of Freedom: Selected Writings of Abraham Lincoln — *Kaplan, Fred*
The New Bohemians: Cool and Collected Homes — *Blakeney, Justina*
The New Book of Optical Illusions — *Ruschemeyer, Georg*
New Catholic Illustrated Bible (Illus. by Fredricksen, Lars) — *Welborn, Amy*
New Challenges for Maturing Democracies in Korea and Taiwan — *Diamond, Larry*
c A New Chick for Chickies (Illus. by Trasler, Janee) — *Trasler, Janee*
The New Christmas Tree: 24 Dazzling Trees and Over 100 Handcrafted Projects for an Inspired Holiday — *Brown, Carrie (b. 1955-)*
The New Class Conflict — *Kotkin, Joel*
New Classics to Moderns Series

The New Confessions of an Economic Hit Man — Perkins, John
New Cthulhu 2: More Recent Weird — Guran, Paula
y A New Darkness — Delaney, Joseph
c New Dawn Raisers — Fuji, Hideaki
The New Deal: A Global History — Patel, Kiran Klaus
New Deal Ruins: Race, Economic Justice, and Public Housing Policy — Goetz, Edward G.
New Developments in Goal Setting and Task Performance — Locke, Edwin A.
c New Developments (Illus. by Spaziante, Patrick) — Lewman, David
New Directions in Children's and Adolescents' Information Behavior Research — Bilal, Dania
The New Encyclopedia of Southern Culture, Volume 23: Folk Art — Crown, Carol
New England Open-House Cookbook: 300 Recipes Inspired by the Bounty of New England — Chase, Sarah Leah
The New Evangelical Social Engagement — Steensland, Brian
c A New Friend for Marmalade (Illus. by McKenzie, Heath) — Reynolds, Alison
c New Friend, Old Friends (Illus. by Pankhurst, Kate) — Jarman, Julia
c A New Friend (Illus. by Bell, Jennifer A.) — Green, Poppy
c New Friend — Steers, Billy
The New Generation Breast Cancer Book: How to Navigate Your Diagnosis and Treatment Options--and Remain Optimistic--in an Age of Information Overload — Port, Elisa
New German Cooking: Recipes for Classics Revisited — Nolen, Jeremy
A New Gospel for Women: Katherine Bushnell and the Challenge of Christian Feminism — Mez, Kristin Kobes Du
y New Guinea Moon — Constable, Kate
y The New Guy (and Other Senior Year Distractions). — Spalding, Amy
A New Heaven and a New Earth: Reclaiming Biblical Eschatology — Middleton, J. Richard
A New Herodotus: Laonikos Chalkokondyles on the Ottoman Empire, the Fall of Byzantium, and the Emergence of the West — Kaldellis, Anthony
New Histories of Pre-Columbian Florida — Wallis, Neill J.
A New History of Life: The Radical New Discoveries about the Origins and Evolution of Life on Earth — Ward, Peter
A New History of Medieval French Literature — Cerquiglini-Toulet, Jacqueline
A New History of Mississippi — Mitchell, Dennis J.
A New History of the Humanities: The Search for Principles and Patterns from Antiquity to the Present — Bod, Rens
A New Hope — Carr, Robyn
c A New Hope — Wang, Jack
y A New Juvenile Justice System: Total Reform for a Broken System — Dowd, Nancy E.
The New Kosher: Simple Recipes to Savor & Share — Kushner, Kim
New Labor in New York: Precarious Workers and the Future of the Labor Movement — Milkman, Ruth
New Leaf — Anderson, Catherine
The New Left, National Identity, and the Break-up of Britain — Matthews, Wade
The New Life: Jewish Students of Postwar Germany — Varon, Jeremy
New Life Stories: Journeys of Recovery in a Mindful Community — Carter, Hilary H.
New Literary Papyri from the Michigan Collection: Mythographic Lyric and a Catalogue of Poetic First Lines — Borges, Cassandra
A New Little Ice Age Has Started: How to Survive and Prosper during the Next 50 Difficult Years — Pierce, Lawrence
New Lives for Ancient and Extinct Crops — Minnis, Paul E.
New Media, Development and Globalization: Making Connections in the Global South — Slater, Don
New Mexico: A Glimpse Into an Enchanted Land — McWilliams, John P.
New Mexico: A History — Gomez, Art
New Mexico: A History — Sanchez, Joseph P.
New Monks in Old Habits: The Formation of the Caulite Monastic Order, 1193-1267 — Adamo, Philip C.
c New Moon, New Moon (Illus. by Alpern, Eliyahu) — Ofanansky, Allison
The New Mutants: Superheroes and the Radical Imagination of American Comics — Fawaz, Ramzi

The New Neighbor — Stewart, Leah
The New Neighborhood Senior Center: Redefining Social and Service Roles for the Baby Boom Generation — Weil, Joyce
New Netherland and the Dutch Origins of American Toleration — Haefeli, Evan
New Netherland Connections: Intimate Networks and Atlantic Ties in Seventeenth-Century America — Romney, Susanah Shaw
The New New Thing: A Silicon Valley Story — Lewis, Michael M.
New Objectivity: Modern German Art in the Weimar Republic 1919-1933 — Barron, Stephanie
The New Old World: An Indian Journalist Discovers the Changing Face of Europe — Aiyar, Pallavi
New Old World: An Indian Journalist Discovers the Changing Face of Europe — Aiyar, Pallavi
New on the Job: A School Librarian's Guide to Success, 2d ed. — Weisberg, Hilda
y The New Order (Read by Julian, Jose). Audiobook Review — Weitz, Chris
New Order — Wolf, Fay
y New Order — Turner, Max
A New Organon: Science Studies in Poland between the Wars
New Organs within Us: Transplants and the Moral Economy — Sanal, Aslihan
The New Orleans Jazz Scene, 1970-2000: A Personal Retrospective — Jacobsen, Thomas W.
c New Orleans Mother Goose (Illus. by Gentry, Marita) — Adam, Ryan
New Orleans Noir — Smith, Julie (b. 1944-)
c New Orleans Saints — Zappa, Marcia
The New Passover Menu — Shoyer, Paula
New Perspectives on Early Korean Art: From Silla to Koryo — Kim, Youn-Mi
New Perspectives on English as a European Linguafranca — Motschenbacher, Heiko
New Perspectives on Safavid Iran: Empire and Society — Mitchell, Colin P.
New Perspectives on the Man of Sorrows — Puglisi, Catherine R.
The New Prophets of Capital — Aschoff, Nicole
A New Republic of Letters: Memory and Scholarship in the Age of Digital Reproduction — McGann, Jerome
New Routes to Library Success: 100+ Ideas from Outside the Stacks — Doucett, Elisabeth
The New Scarlet Letter? Negotiating the U.S. Labor Market with a Criminal Record — Raphael, Steven
The New Scottish Cinema — Murray, Jonathan
New Selected Poems 1988-2013 — Heaney, Seamus
New Selected Poems — Constantine, David
New Selected Poems — Murray, Les
New Selected Poems — Page, Geoff
The New Shade Garden: Creating a Lush Oasis in the Age of Climate Change — Druse, Ken
c New Shoes (Illus. by Velasquez, Eric) — Meyer, Susan Lynn
The New Single: Finding, Fixing and Falling Back in Love with Yourself — Fadal, Tamsen
New Slow City: Living Simply in the World's Fastest City — Powers, William
c The New Small Person (Illus. by Child, Lauren) — Child, Lauren
The New Spymasters: Inside Espionage from the Cold War to Global Terror — Grey, Stephen
The New Statistics with R: An Introduction for Biologists — Hector, Andy
The New Suburban History — Sugrue, Thomas A.
The New Sugar and Spice: A Recipe for Bolder Baking — Seneviratne, Samantha
y New Teen Titans, vol. 2 (Illus. by Romeo, George Perez) — Wolfman, Marv
The New Terrain of International Law: Courts, Politics, Rights — Alter, Karen J.
The New Testament — Brown, Jericho
The New Threat from Islamic Militancy — Burke, Jason
The New Threat: The Past, Present, and Future of Islamic Militancy — Burke, Jason
The New Tsar: The Rise and Reign of Vladimir Putin — Myers, Steven Lee
New Tunisian Cinema — Lang, Robert
New Uses for Old Boyfriends — Kendrick, Beth
The New Wild: Why Invasive Species Will Be Nature's Salvation — Pearce, Fred
New World Companies: The Future of Capitalism — Piasecki, Bruce
New World Drama: The Performative Commons in the Atlantic World, 1649-1849 — Dillon, Elizabeth Maddock

New World Drama: The Performative Commons in the Atlantic World, 1649-1849 — Scott, Helen C.
The New World — Adrian, Chris
The New World — Motion, Andrew
A New World of Labor: The Development of Plantation Slavery in the British Atlantic — Newman, Simon P.
y A New World Order — Hosein-Mohammed, Sherina
New Worlds: A Religious History of Latin America — Lynch, John
c New Year's Eve Thieves — Roy, Ron
New York 1, Tel Aviv 0 — Oria, Shelly
New York and Amsterdam: Immigration and the New Urban Landscape — Foner, Nancy
New York and Los Angeles: The Uncertain Future — Halle, David
New York and Toronto Novels after Postmodernism: Explorations of the Urban — Rosenthal, Caroline
New York at War: Four Centuries of Combat, Fear and Intrigue in Gotham — Jaffe, Steven
New York Family History Research Guide and Gazetteer — New York Genealogical and Biographical Society
New York in a Dozen Dishes — Sietsema, Robert
New York in Fifty Design Icons — Iovine, Julie
The New York Nobody Knows: Walking 6,000 Miles in the City — Helmreich, William B.
New York Noise: Radical Jewish Music and the Downtown Scene — Barzel, Tamar
The New York Pizza Project — Johnson, Nick
The New York School: Photographs, 1936-1963 — Livingston, Jane
New York State Folklife Reader: Diverse Voices — Tucker, Elizabeth
The New York Times Book of Medicine: More Than 150 Years of Reporting on the Evolution of Medicine — Kolata, Gina
New Yorked — Hart, Rob
New York's Poop Scoop Law — Brandow, Michael
c New Zealand — Murray, Julie (b. 1969-)
c The Newbies (Illus. by Catalanotto, Peter) — Catalanotto, Peter
Newcomers' Accomplishments: Jewish Immigrants from Upper Hungary/Slovakia, 1806-1953 — Neurath, A. Robert
A Newly Crimsoned Reliquary — Crow, Donna Fletcher
Newman and His Family — Short, Edward
Newman and Life in the Spirit: Theological Reflections on Spirituality for Today — Connolly, John R.
Newman on Vatican II — Ker, Ian
The Newport Naval Training Station: A Postcard History — Santi, Federico
The News from Waterloo: The Race to Tell Britain of Wellington's Victory — Cathcart, Brian
The News From Waterloo: The Race to Tell Britain of Willington's Victory — Cathcart, Brian
News of the World — Jiles, Paulette
y The News: Poems — Brown, Jeffrey (b. 1956-)
The News Sorority: Diane Sawyer, Katie Couric, Ghristiane Amanpour - and the (Ongoing, Imperfect, Complicated) Triumph of Women in TV News (Read by Hallett, Morgan). Audiobook Review — Weller, Sheila
c Newsom, Fly! — Edwards, Karl
The Newspaper Boy — Isom, Chervis
c Newspaper Hats (Illus. by Swan, Owen) — Cummings, Phil
Newton and the Origin of Civilization — Buchwald, Jed Z.
The Newton Papers — Dry, Sarah
Newton's Apple and Other Myths about Science — Numbers, Ronald L.
y Newt's Emerald — Nix, Garth
y The Next Big Thing: A History of the Boom-or-Bust Moments that Shaped the Modern World (Illus. by Beyer, Ramsey) — Faulk, Richard
The Next Great War? The Roots of World War I and the Risk of U.S.-China Conflict — Miller, Steven E.
The Next Happy: Let Go of the Life You Planned and Find a New Way Forward — Cleantis, Tracey
The Next Next Level — Neyfakh, Leon
Next of Kin — Carter, Maureen
The Next Species: The Future of Evolution in the Aftermath of Man — Tennesen, Michael
The Next Story: Faith, Friends, Family, and the Digital World — Challies, Tim
c Next Time You See a Maple Seed — Morgan, Emily
c Next to You: A Book of Adorableness (Illus. by Hanson, Sydney) — Houran, Lori Haskins
y The Next Together — James, Lauren

c The Next Wave: The Quest to Harness the Power of the Oceans — Rusch, Elizabeth
Nextinction (Illus. by Steadman, Ralph) — Levy, Ceri
Nextinction — Steadman, Ralph
Nexus: Essays in German Jewish Studies, vol. 2 — Donahue, William Collins
c Nez Perce — Tieck, Sarah
NFL Confidential — Anonymous, Johnny
NGSS for All Students — Lee, Okhee
Nibelungenlied und Nibelungensage: Kommentierte Bibliographie 1945-2010 — Kragl, Florian
Nibelungenlied und Nibelungensage: Kommentierte Bibliographie 1945-2010 — Martschini, Elisabeth
Nica of Los Angeles — Perry, Sue
Nicaea Trilogy — Lamb, Warren
Niccolo Machiavelli: An Intellectual Biography — MacMichael, Simon
c Nice Work, Franklin! (Illus. by Day, Larry) — Jurmain, Suzanne Tripp
y Nichiren (Illus. by Tanaka, Ken) — Murakami, Masahiko
Nicholas of Cusa and Islam: Polemic and Dialogue in the Late Middle Ages — Levy, Ian Christopher
Nick and Tesla's Special Effects Spectacular: A Mystery with Animatronics, Alien Makeup, Camera Gear, and Other Movie Magic You Can Make Yourself! (Illus. by Garrett, Scott) — Pflugfelder, Bob
c Nick and Tesla's Special Effects Spectacular: A Mystery with Animatronics, Alien Makeup, Camera Gear, and Other Movie Magic You Can Make Yourself (Illus. by Garrett, Scott) — Pflugfelder, Bob
c Nick and Tesla's Super-Cyborg Gadget Glove: A Mystery with a Blinking, Beeping, Voice-Recording Gadget Glove You Can Build Yourself (Illus. by Garrett, Scott) — Pflugfelder, Bob
Nick Drake: Dreaming England — Wiseman-Trowse, Nathan
The Nick of Time — Levett, John
c Nickerbacher: The Funniest Dragon (Illus. by Sponaugle, Kim) — Barto, Terry John
c Nick's Very First Day of Baseball (Illus. by Tangeman, Dale) — Christofora, Kevin
Nicola Sturgeon: A Political Life — Torrance, David
Nicolas Nabokov: A Life in Freedom and Music — Giroud, Vincent
Nicolas Winding Refn: The Act of Seeing — Jones, Alan
Nicotine — Hens, Gregor
"Nie Wieder Auschwitz!": Die Entstehung eines Symbols und der Alltag einer Gedenkstatte 1945-1955 — Hansen, Imke
Nietzsche and The Birth of Tragedy — Daniels, Paul Raimond
Nietzsche as a Scholar of Antiquity — Jensen, Anthony K.
Nietzsche: Philosopher, Psychologist, Antichrist — Kaufmann, Walter
Nietzsche Versus Paul — Azzam, Abed
Nietzsche, Wagner, Europe — Prange, Martine
Nietzsche's Last Laugh: Ecce Homo as Satire — More, Nicholas D.
Nigeria: A New History of a Turbulent Century — Bourne, Richard
Nigeria — Falola, Toyin
"Night and Fog": A Film in History — Lindeperg, Sylvie
c Night Animals (Illus. by Marino, Gianna) — Marino, Gianna
Night at the Fiestas: Stories — Quade, Kirstin Valdez
c A Night at the Zoo (Illus. by Caple, Kathy) — Caple, Kathy
c The Night before Christmas: A Brick Story (Illus. by Brack, Amanda) — Moore, Clement C.
c The Night before Christmas (Illus. by Duvoisin, Roger) — Moore, Clement C.
c The Night before Christmas (Illus. by Engelbreit, Mary) — Moore, Clement C.
c The Night before Christmas (Illus. by Ercolini, David) — Moore, Clement C.
c The Night before Christmas (Illus. by Reid, Barbara) — Moore, Clement C.
c Night Buddies Go Sky High (Illus. by Love, Jessica) — Hetherington, Sands
Night Bus to the Afterlife — Cooley, Peter
The Night Charter — Hawken, Sam
c The Night Children (Illus. by Bodet, Delphine) — Tsiang, Sarah
The Night Circus — Morgenstern, Erin
c Night Circus (Illus. by Delessert, Etienne) — Delessert, Etienne

c Night Circus — Delessert, Etienne
The Night Clock — Meloy, Paul
c A Night Divided (Read by Sinrses, Kate). Audiobook Review — Nielsen, Jennifer A.
y A Night Divided — Nielsen, Jennifer A.
Night Falling on the Tree of Cups — Margetson, Evan K.
The Night Game — Golden, Frank
Night Games: Sex, Power and a Journey Into the Dark Heart of Sport — Krien, Anna
The Night Garden (Read by Rubinate, Amy). Audiobook Review — Allen, Lisa Van
y The Night Gardener (Read by Crick, Beverley A.). Audiobook Review — Auxier, Jonathan
c The Night Gardener (Illus. by Fan, Eric) — Fan, Terry
y The Night Gardener — Auxier, Jonathan
c The Night Gardener (Illus. by Fan, Eric) — Fan, Terry
The Night Guest — McFarlane, Fiona
Night Hunters: The AC-130s and Their Role in U.S. Airpower — Head, William P.
Night in Erg Chebbi — Hamlin, Edward
Night Is the Hunter — Gore, Steven
Night Life — Taylor, David C.
Night Music: Nocturnes, vol. 2 — Connolly, John
Night Night, Sleep Tight (Read by Lee, Ann Marie). Audiobook Review — Ephron, Hallie
Night Night, Sleep Tight — Ephron, Hallie
Night of the Assassins. E-book Review — Fargo, Ford
The Night of the Cobra — Coughlin, Jack
Night of the Confessor: Christian Faith in an Age of Uncertainty — Halik, Thomas
y Night of the Frightening Fractions — Black, Robert
Night of the Gods: Durga Puja and the Legitimation of Power in Rural Bengal — Nicholas, Ralph W.
Night of the Highland Dragon — Cooper, Isabel
Night of the Jaguar — Gannon, Joe
c Night of the Living Worms: A Speed Bump and Slingshot Misadventure (Illus. by Coverly, Dave) — Coverly, Dave
c Night of the Living Worms (Illus. by Coverly, Dave) — Coverly, Dave
c The Night of the Were-boy (Illus. by Mazali, Gustavo) — Richemont, Enid
Night of the White Buffalo — Coel, Margaret
c Night on Fire — Kidd, Ronald
c The Night Our Parents Went Out (Illus. by Bui, Cat Tuong) — Goodman, Katie
c Night Owl (Illus. by Yuly, Toni) — Yuly, Toni
y Night Owls — Bennett, Jenn
c The Night Parade — Tanquary, Kathryn
c The Night Parade (Illus. by Walker, David) — Roscoe, Lily
Night Post (Illus. by Trinder, Laura) — Read, Benjamin
The Night Searchers — Muller, Marcia
The Night Sister (Read by Campbell, Cassandra). Audiobook Review — McMahon, Jennifer
The Night Sister — McMahon, Jennifer
c Night Sky Dragons (Illus. by Benson, Patrick) — Peet, Mal
c Night Sky — Brockmann, Suzanne
The Night Stages — Urquhart, Jane
c The Night the Lights Went Out on Christmas (Illus. by Brundage, Scott) — Paul, Ellis
y The Night Thief — Fradkin, Barbara
Night Tremors — Coyle, Matt
Night Vision: Nocturnes In American Art, 1860-1960 — Homann, Joachim
Night Vision — Levenson, Christopher
The Night Voice — Hendee, Barb
y The Night Watchman — Fischer, Jeremie
c The Night Watchman (Illus. by Fischer, Jeremie) — Wilson, David Henry
y The Night We Said Yes — Gibaldi, Lauren
The Night We're Not Sleeping In — Bishop, Sean
Night Willow — Igloria, Luisa A.
c The Night World — Gerstein, Mordicai
c The Night World (Illus. by Gerstein, Mordicai) — Gerstein, Mordicai
c The Night World — Gerstein, Mordicai
Nightbird (Read by Lamia, Jenna). Audiobook Review — Hoffman, Alice
y Nightbird — Hoffman, Alice
c Nightborn (Illus. by Gerard, Justin) — Anders, Lou
c Nightborn — Anders, Lou
y Nightfall — Halpern, Jake
The Nightingale (Read by Stone, Polly). Audiobook Review — Hannah, Kristin
Nightingale — Voinov, Aleksandr
y The Nightmare Charade — Arnett, Mindee

The Nightmare Place — Mosby, Steve
y Nightmareland (Illus. by Bruno, Iacopo) — Preller, James
c Nightmares! (Illus. by Kwasny, Karl) — Miller, Kirsten
c Nightmares! (Illus. by Kwasny, Karl) — Segel, Jason
Nightmares of an Ether-Drinker — Lorrain, Jean
Nightmares Unhinged — Viola, Joshua
Nights of the Horns — Sanderson, Douglas
Night's Surrender — Ashley, Amanda
Nightscape: Cynopolis — Edwards, David W.
Nightwalking: A Nocturnal History of London — Beaumont, Matthew
The Nightwatches of Bonaventura — Gillespie, Gerald
The Nightwatches of Bonaventura — Klingemann, August
Nightwise — Belcher, R.S.
c Nighty Night! (Illus. by Argent, Kerry) — Wild, Margaret
Nihilism and Metaphysics: The Third Voyage — Possenti, Vittorio
Niketas Choniates: A Historiographical Study — Simpson, Alicia
Niketas Stethatos: The Life of Saint Symeon the New Theologian — Greenfield, Richard P.H.
Niki de Saint Phalle — de Saint Phalle, Niki
y Nil — Matson, Lynne
y Nil Unlocked — Matson, Lynne
c Nile River — Manning, Paul
y Nimona (Illus. by Stevenson, Noelle) — Stevenson, Noelle
c Nina Goes Barking Mad! (Illus. by Krawczyk, Agata) — Pouroulis, Anita
y Nine Digits — Duret, Jay
Nine Essential Things I've Learned about Life — Kushner, Harold S.
Nine Jewels of Night: One Soul's Journey into God — Lanzetta, Beverly
c The Nine Lives of Jacob Tibbs (Illus. by Kelley, Gerald) — Busby, Cylin
c The Nine Lives of Pinrut the Turnip Boy — Down, Reg
Nine Lives — Staub, Wendy Corsi
Nine New York Poems — Sharma, Yuyutsu
c Nine Open Arms — Lindelauf, Benny
Nine Rabbits — Zaharieva, Virginia
c Ninelands — Boyer, K.E.
Nineteen Eighty-Four — Orwell, George
Nineteenth-Century British Literature Then and Now: Reading with Hindsight — Dentith, Simon
Nineteenth-Century British Travelers in the New World — DeVine, Christine
The Nineteenth-Century Sensation Novel, 2d ed. — Pykett, Lyn
Ninigret, Sachem of the Niantics and Narragansetts: Diplomacy, War, and the Balance of Power in Seventeenth-Century New England and Indian Country — Fisher, Julie A.
Ninigret, Sachem of the Niantics and Narragansetts: Diplomacy, War, and the Balance of Power in Seventeenth-Century New England and Indian Country — Silverman, David J.
c Ninja Baby (Illus. by Goode, Diane) — Zeltser, David
c Ninja Boy Goes to School (Illus. by Harrison, J.J.) — Wilson, N.D.
c Ninja Bunny (Illus. by Olson, Jennifer Gray) — Olson, Jennifer Gray
c Ninja Mouse: Haiku (Illus. by Thomas, J.C.) — Thomas, J.C.
c Ninja! (Illus. by Chung, Arree) — Chung, Arree
c Ninja Red Riding Hood (Illus. by Santat, Dan) — Schwartz, Corey Rosen
c Ninja Timmy (Illus. by Tamm, Henrik) — Tamm, Henrik
c Ninjas — Hyde, Natalie
c Ninjas — Matthews, Rupert
c Nino Wrestles the World (Read by Sananes, Adriana). Audiobook Review — Morales, Yuyi
c Nipper of Drayton Hall (Illus. by McElroy, Gerry) — Lewis, Amey Parsons
c Nirvana: The Angel Dream (Illus. by Johns, Sheridan) — Suzanne, Nicole
c The Nitrogen Cycle — Dakers, Diane
c The Nitty-Gritty Gardening Book: Fun Projects for All Seasons (Illus. by Larson, Jennifer S.) — Cornell, Kari
c Nitty-Gritty Gardening Book: Fun Projects for All Seasons (Illus. by Larson, Jennifer S.) — Cornell, Kari
c The Nitty-Gritty Gardening Book — Cornell, Kari
The Nitty-Gritty Gardening Book (Illus. by Larson, Jennifer S.) — Cornell, Kari

The Nixon Defence: What He Knew and When He Knew It — Dean, John W.
Nixon, Kissinger, and the Shah: The United States and Iran in the Cold War — Alvandi, Roham
The Nixon Tapes: 1971-72 — Brinkley, Douglas
The Nixon Tapes: 1973 — Brinkley, Douglas
The Nixon Tapes: 1973 — Nichter, Luke A.
Nixon's Gamble: How a President's Own Secret Government Destroyed His Administration — Locker, Ray
c Nnewts: Escape from the Lizzarks (Illus. by Garner, Katherine) — TenNapel, Doug
c The No. 1 Car Spotter Goes to School (Illus. by Cadwell, Warwick Johnson) — Atinuke
No. 4 Imperial Lane — Weisman, Jonathan
No Baggage: A Minimalist Tale of Love and Wandering — Bensen, Clara
No Better Friend — Weintraub, Robert
No Better Man — Richardson, Sara
No Billionaire Left Behind: Satirical Activism in America — Hagerud, Angelique
No Book but the World — Cohen, Leah Hager
No Bull Information: A Humorous Practical Guide to Help Americans Adapt to the Information Age — Gamble, John
No-Churn Ice Cream: Over 100 Simply Delicious No-Machine Frozen Treats — Bilderback, Leslie
No Comfort for the Lost — Herriman, Nancy
No Cure for Love — Robinson, Peter
y No Dawn without Darkness — Lorentz, Dayna
c No Dogs Allowed! (Illus. by Muth, Jon J.) — Manzano, Sonia
No End Save Victory: How FDR Led the Nation into War — Kaiser, David
No Excuses Fitness: The 30-Day Plan to Tone Your Body and Supercharge Your Health — Green, Donovan
No Excuses: Growing Up Deaf and Achieving My Super Bowl Dreams — Coleman, Derrick, Jr.
No Freedom without Regulation: The Hidden Lesson of the Subprime Crisis — Singer, Joseph William
No God But Gain: The Untold Story of Cuban Slavery, the Monroe Doctrine, and the Making of the United States — Chambers, Stephen
No Good Deed — Brennan, Allison
No Good Men Among the Living: America, the Taliban, and the War through Afghan Eyes — Gopal, Anand
No Goodbyes: Life-Changing Insights from the Other Side — Eaton, Barry
No Grain, No Pain: A 30-Day Diet for Eliminating the Root Cause of Chronic Pain — Osborne, Peter
No Gun Intended — Burke, Zoe
No Harm Can Come to a Good Man — Smythe, James
No Hero: The Evolution of a Navy SEAL (Read by Michael, Paul). Audiobook Review — Owen, Mark
No Home Like Place: A Christian Theology of Place — Hjalmarson, Leonard
No Hope: Why I Left the GOP (and You Should, Too). — LaSalvia, Jimmy
y No House to Call My Home: Love, Family, and Other Transgressions — Berg, Ryan
No Illusions: The Voices of Russia's Future Leaders — Mickiewicz, Ellen
No Interest in Love. E-book Review — Mae, Cassie
No Irrelevant Jesus: On Jesus and the Church Today — Lohfink, Gerhard
y No Known Grave — Jennings, Maureen
No Land's Man: A Perilous Journey through Romance, Islam, and Brunch (Read by Mandvi, Aasif). Audiobook Review — Mandvi, Aasif
No Limits: The Powerful True Story of Leah Goldstein: World Kickboxing Champion, Israeli Undercover Police and Cycling Champion — Goldstein, Leah
No Makou ka Mana: Liberating the Nation — Beamer, Kamanamaikalani
No Man's Land — Califra, Michael
No Man's Land: Preparing for War and Peace in Post-9/11 America — Elizabeth D. Samet
No Man's Land: Preparing for War and Peace in Post-9/11 America — Samet, Elizabeth D.
No Mission Is Impossible: The Death-Defying Missions of the Israeli Special Forces — Bar-Zohar, Michael
No More Champagne: Churchill and His Money — Lough, David
c No More Cuddles! — Chapman, Jane
The No More Excuses Diet: 3 Days to Bust Any Excuse, 3 Weeks to Easy New Eating Habits, 3 Months to Total Transformation — Kang, Maria
No More Illusions — Babka, Daniel

c No More Pacifier, Duck (Illus. by Vidal, Oriol) — Dahl, Michael
y No Name — Tingle, Tim
c No Nap! Yes Nap! (Illus. by Yaccarino, Dan) — Palatini, Margie
c No, No, Gnome! (Illus. by Anstee, Ashlyn) — Anstee, Ashlyn
c No, No, Kitten! (Illus. by Nichols, Lori) — Thomas, Shelley Moore
The No Nonsense Guide to Green Parenting: How to Raise Your Child, Help Save the Planet and Not Go Mad — Blincoe, Kate
No One Belongs Here More Than You — July, Miranda
y No One Gets Out Alive — Nevill, Adam
"No One Helped": Kitty Genovese, New York City, and the Myth of Urban Apathy — Gallo, Marcia M.
No One Knows — Ellison, J.T.
No One Like You — Angell, Kate
No One Will Let Her Live: Women's Struggle for Well-Being in a Delhi Slum — Snell-Rood, Claire
No Ordinary Billionaire — Scott, J.S.
c No Ordinary Day — Ellis, Deborah
No Ordinary Disruption: The Four Global Forces Breaking All the Trends — Dobbs, Richard
No Ordinary Men: Dietrich Bonhoeffer and Hans von Dohnanyi, Resisters Against Hitler in Church and State — Sifton, Elizabeth
No Other Darkness: A Detective Inspector Marnie Rome Mystery — Hilary, Sarah
y No Parking at the End Times — Bliss, Bryan
c No! (Illus. by Warnes, Tim) — Corderoy, Tracey
No Place to Die — Donoghue, Clare
y No Place to Fall — Brown, Jaye Robin
No Place to Hide — Lewis, Susan
No Place to Hide: Edward Snowden, the NSA, and the U.S. Surveillance State — Greenwald, Glenn
y No Regrets — Karre, Elizabeth
No Requiem for the Space Age: The Apollo Moon Landings and American Culture — Tribbe, Matthew D.
No Room for Dabha — Pai, Raja
No Saddle for the Cowboy — Gurney, George
No Safe House (Read by Winton, Graham). Audiobook Review — Barclay, Linwood
No-See-Me and the Amazing Crimson Stick — Verdick, Mary
No-Sew Fleece Throw — Javier, Nancy
No Shred of Evidence — Todd, Charles
c No, Silly! (Illus. by Krug, Ken) — Krug, Ken
No Simple Highway: A Cultural History of the Grateful Dead — Richardson, Peter
No Solid Ground — Miller, Jeffrey
No Stopping Train — Plesko, Les
y No Such Person (Read by Spencer, Erin). Audiobook Review — Cooney, Caroline B.
y No Such Person — Cooney, Caroline B.
No Such Thing as a Free Gift: The Gates Foundation and the Price of Philanthropy — McGoey, Linsey
No Such Thing As Failure: My Life in Adventure, Exploration, and Survival — Hempleman-Adams, David
y No Such Thing as Free Goldfish — Wittler, Joan
No Sweat: How the Simple Science of Motivation Can Bring You a Lifetime of Fitness — Segar, Michelle
y No True Echo — Jones, Gareth P.
No Turning Back: The Future of Ecumenism — O'Gara, Margaret
c No Two Alike (Illus. by Baker, Keith) — Baker, Keith
No Virgin Island — Dorsey, C. Michele
y No Worse Sin — Bennett, Kyla
c No Yeti Yet (Illus. by Fraser, Mary Ann) — Fraser, Mary Ann
c Noah (AA) Picture story) — Ludy, Mark
c Noah Chases the Wind (Illus. by Cowman, Joseph) — Worthington, Michelle
y Noah Webster: Man of Many Words — Reef, Catherine
c Noah's Ark: Adapted from Genesis, Chapters 6-9 — Falken, Linda
c Noah's Ark — Falken, Linda
Noah's Wife — Starck, Lindsay
Nobility and Kingship in Medieval England: The Earls and Edward I, 1272-1307 — Spencer, Andrew M.
Nobility Lost: French and Canadian Martial Cultures, Indians, and the End of New France — Crouch, Christian A.
Nobility Lost: French and Canadian Martial Cultures, Indians, and the End of New France — Crouch, Christian Ayne

The Noble Hustle: Poker, Beef Jerky and Death — Whitehead, Colson
Noble Power in Scotland from the Reformation to the Revolution — Brown, Keith M.
y Noble Warrior — Sitomer, Alan Lawrence
c Nobody! A Story about Overcoming Bullying in Schools (Illus. by Heaphy, Paula) — Frankel, Erin
Nobody Grew But the Business: On the Life and Work of William Gaddis — Tabbi, Joseph
Nobody Is Ever Missing — Lacey, Catherine
Nobody Walks — Herron, Mick
Nobody's Angel — Hegger, Sarah
Nobody's Child — Hellmann, Libby Fischer
Nobody's Fool — Hegger, Sarah
y Nobody's Goddess — McNulty, Amy
Nobody's Hero — Bailey, J. Leigh
c Nobody's Perfect (Illus. by Zuppardi, Sam) — Elliott, David
Nocni kadrovy dotaznik a jine boje — Benda, Vaclav
Nocturne (Illus. by Hoffmeister, Angie) — Opotowsky, Anne
c Nocturne: Creatures of the Night — Scott, Traer
Nogara: Archeologia e storia di un villaggio medievale, scavi 2003-2008 — Saggioro, Fabio
c Noggin (Read by Heyborne, Kirby). Audiobook Review — Whaley, John Corey
y Noir — Garlick, Jacqueline E.
c Noisy Bird Sing-Along (Illus. by Himmelman, John) — Himmelman, John
c The Noisy Clock Shop (Illus. by Seiden, Art) — Berg, Jean Horton
c Noisy Dinosaurs — Litton, Jonathan
c The Noisy Foxes (Illus. by Husband, Amy) — Husband, Amy
c The Noisy Paint Box: The Colors and Sounds of Kandinsky's Abstract Art (Illus. by GrandPre, Mary) — Rosenstock, Barb
The Nomad Cookbook — Humm, Daniel
y Nomad — Alexander, William
Nomadic Ethics in Contemporary Women's Writing in German: Strange Subjects — Jeremiah, Emily
Nomadism in Iran: From Antiquity to the Modern Era — Potts, D.T.
Nomads as Agents of Cultural Change: The Mongols and Their Eurasian Predecessors — Amitai, Reuven
Non-Dualism in Echart, Julian of Norwich and Traherne: A Theopoetic Reflection — Charlton, James
Nonahere Ori Tahiti: Pipiri Ma — Amaru, Patrick Araia
c None of the Above — Gregario, I.W.
y None of the Above — Gregorio, I.W.
Nong's Thai Kitchen: 84 Classic Recipes That are Quick, Healthy and Delicious — Daks, Nongkran
c Noni the Pony Goes to the Beach (Illus. by Lester, Alison) — Lester, Alison
Nonlinear Dynamics and Chaos: With Applications to Physics, Biology, Chemistry, and Engineering — Strogatz, Steven H.
Nonlinear Physics of Ecosystems — Meron, Ehud
c Nonna Tell Me a Story: Lidia's Egg-citing Farm Adventure (Illus. by Graef, Renee) — Bastianich, Lidia
c Nonna's Hanukkah Surprise (Illus. by Aviles, Martha) — Fisman, Karen
Nonna's House: Cooking and Reminiscing with the Italian Grandmothers of Enoteca Maria — Scaravella, Jody
c Nonsense Limericks (Illus. by Robins, Arthur) — Lear, Edward
c The Nonsense Show (Illus. by Carle, Eric) — Carle, Eric
Nonsense: The Power of Not Knowing — Holmes, Jamie
Nonviolent Action: What Christian Ethics Demands But Most Christians Have Never Really Tried — Sider, Ronald J.
The Nonviolent God — Weaver, Denny J.
c Noodle Magic (Illus. by So, Meilo) — Thong, Roseanne Greenfield
The Noodle Maker of Kalimpong: The Untold Story of My Struggle for Tibet — Thondup, Gyalo
c Noodlehead Nightmares (Illus. by Arnold, Tedd) — Arnold, Tedd
Nookietown — Chickering, V.C.
c Nooks & Crannies (Read by Riddell, Susie). Audiobook Review — Lawson, Jessica
c Nooks & Crannies (Illus. by Andrewson, Natalie) — Lawson, Jessica
Noonday — Barker, Pat
Noontide Toll — Gunesekera, Romesh
Noontime Follies — Gunn, Elizabeth

NOPI: The Cookbook (Illus. by Lovekin, Jonathan) — Ottolenghi, Yotam
y Nora and Kettle — Taylor, Lauren Nicole
Nora Webster (Read by Shaw, Fiona). Audiobook Review — Toibin, Colm
Nora Webster — Toibin, Colm
The Nordic Apocalypse: Approaches to Voluspa and Nordic Days of Judgement — Gunnell, Terry
Nordic Contemporary: Art from Denmark, Finland, Iceland, Norway and Sweden — Amirsadeghi, Hossein
The Nordic Cookbook — Nilsson, Magnus
Nordicana: 100 Icons of Scandi Culture and Nordic Cool — Kinsella, Kajsa
Norfolk Broadsides — Lamont, Brian
Norgeskatalogen Postal II — Anenesn, Peer-Christian
The Norm Chronicles: Stories and Numbers about Danger and Death — Blastland, Michael
The Norm of Belief — Gibbons, John
Norm und Realitat in der Uberlieferung des Fruhen Mittelalters
The Norma Gene — Roufa, M.E.
Normal — Cameron, Graeme
The Norman Campaigns in the Balkans, 1081-1108 — Theotokis, Georgios
Norman Expansion: Connections, Continuities and Contrasts — Stringer, Keith J.
Norman Granz - The Man Who Used Jazz for Justice — Hershorn, Tad
Norman Janes: Wood Engravings and the Man — Grice, Elizabeth
c Norman, Speak! (Illus. by Leng, Qin) — Adderson, Caroline
Norman Tradition and Transcultural Heritage: Exchange of Cultures in the "Norman" Peripheries of Medieval Europe — Foerster, Thomas
The Normans and Empire — Bates, David
Noro Lace: 30 Exquisite Knits — Editors of Sixth&Springs Books
Norse Goddess Magic: Trancework, Mythology, and Ritual — Karlsdottir, Alice
c North American Mammals Series — Johnson, Jinny
North American Odyssey: Historical Geographies for the Twenty-First Century — Colten, Craig E.
North America's Indian Trade in European Commerce and Imagination, 1580-1850 — Colpitts, George
y North and South America — Harris, Tim
North Carolina Women: Their Lives and Times, vol. 1 — Gillespie, Michele
North East — McGrath, Wendy
c The North: From the Arctic Lowlands to Polar Deserts — de Medeiros, Michael
North Korea Confidential: Private Markets, Fashion Trends, Prison Camps, Dissenters and Defectors — Tudor, Daniel
North Korea Undercover: Inside the World's Most Secret State — Sweeney, John
North of the Tension Line — Riordan, J.F.
The North Water — McGuire, Ian
c North Woods Girl (Illus. by McGehee, Claudia) — Bissonette, Aimee
Northanger Abbey (Read by McDermid, Val). Audiobook Review — McDermid, Val
Northeast Asia and the Legacy of Harry S. Truman: Japan, China, and the Two Koreas — Matray, James I.
Northern Armageddon: The Battle of the Plains of Abraham and the Making of the American Revolution — MacLeod, D. Peter
Northern Slave, Black Dakota: The Life and Times of Joseph Godfrey — Bachman, Walt
Northhern Orchards: Places near the Dead — Rogers, James Silas
Northrop Frye's Uncollected Prose — Frye, Northrop
Northwest of Eden — Caruthers, Yancy
The Northwest Passage — Nary, Henry
The Norton Anthology of World Religions, 2 vols. — Miles, Jack
The Norton Anthology of World Religions — Denny, Frederick M.
The Norton Anthology of World Religions — Kinnard, Jacob N.
Norway — Murray, Julie
c Norwegian Folk Tales — Larson, Jean Russell
A Norwegian Tragedy: Anders Behring Breivik and the Massacre on Utoya — Borchgrevink, Aage
Norwegian Wood: Chopping, Stacking, and Drying Wood the Scandinavian Way — Mytting, Lars
c Nose to Toes, You Are Yummy! (Illus. by Harrington, Tim) — Harrington, Tim
c Noses Are Not for Picking — Verdick, Elizabeth

NoSQL for Mere Mortals — Sullivan, Dan
Not a Game: The Incredible Rise and Unthinkable Fall of Allen Iverson — Babb, Kent
c Not a Lot, Robot! (Illus. by Cartwright, Amy) — Powell, Marie
y Not after Everything — Levy, Michelle
Not All Bad Comes to Harm You — Mock, Janice
Not All Bastards Are from Vienna — Molesini, Andrea
Not All Honey — Lumsden, Roddy
c Not As We Know It (Illus. by Grove, Kate) — Avery, Tom
Not Easy Being Green — Gage, Susy
c Not for All the Hamantaschen in Town (Illus. by Chernyak, Inna) — Milhander, Laura Aron
c Not for Hurting (Illus. by Pate, Ashley) — Weber, Alan M.
c Not for Sale (Illus. by Flook, Helen) — Cassidy, Sara
Not from Here — Johnson, Allan G.
y Not Funny Ha-Ha (Illus. by Hayes, Leah) — Hayes, Leah
Not Gay: Sex between Straight White Men — Ward, Jane
Not Going Gently: A Psychologist Fights Back against Alzheimer's for Her Mother ... and Perhaps Herself — Vincent, Constance L.
Not Hollywood: Independent Film at the Twilight of the American Dream — Ortner, Sherry B.
Not I, Not Other Than I: The Life and Teachings of Russel Williams — Williams, Russel
y Not If I See You First — Lindstrom, Eric
Not in God's Name: Confronting Religious Violence — Sacks, Jonathan
Not In God's Name: Making Sense of Religious Conflict — Fouce, Paula
Not in the Pink — Martel, Tina
y Not in the Script — Finnegan, Amy
c Not Me! (Illus. by Gorbachev, Valeri) — Gorbachev, Valeri
Not My Buddy — Berkowitz, Tracey
Not My Father's Son — Cumming, Alan
Not on Fire, but Burning — Hrbek, Greg
Not on the List — Alberts, Heath D.
y Not Otherwise Specified — Moskowitz, Hannah
Not Quite Nice — Imrie, Celia
Not Really Gone — Sharpe, Blaire
Not That Kind of Girl: A Young Woman Tells You What She's "Learned" — Dunham, Lena
c Not This Bear: A First Day of School Story (Illus. by Hussey, Lorna) — Cappucilli, Alyssa Satin
c Not This Bear: A First Day of School Story (Illus. by Hussey, Lorna) — Capucilli, Alyssa Satin
Not Tonight: Migraine and the Politics of Gender and Health — Kempner, Joanna
c The Not Very Merry Pout-Pout Fish (Illus. by Flanna, Dan) — Diesen, Deborah
c The Not Very Merry Pout-Pout Fish (Illus. by Hanna, Dan) — Diesen, Deborah
c Not Very Scary (Illus. by Pizzoli, Greg) — Brendler, Carol
Not What I Expected: Help and Hope for Parents of Atypical Children — Eichenstein, Rita
y Not What I Expected: The Mostly Miserable Life of April Sinclair, Bk. 5 — Friedman, Laurie B.
c Not Your Typical Dragon (Illus. by Bowers, Tim) — Bar-El, Dan
Note Book — Nunokawa, Jeff
The Notebook — Kristof, Agota
Notebooks, English Virtuosi, and Early Modern Science — Yeo, Richard
Notes from a Colored Girl: The Civil War Pocket Diaries of Emilie Francis Davis — Whitehead, Karsonya Wise
Notes from a Dead House — Dostoevsky, Fyodor
c Notes from a Pro (Illus. by Cattish, Anna) — Cobb, Amy
Notes From No Man's Land: American Essays — Biss, Eula
Notes from Underground — Scruton, Roger
Notes on the Assemblage — Herrera, Juan Felipe
Notes on the Death of Culture: Essays on Spectacle and Society — Llosa, Mario Vargas
Notes on the Death of Culture: Essays on Spectacle and Society — Vargas Llosa, Mario
Notes on the Death of Culture — King, John
Notes to Screenwriters: Advancing Your Story, Screenplay, and Career with Whatever Hollywood Throws at You — Peterson, Vicki
Notes to the Nations — Clemans, Ernest G.
Notes Toward a Performative Theory of Assembly — Butler, Judith
c Nothing (Read by Newbern, George). Audiobook Review — Agee, Jon

Nothing — Naseem, Linda
y Nothing Bad Is Going to Happen — Hale, Kathleen
Nothing but Love in God's Water: Black Sacred Music from the Civil War to the Civil Rights Movement — Darden, Robert
Nothing But Love in God's Water, vol. 1: Black Sacred Music from the Civil War to the Civil Rights Movement — Darden, Robert
Nothing Is True and Everything Is Possible: Adventures in Modern Russia — Pomerantsev, Peter
Nothing Is True and Everything Is Possible: The Surreal Heart of the New Russia — Pomerantsev, Peter
y Nothing Left to Burn — Blount, Patty
Nothing Like Love — Ramnanan, Sabrina
Nothing Looks Familiar — Syms, Shawn
Nothing More to Lose — Darwish, Najwan
Nothing Natural Is Shameful: Sodomy and Science in Late Medieval Europe — Cadden, Joan
Nothing to Declare — Cole, Henri
Nothing Ventured — Douglas, Anne
Notice and Note: Strategies for Close Reading — Beers, Kylene
The Notion of Authority — Kojeve, Alexandre
y The Notorious Benedict Arnold: A True Story of Adventure, Heroism and Treachery — Sheinkin, Steve
The Notorious Isaac Earl and His Scouts: Union Soldiers, Prisoners, Spies — Olson, Gordon L.
y The Notorious Pagan Jones — Berry, Nina
Notorious RBG: The Life and Times of Ruth Bader Ginsburg — Carmon, Irin
Notre-Dame de Paris, 1163-2013: Actes du colloque scientifique tenu au College des Bernardins, a Paris, du 12 au 15 decembre 2012 — Giraud, Cedric
y Noughts and Crosses Graphic Novel (Illus. by Aggs, John) — Blackman, Malorie
Nourishing Broth: An Old-Fashioned Remedy for the Modern World — Morell, Sally Fallon
The Nourishing Homestead: One Back-to-the-Land Family's Plan for Cultivating Soil, Skills, and Spirit — Hewitt, Ben
Nova and Quinton: No Regrets — Sorensen, Jessica
y Nova — Fortune, Margaret
Novas y cometas entre 1572 y 1618: Revolucion cosmologica y renovacion politica y religiosa — Granada, Miguel Angel
The Novel: A Biography — Schmidt, Michael
The Novel Habits of Happiness — McCall Smith, Alexander
The Novel in the Age of Disintegration: Dostoevsky and the Problem of Genre in the 1870s — Holland, Kate
Novel Nostalgias: The Aesthetics of Antagonism in Nineteenth-Century U.S. Literature — Funchion, John
Novel of Ancient Sparta — Nicastro, Nick
The Novel of the Future — Nin, Anais
Novel Science: Fiction and the Invention of Nineteenth-Century Geology — Buckland, Adelene
Novels and Stories of the 1940s and 50s — Malamud, Bernard
Novels and Stories of the 1960s — Malamud, Bernard
November 9 — Hoover, Colleen
c November Night (Illus. by Gurney, John Steven) — Roy, Ron
y The Novice — Matharu, Taran
Now and at the Hour of Our Death — Marques, Sandra Moreira
Now I Know Who My Comrades Are: Voices from the Internet Underground — Parker, Emily
Now Is the Time — Bragg, Melvyn
y Now That You're Here — Nichols, Amy K.
Now Then — Stewart, Paul
Now You Hear My Horn: The Journal of James Wilson Nichols, 1820-1887 — McDowell, Catherine W.
c Now You See Them, Now You Don't: Poems About Creatures That Hide (Illus. by Laroche, Giles) — Harrison, David
Nowhere All at Once — Bauer, Grace
y Nowhere but Here — McGarry, Katie
Nowhere Girl — Strecker, Susan
y Nowhere Wild — Beernink, Joe
Nowojorski pasjans: Polski Instytut Naukowy w Ameryce, Jan Lechon, Kazimierz Wierzynski. Studia o wybranych zagadnieniach dzialalnosci 1939-1969 — Dorosz, Beata

NS-Diplomatie und Bundnispolitik 1935-1944: Wipert von Blucher, das Dritte Reich und Finnland — *Jonas, Michael*
NS-Propaganda im 21. Jahrhundert: Zwischen Verbot und öffentlicher Auseinandersetzung — *Kuchler, Christian*
The NSTA Quick-Reference Guide to the NGSS, Elementary School — *Willard, Ted*
The NSTA Quick-Reference Guide to the NGSS: High School — *Willard, Ted*
The Nuclear Age in Popular Media: A Transnational History, 1945-1965 — *van Lente, Dick*
Nuestra Fe: A Latin American Church History Sourcebook — *Gonzalez, Ondina E.*
c Nugget on Top of the World (Illus. by de Beer, Hans) — *de Beer, Hans*
c Nujood Ali and the Fight against Child Marriage — *Don, Katherine*
Null Set — *Mathys, Ted*
c Numbed! — *Lubar, David*
y The Number 7 — *Lidh, Jessica*
Number 11 — *Coe, Jonathan*
y Number 13 (Illus. by Walker, David (b. 1965-)) — *Love, Robert*
Number Fun: Making Numbers with Your Body — *Thomas, Isabel*
Number One Songs: The First Twenty Years — *Irons, Larry*
Number Sense Interventions — *Jordan, Nancy C.*
c Number the Stars — *Lowry, Lois*
c Numbers 1-20 Series — *Salzmann, Mary Elizabeth*
y Numbers — *Poulsen, David A.*
c Numbers — *Poitier, Anton*
c Numbers — *Thurlby, Paul*
c Numbers at the Park — *Ghigna, Charles*

Numbers & Stories: Using Children's Literature to Teach Young Children Number Sense — *Janes, Rita C.*
Numbers: Their Tales, Types, and Treasures — *Posamentier, Alfred S.*
c Numeralia (Illus. by Isol) — *Lujan, Jorge*
A Numerate Life: A Mathematician Explores the Vagaries of Life, His Own and Probably Yours — *Paulos, John Allen*
Numerical Linear Algebra with Application: Using MATLAB — *Ford, William*
Numero Zero — *Eco, Umberto*
Numero Zero (Illus. by Dixon, Richard) — *Eco, Umberto*
Numero Zero — *Eco, Umberto*
c Numerolandia: El Mundo en Mas de 2,000 Cifras y Datos (Illus. by Pinder, Andrew) — *Martin, Steve (b. 1962-)*
Numismatik Lehren in Europa
The Nuns of Sant'Ambrogio: The True Story of a Convent in Scandal (Read by Boehmer, Paul). Audiobook Review — *Wolf, Hubert*
The Nuns of Sant'Ambrogio: The True Story of a Convent in Scandal — *Wolf, Hubert*
The Nuns of Sant'Ambrogio: The True Story of a Convent Scandal — *Wolf, Hubert*
Nuova Germania, antichi timori: Stati Uniti, Ostpolitik e sicurezza europea — *Bernardini, Giovanni*
The Nurses: A Year of Secrets, Drama, and Miracles with the Heroes of the Hospital — *Bobbins, Alexandra*
The Nurses: A Year with the Heroes behind the Hospital Curtain — *Robbins, Alexandra*
c Nut and Bolt (Illus. by de Cock, Nicole) — *de Cock, Nicole*

c Nut and Bolt — *de Cock, Nicole*
Nut Country: Right-Wing Dallas and the Birth of the Southern Strategy — *Miller, Edward H.*
c The Nutcracker Comes to America: How Three Ballet-Loving Brothers Created a Holiday Tradition (Illus. by Gendron, Cathy) — *Baron, Chris*
c The Nutcracker Comes to America: How Three Ballet-Loving Brothers Created a Holiday Tradition (Illus. by Gendron, Cathy) — *Barton, Chris*
c The Nutcracker's Night Before Christmas (Illus. by Cowman, Joseph) — *Brackett, Keith*
c The Nutcracker's Night Before Christmas (Illus. by Cowman, Joseph) — *Brockett, Keith*
y Nutmeg (Illus. by Crofts, Jackie) — *Wright, James F.*
Nutrition and Disease Management for Veterinary Technicians and Nurses — *Burns, Kara M.*
Nutritional Management of Hospitalized Small Animals — *Chan, Daniel L.*
c The Nuts: Bedtime at the Nut House (Illus. by Magoon, Scott) — *Litwin, Eric*
c Nuts in Space (Illus. by Dolan, Elys) — *Dolan, Elys*
c The Nuts: Sing and Dance in Your Polka-Dot Pants (Illus. by Magoon, Scott) — *Litwin, Eric*
y Nuts to You (Read by Almasy, Jessica). Audiobook Review — *Perkins, Lynne Rae*
c Nuts to You (Illus. by Perkins, Lynne Rae) — *Perkins, Lynne Rae*
Nye: The Political Life of Aneurin Bevan — *Thomas-Symonds, Nicklaus*
Nymph: Motif, Phantom, Affect: A Contribution to the Study of Aby Warburg — *Baert, Barbara*
NYPD Green: A Memoir — *Waters, Luke*
The NYPD's First Fifty Years: Politicians, Police Commissioners and Patrolmen — *Bratton, William J.*

O

O, Africa! — *Conn, Andrew Lewis*
The O. Henry Prize Stories 2015 — *Furman, Laura*
O, Louis: In Search of van Gaal — *Borst, Hugo*
O My America! Six Women and Their Seconds Acts in a New World — *Wheeler, Sara*
O Sing Unto the Lord: A History of English Church Music — *Gant, Andrew*
"O, Write My Name": American Portraits, Harlem Heroes — *Pinckney, Darryl*
An Oakwoods Almanac — *Loose, Gerry*
The Oasis Within — *Morris, Tom*
The Oath — *Clark, C.A.*
y The Oathbreaker's Shadow — *McCulloch, Amy*
Oatrageous Oatmeals — *Hester, Kathy*
The Obama Doctrine: American Grand Strategy Today — *Dueck, Colin*
The Obama Doctrine — *Dueck, Colin*
Obama's Challenge to China — *Wang, Chi*
y Obasan — *Kogawa, Joy*
The Obelisk and the Englishman: The Pioneering Discoveries of Egyptologist William Bankes — *Seyler, Dorothy U.*
Oberiu: An Anthology of Russian Absurdism — *Ostashevsky, Eugene*
Oberlin, Hotbed of Abolitionism: College, Community, and the Fight for Freedom and Equality in Antebellum America — *Morris, J. Brent*
Obeying the Truth: Discretion in the Spiritual Writings of Saint Catherine of Siena — *Ragazzi, Grazia Mangano*
Obeying the Truth: Discretion in the Spiritual Writings of Saint Catherine of Sienna — *Ragazzi, Grazia Mangano*
Object and Apparition: Envisioning the Christian Divine in the Colonial Andes — *Stanfield-Mazzi, Maya*
Object Lessons: The Visualisation of Nineteenth-Century Life Sciences — *Loudon, George*
y Objectif Vancouver — *Wesline, Emmie*
Objective Troy: A Terrorist, a President, and the Rise of the Drone — *Shane, Scott*
Objects and Identities: Roman Britain and the North-Western Provinces — *Eckardt, Hella*
Objects of Culture in the Literature of Imperial Spain — *Bernard, Mary E.*
The Oblate's Confession — *Peak, William*
Oblivion — *Lebedev, Sergei*
y Oblivion — *Creagh, Kelly*
Obscurity and Memory in Late Medieval Latin Manuscript Culture: The Case of the Summarium Biblie — *Dolezalova, Lucie*
Obscurity in Medieval Texts — *Dolezalova, Lucie*
Observers and Navigators: And Other Non-Pilot Aircrew in the RFC, RNAS and RAF — *Jefford, C.G.*
An Observer's Guide to Clouds and Weather: A Northeastern Primer on Prediction — *Carlson, Toby*
Obsession Falls — *Dodd, Christina*
Obsession in Death — *Robb, J.D.*
Obsidian Portal — *Preston B.G.*
Obsidian Reflections: Symbolic Dimensions of Obsidian in Mesoamerica — *Levine, Marc N.*
The Obstinate Murderer — *Holding, Elisabeth Sanxay*
Obvious Power: Getting to Know-How — *Moses, Hary Morgan*
The Occasional Diamond Thief — *McLachlan, Jane Ann*
y The Occasional Diamond Thief — *McLachlan, J.A.*

The Occidental Arts & Ecology Center Cookbook: Fresh-from-the-Garden Recipes for Gatherings Large and Small — *Rathbone, Olivia*
The Occupation Trilogy — *Modiano, Patrick*
Occupied Earth: Stories of Aliens, Resistance, and Survival at All Costs — *Brewer, Richard*
Occupied Economies: An Economic History of Nazi-Occupied Europe, 1939-1945 — *Klemann, Hein*
y Occupy Comics: Art + Stories Inspired by Occupy Wall Street — *Pizzolo, Matt*
The Occupy Movement Explained — *Smaligo, Nicholas*
Occupy Spirituality: A Radical Vision for a New Generation — *Bucko, Adam*
Occupying Power: Sex Workers and Servicemen in Postwar Japan — *Kovner, Sarah*
c Ocean: A Visual Encyclopedia — *Woodward, John*
c Ocean Animals around the World — *Uttridge, Sarah*
Ocean Beach — *Cassese, Frank*
Ocean Country: One Woman's Voyage from Peril to Hope in Her Quest to Save the Seas — *Cunningham, Liz*
The Ocean Is a Wilderness: Atlantic Piracy and the Limits of State Authority, 1688-1856 — *Chet, Guy*
Ocean Solutions, Earth Solutions — *Wright, Dawn*
c Ocean Sunlight: How Tiny Plants Feed the Seas (Illus. by Bang, Molly) — *Chisholm, Penny*
The Ocean, the Bird, and the Scholar: Essays on Poets and Poetry — *Vendler, Helen*
The Ocean, the Bird and the Scholar: Essays on Poets and Poetry — *Vendler, Helen*
The Ocean, the Bird, and the Scholar: Essays on Poets and Poetry — *Vendler, Helen*
c Oceans — *Gray, Leon*
c Oceans in 30 Seconds (Illus. by Robins, Wesley) — *Green, Jen*
c Oceans of the World — *Spilsbury, Louise*
Octavio Paz en su siglo — *Dominguez Michael, Christopher*
c The Octopuppy (Illus. by McKenna, Martin) — *McKenna, Martin*
The Octopus Game — *Beer, Nicky*
Octopus Midnight — *Towne, Jonathan*
y The Octopus Scientists: Exploring the Mind of a Mollusk (Illus. by Ellenbogen, Keith) — *Montgomery, Sy*
c Octopuses — *Hansen, Grace*
c Octopuses! Strange and Wonderful (Illus. by Henderson, Meryl) — *Pringle, Laurence*
Oculto a los Ojos Mortales: Introduction a "El Paraiso Perdido" de John Milton — *Nardo, Anna K.*
Odd Couples: The Great Political Pairings of Modern Britain — *Radice, Giles*
Odd Job Man: Some Confessions of a Slang Lexicographer — *Green, Jonathon*
c The Odd Squad: King Karl — *Fry, Michael*
The Odd Woman and the City: A Memoir — *Gornick, Vivian*
The Odd Woman and the City — *Gornick, Vivian*
y Odditorium — *Grim, Alastair*
c Oddly Normal (Illus. by Frampton, Otis) — *Frampton, Otis*
c Oddrey Joins the Team (Illus. by Whamond, Dave) — *Whamond, Dave*
Odds Against Tomorrow — *Rich, Nathaniel*
y The Odds of Getting Even — *Turnage, Sheila*
c Oddsockosaurus (Illus. by Bolton, Bill) — *Mian, Zanib*
Ode to a Commode: Concrete Poems (Illus. by Rowland, Andy) — *Cleary, Brian P.*
Ode to Didcot Power Station — *Wright, Kit*
y Odette Speex — *Lively, Padgett*

Odin's Child — *Macbain, Bruce*
Odiosa Sanctitas: St Peter Damian, Simony, and Reform — *McCready, William D.*
Odrodzenie i Reformacja w Polsce — *Krigseisen, Wojciech*
Odyssean Identities in Modern Cultures: Journey Home — *Gardner, Hunter H.*
Odysseus Abroad (Read by Wyndham, Alex). Audiobook Review — *Chaudhuri, Amit*
Odysseus Abroad — *Chaudhuri, Amit*
The Odyssey. Audiobook Review — *Fitzgerald, Robert*
Odyssey of an Etruscan Noblewoman — *Burgundy, Rosalind*
Oeuvres completes, vol. 5: Histoire naturelle, generale et particuliere, avec la description du Cabinet du Roi — *Buffon, Georges-Louis Leclerc de*
Oeuvres completes, vol. 7: Histoire naturelle, generale et particuliere, avec la description du Cabinet du Roi — *Buffon, Georges-Louis Leclerc de*
Oeuvres: Ethiques, Politique, Rhetoric, Poetique, Metaphysique — *Bodeus, Richard*
Oeuvres — *Tappy, Jose-Flore*
Of All the Gin Joints: Stumbling through Hollywood History (Illus. by Hemingway, Edward) — *Bailey, Mark*
Of Beards and Men: The Revealing History of Facial Hair — *Oldstone-Moore, Christopher*
y Of Beast and Beauty (Read by Whelan, Julia). Audiobook Review — *Jay, Stacey*
Of Beasts and Beauty: Gender, Race, and Identity in Colombia — *Stanfield, Michael Edward*
y Of Better Blood — *Moger, Susan*
Of Bonds and Bondage — *Baker, Rita*
Of Courage and Determination: The First Special Service Force, "The Devil's Brigade," 1942-44 — *Horn, Bernd*
Of Darkest Valor — *Cifichiello, Tom*
y Of Dreams and Rust — *Fine, Sarah*
Of Elephants and Roses: French Natural History, 1790-1830 — *Prince, Sue Ann*
c Of Enemies and Endings — *Bach, Shelby*
Of Entirety Say the Sentence — *Meister, Ernst*
Of Giants and Other Men — *Peek, Caspar*
Of Irish Blood — *Kelly, Mary Pat*
y Of Metal and Wishes — *Fine, Sarah*
c Of Mice and Magic — *Vernon, Ursula*
y Of Monsters and Madness — *Verday, Jessica*
y Of Neptune — *Banks, Anna*
y Of Orcas and Men: What Killer Whales Can Teach Us — *Neiwert, David*
Of Silk and Steam — *McMaster, Bec*
c Of Sorcery and Snow — *Bach, Shelby*
Of Sorrow and Such — *Slatter, Angela*
Of the Laws of Ecclesiastical Polity: A Critical Edition with Modern Spelling — *Hooker, Richard*
Of the Soil: Photographs of Vernacular Architecture and Stories of Changing Times in Arkansas — *Winningham, Geoff*
Of Things That Used to Be: A Childhood on Fox Street in the Bronx in the Early Twentieth Century — *Lobell, Nathan D.*
Of Walking in Ice — *Herzog, Werner*
Off and Running — *Reed, Philip*
Off Balance, the American Way of Health — *Ali, Leyla*
Off-Screen Cinema: Isidore Isou and the Lettrist Avant-Garde — *Cabanas, Kaira M.*
Off the Books — *Zane, J. Peder*
Off the Clock — *Loren, Roni*
Off the Grid — *Box, C.J.*
y Off the Grid — *Choyce, Lesley*

y Off the Page (Read by Various readers). Audiobook Review — Picoult, Jodi
y Off the Page (Illus. by Gilbert, Yvonne) — Picoult, Jodi
Off the Radar: A Father's Secret, a Mother's Heroism, and a Son's Quest — Copeland, Cyrus M.
Off the Reservation — Merzer, Glen
y Off the Rim — Bates, Sonya Spreen
Off to Far Ithicaa — Fraction, Matt
c Off to the Park! — Cheetham, Stephen
Offcomer (Read by Barber, Nicola). Audiobook Review — Baker, Jo
Offcomer — Baker, Jo
Offene Lizenzen in den Digitalen Geisteswissenschaften
The Offense of Love: Ars Amatoria, Remedia Amoris and Tristia — Ovid
Offentlichkeit - Monument - Text: XIV Congressus Internationalis Epigraphiae Graecae et Latinae. 27.-31. Augusti MMXII - Akten — Eck, Werner
The Offering — el Moncef, Salah
An Officer and a Gentlewoman: The Making of a Female British Army Officer — Goodley, Heloise
c Officer Panda: Fingerprint Detective (Illus. by Crowley, Ashley) — Crowley, Ashley
Officers and Accountability in Medieval England, 1170-1300 — Sabapathy, John
The Officer's Prey — Glencross, Michael
Official Stories: Politics and National Narratives in Egypt and Algeria — Brand, Laurie A.
Offshore — Hollinghurst, Alan
OG Dad: Weird Shit Happens When You Don't Die Young — Stahl, Jerry
Ogallala Road — Bair, Julene
Ogling Ladies: Scopophilia in Medieval German Literature — Summers, Sandra Lindemann
Oh, Baby! True Stories About Conception, Adoption, Surrogacy, Pregnancy, Labor, and Love — Gutkind, Lee
Oh Gussie! Cooking and Visiting in Kimberly's Southern Kitchen — Foose, Martha
Oh Joy! 60 Ways to Create and Give Joy — Cho, Joy
c Oh Me, Oh My! (Illus. by Holt, Richard) — Eggleton, Jill
c Oh My, Oh No! (Illus. by Domergue, Agnes) — Rodarmor, William
c Oh No! A Fox! (Illus. by Stoeke, Janet) — Stoeke, Janet
c Oh No, Gotta Go! (Illus. by Karas, G. Brian) — Elya, Susan Middleton
Oh Say Can You Fudge — Coco, Nancy
c Oh So Brave Dragon (Illus. by Kirk, David) — Kirk, David
c Oh That Snow! (Illus. by Ok, SeoJeong) — Kim, JeongHo
y Oh Yeah, Audrey! — Shaw, Tucker
Oh! You Pretty Things — Mahin, Shanna
O'Hearn — Mulcahy, Greg
O'Henry — Brown, T.G.
Oil: A Cultural and Geographic Encyclopedia of Black Gold — Li, Xiaobing
The Oil Cringe of the West: The Collected Essays and Reviews of J.B. Kelly — Kelly, John B.
Oil Culture — Barrett, Ross
Oil, Democracy, and Development in Africa — Heilbrunn, John R.
Oil, Gas and Pipelines: New Perspectives on the Role of Soviet Energy during the Cold War
The Oil Kings: How the U.S., Iran, and Saudi Arabia Changed the Balance of Power in the Middle East — Cooper, Andrew Scott
c The Ojibwa — Lomberg, Michelle
c The Oklahoma City Thunder — Stewart, Mark
The Oklahoma Gamblin' Man — Tanner, Gary Rex
Oklahoma Tough — Padgett, Ron
c Oklahoma's Devasting May 2013 Tornado — Aronin, Miriam
c Oksa Pollock Series — Plichota, Anne
Old 300: Gone to Texas — Spellman, Paul N.
Old Acquaintance — Stacton, David
Old and New New Englanders: Immigration and Regional Identity in the Gilded Age — Adams, Bluford
The Old Boys: The Decline and Rise of the Public School — Turner, David
Old Dog Haven — De Vries, Ardeth
Old English Literature and the Old Testament — Fox, Michael
The Old English Martyrology: Edition, Translation and Commentary — Rauer, Christine
The Old English Poems of Cynewulf — Bjork, Robert E.
Old English Shorter Poems, vol. 2: Wisdom and Lyric — Bjork, Robert E.
Old Fields: Photography, Glamour, and Fantasy Landscape — Stilgoe, John R.

c The Old Fort at St. Augustine — Sipperley, Keli
Old Islam in Detroit: Rediscovering the Muslim American Past — Howell, Sally
c Old King Cole (Illus. by Trapani, Iza) — Trapani, Iza
Old MacDonald Had a Dragon (Illus. by Santoro, Christopher) — Baker, Ken
c Old MacDonald — Brown, Petra
The Old Man and the Bench — Allemann, Urs
The Old Man and the Cat: A Love Story — Uddenberg, Nils
c The Old Man and The Tree (Illus. by Schlatter, Richard) — Schlatter, Richard
c Old Manhattan Has Some Farms (Illus. by Endle, Kate) — Lendroth, Susan
Old Men Forget — Cooper, Duff
Old People and the Things That Pass — Couperus, Louis
Old Saint Peter's, Rome — McKitterick, Rosamond
Old Sparky: The Electric Chair and the History of the Death Penalty — Galvin, Anthony
The Old Straight Track: Its Mounds, Beacons, Moats, Sites and Mark Stones — Watkins, Alfred
Old Testament Pseudepigrapha: More Noncanonical Scriptures, vol. 1 — Bauckham, Richard
Old Three Toes and Other Tales of Survival and Extinction — Kalter, Susan
Old Three Toes and Other Tales of Survival and Extinction — Mathews, John Joseph
Old Venus — Martin, George R.R.
Old Venus — Dozois, Gardner
Old Venus — Martin, George R.R.
The Old Vic: The Story of a Great Theatre from Kean to Olivier to Spacey — Coleman, Terry
c The Old Ways: Inspired by a True Story (Illus. by Mantha, John) — Chapman, Susan Margaret
c Old Wolf (Read by Heyborne, Kirby). Audiobook Review — Avi
c Old Wolf (Illus. by Floca, Brian) — Avi
The Old Woman and the City: A Memoir — Gornick, Vivian
The Old Woman — Kharms, Daniil
Olde Clerkis Speche: Chaucer's Troilus and Criseyde and the Implications of Authorial Recital — Quinn, William A.
c Oldenglen — Mason, Michael
Oldenglen — Mason, Robin
The Oldest Living Things in the World — Sussman, Rachel
Oldsmobile V-8 Engines: How to Build Max Performance — Trovato, Bill
c Olga the Cloud — Costa, Nicoletta
Oligarchy — Winters, Jeffrey
c Olinguito, de la A a la Z!/Olinguito, from A to Z! — Delacre, Lulu
c Olive and the Embarrassing Gift — Freeman, Tor
Olive Marshmallow — Saunders, Katie
c Oliver and His Egg (Illus. by Schmid, Paul) — Schmid, Paul
c Oliver and Patch (Illus. by Hindley, Kate) — Freedman, Claire
c Oliver and the Seawigs Novel) (Illus. by McIntyre, Sarah) — Reeve, Philip
Olivia Manning: A Woman at War — David, Deirdre
c Ollie and the Science of Treasure Hunting: A 14-Day Mystery — Dionne, Erin
c Ollie's Class Trip: A Yes-and-No Book (Illus. by Carter, Abby) — Calmenson, Stephanie
c Ollie's First Year (Illus. by Van Zyle, Jon) — London, Jonathan
Olympia Provisions: Cured Meats and Tales from an American Charcuterie — Cairo, Elias
The Olympic Games and the Environment — Karamichas, John
Omaha Beach on D-Day — Morvan, Jean-David
Omari and the People — Whitfield, Stephen
y Omega City — Peterfreund, Diana
Omens of Adversity: Tragedy, Time, Memory, Justice — Scott, David (b. 1958-)
y The Omnivore's Dilemma: The Secrets behind What You Eat (Read by Andrews, MacLeod). Audiobook Review — Pollan, Michael
y On a Clear Day — Myers, Walter Dean
On a Desert Shore — Rizzolo, S.K.
On a Great Battlefield: The Making, Management, and Memory of Gettysburg National Military Park, 1933-2013 — Murray, Jennifer M.
c On a Slippery Slope — Fitzpatrick, Melody
On a Wing and a Prayer: One Woman's Adventure into the Heart of the Rainforest — Woods, Sarah
On Becoming God: Late Medieval Mysticism and the Modern Western Self — Morgan, Ben
On Behalf of the Family Farm: Iowa Farm Women's Activism since 1945 — Devine, Jenny Barker
On Being an Artist — Craig-Martin, Michael
On Being Here to Stay: Treaties and Aboriginal Rights in Canada — Asch, Michael

On Being Ill — Woolf, Virginia
On Being Rich and Poor: Christianity in a Time of Economic Globalization — Ellul, Jacques
On Bittersweet Place (Read by Lockford, Lesa). Audiobook Review — Wineberg, Ronna
On Cats — Bukowski, Charles
On Cimarron — Lederer, Paul Joseph
On Democracy's Doorstep: The Inside Story of How the Supreme Court Brought "One Person, One Vote" to the United States — Smith, J. Douglas
On Difficulties in the Church Fathers: The Ambigua, vols. 1-2 — Maximos the Confessor
y On Edge — Price, Gin
On Elizabeth Bishop — Toibin, Colm
On Emotions: Philosophical Essays — Deigh, John
On Flinching: Theatricality and Scientific Looking from Darwin to Shell Shock — Smith, Tiffany Watt
On Freedom, Love and Power — Ellul, Jacques
On Further Reflection: 60 Years of Writing — Miller, Jonathan
On Garden Style — Williams, Bunny
On Highway 61 — Mcnally, Dennis
On Hinduism — Doniger, Wendy
On His Own Terms: A Life of Nelson Rockefeller (Read by Michael, Paul). Audiobook Review — Smith, Richard Norton
On His Own Terms: A Life of Nelson Rockefeller — Smith, Richard Norton
On Historical Distance — Phillips, Mark Salber
On History's Trail: Speeches and Essays by the Texas State Historian, 2009-2012 — Townsend, Light
On Immunity: An Inoculation (Read by Marston, Tamara). Audiobook Review — Biss, Eula
On Immunity: An Inoculation — Biss, Eula
On Immunity: An Inoculation — Bliss, Eula
c On Impact! (Illus. by Pamintuan, Macky) — Ball, Nate
On Inequality — Frankfurt, Harry G.
On Intellectual Activism — Collins, Patricia Hill
On Leave (Illus. by Bellos, David) — Anselme, Daniel
On Limited Nuclear War in the 21st Century — Larsen, Jeffrey A.
On Living in an Old Country — Wright, Patrick
On Making Sense: Queer Race Narratives of Intelligibility — Martinez, Ernesto Javier
On Malice — Babstock, Ken
On Married Love: Eridanus — Pontano, Giovanni Gioviano
On Morals — Auvergne, William
On My Ass — Dean, Lou
c On My Beach (Illus. by Siminovich, Lorena) — Gillingham, Sara
On My Own — Rehm, Diane
"On My Way": The Untold Story of Rouben Mamoulian, George Gershwin, and Porgy and Bess — Horowitz, Joseph
c On My Way to School (Illus. by Paraskevas, Michael) — Maizes, Sarah
On n'a pas fini de rire: quelques mots a ma nouvelle famille — Schneidermann, Daniel
On Old Age: Approaching Death in Antiquity and the Middle Ages — Krotzl, Christian
On Point II: Transition to the New Campaign; The United States Army in Operation IRAQI FREEDOM, May 2003-January — Wright, Donald P.
c On Pointe — Berk, Sheryl
On Purpose: How We Create the Meaning of Life — Froese, Paul
On Romantic Love: Simple Truths about a Complex Emotion — Brogaard, Berit
On Shifting Sand — Pittman, Allison
On Stalin's Team: The Years of Living Dangerously in Soviet Politics — Fitzpatrick, Sheila
On Such a Full Sea — Lee, Chang-Rae
On the Arab Revolts and the Iranian Revolution: Power and Resistance Today — Adib-Moghaddam, Arshin
c On the Ball (Illus. by Pinkney, Brian) — Pinkney, Brian
On the Brink: A Trio of Genres — Fitzell, Philip
On the Clock: The Story of the NFL Draft — Wilner, Barry
On the Commodity Trail: The Journey of a Bargain Store Product from East to West — Hulme, Alison
c On the Construction Site (Illus. by Johnson, Bee) — Brown, Carron
On the Cusp: The Yale College Class of 1960 and a World on the Verge of Change — Horowitz, Daniel
On the Doctrine of Election with Special Reference to the 'Aphorisms' of Dr. Bretschneider — Schleiermacher, Friedrich
On the Edge — Chirbes, Rafael
y On the Edge — van Diepen, Allison
c On the Edge of Destiny — Leiner, Jorge

On the Edge: The State and Fate of the World's Tropical Rainforests — Martin, Claude
c On the Farm, At the Market (Illus. by Karas, G. Brian) — Karas, G. Brian
c On the Farm (Illus. by Dogi, Fiammetta) — Riggs, Kate
c On the Farm (Illus. by Kubinyi, Laszlo) — Riggs, Kate
On the Frontier of Science: An American Rhetoric of Exploration and Exploitation — Ceccarelli, Leah
c On the Go — Carpenter, Tad
On the Hunt — Ivy, Alexandra
On the Importance of Being an Individual in Renaissance Italy: Men, Their Professions, and Their Beards — Biow, Douglas
On the Margins of a Minority: Leprosy, Madness, and Disability among the Jews of Medieval Europe — Shoham-Steiner, Ephraim
On the Margins of a Minority: Leprosy, Madness, and Disability among the Jews of Medieval Europe — Watzman, Haim
On the Move: A Life. Audiobook Review — Sacks, Oliver
On the Move: A Life (Read by Woren, Dan). Audiobook Review — Sacks, Oliver
On the Move: A Life — Sacks, Oliver
On the Move for Love: Migrant Entertainers and the U.S. Military in South Korea — Cheng, Sealing
c On the Move (Illus. by Sanders, Allan) — Martin, Ruth
On the Muslim Question — Norton, Anne
On the Organic Law of Change — Costa, James T.
On the Origin of Autonomy — Rosslenbroich, Bernd
On the Origin of Superheroes — Gavaler, Chris
y On the Other Side of the Bridge — Villareal, Ray
On the Rim of the Caribbean: Colonial Georgia and the British Atlantic World — Pressly, Paul M.
y On the Run — Bancks, Tristan
On the Run: Fugitive Life in an American City — Goffman, Alice
On the Run with Mary — Barrow, Jonathan
c On the Sapphire's Trail — Ferrier, Katherine
c On the Shoulder of a Giant (Illus. by Nelson, James) — Christopher, Neil
On the Side of the Poor: The Theology of Liberation — Gutierrez, Gustavo
On the State — Bourdieu, Pierre
On The Street of Divine Love: New and Selected Poems — Hamby, Barbara
On the Town — Bernstein, Leonard
On the Trail of Taro: An Exploration of Natural and Cultural History — Matthews, Peter J.
On the Universal: The Uniform, the Common, and Dialogue Between Cultures — Jullien, Francois
On the Wild West — Twain, Mark
On the Wilder Shores of Love: A Bohemian Life — Blanch, Lesley
c On the Wing (Illus. by Stadtlander, Becca) — Elliott, David
On Their Own Behalf: Ewald Ammende, Europe's National Minorities and the Campaign for Cultural Autonomy, 1920-1936 — Housden, Martyn
On Time: Poems 2005-2014 — Kyger, Joanner
On Time: Technology and Temporality in Modern Egypt — Barak, On
y On Track for Treasure — McClure, Wendy
c On Track — Apel, Kathryn
On Two Feet and Wings (Read by Kazerooni, Abbas). Audiobook Review — Kazerooni, Abbas
On What, There Is for Things to Be — Kramer, Stephan
On Writing — Bukowski, Charles
On Your Case: A Comprehensive, Compassionate (and Only Slightly Bossy) Legal Guide for Every Stage of a Woman's Life — Green, Lisa
y On Your Knees — Moore, Stephanie Perry
Once a Crooked Man — McCallum, David
Once a Fighter Pilot: The Story of Korean War Ace Lt. Gen. Charles G. "Chick" Cleveland — Trest, Warren A.
c Once a Shepherd (Illus. by Lesnie, Phil) — Millard, Glenda
Once and Always — Harper, Julia
The Once and Future King: The Rise of Crown Government in America — Buckley, Frank
The Once and Future World: Nature As It Was, As It Is, As It Could Be — MacKinnon, J.B.
Once Burned — Boyle, Gerry
Once in a Blue Year — Durkota, Michael D.
Once in a Great City: A Detroit Story (Read by Maraniss, David). Audiobook Review — Maraniss, David
Once in a Great City: A Detroit Story — Maraniss, David
Once in the West — Wiman, Christian
Once More into the Breech — Brandvold, Peter

Once Pure — Robson, Cecy
Once Shadows Fall — Daniels, Robert
c Once upon a Cloud (Illus. by Keane, Claire) — Keane, Claire
Once upon a Crime — Brackston, Paula
y Once upon a Kiss — Palmer, Robin
c Once Upon a Line (Illus. by Edwards, Wallace) — Edwards, Wallace
c Once Upon a Line — Edwards, Wallace
c Once upon a Mastodon: All about Prehistoric Mammals (Illus. by Ruiz, Aristides) — Worth, Bonnie
c Once upon a Rainy Day (Illus. by Manceau, Edouard) — Manceau, Edouard
Once upon a Revolution: An Egyptian Story — Cambanis, Thanassis
Once upon a Time: A Short History of Fairy Tale — Warner, Marina
c Once upon a Time in Japan — Pulvers, Roger
Once upon a Time in Russia: The Rise of the Oligarchs: A True Story of Ambition, Wealth, Betrayal, and Murder (Read by Bobb, Jeremy). Audiobook Review — Mezrich, Ben
Once upon a Time in Russia: The Rise of the Oligarchs: A True Story of Ambition, Wealth, Betrayal, and Murder — Mezrich, Ben
c Once upon a Timeless Tale Collection (Read by Margolyes, Miriam). Audiobook Review — Lamond, Margrete
Once upon a Yugoslavia: When the American Way Met Tito's Third Way — Green, Surya
y Once Upon a Zombie, bk, 1: The Color of Fear — Phillips, Billy
c Once upon an Alphabet: Short Stories for All the Letters (Illus. by Jeffers, Oliver) — Jeffers, Oliver
One: A Cook and Her Cupboard — Knight, Florence
y One — Crossan, Sarah
c The One and Only Ivan (Read by Crupper, Adam). Audiobook Review — Applegate, Katherine
c One Bear Extraordinaire (Illus. by McGowan, Jayme) — McGowan, Jayme
c One Big Family (Illus. by Palacios, Sara) — Harshman, Marc
c One Big Pair of Underwear (Illus. by Lichtenheld, Tom) — Gehl, Laura
One Boy Missing — Orr, Stephen
One Breath: Freediving, Death, and the Quest to Shatter Human Limits — Skolnick, Adam
The One by Whom Scandal Comes — Girard, Rene
One Child — Fong, Mei
One Cool Friend (Read by Dean, Robertson). Audiobook Review — Buzzeo, Toni
y One — Crossan, Sarah
c One Day on Our Blue Planetain the Savannah (Illus. by Bailey, Ella) — Bailey, Ella
c One Day, the End: Short, Very Short, Shorter-than-Ever Stories (Illus. by Koehler, Fred) — Dotlich, Rebecca Kai
y One Death, Nine Stories — Aronson, Marc
c One Direction: Popular Boy Band — Diver, Lucas
One Dough, Ten Breads: Making Great Bread by Hand — Black, Sarah
The One-Eyed Man — Modesitt, L.E., Jr.
c One Family (Illus. by Gomez, Blanca) — Shannon, George
One Family under God: Immigration Politics and Progressive Religion in America — Yukich, Grace
One Fish, Two Fish, Red Fish, Blue Fish (Illus. by Dr. Seuss) — Dr. Seuss
One Foot in the Palace: The Habsburg Court of Brussels and the Politics of Access in the Reign of Albert and Isabella, 1598-1621 — Raeymaekers, Dries
One for the Murphys (Read by Hunter, Nora). Audiobook Review — Hunt, Lynda Mullaly
y One Girl, One Dream — Dekker, Laura
c One Good Deed (Illus. by Melmon, Deborah) — Fields, Terri
One Good Life: My Tips, My Wisdom, My Story — Nystul, Jill
c One Hundred Bones — Zommer, Yuval
One Hundred Books Famous in Children's Literature — Loker, Chris
One Hundred Days of Rain — Brooks, Carellin
One Hundred Miles from Manhattan — Orcutt, Chris
One Hundred Years of Servitude: Political Economy of Tea Plantations in Colonial Assam — Behal, Rana Partap
c One Hungry Heron (Illus. by Patkau, Karen) — Beck, Carolyn
One Is a Feast for Mouse: A Thanksgiving Tale (Read by Heyborne, Kirby). Audiobook Review — Cox, Judy
One Islam, Many Muslim Worlds: Spirituality, Identity, and Resistance across Islamic Lands — Baker, Raymond William

One Kick (Read by Lind, Heather). Audiobook Review — Cain, Chelsea
One Kick — Cain, Chelsea
One Killer Force — Fury, Dalton
One Kiss More — Baxter, Mandy
One Less, One More — Vorhaus, Robbie
One Man against the World: The Tragedy of Richard Nixon — Weiner, Tim
y One Man Guy — Barakiva, Michael
One Man's Flag — Downing, David
One Marriage under God: The Campaign to Promote Marriage in America — Heath, Melanie
One Mile Under — Gross, Andrew
One Million Steps: A Marine Platoon at War — West, Bing
One Minute to Ten: Cameron, Miliband and Clegg: Three Men, One Ambition and the Price of Power — Hodges, Dan
One Mississippi, Two Mississippi — George, Carol V.R.
y One Moment in Time — Barnholdt, Lauren
One More Step: My Story of Living with Cerebral Palsy, Climbing Kilimanjaro, and Surviving the Hardest Race on Earth — Paddock, Bonner
One More Thing: Stories and Other Stories — Novak, B. J.
One Morning — Wolff, Rebecca
One Nation under God: How Corporate America Invented Christian America — Kruse, Kevin M.
One Nation, Under Gods: A New American History — Manseau, Peter
One Nation: What We Can All Do to Save America's Future — Carson, Ben
One Nation: What We Can All Do to Save America's Future — Carson, Candy
One Night, Markovitch — Gundar-Goshen, Ayelet
One Night — Dickey, Eric Jerome
y One — Crossan, Sarah
One of the Guys — Aldin, Lisa
One of These Nights — Castle, Kendra Leigh
One of Us — O'Dell, Tawni
y One of Us — Waudby, Jeannie
One of Us: The Story of Anders Breivik and the Massacre in Norway — Seierstad, Asne
One of Us: The Story of Anders Breivik and the Massacre in Norway — Seirstad, Asne
y One of Us — Waudby, Jeannie
One Out of Three: Immigrant New York in the Twenty-First Century — Foner, Nancy
One Out of Two — Sada, Daniel
The One-Page Financial Plan: A Simple Way to Be Smart about Your Money — Richards, Carl
y One Past Midnight — Shirvington, Jessica
One Place: Paul Kwilecki and Four Decades of Photographs — Rankin, Tom
One Place: Paul Kwilecki and Four Decades of Photographs from Decatur County, Georgia (Illus. by Kwilecki, Paul) — Kwilecki, Paul
c One Plastic Bag: Isatou Ceesay and the Recycling Women of the Gambia (Illus. by Zunon, Elizabeth) — Paul, Miranda
c One Plastic Bag: Isatou Ceesay and the Recycling Women of the Gambia (Illus. by Zunon, Elizabeth) — Paui, Miranda
c One Plastic Bag: Isatou Ceesay and the Recycling Women of the Gambia (Illus. by Zunon, Elizabeth) — Paul, Miranda
y One-Punch Man (Illus. by Murata, Yusuke) — One
One Rainy Day in May — Danielewski, Mark Z.
c One Red Shoe (Illus. by Krejtschi, Tobias) — Gruss, Karin
One Righteous Man: Samuel Battle and the Shattering of the Color Line in New York — Browne, Arthur
The One-Sex Body on Trial: The Classical and Early Modern Evidence — King, Helen
One-Skein Wonders for Babies: 101 Knitting Projects for Infants and Toddlers — Durant, Judith
c One Snowy Rescue (Illus. by Macnaughton, Tina) — Butler, M. Christina
c One Step at a Time (Illus. by Heinrich, Sally) — Jolly, Jane
One Step Too Far — Seskis, Tina
One Teacher in Ten in the New Millennium: LGBT Educators Speak Out About What's Gotten Bette ...and What Hasn't — Jennings, Kevin
One Teacher in Ten in the New Millennium: LGBT Educators Speak Out About What's Gotten Better...and What Hasn't — Jennings, Kevin
The One That Got Away — Chase, Bethany
y The One Thing — Curtis, Marci Lyn
y One Thing Stolen — Kephart, Beth
c One Thousand Things (Illus. by Kovecses, Anna) — Kovecses, Anna
One Thousand Things Worth Knowing — Muldoon, Paul

One to the Wolves: On the Trail of a Killer — Duncan, Lois
c One Today (Illus. by Pilkey, Dav) — Blanco, Richard
One Touch More — Baxter, Mandy
y One True Thing — Hayes, Nicole
c One Two, Baa Moo: A Pop-Up Book of Counting (Illus. by Verrall, Lisa) — Litton, Jonathan
One Under — Harrod-Eagles, Cynthia
One Way or Another — Adler, Elizabeth
One Wild Bird at a Time — Heinrich, Bernd
One Wish — Carr, Robyn
c One Witch at a Time — DeKeyser, Stacy
c One Witch At a Time (Illus. by Chaghatzbanian, Sonia) — DeKeyser, Stacy
c One Word from Sophia (Illus. by Ismail, Yasmeen) — Averbeck, Jim
One Year After — Forstchen, William R.
One Year in America — Belliveau, Elisabeth
The Ongoing Burden of Southern History: Politics and Identity in the Twenty-First-Century South — Maxwell, Angie
y The Ongoing Columbian Exchange: Stories of Biological and Economic Transfer in World History — Cumo, Christopher
Ongoingness: The End of a Diary — Manguso, Sarah
O'Nights — Parks, Cecily
The Onlife Manifesto: Being Human in a Hyperconnected Era — Floridi, Luciano
y Online Privacy — Wilcox, Christine
Online Safety for Children and Teens on the Autism Spectrum — Lonie, Nicola
Only a Kiss — Balogh, Mary
Only a Promise — Baiogh, Mary
Only a Promise — Balogh, Mary
c The Only Child (Illus. by Guojing) — Guojing
Only Enchanting (Read by Landor, Rosalyn). Audiobook Review — Balogh, Mary
y Only Ever Yours — O'Neill, Louise
c The Only Game (Read by Nobbs, Keith). Audiobook Review — Lupica, Mike
The Only Game in Town: Central Banks, Instability, and Avoiding the Next Collapse — El-Erian, Mohamed A.
c The Only Game — Lupica, Mike
c The Only Girl in School — Standiford, Natalie
Only in Blood — Down, Therese
The Only Little Prayer You Need: The Shortest Route to a Life of Joy, Abundance, and Peace of Mind — Engle, Debra Landwehr
y Only Love Can Break Your Heart — Tarkington, Ed
Only One Thing Can Save Us: Why America Needs a New Kind of Labor Movement — Geoghegan, Thomas
Only One Thing Can Save Us: Why America Needs a New Kind of Labor Movement — Geoghegan,Thomas
Only One Thing Can Save Us: Why Our Country Needs a New Kind of Labor Movement — Geoghegan, Thomas
The Only Ones — Dibbell, Carola
The Only Street in Paris: Life on the Rue des Martyrs — Sciolino, Elaine
Only the Animals — Dovey, Ceridwen
Only the Longest Threads — Husain, Tasneem Zehra
Only the Strong — Asim, Jabari
y The Only Thing to Fear — Richmond, Caroline Tung
c The Only Thing Worse Than Witches — Magaziner, Lauren
Only Trees Need Roots — Jessen, John
The Only Woman in the Room: Why Science is Still a Boys' Club — Beacon, Eileen Pollack
y The Only Woman in the Room: Why Science Is Still a Boys' Club — Pollack, Eileen
The Only Words That Are Worth Remembering — Rotter, Jeffrey
Only Wounded: Stories of the Irish Troubles — Taylor, Patrick
Ontario Beer: A Heady History of Brewing from the Great Lakes to Hudson Bay — McLeod, Alan
Ontario Boys: Masculinity and the Idea of Boyhood in Postwar Ontario, 1945-1960 — Greig, Christopher J.
Ontology Made Easy — Thomasson, Amie L.
Ontopower: War, Powers, and the State of Perception — Massumi, Brian
c Oona Finds an Egg (Illus. by Wu, Mike) — Griffin, Adele
c Oops, Pounce, Quick, Run! (Illus. by Twohy, Mike) — Twohy, Mike
Op klompen troch de dessa — Speerstra, Hylke
y The Opal Crown — Lundquist, Jenny
c Opal Plumstead — Wilson, Jacqueline
Open Access and the Humanities: Contexts, Controversies and the Future — Eve, Martin Paul
Open Borders to a Revolution: Culture, Politics, and Migration — Arredondo, Jaime Marroquin

Open Education: A Study in Disruption — van Mourik, Pauline
The Open Fields of England — Hall, David
Open Grave — Eriksson, Kjell
Open Letter — Charbonnier, Stephane
Open Letters: Russian Popular Culture and the Picture Postcard, 1880-1922 — Rowley, Alison
The Open Mind: Cold War Politics and the Sciences of Human Nature — Cohen-Cole, Jamie
The Open Mind: Cold War Politics and the Sciences of Human Nature — Cohen-Cole, Jamie Nace
Open Skies: Transparency, Confidence-Building, and the End of the Cold War — Jones, Peter
Open Source Architecture — Ratti, Carlo
Open Standards and the Digital Age: History, Ideology, and Networks — Russell, Andrew L.
Open the Cage, Murphy — O'Grady, Paul
Open to Disruption: Time and Craft in the Practice of Slow Sociology — Garey, Anita Ilta
The Open University: A History — Weinbren, Daniel
c Open Wide! (Illus. by Burks, James) — Krensky, Stephen
Open Your Heart: Religion and Cultural Poetics of Greater Mexico — Sandell, David P.
The Opened Letter: Networking in the Early Modern British World — O'Neill, Lindsay
Opening a Window to the West: The Foreign Concession at Kobe, Japan, 1868-1899 — Ennals, Peter
Opening Belle — Sherry, Maureen
The Opening Statement of Dr. Radovan Karadzic Before the International Criminal Tribunal for the Former Yugoslavia in The Hague March 1-2, 2010 — Karadzic, Radovan
Opening the Field of Practical Theology: An Introduction — Cahalan, Kathleen A.
Opening to Meditation: A Gentle, Guided Approach — Lang, Diana
Openness Unhindered: Further Thoughts of an Unlikely Convert on Sexual Identity and Union with Christ — Butterfield, Rosaria
Openwork: Poetry and Prose — du Bouchet, Andre
Openwork: Poetry and Prose — Du Bouchet, Andre
Opera and the City: The Politics of Culture in Beijing, 1770-1900 — Goldman, Andrea S.
Opera at the Bandstand: Then and Now — Martin, George W.
Opera in the Age of Rousseau: Music, Confrontation, Realism — Charlton, David
Opera Omnia VI.4 — Brown, Andrew J.
The Opera Singer — Costain, Keith M.
The Operas of Giuseppe Verdi — Basevi, Abramo
Operation Greylord: The True Story of an Untrained Undercover Agent and America's Biggest Corruption Bust — Hake, Terrence
c Operation Josh Taylor — Fitzpatrick, Melody
Operation KE: The Cactus Air Force and the Japanese Withdrawal from Guadalcanal — Letourneau, Roger
Operation Long Jump — Yenne, Bill
Operation Nemesis: The Assassination Plot That Avenged the Armenian Genocide — Bogosian, Eric
Operation Nemesis: The Assassination Plot to Avenge the Armenian Genocide — Bogosian, Eric
Operation Paperclip — Jacobsen, Annie
c Operation Pucker Up — Alpine, Rachele
Operation Thunderbolt: Flight 139 and the Raid on Entebbe Airport — David, Saul
Operation Thunderclap and the Black March: Two World War II Stories from the Unstoppable 91st Bomb Group — Allison, Richard
Operation Typhoon: Hitler's March on Moscow, October 1941 — Stahel, David
c Ophelia and the Marvelous Boy (Read by Entwistle, Jayne). Audiobook Review — Foxlee, Karen
y Ophelia: Queen of Denmark — French, Jackie
Opium and Empire: The Lives and Careers of William Jardine and James Matheson — Grace, Richard J.
The Opium War: Drugs, Dreams and the Making of China — Lovell, Julia
The Opposite House — Emerson, Claudia
The Opposite of Everyone — Jackson, Joshilyn
The Opposite of Spoiled: Raising Kids Who Are Grounded, Generous, and Smart about Money — Lieber, Ron
The Opposite of Spoiled: Raising Kids Who Are Grounded, Generous and Smart About Money — Lieber, Ron
Oppressed in the Land? Fatwas on Muslims Living under Non-Muslim Rule from the Middle Ages to the Present — Verskin, Alan
Oprah: The Gospel of an Icon — Loofton, Kathryn
The Optical Lasso — Corwin, Marc

Optics and the Rise of Perspective: A Study in Network Knowledge Diffusion — Raynaud, Dominique
Optimal Aging — Winter, Jerrold
The Optimistic Environmentalist: Progressing Towards a Greener Future — Boyd, David R.
The Optimistic Workplace: Creating an Environment that Energizes Everyone — Murphy, Shawn
Opting for Elsewhere: Lifestyle Migration in the American Middle Class — Hoey, Brian A.
Opting Out: Losing the Potential of America's Young Black Elite — Beasley, Maya A.
y The Option — Brown, Herman
The Oracle — Nika, D.J.
Oracle — Marvin, Cate
Oral History, Community, and Displacement: Imagining Memories in Post-Apartheid South Africa — Field, Sean
Oral History, Community, and Work in the American West — Embry, Jessie
Oral History, Community, and Work in the American West — Embry, Jessie L.
c Orange Animals — Borth, Teddy
c Orangutan: A Day in the Rainforest Canopy — Goldner, Rita
c Orangutan Houdini (Illus. by Kelleher, Kathie) — Neme, Laurel
c Orangutanka: A Story in Poems (Illus. by Kurilla, Renee) — Engle, Margarita
c Orangutanka (Illus. by Kurilla, Renee) — Engle, Margarita
The Orbit Magazine Anthology: Re-Entry — St. Mary, Robert
The Orbital Perspective: Lessons in Seeing the big Picture from a Journey of 71 Million Miles — Garan, Ron
y Orbiting Jupiter — Schmidt, Gary D.
Orbiting Ray Bradbury's Mars: Biographical, Anthropological, Literary, Scientific and Other Perspectives — McMillan, Gloria
The Orchard at the Edge of Town — McCoy, Shirlee
Orchard Grove — Zandri, Vincent
Orchard House: How a Neglected Garden Taught One Family to Grow — Weaver, Tara Austen
The Orchard of Lost Souls — Mohamed, Nadifa
c The Orchestra Pit — Wright, Johanna
Orchestral Conducting in the Nineteenth Century — Illiano, Roberto
Orchestrierte Vertreibung: Unerwunschte Wiener Philharmoniker. Verfolgung, Ermordung und Exil — Mayrhofer, Bernadette
The Orchid Boat — Harwood, Lee
The Ordeal of the Reunion: A New History of Reconstruction — Summers, Mark Wahlgren
The Order of Things: An Archaeology of the Human Sciences — Foucault, Michel
Order within Anarchy: The Laws of War as an International Institution — Morrow, James D.
Ordering Independence: The End of Empire in the Anglophone Caribbean, 1947-69 — Mawby, Spencer
Orderly and Humane: The Expulsion of the Germans after the Second World War — Douglas, R.M.
Ordinaries — Pershing, Douglas
Ordinary Ethics in China — Stafford, Charles
Ordinary Evil — Ferraro, Gene
Ordinary Light — Smith, Tracy K.
Ordinary Lives and Grand Schemes: An Anthropology of Everyday Religion — Schielke, Samuli
Ordinary Lives in the Early Caribbean: Religion, Colonial Competition, and the Politics of Profit — Block, Kristen
An Ordinary Magic — Thibeault, Jason
An Ordinary Marriage: The World of a Gentry Family in Provincial Russia — Antonova, Katherine Pickering
Ordinary Medicine: Extraordinary Treatments, Longer Lives, and Where to Draw the Line — Kaufman, Sharon R.
Ordinary Oblivion and the Self Unmoored: Reading Plato's Phaedrus and Writing the Soul — Rapp, J.R.
Ordinary Oblivion and the Self Unmoored: Reading Plato's "Phaedrus" and Writing the Soul — Rapp, Jennifer R.
The Ordinary Spaceman: From Boyhood Dreams to Astronaut — Anderson, Clayton C.
Ordination of Women to the Diaconate in the Eastern Churches: Essays by Cipriano Vagaggini — Zagano, Phyllis
"Ordo inversus": Formen und Funktionen einer Denkfigur um 1800. Jahrestagung des Zentrums fur Klassikforschung
The Ore Knob Mine Murders: The Crimes, the Investigation and the Trials — Haynes, Rose M.

The Oregon Trail: An American Journey (Read by Buck, Rinker). Audiobook Review — *Buck, Rinker*
The Oregon Trail: An American Journey — *Buck, Rinker*
The Orenda — *Boyden, Joseph*
Oreo — *Ross, Fran*
The Oresteia — *Wright, Angus*
The Organ: An Encyclopaedia — *Kassel, Douglas*
The Organ Broker — *Strumwasser, Stu*
The Organ Takers: A Novel of Surgical Suspense — *Anderson, Richard Van*
The Organic Artist: Make Your Own Paint, Paper, Pigments, Prints, and More from Nature — *Neddo, Nick*
Organic Chemical Toxicology of Fishes — *Tierney, Keith B.*
The Organic Medicinal Herb Farmer: The Ultimate Guide to Producing High-Quality Herbs on a Market Scale — *Carpenter, Jeff*
The Organised Mind: Thinking Straight in the Age of Information Overload — *Levitin, Daniel*
Organizational Change through Individual Empowerment: Applying Social Psychology in Prisons and Policing — *Toch, Hans*
Organizational Climate and Culture: An Introduction to Theory, Research, and Practice — *Ehrhart, Mark G.*
Organizational Myopia: Problems of Rationality and Foresight in Organizations — *Catino, Maurizio*
Organs of Greed — *Fowler, A.A.*
Orhan's Inheritance (Read by Cohen, Assaf). Audiobook Review — *Ohanesian, Aline*
Orhan's Inheritance — *Ohanesian, Aline*
The Orient in Spain: Converted Muslims, the Forged Lead Books of Granada, and the Rise of Orientalism — *Garcia-Arenal, Mercedes*
The Orient in Spain. Converted Muslims, the Forged Lead Books of Granada, and the Rise of Orientalism — *Mediano, Fernando Rodriguez*
Orient — *Bollen, Christopher*
Origami Aircraft — *Packard, Mary*
Origami Bugs — *Ard, Catherine*
The Origami Home: More Than 30 Projects to Craft, Fold, and Create — *Bolitho, Mark*
c Origami Palooza: Dragons, Turtles, Birds, and More! — *Harbo, Christopher*
c Origami Papertainment: Samurai, Owls, Ninja Stars, and More! — *Harbo, Christopher*
Origami Toy Monsters: Easy-to-Assemble Paper Toys That Shudder, Shake, Lurch and Amaze — *Dwar, Andrew*
The Origin of AIDS — *Pepin, Jacques*
The Origin of Heresy: A History of Discourse in Second Temple Judaism and Early Christianity — *Royalty, Robert M., Jr.*
The Origin of Ideas: Blending, Creativity, and the Human Spark — *Turner, Mark*
Original Bavarian Folktales: A Schonwerth Selection — *Schonwerth, Franz Xaver von*
c The Original Cowgirl: The Wild Adventures of Lucille Mulhall (Illus. by Beaky, Suzanne) — *Lang, Heather*
The Original Folk and Fairy Tales of the Brothers Grimm: The Complete First Edition — *Dezso, Andrea*
The Original Folk and Fairy Tales of the Brothers Grimm: The Complete First Edition (Illus. by Dezso, Andrea) — *Zipes, Jack*
The Original Folk and Fairy Tales of the Brothers Grimm: The Complete First Edition (Illus. by Grimm, Jacob) — *Zipes, Jack*
The Original Jesus: Trading the Myths We Create for the Savior Who Is — *Darling, Daniel*
Original Man: The Tautz Compendium of Less Ordinary Gentlemen — *Grant, Patrick*
c Original Recipe (Illus. by Scheret, Jessica) — *Young, Jessica*
Original Rockers — *King, Richard*
Original Spin: Downing Street and the Press in Victorian Britain — *Brighton, Paul*
Originals: How Non-Conformists Move the World — *Grant, Adam*
Origins — *Smiles, Terri-Lynne*
The Origins, History, and Future of the Federal Reserve: A Return to Jekyll Island — *Roberds, William*
The Origins of American Religious Nationalism — *Haselby, Sam*
The Origins of Christian Democracy: Politics and Confession in Modern Germany — *Mitchell, Maria D.*
Origins of Classical Architecture: Architecture Temples, Orders and Gifts to the Gods in Ancient Greece — *Wilson Jones, Mark*
The Origins of Grammar: Language in the Light of Evolution — *Hurford, James*

Origins of Mathematical Words: A Comprehensive Dictionary of Latin, Greek, and Arabic Roots — *Lo Bello, Anthony*
The Origins of Modern Historiography in India: Antiquarianism and Philology, 1780-1880 — *Mantena, Rama Sundari*
The Origins of Museums: The Cabinet of Curiosities in Sixteenth- and Seventeenth-Century Europe — *Impey, Oliver*
c Origins of Olympus — *O'Hearn, Kate*
The Origins of Palestinian Art — *Makhoul, Bashir*
The Origins of Southern Evangelicalism: Religious Revivalism in the South Carolina Lowcountry, 1670-1760 — *Little, Thomas J.*
The Origins of the First World War: Diplomatic and Military Documents — *Mombauer, Annika*
Origins: The Scientific Story of Creation — *Baggott, Jim*
c Orion and the Dark (Illus. by Yarlett, Emma) — *Yarlett, Emma*
The Orion Plan — *Alpert, Mark*
Ormonde — *Lowe, Hannah*
Ornaments of Death — *Cleland, Jane K.*
Ornithological Photographs — *Forsgren, Todd*
Orosius and the Rhetoric of History — *Van Nuffelen, Peter*
c The Orphan and the Mouse (Illus. by McPhail, David) — *Freeman, Martha*
c The Orphan Army — *Maberry, Jonathan*
y Orphan Blade (Illus. by Myler, Jake) — *Almand, M. Nicholas*
Orphan in America — *Avery, Nanette L.*
The Orphan in Eighteenth-Century Fiction: The Vicissitudes of the Eighteenth-Century Subject — *Konig, Eva*
The Orphan of the Rhine — *Sleath, Eleanor*
The Orphan of Torundi — *McCreedy, J.L.*
y The Orphan Queen — *Meadows, Jodi*
The Orphan Scandal: Christian Missionaries and the Rise of the Muslim Brotherhood — *Baron, Beth*
Orphan X — *Hurwitz, Gregg*
Orphans, Assassins and the Existential Eggplant — *Gillett, J.T.*
Orphans — *Steyn, Jan*
The Orpheus Clock: The Search for My Family's Art Treasures Stolen by the Nazis — *Goodman, Simon*
Orpheus in der Spatantike. Studien und Kommentar zuden Argonautika des Orpheus: Ein literarisches, religioses und philosophisches Zeugnis — *Schelske, Oliver*
Orpheus in the Marketplace: Jacopo Peri and the Economy of Late Renaissance Florence — *Carte, Tim*
Orpheus in the Marketplace: Jacopo Peri and the Economy of Late Renaissance Florence — *Carter, Tim*
Orpheus in the Marketplace: Jacopo Peri and the Economy of Late Renaissance Florence — *Goldthwaite, Richard A.*
c Orpheus in the Underworld (Illus. by Pommaux, Yvan) — *Pommaux, Yvan*
c Orpheus in the Underworld — *Pommaux, Yvan*
Orson Welles: One-Man Band — *Callow, Simon*
Orson Welles: Power, Heart & Soul — *Feeney, F.X.*
Orson Welles's Last Movie: The Making of The Other Side of the Wind — *Karp, Josh*
Orson Welles's Last Movie: The Making of "The Other Side of the Wind" — *Karp, Josh*
Orson Welles's Last Movie: The Making of The Other Side of the Wind — *Karp, Josh*
Orte der Varuskatastrophe und der romischen Okkupation in Germanien: Der historisch-archaologische Fuhrer — *Dreyer, Boris*
Orte der Zivilisierungsmission: Franzosische Schulen im Libanon 1909-1943 — *Moller, Esther*
Orthodox Christianity and Nationalism in Nineteenth Century Southeastern Europe — *Leustean, Lucian N.*
Orthodox Christianity and Nationalism in Nineteenth-Century Southeastern Europe — *Leustean, Lucian N.*
Orthodox Christianity in Imperial Russia: A Source Book on Lived Religion — *Coleman, Heather J.*
Orthodox Constructions of the West — *Demacopoulos, George E.*
Orthodoxa Confessio? Konfessionsbildung, Konfessionalisierung und ihre Folgen in der ostlichen Christenheit Europas
Orthodoxy and Controversy in Twelfth-century Religious Discourse: Peter Lombard's Sentences and the Development of Theology — *Monagle, Clare*
y Oryon — *Cooper, T.*
Osbert Lancaster's Cartoons, Columns and Curlicues: Includes "Pillar to Post," "Homes Sweet Homes" and "Drayneflete Revealed" — *Lancaster, Osbert*

c Oscar — *Miles, Ellen*
c Oscar and the Amazing Gravity Repellent — *Peterson, Tina L.*
c Oscar and the Very Hungry Dragon (Illus. by Krause, Ute) — *Krause, Ute*
c Oscar Lives Next Door: A Story Inspired by Oscar Peterson's Childhood (Illus. by Lafrance, Marie) — *Farmer, Bonnie*
c Oscar Lives Next Door: A Story Inspired by Oscar Peterson's Childhood (Illus. by Lafrance, Marie) — *Peterson, Oscar*
Oscar Romero: Love Must Win Out — *Clarke, Kevin*
Oscar Wilde and Ancient Greece — *Ross, Iain*
Oscar Wilde's Chatterton: Literary History, Romanticism, and the Art of Forgery — *Bristow, Joseph*
Oscar Wilde's Scandalous Summer: The 1894 Worthing Holiday and the Aftermath — *Edmonds, Antony*
c Oskar and the Eight Blessings (Illus. by Siegel, Mark) — *Simon, Richard*
Ospedali e citta nel Regno di Napoli: le Annunziate: istituzioni, archivi, e fonti — *Marino, Salvatore*
Ostend: Stefan Zweig, Joseph Roth, and the Summer Before the Dark — *Weidermann, Volker*
"Osterreich wird meine Stimme erkennen lernen wie die Stimme Gottes in der Wuste": Tagebucher 1839-1858, hrsg. v. Franz Adlgasser — *Andrian-Werburg Freiherr, Viktor Franz von*
Osteuropaexperten und Politik im 20. Jahrhundert
Osteuropaische Geschichte und Globalgeschichte — *Aust, Martin*
Ostia in Late Antiquity — *Boin, Douglas*
Ostkrieg: Hitler's War of Extermination in the East — *Fritz, Stephen G.*
Otakar Zich: Vina - Opera in Three Acts Based on the Play by Jaroslav Hilbert: Part 1: Introductory Materials and Act 1 — *Locke, Brian S.*
Otakar Zich: Vina - Opera in Three Acts Based on the Play by Jaroslav Hilbert: Part 2, Act 2 — *Locke, Brian S.*
Otakar Zich: Vina - Opera in Three Acts Based on the Play by Jaroslav Hilbert: Part 3, Act 3 and Critical Report — *Locke, Brian S.*
The Othe Language: Stories — *Marciano, Francesca*
Othello Blues — *Jaffe, Harold*
Othello: The State of Play — *Orlin, Lena Cowen*
The Other Americans in Paris: Businessmen, Countesses, Wayward Youth, 1880-1941 — *Green, Nancy L.*
The Other Blacklist: The African American Literary and Cultural Left of the 1950s — *Washington, Mary Helen*
y Other Broken Things — *Desir, Christa*
The Other Classical Musics: Fifteen Great Traditions — *Church, Michael*
The Other Daughter (Read by Barber, Nicola). Audiobook Review — *Willig, Lauren*
y The Other Daughter — *Willig, Lauren*
Other Dreams of Freedom: Religion, Sex, and Human Trafficking — *Zimmerman, Yvonne C.*
The Other East and Nineteenth-Century British Literature: Imagining Poland and the Russian Empire — *McLean, Thomas*
The Other Four Plays of Sophocles: Ajax, Women of Trachis, Electra, Philoctetes — *Slavitt, R.D.*
Other Fronts, Other Wars? First World War Studies on the Eve of the Centennial — *Egger, Matthias*
Other Fronts, Other Wars? First World War Studies on the Eve of the Centennial — *Burgschwenter, Joachim*
y Other Girl — *Burstein, Nicole*
The Other Great Migration: The Movement of Rural African Americans to Houston, 1900-1941 — *Pruitt, Bernadette*
The Other Joseph — *Horack, Skip*
Other Lives — *Humaydan, Iman*
Other Lives — *Hartman, Michele*
The Other Me — *Garyash, Maha*
The Other Mountain — *Williams, Rowan*
The Other Paris — *Sante, Luc*
Other Pasts, Different Presents, Alternative Futures — *Black, Jeremy*
Other People's Comfort Keeps Me Up at Night — *Parker, Morgan*
Other People's Money: The Real Business of Fame — *Kay, John*
Other People's Money: The Real Business of Finance — *Kay, John*
Other People's Stories — *Elovic, Barbara*
c The Other Rabbit (Illus. by van der Linden, Martijn) — *Rinck, Maranke*
The Other Renaissance: Italian Humanism Between Hegel and Heidegger — *Rubini, Rocco*

The Other School Reformers: Conservative Activism in American Education — Laats, Adam
The Other Serious: Essays for the New American Generation — Wampole, Christy
The Other Shakespeare — Rachel, Lea
The Other Side of the Painting — Rodrigue, Wendy W.
The Other Side of the Sea — Dalembert, Louis-Philippe
y The Other Side of the Wall (Illus. by Schwartz, Simon) — Schwartz, Simon
The Other Solzhenitsyn: Telling the Truth about a Misunderstood Writer and Thinker — Mahoney, Daniel J.
The Other Son (Read by Jackson, Gildart). Audiobook Review — Soderberg, Alexander
The Other Son — Soderberg, Alexander
Other Than War: The American Experience and Operations in the Post-Cold War Decade — Schuber, Frank N.
The Other Zulus: The Spread of Zulu Ethnicity in Colonial South Africa — Mahoney, Michel R.
y Otherbound — Duyvis, Corinne
y Otherwise — Oatman, Linda High
Otherwise Fables — Mandel, Oscar
Otherwise Homeless: Vehicle Living and the Culture of Homelessness — Wakin, Michele
Otherwise Unseeable — Sholl, Betsy
The Otherworld: Music and Song from Irish Tradition — Ogain, Rionach Ui
c Otis and the Scarecrow (Illus. by Long, Loren) — Long, Loren
c Otter in Space (Illus. by Garton, Sam) — Garton, Sam
c Otter Loves Halloween! (Illus. by Garton, Sam) — Garton, Sam
c Otter Loves Halloween (Illus. by Garton, Sam) — Garton, Sam
Otter — Ladouceur, Ben
c Otters Love to Play (Illus. by So, Meilo) — London, Jonathan
Otthon es haza: Tanulmanyok a romaniai magyar kisebbseg torteneterol — Bardi, Nandor
c Otto the Owl Who Loved Poetry — Kousky, Vern
The Ottoman Endgame: War, Revolution, and the Making of the Modern Middle East, 1908-1923 — McMeekin, Sean
Ottoman High Politics and the Ulema Household — Nizri, Michael
Ottoman Imperial Diplomacy: A Political, Social, and Cultural History — Gurpinar, Dogan
Ottoman-Iranian Borderlands: Making a Boundary, 1843-1914 — Ates, Sabri
Ottoman Refugees, 1878-1939: Migration in a Post-Imperial World — Blumi, Isa
The Ottoman Touch: Traditional Decorative Arts and Crafts — Kusoglu, Mehmet Zeki
Ottoman/Turkish Visions of the Nation, 1860-1950 — Gurpinar, Dogan
The Ottoman World — Woodhead, Christine
Ottomans and Armenians: A Study in Counterinsurgency — Erickson, Edward J.
Ottomans Imagining Japan: East, Middle East, and Non-Western Modernity at the Turn of the Twentieth Century — Worringer, Renee
y Otzi the Iceman — Lanser, Amanda
c Ou es-tu, Catherine? (Illus. by Martchenko, Michael) — Munsch, Robert
c Ouch! It Stings! (Illus. by JiSeung, Kook) — JiSeung, Kook
Our Aging Bodies — Merrill, Gary F.
Our America: A Hispanic History of the United States — Fernandez-Armesto, Felipe
Our Ancient National Airs: Scottish Song Collecting from the Enlightenment to the Romantic Era — McAulay, Karen
Our Auntie Rosa: The Family of Rosa Parks Remembers Her Life and Lessons — Keys, Sheila McCauley
c Our Baby (Illus. by Blair, Karen) — Wild, Margaret
y Our Brothers at the Bottom of the Bottom of the Sea — Kranz, Jonathan David
Our Bums: The Brooklyn Dodgers in History, Memory and Popular Culture — Krell, David
y Our Endless Numbered Days — Fuller, Claire
Our Enduring Values Revisited: Librarianship in an Ever-Changing World — Gorman, Michael (b. 1941-)
Our Expanding Universe — Robinson, Alex
c Our Flag: The Story of Canada's Maple Leaf (Illus. by Slavin, Bill) — Owens, Ann-Maureen
Our Gang: A Racial History of 'The Little Rascals' — Lee, Julia
Our Grandchildren Redesigned: Life in the Bioengineered Society of the Near Future — Bess, Michael
c Our Great States Series — Hirsch, Rebecca

c Our Heroes: How Kids Are Making a Difference — Wilson, Janet
Our Ice Is Vanishing/Sikuvut Nunguliqtuq: A History of Inuit, Newcomers, and Climate Change — Wright, Shelley
Our Kids: The American Dream in Crisis — Putnam, Robert D.
Our Lady of the Ice — Clarke, Cassandra Rose
Our Lady of the Nile — Mukasonga, Scholastique
Our Land at War: A Portrait of Rural Britain, 1939-45 — Hart-Davis, Duff
Our Lives, Our Fortunes and Our Sacred Honor: The Forging of American Independence — Beeman, Richard
Our Lost Constitution: The Willful Subversion of America's Founding Document — Lee, Mike
Our Love of Loons — Tekiela, Stan
Our Man in Charleston — Dickey, Christopher
Our Man in Charleston: Britain's Secret Agent in the Civil War South — Dickey, Christopher
Our Mathematical Universe: My Quest for the Ultimate Nature of Reality — Tegmark, Max
c Our Moon: New Discoveries about Earth's Closest Companion — Scott, Elaine
c Our Moon — Graham, Ian
Our Mussequo — Vieira, Jose Luandino
Our Only World: Ten Essays — Berry, Wendell
Our Promised Land: Faith and Militant Zionism in Israeli Settlements — Selengut, Charles
Our Robots, Ourselves: Robotics and the Myths of Autonomy — Mindell, David A.
Our Roots Run Deep as Ironweed: Appalachian Women and the Fight for Environmental Justice — Bell, Shannon Elizabeth
Our Sacred Maiz Is Our Mother: Indigeneity and Belonging in the Americas — Rodriguez, Roberto Cintli
Our School: Searching for Community in the Era of Choice — Chaltain, Sam
c Our Solar System: Updated Edition — Simon, Seymour
Our Souls at Night (Read by Bramhall, Mark). Audiobook Review — Haruf, Kent
Our Souls at Night — Haruf, Kent
Our Spoons Came from Woolworths — Comyns, Barbara
c Our Sun — Graham, Ian
Our Town — McEnroe, Kevin
Our Very Own Tree — Lowery, Lawrence F.
Our Word Is Our Bond: How Legal Speech Acts — Constable, Marianne
Our Young Man — White, Edmund
c Out and About: A First Book of Poems — Hughes, Shirley
Out Came the Sun: Overcoming the Legacy of Mental Illness, Addiction, and Suicide in My Family — Hemingway, Mariel
Out Comes the Evil — Cameron, Stella
y Out in Front: Nujood Ali and the Fight Against Child Marriage — Don, Katherine
y Out in Front Series — Don, Katherine
Out in the Open — Carrasco, Jesus
Out in the Union: A Labor History of Queer America — Frank, Miriam
y Out of Aces (Read by Podehl, Nick). Audiobook Review — Guerra, Stephanie
Out of Ashes: A New History of Europe in the Twentieth Century — Jarausch, Konrad H.
y Out of Control — Alderson, Sarah
y Out of Darkness — Perez, Ashley Hope
y Out of Darkness — Prez, Ashley Hope
Out of Italy: The Story of Italians in North East England — Shankland, Hugh
Out of Nowhere: The Kurds of Syria in Peace and War — Gunter, Michael M.
Out of Orange: A Memoir — Wolters, Cleary
Out of Print: Newspapers, Journalism and the Business of News in the Digital Age — Brock, George
c Out of Shapes — G., Ashley
Out of Sight: The Los Angeles Art Scene of the Sixties — Hackman, William
c Out of Sight till Tonight! All about Nocturnal Animals (Illus. by Mathieu, Joe) — Rabe, Tish
c Out of Sight till Tonight! All About Nocturnal Animals (Illus. by Ruiz, Aristides) — Rabe, Tish
Out of Silence — Matustik, Martin Beck
y Out of Synch — Firschein, Warren
Out of the Blues — Boyce, Trudy Nan
Out of the Box: The Rise of Sneaker Culture — Semmelhack, Elizabeth
y Out of the Dragon's Mouth — Zeiss, Joyce Burns
Out of the Line of Fire — Henshaw, Mark
Out of the Shadows, Into the Streets! Transmedia Organizing and the Immigrant Rights Movement — Costanza-chock, Sasha

Out of the Shadows: The Global Intensification of Supplementary Education — Aurini, Janice
Out of the Woods: A Memoir of Wayfinding — Darling, Lynn
c Out of the Woods: A True Story of an Unforgettable Event (Illus. by Bond, Rebecca) — Bond, Rebecca
Out of the Woods — Carl, William D.
c Out of the Woods (Illus. by Bond, Rebecca) — Bond, Rebecca
y Out of This World — De Lint, Charles
c Out of Tune — Reekles, Beth
y Out on the Water: Twelve Tales of the Sea (Illus. by Potter, Bruce) — Duder, Tessa
Out on the Wire: The Storytelling Secrets of the New Masters of Radio (Illus. by Abel, Jessica) — Abel, Jessica
Out Where the West Begins: Profiles, Vision & Strategies of Early Western Business Leaders — Anscutz, Philip F.
y Outage (Read by Rudd, Kate). Audiobook Review — Barr, Ellisa
The Outbreak of the First World War: Structure, Politics and Decision-Making — Levy, Jack S.
Outcast: A Darkness Surrounds Him (Illus. by Azaceta, Paul) — Kirkman, Robert
c Outdoor Opposites (Illus. by Oldfield, Rachel) — Williams, Brenda
The Outdoor Table: The Ultimate Cookbook for Your Next Backyard BBQ, Front-Porch Meal, Tailgate, or Picnic — McKinney, April
c Outer Space Bedtime Race (Illus. by Won, Brian) — Sanders, Robert L.
c Outer Space (Illus. by Lowery, Mike) — Jennings, Ken
Outland Exile — Boutwell, Clark
c The Outlaw of Sherwood Forest — Seven, John
The Outlaw River Wilde: Sometimes a Man Needs to Journal — Walters, Mike
Outlaw Woman: A Memoir of the War Years, 1960-1975 — Dunbar-Ortiz, Roxanne
Outlawed: Between Security and Rights in a Bolivian City — Goldstein, Daniel M.
c Outlaws 2.0 — Korman, Gordon
c Outlaws and Rebels — Nolan, Frederick
Outlaws — Cercas, Javier
Outlaws of the Atlantic: Sailors, Pirates, and Motley Crews in the Age of Sail — Rediker, Marcus
The Outlaws: Tales of Bad Guys Who Shaped the Wild West — Smith, Robert Barr
Outline (Read by Reading, Kate). Audiobook Review — Cusk, Rachel
Outline — Cusk, Rachel
Outpatients — Issenberg, Sasha
Outpost: Life on the Frontlines of American Diplomacy — Hill, Christopher R.
Outposts of Hope: First Peter's Christ for Culture Strategy — Webster, Douglas D.
y Outrage — Cook, Michele
c Outrageous Car Racing Rivalries — Maurer, Tracy Nelson
c Outrageous Football Rivalries — Doeden, Matt
c Outside (Illus. by Gill, Deirdre) — Gill, Deirdre
y The Outside Circle (Illus. by Mellings, Kelly) — Benson-Laboucane, Patti
Outside Color: Perceptual Science and the Puzzle of Color in Philosophy — Chirimuuta, Mazviita
Outside the Gates of Eden: The Dream of America from Hiroshima to Now — Hales, Peter B.
The Outsider Entrepreneurs — Yavuz, R. Isil
Outsider in the White House — Sanders, Bernie
The Outsider: My Life in Intrigue — Forsyth, Frederick
Outsider Scientists: Routes to Innovation in Biology — Harman, Oren
The Outsiders (Read by Jackson, Gildart). Audiobook Review — Seymour, Gerald
The Outsiders — Seymour, Gerald
The Outskirts of Hope: A Memoir of the 1960s Deep South — Ivester, Jo
Outsmarting Alzheimer's: What You Can Do to Reduce Your Risk — Bowman, Alisa
Outstanding American Gardens: A Celebration — Dickey, Page
c Outstanding in the Rain (Illus. by Viva, Frank) — Viva, Frank
Outstanding Marine Molecules: Chemistry, Biology, Analysis — Barre, Stephane La
The Oval World: A Global History of Rugby — Collins, Tony
Over Here — Hockenberry, James
c Over in the Wetlands (Illus. by Dunlavey, Rob) — Rose, Caroline Starr
c Over On a Mountain: Somewhere in the World (Illus. by Dubin, Jill) — Berkes, Marianne
c Over-Scheduled Andrew (Illus. by Spires, Ashley) — Spires, Ashley

Over the Alleghenies: Early Canals and Railroads of Pennsylvania — Kapsch, Robert J.
c Over the Hills and Far Away: A Treasury of Nursery Rhymes — Hammill, Elizabeth
Over the Hills and Far Away: A Treasury of Nursery Rhymes (Illus. by Bryan, Ashley) — Hammill, Elizabeth
c Over the Hills and Far Away: A Treasury of Nursery Rhymes — Hammill, Elizabeth
c Over the Moon — Dharker, Imtiaz
c Over the River and through the Wood: A Holiday Adventure (Illus. by Smith, Kim) — Ashman, Linda
c Over the River and through the Wood: A Thanksgiving Poem (Illus. by Manson, Christopher) — Child, Lydia Maria
c Over the River and through the Wood (Illus. by Smith, Kim) — Ashman, Linda
Over the Tightrope — Ismael, Asif
Over the Top and Back — Jones, Tom
Over the Top: How the Internet Is (Slowly but Surely) Changing the Television Industry — Wolk, Alan
y Over the Tracks — Stone, Heather Duffy
Over There: Living with the U.S. Military Empire from World War Two to the Present — Hohn, Maria
c Over There (Illus. by Pilcher, Steve) — Pilcher, Steve
Overcoming Anxiety: Self-Help Anxiety Relief — Berndt, David
Overcoming Obamacare: Three Approaches to Reversing the Government Takeover of Health Care — Klein, Philip
Overdevelopment, Overpopulation, Overshoot — Butler, Tom
The Overflowing of Friendship: Love Between Men and the Creation of the American Republic — Godbeer, Richard
The Overparenting Epidemic: Why Helicopter Parenting Is Bad for Your Kids ... and Dangerous for You, Too! — Glass, George S.
Overreach: Delusions of Regime Change in Iraq — MacDonald, Michael
Overruled: The Long War for Control of the U.S. Supreme Court — Root, Damon
Overseas Mailers First Day Covers of Canada — Van der Ven, Jan Pieter
Oversight — Claburn, Thomas
The Oversight — Claburn, Thomas
The Oversight — Fletcher, Charlie
y Overtaken — Kruger, Mark L.
The Overthrow of Hawaii — Radakovich, Tropical Tom
Overture Opera Guide: "Die Meistersinger von Nurnberg" — Whittall, Arnold
Overturning Tables: Freeing Missions from the Christian-Industrial Complex — Bessenecker, Scott A.
y Overturning Wrongful Convictions: Science Serving Justice — Murray, Elizabeth A.
Overview of CIA-Congress Interactions Concerning the Agency's Rendition-Detention-Interrogation Program — Central Intelligence Agency
y Overwhelmed: How to Work, Love, and Play When No One Has the Time — Schulte, Brigid
Ovidian Bibliofictions and the Tudor Book: Metamorphosing Classical Heroines in Late Medieval and Renaissance England — Reid, Lindsay Ann
The Ovidian Vogue: Literary Fashion and Imitative Practice in Late Elizabethan England — Moss, Daniel D.
Ovid's Erotic Poems: Amores and Ars Amatoria — Krisak, Len
Ovid's Erotic Poems: Amores and Ars Amatoria — Ovid
Owen Wester and the West — Scharnhorst, Gary
c The Owl and the Pussy-Cat (Illus. by Galdone, Paul) — Lear, Edward

c The Owl and the Pussy Cat (Illus. by Voake, Charlotte) — Lear, Edward
c Owl Boy (Illus. by Schatell, Brian) — Schatell, Brian
c Owl Diaries: Eva Sees a Ghost — Elliott, Rebecca
c Owl Howl (Illus. by Goossens, Philippe) — Friester, Paul
c Owls — Marsh, Laura
Owning and Using Scholarship: An IP Handbook for Teachers and Researchers — Smith, Kevin L.
Owning the Earth: The Transforming History of Land Ownership — Linklater, Andro
Owning the Past: Why the English Collected Antique Sculpture, 1640-1840 — Guilding, Ruth
Ox in the Culvert — Brence, Gerald
The Oxbow Poems — Burbank, James
The Oxford Anthology of Tudor Drama — Walker, Greg G.
Oxford College Gardens — Richardson, Tim
The Oxford Companion to British History — Cannon, John
c The Oxford Companion to Children's Literature, 2d ed. — Hahn, Daniel
The Oxford Companion to Children's Literature — Hahn, Daniel
The Oxford Companion to Classical Civilization, 2d ed. — Hornblower, Simon
The Oxford Companion to Food, 3d ed. — Davidson, Alan
The Oxford Companion to Pakistani History — Jalal, Ayesha
The Oxford Companion to Sugar and Sweets — Goldstein, Darra
The Oxford Dictionary of Architecture, 3d ed. — Curl, James Stevens
The Oxford Dictionary of Christian Art & Architecture, 2d ed — Murray, Peter (1920-1992)
Oxford Dictionary of Quotations, 8th ed. — Knowles, Elizabeth
The Oxford Edition of the Sermons of John Donne, vol. 3: Sermons Preached at the Court of Charles I — Colclough, David
The Oxford Edition of the Sermons of John Donne. Volume 3: Sermons Preached at the Court of Charles I — Donne, John
The Oxford Edition of the Works of Robert Burns, vol. 1: Commonplace Books, Tour Journals and Miscellaneous Prose — Leask, Nigel
The Oxford Encyclopedia of the Bible and Ethics, 2 vols. — Brawley, Robert L.
The Oxford Encyclopedia of the Bible and Gender Studies, 2 vols. — O'Brien, Julia M.
The Oxford Encyclopedia of the Bible and Law, 2 vols. — Strawn, Brent A.
The Oxford Encyclopedia of the Bible and Theology, 2 vols. — Balentine, Samuel E.
The Oxford Francis Bacon I: Early Writings, 1584-1596 — Stewart, Alan
The Oxford Handbook of Atheism — Bullivant, Stephen
The Oxford Handbook of Children's Musical Cultures — Campbell, Patricia Shehan
The Oxford Handbook of Ecocriticism — Garrard, Greg
The Oxford Handbook of English Prose, 1500u-1640 — Hadfield, Andrew
The Oxford Handbook of Greek and Roman Comedy — Fontaine, Michael
The Oxford Handbook of Holinshed's Chronicles — Kewes, Paulina
The Oxford Handbook of Indigenous American Literature — Cox, James H.
The Oxford Handbook of Late Antiquity — Johnson, Scott Fitzgerald
The Oxford Handbook of Literature and the English Revolution — Knoppers, Laura Lunger
The Oxford Handbook of Martin Luther's Theology — Kolb, Robert

The Oxford Handbook of Modern African History — Parker, John
The Oxford Handbook of Modern and Contemporary American Poetry — Nelson, Cary
The Oxford Handbook of Modern Irish History — Jackson, Alvin
The Oxford Handbook of New Audiovisual Aesthetics — Richardson, John
The Oxford Handbook of Nineteenth-Century American Literature — Castronovo, Russ
The Oxford Handbook of Opera — Greenwald, Helen M.
The Oxford Handbook of Percy Bysshe Shelley — O'Neill, Michael
The Oxford Handbook of Philosophy and Psychiatry — Fulford, Kenneth William Musgrave
The Oxford Handbook of Roman Epigraphy — Bruun, Christer
The Oxford Handbook of the American Revolution — Gray, Edward G.
Oxford Handbook of the British Sermon, 1689-1901 — Francis, Keith A.
The Oxford Handbook of the Economics of the Pacific Rim — Kaur, Inderjit
The Oxford Handbook of the Georgian Theatre 1737-1832 — Swindells, Julia
The Oxford Handbook of the History of Communism — Smith, S.A.
The Oxford Handbook of the History of Consumption — Trentmann, Frank
The Oxford Handbook of the History of International Law — Hogger, Daniel
The Oxford Handbook of the History of Nationalism — Breuilly, John
The Oxford Handbook of the History of Physics — Buchwald, Jed Z.
The Oxford Handbook of the Italian Economy since Unification — Toniolo, Gianni
The Oxford Handbook of the "Psalms" — Brown, William P.
The Oxford Handbook of Women and Gender in Medieval Europe — Bennett, Judith M.
The Oxford Handbook on William Wordsworth — Gravil, Richard
The Oxford History of English: Updated Edition — Mugglestone, Lynda
The Oxford History of the Novel in English, vol. 6: The American Novel 1870-1940 — Wald, Priscilla
The Oxford Illustrated History of the First World War — Strachan, Hew
The Oxford Illustrated History of the Reformation — Marshall, Peter
The Oxford Illustrated History of World War Two — Overy, Richard
Oxford Illustrated Shakespeare Dictionary (Illus. by Bellamy, Kate) — Crystal, David
y Oxford Illustrated Shakespeare Dictionary — Crystal, David
The Oxford Inheritance — McDonald, Ann A.
Oxford Street, Accra: City Life and the Itineraries of Transnationalism — Quayson, Ato
The Oxygen Advantage: The Simple, Scientifically Proven Breathing Techniques for a Healthier, Slimmer, Faster, and Fitter You — McKeown, Patrick
Oy, My Buenos Aires: Jewish Immigrants and the Creation of Argentine National Identity — Nuowen, Mollie Lewis
Oye What I'm Gonna Tell You — Milanes, Cecilia Rodriguez
y Oyster War (Illus. by Towle, Ben) — Towle, Ben
The Oyster War: The True Story of a Small Farm, Big Politics, and the Future of Wilderness in America — Brennan, Summer
The Oz Family Kitchen: More than 100 Simple and Delicious Real-Food Recipes from Our Home to Yours — Oz, Lisa
c Ozark Waltz — Peskanov, Alexander
Ozma of Oz (Read by Yuen, Erin). Audiobook Review — Baum, Frank L

P

P.Cair.Preis.&rqsb; — *Salomons, Robert P.*
c P Is for Pirate: A Pirate Alphabet (Illus. by Manders, John) — *Bunting, Eve*
y P.S. I Still Love You (Read by Keating, Laura Knight). Audiobook Review — *Han, Jenny*
y P.S. I Still Love You — *Han, Jenny*
c P. Zonka Lays an Egg (Read by Morton, Elizabeth). Audiobook Review — *Paschkis, Julie*
c P. Zonka Lays an Egg (Illus. by Paschkis, Julie) — *Paschkis, Julie*
Pablo (Illus. by Oubrerie, Clement) — *Birmant, Julie*
c Pablo & Jane and the Hot Air Contraption (Illus. by Domingo, Jose) — *Domingo, Jose*
Pablo (Illus. by Oubrerie, Clement) — *Birmant, Julie*
Pabst Farms: The History of a Model Farm — *Eastberg, John C.*
Pachucas and Pachucos in Tucson: Situated Border Lives — *Cummings, Laura L.*
Pacific Blitzkrieg: World War II in the Central Pacific — *Lacey, Sharon Tosi*
Pacific Burn — *Lancet, Barry*
Pacific — *Drury, Tom*
Pacific Identities and Well-Being: Cross-Cultural Perspectives — *Agee, Margaret Nelson*
Pacific: Silicon Chips and Surfboards, Coral Reefs and Atom Bombs, Brutal Dictators, Fading Empires, and the Coming Collision of the World's Superpowers (Read by Winchester, Simon). Audiobook Review — *Winchester, Simon*
Pacific: Silicon Chips and Surfboards, Coral Reefs and Atom Bombs, Brutal Dictators, Fading Empires, and the Coming Collision of the World's Superpowers — *Winchester, Simon*
Pacifists in Chains: The Persecution of the Hutterites During the Great War — *Stoltzfus, Duane C.S.*
Pacing: Individual Strategies for Optimal Performance — *Thompson, Kevin G.*
Pack of Lies — *Bellet, Annie*
A Pact with Vichy: Angelo Tasca from Italian Socialism to French Collaboration — *Rota, Emanuel*
c Paddington at the Beach (Illus. by Alley, R.W.) — *Bond, Michael (b. 1926-)*
c Paddington in the Garden (Illus. by Alley, R.W.) — *Bond, Michael (b. 1926-)*
c Paddington (Illus. by Alley, R.W.) — *Bond, Michael (b. 1926-)*
c The Paddington Treasury: Six Classic Bedtime Stories about the Bear from Peru (Illus. by Alley, R.W.) — *Bond, Michael (b. 1926-)*
y Paddle against the Flow: Lessons on Life from Doers, Creators, and Cultural Rebels — *Huck Magazine*
The Pagan Night: Book One of the Hallowed War — *Akers, Tim*
The Pagan Writes Back: When World Religion Meets World Literature — *Ni, Zhange*
Paganism in the Middle Ages: Threat and Fascination — *Steel, Carlos*
Pagans and Philosophers: The Problem of Paganism from Augustine to Leibniz — *Marenbon, John*
Pagans: The End of Traditional Religion and the Rise of Christianity — *O'Donnell, James J.*
Pageants, Parlors, & Pretty Women: Race and Beauty in the Twentieth-Century South — *Roberts, Blain*
c The Pages between Us (Illus. by Dening, Abby) — *Leavitt, Lindsey*
Paginas Criticas: Formas de leer y de narrar de Proust a "Mad Men" — *Schifino, Martin*
Paid For: My Journey through Prostitution — *Moran, Rachel*
Paideia and Cult: Christian Initiation in Theodore of Mopsuetia — *Schwartz, D.L.*

Pain and Compassion in Early Modern Literature and Culture — *Dijkhuizen, Jan Frans van*
Pain Slut — *Rock, J.A.*
c Paine and Jefferson in the Age of Revolutions — *Newman, Simon P.*
Painkillers and Gummi Bears — *Frare, Gail*
y Painless — *Harazin, S.A.*
Paint Like the Masters: An Excellent Way to Learn from Those Who Have Much to Teach — *Brunelle, Michael*
Paint Like the Masters — *Parramon Editorial Team*
Painted Black — *Kihn, Greg*
Painted Fires — *McClung, Nellie L.*
Painted Glories: The Brancacci Chapel in Renaissance Florence — *Eckstein, Nicholas A.*
The Painted Screen of Baltimore: An Urban Folk Art Revealed — *Eff, Elaine*
c Painted Skies (Illus. by Zhao, Amei) — *Mallory, Carolyn*
y The Painter — *Heller, Peter*
y The Painter's Daughter — *Klassen, Julie*
Painting a Map of Sixteenth-Century Mexico City: Land, Writing, and Native Rule — *Miller, Mary E.*
The Painting and the Piano — *Lipscomb, John*
Painting Beyond Pollock — *Falconer, Morgan*
Painting Central Park — *Pasquier, Roger F.*
Painting Death — *Parks, Tim*
c Painting for Peace in Ferguson — *Klein, Carol Swartout*
Painting in Latin America, 1550-1820 — *Alcala, Luisa Elena*
Painting Now — *Hudson, Suzanne*
Painting Successful Watercolours from Photographs — *Kersey, Geoff*
Painting the Moon — *Borum, Traci*
Painting under Pressure: Fame, Reputation and Demand in Renaissance Florence — *O'Malley, Michelle*
Paintings: The James A. de Rothschild Collection at Waddesdon Manor — *Waterhouse, Ellis*
c Pajaros — *Arlon, Penelope*
c Pakistan — *Murray, Julie (b. 1969-)*
c Pakkun the Wolf and His Dinosaur Friends (Illus. by Kimura, Yasuko) — *Kimura, Yasuko*
y Palace of Lies — *Haddix, Margaret Peterson*
c Palace of Stone — *Hale, Shannon*
Palace of Treason (Read by Bobb, Jeremy). Audiobook Review — *Matthews, Jason*
Palace of Treason — *Matthews, Jason*
The Palaces of Memory — *Freedman, Stuart*
A Palazzo in the Stars: Science Fiction Stories — *Di Filippo, Paul*
Pale Highway — *Conley, Nicholas*
Pale Horse: Hunting Terrorists and Commanding Heroes with the 101st Airborne Division — *Blackmon, Jimmy*
y Palefire — *Reed, M.K.*
Paleoclimate — *Bender, Michael L.*
The Paleovedic Diet: A Complete Program to Burn Fat, Increase Energy, and Reverse Disease — *Palanisamy, Akil*
Palermo, City of Kings: The Heart of Sicily — *Dummett, Jeremy*
A Palette for Murder — *Ryan, Vanessa A.*
Palimpsest: A History of the Written Word — *Battles, Matthew*
Palliative Care: The 400-Year Quest for a Good Death — *Vanderpool, Harold Y.*
Palm Beach Nasty — *Turner, Tom*
Palmerston and The Times: Foreign Policy, the Press and Public Opinion in Mid-Victorian Britain — *Fenton, Laurence*

Palookaville, no. 22 — *Seth*
Pan American Women: U.S. Internationalists and Revolutionary Mexico — *Threlkeld, Megan*
c Panda Bear, Panda Bear, What Do You See? (Illus. by Carle, Eric) — *Martin, Bill, Jr.*
Pandemic: Tracking Contagions, from Cholera to Ebola and Beyond — *Shah, Sonia*
Pandora's Box Opened: An Examination and Defense of Historical-Critical Method and Its Master Practitioners — *Harrisville, Roy A.*
y Pandora's Gun — *Van Pelt, James*
Pandora's Promise — *Lance, Kathryn*
Panic Fiction: Women and Antebellum Economic Crisis — *Templin, Mary*
Panic in a Suitcase — *Akhtiorskaya, Yelena*
Panic: One Man's Struggle with Anxiety — *Floyd, Harry*
y Panther — *Owen, David*
c Panther Chameleons: Color-Changing Reptiles — *Hirsch, Rebecca E.*
c Pants for Chuck (Illus. by Schories, Pat) — *Schories, Pat*
The Panza Monologues — *Grise, Virginia*
Paolina's Innocence: Child Abuse in Casanova's Venice — *Wolff, Larry*
Paolo de Matteis: Neapolitan Painting and Cultural History in Baroque Europe — *Pestilli, Livio*
Paolo Rivera — *Nolen-Weathington, Eric*
Paolo Sarpi: A Servant of God and State — *Kainulainen, Jaska*
Pap with an Hatchet: An Annotated Modern-Spelling Edition — *Lyly, John*
c Papa Gave Me a Stick (Illus. by Shin, Simone) — *Levy, Janice*
The Papacy in the Modern World: A Political History — *Coppa, Frank J.*
Papacy, Religious Orders, and International Politics in the Sixteenth and Seventeenth Centuries — *Giannini, Massimo Carlo*
Papal Economics: The Catholic Church on Democratic Capitalism from 'Rerum Novarum' to 'Caritas in Veritate' — *Zieba, Maciej*
c Papa's Backpack: A Tribute to the Bond Between a Child and Military Parent (Illus. by Carroll, James Christopher) — *Carroll, James Christopher*
Papa's War — *van Houten, Therese*
c Papasorsnous de la! (Illus. by Martchenko, Michael) — *Munsch, Robert*
y Paper Airplanes — *O'Porter, Dawn*
Paper and Ink: Stories — *Lubow, Mike*
A Paper Atlas for the Digital Age: Interstellarum Deep Sky Atlas — *Stoyan, Ronald*
Paper Cadavers: The Archives of Dictatorship in Guatemala — *Weld, Kirsten*
Paper Collage — *Perros, Georges*
Paper Contracting — *Mitchell, William D.*
c The Paper Cowboy (Read by Hoppe, Lincoln). Audiobook Review — *Levine, Kristin*
y The Paper Cowboy — *Levine, Kristin*
Paper Craft — *DK Publishing*
y Paper Hearts — *Wiviott, Meg*
Paper Hearts — *Walsh, Courtney*
y Paper Hearts — *Wiviott, Meg*
Paper Knowledge — *Gitelman, Lisa*
Paper Knowledge: Toward a Media History of Documents — *Gitelman, Lisa*
Paper Love: Searching for the Girl My Grandfather Left Behind — *Wildman, Sarah*
y The Paper Magician. Audiobook Review — *Holmberg, Charlie N*

The Paper Museum of Cassiano del Pozzo, Series A: Renaissance and Later Architecture and Ornament, part 10 — *Davies, Paul*
y Paper or Plastic — *Barnes, Vivi*
Paper Pieced Modern: 13 Stunning Quilts - Step-by-Step Visual Guide — *Garro, Amy*
c The Paper Playhouse: Awesome Art Projects for Kids Using Paper, Boxes, and Books — *Rodabaugh, Katrina*
A Paper Son — *Buchholz, Jason*
Paper Sovereigns: Anglo-Native Treaties and the Law of Nations, 1604-1664 — *Glover, Jeffrey*
c Paper Things (Read by Rudd, Kate). Audiobook Review — *Jacobson, Jennifer Richard*
c Paper Things — *Jacobson, Jennifer Richard*
The Paper Trail: An Unexpected History of the World's Greatest Invention — *Monro, Alexander*
Paper Wings — *Clewes, Rosemary*
c Paper Wishes — *Sepahban, Lois*
The Papers of Frederick Law Olmsted, vol. IX: The Last Great Projects, 1890-1895 — *Schuyler, David*
Papers of George Washington: Revolutionary War Series, vol. 21: 1 June-31 July 1779 — *Ferraro, William M.*
The Papers of George Washington: Revolutionary War Series, vol. 22: 1 August-21 October 1779 — *Huggins, Benjamin L.*
The Papers of George Washington, Vol. 17: 1 October 1794-31 March 1795 — *Lengel, Edward G.*
The Papers of Thomas Jefferson, vol. 40: 4 March to 10 July 1803 — *Oberg, Barbara B.*
The Papers of Zebulon Baird Vance, vol. 3: 1864-1865 — *Mobley, Joe A.*
y Paperweight — *Haston, Meg*
Papist Devils: Catholics in British America, 1574-1783 — *Curran, Robert Emmett*
"Papists" and Prejudice: Popular Anti-Catholicism and Anglo-Irish Conflict in the North East of England, 1845-70 — *Bush, Jonathan*
Papstgeschichte des Hohen Mittelalters: Digitale und Hilfswissenschaftliche Zugangsweisen zu einer Kulturgeschichte Europas
c Parade — *Braud, Alexis*
Paradeigma: Die antike Kunstschriftstellerei als Grundlage der fruhneuzeitlichen Kunsttheorie — *Koch, Nadia J.*
Paradigm Busters: Beyond Science, Lost History, Ancient Wisdom — *Kenyon, J. Douglas*
Parading Patriotism: Independence Day Celebrations in the Urban Midwest, 1826-1876 — *Criblez, Adam*
Paradise and Plenty: A Rothschild Family Garden — *Keen, Mary*
Paradise City — *Day, Elizabeth*
Paradise Drive — *Foust, Rebecca*
Paradise Gardens: Spiritual Inspiration and Earthly Expression — *Musgrave, Toby*
Paradise Now: The Story of American Utopianism — *Jennings, Chris*
A Paradise of Blood: The Creek War of 1813-14 — *Weir, Howard T.*
A Paradise of Priests: Singing the Civic and Episcopal Hagiography of Medieval Liege — *Saucier, Catherine*
Paradise of the Pacific: Approaching Hawaii — *Moore, Susanna*
y Paradise Saved: The Remarkable Story of New Zealand's Wildlife Sanctuaries and How They are Stemming the Tide of Extinction — *Butler, Dave (b. 1953-)*
Paradise Sky — *Lansdale, Joe R.*
Paradox — *Fletcher, Charlie*
The Paradox of Evolution: The Strange Relationship Between Natural Selection and Reproduction — *Rothman, Stephen*
The Paradox of Generosity: Giving We Receive, Grasping We Lose — *Smith, Christian*
The Paradox of German Power — *Kundnani, Hans*
The Paradox of Liberation: Secular Revolutions and Religious Counterrevolutions — *Walzer, Michael*
c The Parakeet Named Dreidel (Illus. by Berkson, Suzanne Raphael) — *Singer, Isaac Bashevis*
Parallax and Selected Poems — *Morrissey, Sinead*
Parallel Histories: Muslims and Jews in Inquisitorial Spain — *Amelang, James S.*
Paralysed with Fear: The Story of Polio — *Williams, Gareth*
Paranoid: Exploring Suspicion from the Dubious to the Delusional — *LaPorte, David J.*
y Paranormal — *Robinson, Gary*
Paratexts in English Printed Drama to 1642, 2 vols. — *Berger, Thomas L.*

Paratexts: Thresholds of Interpretation — *Genette, Gerard*
Parchment and Old Lace — *Child, Laura*
Parchment and Old Lace — *Childs, Laura*
Pardon My French: How a Grumpy American Fell in Love with France — *Johnson, Allen (b. 1946-)*
Pardon the Ravens — *Hruska, Alan*
c The Parent Agency — *Baddiel, David*
The Parent App: Understanding Families in the Digital Age — *Clark, Lynn Schofield*
y Parenting — *Musser, Susan*
Parenting, Family Policy, and Children's Well-Being in an Unequal Society: A New Culture War for Parents — *Hartas, Dimitra*
Parents Have the Power to Make Special Education Work: An Insider Guide — *Graves, Judith Canty*
Parfums: A Catalogue of Remembered Smells — *Claudel, Philippe*
The Pariah Problem: Caste, Religion, and the Social in Modern India — *Viswanath, Rupa*
The Pariahs of Yesterday: Breton Migrants in Paris — *Moch, Leslie Page*
A Paris Affair — *de Rosnay, Tatiana*
A Paris Affair — *Taylor, Sam*
Paris and the Fetish: Primal Crime Scenes — *Rolls, Alistair*
Paris at War — *Drake, David*
Paris, Bibliotheque nationale de France, Res. Vm7 674-675: The Bauyn Manuscript - Part I, Works by Jacques Champion de Chambonnieres — *Gustafson, Bruce*
Paris, Bibliotheque nationale de France, Res. Vm7 674-675: The Bauyn Manuscript - Part II, Works by Louis Couperin — *Gustafson, Bruce*
Paris, Bibliotheque nationale de France, Res. Vm7 674-675: The Bauyn Manuscript - Part III, Works by Various Composers — *Gustafson, Bruce*
Paris, Bibliotheque nationale de France, Res. Vm7 674-675: The Bauyn Manuscript - Part IV, Commentary — *Gustafson, Bruce*
Paris Blues: African American Music and French Popular Culture, 1920-1960 — *Fry, Andy*
Paris D.F. — *Wong, Roberto*
Paris: Haussmann and After — *Jordan, David P.*
Paris, He Said — *Sneed, Christine*
The Paris Key (Read by Blackwell, Juliet). Audiobook Review — *Blackwell, Juliet*
The Paris Key — *Blackwell, Juliet*
Paris — *Kharbichi, Amal*
Paris Letters (Read by Gilbert, Tavia). Audiobook Review — *MacLeod, Janice*
Paris Match. Audiobook Review
Paris Nocturne — *Modiano, Patrick*
y Paris Red — *Gibbon, Maureen*
Paris: The 'New Rome' of Napoleon — *Rowell, Diana*
Parisian Palimpsests: Monuments, Ruins, and Preservation in the Long Nineteenth Century — *Oliveira, Patrick Luiz Sullivan De*
The Parker Sisters: A Border Kidnapping — *Maddox, Lucy*
Parker Strip — *Osterhage, Jeff*
Parks, Postmarks & Postmasters: Post Offices within the National Park System — *Lee, Paul R., II*
Parlamentarismuskritik und Antiparlamentarismus in Europa
Parlementer: Assemblees representatives et echange politique en Europe occidentale a la fin du Moyen Age — *Hebert, Michel*
Parliament and the Law — *Horne, Alexander*
Parmigianino's 'Madonna of the Long Neck': A Grace Beyond the Reach of Art — *Olzewski, Edward J.*
Parnell Reconsidered — *Travers, Pauric*
Parodies Lost — *Leaney, Glynn*
Parody and Festivity in Early Modern Art: Essays on Comedy as Social Vision — *Smith, David R.*
Parole, Pardon, Pass and Amnesty Documents of the Civil War: An Illustrated History — *Davis, John M. Jr.*
c Parrot Genius!: And More True Stories of Amazing Animal Talents — *Donohue, Moira Rose*
c Part of Me — *Holt, Kimberly Willis*
Part of Our Lives: A People's History of the American Public Library — *Wiegand, Wayne A.*
Part of the Solution — *Peltzer, Ulrich*
y Part-Time Princesses (Illus. by Galagher, Monica) — *Gallagher, Monica*
y Part-Time Princesses (Illus. by Gallagher, Monica) — *Gallagher, Monica*
Partakers of the Divine: Contemplation and the Practice of Philosophy — *Sherman, Jacob Holsinger*
Partaking of God: Trinity, Evolution, and Ecology — *Edwards, Denis*

Parteidisziplin und Eigenwilligkeit: Das Internationale Komitee Buchenwald-Dora und Kommandos — *Neumann-Thein, Philipp*
Particle Accelerators: From Big Bang Physics to Hadron Therapy — *Amaldi, Ugo*
The Particular Appeal of Gillian Pugsley — *Ornbratt, Susan*
Particulars of Place — *Moore, Richard O.*
Partisan Diary: A Woman's Life in the Italian Resistance — *Gobetti, Ada*
Partitioned Lives: Migrants, Refugees, Citizens in India and Pakistan, 1947-1965 — *Roy, Haimanti*
Partizipation: Metapher, Mimesis, Musik--und die Kunst, Texte bewohnbarzu machen — *Soffner, Jan*
Partners and Rivals: The Uneasy Future of China's Relationship with the United States — *Dobson, Wendy*
Partners in Christ: A Conservative Case for Egalitarianism — *Stackhouse, John G., Jr.*
Partners in Design: Alfred H. Barr Jr. and Philip Johnson — *Albrecht, Donald*
Partners in Spirit: Women, Men, and Religious Life in Germany, 1100-1500 — *Griffiths, Fiona J.*
The Partnership: Brecht, Weill, Three Women, and Germany on the Brink — *Katz, Pamela*
c Parts of a Flower — *Ransom, Candice*
c Parts of Speech Parade: New York City (Illus. by Adams, Mark Wayne) — *Dolinskiy, Irina Gonikberg*
c Party Croc! A Folktale from Zimbabwe (Illus. by Sullivan, Derek) — *MacDonald, Margaret Read*
c Party Drama! — *Siegal, Ida*
y Party Games — *Stine, R.L.*
Party in the Street: The Antiwar Movement and the Democratic Party after 9/11 — *Heaney, Michael T.*
Party Politics and Social Changes in Turkey — *Ozbudun, Ergun*
Party Politics and the Prospects for Democracy in North Africa — *Storm, Lise*
Party School: Crime, Campus, and Community — *Weiss, Karen G.*
c Pas de cadeaux pour les heros! (Illus. by Roux, Paul) — *Lavoie, Michel*
Pas Pleurer — *Salvayre, Lydie*
Pass It On — *Burns, Jim*
Pass on the Cup of Dreams — *Fergusson, Bruce*
Passage to America: Celebrated European Visitors in Search of the American Adventure — *Deak, Gloria*
Passenger 19 — *Larsen, Ward*
The Passenger — *Lutz, Lisa*
The Passenger — *Tallis, F.R.*
y Passenger — *Bracken, Alexandra*
y Passenger on the Pearl: The True Story of Emily Edmonson's Flight from Slavery — *Conkling, Winifred*
The Passenger Pigeon — *Fuller, Errol*
Passing for Human — *Scott, Jody*
The Passion According to G.H. — *Lispector, Clarice*
Passion: Contemporary Writers on the Story of Calvary — *Yarbough, Oliver Larry*
c A Passion for Elephants: The Real Life Adventure of Field Scientist Cynthia Moss (Illus. by Berry, Holly) — *Buzzeo, Toni*
A Passion for Leadership: Lessons on Change and Reform from Fifty Years in Public Service — *Gates, Robert M.*
A Passion for Paris: Romanticism and Romance in the City of Light — *Downie, David*
A Passion for the True and Just: Felix and Lucy Kramer Cohen and the Indian New Deal — *Kehoe, Alice beck*
Passionate Nutrition: A Guide to Using Food as Medicine from a Nutritionist Who Healed Herself from the Inside Out — *Adler, Jennifer*
Passionate Playgoing in Early Modern England — *Hobgood, Allison P.*
Passionately Yours — *Elliott, Cara*
c Passover: Festival of Freedom — *Polak, Monique*
c The Passover Surprise (Illus. by Kauffman, Ronald) — *Heller, Janet Ruth*
Passwords to Paradise — *Ostler, Nicholas*
Past Convictions: The Penance of Louis the Pious and the Decline of the Carolingians — *Booker, Courtney M.*
Past Crimes — *Hamilton, Glen Erik*
Past Futures: Science Fiction, Space Travel, and Postwar Art of the Americas — *Montross, Sarah J.*
The Past — *Hadley, Tessa*
Past Scents: Historical Perspectives on Smell — *Reinarz, Jonathan*
Pasta by Hand: A Collection of Italy's Regional Hand-Shaped Pasta (Illus. by Anderson, Ed) — *Louis, Jenn*

Pasta: The Essential New Collection from the Master of Italian Cookery — Carluccio, Antonio
The Pastor Theologian: Resurrecting an Ancient Vision — Hiestand, Gerald
Pastoral Capitalism: A History of Suburban Corporate Landscapes — Mozingo, Louise A.
Pastoralism and Politics in Northern Kenya and Southern Ethiopia — Schlee, Gunther
Pastrami on Rye: An Overstuffed History of the Jewish Deli — Merwin, Ted
Pasture Art — Barton, Marlin
Pastures Green and Dark Satanic Mills: The British Passion for Landscape — Barringer, Tim
c Pat-a-Cake Baby (Illus. by Dunbar, Polly) — Dunbar, Joyce
c Pat Au Baseball — Dean, James
Patchwerk — Tallerman, David
Patchwork Essentials: The Half-Square Triangle: Foolproof Patterns and Simple Techniques from Basic Blocks — Baker, Jeni
Patently Contestable: Electrical Technologies and Inventor Identities on Trial in Britain — Arapostathis, Stathis
Patently Contestable: Electrical Technologies and Inventor Identities on Trial in Britain — Gooday, Graeme
A Path Appears: Transforming Lives, Creating Opportunity — WuDunn, Sheryl
A Path in the Mighty Waters: Shipboard Life and Atlantic Crossings to the New World — Berry, Stephen R.
The Path of Anger — Rouaud, Antoine
Path of Blood: The Story of Al Qaeda's War on the House of Saud — Small, Thomas
The Path to the Greater, Freer, Truer World: Southern Civil Rights and Anticolonialism, 1937-1955 — Swindall, Lindsey R.
Path toward the Nation: Islam, Community, and Early Nationalist Mobilization in Eritrea, 1941-1961 — Venosa, Joseph L.
c Pathfinder: The Magykal World of Tod Hunter Moon (Illus. by Zug, Mark) — Sage, Angie
The Pathless Sky — Sen, Chaitali
Pathologist of the Mind: Adolf Meyer and the Origins of American Psychiatry — Lamb, S.D.
Paths Out of Dixie: The Democratization of Authoritarian Enclaves in America's Deep South, 1944-1972 — Mickey, Robert
Paths to the Bench: The Judicial Appointment Process in Manitoba, 1870-1950 — Brawn, Dale
Paths toward the Modern Fiscal State: England, Japan, and China — He, Wenkai
Pathways: Novellas and Sstories of New York — Lawenda, Jeff
Pathways to Possibility — Stone, Rosamund Zander
Patience and Fortitude: Power, Real Estate, and the Fight to Save a Public Library — Sherman, Scott
Patience, My Dear — Lewis, Bower
Patience with God: The Story of Zacchaeus — Halik, Thomas
The Patient Will See You Now: The Future of Medicine Is in Your Hands — Topol, Eric
y Patient Zero: Solving the Mysteries of Deadly Epidemics — Peters, Marilee
The Patient's Playbook: How to Save Your Life and the Lives of Those You Love — Michelson, Leslie D.
Patients Teach: The Everyday Ethics of Health Care — Churchill, Larry R.
Patisserie Made Simple — Kimber, Edd
Patmos in the Reception History of the Apocalypse — Boxall, Ian
The Patriarch — Walker, Martin
Patrician Families and the Making of Quebec: The Taschereaus and McCords — Young, Brian
Patrick Conway and His Famous Band — Fonder, Mark
Patrick George — Lambirth, Andrew
The Patriot — Bell, Ted
The Patriot Threat — Berry, Steve
Patriotic Betrayal: The Inside Story of the CIA's Secret Campaign to Enroll American Students in the Crusade against Communism — Paget, Karen M.
The Patriotic Consensus: Unity, Morale, and the Second World War in Winnipeg — Perrun, Jody
c Patriots and Redcoats: Stories of American Revolutionary War Leaders — Otfinoski, Steven
Patron of the Arts — Rotsler, William
The Patron Saint of Dreams — Gerard, Philip

Patronage, Production, and Transmission of Texts in Medieval and Early Modern Jewish Cultures — Alfonso, Esperanza
Patrons of History: Nobility, Capital and Political Transitions in Poland — Jakubowska, Longina
Patrons of History: Nobility, Capital, and Political Transitions in Poland — Jakubowska, Longina
The Pattern Base: Over 550 Contemporary Textile and Surface Designs — O'Meara, Kristi
Pattern of Betrayal — Fox, Mae
A Pattern of Lies (Read by Landor, Rosalyn). Audiobook Review — Todd, Charles
A Pattern of Lies — Todd, Charles
Patternalia: An Unconventional History of Polka Dots, Stripes, Plaid, Camouflage, and Other Graphic Designs — Stewart, Jude
Patterns — Lee Si-young
Patti Smith Collected Lyrics, 1970-2015 — Smith, Patti
y The Patua Pinocchio (Illus. by Chitrakar, Swarna) — Collodi, Carlo
Paul and His Beast — Stup, Sarah
Paul and the Faithfulness of God — Wright, N.T.
Paul and the Restoration of Humanity in Light of Ancient Jewish Traditions — Sherwood, Aaron
Paul Bocuse: Simply Delicious — Bocuse, Paul
The Paul de Man Notebooks — McQuillan, Martin
Paul Durand-Ruel: Memoirs of the First Impressionist Art Dealer — Durand-Ruel, Paul-Louis
Paul for Today's Church: A Commentary on First Corinthians — Marrow, Stanley B.
Paul Lauterbur and the Invention of MRI — Dawson, M. Joan
c Paul Revere — Mara, Wil
Paul Robeson: A Watched Man — Goodman, Jordan
Paul Strand: Master of Modern Photography — Barberie, Peter
Paulina and Fran — Glaser, Rachel B.
y Paulina & Fran — Glaser, Rachel B.
Pauline Hopkins and the American Dream: An African American Writer's Re-Visionary Gospel of Success — Knight, Alisha
Pauline Perspectives: Essays on Paul, 1978-2013 — Wright, N.T.
Paul's Cross and the Culture of Persuasion in England, 1520-1640 — Kirby, Torrance
Paul's Letter to the Philippians: A Socio-Rhetorical Commentary — Witherington, Ben, III
Paul's Summons to Messianic Life: Political Theology and the Coming Awakening — Welborn, L.L.
y The Pause — Larkin, John
Pause and Ponder — Osmani, Rashid
Paw and Order: A Chet and Bernie Mystery — Quinn, Spencer
Pawn Shop — Esposito, Joey
The Pawnbroker — Wallant, Edward Lewis
The Pawnbroker's Daughter: A Memoir — Kumin, Maxine
Pawn's Gambit — Zahn, Timothy
Pawpaw: In Search of America's Forgotten Fruit — Moore, Andrew
c Paws on Ice (Illus. by Reiland, Lizette) — Lozano, Jeff
c Pax (Illus. by Klassen, Jon) — Pennypacker, Sara
Pay Any Price: Greed, Power, and Endless War — Risen, James
c Pay It Forward: Young Readers Edition — Hyde, Catherine Ryan
Payard Cookies — McBride, Anne E.
Payard Cookies — Payard, Francois
Payback — Jacobs, Jonnie
Paying Bribes for Public Services: A Global Guide to Grass Roots Corruption — Rose, Richard
Paying for College Without Going Broke — Chany, Kalman A.
The Paying Guests (Read by Stevenson, Juliet). Audiobook Review — Waters, Sarah
The Paying Guests — Waters, Sarah
Paying With Their Bodies: American War and the Problem of the Disabled Veteran — Kinder, John M.
c PB and J Hooray! (Illus. by Patton, Julia) — Nolan, Janet
The PBIS Tier One Handbook: A Practical Approach to Implementing the Champion Model — Hannigan, Jessica Djabrayan
c The Pea Patch Jig (Illus. by Hurd, Thatcher) — Hurd, Thatcher
Peace and Authority during the French Religious Wars, c. 1560-1600 — Roberts, Penny
Peace Be Still: Modern Black America from World War II to Barack Obama — Whitaker, Matthew C.

c Peace, Bugs, and Understanding: An Adventure in Sibling Harmony (Illus. by Ly, Youme Nguyen) — Silver, Gail
Peace Diplomacy, Global Justice and International Agency: Rethinking Human Security and Ethics in the Spirit of Dag Hammarskjold — Stehn, Carsten
Peace-ing Together Jerusalem — Amos, Clare
c Peace Is an Offering (Illus. by Graegin, Stephanie) — LeBox, Annette
c Peace Is an Offering — LeBox, Annette
The Peace Process — Friedman, Bruce Jay
The Peace Seeker: One Woman's Battle in the Church's War on Homosexuality — Gilmore, Susan E.
c The Peace Tree from Hiroshima (Illus. by Wilds, Kazumi) — Moore, Sandra
c The Peace Tree from Hiroshima: The Little Bonsai with a Big Story (Illus. by Wilds, Kazumi) — Moore, Sandra
Peace Warriors — Huber, Raymond
A Peaceable Economy — Dommen, Edward
Peaceful Parent, Happy Siblings: How to Stop the Fighting and Raise Friends for Life — Markham, Laura
Peacekeepers and Conquerors: The Army Officer Corps on the American Frontier, 1821-1846 — Watson, Samuel J.
Peacekeeping in Africa: The Evolving Security Architecture — Wyss, Marco
Peacekeeping — Berlinski, Mischa
A Peach of a Pair — Boykin, Kim
Peak Season — Widmer, Jeff
Peaks on the Horizon: Two Journeys in Tibet — Carroll, Charlie
Peaks, Politics and Passion: Grand Teton National Park Comes of Age — Righter, Robert W.
c Peanut Butter and Jellyfish (Read by Krosoczka, Jarrett J.). Audiobook Review — Krosoczka, Jarrett J.
c Peanut Butter and Jellyfish (Illus. by Krosoczka, Jarrett J.) — Krosoczka, Jarrett J.
c Peanut Butter and Jellyfish (Illus. by Enik, Ted) — O'Connor, Jane
c Peanut Butter & Brains: A Zombie Culinary Tale (Illus. by Santoso, Charles) — McGee, Joe
c Peanut Butter & Cupcake! (Illus. by Border, Terry) — Border, Terry
c Peanuts: A Charlie Brown Christmas (Illus. by Jeralds, Scott) — Schulz, Charles M.
Peanuts: A Tribute to Charles M. Schulz — Watters, Shannon
c Pearl Harbor — Johnson, Robin
Pearl Harbor: The Missing Motive — O'Connell, Kevin
y Peas and Carrots — Davis, Tanita S.
c Peas in a Pod (Illus. by Snerling, Tina) — McCartney, Tania
c Peas Let Her Be a Princess (Illus. by Mericle, Hannah) — Keyes, Diane E.
c Pebble Plus: Backyard Animals — Schuh, Mari
c Pebble Plus: Birds of Prey — Dunn, Mary R.
c Pebble Plus: Ice Age Animals — Frisch-Schmoll, Joy
c Pebble Plus: Media Literacy for Kids — Rustad, Martha E.H.
c A Pebble Story — Sher, Emil
c A Pebble Story (Illus. by Revell, Cindy) — Sher, Emil
A Peculiar Connection — Hahn, Jan
The Peculiar Life of a Lonely Postman — Thriault, Denis
A Peculiar Mixture: German-Language Cultures and Identities in Eighteenth-Century North America — Stievermann, Jan
A Peculiar People: Anti-Mormonism and the Making of Religion in Nineteenth-Century America — Fluhman, J. Spencer
The Pedagogical Imagination: The Republican Legacy in Twenty-First-Century French Literature and Film — Sachs, Leon
Pedal to the Metal — Thoma, Jesse J.
c The Peddler's Bed (Illus. by Redila, Bong) — Fortino, Lauri
c The Peddler's Road — Cody, Matthew
Pedigree: How Elite Students Get Elite Jobs — Rivera, Lauren A.
Pedigree — Modiano, Patrick
c Pedro and George (Illus. by Perret, Delphine) — Perret, Delphine
Pedro — Martinez, Pedro
Pedro Pietri: Selected Poetry — Pietri, Pedro
Peeing on Hot Coals — Montandon, Pat
c Peek-A-Boo Farm (Illus. by Wan, Joyce) — Wan, Joyce

c Peek-A-Boo — Laden, Nina
c Peek-a-boo Zoo (Illus. by Wan, Joyce) — Wan, Joyce
c Peek-Through Forest — Litton, Jonathan
c Peekaboo Barn (Illus. by Tabor, Nathan) — Sims, Nat
c Peekaboo! (Illus. by Ferri, Giuliano) — Ferri, Giuliano
c Peekaboo! — Ferri, Giuliano
c Peekaboo Presents (Illus. by Lunn, Corey) — Night and Day Studios
c Peep and Ducky Rainy Day (Illus. by Walker, David) — Martin, David (b. 1944-)
Peep and Ducky: Rainy Day (Illus. by Walker, David) — Martin, David (b. 1944-)
c Peep and Egg: I'm Not Hatching (Illus. by Wan, Joyce) — Gehl, Laura
Peers Inc: How People and Platforms Are Inventing the Collaborative Economy and Reinventing Capitalism — Chase, Robin
c Peeve My Parents' Pet (Illus. by Durkin, Kenny) — Ryan, Tom
c Peg + Cat: The Race Car Problem — Oxley, Jennifer
c Peg + Cat: The Race Car Problem (Illus. by Oxley, Jennifer) — Oxley, Jennifer
Peg Plunkett: Memoirs of a Whore — Peakman, Julie
Pegasus Colony — Moore, Phyllis
Peggy Guggenheim: The Shock of the Modern — Prose, Francine
Peiresc's Mediterranean World — Miller, Peter N.
Pelvic Pain Explained: What Everyone Needs to Know — Prendergast, Stephanie A.
Pelvis with Distance — Jacobs, Jessica
Pemmican Empire: Food, Trade, and the Last Bison Hunts in the North American Plains, 1780-1882 — Colpitts, George
Pen and Ink: Tattoos and the Stories Behind Them — Fitzgerald, Isaac
Pen and Ink Witchcraft: Treaties and Treaty-Making in American Indian History — Calloway, Colin G.
Penance in Medieval Europe, 600-1200 — Meens, Rob
The Penderwicks in Spring (Read by Denaker, Susan). Audiobook Review — Birdsall, Jeanne
y The Penderwicks in Spring — Birdsall, Jeanne
c Penelope Crumb Is Mad at the Moon (Illus. by Docampo, Valeria) — Stout, Shawn K.
Penelope Fitzgerald: A Life — Lee, Hermione
c Penelope Perfect (Illus. by Kath, Katie) — Anderson, Shannon
y Penelope Perfect: Project Best Friend — Perry, Chrissie
c Penguin — Murray, Laura K.
c Penguin and Pumpkin (Illus. by Yoon, Salina) — Yoon, Salina
The Penguin Book of British Short Stories, vol. I: From Daniel Defoe to John Buchan — Hensher, Philip
The Penguin Book of British Short Stories, vol. II: From P.G. Wodehouse to Zadie Smith — Hensher, Philip
The Penguin Book of Modern Speeches — MacArthur, Brian
The Penguin Book of Russian Poetry — Chandler, Robert
The Penguin Book of Witches — Howe, Katherine
c A Penguin Named Patience: A Hurricane Katrina Rescue Story (Illus. by Anchin, Lisa) — Lewis, Suzanne
c Penguins — Kuskowski, Alex
c Penguin's Big Adventure (Illus. by Yoon, Salina) — Yoon, Salina
Penguins: Natural History and Conservation — Borboroglu, Pablo Garcia
The Penguin's Song — Daoud, Hassan
Penguins: The Ultimate Guide — De Roy, Tui
Penguins: The Ultimate Guide — Roy, Tui De
A Penny a Kiss — McConnell, Judy
y Penny Chic: How to Be Stylish on a Real Girl's Budget — Miller, Shauna
c Penny Dora and the Wishing Box (Illus. by Bonvillain, Tamra) — Grace, Sina
c Penny Dora and the Wishing Box (Illus. by Grace, Sina) — Stock, Michael
c Penny & Jelly: The School Show (Illus. by Heder, Thyra) — Gianferrari, Maria
The Penny Poet of Portsmouth — Towler, Katherine
c Penny the Palomino Quarter Horse and Her New Shoes (Illus. by Ray, Alex) — Scogin, Gary
c Pennyroyal Academy (Read by Duerden, Susan). Audiobook Review — Larson, M.A.
c Pennyroyal Academy — Larson, M.A.
Penser le lexique-grammaire: perspectives actuelles — Kakoyianni-Doa, Fryni

The Pentagon and the Presidency: Civil-Military Relations from FDR to George W. Bush — Herspring, Dale R.
The Pentagon's Brain: An Uncensored History of DARPA, America's Top-Secret Military Research Agency — Jacobsen, Annie
Pentecostal Mission and Global Christianity — Ma, Wonsuk
Pentecostals, Proselytization, and Anti-Christian Violence in Contemporary India — Bauman, Chad M.
Penthouse Variations on Oral — Pizio, Barbara
y The Peony Lantern — Watts, Frances
People Get Ready: The Future of Jazz Is Now! — Heble, Ajay
The People — Hague, Harlan
People of Print: Innovative, Independent Design and Illustration — Smith, Marcroy
The People of the Abyss — London, Jack
People of the Middle Fraser Canyon: An Archaeological History — Prentiss, Anna Marie
y People of the Plague — Anderson, T. Neill
People of the Songtrail — Gear, W. Michael
c People of the World — Loewen, Nancy
People, Parasites, and Plowshares: Learning from Our Body's Most Terrifying Invaders — Despommier, Dickson D.
People Trees: Worship of Trees in Northern India — Haberman, David L.
c People Who Help: A Kids' Guide to Community Heroes (Illus. by Haggerty, Tim) — Kreisman, Rachelle
The People's Car: A Global History of the Volkswagen Beetle — Rieger, Bernhard
A People's History of Christianity: One Volume Student Edition — Janz, Denis R.
A People's History of the French Revolution — Hazan, Eric
The People's Lawyer: The Life and Times of Frank J. Kelley, the Nation's Longest-Serving Attorney General — Kelley, Frank J.
The People's Martyr: Thomas Wilson Dorr and His 1842 Rhode Island Rebellion — Chaput, Erik J.
The People's Network: The Political Economy of the Telephone in the Gilded Age — MacDougall, Robert
The People's Own Landscape: Nature, Tourism, and Dictatorship in East Germany — Moranda, Scott
The People's Republic of Amnesia: Tiananmen Revisited — Lim, Louisa
A People's War on Poverty: Urban Politics and Grassroots Activists in Houston — Phelps, Wesley G.
c Pepe Camisole: un hiver pas comme les autres (Illus. by Pare-Sorel, Julien) — Desrochers, Pierre
c Peppa Pig and the Day at Snowy Mountain — Candlewick Press
c Pepper & Poe (Illus. by Preston-Gannon, Frann) — Preston-Gannon, Frann
Per Aspera ad Astra - Soziale Hierarchien und Ihre Praxis in der Antike. 3. Gottinger Nachwuchsforum
The Perception of Apartheid in Western Europe, 1960-1990
The Perceptionist — Vohra, Manish
Perchance to Dream — Beaumont, Charles
Percy Jackson and the Lightning Thief — Riordan, Rick
c Percy Jackson's Greek Gods (Read by Bernstein, Jesse). Audiobook Review — Riordan, Rick
c Percy Jackson's Greek Gods (Illus. by Rocco, John) — Riordan, Rick
y Percy Jackson's Greek Heroes (Read by Bernstein, Jesse). Audiobook Review — Riordan, Rick
c Percy Jackson's Greek Heroes (Illus. by Rocco, John) — Riordan, Rick
c Perdidos en NYC: Una aventura en el metro (Illus. by Moral, Lola) — Spiegelman, Nadja
y Perdita — Gardner, Faith
The Peregrine — Baker, J.A.
Peregrine Spring: A Master Falconer's Extraordinary Life with Birds — Cowan, Nancy
Pereira Declares: A Testimony — Tabucchi, Antonio
Perfect — Wickard, Douglas
c Perfect (Illus. by Blackwood, Freya) — Parker, Danny
The Perfect Bet — Kucharski, Adam
y The Perfect Blindside — Wahl, Leslea
y The Perfect Comeback of Caroline Jacobs — Dicks, Matthew
y Perfect Couple — Echols, Jennifer
y Perfect Couple: The Superlatives — Echols, Jennifer
A Perfect Crime — Holmwood, Anna
y A Perfect Crime — Yi, A.
Perfect Days — Montes, Raphael

The Perfect Egg: A Fresh Take on Recipes for Morning, Noon, and Night. — Fisher, Teri Lyn
The Perfect Game — Kirby, Leslie Dana
Perfect Gift Wrapping Ideas: 101 Ways to Personalize Your Gift Using Simple, Everyday Materials — Miyaoka, Hiroe
A Perfect Heritage — Vincenzi, Penny
The Perfect Homecoming — London, Julia
The Perfect Kill: 21 Laws for Assassins — Baer, Robert B.
The Perfect Letter (Read by Eby, Tanya). Audiobook Review — Harrison, Chris
A Perfect Lie: The Hole Truth — Hill, Tom
A Perfect Life — Spring, Joel
c The Perfect Match — Baker, E.D.
The Perfect Metabolism Plan: Restore Your Energy and Reach Your Ideal Weight — Vance, Sara
The Perfect Mother — Darnton, Nina
c The Perfect Percival Priggs (Illus. by Graham, Julie-Anne) — Graham, Julie-Anne
c A Perfect Place for Ted — Rudge, Leila
c The Perfect Place — Harris, Teresa E.
c The Perfect Raisin and Pretzel Cousins Club (Illus. by Sullivan, Ellie) — Tobin, Catherine Sistrunk
Perfect Sins — Bannister, Jo
The Perfect Tea Thief — Chun, Pam
Perfect Touch — Lowell, Elizabeth
c The Perfect Tree (Illus. by Bonfield, Chloe) — Bonfield, Chloe
Perfect Wives in Ideal Homes: The Story of Women in the 1950s — Nicholson, Virginia
c Perfected (Read by Durante, Emily). Audiobook Review — Birch, Kate Jarvik
The Perfection of the Paper Clip: Curious Tales of Invention, Accidental Genius, and Stationery Obsession — Ward, James
y The Perfectionists — Shepard, Sara
Perfectly Broken — Lane, Prescott
Perfectly Feminine Knits: 25 Distinctive Designs — Samsoe, Lene Holme
y Perfectly Good White Boy — Mesrobian, Carrie
c A Perfectly Messed-Up Story (Illus. by McDonnell, Patrick) — McDonnell, Patrick
c A Perfectly Ordinary School (Illus. by Anderson, Scoular) — Strong, Jeremy
The Perfectly Proper Paranormal Museum — Weiss, Kirsten
Performance Artist Database — Miller, Matthew
Performance, Identity, and Immigration Law: A Theatre of Undocumentedness — Guterman, Gad
The Performance of Nationalism: India, Pakistan, and the Memory of Partition — Menon, Jisha
Performance on Behalf of the Environment — Besel, Richard D.
The Performative Presidency: Crisis and Resurrection during the Clinton Years — Mast, Jason L.
Performing Afro-Cuba: Image, Voice, Spectacle in the Making of Race and History — Wirtz, Kristina
Performing Autobiography: Contemporary Canadian Drama — Stephenson, Jenn
Performing Captivity, Performing Escape: Cabarets and Plays from the Terezin/Theresienstadt Ghetto — Peschel, Lisa
Performing Economic Thought: English Drama and Mercantile Writing 1600-1642 — Ryner, Bradley D.
Performing Economic Thought: English Drama and Mercantile Writing, 1600-1642 — Ryner, Bradley D.
Performing Environments: Site-Specificity in Medieval and Early Modern English Drama — Bennett, Susan
Performing Hybridity in Colonial-Modern China — Liu, Siyuan
y Performing Live — Anniss, Matt
Performing Local and Regional Level Administration and Politics: Ceremonies, Rituals and Routines, 16th-18th c.
Performing Medicine: Medical Culture and Identity in Provincial England, c.1760-1850 — Brown, Michael
Performing Place, Practising Memories: Aboriginal Australians, Hippies and the State — Henry, Rosita
Performing Policy: How Contem-Porary Politics and Cultural Programs Redefined U.S. Artists for the Twenty-First Century — Bonin-Rodrigue, Paul
Performing Privacy and Gender in Early Modern Literature — Trull, Mary
Performing Religion in Public — Chambers, Claire Maria
Performing Salome, Revealing Stories — Rowden, Clair
Performing the Temple of Liberty: Slavery, Theater, and Popular Culture in London and Philadelphia, 1760-1850 — Gibbs, Jenna M.

Perfume: Century of Scents — Ostrom, Lizzie
The Perfume Garden — Brown, Kate Lord
c Perhaps (Illus. by van Genechten, Guido) — van Genechten, Guido
Peril by Ponytail — Cohen, Nancy J.
A Perilous Alliance — Buckley, Fiona
y The Perilous Journey of the Not-So-Innocuous Girl — Statham, Leigh
y The Perilous Sea — Thomas, Sherry
The Perils of Normalcy: George L. Mosse and the Remaking of Cultural History — Plessini, Karel
The Perils of Pauline — Yvonne, Collette
The Perils of Peace: The Public Health Crisis in Occupied Germany — Reinisch, Jessica
Period Piece — Raverat, Gwen
c The Periodic Table: Elements with Style — Basher, Simon
Periodic Tales: A Cultural History of the Elements, from Arsenic to Zinc (Read by Ferguson, Antony). Audiobook Review — Aldersey-Williams, Hugh
The Peripheral (Read by King, Lorelei). Audiobook Review — Gibson, William
Peripheral Desires: The German Discovery of Sex — Tobin, Robert Deam
The Peripheral — Gibson, William
Peripheral People — Herbert, Reesa
Periphery: Israel's Search for Middle East Allies — Alpher, Yossi
c Perla Garcia and the Mystery of La Llorona, "The Weeping Woman" (Illus. by Nowakowski, Peter) — Alvarado, Rodolfo
The Permaculture City: Regenerative Design for Urban, Suburban, and Town Resilience — Hemenway, Toby
Perpetrators and Accessories in International Criminal Law: Indivual Modes of Responsibility for Collective Crimes — Jain, Neha
A Perpetual Fire: John C. Ferguson and His Quest for Chinese Art and Culture — Netting, Lara Jaishree
The Perpetual Paycheck: 5 Secrets to Getting a Job, Keeping a Job, and Earning Income for Life in the Loyalty-Free Workplace — Rassas, Lori B.
c Perseverance: I Have Grit! — Shepherd, Jodie
Persia in Crisis: Safavaid Decline and the Fall of Isfahan — Matthee, Rudi
The Persian Interpreter: The Life and Career of Turner Macan — Macan, Turner
Persian Painting: The Arts of the Book and Portraiture — Bayani, Manijeh
Persiana: Recipes from the Middle East and Beyond — Ghayour, Sabrina
y Persist (Illus. by Brett, Cathy) — Burgess, Melvin
The Person Leaders Really Need to Know — Metheny, Richard
Persona — Valentine, Genevieve
The Persona of Ingmar Bergman: Conquering Demons through Film — Young, Barbara
Personal — Child, Lee
The Personal Accountability Code: The Step-by-Step Guide to a Winning Strategy That Transforms Your Goals into Reality with the New Science of Accountability — Worrall, Di
Personal Archiving: Preserving Our Digital Heritage — Hawkins, Donald T.
Personal Characteristics from French History — Rothschild, Ferdinand
Personal Identity: Complex or Simple? — Gasser, Georg
The Personal Librarian: Enhancing the Student Experience — Moniz, Richard
Personal Modernisms: Anarchist Networks and the Later Avant-Gardes — Gifford, James
Personal Names in Ancient Anatolia: Proceedings of the British Academy — Parker, Robert (b. 1950-)
The Personalism of John Henry Newman — Crosby, John F.
Personlicher Einfluss auf den Herrscher in der Romischen Kaiserzeit und dem Fruhen Mittelalter
Persons, Animals, Ourselves — Snowdon, Paul F.
Persons in Relation: An Essay on the Trinity and Ontology — Awad, Najib George
Perspectives on Dodd-Frank and Finance — Schultz, Paul H.
Perspectives on English Revolutionary Republicanism — Weimann, Dirk
Perspectives on English Revolutionary Republicanism — Wiemann, Dirk
Perspectives on European Economic and Social History - Perspektiven der Europaischen Wirtschafts- und Sozialgeschichte — Hesse, Jan-Otmar
Perspectives on Strategy — Gray, Colin S.

Perspectives on Women's Archive — Zanish-Belcher, Tanya
y Persuasion — Boone, Martina
y Persuasion: Heirs of Watson Island — Boone, Martina
Peru: The Cookbook — Acurio, Gatson
c P'esk'a and the First Salmon Ceremony (Illus. by Ritchie, Scot) — Ritchie, Scot
Pesos and Dollars: Entrepreneurs in the Texas-Mexico Borderlands, 1880-1940 — Dewey, Alicia M.
Pesos and Dollars — Dewey, Alicia M.
Pestalozzi and the Educationalization of the World — Trohler, Daniel
Pesticides and Global Health: Understanding Agrochemical Dependence and Investing in Sustainable Solutions — Dowdall, Courtney Marie
Pests in the City: Flies, Bedbugs, Cockroaches, and Rats — Biehler, Dawn Day
c The Pet and the Pendulum (Illus. by Zippardi, Sam) — McAlpine, Gordon
y The Pet and the Pendulum (Illus. by Zuppardi, Sam) — McAlpine, Gordon
Petain's Jewish Children: French Jewish Youth and the Vichy Regime, 1940-42 — Lee, Daniel
c Petal and Poppy and the Mystery Valentine (Illus. by Briant, Ed) — Clough, Lisa
c Petal and Poppy and the Spooky Halloween! (Illus. by Briant, Ed) — Clough, Lisa
c Pete Can Fly! (Illus. by Gordon, John) — Williams, Bonnie
c Pete Makes a Mistake (Illus. by McCully, Emily Arnold) — McCully, Emily Arnold
c Pete Milano's Guide to Being a Movie Star — Greenwald, Tommy
The Pete Seeger Reader — Cohen, Ronald D.
c Pete the Cat and the Bad Banana (Illus. by Dean, James) — Dean, James
c Pete the Cat: And the Bedtime Blues (Illus. by Dean, Kimberly) — Dean, James
c Pete the Cat and the New Guy (Illus. by Dean, James) — Dean, Kimberly
c Pete the Cat's Groovy Guide to Life: Tips from a Cool Cat for Living an Awesome Life — Dean, Kimberly
Pete Von Sholly's History of Monsters — Von Sholly, Pete
c Peter and Lisa: A Mental Illness Children's Story (Illus. by Suico, Mitchi) — Katz, Charles
c Peter Loves Penguin — McPhail, David
Peter of Cornwall's "Book of Revelations": British Writers, 5 — Easting, Robert
c Peter Pan (Illus. by Flyman, Trina Schart) — Barrie, J.M.
Peter Pan Must Die (Read by Fass, Robert). Audiobook Review — Verdon, John
c Peter Puck and the Runaway Zamboni Machine (Illus. by Storey, Geri) — McFarlane, Brian
c Peter Puck and the Stolen Stanley Cup (Illus. by Storey, Geri) — McFarlane, Brian
c Peter the Slug and the Great Forest Race (Illus. by Solyst, Ann) — Schultz, Peter
c Peter's Tree (Illus. by Watts, Bernadette) — Watts, Bernadette
Peterson Field Guide to Finding Mammals in North America — Dinets, Vladimir
Peterson Reference Guide: Birding by Impression - A Different Approach to Knowing and Identifying Birds — Karlson, Kevin T.
Peterson Reference Guide to Owls of North America and the Caribbean — Weidensaul, Scott
Petey & Wolf — Craig, David
c Petite Rouge: A Cajun Twist to an Old Tale (Illus. by Lyne, Alison Davis) — Hebert-Collins, Sheila
c Petlandia (Illus. by Hannan, Peter) — Hannan, Peter
Petra: The Concealed Rose — Nasser, Amjad
Petrarch's Humanist Writing and Carthusian Monasticism: The Secret Language of the Self — Yocum, Demetrio S.
Petrarch's Two Gardens: Landscape and the Image of Movement — Tronzo, William
Petronille — Nothomb, Amelie
Petty: The Biography — Zanes, Warren
The Peyti Crisis — Rusch, Kristine Kathryn
Phantom Angel — Handler, David
c The Phantom Bully (Illus. by Brown, Jeffrey) — Brown, Jeffrey
Phantom Effect — Aronovitz, Michael
Phantom Limb: Amputation, Embodiment, and Prosthetic Technology — Crawford, Cassandra S.
Phantom Limb — Palumbo, Dennis
c The Phantom of Nantucket — Keene, Carolyn
The Phantom Passage — Halter, Paul

The Phantom Punch: The Story behind Boxing's Most Controversial Bout — Sneddon, Rob
Phantom Terror: Political Paranoia and the Creation of the Modern State, 1789-1848 — Zamoyski, Adam
Phantom Terror: The Threat of Revolution and the Repression of Liberty 1789-1848 — Zamoyski, Adam
y Pharaoh's Daughter — Lester, Julius
y Pharrell — Saddleback Educational Publishing
c Pharrell Williams — Morreale, Marie
Phenomenology and Embodiment: Husserl and the Constitution of Subjectivity — Taipale, Joona
Phenomenology in Anthropology: A Sense of Perspective — Ram, Kalpana
Phenomenology of the Spirit — Herder, Johann Gottfried
c Phil Pickle (Illus. by Canby, Kelly) — Herzog, Kenny
The Philanthropic Revolution: An Alternative History of American Charity — Beer, Jeremy
Philanthropy and the Construction of Victorian Women's Citizenship: Lady Frederick Cavendish and Miss Emma Cons — Poole, Andrea Geddes
Philanthropy and Voluntary Action in the First World War — Grant, Peter
Philip Larkin: Life, Art and Love — Booth, James
Philip Roth: Fiction and Power — Hayes, Patrick
Philip Sparrow Tells All: Lost Essays by Samuel Steward, Writer, Professor, Tattoo Artist — Steward, Samuel
Philip Treacy: Hat Designer — Treacy, Philip
Philippe de Commynes: Memory, Betrayal, Text — Kleiman, Irit Ruth
Philippians — Petrus, Kevin A.
Philological and Historical Commentary on Ammianus Marcellinus XXVIII — Den Boeft, Jan
Philologie und Mehrsprachigkeit ed — Dembeck, Till
Philology: The Forgotten Origins of the Modern Humanities — Miller, Peter N.
Philology: The Forgotten Origins of the Modern Humanities — Turner, James (b. 1946-)
The Philosopher Kings — Walton, Jo
Philosopher of History — Voegelin, Eric
The Philosopher, the Priest, and the Painter: A Portrait of Descartes — Nadler, Steven
The Philosophical Life. Biography and the Crafting of Intellectual Identity in Late Antiquity — Urbano, A.P.
Philosophical Psychology in Arabic Thought and the Latin Aristotelianism of the 13th Century — Lopez-Farjeat, Luis Xavier
Philosophical Religions from Plato to Spinoza — Fraenkel, Carlos
Philosophical Toys — Medina, Susana
A Philosophical Walking Tour with C.S. Lewis: Why It Did Not Include Rome — Goetz, Stewart
Philosophie de l'insecte — Drouin, Jean-Marc
Philosophy and "Blade Runner" — Shanahan, Timothy
Philosophy and the Foundations of Dynamics — Sklar, Lawrence
Philosophy Between the Lines: The Lost History of Esoteric Writing — Melzer, Arthur M.
Philosophy in the Hellenistic and Roman Worlds — Adamson, Peter
Philosophy of Biology — Godfrey-Smith, Peter
A Philosophy of Emptiness — Watson, Gay
A Philosophy of Freedom — Svendsen, Lars
The Philosophy of Life and Death: Ludwig Klages and the Rise of a Nazi Biopolitics — Lebovic, Nitzan
The Philosophy of Poetry — Gibson, John
Philosophy of Religion: Towards a More Humane Approach — Cottingham, John
A Philosophy on Life, Family, and Growing Up — Hunter, Troy
Philosophy, Theory and History in Germany since 1945
Philosphy and Non-Philosophy — Laruelle, Francois
c Phineas L. MacGuire ... Gets Cooking! (Illus. by McDaniels, Preston) — Dowell, Frances O'Roark
Phishing for Phools: The Economics of Manipulation and Deception — Akerlof, George A.
Phobias: The Psychology of Irrational Fear — Milosevic, Irena
c Phoebe G. Green: A Passport to Pastries! (Illus. by Dreidemy, Joelle) — Hiranandani, Veera
c Phoebe G. Green: Farm Fresh Fun — Hiranandani, Veera
c Phoebe G. Green: Lunch Will Never Be the Same! — Hiranandani, Veera
Phoenix Claws and Jade Trees: Essential Techniques of Authentic Chinese Cooking — Kho, Kian Lam
y Phoenix Rising — Arielle, Phenice

c Phoenix Rising — Pearce, Bryony
c Phonograph — Salzmann, Mary Elizabeth
Photobiography: Photographic Self-Writing in Proust, Guibert, Ernaux, Mace — Kawakami, Akane
The Photograph and Australia — Annear, Judy
The Photographer and the President: Abraham Lincoln, Alexander Gardner, and the Images That Made a Presidency — Lowry, Richard
The Photographer's Wife — Joinson, Suzanne
Photographing the Female Form with Digital Infrared — Klein, Laurie
Photography and Exploration — Ryan, James R.
Photography and the Art of Chance — Kelsey, Robin
Photography of Personal Adornment — Liu, Robert K.
Photography's Orientalisms: New Essays on Colonial Representation — Behdad, Ali
Photojournalism and the Origins of the French Writer House Museum (1881-1914). — Emery, Elizabeth
c Photos Framed: A Fresh Look at the World's Most Memorable Photographs — Thomson, Ruth
c Phyllis Wong and the Return of the Conjuror — McSkimming, Geoffrey
c Phyllis Wong and the Waking of the Wizard — McSkimming, Geoffrey
Physica Sacra: Wunder, Naturwissenschaft und historischer Schriftsinn zwischen Mittelalter und Fruher Neuzeit — Roling, Bernd
Physical Chemistry for the Chemical Sciences — Chang, Raynod
Physical Expression on Stage and Screen: Using the Alexander Technique to Create Unforgettable Performances — Connington, Bill
The Physician, the Drinker, and the Drunk: Wine's Uses and Abuses in Late Medieval Natural Philosophy — Jaboulet-Vercherre, Azelina
The Physicist and the Philosopher: Einstein, Bergson, and the Debate That Changed Our Understanding of Time — Canales, Jimena
Physics: A Short History from Quintessence to Quarks — Heilbron, John L.
Physics for Gearheads: An Introduction to Vehicle Dynamics, Energy, and Power - with Examples from Motorsports — Beikmann, Randy
The Physics of Sorrow — Gospodinov, Georgi
The Physics of War: From Arrows to Atoms — Parker, Barry
Physics of Wind Instruments and Organ Pipes, 1100-2010: New and Extended Writings — Barbieri, Patrizio
Physics Project Lab — King, John
Phytomedicines, Herbal Drugs, and Poisons — Wyk, Ben-Erik van
Pianist in a Bordello — Erickson, Mike C.
The Piano: An Encyclopaedia, 2d ed. — Palmieri, Robert
The Piano Technique Demystified: Insights Into Problem Solving, 2d ed. — Stannard, Neil
Piccoli Grandi Bronzi — Arbeid, Barbara
Pickett's Charge at Gettysburg — Hessler, James A.
y The Pickle Index — Horowitz, Eli
Picnic in Provence: A Memoir with Recipes (Read by Bard, Elizabeth). Audiobook Review — Bard, Elizabeth
Picnic in Provence: A Memoir with Recipes — Bard, Elizabeth
The Picnic: Recipes and Inspiration from Blanket to Basket — Hanel, Marnie
Pictograph — Kwasny, Melissa
Picture Bride — Hsiung, C. Fong
Picture Titles: How and Why Western Paintings Acquired Their Names — Yeazell, Ruth Bernard
Picture Your Prosperity: Smart Money Moves to Turn Your Vision into Reality (Read by Rogin, Ellen). Audiobook Review — Rogin, Ellen
Picturebooks from 0 to 90: Riveting Reads — Bradnock, Marianne
Picturebooks: Representation and Narration — Kummerling-Meibauer, Bettina
Pictures of Fidelman — Malamud, Bernard
Picturing Frederick Douglass: An Illustrated Biography of the Nineteenth Century's Most Photographed American — Stauffer, John
Picturing People: The New State of the Art — Mullins, Charlotte
Picturing the Apocalypse: The Book of Revelation in the Arts over Two Millennia — O'Hear, Natasha
Pidgin-Knowledge: Wissen und Kolonialismus — Fischer-Tine, Harald
Pidgins and Creoles Beyond Africa-Europe Encounters — Buchstaller, Isabelle
The Pie at Night: in Search of the North at Play — Maconie, Stuart

c Pie for Chuck (Illus. by Schories, Pat) — Schories, Pat
Piece of Mind — Adelman, Michelle
c Pieces and Players (Read by Turpin, Bahni). Audiobook Review — Balliett, Blue
y Pieces and Players — Balliett, Blue
Pieces of My Mother — Cistaro, Melissa
y Pieces of Sky — Doyle, Trinity
y Pieces of Why — Going, K.L.
c The Pied Piper and the Wrong Song — North, Laura
c The Pied Piper of Hamelin (Illus. by Zwerger, Lisbeth) — Bell, Anthea
c Pier 21: Stories From Near and Far, 2d ed. — Renaud, Anne
c The Pier at the End of the World — Erickson, Paul
c The Pier at the End of the World (Illus. by Martinez, Andrew) — Erickson, Paul (b. 1952-)
Piero della Francesca: Artist and Man — Banker, James R.
Pierre Boulez — Barbedette, Sarah
Pierre-Esprit Radisson: The Collected Writings, vol. 2: The Port Nelson Relations, Miscellaneous Writings, and Related Documents — Warkentin, Germaine
Pierre Klossowski: The Pantomime of Spirits — Castanet, Herve
c Pierre the Maze Detective: The Search for the Stolen Maze Stone — Kamigaki, Hiro
Pierre Viret et la diffusion de la Reforme: Pense'e, action, contextes religieux — Crousaz, Karine
Piers Plowman: A Modern Verse Translation — Langland, William
Piet Mondrian: Life and Work — de Jong, Cees W.
Pietro Aretino: Subverting the System in Renaissance Italy — Waddington, Raymond B.
Piety and Persecution in the French Texts of England — Boulton, Maureen B.M.
c Pig and Pug (Illus. by Correll, Gemma) — Berry, Lynne
c Pig and Sheep (Illus. by Berg, Blake) — Breen, Mike
c Pig and Small (Illus. by Latimer, Alex) — Latimer, Alex
c A Pig Called Heather — Oulton, Harry
c Pig in Love (Illus. by Archbold, Tim) — French, Vivian
c Pig Is Big on Books (Illus. by Florian, Douglas) — Florian, Douglas
c Pig Kahuna: Who's That Pig? (Illus. by Sattler, Jennifer) — Sattler, Jennifer
y Pig Park — Martinez, Claudia Guadalupe
Pig Tales: An Omnivore's Quest for Sustainable Meat — Estabrook, Barry
c Pig the Fibber — Blabey, Aaron
c Pig the Pug — Blabey, Aaron
c Piglet Bo Is Not Scared! (Illus. by Van Hemeldonck, Tineke) — De Kockere, Geert
Pigmentocracies: Ethnicity, Race, and Color in Latin America — Telles, Edward E.
c Pigs — Murray, Julie
c Pigsticks and Harold and the Incredible Journey (Illus. by Milway, Alex) — Milway, Alex
c Pigsticks and Harold and the Tuptown Thief — Milway, Alex
y Pike — McGowan, Anthony
c Pilfer Academy: A School So Bad It's Criminal — Magaziner, Lauren
c Pilfer Academy: A School So Bad It's Criminal — Magziner, Lauren
Pilgrim and Preacher: The Audiences and Observant Spirituality of Friar Felix Fabri, 1437/8-1502 — Beebe, Kathryne
Pilgrims of the Air — Foster, John Wilson
Pilgrim's Progress — Bunyan, John
c The Pillars of Ponderay — Cummings, Lindsay
The Pillbox — Hughes, David
Pillow — Battershill, Andrew
y Pills and Starships — Millet, Lydia
The Pilo Traveling Show — Elliot, Will
c The Pilot and the Little Prince: The Life of Antoine de Saint-Exupery (Illus. by Sis, Peter) — Sis, Peter
The Pilots of Borealis — Nabhan, David
Pimp — Bruen, Ken
Pimping the Welfare System: Empowering Participants with Economic, Social, and Cultural Capital — Woodward, Kerry C.
Pinball, 1973 — Goossen, Ted
The Pinch — Stern, Steve
Pindar — Pindar
c Pine and the Winter Sparrow (Illus. by Vidal, Beatriz) — Lumbard, Alexis York
Pine Marten — Swenson, Wallace J.
The Pine Tar Game — Bondy, Filip

The Pine Tar Game: The Kansas City Royals, the New York Yankees, and Baseball's Most Absurd and Entertaining Controversy — Bondy, Filip
c Pineshish: La pie bleue (Illus. by Lavoie, Camille) — Noel, Michel
c Ping and Pong the Penguins (Illus. by Gangloff, Sylvaine) — Gangloff, Sylvaine
c Ping and Pong the Penguins — Gangloff, Sylviane
Ping-Pong Diplomacy: Ivor Montagu and the Astonishing Story Behind the Game that Changed the World — Griffin, Nicholas
c Ping Wants to Play — Gudeon, Adam
y Pink and Green Is the New Black — Greenwald, Lisa
Pink Globalization: Hello Kitty's Trek Across the Pacific — Yano, Christine R.
c Pink Is for Blobfish: Discovering the World's Perfectly Pink Animals (Illus. by DeGrand, David) — Keating, Jess
The Pink Pony — Cutter, Charles
y Pink: Pop Singer and Songwriter — Rowell, Rebecca
c Pink Toys, Yes or No — Picou, Lin
The Pink Trance Notebooks — Koestenbaum, Wayne
c Pinkalicious and the Pink Parakeet (Illus. by Kann, Victoria) — Kann, Victoria
'Pinkoes and Traitors': the BBC and the Nation, 1974-87 — Seaton, Jean
Pinkoes and Traitors: The BBC and the Nation, 1974-1987 — Seaton, Jean
Pinnacle Event — Clarke, Richard A.
c Pinocchio (Illus. by Lemaitre, Pascal) — McMullan, Kate
Pinocchio, Puppets and Modernity: The Mechanical Body — Pizzi, Katia
y Pinstripe Pride: The Inside Story of the New York Yankees — Appel, Marty
The Pioneer Gift: Explorations in Mission — Baker, Jonny
Pioneer Girl: The Annotated Autobiography — Hill, Pamela Smith
Pioneer Girl: The Annotated Autobiography of Laura Ingalls Wilder — Wilder, Laura Ingalls
Pioneer Performances: Staging the Frontier — Rebhorn, Matthew
The Pioneer Woman Cooks: Dinnertime; Comfort Classics... — Drummond, Ree
Pioneers of Neurobiology: My Brilliant Eccentric Heroes — Nicholls, John G.
Pioneers of the Blues Revival — Cushing, Steve
Pious Citizens: Reforming Zoroastrianism in India and Iran — Ringer, Monica M.
The Pious Sex: Catholic Constructions of Masculinity and Femininity in Belgium, c. 1800-1940 — Van Osselaer, Tine
c Pip Bartlett's Guide to Magical Creatures (Read by Morris, Cassandra). Audiobook Review — Pearce, Jackson
c Pip Bartlett's Guide to Magical Creatures (Illus. by Stiefvater, Maggie) — Pearce, Jackson
y Piper Green and the Fairy Tree (Illus. by Leng, Qin) — Potter, Ellen
y Piper Houdini: Apprentice of Coney Island — Herdling, Glenn
y The Piper — Weston, Danny
c Piper's First Show (Illus. by Franson, Leanne) — Hughes, Susan
c Pippa and Pelle in the Winter Snow (Illus. by Drescher, Daniela) — Drescher, Daniela
c Pippa Morgan's Diary (Illus. by Larsen, Kate) — Kelsey, Annie
c Pippi Won't Grow Up (Illus. by Nyman, Ingrid Vang) — Nunnally, Tiina
c Pipsie, Nature Detective: The Disappearing Caterpillar (Illus. by Bishop, Tracy) — DeDonato, Rick
c Pipsie, Nature Detective: The Disappearing Caterpillar (Illus. by Bishop, Tracy) — Dedonato, Rick
The Piracy Crusade: How the Music Industry's War on Sharing Destroys Markets and Erodes Civil Liberties — Sinnreich, Aram
Piranha — Cussler, Clive
c Piranhas — Murray, Julie
c The Pirate Code (Illus. by Hendrix, John) — Schulz, Heidi
Pirate Hunters: Treasure, Obsession, and the Search for a Legendary Pirate Ship (Read by Porter, Ray). Audiobook Review — Kurson, Robert
Pirate Hunters: Treasure, Obsession, and the Search for a Legendary Pirate Ship — Kurson, Robert
Pirate Math: Developing Mathematical Reasoning with Games and Puzzles — Serra, Michael
Pirate Music — Gamble, Miriam

c The Pirate Pie Ship (Illus. by Van Wyk, Rupert) — Guillain, Adam
c The Pirate Pie Ship — Guillain, Charlotte
c The Pirate Pig (Illus. by Meyer, Kerstin) — Funke, Cornelia
c The Pirate Pig (Illus. by Latsch, Oliver) — Meyer, Kerstin
c Pirate Ships — Tucker, Rosalyn
c Pirate Treasure (Illus. by Vaufrey, Delphine) — Miraucourt, Christophe
c Pirate Treasure — Tucker, Rosalyn
c Pirate, Viking and Scientist (Illus. by Chapman, Jared) — Chapman, Jared
c The Pirate Who's Back in Bunny Slippers (Illus. by Holden, Anthony) — Bondor-Stone, Annabeth
Pirate's Alley — Johnson, Suzanne
The Pirates and the Nightmaker — Norcliffe, James
c Pirates Are Stealing Our Cows — Guillain, Adam
c Pirates Are Stealing Our Cows — Remphry, Martin
c Pirates Aren't Afraid of the Dark! (Illus. by Edgson, Alison) — Powell-Tuck, Maudie
c The Pirate's Bed (Illus. by James, Matt) — Winstanley, Nicola
c Pirates Don't Drive Diggers (Illus. by Beedie, Duncan) — English, Alex
c Pirates in Pajamas (Illus. by Knight, Tom) — Crowe, Caroline
c The Pirate's Legacy (Illus. by Marnat, Annette) — Surget, Alain
c Pirate's Lullaby: Mutiny at Bedtime (Illus. by Bowers, Tim) — Wessels, Marcie
c A Pirate's Mother Goose — Sanders, Nancy I.
c Pirates of the Silver Coast (Illus. by Chantler, Scott) — Chantler, Scott
c The Pirates on Holiday (Illus. by Alder, Charlie) — Guillain, Charlotte
c The Pirates on Holiday — Guillain, Charlotte
c Piraye'nin Bir Gunu (Illus. by Ucbasaran, Deniz) — Sayman, Arslan
y Piri's Big All Black Dream (Illus. by Diaz, Jimmy) — Bell, Jared
PISA, Power, and Policy: The Emergence of Global Educational Governance — Meyer, Heinz-Dieter
The Pisces Affair — Auffenorde, Daco
Pitch Black — Onuora, Emy
Pitch by Pitch: My View of One Unforgettable Game — Gibson, Bob
Pitch Imperfect — Alden, Elise
The Pitt Rivers Museum: A World Within — O'Hanlon, Michael
c Pitter and Patter (Illus. by Morrison, Cathy) — Sullivan, Martha
A Pitying of Doves — Burrows, Steve
Pius IV and the Fall of the Carafa: Nepotism and Papal Authority in Counter-Reformation Rome — Pattenden, Miles
A Pius Man: A Holy Thriller — Finn, Declan
Pivot: The Art and Science of Reinventing Your Life — Markel, Adam
c Pizza Is the Best Breakfast: And Other Lessons I've Learned (Illus. by Lewis, Stevie) — Gutknecht, Allison
Place and Replace: Essays on Western Canada — Perry, Adele
Place Attachment: Advances in Theory, Methods and Applications — Manzo, Lynne C.
A Place Called Winter — Gale, Patrick
c A Place for Birds (Illus. by Bond, Higgins) — Stewart, Melissa
c A Place for Elijah (Illus. by Friar, Joanne) — Ruben, Kelly Easton
A Place for Humility: Whitman, Dickinson, and the Natural World — Gerhardt, Christine
A Place for Us — Evans, Harriet
y Place Hacking: Venturing Off Limits — Rosen, Michael J.
The Place I Live, the People I Know: Profiles from the Eastern Mediterranean — Mendel, Lori
c A Place in my Heart (Illus. by Relyea-Parr, Alison) — Grossnickle, Mary
Place-Making for the Imagination — Harney, Marion
Place of the Heart — Siguroardottir, Steinunn
The Place of the Poor in the Biblical Tradition — Anderson, Gary A.
c A Place to Call Home — Lawrence, Ellen
c A Place to Live (Illus. by Jernigan, Case) — Ryman, Kyla
c A Place to Live — Staniford, Linda
c Place Value (Illus. by Miller, Edward) — Adler, David A.
A Place We Knew Well — McCarthy, Susan Carol

c The Place Where You Live / El lugar donde vives (Illus. by Muraida, Thelma) — Luna, James
y Placebo Junkies — Carleson, J.C.
Places of the Heart: The Psychogeography of Everyday Life — Collin, Ellard
c Places We Go: A Kids' Guide to Community Buildings (Illus. by Haggerty, Tim) — Kreisman, Rachelle
Placing Faces: The Portrait and the English Country House in the Long Eighteenth Century — Perry, Gill
Placing Ukraine on the Map: Stepan Rudnytsky's Nation-Building Geography — Stebelsky, Ihor
Plague and Pestilence in Literature and Art — Crawford, Raymond
Plague and Public Health in Early Modern Seville — Bowers, Kristy Wilson
Plague Land — Syke, S.D.
Plague Land — Sykes, S.D.
c A Plague of Bogles (Read by Williams, Mandy). Audiobook Review — Jinks, Catherine
y A Plague of Bogles (Illus. by Watts, Sarah) — Jinks, Catherine
A Plague of Informers: Conspiracy and Political Trust in William III's England — Weil, Rachel
c A Plague of Unicorns — Yolen, Jane
Plagued, with Guilt — Brandt, Michael Jason
Plagues in World History — Aberth, John
Plain Dead — Miller, Emma
Plain Radical — Jensen, Robert
c Plan a Birthday Party. E-book Review — Watson, Stephanie
c Plan a Holiday Party. E-book Review — Braun, Eric
c Plan a Sleepover Party. E-book Review — Watson, Stephanie
c The Plan (Illus. by Lehman, Barbara) — Paul, Alison
c Plan an Outdoor Party. E-book Review — Braun, Eric
The Plan de San Diego: Tejano Rebellion, Mexican Intrigue — Harris, Charles H., III
c Plan, Prepare, Cook Series — Storey, Rita
Planck: Driven by Vision, Broken by War — Brown, Brandon R.
c Planes — Murray, Julie
Planes, Canes, and Automobiles: Connecting with Your Aging Parents through Travel — Grubb, Valerie M.
c Planes Go (Illus. by Light, Steve) — Light, Steve
c Planet Earth (Illus. by Wood, Gerald) — Channing, Margot
A Planet for Rent — Yoss
c Planet Gigantic: New World Home (Illus. by Halverson, David) — Grissom, Eric
c Planet Kindergarten (Illus. by Prigmore, Shane) — Ganz-Schmitt, Sue
c The Planet of Junior Brown — Hamilton, Virginia
The Planet Remade: How Geoengineering Could Change the World — Morton, Oliver
c The Planet Thieves — Krokos, Dan
c Planets — Riggs, Kate
c The Planets and the Solar System (Read by Sillers, Ruth). Audiobook Review — Green, Jen
c Planets Far from Earth — Graham, Ian
c Planets Near Earth — Graham, Ian
y The Planets: The Definitive Visual Guide to Our Solar System — Aderin-Pocock, Maggie
Plankton: Wonders of the Drifting World — Sardet, Christian
Planning Asian Cities: Risks and Resilience — Hamnett, Stephen
Planning Ideas That Matter: Livability, Territoriality, Governance, and Reflective Practice — Sanyal, Bishwapriya
Planning the Home Front: Building Bombers and Communities at Willow Run — Peterson, Sarah Jo
Plans and Views of Public Parks — Olmsted, Frederick Law
c The Plans I Have for You (Illus. by Brantley-Newton, Vanessa) — Parker, Amy
The Plant Lover's Guide to Epidemiums — Gregson, Sally
The Plant Lover's Guide to Ferns — Olsen, Sue
Plant Physics — Niklas, Karl
Plant Power — Atlas, Nava
Plant-Powered for Life — Palmer, Sharon
c Plant Reproduction — Buchanan, Shelly C.
Plant Sensing and Communication — Karban, Richard
Plantation Shudders — Byron, Ellen
Plantation Shuddersy — Byron, Ellen
c Planting My Values (Illus. by Thinkstock) — Powell, Lynn
Planting the Seeds of Algebra, 3-5: Explorations for the Upper Elementary Grades — Neagoy, Monica

c Planting the Wild Garden (Illus. by Halperin, Wendy Anderson) — Galbraith, Kathryn O.
Plants and the Human Brain — Kennedy, David O.
c Plants Feed Me — Rockwell, Lizzy
Plants from Pips: Pots of Plants for the Whole Family to Enjoy — Farrell, Holly
y Plants Vs. Meats: The Health, History, and Ethics of What We Eat — Hughes, Meredith
Plasma Physics: An Introduction — Fitzpatrick, Richard
Plastic Money: Constructing Markets for Credit Cards in Eight Postcommunist Countries — Guseva, Alya
Plastic Money: Constructing Markets for Credit Cards in Eight Postcommunist Countries — Rona-Tas, Akos
Plastic Reality: Special Effects, Technology, and the Emergence of 1970s Blockbuster Aesthetics — Turnock, Julie A.
Plateau Indian Ways with Words: The Rhetorical Tradition of the Tribes of the Inland Pacific Northwest — Monroe, Barbara
Plato and Pythagoreanism — Horky, Phillip Sydney
Plato at the Googleplex: Why Philosophy Won't Go Away — Goldstein, Rebecca Newberger
Plato: Laches — Hardy, Jorg
Platon: La mediation des emotions. L'education du thymos dans les dialogues — Renaut, Olivier
Platonic Dialogue and the Education of the Reader — Cotton, Anne K.
Platonic Drama and its Ancient Reception — Charalabopoulos, Nikos G.
Platonis Gorgias Leonardo Aretino interprete — Venier, Matteo
Plato's Account of Falsehood: A Study of the Sophist — Crivelli, Paolo
Plato's Animals: Gadflies, Horses, Swans, and Other Philosophical Beasts — Bell, Jeremy
Platypus (Illus. by Jackson, Mark) — Whiting, Sue
c Platypus Police Squad: Last Panda Standing — Krosoczka, Jarrett J.
c Platypuses: Web-Footed Billed Mammals — Hirsch, Rebecca E.
c Play (Illus. by Kang, Andrea) — Hutton, John
Play for Me — Keating, Celine
Play Golf Better Faster: The Classic Guide to Optimizing Your Performance and Building Your Best Fast — Barlis, Kalliope
c Play in the Garden: Fun Projects for Kids to Enjoy Outdoors (Illus. by Unka, Vasanti) — O'Neill, Sarah
Play Like Elton John: The Ultimate Piano Lesson — Harrison, Mark
y Play Me Backwards — Selzer, Adam
y Play On — Smith, Michelle
c Play with Your Food — Derrick, David G., Jr.
Players and Pawns: How Chess Builds Community and Culture — Fine, Gary Alan
The Players: Poems — Bialosky, Jill
c Playful Pigs from A to Z (Illus. by Lobel, Anita) — Lobel, Anita
c Playground Math — James, Dawn
The Playground Principle — Smat, David R.
y Playing a Part — Wilke, Daria
Playing against the House — Walsh, James D.
Playing before the Lord: The Life and Work of Joseph Haydn — Stapert, Calvin R.
Playing Dirty — Parker, C.L.
Playing Dirty — Snow, Tiffany
Playing for Keeps — Mello, Deborah Fletcher
Playing for the Commandant (Read by Foster, Emily). Audiobook Review — Zail, Suzy
y Playing for the Commandant — Zail, Suzy
Playing Hard — Scott, Melanie
Playing House in the American West: Western Women's Life Narratives, 1839-1987 — Halverson, Cathryn
Playing in the White: Black Writers, White Subjects — Li, Stephanie
c Playing Juliet — Wetzel, Joanne Stewart
y Playing Pro Baseball — Howell, Brian
c Playing Pro Basketball — Gitlin, Marty
y Playing Pro Football — Bowker, Paul
c Playing Pro Hockey — Hawkins, Jeff
Playing Scared: A History and Memoir of Stage Fright — Solovitch, Sara
Playing Scared — Solovitch, Sara
Playing The Canterbury Tales: The Continuations and Additions — Farnham, Andrew High
Playing to the Gallery: Helping Contemporary Art in Its Struggle to Be Understood — Perry, Grayson

Playing to Win: Raising Children in a Competitive Culture — Friedman, Hilary Levey
Playing with Fire — Mello, Deborah Fletcher
y Playing With Fire — Anderson-Dargatz, Gail
Playing With Fire — Gerritsen, Tess
Playing with Fire — Meader, Kate
y Playing with Fire — Anderson-Dargatz, Gail
Playing with Fire — Gerritsen, Tess
c Playing with Light and Shadows — Boothroyd, Jennifer
y Playing with Matches — Rosen, Suri
Playing with Scales: Piano - A Fresh Way to Practise Scales, Level One — Watson, Alistair
Playing with the Past: Digital Games and the Simulation of History — Kapell, Matthew Wilhelm
y Playlist for the Dead — Falkoff, Michelle
c Playtime — Lee, Fiona
Pleasantville — Locke, Attica
c Please (Illus. by Galloway, Fhiona) — Hegarty, Patricia
Please Don't Bite the Baby: Keeping Your Kids and Your Dogs Safe and Happy Together — Edwards, Lisa
y Please Excuse This Poem: 100 New Poets for the Next Generation — Lauer, Brett Fletcher
Please Forward: How Blogging Reconnected New Orleans after Katrina — Joyce, Cynthia
Please Listen Up Parents — Colan, Cameron
c Please, Mr. Panda (Illus. by Antony, Steve) — Antony, Steve
Please, Mr Postman — Johnson, Alan
c Please, Open This Book! (Illus. by Forsythe, Matthew) — Lehrhaupt, Adam
c Please Share, Aphrodite! — Holub, Joan
Please Stop Helping Us: How Liberals Make It Harder for Blacks to Succeed — Riley, Jason L.
c Please Take Jake! (Illus. by Cartwright, Amy) — Powell, Marie
Please Talk to Me — Heker, Liliana
A Pleasure and a Calling (Read by Page, Michael). Audiobook Review — Hogan, Phil
A Pleasure and a Calling — Hogan, Phil
The Pleasure of Reading: 43 Writers on the Discovery of Reading and the Books that Inspired Them — Fraser, Antonia
The Pleasures of Reading in an Age of Distraction — Jacobs, Alan
A Pledge of Better Times — Porter, Margaret
Plenish: Juices to Boost, Cleanse and Heal — Rosen, Kara M.L.
Plenty Ladylike — McCaskill, Claire
Plenty More: Vibrant Vegetable Cooking from London's Ottolenghi — Ottolenghi, Yotam
Plenus litteris Lucanus: Zur Rezeption der horazischen Oden und Epoden in Lucans Bellum Civile — Gross, Daniel
Pleomorph — Mann, John Paul
Plessner in Wiesbaden — Allert, Tilman
y Plessy v. Ferguson — Hillstrom, Laurie Collier
Plexus — Wilcoxson, Troy T.
The Plimsoll Line — Gracia Armendariz, Juan
Pliny the Younger: A Life in Roman Letters — Winsbury, Rex
Pliny the Younger: Epistles Book II — Whitton, Christopher
Plotinus, Self and the World — Mortley, Raoul
y Plotted: A Literary Atlas — Harmon, Daniel
The Plough that Broke the Steppes: Agriculture and Environment on Russia's Grasslands, 1700-1914 — Moon, David
The Ploughmen — Zupan, Kim
Pluck This — Hartling, Julia
Plucked: A History of Hair Removal — Herzig, Rebecca M.
The Plum in the Golden Vase — Roy, David Tod
c Plum Pudding and Paper Moons — Millard, Glenda
Plunder of the Ancients: A True Story of Betrayal, Redemption, and an Undercover Quest to Recover Sacred Native American Artifacts — Schroeder, Lucinda Delaney
Pluralism: The Future of Religion — Rose, Kenneth
Plutarchi Chaeronensis Vita Dionis et Comparatio et de Bruto ac Dione Iucidium Guarino Veronensi Interprete — Pade, Marianne
c Pluto (Read by Merriman, Scott). Audiobook Review — Palacio, R.J.
c Pluto: The Icy Dwarf Planet — Glaser, Chaya
c Pluto the Starfish: An Undersea Tale for Children 1 to 101 (Illus. by Raines, Malinda) — Anderson, Bonnie M.
Plutocrats United — Hasen, Richard L.
Pnin — Nabokov, Vladimir

c Poached — Gibbs, Stuart
c Pocahontas and the Powhatans — Donaghey, Reese
c A Pocket Full of Murder — Anderson, R.J.
A Pocket Guide to Sharks of the World (Illus. by Dando, Marc) — Ebert, David A.
The Pocket Wife — Crawford, Susan
The Poe Consequence — Steinbaum, Keith
c The Poe Estate — Shulman, Polly
Poem Central: Word Journeys with Readers and Writers — McPhillips, Shirley
c A Poem in Your Pocket (Illus. by Karas, G. Brian) — McNamara, Margaret
c The Poem That Will Not End: Fun with Poetic Forms and Voices — Graham, Joan Bransfield
Poems — Blake, William
The Poems and Letters of Tullia d'Aragona and Others — Hairston, Julia L.
Poems, Emblems, and the Unfortunate Florinda — Pulter, Lady Hester
Poems from the Rio Grande — Anaya, Rudolfo
c Poems in the Attic (Illus. by Zunon, Elizabeth) — Grimes, Nikki
c Poems in the Attic (Illus. by Zunon, Elizabeth) — Grimes, Nikki
The Poems of T.S. Eliot, 2 vols. — Eliot, T.S.
The Poems of T.S. Eliot, vol. 2: Practical Cats and Further Verses — Eliot, T.S.
Poesie Latine a Haute Voix (1500-1700). — Smeesters, Aline
y Poet Anderson ... of Nightmares — Delonge, Tom
The Poet Edgar Allan Poe: Alien Angel — McGann, Jerome
A Poet of the Invisible World — Golding, Michael
The Poet Resigns: Poetry in a Difficult World — Archambeau, Robert
The Poet, the Lion, Talking Pictures, El Farolito, a Wedding in St. Roch, the Big Box Store, the Warp in the Mirror, Spring, Midnights, Fire & All — Wright, C.D.
c Poet: The Remarkable Story of George Moses Horton (Illus. by Tate, Don) — Tate, Don
Poetic License — Fontinel-Gibran, R.J.
Poetic Trespass: Writing between Hebrew and Arabic in Israel/Palestine — Levy, Lital
The Poetic Voices of John Gower: Politics and Personae in the — Irvin, Matthew W.
The Poetics and Politics of Youth in Milton's England — Greteman, Blaine
Poetics in a New Key: Interviews and Essays — Perloff, Marjorie
Poetics of Character: Transatlantic Encounters, 1700-1900 — Manning, Susan
c Poetics of Character: Transatlantic Encounters, 1700-1900 — Philbrick, Rodman
The Poetics of Early Russian Literature — Likhachev, D.S.
The Poetics of Impudence and Intimacy in the Age of Pushkin — Peschio, Joe
The Poetics of Masculinity in Early Modern Italy and Spain — Milligan, Gerry
The Poetics of Phantasia. Imagination in Ancient Aesthetics — Sheppard, Anne D.R.
The Poetics of Piracy: Emulating in English Literature — Fuchs, Barbara
The Poetics of Sight — Lang, Peter
The Poetics of Sleep: From Aristole to Nancy — Wortham, Simon Morgan
Poetics of the Incarnation: Middle English Writing and the Leap of Love — Cervone, Cristina Maria
Poetik des Satyrspiels — Lammle, Rebecca
Poetika slikanice — Haramija, Dragica
Poetiken des Pazifiks
Poetry: A Survivor's Guide — Yakich, Mark
Poetry and Film: Artistic Kinship between Arsenii and Andrei Tarkovsky — Blair, Kitty Hunter
Poetry and Identity in Quattrocento Naples — Soranzo, Matteo
Poetry and Memory in Karaite Prayer: The Liturgical Poetry of the Karaite Poet Moses ben Abraham Dar'I — Yeshaya, Joachim J.M.S.
Poetry for the Rest of Us (Read by Goldenman, Michael). Audiobook Review — Anderson, Benny
Poetry from the Kings' Sagas 1: From Mythical Times to c. 1035 — Whaley, Diana
Poetry Is Useless (Illus. by Nilsen, Anders) — Nilsen, Anders
Poetry Notebook: Reflections on the Intensity of Language — James, Clive
The Poetry of Erasmus Darwin: Enlightened Spaces, Romantic Times — Priestman, Martin
The Poetry of John Milton — Teskey, Gordon

The Poetry of Victorian Scientists: Style, Science and Nonsense — Brown, Daniel (b. 1961-)
Poetry of Witness: The Tradition in English 1500-001 — Forche, Carolyn
The Poetry of Yehuda Amichai — Amichai, Yehuda
Poets and Princes: The Panegyric Poetry of Johannes Michael Nagonius — Gwynne, Paul
Poets and the Peacock Dinner: The Literary History of a Meal — McDiarmid, Lucy
A Poet's Dublin — Boland, Eavan
Poets In Their Youth — Simpson, Eileen
The Poet's Mind: The Psychology of Victorian Poetry 1830-1870 — Tate, Gregory
A Poet's Reich: Politics and Culture in the George Circle — Lane, M.S.
The Poet's Tale: Chaucer and The Year That Made the Canterbury Tales — Strohm, Paul
c Poet's Workshop — Macken, JoAnn Early
c Poet's Workshop Series: Read, Recite, and Write Nursery Rhymes — Macken, JoAnn Early
The Point Is — Eisenberg, Lee
Point of Balance — Jurado, J.G.
Point of Control — Sellers, L.J.
Point of Origin: Gobekli Tepe and the Spiritual Matrix for the World's Cosmologies — Scranton, Laird
The Point of Vanishing: A Memoir of Two Years in Solitude — Axelrod, Howard
Points aveugles de la nature: La rationalite scientifique medievale face a l'occulte, l'attraction magnetique et l'horreur du vide — Weill-Parot, Nicolas
Points of Departure — Dean, Pamela
Points of Inspiration: An Artist's Journey with Painting and Photography — Brook, LeeAnn
The Poison Artist — Moore, Jonathan
c Poison Dart Frogs — Murray, Julie
Poison Ivy — Riggs, Cynthia
y Poison Spring — Boggs, Johnny D.
y Poisoned Apples: Poems for You, My Pretty — Heppermann, Christine
y Poisoned Honey: A Story of Mary Magdalene — Gormley, Beatrice
The Poisoning Angel — Teule, Jean
A Poisonous Thorn in Our Hearts: Sudan and South Sudan's Bitter and Incomplete Divorce — Copnall, James
Poison's Dark Works in Renaissance England — Wilson, Miranda
Pokergeist — Cash, Michael Phillip
c The Poky Little Puppy — Lowrey, Janette Sebring
Pola Negri: Hollywood's First Femme Fatale — Kotowski, Mariusz
Poland, Holy War, and the Piast Monarchy, 1100-1230 — Guttner-Sporzynski, Darius von
Poland in the Modern World: Beyond Martyrdom — Porter-Szucs, Brian
Poland's War on Radio Free Europe, 1950-1989 — Machcewicz, Pawel
c Polar: A Photicular Book — Kainen, Dan
c Polar: A Photicular Book — Kaufmann, Carol
c Polar Bear's Underwear (Illus. by Tupera, Tupera) — Tupera, Tupera
c Polar Bear's Underwear — Tupera Tupera (firm)
c Polar Lands — Gray, Leon
The Polar North: Ways of Speaking, Ways of Belonging — Leonard, Stephen Pax
c Polar Regions (Illus. by Sill, John) — Sill, Cathryn
y Polaris — Arnett, Mindee
Polarized America: The Dance of Ideology and Unequal Riches — McCarty, Nolan
Polemical Austria: The Rhetorics of National Identity - From Empire to the Second Republic — Bushell, Anthony
Policing America's Empire: The United States, the Philippines, and the Rise of the Surveillance State — McCoy, Alfred W.
Policing and Prosecuting Sexual Assault: Inside the Criminal Justice System — Spohn, Cassia
Policing Sexuality: The Mann Act and the Making of the FBI — Pliley, Jessica R.
Policing the Factory: Theft, Private Policing and the Law in Modern England — Godfrey, Barry
Policing the Markets: Inside the Black Box of Securities Enforcement — Williams, James W.
Policing Wars: On Military Intervention in the Twenty-First Century — Holmqvist, Caroline
Polish Cinema in a Transnational Context — Mazierska, Ewa
A Polish Doctor in the Nazi Camps: My Mother's Memories of Imprisonment, Immigration, and a Life Remade — Rylko-Bauer, Barbara

Polish Roots, 2d ed. — Chorzempa, Rosemary A.
Polish vs. American Courtroom Discourse: Inquisitorial and Adversarial Procedures of Witness Examination in Criminal Trials — Bednarek, Grazyna Anna
Political Action in Vaclav Havel's Thought: The Responsibility of Resistance — Popescu, Delia
Political Aid and Arab Activism: Democracy Promotion, Justice, and Representation — Carapico, Sheila
Political Animals: How Our Stone-Age Brain Gets in the Way of Smart Politics — Shenkman, Rick
Political Autobiographies and Memories in Antiquity: A Brill Companion — Marasco, Gabriele
Political Beethoven — Mathew, Nicholas
A Political Biography of Samuel Johnson — Hudson, Nicholas
Political Communication and Political Culture in England 1558-1688 — Shapiro, Barbara J.
The Political Consequences of Motherhood — Greenlee, Jill S.
The Political Cult of the Dead in Ukraine: Traditions and Dimensions from Soviet Time to Today
Political Descent: Malthus, Mutualism, and the Politics of Evolution in Victorian England — Hale, Piers J.
A Political Ecology of Youth and Crime — France, Alan
Political Economies of Empire in Early Modern Mediterranean: The Decline of Venice and the Rise of England, 1450-1700 — Fusaro, Maria
The Political Economy of Human Happiness: How Voters' Choices Determine the Quality of Life — Radcliff, Benjamin
The Political Economy of Iran under the Qajars: Society, Politics, Economics and Foreign Relations 1796-1936 — Amirahmadi, Hooshang
The Political Economy of State-Owned Enterprises in China and India — Yi-Chong, Xu
The Political Economy of Tanzania: Decline and Recovery — Lofchie, Michael F.
The Political Economy of Violence against Women — True, Jacqui
Political Essay on the Island of Cuba — Humboldt, Alexander von
Political Fiction — Levene, Mark
Political Gastronomy: Food and Authority in the English Atlantic World — LaCombe, Michael A.
Political History of Guinea since World War Two — Camara, Mohamed Saliou
Political Illiberalism: A Defense of Freedom — Simpson, Peter L.P.
Political Imprisonment and the Irish, 1912-1921 — Murphy, William
A Political Life in Ming China: A Grand Secretary and His Times — Dardess, John W.
Political Order and Political Decay: From the Industrial Revolution to the Globalisation of Democracy — Fukuyama, Francis
Political Order and Political Decay: From the Industrial Revolution to the Globalization of Democracy — Fukuyama, Francis
Political Power in Medieval Gwynedd: Governance and the Welsh Princes — Stephenson, David
Political Science, 4 vols. — Vanaik, Achin
Political Science, vol. 2: Indian Democracy — Suri, K.C.
Political Science, vol. 3: India Political Thought — Datta, Pradip Kumar
Political Science, vol. 4: India Engages the World — Behera, Navnita Chadha
A Political Theology of Climate Change — Northcott, Michael S.
The Political Thought of Elizabeth Cady Stanton — Davis, Sue
The Political World of Bob Dylan: Freedom and Justice, Power and Sin — Taylor, Jeff
The Political Writings, vol. 2: The Political Regime and Summary of Plato's Laws — Alfarabi
Politically Homeless: A Five-Year Odyssey across Three Continents — Terzian, Mary
Politics and Foreign Policy in the Age of George I, 1714-1727 — Black, Jeremy
Politics and Ideology in Children's Literature — Keyes, Marian Therese
Politics and Letters: Interviews with New Left Review — Williams, Raymond
Politics and Piety: Baptist Social Reform in America, 1770-1860 — Menikoff, Aaron
The Politics and Poetics of Contemporary English Tragedy — Carney, Sean

The Politics and Poetics of Sor Juana Ines de la Cruz — Thomas, George Antony
Politics and the Imagination — Geuss, Raymond
Politics, Faith, and the Making of American Judaism — Adams, Peter
Politics in Color and Concrete: Socialist Materialities and the Middle Class in Hungary — Fehervary, Krisztina
The Politics of Academic Autonomy in Latin America — Beigel, Fernanda
The Politics of Accountability in Southeast Asia: The Dominance of Moral Ideologies — Rodan, Garry
The Politics of Deception: JFK's Secret Decisions on Vietnam, Civil Rights, and Cuba — Sloyan, Patrick J.
The Politics of Dialogic Imagination: Power and Popular Culture in Early Modern Japan — Hirano, Katsuya
The Politics of Energy Dependency: Ukraine, Belarus, and Lithuania between Domestic Oligarchs and Russian Pressure — Balmaceda, Margarita M.
The Politics of Evangelical Identity: Local Churches and Partisan Divides in the United States and Canada — Bean, Lydia
The Politics of Expertise — Turner, Stephen P.
The Politics of Fashion in Eighteenth-Century America — Haulman, Kate
The Politics of Female Households: Ladies-in-Waiting across Early Modern Europe — Akkerman, Nadine
The Politics of Giving in the Viceroyalty of Rio de la Plata: Donors, Lenders, Subjects, and Citizens — Grieco, Viviana L.
The Politics of Giving in the Viceroyalty of the Rio de la Plata: Donors, Lenders, Subjects, and Citizens — Grieco, Viviana L.
The Politics of Industrial Collaboration during World War II: Ford France, Vichy and Nazi Germany — Horn, Martin
The Politics of Industrial Collaboration during World War II: Ford France, Vichy and Nazi Germany — Imlay, Talbot
The Politics of Irony in American Modernism — Stratton, Matthew
The Politics of Judicial Independence in the UK's Changing Constitution — Gee, Graham
The Politics of Language and Nationalism in Modern Central Europe — Kamusella, Tomasz
The Politics of Love: Sexuality, Gender, and Marriage in Syrian Television Drama — Joubin, Rebecca
The Politics of Nation-Building: Making Co-Nationals, Refugees and Minorities — Mylonas, Harris
The Politics of Prohibition: American Governance and the Prohibition Party, 1869-1933 — Andersen, Lisa M.F.
The Politics of Race in Panama: Afro-Hispanic and West Indian Literary Discourses of Contention — Watson, Sonja Stephenson
The Politics of Religion in Early Modern France — Bergin, Joseph
Politics of Security: British and West German Protest Movements and the Early Cold War, 1945-1970 — Nehring, Holger
The Politics of Sorrow: Families, Victims, and the Micro-Organization of Youth Homicide — Martin, Daniel D.
The Politics of Species: Reshaping Our Relationships with Other Animals — Corbey, Raymond
The Politics of State Feminism: Innovation in Comparative Research — Mazur, Amy G.
The Politics of the Black Sea Region: EU Neighbourhood, Conflict Zone or Future Security Community? — Weaver, Carol
The Politics of Time and Youth in Brand India: Bargaining with Capital — Kapur, Jyotsna
The Politics of Washing: Real Life in Venice — White, Paul
The Politics of Wine in Britain: A New Cultural History — Ludington, Charles
The Politics of Wounds: Military Patients and Medical Power in the First World War — Carden-Coyne, Ana
Politik und Versammlung im Fruhmittelalter
Politisierung der Kunst: Avantgarde und US-Kunstwelt — Hieber, Lutz
Polity and Ecology in Formative Period Coastal Oaxaca — Joyce, Arthur A.
Pollution and Religion in Ancient Rome — Lennon, J.L.
Polycentric Monarchies: How Did Early Modern Spain and Portugal Achieve and Maintain a Global Hegemony? — Cardim, Pedro

The Polygamous Wives Writing Club: From the Diaries of Mormon Pioneer Women — Harline, Paula Kelly
Polygamy in Primetime: Media, Gender, and Politics in Mormon Fundamentalism — Bennion, Janet
c Pom Pom Panda Gets the Grumps (Illus. by Henn, Sophy) — Henn, Sophy
The Pomegranate Lady and Her Sons — Taraghi, Goli
y Pompeii — Gimpel, Diane Marczely
c A Pony for Christmas — Pettersen, Bev
c Poo and Puke Eaters of the Animal World — Race, Jody Sullivan
c Poo in the Zoo (Illus. by Grey, Ada) — Smallman, Steve
c Poo in the Zoo! — Smallman, Steve
c Pookie Pop Plays Hide-and-Seek: A Tiny Tab Book (Illus. by Ho, Jannie) — Crow, Nosy
c Pookie Pop Plays Hide-and-Seek (Illus. by Ho, Jannie)
c Pookins Gets Her Way (Illus. by Munsinger, Lynn) — Lester, Helen
c Pool (Illus. by Lee, JiHyeon) — Lee, JiHyeon
c Poop and Puke Eaters of the Animal World — Rake, Jody Sullivan
c Poop-di-doop! (Illus. by Blake, Stephanie) — Blake, Stephanie
c Poop Fountain! — Angleberger, Tom
The Poor and the Perfect: The Rise of Learning in the Franciscan Order, 1209-1310 — Senocak, Neslihan
The Poor Children — Ford, April L.
Poor Man's Feast: Love Story of Comfort, Desire, and the Art of Simple Cooking — Altman, Elissa
Poor Relief in England, 1350-1600 — McInton, Marjorie Keniston
Poor Tom: Living "King Lear" — Palfrey, Simon
Poor Your Soul: A Memoir — Ptacin, Mira
The Poorer Nationa: A Possible History of the Global South
The Poorer Nations: A Possible History of the Global South — Prashad, Vijay
Pop Culture Places: An Encyclopedia of Places in American Popular Culture — Knight, Gladys L.
Pop Goes the Avant-Garde: Experimental Theater in Contemporary China — Ferrari, Rossella
c Pop Goes the Circus! (Illus. by Klise, M. Sarah) — Klise, Kate
Pop Goes the Weasel — Arlidge, M.J.
Pop Grenade: From Public Enemy to Pussy Riot, Despatches from Musical Frontlines — Collin, Matthew
c Pop of the Bumpy Mummy (Illus. by Cummings, Troy) — Cummings, Troy
Pop, Politik und Propaganda: Das Amerika Haus Berlin im Wandel der Zeit — Hiller von Gaertringen, Hans Georg
Pop-Rock Music: Aesthetic Cosmopolitanism in Late Modernity — Rgev, Motti
Pop-Rock Music: Aesthetic Cosmopolitanism in Late Modernity — Roger, Motti
Pop Sonnets: Shakespearean Spins on Your Favorite Songs — Didriksen, Erik
c The Pop Star Pirates (Illus. by Chernett, Dan) — Pearson, Maggie
c Pop-up New York (Illus. by Maizels, Jennie) — Maizels, Jennie
The Popcorn Astronauts: And Other Biteable Rhymes (Illus. by Rankin, Joan) — Ruddell, Deborah
The Pope and Mussolini: The Secret History of Pius XI and the Rise of Fascism in Europe — Kertzer, David I.
Pope Francis among the Wolves: The Inside Story of a Revolution — Politi, Marco
Pope Francis: His Life and Thought — Aguilar, Mario I.
Pope Francis' Little Book of Wisdom: The Essential Teachings — Assaf, Andrea
Pope Francis' Revolution of Tenderness and Love: Theological and Pastoral Perspectives — Kasper, Walter
Pope Francis: The Last Pope? Money, Masons and Occultism in the Decline of the Catholic Church — Zagami, Leo Lyon
c Pope Francis: The Story of Our Pope (Illus. by Carthaigh, Lir Mac) — Travers, Ailis
Pope Francis: The Struggle for the Soul of Catholicism, 2d ed. — Vallely, Paul
Pope Francis: Tradition in Transition — Faggioli, Massimo
Pope Francis: Untying the Knots
Pope Gregory X and the Crusades — Baldwin, Philip B.
The Pope's Daughter — Fo, Dario
POPism: The Warhol Sixties — Warhol, Andy

Popology — *English, Timothy*
c Poppy Cat — *Acton, Sara*
y Poppy in the Field — *Hooper, Mary*
c Poppy Pym and the Pharaoh's Curse — *Wood, Laura*
c Poppy the Pirate Dog and the Missing Treasure (Illus. by Phillips, Mike) — *Kessler, Liz*
y Popular: A Memoir: Vintage Wisdom for a Modern Geek — *van Wagenen, Maya*
Popular Economics: What the Rolling Stones, "Downton Abbey," and LeBron James Can Teach You about Economics — *Tamny, John*
Popular History and Fiction: The Myth of August the Strong in German Literature, Art and Media — *Brook, Madeleine*
Popular Mechanics Robots: A New Age of Bionics, Drones and Artificial Intelligence — *Wilson, Daniel H.*
Popular Muslim Reactions to the Franks in the Levant, 1097-1291 — *Mallet, Alex*
Popular Muslim Reactions to the Franks in the Levant, 1097-1291 — *Mallett, Alex*
Popular Piano Solos for All Piano Methods — *Nyberg, Jason*
Popular: The Ups and Downs of Online Dating from the Most Popular Girl in New York City — *Urasek, Lauren*
c The Popularity Papers: The Less-than-Hidden Secrets and Final Revelations of Lydia Goldblatt and Julie Graham-Chang — *Ignatow, Amy*
y The Popularity Project — *Zeng, Joddie*
c The Popularity Spell — *Gallagher, Toni*
c Popularity Takeover — *de la Cruz, Melissa*
Popularizing Anti-Semitism in Early Modern Spain and Its Empire: Francisco de Torrejoncillo and the Centinela contra Judios 1674 — *Soyer, Francois*
Populating the Barrera: Spanish Immigration Efforts in Colonial Louisiana — *Din, Gilbert C.*
Population Control — *Marrs, Jim*
Population Infographics — *Oxlade, Chris*
Population Wars — *Graffin, Greg*
Populist Cartoons: An Illustrated History of the Third-Party Movement in the 1890s — *Miller, Robert Worth*
Populist Collaborators: The Ilchinhoe and the Japanese Colonization of Korea, 1896-1910 — *Moon, Yumi*
The Porcelain Thief — *Hsu, Huan*
y The Porcupine of Truth — *Konigsberg, Bill*
Porous City: A Cultural History of Rio de Janeiro — *Carvalho, Bruno*
Porphyry in Fragments: Reception of an Anti-Christian Text in Late Antiquity — *Magny, Ariane*
c The Port Chicago 50: Disaster, Mutiny, and the Fight for Civil Rights (Read by Hoffman, Dominic). Audiobook Review — *Sheinkin, Steve*
y The Port Chicago 50: Disaster, Mutiny, and the Fight for Civil Rights — *Sheinkin, Steve*
c The Port Chicago 50: Disaster, Mutiny, and the Fight for Civil Rights — *Shenkin, Steve*
Port Cities and Global Legacies: Hardcover Urban Identity, Waterfront Work, and Radicalism — *Mah, Alice*
Portable Dad: Stuff to Know Without the Lecture — *Palmer, Ocean*
y The Portable Veblen — *McKenzie, Elizabeth*
Portage: A Family, a Canoe, and the Search for the Good Life — *Leaf, Sue*
'The Portals of Sheol' and Other Poems — *Christensen, Bryce*
Portlandia — *Amidsen, Fred*
Portrait inside My Head — *Lopate, Phillip*
Portrait of a Castrato: Politics, Patronage and Music in the Life of Atto Melani — *Freitas, Roger*
Portrait of a Man Known as Il Condottiere — *Perec, Georges*
Portrait of a Secret Agent — *Tamman, Tina*
A Portrait of America: The Demographic Perspective — *Iceland, John*
Portraits at an Exhibition: A Novel — *Horrigan, Patrick E.*
Portraits: John Berger on Artists — *Berger, John*
Portraits of a Mature God: Choices in Old Testament Theology — *McEntire, Mark*
y Portraits of Celina — *Whiting, Sue*
Portraying the Prince in the Renaissance: The Humanist Depiction of Rulers in Historiographical and Biographical Texts — *Lee, Rena*
Ports of Recall — *Lee, Rena*
Portuguese, Dutch, and Chinese in Maritime Asia, c. 1585-1800 — *Souza, George Bryan*
The Poser — *Rubin, Jacob*

y Positive — *Wellington, David*
The Positive Case for Negative Campaigning — *Mattes, Kyle*
Positive Pollutions and Cultural Toxins: Waste and Contamination in US Ethnic Literatures — *Gamber, John Blair*
y Positive: Surviving My Bullies, Finding Hope, and Living to Change the World — *Rawl, Paige*
y Positively Beautiful — *Mills, Wendy*
Possession of a Highlander — *Martin, Madeline*
The Possibilities — *Hemmings, Kaui Hart*
Possibilities of Perception — *Church, Jennifer*
y The Possibility of Now — *Culbertson, Kim*
A Possibility of Violence — *Mishani, D.A.*
c A Possum's Tail (Illus. by Barrow, Alex) — *Dawnay, Gabby*
Post- and Transhumanism: An Introduction — *Ranisch, Robert*
Post-Colonial Germany
Post-Communist Specters: Polish Theatre in the Twenty-First Century — *Illakowicz, Krystyna Lipinska*
The Post-Dictatorship Generation in Argentina, Chile, and Uruguay: Collective Memory and Cultural Production — *Ros, Ana*
Post-Ethical Society: The Iraq War, Abu Ghraib, and the Moral Failure of the Secular — *Porpora, Douglas V.*
Post-Exoticism in Ten Lessons, Lesson Eleven — *Volodine, Antoine*
Post-Islamism: The Changing Faces of Political Islam — *Bayat, Asef*
Post-Panslavismus: Slavizitat, Slavische Idee und Antislavismus im 20. und 21. Jahrhundert — *Gasior, Agnieszka*
The Post-Racial Mystique: Media and Race in the Twenty-First Century — *Squires, Catherine R.*
Post-Roman Transitions: Christian and Barbarian Identities in the Early Medieval West — *Pohl, Walter*
Post-Soul Satire: Black Identity after Civil Rights — *Maus, Derek C.*
Post-Traumatic Church Syndrome: A Memoir of Humor and Healing in 30 Religions — *Riley, Reba*
Post-TV: Piracy, Cord-cutting, and the Future of Television — *Strangelove, Michael*
Post-war Japan as a Sea Power: Imperial Legacy, Wartime Experience and the Making of a Navy — *Patalano, Alessio*
Post-Westerns: Cinema, Region, West — *Campbell, Neil*
The Postage Due Stamps of Zanzibar 1875-1964: The Stamps, the Covers and Their Story — *Griffith-Jones, John*
Postal Censorship in Finland 1914-1918 — *Quinby, Roger P.*
Postal Culture: Writing and Reading Letters in Post-Unification Italy — *Romani, Gabriella*
The Postal History of the Two-Phased Italian Occupation of South-East France 1940-1943 — *Trapnell, David*
The Postal History of the Type Sage Issue of France 1876-1900 — *Kelly, Peter A.*
Postal Pleasures: Sex, Scandal, and Victorian Letters — *Thomas, Kate*
PostCapitalism: A Guide to Our Future — *Mason, Paul (b. 1960-)*
Postcards from Stanland — *Mould, David H.*
Postcards from the Past — *Willett, Marcia*
Postcards from the Rio Bravo Border: Picturing the Place, Placing the Picture, 1900s-1950s — *Arreola, Daniel D.*
Postcolonial Artists and Global Aesthetics — *Adesokan, Akin*
Postcolonial Criticism and Representations of African Dictatorship: The Aesthetics of Tyranny — *Bishop, Cecile*
Postcolonial Fiction and Sacred Scripture: Rewriting the Divine? — *Qadiri, Sura*
Postcolonial Germany: Memories of Empire in a Decolonized Nation — *Schilling, Britta*
The Postcolonial Museum: The Arts of Memory and the Pressures of History — *Chambers, Iain*
The Postcolonial Unconscious. — *Lazarus, Neil*
The Postdoctoral Experience Revisited — *National Research Council (U.S.). Committee to Review the State of Postdoctoral Experience in Scientists and Engineers*
Posthumous Love: Eros and the Afterlife in Renaissance England — *Targoff, Ramie*
The Postman Always Purls Twice — *Canadeo, Anne*

Postmodern Utopias and Feminist Fictions — *Wagner-Lawlor, Jennifer A.*
Postnarrativist Philosophy of Historiography — *Kuukkanen, Jouni-Matti*
Poststructuralism and Critical Theory's Second Generation — *Schrift, Alan D.*
The Postwar Legacy of Appeasement: British Foreign Policy since 1945 — *Hughes, R. Gerald*
Postwar Renoir: Film and the Memory of Violence — *Davis, Colin*
c Posy the Puppy — *Clarke, Jane*
Pot Shards: Fragments of a Life Lived in CIA, the White House, and the Two Koreas — *Gregg, Donald P.*
The Pot Thief Who Studied Georgia O'Keeffe: A Pot Thief Mystery — *Orenduff, J. Michael*
Potamo of Alexandria and the Emergence of Eclecticism in Late Hellenistic Philosophy — *Hatzimichali, M.*
Potato in a Rice Bowl — *Keener, Peggy*
c The Potato King (Illus. by Niemann, Christoph) — *Niemann, Christoph*
c The Potion Diaries — *Alward, Amy*
A Potpourri of Icelandic Poetry through Eleven Centuries — *Hallmundsson, Hallberg*
Potsdam: The End of World War II and the Remaking of Europe — *Neiberg, Michael*
Potter's Field — *Dolan, Chris*
Pound for Pound: A Story of One Woman's Recovery and the Shelter Dogs Who Loved Her Back to Life — *Kopp, Shannon*
Pour les Musulmans — *Plenel, Edwy*
Pour Me: A Life — *Gill, Adrian A.*
Pour Quoi Faire la Revolution — *Chappey, Jean-Luc*
Pour une poesie impure — *Melancon, Robert*
Pourquoi Bologne — *Farah, Alain*
Pourquoi les mathematiques sont-elles difficiles? — *Oumraou, Leny*
Pourtraits divers de Jean de Tournes: Edition critique et fac-simile du tirage de 1556 — *Lejeune, Maud*
Poverty and the Poor Law in Ireland, 1850-1914 — *Crossman, Virginia*
The Poverty of Nations: A Sustainable Solution — *Grudem, Wayne*
The Power and Independence of the Federal Reserve — *Conti-Brown, Peter*
The Power and Intelligence of Karma and Reincarnation — *Dharma*
Power and Pathos: Bronze Sculpture of the Hellenistic World — *Daehner, Jens M.*
Power and Propaganda: Scotland 1306-1488 — *Stevenson, Katie*
The Power Broker: Robert Moses and the Fall of New York — *Caro, Robert*
Power Density: A Key to Understanding Energy Sources and Uses — *Smil, Vaclav*
c Power Down, Little Robot (Illus. by Zeltner, Tim) — *Staniszewski, Anna*
Power Forward: My Presidential Education — *Love, Reggie*
Power Hungry: The Ultimate Energy Bar Cookbook — *Saulsbury, Camilla V.*
Power in Concert: The Nineteenth-Century Origins of Global Governance — *Mitzen, Jennifer*
Power, Law and the End of Privateering — *Lemnitzer, Jan Martin*
Power Lines: Phoenix and the Making of the Modern Southwest — *Needham, Andrew*
The Power of Fifty Bits — *Nease, Bob*
The Power of Gifts: Gift-Exchange in Early Modern England — *Heal, Felicity*
c The Power of Henry's Imagination (Illus. by George, Nic) — *Byrne, Skye*
The Power of Huacas: Change and Resistance in the Andean World of Colonial Peru — *Brosseder, Claudia*
The Power of I Am: Two Words That Will Change Your Life Today — *Osteen, Joel*
The Power of Inaction: Bank Bailouts in Comparison — *Woll, Cornelia*
The Power of Knowledge: How Information and Technology Made the Modern World — *Black, Jeremy*
The Power of Market Fundamentalism: Karl Polanyi's Critique — *Block, Fred*
The Power of Metaphor: Examining Its Influence on Social Life — *Landau, Mark J.*
The Power of Others: Peer Pressure, Groupthink, and How the People Around Us Shape Everything We Do — *Bond, Michael*
The Power of Patience — *Ryan, M.J.*

The Power of Play: Designing Early Learning Spaces — Conner, Marisa
The Power of Questioning — McGough, Julie V.
The Power of Scientific Knowledge: From Research to Public Policy — Grundman, Reiner
The Power of Song: Nonviolent National Culture in the Baltic Singing Revolution — Smidchens, Guntis
The Power of Staying Put — Jimenez, Juan Masullo
The Power of Thanks: How Social Recognition Empowers Employees and Creates a Best Place to Work — Mosley, Eric
The Power of the Past: Understanding Cross-Class Marriages — Streib, Jessi
The Power of Tolerance: A Debate — Brown, Wendy
Power on the Hudson: Storm King Mountain and the Emergence of Modern American Environmentalism — Lifset, Robert D.
Power, Order, and Change in World Politics — Ikenberry, G. John
Power Play — Snow, Tiffany
Power Play — Vilendrer, Nikki
The Power Playbook: Rules for Independence, Money, and Success — Anthony, La La
Power Politics and State Formation in the Twentieth Century: The Dynamics of Recognition — Coggins, Bridget
Power-Relationships in Court Societies: Marriage, Concubinage, Friendship, Kinship, and Patronage in Historical Perspective: International Research Workshop
Power Shift: From Fossil Energy to Dynamic Permanent Power — Stayton, Robert Arthur
y Power Shift: From Fossil Energy to Dynamic Solar Power — Stayton, Robert Arthur
A Power Stronger Than Itself — Lewis, George
Power Surge — Bova, Ben
The Power to Get Things Done (Whether You Feel Like It or Not). — Levinson, Steve
Power to the People: Energy in Europe over the Last Five Centuries — Kander, Astrid
Power to the Poor: Black-Brown Coalition and the Fight for Economic Justice, 1960-1974 — Mantler, Gordon K.
c Power Up! A Visual Exploration of Energy (Illus. by Tse, Glenda) — Paleja, Shaker
Power Up Your Creative Mind — Frazier, Kathy
Power Wars: Inside Obama's Post-9/11 Presidency — Savage, Charlie
c Powerful Muscle Cars — Blackford, Cheryl
Powerful Patriots: Nationalist Protest in China's Foreign Relations — Weiss, Jessica Chen
Powerful Problem Solving — Ray, Max
Powerful Vegan Messages — Dinshah, H. Jay
The Powerhouse: Inside the Invention of a Battery to Save the World — LeVine, Steve
Powering Forward — Ritter, Bill
y Powering Up a Career in Software Development and Programming — Harmon, Daniel
y Powerless — Childs, Tera Lynn
y Powerless — Deebs, Tracy
Powerless — Childs, Tera Lynn
y Powerless — Deebs, Tracy
Powerless Science? Science and Politics in a Toxic World — Boudia, Soraya
Powers: Bureau, Vol 2 (Illus. by Oeming, Michael Avon) — Bendis, Brian Michael
Powers of Possibility: Experimental American Writing since the 1960s — Houen, Alex
Practical Copyright for Library and Information Professionals — Pedley, Paul
A Practical Guide to Government Management — Meconi, Vince
The Practical Past — White, Hayden
Practical Predestinarians in England, c. 1590-1640 — Dixon, Leif
Practical Program Evaluation for Criminal Justice — Vito, Gennaro F.
Practical Sins for Cold Climates — Costa, Shelley
Practice Development in Sport and Performance Psychology — Taylor, Jim
The Practice of Everyday Life — De Certeau, Michel
Practices of Power: Revisiting the Principality and Powers in the Pauline Letters — Moses, Robert Ewusie
The Practices of Structural Policy in Western Market Economies since the 1960s
Practicing Care in Rural Congregations and Communities — Hoeft, Jeanne
Practicing Compassion — Rogers, Frank, Jr.
Practicing Literary Theory in the Middle Ages: Ethics and the Mixed Form in Chaucer, Gower, Usk, and Hoccleve — Johnson, Eleanor

Practicing Piety in Medieval Ashkenaz: Men, Women, and Everyday Religious Observance — Baumgarten, Elisheva
Practicing Stalinism. Bolsheviks, Boyars, and the Persistence of Tradition — Getty, J. Arch
Prae — Szentkuthy, Miklos
The Praetorian Guard: A History of Rome's Elite Special Forces — Bingham, Sandra
Pragmatic Literacy in Medieval Serbia — Bubalo, Djordje
Pragmatischer Standard — Hagemann, Jorg
Prague, Capital of the Twentieth Century: A Surrealist History — Sayer, Derek
c Prairie Dog Song (Illus. by Trumbore, Cindy) — Roth, Susan L.
y Prairie Fire — Johnston, E.K.
A Prairie Food Chain — Tarbox, A.D.
Prairie Forge: The Extraordinary Story of the Nebraska Scrap Metal Drive of World War II — Kimble, James J.
Prairie Man: The Struggle Between Sitting Bull and the Indian Agent James McLaughlin — Matteoni, Norman E.
Prairie Republic: The Political Culture of Dakota Territory, 1879-1889 — Lauck, Jon K.
c The Prairie That Nature Built (Illus. by Morrison, Cathy) — Lorbiecki, Marybeth
A Prairie Year — Rohde, George
The Prank: The Best of Young Chekhov — Chekhov, Anton
The Prank: The Best of Young Chekhov — Bloshteyn, Maria
c Prankenstein (Illus. by Morgan, Richard) — Seed, Andy
Pranksters: Making Mischief in the Modern World — McLeod, Kembrew
Pray Like a Gourmet: Creative Ways to Feed Your Soul — Brazzeal, David
Pray the Gay Away — York, Sara
Pray the Gay Away: The Extraordinary Lives of Bible Belt Gays — Barton, Bernadette
Prayer: Christian and Muslim Perspectives — Marshall, David
Prayer: Experiencing Awe and Intimacy with God — Keller, Timothy
c A Prayer for World Peace (Illus. by Golmohammadi, Feeroozeh) — Goodall, Jane
A Prayer in a Wolf's Mouth: Poems 2013-2014 — Milazzo, Richard
The Prayer Warrior: A Tale of the Last Battle of General Stonewall Jackson — Mellynchuk, Steve
Prayers, Petitions, and Protests: The Catholic Church and the Ontario Schools Crisis in the Windsor Border Region, 1910-1928 — Cecillon, Jack D.
c Prayers That Changed History — Goyer, Tricia
The Preacher's Legacy — Bryant, Walter L.
Preaching and Political Society: From Late Antiquity to the End of the Middle Ages / Depuis l'Antiquite tardive jusqu'a la fin du Moyen — Morenzoni, Franco
Preaching at the Crossroads: How the World--and our Preaching--Is Changing — Lose, David J.
Preaching: Communicating Faith in an Age of Skepticism — Keller, Timothy
Preaching in an Age of Distraction — Kalas, J. Ellsworth
Preaching in Eighteenth-Century London — Farooq, Jennifer
Preaching in Hitler's Shadow: Sermons of Resistance in the Third Reich — Stroud, Dean G.
Preaching on Wax: The Phonograph and the Shaping of Modern African American Religion — Martin, Lerone A.
Preaching the Gospel of Black Revolt: Appropriating Milton in Early African American Literature — Wilburn, Reginald A.
Preaching to Convert: Evangelical Outreach and Performance Activism in a Secular Age — Fletcher, John
Precarious — Peterson, Allan
Precarious Japan — Allison, Anne
Precarious Prescriptions: Contested Histories of Race and Health in North America — Green, Laurie B.
c Precious and the Zebra Necklace — Smith, Alexander McCall
c Precious Bones — Ashley-Hollinger, Mika
The Precious One — de los Santos, Marisa
The Precious One — Santos, Marisa de los
c The Precious Ring (Illus. by Coutts, Lisa) — Branford, Anna
The Precipice (Read by Leyva, Henry). Audiobook Review — Doiron, Paul

The Precipice — Doiron, Paul
The Precolonial State in West Africa: Building Power in Dahomey — Monroe, J. Cameron
The Predator Paradox: Ending the War with Wolves, Bears, Cougars, and Coyotes — Shivik, John A.
Predator: The Secret Origins of the Drone Revolution — Whittle, Richard
Predators: The CIA's Drone War on al Qaeda — Williams, Brian Glyn
y The Predictions — Zander, Bianca
The Preferential Option for the Poor: A Short History and a Reading Based on the Thought of Bernard Lonergan — Curnow, Rohan Michael
The Preferential Option for the Poor Beyond Theology — Groody, Daniel G.
The Pregnant Male as Myth and Metaphor in Classical Greek Literature — Leitao, D.D.
Pregnant on Arrival: Making the Illegal Immigrant — Luibheid, Eithne
Prehension: The Hand and the Emergence of Humanity — McGinn, Colin
c Prehistoric: Follow the Dinosaurs — Owen, John Bailey
c The Prehistoric Games (Illus. by Davey, Martin) — Lawler, Janet
c Prehistoric Mammals (Illus. by Tempesta, Franco) — Zoehfeld, Kathleen Weidner
Prehistoric Materialities: Becoming Material in Prehistoric Britain and Ireland — Jones, Andrew Meirion
y Prehistoric Predators (Illus. by Csotonyi, Julius) — Switek, Brian
A Prehistory of the Cloud — Hu, Tung-Hui
Prejudice and Pride — Messina, Lynn
The Prelate in England and Europe, 1300-1560 — Heale, Martin
Prelude to Baltic Linguistics: Earliest Theories about Baltic Languages — Dini, Pietro U.
Prelude to Blitzkrieg: The 1916 Austro-German Campaign in Romania — Barrett, Michael B.
Prelude to Bruise — Jones, Saeed
Prelude to Genocide — Gavian Rivers, Virginia
Prelude to the Modernist Crisis: The "Firmin" Articles of Alfred Loisy — Thirlway, Christine E.
Prep-Ahead Meals from Scratch: Make Healthy Home Cooking Practically Effortless (Illus. by Holloman, Chris) — Milham, Alea
Prep School Cowboys: Ranch Schools in the American West — Bingmann, Melissa
Preparation for the Next Life — Lish, Atticus
Prepositions in English Grammars until 1801, with a Survey of the Western European Background — Lundskaer-Nielsen, Tom
c Preposterous Rhinoceros (Illus. by Costa, Marta) — Gunaratnam, Tracy
The Prepper's Water Survival Guide — Luther, Daisy
The Preschool Inclusion Toolbox — Barton, Erin E.
The Presence of Medieval English Literature: Studies at the Interface of History, Author, and Text in a Selection of Middle English Literary Landmarks — Fletcher, Alan J.
Present Darkness — Nunn, Malla
Present Perfect: 25 Gifts to Sew and Bestow — White, Betz
A Presentist Path to World Peace — Person, M.G.
The Preservation Management Handbook: A 21st-Century Guide for Libraries, Archives, and Museums — Harvey, Ross
The Preservation Management Handbook: A 21st Century Guide for Libraries, Archives, and Museums — Mahard, Martha
Preserving Family Recipes: How to Save and Celebrate Your Food Traditions — Frey, Valerie J.
Preserving South Street Seaport: The Dream and Reality of a New York Urban Renewal District — Lindgren, James M.
Preserving the Japanese Way: Traditions of Salting, Fermenting, and Pickling for the Modern Kitchen — Hachisu, Nancy Singleton
Preserving the Old City of Damascus — Totah, Faedah M.
The Presidency in Black and White: My Up-Close View of Three Presidents and Race in America — Ryan, April
The President and the Apprentice: Eisenhower and Nixon, 1952-1961 — Gellman, Irwin F.
The President Factor — Obermeier, Pat
President Lincoln Assassinated! The Firsthand Story of the Murder, Manhunt, Trial and Mourning — Holzer, Harold
c President Lincoln (Illus. by Demi) — Demi
c President of the Whole Sixth Grade — Winston, Sherri

c President Squid (Illus. by Varon, Sara) — Reynolds, Aaron
Presidential Campaigning and Social Media: An Analysis of the 2012 Campaign — Hendricks, John Allen
Presidential Declarations — Wood, Douglas J.
Presidential Decrees in Russia: A Comparative Perspective — Remington, Thomas F.
Presidential Faith and Foreign Policy: Jimmy Carter the Disciple and Ronald Reagan the Alchemist — Steding, William
c Presidential Misadventures: Poems That Poke Fun at the Man in Charge (Illus. by Burr, Dan E.) — Raczka, Bob
The Presidential Recordings — Coleman, David
c The Presidential Seal — LaPlante, Walter
Presidents and Terminal Logic Behavior: Term Limits and Executive Action in the United States, Brazil and Argentina — Kehoe, Genevieve M.
The Presidents and UFOs: A Secret History from FDR to Obama — Holcombe, Larry
The President's Book of Secrets — Priess, David
Presidents, Congress, and the Public Schools: The Politics of Education Reform — Jennings, Jack
c Presidents: Follow the Leaders — Owen, John Bailey
The President's Salmon: Restoring the King of Fish and Its Home Waters — Schmitt, Catherine
The President's Shadow — Meltzer, Brad
Presidents & Their Generals: An American History of Command in War — Moten, Matthew
A Press Divided: Newspaper Coverage of the Civil War — Sachsman, David B.
y Press Play — Devine, Eric
Press Start to Play — Wilson, Daniel H.
Pressed for Time: The Acceleration of Life in Digital Capitalism — Wajcman, Judy
Presumed Incompetent: The Intersections of Race and Class for Women in Academia — Gutierrez y Muhs, Gabriella
Presumed Puzzled — Hall, Parnell
Pretend I'm Dead — Beagin, Jen
The Pretender's Lady — Gold, Alan
y Pretending to Be Erica — Painchaud, Michelle
y Pretending to Dance — Chamberlain, Diane
y The Pretty App — Sise, Katie
Pretty Baby (Read by Campbell, Cassandra). Audiobook Review — Kubica, Mary
Pretty Baby — Kubica, Mary
Pretty Birds: 18 Simple Projects to Sew and Love — Lindsay, Virginia
Pretty Funny Tea Cosies and Other Beautiful Knitted Things — Prior, Loani
Pretty/Funny: Women Comedians and Body Politics — Mizejewski, Linda
Pretty Girls — Slaughter, Karin
Pretty Good for a Girl: Women in Bluegrass — Henry, Murphy Hicks
y Pretty Is — Mitchell, Maggie
c Pretty Minnie in Paris (Illus. by Valiant, Kristi) — Steel, Danielle
Pretty Ugly — Butler, Kirker
y Pretty Wanted — Ludwig, Elisa
Preussen, Deutschland und China: Entwicklungslinien und Akteure (1842-1911). — Leutner, Mechthild
Preussens Ruhm Deutschlands Ehre: Zum nationalen Ehrdiskurs im Vorfeld der preussisch-französischen Kriege des 19, Jahrhunderts — Aschmann, Birgit
Prevention Is the Cure! A Scientist's Guide to Extending Your Life — Sancilio, Frederick D.
Preventive Detention: Asking the Fundamental Questions — Keyzer, Patrick
y The Prey — Isbell, Tom
The Price of Blood — Bracewell, Patricia
Price of Fame: The Honorable Clare Boothe Luce — Morris, Sylvia Jukes
Price of Privilege — Dotta, Jessica
The Price of Silence: The Duke Lacrosse Scandal, The Power Elite, and the Corruption of Our Great Universities — Cohan, William D.
The Price of Silence: The Duke Lacrosse Scandal, the Power of the Elite, and the Corruption of Our Great Universities — Cohan, William D.
The Price of Thirst: Global Water Inequality and the Coming Chaos — Piper, Karen
A Price to Pay — Brownjohn, John
c Prices! Prices! Prices! Why They Go Up and Down (Illus. by Miller, Edward) — Adler, David A.
Prices! Prices! Prices!: Why They Go Up and Down (Illus. by Miller, Edward) — Adler, David A.
Pricing Your Portraits: High-Profit Strategies for Photographers — Smith, Jeff

c Prickly Jenny (Illus. by Delacroix, Sibylle) — Delacroix, Sibylle
c Prickly Jenny (Illus. by Prickly Jenny (Picture story)) — Delacroix, Sibylle
c Prickly Jenny — Delacroix, Sibylle
y Pride and Prejudice (Illus. by Deas, Robert) — Austen, Jane
Pride: The Story of the First Openly Gay Navy Seal — Jones, Brett
Pride v. Prejudice: A Claire Malloy Mystery — Hess, Joan
Priest, Politician, Collaborator: Jozef Tiso and the Making of Fascist Slovakia — Ward, James Mace
The Priest, the Prince, and the Pasha: The Life and Afterlife of an Ancient Egyptian Sculpture — Berman, Lawrence M.
Priestly Resistance to the Early Reformation in Germany — Moger, Jourden Travis
Priests of the French Revolution: Saints and Renegades in a New Political Era — Byrnes, Joseph F.
Primacy in the Church from Vatican I to Vatican II: An Orthodox Perspective — Vgenopoulos, Maximos
Primal Force — Ayres, D.D.
c A Primary Source History of Slavery in the United States — Kimmel, Allison Crotzer
c A Primary Source History of U.S. Independence — Goddu, Krystyna Poray
Primate Adaptation and Evolution — Fleagle, John G.
Primate Communication: A Multimodal Approach — Liebal, Katja
Primate Comparative Anatomy — Gebo, Daniel L.
Primate Ecology and Conservation: A Handbook of Techniques — Sterling, Eleanor J.
Primates of Park Avenue — Martin, Wednesday
The Prime of Life: A History of Modern Adulthood — Mintz, Steven
Primed to Perform: How to Build the Highest Performing Cultures Through the Science of Total Motivation — Doshi, Neel
A Primer in Biological Data Analysis and Visualization Using R — Hartvigsen, Gregg
Primitive Minds: Evolution and Spiritual Experience in the Victorian Novel — Neill, Anna
Primitive Passions — Cahill, John M.
Primo Levi's Resistance: Rebels and Collaborators in Occupied Italy — Luzzatto, Sergio
The Prince — Machiavelli
c The Prince and the Porker (Illus. by Roberts, David) — Bently, Peter
The Prince and the Scorpion — Nelson, Dick
c Prince Fly Guy (Illus. by Arnold, Tedd) — Arnold, Tedd
Prince Henry 'The Navigator': A Life — Russell, Peter
Prince Lestat: The Vampire Chronicles (Read by Vance, Simon). Audiobook Review — Rice, Anne
c Prince of a Frog (Illus. by Urbanovic, Jackie) — Urbanovic, Jackie
y Prince of Afghanistan — Nowra, Louis
Prince of Darkness: The Untold Story of Jeremiah G. Hamilton, Wall Street's First Black Millionaire — White, Shane
The Prince of los Cocuyos: A Miami Childhood — Blanco, Richard
The Prince of Medicine: Galen in the Roman Empire — Mattern, Susan P.
The Prince of Minor Writers: The Selected Essays of Max Beerbohm — Beerbohm, Max
Prince of Tyrants — Marcellus, Rabb
The Prince — Appel, Anne Milano
The Prince — Bruschini, Vito
c The Prince Who Was Just Himself (Illus. by Sistig, Heike) — Schnee, Silke
y A Prince Without a Kingdom — Ardizzone, Sarah
A Prince without a Kingdom (Illus. by Ardizzone, Sarah) — de Fombelle, Timothee
y A Prince without a Kingdom — de Fombelle, Timothee
y A Prince without a Kingdom — De Fombelle, Timothee
c Princeless: The Pirate Princess (Illus. by Higgins, Rosy) — Whitley, Jeremy
Princely India and the British: Political Development and the Operation of Empire — Keen, Caroline
Princes at War: The Bitter Battle Inside Britain's Royal Family in the Darkest Days of WWII — Cadbury, Deborah
Princes at War: The British Royal Family's Private Battle in the Second World War — Halliday, Stephen
Prince's Gambit — Pacat, C.S.
c The Princess and the Foal — Gregg, Stacy

c The Princess and the Fog: A Story for Children with Depression (Illus. by Jones, Lloyd) — Jones, Lloyd
c The Princess and the Giant (Illus. by Warburton, Sarah) — Hart, Caryl
c The Princess and the Goblin (Read by Heldman, Brooke). Audiobook Review — MacDonald, George
c The Princess and the Pony (Illus. by Beaton, Kate) — Beaton, Kate
c The Princess and the Presents (Illus. by Warburton, Sarah) — Hart, Caryl
Princess Bari — Sok-yong, Hwang
c Princess Cupcake Jones Won't Go to School (Illus. by LaDuca, Michael) — Fields, Ylleya
c The Princess Curse — Haskell, Marrie
y Princess Decomposia and Count Spatula (Illus. by Watson, Andi) — Watson, Andi
c The Princess in Black and the Hungry Bunny Horde — Hale, Shannon
c The Princess in Black and the Perfect Princess Party (Illus. by Pham, LeUyen) — Hale, Shannon
c The Princess in Black (Illus. by Pham, LeUyen) — Hale, Dean
c Princess in Disguise — Baker, E.D.
c Princess Juniper of the Hourglass — Paquette, Ammi-Joan
c Princess Mirror Belle and the Dragon Pox (Illus. by Monks, Lydia) — Donaldson, Julia
c Princess of the Wild Swans — Zahler, Diane
y Princess of Thorns (Read by Whelan, Julia). Audiobook Review — Jay, Stacey
y Princess of Thorns — Jay, Stacey
c Princess Patty Meets Her Match — Harper, Charise Mericle
c Princess Pistachio and the Pest (Illus. by Gay, Marie-Louise) — Gay, Marie-Louise
c Princess Pistachio and the Pest (Illus. by Gay, Mary-Louise) — Gay, Mary-Louise
Princess Pistachio — Gay, Marie-Louise
c Princess Posey and the First Grade Boys (Read by Nielson, Stina). Audiobook Review — Greene, Stephanie
c Princess Rosie's Rainbows (Illus. by Jacobs, Kim) — Killion, Bette
y Princess Ugg (Illus. by Naifeh, Ted) — Naifeh, Ted
c The Princess Who Had No Kingdom (Illus. by Gibb, Sarah) — Jones, Ursula
c Princesses Don't Wear Jeans (Illus. by Franson, Leanne) — Bellingham, Brenda
Princesses, Dragons and Helicopter Stories — Lee, Trisha
The Princeton Companion to Applied Mathematics — Higham, Nicholas J.
The Princeton Companion to Atlantic History — Miller, Joseph C.
The Princeton Guide to Evolution — Losos, Jonathan B.
The Principal's Office: A Social History of the American School Principal — Rousmaniere, Kate
A Principled Stand: The Story of Hirabayashi v. United States — Hirabayashi, James A.
A Principled Stand: The Story of Hirabayashi v. United States — Hirabayashi, Gordon K.
Principles of Proteomics — Twyman, Richard M.
Principles to Actions: Ensuring Mathematical Success for All — National Council of Teachers of Mathematics
Print and Public Politics in the English Revolution — Peacey, Jason
Print Culture, Crime and Justice in 18th-Century London — Ward, Richard M.
Printed Textiles: British and American Cottons and Linens, 1700-1850 (Illus. by Schneck, Jim) — Eaton, Linda
Printing a Mediterranean World: Florence, Constantinople, and the Renaissance of Geography — Roberts, Sean E.
Printing Ausias March: Material Culture and Renaissance Poetics — Lloret, Albert
Prinz Max von Baden: Der Letzte Kanzler des Kaisers — Machtan, Lothar
Prioners of Geography: Ten Maps That Explain Everything About the World — Marshall, Tim
Prions: Current Progress in Advanced Research — Sakudo, Akikazu
Prioritizing the World: Cost-Benefit to Identify the Smartest Targets for the Next 15 Years — Lomborg, Bjorn
Priscilla: The Hidden Life of an Englishwoman in Wartime France — Shakespeare, Nicholas
y Prism — Walker, Nina

The Prism of Race: W.E.B. Du Bois, Langston Hughes, Paul Robeson, and the Colored World of Cedric Dover — *Slate, Nico*
y Prison Boy — *McKay, Sharon E.*
y Prison Island: A Graphic Memoir (Illus. by Frakes, Colleen) — *Frakes, Colleen*
Prison Ramen: Recipes and Stories From Behind Bars — *Collins, Clifton, Jr.*
Prison Shakespeare: For These Deep Shames and Great Indignities — *Pensalfini, Rob*
A Prisoner in Malta — *DePoy, Phillip*
Prisoner of Belief: One Man's Odyssey to Reclaim His Soul - From Evangelical Minister to Searching Psychologist — *Van Dixhorn, John*
The Prisoner of Kathmandu: Brian Hodgson in Nepal, 1820-43 — *Allen, Charles*
y Prisoner of the Black Hawk — *Tait, A.L.*
c Prisoner of the Penguin! (Illus. by Vecchio, Luciano) — *Sonneborn, Scott*
The Prisoner of Zenda — *Hamid, Omar Shahid*
y The Prisoners of Breendonk — *Deem, James M.*
y The Prisoners of Breendonk: Personal Histories from a World War II Concentration Camp — *Deem, James M.*
Prisons in the Late Ottoman Empire: Microcosms of Modernity — *Schull, Kent F.*
Privacy in the Age of Big Data: Recognizing Threats, Defending Your Rights, and Protecting Your Family — *Payton, Theresa M.*
Privacy in the Modern Age: The Search for Solutions — *Rotenberg, Marc*
Privacy in the New Media Age — *Mills, Jon L.*
y Privacy in the Online World: Online Privacy and Government — *Henderson, Harry*
y Privacy in the Online World: Online Privacy and Health Care — *Abramovitz, Melissa*
y Privacy in the Online World: Online Privacy and Social Media — *Mooney, Carla*
y Private Citizens — *Tulathimutte, Tony*
Private Doubt, Public Dilemma: Religion and Science Since Jefferson and Darwin — *Thomson, Keith*
Private India: City on Fire — *Patterson, James*
Private Island: Why Britain Now Belongs to Someone Else — *Meek, James*
Private Law and the Rule of Law — *Austin, Lisa M.*
Private Life — *de Sagarra, Josep Maria*
Private Life — *Sagarra, Josep Maria de*
The Private Life of General Omar N. Bradley — *Lavoie, Jeffrey D.*
The Private Life of Plants — *Seung-U, Lee*
The Private Life: Why We Remain in the Dark — *Cohen, Josh*
Private Lines — *Gates, Emma*
Private Lives of Trees — *McDowell, Megan*
Private Property and Public Power: Eminent Domain in Philadelphia — *Becher, Debbie*
Private Women and the Public Good: Charity and State Formation in Hamilton, Ontario, 1846-93 — *Nielson, Carmen J.*
Privatization and Transition in Russia in the Early 1990s — *Leonard, Scott Carol*
The Privilege Against Self-Incrimination — *Choo, Andrew L-T*
The Prize — *Bialosky, Jill*
The Prize: Who's in Charge of America's Schools? (Read by Cross, Pete). Audiobook Review — *Russakoff, Dale*
The Prize: Who's in Charge of America's Schools? — *Russakoff, Dale*
Pro Mondo-Pro Domo: The Writings of Alban Berg — *Berg, Alban*
Pro: Reclaiming Abortion Rights — *Pollitt, Katha*
The Pro-War Movement: Domestic Support for the Vietnam War and the Making of Modern American Conservatism — *Scanlon, Sandra*
The Proactive Health Solution — *Cavallini, Nadia Yacoub*
Probable Truth: Editing Medieval Texts from Britain in the Twenty-First Century — *Gillespie, Vincent*
Probate Inventories of French Immigrants in Early Modern London — *Parker, Greig*
The Probiotic Promise: Simple Steps to Heal Your Body from the Inside Out — *Cook, Michelle Schoffro*
The Problem of Animal Pain: A Theodicy for All Creatures Great and Small — *Dougherty, Trent*
The Problem of Democracy in the Age of Slavery: Garrisonian Abolitionists and Transatlantic Reform — *McDaniel, W. Caleb*
The Problem of 'Hamlet' — *Seccombe, Thomas*
The Problem of Slavery in the Age of Emancipation — *Davis, David Brion*

The 'Problem of Women' in Post-War Europe Women's Activism: Global Perspectives from the 1890s to the Present — *Haan, Francisca de*
The Problem with Math Is English: A Language-Focused Approach to Helping All Students Develop a Deeper Understanding of Mathematics — *Molina, Concepcion*
c The Problem with Not Being Scared of Kids (Illus. by Neubecker, Robert) — *Richards, Dan*
c The Problem with Not Being Scared of Monsters (Illus. by Neubecker, Robert) — *Richards, Dan*
y The Problem with the Puddles (Read by Feiffer, Halley). Audiobook Review — *Feiffer, Kate*
Problems and Possibilities of Early Medieval Charters — *Jarrett, Jonathan*
Process and Providence: The Evolution Question at Princeton, 1845-1929 — *Gundlach, Bradley J.*
Process-Tracing Methods: Foundations and Guidelines — *Beach, Derek*
Processes of Social Decline among the European Nobility
Proclus. Commentaire sur le Parmenide de Platon. Tome V: Livre V — *Luna, Concetta*
Prodigal — *Ficklin, Sherry D.*
Prodigal Father Wayward Son: A Roadmap to Reconciliation — *Keen, Sam*
Prodigal: New and Selected Poems, 1976-2014 — *Gregerson, Linda*
Prodigals — *Jackson, Gregg*
Prodigies — *Burke, Sue*
The Prodigy's Cousin — *Ruthsatz, Joanna*
The Producer's Daughter — *Marcott, Lindsay*
Producing and Negotiating Non-Citizenship: Precarious Legal Status in Canada — *Goldring, Luin*
Producing Good Citizens: Literacy Training in Anxious Times — *Wan, Amy J.*
Producing Indonesia: The State of the Field of Indonesian Studies — *Tagliacozzo, Eric*
Producing Power: The Pre-Chernobyl History of the Soviet Nuclear Industry — *Schmid, Sonja D.*
Product Details — *Bhaskar, Sita*
Produkte und Produktinnovationen. 37. Technikgeschichtliche Tagung der Eisenbibliothek
Prof: Alan Turing Decoded — *Turing, Dermot*
Profane Culture — *Willis, Paul E.*
The Professor and the President: Daniel Patrick Moynihan in the Nixon White House — *Hess, Stephen*
The Professor in the Cage: Why Men Fight and Why We Like To Watch (Read by Dunn-Baker, Quincy) — *Gottschall, Jonathan*
The Professor in the Cage: Why Men Fight and Why We Like to Watch — *Gottschall, Jonathan*
The Professor Is In: The Essential Guide to Turning Your Ph.D. into a Job — *Kelsky, Karen*
Professor Porsche's Wars — *Ludvigsen, Karl*
Professor Stewart's Incredible Numbers — *Stewart, Ian*
Professors and Their Politics — *Gross, Neil*
Profiling and Criminal Justice in America, 2d ed. — *Bumgarner, Jeff*
Profiling: Latinos, Asian Americans and the Achievement Gap — *Ochoa, Gilda L.*
The Profiteers: Bechtel and the Men Who Built the World — *Denton, Sally*
The Profligate Son: Or, A True Story of Family Conflict, Fashionable Vice, and Financial Ruin in Regency Britain — *Phillips, Nicola*
Progress for the Poor — *Kenworthy, Lane*
Progress in Bioethics: Science, Policy and Politics — *Moreno, Jonathan D.*
A Progressive Education — *Howard, Richard*
Progressive Enlightenment: The Origins of the Gaslight Industry, 1780-1820 — *Tomory, Leslie*
The Progressive Era — *Sicius, Francis J.*
Progressive Evangelicals and the Pursuit of Social Justice — *Gasaway, Brantley W.*
Progressive Inequality: Rich and Poor in New York, 1890-1920 — *Huyssen, David*
The Progressive Poetics of Confusion in the French Enlightenment — *O'Neal, John c*
Progressives at War: William G. McAdoo and Newton D. Baker, 1863-1941 — *Craig, Douglas B.*
Proiectul Feroviar Romanesc — *Popescu, Toader*
c Project Alpha — *MacHale, D.J.*
c Project Alpha — *Machale, D.J.*
Project Animal Farm: An Accidental Journey into the Secret World of Farming and the Truth about Our Food — *Faruqi, Sonia*
y Project Disclosure: Revealing Government Secrets and Breaking the Truth Embargo — *Dolan, Richard M.*

Project Fatherhood: A Story of Courage and Healing in One of America's Toughest Communities — *Leap, Jorja*
Project Holiness: Marriage as a Workshop for Everyday Saints — *Ravizza, Bridget Burke*
c Project Kid: 100 Ingenious — *Kingloff, Amanda*
Project Nephili — *Farmer, T.L.*
Project Puffin: The Improbable Quest to Bring a Beloved Seabird Back to Egg Rock — *Kress, Stephen W.*
Projecting Tomorrow: Science Fiction and Popular Cinema — *Chapman, James*
y Prom Date — *Carlson, Melody*
y The Prom Goer's Interstellar Excursion — *McCoy, Chris*
Prometheus in the Nineteenth Century: From Myth to Symbol — *Corbeau-Parsons, Caroline*
Prometheus Rebound — *Akers, R.L.*
Prometheus Shackled: Goldsmith Banks and England's Financial Revolution after 1700 — *Voth, Hans-Joachim*
The Promise — *Crais, Robert*
c Promise — *Young, Judy (b. 1956-)*
Promise and Challenge: Catholic Women Reflect on Feminism, Complementarity, and the Church — *Hasson, Mary Rice*
c The Promise (Illus. by Carlin, Laura) — *Davies, Nicola*
Promise Land: My Journey through America's Self-Help Culture — *Lamb-Shapiro, Jessica*
The Promise of a Child — *Toner, Tom*
c The Promise of Amazing — *Constantine, Robin*
A Promise of Forever — *Pappano, Marilyn*
The Promise of Francis: The Man, the Pope, and the Challenge of Change — *Willey, David*
The Promise of Francis: The Man, the Pope, and the Challenge of Change — *Wiley, David*
The Promise of Home — *Chan, Darcie*
The Promise of Hope: New and Selected Poems, 1964-2013 — *Awoonor, Kofi*
The Promise of Power: The Origins of Democracy in India and Autocracy in Pakistan — *Tudor, Maya*
y Promise of Shadows — *Ireland, Justina*
The Promise of Wilderness: American Enviromental Politics since 1964 — *Turner, James Morton*
A Promise to Die For — *Pelham, Jacqueline*
y Promise, vol. 12 — *Bracken, Beth*
Promised Bodies: Time, Language, and Corporeality in Medieval Women's Mystical Texts — *Dailey, Patricia*
Promised by Heaven: A Doctor's Return from the Afterlife to a Destiny of Love and Healing — *Hensley, Mary Helen*
The Promised Land — *Remarque, Erich Maria*
Promised You a Miracle: UK 80-82 — *Beckett, Andy*
y Promises I Made — *Zink, Michelle*
Promises to Keep — *Beaumont, Maegan*
Promoting Peace, Inciting Violence: The Role of Religion and the Media — *Mitchell, Jolyon*
y Promposal — *Helms, Rhonda*
The Proof — *Kristof, Agota*
y Proof of Forever (Read by Zeller, Emily Woo). Audiobook Review — *Hillyer, Lexa*
y Proof of Forever — *Hillyer, Lexa*
Proof of Guilt: Barbara Graham and the Politics of Executing Women in America — *Cairns, Kathleen A.*
Proof Positive — *Mayor, Archer*
Propaganda and Intelligence in the Cold War: The NATO Information Service — *Risso, Linda*
Propaganda im Ersten Weltkrieg — *Bremm, Klaus-Jurgen*
Properties — *Edwards, Douglas*
Prophecies and Providence: A Biblical Approach to Modern Jewish History — *Pfeffer, Yehoshua*
Prophecy and Kingship in Adomnan's "Life of Saint Columba" — *Enright, Michael J.*
The Prophet of Cuernavaca: Ivan Illich and the Crisis of the West — *Hartch, Todd*
Prophetic Rage: A Postcolonial Theology of Liberation — *Hill, Johnny Bernard*
A Prophetic Trajectory: Ideologies of Place, Time and Belonging in an Angolan Religious Movement — *Blanes, Ruy Llera*
Prophetic Visions of the Past: Pan-Caribbean Representations of the Haitian Revolution — *Figueroa, Victor*
Prophets of Eternal Fjord — *Aitken, Martin*
The Prophets of Eternal Fjord — *Leine, Kim*
ProQuest Statistical Abstract of the United States, 2015

The Prose of Sasha Sokolov: Reflections on/of the Real — *Kravchenko, Elena*
Prosopopee et persona a la Renaissance — *Perona, Blandine*
Prostitution and the Ends of Empire: Scale, Governmentalities, and Interwar India — *Legg, Stephen*
Prostitution, Modernity, and the Making of the Cuban Republic, 1840-1920 — *Sippial, Tiffany A.*
Protagoras of Abdera: the Man, His Measure — *Ophuijsen, J.M. van*
Protecting Caroline — *Stoker, Susan*
Protecting Patron Privacy: Safe Practices for Public Computers — *Beckstrom, Matthew*
Proteinaholic: How Our Obsession with Meat is Killing Us and What We Can Do about It — *Davis, Garth*
Protest and Propaganda: W. E. B. Du Bois, the Crisis, and American History — *Sinitiere, Phillip Luke*
Protest and Propaganda: W.E.B. Du Bois, "The Crisis," and American History — *Kirschke, Amy Helene*
Protest, Reform and Repression in Khrushchev's Soviet Union — *Hornsby, Robert*
Protestant-Catholic Conflict from the Reformation to the 21st Century: The Dynamics of Religious Difference — *Wolffe, John*
Protestant Cosmopolitanism and Diplomatic Culture: Brandenburg-Swedish Relations in the Seventeenth Century — *Riches, Daniel*
The Protestant Ethic and Spirit of Sport: How Calvinism and Capitalism Shaped America's Games — *Overman, Steven J.*
Protestantische Selbstverortung: Die Rezensionen Ernst Troeltschs — *Bienert, Maren*
Protestantism, Politics, and Women in Britain, 1660-1714 — *Zook, Melinda S.*
Protestantismus im geteilten Deutschland. Forschungsperspektiven
Protocol Zero — *Abel, James*
Protocols of Liberty: Communication Innovation and the American Revolution — *Warner, William B.*
y Proud Heritage: People, Issues, and Documents of the LGBT Experience — *Stewart, Chuck*
c Proud to Be an American (Illus. by Sekulow, Amanda) — *Greenwood, Lee*
Proust Pluriel — *Naturel, Mireille*
Proust: The Search — *Taylor, Benjamin*
Proust's Latin Americans — *Gallo, Ruben*
Proven Programs in Education: Science, Technology, and Mathematics — *Slavin, Robert E.*
Proverbs and Ecclesiastes: A Theological Commentary on the Bible — *Pauw, Amy Plantinga*
Providence Noir — *Hood, Ann*
y Providential — *Channer, Colin*
Providing for National Security: A Comparative Analysis — *Dorman, Andrew M.*
Provincializing the Social Sciences: International Workshop
Proxima (Read by McCarley, Kyle). Audiobook Review — *Baxter, Stephen*
Prozessionen in Preussen: Katholisches Leben in Berlin, Breslau, Essen und Munster im 19. Jahrhundert — *Krull, Lena*
Prudence — *Treuer, David*
Prudence (Read by Quirk, Moira). Audiobook Review — *Carriger, Gail*
Prudence Crandall's Legacy: The Fight for Equality in the 1830s, Dred Scott, and Brown v. Board of Education — *Williams, Donald E., Jr.*
y Prudence — *Carriger, Gail*
Prudes on the Prowl: Fiction and Obscenity in England, 1850 to the Present Day — *Bradshaw, David*
Prune — *Hamilton, Gabrielle*
Przesniona rewolucja: Cwiczenie z logiki historycznej — *Leder, Andrzej*
Psalm of My Heart: Who We Are in Christ — *Phelps, Rebekah Lea*
Psalmandala — *Collins, Michael Patrick*
Psalms 1-72 — *Kidner, Derek*
Psalms — *Brueggemann, Walter*
The Pseudo-Bonaventuran Lives of Christ: Exploring the Middle English Tradition — *Johnson, Ian*
Pseudo-Kodinos and the Constantinopolitan Court: Offices and Ceremonies — *Macrides, Ruth*
Pseudoisidor und das Papsttum: Funktion und Bedeutung des apostolischen Stuhls in den pseudoisidorischen Falschungen — *Harder, Clara*
Psychedelia and Other Colours — *Chapman, Rob*

Psychedelic Bubble Gum: Boyce and Hart, the Monkees, and Turning Mayhem into Miracles — *Hart, Bobby*
Psychological Testing of Hispanics: Clinical and Intellectual Assessment — *Geisinger, Kurt F.*
Psychological Warfare in the Arab-Israeli Conflict — *Schleifer, Ron*
The Psychologically Healthy Workplace: Building a Win-Win Environment for Organizations and Employees — *Grawitch, Matthew J.*
Psychology Comes to Harlem: Rethinking the Race Question in Twentieth-Century America — *Garcia, Jay*
The Psychology of the Athenian Hoplite: The Culture of Combat in Classical Athens — *Crowley, Jason*
Psychology Today: An Introduction, 2d ed. — *Asimov, Isaac*
Psychopath Free (Expanded Edition): Recovering from Emotionally Abusive Relationships with Narcissists, Sociopaths, and Other Toxic People — *Mackenzie, Jackson*
Psychopharmacology: Drugs, the Brain, and Behavior — *Meyer, Jerrold S.*
PT 109: An American Epic of War, Survival, and the Destiny of John F. Kennedy — *Doyle, William*
c Pteranodon — *Lennie, Charles*
c Pterosaur — *Zeiger, Jennifer*
Pterosaurs: Natural History, Evolution, Anatomy — *Witton, Mark P.*
The Public and Its Possibilities: Triumphs and Tragedies in the American City — *Fairfield, John D.*
Public Buildings in Early Modern Europe — *Ottenheym, Koen*
Public Capitalism: The Political Authority of Corporate Executives — *McMahon, Christopher*
A Public Empire: Property and the Quest for the Common Good in Imperial Russia — *Pravilova, Ekaterina*
y Public Enemies — *Aguirre, Ann*
Public Enemy: Inside the Terrordome — *Grierson, Tim*
Public Libraries, Public Policies, and Political Processes: Serving and Transforming Communities in Times of Economic and Political Restraint — *Jaeger, Paul T.*
Public Natures: Evolutionary Infrastructures — *Weiss, Marion*
The Public Professor: How to Use Your Research to Change the World — *Badgett, M.V. Lee*
Public Properties: Museums in Imperial Japan — *Aso, Noriko*
The Public School Advantage: Why Public Schools Outperform Private Schools — *Lubienski, Christopher A.*
c Public School Superhero (Read by Boone, Joshua). Audiobook Review — *Patterson, James*
c Public School Superhero (Illus. by Thomas, Cory) — *Tebbetts, Chris*
c Public School Superhero (Illus. by Thomas, Cory) — *Patterson, James*
Public Space Acupuncture — *Casanova, Helena*
The Public Value of the Social Sciences — *Brewer, John D.*
The Public Wealth of Nations — *Detter, Dag*
Publishing: A Writer's Memoir — *Godwin, Gail*
Publishing — *Godwin, Gail*
Publishing Business in Eighteenth-Century England — *Raven, James*
Publishing the Stage: Print and Performance in Early Modern Japan — *Kimbrough, R. Keller*
c Puck of Pook's Hill (Read by Kenny, Peter). Audiobook Review — *Kipling, Rudyard*
c Pucker Power: The Super-Powered Superpug (Illus. by Dempsey, Sheena) — *Stevens, Kevin*
c Puckster Plays the Hockey Mascots — *Schultz Nicholson, Lorna*
c Puckster's Christmas Hockey Tournament — *Schultz Nicholson, Lorna*
c Puddle (Illus. by Yum, Hyewon) — *Yum, Hyewon*
c Puddle Jumpers — *Lewis, Anne Margaret*
c Puddles Are for Jumping (Illus. by Dunstan, Kylie) — *Dunstan, Kylie*
c Puddles or Lunch? (Illus. by Makonin, Anna) — *Makonin, Anna*
Pudge: The Biography of Carlton Fisk — *Wilson, Doug*
Pueblo Indians and Spanish Colonial Authority in Eighteenth-Century New Mexico — *Brown, Tracy L.*

A Pueblo Social History: Kinship, Sodality, and Community in the Northern Southwest — *Ware, John A.*
Puer Tea: Ancient Caravans and Urban Chic — *Zhang, Jinghong*
c Puff — *Wondriska, William*
The Puffin of Death — *Webb, Betty*
c A Puffin Playing by the Sea: The Twelve Days of Christmas in Newfoundland and Labrador (Illus. by Peddle, Derek) — *Noordhof, Gina*
Puglia — *Silver Spoon Kitchen*
c Pugs of the Frozen North (Illus. by McIntyre, Sarah) — *Reeve, Philip*
Puke Force — *Chippendale, Brian*
y Pull — *Waltman, Kevin*
c Pull (Illus. by Kumar, Rohit) — *Murphy, Jonell Patricia*
Pulled Over: How Police Stops Define Race and Citizenship — *Epp, Charles R.*
Pulling The Dragon's Tail — *Kauffman, Kenton*
The Pullman Porter: An American Journey (Illus. by Blanc, Mike) — *Oelschlager, Vanita*
The Pulpit and the Press in Reformation Italy — *Michelson, Emily*
Pulse: A National Security Thriller — *Cook, Robert*
The Puma Blues: The Complete Saga — *Murphy, Stephen*
c Pumpkin Day! (Illus. by Meza, Erika) — *Ransom, Candice*
c Pumpkin Party! (Illus. by Guile, Gill) — *Powell-Tuck, Maudie*
c Pumpkin Time! (Illus. by Cushman, Doug) — *Deak, Erzsi*
c Pumpkins, Pumpkins Everywhere (Illus. by Alvarez, Lorena) — *Prasadam-Halls, Smitri*
y Punch Like a Girl — *Krossing, Karen*
c Punishing Bullies: Zero Tolerance vs. Working Together — *Owings, Lisa*
Punishment and Penance: Two Phases in the History of the Bishop's Tribunal of Novara — *Deutscher, Thomas B.*
A Punishment for Each Criminal: Gender and Crime in Swedish Medieval Law — *Ekholst, Christine*
The Punishment Imperative: The Rise and Failure of Mass Incarceration in America — *Clear, Todd R.*
The Punitive Turn: New Approaches to Race and Incarceration — *McDowell, Deborah E.*
Punjab Reconsidered: History, Culture, and Practice — *Malhotra, Anshu*
Punjabi Immigrant Mobility in the United States: Adaptation through Race and Class — *Mitra, Diditi*
Punk Rock Blitzkrieg: My Life as a Ramone — *Ramone, Marky*
c Punk Science: The Intergalactic, Supermassive Space Book (Illus. by Hope, Dan) — *Milton, Jon*
c Punk Skunks (Illus. by Shaskan, Stephen) — *Shaskan, Trisha Speed*
c Punky Brewster (Illus. by Vamos, Lesley) — *Sellner, Joelle*
c The Punkydoos Take the Stage (Illus. by Andreasen, Dan) — *Jackson, Jennifer*
c Pup and Hound's Big Book of Stories (Illus. by Hendry, Linda) — *Hood, Susan*
c Pup Patrol: Farm Rescue (Illus. by Dawson, Janine) — *Odgers, Darrel*
Puppets in the Wind — *Krolow, Karl*
The Puppet's Tattered Clothes — *Bray, Alan*
c Puppy! (Illus. by Graves, Keith) — *Graves, Keith*
c Puppy Love: True Stories of Doggie Devotion — *Gerry, Lisa M.*
c Puppy Love: True Stories of Doggy Devotion — *Gerry, Lisa M.*
c Pura Vida Mae!: An Original Story for Children — *Biddle, Buffie*
Purchasing Whiteness: Pardos, Mulattos, and the Quest for Social Mobility in the Spanish Indies — *Twinam, Ann*
Pure Act: The Uncommon Life of Robert Lax — *McGregor, Michael N.*
Pure and Modern Milk: An Environmental History since 1900 — *Smith-Howard, Kendra*
Pure Intelligence: The Life of William Hyde Wollaston — *Usselman, Melvyn C.*
Pure Pork Awesomeness: Totally Cookable Recipes from Around the World — *Gillespie, Kevin*
Purebred Dead — *Delaney, Kathleen*
Purging the Empire: Mass Expulsions in Germany, 1871-1914 — *Fitzpatrick, Matthew P.*
Purging the Poorest: Public Housing and the Design Politics of Twice-Cleared Communities — *Vale, Lawrence J.*
Purity — *Franzen, Jonathan*

Purity and Danger: An Analysis of Concepts of Pollution and Taboo — *Douglas, Mary*
Purity, Body, and Self in Early Rabbinic Literature — *Balberg, Mira*
Purity — *Franzen, Jonathan*
Purl Up and Die — *Sefton, Maggie*
Puro Arte: Filipinos on the Stages of Empire — *Burns, Lucy Mae San Pablo*
The Purpose-Based Library: Finding Your Path to Survival, Success, and Growth — *Huber, John J.*
c **The Purpose Driven Life Devotional for Kids** — *Warren, Rick*
The Purpose of Rhetoric in Late Antiquity: From Performance to Exegesis — *Quiroga Puertas, A.J.*
The Purposeful Graduate: Why Colleges Must Talk to Students About Vocation — *Clydesdale, Tim*
Pursuing Meaning — *Borg, Emma*
Pursuing the Spiritual Roots of Protest: Merton, Berrigan, Yoder, and Muste at the Gethsemani Abbey Peacemakers Retreat — *Oyer, Gordon*
Pursuit — *Taylor, Harry*
Pursuit in Provence — *Gobbell, Phyllis*
The Pursuit of Justice — *Matthews, Ben*
Pursuit of Power: NASA's Propulsion Systems Laboratory No. 1 and 2 — *Arrighi, Robert S.*
The Pursuit of the Nazi Mind: Hitler, Hess, and the Analysts — *Pick, Daniel*
y **Push** — *Silver, Eve*
Push Me, Pull You, 2 vols. — *Blick, Sarah*

The Pushcart Prize XL: Best of the Small Presses — *Henderson, Bill*
c **The Pushcart War (Illus. by Solbert, Ronni)** — *Merrill, Jean*
Pushing the Limits: The Remarkable Life and Times of Adm. Allan Rockwell McCann, USN — *LaVO, Carl*
Pushkin Hills — *Dovlatov, Sergei*
c **Pussycat, Pussycat and More: Purrfect Nursery Rhymes (Illus. by Bixley, Donovan)** — *Bixley, Donovan*
c **Pussycat, Pussycat (Illus. by van Hout, Mies)** — *van Hout, Mies*
Put a Ring on It — *Kendrick, Beth*
Put This On, Please: New and Selected Poems — *Trowbridge, William*
Put Up Your Duke — *Frampton, Megan*
Putin and the Oligarch: The Khodorkovsky-Yukos Affair — *Sakwa, Richard*
Putin Country: A Journey into the Real Russia — *Garrels, Anne*
Putin kaputt!? Russlands neue Protestkultur — *Gabowitsch, Mischa*
Putinism: Russia and Its Future with the West — *Laquer, Walter*
Putinism: Russia and Its Future with the West — *Laqueur, Walter*
Putin's Kleptocracy: Who Owns Russia? — *Dawisha, Karea*

Putin's Kleptocracy: Who Owns Russia? — *Dawisha, Karen*
Putting a Name to It: Diagnosis in Contemporary Society — *Jute, Annemarie Goldstein*
Putting Essential Understanding into Practice: Statistics, 9-12 — *Crites, Terry*
Putting Essential Understanding of Addition and Subtraction into Practice, Pre-K-Grade 2 — *Dougherty, Barbara J.*
Putting Essential Understanding of Fractions into Practice in Grades 9-12 — *Ronau, Robert N.*
Putting God Second: How to Save Religion from Itself — *Hartman, Donniel*
c **Putting the Monkeys to Bed (Illus. by Davis, Jack E.)** — *Choldenko, Gennifer*
Putting the Practices Into Action: Implementing the Common Core Standards for Mathematical Practice K-8 — *O'Connell, Susan*
Putting the User First: 30 Strategies for Transforming Library Services — *McDonald, Courtney Greene*
Puzzled Indemnity — *Hall, Parnell*
c **Puzzling Cats** — *Falken, Linda*
c **Puzzling Dogs** — *Falken, Linda*
c **Pyjama Day (Illus. by Martchenko, Michael)** — *Munsch, Robert*
Pyrite: A Natural History of Fool's Gold — *Rickard, David*
Pythagorean Women: Their History and Writings — *Pomeroy, S.B.*

Q R

c Q Is for Quinoa: A Modern Parent's ABC (Illus. by Wilson, Spencer) — *Rickett, Joel*
Q Island — *James, Russell*
Q Tasks: How to Empower Students to Ask Questions and Care About the Answers, 2d ed. — *Koechlin, Carol*
Qaqamiigux: Traditional Foods and Recipes from the Aleutian and Pribilof Islands — *Unger, Suanne*
c Quackers Wants to Fly (Illus. by Currie, Justin) — *Wolff, Susan*
y Quake — *Carman, Patrick*
Quaker Brotherhood: Interracial Activism and the American Friends Service Committee, 1917-1950 — *Austin, Allan W.*
Quakers and Abolition — *Carey, Brycchan*
Quakers and Abolition — *Casey, Brycchan*
c Quaky Cat Helps Out (Illus. by Bishop, Gavin) — *Noonan, Diana*
The Quality of Silence — *Lupton, Rosamund*
'Quand la folie parle': The Dialectic Effect of Madness in French Literature since the Nineteenth Century — *Cheallaigh, Gillian Ní*
Quantitative Plate Tectonics: Physics of the Earth - Plate Kinematics - Geodynamics — *Schettino, Antonio*
The Quantum Deception — *Acey, Denver*
Quantum Economics: Unleashing the Power of an Economics of Consciousness — *Goswami, Amit*
Quantum Holographic Criminology: Paradigm Shift in Criminology, Law, and Transformative Justice — *Milovanovic, Dragan*
The Quantum Moment: How Planck, Bohr, Einstein, and Heisenberg Taught Us to Love Uncertainty — *Crease, Robert P.*
Quantum Poetics: Newcastle/Bloodaxe Poetry Lectures — *Lewis, Gwyneth*
Quantum Theory for Mathematics — *Hall, Brian*
y Quarantine: The Burnouts — *Thomas, Lex*
The Quarry — *Howe, Susan*
Quarry Light — *Smith, Claudia*
Quarry's Choice — *Collins, Max Allan*
c Quarterback Rush (Illus. by Garcia, Eduardo) — *Bowen, Carl*
Quartet for the End of Time — *Skibsrud, Johanna*
The Quartet — *Ellis, Joseph J.*
The Quartet: Orchestrating the Second American Revolution, 1783-1789 (Read by Dean, Robertson). Audiobook Review — *Ellis, Joseph J.*
The Quartet: Orchestrating the Second American Revolution, 1783-1789 — *Ellis, Joseph J.*
Quartz and Feldspar: Dartmoor - A British Landscape in Modern Times — *Kelly, Matthew*
Quatermass and the Pit: Five Million Years to Earth — *Newman, Kim*
c The Quayside Cat (Illus. by Brown, Ruth) — *Forward, Toby*
Quebec Women and Legislative Representations — *Tremblay, Manon*
The Queen and I — *Townsend, Sue*
Queen Anne: Patroness of Arts — *Winn, James Anderson*
Queen Caroline: Cultural Politics at the Early Eighteenth-Century Court — *Marschner, Joanna*
Queen for a Day: Transformistas, Beauty Queens, and the Performance of Femininity in Venezuela — *Ochoa, Marcia*
Queen For Power: European Imperialism and the Making of Chinese Statecraft — *Halsey, Stephen R.*
Queen Lear — *Conley, Ellen Alexander*
y The Queen of Bright and Shiny Things — *Aguirre, Ann*
Queen of Flowers and Pearls — *Ghermandi, Gabriella*

Queen of Hearts — *Bowen, Rhys*
y Queen of Shadows — *Maas, Sarah J.*
The Queen of Sparta — *Chaudhry, T.S.*
A Queen of Sparta — *Chaudhry, Tariq*
Queen of Spies: Daphne Park, Britain's Cold War Spy Master — *Hayes, Paddy*
c Queen of the Diamond: The Lizzie Murphy Story (Illus. by McCully, Emily Arnold) — *McCully, Emily Arnold*
Queen of the Fall: A Memoir of Girls and Goddesses — *Livingston, Sonja*
Queen of the Hurricanes: The fearless Elsie MacGill — *Sissons, Crystal*
Queen of the Night — *Chee, Alexander*
y Queen of the Night — *Hall, Leanne*
The Queen of the Tearling (Read by Kellgren, Katherine). Audiobook Review — *Johansen, Erika*
The Queen of the Tearling — *Johansen, Erika*
y Queen of Tomorrow — *Ficklin, Sherry D.*
c The Queen of Zombie Hearts — *Showalter, Gena*
Queen Victoria: Gender and Empire — *Kent, Susan Kingsley*
Queen Victoria's Mysterious Daughter: A Biography of Princess Louise — *Hawksley, Lucinda*
Queens and Mistresses of Renaissance France — *Wellman, Kathleen*
The Queen's Caprice — *Echenoz, Jean*
Queen's Caprice — *Coverdale, Linda*
The Queen's Dumbshows: John Lydgate and the Making of Early Theater — *Sponsler, Claire*
c The Queen's Hat (Illus. by Antony, Steve) — *Antony, Steve*
The Queen's Play — *Kaul, Aashish*
The Queens Regnant of Navarre: Succession, Politics, and Partnership, 1274-1512 — *Woodacre, Elena*
c The Queen's Shadow: A Story about How Animals See — *Young, Cybele*
y The Queen's Shadow: A Story about How Animals See (Illus. by Young, Cybele) — *Young, Cybele*
Queensboro — *Drago, Thomas*
Queenship in Medieval Europe — *Earenfight, Theresa*
Queequeg's Coffin: Indigenous Literacies and Early American Literature — *Rasmussen, Birgit Brander*
Queer Activism in India: A Story in the Anthropology of Ethics — *Dave, Naisargi N.*
Queer BDSM Intimacies: Critical Consent and Pushing Boundaries — *Bauer, Robin*
Queer Domesticities: Homosexuality and Home Life in Twentieth-Century London — *Cook, Matt*
Queer Enchantments: Gender, Sexuality, and Class in the Fairy-Tale Cinema of Jacques Demy — *Duggan, Anne E.*
Queer Environmentality: Ecology, Evolution, and Sexuality in American Literature — *Azzarello, Robert*
Queer Events: Post-Deconstructive Subjectivities in Spanish Writing and Film, 1960s to 1990s — *Vilaseca, David*
The Queer Limit of Black Memory: Black Lesbian Literature and Irresolution — *Richardson, Matt*
Queer Migration Politics: Activist Rhetoric and Coalitional Possibilities — *Chavez, Karma R.*
Queer Others in Victorian Gothic: Transgressing Monstrosity — *Thomas, Ardel Haefele*
Queer Saint: The Cultured Life of Peter Watson, Who Shook Twentieth-Century Art and Shocked High Society — *Clark, Adrian*
Queering Marriage Challenging Family Formation in the United States — *Kimport, Katrina*
Queering Marriage: Challenging Family Formation in the United States — *Kimport, Katrina*

Quellen zur Nationalen und Internationalen Schulgesundheitspflege Wahrend der Weimarer Republik — *Forster, Gabriele*
Quench Your Own Thirst: Business Lessons Learned over a Beer or Two — *Koch, Jim*
The Quest for Mastery: Positive Youth Development Through Out-of-School Programs — *Intrator, Sam M.*
c The Quest for Screen Time (Illus. by Muravski, Mari) — *Dumas, Marti*
c A Quest for Shiny Purple Crystals: Johnny and Max's Rock Hunting Adventure — *Rakovan, Monica Tsang*
The Quest for Socialist Utopia: The Ethiopian Student Movement, c. 1960-1974 — *Zewde, Bahru*
The Quest for the Historical Satan — *De La Torre, Miguel A.*
c Quest Maker — *McKay, Laurie*
y Quest of a Bipolar Soldier — *Redman, Winston K.*
c Quest (Illus. by Becker, Aaron) — *Becker, Aaron*
c The Quest to End World Hunger — *Kjelle, Marylou*
c Question It! — *Sharkaway, Azza*
A Question of Bounty: The Shadow of Doubt — *Colt, Paul*
A Question of Genocide: Armenians and Turks at the End of the Ottoman Empire — *Suny, Ronald Grigor*
c The Question of Miracles — *Arnold, Elana K.*
The Question of the Unfamiliar Husband — *Copperman, E.J.*
Questiones Libri Porphirii — *Manlevelt, Thomas*
Questioning Science in East Asian Contexts: Essays on Science, Confucianism, and the Comparative History of Science — *Kim, Yung Sik*
Questioning the Human: Toward a Theological Anthropology for the Twenty-First Century — *Boeve, Lieven*
Questions Jesus Asks: Where Divinity Meets Humanity — *Wayne, Israel*
Questions of Gender in Byzantine Society — *Neil, Bronwen*
c Qui aidera le pere Noel? (Illus. by Biedrzycki, David) — *Pallotta, Jerry*
Qui est Charlie? Sociologie d'une crise religieuse — *Todd, Emmanuel*
y Qui est le plus fort? (Illus. by Boudreau, Joel) — *Ancelet, Barry Jean*
c Qui EsTu? (Illus. by Perreault, Guillaume) — *Gagnon, Cecile*
The Quick — *Owen, Lauren*
The Quick — *Sail, Lawrence*
Quick Check Guide to Organic Foods — *Wexler, Barbara*
Quick Crocheted Accessories — *Zientara, Sharon*
c Quick, Little Monkey! (Illus. by Judge, Lita) — *Thomson, Sarah L.*
Quicksand — *Baugh, Carolyn*
Quicksand — *Toltz, Steve*
Quickstart Molecular Biology: An Introduction for Mathematics, Physicists, and Computational Scientists — *Benfey, Philip N.*
The Quiet American — *Greene, Graham*
The Quiet Man: The Indispensable Presidency of George H.W. Bush — *Sununu, John H.*
Quiet: The Power of Introverts in a World That Can't Stop Talking — *Cain, Susan*
The Quiet Tides of Bordeaux — *Lambert, J.L.F.*
Quilled Animals — *Boden, Diane*
The Quilt Calendar 2016 — *That Patchwork Place*
A Quilt for Christmas — *Dallas, Sandra*
Quilt Local: Finding Inspiration in the Everyday — *Jones, Heather*
Quilt Lovely: 15 Vibrant Projects Using Piecing and Applique — *Kingwell, Jen*

The Quilter's Practical Guide to Color — Goldsmith, Becky
Quilts du Jour: Make it Your Own with a la Carte Blocks and Settings — Buck, Marny
c Quinito, Day and Night / Quinito, dia y noche (Illus. by Ramirez, Jose) — Cumpiano, Ina
Quintessential Style — Beatty, Janna
c The Quirks and the Quirkalicious Birthday (Illus. by Jack, Colin) — Soderberg, Erin
c Quit It! (Illus. by Cartwright, Amy) — Powell, Marie
Quite a Good Time to Be Born: A Memoir, 1935-1975 — Lodge, David
Quite Contrary: The Litigious Life of Mary Bennett Love — Bakken, Gordon Morris
Quite Contrary: The Litigious Life of Mary Bennett Love — Langum, David J., Sr.
Quite Happy — Williams, L.C.
The Quilter's Practical Guide to Color — Goldsmith, Becky
Quitting Certainties: A Bayesian Framework Modeling Degrees of Belief — Titelbaum, Michael C.
Quiver of the Pure Heart — Bluitt, Burnita
Quixote: The Novel and the World — Stavans, Ilan
Quo vadis Zeitgeschichte?/L'histoire du Temps Present et ses Defis au XXIe Siecle
The Quotable Feynman — Feynman, Richard P.
The Qur'an's Legal Culture: The Didascalia Apostolorum as a Point of Departure — Zellentin, Holger Michael
Qviet — Burkholder, Andy
R.E.A.D. Dogs — Goldish, Meish
R.I.P. — Williams, Nigel
c R Is for Rocket: An ABC Book (Illus. by Hills, Tad) — Hills, Tad
(R)Evolution — Manney, P.J.
Rab Butler: The Best Prime Minister We Never Had? — Jago, Michael
c Rabbi Benjamin's Buttons (Illus. by Reinhardt, Jennifer Black) — McGinty, Alice B.
Rabbinic Creativity in the Modern Middle East — Zohar, Zvi
Rabbit — Dickenson, Victoria
y The Rabbit Ate My Homework (Illus. by Dionne, Deanna) — Cole, Rachel Elizabeth
c The Rabbit Who Wants to Fall Asleep: A New Way of Getting Children to Sleep (Illus. by Maununen, Irina) — Ehrlin, Carl-Johan Forssen
Rac(e)ing to Class: Confronting Poverty and Race in Schools and Classrooms — Milner, H. Richard
Raccogliamo le vele — Servadio, Gaia
Race after the Internet — Nakamura, Lisa
Race and Displacement: Nation, Migration, and Identity in the Twenty-First Century — Marouan, Maha
Race and Masculinity in Southern Memory: History of Richmond, Virginia's Monument Avenue, 1948-1996 — Barbee, Matthew Mace
Race and Multiculturalism in Malaysia and Singapore — Goh, Daniel P.S.
Race and Racism in International Relations: Confronting the Global Colour Line — Anievas, Alexander
Race and Racism in the United States: An Encyclopedia of the American Mosaic — Gallagher, Charles A.
Race and Rights: Fighting Slavery and Prejudice in the Old Northwest, 1830-1870 — Weiner, Dana Elizabeth
Race and the Chilean Miracle: Neoliberalism, Democracy, and Indigenous Rights — Richards, Patricia
Race and the Modernist Imagination — Seshagiri, Urmila
Race: Antiquity and Its Legacy — McCoskey, Denise Eileen
c Race Car Count — Dotlich, Rebecca Kai
c Race Car Count (Illus. by Slack, Michael) — Dotlich, Rebecca Kai
Race Decoded: The Genomic Fight for Social Justice — Bliss, Catherine
Race, Ethnicity, and Nuclear War: Representations of Nuclear Weapons and Post-Apocalyptic Worlds — Williams, Paul (b. 1979-)
y The Race for Boatlantis — Roman, Dave
Race for Empire: Koreans as Japanese and Japanese as Americans during World War II — Fujitani, Takashi
The Race for Paris — Clayton, Meg Waite
The Race for Paris — Clayton, Mega Waite
c Race from A to Z (Illus. by Shannon, David) — Scieszka, Jon

Race, Gender and Empire in American Detective Fiction — Gruesser, John Cullen
Race, Gender, and Military Heroism in U.S. History: From World War I to 9/11
Race Harmony and Black Progress: Jack Woofter and the Interracial Cooperation Movement — Ellis, Mark
Race Horse Men: How Slavery and Freedom Were Made at the Racetrack — Mooney, Katherine C.
Race in Cuba: Essays on the Revolution and Racial Inequality — Morales Dominguez, Esteban
Race in Mind: Critical Essays — Spickard, Paul
Race Migrations: Latinos and the Cultural Transformation of Race — Roth, Wendy
Race, Multiculture and Social Policy — Bloch, Alice
Race on the QT: Blackness and the Films of Quentin Tarantino — Nama, Adilifu
Race, Romance, and Rebellion: Literatures of the Americas in the Nineteenth Century — O'Brien, Colleen C.
Race to Revolution: The United States and Cuba during Slavery and Jim Crow — Horne, Gerald
c The Race to the Beach! (Illus. by Shuttlewood, Anna) — Shuttlewood, Anna
y Race to the End of the World — Tait, A.L.
c Race to the Moon — Parker, Steve
Race to Tibet — Schiller, Sophie
Race Unmasked: Biology and Race in the Twentieth Century — Yudell, Michael
c Racehorses — Turnbull, Stephanie
The Racer — Millar, David
Rache und Triumph: Krieg, Gefuhle und Gedenken in der Moderne — de Libero, Loretana
Rachel Carson and Her Sisters: Extraordinary Women Who Have Shaped America's Environment — Musil, Brian
c Rachel Carson: Environmental Crusader — Dickmann, Nancy
y Rachel Maddow: Primetime Political Commentator — Houts, Amy
Rachmaninoff's Cape: A Nostalgia Memoir — Rousseau, George
Racial Asymmetries: Asian American Fictional Worlds — Sohn, Stephen Hong
Racial Cleansing in Arkansas, 1883-1924: Politics, Land, Labor, and Criminality — Lancaster, Guy
Racial Imperatives: Discipline, Performativity, and Struggles against Subjection — Ehlers, Nadine
y Racial Profiling and Discrimination: Your Legal Rights — Grinapol, Corinne
Racial Reckoning: Prosecuting America's Civil Rights Murders — Romano, Renee C.
Racialised Correctional Governance: The Mutual Constructions of Race and Criminal Justice — Spivakovsky, Claire
y Racing the Rain — Parker, John L.
y Racing the Waves (Illus. by Neubecker, Robert) — Neubecker, Robert
Racism and Ethnic Relations in the Portuguese-Speaking World — Bethencourt, Francisco
Racism in the Nation's Service: Government Workers and the Color Line in Woodrow Wilson's America — Yellin, Eric S.
The Racket: A Rogue Reporter vs. the Masters of the Universe — Kennard, Matt
y Rad American Women A-Z: Rebels, Trailblazers, and Visionaries who Shaped Our History ... and Our Future! (Illus. by Stahl, Miriam Klein) — Schatz, Kate
Radiance — Valente, Catherynne M.
Radiance from Halcyon: A Utopian Experiment in Religion and Science — Ivey, Paul Eli
Radiance — Valente, Catherynne M.
Radiance — Kissane, Andy
Radiant Angel (Read by Brick, Scott). Audiobook Review — DeMille, Nelson
Radiant Angel — DeMille, Nelson
y The Radiant Road — Catmull, Katherine
Radical Chic and Mau Mauing the Flak Catchers — Wolfe, Tom
Radical Chicana Poetics — Vivancos Perez, Ricardo F.
Radical Feminism: Feminist Activism in Movement — Mackay, Finn
Radical History and the Politics of Art — Rockhill, Gabriel
Radical Marriage — Steele, David
Radical Pedagogies: Architectural Education and the British Tradition — Harriet Harriss, Daisy
Radical Political Theology: Religion and Politics after Liberalism — Crockett, Clayton

Radical Prototypes: Allan Kaprow and the Invention of Happenings — Rodenbeck, Judith F.
Radical Sensations: World Movements, Violence, and Visual Culture — Streeby, Shelley
Radical Shakespeare: Politics and Stagecraft in the Early Career — Fitter, Chris
Radical Survivor: One Woman's Path through Life, Love, and Uncharted Tragedy — Saltzman, Nancy
Radicals on the Road: Internationalism, Orientalism, and Feminism during the Vietnam Era — Wu, Judy Tzu-Chun
Radikalisierung des Antisemitismus wahrend des Ersten Weltkrieges? Antisemitische Akteure und judische Kriegserfarungen im europaischen Vergleich
c Radio Active (Illus. by Pamintuan, Macky) — Ball, Nate
Radio Benjamin — Benjamin, Walter
Radio Benjamin — Rosenthal, Lecia
Radio Fields: Anthropology and Wireless Sound in the 21st Century — Bessire, Lucas
Radio Rides the Range: A Reference Guide to Western Drama on the Air, 1929-1967 — French, Jack
y Radioactive! How Irene Curie and Lise Meitner Revolutionized Science and Changed the World — Conkling, Winifred
Radioland — McHugh, Matt
Radiomen — Lerman, Eleanor
Radium and the Secret of Life — Campos, Luis A.
Radovan Karadzic: Architect of the Bosnian Genocide — Donia, Robert J.
Raed and Frofer: Christian Poetics in the Old English "Froferboc" Meters — Lenz, Karmen
c Rafa Was My Robot (Illus. by Turner, Ken) — Dellevoet, Alexandra
Rafiki — Minier, David
The Rag Race: How Jews Sewed Their Way to Success in America and the British Empire — Mendelsohn, Adam D.
Rage — Shufeldt, Ken
Rage Ignition — Miner, Matt
Rage Master — Clark, Simon (b. 1958-)
Rage to Redemption in the Sterilization Age: A Confrontation with American Genocide — Railey, John
The Ragged Road to Abolition: Slavery and Freedom in New Jersey, 1775-1865 — Gigantino, James J., II
The Ragged Road to Abolition: Slavery and Freedom in New Jersey, 1775-1865 — Gigantino, James J., III
Raging Sea — Brisbin, Terri
y Raging Sea — Buckley, Michael
The Raging Skillet: The True Life Story of Chef Rossi: A Memoir with Recipes — Rossi, Chef
c Raging Star (Read by Lind, Heather). Audiobook Review — Young, Moira
y Raging Star — Young, Moira
Ragtime Cowboys — Estleman, Loren D.
c Ragweed's Farm Dog Handbook (Illus. by Kennedy, Anne Vittur) — Kennedy, Anne Vittur
A Raid Too Far: Operation Lam Son 719 and Vietnamization in Laos — Willbanks, James H.
c Raiders of the Lost Shark — Gardner, Lyn
Raiding with Morgan — Woolard, Jim R.
y Railhead — Reeve, Philip
Railing, Reviling and Invective in English Literary Culture, 1588-1617: The Anti-Poetics of Theater and Print — Prendergast, Maria Theresa Micaela
Railroad Radicals in Cold War Mexico: Gender, Class, and Memory — Alegre, Robert F.
Railroaders: Jack Delano's Homefront Photography — Gruber, John
c A Railway ABC (Illus. by Townend, Jack) — Townend, Jack
The Railways: Nation, Network and People — Bradley, Simon
Rain: A Natural and Cultural History — Barnett, Cynthia
c The Rain Dragon Rescue (Illus. by Santat, Dan) — Selfors, Suzanne
c Rain Forest Colors (Illus. by Laman, Tim) — Lawler, Janet
c Rain Forest (Illus. by Scrace, Carolyn) — Channing, Margot
c Rain Forest Relay — Earhart, Kristin
c Rain of Blood — Veys, Pierre
c Rain Reign (Read by Hamilton, Laura). Audiobook Review — Martin, Ann M.
c Rain Reign — Martin, Ann M.
y Rain Shadow — Sherrard, Valerie
y The Rain Wizard: The Amazing, Mysterious, True Life of Charles Mallory Hatfield — Brimner, Larry Dane

The Rainborowes: One Family's Quest to Build a New England — Tinniswood, Adrian
c The Rainbow Dancer — Hirsch, Allan
Rainbow Dust: Three Centuries of Delight in British Butterflies — Marren, Peter
c Rainbow of Friendship (Illus. by Goldenberg, Eileen) — Kelin-Higger, Joni
The Rainbow Piano: A Method for Children 4-7 Years Old — Muller-Simmerling, Chantal
c The Rainbow Serpent (Illus. by Greene, Sanford) — Pryce, Trevor
c Rainbows Never End: And Other Fun Facts (Illus. by Oswald, Pete) — DiSiena, Laura Lyn
Raincoast Chronicles 23 — Robson, Peter A.
c Raindrops Fall All Around (Illus. by Watson, Laura) — Ghigna, Charles
c Raindrops Roll — Sayre, April Pulley
The Rainman's Third Cure: An Irregular Education — Coyote, Peter
Rainy Day Sisters — Hewitt, Kate
c Rainy, Sunny, Blowy, Snowy: What Are Seasons? — Brocket, Jane
y Raise the Stakes — Atwood, Megan
Raised Up down Yonder: Growing up Black in Rural Alabama — Howell, Angela McMillan
Raising Aphrodite — Curnutt, Kirk
Raising Caine — Gannon, Charles E.
Raising Can-Do Kids: Giving Children the Tools to Thrive in a Fast-Changing World — Rende, Richard
Raising Generation Rx — Blum, Linda M.
y Raising Heaven — Jones, Patrick
y Raising Rufus — Fulk, David
Raising Ryland: Our Story of Parenting a Transgender Child with No Strings Attached — Whittington, Hillary
Raising Self-Esteem in Adults: An Eclectic Approach with Art Therapy, CBT and DBT Based Techniques — Buchalter, Susan
Raising Steam — Prachett, Terry
Raising the Barre: Big Dreams, False Starts, and My Midlife Quest to Dance the Nutcracker — Kessler, Lauren
c Raising the Stakes — Romanek, Trudee
Raising the World: Child Welfare in the American Century — Fieldston, Sara
The Raj at War: A People's History of India's Second World War — Khan, Yasmin
c Rajon Rondo — Jackson, Aurelia
Rally the Scattered Believers: Northern New England's Religious Geography — Balik, Shelby M.
Ralph Ellison and Kenneth Burke: At the Roots of the Racial Divide — Crable, Bryan
Ralph Vaughan Williams: Bucolic Suite - Study Score — Rushton, Julian
Ralph Vaughan Williams: Burley Heath - Study Score — Brown, James Francis
Ralph Vaughan Williams: Fantasia for Piano and Orchestra - Study Score — Parlett, Graham
Ralph Vaughan Williams: Harnham Down - Study Score — Brown, James Francis
Ralph Vaughan Williams: Serenade in A Minor (1898) - Study Score — Rushton, Julian
Ralph Vaughan Williams: The Solent - Study Score — Brown, James Francis
RAM-2050 — Roughgarden, Joan
The Ramblers — Rowley, Aidan Donnelley
Rameau's Nephew: A Multi-Media Edition — Diderot, Denis
y Ramona the Pest (Read by Channing, Stockard). Audiobook Review — Cleary, Beverly
y Random — Leveen, Tom
y Random Acts — Sharrard, Valerie
c Random Body Parts: Gross Anatomy Riddles in Verse (Illus. by Lowery, Mike) — Bulion, Leslie
Random Shootings — Drury, Frank
y Randoms — Liss, David
Randy Lopez Goes Home — Anaya, Rudolfo
c Randy Orton — Scheff, Matt
The Range War of '82 — Wolfe, Ethan J.
Range Wars: The Environmental Contest for White Sands Missile Range — Edgington, Ryan H.
The Range Wolf — Fenady, Andrew J.
Ranger Creek Guest Ranch — Comisford, Sue
c Ranger in Time: Rescue on the Oregon Trail — Messner, Kate
c A Ranger to Fight With — Griffin, James J.
c A Ranger to Reckon With — Griffin, James J.
c A Ranger to Ride With — Griffin, James J.
c A Ranger to Stand With — Griffin, James J.
c Ranger's Apprentice: The Early Years — Flanagan, John

c A Ranger's Christmas — Griffin, James J.
c Rani in Search of a Rainbow: A Natural Disaster Survival Tale (Illus. by Samaddar, Bijan) — Abdullah, Shaila
Ranking Faiths: Religious Stratification in America — Davidson, James D.
The Ransom of the Soul: Afterlife and Wealth in Early Western Christianity — Brown, Peter (b. 1935-)
Raoul Wallenberg: The Heroic Life and Mysterious Disappearance of the Man Who Saved Thousands of Hungarian Jews from the Holocaust — Carlberg, Ingrid
Rap Tees: A Collection of Hip-Hop T-Shirts 1980-1999 — DJ Ross One
The Rape of Europa: The Intriguing History of Titian's Masterpiece — FitzRoy, Charles
Rape: Weapon of War and Genocide — Rittner, Carol
The Raping of Ava DeSantis — Carbia, Mylo
c Rappy the Raptor (Illus. by Bowers, Tim) — Gutman, Dan
c Rapunzel and the Prince of Pop — Gorman, Karyn
c Rapunzel (Illus. by Rossi, Francesca) — Francia, Giada
Rare Birds of North America — Howell, Steve N.G.
Rare Books and Special Collections — Berger, Sidney E.
Rare: The High-Stakes Race to Satisfy Our Need for the Scarcest Metals on Earth — Veronese, Keith
The Rarest Bird in the World: The Search for the Nechisar Nightjar — Head, Vernon R.L.
Rasende Reporter: Eine Kulturgeschichte des Fotojournalismus. Fotografie, Presse und Gesellschaft in Osterreich 1890 bis 1945 — Holzer, Anton
Raspberry Pi for Dummies — McManus, Sean
c The Rat — Gravel, Elise
y Rat Runners — McGann, Oisin
c The Rat with the Human Face (Read by Turetsky, Mark). Audiobook Review — Angleberger, Tom
c The Rat with the Human Face (Illus. by Angleberger, Tom) — Angleberger, Tom
The Rataban Betrayal — Alter, Stephen
Rational Expectations: Asset Allocation for Investing Adults — Bernstein, William J.
Rationality through Reasoning — Broome, John
c Rats! (Illus. by Bixley, Donovan) — Mewburn, Kyle
c Ratscalibur (Read by Ballerini, Edoardo). Audiobook Review — Lieb, Josh
c Ratscalibur (Illus. by Lintern, Tom) — Lieb, Josh
Rattlesnakes and Bald Eagles: Hiking the Pacific Crest Trail — Townsend, Chris
"Rattraper et depasser la Suisse": Histoire de l'industrie horlogere japonaise de 1850 a nos jours — Donze, Pierre-Yves
Raub, Raubkunst und Verwertung Judischen Eigentums. 26. Tagung zur Geschichte und Kultur der Juden in Schwaben
Raum - Ort - Ding: Kultur- und Sozialwissenschaftliche Perspektiven
Raum und Nation in der polnischen Westforschung 1918-1948: Wissenschaftsdiskurse, Raumdeutungen und geopolitische Visionen im Kontext der deutsch-polnischen Beziehungsgeschichte — Briesewitz, Gernot
Raume, Orte, Konstruktionen. (Trans)Lokale Wirklichkeiten im Mittelalter und der Fruhen Neuzeit
Raumzeitlichkeit des Imperialen
Raven: The Turbulent World of Baron Corvo — Scoble, Robert
The Raven Watched — Weiss, Karin E.
c Ravenbach's Way — Akers, William M.
y Ravencliffe — Goodman, Carol
c Ravenous — Connolly, MarcyKate
The Ravens — Sundstol, Vidar
Ravensbruck: Life and Death in Hitler's Concentration Camp for Women — Helm, Sarah
Ravenscrag — Farah, Alain
The Ravine — Pascuzzi, Robert
Raw Deal: How the "Uber Economy" and Runaway Capitalism Are Screwing American Workers — Hill, Steven
Raw Material — Bulloch, Jamie
Raw Organic Goodness: 100 Recipes, 100 Percent Raw and Plant Based, for Everyone Who Loves Food — May, Megan
Raw Spirit: In Search of the Perfect Dram — Banks, Iain
y Ray Bradbury and the Cold War — Kampff, Joseph
Ray Bradbury Unbound — Eller, Jonathan R.
Ray Davies: A Complicated Life — Roganm, Johnny

Ray of Sunlight — Stein, Brynn
Raymundo Gonzalez: Magical Realism in Mexico — Oettinger, Marion
y Razorhurst — Larbalestier, Justine
Razzle Dazzle: The Battle for Broadway — Riedel, Michael
y RDA Made Simple: A Practical Guide to the New Cataloging Rules — Hart, Amy
Re-collecting Black Hawk: Landscape, Memory, and Power in the American Midwest — Brown, Nicholas A.
Re-Collection: Art, New Media, and Social Memory — Rinehart, Richard
y Re Jane — Park, Patricia
Re-Viewing Thomas Holcroft, 1745-1809: Essays on His Works and Life — Wallace, Miriam L.
(Re)Constructing Maternal Performance In Twentieth-Century American Drama — McDaniel, L. Bailey
Reach: 40 Black Men Speak on Living, Leading, and Succeeding — Jealous, Benjamin Todd
Reacher Said Nothing: Lee Child and the Making of "Make Me" — Martin, Andy
Reaching Down the Rabbit Hole: A Renowned Neurologist Explains the Mystery and Drama of Brain Disease (Read by Boehmer, Paul). Audiobook Review — Ropper, Allan H.
Reaching Down the Rabbit Hole: A Renowned Neurologist Explains the Mystery and Drama of Brain Disease — Ropper, Allan H.
Reactor Agenda — Sales, Michael A.
c Read and Discover Series — Lindeen, Mary
y Read Between the Lines — Knowles, Jo
y Read Me Like A Book — Kessler, Liz
Read On ... Romance: Reading Lists for Every Taste — Quillen, C.L.
c Read, Recite, and Write Cinquains — Macken, JoAnn Early
c Read, Recite, and Write Concrete Poems — Macken, JoAnn Early
c Read, Recite, and Write Free Verse Poems — Macken, JoAnn Early
c Read, Recite, and Write Haiku — Macken, JoAnn Early
c Read, Recite, and Write Limericks — Macken, JoAnn Early
c Read, Recite, and Write List Poems — Macken, JoAnn Early
c Read, Recite, and Write Narrative Poems — Macken, JoAnn Early
The Readable Darwin: The Origin of Species: Edited for Modern Readers — Pechenik, Jan A.
The Readaholics and the Poirot Puzzle — DiSilverio, Laura
The Reader in the Book — Orgel, Stephen
The Readers' Advisory Guide to Genre Blends — McArdle, Megan M.
The Readers' Advisory Guide to Historical Fiction — Baker, Jennifer S.
The Reader's Brain: How Neuroscience Can Make You a Better Writer — Douglas, Yellowlees
The Readers of Broken Wheel Recommend — Bivald, Katarina
The Readers of "Novyi Mir": Coming to Terms with the Stalinist Past — Kozlov, Denis
Readers Writing: Strategy Lessons for Responding to Narrative and Informational Text — Hale, Elizabeth
Reading 1-2 Peter and Jude: A Resource for Students — Mason, Eric E.
Reading and Writing during the Dissolution: Monks, Friars, and Nuns 1530-1558 — Erler, Mary C.
Reading and Writing in Science: Tools to Develop Disciplinary Literacy — Grant, Maria C.
Reading Arabia: British Orientalism in the Age of Mass Publication, 1880-1930 — Nash, Geoffrey P.
Reading Augustine in the Reformation: The Flexibility of Intellectual Authority in Europe, 1500-1620 — Visser, Arnoud S.Q.
Reading Authority and Representing Rule in Early Modern England — Sharpe, Kevin
Reading Backwards: Figural Christology and the Fourfold Gospel Witness — Hays, Richard B.
Reading Basics for All Teachers: Supporting the Common Core — Carver, Lin
Reading Champs — Wirtz, Rita M.
Reading Chaucer: Selected Essays — Brown, Peter (b. 1948-)
Reading Claude Cahun's 'Disavowals' — Shaw, Jennifer L.
Reading Claudius: A Memoir in Two Parts — Heller, Caroline

Reading Dante: From Here to Eternity — *Shaw, Prue*
Reading Darwin in Arabic, 1860-1950 — *Elshakry, Marwa*
Reading for Liberalism: The Overland Monthly and the Writing of the Modern American West — *Mexal, Stephen J.*
Reading for Preaching: The Preacher in Conversation with Storytellers, Biographers, Poets, and Journalists — *Plantinga, Cornelius, Jr.*
Reading Green in Early Modern England — *Knight, Leah*
Reading Hosea-Micah: A Literary and Theological Commentary — *Fretheim, Terence E.*
Reading Like a Girl: Narrative Intimacy in Contemporary American Young Adult Literature — *Day, Sara K.*
Reading Literature Cognitively — *Cave, Terence*
Reading Lucretius in the Renaissance — *Palmer, Ada*
Reading "Matthew" for the First Time — *Harrington, Wilfrid*
Reading Medbh McGuckian — *Flynn, Leontia*
Reading Medieval Anchoritism: Ideology and Spiritual Practices — *Hughes-Edwards, Mari*
Reading Onora O'Neill — *Archard, David*
Reading Picture Books with Children — *Lambert, Megan Dowd*
Reading "Piers Plowman" — *Steiner, Emily*
Reading Prisoners: Literature, Literacy, and the Transformation of American Punishment, 1700-1845 — *Schorb, Jodi*
Reading Publics: New York City's Public Libraries, 1754-1911 — *Glynn, Tom*
c Reading Science Stories: Narrative Tales of Science Adventurers — *Hakim, Joy*
Reading Skin in Medieval Literature and Culture — *Walter, Katie L.*
Reading the Art in Caldecott Award Books: A Guide to the Illustrations — *Hammond, Heidi K.*
Reading the Bromance: Homosocial Relationships in Film and Television — *DeAngelis, Michael*
Reading the Comments: Likers, Haters, and Manipulators at the Bottom of the Web — *Reagle, Joseph M., Jr.*
Reading the Parables: Interpretation: Resources for the Use of Scripture in the Church — *Lischer, Richard*
Reading the Rabbis: Christian Hebraism in the Works of Herbert of Bosham — *De Visscher, Eva*
Reading the Ruins: Modernism, Bombsites and British Culture — *Mellor, Leo*
Reading the Streets — *Riley, Michael*
Reading the Wampum: Essay on Hodinohsoni' Visual Code Epistemological Recovery — *Kelsey, Penelope Myrtle*
Reading the World: Confessions of Literary Explorer — *Morgan, Ann*
Reading Unruly: Interpretation and its Ethical Demands — *Zalloua, Zahi*
Reading Up: Middle-Class Readers and the Culture of Success in the Early Twentieth-Century United States — *Blair, Amy L.*
Reading What's There: Essays on Shakespeare in Honor of Stephen Booth — *Collins, Michael J.*
Reading William Blake — *Makdisi, Saree*
c Reading with Pictures: Comics That Make Kids Smarter (Illus. by McMeel, Andrews) — *Elder, Josh*
Reading Writing Interfaces: From the Digital to the Bookbound — *Emerson, Lori*
Readings in Wood: What the Forest Taught Me — *Leland, John*
c Ready for Math Series — *Wingard-Nelson, Rebecca*
c Ready for Military Action — *Bell, Samantha S.*
c Ready for School, Murphy? (Illus. by Murphy, Brendan) — *Murphy, Brendan*
c Ready Rabbit Gets Ready! (Illus. by Kennedy, Chuck) — *Maloney, Brenna*
c Ready, Set, Kindergarten! (Illus. by Arbour, Danielle) — *Ayer, Paula*
Ready, Set, Learn: Integrating Powerful Learning Skills and Strategies into Daily Instruction — *Dzaldov, Brenda Stein*
c Ready, Set, Rhythm! Sequential Lessons to Develop Rhythmic Reading — *Easter-Clutter, Melody*
c Ready, Steady, Ghost! (Illus. by Lindsay, Marion) — *Baguley, Elizabeth*
c Ready, Steady, Jump! (Illus. by Reynolds, Adrian) — *Willis, Jeanne*
Ready to Burst — *Franketienne*
Reagan and Pinochet: The Struggle over U.S. Policy toward Chile — *Morley, Morris H.*
Reagan: The Life — *Brands, H.W.*

Real and Phantom Pains: An Anthology of New Russian Drama — *Freedman, John*
Real Baby Food: Easy, All-Natural Recipes for Your Baby and Toddler — *Helwig, Jenna*
The Real Cost of Fracking: How America's Shale Gas Boom Is Threatening Our Families, Pets, and Food — *Bamberger, Michelle*
The Real Deal: the Autobiography of Britain's Most Controversial Media Mogul — *Desmond, Richard*
The Real Doctor Will See You Shortly: A Physician's First Year — *McCarthy, Matt*
Real Estate Development: Principles and Process — *Schmitz, Adrienne*
y Real Justice: A Police Mr. Big Sting Goes Wrong: The Story of Kyle Unger — *Brignall, Richard*
y Real Justice: Jailed for Life for Being Black - The Story of Rubin "Hurricane" Carter — *Swan, Bill*
y Real Justice: Jailed for Life for Being Black: The Story of Rubin "Hurricane" Carter — *Swan, Bill*
The Real Justine — *Amidon, Stephen*
Real Lawyers — *Farmer, Kenneth*
The Real-Life MBA: Your No-BS Guide to Winning the Game, Building a Team, and Growing Your Career — *Welch, Jack*
Real Life Rock: The Complete Top Ten Columns — *Marcus, Greil*
The Real Lives of Roman Britain — *de la Bedoyere, Guy*
c The Real Man of Steel (Illus. by Vecchio, Luciano) — *Sutton, Laurie S.*
Real Men Don't Sing: Crooning in American Culture — *McCracken, Allison*
Real Native Genius: How an Ex-Slave and a White Mormon Became Famous Indians — *Hudson, Angela Pulley*
The Real North Korea: Life and Politics in the Failed Stalinist Utopia — *Lankov, Andrei*
Real People and the Rise of Reality Television — *McKenna, Michael*
The Real Planet of the Apes: A New Story of Human Origins — *Begun, David R.*
Real Solutions Weight Loss Workbook, 2d ed. — *Piechota, Toni*
A Real Southern Cook in Her Savannah Kitchen — *Charles, Dora*
y Real Stories about Werewolves — *Mercier, Deb*
Real Sweet: More Than 80 Crave-Worthy Treats Made with Natural Sugars - Fun with Coconut Sugar, Muscovado, Turbinado, Honey, Maple Syrup, Agave Nectar, and Many More! — *Sever, Shauna*
The Real Thing: Essays on Making in the Modern World — *Harrod, Tanya*
The Real Thing: Lessons on Love and Life from a Wedding Reporter's Notebook — *McCarthy, Ellen*
The Real Thing. E-book Review — *Rettstatt, Linda*
Real Tigers — *Herron, Mick*
The Real Traviata: The Song of Marie Duplessis — *Weis, Rene*
The Real Watergate Scandal: Collusion, Conspiracy, and the Plot to Bring Nixon Down — *Shepard, Geoff*
The Realignment Case — *Dearden, R.J.*
Realism and Romanticism in German Literature — *Gottsche, Dirk*
The Realism Challenge: Drawing and Painting Secrets from a Modern Master of Hyperrealism — *Crilley, Mark*
The Realist Author and Sympathetic Imagination — *Paraschas, Sotirios*
Realistic Retirement for Realistic People: Look Before You Leap — *Martin, Randolph M.*
c Reality Check — *Harding, David*
c Reality Check in Detroit — *MacGregor, Roy*
The Reality of God: The Layman's Guide to Scientific Evidence for the Creator — *Hemler, Steven R.*
Reality Show — *Sullivan, Jazmine*
y Really Professional Internet Person — *McAllister, Jenn*
Reap the Wind — *Chance, Karen*
The Reaper: Autobiography of One of the Deadliest Special Ops Snipers — *Brozek, Gary*
Reason, Faith, and Otherness in Neoplatonic and Early Christian Thought — *Corrigan, Kevin*
The Reason for Flowers: Their History, Culture, Biology, and How They Change Our Lives — *Buchmann, Stephen*
Reasoned and Unreasoned Images: The Photography of Bertillon, Galton, and Marey — *Ellenbogen, Josh*
Reasons as Defaults — *Horty, John F.*
Reasons of Conscience: The Bioethics Debate in Germany — *Sperling, Stefan*
Reasons to Stay Alive — *Haig, Matt*

y Reawakened — *Houck, Colleen*
y Reawakened (Read by Strole, Phoebe). Audiobook Review — *Houck, Colleen*
y Reawakened — *Houck, Colleen*
Rebalancing U.S. Forces: Basing and Forward Presence in the Asia-Pacific — *Lord, Carnes*
Rebecca Dickinson: Independence for a New England Woman — *Miller, Marla*
Rebecca Ringquist's Embroidery Workshops: A Bend-the-Rules Primer — *Ringquist, Rebecca*
c A Rebel among Redcoats — *Gunderson, Jessica*
c Rebel Belle (Read by Rubinate, Amy). Audiobook Review — *Hawkins, Rachel*
y Rebel, Bully, Geek, Pariah — *Lange, Erin Jade*
Rebel Cowboy — *Helm, Nicole*
Rebel Footprints: A Guide to Uncovering London's Radical History — *Rosenberg, David*
y Rebel Mechanics — *Swendson, Shanna*
Rebel Music: Race, Empire, and the New Muslim Youth Culture — *Aidi, Hisham D.*
The Rebel of Rangoon: A Tale of Defiance and Deliverance in Burma — *Schrank, Delphine*
y Rebel of the Sands — *Hamilton, Alwyn*
y Rebel of the Sands — *Hammilton, Alwyn*
Rebel Queen — *Moran, Michelle*
Rebel Souls: Walt Whitman and America's First Bohemians — *Martin, Justin*
The Rebel: The Complete Series: The Collectors Edition — *Joyner, C. Courtney*
c Rebel with a Cause: The Daring Adventure of Dicey Langston, Girl Spy of the American Revolution (Illus. by Faber, Rudy) — *Kudlinski, Kathleen V.*
Rebel Yell: The Violence, Passion, and Redemption of Stonewall Jackson. Audiobook Review — *Gwynne, S.C.*
Rebel Yell: The Violence, Passion, and Redemption of Stonewall Jackson — *Gwynne, S.C.*
Rebel Youth: 1960s Labour Unrest, Young Workers, and New Leftists in English Canada — *Milligan, Ian*
y Rebellion — *Diaz, Stephanie*
The Rebellion of Miss Lucy Ann Lobdell — *Klaber, William*
Rebellion: The History of England from James I to the Glorious Revolution (Read by Chafer, Clive). Audiobook Review — *Ackroyd, Peter*
Rebellion: The History of England from James I to the Glorious Revolution — *Ackroyd, Peter*
The Rebellious No: Variations on a Secular Theology of Language — *Vahanian, Noelle*
Rebellious Spirits: The Illicit History of Booze in Britain — *Ball, Ruth*
Rebels at the Bar: The Fascinating, Forgotten Stories of America's First Women Lawyers — *Norgren, Jill*
Rebels in Paradise: The Los Angeles Art Scene and the 1960s — *Drohojowska-Philp, Hunter*
y Rebels of the Lamp — *Galvin, Michael M.B.*
Rebirth — *Walker, Landry Q.*
The Rebirth of Latin American Christianity — *Hartch, Todd*
The Rebirthing of God: Christianity's Struggle for New Beginnings — *Newell, John Philip*
Rebound Remedy — *d'Abo, Christine*
Rebozos De Palabras: An Helena Maria Viramontes Critical Reader — *Muhs, Gabriella Gutierrez*
Rebranding Rule: The Restoration and Revolution Monarchy, 1660-1714 — *Sharpe, Kevin*
Rebuilding a Dream: Partnership for Sustainable Communities — *Shashaty, Andre F.*
Rebuilding Anatolia after the Mongol Conquest: Islamic Architecture in the Lands of Rum, 1240-1330 — *Blessing, Patricia*
Recalled to Death — *Masters, Priscilla*
Recalling Deeds Immortal: Florida Monuments to the Civil War — *Lees, William B.*
Recalling Deeds Immortal: Florida Monuments to the Civil War — *Lees William B.*
Recapitulations — *Crapanzano, Vincent*
Recapturing the Oval Office: New Historical Approaches to the American Presidency — *Balogh, Brian*
Recasting India: How Entrepreneurship is Revolutionising the World's Largest Democracy — *Sengupta, Hindol*
Recent Advances in Predicting and Preventing Epileptic Seizures — *Tetzlaff, Ronald*
The Reception of Machiavelli in Early Modern Spain — *Howard, Keith David*
Recharge Your Library Programs with Pop Culture and Technology: Connect with Today's Teens — *Behen, Linda D.*
c The Rechargeables: Eat Move Sleep — *Rath, Tom*

Recht und Politik in der Transnationalen Konstellation — *Franzius, Claudio*
c Recipe for a Story — *Burfoot, Ella*
c A Recipe for Bedtime (Illus. by Massini, Sarah) — *Bently, Peter*
   Recipes for a Beautiful Life: A Memoir in Stories — *Barry, Rebecca*
   Recipes for Love and Murder — *Andrew, Sally*
   Recipes from Italy — *Rau, Dana Meachen*
   Reckless — *Toptas, Hasan Ali*
y Reckless Hearts — *Olin, Sean*
   Reckless: My Life as a Pretender (Read by Arquette, Rosanna). Audiobook Review — *Hynde, Chrissie*
   Reckless: My Life as a Pretender — *Hynde, Chrissie*
   Reckless — *Kincaid, Kimberly*
   Reckoning Day: Race, Place, and the Atom Bomb in Postwar America — *Foertsch, Jacqueline*
   The Reckoning: Death and Intrigue in the Promised Land: A True Detective Story — *Bishop, Patrick*
   The Reckoning: Financial Accountability and the Rise and Fall of Nations — *Soll, Jacob*
   The Reckoning Stones — *DiSilverio, Laura*
   The Reckoning — *Stroud, Carsten*
   Reclaim the Magic: The Real Secrets to Manifesting Anything You Want — *Milteer, Lee*
   Reclaim Your Brain — *Annibali, Joseph A.*
   Reclaiming American Virtue: The Human Rights Revolution of the 1970s — *Keys, Barbara J.*
   Reclaiming Conversation: The Power of Talk in a Digital Age — *Turkle, Sherry*
   Reclaiming Food Security — *Carolan, Michael*
   Reclaiming Late-Romantic Music: Singing Devils and Distant Sounds — *Franklin, Peter*
   Reclaiming Pietism: Retrieving an Evangelical Tradition — *Olson, Roger E.*
   Reclaiming the Don: An Environmental History of Toronto's Don River Valley — *Bonnell, Jennifer*
   Reclaiming Travel — *Stavans, Ilan*
   Recognizing Heritage: The Politics of Multiculturalism in New Mexico — *Guthrie, Thomas H.*
   Recollecte super Poetria magistri Gualfredi — *da Bologna, Guizzardo*
   Recollecting Resonances: Indonesian-Dutch Musical Encounters — *Barendregt, Bart*
   Recollections of a Tejano Life: Antonio Menchaca in Texas History — *Matovina, Timothy*
   ReCombinatorics: The Algorithms of Ancestral Recombination Graphs and Explicit Phylogenetic Networks — *Yufeng Wu*
   Recommended Reference Books for Small and Medium-Sized Libraries and Media-Centers, 2015 ed. — *Hysell, Shannon G.*
   Reconceiving Infertility: Biblical Perspective on Procreation and Childlessness — *Moss, Candida R.*
   Reconciling Canada: Critical Perspectives on the Culture of Redress — *Wakeham, Pauline*
   Reconnaisance — *Phillips, Carl*
   Reconnaissance and Bomber Aces of World War 1 — *Guttman, Jon*
   Reconnaissance on Sonora: Charles D. Poston's 1854 Exploration of Mexico and the Gadsden Purchase — *Storms, G. Gilbert*
   The Reconnected Leader: An Executive's Guide to Creating Responsible, Purposeful and Valuable Organizations — *Pickavance, Norman*
   Reconsidering the American Way of War: US Military Practice from the Revolution to Afghanistan — *Echevarria, Antulio J., II*
   Reconsidering the American Way of War: US Military Practice from the Revolution to Afghanistan — *Echevarria, Antulio J., III*
   Reconsidering the Date and Provenance of the Book of Hosea: The Case for Persian-Period Yehud — *Bos, James M.*
   Reconsidering the Relationship between Biblical and Systematic Theology in the New Testament — *Reynolds, Benjamin E.*
   Reconstructing a Shattered Egyptian Army: War Minister Gen. Mohamed Fawzi's Memoirs, 1967-1971 — *Aboul-Enein, Youssef H.*
   Reconstructing Memory: The Holocaust in Polish Public Debates — *Forecki, Piotr*
   Reconstructing Obesity: The Meaning of Measures and the Measure of Meanings — *McCullough, Megan B.*
   Reconstructing Rage: Transformative Reentry in the Era of Mass Incarceration — *Price-Spratlen, Townsand*
   Reconstructing Strategy — *Qureshi, Saqib*
   Reconstructing the Theology of Evagrius Ponticus: Beyond Heresy — *Casiday, Augustine*
c The Reconstruction Era — *Latta, Susan M.*

   Reconstruction: First A Body, Then A Life — *Ashburne, Ara Lucia*
y The Reconstruction of the South after the Civil War — *Ziff, Marsha*
c Record-Breaking Animals (Illus. by Simkins, Ed) — *Richards, Jon*
c Record-Breaking Earth and Space Facts — *Richards, Jon*
c Record-Breaking People — *Richards, Jon*
   Records of the Moravians Among the Cherokees, vol. 5: The Anna Rosina Years, Part 3: Farewell to Sister Gambold, 1817-1821 — *Crews, C. Daniel*
   Records Ruin the Landscape: John Cage, the Sixties, and Sound Recording — *Grubbs, David*
   Recovering Joy: A Mindful Life After Addiction — *Griffin, Kevin*
   Recovering Liberties: Indian Thought in the Age of Liberalism and Empire — *Bayly, Christopher Alan*
   Recovering the Piedmont Past: Unexplored Moments in Nineteenth-Century Upcountry South Carolina History — *Grady, Timothy P.*
   Recreating First Contact: Expeditions, Anthropology, and Popular Culture — *Bell, Joshua A.*
   Recursive Origins: Writing at the Transition to Modernity — *Kuskin, William*
c Recycling — *Mooney, Carla*
c Recycling Day (Illus. by Miller, Edward) — *Miller, Edward*
   Recycling Reconsidered: The Present Failure and Future Promise of Environmental Action in the United States — *MacBride, Samantha*
   Recycling, Yes or No — *Palmer, Erin*
c Red: A Crayon's Story (Illus. by Hall, Michael) — *Hall, Michael*
c Red, A Crayon's Story (Illus. by Hall, Michael) — *Hall, Michael*
c Red: A Crayon's Story (Illus. by Hall, Michael) — *Hall, Michael*
   Red: A Haida Manga — *Yahgulanaas, Michael Nicoll*
   Red: A History of the Redhead — *Harvey, Jacky Colliss*
   Red: A Natural History of the Redhead — *Harvey, Jacky Colliss*
c Red (Illus. by De Kinder, Jan) — *De Kinder, Jan*
c Red and Green in Spring — *Carole, Bonnie*
   The Red and the White: A Family Saga of the American West — *Graybill, Andrew R.*
c Red Animals — *Borth, Teddy*
   Red Apple: Communism and McCarthyism in Cold War New York — *Deery, Phillip*
c The Red Apple — *Oral, Feridun*
   The Red Atlantic: American Indigenes and the Making of the Modern World, 1000-1927 — *Weaver, Jace*
   The Red Bekisar — *Tohari, Ahmad*
c Red Berries, White Clouds, Blue Sky (Read by Ikeda, Jennifer). Audiobook Review — *Dallas, Sandra*
y Red Berries, White Clouds, Blue Sky — *Dallas, Sandra*
   The Red Bicycle: The Extraordinary Story of One Ordinary Bicycle (Illus. by Shin, Simone) — *Isabella, Jude*
   The Red Bird All-Indian Traveling Band — *Washburn, Frances*
y Red Butterfly (Illus. by Bates, Amy June) — *Sonnichsen, A.L.*
c Red Butterfly — *Sonnichsen, A.L.*
c Red Butterfly (Illus. by Bates, Amy June) — *Sonnichsen, A.L.*
c Red Butterfly (Illus. by June, Amy) — *Sonnichsen, A.L.*
c Red Car, Blue Car (Illus. by Verrall, Lisa) — *Litton, Jonathan*
   Red Cavalry — *Babel, Isaac*
   Red Cavalry — *Babel, Nathalie*
   Red Cavalry — *Dralyuk, Boris*
   Red Cloud: Oglala Legend — *McDermott, John D.*
   Red Cloud: The Greatest Warrior Chief of the American West — *Drury, Bob*
c Red Cloud's War: Brave Eagle's Account of the Fetterman Fight December 21, 1866 — *Goble, Paul*
c Red Cloud's War: Brave Eagle's Account of the Fetterman Fight (Illus. by Goble, Paul) — *Goble, Paul*
c Red Cloud's War — *Goble, Paul*
   The Red Collar — *Rufin, Jean-Christophe*
   Red Deer — *Macari, Anne Marie*
   Red Dreams, White Nightmares: Pan-Indian Alliances in the Anglo-Indian Mind, 1963-1815 — *Owens, Robert M.*
   Red Dust Road — *Kay, Jackie*
   The Red Earl — *Hastings, Selina*

y Red Eggs and Good Luck — *Lam, Angela*
   The Red: First Light — *Nagata, Linda*
   Red Flags: How to Spot Frenemies, Underminers, and Toxic People in Your Life — *Patrick, Wendy L.*
   Red Fortress: The Secret Heart of Russia's History — *Merridale, Catherine*
   Red Gas: Russia and the Origins of European Energy Dependence — *Hogselius, Per*
y Red Girl, Blue Boy — *Baratz-Logsted, Lauren*
y Red Girls: The Legend of the Akakuchibas — *Sakuraba, Kazuki*
   Red Globalization: The Political Economy of the Soviet Cold War from Stalin to Khrushchev — *Sanchez-Sibony, Oscar*
   The Red Handkerchief and Other Poems — *Shapiro, Daniel*
c Red Hat (Illus. by Portis, Antoinette) — *Teague, David*
   Red Hot Chili Grower: The Complete Guide to Planting, Picking, and Preserving Chilis — *Maguire, Kay*
   Red Icon — *Eastland, Sam*
y Red Ink — *Mayhew, Julie*
   Red Juice — *Nguyen, Hoa*
c Red Knit Cap Girl and the Reading Tree — *Stoop, Naoko*
   The Red Land to the South: American Indian Writers and Indigenous Mexico — *Cox, James H.*
y Red Leaves — *Brahmachari, Sita*
c Red Light, Green Light (Illus. by Heo, Yumi) — *Heo, Yumi*
   The Red Light in the Ivory Tower: Contexts and Implications of Entrepreneurial Education — *Breault, Donna Adair*
   Red Light to Starboard: Recalling the Exxon Valdez Disaster — *Day, Angela*
   Red Lighting — *Pritchett, Laura*
   Red Lightning — *Pritchett, Laura*
   Red Line — *Thiem, Brian*
   Red Mars — *Robinson, Kim Stanley*
   Red Nations: The Nationalities Experience in and after the USSR — *Smith, Jeremy (b. 1964-)*
   The Red Notebook — *Laurain, Antoine*
   Red Notice: A True Story of High Finance, Murder, and One Man's Fight for Justice (Read by Grupper, Adam). Audiobook Review — *Browder, Bill*
   Red Notice: A True Story of High Finance, Murder, and One Man's Fight for Justice — *Browder, Bill*
   Red Notice: How I Became Putin's No 1 Enemy — *Browder, Bill*
y The Red Pencil (Illus. by Evans, Shane W.) — *Pinkney, Andrea Davis*
c Red (Illus. by De Kinder, Jan) — *De Kinder, Jan*
c Red — *De Kinder, Jan*
y Red Queen — *Aveyard, Victoria*
   Red Rising — *Brown, Pierce*
   The Red Road — *Mina, Denise*
   Red Sails: Prose — *Enniss, Stephen*
y The Red Sheet — *Kerick, Mia*
   The Red Shoe — *Dubosarsky, Ursula*
c The Red Shoes and Other Tales (Illus. by Metaphrog) — *Metaphrog*
   Red Skin, White Masks: Rejecting the Colonial Politics of Recognition — *Coulthard, Glen Sean*
c Red Socks (Illus. by Hu, Ying-Hwa) — *Mayer, Ellen*
c Red Spider Hero (Illus. by Cucco, Giuliano) — *Miller, John (b. 1934-)*
   Red Stamps and Gold Stars: Fieldwork Dilemmas in Upland Socialist Asia — *Turner, Sarah*
   Red State Religion: Faith and Politics in America's Heartland — *Wuthnow, Robert*
   Red Storm Rising — *Bywaters, Grant*
   Red Sulphur — *Bosnak, Robert*
y The Red Sun — *Adams, Alane*
   Red Tape: Bureaucracy, Structural Violence, and Poverty in India — *Gupta, Akhil*
   Red Team: How to Succeed by Thinking like the Enemy — *Zenko, Micah*
   The "Red Terror" and the Spanish Civil War: Revolutionary Violence in Madrid — *Ruiz, Julius*
y The Red Thirst (Illus. by Evergreen, Nelson) — *Hulme-Cross, Benjamin*
   Red Tide — *Niven, Larry*
   Red Tide — *Lindsay, Jeff*
   The Red Web: The Struggle between Russia's Digital Dictators and the New Online Revolutionaries — *Soldatov, Andrei*
   Red, White and Army Blue — *Decker, Peter R.*
   Red, White, and Black Make Blue: Indigo in the Fabric of Colonial South Carolina Life — *Feeser, Andrea*
y Red Zone Rivals — *Howling, Eric*

Redbrick: A Social and Architectural History of Britain's Civic Universities — *Whte, William*
Redburn: His First Voyage — *Melville, Herman*
Redcoats: The British Soldiers of the Napoleonic Wars — *Haythornthwaite, Philip*
Redeemable: A Memoir of Darkness and Hope — *James, Erwin*
c Redeemed — *Cast, P.C.*
c Redeemed — *Haddix, Margaret Peterson*
Redeemer: The Life of Jimmy Carter — *Balmer, Randall*
The Redeemers — *Atkins, Ace*
Redeeming Fear: A Constructive Theology for Living into Hope — *Whitehead, Jason C.*
Redeeming Our Sacred Story: The Death of Jesus and Relations between Jews and Christians — *Boys, Mary C.*
Redeeming the Dream: The Case for Marriage Equality — *Olson, Theodore B.*
Redeeming the Great Emancipator — *Guelzo, Allen C.*
Redeeming "The Prince": The Meaning of Machiavelli's Masterpiece — *Viroli, Maurizio*
Redefining Ancient Orphism: A Study in Greek Religion — *Edmonds, Radcliffe G., III*
Redefining Hungarian Music from Liszt to Bartok — *Hooker, Lynn M.*
Redefining Mainstream Popular Music — *Baker, Sarah*
Redefining Rape: Sexual Violence in the Era of Suffrage and Segregation — *Freedman, Estelle B.*
Redemption Bay — *Thayne, RaeAnne*
Redemption Road — *Ashley, Katie*
Redemption Songs: Suing for Freedom before Dred Scott — *VanderVelde, Lea*
Reden und Schweigen uber religiose Differenz: Tolerieren in epochenubergreifender Perspektive — *Huchtker, Dietlind*
Redeployment — *Lahiri, Jhumpa*
Redeployment (Read by Klein, Craig). Audiobook Review — *Klay, Phil*
Redeployment — *Klay, Phil*
Redes de nacion y espacios de poder. La Comunidad irlandesa en Espana y la America Espanola, 1600-1825 — *Morales, Oscar Recio*
Redevelopment and Race: Planning a Finer City in Postwar Detroit — *Thomas, June Manning*
Redeye Fulda Cold — *Fortin, Bill*
Rediscovering the Umma: Muslims in the Balkans between Nationalism and Transnationalism — *Merdjanova, Ina*
Rednecks, Queers, and Country Music — *Hubbs, Nadine*
y Red's Untold Tale: Once upon a Time — *Toliver, Wendy*
Redskins: Insult and Brand — *King, C. Richard*
Redzone — *Dietz, William C.*
The Reef: A Passionate History — *McCalman, Iain*
Reef Libre: Cuba-The Last, Best Reefs in the World — *Wintner, Robert*
Reeling through Life: How I Learned to Live, Love, and Die at the Movies — *Ison, Tara*
Reeling with Laughter: American Film Comedies-from Anarchy to Mockumentary — *Tueth, Michael V.*
The Reference Guide to Data Sources — *Bauder, Julia*
Referendariat Geschichte: Kompaktwissen fur Berufseinstieg und Examensvorbereitung — *Berger, Jutta*
Refiguring the Spiritual: Beuys, Barney, Turrell, Goldsworthy — *Taylor, Mark C.*
Refining Fire — *Peterson, Trade*
Refire! Don't Retire: Make the Rest of Your Life the Best of Your Life — *Blanchard, Ken*
The Reflection — *Wilcken, Hugo*
Reflection from Pope Francis: An Invitation to Journaling, Prayer, and Action — *Stark, Susan*
Reflections of a Metaphysical Flaneur and Other Essays — *Tallis, Raymond*
Reflections on Progress, Coexistence, and Intellectual Freedom — *Sakharov, Andrei*
Reflections on the Revolution in France — *Burke, Edmund*
Reflective Teaching in Higher Education — *Ashwin, Paul*
Reflexion von ethnischer Identitat(szuweisung) im deutschen Gegenwarts-theater — *Voss, Hanna*
Reflexology Made Easy: Self-Help Techniques for Everyday Ailments — *Kliegel, Ewald*
Refocusing Chaplin: A Screen Icon through Critical Lenses — *Howe, Lawrence*
Reforging the Bible: More Biblical Stories and Their Literary Reception — *Swindell, Anthony C.*

Reform Acts: Chartism, Social Agency, and the Victorian Novel, 1832-1867 — *Bossche, Chris R. Vanden*
The Reform of the English Parish Church — *Whiting, Robert*
The Reformation as Christianization: Essays on Scott Hendrix's Christianization Thesis — *Johnson, Anna Marie*
Reformation Faith: Exegesis and Theology in the Protestant Reformations — *Parsons, Michael*
Reformation vor Ort. Zum Quellenwert von Visitationsprotokollen
Reformationsgeschichte und Kulturgeschichte der Reformation. Symposium zum Gedenken an Ernst Walter Zeeden
Reforme catholique, religion des pretres et "foi des simples": Etudes d'anthropologie religieuse — *Julia, Dominique*
Reformed Confessions of the 16th and 17th Centuries in English Translation, vol. 4, 1600-1693 — *Dennison, James T., Jr.*
Reformed Means Missional: Following Jesus into the World — *Logan, Samuel T., Jr.*
Reformers to Radicals: The Appalachian Volunteers and the War on Poverty — *Kiffmeyer, Thomas*
Reforming Asian Labor Systems: Economic Tensions and Worker Dissent — *Deyo, Frederic C.*
Reforming Ideas in Britain: Politics and Language in the Shadow of the French Revolution, 1789-1815 — *Philp, Mark*
Reforming Japan: The Women's Christian Temperance Union in the Meiji Period — *Lublin, Elizabeth Dorn*
Reforming Ottoman Governance: Success, Failure and the Path to Decline — *Andic, Fuat*
Reforming Reformation — *Mayer, Thomas F.*
Reforming the World Monetary System: Fritz Machlup and the Bellagio Group — *Connell, Carol M.*
Reforming Trollope: Race, Gender, and Englishness in the Novels of Anthony Trollope — *Morse, Deborah Denenholz*
The Refrain and the Rise of the Vernacular in Medieval French Music and Poetry — *Saltzstein, Jennifer*
Refrains for Moving Bodies: Experience and Experiment in Affective Spaces — *McCormack, Derek P.*
Reframing Antifascism: Memory, Genre and the Life Writings of Greta Kuckhoff — *Sayner, Joanne*
Reframing the Feudal Revolution: Political and Social Transformation between Marne and Moselle, c.800-c.1100 — *West, Charles*
Reframing Yeats: Genre, Allusion and History — *Armstrong, Charles I.*
Refrigeration: A History — *Gantz, Carroll*
The Refuge — *Mackenzie, Kenneth*
The Refugee Centaur — *Robles, Antonio J.*
Refugee Performance: Practical Encounters — *Balfour, Michael*
Refugees, Capitalism and the British State: Implications for Social Workers, Volunteers and Activists — *Vickers, Tom*
Refund — *Bender, Karen E.*
c Reg Saunders: An Indigenous War Hero (Illus. by Barbu, Adrian) — *Dolan, Hugh*
Regarding Lost Time: Photography, Identity, and Affect in Proust, Benjamin, and Barthes — *Haustein, Katja*
Regenerations: Canadian Women's Writing — *Carriere, Marie*
Regenerative Biology of the Eye — *Pebay, Alice*
y Regenesis — *Walters, Eric*
Regesta Regum Scottorum IV, Pt 1: The Acts of Alexander III — *Neville, Cynthia J.*
Reggie & Me — *Yates, Marie*
"Regimental Practice". E-book Review — *Kopperman, Paul*
Region, Religion and English Renaissance Literature — *Coleman, David*
Regional Integration in East Asia: Theoretical and Historical Perspectives — *Amako, Satoshi*
Regionale Produzenten oder Global Player? Zur Internationalisierung der Wirtschaft im 19. und 20. Jahrhundert
Regionalists on the Left: Radical Voices from the American West — *Steiner, Michael C.*
Regionalists on the Left: Radical Voices from the American West — *Steiner, Micheal C.*
Regionalizing Culture: The Political Economy of Japanese Popular Culture in Asia — *Otmazgin, Nissim Kadosh*

Registres du Consistoire de Geneve au Temps de Calvin: Tome VIII, 25 mars 1553-1 fevrier 1554 — *Watt, Isabella M.*
Regrets Only — *Pullen, M.J.*
Regulating Desire: From the Virtuous Maiden to the Purity Princess — *Ehrlich, J. Shoshanna*
Regulating Passion: Sexuality and Patriarchal Rule in Massachusetts, 1700-1830 — *Ryan, Kelly A.*
Regulating Prostitution in China: Gender and Local Statebuilding, 1900-1937 — *Remick, Elizabeth J.*
Regulation between Legal Norms and Economic Reality: Intentions, Effects, and Adaption - the German and American Experiences — *Schulz, Gunther*
The Regulator — *Wolfe, Ethan J.*
Reguliertes Abenteuer: Missionarinnen in Sudafrika nach 1945 — *Gugglberger, Martina*
The Reharkening — *Booker, Stephen Todd*
Reichsgewalt Bedeutet Seegewalt: Die Kreuzergeschwader der Kaiserlichen Marine als Instrument der Deutschen Kolonial- und Weltpolitik 1885 bis 1914 — *Herold, Heiko*
The Reign of Greed — *Rizal, Jose*
y Reign of Shadows — *Jordan, Sophie*
Reimagining Business History — *Scranton, Philip*
Reimagining Business History — *Fridenson, Patrick*
Reimagining Business History — *Scranton, Philip*
Reimagining Courts: A Design for the Twenty-First Century — *Flango, Victor E.*
Reimagining the Sacred: Richard Kearney Debates God — *Kearney, Richard*
Reincarnation, Oblivion, or Heaven? An Exploration from a Christian Perspective — *Bose, Bobby*
c Reindeer Dust (Illus. by Lew-Vriethoff, Joanne) — *Dwyer, Kate*
c The Reindeer Wish (Illus. by Breiehagen, Per) — *Evert, Lori*
c The Reindeer Wish — *Evert, Lori*
c Reindeer's Christmas Surprise (Illus. by deGennaro, Sue) — *Dubosarsky, Ursula*
Reining in the State: Civil Society and Congress in the Vietnam and Watergate Eras — *Scott, Katherine A.*
Reinventing Citizenship: Black Los Angeles, Korean Kawasaki, and Community Participation — *Tsuchiya, Kazuyo*
Reinventing Dixie: Tin Pan Alley's Songs and the Creation of the Mythic South — *Jones, John Bush*
Reinventing Race, Reinventing Racism — *Betancur, John J.*
Reinventing Reference: How Libraries Deliver Value in the Age of Google — *Anderson, Katie Elson*
Reinventing State Capitalism: Leviathan in Business, Brazil and Beyond — *Musacchio, Aldo*
Rejection Proof: How I Beat Fear and Became Invincible through 100 Days of Rejection — *Jiang, Jia*
Rejoicing in Lament: Wrestling with Incurable Cancer and Life in Christ — *Bilings, J. Todd*
Rejoicing in Lament: Wrestling with Incurable Cancer and Life in Christ — *Billings, J. Todd*
Rekonstruktive Wissensbildung. Historische und gegenwartige Perspektiven einer gegenstandsbezogenen Theorie der Sozialen Arbeit
Relationship Skills 101 for Teens: Your Guide to Dealing with Daily Drama, Stress, and Difficult Emotions Using DBT — *van Dijk, Sheri*
Relationship Thinking: Agency, Enchrony, and Human Sociality — *Enfield, Nick J.*
Relationships/Beziehungsgeschichten: Austria and the United States in the Twentieth Century — *Bischof, Gunter*
Relationships / Beziehungsgeschichten: Austria and the United States in the Twentieth Century — *Bischof, Gunter*
Relativity: The Special and the General Theory — *Einstein, Albert*
Relax, It's Just God: How and Why to Talk to Your Kids about Religion When You're Not Religious — *Russell, Wendy Thomas*
Release — *Nunki, Hope Russell*
c Release the Beast (Illus. by Merkens, Cinzah) — *Zunde, Romy Sai*
Relentless Reformer: Josephine Roche and Progressivism in Twentieth Century America — *Muncy, Robyn*
Relentless Strike: The Secret History of Joint Special Operations Command — *Naylor, Sean*
The Relevance of Religion: How Faithful People Can Change Politics — *Danforth, John*
The Relic Master — *Buckley, Christopher*
c The Relic of Perilous Falls — *Arroyo, Raymond*

Relics and Writing in Late Medieval England — Malo, Robyn
Relics of the Past: The Collecting and Studying of Pre-Columbian Antiquities in Peru and Chile, 1837-1911 — Ganger, Stefanie
Relief Map — Knecht, Rosalie
Religio Medici and Urne-Buriall — Browne, Thomas
y Religion: A Discovery in Comics — De Heer, Margareet
Religion: A Discovery in Comics — De Heer, Margreet
Religion: A Discovery in Comics — de Heer, Margreet
Religion and AIDS in Africa — Trinitapoli, Jenny
Religion and American Cultures: Tradition, Diversity, and Popular Expression, 2d ed. — Leon, Luis
Religion and Authoritarianism: Cooperation, Conflict, and the Consequences — Koesel, Karrie J.
Religion and Competition in Antiquity — Engels, David
Religion and Enlightenment in Catherinian Russia: The Teachings of Metropolitan Platon — Wirtschafter, Elise Kimerling
Religion and Identity in Porphyry of Tyre: The Limits of Hellenism in Late Antiquity — Johnson, A.P.
Religion and Knowledge: Sociological Perspectives — Guest, Mathew
Religion and Man: Our Story — Guiteau, Leif
Religion and Politics in America: Faith, Culture, and Strategic Choices — Fowler, Robert Booth
Religion and Politics in Post-Socialist Central and Southeastern Europe: Challenges since 1989 — Ramet, Sabrina P.
Religion and Politics in the United States, 7th ed. — Wald, Kenneth D.
Religion and Psychotherapy in Modern Japan — Harding, Christopher
Religion and Rabindranath Tagore: Select Discourses, Addresses, and Letters in Translation — Sen, Amiya P.
Religion and Regimes: Support, Separation, and Opposition — Tamadonfar, Mehran
Religion and Social Transformations in Cyprus: From the Cypriots Basileis to the Hellenistic Strategos — Papantoniou, G.
Religion and sports in American Culture — Oca, Jeffrey Montez
Religion and State Formation in Postrevolutionary Mexico — Fallaw, Ben
The Religion and the American Moral Tradition: Seven Liberals and the American Moral Tradition — Kittelstrom, Amy
Religion and Trade: Cross-Cultural Exchanges in World History, 1000-1900 — Trivellato, Francesca
Religion Around Shakespeare — Kaufman, Peter Iver
Religion as Metaphor: Beyond Literal Belief — Tacey, David
Religion, Identity and Conflict in Britain: From the Restoration to the Twentieth Century: Essays in Honour of Keith Robbins — Brown, Stewart J.
Religion in China and Its Modern Fate — Katz, Paul R.
Religion in Public Spaces: A European Perspective — Ferrari, Silvio
Religion in Republican Rome. Rationalization and Ritual Change — Rupke, J.
Religion in Science Fiction: The Evolution of an Idea and the Extinction of a Genre — Hrotic, Steven
y Religion in Southeast Asia: An Encyclopedia of Faiths and Culture — Athyal, Jesudas M.
Religion in the British Navy, 1815-1879: Piety and Professionalism — Blake, Richard
Religion in the Oval Office: The Religious Lives of American Presidents — Smith, Gary Scott
Religion in the Public Schools: Negotiating the New Commons — Waggoner, Michael D.
Religion, Law and Society — Sandberg, Russell
Religion, Macht, Politik: Hofgeistlichkeit im Europa der Fruhen Neuzeit — Meinhardt, Matthias
Religion, Migration, Settlement: Reflections on Post-1990 Immigration to Finland — Martikainen, Tuomas
Religion, Nation, Krieg: Der Lutherchoral zwischen Befreiungskriegen und Erstem Weltkrieg — Fischer, Michael
The Religion of Democracy: Seven Liberals and the American Moral Tradition — Kittelstrom, Amy
The Religion of the Future — Irvine, Andrew B.
The Religion of the Future — Mangabeira, Roberto
The Religion of the Future — Unger, Roberto Mangabeira
Religion Out Loud: Religious Sound, Public Space, and American Pluralism — Weiner, Isaac

Religion, Politics, and Polarization: How Religiopolitical Conflict Is Changing Congress and American Democracy — D'Antonio, William V.
Religion, Politics and Society in Britain, 1066-1272 — Mayr-Harting, Henry
Religion, Politics, and the Origins of Palestine Refugee Relief — Romirowsky, Asaf
Religion, Race, and the Making of Confederate Kentucky, 1830-1880 — Harlow, Luke E.
Religion, Reason, and Culture in the Age of Goethe — Krimmer, Elisabeth
Religion, Reason, and Culture in the Age of Goethe — Simpson, Patricia Anne
Religion, Rights and Secular Society: European Perspectives — Cumper, Peter
Religions in Movement: The Local and the Global in Contemporary Faith Traditions — Hefner, Robert
Religious and Sexual Identities: A Multi-faith Exploration of Young Adults — Yip, Andrew Kam-Tuck
The Religious and Spiritual Life of the Jews of Medina — Hughes, Aaron W.
Religious Diaspora in Early Modern Europe: Strategies of Exile — Fehler, Timothy G.
Religious Diversity: Philosophical and Political Dimensions — Trigg, Roger
Religious Education and the Challenge of Pluralism — Seligman, Adam B.
Religious Education in a Multicultural Europe: Children, Parents and Schools — Smyth, Emer
The Religious Elite of the Early Islamic Hijaz: Five Prosopographical Case Studies — Ahmed, Asad Q.
Religious Freedom: Jefferson's Legacy, America's Creed — Ragosta, John
Religious Internationals in the Modern World: Globalization and Faith Communities Since 1750 — Green, Abigail
Religious Men and Masculine Identity in the Middle Ages — Cullum, Patricia H.
Religious Minorities and Cultural Diversity in the Dutch Republic: Studies Presented to Piet Visser on the Occasion of His 65th Birthday — Noord, Alex
Religious Networks in the Roman Empire: The Spread of New Ideas — Collar, Anna
The Religious Philosophy of Simone Weil: An Introduction — McCullough, Lissa
Religious Poverty, Visual Riches: Art in the Dominican Churches of Central Italy in the Thirteenth and Fourteenth Centuries — Cannon, Joanna
Religious Press and Print Culture
A Reluctant Bride — Fuller, Kathleen
The Reluctant Cannibals — Flitcroft, Ian
The Reluctant Duchess — Cullen, Sharon
The Reluctant Matador — Pryor, Mark
Reluctant Meister: How Germany's Past in Shaping Its European Future — Green, Stephen
The Reluctant Midwife — Harman, Patricia
y Reluctantly Charmed — O'Neill, Ellie
Remain in Your Calling: Paul and the Continuation of Social Identity in 1 Corinthians — Tucker, J. Brian
Remains of Innocence — Jance, J.A.
Remake — Todd, Ilima
Remaking history: The Past in Contemporary Historical Fictions — Groot, Jerone de
Remaking the American Patient: How Madison Avenue and Modern Medicine Turned Patients into Consumers — Tomes, Nancy
Remaking the Heartland: Middle America since the 1950s — Wuthnow, Robert
y Remaking the John: The Invention and Reinvention of the Toilet — DiPiazza, Francesca Davis
Remaking the Male Body: Masculinity and the uses of Physical Culture in Interwar and Vichy France — Tumblety, Joan
Remaking the Rhythms of Life: German Communities in the Age of the Nation-State — Zimmer, Oliver
c The Remarkable Journey of Charlie Price — Maschari, Jennifer
A Remarkable Kindness — Bletter, Diana
y Remarkable Minds: 17 More Pioneering Women in Science & Medicine — Noyce, Pendred E.
The Remarkable Rise of Eliza Jumel: A Story of Marriage and Money in the Early Republic — Oppenheimer, Margaret A.
c Remarkably Rexy — Smith, Craig
Rembrandt's Eyes — Schama, Simon
y The Remedy — Young, Suzanne
Remedy and Reaction: The Peculiar American Struggle over Health Care Reform — Starr, Paul
y Remember — Cook, Eileen
Remember Me Like This — Johnston, Anthony

y Remember Me — Bernard, Romily
Remember Me This Way — Durrant, Sabine
Remember, Remember — Cutts, Lisa
c Remember When ... (Illus. by Lehman, Judy) — Lehman, Dana
Rememberers — Baldwin, C. Edward
Remembering Africa: The Rediscovery of Colonialism in Contemporary German Literature — Gottsche, Dirk
Remembering and Rethinking the GDR: Multiple Perspectives and Plural Authenticities — Saunders, Anna
Remembering Armageddon: Religion and the First World War — Jenkins, Philip
Remembering Chris — Calabrese, Rosalie
Remembering Communism: Private and Public Recollections of Lived Experience in Southeast Europe — Todorova, Maria
c The Remembering Day / El Dia de Los Muertos (Illus. by Casilla, Robert) — Mora, Pat
c The Remembering Day / El Dia de Los Muertos — Mora, Pat
Remembering England: New and Selected Poems — Bland, Peter
Remembering God's Mercy: Redeem the Past and Free Yourself from Painful Memories — Eden, Dawn
Remembering Inez: The Last Campaign of Inez Milholland, Suffrage Martyr — Cooney, Robert
Remembering Parthenope: The Reception of Classical Naples from Antiquity to the Present — Hughes, Jessica
Remembering Paul: Ancient and Modern Contests over the Image of the Apostle — White, Benjamin L.
Remembering the Civil War: Reunion and the Limits of Reconciliation — Janney, Caroline E.
Remembering the Modoc War: Redemptive Violence and the Making of American Innocence — Cothran, Boyd
Remembering the Revolution: Memory, History, and Nation Making from Independence to the Civil War — Mcdonnell, Michael A.
Remembrance — Cabot, Meg
Remembrances in Black: Personal Perspective of the African American Experience at the University of Arkansas 1940-2000s — Robinson, Charles R., II
The Remittance Landscape: Spaces of Migration in Rural Mexico and Urban USA — Lopez, Sarah Lynn
y Remix — Pratt, Non
Remnants: A Memoir of Spirit, Activism, and Mothering — Harding, Rachel Elizabeth
Remnants: A Memoir of Spirit, Activism, and Mothering — Harding, Rosemarie Freeney
Remontagen der Erlittenen Zeit: Das Auge der Geschichte 2 — Didi-Huberman, Georges
Removing Mountains: Extracting Nature and Identity in the Appalachian Coalfields — McNeil, Bryan T.
Removing Mountains: Extracting Nature and Identity in the Appalachian Coalfields — Scott, Rebecca R.
c Remy and Lulu (Illus. by Harrison, Hannah E.) — Hawkes, Kevin
Renaissance and Baroque Bronzes in and around the Peter Marino Collection — Warren, Jeremy
Renaissance Drama on the Edge — Hopkins, Lisa
Renaissance Dynasticism and Apanage Politics: Jacques de Savoie-Nemours 1531-1585 — Vester, Matthew
Renaissance Humanism: An Anthology of Sources — King, Margaret L.
Renaissance Humanism and Ethnicity before Race: The Irish and the English in the Seventeenth Century — Campbell, Ian
The Renaissance in Italy: A Social and Cultural History of the Rinascimento — Ruggiero, Guido
Renaissance Keywords — Carthy, Ita Mac
The Renaissance of Empire in Early Modern Europe — Dandelet, Thomas James
Renaissance Retrospections: Tudor Views of the Middle Ages — Kelen, Sarah A.
Renaissance Truths: Humanism, Scholasticism and the Search for the Perfect Language — Perreiah, Alan R.
The Renaissance Utopia: Dialogue, Travel and the Ideal Society — Houston, Chloe
Rendez-vous avec l'heure qui blesse — Effa, Gaston-Paul
Rendez-vous with Art — Montebello, Philippe de
Rendezvous at the Russian Tea Rooms: The Spy Hunter, the Fashion Designer and the Man from Moscow — Willetts, Paul

Rendezvous mit dem Realen: Die Spur des Traumas in den Kunsten — Assmann, Aleida
Rene Girard and Secular Modernity: Christ, Culture, and Crisis — Cowdell, Scott
y Renegade — Wilkinson, Kerry
Renegade Amish: Beard Cutting, Hate Crimes, and the Trial of the Bergholz Barbers — Kraybill, Donald B.
y Renegade: An Elemental Novel — John, Anthony
Renegade Revolutionary: The Life of General Charles Lee — Papas, Phillip
Renegade Son — Jackson, Lisa
Renegades of Perdition Range — Paine, Lauran
The Renewal of the Kibbutz: From Reform to Transformation — Russell, Raymond
Renewing Christian Theology: Systematics for a Global Christianity — Anderson, Jonathan A.
Renewing Moral Theology: Christian Ethics as Action, Character and Grace — Westberg, Daniel A.
Renishaw Hall: The Story of the Sitwells — Seward, Desmond
Reno, Las Vegas, and the Strip: A Tale of Three Cities — Moehring, Eugene P.
Renovation — Robins, Lane
Reorienting the East: Jewish Travelers to the Medieval Muslim World — Jacobs, Martin
Repercussions — Schneider, Anthony
Repertorium poenitentiariae Germanicum: Verzeichnis der in den Supplikenregistern der Ponitentiarie Kirchen, und Orte des Deutschen Reiches — Schmugge, Ludwig
y The Replaced — Derting, Kimberly
A Replacement Life — Fishman, Boris
The Replacements — Putnam, David
Reply All...and Other Ways to Tank Your Career — Frieman, Richie
Reporting Always: Writings from The New Yorker — Ross, Lillian
Repositioning Race: Prophetic Research in a Postracial Obama Age — Barnes, Sandra L.
Repositioning Reference: New Methods and New Services for a New Age — Saunders, Laura
Representation in Western Music — Walden, Joshua
Representatives of Roman Rule: Roman Provincial Governors in Luke-Acts — Yoder, Joshua
Representing Argentinian Mothers; Medicine, Ideas and Culture in the Modern Era, 1900-1946 — Eraso, Yolanda
Representing Avarice in Late Renaissance France — Patterson, Jonathan
Representing Judith in Early Modern French Litterature — Llewellyn, Kathleen M.
Representing Violence in France 1760-1820 — Wynn, Tom
Repression, Haft und Geschlecht: Die Untersuchungshaftanstalt des Ministeriums fur Staatssicherheit Magdeburg-Neustadt 1958-1989 — Bastian, Alexander
The Reproach of Hunger: Food, Justice, and Money in the Twenty-First Century — Rieff, David
The Reproach of Hunger: Food, Justice, and Money in the Twenty-First Century — Verso, David Rieff
Reproducing Race: An Ethnography of Pregnancy as a Site of Racialization — Hinkson, Leslie
Reproducing the British Caribbean: Sex, Gender, and Population Politics after Slavery — De Barros, Juanita
Reproduction and Society: Interdisciplinary Readings — Ioffe, Carole
Reproductive Justice: The Politics of Health Care for Native American Women — Gurr, Barbara
y Reproductive Rights — Wittenstein, Vicki Oransky
c Reptile Flu: A Story about Communication (Illus. by Leng, Qin) — Cole, Kathryn
Reptile House — McLean, Robin
c Reptiles — Royston, Angela
c Reptiles Series — Hansen, Grace
The Republic — Plato
A Republic No More: Big Government and the Rise of American Political Corruption — Cost, Jay
The Republic of Conscience — Hart, Gary
The Republic of Imagination: A Case for Fiction — Nafisi, Azar
The Republic of Imagination: A Life in Books — Nafisi, Azar
The Republic of Imagination: America in Three Books — Nafisi, Azar
The Republic of Rock: Music and Citizenship in the Sixties Counterculture — Kramer, Michael J.
Republic of Spin: An Inside History of the American Presidency — Greenberg, David
The Republic of Virtue — Flanders, Jefferson

Republic of Women: Rethinking the Republic of Letters in the Seventeenth Century — Pal, Carol
The Republic: The Fight for Irish Independence — Townshend, Charles
The Republic Unsettled: Muslim French and the Contradictions of Secularism — Vince, Natalya
The Republican Army in the Spanish Civil War, 1936-1939 — Alpert, Michael
The Republican Party in the Age of Roosevelt: Sources of Anti-Government Conservatism in the United States — Rosen, Elliot A.
Republican Theology: The Civil Religion of American Evangelicals — Lynerd, Benjamin T.
Republicans and Race: The GOP's Frayed Relationship with African Americans, 1945-1974 — Thurber, Timothy N.
Requiem: A Hallucination — Tabucchi, Antonio
Requiem for a Soldier — Pavlov, Oleg
Requiem for Rosco — Gallagher, Peter
Requiem for the Santa Cruz: An Environmental History of an Arizona River — Webb, Robert H.
The Requiem Shark — Burnette, W.E.
Rereading the Fossil Record: The Growth of Paleobiology as an Evolutionary Discipline — Sepkoski, David
Rescue at Los Banos: The Most Daring Prison Camp Raid of World War II — Henderson, Bruce
Rescue Road: One Man, Thirty Thousand Dogs, and a Million Miles on the Last Hope Highway — Zheutlin, Peter
Rescued — Rettstatt, Linda
Rescuing Garden: Preserving America's Historic Gardens — Seebohm, Caroline
Rescuing Jesus: How People of Color, Women, and Queer Christians Are Reclaiming Evangelicalism — Jian Lee, Deborah
Rescuing Jesus: How People of Color, Women, and Queer Christians Are Reclaiming Evangelicalism — Lee, Deborah Jian
Rescuing the Gospel from the Cowboys: A Native American Expression of the Jesus Way — Twiss, Richard
Research Theatre, Climate Change, and the Ecocide Project: A Casebook — Chaudhuri, Una
Reset Your Child's Brain: A Four-Week Plan to End Meltdowns, Raise Grades, and Boost Social Skills by Reversing the Effects of Electronic Screen Time — Dunckley, Victoria L.
Reshaw: The Life and Times of John Baptiste Richard — Glass, Jefferson
The Residence: Inside the Private World of the White House — Brower, Kate Andersen
Resilience: Hard-Won Wisdom for Living a Better Life — Greitens, Eric
The Resilience of the Latin American Right — Luna, Juan Pablo
Resilience: Two Sisters and a Story of Mental Illness (Read by Close, Jessie). Audiobook Review — Close, Jessie
Resilience: Two Sisters and a Story of Mental Illness (Read by Close, Jessie). Audiobook Review — Earley, Pete
Resilience: Two Sisters and a Story of Mental Illness — Close, Jessie
Resilient America: Electing Nixon in 1968, Channeling Dissent, and Dividing Government — Nelson, Michael
Resilient America: Electing Nixon in 1968, Channeling Dissent, and Dividing Government — Nelson, Michael (b. 1949-)
Resilient Life: The Art of Living Dangerously — Evans, Brad
The Resilient Woman: Mastering the 7 Steps to Personal Power — O'Gorman, Patricia
Resistance: Jews and Christians Who Defied the Nazi Terror — Tec, Nechama
Resisting Gendered Norms: Civil Society, the Juridical and Political Space in Cambodia — Lilja, Mona
Resisting Structural Evil: Love as Ecological-Economic Vocation — Moe-Lobeda, Cynthia D.
Resisting Work: The Corporatization of Life and Its Discontents — Fleming, Peter
Resocialising Europe in a Time of Crisis — Contouris, Nicola
y Resonance — Kiernan, Celine
y Resonance — O'Rourke, Erica
Resonances of the Raj: India in the English Musical Imagination, 1897-1947 — Ghuman, Nalini
Resorting to Murder — Edwards, Martin

Respecifying Lab Ethnography: An Ethnomethodological Study of Experimental Physics — Sormani, Philippe
Respect: The Life of Aretha Franklin — Ritz, David
y Respect: The Walter Tull Story — Morgan, Michaela
Respect Yourself, Protect Yourself: Latina Girls and Sexual Identity — Garcia, Lorena
Respect Yourself: Stax Records and the Soul Explosion — Gordon, Robert
Responding to School Violence: Confronting the Columbine Effect — Muschert, Glenn W.
The Responsible Leader: Developing a Culture of Responsibility in an Uncertain World — Richardson, Tim
The Rest Is Silence — Benn, James R.
y The Rest of Us Just Live Here — Ness, Patrick
Rest Ye Murdered Gentlemen — Delany, Vicki
Restart: The Last Chance for the Indian Economy — Sharma, Mihir
Restating the Catholic Church's Relationship with the Jewish People: The Challenge of Super-Sessionary Theology — Pawlikowski, John T.
The Restaurant Critic's Wife — LaBan, Elizabeth
A Restful Mind — Zabawa, Mark Allen
Restitution: Civil Liability for Unjust Enrichment — Farnsworth, Ward
Restless Ambition: Grace Hartigan, Painter — Curtis, Cathy
The Restless City: A Short History of New York from Colonial Times to the Present — Reitano, Joanne
Restless Creatures — Wilkinson, Matt
Restless Empire: A Historical Atlas of Russia — Barnes, Ian
Restless Empire: A Historical Atlas of Russia — Westad, Odd Arne
Restless Mind: "Curiositas" & the Scope of Inquiry in St. Augustine's Psychology — Torchia, Joseph
The Restless Supermarket — Vladislavic, Ivan
The Restoration of Otto Laird — Packer, Nigel
Restoration: The Legacy — Walsh, Dan
Restored to Earth: Christianity, Environmental Ethics, and Ecological Restoration — Van Wieren, Gretel
Restoring Independence and Abundance on the Kulaiwi and Aina Momona — Fujikane, Candace
Restoring the Shattered Self: A Christian Counselor's Guide to Complex Trauma — Gingrich, Heather Davediuk
Restraint: A New Foundation for U.S. Grand Strategy — Posen, Barry R.
The Resurrected Skeleton: From Zhuangzi to Lu Xun — Idema, Wilt Lukas
Resurrecting Democracy: Faith, Citizenship, and the Politics of a Common Life — Bretherton, Luke
Resurrection Dialogues with Skeptics and Believers — Keire, Anita E.
y Resurrection — Hager, Mandy
The Resurrection Maker — Cooper, Glenn
Resurrection Science: Conservation, De-Extinction and the Precarious Future of Wild Things — O'Connor, M.R.
The Retail — Danker-Dake, Joshua
Rethinking Agency: Developmentalism, Gender and Rights — Madhok, Sumi
Rethinking Chaucer's Legend of Good Women — Collette, Carolyn P.
Rethinking Collection Development and Management — Albitz, Becky
Rethinking Everything: Personal Growth through Transactional Analysis — Bright, Neil
Rethinking Journalism: Trust and Participation in a Transformed News Landscape — Peters, Chris
Rethinking Library Technical Services: Redefining Our Profession for the Future — Weber, Mary Beth
Rethinking Modern European Intellectual History — McMahon, Darrin M.
Rethinking Narcissism: The Bad--and Surprising Good--about Feeling Special — Malkin, Craig
y Rethinking Normal: A Memoir in Transition — Hill, Katie Rain
Rethinking Poverty: Income, Assets, and the Catholic Social Justice Tradition — Bailey, Janies P.
Rethinking Professionalism: Women and Art in Canada, 1850-1970 — Huneault, Kristina
Rethinking Reference for Academic Libraries: Innovative Developments and Future Trends — Forbes, Carrie
Rethinking Rural: Global Community and Economic Development in the Small Town West — Albrecht, Don E.
Rethinking the American City: An International Dialogue — Orvell, Miles

Rethinking the Law School: Education, Research, Outreach and Governance — *Stolker, Carel*
Rethinking the Weimar Republic: Authority and Authoritarianism, 1916-1936 — *McElligott, Anthony*
Rethinking Transnational Men: Beyond, Between, and Within Nations — *Hearn, Jeff*
Rethinking Unemployment and the Work Ethic: Beyond the 'Quasi-Titmuss' Paradigm — *Dunn, Andrew*
Rethinking Virtue, Reforming Society: New Directions in Renaissance Ethics, c.1350 - c.1650 — *Lines, David A.*
Retired Broke — *Kirk, Randy*
Retiring? Beware!! Don't Run Out of Money and Don't Become Bored — *Bivona, Michael*
Retox: Healthy Solutions for Real Life — *Imparato, Lauren*
c Retribution — *Walden, Mark*
y The Retribution of Mara Dyer — *Hodkin, Michelle*
Retrieving Realism — *Dreyfus, Hubert*
The Retrospect As Prospect: Seamus Heaney's Regions — *Russell, Richard Rankin*
Return: A Palestinian Memoir — *Karmi, Ghada*
c The Return — *Torres, Jennifer*
Return from the Natives: How Margaret Mead Won the Second World War and Lost the Cold War — *Mandler, Peter*
Return: Nationalizing Transnational Mobility in Asia — *Xiang, Biao*
The Return of Ancestral Gods: Modern Ukrainian Paganism as an Alternative Vision for a Nation — *Lesiv, Mariya*
The Return of Comrade Ricardo Flores Magon — *Lomnitz, Claudio*
The Return of George Washington, 1783-1789 — *Larson, Edward J.*
Return of the Dragon: Rising China and Regional Security — *Roy, Denny*
c Return of the Forgotten (Illus. by To, Vivienne) — *Fiedler, Lisa*
Return of the Gar — *Spitzer, Mark*
y Return of the Geek: The Private Blog of Joe Cowley — *Davis, Ben*
Return of the Jew: Identity Narratives of the Third Post-Holocaust Generation of Jews in Poland — *Reszke, Katka*
Return of the Native — *Hardy, Thomas*
Return of the Outlaw — *Curtis, Craig M.*
c The Return of the Psammead — *Creswell, Helen*
Return of the Queen (Illus. by YoYo) — *YoYo*
c Return to Augie Hobble (Illus. by Smith, Lane) — *Smith, Lane*
Return to Aztlan: Indians, Spaniards, and the Invention of Nuevo Mexico — *Levin Rojo, Danna A.*
Return to Aztlan: Indians, Spaniards, and the Invention of Nuevo Mexico — *Rojo, Danna A. Levin*
Return to Dust — *Lanh, Andrew*
c Return to Earth! (Illus. by Kraft, Jason) — *O'Ryan, Ray*
Return to Eden — *Taylor, Richard*
Return to Mateguas Island — *Watkins, Linda*
Return to Me — *Moran, Kelly*
Return to Order: From a Frenzied Economy to an Organic Christian Society - Where We've Been, How We Got Here, and Where We Need to Go — *Horvat, John*
y Return to Planet Tad (Illus. by Holgate, Douglas) — *Carvell, Tim*
Return to Roswell — *Rosen, Martin A.*
Return to Sender — *Halleck, Mindy*
Return to Silver Creek — *Tyrell, Chuck*
y Return to the Crows, vol. 11 — *Bracken, Beth*
Return to the Land of the Head Hunters: Edward S. Curtis, the Kwakwaka'wakw and the Making of Modern Cinema — *Evans, Brad*
Return to the Land of the Head Hunters: Edward S. Curtis, the Kwakwaka'wakw and the Making of the Modern Cinema — *Evans, Brad*
Return to You — *Chase, Samantha*
Return to Zion — *Gartman, Eric*
Return to Zion: The History of Modern Israel — *Gartman, Eric*
Returning Home: Reintegration after Prison or Jail — *Bahr, Stephen J.*
Returns: Becoming Indigenous in the Twenty-First Century — *Clifford, James*
c Reuben — *Borntrager, Mary Christner*
A Reunion of Ghosts — *Mitchell, Judith Claire*
Rev Up Your Writing Series (Illus. by Gallagher-Cole, Mernie) — *Owings, Lisa*
c Revealed (Read by Sorensen, Chris). Audiobook Review — *Haddix, Margaret Peterson*

c Revealed — *Haddix, Margaret*
Revealed to Him — *Frederick, Jen*
Revealing Hannah — *Fedolfi, Laura*
Revelation and Authority: Sinai in Jewish Scripture and Tradition — *Sommer, Benjamin D.*
Revelation — *Covington, Dennis*
y The Revelation of Louisa May — *MacColl, Michaela*
Revelations of the Ruby Crystal — *Clow, Barbara Hand*
The Revelator — *Kloss, Robert*
y Revenge and the Wild — *Modesto, Michelle*
y Revenge, Ice Cream, and Other Things Best Served Cold — *Finn, Katie*
y The Revenge of Seven — *Lore, Pittacus*
y Revenge of Superstition Mountain (Illus. by Ivanov, Olga) — *Broach, Elise*
c Revenge of the Angels — *Ziegler, Jennifer*
c Revenge of the Bully — *Starkey, Scott*
The Revenge of the Golf Gods — *Jahre, Howard*
y The Revenge Playbook — *Allen, Rachael*
Reverend Colt — *Clay, James*
The Reverend Jennie Johnson and African Canadian History, 1868-1967 — *Reid-Maroney, Nina*
Reverse Genetics of RNA Viruses: Applications and Perspectives — *Bridgen, Anne*
Review of Linked Data for Libraries, Archives and Museums: How to Clean, Link and Publish Your Metadata — *Hooland, Seth van*
Review of Pharmaceutical Research, Democracy and Conspiracy: International Clinical Trials in Local Medical Institutions — *Bicudo, Edison*
Revision — *Phillips, Andrea*
Revisiting Humboldtian Science
Revisiting Napoleon's Continental System: Local, Regional and European Experiences — *Aaslestad, Katherine B.*
Revisiting the Poetic Edda: Essays on Old Norse Heroic Legend — *Acker, Paul*
Revisiting the Sixties: Interdisciplinary Perspectives on America's Longest Decade — *Bieger, Laura*
Revisiting The Tempest: The Capacity to Signify — *Bigliazzi, Silvia*
Revival and Awakening: American Evangelical Missionaries in Iran and the Origins of Assyrian Nationalism — *Becker, Adam H.*
Revival (Read by Morse, David). Audiobook Review — *King, Stephen*
Revival — *King, Stephen*
Reviving the Eternal City: Rome and the Papal Court, 1420-1447 — *McCahill, Elizabeth*
Revolt at Taos: The New Mexican and Indian Insurrection of 1847 — *Crutchfield, James A.*
The Revolt of Owain Glynd?r in Medieval English Chronicles — *Marchant, Alicia*
Revolting Families: Toxic Intimacy, Private Politics, and Literary Realisms in the German Sixties — *Smith-Prei, Carrie*
c Revolution. Audiobook Review — *Wiles, Deborah*
y Revolution (Read by several narrators). Audiobook Review — *Wiles, Deborah*
y Revolution — *Wiles, Deborah*
Revolution at Point Zero: Housework, Reproduction, and Feminist Struggle — *Federici, Silvia*
Revolution in Higher Education: How a Small Band of Innovators Will Make College Accessible and Affordable — *DeMillo, Richard A.*
Revolution in Higher Education: How a Small Band of Innovators Will Make College Accessible and Affordable — *DeMillo, Rivhard A.*
Revolution in the Andes: The Age of Tupac Amaru — *Serulnikov, Sergio*
The Revolution Is for the Children: The Politics of Childhood in Havana and Miami, 1959-1962 — *Bradford, Anita Casavantes*
The Revolution Is for the Children: The Politics of Childhood in Havana and Miami, 1959-1962 — *Bradford, Anita Casavantes*
Revolution — *Manney, P.J.*
Revolution — *Brown, Richard H.*
Revolution — *Black, Jenna*
y The Revolution of Ivy — *Engel, Amy*
Revolutionary Atmosphere, NASA SP 2010-4319 — *Arrighi, Robert S.*
Revolutionary Beauty: The Radical Photomontages of John Heartfield — *Kriebel, Sabine T.*
Revolutionary Emancipation: Slavery and Abolitionism in the British West Indies — *Fergus, Claudius*
Revolutionary Experiments: The Quest for Immortality in Bolshevik Science and Fiction — *Krementsov, Nikolai*

Revolutionary Ideas - An Intellectual History of the French Revolution from the 'Rights of Man' to Robespierre — *Israel, Jonathan*
Revolutionary Medicine: The Founding Fathers and Mothers in Sickness and in Health — *Abrams, Jeanne E.*
c The Revolutionary War: A Chronology of America's Fight for Independence — *Smith-Llera, Danielle*
Revolutionary Womanhood: Feminism, Modernity, and the State in Nasser's Egypt — *Bier, Laura*
Revolutionary Womanhood: Feminisms, Modernity, and the State in Nasser's Egypt — *Bier, Laura*
Revolutionizing Expectations: Women's Organizations, Feminism, and American Politics, 1965-1980 — *Blair, Melissa Estes*
Revolutionizing Romance: Interracial Couples in Contemporary Cuba — *Fernandez, Nadine T.*
Revolutions: A Very Short Introduction — *Goldstone, Jack A.*
Revolutions from Grub Street: A History of Magzine Publishing in Britain — *Cox, Howard*
Revolutions without Borders: The Call to Liberty in the Atlantic World — *Polasky, Janet*
Rewire: Digital Cosmopolitans in the Age of Connection — *Zuckerman, Ethan*
Rewiring the Real: In Conversation with William Gaddis, Richard Powers, Mark Danielewski, and Don DeLillo — *Taylor, Mark C.*
Rewriting Arthurian Romance in Renaissance France: From Manuscript to Printed Book — *Taylor, Jane H.M.*
Rewriting Marpole: The Path to Cultural Complexity in the Gulf of Georgia — *Clark, Terence N.*
Rewriting Saints and Ancestors: Memory and Forgetting in France, 500-1200 — *Bouchard, Constance Brittain*
Rewriting the Rules of the American Economy: An Agenda for Growth and Shared Prosperity — *Stiglitz, Joseph E.*
Rewriting Wrongs: French Crime Fiction and the Palmpsest — *Kimyongur, Angela*
c Rex Finds an Egg! Egg! Egg! — *Weinberg, Steven*
Rex Ingram: Visionary Director of the Silent Screen — *Barton, Ruth*
Rex Whistler: Inspirations, 2 vols. — *Cecil, Hugh*
Rex Whistler: Inspirations: Family, Friendships, Landscapes — *Cecil, Hugh*
Rex Whistler: Inspirations: Love and War — *Cecil, Hugh*
c Rex Wrecks It! (Illus. by Clanton, Ben) — *Clanton, Ben*
c Rey Mysterio — *Markegard, Blake*
Reykjavik Nights — *Indridason, Arnaldur*
Reynard the Fox: A New Translation — *Simpson, James*
RFK, Jr.: Robert F. Kennedy, Jr. and the Dark Side of the Dream — *Oppenheimer, Jerry*
The Rhetoric of Sincerity — *Van Alphen, Ernst*
The Rhetorical Leadership of Fulton J. Sheen, Norman Vincent Peale, and Billy Graham in the Age of Extremes — *Sherwood, Timothy H.*
Rhett Butler's People — *McCaig, Donald*
c Rhinos Don't Eat Pancakes (Illus. by Ogilvie, Sara) — *Kemp, Anna*
c Rhoda's Rock Hunt (Illus. by Bell, Jennifer A.) — *Griffin, Molly Beth*
c Rhyme Schemer — *Holt, K.A.*
c Rhymoceros — *Coat, Janik*
c Rhymoceros (Illus. by Coat, Janik) — *Coat, Janik*
Rhythm Makers: The Drumming Legends of Nashville in Their Own Words — *Artimsi, Tony*
The Rhythm of the August Rain — *Royes, Gillian*
Rhythm of the Imperium — *Nye, Jody Lynn*
Rhythm of the Wild: A Life Inspired by Alaska's Denali National Park — *Heacox, Kim*
y Rhythm Ride: A Road Trip through the Motown Sound — *Pinkney, Andrea Davis*
The Rhythms of Jewish Living: A Sephardic Exploration of the Basic Teachings of Judaism — *Angel, Marc D.*
Rhythms of the Pachakuti: Indigenous Uprising and State Power in Bolivia — *Aguilar, Raquel Gutierrez*
c Ribblestrop — *Mulligan, Andy*
Ribbon of Fire: How Europe Adopted and Developed US Strip Mill Technology (1920-2000). — *Aylen, Jonathan*
Rice and Beans (Illus. by Cerato, Mattia) — *Blevins, Wiley*
Rice, Noodle, Fish: Deep Travels Through Japan's Food Culture — *Goulding, Matt*
y Rich and Rare: A Collection of Australian Stories, Poetry and Artwork — *Collins, Paul*

Rich Is Not a Four-Letter Word: How to Survive Obamacare, Trump Wall Street, Kick-Start Your Retirement, and Achieve Financial Success — Willis, Gerri
Richard Aldington: Poet, Soldier and Lover, 1911-29 — Whelpton, Vivien
Richard: Blue's Point — Ferguson, Richard
Richard E. Norman and Race Filmmaking — Lupack, Barbara Tepa
Richard Hakluyt and Travel Writing in Early Modern Europe — Carey, Daniel
Richard Hooker: Of the "Laws of Ecclesiastical Polity" - A Critical Edition with Modern Spelling — McGrade, Arthur Stephen
Richard III: A Ruler and His Reputation — Horspool, David
Richard III (Read by Various readers). Audiobook Review — Shakespeare, William
Richard John Neuhaus: A Life in the Public Square — Boyagoda, Randy
c Richard M. Nixon — Hasselius, Michelle M.
Richard Morris's Prick of Conscience: A Corrected and Amplified Reading Text — Hanna, Ralph
Richard Nixon and the Vietnam War: The End of the American Century — Schmitz, David F.
Richard Nixon — Coppolani, Antoine
Richard Rowlands Verstegan: A Versatile Man in an Age of Turmoil — Zacchi, Romana
Richard Wilson and the Transformation of European Landscape Painting — Postle, Martin
Richardson and the Philosophers — Fowler, James
The Richest Man Who Ever Lived: The Life and Times of Jacob Fugger — Steinmetz, Greg
Richie — Bacque, Raphaelle
Richmond Must Fall: The Richmond-Petersburg Campaign, October 1864 — Newsome, Hampton
c Ricky Ricotta's Mighty Robot vs. the Jurassic Jackrabbits from Jupiter (Illus. by Santat, Dan) — Pilkey, Dav
c Ricky Ricotta's Mighty Robot vs. the Mecha-Monkeys from Mars (Illus. by Santat, Dan) — Pilkey, Dav
c Ricky Ricotta's Mighty Robot vs. the Mutant Mosquitoes from Mercury (Illus. by Santat, Dan) — Pilkey, Dav
c Ricky Ricotta's Mighty Robot vs. the Stupid Stinkbugs from Saturn (Illus. by Santat, Dan) — Pilkey, Dav
c Ricky Ricotta's Mighty Robot vs. the Voodoo Vultures from Venus (Illus. by Santat, Dan) — Pilkey, Dav
Ricoeur, Literature and Imagination — Vlacos, Sophie
c A Riddle in Ruby — Davis, Kent
The Riddle of the Image: The Secret Science of Medieval Art — Bucklow, Spike
Riddley Walker — Hoban, Russell
c The Ride-by-Nights (Illus. by Rabei, Carolina) — de la Mare, Walter
y Ride, Ricardo, Ride! (Illus. by Devries, Shane) — Cummings, Pat
Ride Steady — Ashley, Kristen
c Ride the Big Machines Across Canada (Illus. by Mok, Carmen) — Mok, Carmen
Ride Your Heart 'Til It Breaks — Hawkins, Deborah
y Riders — Rossi, Veronica
Riders of Purple Sage (Read by Lackey, Michael). Audiobook Review — Grey, Zane
Riders of the Apocalypse: German Cavalry and Modern Warfare, 1870-1945 — Dorondo, David R.
Ridgeline — Foster, Pamela
Riding Home: The Power of Horses to Heal — Hayes, Tim
Riding on Comets — Pleska, Cat
Riel's Defence: Perspectives on His Speeches — Hansen, Hans V.
c Riette l'assiette — Sirois, Anne-Marie
c Riff Raff Sails the High Cheese (Illus. by Kennedy, Anne) — Schade, Susan
The Rift: A New Africa Breaks Free — Perry, Alex
y The Rig — Ducie, Joe
The Right and Labor in America: Politics, Ideology, and Imagination — Lichtenstein, Nelson
The Right in France from the Third Republic to Vichy — Passmore, Kevin
Right of Boom: The Aftermath of Nuclear Terrorism — Schwartz, Benjamin E.
Right Out of California: The 1930s and the Big Business Roots of Modern Conservatism — Olmsted, Kathryn S.
y The Right Side of History: 100 Years of LGBTQI Activism — Brooks, Adrian
The Right Spouse: Preferential Marriages in Tamil Nadu — Clark-Deces, Isabelle
The Right to Be Cold: One Woman's Story of Protecting Her Culture, the Arctic and the Whole Planet — Watt-Cloutier, Sheila

The Right to Try: How the Federal Government Prevents Americans from Getting the Life-Saving Treatments They Need — Olsen, Darcy
The Right Way To Lose a War: America in an Age of Unwinnable Conflicts — Tierney, Dominic
Right-Wing Spain in the Civil War Era: Soldiers of God and Apostles of the Fatherland, 1914-45 — Quiroga, Alejandro
c The Right Word: Roget and His Thesaurus (Illus. by Sweet, Melissa) — Bryant, Jen
The Right Wrong Man — Douglas, Lawrence
The Right Wrong Thing — Kirschman, Ellen
The Righteous of the Wehrmacht — Malkes, Simon
Righteous Release — Gardner, Richard
Righteous Republic: The Political Foundations of Modern India — Vajpeyi, Ananya
The Righteous Revenge of Lucy Moon — Brooks, Bill
Righteous Rhetoric: Sex, Speech, and the Politics of Concerned Women for America — Smith, Leslie Dorrough
Rightsizing the Academic Library Collection — Ward, Suzanne M.
y Rihanna: Grammy-Winning Superstar — Herringshaw, Deann
The Rim of Morning — Sloane, William
Rime — Boccaccio, Giovanni
Rina — Kang, Yong-sook
Ring, Dance, Play: First Experiences with Choirchimes and Orff Schulwerk — Gall, Griff
Ring of Steel: Germany and Austria-Hungary in World War I — Watson, Alexander
Ring Shout, Wheel About: The Racial Politics of Music and Dance in North American Slavery — Thompson, Katrina Dyonne
Ringo: With a Little Help — Starr, Michael Seth
c Rio de Janeiro! (Illus. by Gambatesa, Francesca) — De Laurentiis, Giada
Rio — Morton, Orde
Riot Most Uncouth — Friedman, Daniel
Riot: Witness to Anger and Change — Meek, Edwin E.
Riotous Flesh: Women, Physiology, and the Solitary Vice in Nineteenth-Century America — Haynes, April R.
Riots in Regions of Heavy Industry: Violence, Conflict and Protest in the 20th Century
y Rip Van Winkle, The Legend of Sleepy Hollow, The Pride of the Village & Spectre Bridegroom (Illus. by Smith, Tod) — Irving, Washington
y Rip Van Winkle, The Legend of Sleepy Hollow, The Pride of the Village & The Spectre Bridegroom (Read by Sims, Adam). Audiobook Review — Irving, Washington
Ripe for Change: Garden-Based Learning in Schools — Hirschi, Jane S.
Ripeness Is All: A Boomer's Mirthful, Spiritual Journey — Carrier, Henry
c Ripley's Believe It or Not! Special Edition 2015 — Ripley's Entertainment, Inc.
Ripped from the Pages (Read by Berneis, Susie). Audiobook Review — Carlisle, Kate
Ripped from the Pages — Carlisle, Kate
Ripped Off: A Serviceman's Guide to Common Scams, Frauds, and Bad Deals — Archer, Michael A.
The Ripper Gene — Ransom, Michael
c Ripple Effect — Taekema, Sylvia
Rise Again Songbook: Words and Chords to Nearly 1,200 Songs — Blood, Peter
The Rise and Decline of Faculty Governance — Gerber, Larry G.
The Rise and Decline of Faculty Governance: Professionalization and the Modern American University — Gerber, Larry G.
The Rise and Decline of the Redneck Riviera: An Insider's History of the Florida-Alabama Coast — Jackson, Harvey H., III
c Rise and Fall — Schrefer, Eliot
The Rise and Fall of American Growth: The U.S. Standard of Living since the Civil War — Gordon, Robert J.
The Rise and Fall of Arab Presidents for Life — Owen, Roger
The Rise and Fall of Classical Greece — Ober, Josiah
The Rise and Fall of Human Rights: Cynicism and Politics in Occupied Palestine — Allen, Lori
The Rise and Fall of Intelligence: An International Security History — Warner, Michael
c The Rise and Fall of Oscar the Magician (Illus. by Porter, Matthew) — Porter, Matthew
The Rise and Fall of Radical Westminster, 1780-1890 — Baer, Marc
y The Rise and Fall of the Gallivanters — Beaufrand, M.J.
The Rise and Fall of Triumph: The History of a Radical Roman Catholic Magazine, 1966-1976 — Popowski, Mark D.

Rise and Fire: The Origins, Science, and Evolution of the Jump Shot--and How It Transformed Basketball Forever — Fury, Shawn
The Rise, Fall, and Return of Michigan Football — Bacon, John U.
Rise — Campbell, Karen
Rise of a Japanese Chinatown: Yokohama, 1894-1972 — Han, Eric C.
The Rise of a Prairie Statesman — Knock, Thomas J.
The Rise of Germany, 1939-1941: The War in the West, vol. 1 — Holland, James
The Rise of Heritage: Preserving the Past in France, Germany, and England, 1789-1914 — Swenson, Astrid
c The Rise of Humans — West, David
The Rise of Islamic State: ISIS and the New Sunni Revolution — Cockburn, Patrick
The Rise of Liberal Religion: Book Culture and American Spirituality in the Twentieth Century — Hedstrom, Matthew
The Rise of Market Society in England 1066-1800 — Eisenberg, Christine
The Rise of the Automated Aristocrats — Hodder, Mark
y Rise of the Earth Dragon (Illus. by Howells, Graham) — West, Tracey
y The Rise of the Nazis — Marcovitz, Hal
The Rise of the Public Authority: Statebuilding and Economic Development in Twentieth-Century America — Radford, Gail
c Rise of the Ragged Clover — Durham, Paul
Rise of the Robots: Technology and the Threat of a Jobless Future — Ford, Martin
c Rise of the Wolf — Nielsen, Jennifer A.
y Rise of the Zombie Scarecrows — Loughead, Deb
The Rise of Turkey: The Twenty-First Century's First Muslim Power — Cagaptay, Soner
The Rise of Women: The Growing Gender Gap in Education and What It Means for American Schools — DiPrete, Thomas A.
The Rise of Women's Transnational Activism: Identity and Sisterhood Between the World Wars — Sandell, Marie
Rise to Greatness: The History of Canada from the Vikings to the Present — Black, Conrad
Risen II--The Progeny — Lawrence, Krystal
The Rising — Tregillis, Ian
The Rising — D'Agostino, Ryan
Rising Fire — Brisbin, Terri
Rising from the Mire — Grace, Christine
Rising Ground: A Search for the Spirit of Place — Marsden, Philip
Rising Inequality in China: Challenges to a Harmonious Society — Shi, Li
The Rising: Murder, Heartbreak, and the Power of Human Resilience in an American Town — D'Agostino, Ryan
The Rising — D'Agostino, Ryan
y The Rising of the Shield Hero (Illus. by Minami, Seira) — Yusagi, Aneko
Rising Star — Lawrence, Kendra
Rising Strong — Brown, Brene
Rising Tide — Ryan, Patricia Twomey
The Rising Tide of Color: Race, State Violence, and Radical Movements across the Pacific — Jung, Moon-Ho
Rising Tide — Khanna, Rajan
Rising to the Challenge: My Leadership Journey — Fiorina, Carly
Risk — Skeen, Tim
Risk and Portfolio Analysis: Principles and Methods — Hult, Henrik
y Risk — Ferris, Fleur
The Risk of Brexit — Liddle, Roger
Risk/Reward: Why Intelligent Leaps and Daring Choices Are the Best Career Moves You Can Make — Kreamer, Anne
The Risk Society Revisited: Social Theory and Governance — Rosa, Eugene A.
Risking Everything: A Freedom Summer Reade — Edmonds, Michael
Risking It All — Bailey, Tessa
The Risky Business of French Feminism: Publishing, Politics and Artistry — Sweatman, Jennifer L.
c Rita and the Firefighters (Illus. by Cowman, Joseph) — Huber, Mike
c Rita's Rhino (Illus. by Ross, Tony) — Ross, Tony
y Rites of Passage — Hensley, Joy N.
Riti proibiti: Liturgia e inquisizione nella Francia del Settecento — Fontana, Paolo
Ritter Runkel in seiner Zeit. Mittelalter und Zeitgeschichte im Spiegel eines Geschichtscomics
Rittersagas: Ubersetzung, Uberlieferung, Transmission — Glauser, Jurg

Ritual and Conflict: The Social Relations of Childbirth in Early Modern England — Wilson, Adrian
Ritual and Recovery in Post-Conflict Sri Lanka — Derges, Jane
Ritual, Performance, and Politics in the Ancient Near East — Ristvet, Lauren
Ritual Textuality: Pattern and Motion in Performance — Tomlinson, Matt
The Rival Queen: Catherine de' Medici, Her Daughter Marguerite of Valois, and the Betrayal That Ignited a Kingdom — Goldstone, Nancy
The Rival Queens: Catherine de' Medici, Her Daugher Marguerite de Valois, and the Betrayal That Ignited a Kingdom — Goldstone, Nancy
The Rival Queens: Catherine de' Medici, Her Daughter Marguerite de Valois, and the Betrayal That Ignited a Kingdom — Goldstone, Nancy
The Rival Queens — Goldstone, Nancy
y Rivals in the City — Lee, Y.S.
The Rivals of Dracula — Rennison, Nick
Riven — Ficklin, Sherry D.
y The River and the Book — Croggon, Allison
y River Music — Sauerwein, Leigh
River of Dark Dreams: Slavery and Empire in the Cotton Kingdom — Johnson, Walter
River of Ghosts: A Cedar Valley Odyssey — Gish, Robert F.
River of Ghosts — Gish, Robert F.
River of Glass — Terrell, Jaden
River of Hope: Black Politics and the Memphis Freedom Movement, 1865-1954 — Gritter, Elizabeth
River of Hope: Forging Identity and Nation in the Rio Grande Borderlands — Valerio-Jimenez, Omar S.
River of Ink — Cooper, Paul M.M.
The River of Life: Changing Ecosystems of the Mekong Region — Santasombat, Yos
The River of No Return — Bertsch, David Riley
The River People in Flood Time: The Civil Wars in Tabasco, Spoiler of Empires — Rugeley, Terry
c A River (Illus. by Martin, Marc) — Martin, Marc
The River Pollution Dilemma in Victorian England: Nuisance Law versus Economic Efficiency — Rosenthal, Leslie
River Road — Goodman, Carol
A River Runs Again: India's Natural World in Crisis, from the Barren Cliffs of Rajasthan to the Farmlands of Karnataka — Subramanian, Meera
y River Runs Deep — Bradbury, Jennifer
River Song: Naxiyamtama (Snake River-Palouse) Oral Traditions from Mary Jim, Andrew George, Gordon Fisher, and Emily Peone — Scheuerman, Richard D.
River Story (Illus. by Willey, Bee) — Hooper, Meredith
The River Was Dyed with Blood: Nathan Bedford Forrest and Fort Pillow — Wills, Brian Steel
Rivers — Teru, Miyamoto
c Rivers — Feldman, Llewellyn
Rivers: Recipes and Memories of the Himalayan River Valleys — Khanna, Vikas
River's Song — Lim, Suchen Christine
Riversong of the Rhone — Ramuz, Charles-Ferdinand
Riveting Reads: World War I — Dubber, Geoff
The Road Back to Sweetgrass — Grover, Linda LeGarde
The Road Headed West: A 6,000-Mile Cycling Odyssey Through North America — McCarron, Leon
The Road Home: A Contemporary Exploration of the Buddhist Path — Nichtern, Ethan
The Road In Is Not the Same Road Out — Solie, Karen
The Road Not Taken: Finding America in the Poem Everyone Loves and Almost Everyone Gets Wrong — Orr, David
The Road Taken: The History and Future of America's Infrastructure — Petroski, Henry
The Road to Black Ned's Forge: A Story of Race, Sex, and Trade on the Colonial American Frontier — McCleskey, Turk
The Road to Character — Brook, David
The Road to Character — Brooks, David
The Road to Chinese Exclusion: The Denver Riot, 1880 Election and the Rise of the West — Zhu, Liping
The Road to Emmaus — Reece, Spencer
The Road to Iraq: The Making of a Neoconservative War — Ahmad, Muhammad Idrees
The Road to Little Dribbling: Adventures of an American in Britain — Bryson, Bill
The Road to Little Dribbling: More Notes from a Small Island — Bryson, Bill
Road to Power: How GM's Mary Barra Shattered the Glass Ceiling — Colby, Laura

The Road to Social Europe: A Contemporary Approach to Political Cultures and Diversity in Europe — Barbier, Jean-Claude
The Road to the Winter Palace — Grecian, Alex
The Road to the Winter Palace (Illus. by Rossmo, Riley) — Grecian, Alex
y The Road to You — Whitaker, Alecia
Road Trip — Rozema, Mark
Road Trip USA: Cross-Country Adventures on America's Two-Lane Highways — Jensen, Jamie
c The Roadman Boogie (Illus. by Robinson, Nikki Slade) — Robinson, Nikki Slade
Roadmap: The Get-It-Together Guide for Figuring Out What to Do with Your Life — Roadmap Nation
Roadmap to Reconciliation: Moving into Unity, Wholeness and Justice — McNeil, Brenda Salter
Roads in the Wilderness: Conflict in Canyon Country — Rogers, Jedediah S.
Roads Taken: The Great Jewish Migrations to the New World and the Peddlers Who Forged the Way — Diner, Hasia R.
Roads Were Not Built for Cars — Reid, Carlton
Roadside Magic — Saintcrow, Lillith
Roadside Survival: Low-tech Solutions to Automobile Breakdowns — Brinker, Walt
Roadtrip with a Raindrop — Harper, Gayle
The Roar of Morning — Marugg, Tip
The Roar of the Lion: The Untold Story of Churchill's World War — Toye, Richard
c Roar! (Illus. by Bayless, Julie) — Bayless, Julie
c Roar! (Illus. by Starin, Liz) — Sauer, Tammi
Robert A. Heinlein in Dialogue with His Century, vol. 2, 1948-88: The Man Who Learned Better — Patterson, William H., Jr.
Robert B. Parker's Blackjack — Knott, Robert
Robert B. Parker's Blind Spot — Coleman, Reed Farrel
Robert B. Parker's Cheap Shot — Atkins, Ace
Robert B. Parker's Kickback — Atkins, Ace
Robert B. Parker's The Devil Wins — Coleman, Reed Farrel
Robert Bruce and the Community of the Realm of Scotland — Barrow, G.W.S.
Robert Cantwell and the Literary Left: A Northwest Writer Reworks American Fiction — Reed, T.V.
c Robert Crowther's Pop-Up Dinosaur ABC (Illus. by Crowther, Robert) — Crowther, Robert
Robert Elsmere — Burstein, Elizabeth
Robert Graves: Selected Poems — Longley, Michael
c Robert Griffin III — Yomtov, Nel
Robert Love's Warnings: Searching for Strangers in Colonial Boston — Dayton, Cornelia H.
Robert Lowell in Love — Meyers, Jeffrey
Robert Ludlum's The Janson Equation — Corleone, Douglas
Robert Morrison and the Protestant Plan for China — Daily, Christopher A.
Robert Morris's Folly: The Architectural and Financial Failures of an American Founder — Smith, Ryan K.
Robert Moses: The Master Builder of New York City (Illus. by Balez, Olivier) — Christin, Pierre
Robert Motherwell: The Making of an American Giant — Jacobson, Bernard
Robert Oppenheimer: A Life inside the Center — Monk, Ray
Robert Recorde: The Life and Times of a Tudor Mathematician — Roberts, Gareth
Robert Thornton and His Books: Essays on the Lincoln and London Thornton Manuscripts — Fein, Susanna
Roberto Bolano's Fiction: An Expanding Universe — Andrews, Chris
Roberto's New Vegan Cooking: 125 Easy, Delicious, Real Food Recipes — Martin, Roberto
c Robin Hood — Gagne, Tammy
Robin Robertson's Vegan without Borders: Easy Everyday Meals from around the World — Robertson, Robin
Robinson Crusoe — Defoe, Daniel
c Robinson Crusoe (Illus. by Wyeth, N.C.) — Defoe, Daniel
Robinson Jeffers: Poet and Prophet — Karman, James
c Robo-Sauce (Illus. by Salmieri, Daniel) — Rubin, Adam
y Robogenesis — Wilson, Daniel H.
c Robot Girl — Blackman, Malorie
c Robot Smash! (Illus. by Solon, Juan Carlos) — Martin, Stephen W.
c Robotics — Peppas, Lynn
y Robotics: From Automatons to the Roomba — Foran, Racquel
y Robotics: From Concept to Consumer — Mara, Wil
c Robots in Industry — Spilsbury, Louise
c Robots in Law Enforcement — Spilsbury, Louise

c Robots in Risky Jobs: On the Battlefield and Beyond — Clay, Kathryn
c Robots in Space — Spilsbury, Louise
c Robots: Watch Out, Water About! (Illus. by Hall, Cynthia) — Ug, Philippe
c Roc and Roe's Twelve Days of Christmas (Illus. by Ford, A.G.) — Cannon, Nick
The Rocheforts — Laborie, Christian
c Rock-A-Bye Romp (Illus. by Mulazzani, Simona) — Ashman, Linda
c The Rock — Scheff, Matt
Rock Art! Painting and Crafting with the Humble Pebble — Scicluna, Denise
c A Rock Can Be ... (Illus. by Dabija, Violeta) — Salas, Laura Purdie
A Rock Fell on the Moon: Dad and the Great Yukon Silver Ore Heist — Priest, Alicia
The Rock House Method: The Only Chord Book You Will Ever Need! — Gorenberg, Steve
The Rock Jaw Ladies Club: A Memoir of Vietnam, the Sick Crazy One! — Baysden, E.T.
Rock Me Two Times — Ryder, Dawn
Rock, Meet Window: A Father-Son Story — Good, Jason
Rock 'n' Roll Soccer: The Short Life and Fast Times of the North American Soccer League — Plenderleith, Ian
Rock 'n' Soul — Sattersby, Lauren
Rock, Paper, Scissors — Aidt, Naja Marie
Rock, Paper, Scissors — Marie, Naja
c Rock & Roll Highway: The Robbie Robertson Story (Illus. by Gustavson, Adam) — Robertson, Sebastian
Rock Star: The Making of Musical Icons from Elvis to Springsteen — Shumway, David R.
Rock That Quilt Block: Weathervane — Hahn, Linda J.
y Rock the Boat — Brouwer, Sigmund
Rock with Wings — Hillerman, Anne
Rocket and Lightship: Essays on Literature and Ideas — Kirsch, Adam
c Rocket et ses mots preferes — Hills, Tad
y Rocket Science for the Rest of Us — Gilliland, Ben
c Rocket's 100th Day of School (Illus. by Hills, Tad) — Hills, Tad
The Rockets' Red Glare — Darrin, John
Rockhounding New England: A Guide to 100 of the Region's Best Rockhounding Sites — Cristofono, Peter
y Rockin' the Boat: 50 Iconic Rebels and Revolutionaries-from Joan of Arc to Malcolm X — Fleischer, Jeff
c Rockin' the Boat — Fleischer, Jeff
The Rocks — Nichols, Peter
c Rocks and Minerals — Lawrence, Ellen
Rocks and Minerals — Pellant, Chris
c Rocks and Soil — Riley, Peter
c The Rocky Road of Love — Hosannah, Vernon
The Rocky Road to the Great War: The Evolution of the Trench Warfare to 1914 — Murray, Nicholas
y Rodeo Princess — Higgins, M.G.
y Rodeo Princess — Higgns, M.G.
Rodeo Ranch — Brand, Max
c Rodeo Red (Illus. by Idle, Molly) — Perkins, Maripat
Roger Bacon and the Defence of Christendom — Power, Amanda
c Roger Is Reading a Book (Illus. by Van Biesen, Koen) — Van Biesen, Koen
y Rogue — Kagawa, Julie
Rogue Knight (Read by Nobbs, Keith). Audiobook Review — Mull, Brandon
c Rogue Knight — Mull, Brandon
Rogue Lawyer — Grisham, John
The Rogue Not Taken — MacLean, Sarah
The Rogue Queen — Maxwell, Marcia
Rogue Spy — Bourne, Joanna
y Rogue Wave — Donnelly, Jennifer
The Rogue You Know — Galen, Shana
Rogues, Riches and Retribution — Taylor, Harry
Rohstoffgewinnung im Strukturwandel: Der Deutsche Bergbau im 20. Jahrhundert — Ziegler, Dieter
Roland Barthes: Biographie — Samoyault, Tiphaine
The Role of American NGOs in China's Modernization: Invited Influence — Wheeler, Norton
The Role of Business in the Development of the Welfare State and Labor Markets in Germany: Containing Social Reforms — Paster, Thomas
The Role of Central Banks in Financial Stability: How Has It Changed? — Evanoff, Douglas D.
y Roll Call — Mansfield, Gwen
Roll Deep: Poems — Jackson, Major
Roll Over Tchaikovsky! Russian Popular Music and Post-Soviet Homosexuality — Amico, Stephen
c Roller Coasters — Pettiford, Rebecca
c Roller Derby Rivals (Illus. by Collins, Matt) — Macy, Sue

c Roller Girl (Illus. by Jamieson, Victoria) — Jamieson, Victoria
Rolling in the Deep — Grant, Mira
The Rolling Stones — Heinlein, Robert A.
c Rolly the Anzac Donkey (Illus. by Cooper, Jenny) — Harper, Glyn
Rom am Bodensee: Die Zeit des Konstanzer Konzils — Volkart, Silvia
The Roma: A Balkan Underclass — Cvorovic, Jelena
Roma medica: Anatomie d'un systeme medical au XVIe siecle — Andretta, Elisa
Romaine Brooks: A Life — Langer, Cassandra
Roman Antiquities in Renaissance France, 1515-65 — Cooper, Richard
The Roman Army and the Expansion of the Gospel: The Role of the Centurion in Luke-Acts — Kyrychenko, Alexander
The Roman Crucible: The Artistic Patronage of the Papacy, 1198-1304 — Gardner, Julian
Roman Disasters — Toner, Jerry
The Roman History: From Romulus and the Foundation of Rome to the Reign of the Emperor Tiberius — Paterculus, Velleius
Roman Imperial Chronology and Early-Fourth-Century Historiography: The Regnal Durations of the So-Called "Chronica urbis Romae" of the "Chronograph of 354" — Burgess, Richard W.
The Roman Inquisition: A Papal Bureaucracy and Its Laws in the Age of Galileo — Mayer, Thomas F.
The Roman Inquisition on the Stage of Italy, c. 1590-1640 — Mayer, Thomas F.
The Roman Inquisition: Trying Galileo — Mayer, Thomas F.
Roman Law in the State of Nature — Straumann, Benjamin
The Roman Law of Obligations — Birks, Peter
The Roman Market Economy — Temin, Peter
The Roman Monster: An Icon of the Papal Antichrist in Reformation Polemics — Buck, Lawrence P.
The Roman Poetry of Love. Elegy and Politics in a Time of Revolution — Spentzou, Efrossini
Roman Republican Villas: Architecture, Context, and Ideology — Becker, Jeffrey A.
Roman Splendour, English Arcadia: The English Taste for Pietre Dure and the Sixtus Cabinet at Stourhead — Jervis, Simon Swynfen
Roman Warfare — Goldsworthy, Adrian
Romance and the Gentry in Late Medieval England — Johnston, Michael
Romance Is My Day Job: A Memoir of Finding Love at Last (Read by Bloom, Patience). Audiobook Review — Bloom, Patience
The Romance of Race: Incest, Miscegenation, and Multiculturalism in the United States, 1880-1930 — Sheffer, Jolie A.
The Romance of Teresa Hennert — Nalkowska, Zofia
Romance of the Grail: The Magic and Mystery of Arthurian Myth — Campbell, Joseph
The Romance of Tristan and Iseut — Bedier, Joseph
Romance on Four Worlds: A Casanova Quartet — Purdom, Tom
y Romancing the Dark in the City of Light — Jacobus, Ann
Romancing the Self in Early Modern Englishwomen's Life Writing — Eckerle, Julie A.
Romancing the Self in Early Modern Englishwomen's Life Writing — Eckerle, Julie A.
Romancing the Wild: Cultural Dimensions of Ecotourism — Fletcher, Robert
Romanesque and the Past: Retrospection in the Art and Architecture of Romanesque Europe — McNeill, John
Romanesque Architecture: The First Style of the European Age — Fernie, Eric
The Romani Gypsies — Matras, Varon
Romantic Anatomies of Performance — Davies, J.Q.
Romantic Catholics: France's Postrevolutionary Generation in Search of a Modern Faith — Harrison, Carol E.
Romantic Feuds: Transcending the 'Age of Personality' — Wheatley, Kim
The Romantic Machine: Utopian Science and Technology after Napoleon — Tresch, John
Romantic Naturalists, Early Environmentalists: An Ecocritical Study, 1789-1912 — Hall, Dewey W.
Romantic Outlaws: The Extraordinary Lives of Mary Wollstonecraft and Her Daughter Mary Shelley — Gordon, Charlotte
Romantic Outlaws: The Extraordinary Lives of Mary Wollstonecraft and Mary Shelley — Gordon, Charlotte
Romantic Readers and Transatlantic Travel: Expeditions and Tours in North America, 1760-1840 — Jarvis, Robin
Romantic Reformers and the Antislavery Struggle in the Civil War Era — Kytle, Ethan J.

Romantic Violence: Memoirs of an American Skinhead — Picciolin, Christian
Romanticism: A German Affair — Safranski, Rudiger
Romanticism in the Shadow of War: Literary Culture in the Napoleonic War Years — Cox, Jeffrey N.
c Rome — Bodden, Valerie
Rome in Love — Hughes, Anita
Rome, Pollution, and Propriety: Dirt, Disease and Hygiene in the Eternal City from Antiquity to Modernity — Bradley, Mark (b. 1977-)
Romeo and Juliet in Palestine: Teaching under Occupation — Sperlinger, Tom
y Romeo and Juliet — Shakespeare, William
c Romeo et Juliette (Illus. by Rovira, Francesc) — Shakespeare, William
Rome's Economic Revolution — Kay, Philip
Rome's Revolution: Death of the Republic and Birth of the Empire — Alston, Richard
Rome's Wreck — Joyce, Trevor
Romische Militargeschichte — Nemeth, Eduard
Ronald Reagan — Weisberg, Jacob
c Ronald Reagan — Tucker, Rosalyn
Ronald Reagan: Decisions of Greatness — Anderson, Martin
Ronin: The Deluxe Edition — Miller, Frank
Ronnie Gilbert: A Radical Life in Song — Gilbert, Ronnie
The Roof Walkers — Henderson, Keith
y Rook — Cameron, Sharon
c The Rookie Blue Jay (Illus. by Meyers, Mark) — Kelly, David A.
c The Rookie Bookie (Illus. by Swaab, Neil) — Wertheim, L. Jon
The Room — Smith, Neil
c Room for Bear (Illus. by Gavin, Ciara) — Gavin, Ciara
Room for Bear — Gavin, Ciara
Room for Love (Illus. by Ilya) — Ilya
The Room — Karlsson, Jonas
c The Room of Woe (Illus. by Flores, Jose Emroca) — Wallace, Rich
c Roosevelt (Illus. by Sodt, Fred) — Frost, Allen
Roosevelt and Stalin: Portrait of a Partnership — Butler, Susan
Root to Leaf: A Southern Chef Cooks through the Seasons — Satterfield, Steven
Rooted in Design: Sprout Home's Guide to Creative Indoor Planting — Heibel, Tara
c The Rootlets: Super Rootabilities (Illus. by Russnak, Jeremy) — Marquez, Vicki
The Roots of Conservatism in Mexico: Catholicism, Society, and Politics in the Mixteca Baja, 1750-1962 — Smith, Benjamin T.
The Roots of Terrorism in Indonesia: From Darul Islam to Jema'ah Islamiyah — Solahudin
Roots of the Revival: American and British Folk Music in the 1950s — Cohen, Ronald D.
Rootwork — Golos, Veronica
Rope and Bone — Howard, Ginnah
Rori's Healing — Hiers, Dora
c Rory McIlroy: Golf Champion — Logothetis, Paul
c Rory the Dinosaur: Me and My Dad (Illus. by Climo, Liz) — Climo, Liz
c Rory the Dinosaur: Me and My Dad — Climo, Liz
c Rory's Promise — MacColl, Michaela
c Rosa Blooms (Illus. by Batcheller, Lori) — Batcheller, Lori
c Rosa Parks — Taylor-Butler, Christine
Rosalie Lightning: A Graphic Memoir (Illus. by Hart, Tom) — Hart, Tom
c Rosario's Fig Tree (Illus. by Melanson, Luc) — Wahl, Charis
Rosa's Gift and Other Stories — Cantwell, Michael
Rosa's Thai Cafe — Moore, Saiphin
The Rose and Geryon: The Poetics of Fraud and Violence in Jean De Meun and Dante — Baika, Gabriella I.
c Rose and the Wish Thing — Magerl, Caroline
y Rose Bliss Cooks Up Magic — Littlewood, Kathryn
Rose Gold (Read by Jackson, J.D.). Audiobook Review — Mosley, Walter
Rose Gold — Mosley, Walter
Rose Heilbron: The Story of England's First Woman Queen's Counsel and Judge — Heilbron, Hilary
The Rose Hotel: A Memoir of Secrets, Loss, and Love from Iran to America — Andalibian, Rahimeh
y The Rose Society — Lu, Marie
c Rose under Fire — Wein, Elizabeth
Rose Water and Orange Blossoms: Fresh and Classic Recipes from My Lebanese Kitchen — Abood, Maureen
y The Rosemary Spell — Zimmerman, Virginia
Rosemary: The Hidden Kennedy Daughter — Larson, Kate Clifford
Rosen Digital's Spotlight on Science and Social Studies Series. Audiobook Review

Roses without Chemicals: 150 Disease-Free Varieties That Will Change the Way You Grow Roses — Kukielski, Peter
c Rosie and Rolland in the Legendary Show-and-Tell (Illus. by Berg, Jon) — Berg, Jon
The Rosie Effect (Read by O'Grady, Dan). Audiobook Review — Simsion, Graeme
The Rosie Effect — Simsion, Graeme
c Rosie Goes to Preschool (Illus. by Katz, Karen) — Katz, Karen
c Rosie the Reindeer (Illus. by Tenney, Shawna J.C.) — Taylor, Chantell
c Rosie's Radical Rescue Ride — Mewburn, Kyle
c Rosie's Special Present (Illus. by Millward, Gwen) — Millward, Myfanwy
c Rosie's Walk — Hutchins, Pat
c Ross Lynch: Disney Channel Actor — Diver, Lucas
Rot, Riot, and Rebellion: Mr. Jefferson's Struggle to Save the University That Changed America — Bowman, Rex
y Rot & Ruin: Warrior Smart (Illus. by Vargas, Tony) — Maberry, Jonathan
Rothaker — Ruff, Jenifer
A Rothschild Renaissance: Treasures from the Waddesdon Bequest — Thornton, Dora
The Rothschilds at Waddesdon Manor — Rothschild, James de, Mrs.
c Rotten Ralph's Rotten Family (Illus. by Rubel, Nicole) — Gantos, Jack
Rough and Tumble: Aggression, Hunting, and Human Evolution — Pickering, Travis Rayne
Rough Country: How Texas Became America's Most Powerful Bible-Belt State — Wuthnow, Robert
Rough Cut — Orvis, Linda
Rough Justice — Castille, Sarah
Rough Justice — Smith, Brad
Rough Justice — Paine, Lauran
Rough Knowledge — Poreba, Christine
A Rough Ride to the Future — Lovelock, James
Rough Road — North, Vanessa
The Roughest Riders: The Untold Story of the Black Soldiers in the Spanish American War — Tuccille, Jerome
Rounding Wagner's Mountain: Richard Strauss and Modern German Opera — Gilliam, Bryan
Roundtower — Von Osten, Hans
Rousseau's Hand: The Crafting of a Writer — Goodden, Angelica
Rousseau's Social Contract: An Introduction — Williams, David Lay
Routes and Realms: The Power of Place in the Early Islamic World — Antrim, Zayde
Routes of Power: Energy and Modern America — Jones, Christopher F.
Routes of War: The World of Movement in the Confederate South — Sternhell, Yael A.
The Routledge Companion to Accounting Education — Wilson, Richard M.S.
The Routledge Companion to Dramaturgy — Romanska, Magda
The Routledge Companion to Music and Visual Culture; Representation in Western Music — Shephard, Tim
The Routledge Companion to Puppetry and Material Performance — Posner, Dassia N.
The Routledge Guidebook to Galileo's "Dialogue" — Finocchiaro, Maurice A.
Routledge Handbook of African Politics — Cheeseman, Nic
The Routledge Handbook of American Military and Diplomatic History: 1865 to the Present — Thompson, Antonio S.
The Routledge Handbook of German Politics and Culture — Colvin, Sarah
A Roving Eye: Head to Toe in Egyptian Arabic Expressions — Ateek, Mona
c Row, Row, Row Your Boat (Illus. by Cabrera, Jane) — Cabrera, Jane
c Row, Row, Row Your Boat — Cabrera, Jane
c Rowan Blanchard: Star of Girl Meets World — Diver, Lucas
Rows of Memory: Journeys of a Migrant Sugar-Beet Worker — Sanchez, Saul
Roy Wilkins: The Quiet Revolutionary and the NAACP — Ryan, Yvonne
The Royal Assassin — Parker, Kate
y The Royal Cup (Illus. by Vives, Bastien) — Vives, Bastien
A Royal Experiment: The Private Life of King George III — Hadlow, Janice
c A Royal Tea (Illus. by Avakyan, Tatevik) — Dadey, Debbie
The Royal We — Cocks, Heather
The Royal We — Morgan, Jessica
y Royal Wedding — Cabot, Meg

The Royalist Republic: Literature, Politics and Religion in the Anglo-Dutch Public Sphere, 1639-1660 — Helmers, Helmer J.
The Royalist Revolution: Monarchy and the American Founding — Nelson, Eric
The Royalist Revolution: Monarchy and the American Founding — Nelson, Eric (b. 1977-)
Royalists at War in Scotland and Ireland, 1638-1650 — Robertson, Barry
An RTI Guide to Improving the Performance of African American Students — Williams, Dwayne D.
RtI in Math: Evidence-Based Interventions for Struggling Students — Forbringer, Linda L.
Rubbernecker — Bauer, Belinda
Rubble Fever — Pounds, Robbi
Rubens, Velasquez, and the King of Spain — Silver, Larry
Rubens, Velazquez, and the King of Spain — Georgievska-Shine, Aneta
c The Ruby Airship — Gosling, Sharon
c Ruby and Grub (Illus. by Warburton, Sarah) — Burlingham, Abi
Ruby (Read by Bond, Cynthia). Audiobook Review — Bond, Cynthia
c Ruby Lee and Me — Hitchcock, Shannon
c Ruby Lee & Me — Hitchcock, Shannon
Ruby — Bond, Cynthia
Ruby on Rails Tutorial, 3d ed. — Hartl, Michael
Ruby on the Outside — Baskin, Nora Raleigh
c Ruby Redfort: Catch Your Death — Child, Lauren
c Ruby Redfort: Look into My Eyes (Read by Stirling, Rachel). Audiobook Review — Child, Lauren
c Ruby Reinvented — Arno, Ronni
c Ruby Valentine and the Sweet Surprise (Illus. by Avril, Lynne) — Friedman, Laurie
The Ruby Way, 3d ed. — Arko, Andre
c Ruby Wizards — Weinstein, Eric
Rudder: From Leader to Legend — Hatfield, Thomas M.
c Rude Cakes (Illus. by Watkins, Rowboat) — Watkins, Rowboat
Rudolf Bultmann: A Biography — Hammann, Konrad
c Rudolfo Anaya's The Farolitos of Christmas (Illus. by Cordova, Amy) — Anaya, Rudolfo
c Rudolph Shines Again (Illus. by Caparo, Antonio Javier) — May, Robert L.
c Rudolph the Red-Nosed Reindeer (Illus. by Caparo, Antonio Javier) — May, Robert L.
c Rudolph the Red-Nosed Reindeer: The Classic Story (Illus. by Madrid, Erwin) — Feldman, Thea
c Rudy Toot Toots and His Cowboy Boots — Scholz, Paul
c Rudy's Windy Christmas (Illus. by Mantle, Ben) — Baugh, Helen
Rue — Bull, Melissa
Ruffer's Birthday Party — Shin, Soon-jae
c Ruffleclaw (Illus. by Funke, Cornelia) — Funke, Cornelia
c Ruffleclaw — Funke, Cornelia
c Ruffleclaw (Illus. by Funke, Cornelia) — Funke, Cornelia
c Rufus Goes to Sea (Illus. by Gorbachev, Valeri) — Griswell, Kim T.
c Rufus the Writer (Illus. by Groenink, Chuck) — Bram, Elizabeth
Ruhlman's How to Braise: Foolproof Techniques and Recipes for the Home Cook — Ruhlman, Michael
Ruhlman's How to Roast: Foolproof Techniques and Recipes for the Home Cook — Ruhlman, Michael
Ruin and Redemption: The Struggle for a Canadian Bankruptcy Law, 1867-1919 — Telfer, Thomas G.W.
Ruin and Redemption: The Struggle for Canadian Bankruptcy Law, 1867-1919 — Telfer, Thomas G.W.
Ruin: Essays in Exilic Living — Kalfopoulou, Adrianne
Ruin Falls — Milchman, Jenny
Ruin Memories: Materialities, Aesthetics and the Archaeology of the Recent Past — Olsen, Bjornar
Ruined Abbey — Emery, Anne
Ruined by this Miserable War: The Dispatches of Charles Prosper Fauconnet, a French Diplomat in New Orleans, 1863-1868 — Brasseux, Carl A.
Ruins (Illus. by Kuper, Peter) — Kuper, Peter
c The Ruins — Smith, Scott
Ruins and Fragments: Tales of Loss and Rediscovery — Harbison, Robert
Ruins of War — Connell, John A.

Rule and Ruin: The Downfall of Moderation and the Destruction of the Republican Party, from Eisenhower to the Tea Party — Kabaservice, Geoffrey
A Rule of Law: Elite Political Authority and the Coming of the Revolution in the South Carolina Lowcountry, 1763-1776 — Palmer, Aaron J.
The Rule of Law in Action in Democratic Athens — Harris, Edward Monroe
y The Rule of Mirrors — O'Brien, Caragh M.
y The Rule of Thoughts — Dashner, James
A Ruler's Consort in Early Modern Germany: Aemilia Juliana of Schwarzburg-Rudolstadt — Aikin, Judith P.
c The Rules — Lord, Cynthia
y The Rules — Viguie, Debbie
Rules and Observance: Devising Forms of Communal Life — Breitenstein, Mirak
y The Rules (Read by Daymond, Robbie). Audiobook Review — Holder, Nancy
c Rules for 50/50 Chances — McGovern, Kate
y Rules for a Knight — Hawke, Ethan
c Rules for Stealing Stars — Haydu, Corey Ann
Rules for the Perpetual Diet — Burns, K.S.R.
Rules for Werewolves — Lynn, Kirk
y The Rules — Holder, Nancy
y The Rules of Ever After — Brewer, Killian B.
The Rules of Isabelle of France: An English Translation with Introductory Study — Field, Sean L.
The Rules of Perspective — Thorpe, Adam
The Rules of Riding: An Edited Translation of the First Renaissance Treatise on Classical Horsemanship — Grisone, Federico
c Rules of Summer — Tan, Shaun
Rum Maniacs: Alcoholic Insanity in the Early American Republic — Osborn, Matthew Warner
Rumble (Read by Heyborne, Kirby). Audiobook Review — Hopkins, Ellen
y Rumble — Hopkins, Ellen
y Rumble with the Romans! — Northfield, Gary
y The Rumor (Read by McInerney, Kathleen). Audiobook Review — Hilderbrand, Elin
Rumor, Diplomacy and War in Enlightment Paris — Ewing, Tabetha Leigh
Rumor Has It — Hodges, Cheris
The Rumor — Hilderbrand, Elin
c Rumpelstiltskin Returns — Guillain, Charlotte
c Rumpelstiltskin Returns (Illus. by Stone, Steve) — Pearson, Maggie
Rumpled Stilton Skin — Postgate, Daniel
c Run for Your Life! Predators and Prey on the African Savanna (Illus. by Meisel, Paul) — Schaefer, Lola M.
Run like Crazy, Run like Hell — Tardi, Jacques
c Run, Pip, Run — Jones, J.C.
c Run, Run Piglet (Illus. by Ng, Neiko) — Schwartz, Betty Ann
Run You Down (Read by Arndt, Andi). Audiobook Review — Dahl, Julia
Run You Down — Dahl, Julia
c Run Your Own Babysitting Business — Berne, Emma Carlson
Runaway — May, Peter
c The Runaway Pumpkin (Illus. by Schindler, S.D.) — Lewis, Anne Margaret
c The Runaway Pumpkin (Illus. by Zenz, Aaron) — Margaret, Anne
Runaway Radical: A Young Man's Reckless Journey to Save the World — Hollingsworth, Amy
c The Runaway Santa: A Christmas Adventure Story (Illus. by Zenz, Aaron) — Lewis, Anne Margaret
c The Runaway Tortilla — Kimmel, Eric A.
Runaway Train: Saved by Belle of the Mines and Mountains (Illus. by Renaud, Joanne) — Coleman, Wim
c The Runaway's Gold — Burack, Emilie Christie
Runes — Findell, Martin
Runner's World: The Runner's Brain: How to Think Smarter to Run Better — Brown, Jeff (b. 1969-)
y Running Dry: The Global Water Crisis — Kallen, Stuart A.
Running Fire — McKenna, Lindsay
Running for the House — Kleinhendler, Howard
Running from Office: Why Young Americans Are Turned Off to Politics — Lawless, Jennifer L.
c Running Out of Night — Lovejoy, Sharon

Running to the Fire: An American Missionary Comes of Age in Revolutionary Ethiopia — Bascom, Tim
y Running Wide Open — Nowak, Lisa
Running Wild — Anderson, Susan
y Running with Cosmos Flowers: The Children of Hiroshima — Manale, Shizumi Shigeto
Running with the Hounds — Wingfield, David
c Rupert Can Dance (Illus. by Feiffer, Jules) — Feiffer, Jules
c Rupert's Parchment: Story of Magna Carta (Illus. by Ettlinger, Doris) — Cameron, Eileen
Rural Fictions, Urban Realities: A Geography of Gilded Age American Literature — Storey, Mark
Rural Unrest during the First Russian Revolution: Kursk Province, 1905-1906 — Miller, Burton Richard
Rural Women's Health — Leipert, Beverly
Rush — Gordon, Gina
Rush Hour: How 500 Million Commuters Survive the Daily Journey to Work — Gately, Iain
Rush Hour: How 500 Million Commuters Survive the Daily Journey to Work — Gately, Ian
Rush to Gold: The French and the California Gold Rush, 1848-1854 — Rohrbough, Malcolm J.
Ruskin's Venice: The Stones Revisited — Quill, Sarah
Russell Brand's Trickster Tales: The Pied Piper of Hamelin (Read by Brand, Russell). Audiobook Review — Brand, Russell
c Russell Brand's Trickster Tales: The Pied Piper of Hamelin (Illus. by Riddell, Chris) — Brand, Russell
Russell Kirk: American Conservative — Birzer, Bradley J.
Russia and Britain in Persia: Imperial Ambitions in Qajar Iran — Kazemzadeh, Firuz
Russia and the Making of Modern Greek Identity, 1821-1844 — Frary, Lucien J.
Russia and the New World Disorder — Lo, Bobo
Russia at War: From the Mongol Conquest to Afghanistan, Chechnya, and Beyond — Dowling, Timothy C.
Russia in Private — Yatzek, Richard
Russia in the Microphone Age: A History of Soviet Radio — Lovell, Stephen
Russia vs. the EU: The Competition for Influence in Post-Soviet States — Tolstrup, Jakob
The Russian Army in the Great War: The Eastern Front, 1914-1917 — Stone, David R.
The Russian Bride — Kavacs, Ed
The Russian Bride — Kovacs, Ed
Russian Cross-Currents of German and Russian Art, 1907-1917 — Akinsha, Konstantin
Russian Energy and Security up to 2030 — Oxenstierna, Susanne
y The Russian Federation: Then and Now — Allen, John
The Russian Gas Matrix: How Markets are Driving Change — Pirani, Simon
Russian Idea, Jewish Presence: Essays on Russian-Jewish Intellectual Life — Horowitz, Brian
Russian Modernism: Cross-Currents of German and Russian Art, 1907-1917 — Akinsha, Konstantin
Russian Monarchy: Representation and Rule; Collected Articles — Wortman, Richard
Russian Optimism: Dark Nursery Rhymes to Cheer You Right Up — Rosenfeld, Ben
The Russian Revolution of 1905 in Transcultural Perspective: Identities, Peripheries, and the Flow of Ideas — Felicitas Fischer von Weikersthal
Russian Tattoo — Gorokhova, Elena
Russlands Imperiale Macht: Integrationsstrategien und Ihre Reichweite in Transnationaler Perspektive — Pietrow-Ennker, Bianca
Rust: The Longest War — Waldman, Jonathan
Rustic: Simple Food and Drink, from Morning to Night — Fernandez, Jorge
c Rustle Up a Rhythm (Illus. by Anderson, Sarah Nelisiwe) — Malam, Rosalind
y Rusty Summer — McKinley, Mary
Rutabaga: The Adventure Chef (Illus. by Colossal, Eric) — Colossal, Eric
y Ruthless — Adams, Carolyn Lee
Ruthless — Rector, John
Rywka's Diary: The Writings of a Jewish Girl from the Lodz Ghetto — Lipszyc, Rywka

S

S. — *Abrams, J.J.*
c S Is for Sleeping Bear Dunes: A National Lakeshore Alphabet (Illus. by Frankenhuyzen, Gijsbert van) — *Wargin, Kathy-jo*
S.N.U.F.F.: A Utopia — *Pelevin, Victor*
Saban: The Making of a Coach — *Burke, Monte*
c Saber-Toothed Cat — *Zeiger, Jennifer*
Saberes Humanisticos — *Strosetzki, Christoph*
Sabotage, Sedition and Sundry Acts of Rebellion — *Aretha, David*
Sabotaged — *Pettrey, Dani*
c Sacagawea — *Shepherd, Jodie*
c Sacajawea (Illus. by Collins, Matt) — *Krull, Kathleen*
Sacral Kingship between Disenchantment and Re-Enactment: The French and English Monarchies, 1587-1688 — *Asch, Ronald G.*
The Sacrament of Penance and Religious Life in Golden Age Spain — *O'Banion, Patrick J.*
A Sacramental-Prophetic Vision: Christian Spirituality in a Suffering World — *Eggemeier, Matthew T.*
Sacramental Shopping: Louisa May Alcott, Edith Wharton, and the Spirit of Modern Consumerism — *Sherman, Sarah Way*
Sacrati — *Sherwood, Kate*
The Sacred Architecture of Byzantium: Art, Liturgy and Symbolism in Early Christian Churches — *Patricios, Nicholas N.*
Sacred Authority and Temporal Power in the Writings of Bernard of Clairvaux — *Chapman, Alice*
Sacred Communities, Shared Devotions: Gender, Material Culture, and Monasticism in Late Medieval Germany — *Mecham, June L.*
Sacred Divorce: Religion, Therapeutic Culture, and Ending Life Partnerships — *Jenkins, Kathleen E.*
The Sacred Encounter: Jewish Perspectives on Sexuality — *Grushcow, Rabbi Lisa J.*
Sacred Landscape in Medieval Afghanistan: Revisiting the Fada'il-i Balkh — *Azad, Arezou*
y The Sacred Lies of Minnow Bly — *Oakes, Stephanie*
Sacred Mountains of China — *Pyle, Ryan*
Sacred Music in Secular Society — *Arnold, Jonathan*
Sacred Pause: A Creative Retreat for the Word-Weary Christian — *Hackenberg, Rachel G.*
The Sacred Project of American Sociology — *Smith, Christian*
Sacred Relics: Pieces of the Past in Nineteenth-Century America — *Barnett, Teresa*
Sacred River — *Cheney-Coker, Syl*
Sacred Scripture, Sacred War: The Bible and the American Revolution — *Byrd, James P.*
Sacred Sense: Discovering the Wonder of God's Word and World — *Brown, William P.*
Sacred Stiches: Ecclesiastical Textiles in the Rothschild Collection at Waddesdon Manor — *Boak, Rachel*
Sacred Stories, Spiritual Tribes: Finding Religion in Everyday Life — *Ammerman, Nancy Tatom*
Sacrifice — *Freeman, Philip*
The Sacrifice — *Oates, Joyce Carol*
Sacrifice and Modern Thought — *Mezaros, Julia*
Sacrifice — *Girard, Rene*
Sacrificial Lamb Cake — *Monroe, Katrina*
Sacrificing Families: Navigating Laws, Labor, and Love Across Borders — *Abrego, Leisy J.*
Sacrificing Families: Negotiating Laws, Labor, and Love Across Borders — *Abrego, Leisy J.*
Sacrificing Soldiers on the National Mall — *Hass, Kristin Ann*
c Sad, the Dog — *Fussell, Sandy*
c Sad, the Dog (Illus. by Suwannakit, Tull) — *Fussell, Sandy*

c Sadako's Cranes (Illus. by Loske, Judith) — *Loske, Judith*
Sade's Sensibilities — *Parker, Kate*
c Sadie and Ori and the Blue Blanket (Illus. by Fortenberry, Julie) — *Korngold, Jamie*
c Sadie, Ori, and Nuggles Go to Camp (Illus. by Fortenberry, Julie) — *Korngold, Jamie*
c Sadie: The Dog Who Finds the Evidence — *Feldman, Thea*
c Sadie's Big Steal — *McKenna, Marla*
c Saeurs — *Telgemeier, Raina*
Safari (Read by Graham, Dion). Audiobook Review — *Tuchman, Gail*
Safe as Houses — *Glickman, Susan*
Safe as Houses — *Hutchison, Michele*
Safe as Houses — *Van der Vlugt, Simone*
Safe Dance Practice — *Quin, Edel*
Safe Space: Gay Neighborhood History and the Politics of Violence — *Hanhardt, Christina B.*
The Safeguard of Liberty and Property: The Supreme Court, Kelo v. New London, and the Takings Clause — *Burnett, Guy F.*
Safekeeping — *Hope, Jessamyn*
c The Safest Lie — *Cerrito, Angela*
y Safety Stars: Players Who Fought to Make the Hard-Hitting Game of Professional Hockey Safer — *Irwin, Sue*
Saffron — *Warren, Vic*
The Saffron Road: A Journey with Buddha's Daughters — *Toomey, Christine*
y The Saga of Gudrid the Far-Traveler — *Brown, Nancy Marie*
The Saga of the Pony Express — *Di Certo, Joseph J.*
Sagan, Paris 1954 — *Berest, Anne*
c Sage and the Journey to Wishworld — *Zappa, Shana Muldoon*
The SAGE Encyclopedia of Action Research — *Coghlan, David*
The SAGE Encyclopedia of Educational Technology, 2 vols. — *Spector, J. Michael*
The SAGE Encyclopedia of Intercultural Competence, 2 vols. — *Bennett, Janet M.*
The SAGE Encyclopedia of Stem Cell Research, 2d ed. — *Bouhassira, Eric E.*
c Sage: I am the Middle Sister — *Azaro, Victoria M.*
The Sage of Waterloo — *Francombe, Leona*
Sagrada Familia: Gaudi's Unfinished Masterpiece, Geometry, Construction and Site — *Ojeda, Oscar Riera*
Saharan Jews and the Fate of French Algeria — *Stein, Sarah Abrevaya*
Saigon's Edge — *Harms, Erik*
c Sail Away (Illus. by Bryan, Ashley) — *Hughes, Langston*
Sail upon the Land — *Young, Josa*
c Sailing Away on a Windy Day (Illus. by Kudemus, Raynald) — *Napoli, Linda*
Sailing Close to the Wind: Reminiscences — *Skinner, David*
Sailing the Forest: Selected Poems — *Robertson, Robin*
Sailor and Fiddler — *Wouk, Herman*
Sailor Man: The Troubled Life and Times of J.P. Nunnally, USN — *Staecker, Del*
c A Sailor Went to Sea, Sea, Sea (Illus. by Pearse, Asha) — *Bell, Lucy*
A Sailor's Story (Illus. by Glanzman, Sam) — *Glanzman, Sam*
The Saint and the Chopped-Up Baby: The Cult of Vincent Ferrer in Medieval and Early Modern Europe — *Smoller, Laura Ackerman*
c Saint Anthony the Great (Illus. by Brent, Isabelle) — *Chryssavgis, John*

y Saint Anything (Read by Meskimen, Taylor). Audiobook Review — *Dessen, Sarah*
y Saint Anything (Read by Meskimen, Taylor) — *Dessen, Sarah*
y Saint Anything (Read by Meskimen, Taylor). Audiobook Review — *Dessen, Sarah*
y Saint Anything — *Dessen, Sarah*
Saint Augustine of Hippo: An Intellectual Biography — *Hollingworth, Miles*
The Saint-Fiacre Affair — *Simenon, Georges*
Saint Mazie — *Attenberg, Jami*
Saint Odd (Read by Baker, David Aaron). Audiobook Review — *Koontz, Dean*
Saintly Spouses: Chaste Marriage in Sacred and Secular Narrative from Medieval Germany (12th and 13th Centuries). — *Bornholdt, Claudia*
Saints and Citizens: Indigenous Histories of Colonial Missions and Mexican California — *Haas, Lisbeth*
Saints' Lives, 2 vols. — *Henry of Avranches*
Saints Observed: Studies of Mormon Village Life, 1850-2005 — *Bahr, Howard M.*
Saints of New York — *Ellory, R.J.*
Saints of New York — *Ellory, Roger Jon*
Saints of the Shadow Bible — *Rankin, Ian*
Saints or Devils Incarnate? Studies in Jesuit History — *O'Malley, John W.*
Sairseal agus Dill, 1947-1981: Sceal foilsitheora — *O hEigeartaigh, Cian*
Sakramentale Reprasentation: Substanz, Zeichen und Prasenz in der fruhen Neuzeit — *Oster, Carolin*
Salad Samurai — *Romero, Terry Hope*
Saladin: The Life, the Legend and the Islamic Empire — *Man, John*
c Salamander Season (Illus. by Bersani, Shennen) — *Curtis, Jennifer Keats*
Salamander Sun — *Tafdrup, Pia*
Salami Tactics Revisited: Hungarian Communists on the Road to Power — *Rieber, Alfred J.*
Salem Health: Psychology and Behavioral Health, 4th ed. — *Moglia, Paul*
c The Salem Witch Trials — *Johnson, Robin*
c The Salem Witchcraft Trials: Would You Join the Madness? — *Landau, Elaine*
Salinger — *Salerno, Shane*
Sally McFague: Collected Readings — *Lott, David B.*
c Sally Poor Doreen: A Fishy Tale (Illus. by Boiger, Alexandra) — *Lloyd-Jones, Sally*
c Sally Ride: A Photobiography of America's Pioneering Woman in Space — *O'Shaughnessy, Tam*
Sally Ride: America's First Woman in Space (Read by Ward, Pam). Audiobook Review — *Sherr, Lynn*
c Sally Ride: Life on a Mission — *Macy, Sue*
c Sally Ride — *Edison, Erin*
Salman Rushdie in the Cultural Marketplace — *Mendes, Ana Cristina*
Salmon Is Everything: Community-Based Theatre in the Klamath Watershed — *May, Theresa*
Salmon Maerins Gediehtsammlungen von 1538 bis 1546 — *Schumann, Marie, Francoise*
y Salmon River Kid — *Dorris, Joseph*
y Salome — *Gormley, Beatrice*
The Salon Dore from the Hotel de la Tremoille — *Chapman, Martin*
The Saloon and the Mission: Addiction, Conversion and the Politics of Redemption in American Culture — *Cannon, Eoin F.*
Saloons, Prostitutes, and Temperance in Alaska Territory — *Spude, Catherine Holder*
Salsa Crossings: Dancing Latinidad in Los Angeles — *Garcia, Cindy*
Salsa, Language and Transnationalism — *Schneider, Britta*

c Salsa: Un Poema Para Cocinar/A Cooking Poem (Illus. by Tonatiuh, Duncan) — Argueta, Jorge
Salsa with the Pope — Anderson, Samantha Wren
Salt: A Story of Friendship in a Time of War — Frost, Helen
y Salt and Stone — Scott, Victoria
y Salt & Storm — Kulper, Kendall
y Salt to the Sea — Sepetys, Ruta
Saltair Saíochta, Sanasaíochta agus Seanchais: A Festschrift for Gearóid Mac Eoin — O Baoill, Donall
Saltpeter: The Mother of Gunpowder — Cressy, David
Saltwater Cowboy: The Rise and Fall of a Marijuana Empire — McBride, Tim
Saltwater Cowboys — Furlong, Dayle
The Saltwater Frontier: Indians and the Contest for the American Coast — Lipman, Andrew
SaltWater — Ashfeldt, Lane
Salvage — Warren, Rosie
y The Salvation of Gabriel Adam — Duncan, S.L.
y The Salvation of Miss Lucretia — Dunagan, Ted M.
Salvation through Dissent: Tonghak Heterodoxy and Early Modern Korea — Kallander, George L.
Salvation with a Smile: Joel Osteen, Lakewood Church, and American Christianity — Sinitiere, Phillip Luke
c Sam and Dave Dig a Hole (Illus. by Klassen, Jon) — Barnett, Mac
Sam Dunn Is Dead — Corra, Bruno
Sam Phillips: The Man Who Invented Rock 'n' Roll — Guralnick, Peter
Sam Zabel and the Magic Pen — Horrocks, Dylan
Sam(uel). — Gareau, Colleen
c Samantha Sanderson: Off the Record — Caroll, Robin
The Samaritan — Cross, Mason
y Same But Different: Teen Life on the Autism Express — Peete, Holly Robinson
The Same City — Martin, Luisge
Same-Sex Desire in Early Modern England, 1550-1735: An Anthology of Literary Texts and Contexts — Loughlin, Marie H.
The Same Sky — Ward, Amanda Eyre
Same Time Next Week: True Stories of Working through Mental Illness — Gutkind, Lee
The Sami Peoples of the North: A Social and Cultural History — Kent, Neil
c Sami the Magic Bear: No to Bullying! (Illus. by Bourdon, Murielle) — Bourdon, Murielle
c Sammy Keyes and the Kiss Goodbye — Van Draanen, Wendelin
Sammy Keyes and the Night of the Skulls (Read by Sands, Tara). Audiobook Review — Van Draanen, Wendelin
c Sammy Spider's First Mitzvah (Illus. by Kahn, Katherine Janus) — Rouss, Sylvia A.
c Sammy Spider's First Taste of Hanukkah: A Cookbook (Illus. by Kahn, Katherine Janus) — Rouss, Sylvia A.
c Sammy Spider's First Taste of Hanukkah (Illus. by Kahn, Katherine Janus) — Rouss, Sylvia A.
c Sam's Big Deer (Illus. by King, Jason) — Stearns, James
c Sam's Pet Temper (Illus. by Arbona, Marion) — Bhadra, Sangeeta
Sams Teach Yourself Javascript in 24 Hours, 6th ed. — Ballard, Phil
Samtliche Werke, vol. 3: Dramen, part. 3: Kommentar zu Priscianus Vapulans und Iulius Redivivus — Frischlin, Nicodemus
Samuel Beckett's Library — Nixon, Mark
Samuel Johnson and the Journey into Words — Mugglestone, Lynda
Samuel Johnson: New Contexts for a New Century — Weinbrot, Howard D.
Samuel Palmer: Shadows on the Wall — Vaughan, William
Samuel Pepys and His Books: Reading, Newsgathering, and Sociability, 1660-1703 — Loveman, Kate
Samuel Taylor's Last Night — Amato, Joe
y Samurai Rising: The Epic Life of Minamoto Yoshitsune (Illus. by Hinds, Gareth) — Turner, Pamela S.
c Samurai Santa: A Very Ninja Christmas (Illus. by Pingk, Rubin) — Pingk, Rubin
c The San Antonio Spurs — Stewart, Mark
c Sana fi Qina (Illus. by Gueissa, Yasser) — Ghoneim, Hadil
Sanaaq: An Inuit Novel — Nappaaluk, Mitiarjuk Attasie

Sancta Sedes Apostolica et Cardinalis Ioseph Mindszenty, II: Documenta 1956-1963 — Somorjai, Adam
Sancta Sedes Apostolica et Cardinalis Joseph Mindszenty, III/1.: Documenta 1963-1966 — Somorjai, Adam
Sancta Sedes Apostolica et Cardinalis Joseph Mindszenty, III/2: Documenta 1967-1971 — Somorjai, Adam
Sanctity and Pilgrimage in Medieval Southern Italy, 1000-1200 — Oldfield, Paul
The Sanctity of Louis IX: Early Lives of Saint Louis by Geoffrey of Beaulieu and William of Chartres — Field, Larry F.
Sanctuary: A Novel — Edric, Robert
y Sanctuary — McKissack, Jennifer
y Sanctuary Bay — Burns, Laura J.
Sanctuary: Creating a Space for Grace in Your Life — Hershey, Terry
y Sanctum — Roux, Madeleine
Sand Castles: Interiors Inspired by the Coast — Neve, Tim
The Sand Men — Fowler, Christopher
y Sand Spider (Illus. by Fuentes, Benny) — Bowen, Carl
c Sand Swimmers: The Secret Life of Australia's Desert Wilderness (Illus. by Oliver, Narelle) — Oliver, Narelle
c SandCastle: Zoo Animals — Kuskowski, Alex
The Sandman: Overture — Klein, Todd
The Sandman: Overture — Williams, J.H., III
The Sandman: Overture — Gaiman, Neil
c Sandrider — Sage, Angie
The Sandzak: A History — Morrison, Kenneth
The Sandzak: A History — Roberts, Elizabeth
Sangama — Hernandez, Arturo D.
Sangre de Cristo: The Blood of Christ — Redfield, Wesley
Sanierung - Rekonstruktion - Neugestaltung: Zum Umgang mit historischen Bauten in Gedenkstätten — Hammermann, Gabriele
Sanitation, Latrines and Intestinal Parasites in Past Populations — Mitchell, Piers D.
c Sanitized for Your Protection (Illus. by Pastis, Stephan) — Pastis, Stephan
Sanspell — Pulford, Elizabeth
The Santa Claus Man: The Rise and Fall of a Jazz Age Con Man and the Invention of Christmas in New York — Palmer, Alex
c Santa Clauses: Short Poems from the North Pole (Illus. by Groenink, Chuck) — Raczka, Bob
The Santa Klaus Murder — Hay, Mavis Doriel
Santa Rita Stories — Rodriguez, Andrew J.
c The Santa Shimmy — Jones, Christianne C.
The Santa Shimmy (Illus. by Randall, Emma) — Jones, Christianne C.
The Santangelos — Collins, Jackie
c Santa's Search for the Perfect Child (Illus. by Chadwell, Dennis) — Schulte, Donna Faulkner
c Santa's Secret (Illus. by Hoover, Sunny) — Hoover, Sunny
Sante Militaire, Sante Coloniale. Guerres, Maladies et Empires au long XIXe Siecle
The Santero — Vincenti, F.R.
Sapiens: A Brief History of Humankind — Harari, Yuval Noah
Sapient — Kaczmarowski, Jerry
Sapphic Fathers: Discourses of Same-Sex Desire from Nineteenth-Century France — Schultz, Gretchen
Sapphire: A Tale of the Cold War — Graham, Thomas, Jr. (b. 1933-)
Sappho: A New Translation of the Complete Works — Rayor, Diane J.
Sappho's Agency — Newell, Lizzie
Saqueo en el archivo: El paradero de los tesoros documentales guatemaltecos — Kramer, Wendy
Sara Coleridge: Her Life and Thought — Barbeau, Jeffrey W.
c Sara Lost and Found — Castleman, Virginia
Sarah Charlesworth: Stills — Witkovsky, Matthew S.
c Sarah in the City of Moon (Illus. by Qutob, Dalia) — Qutob, Fida Fayez
Sarah Waters: Contemporary Critical Perspectives — Mitchell, Kaye
The Sarashina Diary: A Woman's Life in Eleventh-Century Japan — Sugawara no Takasue no Musume
The Sarashina Diary: A Woman's Life in Eleventh-Century Japan — Arntzen, Sonja
The Sarcastic Lens — Lynn, Richard
c Sardines of Love (Illus. by Aguirre, Zurine) — Aguirre, Zurine

Sargent: Portraits of Artists and Friends — Ormond, Richard
Sartre: A Philosophical Biography — Flynn, Thomas R.
The Sasanian World through Georgian Eyes: Caucasia and the Iranian Commonwealth in Late Antique Georgian Literature — Rapp, Stephen H., Jr.
c Sashi Adopts a Brother (Illus. by Spicer, Morgan) — Greiner, Linda
The Sasquatch Hunter's Almanac — Shields, Sharma
y Sasquatch — Hirsch, Andrea Schicke
Sassy Gal's How to Lose the Last Damn 10 Pounds or 15, 20, 25.... — Helbert, Sharon
Satan and Salem: The Witch-Hunt Crisis of 1692 — Ray, Benjamin C.
Satin Island — McCarthy, Tom
Satisfying Clicking Sound — Guriel, Jason
Satoshi Kon's Opus — Kon, Satoshi
y Saturday Night Live: Shaping TV Comedy and American Culture — Kaplan, Arie
c Saturn — Roumanis, Alexis
Saturn: Amazing Rings — Glaser, Chaya
c Saturn Could Sail: And Other Fun Facts (Illus. by Oswald, Pete) — DiSiena, Laura Lyn
Saturn Run — Ctein
Saturn Run — Sandford, John
Satyre seconde: le neveu de Rameau — Hobson, Marian
Satyric Play: The Evolution of Greek Comedy and Satyr Drama — Shaw, C.A.
Saudi-Arabien: Politik, Geschichte, Religion — Steinberg, Guido
Saul Bellow: Novels, 1944-1953 — Bellow, Saul
Saul Bellow: Novels, 1956-1964 — Bellow, Saul
Saul Bellow: Novels, 1970-1982 — Bellow, Saul
Saul Bellow: Novels, 1984-2000 — Bellow, Saul
Saul Leiter: Early Black and White, 2 vols. — Kozloff, Max
Saul Leiter: Early Color — Harrison, Martin
Saul Leiter: Retrospektive — Taubhorn, Ingo
Savage Chains — Roane, Caris
y Savage Drift — Laybourne, Emmy
Savage Lane — Starr, Jason
c Savage Mountain — Smelcer, John
Savage Portrayals: Race, Media, and the Central Park Jogger Story — Byfield, Natalie P.
Savage Preservation: The Ethnographic Origins of Modern Media Technology — Hochman, Brian
Savages — Parker, K.J.
Savaging the Dark — Conlon, Christopher
The Savants — Kendrick, Patrick
y Save Me, Kurt Cobain — Manzer, Jenny
y Save Me — Elliott, Jenny
c Save Money — Reina, Mary
Saveur: The New Classics Cookbook
Saveur: The New Classics Cookbook — Saveur editors
Saving Alex — Cooper, Alex
Saving America Now: The Buffet Syndrome — Slover, Ron
c Saving Annie's Mountain — Children of Wild Dance Farm
Saving Capitalism: For the Many, Not the Few — Reich, Robert B.
Saving Cecil — Mims, Lee
Saving Community Journalism: The Path to Profitability — Abernathy, Penelope Muse
Saving Congress from Itself: Emancipating the States and Empowering Their People — Buckley, James L.
c Saving Crazy — Hood-Caddy, Karen
c Saving Eyesight: Adventures of Seva around the World — Pruessen, Linda
Saving Face: Disfigurement and the Politics of Appearance — Talley, Heather Laine
Saving Gotham: A Billionaire Mayor, Activist Doctors, and the Fight for Eight Million Lives — Farley, Tom
Saving Grace (Read by Green, Jane). Audiobook Review — Green, Jane
Saving Grapes — Lundy, J.T.
Saving Jason — Sears, Michael
Saving Karl Barth: Hans Urs von Balthasar's Preoccupation — Long, D. Stephen
Saving Karl Barth: Hans Urs von Balthasars Preoccupation — Long, Stephen D.
Saving Lake Tahoe: An Environmental History of a National Treasure — Makley, Michael J.
c Saving Mim (Illus. by Bickel, Chuck) — McAdam, Nan
c Saving Montgomery Sole — Tamaki, Mariko
y Saving Mr. Terupt — Buyea, Rob
Saving Our Skins: Building a Vineyard Dream in France — Feely, Caro

Saving Place: 50 Years of New York City Landmarks — *Stern, Robert A.M.*
Saving Sex: Sexuality and Salvation in American Evangelism — *Derogatis, Amy*
Saving Sophie — *Balson, Ronald H.*
Saving the Original Sinner: How Christians Have Used the Bible's First Man to Oppress, Inspire, and Make Sense of the World — *Giberson, Karl W.*
Saving the Original Sinner — *Giberson, Karl W.*
c Saving the Persecuted — *Williams, Brian*
Saving the Soul of Georgia: Donald L. Hollowell and the Struggle for Civil Rights — *Daniels, Maurice C.*
c Saving the Sun Dragon (Illus. by Howells, Graham) — *West, Tracey*
Saving Turtles: A Kid's Guide to Helping Endangered Creatures — *Carstairs, Sue*
c Saving Wonder — *Knight, Mary*
Savoia-Marchetti S.79 Sparviero Torpedo-Bomber Units — *Mattioli, Marco*
The Savonnerie: The James A. de Rothschild Collection at Waddesdon Manor — *Verlet, Pierre*
Savoring Gotham: A Food Lover's Companion to New York City — *Smith, Andrew F.*
Savoring Power, Consuming the Times: The Metaphors of Food in Medieval and Renaissance Italian Literature — *Palma, Pina*
Say Good-bye to Dork City — *Peirce, Lincoln*
c Say Hello! (Illus. by Davick, Linda) — *Davick, Linda*
c Say It! (Illus. by Stevenson, James) — *Zolotow, Charlotte*
Say No to the Devil: The Life and Musical Genius of Rev. Gary Davis — *Zack, Ian*
y Say You Will — *Walters, Eric*
Say You're One of Them — *Akpan, Uwem*
Saying Is Believing: The Necessity of Testimony in Adolescent Spiritual Development — *Drury, Amanda Hontz*
Saying No to Say Yes: Everyday Boundaries and Pastoral Excellence — *Olsen, David C.*
Sayonara Amerika, Sayonara Nippon: A Geopolitical Prehistory of J-Pop — *Bourdaghs, Michael K.*
Sayyid Qutb: The Life and Legacy of a Radical Islamic Intellectual — *Toth, James*
Scalawag: A White Southerner's Journey through Segregation to Human Rights Activism — *Peeples, Edward H.*
Scale and Scale Change in the Early Middle Ages: Exploring Landscape, Local Society, and the World Beyond — *Escalona, Julio*
Scale-Bright — *Sriduangkaew, Benjanun*
Scales on Censorship: Real Life Lessons from School Library Journal — *Scales, Pat R.*
Scalp Dance — *Clifton, Lu*
Scalping Columbus and Other Damn Indian Stories: Truths, Half-Truths and Outright Lies — *Eagle, Adam Fortunate*
Scalping Columbus and Other Damn Indian Stories: Truths, Half-Truths, and Outright Lies — *Eagle, Adam Fortunate*
Scam Chowder — *Corrigan, Maya*
Scammed: Team from the Biggest Consumer and Money Frauds How Not to Be a Victim — *Scott, Gini Graham*
The Scamp — *Pashley, Jennifer*
y Scan (Read by Daniels, Luke). Audiobook Review — *Jury, Walter*
c Scandal — *Ockler, Sarah*
Scandal Takes the Stage — *Leigh, Eva*
Scandalous Behavior — *Woods, Stuart*
y The Scandalous Sisterhood of Prickwillow Place (Read by Entwistle, Jayne). Audiobook Review — *Berry, Julie*
y The Scandalous Sisterhood of Prickwillow Place — *Berry, Julie*
Scandals and Abstraction: Financial Fiction of the Long 1980s — *La Berge, Leigh Claire*
Scandal's Heiress — *Smith, Amelia*
Scandinavia in the Age of Revolution: Nordic Political Cultures, 1740-1820 — *Ihalainen, Pasi*
Scandinavian Baking — *Hahnemann, Trine*
Scandinavian Home: A Comprehensive Guide to Mid-Century Modern Scandinavian Designers — *Wilhide, Elizabeth*
The Scapegoat — *Nikolaidou, Sophia*
Scapegoat — *Gillis, Alan*
Scapegoats: Thirteen Victims of Military Injustice — *Scott, Michael*
c The Scar (Illus. by Tallec, Olivier)
y Scar Girl — *Vlahos, Len*
Scarback — *Corea, Roger*
The Scarborough — *Lista, Michael*
c Scare Scape (Illus. by Bosma, Sam) — *Fisher, Sam*

y Scare Scape: The Midnight Door — *Fisher, Sam*
c Scarecrow Magic (Illus. by Myers, Matt) — *Masessa, Ed*
c The Scarecrows' Wedding (Illus. by Scheffler, Axel) — *Donaldson, Julia*
c Scaredy-Cat, Splat! (Illus. by Scotton, Rob) — *Scotton, Rob*
The Scarlet Gospels — *Barker, Clive*
y The Scarlet Letter: Manga Classics (Illus. by Lee, SunNeko) — *Hawthorne, Nathaniel*
Scarlet Women: The Scandalous Lives of Courtesans, Concubines, and Royal Mistresses — *Graham, Ian*
c Scarlett and Sam: Escape from Egypt (Illus. by Stevanovic, Ivica) — *Kimmel, Eric A.*
y Scarlett Undercover — *Latham, Jennifer*
Scarpia — *Read, Piers Paul*
Scarred Hearts — *Tiner, Billi*
The Scars of Project 459: The Environmental Story of the Lake of the Ozarks — *Angel, Traci*
Scarsdale — *O'Brien, Dan*
Scary Close: Dropping the Act and Finding True Intimacy — *Miller, Donald*
The Scary Girls — *Kaplan, J.D.*
Scary Old Sex — *Heyman, Arlene*
The Scatter Here is Too Great — *Tanweer, Bilal*
Scattered at Sea — *Gerstler, Amy*
c The Scavengers (Read by Rustin, Sandy). Audiobook Review — *Perry, Michael*
c The Scavengers — *Perry, Michael*
Scenario-Focused Engineering: A Toolbox for Innovation and Customer-Centricity — *De Bonte, Austina*
Scenes for Teens: 50 Original Comedy and Drama Scenes for Teenage Actors — *Kimmel, Mike*
The Scent of Eternity — *McKean, Alan T.*
Scent of Murder — *Born, James O.*
The Scent of Pine — *Vapnyar, Lara*
The Scent of Secrets — *Thynne, Jane*
Scent of Triumph — *Moran, Jan*
Scents and Sensibility — *Quinn, Spencer*
The Sceptical Gardener: The Thinking Person's Guide to Good Gardening — *Thompson, Ken*
The Sceptical Optimist: Why Technology Isn't the Answer to Everything — *Agar, Nicholas*
Schafe fur die Ewigkeit: Handschriften und ihre Herstellung: Katalog zur Jahresausstellung in der Stiftsbibliothek St. Gallen — *Schnoor, Franziska*
Schattengefechte: Genealogische Praktiken in Nachrufen auf Naturwissenschaftler — *Echterholter, Anna*
Schattengefechte: Generalogische Praktiken in Nachrufen auf Naturwissenschaftler, 1710-1860 — *Echterholter, Anna*
Schatz Images: 25 Years — *Schatz, Howard*
Schaufeln - Schubkarren - Stacheldraht: Peter Demant - Erinnerungen eines Osterreichers an Zwangsarbeitslager und Verbannung in der Sowjetunion — *Scharr, Kurt*
Schedule of Unrest: Selected Poems — *Wilkinson, John*
Scheitert Europa? — *Fischer, Joschka*
Schicksal: Based on a True Story: Two Lives Torn Apart by War, Cradled in the Palm of Fate — *Jackson, Merima*
y Schindler, Wallenberg, Miep Gies: The Holocaust Heroes — *Fremon, David K.*
Schirmer Performance Editions: Burgmuller: 25 Progressive Studies, Opus 100 — *Otwell, Margaret*
Schirmer Performance Editions: Kabalevsky: 24 Pieces for Children, Opus 39 — *Otwell, Margaret*
y Schizo — *Sheff, Nic*
The Schizophrenic Society: Lost in a Make-Believe World While We Destroy the Real One — *Boyd, Roger*
A Schizophrenic Will: A Story of Madness, a Story of Hope — *Jiang, William*
Schizophrenics Can Be Good Mothers Too — *Lam, Q.S.*
The Schlieffen Plan: International Perspectives on the German Strategy for World War I — *Ehlert, Hans*
Schlump — *Grimm, Hans Herbert*
Schmuck — *Kushner, Seth*
c The Schnoz of Doom (Illus. by Santat, Dan) — *Beaty, Andrea*
Schoenberg and Redemption — *Brown, Julie*
The Scholar Denied: W.E.B. Du Bois and the Birth of Modern Sociology — *Morris, Aldon D.*
Scholarly Metrics under the Microscope: From Citation Analysis to Academic Auditing — *Sugimoto, Cassidy R.*
Scholarly Metrics Under the Microscope — *Cronin, Blaise*

Scholars, Poets and Radicals: Discovering Forgotten Lives in Blackwell Collections — *Ricketts, Rita*
Scholarship in Software - Software as Scholarship. From Genesis to Peer Review
c Scholastic Discover More: Hurricane Katrina — *Callery, Sean*
Scholastic Metaphysics: A Contemporary Introduction — *Feser, Edward*
Scholia to an Implicit Text — *Gomez-Davila, Nicolas*
Scholies a Pindare — *Daude, Cecile*
c School Days around the World (Illus. by Feagan, Alice) — *Ruurs, Margriet*
y A School for Brides: A Story of Maidens, Mystery, and Matrimony — *Kindl, Patrice*
y A School for Brides — *Kindi, Patrice*
y A School for Brides — *Kindl, Patrice*
A School for Fools — *Boguslawski, Alexander*
y School for Sidekicks — *McCullough, Kelly*
c School for Sidekicks — *McCulough, Kelly*
y A School for Unusual Girls — *Baldwin, Kathleen*
School Librarians and the Technology Department: A Practical Guide for Successful Collaboration — *Bell, Mary Ann*
y School Libraries 3.0: Principles and Practices for the Digital Age — *Butler, Rebecca P.*
School Libraries Matter: Views from the Research — *Dow, Mirah J.*
School Library Management, 7th ed. — *Dickinson, Gail K.*
School Lunches: Healthy Choices vs. Crowd Pleasers — *Lanser, Amanda*
c The School of Art: Learn How to Make Great Art with 40 Simple Lessons (Illus. by Frost, Daniel) — *Triggs, Teal*
The School of Sophisticated Drinking: An Intoxicating History of Seven Spirits — *Ehmer, Kerstin*
c The School Show (Illus. by Heder, Thyra) — *Gianferrari, Maria*
School Spirits — *Davidson, Anya*
c School Uniforms, Yes or No — *Carole, Bonnie*
c Schooled — *Korman, Gordon*
The Schooled Society: The Educational Transformation of Global Culture — *Baker, David P.*
Schooling, Childhood, and Bureaucracy: Bureaucratizing the Child — *Waters, Tony*
The Schooling of Girls in Britain and Ireland, 1800-1900 — *McDermid, Jane*
Schools on Trial — *Goyal, Nikhil*
School's Out: Gay and Lesbian Teachers in the Classroom — *Connell, Catherine*
Schopenhauer and the Aesthetic Standpoint: Philosophy as a Practise of the Sublime — *Vasalou, Sophia*
Schopenhauer's Encounter with Indian Thought: Representation and Will and Their Indian Parallels — *Cross, Stephen*
Schreibschulen und Buchmalerei: Handschriften und Texte des 9.-11. Jahrhunderts — *Hoffmann, Hartmut*
Schriften zur Erkenntnisschulung: Wie Erlangt man Erkenntnisse der Hoheren Welten. Die Stufen der Hoheren Erkenntnis, hrsg. u. Kommentiert von Christian Clement — *Steiner, Rudolf*
Schubert: Interpretationen — *Pietschmann, Klaus*
Schubert's Winter Journey: Anatomy of an Obsession — *Bostridge, Ian*
Schwarze Flamme: Revolutionare Klassenpolitik des Anarchismus und Syndikalismus — *Schmidt, Michael*
Sci-Fi Chronicles — *Haley, Guy*
y Science — *Gigliotti, Jim*
Science and Faith: A New Introduction — *Haught, John F.*
Science and Hope: A Forest History — *Dargavel, John*
Science and Religion in Mamluk Egypt: Ibn al-Nafis, Pulmonary Transit and Bodily Resurrection — *Fancy, Emillie*
Science and Spirituality: Making Room for Faith in the Age of Science — *Ruse, Michael*
Science before Socrates: Parmenides, Anaxagoras and the New Astronomy — *Graham, Daniel W.*
Science Education and Citizenship: Fairs, Clubs and Talent Searches for Amerian Youth, 1918-1958 — *Terzian, Sevan G.*
Science Fiction: A Guide for the Perplexed — *Vint, Sherryl*
Science Fiction, Alien Encounters, and the Ethics of Posthumanism: Beyond the Golden Rule — *Gomel, Elana*
Science Fiction and Digital Technologies in Argentine and Brazilian Culture — *King, Edward*

The Science Fiction of Phyllis Gotlieb — Grace, Dominick
Science Fiction TV — Telotte, J.P.
Science Formative Assessment, vol. 2 — Keeley, Page
Science from Sight to Insight: How Scientists Illustrate Meaning — Gross, Alan G.
c Science Gets It Wrong Series — Zuchora-Walske, Christine
Science in the Nation-State: Historic and Current Configurations in Global Perspective, 1800-2010
Science in Wonderland: The Scientific Fairy Tales of Victorian Britain — Keene, Melanie
Science Myths We Tell Ourselves — Barbat, William N.
c The Science of a Flood — Marquardt, Meg
c The Science of a Nuclear Plant Explosion — Marquardt, Meg
c The Science of a Sinkhole — Koontz, Robin
c The Science of a Triple Axel — Labrecque, Ellen
c The Science of a Tsunami — Koontz, Robin
c The Science of Computers — Gifford, Clive
The Science of Deception: Psychology and Commerce in America — Pettit, Michael
The Science of Interstellar — Thorne, Kip
The Science of Language: Interviews with James McGilvray — Chomsky, Noam
The Science of Open Spaces: Theory and Practice for Conserving Large Complex Systems — Curtin, Charles G.
y The Science of Soccer: A Bouncing Ball and a Banana Kick — Taylor, John
Science of the Magical: From the Holy Grail to Love Potions to Superpowers — Kaplan, Matt
The Science of the Perfect Swing — Dewhurst, Peter
The Science of the Rishis: The Spiritual and Material Discoveries of the Ancient Sages of India — Vanamali
The Science of the Soul in Colonial New England — Rivett, Sarah
Science Policy Up Close — Marburger, John H., III
c Science Sleuths Series, 4 vols. — Sharkaway, Azza
c Science Stunts: Fun Feats of Physics (Illus. by Owsley, Anthony) — Brown, Jordan D.
y Science Surprises: Exploring the Nature of Science — Flammer, Lawrence
Science Unshackled: How Obscure, Abstract, Seemingly Useless Scientific Research Turned Out to Be the Basis for Modern Life — Jones, C. Renee
Sciences of Modernism: Ethnography, Sexology, and Psychology — Peppis, Paul
Sciences of the Ancient Hindus: Unlocking Nature in the Pursuit of Salvation — Kumar, Alok
Scientific Babel: The Language of Science from the Fall of Latin to the Rise of English — Gordin, Michael
Scientific Babel: The Language of Science from the Fall of Latin to the Rise of English — Gordin, Michael D.
The Scientific Buddha: His Short and Happy Life — Lopez, Donald S., Jr.
The Scientist and the Forger: Insights into the Scientific Detection of Forgery in Paintings — Ragai, Jehane
A Scientist in Wonderland: A Memoir of Searching for Truth and Finding Trouble — Ernst, Edzard
Scientists at War: The Ethics of Cold War Weapons Research — Bridger, Sarah
Scienza, patria, religione: Antonio Stoppani e la cultura italiana dell'Ottocento — Zanoni, Elena
c Sciku: The Wonder of Science - In Haiku! — Flynn, Simon
c Scooby-Doo! and the Truth Behind Ghosts — Cornia, Christian
c Scooby-Doo Team-Up (Illus. by Brizuela, Dario) — Fisch, Sholly
c Scooby-Doo! Unmasking Monsters Series (Illus. by Neely, Scott) — Collins, Terry
c The Scoop on Ice Cream! (Illus. by Burroughs, Scott) — Williams, Bonnie
y The Scorch of a Skilten — Zaman, Nashat
c Scorched — Mancusi, Mari
The Score — Swinson, Kiki
c Score One for the Sloths (Illus. by Munsinger, Lynn) — Lester, Helen
y Scorpion Mountain — Flanagan, John
y The Scorpion Rules — Bow, Erin
The Scorpion's Sting: Antislavery and the Coming of the Civil War — Oakes, James
Scotland and the British Army, 1700-1750: Defending the Union — Henshaw, Victoria
Scotland's Pariah: The Life and Work of John Pinkerton, 1759-1826 — O'Flaherty, Patrick

The Scots in Victorian and Edwardian Belfast: A Study in Elite Migration — Hughes, Kyle
Scott on Waterloo — Scott, Walter
The Scottie Barked at Midnight — Dunnett, Kaitlyn
Scottish Baking — Lawrence, Sue
The Scottish Enlightenment: Race, Gender, and the Limits of Progress — Sebastiani, Silvia
Scottish Independence and the Idea of Britain: From the Picts to Alexander III — Broun, Dauvit
Scottish Mandarin: The Life and Times of Sir Reginald Johnston — Airlie, Shiona
Scottish Theology — MacLeod, John
Scottish Witches and Witch-Hunters — Goodare, Julian
The Scoundrel and the Debutante — London, Julia
A Scoundrel by Moonlight — Campbell, Anna
A Scourge of Vipers — DeSilva, Bruce
Scouting for the Reaper — Appel, Jacob M.
c Scowl (Illus. by Watson, Richard) — Smallman, Steve
The Scramble for Citizens: Dual Nationality and State Competition for Immigrants — Cook-Martin, David
Scrambling for Africa: AIDS, Expertise, and the Rise of American Global Health Science — Crane, Joanna Tayloe
c Scrap City — Thornton, D.S.
A Scrap of Paper: Breaking and Making International Law during the Great War — Hull, Isabel V.
c Scrapes with Snakes! True Stories of Adventures with Animals — Barr, Brady
Scrapper — Bell, Matt
c Scratch — Benson, Pete
Scream: Chilling Advebture in the Science of Fear — Kerr, Margee
Scream: Chilling Adventures in the Science of Fear — Kerr, Margee
Scream from the Shadows: The Women's Liberation Movement in Japan — Shigematsu, Setsu
y Screaming Divas — Kamata, Suzanne
Screen Nazis: Cinema, History, and Democracy — Hake, Sabine
Screening Early Modern Drama: Beyond Shakespeare — Aebischer, Pascale
Screening Neoliberalism: Transforming Mexican Cinema 1988-2012 — Prado, Ignacio M. Sanchez
Screening Room: Family Pictures — Lightman, Alan
c Screening Silk — Luidens, Lyz
Scribal Correction and Literary Craft: English Manuscripts 1375-1510 — Wakelin, Daniel
c Scribblenauts Unmasked: A DC Comics Adventure (Illus. by Archer, Adam) — Elder, Josh
The Scribe — Guinn, Matthew
Scribes and Scholars: a Guide to the Transmission of Greek and Latin Literature — Reynolds, L.D.
Scribes and the City: London Guildhall Clerks and the Dissemination of Middle English Literature 1375-1425 — Mooney, Linne R.
Scribit Mater: Mary and the Language Arts in the Literature of Medieval England — Donavin, Georgiana
y Scripted (Read by Almasy, Jessica). Audiobook Review — Rock, Maya
y Scripted — Rock, Maya
The Scripting of the Germanic Languages: A Comparative Study of "Spelling Difficulties" in Old English, Old High German and Old Saxon — Seiler, Annina
Scripture: A Guide for the Perplexed — Lamb, William
c Scritch Scratch Scraww Plop (Illus. by Crowther, Kitty) — Crowther, Kitty
c Scritch Scratch Scraww Plop (Illus. by Crowther, Kitty)
Scrivere la storia a Napoli tra Medioevo e prima et a moderna — Caprio, Chiara De
Scugnizzi — Lloyd, Brett
The Sculptor (Illus. by McCloud, Scott) — McCloud, Scott
Sculpture Collections in Early Modern Spain — Helmstutler Di Dio, Kelley
The Sculpture of Tullio Lombardo — Schulz, Anne Markham
Scupture: The James A. de Rothschild Collection at Waddesdon Manor — Hodgkinson, Terrence
The Sea — Tennent, Martha
The Sea Beach Line — Nadler, Ben
c Sea Bones (Illus. by Barner, Bob) — Barner, Bob
c Sea Dragons — Meister, Cari
Sea Fever: The True Adventures That Inspired Our Greatest Maritime Authors, from Conrad to Masefield, Melville and Hemingway — Jefferson, Sam
The Sea House — Gifford, Elisabeth

The SEA Is Ours: Tales from Steampunk Southeast Asia — Goh, Jaymee
The Sea Keeper's Daughters — Wingate, Lisa
Sea-Level Science: Understanding Tides, Surges, Tsunamis and Mean Sea-Level Changes — Pugh, David
c Sea Lions — Riggs, Kate
Sea Lovers: Selected Stories — Martin, Valerie
c Sea Monster! (Illus. by McPhillips, Robert) — Quinn, Jordan
Sea Monsters: A Voyage around the World's Most Beguiling Map — Nigg, Joseph
Sea Monsters on Medieval and Renaissance Maps — Van Duzer, Chet
A Sea of Languages: Rethinking the Arabic Role in Medieval Literary History — Akbari, Suzanne Conklin
A Sea of Misadventures: Shipwreck and Survival in Early America — Mitchell-Cook, Amy
Sea of Storms: A History of Hurricanes in the Greater Caribbean from Columbus to Katrina — Schwartz, Stuart B.
c Sea Otters — Marsh, Laura
c Sea Rex (Illus. by Idle, Molly) — Idle, Molly
Sea Salt Sweet: The Art of Using Salts for the Ultimate Dessert Experience — Baird, Heather
c Sea Slime: It's Eeuwy, Gooey, and Under the Sea (Illus. by Bersani, Shennen) — Prager, Ellen
The Sea: Thalassography and Historiography — Miller, Peter N.
c The Sea Tiger (Illus. by Turnbull, Victoria) — Turnbull, Victoria
c Sea Turtles — Riggs, Kate
The Sea Wolves: A History of the Vikings (Read by Barrett, Joe). Audiobook Review — Brownworth, Lars
c SeaBEAN: The SeaBEAN Trilogy, vol. 1 — Holding, Sarah
c Seacrow Island — Ramsden, Evelyn
The Seafront Tearoom — Greene, Vanessa
c Seagull — Snell, Danny
Seahorse — Pariat, Janice
c Seahorses — Hansen, Grace
A SEAL Forever — Elizabeth, Anne
The Seal — Koulias, Adriana
SEAL Survival Guide: A Navy SEAL'S Secrets to Surviving Any Disaster (Read by Bray, R.C.). Audiobook Review — Courtley, Cade
Seal Team Six: Hunt the Fox — Mann, Don
c Sealed with a Lie — Carlton, Kat
y Sean Combs — Saddleback Educational Publishing
Sean Keating: Art, Politics and Building the Irish Nation — O'Connor, Eimear
Sean O'Faolain: Literature, Inheritance and the 1930s — Delaney, Paul
Search and Recovery — Rusch, Kristine Kathryn
c Search and Spot: Animals! (Illus. by Ljungkvist, Laura) — Ljungkvist, Laura
The Search for a Socialist El Dorado: Finnish Immigration to Soviet Karelia from the United States and Canada in the 1930s — Golubev, Alexey
The Search for Authority in Reformation Europe — Parish, Helen
c The Search for Baby Ruby — Shreve, Susan
The Search For Hidden Sacred Knowledge — Cannon, Dolores
The Search for the Man in the Iron Mask: A Historical Detective Story — Sonnino, Paul
c The Search for Treasure: The Sixth Adventure in the Kingdom of Fantasy — Stilton, Geronimo
The Searcher — Toyne, Simon
Searching for Golden Empires: Epic Cultural Collisions in Sixteenth-Century America — Hartmann, William K.
Searching for Marquette: A Pilgrimage in Art — Nelson, Ruth D.
Searching for Sappho: The Lost Songs and World of the First Woman Poet — Freeman, Philip
y Searching for Sarah Rector: The Richest Black Girl in America — Bolden, Tonya
Searching for Sasquatch: Crackpots, Eggheads, and Cryptozoology — Regal, Bryan
Searching for Scientific Womanpower: Technocratic Feminism and the Politics of National Security, 1940-1980 — Puaca, Laura Micheletti
c Searching for Silverheels — Mobley, Jeannie
Searching for Sitala Mata — Davis, Cornelia E.
Searching for Sunday: Loving, Leaving and Finding the Church — Evans, Rachel Held
y Searching for Super — Jensen, Marion
Searching for the Oldest Stars: Ancient Relics from the Early Universe — Frebel, Anna

Searching for Wallenberg — *Lelchuk, Alan*
c Searchlight Books: What Are Energy Sources? Series — *Doeden, Matt*
c SeaRISE: The SeaBEAN Trilogy, vol. 3 — *Holding, Sarah*
c Seas and Oceans (Illus. by Scrace, Carolyn) — *Channing, Margot*
The Season of Delicate Hunger — *Stoykova-Klemer, Katerina*
Season of Fear — *Freeman, Brian*
Season of Fire — *Bergren, Lisa T.*
The Season of Migration — *Hermann, Nellie*
Season of Salt and Honey — *Tunnicliffe, Hannah*
Season of the Crow — *Yelton, Barry D.*
Season of the Witch: How the Occult Saved Rock and Roll — *Bebergal, Peter*
The Seasonal Jewish Kitchen: A Fresh Take on Tradition — *Saltsman, Amelia*
Seasonal Tales: Memoir — *Shea, Erin*
Seasonal Works with Letters on Fire — *Hillman, Brenda*
Seasoned with Grace — *Lockley, Nigeria*
Seasons of Change: Labor, Treaty Rights, and Ojibwe Nationhood — *Norrgard, Chantal*
Seasons of Change: Labour, Treaty Rights, and Ojibwe Nationhood — *Lakomaki, Sami*
Seasons of Misery: Catastrophe and Colonial Settlement in Early America — *Donegan, Kathleen*
Seasons of the Maple on First Day Covers — *Dickinson, Gary*
Seasons of the Tallgrass Prairie: A Nebraska Year — *Johnsgard, Paul A.*
The Seasons of Trouble: Life amid the Ruins of Sri Lanka's Civil War — *Mohan, Rohini*
c Seattle Seahawks — *Zappa, Marcia*
c Seaver the Weaver (Illus. by The Brothers Hilts) — *Czajak, Paul*
c SeaWAR: The SeaBEAN Trilogy, vol. 2 — *Holding, Sarah*
Seaweed in the Kitchen — *Bird, Fiona*
y Seb Cage Begins His Adventures — *Tumbler, Terry*
Sebald's Vision — *Jacobs, Carol*
c Sebastian and the Balloon (Illus. by Stead, Philip C.) — *Stead, Philip C.*
Secessia — *Wascom, Kent*
Secession Winter: When the Union Fell Apart — *Cook, Robert J.*
c Second Banana — *Graves, Keith*
The Second British Empire: In the Crucible of the Twentieth Century — *Parsons, Timothy H.*
Second Chance — *Miesnik, Liz*
c Second-Chance Soccer — *Maddox, Jake*
Second Chance Summer — *Shalvis, Jill*
The Second Chances of Priam Wood — *Rigby, Alexander*
Second Chances: Surviving Aids in Uganda — *Whyte, Susan Reynolds*
Second Childhood — *Howe, Fanny*
Second Chronicles of Illumination — *Pack, C.A.*
Second-Class Sailors — *Garland, Lance*
The Second Coming of Jesus Christ — *Toney, David L.*
The Second Creek War: Interethnic Conflict and Collusion on a Collapsing Frontier — *Ellisor, John T.*
The Second Deadly Sin — *Thompson, Laurie*
The Second Decison — *Nelson, Randy H.*
Second Empire — *Hofmann, Richie*
Second-Generation Transnationalism and Roots Migration: Cross-Border Lives — *Wessendorf, Susanne*
y The Second Guard — *Vaughn, J.D.*
Second-Hand Time — *Alexievich, Svetlana*
Second Helpings at the Serve You Right Cafe — *Jacobs, Tilia*
c Second Kiss — *Priest, Robert*
Second Life — *Watson, S.J.*
The Second Machine Age — *Brynjolfsson, Erik*
The Second Machine Age: Work, Progress, and Prosperity in a Time of Brilliant Technologies — *McAfee, Andrew*
Second Nature: An Environmental History of New England — *Judd, Richard W.*
Second Person Singular: Late Victorian Poets and the Bonds of Verse — *Harrington, Emily*
The Second Red Scare and the Unmaking of the New Deal Left — *Storrs, Landon R.Y.*
A Second Shot of Coffee with Jesus (Illus. by Wilkie, David J.) — *Wilkie, David J.*
The Second Sister — *Bostwick, Marie*
Second Skin — *Wiley, Michael*
Second Street Station — *Levy, Lawrence H.*

Second Suburb: Levittown, Pennsylvania — *Harris, Dianne*
Second to Nun — *Loweecey, Alice*
The Second Vatican Council: Message and Meaning — *O'Collins, Gerald*
The Second Vatican Council on Other Religions — *O'Collins, Gerald*
The Second World War and the Baltic States — *Corum, James S.*
Secondhand Souls (Read by Stevens, Fisher). Audiobook Review — *Moore, Christopher*
Secrecy in the Sunshine Era: The Promise and Failures of U.S. Open Government Laws — *Arnold, Jason Ross*
The Secret Adversary (Read by Larkin, Alison). Audiobook Review — *Christie, Agatha*
c Secret Agent Derek 'Danger' Dale: The Case of the Really, Really Scary Things (Illus. by Bauer, Joe) — *Bauer, Michael Gerard*
c Secret at Mystic Lake — *Keene, Carolyn*
c The Secret Bay (Illus. by Raye, Rebekah) — *Ridley, Kimberly*
Secret Cables of the Comintern, 1933-1943 — *Firsov, Fridrikh I.*
The Secret Chamber of Osiris: Lost Knowledge of the Sixteen Pyramids — *Creighton, Scott*
The Secret Chord — *Brooks, Geraldine*
c The Secret Cipher — *Ringwald, Whitaker*
c Secret Coders (Illus. by Holmes, Mike) — *Yang, Gene Luen*
c The Secret Cookie Club — *Freeman, Martha*
y The Secret Diary of Lizzie Bennet — *Rorick, Kate*
c The Secret Files of Fairday Morrow (Illus. by Muradov, Roman) — *Haight, Jessica*
y The Secret Fire — *Daugherty, C.J.*
c The Secret Galaxy (Illus. by Taylor, Mike) — *Hodgkins, Fran*
y The Secret Game: A Basketball Story in Black and White — *Ellsworth, Scott*
The Secret Game — *Ellsworth, Scott*
The Secret Gift — *Somers, Ian*
Secret Harbor — *Sullivan, Anna*
Secret History: Conspiracies from Ancient Aliens to the New World Order — *Redfern, Nick*
The Secret History of Kindness: Learning from How Dogs Learn. — *Pierson, Melissa Holbrook*
The Secret History of Wonder Woman (Read by Lepore, Jill). Audiobook Review — *Lepore, Jill*
The Secret History of Wonder Woman — *Lepore, Jill*
The Secret Knowledge — *Cruney, Andrew*
The Secret Language of Doctors: Cracking the Code — *Goldman, Brian*
y The Secret Language of Sisters — *Rice, Luanne*
The Secret Life of Anna Blanc — *Kincheloe, Jennifer*
The Secret Life of Puppets — *Nelson, Victoria*
c The Secret Life of Squirrels (Illus. by Rose, Nancy) — *Rose, Nancy*
The Secret Life of Stories: From Don Quixote to Harry Potter, How Understanding Intellectual Disability Transforms the Way We Read — *Berube, Michael*
The Secret Life of the American Musical: How Broadway Shows Are Built — *Viertel, Jack*
c The Secret Life of the Woolly Bear Caterpillar (Illus. by Paley, Joan) — *Pringle, Laurence*
The Secret Life of Violet Grant (Read by McInerney, Kathleen). Audiobook Review — *Williams, Beatriz*
The Secret Lives of Bats: My Adventures with the World's Most Misunderstood Mammals — *Tuttle, Merlin*
Secret Lives of the Underground Railroad in New York City: Sydney Howard Gay, Louis Napoleon and the Record of Fugitives — *Papson, Don*
c The Secret Mission of William Tuck — *Pierpoint, Eric*
The Secret Of Chabad — *Eliezrie, David*
The Secret of Evil — *Bolano, Roberto*
The Secret of Golf: The Story of Tom Watson and Jack Nicklaus — *Posnanski, Joe*
The Secret of Our Success: How Culture Is Driving Human Evolution, Domesticating Our Species, and Making Us Smarter — *Henrich, Joseph*
y The Secret of the Golden Flower — *Stellings, Caroline*
c The Secret of the Key (Read by Campbell, Cassandra). Audiobook Review — *Malone, Marianne*
c The Secret of the Key (Illus. by Call, Greg) — *Malone, Marianne*
y Secret of the Mountain Dog — *Kimmel, Elizabeth Cody*
y Secret of the Seeds — *Muus, Kate*
y Secret of the Sevens — *Lindquist, Lynn*
c The Secret of the Snow — *Stilton, Thea*

Secret of the Thorns — *Haase, Tom*
Secret of the Warlock's Crypt — *Hayes, Tom*
c Secret of the Water Dragon (Illus. by Howells, Graham) — *West, Tracey*
The Secret of Your Immortal Self: Key Lessons for Realizing the Divinity Within — *Finley, Guy*
Secret Paris: Colour Your Way to Calm — *de las Cases, Zoe*
c The Secret Path — *Pike, Christopher*
The Secret Place — *French, Tana*
The Secret Rebellion — *Baggen, Martin*
Secret Science: A Century of Poison Warfare and Human Experiments — *Schmidt, Ulf*
The Secret Shelter — *Gittins, Rob*
y Secret Side of Empty — *Andreu, Maria E.*
The Secret Sister — *Novak, Brenda*
The Secret Sister — *Tsalikoglou, Fotini*
Secret Sisters — *Krentz, Jayne Ann*
y The Secret Sky: A Novel of Forbidden Love in Afghanistan (Read by Delwari, Ariana). Audiobook Review — *Abawi, Atia*
The Secret Sky: A Novel of Forbidden Love in Afghanistan — *Abawi, Atia*
c The Secret Sock Club (Illus. by Conway, Michael P.) — *Werchinski-Yates, Janine*
c The Secret Subway — *Corey, Shana*
The Secret Teachers of the Western World — *Lachman, Gary*
c The Secret Throne — *Hamilton, Peter F.*
The Secret War for the Middle East: The Influence of Axis and Allied Intelligence Operations during World War II — *Aboul-Enein, Youssef*
The Secret War: Spies, Codes and Guerillas, 1939-1945 — *Hastings, Max*
Secret Warriors: Key Scientists, Code Breakers and Propagandists of the Great War — *Downing, Taylor*
Secret Warriors: The Spies, Scientists and Code Breakers of World War I — *Downing, Taylor*
Secret Wars — *Shooter, Jim*
The Secret Wisdom of the Earth — *Scotton, Christopher*
The Secret Within: Hermits, Recluses, and Spiritual Outsiders in Medieval England — *Riehle, Wolfgang*
Secret World — *Trow, M.J.*
c The Secret World of Walter Anderson (Illus. by Lewis, E.B.) — *Bass, Hester*
Secrets and Leaks: The Dilemma of State Secrecy — *Sagar, Rahul*
Secrets and Truths: Ethnography in the Archive of Romania's Secret Police — *Verdery, Katherine*
c Secrets Beneath the Sea (Illus. by Wood, Katie) — *Gurtler, Janet*
Secrets from Sesame Street's Pioneers: How They Produced a Successful Television Series — *Burbank, Lucille*
Secrets from the Eating Lab: The Science of Weight Loss, the Myth of Willpower, and Why You Should Never Diet Again — *Mann, Traci*
Secrets in a Dead Fish: The Spying Game in the First World War — *King, Melanie*
The Secrets Men Keep — *Sampson, Mark*
Secrets of a Charmed Life — *Meissner, Susan*
Secrets of a Dog Trainer — *Schade, Victoria*
The Secrets of Alchemy — *Principe, Lawrence*
y The Secrets of Attraction — *Constantine, Robin*
c Secrets of Bearhaven (Illus. by Dearsley, Ross) — *Rocha, K.E.*
The Secrets of Blood and Bone — *Alexander, Rebecca*
y The Secrets of Blueberries, Brothers, Moose & Me — *Nickerson, Sara*
c The Secrets of Eastcliff-by-the-Sea — *Beha, Eileen*
c The Secrets of Flamant Castle: The Complete Adventures of Sword Girl and Friends — *Watts, Frances*
The Secrets of Lake Road — *Katchur, Karen*
y The Secrets of Love and Death — *Van Lowe, E.*
y Secrets of Neverak — *Gowans, Jacob*
The Secrets of Sand: A Journey into the Amazing Microscopic World of Sand — *Greenberg, Gary*
y Secrets of Selkie Bay — *Thomas, Shelley Moore*
The Secrets of Sir Richard Kenworthy — *Quinn, Julia*
y The Secrets of Solace — *Johnson, Jaleigh*
Secrets of State — *Palmer, Matthew*
c Secrets of the Dragon Tomb (Illus. by Holmes, Jeremy) — *Samphire, Patrick*
c The Secrets of the Greaser Hotel — *Fuqua, J. Scott*
Secrets of the Greatest Snow on Earth: Weather, Climate Change, and Finding Deep Powder in Utah's Wasatch Mountains and around the World — *Steenburgh, Jim*

Secrets of the Nanny Whisperer: A Practical Guide for Finding and Achieving the Gold Standard of Care for Your Child — *Gold, Tammy*
c Secrets of the Rain Forest (Illus. by Nassner, Alyssa) — *Brown, Carron*
c Secrets of the Rainforest: A Shine-a-Light Book (Illus. by Nassner, Alyssa) — *Brown, Carron*
c Secrets of the Rainforest (Illus. by Nassner, Alyssa) — *Brown, Carron*
c Secrets of the Seashore (Illus. by Nassner, Alyssa) — *Brown, Carron*
c The Secrets of the Storm Vortex (Illus. by Jamieson, Victoria) — *Cameron, Anne*
y The Secrets of the Storm Vortex: The Lightning Catcher, Book 3 (Illus. by Jamieson, Victoria) — *Cameron, Anne*
The Secrets of the Universe in 100 Symbols — *Bartlett, Sarah*
The Secrets of the Wild Wood — *Dragt, Tonke*
c Secrets of Valhalla — *Richards, Jasmine*
c Secrets of Winter (Illus. by Johnson, Bee) — *Brown, Carron*
c Secrets of Winter (Illus. by Tee, Georgina) — *Brown, Carron*
c Secrets Out! (Illus. by Wright, Johanna) — *Sternberg, Julie*
y Secrets, Schemes and Sewing Machines — *Cannon, Katy*
The Secrets She Keeps — *Caletti, Deb*
c The Secrets to Ruling School (without Even Trying). — *Swaab, Neil*
c The Secrets to Ruling School (without Even Trying). (Illus. by Swaab, Neil) — *Swaab, Neil*
y The Secrets We Keep (Read by Rudd, Kate). Audiobook Review — *Leaver, Trisha*
The Secrets We Keep — *Butland, Stephanie*
y The Secrets We Keep — *Leaver, Trisha*
The Secrets We Left Behind — *Wright, Susan Elliot*
Sectarian Politics in the Gulf: From the Iraq War to the Arab Upsprings — *Wehrey, Frederic M.*
The Secular Clergy in England, 1066-1216 — *Thomas, Hugh M.*
Secular Faith: Why Culture Trumps Religion in American Politics — *Smith, Mark A.*
The Secular Spectacle: Performing Religion in a Southern Town — *Seales, Chad E.*
Secularism and Religion in Nineteenth-Century Germany: The Rise of the Fourth Confession — *Weir, Todd H.*
Secularism, Assimilation, and the Crisis of Multiculturalism — *Jansen, Yolande*
Secularism, Catholicism, and the Future of Public Life — *Kmiec, Douglas*
Secularism in Question: Jews and Judaism in Modern Times — *Joskowicz, Ari*
Secure Development for Mobile Apps: How to Design and Code Secure Mobile Applications with PHP and JavaScript — *Glaser, J.D.*
Secure the Soul: Christian Piety and Gang Prevention in Guatemala — *O'Neill, Kevin Lewis*
Securing Paradise: Tourism and Militarism in Hawai'i and the Philippines — *Gonzalez, Vernadette Vicuna*
Securing the West: Politics, Public Lands, and the Fate of the Old Republic, 1785-1850 — *Van Atta, John R.*
Securing the World Economy: The Reinvention of the League of Nations, 1920-1946 — *Clavin, Patricia*
Securitizing Islam: Identity and the Search for Security — *Croft, Stuart*
Security and Profit in China's Energy Policy: Hedging Against Risk — *Tunsjo, Oystein*
The Security Archipelago: Human-Security States, Sexuality Politics and the End of Neoliberalism — *Amar, Paul*
Security, Democracy and War Crimes: Security Sector Transformation in Serbia — *Gow, James*
Sedition — *Grant, Katherine*
Seduced by Sunday — *Bybee, Catherine*
Seduction Game — *Clare, Pamela*
c Seduction — *Cochran, Molly*
See Also Murder — *Sweazy, Larry D.*
See for Yourself: A Visual Guide to Beauty — *Forbes, Rob*
See How Small — *Blackwood, Scott*
c See How They Work and Look inside Big Rigs (Illus. by Tegg, Simon) — *Paiva, Johannah Gilman*
c See How They Work and Look inside Diggers (Illus. by Tegg, Simon) — *Paiva, Johannah Gilman*
c See How They Work and Look inside Farm Equipment (Illus. by Tegg, Simon) — *Paiva, Johannah Gilman*

c See How They Work and Look inside Fire Trucks — *Paiva, Johannah Gilman*
c See It Grow Series — *Lee, Jackie*
y See No Color — *Gibney, Shannon*
See You in Paradise: Stories — *Lennon, J. Robert*
c See You Next Year (Illus. by Stewart, Todd) — *Larsen, Andrew*
c See You Next Year (Illus. by Stewart, Todd) — *Stewart, Todd*
See You Tomorrow — *Renberg, Tore*
y Seed — *Heathfield, Lisa*
Seed Bead Chic: 25 Elegant Projects Inspired by Fine Jewelry — *Katz, Amy*
The Seed Collectors — *Thomas, Scarlett*
y Seed — *Heathfield, Lisa*
Seed Libraries and Other Means of Keeping Seeds in the Hands of the People — *Conner, Cindy*
Seed — *Crawford, Stanley*
y The Seedless Trees (Illus. by Nikolouzos, John) — *Waymreen, Christina*
c Seedlings — *Riggs, Kate*
Seeds of Freedom: Liberating Education in Guatemala — *Taylor, Clark*
c Seeds of Freedom (Illus. by Lewis, E.B.) — *Bass, Henry*
c The Seeds of Friendship (Illus. by Foreman, Michael) — *Foreman, Michael*
Seeing Beauty, Sensing Race in Transnational Indonesia — *Saraswati, L. Ayu*
Seeing Evil — *Parent, Jason*
Seeing Green: The Use and Abuse of American Environmental Images — *Dunaway, Finis*
Seeing Home: The Ed Lucas Story: A Blind Broadcaster's Story of Overcoming Life's Greatest Obstacles — *Lucas, Ed*
c Seeing Is Believing (Illus. by Moore, Gareth) — *Moore, Gareth*
Seeing Israeli and Jewish Dance — *Ingber, Judith Brin*
Seeing Like a Rover: How Robots, Teams, and Images Craft Knowledge of Mars — *Vertesi, Janet*
y Seeing off the Johns — *Perez, Rene S., II*
Seeing Race in Modern America — *Guterl, Matthew Pratt*
Seeing Red — *Meruane, Lina*
Seeing Seeds: A Journey Into the World of Seedheads, Pods, and Fruit — *Chace, Teri Dunn*
Seeing Sodomy in the Middle Ages — *Mills, Robert*
Seeing the World and Knowing God: Hebrew Wisdom and Christian Doctrine in a Late-Modern Context — *Fiddes, Paul S.*
Seeing Things as They Are: A Theory of Perception — *Searle, John R.*
Seeing Things as They Are: Selected Journalism and Other Writings — *Orwell, George*
Seeing Things Politically — *Manent, Pierre*
Seeing through the Eyes of the Polish Revolution: Solidarity and the Struggle Against Communism in Poland — *Bloom, Jack*
Seeing Transnationally: How Chinese Migrants Make Their Dreams Come True — *Minghuan, Li*
Seeing Underground: Maps, Models, and Mining Engineering in America — *Nystrom, Eric C.*
Seek Justice That You May Live: Reflections and Resources on the Bible and Social Justice — *Donahue, John R.*
y Seeker (Read by McEwan, Katharine). Audiobook Review — *Dayton, Arwen Elys*
y Seeker — *Dayton, Arwen Elys*
Seeking a New Majority: The Republican Party and American Politics, 1960-1980 — *Mason, Robert*
Seeking Jordan: How I Learned the Truth about Death and the Invisible Universe — *McKay, Matthew*
Seeking Our Eden: The Dreams and Migrations of Sarah Jameson Craig — *Findon, Joanne*
Seeking Serenity: The 10 New Rules for Health and Happiness in the Age of Anxiety — *Enayati, Amanda*
Seeking the Face of Love — *Bradley, Hadrian*
Seeking the Promised Land: Mormons and American Politics — *Campbell, David E.*
Seelsorge, Frommigkeit und Kriegserfahrungen im Ersten Weltkrieg: Feldpost an den Pfarrer zu Brochterbeck — *Chaoui, Maren*
Seems Like Scrappy: The Look You Love with Fat Quarters and Precuts — *Silbaugh, Rebecca*
Seen and Heard in Mexico: Children and Revolutionary Cultural Nationalism — *Albarran, Elena Jackson*
Seen and Heard in Mexico: Children and Revolutionary Cultural Nationalism — *Jackson Albarran, Elena*

c Seen and Not Heard (Illus. by Green, Katie May) — *Green, Katie May*
The Seer — *Lyris, Sonia Orin*
The Seer of Bayside: Veronica Lueken and the Struggle to Define Catholicism — *Laycock, Joseph P.*
Seeraub im Mittelmeerraum: Piraterie, Korsarentum und maritime Gewalt von der Antike bis zur Neuzeit — *Jaspert, Nikolas*
Seiobo There Below — *Mulzet, Ottilie*
c Seismology: Our Violent Earth — *Baxter, Roberta*
Seize the Night: New Tales of Vampiric Terror — *Golden, Christopher*
Seizing Freedom: Slave Emancipation and Liberty for All — *Roediger, David*
Seizing the Means of Reproduction — *Murphy, Michelle*
y Sekret — *Smith, Lindsay*
Selbst-Bildungen: Soziale und kulturelle Praktiken der Subjektivierung — *Alkemeyer, Thomas*
Selbstaufklarung theologischer Ethik: Themen-Thesen-Perspektiven — *Demmer, Klaus*
Selected Essays of Malcolm Bowie — *Finch, Alison*
Selected Later Poems — *Williams, C.K.*
Selected Letters of Langston Hughes — *Fratantoro, Christa*
Selected Letters of Langston Hughes — *Hughes, Langston*
The Selected Letters of Langston Hughes — *Rampersad, Arnold*
The Selected Letters of Lewis Carroll — *Cohen, Morton*
Selected Poems, 1988-2013 — *Heaney, Seamus*
c Selected Poems — *Lux, Thomas*
The Selected Poems of Donald Hall — *Hall, Donald*
Selected Poems — *Bowling, Tim*
Selected Poems — *Updike, John*
c Selected Tales of the Brothers Grimm — *Wortsman, Peter*
Self and Society: Essays on Pali Literature and Social Theory, 1988-2010 — *Collins, Steven*
Self and Soul: A Defense of Ideals — *Edmundson, Mark*
Self-Consciousness and the Critique of the Subject: Hegel, Heidegger, and the Poststructuralists — *Lumsden, Simon*
The Self Esteem Team's Guide to Sex, Drugs and WTFs?!! — *Devon, Natasha*
A Self-Evident Lie: Southern Slavery and the Threat to American Freedom — *Tewell, Jeremy J.*
Self-Knowledge for Humans — *Cassam, Quassim*
Self-Made: How to Become Self-Reliant, Self-Realized, and Rich in Every Way — *Galan, Nely*
Self-Portrait in Green — *NDiaye, Marie*
Self-Portrait with the Happiness — *Tait, David*
Self-Projection: The Director's Image in Art Cinema — *Rugg, Linda Haverty*
The Self-Propelled Island — *Verne, Jules*
Self, World, and Time: Ethics as Theology — *O'Donovan, Oliver*
Selfish — *West, Kim Kardashian*
Selfish — *Kardashian West, Kim*
c The Selfish Giant (Illus. by Zwerger, Lisbeth) — *Wilde, Oscar*
Selfish — *Kardashian West, Kim*
Selfish — *Goldbarth, Albert*
Selfish, Shallow, and Self-Absorbed — *Daum, Meghan*
Selfish, Shallow, and Self-Absorbed: Sixteen Writers on the Decision Not to Have Kids — *Daum, Meghan*
Selfish, Shallow and Self-Absorbed: Sixteen Writers on the Decision Not to Have Kids — *Daum, Meghan*
Selfish, Shallow, and Self-Absorbed: Sixteen Writers on the Decision Not to Have Kids — *Daum, Meghan*
c The Selkie Girl (Illus. by Mhasane, Ruchi) — *Mackay, Janis*
The Selling of the Babe: The Deal That Changed Baseball and Created a Legend — *Stout, Glenn*
c Selling Ourselves: Marketing Body Images — *Palser, Barb*
Selling under the Swastika: Advertising and Commercial Culture in Nazi Germany — *Swett, Pamela E.*
The Sellout — *Beatty, Paul*
Selma — *DuVernay, Ava*
Selma to Saigon: The Civil Rights Movement and the Vietnam War — *Lucks, Daniel S.*
Semiotics of Happiness: Rhetorical Beginnings of a Public Problem — *Frawley, Ashley*

Semitic Languages: Features, Structures, Relations, Processes — Goldenberg, Gideon
c The Senate — Rose, Simon
Senate Intelligence Committee Report on Torture: Committee Study of the Central Intelligence Agency's Detention and Interrogation Program — Feinstein, Dianne
Senator Benton and the People: Master Race Democracy on the Early American Frontiers — Mueller, Ken S.
The Senator Next Door: A Memoir from the Heartland — Klobuchar, Amy
Send More Idiots — Perez-Giese, Tony
Seneca: A Life — Wilson, Emily
Seneca Falls and the Origins of the Women's Rights Movement — McMillen, Sally G.
Senecas Schrift und der Wandel im Romischen Benefizienwesen — Wolkenhauer, Jan
Seneca's Tragedies and the Aesthetics of Pantomime — Zanobi, Alessandra
Senfl-Studien I — Gasch, Stefan
Senior Citizens Behind Bars: Challenges for the Criminal Justice System — Kerbs, John J.
Sennacherib at the Gates of Jerusalem: Story, History and Historiography — Kalimi, Isaac
Sensation Comics Featuring Wonder Woman, vol. 1 — Simone, Gail
Sensation & Perception — Wolfe, Jeremy M.
Sensational Religion: Sensory Cultures in Material Practice — Promey, Sally
c Sensational Senses — Abbott, Simon
Sense of Deception — Laurie, Victoria
The Sense of Sight in Rabbinic Culture: Jewish Ways of Seeing in Late Antiquity — Neis, Rachel
The Sense of Style: The Thinking Person's Guide to Writing in the 21st Century — Pinker, Steven
A Sense of the Enemy: The High-Stakes History of Reading Your Rival's Mind — Shore, Zachary
y A Sense of the Infinite — Smith, Hilary T.
c SENSEational Illusions — DK Publishing
Senses of the Subject — Butler, Judith
Sensing the Scriptures: Aminadab's Chariot and the Predicament of Biblical Interpretation — Froehlich, Karlfried
Sensory Ecology, Behaviour, and Evolution — Stevens, Martin
The Sensual God: How the Senses Make the Almighty Senseless — Kleinberg, Aviad M.
The Sensual Icon: Space, Ritual, and the Senses in Byzantium — Pentcheva, Bissera V.
Sentenced to Life — James, Clive
Sentences and Rain — Equi, Elaine
Sentimental Memorials: Women and the Novel in Literary History — Sodeman, Melissa
Sentimental Readers: The Rise, Fall, and Revival of a Disparaged Rhetoric — Halpern, Faye
The Sentimental Touch: The Language of Feeling in the Age of Managerialism — Ritzenberg, Aaron
Separado — Cox, Paul
c Separate Is Never Equal: Sylvia Mendez and Her Family's Fight for Desegregation (Illus. by Tonatiuh, Duncan) — Tonatiuh, Duncan
Separating Fools from their Money — MacDonald, Scott B.
Sephardi Lives: A Documentary History, 1700-1950 — Cohen, Julia Phillips
c Sequoia (Illus. by Minor, Wendell) — Johnston, Tony
c Sequoyah and His Talking Leaves: A Play about the Cherokee Syllabary (Illus. by Feeney, Siri Weber) — Coleman, Wim
Ser Mujer En La Ciudad Medieval Europea — Telechea, Jesus A. Solorzano
c Serafina and the Black Cloak (Read by Campbell, Cassandra). Audiobook Review — Beatty, Robert
c Serafina and the Black Cloak — Beatty, Robert
y Seraphina — Hartman, Rachel
y Serendipity's Footsteps — Nelson, Suzanne
The Serengeti Rules: The Quest to Discover How Life Works and Why It Matters — Carroll, Sean B.
Sergi Belbel and Catalan Theatre: Text, Performance and Identity — George, David
Serial Fu Manchu: The Chinese Supervillain and the Spread of Yellow Peril Ideology — Mayer, Ruth
Serial/ Portable Classic: The Greek Canon and Its Mutations — Settis, Salvatore
y A Series of Small Maneuvers — Treichel, Eliot
A Serious Call — Coles, Don
y Seriously Wicked — Connolly, Tina
c Seriously, You Have to Eat (Illus. by Brozman, Owen) — Mansbach, Adam

Sermo doctorum: Compilers, Preachers, and Their Audiences in the Early Medieval West — Diesenberger, Maximilian
A Sermon Workbook: Exercises in the Art and Craft of Preaching — Tisdale, Lenora Tubbs
y The Serpent King — Zentner, Jeff
y Serpentine — Pon, Cindy
c The Serpent's Curse (Illus. by Perkins, Bill) — Abott, Tony
Serpents in Paradise — Edwards, Martin
Serpents in the Cold — O'Malley, Thomas
Servant of the Crown — McShane, Melissa
Servants: A Downstairs History of Britain from the Nineteenth Century to Modern Times — Lethbridge, Lucy
y Servants of the Storm — Dawson, Delilah S.
c Serving in the Military Series — Bozzo, Linda
Serving the Reich: The Struggle for the Soul of Physics Under Hitler — Ball, Philip
Set in Stone: The Petralist — Morin, Frank
y Set You Free — Ross, Jeff
Seth: Conversations — Hoffman, Eric
Setting All the Captives Free: Capture, Adjustment, and Recollection in Allegheny Country — Steele, Ian K.
Setting Aside All Authority: Giovanni Battista Riccioli and the Science against Copernicus in the Age of Galileo — Graney, Christopher M.
Settler Common Sense: Queerness and Everyday Colonialism in the American Renaissance — Rifkin, Mark
The Settlers' Empire: Colonialism and State Formation in America's Old Northwest — Saler, Bethel
Settling Saskatchewan — Anderson, Alan B.
c Seuss-isms! — Seuss, Dr.
y Seven Ancient Wonders of the World — McHugh, Arianne
y Seven Black Diamonds — Marr, Melissa
Seven Brief Lessons on Physics — Rovelli, Carlo
Seven Days — Nixon, Sterling
c Seven Dead Pirates — Bailey, Linda
Seven Dirty Words: The Life and Crimes of George Carlin — Sullivan, James
The Seven Good Years: A Memoir (Read by Karpovsky, Alex). Audiobook Review — Keret, Etgar
The Seven Good Years: A Memoir — Keret, Etgar
Seven Last Words: An Invitation to a Deeper Friendship with Jesus — Martin, James (b. 1960-)
Seven Last Words — Minchow-Proffitt, Terry
Seven New Generation African Poets — Dawes, Kwame
Seven Nights to Surrender — Grey, Jeanette
c Seven Orange Pumpkins (Illus. by Savage, Stephen) — Savage, Stephen
Seven Schools of Macroeconomic Thought — Phelps, Edmund S.
y Seven Second Delay — Easton, Tom
The Seven Sisters (Read by Lucienne, Emily). Audiobook Review — Riley, Lucinda
The Seven Sisters — Riley, Lucinda
Seven Spoons: My Favorite Recipes for Any and Every Day — O'Brady, Tara
Seven Steps to Spiritual Intelligence — Hussain, Musharraf
Seven Steps to Train Your Mind — Tulku, Gomo
Seven Tales for the Seven Dark Seas — Morris, Harold C.
y Seven Tears at High Tide — Lee, C.B.
c Seven Viking Days (Illus. by Hocking, Mia) — Cuesta, Lee
c The Seven Voyages of Sinbad the Sailor (Illus. by Rashin) — Said
y Seven Ways We Lie — Redgate, Riley
The Seven Years' War: Global Views — Danley, Mark H.
Seveneves (Read by Kowal, Mary Robinette). Audiobook Review — Stephenson, Neal
Seveneves — Stephenson, Neal
y Seventeen Ultimate Guide to College: Everything You Need to Know to Walk onto Campus and Own It! — Shoket, Ann
Seventh. E-book Review — White, Rachel
y The Seventh Crow — Ramsey, Sherry D.
The Seventh Day — Hua, Yu
The Seventh Day — Yu, Hua
The Seventh Holy Man — Brazzel, William
y The Seventh Kingdom, vol. 10 — Bracken, Beth
c The Seventh Most Important Thing — Pearsall, Shelley
The Seventh Seal — Heiberger, Frank

Severally Seeking Sartre — O'Donohoe, Benedict
Severed: A History of Heads Lost and Heads Found — Larson, Frances
The Severed Head and the Grafted Tongue: Literature, Translation and Violence in Early Modern Ireland — Palmer, Patricia
Severina — Rey Rosa, Rodrigo
Sew Cute and Collectible Sock Monkeys: For Red-Heel Sock Monkey Crafters and Collectors — Lindner, Dee
Sew Organized for the Busy Girl: Tips to Make the Most of Your Time & Space: 23 Quick & Clever Sewing Projects You'll Love — Staples, Heidi
Sew & Play Puzzle Ball Animals: 6 Little Pets with Big Personalities — Glassenberg, Abby
c Sew Zoey Series (Illus. by Zhang, Nancy) — Taylor, Chloe
Sewing for Your Girls: Easy Instructions for Dresses, Smocks and Frocks — Tsukiori, Yoshiko
Sewing Pretty Bags: Boutique Designs to Stitch and Love — Valencia, Debra
c Sewing Stories: Harriet Powers' Journey from Slave to Artist (Illus. by Brantley-Newton, Vanessa) — Herkert, Barbara
c Sewing Stories: Harriet Powers' Journey from Slave to Artist (Illus. by Newton, Vanessa) — Herkert, Barbara
Sex Addiction: A Critical History — Reay, Barry
y Sex: An Uncensored Introduction (Illus. by Capozzola, Michael) — Hasler, Nikol
y Sex: An Uncensored Introduction — Hasler, Nikol
Sex and Film: The Erotic in British, American and World Cinema — Forshaw, Barry
Sex and the Founding Fathers: The American Quest for a Relatable Past — Foster, Thomas A.
Sex and the Office: A History of Gender, Power, and Desire — Berebitsky, Julie
Sex and the Office: Women, Men, and the Sex Partition That's Dividing the Workplace — Elsesser, Kim
Sex and Unisex: Fashion, Feminism, and the Sexual Revolution — Paoletti, Jo B.
Sex as a Political Condition — Flores, Carlos Nicolas
Sex Becomes Her — Cole, Regina
Sex before Sex: Figuring the Act in Early Modern England — Bromley, James M.
Sex by Numbers: What Statistics Can Tell Us about Sexual Behaviour — Spiegelhalter, David
Sex Criminals: Two Worlds, One Cop — Fraction, Matt
Sex Criminals, vol. 2: Two Worlds, One Cop (Illus. by Zdarsky, Chip) — Fraction, Matt
Sex Difference in Christian Theology: Male, Female and Intersex in the Image of God — DeFranza, Megan K.
Sex, Drugs and Rock 'n' Roll: The Science of Hedonism and the Hedonism of Science — Cormier, Zoe
Sex, Freedom, and Power in Imperial Germany, 1880-1914 — Dickinson, Edward Ross
Sex in China — Jeffreys, Elaine
Sex in the Sea: Our Intimate Connection with Sex-Changing Fish, Romantic Lobsters, Kinky Squid, and Other Salty Erotica of the Deep — Hardt, Marah J.
c Sex Is a Funny Word: A Book about Bodies, Feelings, and You (Illus. by Smyth, Fiona) — Silverberg, Cory
Sex Itself: The Search for Male and Female in the Human Genome — Richardson, Sarah S.
Sex, Lies and Pharmaceuticals: How Drug Companies Plan to Profit from Female Sexual Dysfunction — Moynihan, Ray
Sex, Lies and the Ballot Box — Cowley, Philip
The Sex Lives of Siamese Twins — Welsh, Irvine
The Sex Myth: The Gap Between Our Fantasies and Reality — Hills, Rachel
Sex on Earth: A Celebration of Animal Reproduction — Howard, Jules
Sex Outside the Lines: Authentic Sexuality in a Sexually Dysfunctional Culture — Donaghue, Chris
Sex, Politics and Putin: Political Legitimacy in Russia — Sperling, Valerie
Sex Tourism in Bahia: Ambiguous Entanglements — Williams, Erica Lorraine
Sex versus Survival: The Life and Ideas of Sabina Spielrein — Launer, John
Sex, Violence, and Justice: Contraception and the Catholic Church — Kalbian, Aline H.
Sex Work Politics: From Protest to Service Provision — Majic, Samantha

Sex Workers Unite: A History of the Movement from Stonewall to SlutWalk — *Chateauvert, Melinda*
Sexcastle — *Starks, Kyle*
Sexting Panic: Rethinking Criminalization, Privacy, and Consent — *Hasinoff, Amy Adele*
Sexual Assault in Canada: Law, Legal Practice and Women's Activism — *Sheehy, Elizabeth A.*
y Sexual Content in Young Adult Literature: Reading Between the Sheets — *Gillis, Bryan*
Sexual Diversity in Africa: Politics, Theory, and Citizenship — *Nyeck, S.N.*
Sexual Fields: Towards a Sociology of Collective Social Life — *Green, Adam Isaiah*
The Sexual Life of English: Languages of Caste and Desire in Colonial India — *Chandra, Shefali*
c Sexual Orientation and Gender Identity — *Stuckey, Rachel*
Sexual Politics in Modern Iran — *Afary, Janet*
Sexual Politics in the Work of Tennessee Williams: Desire Over Protest — *Hooper, Michael S.D.*
Sexual Selection: Perspectives and Models from the Neotropics — *Macedo, Regina H.*
Sexualities, Textualities, Art and Music in Early Modern Italy: Playing with Boundaries — *Marshall, Melanie L.*
Sexuality in Role-Playing Games — *Brown, Ashley M.L.*
The Sexuality of History: Modernity and the Sapphic, 1565-1830 — *Lanser, Susan S.*
Sexuality Studies — *Srivastava, Sanjay*
Sexy Serenity: A Memoir — *Simon, Miranda K.*
Seymour Hersh, Scoop Artist — *Miraldi, Robert*
The SG Guitar Book: 50 Years of Gibson's Stylish Solid Guitar — *Bacon, Tony*
c Shabbat Shalom, Hey! (Illus. by Koffsky, Ann D.) — *Koffsky, Ann D.*
c Shabbat Shalom, Hey! (Illus. by Koffsky, Ann D) — *Koffsky, Ann D.*
c Shabbat Shalom, Hey! (Illus. by Koffsky, Ann D.) — *Koffsky, Ann D.*
c Shack Island Summer — *Chamberlain, Penny*
y Shackled — *Leveen, Tom*
Shackleton: By Endurance We Conquer — *Smith, Michael (b. 1946-)*
Shade-Grown Slavery: The Lives of Slaves on Coffee Plantations in Cuba — *Van Norman, William C.*
y Shade Me — *Brown, Jennifer*
Shades of Africa — *Loshe, Toko*
Shades of Artemis — *Martin, Jon Edward*
Shades of Blue: Writers on Depression, Suicide, and Feeling Blue — *Ferris, Amy*
y Shades of Darkness — *Kahler, A.R.*
y Shades of Doon — *Corp, Carey*
Shades of Greene: One Generation of an English Family — *Lewis, Jeremy*
Shades: The Gehenna Dilemma — *Dallaire, Eric*
y The Shadow Behind the Stars — *Hahn, Rebecca*
The Shadow Broker — *Conger, Trace*
y The Shadow Cabinet — *Johnson, Maureen*
y The Shadow Cabinet (Read by Barber, Nicola). Audiobook Review — *Johnson, Maureen*
y The Shadow Cabinet — *Johnson, Maureen*
c Shadow Cat — *Cross, Gillian*
c Shadow Catcher: How Edward S. Curtis Documented American Indian Dignity and Beauty — *Burgan, Michael*
c Shadow Chasers — *MacKay, Elly*
y Shadow Creatures — *Lane, Andrew*
y The Shadow Hero — *Yang, Gene Luen*
A Shadow in Summer (Read by Shah, Neil). Audiobook Review — *Abraham, Daniel*
c The Shadow Lantern — *Flavin, Teresa*
The Shadow Man: At the Heart of the Cambridge Spy Circle — *Andrews, Geoff*
y The Shadow Mother (Illus. by Perez, Javier Serrano) — *Virgo, Sean*
Shadow Nations: Tribal Sovereignty and the Limits of Legal Pluralism — *Duthu, N. Bruce*
Shadow of a Doubt — *Snow, Tiffany*
The Shadow of a Year: The 1641 Rebellion in Irish History and Memory — *Gibney, John*
The Shadow of Arms — *Hwang, Sog-Yong*
The Shadow of Colonialism on Europe's Modern Past — *Healy, Roisin*
Shadow of Empire — *Allan, Jay*
y The Shadow of Seth — *Llewellyn, Tom*
The Shadow of the Crescent Moon — *Bhutto, Fatima*
Shadow of the Raven (Read by Vance, Simon). Audiobook Review — *Harris, Tessa*
y Shadow of the War Machine — *Bailey, Kristin*
y Shadow of the Wolf — *Hall, Tim*
Shadow on the Mesa — *Martin, Lee*

Shadow Play: An Eve Duncan Novel — *Johansen, Iris*
y The Shadow Queen — *Redwine, C.J.*
Shadow Ritual — *Giacometti, Eric*
Shadow Ritual — *Ravenne, Jacques*
y Shadow Scale (Read by Williams, Mandy). Audiobook Review — *Hartman, Rachel*
y Shadow Scale — *Hartman, Rachel*
Shadow Trails — *Flowers, Graham J.*
Shadow Wars: Chasing Conflict in an Era of Peace — *Axe, David*
Shadow Work: The Unpaid, Unseen Jobs That Fill Your Day — *Lambert, Craig*
c Shadow Wrack — *Thompson, Kim*
A Shadowed Evil — *Clare, Alys*
Shadowlands — *Prior, Mark E.*
c Shadows at Predator Reef — *Dixon, Franklin W.*
c The Shadows (Read by Peakes, Karen). Audiobook Review — *Chance, Megan*
y The Shadow's Curse — *McCulloch, Amy*
Shadows in the Fire — *Basnight, Gray*
Shadows in the Fog: The True Story of Major Suttill and the Prosper French Resistance Network — *Suttill, Francis J.*
Shadows of Doubt: Language and Truth in Post-Reformation Catholic Culture — *Tutino, Stefania*
Shadows of Ladenbrooke Manor — *Dobson, Melanie*
Shadows of Self — *Sanderson, Brandon*
c Shadows of Sherwood — *Magoon, Kekla*
Shadows of the New Sun — *Mooney, J.E.*
The Shadows of the Past: A Study of Life-World and Identity of Serbian Youth after the Milosevic Regime — *Spasenic, Jelena*
c Shadows of the Silver Screen — *Edge, Christopher*
Shadows of the Slave Past: Memory, Heritage, and Slavery — *Araujo, Ana Lucia*
Shadows of Us — *Stowers, Sylvia C.*
Shadows over Paradise — *Wolff, Isabel*
y Shadowshaper — *Older, Daniel Jose*
Shady Cross — *Hankins, James*
Shaggy Crowns: Ennius' Annales and Virgil's Aeneid — *Goldschmidt, Nora*
Shaker — *Frank, Scott*
Shakespeare and Abraham — *Jackson, Ken*
Shakespeare and Classical Antiquity — *Burrow, Colin*
Shakespeare and Costume — *Lennox, Patricia*
Shakespeare and Ecology — *Martin, Randall*
Shakespeare and I — *McKenzie, William*
Shakespeare and Immigration — *Espinosa, Ruben*
Shakespeare and Impure Aesthetics — *Grady, Hugh*
Shakespeare and the Body Politic — *Dobski, Bernard J.*
Shakespeare and the Countess: The Battle That Gave Birth to the Globe — *Laoutaris, Chris*
Shakespeare and the Culture of Romanticism — *Ortiz, Joseph M.*
Shakespeare and the Eighteenth Century — *Caines, Michael*
Shakespeare and the English-Speaking Cinema — *Jackson, Russell*
Shakespeare and the Remains of Richard III — *Schwyzer, Philip*
Shakespeare and the Versification of English Drama, 1561-1642 — *Tarlinskaja, Marina*
Shakespeare Basics for Grown-Ups: Everything You Need to Know About the Bard — *Foley, Elizabeth*
y The Shakespeare Book: Big Ideas Simply Explained — *Wells, Stanley*
y The Shakespeare Book — *Wells, Stanley*
Shakespeare — *Edmondson, Paul*
The Shakespeare Circle: An Alternative Biography — *Edmondson, Paul*
Shakespeare, Dissent, and the Cold War — *Thomas, Alfred*
Shakespeare in America — *Vaughan, Alden T.*
Shakespeare in Company — *van Es, Bart*
Shakespeare in London — *Crawforth, Hannah*
Shakespeare in the Nineteenth Century — *Marshall, Gail*
Shakespeare No More — *Hays, Tony*
Shakespeare — *Edmondson, Paul*
Shakespeare Performance Studies — *Worthen, William B.*
c Shakespeare Saves the Globe (Illus. by Bernard, Courtney) — *Mullarkey, Lisa*
Shakespeare, Time and the Victorians: A Pictorial Exploration — *Sillars, Stuart*
Shakespearean Sensations: Experiencing Literature in Early Modern England — *Craik, Katharine A.*
Shakespeare's Anti-Politics: Sovereign Power and the Life of the Flesh — *Gil, Daniel Juan*

Shakespeare's Boys: A Cultural History — *Knowles, Katie*
Shakespeare's Curse: The Aporias of Ritual Exclusion in Early Modern Royal Drama — *Quiring, Bjorn*
Shakespeare's Demonology: A Dictionary — *Gibson, Marion*
Shakespeare's Medical Language: A Dictionary — *Iyengar, Sujata*
Shakespeare's Medieval Craft: Remnants of the Mysteries on the London Stage — *Schreyer, Kurt A.*
Shakespeare's Nature: From Cultivation to Culture — *Scott, Charlotte*
Shakespeare's Possible Worlds — *Palfrey, Simon*
Shakespeare's Princes of Wales: English Identity and the Welsh Connection — *Cull, Marisa R.*
Shakespeare's Restless World: A Portrait of an Era in Twenty Objects — *MacGregor, Neil*
Shakespeare's Sense of Character: On the Page and from the Stage — *Shurgot, Michael W.*
Shakespeare's Stage Traffic: Imitation, Borrowing and Competition in Renaissance Theatre — *Clare, Janet*
Shakespeare's Surrogates: Rewriting Renaissance Drama — *Loftis, Sonya Freeman*
Shakespeare's Theatres and the Effects of Performance — *Karim-Cooper, Farah*
Shakin' All Over: Popular Music and Disability — *McKay, George*
Shaky Foundations: The Politics-Patronage-Social Science Nexus in Cold War America — *Solovey, Mark*
Shaky Ground: Context, Connoisseurship and the History of Roman Art — *Marlowe, Elizabeth*
Shaky Ground: The Strange Saga of the U.S. Mortgage Giants — *McLean, Bethany*
y Shallow Graves — *Wallace, Kali*
c Shalom Everybodeee! (Illus. by Fischer, Ellen) — *Balsley, Tilda*
The Shaman's Mate — *McDonald, Donna*
y Shamans, Witch Doctors, Wizards, Sorcerers, and Alchemists — *Kavanaugh, Dorothy*
Shame and the Captives — *Keneally, Thomas*
Shame and Wonder: Essays — *Searcy, David*
Shame: How America's Past Sins Have Polarized Our Country — *Steele, Shelby*
Shame - Shame: Poems — *Becker, Devin*
The Shameful Act: The Armenian Genocide and the Question of Turkish Responsibility — *Ackam, Taner*
A Shameful Murder — *Harrison, Cora*
Shameless — *Johnston, Joan*
Shameless: The Canine and the Feminine in Ancient Greece — *Franco, Cristiana*
c Shang Dynasty China — *Hile, Lori*
Shanghai, 1937: Stalingrad on the Yangtze — *Harmsen, Peter*
Shanghai Gone: Domicile and Defiance in a Chinese Megacity — *Shao, Qin*
Shanghai Homes: Palimpsests of Private Life — *Li, Jie*
Shanghai Redemption — *Qiu, Xiaolong*
Shanghai Redemption — *Xiaolong, Qiu*
Shanghai Sanctuary: Chinese and Japanese Policy toward European Jewish Refugees during World War II — *Gao, Bei*
c Shanghai Sukkah (Illus. by Tsong, Jing) — *Hyde, Heidi Smith*
c Shanghai Sukkah (Illus. by Tsong, Jing Jing) — *Hyde, Heidi Smith*
Shanghai (Urban Public) Space — *Haarmann, Anke*
c Shantideva: How to Wake Up a Hero (Illus. by Norbu, Tenzin) — *Townsend, Dominique*
The Shantyman — *Spilman, Rick*
The Shaolin Cowboy: Shemp Buffet — *Doherty, Peter*
The Shape and Shaping of the Book of Psalms: The Current State of Scholarship — *deClaisse-Walford, Nancy L.*
The Shape of Script: How and Why Writing Systems Change — *Houston, Stephen*
The Shape of the New: Four Big Ideas and How They Made the Modern World — *Montgomery, Scott L.*
The Shape of the New — *Montgomery, Scott L.*
c Shape Shift (Illus. by Hesselberth, Joyce) — *Hesselberth, Joyce*
c Shape-Shifting Animals — *Lunis, Natalie*
c Shapes are Everywhere! — *Ghigna, Charles*
Shapes of Apocalypse: Arts and Philosophy in Slavic Thought — *Oppo, Andrea*
The Shapeshifters — *Spjut, Stefan*
Shaping Europe: France, Germany, and Embedded Bilateralism from the Elysee Treaty to Twenty-First Century Politics — *Krotz, Ulrich*
Shaping Immigration News: A French-American Comparison — *Benson, Rodney*

Shaping Public Theology: Selections from the Writings of Max L. Stackhouse — *Paeth, Scott R.*
Shaping the Motherhood of Indigenous Mexico — *Smith-Oka, Vania*
Shaping US Military Forces for the Asia-Pacific: Lessons from Conflict Management in Past Great Power Eras — *Kraig, Michael R.*
The Shards of Heaven — *Livingston, Michael*
Shards of History — *Roland, Rebecca*
Shards of Hope — *Singh, Nalini*
c Share! (Illus. by Birkett, Georgie) — *Simmons, Anthea*
Sharecropper's Troubadour: John L. Handcox, the Southern Tenant Farmers' Union, and the African American Song Tradition — *Honey, Michael K.*
Shared Agency: A Planned Theory of Acting Together — *Bratman, Michael E.*
Shared Stories, Rival Tellings: Early Encounters of Jews, Christians, and Muslims — *Gregg, Robert C.*
Sharing Cities: A Case for Truly Smart and Sustainable Cities — *Agyeman, Julian*
c Sharing God's Love: The Jesus Creed for Children (Illus. by Hill, Dave) — *McKnight, Scott*
c Sharing the Bread: An Old-Fashioned Thanksgiving Story (Illus. by McElmurry, Jill) — *Miller, Pat Zietlow*
Sharing the Sacra: The Politics and Pragmatics of Inter-Communal Relations Around Holy Places — *Bowman, Glenn*
Sharing the Truth in Love — *Fernando, Ajith*
Shark — *Self, Will*
c Shark Bite! (Illus. by Costamagna, Beatrice) — *Costamagna, Beatrice*
y Shark Bite! — *Costamagna, Beatrice*
y The Shark Curtain — *Scofield, Chris*
c Shark Detective! (Illus. by Olien, Jessica) — *Olien, Jessica*
c Shark Island (Illus. by Marnat, Annette) — *Lewin, Jill*
c Shark School Series (Illus. by Blecha, Aaron) — *Ocean, Davy*
Shark Skin Suite — *Dorsey, Tim*
The Shark Warrior of Alewai: A Phenomenology of Melanesian Identity — *Van Heekeren, Deborah*
c Shark Wars: Creatures of the Deep Go Head to Head — *Woodward, John*
c Shark Wars: Creatures of the Deep Go Head-to-Head — *Woodward, John*
c Sharkie and the Haunted Cat Box — *Bergmann, Daniel*
y Sharkman — *Alten, Steve*
c Sharks and Sea Creatures around the World — *Alderton, David*
c Sharks Have Six Senses (Illus. by Barner, Bob) — *Waters, John F.*
The Shark's Paintbrush: Biomimicry and How Nature is Inspiring Innovation — *Harman, Jay*
c Sharks Series — *Barnes, Nico*
The Sharon Springs Timeline: A Microcosm of American History - with Dates Relating to a Remarkable Village and Neighboring Regions, from the 16th Century to Modern Times — *Waldman, Carl*
Sharon Tate: A Life — *Sanders, Ed*
c Sharp Sisters Series — *Moore, Stephanie*
Sharpie Art Workshop: Techniques and Ideas for Transforming Your World — *Goodman, Timothy*
Shasta and Her Cubs — *Robson, Lane*
y Shattered Blue — *Horowitz, Lauren Bird*
The Shattered Court — *Scott, M.J.*
Shattered Dreams — *Senocak, Bulent*
Shattered Dreams of Revolution: From Liberty to Violence in the Late Ottoman Empire — *Der Matossian, Bedross*
Shattered Dreams of Revolution: From Liberty to Violence in the Late Ottoman Empire — *Matossian, Bedross Der*
Shattered Duty — *Reus, Katie*
Shattered Families, Broken Dreams: Little-Known Episodes from the History of the Persecution of Chinese Revolutionaries in Stalin's Gulag — *Sin-Lin*
y Shattered Glass — *Toten, Teresa*
Shattered Hand: Sarah's Secret War — *Liddle, J.D.*
Shattered Mirror: The Problem of Identity in the Post-Yugoslav Documentary — *Tutka-Gwozdz, Magdalena*
A Shattered Moment — *King, Tiffany*
Shaw and Feminisms: On Stage and Off — *Hadfield, Dorothy A.*
c Shawnee — *Tieck, Sarah*
Shaw's Settings: Gardens and Landscapes — *Stafford, Tony Jason*
She Came from Beyond! — *Darling, Nadine*

y She Is Not Invisible — *Sedgwick, Marcus*
She of the Mountains (Illus. by Biesinger, Raymond) — *Shraya, Vivek*
'She Said She Was in the Family Way': Pregnancy and Infancy in Modern Ireland — *Farrell, Elaine*
y She Takes a Stand: 16 Fearless Activists Who Have Changed the World — *Ross, Michael Elsohn*
She Wears the Pants: Easy Sew-It-Yourself Fashion with an Edgy Urban Style — *Takada, Yuko*
She Weeps Each Time You're Born — *Barry, Quan*
She will Build Him a City — *Jha, Raj Kamal*
c She Yelled, I Screamed ... She Pulled My Hair! — *Leshay, Tracy*
c She Yelled, I Screamed ... She Pulled My Hair! (Illus. by Renald, James) — *Leshay, Tracy*
c Sheamus — *Markegard, Blake*
Shed Decor: How to Decorate and Furnish Your Favorite Garden Room — *Coulthard, Sally*
The Shed that Fed a Million Children: The Extraordinary Story of Mary's Meals — *MacFarlane-Barrow, Magnus*
c Sheep — *Murray, Julie*
c The Sheep Go On Strike (Illus. by Dumont, Jean-Francois) — *Dumont, Jean-Francois*
c The Sheep Go on Strike — *Dumont, Jean-Francois*
c Sheep Go to Sleep (Illus. by Apple, Margot) — *Shaw, Nancy*
c Sheep in the Closet (Illus. by Cerato, Mattia) — *Cerato, Mattia*
c The Sheep in Wolf's Clothing (Illus. by Munsinger, Lynn) — *Lester, Helen*
c SheHeWe (Illus. by Bosch, Meritxell) — *Nordling, Lee*
Sheila — *Caldwell, Shawn*
Sheila Watson: Essays on Her Works — *Pivato, Joseph*
c Shelby the Flying Snail (Illus. by Piu, Amandine) — *Hanna, Virginia*
c Sheldon: The Antioxidant Super Hero of Jaloonsville — *Jones, Melissa*
Shell Shock — *Stahl, Steve*
c Shelter — *Aust, Patricia H.*
Shelter — *Jung, Yun*
Shelterbelts — *Simar, Candace*
Shenandoah, 1864: Sheridan's Valley Campaign — *Lardas, Mark*
c Shenandoah — *Johnson, Nancy*
Shenandoah Valley Apples — *Jost, Scott*
Shepherd's Crook — *Boneham, Sheila Webster*
y The Shepherd's Crown (Read by Briggs, Stephen). Audiobook Review — *Pratchett, Terry*
y The Shepherd's Crown — *Pratchett, Terry*
The Shepherd's Life: A Tale of the Lake District — *Rebanks, James*
The Shepherd's Life: Modern Dispatches from an Ancient Landscape — *Rebanks, James*
Shepherds of the Empire: Germany's Conservative Protestant Leadership, 1888-1919 — *Correll, Mark R.*
Sheppard of the Argonne — *Weatherly, G. William*
Sherds of History: Domestic Life in Colonial Guadeloupe — *Arcangeli, Myriam*
Sherlock Holmes and the Mystery of Einstein's Daughter — *Symonds, Tim*
Sherlock Holmes and the Unholy Trinity — *Gilbert, Paul D.*
y Sherlock Holmes in a Study in Scarlet — *Doyle, Arthur Conan*
Sherlock Holmes: The London Terrors — *Meikle, William*
Sherlock Holmes, the Missing Years: Japan — *Murthy, Vasudev*
Sherlock Holmes, the Missing Years: Timbuktu — *Murthy, Vasudev*
c Sherman and the Sheep Shape Contest (Illus. by Nadeau, Sonia) — *Zaidman, Harriet*
Sherman's Ghosts: Soldiers, Civilians, and the American Way of War — *Carr, Matthew*
She's Not into Poetry: Mini Comics 1991-1996 — *Hart, Tom*
She's Not There — *Fielding, Joy*
Shetani's Sister — *Slim, Iceberg*
The Sheynan Trilogy — *Birtolo, Dylan*
c Shh! Bears Sleeping (Illus. by Johnson, Steve) — *Martin, David (b. 1944-)*
c Shh! We Have a Plan (Illus. by Haughton, Chris) — *Haughton, Chris*
Shhh: It's a Secret BDSM — *Ferrer, Charley*
c Shield of God (Illus. by Delacruz, Nikki) — *Delacruz, Nikki*
The Shift: One Nurse, Twelve Hours, Four Patients' Lives — *Brown, Theresa*

Shifting Gears to Your Life and Work After Retirement — *Duckworth, Carolee*
Shifting Ground: People, Mobility, and Animals in India's Environmental Histories — *Rangarajan, Mahesh*
Shifting Shadows (Read by King, Lorelei). Audiobook Review — *Briggs, Patricia*
Shifting Standards: Experiments in Particle Physics in the Twentieth Century — *Franklin, Allan*
Shifting Stones, Shaping the Past: Sculpture from the Buddhist Stupas of Andhra Pradesh — *Becker, Catherine*
The Shifts and the Shocks: What We've Learned - and Have Still to Learn - from the Financial Crisis — *Wolf, Martin*
Shigeru Mizuki's Hitler — *Mizuki, Shigeru*
The Shiites of Lebanon under Ottoman Rule, 1516-1788 — *Winter, Stefan*
c A Shiloh Christmas — *Naylor, Phyllis Reynolds*
Shiloh: Conquer or Perish — *Smith, Timothy B.*
y Shimmey — *Jones, Kari*
c Shine: A Story About Saying Goodbye (Illus. by Balla, Trace) — *Balla, Trace*
c Shine Izzy Shine — *Daines, Ellie*
c Shingaling (Read by Krahn, Taylor Ann). Audiobook Review — *Palacio, R.J.*
Shingle Street — *Morrison, Blake*
c The Ship Captain's Tale (Illus. by Yesh, Jeff) — *Boeholt, Veronica*
Ship of Death: A Voyage that Changed the Atlantic World — *Smith, Billy G.*
y Ship of Death (Illus. by Evergreen, Nelson) — *Hulme-Cross, Benjamin*
c Ship of Dolls (Read by Reinders, Kate). Audiobook Review — *Parenteau, Shirley*
y Ship of Dolls — *Parenteau, Shirley*
Ships and Silver, Taxes and Tribute: A Fiscal History of Archaic Athens — *van Wees, Hans*
c Shipwreck Island (Read by Heyborne, Kirby). Audiobook Review — *Bodeen, S.A.*
y Shipwreck Island — *Bodeen, S.A.*
The Shipwrecked: Contemporary Stories by Women from Iran — *Nouraie-Simone, Fereshteh*
y Shipwrecked! The True Adventures of a Japanese Boy — *Blumberg, Rhoda*
Shirin Neshat: Facing History — *Chiu, Melissa*
Shirley, I Jest! A Storied Life — *Williams, Cindy*
Shirt in Heaven — *Valentine, Jean*
c Shivers! The Pirate Who's Afraid of Everything (Illus. by Holden, Anthony) — *Bondor-Stone, Annabeth*
c Shivery Shades of Halloween: A Spooky Book of Colors (Illus. by Pickering, Jimmy) — *Siddals, Mary McKenna*
c Shmulik Paints the Town (Illus. by Echeverri, Catalina) — *Rose, Lisa*
Shock by Shock — *Young, Dean*
The Shock of America: Europe and the Challenge of the Century — *Ellwood, David W.*
Shocked: Adventures in Bringing Back the Recently Dead — *Casarett, David*
Shocking Paris: Soutine, Chagall, and the Outsiders of Montparnasse — *Meisler, Stanley*
A Shocking Reunion — *Booth-Lynch, Pat*
Shockwaves of Possibility: Essays on Science Fiction, Globalization, and Utopia — *Wegner, Philip E.*
c Shoe Dog (Illus. by Tillotson, Katherine) — *McDonald, Megan*
The Shoemaker's Daughter — *Block, Helen Martin*
Shogun (Read by Lister, Ralph). Audiobook Review — *Clavell, James*
c Shoo, Fly! You Can't Eat Here! (Illus. by Switzer, Bobbi) — *Hamilton, Liller*
Shoot — *Estleman, Loren D.*
Shoot the Conductor — *Brusilow, Anshel*
y Shoot to Kill — *Cole, Steve*
Shooting Arrows and Slinging Mud: Custer, the Press, and the Little Bighorn — *Mueller, James E.*
c Shooting at the Stars (Illus. by Hendrix, John) — *Hendrix, John*
Shooting for the Stars — *Belsky, R.G.*
c Shooting Stars Soccer Team (Illus. by Lee, Hyeongjin) — *Kim, YeoengAh*
The Shootout Solution — *Underwood, Michael R.*
Shop Girl — *Portas, Mary*
y Shopaholic to the Stars (Read by Corbett, Clare). Audiobook Review — *Kinsella, Sophie*
y Shopaholic to the Stars — *Kinsella, Sophie*
The Shopkeeper's Daughter — *Baxter, Lily*
The Shore (Read by Lamia, Jenna, with MacLeod Andrews). Audiobook Review — *Taylor, Sara*
The Shore — *Taylor, Sara*
The Shores of Spain — *Cheney, J. Kathleen*

Short: An International Anthology of Five Centuries of Short-Stories Prose Poems, Brief Essays, & Other Short Prose Forms — *Zeigler, Alan*
The Short and Tragic Life of Robert Peace: A Brilliant Young Man Who Left Newark for the Ivy League — *Hobbs, Jeff*
Short Bus Hero — *Giglio, Shannon*
The Short Drop — *FitzSimmons, Matthew*
Short Flights: Thirty-Two Modern Writers Share Aphorisms of Insight, Inspiration, and Wit — *Lough, James*
A Short History of Ancient Greece — *Rhodes, P.J.*
A Short History of the Twentieth Century — *Lukacs, John*
A Short History of the Weimar Republic — *Storer, Colin*
A Short Path to Change: 30 Ways to Transform Your Life — *Mannion, Jenny*
Short Scottish Prose Chronicles — *Embree, Dan*
Short Selling: Finding Uncommon Short Ideas — *Kumar, Amit*
Short Stories by Jesus: The Enigmatic Parables of a Controversial Rabbi — *Levine, Amy-Jill*
Short Stories (Illus. by Henry, Matt) — *Henry, Matt*
Short Talks — *Carson, Anne*
Shot Down: The True Story of Pilot Howard Snyder and the Crew of the B-17 Susan Ruth — *Snyder, Steve*
y Shot in the Dark — *Whyte, Janet M.*
Shotgun Lovesongs (Read by Sowers, Scott). Audiobook Review — *Butler, Nickolas*
Shotgun Lovesongs — *Butler, Nickolas*
Shots on the Bridge: Police Violence and Cover-Up in the Wake of Katrina — *Greene, Ronnie*
Should I Scoop Out My Bagel? And 99 Other Answers to Your Everyday Diet and Nutrition Questions to Help You Lose Weight, Feel Great, and Live Healthy — *Schapiro, Ilyse*
c Should You Be a River: A Poem about Love — *Young, Ed*
c Shouldn't You Be in School? All the Wrong Questions (Illus. by Seth) — *Snicket, Lemony*
The Shouting in the Dark — *Boehmer, Elleke*
Shouting Your Name Down the Well: Tankas and Haiku — *McFadden, David W.*
c Shouty Arthur — *Morgan, Angie*
y Show and Prove — *Quintero, Sofia*
c Show-and-Tell, Flat Stanley! (Illus. by Pamintuan, Macky) — *Brown, Jeff*
c Show Horses — *Turnbull, Stephanie*
c Show Me Happy (Illus. by Futran, Eric) — *Allen, Kathryn Madeline*
Show Me The Ashes — *Mulford, Carolyn*
A Show of Hands for the Republic: Opinion, Information, and Repression in Eighteenth-Century Rural France — *Walshaw, Jill Maciak*
Showa 1944-1953: A History of Japan (Illus. by Mizuki, Shigeru) — *Mizuki, Shigeru*
Showa 1953-1989: A History of Japan (Illus. by Mizuki, Shigeru) — *Mizuki, Shigeru*
Showdown in the Big Quiet: Land, Myth, and Government in the American West — *Bieter, John P., Jr.*
Showdown: The Looming Crisis over Gun Control — *Eakin, Lenden*
Showdown: Thurgood Marshall and the Supreme Court Nomination That Changed America — *Haygood, Wil*
Showdown: Thurgood Marshall and the Supreme Court Nomination that Changed America — *Haywood, Wil*
Shower of Stones — *Jernigan, Zachary*
Showman Killer: Heartless Hero — *Jodorowsky, Alejandro*
Shows and Tales: On Jewelry Exhibition-Making — *Lignel, Benjamin*
c Showstopper — *Berk, Sheryl*
The Shred Power Cleanse: Eat Clean, Get Lean, Burn Fat — *Smith, Ian K.*
c Shredding with the Geeks (Illus. by Cattish, Anna) — *Cobb, Amy*
Shrill Hurrahs: Women, Gender, and Racial Violence in South Carolina, 1865-1900 — *Gillin, Kate Cote*
Shrinking the Earth: The Rise and Decline of American Abundance — *Worster, Donald*
Shrinks: The Untold Story of Psychiatry — *Lieberman, Jeffrey A.*
Shriver — *Belden, Chris*
Shroud of Roses — *Ferris, Gloria*
The Shrunken Head (Read by Steinbruner, Greg). Audiobook Review — *Oliver, Lauren*

c The Shrunken Head (Illus. by Lacombe, Benjamin) — *Oliver, Lauren*
c The Shrunken Head — *Oliver, Lauren*
The Sh!t No One Tells You About Toddlers: A Guide to Surviving the Toddler Years — *Dais, Dawn*
y Shtetl: A Vernacular Intellectual History — *Shandler, Jeffrey*
Shtetl: The Golden Age: A New History of Jewish Life in East Europe — *Petrovsky-Shtern, Yohanan*
The Shut Eye — *Bauer, Belinda*
Shutter Man — *Montanari, Richard*
c Shutter — *Alameda, Courtney*
Shutter, vol 1: Wanderlost (Illus. by Duca, Leila Del) — *Keatinge, Joe*
Shylock Is My Name — *Jacobson, Howard*
Shyness: The Ultimate Teen Guide — *Carducci, Bernardo J.*
Si Ja, Say Yes to Better Life and Death: An Introduction to Health Literacy and Meditation — *Holmene Pelaez, Annelie*
c Sian, a New Australian — *Luckett, Dave*
Siberia: A History of the People — *Hartley, Janet M.*
y Siberiak: My Cold War Adventure on the River Ob (Illus. by Jaeckel, Jenny) — *Jaeckel, Jenny*
c Siblings, Curfews, and How to Deal: Questions and Answers about Family Life (Illus. by Mora, Julissa) — *Loewen, Nancy*
Sibyls: Prophecy and Power in the Ancient World — *Guillermo, Jorge*
Sicherheitskulturen im Vergleich: Deutschland und Russland/UdSSR seit dem Spaten 19. Jahrhundert — *Bauerkamper, Arnd*
Sicily: A Short History from the Ancient Greeks to Cosa Nostra — *Norwich, John Julius*
Sicily: An Island at the Crossroads of History — *Norwich, John Julius*
c A Sick Day for Amos McGee (Illus. by Stead, Erin E.) — *Stead, Philip C.*
Sick from Freedom: African-American Illness and Suffering during the Civil War and Reconstruction — *Downs, Jim*
y Sick in the Head: Conversations about Life and Comedy — *Apatow, Judd*
The Sick Rose or: Disease and the Art of Medical Illustration — *Barnett, Richard*
c Sick Simon (Illus. by Krall, Dan) — *Krall, Dan*
Sickness, Suffering and the Sword: The British Regiment on Campaign, 1808-1815 — *Bamford, Andrew*
Sid — *Feng, Anita M.*
c Side by Side (Illus. by Gliori, Debi) — *Bright, Rachel*
Side Effects — *Powell, V.K.*
Side Show — *Krieger, Henry*
Sideswiped — *Riley, Lia*
c Sidewalk Flowers (Illus. by Smith, Sydney) — *Lawson, JonArno*
c Sidewalk Flowers — *Smith, Sydney*
Sidewalking — *Ulin, David L.*
The Sidhe — *Ashe, Charlotte*
Sidney Chambers and the Forgiveness of Sins — *Runcie, James*
c Sidney Crosby — *Burgan, Michael*
The Siege of Jerusalem — *Boyarin, Adrienne Williams*
The Siege of Kut-al-Amara: At War in Mesopotamia 1915-1916 — *Gardner, Nikolas*
The Siege of Kut-al-Amara: At War in Mesopotamia, 1915-1916 — *Gardner, Nikolas*
The Siege of Petersburg: The Battles for the Weldon Railroad, August 1864 — *Horn, John*
The Siege of Strasbourg — *Chrastil, Rachel*
Siege Warfare and Military Organization in the Successor States (400-800 AD): Byzantium, the West and Islam — *Petersen, Leif Inge Ree*
The Siege Winter — *Franklin, Ariana*
Siegerwald und Westerwald: Bergbaugschichte - Mineralienschatze - Fundorte — *Golze, Rolfe*
Siena: City of Secrets — *Tylus, Jane*
Sighing Women Tea — *Seiler, Mark Daniel*
y Sight: The Delta Girls — *Madison, Juliet*
Sightseeing in the Undiscovered Country — *Green, Louisa Oakley*
A Sign Catalog: Glyphs in Selected Text-Like Layouts at Teotihuacan — *Guerrero, Joanne Michel*
c The Sign of the Black Dagger — *Lingard, Joan*
c The Sign of the Cat (Illus. by Jonell, Lynne) — *Jonell, Lynne*
Signa Vides--Researching and Recording Printers' Devices: Current Activities and New Perspectives
Signal — *Lee, Patrick*
The Signal and the Noise: Why So Many Predictions Fail - But Some Don't — *Silver, Nate*
Signal Boost — *Cole, Alyssa*

Signal Fires — *Baldwin, Sy Margaret*
Signal to Noise — *Moreno-Garcia, Silvia*
Signature Kill — *Levien, David*
Signed, Sealed, Delivered: Celebrating the Joys of Letter Writing — *Sankovitch, Nina*
y Signed, Skye Harper — *Williams, Carol Lynch*
The Significance of Moths — *Camia, Shirley*
Signifying without Specifying: Racial Discourse in the Age of Obama — *Li, Stephanie*
Signs for Lost Children — *Moss, Sarah*
Signs in Life: Finding Direction in Our Travels with God — *Nowadnick, Deanna*
y Signs Point to Yes — *Hall, Sandy*
Signs Preceding the End of the World — *Herrera, Yuri*
SignWave — *Vachss, Andrew*
Silabas De Viento/Syllables Of Wind — *Caraza, Xanath*
Silence: A Christian History — *MacCulloch, Diarmaid*
y Silence — *Lytton, Deborah*
Silence and Song — *Thon, Melanie Rae*
Silence in Catullus — *Stevens, B.E.*
y Silence Is Goldfish — *Pitcher, Annabel*
y The Silence of Six — *Myers, E.C.*
The Silence of Stones — *Westerson, Jeri*
The Silence of the Lambs — *Harris, Thomas*
The Silence of the Sea — *Sigurdardottir, Yrsa*
Silence Once Begun — *Ball, Jesse*
The Silence That Speaks — *Kane, Andrea*
The Silence That Speaks (Read by Huber, Hillary). Audiobook Review — *Kane, Andrea*
The Silence That Speaks — *Kane, Andrea*
Silence: The Power of Quiet in a World Full of Noise — *Hanh, Thich Nhat*
Silence was Salvation: Child Survivors of Stalin's Terror and World War II in the Soviet Union — *Frierson, Cathy A.*
The Silencing: How the Left Is Killing Free Speech — *Powers, Kirsten*
Silencing the Sea: Secular Rhythms in Palestinian Poetry — *Furani, Khaled*
y Silent Alarm — *Banash, Jennifer*
The Silent Boy — *Taylor, Andrew*
Silent City — *Smith, Carrie*
The Silent Deep: The Royal Navy Submarine Service since 1945 — *Hennessy, Peter*
Silent Film Comedy and American Culture — *Bilton, Alan*
Silent Highway — *Howell, Anthony*
The Silent History — *Horowitz, Eli*
Silent Nights: Christmas Mysteries — *Edwards, Martin*
Silent Running — *Kermode, Mark*
Silent Running — *Rowson, Pauline*
The Silent Sex: Gender, Deliberation and Institutions — *Karpowitz, Christopher F.*
The Silent Sister (Read by Bennett, Susan). Audiobook Review — *Chamberlain, Diane*
c Silent Soldiers (Illus. by Juta, Jason) — *Chambers, Catherine*
Silent Spring — *Carson, Rachel*
y Silent Symmetry — *Dutton, J.B.*
The Silk Road: Taking the Bus to Pakistan — *Porter, Bill*
Silk Road: The Journey — *Canatsey, Kenneth*
The Silk Roads: A New History of the World — *Frankopan, Peter*
The Silkworm (Read by Glenister, Robert). Audiobook Review — *Galbraith, Robert*
c The Silly Book of Weird and Wacky Words (Illus. by Garrett, Scott) — *Seed, Andy*
c Silly Cat Jokes to Tickle Your Funny Bone — *Gonzales, Doreen*
c Silly Shoes: Poems to Make You Smile (Illus. by Guillory, Mike) — *Gow, Lawson*
c Silly Squid! Poems About the Sea (Illus. by Johns, Cheryll) — *Brian, Janeen*
c Silly Wonderful You (Illus. by McDonnell, Patrick) — *Rinker, Sherri Duskey*
The Silo Effect: The Peril of Expertise and the Promise of Breaking Down Barriers — *Tett, Gillian*
The Silo Effect: Why Putting Everything in Its Place Isn't Such a Bright Idea — *Tett, Gillian*
Silver Bullets — *Mendoza, Elmer*
c Silver Bunny and the Secret Fort Chop (Illus. by Spurging, Curt) — *Wacker, Eileen*
The Silver Fork Novel: Fashionable Fiction in the Age of Reform — *Copeland, Edward*
y Silver in the Blood — *George, Jessica Day*
Silver Linings — *Macomber, Debbie*
Silver on the Road — *Gilman, Laura Anne*
c Silver Penny Stories (Illus. by Olafsdottir, Linda) — *Olmstead, Kathleen*
c Silver People — *Engle, Margarita*

Silver Screen Fiend: Learning about Life from an Addiction to Film (Read by Oswalt, Patton). Audiobook Review — Oswalt, Patton
Silver Screen Fiend: Learning about Life from an Addiction to Film — Oswalt, Patton
c Silver Shoes, Book 1: And All the Jazz (Illus. by Bound, Samantha-Ellen) — Bound, Samantha-Ellen
c Silver Shoes, Book 2: Hit the Streets (Illus. by Bound, Samantha-Ellen) — Bound, Samantha-Ellen
The Silver Swan — Delbanco, Elena
The Silver Swan — Delbanco, Elena
Silver Voyage — Mason, Sandy
The Silver Witch — Brackston, Paula
Silvertown: The Lost Story of a Strike that Shook London and Helped Modern Labour Movement — Tully, John
Silvina Ocampo — Ocampo, Silvina
Silvina Ocampo — Weiss, Jason
Simmer and Smoke — Lampman, Peggy
y Simon — Mullin, Michael
c Simon and the Bear (Illus. by Trueman, Matthew) — Kimmel, Eric A.
c Simon Thorn and the Wolf's Den — Carter, Aimee
y Simon vs. the Homo Sapiens Agenda — Albertalli, Becky
Simone — Frye, David
Simone — Lalo, Eduardo
Simone Weil: Late Philosophical Writings — Weil, Simone
c Simon's New Bed (Illus. by Van der Paardt, Melissa) — Trimmer, Christian
c A Simple Case of Angels — Adderson, Caroline
Simple Habits for Complex Times — Garvey Berger, Jennifer
Simple Lessons for a Better Life — Dodgen, Charles E.
Simple Lessons for a Better Life: Unexpected Inspiration from Inside the Nursing Home — Dodgen, Charles E.
c Simple Machines: Wheels, Levers, and Pulleys (Illus. by Raff, Anna) — Adler, David A.
Simple Witness — Siqveland, Bob
Simpler: The Future of Government — Sunstein, Cass R.
Simplicity: A Meta-Metaphysics — Dilworth, Craig
The Simplicity Cycle: A Field Guide to Making Things Better Without Making Them Worse — Ward, Dan
The Simplicity of Stillness Method: 3 Steps to Rewire Your Brain and Access Your Highest Potential — Karlin, Marlise
Simplicius on the Planets and Their Motions: In Defense of a Heresy — Bowen, Alan C.
Simply Ancient Grains: Fresh and Flavorful Whole Grain Recipes for Living Well — Speck, Maria
Simply Anna — Moore, Jennifer
Simply Scratch: 120 Wholesome Recipes Made Easy — McNamara, Laurie
Simply Stitched Gifts: 21 Fun Projects Using Free-Motion Stitching — Shaffer, Cynthia
Simply to Know Its Name — McNally, Robert Aquinas
Simply Vegan — Wasserman, Debra
Simulated Environment for Theatre — Roberts-Smith, Jennifer
Sin — Rand, Violetta
Sin and Confession in Colonial Peru: Spanish-Quechua Penitential Texts, 1560-1650 — Harrison, Regina
Sin and Filth in Medieval Culture: The Devil in the Latrine — Bayless, Martha
y The Sin Eater's Daughter (Read by Shields, Amy). Audiobook Review — Salisbury, Melinda
y The Sin Eater's Daughter — Salisbury, Melinda
Sinatra 100 — Pignone, Charles
Sinatra — Erlinger, Amanda
Sinatra: The Chairman — Kaplan, James
Sinatra's Century: One Hundred Notes on the Man and His World — Lehman, David
Sinews of the Nation: Constructing Irish and Zionist Bonds in the United States — Lainer-Vos, Dan
Sinful — Johnston, Joan
y Sing a Rebel Song — Rushby, Pamela
c Sing a Season Song (Illus. by Ashlock, Lisel Jane) — Yolen, Jane
Sing a Worried Song — Deverell, William
y Sing Down the Stars — Hatton, L.J.
Sing What You Cannot Say — Raymond, Cathy
c The Singer in the Stream: A Story of American Dippers — Hocker, Katherine
Singers and Tales: Oral Tradition and the Roots of Literature (Read by Drout, Michael D.C.). Audiobook Review — Drout, Michael D.C.

The Singing Bone — Hahn, Beth
y The Singing Bones — Tan, Shaun
Singing for Equality: Hymns in the American Antislavery and Indian Rights Movements — Boots, Cheryl C.
Singing from the Floor: A History of British Folk Clubs — Hawley, Richard
Singing Jeremiah: Music and Meaning in Holy Week — Kendrick, Robert L.
Singing with Starlings — Altshul, Victor
Single: Arguments for the Uncoupled — Cobb, Michael
Single, Carefree, Mellow: Stories — Heiny, Katherine
Single Digits: In Praise of Small Numbers — Chamberland, Marc
The Single Guy Cookbook — Shemtov, Avi
Single Jewish Male Seeking Soul Mate — Pogrebin, Letty Cottin
y A Single Stone — McKinlay, Meg
The Single Undead Moms Club — Harper, Molly
Singular Pertubations: Introduction to Sysytem Order Reduction Methods with Applications — Shchepakina, Elena
The Singular Universe and the Reality of Time: A Proposal in Natural Philosophy — Turney, Jon
The Singular Universe and the Reality of Time — Unger, Roberto Mangabeira
Singularities: Technoculture, Transhumanism, and Science Fiction in the 21st Century — Raulerson, Joshua
A Singularly Unfeminine Profession: One Woman's Journey in Physics — Gaillard, Mary K.
Sinicizing International Relations: Self, Civilization and Intellectual Politics in Subaltern East Asia — Shih, Chih-Yu
Sinking Suspicions — Hoklotubbe, Sara Sue
y Sinner — Stiefvater, Maggie
Sinner's Steel — Castille, Sarah
The Sino-Russian Challenge to the World Order: National Identities, Bilateral Relations, and East Versus West in the 2010s — Rozman, Gilbert
The Sino-Soviet Alliance: An International History — Jersild, Austin
Sinophone Malaysian Literature: Not Made in China — Groppe, Alison M.
Sins of a Wicked Princess — Randol, Anna
Sins of Our Fathers — Otto, Shawn Lawrence
The Sins of Soldiers — Lea, S.J. Hardman
Sinti und Roma: Die unerwunschte Minderheit - Uber das Vorurteil Antiziganismus — Benz, Wolfgang
Sipping Whiskey in a Shallow Grave — Mitten, Mark
Sir Cumference and the Off-the-Charts Dessert (Illus. by Geehan, Wayne) — Neuschwander, Cindy
c Sir Cumference and the Roundabout Battle: A Math Adventure (Illus. by Geehan, Wayne) — Neuschwander, Cindy
Sir Gawain and the Green Knight — Battles, Paul
c Sir Henry Morgan — Nardo, Don
c Sir John the (Mostly) Brave (Illus. by Anderson, Laura Ellen) — Smith, Johnny
Sir John's Table: The Culinary Life and Times of Canada's First Prime Minister — Mechefske, Lindy
Sir Robert Filmer (1588-1653) and the Patriotic Monarch: Patriarchalism in Seventeenth-Century Political Thought — Cuttica, Cesare
Sir Thomas Browne: A Life — Barbour, Reid
Sir Thomas Elyot as Lexicographer — Stein, Gabriele
Sir Thomas Malory: Le Morte Darthur, 2 vols. — Field, P.J.C.
c Sir Tony Robinson's Weird World of Wonders: Pets (Illus. by Thorpe, Del) — Robinson, Tony
Sir Williams — Stacton, David
y Sired by Stone — Post, Andrew
Siren Song — Greenwood, Jo
The Sirena Quest — Kahn, Michael A.
Siren's Call — Castle, Jayne
y Siren's Fury — Weber, Mary
Sister Churches: American Congregations and Their Partners Abroad — Bakker, Janel Kragt
y Sister Heart — Morgan, Sally
The Sister Pact — Ramey, Stacie
c The Sister Solution — Trueit, Trudi
Sister Thorn and Catholic Mysticism in Modern America — Kane, Paula M.
A Sisterhood of Sculptors: American Artists in Nineteenth-Century Rome — Dabakis, Melissa
The Sisters Are Alright: Changing the Broken Narrative of Black Women in America — Winfrey-Harris, Tamara L.
c Sisters (Illus. by Lamb, Braden) — Telgemeier, Raina
y Sisters' Fate — Spotswood, Jessica

Sisters in Law: How Sandra Day O'Connor and Ruth Bader Ginsburg Went to the Supreme Court and Changed the World — Hirshman, Linda
y Sisters of Blood and Spirit — Cross, Kady
Sisters of Heart and Snow (Read by Cronyn, Tandy). Audiobook Review — Dilloway, Margaret
Sisters of Heart and Snow — Dilloway, Margaret
Sisters of Shiloh — Hepinstall, Becky
Sisters of Shiloh — Hepinstall, Kathy
y Sisters of the Revolution: A Feminist Speculative Fiction Anthology — VanderMeer, Ann
Sisters of the Wyoming Mountains: Book I — McCarthy, Gary
Sisters of the Wyoming Plains: Book II — McCarthy, Gary
Sistina — Swain, Brian
Sit! Stay! Speak! — Noblin, Annie England
Sites of Slavery: Citizenship and Racial Democracy in the Post-Civil Rights Imagination — Tillet, Salamishah
c Sitting Bull: Lakota Warrior and Defender of His People (Illus. by Nelson, S.D.) — Nelson, S.D.
Situation Momedy — von Oy, Jenna
SIV & the Blood Moon — Leigh, Geoffrey
c Siver Eve — Waugh, Sandra
y The Six — Alpert, Mark
y Six — Vaughan, M.M.
Six and a Half Deadly Sins — Cotterill, Colin
The Six-Day War and Israeli Self-Defense: Questioning the Legal Basis for Preventive War — Quigley, John
The Six-Degree Conspiracy, vol. 1: — Shear, Jeff
c Six Degrees of LeBron James: Connecting Basketball Stars — Lohre, Mike
c Six Degrees of Peyton Manning: Connecting Football Stars — Hetrick, Hans
y Six Feet over It — Longo, Jennifer
Six-Gun Snow White — Valente, Catherynne M.
y Six Impossible Things — Wood, Fiona
Six Moments of Crisis: Inside British Foreign Policy — Bennett, Gill
The Six — Alpert, Mark
y Six of Crows — Bardugo, Leigh
Six-Shooters and Shifting Sands — Alexander, Bob
c The Six Swans (Illus. by Raidt, Gerda) — Grimm, Wilhelm
Six years of re:work. A conference in Berlin
Sixteen for '16: A Progressive Agenda for a Better America — Babones, Salvatore
The Sixteenth of June (Read by Whelan, Julia). Audiobook Review — Lang, Maya
y Sixteenth Summer — Dalton, Michelle
The Sixth Extinction: An Unnatural History — Kolbert, Elizabeth
The Sixth Form MBA — Croft, Susan
y The Sixth Man — Feinstein, John
The Sixth — Hays, Avery
Sixties Radicalism and Social Movement Activism: Retreat or Resurgence? — Jones, Bryn
Sixty Degrees North: Around the World in Search of Home — Tallack, Malachy
The Size of Others' Burdens: Barack Obama, Jane Addams, and the Politics of Helping Others — Schneiderhan, Erik
y Skandal — Smith, Lindsay
Skandal und Nation: Politische Deutungskampfe in der Schweiz 1988-1991 — Liehr, Dorothee
Skandalon: Poems — Hummer, T.R.
c Skara Brae — Finch, Dawn
c Skateboard Party (Illus. by Freeman, Laura) — English, Karen
Skateboarding: Zwischen Urbaner Rebellion und Neoliberalem Selbstentwurf — Schweer, Sebastian
Skeletal — Hayton, Katherine
The Skeleton Cupboard — Byron, Tanya
Skeleton Plot — Gregson, J.M.
The Skeleton Road — McDermid, Val
c The Skeleton Tree — Lawrence, Iain
Skeptic: Viewing the World with a Rational Eye — Shermer, Michael
Sketch City: Tips and Inspiration for Drawing on Location — Dopress Books
The Sketchbook Project World Tour — Peterman, Steven
y Sketches from a Nameless Land: The Art of The Arrival — Tan, Shaun
Sketches from the Sierra De Tejada — Fuller, John
y Skies Like These — Hilmo, Tess
Skies of Ash — Hall, Rachel Howzell
Skiing into Modernity: A Cultural and Environmental History — Denning, Andrew

Skilled and Resolute: A History of the 12th Evacuation Hospital and the 212th MASH, 1917-2006 — Marble, Sanders
The Skin Collector — Deaver, Jeffery
y Skin Deep — Jarratt, Laura
Skin Effect: More Science Fiction and Fantasy Erotica — Christian, M.
Skin Like Silver — Nickson, Chris
Skinhead: An Archive — Mott, Toby
y Skinhead Birdy — Jacobs, Evan
c Skink-No Surrender (Read by Heyborne, Kirby). Audiobook Review — Hiaasen, Carl
c Skink-No Surrender. Audiobook Review — Hiaasen, Carl
y Skink-No Surrender — Hiaasen, Carl
Skinner Luce — Ward, Patricia
Skinny Dipping with Murder — Wallace, Auralee
Skinny Habits: The Six Secrets of Thin People — Harper, Bob
Skintight — Beauchamp, Wade
c Skip School, Fly to Space (Illus. by Pastis, Stephan T.) — Pastis, Stephan T.
c Skip to the Loo, My Darling! A Potty Book (Illus. by Jeram, Anita) — Lloyd-Jones, Sally
Skip Trace. E-book Review — Jensen, Kelly
Skull Fragments — Williams, Tim L.
Skull in the Ashes: Murder, a Gold Rush Manhunt, and the Birth of Circumstantial Evidence in America — Kaufman, Peter
The Skull of Pancho Villa and Other Stories — Ramos, Manuel
Skullduggery, Secrets, and Murders: The 1894 Wells Fargo Scam That Backfired — Neal, Bill
Skully: Perdition Games — Fraser, L.E.
c Skunk on a String (Illus. by Lam, Thao) — Lam, Thao
c The Skunk (Illus. by McDonnell, Patrick) — Barnett, Mac
Sky Blue Stone: The Turquoise Trade in World History — Khazeni, Arash
The Sky Detective — Tabazadeh, Azadeh
c Sky in Stereo (Illus. by Mardou) — Mardou
c The Sky is Falling — Pearson, Kit
c The Sky Is Falling! (Illus. by Teague, Mark) — Teague, Mark
y Sky Key — Frey, James
y Sky Key — Johnson-Shelton, Nils
Sky Lantern: The Story of a Father's Love for His Children and the Healing Power of the Smallest Act of Kindness — Mikalatos, Matt
c A Sky of Diamonds — Gibbs, Camille
c The Sky Painter: Louis Fuertes, Bird Artist (Illus. by Bereghici, Aliona) — Engle, Margarita
Sky People: Untold Stories of Alien Encounters in Mesoamerica — Clarke, Ardy Sixkiller
Skyborn — Dalglish, David
c Skydiving Dogs — Goldish, Meish
c Skydiving — Bailey, Diane
Skyfaring: A Journey with a Pilot — Vanhoenacker, Mark
Skylark — Morgan, Ruthie
Skylight — Costa, Margaret Jull
Skylight — Saramago, Jos
y The Skylighter — Wallace, Becky
y Skyscraping — Jensen, Cordelia
Slade House — Michell, David
Slade House — Mitchell, David
Slade House — Mitchell, David Stephen
The Slain God: Anthropologists and the Christian Faith — Larsen, Timothy
y Slam a tout vent! — Lavoie, Michel
Slandering the Jew: Sexuality and Difference in Early Christian Texts — Drake, Susanna
A Slant of Light — Lent, Jeffrey
Slant Six — Belieu, Erin
Slanting I, Imagining We: Asian Canadian Literary Production in the 1980s and 1990s — Lai, Larissa
c Slappy's Tales of Horror (Illus. by Roman, Dave) — Stine, R.L.
y Slasher Girls and Monster Boys (Read by Daymond, Robbie). Audiobook Review — Tucholke, April Genevieve
y Slasher Girls and Monster Boys — Tucholke, April Genevieve
Slashtag — Thiede, Todd M.
Slated for Death (Read by Flosnik, Anne). Audiobook Review — Duncan, Elizabeth J.
Slated for Death — Duncan, Elizabeth J.
The Slaughter Man — Parsons, Tony
A Slaughtered Lamb: Revelation and the Apocalyptic Response to Evil and Suffering — Stevenson, Gregory

Slaughterhouse-Five — Packer, Ann
Slave and Sister — Waldfogel, Sabra
Slave Breeding: Sex, Violence, and Memory in African American History — Smithers, Gregory D.
Slave Portraiture in the Atlantic World — Lugo-Ortiz, Agnes
A Slaveholders' Union: Slavery, Politics, and the Constitution in the Early American Republic — Van Cleve, George William
Slavery and Antislavery in Spain's Atlantic Empire — Fradera, Josep M.
Slavery and Emancipation in Islamic East Africa: From Honor to Respectability — McMahon, Elisabeth
Slavery and Freedom in Savannah — Harris, Leslie M.
Slavery and the Enlightenment in the British Atlantic, 1750-1807 — Roberts, Justin
Slavery and War in the Americas: Race, Citizenship, and State Building in the United States and Brazil, 1861-1870 — Izecksohn, Vitor
Slavery in American Children's Literature, 1790-2010 — Connolly, Paula T.
Slavery in Medieval and Early Modern Iberia — Phillips, William D.
Slavery in Medieval and Early Modern Iberia — Phillips, William D., Jr.
Slavery in Mississippi — Sydnor, Charles S.
Slavery, Race, and Conquest in the Tropics: Lincoln, Douglas, and the Future of Latin America — May, Robert E.
Slavery, the State, and Islam — Ennaji, Mohammed
y Slavery through the Ages — Nardo, Don
Slavery's Borderland: Freedom and Bondage along the Ohio River — Salafia, Matthew
Slavery's Exiles: The Story of the American Maroons — Diouf, Sylviane A.
Slaves and Englishmen: Human Bondage in the Early Modern Atlantic World — Guasco, Michael
Slaves and Englishmen: Human Bondage in the Early Modern Atlantic World — Guasco, Michael
Slaves and Englishmen: Human Bondage in the Early Modern Atlantic World — Guasco, Michael
The Slave's Cause — Sinha, Manisha
Slaves Waiting for Sale: Abolitionist Art and the American Slave Trade — McInnis, Maurie D.
Slay Bells — Mahon, Annette
Slaying Dragons — Miller, Sasha L.
Slaying the Tiger: A Year Inside the Ropes on the New PGA Tour — Ryan, Shane
Sleep and Your Special Needs Child — Chitty, Antonia
Sleep Around the World: Anthropological Perspectives — Glaskin, Katie
The Sleep Garden — Krusoe, Jim
Sleep in Peace Tonight — MacManus, James
The Sleep of Behemoth: Disputing Peace and Violence in Medieval Europe, 1000-1200 — Malegam, Jehangir Yezdi
The Sleep of the Righteous — Cole, Isabel Fargo
y Sleep Problems — Nardo, Don
c Sleep Softly (Illus. by Nouren, Elodie) — Pastor, David
c Sleep Tight, Anna Banana! (Illus. by Dormal, Alexis) — Roques, Dominique
c Sleep Tight, Little Bear (Illus. by Teckentrup, Britta) — Teckentrup, Britta
y The Sleeper and the Spindle (Read by Rhind-Tutt, Julian). Audiobook Review — Gaiman, Neil
y The Sleeper and the Spindle (Illus. by Riddell, Chris) — Gaiman, Neil
y The Sleeper and the Spindle — Gaiman, Neil
y The Sleeper and the Spindle (Illus. by Riddell, Chris) — Gaiman, Neil
c The Sleeper and the Spindle (Illus. by Riddell, Chris)
Sleeper — Janes, J. Robert
Sleeping Beauties in Theoretical Physics: 26 Surprising Insights — Padmanahan, Thanu
c Sleeping Beauty (Illus. by Gibb, Sarah) — Gibb, Sarah
c Sleeping Beauty (Illus. by Gibbs, Sarah) — Sage, Alison
c Sleeping Beauty's Daughters — Zahler, Diane
c Sleeping Cinderella and Other Princess Mix-Ups (Illus. by Barrager, Brigette) — Clarkson, Stephanie
Sleeping Dogs — Mogford, Thomas
Sleeping Embers of an Ordinary Mind — Charnock, Anne
Sleeping in Trees — Brown, Keith Ballard
Sleeping on Jupiter — Roy, Anuradha
c Sleeping to Death — Baum, G.D.
Sleeping Truth — Vesole, Martin
Sleeping with Other People — Sudeikis, Jason

Sleeping with the Enemy — Solheim, Tracy
A Sleepless Eye: Aphorisms from the Sahara — Koni, Ibrahim al-
c Sleepless Knight (Illus. by Sturm, James) — Sturm, James
c Sleepover with Beatrice and Bear (Illus. by Carnesi, Monica) — Carnesi, Monica
Sleepwalker: The Mysterious Makings and Recovery of a Somnambulist — Frazier, Kathleen
c The Sleepwalker Tonic (Read by Segel, Jason). Audiobook Review — Segel, Jason
c The Sleepwalker Tonic — Segel, Jason
The Sleepwalkers: How Europe Went to War in 1914 — Clark, Christopher
The Sleepwalkers: How Europe Went to War in 1914 — Clarke, Christopher
c Sleepy Dog, Wake Up! (Illus. by Gorbaty, Norman) — Ziefert, Harriet
c Sleepy Kitty — Sterling Children's Books
c Sleepy Puppy
c Sleepy Snoozy Cozy Coozy: A Book of Animal Beds (Illus. by Monroe, Michael Glenn) — Young, Judy (b. 1956-)
c Sleepy Snoozy, Cozy Coozy (Illus. by Monroe, Michael Glenn) — Young, Judy (b. 1956-)
c Sleepy Snoozy Cozy Coozy (Illus. by Monroe, Michael Glenn) — Young, Judy (b. 1956-)
c The Sleepy Songbird — Barton, Suzanne
Sleet: Selected Stories — Dagerman, Stig
y Sleight of Hand — Deen, Natasha
c Sleuth on Skates (Illus. by Horne, Sarah) — Beauvais, Clementine
Slice Harvester: A Memoir in Pizza — Hagendorf, Colin Atrophy
Sliced Vegetarian — Malik, Liesa
Slick Water: Fracking and One Insider's Stand against the World's Most Powerful Industry — Greystone, Andrew Nikiforuk
c Slickety Quick: Poems About Sharks (Illus. by Kolar, Bob) — Brown, Skila
Slimy Science and Awesome Experiments (Illus. by Ursell, Martin) — Martineau, Susan
c Slimy Spawn and Other Gruesome Life Cycles — Taylor, Barbara
A Slip of the Keyboard: Collected Nonfiction — Pratchett, Terry
c Slipper and Flipper in the Quest for the Golden Sun (Illus. by Reagan, Susan) — Reagan, Susan
c The Slippers' Keeper (Illus. by Wallace, Ian) — Wallace, Ian
Slippery Noodles: A Culinary History of China — Lin, Hsiang-ju
c A Sliver of Stardust — Burt, Marissa
c Sloth Slept On — Preston-Gannon, Frann
c Sloths — Gregory, Josh
c Sloths — Murray, Julie
Slow and Steady Rush. E-book Review — Trentham, Laura
Slow Bullets — Reynolds, Alastair
Slow Fires: Mastering New Ways to Braise, Roast, and Grill — Smillie, Justin
Slow Pilgrim: The Collected Poems — Cairns, Scott
The Slow Regard of Silent Things (Read by Rothfuss, Patrick). Audiobook Review — Rothfuss, Patrick
The Slow Regard of Silent Things — Rothfuss, Patrick
Slow River — Griffith, Nicola
c Slug Needs a Hug! (Illus. by Ross, Tony) — Willis, Jeanne
c The Slug — Gravel, Elise
The Slumbering Masses: Sleep, Medicine, and Modern American Life — Wolf-Meyer, Matthew J.
y Slump — Waltman, Kevin
The Slums of Palo Alto — Fussell, Mark L.
Slur Exercises, Trills, and Chromatic Octaves — Segovia, Andres
The Slush Pile Brigade — Marquis, Samuel
Slut: A Play and Guidebook for Combating Sexism and Sexual Violence — Cappiello, Katie
Slutwalk: Feminism, Activism and Media — Mendes, Kaitlynn
c Small and Big (Illus. by Wood, Ben) — Collum, Karen
The Small Backs of Children — Yuknavitch, Lidia
The Small Big: Small Changes That Spark Big Influence (Read by Chamberlain, Mike). Audiobook Review — Martin, Steve J.
Small Blessings (Read by King, Lorelei). Audiobook Review — Woodroof, Martha
c Small Blue and the Deep Dark Night — Davis, Jon
y Small Bones — Grant, Vicki
A Small Circus — Fallada, Hans
Small Data: The Tiny Clues That Uncover Huge Trends — Lindstrom, Martin

c Small Elephant's Bathtime — *Feeney, Tatyana*
Small Enterprise — *Biddinger, Betty*
Small Fires in the Sun — *Metoyer, Herbert R., Jr.*
Small Government My A** — *Loesch, Kevin*
Small, Gritty and Green: The Promise of America's Smaller Industrial Cities in a Low Carbon World — *Tumber, Catherine*
The Small House at Allington — *Birch, Dinah*
The Small Library Manager's Handbook — *Graves, Alice*
y A Small Madness — *Touchell, Dianne*
Small Mercies — *Joyce, Eddie*
Small Navies: Strategy and Policy for Small Navies in War and Peace — *Mulqueen, Michael*
Small Navies: Strategy and Policy for Small Navies in War and Peace — *Milqueen, Michael*
c Small Smaller Smallest (Illus. by Marshall, Natalie) — *Fletcher, Corina*
A Small Story about the Sky — *Rios, Alberto*
Small-Town America: Finding Community, Shaping the Future — *Wuthnow, Robert*
Small Town Talk: Bob Dylan, The Band, Van Morrison, Janis Joplin, Jimi Hendrix and Friends in the Wild Years of Woodstock — *Hoskyns, Barney*
Small Victories. Audiobook Review
Small Victories — *Williams, Dave H.*
Small Victories: Spotting Improbable Moments of Grace (Read by Lamott, Anne). Audiobook Review — *Lamott, Anne*
c Small Wonders: Jean-Henri Fabre and His World of Insects (Illus. by Ferri, Giuliano) — *Smith, Matthew Clark*
Small Wonders — *Lux, Courtney*
c The Small World of Paper Toys — *Lo Monaco, Gerard*
Smaller and Smaller Circles — *Batacan, F.H.*
y Smart and Spineless: Exploring Invertebrate Intelligence — *Downer, Ann*
Smart Cities: Big Data, Civic Hackers, and the Quest for a New Utopia — *Townsend, Anthony*
Smart Girl — *Hollis, Rachel*
c Smart Girl: Yoga for Brain Power — *Rissman, Rebecca*
y The Smart Girl's Guide to Privacy: Practical Tips for Staying Safe Online — *Blue, Violet*
c The Smart Kid's Guide to Everyday Life Series
Smart Money: How High-Stakes Financial Innovation Is Reshaping Our World--for the Better — *Palmer, Andrew*
The Smart Palate: Delicious Recipes for a Healthy Lifestyle — *Abbey, Tina Landsman*
A Smarter, Greener Grid: Forging Environmental Progress through Smart Energy Policies and Technologies — *Jones, Kevin B.*
The Smarter Screen: Surprising Ways to Influence and Improve Online Behavior — *Benartzi, Shlomo*
Smarter Than We Think: More Messages about Math, Teaching, and Learning in the 21st Century — *Seeley, Cathy L.*
c Smartest Animals Series — *Gagne, Tammy*
The Smartest Book in the World: A Lexicon of Literacy, a Rancorous Reportage, a Concise Curriculum of Cool (Read by Proops, Greg). Audiobook Review — *Proops, Greg*
The Smartest Book in the World: A Lexicon of Literacy, a Rancorous Reportage, a Concise Curriculum of Cool — *Proops, Greg*
Smash Cut: A Memoir of Howard & Art & the '70s & the '80s — *Gooch, Brad*
Smash Cut — *Gooch, Brad*
c Smashie McPerter and the Mystery of Room 11 (Illus. by Hindley, Kate) — *Griffin, N.*
y Smashie McPerter and the Mystery of Room 11 (Illus. by Hindley, Kate) — *Griffin, N.* Smashie
The Smashwords Style Guide — *Coker, Mark*
y Smek for President! (Read by Turpin, Bahni). Audiobook Review — *Rex, Adam*
c Smek for President! — *Rex, Adam*
y Smek for President (Illus. by Rex, Adam) — *Rex, Adam*
The Smell of Battle, the Taste of Siege: A Sensory History of the Civil War — *Smith, Mark M.*
y The Smell of Other People's Houses — *Hitchcock, Bonnie-Sue*
c Smelly Farts and Other Body Horrors — *Claybourne, Anna*
c Smick! (Illus. by Medina, Juana) — *Cronin, Doreen*
y Smile and Succeed for Teens: A Crash Course in Face-to-Face Communication — *Manecke, Kirt*
Smile of a Midsummer Night: A Picture of Sweden — *Gustafsson, Lars*
The Smile Revolution in Eighteenth-Century Paris — *Jones, Colin*

c The Smile That Went Around the World (Illus. by Christy, Jana) — *Karst, Patrice*
c A Smile/Una Sonrisa (Illus. by Aguiler, Manny) — *Smith, Michael*
c Smiles: The Sound of Long I — *Noyed, Robert B.*
c Smithsonian Readers: Seriously Amazing, Level 2 — *Scott-Royce, Brenda*
Smithsonian Stories: Chronicle of a Golden Age, 1964-1984 — *Dillon, Wilton S.*
The Smithsonian's History of America in 101 Objects — *Kurin, Richard*
Smoke — *McKenzie, Catherine*
Smoke Gets in Your Eyes: And Other Lessons from the Crematorium — *Doughty, Caitlin*
Smoke Gets in Your Eyes: And Other Lessons from the Crematory — *Doughty, Caitlin*
Smoke Gets in Your Eyes: And Other Lessons from the Crematory. Audiobook Review — *Doughty, Caitlin*
Smoke — *Benton, Gregory*
y Smoked — *Mancusi, Mari*
Smokejumper: A Memoir by One of America's Most Select Airborne Firefighters — *Ramos, Jason*
c Smokejumpers — *Goldish, Meish*
c Smoking — *Parks, Peggy J.*
Smoking Cigarettes, Eating Glass: A Psychologist's Memoir — *Sawyer, Annita Perez*
y The Smoking Mirror — *Bowles, David*
Smolensk under the Nazis: Everyday Life in Occupied Russia — *Cohen, Laurie R.*
SMS communication: A Linguistic Approach — *Cougnon, Louise-Amelie*
Smuggler Nation: How Illicit Trade Made America — *Andreas, Peter*
Smugglers and Saints of the Sahara: Regional Connectivity in the Twentieth Century — *Scheele, Judith*
y The Smuggler's Gambit — *Whitford, Sara*
Smugglers — *Debeljak, Alex*
c Snail, Where Are You? (Illus. by Ungerer, Tomi) — *Ungerer, Tomi*
c Snake — *Bodden, Valerie*
y Snake Bite — *Lane, Andrew*
Snake Box — *Mandel, Harvey*
Snake Pass — *Campbell, Colin*
y The Snake Trap — *Brooks, Kevin*
The Snake Who Said Shh ... — *Parachini, Jodie*
c Snakes, Alligators, and Broken Hearts: Journeys of a Biologist's Son — *Collard, Sneed B., III*
c Snakes and Reptiles around the World — *Alderton, David*
Snakes! Guillotines! Electric Chairs! My Adventures in the Alice Cooper Group — *Dunaway, Dennis*
Snakes of the World: A Catalogue of Living and Extinct Species — *Wallach, Van*
Snakes, Sunrises, and Shakespeare: How Evolution Shapes Our Loves and Fears — *Orians, Gordon H.*
c Snap (Illus. by Galloway, Fhiona) — *Litton, Jonathan*
c Snap Decision — *Whitaker, Nathan*
c Snap! (Illus. by Petricic, Dusan) — *Hutchins, Hazel*
c Snappsy the Alligator (Did Not Ask to Be in This Book). (Illus. by Miller, Tim) — *Falatko, Julie*
Snapshot Photography: The Lives of Images — *Zuromskis, Catherine*
Snapshots from My Uneventful Life — *Aboulafia, David I.*
Snarl: In Defense of Stalled Traffic and Faulty Networks — *Miller, Ruth A.*
y Snaygill — *Assor, Michelle B.*
y Sneaker Century: A History of Athletic Shoes — *Keyser, Amber J.*
Sneaky Math: A Graphic Primer with Projects — *Tymony, Cy*
Sneezes, Snorts and Sniffles: 7 Piano Pieces with Extra-musical Sounds — *Stevens, Wendy*
c A Snicker of Magic (Read by Morris, Cassandra). Audiobook Review — *Lloyd, Natalie*
c The Snickerblooms and the Age Bug (Illus. by Laughead, Mike) — *Perritano, John*
c Sniff a Skunk! (Illus. by Marble, Abigail) — *Amato, Mary*
c Sniff! Sniff! (Illus. by Sias, Ryan) — *Sias, Ryan*
y Sniffer Dogs: How Dogs (and Their Noses) Save the World — *Castaldo, Nancy F.*
c Snip Snap Pop-Up Fun (Illus. by Nowowiejska, Kasia) — *Litton, Jonathan*
The Sniper and the Wolf: A Sniper Elite Novel — *McEwen, Scott*
Sniper — *Rusch, Kristine Kathryn*
c Snoozefest (Illus. by Litten, Kristyna) — *Berger, Samantha*
c Snow (Illus. by Rabei, Carolina) — *de la Mare, Walter*

c Snow (Illus. by Thompson, Carol) — *Thompson, Carol*
c Snow (Illus. by Usher, Sam) — *Usher, Sam*
Snow and Shadow — *Tse, Dorothy*
Snow and Steel: The Battle of the Bulge, 1944-45 — *Caddick-Adams, Peter*
c Snow Babies — *de la Bedoyere, Camilla*
c Snow Babies — *Anderson, Laura Ellen*
y The Snow Baby: The Arctic Childhood of Robert E. Peary's Daring Daughter — *Kirkpatrick, Katherine*
c The Snow Beast (Illus. by Judge, Chris) — *Judge, Chris*
Snow Bunny's Christmas Gift (Illus. by Harry, Rebecca) — *Harry, Rebecca*
c The Snow Girl (Illus. by Muller, Hlne) — *Giraud, Robert*
Snow Hunters — *Yoon, Paul*
y Snow Job — *Benoit, Charles*
c Snow Joke — *Degen, Bruce*
The Snow Kimono — *Henshaw, Mark*
c Snow Leopards — *Esbaum, Jill*
y Snow Like Ashes — *Raasch, Sara*
Snow Men — *Ceroni, Andrew*
c The Snow Princess (Illus. by Sanderson, Ruth) — *Sanderson, Ruth*
c The Snow Queen (Read by Kellgren, Katherine). Audiobook Review — *Andersen, Hans Christian*
c The Snow Queen (Read by Yuen, Erin). Audiobook Review — *Andersen, Hans Christian*
The Snow Queen — *Cunningham, Michael*
c The Snow Queen (Illus. by Sedova, Yana) — *Andersen, Hans Christian*
c The Snow Queen (Illus. by Arnoux, Lucie) — *Hoekstra, Misha*
c The Snow Rabbit (Illus. by Garoche, Camille) — *Garoche, Camille*
c Snow White and the 77 Dwarfs (Illus. by Barbanegre, Raphaelle) — *Cali, Davide*
c Snow White and the 77 Dwarves (Illus. by Barbanegre, Raphaelle) — *Cali, Davide*
c Snow White and the Magic Mirror (Illus. by Warburton, Sarah) — *Bradman, Tony*
c Snow White (Illus. by Rossi, Francesca) — *Francia, Giada*
c Snow White (Illus. by Bryan, Ed). E-book Review
c Snow White Sees the Light — *Wallace, Karen*
Snowball: Chronicles of a Wererabbit — *Zeman, M.Y.*
Snowball in a Blizzard — *Hatch, Steven*
The Snowball: Warren Buffett and the Business of Life — *Schroeder, Alice*
c The Snowbirds — *Fitzsimmons, Jim*
Snowblind — *Arnold, Daniel*
Snowden — *Rail, Ted*
The Snowden Reader — *Fidler, David P.*
The Snowflake: Winter's Frozen Artistry — *Libbrecht, Kenneth*
c The Snowman and the Snowdog — *Briggs, Raymond*
c Snowman's Story — *Hillenbrand, Will*
c Snowshoe Hare — *Phillips, Dee*
c Snowy Bear (Illus. by Brown, Alison) — *Mitton, Tony*
c The Snowy Day (Illus. by Keats, Ezra Jack) — *Keats, Ezra Jack*
c Snowy Sunday (Illus. by Craig, Helen) — *Root, Phyllis*
So As I Was Saying ... My Somewhat Eventful Life — *Mankiewicz, Frank*
So Buttons — *Baylis, Jonathan*
c So Cozy (Illus. by Korda, Lerryn) — *Korda, Lerryn*
y So Cute It Hurts!! — *Ikeyamada, Go*
y So Cute It Hurts!!, vol. 1 — *Ikeyamada, Go*
So Far from Spring — *Curry, Peggy Simson*
So, How Long Have You Been Native? Life as an Alaska Native Tour Guide — *Bunten, Alexis C.*
c So Many Babies (Illus. by Watson, Laura) — *Crozier, Lorna*
So Many Roads: The Life and Times of the Grateful Dead (Read by Runnette, Sean). Audiobook Review — *Browne, David*
So Many Roads: The Life and Times of the Grateful Dead — *Browne, David*
So Many Shapes! A Spot-It, Learn-It Challenge — *Schuette, Sarah L.*
So Nude, So Dead — *McBain, Ed*
So Sad Today: Personal Essays — *Broder, Melissa*
So the New Could be Born: The Passing of a Country Grammar School — *Housden, Peter*
So This Is Permanence: Joy Division Lyrics and Notebooks — *Curtis, Ian*
So viel Wende war nie: Zur Geschichte des Projekts "Asthetische Grundbegriffe" - Stationen zwischen 1983 und 2000 — *Boden, Petra*
So What's Next! — *Griffiths, G.J.*
So You Don't Get Lost in the Neighborhood — *Modiano, Patrick*

So You Think You Know Gettysburg? The Stories Behind the Monuments and the Men Who Fought One of America's Most Epic Battles, vol. 2 — *Gindlesperger, James*
y So, You Want To Be a Dancer? The Ultimate Guide to Exploring the Dance Industry — *Van der Linde, Laurel*
c So, You Want to Be a Dancer? The Ultimate Guide to Exploring the Dance Industry — *Van Der Linde, Laurel*
So You Want to Be a Music Major: A Guide for High School Students, Their Parents, Guidance Counselors, and Music Teachers — *Franzblau, Robert*
c So, You Want to Work in Fashion? How to Break into the World of Fashion and Design — *Wooster, Patricia*
y So, You Want to Work with the Ancient and Recent Dead? Unearthing Careers from Paleontology to Forensic Science — *Bedell, J.M.*
So You've Been Publicly Shamed (Read by Ronson, Jon). Audiobook Review — *Ronson, Jon*
So You've Been Publicly Shamed — *Jacquet, Jennifer*
So You've Been Publicly Shamed — *Ronson, Jon*
c Soar — *Bauer, Joan*
c Soccer: A Nonfiction Companion to Soccer on Sunday (Illus. by Murdocca, Sal) — *Osborne, Mary Pope*
Soccer FAQ: All That's Left to Know about the Clubs, the Players, and the Rivalries — *Thompson, Dave*
Soccer Speed — *Bate, Dick*
The Sociable Sciences: Darwin and His Contemporaries in Chile — *Schell, Patience A.*
Social Analysis of Security: Financial, Economic and Ecological Crime - Crime, (In)security and (Dis)trust - Public and Private Policing — *Ponsaers, Paul*
Social and Economic Life in Second Temple Judea — *Adams, Samuel L.*
The Social Architecture of French Cinema: 1929-1939 — *Flinn, Margaret C.*
The Social Cancer — *Rizal, Jose*
Social Capital and Health Inequality in European Welfare States — *Rostila, Mikael*
Social Capital and Institutional Constraints: A Comparative Analysis of China, Taiwan and the US — *Routledge, Joonmo Son*
Social Class in Applied Linguistics — *Block, David*
Social Class in the 21st Century — *Savage, Mike*
Social Concern and Left Politics in Jewish American Art: 1880-1940 — *Baigell, Matthew*
Social Democratic America — *Kenworthy, Lane*
Social-Ecological Resilience and Law — *Garmestani, Ahjond S.*
A Social History of Hebrew: Its Origins through the Rabbinic Period — *Schniedewind, William*
Social Imagery in Middle Low German: Didactical Literature and Metaphorical Representation, 1470-1517 — *Hess, Cordelia*
Social Inquiry after Wittgenstein and Kuhn: Leaving Everything As It Is — *Gunnell, John*
Social Issues in Diagnosis: An Introduction for Students and Clinicians — *Jutel, Annemarie Goldstein*
The Social Life of DNA — *Nelson, Alondra*
The Social Life of Hagiography in the Merovingian Kingdom — *Kreiner, Jamie*
The Social Life of Money — *Dodd, Nigel*
The Social Lives of Forests: Past, Present, and Future of Woodland Resurgence — *Hecht, Susanna B.*
c Social Media: Like It or Leave It — *Rowell, Rebecca*
Social Media Marketing Workbook — *McDonald, Jason*
The Social Media President: Barack Obama and the Politics of Digital Engagement — *Katz, James E.*
The Social Order of the Underworld: How Prison Gangs Govern the American Penal System — *Skarbek, David*
Social Predation: How Group Living Benefits Predators and Prey — *Beauchamp, Guy*
Social Psychology of Musicianship — *Woody, Robert H.*
Social Radicalism and Liberal Education — *Paterson, Lindsay*
Social Relations and Urban Space: Norwich, 1600-1700 — *Williamson, Fiona*
The Social Roots of Risk: Producing Disasters, Promoting Resilience — *Tierney, Kathleen J.*
Social Science in Context: Historical, Sociological, and Global Perspectives — *Danell, Rickard*
Social Security for Dummies, 2d ed. — *Peterson, Jonathan*

Social Security Handbook 2015: Overview of Social Security Programs — *Social Security Administration*
Social Security Works! Why Social Security Isn't Going Broke and How Expanding It Will Help Us All — *Altman, Nancy J.*
y The Social Sex: A History of Female Friendship — *Yalom, Marilyn*
Social-Spatial Segregation: Concepts, Processes and Outcomes — *Lloyd, Christopher D.*
Social Theory and Regional Studies in the Global Age — *Arjomand, Said Amir*
Social Tragedy: The Power of Myth, Ritual, and Emotion in the New Media Ecology — *Baker, Stephanie Alice*
Social Trends in American Life: Findings from the General Social Survey since 1972 — *Marsden, Peter*
Social Unrest and American Military Bases in Turkey and Germany since 1945 — *Holmes, Amy Austin*
The Social Value of Drug Addicts: Uses of the Useless — *Singer, Merrill*
Social Work Practice with Veterans — *Dick, Gary L.*
The Social World of Intellectuals in the Roman Empire: Sophists, Philosophers, and Christians — *Eshelman, Kendra*
Socialising Children — *James, Allison*
The Socialist Car: Automobility in the Eastern Bloc — *Siegelbaum, Lewis H.*
A Socialist History of the French Revolution — *Jaures, Jean*
Sociality: New Directions — *Long, Nicholas J.*
Societe — *Helas, Alexander*
Societies under Occupation in World War II: Supply, Shortage, Hunger
Society in an Age of Plague — *Clark, Linda*
The Society of Genes — *Yanai, Itai*
The Society of the Crossed Keys — *Zweig, Stefan*
A Society of Young Women: Opportunities of Place, Power, and Reform in Saudi Arabia — *Le Renard, Amelie*
A Society of Young Women: Oppurtunities of Place, Power and Reform in Saudi Arabia — *Renard, Amelie Le*
Sociolinguistic Fieldwork — *Schilling, Natalie*
Sociolinguistics in Scotland — *Lawson, Robert*
Sociologica de Lima — *Capelo, Joaquin*
y The Sociology Book: Big Ideas Simply Explained — *Atkinson, Sam*
The Sociology Book: Big Ideas Simply Explained — *Hobbs, Mitchell*
Sociology & Empire: The Imperial Entanglements of a Discipline — *Steinmetz, George*
The Sociology of Military Science: Prospects for Postinstitutional Military Design — *Paparone, Chris*
The Sociology of Wind Bands: Amateur Music Between Cultural Domination and Autonomy — *Dubois, Vincent*
Sock Monkey into the Deep Woods — *Danner, Matt*
c Sock Monster (Illus. by Thieme, Elizabeth) — *Campbell, Stacey R.*
c The Sock Thief (Illus. by Gonzalez, Nana) — *Crespo, Ana*
Sock-Yarn Shawls II: 16 Patterns for Lace Knitting — *Lucas, Jen*
Sod Busting: How Families Made Farms on the 19th-Century Plains — *Danbom, David*
Sod Busting: How Families Made Farms on the 19th-Century Plains — *Danbom, David B.*
c The Soda Bottle School: A True Story of Recycling, Teamwork, and One Crazy Idea (Illus. by Darragh, Aileen) — *Kutner, Laura*
Soda Politics: Taking on Big Soda (and Winning). — *Nestle, Marion*
c Sofi and the Magic, Musical Mural/Sofi y el magico mural musical (Illus. by Dominguez, Maria) — *Ortiz, Raquel M.*
Sofrito — *Diederich, Phillippe*
Soft Circuits: Crafting e-Fashion with DIY Electronics — *Peppler, Kylie*
Soft Force: Women in Egypt's Islamic Awakening — *McLarney, Ellen Anne*
Softly, with Feeling: Joe Wilder and the Breaking of Barriers in American Music — *Berger, Edward*
Soil — *Kornegay, Jamie*
Soil (Read by Hutchinson, Brian). Audiobook Review — *Kornegay, Jamie*
Soixante-trois: La peur de la grande annee climacterique a la Renaissance — *Engammare, Max*
Sojourning for Freedom: Black Women, American Communism, and the Making of Black Left Feminism — *McDuffie, Erik S.*
Solar Express — *Modesitt, L.E., Jr.*

Solar Living Sourcebook, 14th ed. — *Schaeffer, John*
Soldier Girls: The Battles of Three Women at Home and at War (Read by Postel, Donna). Audiobook Review — *Thorpe, Helen*
The Soldier in Later Medieval England — *Bell, Adrian R.*
Soldier of Christ: The Life of Pope Pius XII — *Ventresca, Robert A.*
A Soldier on the Southern Front: The Classic Italian Memoir of World War I — *Lussu, Emilio*
Soldier, Sailor, Beggarman, Thief: Crime and the British Armed Services since 1914 — *Emsley, Clive*
Soldiering for Freedom: How the Union Army Recruited, Trained, and Deployed the U.S. Colored Troops — *Luke, Bob*
Soldiering in Britain and Ireland, 1750-1850: Men of Arms — *Kennedy, Catriona*
Soldiers out of Time — *White, Steve*
Soldiers' Stories: Military Women in Cinema and Television since World War II — *Tasker, Yvonne*
Solecism — *Ben-Oni, Rosebud*
Soleil's Star — *Bonner, Larry*
A Solemn Pleasure: To Imagine, Witness, and Write — *Pritchard, Melissa*
Solemn Pleasure: To Imagine, Witness, and Write — *Pritchard, Melissa*
Solidarity Ethics: Transformation in a Globalized World — *Peters, Rebecca Todd*
y Solitaire — *Oseman, Alice*
Solitude Creek — *Deaver, Jeffery*
Solo cuento VI — *Santos-Febres, Mayra*
The Solomon Curse — *Blake, Russell*
The Solomon Curse — *Cussler, Clive*
Solomon's Arrow — *Jennings, J. Dalton*
Solomon's Secret Arts: The Occult in the Age of Enlightenment — *Monod, Paul Kleber*
The Solution: A Blueprint for Change and Happiness — *Matta, William*
Solutions to Thirty-Eight Questions. Cistercian Studies, 253 — *Mayne, Kienzle*
Solutions to Thirty-Eight Questions — *Hildegard of Bingen*
y Solve a Crime (Illus. by Aleksic, Vladimir) — *Koll, Hilary*
Solve Common Teaching Challenges in Children with Autism: 8 Essential Strategies for Professionals and Parents — *Delmolino, Lara*
Solving for Y — *Barrows, Frederick*
c Solving the Puzzle Under the Sea: Marie Tharp Maps the Ocean Floor (Illus. by Colon, Raul) — *Burleigh, Robert*
Solving the Strategy Delusion: Mobilizing People and Realizing Distinctive Strategies — *Stigter, Marc*
Somalia in Transition Since 2006 — *Shay, Shaul*
y Some Assembly Required: The Not-So-Secret Life of a Transgender Teen — *Andrews, Arin*
Some Desperate Glory: The First World War the Poets Knew — *Egremont, Max*
y Some Fine Day (Read by Kowal, Mary Robinette). Audiobook Review — *Ross, Kat*
Some Here among Us — *Walker, Peter*
c Some Kind of Courage — *Gemeinhart, Dan*
Some Kind of Ending — *Parks, Conon*
y Some Kind of Magic — *Fogelin, Adrian*
y Some Kind of Normal — *Stone, Juliana*
Some Like It Scot — *Enoch, Suzanne*
Some Luck — *Smiley, Jane*
Some of the Best from Tor.com: 2014 — *Datlow, Ellen*
y Some of the Parts — *Barnaby, Hannah*
Some Other Town — *Collison, Elizabeth*
c Some Other War — *Newbery, Linda*
Some Talk of Being Human — *Farina, Laura*
y Some Things I've Lost (Illus. by Young, Cybele) — *Young, Cybele*
Somebody I Used to Know — *Bell, David*
y Somebody on This Bus Is Going to Be Famous — *Cheaney, J.B.*
Somebody's Children: The Politics of Transracial and Transnational Adoption — *Briggs, Laura*
The Someday File: Deuce Mora Series, vol. 1 — *Heller, Jean*
Someday Is Now: The Art of Corita Kent — *Berry, Ian*
Someone Is Watching (Read by Traister, Christina). Audiobook Review — *Fielding, Joy*
Someone Is Watching — *Fielding, Joy*
Someone to Watch over Me — *Sigurdardottir, Thora*
c Something about a Bear — *Morris, Jackie*
Something Extraordinary (Illus. by Clanton, Ben) — *Clanton, Ben*
c Something Extraordinary — *Clanton, Ben*

Something Must Be Done about Prince Edward County: A Family, a Virginia Town, a Civil Rights Battle — Green, Kristen
Something of a Peasant Paradise?: Comparing Rural Societies in Acadie and the Loudunais, 1604-1755 — Kennedy, Gregory M.W.
Something Rich and Strange: Selected Stories — Rash, Ron
c Something Sure Smells Around Here: Limericks (Illus. by Rowland, Andy) — Cleary, Brian P.
Something Sure Smells Around Here (Illus. by Rowland, Andy) — Cleary, Brian P.
c Something True — Scott, Kieran
c Something Wiki — Sutherland, Suzanne
Somethingtofoodabout — Thompson, Ahmir
Sometimes an Art: Nine Essays on History — Bailyn, Bernard
c Sometimes I Feel Like a Fox (Illus. by Daniel, Danielle) — Daniel, Danielle
Sometimes I Lie and Sometimes I Don't — Spiegel, Nadja
c Sometimes We Think You Are A Monkey (Illus. by Morstad, Julie) — Skibsrud, Johanna
c Sometimes You Barf (Illus. by Carlson, Nancy) — Carlson, Nancy
c Sometimes You Win--Sometimes You Learn (Illus. by Bjorkman, Steve) — Maxwell, John C.
Somewhere between War and Peace — Hill, James
y Somewhere There Is Still a Sun: A Memoir of the Holocaust — Gruenbaum, Michael
The Son Also Rises: Surnames and the History of Social Mobility — Clark, Gregory
The Son — Barslund, Charlotte
Son of a Son — Gould, Marilyn Amster
Son of Man — Mun-yol, Yi
Son of the Morning — Alder, Mark
c Sona and the Wedding Game (Illus. by Jaeggi, Yoshiko) — Sheth, Kashmira
y Sondheim: The Man Who Changed Musical Theater — Rubin, Susan Goldman
c Song for a Scarlet Runner — Hunt, Julie
c Song for a Summer Night: A Lullaby (Illus. by Leng, Qin) — Heidbreder, Robert
c Song for a Summer Night (Illus. by Leng, Qin) — Heidbreder, Robert
y A Song for Ella Grey — Almond, David
A Song for the Brokenhearted — Shaw, William
A Song for the Dying — MacBride, Stuart
The Song Machine: Inside the Hit Factory (Read by Graham, Dion). Audiobook Review — Seabrook, John
The Song Machine: Inside the Hit Factory — Seabrook, John
The Song of a Crooked River — Singh, Ajit
c The Song of Delphine (Illus. by Kraegel, Kenneth) — Kraegel, Kenneth
Song of Dewey Beard — Burnham, Philip
The Song of Hartgrove Hall — Solomons, Natasha
Song of Moving Water — Schmidt, Susan
c Song of Remembrance — Peskanov, Alexander
The Song of Sarah — Little, Charlene Pillow
A Song of Shadows — Connolly, John
The Song of Synth — Doubinsky, Seb
The Song of the Lark — Ronning, Kari A.
Song of the Shank — Allen, Jeffery Renard
The Song of the Shirt: The High Price of Cheap Garments, from Blackburn to Bangladesh — Seabrook, Jeremy
Song of the Wild — MacAfee, M.A.
The Song That Seduced Paris — Irish, Cindy
c The Song within My Heart (Illus. by Sapp, Allen) — Bouchard, David
The Songbirds of Pain — Kilworth, Garry
Songs of a Dead Dreamer and Grimscribe — Ligotti, Thomas
Songs of Seoul: An Ethnography of Voice and Voicing in Christian South Korea — Harkness, Nicholas
c The Songs of Stones River: A Civil War Novel — Gunderson, Jessica
Songs of the Factory: Pop Music, Culture, and Resistance — Korczynski, Marek
Sonia Delaunay — Montfort, Anne
c Sonia Sotomayor (Illus. by Dominguez, Angela) — Krull, Kathleen
Sonic Possible Worlds: Hearing the Continuum of Sound — Vogelin, Salome
Sonic Wind: The Story of John Paul Stapp and How a Renegade Doctor Became the Fastest Man on Earth — Ryan, Craig
Sonne, Mond und Venus: Visualisierungen astronomischen Wissens im fruhneuzeitlichen Rom — Feist, Ulrike

Sonnets for an Analyst — Schmitt, Gladys
Sono il fratello di XX — Jaeggy, Fleur
Sonoran Strange — Phillips, Logan
Sons + Fathers: An Anthology of Words and Images — Gilfillan, Kathy
The Sons of Sora — Tassi, Paul
Sons of the Dawn: A Basque Odyssey — Nuwer, Hank
Sons of the Father: George Washington and His Proteges — McDonald, Robert M.S.
Sons Without Fathers: What Every Mother Needs to Know — Allen, Mardi
c Sonya's Chickens (Illus. by Wahl, Phoebe) — Wahl, Phoebe
c Soon (Illus. by Benson, Patrick) — Knapman, Timothy
y Soon — Gleitzman, Morris
c Soon (Illus. by Benson, Patrick) — Knapman, Timothy
Soothe Your Soul: Meditations to Help You through Life's Painful Moments — Vredeveld, Margaret
Sophia — Bible, Michael
Sophia: Princess, Suffragette, Revolutionary — Anand, Anita
y Sophia's War: A Tale of Revolution — Avi
Sophie — Sargam, Jennie
Sophie and the Sibyl: A Victorian Romance — Duncker, Patricia
Sophie and the Sibyl — Duncker, Patricia
y Sophie Someone — Long, Hayley
c Sophie's Animal Parade (Illus. by Wish, Katia) — Dixon, Amy
c Sophie's Big Noisy Day Book — DK Publishing
Sophist Kings: Persians as Other in Herodotus — Provencal, Vernon L.
Sophocles: Four Tragedies: "Oedipus the King," "Aias," "Philoctetes," "Oedipus at Colonus" — Taplin, Oliver
Sophocles: Philoctetes — Schein, Seth L.
Sophocles: Philoctetes — Schein, S.L.
y Sophomore Year Is Greek to Me — Zeitlin, Meredith
y Sophomores and Other Oxymorons (Read by Goldstrom, Michael). Audiobook Review — Lubar, David
y Sophomores and Other Oxymorons — Lubar, David
c The Soprano's Last Song (Illus. by Bruno, Iacopo) — Adler, Irene
Sor Juana Ines De La Cruz: Selected Works — Grossman, Edith
The Sorcerer of the Wildeeps — Wilson, Kai Ashante
Sorcerer to the Crown — Cho, Zen
y Sorceress — Gray, Claudia
Sorrow Bound — Mark, David
The Sorrow Proper — Drager, Lindsey
Sorrows of a Century: Interpreting Suicide in New Zealand, 1900-2000 — Weaver, John C.
Sorrow's Point — DeVor, Danielle
Sorry about That: The Language of Public Apology — Battistella, Edwin L.
Sorry I Don't Dance: Why Men Refuse to Move — Craig, Maxine Leeds
c Sorry I'm Not Sorry — Rue, Nancy
c The Sorta Sisters — Fogelin, Adrian
Sorting Out Catholicism: A Brief History of the New Ecclesial Movements — Faggioli, Massimo
SOS: Poems, 1961-2013 — Baraka, Amiri
The Soteriology of James Ussher: The Act and Object of Saving Faith — Snoddy, Richard
Sottsass — Thome, Philippe
The Soul Continuum — West-Bulford, Simon
Soul External: Rediscovering The Great Blue Heron — Semken, Steven H.
Soul Food Love: Healthy Recipes Inspired by One Hundred Years of Cooking in a Black Family — Randall, Alice
Soul Food — Miller, Adrian
Soul Food Odyssey — Tyson, Stephanie L.
Soul Machine: The Invention of the Modern Mind — Makari, George
Soul Mates — Little, John R.
Soul Mothers' Wisdom — Freedson, Bette J.
y The Soul of an Octopus: A Surprising Exploration into the Wonder of Consciousness (Read by Montgomery, Sy). Audiobook Review — Montgomery, Sy
y The Soul of an Octopus: A Surprising Exploration into the Wonder of Consciousness — Montgomery, Sy
The Soul of Anime: Collaborative Creativity and Japan's Media Success Story — Condry, Ian
The Soul of Discretion — Hill, Susan
The Soul of Shame: Retelling the Stories We Believe about Ourselves — Thompson, Curt
Soul of the Fire — Pattison, Eliot
The Soul of the Marionette: A Short Inquiry into Human Freedom — Gray, John

The Soul of the World — Scruton, Roger
Soul Repair: Recovering from Moral Injury After War — Brock, Rita Nakashima
The Soul Searcher's Handbook: The Modern Girl's Guide to the New Age World — Mildon, Emma
Soul Serenade: Rhythm, Blues and Coming of Age through Vinyl — Ollison, Rashod
Soul Splitting, vol. 1 — Flemming, LeRoy
Soul Unsung: Reflections on the Band in Black Popular Music — Le Gendre, Kevin
Soul, World, and Idea. An Interpretation of Plato's Republic and Phaedo — Sherman, Daniel
Soul Writer — Brooks, Leslie
Soulbound — Callihan, Kristen
Soulmate — Lowell, D.L.
SoulMating: The Secret to Finding Everlasting Love and Passion — Kaplan, Basha
Soulminder — Zahn, Timothy
y Soulprint — Miranda, Megan
SoulServe — Wilson, Robert S.
y Soulshifter — Pietron, Barbara
Soumission — Flammarion, Michel Houllebecq
Soumission — Houellebecq, Michel
c Sound — Lawrence, Ellen
y The Sound — Alderson, Sarah
Sound and Safe: A History of Listening behind the Wheel — Bijsterveld, Karin
Sound Communication in Fishes — Ladich, Friedrich
Sound Intentions: The Workings of Rhyme in Nineteenth-Century Poetry — McDonald, Peter
Sound Man: A Life Recording Hits with the Rolling Stones, the Who, Led Zeppelin, the Eagles, Eric Clapton, the Faces (Read by Vance, Simon). Audiobook Review — Johns, Glyn
y Sound — Duncan, Alexandra
The Sound of Glass — White, Karen
The Sound of Gravel: A Memoir — Wariner, Ruth
c The Sound of Life and Everything — Dolzer, Krista Van
c The Sound of Life and Everything — Van Dolzer, Krista
The Sound of Music FAQ: All That's Left to Know About Maria, the Von Trapps, and Our Favorite Things — Monush, Barry
The Sound of Music Story: How a Beguiling Young Novice, a Handsome Austrian Captain, and Ten Singing Von Trapp Children Inspired the Most Beloved Film of All Time (Read by Summerer, Eric Michael). Audiobook Review — Santopietro, Tom
The Sound of Music Story: How a Beguiling Young Novice, a Handsome Austrian Captain, and Ten Singing Von Trapp Children Inspired the Most Beloved Film of All Time — Santopietro, Tom
The Sound of Our Steps — Matalon, Ronit
The Sound of the Liturgy: How Words Work in Worship — Hammond, Cally
c The Sound of Thunder (Illus. by Hicks, Faith Erin) — Torres, J. (b. 1969-)
The Sound of Water — Linden, Joshua
c The Sound of Whales — Thomson, Kerr
Sound Play: Video Games and the Musical Imagination — Cheng, William
y Sound: Salvage, Book 2 — Duncan, Alexandra
Sound, Speech, Music in Soviet and Post-Soviet Cinema — Kaganovsky, Lilya
Sounding Out Heritage: Cultural Politics and the Social Practice of Quan Ho Folk Song in Northern Vietnam — Meeker, Lauren
Sounding the Modern Woman: The Songstress in Chinese Cinema — Ma, Jean
y Soundless — Mead, Richelle
Sounds Like Me: My Life (So Far) in Song — Bareilles, Sara
c Sounds of the Savanna — Jennings, Terry Catasus
The Sounds of the Silents in Britain — Brown, Julie
Sounds of War: Music in the United States during World War II — Fauser, Annegret
c Sounds (Illus. by Parker, Ant) — Mitton, Tony
The Soup Cleanse: A Revolutionary Detox from Nourishing Soups and Healing Broths from the Founders of Soupure — Blatteis, Angela
Soup for Syria: Recipes to Celebrate Our Shared Humanity — Massaad, Barbara Abdeni
The Sources of Social Power, vol. 1: A History of Power from the Beginning to AD 1760 — Mann, Michael
The Sources of Social Power, vol. 2: The Rise of Classes and Nation-States, 1760-1914 — Mann, Michael
The Sources of Social Power, vol. 3: Global Empires and Revolution, 1890-1945 — Mann, Michael

The Sources of Social Power, vol. 4: Globalizations, 1945-2011 — Mann, Michael
c Souris Cendrillon — Smallman, Steve
c Souris, tu viens au cinema? (Illus. by Bond, Felicia) — Numeroff, Laura
Sous Chef: 24 Hous on the Line — Gibney, Michael
c South Africa — Senker, Cath
South Africa: Inventing the Nation — Johnston, Alexander
c South American Animals: Toucans — Murray, Julie
y South and Central Asia — Harris, Tim
South by Southwest: Katherine Anne Porter and the Burden of Texas History — Stout, Janis
South Carolina Fire-Eater: The Life of Laurence Massillon Keitt, 1824-1864 — Merchant, Holt
The South China Sea: The Struggle for Power in Asia — Hayton, Bill
y South Korea — Somervill, Barbara A.
South of Nowhere — Koenig, Minerva
South of the Clouds: Travels in Southwest China — Porter, Bill
South Pacific: The Complete Book and Lyrics of the Broadway Musical — Rodgers, Richard
South Pass: Gateway to a Continent — Bagley, Will
South Side Girls: Growing Up in the Great Migration — Chatelain, Marcia
South Sudan: A Slow Liberation — Thomas, Edward
South toward Home: Travels in Southern Literature — Eby, Margaret
South Toward Home: Travels in Southern Literature — Margaret, Eby
Southeast Foraging: 120 Wild and Flavorful Edibles from Angelica to Wild Plums — Bennett, Chris
Southeaster — Miles, Jon Lindsay
The Southern African Historical Society: 25th Biennial Conference "Unsettling Stories and Unstable Subjects"
The Southern Exodus to Mexico: Migration across the Borderlands after the American Civil War — Wahlstrom, Todd W.
The Southern Flank of NATO, 1951-1959: Military Strategy or Political Stabilization — Chourchoulis, Dionysios
The Southern Garden Poetry Society: Literary Culture and Social Memory in Guangdong — Honey, David B.
The Southern Manifesto: Massive Resistance and the Fight to Preserve Segregation — Day, John Kyle
Southern Provisions: The Creation and Revival of a Cuisine — Shields, David S.
Southern Rites — Laub, Gillian
Southern Rocky Mountain Wildflowers — Robertson, Leigh
Southern Soups and Stews: More Than 75 Recipes from Burgoo and Gumbo to Etouffee and Fricassee — McDermott, Nancie
Southern Women Novelists and the Civil War: Trauma and Collective Memory in the American Literary Tradition since 1861 — Talley, Sharon
Southerner's Cookbook: Recipes, Wisdom, and Stories — DiBenedetto, David
Southside Provisional — Conway, Kieran
c The Southwest — Bartley, Niccole
Souvenir Nation: Relics, Keepsakes, and Curios from the Smithsonian's National Museum of American History — Bird, William L., Jr.
Souveraine Magnifique — Ebode, Eugene
Souveranitat-Feindschaft-Masse: Theatralikund Rhetorikdes Politischen in den Dramen Christian Dietrich Grabbes — Maes, Sientje
Sovereign Feminine: Music and Gender in Eighteenth-Century Germany — Head, Matthew
Sovereign Screens: Aboriginal Media on the Canadian West Coast — Dowell, Kristin L.
Sovereign Sugar: Industry and Environment in Hawai'i — MacLennan, Carol A.
Sovereignty Betrayed: Imperium Proditum — Morrison, Richard T.
Soviet Bus Stops — Herswig, Christopher
Soviet Consumer Culture in the Brezhnev Era — Chernyshova, Natalya
The Soviet Counterinsurgency in the Western Borderlands — Statiev, Alexander
Soviet Heroic Poetry in Context: Folklore or Fakelore — Ziolkowski, Margaret
Soviet Jews in World War II: Fighting, Witnessing, Remembering — Murav, Harriet
Soviet Postal Censorship during World War II — Wallen, Per-Christian
The Soviet Theater: A Documentary History — Senelick, Laurence

Sowing the Seeds of Victory: American Gardening Programs of World War I — Hayden-Smith, Rose
Sowing the Wind — Linton, Eliza Lynn
Soziale Ungleichheit im Visier. Images von 'Armut' und 'Reichtum' in West und Ost nach 1945
Sozialgeschichte des Todes
Sozialstaat und Gesellschaft: Das Deutsche Kaiserreich in Europa — Kott, Sandrine
c Space and Other Flying Machines — Channing, Margot
Space and Self in Early Modern European Cultures — Sabean, David Warren
c Space Boy and His Dog (Illus. by Neubecker, Robert) — Regan, Dian Curtis
c Space Boy and His Sister Dog (Illus. by Neubecker, Robert) — Regan, Dian Curtis
c Space Boy and the Space Pirate — Regan, Dian Curtis
c Space Case — Gibbs, Stuart
c Space Dog (Illus. by Grey, Mini) — Grey, Mini
c Space Dumplins (Illus. by Thompson, Craig) — Thompson, Craig
c Space Exploration: Science, Technology, and Engineering — Mara, Wil
Space, Hope and Brutalism: English Architecture, 1945-1975 — Harwood, Elaine
c Space Hostages — McDougall, Sophia
Space in the Medieval West: Places, Territories, and Imagined Geographies — Cohen, Meredith
y Space Junk: The Dangers of Polluting Earth's Orbit — Young, Karen Romano
Space of Detention: The Making of a Transnational Gang Crisis between Los Angeles and San Salvador — Zilberg, Elana
Space, Place and Identity in Northern Anatolia — Bekker-Nielsen, Tonnes
c Space Song Rocket Ride (Illus. by Sim, David) — Scribens, Sunny
c Space Taxi: Archie Takes Flight — Mass, Wendy
The Space That Remains: Reading Latin Poetry in Late Antiquity — Pelttari, Aaron
Space Traveler — Grossberg, Benjamin S.
c Spaced Out — Gibbs, Stuart
Spacefarers: Images of Astronauts and Cosmonauts in the Heroic Era of Spaceflight — Neufeld, Michael J.
c Spacejackers — Powell, Huw
Spaces and Places in Central and Eastern Europe: Historical Trends and Perspectives — Horvath, Gyula
Spaces of Aid: How Cars, Compounds and Hotels Shape Humanitarianism — Smirl, Lisa
Spaceship Earth in the Environmental Age 1960-1990 — Hohler, Sabine
c Spaceships — Murray, Julie
SpaceX and Tesla Motors Engineer Elon Musk — Doeden, Matt
A Spacious Life: Memoir of a Meditator — Doumani, Narissa
c Spaghetti Smiles (Illus. by Harrington, David) — Sorenson, Margo
c The Spaghetti Yeti (Illus. by Pankhurst, Kate) — Pankhurst, Kate
Spain: The Center of the World, 1519-1682 — Goodwin, Robert
Spain: The Centre of the World 1519-1682 — Goodwin, Robert
Spain: The Centre of the World, 1519-1682 — Goodwin, Robert
Spain: The Centre of the World, 1519-1862 — Goodwin, Robert
Spaniens Stadte - Moderne Urbanitat seit 2000 Jahren (II): Mittelalter und Fruhe Neuzeit
The Spanish Arcadia: Sheep Herding, Pastoral Discourse, and Ethnicity in Early Modern Spain — Irigoyen-Garcia, Javier
The Spanish Atlantic World in the Eighteenth Century: War and the Bourbon Reforms, 1713-1796 — Kuethe, Allan J.
Spanish Cedar — Adams, Christopher Robin
Spanish Female Writers and the Freethinking Press, 1879-1926 — Arkinstall, Christine
Spanish in the USA — Fuller, Janet M.
Spanish Milan: A City within the Empire, 1535-1706 — D'Amico, Stefano
The Spanish Tragedy — Neill, Michael
c Spare Dog Parts (Illus. by Spires, Ashley) — Hughes, Alison
Spare Not the Brave: The Special Activities Group in Korea — Kiper, Richard L.
Spare Parts: Four Undocumented Teenagers, One Ugly Robot, and the Battle for the American Dream — Davis, Joshua
c Spare Parts (Illus. by Emberley, Ed) — Emberley, Ed

c Spare Parts (Illus. by Emberley, Ed) — Emberley, Rebecca
Spark (Read by Brick, Scott). Audiobook Review — Twelve Hawks, John
Spark (Read by Brick, Scott). Audiobook Review — Hawks, John Twelve
Spark Joy — Rondo, Marie
Spark Rising — Corcino, Kate
c Sparkers — Glewwe, Eleanor
c Sparkling Princess Opposites (Illus. by Perrett, Lisa) — Perrett, Lisa
c The Sparrow and the Trees (Illus. by Detwiler, Susan) — Chriscoe, Sharon
Sparrow Hill Road — McGuire, Seanan
Spartan — Manfredi, Valerio Massimo
Sparta's German Children: The Ideal of Ancient Sparta in the Royal Prussian Cadet Corps, 1818-1920, and in National Socialist Elite Schools (the Napolas), 1933-1945 — Roche, Helen
Spatial Justice and the Irish Crisis — Kearns, Gerry
Spawn of Mars (Illus. by Wood, Wallace) — Feldstein, Al
y Speak a Word for Freedom: Women against Slavery — Willen, Janet
Speak — Hall, Louisa
Speak Easy — Valente, Catherynne M.
Speak — Hall, Louisa
Speak Now: Marriage Equality on Trial: The Story of Hollingsworth v. Perry — Yoshino, Kenji
Speak of the Devil — Holding, Elisabeth Sanxay
Speak the Dead — McKenzie, Grant
y Speak Up! A Guide to Having Your Say and Speaking Your Mind — Bondy, Halley
Speakers' Corner at Simon Balle School — Syme, Janet
Speakers of the Dead — Sanders, J. Aaron
Speaking in Bones — Reichs, Kathy
Speaking of Flowers: Student Movements and the Making and Remembering of 1968 in Military Brazil — Langland, Victoria
Speaking Our Minds — Scott-Phillips, Thom
c Speaking Up for Women: Clarina Nichols and the World's First Women's Rights Campaign — Eickhoff, Diane
Speaking with Nature: Awakening to the Deep Wisdom of the Earth — Ingerman, Sandra
Speaking with the People's Voice: How Presidents Invoke Public Opinion — Mehltretter, Jeffrey P.
The Spear of Longinus — Levocz, Reynold J.
c Spearfishing — Hamilton, S.L.
c Special Deliver (Illus. by Cordell, Matthew) — Stead, Philip C.
c Special Delivery (Illus. by Cordell, Matthew) — Stead, Philip C.
Special Deluxe: A Memoir of Life and Cars (Read by Young, Neil). Audiobook Review — Young, Neil
c Special Edition 2015 of Ripley's Believe It Or Not! — Ripley's Entertainment Inc.
A Special Hell: Institutional Life in Alberta's Eugenic Years — Malacrida, Claudia
Special Interest Society: How Membership-Based Organizations Shape America — Hudson, James R.
Special Needs and Legal Entitlement: The Essential Guide to Getting Out of the Maze — Nettleton, Melinda
c The Specific Ocean (Illus. by Maurey, Katty) — Maclear, Kyo
Specimen: Stories — Kovalyova, Irina
c Specs for Rex (Illus. by Ismail, Yasmeen) — Ismail, Yasmeen
c Specs for Rex — Ismail, Yasmeen
y Spectaccolo: A Tale of Darkness and Light — Catlin, Christine
Spectacle and the City: Chinese Urbanities in Art and Popular Culture — Jeroen de Kloet
The Spectacle of Skill: New and Selected Writings of Robert Huges — Hughes, Robert
The Spectacle of Skill: New and Selected Writings of Robert Hughes — Hughes, Robert
Spectacle: The Astonishing Life of Ota Benga (Read by Turpin, Bahni). Audiobook Review — Newkirk, Pamela
Spectacle: The Astonishing Life of Ota Benga — Newkirk, Pamela
Spectacles of Reform: Theater and Activism in Nineteenth-Century America — Hughes, Amy E.
The Spectacular Few: Prisoner Radicalization and the Evolving Terrorist Threat — Hamm, Mark S.
Spectacular Girls: Media Fascination and Celebrity Culture — Projansky, Sarah

A Spectacular Leap: Black Women Athletes in Twentieth-Century America — *Lansbury, Jennifer H.*

Spectacular Mexico: Design, Propaganda, and the 1968 Olympics — *Castaneda, Luis M.*

Spectacular Performances: Essays on Theatre, Imagery, Books, and Selves in Early Modern England — *Orgel, Stephen*

c A Spectacular Selection of Sea Critters: Concrete Poems (Illus. by Wertz, Michael) — *Franco, Betsy*

c Spectacular Spots (Illus. by Stockdale, Susan) — *Stockdale, Susan*

Spectacular Wickedness: Sex, Race, and Memory in Storyville, New Orleans — *Landau, Emily Epstein*

Spectateurs de paroles! Deliberation democratique et theatre a Athenes a l'e'poque classique — *Villaceque, N.*

The Spectators (Illus. by Hussenot, Victor) — *Hussenot, Victor*

A Specter of Justice — *De Castrique, Mark*

The Specter of "The People": Urban Poverty in Northeast China — *Cho, Mun Young*

The Spectral Wilderness — *Bendorf, Oliver*

Spectrometric Identification of Organic Compounds, 8th ed. — *Silverstein, Robert M.*

Spectrum of Mind: An Inquiry into the Principles of the Mind and the Meaning of Life — *Yang, J. Michael*

Speculative Markets: Drug Circuits and Derivative Life in Nigeria — *Peterson, Kristin*

Speech Analysis in Financial Markets — *Mayew, William J.*

Speech communities — *Morgan, Marcyliena H.*

Speech Matters: On Lying, Morality, and the Law — *Shiffrin, Seana Valentine*

The Speechwriter: A Brief Education in Politics (Read by Yen, Jonathan). Audiobook Review — *Swaim, Barton*

The Speechwriter: A Brief Education in Politics — *Swaim, Barton*

The Speechwriter — *Swaim, Barton*

Speed Brewing: Techniques and Recipes for Fast-Fermenting Beers, Ciders, Meads, and More — *Izett, Mary*

Speed Kings: The 1932 Winter Olympics and the Fastest Men in the World — *Bull, Andy*

Speed Limits: Where Time Went and Why We Have So Little Left — *Taylor, Mark C.*

Speer: Hitler's Architect — *Kitchen, Martin*

y The Spell Bind (Illus. by Halpin, Abigail) — *Brauner, Barbara*

y Spelled — *Schow, Betsy*

Spells, Images, and Mandalas: Tracing the Evolution of Esoteric Buddhist Rituals — *Shinohara, Koichi*

Spenser's Images of Life — *Lewis, C.S.*

Spenser's Ruins and the Art of Recollection — *Helfer, Rebecca*

c The Sphere of Septimus — *Rose, Simon*

The Sphinx: Franklin Roosevelt, the Isolationists, and the Road to World War II — *Wapshott, Nicholas*

Sphinx — *Garreta, Anne*

c Spic-and-Span! Lillian Gilbreth's Wonder Kitchen (Illus. by Parkins, David) — *Kulling, Monica*

Spice — *Suzanne, Lilah*

c The Spider (Illus. by Gravel, Elise) — *Gravel, Elise*

c Spider — *Bodden, Valerie*

c The Spider (Illus. by Gravel, Elise) — *Gravel, Elise*

c The Spider Ring — *Harwell, Andrew*

c Spider Sandwiches (Illus. by Hendra, Sue) — *Freedman, Claire*

Spider Woman's Daughter — *Hillerman, Anne*

c Spidermania: Friends on the Web

c Spidermania: Friends on the Web (Illus. by Kunkel, Dennis) — *Siy, Alexandra*

c Spiders — *Murray, Laura K.*

c Spiders and Bugs around the World — *Martin, Claudia*

c Spiders: Deadly Predators — *Llewellyn, Claire*

Spider's Trap — *Estep, Jennifer*

Spiele und Machtspiele in der Vormoderne. Politische und soziale Aspekte von Geselligkeit in hiofischen Gesellschaften — *Kopp, Vanina*

Spies and Shuttles: NASA's Secret Relationships with the DOD and CIA — *David, James E.*

Spies In Our Midst — *Reynolds, L.M.*

Spill Simmer Falter Wither — *Baume, Sara*

Spilt Milk: A Collection of Stories — *Cassidy, D.K.*

Spinglish: The Definitive Dictionary of Deliberately Deceptive Language — *Cerf, Christopher*

Spinglish: The Definitive Dictionary of Deliberately Deceptive Language — *Beard, Henry*

y Spinning Starlight — *Lewis, R.C.*

Spinoza Contra Phenomenology: French Rationalism from Cavailles to Deleuze — *Peden, Knox*

Spinoza for our Time: Politics and Postmodernity — *Negri, Antonio*

y Spinoza: The Outcast Thinker — *Lehmann, Devra*

Spinoza's Metaphysics: Substance and Thought — *Fraser, Steve*

Spinster: Making a Life of One's Own (Read by Bolick, Kate). Audiobook Review — *Bolick, Kate*

y Spinster: Making a Life of One's Own — *Bolick, Kate*

The Spinster's Guide to Scandalous Behavior — *McQuiston, Jennifer*

y The Spiral Notebook: The Aurora Theater Shooter and the Epidemic of Mass Violence Committed by American Youth — *Singular, Stephen*

The Spiralized Kitchen: Transform Your Vegetables into Fresh and Surprising Meals — *Bilderback, Leslie*

Spirals in Time: The Secret Life and Curious Afterlife of Seashells — *Scales, Helen*

The Spirit: A Celebration of 75 Years — *Eisner, Will*

Spirit and Trauma: A Theology of Remaining — *Rambo, Shelly*

y Spirit Level — *Harvey, Sarah N.*

The Spirit Moves West: Korean Missionaries in America — *Kim, Rebecca Y.*

The Spirit of '74: How the American Revolution Began — *Raphael, Ray*

The Spirit of 1976: Commerce, Community, and the Politics of Commemoration — *Gordon, Tammy S.*

The Spirit of Adoption: Writers on Religion, Adoption, Faith, and More — *Mock, Melanie Springer*

The Spirit of an Activist: The Life and Work of I. DeQuincey Newman — *Logan, Sadye L.M.*

The Spirit of Attack: Fighter Pilot Stories — *Gordon, Bruce*

c The Spirit of Christmas: A Giving Tradition (Illus. by Cockroft, Jason) — *Benson, Nicky*

The Spirit of Flamenco: From Spain to New Mexico — *Chavez, Nicolasa*

The Spirit of Grace: A Guide for Study and Devotion — *McGrath, Alister E.*

The Spirit of New York: Defining Events in the Empire State's History — *Dearstyne, Bruce W.*

The Spirit of Saint Francis: Inspiring Words from Pope Francis — *Francis, Pope*

c The Spirit of the Sea (Illus. by Lim, Hwei) — *Hainnu, Rebecca*

Spirit of the Valley — *Shoup, Jane*

Spirit Talker: The Legend of Nakosis — *Coles, Tom*

y Spirit Training: A Book of Ethics for Black Teens — *Conwill, William L.*

c Spirit Week Showdown (Illus. by Kaban, Eda) — *Allen, Crystal*

y The Spiritglass Charade — *Gleason, Colleen*

The Spirits: A Guide to Modern Cocktailing — *Godwin, Richard*

y Spirit's Key — *Cohn, Edith*

Spirits of the Rockies: Reasserting an Indigenous Presence in Banff National Park — *Mason, Courtney W.*

Spirits Rejoice! Jazz and American Religion — *Bivins, Jason C.*

The Spirit's Tether: Family, Work, and Religion among American Catholics — *Konieczny, Mary Ellen*

The Spiritual Awakening Guide: Kundalini, Psychic Abilities, and the Conditioned Layers of Reality — *Shutan, Mary Mueller*

The Spiritual Child: The New Science on Parenting for Health and Lifelong Thriving — *Miller, Lisa*

Spiritual Companioning: A Guide to Protestant Theology and Practice — *Smucker, Marcus G.*

Spiritual Currency in Northeast Brazil — *King, Lindsey*

Spiritual Defiance: Building a Beloved Community of Resistance — *Meyers, Robin*

The Spiritual Expansion of Medieval Latin Christendom: The Asian Missions — *Ryan, James D.*

Spiritual Leadership for Challenging Times: Presidential Addresses from the Leadership Conference of Women Religious — *Sanders, Annmarie*

The Spiritual Vision of Frank Buchman — *Boobbyer, Philip*

y Spirituality in Young Adult Literature: The Last Taboo — *Campbell, Patty*

Spirituality of Gratitude: The Unexpected Blessings of Thankfulness — *Kang, Joshua Choonmin*

The Spirituality of the Second Vatican Council — *O'Collins, Gerald*

Spirituality Seeking Theology — *Haight, Roger*

c Spit and Sticks: A Chimney Full of Swifts (Illus. by Gsell, Nicole) — *Evans, Marilyn Grohoske*

c A Splash of Red: The Life and Art of Horace Pippin — *Sweet, Melissa*

c Splat the Cat and the Hotshot (Illus. by Eberz, Robert) — *Scotton, Rob*

c Splat the Cat: Christmas Countdown (Illus. by Scotton, Rob) — *Scotton, Rob*

c Splat the Cat: I Scream for Ice Cream (Illus. by Eberz, Robert) — *Scotton, Rob*

c Splat the Cat: Splat and Seymour, Best Friends Forevermore (Illus. by Eberz, Robert) — *Scotton, Rob*

Splendid Cities: Colour Your Way to Calm (Illus. by Chadwick, Alice) — *Goodwin, Rosie*

A Splendid Savage: The Restless Life of Frederick Russell Burnham — *Kemper, Steve*

The Splendid Things We Planned: A Family Portrait — *Bailey, Blake*

The Splendors and Miseries of Ruling Alone. Encounters with Monarchy from Archaic Greece to the Hellenistic Mediterranean — *Luraghi, Nino*

Splinter the Silence — *McDermid, Val*

Splintered Soul — *Dean, Erika Lucke*

Split — *Dispenza, Mary*

Split Screen Korea: Shin Sang-ok and Postwar Cinema — *Chung, Steven*

Split Screen Korea: Shin Sang-ok and Postwar Cinema — *Steven Chung*

Split Season, 1981: Fernandomania, the Bronx Zoo, and the Strike That Saved Baseball — *Katz, Jeff*

Splitting an Order — *Kooser, Ted*

Spoiled Brats: Stories — *Rich, Simon*

Spoils of Olympus: By the Sword — *Kachel, Christian*

Spoils of Truce: Corruption and State-Building in Postwar Lebanon — *Leenders, Reinoud*

Spoils of Victory — *Connell, John A.*

Spokojnie, to tylko rewolucja — *Beylin, Marek*

c Spook the Halloween Cat (Illus. by Norman, Dean) — *Norman, Dean*

Spooky Action at a Distance: The Phenomenon That Reimagines Space and Time--and What It Means for Black Holes, the Big Bang, and Theories of Everything — *Musser, George*

c Spooky House (Illus. by Fukuoka, Aki) — *Rippin, Sally*

c Spooky Pookie — *Boynton, Sandra*

c Spooky & Spookier: Four American Ghost Stories (Illus. by Diaz, Viviana) — *Haskins, Lori*

A Spool of Blue Thread (Read by Farr, Kimberly). Audiobook Review — *Tyler, Anne*

A Spool of Blue Thread — *Tyler, Anne*

The Spoonflower Handbook: A DIY Guide to Designing Fabric, Wallpaper and Gift Wrap — *Fraser, Stephen*

A Sport and a Pastime — *Salter, James*

Sport and Christianity: A Sign of the Times in the Light of Faith — *Lixey, Kevin*

Sport and the Shaping of Italian-American Identity — *Gems, Gerald R.*

Sport and the Shaping of Italian American Identity — *Gems, Gerald R.*

Sport, Gender and Power: The Rise of Roller Derby — *Pavlidis, Adele*

Sport im Abseits: Die Geschichte der Judischen Sportbewegung im Nationalsozialistischen Deutschland — *Wahlig, Henry*

Sport in Ireland, 1600-1840 — *Kelly, James*

c Sport-O-Rama (Illus. by Tardif, Benoit) — *Tardif, Benoit*

Sport, Spectacle, and NASCAR Nation: Consumption and the Cultural Politics of Neoliberalism — *Newman, Joshua I.*

Sporting Gender: Women Athletes and Celebrity-Making during China's National Crisis, 1931-45 — *Gao, Yunxiang*

c Sports Horses — *Turnbull, Stephanie*

c Sports Illustrated Kids: Football Cookbooks — *Jorgensen, Katrina*

y Sports Nutrition — *MacKay, Jennifer*

Sports, Peacebuilding and Ethics — *Johnston, Linda M.*

c Sports Top Tens — *Donovan, Sandy*

c SportsZone: Speed Machines — *Scheff, Matt*

c A Spot of Bother (Illus. by Cabban, Vanesa) — *Emmett, Jonathan*

c Spot, the Cat (Illus. by Cole, Henry) — *Cole, Henry*

c Spotlight on Space Science

y Spotlight on Sunny — *Stainton, Keris*

c Spots in a Box (Illus. by Ward, Helen) — Ward, Helen
The Spotted Hyena: A Study of Predation and Social Behavior — Kruuk, Hans
SPQR: A History of Ancient Rome — Beard, Mary
Spring 1865: The Closing Campaigns of the Civil War — Jamieson, Perry D.
Spring — Jackson, Vina
The Spring Bride — Gracie, Anne
The Spring Bride — Grade, Anne
Spring Chicken — Gifford, Bill
Spring Chicken: Stay Young Forever (or Die Trying). — Gifford, Bill
Spring Remains — Kallentoft, Mons
c Spring Walk (Illus. by Snow, Virginia Brimhall) — Snow, Virginia Brimhall
c Spring's Sparkle Sleepover (Illus. by Pooler, Paige) — Allen, Elise
c Springtime Dance (Illus. by Hopkins, Kimberly) — Smallkin, Valerie Leonhart
c Sprout Street Neighbors: Five Stories (Illus. by Alter, Anna) — Alter, Anna
The Sprouted Kitchen Bowl and Spoon: Simple and Inspired Whole Foods Recipes to Savor and Share — Forte, Hugh
The Sprouted Kitchen Bowl and Spoon: Simple and Inspired Whole Foods Recipes to Savor and Share — Forte, Sara
Spuntino: Comfort Food — Norman, Russell
A Spy among Friends: Kim Philby and the Great Betrayal — Macintyre, Ben
c Spy Camp — Gibbs, Stuart
Spy Games — Brookes, Adam
c Spy Guy: The Not-So-Secret Agent (Illus. by Santoso, Charles) — Young, Jessica
The Spy House — Dunn, Matthew
A Spy in the Archive: A Memoir of Cold War Russia — Fitzpatrick, Sheila
The Spy on the Tennessee Walker — Peterson, Linda Lee
c Spy School — Gibbs, Stuart
Spy Secrets That Can Save Your Life: A Former CIA Officer Reveals Safety and Survival Techniques To Keep You and Your Family Protected — Hanson, Jason
The Spy Who Knew Nothing — Boland, John C.
The Spy with 29 Names: The Story of the Second World War's Most Audacious Double Agent — Webster, Jason
Spying for the People: Mao's Secret Agents, 1949-1967 — Schoenhals, Michael
c Spymaster — Chancellor, Deborah
The Spy's Son — Denson, Bryan
The Spy's Son: The True Story of the Highest-Ranking CIA Officer Ever Convicted of Espionage and the Son He Trained to Spy for Russia — Benson, Bryan
The Squandered — Putnam, David
Squandering America's Future: Why ECE Policy Matters for Equality, Our Economy, and Our Children — Ochshorn, Susan
The Square — Choe, In-hun
Square Affair — Holt, Timmothy J.
c Square Cat ABC (Illus. by Schoonmaker, Elizabeth) — Schoonmaker, Elizabeth
Square Wave — de Silva, Mark
c Squares (Illus. by Yonezu, Yusuke) — Yonezu, Yusuke
Squatters into Citizens: The 1961 Bukit Ho Swee Fire and the Making of Modern Singapore — Loh, Kah Seng
A Squatter's Republic: Land and the Politics of Monopoly in California, 1850-1900 — Shelton, Tamara Venit
c Squid Kid the Magnificent (Illus. by LaMarca, Luke) — Berry, Lynne
c Squishy Squashy Birds (Illus. by Van Wijk, Carl) — Munday, Alicia
y Srsly Hamlet — Shakespeare, William
St. Anne in Renaissance Music: Devotion and Politics — Anderson, Michael Alan
St. Catherine of Alexandria in Renaissance Roman Art: Case Studies in Patronage — Stollhans, Cynthia
St. Elmo's Ghost — Schmid, Vernon
St. Francis of America: How a Thirteenth-Century Friar Became America's Most Popular Saint — Appelbaum, Patricia
St George: A Saint for All — Riches, Samantha
St. John and the Victorians — Wheeler, Michael
St. Marks Is Dead: The Many Lives of America's Hippest Street — Calhoun, Ada
St. Nic, Inc. — Staley, S.R.

St. Paul: The Apostle We Love to Hate — Armstrong, Karen
St Paul: The Misunderstood Apostle — Armstrong, Karen
St Petersburg: Shadows of the Past — Kelly, Catriona
The St. Simons Island Club: A John Le Brun Novel — Monahan, Brent
Staat, Gesellschaft und Demokratisierung. Luxemburg im Kurzen 20. Jahrhundert
Staat und Politische Bildung: Von der "Zentrale fur Heimatdienst" zur "Bundeszentrale fur Politische Bildung" — Hentges, Gudrun
Staatsaktion im Wunderland: Oper und Festspiel als Medien politischer Reprasentation, 1890-1930
Stability of Functional Equations in Random Normed Spaces — Cho, Yeol Je
Stad i rorelse: Stadsomvandlingen och striderna om Haga och Christiania — Thorn, Hakan
Stadtentwicklung im Doppelten Berlin: Zeitgenossenschaft und Erinnerungsorte — Schlusche, Gunter
Stage Designers in Early Twentieth-Century America: Artists, Activists, Cultural Critics — Essin, Christin
Stagecoach Robberies in California: A Complete Record, 1856-1913 — Wilson, R. Michael
Staged Transgression in Shakespeare's England — Loughnane, Rory
The Stager — Coll, Susan
The Stages — Satterlee, Thom
Stages of Occupational Regulation: Analysis of Case Studies — Kleiner, Morris M.
c Stagestruck: Curtain Up — Fiedler, Lisa
Stagestruck: The Business of Theater in Eighteenth-Century France and Its Colonies — Clay, Lauren R.
Staging Conventions in Medieval English Theatre — Butterworth, Philip
Staging England in the Elizabethan History Play: Performing National Identity — Hertel, Ralf
Staging Faith: Religion and African American Theater from the Harlem Renaissance to World War II — Prentiss, Craig R.
Staging Race: Black Performers in Turn of the Century America — Sotiropoulos, Karen
Staging the Blazon in Early Modern English Theater — Uman, Deborah
Staging the Blues: From Tent Shows to Tourism — McGinley, Paige A.
Staging Women and the Soul-Body Dynamic in Early Modern England — Johnson, Sarah E.
Stairway of the Gods — Warren, Vic
Stairway to Heaven: The Functions of Medieval Upper Spaces — Huitson, Toby
The Stairwell — Longley, Michael
Stalin and Europe: Imitation and Domination, 1928-1953 — Snyder, Timothy
Stalin: New Biography of a Dictator — Khlevniuk, Oleg V.
Stalin, vol. 1: Paradoxes of Power, 1878-1928 — Kotkin, Stephen
Stalin, vol. I: Paradoxes of Power, 1878-1928 — Kotkin, Stephen
The Stalingrad Trilogy, vol. 3: Endgame at Stalingrad, Book One: November 1942 — Glantz, David M.
The Stalingrad Trilogy, vol. 3: Endgame at Stalingrad, Book Two: December 1942-February 1943 — Glantz, David M.
Stalinist City Planning: Professionals, Performance, and Power — DeHaan, Heather D.
Stalin's Agent: The Life and Death of Alexander Orlov — Volodarsky, Boris
Stalin's Curse: Battling for Communism in War and Cold War — Gellately, Robert
Stalin's Daughter: The Extraordinary and Tumultuous Life of Svetlana Alliluyeva — Sullivan, Rosemary
Stalin's Englishman: The Lives of Guy Burgess — Lownie, Andrew
Stalins Nomaden: Herrschaft und Hunger in Kasachstan — Kindler, Robert
Stalin's World: Dictating the Soviet Order — Davies, Sarah
Stamp Stencil Paint: Making Extraordinary Patterned Projects by Hand — Joyce, Anna
c Stan the Van Man (Illus. by Webb, Philip) — Vere-Jones, Emma
Stand By Me — Downs, Jim
y Stand-Off (Illus. by Bosma, Sam) — Smith, Andrew Anselmo
y Stand-Off — Smith, Andrew Anselmo
Stand Out: How to Find Your Breakthrough Idea and Build a Following around It — Clark, Dorie

c Stand Tall! A Book about Integrity (Illus. by Allen, Elizabeth) — Meiners, Cheri J.
c Stand There! She Shouted: The Invincible Photographer Julia Margaret Cameron (Illus. by Ibatoulline, Bagram) — Rubin, Susan Goldman
Stand Your Ground: Black Bodies and the Justice of God — Douglas, Kelly Brown
Stand Your Ground — Lomax, Raeder
y Stand Your Ground — Murray, Victoria Christopher
Standard Cataloging for School and Public Libraries, 5th ed. — Intner, Sheila S.
Standesgemasse Ordnung in der Moderne: Adlige Familienstrategien und Gesellschaftsentwurfe in Deutschland 1840-1945 — Menning, Daniel
Standing in the Need: Culture, Comfort, and Coming Home After Katrina — Browne, Katherine E.
Standing Naked Before God: The Art of Public Confession — Baskette, Molly Phinney
Standing on Common Ground — Cadava, Geraldo L.
Standing Their Ground: Small Farmers in North Carolina since the Civil War — Petty, Adrienne Monteith
Stanislavsky: A Life In Letters — Senelick, Laurence
c Stanley at School (Illus. by Slavin, Bill) — Bailey, Linda
c Stanley the Builder (Illus. by Bee, William) — Bee, William
c Stanley the Farmer (Illus. by Bee, William) — Bee, William
c Stanley's Cafe (Illus. by Bee, William) — Bee, William
c Stanley's Diner (Illus. by Bee, William) — Bee, William
c Stanley's Garage (Illus. by Bee, William) — Bee, William
c Stanley's Plan: The Birthday Surprise (Illus. by Green, Ruth) — Green, Ruth
The Star and the Stripes: A History of the Foreign Policies of American Jews — Barnett, Michael N.
c Star Bright: A Christmas Story (Illus. by Reynolds, Peter H.) — McGhee, Alison
A Star Called Lucky — Jain, Bapsy
A Star Called the Sun — Gamow, George
c Star Child — Nivola, Claire A.
Star Fall — Harrod-Eagles, Cynthia
Star of Deltora: Shadows of the Master — Rodda, Emily
c Star Rise — Lasky, Kathryn
Star Shrines and Earthworks of the Desert Southwest — David, Gary A.
y The Star Side of Bird Hill — Jackson, Naomi
Star-Spangled Banner: The Unlikely Story of America's National Anthem — Ferris, Marc
c Star Stuff: Carl Sagan and the Mysteries of the Cosmos (Illus. by Sisson, Stephanie Roth) — Sisson, Stephanie Roth
c Star Wars: A New Hope: The Princess, the Scoundrel, and the Farm Boy (Illus. by McQuarrie, Ralph) — Bracken, Alexandra
c Star Wars: Jedi Academy: Return of the Padawan — Brown, Jeffrey
c Star Wars--L'Academie Jedi--Le retour du Padawan — Brown, Jeffrey
c Star Wars - Return of the Jedi: Beware the Power of the Dark Side! (Illus. by Johnston, Joe) — Angleberger, Tom
c Star Wars: The Adventures of Luke Skywalker, Jedi Knight (Illus. by McQuarrie, Ralph) — DiTerlizzi, Tony
c Star Wars: The Empire Strikes Back: So You Want to Be a Jedi? (Illus. by McQuarrie, Ralph) — Gidwitz, Adam
Starblind — Dyllin, D.T.
c Starbounders — Epstein, Adam
c Starbreak — North, Phoebe
c Stardragon (Illus. by Serra, Adolfo) — Butterfield, Moira
c Starfire — Alvarez, Jennifer Lynn
Starfish: Biology and Ecology of the Asteroidea — Lawrence, John M.
y Starflight — Landers, Melissa
The Stargazer's Sister — Brown, Carrie (b. 1959-)
y Starley's Rust — Dutton, J.B.
Starlight on Willow Lake — Wiggs, Susan
The Starlight Years: Love and War at Kelmscott Manor, 1940-1948 — Godwin, Joscelyn
y Starlight's Edge — Waggoner, Susan
The Starling Project (Read by Molina, Alfred). Audiobook Review — Deaver, Jeffery
Starlost Child: Adventures of a Space Bum — Batson, Jon
c Starr Blue Birds — Rose, Caroline

c Starring Jules (Third Grade Debut). (Illus. by Higgins, Anne Keenan) — Ain, Beth
Starring New York: Filiming the Grime and the Glamour of the Long 1970s — Corkin, Stanley
c Starring Shapes! (Illus. by Howells, Tania) — Howells, Tania
y Starry Night — Gillies, Isabel
The Starry Sky Within: Astronomy and the Reach of the Mind in Victorian Literature — Henchman, Anna
y Stars — Oakes, Colleen
c Stars and Planets (Illus. by Donohoe, Bill) — Channing, Margot
Stars Between the Sun and Moon: One Woman's Life in North Korea and Escape to Freedom (Read by Song, Janet). Audiobook Review — Jang, Lucia
Stars Between the Sun and Moon: One Woman's Life in North Korea and Escape to Freedom — Jang, Lucia
y The Stars Never Rise — Vincent, Rachel
Stars of Fortune — Roberts, Nora
y The Stars of Summer — Dairman, Tara
c Stars of the Rock 'N' Roll Highway — Pasmore, Victoria Micklish
Stars over Sunset Boulevard — Meissner, Susan
c Stars Shall Be Bright — MacPhail, Catherine
Stars Wars FAQ: Everything Left to Know about the Trilogy That Changed the Movies — Clark, Mark
Start a Community Food Garden: The Essential Handbook. — Joy, LaManda
Start a Revolution: Stop Acting Like a Library — Bizzle, Ben
Start Me Up — Michaels, Nicole
y The Start of Me and You — Lord, Emery
c Start to Finish, Second Series: Nature's Treasures — Owings, Lisa
c Start to Finish: Sports Gear Series — Nelson, Robin
Starting with Max: How a Wise Stray Dog Gave Me Strength and Inspiration — Ying Ying
Starts with Trouble: William Goyen and the Life of Writing — Davis, Clark
Starvation and the State: Famine, Slavery, and Power in Sudan, 1883-1956 — Serels, Steven
Starve and Immolate: The Politics of Human Weapons — Bargu, Banu
State and Citizen: British America and the Early United States — Thompson, Peter
State and Nation Making in Latin America and Spain: Republics of the Possible — Centeno, Miguel A.
State Behavior and the Nuclear Nonproliferation Regime — Fields, Jeffrey R.
State-Building and Multilingual Education in Africa — Albaugh, Ericka A.
State Correspondence in the Ancient World: From New Kingdom Egypt to the Roman Empire — Radner, Karen
State, Faith and Nation in Ottoman and Post-Ottoman Lands — Anscome, Frederick F.
State of Defiance: Challenging the Johns Committee's Assault on Civil Liberties — Poucher, Judith G.
The State of Freedom: A Social History of the British State since 1800 — Joyce, Patrick
y State of Grace — Badger, Hilary
A State of Play: British Politics on Screen, Stage and Page, from Anthony Trollope to the Thick of It — Fielding, Steven
The State of Play: Creators and Critics on Video Game Culture — Goldberg, Daniel
The State of Play: Sixteen Voices on Video Games — Goldberg, Daniel
The State of Post-conflict Reconstruction: Land, Urban Development and State-Building in Juba, Southern Sudan — Badiey, Naseem
The State of the American Mind: 16 Leading Critics on the New Anti-Intellectualism — Bauerlein, Mark
The State of the American Mind: 16 Leading Critics on the New Anti-Intellectualism — Bauerlein, Mark
State of the Apes 2013 — Rainer, Helga
The State of the Art: A Chronicle of American Poetry, 1988-2014 — Lehman, David
State of the Marital Union: Rhetoric, Identity, and Nineteenth-Century Marriage Controversies — Harris, Leslie J.
State, Religion, and Revolution in Iran, 1796 to the Present — Moazami, Behrooz
State Responses to Minority Religions — Kirkham, David M.
The State We're In: Maine Stories — Beattie, Ann
Statebuilding from the Margins: Between Reconstruction and the New Deal — Nackenoff, Carol
States at Work: Dynamics of African Bureaucracies — Bierschenk, Thomas
States, Debt, and Power: "Saints" and "Sinners" in European History and Integration — Dyson, Kenneth

States of Delinquency: Race and Science in the Making of California's Juvenile Justice System — Chavez-Garcia, Miroslava
States of Desire Revisited: Travels in Gay America — White, Edmund
States of Division: Border and Boundary Formation in Cold War Rural Germany — Schaefer, Sagi
States of Union: Family and Change in the American Constitutional Order — Brandon, Mark E.
Station 16 — Huppen, Hermann
Station Eleven (Read by Potter, Kirsten). Audiobook Review — Mandel, Emily St. John
y Station Eleven — Mandel, Emily St. John
Station to Station — Aitken, Doug
Station to Station: Searching for Stories on the Great Western Line — Attlee, James
Station Zed — Sleigh, Tom
The Stationers' Company and the Printers of London: 1501-57 — Blayney, Peter
c Statues of Easter Island — Raum, Elizabeth
Status Interaction During the Reign of Louis XIV — Sternberg, Giora
The Status of All Things — Fenton, Liz
Status, Power and Ritual Interaction: A Relational Reading of Durkheim, Goffman, and Collins — Kemper, Theodore D.
Status Update — Albert, Annabeth
c Stay! A Top Dog Story (Illus. by Latimer, Alex) — Latimer, Alex
Stay — Gischler, Victor
Stay, Illusion — Brock-Broido, Lucie
y Stay in the Game — Atwood, Megan
c Stay, Kay! — Powell, Marie
Stay: Lessons My Dogs Taught Me About Life, Loss, and Grace — Burchett, Dave
Stay — Gischler, Victor
y Stay Strong: A Musician's Journey from Congo — Hyde, Natalie
Stay the Distance: The Life and Times of Marshal of the Royal Air Force Sir Michael Beetham — Jacobs, Peter
Staying Alive: Personal Identity, Practical Concerns and the Unity of a Life — Schechtman, Marya
Staying on Track: The Autobiography — Mansell, Nigel
Staying Sharp: 9 Keys for a Youthful Brain through Modern Science and Ageless Wisdom — Emmons, Henry
Steal It Back — Simonds, Sandra
Steal Me — Layne, Lauren
Steal the North — Bergstrom, Heather Brittain
Stealing America: What My Experience with Criminal Gangs Taught Me About Obama, Hillary, and the Democratic Party — D'Souza, Dinesh
Stealing Cars: Technology and Society from the Model T to the Gran Torino — Heitmann, John A.
Stealing Obedience: Narratives of Agency and Identity in Later Anglo-Saxon England — O'Keeffe, Katherine O'Brien
Stealing Propeller Hats from the Dead — Keaton, David James
Stealing Rose — Murphy, Monica
Stealing Shiva — Ortner, Kathleen
Stealing Sisi's Star — Bowers Bahney, Jennifer
c Stealing the Game — Abdul-Jabbar, Kareem
Steam Me Up, Rawley — Quarles, Angela
The Steamboat Bertrand and Missouri River Commerce — Switzer, Ronald R.
Steamboats on the Indus: The Limits of Western Technological Superiority in South Asia — Dewey, Clive
Steaming to the North: The First Summer Cruise of the US Revenue Cutter Bear, Alaska and Chukotka, Siberia, 1886 — Donahue, Katherine C.
y Steampunk Fables — Espinosa, Rod
c Steampunk Lego: The Illustrated Researches of Various Fantastical Devices by Sir Herbert Jobson, with Epistles to the Crown, Her Majesty Queen Victoria — Himber, Guy
Steel Barrio: The Great Mexican Migration to South Chicago, 1915-1940 — Innis-Jimenez, Michael
Steel Closets: Voices of Gay, Lesbian, and Transgender Steelworkers — Balay, Anne
Steel Victory — Gribble, J.L.
Steele Resolve — Amato, Kimberly
y The Steep and Thorny Way — Winters, Cat
Steering Clear: How to Avoid a Debt Crisis and Secure Our Economic Future — Peterson, Peter G.
Steering the Craft: A 21st-Century Guide to Sailing the Sea of Story — Le Guin, Ursula K.
Stefan Wolpe and the Avant-Garde Diaspora — Cohen, Brigid
c Stegosaurus — Lennie, Charles
Stella: A Novel of the Haitian Revolution — Bergeaud, Emeric

c Stella and Charlie, Friends Forever (Illus. by Murphy, Liz) — Peters, Bernadette
c Stella Brings the Family (Illus. by Clifton-Brown, Holly) — Schiffer, Miriam B.
Stella By Starlight — Draper, Sharon M.
c Stella By Starlight — Draper, Sharon
y Stella by Starlight — Draper, Sharon M.
Stella Mia — Chiofalo, Rosanna
c Stellar Space: 250 Facts Kids Want to Know — TIME for Kids Magazine editors
y The Stellow Project (Read by Rudd, Kate). Audiobook Review — Becker, Shari
y The Stellow Project — Becker, Shari
Stem Cell Dialogues: A Philosophical and Scientific Inquiry into Medical Frontiers — Krimsky, Sheldon
The Stem Shift: A Guide for School Leaders — Myers, Ann
y Step Aside, Pops: A Hark! A Vagrant Collection (Illus. by Beaton, Kate) — Beaton, Kate
Step-by-Step Free-Motion Quilting: Turn 9 Simple Shapes into 80+ Distinctive Designs — Cameli, Christina
Step Dancing in Ireland: Culture and History — Foley, Catherine E.
Step into Nature: Nurturing Imagination and Spirit in Everyday Life — Vecchione, Patrice
STEP into Storytime: Using StoryTime Effective Practice to Strengthen the Development of Newborns to Five-Year-Olds — Nadkarni, Saroj
y A Step toward Falling — McGovern, Cammie
Stepan Bandera: The Life and Afterlife of a Ukrainian Nationalist: Fascism, Genocide, and Cult — Rossoliski-Liebe, Grzegorz
Stepdog: A Memoir — Navarro, Mireya
Stepdog — Galland, Nicole
Stephen Crane: A Life of Fire — Sorrentino, Paul
c Stephen Harper — Yasuda, Anita
c Stephen Hawking — Senker, Cath
The Stephen Hawking Death Row Fan Club — Goodwin, R.C.
c Stephen Hawking: Extraordinary Theoretical Physicist — Kenney, Karen Latchana
The Stephen King Companion: Four Decades of Fear from the Master of Horror, 3d ed. (Illus. by Whelan, Michael) — Beahm, George
Stephen Larigaudelle Dubuisson, S.J. (1786-1864), and the Reform of the American Jesuits — Buckley, Cornelius Michael
Stephen Sondheim: A Life — Secrest, Meryle
Steppes: The Plants and Ecology of the World's Semi-Arid Regions — Bone, Michael
y Stepping Out — Langston, Laura
y Stessed-Out Girl?: Girls Dealing with Feelings — Snyder, Gail
Steve Jobs: A Biography — Hartland, Jessie
Steve Jobs and Philosophy: For Those Who Think Different — Klein, Shawn E.
Steve Jobs: Insanely Great (Illus. by Hartland, Jessie) — Harland, Jessie
y Steve Jobs: Insanely Great (Illus. by Hartland, Jessie) — Hartland, Jessie
c Steve, Raised by Wolves (Illus. by Chapman, Jared) — Chapman, Jared
Steven Holl — McCarter, Robert
Stewards of the Mysteries of God: Preaching the Old Testament and the New — Miller, Patrick D.
Stewie Boom! Boss of the Big Boy Bed (Illus. by Young, Karen) — Bronstein, Christine
c Stick and Stone (Illus. by Lichtenheld, Tom) — Ferry, Beth
c Stick Cat: A Tail of Two Kitties (Illus. by Watson, Tom) — Watson, Tom
c Stick Dog Chases a Pizza (Illus. by Long, Ethan) — Watson, Tom
c Stick Dog Dreams of Ice Cream (Illus. by Watson, Tom) — Watson, Tom
y Stick — Harmon, Michael
c Stickiest, Fluffiest, Crunchiest: Super Superlatives (Illus. by Brocket, Jane) — Brocket, Jane
c Stickley Sticks To It! A Frog's Guide to Getting Things Done (Illus. by Mack, Steve) — Miles, Brenda S.
c Stickmen's Guide to Watercraft — Farndon, John
The Stickup Kids: Race, Drugs, Violence and the American Dream — Contreras, Randol
The Stickup Kids: Race, Drugs, Violence and the American Dream — Contreras, Randol
Stiff Penalty — Ryan, Annelise
Stiftungen und Stiften im Wandel der Zeiten - Internationale Winterschule
A Still and Quiet Conscience: The Archbishop Who Challenged a Pope, a President, and a Church — McCoy, John A.
y Still Falling — Wilkinson, Sheena

y Still Life Las Vegas (Illus. by Choi, Sungyoon) — Sie, James
c Still Life (Illus. by Bernatene, Poly) — West, Jacqueline
   Still Lives: Death, Desire, and the Portrait of the Old Master — Loh, Maria H.
   Still Night in L.A. — Saroyan, Aram
   Still the One — Shalvis, Jill
   Still Time — Hegland, Jean
y Still Waters — Parsons, Ash
   Stillwell: A Haunting on Long Island — Cash, Michael Phillip
   Sting and the Police: Walking in Their Footsteps — West, Aaron J.
c Stingrays! Underwater Fliers (Illus. by Mones, Isidre) — Gerber, Carole
c Stink Moody in Master of Disaster (Illus. by Madrid, Erwin) — McDonald, Megan
   Stinking Stones and Rocks of Gold: Phosphate, Fertilizer, and Industrialization in Postbellum South Carolina — McKinley, Shepherd W.
c Stinky Cecil in Operation Pond Rescue — Braddock, Paige
c Stinky (Illus. by Elkerton, Andy) — Byant, Ann
c Stinky! (Illus. by Elkerton, Andy) — Guillain, Charlotte
c Stinky Skunks and Other Animal Adaptations — Taylor, Barbara
c Stinky Spike the Pirate Dog (Illus. by Meisel, Peter) — Meisel, Peter
   Stir: My Broken Brain and the Meals That Brought Me Home — Fechtor, Jessica
   A Stitch in Crime — Yost, Ann
   Stitch, Wear, Play: 20 Charming Patterns for Boys & Girls — Nakamura, Mariko
   Stitches in Time: The Story of the Clothes We Wear — Adlington, Lucy
   Stitches to Savor — Spargo, Sue
   Stitching Resistance: Women, Creativity, and Fiber Arts — Agosin, Marjorie
y Stitching Snow — Lewis, R.C.
   Stochastic Chemical Kinetics: Theory and (Mostly) Systems Biology Applications — Erdi, Peter
   Stochastic Processes — Bass, Richard F.
   The Stockholm Castle Mystery — Moore, Joyce Elson
   Stockholm Noir — Larson, Nathan
   Stocks, Bonds and Soccer Moms — Higgins, Michelle Perry
   Stocks for the Long Run: The Definitive Guide to Financial Market Returns and Long-Term Investment Strategies — Siegel, Jeremy J.
   Stokely: A Life — Joseph, Peniel E.
c The Stolen Chapters — Riley, James
   Stolen Identity — Banister, Michael
   The Stolen Mackenzie Bride — Ashley, Jennifer
y Stolen Magic — Levine, Gail Carson
c The Stolen Moon — Searles, Rachel
y Stolen — de la Cruz, Melissa
   The Stolen Ones — Laukkanen, Owen
   A Stolen Season — Hamilton, Steve
   Stolen, Smuggled, Sold: On the Hunt for Cultural Treasures — Moses, Nancy
   Stolen Words — Glickman, Mark
c Stoll Balancing Act — Walsh, Ellen Stoll
c Stone Angel (Read by Botchan, Rachel). Audiobook Review — Yolen, Jane
c Stone Angel (Illus. by Green, Katie May) — Yolen, Jane
   Stone Blood — Green, R.M.
   The Stone-Campbell Movement: A Global History — Williams, D. Newell
   Stone Cold Case — Dilts, Catherine
   Stone Cold Dead — Ziskin, James W.
   Stone Cold — Box, C.J.
y Stone Cove Island — Myers, Suzanne
y Stone Field — Lenzi, Christy
y Stone in the Sky — Castellucci, Cecil
   The Stone Reader: Modern Philosophy in 133 Arguments — Catapano, Peter
y Stone Rider (Read by Morgan, Matthew). Audiobook Review — Hofmeyr, David
y Stone Rider — Hofmeyr, David
   Stone Song: A Novel of the Life of Crazy Horse — Blevins, Win
c Stonebird — Revell, Mike
   Stoned: A Doctor's Case for Medical Marijuana — Casarett, David
   Stoned: Jewelry, Obsession, and How Desire Shapes the World — Raden, Aja
c Stonehenge — Raum, Elizabeth
   Stoner Mug Cakes — Noon, Dane
   Stones in the Road — Moore, E.B.
   Stones of Contention: A History of Africa's Diamonds — Cleveland, Todd
   The Stones of Kaldaar — Etherton, Tameri
y Stones on a Grave — Kacer, Kathy

   Stones Tell Stories at Osu: Memories of a Host Community of the Danish Trans-Atlantic Slave Trade — Wellington, H. Nii-Adziri
y Stonewall: Breaking Out in the Fight for Gay Rights (Read by Federle, Tim). Audiobook Review — Bausum, Ann
y Stonewall: Breaking Out in the Fight for Gay Rights — Bausum, Ann
y Stonger Than You Know — Perry, Jolene
   Stony Kill — Small, Marie White
   Stop at Nothing — SeRine, Kate
c Stop the Presses! — Wise, Rachel
   Stop the Stress in Schools: Mental Health Strategies Teachers Can Use to Build a Kinder Gentler Classroom — Mandel, Joey
c Stop, Thief! (Illus. by Pratt, Pierre) — Tekavec, Heather
c Stop Those Monsters — Cole, Steve
   A Stopinder Anthology — Kherdian, David
   Stopping the Panzers: The Untold Story of D-Day — Milner, Marc
   A Store Almost in Sight: The Economic Transformation of Missouri from the Louisiana Purchase to the Civil War — Bremer, Jeff
   Store Front II: A History Preserved: The Disappearing Face of New York — Murray, James T.
c Store Math — James, Dawn
   Storia della lingua italiana e storia dell'Italia unita: l'italiano e lo stato nazionale — Nesi, Annalisa
   Storia di una doppia censura: Gli Strategemmi di Satana di Giacomo Aconcio nell'Europa del Seicento — Caravale, Giorgio
   The Storied Ice: Exploration, Discovery, and Adventure in Antarctica's Peninsula Region — Boothe, Joan N.
   Stories — Srodek-Hart, Guillermo
   Stories About Stories: Fantasy and the Remaking of Myth — Attebery, Brian
   Stories for Chip: A Tribute to Samuel R. Delany — Shawl, Nisi
   Stories for Simon (Illus. by Briggs, Lauren) — Sarzin, Lisa Miranda
c Stories from Bug Garden (Illus. by Millward, Gwen) — Moser, Lisa
   Stories from the Kitchen — Tesdeli, Diana Seeker
   Stories from the Polycule: Real Life in Polyamorous Families — Sheff, Elisabeth
   Stories I Tell — D'Angelo, Paul
   Stories I Tell Myself: Growing Up with Hunter S. Thompson — Thompson, Juan F.
   Stories in the Stars: An Atlas of Constellations — Hislop, Susanna
   Stories My Father Never Finished Telling Me: Living with the Armenian Legacy of Loss and Silence — Kalajian, Douglas
   The Stories of Frederick Busch — Strout, Elizabeth
   Stories of My Life (Read by Birmingham, Laurie). Audiobook Review — Paterson, Katherine
y Stories of My Life — Paterson, Katherine
   Stories of the South: Race and the Reconstruction of Southern Identity, 1865-1915 — Prince, K. Stephen
y Stories of Women During the Industrial Revolution: Changing Roles, Changing Lives — Hubbard, Ben
c Stories of Women in the 1960s: Fighting for Freedom — Senker, Cath
   Stories of Women in World War II: We Can Do It! — Langley, Andrew
y Stories of Women's Suffrage: Votes for Women! — Hubbard, Ben
c Stories of Women's Suffrage: Votes for Women! — Guillain, Charlotte
   Stork Mountain — Penkov, Miroslav
c Stork's Landing (Illus. by Shuttlewood, Anna) — Lehman-Wilzig, Tami
c Storm — Kemmerer, Brigid
y Storm — Napoli, Donna Jo
   Storm and Steel — Sprunk, Jon
   Storm Bride — Bangs, J.S.
   The Storm Dragon's Heart — Hayden, David Alastair
   The Storm Murders — Farrow, John
c Storm of Dogs — Hunter, Erin
   The Storm Of Steel — Junger, Ernst
   The Storm of the Century: Tragedy, Heroism, Survival, and the Epic True Story of America's Deadliest Natural Disaster: The Great Gulf Hurricane of 1900 — Roker, Al
   A Storm of Witchcraft: The Salem Trials and the American Experience — Baker, Emerson W.
   A Storm over This Court: Law, Politics and Supreme Court Decision Making in Brown v. Board of Education — Hockett, Jeffrey D.
   Storm Siren (Read by Stevens, Christine). Audiobook Review — Weber, Mary
y Storm Siren — Weber, Mary

c The Storm Whale (Illus. by Davies, Benji) — Davies, Benji
y Stormbound — Alvarez, Jennifer Lynn
   Storme Warning — Ripley, W.L.
   Storms of Lazarus — Kincy, Karen
   The Storms of War — Williams, Kate
y The Storms of War — Williams, Kate (b. 1974-)
c Stormstruck! — MacFarlane, John
c Stormstruck! — MacFfarlane, John
   Stormtrooper Families: Homosexuality and Community in the Early Nazi Movement — Wackerfuss, Andrew
c Stormy Night — Yoon, Salina
   The Story: A Reporter's Journey — Miller, Judith
   The Story: An Autobiography — Story, James B.
   A Story as Sharp as a Knife: The Classical Haida Mythtellers and Their World — Bringhurst, Robert
   The Story Hour (Read by Mathan, Sneha). Audiobook Review — Umrigar, Thrity
c The Story I'll Tell (Illus. by Lanan, Jessica) — Ling, Nancy Tupper
   The Story of Alice: Lewis Carroll and the Secret History of Wonderland — Douglas-Fairhurst, Robert
y The Story of AT&T — Murray, Laura K.
c The Story of Britain — Manning, Mick
c The Story of Crime and Punishment (Illus. by Bougaeva, Sonja) — Schoffman, Stuart
c The Story of Diva and Flea (Illus. by DiTerlizzi, Tony) — Willems, Mo
c The Story of Fossil Fuels — Rice, William B.
c The Story of Hurry (Illus. by Quraishi, Ibrahim) — Williams, Emma
c The Story of Ironman (Illus. by Rousseau, Craig) — Macri, Thomas
   The Story of Jesus in History and Faith: An Introduction — McDonald, Lee Martin
c The Story of Juneteenth: An Interactive History Adventure — Otfinoski, Steven
c The Story of King Jesus (Illus. by Lee, Nick) — Irwin, Ben
c The Story of Life: A First Book about Evolution (Illus. by Husband, Amy) — Barr, Catherine
   The Story of Life in 25 Fossils — Prothero, Donald R.
   The Story of Life in 25 Fossils: Tales of Intrepid Fossil Hunters and the Wonders of Evolution — Prothero, Donald R.
   The Story of Manu — Peddana, Allasani
   The Story of Monasticism: Retrieving an Ancient Tradition for Contemporary Spirituality — Peters, Greg
c The Story of MTV — Gilbert, Sara
   The Story of My Teeth — Luiselli, Valeria
   The Story of My Tits (Illus. by Hayden, Jennifer) — Hayden, Jennifer
   The Story of N: A Social History of the Nitrogen Cycle and the Challenge of Sustainability — Gorman, Hugh S.
c The Story of Owen: Dragon Slayer of Trondheim — Johnston, E.K.
   The Story of Pain: From Prayer to Painkillers — Bourke, Joanna
c The Story of Paul Bunyan (Illus. by Emberley, Ed) — Emberley, Barbara
   The Story of Science: From the Writings of Aristotle to the Big Bang Theory — Bauer, Susan Wise
y The Story of Seeds — Castaldo, Nancy F.
   A Story of Six Rivers: History, Culture and Ecology — Coates, Peter
c The Story of Snowflake and Inkdrop (Illus. by Mulazzani, Simona) — Gatti, Alessandro
c The Story of Snowflake and Inkdrop (Illus. by Mulazzini, Simona) — Gatti, Alessandro
c The Story of Spider-Man — Macri, Thomas
c The Story of the Avengers (Illus. by Olliffe, Pat) — Macri, Thomas
   The Story of the British and Their Weather — Moore, Peter (b. 1983-)
c The Story of the Civil Rights Movement in Photographs Series
c The Story of the Indiana Pacers — Frisch, Nate
c The Story of the Los Angeles Clippers — Whiting, Jim
   The Story of the Lost Child — Ferrante, Elena
c The Story of the Miami Heat — Frederick, Shane
c The Story of the Oklahoma City Thunder — LeBoutillier, Nate
c The Story of the San Antonio Spurs — Frederick, Shane
   The Story of Us — Atkins, Dani
   The Story of Vicente, Who Murdered His Mother, His Father, and His Sister: Life and Death in Juarez — Nieto, Sandra Rodriguez
c The Story Starts Here! (Illus. by Merola, Caroline) — Merola, Caroline
c Story Thieves — Riley, James
   Story/Time: The Life of an Idea — Jones, Bill T.

StoryCorps OutLoud: Voices of the LGBTQ Community from Across America (Read by Shapiro, Ari). Audiobook Review — Isay, Dave
c Storyline — Moyson, Graham
The StorySellers — Bender, Mickey
y The Storyspinner — Wallace, Becky
c The Storyteller — Starmer, Aaron
The Storyteller of Jerusalem: The Life and Times of Wasif Jawhariyyeh, 1904-1948 — Nassar, Issam
Storyteller: The Photographs of Duane Michals — Benedict-Jones, Linda
Storyteller's Sampler: Tales from Tellers around the World — MacDonald, Margaret R.
The Storyteller's Secret: From TED Speakers to Business Legends, Why Some Ideas Catch On and Others Don't — Gallo, Carmine
Storytelling and the Sciences of Mind — Herman, David
The Storytelling Animal: How Stories Make Us Human — Gottschall, Jonathan
Storytelling Apes: Primatology Narratives Past and Future — Pollock, Mary Sanders
Storytelling, History, and the Postmodern South — Phillips, Jason
Stowaway: Curse of the Red Pearl — Fobes, Tracy
Stowe Away — Rippon, Blythe
Straddle — Cavanagh, David
The Straight State: Sexuality and Citizenship in Twentieth-Century America — Canaday, Margot
y Straight Talk about ... Binge Drinking — Bow, James
y Straight Talk about...Dealing with Loss — Bow, James
y Straight Talk about ... Dealing with Loss — Bow, James
y Straight Talk about ... Digital Dangers — Stuckey, Rachel
y Straight Talk about ... Sexual Orientation and Gender Identity — Stuckey, Rachel
Straight to Hell: True Tales of Deviance, Debauchery, and Billion-Dollar Deals — LeFevre, John
Straight Up Tasty — Richman, Adam
Straights: Heterosexuality in Post-Closeted Culture — Dean, James Joseph
Straining at the Oars: Case Studies in Pastoral Leadership — Fearon, H. Dana
Straits of Hell — Anderson, Taylor
y Stranded — Braun, Melinda
y Stranded — Huffaker, Nathan
c Stranded on Planet Stripmall! — Angleberger, Tom
c The Stranded Whale (Illus. by Cataldo, Melanie) — Yolen, Jane
y The Strange and Beautiful Sorrows of Ava Lavender (Read by Campbell, Cassandra). Audiobook Review — Walton, Leslye
The Strange and Terrible Visions of Wilhelm Friess: The Paths of Prophecy in Reformation Europe — Green, Jonathan
A Strange Business: A Revolution in Art, Culture, and Commerce in Nineteenth Century London — Hamilton, James
y The Strange Case of Dr. Jekyll and Mr. Hyde (Illus. by Ferran, Daniel) — Stevenson, Robert Louis
The Strange Case of Rachel K. — Kushner, Rachel
The Strange Case of the Rickety Cossack and Other Cautionary Tales from Human Evolution — Tattersall, Ian
Strange Country: Why Australian Painting Matters — Gruber, Fiona
The Strange Death of Fiona Griffiths — Bingham, Harry
Strange Electromagnetic Dimensions: The Science of the Unexplainable — Proud, Louis
y Strange Girl — Pike, Christopher
Strange Glory: A Life of Dietrich Bonhoeffer — Marsh, Charles
Strange Glow: The Story of Radiation — Jorgensen, Timothy J.
Strange Gods: A Secular History of Conversion — Jacoby, Susan
The Strange History of the American Quadroon: Free Women of Color in the Revolutionary Atlantic World — Clark, Emily
"Strange Lands and Different Peoples": Spaniards and Indians in Colonial Guatemala — Lovell, W. George
The Strange Library (Read by Heyborne, Kirby). Audiobook Review — Murakami, Haruki
The Strange Library — Murakami, Haruki
Strange Material: Storytelling through Textiles — Prain, Leanne
Strange Natures: Futurity, Empathy, and the Queer Ecological Imagination — seymour, Nicole
Strange Rebels: 1979 and the Birth of the 21st Century — Caryl, Christian
Strange Shores — Indridason, Arnaldur
The Strange Side of the Tracks — Avant, George
y Strange Skies — Heivig, Kristi
y Strange Skies — Helvig, Kristi

Strange Tools: Art and Human Nature — Noe, Alva
Strange Visitors: Documents in Indigenous-Settler Relations in Canada from 1876 — Smith, Keith D.
A Strangeness in My Mind — Oklap, Ekin
A Strangeness in My Mind — Pamuk, Orhan
y The Stranger (Illus. by Vives, Bastien) — Vives, Bastien
The Stranger (Read by Newbern, George). Audiobook Review — Cohen, Harlan
c The Stranger Box — Cuming, Pamela
y Stranger — Brown, Rachel Manija
The Stranger — Coben, Harlan
y The Stranger (Illus. by Balak) — Balak
A Stranger in My Own Country: The 1944 Prison Diary — Fallada, Hans
A Stranger in My Own Country: The 1944 Prison Diary — Williams, Jenny
Stranger Intimacy: Contesting Race, Sexuality and the Law in the North American West — Shah, Nayan
c Stranger — Brown, Rachel Manija
The Stranger on the Train — Taylor, Abbie
The Stranger She Loved: A Mormon Doctor, His Beautiful Wife, and an Almost Perfect Murder — Hogan, Shanna
Stranger than Fiction: The Life of Edgar Wallace, the Man Who Created King Kong — Clark, Neil
Stranger Than We Can Imagine: Making Sense of the Twentieth Century — Higgs, John
A Stranger to the Darklands — Blackehart, Stephen
The Stranger — Coben, Harlan
Strangers and Neighbors: Multiculturalism, Conflict, and Community in America — Voyer, Andrea M.
Strangers at the Gates: Movements and States in Contentious Politics — Tarrow, Sidney
Strangers Drowning: Grappling with Impossible Idealism, Drastic Choices, and the Overpowering Urge to Help (Read by MacFarquhar, Larissa). Audiobook Review — MacFarquhar, Larissa
Strangers Drowning: Grappling with Impossible Idealism, Drastic Choices, and the Overpowering Urge to Help — MacFarquhar, Larissa
Strangers, Lovers and the Winds of Time — Lovin, Dale
A Stranger's Mirror: New and Selected Poems, 1994-2014 — Hacker, Marilyn
Strangers No More: Immigration and the Challenges of Integration in North America and Western Europe — Alba, Richard
Strangers on a Train (Read by Pinchot, Bronson). Audiobook Review — Highsmith, Patricia
Strangers on Familiar Soil: Rediscovering the Chile-California Connection — Melillo, Edward Dallam
The Strangest — Seidlinger, Michael J.
c The Strangest Animals in the World — Gagne, Tammy
y Strangled Silence — McGann, Oisin
The Strangler Vine — Carter, M.J.
The Strangler Vine — Carter, Miranda J.
The Strangler Vine — Watchulonis, Michael
Strategic Cooperation: Overcoming the Barriers of Global Anarchy — Slobodchikoff, Michael O.
Strategic Failure: How President Obama's Drone Warfare, Defense Cuts, and Military Amateurism Have Imperiled America — Moyar, Mark
Strategic Thinking in 3D: A Guide for National Security, Foreign Policy, and Business Professionals — Harrison, Ross
Strategies of Symbolic Nation Building in South Eastern Europe — Kolsto, Pal
The Strategist: Brent Scowcroft and the Call of National Security — Sparrow, Bartholomew
Strategy and Defence Planning: Meeting the Challenge of Uncertainty — Gray, Colin S.
The Strategy Bridge: Theory for Practice — Gray, Colin S.
Strategy in Asia: The Past, Present, and Future of Regional Security — Mahnken, Thomas G.
The Strategy of Defeat at the Little Big Horn: A Military and Timing Analysis of the Battle — Wagner, Frederic C., III
Strategy Rules: Five Timeless Lessons from Bill Gates, Andy Grove, and Steve Jobs — Yoffie, David B.
c The Stratford Zoo Midnight Revue Presents Romeo and Juliet (Illus. by Giallongo, Zack) — Lendler, Ian
Strawberry Pie — Cote, Lynne Kathryn
y Stray — Sussman, Elissa
The Stray Bullet: William S. Burroughs in Mexico — Garcia-Robles, Jorge
y Stray — Craw, Rachael
Stray Dogs: Writing from the Other America — Hastings, William
Strayhorn: An Illustrated Life — Claerbaut, A. Alyce
c Strays — Caloyeras, Jennifer
The Stream of Life — Tobler, Stefan
Streaming — Hedge Coke, Allison Adelle

Streamlined Library Programming: How to Improve Services and Cut Costs — Porter-Reynolds, Daisy
Streb: How to Become an Extreme Action Hero — Streb, Elizabeth
Street Corner Secrets: Sex, Work, and Migration in the City of Mumbai — Shah, Svati P.
Street Craft: Guerilla Gardening, Yarnbombing, Light Graffiti, Street Sculpture, and More — Kuittinen, Riikka
A Street Divided — Nissenbaum, Dion
Street God: The Explosive True Story of a Former Drug Boss on the Run from the Hood - and the Courageous Mission That Drove Him Back — Salaberrios, Dimas
Street Life in London: Context and Commentary — Morgan, Emily Kathryn
Street of Thieves — Enard, Mathias
The Street of Wonderful Possibilities: Whistler, Wilde and Sargent in Tite Street — Cox, Devon
Street Poison: The Biography of Iceberg Slim (Read by Jackson, J.D.). Audiobook Review — Gifford, Justin
Street Poison: The Biography of Iceberg Slim — Gifford, Justin
The Street Politics of Abortion: Speech, Violence, and America's Culture Wars — Wilson, Joshua C.
Street Smart: The Rise of Cities and the Fall of Cars — Schwartz, Samuel I.
The Streets of San Francisco: Policing and the Creation of a Cosmopolitan Liberal Politics, 1950-1972 — Agee, Christopher Lowen
Strength in Numbers: The Political Power of Weak Interests — Trumbull, Gunnar
Strength of Conviction — Mulcair, Thomas
A Strengths-Based Approach for Intervention with At-Risk Youth — Powell, Kevin M.
Stresemann Workshop 2015: Illusionary Visions or Policy Options? Discontent over Cold War Security Architecture in Europe and the Search for Alternatives
Stress Biology of Cyanobacteria: Molecular Mechanisms to Cellular Responses — Srivastava, Ashish Kumar
The Stress Cure: How to Resolve Stress, Build Resilience, and Boost Your Energy — Holford, Patrick
Stress Test: Reflections on Financial Crises — Geithner, Timothy F.
Stretch: How to Future-Proof Yourself for Tomorrow's Workplace — Willyerd, Karie
Stricken by Sin, Cured by Christ: Agency, Necessity, and Culpability in Augustinian Theology — Couenhoven, Jesse
c Strictly No Elephants (Illus. by Yoo, Taeeun) — Mantchev, Lisa
Strider: The Story of a Horse — Tolstoy, Leo
Strike a Poser — Asher, Dylan Edward
y Strike! The Farm Workers' Fight for Their Rights — Brimmer, Larry
y Strike! The Farm Workers' Fight for Their Rights — Brimner, Larry Dane
Striking Beauty: A Philosophical Look at the Asian Martial Arts — Allen, Barry
The String Diaries — Jones, Stephen Lloyd
A String of Beads (Read by Bean, Joyce). Audiobook Review — Perry, Thomas
A String of Beads — Perry, Thomas
The String Quartets of Bela Bartok: Tradition and Legacy in Analytical Perspective — Biro, Daniel Peter
Strip Cultures: Finding America in Las Vegas — Jameson, Stacy M.
Strip Cultures: Finding America in Las Vegas — Willis, Susan
Strip Your Stash: Dynamic Quilts Made from Strips: 12 Projects in Multiple Sizes from GE Designs — Erla, Gudrun
Striving in the Path of God: Jihad and Martyrdom in Islamic Thought — Afsaruddin, Asma
Stroke Victor: How to Go From Stroke Victim to Stroke Victor — Mandell, Bob
Strom Thurmond's America — Crespino, Joseph
Strong as Death Is Love: The Song of Songs, Ruth, Esther, Jonah, Daniel — Alter, Robert
Strong Boy: The Life and Times of John L. Sullivan, America's First Sports Hero — Klein, Christopher
Strong Darkness — Land, Jon
Strong Enough — Leighton, M.
Strong Light of Day — Land, Jon
Strong, My Love — Fallon, Peter
Strong: Nine Next-Level Workout Programs for Women — Schuler, Lou
The Strong Spirit: History, Politics, and Aesthetics in the Writings of James Joyce, 1898-1915 — Gibson, Andrew

c Strongheart: The World's First Movie Star Dog — McCully, Emily Arnold
Stroppy (Illus. by Bell, Marc) — Bell, Marc
Structure and Method in Aristotle's Meteorologica: A More Disorderly Nature — Wilson, Malcolm
The Structure of Cuban History: Meanings and Purpose of the Past — Perez, Louis A., Jr.
The Structure of World History: From Modes of Production to Modes of Exchange — Karatani, Kojin
Structured Worlds: The Archaeology of Hunter-Gatherer Thought and Action — Cannon, Aubrey
Struggle, Condemnation, Vindication: John Courtney Murray's Journey toward Vatican II — Hudock, Barry
The Struggle for America's Promise: Equal Opportunity at the Dawn of Corporate Capital — Goldstene, Claire
The Struggle for Black Freedom in Miami: Civil Rights and America's Tourist Paradise, 1896-1968 — Rose, Chanelle N.
The Struggle for Equal Adulthood: Gender, Race, Age, and the Fight for Citizenship in Antebellum America — Field, Corinne T.
The Struggle for Form: Perspectives on Polish Avant-Garde Film 1916-1989 — Kuc, Kamila
The Struggle for Mastery in Europe, 1848-1918 — Taylor, A.J.P.
The Struggle for Pakistan: A Muslim Homeland and Global Politics — Jalal, Ayesha
The Struggle for Roman Citizenship: Romans, Allies, and the Wars of 91-77 BCE — Kendall, Seth
The Struggle for Sea Power: A Naval History of the American Revolution — Willis, Sam
The Struggle for the Eurasian Borderlands: From the Rise of Early Modern Empires to the End of the First World War — Rieber, Alfred J.
c The Struggles of Johnny Cannon — Campbell, Isaiah
Struggling Giants: City-Region Governance in London, New York, Paris and Tokyo — Kantor, Paul
Struggling in Good Faith: LGBTQI Inclusion from 13 American Religious Perspectives — Copeland, Mychal
Stuck in Place: Urban Neighborhoods and the End of Progress toward Racial Equality — Sharkey, Patrick
Stuck in the Passing Lane: A Memoir — Ringel, Jed
The Student Loan Scam: The Most Oppressive Debt in U.S. History--and How We Can Fight Back — Collinge, Alan Michael
Student Voice: Turn Up the Volume K-8 Activity Book — Quaglia, Russell J.
Student's Essential Studies for Clarinet: A Sequential Collection of 40 Standard Etudes for the Advancing Student — Wright, Scott
The Students of Sherman Indian School: Education and Native Identity since 1892 — Bahr, Diana Meyers
The Student's Survival Guide to Research — McAdoo, Monty L.
Studies in Ancient Oracles and Divination — Kajava, Mika
Studies in Ephemera: Text and Image in Eighteenth-Century Print — Murphy, Kevin D.
Studies in Italian History in the Middle Ages and the Renaissance, Volume 3: Humanists, Machiavelli, Guicciardini — Rubinstein, Nicolai
Studies in Medieval Muslim Thought and History — Madelung, Wilferd
Studies in Medievalism XXIII: Ethics and Medievalism — Fugelso, Karl
Studies in the Hereafter — Bernard, Sean
Studies in Urbanormativity: Rural Communities in Urban Society — Fulkerson, Gregory M.
Studies of Communication in the 2012 Presidential Campaign — Denton, Robert E., Jr.
Studii su la storia di Sicilia dalla meta del XVIII secolo al 1820 di Michele Amari — Crisantino, Amelia
Studio Grace: The Making of a Record — Siblin, Eric
c Study Hall of Justice — Fridolfs, Derek
y A Study in Charlotte — Cavallaro, Brittany
A Study in Death — Huber, Anna Lee
Study in Perfect — Gorham, Sarah
The Study of Seduction — Jeffries, Sabrina
Study & Other Poems of Art — Otomo, Yuko
Studying Human Behavior: How Scientists Investigate Aggression and Sexuality — Longino, Helen E.
Studying Popular Music — Middleton, Richard
Studying Vibrational Communication — Cocroft, Reginald B.
Stuff and Money in the Time of the French Revolution — Spang, Rebecca L.

Stuff Brits Like: A Guide to What's Great About Great Britain — McAlpine, Fraser
c Stuff You Need to Know! — Farndon, John
Stuffocation: Why We've Had Enough of Stuff and Need Experience More Than Ever — Wallman, James
Stuffology 101: Get Your Mind Out of the Clutter — Avadian, Brenda
c Stunno's Surf Adventure (Illus. by Jacobson, Tina) — Reside, Mark
c Stunt Cat to the Stars (Illus. by Lombardo, Constance) — Lombardo, Constance
c Stuntboy: The Fincredible Diary of Fin Spencer (Illus. by Wesson, Tim) — Murtagh, Ciaran
Stuntwomen: The Untold Hollywood Story — Gregory, Mollie
Style and Swing: 12 Structured Handbags for Beginners and Beyond — Dunlop, Susan
Style Icons: Golden Boys — Roberts, Paul G.
Stylish Remakes: Upcycle Your Old T's, Sweats and Flannels into Trendy Street Fashion Pieces — Violette Room
Styx — Dhooge, Bavo
y Sublime — Lauren, Christina
Sublime Physick: Essays — Madden, Patrick
The Sublime Seneca: Ethics, Literature, Metaphysics — Gunderson, Erik
c Submarines: 1940 to Today — Jackson, Robert
c Submarines (Illus. by West, David) — West, David
Submission — Houellebecq, Michel
Submission — Stein, Lorin
Submission — Houellebecq, Michel
The Subprimes — Greenfeld, Karl Taro
The Subprimes — Greenfield, Karl Taro
The Subs Club — Rock, J.A.
c The Substitutes (Illus. by Calo, Marcos) — Lay, Kathryn
Subterranean Struggles: New Dynamics of Mining, Oil, and Gas in Latin America — Bebbington, Anthony
The Suburb Reader — Nicolaides, Becky M.
Suburban Christianity: God's Work in Unhip Places — Miller, Keith
Suburban Wonder: Wandering the Margins of Paris — Tabouret, Francis
Subversion, Conversion, Development: Cross-Cultural Knowledge and the Politics of Design — Leach, James
Subversive Networks: Agents of Change in International Organizations, 1920-1960
Subverting Aristotle: Religion, History, and Philosophy in Early Modern Science — Martin, Craig
The Success of the Left in Latin America: Untainted Parties, Market Reforms, and Voting Behavior — Queirolo, Rosario
Successfully Serving the College Bound — Hands, Africa S.
Succession — Michael, Livi
Succulent Wild Love: Six Powerful Habits for Feeling More Love More Often — Waddell, John
c Such a Little Mouse (Illus. by Yue, Stephanie) — Schertle, Alice
Sucker — Lingane, Mark
Suckered: The History of Sugar, Our Toxic Addiction, Our Power to Change — Eisenberg, Jeffrey
Suckered: The History of Sugar, Our Toxic Addiction, Our Power to Change — Eisenberg, Jeffrey
Suckers — Rider, Z.
Sudden Death — Enrigue, Alvaro
Sudden Death — Enrique, Alvaro
Sudden Death — Wimmer, Natasha
Sudden Justice: America's Secret Drone Wars — Woods, Chris
y A Sudden Light (Read by Numrich, Seth). Audiobook Review — Stein, Garth
A Sudden Sun — Morgan-Cole, Trudy J.
Suddenly One Summer (Read by White, Karen). Audiobook Review — James, Julie
Suddenly One Summer — James, Julie
Sudlich der Sahara: Afrikanische Literatur in franzosischer Sprache — Riesz, Janos
Suetonius the Biographer: Studies in Roman Lives — Power, Tristan
Suffer and Grow Strong: The Life of Ella Gertrude Clanton Thomas, 1834-1907 — Curry, Carolyn Newton
Suffering and Sunset: World War I in the Art and Life of Horace Pippin — Bernier, Celeste-Marie
y The Suffering — Chupeco, Rin
Suffrage Sisters: The Fight for Liberty (Illus. by Feeney, Siri Weber) — Mead, Maggie
Suffragette: My Own Story — Pankhurst, Emmeline
Sufism in the Secret History of Persia — Milani, Milad
y Sugar — Hall, Deirdre Riordan

y Sugar — Riordan Hall, Deirdre
y Sugar (Read by Sands, Tara). Audiobook Review — Hall, Deirdre Riordan
The Sugar Book — Goransson, Johannes
Sugar Burn — Kurr, Ryan
y The Sugar Mountain Snow Ball — Atkinson, Elizabeth
y Sugar — Hall, Deirdre Riordan
The Sugar Trade: Brazil, Portugal and the Netherlands (1595-1630). — Strum, Daniel
c Sugar White Snow and Evergreens: A Winter Wonderland of Color (Illus. by Swan, Susan) — Chernesky, Felicia Sanzari
The Suicide Club — Graham, Toni
The Suicide Exhibition — Richards, Justin
Suicide Forest — Bates, Jeremy
Suicide Movies: Social Patterns 1900-2009 — Stack, Steven
Suicide — Critchley, Simon
y Suicide Notes from Beautiful Girls — Weingarten, Lynn
The Suicide of Claire Bishop — Banasky, Carmiel
Suicide of the West: An Essay on the Meaning and Destiny of Liberalism — Burnham, James
Suicide Pact: The Radical Expansion of Presidential Powers and the Lethal Threat to American Liberty — Napolitano, Andrew P.
Suitcase City — Watson, Sterling
Suite for Barbara Loden — Leger, Nathalie
Suite Seventeen — Da Costa, Portia
Suite Venitienne — Calle, Sophie
y The Summer After You and Me — Doktorski, Jennifer Salvato
y The Summer after You + Me — Doktorski, Jennifer Salvato
Summer at the Shore — Sykes, V.K.
The Summer before the War — Simonson, Helen
The Summer Book — Jansson, Tove
y Summer by Summer — Burch, Heather
Summer Cocktails: Margaritas, Mint Juleps, Punches, Party Snacks, and More (Illus. by Striano, Tara) — Sacasa, Maria del Mar
Summer Cooking: Kitchen-Tested Recipes for Picnics, Patios, Grilling and More — Chicago Tribune Staff
c The Summer Experiment — Pelletier, Cathie
Summer in the City: John Lindsay, New York, and the American Dream — Viteritti, Joseph P.
y Summer Love: An LGBTQ Collection — Harper, Annie
y The Summer of Chasing Mermaids — Ockler, Sarah
The Summer of Good Intentions — Francis, Wendy
The Summer of the Crow — Boeve, Eunice
y Summer of the Oak Moon — Templeton, Laura
Summer School "Political Participation: Ideas, Forms and Modes since Antiquity"
Summer Secrets — Green, Jane
Summer Shadows — Traynor, Killarney
The Summer Table: Recipes and Menus for Casual Outdoor Entertaining — Lemke, Lisa
y The Summer We Saved the Bees — Stevenson, Robin
Summer with My Sisters — Chamberlin, Holly
Summerlong — Bakopoulos, Dean
c Summerlost — Condie, Ally
The Summit: Bretton Woods, 1944: J.M. Keynes and the Reshaping of the Global Economy — Conway, Ed
Summit Lake — Donlea, Charlie
The Summits of Modern Man: Mountaineering after the Enlightenment — Hansen, Peter H.
y Summoned — Pillsworth, Anne M.
Summoning the Ghosts of Detroit — Flournoy, Angela
c The Sun: A Super Star — Glaser, Chaya
c The Sun — Riggs, Kate
c Sun Above and Blooms Below: A Springtime of Opposites (Illus. by Swan, Susan) — Chernesky, Felicia Sanzari
Sun Above and Blooms Below: A Springtime of Opposites (Illus. by Swan, Susan) — Sanzari, Felicia
c Sun Above and Blooms Below: A Springtime of Opposties (Illus. by Swan, Susan) — Chernesky, Felicia Sanzari
c The Sun: All about Solar Flares, Eclipses, Sunspots, and More! — Simon, Seymour
c Sun and Moon (Illus. by Yankey, Lindsey) — Yankey, Lindsey
The Sun between Their Fleet — Lessing, Doris
The Sun King — O'Callaghan, Conor
c Sun, Moon, and Stars — Wilson, Hannah
The Sun Never Sets: South Asian Migrants in an Age of U.S. Power — Bald, Vivek
Sun Up, Sun Down — Gibbons, Gail
Sundance — Fuller, David
Sunday Morning, Shamwana — Robinson, Linda Orst
c Sunday Shopping (Illus. by Strickland, Shadra) — Derby, Sally

c Sunday Shopping (Illus. by Strickland, Shandra) — Derby, Sally
Sunday's on the Phone to Monday — Reilly, Christine
y Sundberg — Grainger, A.J.
The Sundown Speech — Estleman, Loren D.
Sunfail — Savile, Steven
Sunflower Justice: A New History of the Kansas Supreme Court — Lee, R. Alton
Sunk! — Hitchcock, Fleur
The Sunken Cathedral — Walbert, Kate
y Sunker's Deep — Tanner, Lian
y Sunkissed — McLachlan, Jenny
The Sunlit Night — Dinerstein, Rebecca
Sunny 101: The 10 Commandments of a Boss Chick — Smith-Williams, Sunshine
c Sunny Side Up (Illus. by Holm, Matthew) — Holm, Jennifer L.
c Sunny Side Up (Illus. by Holm, Matthew) — Holm, Matthew
c Sunny Side Up (Illus. by Holm, Matthew) — Holm, Jennifer L.
c Sunny Side Up (Illus. by Holm, Matthew) — Holm, Matthew
y Sunny Sweet Can So Get Lost — Mann, Jennifer Ann
Sunny's Nights: Lost and Found at a Bar on the Edge of the World — Sultan, Tim
c The Sunrise Band (Illus. by Palen, Debbie) — Dinardo, Jeff
The Sunrise — Hislop, Victoria
The Suns Gods — Rubin, Jay
y Sunset Ranch — Destiny, A.
The Sunshine Crust Baking Factory — Wakefield, Stacy
Sunshine on Scotland Street (Read by Mackenzie, Robert Ian). Audiobook Review — Smith, Alexander McCall
Sunshine Was Never Enough: Los Angeles Workers, 1880-2010 — Laslett, John
c Super Baseball Infographics (Illus. by Westlund, Laura) — Braun, Eric
c Super Baseball Infographics (Illus. by Westlund, Laura) — Graun, Eric
c Super Baseball Infographics (Illus. by Westlund, Laura) — Braun, Eric
c Super Basketball Infographics (Illus. by Schuster, Rob) — Savage, Jeff
c Super Bunny (Illus. by Blake, Stephanie) — Blake, Stephanie
c Super Cool Forces and Motion Activities with Max Axiom — Biskup, Agnieszka
c Super Cool Mechanical Activities with Max Axiom — Enz, Tammy
Super Fly: The World's Smallest Superhero! — Doodler, Todd H.
c Super Fly: The World's Smallest Superhero! (Illus. by Doodler, Todd H.) — Doodler, Todd H.
c Super Football Infographics (Illus. by Westlund, Laura) — Braun, Eric
Super Genes: Unlock the Astonishing Power of Your DNA for Optimum Health and Well-Being — Chopra, Deepak
c The Super Gifts of Spring (Illus. by Blackmore, Katherine) — Mackall, Dandi Daley
c Super Happy Magic Forest — Long, Matty
c Super Hockey Infographics (Illus. by Kulihin, Vic) — Savage, Jeff
Super House: Design Your Dream Home for Super Energy Efficiency, Total Comfort, Dazzling Beauty, Awesome Strength, and Economy — Wulfinghoff, Donald R.
Super Indian: Fritz Scholder, 1967-1980 — Scholder, Fritz
Super Job Search IV: The Complete Manual for Job Seekers and Career Changers — Studner, Peter K.
c Super Jumbo (Illus. by Koehler, Fred) — Koehler, Fred
y Super Mutant Magic Academy (Illus. by Tamaki, Jillian) — Tamaki, Jillian
The Super Natural — Kripal, Jeffrey J.
c Super Red Riding Hood (Illus. by Davila, Claudia) — Davila, Claudia
c Super SandCastle: Super Simple Gardening — Kuskowski, Alex
c Super Sasquatch Showdown (Illus. by Harper, Charise Mericle) — Harper, Charise Mericle
c Super Schnoz and the Invasion of the Snore Snatchers (Illus. by Frawley, Keith) — Urey, Gary
c Super Scorers — Zweig, Eric
c Super Secret Surprise Party (Illus. by Enik, Ted) — O'Connor, Jane
c Super Shark Encyclopedia and Other Creatures of the Deep — Harvey, Derek
c Super Simple Australian Art: Fun and Easy Art from around the World — Kuskowski, Alex
c Super Simple European Art: Fun and Easy Art from around the World — Kuskowski, Alex

c Super Simple Hanging Gardens: A Kid's Guide to Gardening — Kuskowski, Alex
c Super Simple Indian Art: Fun and Easy Art from around the World — Kuskowski, Alex
c Super Simple Japanese Art: Fun and Easy Art from around the World — Kuskowski, Alex
c The Super-Smelly Moldy Blob — Stadelmann, Amy Marie
c Super Sniffers: Dog Detectives on the Job — Patent, Dorothy Hinshaw
y SuperBetter: A Revolutionary Approach to Getting Stronger, Happier, Braver and More Resilient: Powered by the Science of Games — McGonigal, Jane
c Superbrain: The Insider's Guide to Getting Smart (Illus. by Whamond, Dave) — Toronto Public Library
The Supercarriers: The Forrestal and Kitty Hawk Classes — Faltum, Andrew
c Supercat vs. the Fry Thief (Illus. by Field, Jim) — Willis, Jeanne
c SuperCat vs the Pesky Pirate (Illus. by Field, Jim) — Willis, Jeanne
Superdads: How Fathers Balance Work and Family in the 21st Century — Kaufman, Gayle
c Superfab Saves the Day (Illus. by Delaporte, Berengere) — Delaporte, Berengere
Superfluous Women — Dunn, Carola
Superforecasting: The Art and Science of Prediction — Tetlock, Philip E.
c Superheroes Don't Eat Veggie Burgers — Kelley, Gretchen
The Superhuman Mind: Free the Genius in Your Brain — Brogaard, Berit
A Superior Man — Yee, Paul
Superior Packets — Timmons, Susie
c Superlove (Illus. by Chambers, Mark) — Harper, Charise Mericle
c Superman: A Giant Attack (Illus. by Ferguson, Lee) — Lemke, Donald
c Supermom and the Big Baby (Illus. by Laird, Guy) — Driver, Dave
The Supermom Myth — Kopitzke, Becky
y SuperMutant Magic Academy — Tamaki, Jillian
Supernotes — Kasper, Agent
Superposition — Walton, David
Superpower: Three Choices for America's Role in the World — Bremmer, Ian
c Supersonic — Zucker, Jonny
c Superstats: Amazing Body — Butterfield, Moira
c Superstats: Extreme Planet — Butterfield, Moira
Supersymmetry — Walton, David
c Supertruck (Illus. by Savage, Stephen) — Savage, Stephen
The SuperWoman's Guide to Super Fulfillment — Kulaga, Jaime
The Superyogi Scenario — Connor, James
The Supplement Handbook: A Trusted Expert's Guide to What Works and What's Worthless for More Than 100 Conditions — Moyad, Mark
Supplication: Selected Poems of John Wieners — Wieners, John
Supply Shock: Economic Growth at the Crossroads and the Steady State Solution — Czech, Brian
Supporting the Dream: High School-College Partnerships for College and Career Readiness — McGaughy, Chris
Supposed to Die — Dutton, Hugh
Suppressed Terror: History and Perception of Soviet Special Camps in Germany — Greiner, Bettina
Supreme City: How Jazz Age Manhattan Gave Birth to Modern America — Miller, Donald L.
Surabaya, 1945-2010: Neighbourhood, State and Economy in Indonesia's City of Struggle — Peters, Robbie
Surface — Robinson, Stacy
Surface Imaginations: Cosmetic Surgery, Photography, and Skin — Hurst, Rachel Alpha Johnston
The Surfacing — James, Cormac
y Surfacing — Magro, Mark
Surfing about Music — Cooley, Timothy J.
Surfing Uncertainty: Prediction, Action, and the Embodied Mind — Clark, Andy
c Surf's Up (Illus. by Miyares, Daniel) — Alexander, Kwame
The Surgeon of Crowthorne. A tale of murder, madness and the love of Words — Winchester, Simon
A Surgical Temptation: The Demonization of the Foreskin and the Rise of Circumcision in Britain — Darby, Robert
Suriname in the Long Twentieth Century: Domination, Contestation, Globalization — Hoefte, Rosemarijn
Suri's Wall (Illus. by Ottley, Matt) — Estella, Lucy

c Surprise (Illus. by Van Hout, Mies) — Van Hout, Mies
Surprise Attack: From Pearl Harbor to 9/11 to Benghazi — Hancock, Larry
Surprise: Embrace the Unpredictable and Engineer the Unexpected — Luna, Tania
c A Surprise for Giraffe and Elephant (Illus. by Gude, Paul) — Gude, Paul
c A Surprise for Tiny Mouse (Illus. by Horacek, Petr) — Horacek, Petr
c Surprise in the Meadow (Illus. by Vojtech, Anna) — Vojtech, Anna
Surprise: The Poetics of the Unexpected from Milton to Austen — Miller, Christopher R.
Surprise the World — Frost, Michael
Surprised at Being Alive: An Accidental Helicopter Pilot in Vietnam and Beyond — Curtis, Robert F.
Surprised by Scripture: Engaging with Contemporary Issues — Wright, Tom
Surprised by Sin: The Reader in Paradise Lost — Fish, Stanley
c Surprisingly Scary! — Austen, Amy
Surreality: Strange Tales of a Man Sitting Down the Bar from You — Bradley, J.D.
Surrounded by Friends — Rohrer, Matthew
c Surrounded by Sharks — Northrop, Michael
Surveillance Cinema — Zimmer, Catherine
The Surveillance-Industrial Complex: A Political Economy of Surveillance — Ball, Kirstie
Survey of Historic Costume, 6th ed. — Tortora, Phyllis G.
Survival and Success on Medieval Borders: Cistercian Houses in Medieval Scotland and Pomerania from the Twelth to the Late Fourteenth Century — Jamroziak, Emilia
Survival — Casden, Mahra
c Survival Challenge — Turnbull, Stephanie
y Survival Colony 9 — Bellin, Joshua David
The Survival Guide for Kids with Physical Disabilities and Challenges — Moss, Wendy L.
c The Survival Guide for Making and Being Friends — Crist, James J
c The Survival Guide for School Success: Use Your Brain's Built-In Apps to Sharpen Attention, Battle Boredom, and Build Mental Muscle — Shumsky, Ron
y The Survival Guide to Bullying: Written by a Teen — Mayrock, Aija
Survival Schools: The American Indian Movement and Community Education in the Twin Cities — Davis, Julie L.
y Survival Strategies of the Almost Brave — White, Jen
Survival Time: A Handbook for Surviving a Violent Incident — Olivas, Aimee
y Survivants - 1912: Le naufrage du Titanic (Illus. by Dawson, Scott) — Tarshis, Lauren
y Survive the Night — Vega, Daniella
y Survive the Night — Vega, Danielle
c Surviving Bear Island — Greci, Paul
Surviving Desires: Making and Selling Native Jewellery in the American Southwest — Lidchi, Henrietta
Surviving Incarceration: Inside Canadian Prisons — Ricciardelli, Rose
Surviving Katrina: The Experiences of Low-Income African American Women — Pardee, Jessica Warner
Surviving Puberty: Erecting Your Future and Making the Breast Decisions — Bishoff, Chad
y Surviving Santiago — Miller-Lachmann
y Surviving Santiago — Miller-Lachmann, Lyn
Surviving Wounded Knee: The Lakotas and the Politics of Memory — Grua, David W.
The Survivor — Flynn, Vince
A Survivor from Warsaw, Opus 46 — Schonberg, Arnold
The Survivors — Palmer, Robert L.
Survivors and Exiles: Yiddish Culture After the Holocaust — Schwarz, Jan
Survivors: Hungarian Jewish Poets of the Holocaust — Orszag-Land, Thomas
Survivors: Politics and Semantics of a Concept
A Survivor's Tale: The Titanic 1912-2012 — Thayer, John B.
Susan B. Anthony and the Struggle for Equal Rights — Ridarsky, Christine L.
Susan Mallery — Mallery, Susan
Susan Sontag: A Biography — Schreiber, Daniel
Susan Sontag — Maunsell, Jerome Boyd
Susana and the Scot — York, Sabrina
c The Suspended Castle (Illus. by Kutner, Richard) — Fred
Suspended Sentences: Three Novellas — Modiano, Patrick
Suspicion — Finder, Joseph
y Suspicion — Monir, Alexandra
y The Suspicion at Sanditon — Bebris, Carrie

Suspicion at Seven — *Purser, Ann*
Suspicion — *Finder, Joseph*
Suspicious Gifts: Bribery, Morality, and Professional Ethics — *Akerstrom, Malin*
Suspicious Minds: Why We Believe Conspiracy Theories — *Brotherton, Rob*
The Sussex Downs Murder — *Bude, John*
Sustainability of Scholarly Information — *Chowdhury, G.G.*
Sustainable Happiness: Live Simply, Live Well, Make a Difference — *Van Gelder, Sarah*
Sustainable Luxury: The New Singapore House, Solutions for a Livable Future — *McGillick, Paul*
Sustaining Activism: A Brazilian Women's Movement and a Father-Daughter Collaboration — *Rubin, Jeffrey W.*
Sveti Pavao Shipwreck: A 16th Century Venetian Merchantman from Mljet, Croatia, With Italian and Croatian Abstracts — *Beltrame, Carlo*
Swag Bags and Swindlers — *Howell, Dorothy*
y The Swallow: A Ghost Story — *Cotter, Charis*
Swallow This: Serving Up the Food Industry's Darkest Secrets — *Blythman, Joanna*
y Swallowdale — *Ransome, Arthur*
Swallows and Waves — *Bohince, Paula*
Swan Feast — *Eilbert, Natalie*
c Swan: The Life and Dance of Anna Pavlova (Illus. by Morstad, Julie) — *Snyder, Laurel*
c Swan: The Life and Dance of Anna Pavlova (Illus. by Morstad, Julie) — *Snydr, Laurel*
The Swans of Fifth Avenue — *Benjamin, Melanie*
Swansong 1945: A Collective Diary of the Last Days of the Third Reich — *Kempowski, Walter*
Swansong 1945 — *Kempowski, Walter*
c Swap! (Illus. by Light, Steve) — *Light, Steve*
c The Swap — *Shull, Megan*
A Swarm of Bees in High Court — *Foster, Tonya M.*
y Swashbuckling Scoundrels — *Kaplan, Arie*
c Swatch: The Girl Who Loved Color — *Denos, Julia*
c Sway (Read by Podehl, Nick). Audiobook Review — *Spears, Kat*
y Sway — *Spears, Kat*
c Sweaterweather and Other Short Stories (Illus. by Varan, Sara) — *Varan, Sara*
c Sweaterweather and Other Short Stories (Illus. by Varon, Sara) — *Varon, Sara*
The Swede (Read by Harding, Jeff). Audiobook Review — *Karjel, Robert*
The Swede — *Karjel, Robert*
The Sweden File: Memoir of an American Expatriate — *Proctor, Alan Robert*
Swedish Naval Administration, 1521-1721: Resource Flows and Organisational Capabilities — *Glete, Jan*
Sweep Rowing — *Cherry, Dave*
c Sweep Up the Sun (Illus. by Lieder, Rick) — *Frost, Helen*
y Sweet — *Laybourne, Emmy*
Sweet and Tart: 70 Irresistible Recipes with Citrus — *Snyder, Carla*
Sweet as Sin — *Geissinger, J.T.*
Sweet Caress — *Boyd, William*
c Sweet Child of Mine (Illus. by Church, Caroline Jayne) — *Caroline Jayne Church*
c Sweet Child of Mine (Illus. by Church, Caroline Jayne) — *Church, Caroline Jayne*
c Sweet Dreams: 5-Minute Bedtime Stories — *Rey, Margret*
Sweet Dreams — *Potter, Joan Monk*
c Sweet Dreams, Wild Animals! A Story of Sleep (Illus. by Caple, Laurie) — *Meyer, Eileen R.*
Sweet Envy: Deceptively Easy Desserts, Designed to Steal the Show — *Rossini, Seton*
Sweet Forgiveness — *Spielman, Lori Nelson*
Sweet Holy Motherfucking Everloving Delusional Bastard — *Segundo, Jerome*
c Sweet Home Alaska — *Dagg, Carole Estby*
Sweet Lamb of Heaven — *Millet, Lydia*
Sweet Lechery — *Heer, Jeet*
y Sweet Madness — *Currie, Lindsay*

y Sweet Madness — *Leaver, Trisha*
Sweet — *Constantine, Alysia*
c Sweet Secrets (Illus. by Waters, Erica-Jane) — *Perelman, Helen*
c The Sweet Story of Hot Chocolate! (Illus. by McClurkan, Rob) — *Krensky, Stephen*
Sweet Sunday — *Lawton, John*
Sweet Surprise — *Terry, Candis*
y Sweet Temptation — *Higgins, Wendy*
Sweet Treats around the World: An Encyclopedia of Food and Culture — *Roufs, Kathleen S.*
Sweetbitter — *Danler, Stephanie*
The Sweetest Dream — *Lessing, Doris*
c The Sweetest Heist in History (Illus. by Spencer, Octavia). Audiobook Review — *Spencer, Octavia*
c The Sweetest Heist in History (Illus. by To, Vivienne) — *Spencer, Octavia*
c Sweetest Kulu (Illus. by Neonakis, Alexandra) — *Kalluk, Celina*
y The Sweetest Thing You Can Sing — *Martin, C.K. Kelly*
c The Sweetest Witch Around (Illus. by Bliss, Harry) — *McGhee, Alison*
y Sweetgirl — *Muihauser, Travis*
Sweetgirl — *Mulhauser, Travis*
Sweetheart Deal — *Dugan, Polly*
The Sweetheart Deal — *Dugan, Polly*
y Sweetheart Deal — *Hull, Linda Joffe*
Sweetheart — *Cain, Chelsea*
c Sweetie (Illus. by Jessell, Tim) — *Klimo, Kate*
Sweetland (Read by Lee, John). Audiobook Review — *Crummey, Michael*
Sweetland — *Crummey, Michael*
The Sweetness of Honey (Read by Ross, Natalie). Audiobook Review — *Kent, Alison*
Sweets and Treats with Six Sisters' Stuff: 100+ Desserts, Gift Ideas, and Traditions for the Whole Family — *Six Sisters' Stuff*
Sweetwater Blues — *Atkins, Raymond L.*
y Swept Away: A Sixteenth Summer Novel — *Dalton, Michelle*
y Swept Away — *Dalton, Michelle*
Swerve — *Pettersson, Vicki*
Swift and Others — *Rawson, Claude*
Swift to Wrath: Lynching in Global Historical Perspective — *Carrigan, William D.*
Swift's Angers — *Rawson, Claude*
c Swim, Fish!: Explore the Coral Reef — *Neuman, Susan B.*
Swim to Me — *Carter, Betsy*
The Swimmer — *Zander, Joakim*
The Swimmer — *Koethe, John*
The Swimmer — *Zander, Joakim*
c Swimming Home (Illus. by Raye, Rebekah) — *Shetterly, Susan Hand*
Swimming in the Dark — *Richardson, Paddy*
Swimming in the Rain: New and Selected Poems, 1980-2015 — *Bloch, Chana*
c Swimming, Swimming (Illus. by Clement, Gary) — *Clement, Gary*
c Swimming, Swimming — *Clement, Gary*
Swimming the Elements — *Rosta, Joseph*
Swimming with Turtles: Travel Narratives, Spirit of Place — *Beardsley, Doug*
c Swimmy — *Lionni, Leo*
Swing — *Beard, Philip*
Swing in the House and Other Stories — *Anand, Anita*
c Swing Sisters: The Story of the International Sweethearts of Rhythm (Illus. by Cepeda, Joe) — *Deans, Karen*
Swing, Sloth!: Explore the Rain Forest — *Neuman, Susan B.*
Swiped: How to Protect Yourself in a World Full of Scammers, Phishers, and Identity Thieves — *Levin, Adam*
y Switch — *Davey, Douglas*
y Switch — *Law, Ingrid*
Switchback — *Dunlap, Susan*
Switched On — *Robison, John*

The Sword and the Pen: Women, Politics, and Poetry in Sixteenth-Century Siena — *Eisenbichler, Konrad*
y Sword and Verse — *MacMillan, Kathy*
A Sword for His Lady — *Wine, Mary*
The Sword of Agrippa: Antioch. E-book Review — *Ness, Gregory*
Sword of Honor — *Kirk, David*
y The Sword of Summer — *Riordan, Rick*
Sword of Zen: Master Takuan and His Writings on Immovable Wisdom and the Sword Tale — *Haskel, Peter*
y Swords and Scoundrels — *Knight, Julia*
c The Swords of Glass (Illus. by Zuccheri, Laura) — *Corgiat, Sylviane*
c Sybil the Backpack Fairy 5: The Dragon's Dance (Illus. by Dalena, Antonello) — *Rodrigue, Michel*
c Sydney & Simon: Full Steam Ahead! (Illus. by Reynolds, Peter H.) — *Reynolds, Paul A.*
c Sydney & Simon: Go Green! (Illus. by Reynolds, Peter H.) — *Reynolds, Paul A.*
c Sydney the Monster Stops Bullies (Illus. by Barrows, Laurie) — *DePaoli, Tom*
Syllabus: Notes from an Accidental Professor — *Barry, Lynda*
Syllabus of Errors: Poems — *Jollimore, Troy*
y Sylo (Read by Bates, Andrew S.). Audiobook Review — *MacHale, D.J.*
c Sylvia and Aki — *Conkling, Winifred*
Symbiosis in Fishes: The Biology of Interspecific Partnerships — *Karplus, Ilan*
Symbol and Intuition: Comparative Studies in Kantian and Romantic-Period Aesthetics — *Huhn, Helmut*
Symbolic Power, Politics, and Intellectuals: The Political Sociology of Pierre Bourdieu — *Swartz, David L.*
Symbolische Formung und die gesellschaftliche Konstruktion von Wirklichkeit — *Schramm, Michael W.*
Symmetry: A Very Short Introduction — *Stewart, Ian*
The Sympathetic State: Disaster Relief and the Origins of the American Welfare State — *Dauber, Michele Landis*
The Sympathizer — *Nguyen, Viet Thanh*
Sympathy for the Devil: Four Decades of Friendship with Gore Vidal — *Mewshaw, Michael*
Sympathy for the Devil — *McCauley, Terrence*
y Symphony for the City of the Dead: Dmitri Shostakovich and the Siege of Leningrad — *Anderson, M.T.*
Symposius: The Aenigmata: An Introduction, Text and Commentary — *Leary, Timothy John*
y Symptoms of Being Human — *Garvin, Jeff*
Syren's Song — *Berube, Claude*
Syria: A History of the Last Hundred Years — *McHugo, John*
Syria and Lebanon: International Relations and Diplomacy in the Middle East — *Osoegawa, Taku*
Syria and the USA: Washington's Relations with Damascus from Wilson to Eisenhower — *Moubayed, Sami*
Syria Burning: ISIS and the Death of the Arab Spring — *Glass, Charles*
Syrian Identity in the Greco-Roman World — *Andrade, Nathanael J.*
The Syrian Jewelry Box: A Daughter's Journey for Truth — *Burns, Carina Sue*
The Syrian Jihad: Al-Qaeda, the Islamic State and the Evolution of an Insurgency — *Lister, Charles R.*
Syrian Notebooks: Inside the Homs Uprising — *Littell, Jonathan*
Syrian Notebooks: Inside the Homs Uprising — *Mandell, Charlotte*
The System of Dante's Hell — *Baraka, Amiri*
The System Worked: How the World Stopped Another Great Depression — *Drezner, Daniel W.*
Systematic Theology — *Sonderegger, Katherine*
Systematicity: The Nature of Science — *Hoyningen-Huene, Paul*

T

T.D. Jakes Speaks to Men — *Jakes, T.D.*
T.E. Lawrence and the Red Sea Patrol: The Royal Navy's Role in Creating the Legend — *Johnson-Allen, John*
c T Is for Time (Illus. by Graef, Renee) — *Smith, Roland*
c T Is for Time (Illus. by Graef, Renee) — *Smith, Marie*
Taboo: Corporeal Secrets in Nineteenth-Century France — *Thompson, Hannah*
y Tabula Rasa (Read by Rudd, Kate). Audiobook Review — *Lippert-Martin, Kristen*
y Tabula Rasa — *Lippert-Martin, Kristen*
Tacit Subjects: Belonging and Same-Sex Desire among Dominican Immigrant Men — *Decena, Carlos Ulises*
Tacito: Il libro quarto degli Annales — *Formicola, Crescenzo*
Tacitus — *Ash, Rhiannon*
c Tacky and the Haunted Igloo (Illus. by Munsinger, Lynn) — *Lester, Helen*
Taconite Creek — *Luthens, John*
c Tad and Dad (Illus. by Stein, David Ezra) — *Stein, David Ezra*
c Tae Kwon Do — *Adamson, Thomas K.*
c Taffy Time (Illus. by Lee, Jacqui) — *Lloyd, Jennifer*
Tagebuch 1944: Und 46 Sonette — *Keilson, Hans*
Tagebucher 2002-2012 — *Raddatz, Fritz J.*
Tagebucher: Band 6, 1919 — *Muhsam, Erich*
y Tagged — *Mullen, Diane C.*
Tagung Lutherbilder - Lutherbildprojektionen und ein Okumenischer Luther. Katholische und Evangelische Entwurfe Martin Luthers in Fruher Neuzeit und Moderne
Taiko Boom: Japanese Drumming in Place and Motion — *Bender, Shawn*
The Tail: How England's Schools Fail One Child in Five And What Can be Done — *Marshall, Paul*
c The Tail of the Christmas Cat (Illus. by Rodriguez, Raquel) — *Allen, Sally A.*
The Tail Wags the Dog: International Politics and the Middle East — *Karsh, Efraim*
Tailings: A Memoir — *Schwehn, Kaethe*
Tails from the Booth — *Terry, Mark*
Tainted Glory in Handel's Messiah: The Unsettling History of the World's Most Beloved Choral Work — *Marissen, Michael*
Tainted Heart — *Graves, Melissa*
Taiwan Straits: Crisis in Asia and the Role of the U.S. Navy — *Elleman, Bruce A.*
c Taj Mahal — *Raum, Elizabeth*
Take 5 Fat Quarters: 15 Easy Quilt Patterns — *Brown, Kathy (b. 1955-)*
Take 5! for Science: 150 Prompts That Build Writing and Critical-Thinking Skills — *Hagler, Kaye*
c Take Away the A: An Alphabeast of a Book (Illus. by Di Giacomo, Kris) — *Escoffier, Michael*
c Take Away the A (Illus. by Di Giacomo, Kris) — *Escoffier, Michael*
Take Me All the Way — *Blake, Toni*
Take My Hand Again: A Faith-Based Guide for Helping Aging Parents — *Brummett, Nancy Parker*
Take on Me — *Zimmerman, Minerva*
c Take Shelter: At Home and Around the World — *Tate, Nikki*
y Take the Fall — *Hainsworth, Emily*
Take the Fall — *Valentine, Marquita*
Take This Man — *Plakcy, Neil*
c Take Your Last Breath (Read by Stirling, Rachael). Audiobook Review — *Child, Lauren*
Taken — *Massey, David*
y Taken at the Flood: The Roman Conquest of Greece — *Waterfield, Robin*
Taken — *Henderson, Dee*
Taking a Stand: Moving Beyond Partisan Politics to Unite America — *Paul, Rand*
y Taking Aim: Power and Pain, Teens and Guns — *Cart, Michael*
Taking Care of Your Child: A Parent's Illustrated Guide to Complete Medical Care — *Pantell, Robert H.*
Taking Criminal Justice: Language and the Just Society — *Coyle, Michael J.*
Taking Fire — *Gerard, Cindy*
Taking Fire — *McKenna, Lindsay*
y Taking Flight: From War Orphan to Star Ballerina — *DePrince, Michaela*
y Taking Flight — *Wilkinson, Sheena*
y Taking Hold: From Migrant Childhood to Columbia University — *Jimenez, Francisco*
Taking Liberties: A History of Human Rights in Canada — *Goutor, David*
Taking on Diversity: How We Can Move from Anxiety to Respect; A Diversity Doctor's Best Lessons from the Campus — *Nacoste, Rupert W.*
Taking on Theodore Roosevelt: How One Senator Defied the President on Brownsville and Shook American Politics — *Lembeck, Harry*
Taking Pity — *Mark, David*
Taking Sides: A Memoir in Stories — *Green, Philip*
y Taking Sides — *Jones, Patrick*
Taking Socialism Seriously — *Anton, Anatole*
Taking the Back Off the Watch: A Personal Memoir — *Gold, Thomas*
Taking the Heat — *Dahl, Victoria*
Taking the Measure: The Presidency of George W. Bush — *Kelley, Donald R.*
Taking to the Streets: The Transformation of Arab Activism — *Khatib, Lina*
Tal Farlow: A Life In Jazz Guitar — *Katchoura, Jean-Luc*
A Tale for the Time Being — *Ozeki, Ruth*
The Tale of Genji: Translation, Canonization, and World Literature by — *Emmerich, Michael*
c A Tale of Highly Unusual Magic — *Papademetriou, Lisa*
A Tale of Life & War — *Morin, Christopher*
A Tale of Light and Shadow — *Gowans, Jacob*
Tale of Miss Susie and Her Steamboat: And Other Songs from your Childhood Explained — *Kreps, Sonja N.*
A Tale of Monstrous Extravagance — *Highway, Tomson*
The Tale of Nottingswood — *Young, J.R.*
c The Tale of Rescue (Illus. by Fellows, Stan) — *Rosen, Michael J.*
A Tale of Seven Elements — *Scerri, Eric*
c The Tale of Tam Linn (Illus. by Longson, Philip) — *Don, Lari*
c The Tale of the Little, Little Old Woman — *Beskow, Elsa*
c The Tale of Tumeleng — *Douglas, Ryke Leigh*
c A Tale of Two Beasts (Illus. by Roberton, Fiona) — *Roberton, Fiona*
c A Tale of Two Besties (Read by Brisbin, Anna, with Nora Hunter). Audiobook Review — *Rossi, Sophia*
y A Tale of Two Besties — *Rossi, Sophia*
A Tale of Two Plantations: Slave Life and Labor in Jamaica and Virginia — *Dunn, Richard S.*
c A Tale of Two Sisters (Illus. by Avakyan, Tatevik) — *Dadey, Debbie*
A Talent for Friendship: Rediscovery of a Remarkable Trait — *Terrell, John Edward*
A Talent for Murder — *LaRue, Teresa*
A Talent for Trickery — *Johnson, Alissa*
Tales and Trials of Love, Concerning Venus's Punishment of Those Who Scorn True Love and Denounce Cupid's Sovereignty: A Bilingual Edition and Study — *Flore, Jeanne*
Tales — *Baraka, Amiri*
c Tales from a Not-So-Glam TV Star — *Russell, Rachel Renee*
Tales from Both Sides of the Brain: A Life in Neuroscience — *Gazzaniga, Michael S.*
Tales from Both Sides of the Brain: A Life in Neuroscience — *Gazzinga, Michael S.*
Tales from Both Sides of the Brain: A Life in Neuroscience — *Gazzaniga, Michael S.*
Tales from Concrete Jungles: Urban Birding around the World — *Linda, David*
Tales from Corral Fences — *Duncklee, John*
c Tales from Shakespeare (Illus. by Williams, Marcia) — *Williams, Marcia*
Tales from Shakespeare: Creative Collections — *Holderness, Graham*
Tales from the Back Row: An Outsider's View from Inside the Fashion Industry — *Odell, Amy*
c Tales from the Brothers Grimm (Illus. by Leupin, Herbert) — *Grimm, Jacob*
Tales of a Female Nomad: Living at Large in the World (Read by Gelman, Rita Golden). Audiobook Review — *Gelman, Rita Golden*
Tales of a Hamptons Sailor — *Catalano, Nick*
Tales of Accidental Genius — *Van Booy, Simon*
c Tales of Bunjitsu Bunny (Illus. by Himmelman, John) — *Himmelman, John*
Tales of High Hallack: The Collected Short Stories — *Norton, Andre*
Tales of Iran — *Rashidi, Feridon*
Tales of Iran 2 — *Rashidi, Feridon*
c Tales of Mr. Snuggywhiskers: The Autumn Tales (Illus. by Crawford, L.H.) — *Crawford, C.F.*
y Tales of Remarkable Birds — *Couzens, Dominic*
c Tales of the Great Beasts: Special Edition — *Mull, Brandon*
Tales of the Marvellous and News of the Strange — *Lyons, Malcolm C.*
Tales of the Primal Land — *Lumley, Brian*
Tales of Three Cities: Urban Jewish Cultures in London, Berlin, and Paris — *Metzler, Tobias*
Tales of Time and Space — *Steele, Allen*
c Talia and the Very Yum Kippur (Illus. by Assirelli, Francesca) — *Marshall, Linda Elovitz*
Talk — *Rosenkrantz, Linda*
Talk at the Brink: Deliberation and Decision during the Cuban Missile Crisis — *Gibson, David R.*
The Talk of the Town — *Mosca, Sal*
Talk Talk — *Boyle, T. Coraghessan*
Talk to God — *Verus, DeiAmor*
y Talk under Water — *Lomer, Kathryn*
c Talkin' Guitar: A Story of Young Doc Watson (Illus. by Gourley, Robbin) — *Gourley, Robbin*
c Talkin' Guitar: A Story of Young Doc Watson — *Gourley, Robbin*
c Talkin' Guitar: A Story of Young Doc Watson (Illus. by Gourley, Robbin) — *Gourley, Robbin*
Talking Story: One Woman's Quest to Preserve Ancient Spiritual and Healing Traditions — *Phan-Le, Marie-Rose*
Talking to Terrorists: How to End Armed Conflicts — *Powell, Jonathan*
Talking to the Dead: Religion, Music, and Lived Memory among Gullah/Geechee Women — *Manigault-Bryant, LeRhonda S.*
Talking with Catholics About the Gospel: A Guide for Evangelicals — *Castaldo, Chris*

Talking with Dogs and Cats: Joining the Conversation to Improve Behavior and Bond with Your Animals — *Link, Tim*
Talking with: Lorenzo Pace — *Kraus, Daniel*
Tall, Dark, and Wicked — *Hunter, Madeline*
c Tallulah: Mermaid of the Great Lakes (Illus. by Hartung, Susan Kathleen) — *Brennan-Nelson, Denise*
c Tallulah's Tap Shoes (Illus. by Boiger, Alexandra) — *Singer, Marilyn*
The Talmud: A Biography — *Freedman, Harry*
c Talon — *Kagawa, Julie*
c Tamar's Sukkah (Illus. by Kahn, Katherine) — *Gellman, Ellie B.*
c Tamar's Sukkah (Illus. by Kahn, Katherine Janus) — *Gellman, Ellie B.*
Tambora: The Eruption That Changed the World — *Wood, Gillen D'Arcy*
The Tamburitza Tradition: From the Balkans to the American Midwest — *March, Richard*
Tamil Folk Music as Dalit Liberation Theology — *Sherinian, Zoe C.*
Taming China's Wilderness: Immigration, Settlement and the Shaping of the Heilongjiang Frontier, 1900-1931 — *Shan, Patrick Fuliang*
Taming Lust: Crimes against Nature in the Early Republic — *Ben-Atar, Doron S.*
Taming Lust: Crimes against Nature in the Early Republic — *Brown, Richard D.*
Taming Manhattan: Environmental Battles in the Antebellum City — *McNeur, Catherine*
The Taming of Malcolm Grant — *Quinn, Paula*
The Taming of the Queen (Read by Amato, Bianca). Audiobook Review — *Gregory, Philippa*
The Taming of the Queen — *Gregory, Philippa*
Taming the Legend — *Latham, Kat*
Taming the Tiger Parent — *Carey, Tanith*
Taming Tibet: Landscape Transformation and the Gift of Chinese Development — *Yeh, Emily T.*
Taming Time, Timing Death: Social Technologies and Ritual — *Christensen, Dorthe Refslund*
Tan Men/Pale Women: Color and Gender in Archaic Greece and Egypt. A Comparative Approach — *Eaverly, M. A.*
Tang China in Multi-Polar Asia: A History of Diplomacy and War — *Wang, Zhenping*
y A Tangle of Gold — *Moriarty, Jaclyn*
Tangled Ribbons — *Strock, Carren*
Tangled Roots: The Appalachian Trail and American Environmental Politics — *Mittlefehldt, Sarah*
y Tangled Secrets — *Conway, Anne-Marie*
A Tangled Thread — *Fraser, Anthea*
Tangled Vines: Greed, Murder, Obsession, and an Arsonist in the Vineyards of California — *Dinkelspiel, Frances*
y Tangled Webs — *Bross, Lee*
Tanglewood — *Bolger, Dermot*
Tango Lessons: Movement, Sound, Image, and Text in Contemporary Practice — *Miller, Marilyn G.*
y Tango — *Thomas, Wendell*
Tango Nuevo — *Merritt, Carolyn*
The Tank Man's Son — *Bouman, Mark*
c Tanks (Illus. by West, David) — *West, David*
Tantra for the West: A Direct Path to Living the Life of Your Dreams — *Allen, Mark*
The Tao of Happiness: Stories from Chuang Tzu for Your Spiritual Journey — *Lin, Derek*
y Tap Out — *Rodman, Sean*
c Tap to Play! — *Yoon, Salina*
The Tapestry — *Bilyeau, Nancy*
The Tapestry (Read by Barber, Nicola). Audiobook Review — *Bilyeau, Nancy*
Tapestry Weaving — *Glasbrook, Kirsten*
The Tapper Twins Go to War (with Each Other). — *Rodkey, Geoff*
c The Tapper Twins Go to War — *Rodkey, Geoff*
c The Tapper Twins Go to War with Each Other — *Rodkey, Geoff*
y The Tapper Twins Go to War (with Each Other). — *Rodkey, Geoff*
c The Tapper Twins Tear Up New York — *Rodkey, Geoff*
Tapping Into Wealth: How Emotional Freedom Techniques (EFT) Can Help You Clear the Path to Making More Money — *Lynch, Margaret M.*
Tapping Philanthropy for Development: Lessons Learned from a Public-Private Partnership in Rural Uganda — *Butler, Lorna Michael*
c Tarantula Spiders — *Archer, Claire*
The Target — *Sellers, L.J.*
Target America — *McEwen, Scott*
Target Citadel — *Adrian, Robert*
Target Engaged — *Buchman, M.L.*

Target Tokyo: Jimmy Doolittle and the Raid That Avenged Pearl Harbor — *Scott, James*
Target Tokyo: Jimmy Doolittle and the Raid That Avenged Pearl Harbor — *Scott, James M.*
A Taste for Brown Sugar: Black Women in Pornography — *Miller-Young, Mireille*
A Taste for Chaos: The Art of Literary Improvisation — *Fertel, Randy*
A Taste for Happiness — *David-Weill, Michel*
A Taste for Nightshade — *Bailey, Martine*
The Taste of Belgium — *Waerebeek, Ruth van*
A Taste of Cowboy: Ranch Recipes and Tales from the Trail — *Rollins, Kent*
A Taste of Pleasure — *Antoinette*
A Taste of Sugar — *Adair, Marina*
Taste: The Infographic Book of Food — *Rowe, Laura*
The Tastemaker: Carl Van Vechten and Birth of Modern America — *White, Edward*
c Tastes Like Music: 17 Quirks of the Brain and Body (Illus. by Melnychuk, Monika) — *Birmingham, Maria*
Tasting Wine and Cheese: An Insider's Guide to Mastering the Principles of Pairing — *Centamore, Adam*
Tasty: The Art and Science of What We Eat (Read by Perkins, Tom). Audiobook Review — *McQuaid, John*
Tasty: The Art and Science of What We Eat — *John, McQuaid*
Tasty: The Art and Science of What we Eat — *McQuaid, John*
y Tasunka: A Lakota Horse Legend (Illus. by Montileaux, Donald F.) — *Montileaux, Donald F.*
Tata Dada: The Real Life and Celestial Adventures of Tristan Tzara — *Hentea, Marius*
TaTa Dada: The Real Life and Celestial Adventures of Tristan Tzara — *Dayan, Peter*
Tatiana: An Arkady Renko Novel — *Smith, Martin Cruz*
c Tator's Swamp Fever — *Shapley-Box, Diane*
Tatort Germany: The Curious Case of German-Language Crime Fiction — *Kutch, Lynn M.*
Tattered and Mended: The Art of Healing the Wounded Soul — *Ruchti, Cynthia*
Tattered Legacy — *Baker, Shannon*
The Tattooed Arm — *Simpson, M.*
y The Tattooed Heart: A Messenger of Fear — *Grant, Michael*
y The Tattooed Heart: A Messenger of Fear Novel — *Grant, Michael*
The Tattoorialist: Tattoo Street Style — *Brulez, Nicolas*
Tavern Tales 2004-2014 — *Frank, Wayne*
Taxation for and against Redistribution since 1945
Taxifornia 2016: 14 Essays on the Future of California — *Lacy, James V.*
Taxing Colonial Africa: The Political Economy of British Imperialism — *Gardner, Leigh A.*
Taxing the Poor: Doing Damage to the Truly Disadvantaged — *Newman, Katherine S.*
The Taymouth Hours: Stories and the Construction of the Self in Late Medieval England — *Smith, Kathryn A.*
c !Te amo, te abrazo, leo contigo! Love You, Hug You, Read to You! (Illus. by Endersby, Frank) — *Rabe, Tish*
Tea on the Great Wall: An American Girl in War-Torn China — *Chapman, Patricia Luce*
c The Tea Party in the Woods (Illus. by Miyakoshi, Akiko) — *Miyakoshi, Akiko*
Teach Me to Applique: Fusible Applique That's Soft and Simple — *Sloan, Pat*
c Teach Me to Love (Illus. by Brennan-Nelson, Denise) — *Brennan-Nelson, Denise*
Teach, Reflect, Learn: Building Your Capacity for Success in the Classroom — *Hall, Peter A.*
Teach Your Herding Breed to Be a Great Companion Dog: From Obsessive to Outstanding — *Antoniak-Mitchell, Dawn*
Teach Your Kids to Code: A Parent-Friendly Guide to Python Programming — *Payne, Bryson*
The Teacher Wars: A History of America's Most Embattled Profession — *Goldstein, Dana*
c The Teacher Who Would Not Retire Loses Her Ballet Slippers (Illus. by Bone, Thomas H., III) — *Sustrin, Letty*
A Teacher's Guide to Using the Common Core State Standards with Mathematically Gifted and Advanced Learners — *Johnsen, Susan K.*

A Teacher's Guide to Using the Next Generation Science Standards with Gifted and Advanced Learners — *Adams, Cheryll M.*
c Teacher's Pets (Illus. by Ross, Heather) — *Calmenson, Stephanie*
c Teacher's Pets — *Meddaugh, Susan*
y Teacher's Pets — *Hurdle, Crystal*
Teachers versus the Public: What Americans Think about Schools and How to Fix Them — *West, Martin R.*
Teaching All Nations: Interrogating the Matthean Great Commission — *Smith, Mitzi J.*
Teaching and Learning in Bilingual Classrooms: New Scholarship — *Mulrooney, Kristin J.*
Teaching Arguments: Rhetorical Comprehension, Critique, and Response — *Fletcher, Jennifer*
The Teaching Brain — *Rodriguez, Vanessa*
Teaching Dilemmas and Solutions in Content-Area Literacy, Grades 6-12 — *Smagorinsky, Peter*
Teaching for a Culturally Diverse and Racially Just World — *Fernandez, Eleazar S.*
Teaching for Conceptual Understanding in Science — *Konicek-Moran, Richard*
Teaching French through Drama: A Teacher Resource — *Williamson, Denise Gagne*
Teaching French Women Writers of the Renaissance and Reformation — *Winn, Colette H.*
Teaching Gender — *Ferrebe, Alice*
Teaching Internet Basics: The Can-Do Guide — *Nichols, Joel A.*
Teaching Machines: Learning from the Intersection of Education and Technology — *Ferster, Bill*
Teaching Marianne and Uncle Sam: Public Education, State Centralization, and Teacher Unionism in France and United States — *Touloudis, Nicolas*
Teaching Math, Science, and Technology in Schools Today: Guidelines for Engaging Both Eager and Reluctant Learners — *Adams, Dennis*
Teaching Plato in Palestine: Philosophy in a Divided World — *Fraenkel, Carlos*
Teaching Science for Understanding in Elementary and Middle Schools — *Harlen, Wynne*
Teaching Student-Centered Mathematics: Developmentally Appropriate Instruction for Grades 3-5 — *Van de Walle, John A.*
Teaching Student-Centered Mathematics: Developmentally Appropriate Instruction for Grades Pre-K-2 — *Van de Walle, John A.*
Teaching the Dog to Read — *Carroll, Jonathan*
Teaching the Social Skills of Academic Interaction: Step-by-Step Lessons for Respect, Responsibility, and Results — *Daniels, Smokey*
Teaching Will — *Ryane, Mel*
A Teacup Collection: Paintings of Porcelain Treasures — *Hatch, Molly*
y Teacup (Illus. by Ottley, Matt) — *Young, Rebecca*
Team Dog: How to Train Your Dog - the Navy SEAL Way — *Ritland, Mike*
Team Genius: The New Science of High-Performing Organizations — *Karlgaard, Rich*
Team of Teams: New Rules of Engagement for a Complex World — *McChrystal, Stanley*
y Tear You Apart — *Cross, Sarah*
The Tears of Angels — *Ramsay, Caro*
The Tears of Dark Water — *Addison, Corban*
Tears of Innocence — *Rapp, Bill*
Tears of Innocense — *Rapp, Bill*
Tears of Repentance: Christian Indian Identity and Community in Colonial Southern New England — *Rubin, Julius H.*
The Tears of the Rajas: Mutiny, Money and Marriage in India 1805-1905 — *Mount, Ferdinand*
Tears to Triumph — *Williamson, Marianne*
Teatime in Paris! A Walk through Easy French Patisserie Recipes — *Colonna, Jill*
Technikstudien als Teildisziplin der Japanforschung - Japanisch-Deutsche Perspektiven der Science and Technology Studies
Techniques for Virtual Palaeontology — *Sutton, Mark D.*
The Technological Singularity — *Shanahan, Murray*
Technologies of Sexiness: Sex, Identity and Consumer Culture — *Evans, Adrienne*
Technologies of Spectacle - Knowledge Transfer in Early Modern Theater Cultures. Workshop
y Technology — *Buckley, James, Jr.*
Technology and Identity in Young Adult Fiction: The Posthuman Subject — *Flanagan, Victoria*
Technology as Human Social Tradition: Cultural Transmission among Hunter-Gatherers — *Jordan, Peter*

c Technology: Cool Women Who Code (Illus. by Chandhok, Lena) — Diehn, Andi
Technology Disaster Response and Recovery Planning: A LITA Guide — Mallery, Mary
Technology Distribution Channels: Understanding and Managing Channels to Market — Dent, Julian
Technology Handbook for School Librarians — Scheeren, William O.
The Technology of Nonviolence: Social Media and Violence Prevention — Bock, Joseph G.
Technology, Skills and the Pre-Modern Economy in the East and the West — Prak, Maarten
c Technology Top Tens — Donovan, Sandy
TechnoSpaces: Persistence - Practices - Performance - Power
Ted Browning's Dracula — Rhodes, Gary D.
Ted Hughes, Class and Violence — Bentley, Paul
Ted Hughes: The Unauthorised Life — Bate, Jonathan
c Ted Rules the World (Illus. by Riddell, Chris) — Cottrell Boyce, Frank
c Teddy Bear Addition (Illus. by Nihoff, Tim) — McGrath, Barbara Barbieri
c Teddy Bear Doctor: Be a Vet and Fix the Boo-Boos of Your Favorite Stuffed Animals — Cook, Deanna F.
c Teddy Bedtime (Illus. by Birkett, Georgie) — Birkett, Georgie
c Teddy Mars: Almost a World Record Breaker (Illus. by Spencer, Trevor) — Burnham, Molly B.
c The Teddy Potty Book — Channing, Margot
Teddy Roosevelt and Leonard Wood: Partners in Command — Eisenhower, John S.D.
c Teddy Took the Train (Illus. by Greenberg, Nicki) — Greenberg, Nicki
c Teen Boat! The Race for Boatlantis (Illus. by Green, John) — Roman, Dave
y Teen Frankenstein — Baker, Chandler
y Teen Pregnancy — Kenney, Karen Latchana
y Teen Reads: Home — Donbavand, Tommy
y Teen Rights and Freedoms: Drugs — Merino, Noel
y Teen Rights and Freedoms: Emancipation — Merino, Noel
y Teen Rights and Freedoms: Health Care — Merino, Noel
y Teen Self-Injury — Higgins, Melissa
y Teen Services 101: A Practical Guide for Busy Library Staff — Fink, Megan P.
c Teen Titans Go! Party, Party! (Illus. by Hernandez, Lea) — Fisch, Sholly
y Teen Titans (Illus. by Dodson, Terry) — Fletcher, Jared
The Teenage Brain: A Neuroscientist's Survival Guide to Raising Adolescents and Young Adults — Nutt, Amy Ellis
Teenage Citizens: The Political Theories of the Young — Flanagan, Constance A.
y Teenage Diaries Then and Now. Audiobook Review — Richman, Joe
c Teenage Rebels: Successful High School Activists, from the Little Rock 9 to the Class of Tomorrow — Barrett, Dawson
y Teens and LGBT Issues — Wilcox, Christine
y Teens and Marijuana — Currie-McGhee, Leanne
y Teens and Sex — Nakaya, Andrea C.
y Teens and Sexting — Netzley, Patricia D.
Tehran Noir — Abdoh, Salar
c Telephone (Illus. by Corace, Jen) — Barnett, Mac
The Telescopic Polity: Andean Patriarchy and Materiality — Dillehay, Tom D.
Television Is the New Television: The Unexpected Triumph of Old Media in the Digital Age — Wolff, Michael
Tell — Itani, Frances
c Tell Me a Picture — Blake, Quentin
Tell Me a Story In the Dark: A Guide to Creating Magical Bedtime Stories for Young Children — Olive, John
y Tell Me Again How a Crush Should Feel (Read by Farsad, Negin). Audiobook Review — Farizan, Sara
y Tell Me Again How a Crush Should Feel — Farizan, Sara
c Tell Me — Bauer, Joan
c Tell Me What to Dream About (Illus. by Potter, Giselle) — Potter, Giselle
"Tell Me Why I Shouldn't Kill You": On Johanna Dubrow's The Arranged Marriage — Dubrow, Jehanne
The Tell-Tale Heart — Dawson, Jill
Tell Tchaikovsky the News: Rock 'n' Roll, the Labor Question, and the Musicians' Union, 1942-1968 — Roberts, Michael James
y Tell the Story to Its End — Clark, Simon P.

Tell This in My Memory: Stories of Enslavement from Egypt, Sudan, and the Ottoman Empire — Powell, Eve Troutt
The Teller — Stone, Jonathan
The Telling — Baker, Jo
Telling Genes: The Story of Genetic Counseling in America — Stern, Alexandra Minna
y The Telling Stone — McQuerry, Maureen Doyle
Telling the Whole Story: Reading and Preaching Old Testament Stories — Holbert, John
c Telling Time (Illus. by Longhi, Katya) — Heos, Bridget
The Temp Economy: From Kelly Girls to Permatemps in Postwar America — Hatton, Erin
Temperature and Plant Development — Franklin, Keara A.
Tempest — Rock, J.A.
c Tempete — Tamburini, Arianna
y Temple Boys — Buxton, Jamie
Temple Grandin: How the Girl Who Loved Cows Embraced Autism and Changed the World — Montgomery, Sy
c Temple Grandin: Inspiring Animal-Behavior Scientist — Sepahban, Lois
y The Temple of Doubt — Levy, Anne Boles
The Temple of Light — Piazza, Daniela
The Temple of Perfection: A History of the Gym — Chaline, Eric
Templerburgen — Biller, Thomas
Temples for a Modern God: Religious Architecture in Postwar America — Price, Jay M.
c Templeton Gets His Wish (Illus. by Pizzoli, Greg) — Pizzoli, Greg
A Temporary Future: The Fiction of David Mitchell — O'Donnell, Patrick
The Temporary Gentleman (Read by Grimes, Frank). Audiobook Review — Barry, Sebastian
Temporary Superheroine — Vartanoff, Irene
Temptation in the Archives: Essays in Golden Age Dutch Culture — Jardine, Lisa
The Temptation of Elizabeth Tudor: Elizabeth I, Thomas Seymour, and the Making of a Virgin Queen — Norton, Elizabeth
Temptations Behind Stained Glass — Crangle, Richard
The Tempting of Thomas Carrick — Laurens, Stephanie
Ten African Cardinals — Ninham, Sally
Ten Bedtime Poems, vol. 2 — Greer, Germaine
Ten Billion Tomorrows: How Science Fiction Technology Became a Reality and Shapes the Future — Clegg, Brian
Ten Billion Tomorrows: How Science Fiction Technology Became Reality and Shapes the Future — Clegg, Brian
Ten Cocktails: The Art of Convivial Drinking — Lascalles, Alice
The Ten Commandments: A Short History of an Ancient Text — Coogan, Michael
The Ten Commandments: Interpreting the Bible in the Medieval World — Smith, Lesley
y Ten Days a Madwoman: The Daring Life and Turbulent Times of the Original "Girl" Reporter Nellie Bly — Noyes, Deborah
c Ten Easter Eggs (Illus. by Logan, Laura) — Bodach, Vijaya
Ten Good Reasons — Christopher, Lauren
c Ten Kisses for Sophie — Wells, Rosemary
Ten Million Aliens: A Journey through the Entire Animal Kingdom — Barnes, Simon
c Ten Monsters in the Bed (Illus. by Blecha, Aaron) — Cotton, Katie
c Ten — Flint, Shamini
c Ten of the Best God and Goddess Stories (Illus. by West, David) — West, David
c Ten of the Best: Myths, Legends and Folk Stones Series, 8 vols. — West, David
Ten Percent: Hollywood Can Be Murder — Bruin, D.L.
c Ten Pigs: An Epic Bath Adventure — Anderson, Derek
c Ten Playful Penguins — Ford, Emily
c Ten Playful Tigers: A Back-and-Forth Counting Book (Illus. by Powell, Luciana Navarro) — Schwartz, Betty Ann
Ten Prayers That Changed the World: Extraordinary Stories of Faith That Shaped the Course of History — Isbouts, Jean-Pierre
c Ten Rules of Being a Superhero — Pilutti, Deb
c Ten Thank-You Letters — Kirk, Daniel
c Ten: The New Wave — Woolf, Karen McCarthy
Ten Thousand Birds: Ornithology since Darwin — Montgomerie, Bob
y Ten Thousand Skies above You — Gray, Claudia

Ten Thousand Waves — Wang, Ping
Ten Windows: How Great Poems Transform the World — Hirshfield, Jane
c Ten Zany Birds (Illus. by Jain, Charu) — Ellis, Sherry
Tenacity — Law, J.S.
Tender — McKeon, Belinda
Tender Data — McClure, Monica
The Tender Friendship and the Charm of Perfect Accord: Nabokov and His Father — Shapiro, Gavriel
Tender the Maker — Hutchins, Christina
y The Tenderness of Thieves — Freitas, Donna
Tending the Epicurean Garden — Crespo, Hiram
Tennesseans at War, 1812-1815: Andrew Jackson, the Creek War, and the Battle of New Orleans — Kanon, Tom
Tennessee Williams: Mad Pilgrimage of the Flesh — Lahr, John
Tennyson and the Fabrication of Englishness — Sherwood, Marion
y The Tenth Doctor: Revolutions of Terror (Illus. by Casagrande, Elena) — Abadzis, Nick
c Teo (Illus. by Pineiro, Azul) — Jurado, Anabel
Tequila! Distilling the Spirit of Mexico — Gaytan, Marie Sarita
Teratology: Poems — Nevison, Susannah
Teresa, My Love: An Imagined Life of the Saint of Avila — Kristeva, Julia
y Terminal — Reichs, Kathy
Terminal City — Fairstein, Linda
Terminal Innocence — Rifbjerg, Klaus
y The Terminals — Buckingham, Royce Scott
Terms of Service: Social Media and the Price of Constant Connection — Silverman, Jacob
Terms of Surrender — Farrelly, Lorrie
Terms of Use — Morrison, Scott Allan
Terra Incognita: An Annotated Bibliography of the Great Smoky Mountains, 1544-1934 — Bridges, Anne
Terrariums: Gardens under Glass: Designing, Creating, and Planting Modern Indoor Gardens — Colletti, Maria
Terra's World — Benn, Mitch
c Terremoto — Markovics, Joyce
Terrence Davies — Koresky, Michael
A Terrible Beauty: The Wilderness of American Literature — Raskin, Jonah
c Terrible Lizard (Illus. by Moss, Drew) — Bunn, Cullen
c The Terrible Two (Read by Verner, Adam). Audiobook Review — Barnett, Mac
c The Terrible Two Get Worse (Illus. by Cornell, Kevin) — Barnett, Mac
c The Terrible Two (Illus. by Cornell, Kevin) — Barnett, Mac
c The Terrible Two (Illus. by Cornell, Kevin) — John, Jory
y Terrible Typhoid Mary: A True Story of the Deadliest Cook in America (Read by Postel, Donna). Audiobook Review — Bartoletti, Susan Campbell
y Terrible Typhoid Mary: A True Story of the Deadliest Cook in America — Bartoletti, Susan Campbell
Terrific (Read by Heyborne, Kirby). Audiobook Review — Agee, Jon
c Terrifying Tales — Scieszka, Jon
The Territories of Science and Religion — Harrison, Peter
Territory, Authority, Rights: From Medieval to Global Assemblages — Sassen, Saskia
Terror and Democracy in West Germany — Hanshew, Karrin
c Terror at Bottle Creek — Key, Watt
y The Terror of the Southlands (Illus. by Phillips, Dave) — Carlson, Caroline
c The Terror of the Tengu — Seven, John
y Terrorist: Gavrilo Princip, the Assassin Who Ignited World War I (Illus. by Rehr, Henrik) — Rehr, Henrik
y Terrorist: Gavrilo Princip, the Assassin Who Ignited World War I — Schwartz, Simon
y Terrorist: Gavrilo Princip, the Assassin Who Ignited World War I (Illus. by Rehr, Henrik) — Rehr, Henrik
Terrorists at the Table: Why Negotiating is the Only Way to Peace — Powell, Jonathan
c Terry Perkins and his Upside Down Frown — Massie, Felix
Tesla: Inventor of the Electrical Age — Carlson, W. Bernard
Test, Evaluate and Improve Your Chess: A Knowledge-Based Approach — Kopec, Danny
The Test: My Life, and the Inside Story of the Greatest Ashes Series — Jones, Simon

The Test: Why Our Schools Are Obsessed With Standardized Testing - But You Don't Have to Be — Kamenetz, Anya
The Testament of Gideon Mack — Robertson, James
The Testament of James — Suprynowicz, Vin
Testament of Youth — Brittain, Vera
Testament of Youth — Kent, James
Testimonial Plays in Contemporary American Theater — Forsyth, Alison
The Testimonies of Indian Soldiers and the Two World Wars: Between Self and Sepoy — Singh, Gajendra
Testimony of the Protected — Milliken, Doug
y Testing the Truth — Knudsen, Shannon
Testing Wars in the Public Schools: A Forgotten History — Reese, William J.
Testosterone: Sex, Power, and the Will to Win — Herbert, Joe
y Tether — Jarzab, Anna
Tethered Worlds: Unwelcome Star — Faccone, Gregory
Tetralogue: I'm Right, You're Wrong — Williamson, Timothy
'Teutsche Liedlein' des 16. Jahrhunderts. Jahrestagung des Wolfenbutteler Arbeitskreises fur Renaissanceforschung
Tex-Mex from Scratch — Cramby, Jonas
Texas Adoption Activist Edna Gladney: A Life and Legacy Of Love — McLeRoy, Sherrie S.
Texas BBQ: Meat, Smoke, and Love — Cramby, Jonas
Texas Ranch Women: Three Centuries of Mettle and Moxie — Goldthwaite, Carmen
Texas Ranger N.O. Reynolds, The Intrepid — Parsons, Chuck
The Texas Right: The Radical Roots of Lone Star Conservatism — Cullen, David O'Donald
Texas Rising — Moore, Stephen L.
Texas Seashells: A Field Guide — Barrera, Noe C.
Texas Takes Wing: A Century of Flight in the Lone Star State — Ganson, Barbara
Texas Takes Wing: A Century of Flight in the Lone Star State — Ganson, Barbara Anne
c Texas Tales Illustrated: The Trail Drives (Illus. by White, Mack) — Kearby, Mike
Texas Thunder — Raye, Kimberly
Text and Authority in the South African Nazaretha Church — Cabrita, Joel
c Text Styles: How to Write Science Fiction — Kopp, Megan
Textiles and the Medieval Economy: Production, Trade, and Consumption of Textiles, 8th-16th Centuries — Huang, Angela Ling
Texting toward Utopia: Kids, Writing, and Resistance — Agger, Ben
Texts from Jane Eyre: And Other Conversations with Your Favorite Literary Characters (Read by Landon, Amy). Audiobook Review — Ortberg, Mallory
Texts in Transit: Manuscript to Proof and Print in the Fifteenth Century — Hellinga, Lotte
Textual Agency: Writing Culture and Social Networks in Fifteenth-Century Spain — Gomez-Bravo, Ana M.
Textual Rivals: Self-Presentation in Herodotus' Histories — Branscome, David
Textual Warfare and the Making of Methodism — McInelly, Brett C.
Textualizing Illness: Medicine and Culture in New England, 1620-1730 — Priewe, Marc
Textured Bead Embroidery: Learn to Make Inspired Pins, Pendants, Earrings, and More — Landy, Linda
The Textures of Time: Agency and Temporal Experience — Flaherty, Michael G.
Thackeray's Angel: A Life of Jane Octavia Brookfield 1821-1896 — Beales, Sally
Thai Stick: Surfers, Scammers, and the Untold Story of the Marijuana Trade — Farber, David
The Thai Way of Counterinsurgency — Moore, Jeff M.
Thalassokratographie - Rezeption und Transformation Antiker Seeherrschaft
c Thank You and Good Night (Illus. by McDonnell, Patrick) — McDonnell, Patrick
Thank You For the Shoes — Rizzo, Raffaela Marie
Thank You for This Moment — Trierweiler, Valerie
c Thank You, God (Illus. by Jago) — Wigger, J. Bradley
Thank You, Goodnight — Abramowitz, Andy
c Thank You, Jackson: How One Little Boy Makes a Big Difference — Daly, Jude
c Thank you, Jackson: How One Little Boy Makes a Big Difference (Illus. by Daly, Jude) — Daly, Niki

c Thank You, Jackson: How One Little Boy Makes a Big Difference — Daly, Niki
Thank You, Madagascar: The Conservation Diaries of Alison Jolly — Jolly, Alison
c Thankful (Illus. by Preston, Archie) — Spinelli, Eileen
y Thanks for the Trouble — Wallach, Tommy
y Thanksgiving Angels — Duncan, Alice
c Thanksgiving — Dash, Meredith
That Chesapeake Summer — Stewart, Mariah
c That Day in September and Other Rhymes for the Times — Lime, Liz
That Devil's Trick: Hypnotism in the Victorian Popular Imagination — Hughes, William
c That Dog! (Illus. by Johnson-Isaacs, Cally) — Shields, Gillian
That Dream Shall Have a Name: Native Americans Rewriting America — Moore, David L.
c That Is a Hat (Illus. by Casey, Betty Selakovich) — Casey, Betty Selakovich
That Old Bilbao Moon: The Passion and Resurrection of a City — Zulaika, Joseba
That Other Me — Gargash, Maha
That Pride of Race and Character: The Roots of Jewish Benevolence in the Jim Crow South — Light, Caroline E.
That Religion in Which All Men Agree: Freemasonry in American Culture — Hackett, David G.
c That Squeak (Illus. by Thisdale, Francois) — Beck, Carolyn
That Sugar Film — Gameau, Damon
That the Blood Stay Pure: African Americans, Native Americans, and the Predicament of Race and Identity in Virginia — Coleman, Arica L.
"That the People Might Live": Loss and Renewal in Native American Elegy — Krupat, Arnold
That Thing You Do with Your Mouth — Matthews, Samantha
That Winter the Wolf Came — Spahr, Juliana
Thatcher's Trial: 180 Days That Created a Conservative Icon — Kwarteng, Kwasi
c That's Deadly — Boyer, Crispin
That's Entertainment: My Life in the Jam — Buckler, Rick
c That's Not Bunny! (Illus. by Jack, Colin) — Barton, Chris
That's Not English: Britishisms, Americanisms, and What Our English Says About Us — Moore, Erin
c That's (Not) Mine (Illus. by Weyant, Christopher) — Kang, Anna
That's Racist!: How the Regulation of Speech and Thought Divides Us All — Hart, Adrian
c That's Sneaky! — Boyer, Crispin
That's the Way It Is: A History of Television News in America — de Leon, Charles L. Ponce
That's the Way It Is: A History of Television News in America — Ponce de Leon, Charles L.
That's What Fashion Is — Zee, Joe
c That's What Wings Are For (Illus. by Germain, Daniella) — Guest, Patrick
That's What You Think!: A Mind-Boggling Guide to the Brain — Von Holleben, Jan
The Thaw: Soviet Society and Culture during the 1950s and 1960s — Kozlov, Denis
Theater & Animals — Orozco, Lourdes
A Theater of Our Own: A History and a Memoir of 1,001 Nights in Chicago — Christiansen, Richard
The Theater of War: What Ancient Greek Tragedies Can Teach Us Today — Doerries, Bryan
Theater und Offentlichkeit im Vormarz. Berlin, Munchen und Wien als Schauplatze burgerlicher Medienpraxis — Wagner, Meike
Theatergeschichte: Eine Einfuhrung — Kotte, Andreas
Theatre and Testimony in Shakespeare's England: A Culture of Mediation — Syme, Holger Schott
Theatre de femmes de l'Ancien Regime — Evain, Aurore
The Theatre of Cornwall: Space, Place and Performance — Kent, Alan M.
Theatre of Good Intentions: Challenges and Hopes for Theatre and Social Change — Snyder-Young, Dani
The Theatre of War: What Ancient Greek Tragedies Can Teach Us Today — Doerries, Bryan
Theatres of Affect — Hurley, Erin
Theatres of Life: Drawings from the Rothschild Collection at Waddesdon Manor — Carey, Juliet
The Theatrical Public Sphere — Balme, Christopher B.
Theatricality, Dark Tourism and Ethical Spectatorship: Absent Others — Willis, Emma
Theatrum Humanum: Illustrierte Flugblatter und Druckgrafik des 17. Jahrhunderts als Spiegel der Zeit: Beispiele aus dem Bestand der Sammlung Valvasor des Zagreber Erzbistum — Pelc, Milan

The Theft of Memory: Losing My Father, One Day at a Time — Kozol, Jonathan
c Their Great Gift: Courage, Sacrifice, and Hope in a New Land (Illus. by Huie, Wing Young) — Coy, John
Their Last Full Measure — Wheelan, Joseph
Their Lives, Their Wills: Women in the Borderlands, 1750-1846 — Porter, Amy M.
Their Name Is Today: Reclaiming Childhood in a Hostile World — Arnold, Johann Christoph
Their Promised Land: My Grandparents in Love and War — Buruma, Ian
c Theis Rags, Hero Dog of WWI: A True Story (Illus. by Brown, Petra) — Raven, Margot
c Thelma the Unicorn (Illus. by Blabey, Aaron) — Blabey, Aaron
Thematisierte Welten: Uber Darstellungspraxen in Zoologischen Garten und Vergnugungsparks — Steinkruger, Jan-Erik
Themes in Roman Society and Culture: An Introduction to Ancient Rome — Gibbs, Matt
Then Comes Marriage: United States v. Windsor and the Defeat of DOMA — Dickey, Lisa
Then Comes Marriage: United States v. Windsor and the Defeat of Doma — Kaplan, Roberta
Theo Chocolate: Recipes and Sweet Secrets from Seattle's Favorite Chocolate Maker — Music, Debra
Theodahad: A Platonic King at the Collapse of Ostrogothic Italy — Vitiello, Massimiliano
Theoderic and the Roman Imperial Restoration — Arnold, Jonathan J.
Theodor Eschenburg: Biographie einer Politischen Leitfigur 1904-1999 — Wengst, Udo
Theodor Fontane: Angstliche Moderne - Uber das Imaginare — Graevenitz, Gerhart von
Theodora: Actress, Emperor, Saint — Potter, David S. (b. 1957-)
Theodora: Actress, Empress, Saint — Potter, David S. (b. 1957-)
y Theodore Boone — Grisham, John
Theodosius II: Rethinking the Roman Empire in Late Antiquity — Kelly, Christopher
Theologe, Erbauungsschriftsteller, Hofprediger: Joachim Lutkemann in Rostock und Wolfenbuttel — Deurper, Christian
Theological Reflection Across Religious Traditions: The Turn to Reflective Believing — Foley, Edward
The Theological Vision of Reinhold Niebuhr's "In the Battle and Above It" — Erwin, Scott R.
Theologie in der jemenitischen Zaydiyya. Die naturphilosophischen Uberlegungen des al-Hasan ar-Rassas — Thiele, Jan
Theologie und Vergangenheitsbewaltigung VI: Diskurse uber "Form," "Gestalt" und "Stil" in den 20er und 30er Jahren
Theology after the Birth of God: Atheist Conceptions in Cognition and Culture — Shults, F. LeRon
Theology against religion: Constructive Dialouges with Bonhoeffer and Barth — Greggs, Tom
Theology and Society in Three Cities: Berlin, Oxford, and Chicago, 1800-1914 — Chapman, Mark D.
Theology and the End of Doctrine — Helmer, Christine
Theology as Science in Nineteenth-Century Germany — Zachhuber, Johannes
Theology for Liberal Protestants: God the Creator — Ottati, Douglas F.
Theology for Ministry: An Introduction for Lay Ministers — Hahnenberg, Edward P.
c Theology of the Body Series (Illus. by Kaminski, Karol) — Ashour, Monica
y Theophilus Grey and the Demon Thief — Jinks, Catherine
The Theoretical Foot — Fisher, M.F.K.
c Theoretical Physicist Brian Greene — Doeden, Matt
Theoretische Ansatze und Konzepte der Forschung uber soziale Bewegungen in der Geschichtswissenschaft — Mittag, Jurgen
Theoretische und Methodische Zugriffe auf die Spatmittelalterliche Wirtschaftsgeschichte am Beispiel von Quellen zum Rechnungswesen
Theories of Practice: Raising the Standards of Early Childhood Education — Mooney, Carol Garhart
Theorizing Cultural Work: Labour, Continuity and Change in the Cultural and Creative Industries — Banks, Mark
Theorizing in Social Science: The Context of Discovery — Swedberg, Richard
Theorizing Native Studies — Simpson, Audra

Theorizing NGOs: States, Feminisms, and Neoliberalism — Bernal, Victoria
Theory at Yale: The Strange Case of Deconstruction in America — Redfield, Mark
A Theory of Character in New Testament Narrative — Bennema, Cornelis
The Theory of Death — Kellerman, Faye
A Theory of Expanded Love — Hicks, Caitlin
The Theory of Light at Midnight — Ukrainetz, Elizabeth
The Theory of Opposites (Read by Traister, Christina). Audiobook Review — Scotch, Allison Winn
A Theory of the Drone — Chamayou, Gregoire
Theosis, Sino-Christian Theology, and the Second Chinese Enlightenment: Heaven and Humanity in Unity — Chow, Alexander
Therapeutic Gardens: Design for Healing Spaces — Winterbottom, Daniel
Therapeutic Revolutions: Medicine, Psychiatry, and American Culture, 1945-1970 — Halliwell, Martin
The Therapeutic Turn: How Psychology Altered Western Culture — Madsen, Ole Jacob
Theravada Buddhism: Continuity, Diversity, and Identity — Heim, Maria
There Are No Solid Gold Dancers Anymore — Weiss, Adrienne
There Can Never Be Enough — Arnason, David
c There Goes Ted Williams: The Greatest Hitter Who Ever Lived (Illus. by Tavares, Matt) — Tavares, Matt
There Goes the Gayborhood? — Ghaziani, Amin
c There Is a Crocodile under My Bed! (Illus. by Schubert, Dieter) — Schubert, Ingrid
There Is No Such Thing as a Social Science — Hutchinson, Phil
There Is No Us (Illus. by Dragotta, Nick) — Hickman, Jonathan
There Is Simply Too Much to Think About: Collected Nonfiction — Bellow, Saul
There Is Still Time: To Look at the Big Picture ... and Act — Seidel, Peter
c There Once Was A Dog (Illus. by Vaz de Carvalho, Joao) — Carvalho, Adelia
c There Was an Old Dragon Who Swallowed a Knight (Illus. by Mantle, Ben) — Klostermann, Penny Parker
c There Was an Old Lady Who Gobbled a Skink — Wissinger, Tammera Will
c There Was an Old Lady Who Swallowed a Frog! (Illus. by Lee, Jared) — Colandro, Lucille
c There Was an Old Lady Who Swallozved a Fly (Illus. by Rashin) — Rashin
c There Was an Old Martian Who Swallowed the Moon (Illus. by Gray, Steve) — Ward, Jennifer (b. 1963-)
c There Was an Old Mummy Who Swallowed a Spider (Illus. by Gray, Steve) — Ward, Jennifer (b. 1963-)
There Was and There Was Not: A Journey through Hate and Possibility in Turkey, Armenia, and Beyond — Toumani, Meline
y There Will Be Lies — Lake, Nick
There's a Bug in the Tub and It Won't Get Out — Allen, J.J.
c There's a Giraffe in My Soup (Illus. by Burach, Ross) — Burach, Ross
c There's a Lion in My Cornflakes (Illus. by Field, Jim) — Robinson, Michelle
c There's a Little Black Spot on the Sun Today (Illus. by Volker, Sven) — Sting
There's a Man with a Gun over There — Ryan, R.M.
c There's a Monster in the Garden — Harmer, David
c There's a Mouse Hiding in This Book (Illus. by Perez, Carmen) — Bird, Benjamin
c There's a Pig in My Class! (Illus. by Ramel, Charlotte) — Thydell, Johanna
There's a Woman in the Pulpit: Christian Clergywomen Share Their Hard Days, Holy Moments and the Healing Power of Humor — Spong, Martha
c There's No Such Thing as Little (Illus. by Pham, LeUyen) — Pham, LeUyen
There's No Time Like the Present — Rainey, Paul B.
There's Something I Want You to Do — Baxter, Charles
c There's This Thing (Illus. by Brecon, Connah) — Brecon, Connah
Therese of Lisieux — Wallace, Susan Helen
Therigatha: Poems of the First Buddhist Women — Hallisey, Charles
Thermodynamics: For Physicists, Chemists and Materials Scientists — Hentschke, Reinhard
These Are the Names — Wieringa, Tommy

These Boots Are Made for Butt Kickin' — Lloyd, Kalan Chapman
y These Broken Stars — Kaufman, Amie
These Kids: Identity, Agency, and Social Justice at a Last Chance High School — Nygreen, Kysa
y These Shallow Graves — Donnelly, Jennifer
These United States: A Nation in the Making, 1890 to the Present — Gilmore, Glenda Elizabeth
These United States — Gilmore, Glenda Elizabeth
c Theseus and the Minotaur (Illus. by Pommaux, Yvan) — Kutner, Richard
The Theta Prophecy — Dietzel, Chris
y They All Fall Down — St. Claire, Roxanne
They All Love Jack: Busting the Ripper — Robinson, Bruce
They Are All My Family: A Daring Rescue in the Chaos of Saigon's Fall — Riordan, John P.
They Can Live in the Desert but Nowhere Else: A History of the Armenian Genocide
"They Can Live in the Desert but Nowhere Else": A History of the Armenian Genocide — Suny, Ronald Grigor
They Can Live in the Desert but Nowhere Else: A History of the Armenian Genocide — Suny, Ronald Grigor
"They Can Live in the Desert But Nowhere Else": A History of the Armenian Genocide — Suny, Ronald Grigor
They Drew as They Pleased: The Hidden Art of Disney's Golden Age: The 1930s — Ghez, Didier
They Eat Horses, Don't They? The Truth About the French — Eatwell, Piu Marie
c They Just Know (Illus. by Klein, Laurie Allen) — Yardi, Robin
They Know Everything about You: How Data-Collecting Corporations and Snooping Government Agencies Are Destroying Democracy — Scheer, Robert
They Laughed at Galileo: How the Great Inventors Proved Their Critics Wrong — Jack, Albert
They Left Us Everything: A Memoir — Johnson, Plum
They Told Me Not to Take That Job: Tumult, Betrayal, Heroics, and the Transformation of Lincoln Center — Levy, Reynold
c They're There on Their Vacation (Illus. by Paillot, Jim) — Cleary, Brian P.
y Thick as Thieves — Marlow, Susan K.
Thicker Than Blood — Leary, Jan English
y Thicker Than Water — Fiore, Kelly
y Thicker Than Water — Kemmerer, Brigid
Thicker Than Water — Spencer, Sally
y The Thickety: The Whispering Trees (Illus. by Offermann, Andrea) — White, J.A.
c The Thief and the Sword (Illus. by Maihack, Mike) — Maihack, Mike
Thief in the Interior — Williams, Philip B.
Thieves Fall Out — Vidal, Gore
y The Thieves of Pudding Lane — Eyers, Jonathan
Thieves of State: Why Corruption Threatens Global Security — Chayes, Sarah
Thieves' Road: The Black Hills Betrayal and Custer's Path to Little Bighorn — Mort, Terry
Thieving Forest — Conway, Martha
Thin Air: A Shetland Mystery — Cleeves, Anne
Thin Air — Cleeves, Ann
Thin from Within: The Powerful Self-Coaching Program for Permanent Weight Loss — Luciani, Joseph J.
The Thin Green Line: The Money Secrets of the Super Wealthy — Sullivan, Paul
c The Thing About Jellyfish (Read by Franco, Sarah). Audiobook Review — Benjamin, Ali
y The Thing about Jellyfish — Benjamin, Ali
c The Thing about Spring (Illus. by Kirk, Daniel) — Kirk, Daniel
c The Thing about Yetis (Illus. by Vogel, Vin) — Vogel, Vin
Thing Explainer: Complicated Stuff in Simple Words — Monroe, Randall
Thing Explainer: Complicated Stuff in Simple Words — Munroe, Randall
c Things Ellie Likes — Reynolds, Kate E.
y Things I Can't Explain — Kriegman, Mitchell
Things I Don't Want to Know: On Writing — Levy, Deborah
The Things I Heard about You — Leslie, Alex
Things I Wish I'd Known: Cancer and Kids — Cornwall, Deborah J.
y Things I'll Never Say: Stories About Our Secret Selves — Angel, Ann
Things Lost In The Fire — Jennings, Katie

Things No One Will Tell Fat Girls: A Handbook for Unapologetic Living — Baker, Jes
c Things That Go Burp! in the Night — Moerder, Lynne
c Things That Go — Jones, Frankie
The Things They Carried (Read by Cranston, Bryan). Audiobook Review — O'Brien, Tim
Things to Do in a Retirement Home Trailer Park ... When You're 29 and Unemployed — Wright, Aneurin
Things to Make and Do in the Fourth Dimension: A Mathematician's Journey through Narcissistic Numbers, Optimal Dating Algorithms, at Least Two Kinds of Infinity, and More — Parker, Matt
c Things We Do: A Kids' Guide to Community Activity (Illus. by Haggerty, Tim) — Kreisman, Rachelle
The Things We Don't Do — Neuman, Andres
The Things We Keep — Hepworth, Sally
y Things We Know by Heart — Kirby, Jessi
y The Things You Kiss Goodbye — Connor, Leslie
Things You Won't Say — Pekkanen, Sarah
c Thingy Things Series (Illus. by Raschka, Chris) — Raschka, Chris
c Think About Series (Illus. by Bolam, Emily) — Ziefert, Harriet
Think Again: Contrarian Reflections on Life, Culture, Politics, Religion, Law, and Education — Fish, Stanley
Think Agile: How Smart Entrepreneurs Adapt in Order to Succeed — Williams, Taffy
Think! Eat! Act! — Tolicetti, Raffaella
Think Like a Baby: 33 Simple Research Experiments You Can Do at Home to Better Understand Your Child's Developing Mind — Ankowski, Amber
Think Like a Commoner: A Short Introduction to the Life of the Commons — Bolder, David
c Think Like Churchill (Illus. by Huxable, Jaime). E-book Review — Johnson, Boris
Think South: How We Got Six Men and Forty Dogs Across Antarctica — Moll, Cathy de
Think Tank Library: Brain-Based Learning Plans for New Standards, Grades K-5 (Illus. by #) — Jaeger, Paige
Think Tank Library: Brain-Based Learning Plans for New Standards, Grades K-5 — Jaeger, Paige
Think Tank — Carr, Julie
Thinking about Cybersecurity: From Cyber Crime to Cyber Warfare (Read by Rosenzweig, Paul). Audiobook Review — Rosenzweig, Paul
Thinking about Video Games: Interviews with the Experts — Heineman, David S.
Thinking beyond Boundaries: Transnational Challenges to US Foreign Policy — Liebert, Hugh
y Thinking Critically: Biofuels — Dudley, William
y Thinking Critically: Cyberbullying — Currie, Stephen
y Thinking Critically: Mass Shootings — Nakaya, Andrea C.
The Thinking Drinker's Guide to Alcohol: A Cocktail of Amusing Anecdotes and Opinion on the Art of Imbibing — McFarland, Ben
Thinking Good Thoughts about Me — McGranaghan, Mary K.
Thinking In Numbers: On Life, Love, Meaning, and Math — Tammet, Daniel
Thinking in Pictures — Grandin, Temple
Thinking Its Presence: Form, Race, and Subjectivity in Contemporary Asian American Poetry — Wang, Dorothy J.
Thinking Orthodox in Modern Russia: Culture, History, Context — Michelson, Patrick Lally
Thinking Outside the Book — Rohrbach, Augusta
Thinking Sex with the Early Moderns — Traub, Valerie
Thinking Women and Health Care Reform in Canada — Armstrong, Pat
Thinning the Herd — Phoenix, Adrian
y The Third Chimpanzee for Young People: On the Evolution and Future of the Human Animal — Diamond, Jared
The Third Coast: When Chicago Built the American Dream — Dyja, Thomas
Third Daughter — Quinn, Susan Kaye
The Third Lie — Kristof, Agota
The Third Place: A Viennese Mystery — Jones, J. Sydney
The Third Plate: Field Notes on the Future of Food — Barber, Dan
The Third Plate — Barber, Dan
The Third Reconstruction — Barber, William J., II
The Third Reich in History and Memoryq — Evans, Richard J.
y The Third Twin — Omololu, C.J.
The Third Wife — Jewell, Lisa

y Thirst — Wilcock, Lizzie
c A Thirst for Home: A Story of Water across the World (Illus. by Velasquez, Eric) — Ieronimo, Christine
  Thirsty Dragon: China's Lust for Bordeaux and the Threat to the World's Best Wines — Mustacich, Suzanne
y Thirteen — Hoyle, Tom
  Thirteen — Morgan, Richard
y Thirteen Chairs (Illus. by Shelton, Dave) — Shelton, Dave
c Thirteen Chairs — Shelton, Dave
y Thirteen Chairs (Illus. by Shelton, Dave) — Shelton, Dave
  Thirteen Days in September: Carter, Begin, and Sadat at Camp David (Read by Bramhall, Mark). Audiobook Review — Wright, Lawrence
  Thirteen Days in September: The Dramatic Story of the Struggle for Peace — Wright, Lawrence
y Thirteen Days of Midnight — Hunt, Leo
  Thirteen Guests — Farjeon, J. Jefferson
y Thirteen — Hoyle, Tom
  Thirteen Months at Manassas/Bull Run: The Two Battles and the Confederate and Union Occupations — Johnson, Don
y Thirteen — Hoyle, Tom
  Thirteen Ways of Looking (Read by McCann, Colum). Audiobook Review — McCann, Colum
  Thirteen Ways of Looking — McCann, Colum
  Thirteeners: Why Only 13 Percent of Companies Successfully Execute Their Strategy--and How Yours Can Be One of Them — Prosser, Daniel F.
  The Thirteenth Step: Addiction in the Age of Brain Science — Heilig, Markus
  Thirty Girls — Minot, Susan
  Thirty Million Words: Building a Child's Brain — Suskind, Dana
  Thirty-Three Good Men: Celibacy Obedience and Identity — Weafer, John A.
  This Ain't Chicago: Race, Class, and Regional Identity in the Post-Soul South — Robinson, Zandria F.
c This and That (Illus. by Horacek, Judy) — Fox, Mem
  This Angel on My Chest — Pietrzyk, Leslie
  This Blue — McLane, Maureen N.
y This Book Is Gay (Illus. by Gerrell, Spike) — Dawson, James
y This Book Is Gay — Dawson, James
c This Book Just Ate My Dog! (Illus. by Byrne, Richard) — Byrne, Richard
c This Bridge Will Not Be Gray (Illus. by Nichols, Tucker) — Eggers, Dave
y This Broken Wondrous World (Read by Skovron, Jon). Audiobook Review — Skovron, Jon
y This Broken Wondrous World — Skovron, Jon
  This Census-Taker — Mieville, China
  This Changes Everything: Capitalism vs. the Climate (Read by Archer, Ellen). Audiobook Review — Klein, Naomi
  This Changes Everything: Capitalism vs. The Climate — Klein, Naomi
  This Day: Collected and New Sabbath Poems — Berry, Wendell
  This Dialogue of One: Essays on Poets from John Dunne to Joan Murray — Ford, Mark
  This Divided Island: Stories from the Sri Lankan War — Peake, Ernest Cromwell
  This Divided Island: Stories from the Sri Lankan War — Subramanian, Samanth
  This Gulf of Fire: The Destruction of Lisbon, or Apocalypse in the Age of Science and Reason — Molesky, Mark
  This Gun for Hire — Goodman, Jo
y This Heart of Mine — Novak, Brenda
  This House of Grief: The Story of a Murder Trial — Gamer, Helen
  This House of Grief: The Story of a Murder Trial — Garner, Helen
  This Idea Must Die: Scientific Theories That Are Blocking Progress — Brockman, John
c This Is a Ball (Illus. by Stanton, Beck) — Stanton, Beck
  This Is All a Dream We Dreamed: An Oral History of the Grateful Dead — Jackson, Blair
y This Is All: The Pillow Book of Cordelia Kenn — Chambers, Aidan
  This Is an Uprising — Engler, Mark
  This Is Awkward: How Life's Uncomfortable Moments Open the Door to Intimacy and Connection — Rhodes, Sammy
  This Is Camino — Moore, Russell

c This is Captain Cook (Illus. by Booth, Christina) — McCartney, Tania
y This Is Dali (Illus. by Rae, Andrew) — Ingram, Catherine
  This is Happy: A Memoir — Gibb, Camilla
y This Is How It Ends — Nadol, Jen
  This Is How It Really Sounds — Cohen, Stuart Archer
  This Is Jerusalem Calling: State Radio in Mandate Palestine — Stanton, Andrea
  This Is My Body: From Obesity to Ironman, My Journey into the True Meaning of Flesh, Spirit, and Deeper Faith — Sutterfield, Ragan
c This Is My Home, This Is My School (Illus. by Bean, Jonathan) — Bean, Jonathan
c This Is Not a Love Story — Brown, Judy
c This Is Not a Photo Opportunity: The Street Art of Banksy — Bull, Martin
  This Is Not a Test: A New Narrative on Race, Class, and Education — Vilson, Jose Luis
  This Is Only a Test — Hollars, B.J.
y This Is Pollock (Illus. by Arkle, Peter) — Ingram, Catherine
c This Is Sadie — Morstad, Julie
y This Is Sadie (Illus. by Morstad, Julie) — O'Leary, Sara
  This Is the City: Making Model Citizens in Los Angeles — Schmidt, Ronald J, Jr.
c This Is the Earth (Illus. by Minor, Wendell) — Shore, Diane Z.
  This Is the Night — Sirott, Jonah C.
  This Is the Rope: A Story from the Great Migration (Read by Waites, Channie). Audiobook Review — Woodson, Jacqueline
  This Is the Story of A Happy Marriage (Read by Patchett, Ann). Audiobook Review — Patchett, Ann
c This Is the World: A Global Treasury — Sasek, Miroslav
y This Is Warhol (Illus. by Rae, Andrew) — Ingram, Catherine
y This Is What You Want, This Is What You Get — Scheers, Jim
y This Is Where It Ends — Nijkamp, Marieke
y This Is Where It Ends — Nukamp, Marieke
y This Is Where the World Ends — Zhang, Amy
y This Is Who We Were: 1880-1899 — Derks, Scott
  This Is Why I Came — Rakow, Mary
  This Is Why We Can't Have Nice Things: Mapping the Relationship between Online Trolling and Mainstream Culture — Phillips, Whitney
  This Is Woman's Work: Calling Forth Your Inner Council of Wise, Brave, Crazy, Rebellious, Loving, Luminous Selves — Christina, Dominique
  This Is Your Brain on Sports: The Science of Underdogs, the Value of Rivalry, and What We Can Learn from the T-shirt Cannon — Wertheim, L. Jon
  This Is Your Life, Harriet Chance! — Evison, Jonathan
c This Kid Can Fly: It's about Ability (Not Disability). — Philip, Aaron
c This Land Is Your Land (Illus. by Morrison, Cathy) — Ciocchi, Catherine
  This Life — Schoeman, Karel
c This Little Light of Mine — Kolanovic, Dubravka
  This Little Piggy — Davenport, Bea
c This Little Piggy — Marshall, Natalie
c This Little Piggy Went Dancing (Illus. by Niland, Deborah) — Wild, Margaret
y This May Sound Crazy — Breslin, Abigail
y This Monstrous Thing — Lee, Mackenzi
  This Muslim American Life: Dispatches from the War on Terror — Bayoumi, Moustafa
  This New Noise: The Extraordinary Birth and Troubled Life of the BBC — Higgins, Charlotte
  This Nonviolent Stuff'll Get You Killed: How Guns Made the Civil Rights Movement Possible — Cobb, Charles E., Jr.
  This Nonviolent Stuff'll Get You Killed: How Guns Made the Civil Rights Movement Possible — Umoja, Akinyele Omowale
  This Old Man: All in Pieces — Angell, Roger
c This Old Van (Illus. by Conahan, Carolyn) — Norman, Kim
  This One Summer — Tamaki, Jillian
y This One Summer (Illus. by Tamaki, Jillian) — Tamaki, Mariko
  This One Thing — Maher, Damian
  This One's Trouble — Sellers, Peter
c This or That? 2: More Wacky Choices to Reveal the Hidden You — Mortimer, J.R.
y This Ordinary Life — Walkup, Jennifer

c This Orq. (He Cave Boy.). (Illus. by Nichols, Lori) — Elliott, David
c This Orq (He Cave Boy.). (Illus. by Nichols, Lori) — Elliott, David
c This Orq. (Illus. by Nichols, Lori) — Elliott, David
c This Orq: He Say "Ugh!" (Illus. by Nichols, Lori) — Elliott, David
  This Picture I Gift: An Armenian Memoir — Andonian, Michelle
  This Present Moment — Snyder, Gary
y This Raging Light — Laure, Estelle
y This Shattered World (Read by Various readers). Audiobook Review — Kaufman, Amie
y This Shattered World — Kaufman, Amie
y This Shattered World — Spooner, Meagan
  This Should Be Written in the Present Tense — Helle, Helle
y This Side of Home — Watson, Renee
  This Side of Midnight — Lamanda, Al
  This Side of the River — Stayton, Jeffrey
c This Side of Wild: Mutts, Mares, and Laughing Dinosaurs (Read by Sanders, Fred). Audiobook Review — Paulsen, Gary
c This Side of Wild: Mutts, Mares, and Laughing Dinosaurs (Illus. by Jessell, Tim) — Paulsen, Gary
y This Song Will Save Your Life (Read by Lowman, Rebecca). Audiobook Review — Sales, Leila
  This Spy in France — Angliss, Michael
  This Strange and Sacred Scripture: Wrestling with the Old Testament and Its Oddities — Schlimm, Matthew Richard
y This Strange Wilderness: The Life and Art of John James Audubon — Plain, Nancy
  This Tattooed Land — Parker, Derek
  This Thing Called Literature: Reading, Thinking, Writing — Bennett, Andrew
  This Thing Called Love — Liasson, Miranda
  This Time It's Not Personal: Why Science Says Get Over Yourself — Hicken, Sam
  This Was Not the Plan — Alger, Cristina
y This Way Home — Moore, Wes
  The Thiselton Companion to Christian Theology — Thiselton, Anthony C.
  This'll Be the Day That I Die — Griffin, John Michael
  Thomas Aquinas: A Portrait — Turner, Denys
  Thomas Aquinas's Summa Theologiae: A Biography — McGinn, Bernard
  Thomas Berry: Selected Writings on the Earth Community — Tucker, Marilyn Evelyn
  Thomas Browne — Killeen, Kevin
  Thomas Cromwell: The Untold Story of Henry VIII's Most Faithful Servant — Borman, Tracy
  Thomas Dekker and the Culture of Pamphleteering in Early Modern London — Bayman, Anna
  Thomas Harriot and His World: Mathematics, Exploration, and Natural Philosophy in Early Modern England — Fox, Robert
  Thomas Hart Benton: Discoveries and Interpretations — Adams, Henry
  Thomas Jefferson and the Tripoli Pirates: The Forgotten War That Changed American History — Kilmeade, Brian
c Thomas Jefferson Grows a Nation (Illus. by Innerst, Stacy) — Thomas, Peggy
  Thomas Jefferson: Life, Liberty and the Pursuit of Everything — Kalman, Maira
c Thomas Jefferson: President and Philosopher (Read by Hermann, Edward). Audiobook Review — Meacham, Jon
y Thomas Jefferson: President and Philosopher — Meacham, Jon
  Thomas Jefferson's Ethics and the Politics of Human Progress: The Morality of a Slaveholder — Helo, Ari
  Thomas Jefferson's Haitian Policy: Myths and Realities — Scherr, Arthur
  Thomas Killigrew and the Seventeenth-Century English Stage: New Perspectives — Major, Philip
  Thomas Morley: Elizabethan Music Publisher — Murray, Tessa
  Thomas Murphy — Rosenblatt, Roger
  Thomas Nast: The Father of Modern Political Cartoons — Halloran, Fiona Deans
c Thomas Paine: Crusader for Liberty: How One Man's Ideas Helped Form a New Nation — Marrin, Albert
  Thomas Sackville and the Shakespearean Glass Slipper — Feldman, Sabrina
c Thor Is Locked in My Garage — Harris, Robert J. (b. 1955-)

c   Thor Speaks! A Guide to the Realms by the Norse
       God of Thunder (Illus. by Larson, J.E.) — Shecter,
       Vicky Alvear
y   Thor: The Goddess of Thunder (Illus. by Dauterman,
       Russell) — Aaron, Jason
    Thoreau in Phantom Bog — Oak, B.B.
    A Thorn among the Lilies — Hiebert, Michael
    Thorns in the Flesh: Illness and Sanctity in Late
       Ancient Christianity — Crislip, Andrew
y   Thorny — Eye, Lelia
    Those Girls (Read by Marie, Jorjeana). Audiobook
       Review — Stevens, Chevy
    Those Girls — Stevens, Chevy
y   Those Girls — Saft, Lauren
    Those Girls — Stevens, Chevy
    Those Girls: Single Women in Sixties and Seventies
       Popular Culture — Lehman, Katherine
c   Those Magnificent Sheep in Their Flying Machine
       (Illus. by Roberts, David) — Bently, Peter
    Those Secrets We Keep — Liebert, Emily
    Those We Left Behind — Neville, Stuart
    Those Who Hold Bastogne: The True Story of the
       Soldiers and Civilians Who Fought in the Biggest
       Battle of the Bulge — Schrijvers, Peter
    Those Who Leave and Those Who Stay — Ferrante,
       Elena
    Those Who Wish Me Dead — Koryta, Michael
    Those Who Write for Immortality: Romantic
       Reputations and the Dream of Lasting Fame
       — Jackson, H.J.
    Those Who Write for Immortality. Romantic
       Reputations and the Dream of Lasting Fame
       — Jackson, H.J.
    Thought and World: The Hidden Necessities — Ross,
       James
    The Thought Remolding Campaign of the Chinese
       Communist Party-State — Hu, Ping
    Thoughtful — Stephens, S.C.
    Thoughts and Things — Bersani, Leo
    The Thousand and One Nights (Alf Layla Wa-Layla),
       2 vols. — Mahdi, Musin
    The Thousand Dollar Dinner: America's First Great
       Cookery Challenge — Diamond, Becky Libourel
    A Thousand Falling Crows — Sweazy, Larry D.
    A Thousand Forests in One Acorn: An Anthology of
       Spanish-Language Fiction — Miles, Valerie
    A Thousand Miles to Freedom: My Escape from
       North Korea (Read by Zeller, Emily Woo).
       Audiobook Review — Kim, Eunsun
    A Thousand Miles to Freedom: My Escape from
       North Korea — Eunsun Kim
    A Thousand Miles to Freedom: My Escape from
       North Korea — Falletti, Sebastien
    A Thousand Miles to Freedom: My Escape from
       North Korea — Kim, Eunsun
    A Thousand Naked Strangers: A Paramedic's Wild
       Ride to the Edge and Back — Hazzard, Kevin
y   A Thousand Nights — Johnston, E.K.
y   A Thousand Pieces of You — Gray, Claudia
    Thousand Times Broken, 3 vols. — Michaux, Henri
    Thrace - Local Coinage and Regional Identity:
       Numismatic Research in the Digital Age
    Thread and Gone — Wait, Lea
    Thread Stories: A Visual Guide to Creating Stunning
       Stitched Portrait Quilts — Day, Jennifer
    Threads of Deceit — Fox, Mae
    Threads: The Delicate Life of John Craske
       — Blackburn, Julia
y   Threats to Privacy and Security — Nakaya, Andrea C.
    The Three Battles of Wanat and Other True Stories
       — Bowden, Mark
c   Three Bears in a Boat (Illus. by Soman, David)
       — Soman, David
c   The Three Billy Goats Gruff (Illus. by Pankhurst,
       Kate) — Alperin, Mara
c   The Three Billy Goats Gruff/Ttizi Chqqh Chq'i Taa'ii
       (Illus. by Hu, Ying-Hwa) — Wright, Rebecca
       Hu-Van
    The Three-Body Problem — Liu, Cixin
c   The Three Cattle Dogs Gruff (Illus. by Lawford,
       Myles) — Gurney, Chris
    Three Day Summer — SarvenazTash
y   Three Day Summer — Tash, Sarvenaz
    Three Days of Anna Madrigal — Maupin, Armistead
    Three Faces of an Angel — Pehe, Jiri
c   The Three Frilly Goats Fluff — Guillain, Charlotte
y   Three Good Things — Peterson, Lois
    The Three Graces — Wolfe, Michele
    Three Great Lies — MacLellan, Vanessa
    Three Kinds of Motion: Kerouac, Pollock, and the
       Making of American Highways — Hanick, Riley
    The Three Leaps of Wang-lun — Doblin, Alfred

y   Three-Legged Horse — Hall, Russ
c   Three Little Peas — Rivoal, Marine
    The Three Little Pigs Count to 100 (Illus. by
       Pistacchio) — Maccarone, Grace
c   The Three Little Pigs/Los tres cerditos (Illus. by
       Cuellar, Olga) — Mlawer, Teresa
c   Three Little Words (Illus. by Beardshaw, Rosalind)
       — Pearce, Clemency
    Three Lullabies for Two Pianos — Liebermann, Lowell
    Three Many Cooks: One Mom, Two Daughters, Their
       Shared Stories of Food, Faith, and Family
       — Anderson, Pam
    Three Men and a Bradshaw: An Original Victorian
       Travel Journal — Scott, Ronnie
    Three Minutes in Poland: Discovering a Lost World in
       a 1938 Family Film — Kurtz, Glenn
    Three Moments of an Explosion — Mieville, China
    Three Moments of an Explosion — Miville, China
y   Three More Words — Rhodes-Courter, Ashley
c   The Three Mouths of Little Tom Drum (Illus. by
       Hawkes, Kevin) — Willard, Nancy
    The Three-Nine Line — Freed, David
c   Three Pickled Herrings (Illus. by Roberts, David)
       — Gardner, Sally
c   The Three Pig Sisters (Illus. by Park, Keun) — Kim,
       Cecil
    Three Promises — Everett, Lily
c   Three-Ring Rascals, Books 1-2: The Show Must Go
       On! - The Greatest Star on Earth. Audiobook
       Review — Klise, Kate
c   Three-Ring Rascals, Books 3-4: The Circus Goes to
       Sea - Pop Goes the Circus!. Audiobook Review
       — Klise, Kate
    Three Rivers — Tyson, Tiffany Quay
    Three Songs, Three Singers, Three Nations: The
       William E. Massey Sr. Lectures in the History of
       American Civilization, 2013 — Marcus, Greil
c   The Three Wise Men — Koopmans, Loek
y   The Three-Year Swim Club: The Untold Story of
       Maui's Sugar Ditch Kids and Their Quest for
       Olympic Glory — Checkoway, Julie
    Threshold — Ford, G.M.
    Thrift: The History of an American Cultural
       Movement — Yarrow, Andrew L.
    Thrill Me — Mallery, Susan
    The Thrill of the Krill: What You Should Know
       About Krill Oil — Goodman, Dennis
    The Thrilling Adventures of Lovelace and Babbage:
       The (Mostly) True Story of the First Computer
       — Padua, Sydney
    Thrive: 5 Ways to (Re)Invigorate Your Teaching
       — Heinemann, Meenoo Rami
    Thrive: How Better Mental Health Care Transforms
       Lives and Saves Money — Layard, Richard
    Thriving with Chronic Pain : A Holistic Guide to
       Reclaiming Your Life — Meshorer, Sean
    Throne of Darkness — Nicholas, Douglas
    Throne of Ice — Paris, Alain
    Through a Screen Darkly: Popular Culture, Public
       Diplomacy, and Americas Image Abroad — Bayles,
       Martha
    Through My Eyes — Delinsky, Barbara
    Through the Glass — Moroney, Shannon
    Through the Heart of Dixie: Sherman's March and
       American Memory — Rubin, Anne Sarah
    Through the Looking-Glass and What Alice Found
       There — Carroll, Lewis
c   Through the Town (Illus. by Shuttlewood, Craig)
       — Haworth, Katie
c   Through the Town (Illus. by Shuttlewood, Craig)
       — Shuttlewood, Craig
    Through the Window: Seventeen Essays and a Short
       Story — Barnes, Julian
c   Through the Woods — Carroll, Emily
c   Through the Years: How Having Fun Has Changed in
       Living Memory — Lewis, Clare
y   Through to You — Barnholdt, Lauren
    Through Waters Deep — Sundin, Sarah
    The Throwback Special — Bachelder, Chris
    Throwing Rocks at the Google Bus — Rushkoff,
       Douglas
    Thrown — Howley, Kerry
    Thrown under the Omnibus: A Reader — O'Rourke,
       P.J.
    Thucydides and the Idea of History — Morley, Neville
    Thucydides on Politics: Back to the Present
       — Hawthorn, Geoffrey
c   Thumbelina (Illus. by Vivanco, Kelly) — Andersen,
       Hans Christian
c   Thump, Quack, Moo (Read by England, Maurice).
       Audiobook Review — Cronin, Doreen

    Thunder and Flames: Americans in the Crucible of
       Combat, 1917-1918 — Lengel, Edward G.
c   Thunder and Lightning — Hansen, Grace
    Thunder and Lightning: Weather Past, Present,
       Future — Redniss, Lauren
c   The Thunder Egg (Illus. by Coleman, Winfield)
       — Myers, Tim J.
    The Thunder of Giants — Fishbane, Joel
    Thunder on the Plains — Bittner, Rosanne
    Thunder over the Superstitions — Brandvold, Peter
y   Thunderbirds — Anderson, Gerry
c   Thunderstorm Dancing (Illus. by Watson, Judy)
       — Germein, Katrina
    Thunderstruck and Other Stories — McCracken,
       Elizabeth
    Thurgood Marshall: Race, Rights, and the Struggle
       for a More Perfect Union — Zelden, Charles L.
    Thursdays with the Crown (Read by Jackson, Suzy).
       Audiobook Review — George, Jessica Day
c   Thursdays with the Crown — George, Jessica Day
    Thus Were Their Faces: Selected Stories — Ocampo,
       Silvina
c   Tia Isa Wants a Car (Illus. by Munoz, Claudio)
       — Medina, Meg
c   The Tiara on the Terrace — Kittscher, Kristen
c   Tiara Saurus Rex (Illus. by Boldt, Mike) — Sayres,
       Brianna Caplan
    Tibetan Folktales — Yuan, Haiwang
    The Tick Rider: A Story of Families, Homelands,
       Drugs, Redemption, and the Dividing Rio Grande
       — Street, William
c   A Ticket around the World (Illus. by Owens, Melissa)
       — Diaz, Natalia
c   A Ticket around the World (Illus. by Smith, Kim)
       — Diaz, Natalia
c   A Ticket around the World (Illus. by Smith, Kim (b.
       1986-)) — Diaz, Natalia
    The Ticket — Schutte, Karen
    Ticket Stub — Hensley, Tim
c   Ticket to India — Senzai, N.H.
c   Tickle Monster (Illus. by Manceau, Edouard)
       — Manceau, Edouard
c   Tickly Toes — Hood, Susan
    The Tide of War — Witt, Lori A.
    The Tide Tarrieth No Man — Happe, Peter
    The Tide Watchers — Chaplin, Lisa
    The Tides of Mind: Uncovering the Spectrum of
       Consciousness — Gelernter, David
    The Tie That Bound Us: The Women of John Brown's
       Family and the Legacy of Radical Abolitionism
       — Laughlin-Schultz, Bonnie
    Tiere und Geschichte: Konturen einer "Animate
       History" — Clemens Wischermann
    "Tiere Unserer Heimat": Auswirkungen der
       SED-Ideologie auf Gesellschaftliche
       Mensch-Tier-Verhaltnisse in der DDR
    Tiffany Girl (Read by Botchan, Rachael). Audiobook
       Review — Gist, Deeanne
y   Tiffany Girl — Gist, Deeanne
c   Tiffany la fee du tennis: Les fees des sports
       — Meadows, Daisy
c   Tig and Tog's Dinosaur Discovery (Illus. by Garland,
       Sally) — Garland, Sally
c   Tiger — Eszterhas, Suzi
c   Tiger and Badger (Illus. by Gay, Marie-Louise)
       — Jenkins, Emily
    Tiger Boy (Illus. by Hogan, Jamie) — Perkins, Mitali
    Tiger Pelt — Kim, Annabelle J.
c   The Tiger Who Would Be King (Illus. by Moon,
       JooHee) — Moon, JooHee
c   The Tiger Who Would Be King (Illus. by Yoon,
       JooHee) — Thurber, James
c   Tiger Woods Makes Masters History — Williams,
       Doug
    Tigerman (Read by Bates, Matt). Audiobook Review
       — Harkaway, Mick
c   Tigers — Markert, Jenny
    Tightrope — Mawer, Simon
y   The Tightrope Walkers — Almond, David
    The Tijuana Book of the Dead — Urrea, Luis Alberto
    Tikal Report 20A: Excavations in Residential Areas of
       Tikal: Non-elite Groups without Shrines: The
       Excavations — Haviland, William A.
    Tikal Report 20B: Excavations in Residential Areas of
       Tikal: Non-elite Groups without Shrines: Analysis
       and Conclusions — Haviland, William A.
    Tiki Pop: America Imagines Its Own Polynesian
       Paradise — Kirsten, Sven
    'Til Death Do Us Part — Oortman, Annie
    'Til Faith Do Us Part: How Interfaith Marriage Is
       Transforming America — Riley, Naomi Schaefer

'Til Faith Do Us Part: How Interfaith Marriage Is Transforming America — Schaefer Riley, Naomi
Til the Well Runs Dry — Francis-Sharma, Lauren
Tile Makes the Room: Good Design from Heath Ceramics — Petravic, Robin
Till the Dark Angel Comes: Abolitionism and the Road to the Second American Revolution — King, William S.
c Tillie and Clementine Noises in the Night (Illus. by Killeen, Dan) — Killeen, Dan
c Tillie and P-Trap the Plumber (Illus. by Chamness, Julia) — Foley, Patrick C.
c Tilly's Staycation — Hibbs, Gillian
c Tilt Your Head, Rosie the Red (Illus. by Cathcart, Yvonne) — McCarney, Rosemary
c Tim and Ed (Illus. by Joyner, Andrew) — Dubosarsky, Ursula
Tim and Eric's Zine Theory — Wareheim, Eric
Tim Ginger (Illus. by Hanshaw, Julian) — Hanshaw, Julian
Tim Gunn: The Natty Professor: A Master Class on Mentoring, Motivating, and Making It Work! (Read by Gunn, Tim). Audiobook Review — Gunn, Tim
Tim Gunn: The Natty Professor: A Master Class on Mentoring, Motivating, and Making It Work (Read by Gunn, Tim). Audiobook Review — Gunn, Tim
y Timber Creek Station — Lewis, Ali
The Timber Press Guide to Vegetable Gardening in the Midwest — VanderBrug, Michael
c Time — Feldman, Thea
Time Ages in a Hurry — Tabucchi, Antonio
Time and the Science of the Soul in Early Modern Philosophy — Edwards, Michael
Time and Time Again — Elton, Ben
Time, Astronomy, and Calendars in the Jewish Tradition — Stern, Sacha
y The Time Box — Capetanos, Leon
Time Cat: The Remarkable Journeys of Jason and Gareth — Staub, Wendy Corsi
Time Down to Mind — Foust, Graham
Time Flies — Kaufman, Alex
c Time for a Bath (Illus. by Walker, David) — Gershator, Phillis
c Time for Cranberries (Illus. by Henry, Jed) — Detlefsen, Lisl
c Time for Cranberries (Illus. by Henry, Jed) — Detlefsen, Lisl H.
A Time for Hope — Jacobs, Anna
A Time for Truth: Reigniting the Promise of America — Cruz, Ted
Time, History and Literature: Selected Essays of Erich Auerbach — Porter, James
y The Time Hunters — Ashmore, Carl
Time in Early Modern Islam: Calendar, Ceremony, and Chronology in the Safavid, Mughal, and Ottoman Empires — Blake, Stephen P.
Time in Eternity: Pannenberg, Physics, and Eschatology in Creative Mutual Interaction — Russell, Robert John
The Time Is Always Now: Black Thought and the Transformation of US Democracy — Bromell, Nick
The Time Mom Met Hitler, Frost Came to Dinner, and I Heard the Greatest Story Ever Told — Eberhart, Dikkon
Time of Death — Billingham, Mark
Time of Departure — Schofield, Douglas
Time of Fog and Fire — Bowen, Rhys
The Time of Our Lives: Collected Writings — Noonan, Peggy
c The Time of the Fireflies — Little, Kimberley Griffiths
Time Out of Mind — Gere, Richard
c Time Sailors of Pizzolungo — Abrams, Scott
Time Salvager — Chu, Wesley
The Time Slip Girl — Andre, Elizabeth
The Time the Water Rose — Ruffin, Paul
c Time to Build (Illus. by Dogi, Fiammetta) — Riggs, Kate
y A Time to Dance — Venkatraman, Padma
Time to Get Tough: Make America Great Again! — Trump, Donald J.
c Time to Play — Lawrence, Ellen
c Time to Start a Brand New Year (Illus. by Scheinberg, Shepsil) — Vorst, Rochel Groner
Time to Think: Listening to Ignite the Human Mind — Kline, Nancy
Time Travel: The Popular Philosophy of Narrative — Wittenberg, David
The Time Traveller's Guide to British Theatre: The First Four Hundred Years (Illus. by Illman, James) — Sierz, Aleks
y Time Warper: Fated — Martinez, Peggy

Timelapse — Farrelly, Lorrie
Timeless: Love, Morgenthau, and Me — Franks, Lucinda
The Timeless Love of Twin Souls — Darling, Janet Kay
c A Timeline History of Early American Indian Peoples — Gimpel, Diane Marczely
c A Timeline History of the Declaration of Independence — Morey, Allan
c A Timeline History of the Early American Republic — Morey, Allan
c A Timeline History of the Thirteen Colonies — Pratt, Mary K.
Time's Edge (Read by Rudd, Kate). Audiobook Review — Walker, Rysa
The Times Guide to the House of Commons 2015 — Brunskill, Ian
The Times-Picayune in a Changing Media World: The Transformation of an American Newspaper — Alexander, S.L.
Time's Up — Mack, Janey
A Timeshare — Ross, Margaret
c Timmy Failure: Sanitized for Your Protection (Illus. by Pastis, Stephan) — Pastis, Stephan
c Timmy Failure: We Meet Again — Pastis, Stephan
c Timo's Garden (Illus. by Griffiths, Dean) — Allenby, Victoria
Timothee de Milet : le poete et le musicien — Lambin, Gerard
Tin Cup — Deason, Jude
Tin Men — Golden, Christopher
The Tin Men — Golden, Christopher
Tin Pan Alley and the Philippines: American Songs of War and Love, 1898-1946 - A Resource Guide — Walsh, Thomas P.
c Tin — Judge, Chris
Tin Sky — Pastor, Ben
c The Tin Snail (Illus. by Usher, Sam) — McAllister, Cameron
c Tino the Tortoise: Adventures in the Grand Canyon (Illus. by Brooks, Erik) — Ahern, Carolyn L.
Tintin: Herge's Masterpiece — Sterckx, Pierre
c Tiny Creatures: The World of Microbes (Illus. by Sutton, Emily) — Davies, Nicola
c Tiny Hamster Is a Giant Monster — Jenson, Joel
Tiny Little Thing — Williams, Beatriz
A Tiny Piece of Sky — Stout, Shawn K.
Tiny Pieces of Skull: A Lesson in Manners — Kaveney, Roz
The Tiny Portrait (Illus. by Cinquanta, Karla) — Carla, Heidi
y Tiny Pretty Things — Charaipotra, Sona
y Tiny Pretty Things — Clayton, Dhonielle
y Tiny Pretty Things — Sharaipotra, Sona
c Tiny Titans: Return to the Treehouse (Illus. by Franco) — Baltazar, Art
c The Tiny Wish (Illus. by Breiehagen, Per) — Evert, Lori
Tipping Point — Poyer, David
Tipping the Valet — Beck, K.K.
The Tippling Bros.: A Lime and a Shaker: Discovering Mexican-Inspired Cocktails — Carducci, Tad
c Tiptoe Tapirs (Illus. by Hanmin Kim) — Hanmin Kim
c Tiptoe Tapirs (Illus. by Kim, Hanmin) — Kim, Hanmin
c Tiptoe Tapirs (Illus. by Kim, Hanmin) — Lee, Sera
c Tiptop Cat (Read by Mitchell, Lizan). Audiobook Review — Mader, C. Roger
c Tiptop Cat (Illus. by Mader, C. Roger) — Mader, C. Roger
'Tis the Season to Be Felt-y: Over 40 Handmade Holiday Decorations — Sheldon, Kathy
c Titanic Disaster! Nickolas Flux and the Sinking of the Great Ship (Illus. by Simmons, Mark) — Yomtov, Nel
c The Titans — Scott, Victoria
c Titch (Illus. by Hutchins, Pat) — Hutchins, Pat
Titos Gulag auf der Insel Goli Otok — Jezernik, Bozidar
c Tiz and Ott's Big Draw (Illus. by Marzo, Bridget) — Marzo, Bridget
To All Nations from All Nations: A History of the Christian Missionary Movement — Cardoza-Orlandi, Carlos F.
To Be a Soldier — Olejniczak, Julian M.
To Capture Her Heart — DeMarino, Rebecca
To Carl Schmitt: Letters and Reflections — Taubes, Jacob
c To Catch a Cheat — Johnson, Varian
To Conserve Unimpaired: The Evolution of the National Park Idea — Keiter, Robert B.

To Crown the Waves: The Great Navies of the First World War — O'Hara, Vincent P.
To Defend the Revolution Is to Defend Culture: The Cultural Policy of the Cuban Revolution — Gordon-Nesbitt, Rebecca
To Desire a Highlander — Welfonder, Sue-Ellen
To Die For — Hunter, Phillip
To Dwell in Darkness — Crombie, Deborah
To Explain the World: The Discovery of Modern Science — Weinberg, Steven
To Fight Aloud Is Very Brave: American Poetry and the Civil War — Barrett, Faith
To Follow in Their Footsteps: The Crusades and Family Memory in the High Middle Ages — Paul, Nicholas L.
To Govern the Devil in Hell: The Political Crisis in Territorial Kansas — Ponce, Pearl T.
To Hell and Back: Europe 1914-1949 — Kershaw, Ian
To Hell and Back: The Last Train from Hiroshima — Pellegrino, Charles
y To Hold the Bridge — Nix, Garth
To Journey in the Year of the Tiger — Dickson, H. Leighton
To Kill a Mockingbird — Lee, Harper
To Kill the Valko Kid — George, Michael D.
To Light a Fire: 20 Years with the InsideOut Literary Arts Project — Blackhawk, Terry
To Live an Antislavery Life: Personal Politics and the Antebellum Black Middle Class — Ball, Erica L.
To Live and Dine in Dixie: The Evolution of Urban Food Culture in the Jim Crow South — Cooley, Angela Jill
To Make Men Free: A History of the Republican Party — Richardson, Heather Cox
To March for Others: The Black Freedom Struggle and the United Farm Workers — Araiza, Lauren
To Mourn a Child: Jewish Responses to Neonatal and Childhood Death — Saks, Jeffrey
To Overcome Oneself: The Jesuit Ethic and Spirit of Global Expansion, 1520-1767 — Molina, Michelle
To Plead Our Own Cause: African Americans in Massachusetts and the Making of the Antislavery Movement — Cameron, Christopher
To Raise Up a Nation: John Brown, Frederick Douglass, and the Making of a Free Country — King, William S.
To Render Invisible: Jim Crow and Public Space in New South Jacksonville — Cassanello, Robert
To Ride a White Horse — Ford, Pamela
y To Rise Again at a Decent Hour — Ferris, Joshua
To Save the Children of Korea: The Cold War Origins of International Adoption — Oh, Arissa H.
To Tell Their Children: Jewish Communal Memory in Early Modern Prague — Greenblatt, Rachel L.
To the Bitter End: Appomattox, Bennett Place, and the Surrenders of the Confederacy — Dunkerly, Robert M.
To the Cloud: Big Data in a Turbulent World — Mosco, Vincent
To the End of June: The Intimate Life of American Foster Care — Beam, Cris
To the Ends of the Earth: Pentecostalism and the Transformation of World Christianity — Anderson, Allan Heaton
To the Fullest: The Clean Up Your Act Plan to Lose Weight, Rejuvenate, and Be the Best You Can Be — Bracco, Lorraine
To the Gates of Jerusalem: The Diaries and Papers of James G. McDonald, 1945-1947 — Goda, Norman J.W.
To the Harvest — Duncklee, John
To the House of the Sun — Miller, Tim
To the Klondike and Back 1894-1901 — Shaw, George G.
To the Letter: A Celebration of the Lost Art of Letter Writing — Garfield, Simon
c To the Rescue! Garrett Morgan Underground (Illus. by Parkins, David) — Kulling, Monica
c To the Sea (Illus. by Atkinson, Cale) — Atkinson, Cale
c To the Sea (Illus. by Tugeau, Jeremy) — Grant, Callie
c To the Stars! The First American Woman to Walk in Space (Illus. by Wong, Nicole) — Van Vleet, Carmella
y To This Day: For the Bullied and Beautiful — Koyczan, Shane
To Touch the Face of God: The Sacred, the Profane, and the American Space Program, 1957-1975 — Oliver, Kendrick
To Walk with the Devil: Slovene Collaboration and Axis Occupation, 1941-1945 — Kranjc, Gregor Joseph

To Whom Does Christianity Belong? Critical Issues in World Christianity — *Daughrity, Dyron B.*
To Win Her Favor — *Alexander, Tamera*
To Win the Indian Heart: Music at Chemawa Indian School — *Parkhurst, Melissa*
c Toad Chicken Jokes to Tickle Your Funny Bone — *LaRoche, Amelia*
c Toad Weather (Illus. by Gonzalez, Thomas) — *Markle, Sandra*
c Tobby's Day at the Beach — *Charlet, Izabella*
c Toby and the Ice Giants (Illus. by Lillington, Joe) — *Lillington, Joe*
Tocqueville's Nightmare: The Administrative State Emerges in America, 1900-1940 — *Ernst, Daniel R.*
Tod auf der Piste — *Forg, Nicola*
Today I Wrote Nothing: The Selected Writings of Daniil Kharms — *Yankelevich, Matvei*
Today Is Not Your Day — *Thurm, Marian*
c Today Is the Day (Illus. by Fernandes, Eugenie) — *Walters, Eric*
c Toes, Ears, and Nose! (Illus. by Katz, Karen) — *Bauer, Marion Dane*
c Tofu Power: What Does Tofu Have to Do With Kung Fu? (Illus. by Yumul, Anthony) — *Hu, Eileen*
Together with You — *Bylin, Victoria*
Togetherness — *Duplass, Mark*
c Toilet — *Macaulay, David*
A Token of Elegance: Cigarette Holders in Vogue — *Lorber, Martin Barnes*
c Tokyo Digs a Garden (Illus. by Hatanaka, Kellen) — *Lappano, Jon-Erik*
Tokyo Ghoul, vol. 1 — *Ishida, Sui*
The Tokyo Rose Case: Treason on Trial, by Aiko Takeuchi-Demirci — *Kawashima, Yasuhide*
Tokyo Tales — *Lucas-Hall, Renae*
Tokyo Vernacular: Common Spaces, Local Histories, Found Objects — *Sand, Jordan*
Tokyo Void: Possibilities in Absence — *Jonas, Marieluise*
Told Again: Old Tales Told Again — *de la Mare, Walter*
Toledo's Peru: Vision and Reality — *St. John, Ronald Bruce*
Tolerance and Coexistence in Early Modern Spain: Old Christians and Moriscos in the Campo de Calatrava — *Dadson, Trevor J.*
Tolerance, Intolerance and Respect: Hard to Accept? — *Dobbernack, Jan*
The Tolerance Trap: How God, Genes, and Good Intentions are Sabotaging Gay Equality — *Walters, Suzanna Danuta*
Toleration in Conflict: Past and Present — *Forst, Rainer*
Tolkien und der Erste Weltkrieg: Das Tor zu Mittelerde — *Garth, John*
Tolstoy's False Disciple: The Untold Story of Leo Tolstoy and Vladimir Chertkov — *Popoff, Alexandra*
The Toltec Art of Life and Death: A Story of Discovery — *Ruiz, Don Miguel*
Tom and Lucky (and George and Cokey Flo). — *Greaves, C. Joseph*
Tom and Lucky and George and Cokey Flo — *Greaves, C. Joseph*
Tom Clancy's Op-Center: Into the Fire — *Couch, Dick*
c Tom Gates Absolutely Brilliant Book — *Pichon, Liz*
c Tom Gates: Excellent Excuses and Other Good Stuff (Illus. by Pichon, L.) — *Pichon, L.*
c Tom Gates: Excellent Excuses (and Other Good Stuff). — *Pichon, Liz*
c Tom Gates: Excellent Excuses (and Other Good Stuff). (Illus. by Pichon, Liz) — *Pichon, Liz*
Tom Harper's A History of the Twentieth Century in 100 Maps — *Bryars, Tim*
Tom Horn in Life and Legend — *Ball, Larry D.*
c Tom Monaghan: Domino's Pizza Innovator — *Lianas, Sheila Griffin*
c Tomas Loves ... a Rhyming Book about Fun, Friendship--and Autism (Illus. by Telford, Jane) — *Welton, Jude*
Tomas Transtromer's First Poems and Notes From the Land of Lap Fever — *Transtromer, Tomas*
The Tomb — *Landsem, Stephanie*
The Tomb in Turkey — *Brett, Simon*
c The Tomb Robber and King Tu (Illus. by Garns, Allen) — *Gauch, Sarah*
c The Tomb Robber and King Tut (Illus. by Garns, Allen) — *Gauch, Sarah*
y Tomboy: A Graphic Memoir (Illus. by Prince, Liz) — *Prince, Liz*
c Tombquest: Book of the Dead — *Northrup, Michael*

Tomlinson Hill: The Remarkable Story of Two Families Who Share the Tomlinson Name - One White, One Black (Read by Drummond, David). Audiobook Review — *Tomlinson, Chris*
c Tommy Can't Stop! (Illus. by Fearing, Mark) — *Federle, Tim*
y Tommy: The Gun that Changed America — *Blumenthal, Karen*
Tomorrow and Tomorrow — *Sweterlitsch, Thomas*
Tomorrow I'm Dead — *Yom, Bun*
c Tomorrow Is a Chance to Start Over — *Grist, Hilary*
Tomorrow War — *Bourne, J.L.*
Tomorrowland: Our Journey from Science Fiction to Science Fact (Read by Parks, Tom). Audiobook Review — *Kotler, Steven*
Tomorrowland: Our Journey from Science Fiction to Science Fact — *Kotler, Steven*
Tomorrow's Parties: Sex and the Untimely in Nineteenth-Century America — *Coviello, Peter*
Tom's River: A Story of Science and Salvation — *Fagin, Dan*
c Tom's Sunflower (Illus. by Stanley, Mandy) — *Robinson, Hilary*
Tone It Up: 28 Days to Fit, Fierce, and Fabulous — *Scott, Katrina*
y Tonight the Streets Are Ours — *Sales, Leila*
Tonio: A Requiem Memoir — *van der Heijden, Adri*
c Tony Baloney: Pen Pal (Illus. by Fotheringham, Edwin) — *Ryan, Pam Munoz*
c Tony Baroni Loves Macaroni (Illus. by Crovatto, Lucie) — *Sadler, Marilyn*
c Tony Hawk — *Scheff, Matt*
Too Bad to Die (Read by Brenher, Matthew). Audiobook Review — *Mathews, Francine*
Too Bad to Die (Read by Brenner, Matthew). Audiobook Review — *Mathews, Francine*
Too Bad to Die — *Mathews, Francine*
Too Big to Jail: How Prosecutors Compromise with Corporations — *Garrett, Brandon L.*
c Too Busy Sleeping (Illus. by Pignataro, Anna) — *Louise, Zanni*
Too Close — *Krall, Elizabeth*
Too Close to Home — *Lewis, Susan*
y Too Close to Home — *Walsh, Aoife*
Too Dangerous for a Lady — *Beverley, Jo*
Too Fast to Live, Too Young to Die: James Dean's Final Hours — *Greenberg, Keith Elliot*
Too Hard to Handle — *Walker, Julie Ann*
c Too Hot For Spots — *Goss, Mini*
Too Hot to Handle: A Global History of Sex Education — *Zimmerman, Jonathan*
c Too Hot to Moo — *Henwood, Karyn*
c The Too Little Fire Engine — *Flory, Jane*
c Too Many Carrots (Illus. by Hudson, Katy) — *Hudson, Katy*
Too Many Cooks — *Bate, Dana*
c Too Many Tables (Illus. by Monkey, Micah) — *Schroeder, Abraham*
c Too Many Toys (Illus. by Deedman, Heidi) — *Deedman, Heidi*
Too Much of a Good Thing: How Four Key Survival Traits Are Now Killing Us — *Goldman, Lee*
c Too Shy for Show and Tell (Illus. by Bell, Jennifer) — *Bracken, Beth*
c Took: A Ghost Story — *Hahn, Mary Downing*
c Took — *Hahn, Mary Downing*
c Tooling Around: Crafty Creatures and the Tools They Use (Illus. by Benoit, Renne) — *Jackson, Ellen*
A Toolkit for Department Chairs — *Buller, Jeffrey L.*
c Tools and Weapons — *McDowell, Pamela*
c Toot: The World's Tiniest Whale (Illus. by Chapman, Mike) — *Ramirez, Joy*
c Tooth by Tooth (Illus. by Spookytooth, T. S.) — *Levine, Sarah*
Tooth Development in Human Evolution and Bioarchaeology — *Hillson, Simon*
c The Tooth Fairy Wars (Illus. by Parker, Jake) — *Coombs, Kate*
y Top 250 LGBTQ Books for Teens: Coming Out, Being Out, and the Search for Community — *Cart, Michael*
The Top of His Game: The Best Sportswriting of W.C. Heinz. — *Littlefield, Bill*
The Top of His Game: The Best Sportswriting of W. C. Heinz — *Littlefield, Bill*
Top Student, Top School?: How Social Class Shapes Where Valedictorians Go to College — *Radford, Alexandria Walton*
Top Technologies Every Librarian Needs to Know: A LITA Guide — *Varnum, Kenneth J.*

y Top Ten Clues You're Clueless — *Czukas, Liz*
Topless Cellist: The Improbable Life of Charlotte Moorman — *Rothfuss, Joan*
Topographies of Fascism: Habitus, Space, and Writing in Twentieth-Century Spain — *Nil, Santianez*
Topographies of the Imagination: New Approaches to Daniel Defoe — *Ellison, Katherine*
c Torah Bright — *Scheff, Matt*
c Tormenta De Nieve — *Markovics, Joyce*
Torn by War: The Civil War Journal of Mary Adelia Byers — *Phillips, Samuel R.*
y Torn — *Hastings, Avery*
Torn Together: One Family's Journey through Addiction, Treatment, and the Restaurant Industry — *Pine, Shaaren*
c Tornado — *Rudolph, Jessica*
c Tornadoes: Be Aware and Prepare — *Rustad, Martha E.H.*
c Toronto ABC — *Covello, Paul*
Toronto: Biography of a City — *Levine, Allan*
Toronto, the Belfast of Canada: The Orange Order and the Shaping of Municipal Culture — *Smyth, William J.*
Torpedo: Inventing the Military-Industrial Complex in the United States and Great Britain — *Epstein, Katherine*
Torpedo: Inventing the Military Industrial Complex in the United States and Great Britain — *Epstein, Katherine C.*
Torpedo: Inventing the Military-Industrial Complex in the United States and Great Britain — *Epstein, Katherine C.*
c Tortillas and Lullabies / Tortillas y cancioncitas (Illus. by Valientes, Corazones) — *Reiser, Lynn*
c Tortoise and Hare's Amazing Race (Illus. by Morrison, Cathy) — *Berkes, Marianne*
c The Tortoise and the Hare: An Aesop Fable (Illus. by Watts, Bernadette) — *Watts, Bernadette*
c The Tortoise and the Hare (Illus. by Noj, Nahta) — *Ritchie, Alison*
c The Tortoise and the Soldier: A Story of Courage and Friendship in World War I (Illus. by Foreman, Michael) — *Foreman, Michael*
c Tortoises — *Riggs, Kate*
Torture and Brutality in Medieval Literature: Negotiations of National Identity — *Tracy, Larissa*
The Tortured Life of Scofield Thayer — *Dempsey, James*
Total State Machine — *Cunnington, Graham*
c Total Tractor! — *Roberts, Josephine*
Total War Rome: The Sword of Attila — *Gibbins, David*
The Total Work of Art in European Modernism — *Roberts, David*
Totale Erziehung in Europaischer und Amerikanischer Literatur — *Faber, Richard*
y The (Totally Not) Guaranteed Guide to Friends, Foes, & Faux Friends — *McCafferty, Megan*
c The Totally Secret Secret (Illus. by Shea, Bob) — *Shea, Bob*
c Totally Tardy Marty (Illus. by Krosoczka, Jarrett J.) — *Perl, Erica S.*
TotIs — *Kazden, J. Joseph*
c Toucan Can! (Illus. by Davis, Sarah) — *MacIver, Juliette*
Touch — *North, Claire*
c Touch and Feel ABC — *Scholastic Inc.*
c Touch and Feel Baby Animals — *Scholastic Inc.*
"A Touch of Greatness": A History of Tennessee State University — *Lovett, Bobby L.*
A Touch of Stardust (Read by Campbell, Cassandra). Audiobook Review — *Alcott, Kate*
A Touch of Stardust — *Alcott, Kate*
c Touch the Brightest Star (Illus. by Matheson, Christie) — *Matheson, Christie*
Touch: The Science of Hand, Heart, and Mind — *Linden, David J.*
Touche: The Duel in Literature — *Leigh, John*
Touched by the Extraordinary: Healing Stories of Love, Loss and Hope — *Apollon, Susan Barbara*
Touching America's History: From the Pequot War through World War II — *Brown, Meredith Mason*
Touching the Hem of Heaven — *Desind, Jay*
c Tough Cookie (Illus. by Sandford, Grace) — *Louise, Kate*
c Tough Guys Have Feelings Too (Illus. by Negley, Keith) — *Negley, Keith*
A Tough Little Patch of History: Gone with the Wind and the Politics of Memory — *Dickey, Jennifer W.*
A Tough Little Patch of History: "Gone with the Wind" and the Politics of Memory — *Dickey, Jennifer W.*

A Tough Little Patch of History: Gone with the Wind and the Politics of Memory — Dickey, Jennifer W.
Tough Love — Foster, Lori
A Tour of Bones: Facing Fear and Looking for Life — Inge, Denise
Toured to Death — Conrad, Hy
Tourism Enterprise: Developments, Management and Sustainability — Leslie, David
The Tournament (Read by Firth, Katie). Audiobook Review — Reilly, Matthew
The Tournament — Reilly, Matthew
y The Tournament at Gorlan — Flanagan, John
Toussaint Louverture: The Story of the Only Successful Slave Revolt in History; A Play in Three Acts — James, C.L.R.
Toward A Female Genealogy of Transcendentalism — Argersinger, Jana L.
Toward a More Perfect University — Cole, Jonathan R.
Toward an African Church in Mozambique: Kamba Simango and the Protestant Community in Manica and Sofala, 1892-1945 — Spencer, Leon P.
Toward an Ecology of Transfiguration: Orthodox Christian Perspectives on Environment, Nature, and Creation — Chryssavgis, John
Toward Spatial Humanities: Historical GIS & Spatial History — Gregory, Ian N.
Toward the Future: Essays on Catholic-Jewish Relations in Memory of Rabbi Leon Klenicki — Deutsch, Celia M.
Toward the Geopolitical Novel: U.S. Fiction in the Twenty-First Century — Irr, Caren
Toward the Light: Rescuing Spirits, Trapped Souls, and Earthbound Ghosts — Major, Amy
Towards the Flame: Empire, War and the End of Tsarist Russia — Lieven, Dominic
c A Tower of Giraffes: Animals in Groups (Illus. by Wright, Anna) — Wright, Anna
The Tower of London — Flanagan, Damian
Tower of Thorns — Marillier, Juliet
c The Town Musicians of Bremen — Muller, Gerda
The Town That Forgot How to Breathe — Harvey, Kenneth J.
Townships — Messier, William S.
y Toxic — Shepard, Sara
Toxic Aid: Economic Collapse and Recovery in Tanzania — Edwards, Sebastian
Toxic Charity: How Churches and Charities Hurt Those They Help (and How to Reverse It). (Read by Lawlor, Patrick). Audiobook Review — Lupton, Robert D.
Toxic Schools: High-Poverty Education in New York and Amsterdam — Paulle, Bowen
Toxic Town: IBM, Pollution, and Industrial Risks — Little, Peter C.
y The Toymaker's Apprentice — Smith, Sherri L.
c Toys — Stewart, David
c Toys Meet Snow (Illus. by Zelinsky, Paul O.) — Jenkins, Emily
c Trace, Lift, and Learn — Scholastic Inc.
Trace: Memory, History, Race, and the American Landscape — Savoy, Lauret
The Trace — Gander, Forrest
y Tracers — Howard, J.J.
Traces of the Trinity: Signs, Sacraments, and Sharing God's Life — Robinson, Andrew
Traces of Time — Mariani, Lucio
Traces of Time — Molino, Anthony
Tracing Childhood: Bioarchaeological Investigations of Early Lives in Antiquity — Thompson, Jennifer L.
Track-Two Diplomacy toward an Israeli-Palestinian Solution, 1978-2014 — Hirschfeld, Yair
Track-Two Diplomacy: Toward an Israeli-Palestinian Solution 1978-2014 — Hirschfeld, Yair
y Tracked — Martin, Jenny
Tracker's End — Fernando, Chantal
c Tracking Animal Movement — Jackson, Tom
Tracking the Beast — Kisor, Henry
Tractatus de Signis: The Semiotic of John Poinsot, 2d ed. — Deely, John
c Tractor Mac Saves Christmas — Steers, Billy
Tractor: The Definitive Visual History — Dorling Kindersley Publishing, Inc
Trade and Institutions in the Medieval Mediterranean: The Geniza Merchants and Their Business World — Goldberg, Jessica L.
Trade and Poverty: When the Third World Fell Behind — Williamson, Jeffrey G.
Trade and Romance — Murrin, Michael
Trade and Shipping in the Medieval West: Portugal, Castile and England — Childs, Wendy R.
Trade, Land, Power: The Struggle for Eastern North America — Richter, Daniel K.
Trade Secrets — Wishart, David
Trade Union Bill — Great Britain: Parliament: House of Commons
Traders and Raiders: The Indigenous World of the Colorado Basin, 1540-1859 — Zappia, Natale A.
Trading Tongues: Merchants, Multilingualism, and Medieval Literature — Hsy, Jonathan
Trading with the Enemy: The Covert Economy During the American Civil War — Leigh, Philip
Tradition and Influence in Anglo-Saxon Literature: An Evolutionary, Cognitivist Approach — Drout, Michael D.C.
Tradition and the Formation of the Talmud — Vidas, Moulie
The Tradition of the Actor-Author in Italian Theatre — Fisher, Donatella
Traditional Japanese Origami Kit — Robinson, Nick
Traditional Subjectivities: The Old English Poetics of Mentality — Mize, Britt
Traditional Weavers of Guatemala: Their Stories, Their Lives — Chandler, Deborah
Traditions and Transformations in the History of Quantum Physics — Katzir, Shaul
The Traffic in Babies: Cross-Border Adoption and Baby-Selling Between the United States and Canada, 1930-1972 — Balcom, Karen A.
y Traffick — Hopkins, Ellen
Trafficking Justice — McCarthy, Lauren A.
Tragedy and Archaic Greek Thought — Cairns, Douglas L.
c Tragedy at the Triangle — Doman, Mary Kate
Tragedy in Hegel's Early Theological Writings — Wake, Peter
The Tragedy of a Generation: The Rise and Fall of Jewish Nationalism in Eastern Europe — Karlip, Joshua M.
The Tragedy of Religious Freedom — DeGirolami, Marc O.
y The Tragic Age — Metcalfe, Stephen
"The Tragic Couple": Encounters between Jews and Jesuits — Bernauer, James W.
Tragic Encounter — Smith, Page
Tragic Modernities — Leonard, Miriam
Tragic Spirits: Shamanism, Memory, and Gender in Contemporary Mongolia — Buyandelger, Manduhai
c The Trail Game (Illus. by Tullet, Herve) — Tullet, Herve
The Trail Home — Daniel, John
Trail of Deceit — House, John C.
Trail of Evil — Taylor, Travis S.
Trail of Hope: The Anders Army, an Odyssey Across Three Continents — Davies, Norman
y Trail of the Dead — Bruchac, Joseph
Trail Sisters: Freedwomen in Indian Territory, 1850-1890 — Reese, Linda Williams
y Trailblazers in Medicine — Aldridge, Susan
c Trailblazing the Way West — Nolan, Frederick
Trails — Ross, Don
Trails of Bronze Drums Across Early Southeast Asia: Exchange Routes and Connected Cultural Spheres — Calo, Ambra
c Train (Illus. by Abbot, Judi) — Abbot, Judi
The Train Doesn't Stop Here Anymore: An Illustrated History of Railway Stations in Canada — Brown, Ron
c Train Is on Track — Bently, Peter
c Train (Illus. by Abbot, Judi) — Abbot, Judi
Train: Riding the Rails That Created the Modern World - from the Trans-Siberian to the 'Southwest Chief' — Zoellner, Tom
The Train to Crystal City: FDR's Secret Prisoner Exchange Program and America's Only Family Internment Camp During World War II — Russell, Jan Jarboe
Training Students to Extract Value from Big Data: Summary of a Workshop — Mellody, Maureen
c Trains Can Float: And Other Fun Facts (Illus. by Oswald, Pete) — DiSiena, Laura Lyn
The Trains Now Departed: Sixteen Excursions into the Lost Delights of Britain's Railways — Williams, Michael
The Traitor Baru Cormorant — Dickinson, Seth
y The Traitor: Boy Nobody — Zadoff, Allen
The Traitor — Horler, Sydney
c Traitor's Chase — Gibbs, Stuart
Traitor's Gate — Newton, Charlie
The Traitor's Mark — Wilson, D.K.
Trajectories of Religion in Africa: Essays in Honour of John S. Pobee — Omenyo, Cephas N.
Tram 83 — Mujila, Fiston Mwanza
y Trampoline: An Illustrated Novel (Illus. by Gipe, Robert) — Gipe, Robert
Trams or Tailfins? Public and Private Prosperity in Postwar West Germany and the United States — Logemann, Jan L.
Trance-Migrations: Stories of India, Tales of Hypnosis — Siegel, Lee
Tranquility: Cultivating a Quiet Soul in a Busy World — Henderson, David W.
Trans: A Memoir — Jacques, Juliet
Trans-Americanity: Subaltern Modernities, Global Coloniality, and the Cultures of Greater Mexico — Saldivar, Jose David
Trans/Portraits: Voices from Transgender Communities — Shultz, Jackson Wright
Transatlantic Abolitionism in the Age of Revolution: An International History of Anti-Slavery, c.1787-1820 — Oldfield, J.R.
A Transatlantic History of the Social Sciences: Robber Barons, the Third Reich and the Invention of Empirical Social Research — Fleck, Christian
Transatlantic Methodists: British Wesleyanism and the Formation of an Evangelical Culture in Nineteenth-Century Ontario and Quebec — Webb, Todd
Transatlantic Renaissances: Literature of Ireland and the American South — Artuso, Kathryn Stelmach
Transatlantic Spectacles of Race: The Tragic Mulatta and the Tragic Muse — Manganelli, Kimberly Snyder
Transatlantic Theory Transfer: Missed Encounters?
Transatlantic Travels in Nineteenth-Century Latin America: European Women Pilgrims — Rodenas, Adriana Mendez
The Transatlantic World of Higher Education: Americans at German Universities, 1776-1914 — Werner, Anja
Transatlantische Germanistik. Kontakt, Transfer, Dialogik — Lutzeler, Paul Michael
y Transcendent: A Starling Novel — Livingston, Lesley
y Transcendent: A Starling Novel — Livington, Lesley
The Transcriptionist — Rowland, Amy
Transfeminist Perspectives: In and Beyond Transgender and Gender Studies — Enke, Anne
Transformation Now! Toward a Post-Oppositional Politics of Change — Keating, Ana Louise
Transformation of the African American Intelligentsia, 1880-2012 — Kilson, Martin
The Transformation of the World: A Global History of the Nineteenth Century — Osterhammel, Jurgen
Transformations in Biblical Literary Traditions: Incarnation, Narrative, and Ethics: Essays in Honor of David Lyle Jeffrey — Williams, D.H.
The Transformations of Magic: Illicit Learned Magic in the Later Middle Ages and the Renaissance — Klaassen, Frank
Transformations of Retailing in Europe after 1945 — Jessen, Ralph
Transformations of the Classics via Early Modern Commentaries — Enenkel, Karl A.E.
Transformations of Time and Temporality in Medieval and Renaissance Art — Cohen, Simona
Transformative Experience — Paul, L.A.
Transforming Archaeology: Activist Practices and Prospects — Atalay, Sonya
Transforming Civil War Prisons: Lincoln, Lieber, and the Politics of Captivity — Springer, Paul J.
Transforming Faith: Stories of Change from a Lifelong Spiritual Seeker — Howard, Fred
Transforming the South: Federal Development in the Tennessee Valley 1915-1960 — Downs, Matthew L.
Transforming Work: Early Modern Pastoral and Late Medieval Poetry — Little, Catherine C.
Transgender China — Chiang, Howard
y Transgender Lives: Complex Stories, Complex Voices — Cronn-Mills, Kirstin
Transgression, Tragik und Metatheater: Versuch einer Neuinterpretation des antiken Dramas — Willms, Lothar
Transgressions and Other Stories — Orbach, Hilary
Transgressive Theatricality, Romanticism, and Mary Wollstonecraft — Crafton, Lisa Plummer
Transient Apostle: Paul, Travel, and the Rhetoric of Empire — Marquis, Timothy Luckritz
Transient Workspaces: Technologies of Everyday Innovation in Zimbabwe — Mavhunga, Clapperton Chakanetsa
Transit of Venus: Travels in the Pacific — Evans, Julian
Transition Metal Compounds — Khomskii, Daniel I.
Transition to an Industrial South: Athens, Georgia, 1830-1870 — Gagnon, Michael J.

The Transition to Democracy in Hungary: Arpad Goncz and the Post-Communist Hungarian Presidency — *Kim, Dae Soon*
Transitional Justice in der Weltgesellschaft — *Kastner, Fatima*
Transitional Justice in Post-Communist Romania: The Politics of Memory — *Stan, Lavinia*
Transitional Justice - The Role of Historical Narrative in Times of Transitions
Transitions and Non-Transitions from Communism: Regime Survival in China, Cuba, North Korea, and Vietnam — *Saxonberg, Steven*
Transitions: Emerging Women Writers in German-Language Literature — *Heffernan, Valerie*
Translated Christianities: Nahuatl and Maya Religious Texts — *Christensen, Mark Z.*
Translating Apollinaire — *Scott, Clive*
Translating the Past: Essays on Medieval Literature in Honor of Marijane Osborn — *Beal, Jane*
Translating Troy: Provincial Politics in Alliterative Romance — *Mueller, Alex*
Translation as Collaboration: Virginia Woolf, Katherine Mansfield and S.S. Koteliansky — *Davison, Claire*
Translingual Identities: Language and the Self in Stefan Heym and Jakov Lind — *Steinitz, Tamar*
Translucence — *Stevens, Jeremy*
Transnational Crossroads: Remapping the Americas and the Pacific — *Fojas, Camilla*
Transnational France: The Modern History of a Universal Nation — *Stovall, Tyler*
Transnational Lives in China: Expatriates in a Globalizing City — *Lehmann, Angela*
A Transnational Poetics — *Ramazani, Jahan*
Transnational Sport: Gender, Media, and Global Korea — *Joo, Rachael Miyung*
Transnational Tolstoy: Between the West and the World — *Foster, John Burt, Jr.*
Transnational Traditions: New Perspectives on American Jewish History — *Kahn, Ava Fran*
Transnationale Praktiken der Konstruktion Europas
Transpacific Antiracism: Afro-Asian Solidarity in 20th-Century Black America, Japan, and Okinawa — *Onishi, Yuichiro*
Transpacific Articulations: Student Migration and the Remaking of Asian America — *Wang, Chih-ming*
Transpacific Femininities: The Making of the Modern Filipina — *Cruz, Denise*
The Transplant Imaginary: Mechanical Hearts, Animal Parts, and Moral Thinking in Highly Experimental Science. — *Sharp, Lesley A.*
Transplantation Ethics, 2d ed. — *Veatch, Robert M.*
Transplantierte Alltage: Zur Produktion von Normalitat nach einer Organtransplantation — *Amelang, Katrin*
Transporting Chaucer — *Barr, Helen*
The Transregional Production, Translation, and Appropriation of Knowledge: Actors, Institutions, and Discourses
y The Trap — *Arntson, Steven*
Trap — *Tanenbaum, Robert K.*
c The Trap — *Arntson, Steven*
c Trapped! A Whale's Rescue (Illus. by Minor, Wendell) — *Burleigh, Robert*
Trapped at the Altar (Read by Tanner, Jill). Audiobook Review — *Feather, Jane*
Trapped by Scandal — *Feather, Jane*
c Trapped in Antarctica! Nickolas Flux and the Shackleton Expedition (Illus. by Simmons, Mark) — *Yomtov, Nel*
Trash — *Hoover, Laurie*
y Trash Can Nights — *Steinkellner, Teddy*
Trash Market — *Tsuge, Tadao*
c Trash Mountain (Illus. by Monroe, Chris) — *Yolen, Jane*
c Trash Talk: Moving toward a Zero-Waste World — *Mulder, Michelle*
y Trashed — *Backderf, Derf*
Trauma — *Palmer, Daniel*
The Traumatic Colonel: The Founding Fathers, Slavery, and the Phantasmatic Aaron Burr — *Drexler, Michael J.*
The Traumatic Colonel: The Founding Fathers, Slavery, and the Phantasmic Aaron Burr — *Drexler, Michael J.*
The Traumatized Brain: A Family Guide to Understanding Mood, Memory, and Behavior After Brain Injury — *Rao, Vani*
Travel and Religion in Antiquity — *Harland, Philip A.*
Travel, Collecting, and Museums of Asian Art in Nineteenth-Century Paris — *Chang, Ting*
Travel Every Day — *Ennis, John*

A Travel Guide to Homer: On the Trail of Odysseus through Turkey and the Mediterranean — *Freely, John*
Travel, Modernism and Modernity — *Burden, Robert*
Travel Narrative and the Ends of Modernity — *Buron, Stacy*
A Traveled First Lady: Writings of Louisa Catherine Adams — *Adams, Louisa Catherine*
A Traveled First Lady: Writings of Louisa Catherine Adams — *Hogan, Margaret A.*
Travelers Rest — *Morris, Keith Lee*
c Traveling Butterflies (Illus. by Shingu, Susumu) — *Shingu, Susumu*
c Traveling Butterflies (Illus. by Susumu, Shingu) — *Susumu, Shingu*
c The Traveling Circus (Illus. by Gay, Marie-Louise) — *Gay, Marie-Louise*
c The Traveling Circus — *Gay, Marie-Louise*
c The Traveling Circus (Illus. by Gay, marie-Louise) — *Gay, Marie-Louise*
A Traveling Homeland: The Babylonian Talmud as Diaspora — *Boyarin, Daniel*
Travellers' Accounts as Source-Material for Irish Historians — *Woods, C.J.*
Travelling to Work: Diaries 1988-1998 — *Palin, Michael*
Travels in Vermeer: A Memoir — *White, Michael*
c Travels of an Extraordinary Hamster (Illus. by Martin, Pauline) — *Desbordes, Astrid*
The Travels of Daniel Ascher — *Levy-Bertherat, Deborah*
y Travels with Gannon and Wyatt: Ireland — *Hemstreet, Keith*
Travels with Gannon and Wyatt: Ireland — *Wheeler, Patti*
Treacherous Faith: The Specter of Heresy in Early Modern English Literature and Culture — *Loewenstein, David*
The Treacherous Net — *Tursten, Helene*
Treacherous Subjects: Gender, Culture, and Trans-Vietnamese Feminism — *Duong, Lan P.*
Treacherous Subjects: Gender, Culture, and Trans-Vietnamese Feminism — *Duong, Lan P*
Treacherous Translation: Culture, Nationalism, and Colonialism in Korea and Japan from the 1910s to the 1960s — *Suh, Serk-Bae*
Treadmill — *Adler, Warren*
The Treason of the Intellectuals — *Benda, Julien*
c The Treasure Hunt Stunt at Fenway Park — *Aretha, David*
c Treasure Hunters: Danger Down the Nile (Illus. by Neufeld, Juliana) — *Patterson, James*
c Treasure Hunter's Handbook — *Walsh, Liza Gardner*
c Treasure Hunters: Secret of the Forbidden City (Read by Kennedy, Bryan). Audiobook Review — *Patterson, James*
c Treasure in Trident City (Illus. by Avakyan, Tatevik) — *Dadey, Debbie*
Treasure Neverland: Real and Imaginary Pirates — *Rennie, Neil*
c The Treasure of the Viking Ship (Illus. by Frare, Michela) — *Stilton, Thea*
Treasure State Justice: Judge George M. Bourquin, Defender of the Rule of Law — *Gutfeld, Arnon*
Treasured by Thursday — *Bybee, Catherine*
Treasured Possessions: Indigenous Interventions into Cultural and Intellectual Property — *Geismar, Haidy*
c Treasury of Norse Mythology: Stories of Intrigue, Trickery, Love, and Revenge (Illus. by Balit, Christina) — *Napoli, Donna Jo*
y A Treasury of Victorian Murder Compendium II — *Geary, Rick*
c A Treasury of Wintertime Tales (Illus. by Anglund, Joan Walsh) — *Anglund, Joan Walsh*
c A Treasury of Wisdom — *Joslin, Mary*
c Treat — *Sullivan, Mary*
Treating AIDS: Politics of Difference, Paradox of Prevention — *Sangaramoorthy, Thurka*
The Treatment of Armenians in the Ottoman Empire, 1915-1916: Documents Presented to Viscount Grey of Fallodon by Viscount Bryce — *Toynbee, Arnold*
c Tree: A Peek-Through Picture Book (Illus. by Teckentrup, Britta) — *Teckentrup, Britta*
c Tree — *Teckentrup, Britta*
Tree of Salvation: Yggdrasil and the Cross in the North — *Murphy, G. Ronald*
y The Tree of Water — *Haydon, Elizabeth*
c Tree of Wonder: The Many Marvelous Lives of a Rainforest Tree (Illus. by Mulazzani, Simona) — *Messner, Kate*
The Tree of Young Dreamers — *Sousa, Frank*

The Tree: Symbol, Allegory, and Mnemonic Device in Medieval Art and Thought — *Salonius, Pippa*
c Trees: A Compare and Contrast Book — *Hall, Katharine*
Trees and Timber in the Anglo-Saxon World — *Bintley, Michael D.J.*
Trees in Paradise: A California History — *Farmer, Jared*
Trees of Western North America — *Spellenberg, Richard*
Trees, vol. 1: In Shadow — *Ellis, Warren*
Trees, Woods and Forests: A Social and Cultural History — *Watkins, Charles*
Tremaine's True Love — *Burrowes, Grace*
The Trench Angel — *Gutierrez, Michael Keenan*
Trends and Traditions in Southeastern Zooarchaeology — *Peres, Tanya M.*
Trent: What Happened at the Council — *O'Malley, John W.*
Trepanation of the Skull — *Gandlevsky, Sergey*
Tres Green, Tres Clean, Tres Chic: Eat (and Live!) the New French Way with Plant-Based, Gluten-Free Recipes for Every Season — *Leffler, Rebecca*
The Trespasser — *Wynn, Todd*
The Tri-State Gang in Richmond: Murder and Robery in the Great Depression — *Richardson, Selden*
Trial by Fire — *Clegg, Bill*
Trial by Fire — *Angelini, Josephine*
y Trial by Fire — *Angelini, Josephine*
Trial by Gas: The British Army at the Second Battle of Ypres — *Cassar, George H.*
The Trial of Galileo: Essential Documents — *Finocchiaro, Maurice A.*
Trial of Intentions — *Orullian, Peter*
The Trial of Jan Hus: Medieval Heresy and Criminal Procedure — *Fudge, Thomas A.*
Trialer Park Fae — *Saintcrow, Lilith*
Trials and Triumphs: The Gordons of Huntly in Sixteenth-Century Scotland — *Forbes, Anne L.*
Trials of Arab Modernity: Literary Affects and the New Political — *El-Ariss, Tarek*
The Trials of Christopher Mann — *Charles, Casey*
The Trials of Laura Fair: Sex, Murder, and Insanity in the Victorian West — *Haber, Carole*
The Trials of Laura Lair: Sex, Murder, and Insanity in the Victorian West — *Carole Haber*
Trials of Passion: Crimes Committed in the Name of Love and Madness — *Appignanesi, Lisa*
Trials of Passion: Crimes in the Name of Love and Madness — *Appignanesi, Lisa*
c Triangles (Illus. by Miller, Edward) — *Adler, David A.*
c Triangles — *Yonezu, Yusuke*
Triangular Landscapes: Environment, Society, and the State in the Nile Delta under Roman Rule — *Blouin, Katherine*
Tribal: College Football and the Secret Heart of America — *Roberts, Diane*
Tribal Modern: Branding New Nations in the Arab Gulf — *Cooke, Miriam*
Tribal Worlds: Critical Studies in American Indian Nation Building — *Hosmer, Brian*
Tributaries — *Da, Laura*
Tribute: The Complete Collection — *Pearce, Kate*
c Triceratops — *Lennie, Charles*
c Trick ARRR Treat: A Pirate Halloween (Illus. by Monlongo, Jorge) — *Kimmelman, Leslie*
c Trick or Treat? (Illus. by Rigo, Laura) — *Lorini, Andrea*
c Trick Out My School! (Illus. by Gilpin, Stephen) — *Mellom, Robin*
c The Tricks and Treats of Halloween! (Illus. by Wake, Rich) — *Murphy, Angela*
Tricks of the Trade: Confessions of a Bookbinder — *Kamph, Jamie*
The Trickster Figure in American Literature — *Morgan, Winifred*
The Tricky Art of Co-Existing: How to Behave Decently No Matter What Life Throws Your Way — *Toksvig, Sandi*
c Tricky Vic: The Impossibly True Story of the Man Who Sold the Eiffel Tower (Illus. by Pizzoli, Greg) — *Pizzoli, Greg*
Trieglaff: Balancing Church and Politics in a Pomeranian World, 1807-1948 — *von Thadden, Rudolf*
Trieste — *Drndic, Dasa*
Trigger Mortis: A James Bond Novel — *Horowitz, Anthony*
Trigger Warning: Is the Fear of Being Offensive Killing Free Speech? — *Hume, Mick*

Trigger Warning: Short Fictions and Disturbances (Read by Gaiman, Neil). Audiobook Review — Gaiman, Neil
y Trigger Warning: Short Fictions and Disturbances — Gaiman, Neil
Trillion Dollar Economists: How Economists and Their Ideas Have Transformed Business — Litan, Robert E.
y The Trilogy of Two (Illus. by Malouf, Juman) — Malouf, Juman
A Trinitarian Theology of Religions: An Evangelical Proposal — McDermott, Gerald R.
Trinity and Revelation, vol. 2 — Karkkainen, Veli-Matti
Trio for Horn, Violin, and Piano — Ewazen, Eric
The Trip to Echo Spring: On Writers and Drinking — Laing, Olivia
Triphiodorus, the Sack of Troy: A General Study and a Commentary — Miguelez-Cavero, Laura
c Triple H — Scheff, Matt
y Triple Moon — de la Cruz, Melissa
y Tripping Back Blue — Storti, Kara
Trisha's Table: My Feel-Good Favorites for a Balanced Life — Yearwood, Trisha
Tristana — Galdos, Benito Perez
Tristano Dies — Harris, Elizabeth
Tristano Dies — Tabucchi, Antonio
Tristram Shandy — Sterne, Laurence
Triumph in Defeat: Military Loss and the Roman Republic — Clark, Jessica Homan
A Triumph of Genius: Edwin Land, Polaroid, and the Kodak Patent War — Fierstein, Ronald
The Triumph of Human Empire: Verne, Morris, and Stevenson at the End of the World — Williams, Rosalind
The Triumph of Improvisation: Gorbachev's Adaptability, Reagan's Engagement, and the End of the Cold War — Wilson, James Graham
The Triumph of Seeds: How Grains, Nuts, Kernels, Pulses, and Pips Conquered the Plant Kingdom and Shaped Human History — Hanson, Thor
Triumph of the Absurd: A Reporter's Love for the Abandoned People of Vietnam — Siemon-Netto, Uwe
Triumph of the Heart: Forgiveness in an Unforgiving World — Bettencourt, Megan Feldman
The Triumph of William McKinley: Why the Election of 1896 Still Matters — Rove, Karl
The Triumph & Tragedy of Lyndon Johnson: The White House Years — Califano, Joseph A.
c Triumphant Journey — Rossi, Wynn-Anne
Troilus and Criseyde in Modern Verse — Chaucer, Geoffrey
The Trojan Legend in Medieval Scottish Literature — Wingfield, Emily
c The Trojan War: A Graphic Retelling (Illus. by Haus, Estudio) — Chandler, Matt
c Trojans! The Story of the Trojan Horse (Illus. by Jones, Dani) — Holub, Joan
c Troll and the Oliver (Illus. by Stower, Adam) — Stower, Adam
y Troll Hunters (Illus. by Murray, Sean) — Del Toro, Guillermo
c The Troll Who Cried Wolf — Harrell, Rob
The Trolley Problem Mysteries — Kamm, F.M.
y Trollhunters (Read by Heyborne, Kirby). Audiobook Review — del Toro, Guillermo
c Trollhunters (Illus. by Murray, Sean) — del Toro, Guillermo
c Trollhunters (Illus. by Murray, Sean) — Kraus, Daniel
The Trombone in the Attic, 20 Short Recital and Study Pieces for the Intermediate Player — Walker, John
c Trombone Shorty (Illus. by Collier, Bryan) — Andrews, Troy
Trompe l'Oeil — Reisman, Nancy
Trop de lumiere pour Samuel Gaska — Beaulieu, Etienne
Tropic of Hopes: California, Florida, and the Selling of American Paradise, 1869-1929 — Knight, Henry
c Tropical Fish — Hansen, Grace
Tropical Judgments — Robinson, David Myles
c Tropical Rain Forests — Gray, Leon
Tropical Whites: The Rise of the Tourist South in the Americas — Cocks, Catherine
Tropics of Savagery: The Culture of Japanese Empire in Comparative Frame — Tierney, Robert Thomas
Trosley's How to Draw Cartoon Cars — Trosley, George
c Troto and the Trucks (Illus. by Shulevitz, Uri) — Shulevitz, Uri
Trouble at Work — Fevre, Ralph
y Trouble from the Start — Hawthorne, Rachel

Trouble in Goshen: Plain Folk, Roosevelt, Jesus, and Marx in the Great Depression South — Smith, Fred C.
y The Trouble in Me (Read by Gantos, Jack). Audiobook Review — Gantos, Jack
y The Trouble in Me — Gantos, Jack
Trouble in Paradise: From the End of History to the End of Capitalism — Zizek, Slavoj
Trouble in Rooster Paradise — Emory, T.W.
y Trouble Is a Friend of Mine (Read by McInerney, Kathleen). Audiobook Review — Tromly, Stephanie
y Trouble Is a Friend of Mine — Tromly, Stephanie
c Trouble Is My Beeswax — Hale, Bruce
Trouble I've Seen — Hart, Drew G.I.
y Trouble on Cable Street — Lingard, Joan
Trouble on the Thames — Bridges, Victor
c The Trouble with Ants (Illus. by Kath, Katie) — Mills, Claudia
y The Trouble with Destiny — Morrill, Lauren
c The Trouble with Fuzzwonker Fizz — Carman, Patrick
The Trouble With History: Morality, Revolution, and Counterrevolution — Michnik, Adam
The Trouble with History: Morality, Revolution, and Counterrevolution — Gross, Irena Grudzinska
The Trouble with Honor (Read by Landor, Rosalyn). Audiobook Review — London, Julia
The Trouble with Patience — Brendan, Maggie
y The Trouble with Peer Pressure: A Simple "My ADHD Story" for Young Teens (Illus. by Guiza, Victor) — Wood, Darlene R.
The Trouble with the Truth — Robinson, Edna
Troubled Geographies: A Spatial History of Religion and Society in Ireland — Ell, Paul S.
y The Troubles of Johnny Cannon — Campbell, Isaiah
A Troublesome Inheritance: Genes, Race and Human History — Wade, Nicholas
c Tru and Nelle — Neri, G.
y Tru Detective (Illus. by Hughes, Steven P.) — McClintock, Norah
c Trucks — Gillingham, Sara
True Alignment: Linking Company Culture with Customer Needs for Extraordinary Results — Papke, Edgar
The True American: Murder and Mystery in Texas — Giridharadas, Anand
True and Holy: Christian Scripture and Other Religions — Lefebure, Leo D.
c True Blue (Read by Goethals, Angela). Audiobook Review — Smiley, Jane
c A True Book: Biographies — Doak, Robin S.
c True Colors — Santopolo, Jill
True Crimes — Harrison, Kathryn
True Emotions — Salmela, Mikko
True False — Klee, Miles
True Grit — Bunker, Jack
c True Grit — Grylls, Bear
The True Herod — Vermes, Geza
c True Heroes: A Treasury of Modern-Day Fairy Tales Written by Best-Selling Authors (Illus. by Diaz, Jonathan) — Diaz, Jonathan
c True Heroes — Diaz, Jonathan
The True History of Merlin the Magician — Lawrence, Anne
The True History of the Conquest of New Spain — Humphrey, Ted
True Love's Kiss — Rustad, Robert
True North: Tice's Story — Leslie, Mark Alan
A True Novel — Mizumura, Minae
True Relations: Reading, Literature, and Evidence in Seventeenth-Century England — Dolan, Frances E.
y True Son — Krumwiede, Lana
c The True Spirit of Christmas (Illus. by Manning, Dorothy Thurgood) — Manning, Dorothy Thurgood
y The True Story of Spit MacPhee — Aldridge, James
True Style: The History and Principles of Classic Menswear — Boyer, G. Bruce
c True Tails from the Dog Park (Illus. by Stricklin, Julie Ann) — Max
y Truest — Sommers, Jackie Lea
Truly Human Enhancement: A Philosophical Defense of Limits — Agar, Nicholas
Truly Madly Pizza: One Incredibly Easy Crust, Countless Inspired Combinations and Other Irresistible Tidbits to Make Handmade Pizza a Nightly Affair — Lenzer, Suzanne
Truly Sweet — Terry, Candis
Truly Texas Mexican: A Native Culinary Heritage in Recipes — Medrano, Adan
Truman Capote: A Literary Life at the Movies — Pugh, Tison

Trumbo: A Biography of the Oscar-Winning Screenwriter Who Broke the Hollywood Blacklist (Read by Daniels, Luke). Audiobook Review — Cook, Bruce
The Trumpet in the Attic, 20 Short Recital and Study Pieces for the Intermediate Player — Walker, John
Trumpets in the Mountains: Theater and the Politics of National Culture in Cuba — Frederik, Laurie
Trust in Food: A Comparative and Institutional Analysis — Kjaernes, Unni
y Trust Me, I'm Lying — Summer, Mary Elizabeth
y Trust Me, I'm Trouble — Summer, Mary Elizabeth
Trust Me — Lorrimer, Claire
Trust No One — Cleave, Paul
Trust of People, Words, and God: A Route for Philosophy of Religion — Godfrey, Joseph J.
Trust: The Spiritual Impulse After Darwin — Fishman, Loren M.
Trusting Liam — McAdams, Molly
y The Truth about Alice (Read by several narrators). Audiobook Review — Mathieu, Jennifer
The Truth about Caroline — Sherman, Randi M.
The Truth about Him — O'Keefe, Molly
y The Truth about My Success (Read by Sands, Tara). Audiobook Review — Sheldon, Dyan
y The Truth about My Success — Sheldon, Dyan
Truth about Nature: A Family's Guide to 144 Common Myths about the Great Outdoors — Tornio, Stacy
y The Truth about Peacock Blue — Hawke, Rosanne
The Truth About Tesla: The Myth of the Lone Genius in the History of Innovation — Cooper, Christopher
y The Truth about Twinkie Pie — Yeh, Kat
y The Truth about Us — Gurtler, Janet
The Truth According to Us (Read by Lee, Ann Marie). Audiobook Review — Barrows, Annie
y The Truth According to Us — Barrows, Annie
The Truth: An Uncomfortable Book about Relationships — Strauss, Neil
Truth and Kisses — Friedman, Laurie B.
y The Truth and Other Lies — Arango, Sascha
Truth and Relevance: Catholic Theology in French Quebec Since the Quiet Revolution — Baum, Gregory
Truth Be Told (Read by Sands, Xe). Audiobook Review — Ryan, Hank Phillippi
Truth Be Told — Ryan, Hank Phillippi
y The Truth Commission. Audiobook Review — Juby, Susan
y The Truth Commission — Juby, Susan
y The Truth Commission (Illus. by Cooper, Trevor) — Juby, Susan
y The Truth Commission — Juby, Susan
The Truth Commissioner — Park, David
Truth Evolves — Arand, Dustin
Truth Insurrected: The Saint Mary Project — Douglas, Daniel P.
Truth of My Songs: Poems of the Trobairitz — Keelan, Claudia
Truth or Die (Read by Ballerini, Edoardo). Audiobook Review — Patterson, James
Truth Overruled: The Future of Marriage and Religious Freedom — Anderson, Ryan T.
Truth Seeker — O'Connor, J. Patrick
A Truth Stranger Than Fiction — Orcutt, Chris
Truth Will Out: Indonesian Accounts of the 1965 Mass Violence — Wardaya, Baskara T.
The Truth Within: A History of Inwardness in Christianity, Hinduism, and Buddhism — Flood, Gavin
Truth's Ragged Edge: The Rise of the American Novel — Gura, Philip E.
y Truthwitch — Dennard, Susan
Try Not to Breathe — Seddon, Holly
c Try This! 50 Fun Experiments for the Mad Scientist in You — Young, Karen Romano
Trying: Love, Loose Pants & the Quest for a Baby — Cossey, Mark
Trying to Please: A Memoir — Norwich, John Julius
Tryst — Jennings, S.L.
Tsai Ming-liang and a Cinema of Slowness — Lim, Song Hwee
The Tsar of Love and Techno: Stories — Marra, Anthony
The Tsarnaev Brothers: The Road to a Modern Tragedy — Gessen, Masha
Tschechische, Slowakische und Tschechoslowakische Geschichte des 20. Jahrhunderts
c Tsunami — Markovics, Joyce
Tsunami: Images of Resilience — Root, Dan
c Tsunami — Markovics, Joyce
c Tuataras: Dinosaur-Era Reptiles — Hirsch, Rebecca E.

Tuberculosis and the Victorian Literary Imagination — Byrne, Katherine
c   Tuck Everlasting — Babbitt, Natalie
c   Tuck-in Time (Illus. by Pearson, Tracey Campbell) — Gerber, Carole
c   Tucky Jo and Little Heart (Illus. by Polacco, Patricia) — Polacco, Patricia
    The Tudor Discovery of Ireland — Wooding, Lucy
c   The Tudors: Kings, Queens, Scribes and Ferrets! (Illus. by Williams, Marcia) — Williams, Marcia
c   Tuesday Tucks Me In: The Loyal Bond Between a Soldier and His Service Dog — Witter, Bret
c   Tuky — Rosenfeld, Shterni
c   Tulip and Rex Write a Story (Illus. by Massini, Sarah) — Capucilli, Alyssa Satin
c   Tuma: The Tribe's Little Princess (Illus. by Violante, Susan) — Violante, Susan
c   Tumbleiveed Baby (Illus. by Vess, Charles) — Myers, Anna
y   Tumbleweed Baby (Illus. by Vess, Charles) — Myers, Anna
    Tundra Kill — Jones, Stan
c   Tuniit: Mysterious People of the Arctic (Illus. by Brigham, Sean) — Qitsualik-Tinsley, Sean
c   Tuniit — Qitsualik-Tinsley, Rachel
    Tunnel Vision, A Focused Life — Beauregard, Isadora
y   Tunnel Vision — Adrian, Susan
    Tunnel Visions: The Rise and Fall of the Superconducting Super Collider — Riordan, Michael
    The Tupac Amaru Rebellion — Walker, Charles F.
    Turbo-Folk Music and Cultural Representations of National Identity in Former Yugoslavia — Cvoro, Uros
c   The Turbulent Term of Tyke Tiler — Kemp, Gene
    Turing: Pioneer of the Information Age — Copeland, B. Jack
c   Turkey Trouble (Illus. by Kerber, Kathy) — Walker, Judy
    Turkish Berlin: Integration Policy and Urban Space — Hinze, Annika Marlen
    Turkish German Cinema in the New Millennium: Sites, Sounds, and Screens — Hake, Sabine
c   The Turn of the Tide — Parry, Rosanne
c   Turn Off That Light! — Crossingham, John
    Turn the Ship Around! A True Story of Turning Followers into Leaders — Marquet, L. David
    Turn Your Mate into Your Soulmate: A Practical Guide to Happily Ever After — Ford, Arielle
    The Turner House — Flournoy, Angela
y   Turning 15 on the Road to Freedom: My Story of the 1965 Selma Voting Rights March (Illus. by Loughran, P.J.) — Lowery, Lynda Blackmon
    Turning Into Dwelling: Poems — Gilbert, Christopher
    Turning into Dwelling — Gilbert, Christopher
    Turning Over a New Leaf: Change and Development in the Medieval Book — Kwakkel, Erik
    Turning Prayers into Protests: Religious-Based Activism and Its Challenge to State Power in Socialist Slovakia and East Germany — Doellinger, David
    Turning Texas Blue: What It Will Take to Break the GOP Grip on America's Reddest State — Rogers, Mary Beth
    Turning the Tide: The University of Alabama in the 1960s — Tilford, Earl H.
    Turning to Tradition: Converts and the Making of an American Orthodox Church — Herbel, D. Oliver
c   The Turnip (Illus. by Brett, Jan) — Brett, Jan
c   The Turnip Princess and Other Newly Discovered Fairy Tales — Schonwerth, Franz Xaver von
c   Turtle and Me (Illus. by Freeman, Tor) — Harris, Robie H.
c   Turtle Island — Sherry, Kevin
c   The Turtle of Oman (Illus. by Peterschmidt, Betsy) — Nye, Naomi
    Turtleface and Beyond — Bradford, Arthur
    The Turtles of Mexico: Land and Freshwater Forms — Legler, John M.
c   Turvytops: A Really Wild Island — Brasher, Cecil
    The Tuscarora War: Indians, Settlers, and the Fight for the Carolina Colonies — La Vere, David
    The Tusk That Did the Damage — James, Tania
    The Tuskegee Airmen: An Illustrated History, 1939-1949 — Caver, Joseph
c   The Tuskegee Airmen — Gagne, Tammy
y   Tut: The Story of My Immortal Life — Hoover, P.J.
    The Tutor — Chapin, Andrea
    TuTu Thin — Smith-Theodore, Dawn
    Twain and Stanley Enter Paradise — Hijuelos, Oscar
    Twain's End — Cullen, Lynn

c   'Twas Nochebuena (Illus. by Palacios, Sara) — Thong, Roseanne Greenfield
c   'Twas the Night before Christmas (Illus. by Kirk, Daniel) — Moore, Clement C.
c   'Twas the Night before Christmas (Illus. by Marshall, Mark) — Moore, Clement C.
    Twee: The Gentle Revolution in Music, Books, Television, Fashion, and Film — Spitz, Marc
c   The Tweedles Go Electric (Illus. by Lafrance, Marie) — Kulling, Monica
c   The Tweedles Go Online (Illus. by Lafrance, Marie) — Kulling, Monica
c   The Tween Book: A Growing-Up Guide for the Changing You — Moss, Wendy L.
y   The Tween Scene: A Year of Programs for 10- to 14-Year Olds — Balducci, Tiffany
c   Tweezle into Everything (Illus. by Griffiths, Dean) — McLellan, Stephanie
c   Twelve Dancing Unicorns (Illus. by Gerard, Justin) — Heyman, Alissa
    Twelve Days (Read by Guidall, George). Audiobook Review — Berenson, Alex
    Twelve Days — Berenson, Alex
c   The Twelve Days of Christmas in New England (Illus. by Woodruff, Liza) — Buzzeo, Toni
c   The Twelve Days of Christmas in Ohio (Illus. by Ebbeler, Jeffrey) — Gerber, Carole
c   The Twelve Days of Christmas in Oregon (Illus. by Conahan, Carolyn) — Blackaby, Susan
c   The Twelve Days of Christmas in Pennsylvania (Illus. by Dougherty, Rachel) — Levine, Martha Peaslee
c   The Twelve Days of Christmas in Indiana (Illus. by Cummings, Troy) — Griffin, Donna
c   The Twelve Days of Christmas (Illus. by Griffin, Rachel) — Griffin, Rachel
c   The Twelve Days of Christmas (Illus. by Pham, LeUyen) — Pham, LeUyen
    Twelve Kings in Sharakhai — Beaulieu, Bradley P.
    Twelve Recipes — Peternell, Cal
    Twelve Stations — Rozycki, Tomasz
c   The Twelve Tasks of Hercules (Illus. by Kelly, Gerald) — Pirotta, Saviour
    Twelve Tomorrows — Sterling, Bruce
    Twelve Voices from Greece and Rome: Ancient Ideas for Modern Times — Pelling, Christopher
    Twelve Yards: The Art and Psychology of the Perfect Penalty Kick — Lyttleton, Ben
    Twentieth-Century Sentimentalism: Narrative Appropriation in American Literature — Williamson, Jennifer A.
    Twentieth-Century Spain: A History — Casanova, Julian
    Twentieth-Century War and Conflict: A Concise Encyclopedia — Martel, Gordon
    Twenty-Eight and a Half Wishes — Swank, Denise Grover
    Twenty-First-Century Fiction: A Critical Introduction — Boxall, Peter
    Twenty Trillion Leagues under the Sea — Roberts, Adam
c   Twenty-two Cents: Muhammad Yunus and the Village Bank (Illus. by Akib, Jamel) — Yoo, Paula
    The Twenty-Year Death: Malniveau Prison — Winter, Ariel S.
    The Twenty-Year Death: Police at the Funeral — Winter, Ariel S.
    The Twenty-Year Death: The Falling Star — Winter, Ariel S.
    Twenty Years After Communism: The Politics of Memory and Commemoration — Bernhard, Michael H.
    Twice a Texas Bride — Broday, Linda
    Twice in a Lifetime — Garlock, Dorothy
    The Twilight of Human Rights Law — Posner, Eric
    The Twilight of Social Conservatism: American Culture Wars in the Obama Era — Dombrink, John
    The Twilight of the American Enlightenment: The 1950s and the Crisis of Liberal Belief — Marsden, George M.
    Twilight of the Belle Epoque: The Paris of Picasso, Stravinsky, Proust, Renault, Marie Curie, Gertrude Stein, and Their Friends through the Great War — McAuliffe, Mary
    Twilight of the Eastern Gods — Kadare, Ismail
    The Twilight of the Mission Frontier: Shifting Interethnic Alliances and Social Organization in Sonora, 1768-1855 — de la Torre Curiel, Jose Refugio
    Twilight of the Saints: Everyday Religion in Ottoman Syria and Palestine — Grehan, James
    Twillyweed: A Claire Breslinsky Mystery — Kelly, Mary Anne

    The Twin Powers — Lipsyte, Robert
    Twin Reflections — Joseph, Elizabeth R.
    Twin River II — Fields, Michael
    Twin Tracks: The Autobiography — Bannister, Roger
c   Twinkle, Twinkle, I Love You (Illus. by Corke, Estelle) — Metzger, Steve
c   Twinkle, Twinkle, Little Star: A Collection of Bedtime Rhymes (Illus. by Galloway, Fhiona) — Galloway, Fhiona
c   Twinkle, Twinkle, Little Star (Illus. by Van Hout, Mies) — van Hout, Mies
y   Twintuition: Double Vision — Mowry, Tia
c   Twist My Charm: The Popularity Spell — Gallagher, Toni
y   Twist — Akins, Karen
y   Twist of the Blade — Willett, Edward
    Twisted — Ashe, Bert
y   Twisted Dark, vol. 1 — Gibson, Neil
y   Twisted Fate — Olson, Norah
y   Twisted — Harrington, Lisa
    Twisted — Ashe, Bert
    Twisted Reunion — Tullius, Mark
    Twisted River — MacDonald, Siobhan
    Twisted Whispers — Wohl, Sheri Lewis
    Twisting My Kaleidoscope — Love, Shannon
    Two (Illus. by Otoshi, Kathryn) — Otoshi, Kathryn
    Two — Pinney, Melissa Ann
y   Two Across — Bartsch, Jeff
    Two Aelfric Texts: The Twelve Abuses and the Vices and Virtues — Clayton, Mary
    Two Arabic Travel Books: Accounts of China and India and Mission to the Volga — Sirafi, Abu Zayd Hasan ibn Yazid
    Two Armies on the Rio Grande: The First Campaign of the US-Mexican War — Murphy, Douglas A.
    Two Bronze Pennies — Nickson, Chris
    Two Brothers — Ba, Gabriel
y   Two Cool for School — Payton, Belle
    Two-Dollar Pistol — Cogburn, Brett
    The Two-Family House — Loigman, Lynda Cohen
c   Two for Joy (Illus. by Marble, Abigail) — Amateau, Gigi
c   Two Friends: Susan B. Anthony and Frederick Douglass (Illus. by Qualls, Sean) — Robbins, Dean
y   Two Girls: Staring at the Ceiling — Frank, Lucy
c   Two Girls Want a Puppy (Illus. by Lam, Maple) — Cordell, Evie
    Two Girls Want a Puppy (Illus. by Lam, Maple) — Cordell, Ryan
y   Two Hours: The Quest to Run the Impossible Marathon — Caesar, Ed
    Two If by Sea — Mitchard, Jacquelyn
c   Two Is Enough (Illus. by Mourning, Tuesday) — Matthies, Janna
    The Two Koreas and the Politics of Global Sport — Bridges, Brian
c   Two Mice (Illus. by Ruzzier, Sergio) — Ruzzier, Sergio
    Two-Minute Silence — Khatri, Chhote La
    Two Moms in the Raw: Simple, Clean, Irresistible Recipes for Your Family's Health — Leidich, Shari Koolik
    Two Mothers One Prayer — Lane, Laura
    Two of Hearts — Lee, Christina
    The Two of Us — Jones, Andy
    Two Percent Solutions for the Planet: 50 Low-Cost, Low-Tech, Nature-Based Practices for Combating Hunger, Drought, and Climate Change — White, Courtney
c   Two Renegade Realms — Paul, Donita K.
    Two Revisions of Rolle's English Psalter Commentary and the Related Canticles — Hudson, Anne
    Two Revisions of Rolle's English Psalter Commentary and the Related Canticles, vol. 2 — Hudson, Anne
    The Two-State Delusion: Israel and Palestine--a Tale of Two Narratives — O'Malley, Padraig
    The Two-State Delusion: Israel and Palestine -- a Tale of Two Narratives — O'Malley, Padraig
c   The Two Trees (Illus. by Olfert, Trudi) — Meadows, Sally
    Two Troubled Souls: An Eighteenth-Century Couple's Spiritual Journey in the Atlantic World — Fogleman, Aaron Spencer
    Two Troubled Souls: An Eighteenth-Century Couple's Spiritual Journey in the Atlantic World — Bryant, Sherwin K.
    Two Troubled Souls: An Eighteenth-Century Couple's Spiritual Journey in the Atlantic World — Fogleman, Aaron Spencer
c   Two White Rabbits (Illus. by Yockteng, Rafael) — Buitrago, Jairo
    Two Women: Anyentuyuwe and Ekakise — Bucher, Henry H.

Two Years Eight Months and Twenty-Eight Nights — *Rushdie, Salman*
y The Twyning — *Blacker, Terence*
y Ty Cobb: A Terrible Beauty — *Leerhsen, Charles*
Tycoon Takedown — *Cardello, Ruth*
Tyler Alexander: A Life and Times with McLaren — *Alexander, Tyler*
Tyndale's Bible: Saint Matthew's Gospel (Read by Crystal, David). Audiobook Review — *Crystal, David*
The Type B Manager: Leading Successfully in a Type A World — *Lipman, Victor*
Types of Pentecostal Theology: Methods, Systems, and Spirit — *Stephenson, Christopher A.*

c The Typewriter (Illus. by Thomson, Bill) — *Thomson, Bill*
y The Typewriter Revolution: A Typist's Companion for the 21st Century — *Polt, Richard*
Typewriter: The History, the Machine, the Writer — *Allan, Tony*
Typo — *Mayer, Hansjorg*
Typologie in der fruhen Neuzeit: Genese und Semantik heilsgeschichtlicher Bildprogramme von der Cappella Sistina (1480) bis San Giovanni in Laterano, 1650 — *Linke, Alexander*
Typology and Iconography in Donne, Herbert, and Milton: Fashioning the Self after Jeremiah — *Sanchez, Reuben*
Tyrannicide: Forging an American Law of Slavery in Revolutionary South Carolina and Massachusetts — *Blanck, Emily*
Tyranno-sort-of-Rex (Illus. by Tulloch, Scott) — *Llewelyn, Christopher*
The Tyranny of Experts: Economists, Dictators, and the Forgotten Rights of the Poor — *Easterly, William*
y A Tyranny of Petticoats: 15 Stories of Belles, Bank Robbers & Other Badass Girls — *Spotswood, Jessica*
The Tyranny of the Meritocracy: Democratizing Higher Education in America — *Guinier, Lani*
Tyranny of the Weak: North Korea and the World, 1950-1992 — *Armstrong, Charles K.*
Tyrone: The Irish Revolution, 1912-23 — *McCluskey, Fergal*
c The Tzvin's Little Sister — *Yum, Hyewon*

U

U and I — *Smith, Cassandra*
U Chic: College Girls' Real Advice for Your First Year — *Garton, Christie*
The U.S. Army and Counterinsurgency in the Philippine War — *Linn, Brian McAllister*
c The U.S. Civil War: A Chronology of a Divided Nation — *Peterson, Amanda*
U.S. Foreign Policy and the Other: Transatlantic Perspectives — *Ryan, David*
U.S.-Habsburg Relations from 1815 to the Paris Peace Conference: Sovereignty Transformed — *Phelps, Nicole M.*
U.S. History for Dummies, 3d ed. — *Wiegand, Steve*
The U.S. House of Representatives — *Spieler, Matthew*
U.S. Immigration in the Twenty-First Century: Making Americans, Remaking America — *DeSipio, Louis*
U.S. Latinos and Educational Policy: Research-Based Directions for Change — *Portes, Pedro R.*
U.S. Lesbian, Gay, Bisexual, and Transgender History — *Rupp, Leila J.*
U.S. Mica Industry Pioneers: The Ruggles and Bowers Families — *Davis, Fred E.*
The U.S. Naval Institute on Naval Tactics — *Hughes, Wayne P.*
c The U.S. Presidency — *Cane, Ella*
The U.S. South and Europe: Transatlantic Relations in the Nineteenth and Twentieth Centuries — *van Minnen, Cornelis A.*
The U.S. South in the Black Atlantic: Transnational Histories of the Jim Crow South Since 1865 — *Engel, Elisabeth*
c The U.S. Supreme Court — *Cane, Ella*
c U2: Changing the World through Rock 'n' Roll — *Huston, Jennifer L.*
Ubungswissen in Religion und Philosophie: Produktion, Weitergabe, Wandel
Ubuntu, Migration, and Ministry: Being Human in a Johannesburg Church — *Hankela, Elina*
y The UFO Dossier: 100 Years of Government Secrets, Conspiracies, and Cover-Ups — *Randle, Kevin D.*
Ugliness: A Cultural History — *Henderson, Gretchen E.*
c The Ugly Duckling Returns (Illus. by Warburton, Sarah) — *Bradman, Tony*
The Ugly Game: The Corruption of FIFA and the Qatari Plot to Buy the World Cup — *Blake, Heidi*
The Ugly Laws: Disability in Public — *Schweik, Susan M.*
The Ugly Renaissance: Sex, Greed, Violence and Depravity in an Age of Beauty (Read by Morey, Arthur). Audiobook Review — *Lee, Alexander*
The Ugly Renaissance: Sex, Greed, Violence and Depravity in an Age of Beauty — *Lee, Alexander*
c Ugly: Young Reader's Edition — *Hoge, Robert*
c Uh-Oh Octopus! (Illus. by van Hout, Mies) — *van Lieshout, Elle*
c Uh-Oh Octopus! (Illus. by van Hout, Mies) — *van Lieshout, Ellie*
c Uh-Oh! (Illus. by Barton, Patrice) — *Crum, Shutta*
c Ukraine — *Savery, Annabel*
y Ukraine: Then and Now — *Stewart, Gail B.*
Ukrainian Nationalism: Politics, Ideology, and Literature, 1929-1956 — *Shkandrij, Myroslav*
Ulrich Richental: Chronik des Konzils zu Konstanz, 1414-1418 — *Klockler, Jurgen*
Ulster and the City of Belfast — *Hayward, Richard*
Ultima — *Baxter, Stephen*
The Ultimate Betrayal — *Roby, Kimberla Lawson*
c Ultimate Bodypedia (Illus. by Turner, Cynthia) — *Wilsdon, Christina*

c The Ultimate Book of Randomly Awesome Facts — *Arlon, Penelope*
The Ultimate Dehydrator Cookbook: The Complete Guide to Drying Food, Plus 398 Recipes, Including Making Jerky, Fruit Leather and Just-Add Water Meals — *Gangloff, Tammy*
c The Ultimate Disney Party Book — *Ward, Jessica*
c Ultimate Explorer Guide for Kids — *Miles, Justin*
The Ultimate Guide to Sex after Fifty: How to Maintain--or Regain--a Spicy, Satisfying Sex Life — *Price, Joan*
The Ultimate Mediterranean Diet Cookbook: Harness the Power of the World's Healthiest Diet to Live Better, Longer — *Riolo, Amy*
c The Ultimate Pirate Handbook (Illus. by Leyssenne, Matheiu) — *Hamilton, Libby*
y Ultimate Spy: Inside the Secret World of Espionage, 4th ed. — *Melton, H. Keith*
The Ultimatum — *Wolf, Dick*
The Ultra Fabulous Glitter Squadron Saves the World Again — *Wise, A.C.*
The Ultra Thin Man — *Swenson, Peter*
Ultrasonic: Essays — *Church, Steven*
Ulysses — *Joyce, James*
Umami: Unlocking the Secrets of the Fifth Taste — *Mouritsen, Ole G.*
c The Umbrella Book — *Schubert, Ingrid*
The Umbrella Mender — *Guy, Christine Fischer*
Umweltgeschichte(n): Ostmitteleuropa von der Industrialisierung bis zum Postsozialismus — *Forster, Horst*
Un-American: W.E.B. Du Bois and the Century of World Revolution — *Mullen, Bill V.*
c Un Arbre (Illus. by Pallegoix, Luc) — *Dodier, Sylvain*
y Un gouffre sous mon lit — *Labrie, Pierre*
Un Monde de camps — *Agier, Michel*
Un paese senza eroi: L'Italia da Jacopo Ortis a Montalbano — *Jossa, Stefano*
c Un Papillon (Illus. by Dechassey, Laurence) — *Delaunois, Angele*
Un "plan Marshall juif": La presence juive americaine en France apres la Shoah, 1944-1954 — *Hobson Faure, Laura*
Un siecle d'oubli: Les Canadiens et la Premiere Guerre mondiale, 1914-2014 — *Martin, Jean*
The (Un)Documented Mark Steyn: Don't Say You Weren't Warned — *Steyn, Mark*
Unabrow: Misadventures of a Late Bloomer — *LaMarche, Una*
The Unaccountable & Ungovernable Corporation: Companies' Use-By Dates Close In — *Clarke, Frank*
Unattached — *Johnson, Kristin Lee*
The Unbeatable Squirrel Girl, vol. 1: Squirrel Power (Illus. by Henderson, Erica) — *North, Ryan*
Unbecoming (Read by Taber, Catherine). Audiobook Review — *Scherm, Rebecca*
y Unbecoming — *Downham, Jenny*
Unbecoming — *Scherm, Rebecca*
Unbecoming Americans: Writing Race and Nation from the Shadows of Citizenship, 1945-1960 — *Keith, Joseph*
Unbelievable Me — *Lowell, David W.*
c The Unbelievable Top Secret Diary of Pig (Illus. by Stamp, Emer) — *Stamp, Emer*
Unbelievable: Why We Believe and Why We Don't — *Ward, Graham*
Unbeugsam - Ein Pionier des Rumanischen Anarchismus: Panait Musoiu — *Veith, Martin*
Unbought and Unbossed: Transgressive Black Women, Sexuality, and Representation — *Melancon, Trimiko*
y Unbound — *Shusterman, Neal*

Unbounded Attachment: Sentiment and Politics in the Age of the French Revolution — *Guest, Harriet*
An Unbowed Warriot — *DeVita, Vincent T.*
Unbreakable: A Navy SEAL'S Way of Life — *Shea, Tom*
y Unbreakable — *Garcia, Kami*
y Unbroken: An Olympian's Journey from Airman to Castaway to Captive (Read by Herrmann, Edward). Audiobook Review — *Hillenbrand, Laura*
y Unbroken: An Olympian's Journey from Airman to Castaway to Captive — *Hillenbrand, Laura*
y Unbroken (Read by Herrmann, Edward). Audiobook Review — *Hillenbrand, Laura*
Unbuttoning America: A Biography of Peyton Place — *Cameron, Ardis*
y Uncaged (Read by Cook, Michele). Audiobook Review — *Sandford, John*
y Uncaged — *Cook, Michele*
An Uncanny Era: Conversations between Vaclav Havel and Adam Michnik — *Matynia, Elzbieta*
The Uncanny Reader: Stories from the Shadows — *Sandor, Marjorie*
The Uncanny Valley in Games and Animation — *Tinwell, Angela*
An Uncertain Choice — *Hedlund, Jody*
Uncertain Empire: American History and the Idea of the Cold War — *Isaac, Joel*
Uncertain Glory — *Sales, Joan*
Uncertain Knowledge: Scepticism, Relativism and Doubt in the Middle Ages — *Denery, Dallas G., II*
Uncertain Knowledge: Scepticism, Relativism, and Doubt in the Middle Ages — *Denery II, Dallas G.*
The Uncertain Legacy of Crisis: European Foreign Policy Faces the Future — *Youngs, Richard*
y Uncertain Soldier — *Bass, Karen*
Uncharted Strait: The Future of China-Taiwan Relations — *Bush, Richard C.*
y Unclaimed — *Wetzel, Laurie*
c Uncle Eli's Wedding (Illus. by Isik, Sernur) — *Newman, Tracy*
Uncle Janice (Read by Fulginiti, Rachel). Audiobook Review — *Burgess, Matt*
Uncle John's Robotica — *Bathroom Readers Institute*
c Uncle Vic's Farm (Illus. by Allen, Lisa) — *Caisley, Raewyn*
Unclean Lips: Obscenity, Jews, and American Culture — *Lambert, Josh*
c Uncles and Antlers (Illus. by Floca, Brian) — *Wheeler, Lisa*
The Uncollected David Rakoff: Including the Entire Text of Love, Dishonor, Marry, Die, Cherish, Perish — *Rakoff, David*
Uncommon Contexts: Encounters Between Science and Literature, 1800-1914 — *Marsden, Ben*
Uncommon Ground: A Word-lover's Guide to the British Landscape — *Tyler, Dominick*
Uncommon Grounds: New Media and Critical Practices in the Middle East and North Africa — *Downey, Anthony*
Uncommon Prayer — *Johnson, Kimberly*
Uncommon Tongues: Eloquence and Eccentricity in the English Renaissance — *Nicholson, Catherine*
Uncommonly Savage: Civil War and Remembrance in Spain and the United States — *Escott, Paul D.*
An Uncomplicated Life: A Father's Memoir of His Exceptional Daughter — *Daugherty, Paul*
Uncomplicating Fractions to Meet Common Core Standards in Math, K-7 — *Small, Marian*
An Unconventional Leader — *Wallace, Neill*
Uncovered: How I Left Hasidic Life and Finally Came Home — *Lax, Leah*

Uncovering Spiritual Narratives: Using Story in Pastoral Care and Ministry — Coyle, Suzanne M.
Uncovering Student Ideas in Physical Science: 39 New Electricity and Magnetism Formative Assessment Probes — Keeley, Page
Uncovering the Germanic Past: Merovingian Archaeology in France, 1830-1914 — Effros, Bonnie
Uncovering the Hidden: The Works and Life of Der Nister — Estraikh, Gennady
c Uncovering the Past Series
Undaunted Courage — Ambrose, Stephen
Undaunted Hope — Hedlund, Jody
Undaunted — Douglas, Ronnie
Undead and Unforgiven — Davidson, Mary Janice
Undead and Unforgiven — Davidson, MaryJanice
Undead Obsessed: Finding Meaning in Zombies — Robinson, Jessica
The Undead President — Richardson, Todd
Undeceived — Cox, Karen M.
The Undecided College Student: An Academic and Career Advising Challenge, 4th ed. — Gordon, Virginia N.
The Undelightened — Deyo, Bentz
Undeniable — Bankes, Liz
Under a Dark Summer Sky — Lafaye, Vanessa
y Under a Painted Sky — Lee, Stacey
c Under a Pig Tree: A History of the Noble Fruit (Illus. by Groenink, Chuck) — Palatini, Margie
Under an English Heaven — Boatwright, Alice K.
Under Another Sky: Journeys in Roman Britain — Higgins, Charlotte
y Under Different Stars (Read by Rudd, Kate). Audiobook Review — Bartol, Amy A.
Under Household Government: Sex and Family in Puritan Massachusetts — Morris, M. Michelle Jarrett
Under Household Government: Sex and Family in Puritan Massachusetts — Morris, Michelle Jarrett
Under Lock and Key — Geesman, Robin
y Under My Skin — Dawson, James
Under My Skin — Kenner, Julie
Under Paris Rooftops — Shabel, Arleen
Under Postcolonial Eyes: Figuring the 'Jew' in Contemporary British Writing — Sicher, Efraim
y Under Pressure — Chambers, Catherine
Under Strange Suns — Lizzi, Ken
Under the Affluence: Shaming the Poor, Praising the Rich and Sacrificing the Future of America — Wise, Tim
c Under the Blood-Red Sun (Read by Watanabe, Greg). Audiobook Review — Salisbury, Graham
Under the Bus: How Working Women Are Being Run Over — Fredrickson, Caroline
Under the Channel — Petel, Gilies
y Under the Dusty Moon — Sutherland, Suzanne
c Under the Egg (Read by Almasy, Jessica). Audiobook Review — Fitzgerald, Laura Marx
Under the Hood: Fire Up and Fine-Tune Your Employee Culture — Slap, Stan
Under the Influence — Maynard, Joyce
Under the Lights — Stacey, Shannon
y Under the Lights — Adler, Dahlia
Under the Radar Michigan: The First 50 — Daldin, Tom
Under the Same Blue Sky — Schoenewaldt, Pamela
Under the Same Sky: From Starvation in North Korea to Salvation in America — Kim, Joseph
c Under the Sea (Illus. by Daubney, Kate) — Goldsmith, Mike
c Under the Sleepy Stars (Illus. by Harry, Rebecca) — Shaw, Stephanie
Under the Sour Sun: Hunger through the Eyes of a Child — Campos, Elmer Hernan Rodriguez
y Under the Spotlight: A Jamieson Brothers Novel — Stanton, Angie
y Under the Spotlight — Stanton, Angie
Under the Tripoli Sky — Hunter, Adriana
y Under the Udala Trees — Okparanta, Chinelo
Under the Volcano — Lowry, Malcolm
Under the Volcano: Revolution in a Sicilian Town — Riall, Lucy
c Under Their Skin — Haddix, Margaret Peterson
Under This Beautiful Dome: A Senator, A Journalist, and the Politics of Gay Love in America — Mutchler, Terry
Under Tiberius — Tosches, Nick
Under Your Skin — Durant, Sabine
c Undercover Story: The Hidden Story of Eating Disorders — Levete, Sarah
Undercurrent — Wong, Rita
y The Underdogs (Read by Wemyss, Stig). Audiobook Review — Zusak, Markus

The Underdogs — Azuela, Mariano
Underdogs: The Making of the Modern Marine Corps — O'Connell, Aaron B.
Undergraduate Mathematics for the Life Sciences: Models, Processes, and Directions — Ledder, Glenn
The Underground Girls of Kabul: In Search of a Hidden Resistance in Afghanistan — Nordberg, Jenny
Underground in Berlin: A Young Woman's Extraordinary Tale of Survival in the Heart of Nazi Germany — Simon, Marie Jalowicz
c The Underground Labyrinth — Dizon, Louella
Underground Movements: Modern Culture on the New York City Subway — Stalter-Pace, Sunny
c The Underground Railroad — Allen, Nancy
c The Underground Railroad — Hyde, Natalie
c The Underground Railroad: Would You Help Them Escape? — Landau, Elaine
Undermajordomo Minor (Read by Prebble, Simon). Audiobook Review — deWitt, Patrick
y Undermajordomo Minor — deWitt, Patrick
c Underneath a Cow (Illus. by Wood, Ben) — Martin, Carol Ann
y Underneath Everything — Paul, Marcy Beller
The Undersea Network — Starosielski, Nicole
Understanding and Negotiating 360 Ancillary Rights Deals — Minter, Kendall
Understanding and Overcoming Temptation — Morris, Daniel
Understanding Autism: The Essential Guide for Parents — Williams, Katrina
Understanding China: There Is Reason for the Difference — Moreau, Gary
Understanding Chronic Fatigue Syndrome: An Introduction for Patients and Caregivers — Ali, Naheed
Understanding Clarence Thomas: The Jurisprudence of Constitutional Restoration — Rossum, Ralph A.
c Understanding Computer Safety — Mason, Paul (b. 1967-)
c Understanding Computing Series — Mason, Paul (b. 1967-)
Understanding Digital Humanities — Berry, David M.
Understanding Ethnopolitical Conflict: Karabakh, South Ossetia, and Abkhazia Wars Reconsidered — Souleimanov, Emil
Understanding Evolution — Kampourakis, Kostas
Understanding Families Over Time — Holland, Janet
Understanding Fandom: An Introduction to the Study of Media Fan Culture — Duffett, Mark
Understanding Fetal Alcohol Spectrum Disorder: A Guide to FASD for Parents, Carers and Professionals — Catterick, Maria
Understanding Interreligious Relations — Cheetham, David
Understanding ISIS and the New Global War on Terror: A Primer — Bennis, Phyllis
Understanding Mass Incarceration: A People's Guide to the Key Civil Rights Struggle of Our Time — Kilgore, James
Understanding Mental Disorders — American Psychiatric Association
Understanding Michael Chabon — Dewey, Joseph
Understanding Monastic Practices of Oral Communication (Western Europe, Tenth Thirteenth Centuries). — Vanderputten, Steven
Understanding Multiculturalism: The Habsburg Central European Experience — Cohen, Gary B.
Understanding Namibia: The Trials of Independence — Melber, Henning
Understanding Pain: An Introduction for Patients and Caregivers — Ali, Naheed
Understanding Ron Rash — Lang, John
Understanding Roots: Discover How to Make Your Garden Flourish — Kourik, Robert
Understanding Shiite Leadership: The Art of the Middle Ground in Iran and Lebanon — Mishal, Shaul
Understanding Social Media: How to Create a Plan for Your Business that Works — Ryan, Damian
Understanding the Political Economy of the Arab Uprisings — Diwan, Ishac
Understanding Truman Capote — Fahy, Thomas
c Undertaker — Scheff, Matt
The Undertaker's Daughter — Mayfield, Kate
Undertones of War — Blunden, Edmund
y Undertow (Read by Grace, Jennifer). Audiobook Review — Buckley, Michael
y Undertow — Buckley, Michael
y Underwater — Reichardt, Marisa
Underwater Babies — Casteel, Seth

c The Underwater Fancy Dress Parade (Illus. by Colpoys, Allison) — Bell, Davina
Underworld — Strieber, Whitley
The Underwriting — Miller, Michelle
The Undeserving Rich: American Beliefs about Inequality, Opportunity, and Redistribution — McCall, Leslie
"Undetermined" Ukrainians: Post-War Narratives of the Waffen SS "Galicia" Division — Khromeychuk, Olesya
Undiluted Hocus-Pocus: The Autobiography of Martin Gardner — Gardner, Martin
Undisciplining Knowledge: Interdisciplinary in the Twentieth Century — Graff, Harvey J.
The Undiscovered Country: Text, Translation, and Modernity in the Work of Yanagita Kunio — Ortabasi, Melek
An Undisturbed Peace — Glickman, Mary
Undivided: A Muslim Daughter, Her Christian Mother, Their Path to Peace (Read by Althens, Suzie). Audiobook Review — Raybon, Patricia
Undivided: A Muslim Daughter, Her Christian Mother, Their Path to Peace — Raybon, Patricia
y UnDivided — Shusterman, Neal
y Undocumented: A Dominican Boy's Odyssey from a Homeless Shelter to the Ivy League — Peralta, Dan-el Padilla
The Undoing — Dean, Averil
Undoing Time: The Life and Work of Samuel Beckett — Birkett, Jennifer
c Une etoile sur la dune — Loranger, Danielle
Une Mairie dans la France Coloniale: Kone, Nouvelle Caledonie — Trepied, Benoit
Une politique pontificale en temps de crise: Clement VII d'Avignon et les premieres annees du grand Schisme d'Occident — Genequand, Philippe
Unearthing the Changes: Recently Discovered Manuscripts of the Yi Jing (I Ching) and Related Texts — Shaughnessy, Edward L.
Unearthing the Nation: Modern Geology and Nationalism in Republican China — Shen, Grace Yen
An Uneasy Alliance — March, JD
Unemployment and the State in Britain: The Means Test and Protest in 1930s South Wales and North-East England — Ward, Stephanie
Unequal Time: Gender, Class, and Family in Employment Schedules — Clawson, Dan
The Unexpected Consequences of Love — Mansell, Jill
The Unexpected Inheritance of Inspector Chopra: A Baby Ganesh Agency Investigation — Khan, Vaseem
The Unexpected Inheritance of Inspector Chopra — Khan, Vaseem
Unfair: The New Science of Criminal Injustice (Read by Barrett, Joe). Audiobook Review — Benforado, Adam
Unfair: The New Science of Criminal Injustice — Benforado, Adam
Unfaithful Music & Disappearing Ink (Read by Costello, Elvis). Audiobook Review — Costello, Elvis
Unfaithful Music & Disappearing Ink — Costello, Elvis
Unfaithful Music & Disappearing Ink — The Maccabees
Unfaithful Music & Disappearing Ink — Costello, Elvis
y Unfed (Read by Shindler, Amy). Audiobook Review — McKay, Kirsty
Unfinished Business: Paid Family Leave in California and the Future of U.S. Work-Family Policy — Milkman, Ruth
Unfinished Business: Women Men Work Family — Slaughter, Anne-Marie
y The Unfinished Life of Addison Stone — Griffin, Adele
Unfinished Utopia: Nowa Huta, Stalinism, and Polish Society, 1949-56 — Lebow, Katherine
The Unfinished World — Sparks, Amber
Unflattening — Sousanis, Nick
Unforgettable: A Son, a Mother, and the Lessons of a Lifetime (Read by Simon, Scott). Audiobook Review — Simon, Scott
Unforgettable: A Son, a Mother, and the Lessons of a Lifetime — Simon, Scott
y Unforgiven — Kate, Lauren
Unforgiving — Oldham, Nick
y Unforgotten (Illus. by Riddle, Tohby) — Riddle, Tohby
Unforgotten New York: Legendary Spaces of the Twentieth-Century Avant-Garde — Brun-Lambert, David

y The Unfortunate Decisions of Dahlia Moss — Wirestone, Max
The Unfortunate Importance of Beauty (Read by Delaine, Christina). Audiobook Review — Filipacchi, Amanda
y The Unfortunate Importance of Beauty — Filipacchi, Amanda
The Unfortunates — Johnson, Bryan Stanley
The Unfortunates — McManus, Sophie
y Unfriended (Read by Allen, Corey). Audiobook Review — Vail, Rachel
y Unfriended — Vail, Rachel
c Ungifted — Korman, Gordon
y Ungodly — Blake, Kendare
Unhappiness of Being Greek — Dimou, Nikos
Unhealthy Pharmaceutical Regulation: Innovation, Politics, and Promissory Science — Davis, Courtney
Unhinge — Read, Calia
Unholy Fury: Whitlam and Nixon at War — Curran, James
Unholy Innocents — Heagerty Marton
y Unhooked — Maxwell, Lisa
c Uni the Unicorn (Illus. by Barrager, Brigette) — Rosenthal, Amy Krouse
y The Unicorn Hunter — Golden, Che
c Unicorn on a Roll: Another Phoebe and Her Unicorn Adventure (Illus. by Simpson, Dana) — Simpson, Dana
y Unicorn vs. Goblins — Simpson, Dana
Unidentified Woman #15 — Housewright, David
Unidentified Woman # 15 — Housewright, David
Unidentified Woman #15 — Housewright, David
c Uniforms: 1944 to Today — McNab, Chris
The Unintended Reformation: How a Religious Revolution Secularized Society — Gregory, Brad
Unintimidated: A Governor's Story and a Nation's Challenge — Walker, Scott
y The Uninvited — Winters, Cat
c Uninvited — Jordan, Sophie
Uninvited Neighbors: African Americans in Silicon Valley, 1769-1990 — Ruffin, Herbert G.
Union and States' Rights: A History and Interpretation of Interposition, Nullification, and Secession 150 Years After Sumter — Cogan, Neil H.
A Union Forever: The Irish Question and U.S. Foreign Relations in the Victorian Age — Sim, David
A Union Forever: The Irish Question and U.S. Foreign Relations in the Viphet — Brady, Ciaran
Union Heartland: The Midwestern Home Front during the Civil War — Aley, Ginette
Union Made: Working People and the Rise of Social Christianity in Chicago — Carter, Heath W.
Unions, Equity and the Path to Renewal — Foley, Janice R.
Unions — Corn, Alfred
Uniquely Human: A Different Way of Seeing Autism (Read by Ochlan, P.J.). Audiobook Review — Prizant, Barry M.
Uniquely Human: A Different Way of Seeing Autism — Prizant, Barry M.
y The Uniquiet — Everett, Mikaela
c Unite speciale (Illus. by Leong, Sonia) — Barlow, Steve
c The United Empire Loyalists — Mitchell, Sara
The United Nations at 70: Restoration and Renewal — Ahtisaari, Martti
c United States Air Force — Murray, Julie
The United States Army in China 1900-1938: A History of the 9th, 14th, 15th and 31st Regiments in the East — Cornebise, Alfred Emile
c United States Army — Murray, Julie
The United States, Italy, and the Origins of the Cold War: Waging Political Warfare, 1945-1950 — Mistry, Kaeten
c United States Marine Corps — Murray, Julie
c United States Navy — Murray, Julie
c United States of America — Ganeri, Anita
United States of Cakes: Tasty Traditional American Cakes, Cookies, Pies, and Baked Goods — Fares, Roy
The United States of Incarceration — Anderson, Tim
The United States of Pizza: America's Favorite Pizzas, from Thin Crust to Deep Dish, to Sourdough and Gluten-Free — Priebe, Craig
United States Postal Card Catalog — Bussey, Lewis E.
Unity and Diversity in the Gospels and Paul: Essays in Honor of Frank J. Matera — Skinner, Christopher W.
Universal Man: The Lives of John Maynard Keynes — Davenport-Hines, Richard

Universal Man: The Seven Lives of John Maynard Keynes — Davenport-Hines, Richard
The Universal Man: The Seven Lives of John Maynard Keynes — Davenport-Hines, Richard
Universal Meaning: In Search of the Reason for Our Existence — Brown, Floyd
The Universal Tone: Bringing My Story to Light (Read by Davis, Jonathan). Audiobook Review — Santana, Carlos
The Universe in Your Hand: A Journey Through Space, Time and Beyond — Galfard, Christophe
The Universe: Leading Scientists Explore the Origin, Mysteries, and Future of the Cosmos (Read by Campbell, Danny). Audiobook Review — Brockman, John
The Universe of Things: On Speculative Realism — Shaviro, Steven
The Universe Wreckers — Hamilton, Edmond
Universities at War — Docherty, Thomas
Universities for a New World: Making a Global Network in International Higher Education, 1913-2013 — Schreuder, Deryck M.
University Control — Cattell, James McKeen
The University of Chicago: A History — Boyer, John W.
The University Socialist Club and the Contest for Malaya: Tangled Strands of Modernity — Loh, Kah Seng
Unknown Soldiers — Linna, Vaino
The Unknown Travels and Dubious Pursuits of William Clark — Trogdon, Jo Ann
The Unknown Universe: What We Don't Know About Time and Space in Ten Chapters — Clark, Stuart
Unlawful Combatants: A Genealogy of the Irregular Fighter — Scheipers, Sibylle
c Unleashed (Read by Ross, Jonathan Todd). Audiobook Review — Korman, Gordon
y Unleashed — Brouwer, Sigmund
Unleashed — Korman, Gordon
y Unleashed — Brouwer, Sigmund
y Unleashed — Jordan, Sophie
c Unleashed — Korman, Gordon
Unleashed — Brady, Eileen
y Unleashed — Brouwer, Sigmund
The Unleashing — Laurenston, Shelly
c The Unlikely Adventures of Mabel Jones (Illus. by Collins, Ross) — Mabbitt, Will
y The Unlikely Hero of Room 13B (Read by McClain, Jonathan). Audiobook Review — Toten, Teresa
y The Unlikely Hero of Room 13B — Toten, Teresa
The Unlikely Lady — Bowman, Valerie
c The Unlikely Outlaws (Illus. by Jones, Tom Morgan) — Ardagh, Philip
Unlikely: Setting Aside Our Differences to Live Out the Gospel — Palau, Kevin
c The Unlikely Story of Bennelong and Phillip (Illus. by Emmerichs, Bern) — Sedunary, Michael
An Unlikely Union: The Love-Hate Story of New York's Irish and Italians — Moses, Paul
y Unlikely Warrior: A Jewish Soldier in Hitler's Army — Rauch, Georg
Unlocking the Mysteries of Cataloging: A Workbook of Examples — Haynes, Elizabeth
The Unloved — Levy, Deborah
c Unlovely — Conway, Celeste
y Unmade — Brennan, Sarah Rees
y Unmade — Capetta, Amy Rose
Unmaking the Bomb: A Fissile Material Approach to Nuclear Disarmament and Nonproliferation — Feiveson, Harold A.
Unmanly Men: Refigurations of Masculinity in Luke-Acts — Wilson, Brittany W.
Unmanned: Drones, Data, and the Illusion of Perfect Warfare — Arkin, William M.
y Unmarked — Garcia, Kami
c Unmoored — Parker, Jeri
Unnatural Frenchmen: The Politics of Priestly Celibacy and Marriage — Cage, E. Claire
Unnatural Habits (Read by Daniel, Stephanie). Audiobook Review — Greenwood, Kerry
c Unnatural Selections — Edwards, Wallace
c Unnaturals: The Battle Begins (Illus. by Richardson, Owen) — Hughes, Devon
An Unnecessary Woman — Alameddine, Rabih
The Unnoticeables — Brockway, Robert
Unpacking the Boxes: A Memoir of a Life in Poetry — Hall, Donald
Unpaid Debts — Barca, Antonio Jimenez
Unpeopled Eden — Gonzalez, Rigoberto
Unplayable Lies: (The Only Golf Book You'll Ever Need). — Jenkins, Dan

The Unpleasantness at Baskerville Hall — Dolley, Chris
Unpolitische Wissenschaft? Wilhelm Reich und die Psychoanalyse im Nationalsozialismus — Peglau, Andreas
The Unprofessionals: New American Writing from The Paris Review — Stein, Lorin
The Unquiet Dead. Audiobook Review — Khan, Ausma Zehanat
The Unquiet Frontier: Rising Rivals, Vulnerable Allies, and the Crisis of American Power — Grygiel, Jakub J.
y The Unquiet — Everett, Mikaela
The Unquiet Ones: A History of Pakistan Cricket — Samiuddin, Osman
y The Unquiet Past — Armstrong, Kelley
y Unravel — Howson, Imogen
y Unraveled — Albin, Gennifer
y Unraveling (Illus. by Hagel, Brooke) — Gurevich, Margaret
The Unraveling: High Hopes and Missed Opportunities in Iraq — Sky, Emma
y The Unraveling of Mercy Louis — Parssinen, Keija
Unreasonable Behavior: The Updated Autobiography — McCullin, Don
Unreasonable Doubt — Delany, Vicki
Unreliable Memoirs — James, Clive
Unremarried Widow: A Memoir — Henderson, Artis
The Unremembered — Orullian, Peter
Unrequited: Women and Romantic Obsession — Phillips, Lisa A.
The Unruly PhD: Doubts, Detours, Departures, and Other Success Stories — Peabody, Rebecca
Unruly Places: Lost Spaces, Secret Cities, and Other Inscrutable Geographies (Read by Perkins, Derek). Audiobook Review — Bonnett, Alastair
Unruly Women: Performance, Penitence, and Punishment in Early Modern Spain — Boyle, Margaret E.
Unruly Words — Raffman, Diana
Unsafe Abortion and Women's Health: Change and Liberation — Francome, Colin
Unscripted: My Ten Years in Telly — Sugar, Alan
An Unseemly Wife — Moore, E.B.
The Unsettlement of America: Translation, Interpretation, and the Story of Don Luis de Velasco, 1560-1945 — Brickhouse, Anna
Unsettling Montaigne — Guild, Elizabeth
Unsingle: The Art and Science of Finding True Love — Gabriel, Louise
Unsinn auf Stelzen: Schriften zur Französischen Revolution — Bentham, Jeremy
y UnSlut: A Diary and a Memoir — Linden, Emily
y UnSlut: A Diary and a Memoir — Lindin, Emily
c Unsolved — Powell, Marie
c Unsolved Crimes — Dicker, Katie
Unspeakable — Pickett, Michelle K.
y Unspeakable — Rushton, Abbie
The Unspeakable: And Other Subjects of Discussion (Read by Daum, Meghan). Audiobook Review — Daum, Meghan
Unspeakable Things — Spivack, Kathleen
y Unspoken: Shadow Falls — Hunter, C. C.
Unspoken Valor — Abernathy, Steven
Unstoppable: Harnessing Science to Change the World — Powell, Corey S.
c Unstoppable Octobia May (Read by Turpin, Bahni). Audiobook Review — Flake, Sharon G.
c Unstoppable Octobia May — Flake, Sharon G.
Unstoppable: The Emerging Left-Right Alliance to Dismantle the Corporate State — Nader, Ralph
Unstuffed — Soukup, Ruth
The Unsubstantial Air: American Fliers in the First World War — Hynes, Samuel
Untamed — Palmer, Diana
y Untamed City: Carnival of Secrets — Marr, Melissa
An Untamed State (Read by Miles, Robin). Audiobook Review — Gay, Roxane
An Untamed State — Gay, Roxane
c Untamed: The Wild Life of Jane Goodall — Silvey, Anita
Untangled: Guiding Teenage Girls through the Seven Transitions into Adulthood — Damour, Lisa
Untangling the Knot: Queer Voices on Marriage, Relationships, and Identity — Sickels, Carter
Unter dem roten Wunderschirm: Lesarten klassischer Kinder- und Jugendliteratur — Brauer, Christoph
Unter Zions Panier: Mormonism and Its Interaction with Germany and Its People, 1840-1990 — Widmer, Kurt

Unternehmer - Fakten und Fiktionen: Historisch-biographische Studien — *Plumpe, Werner*
Unterwegs auf Pilgerstrassen. Pilger aus dem Polnischen und Deutschen Raum im Spatmittelalter und der Fruhen Neuzeit
Unterwegs im Namen der Religion II: Wege und Ziele in Vergleichender Perspektive - das Mittelalterliche Europa und Asien
y Until Beth — *Amowitz, Lisa*
Until Choice Do Us Part: Marriage Reform in the Progressive Era — *Eby, Clare Virginia*
Until Darwin, Science, Human Variety and the Origins of Race — *Brown, Ricardo*
y Until Friday Night — *Glines, Abbi*
c Until I Find Julian — *Giff, Patricia Reilly*
c Until I Find Julian — *Giff, Patricia Reilly*
Until My Heart Stops — *Currier, Jameson*
Until September — *Scully, Chris*
y Until the Beginning — *Plum, Amy*
Until the Dawn — *Camden, Elizabeth*
y Until the Day Arrives — *Machado, Ana Maria*
y Until the End — *Glines, Abbi*
Until the Harvest — *Thomas, Sarah Loudin*
Until Thy Wrath Be Past — *Larsson, Asa*
Until We Are Free — *Ebadi, Shirin*
y Until We Meet Again — *Collins, Renee*
Untimely Death — *Duncan, Elizabeth J.*
y The Untold History of the United States: Young Readers Edition, vol. 1: 1898-1945 — *Stone, Oliver*
Untold Stories: Life, Love, and Reproduction — *Cockrill, Kate*
Untold Story — *Ali, Monica*
c The Untold Story of the Battle of Saratoga: A Turning Point in the Revolutionary War — *Burgan, Michael*
c The Untold Story of the Black Regiment: Fighting in the Revolutionary War — *Burgan, Michael*
Untouchable — *Marsh, Ava*
Untouchable — *Anand, Mulk Raj*
The Untranslatable Image: A Mestizo History of the Arts in New Spain — *Russo, Alessandra*
y Untwine — *Danticat, Edwidge*
c Unusual and Awesome Jobs Using Science: Food Taster, Human Lie Detector, and More — *Wendinger, Jennifer*
c Unusual and Awesome Jobs Using Technology: Roller Coaster Designer, Space Robotics Engineer, and More — *LeBoutillier, Linda*
y Unusual Chickens for the Exceptional Poultry Farmer (Illus. by Kath, Katie) — *Jones, Kelly*
c Unusual Chickens for the Exceptional Poultry Farmer (Illus. by Kath, Katie) — *Jones, Kelly (b. 1976-)*
c Unusual Chickens for the Exceptional Poultry Farmer (Illus. by Kath, Katie) — *Knopf, Kelly Jones*
Unveiling Emotions II: Emotions in Greece and Rome - Texts, Images, Material Culture — *Chaniotis, Angelos*
Unwanted Girl — *Schiller, M.K.*
y Unwanted — *Holohan, Amanda*
Unwanted: Muslim Immigrants, Dignity, and Drug Dealing — *Bucerius, Sandra M.*
Unwanted Visionaries: The Soviet Failure in Asia at the End of the Cold War — *Radchenko, Sergey*
The Unwieldy American State: Administrative Politics since the New Deal — *Grisinger, Joanna L.*
An Unwilling Accomplice — *Todd, Charles*
Up Against the Night — *Cartwright, Justin*
c Up & Down: A Lift-the-Flap Book — *Teckentrup, Britta*
c Up Down Across (Illus. by Marshall, Natalie) — *Fletcher, Corina*
y Up for Sale: Human Trafficking and Modern Slavery — *Behnke, Alison Marie*
Up from Generality: How Inorganic Chemistry Finally Became a Respectable Field — *Labinger, Jay A.*
y Up from the Sea — *Lowitz, Leza*
Up Ghost River: A Chief's Journey through the Turbulent Waters of Native History — *Metatawabin, Edmund*
c Up Hamster, Down Hamster (Illus. by Reich, Kass) — *Reich, Kass*
c Up in the Garden and Down in the Dirt (Illus. by Neal, Christopher Silas) — *Messner, Kate*

c Up in the Garden and Down in ther Dirt (Illus. by Neal, Christopher Silas) — *Messner, Kate*
Up in the Old Hotel — *Mitchell, Joseph*
Up the Hill to Home — *Yacovissi, Jennifer Bort*
Up to the Mountains and Down to the Countryside — *Carroll, Quincy*
y Up to This Pointe — *Longo, Jennifer*
Updike — *Begley, Adam*
y Updraft — *Wilde, Fran*
Upgraded — *Clarke, Neil*
Upon Provincialism: Southern Literature and National Periodical Culture, 1870-1900 — *Hardwig, Bill*
Upper Canada: The Formative Years, 1784-1841 — *Craig, Gerald M.*
The Uppsala Edda: DG 11 4T0 — *Faulkes, Anthony*
Upright Beast — *Michel, Lincoln*
Upright Beasts: Stories — *Michel, Lincoln*
The Upright Thinkers: The Human Journey from Living in Trees to Understanding the Cosmos (Read by Mlodinow, Leonard). Audiobook Review — *Mlodinow, Leonard*
The Upright Thinkers: The Human Journey from Living in Trees to Understanding the Cosmos — *Mlodinow, Leonard*
Uprise: Back Pain Liberation, by Tuning Your Body Guitar — *Wheeler, Sean M.*
Uprising at Bowling Green: How the Quiet Fifties Became the Political Sixties — *Wiley, Norbert*
Uprising of Goats — *Glancy, Diane*
Uprooted (Read by Emelin, Julia). Audiobook Review — *Novik, Naomi*
Uprooted — *Novik, Naomi*
y Uprooted — *Banks, Lynne Reid*
Upside Down — *Riley, Lia*
c Upside-Down Magic — *Mlynowski, Sarah*
The Upside of Stress: Why Stress Is Good for You and How to Get Good at It — *McGonigal, Kelly*
Upside: The New Science of Post-Traumatic Growth — *Rendon, Jim*
Upsidedown and Backwards — *Rawlings, Annette*
The Upstairs Wife: An Intimate History of Pakistan — *Zakaria, Rafia*
Upstyle Your Furniture: Techniques and Creative Inspiration to Style Your Home — *Jones, Stephanie*
Upton Sinclair: California Socialist, Celebrity Intellectual — *Coodley, Lauren*
Uptown Special — *Ronson, Mark*
Upward: Faith, Church, and the Ascension of Christ — *Kelly, Anthony J.*
Ur: The City of the Moon God — *Crawford, Harriet*
c Uranus: Cold and Blue — *Glaser, Chaya*
Urban and Amish: Classic Quilts and Modern Updates — *Harder, Myra*
Urban Appetites: Food and Culture in Nineteenth-Century New York — *Lobel, Cindy R.*
Urban Bodies: Communal Health in Late Medieval English Towns and Cities — *Rawcliffe, Carole*
y The Urban Boys — *Smith, K.N.*
Urban Ecosystems: Ecological Principles for the Built Environment — *Adler, Frederick R.*
The Urban Homesteading Cookbook: Forage, Farm, Ferment and Feast for a Better World — *Nelson, Michelle*
Urban Jewish Transformations — *Goldstone, Genevieve Okada*
y Urban Legends — *Grant, Helen*
Urban Magic in Early Modern Spain: Abracadabra Omnipotens — *Tausiet, Maria*
Urban Nightlife: Entertaining Race, Class, and Culture in Public Space — *May, Reuben A. Buford*
Urban Origins of American Judaism — *Moore, Deborah Dash*
y Urban Tribes: Native Americans in the City — *Charleyboy, Lisa*
Urbanism and Cultural Landscapes in Northeastern Syria: The Tell Hamoukar Survey 1999-2001 — *Ur, Jason A.*
Urbanization, Urbanism and Urbanity in an African City: Home Spaces and House Cultures — *Jenkins, Paul*
Urgency and Patience — *Toussaint, Jean-Philippe*
Urgent Interventional Therapies — *Kopshidze, Nicholas*
Us (Read by Haig, David). Audiobook Review — *Nicholls, David*

Us — *Nicholls, David*
y The US Air Force — *Grayson, Robert*
y The US Army — *Pratt, Mary K.*
y The US Coast Guard — *Marciniak, Kristin*
Us Conductors — *Michaels, Sean*
The US Congress for Kids: Over 200 Years of Lawmaking, Deal Breaking, and Compromising, with 21 Activities — *Reis, Ronald A.*
c US Culture Through Infographics (Illus. by Westlund, Laura) — *Higgins, Nadia*
US Foreign Policy and the Iranian Revolution: The Cold War Dynamics of Engagement and Strategic Alliance — *Emery, Christian*
c US Geography Through Infographics (Illus. by Westlund, Laura) — *Higgins, Nadia*
c US Government through Infographics (Illus. by Westlund, Laura) — *Higgins, Nadia*
US Guided Missiles: The Definitive Reference Guide — *Yenne, Bill*
c US History Through Infographics (Illus. by Westlund, Laura) — *Kenney, Karen Latchana*
y US-Led Wars in Iraq: 1991-Present — *Gallagher, Jim*
y The US National Guard — *Lusted, Marcia Amidon*
c US Women Win the World Cup — *Trusdell, Brian*
The US Women's Jury Movements and Strategic Adaptation: A More Just Verdict — *McCammon, Holly J.*
Usability and the Mobile Web: A UTA Guide — *Tidal, Junior*
Usable History: Representations of Yugoslavia's Difficult Past from 1945 to 2002 — *Sindbaek, Tea*
The Use of Man — *Tisma, Aleksandar*
c Use Your Imagination (Illus. by O'Byrne, Nicola) — *O'Byrne, Nicola*
c Use Your Words, Sophie! (Illus. by Wells, Rosemary) — *Wells, Rosemary*
Useful, Usable, Desirable: Applying User Experience Design to Your Library — *Schmidt, Aaron*
A Useless Man: Selected Stories — *Abasiyanik, Sait Faik*
The Uses of Literacy — *Hoggart, Richard*
The Uses of the Body — *Landau, Deborah*
Uses of the Written Word in Medieval Towns: Medieval Urban Literacy, 2 vols. — *Mostert, Marco*
Using Children's Literature to Teach Problem Solving in Math: Addressing the Common Core in K-2 — *White, Jeanne*
Using Images in Late Antiquity — *Birk, Stine*
Using Physical Science Gadgets and Gizmos, Grades 3-5: Phenomenon-Based Learning — *Bobrowsky, Mathew*
Using Research to Improve Instruction — *Karp, Karen S.*
Using RTI in Secondary Schools: A Training Manual for Successful Implementation — *Callender, Wayne A.*
Usos politicos de la historia: Lenguaje de clases y revisionismo historico — *Chiaramonte, Jose Carlos*
The USPS 2014 Stamp Yearbook — *United States Postal Service*
Utilitarianism and the Art School in Nineteenth-Century Britain — *Quinn, Malcolm*
The Utopia Experiment — *Evans, Dylan*
Utopia in the Age of Globalization: Space, Representation, and the World-System — *Tally, Robert T., Jr*
y Utopia, Iowa — *Yansky, Brian*
Utopia, Limited: Romanticism and Adjustment — *Nersessian, Anahid*
The Utopia of Rules: On Technology, Stupidity, and the Secret Joys of Bureaucracy — *Graeber, David*
The Utopia of Rules: On Technology, Stupidity, and the Secret Joys of Bureaucracy — *Graeber, David*
The Utopia of Rules: On Technology, Stupidity, and the Secret Joys of Bureaucracy — *Graeber, David*
The Utopia of Rules: On Technology, Stupidity, and the Secret Joys of Bureaucracy — *Graeber, David*
Utopianism, Modernism, and Literature in the Twentieth Century — *Reeve-Tucker, Alice*
Utopias: A Brief History from Ancient Writings to Virtual Communities — *Segal, Howard P.*
Utopie und Alltag. Perspektiven auf Ideal und Praxis im 20. Jahrhundert
Utoya: Norvege, 22 juillet 2011, 77 morts — *Obertone, Laurent*
c Utterly Amazing Human Body — *Walker, Richard*

V

V Is for Vegetables: Inspired Recipes and Techniques for Home Cooks from Artichokes to Zucchini — *Anthony, Michael*
y The V-Word: True Stories About First-Time Sex — *Keyser, Amber J.*
c Vacancy (Illus. by Lee, Jen) — *Lee, Jen*
The Vacationers — *Straub, Emma*
Vacationland: Tourism and Environment in the Colorado High Country — *Philpott, William*
Vaccine Injuries: Documented Adverse Reactions to Vaccines — *Conte, Louis*
The Vagabond — *Seymour, Gerald*
Vagabonding through Retirement: Unusual Wanders Far From Our Paris Houseboat — *Mahoney, Bill*
Vainglory: The Forgotten Vice — *DeYoung, Rebecca Konyndyk*
A Valediction — *Friedman, Ellis*
c Valentine's Day and the Lunar New Year (Illus. by Nguyen, Dustin) — *Nguyen, Dustin*
Valentine's Day — *Kelly, April*
The Valiant — *Lemire, Jeff*
y Valiant — *McGuire, Sarah*
c Valkyrie — *O'Hearn, Kate*
The Valley — *Renehan, John*
Valley Fever — *Taylor, Katherine*
c Valley of Fires — *Mitchell, J. Barton*
The Valley of the Shadow of Death: A Tale of Tragedy and Redemption — *Alexander, Kermit*
Valley of the Shadow — *Peters, Ralph*
The Valley of Two Moons — *Berthard, Wayne*
The Value of Debt in Retirement — *Anderson, Thomas J.*
The Value of Living Well — *Lebar, Mark*
The Value of the Humanities — *Small, Helen*
Valuing Life: Humanizing the Regulatory State — *Sunstein, Cass R.*
c Vamonos! Let's Go! (Illus. by Cepeda, Joe) — *Colato Lainez, Rene*
y The Vampire Book of the Month Club — *Fischer, Rusty*
Vampire Jacques, the Last Templar — *2-Shirt, Charlie*
The Vampyre Family: Passion, Envy and the Curse of Byron — *Stott, Andrew McConnell*
Van Gogh: A Power Seething — *Bell, Julian*
y Van Gogh — *Bailey, Jessica*
Van Halen Rising: How a Southern California Backyard Party Band Saved Heavy Metal — *Renoff, Greg*
Van Leeuwen Artisan Ice Cream: Classic Flavors and New Favorites: 100 Recipes Made in Brooklyn (Illus. by Bensimon, Sidney) — *O'Neill, Laura*
Van Leeuwen Artisan Ice Cream: Classic Flavors and New Favorites: 100 Recipes Made in Brooklyn — *O'Neill, Laura*
Vandal Confession — *Gauvin, Mitchell*
Vanessa and Her Sister (Read by Fox, Emilia). Audiobook Review — *Parmar, Priya*
Vanessa and Her Sister (Read by Fox Emilia). Audiobook Review — *Parmar, Priya*
Vanessa and Her Sister — *Parmar, Priya*
Vanessa and Her Sister. Audiobook Review — *Parmar, Priya*
Vanessa and Her Sister — *Parmar, Priya*
Vango: Between Sky and Earth — *de Fombelle, Timothee*
Vango: Between Sky and Earth — *De Fombelle, Timothee*
y Vango: Between Sky and Earth — *de Fombelle, Timothee Vango*
c Vanilla Ice Cream — *Graham, Bob*
Vanilla Table: The Essence of Exquisite Cooking from the World's Best Chefs — *MacAller, Natasha*

y Vanished — *Cooper, E.E.*
Vanished History: The Holocaust in Czech and Slovak Historical Culture — *Sniegon, Tomas*
y Vanished — *Cooper, E.E.*
Vanishing — *Woodward, Gerard*
c The Vanishing Coin (Illus. by Wight, Eric) — *Egan, Kate*
Vanishing for the Vote: Suffrage, Citizenship and the Battle for the Census — *Liddington, Jill*
Vanishing Games (Read by Weber, Jake). Audiobook Review — *Hobbs, Roger*
Vanishing Games — *Hobbs, Roger*
y Vanishing Girls (Read by Maarleveld, Saskia). Audiobook Review — *Oliver, Lauren*
y Vanishing Girls — *Oliver, Lauren*
Vanishing Ice: Alpine and Polar Landscapes in Art, 1775-2012 — *Matilsky, Barbara C.*
c The Vanishing Island — *Wolverton, Barry*
y The Vanishing — *Gazotti, Bruno*
The Vanishing Point That Whistles: An Anthology of Contemporary Romanian Poetry — *Mugur, Paul Doru*
y The Vanishing Season — *Anderson, Jodi Lynn*
c Vanishing Trick (Illus. by Asquith, Ros) — *Asquith, Ros*
The Vanishing Velazquez — *Cumming, Laura*
Vano and Niko — *Akhvlediani, Erlom*
Variation and Change in English: An Introduction — *Schreier, Daniel*
Variation and Change in French Morphosyntax: The Case of Collective Nouns — *Tristram, Anna*
Variations on a Rectangle: Thirty Years of Graphic Design from Texas Monthly to Pentagram — *Stout, D.J.*
Variations sur l'Amour et le Graal — *Mela, Charles*
The Variety of Values: Essays on Morality, Meaning, and Love — *Wolf, Susan*
A Variorum Edition of the Works of Geoffrey Chaucer, vol. 2: The Canterbury Tales: The Wife of Bath's Prologue and Tale, Parts 5A and 5B — *Chaucer, Geoffrey*
y Varsity 170 — *Jacobs, Evan*
c Vasilisa the Beautiful (Illus. by Morgunova, Anna) — *Bell, Anthea*
y The Vast and Brutal Sea — *Cordova, Zoraida*
Vater, Tochter, Schwiegersohn: Die erzahlerische Ausgestaltung einer familiaren Dreierkonstellation im Artusroman franzosischer und deutscher Sprache um 1200 — *Quinlan, Jessica*
The Vatican and Catholic Activism in Mexico and Chile: The Politics of Transnational Catholicism, 1920-1940 — *Andes, Stephen J.C.*
The Vatican Files — *Knuteman, Jerzy*
Vatican II: Catholic Doctrines on Jews and Muslims — *D'Costa, Gavin*
The Vatican Princess — *Gortner, C.W.*
The Vatican Prophecies: Investigating Supernatural Signs, Apparitions, and Miracles in the Modern Age — *Thavis, John*
Vatikan und aRassendebatteo in der Zwischenkriegszeit - Stand und Perspektiven der Forschung
y Vault of Dreamers (Read by Zeller, Emily Woo). Audiobook Review — *O'Brien, Caragh M.*
y The Vault of Dreamers — *O'Brien, Caragh M.*
Vdlkommen hem Mr. Swanson: Svenska emigranter och svenskhet pa film — *Merton, Charlotte*
y Veda: Assembly Required — *Teer, Samuel*
Vegan al Fresco — *Kelly, Carla*
Vegan Finger Foods — *Steen, Celine*
Vegan Handbook — *Wasserman, Debra*

Vegan Holiday Cooking from Candle Cafe: Celebratory Menus and Recipes from New York's Premier Plant-Based Restaurants — *Pineda, Jorge*
Vegan in Volume — *Berkoff, Nancy*
Vegan Meals for One or Two--Your Own Personal Recipes — *Berkoff, Nancy*
Vegan Menu for People with Diabetes — *Berkoff, Nancy*
Vegan Microwave Cookbook — *Berkoff, Nancy*
Vegan Passover Recipes — *Berkoff, Nancy*
Vegan Pressure Cooking: Delicious Beans, Grains, and One-Pot Meals in Minutes — *Fields, J.L.*
Vegan Soul Kitchen — *Terry, Bryant*
Vegan Tacos — *Wyrick, Jason*
Vegan Vegetarian Omnivore: Dinner for Everyone at the Table — *Thomas, Anna*
Vegans Know How to Party — *Berkoff, Nancy*
The Vegetable Butcher: How to Select, Prep, Slice, Dice, and Masterfully Cook Vegetables from Artichokes to Zucchini — *Mangini, Cara*
c Vegetables in Underwear (Illus. by Chapman, Jared) — *Chapman, Jared*
The Vegetarian — *Han, Kang*
The Vegetarian Crusade: The Rise of an American Reform Movement, 1817-1921 — *Shprintzen, Adam D.*
Vegetarian India: A Journey through the Best of Indian Home Cooking — *Jaffrey, Madhur*
The Vegetarian — *Kang, Han*
y Vegetarian Nutrition for Teenagers — *Vegetarian Resource Group*
c Veggie Rhapsody: I Want You in My Lunch (Illus. by Jackson, Sommer) — *James, Ray Anthony*
The Vegiterranean Diet: The New and Improved Mediterranean Eating Plan--with Deliciously Satisfying Vegan Recipes for Optimal Health — *Hever, Julieanna*
A vegso kocsma — *Kertesz, Imre*
Vehicles (Illus. by Deneux, Xavier) — *Deneux, Xavier*
The Veil — *Neill, Chloe*
Veiled — *Jacka, Benedict*
Veiled Spill: A Sequence — *Clausen, Jan*
Veiled Warriors: Allied Nurses of the First World War — *Hallett, Christine E.*
y Velociraptor — *Riehecky, Janet Ellen*
y Velocity — *Wooding, Chris*
y Velvet — *West, Temple*
y Velvet Undercover — *Brown, Teri*
c The Velveteen Rabbit (Read by Bond, Jilly). Audiobook Review — *Williams, Margery*
y Vendetta (Read by Bouvard, Laurence). Audiobook Review — *Doyle, Catherine*
y The Vendetta — *Doyle, Catherine*
Vendetta: Bobby Kennedy Versus Jimmy Hoffa — *Neff, James*
y Vendetta — *Doyle, Catherine*
Vendetta — *Harris, Lisa*
Vendetta — *Neff, James*
The Vendetta of Felipe Espinosa — *Jones, Adam James*
The Venetian Origins of the Commedia dell'Arte — *Jordan, Peter*
Venezuela: What Everyone Needs to Know — *Salas, Miguel Tinker*
Vengeance at Sundown — *Sweazy, Larry D.*
y Vengeance Road — *Bowman, Erin*
Venice: A Contested Bohemia in Los Angeles — *Deener, Andrew*
Venice: A Travel Guide to Murano Glass, Carnival Masks, Gondolas, Lace, Paper, and More — *Morelli, Laura*
Venice: Cult Recipes — *Zavan, Laura*

The Venice Myth: Culture, Literature, Politics, 1800 to the Present — Barnes, David
Venice: Recipes Lost and Found — Caldesi, Katie
Venture Mom: From Idea to Income in Just 12 Weeks — Hurd, Holly
c Venus — Bloom, J.P.
c Venus: Goddess of Love and Beauty (Illus. by Young, Eric) — Temple, Emily
c Venus: Super Hot — Oldfield, Dawn Bluemel
The Venusian Gambit — Martinez, Michael J.
Vera Brittain and the First World War: The Story of Testament of Youth — Bostridge, Mark
Veracruz 1519: Los bombres de Cortes — Martinez, Maria Del Carmen
Verbum Domini and the Complementarity of Exegesis and Theology — Carl, Scott
The Verdict — Stone, Nick
Verdun: The Longest Battle of the Great War — Jankowski, Paul
Verdun: The Lost History of the Most Important Battle of the World War I, 1914-1918 — Mosier, John
c Verduras/Vegetables — Anderson, Sara
Verfolgte Schuler: Ursachen und Folgen von Diskriminierung im Schulwesen der DDR — Kwiatkowski-Celofiga, Tina
Vergangenes Unrecht: Entschadigung und Restitution in einer Globalen Perspektive — Unfried, Berthold
c Verity Sparks and the Scarlet Hand — Green, Susan
Verliebt, Verlobt, Verheiratet. Eine Geschichte der Ehe seit der Romantik — Wienfort, Monika
The Vermeer Conspiracy — Halaban, Eytan
Vermeer in Hell: Poems — White, Michael
Vermilion: The Adventures of Lou Merriwether, Psychopomp — Tanzer, Molly
Vermittlungspotenzial der "NS-Volksgemeinschaft" - Der Fachdidaktische Gehalt eines Wissenschaftlichen Analysekonzepts
Vernunft und Imperium: Die Societas Jesu in Indien und Japan, 1542-1574 — Winnerling, Tobias
Veronese — Salomon, Xavier F.
A Versatile American Institution: The Changing Ideals and Realities of Philanthropic Foundations — Hammack, David C.
Verse and Transmutation: A Corpus of Middle English Alchemical Poetry — Timmermann, Anke
Verse Saints' Lives, Written in the French of England: Saint Giles by Guillaume de Berneville, Saint George by Simund de Freine, Saint Faith of Agen by Simon of Walsingham, Saint Mary Magdalene by Guillaume Le Clerc de Normandie — Russell, Delbert W.
The Verses in Eric the Red's Saga, and Again: Norse Visits to America — Perkins, Richard
Version Control — Palmer, Dexter
Versions of Academic Freedom: From Professionalism to Revolution — Fish, Stanley
The Versions of Us — Barnett, Laura
Verso il centenario del Boccaccio: Presenze classiche e tradizione biblica — Ballarini, Marco
Vertigo 42 — Grimes, Martha
Vertigo — Walsh, Joanna
Vertigo! When the World Spins out of Control — Zonana, Linda Howard
Verwaltete Erinnerung - Symbolische Politik: Die Heimatsammlungen der Deutschen Fluchtlinge, Vertriebenen und Aussiedler — Eisler, Cornelia
y Very Bad Things — McBride, Susan
The Very Best of Kate Elliott — Elliott, Kate
A Very British Coup — Mullin, Chris
c The Very Cold, Freezing, No-Numbers Day (Illus. by Miles, David W.) — Sorenson, Ashley
A Very Courageous Decision: The Inside Story of Yes Minister — McCann, Graham
c The Very Cranky Bear (Illus. by Bland, Nick) — Bland, Nick
A Very Dangerous Woman: The Lives, Loves and Lies of Russia's Most Seductive Spy — McDonald, Deborah
Very Different, But Much the Same: The Evolution of English Society since 1714 — Runciman, W.G.
The Very Fairy Princess: A Spooky, Sparkly Halloween (Read by Cordaro, Alison). Audiobook Review — Andrews, Julie
The Very Fairy Princess: A Spooky, Sparkly Halloween (Illus. by Davenier, Christine) — Andrews, Julie
c The Very Fairy Princess: A Spooky, Sparkly Halloween (Illus. by Davenier, Christine) — Hamilton, Emma Walton
c Very First Book of Things to Spot — Watt, Fiona
Very Good Lives — Rowling, J.K.

y Very in Pieces — Blakemore, Megan Frazer
Very Late Diagnosis of Asperger Syndrome, Autism Spectrum Disorder: How Seeking a Diagnosis in Adulthood Can Change Your Life — Wylie, Philip
The Very Late Goethe: Self-Consciousness and the Art of Ageing — Lee, Charlotte
c Very Little Cinderella (Illus. by Heap, Sue) — Heapy, Teresa
c Very Little Red Riding Hood (Illus. by Heap, Sue) — Heapy, Teresa
c A Very Merry Christmas Prayer (Illus. by Moore, Natalia) — Jensen, Bonnie Rickner
c The Very Noisy Bear — Bland, Nick
c A Very Pirate Christmas (Illus. by Ayto, Russell) — Knapman, Timothy
A Very Principled Boy: The Life of Duncan Lee, Red Spy and Cold Warrior — Bradley, Mark A.
A Very Private Celebrity: The Nine Lives of John Freeman — Purcell, Hugh
A Very Private Public Citizen: The Life of Grenville Clark — Hill, Nancy Peterson
c The Very Stuffed Turkey (Illus. by Talib, Binny) — Kenah, Katharine
c A Very Top Secret Mission — Eastland, Sue
c The Very Worried Sparrow (Illus. by Hansen, Gaby) — Doney, Meryl
y Vessel — Cresswell, Lisa T.
Vessel — Jones, Parneshia
Vessels: A Love Story — Raeburn, Daniel
Vestiges of Flames — McConchie, Lyn
y Veterinarian — Trueit, Trudi Strain
c Vibrations Make Sound — Boothroyd, Jennifer
The Vice of Luxury: Economic Excess in a Consumer Age — Cloutier, David
The Viceroys — De Roberto, Federico
The Vices of Learning: Morality and Knowledge at Early Modern Universities — Kivisto, Sari
c Vicious — Shepard, Sara
Vicious Cycle — Ashley, Katie
The Vicksburg Campaign, March 29-May 18, 1863 — Woodworth, Steven E.
Victor Fenigstein: Lebensprotokoll, Werkkommentare, Kataloge — Hennenberg, Fritz
Victoria: A Life — Wilson, A.N.
Victoria: Queen, Matriarch, Empress — Ridley, Jane
Victorian Bloomsbury — Ashton, Rosemary
Victorian Celebrity Culture and Tennyson's Circle — Boyce, Charlotte
The Victorian Empire and Britain's Maritime World, 1837-1901: The Sea and Global History — Taylor, Miles
The Victorian Gothic: An Edinburgh Companion — Smith, Andrew (b. 1964-)
The Victorian Internet: The Remarkable Story of the Telegraph and the Nineteenth Century's On-line Pioneers (Read by Perkins, Derek). Audiobook Review — Standage, Tom
Victorian Parables — Colon, Susan E.
Victorian Poets: A Critical Reader — Cunningham, Valentine
Victorian Radicals and Italian Democrats — Sutcliffe, Marcella Pellegrino
Victorian Reformations: Historical Fiction and Religious Controversy, 1820-1900 — Burstein, Miriam Elizabeth
The Victorian Reinvention of Race: New Racisms and the Problem of Grouping in the Human Sciences — Beasley, Edward
Victorian Time: Technologies, Standardizations, Catastrophes — Ferguson, Trish
Victorian Women and the Economies of Travel, Translation and Culture, 1830-1870 — Johnston, Judith
Victorian Women, Unwed Mothers and the London Foundling Hospital — Sheetz-Nguyen, Jessica A.
Victorian Yankees at Queen Victoria's Court: American Encounters with Victoria and Albert — Weintraub, Stanley
c The Victorians — Cooke, Tim
Victoria's Cross — Mead, Gary
y Victories — Edghill, Rosemary
Victory Fever on Guadalcanal: Japan's First Land Defeat of WWII — Bartsch, William H.
Victory — Conrad, Joseph
The Victory with No Name: The Native American Defeat of the First American Army — Buss, James Joseph
y Video Games and Youth — Nakaya, Andrea C.
c Video Games: Design and Code Your Own Adventure (Illus. by Crosier, Mike) — Ceceri, Kathy
y Video Games, Violence, and Crime — Netzley, Patricia D.

Video Revolutions. On the History of a Medium — Newman, Michael Z.
Videoland: Movie Culture at the American Video Store — Herbert, Daniel
Vidi et intellexi: Die Schrifthermeneutik in der Visionstrilogie Hildegards von Bingen — Zantonyi, Maura
Vie de saint Jerome — Erasmus, Desiderius
Vie et miracles de Berard, eveque de Marses — Dalarun, Jacques
Vie et miracles de Berard eveque des Marses — Dalarun, Jacques
Vienna 1815: The Making of a European Security Culture
The Vienna Melody — Lothar, Ernst
Vienna — Kirby, William S.
Vienna Tales — Constantine, Helen
Vierte Mitteldeutsche Konferenz fur Medizin- und Wissenschaftsgeschichte
Viet Man — Lliteras, D.S.
Vietnam and Beyond: Tim O'Brien and the Power of Storytelling — Ciocia, Stefania
Vietnam Rough Riders: A Convoy Commander's Memoir — McAdams, Frank
y The Vietnam War — Rice, Earle
c Vietnamese Children's Favorite Stories — Thi Minh Tran, Phuoc
Vietnamese Colonial Republican: The Political Vision of Vu Trong Phung — Zinoman, Peter
The View from Above: The Science of Social Space — Haffner, Jeanne
The View from Here: On Affirmation, Attachment and the Limits of Regret — Wallace, R. Jay
The View from Prince Street — Taylor, Mary Ellen
The View from Saturn — Friman, Alice
A View from the Bottom: Asian American Masculinity and Sexual Representation — Nguyen Tan Hoang
A View from the Porch: Rethinking Home and Community Design — Friedman, Avi
y The View from Who I Was — Sappenfield, Heather
A View of the Harbour — Taylor, Elizabeth
Vigilant Faith: Passionate Agnosticism in a Secular World — Boscaljon, Daniel
y The Vigilante Poets of Selwyn Academy — Hattemer, Kate
Viking Archaeology in Iceland: Mosfell Archaeological Project — Zori, Davide
Viking Myths and Sagas: Retold from Ancient Norse Texts — Kerven, Rosalind
The Vikings and Their Age — Somerville, Angus A.
Vikings: Life and Legend — Williams, Gareth
Viktor Frankl's Search for Meaning: An Emblematic 20th-Century Life — Pytell, Timothy E.
Viktor Wynd's Cabinet of Wonders — Wynd, Viktor
Villa America — Klaussmann, Liza
The Village: 400 Years of Beats and Bohemians, Radicals and Rogues: A History of Greenwich Village — Strausbaugh, John
c Village Christmas: And Other Notes on the English Year — Lee, Laurie
y Villain Keeper — McKay, Laurie
Villainous — Cody, Matthew
The Ville: Cops and Kids in Urban America — Danaldson, Greg
The Ville — Donaldson, Greg
The Ville Rat — Limon, Martin
Villette — Bronte, Charlotte
The Vilna Vegetarian Cookbook: Garden-Fresh Recipes Rediscovered and Adapted for Today's Kitchen — Lewando, Fania
Vincent (Illus. by Stok, Barbara) — Stok, Barbara
c Vincent and the Night (Illus. by Enersen, Adele) — Enersen, Adele
c Vincent and the Night — Enersen, Adele
c Vincent Paints His House (Illus. by Arnold, Tedd) — Arnold, Tedd
Vincenzo Scamozzi and the Chorography of Early Modern Architecture — Borys, Ann Marie
Vines of Entanglemento — Carter, Lisa
The Vineyard — Hurley, Michael
Vingt-Cinq poemes — Tzara, Tristan
Vino Business: The Cloudy World of French Wine — Saporta, Isabelle
Vintage Crochet: 30 Specially Commissioned Patterns (Illus. by Perers, Kristin) — Cropper, Susan
Vintage Fashion Complete — Albrechtsen, Nicky
Vintage — Baker, David
Vintage Visions: Essays on Early Science Fiction — Evans, Arthur B.
Vinyl: The Analogue Record in the Digital Age — Bartmanski, Dominik
Violation: Collected Essays — Tisdale, Sallie

Violence: A Modern Obsession — Bessel, Richard
Violence After War: Explaining Instability in Post-Conflict States — Boyle, Michael J.
Violence Against Women in Kentucky: A History of U.S. and State Legislative Reform — Jordan, Carol E.
Violence and the State in Languedoc, 1250-1400 — Firnhaber-Baker, Justine
Violence and the Writing of History in the Medieval Francophone World — Guynn, Noah D.
Violence and Visibility in Modern History — Martschukat, Jurgen
Violence and Warfare among Hunter-Gatherers — Allen, Mark W.
Violence in Roman Egypt: A Study in Legal Interpretation — Bryen, Ari Z.
Violent Capitalism and Hybrid Identity in the Eastern Congo: Power to the Margins — Raeymaekers, Timothy
The Violent Century — Tidhar, Lavie
Violent Crimes — Margolin, Phillip
Violent Delights, Violent Ends: Sex, Race, and Honor in Colonial Cartagena de Indias — Germeten, Nicole von
y Violent Ends — Hutchinson, Shaun David
Violent Intermediaries: African Soldiers, Conquest, and Everyday Colonialism in German East Africa — Moyd, Michelle R.
Violent Masculinities: Male Aggression in Early Modern Texts and Culture — Feather, Jennifer
Violent Protest, Contentious Politics, and the Neoliberal State — Seferiades, Seraphim
c Violet and Victor Write the Best-Ever Bookworm Book (Illus. by Murguia, Bethanie Deeney) — Kuipers, Alice
c Violet and Victor Write the Most Fabulous Fairy Tale (Illus. by Murguia, Bethanie Deeney) — Kuipers, Alice
The Violet Bakery Cookbook: Baking All Day on Wilton Way — Ptak, Claire
The Violet Bakery Cookbook — Ptak, Claire
The Violet Hour: Great Writers at the End — Roiphe, Katie
c Violet Mackerel's Formal Occasion (Illus. by Davis, Sarah) — Branford, Anna
c Violet Mackerel's Pocket Protest — Branford, Anna
c A Violin for Elva (Illus. by Tusa, Tricia) — Ray, Mary Lyn
The Violinist of Venice — Palombo, Alyssa
c VIP: I'm with the Band (Illus. by Gudsnuk, Kristen) — Calonita, Jen
Viper Wine — Eyre, Hermione
Vipers Rule — Tyler, Stephanie
Viral: Stories — Mitchell, Emily
The Virgil Encyclopedia — Thomas, Richard F.
Virgil, Father of the West — Haecker, Theodor
c Virgil & Owen (Illus. by Bogan, Paulette) — Bogan, Paulette
c Virgil & Owen Stick Together (Illus. by Bogan, Paulette) — Bogan, Paulette
Virgil Thomson: Music Chronicles, 1940-1954 — Thomson, Virgil
The Virgin Mary and Catholic Identities in Chinese History — Clarke, Jeremy
Virgin Nation: Sexual Purity and American Adolescence — Moslener, Sara
The Virgin of Guadalupe and the Conversos: Uncovering Hidden Influences from Spain to Mexico — Hernandez, Marie-Theresa
The Virgin Way: Everything I Know About Leadership — Branson, Richard
Virginia in the War Years, 1938-1945: Military Bases, the U-Boat War and Daily Life — Freitus, Joe
Virginia Woolf & 20th Century Women Writers — Artuso, Kathryn Stelmach
Virginia Woolf: A Portrait — Forrester, Viviane
Virginia Woolf, Jane Ellen Harrison and the Spirit of Modernist Classicism — Mills, Jean
A Virtual Love — Blackman, Andrew
Virtual Modernism: Writing and Technology in the Progressive Era — Biers, Katherine
y Virtual Reality — Perritano, John
Virtual War and Magical Death: Technologies and Imaginaries for Terror and Killing — Whitehead, Neil L.
Virtue and Happiness: Essays in Honour of Julia Annas — Kamteka, Rachana
Virtue and the Moral Life: Theological and Philosophical Perspectives — Werpehowski, William
Virtue Falls (Read by Soler, Rebecca). Audiobook Review — Dodd, Christina

Virtue Is Knowledge. The Moral Foundations of Socratic Political Philosophy — Pangle, Lorraine Smith
The Virtues of Abandon: An Anti-Individualist History of the French Enlightenment — Coleman, Charly
The Virtues of the Table — Baggini, Julian
Virtues of Thought: Essays on Plato and Aristotle — Kosman, Aryeh
Virtuosen der Öffentlichkeit? Friedrich von Gentz, 1764-1832: im globalen intellektuellen Kontext seiner Zeit
The Virtuoso Circle: Competition, Collaboration, and Complexity in Late Medieval French Poetry — Armstrong, Adrian
The Virtuous Citizen: Patriotism in a Multicultural Society — Soutphommasane, Tim
The Virtuous Feats of the Indomitable Miss Trafalgar and the Erudite Lady Boone — Cannon, Geonn
Virtuous Violence: Hurting and Killing To Create, Sustain, End, and Honor Social Relationships — Fiske, Alan Page
Visibly Canadian: Imaging Collective Identities in the Canadas, 1820-1910 — Stanworth, Karen
Vision, Devotion, and Self-Representation in Late Medieval Art — Sand, Alexa
Vision in Silver — Bishop, Anne
A Vision of Voices: John Crosby and the Santa Fe Opera — Smith, Craig A.
Visionary Philology: Geoffrey Hill and the Study of Words — Sperling, Matthew
The Visioneers: How a Group of Elite Scientists Pursued Space Colonies, Nanotechnologies, and a Limitless Future — McCray, W. Patrick
The Visionist — Urquhart, Rachel
Visions and Revisions: Coming of Age in the Age of AIDS (Read by Woodman, Jeff). Audiobook Review — Peck, Dale
Visions and Revisions: Coming of Age in the Age of AIDS — Peck, Dale
Visions from the Forests: The Art of Liberia and Sierra Leone — Grootaers, Jan-Lodewijk
Visions of Amen: The Early Life and Music of Olivier Messiaen — Schloesser, Stephen
Visions of Blake: William Blake in the Art World 1830-1930 — Trodd, Colin
Visions of Community in Nazi Germany: Social Engineering and Private Lives — Steber, Martina
Visions of Dystopia in China's New Historical Novels — Kinkley, Jeffrey C.
Visions of Music: Sheet Music in the Twentieth Century — Walas, Tony
Visions of Power in Cuba: Revolution, Redemption, and Resistance, 1959-1971 — Guerra, Lillian
Visions of Queer Martyrdom from John Henry Newman to Derek Jarman — Janes, Dominic
Visions of the Apocalypse: Receptions of John's Revelation in Western Imagination — Chilton, Bruce
Visions of the Ottoman World in Renaissance Europe — Pippidi, Andrei
c A Visit from St. Nicholas — Moore, Clement C.
c Visit the Bhil Carnival (Illus. by Amaliyar, Subhash) — Wolf, Gita
c A Visit to Dr. Duck (Illus. by Wells, Rosemary) — Wells, Rosemary
c A Visit to the Space Station — Throp, Claire
Visiting Hours: A Memoir of Friendship and Murder — Butcher, Amy
The Visiting Privilege: New and Collected Stories — Williams, Joy
Visiting the Sins — Denman, Melanie
The Visitor: Andre Palmeiro and the Jesuits in Asia — Brockey, Liam Matthew
y The Visitors — Sylvester, Simon
y Visitors — Card, Orson Scott
The Visitors — Beauman, Sally
Visits - Bilateral Relations and Personal Encounters in Israel, Germany and Beyond. International Workshop marking 50 Years of Israeli-German Diplomatic Relations 1965-2015
Visual Culture in the Modern Middle East: Rhetoric of the Image — Gruber, Christiane
The Visual Culture of Catholic Enlightenment — Johns, Christopher M. S.
Visual Cultures of Secrecy in Early Modern Europe — Roberts, Sean E.
Visual Judaism in Late Antiquity: Historical Contexts of Jewish Art — Levine, Lee I.
Visual Leap: A Step-by-Step Guide to Visual Learning for Teachers and Students — Berg, Jesse

Visual Rhetoric and Early Modern English Literature — Acheson, Katherine
The Visual World of Muslim India: The Art, Culture and Society of the Deccan in the Early Modern Era — Parodi, Laura E.
Visuality and Materiality in the Story of Tristan and Isolde — Eming, Jutta
Visualizing Guadalupe: From Black Madonna to Queen of the Americas — Peterson, Jeanette Favrot
Visualizing the Past: The Power of the Image in German Historicism — Maurer, Kathrin
The Vital Question: Energy, Evolution, and the Origins of Complex Life — Lane, Nick
The Vital Question: Why Is Life the Way It Is? — Lane, Nick
Vital Signs — De Jesus, Pedro
Vital Signs, Volume 20 — Renner, Michael
Vitals — Meany, Paul
Vitamania: Our Obsessive Quest for Nutritional Perfection — Price, Catherine
Vittoria Colonna: Selections from the Rime Spirituali (Illus. by Moody, Robert) — Zwicky, Jan
c Viva Frida (Illus. by O'Meara, Tim) — Morales, Yuyi
Vivas to Those Who Have Failed — Espada, Martin
Vivian and Victor Learn About Verbs (Illus. by Prater, Linda) — Malaspina, Ann
y Vivian Apple at the End of the World (Read by Whelan, Julia). Audiobook Review — Coyle, Katie
y Vivian Apple at the End of the World — Coyle, Katie
y Vivian Apple Needs a Miracle — Coyle, Katie
Vivid Faces: The Revolutionary Generation in Ireland, 1890-1923 — Foster, R.F.
Vivienne's Blog — Leaton, Stephen K.
The Vivisection Mambo — Lark, Lolita
The Vixen — Pronzini, Bill
Vizual'nyi arkhetip — Malaev, Alibek Kazhgalievich
Vladimir Sorokin's Languages — Roesen, Tine
y The Vo-Tech Track to Success in Information Technology — Meyer, Terry Teague
Vocabularians: Integrated Word Study in the Middle Grades — Overturf, Brenda J.
A Vocabulary of Desire: The Song of Songs in the Early Synagogue — Lieber, Laura Suzanne
Vocation to Virtue: Christian Marriage as a Consecrated Life — Lasnoski, Kent J.
Vodka Politics: Alcohol, Autocracy, and the Secret History of the Russian State — Schrad, Mark Lawrence
A Voice from the Field — Griffin, Neal
c Voice of Freedom: Fannie Lou Hamer, Spirit of the Civil Rights Movement (Illus. by Holmes, Ekua) — Weatherford, Carole Boston
y Voice of Freedom: Fannie Lou Hamer, Spirit of the Civil Rights Movement (Illus. by Holmes, Ekula) — Weatherford, Carole Boston
A Voice Still Heard: Selected Essays of Irving Howe — Howe, Nina
A Voice Still Heard: Selected Essays of Irving Howe — Howe, Irving
The Voice That Challenged a Nation: Marion Anderson and the Struggle for Equal Rights — Freedman, Russell
A Voice That Could Stir an Army: Fannie Lou Hamer and the Rhetoric of the Black Freedom Movement — Brooks, Maegan Parker
The Voiceover Artist — Reidy, Dave
The Voices (Read by Jackson, Gildart). Audiobook Review — Tallis, F.R.
c Voices across the Lakes (Illus. by Hall, Emmeline) — Pinson, Anita
y Voices Against Silence — Holder, Alan
c Voices Are Not for Yelling (Illus. by Heinlen, Marieka) — Verdick, Elizabeth
Voices at Work: Continuity and Change in the Common Law World — Bogg, Alan
Voices Beyond Bondage: An Anthology of Verse by African Americans of the 19th Century — DeSimone, Erika
Voices Bright Flags — Brock, Geoffrey
Voices from Labour's Past — Clark, David
Voices from the Canefields: Folksongs from Japanese Immigrant Workers in Hawai'i — Odo, Franklin
c Voices from the March on Washington — Lyon, George Ella
Voices from the Rainbow — Taylor, Traci Leigh
Voices from Tibet: Selected Essays and Reportage — Woeser, Tsering
Voices in the Band: A Doctor, Her Patients, and How the Outlook on AIDS Care Changed from Doomed to Hopeful — Ball, Susan C.
Voices in the Night — Millhauser, Steven
Voices in the Night: Stories — Millhauser, Steven

Voices in the Ocean: A Journey into the Wild and Haunting World of Dolphins (Read by Campbell, Cassandra). Audiobook Review — *Casey, Susan*

Voices in the Ocean: A Journey into the Wild and Haunting World of Dolphins — *Casey, Susan*

The Voices of Baseball: The Game's Greatest Broadcasters Reflect on America's Pastime — *McKnight, Kirk*

Voices of Cherokee Women — *Johnston, Carolyn Ross*

Voices of Fire: Reweaving the Literary Lei of Pele and Hi'iaka — *Ho'omanawanui, Ku'ualoha*

Voices of the Arab Spring: Personal Stories from the Arab Revolutions — *Al-Saleh, Asaad*

c Voices of the Civil Rights Movement: A Primary Source Exploration of the Struggle for Racial Equality — *Mortensen, Lori*

Voices of the People in Nineteenth-Century France — *Hopkin, David*

Voices of the Reformation: Contemporary Accounts of Daily Life — *Wagner, John A.*

c Voices of the Western Frontier (Illus. by Buckner, Julie) — *Garland, Sherry*

c Voici l'automne — *Cocca-Leffler, Maryann*

c Voici le printemps — *Cocca-Leffler, Maryann*

c Voici l'hiver — *Cocca-Leffler, Maryann*

The Void — *Johnston, Timothy S.*

VOKS: Le laboratoire helvetique. Histoire de la diplomatie culturelle sovietique durant l'entre-deux-guerres — *Fayet, Jean-Francois*

c Volcanologists — *Koontz, Robin*

Volkermord zur Primetime. Der Holocaust im Fernsehen. Simon Wiesenthal Conference 2014

"Volksgemeinschaft" unter Vorbehalt: Gesinnungskontrolle und Politische Mobilisierung in der Herrschaftspraxis der NSDAP-Kreisleitung Gottingen — *Thieler, Kerstin*

Voltaire und Friedrich der Grosse — *Stackelberg, Jurgen von*

The Volume of Possible Endings (Illus. by Broad, Sam) — *Else, Barbara*

Volume the First: In Her Own Hand — *Austen, Jane*

Volume the Second: In Her Own Hand — *Austen, Jane*

Volume the Third: In Her Own Hand — *Austen, Jane*

Vom (Be-)Nutzen der Bucher. Praktiken des Buchgebrauchs in der Fruhen Neuzeit

Vom Kaffeehaus zum Furstenhof: Johann Sebastian Bachs weltliche Kantaten — *Schleuning, Peter*

Von Bregenz bis Brody - von Zara bis Znojmo

Von Daten zu Erkenntnissen: Digitale Geisteswissenschaften als Mittler zwischen Information und Interpretation. DHd-Jahrestagung 2015

Von der Entstehung des Geldes zur Sicherung der Wahrung: Die Theorien von Bernhard Laum und Wilhelm Gerloff zur Genese des Geldes — *Brandl, Felix*

Von der Shoa eingeholt: Auslandische judische Fluchtlinge im ehemaligen Jugoslawien 1933-1945 — *Grunfelder, Anna Maria*

Von der Stern-Schnuppe zum Fix-Stern: Zwei Deutsche Illustrierte und Ihre Gemeinsame Geschichte vor und nach 1945 — *Tolsdorff, Tim*

Von Kafern, Markten und Menschen: Kolonialismus und Wissen in der Moderne — *Habermas, Rebekka*

Von Kunstworten und -werten: Die Entstehung der deutschen Kunstkritik in Periodika der Aufklarung — *Vogt, Margrit*

Von Kuste zu Kuste - der Westliche Ostseeraum als Kontaktzone vom Fruhmittelalter bis zur Fruhen Neuzeit

Von Ulfila bis Rekkared: Die Goten und Ihr Christentum — *Faber, Eike*

Vor der Mauer. Berlin in der Ost-West-Konkurrenz 1948 bis 1961 — *Lemke, Michael*

Voracious: A Hungry Reader Cooks Her Way through Great Books — *Nicoletti, Cara*

Vorbilder: Partisanenprofessoren im geteilten Deutschland — *Hermand, Jost*

Vormarz und Revolution: Die Tagebucher des Grossherzogs Friedrich Franz II. von Mecklenburg-Schwerin 1841-1854, kommentiert, eingeleitet und hrsg. v. Rene Wiese — *Mecklenburg-Schwerin, Friedrich Franz von, II*

The Vorrh — *Catling, B.*

Vorsorgen in der Moderne. Akteure - Raume - Praktiken

Vorwarts zum neuen Menschen? Die sozialistische Erziehung in der DDR 1949-1989 — *Droit, Emmanuel*

c Vote — *Paulsen, Gary*

c The Voting Rights Act of 1965: An Interactive History Adventure — *Burgan, Michael*

The Voting Wars: From Florida 2000 to the Next Election Meltdown — *Hasen, Richard L.*

The Vows Book: Anglican Teaching on the Vows of Obedience, Poverty, and Chastity — *Berge, Clark*

c The Voyage of Lucy P. Simmons: The Emerald Shore — *Mariconda, Barbara*

Voyage of the Basilisk — *Brennan, Marie*

The Voyage of the Komagata Maru: The Sikh Challenge to Canada's Colour Bar, 3d ed. — *Johnston, Hugh J.M.*

Voyage of the Sable Venus and Other Poems — *Coste, Robin*

Voyage of the Sable Venus and Other Poems — *Lewis, Robin Coste*

Voyage (Illus. by Romagna, Karen) — *Collins, Billy*

Voyage to Gallipoli — *Plowman, Peter*

c Voyagers: Project Alpha — *MacHale, D.J.*

Voyaging with Kids: A Guide to Family Life Afloat — *Gifford, Behan*

A Vulgar Art: A New Approach to Stand-up Comedy — *Brodie, Ian*

Vulnerability and Young People: Care and Social Control in Policy and Practice — *Brown, Kate*

Vulnerability in Technological Cultures: New Directions in Research and Governance — *Hommels, Anique*

Vulnerability: New Essays in Ethics and Feminist Philosophy — *Mackenzie, Catriona*

Vulnerable Faith: Missional Living in the Radical Way of St. Patrick — *Arpin-Ricci, Jamie*

The Vulture — *Ramsay, Frederick*

W

W.E.B. Du Bois and The Souls of Black Folk — *Shaw, Stephanie J.*
W.G. Grace: In the Steps of a Legend — *Meredith, Anthony*
W.H. Davies: Man and Poet: A Reassessment — *Cullup, Michael*
c W Is for Webster: Noah Webster and His American Dictionary (Illus. by Kulikov, Boris) — *Fern, Tracey*
c W Is for Webster (Illus. by Kulikov, Boris) — *Fern, Tracey*
c The Wacky and Wonderful World through Numbers: Over 2,000 Figures and Facts — *Martin, Steve*
c Waddle! Waddle! (Illus. by Proimos, James) — *Proimos, James*
Wading into the Stream of Wisdom: Essays in Honor of Leslie Kawamura — *Haynes, Sarah F.*
The Wages of Oil: Parliaments and Economic Development in Kuwait and the UAE — *Herb, Michael*
Wages of Rebellion — *Hedges, Chris*
The Wages of Relief: Cities and the Unemployed in Prairie Canada, 1929-39 — *Strikwerda, Erik*
The Wagner Experience and Its Meaning to Us — *Dawson-Bowling, Paul*
Wagner's Melodies: Aesthetics and Materialism in German Musical Identity — *Trippett, David*
Wagner's Visions: Poetry, Politics, and the Psyche in the Operas through Die Walkure — *Syer, Katherine R.*
Wagners Welttheater: Die Geschichte der Bayreuther Festspiele zwischen Kunst und Politik — *Buchner, Bernd*
Wagstaff: Before and After Mapplethorpe: A Biography — *Gefter, Philip*
Wail: The Life of Bud Powell — *Pullman, Peter*
c The Wainscott Weasel (Illus. by Marcellino, Fred) — *Seidler, Tor*
y Waistcoats and Weaponry — *Carriger, Gail*
c Wait (Illus. by Portis, Antoinette) — *Portis, Antoinette*
Wait for Signs — *Johnson, Craig*
c Waitangi Day: The New Zealand Story — *Werry, Philippa*
Waiter to the Rich and Shameless — *Hartford, Paul*
c Waiting (Illus. by Henkes, Kevin) — *Henkes, Kevin*
y Waiting for a Sign — *Schachter, Esty*
Waiting for Electricity — *Nichol, Christina*
Waiting for Jose: The Minutemen's Pursuit of America — *Shapira, Harel*
Waiting for Paint to Dry — *Mack, Lia*
c Waiting for Santa (Illus. by Edgson, Alison) — *Metzger, Steve*
Waiting for the Cool Kind of Crazy — *Moore, M.D.*
c Waiting for Unicorns — *Hautala, Beth*
c Waiting Is Not Easy! (Illus. by Willems, Mo) — *Willems, Mo*
c Waiting (Illus. by Henkes, Kevin) — *Henkes, Kevin*
y Wakanabi Blues — *Zobel, Melissa Tantaquidgeon*
The Wake — *Kingsnorth, Paul*
Wake of Vultures — *Bowen, Lila*
Wake Up Happy Every Day — *May, Stephen*
Wake Up Happy: The Dream Big, Win Big Guide to Transforming Your Life — *Strahan, Michael*
c Wake Up, Island (Illus. by Wroblewski, Nick) — *Casanova, Mary*
Wake Up, Sir! — *Ames, Jonathan*
c Wake Up, Spring — *Ferrier, Katherine*
Waking from the Dream: The Struggle for Civil Rights in the Shadow of Martin Luther King, Jr. — *Chappell, David L.*
Waking the Merrow — *Rigney, Heather*

Waking Up: A Guide to Spirituality Without Religion — *Harris, Sam*
Waking Up from War: A Better Way Home for Veterans and Nations — *Bobrow, Joseph*
Waking Up to the Dark — *Strand, Clark*
Wal-Mart Wars: Moral Populism in the Twenty-First Century — *Messengill, Rebekah Peeples*
Walden on Wheels: On the Open Road from Debt to Freedom — *Ilgunas, Ken*
Walden Warming: Climate Change Comes to Walden Woods — *Primack, Richard B.*
Walden's Shore: Henry David Thoreau and Nineteenth Century Science — *Thorson, Robert M.*
c Waldo, Blue, and Glad Max Too! (Illus. by Crank, Donny) — *Kruse, Donald W.*
Wales and the Medieval Colonial Imagination: The Matters of Britain in the Twelfth Century — *Faletra, Michael A.*
Wales: Die Entdeckung einer Landschaft und eines Volkes durch Deutsche Reisende (1780-1860). — *Maurer, Michael*
y Walk on Earth a Stranger — *Carson, Rae*
c The Walk On — *Feinstein, John*
c Walk on the Wild Side (Illus. by Oldland, Nicholas) — *Oldland, Nicholas*
Walk-Up Music — *Watsky, Paul*
Walker on Water — *Ehin, Kristiina*
Walking a Tightrope: Defending Human Rights in China — *Nielsen, Gert Holmgaard*
Walking Away: Further Travels with a Troubadour on the South West Coast Path — *Armitage, Simon*
Walking Backwards to Christmas — *Cottrell, Stephen*
Walking by Night — *Ellis, Kate*
Walking Home: My Family and Other Rambles — *Wheeler, Sharon*
Walking in Credence: An Administrative History of George Washington Carver National Monument — *Krache, Diane L.*
Walking in Grace with Grief: Meditations for Healing after Loss — *Temple, Della*
Walking New York: Reflections of American Writers from Walt Whitman to Teju Cole — *Miller, Stephen*
Walking on Custard and the Meaning of Life: A Guide for Anxious Humans — *Hughes, Neil*
Walking on the Wild Side: Long-Distance Hiking on the Appalachian Trail — *Fondren, Kristi M.*
Walking on Trampolines — *Whiting, Frances*
Walking St. Augustine: An Illustrated Guide and Pocket History to America's Oldest City — *Gordon, Elsbeth "Buff*
Walking the Kiso Road: A Modern-Day Exploration of Old Japan — *Wilson, William Scott*
Walking the Night Road: Coming of Age in Grief — *Butler, Alexandra*
Walking the Nile — *Wood, Levison*
y Walking Two Worlds — *Bruchac, Joseph*
The Walking Whales: From Land to Water in Eight Million Years — *Thewissen, J.G.M.*
Walking Where Jesus Walked: American Christians and Holy Land Pilgrimage — *Kaell, Hillary*
Walking with Abel: Journeys with the Nomads of the African Savannah (Illus. by #) — *Badkhen, Anna*
Walking with Abel: Journeys with the Nomads of the African Savannah — *Badkhen, Anna*
Walking with Gosse: Natural History, Creation and Religious Conflicts — *Wotton, Roger S.*
c Walking with Herb: A Spiritual Golfing Journey to the Masters — *Bullock, Joe S.*
Walking with Spirit: Consciously Continuing Your Spiritual Journey — *Maddox, Cynthia*
y Walking Wounded — *Lynch, Chris*

Walking Wounded: Uncut Stories from Iraq (Illus. by Mael) — *Morel, Olivier*
The Wall between Us: Notes from the Holy Land — *Small, Matthew*
c The Wall People: In Search of a Home — *Di Certo, Joseph J.*
c Wall (Illus. by Cole, Tom Clohosy) — *Cole, Tom Clohosy*
Wall Street Women — *Fisher, Melissa*
Wall Streeters: The Creators and Corruptors of American Finance — *Morris, Edward L.*
The Wall, the Mount, and the Mystery of the Red Heifer — *Silverman, Sidney B.*
Wallace, Darwin, and the Origin of Species — *Costa, James T.*
The Wallcreeper — *Zink, Nell*
y The Walled City — *Graudin, Ryan*
y The Walls around Us (Read by King, Georgia, with Sandy Rustin). Audiobook Review — *Suma, Nova Ren*
y The Walls around Us (Read by King, Georgia). Audiobook Review — *Suma, Nova Ren*
y The Walls around Us (Read by King, Georgia, with Sandy Rustin). Audiobook Review — *Suma, Nova Ren*
y The Walls around Us — *Suma, Nova Ren*
The Walls of Delhi — *Prakash, Uday*
c Wally McBap Needs a Nap! (Illus. by Teets, Ashley) — *Arco-Mastromichalis, Andrea N.*
c The Walrus Who Escaped (Illus. by Brennan, Anthony) — *Qitsualik-Tinsley, Sean*
c The Walrus who Escaped (Illus. by Brennan, Anthony) — *Qitsualik-Tinsley, Rachel*
Walsingham and the English Imagination — *Waller, Gary*
c Walt Disney: Animator & Founder — *Hansen, Grace*
c Walt Disney (Illus. by Irvin, Frank) — *Hammontree, Marie*
c Walt Disney: Drawn from Imagination — *Scollon, Bill*
Walt Disney's Uncle Scrooge: The Seven Cities of Gold — *Barks, Carl*
c Walt Whitman (Illus. by Day, Rob) — *Loewen, Nancy*
Walter Benjamin: A Critical Life — *Eiland, Howard*
Walter Benjamin's Archive: Images, Texts, Signs — *Marx, Ursula*
Walter Lippmann: Public Economist — *Goodwin, Craufurd D.*
Walter Mehring — *Schulz, Georg-Michael*
Walter Ralegh's "History of the World" and the Historical Culture of the Late Renaissance — *Popper, Nicholas*
c Walter the Baker — *Carle, Eric*
Walter Wink: Collected Readings — *French, Henry*
Walter's Way — *Scherr, Walter J.*
c Walter's Wheels — *Dingeldein, Noelle*
Wampum and the Origins of American Money — *Shell, Marc*
c The Wand and the Sea — *Caterer, Claire M.*
y The Wanderers — *Ormand, Kate*
The Wanderer's Children — *O'Connor, Liz Gelb*
Wandering Greeks: The Ancient Greek Diaspora from the Age of Homer to the Death of Alexander the Great — *Garland, Robert*
The Wandering Mind: What the Brain Does When You're Not Looking — *Corballis, Michael*
Wandering: Philosophical Performances of Racial and Sexual Freedom — *Cervenak, Sarah Jane*
The Wandering Pine — *Enquist, Per Olov*
y Wandering Star — *Russell, Romina*
c Wandering Whale Sharks (Illus. by Shingu, Susumu) — *Shingu, Susumu*
Wandering Whale Sharks — *Shingu. Susumu*

c Wandering Woolly (Illus. by Gabriel, Andrea) — Gabriel, Andrea
Wanderjahre: A Reporter's Journey in a Mad World — Kleveman, Lutz
Wanderlust: A Modern Yogi's Guide to Discovering Your Best Self — Krasno, Jeff
Wanderlust — Schout, Dawn
Wanderlust Quilts: 10 Modern Projects Inspired by Classic Art and Architecture — Leins, Amanda
Wanderlust — Black, Kojo
Wang Renmei: The Wildcat of Shanghai — Meyer, Richard J.
c Wangari Maathai: The Woman Who Planted Millions of Trees (Illus. by Fronty, Aurelia) — Prevot, Franck
c Wangari Maathai: The Woman Who Planted Millions of Trees (Illus. by Clement, Dominique) — Prevot, Franck
c Wangari Maathai: The Woman Who Planted Millions of Trees (Illus. by Fronty, Aurelia) — Prevot, Franck
c Want to Play? (Illus. by Ng-Benitez, Shirley) — Yoo, Paula
Want to Wake Alive: Selected Poems/ K.B. Aussi petit que mon prochain — Barnes, Keith
Want You Dead — James, Peter
Wanted: A Spiritual Pursuit Through Jail, Among Outlaws, and Across Borders — Hoke, Chris
Wanted — Utley, Robert M.
c Wanted: Prince Charming (Illus. by Fiofin, Fabiano) — Benjamin, A.H.
c Wanted Prince Charming (Illus. by Fiorin, Fabiano) — Remphry, Martin
c Wanted! Ralfy Rabbit, Book Burglar — Mackenzie, Emily
Wanted Sam Bass — Colt, Paul
War: A Crime against Humanity — Vivo, Roberto
War Against All Puerto Ricans — Denis, Nelson A.
War Against All Puerto Ricans: Revolution and Terror in America's Colony — Denis, Nelson A.
War, Agriculture, and Food: Rural Europe from the 1930s to the 1950s — Brassley, Paul
War and Health Insurance Policy in Japan and the United States: World War II to Postwar Reconstruction — Yamagishi, Takakazu
War and Literature — Ashe, Laura
War and Nationalism: The Balkan Wars, 1912-1913, and Their Sociopolitical Implications — Yavuz, M. Hakan
War and Revolution in Russia, 1914-22: The Collapse of Tsarism and the Establishment of Soviet Power — Read, Christopher
War and State Formation in Syria: Cemal Pasha's Governorate during World War I, 1914-1917 — Cicek, M. Talha
War and Warfare in Late Antiquity: Current Perspectives — Sarantis, Alexander Constantine
War at the Edge of the World — Ross, Ian James
War at the End of the World: Douglas MacArthur and the Forgotten Fight for New Guinea, 1942-1945 — Duffy, James P.
War Babies: The Generation That Changed America — Pells, Richard
y War Brothers: The Graphic Novel (Illus. by Lafrance, Daniel) — McKay, Sharon E.
The War Came Home with Him: A Daughter's Memoir — Madison, Catherine
War, Clausewitz, and the Trinity — Waldman, Thomas
War, Climate Change and Catastrophe in the Seventeenth Century — Parker, Geoffrey
War Crimes Tribunals and Transitional Justice: The Tokyo Trial and the Nuremburg Legacy — Futamura, Madoka
War Dogs — Bear, Greg
War Echoes: Gender and Militarization in U.S. Latina/o Cultural Production — Vigil, Ariana E.
War Finance and Logistics in Late Imperial China: A Study of the Second Jinchuan Campaign, 1771-1776 — Theobald, Ulrich
The War for Korea, 1950-1951: They Came from the North — Millett, Allan R.
A War for the Soul of America: A History of the Culture Wars — Hartman, Andrew
War, Guilt, and World Politics after World War II — Berger, Thomas U.
The War Has Brought Peace to Mexico: World War II and the Consolidation of the Post-Revolutionary State — Jones, Halbert
y War in My Town — Graziani, E.
War in Peace: Paramilitary Violence in Europe after the Great War — Horne, John

War in Social Thought: Hobbes to the Present — Joas, Hans
War Is Beautiful: The 'New York Times' Pictorial Guide to the Glamour of Armed Conflict — Shields, David
A War Like No Other: The Constitution in a Time of Terror — Fiss, Owen
War Music — Logue, Christopher
The War of 1812: Conflict for a Continent — Stagg, J.C.A.
The War of My Generation: Youth Culture and the War on Terror — Kieran, David
y War of Rain — Vivian, H.W.
War of the Encyclopaedists (Read by Robinson, Christopher). Audiobook Review — Robinson, Christopher
War of the Encyclopaedists — Kovite, Gavin
War of the Encyclopaedists — Robinson, Christopher
War of the Foxes — Siken, Richard
The War of the Roses: The Fall of the Plantagenets and the Rise of the Tudors — Jones, Dan
War of the Wives — Cohen, Tamar
c War of the World Records (Read by Crossley, Steven). Audiobook Review — Ward, Matthew
c War of the World Records — Ward, Matthew
War of Two: Alexander Hamilton, Aaron Burr, and the Duel That Stunned the Nation — Sedgwick, John
War of Words: Culture and the Mass Media in the Making of the Cold War in Europe — Devlin, Judith
The War of Words — Neftzger, Amy
The War on Alcohol: Prohibition and the Rise of the American State — McGirr, Lisa
The War on Leakers — Gardner, Lloyd C.
The War on Slums in the Southwest: Public Housing and Slum Clearance in Texas, Arizona, and New Mexico, 1935-1965 — Fairbanks, Robert B.
War on the Silver Screen: Shaping Americas Perception of History — Jeansonne, Glen
War on the Waters: The Union and Confederate Navies, 1861-1865 — McPherson, James M.
War, Pacification, and Mass Murder, 1939: The Einsatzgruppen in Poland — Matthaus, Jurgen
The War Reporter — Fletcher, Martin
War Room — Fabry, Chris
War, So Much War — Rodoreda, Merce
War Stories: Suffering and Sacrifice in the Civil War North — Clarke, Frances M.
The War That Ended Peace — MacMillan, Margaret
The War That Forged a Nation: Why the Civil War Still Matters — McPherson, James M.
y The War That Saved My Life (Read by Entwistle, Jayne). Audiobook Review — Bradley, Kimberly Brubaker
c The War that Saved My Life — Bradley, Kimberly Brubaker
The War That Used Up Words: American Writers and the First World War — Hutchison, Hazel
War Time: An Idea, Its History, Its Consequences — Dudziak, Mary L.
War! What Is It Good For? Conflict and the Progress of Civilization from Primates to Robots — Morris, Ian
The War with God: Theomachy in Roman Imperial Poetry — Chaudhuri, Pramit
Warbird Factory: North American Aviation in World War II — Fredrickson, John M.
y The Warbler Guide. E-book Review — Stephenson, Tom
Warburg in Rome (Read by Doersch, David). Audiobook Review — Carroll, James
The Ward: The Life and Loss of Toronto's First Immigrant Neighbourhood — Lorinc, John
The Warden — Shrimpton, Nicholas
Warfare in the Old Testament: The Organization, Weapons, and Tactics of Ancient Near Eastern Armies — Seevers, Boyd
Warlords, Inc.: Black Markets, Broken States, and the Rise of the Warlord Entrepreneur — Raford, Noah
The Warming: Speculative Fiction about the Human Impact of the Climate Crisis — Robinson, Lorin R.
y Warren the 13th and the All-Seeing Eye (Illus. by Staehle, Will) — del Rio, Tania
c Warren the Honking Cat Saves the Day (Illus. by Ugang, Rosauro) — White, Virginia K.
A Warring Nation: Honor, Race, and Humiliation in America and Abroad — Wyatt-Brown, Bertram
Warrior: A Memoir — Larson, Theresa
c Warrior Heroes Series — Hulme-Cross, Benjamin
Warrior — Irving, Terry

Warrior Nations: The United States and Indian Peoples — Nichols, Roger L.
The Warrior State: Pakistan in the Contemporary World — Paul, T.V.
The Warrior Vampire — Baxter, Kate
Warrior Women — Guran, Paula
Warrior Women: Gender, Race, and the Transnational Chinese Action Star — Funnell, Lisa
c Warriors — Turner, Tracey
Warriors and Worriers: The Survival of the Sexes — Benenson, Joyce F.
Warriors of the Cloisters: The Central Asian Origins of Science in the Medieval World — Beckwith, Christopher I.
Warriors of the Storm — Cornwell, Bernard
c Warriors Super Edition: Bramblestar's Storm — Hunter, Erin
The Wars Before the Great War: Conflict and International Politics before the Outbreak of the First World War — Geppert, Dominik
The Wars before the Great War: Conflict and International Politics before the Outbreak of the First World War — Rose, Andreas
Wars Don't Happen Anymore — White, Sarah
War's Ends: Human Rights, International Order, and the Ethics of Peace — Murphy, James G.
The Wars for Asia, 1911-1949 — Paine, S.C.M.
The Wars of Justinian — Dewing, Henry B.
The Wars of Reconstruction: The Brief, Violent History of America's Most Progressive Era — Egerton, Douglas R.
Wars of the Roses: Margaret of Anjou — Iggulden, Conn
Wars of the Roses: Stormbird (Read by Curless, John). Audiobook Review — Iggulden, Conn
The Wars of the Roses: The Fall of the Plantagenets and the Rise of the Tudors (Read by Curless, John). Audiobook Review — Jones, Dan
y Warsaw, Lodz, Vilna: The Holocaust Ghettos — Altman, Linda Jacobs
Was der Mensch Essen Darf: Okonomischer Zwang, Okologisches Gewissen und Globale Konflikte — Hirschfelder, Gunther
Was Hitler a Darwinian? Disputed Questions in the History of Evolutionary Theory — Richards, Robert J.
Was wird, wenn die Zeitbombe hochgeht? Eine sozialgeschichtliche Analyse der fremdenfeindlichen Ausschreitungen in Hoyerswerda im September 1991 — Wowtscherk, Christoph
Washday (Read by Cottle, Elizabeth). Audiobook Review — Bunting, Eve
Washing the Dead — Brafman, Michelle
Washington: A History of Our National City — Lewis, Tom
Washington and Hamilton: The Alliance That Forged America — Knott, Stephen F.
Washington Brotherhood: Politics, Social Life, and the Coming of the Civil War — Shelden, Rachel A.
The Washington Dissensus: A Privileged Observer's Perspective on US-Brazil Relations — Barbosa, Rubens
Washington Journal: Reporting Watergate and Richard Nixon's Downfall — Drew, Elizabeth
Washington Merry-Go-Round — Pearson, Drew
c Washington Redskins — Zappa, Marcia
The Washington Stratagem — LeBor, Adam
Washington's Circle: The Creation of the President — Heidler, David S.
The Washingtons: George and Martha, Join'd by Friendship, Crown'd by Love — Fraser, Flora
Washington's Immortals: The Untold Story of an Elite Regiment Who Changed the Course of the Revolution — O'Donnell, Patrick K.
Washington's Monument: And the Fascinating History of the Obelisk — Gordon, John Steele
Washington's Rebuke to Bigotry: Reflections on Our First President's Famous 1790 Letter to the Hebrew Congregation in Newport, Rhode Island — Hebrew Congregation
Washington's Rebuke to Bigotry: Reflections on Our First President's Famous 1790 Letter to the Hebrew Congregation In Newport, Rhode Island — Strom, Adam
y Washington's Revolution: The Making of America's First Leader — Middlekauff, Robert
Washita — Lane, Patrick
Waste: A Philosophy of Things — Viney, William
Waste to Wealth: The Circular Economy Advantage — Lacy, Peter
Wasted: How Misunderstanding Young Britain Threatens Our Future — Gould, Georgia

Watch My Baby Grow: One Baby, One Year, One Extraordinary Project — Bhattacharya, Shaoni
c Watch Out for Flying Kids! How Two Circuses, Two Countries, and Nine Kids Confront Conflict and Build Community — Levinson, Cynthia
c Watch Out for the Crocodile (Illus. by Eriksson, Eva) — Moroni, Lisa
c Watch Out, Hollywood!: More Confessions of a So-Called Middle Child — Lennon, Maria T.
Watch over Me — Landon, Sydney
The Watch — Roy-Bhattacharya, Joydeep
Watch the Lady — Fremantle, Elizabeth
c Watch the Sky — Hubbard, Kirsten
c Watch Your Step — Burns, T.R.
The Watchdog That Didn't Bark: The Financial Crisis and the Disappearance of Investigative Journalism — Starkman, Dean
Watchdogs and Whistleblowers: A Reference Guide to Consumer Activism — Brobeck, Stephen
y Watched — Lyons, C.J.
y Watched — Baker, Tihema
y The Watcher — Harlow, Joan
c The Watcher — Hiatt, Joan
Watcher in Black and Other Poems — Boucher, Stanley
The Watcher in the Wall — Laukkanen, Owen
The Watchful Clothier: The Life of an Eighteenth-Century Protestant Capitalist — Kadane, Matthew
Watching Weimar Dance — Elswit, Kate
Watching Women's Liberation, 1970: Feminism's Pivotal Year on the Network News — Dow, Bonnie J.
Watchlist — Hurt, Bryan
y The Watchmaker of Filigree Street — Pulley, Natasha
The Watchmen in Pieces: Surveillance, Literature, and Liberal Personhood — Rosen, David
c The Watchmen of Port Fayt — Mason, Conrad
Water 4.0: The Past, Present, and Future of the World's Most Vital Resource — Sedlak, David
Water: A Global History — Miller, Ian
c Water — Stewart, Melissa
y The Water and the Wild — Ormsbee, K.E.
Water and What We Know: Following the Roots of a Northern Life — Babine, Karen
The Water-Babies: A Fairy Tale for a Land Baby — Kingsley, Charles
Water, Earth, Air, Fire, and Picket Fences — Smallwood, Carol
Water for the City, Fountains for the People: Monumental Fountains in the Roman East. An Archaeological Study of Water Management — Richard, Julian
y Water Ghosts — Collison, Linda
c The Water Horse — Webb, Holly
c Water Is Water: A Book About the Water Cycle (Illus. by Chin, Jason) — Paul, Miranda
y The Water Knife (Read by Guerra, Almarie). Audiobook Review — Bacigalupi, Paolo
y The Water Knife — Bacigalupi, Paolo
Water Lessons — Wall, Chadwick
The Water Museum — Urrea, Luis Alberto
Water Music — Gouveia, Georgette
c Water Planet Rescue (Illus. by Gravel, Elise) — Mass, Wendy
c Water Rolls, Water Rises / El agua rueda, el agua sube (Illus. by So, Meilo) — Mora, Pat
The Water-Saving Garden: How to Grow a Gorgeous Garden with a Lot Less Water — Penick, Pam
Water to the Angels: William Mulholland, His Monumental Aqueduct, and the Rise of Los Angeles — Standiford, Les
y The Water Urn — Kermani, Houshang Moradi
c Water! Water! Water! — Wallace, Nancy Elizabeth
y The Water-Wise Home — Allen, Laura
Waterborne Pageants and Festivities in the Renaissance: Essays in Honour of J.R. Mulryne — Shewring, Margaret
The Watercolor Course You've Always Wanted: Guided Lessons for Beginners and Experienced Artists — Frontz, Leslie
y Waterfall — Lauren, Kate
Waterfalls and Wildflowers in the Southern Appalachians: Thirty Great Hikes — Spira, Timothy P.
Waterfire Saga: 02: Rogue Wave. Audiobook Review — Jennifer, Donnelly
Waterlog — Deakin, Roger
Waterloo — Forrest, Allan
The Waterloo Archive, vol. 5: German Sources — Glover, Gareth

Waterloo: Four Days That Changed Europe's Destiny — Clayton, Tim
Waterloo — Forrest, Alan
Waterloo: The Aftermath — O'Keefe, Paul
Waterloo: The Aftermath — O'Keeffe, Paul
Waterloo: The Decisive Victory — Lipscombe, Nick
Waterloo: The History of Four Days, Three Armies and Three Battles — Cornwell, Bernard
Watermark — O'Reilly, Sean
The Waters of Eternal Youth — Leon, Donna
The Waters of Rome: Aqueducts, Fountains, and the Birth of the Baroque City — Rinne, Katherine Wentworth
Waterside Modern — Bradbury, Dominic
The Wax Bullet War: Chronicles of a Soldier and Artist — Davis, Sean
y The Way Around: Finding My Mother and Myself among the Yanomami — Good, David
y The Way Back from Broken — Keyser, Amber J.
c Way Back Then (Illus. by Arnaktauyok, Germaine) — Christopher, Neil
c Way Down Below Deep (Illus. by Sheldon, David) — Day, Nancy Raines
y Way Down Dark — Smythe, J.P.
The Way Forward: Renewing the American Idea — Ryan, Paul
c The Way Home Looks Now — Shang, Wendy Wan-Long
y The Way I Used to Be — Smith, Amber
The Way into Chaos — Connolly, Harry
The Way Into Darkness — Connolly, Harry
The Way into Magic — Connolly, Harry
Way of Love — Wirzba, Norman
The Way of Science: Finding Truth and Meaning in a Scientific Worldview — Trumble, Dennis R.
The Way of Sorrows — Steele, Jon
The Way of Tenderness: Awakening Through Race, Sexuality, and Gender — Manuel, Zenju Earthlyn
Way of the Bushman as Told by the Tribal Elders: Spiritual Teachings and Practices of the Kalahari Jul'hoansi — Keeney, Bradford
Way of the Warrior — Brockmann, Suzanne
The Way: Religious Thinkers of the Russian Emigration in Paris and Their Journal 1925-1940 — Arjakovsky, Antoine
The Way Things Were — Taseer, Aatish
c The Way to School — McCarney, Rosemary
c The Way to School — Mccarney, Rosemary
c The Way to Stay in Destiny (Read by Crouch, Michael). Audiobook Review — Scattergood, Augusta
c The Way to Stay in Destiny — Scattergood, Augusta
c The Way to the Zoo (Illus. by Burningham, John) — Burningham, John
y The Way We Bared Our Souls — Strayhorn, Willa
The Way We Live Now — Trollope, Anthony
The Way We Were — Forss, George
The Way We Weren't: A Memoir — Talbot, Jill Lynn
Wayfaring Stranger — Burke, James Lee
Wayfaring Strangers: The Musical Voyage from Scotland and Ulster to Appalachia — Ritchie, Fiona
Ways of Curating — Obrist, Hans Ulrich
The Ways of Evil Men — Gage, Leighton
Ways of Going Home — Zambra, Alejandro
Ways of Making and Knowing: The Material Culture of Empirical Knowledge — Smith, Pamela H.
Ways of Sensing: Understanding the Senses in Society — Howes, David
The Ways of the World: A James Maxted Thriller — Goddard, Robert
The Ways of the World (Read by Perkins, Derek). Audiobook Review — Goddard, Robert
The Ways of the World — Harvey, David
The Ways of the World — Goddard, Robert
Ways of War: American Military History from the Colonial Era to the Twenty-First Century — Muehlbauer, Matthew S.
Ways to Disappear — Novey, Idra
c Wazdot? (Illus. by Slack, Michael) — Slack, Michael
We All Become Stories — Carson, Ann Elizabeth
y We All Looked Up — Wallach, Tommy
c We All Sleep (Illus. by Morgan, Sally) — Kwaymullina, Ezekiel
We Are Afghan Women — George W. Bush Presidential Center
We Are All Children of God: The Story of the Forty Young Martyrs of Buta-Burundi — Bukuru, Zacharie
We Are All Completely Beside Ourselves — Fowler, Karen Joy
y We Are All Made of Molecules (Read by Bernstein, Jesse). Audiobook Review — Nielsen, Susin

y We Are All Made of Molecules — Nielsen, Susin
We Are All Stardust — Klein, Stefan
We Are Better Than This: How Government Should Spend Our Money — Kleinbard, Edward D.
c We Are in a Book! — Willems, Mo
We Are Market Basket: The Story of the Unlikely Grassroots Movement that Saved a Beloved Business — Korschun, Daniel
We Are Monsters — Kirk, Brian
We Are Not Ourselves — Thomas, Matthew
"We Are Now the True Spaniards": Sovereignty, Revolution, Independence, and the Emergence of the Federal Republic of Mexico, 1808-1824 — Rodriguez O., Jaime E.
We Are Pirates — Handler, Daniel
c We Are Proud of You (Illus. by The Pope Twins) — Kim, YeShil
We Are Strong, But We Are Fragile — Mustin, Bob
y We Are the Ants — Hutchinson, Shaun David
We Are the Birds of the Coming Storm — Lafon, Lola
y We Are the Rebels: The Women and Women Who Made Eureka — Wright, Clare
We Believe the Children: A Moral Panic in the 1980s — Beck, Richard
We Bought a WWII Bomber: The Untold Story of a Michigan High School, a B-17 Bomber, and the Blue Ridge Parkway! — Warren, Sandra
We British: The Poetry of a People — Marr, Andrew
c We Can Get Along: A Child's Book of Choices (Illus. by Iwai, Melissa) — Payne, Lauren Murphy
We Can Make the World Economy a Sustainable Global Home — Mudge, Lewis S.
y We Can Work It Out — Eulberg, Elizabeth
We - Commerce: How to Create, Collaborate, and Succeed in the Sharing Economy — Howard, Billee
We Could Not Fail: The First African Americans in the Space Program — Paul, Richard
We Created Chavez: A People's History of the Venezuelan Revolution — Ciccariello-Maher, George
c We Dig Worms! — McCloskey, Kevin
c We Dig Worms! (Illus. by McCloskey, Kevin) — McCloskey, Kevin
c We Dig Worms! — McCloskey, Kevin
We Don't Know What We're Doing — Morris, Thomas
We Don't Need Roads: The Making of the Back to the Future Trilogy (Read by Butler, Ron). Audiobook Review — Gaines, Caseen
We Don't Need Roads: The Making of the Back to the Future Trilogy — Gaines, Caseen
We Fight for Peace: Twenty-Three American Soldiers, Prisoners of War and 'Turncoats' in the Korean War — McKnight, Brian D.
We Five — Dunn, Mark
c We Forgot Brock! (Illus. by Goodrich, Carter) — Goodrich, Carter
We Gather Together: The Religious Right and the Problem of Interfaith Politics — Young, Neil J.
We Have Raised All of You: Motherhood in the South, 1750-1835 — Smith, Katy Simpson
We Have the Technology: How Biohackers, Foodies, Physicians, and Scientists Are Transforming Human Perception, One Sense at a Time — Platoni, Kara
We Install and Other Stories — Turtledove, Harry
We Just Keep Running the Line: Black Southern Women and the Poultry Processing Industry — Gray, LaGuana
We Kill Because We Can: From Soldiering to Assassination in the Drone Age — Calhoun, Laurie
We Killed: The Rise of Women in American Comedy — Kohen, Yael
We Know How This Ends: Living While Dying — Kramer, Bruce H.
'We Love Death as You Love Life': Britain's Suburban Terrorists — Pantucci, Raffaello
c We Love to Craft: Christmas Fun Stuff for Kids: 17 Handmade Fabric and Paper Projects — Wrigley, Annabel
We Love You, Charlie Freeman — Greenidge, Kaitlyn
c We Love You, Hugless Douglas! — Melling, David
We Mammals in Hospitable Times — Martin, Jynne Dilling
We Meet Again (Read by Goldsmith, Jared). Audiobook Review — Pastis, Stephan
We Modern People: Science Fiction and the Making of Russian Modernity — Banerjee, Anindita
We Need Another Revolution: Five Decades of Mathematics Curriculum Papers by Zalman Usiskin — Reys, Barbara J.
We Need New Names — Bulawayo, NoViolet

We Need Silence to Find Out What We Think: Selected Essays — Hazzard, Shirley
We Never Asked for Wings (Read by Bering, Emma). Audiobook Review — Diffenbaugh, Vanessa
We Never Asked for Wings — Diffenbaugh, Vanessa
"We Never Retreat": Filibustering Expeditions into Spanish Texas, 1812-1822 — Bradley, Ed
y We Sang in Hushed Voices — Jockel, Helena
We Sell Drugs: The Alchemy of US Empire — Reiss, Suzanna
We Share Our Matters: Two Centuries of Writing and Resistance at Six Nations of the Grand River — Monture, Rick
We Should All Be Feminists — Adichie, Chimamanda Ngozi
y We Should Hang Out Sometime: Embarrassingly, a True Story — Sundquist, Josh
We That Are Left — Clark, Clare
c We the People: The Constitution of the United States — Spier, Peter
We the People, vol. 3: The Civil Rights Revolution — Ackerman, Bruce
We Too Sing America: South Asian, Arab, Muslim, and Sikh Immigrants Shape Our Multiracial Future — Iyer, Deepa
y We Were Brothers — Moser, Barry
c We Were Liars (Read by Meyers, Ariadne). Audiobook Review — Lockhart, E.
y We Were Liars — Lockhart, E.
y We Will Be Crashing Shortly — Gillespie, Hollis
We Will Shoot Back: Armed Resistance in the Mississippi Freedom Movement — Cobb, Charles E.
Weak Messages Create Bad Situations — Shrigley, David
Wealth and Power: China's Long March to the Twenty-First Century — Schell, Orville
The Wealth of Communities: War, Resources and Cooperation in Renaissance Lombardy — Di Tullio, Matteo
Wealth, Poverty and Politics: An International Perspective — Sowell, Thomas
Wealth Secrets of the One Percent: A Modern Manual to Getting Marvelously, Obscenely Rich — Wilkin, Sam
Wealth, Whiteness, and the Matrix of Privilege: The View from the Country Club — Sherwood, Jessica Holden
Weapons of Fitness: The Women's Ultimate Guide to Fitness, Self-Defense, and Empowerment — Zeisler, Avital
Weapons of Mass Destruction — Vandenburg, Margaret
Wearable Technology — Bruno, Tom
Wearing God: Clothing, Laughter, Fire, and Other Overlooked Ways of Meeting God — Winner, Lauren F.
The Weary Blues — Hughes, Langston
The Weather Experiment: The Pioneers Who Sought to See the Future — Moore, Peter
c Weather Wise Series
c Weatherboy (Illus. by Devos, Kristof) — Van Hest, Pimm
Weathering — Wood, Lucy
Weatherland: Writers and Artists Under English Skies — Harris, Alexandra
The Weave — Moore, Nancy Jane
Weavers — Davis, Aric
y The Web (Read by Peakes, Karen). Audiobook Review — Chance, Megan
Web of Deceit — Howell, Katherine
A Web of Evil — McMahon, Richard
Web Security: A WhiteHat Perspective — Hanqing, Wu
c Webster: Tale of an Outlaw — White, Ellen Emerson
Wedding Cake Murder — Fluke, Joanne
The Wedding Chapel — Hauck, Rachel
Wedding Night with the Earl — Grey, Amelia
A Wedding on Primrose Street — Roberts, Sheila
A Wedding Song for Poorer People — DePew, Alfred
The Wedding Tree — Wells, Robin
The Wedge — Weber, Alan M.
The Wednesday Group — True, Sylvia
c Wednesday (Illus. by Berber, Anne) — Berber, Anne
Wednesdays in Mississippi: Proper Ladies Working for Radical Change, Freedom Summer 1964 — Harwell, Debbie Z.
Weed the People: The Future of Legal Marijuana in America — Barcott, Bruce
The Weeding Handbook: A Shelf-by-Shelf Guide — Vnuk, Rebecca

The Weegee Guide to New York: Roaming the City with Its Greatest Tabloid Photographer — Mariani, Philomena
A Week at the Lake — Wax, Wendy
A Week from Next Tuesday: Joy Keeps Showing Up (Because Christ Keeps Showing Up). — Rich, Matthew A.
c A Week without Tuesday (Illus. by Lewis, Stevie) — Banks, Angelica
c A Weekend with Dinosaurs — Throp, Claire
c Weekends with Max and His Dad — Urban, Linda
Weeping Britannia: Portrait of a Nation in Tears — Dixon, Thomas
Wehrmacht Priests: Catholicism and the Nazi War of Annihilation — Rossi, Lauren Faulkner
Weighing In: Obesity, Food Justice, and the Limits of Capitalism — Guthman, Julie
Weighing Shadows — Goldstein, Lisa
Weight of Chains — Conner, Lester
y The Weight of Feathers — McLemore, Anna-Marie
The Weight of Things — Fritz, Marianne
y Weightless — Bannan, Sarah
Weihgeschenke aus dem Heiligtum der Aphrodite in Alt-Paphos. Terrakotten, Skulpturen und andere figurliche Kleinvotive — Weiland, Leibundgut D.
The Weimar Century — Greenberg, Uri
Weimar Colonialism: Discourses and Legacies of Post-Imperialism in Germany after 1918 — Krobb, Florian
Weimar Culture: The Outsider as Insider — Gay, Peter
Weimar Thought: A Contested Legacy — Gordon, Peter E.
c Weird and Wild Animal Facts (Illus. by Loy, Jessica) — Loy, Jessica
Weird Birds — Earley, Chris
c Weird But True! Food: 300 Bite-Sized Facts About Incredible Edibles! — Flynn, Sarah Wassner
Weird Frogs — Earley, Chris
c Weird Frogs — Early, Chris
y Weird Girl and What's His Name — Brothers, Meagan
Weird John Brown: Divine Violence and the Limits of Ethics — Smith, Ted A.
y Weird Sports and Wacky Games around the World: From Buzkashi to Zorbing — Williams, Victoria
Weisskittel und Braunhemd: Der Gottinger Mediziner Rudolf Stich im Kaleidoskop — Trittel, Katharina
c Welcome Home, Bear: A Book of Animal Habitats — Na, Il Sung
c Welcome Home, Bear: A Book of Animal Habitats (Illus. by Na, Il Sung) — Na, Il Sung
Welcome Home! — Earhart, Kristin
Welcome Home, Mr. Swanson: Swedish Emigrants and Swedishness on Film — Wallengren, Ann-Kristin
c Welcome Home! — Earhart, Kristin
c Welcome Home! (Illus. by Geddes, Serena) — Earhart, Kristin
Welcome Thieves — Beaudoin, Sean
Welcome to Braggsville — Johnson, T. Geronimo
c Welcome to Lovecraft — Hill, Joe
c Welcome to Mars: Making a Home on the Red Planet — Aldrin, Buzz
Welcome to Marwencol — Hogancamp, Mark
c Welcome to New Zealand: A Nature Journal (Illus. by Morris, Sandra) — Morris, Sandra
Welcome to Night Vale — Fink, Joseph
Welcome to PlanitDo! — Fraser, Melissa
Welcome to Resistervilk: American Dissidents in British Columbia — Rodgers, Kathleen
Welcome to Subirdia: Sharing Our Neighborhoods with Wrens, Robins, Woodpeckers, and Other Wildlife — Marzluff, John
Welcome to the Bike Factory — Buttress, Derrick
Welcome to the Circus — Douglas, Rhonda
y Welcome to the Dark House — Stolarz, Laurie Faria
c Welcome to the Family (Illus. by Asquith, Ros) — Hoffman, Mary
c Welcome to the Jungle — London, Matt
Welcome to the Madhouse — Sasaki, S.E.
Welcome to the Microbiome: Getting to Know the Trillions of Bacteria and Other Microbes in, on, and Around You — DeSalle, Rob
c Welcome to the Neighborwood (Illus. by Sheehy, Shawn) — Sheehy, Shawn
The Welfare State and the 'Deviant Poor' in Europe: 1870-1933 — Althammer, Beate
The Well at the World's End — Morris, William
The Well — Chanter, Catherine
The Well-Educated Mind — Bauer, Susan Wise
Well-Heeled: An Emily's Place Mystery — Siegel, Roz
A Well-Made Bed — Frucht, Abby

Well-Mannered Medicine: Medical Ethics and Etiquette in Classical Ayurveda — Wujastyk, Dagmar
y We'll Never Be Apart — Jean, Emiko
The Well — Chanter, Catherine
The Well of Ascension — Sanderson, Brandon
y Well of Witches — White, J.A.
Well Played: Building Mathematical Thinking through Number Games and Puzzles Grades 3-5 — Dacey, Linda
The Well-Tuned Brain: Neuroscience and the Life Well Lived — Whybrow, Peter C.
Wellington and Waterloo: The Duke, the Battle and Posterity, 1815-2015 — Foster, Ruscombe
Wellington: Waterloo and the Fortunes of Peace, 1814-1852 — Muir, Rory
Wellington's Guns: The Untold Story of Wellington and His Artillery in the Peninsula and at Waterloo — Lipscombe, Nick
Wellington's War: The Making of a Military Genius — Davies, Huw J.
The Wellness Syndrome — Cederstrom, Carl
The Welsh and the Shaping of Early Modern Ireland — Morgan, Rhys
A Welsh Dawn — Thomas, Gareth
Welteis: Eine Wahre Geschichte — Wessely, Christina
Weltmeere: Wissen und Wahrnehmung im Langen 19. Jahrhundert — Kraus, Alexander
Weltmeister im Schatten Hitlers: Deutschland und die Fussball-Weltmeisterschaft 1954 — Bruggemeier, Franz-Josef
c Welwyn Ardsley and the Cosmic Ninjas: Preparing Your Child, and Yourself for Anesthesia and Surgery — Rosenblum, David
Wendell Fertig and His Guerrilla Forces in the Philippines: Fighting the Japanese Occupation, 1942-1945 — Holmes, Kent
c Wendell the Narwhal (Illus. by Dove, Emily) — Dove, Emily
"Wenn das Erbe in die Wolke Kommt": Digitalisierung und Kulturelles Erbe
Went the Day Well? Witnessing Waterloo — Crane, David
c We're All Friends Here (Illus. by Goldsmith, Tom) — Wilcox Richards, Nancy
c We're Going on a Moa Hunt — MacDonald, Patrick
We're in this Together: Public-Private Partnerships in Special and At-Risk Education — Claypool, Mark K.
"We're People Who Do Shows": Back to Back Theatre: Performance, Politics, Visibility — Grehan, Helena
We're Still Here Ya Bastards: How the People of New Orleans Rebuilt Their City — Brandes, Roberta
We're Still Here Ya Bastards: How the People of New Orleans Rebuilt Their City — Gratz, Roberta Brandes
Weresisters — Kennedy, John Patrick
Werewolf Cop — Klavan, Andrew
The Werewolf of Bamberg — Potzsch, Oliver
Werkstatt Wissenschaftsgeschichte
Werkstattgesprach Lehre in der Technik - und Wissenschaftsgeschichte
Werner Herzog: A Guide for the for the Perplexed — Cronin, Paul
Werner Herzog: Interviews — Ames, Eric
Werner Scholem: Eine Politische Biographie — Hoffrogge, Ralf
Wertewandel in Wirtschaft und Arbeitswelt? Arbeit, Leistung und Fuhrung in den 1970er und 1980er Jahren in der Bundesrepublik Deutschland
Wertheim 1628: Eine Stadt in Krieg und Hexenverfolgung — Meier, Robert
c Wesley Booth Super Sleuth (Illus. by Streich, Michel) — Cece, Adam
West — Franck, Julia
West African Drumming and Dance in North American Universities: An Ethnomusicological Perspective — Dor, George Worlasi Kwasi
c West Coast Wild: A Nature Alphabet (Illus. by Reczuch, Karen) — Hodge, Deborah
West for the Black Hills — Leavell, Peter
West from Yesterday — Harrison, Randolph Carter
West Indian Women's Experience in Los Angeles: The Impact of Politics and the Global Economy — Squires, Stacey
West of Eden: An American Place — Stein, Jean
West of Eden — Harrison, Harry
West of Sunset (Read by Lane, Christopher). Audiobook Review — O'Nan, Stewart
West of Sunset — O'Nan, Stewart
c West of the Big River: The Ranger — Griffin, James J.

y West of the Moon — Preus, Margi
West of the Revolution: An Uncommon History of 1776 — Saunt, Claudio
West Point History of World War II, vol. 1 — U.S. Military Academy
West Texas: A History of the Giant Side of the State — Carlson, Paul H.
Western Anti-Communism and the Interdoc Network: Cold War Internationale — Scott-Smith, Giles
Western Daughters in Eastern Lands: British Missionary Women in Asia — Seton, Rosemary
The Western Flyer: Steinbeck's Boat, the Sea of Cortez, and the Saga of Pacific Fisheries — Bailey, Kevin M.
Western Union and the Creation of the American Corporate Order, 1848-1893 — Wolff, Joshua D.
Western Women Travelling East, 1716-1916 — Tuson, Penelope
WesternLore — Braun, Matt
c Westly: A Spider's Tale (Illus. by Beus, Bryan) — Beus, Bryan
Westminster 1640-60: A Royal City in a Time of Revolution — Merritt, J.F.
Westphalia: The Last Christian Peace — Croxton, Derek
c Wet Cement: A Mix of Concrete Poems — Raczka, Bob
c Wet Hen: A Short Vowel Adventure (Illus. by Coxe, Molly) — Coxe, Molly
Wet Prairie: People, Land, and Water in Agricultural Manitoba — Bower, Shannon Stunden
We've Already Gone This Far — Dacey, Patrick
c Whack of the P-Rex (Illus. by Cummings, Troy) — Cummings, Troy
The Whale Chaser — Ardizzone, Tony
c The Whale in My Swimming Pool (Illus. by Wan, Joyce) — Wan, Joyce
The Whale Savers: Returning Wera to the Ocean (Illus. by Potter, Bruce) — Roberts, Linda
c Whale Trails: Before and Now (Illus. by Karas, G. Brian) — Cline-Ransome, Lesa
c The Whale Who Won Hearts!: And More True Stories of Adventures with Animals — Skerry, Brian
Whales and Nations: Environmental Diplomacy on the High Seas — Dorsey, Kurkpatrick
c Whales: Ocean Life — Hansen, Grace
y Whasian — Stoffers, Joy Huang
c What a Hoot! — Preston-Gannon, Frann
c What a Wonderful World (Illus. by Hopgood, Tim) — Thiele, Bob
c What a Wonderful World (Illus. by Hopgood, Tim) — Weiss, George David
What about Me? The Struggle for Identity in a Market-Based Societ — Verhaeghe, Paul
c What about Moose? (Illus. by Yamaguchi, Keika) — Schwartz, Corey Rosen
What About Mozart? What About Murder? Reasoning from Cases — Becker, Howard S.
What about This: Collected Poems of Frank Stanford — Stanford, Frank
What about This: Collected Poems of Frank Stanford — Wiegers, Michael
c What Are Fiction Genres? — Bodden, Valerie
c What Are Graphic Novels? — Berne, Emma Carlson
c What Are Legends, Folktales, and Other Classic Stories? — Owings, Lisa
c What Are Nonfiction Genres? — Bodden, Valerie
c What Are Plays? — Owings, Lisa
y What Are Sleep Disorders? — Currie-McGhee, Leanne
c What Are the Three Branches of Government? And Other Questions about the U.S. Constitution — Richmond, Benjamin
What Are They Saying About Augustine? — Kelley, Joseph T.
What Are We Doing on Earth for Christ's Sake? — Leonard, Richard
c What Are You Glad About? What Are You Mad About? Poems for When a Person Needs a Poem (Illus. by White, Lee) — Viorst, Judith
c What are You Scared of, Little Mouse? (Illus. by Hilb, Nora) — Isern, Susanna
What Art Is Like, in Constant Reference to the Alice Books — Tamen, Miguel
What Became of the White Savage — Garde, Francois
What Belongs to You — Greenwell, Garth
What Children Can Teach Adults About Mathematics — Hunting, Robert P.
What Color Is Your Parachute? 2015 — Bolles, Richard N.
What Comes Next and How to Like It — Thomas, Abigail

What Do Cats Have Tails? (Illus. by Thatcher, Stephanie) — Ling, David
What Do I Know? People, Politics and the Arts — Eyre, Richard
c What Do You Wish For? (Illus. by Walker, Anna) — Godwin, Jane
What Does a Black Hole Look Like? — Bailyn, Charles D.
c What Does Baby Love? (Illus. by Katz, Karen) — Katz, Karen
c What Does It Mean to Be Kind? (Illus. by Jorisch, Stephane) — DiOrio, Rana
c What Does Super Jonny Do When Mum Gets Sick? (Illus. by Ting, Jasmine) — Colwill, Simone
What Does the Bible Really Teach about Homosexuality? — DeYoung, Kevin
What Doesn't Kill Her (Read by Delaine, Christina). Audiobook Review — Norton, Carla
What Doesn't Kill Her — Norton, Carla
What Doesn't Kill Us — Joseph, Stephen
c What Flowers Say: And Other Stories (Illus. by Crabapple, Molly) — Sand, George
What Flows across the Glass — Moulson, Roger
c What Forest Knows (Illus. by Hall, August) — Lyon, George Ella
What Fresh Hell: The Best of Levees Not War: Blogging on Post-Katrina New Orleans and America, 2005-2015 — LaFleur, Mark
What Good Is Grand Strategy? Power and Purpose in American Statecraft from Harry S. Truman to George W. Bush — Brands, Hal
What Have We Learned? Macroeconomic Policy After the Crisis — Akerlof, George A.
What I Know for Sure (Read by Winfrey, Oprah). Audiobook Review — Winfrey, Oprah
What I Tell You in the Dark — Samuel, John
y What I Thought was True (Read by Spencer, Erin). Audiobook Review — Fitzpatrick, Huntley
What If Everybody Understood Child Development? Straight Talk about Bettering Education and Children's Lives — Pica, Rae
What If I'm an Atheist? A Teen's Guide to Exploring a Life without Religion — Seidman, David
c What if...? (Illus. by Browne, Anthony) — Browne, Anthony
What If?: Serious Scientific Answers to Absurd Hypothetical Questions — Munroe, Randall
c What If You Had Animal Feet!? (Illus. by McWilliam, Howard) — Markle, Sandra
c What in the World? Fantastic Photo Puzzles for Curious Minds — Agnone, Julie Vosburgh
What in the World Is Going On? Wisdom Teachings for Our Time — Gill, Penny
c What in the World? Numbers in Nature (Illus. by Cyrus, Kurt) — Day, Nancy Raines
c What Is a Graphic Novel? — Guillain, Charlotte
c What Is a Poem? — Guillain, Charlotte
y What Is Anxiety Disorder? — Mooney, Carla
What Is History For? Johann Gustav Droysen and the Functions of Historiography — Assis, Arthur Alfaix
c What Is Inside the Lincoln Memorial? (Illus. by Poling, Kyle) — Rustad, Martha E.H.
What Is Islam? The Importance of Being Islamic — Ahmed, Shahab
c What Is Literary Non-Fiction? — Guillain, Charlotte
y What Is Lost — Skidmore, Lauren
c What Is Love? (Illus. by Smith, Shane) — Smith, Shane
What Is Not Sacred? African Spirituality — Magesa, Laurenti
What Is Not Yours Is Not Yours — Oyeyemi, Helen
y What Is Panic Disorder? — Mooney, Carla
c What Is Poetry? — Trueit, Trudi Strain
c What Is Punk? (Illus. by Yi, Anny) — Morse, Eric
y What Is Self-Injury Disorder? — Yuwiler, Janice M.
What Is Your Quest? From Adventure Games to Interactive Books — Salter, Anastasia
What It Looks Like — Maranda, Marta
What It Takes — Sierra, Jude
What I've Learned — Heist, Christopher T.
c What James Said (Illus. by Myers, Matt) — Rosenberg, Liz
What Katie Ate on the Weekend — Davies, Katie Quinn
What Kind of Creatures are We? — Chomsky, Noam
c What Kinds of Coverings Do Animals Have? — Kalman, Bobbie
What Lies Across the Water: The Real Story of the Cuban Five — Kimber, Stephen
What Lies Behind — Ellison, J.T.
What Lies between Us — Munaweera, Nayomi
c What Makes a Rainbow? — Van Dusen, Ross

c What Makes a Tornado Twist?: And Other Questions about Weather — Carson, Mary Kay
What Makes Law: An Introduction to the Philosophy of Law — Murphy, Liam
c What Makes Sports Gear Safer? — Kurtz, Kevin
What Middletown Read: Print Culture in an American Small City — Felsenstein, Frank
What Nature Does for Britain — Juniper, Tony
c What Pet Should I Get? and One Fish Two Fish Red Fish Blue Fish (Read by Wilson, Rainn, with David Hyde Pierce). Audiobook Review — Dr. Seuss
c What Pet Should I Get? (Illus. by Dr. Seuss) — Dr. Seuss
c What Pet Should I Get? — Dr. Seuss
What Philosophy Can Do — Gutting, Gary
y What Remains — Dunbar, Helene
What Remains of Me — Gaylin, Alison
What Shakespeare Teaches Us about Psychoanalysis: A Local Habitation and a Name — Grunes, Dorothy T.
What She Knew — Macmillan, Gilly
y What She Left — Richmond, T.R.
c What Ship Is Not a Ship? (Illus. by Masse, Josee) — Ziefert, Harriet
What So Proudly We Hailed: Essays on the Contemporary Meanings of the War of 1812 — Nivola, Pietro S.
What Soldiers Do: Sex and the American GI in World War II France — Roberts, Mary Louise
What Stands in a Storm: Three Days in the Worst Superstorm to Hit the South's Tornado Valley — Cross, Kim
c What the Dinosaurs Did Last Night: A Very Messy Adventure (Illus. by Tuma, Refe) — Tuma, Refe
What the Eye Hears: A History of Tap Dancing — Seibert, Brian
y What the Fly Saw — Bailey, Frankie Y.
c What the Jackdaw Saw (Illus. by Sharratt, Nick) — Donaldson, Julia
c What the Ladybird Heard Next (Illus. by Monks, Lydia) — Donaldson, Julia
c What the Ladybird Heard (Illus. by Monks, Lydia) — Donaldson, Julia
c What the Moon Said (Read by Merlington, Laural). Audiobook Review — Rosengren, Gayle
What the Mystics Know: Seven Pathways to Your Deeper Self — Rohr, Richard
c What the Shepherd Saw (Illus. by Dusikova, Maja) — Lagerlof, Selma
What the Waves Know — Valentine, Tamara
c What There Is Before There Is Anything There: A Scary Story (Illus. by Liniers) — Liniers
What They Didn't Teach You in Photo School: What You Actually Need to Know to Succeed in the Industry — Fordham, Demetrius
What They Wished For: American Catholics and American Presidents, 1960-2004 — McAndrews, Lawrence J.
c What This Story Needs Is a Hush and a Shush (Illus. by Virjan, Emma J.) — Virjan, Emma J.
c What This Story Needs Is a Pig in a Wig (Illus. by Virjan, Emma J.) — Virjan, Emma J.
What to Bake & How to Bake It — Hornby, Jane
What To Do — Katchadjian, Pablo
What to Do to Retire Successfully: Navigating Psychological, Financial, and Lifestyle Hurdles New Horizon — Goldstein, Martin B.
What to Do to Retire Successfully: Navigating Psychological, Financial, and Lifestyle Hurdles — Goldstein, Martin B.
c What to Do When Mistakes Make You Quake: A Kid's Guide to Accepting Imperfection — Freeland, Claire A.B.
c What to Do When You're Sent to Your Room (Illus. by Gilpin, Stephen) — Stott, Ann
What to Do with a Duke — Mackenzie, Sally
What to Think About Machines That Think: Today's Leading Thinkers on the Edge of Machine Intelligence — Brockman, John
What Unions No Longer Do — Rosenfeld, Jake
y What Waits in the Woods — Scott, Kieran
c What Was It Like, Mr. Emperor? Life in China's Forbidden City — Kwong-chiu, Chiu
What Was Mine — Ross, Helen Klein
c What We Eat — Stones, Brenda
What We Gain as We Grow Older: On Gelassenheit — Schmid, Wilhelm
c What We Get from Norse Mythology — Krieg, Katherine
What We Have Done, What We Have Failed to Do: Assessing the Liturgical Reforms of Vatican II — Irwin, Kevin W.

y What We Knew — Stewart, Barbara
y What We Left Behind — Talley, Robin
y What We Saw — Hartzler, Aaron
What We Think About When We Try Not to Think about Global Warming: Toward a New Psychology of Climate Action — Stoknes, Per Espen
y What We're Fighting for Now Is Each Other: Dispatches from the Front Lines of Climate Justice — Stephenson, Wen
c What Will I Be? (Illus. by Lycett-Smith, Jon) — Sinclair, Richard
What Works for Workers? Public Policies and Innovative Strategies for Low-Wage Workers — Luce, Stephanie
What Works — Bohnet, Iris
What Would Jesus Read? Popular Religious Books and Everyday Life in Twentieth-Century America — Smith, Erin A.
What Would You Do? Words of Wisdom about Doing the Right Thing — Quinones, John
y What You Always Wanted — Rae, Kristin
What You Can Learn From Your Teenager — Kallanian, Jean-Pierre
What You Left Behind (Read by Bentinck, Anna). Audiobook Review — Hayes, Samantha
What You Left Behind — Hayes, Samantha
y What You Left Behind — Verdi, Jessica
c What You Need to Know About Cancer — Forest, Christopher
What You Need to Know about Privacy Law: A Guide for Librarians and Educators — McCord, Gretchen
What You See — Ryan, Hank Phillippi
What You Will on Capitol Hill — Tillotson, Richard
Whatever Arises, Love That: A Love Revolution that Begins with You — Kahn, Matt
Whatever Happened to Class? Reflections from South Asia — Agarwala, Rina
Whatever Happened to Molly Bloom? — Stirling, Jessica
c Whatever Happened to My Sister? (Illus. by Ciraolo, Simona) — Ciraolo, Simona
c Whatever Happened to My Sister? — Ciraolo, Simona
Whatever Happened to the Metric System?: How America Kept Its Feet — Marciano, John Bemelmans
y Whatever Life You Wear — Kennedy, Cecilia
c Whatever Wanda! (Illus. by Billin-Frye, Paige) — Ziglar, Christy
y What's Broken Between Us — Bass, Alexis
What's for Lunch? — Curtis, Andrea
What's Gone Wrong? South Africa on the Brink of Failed Statehood — Boraine, Alex
c What's Great about Arizona? — Hirsch, Rebecca E.
c What's Great about Colorado? — Meinking, Mary
c What's Great about Georgia? — Wang, Andrea
c What's Great about Maine? — Wang, Andrea
c What's Great about Mississippi? — Yasuda, Anita
c What's Great about Montana? — Bailer, Darice
c What's Great about New Mexico? — VanVoorst, Jenny Fretland
c What's Great about Oregon? — Felix, Rebecca
c What's Great about South Dakota? — Meinking, Mary
c What's Great about Virginia? — Kallio, Jamie
c What's Great about Washington, DC? — Hirsch, Rebecca E.
c What's Happening to Ellie? — Reynolds, Kate E.
c What's In My Truck? (Illus. by Bleck, Linda) — Bleck, Linda
What's Never Said — Shapiro, Susan
c What's So Yummy? All About Eating Well and Feeling Good (Illus. by Westcott, Nadine Bernard) — Harris, Robie H.
c What's That in the Water? — Norris, Eryl
c What's That Smell? A Kids' Guide to Keeping Clean (Illus. by Haggerty, Tim) — Kreisman, Rachelle
c What's the Buzz? Keeping Bees in Flight — Wilcox, Merrie-Ellen
c What's the Time Clockodile? — Litton, Jonathan
c What's the Time, Dinosaur? (Illus. by Paul, Ruth) — Paul, Ruth
c What's the Time, Wilfred Wolf? (Illus. by Smallman, Steve) — Barrah, Jessica
c What's Up in the Amazon Rainforest — Clarke, Ginjer L.
What's Wrong with Fat? — Saguy, Abigail C.
What's Wrong with My Houseplant? — Deardroff, David
What's Wrong with the Poor? Psychiatry, Race, and the War on Poverty — Raz, Mical
c What's Your Favorite Animal? (Illus. by Carle, Eric) — Carle, Eric

Wheat Belly: 10-Day Grain Detox: Reprogram Your Body for Rapid Weight Loss and Amazing Health — Davis, William
Wheel of Fortune: The Battle for Oil and Power in Russia — Gustafson, Thane
The Wheel of Healing with Ayurveda: An Easy Guide to a Healthy Lifestyle — Fondin, Michelle S.
y The Wheel of Life and Death: Mysterium — Sedgwick, Julian
c The Wheels on the Tuk Tuk (Illus. by Golden, Jess) — Sehgal, Kabir
When (Read by Dykhouse, Whitney). Audiobook Review — Laurie, Victoria
y When — Laurie, Victoria
c When a Dragon Moves in Again (Illus. by McWilliam, Howard) — Moore, Jodi
c When a Grandpa Says "I Love You" (Illus. by Bell, Jennifer A.) — Wood, Douglas
When a Rake Falls — Orr, Sally
When a Scot Ties the Knot — Dare, Tessa
"When All of Rome Was Under Construction": The Building Process in Baroque Rome — Habel, Dorothy Metzger
When All the Saints Come Marching In — Edkins, Rita
c When Andy Met Sandy (Illus. by dePaola, Tomie) — dePaola, Tomie
c When Aunt Mattie Got Her Wings (Illus. by Mathers, Petra) — Mathers, Petra
When Bad Things Happen to Good Quilters: Survival Guide for Fixing and Finishing Any Quilting Project — Ford, Joan
When Ballet Became French: Modern Ballet and the Cultural Politics of France, 1909-1939 — Karthas, Ilyana
When Biometrics Fail: Gender, Race and the Technology of Identity — Magnet, Shoshana Amielle
When Books Went to War: The Stories That Helped Us Win World War II (Read by Dunne, Bernadette). Audiobook Review — Manning, Molly Guptill
When Books Went to War: The Stories that Helped Us Win World War II — Manning, Molly Guptill
When Boys Become Boys: Development, Relationships and Masculinity — Chu, Judy Y.
When Breath Becomes Air — Kalanithi, Paul
When Bunnies Go Bad — Simon, Clea
c When Butterflies Cross the Sky: The Monarch Butterfly Migration (Illus. by Brunet, Joshua S.) — Cooper, Sharon Katz
When Camels Fly — Horton, NLB
When Christians First Met Muslims: A Sourcebook of the Earliest Syriac Writings on Islam — Penn, Michael Philip
When Clouds Fell from the Sky — Carmichael, Robert
When Colleges Sang: The Story of Singing in American College Life — Winstead, J. Lloyd
c When Dad Showed Me the Universe (Illus. by Eriksson, Eva) — Stark, Ulf
When Dreams Touch — Hanrahan, Rosemary
When Eagles Roar: The Amazing Journey of an African Wildlife Adventurer — Currie, James Alexander
y When Everything Feels Like the Movies — Reid, Raziel
When Falcons Fall — Harris, C.S.
When Fraser Met Billy: An Autistic Boy, a Rescue Cat, and the Transformative Power of Animal Connections — Booth, Louise
c When Fred the Snake Got Squished and Mended (Illus. by Lemaire, Bonnie) — Cotton, Peter B.
When Globalization Fails: The Rise and Fall of Pax Americana — Macdonald, James
When God Is a Traveller — Subramaniam, Arundhathi
When God Isn't Green: A World-Wide Journey to Places Where Religious Practice and Environmentalism Collide — Wexler, Jay
When God Spoke Greek: The Eptuagint and the Making of the Christian Bible — Law, Timothy Michael
When Good Men Die — Horn, Steven W.
When Google Met WikiLeaks — Assange, Julian
c When Grandma Saved Christmas (Illus. by Pedler, Caroline) — Hubery, Julia
c When Green Becomes Tomatoes: Poems for All Seasons (Illus. by Morstad, Julie) — Fogliano, Julie
When Helping Hurts: How to Alleviate Poverty without Hurting Poor...and Yourself — Corbett, Steve
When Hitler Took Cocaine and Lenin Lost His Brain — Milton, Giles

c When I Am Happiest (Illus. by Eriksson, Eva) — Lagercrantz, Rose
c When I Grow Up I Want to Be ... a Nurse! Amber's Accidental Journey — Wigu Publishing
c When I Grow Up I Want To Be ... a Veterinarian! — Ressler, Kim
c When I Grow Up (Illus. by Dodd, Emma) — Dodd, Emma
When I Grow Up — McLean, Gill
When I Set Myself on Fire — Singer, W.W.
y When I Was Me — Freeman, Hilary
c When I was the Greatest (Read by Adkins, J.B.). Audiobook Review — Reynolds, Jason
When I Wear My Alligator Boots: Narco-Culture in the U.S.-Mexico Borderlands — Muehlmann, Shaylih
When It Was Just a Game: Remembering the First Super Bowl — Frommer, Harvey
When It's Right — Ryan, Jennifer
When Joss Met Matt — Cahill, Ellie
y When Kacey Left — Green, Dawn
When Kids Call the Shots: How to Seize Control from Your Darling Bully--and Enjoy Being a Parent Again — Grover, Sean
c When Lunch Fights Back: Wickedly Clever Animal Defenses (Illus. by Johnson, Rebecca L.) — Johnson, Rebecca L.
c When Lyla Got Lost — Schiller, Abbie
c When Marnie Was There (Read by Duerden, Susan). Audiobook Review — Robinson, Joan G.
When Mexicans Could Play Ball: Basketball, Race, and Identity in San Antonio, 1928-1945 — Garcia, Ignacio M.
When Mexico Recaptures Texas: Essays — Boullosa, Carmen
c When Mischief Came to Town — Nannestad, Katrina
When Money Grew on Trees: A. B. Hammond and the Age of the Timber Baron — Gordon, Greg
When Money Grew on Trees: A.B. Hammond and the Age of the Timber Baron — Gordon, Greg
When Money Grew on Trees: A.B. Hammond and the Age of Timber Baron — Gordon, Greg
y When My Heart Was Wicked — Stirling, Tricia
y When on Earth? History as You've Never Seen it Before! — Houston, Rob
c When Otis Courted Mama (Illus. by McElmurry, Jill) — Appelt, Kathi
When Parents Part: How Mothers and Fathers Can Help Their Children Deal with Separation and Divorce — Leach, Penelope
When Peace Is Not Enough: How the Israeli Peace Camp Thinks about Religion, Nationalism, and Justice — Omer, Atalia
When Private Talk Goes Public: Gossip in American History — Feeley, Kathleen A.
When Rains Became Floods: A Child Soldier's Story — Gavilan Sanchez, Lurgio
y When Reason Breaks — Rodriguez, Cindy L.
When Robots Kill: Artificial Intelligence Under Criminal Law — Hallevy, Gabriel
When Saint Francis Saved the Church: How A Converted Medieval Troubadour Created a Spiritual Vision for the Ages — Sweeney, Jon M.
c When Santa Was a Baby (Illus. by Godbout, Genevieve) — Bailey, Linda
When Secrets Strike — Perry, Marta
When Soldiers Fall: How Americans Have Confronted Combat Losses from World War I to Afghanistan — Casey, Steven
When Somebody Kills You — Randisi, Robert J.
When Somebody Loves You — Jump, Shirley
c When Sophie's Feelings Are Really, Really Hurt (Illus. by Bang, Molly) — Bang, Molly
c When Spring Comes (Illus. by Dronzek, Laura) — Henkes, Kevin
When Tenants Claimed the City: The Struggle for Citizenship in New York City Housing — Gold, Roberta
c When the Anger Ogre Visits (Illus. by Salom, Ivette) — Salom, Andree
c When the Animals Saved Earth (Illus. by Demi) — Lumbard, Alexis York
When the Balls Drop — Garrett, Brad
When The Balls Drop: How I Learned to Get Real and Embrace Life's Second Half — Garrett, Brad
c When the Curtain Rises — Muller, Rachel Dunstan
When the Devil Flies — McGowan, Michael
When the Devil's Idle — Serafim, Leta
When the Diamonds Were Gone — Padowicz, Julian
When the Doves Disappeared — Oksanen, Sofi
When the Doves Disappeared — Rogers, Lola

c   When the Earth Shakes: Earthquakes, Volcanoes, and Tsunamis — Winchester, Simon
    When the Facts Change: Essays, 1995-2010 — Judt, Tony
    When the Heavens Fall — Turner, Marc
    When the Invasion of Land Failed: The Legacy of the Devonian Extinctions — McGhee, George R., Jr.
    When the Lights Went Out: Britain in the Seventies — Beckett, Andy
y   When the Moon Is Low — Hashimi, Nadia
    When the Night Comes — Parrett, Favel
    When the Professor Got Stuck in the Snow — Rhodes, Dan
y   When the River Rises (Illus. by Oliveira, Bruno) — Walker, D.C.
    When the Serpent Bites — Clerge, Nesly
    When the Sick Rule the World — Bellamy, Dodie
c   When the Slave Esperanca Garcia Wrote a Letter (Illus. by Hees, Luciana Justiniani) — Rosa, Sonia
    When the Sun Bursts: The Enigma of Schizophrenia — Bollas, Christopher
    When the Sun Danced: Myth, Miracles, and Modernity in Early Twentieth-Century Portugal — Bennett, Jeffrey S.
c   When the Sun Shines on Antarctica: And Other Poems About the Frozen Continent (Illus. by Wadham, Anna) — Latham, Irene
    When the United States Invaded Russia: Woodrow Wilson's Siberian Disaster — Richard, Carl J.
    When the United States Spoke French: Five Refugees Who Shaped a Nation — Furstenberg, Francois
c   When the Wind Blows (Illus. by Sneed, Brad) — Clark, Stacy
c   When the Wind Blows (Illus. by Christy, Jana) — Sweeney, Linda Booth
    When the Wolf Came: The Civil War and the Indian Territory — Warde, Mary Jane
    When the World Becomes Female: Guises of a South Indian Goddess — Flueckiger, Joyce Burkhalter
    When the World Breaks Open — Reza, Seema
    When These Things Begin: Conversation with Michel Treguer — Girard, Rene
    When to Hold Them — Gordon, G.B.
    When to Rob a Bank ... and 131 More Warped Suggestions and Well-Intended Rants — Levitt, Steven D.
y   When to Rob a Bankaand 131 More Warped Suggestions and Well-Intended Rants — Dubner, Stephen J.
    When Tobacco Was King: Families, Farm Labor, and Federal Policy in the Piedmont — Bennett, Evan P.
    When Washington Burned: An Illustrated History of the War of 1812 — Blumberg, Arnold
    When We Are No More: How Digital Memory Is Shaping Our Future — Rumsey, Abby Smith
    When We Fight, We Win! — Jobin-Leeds, Greg
y   When We Were Animals — Gaylord, Joshua
c   When Whales Cross the Sea: The Grey Whale Migration (Illus. by Leonard, Tom) — Cooper, Sharon Katz
    When Women Win — Malcolm, Ellen R.
c   When You Give an Imp a Penny — Herz, Henry
c   When You Just Have to Roar! (Illus. by Prentice, Priscilla) — Robertson, Rachel
y   When You Leave — Ropal, Monica
    When You Need a Friend (Illus. by Pedler, Caroline) — Chiew, Suzanne
c   When You Were Born (Illus. by Dodd, Emma) — Dodd, Emma
c   When You Were Born — Dodd, Emma
    When Young Children Need Help: Understanding and Addressing Emotional, Behavioral, and Developmental Challenges — Hirschland, Deborah
    When Your Child Hurts: Effective Strategies to Increase Comfort, Reduce Stress, and Break the Cycle of Chronic Pain — Coakley, Rachael
    When Your Life is on Fire, What Would You Save? — Kolbell, Erik
    When Your Life Is Touched by Cancer: Practical Advice and Insights for Patients, Professionals and Those Who Care — Riter, Bob
    Whenever You Come Around — Hatcher, Robin Lee
    Where — Reed, Kit
    Where All Light Tends to Go — Joy, David
    Where Are My Books? (Illus. by Ohi, Debbie Ridpath) — Ohi, Debbie Ridpath
    Where Are the Trees Going? — Khoury-Ghata, Venus
c   Where Are You, Blue? (Illus. by Clifton-Brown, Holly) — Fry, Sonali
c   Where Bear? (Illus. by Henn, Sophy) — Henn, Sophy
    Where Chefs Eat: A Guide to Chefs' Favourite Restaurants — Warwick, Joe

c   Where Did My Clothes Come From? (Illus. by Gaggiotti, Lucia) — Butterworth, Chris
    Where Did You Sleep Last Night? — Crosbie, Lynn
c   Where Do Babies Come From? Our First Talk about Birth (Illus. by Revell, Cindy) — Roberts, Jillian
c   Where Do I End and You Begin? (Illus. by Felix, Monique) — Oppenheim, Shulamith
c   Where Do I Sleep? A Pacific Northwest Lullaby (Illus. by Gabriel, Andrea) — Blomgren, Jennifer
c   Where Does Our Food Come From? Series — Lassieur, Allison
y   Where Everybody Looks like Me: At the Crossroads of America's Black Colleges and Culture — Stodghill, Ron
y   Where Futures End — Peevyhouse, Parker
    Where Have the Dead Gone? And Other Poems — Kumar, Shiv K.
    Where Have You Been? Selected Essays — Hofmann, Michael
c   Where I Belong — Hahn, Mary
y   Where I Belong — White, Tara
    Where I Lost Her — Greenwood, T.
    Where I Stand: On the Signing Community and My DeafBlind Experience — Clark, John Lee
    Where I Was From — Didion, Joan
    Where I'm Reading From: The Changing World of Books — Parks, Tim
c   Where Is Fluffy? (Illus. by Ho, Jannie) — Bulion, Leslie
c   Where Is Galah? — Morgan, Sally
c   Where Is Jumper? (Illus. by Walsh, Ellen Stoll) — Walsh, Ellen Stoll
    Where Is Mount Rushmore? (Illus. by Hinderliter, John) — Kelley, True
y   Where Is Pidge? (Illus. by DeOre, Bill) — Grimes, Michelle
c   Where Is Pim? (Illus. by Landstrom, Olof) — Landstrom, Lena
c   Where Is Pim? (Illus. by Landstrom, Olof) — Marshall, Julia
c   Where Is Rusty? (Illus. by Posthuma, Sieb) — Posthuma, Sieb
    Where Is the Grand Canyon? (Illus. by Colon, Daniel) — O'Connor, Jim
c   Where Is the Great Wall? (Illus. by Hoare, Jerry) — Demuth, Patricia Brennan
c   Where Is the Rocket? — Ziefert, Harriet
c   Where Is the White House? (Illus. by Groff, David) — Stine, Megan
    Where It Hurts — Coleman, Reed Farrel
c   Where My Feet Go — Sif, Birgitta
    Where My Heart Used to Beat — Faulks, Sebastian
c   Where, Oh Where, Is Rosie's Chick? — Hutchins, Pat
    Where Pigeons Don't Fly — Al-Mohaimeed, Yousef
    Where Rivers Part — Gilbert, Kellie Coates
    Where Secrets Sleep — Perry, Marta
    Where Shadows Linger — Brooks, Mary D.
    Where the Bird Sings Best — Jodorowsky, Alejandro
    Where the Bodies Were Buried: Whitey Bulger and the World That Made Him — English, T.J.
    Where the Bones of a Buried Rat Lie — Ekemar, Kim
c   Where the Bugaboo Lives (Illus. by Layton, Neal) — Taylor, Sean (b. 1965-)
    Where the Cherry Tree Grew: The Story of Ferry Farm, George Washington's Boyhood Home — Levy, Philip
    Where the Dead Pause, and the Japanese Say Goodbye — Mockett, Marie Mutsuki
    Where the Negroes are Masters: An African Port in the Era of the Slave Trade — Sparks, Randy J.
    Where the Red Fern Grows — Rawls, Wilson
    Where the River Ends: Contested Indigeneity in the Mexican Colorado Delta — Muehlmann, Shaylih
    Where the Staircase Ends — Stokes, Stacy A.
y   Where the Words End and My Body Begins — Dawn, Amber
    Where They Found Her — McCreight, Kimberly
c   Where Triplets Go, Trouble Follows (Illus. by Jamieson, Victoria) — Poploff, Michelle
    Where We Belong — Kotb, Hoda
    Where We Want to Live: Reclaiming Infrastructure for a New Generation of Cities — Gravel, Ryan
    Where Women Are Kings — Watson, Christie
    Where Women Are Kings — Watson, Christine
    Where You Are: A Book of Maps That Will Leave You Completely Lost — Aridjis, Chloe
y   Where You End — Pellicioli, Anna
y   Where You Go Is Not Who You'll Be: An Antidote to the College Admissions Mania — Bruni, Frank
y   Where You'll Find Me — Friend, Natasha
    Where'd You Get Those? New York City's Sneaker Culture, 1960-1987 — Garcia, Bobbito

c   Where's Glimmer? (Illus. by Ying, Victoria) — Burkhart, Jessica
c   Where's My Fnurgle? — Benton, Jim
c   Where's Santa? (Illus. by Whelon, Chuck) — Jones, Bryony
    Where's Stephanie? A Story of Love, Faith, and Courage — Livingston, Lenora
c   Where's the Baboon? (Illus. by Di Giacomo, Kris) — Escoffier, Michael
c   Where's the Baboon? (Illus. by Giacomo, Kris Di) — Escoffier, Michael
c   Where's the Elephant? — Barroux
c   Where's the Fairy? (Illus. by Harris, Nick) — Moseley, Keith
c   Where's the Pair? A Spotting Book — Teckentrup, Britta
c   Where's the Pair? (Illus. by Teckentrup, Britta) — Teckentrup, Britta
c   Where's Walrus? And Penguin? (Illus. by Savage, Stephen) — Savage, Stephen
    Wherever There Is Light — Golden, Peter
c   Wherever We Go! (Illus. by Lumer, Marc) — Altein, Chani
c   Wherever You Go — Miller, Pat Zietlow
c   Wherever You Go (Illus. by Wheeler, Eliza) — Miller, Pat Zietlow
c   Which Endangered Animal Lives in Mongolia? (Illus. by Smith, Dawn) — Tulip, Jenny
    Which Sin to Bear? Authenticity and Compromise in Langston Hughes — Chinitz, David E.
    Which Way Did She Go? — Perkovich, Beth
c   Which Way to Freedom? And Other Questions about the Underground Railroad — Carson, Mary Kay
c   Whiffy Wilson The Wolf Who Wouldn't Go to School (Illus. by Lord, Leonie) — Hart, Caryl
    While Glaciers Slept: Being Human in a Time of Climate Change — Jackson, M.
    While the City Slept: A Love Lost to Violence and a Young Man's Descent into Madness — Sanders, Eli
    While the Gods Were Sleeping — Mortier, Erwin
y   While You Were Gone — Nichols, Amy K.
c   While You Were Napping (Illus. by Blitt, Barry) — Offill, Jenny
    Whipping Boy: The Forty-Year Search for My Twelve-Year-Old Bully — Kurzweil, Allen
y   Whippoorwill — Monninger, Joseph
    Whirlgig — Macintyre, Magnus
    Whirligig — Macintyre, Magnus
    Whirlwind: The American Revolution and the War That Won It — Ferling, John
    Whiskers of the Lion — Gaus, Paul L.
    Whiskey and Charlie — Smith, Annabel
    The Whiskey Baron — Sealy, Jon
    Whiskey Bottles and Brand-New Cars: The Fast Life and Sudden Death of Lynyrd Skynyrd — Ribowsky, Mark
    Whiskey Cocktails: Rediscovered Classics and Contemporary Craft Drinks Using the World's Most Popular Spirit — Bobrow, Warren
    Whiskey Tango Foxtrot — Shafer, David
    Whiskey: What to Drink Next: Craft Whiskeys, Classic Flavors, New Distilleries, Future Trends — Roskrow, Dominic
c   The Whisper (Read by Halstead, Graham). Audiobook Review — Starmer, Aaron
y   The Whisper — Starmer, Aaron
c   The Whisper (Illus. by Zagarenski, Pamela) — Zagarenski, Pamela
    Whisper Beach — Noble, Shelley
y   The Whisper — Clayton, Emma
    Whisper Hollow — Cander, Chris
y   Whisper — Keighery, Chrissie
c   A Whisper of Wolves — Humphrey, Kris
y   Whisper the Dead — Harvey, Alyxandra
c   Whisper, Whisper: Learning about Church (Illus. by Aviles, Martha) — Moerbe, Mary J.
    Whispered Words — Ikeda, Takashi
y   The Whisperer — McIntosh, Fiona
    The Whispering City — Moliner, Sara
    Whispering Shadows — Sendker, Jan-Philipp
c   The Whispering Skull (Read by Lyons, Katie). Audiobook Review — Stroud, Jonathan
c   The Whispering Skull — Stroud, Jonathan
    The Whispering Swarm — Moorcock, Michael
c   The Whispering Town (Read by Cottle, Elizabeth). Audiobook Review — Elvgren, Jennifer
    The Whispering Voice — Oby, Maduka Sunny
    Whispers from Eternity — Buchmann, Jacinda
    Whispers in the Reading Room — Gray, Shelley
    The Whispers of Cities: Information Flows in Istanbul, London, and Paris in the Age of William Trumbull — Ghobrial, John-Paul A.

c Whispers of the Wolf (Illus. by Ts'o, Pauline) — Ts'o, Pauline
y Whistle-Blowers: Exposing Crime and Corruption — Doeden, Matt
Whistle Stop — White, Philip
Whistleblower — Gerritsen, Tess
The Whistleblower's Dilemma: Snowden, Silkwood and Their Quest for the Truth — Rashke, Richard
c Whistling in the Dark — Hughes, Shirley
c Whistling Willie from Amarillo, Texas (Illus. by Harrington, David) — Harper, Josephine
Whistling Women — Romo, Kelly A.
c Whit the Clockleddy Heard: What the Ladybird Heard in Scots — Donaldson, Julia
c White Animals — Borth, Teddy
White Backlash — Abrajano, Marisa
c The White Book (Illus. by Borando, Silvia) — Borando, Silvia
c A White Butterfly (Illus. by Ortelli, Barbara) — Cohen, Laurie
c A White Butterfly (Illus. by Ortelli, Barbara) — Cohen, Laurie (b. 1988-)
White City, Black City: Architecture and War in Tel Aviv and Jaffa — Rotbard, Sharon
White Collar Girl — Rosen, Renee
White Crocodile — Medina, K.T.
White Devil: The True Story of the First White Asian Crime Boss — Halloran, Bob
White Dresses — Peterson, Mary Pflum
White Elephants on Campus: The Decline of the University Chapel in America, 1920-1960 — Grubiak, Margaret M.
White Elephants on Campus: The Decline of the University Chapel in America, 1920-1960 — Molina, Natalia
White Eskimo: Knud Rasmussen's Fearless Journey into the Heart of the Arctic — Bown, Stephen R.
White Gardenia — Alexandra, Belinda
The White Ghost — Benn, James R.
White Ghost — Benn, James R.
The White Ghost — Benn, James R.
y White Hat Hacking — Smith, Jonathan
c The White House Is Burning: August 24, 1814 — Sutcliffe, Jane
c The White House — Sabuda, Robert
White Hunger — Ollikainen, Aki
White Leopard — Guillaume, Laurent
White Light — Garcia, Vanessa
White Lines III: All Falls Down — Brown, Tracy (b. 1974-)
White Lotus Rebels and South China Pirates: Crisis and Reform in the Qing Empire — Wang, Wensheng
White Lotus Rebels and South China Pirates: Crisis and Reform in the Qing Empire — Wensheng, Wang
White Magic: The Age of Paper — Muller, Lothar
White Magic: The Age of Paper — Spengler, Jessica
White Man, Yellow Man: Two Novellas — Endo, Shusaku
The White Mouse: The Story of Nancy Wake — Gouldthorpe, Peter
The White Nile Diaries — Hopkins, John
White Parents, Black Children: Experiencing Transracial Adoption — Smith, Darron T.
White Plague (Read by Porter, Ray). Audiobook Review — Abel, James
White Race Discourse: Preserving Racial Privilege in a Post-Racial Society — Foster, John D.
The White Road: A Pilgrimage of Sorts — de Waal, Edmund
The White Road: Journey into an Obsession — de Waal, Edmund
The White Road — de Waal, Edmund
White Robes and Burning Crosses: A History of the Ku Klux Klan from 1866 — Newton, Michael
y The White Rose — Ewing, Amy
y The White Rose: Jewel, Book 2 — Ewing, Amy
White Sails — Yu Huang, Ann
The White Savior Film: Content, Critics, and Consumption — Hughey, Matthew W.
The White Sea — Johnston, Paul
The White Shepherd — Dalton, Annie
c White Space (Read by McInerney, Kathleen). Audiobook Review — Bick, Ilsa J.
y White Space — Bick, Ilsa J.
c The White Umbrella (Illus. by Lasson, Sally Ann) — Sewell, Brian
White Walls: A Memoir about Motherhood, Daughterhood, and the Mess in Between — Batalion, Judy
y Whitebeam — del Mara, K.M.

The Whites — Brandt, Harry
The Whites — Price, Richard
The Whites (Read by Fliakos, Ari). Audiobook Review — Brandt, Harry
The Whites — Brandt, Harry
Whitewash — Gordon, Stan
Whither the Child?: Causes and Consequences of Low Fertility — Kaufmann, Eric
Whither the World: The Political Economy of the Future, Volume I — Kolodko, Grzegorz
Whither the World: The Political Economy of the Future, Volume II — Kolodko, Grzegorz
Whiting Up: Whiteface Minstrels and Stage Europeans in African American Performance — McAllister, Marvin
c Who Built That? Modern Houses: An Introduction to Modern Houses and Their Architects — Cornille, Didier
c Who Built That? Skyscrapers: An Introduction to Skyscrapers and Their Architects — Cornille, Didier
Who Buries the Dead — Harris, C.S.
Who Can Afford to Improvise? James Baldwin and Black Music, the Lyric and the Listeners — Pavlic, Ed
Who Cares? Public Ambivalence and Government Activism from the New Deal to the Second Gilded Age — Newman, Kathryn
Who Cooked Adam Smith's Dinner? — Marcal, Katrine
Who Did It First? Great Pop Cover Songs and Their Original Artists — Leszczak, Bob
Who Died — Barbour, Kathryn
Who Do People Say I Am? Rewriting Gospel in Emerging Christianity — Robbins, Vernon K.
y Who Do You Love — Weiner, Jennifer
c Who Done It? (Illus. by Tallec, Olivier) — Tallec, Olivier
c Who Eats First? (Illus. by Yang, Hae-won) — Yoon, Ae-hae
c Who Flies, Cat the Cat? (Illus. by Willems, Mo) — Willems, Mo
Who Freed the Slaves? — Richards, Leonard
Who Gets What--and Why: The New Economics of Matchmaking and Market Design (Read by Berkrot, Peter). Audiobook Review — Roth, Alvin E.
Who Gets What--and Why: The New Economics of Matchmaking and Market Design — Roth, Alvin E.
Who Governs Britain? — King, Anthony
c Who Handles Retruns? And, Maybe Repayment? (Illus. by Scratchmann, Max) — Gherghel, Daniela
Who Is Allah? — Lawrence, Bruce B.
Who Is Charlie? Xenophobia and the New Middle Class — Todd, Emmanuel
c Who Is Happy? (Illus. by Jarvis) — Jarvis
c Who Is King? Ten Magical Stories from Africa (Illus. by Grobler, Piet) — Naidoo, Beverley
y Who Is Mackie Spence? — Kaymer, Lin
Who Is Martha? — Gaponenko, Marjana
Who Is the Church? An Ecclesiology for the Twenty-First Century — Peterson, Cheryl
Who Let the Dog Out? — Rosenfelt, David
Who Made Early Christianity? The Jewish Lives of the Apostle Paul — Gager, John G.
y Who Needs a Bath? (Illus. by Mack, Jeff) — Mack, Jeff
Who Owns America's Past? The Smithsonian and the Problem of History — Post, Robert C.
y Who R U Really? — Kelly, Margo
Who Rules Japan? Popular Participation in the Japanese Legal Process — Nottage, Luke
Who Rules the Earth?: How Social Rules Shape Our Planet and Our Lives — Steinberg, Paul F.
Who Should Sing Ol' Man River: The Lives of an American Song — Decker, Tod
c Who Sleeps, Cat the Cat? (Illus. by Willems, Mo) — Willems, Mo
c Who Stole Uncle Sam? — Freeman, Martha
c Who Wants a Hug? (Illus. by Mack, Jeff) — Mack, Jeff
c Who Wants Broccoli? (Illus. by Jones, Val) — Jones, Val
Who Wants to be a Batsman? The Analyst Unveils the Secrets of Batting — Hughes, Simon
c Who Was Here? Discovering Wild Animal Tracks (Illus. by Posada, Mia) — Posada, Mia
c Who We Are!: All About Being the Same and Being Different (Illus. by Westcott, Nadine Bernard) — Harris, Robie H.
Who We Be: The Colorization of America — Chang, Jeff

Who Will Die Last — Ehrlich, David
c Who Woke the Baby? (Illus. by Fuge, Charles) — Clarke, Jane
The Whole and Rain-Domed Universe — Bryce, Colette
The Whole Enchilada: Fresh and Nutritious Southwestern Cuisine — LaRue, Angelina
The Whole Harmonium: The Life of Wallace Stevens — Mariani, Paul
The Whole Library Handbook: Teen Services — Booth, Heather
The Whole Life Fertility Plan: Understanding What Affects Your Fertility to Help You Get Pregnant When You Want To — Phillips, Kyra
A Whole Life — Seethaler, Robert
c A Whole New Ballgame (Illus. by Probert, Tim) — Bildner, Phil
y A Whole New World: A Twisted Tale — Braswell, Liz
y A Whole New World — Braswell, Liz
c Whoops! (Illus. by Ayto, Russell) — Moore, Suzi
Whore — Arcan, Nelly
Who's Afraid of Academic Freedom? — Bilgrami, Akeel
Who's Afraid of Academic Freedom? — Cole, Jonathan R.
Who's Afraid of Meryl Streep? — Daif, Rashid al-
Who's Afraid of Relativism? Community, Contingency, and Creaturehood — Smith, James K.A.
y Who's Afraid of the Big Bad Dragon: Why China Has the Best (and Worst) Education System in the World — Zhao, Yong
c Who's Coming Tonight? (Illus. by Gang, Minjeong) — Choi, Jeonglm
Who's Going to Watch My Kids? Working Mothers' Humorous and Heartfelt Struggles to Find and Hold on to the Elusive Perfect Nanny — Lesser, Rachel Levy
Who's Got Time? Spirituality for a Busy Generation — Peterson, Teri
c Who's Hiding? — Baruzzi, Agnese
c Who's Hungry? (Illus. by Scharschmidt, Sherry) — Hacohen, Dean
y Who's Ju? — Ramos, Dania
c Who's Next Door? (Illus. by Takabakate, Jun) — Kishira, Mayuko
Who's the New Kid? — Bond, Heidi
c Who's There? Beware! (Illus. by Truong, Tom) — Hegarty, Patricia
c Who's There? — Crozon, Alain
Who's Who in Thomas Hardy — Rahane, Huw Barker
Who's Your Paddy? Racial Expectations and the Struggle for Irish American Identity — Duffy, Jennifer Nugent
c Whose Eye Am I? (Illus. by Rotner, Shelley) — Rotner, Shelley
Whose Flesh Is Flame, Whose Bone Is Time — Pelizzon, V. Penelope
c Whose Hands Are These? — Paul, Miranda
c Whose Shoe? (Illus. by Ruzzier, Sergio) — Bunting, Eve
c Whose Tools? (Illus. by Datz, Jim) — Buzzeo, Toni
c Whose Tools? (Illus. by Datz, Jim)
c Whose Truck? (Illus. by Datz, Jim) — Buzzeo, Toni
c Why? (Illus. by Warnes, Tim) — Corderoy, Tracey
Why Acting Matters — Thomson, David
Why America Misunderstands the World — Pillar, Paul R.
c Why and Where Are Animals Endangered? — Kalman, Bobbie
Why Are Professors Liberal and Why Do Conservatives Care? — Gross, Neil
c Why Are There Stripes on the American Flag? (Illus. by Poling, Kyle) — Rustad, Martha E.H.
Why Are We Waiting? The Logic, Urgency, and Promise of Tackling Climate Change — Stern, Nicholas
Why Are Women More Religious Than Men? — Trzebiatowska, Marta
Why Australia Prospered: The Shifting Sources of Economic Growth — McLean, Ian W.
Why Be Afraid? — McManaman, Doug
Why Be Happy When You Could Be Normal? — Winterson, Jeanette
Why Be Jewish? — Bronfman, Edgar M.
Why Believe the Bible? — MacArthur, John
Why Can the Dead Do Such Great Things? Saints and Worshippers from the Martyrs to the Reformation — Bartlett, Robert
Why Communism Did Not Collapse: Understanding Authoritarian Regime Resilience in Asia and Europe — Dimitrov, Martin K.

c Why Couldn't Susan B. Anthony Vote? And Other Questions about Women's Suffrage — *Carson, Mary Kay*
Why Did Europe Conquer the World? — *Hoffman, Philip T.*
c Why Did T. Rex Have Short Arms?: And Other Questions about Dinosaurs — *Stewart, Melissa*
Why Did the Chicken Cross the World? The Epic Saga of the Bird That Powers Civilization — *Lawler, Andrew*
c Why Do I Burp? — *Kolpin, Molly*
c Why Do I Hiccup? — *Kolpin, Molly*
c Why Do I Sing? Animal Songs of the Pacific Northwest (Illus. by Gabriel, Andrea) — *Blomgren, Jennifer*
Why Do Monkeys and Other Animals Have Fur? — *Beaumont, Holly*
c Why Do Tractors Have Such Big Tires? (Illus. by Fabbri, Daniele) — *Shand, Jennifer*
c Why Dogs Have Wet Noses (Illus. by Torseter, Oyvind) — *Steven, Kenneth*
Why God Is a Woman — *Andrews, Nin*
Why, God? Suffering through Cancer into Faith — *Cupit, Margaret Caslisle*
Why "Good Kids" Turn into Deadly Terrorists: Deconstructing the Accused Boston Marathon Bombers and Others Like Them — *LoCicero, Alice*
Why Government Fails so Often: And How It Can Do Better — *Schuck, Peter H.*
Why Grow Up? Subversive Thoughts for an Infantile Age — *Neiman, Susan*
Why I Am a Salafi — *Knight, Michael Muhammad*
Why I Live Where I Live — *Welty, Eudora*
c Why I Love Footy (Illus. by Jellett, Tom) — *Wagner, Michael*
c Why I Love My Dad (Illus. by Geddes, Serena) — *Reynolds, Alison*
c Why I Love Nova Scotia — *Howarth, Daniel*
Why I Read: The Serious Pleasure of Books — *Lesser, Wendy*
Why Information Grows: The Evolution of Order, from Atoms to Economies — *Hidalgo, Cesar*
Why Is Mid-Life Mooching Your Mojo? Solutions to Banish Fuzziness and Fatigue Forever! — *Labbe, Joni*
c Why Is the Sea Salty?: And Other Questions About Oceans — *Richmond, Benjamin*
c Why Is the Statue of Liberty Green? (Illus. by Conger, Holli) — *Rustad, Martha E.H.*
y Why Is This Night Different from All Other Nights? (Read by Aiken, Liam). Audiobook Review — *Snicket, Lemony*
'Why Is Your Axe Bloody?': A Reading of Njal's Saga — *Miller, William Ian*
Why Jazz Happened — *Myers, Marc*
c Why Johnny Doesn't Flap: NT is OK! — *Morton, Clay*
Why Kids Make You Fat ... And How to Get Your Body Back — *Macdonald, Mark*
Why Liberals Win the Culture Wars (Even When They Lose Elections): The Battles That Define America from Jefferson's Heresies to Gay Marriage — *Prothero, Stephen*
Why Look at Animals? — *Berger, John*
Why Mars: NASA and the Politics of Space Exploration — *Lambright, W. Henry*
Why Motivating People Doesn't Work...and What Does: The New Science of Leading, Energizing and Engaging — *Fowler, Susan*
Why Music Matters — *Hesmondhalgh, David*
Why Not Capitalism? — *Brennan, Jason*
Why Not? Conquering The Road Less Traveled — *Brown, John*
Why Not Me? (Read by Kaling, Mindy). Audiobook Review — *Kaling, Mindy*
Why Not Say What Happened: A Sentimental Education — *Dickstein, Morris*
Why on Earth Would Anyone Build That: Modern Architecture Explained — *Zukowsky, John*
Why Place Matters: Geography, Identity, and Civic Life in Modern America — *McClay, Wilfred M.*
Why Race and Culture Matters in Schools: Closing the Achievement Gap in America's Classrooms — *Howard, Tyrone C.*
Why Religion Is Natural and Science Is Not — *McCauley, Robert N.*
Why South Vietnam Fell — *Joes, Anthony James*
Why Spy? The Art of Intelligence — *Stewart, Brian*
Why States Recover: Changing Walking Societies into Winning Nations, from Afghanistan to Zimbabwe — *Mills, Greg*

Why Taiwan? Geostrategic Rationales for China's Territorial Integrity — *Wachman, Alan M.*
Why the Germans? Why the Jews? Envy, Race Hatred, and the Prehistory of the Holocaust — *Aly, Gotz*
Why the Right Went Wrong: Conservatism--from Goldwater to the Tea Party and Beyond — *Dionne Jr., E.J.*
Why the Romantics Matter — *Gay, Peter*
Why the Social Sciences Matter — *Michie, Jonathan*
Why the West Fears Islam: An Exploration of Muslims in Liberal Democracies — *Cesari, Jocelyne*
Why the World Does Not Exist — *Gabriel, Markus*
Why Therapy Works: Using Our Minds to Change Our Brains — *Cozolino, Louis*
Why They Run the Way They Do — *Perabo, Susan*
Why This Jubilee? Advent Reflections on Songs of the Seasons — *Howell, James C.*
Why Torture Doesn't Work: The Neuroscience of Interrogation — *O'Mara, Shane*
Why Walls Won't Work: Repairing the US-Mexico Divide — *Dear, Michael*
Why We Bite the Invisible Hand — *Foster, Peter*
Why We Came to the City — *Jansma, Kristopher*
Why We Can't Afford the Rich — *Sayer, Andrew*
Why We Make Things and Why It Matters: The Education of a Craftsman — *Korn, Peter*
Why We Snap: Understanding the Rage Circuit in Your Brain — *Fields, R. Douglas*
Why We Work — *Schwartz, Barry*
Why We Write About Ourselves: Twenty Memoirists on Why They Expose Themselves (and Others) in the Name of Literature — *Maran, Meredith*
Why You Can Build it Like That: Modern Architecture Explained — *Zukowsky, John*
y Why'd They Wear That? — *Albee, Sarah*
y The Wicked Awakening of Anne Merchant — *Wiebe, Joanna*
c Wicked Games — *Olin, Sean*
Wicked Lies — *Leigh, Lora*
Wicked, My Love — *Ives, Susanna*
Wicked Release — *Collins, Katana*
Wicked Sexy Liar — *Lauren, Christina*
Wicked Temper — *Thornhorn, Randy*
The Wicked + The Divine, vol. 1: The Faust Act — *Gillan, Kieron*
y A Wicked Thing — *Thomas, Rhiannon*
c The Wicked Tricks of Till Owlyglass (Illus. by Wenger, Fritz) — *Rosen, Michael*
A Wicked Way to Win an Earl — *Bradley, Anna*
y The Wicked Will Rise — *Paige, Danielle*
Wickedly Powerful — *Blake, Deborah*
Wide Awake in Slumberland: Fantasy, Mass Culture, and Modernism in the Art of Winsor McCay — *Roeder, Katherine*
Wide Rivers Crossed: The South Platte and Illinois of the American Prairie — *Wohl, Ellen*
Wide Welcome: How the Unsettling Presence of Newcomers Can Save the Church — *Duckworth, Jessicah Krey*
Widerstand, Repression und Verfolgung: Beitrage zur Geschichte des Nationalsozialismus an der Saar — *Herrmann, Hans-Christian*
Widerstand und Auswartiges Amt. Diplomaten gegen Hitler — *Schulte, Jan Erik*
Widgets: The 12 New Rules for Managing Your Employees As If They're Real People — *Wagner, Rod*
Widows and Orphans — *Arditti, Michael*
Widukind of Corvey: Deeds of the Saxons — *Bachrach, Bernard S.*
Wie Pietistisch Kann Adel Sein? Hallescher Pietismus und Adel im Langen 18. Jahrhundert. 4. Tag der Sachsen-Anhaltischen Landesgeschichte
Wiederaufnahme? Ruckkehr aus dem Exil und das Westdeutsche Musikleben nach 1945 — *Pasdzierny, Matthias*
Wiederhergestellte Synagogen. Raum - Geschichte - Wandel durch Erinnerung
Wien in der Weltwirtschaft: Die Positionsbestimmung der Stadtregion Wien in der Internationalen Stadtehierarchie — *Musil, Robert*
y Wiesel, Wiesenthal, Klarsfeld: The Holocaust Survivors — *Yeatts, Tabatha*
Wife of the Deceased: A Memoir of Love, Loss, and Learning to Live Again — *Bell, Dawn M.*
c Wiggle Waggle Woof 1, 2, 3: A Counting Book — *Stihler, Cherie B.*
Wiki at War: Conflict in a Socially Networked World — *Carafano, James Jay*
The WikiLeaks Files — *WikiLeaks*

Wikipedia and the Politics of Openness — *Tkacz, Nathaniel*
Wikipedia U: Knowledge, Authority and Liberal Education in the Digital Age — *Leitch, Thomas*
Wil Usdi: Thoughts from the Asylum — *Conley, Robert J.*
y Wilberforce — *Cross, H.S.*
Wilber's War — *Bradt, Hale*
y Wild — *Mallory, Alex*
c Wild About Bears (Illus. by Brett, Jeannie) — *Brett, Jeannie*
c Wild About Shapes — *Fischer, Jeremie*
Wild about the Wrangler — *Thompson, Vicki Lewis*
c Wild about Us! (Illus. by Stevens, Janet) — *Beaumont, Karen*
c Wild About Wheels — *Clay, Kathryn*
c Wild Adventures: Look, Make, Explore--in Nature's Playground (Illus. by Manning, Mick) — *Manning, Mick*
c Wild Adventures (Illus. by Manning, Mick) — *Granstrom, Brita*
Wild Animal Skins in Victorian Britain: Zoos, Collections, Portraits, and Maps — *Colley, Ann C.*
c Wild Animals! (Illus. by Ryser, Nicolas) — *Richard, Laurent*
c Wild at Heart: Mustangs and the Young People Fighting to Save Them (Illus. by Farlow, Melissa) — *Farley, Terri*
Wild Bill Wellman: Hollywood Rebel — *Wellman, William, Jr.*
y Wild Born (Read by Barber, Nicola). Audiobook Review — *Mull, Brandon*
y Wild Boy and the Black Terror (Read by Clamp, James). Audiobook Review — *Jones, Rob Lloyd*
y Wild Boy and the Black Terror — *Jones, Rob Lloyd*
Wild by Nature: From Siberia to Australia, Three Years Alone in the Wilderness on Foot — *Marquis, Sarah*
c Wild Cats: Around the Globe with Suki & Finch — *Murdock, Rebecca Merry*
c Wild Cats Series — *Ringstad, Arnold*
c Wild Child (Illus. by Salerno, Steven) — *Salerno, Steven*
Wild Cowboy Ways — *Brown, Carolyn*
c Wild Dolphin Rider (Illus. by Spellman, Susan) — *Donovan, Nancy*
c Wild Feelings (Illus. by Milgrim, David) — *Milgrim, David*
Wild Frenchmen and Frenchified Indians: Material Culture and Race in Colonial Louisiana — *White, Sophie*
Wild Game — *Davis, Blayne*
The Wild Girl — *Forsyth, Kate*
Wild Gourmet: Naturally Healthy Game, Fish and Fowl Recipes for Everyday Chefs — *Nelson, Daniel*
Wild Gourmet — *Chiarello, Michael*
Wild Grass on the Riverbank — *Angles, Jeffrey*
y Wild Hearts — *Burkhart, Jessica*
Wild Heat — *Monroe, Lucy*
c Wild Horses — *Turnbull, Stephanie*
Wild Horses — *Daniels, B.J.*
Wild Hundreds — *Marshall, Nate*
Wild Idea: Buffalo and Family in a Difficult Land — *O'Brien, Dan*
c Wild Ideas: Let Nature Inspire Your Thinking (Illus. by Kim, Soyeon) — *Kelsey, Elin*
Wild in the Hollow — *Haines, Amber C.*
The Wild Inside — *Carbo, Christine*
Wild Justice — *McCormac, P.*
c The Wild Life of Bears — *de la Bedoyere, Camilla*
c The Wild Life of Lizards — *de la Bedoyere, Camilla*
c The Wild Life of Owls — *de la Bedoyere, Camilla*
c The Wild Life of Sharks — *de la Bedoyere, Camilla*
Wild Life: The Institution of Nature — *Braverman, Irus*
Wild Man from Borneo: A Cultural History of the Orangutan — *Cribb, Robert*
The Wild Oats Project: One Woman's Midlife Quest for Passion at Any Cost — *Rinaldi, Robin*
The Wild One — *Burgess, Gemma*
c The Wild Ones — *London, C. Alexander*
c Wild Ones: Critters in the City (Illus. by Morrison, Cathy) — *Malnor, Carol L.*
y The Wild Piano (Illus. by Kutner, Richard) — *Fred*
Wild Ran the Rivers — *Crownover, James D.*
Wild Religion: Tracking the Sacred in South Africa — *Chidester, David*
c A Wild Ride on the Water Cycle (Illus. by Guillory, Mike) — *Yanez, Anthony*
Wild Rose — *Sun Yu*

y Wild Rover No More: Being the Last Recorded Account of the Life and Times of Jacky Faber — Meyer, L.A.
Wild Rover No More: Being the Last Recorded Account of the Life & Times of Jacky Faber (Read by Kellgren, Katherine). Audiobook Review — Meyer, L.A.
y Wild Sky — Brockmann, Suzanne
y A Wild Swan and Other Tales (Illus. by Shimizu, Yuko) — Cunningham, Michael
y Wild Things! Acts of Mischief in Children's Literature — Bird, Betsy
Wild Tongues: Transnational Mexican Popular Culture — Urquijo-Ruiz, Rita E.
c Wild Water Magic (Illus. by Dorman, Brandon) — Jonell, Lynne
Wild West Detective — Clay, James
c The Wild West: Native Peoples — Nolan, Frederick
Wild Wood — Graeme-Evans, Posie
Wildalone — Zourkova, Krassi
y Wildboy: An Epic Trek Around the Coast of New Zealand — Yelavich, Brando
Wildcat Currency: How the Virtual Money Revolution Is Transforming the Economy — Castronova, Edward
Wilde in America: Oscar Wilde and the Invention of Modern Celebrity — Friedman, David M.
Wilde Stories — Berman, Steve
c Wilder Boys — Wallace, Brandon
A Wilder Rose (Read by Kowal, Mary Robinette). Audiobook Review — Albert, Susan Wittig
Wilderburbs: Communities on Nature's Edge — Bramwell, Lincoln
Wilderburbs: Communities on Nature's Edge — Cronon, William
Wilderness — Weller, Lance
The Wilderness — Lim, Sandra
Wilderness and Waterpower: How Banff National Park Became a Hydro-Electric Storage Reservoir — Armstrong, Christopher
The Wilderness: Deep Inside the Republican Party's Combative, Contentious, Chaotic Quest to Take Back the White House — Coppins, McKay
A Wilderness of Mirrors: Trusting Again in a Cynical World — Meynell, Mark
The Wilderness of Ruin: A Tale of Madness, Boston's Great Fire, and the Hunt for America's Youngest Serial Killer — Montillo, Rosearme
The Wilderness of Ruin: A Tale of Madness, Fire and the Hunt for America's Youngest Serial Killer (Read by Zeller, Emily Woo). Audiobook Review — Montillo, Roseanne
The Wilderness of Ruin: A Tale of Madness, Fire, and the Hunt for America's Youngest Serial Killer — Montillo, Roseanne
The Wilderness of Ruin — Montillo, Roseanne
The Wilderness of the Upper Yukon — Sheldon, Charles
Wilderness Rising — Shields, A.L.
Wilde's Women: How Oscar Wilde Was Shaped by the Women of His Life — Fitzsimons, Eleanor
Wildest Dreams — Carr, Robyn
c The Wildest Race Ever: The Story of the 1904 Olympic Marathon (Illus. by McCarthy, Meghan) — McCarthy, Meghan
Wildfire in His Arms (Read by Branson, Ted). Audiobook Review — Lindsey, Johanna
y Wildflower — Barrymore, Drew
y Wildflower — Whitaker, Alecia
The Wilding Eye — Byard, Olivia
y Wildlife — Wood, Fiona
Wildlife, Conservation, and Conflict in Quebec, 1840-1914 — Ingram, Darcy
Wildlife Conservation on Framland — Macdonald, David W.
Wildlife in the Anthropocene — Lorimer, Jamie
Wildlife Management and Conservation: Contemporary Principles and Practices — Krausman, Paul R.
c Wildlife of the World — Wilson, Don E.
y Wilds of the Wolf — Backshall, Steve
The Wilds — Elliott, Julia
The Wiley-Blackwell Handbook of the Psychology of Coaching and Mentoring — Passmore, Jonathan
The Wiley Kids in the Adventure of Cottonwood Canyon. E-book Review — Wiley Kids
c Wilf the Mighty Worrier: Saves the World (Illus. by Littler, Jamie) — Pritchett, Georgia
Wilfrid: Abbot, Bishop, Saint: Papers from the 1300th Anniversary Conferences — Higham, N.J.
Wilhelm II: Into the Abyss of War and Exile, 1900-41 — Rohl, John

Wilhelm Lohe: Theologie und Geschichte — Blaufuss, Dietrich
Wilkie Collins: A Brief Life — Ackroyd, Peter
Will Africa Feed China? — Brautigam, Deborah
Will Bonsall's Essential Guide to Radical, Self-Reliant Gardening — Bonsall, Will
Will College Pay Off? A Guide to the Most Important Financial Decision You'll Ever Make (Read by Perkins, Tom). Audiobook Review — Cappelli, Peter
Will College Pay Off? A Guide to the Most Important Financial Decision You'll Ever Make — Cappelli, Peter
Will Eisner: A Spirited Life — Andelman, Bob
y Will Poole's Island — Weed, Tim
A Will to Believe: Shakespeare and Religion — Kastan, David Scott
y Willa Cather and Westward Expansion — Clinton, Greg
c Willamina Mermaid & the Quest for the Crystal of Light — Kelly, J.A.
Willard Boepple Sculpture: The Sense of Things — Wilkin, Karen
Willful Disregard — Anderson, Lena
Willful Disregard — Andersson, Lena
y Willful Machines — Floreen, Tim
William Beckford: First Prime Minister of the London Empire — Gauci, Perry
William Blake and the Productions of Time — Cooper, Andrew M.
William Blake: The Drawings for Dante's Divine Comedy — Schutze, Sebastian
William Cameron Menzies: The Shape of Films to Come — Curtis, James
c William Caxton and Tim Berners-Lee — Hunter, Nick
William Cobbett, the Press and Rural England: Radicalism and the Fourth Estate, 1792-1835 — Grande, James
William Faulkner in Context — Matthews, John T.
William Gladstone: New Studies and Perspectives — Quinault, Roland
William Howard Taft: The Travails of a Progressive Conservative — Lurie, Jonathan
c The William Hoy Story: How a Deaf Baseball Player Changed the Game (Illus. by Tuya, Jez) — Churnin, Nancy
William III and Mary II: Partners in Revolution — Keates, Jonathan
William James and the Transatlantic Conversation: Pragmatism, Pluralism, and Philosophy of Religion — Halliwell, Martin
c William Kidd — Derovan, David
William Lloyd Garrison and Giuseppe Mazzini: Abolition, Democracy, and Radical Reform — Dal Lago, Enrico
William Perkins and the Making of a Protestant England — Patterson, W.B.
c William Shakespeare (Illus. by Imsand, Marcel) — Fandel, Jennifer
y William Shakespeare: Scenes from the Life of the World's Greatest Writer (Illus. by Manning, Mick) — Manning, Mick
c William Shakespeare's Star Wars Collection (Read by Various readers). Audiobook Review — Doescher, Ian
William Shakespeare's Star Wars: William Shakespeare's Star Wars, William Shakespeare's The Empire Striketh Back, and William Shakespeare's The Jedi Doth Return (Read by Davis, Daniel). Audiobook Review — Doescher, Ian
William Shakespeare's Tragedy of the Sith's Revenge: Star Wars Part the Third — Doescher, Ian
William T. Vollmann: A Critical Companion — Coffman, Christopher K.
William the Conqueror vs. King Harold — Vint, Jesse Lee
c William & the Missing Masterpiece (Illus. by Hancocks, Helen) — Hancocks, Helen
William Washington, American Light Dragoon: A Continental Cavalry Leader in the War of Independence — Murphy, Daniel
William Wells Brown: An African American Life — Greenspan, Ezra
William Wordsworth and the Invention of Tourism, 1820-1900 — Yoshikawa, Saeko
William Wordsworth in Context — Bennett, Andrew
y Williams the Sorcerer Heir — Chima, Cinda
The Williamston Freedom Movement: A North Carolina Town's Struggle for Civil Rights, 1957-1970 — Smith, Amanda Hilliard

c Willie & Me: A Baseball Card Adventure (Read by Heller, Johnny). Audiobook Review — Gutman, Dan
c Willie & Me: A Baseball Card Adventure — Gutman, Dan
The Willing Spirit — Camp, Greg
The Willing Widow — LeCoeur, Ursula
Willoughbyland: England's Lost Colony — Parker, Matthew
Willow Brook Road — Woods, Sherryl
y Willowgrove — Peacock, Kathleen
c Willy Maykit in Space (Illus. by Burks, James) — Trine, Greg
Willy's Stories (Illus. by Browne, Anthony) — Browne, Anthony
The Wilmington Ten: Violence, Injustice, and the Rise of Black Politics in the 1970s — Janken, Kenneth Robert
The Wilson Deception — Stewart, David O.
Win Friends and Customers — Bookbinder, Lawrence J.
c Win or Lose, I Love You (Illus. by Christy, Jana) — TerKeurst, Lysa
c Win or Lose, I Love You! (Illus. by Christy, Jana) — TerKeurst, Lysa
y Win the Rings — Van Brunt, K.D.
Winchester 1886 — Johnstone, William W.
Winckelmann and the Invention of Antiquity — Harloe, Katherine
y Wind Energy — Newton, David E.
The Wind in the Reeds: A Storm, a Play, and the City That Would Not Be Broken — Pierce, Wendell
Wind Over Water: Migration in an East Asian Context — Haines, David W.
Wind/Pinball (Read by Heyborne, Kirby). Audiobook Review — Murakami, Haruki
Wind/Pinball — Murakami, Haruki
Wind River — Reasoner, James
The Wind-Up Bird Chronicle — Murakami, Haruki
Wind Wizard: Alan G. Davenport and the Art of Wind Engineering — Roberts, Siobhan
Windigo Island — Krueger, William Kent
Winding Up the British Empire in the Pacific Islands — McIntyre, W. David
c Windmill Dragons (Illus. by Nytra, David) — Nytra, David
y A Window Opens — Egan, Elisabeth
A Window Opens — Egan, Elizabeth
A Window to the Soul — Dickie, William
Window Wall — Rawn, Melanie
Winds from the North: Tewa Origins and Historical Anthropology — Ortman, Scott G.
The Wine Bible, 2d ed. — MacNeil, Karen
The Winemaker Detective — Alaux, Jean-Pierre
c Winfield Day Dreamers: A Journey of Imagination — Martin, Emily
y Wing Commander: Freedom Flight — Jones, Patrick
y Wing Commander: Freedom Flight
c The Wing Wing Brothers Geometry Palooza! — Long, Ethan
The Winged Histories — Samatar, Sofia
Wings of the Navy: Testing British and U.S. Carrier Aircraft — Brown, Eric
y Wink Poppy Midnight — Tucholke, April Genevieve
Winner-Take-All Politics: How Washington Made the Rich Richer--and Turned Its Back on the Middle Class — Pierson, Paul
Winner Take None — Comer, Greg
Winners and How They Succeed — Campbell, Alastair
y The Winner's Crime — Rutkoski, Marie
y The Winner's Curse — Rutkoski, Marie
Winnie and the Red Winniebago — Domeny, Lisa
c Winnie and Waldorf — Hites, Kati
Winnie Davis: Daughter of the Lost Cause — Lee, Heath Hardage
c Winnie: The True Story of the Bear Who Inspired Winnie-the-Pooh (Illus. by Voss, Jonathan D.) — Walker, Sally M.
Winning Marriage: The Inside Story of How Same-Sex Couples Took on the Politicians and Pundits--and Won — Solomon, Marc
Winning the Money Game in College, Book 1: Finance — Roberts, Steven C.
Winning the West with Words: Language and Conquest in the Lower Great Lakes — Buss, James Joseph
Winning While Losing: Civil Rights, the Conservative Movement, and the Presidency from Nixon to Obama — Osgood, Kenneth
A Winsome Murder — DeVita, James

Winston Churchill and the Islamic World: Orientalism, Empire and Diplomacy in the Middle East — Dockter, Warren
Winston Churchill: Der Spate Held — Kielinger, Thomas
Winston Churchill Reporting: Adventures of a Young War Correspondent — Read, Simon
Winston Churchill's Last Campaign: Britain and the Cold War, 1951-55 — Young, John
Winter — Jackson, Vina
y Winter — Meyer, Marissa
Winter — Nicholson, Christopher
c Winter — Busby, Ailie
Winter at the Door — Graves, Sarah
Winter Ball — Lane, Amy
c Winter Bees and Other Poems of the Cold (Illus. by Allen, Rick) — Sidman, Joyce
c Winter Break Wipeout (Illus. by St. Aubin, Bruno) — Tibo, Gilles
The Winter Family — Jackman, Clifford
The Winter Foundlings — Rhodes, Kate
The Winter Girl — Marinovich, Matt
c The Winter Horses — Kerr, Philip
c Winter Is Coming (Illus. by LaMarche, Jim) — Johnston, Tony
Winter Is Coming: Why Vladimir Putin and the Enemies of the Free World Must Be Stopped — Kasparov, Garry
Winter — Jackson, Vina
c Winter Moon Song (Illus. by Ruifernandez, Leticia) — Brooks, Martha
Winter Oranges — Sexton, Marie
c Winter — Carter, David A.
y The Winter Place — Yates, Alexander
Winter Stroll — Hilderbrand, Elin
Winter Symphony on Lake Mattamuskeet: A Love Story — Warren, Georgia Denton
The Winter War — Teir, Philip
c The Winter Wolf — Webb, Holly
y Winterfrost (Read by McFadden, Amy) — Houts, Michelle
y Winterfrost — Houts, Michelle
c Winterkill — Boorman, Kate A.
y Winter's Bullet — Osborne, William
c Winter's Child (Illus. by Baker-Smith, Grahame) — McAllister, Angela
c Winter's Coming (Illus. by Bisaillon, Josee) — Thornhill, Jan
c Winter's Tlurry Adventure (Illus. by Pooler, Paige) — Allen, Elise
y Winterspell — Legrand, Claire
The Winthrop Woman (Read by James, Corrie). Audiobook Review — Seton, Anya
The Winthrop Woman (Read by James, Corrie). Audiobook Review — The winthrop woman.(Spotlight on Historical Fiction)(Brief article)(Audiobook review)
"Wir sind Frauen wie andere auch!" Prostituierte und ihre Kampfe — Biermann, Pieke
c The Wired Bunch Series. E-book Review
Wired for Dating: How Understanding Neurobiology and Attachment Style Can Help You Find Your Ideal Mate — Tatkin, Stan
Wired for Story — Cron, Lisa
Wired to Create: Unraveling the Mysteries of the Creative Mind — Kaufman, Scott Barry
Wirstanden nicht Abseits: Frauen im Widerstandgegen Hitler — Geyken, Frauke
Wirtschaftsgeschichte des Ersten Weltkriegs. Okonomische Ordnung und Handeln der Unternehmen
Wisconsin's Flying Trees in World War II: A Victory for American Forest Products and Allied Aviation — Connor, Sara Witter
Wisden Cricketers' Almanack 2015 — Booth, Lawrence
y Wisdom from Our First Nations — Ernst, Lyle
Wisdom, Justice, and Charity: Canadian Social Welfare through the Life of Jane B. Wisdom, 1884-1975 — Morton, Suzanne
The Wisdom of Animals: Creatureliness in Early Modern French Spirituality — Randall, Catharine
c Wisdom of Merlin: 7 Magical Words for a Meaningful Life — Barron, T.A.
The Wisdom of Perversity — Yglesias, Rafael
The Wisdom of the Beguines: The Forgotten Story of a Medieval Women's Movement — Swan, Laura
The Wisdom of the Liminal: Evolution and Other Animals in Human Becoming — Deane-Drummond, Celia
The Wisdom of Trees — Adams, Max

Wisdom's Wonder: Character, Creation, and Crisis in the Bible's Wisdom Literature — Brown, William P.
Wisdom's Workshop — Axtell, James
The Wise and Foolish Builders: Poems — Teague, Alexandra
The Wise King: A Christian Prince, Muslim Spain, and the Birth of the Renaissance — Doubleday, Simon R.
Wisent-Reservat und UNESCO-Welterbe. Referenzen fur den Bia?owie?a-Nationalpark
Wiser: Getting Beyond Groupthink to Make Groups Smarter — Sunstein, Cass R.
The Wisest One in the Room — Gilovich, Thomas
y The Wish — Hueller, R.W.
c Wish — Dodd, Emma
y Wish Girl — Loftin, Nikki
c The Wish of the Well-Witcher — Harris, Julie Mahler
c Wish (Illus. by Cordell, Matthew) — Cordell, Matthew
A Wish Your Heart Makes — Solomon, Charles
c The Wishbone Wish (Illus. by Reynolds, Peter H.) — McDonald, Megan
c The Wishgranter's Babies Tucca and Tucco (Illus. by Winburn, Sean) — Allwell-Brown, Kiru
c Wishworks, Inc. (Illus. by Bates, Amy June) — Tolan, Stephanie
Wissens-Ordnungen: Zu einer historischen Epistemologie der Literatur — Gess, Nicola
Wissenschaft fur den Krieg: Die geheimen Arbeiten des Heereswaffenamtes — Nagel, Gunter
Wissenschaftliches Netzwerk: Toletum. Netzwerk zur Erforschung der Iberischen Halbinsel in der Antike - Network para la Investigacion sobre la Peninsula Iberica en la Antiguedad. 5. Workshop
Wissenschaftspolitik, Forschungspraxis und Ressourcenmobilisierung im NS-Herrschaftssystem
Wissensregulierung und Regulierungswissen — Alfons, Bora
The Wister Trace: Assaying Classic Western Fiction, 2d ed. — Estleman, Loren D.
The Wister Trace: Assaying Classic Western Fiction — Estleman, Loren D.
c Wisteria Jane (Illus. by Hoyt, Ard) — Harris, Amber
c The Witch at the Window — Chew, Ruth
The Witch-Hunt Narrative: Politics, Psychology, and the Sexual Abuse of Children — Cheit, Ross E.
y The Witch Hunter — Boecker, Virginia
The Witch of Bourbon Street — Palmieri, Suzanne
The Witch of Lime Street: Seance, Seduction, and Houdini in the Spirit World — Jaher, David
The Witch of Lime Street: Seance, Seduction, and Houdini in the Spirit World — Jalier, David
The Witch of Napoli — Schmicker, Michael
The Witch of Painted Sorrows (Read by Ross, Natalie). Audiobook Review — Rose, M.J.
y The Witch of Painted Sorrows — Rose, M.J.
Witch upon a Star — Harlow, Jennifer
c Witch Wars (Illus. by Anderson, Laura Ellen) — Pounder, Sibeal
Witchcraft and Magic in the Nordic Middle Ages — Mitchell, Stephen A.
Witchcraft and the Rise of the First Confucian Empire — Cai, Liang
y Witchcraft — Pizer, Carol
c Witches and Wicca — Alexander, Audrey
Witches of America — Mar, Alex
The Witches of Cambridge — Van Praag, Menna
Witches of Lychford — Cornell, Paul
Witches Protection Program — Cash, Michael Phillip
The Witches: Salem, 1692 — Schiff, Stacy
Witches, Tea Plantations, and Lives of Migrant Laborers in India: Tempest in a Teapot — Chaudhuri, Soma
The Witching Hour and Other Plays — Sadur, Nina
y Witchrise — Lamb, Victoria
c The Witch's Boy — Barnhill, Kelly
c The Witch's Curse (Illus. by McPhillips, Robert) — Quinn, Jordan
The Witch's Oracle — Brooks, Marla
c Witchworld (Illus. by Riddell, Chris) — Fischel, Emma
c With a Friend by Your Side — Kerley, Barbara
With a Voice That Is Often Still Confused But Is Becoming Ever Louder and Clearer — Hamantaschen, J.R.
c With Books and Bricks: How Booker T. Washington Built a School (Illus. by Tadgell, Nicole) — Slade, Suzanne
With Dogs at the Edge of Life — Dayan, Colin
With Every Breath — Riley, Lia
y With Fearful Bravery — Kositsky, Lynne
With Friends Like These ... Why Britain Should Leave the EU-and How — Conway, David

c With Love (Illus. by Marks, Alan) — Goodall, Jane
With Malice toward Some: Treason and Loyalty in the Civil War Era — Blair, William
With Malice toward Some: Treason and Loyalty in the Civil War Era — Blair, William A.
With Sails Whitening Every Sea: Mariners and the Making of an American Maritime Empire — Rouleau, Brian
With the Children — Webb, Henry
c Withering-by-Sea — Rossell, Judith
c Witherwood Reform School (Illus. by Thompson, Keith) — Skye, Obert
Within These Walls (Read by Bray, R.C.). Audiobook Review — Ahlborn, Ania
Within These Walls — Ahlborn, Ania
Without Consent — Degner, Virginia R.
Without Copyrights: Piracy, Publishing, and the Public Domain — Spoo, Robert
Without Ground: Lacanian Ethics and the Assumption of Subjectivity — Neill, Calum
Without Limits — Grinnell, Dustin
Without Mercy: The Stunning True Story of Race, Crime, and Corruption in the Deep South — Beasley, David
Without Restraint — Knight, Angela
Without You, There Is No Us: My Time with the Sons of North Korea's Elite — Kim, Suki
Witness: A Hunkpapha Historian's Strong-Heart Song of the Lakotas — Waggoner, Josephine
y Witness: Passing the Torch of the Holocaust Memory to New Generations — Rubenstein, Eli
Witness to Change — Morial, Sybil Haydel
Witness: Two Hundred Years of African-American Faith and Practice at the Abyssinian Baptist Church of Harlem, New York — Dixie, Quinton Hosford
Witness: Two Hundred Years of African-American Faith and Practice at the Abyssinian Baptist Church of Harlem, New York — McNeil, Genna Rae
Witnesses, Neighbors, and Community in Late Medieval Marseille: The New Middle Ages — McDonough, Susan Alice
Witnessing the Revolutionary and Napoleonic Wars in German Central Europe — James, Leighton S.
Witnessing Witnessing: On the Reception of Holocaust Survivor Testimony — Trezise, Thomas
Wives, Husbands, and Lovers: Marriage and Sexuality in Hong Kong, Taiwan, and Urban China — Friedman, Sara L.
The Wives of Los Alamos — Nesbit, TaraShea
c The Wizard and the Quient — Lemmer, T.J.
The Wizard of Oz Counting — McCurry, Kristen
c The Wizard of Oz (Illus. by Zwerger, Lisbeth) — Baum, L. Frank
The Wizard of Oz Shapes — Harbo, Christopher L.
Wizard of Their Age: Critical Essays from the Harry Potter Generation — Farr, Cecilia Konchar
c The Wizard, the Fairy, and the Magic Chicken (Illus. by Munsinger, Lynn) — Lester, Helen
c The Wizardling (Illus. by Schroeder, Binette) — Schroeder, Binette
Wizards, Aliens, and Starships: Physics and Math in Science Fiction — Adler, Charles L.
The Wobblies in Their Heyday: The Rise and Destruction of the Industrial Workers of the World During the World War I Era — Chester, Eric Thomas
c Wobbling Whiskers (Illus. by Rumsey, Ricky) — Eggleton, Jill
Wohnen und die Okonomie des Raums - L'habitat et l'economie de l'espace — Conrad, Christoph
Wolf and Iron — Dickson, Gordon R.
The Wolf and the Buffalo — Kelton, Elmer
c A Wolf at the Gate (Illus. by Hedstrom, Joel) — Van Steenwyk, Mark
A Wolf at the Gate — Van Steenwyk, Mark
c The Wolf-Birds (Illus. by Dawson, Willow) — Dawson, Willow
The Wolf Border — Hall, Sarah
Wolf Bride — Moss, Elizabeth
y Wolf by Wolf — Graudin, Ryan
Wolf Creek — Fargo, Ford
Wolf — Hayder, Mo
y Wolf High — Hueller, R.W.
Wolf in White Van — Darnielle, John
The Wolf in Winter — Connolly, John
Wolf Land — Janz, Jonathan
Wolf Point — Thompson, Mike
Wolf Skin — McMyne, Mary
c Wolf Spiders — Archer, Claire
Wolf Trouble — Tyler, Paige

c The Wolf Who Travels Back in Time (Illus. by Thuillier, Eleonore) — *Lallemand, Orianne*
c The Wolf Who Wanted to Change His Color (Illus. by Thuillier, Eleonore) — *Lallemand, Orianne*
y The Wolf Wilder — *Rundell, Katherine*
   Wolf Winter: A Novel — *Ekback, Cecilia*
   Wolf Winter — *Ekback, Cecilia*
   Wolf, Wolf — *Venter, Eben*
c Wolfie the Bunny (Illus. by OHora, Zachariah) — *Dyckman, Ame*
c Wolfie the Bunny (Illus. by OHora, Zachariah) — *Dyckman, Anne*
c Wolfie the Bunny (Illus. by OHora, Zachariah) — *Dyckman, Arne*
c Wolfie the Bunny (Illus. by OHora, Zachariah) — *Dykeman, Arne*
y The Wollenstonecraft Detective Agency — *Stratford, Jordan*
   Wolseley — *le Grange, J. John*
   Wolves — *Berenson, Alex*
   Wolves — *Ings, Simon*
   The Wolves — *Berenson, Alex*
   Wolves of the Northern Rift — *Messenger, Jon*
   A Woman in Arabia: The Writings of the Queen of the Desert — *Bell, Gertrude*
   Woman in Battle Dress — *Benitez-Rojo, Antonio*
c A Woman in the House (and Senate): How Women Came to the United States Congress, Broke Down Barriers, and Changed the Country (Illus. by Baddeley, Elizabeth) — *Cooper, Ilene*
   The Woman in the Movies Star Dress — *Asthana, Praveen*
   A Woman Loved — *Makine, Andrei*
   The Woman of Porto Pim — *Parks, Tim*
   Woman of the Dead — *Aichner, Bernhard*
   Woman-Powered Farm: Manual for a Self-Sufficient Lifestyle from Homestead to Field — *Levatino, Audrey*
   A Woman Unknown — *Brody, Frances*
   The Woman Who Did — *Allin, Lou*
   The Woman Who Lost Her Soul — *Shacochis, Bob*
   The Woman Who Read too Much: A Novel — *Nakhjavani, Bahlyylh*
   The Woman Who Read Too Much — *Nakhjavani, Bahiyyih*
   The Woman Who Stole My Life (Read by McMahon, Aoife). Audiobook Review — *Keyes, Marian*
   The Woman Who Stole My Life — *Keyes, Marian*
   The Woman Who Walked in Sunshine — *Smith, Alexander McCall*
   The Woman Who Would Be King: Hatshepsut's Rise to Power in Ancient Egypt (Read by Cooney, Kara). Audiobook Review — *Cooney, Kara*
   The Woman Who Would Be King: Hatshepsut's Rise to Power in Ancient Egypt — *Cooney, Kara*
   Woman with a Blue Pencil — *McAlpine, Gordon*
   Woman with a Gun (Read by Huber, Hillary). Audiobook Review — *Margolin, Phillip*
   Woman with a Secret — *Hannah, Sophie*
   A Woman without a Country — *Boland, Eavan*
   Woman, Women, and the Priesthood in the Trinitarian Theology of Elisabeth Behr-Sigel — *Wilson, Sarah Hinlicky*
   A Woman's Guide to the Sailing Lifestyle — *Picchi, Debra*
   The Woman's National Indian Association: A History — *Mathes, Valerie Sherer*
   A Woman's Story — *Ernaux, Annie*
c Wombat Wins (Illus. by Whatley, Bruce) — *French, Jackie*
   Wombs in Labor: Transnational Commercial Surrogacy in India — *Pande, Amrita*
   Women After All: Sex, Evolution, and the End of Male Supremacy — *Konner, Melvin*
   Women Aging in Prison: A Neglected Population in the Correctional System — *Aday, Ronald H.*
   Women and Casualisation: Women's Experiences of Job Insecurity — *Dewar, Laura*
   Women and English Piracy, 1540-1720: Partners and Victims of Crime — *Appleby, John C.*
   Women and Gender in Postwar Europe: From Cold War to European Union — *Regulska, Joanna*
   Women and Literary Celebrity in the Nineteenth Century: The Transatlantic Production of Fame and Gender — *Weber, Brenda R.*
   Women and Mass Consumer Society in Postwar France — *Pulju, Rebecca J.*
   Women and Religion in the Atlantic Age, 1550-1900 — *Clark, Emily*
   Women and Slavery in Nineteenth-Century Colonial Cuba — *Franklin, Sarah L.*

   Women and States: Norms and Hierarchies in International Society — *Towns, Ann E.*
   Women and the Bible in Early Modern England: Religious Reading and Writing — *Molekamp, Femke*
   Women and the Birth of Russian Capitalism. A History of the Shuttle Trade — *Mukhina, Irina*
   Women and the City, Women in the City: A Gendered Perspective of Ottoman Urban History — *Maksudyan, Nazan*
   Women and the Counter-Reformation in Early Modern Munster — *Laqua-O'Donnell, Simone*
   Women and the Gift: Beyond the Given and the All-Giving — *Joy, Morny*
   Women and the Reinvention of the Political: Feminism in Italy, 1968-1983 — *Bracke, Maud*
   Women and the Roman City in the Latin West — *Hemelrijk, Emily A.*
   Women and the Transmission of Religious Knowledge in Islam — *Sayeed, Asma*
   Women and the Vote: A World History — *Adams, Jad*
   Women and Tudor Tragedy: Feminizing Counsel and Representing Gender — *Ward, Allyna E.*
   Women and Work in Eighteenth-Century France — *Hafter, Daryl M.*
   Women and Work in Eighteenth-Century France — *Kushner, Nina*
   Women Artists: The Linda Nochlin Reader — *Reilly, Maura*
   Women Attorneys and the Changing Workplace: High Hopes, Mixed Outcomes — *Kitzerow, Phyllis*
   Women Chefs of New York — *Arumugam, Nadia*
   Women Crime Writers: Eight Suspense Novels of the 1940s and 1950s — *Weinman, Sarah*
   Women Drummers: A History from Rock and Jazz to Blues and Country — *Smith, Angela*
   Women Exiting Prison: Critical Essays on Gender, Post-Release Support and Survival — *Carlton, Bree*
   Women, Food, and Desire: Embrace Your Cravings, Make Peace with Food, Reclaim Your Body — *Jamieson, Alexandra*
   Women, Gender, and the Palace Households in Ottoman Tunisia — *Kallander, Amy Aisen*
y Women Heroes of the American Revolution: 20 Stories of Espionage, Sabotage, Defiance, and Rescue — *Casey, Susan*
   Women in Ancient Rome — *Chrystal, Paul*
   Women in Ancient Rome: A Sourcebook — *MacLachlan, Bonnie*
c Women in Black History: Stories of Courage, Faith, and Resilience — *Jackson, Tricia Williams*
   Women in Christian Traditions — *Moore, Rebecca*
   Women in Conflict in the Middle East: Palestinian Refugees and the Response to Violence — *Holt, Maria*
   Women in Dark Times — *Rose, Jacqueline*
   Women in Early America — *Foster, Thomas A.*
   Women in Early Indian Buddhism: Comparative Textual Studies — *Collett, Alice*
   Women in Industrial Research — *Tobies, Renate*
   Women in Iraq: Past Meets Present — *Efrati, Noga*
   Women in Love — *Lawrence, D.H.*
y Women in Medicine — *Etingoff, Kim*
   Women in My Rose Garden: The History, Romance and Adventure of Old Roses — *Chapman, Ann*
   Women in Old Norse Literature: Bodies, Words, and Power — *Fridriksdottir, Johanna Katrin*
   Women in Pastoral Office: The Story of Santa Prassede, Rome — *Schaefer, Mary M.*
   Women in Philosophy: What Needs to Change? — *Hutchison, Katrina*
   Women in Revolutionary Debate: Female Novelists from Burney to Austen — *Russo, Stephanie*
   Women in the Ancient Near East: A Sourcebook — *Chavals, Mark*
   Women in the Peninsular War — *Esdaile, Charles J.*
   Women in the Weimar Republic — *Boak, Helen*
   Women in War: The Micro-processes of Mobilization in El Salvador — *Viterna, Jocelyn*
   Women, Incarceration and Human Rights Violations: Feminist Criminology and Corrections — *Van Gundy, Alana*
   Women, Islam, and Resistance in the Arab World — *Holt, Maria*
   Women Making Shakespeare: Text, Reception and Performance — *Gordon McMullan,*
   Women, Manuscripts and Identity in Northern Europe, 1350-1550 — *Hand, Joni M.*
   Women, Men and Everyday Talk — *Coates, Jennifer*
   Women, Money and Prosperity: A Sister's Perspective on How to Retire Well — *Phelan, Donna M.*

   Women of Colonial America: 13 Stories of Courage and Survival in the New World — *Miller, Brandon Marie*
   Women of Faith: The Chicago Sisters of Mercy and the Evolution of a Religious Community — *Connolly, Mary Beth Fraser*
   Women of Faith: The Chicago Sisters of Mercy and the Evolution of a Religious Community — *Fraser, Mary Beth*
   The Women of Pliny's Letters — *Shelton, J.A.*
   Women of the Nation: Between Black Protest and Sunni Islam — *Gibson, Dawn-Marie*
   Women of Will: Following the Feminine in Shakespeare's Plays — *Packer, Tina*
   Women on Ice: Methamphetamine Use Among Suburban Women — *Boeri, Miriam*
   Women on the North American Plains — *Jensen, Joan M.*
   Women, Pleasure, Film: What Lolas Want — *Richter, Simon*
   Women, Rank, and Marriage in the British Aristocracy, 1485-2000: An Open Elite? — *Schutte, Kimberly*
   Women, Terrorism, and Trauma in Italian Culture — *Glynn, Ruth*
   Women, Travel and Identity: Journeys by Rail and Sea, 1870-1940 — *Robinson-Tomsett, Emma*
   Women Warriors in Romantic Drama — *Nielsen, Wendy C.*
   Women, Work and Sociability in Early Modern London — *Reinke-Williams, Tim*
   Women, Work, and the Web: How the Web Creates Entrepreneurial Opportunities — *Smallwood, Carol*
   Women Writers and the Artifacts of Celebrity in the Long Nineteenth Century — *Hawkins, Ann R.*
   Women Writing Crime Fiction, 1860-1880: Fourteen American, British and Australian Authors — *Watson, Kate*
   Women's Cinema, World Cinema: Projecting Contemporary Feminisms — *White, Patricia*
   Women's Rights in the United States: A Comprehensive Encyclopedia of Issues, Events, and People, 4 vols. — *Wayne, Tiffany K.*
   The Women's War of 1929: Gender and Violence in Colonial Nigeria — *Matera, Marc*
c Won Ton and Chopstick (Illus. by Yelchin, Eugene) — *Wardlaw, Lee*
c The Wonder (Illus. by Hanson, Faye) — *Hanson, Faye*
   Wonder and Exile in the New World — *Nava, Alex*
c Wonder at the Edge of the World — *Helget, Nicole*
   The Wonder Garden — *Acampora, Lauren*
c The Wonder Garden (Illus. by Williams, Kristjana S.) — *Broom, Jenny*
   The Wonder Garden — *Acampora, Lauren*
c Wonder Horse — *Dahar, Anita*
   The Wonder of All Things (Read by Whelan, Julia). Audiobook Review — *Mott, Jason*
c The Wonder (Illus. by Hanson, Faye) — *Hanson, Faye*
   Wonder Woman: Bondage and Feminism in the Marston/Peter Comics, 1941-1948 — *Berlatsky, Noah*
c The Wonderful Fluffy Little Squishy (Illus. by Alemagna, Beatrice) — *Alemagna, Beatrice*
c The Wonderful Habits of Rabbits (Illus. by Sanchez, Sonia) — *Florian, Douglas*
c The Wonderful Things You Will Be (Illus. by Martin, Emily Winfield) — *Martin, Emily Winfield*
c A Wonderful Year (Illus. by Bruel, Nick) — *Bruel, Nick*
   Wondering Boy — *Kern, Ronni*
   Wondering Who You Are (Read by Lea, Sonya). Audiobook Review — *Lea, Sonya*
   Wondering Who You Are — *Lea, Sonya*
y Wonders of the Invisible World — *Barzak, Christopher*
c Wonders of the World — *Bergin, Mark*
y The Wondrous and the Wicked — *Morgan, Page*
   Wondrous Brutal Fictions: Eight Buddhist Tales from the Early Japanese Puppet Theater — *Kimbrough, R. Keller*
   A Wong: The Cookbook — *Wong, Andrew*
y Wonton Soup (Illus. by Stokoe, James) — *Stokoe, James*
   Wood, Whiskey and Wine: A History of Barrels — *Work, Henry H.*
   Wooden Os: Shakespeare's Theatres and England's Trees — *Nardizzi, Vin*
c The Wooden Prince — *Bemis, John Claude*
c Woodford Brave (Illus. by Whipple, Kevin) — *Jones, Marcia Thornton*
c Woodford Brave (Illus. by Whipple, Kevin) — *Jones, Martha Thornton*

c Woodpecker Wham! (Illus. by Jenkins, Steve) — Sayre, April Pulley
Woodrow Wilson and World War I: A Burden too Great to Bear — Striner, Richard
The Woods of Ireland: A History, 700-1800 — Everett, Nigel
Woody Allen: A Retrospective — Shone, Tom
Woody Allen: Film by Film — Solomons, Jason
Woody — Evanier, David
Woody: The Biography — Evanier, David
c Woof (Read by Frangione, Jim). Audiobook Review — Quinn, Spencer
c Woof — Quinn, Spencer
The Woolly Monkey: Behavior, Ecology, Systematics, and Captive Research — Defler, Thomas R.
Word and Image: Art, Books and Design from the National Art Library — Watson, Rowan
Word and Image: The Hermeneutics of the Saint John's Bible — Patella, Michael
The Word — Crouch, Hubert
y The Word for Yes — Needell, Claire
A Word from Our Sponsor: Admen, Advertising, and the Golden Age of Radio — Meyers, Cynthia B.
The Word Kingdom — Gordon, Noah Eli
Word Nerd: Dispatches from the Games, Grammar, and Geek Underground — Williams, John D.
The Word — Crouch, Hubert
The Word Window: Black History and the Bible Reference Book, vol. 2 — Harris, Lionel, Jr.
Word Without Music — Glass, Philip
c Word Wizard Series, 4 vols. — Johnson, Robin
c The Word Wizard Series
c The Word Wizard's Book of Adjectives — Johnson, Robin
c The Word Wizard's Book of Adverbs — Johnson, Robin
c The Word Wizard's Book of Homonyms — Johnson, Robin
c The Word Wizard's Book of Nouns — Johnson, Robin
c The Word Wizard's Book of Prefixes and Suffixes — Johnson, Robin
c The Word Wizard's Book of Pronouns — Johnson, Robin
c The Word Wizard's Book of Synonyms and Antonyms — Johnson, Robin
c The Word Wizard's Book of Verbs — Johnson, Robin
Word World — Ivory, Vincent H.
Words of Command — Mallinson, Allan
The Words of Langston Hughes: Modernism and Translation in the Americas — Kutzinski, Vera M.
Words of Protest, Words of Freedom: Poetry of the American Civil Rights Movement and Era — Coleman, Jeffrey Lamar
Words Onscreen: The Fate of Reading in a Digital World — Baron, Naomi S.
Words to Die For — Kostoff, Lynn
Words Without Music: A Memoir — Glass, Philip
y Words Without Music — Glass, Philip
y The Wordsmith — Forde, Patricia
Wordsworth and the Enlightenment Idea of Pleasure — Boyson, Rowan
c Work: An Occupational ABC — Hatanaka, Kellen
Work and Leisure in Late Nineteenth-Century French Litterature and Visual Culture: Time, Politics and Class — White Claire
c Work and More Work (Illus. by Perez, Oscar T.) — Little, Linda
y Work Boots and Tees — Ramsey, Jo
Work, Class, and Power in the Borderlands of the Early American Pacific: The Labors of Empire — Lampe, Evan
c Work, Dogs, Work: A Highway Tail — Horvath, James
A Work in Progress — Franta, Connor
Work Like Any Other — Reeves, Virginia
The Work: My Search for a Life That Matters (Read by Moore, Wes). Audiobook Review — Moore, Wes
y A Work of Art — Maysonet, Melody
The Work of Recognition: Caribbean Colombia and the Postemancipation Struggle for Citizenship — McGraw, Jason
The Work of the Dead: A Cultural History of Mortal Remains — Laqueur, Thomas W.
The Work of Theology — Hauerwas, Stanley
Work. Pump. Repeat: How to Survive Breastfeeding and Going Back to Work — Shortall, Jessica
Work, Regulation, and Identity in Provincial France: The Bordeaux Leather Trades, 1740-1815 — Heimmermann, Daniel
Work Rules! Insights from Inside Google that Will Transform How You Live and Lead (Read by Bock, Laszlo). Audiobook Review — Bock, Laszlo

Work Rules! Insights from Inside Google that Will Transform How You Live and Lead — Bock, Laszlo
Workers Go Shopping in Argentina: The Rise of Popular Consumer Culture — Milanesio, Natalia
Workers in Hard Times: A Long View of Economic Crises — Fink, Leon
y Working as a Tattoo Artist in Your Community — Porterfield, Jason
Working for Bigfoot: Stories from the Dresden Files — Butcher, Jim
Working in the Big Easy: The History and Politics of Labor in New Orleans — Adams, Thomas J.
The Working Man's Reward: Chicago's Early Suburbs and the Roots of American Sprawl — Lewinnek, Elaine
Working Men's Bodies: Work Camps in Britain, 1880-1940 — Field, John
Working Stiff: Two Years, 262 Bodies, and the Making of a Medical Examiner (Read by Eby, Tanya). Audiobook Review — Melinek, Judy
Working with Nineteenth-Century Medical and Health Periodicals
Working with the Math Balance — Marolda, Maria
Working with Written Discourse — Cameron, Deborah
Working Women into the Borderlands — Evans, Sterling D.
Working Women into the Borderlands — Hernandez, Sonia
Works in Progress: Plans and Realities on Soviet Farms, 1930-1963 — Smith, Jenny Leigh
The Works of Thomas Traherne, vol. 6 — Traherne, Thomas
The Works of Tim Burton: Margins to Mainstream — Weinstock, Jeffrey Andrew
Works Well with Others: An Outsider's Guide to Shaking Hands, Shutting Up, Handling Jerks, and Other Crucial Skills in Business That No One Ever Teaches You — McCammon, Ross
Workshop Biographie-Forschung
Workshop Historisch-Biographisches Informationssystem
Workshop: Public History in Studium und Ausbildung
Workshops of Empire: Stegner, Engle, and American Creative Writing During the Cold War — Bennett, Eric
c The World According to Musk Ox (Illus. by Myers, Matthew) — Cabatingan, Erin
The World Almanac and Book of Facts 2015 — Janssen, Sarah
World Antiquarianism: Comparative Perspectives — Schnapp, Alain
The World as We Know It — Krusie, Curtis
The World Atlas of Whiskey — Broom, Dave
The World Atlas of Whisky — Broom, Dave
The World Before Us (Read by Hardingham, Fiona). Audiobook Review — Hunter, Aislinn
The World Before Us — Hunter, Aislinn
y The World Beneath: One Boy's Struggle to Be Free — Warman, Janice
The World between Two Covers: Reading the Globe — Morgan, Ann
The World beyond Europe in the Romance Epics of Boiardo and Ariosto — Cavallo, Jo Ann
The World beyond Your Head: How to Flourish in an Age of Distraction — Crawford, Matthew B.
The World beyond Your Head: On Becoming an Individual in an Age of Distraction — Crawford, Matthew B.
World Cheese Book — Harbutt, Juliet
A World Elsewhere: An American Woman in Wartime Germany — MacRae, Sigrid von Hoyningen-Huene
c The World-Famous Cheese Shop Break-In (Illus. by Shaw, Hannah) — Taylor, Sean (b. 1965-)
c The World Famous Cheese Shop Break-In (Illus. by Shaw, Hannah) — Taylor, Sean (b. 1965-)
c The World-Famous Cheese Shop Break-in (Illus. by Shaw, Hannah) — Taylor, Sean (b. 1965-)
c World Fishing — Pissock, Jonathan
y The World Forgot — Leicht, Martin
c World Geography through Infographics (Illus. by Stankiewicz, Steven) — Kenney, Karen Latchana
The World Goes Pop — Frigeri, Flavia
World Gone By (Read by Frangione, Jim). Audiobook Review — Lehane, Dennis
World Gone By — Lehane, Dennis
World Gone Water — Clarke, Jaime
World History of Design, 2 vols. — Margolin, Victor
c The World in a Second (Illus. by Carvalho, Bernardo) — Martins, Isabel Minhos
The World is a Wedding — Jones, Wendy
The World Is on Fire: Scrap, Treasure, and Songs of A — Tevis, Joni

The World Is on Fire: Scrap, Treasure, and Songs of Apocalypse — Tevis, Joni
The World is Waiting for You — Grove, Tara
c World Money (Illus. by Beech, Mark) — Bailey, Gerry
A World More Concrete: Real Estate and the Remaking of Jim Crow South Florida — Connolly, N.D.B.
A World Not to Come: A History of Latino Writing and Print Culture — Coronado, Raul
c The World of Endangered Animals: South and Central Asia — Harris, Tim
A World of Homeowners: American Power and the Politics of Housing Aid — Kwak, Nancy H.
The World of Late Antiquity: AD 150-170 — Brown, Peter (b. 1935-)
c The World of Mamoko in the Time of Dragons — Mizielinska, Aleksandra
c The World of Mamoko in the Time of Dragons (Illus. by Mizielinski, Daniel) — Mizielinska, Aleksandra
The World of Persian Literary Humanism — Dabashi, Hamid
The World of Raymond Chandler: In His Own Words — Day, Barry
The World of the Fullo: Work, Economy, and Society in Roman Italy — Flohr, Miko
The World of the John Birch Society: Conspiracy, Conservatism, and the Cold War — Mulloy, D.J.
The World of the New Testament: Cultural, Social, and Historical Contexts — Green, Joel B.
The World of the Revolutionary American Republic: Land, Labor, and the Conflict for a Continent — Shankman, Andrew
A World of Their Own: A History of South Africa Women's Education — Healy-Clancy, Meghan
The World on a Plate: 40 Cuisines, 100 Recipes, and the Stories Behind Them — Holland, Mina
The World on a Plate — Holland, Mina
World Order — Kissinger, Henry
World Religions in Dialogue: A Comparative Theological Approach — Valkenberg, Pim
c World Soccer Legends Series — Jokulsson, Illugi
The World Split Open: Great Authors on How and Why We Write — Raymond, Jon
The World the Railways Made — Faith, Nicholas
The World Turned Upside Down — Hill, Christopher
World War I and Propaganda — Paddock, Troy R.E.
World War I and the Triumph of a New Japan, 1919-1930 — Dickinson, Frederick R.
y World War I by the Numbers — Lanser, Amanda
World War I Companion — Strohn, Matthias
The World War I Diary of Jose de la Luz Saenz — Zamora, Emilio
World War I in American Fiction: An Anthology of Short Stories — Emmert, Scott D.
World War I — Dubber, Geoff
World War I: The Definitive Encyclopedia and Document Collection, 5 vols. — Tucker, Spencer C.
c World War II — Adamson, Thomas K.
y World War II by the Numbers — Lanser, Amanda
y World War II — Corrigan, Jim
y World War II: Step into the Action and Behind Enemy Lines from Hitler's Rise to Japan's Surrender — Murray, Stuart A.P.
y World War II: The Definitive Visual History — DK
c World War II U.S. Homefront: A History Perspectives Book — Gitlin, Martin
y World War Moo — Logan, Michael
y The World Within: A Novel of Emily Bronte — Eagland, Jane
y The World Within — Eagland, Jane
A World without Boundaries — Xiong, Ge
World without End: Spain, Philip II, and the First Global Empire — Thomas, Hugh (b. 1931-)
World without End: The Global Empire of Philip II — Thomas, Hugh (b. 1931-)
A World without Jews: The Nazi Imagination from Persecution to Genocide — Alon Confino
A World without Jews: The Nazi Imagination from Persecution to Genocide — Confino, Alon
y The World Without Us — Stevenson, Robin
Worldchanging 101: Challenging the Myth of Powerlessness — LaMotte, David
Worldly Philosopher: The Odyssey of Albert O. Hirschman — Adelman, Jeremy
Worldmaking: The Art and Science of American Diplomacy — Milne, David
Worlds Apart: A Memoir — Plante, David
Worlds Apart — Earlstone, Allen J.
c The World's Best Noses, Ears, and Eyes (Illus. by Arrhenius, Ingela P.) — Rundgren, Helen
Worlds Elsewhere: Journeys Around Shakespeare's Globe — Dickson, Andrew

World's Fairs in a Southern Accent: Atlanta, Nashville, and Charleston, 1895-1902 — *Harvey, Bruce G.*
The World's First Stock Exchange — *Petram, Lodewijk*
The World's Largest Man — *Key, Harrison Scott*
c   The World's Oddest Inventions — *Higgins, Nadia*
Worlds of Dissent: Charter 77, the Plastic People of the Universe, and Czech Culture under Communism — *Bolton, Jonathan*
y   Worlds of Ink and Shadow — *Coakley, Lena*
The Worlds of Langston Hughes: Modernism and Translation in the Americas — *Kutzinski, Vera M.*
Worlds of Learning: The Library and World Chronicle of the Nuremberg Physician Hartmann Schedel — *Wagner, Bettina*
The Worlds of Russian Village Women: Tradition, Transgression, Compromise — *Olson, Laura J.*
The Worlds of the Seventeenth-Century Hudson Valley — *Jacobs, Jaap*
The World's Population: An Encyclopedia of Critical Issues, Crises, and Ever-Growing Countries — *Shelley, Fred M.*
The World's Rarest Birds — *Hirschfeld, Erik*
The Worlds the Shawnees Made: Migration and Violence in Early America — *Warren, Stephen*
Worlds without End: The Many Lives of Multiverse — *Rubenstein, Mary-jane*
The World's Your Stage: How Performing Artists Can Make a Living While Still Doing What They Love — *Baker, William F.*
The Worm at the Core: On the Role of Death in Life — *Solomon, Sheldon*
c   Worm Loves Worm (Illus. by Curato, Mike) — *Austrian, J.J.*
c   The Worm Who Knew Karate! (Illus. by Denton, Terry) — *Lever, Jill*
y   Wormholes — *Perritano, John*
c   Worms — *Murray, Laura K.*
c   Worms (Illus. by Guillerey, Aurelie) — *Friot, Bernard*
y   The Worrier's Guide to Life — *Correll, Gemma*
Worrying: A Literary and Cultural History — *O'Gorman, Francis*
Worship and Culture: Foreign Country or Homeland? — *Wilkey, Glducia Vasconcelos*
Worship and the Parish Church in Early Modern Britain — *Mears, Natalie*
The Worship Piano Method Songbook — *Stevens, Wendy*
c   The Worst-Case Scenario Handbook (Illus. by Gonzales, Chuck) — *Borgenicht, David*
c   The Worst Class Trip Ever (Read by Haberkorn, Todd). Audiobook Review — *Barry, Dave*
y   The Worst Class Trip Ever (Illus. by Cannell, Jon) — *Barry, Dave*
c   The Worst Day Ever! (Illus. by Head, Ron) — *Reece, Debbie*
c   Worst in Show (Illus. by Hindley, Kate) — *Bee, William*
The Worst of Times: How Life on Earth Survived Eighty Million Years of Extinctions — *Wignall, Paul B.*
c   The Worst Witch to the Rescue — *Murphy, Jill*
Worte - Konzepte - Bedeutungen. Welche Historische Semantik fur das Mittelalter? Abschlusstagung des Leibniz-Projekts "Politische Sprache im Mittelalter. Semantische Zugange"
Worth Fighting For — *Fanning, Rory*
The Worth of War — *Ginsberg, Benjamin*
Worth the Trouble — *Beck, Jamie*
Worth Writing About: Exploring Memoir with Adolescents — *Wizner, Jake*
Worthy Fights: A Memoir of Leadership in War and Peace — *Panetta, Leon*
A Worthy Heart — *Mason, Susan Anne*
A Worthy Pursuit — *Witemeyer, Karen*
c   The Would-Be Witch — *Chew, Ruth*
Would I Like Jesus? A Casual Walk through the Life of Jesus — *Fleming, Peter*
c   Would the Real Stanley Carrot Please Stand Up? — *Stevens, Rob*
Would they Lie to You? How to Spin Friends and Manipulate People — *Hotton, Robert*
Would They Lie to You? How to Spin Friends and Manipulate People — *Hutton, Robert*
c   Would You Rather...Dine with a Dung Beetle or Lunch with a Maggot? (Illus. by Howells, Mel) — *de la Bedoyere, Camilla*
y   The Wound Is Mortal: The Story of the Assassination of Abraham Lincoln — *Gunderson, Jessica*

c   Woundabout (Illus. by Rosen, Ellis) — *Rosen, Lev*
Wounded: A New History of the Western Front in World War I — *Mayhew, Emily*
The Wounded Thorn — *Sampson, Fay*
Wounded Tiger: A History of Cricket in Pakistan — *Oborne, Peter*
The Wounded World — *Sieling, Ariele*
The Wounded Yellow Butterfly — *Diaz, Linda*
Wounds in the Middle Ages — *Kirkham, Anne*
Woven Miniatures of Buddhist Art: Sazigyo, Burmese Manuscript Binding Tapes — *Isaacs, Ralph*
y   Woven — *Jensen, Michael*
y   Woven — *King, David Powers*
c   Wow! I Didn't Know That: Surprising Facts About Pirates (Illus. by Aspinall, Marc) — *Steele, Philip*
c   Wow Wow and Haw Haw (Illus. by Pittman, Michael) — *Murray, George*
Wrapped in Color: 30 Shawls to Knit — *Landra, Maie*
y   The Wrath and the Dawn (Read by Delawari, Ariana). Audiobook Review — *Ahdieh, Renee*
y   The Wrath and the Dawn — *Ahdieh, Renee*
The Wrath of Capital: Neoliberalism and Climate Change Politics — *Parr, Adrian*
y   Wrath of the Caid — *O'Neill, Joe*
Wrath of the Dixie Mafia — *Sinor, Paul*
Wrath of the Furies — *Saylor, Steven*
Wreck and Order — *Tennant-Moore, Hannah*
Wrecks of Human Ambition: A History of Utah's Canyon Country to 1936 — *Nelson, Paul T.*
c   The Wren and the Sparrow (Illus. by Nayberg, Yevgenia) — *Lewis, J. Patrick*
Wrestlers, Pigeon Fanciers and Kite Flyers: Traditional Sports and Pastimes in Lahore — *Frembgen, Jurgen Wasim*
Wrestling for My Life: The Legend, the Reality, and the Faith of a WWE Superstar — *Michaels, Shawn*
Wrestling On and Off the Mat — *Baughman, R. Wayne*
Wrestling With God: Stories of Doubt and Faith — *Newhall Barbara Falconer*
The Wright Brothers. Audiobook Review — *McCullough, David*
y   The Wright Brothers — *McCullough, David*
The Wright Company: From Invention to Industry — *Roach, Edward J.*
Wrightslaw: All about Tests and Assessments — *Farrall, Melissa Lee*
c   The Wrinkled Crown — *Nesbet, Anne*
y   Wrinkles — *Roca, Paco*
Write, If You Live to Get There — *Sonntag, Mary K.*
Write On! Math — *Gerver, Robert*
Write Your Own Fairy Tale: The New Rules for Dating, Relationships, and Finding Love on Your Terms — *Flicker, Siggy*
y   Writer to Writer: From Think to Ink — *Levine, Gail Carson*
The Writers: A History of American Screenwriters and Their Guild — *Banks, Miranda J.*
Writing Across the Landscape: Travel Journals, 1960-2010 — *Ferlinghetti, Lawrence*
Writing America: Literary Landmarks from Walden Pond to Wounded Knee — *Fishkin, Shelley Fisher*
Writing and Reading Byzantine Secular Poetry, 1025-1081 — *Bernard, Floris*
Writing and Reading in Medieval Manuscript Culture: The Translation and Transmission of the Story of Elye in Old French and Old Norse Literary Texts — *Eriksen, Stefka Georgieva*
Writing as Poaching: Interpellation and Self-Fashioning in Colonial Relaciones de meritos y servicios — *Folger, Robert*
Writing Down the Myths — *Nagy, J.F.*
Writing Faith and Telling Tales: Literature, Politics, and Religion in the Work of Thomas More — *Betteridge, Thomas*
c   Writing Fantastic Fiction — *Anderson, Jennifer Joline*
Writing Fashion in Early Modern Italy: From Sprezzatura to Satire — *Paulicelli, Eugenia*
Writing for the "New Yorker": Critical Essays on an American Periodical — *Green, Fiona*
Writing History for the King: Henry II and the Politics of Vernacular Historiography — *Urbanski, Charity*
Writing History in the Age of Biomedicine — *Cooter, Roger*
Writing History in the Global Era — *Hunt, Lynn*
Writing in the Air: Heterogeneity and the Persistence of Oral Tradition in Andean Literature — *Polar, Antonio Cornejo*
Writing in the Kitchen: Essays on Southern Literature and Foodways — *Davis, David A.*

Writing Local History Today: A Guide to Researching, Publishing, and Marketing Your Book — *Mason, Thomas A.*
Writing Material Culture History — *Gerritsen, Anne*
Writing on the Wall — *Abu-Jamal, Mumia*
Writing Postcommunism: Towards a Literature of the East European Ruins — *Williams, David (b. 1976-)*
Writing, Reading, Grieving: Essays in Memory of Suzanne Dow — *Cruickshank, Ruth*
Writing Royal Entries in Early Modern Europe — *Canova-Green, Marie-Claude*
Writing Short Stories — *Newland, Courttia*
Writing the Early Crusades: Text, Transmission and Memory — *Bull, Marcus*
Writing the Future: Prognostic Texts of Medieval England — *Hunt, Tony*
Writing the Gettysburg Address — *Johnson, Martin P.*
Writing the Rebellion: Loyalists and the Literature of Politics in British America — *Gould, Philip*
Writing the Record: The Village Voice and the Birth of Rock Criticism — *Powers, Devon*
Writing the Seaman's Tale in Law and Literature: Dana, Melville, and Justice Story — *Mudgett, Kathryn*
Writing the War: Chronicles of a World War II Correspondent — *Kiley, Charles*
Writing Travel in Central Asian History — *Green, Nile*
Writing War: Soldiers Record the Japanese Empire — *Moore, Aaron William*
Writing Workouts to Develop Common Core Writing Skills: Step by Step Exercises, Activities, and Tips for Student Success, Grades 2-6 — *Haven, Kendall*
Writing Workouts to Develop Common Core Writing Skills: Step by Step Exercises, Activities, and Tips for Student Success, Grades 7-12 — *Haven, Kendall*
Writings on Medicine — *Canguilhem, Georges*
c   Written and Drawn by Henrietta (Illus. by Liniers) — *Liniers*
Written in Fire — *Sakey, Marcus*
Written in My Own Heart's Blood — *Gabaldon, Diana*
Written in Stone: A Journey through the Stone Age and the Origins of Modern Language — *Stevens, Christopher*
Written in the Blood — *Jones, Stephen Lloyd*
y   Written in the Stars — *Saeed, Aisha*
Written in the Stars — *McLane, LuAnn*
y   Written in the Stars — *Saeed, Aisha*
The Written Word in the Medieval Arabic Lands: A Social and Cultural History of Reading Practices. — *Hirschiler, Konrad*
y   Wrong about the Guy — *LaZebnik, Claire*
The Wrong Bride — *Callen, Gayle*
The Wrong Enemy: America in Afghanistan, 2001-2014 — *Gall, Carlotta*
The Wrong Hands: Popular Weapons Mannuals and Their Historic Challenges to a Democratic Society — *Larabee, Ann*
The Wrong Man (Read by Bennett, Erin). Audiobook Review — *White, Kate*
The Wrong Man — *White, Kate*
Wrong: Nine Economic Policy Disasters and What We Can Learn from Them — *Grossman, Richard S.*
c   The Wrong Pong (Illus. by Fisher, Chris) — *Butler, Steven*
y   The Wrong Side of Right — *Thorne, Jenn Marie*
c   The Wrong Side of the Bed (Illus. by Raff, Anna) — *Bakos, Lisa M.*
Wrong Side of the Grave — *Butler, Bryna*
Wrongful Conviction — *Heijens, Janet*
Wrongful Death — *Sellers, L.J.*
Wrongful Deaths: Selected Inquest Records from Nineteenth-Century Korea — *Kim, Sun Joo*
Wrongly Charged: A Look at the Legal System — *Merkatz, David*
Wrote for Luck — *Taylor, D.J.*
Wurttemberger in Nordamerika: Migration von der Schwabischen Alb im 19. Jahrhundert — *Krebber, Jochen*
Wurzel, Stamm, Krone: Furstliche Genealogie in Fruhneuzeitlichen Druckwerken — *Bauer, Volker*
Wuvable Oaf — *Luce, Ed*
Wyatt Abroad: Tudor Diplomacy and the Translation of Power — *Rossiter, William T.*
c   Wyatt Earp — *Mattern, Joanne*
Wyatt in Wichita — *Shirley, John*
Wylding Hall — *Hand, Elizabeth*
Wytches (Illus. by Jock) — *Snyder, Scott*
Wytchfire — *Meyerhofer, Michael*
y   WYW — *Dollahite, Derek*

X Y Z

X-15 Rocket Plane: Plying the First Wings into Space — *Evans, Michelle*
y **X** — *Magoon, Kekla*
y **X** — *Shabazz, Ilyasah*
X — *Groarke, Vona*
c **X Marks the Spot** (Illus. by Whamond, Dave) — *Szpinglas, Jeff*
X — *Grafton, Sue*
X — *Shabazz, Ilyasah*
Xbox Revisited: A Game Plan for Corporate and Civic Renewal — *Bach, Robbie*
Xerxes: A Persian Life — *Stoneman, Richard*
Xi Jingping: The Governance of China — *Jingping, Xi*
y **XIII Mystery: The Mongoose** (Illus. by Dorison, Xavier) — *Meyer, Ralph*
XML for Catalogers and Metadata Librarians — *Cole, Timothy W.*
y **Xodus** — *McPike, K.J.*
c **Xtreme Fish Series** — *Hamilton, S.L.*
c **Xtreme Insects** — *Hamilton, S.L.*
c **The XYZs of Being Wicked** — *Chapman, Lara*
Y Negative — *Haworth, Kelly*
Y no se lo Trago la Tierra / And the Earth Did Not Devour Him — *Rivera, Tomas*
Yahweh to Hell: Why We Need Jesus Out of Politics! — *Woods, Rich*
c **Yak and Gnu** (Illus. by Chapman, Cat) — *MacIver, Juliette*
c **Yaks Yak: Animal Word Pairs** (Illus. by Reinhardt, Jennifer Black) — *Park, Linda Sue*
Yamasaki in Detroit — *Gallagher, John*
A Yankee in De Valera's Ireland: The Memoir of David Gray — *Henry, Paul*
c **Yankees and Rebels: Stories of the U.S. Civil War Leaders** — *Otfinoski, Steven*
Yankel's Tavern: Jews, Liquor, and Life in the Kingdom of Poland — *Dynner, Glenn*
Yanks and Limeys: Alliance Warfare in the Second World War — *Barr, Niall*
y **Yappy Hour** — *Orgain, Diana*
The Yaquis and the Empire: Violence, Spanish Imperial Power, and Native Resilience in Colonial Mexico — *Folsom, Raphael Brewster*
c **Yard Sale** (Illus. by Castillo, Lauren) — *Bunting, Eve*
c **Yard War** — *Kitchings, Taylor*
Yarn Happy: Traditional Norwegian Designs for Modern Knit and Crochet — *Lindeland, Turid*
Yarned and Dangerous — *Hartwell, Sadie*
A Year in China: Bill Wong's Diaries in His Father's Home Village 1936-37 — *Wong, Bill*
y **A Year in the Life of a Complete and Total Genius** — *Matson, Stacey*
The Year My Mother Came Back — *Cohen, Alice Eve*
y **The Year of Chasing Dreams** — *McDaniel, Lurlene*
The Year of Fear: Machine Gun Kelly and the Manhunt That Changed the Nation — *Urschel, Joe*
The Year of Fear — *Urschel, Joe*
The Year of Indecision, 1946: A Tour through the Crucible of Harry Truman's America — *Weisbrode, Kenneth*
y **The Year of Lear: Shakespeare in 1606** — *Shapiro, James*
A Year of Learning, Laughter, and Life: 365 Motivational Parables — *Rajah, Jaishen*
A Year of Living Prayerfully: How a Curious Traveler Met the Pope, Walked on Coals, Danced with Rabbis, and Revived His Prayer Life (Read by Brock, Jared). Audiobook Review — *Brock, Jared*
A Year of Living Prayerfully: How A Curious Traveler Met the Pope, Walked on Coals, Danced with Rabbis, and Revived His Prayer Life — *Brock, Jared*

Year of the Cow: How 420 Pounds of Beef Built a Better Life for One American Family — *Stone, Jared*
c **The Year of the Dog** (Read by Wu, Nancy). Audiobook Review — *Lin, Grace*
Year of the Dunk: A Modest Defiance of Gravity — *Price, Asher*
Year of the Fat Knight: The Falstaff Diaries — *Sher, Antony*
The Year of the Rat. Audiobook Review — *Furniss, Clare*
y **The Year of the Rat** — *Furniss, Clare*
The Year of the Runaways — *Sahota, Sunjeev*
c **The Year of the Sheep: Tales from the Chinese Zodiac** (Illus. by Chau, Alina) — *Chin, Oliver*
c **The Year of the Three Sisters** (Illus. by Barton, Patrice) — *Cheng, Andrea*
Year-Round Indoor Salad Gardening: How to Grow Nutrient-Dense, Soil-Sprouted Greens in Less Than 10 Days — *Burke, Peter*
The Year She Left Us — *Ma, Kathryn*
A Year Unplugged: A Family's Life without Technology — *Kolberg, Sharael*
y **The Year We Fell Apart** — *Martin, Emily (b. 1987-)*
c **The Year We Sailed the Sun** — *Nelsn, Theresa*
c **The Year We Sailed the Sun** — *Nelson, Theresa*
The Year Without a Purchase: One Family's Quest to Stop Shopping and Start Connecting — *Dannemiller, Scott*
c **A Year without Mom** (Illus. by Tolstikova, Dasha) — *Tolstikova, Dasha*
The Year Yellowstone Burned: A Twenty-Five-Year Perspective — *Henry, Jeff*
Year Zero: A History of 1945 — *Buruma, Ian*
y **The Yearbook** — *Masciola, Carol*
The Yearling — *Mei-en, Lo Kwa*
Yearning for Normal — *Busch, Susan Ellison*
Yearning for the New Age: Laura Holloway-Langford and Late Victorian Spirituality — *Sasson, Diane*
Yearning: Race, Gender and Cultural Politics — *Hooks, Bell*
The Year's Best Military SF and Space Opera — *Afsharirad, David*
The Year's Best Science Fiction, 2015 — *Dozois, Gardner*
The Year's Best Science Fiction and Fantasy Novellas 2015 — *Guran, Paula*
y **Year's Best Young Adult Speculative Fiction 2014** — *Rios, Julia*
The Years — *Delbanco, Nicholas*
Years of Plenty, Years of Want: France and the Legacy of the Great War — *Martin, Benjamin Franklin*
The Years of Zero: Coming of Age under the Khmer Rouge — *Ty, Seng*
The Year's Work at the Zombie Research Center — *Comentale, Edward P.*
Yeats and Afterwords: Christ, Culture, and Crisis — *Howes, Marjorie*
Yee? Baw for Bokes: Essays on Medieval Manuscripts and Poetics in Honor of Hoyt N. Duggan — *Calabrese, Michael*
Yell Less, Love More: How the Orange Rhino Mom Stopped Yelling at Her Kids--and How You Can Too! — *McCraith, Sheila*
c **The Yelling Stones** — *Jensen, Oscar*
Yellow and Blue — *Clark, Thomas A.*
c **Yellow Animals** — *Borth, Teddy*
The Yellow Birds — *Powers, Kevin*
c **Yellow Copter** (Illus. by Petrone, Valeria) — *Hamilton, Kersten*

The Yellow Peril: Dr. Fu Manchu and the Rise of Chinaphobia — *Frayling, Christopher*
The Yellow River: The Problem of Water in Modern China — *Pietz, David A.*
The Yellow Table: A Celebration of Everyday Gatherings (Illus. by Birck, Signe) — *Carl, Anna Watson*
The Yellowhammer War: The Civil War and Reconstruction in Alabama — *Noe, Kenneth W.*
Yellowstone Wildlife: Ecology and Natural History of the Greater Yellowstone Ecosystem — *Johnsgard, Paul A.*
The Yeomen of the Guard and the Early Tudors: The Formation of a Royal Bodyguard — *Hewerdine, Anita*
Yes, My Accent Is Real: And Some Other Things I Haven't Told You — *Nayyar, Kunal*
Yes! My Improbable Journey to the Main Event of WrestleMania — *Bryan, Daniel*
y **Yes!: My Improbable Journey to the Main Event of Wrestlemania** — *Tello, Craig*
c **The Yes** (Illus. by Kitamura, Satoshi) — *Bee, Sarah*
Yes Please (Read by Poehler, Amy). Audiobook Review — *Poehler, Amy*
Yes! Poems and Paintings by Michael Robbins — *Robbins, Michael*
Yes, You Can! — *Thompson, Gail L.*
Yeshu — *Kleymeyer, Charles David*
Yesterday Came Suddenly — *King, Francis*
c **Yesterday's Voices Series** — *Phillips, Dee*
Yet All Shall Be Well — *Heisey, Daniel J.*
Yet More Mind-Bending Puzzles and Fascinating Facts — *Williams, Paul*
Yet One More Spring: A Critical Study of Joy Davidman — *King, Don W.*
c **Yeti and the Bird** (Illus. by Shireen, Nadia) — *Shireen, Nadia*
Yiayia Visits Amalia — *Mackavey, Maria G.*
The Yid — *Goldberg, Paul*
The Yiddish Fish — *Cohen, Santiago*
The Yilna Vegetarian Cookbook: Garden-Fresh Recipes Rediscovered and Adapted for Today's Kitchen — *Jochnowitz, Eve*
Yin Xiuzhen — *Eungie Joo*
Yinyang: The Way of Heaven and Earth in Chinese Thought and Culture — *Wang, Robin R.*
y **Ylsnavan, Realms of Elsvanische** — *Loveland, Helena*
Yo Miss: A Graphic Look at High School — *Wilde, Lisa*
Yo Miz! — *Rose, Elizabeth*
Yo Soy Negro: Blackness in Peru — *Golash-Boza, Tanya*
c **Yoda: The Story of a Cat and His Kittens** (Illus. by Crane, Devin) — *Stern, Beth*
Yoga for Cancer: A Guide to Managing Side Effects, Boosting Immunity, and Improving Recovery for Cancer Survivors — *Prinster, Tari*
c **Yoga for Kids: Simple Animal Poses for Any Age** (Illus. by Forlati, Anna) — *Pajalunga, Lorena V.*
y **Yoga for You** — *Rissman, Rebecca*
y **Yoga for Your Mind and Body: A Teenage Practice for a Healthy, Balanced Life** — *Rissman, Rebecca*
Yoga Therapy for Stress and Anxiety: Create a Personalized Holistic Plan to Balance Your Life — *Butera, Robert*
Yogurt Culture: A Global Look at How to Make, Bake, Sip and Chill the World's Creamiest, Healthiest Food — *Rule, Cheryl Sternman*
c **Yoko** (Illus. by Wells, Rosemary) — *Wells, Rosemary*
Yokohama, California — *Mori, Toshio*
y **YOLO Juliet** — *Shakespeare, William*
c **Yolo** — *Jones, Sam*

y Yolo — Myracle, Lauren
Yoruba Art and Language: Seeking the African in African Art — Abiodun, Rowland
Yoruba Elites and Ethnics Politics in Nigeria: Obafemi Awolowo and Corporate Agency — Adebanwi, Wale
Yoruba Traditions and African American Religious Nationalism — Hucks, Tracey E.
Yosef Haim Brenner: A Life — Shapira, Anita
y You and Me and Him — Dinnison, Kris
c You and Me (Illus. by Reynolds, Peter H.) — Verde, Susan
c You Are a Powerful Creator, My Little One: Creating Happiness (Illus. by Matheus, Robert Paul) — Iglesias, Monica
You Are Dead — James, Peter
You Are Here: Around the World in 92 Minutes - Photographs from the International Space Station — Hadfield, Chris
You. Are. Not. Alone. — Watkins, W.R.
c You Are Not My Friend, But I Miss You (Illus. by Kirk, Daniel) — Kirk, Daniel
You Are Woman, You Are Divine: The Modern Woman's Journey Back to The Goddess — Starr, Renee
c You Call That Brave? (Illus. by Scharer, Kathrin) — Pauli, Lorenz
c You Call That Brave? (Illus. by Scharer, Kathrin) — Wilson, David Henry
c You Can Do It, Bert! (Illus. by Konnecke, Ole) — Konnecke, Ole
You Can Leave Anytime — Dinsmoor, Rob
You Can Trust Me — McKenzie, Sophie
You Can Trust Me — MeKenzie, Sophie
c You Can't Build a House If You're a Hippo!: A Book about All Kinds of Houses (Illus. by Haley, Amanda) — Ehrlich, Fred
y You Can't See the Elephants — Kreller, Susan
c You Can't Sit with Us — Rue, Nancy
c You Can't Take Your Body to a Car Mechanic! A Book About What Makes You Sick (Illus. by Haley, Amanda) — Ehrlich, Fred
You Come Too — Francis, Lesley Lee
You Could Look It Up: The Reference Shelf from Ancient Babylon to Wikipedia — Lynch, Jack
You Deserve a Drink: Boozy Misadventures and Tales of Debauchery — Hart, Mamrie
c You Do the Math Series — Koll, Hilary
You Don't Die of Love — Thonson, Thomas
You Don't Have to Like Me: Essays on Growing Up, Speaking Out, and Finding Feminism — Nugent, Alida
You Don't Have to Live Like This — Markovits, Benjamin
y You Don't Say: Stories 2004-2013 (Illus. by Powell, Nate) — Powell, Nate
You Fascinate Me So: The Life and Times of Cy Coleman — Propst, Andy
c You Have a Pet What?! Hedgehog — Matzke, Ann
c You Have a Pet What?! Mini Horse — Matzke, Ann
c You Have a Pet What?! Mini Pig — Reed, Cristie
c You Have a Pet What?! Sugar Glider — Kenney, Karen Latchana
You Have It Made: Delicious, Healthy, Do-Ahead Meals — Krieger, Ellie
You Have Never Been Here — Rickert, Mary
You Know Who Killed Me — Estleman, Loren D.
You Look Like That Girl: A Child Actor Stops Pretending and Finally Grows Up — Jakub, Lisa
c You Look Yummy! (Illus. by Miyanishi, Tatsuya) — Miyanishi, Tatsuya
c You Make Me Happy (Illus. by Bakker, Jenny) — Swerts, An
c You Nest Here with Me (Illus. by Sweet, Melissa) — Stemple, Heidi E. Y.
c You Nest Here with Me (Illus. by Sweet, Melissa) — Yolen, Jane
c You Never Heard of Casey Stengel?! (Illus. by Blitt, Barry) — Winter, Jonah
You Only Live Once: A Lifetime of Experiences for the Explorer in All of Us — Lonely Planet
You Rule! A Practical Guide to Creating Your Own Kingdom — Forbes, Scott
You Should Pity Us Instead — Gustine, Amy
c You Tell Me (Illus. by Paul, Korky) — McGough, Roger
You Too Can Have a Body Like Mine — Kleeman, Alexandra
y You Were Here — McCarthy, Cori
You Will Never Find Me — Wilson, Robert (b. 1957-)
c You Wouldn't Want to Live without Dentists! (Illus. by Antram, David) — MacDonald, Fiona

The Young Ataturk: From Ottoman Soldier to Statesman of Turkey — Gawrych, George W.
Young Catholic America: Emerging Adults In, Out of, and Gone from the Church — Smith, Christian
c Young Charlotte, Filmmaker (Illus. by Viva, Frank) — Viva, Frank
Young Eliot: From St. Louis to The Waste Land — Crawford, Robert
Young Eliot: From St. Louis to The Waste Land — Crawford, Robert (b. 1959-)
y The Young Elites — Lu, Marie
Young Elizabeth: The Making of the Queen — Williams, Kate (b. 1974-)
Young Enough to Change the World: Stories of Kids and Teens Who Turned Their Dreams into Actions — Connolly, Michael P.
c Young-hee and the Pullocho — Russell, Mark James
Young Irelanders — Lordan, Dave
y Young Jane Austen: Becoming a Writer (Illus. by Mongiardo, Massimo) — Pliscou, Lisa
Young Lawrence: A Portrait of the Legend as a Young Man — Sattin, Anthony
y Young Man with Camera — Sher, Emil
Young Men, Time, and Boredom in the Republic of Georgia — Frederiksen, Martin Demant
Young Milton: The Emerging Author, 1620-1642 — Jones, Edward
Young Once — Modiano, Patrick
Young Orson: The Years of Luck and Genius on the Path to Citizen Kane — McGilligan, Patrick
Young Ovid: A Life Recreated — Middlebrook, Diana
Young People and the Shaping of Public Space in Melbourne, 1870-1914 — Sleight, Simon
Young Skins — Barrett, Colin
The Young T.E. Lawrence — Sattin, Anthony
Young Titan: The Making of Winston Churchill — Shelden, Michael
The Young Turks' Crime Against Humanity: The Armenian Genocide and the Ethnic Cleansing in the Ottoman Empire — Ackam, Taner
Young, Well-Educated, and Adaptable: Chilean Exiles in Ontario and Quebec, 1973-2010 — Peddle, Francis
y Young Widows Club — Coutts, Alexandra
y The Young World (Read by Julian, Jose). Audiobook Review — Weitz, Chris
y The Young World — Weitz, Chris
Youngblood — Gallagher, Matt
Younger-Generation Korean Experiences in the United States: Personal Narratives on Ethnic and Racial Identities — Chung, Thomas
c Your Alien (Illus. by Fujita, Goro) — Sauer, Tammi
c Your Baby's First Word Will be Dada (Illus. by Ordonez, Miguel) — Fallon, Jimmy
Your Band Sucks: What I Saw at Indie Rock's Failed Revolution (But Can No Longer Hear). — Fine, Jon
Your Band Sucks: What I Saw at Indie Rock's Failed Revolution (but Can No Longer Hear). (Read by Fine, Jon). Audiobook Review — Fine, Jon
Your Cash Is Flowing: Why Every Entrepreneur Needs to Think Like a CFO — Homza, Kenneth M.
Your Child in the Hospital: A Practical Guide for Parents. 3d ed. — Keene, Nancy
Your Dog and You — Walters, Tom
Your Dream Job: Use Dating Secrets to Get Hired and Build a Career You Love — Bokich, Dom
y Your Father Sends His Love — Evers, Stuart
c Your Hand in My Hand (Illus. by Teckentrup, Britta) — Sperring, Mark
c Your Head Shape Reveals Your Personality: Science's Biggest Mistakes about the Human Body — Zuchora-Walske, Christine
Your Healthy Brain — Kiraly, Stephen J.
Your Heart Is a Muscle the Size of a Fist — Yapa, Sunil
y Your Kids: Cooking! A Recipe for Turning Ordinary Kids into Extraordinary Cooks — Brandt, Barbara
Your Life Idyllic — Bernier, Craig
c Your Money: How You Spend Your Money and Why (Illus. by Beech, Mark) — Bailey, Gerry
Your New Pregnancy Bible: The Experts' Guide to Pregnancy and Early Parenthood, 4th ed. — Stone, Joanne
Your New Prime: 30 Days to Better Sex, Eternal Strength, and a Kick-Ass Life After 40 — Cooper, Craig
Your Next Breath — Johansen, Iris
Your Next Mission: A Personal Branding Guide for the Military-to-Civilian Transition — Citroen, Lida D.

Your Own Terms: A Woman's Guide to Taking Charge of Any Negotiation — Davidds, Yasmin
Your Personal Hang-Ups — Standish, Stephanie
Your Smallest Bones — Taylor, Sean D.
Your Strategy Needs a Strategy — Reeves, Martin
y Your Voice Is All I Hear — Scheier, Leah
y Your Water Footprint — Leahy, Stephen
Your Weight or Your Life?: Balancing the Scale for A Healthy Life — McCalmon, Barbara
c You're a Crab! A Moody Day Book (Illus. by Whitehead, Jenny) — Whitehead, Jenny
You're Better Than Me: A Memoir — McFarlane, Bonnie
c You're Here for a Reason (Illus. by Tillman, Nancy) — Tillman, Nancy
y You're Invited — Malone, Jen
y You're Invited Too — Malone, Jen
You're Loved No Matter What: Freeing Your Heart from the Need to Be Perfect — Gerth, Holley
You're Never Weird on the Internet (Almost). (Read by Day, Felicia). Audiobook Review — Day, Felicia
You're Never Weird on the Internet — Day, Felicia
You're Never Weird on the Internet (Almost). — Day, Felicia
y You're Never Weird on the Internet — Day, Felicia
You're Not Edith — Gruber, Allison
c You're Pulling My Leg! (Illus. by Brace, Eric) — Street, Pat
You're the Earl That I Want — Bowen, Kelly
y You're the Kind of Girl I Write Songs About — Herborn, Daniel
You're the One That I Want — Warren, Susan May
Yours in Haste and Adoration: Selected Letters of Terry Southern — Southern, Nile
y Youth Activism in an Era of Education Inequality — Kirshner, Ben
Youth: Autobiographical Writings — Koeppen, Wolfgang
Youth Gangs, Violence and Social Respect — White, Rob
Youth Work: An Institutional Ethnography of Youth Homelessness — Nichols, Naomi
c YouTube Founders Steve Chen, Chad Hurley, and Jawed Karim — Wooster, Patricia
You've Heard These Hands: From the Wall of Sound to the Wrecking Crew and Other Incredible Stories — Randi, Don
c The Yoyo and the Piggy Bank (Illus. by Eveland, Keith) — Thoresen, Susan Werner
Ysengrimus — Mann, Jill
Yucatan Is Murder — Wyle, Dirk
Yuchi Folklore: Cultural Expression in a Southeastern Native American Community — Jackson, Jason Baird
c Yuck! Said the Yak (Illus. by Levey, Emma) — English, Alex
y Yukarism (Illus. by Shiomi, Chika) — Shiomi, Chika
Yukio Mishima — Flanagan, Damian
c The Yule Tomte and the Little Rabbits: A Christmas Story for Advent (Illus. by Eriksson, Eva) — Stark, Ulf
Yum — Nicassio, Theresa
YumUniverse: Infinite Possibilities for a Gluten-Free, Plant-Powerful, Whole-Food Lifestyle — Crosby, Heather
Yves Saint Laurent's Studio: Mirror and Secrets — Savignon, Jeromine
Zac & Mia (Read by Mondelli, Nicholas, with Kristin Condon) — Betts, A.J.
y Zac & Mia — Betts, A.J.
c Zac Power: Mission Swamp Race (Illus. by Hook, Andy) — Larry, H.I.
c Zack Delacruz: Me and My Big Mouth — Anderson, Jeff
c Zacktastic (Illus. by Crosby, Jeff) — Sheimel, Courtney
y Zafir: Through My Eyes — Mason, Prue
Zagreb Cowboy — Mattich, Alen
Zagreb Noir — Srsen, Ivan
Zahav: A World of Israeli Cooking — Solomonov, Michael
Zahnarzte und Dentisten vor, wahrend und nach der Zeit des Nationalsozialismus
Zakotrljaj me oko sveta — Radojicic, Snezana
c Zak's King Arthur Adventure (Illus. by Alder, Charlie) — Guillain, Adam
Zambia: Building Prosperity from Resource Wealth — Adam, Christopher S.
Zambia: The First 50 Years: Reflections of an Eyewitness — Sardanis, Andrew
c Zapato Pozver: Freddie Ramos Stomps the Snow (Illus. by Benitez, Miguel) — Jules, Jacqueline

c Zar and the Broken Spaceship (Illus. by Germano, Santiago) — *O'Dell, Dino*
c Zazette, la chatte des ouendats (Illus. by Lamarre, Adeline) — *Marchildon, Daniel*
Zeitenwende 1914: Kunstler, Dichter und Denker im Ersten Weltkrieg — *Bruendel, Steffen*
Zeitgenossenschaft: Zum Auschwitz-Prozess 1964 — *Warnke, Martin*
c Zeke Meeks vs. the Annoying Princess Sing-Along (Illus. by Alves, Josh) — *Green, D.L.*
c Zeke Meeks vs. the Crummy Class Play (Illus. by Alves, Josh) — *Green, D.L.*
Zen Anarchism: The Egalitarian Dharma of Uchiyama Gudo — *Rambelli, Fabio*
Zen and the Art of Cannibalism — *Younger, Daniel*
Zen and the Art of Local History — *Kammen, Carol*
Zen and the Spiritual Exercises: Paths of Awakening and Transformation — *Habito, Ruben L.F.*
Zen And The White Whale: A Buddhist Rendering of Moby-Dick — *Herman, Daniel*
Zen Doodle: Oodles of Doodles — *Jenny, Tonia*
Zen Koans — *Heine, Steven*
Zen of the Plains: Experiencing Wild Western Places — *Olstad, Tyra A.*
c Zen Socks (Illus. by Muth, Jon J.) — *Muth, Jon J.*
Zen: The Authentic Gate — *Yamada, Koun*
c Zendaya: Disney Channel Actress — *Diver, Lucas*
Zensur im Vormarz: Pressefreiheit und Informationskontrolle in Europa — *Clemens, Gabriele B.*
Zentrum Revisited. Bilanz und Perspektiven der Forschung zum Politischen Katholizismus im Kaiserreich
y Zer0es (Read by Benson, Amber). Audiobook Review — *Biancotti, Deborah*
y Zer0es — *Biancotti, Deborah*
Zer0es — *Wendig, Chuck*
y Zero Day — *Gangsei, Jan*
c The Zero Degree Zombie Zone (Illus. by Craft, Jerry) — *Bass, Patrik Henry*
Zero Footprint — *Chase, Simon*
y Zero Hour: Department 19, Book 4 — *Hill, Will*
Zero Hunger: Political Culture and Antipoverty Policy in Northeast Brazil — *Ansell, Aaron*
Zero K — *DeLillo, Don*
Zero Night — *Felton, Mark*
Zero to One: Notes on Startups, or How to Build the Future — *Masters, Blake*
Zero to One: Notes on Startups, or How to Build the Future — *Thiel, Peter*
Zero World — *Hough, Jason M.*
y Zeroboxer — *Lee, Fonda*
y Zeroes — *Westerfeld, Scott*
ZeroZeroZero — *Saviano, Roberto*
Zerrissene Loyalitaten. Politische und kulturelle Orientierungen im Ersten Weltkrieg: Bukowina, Galizien, Bessarabien — *Coles, Anthony*
c Zheng He, the Great Chinese Explorer: A Bilingual Story of Adventure and Discovery — *Jian, Li*

c Zheng He, the Great Chinese Explorer: A Bilingual Story of Adventure and Discovery (Illus. by Jian, Li) — *Jian, Li*
The Zhivago Affair: The Kremlin, the CIA, and the Battle Over a Forbidden Book — *Finn, Peter*
Zibaldone — *Rucellai, Giovanni di Pagolo*
Ziegfeld and His Follies: A Biography of Broadway's Greatest Producer — *Brideson, Cynthia*
Zielregion Ostmitteleuropa - Migration im 20. Jahrhundert
c Zig and the Magic Umbrella (Illus. by Kantorovitz, Sylvie) — *Kantorovitz, Sylvie*
c Zig Zag et Frankenmouche — *Arnold, Tedd*
c Zig Zag et Zazie (Illus. by Arnold, Tedd) — *Arnold, Tedd*
The Zig Zag Girl (Read by Langton, James). Audiobook Review — *Griffiths, Elly*
The Zig Zag Girl — *Griffiths, Elly*
Zigaretten-Fronten: Die politischen Kulturen des Rauchens in der Zeit des Ersten Weltkriegs — *Schindelbeck, Dirk*
Zillow Talk: The New Rules of Real Estate — *Humphries, Stan*
Zing! By Gorji — *Chef Gorji*
Zip It: A Fancy Book of Fastenings (Illus. by Galloway, Fhiona) — *Hogarty, Patricia*
c Zip It: A First Book of Fasteners (Illus. by Galloway, Fhiona) — *Hegarty, Patricia*
c Zippy the Runner (Illus. by Seon, Jeong-Hyeon) — *Kim, JiYu*
y Zodiac — *Russell, Romina*
The Zodiac Recipe: An Effortless Recipe That is Certain to Help You Better Understand Your Partners, Friends and Ourselves — *Wiersma, Jacquelyn*
Zodiac Station — *Harper, Tom*
c Zombelina Dances The Nutcracker (Illus. by Idle, Molly) — *Crow, Kristyn*
The Zombie Book: The Encyclopedia of the Living Dead — *Redfern, Nick*
c The Zombie Combat Field Guide — *Ma, Roger*
c Zombie in Love 2 + 1 (Illus. by Campbell, Scott) — *DiPucchio, Kelly*
Zombie Loyalists: Using Great Service To Create Rabid Fans. Audiobook Review — *Shankman, Peter*
Zombie Moose of West Bath, Maine — *Hinton, Marsha*
Zombies: A Cultural History — *Luckhurst, Roger*
Zombies and Calculus — *Adams, Colin*
c Zombies in Nature — *Larson, Kirsten W.*
c Zombies of the Carribbean (Illus. by DeGrand, David) — *Kloepfer, John*
The Zone: A Prison Camp Guard's Story — *Dovlatov, Sergei*
The Zone of Interest — *Amis, Martin*
Zone: Selected Poems — *Apollinaire, Guillaume*
Zoned in the USA: The Origins and Implications of American Land-Use Regulation — *Hirt, Sonia*
Zong! — *Philip, M. NourbeSe*

Zoo Animals: Behaviour, Management and Welfare — *Pankhurst, Sheila*
c The Zoo at the Edge of the World (Read by Elfer, Julian). Audiobook Review — *Gale, Eric Kahn*
c The Zoo at the Edge of the World (Illus. by Nielson, Sam) — *Gale, Eric Kahn*
c Zoo Clues Series — *Rudolph, Jessica*
c A Zoo Field Trip (Illus. by Martin, Isabel) — *Martin, Isabel*
c The Zoo Is Closed Today!: Until Further Notice (Illus. by Kennedy, Arme) — *Beilenson, Evelyn*
c Zoo Train (Illus. by Parton, Daron) — *Sutton, Sally*
c Zoo Zoom! (Illus. by Pamintuan, Macky) — *Ryan, Candace*
c Zoology for Kids: Understanding and Working with Animals — *Hestermann, Bethanie*
c Zoology for Kids: Understanding and Working with Animals — *Hestermann, Josh*
c Zora's Zucchini (Illus. by Raff, Anna) — *Pryor, Katherine*
Zorba the Greek — *Bien, Peter A.*
c Zorgoochi Intergalactic Pizza: Delivery of Doom — *Yaccarino, Dan*
Zoroaster's Children — *Kociejowski, Marius*
The Zukofsky Era: Modernity, Margins, and the Avant-Garde — *Jennison, Ruth*
Zukunft am Ende: Autobiographische Sinnstiftungen von DDR-Geisteswissenschaftlern nach 1989 — *Lahusen, Christiane*
Zulu Warriors: The Battle for the South African Frontier — *Laband, John*
Zundel's Exit — *Werner, Markus*
Zundfunke aus Prag: Wie 1989 der Mut zur Freiheit die Geschichte Veranderte — *Genscher, Hans-Dietrich*
Zur Kulturgeschichte Osterreichs und Ungarns 1890-1938: Auf der Suche nach Verborgenen Gemeinsamkeiten — *Johnston, William M.*
Zurcher Werkstatt Historische Bildungsforschung
c Zuri Pi Wonders Why: Do I Have to Go to School? (Illus. by Gonzales, Chuck) — *Perez-Brown, Maria*
Zwischen Kaisern und Aposteln: Das Akakianische Schisma (484-519) als Kirchlicher Ordnungskonflikt der Spatantike — *Kotter, Jan-Markus*
Zwischen Osterreich und Grossdeutschland: Eine politische Geschichte der Salzburger Festspiele, 1933-1944 — *Kriechbaumer, Robert*
Zwischen Princeps und Res Publica: Tacitus, Plinius und die senatorische Selbstdarstellung in der Hohen Kaiserzeit — *Geisthardt, Johannes*
Zwischen Republik und Kaiserzeit: Die Munzmeisterpragung unter Augustus — *Kuter, Alexa*
Zwischen Sprache und Geschichte: Zum Werk Reinhart Kosellecks — *Dutt, Carsten*
Zwischen Utopie und Apokalypse. Nukleare technopolitics in der Sowjetunion
Zygmunt Bauman: Why Good People Do Bad Things — *Best, Shaun*